W9-CJB-538

The New International Atlas
Der Neue Internationale Atlas
El Nuevo Atlas Internacional
Le Nouvel Atlas International
O Nôvo Atlas Internacional

RAND McNALLY & COMPANY CHICAGO / NEW YORK / SAN FRANCISCO

ADVISERS AND CONSULTANTS

The editors wish to express their special appreciation to these geographers, cartographers, and regional specialists who assisted in the refinement of the basic concepts of the atlas or who participated in the review of many of the regional maps.

ALLGEMEINE UND KARTOGRAPHISCHE BERATER

Die Herausgeber möchten ihren besonderen Dank den Geographen, Kartographen und Landeskundlern aussprechen, die mitgeholfen haben bei der Klärung des Atlaskonzepts oder beteiligt waren an der Durchsicht vieler Regionalkarten.

ASESORES Y CONSULTORES

Los redactores quieren expresar su más profundo agradecimiento a los geógrafos, cartógrafos y especialistas en mapas regionales, que han colaborado en la determinación exacta de los conceptos básicos del atlas o que han participado en la revisión de gran número de los mapas regionales.

CONSEILLERS ET CONSULTANTS

Les éditeurs veulent exprimer ici leur gratitude aux géographes, cartographes et spécialistes régionaux qui ont collaboré à la mise au point de la conception de base de l'Atlas ou qui ont participé à la révision de nombreuses cartes régionales.

CONSELHEIROS E CONSULTORES

Os editores desejam expressar seu profundo agradecimento aos geógrafos, cartógrafos e especialistas regionais que assistiram no refinamento dos conceitos básicos do atlas ou que tenham participado na revisão de um grande número de mapas regionais.

International Planning Conference
Internationale Planungskonferenz
Conferencia Internacional de Consultores
Conférence Internationale de Planning
Conferência Internacional de Consultores

Dr. MANLIO CASTIGLIONI (deceased)
Italy

Dr. ARCH C. GERLACH (deceased)
United States

Dr. Ir. CORNELIS KOEMAN
Netherlands

Dr. ANDRÉ LIBAULT
Brazil

Brig. D. E. O. THACKWELL
United Kingdom

ROBERT J. VOSKUIL
United States

Dr. AKIRA WATANABE
Japan

Map Advisers
Kartographische Berater
Consejeros Cartográficos
Conseillers Cartographes
Conselheiros Cartográficos

Europe
Prof. Dr. EMIL MEYNEN
Germany

Dr. SANDOR RADO
Hungary

Asia
Dr. HISASHI SATO
Japan

Australia
R. O. BUCHANAN
United Kingdom

Anglo-America
Dr. ARCH C. GERLACH (deceased)
United States

Latin America
Dr. ANDRÉ LIBAULT
Brazil

Dra. CONSUELO SOTO MORA
Mexico

Dr. JORGE A. VIVÓ ESCOTO
Mexico

Metropolitan Area Maps
Prof. HAROLD M. MAYER
United States

Library of Congress Catalog Card Number: 80-51969
Printed in the United States of America

International Atlas Staff
Redaktion des Internationalen Atlasses
Personal del Atlas Internacional
Personnel de l'Atlas International
Redação do Atlas Internacional

RAND McNALLY & COMPANY, Chicago

Publisher
Andrew McNally III

Editorial and Cartographic Direction
Russell L. Voisin
Jon M. Leverenz

Art and Design Direction
Chris Arvetis
Gordon Hartshorne

Coordination
Victor P. Healy
John E. Zych
David B. Gattorna

Geographic Research
Joseph C. Smutnik
Kerstin Thielen
Keith Jennerjohn

Cartographic Editorial
Visvaldis Smits (deceased)
Robert K. Argersinger
William L. Abel

Cartographic Compilation
Esther A. Grene, Lynn N. Jasmer,
Ernest A. Dahl, Han Sik Lee,
Larry K. Tyler

Cartographic Production
Raymond J. Nitch, Wasyl Szwec,
Adolph Bravi, Ronald Peters,
Walter E. Erck, Dorothy M. Cundiff,
Robert Mancic, Joseph H. Funke,
Ruth Garner

Index
Donald R. Schultz

Terrain Illustrators
Ivan Barcaba
Evelyn Mitchell

Corporate Advisory Group
Thomas J. Hermes
Dennis O'Shea
Carl Mapes (deceased)
Bruce C. Ogilvie
Paul T. Tiddens

MONDADORI McNALLY GmbH, Stuttgart

General Manager
Helmut Schaub
and Cartographic Staff

CARTOGRAPHIA, Budapest

Coordinator
Ervin Földi
and Cartographic Staff

ESSELTE MAP SERVICE, Stockholm

Editorial and Cartographic Direction
Paul R. Kraske,
Jürgen Jansch,
and Cartographic Staff

GEORGE PHILIP & SON, London

Editorial and Cartographic Direction
Harold Fullard,
A. G. Poynter,
and Cartographic Staff

TEIKOKU-SHOIN CO., LTD., Tokyo

Supervisor
Kimio Moriya
and Cartographic Staff

Foreword

THE HISTORY OF MAPS is as old as travel, discovery, and curiosity about the world. Since the earliest times, cartographers have served mariners with guidance for their explorations, monarchs with portraits of their territories, and scholars with a record of the earth's surface. Today, maps play an even more important role by providing men with the evidence of the ties which link the world's countries and peoples to one another.

The prime function of a map is to portray the earth's surface and the patterns of human occupance that have developed upon it. If a map were no more than an objective record, it would not need revision; however, a map is more than just a simple picture. Greatly reduced in scale from the reality it represents, it must abstract and generalize from that reality, selecting and interpreting the facts deemed to be of greatest significance. Thus, not only must cartography map new regions of the world, but it must also reflect a steady improvement in the techniques of portraying geographic information for the user.

The present century has offered a great challenge to map makers. Not only has it witnessed the increasing demand for specialized map information from governments, teachers, and scientists, it has also seen growing numbers of non-specialists eager to use maps in their business, for travel, or simply for enjoyment.

The Editors of *The International Atlas* feel, then, that a new work should be more than an updated version of older ones. The goal should be to produce an atlas of the greatest possible value and interest to a wide range of specialists and laymen. In this Foreword, we call the attention of users to several aspects which are new to the traditional framework of atlas publishing. The two most significant of these are the internationality of its planning and execution, and the designing of the maps as components of five distinctive series.

From the beginning, this Atlas has been international in concept, planning, editorial policy, and production. It was felt by Rand McNally & Company that there would be important gains in source material and expertise from the participation of organizations with previous cartographic experience in widely varying regions of the world. The advice and guidance of the senior personnel of these organizations has borne out this belief, although Rand McNally & Company as publisher has retained prime responsibility.

The editorial policies of the Atlas have been established with international use in mind, being designed for those whose native tongue is German, Spanish, French or Portuguese, as well as English. This international approach has been carried into the maps through the utilization of the metric system of measurement, and particularly by a strong emphasis on the use of local forms for geographic names. Essentially all names are in the local language, and English is used only for names of major features which extend across international borders. The names of countries appear on most of the maps both in English and in the locally official forms.

Generic terms for physical features (mountain, island, cape, etc.) also appear in their local forms, not in English. Short glossaries translating the most common of these terms appear in the margins of most maps. There is also a comprehensive glossary of all the generic terms. In the index to the Atlas, translation of generic terms is aided by the use of a system of symbols.

The coverage of the world's regions has also been planned with international utilization in mind. The space allotted to each region reflects its relative economic and cultural significance on the world scene, as well as its total population and area. There is an approximate balance between Anglo-America, Europe, and Asia, each with over one-fifth of the total map pages. Africa, Oceania, and Latin America together account for the remaining one-third. The index maps on pages xiii-xv show the map coverage according to scale.

The second of the Atlas' significant new aspects is the planning of the maps as components of five separate series. Each series has a distinctive style and content. In the first of these series, the continents are portrayed at 1:24,000,000 in natural colors, as they might appear from about 4,000 miles in space. The series also includes maps of the oceans at 1:48,000,000 and the world at 1:75,000,000.

In the next series, the major world regions are uniformly portrayed at 1:12,000,000 (190 miles to the inch). These maps are primarily political in style and content. The third series covers virtually the entire inhabited area of the earth at either 1:6,000,000 (95 miles to the inch), for the less dense regions, or 1:3,000,000 (47 miles to the inch), for Europe, most of North America, and the densest portions of South and East Asia. Physical and cultural detail are given approximately equal emphasis in this series.

In the fourth series, the scale of 1:1,000,000 (16 miles to the inch) has been used to portray key regions in each continent, selected for their exceptional importance, high population density, or complexity of development. The emphasis is on cultural detail, though shaded relief also appears. A final series maps the world's major urban areas at 1:300,000 (4.7 miles to the inch). This series emphasizes the complex patterns characteristic of large urban areas, omitting relief portrayal.

Each of the map series is comprehensive in a significant sense. The first three are territorially comprehensive, except for a few remote areas, and the last two are comprehensive for the most densely settled regions of the earth.

The sequence of maps in the Atlas begins with the series of world, continent, and ocean maps. Next are the three series of regional maps, arranged within major regions from smallest scale (1:12,000,000) to largest scale (1:1,000,000). The metropolitan map series (1:300,000) are kept together in one section following the regional maps.

The individual map layouts have usually been planned to portray geographic and economic regions rather than individual countries. Thus there are maps of the Iberian Peninsula and of Southeastern Europe, but no separate maps of Portugal or Romania. In a few instances, this has necessitated the omission of some small portion of the region or country described in the map title. Inset maps have also been avoided, though exceptions have been made to portray some isolated islands or island groups.

The map symbols used for given features (Legend to Maps, pages x-xii) are generally alike on all of the map scales, though reduced in size on smaller scales. The symbols most often used have been arranged on page xi.

No aspect of map design has shown more dramatic advances in recent years than the cartographic rendering of relief. The Editors believe that the most effective method to depict this is the bird's-eye view or hill shading technique, which uses variation from light through dark tones to indicate slope and shape of relief features pictorially. This Atlas uses shaded relief on all but one of its five map series. On the 1:6,000,000 and 1:3,000,000 maps, it appears in combination with altitude tints, which show variations in elevation by means of light reflection, hue and intensity.

In the concluding portion of the Atlas are various tables and summaries for general reference. The World Scene (pages 289-320) is a separate section of topical maps. These maps summarize the patterns of man's physical environment and some of his more important economic activities, political alignments, and cultural distributions. This section is based on the most recent information available, taken from a variety of sources and adapted by the editors. Next is the comprehensive glossary of geographic terms (pages ***I•1–I•7***). The tables on pages ***I•8–I•9***, Major Geographic Changes Since 1969, show a selection of the many map revisions since the first edition of the Atlas. The World Information Table (pages ***I•10–I•13***) lists the area, population, and political status for each major political unit. The world's largest metropolitan areas are listed on page ***I•14***, followed by a comprehensive list of the world's major cities with population (pages ***I•15–I•27***). Finally, the Index provides map location references—map page, latitude and longitude—for more than 160,000 names.

Vorwort

DIE GESCHICHTE DER KARTE ist so alt wie das Reisen, die Entdeckungsfahrten und die Wissbegier über die Welt. Seit alten Zeiten haben Kartographen den Seefahrern mit Unterlagen für ihre Erkundungen gedient, den Herrschern Aufnahmen ihres Besitzes und den Gelehrten Darstellungen der Erdoberfläche geliefert. Heute spielen Karten eine noch bedeutendere Rolle, weil sie den Menschen vor Augen führen, wie eng die Länder und Völker der Welt miteinander verbunden sind.

Wichtigste Aufgabe einer Karte ist es, die Oberfläche der Erde und die vom Menschen geschaffenen Formen darzustellen. Wäre eine Karte nichts anderes als eine objektive Bestandsaufnahme, brauchte sie nicht bearbeitet zu werden; eine Karte ist jedoch mehr als nur ein Bild. Da sie eine vielfache Verkleinerung der Wirklichkeit wiedergibt, muss sie abstrahieren und durch Auswahl und Symbolisierung der wesentlichsten Tatsachen vereinfachen. So hat die Kartographie neue Regionen der Erde aufzunehmen und den neuesten Stand der Darstellung geographischer Informationen für den Benutzer aufzuzeigen.

Unser Jahrhundert bedeutet für die Kartographen eine grosse Herausforderung. Karten werden nicht nur in zunehmendem Masse von Regierungen, Wissenschaftlern und Pädagogen gefordert, sondern auch von interessierten Laien, die in ihrem Beruf, auf Reisen oder einfach zu ihrer Freude Karten benutzen.

Die Herausgeber des *Internationalen Atlas* meinen, dass ein neues Atlaswerk mehr sein sollte als nur die laufend gehaltene Ausgabe eines alten. Das Ziel sollte sein, einen Atlas von höchstem Gebrauchswert und Interesse sowohl für Fachleute wie auch Laien zu schaffen.

In diesem Sinne möchten wir auf Besonderheiten hinweisen, die sich von dem traditionellen Aufbau eines Atlas wesentlich unterscheiden. Die beiden wichtigsten sind die Internationalität in Planung und Ausführung sowie die einheitliche Gestaltung der Karten zu fünf Gruppen.

Von Anfang an war dieser Atlas international in Planung, Redaktion und Herstellung. Rand McNally & Company war überzeugt, dass die Beteiligung von Partnern aus verschiedenen Teilen der Welt mit ihrer kartographischen Erfahrung einen grossen Gewinn an Quellen und Rat ergeben würde. Der Rat und die Mitarbeit dieser Fachleute haben diese Ansicht voll bestätigt, wobei Rand McNally als Verleger die letzte Entscheidung zufiel.

Die redaktionelle Bearbeitung des Atlas erfolgte mit Blick auf einen internationalen Interessentenkreis, vor allem aber für Benutzer, deren Muttersprache Deutsch, Spanisch, Französisch, Portugiesisch oder Englisch ist. Diese internationale Einstellung zeigt sich im Karteninhalt selbst, in der Benutzung des metrischen Masssystems und vor allem in der Bevorzugung der lokalen Schreibweise geographischer Namen. Grundsätzlich werden alle Namen in der Landessprache wiedergegeben; nur Namen grösserer Objekte, die sich über nationale Grenzen erstrecken, erscheinen in Englisch. Die Ländernamen stehen auf den meisten Karten sowohl in Englisch als auch in der offiziellen nationalen Form.

Namen für physische Objekte (Berg, Insel, Kap usw.) sind ebenfalls in ihrer lokalen Form wiedergegeben, nicht in Englisch. Die am häufigsten vorkommenden Begriffe stehen am Rande der meisten Karten erläutert. Der Atlas enthält ausserdem ein umfangreiches Verzeichnis aller Gattungsbegriffe. Im Register wird das Verständnis dieser Gattungsbegriffe durch ein System von Symbolen erleichtert.

Die Kartenausschnitte der verschiedenen Regionen der Erde wurden gleichfalls mit Blick auf einen internationalen Benutzerkreis gewählt. In diesem Atlas entspricht der einer Region zugemessene Kartenanteil ihrer relativen wirstshaftlichen und kulturellen Bedeutung in der Welt wie ihrer Gesamtbevölkerung und Fläche. Auf Anglo-Amerika, Europa und Asien entfällt mit je etwas mehr als einen Fünftel der Gesamtkartenzahl ungefähr der gleiche Anteil. Das verbleibende Drittel teilen sich Afrika, Australien, Ozeanien und Lateinamerika. Auf den Seiten XIII-XV sind die Kartenschnitte den Massstäben entsprechend auf Übersichtskarten ersichtlich.

Die zweite wesentliche Besonderhiet des Atlas ist seine Gliederung der Karten in fünf charakteristische Gruppen. Jede Gruppe ist gekennzeichnet durch einen bestimmten Stil und Inhalt. In der ersten Gruppe werden die Kontinente (1:24 Mill.) abgebildet, wie sie sich aus einer ungefähren Entfernung von 6 500 km aus dem Weltraum darbieten. Diese Gruppe schliesst Karten der Ozeane (1:48 Mill.) und der Erde (1:75 Mill.) ein. In der folgenden Gruppe werden Grossregionen einheitlich (1:12 Mill.) dargestellt. Diese Karten sind in erster Linie politische Karten. Die dritte Serie deckt im wesentlichen das bewohnte Gebiet der Erde, entweder 1:6 Mill. für weniger dicht besiedelte Gebiete oder 1:3 Mill. für Europa, den Grossteil von Nordamerika und die dichtest besiedelten Teile Süd- und Ostasiens. Physische und kulturgeographische Einzelheiten werden in ungefähr gleichem Umfang wiedergegeben.

Für die vierte Gruppe wurde der Massstab 1:1 Mill. gewählt, um zentrale Räume jedes Kontinents abzubilden; sie sind entsprechend ihrer aussergewöhnlichen Bedeutung, hohen Bevölkerungsdichte oder komplexen Entwicklung gewählt. Betont werden kulturgeographische Einzelheiten, dazu enthalten die Karten eine Reliefschummerung. Die letzte Gruppe umfasst die bedeutendsten Stadtregionen der Erde (1:300 000). Diese Serie hebt das charakteristische, komplexe Gefüge grosser städtischer Ballungsgebiete hervor; auf Reliefdarstellung wurde verzichtet.

Jede der Kartenserien ist in sich abgeschlossen: Die ersten drei sind in Bezug auf die Landflächen umfassend, ausgenommen einige entlegene Gebiete; die zwei letzten sind es hinsichtlich der Darstellung der dichtest besiedelten Räume der Erde.

Der Atlas beginnt mit der Gruppe der Welt-, Kontinent- und Ozeankarten. Es folgen drei Gruppen Regionalkarten, innerhalb jeder Grossregion geordnet vom kleinsten Massstab (1:12 Mill.) zum grössten (1:1 Mill.). Die Serie der Stadtregionen (1:300 000) wurde in einem einzigen Kapitel zusammengefasst, im Anschluss an die Regionalkarten.

Die Festlegung der einzelnen Kartenausschnitte zielte gewöhnlich mehr darauf ab, geographische und wirtschaftliche Regionen darzustellen als einzelne Staaten. Es gibt daher eine Karte der Iberischen Halbinsel oder von Südosteuropa, aber keine Einzelkarte von Portugal oder Rumänien. In einigen Fällen sind hierdurch kleinere Flächen des Landes oder der Region nicht erfasst, die im Kartentitel genannt sind. Die Verwendung von Einsatzkärtchen wurde möglichst vermieden, dennoch waren Ausnahmen erforderlich, um entlegene Inseln oder Inselgruppen darstellen zu können.

Die Kartensignaturen für bestimmte Objekte (Zeichenerklärung Seite X-XII) gleichen sich im allgemeinen in allen Massstäben, auch wenn sie in Karten kleinerer Massstäbe verkleinert sind. Die am häufigsten vorkommenden Signaturen sind auf Seite XI dargestellt.

Auf kaum einem Gebiet der Kartengestaltung gab es in den vergangenen Jahren so eindrucksvolle Fortschritte wie auf dem der Geländedarstellung. Die Herausgeber glauben, dass die wirkungsvollste Darstellungsmethode die Reliefschummerung ist. Sie benutzt Tonabstufungen von Hell zu Dunkel, um Neigungen und Geländeformen plastisch hervorzuheben. Dieser Atlas bringt die Schummerung bei vier der fünf Kartenserien. In den Karten 1:6 und 1:3 Mill. wird sie kombiniert mit farbigen Höhenschichten, die unterschiedliche Höhenlagen durch ihren Farb- und Tonwert abgestuft wiedergeben.

Der letzte Teil des Atlas enthält zahlreiche Tabellen und Übersichten. Die Welt von Heute (Seite 289-320) ist ein selbständiges Kapitel mit thematischen Karten. Sie geben einen Überblick über die physichen Grundlagen des Siedlungsraumes des Menschen, seine wichtigsten wirtschaftlichen Tätigkeiten, die politischen Grenzen und Gruppierungen und sonstige Kulturgeographische Erscheinungen. Als Grundlage dienten die neuesten erhältlichen Daten verschiedenster Herkunft. Auf Seite *I•1–I•7* folgt eine Zusammenstellung geographischer Begriffe. Die Tabellen auf den Seiten *I•8–I•9*, "Wichtige geographische Veränderungen seit 1969," zeigt eine Auswahl aus den vielen, seit der ersten Ausgabe des Atlas erforderlich gewordenen Kartenüberarbeitungen. In einer Länderübersicht (Seite *I•10–I•13*) sind Daten über Fläche, Bevölkerung und politischen Status der wichtigsten politischen Einheiten zusammengefasst. Die grössten Stadtregionen der Erde werden auf Seite *I•14*. Weiter folgt eine umfangreiche Liste der wichtigsten Weltstädte mit Einwohnerzahlen (Seite *I•15–I•27*). Im Register werden für über 160 000 Namen die Kartenseite sowie die geographische Länge und Breite aufgeführt.

Prefacio

LA HISTORIA DE LOS MAPAS es tan antigua como la de los viajes, los descubrimientos y la curiosidad del hombre por el mundo. Desde hace mucho tiempo los cartógrafos han proporcionado guías a los navegantes en sus exploraciones, descripciones de sus territorios a los monarcas y registros de la superficie de la tierra a los eruditos. Más importante todavía es el papel que desempeñan los mapas en la actualidad, proporcionando al hombre en todas partes prueba de los lazos que vinculan entre sí a los diferentes países y pueblos del globo.

La función primordial de un mapa es la representación de la superficie de la tierra y de los patrones de ocupación humana que se han desarrollado sobre ella. Si un mapa no fuera sino un registro objetivo, no necesitaría ser revisado; sin embargo, un mapa es algo más que una simple representación gráfica. Representando una realidad enormemente reducida a escala, el mapa, forzosamente, debe abstraer y generalizar de esa realidad, seleccionando e interpretando los hechos que se juzguen de mayor significación. En consecuencia, la cartografía no debe limitarse al trazo de mapas de las nuevas regiones del mundo, sino que debe reflejar en ellos un continuo adelanto en las técnicas de representación de la información geográfica en provecho de quien los utiliza.

El siglo actual ha venido a presentar a los cartógrafos una desafiante tarea. Es época que no sólo ha presenciado una creciente demanda de información cartográfica especializada por parte de los gobiernos, maestros y científicos, sino que durante ella ha surgido un público cada vez mayor de gentes no especializadas, ávidas de aprovechar los mapas en sus negocios y viajes o que los adquieren simplemente por placer.

Los directores del *Atlas Internacional* consideran, por lo tanto, que una nueva obra debe ser algo más que una versión al día de trabajos anteriores. El objetivo debe ser producir un atlas del mayor valor e interés posibles para un vasto número de especialistas y de legos en la materia. En este prefacio, queremos llamar la atención de quienes consulten esta obra sobre varias innovaciones introducidas en el diseño tradicional de un atlas. De ellas, las más significativas son la internacionalidad de su preparación, y el diseño de los mapas como componentes de cinco series con características propias.

Desde un principio, este atlas ha tenido carácter internacional en cuanto a su concepto básico, su planeamiento, política editorial y producción. Rand McNally y Compañía consideró que con la participación de organizaciones con experiencia en cartografía en una gran variedad de regiones del mundo, se obtendría importante progreso en cuanto a fuentes de material y de conocimientos. Esta creencia originó el asesoramiento y guía recibidos del personal directivo de estas organizaciones, aunque Rand McNally y Compañía ha retenido la responsabilidad principal como casa editora.

Las normas o política editorial del atlas se ha establecido teniendo en cuenta su uso internacional, y éste ha sido diseñado para el público de habla alemana, española, francesa, portuguesa e inglesa. Este carácter internacional se introdujo en los mapas mediante la utilización del sistema métrico y en particular, dando marcada preferencia al uso de vocablos locales en la nomenclatura. Virtualmente todo nombre se da en el idioma de la localidad, usándose el inglés únicamente en la identificación de elementos geográficos de mayor importancia que se extienden a través de las fronteras internacionales. En la mayoría de los mapas, los nombres de los países aparecen en inglés y en la forma oficial localmente utilizada.

Los términos genéricos de geografía física (montañas, islas, cabos, etc.), también aparecen en el idioma local, no en inglés. Al margen de la mayoría de los mapas se incluyen breves glosarios con la traducción de los más comunes de dichos términos. Se incluye también un glosario completo de los términos genéricos y en el índice del atlas, mediante un sistema de símbolos, se facilita la traducción de los mismos.

Igualmente, la amplitud que el atlas da a las distintas regiones del mundo, fue preparada con un criterio de utilización internacional. El espacio asignado a cada región refleja su posición económica y cultural relativa dentro del escenario mundial, así como su población y superficie. El resultado de esto ha sido el equilibrio aproximado resultante entre Angloamérica, Europa y Asia, ocupando, cada cual, más de la quinta parte del total de páginas dedicadas a mapas. Africa, Oceanía y América Latina juntas, cubren el resto del volumen. Los mapas índices, en las páginas xiii a xv, muestran, a escala, la extensión de las regiones que los mapas comprenden.

El segundo de los nuevo aspectos significativos del atlas, es el planeamiento de los mapas como componentes de cinco series separadas. Cada serie tiene un estilo y contenido propios. En la primera de estas series, los continentes están representados a una escala de 1:24 000 000, en colores naturales, como aparecerían al observar la tierra desde el espacio a una distancia de cerca de 6 500 kilómetros. La serie incluye también mapas de los océanos a escala 1:48 000 000 y del mundo a escala 1:75 000 000.

En la serie siguiente, las principales regiones del mundo están uniformemente representadas a escala 1:12 000 000 (120 km por cm). Estos mapas son básicamente políticos en su estilo y contenido. La tercera serie cubre prácticamente el total de la superficie habitada de la tierra, a una de dos escalas: 1:6 000 000 (60 km por cm), para las regiones menos densas, o 1:3 000 000 (30 km por cm), para Europa, la mayor parte de Norteamérica y las regiones de mayor densidad de población del Sur y Sureste de Asia. En esta serie se hace aproximadamente igual énfasis a los detalles de orden físico y cultural.

En la cuarta serie se ha usado la escala 1:1 000 000 (10 km por cm), para representar las regiones más notables en cada continente, seleccionadas por su excepcional importancia, alta densidad de población o complejidad de desarrollo. Acá, el énfasis es en el detalle cultural aunque también aparece el relieve utilizando la técnica de sombreado. La serie final la componen los mapas de las principales áreas urbanas del mundo a una escala de 1:300 000 (3 km por cm). Esta serie recalca los complejos patrones culturales característicos de las grandes áreas urbanas, omitiendo la representación del relieve.

Cada una de las series es en sí una serie integral desde el punto de vista de significación. Las tres primeras, con excepción de unas cuantas áreas remotas, son territorialmente completas; las dos últimas, son completas en cuanto a las regiones más densamente pobladas de la tierra.

La sucesión de los mapas en el atlas principia con la serie del mundo, los continentes y los océanos. Luego vienen las tres series de mapas regionales distribuídos dentro de cada región principal, de la escala menor, (1:12 000 000), a la escala mayor, (1:1 000 000). La serie de mapas de áreas metropolitanas (1:300 000), se ofrece en una sección, inmediatamente después de los mapas regionales.

En general, el trazado de cada mapa se hizo con miras a representar regiones geográficas y económicas, y no necesariamente países individuales. Así, el atlas contiene mapas de la Península Ibérica y de Europa Sudoriental, pero no mapas separados de Portugal o de Rumania. En unos pocos casos, esto impuso la necesidad de omitir alguna pequeña porción de la región o país descrito en el título del mapa. También se evitó la inserción de mapas detallando determinada área, aunque se hicieron excepciones para representar algunas islas o grupos de islas.

Los símbolos utilizados para ciertos elementos (Leyenda para Mapas, páginas x a xii), son en general similares en todas las escalas, aunque reducidos en tamaño en los mapas de escala más pequeña. Los usados más frecuentemente se encuentran en la página xi.

En ningún aspecto del diseño cartográfico se han hecho progresos tan notables en años recientes como en la representación del relieve del terreno. Los editores opinan, sin embargo, que el método más efectivo en este sentido es la vista a vuelo de pájaro o técnica de sombreado: la variación de tonos claros a obscuros indica gráficamente la pendiente y la configuración del relieve. Este atlas utiliza el sombreado en cuatro de las cinco series de mapas. En los mapas a escala 1:6 000 000 y 1:3 000 000, el sombreado se combina con tintes que indican los cambios de altitud mediante reflexión de la luz, colorido e intensidad variables.

En la última parte del atlas se ofrecen varias tablas y resúmenes para consulta. La Escena Mundial, (páginas 289 a 320), es una sección separada de mapas los cuales resumen los patrones del medio ambiente del hombre y algunas de sus más importantes actividades, alineaciones políticas y distribuciones culturales. Esta sección se basa en la información disponible más reciente tomada de diversas fuentes y compendiada por los editores. En seguida se encuentra un glosario completo de términos geográficos (páginas *I•1–I•7*). Las tablas de las páginas *I•8–I•9*, "Cambios Geográficos Importantes desde 1969," muestra una selección de la gran cantidad de revisiones que se han hecho a los mapas desde la primera edición del Atlas. La Tabla de Información Mundial, (páginas *I•10* a *I•13*), muestra el área, la población y la situación de cada una de las principales unidades políticas. La lista de las áreas metropolitanas más grandes del mundo aparece en la página *I•14*, y está seguida por una lista completa de las principales ciudades del mundo con indicación del número de habitantes, (páginas *I•15* a *I•27*). Finalmente, el índice ofrece referencias para localizar en los mapas más de 160 000 nombres: página del mapa, latitud y longitud.

Avant-propos

L'HISTOIRE DES CARTES géographiques remonte aussi loin que celle des voyages, des découvertes et du sentiment de curiosité touchant le globe terrestre. Depuis les temps les plus reculés, les cartographes ont servi les marins en les aidant à s'orienter dans leurs voyages d'explorations, les monarques en leur fournissant des représentations de leurs territoires, les savants en les documentant sur la surface terrestre. De nos jours, les cartes jouent un rôle plus important encore, en ce qu'elles procurent aux hommes l'évidence tangible des liens joignant les uns aux autres peuples et nations du monde.

La fonction primordiale d'une carte consiste à représenter la surface du globe et la répartition des concentrations humaines qui s'y sont développées. Une carte ne fût-elle qu'un document objectif, point ne serait besoin de la réviser; mais justement, elle constitue bien davantage qu'une simple image. Considérablement réduite relativement à la réalité qu'elle représente, elle doit abstraire et généraliser à partir de cette réalité, par la sélection et l'interprétation des données jugées les plus significatives. De sorte que la cartographie doit non seulement établir les cartes des nouvelles régions du globe, mais il lui faut en outre refléter les progrès constants des techniques d'exposé de la documentation géographique à l'intention du lecteur.

Le siècle actuel a porté un défi suprême aux cartographes. Non seulement en ce que l'on y est témoin d'une demande toujours croissante de cartes à l'usage des spécialistes, de la part des gouvernements, des professeurs et des savants, mais aussi bien en ce que l'on y constate une proportion de plus en plus élevée de non-initiés avides d'utiliser des cartes de vulgarisation pour leurs affaires, leurs voyages, ou simplement leur plaisir.

Les Editeurs de *L'Atlas International* estiment, dès lors, qu'un nouvel ouvrage se doit d'être plus qu'une ancienne version mise à jour. Le but qu'ils se proposent consiste à sortir un atlas qui soit du plus haut intérêt et de la plus profonde valeur pour un vaste public de spécialistes et de profanes. Les Editeurs attirent l'attention des lecteurs sur plusieurs innovations apportées ici au cadre traditionnel de publication des atlas. Deux des plus significatives de ces innovations résident dans l'internationalisation de la conception et de l'exécution d'une part, d'autre part dans la disposition des cartes réparties en cinq séries distinctives.

Envisagé et entrepris sur un mode international dès le début, cet Atlas s'est développé selon une conception, une forme éditoriale et une réalisation du même ordre. Rand McNally & Company jugeait que de sérieux avantages—apports importants en matériaux de documentation et en connaissances spécialisées faisant autorité—résulteraient d'une collaboration avec des organisations possédant de longue date une expérience cartographique des régions les plus diversifiées du globe. Les avis et les opinions émanant du personnel de cadres de ces organisations ont corroboré cette conviction, encore que Rand McNally en tant que société d'édition en assume la responsabilité principale.

D'usage international, destiné à des lecteurs de langue allemande, espagnole , française ou portugaise, tout autant qu'anglaise, cet Atlas a dû être édité sous une forme qui tînt compte de sa raison d'être. Cette conception internationale de l'Atlas a été réalisée sur les cartes elles-mêmes avec d'une part l'utilisation du système métrique, avec d'autre part l'emploi délibéré des noms géographiques sous leur forme nationale. Essentiellement, tous les noms apparaissent sous leur forme nationale, l'anglais n'étant utilisé que pour les noms d'importantes structures du relief qui s'étendent par-delà les frontières internationales. Sur la plupart des cartes, les noms des pays apparaissent à la fois en anglais et sous leur forme nationale officielle.

Les termes génériques désignant des structures de relief (montagne, île, cap, etc.) apparaissent également sous leur forme nationale, et non pas en anglais. En marge de la plupart des cartes, de courtes listes lexicales donnent la traduction des plus communs de ces termes. En outre, un glossaire donne tous les termes génériques dont la traduction se trouve par ailleurs facilitée grâce au système de symboles décrit dans l'Index de l'Atlas.

La répartition des régions du globe a été également déterminée en tenant compte de l'usage international qu'il sera fait de l'Atlas. L'espace attribué à chaque région reflète son importance économique et culturelle relative dans le monde, aussi bien que sa superficie et sa population. Il y a un équilibre approximatif entre l Amérique du Nord, l'Europe et l'Asie, chacune avec plus d'un cinquième de la totalité des pages. L'Afrique, l'Océanie et l'Amérique du Sud occupent le tiers restant. Les cartes index des pages xiii-xv présentent la répartition des cartes en fonction de l'échelle à laquelle elles sont reproduites.

La seconde des innovations importantes de cet Atlas réside dans la conception des cartes en tant qu'éléments constitutifs de cinq séries séparées. Style et contenu distinctifs caractérisent nettement chacune de ces cinq séries. Dans la première, les continents sont représentés à l'échelle de 1:24 000 000, en couleurs naturelles, tels qu'ils apparaîtraient, vus de l'espace, à 6 500 km. Cette série comprend également les cartes de océans à l'échelle de 1:48 000 000 et du monde à l'échelle de 1:75 000 000.

Dans la série suivante, les régions majeures du globe sont représentées de facon uniforme à l'échelle de 1:12 000 000 (120 km au cm). Par leur style et leur contenu, celles-ci sont essentiellement des cartes politiques. Dans la troisième série, virtuellement toute las surface habitée de la terre est représentée, soit à l'échelle de 1:6 000 000 (60 km au cm) pour les régions de moindre densité de population, soit à l'échelle de 1:3 000 000 (30 km au cm) pour l'Europe, la plus grande partie de l'Amérique du Nord et les portions de plus forte densité du Sud et de l'Est de l'Asie. Dans cette série, une importance à peu près égale a été accordée aux détails physiques et aux détails culturels.

Dans la quatrième série, l'échelle de 1:1 000 000 (10 km au cm) a été employée pour représenter certaines régions-clefs de chaque continent, choisies pour leur importance exceptionnelle, leur densité de population, ou la complexité de leur développement. L'accent porte sur les détails culturels, bien que le relief ombré apparaisse également. Une série finale souligne la répartition culturelle complexe, caractéristique des vastes zones urbaines, omettant le relief.

Chacune de ces séries est complète dans un mode significatif. Les trois premières sont complètes du point de vue territorial, exception faite de quelques lointaines contrées, et les deux dernières sont complètes en ce qui concerne les régions du globe de plus forte densité de population.

La succession des cartes de l'Atlas s'ouvre avec la série qui comprend les cartes du monde, des continents, et des océans. A sa suite, viennent les trois séries de cartes régionales disposées pour chaque région principale depuis les plus petites échelles (1:12 000 000), aux plus grandes (1:1 000 000). La série des cartes métropolitaines est groupée en une section qui fait suite aux cartes régionales.

La répartition individuelle des cartes a généralement été conçue en fonction des régions géographiques et économiques, plutôt qu'en fonction des frontières politiques nationales. De sorte qu'il y a des cartes de la Péninsule Ibérique et de l'Europe du Sud-Est, mais pas de cartes séparées pour le Portugal ou la Roumanie. Dans quelques cas, ceci a nécessité l'omission de quelque petite portion de la région ou du pays décrit dans le titre de la carte. Les insertions d'extensions ont également été évitées, encore que plusieurs exceptions aient été faites pour représenter certaines îles isolées ou certains groupes d'îles.

Les symboles employés sur les cartes sont en général identiques pour toutes les échelles de cartes, quoique de taille réduite sur les cartes à petite échelle. Les symboles les plus fréquemment employés ont été réunis à la page xi.

Aucun de aspects de la réalisation des cartes n'a fait de progrès plus prodigieux durant ces dernières années que la représentation cartographique du relief. Les Editeurs estiment que la méthode la plus efficace est celle de la "vue à vol d'oiseau", ou technique du relief ombré; celle-ci utilise toute la gamme des tons, des plus clairs aux plus foncés, pour indiquer picturalement l'inclinaison des pentes et la forme des structures du relief. Le relief ombré apparaît sur quatre des cinqu séries de cartes. Sur les cartes au 1:6 000 000e et au 1:3 000 000e, il apparaît en combinaison avec les teintes d'altitude qui indiquent les variations d'élévation au moyen de la réflexion de la lumière, de la nuance et de l'intensité.

Dans la dernière partie de l'Atlas, qui constitue sa conclusion, se trouvent divers tableaux de récapitulations et de références. La Scène du Monde (pages 289-320) occupe une section à part avec se cartes de sujets particuliers. Ces carte récapitulent les répartitions de l'environnement physique de l'homme, ainsi que certaines de ses activités économiques les plus importantes, les limite politiques et les distributions culturelles. Cette section s'appuie sur la plus récente documentation disponible provenant de sources diverses et adaptée par les editeurs. A sa suite se trouve le lexique complet des termes géographiques (pages *I•1–I•7*). Tableaux pages *I•8* et *I•9*, "Principales Modifications Géographiques depuis 1969," indiquent les principales modifications cartographiques depuis la première édition de cet Atlas. Puis une table d'informations mondiales donne la liste de toutes les unités politiques principales, avec superficie, population et statut politique de chacune (pages *I•10–I•13*). La liste des plus importants centres urbains du monde est à la page *I•14*. A la suite de cette table se trouve une liste complète des principales villes du monde avec leur population (pages *I•15–I•27*). Enfin, l'Index fournit des références de cartes—numéros de pages, longitude et latitude—pour permettre de situer plus de 160 000 noms géographiques.

Prefácio

A HISTÓRIA DOS MAPAS é tão antiga quanto as das viagens, descobertas, e curiosidades sobre o mundo. Desde os primórdios tempos, cartógrafos têm servido à marinheiros orientando-os em suas explorações, monarcas com reproduções dos seus territórios, e acadêmicos com o registro da superfície da terra. Hoje, os mapas têm um papel mais importante-ainda, fornecendo ao homem provas das ligações que unem os países e os povos do mundo.

A função fundamental do mapa é de retratar a superfície da terra e os padrões da ocupação humana que sobre ela se desenvolveu. Se o mapa não fosse nada mais que um registro objetivo, não necessitaria de revisão; contudo, um mapa é mais do que um simples retrato. Grandemente reduzido em escala, em relação à realidade que representa, ele deve absorver e ao mesmo tempo generalizar a realidade, selecionando e interpretando os fatos supostamente de maior significado. Portanto, não somente é preciso que o cartógrafo registre novas regiões do mundo, mas também tente refletir um melhoramento contínuo nas técnicas de retratamento de informação geográfica para o usuário.

O século atual tem oferecido um grande desafio para confeccionadores de mapas. Não há somente o testemunho da crescente demanda por mapas de informações especializadas, pelos governos, professores e cientistas, mas também tem-se notado um número crescente de leigos, ansiosos em usar mapas em seus negócios, viagens, ou simplesmente como-passatempo.

Os Editores do *Atlas Internacional* sentem, que um novo trabalho deveria ser mais do que uma versão renovada dos trabalhos anteriores. O objetivo deveria ser de produzir um atlas de máximo valor e interêsse possível, para uma grande gama de especialistas e leigos. Neste prefácio, chamamos a atenção dos usuários para os vários aspectos-que são novos para os esquemas tradicionais de publicação de atlas. Os dois mais significantes são: a internacionalidade do seu planejamento e execução, e o arranjo de mapas como componentes de cinco séries distintas.

Desde o início, o atlas tem sido internacional em conceito, planejamento, política editorial e produção. Rand McNally & Company sentiu que haveriam ganhos importantes na fonte de material e conhecimento, pela participação de organizações com experiências cartográficas anteriores, nas mais diversas regiões do mundo. O conselho e orientação do quadro pessoal dessas organizações têm comprovado esta crença, apesar da Rand McNally & Company, como editor, ter retido a responsabilidade principal.

As políticas editoriais do Atlas têm sido estabelecidas visando o uso internacional, sendo designado para aqueles cuja língua nativa é Alemão, Espanhol, Francês ou Português, bem como Inglês. Essa técnica internacional tem sido executada em mapas, através da utilização do sistema métrico de medidas, e particularmente, pela grande ênfase no uso dos estilos locais para nomes geográficos. Essencialmente, todos os nomes estão em linguagem local, e o Inglês é usado somente para nomes de acidentes geográficos importantes, que se extendam através de fronteiras internacionais. Os nomes dos países-aparecem na maioria dos mapas, em Inglês, e em linguagem oficial local.

Termos genéricos para características físicas (montanhas, ilhas, cabos, etc.) aparecem também nas suas formas locais, não em Inglês. Pequenos glossários traduzindo estes têrmos mais comuns aparecem nas margens da maioria dos mapas. Há também um glossário completo de todos os termos genéricos. No índice dos atlas, a tradução dos termos genéricos é auxiliada pelo uso de um sistema de símbolos.

A cobertura das regiões do mundo tem sido visando a utilização internacional. O espaço atribuído para cada região reflete seu relativo significado econômico e cultural no cenário mundial, bem como sua população e área. Há um balanço aproximado entre Anglo-América, Europa e Ásia, cada qual com mais de um quinto do total de páginas. África, Oceania e América Latina, juntos, contam com o restante um terço. O mapa índice nas páginas xiii-xv mostra a cobertura do mapa de acordo com a escala.

Um novo aspecto secundário do Atlas, é o planejamento de mapas como componentes de cinco séries separadas. Cada série tem um estilo e conteúdo distinto. Na primeira dessas séries, os continentes são ilustrados em 1:24 000 00 em cores naturais, tal como elas apareceriam a 6.500 km de espaço. A série também inclui mapas dos oceanos em 1:48 000 000 e do mundo em 1:75 000 000.

Na série seguinte, as regiões principais do mundo estão uniformemente ilustradas em 1:12 000 000 (120 km por cm). Estes mapas são principalmente políticos no estilo e conteúdo. A terceira série virtualmente, cobre toda a área habitada da terra em 1:6 000 000 (60 km por cm) para as regiões menos densas, ou 1:3 000 000 (47 km por cm) para Europa, maioria da América do Norte, e a mais densa porção do Sul e Leste da Ásia. É dado ênfase de igual valor aos detalhes físicos e culturais nesta série.

Na quarta série, a escala de 1:1 000 000 (10 km por cm) tem sido usada para ilustrar regiões chaves em cada continente, selecionado pela sua excepcional importância, alta densidade populacional ou complexidade de desenvolvimento. A ênfase está no detalhe cultural, apesar de relêvo sombreado também aparecer. A série final mapeia as principais áreas urbanas mundiais em 1:300 000 (3 km por cm). Esta série enfatiza padrões complexos característicos de grandes áreas urbanas, omitindo a ilustração do relêvo.

Cada série de mapas é completa em um determinado senso. As três primeiras são territorialmente completas, exceto as poucas áreas remotas, e as duas últimas são também completas para as regiões mais densamente habitadas da terra.

A sequência de mapas no Atlas começa com a série de mapas do mundo, continentes e oceanos. Em seguida, estão as três séries de mapas regionais, arranjados dentro de regiões principais de escala mínima (1:12 000 000) para escala máxima (1:1 000 000). As séries de mapas metropolitanos (1:300 000) têm sido mantidas juntas em uma secção seguindo os mapas regionais.

As apresentações individuais dos mapas têm sido normalmente planejadas para ilustrar regiões geográficas e econômicas em vez de países individuais. Portanto, existem mapas da Península Ibérica e do Sudeste Europeu, mas não existem mapas separados para Portugal ou Romênia. Em alguns casos, foi necessária a omissão de pequena porção de uma região ou país, descrito no título do mapa. Têm sido evitados os mapas embutidos, apesar de terem sido feitas exceções para ilustrar algumas ilhas ou grupos de ilhas isolados.

Os símbolos dos mapas usados para as características dadas (legendas para mapas, páginas x-xii) são geralmente semelhantes em todas as escalas dos mapas, apesar de serem reduzidos em tamanho nas escalas menores. Os símbolos mais usados foram dispostos na página xi.

Nenhum aspecto de apresentação de mapas, mostrou-se mais dramático recentemente, do que a reprodução cartográfica do relêvo. Os editores acreditam que o método mais efetivo para representá-lo é a reprodução vista do alto ou a técnica do sombreamento das colinas, que usa variações de tonalidades claras para escuras, para indicar o declive e a forma dos aspectos dos relêvos, por meio de ilustrações. Este Atlas usa relêvo sombreado em todas as cinco séries de mapas, com exceção de uma. Nos mapas de 1:6 000 000 e 1:3 000 000, aparece em combinação com variações de cores das altitudes, que mostram variações em elevação por meio de reflexão da luz, matiz e intensidade.

Na porção conclusiva do Atlas, estão várias tabelas e sumários para referências gerais. O cenário do mundo (páginas 289-320) é uma secção separada dos mapas especializados. Estes mapas sintetizam os padrões do ambiente físico do homem e alguma das suas mais importantes atividades econômicas, tendências políticas e distribuições culturais. Esta secção está baseada nas mais recentes informações disponíveis, tomadas de uma variedade de fontes, e adaptadas pelos editores. Em seguida, está um glossário completo de termos geográficos (páginas *I•1–I•7*). As tabelas das páginas *I•8–I•9*, "Principais Mudanças Geográficas desde 1969," apresentam uma seleção das numerosas revisões de mapas feitas desde a primeira edição do Atlas. A tabela de informação mundial (páginas *I•10–I•13*) registra a área, população e "status" político para cada unidade política principal. As maiores áreas metropolitanas do mundo, estão relacionadas na página *I•14*. É seguido por uma lista completa das principais cidades do mundo, com as respectivas populações (páginas *I•15–I•27*). Finalmente, o índice dá referências para a localização do mapa—página do mapa, latitude e longitude—com mais de 160 000 nomes.

SUMMARY OF CONTENTS

ADVISERS, CONTRIBUTORS, EDITORS AND STAFF ii
FOREWORD iii
SUMMARY OF CONTENTS vi
LIST OF MAPS vi–vii
LEGEND TO MAPS x–xii
WORLD AND REGIONAL INDEX MAPS xiii–xv
SELECTED MAP REFERENCES xvi
MAPS (see *List of Maps,* vi–vii) 1–288
World, Ocean, and Continent Maps 1–19
Regional Maps 20–258
Metropolitan Area Maps 259–288
WORLD SCENE 289–320
GLOSSARY AND ABBREVIATIONS OF GEOGRAPHICAL TERMS *I·1—I·7*
MAJOR GEOGRAPHIC CHANGES SINCE 1969 *I·8—I·9*
WORLD INFORMATION TABLE *I·10—I·13*
METROPOLITAN AREAS TABLE *I·14*
POPULATION OF CITIES AND TOWNS *I·15—I·27*
INDEX *I·28*

INHALTSVERZEICHNIS

BERATER, MITARBEITER, HERAUSGEBER UND REDAKTION ii
VORWORT iii–iv
INHALTSVERZEICHNIS vi
KARTENVERZEICHNIS vii
ZEICHENERKLÄRUNG x–xii
WELT- UND REGIONALE INDEXKARTEN xiii–xv
REGISTER WICHTIGER GEOGRAPHISCHER NAMEN xvi
KARTEN (siehe *Kartenverzeichnis,* vii) 1–288
Weltkarten, Karten der Ozeane und Erdteile 1–19
Regionalkarten 20–258
Karten von Stadtregionen 259–288
WELT-PANORAMA 289–320
VERZEICHNIS UND ABKÜRZUNGEN GEOGRAPHISCHER BEGRIFFE *I·1—I·7*
WICHTIGE GEOGRAPHISCHE VERÄNDERUNGEN SEIT 1969 *I·8—I·9*
WELT-INFORMATIONSTABELLE *I·10—I·13*
TABELLE DER STADTREGIONEN *I·14*
EINWOHNERZAHLEN VON GROSS-STÄDTEN *I·15—I·27*
REGISTER *I·28*

SUMARIO DEL CONTENIDO

ASESORES, COLABORADORES, REDACTORES Y AYUDANTES ii
PREFACIO iv
SUMARIO DEL CONTENIDO vi
LISTA DE MAPAS vii–viii
LEYENDAS PARA MAPAS x–xii
INDICE DE LOS MAPAS DEL MUNDO Y REGIONALES xiii–xv
SELECCIONES DE REFERENCIAS DE LOS MAPAS xvi
MAPAS (véase *Lista de Mapas,* vii–viii) 1–288
Mapas del Mundo, Océanos y Continentes 1–19
Mapas Regionales 20–258
Mapas de las Áreas Metropolitanas 259–288
PERSPECTIVA DEL MUNDO 289–320
GLOSARIO Y ABREVIACIONES DE TÉRMINOS GEOGRÁFICOS *I·1—I·7*
CAMBIOS GEOGRÁFICOS IMPORTANTES DESDE 1969 *I·8—I·9*
TABLA DE INFORMACIÓN MUNDIAL *I·10—I·13*
TABLA DE LAS ÁREAS METROPOLITANAS *I·14*
HABITANTES EN LAS CIUDADES Y POBLACIONES *I·15—I·27*
INDICE *I·28*

TABLE DES MATIÈRES

CONSEILLERS, COLLABORATEURS, RÉDACTEURS ET PERSONNEL ii
AVANT-PROPOS iv–v
TABLE DES MATIÈRES vi
LISTE DES CARTES viii–ix
LÉGENDE DES CARTES x–xii
INDEX DES CARTES DU MONDE ET DES CARTES RÉGIONALES xiii–xv
INDEX CARTOGRAPHIQUE ABRÉGÉ xvi
CARTES (voir *Liste des Cartes,* viii–ix) 1–288
Cartes du Monde, des Océans et des Continents 1–19
Cartes Régionales 20–258
Cartes des Zones Métropolitaines 259–288
LE MONDE AUJOURD'HUI 289–320
GLOSSAIRE ET ABRÉVIATIONS DE TERMES GÉOGRAPHIQUES *I·1—I·7*
PRINCIPALES MODIFICATIONS GÉOGRAPHIQUES DEPUIS 1969 *I·8—I·9*
TABLE D'INFORMATIONS MONDIALES *I·10—I·13*
TABLE DES ZONES MÉTROPOLITAINES *I·14*
POPULATION DES GRANDS CENTRES ET DES VILLES *I·15—I·27*
INDEX *28*

SUMÁRIO

EDITORES, ASSESSORES E COLABORADORES ii
PREFÁCIO v
SUMÁRIO vi
LISTA DE MAPAS ix
LEGENDAS DOS MAPAS x–xii
ÍNDICE DES MAPAS DO MUNDO E REGIONAIS xiii–xv
REFERÊNCIAS A MAPAS SELECIONADAS xvi
MAPAS (ver a *Lista de Mapas,* ix) 1–288
Mapas do mundo, dos oceanos e dos continentes 1–19
Mapas regionais 20–258
Mapas das áreas metropolitanas 259–288
PERSPECTIVA DO MUNDO 289–320
GLOSSÁRIO E ABREVIAÇÕES DE TERMOS GEOGRÁFICOS *I·1—I·7*
PRINCIPAIS MUDANÇAS GEOGRÁFICAS DESDE 1969 *I·8—I·9*
TABELA DE INFORMAÇÕES MUNDIAIS *I·10—I·13*
TABELA DAS ÁREAS METROPOLITANAS *I·14*
POPULAÇAÕ DOS CENTROS URBANOS *I·15—I·27*
ÍNDICE *I·28*

List of Maps

WORLD, OCEAN, and CONTINENT MAPS

* Introduction 1
1:75 World: Political 2–3
1:75 World: Physical 4–5
1:48 Pacific and Indian Oceans 6–7
1:48 Atlantic Ocean 8
1:24 Antarctica 9
1:24 Europe and Africa 10–11
1:24 Asia 12–13
1:24 Australia and Oceania 14–15
1:24 North America 16–17
1:24 South America 18–19

REGIONAL MAPS

Introduction 20–21

Europe

1:12 Europe 22–23
1:6 Northern Europe 24–25
1:3 Southern Scandinavia 26–27
1:3 British Isles 28–29
1:3 Central Europe 30–31
1:3 France and the Alps 32–33
1:3 Spain and Portugal 34–35
1:3 Italy 36–37
1:3 Southeastern Europe 38–39
1:1 Stockholm - Karlstad 40
1:1 København - Malmö - Kiel 41
1:1 London - Birmingham - Cardiff 42–43
1:1 Dublin - Manchester - Newcastle upon Tyne 44–45
1:1 Glasgow - Edinburgh - Aberdeen 46–47
1:1 Dublin - Belfast - Cork 48–49
1:1 Paris - London - Bruxelles 50–51
1:1 Amsterdam - Düsseldorf - Hamburg 52–53
1:1 Berlin - Hamburg - Praha 54–55
1:1 Bruxelles - Frankfurt - Stuttgart 56–57
1:1 Zürich - Genève - Strasbourg 58–59
1:1 Nürnberg - München 60
1:1 Wien - Brno - Linz 61
1:1 Lyon - Marseille - Milano 62–63
1:1 München - Venezia - Firenze 64–65
1:1 Roma - Firenze - Napoli 66–67
1:1 Napoli - Messina - Bari 68–69
1:1 Palermo - Catania - Messina 70
1:1 Cagliari - Sassari 71

Union of Soviet Socialist Republics

1:12 Western and Central Soviet Union 72–73
1:12 Eastern and Central Soviet Union 74–75
1:3 Baltic and Moscow Regions 76–77
1:3 Ukraine 78–79
1:3 Volga Region 80–81
1:1 Moskva - Tula - Kalinin 82
1:1 Doneck - Vorošilovgrad - Rostov 83
1:3 Caucasus and Transcaucasia 84
1:3 Eastern Soviet Central Asia 85
1:6 Central Soviet Union 86–87
1:6 Lake Baikal Region 88
1:6 Soviet Far East 89

Asia

1:12 China, Japan and Korea 90–91
1:3 Japan 92–93
1:1 Tōkyō - Nagoya - Kyōto 94–95
1:1 Ōsaka - Hiroshima - Fukuoka 96–97
1:3 Northeast China and Korea 98–99
1:3 East and Southeast China 100–101
1:6 Interior China 102–103
1:1 Shenyang - Fushun (Mukden - Fushun) 104
1:1 Beijing - Tianjin (Peking - Tientsin) 105
1:1 Shanghai - Nanjing (Shanghai - Nanking) 106
1:1 Chongqing - Chengdu (Chungking - Chengtu) 107
1:12 Southeast Asia 108–109
1:6 Burma, Thailand and Indochina 110–111
1:6 Malaysia and Western Indonesia 112–113
1:3 Malaya, Singapore and Northern Sumatra 114
1:3 Java • Lesser Sunda Islands 115
1:3 Philippines 116–117
1:12 India, Pakistan and Southwest Asia 118–119
1:6 Northern India and Pakistan 120–121
1:6 Southern India and Sri Lanka 122
1:3 Punjab and Kashmir 123
1:3 Ganges Lowland and Nepal 124–125
1:1 Calcutta - Dacca - Jamshedpur 126–127
1:6 The Middle East 128–129
1:3 Turkey and Cyprus 130–131
1:1 Yerushalayim - Dimashq (Jerusalem - Damascus) 132–133

Africa

1:12 Western North Africa 134–135
1:12 Eastern North Africa 136–137
1:12 Southern Africa 138–139
1:6 Egypt and Sudan 140–141
1:1 Al-Qāhirah - As-Suways (Cairo - Suez) 142–143
1:6 Ethiopia, Somalia and Yemen 144–145
1:6 Libya and Chad 146–147
1:6 Northwestern Africa 148–149
1:6 West Africa 150–151
1:6 Western Congo Basin 152–153
1:6 East Africa and Eastern Congo Basin 154–155
1:6 Southern Africa and Madagascar 156–157
1:3 South Africa 158–159

Australia/Oceania

1:12 Australia 160–161
1:6 Western and Central Australia 162–163
1:6 Northern Australia and New Guinea 164–165
1:6 Eastern Australia 166–167
1:1 Perth • Adelaide 168
1:1 Melbourne - Geelong - Ballarat 169
1:1 Sydney - Newcastle 170
1:1 Brisbane • Canberra 171
1:3 New Zealand 172–173
Various Scales
Islands of the Pacific 174–175

Anglo America

1:12 Canada 176–177
1:12 United States 178–179
1:6 Alaska and Yukon 180–181
1:3 Southwestern Canada 182–183
1:3 South-Central Canada 184–185
1:3 Southeastern Canada 186–187
1:3 Northeastern United States 188–189
1:3 Great Lakes Region 190–191
1:3 Southeastern United States 192–193
1:3 Mississippi Valley 194–195
1:3 Southern Great Plains 196–197
1:3 Northern Great Plains 198–199
1:3 Southern Rocky Mountains 200–201
1:3 Northwestern United States 202–203
1:3 California and Nevada 204–205
1:1 Montréal - Québec 206
1:1 Boston - New York - Albany 207
1:1 New York - Philadelphia - Washington - Norfolk 208–209
1:1 New York - Buffalo 210–211
1:1 Toronto - Ottawa 212–213
1:1 Pittsburgh - Cleveland - Detroit 214–215
1:1 Chicago - Detroit - Milwaukee 216–217
1:1 Indianapolis - Cincinnati - Louisville 218
1:1 St. Louis - Springfield 219
1:1 Miami - Tampa - Orlando 220–221
1:1 Houston - Dallas - Austin 222–223
1:1 Vancouver - Seattle - Portland 224–225
1:1 San Francisco - Reno - Bakersfield 226–227
1:1 Los Angeles - San Diego 228
Various Scales
Hawaii 229

Latin America

1:12 Middle America 230–231
1:6 Mexico 232–233
1:3 Central Mexico 234–235
1:3 Central America 236–237
1:6 Caribbean Region 238–239
Various Scales
Islands of the West Indies 240–241
1:12 Northern South America 242–243
1:12 Southern South America 244–245
1:6 Columbia, Ecuador, Venezuela and Guyana 246–247
1:6 Peru, Bolivia and Western Brazil 248–249
1:6 Northeastern Brazil 250–251
1:6 Central Argentina and Chile 252–253
1:6 Southern Argentina and Chile 254
1:6 Southeastern Brazil 255
1:1 Rio de Janeiro - São Paulo 256–257
1:1 Buenos Aires - Montevideo 258

METROPOLITAN AREA MAPS (1:300,000)

Introduction 259
London 260
Paris 261
Manchester - Liverpool 262
Ruhr Area 263

*Scale in millions

Berlin 264
Wien 264
Budapest 264
Leningrad 265
Moskva 265
Madrid 266
Milano 266
Lisboa 266
Barcelona 266
Roma 267
Athínai 267
İstanbul 267
Tehrān 267
Tōkyō - Yokohama 268
Krung Thep (Bangkok) 269
Thanh-pho Ho Chi Minh (Sai-gon) 269
Jakarta 269
Shanghai 269
T'aipei 269
Manila 269
Ōsaka - Kōbe - Kyōto 270
Beijing (Peking) 271
Sŏul 271
Singapore 271
Hong Kong 271
Delhi 272
Bombay 272
Calcutta 272
Lagos 273
Kinshasa - Brazzaville 273
Al-Qāhirah (Cairo) 273
Johannesburg 273
Sydney 274
Melbourne 274
Montréal 275
Toronto 275
New York 276–277
Chicago 278
Cleveland 279
Pittsburgh 279
Los Angeles 280
Detroit - Windsor 281
San Francisco - Oakland - San Jose 282
Boston 283
Buffalo - Niagara Falls 284
Baltimore 284
Washington 284
Philadelphia 285
Ciudad de México 286
La Habana 286
Caracas 286
Lima 286
Santiago 286
Rio de Janeiro 287
São Paulo 287
Buenos Aires 288

Kartenverzeichnis

WELTKARTEN, KARTEN DER OZEANE UND ERDTEILE

* Einleitung 1
1:75 Erde: Politisch 2–3
1:75 Erde: Physisch 4–5
1:48 Pazifischer und Indischer Ozean 6–7
1:48 Atlantischer Ozean 8
1:24 Antarktis 9
1:24 Europa und Afrika 10–11
1:24 Asien 12–13
1:24 Australien und Ozeanien 14–15
1:24 Nordamerika 16–17
1:24 Südamerika 18–19

REGIONALKARTEN

Einleitung 20–21

EUROPA

1:12 Europa 22–23
1:6 Nordeuropa 24–25
1:3 Südskandinavien 26–27
1:3 Britische Inseln 28–29
1:3 Mitteleuropa 30–31
1:3 Frankreich und die Alpen 32–33
1:3 Spanien und Portugal 34–35
1:3 Italien 36–37
1:3 Südosteuropa 38–39
1:1 Stockholm - Karlstad 40
1:1 København - Malmö - Kiel 41
1:1 London - Birmingham - Cardiff 42–43
1:1 Dublin - Manchester - Newcastle upon Tyne 44–45
1:1 Glasgow - Edinburgh - Aberdeen 46–47
1:1 Dublin - Belfast - Cork 48–49
1:1 Paris - London - Bruxelles 50–51
1:1 Amsterdam - Düsseldorf - Hamburg 52–53
1:1 Berlin - Hamburg - Praha 54–55
1:1 Bruxelles - Frankfurt - Stuttgart 56–57
1:1 Zürich - Genève - Strasbourg 58–59
1:1 Nürnberg - München 60
1:1 Wien - Brno - Linz 61
1:1 Lyon - Marseille - Milano 62–63
1:1 München - Venezia - Firenze 64–65
1:1 Roma - Firenze - Napoli 66–67
1:1 Napoli - Messina - Bari 68–69
1:1 Palermo - Catania - Messina 70
1:1 Cagliari - Sassari 71

Union der Sozialistischen Sowjetrepubliken

1:12 Westliche und zentrale Sowjetunion 72–73
1:12 Östliche und zentrale Sowjetunion 74–75
1:3 Baltenland und Mittelrussland 76–77
1:3 Ukraine 78–79
1:3 Wolgagebiet 80–81
1:1 Moskva - Tula - Kalinin 82
1:1 Doneck - Vorošilovgrad - Rostov 83
1:3 Kaukasus und Transkaukasien 84
1:3 Östliches Sowjet-Mittelasien 85
1:6 Sowjet-Mittelasien 86–87
1:6 Baikalseegebiet 88
1:6 Sowjet-Ostasien 89

Asien

1:12 China, Japan und Korea 90–91
1:3 Japan 92–93
1:1 Tōkyō - Nagoya - Kyōto 94–95
1:1 Ōsaka - Hiroshima - Fukuoka 96–97
1:3 Nordostchina und Korea 98–99
1:3 Ost- und Südostchina 100–101
1:6 Innerchina 102–103
1:1 Shenyang - Fushun (Mukden - Fushun) 104
1:1 Beijing - Tianjin (Peking - Tientsin) 105
1:1 Shanghai - Nanjing (Shanghai - Nanking) 106
1:1 Chongqing - Chengdu (Chungking - Chengtu) 107
1:12 Südostasien 108–109
1:6 Burma, Thailand und Indochina 110–111
1:6 Malaysia und Westliches Indonesien 112–113
1:3 Malaya, Singapur und Nordsumatra 114
1:3 Java • Kleine Sundainseln 115
1:3 Philippinen 116–117
1:12 Indien, Pakistan und Südwestasien 118–119
1:6 Nordindien und Pakistan 120–121
1:6 Südindien und Sri Lanka 122
1:3 Pandschab und Kaschmir 123
1:3 Gangestiefland und Nepal 124–125
1:1 Calcutta - Dacca - Jamshedpur 126–127
1:6 Vorderasien 128–129
1:3 Türkei und Zypern 130–131
1:1 Yerushalayim - Dimashq (Jerusalem - Damascus) 132–133

Afrika

1:12 West Nordafrika 134–135
1:12 Ost Nordafrika 136–137
1:12 Südafrika 138–139
1:6 Ägypten und Sudan 140–141
1:1 Al-Qāhirah - As-Suways (Cairo - Suez) 142–143
1:6 Äthiopien, Somalia und Jemen 144–145
1:6 Libyen und Tschad 146–147
1:6 Nordwestafrika 148–149
1:6 Westafrika 150–151
1:6 Westliches Kongobecken 152–153
1:6 Ostafrika und Östliches Kongobecken 154–155
1:6 Südafrika und Madagaskar 156–157
1:3 Republik Südafrika 158–159

Australien/Ozeanien

1:12 Australien 160–161
1:6 West- und Mittelaustralien 162–163
1:6 Nordaustralien und Neuguinea 164–165
1:6 Ostaustralien 166–167
1:1 Perth • Adelaide 168
1:1 Melbourne - Geelong - Ballarat 169
1:1 Sydney - Newcastle 170
1:1 Brisbane • Canberra 171
1:3 Neuseeland 172–173
verschiedene Massstäbe Pazifische Inseln 174–175

Anglo-Amerika

1:12 Kanada 176–177
1:12 Vereinigte Staaten 178–179
1:6 Alaska und Yukon 180–181
1:3 Südwestkanada 182–183
1:3 Südliches Mittelkanada 184–185
1:3 Südostkanada 186–187
1:3 Nordöstliche Vereinigte Staaten 188–189
1:3 Grosse Seen-Region 190–191
1:3 Südöstliche Vereinigte Staaten 192–193
1:3 Mississippi-Tiefland 194–195
1:3 Südliche Grosse Ebenen 196–197
1:3 Nördliche Grosse Ebenen 198–199
1:3 Südliches Felsengebirge 200–201
1:3 Nordwestliche Vereinigte Staaten 202–203
1:3 Kalifornien und Nevada 204–205
1:1 Montréal - Québec 206
1:1 Boston - New York - Albany 207
1:1 New York - Philadelphia - Washington - Norfolk 208–209
1:1 New York - Buffalo 210–211
1:1 Toronto - Ottawa 212–213
1:1 Pittsburgh - Cleveland - Detroit 214–215
1:1 Chicago - Detroit - Milwaukee 216–217
1:1 Indianapolis - Cincinnati - Louisville 218
1:1 St. Louis - Springfield 219
1:1 Miami - Tampa - Orlando 220–221
1:1 Houston - Dallas - Austin 222–223
1:1 Vancouver - Seattle - Portland 224–225
1:1 San Francisco - Reno - Bakersfield 226–227
1:1 Los Angeles - San Diego 228
verschiedene Massstäbe Hawaii 229

Latein-Amerika

1:12 Mittelamerika 230–231
1:6 Mexiko 232–233
1:3 Mittelmexiko 234–235
1:3 Zentralamerika 236–237
1:6 Mittelamerikanische Inselwelt 238–239
verschiedene Massstäbe Westindische Inseln 240–241
1:12 Südamerika, nördlicher Teil 242–243
1:12 Südamerika, südlicher Teil 244–245
1:6 Kolumbien, Ecuador, Venezuela und Guayana 246–247
1:6 Peru, Bolivien und Westliches Brasilien 248–249
1:6 Nordostbrasilien 250–251
1:6 Mittelargentinien und Mittelchile 252–253
1:6 Südliches Argentinien und Südliches Chile 254
1:6 Südostbrasilien 255
1:1 Rio de Janeiro - São Paulo 256–257
1:1 Buenos Aires - Montevideo 258

KARTEN VON STADTREGIONEN (1:300 000)

Einleitung 259
London 260
Paris 261
Manchester - Liverpool 262
Ruhr Area 263
Berlin 264
Wien 264
Budapest 264
Leningrad 265
Moskva 265
Madrid 266
Milano 266
Lisboa 266
Barcelona 266
Roma 267
Athínai 267
İstanbul 267
Tehrān 267
Tōkyō - Yokohama 268
Krung Thep (Bangkok) 269
Thanh-pho Ho Chi Minh (Sai-gon) 269
Jakarta 269
Shanghai 269
T'aipei 269
Manila 269
Ōsaka - Kōbe - Kyōto 270
Beijing (Peking) 271
Sŏul 271
Singapore 271
Hong Kong 271
Delhi 272
Bombay 272
Calcutta 272
Lagos 273
Kinshasa - Brazzaville 273
Al-Qāhirah (Cairo) 273
Johannesburg 273
Sydney 274
Melbourne 274
Montréal 275
Toronto 275
New York 276–277
Chicago 278
Cleveland 279
Pittsburgh 279
Los Angeles 280
Detroit - Windsor 281
San Francisco - Oakland - San Jose 282
Boston 283
Buffalo - Niagara Falls 284
Baltimore 284
Washington 284
Philadelphia 285
Ciudad de México 286
La Habana 286
Caracas 286
Lima 286
Santiago 286
Rio de Janeiro 287
São Paulo 287
Buenos Aires 288

***Im massstäb millionen**

Lista de Mapas

MAPAS DEL MUNDO, OCÉANOS Y CONTINENTES

* Introducción 1
1:75 Mundo: Político 2–3
1:75 Mundo: Físico 4–5
1:48 Oceános Pacífico e Indico 6–7
1:48 Oceáno Atlántico 8
1:24 Antártida 9
1:24 Europa y África 10–11
1:24 Asia 12–13
1:24 Australia y Oceanía 14–15
1:24 América del Norte 16–17
1:24 América del Sur 18–19

***Escala en millones**

MAPAS REGIONALES

Introducción 20–21

Europa

1:12 Europa 22–23
1:6 Europa Septentrional 24–25
1:3 Escandinavia Meridional 26–27
1:3 Islas Británicas 28–29
1:3 Europa Central 30–31
1:3 Francia y los Alpes 32–33
1:3 España y Portugal 34–35
1:3 Italia 36–37
1:3 Europa Sud-oriental 38–39
1:1 Stockholm - Karlstad 40
1:1 København - Malmö - Kiel 41
1:1 London - Birmingham - Cardiff 42–43
1:1 Dublin - Manchester - Newcastle upon Tyne 44–45
1:1 Glasgow - Edinburgh - Aberdeen 46–47
1:1 Dublin - Belfast - Cork 48–49
1:1 Paris - London - Bruxelles 50–51
1:1 Amsterdam - Düsseldorf - Hamburg 52–53
1:1 Berlin - Hamburg - Praha 54–55
1:1 Bruxelles - Frankfurt - Stuttgart 56–57
1:1 Zürich - Genève - Strasbourg 58–59
1:1 Nürnberg - München 60
1:1 Wien - Brno - Linz 61
1:1 Lyon - Marseille - Milano 62–63
1:1 München - Venezia - Firenze 64–65
1:1 Roma - Firenze - Napoli 66–67
1:1 Napoli - Messina - Bari 68–69
1:1 Palermo - Catania - Messina 70
1:1 Cagliari - Sassari 71

Unión de Repúblicas Socialistas Soviéticas

1:12 Unión Soviética Occidental y Central 72–73
1:12 Unión Soviética Oriental y Central 74–75
1:3 Regiones del Báltico y de Moscú 76–77
1:3 Ucrania 78–79
1:3 Región del Volga 80–81
1:1 Moskva - Tula - Kalinin 82
1:1 Doneck - Vorošilovgrad - Rostov 83
1:3 Cáucaso y Transcaucasia 84
1:3 Asia Central Soviética: zona oriental 85

1:6 Unión Soviética Central 86–87
1:6 Región del Lago Baikal 88
1:6 Extremo Oriental Soviético 89

Asia

1:12 China, Japón y Corea 90–91
1:3 Japón 92–93
1:1 Tōkyō - Nagoya - Kyōto 94–95
1:1 Ōsaka - Hiroshima - Fukuoka 96–97
1:3 China Nor-oriental y Corea 98–99
1:3 Este y Sudeste de la China 100–101
1:6 China Interior 102–103
1:1 Shenyang - Fushun (Mukden - Fushun) 104
1:1 Beijing - Tianjin (Peking - Tientsin) 105
1:1 Shanghai - Nanjing (Shanghai - Nanking) 106
1:1 Chongqing - Chengdu (Chungking - Chengtu) 107
1:12 Asia Sud-oriental 108–109
1:6 Birmania, Siam e Indochina 110–111
1:6 Malasia e Indonesia Occidental 112–113
1:3 Malaya, Singapur y Sumatra Septentrional 114
1:3 Java • Islas Menores de la Sonda 115
1:3 Filipinas 116–117
1:12 India, Pakistán y Asia Sud-occidental 118–119
1:6 India Septentrional y Pakistán 120–121
1:6 India Meridional y Sri Lanka 122
1:3 Punjab y Cachemira 123
1:3 Llanuras del Ganges y Nepal 124–125
1:1 Calcutta - Dacca - Jamshedpur 126–127
1:6 El Medio Oriente 128–129
1:3 Turquía y Chipre 130–131
1:1 Yerushalayim - Dimashq (Jerusalem - Damascus) 132–133

África

1:12 Región Occidental de África Septentrional 134–135
1:12 Región Oriental de África Septentrional 136–137
1:12 África Meridional 138–139
1:6 Egipto y Sudán 140–141
1:1 Al-Qāhirah - As-Suways (Cairo - Suez) 142–143
1:6 Etiopía, Somalía y Yemen 144–145
1:6 Libia y el Chad 146–147
1:6 África Nor-occidental 148–149
1:6 África Occidental 150–151
1:6 Cuenca Occidental del Congo 152–153
1:6 África Oriental y Cuenca Oriental del Congo 154–155
1:6 África Meridional y Madagascar 156–157
1:3 Sudáfrica 158–159

Australia/Oceanía

1:12 Australia 160–161
1:6 Australia Centro-occidental 162–163
1:6 Australia Septentrional y Nueva Guinea 164–165
1:6 Australia Oriental 166–167
1:1 Perth • Adelaide 168
1:1 Melbourne - Geelong - Ballarat 169
1:1 Sydney - Newcastle 170
1:1 Brisbane • Canberra 171
1:3 Nueva Zelanda 172–173
Varias Escalas
Islas del Pacífico 174–175

América Anglosajona

1:12 Canadá 176–177
1:12 Estados Unidos 178–179
1:6 Alaska y Yukón 180–181
1:3 Canadá Sud-occidental 182–183
1:3 Centro Meridonal del Canadá 184–185
1:3 Canadá Sud-oriental 186–187
1:3 Nor-este de los Estados Unidos 188–189
1:3 Región de los Grandes Lagos 190–191
1:3 Sud-este de los Estados Unidos 192–193
1:3 Valle del Misisipi 194–195
1:3 Grandes Llanos: zona meridional 196–197
1:3 Grandes Llanos: zona septentrional 198–199
1:3 Montañas Rocosas: zona meridional 200–201
1:3 Nor-oeste de los Estados Unidos 202–203
1:3 California y Nevada 204–205
1:1 Montréal - Québec 206
1:1 Boston - New York - Albany 207
1:1 New York - Philadelphia - Washington - Norfolk 208–209
1:1 New York - Buffalo 210–211
1:1 Toronto - Ottawa 212–213
1:1 Pittsburgh - Cleveland - Detroit 214–215
1:1 Chicago - Detroit - Milwaukee 216–217
1:1 Indianapolis - Cincinnati - Louisville 218
1:1 St. Louis - Springfield 219
1:1 Miami - Tampa - Orlando 220–221
1:1 Houston - Dallas - Austin 222–223
1:1 Vancouver - Seattle - Portland 224–225
1:1 San Francisco - Reno - Bakersfield 226–227
1:1 Los Angeles - San Diego 228
Varias Escalas
Hawaii 229

América Latina

1:12 México, Centroamérica y Las Antillas 230–231
1:6 México 232–233
1:3 México Central 234–235
1:3 América Central 236–237
1:6 Región del Caribe 238–239
Varias Escalas
Islas de las Antillas 240–241
1:12 América del Sur: zona septentrional 242–243
1:12 América del Sur: zona meridional 244–245
1:6 Colombia, Ecuador, Venezuela y Guyana 246–247
1:6 Perú, Bolivia y Brasil Occidental 248–249
1:6 Brasil Nor-oriental 250–251
1:6 Argentina y Chile: zonas centrales 252–253
1:6 Argentina y Chile: zonas meridionales 254
1:6 Brasil Sud-oriental 255
1:1 Rio de Janeiro - São Paulo 256–257
1:1 Buenos Aires - Montevideo 258

MAPAS DE LAS ÁREAS METROPOLITANAS (1:300 000)

Introducción 259
London 260
Paris 261
Manchester - Liverpool 262
Ruhr Area 263
Berlin 264
Wien 264
Budapest 264
Leningrad 265
Moskva 265
Madrid 266
Milano 266
Lisboa 266
Barcelona 266
Roma 267
Athínai 267
İstanbul 267
Tehrān 267
Tōkyō - Yokohama 268
Krung Thep (Bangkok) 269
Thanh-pho Ho Chi Minh (Sai-gon) 269
Jakarta 269
Shanghai 269
T'aipei 269
Manila 269
Ōsaka - Kōbe - Kyōto 270
Beijing (Peking) 271
Sŏul 271
Singapore 271
Hong Kong 271
Delhi 272
Bombay 272
Calcutta 272
Lagos 273
Kinshasa - Brazzaville 273
Al-Qāhirah (Cairo) 273
Johannesburg 273
Sydney 274
Melbourne 274
Montréal 275
Toronto 275
New York 276–277
Chicago 278
Cleveland 279
Pittsburgh 279
Los Angeles 280
Detroit - Windsor 281
San Francisco - Oakland - San Jose 282
Boston 283
Buffalo - Niagara Falls 284
Baltimore 284
Washington 284
Philadelphia 285
Ciudad de México 286
La Habana 286
Caracas 286
Lima 286
Santiago 286
Rio de Janeiro 287
São Paulo 287
Buenos Aires 288

Liste des Cartes

CARTES DU MONDE, DES OCÉANS ET DES CONTINENTS

* Introduction 1
1:75 Monde: Politique 2–3
1:75 Monde: Physique 4–5
1:48 Océans Pacifique et Indien 6–7
1:48 Océan Atlantique 8
1:24 Antarctique 9
1:24 Europe et Afrique 10–11
1:24 Asie 12–13
1:24 Australie et Océanie 14–15
1:24 Amérique du Nord 16–17
1:24 Amérique du Sud 18–19

CARTES RÉGIONALES

Introduction 20–21

Europe

1:12 Europe 22–23
1:6 Europe Septentrionale 24–25
1:3 Scandinavie Méridionale 26–27
1:3 Îles Britanniques 28–29
1:3 Europe Centrale 30–31
1:3 France et Alpes 32–33
1:3 Espagne et Portugal 34–35
1:3 Italie 36–37
1:3 Europe du Sud-Est 38–39
1:1 Stockholm - Karlstad 40
1:1 København - Malmö - Kiel 41
1:1 London - Birmingham - Cardiff 42–43
1:1 Dublin - Manchester - Newcastle upon Tyne 44–45
1:1 Glasgow - Edinburgh - Aberdeen 46–47
1:1 Dublin - Belfast - Cork 48–49
1:1 Paris - London - Bruxelles 50–51
1:1 Amsterdam - Düsseldorf - Hamburg 52–53
1:1 Berlin - Hamburg - Praha 54–55
1:1 Bruxelles - Frankfurt - Stuttgart 56–57
1:1 Zürich - Genève - Strasbourg 58–59
1:1 Nürnberg - München 60
1:1 Wien - Brno - Linz 61
1:1 Lyon - Marseille - Milano 62–63
1:1 München - Venezia - Firenze 64–65
1:1 Roma - Firenze - Napoli 66–67
1:1 Napoli - Messina - Bari 68–69
1:1 Palermo - Catania - Messina 70
1:1 Cagliari - Sassari 71

Union des Républiques Socialistes Soviétiques

1:12 Union Soviétique Occidentale et Centrale 72–73
1:12 Union Soviétique Orientale et Centrale 74–75
1:3 Républiques Baltes et la Région de Moscou 76–77
1:3 Ukraine 78–79
1:3 Région de la Volga 80–81
1:1 Moskva - Tula - Kalinin 82
1:1 Doneck - Vorošilovgrad - Rostov 83
1:3 Caucasie et Transcaucasie 84
1:3 Asie Centrale Soviétique, partie Orientale 85
1:6 Union Soviétique Centrale 86–87
1:6 Région du Lac Baïkal 88
1:6 Extrême Orient Soviétique 89

Asie

1:12 Chine, Japon et Corée 90–91
1:3 Japon 92–93
1:1 Tōkyō - Nagoya - Kyōto 94–95
1:1 Ōsaka - Hiroshima - Fukuoka 96–97
1:3 Nord-Est de la Chine et Corée 98–99
1:3 Chine de l'Est et du Sud-Est 100–101
1:6 Chine Intérieure 102–103
1:1 Shenyang - Fushun (Mukden - Fushun) 104
1:1 Beijing - Tianjin (Peking - Tientsin) 105
1:1 Shanghai - Nanjing (Shanghai - Nanking) 106
1:1 Chongqing - Chengdu (Chungking - Chengtu) 107
1:12 Asie du Sud-Est 108–109
1:6 Birmanie, Thaïlande et Indochine 110–111
1:6 Malaisie et Indonésie Occidentale 112–113
1:3 Malaya, Singapour et Sumatra Septentrional 114
1:3 Java • Petites Îles de la Sonde 115
1:3 Philippines 116–117
1:12 Inde, Pakistan et Asie du Sud-Ouest 118–119
1:6 Inde Septentrionale et Pakistan 120–121
1:6 Inde Méridionale et Sri Lanka 122
1:3 Punjab et Cachemire 123
1:3 Plaine du Grange et Népal 124–125
1:1 Calcutta - Dacca - Jamshedpur 126–127
1:6 Le Moyen - Orient 128–129
1:3 Turquie et Chypre 130–131
1:1 Yerushalayim - Dimashq (Jerusalem - Damascus) 132–133

Afrique

1:12 Afrique du Nord Occidentale 134–135
1:12 Afrique du Nord Orientale 136–137
1:12 Afrique Méridionale 138–139
1:6 Égypte et Soudan 140–141
1:1 Al-Qāhirah - As-Suways (Cairo - Suez) 142–143
1:6 Ethiopie, Somalie et Yemen 144–145
1:6 Libye et Tchad 146–147
1:6 Afrique du Nord-Ouest 148–149
1:6 Afrique Occidentale 150–151
1:6 Bassin du Congo, partie Occidentale 152–153
1:6 Afrique Orientale et Bassin du Congo, partie Orientale 154–155
1:6 Afrique Méridionale et Madagascar 156–157
1:3 Afrique du Sud 158–159

Australie/Océanie

1:12 Australie 160–161
1:6 Australie Occidentale et Centrale 162–163
1:6 Australie Septentrionale et Nouvelle Guinée 164–165
1:6 Australie Orientale 166–167
1:1 Perth • Adelaide 168
1:1 Melbourne - Geelong - Ballarat 169
1:1 Sydney - Newcastle 170
1:1 Brisbane • Canberra 171
1:3 Nouvelle Zélande 172–173
Echelles Variées
Îles du Pacifique 174–175

Amérique Anglo-Saxonne

1:12 Canada 176–177
1:12 États-Unis 178–179
1:6 Alaska et Yukon 180–181
1:3 Sud-Ouest du Canada 182–183
1:3 Canada Central, partie Méridionale 184–185
1:3 Sud-Est du Canada 186–187
1:3 Nord-Est des États-Unis 188–189
1:3 Région des Grands Lacs 190–191
1:3 Sud-Est des États-Unis 192–193
1:3 Vallée du Mississippi 194–195
1:3 Grandes Plaines, partie Méridionale 196–197
1:3 Grandes Plaines, partie Septentrionale 198–199
1:3 Montagnes Rocheuses, partie Méridionale 200–201

*Echelle en millions

1:3 Nord-Ouest des États-Unis 202–203
1:3 Californie et Névada 204–205
1:1 Montréal - Québec 206
1:1 Boston - New York - Albany 207
1:1 New York - Philadelphia - Washington - Norfolk 208–209
1:1 New York - Buffalo 210–211
1:1 Toronto - Ottawa 212–213
1:1 Pittsburgh - Cleveland - Detroit 214–215
1:1 Chicago - Detroit - Milwaukee 216–217
1:1 Indianapolis - Cincinnati - Louisville 218
1:1 St. Louis - Springfield 219
1:1 Miami - Tampa - Orlando 220–221
1:1 Houston - Dallas - Austin 222–223
1:1 Vancouver - Seattle - Portland 224–225
1:1 San Francisco - Reno - Bakersfield 226–227
1:1 Los Angeles - San Diego 228
Echelles Variées
Hawaï 229

Amérique Latine

1:12 Mexique, Amérique Centrale et Région des Caraïbes 230–231
1:6 Mexique 232–233
1:3 Mexique Central 234–235
1:3 Amérique Centrale 236–237
1:6 Région des Caraïbes 238–239
Echelles Variées
Îles des Antilles 240–241
1:12 Amérique du Sud Septentrionale 242–243
1:12 Amérique du Sud Méridionale 244–245
1:6 Colombie, Équateur, Venezuela et Guyane 246–247
1:6 Pérou, Bolivie et Brésil Occidental 248–249
1:6 Nord-Est du Brésil 250–251
1:6 Argentine et Chili, parties Centrales 252–253
1:6 Argentine et Chili, parties Méridionales 254
1:6 Sud-Est du Brésil 255
1:1 Rio de Janeiro - São Paulo 256–257
1:1 Buenos Aires - Montevideo 258

CARTES DES ZONES MÉTROPOLITAINES (1:300 000)

Introduction 259
London 260
Paris 261
Manchester - Liverpool 262
Ruhr Area 263
Berlin 264
Wien 264
Budapest 264
Leningrad 265
Moskva 265
Madrid 266
Milano 266
Lisboa 266
Barcelona 266
Roma 267
Athínai 267
İstanbul 267
Tehrān 267
Tōkyō - Yokohama 268
Krung Thep (Bangkok) 269
Thanh-pho Ho Chi Minh (Sai-gon) 269
Jakarta 269
Shanghai 269
T'aipei 269
Manila 269
Ōsaka - Kōbe - Kyōto 270
Beijing (Peking) 271
Sŏul 271
Singapore 271
Hong Kong 271
Delhi 272
Bombay 272
Calcutta 272
Lagos 273
Kinshasa - Brazzaville 273
Al-Qāhirah (Cairo) 273
Johannesburg 273
Sydney 274
Melbourne 274
Montréal 275
Toronto 275
New York 276–277
Chicago 278
Cleveland 279
Pittsburgh 279
Los Angeles 280
Detroit - Windsor 281
San Francisco - Oakland - San Jose 282
Boston 283
Buffalo - Niagara Falls 284
Baltimore 284
Washington 284
Philadelphia 285
Ciudad de México 286
La Habana 286
Caracas 286
Lima 286
Santiago 286
Rio de Janeiro 287
São Paulo 287
Buenos Aires 288

Lista de Mapas

MAPAS DO MUNDO, DOS OCEANOS E DOS CONTINENTES

* Introdução 1
1:75 Mundo Político 2–3
1:75 Mundo Físico 4–5
1:48 Oceanos Pacífico e Índico 6–7
1:48 Oceano Atlântico 8
1:24 Antártida 9
1:24 Europa e África 10–11
1:24 Ásia 12–13
1:24 Austrália e Oceania 14–15
1:24 América do Norte 16–17
1:24 América do Sul 18–19

MAPAS REGIONAIS

Introdução 20–21

Europa

1:12 Europa 22–23
1:6 Europa Setentrional 24–25
1:3 Escandinávia Meridional 26–27
1:3 Ilhas Britânicas 28–29
1:3 Europa Central 30–31
1:3 França e os Alpes 32–33
1:3 Espanha e Portugal 34–35
1:3 Itália 36–37
1:3 Europa: Sul-oriental 38–39
1:1 Stockholm - Karlstad 40
1:1 København - Malmö - Kiel 41
1:1 London - Birmingham - Cardiff 42–43
1:1 Dublin - Manchester - Newcastle upon Tyne 44–45
1:1 Glasgow - Edinburgh - Aberdeen 46–47
1:1 Dublin - Belfast - Cork 48–49
1:1 Paris - London - Bruxelles 50–51
1:1 Amsterdam - Düsseldorf - Hamburg 52–53
1:1 Berlin - Hamburg - Praha 54–55
1:1 Bruxelles - Frankfurt - Stuttgart 56–57
1:1 Zürich - Genève - Strasbourg 58–59
1:1 Nürnberg - München 60
1:1 Wien - Brno - Linz 61
1:1 Lyon - Marseille - Milano 62–63
1:1 München - Venezia - Firenze 64–65
1:1 Roma - Firenze - Napoli 66–67
1:1 Napoli - Messina - Bari 68–69
1:1 Palermo - Catania - Messina 70
1:1 Cagliari - Sassari 71

União das Repúblicas Socialistas Soviéticas

1:12 União Soviética Ocidental e Central 72–73
1:12 União Soviética Oriental e Central 74–75
1:3 Regiões do Báltico e de Moscou 76–77
1:3 Ucrânia 78–79
1:3 Região do Volga 80–81
1:1 Moskva - Tula - Kalinin 82
1:1 Doneck - Vorošilovgrad - Rostov 83
1:3 Cáucaso e Transcaucásia 84
1:3 Ásia Central Soviética: zona parte 85
1:6 União Soviética Central 86–87
1:6 Região do Lago Baikal 88
1:6 Extremo-Oriente Soviético 89

Ásia

1:12 China, Japão e Coréia 90–91
1:3 Japão 92–93
1:1 Tōkyō - Nagoya - Kyōto 94–95
1:1 Ōsaka - Hiroshima - Fukuoka 96–97
1:3 Nordeste da China e Coréia 98–99
1:3 Leste e Sudeste da China 100–101
1:6 China Interior 102–103
1:1 Shenyang - Fushun (Mukden - Fushun) 104
1:1 Beijing - Tianjin (Peking - Tientsin) 105
1:1 Shanghai - Nanjing (Shanghai - Nanking) 106
1:1 Chongqing - Chengdu (Chungking - Chengtu) 107
1:12 Sudeste Asiático 108–109
1:6 Birmânia, Tailândia e Indochina 110–111
1:6 Malásia e Indonésia Ocidental 112–113
1:3 Malaia, Cingapura e Sumatra Setentrional 114
1:3 Java • Ilhas Menores da Sonda 115
1:3 Filipinas 116–117
1:12 Índia, Paquistão e Ásia do Sudoeste 118–119
1:6 Índia Setentrional e Paquistão 120–121
1:6 Índia Meridional e Sri Lanka 122
1:3 Punjab e Cachemira 123
1:3 Planície do Ganges e Nepal 124–125
1:1 Calcutta - Dacca - Jamshedpur 126–127
1:6 Oriente Médio 128–129
1:3 Turquia e Chipre 130–131
1:1 Yerushalayim - Dimashq (Jerusalem - Damascus) 132–133

África

1:12 África do Norte Ocidental 134–135
1:12 África do Norte Oriental 136–137
1:12 África Meridional 138–139
1:6 Egito e Sudão 140–141
1:1 Al-Qāhirah - As-Suways (Cairo - Suez) 142–143
1:6 Etiópia, Somália e Iêmen 144–145
1:6 Líbia e Tchad 146–147
1:6 África Norte-ocidental 148–149
1:6 África Ocidental 150–151
1:6 Bacia Ocidental do Congo 152–153
1:6 África Oriental e Bacia Oriental do Congo 154–155
1:6 África Meridional e Madagascar 156–157
1:3 África do Sul 158–159

Austrália/Oceania

1:12 Austrália 160–161
1:6 Austrália Centro-ocidental 162–163
1:6 Austrália Setentrional e Nova Guiné 164–165
1:6 Austrália Oriental 166–167
1:1 Perth • Adelaide 168
1:1 Melbourne - Geelong - Ballarat 169
1:1 Sydney - Newcastle 170
1:1 Brisbane • Canberra 171
1:3 Nova Zelândia 172–173
Várias Escalas
Ilhas do Pacífico 174–175

América Anglosaxônica

1:12 Canadá 176–177
1:12 Estados Unidos 178–179
1:6 Alasca e Yukon 180–181
1:3 Canadá: Sul-oriental 182–183
1:3 Canadá Central, parte meridional 184–185
1:3 Canadá: Sul-ocidental 186–187
1:3 Estados Unidos: Nordeste 188–189
1:3 Região dos Grandes Lagos 190–191
1:3 Estados Unidos: Sudeste 192–193
1:3 Vale do Mississippi 194–195
1:3 Grandes Planícies: zona meridional 196–197
1:3 Grandes Planícies: zona setentrional 198–199
1:3 Montanhas Rochosas: Sul 200–201
1:3 Noroeste dos Estados Unidos 202–203
1:3 Califórnia e Nevada 204–205
1:1 Montréal - Québec 206
1:1 Boston - New York - Albany 207
1:1 New York - Philadelphia - Washington - Norfolk 208–209
1:1 New York - Buffalo 210–211
1:1 Toronto - Ottawa 212–213
1:1 Pittsburgh - Cleveland - Detroit 214–215
1:1 Chicago - Detroit - Milwaukee 216–217
1:1 Indianapolis - Cincinnati - Louisville 218
1:1 St. Louis - Springfield 219
1:1 Miami - Tampa - Orlando 220–221
1:1 Houston - Dallas - Austin 222–223
1:1 Vancouver - Seattle - Portland 224–225
1:1 San Francisco - Reno - Bakersfield 226–227
1:1 Los Angeles - San Diego 228
Várias Escalas
Havaí 229

América Latina

1:12 México, América Central e Antilhas 230–231
1:6 México 232–233
1:3 México Central 234–235
1:3 América Central 236–237
1:6 Região do Caribe 238–239
Várias Escalas
Ilhas do Caribe (Índias Ocidentais) 240–241
1:12 América do Sul: Norte 242–243
1:12 América do Sul: Sul 244–245
1:6 Colômbia, Equador, Venezuela e Guiana 246–247
1:6 Peru, Bolívia e Brasil Ocidental 248–249
1:6 Brasil Nordeste 250–251
1:6 Argentina e Chile: Centro 252–253
1:6 Argentina e Chile: Sul 254
1:6 Brasil Sudeste 255
1:1 Rio de Janeiro - São Paulo 256–257
1:1 Buenos Aires - Montevideo 258

MAPAS DAS ÁREAS METROPOLITANAS (1:300 000)

Introdução 259
London 260
Paris 261
Manchester - Liverpool 262
Ruhr Area 263
Berlin 264
Wien 264
Budapest 264
Leningrad 265
Moskva 265
Madrid 266
Milano 266
Lisboa 266
Barcelona 266
Roma 267
Athínai 267
İstanbul 267
Tehrān 267
Tōkyō - Yokohama 268
Krung Thep (Bangkok) 269
Thanh-pho Ho Chi Minh (Sai-gon) 269
Jakarta 269
Shanghai 269
T'aipei 269
Manila 269
Ōsaka - Kōbe - Kyōto 270
Beijing (Peking) 271
Sŏul 271
Singapore 271
Hong Kong 271
Delhi 272
Bombay 272
Calcutta 272
Lagos 273
Kinshasa - Brazzaville 273
Al-Qāhirah (Cairo) 273
Johannesburg 273
Sydney 274
Melbourne 274
Montréal 275
Toronto 275
New York 276–277
Chicago 278
Cleveland 279
Pittsburgh 279
Los Angeles 280
Detroit - Windsor 281
San Francisco - Oakland - San Jose 282
Boston 283
Buffalo - Niagara Falls 284
Baltimore 284
Washington 284
Philadelphia 285
Ciudad de México 286
La Habana 286
Caracas 286
Lima 286
Santiago 286
Rio de Janeiro 287
São Paulo 287
Buenos Aires 288

***Escalas em milhões**

Legend to Maps/Zeichenerklärung
Leyendas Para Mapas/Légende des Cartes/Legendas dos Mapas

The design and color of the map symbols are consistent throughout the Regional and Metropolitan Area maps, although the size of the symbol varies with scale. An asterisk marks those symbols which appear only on the 1:300,000 scale maps. Symbols for inhabited localities, boundaries, and capitals are given on page xi.

The symbol 80-81 in the margin of a map directs the reader to a map of the adjoining area.

A separate legend on page 1 identifies the land and submarine features which appear on the World, Ocean, and Continent maps.

Der Entwurf und die Farbe der Kartensymbole sind einheitlich für alle Regionalkarten und Karten von Stadtregionen, während die Grösse des Symbols sich mit dem Massstab ändert. Ein Stern kennzeichnet diejenigen Symbole, welche nur auf den Karten im Massstab 1:300 000 erscheinen. Symbole für bewohnte Orte, für Grenzen und Hauptstädte sind auf Seite xi angeführt.

Kennzeichen 80-81 am Rande einer Karte ist ein Hinweis für den Leser, die Karte eines angrenzenden Gebietes nachzuschlagen.

Eine andere Legende auf Seite 1 identifiziert die Land- und untermeerischen Phänomene, die auf den Weltkarten, Karten der Ozeane und Erdteile erscheinen.

El diseño y el color de los símbolos cartográficos son uniformes para todas los mapas regionales y de las áreas metropolitanas, aunque el tamaño del símbolo varía según la escala. Un asterisco distingue los símbolos que aparecen sólo en los mapas a 1:300 000. Los símbolos de lugares poblados, de límites y de capitales se hallan en la página xi.

El símbolo 80-81 al margen de un mapa dirige al lector a un mapa del área adyacente.

Otra leyenda, en la página 1, identifica la topografía terrestre y submarina que se encuentra en los mapas del Mundo, Océanos y Continentes.

La couleur et la forme des symboles cartographiques des cartes régionales et des cartes des zones métropolitaines sont identiques, bien que la grandeur des signes varie selon l'échelle. Un astérisque accompagne les symboles qui n'apparaissent que sur les cartes au 1:300 000*. La légende des signes conventionnels pour les lieux habités, les frontières et les capitales se trouve à la page xi.

Le symbole 80-81 en marge d'une carte renvoie le lecteur à une carte de la région voisine.

Pour les cartes du monde, des océans et des continents une légende séparée, à la page 1, donne le sens des symboles représentant les paysages continentaux et les formes de relief sous-marin.

A cor e a forma dos símbolos cartográficos dos mapas regionais e das áreas metropolitanas são idênticos, ainda que a dimensão do símbolo varie segundo a escala. Um asterisco distingue os símbolos que só aparecem nos mapas da escala de 1:300 000. As legendas dos símbolos convencionais dos lugares povoados, fronteiras e capitais encontram-se à pág. xi.

O símbolo 80-81 à margem de um mapa, remete o leitor a um mapa da região vizinha.

Nos mapas do mundo, dos oceanos e dos continentes uma legenda separada, na pág. 1, indica o sentido dos símbolos representativos das paisagens continentais e das formas do relevo submarino.

Hydrographic Features / Hydrographische Objekte / Elementos Hidrográficos
Données Hydrographiques / Acidentes Hidrográficos

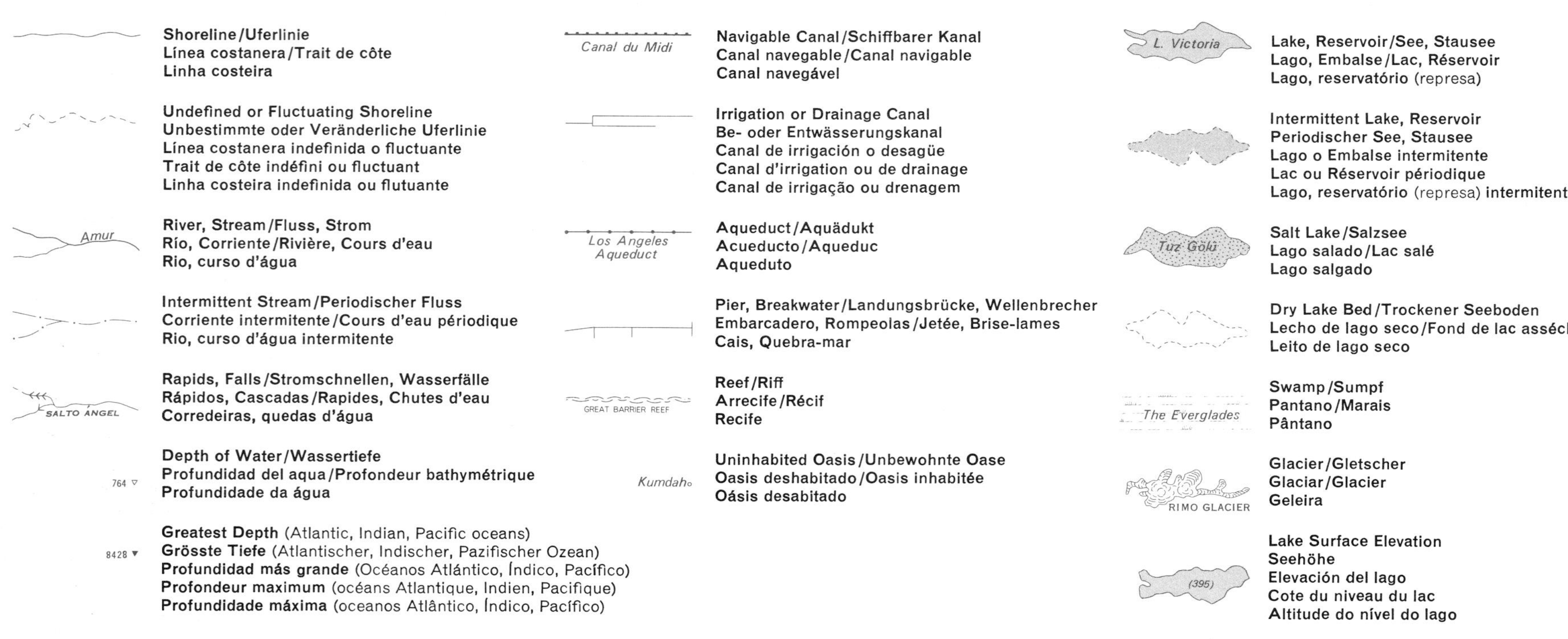

Topographic Features / Topographische Objekte / Elementos Topográficos
Données Topographiques / Acidentes Topográficos

Matterhorn 4478 △
Elevation Above Sea Level
Höhe über dem Meeresspiegel
Elevatión sobre el nivel del mar
Cote au-dessus du niveau de la mer
Altitude acima do nível do mar

76 ▽
Elevation Below Sea Level
Höhe unter dem Meeresspiegel
Elevación bajo del nivel del mar
Cote au-dessous du niveau de la mer
Altitude abaixo do nível do mar

Mount Cook 3764 ▲
Highest Elevation in Country
Höchster Punkt des Landes
Elevación más alta en el país
Cote la plus élevée d'un pays
Altitude mais elevada de um país

133 ▼
Lowest Elevation in Country
Tiefster Punkt des Landes
Elevación más baja en el país
Cote la plus basse d'un pays
Altitude mais baixa de um país

(106)
Elevation of City
Höhenangabe einer Stadt
Elevación de ciudad
Altitude d'une ville
Altitude de uma cidade

Khyber Pass 1067
Mountain Pass/Pass
Paso/Col de montagne
Passo (de montanha)

Rock/Fels
Roca/Rocher
Rocha

Lava/Lava
Lava/Lave
Lava

Sand Area/Sandgebiet
Area de arena/Région sableuse, Erg
Região arenosa, Erg

Salt Flat/Salzebene
Salar/Dépression salée
Depressão salgada

A N D E S
KUNLUNSHANMAI
Mountain Range, Plateau, Valley, etc.
Gebirge, Hochebene, Tal, usw.
Sierra, Meseta, Valle, etc.
Chaîne de montagnes, Plateau, Vallée, etc.
Cadeia de montanhas. Planalto, Vale etc.

BAFFIN ISLAND
NUNIVAK ISLAND
Island
Insel
Isla
Île
Ilha

POLUOSTROV KAMČATKA
CABO DE HORNOS
Peninsula, Cape, Point, etc.
Halbinsel, Kap, Landspitze, usw.
Península, Cabo, Punta, etc.
Péninsule, Cap, Pointe, etc.
Península, Cabo, Ponta etc.

Elevations and depths are given in meters
Höhen und Tiefen sind in Metern angegeben
Elevaciones y profundidades se dan en metros
Cotes et profondeurs sont indiquées en mètres
Altitudes e profundidades são apresentadas em metros

Highest Elevation and Lowest Elevation of a continent are underlined
Höchster und tiefster Punkt innerhalb eines Erdteils sind unterstrichen
Elevación más alta y más baja de un continente se subrayan
La cote la plus haute et la cote la plus basse d'un continent sont soulignées
As altitudes mais e menos elevadas de um continente são sublinhadas

Legend to Maps/Zeichenerklärung
Leyendas Para Mapas/Légende des Cartes/Legendas dos Mapas

Inhabited Localities / Bewohnte Orte / Lugares Poblados / Lieux Habités / Lugares Habitados

The symbol represents the number of inhabitants within the locality/Die Signatur entspricht der Einwohnerzahl des Ortes
El símbolo representa el número de habitantes dentro del lugar/Le symbole représente le nombre d'habitants de la localité
O símbolo representa o número de habitantes do lugar

1:300,000 / 1:3,000,000 — 1:1,000,000 / 1:6,000,000
- 0—10,000
- 10,000—25,000
- 25,000—100,000
- 100,000—250,000
- 250,000—1,000,000
- >1,000,000

1:12,000,000
- 0—50,000
- 50,000—100,000
- 100,000—250,000
- 250,000—1,000,000
- >1,000,000

1:24,000,000 / 1:48,000,000
- 0—100,000
- 100,000—1,500,000
- >1,500,000

The size of type indicates the relative economic and political importance of the locality
Die Schriftgrösse entspricht der relativen wirtschaftlichen und politischen Bedeutung des Ortes
El tamaño del tipo de imprenta indica la relativa importancia económica y política del lugar
La dimension des caractères indique l'importance économique et politique relative d'une localité
A dimensão dos caracteres tipográficos indica a importância econômica e política relativa do lugar

Écommoy Lisieux **Rouen**
Trouville Orléans **PARIS**

Hollywood / *Westminster* — **Section of a City, Neighborhood/Stadtteil, Nachbarschaft**
Sección de una ciudad, Barrio/Arrondissement, Quartier
Seção de uma cidade, Bairro

Northland Center — * **Major Shopping Center/Haupteinkaufszentrum/Mercado principal**
Centre commercial important/Centro comercial importante

BYRD — **Scientific Station/Wissenschaftliche Station/Estación científica**
Station scientifique/Estação científica

Bi'r Safājah — **Inhabited Oasis/Bewohnte Oase/Oasis habitado**
Oasis habitée/Oásis habitado

Kumdah — **Uninhabited Oasis/Unbewohnte Oase/Oasis deshabitado**
Oasis inhabitée/Oásis desabitado

Urban Area (area of continuous industrial, commercial, and residential development)
Stadtgebiet (ausgedehntes industrie-, Geschäfts- und Wohngebiet)
Zona urbanizada (área de desarrollo industrial, comercial y residencial)
Zone urbanisée (zone d'occupation continue par des industries, des commerces, des habitations)
Zona urbanizada (área de ocupação contínua por indústrias, estabelecimentos comerciais e habitações)

* **Major Industrial Area/Hauptindustriegebiet/Zona principal industrial**
Région industrielle importante/Zona industrial importante

* **Wooded Area/Wald/Área de bosque**
Région boisée/Área verde

* **Local Park or Recreational Area/Park oder Erholungsgebiet**
Parque municipal o área de recreo/Parc municipal ou zone de loisirs
Parque municipal ou área de lazer

Political Boundaries / Politische Grenzen / Límites Políticos / Frontières Politiques / Fronteiras e Limites

International (First-order political unit) **/Staatsgrenze** (Politische Einheit erster Ordnung)
Internacionales (Unidad política de primer orden) **/Internationales** (Entités politiques de premier ordre)
Internacionais (Unidade política de primeiro nível)

1:300,000 / 1:1,000,000 / 1:3,000,000 / 1:6,000,000 — 1:24,000,000 / 1:48,000,000 — 1:12,000,000

HUNGARY — **Demarcated, Undemarcated, and Administrative**
Markiert, unmarkiert, verwaltungstechnisch
Demarcado, No demarcado, y Administrativo
Délimitées, Non-délimitées, Administratives
Delimitados, Não delimitados, Administrativos

Disputed de facto/Umstritten de facto
Disputado de hecho/Contestées de facto
Contestados de fato

Disputed de jure/Umstritten de jure
Disputado de derecho/Contestées de jure
Contestados de direito

Indefinite or Undefined/Unklar oder Unbestimmt
Indefinido o No determinado/Imprécises ou Non définies
Imprecisos ou Não definidos

Demarcation Line/Demarkationslinie
Línea de demarcación/Ligne de démarcation
Linha de demarcação (utilizada na Coréia)

Capitals of Political Units
Hauptstädte politischer Einheiten
Capitales de Unidades Políticas
Capitales d'Entités Politiques
Capitais de Unidades Políticas

BUDAPEST — **Independent Nation**
Unabhängiger Staat
Nación independiente
État indépendant
Estado independente

Cayenne — **Dependency** (Colony, protectorate, etc.)
Abhängiges Gebiet (Kolonie, Protektorat, usw.)
Dependencia (Colonia, protectorado, etc.)
Territoire dépendant (Colonie, protectorat, etc.)
Dependência (Colônia, protetorado, etc.)

GALAPAGOS (Ecuador) — **Administering Country**
Verwaltender Staat
País administrador
Pays administrateur
País administrador

Internal/Verwaltungsgrenze/Internos/Intérieures/Limites Internos

PERNAMBUCO — **State, Province, etc.** (Second-order political unit)
Land, Provinz, usw. (Politische Einheit zweiter Ordnung)
Estado, Provincia, etc. (Unidad política de segundo orden)
État, Province, etc. (Subdivision administrative de deuxième ordre)
Estado, Província, etc. (Unidade política de segundo nível)

Recife — **State, Province, etc./Land, Provinz, usw.**
Estado, Provincia, etc./État, Province, etc.
Estado, Província, etc.

WESTCHESTER — **County, Oblast, etc.** (Third-order political unit)**/Grafschaft, Oblast, usw.** (Politische Einheit dritter Ordnung)
Condado, Oblast, etc. (Unidad política de tercer orden)
Comté, Oblast, etc. (Subdivision administrative de troisième ordre)
Condado, Oblast, etc. (Unidade política de terceiro nível)

White Plains — **County, Oblast, etc./Grafschaft, Oblast, usw.**
Condado, Oblast, etc./Comté, Oblast, etc.
Condado, Oblast, etc.

ISERLOHN — **Okrug, Kreis, etc.** (Fourth-order political unit)**/Okrug, Kreis, usw.** (Politische Einheit vierter Ordnung)
Okrug, Kreis, etc. (Unidad política de cuarto orden)
Okrug, Kreis, etc. (Subdivision administrative de quatrième ordre)
Okrug, Kreis, etc. (Unidade política de quarto nível)

Iserlohn — **Okrug, Kreis, etc./Okrug, Kreis, usw.**
Okrug, Kreis, etc./Okrug, Kreis, etc.
Okrug, Kreis, etc.

City or Municipality (may appear in combination with another boundary symbol)
Stadt oder Gemeinde (kann zusammen mit einem anderen Begrenzungssymbol erscheinen)
Ciudad o Municipio (puede aparecer en combinación con otro símbolo de límite)
Ville ou Municipalité (peut paraître en combinaison avec un autre symbole de limites politiques)
Cidade ou Municipalidade (Pode aparecer em combinação com outro símbolo de limite político)

ANDALUCÍA — **Historical Region** (No boundaries indicated)
Historische Landschaft (Grenzen werden nicht gezeigt)
Región Histórica (Sin indicación de límites)
Région Historique (Sans indication de frontières)
Região Histórica (Sem indicação de fronteiras)

Legend to Maps/Zeichenerklärung
Leyendas Para Mapas/Légende des Cartes/Legendas dos Mapas

Transportation / Verkehr / Transporte / Transports / Transporte

Road/Strasse/Camino/Route/Rodovia	1:300,000	1:1,000,000	1:3,000,000 1:6,000,000	1:12,000,000
Primary/Erster Ordnung/Principal/de premier ordre/Principal	PASSAIC EXPWY. (I-80)	PENNSYLVANIA TURNPIKE		
Secondary/Zweiter Ordnung/Secundario/de second ordre/Secundária	BERLINER RING			
Tertiary/Dritter Ordnung/Terciario/de troisième ordre/Terciária				
Minor Road, Trail/Weg, Pfad Rodera, Vereda/Route secondaire, Piste/Caminho, trilha				

Railway/Eisenbahn/Ferrocarril/Voie ferrée/Ferrovia				
Primary/Hauptbahn/Principal/Principale/Principal	CANADIAN NATIONAL	SANTA FE		
Secondary/Sonstige Bahn/Secundario/Secondaire/Secundária				
*Rapid Transit/Schnellverkehr/Tránsito rápido/Métro/Trânsito rápido (metrô)				
Airport/Flughafen/Aeropuerto/Aéroport/Aeroporto	LONDON (HEATHROW) AIRPORT	DULLES INTERNATIONAL AIRPORT		
*Rail or Air Terminal/Bahnhof oder Flughafengebäude Terminal ferroviaria o aéro/Gare ou aérogare Terminal ferroviário ou aéreo (estação)	SÜD-BAHNHOF			

REICHS-BRÜCKE — Bridge/Brücke/Puente/Pont/Ponte

GREAT ST. BERNARD TUNNEL — Tunnel/Tunnel/Túnel/Tunnel/Túnel

Houston Ship Channel — Shipping Channel/Schiffahrtsrinne
Canal maritimo/Chenal maritime
Canal marítimo

Canal du Midi — Navigable Canal/Schiffbarer Kanal
Canal navegable/Canal navigable
Canal navegável

Intracoastal Waterway/Küstenschiffahrtsweg
Via fluvial Intracostera/Canal côtier
Via costeira interna

TO MALMÖ — Ferry/Fähre
Balsadera/Bac
Balsa

Miscellaneous Cultural Features / Sonstige Objekte / Elementos Culturales Misceláneos
Éléments Culturels Divers / Acidentes Culturais Diversos

PARQUE NACIONAL LANIN — National or State Park or Monument
National- oder Naturpark oder Denkmal
Parque o Monumento nacional o provincial
Parc ou Monument national ou régional
Parque ou Monumento nacional ou regional

EDISON NAT. HIST. SITE — National or State Historic(al) Site, Memorial
Historische Stätte, Gedenkstätte
Sitio histórico nacional o provincial, Monumento
Site historique national ou régional, Mémorial
Sítio histórico nacional ou regional, Monumento histórico

SEMINOLE IND. RES. — Indian Reservation/Indianerreservation
Reserva de indios/Réserve indienne
Reserva indígena

FORT DIX — Military Installation/Militäranlage
Instalación militar/Installation militaire
Instalação militar

GREENWOOD CEMETERY — * Cemetery/Friedhof
Cementerio/Cimetière/Cemitério

SORBONNE — Point of Interest (Battlefield, museum, temple, university, etc.)
Sehenswürdigkeit (Schlachtfeld, Museum, Tempel, Universität, usw.)
Punto de interés (Campo de batalla, museo, templo, universidad, etc.)
Curiosité (Champ de bataille, musée, temple, université, etc.)
Pontos de interesse (Campo de batalha, museu, templo, universidade, etc.)

STEPHANSDOM — Church, Monastery/Kirche, Kloster
Iglesia, Monasterio/Église, Monastère
Igreja, Mosteiro

UXMAL — Ruins/Ruinen/Ruinas/Ruines/Ruínas

WINDSOR CASTLE — Castle/Burg, Schloss/Castillo/Château/Castelo

* Lighthouse/Leuchtturm
Faro/Phare/Farol

ASWĀN DAM — Dam/Damm/Presa/Barrage
Represa (barragem)

* Lock/Schleuse/Esclusa
Écluse/Eclusa

Crib — * Water Intake Crib/Wasseraufnahmestation
Toma de agua/Prise d'eau/Captação de água

Quarry or Surface Mine
Steinbruch oder Tagebau
Cantera o Mina de hoyo abierto
Carrière ou Mine à ciel ouvert
Pedreira ou mina a céu aberto

Subsurface Mine/Bergwerk
Mina subterránea/Mine souterraine
Mina subterrânea

* Oil Well/Ölbohrturm
Pozo de petróleo/Puits de pétrole
Poço de petróleo

Metric-English Equivalents / Umrechnung metrischer Masse in englische Masse / Métrico-Equivalentes Ingleses
Equivalences métriques des mesures anglaises / Equivalentes métricos das medidas inglesas

Areas represented by one square centimeter at various map scales
Flächen die einem cm² in den verschiedenen Kartenmassstäben entsprechen
Áreas representados por un centímetro cuadrado a varias escalas de mapas
Surface représentée par un cm² aux échelles indiquées
Áreas representadas por cm² nas escalas indicadas nos mapas

Meter=3.28 feet — Meter² (m²)=10.76 square feet
Kilometer=0.62 mile — Kilometer² (km²)=0.39 square mile

1:300,000	9 km²	3.48 square miles
1:1,000,000	100 km²	39 square miles
1:3,000,000	900 km²	348 square miles
1:6,000,000	3,600 km²	1,390 square miles
1:12,000,000	14,400 km²	5,558 square miles
1:24,000,000	57,600 km²	22,234 square miles
1:48,000,000	230,400 km²	88,934 square miles

Elevation tints shown only on 1:3,000,000 and 1:6,000,000 scale maps
Höhenschichten erscheinen nur auf Karten im Massstab 1:3 000 000 und 1:6 000 000
Se indica las tintas de elevación sólo en los mapas de escala 1:3 000 000 y 1:6 000 000
Teintes hypsométriques exprimées seulement sur cartes à 1:3 000 000 et 1:6 000 000
Indicaram-se as graduações de cor hipsométricas somente nos mapas de escalas 1:3 000 000 e 1:6 000 000

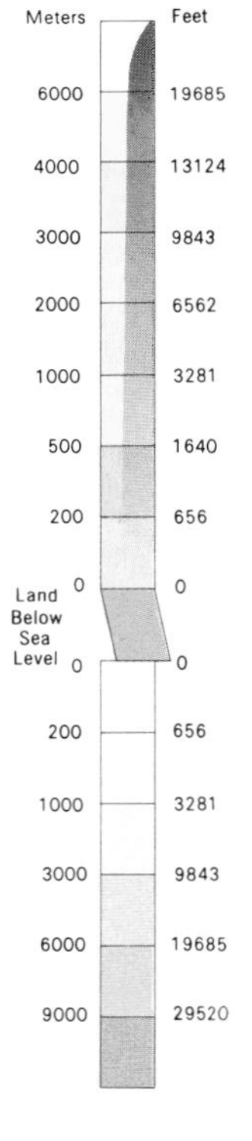

Meters	Feet
6000	19685
4000	13124
3000	9843
2000	6562
1000	3281
500	1640
200	656
0	0
Land Below Sea Level 0	0
200	656
1000	3281
3000	9843
6000	19685
9000	29520

Alternate Names / Alternative Namensformen / Nombres Alternativos
Variantes Toponymiques / Variantes Toponímicas

MOSKVA
MOSCOW

Basel
Bâle

English or second official language names are shown in reduced size lettering
Englische Namen oder Namen in einer zweiten offiziellen Sprache erscheinen in kleineren Schriftgrössen
Los nombres en inglés o un segundo idioma oficial se muestran en tipo de imprenta mas pequeño
Les toponymes en anglais ou dans la seconde langue officielle sont indiqués en caractères plus petits
Os topônimos em inglês ou num segundo idioma oficial aparecem em tipologia menor

VOLGOGRAD
(STALINGRAD)

Ventura
(San Buenaventura)

Historical or other alternates in the local language are shown in parentheses
Historische oder alternative Namensformen einheimischen Sprache erscheinen in Klammern
Los nombres históricos y alternativos locales se muestran en paréntesis
Les noms historiques de lieux ou les variantes toponymiques locales sont mis entre parenthèses
Os topônimos históricos ou as variantes toponimicas locais aparecem entre parênteses

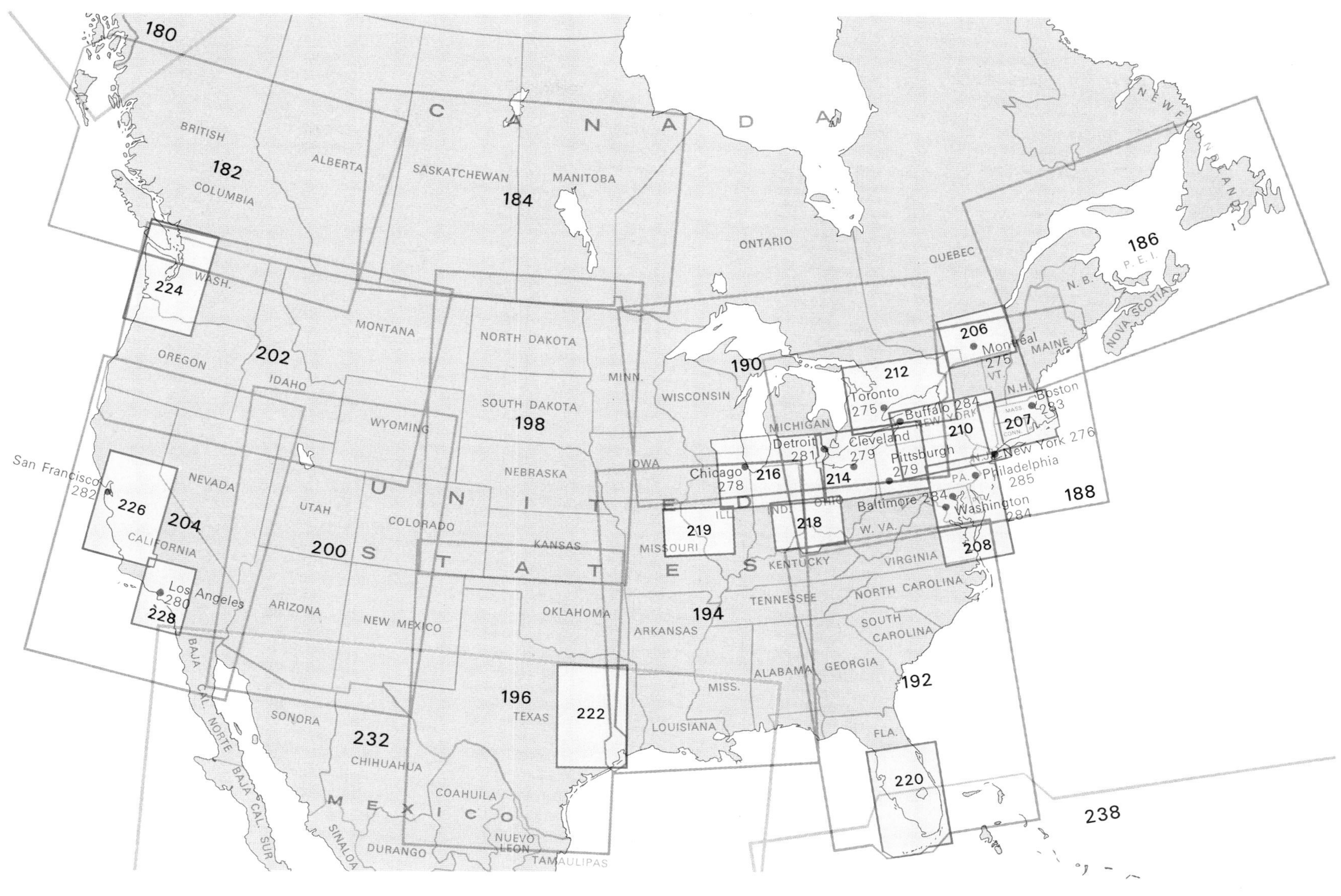
180
BRITISH
182
COLUMBIA
ALBERTA
C A N A D A
SASKATCHEWAN
MANITOBA
184
ONTARIO
QUEBEC
186
N. B.
P. E. I.
NOVA SCOTIA
224
WASH.
MONTANA
NORTH DAKOTA
MINN.
OREGON
202
IDAHO
WYOMING
SOUTH DAKOTA
198
WISCONSIN
190
MICHIGAN
212
Toronto
275
206
Montréal
275
MAINE
VT.
N.H.
Boston
283
Buffalo 284
NEW YORK
210
207
Detroit
281
Cleveland
279
Pittsburgh
279
New York 276
Philadelphia
285
San Francisco
282
NEVADA
226
204
CALIFORNIA
UTAH
200
COLORADO
U N I T E D S T A T E S
NEBRASKA
IOWA
Chicago
278
216
214
PA.
N.J.
Baltimore 284
Washington
284
188
219
ILL.
IND.
218
OHIO
W. VA.
208
KANSAS
MISSOURI
KENTUCKY
VIRGINIA
Los Angeles
280
228
ARIZONA
NEW MEXICO
OKLAHOMA
ARKANSAS
194
TENNESSEE
NORTH CAROLINA
SOUTH CAROLINA
BAJA CAL. NORTE
MISS.
ALABAMA
GEORGIA
192
196
TEXAS
222
LOUISIANA
SONORA
232
CHIHUAHUA
FLA.
220
COAHUILA
M E X I C O
BAJA CAL. SUR
SINALOA
DURANGO
NUEVO LEON
TAMAULIPAS
238

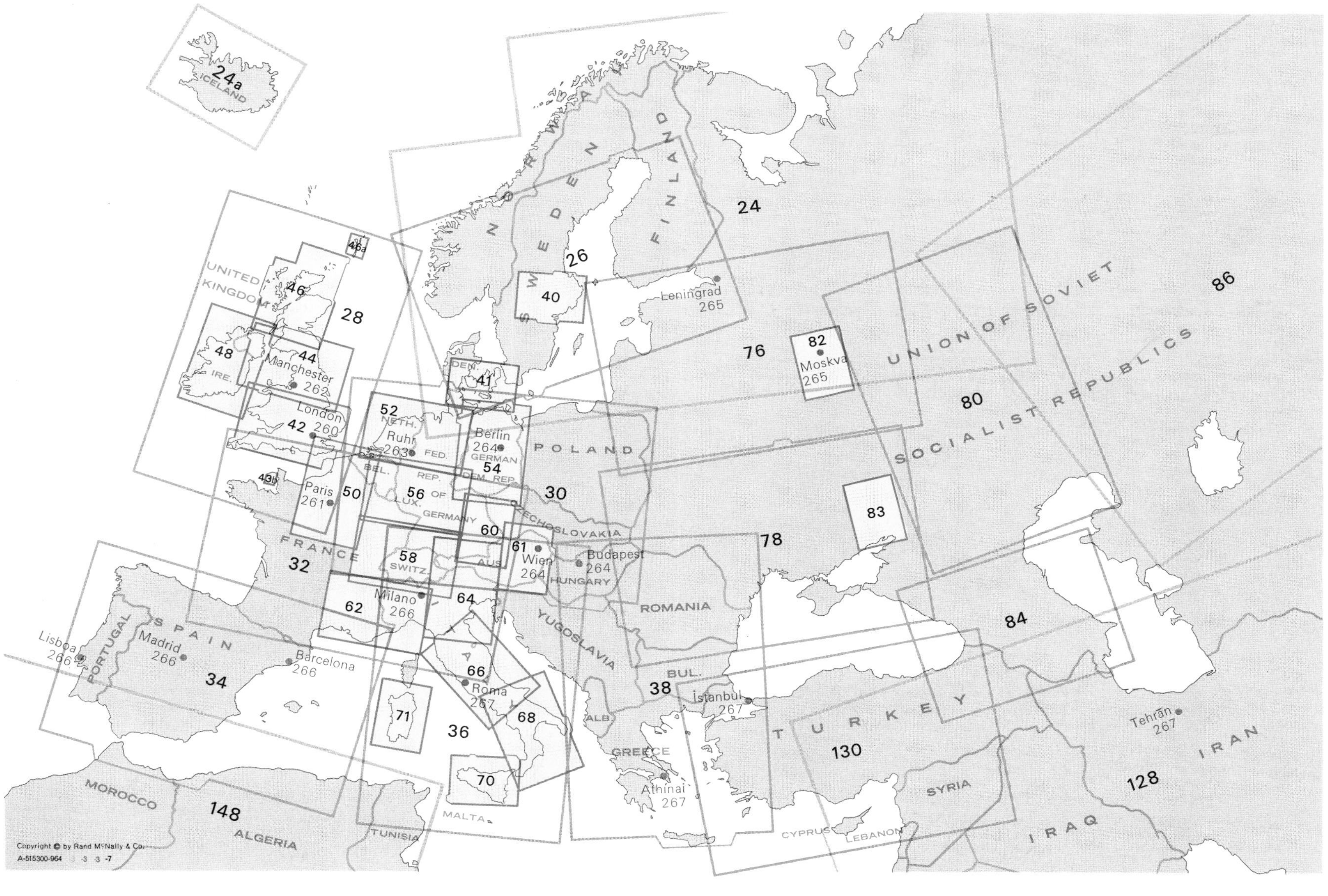

24a
ICELAND
N O R W A Y
S W E D E N
F I N L A N D
24
26
40
Leningrad
265
UNITED KINGDOM
46
48a
28
48
IRE.
44
Manchester
262
London
260
42
DEN.
41
52
NETH.
Ruhr
263
BEL.
FED. REP. OF GERMANY
Berlin
264
GERMAN DEM. REP.
54
POLAND
30
49b
Paris
261
50
56
LUX.
76
82
Moskva
265
UNION OF SOVIET SOCIALIST REPUBLICS
86
80
83
CZECHOSLOVAKIA
60
61
Wien
264
Budapest
264
HUNGARY
78
F R A N C E
32
58
SWITZ.
AUS.
62
Milano
266
64
ROMANIA
YUGOSLAVIA
84
Lisboa
266
PORTUGAL
S P A I N
Madrid
266
34
Barcelona
266
66
Roma
267
BUL.
38
İstanbul
267
71
36
68
ALB.
T U R K E Y
130
Tehrān
267
I R A N
GREECE
Athínai
267
SYRIA
128
70
MOROCCO
148
ALGERIA
TUNISIA
MALTA
CYPRUS
LEBANON
I R A Q

MAP COVERAGE / KARTENAUSSCHNITTE
CONTENIDO DEL ATLAS / TABLEAU D'ASSEMBLAGE
ABRANGÊNCIA DO MAPA

Map Scale

Manila 269 • 1:300,000

1:1,000,000 — 1:6,000,000

1:3,000,000 — 1:12,000,000

148 **Page Reference / Seitenangabe**
Página de Referencia / Page de Référence / Página de Referência

Enlarged maps of Anglo-America and Europe on page xiii.
Vergrösserte Karten von Anglo-Amerika und Europa auf Seite xiii.
Mapas aumentados de América Anglosajona y Europa, página xiii.
Cartes à grande échelle de l'Amérique anglo-saxonne et de l'Europe à la page xiii.
Mapas ampliados da América Anglo-saxônica e da Europa, página xiii.

World, Ocean, and Continent maps on pages 2-19.
Weltkarten, Karten der Ozeane und Erdteile auf Seiten 2-19.
Mapas del Mundo, Océanos y Continentes, páginas 2-19.
Cartes du Monde, des Océans et des Continents aux pages 2-19.
Mapas do Mundo, dos Oceanos e dos Continentes, páginas 2-19.

Additional Pacific Ocean Island maps on pages 174-175.
Zusätzliche Karten der Inseln des Pazifischen Ozeans auf Seite 174-175.
Mapas adicionales de las Islas del Océano Pacifico, páginas 174-175.
Cartes supplémentaires des Îles de l'Océan Pacifique aux pages 174-175.
Mapas suplementares das ilhas do Oceano Pacífico, páginas 174-175.

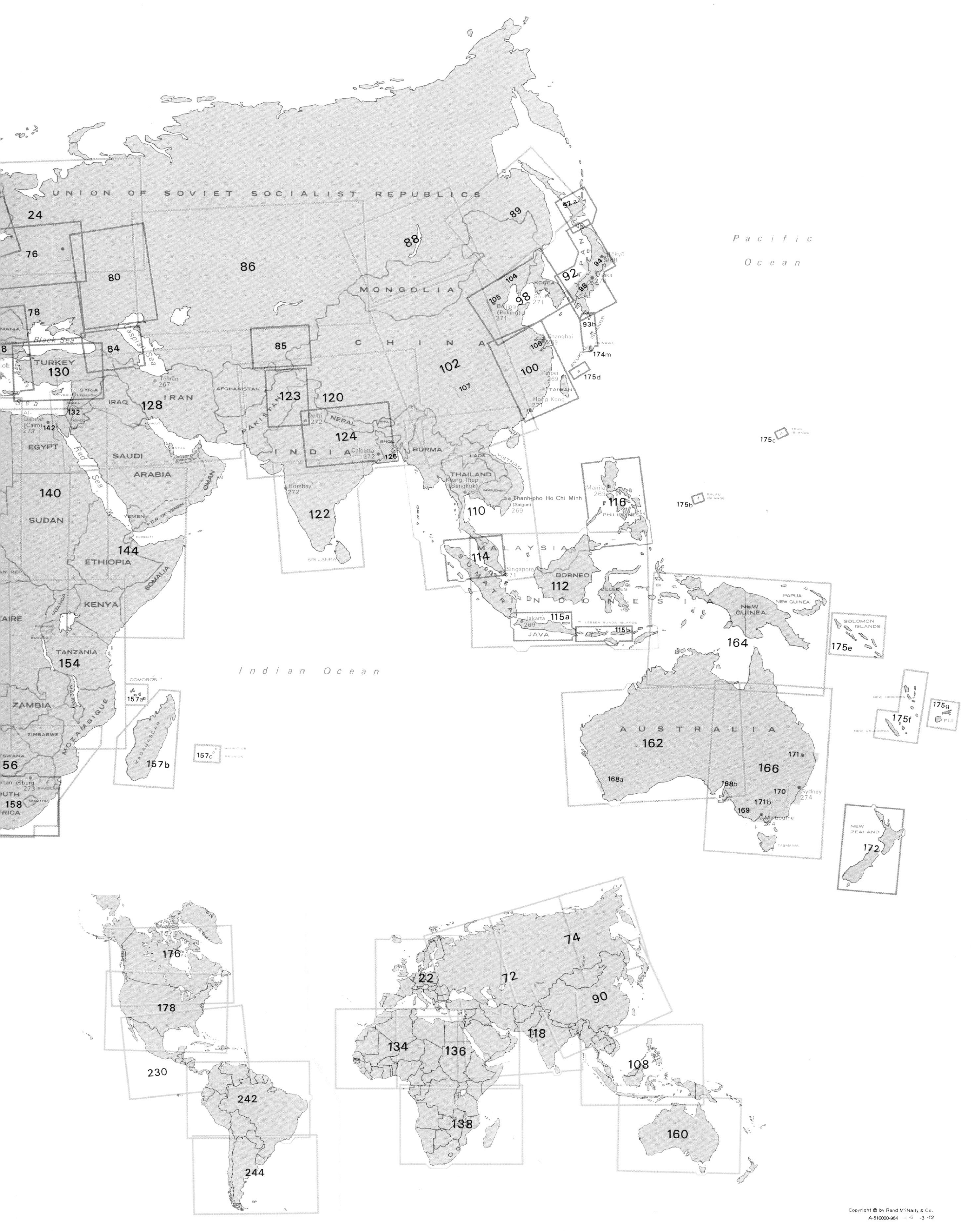
UNION OF SOVIET SOCIALIST REPUBLICS
Pacific Ocean
Indian Ocean
MONGOLIA
CHINA
KOREA
JAPAN
TURKEY
SYRIA
IRAQ
IRAN
AFGHANISTAN
PAKISTAN
INDIA
NEPAL
BURMA
LAOS
VIETNAM
THAILAND
KAMPUCHEA
MALAYSIA
SUMATRA
BORNEO
CELEBES
INDONESIA
JAVA
PHILIPPINES
TAIWAN
NEW GUINEA
PAPUA NEW GUINEA
SOLOMON ISLANDS
AUSTRALIA
TASMANIA
NEW ZEALAND
FIJI
EGYPT
SAUDI ARABIA
OMAN
YEMEN
P.D.R. OF YEMEN
SUDAN
ETHIOPIA
SOMALIA
KENYA
UGANDA
TANZANIA
ZAIRE
ZAMBIA
ZIMBABWE
MOZAMBIQUE
MADAGASCAR
COMOROS
Black Sea
Caspian Sea
Red Sea
SRI LANKA
Tehrān 267
Al-Qāhirah (Cairo) 273
Delhi 272
Calcutta 272
Bombay 272
Beijing (Peking) 271
Seoul 271
Shanghai 269
Taipei 269
Hong Kong 271
Krung Thep (Bangkok) 269
Thanh-pho Ho Chi Minh (Saigon) 269
Manila 269
Singapore 271
Jakarta 269
Sydney 274
Melbourne
Johannesburg 273
24
76
80
86
88
89
78
84
85
128
130
132
142
140
144
154
56
158
157a
157b
157c
120
123
124
126
122
92a
92
93b
94
96
98
102
104
105
106
107
100
174m
175d
175c
175b
116
110
114
112
115a
115b
164
175e
175f
175g
162
166
168a
168b
169
170
171a
171b
172
176
178
230
242
244
22
72
74
90
118
134
136
138
108
160

Adriatic Sea 22
Aegean Sea 39
Afars and Issas, see Djibouti
Afghanistan 120, 129
Africa 10-11
Alabama 195
Alaska 180-181
Albania 38-39
Alberta 183-184
Aleutian Islands 180-181
Algeria 148-149
Alps 33
American Samoa 175
Andaman and Nicobar Islands 110-111
Andes 18-19
Andorra 35
Angola 153
Anguilla 239
Antarctica 9
Antigua 240c
Arabian Peninsula 118
Arabian Sea 118-119
Aral Sea 86
Arctic Ocean 12, 16
Arizona 201
Arkansas 194-195
Armenia 84
Argentina 252-254
Aruba 241s
Ascension 11
Asia 12-13
Atlantic Ocean 8
Australia 162-167
Australian Capital Territory 171b
Austria 30-31
Azerbajdžanskaja S.S.R. 84
Azores 148a
Bahamas 238-239
Bahrain 129
Baikal, Lake 88
Balearic Islands 35
Balkhash, Lake 87
Baltic Sea 24
Bangladesh 121
Barbados 241g
Basutoland, see Lesotho
Bechuanaland, see Botswana
Belgium 30
Belize 233
Belorusskaja S.S.R. 76-77
Bengal, Bay of 13
Benin 151
Bering Sea 16
Bermuda 240a
Bhutan 121
Bioko 152
Bismarck Archipelago 165
Black Sea 23
Bolivia 248-249
Borneo 112-113
Botswana 156-157
Brazil 246-251, 253, 255
British Antarctic Territory 9
British Columbia 181-183
British Indian Ocean Territory 13
British Virgin Islands 240m
Brunei 113
Bulgaria 38-39
Burma 110-111
Burundi 154
California 204-205
Cambodia, see Kampuchea
Cameroon 147, 152
Canada 176-177
Canary Islands 148
Canton and Enderbury 15
Cape Verde 150a
Caribbean Sea 238-239
Caroline Islands 14-15
Caspian Sea 72
Cayman Islands 238
Celebes 113
Central African Republic 141, 147, 152, 154
Central America 236-237
Chad 146-147
Chile 248-249, 251, 254
China 90-91
Christmas Island 112
Cocos (Keeling) Islands 13
Colombia 246-247
Colorado 199-201
Comoros 157a
Congo 152
Congo, Democratic Republic of the, see Zaire
Connecticut 207
Cook Islands 15
Corsica 36-37
Costa Rica 237
Crete 39
Cuba 240p
Curaçao 241s
Cyprus 130-131
Czechoslovakia 30-31
Dahomey, see Benin
Delaware 208-209
Denmark 26
Djibouti 144
Dominica 240d
Dominican Republic 239
Ecuador 246
Egypt 140
El Salvador 236
England 28-29
Equatorial Guinea 152
Erie, Lake 214-215
Estonia 76
Ethiopia 144-145
Europe 22-23
Faeroe Islands 22
Falkland Islands (Is. Malvinas) 254
Fiji 175g
Finland 24-25
Florida 193
Formosa 101
France 32-33
French Guiana 250
French Polynesia 15
French Somaliland, see Djibouti
French Southern and Antarctic Territories 6
Gabon 152
Galápagos Islands 246a
Gambia 150
Georgia, U.S.S.R. 84
Georgia, U.S. 192-193
German Democratic Republic 30–31
Germany, Federal Republic of 30–31
Ghana 151
Gibraltar 34
Gobi Desert 90-91
Great Lakes 190-191
Greece 39
Greenland 16
Grenada 241k
Guadeloupe 241o
Guam 174p
Guatemala 233
Guernsey 29
Guinea 150
Guinea-Bissau 150
Gulf of Mexico 230
Guyana 247, 250
Haiti 238-239
Hawaii 229d
Himalayas 120-121
Hispaniola 238-239
Honduras 236-237
Hong Kong 271d
Hudson Bay 176-177
Hungary 31
Huron, Lake 191
Iceland 24a
Idaho 202-203
Illinois 190, 194
India 120-122
Indiana 194
Indian Ocean 6
Indonesia 111-113, 164
Inner Mongolia 90-91
Iowa 190, 199
Iran 128-129
Iraq 128
Ireland 28-29
Isle of Man 44
Israel 132-133
Italy 36-37
Ivory Coast 150-151
Jamaica 241q
Japan 92-93
Java 115a
Jersey 29
Jordan 128
Kampuchea 110-111
Kansas 199
Kazachskaja S.S.R. 72-73
Kentucky 192, 194
Kenya 154
Kerguelen 6
Kirgizskaja S.S.R. 72
Kiribati 15
Korea, North 99
Korea, South 99
Kuwait 128
Labrador 177
Laos 200
Latvia 76
Lebanon 128
Lesotho 159
Liberia 150
Libya 146-147
Liechtenstein 59
Lithuania 76
Louisiana 195
Luxembourg 56
Macau 101
Madagascar 157b
Madeira Islands 148
Maine 186
Malawi 155
Malaysia 112-113
Maldives 13
Mali 148-151
Malta 37
Manchuria 91
Manitoba 184-185
Mariana Islands 14
Marshall Islands 15
Martinique 240e
Maryland 188-189
Massachusetts 207
Mauritania 148, 150
Mauritius 157c
Mayotte 157a
Mediterranean Sea 10
Melanesia 14-15
Mexico 232-233
Michigan 190-191
Michigan, Lake 190-191
Micronesia 14-15
Middle East 128-129
Midway Islands 174g
Minnesota 190, 198
Mississippi 195
Missouri 194
Moldavia 78
Monaco 63
Mongolia 90-91
Montana 198, 202-203
Montserrat 239
Morocco 148-149
Mozambique 155, 157
Namibia 156
Nauru 174b
Nebraska 199
Nepal 124-125
Netherlands 30
Netherlands Antilles 241s
Nevada 204-205
New Brunswick 186
New Caledonia 175f
Newfoundland 187
New Guinea 164-165
New Hampshire 188
New Hebrides 175f
New Jersey 189
New Mexico 196, 201
New South Wales 166-167
New York 188-189
New Zealand 172-173
Nicaragua 236-237
Niger 146-147, 151
Nigeria 146, 151
Niue 174v
Norfolk Island 174c
North America 16-17
North Carolina 192
North Dakota 198
Northern Ireland 28-29
Northern Rhodesia, see Zambia
Northern Territory 160-161
North Sea 22
Northwest Territories 176-177
Norway 24
Nova Scotia 186-187
Nyasa, Lake 155
Nyasaland, see Malawi
Ohio 188
Oklahoma 196
Oman 118
Ontario 176-177
Ontario, Lake 212-213
Oregon 202
Orkney Islands 28
Pacific Islands Trust Territory 14-15
Pacific Ocean 6-7
Pakistan 120, 129
Palestine 132-133
Panama 246
Papua New Guinea 165
Paraguay 249, 252-253
Pennsylvania 188-189
Peru 246, 248
Persian Gulf 128-129
Philippines 116-117
Pitcairn 174e
Poland 31
Polynesia 15
Portugal 34
Portuguese Guinea, see Guinea-Bissau
Prince Edward Island 186
Puerto Rico 240m
Qatar 129
Quebec 177
Queensland 160-161
Red Sea 137
Reunion 157c
Rhode Island 207
Rhodesia, see Zimbabwe
Rocky Mountains 16-17
Romania 38
Russian S.F.S.R. 72-75
Rwanda 154
Sahara Desert 134-135
St. Helena 8
St. Kitts-Nevis 239
Saint Lucia 241f
St. Pierre and Miquelon 187
St. Vincent 241h
San Marino 66
Sao Tome and Principe 152
Sardinia 37
Saskatchewan 184-185
Saudi Arabia 118
Scotland 28
Senegal 150
Seychelles 139
Shetland Islands 28
Siberia 74-75
Sicily 37
Sierra Leone 150
Singapore 271c
Sinkiang 90
Solomon Islands 175e
Somalia 144-145
South Africa 156-157
South America 18-19
South Australia 163
South Carolina 192
South Dakota 198-199
South Georgia 245
Soviet Union, see Union of Soviet Socialist Republics
Spain 34-35
Spanish North Africa 34-35
Spanish Sahara, see Western Sahara
Sri Lanka 122
Sudan 140-141
Sumatra 111-112
Superior, Lake 190-191
Suriname 250
Svalbard and Jan Mayen 10
Swaziland 159
Sweden 24
Switzerland 58-59
Syria 128
Tadžikskaja S.S.R. 72
Taiwan 101
Tanganyika, Lake 154-155
Tanzania 154-155
Tasmania 167
Tennessee 192, 194-195
Texas 196-197
Thailand 200-201
Tibet 121
Tierra del Fuego 254
Togo 151
Tokelau Islands 15
Tonga 15
Transvaal 156-157
Trinidad and Tobago 241r
Tristan da Cunha 8
Tunisia 149
Turkey 130-131
Turkmenskaja S.S.R. 72
Turks and Caicos Islands 238-239
Tuvalu 15
Uganda 154
Ukraine 78-79
Union of Soviet Socialist Republics 72-75
United Arab Emirates 129
United Kingdom 28-29
United States 178-181, 229
Upper Volta 150-151
Ural Mountains 72
Uruguay 253
Utah 200-201
Uzbekskaja S.S.R. 72
Vatican City 267a
Venezuela 246-247
Vermont 188
Victoria 167
Victoria, Lake 154
Vietnam 200-201
Virginia 192
Virgin Islands 240m
Wake Island 174a
Wales 28-29
Wallis and Futuna 15
Washington 202
Western Australia 160
Western Sahara 148
Western Samoa 175a
West Indies 238-239
West Virginia 188-189
White Sea 25
Wisconsin 190
Wyoming 198-200, 202
Yellow Sea 91
Yemen 144
Yemen, People's Democratic Republic of 144
Yugoslavia 36, 38-39
Yukon 181
Zaire 152-155
Zambia 153, 155
Zanzibar 154
Zimbabwe 155

THIS SECTION OPENS with World Political and World Physical maps at the scale of 1:75,000,000. There follow maps of the Pacific, Indian, and Atlantic oceans at the scale 1:48,000,000, the largest scale at which the total expanse of these bodies of water could be portrayed. Finally, a series of continent relief maps at the scale of 1:24,000,000 show a global view of the earth as it would appear from about 4,000 miles in space. The Azimuthal Equal-Area projection is used for the 1:24,000,000 maps, the scale being approximately that of a globe 20 inches in diameter.

The colors of the continent maps portray the land areas as if viewed from space during the growing season, without regard to the fact that the growing seasons are not concurrent in all areas. Underwater features and varying water depths are represented by shaded relief and different color tones. The result is a strong physical portrait of the earth's major land and submarine forms. The legend below shows how these different kinds of terrain and vegetation have been represented. The names of physical features—plateaus, basins, mountain ranges, seas, rivers, lakes, gulfs, trenches, bays, islands—predominate on these maps.

DIESER KARTENTEIL BEGINNT mit politischen und physischen Weltkarten im Massstab 1:75 Millionen. Dann folgen Karten des Pazifischen, Indischen und Atlantischen Ozeans in 1:48 Millionen, dem grössten Massstab, in dem diese Wasserflächen in ihrer ganzen Ausdehnung abgebildet werden konnten. Schliesslich folgt eine Reihe von Reliefkarten der Erdteile in 1:24 Millionen. Sie geben eine Übersicht der Erde, wie sie aus einer Entfernung von ungefähr 6 400 Kilometer aus dem Weltraum gewonnen würde. Den Karten im Massstab 1:24 Millionen liegt ein flächentreuer azimutaler Entwurf zugrunde, dieser Massstab entspricht ungefähr dem eines Globus von 50 cm Durchmesser.

Die Farben der Erdteilkarten bilden jedes Landgebiet so ab, wie es in der Vegetationsperiode aus der Vogelperspektive erschiene, ohne zu berücksichtigen, dass die Vegetationsperioden nicht in allen Gebieten gleichzeitig eintreten. Die Gliederung des Meeresbodens und die unterschiedlichen Meerestiefen werden durch Schummerung und verschiedene Farbstufen dargestellt. Das Ergebnis ist eine anschauliche physische Darstellung der wichtigsten terrestrischen und untermeerischen Formen der Erde. Die untenstehende Zeichenerklärung zeigt, wie diese verschiedenen Geländeformen und Vegetationsgebiete veranschaulicht werden. Namen physischer Objekte—Hochebenen, Becken, Gebirgszüge, Meere, Flüsse, Seen, Buchten, Gräben, Inseln—herrschen in diesen Karten vor.

ESTA SECCIÓN DA PRINCIPIO con los Mapas Políticos y Físicos del Mundo, a una escala de 1:75 000 000. A continuación están los mapas de los océanos Pacífico, Indico y Atlántico a una escala de 1:48 000 000, que es la mayor escala utilizable para la representación de esas masas de agua en toda su extensión. Por último, una serie de mapas del relieve de los continentes, a una escala de 1:24 000 000, proporcionan una vista global de la tierra tal como se apreciaría desde el espacio a una distancia aproximada de 6 400 kilómetros. La proyección azimutal equiárea se usa, para los mapas de 1:24 000 000, a una escala según la cual la tierra se reduciría a un globo de unos 50 cm de diámetro.

Los colores utilizados en los mapas de los continentes representan las diversas regiones de la tierra tal como se verían desde el espacio durante la estación en que la vegetación se desarrolla, sin tomar en cuenta que este fenómeno no se produce simultáneamente en todas las áreas. Las estructuras características del fondo marino y las variaciones de profundidad de los océanos se representan mediante relieve sombreado y distintos matices de color. El resultado es una imagen elocuente de las formas terrestres y submarinas más notables del planeta. La leyenda abajo explica cómo se representan estos diferentes tipos de terreno y vegetación. En estos mapas predomina la nomenclatura de elementos físicos: mesetas, cuencas, sierras, mares, ríos, lagos, golfos, bahías, trincheras, islas.

CETTE PARTIE comprend d'abord des cartes du monde politique et du monde physique à l'échelle de 1:75 000 000. Viennent ensuite les cartes des océans Pacifique, Indien et Atlantique à l'échelle de 1:48 000 000, la plus grande échelle qui a permis la reproduction complète de ces étendues d'eau. Pour terminer, une série de cartes en relief des continents à l'échelle de 1:24 000 000 donne une vue globale de la terre, telle qu'elle apparaîtrait vue de l'espace à une distance d'environ 6 400 kilomètres. La projection azimutale équivalente a été utilisée pour les cartes au 1:24 000 000ᵉ, dont l'échelle équivaut à celle d'un globe de 50 cm de diamètre environ.

Les couleurs des cartes font apparaître les continents tels qu'on les verrait de l'espace, pendant la saison de croissance végétale, mais sans tenir compte du fait que cette saison n'apparaît pas partout simultanément. Le relief sous-marin est représenté par un estompage et la profondeur des océans par une variation de la couleur. Il en résulte une reproduction vigoureuse des principaux paysages continentaux et des principales formes sous-marines. La légende ci-dessous indique de quelle façon ils sont cartographiés. Les noms d'éléments topographiques tels que plateaux, bassins, chaînes de montagnes, mers, cours d'eau, lacs, golfes, baies, crêtes, îles et fosses océaniques, prédominent dans ces cartes.

ESTA SEÇÃO PRINCIPIA com os mapas políticos e físicos do Mundo, em escala de 1:75 000 000. Seguem-se os mapas dos oceanos Pacífico, Índico e Atlântico na escala de 1:48 000 000, a maior escala que se pode utilizar para a representação dessas massas de água em toda a sua extensão. Finalmente, uma série de mapas de relevo dos continentes, na escala de 1:24 000 000, proporciona uma visão global da Terra tal como apareceria do espaço a uma distância aproximada de cerca de 6 400 km. A projeção azimutal equiárea foi usada para os mapas da escala de 1:24 000 000, segundo a qual a Terra se apresentaria como um globo de cerca de 50 cm de diâmetro.

As cores utilizadas nos mapas dos continentes representam as massas terrestres tal como apareceriam vistas do espaço durante a estação do crescimento vegetal, sem levar em conta que este fenômeno não se produz simultaneamente em todas as regiões. As características do fundo do mar e as variações de profundidade das águas são representadas por um relevo sombreado e por diferentes matizes de cor. O resultado proporciona uma imagem física eloqüente das principais formas terrestres e submarinas da Terra. As legendas abaixo explicam como foram representados os diversos tipos de terreno e de vegetação. Nestes mapas predomina a nomenclatura dos elementos físicos: planaltos, bacias, cadeias de montanhas, mares, rios, lagos, golfos, baías, fossas, ilhas.

Land Features / Land Phänomene / Elementos de la Tierra
Paysages Continentaux / Elementos da Terra

Ice and Snow
Eis und Schnee
Hielo y nieve
Glace et neige
Gelo e neve

High Barren Area
Hochgebirgswüste
Alta zona árida
Région haute et aride
Alta zona árida

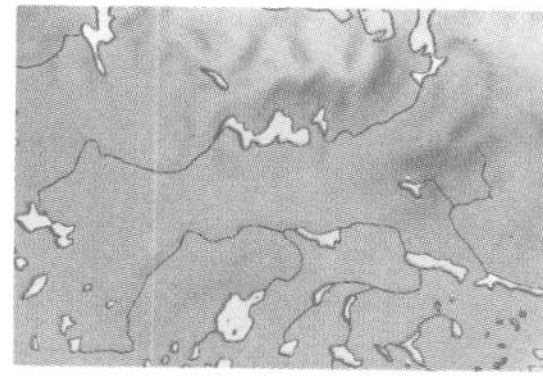
Tundra and Alpine
Tundra und Alpine Vegetation
Tundra y alpina
Toundra et végétation alpine
Tundra e vegetação alpina

Needleleaf Trees
Nadelwälder
Coníferas
Forêt de conifères
Coníferas

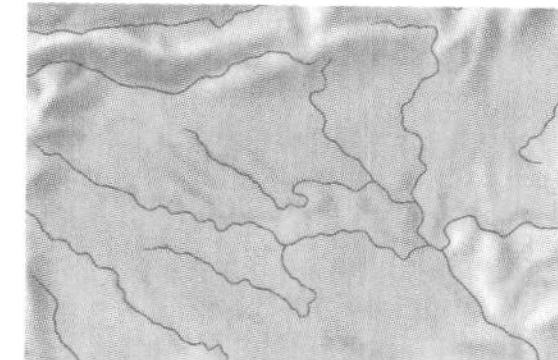
Broadleaf Trees
Laubwälder
Árboles de hojas anchas
Forêt à feuilles caduques
Árvores de folhas caducas

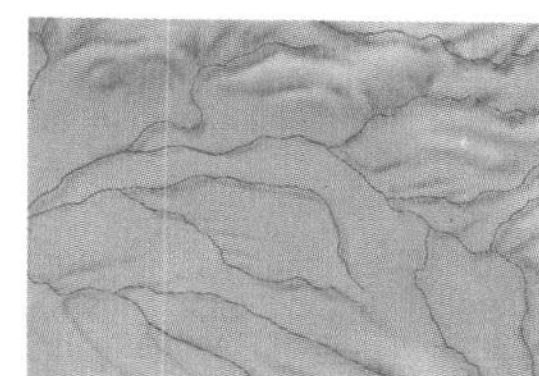
Tropical Rainforest
Tropischer Regenwald
Bosque tropical lluvioso
Forêt tropicale humide
Floresta tropical úmida

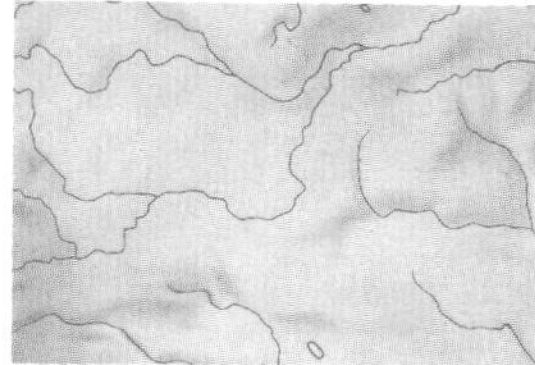
Grassland
Grasland
Pradera
Formations herbacées
Pradaria

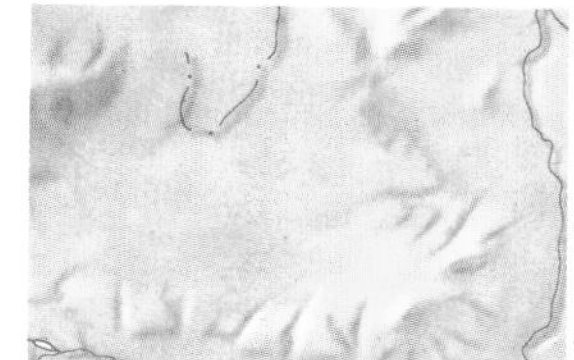
Dry Scrub
Trockenes Buschland
Matorral
Brousse sèche
Caatinga

Desert
Wüste
Desierto
Désert
Deserto

Submarine Features / Untermeerische Phänomene
Elementos Submarinos / Formes de Relief Sous-marin / Elementos Submarinos

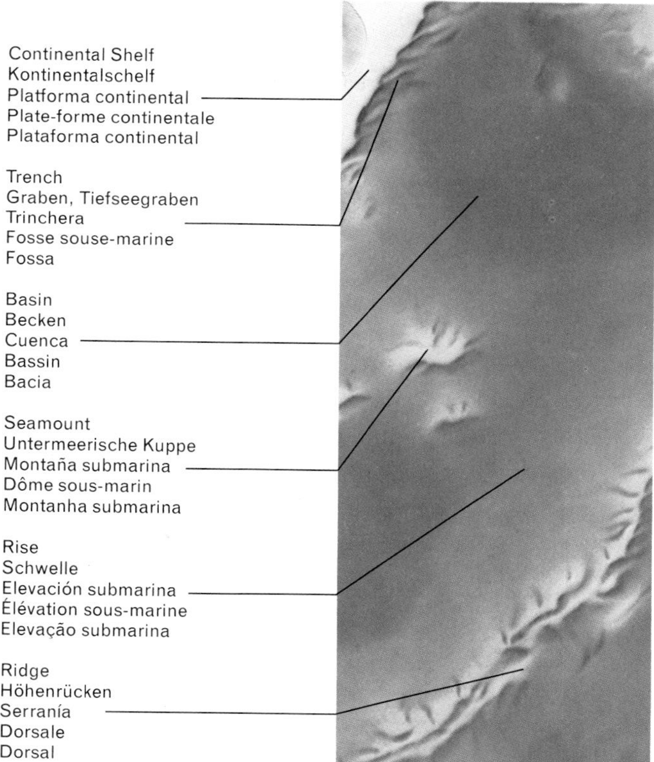

ARCTIC OCEAN
Beaufort Sea
GREENLAND
(Den.)
Baffin Bay
BAFFIN ISLAND
Thule
Godhavn
Godthåb
Angmagssalik
Reykjavík
ICELAND
FAEROE ISLANDS
(Den.)
U.S.S.R.
UNITED STATES
Nome
Fairbanks
Anchorage
Mount McKinley
6194
Inuvik
VICTORIA ISLAND
Yellowknife
Bering Sea
Gulf of Alaska
ALEUTIAN ISLANDS
Juneau
ROCKY MOUNTAINS
C A N A D A
Edmonton
Churchill
Hudson Bay
Goose Bay
Calgary
Winnipeg
Vancouver
Seattle
NEWFOUNDLAND
St. John's
Portland
Minneapolis
Ottawa
Montréal
Québec
Halifax
Glasgow
Dublin
IRELAND
NORTH AMERICA
CHICAGO
DETROIT
Toronto
Boston
NEW YORK
PHILADELPHIA
Washington
APPALACHIAN MOUNTAINS
Salt Lake City
Denver
St. Louis
UNITED STATES
SAN FRANCISCO
LOS ANGELES
San Diego
Phoenix
El Paso
Dallas
Atlanta
Houston
New Orleans
ATLANTIC OCEAN
AÇORES AZORES
(Port.)
Porto
PORTUGAL
Lisboa
GIBRALTAR
(U.K.)
Rabat
Casablanca
MOROCCO
ARQUIPÉLAGO DA MADEIRA
(Port.)
BERMUDA
(U.K.)
ISLAS CANARIAS
CANARY ISLANDS
(Sp.)
P A C I F I C
O C E A N
MIDWAY ISLANDS
(U.S.)
Tropic of Cancer
Gulf of Mexico
Miami
BAHAMAS
Monterrey
WESTERN SAHARA
HAWAIIAN ISLANDS
(U.S.)
Honolulu
CABO SAN LUCAS
MEXICO
La Habana
CUBA
DOMINICAN REPUBLIC
HAITI
Port-au-Prince
Santo Domingo
San Juan
PUERTO RICO (U.S.)
MAURITANIA
Nouakchott
Guadalajara
CIUDAD DE MÉXICO
JAMAICA
Kingston
GUADELOUPE (Fr.)
CAPE VERDE
SENEGAL
Dakar
GAMBIA
Banjul
GUINEA-BISSAU
JOHNSTON ATOLL
(U.S.)
GUATEMALA
BELIZE
(U.K.)
HONDURAS
Guatemala
Tegucigalpa
San Salvador
EL SALVADOR
Caribbean Sea
MARTINIQUE (Fr.)
BARBADOS
TRINIDAD AND TOBAGO
Port of Spain
NICARAGUA
Managua
San José
Panamá
COSTA RICA
PANAMA
CLIPPERTON
Caracas
VENEZUELA
GUYANA
Georgetown
Paramaribo
SURINAME
FRENCH GUIANA
Medellín
Bogotá
Cali
COLOMBIA
GUINEA
Conakry
Freetown
SIERRA LEONE
Monrovia
LIBERIA
Bamako
Tombouctou
IVORY COAST
Abidjan
P O L Y N E S I A
LINE ISLANDS
Equator
Quito
ECUADOR
Guayaquil
ARCHIPIÉLAGO DE COLÓN
GALAPAGOS ISLANDS
(Ec.)
Manaus
Belém
Fortaleza
CABO DE SÃO ROQUE
Natal
Recife
CANTON AND ENDERBURY (U.K.-U.S.)
PHOENIX ISLANDS
Iquitos
ANDES
PERU
B R A Z I L
Trujillo
Lima
TOKELAU ISLANDS
(N.Z.)
ÎLES MARQUISES
WALLIS AND FUTUNA
(Fr.)
W. SAMOA
AM. SAMOA
Apia
SOUTH AMERICA
Salvador
ATLANTIC OCEAN
ÎLES TUAMOTU
FIJI
ÎLES DE LA SOCIÉTÉ
SOCIETY ISLANDS
NIUE
(N.Z.)
COOK ISLANDS
(N.Z.)
FRENCH POLYNESIA
Arequipa
La Paz
BOLIVIA
Sucre
Goiânia
Brasília
Belo Horizonte
TONGA
PARAGUAY
SÃO PAULO
RIO DE JANEIRO
Santos
Curitiba
Tropic of Capricorn
PITCAIRN
(U.K.)
Antofagasta
Asunción
ISLA DE PASCUA
EASTER ISLAND
(Chile)
ISLA SAN AMBROSIO
(Chile)
CHILE
International Date Line
Co. Aconcagua
6959
Córdoba
Pôrto Alegre
Valparaíso
Santiago
Rosario
URUGUAY
BUENOS AIRES
Montevideo
ISLAS JUAN FERNÁNDEZ
(Chile)
P A C I F I C
Concepción
ARGENTINA
Mar del Plata
Bahía Blanca
O C E A N
CHATHAM ISLAND
(N.Z.)
FALKLAND ISLANDS
ISLAS MALVINAS
(U.K.)
Punta Arenas
CABO DE HORNOS
CAPE HORN
SOUTH GEORGIA
(Falk. Is.)
SOUTH ORKNEY ISLANDS
(B.A.T.)
Antarctic Circle
ANTARCTIC PENINSULA
Bellingshausen Sea
Weddell Sea
Ross Sea
Vinson Massif
5140
A N T A R

Kilometers 0 1000 2000 3000 Km.
Statute Miles 0 1000 2000 3000 Mi.

One centimeter represents 750 kilometers.
One inch represents approximately 1200 miles.
Robinson Projection
Scale 1:75,000,000

World: Physical / Erde: Physisch / Mundo: Físico
Monde: Physique / Mundo: Físico

One centimeter represents 750 kilometers.
One inch represents approximately 1200 miles.
Robinson Projection
Scale 1:75,000,000

GREENLAND
Greenland Sea
Barents Sea
Arctic Circle
Norwegian Sea
ICELAND
FINLAND
UNION OF SOVIET SOCIALIST REPUBLICS
ZAPADNO-SIBIRSKAJA NIZMENNOST'
SREDNESIBIRSKOJE PLOSKOGORJE
URAL'SKIJE GORY
URAL MOUNTAINS
Sea of Okhotsk
UNITED KINGDOM
IRELAND
North Sea
Baltic Sea
EUROPE
FRANCE
POLAND
HUNGARY
ROMANIA
BULGARIA
YUGO.
ALB.
GREECE
TURKEY
ASIA MINOR
Black Sea
Caspian Sea
Aral'skoje More
MONGOLIA
GOBI
CHINA
ASIA
TIEN SHAN
PAMIR
HINDU KUSH
AFGHANISTAN
IRAN
IRAQ
SYRIA
JORDAN
ISRAEL
LEBANON
CYPRUS
KUWAIT
SAUDI ARABIA
QATAR
UNITED ARAB EMIRATES
OMAN
YEMEN
P.D.R. OF YEMEN
PAKISTAN
INDIA
NEPAL
BHUTAN
BNGL.
BURMA
THAILAND
LAOS
VIET-NAM
KAMPUCHEA
MALAYSIA
INDONESIA
PHILIPPINES
TAIWAN
KOREA
JAPAN
Sea of Japan
Yellow Sea
East China Sea
South China Sea
Philippine Sea
HIMALAYAS
Mount Everest
MEDITERRANEAN SEA
TUNISIA
LIBYA
EGYPT
SAHARA
Tropic of Cancer
SUDAN
ETHIOPIA
DJIBOUTI
SOMALIA
KENYA
UGANDA
RWANDA
BURUNDI
TANZANIA
ZAIRE
ZAMBIA
MALAWI
MOZAMBIQUE
ZIMBABWE
BOTSWANA
NAMIBIA
SOUTH AFRICA
LESOTHO
SWAZILAND
MADAGASCAR
AFRICA
Equator
Red Sea
Gulf of Aden
ARABIAN SEA
Bay of Bengal
Andaman Sea
SRI LANKA
MALDIVES
SEYCHELLES
MAURITIUS
REUNION
COMOROS
Mozambique Channel
INDIAN OCEAN
CENTRAL BASIN
MID-INDIAN RIDGE
EAST INDIAN RIDGE
WEST AUSTRALIAN BASIN
COCOS BASIN
Tropic of Capricorn
MASCARENE BASIN
CROZET BASIN
AGULHAS BASIN
ATLANTIC-INDIAN RIDGE
ATLANTIC-INDIAN BASIN
AUSTRALIAN - ANTARCTIC RISE
SOUTH INDIAN BASIN
KERGUELEN-GAUSSBERG RIDGE
JAVA TRENCH
GREATER SUNDA ISLANDS
BORNEO
SUMATRA
JAWA
SULAWESI
NEW GUINEA
PAPUA NEW GUINEA
Timor Sea
Arafura Sea
Gulf of Carpentaria
AUSTRALIA
GREAT SANDY DESERT
GREAT VICTORIA DESERT
GREAT DIVIDING RANGE
Great Australian Bight
SOUTH AUSTRALIAN BASIN
TASMANIA
CORAL SEA
Antarctic Circle
ANTARCTICA
ENDERBY LAND
WILKES LAND
QUEEN MAUD LAND
AMERICAN HIGHLAND

Pacific and Indian Oceans / Pazifischer und Indischer Ozean
Océanos Pacífico e Indico / Océans Pacifique et Indien
Oceanos Pacífico e Indico

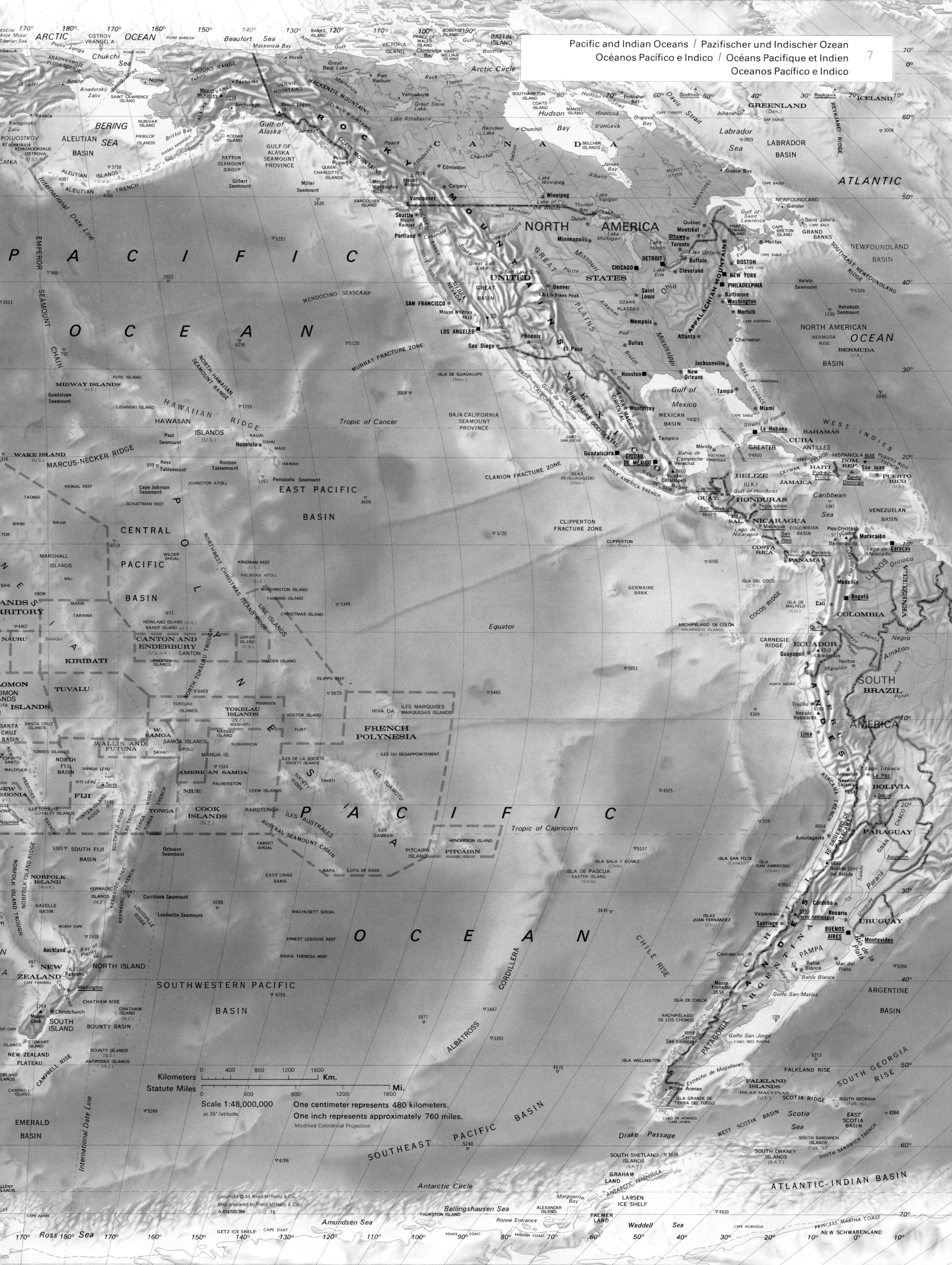

8
Atlantic Ocean / Atlantischer Ozean
Océano Atlántico / Océan Atlantique
Oceano Atlântico
NORTH AMERICA
CANADA
UNITED STATES
GREENLAND
ICELAND
Hudson Bay
Labrador Sea
LABRADOR BASIN
Baffin Bay
Davis Strait
Norwegian Sea
Greenland Sea
ARCTIC OCEAN
Barents Sea
North Sea
UNITED KINGDOM
IRELAND
FRANCE
SPAIN
PORTUGAL
UNION OF SOVIET SOCIALIST REPUBLICS
EUROPE
Mediterranean Sea
Black Sea
Caspian Sea
ATLANTIC OCEAN
WEST EUROPEAN BASIN
NEWFOUNDLAND BASIN
AZORES
MID-ATLANTIC RIDGE
NORTH AMERICAN BASIN
BERMUDA
BAHAMAS
Tropic of Cancer
Gulf of Mexico
MEXICO
Caribbean Sea
WEST INDIES
CANARY BASIN
CAPE VERDE BASIN
CAPE VERDE
AFRICA
SAHARA
ALGERIA
LIBYA
EGYPT
MOROCCO
MAURITANIA
MALI
NIGER
CHAD
SUDAN
NIGERIA
ZAIRE
ANGOLA
NAMIBIA
BOTSWANA
SOUTH AFRICA
GUIANA BASIN
Equator
SOUTH AMERICA
BRAZIL
COLOMBIA
VENEZUELA
PERU
BOLIVIA
PARAGUAY
URUGUAY
ARGENTINA
CHILE
PACIFIC OCEAN
Tropic of Capricorn
BRAZIL BASIN
ANGOLA BASIN
CAPE BASIN
ARGENTINE BASIN
AGULHAS BASIN
INDIAN OCEAN
Scotia Sea
Weddell Sea
Drake Passage
Antarctic Circle
ANTARCTICA
Kilometers 0 400 800 1200 1600 Km.
Statute Miles 0 200 400 800 1200 1600 Mi.
Scale 1:48,000,000
at 35° latitude
One centimeter represents 480 kilometers.
One inch represents approximately 760 miles.
Modified Cylindrical Projection
Copyright © by Rand McNally & Co.
Map prepared by Rand McNally & Co.
A-513700-764 -15

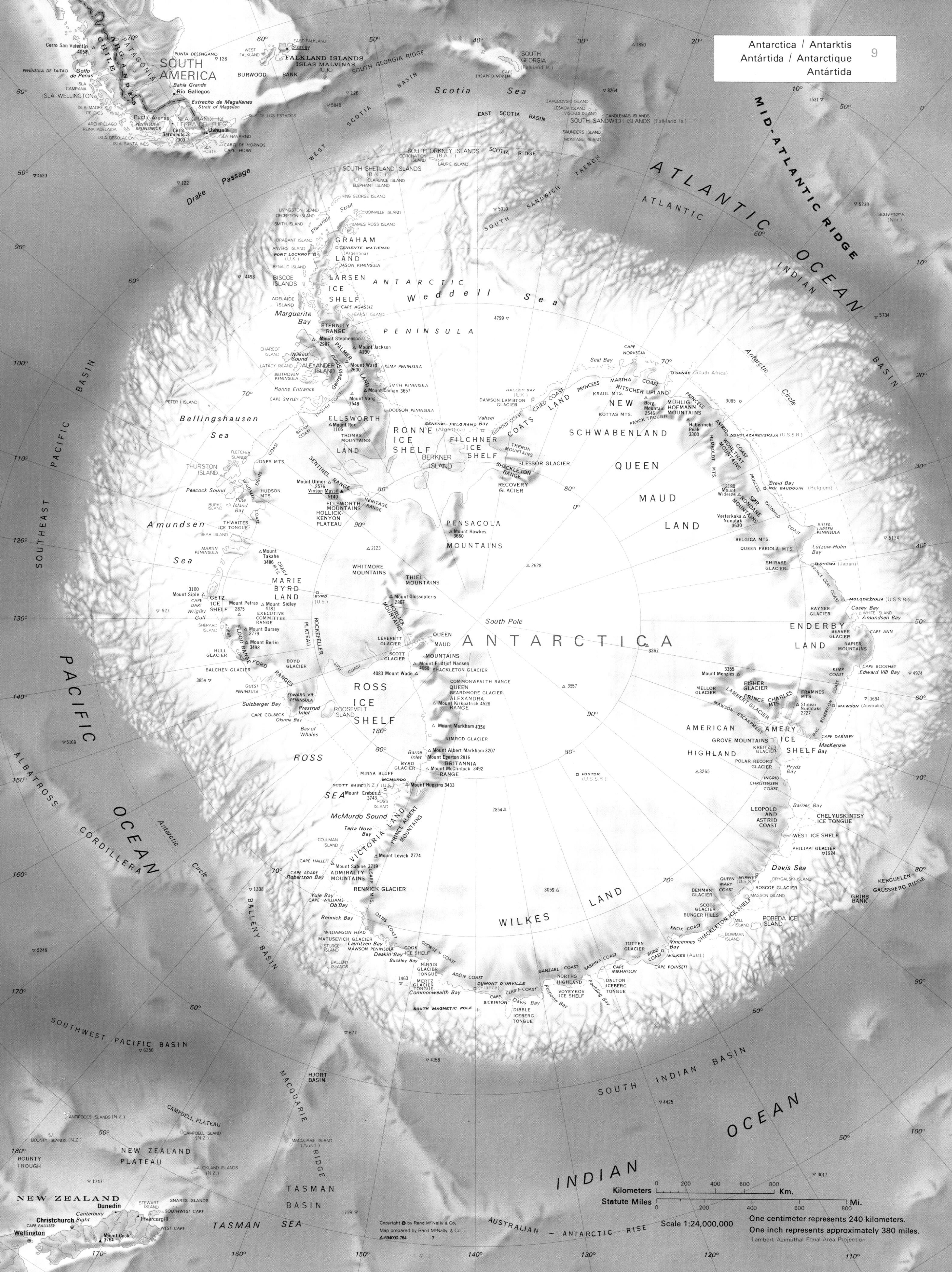
SOUTH AMERICA
PATAGONIA
CHILE
ARGENTINA
ANDES
Cerro San Valentín 4058
Golfo de Penas
ISLA WELLINGTON
Bahía Grande
Río Gallegos
Estrecho de Magallanes
Strait of Magellan
Punta Arenas
ISLA GRANDE DE TIERRA DEL FUEGO
Ushuaia
ISLA DE LOS ESTADOS
CABO DE HORNOS
CAPE HORN
FALKLAND ISLANDS
ISLAS MALVINAS
(U.K.)
Stanley
BURWOOD
BANK
SOUTH GEORGIA RIDGE
SOUTH GEORGIA
(Falkland Is.)
Scotia
Sea
EAST
SCOTIA
BASIN
SOUTH SANDWICH ISLANDS (Falkland Is.)
WEST
SCOTIA
BASIN
Drake
Passage
SOUTH ORKNEY ISLANDS
(B.A.T.)
SCOTIA
RIDGE
SOUTH SHETLAND ISLANDS
SOUTH SANDWICH TRENCH
SOUTH
ATLANTIC
ATLANTIC OCEAN
MID-ATLANTIC RIDGE
INDIAN
BOUVETØYA
(Nor.)
Bransfield Strait
GRAHAM
LAND
LARSEN
ICE
SHELF
ANTARCTIC
PENINSULA
Weddell
Sea
Marguerite Bay
ETERNITY RANGE
Mount Stephenson 2987
Mount Jackson 4190
Wilkins Sound
ALEXANDER ISLAND
PALMER LAND
George VI Sound
Mount Coman 3657
Ronne Entrance
Mount Vang 1548
ELLSWORTH LAND
Mount Rex 1105
Bellingshausen
Sea
RONNE
ICE
SHELF
FILCHNER
ICE
SHELF
BERKNER ISLAND
THURSTON ISLAND
Peacock Sound
Amundsen
Sea
SENTINEL RANGE
Mount Ulmer 2576
Vinson Massif 5140
ELLSWORTH MOUNTAINS
HERITAGE RANGE
HOLLICK-KENYON PLATEAU
PENSACOLA
MOUNTAINS
Mount Hawkes 3660
WHITMORE MOUNTAINS
THIEL MOUNTAINS
MARIE
BYRD
LAND
Mount Takahe 3486
Mount Sidley 4181
EXECUTIVE COMMITTEE RANGE
GETZ ICE SHELF
ROCKEFELLER PLATEAU
FLOOD RANGE
FORD RANGES
Sulzberger Bay
Mount Glossopteris 2867
HORLICK MOUNTAINS
South Pole
ANTARCTICA
QUEEN MAUD MOUNTAINS
Mount Fridtjof Nansen 4068
4083 Mount Wade
SHACKLETON GLACIER
ROSS
ICE
SHELF
ROOSEVELT ISLAND
Bay of Whales
ROSS
SEA
COMMONWEALTH RANGE
QUEEN ALEXANDRA RANGE
BEARDMORE GLACIER
Mount Kirkpatrick 4528
Mount Markham 4350
NIMROD GLACIER
Mount Albert Markham 3207
Mount Egerton 2816
BRITANNIA RANGE
Mount McClintock 3492
MINNA BLUFF
McMURDO
SCOTT BASE (N.Z.) (U.S.)
Mount Huggins 3433
Mount Erebus 3743
ROSS ISLAND
McMurdo Sound
Terra Nova Bay
VICTORIA LAND
PRINCE ALBERT MOUNTAINS
Mount Levick 2774
Mount Sabine 3719
ADMIRALTY MOUNTAINS
Robertson Bay
RENNICK GLACIER
USARP MTS.
Yule Bay
Ob' Bay
Rennick Bay
OATES COAST
Lauritzen Bay
COOK ICE SHELF
GEORGE V COAST
Deakin Bay
Buckley Bay
NINNIS GLACIER TONGUE
MERTZ GLACIER TONGUE
Commonwealth Bay
ADÉLIE COAST
DUMONT D'URVILLE (France)
CLARIE COAST
Davis Bay
DIBBLE ICEBERG TONGUE
SOUTH MAGNETIC POLE
BANZARE COAST
SABRINA COAST
NORTHS HIGHLAND
VOYEYKOV ICE SHELF
DALTON ICEBERG TONGUE
Porpoise Bay
Paulding Bay
WILKES
LAND
TOTTEN GLACIER
BUDD COAST
WILKES (Austl.)
Vincennes Bay
KNOX COAST
SHACKLETON ICE SHELF
QUEEN MARY COAST
MIRNYY (U.S.S.R.)
DENMAN GLACIER
SCOTT GLACIER
BUNGER HILLS
POBEDA ICE ISLAND
Davis Sea
WEST ICE SHELF
PHILIPPI GLACIER
LEOPOLD AND ASTRID COAST
CHELYUSKINTSY ICE TONGUE
Barrier Bay
INGRID CHRISTENSEN COAST
Prydz Bay
AMERY ICE SHELF
AMERICAN HIGHLAND
GROVE MOUNTAINS
MacKenzie Bay
VOSTOK (U.S.S.R.)
PRINCE CHARLES MTS.
LAMBERT GLACIER
FISHER GLACIER
MELLOR GLACIER
MAWSON ESCARPMENT
FRAMNES MTS.
MAWSON (Australia)
Edward VIII Bay
KEMP COAST
NAPIER MOUNTAINS
ENDERBY
LAND
Amundsen Bay
Casey Bay
MOLODEZHNAJA (U.S.S.R.)
RAYNER GLACIER
PRINCE OLAV COAST
SHOWA (Japan)
Lützow-Holm Bay
SHIRASE GLACIER
QUEEN FABIOLA MTS.
BELGICA MTS.
RIISER-LARSEN PENINSULA
SØR RONDANE MOUNTAINS
Breid Bay
ROI BAUDOUIN (Belgium)
PRINCESS RAGNHILD COAST
PRINCESS ASTRID COAST
WOHLTHAT MOUNTAINS
HUMBOLDT MTS.
NOVOLAZAREVSKAJA (U.S.S.R.)
MÜHLIG-HOFMANN MOUNTAINS
Habermehl Peak 3300
QUEEN
MAUD
LAND
NEW
SCHWABENLAND
RITSCHER UPLAND
Borg Mountain 2546
PRINCESS MARTHA COAST
SANAE (South Africa)
Seal Bay
CAPE NORVEGIA
HALLEY BAY (U.K.)
CAIRD COAST
COATS LAND
LUITPOLD COAST
Vahsel Bay
GENERAL BELGRANO (Argentina)
THERON MOUNTAINS
SHACKLETON RANGE
SLESSOR GLACIER
RECOVERY GLACIER
Antarctic Circle
SOUTHEAST PACIFIC BASIN
PACIFIC OCEAN
ALBATROSS CORDILLERA
BALLENY BASIN
BALLENY ISLANDS
SOUTHWEST PACIFIC BASIN
MACQUARIE RIDGE
HJORT BASIN
CAMPBELL PLATEAU
NEW ZEALAND PLATEAU
BOUNTY TROUGH
TASMAN BASIN
TASMAN SEA
NEW ZEALAND
Christchurch
Dunedin
Wellington
Invercargill
Mount Cook 3764
AUSTRALIAN – ANTARCTIC RISE
SOUTH INDIAN BASIN
INDIAN OCEAN
KERGUELEN-GAUSSBERG RIDGE
GRIBB BANK
Kilometers 0 200 400 600 800 Km.
Statute Miles 0 200 400 600 800 Mi.
Scale 1:24,000,000
One centimeter represents 240 kilometers.
One inch represents approximately 380 miles.
Lambert Azimuthal Equal-Area Projection
Copyright © by Rand McNally & Co.
Map prepared by Rand McNally & Co.
A-594000-764

ATLANTIC OCEAN
EUROPE
ASIA
UNION OF SOVIET SOCIALIST REPUBLICS
CANADA
GREENLAND (Den.)
ICELAND
Reykjavík
FAEROE ISLANDS (Den.)
NORWAY
SWEDEN
FINLAND
DENMARK
UNITED KINGDOM
IRELAND
FRANCE
SPAIN
PORTUGAL
ITALY
POLAND
CZECHOSLOVAKIA
AUSTRIA
HUNGARY
ROMANIA
YUGOSLAVIA
BULGARIA
ALBANIA
GREECE
TURKEY
SYRIA
IRAQ
IRAN
JORDAN
LEBANON
ISRAEL
CYPRUS
KUWAIT
SAUDI ARABIA
BAHRAIN
QATAR
UNITED ARAB EMIRATES
OMAN
EGYPT
LIBYA
TUNISIA
ALGERIA
MOROCCO
WESTERN SAHARA
MAURITANIA
SAHARA
LONDON
PARIS
MADRID
Lisboa
ROMA
BERLIN
Warszawa
Praha
WIEN
BUDAPEST
Beograd
Bucuresti
Sofija
Tiranë
Athínai
İSTANBUL
Ankara
MOSKVA
LENINGRAD
Helsinki
Stockholm
Oslo
København
Amsterdam
Bruxelles
Bern
Dublin
Alger
Tunis
Tarābulus
Rabat
AL-QĀHIRAH
Baghdād
TEHRĀN
Dimashq
Bayrūt
Ammān
Yerushalayim
Ar-Riyāḍ
Al-Kuwayt
Norwegian Sea
North Sea
Baltic Sea
Barents Sea
Greenland Sea
Labrador Sea
Mediterranean Sea
Black Sea
Caspian Sea
Adriatic Sea
Aegean Sea
Tyrrhenian Sea
Ionian Sea
Red Sea
Persian Gulf
Bay of Biscay
English Channel
Davis Strait
Denmark Strait
Strait of Gibraltar
Gulf of Bothnia
Gulf of Finland
URAL'SKIJE GORY
URAL MOUNTAINS
ALPS
CARPATHIAN MOUNTAINS
ATLAS MOUNTAINS
PYRENEES
APPENNINO
BOL'ŠOJ KAVKAZ
MID-ATLANTIC RIDGE
REYKJANES RIDGE
WEST EUROPEAN BASIN
AZORES-GIBRALTAR RIDGE
CANARY BASIN
LABRADOR BASIN
NORWEGIAN BASIN
LOFOTEN BASIN
GREENLAND BASIN
MOHNS RIDGE
ROCKALL RISE
ZAPADNO-SIBIRSKAJA NIZMENNOST'
ARABIAN PENINSULA
Arctic Circle
Tropic of Cancer

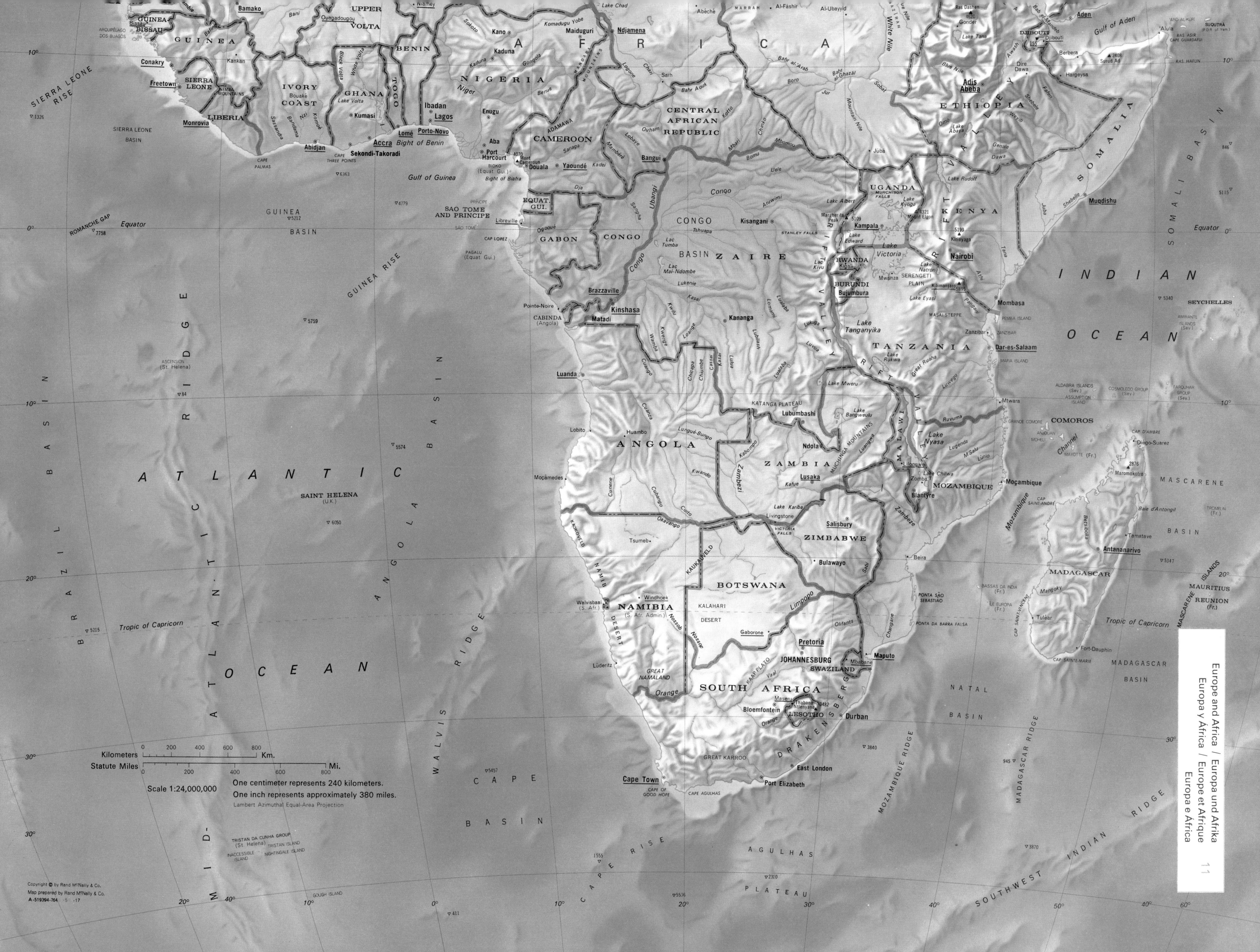
AFRICA
INDIAN OCEAN
ATLANTIC OCEAN
ETHIOPIA
SOMALIA
DJIBOUTI
KENYA
UGANDA
TANZANIA
RWANDA
BURUNDI
ZAIRE
CONGO
GABON
EQUAT. GUI.
CAMEROON
CENTRAL AFRICAN REPUBLIC
NIGERIA
BENIN
TOGO
GHANA
UPPER VOLTA
IVORY COAST
LIBERIA
SIERRA LEONE
GUINEA
GUINEA-BISSAU
SAO TOME AND PRINCIPE
ANGOLA
ZAMBIA
MALAWI
MOZAMBIQUE
ZIMBABWE
BOTSWANA
NAMIBIA
SOUTH AFRICA
LESOTHO
SWAZILAND
MADAGASCAR
COMOROS
MAURITIUS
REUNION (Fr.)
SEYCHELLES
SAINT HELENA (U.K.)
Equator
Tropic of Capricorn
Gulf of Guinea
Gulf of Aden
Bight of Benin
Bight of Biafra
Mozambique Channel
GUINEA BASIN
ANGOLA BASIN
CAPE BASIN
NATAL BASIN
MADAGASCAR BASIN
MASCARENE BASIN
SOMALI BASIN
BRAZIL BASIN
SIERRA LEONE BASIN
MID-ATLANTIC RIDGE
WALVIS RIDGE
GUINEA RISE
CAPE RISE
SIERRA LEONE RISE
MOZAMBIQUE RIDGE
MADAGASCAR RIDGE
SOUTHWEST INDIAN RIDGE
AGULHAS PLATEAU
Kilometers 0 200 400 600 800 Km.
Statute Miles 0 200 400 600 800 Mi.
Scale 1:24,000,000
One centimeter represents 240 kilometers.
One inch represents approximately 380 miles.
Lambert Azimuthal Equal-Area Projection
Copyright © by Rand McNally & Co.
Map prepared by Rand McNally & Co.
A-519394-764

ARCTIC
OCEAN
ATLANTIC
OCEAN
North Pole
GREENLAND
(Den.)
ICELAND
Reykjavík
Greenland
Sea
Norwegian
Sea
Barents
Sea
Karskoje
More
Kara Sea
More
Laptevych
Laptev Sea
Vostočno-Sibirskoje More
East Siberian Sea
Chukchi
Sea
Bering
Sea
ALEUTIAN
BASIN
UNITED STATES
Bering Strait
Arctic Circle
SVALBARD
ZEML'A FRANCA-IOSIFA
FRANZ JOSEPH LAND
SEVERNAJA
ZEML'A
NOVOSIBIRSKIJE
OSTROVA
OSTROV
VRANGEL'A
NOVAJA ZEML'A
FAEROE
ISLANDS
(Den.)
IRELAND
UNITED
KINGDOM
North
Sea
NORWAY
SWEDEN
FINLAND
Gulf of Bothnia
DENMARK
Baltic
Sea
POLAND
CZECHOSLOVAKIA
HUNGARY
ROMANIA
BULGARIA
TURKEY
ASIA
MINOR
SYRIA
IRAQ
IRAN
AFGHANISTAN
SAUDI
ARABIA
Black
Sea
Caspian
Sea
Aral'skoje
More
BOL'SOJ KAVKAZ
CAUCASUS
URAL'SKIJE GORY
URAL MOUNTAINS
UNION
OF
SOVIET
SOCIALIST
REPUBLICS
EUROPE
ZAPADNO-SIBIRSKAJA
NIZMENNOST'
SREDNESIBIRSKOJE
PLOSKOGORJE
CHREBET ČERSKOGO
MONGOLIA
GOBI
ASIA
TIEN SHAN
PAMIR
HINDU KUSH
TALIMUPENDI
TAKLA MAKAN
KUNLUNSHANMAI
CHINA
NORTH KOREA
SOUTH KOREA
JAPAN
HONSHU
KYUSHU
HOKKAIDO
Sea of
Japan
Yellow
Sea
EAST
CHINA
SEA
Sea of
Okhotsk
OSTROV
SACHALIN
KURIL'SKIJE OSTROVA
KURIL ISLANDS
POLUOSTROV
KAMČATKA
LONDON
Dublin
Glasgow
Edinburgh
Manchester
Birmingham
Cardiff
Oslo
Bergen
Trondheim
Stockholm
Göteborg
København
Malmö
Helsinki
Amsterdam
Bruxelles
Hamburg
BERLIN
Leipzig
Frankfurt
Stuttgart
MÜNCHEN
Praha
WIEN
BUDAPEST
Beograd
Bucuresti
Sofija
Warszawa
Kraków
Katowice
Gdańsk
Kaliningrad
Riga
Tallinn
Vilnius
Minsk
LENINGRAD
MOSKVA
Murmansk
Archangel'sk
Kijev
Char'kov
ODESSA
Kišin'ov
L'vov
Dnepropetrovsk
Doneck
Rostov-na-Donu
VOLGOGRAD
Saratov
Kujbyšev
Kazan'
Gor'kij
Perm'
SVERDLOVSK
Čel'abinsk
Magnitogorsk
Ufa
Orenburg
Orsk
Omsk
Novosibirsk
Tomsk
Krasnojarsk
Irkutsk
Ulan-Ude
Čita
Jakutsk
Magadan
Chabarovsk
Vladivostok
Noril'sk
Dikson
ISTANBUL
Ankara
Izmir
TBILISI
Jerevan
BAKU
TEHRĀN
Baghdād
Dimashq
Bayrūt
Ammān
Yerushalayim
Tel Aviv-Yafo
Al-Kuwayt
Kābul
Herāt
Taškent
Samarkand
Dušanbe
Alma-Ata
Frunze
Karaganda
Celinograd
Semipalatinsk
Ulaan Baatar
BEIJING
PEKING
TIANJIN
SHENYANG
MUKDEN
P'YŎNGYANG
SŎUL
SHANGHAI
WUHAN
Xi'an
Lanzhou
Wulumuqi
Harbin
Changchun
Sapporo
Sendai
Nagoya
ŌSAKA
Kyōto
Hiroshima
Fukuoka
Kagoshima
Petropavlovsk-Kamčatskij
Lena
Ob'
Jenisej
Amur
Volga
Ozero
Bajkal
Ozero
Balchaš

INDIAN OCEAN
ARABIAN SEA
Bay of Bengal
Andaman Sea
SOUTH CHINA SEA
Philippine Sea
Sulu Sea
Celebes Sea
Java Sea
Laccadive Sea
Red Sea
Gulf of Aden
Gulf of Oman
Gulf of Thailand
Gulf of Tonkin
Gulf of Martaban
Gulf of Mannar
INDIA
PAKISTAN
NEPAL
BHUTAN
BANGLADESH
BURMA
THAILAND
LAOS
KAMPUCHEA
VIETNAM
MALAYSIA
INDONESIA
PHILIPPINES
BRUNEI
SINGAPORE
SRI LANKA
MALDIVES
OMAN
YEMEN
P.D.R. OF YEMEN
DJIBOUTI
SOMALIA
ETHIOPIA
MADAGASCAR
MAURITIUS
SEYCHELLES
AUSTRALIA
ARABIAN PENINSULA
AR-RUB' AL-KHĀLĪ
SUMATERA
BORNEO
JAWA
SULAWESI
MID-INDIAN BASIN
WEST AUSTRALIAN BASIN
ARABIAN BASIN
SOMALI BASIN
MADAGASCAR BASIN
MASCARENE BASIN
COCOS BASIN
NINETY EAST RIDGE
BROKEN RIDGE
CARLSBERG RIDGE
MID-INDIAN RIDGE
SOUTHWEST INDIAN RIDGE
CHAGOS-LACCADIVE PLATEAU
MASCARENE PLATEAU
JAVA TRENCH
Tropic of Cancer
Equator
Tropic of Capricorn
DELHI
BOMBAY
CALCUTTA
MADRAS
Bangalore
Hyderābād
KARĀCHI
Dacca
Rangoon
KRUNG THEP (BANGKOK)
Ha-noi
Phnum Pénh
Kuala Lumpur
JAKARTA
MANILA
HONG KONG
VICTORIA
Colombo
Muqdisho
Antananarivo
Perth
Scale 1:24,000,000
Kilometers 0 200 400 600 800
Statute Miles 0 200 400 600 800
One centimeter represents 240 kilometers.
One inch represents approximately 380 miles.
Lambert Azimuthal Equal-Area Projection
Copyright © by Rand McNally & Co.
Map prepared by Rand McNally & Co.

CHONGQING
Changsha
Nanchang
East China Sea
HIMALAYAS
INDIA
CHINA
ASIA
Guiyang
Fuzhou
Wenzhou
Naha
OKINAWA-JIMA
Kunming
Liuzhou
Xiamen
Amoy
Formosa Strait
T'aipei
TAIWAN
RYUKYU TRENCH
NANSEI-SHOTŌ
RYUKYU ISLANDS
(Japan)
OGASAWARA-GUNTŌ
BONIN ISLANDS
(Jap.)
Tropic of Cancer
Mekong
Brahmaputra
Irrawaddy
GUANGZHOU
CANTON
VICTORIA
HONG KONG
(U.K.)
Macau
(Port.)
Nanning
Luzon Strait
Zhanjiang
Mandalay
BURMA
Ha-noi
Hai-phong
Haikou
HAINANDAO
Gulf of Tonkin
LAOS
Viangchan
Udon Thani
Hue
Da-nang
VIETNAM
PARACEL ISLANDS
LUZON
Lingayen Gulf
SIERRA MADRE
Quezon City
MANILA
PHILIPPINE SEA
PHILIPPINE BASIN
PALAU KYUSHU RIDGE
HONSHU RIDGE
MARIANA RIDGE
MARIANA ISLANDS
MARIANA TRENCH
GUAM
(U.S.)
MARIANA BASIN
Moulmein
THAILAND
KRUNG THEP
BANGKOK
SOUTH CHINA SEA
KAMPUCHEA
Tônlé Sab
Phnum Penh
THANH-PHO HO CHI MINH
(SAI-GON)
BASIN
PHILIPPINES
PHILIPPINE TRENCH
Cebu
Mindanao Sea
MINDANAO
Davao
Sulu Sea
SULU SEA BASIN
Zamboanga
SOUTH
CAROLINE
WEST CAROLINE BASIN
EAST CAROLINE BASIN
EAURIPIK RIDGE
PALAU ISLANDS
TRUK ISLANDS
HALL ISLANDS
ISTHMUS OF KRA
Gulf of Thailand
Balabac Strait
Kota Kinabalu
Gunong Kinabalu
Bandar Seri Begawan
BRUNEI
(U.K.)
Celebes Sea
CELEBES BASIN
MALAYSIA
George Town
MALAY PENINSULA
Manado
Medan
Kuala Lumpur
SINGAPORE
Strait of Malacca
Kuching
BORNEO
KALIMANTAN
Balikpapan
Equator
SUMATERA
SUMATRA
GREATER SUNDA ISLANDS
Banjarmasin
SULAWESI
CELEBES
MALUKU
MOLUCCAS
SERAM
Laut Seram
Laut Maluku
Jayapura
PEGUNUNGAN MAOKE
Puncak Jaya
NEW GUINEA
Bismarck Sea
PAPUA NEW GUINEA
Mount Wilhelm
Rabaul
NEW BRITAIN
BOUGAINVILLE
NEW BRITAIN TRENCH
SOLOMON BASIN
Padang
Palembang
Selat Karimata
INDONESIA
Laut Jawa
Java Sea
Ujung Pandang
SOUTH BANDA BASIN
ARU BASIN
PULAU YOS SUDARSA
Gulf of Papua
Port Moresby
OWEN STANLEY RANGE
Torres Strait
Arafura Sea
JAKARTA
Bandung
JAWA
JAVA
Surabaya
Laut Flores
NUSA TENGGARA
Dili
Laut Sawu
SAVU BASIN
TIMOR
TIMOR TROUGH
Timor Sea
CAPE YORK
CAPE YORK PENINSULA
CORAL SEA BASIN
CAPE WESSEL
CAPE ARNHEM
Gulf of Carpentaria
GROOTE EYLANDT
ARNHEM LAND
Darwin
SAHUL SHELF
JAVA TRENCH
Joseph Bonaparte Gulf
WELLESLEY ISLANDS
GREAT BARRIER REEF
CORAL SEA PLATEAU
Cairns
Townsville
CHRISTMAS ISLAND
(Austl.)
KIMBERLEY PLATEAU
Birdum
BARKLY TABLELAND
GREAT DIVIDING RANGE
Collier Bay
Broome
Fitzroy
WHARTON BASIN
COCOS ISLANDS
(Austl.)
Mount Isa
SELWYN RANGE
TANAMI DESERT
GREAT SANDY DESERT
Rockhampton
MACDONNELL RANGES
Alice Springs
SIMPSON DESERT
AUSTRALIA
Brisbane
WEST AUSTRALIAN BASIN
INDIAN OCEAN
Mount Bruce
GIBSON DESERT
Mount Woodroffe
NORTH WEST CAPE
Lake Eyre
STURT DESERT
Lake Macleod
GREAT VICTORIA DESERT
Lake Torrens
Lake Frome
Broken Hill
Carnarvon
Shark Bay
Newcastle
SYDNEY
NULLARBOR PLAIN
Lake Everard
Lake Gairdner
Kalgoorlie
Adelaide
Canberra
Mount Kosciusko
Tropic of Capricorn
MELBOURNE
Perth
DARLING RANGE
Great Australian Bight
SOUTH AUSTRALIAN BASIN
Bass Strait
Launceston
Hobart
TASMAN
Geographe Bay
CAPE LEEUWIN
NINETY EAST RIDGE
BROKEN RIDGE
DIAMANTINA TROUGH
OBI TROUGH
SOUTH TASMANIA RISE
Kilometers
Km.
Statute Miles
Mi.
Scale 1:24,000,000
One centimeter represents 240 kilometers.
One inch represents approximately 380 miles.
Lambert Azimuthal Equal-Area Projection

HAWAIIAN ISLANDS
HAWAIIAN RIDGE
MIDWAY ISLANDS
(U.S.)
PEARL AND HERMES REEF
LISIANSKI ISLAND
LAYSAN ISLAND
Gardner Pinnacles
Guadalupe Seamount
International Date Line
Paul Seamount
FRENCH FRIGATE SHOALS
NECKER ISLAND
NIHOA
NECKER RIDGE
Tropic of Cancer
KAUAI
NIIHAU
OAHU
Honolulu
MOLOKAI
LANAI
MAUI
KAHOOLAWE
Hilo
Mauna Kea
4205
HAWAII
KA LAE
Swordfish Seamount
Pensacola Seamount
Horizon Tablemount
Karin Seamount
JOHNSTON ATOLL
(U.S.)
WAKE ISLAND
(U.S.)
MID PACIFIC MOUNTAINS
Hess Tablemount
Cape Johnson Seamount
RIONAL REEF
RENE REEF
SCHJETMAN REEF
PACIFIC ISLANDS TRUST TERRITORY
(U.S.)
RATAK CHAIN
RALIK CHAIN
MARSHALL ISLANDS
BIKINI
ENIWETOK
RONGELAP
UTIRIK
WOTHO
AILUK
UJAE
KWAJALEIN
WOTJE
MALOELAP
LAE
LIB
NAMU
AILINGLAPALAP
ARNO
MAJURO
MILI
JALUIT
KILI
EBON
NAMORIK
PINGELAP
KUSAIE
CENTRAL PACIFIC BASIN
WILDER SHOAL
P A C I F I C
O C E A N
EAST PACIFIC BASIN
CHRISTMAS RIDGE
LINE ISLANDS
KINGMAN REEF
PALMYRA ATOLL
(U.S.)
WASHINGTON ISLAND
FANNING ISLAND
CHRISTMAS ISLAND
JARVIS ISLAND
(U.S.)
MALDEN ISLAND
STARBUCK ISLAND
FILIPPO REEF
PENRHYN
Merlin Seamount
VOSTOK ISLAND
CAROLINE ATOLL
FLINT
Equator
MAKIN
TARAWA
ABEMAMA
KURIA
KIRIBATI
NAURU
BANABA
NONOUTI
BERU
TABITEUEA
NIKUNAU
ONOTOA
TAMANA
ARORAE
Winslow Seamount
HOWLAND ISLAND (U.S.)
BAKER ISLAND (U.S.)
CANTON AND ENDERBURY
(U.K.-U.S.)
CANTON
ENDERBURY
BIRNIE
PHOENIX
HULL
SYDNEY
GARDNER
PHOENIX ISLANDS
PHOENIX TROUGH
NORTH TOKELAU TROUGH
SOLOMON ISLANDS
TUVALU
NANUMEA
NIUTAO
NANUMANGA
NUI
VAITUPU
NUKUFETAU
FUNAFUTI
NUKULAILAI
MELANESIAN BORDER PLATEAU
NURAKITA
TOKELAU ISLANDS
(N.Z.)
ATAFU
NUKUNONU
FAKAOFO
SWAINS ISLAND
AMERICAN SAMOA
SAMOA ISLANDS
NASSAU ISLAND
MANIHIKI
GUADALCANAL
SAN CRISTOBAL
NENDÖ
SANTA CRUZ ISLANDS
UTUPUA
VANIKORO
SANTA CRUZ BASIN
RENNELL
TORRES ISLANDS
BANKS ISLANDS
VANUA LAVA
SANTA MARÍA ISLAND
ESPÍRITU SANTO
NEW HEBRIDES BASIN
NEW HEBRIDES
(Fr.-U.K.)
MAEWO
PENTECOST ISLAND
AMBRIM
MALEKULA
EPI
EFATE
ERROMANGA
TANA
ANEITYUM
NEW HEBRIDES TRENCH
ROTUMA
Combe Seamount
ÎLES WALLIS
FUTUNA
WALLIS AND FUTUNA
(Fr.)
Home Seamount
Pasco Seamount
WESTERN SAMOA
SAVAII
Apia
UPOLU
Pago Pago
TUTUILA
MANUA ISLANDS
SUWARROW
FIJI ISLANDS
VANUA LEVU
VANUAMBALAVU
TAVEUNI
LAU GROUP
VITI LEVU
Suva
Koro Sea
KANDAVU
FIJI
LAU TROUGH
TAFAHI
TOKU
VAVAU
VAVAU GROUP
TONGA ISLANDS
NIUE
(N.Z.)
COOK ISLANDS
(N.Z.)
PALMERSTON
AITUTAKI
MANUAE
TAKUTEA
ATIU
MITIARO
MAUKE
COOK ISLANDS
RAROTONGA
MANGAIA
LOYALTY ISLANDS
ÎLE OUVÉA
ÎLE LIFOU
ÎLES LOYAUTÉ
ÎLE MARÉ
NEW CALEDONIA
(Fr.)
Nouméa
HUNTER ISLAND
HUNTER ISLAND RIDGE
ONO-I-LAU
TONGATAPU GROUP
TONGA TAPU
Nukualofa
EUA
ATA
TONGA
TONGA RIDGE
TONGA TRENCH
LAU RIDGE
SOUTH FIJI RIDGE
SOUTH FIJI BASIN
Monongahela Seamount
Ozbourn Seamount
BELLINGSHAUSEN
SCILLY
MOPELIA
TUPAI
BORA BORA
RAIATEA
MAKATEA
MATAIVA
KAUKURA
FAKARAVA
TAKAPOTO
MOOREA
ÎLES DE LA SOCIÉTÉ
SOCIETY ISLANDS
SOCIETY RIDGE
TETIAROA
Papeete
TAHITI
MEHETIA
ANAA
HARAIKI
MARUTEA
RAVAHERE
HIKUERU
AMANU
NENGONENGO
HAO
MANUHANGI
AHUNUI
VANAVANA
ÎLES DU DÉSAPPOINTEMENT
ÎLES DU ROI GEORGES
TIKEI
RAROIA
MAKEMO
TAROIA
ÎLES TUAMOTU
TUAMOTU ARCHIPELAGO
FRENCH POLYNESIA
MARIA
RIMATARA
RURUTU
ÎLE TUPUAI
ÎLES AUSTRALES
RAEVAVAE
TEMATANGI
ÎLES GAMBIER
Tropic of Capricorn
AUSTRAL SEAMOUNT CHAIN
FABERT SHOAL
RAPA
ÎLOTS DE BASS
E. ORNE BANK
LORD HOWE RISE
NEW CALEDONIA BASIN
NORFOLK RIDGE
NORFOLK ISLAND
(Austl.)
LORD HOWE ISLAND
(Austl.)
WANGANELLA BANK
RAOUL ISLAND
KERMADEC ISLANDS
CURTIS ISLAND
KERMADEC RIDGE
KERMADEC TRENCH
Curritiuck Seamount
Seafox Seamount
Louisville Seamount
Burton Seamount
LOUISVILLE RIDGE
THREE KINGS IS.
NORTH CAPE
TAUROA POINT
GREAT BARRIER ISLAND
Auckland
Bay of Plenty
EAST CAPE
NORTH ISLAND
NEW ZEALAND
New Plymouth
Ruapehu
2797
CAPE EGMONT
Napier
Hawke Bay
CAPE FAREWELL
Wellington
CAPE PALLISER
Cook Strait
Tasman Sea
Mount Cook
3764
Christchurch
SOUTH ISLAND
Canterbury Bight
CHATHAM RISE
CHATHAM ISLAND
CHATHAM ISLANDS
(N.Z.)
WEST CAPE
Dunedin
Invercargill
SOUTHWEST CAPE
STEWART ISLAND
BOUNTY TROUGH
SNARES ISLANDS
CAMPBELL PLATEAU
BOUNTY ISLANDS
(N.Z.)
ANTIPODES ISLANDS
(N.Z.)
WACHUSETT SHOAL
ERNEST LEGOUVE REEF
MARIA THERESA REEF
SOUTHWEST PACIFIC BASIN
6890
1316
1477
859
1057
4809
6519
4462
5349
1737
6469
6879
1188
7314
4846
3580
10882
5303
10047
1518
8009
1088
497
5267
160°
170°
180°
150°
140°
130°
40°
30°
20°
10°
0°

ARCTIC
OCEAN
North Pole
ASIA
UNION OF SOVIET SOCIALIST REPUBLICS
ZAPADNO-SIBIRSKAJA NIZMENNOST'
URAL'SKIJE GORY
EUROPE
MOSKVA
MOSCOW
LENINGRAD
FINLAND
SWEDEN
NORWAY
Helsinki
Stockholm
Oslo
København
Göteborg
Trondheim
Bergen
Stavanger
DENMARK
Riga
Tallinn
Minsk
Vilnius
Klaipeda
Kaliningrad
Tula
Char'kov
Doneck
Rostov-na-Donu
Gor'kij
Rybinsk
Kirov
Kotlas
Archangel'sk
Murmansk
Hammerfest
Narvik
Kiruna
Vaasa
Gulf of Bothnia
Gulf of Finland
Baltic Sea
North Sea
Norwegian Sea
LOFOTEN BASIN
NORWEGIAN BASIN
MIDOCEAN RIDGE
MOHNS RIDGE
Greenland Sea
GREENLAND BASIN
SVALBARD
SPITSBERGEN
BJØRNØYA
BEAR ISLAND
SPITSBERGEN BANK
BARENTS TROUGH
Barents Sea
MURMANSK RISE
ZEML'A FRANCA-IOSIFA
FRANZ JOSEPH LAND
NOVAJA ZEML'A
Karskoje More
Kara Sea
SEVERNAJA ZEML'A
Dikson
Noril'sk
Dudinka
Salechard
Vorkuta
Narjan-Mar
Ob'
Jenisej
Arctic Circle
PLATO PUTORANA
SEVERO-SIBIRSKAJA NIZMENNOST
POLUOSTROV TAJMYR
Chatanga
Nordvik
Tiksi
Lena
More Laptevych
Laptev Sea
NOVOSIBIRSKIJE OSTROVA
Vostočno-Sibirskoje More
East Siberian Sea
VERCHOJANSKIJ CHREBET
CHREBET ČERSKOGO
Verchojansk
Kazačje
Jakutsk
Aldan
Žigansk
Srednekolymsk
Ambarčik
OSTROV VRANGEL'A
Chukchi Sea
Anadyr'
Uel'kal'
Uelen
Markovo
Kavača
Magadan
Ochotsk
Ajan
Sea of Okhotsk
Ochotskoje More
OKHOTSK BASIN
Zaliv Šelichova
Jamsk
Petropavlovsk-kamčatskij
SREDINNYJ CHREBET
Komsomol'sk-na-Amure
Chabarovsk
Amur
SICHOTE-ALIN
OSTROV SACHALIN
Ocha
ALDANSKOJE NAGORJE
STANOVOJ CHREBET
CHREBET DŽUGDŽUR
Anadyrskij Zaliv
BERING SEA
Bering Strait
ALEUTIAN BASIN
BOWERS RIDGE
ALEUTIAN ISLANDS
ALEUTIAN TRENCH
Unalaska
Bethel
Nome
Norton Sound
SAINT LAWRENCE ISLAND
SAINT MATTHEW ISLAND
PRIBILOF ISLANDS
Bristol Bay
Barrow
POINT BARROW
POINT HOPE
BROOKS RANGE
UNITED STATES
Yukon
Fairbanks
Anchorage
ALASKA RANGE
Seward
Gulf of Alaska
GULF OF ALASKA SEAMOUNT PROVINCE
PATTON SEAMOUNT GROUP
Juneau
Whitehorse
Beaufort Sea
Inuvik
MACKENZIE MOUNTAINS
Mackenzie
Norman Wells
Great Bear Lake
Great Slave Lake
Yellowknife
Fort Nelson
Dawson Creek
Prince George
Prince Rupert
QUEEN CHARLOTTE ISLANDS
ROCKY
CARIBOU MOUNTAINS
HORN PLATEAU
Lake Athabasca
Uranium City
CANADA
Hudson Bay
Churchill
York Factory
SOUTHAMPTON ISLAND
COATS ISLAND
MANSEL ISLAND
Foxe Basin
BAFFIN ISLAND
Baffin Bay
BAFFIN BASIN
Davis Strait
Labrador Sea
LABRADOR BASIN
Hudson Strait
Ungava Bay
PÉNINSULE D'UNGAVA
Schefferville
Goose Bay
John's
ATLANTIC OCEAN
FLEMISH CAP
QUEEN ELIZABETH ISLANDS
ELLESMERE ISLAND
DEVON ISLAND
VICTORIA ISLAND
BANKS ISLAND
MELVILLE ISLAND
PRINCE PATRICK ISLAND
PRINCE OF WALES ISLAND
SOMERSET ISLAND
KING WILLIAM ISLAND
Viscount Melville Sound
Lancaster Sound
Gulf of Boothia
NORTH MAGNETIC POLE
Amundsen Gulf
Coronation Gulf
Cambridge Bay
Repulse Bay
Lincoln Sea
PEARY LAND
GREENLAND
Thule
Godthåb
Godhavn
Angmagssalik
Gunnbjørn Fjeld
Denmark Strait
ICELAND
Reykjavík
FAEROE ISLANDS
SHETLAND ISLANDS
UNITED KINGDOM
Edinburgh
Glasgow
ROCKALL RISE
REYKJANES RIDGE
JAN MAYEN
WEST JAN MAYEN RIDGE
SOUTH JAN MAYEN RIDGE

NORTH AMERICA
UNITED STATES
MEXICO
ATLANTIC OCEAN
NORTH AMERICAN BASIN
PACIFIC OCEAN
GULF OF MEXICO
MEXICO BASIN
CARIBBEAN SEA
SOUTH AMERICA
COLOMBIA
VENEZUELA
ECUADOR
PERU
BRAZIL
PANAMA
COSTA RICA
NICARAGUA
HONDURAS
EL SALVADOR
GUATEMALA
BELIZE (U.K.)
CUBA
JAMAICA
HAITI
DOMINICAN REPUBLIC
PUERTO RICO
BAHAMAS
WEST INDIES
APPALACHIAN MOUNTAINS
GREAT PLAINS
ROCKY MOUNTAINS
SIERRA MADRE OCCIDENTAL
SIERRA MADRE ORIENTAL
SIERRA MADRE DEL SUR
BAJA CALIFORNIA
MIDDLE AMERICA TRENCH
EAST PACIFIC RISE
GUATEMALA BASIN
GALAPAGOS RISE
COCOS RIDGE
CLIPPERTON FRACTURE ZONE
CLARION FRACTURE ZONE
MURRAY FRACTURE ZONE
BAJA CALIFORNIA SEAMOUNT PROVINCE
MATHEMATICIANS SEAMOUNT GROUP
VENEZUELAN BASIN
Tropic of Cancer
Equator
WASHINGTON
NEW YORK
PHILADELPHIA
BOSTON
MONTRÉAL
TORONTO
Ottawa
CHICAGO
DETROIT
CLEVELAND
ST. LOUIS
LOS ANGELES
SAN FRANCISCO
Houston
New Orleans
Miami
CIUDAD DE MÉXICO
MEXICO CITY
La Habana
CARACAS
BOGOTÁ
Quito
Panamá
Kilometers
Statute Miles
Scale 1:24,000,000
One centimeter represents 240 kilometers.
One inch represents approximately 380 miles.
Lambert Azimuthal Equal-Area Projection

NORTH AMERICA
UNITED STATES
ROCKY MTS.
APPALACHIAN MOUNTAINS
GREAT PLAINS
OZARK PLATEAU
EDWARDS PLATEAU
Denver
Omaha
Des Moines
CHICAGO
CLEVELAND
Pittsburgh
NEW YORK
PHILADELPHIA
Baltimore
WASHINGTON
Richmond
Norfolk
Raleigh
Cincinnati
Charleston
Louisville
Nashville
Memphis
Atlanta
Birmingham
Montgomery
Savannah
Charleston
Jacksonville
Tampa
Miami
Kansas City
ST. LOUIS
Wichita
Oklahoma City
Little Rock
Dallas
Fort Worth
Jackson
Mobile
New Orleans
Houston
San Antonio
Laredo
Brownsville
Albuquerque
El Paso
MEXICO
SIERRA MADRE ORIENTAL
SIERRA MADRE DEL SUR
Monterrey
Matamoros
Torreón
Tampico
Guadalajara
CIUDAD DE MÉXICO
Puebla
Veracruz
Oaxaca
Acapulco
Villahermosa
Mérida
GULF OF MEXICO
MEXICO BASIN
Bahía de Campeche
YUCATAN PENINSULA
Yucatan Channel
Straits of Florida
BAHAMAS
Nassau
CUBA
La Habana
Havana
Santiago de Cuba
Guantánamo
CAYMAN ISLANDS
JAMAICA
Kingston
HAITI
Port-au-Prince
HISPANIOLA
DOMINICAN REPUBLIC
Santo Domingo
PUERTO RICO
San Juan
VIRGIN ISLANDS
ANTIGUA
GUADELOUPE
DOMINICA
MARTINIQUE
Fort-de-France
SAINT LUCIA
BARBADOS
Bridgetown
SAINT VINCENT
GRENADA
TRINIDAD AND TOBAGO
Port of Spain
WEST INDIES
GREATER ANTILLES
LESSER ANTILLES
NETHERLANDS ANTILLES
CARIBBEAN SEA
VENEZUELAN BASIN
BELIZE
Gulf of Honduras
GUATEMALA
Guatemala
EL SALVADOR
San Salvador
HONDURAS
Tegucigalpa
NICARAGUA
Managua
COSTA RICA
San José
PANAMA
Panama
MIDDLE AMERICA TRENCH
VENEZUELA
CARACAS
Maracaibo
Barquisimeto
Ciudad Bolívar
Ciudad Guayana
COLOMBIA
BOGOTÁ
Medellín
Cali
Barranquilla
Cartagena
Cúcuta
Bucaramanga
LLANOS
GUYANA
Georgetown
SURINAME
Paramaribo
FRENCH GUIANA
Cayenne
ECUADOR
Quito
Guayaquil
Cuenca
PERU
LIMA
Trujillo
Chiclayo
Iquitos
ANDES
SOUTH AMERICA
BRAZIL
SELVAS
Manaus
Belém
São Luís
Fortaleza
Teresina
Natal
João Pessoa
Recife
Maceió
Aracaju
Salvador
Campina Grande
Amazon
Orinoco
Negro
Equator
Tropic of Cancer
ATLANTIC OCEAN
NORTH AMERICAN BASIN
MID-ATLANTIC RIDGE
AZORES RIDGE
BERMUDA
CAPE VERDE BASIN
GUIANA BASIN
GUATEMALA BASIN
COCOS RIDGE
GALAPAGOS RISE
CARNEGIE RIDGE
PERU BASIN
PERU-CHILE TRENCH
ARCHIPIÉLAGO DE COLÓN

MID-ATLANTIC RIDGE
ATLANTIC OCEAN
BROMLEY PLATEAU
ARGENTINE BASIN
PACIFIC OCEAN
SOUTHEAST PACIFIC BASIN
CHILE RISE
EAST PACIFIC RISE
SALA Y GOMEZ RIDGE
CHILE TRENCH
Tropic of Capricorn
ANTARCTICA
Weddell Sea
Scotia Sea
Drake Passage
Bellingshausen Sea
Amundsen Sea
Antarctic Circle
SOUTH GEORGIA
SOUTH SANDWICH ISLANDS
SOUTH ORKNEY ISLANDS
SOUTH SHETLAND ISLANDS
FALKLAND ISLANDS
ISLAS MALVINAS
BURDWOOD BANK
ISLA GRANDE DE TIERRA DEL FUEGO
ALEXANDER ISLAND
LARSEN ICE SHELF
PARAGUAY
URUGUAY
PAMPA
PATAGONIA
ANDES
GRAN CHACO
BUENOS AIRES
Montevideo
SANTIAGO
Asunción
Córdoba
Rosario
Mendoza
Mar del Plata
Bahía Blanca
Valparaíso
Concepción
Antofagasta
SÃO PAULO
RIO DE JANEIRO
Belo Horizonte
Porto Alegre
Curitiba
Florianópolis
Kilometers
Statute Miles
Scale 1:24,000,000
One centimeter represents 240 kilometers.
One inch represents approximately 380 miles.
Lambert Azimuthal Equal-Area Projection

THE REGIONAL MAPS consist of three basic series, each distinctive in style, but using common symbols to ensure ease of understanding (see Legend to Maps, pages x-xii). Every major land region, continent or subcontinent, is introduced by one or more maps at the scale of 1:12,000,000. There follow maps at 1:6,000,000 and 1:3,000,000 which cover the region in sections, in greater detail. Except for scale, the 1:6,000,000 and 1:3,000,000 maps are alike. Finally, selected areas of special importance in the region are shown at 1:1,000,000. Each scale is identified by a color bar, and a locater map with the same color may be found in the margin of the map page. A sample area at each of the scales, including centimeter-kilometer and inch-mile equivalents, appears on page 21.

The three basic series differ in content and emphasis. The 1:12,000,000 maps, which are primarily political, present an overview of each region. They show national boundaries and, in some cases, subordinate administrative subdivisions as well. These introductory maps make it possible to compare location, areal extent, and shape among the nations of the world. The distribution of cities, towns and metropolitan areas is shown in the context of broad physical configurations. A selection of the most important railways and highways also appears.

The 1:6,000,000 and 1:3,000,000 maps together constitute about half of the map pages and provide the basic reference coverage of the Atlas. They show sections of regions in great detail—in some cases individual countries (Japan and New Zealand), in others, parts of countries (central Mexico), in still others, larger regions (the Middle East). The more densely settled areas appear at the larger 1:3,000,000 scale, the remaining areas at 1:6,000,000. Maps at these two scales present political and cultural information against the background of a detailed physical portrait of the terrain, which is depicted by both shaded relief and a spectrum of altitude tints. Bathymetric tints are used to show offshore water depths. The transportation pattern shown includes major railways, two classes of roads, and airports that offer either international or jet service. The names and boundaries of political subdivisions are given for selected countries.

In the 1:1,000,000 series, strategic areas that are of special interest because of economic importance, dense settlement, or both, appear in even greater detail. This series is designed to show the pattern of cities, towns, roads, railways, bridges, airports, dams, reservoirs, and other interrelated features reflecting man's dense occupancy in these areas. The most important parks, places of historical interest, and recreational facilities are indicated. Three classes of highways and two classes of railways are shown, and major roads are named. All features are portrayed against a topographic background of shaded relief.

Inhabited places on the regional maps are classified in two distinct ways. Cities and towns of different *population size* are distinguished by the *size and shape of the symbol* that locates the place. The symbol reflects the population within the municipal or corporate limits, exclusive of any suburbs. In countries where the limits of a municipality include rural areas, the symbol represents only the urban or agglomerated population. The *relative political and economic importance* of a place which may be independent of the number of its inhabitants, is indicated by the *size of type* in which its name appears.

A key to all symbols and type sizes is shown on page xi of the Legend to Maps.

DIE REGIONALKARTEN bestehen aus drei Serien, die im Stil verschieden sind, der besseren Lesbarkeit halber aber gemeinsame Kartensignaturen verwenden (siehe "Zeichenerklärung" S. x-xii). Jede Grossregion, jeder Kontinent oder Subkontinent wird durch eine oder mehrere Karten im Massstab 1:12 Millionen eingeleitet. Es folgen sodann Karten in den Massstäben 1:6 und 1:3 Millionen, welche die Region in Teilen und grösseren Einzelheiten darstellen. Die Karten in 1:6 Millionen und 1:3 Millionen unterscheiden sich nur im Massstab. Schliesslich werden ausgewählte Gebiete von besonderer Bedeutung innerhalb der Region in 1:1 Million dargestellt. Jede Massstabsangabe ist durch ein Farbfeld gekennzeichnet, und ein Lagekärtchen in derselben Farbe erscheint am Rand der Kartenseite. Kartenausschnitte als Beispiele für jeden dieser Massstäbe mit Angabe des Verhältnisses Zentimeter zu Kilometer und Zoll zu Meilen sind auf Seite 21 aufgeführt.

Die drei Kartenreihen unterscheiden sich in Inhalt und Betonung. Die Karten in 1:12 Millionen, die vor allem politische Karten sind, geben einen Überblick über jede Region. Sie zeigen die Staatsgrenzen und in manchen Fällen auch die Grenzen von nachgeordneten Verwaltungseinheiten. Diese einführenden Karten ermöglichen einen Vergleich der Lage, Ausdehnung und Gestalt der Staaten der Erde. Die Verteilung der städtischen Ballungsgebiete, Grossstädte und Städte wird in ihrem Zusammenhang mit dem grossräumigen Formenschatz des Reliefs gezeigt. Gezeigt wird auch eine Auswahl der wichtigsten Eisenbahnlinien und Fernverkehrsstrassen.

Die Karten 1:6 Millionen und 1:3 Millionen machen zusammen mehr als die Hälfte der Kartenseiten aus und bilden den grundlegenden Teil des Atlasses. Sie zeigen sehr inhaltsreiche Ausschnitte von Regionen—in einigen Fällen einzelne Länder (Japan und Neuseeland), in anderen Landesteile (Zentralmexiko) und weider anderen Grossräume (Mittlerer Osten).

Die dichter besiedelten Gebiete sind in 1:3 Millionen dargestellt, die übrigen Gebiete in 1:6 Millionen. Die Karten in diesen beiden Massstäben liefern politische und kulturgeographische Informationen vor dem Hintergrund einer detaillierten Geländedarstellung, gekennzeichnet durch Reliefschummerung und eine Skala von Höhenschichten. Tiefenstufen werden verwendet, um die Wassertiefen jenseits der Küsten zu gliedern. Das abgebildete Verkehrsnetz umfasst wichtige Eisenbahnlinien, zwei Klassen von Strassen und Flughäfen, die entweder im internationalen Verkehr oder von Düsenflugzeugen angeflogen werden. Die Verwaltungsgliederung wird für eine grosse Zahl von Staaten gezeigt.

In der Kartenserie 1:1 Million sind mit noch zahlreicheren Einzelheiten zentrale Räume dargestellt, denen infolge ihrer wirtschaftlichen Bedeutung, dichten Besiedlung oder durch beide Faktoren bedingt, besonderes Interesse zukommt. Diese Kartenserie wurde entwickelt, um die Verteilung der Grossstädte, Städte, Strassen, Eisenbahnen, Brücken, Flughäfen, Dämme, Stauseen und anderer Objekte zu zeigen, die Ausdruck sind für die dichte Besiedlung. Verzeichnet sind auch die wichtigsten Parks, Örtlichkeiten von historischem Interesse und Erholungsstätten. Drei Strassenklassen und zwei Klassen von Eisenbahnlinien werden unterschieden. Die Darstellung ist unterlegt durch eine Reliefschummerung.

Die Siedlungen auf den Regionalkarten sind auf zwei bestimmte Arten klassifiziert. Grossstädte und Städte unterschiedlicher *Einwohnerzahl* sind durch *Grösse und Form der Signatur* unterschieden, die den Ort lokalisiert. Die Signatur entspricht der Zahl der Einwohner innerhalb der Stadtgrenzen, schliesst also nicht eingemeindete Vororte aus. In Staaten, in denen ländliche Gebiete in die Stadtgemeinden einbezogen sind, entsprechen die Signaturen nur der in den zentralen Siedlungen ansässigen Bevölkerung. Die *relative politische und wirtschaftliche Bedeutung* eines Ortes, die von der Zahl seiner Einwohner unabhängig sein kann, ist ausgedrückt durch die *Schriftgrösse*, in welcher der Ortsname erscheint.

Ein Schlüssel zu allen Signaturen und Schriftgrössen findet sich auf Seite xi der "Zeichenerklärung".

LOS MAPAS REGIONALES integran tres series básicas, cada una con su estilo propio; pero los símbolos usados son en todas los mismos para facilitar su comprensión (véanse las Leyendas para Mapas, páginas x-xii). Cada una de las grandes regiones, continentes o subcontinentes, se presenta a través de uno o varios mapas a la escala de 1:12 000 000. A continuación hay mapas a escalas de 1:6 000 000 y 1:3 000 000 que presentan la región correspondiente en secciones, con mayores detalles. Con excepción de su escala, los mapas de 1:6 000 000 y 1:3 000 000 tienen las mismas características. Por ultimo, aparecen a la escala de 1:1 000 000 áreas de cada región seleccionadas por su importancia. Cada escala se identifica por una barra de color, y un mapa-guía con el mismo color se presenta en el margen de la página de cada mapa. La página 21 ofrece como ejemplo un área-muestra a cada una de las escalas, incluyendo equivalentes en centímetros-kilómetros y pulgadas-millas.

Las tres series básicas son diferentes en contenido y en énfasis. Los mapas a escala de 1:12 000 000, fundamentalmente políticos, ofrecen una vista general de cada región. Indican las fronteras nacionales y, en algunos casos, las subdivisiones administrativas secundarias. Son mapas introductivos que permiten comparar la ubicación, extensión territorial y forma de las distintas naciones. La distribución de ciudades, poblados y áreas metropolitanas se aprecia en un contexto físico esbozado a grandes rasgos. Los detalles incluyen una selección de las vías férras y las carreteras más importantes.

Las series de mapas a 1:6 000 000 y a 1:3 000 000 ocupan entre ambas cerca de la mitad de los mapas del atlas y en ellas se concentra el material de consulta básico de la obra. Los mapas muestran secciones de regiones en gran detalle: en algunos casos países enteros, como Japón y Nueva Zelandia; en otros, partes de países, como el centro de México; y en otros, regiones mas extensas, como el Medio Oriente. Las áreas con mayor densidad de establecimientos humanos se presentan a una escala mayor, la de 1:3 000 000, y las demás a la escala de 1:6 000 000. En estas dos escalas los mapas contienen información política y cultural, sobre un fondo que ilustra en detalle la configuración física del terreno, utilizando sombreado para el relieve y toda una gama de tintes para indicar las altitudes. Un colorido batimétrico señala las variaciones de profundidad en el suelo marino. El esquema de las vías de comunicación incluye las principales vías férreas, dos clases de caminos, y los aeropuertos que ofrecen servicio nacional o internacional de jets. Las subdivisiones políticas secundarias se dan para una selección de varios países.

En la serie de mapas de 1:1 000 000, las áreas estratégicas de especial interés por su importancia económica, su densidad de población, o ambos factores combinados, aparecen aún con mayor detalle. Esta serie se diseñó para mostrar la distribución de ciudades, poblados, caminos, vías férreas, puentes, aeropuertos, presas, embalses y otros elementos similares, que reflejan la densidad de la ocupación humana. También se consignan los parques más importantes, los sitios de interés histórico, los campos de recreo, tres clases de carreteras, y dos de ferrocarriles, se da los nombres de los caminos más importantes. Todos estos elementos aparecen sobre un fondo topográfico de relieve sombreado.

En los mapas regionales se hacen dos clasificaciones distintas de los lugares habitados. Las ciudades y las poblaciones *de diferente densidad de habitantes* se distinguen por la *forma y tamaño del símbolo* que las localiza en el mapa. Este símbolo refleja el tamaño de la poblacióin dentro de sus límites municipales, sin tomar en cuenta los suburbios. En los países donde los límites de una municipalidad incluyen áreas rurales, el símbolo se limita a representar el conglomerado urbano de habitantes. La *importancia económica y política de un lugar,* la cual puede ser independiente del número de sus habitantes, se indica mediante el *tamaño del tipo de imprenta* en que aparece su nombre.

La clave de los símbolos y el valor de los tamaños de las letras se dan en la página xi de las Leyendas para Mapas.

LES CARTES RÉGIONALES sont de trois types principaux, chacun d'un style différent mais avec des symboles communs pour faciliter la compréhension (voir la légende des cartes pages x-xii). Chaque grande région, continent ou subcontinent, est représentée par une ou plusieurs cartes à l'échelle de 1:12 000 000e. Viennent ensuite des cartes au 1:6 000 000e et au 1:3 000 000e qui couvrent la région par sections plus détaillées; hormis la différence d'échelle, ces cartes sont semblables. Enfin, des secteurs particulièrement importants sont représentés au 1:1 000 000e. À chaque échelle correspond une bande colorée et une carte repère de même couleur, dans la marge de chaque page. Un échantillon de cartes aux diverses échelles est représenté à droite. Chaque carte est accompagnée d'une double échelle graphique donnant les rapports centimètre/kilomètre et inch/mille correspondants.

Les trois catégories de cartes diffèrent par le contenu et par ce qu'elles mettent en relief. Les cartes au 1:12 000 000e, qui sont essentiellement politiques, donnent un apercu général de chaque région. Elles indiquent les frontières nationales et, dans certains cas, les subdivisions administratives intérieures. Ces cartes d'introduction permettent de comparer la localisation, la superficie et la forme des pays du monde. La répartition des villes et des zones métropolitaines y apparaît dans le cadre des grandes régions naturelles. Les routes et les voies ferrées les plus importantes y figurent également.

Les cartes au 1:6 000 000e et au 1:3 000 000e forment la moitié de l'Atlas et en constituent la série cartographique essentielle. Elles représentent de façon plus détaillée une partie de pays (centre du Mexique), ou encore des régions plus vestes (Moyen-Orient) ou, parfois, des pays entiers (Japon, Nouvelle-Zélande). Les régions les plus peuplées sont représentées à plus grande échelle (1;3 000 000e) que les autres (1:6 000 000e). Ces cartes offrent des informations d'ordre politique et culturel sur un fond topographique précis où le relief est indiqué à la fois par un estompage et par des variations de couleur. Différentes teintes de bleu sont utilisées pour symboliser les profondeurs marines. Les réseaux de transport représentés comprennent les principales voies ferrées, deux catégories de routes et les aéroports internationaux ou desservis par des avions à réaction. Les subdivisions politiques d'un certain nombre de pays sont aussi tracées.

Dans la série de cartes au 1:1 000 000e, des régions très importantes, soit du fait de leur densité de population, soit du fait de leur rôle économique, sont représentées d'une manière encore plus détaillée. L'objectif de cette série de cartes est de montrer la répartition des villes, routes, voies ferrées, ponts, aéroports, barrages, lacs de barrages et autres données associées qui traduisent la densité de l'occupation humaine dans ces régions. Les parcs les plus importants, les sites historiques essentiels et les centres de loisirs sont indiqués. Toutes les informations se détachent sur un fond topographique où le relief apparaît en estompage.

Les centres urbains des cartes régionales sont classés de deux manières différentes. *L'importance de la population* des villes est indiquée par *la dimension et la forme du symbole* qui les situe sur la carte. Seule la population comprise dans les limites municipales est prise en considération; dans les pays où des espaces ruraux sont inclus dans les limites d'une municipalité, seule la population urbaine entre en ligne de compte. *L'importance politique et économique relative* d'une ville, qui n'est pas nécessairement liée au nombre d'habitants, est indiquée par la dimension des caractères qui composent son nom.

La signification de tous les symboles utilisés dans les cartes régionales est donnée par la légende des cartes aux pages x-xii.

OS MAPAS REGIONAIS compreendem três séries básicas, cada uma em estilo diferente, mas que empregam os mesmos símbolos para facilitar sua compreensão (Ver as *Legendas dos mapas*, pág. x-xii). Os mapas de cada uma das principais regiões terrestres, continentes ou subcontinentes, são introduzidos por um ou mais mapas na escala 1:12 000 000. Em seguida, vêm mapas, nas escalas de 1:6 000 000 e 1:3 000 000, que apresentam, com maiores detalhes, seções da região considerada. Exceto quanto à escala, os mapas de 1:6 000 000 e 1:3 000 000 têm as mesmas características. Finalmente, aparecem, na escala de 1:1 000 000, os mapas das áreas mais importantes da região considerada. A cada escala corresponde uma barra colorida e um indicador da mesma cor, que se encontra à margem da página de cada mapa. À página 21, acha-se um exemplo de cada escala, bem como a equivalência das relações centímetro/quilômetro e polegada/milha.

As três séries básicas de mapas são diferentes quanto ao conteúdo e à apresentação. Os mapas em escala de 1:12 000 000, que são essencialmente políticos, oferecem uma visão geral de cada região. Indicam as fronteiras nacionais e, em alguns casos, as subdivisões administrativas internas. Esses mapas servem de introdução e permitem avaliar e comparar a posição, superfície e forma dos países do Mundo. Neles está claramente indicada a distribuição das cidades e outros centros urbanos, bem como as principais características da configuração do solo. Encontra-se neles também uma seleção das ferrovias e rodovias mais importantes.

A série de mapas das escalas de 1:6 000 000 e de 1:3 000 000 constituem o principal material de referência do Atlas e representa cerca de metade do conjunto de mapas. Entre eles há mapas detalhados de parte de um país (centro do México), de um país inteiro (Japão e a Nova Zelândia) ou de uma região mais extensa (Oriente Médio). As áreas de maior densidade demográfica são apresentados em escala maior, a de 1:3 000 000, e as demais, na de 1:6 000 000. Nessas duas escalas, os mapas fornecem informações de ordem política e cultural sobre um fundo que indica a configuração detalhada das particularidades físicas do solo, cujo relevo se destaca por contrastes de sombras e cores. Diversos matizes do azul traduzem o mapa batimétrico da profundidade ao largo das costas. Indicam também os aeroportos internacionais, as principais ferrovias, duas categorias de rodovias. As subdivisões políticas internas de numerosos países estão igualmente assinalados.

Na série de mapas da escala de 1:1 000 000, certas áreas, de interesse estratégico conjugado à importância econômica, densidade demográfica, ou ambos os elementos combinados, aparecem em forma ainda mais detalhada. O objetivo dessa série é representar a distribuição dos grandes centros urbanos, cidades, rodovias, ferrovias, pontes, aeroportos, represas, reservatórios e outras características associadas às grandes densidades demográficas. Indicam-se, também, os parques mais importantes, os lugares de interesse histórico, as áreas de lazer, três categorias de rodovias, e duas de ferrovias; e a nomenclatura dos grandes itinerários rodoviários. Todos esses elementos destacam-se sobre um fundo topográfico do relevo, executado em matizes das diversas cores.

Nos mapas regionais, assinalam-se os centros urbanos de dois modos. A *grandeza da população* das grandes cidades e dos centros urbanos secundários é representada pela *dimensão e forma do símbolo* que as localiza no mapa. O símbolo só reflete a população situada dentro de limites administrativos, sem levar em conta os subúrbios. Nos países onde os limites de uma municipalidade incluem zonas rurais, o símbolo representa apenas a população. A *importância política e econômica* de uma cidade, que não se relaciona necessariamente com o número de seus habitantes, é indicada pela *dimensão* dos caracteres tipográficos com que se compõe o seu nome.

A chave dos símbolos e caracteres tipográficos empregados figura na pág. xi, nas *Legendas dos mapas*.

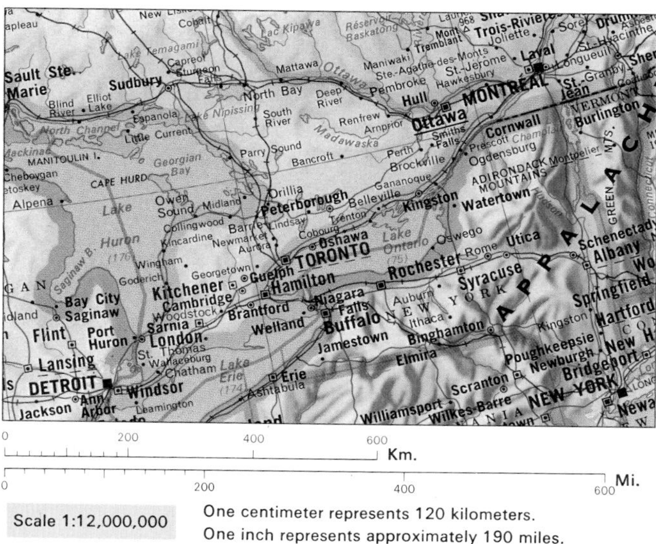

Scale 1:12,000,000 One centimeter represents 120 kilometers. One inch represents approximately 190 miles.

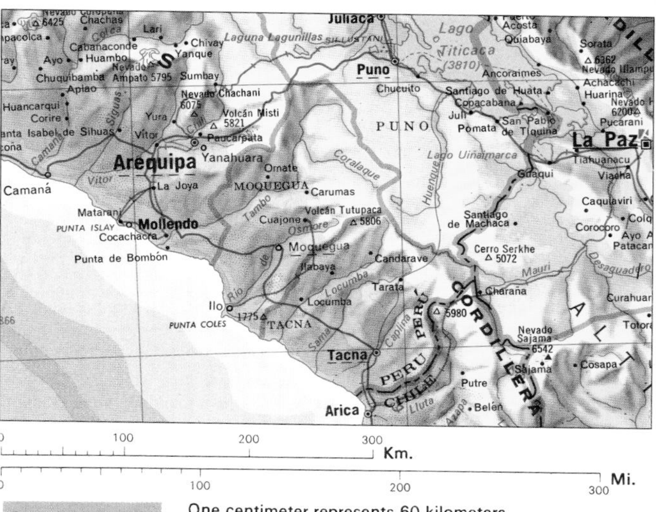

Scale 1:6,000,000 One centimeter represents 60 kilometers. One inch represents approximately 95 miles.

Scale 1:3,000,000 One centimeter represents 30 kilometers. One inch represents approximately 47 miles.

Scale 1:1,000,000 One centimeter represents 10 kilometers. One inch represents approximately 16 miles.

134 - 137

MAP FORM	-älven	gora	île	islands	-øya	ozero	sea	vodochranilišče
ENGLISH	river	mountain	island	islands	island	lake	sea	reservoir
DEUTSCH	Fluss	Berg	Insel	Inseln	Insel	See	Meer	Stausee
ESPAÑOL	río	montaña	isla	islas	isla	lago	mar	embalse
FRANÇAIS	rivière	montagne	île	îles	île	lac	mer	réservoir
PORTUGUÊS	rio	montanha	ilha	ilhas	ilha	lago	mar	reservatório

For complete glossary see page *I • 1*.

Kilometers 0 200 400 600 Km.
Statute Miles 0 200 400 600 Mi.

Scale 1:12,000,000

One centimeter represents 120 kilometers.
One inch represents approximately 190 miles.
Miller Oblated Stereographic Projection

72-75
118-119

MAP FORM	-älven	-fjorden	guba	-joki	-jökull	lääni	-øya	ozero
ENGLISH	river	fjord, lake	bay	river	glacier	province	island	lake
DEUTSCH	Fluss	Fjord, See	Bucht	Fluss	Gletscher	Provinz	Insel	See
ESPAÑOL	río	fiordo, lago	bahía	río	glaciar	provincia	isla	lago
FRANÇAIS	rivière	fjord, lac	baie	rivière	glacier	province	île	lac
PORTUGUÊS	rio	fiorde, lago	baía	rio	geleira	província	ilha	lago

For complete glossary see page *I • 1*.

BARENTS SEA
BARENC'OVO MORE
PEČORSKOJE MORE
OSTROV KOLGUJEV
Češskaja Guba
Mezenskaja Guba
White Sea
Beloje More
Onežskaja Guba
Dvinskaja Guba
Arctic Circle
URAL MOUNTAINS
URAL'SKIJE GORY
Murmansk
Severomorsk
Kandalakša
Archangel'sk
Severodvinsk
Onega
Petrozavodsk
Naŕjan Mar
Uchta
Sosnogorsk
Pečora
Inta
Vorkuta
Syktyvkar
Kotlas
Vologda
Čerepovec
Rybinsk
Jaroslavl'
Kostroma
Ivanovo
Kirov
Kirovo-Čepeck
Glazov
Iževsk
Kazan'
Čeboksary
Joškar-Ola
GOR'KIJ GORKY
Dzeržinsk
Vladimir
Kalinin
MOSKVA MOSCOW
Tula
Kaluga
Smolensk
R'azan'
Saransk
Uljanovsk
Kujbyšev
Toljatti
Syzran'
Penza
Kuzneck
Sarapul
Nižnekamsk
Al'metjevsk
Kubyšev
Lake Ladoga
Ladožskoje Ozero
Dvina
Volga
Oka
Kama
Pečora
Mezen'
Vyčegda
Rybinskoje Vodochranilišče
Gor'kovskoje Vodochranilišče
Kujbyševskoje Vodochranilišče
Map compiled by Rand McNally & Co.
Map compiled by Rand McNally GmbH, Stuttgart.
Map edited by Rand McNally & Co.
76-77
86-87
32° 34° 36° 38° 40° 42° 44° 46° 48° 50° 52° 54° 56° 58° 60° 62° 64° 66°
Kilometers 0 100 200 300 Km.
Statute Miles 0 100 200 300 Mi.
Scale 1:6,000,000
One centimeter represents 60 kilometers.
One inch represents approximately 95 miles.
Lambert Conformal Conic Projection

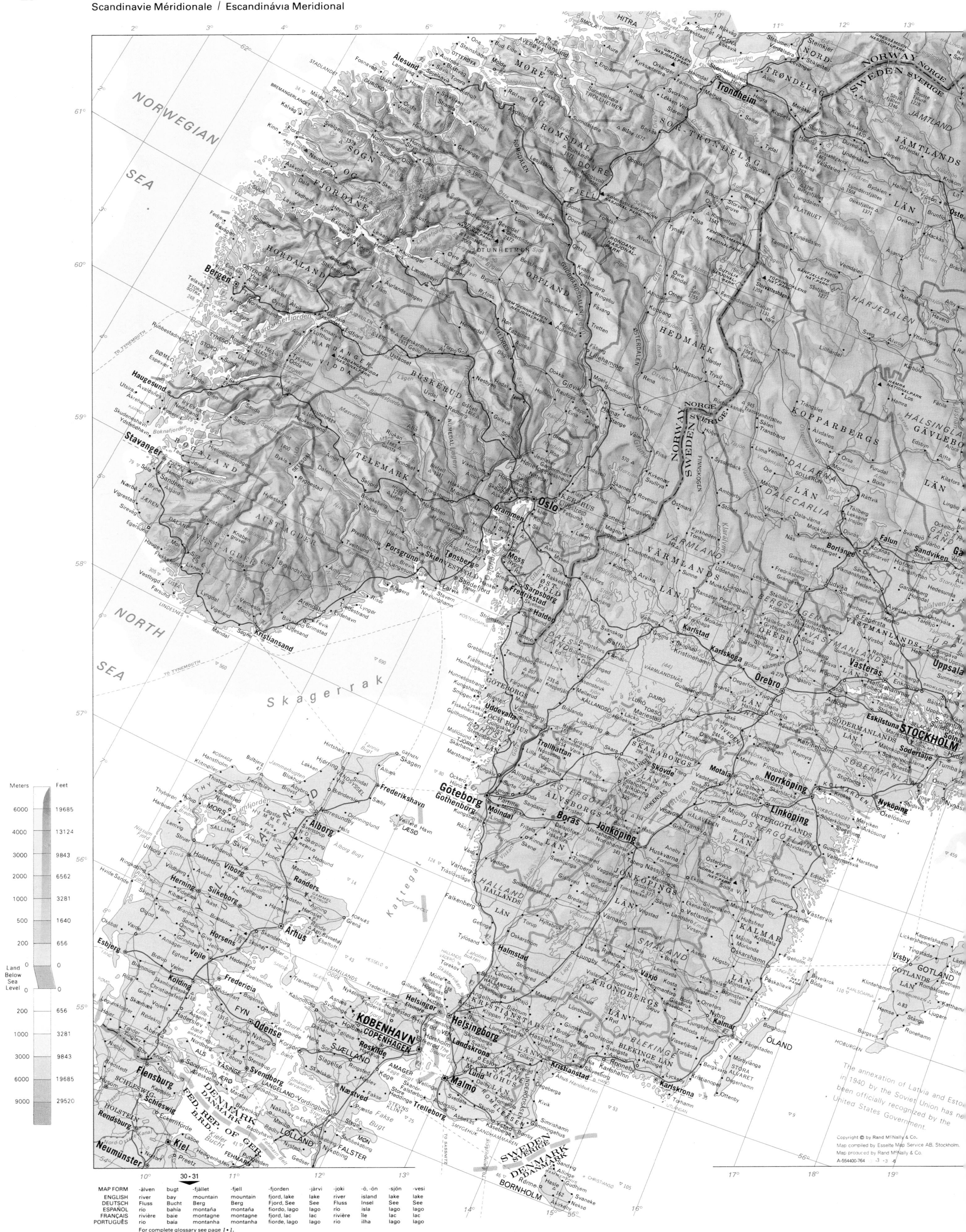

MAP FORM	-älven	bugt	-fjället	-fjell	-fjorden	-järvi	-joki	-ö, -ön	-sjön	-vesi
ENGLISH	river	bay	mountain	mountain	fjord, lake	lake	river	island	lake	lake
DEUTSCH	Fluss	Bucht	Berg	Berg	Fjord, See	See	Fluss	Insel	See	See
ESPAÑOL	río	bahía	montaña	montaña	fiordo, lago	lago	río	isla	lago	lago
FRANÇAIS	rivière	baie	montagne	montagne	fjord, lac	lac	rivière	île	lac	lac
PORTUGUÊS	rio	baía	montanha	montanha	fiorde, lago	lago	rio	ilha	lago	lago

For complete glossary see page I • 1.

30 • 31

Scale 1:3,000,000

One centimeter represents 30 kilometers.
One inch represents approximately 47 miles.
Conic Projection, Two Standard Parallels

NORWAY
ATLANTIC OCEAN
NORTH SEA
SHETLAND ISLANDS
Lerwick
ORKNEY ISLANDS
Kirkwall
Stromness
John o' Groats
Thurso
Wick
OUTER HEBRIDES
ISLE OF LEWIS
Stornoway
ISLAND OF SKYE
The Minch
Little Minch
Inverness
Aberdeen
Peterhead
Fraserburgh
GRAMPIAN MOUNTAINS
Fort William
Oban
ISLAND OF MULL
ISLAY
Dundee
Perth
St. Andrews
GLASGOW
Edinburgh
Paisley
Kilmarnock
Ayr
Campbeltown
Dumfries
Carlisle
Newcastle upon Tyne
Sunderland
South Shields
Tynemouth
Durham
Hartlepool
Middlesbrough
Workington
Whitehaven
Berwick-upon-Tweed
Londonderry
Belfast
Bangor
Newtownabbey
Carrickfergus
Larne
DONEGAL
Donegal Bay
SAINT KILDA

ATLANTIC OCEAN
IRISH SEA
St. George's Channel
Bristol Channel
English Channel
La Manche
30-31
32-33
Meters
Feet
Land Below Sea Level
MAP FORM: bay, ben, head, hills, island, loch, mountains, point, sound
ENGLISH: bay, mountain, head, hills, island, lake; inlet, mountains, point, sound
DEUTSCH: Bucht, Berg, Landspitze, Hügel, Insel, See; Einfahrt, Berge, Landspitze, Sund
ESPAÑOL: bahía, montaña, promontorio, colinas, isla, lago; abra, montañas, punta, canal
FRANÇAIS: baie, montagne, promontoire, collines, île, lac; bras de mer, montagnes, pointe, détroit
PORTUGUÊS: baía, montanha, promontório, colinas, ilha, lago; braço de mar, montanhas, ponta, canal
For complete glossary see page I·1.
Kilometers
Statute Miles
Scale 1:3,000,000
One centimeter represents 30 kilometers.
One inch represents approximately 47 miles.
Conic Projection, Two Standard Parallels

26-27
28-29
36-37

MAP FORM	Bucht	Gebirge	jezioro	Kanal	park narodowy	See	Wald
ENGLISH	bay	range	lake, lagoon	canal	national park	lake	forest, mountains
DEUTSCH	Bucht	Gebirge	See, Haff	Kanal	Nationalpark	See	Wald
ESPAÑOL	bahía	sierra	lago, laguna	canal	parque national	lago	bosque, montañas
FRANÇAIS	baie	chaîne	lac, lagune	canal	parc national	lac	forêt, montagnes
PORTUGUÊS	baía	serra	lago, laguna	canal	parque nacional	lago	bosque, montanhas

For complete glossary see page *I • 1*.
For Budapest and Wien metropolitan maps see page 264.

Kilometers 0 50 100 150 Km.
Statute Miles 0 50 100 150 Mi.

Scale 1:3,000,000

One centimeter represents 30 kilometers.
One inch represents approximately 47 miles.
Conic Projection, Two Standard Parallels.

BALTIC SEA
Gulf of Danzig
Kaliningrad
(Königsberg)
Gdańsk
(Danzig)
Gdynia
Szczecin
(Stettin)
Poznań
Bydgoszcz
Toruń
Włocławek
Płock
WARSZAWA WARSAW
Łódź
Wrocław
(Breslau)
Częstochowa
Kraków
Katowice
Lublin
Białystok
Kielce
Radom
Rzeszów
Przemyśl
Dresden
Görlitz
Frankfurt an der Oder
Eisenhüttenstadt
Cottbus
Neubrandenburg
PRAHA
PRAGUE
Plzeň
Brno
Olomouc
Ostrava
Gottwaldov
Žilina
Košice
Prešov
Bratislava
WIEN
VIENNA
Linz
Graz
Klagenfurt
BUDAPEST
Győr
Miskolc
Debrecen
Szeged
Pécs
Kecskemét
Oradea
Arad
Mukačevo
Užgorod
Brest
Grodno
C A R P A T H I A N   M O U N T A I N S
POLAND
U.S.S.R.
CZECHOSLOVAKIA
HUNGARY
ROMANIA
YUGOSLAVIA
ÖSTERREICH
76-77
78-79

MAP FORM	canal	cap	île	lago	mont (e)	monts	pointe	See
ENGLISH	canal	cape	island	lake	mount	mountains	point	lake
DEUTSCH	Kanal	Kap	Insel	See	Berg	Berge	Landspitze	See
ESPAÑOL	canal	cabo	isla	lago	monte	montes	punta	lago
FRANÇAIS	canal	cap	île	lac	mont	monts	pointe	lac
PORTUGUÊS	canal	cabo	ilha	lago	monte	montes	ponta	lago

For complete glossary see page *I • 1*.

30 - 31
36 - 37
Köln
Bonn
Koblenz
Frankfurt a. M.
Wiesbaden
Mainz
Darmstadt
Mannheim
Ludwigshafen
Heidelberg
Karlsruhe
Stuttgart
Würzburg
Nürnberg
Regensburg
Augsburg
München
Ulm
Freiburg
Saarbrücken
Luxembourg
Liège
Aachen
Metz
Nancy
Strasbourg
Mulhouse
Basel
Zürich
Bern
Lausanne
Genève
Dijon
Besançon
Lyon
Grenoble
Torino
Milano
Genova
Venezia
Verona
Bologna
Firenze
Pisa
Livorno
Ancona
Trieste
Innsbruck
Salzburg
Linz
Plzeň
Praha
Karl-Marx-Stadt
Erfurt
Marseille
Toulon
Nice
Cannes
Avignon
Bastia
CORSE
CORSICA
LIGURIAN SEA
MEDITERRANEAN SEA
ADRIATIC SEA
Gulf of Venice
ALPS
Copyright © by Rand McNally & Co.
Map prepared by Rand McNally GmbH, Stuttgart.
A-559495-764
Kilometers 0 50 100 150 Km.
Statute Miles 0 50 100 150 Mi.
Scale 1:3,000,000
One centimeter represents 30 kilometers.
One inch represents approximately 47 miles.
Lambert Conformal Conic Projection

Bay of Biscay
ATLANTIC
OCEAN
ATLANTIC
OCEAN
Golfo de Cádiz
MADRID
LISBOA LISBON
Porto
Vila Nova de Gaia
Coimbra
Braga
Santander
Bilbao
San Sebastián
Vitoria
Oviedo
Gijón
Avilés
La Coruña
El Ferrol del Caudillo
Santiago de Compostela
Lugo
Orense
Pontevedra
Vigo
León
Ponferrada
Burgos
Palencia
Valladolid
Zamora
Salamanca
Segovia
Ávila
Guadalajara
Alcalá de Henares
Getafe
Aranjuez
Toledo
Talavera de la Reina
Plasencia
Cáceres
Badajoz
Mérida
Ciudad Real
Puertollano
Valdepeñas
Tomelloso
Linares
Jaén
Córdoba
Sevilla
Huelva
Cádiz
Jerez de la Frontera
Granada
Málaga
Almería
Algeciras
La Línea
Gibraltar (U.K.)
Ceuta (Sp.)
Tanger
Tétouan
Melilla (Sp.)
Logroño
Soria
Setúbal
Barreiro
Almada
Évora
Faro
Leiria
Santarém
Viseu
Guarda
Covilhã
Castelo Branco
Bragança
Vila Real
Viana do Castelo
CORDILLERA CANTÁBRICA
SISTEMA IBÉRICO
SISTEMA CENTRAL
SIERRA MORENA
SISTEMAS BÉTICOS
MONTES DE TOLEDO
TIERRA DE CAMPOS
LA MANCHA
EXTREMADURA
ESTREMADURA
ALENTEJO
ALGARVE
GALICIA
ASTURIAS
PROVINCIAS VASCONGADAS
ANDALUCÍA
CASTILLA LA NUEVA
CASTILLA LA VIEJA
TRÁS-OS-MONTES
MINHO
BEIRA
LITORAL
BAIXA
MOROCCO AL-MAGREB
RIF
SPAIN ESPAÑA
PORTUGAL
Meters Feet
6000 19685
4000 13124
3000 9843
2000 6562
1000 3281
500 1640
200 656
0 0
Land Below Sea Level
0
200 656
1000 3281
3000 9843
6000 19685
9000 29520
Copyright © by Rand McNally & Co.
Map prepared by Rand McNally GmbH, Stuttgart.
A-559900-764
ESPAÑOL bahía cabo isla embalse puerto punta ría sierra
ENGLISH bay cape island reservoir pass point estuary mountains
DEUTSCH Bucht Kap Insel Stausee Pass Landspitze Trichtermündung Berge
FRANÇAIS baie cap île réservoir col pointe estuaire montagnes
PORTUGUÊS baía cabo ilha reservatório porto ponta estuário serra
For complete glossary see page I·I.
For Madrid, Barcelona and Lisboa metropolitan maps see page 266.

32-33
Toulouse
Montauban
Albi
AVEYRON
Nîmes
Avignon
Montpellier
Marseille
Toulon
Nice
Cannes
Antibes
Grasse
MONACO
Arles
Aix-en-Provence
Béziers
Sète
Narbonne
Carcassonne
Perpignan
Tarbes
Pau
Bayonne
Golfe du Lion
PYRÉNÉES
ANDORRA
Andorra
Huesca
Zaragoza
Lérida
Gerona
Vich
Manresa
Sabadell
Tarrasa
Mataró
Badalona
BARCELONA
Hospitalet
Prat de Llobregat
Villanueva y Geltrú
Reus
Tarragona
DELTA DEL EBRO
Tortosa
Amposta
Vinaroz
Benicarló
Peñíscola
Teruel
CASTELLÓN
Castellón de la Plana
Burriana
Sagunto
Valencia
Golfo de Valencia
Gandía
Alcoy
Elda
Alicante
Elche
Murcia
Torrevieja
Cartagena
La Unión
Benidorm
MENORCA
Ciudadela
Mahón
MALLORCA
Palma
Manacor
Lluchmayor
IBIZA
Ibiza
FORMENTERA
BALEARES
ISLAS BALEARES
BALEARIC ISLANDS
MEDITERRANEAN SEA
ALGER
ALGIERS
Blida
Tizi-Ouzou
Bejaïa (Bougie)
Djidjelli
Sétif
El Eulma
Médéa
El Asnam (Orléansville)
Mostaganem
Oran (Ouahran)
Sidi bel Abbès
Tiaret
Batna
Bou Saâda
ALGERIA
ALGÉRIE
MOUNTAINS
ATLAS TELLIEN
148-149
Kilometers
Km.
Statute Miles
Mi.
Scale 1:3,000,000
One centimeter represents 30 kilometers.
One inch represents approximately 47 miles.
Conic Projection, Two Standard Parallels

Italy / Italien / Italia
Italie / Itália

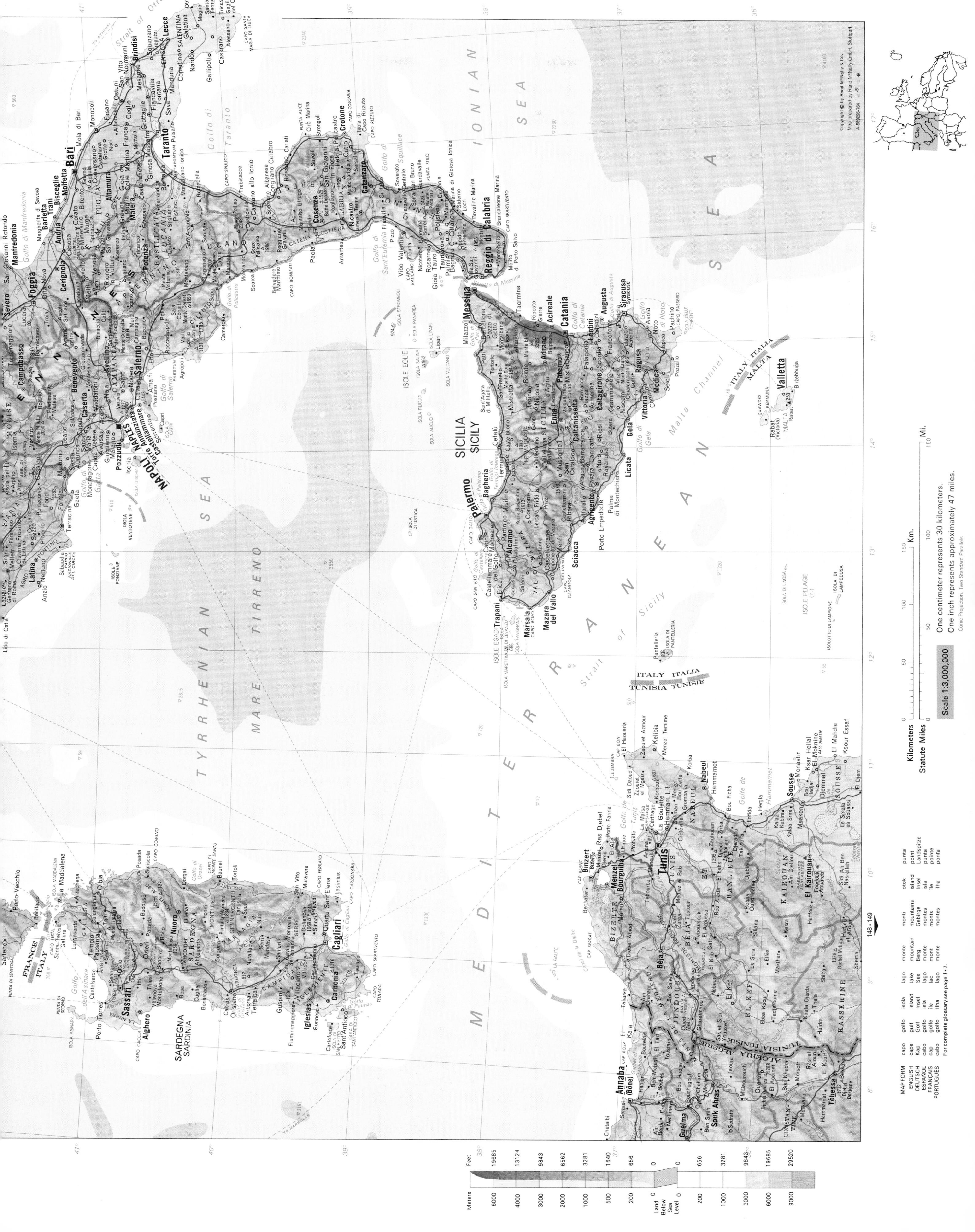

TYRRHENIAN SEA
MARE TIRRENO
IONIAN SEA
MEDITERRANEAN SEA
SICILIA
SICILY
SARDEGNA
SARDINIA
Strait of Sicily
Malta Channel
Strait of Otranto
ITALY ITALIA
MALTA
TUNISIA TUNISIE
FRANCE
ITALY

Kilometers 0 50 100 150 Km.
Statute Miles 0 50 100

Scale 1:3,000,000

One centimeter represents 30 kilometers.
One inch represents approximately 47 miles.
Conic Projection, Two Standard Parallels

Meters	Feet
6000	19685
4000	13124
3000	9843
2000	6562
1000	3281
500	1640
200	656
0	0
Land Below Sea Level 0	0
200	656
1000	3281
3000	9843
6000	19685
9000	29520

MAP FORM	capo	golfo	isola	lago	monte	monti	otok	punta
ENGLISH	cape	gulf	island	lake	mountain	mountains	island	point
DEUTSCH	Kap	Golf	Insel	See	Berg	Gebirge	Insel	Landspitze
ESPAÑOL	cabo	golfo	isla	lago	monte	montes	isla	punta
FRANÇAIS	cap	golfe	île	lac	mont	monts	île	pointe
PORTUGUÊS	cabo	golfo	ilha	lago	monte	montes	ilha	ponta

For complete glossary see page *I • 1*.

148-149

MAP FORM ákra kólpos lacul límni manastir munţii prohod sea
ENGLISH cape bay lake lake monastery mountains pass sea
DEUTSCH Kap Bucht See See Kloster Berge Pass Meer
ESPAÑOL cabo bahía lago lago monasterio montañas paso mar
FRANÇAIS cap baie lac lac monastère montagnes col mer
PORTUGUÊS cabo baía lago lago mosteiro montanhas passo mar
For complete glossary see page I • I.
For Athinai and İstanbul metropolitan maps, see page 267; Budapest, page 264.
Kilometers
Statute Miles
Km.
Mi.
Scale 1:3,000,000
One centimeter represents 30 kilometers.
One inch represents approximately 47 miles.
Conic Projection. Two Standard Parallels
30 • 31
78 • 79
36 • 37
BLACK SEA
CARPATHIAN MOUNTAINS
BUDAPEST
BUCUREŞTI
BUCHAREST
Beograd
Belgrade
Sofija
Sofia
Mouths of the Danube

130 • 131
ADRIATIC SEA
IONIAN SEA
AEGEAN SEA
MEDITERRANEAN SEA
Strait of Otranto
ITALY
İSTANBUL
Thessaloniki
Salonika
ATHÍNAI
ATHENS
Piraiévs
Pátrai
İzmir
Marmara Denizi
Sea of Marmara
KIKLÁDHES
CYCLADES
DHODHEKÁNISOS
DODECANESE
KRÍTI
CRETE
Kritikón Pélagos
Sea of Crete
LÉSVOS
LESBOS
RÓDHOS
RHODES
Meters
Feet
Land
Below
Sea
Level
Copyright © by Rand McNally & Co.
Map prepared by Rand McNally GmbH, Stuttgart.

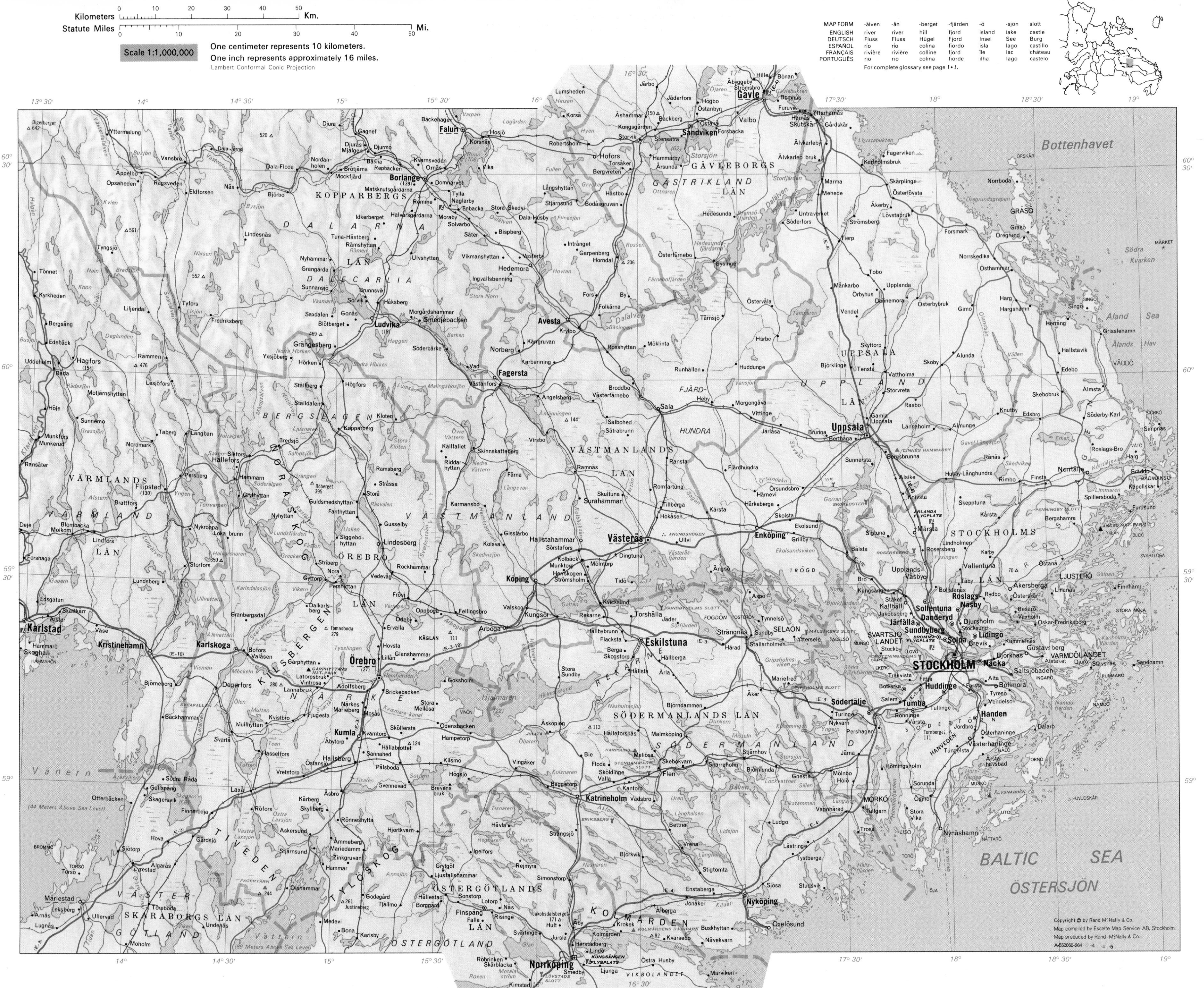
Kilometers
Statute Miles
Km.
Mi.
Scale 1:1,000,000
One centimeter represents 10 kilometers.
One inch represents approximately 16 miles.
Lambert Conformal Conic Projection
MAP FORM -älven -ån -berget -fjärden -ö -sjön slott
ENGLISH river river hill fjord island lake castle
DEUTSCH Fluss Fluss Hügel Fjord Insel See Burg
ESPAÑOL río río colina fiordo isla lago castillo
FRANÇAIS rivière rivière colline fjord île lac château
PORTUGUÊS rio rio colina fiorde ilha lago castelo
For complete glossary see page I•1.
Bottenhavet
BALTIC SEA
ÖSTERSJÖN
STOCKHOLM
Uppsala
Västerås
Örebro
Karlstad
Gävle
Norrköping
Nyköping
Eskilstuna
Vänern
Hjälmaren
Copyright © by Rand McNally & Co.
Map compiled by Esselte Map Service AB, Stockholm.
Map produced by Rand McNally & Co.

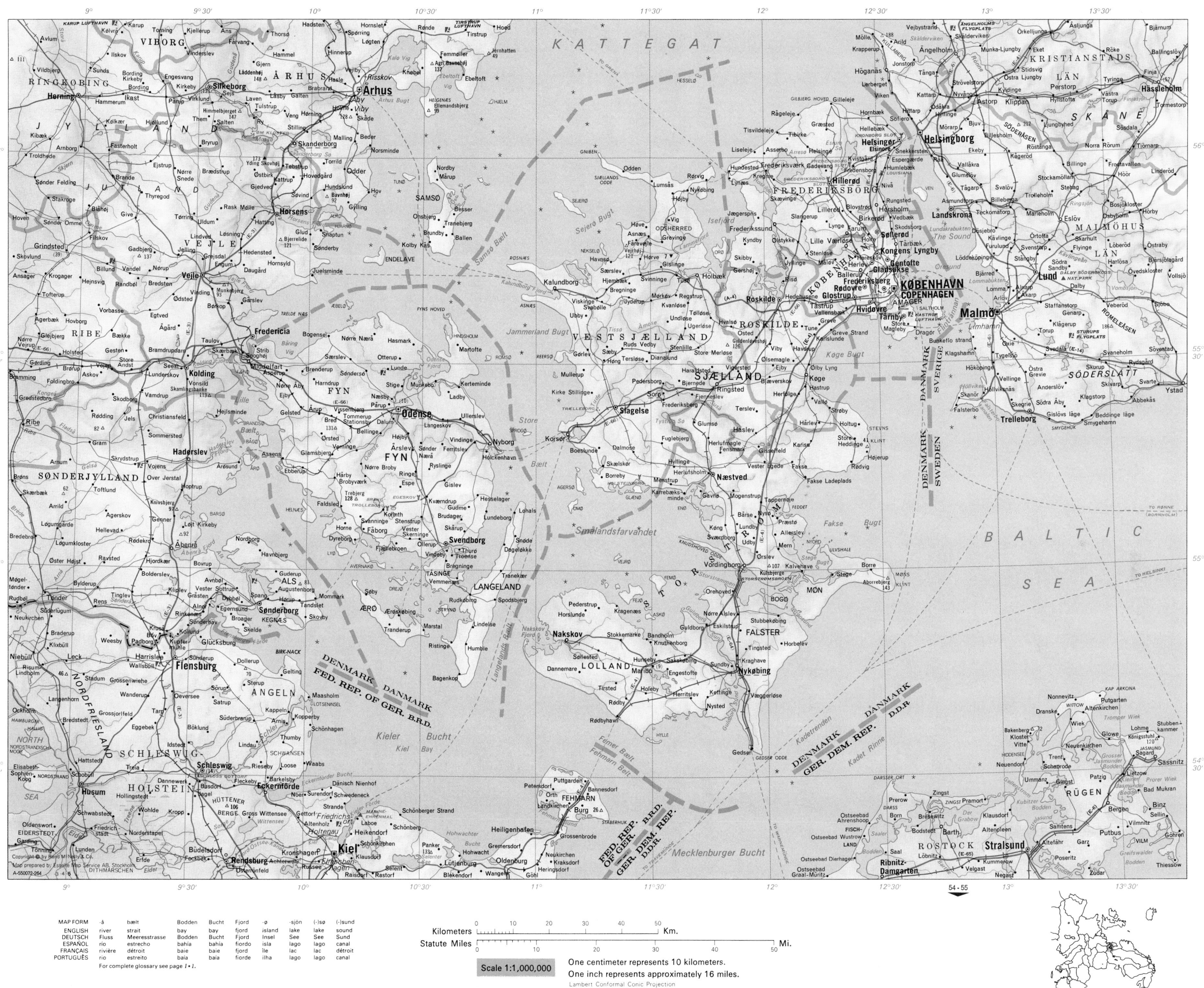

MAP FORM	-å	bælt	Bodden	Bucht	Fjord	-ø	-sjön	(-)sø	(-)sund
ENGLISH	river	strait	bay	bay	fjord	island	lake	lake	sound
DEUTSCH	Fluss	Meeresstrasse	Bodden	Bucht	Fjord	Insel	See	See	Sund
ESPAÑOL	rio	estrecho	bahia	bahia	fiordo	isla	lago	lago	canal
FRANÇAIS	rivière	détroit	baie	baie	fjord	île	lac	lac	détroit
PORTUGUÊS	rio	estreito	baia	baia	fiorde	ilha	lago	lago	canal

For complete glossary see page I • I.

Kilometers 0 10 20 30 40 50 Km.
Statute Miles 0 10 20 30 40 50 Mi.

Scale 1:1,000,000

One centimeter represents 10 kilometers.
One inch represents approximately 16 miles.
Lambert Conformal Conic Projection

Saint George's Channel
Cardigan Bay
Tremadoc Bay
Carmarthen Bay
Bristol Channel
Bridgwater Bay
Lyme Bay
LLEYN PENINSULA
SNOWDONIA NATIONAL PARK
CAMBRIAN MOUNTAINS
BERWYN
BLACK MOUNTAINS
BRECON BEACONS NATIONAL PARK
PEMBROKESHIRE COAST NATIONAL PARK
EXMOOR
DARTMOOR
BODMIN MOOR
QUANTOCK HILLS
BLACKDOWN HILLS
NORTH DORSET DOWNS
Wrexham
Shrewsbury
Wolverhampton
Kidderminster
Worcester
Hereford
Gloucester
Tewkesbury
Aberystwyth
Cardigan
Carmarthen
Haverfordwest
Pembroke
Llanelli
Swansea
Neath
Port Talbot
Rhondda
Merthyr Tydfil
Aberdare
Ebbw Vale
Pontypool
Pontypridd
Caerphilly
Newport
Bridgend
Llandaff
Cardiff
Penarth
Barry
Bristol
Bath
Trowbridge
Weston-super-Mare
Bridgwater
Taunton
Yeovil
Dorchester
Weymouth
Barnstaple
Bideford
Exeter
Exmouth
Newton Abbot
Torquay (Torbay)
Plymouth
Newquay
Truro
Saint Austell
Falmouth
Camborne
Penzance
Helston
Lizard
LUNDY
a
ISLES OF SCILLY
Hugh Town
ATLANTIC OCEAN
E N G
Copyright © by Rand McNally & Co.
Map prepared by Rand McNally & Co.
A-556900-264
ENGLISH bay drain forest head hill isle marsh point vale
DEUTSCH Bucht Abzugsgraben Wald Landspitze Hügel Insel Marsch Landspitze Tal
ESPAÑOL bahía acquia bosque promontorio colina isla pantano punta valle
FRANÇAIS baie drainage forêt promontoire colline île marais pointe dépression
PORTUGUÊS baía drenagem bosque promontório colina ilha pântano ponta vale
For complete glossary see page I · 1.
For London metropolitan map, see page 260.

44 - 45
50 - 51
NORTH SEA
ENGLISH CHANNEL
The Wash
Holland Fen
Brancaster Roads
Strait of Dover
Nottingham
Derby
Leicester
Coventry
Nuneaton
Rugby
Northampton
Peterborough
Boston
Grantham
King's Lynn
Norwich
Great Yarmouth
Lowestoft
Cambridge
Bedford
Luton
Oxford
Swindon
Reading
LONDON
Ipswich
Colchester
Chelmsford
Southend-on-Sea
Chatham
Maidstone
Canterbury
Margate
Ramsgate
Dover
Folkestone
Hastings
Eastbourne
Brighton
Worthing
Portsmouth
Southampton
Winchester
Salisbury
Guildford
Reigate
Aldershot
High Wycombe
Aylesbury
Hertford
Stevenage
Newmarket
Bury Saint Edmunds
Tunbridge Wells
Crawley
Horsham
Chichester
Bognor Regis
Newport
ISLE OF WIGHT
ISLE OF SHEPPEY
ISLE OF ELY
CAMBRIDGESHIRE
LEICESTERSHIRE
WARWICKSHIRE
HAMPSHIRE
WEALD
SOUTH DOWNS
GUERNSEY (U.K.)
St. Peter Port
JERSEY (U.K.)
St. Helier
ALDERNEY
St. Anne
SARK
CHANNEL ISLANDS
Passage de la Déroute
b
1° 30′
1°
0° 30′ West
0°
0° 30′ East
2° 30′ West
2°
53°
52° 30′
52°
51° 30′
51°
50° 30′
49° 30′
Kilometers 0 10 20 30 40 50 Km.
Statute Miles 0 10 20 30 40 50 Mi.
Scale 1:1,000,000
One centimeter represents 10 kilometers.
One inch represents approximately 16 miles.
Lambert Conformal Conic Projection

MAP FORM	bay	dale	firth	forest	head	loch	moor	water
ENGLISH	bay	dale	estuary	forest	head	lake; inlet	moor	water (lake, river)
DEUTSCH	Bucht	Weites Tal	Trichtermündung	Wald	Landspitze	See; Einfahrt	Moor	See, Fluss
ESPAÑOL	bahía	valle	estuario	bosque	promontorio	lago; abra	páramo	lago, río
FRANÇAIS	baie	vallée	estuaire	forêt	promontoire	lac; bras de mer	lande	lac, rivière
PORTUGUÊS	baía	vale	estuário	bosque	promontório	lago; braço de mar	charco	lago, rio

For complete glossary see page *I • 1*.
For Manchester-Liverpool metropolitan map see page 262.

Kilometers 0 10 20 30 40 50 Km.
Statute Miles 0 10 20 30 40 50 Mi.

Scale 1:1,000,000

One centimeter represents 10 kilometers.
One inch represents approximately 16 miles.
Lambert Conformal Conic Projection

ATLANTIC
OCEAN
NORTH
SEA
ORKNEY ISLANDS
SHETLAND ISLANDS
MAINLAND
HIGHLAND
HEBRIDES
LEWIS
HARRIS
The Minch
Little Minch
BLACK ISLE
Moray Firth
Pentland Firth
Kirkwall
Stornoway
Thurso
Wick
Lerwick
Copyright © by Rand McNally & Co.

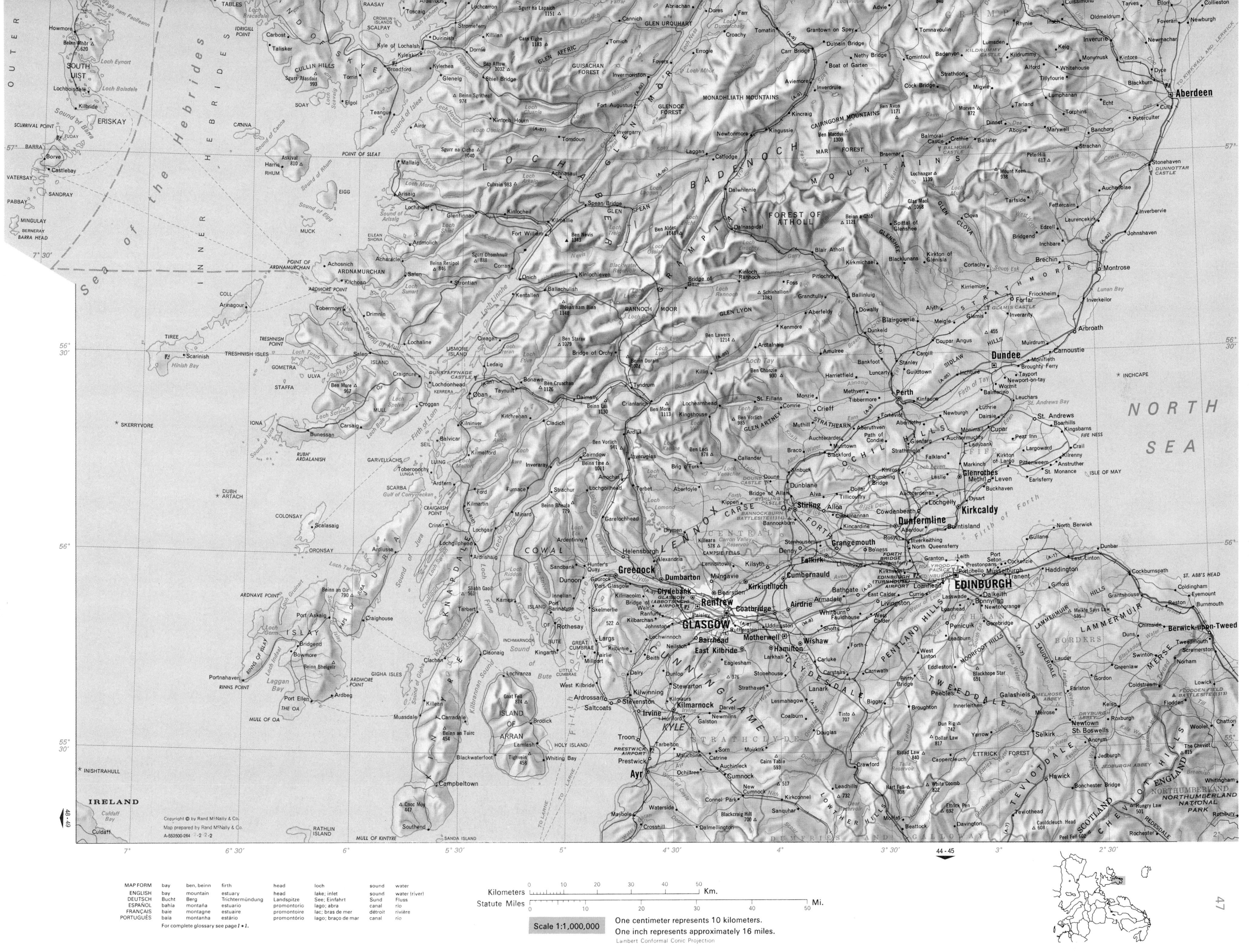
NORTH SEA
OUTER HEBRIDES
INNER HEBRIDES
Sea of the Hebrides
IRELAND
Aberdeen
Dundee
Perth
EDINBURGH
GLASGOW
Greenock
Kirkcaldy
Dunfermline
Stirling
Ayr
Kilmarnock
Berwick-upon-Tweed
GRAMPIAN MOUNTAINS
MONADHLIATH MOUNTAINS
CAIRNGORM MOUNTAINS
LOCHABER
BADENOCH
FOREST OF ATHOLL
STRATHMORE
LENNOX
CUNNINGHAME
KYLE
LAUDERDALE
TWEEDDALE
TEVIOTDALE
CHEVIOT HILLS
LAMMERMUIR
PENTLAND HILLS
OCHIL HILLS
KNAPDALE
KINTYRE
COWAL
ISLAY
JURA
ISLAND OF ARRAN
SKYE
MULL
NORTHUMBERLAND NATIONAL PARK
SCOTLAND
ENGLAND
44-45
48-49
Copyright © by Rand McNally & Co.
Map prepared by Rand McNally & Co.
A-553500-264 -2-2-2
MAP FORM bay ben, beinn firth head loch sound water
ENGLISH bay mountain estuary head lake; inlet sound water (river)
DEUTSCH Bucht Berg Trichtermündung Landspitze See; Einfahrt Sund Fluss
ESPAÑOL bahía montaña estuario promontorio lago; abra canal río
FRANÇAIS baie montagne estuaire promontoire lac; bras de mer détroit rivière
PORTUGUÊS baía montanha estário promontório lago; braço de mar canal rio
For complete glossary see page I • 1.
Kilometers 0 10 20 30 40 50 Km.
Statute Miles 0 10 20 30 40 50 Mi.
Scale 1:1,000,000
One centimeter represents 10 kilometers.
One inch represents approximately 16 miles.
Lambert Conformal Conic Projection

ATLANTIC
OCEAN
NORTH
CHANNEL
IRISH
SEA
SCOTLAND
NORTHERN IRELAND
U.K.
IRELAND
EIRE
ULSTER
CONNAUGHT
LEITRIM
SLIGO
ROSCOMMON
LONGFORD
CAVAN
MONAGHAN
LOUTH
MEATH
DONEGAL
MAYO
Belfast
Londonderry
Lough Neagh
Lough Foyle
Donegal Bay
Clew Bay
SPERRIN MTS.
MOURNE MTS.
BLUE STACK MTS.
NEPHIN BEG RANGE
SLIEVE GAMPH
INISHOWEN PEN.
ACHILL ISLAND
CLARE ISLAND
46 - 47
44 - 45

42 - 43
MAP FORM / ENGLISH / DEUTSCH / ESPAÑOL / FRANÇAIS / PORTUGUÊS
bay / bay / Bucht / bahía / baie / baía
harbour / harbor, harbour / Hafen / puerto / port / porto
head / head / Landspitze / promontorio / promontoire / promontório
lough / lake; inlet / See; Einfahrt / lago; abra / lac; bras de mer / lago; braço de mar
mountains, mts. / mountains / Berge / montañas / montagnes / montanhas
point / point / Landspitze / punta / pointe / ponta
slieve / mountain, mountains / Berg, Berge / montaña, montañas / montagne, montagnes / montanha, montanhas
For complete glossary see page I • I.
Kilometers
Statute Miles
Scale 1:1,000,000
One centimeter represents 10 kilometers.
One inch represents approximately 16 miles.
Lambert Conformal Conic Projection
Copyright © by Rand McNally & Co.
Map prepared by Rand McNally & Co.

52-53
56-57
42-43
NORTH SEA
ENGLISH CHANNEL
LA MANCHE
Strait of Dover
Pas de Calais
UNITED KINGDOM
FRANCE
BELGIUM
NETHERLANDS
LONDON
BRUXELLES
BRUSSEL
LILLE
Calais
Dover
Boulogne-sur-Mer
Dunkerque
Oostende
Brugge
Gent
ANTWERPEN
Amiens
Le Havre

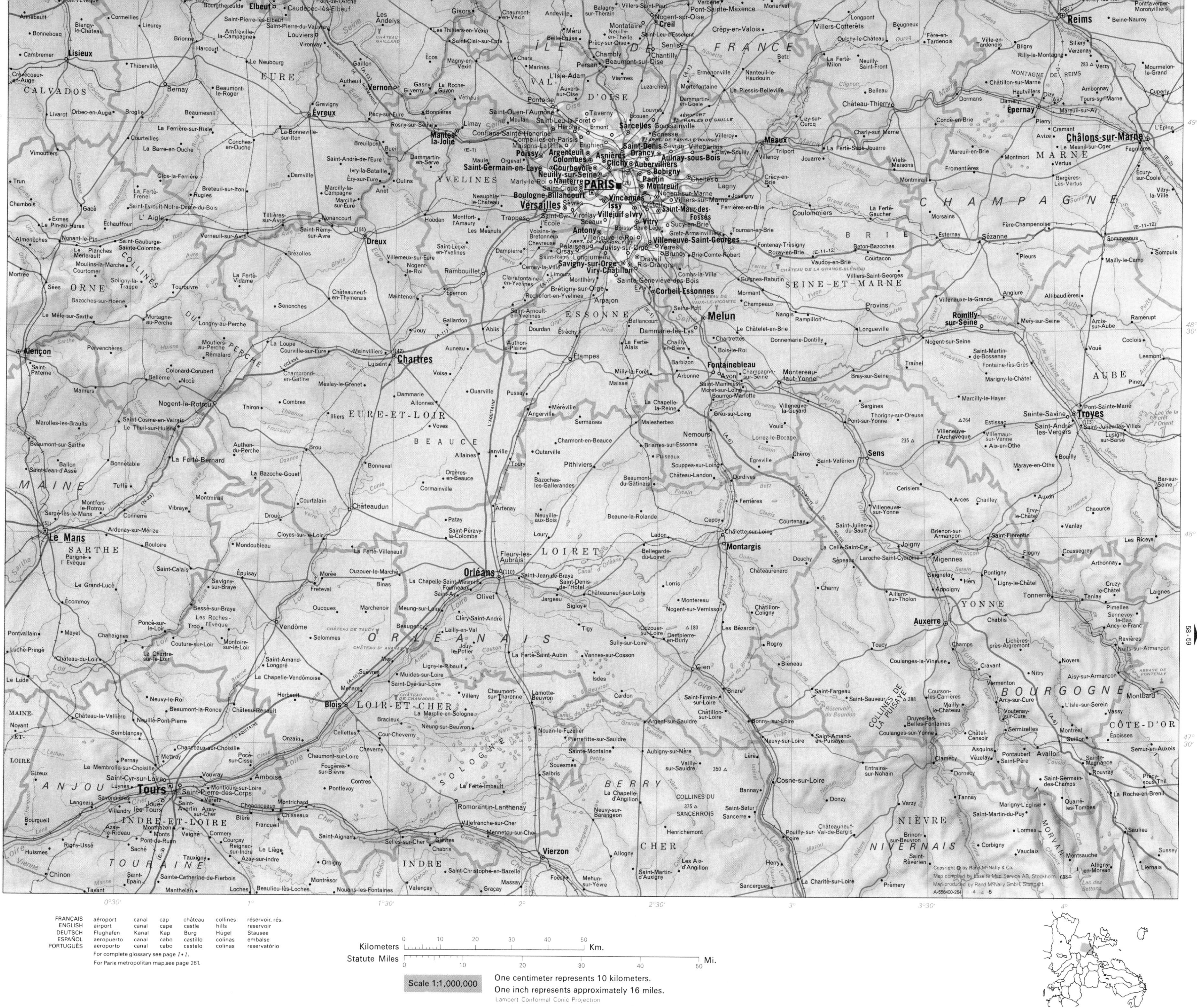
58-59
Reims
Châlons-sur-Marne
Épernay
Troyes
Sens
Auxerre
Melun
Fontainebleau
Meaux
Montargis
PARIS
Versailles
Chartres
Dreux
Évreux
Orléans
Blois
Tours
Vierzon
Le Mans
Alençon
Lisieux
CHAMPAGNE
BRIE
BEAUCE
SOLOGNE
BERRY
BOURGOGNE
MAINE
ANJOU
TOURAINE
ORLÉANAIS
FRANÇAIS aéroport canal cap château collines réservoir, rés.
ENGLISH airport canal cape castle hills reservoir
DEUTSCH Flughafen Kanal Kap Burg Hügel Stausee
ESPAÑOL aeropuerto canal cabo castillo colinas embalse
PORTUGUÊS aeroporto canal cabo castelo colinas reservatório
For complete glossary see page I • I.
For Paris metropolitan map see page 261.
Kilometers
Statute Miles
Km.
Mi.
Scale 1:1,000,000
One centimeter represents 10 kilometers.
One inch represents approximately 16 miles.
Lambert Conformal Conic Projection

DEUTSCH	Gebirge	Kanal	Moor	Naturpark	Stausee	Talsperre	Wald
ENGLISH	range	canal	moor	reserve	reservoir	dam	forest, mountains
ESPAÑOL	sierra	canal	páramo	reserva	embalse	presa	bosque, montañas
FRANÇAIS	chaîne	canal	lande	réserve	réservoir	barrage	forêt, montagnes
PORTUGUÊS	serra	canal	charco	reserva	reservatório	represa	bosque, montanhas

For complete glossary see page I·1.
For Ruhr metropolitan map see page 263.

50-51
56-57

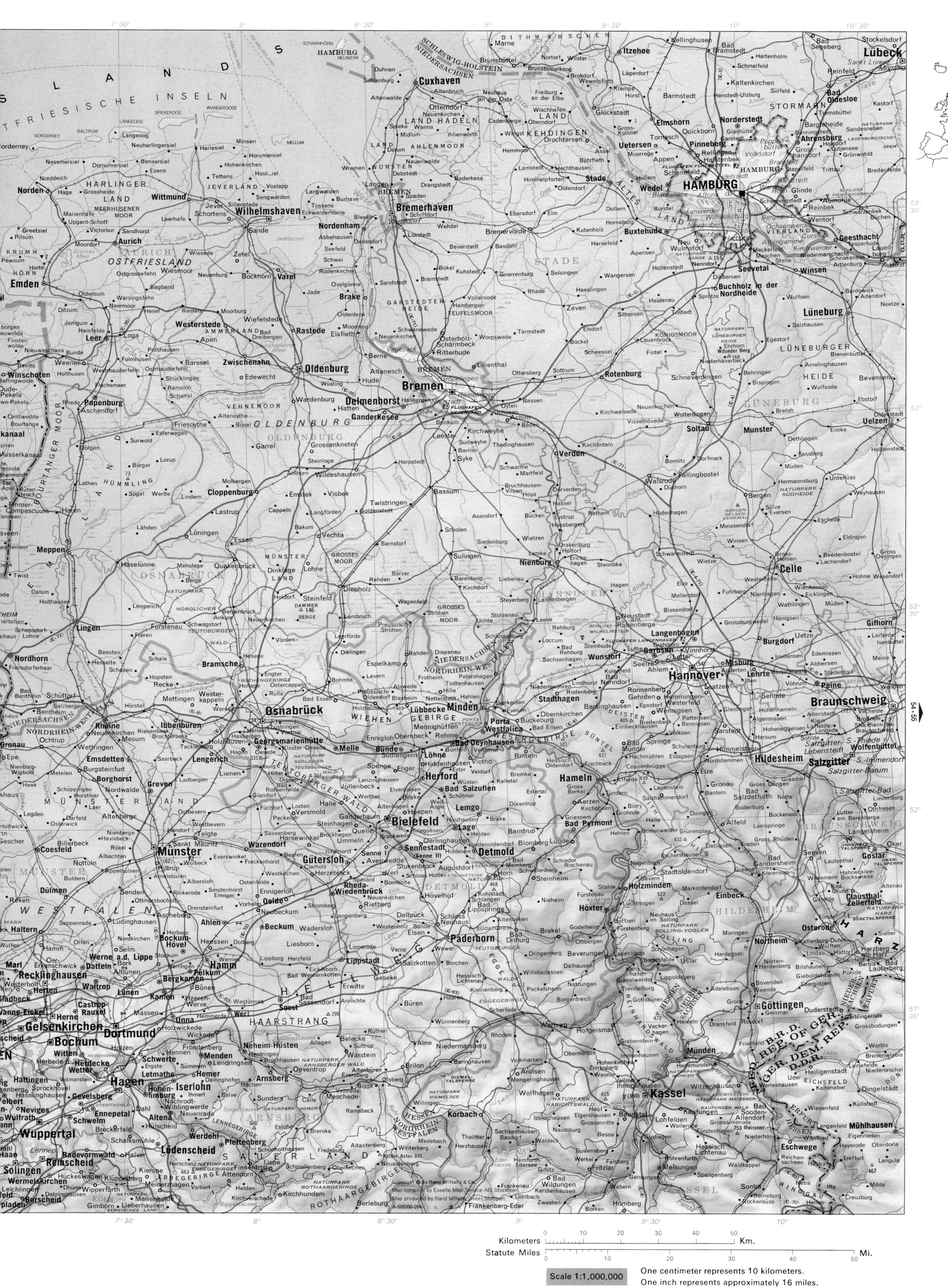

Kilometers 0 10 20 30 40 50 Km.

Statute Miles 0 10 20 30 40 50 Mi.

Scale 1:1,000,000

One centimeter represents 10 kilometers.
One inch represents approximately 16 miles.

Lambert Conformal Conic Projection

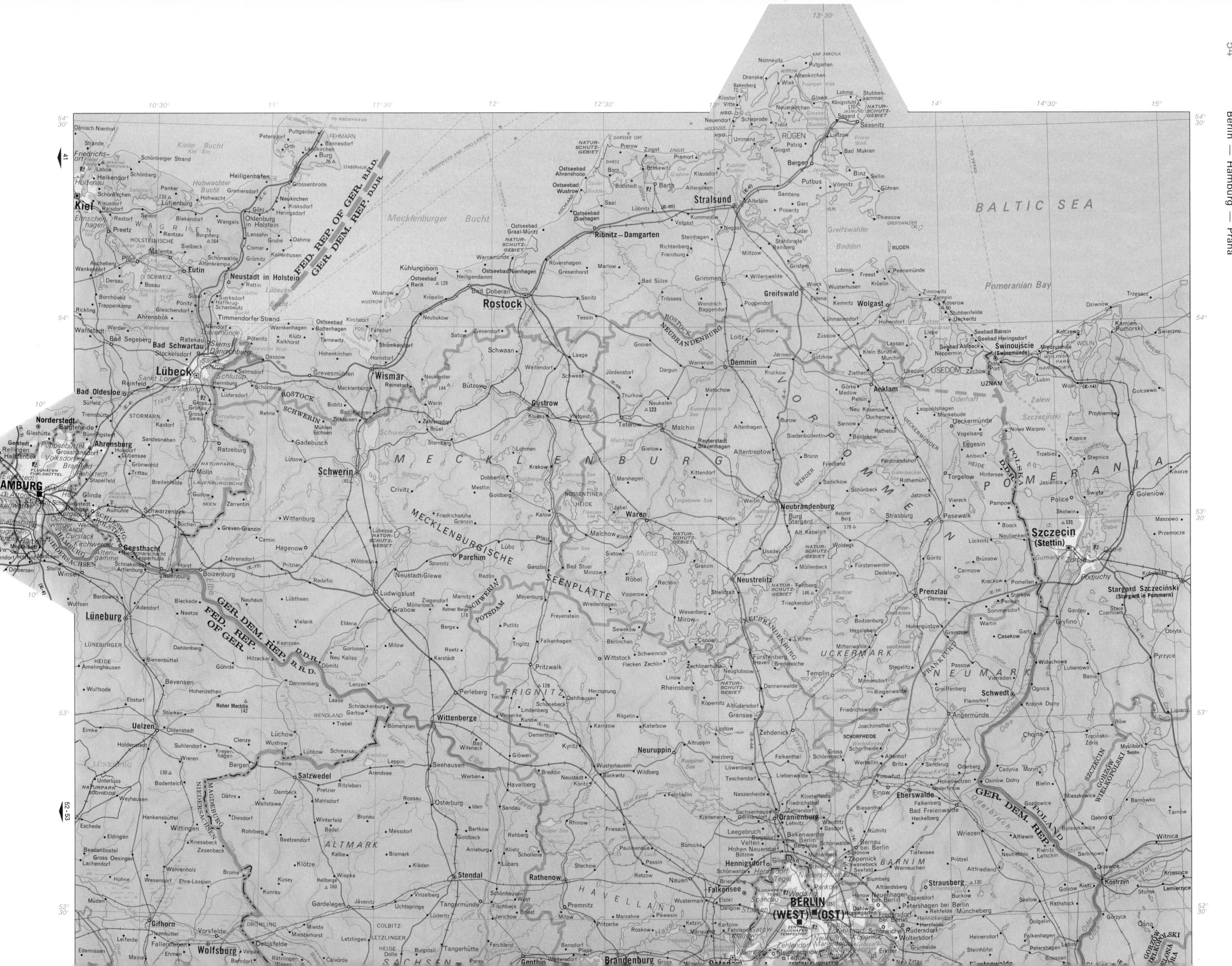
BALTIC SEA
Pomeranian Bay
Mecklenburger Bucht
Kieler Bucht
RÜGEN
USEDOM
WOLIN
POMERANIA
VORPOMMERN
MECKLENBURG
MECKLENBURGISCHE SEENPLATTE
UCKERMARK
NEUMARK
PRIGNITZ
HAVELLAND
BARNIM
ALTMARK
FED. REP. OF GER. B.R.D.
GER. DEM. REP. D.D.R.
GER. DEM. REP.
POLAND
Szczecin
(Stettin)
Rostock
Stralsund
Greifswald
Neubrandenburg
Schwerin
Wismar
Lübeck
Kiel
Lüneburg
HAMBURG
BERLIN (WEST) (OST)
Brandenburg
Stendal
Wittenberge
Salzwedel
Uelzen
Wolfsburg
Gifhorn
Neuruppin
Neustrelitz
Prenzlau
Pasewalk
Anklam
Demmin
Güstrow
Parchim
Ludwigslust
Waren
Wolgast
Eberswalde
Oranienburg
Kostrzyn
Stargard Szczeciński
41
52-53

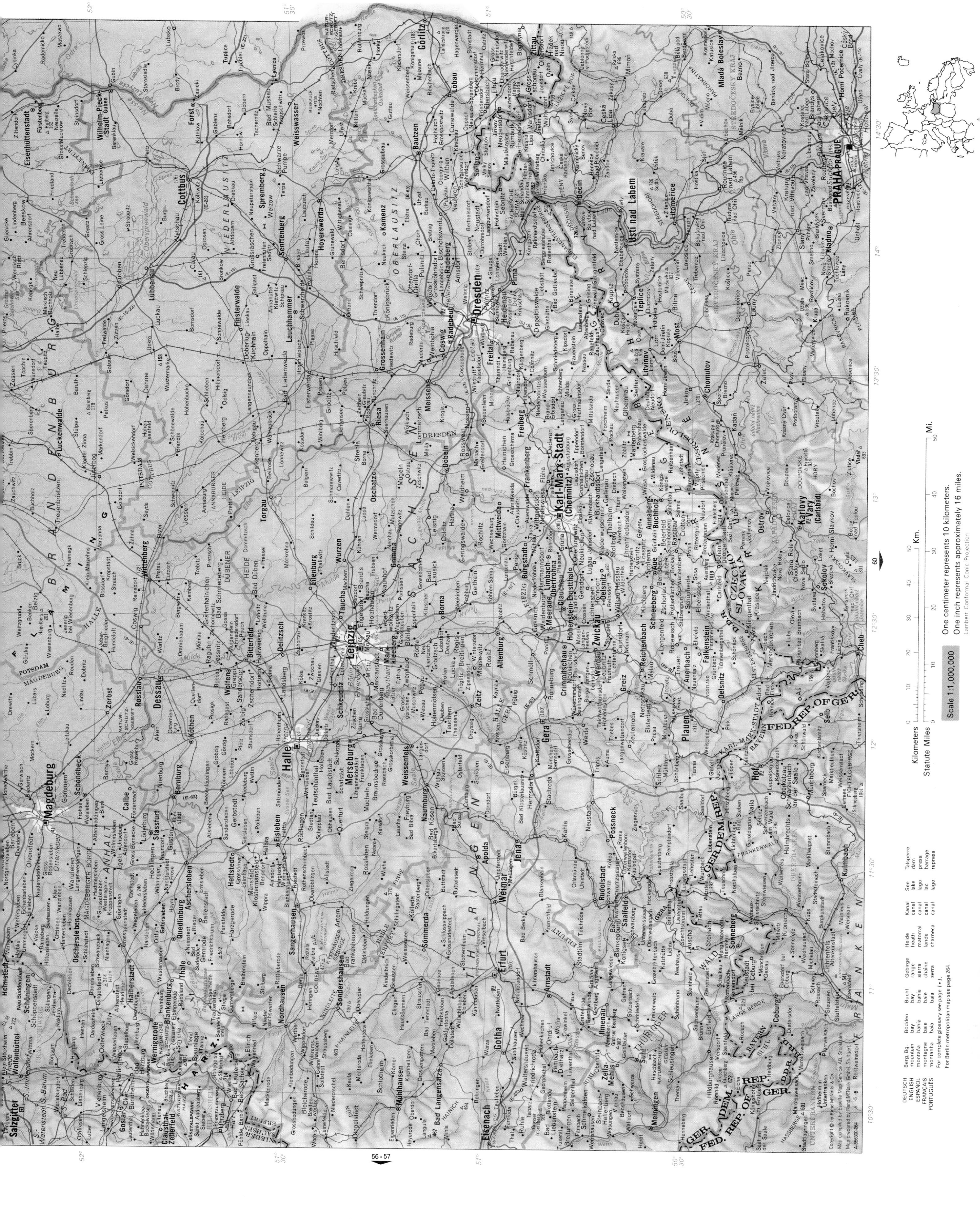

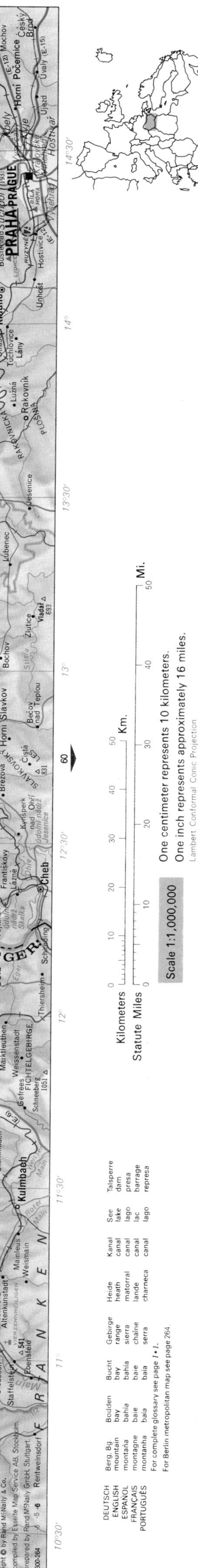
Scale 1:1,000,000
One centimeter represents 10 kilometers.
One inch represents approximately 16 miles.
Lambert Conformal Conic Projection
Kilometers
Statute Miles

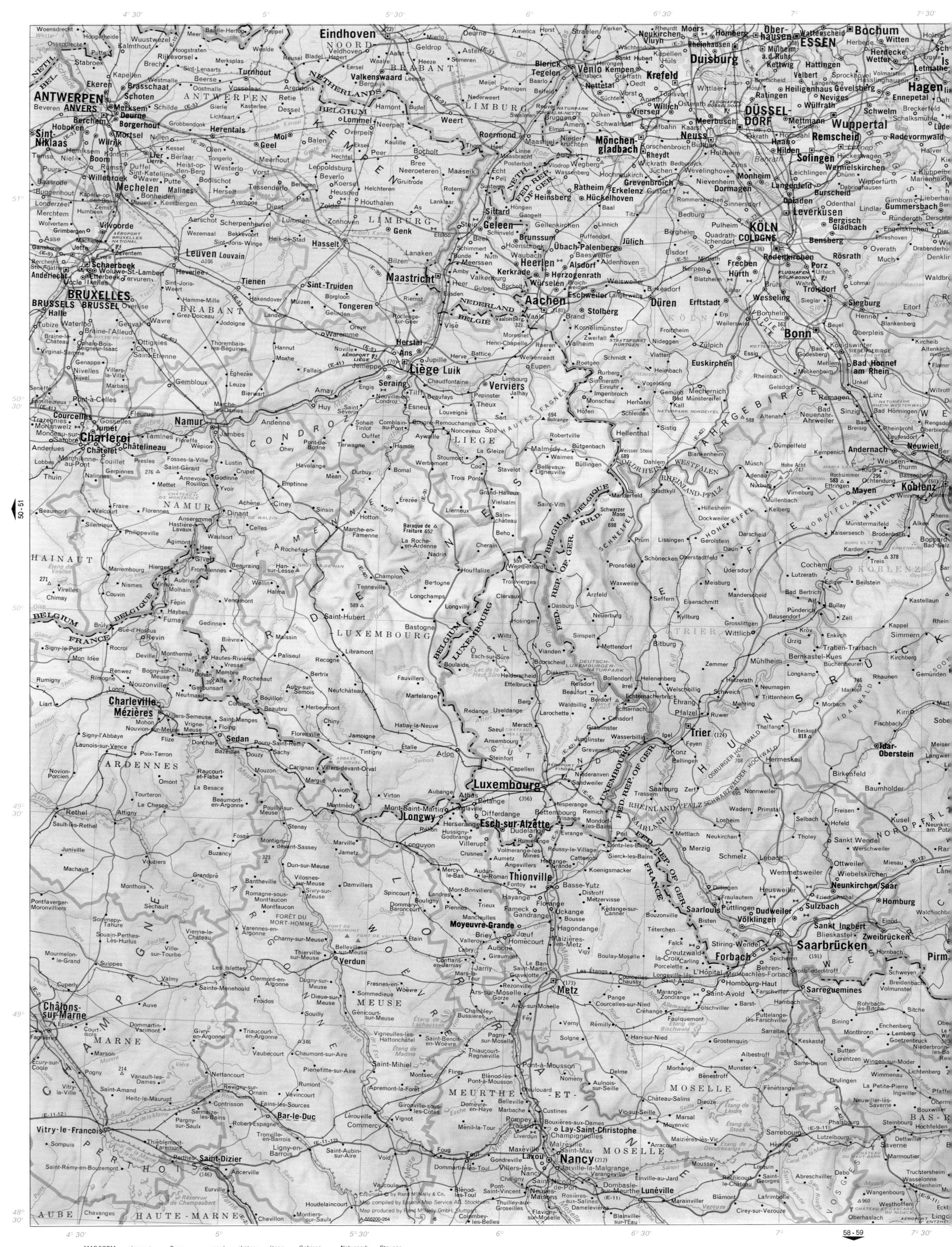

MAP FORM	aéroport	Berg	canal	chateau	étang	Gebirge	Naturpark	Stausee
ENGLISH	airport	mountain	canal	castle	pond	range	reserve	reservoir
DEUTSCH	Flughafen	Berg	Kanal	Burg	Teich	Gebirge	Naturpark	Stausee
ESPAÑOL	aeropuerto	montaña	canal	castillo	charca	cordillera	reserva	embalse
FRANCAIS	aéroport	montagne	canal	château	étang	chaîne	réserve	réservoir
PORTUGUÊS	aeroporto	montanha	canal	castelo	lagoa	cordilheira	reserva	reservatório

For complete glossary see page I • 1.
For Ruhr metropolitan map see page 263.

52-53
54-55
60
Kassel
Marburg an der Lahn
Giessen
Wetzlar
Fulda
Bad Hersfeld
Eisenach
Gotha
Erfurt
Siegen
Wiesbaden
Mainz
FRANKFURT AM MAIN
Offenbach
Hanau
Aschaffenburg
Darmstadt
Würzburg
Schweinfurt
Bamberg
Erlangen
Fürth
Nürnberg
Worms
MANNHEIM
Ludwigshafen
Heidelberg
Heilbronn
Karlsruhe
Pforzheim
STUTTGART
Esslingen
Baden-Baden
Strasbourg
Ansbach
Crailsheim
Aalen
Heidenheim an der Brenz
Schwäbisch Hall
Schwäbisch Gmünd
Ludwigsburg
Kilometers 0 10 20 30 40 50 Km.
Statute Miles 0 10 20 30 40 50 Mi.
Scale 1:1,000,000
One centimeter represents 10 kilometers.
One inch represents approximately 16 miles.
Lambert Conformal Conic Projection

MAP FORM	col	Horn	lago	mont	passo	piz, -zo	See	Spitze	val
ENGLISH	pass	peak	lake	mount	pass	peak	lake	peak	valley
DEUTSCH	Pass	Horn	See	Berg	Pass	Gipfel	See	Spitze	Tal
ESPAÑOL	paso	pico	lago	monte	paso	pico	lago	pico	valle
FRANÇAIS	col	cime	lac	mont	col	cime	lac	cime	val
PORTUGUÊS	passo	pico	lago	monte	passo	pico	lago	pico	vale

For complete glossary see page I • 1.

56-57
60
64-65
62-63
Strasbourg
Offenburg
Freiburg im Breisgau
Tübingen
Reutlingen
Göppingen
Heidenheim an der Brenz
Ulm
Neu-Ulm
Augsburg
Memmingen
Kempten
Kaufbeuren
Biberach an der Riss
Ravensburg
Friedrichshafen
Konstanz
Lindau
Bregenz
Dornbirn
Feldkirch
Vaduz
LIECHTENSTEIN
Sankt Gallen
Winterthur
Schaffhausen
Zürich
Baden
Aarau
Luzern
Zug
Schwyz
Chur
Davos
Bellinzona
Locarno
Lugano
Como
Varese
Lecco
Sondrio
Domodossola
Verbania
SCHWÄBISCHE ALB
SCHWARZWALD
BODENSEE
Lake Constance
FED. REP. OF GER.
SWITZERLAND
AUSTRIA
ITALY
FRANCE
TIROL
VORARLBERG
GRAUBÜNDEN
RHAETIAN ALPS
TICINO
GLARUS
URI
SCHWYZ
THURGAU
AARGAU
ZÜRICH
LUZERN
APPENZELL
UNTERWALDEN
ALPEN
Kilometers 0 10 20 30 40 50 Km.
Statute Miles 0 10 20 30 40 50 Mi.
Scale 1:1,000,000
One centimeter represents 10 kilometers.
One inch represents approximately 16 miles.
Lambert Conformal Conic Projection

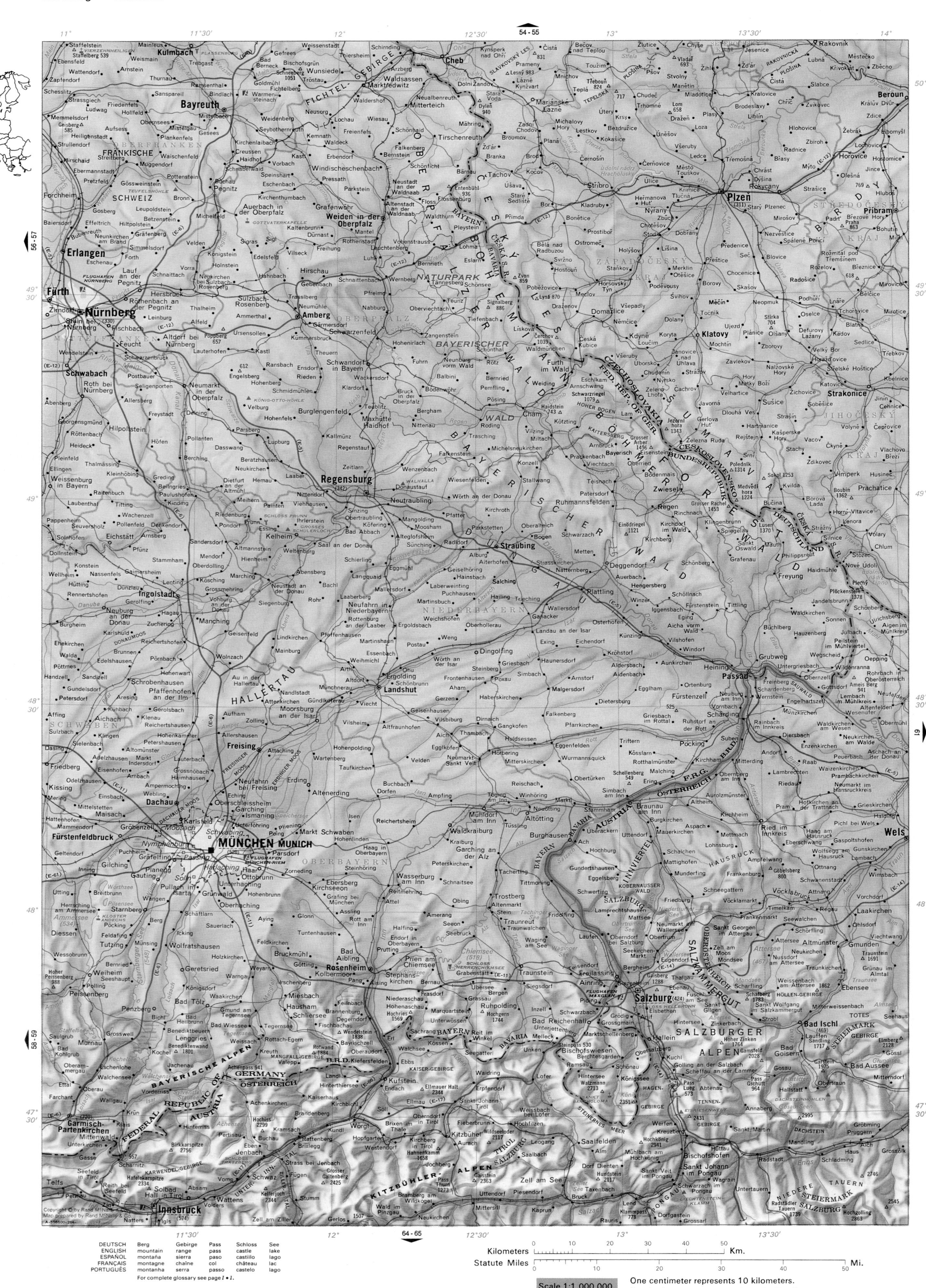
54-55
56-57
58-59
61
64-65
11°
11°30'
12°
12°30'
13°
13°30'
14°
50°
49° 30'
49°
48° 30'
48°
47° 30'
Nürnberg
Fürth
Erlangen
Bayreuth
Kulmbach
Amberg
Regensburg
Straubing
Deggendorf
Passau
Landshut
Ingolstadt
Freising
Dachau
MÜNCHEN MUNICH
Rosenheim
Salzburg
Innsbruck
Kufstein
Cheb
Plzeň
Klatovy
Strakonice
Příbram
Beroun
Rakovník
Wels
Bad Ischl
Schwabach
Weiden in der Oberpfalz
Fürstenfeldbruck
Garmisch-Partenkirchen
Mittenwald
Bad Tölz
Traunstein
Bad Reichenhall
Hallein
Kitzbühel
Wörgl
Schwaz
Braunau am Inn
Ried im Innkreis
FRÄNKISCHE SCHWEIZ
FICHTEL-GEBIRGE
OBERPFÄLZER WALD
BAYERISCHER WALD
ŠUMAVA
BÖHMER WALD
HALLERTAU
NIEDERBAYERN
OBERBAYERN
OBERPFALZ
MITTELFRANKEN
SCHWABEN
NATURPARK BAYERISCHER WALD
BAYERISCHE ALPEN
SALZBURGER ALPEN
KITZBÜHLER ALPEN
SALZKAMMERGUT
HAUSRUCK
INNVIERTEL
ZÁPADOČESKÝ KRAJ
STŘEDOČESKÝ KRAJ
JIHOČESKÝ KRAJ
BRDY
ČESKOSLOVENSKO
CZECHOSLOVAKIA
FED. REP. OF GER.
BUNDESREPUBLIK DEUTSCHLAND
FEDERAL REPUBLIC OF GERMANY
B.R.D.
AUSTRIA
ÖSTERREICH
F.R.G.
BAVARIA
BAYERN
TIROL
STEIERMARK
Danube
Donau
Isar
Inn
Regen
Chiemsee
Starnberger See
Ammersee
Copyright © by Rand McNally & Co.
Map prepared by Rand McNally & Co.
DEUTSCH Berg Gebirge Pass Schloss See
ENGLISH mountain range pass castle lake
ESPAÑOL montaña sierra paso castillo lago
FRANÇAIS montagne chaîne col château lac
PORTUGUÊS montanha serra passo castelo lago
For complete glossary see page I • 1.
Kilometers 0 10 20 30 40 50 Km.
Statute Miles 0 10 20 30 40 50 Mi.
Scale 1:1,000,000
One centimeter represents 10 kilometers.
One inch represents approximately 16 miles.
Modified Polyconic Projection

DEUTSCH	Alpe, -n	Berg	Gebirge	Sattel	Schloss	Wald
ENGLISH	mountains	mountain	range	saddle	castle	forest; mountains
ESPAÑOL	montañas	montaña	sierra	paso	castillo	bosque; montañas
FRANÇAIS	montagnes	montagne	chaîne	col	château	forêt; montagnes
PORTUGUÊS	montanhas	montanha	serra	passo	castelo	Floresta; montanhas

For complete glossary see page I • 1.

Kilometers 0 10 20 30 40 50 Km.

Statute Miles 0 10 20 30 40 50 Mi.

Scale 1:1,000,000

One centimeter represents 10 kilometers.
One inch represents approximately 16 miles.

Lambert Conformal Conic Projection

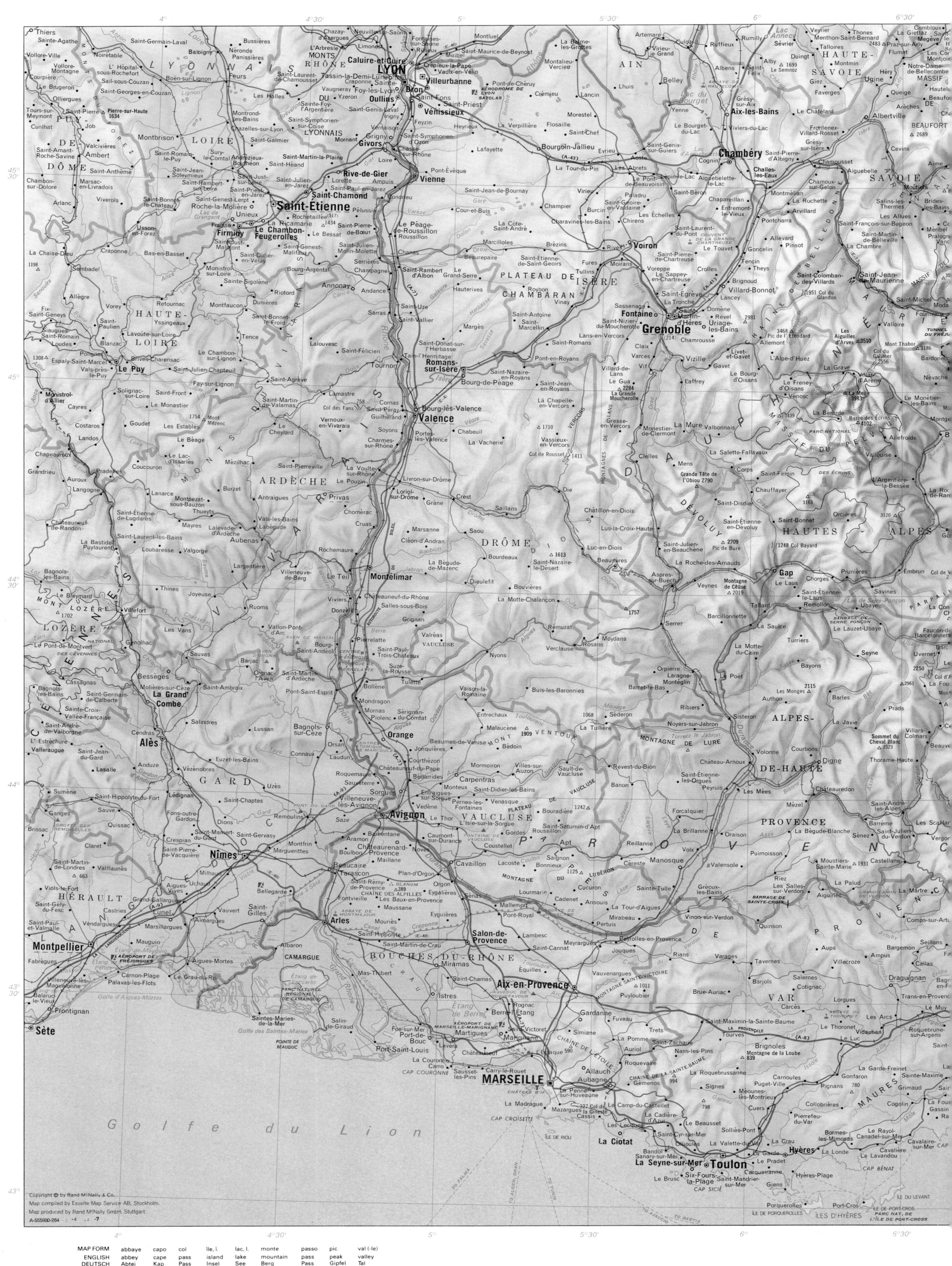

Map compiled by Esselte Map Service AB, Stockholm.
Map produced by Rand McNally GmbH, Stuttgart.
A-555600-264

MAP FORM	abbaye	capo	col	île, î.	lac, l.	monte	passo	pic	val (-le)
ENGLISH	abbey	cape	pass	island	lake	mountain	pass	peak	valley
DEUTSCH	Abtei	Kap	Pass	Insel	See	Berg	Pass	Gipfel	Tal
ESPAÑOL	abadia	cabo	paso	isla	lago	montaña	paso	pico	valle
FRANÇAIS	abbaye	cap	col	île	lac	montagne	col	cime	val
PORTUGUÊS	abadia	cabo	passo	ilha	lago	montanha	passo	pico	vale

For complete glossary see page *I • 1*.
For Milano metropolitan map see page 266.

58-59
64-65
Ligurian Sea
Mar Ligure
MEDITERRANEAN SEA
Golfo di Genova
RIVIERA DI PONENTE
RIVIERA DI LEVANTE
CÔTE D'AZUR
APPENNINO LIGURE
ALPI MARITTIME
ALPES MARITIMES
MONFERRATO
LANGHE
LOMELLINA
BRIANZA
PIEMONTE
LIGURIA
LOMBARDIA
EMILIA-ROMAGNA
TOSCANA
MONACO
CORSE CORSICA
HAUTE-CORSE (Fr.)
MILANO MILAN
TORINO TURIN
GENOVA GENOA
Aosta
Biella
Novara
Vercelli
Varese
Como
Lecco
Bergamo
Monza
Pavia
Piacenza
Alessandria
Asti
Cuneo
Savona
Imperia
San Remo
Ventimiglia
Monaco
Nice
Cannes
Antibes
La Spezia
Chiavari
Rapallo
Sestri Levante
Voghera
Tortona
Novi Ligure
Acqui Terme
Alba
Bra
Pinerolo
Ivrea
Chivasso
Moncalieri
Vigevano
Casale Monferrato
Lodi
Crema
Kilometers 0 10 20 30 40 50 Km.
Statute Miles 0 10 20 30 40 50 Mi.
Scale 1:1,000,000
One centimeter represents 10 kilometers.
One inch represents approximately 16 miles.
Lambert Conformal Conic Projection

60

61

58-59

MAP FORM	Alpen	Berg	cima	Gebirge	monte	piz	Schloss	See	Spitze
ENGLISH	mountains	mountain	peak	range	mountain	peak	castle	lake	peak
DEUTSCH	Alpen	Berg	Gipfel	Gebirge	Berg	Gipfel	Schloss	See	Spitze
ESPAÑOL	montañas	montaña	pico	sierra	montaña	pico	castillo	lago	pico
FRANÇAIS	montagnes	montagne	cime	chaîne	montagne	cime	château	lac	cime
PORTUGUÊS	montanhas	montanha	pico	serra	montanha	pico	castelo	lago	pico

For complete glossary see page I•1.

Kilometers 0 10 20 30 40 50 Km.
Statute Miles 0 10 20 30 40 50 Mi.

Scale 1:1,000,000

One centimeter represents 10 kilometers.
One inch represents approximately 16 miles.
Lambert Conformal Conic Projection

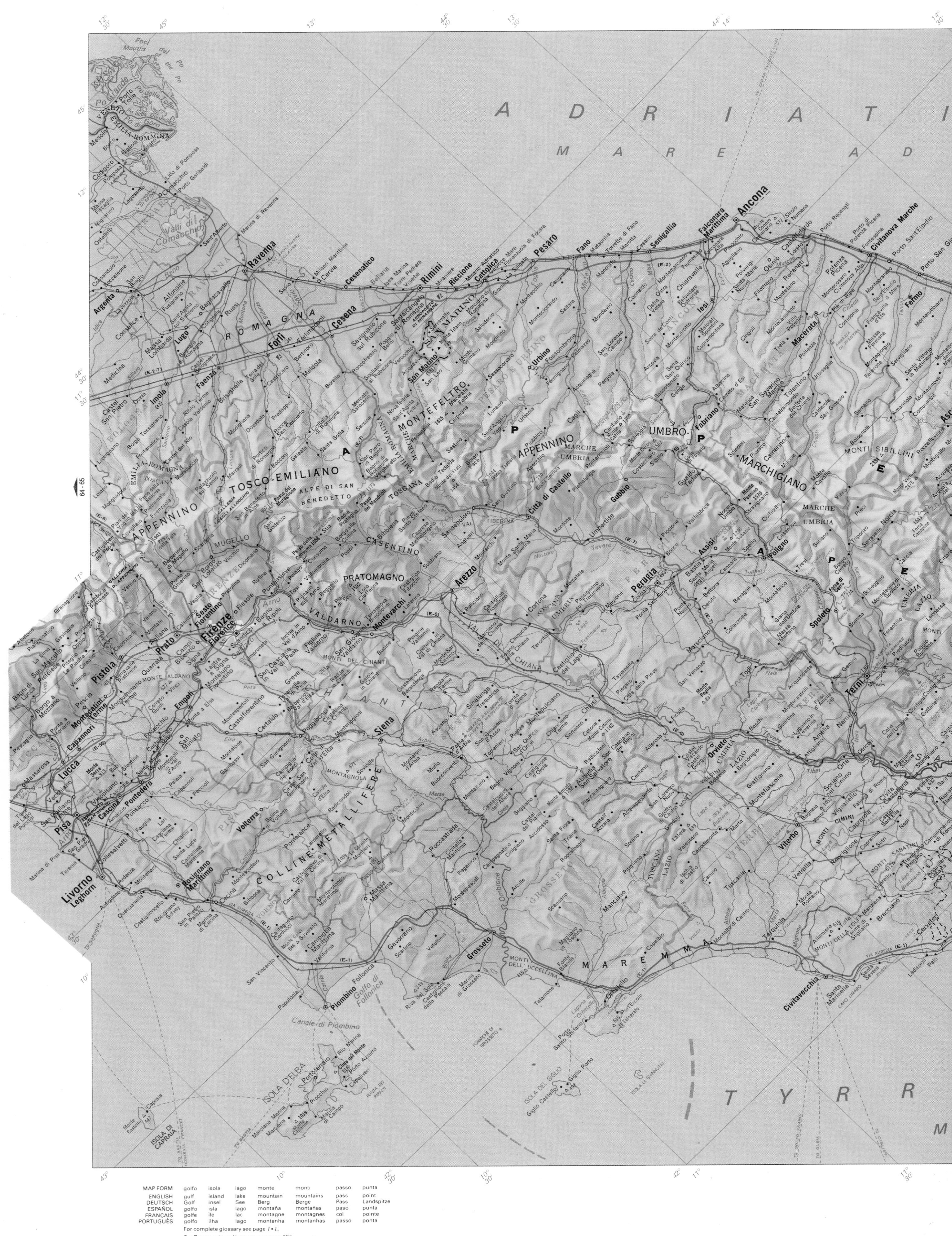

MAP FORM	golfo	isola	lago	monte	monti	passo	punta
ENGLISH	gulf	island	lake	mountain	mountains	pass	point
DEUTSCH	Golf	Insel	See	Berg	Berge	Pass	Landspitze
ESPAÑOL	golfo	isla	lago	montaña	montañas	paso	punta
FRANÇAIS	golfe	île	lac	montagne	montagnes	col	pointe
PORTUGUÊS	golfo	ilha	lago	montanha	montanhas	passo	ponta

For complete glossary see page *I • 1*.
For Roma metropolitan map see page 267.

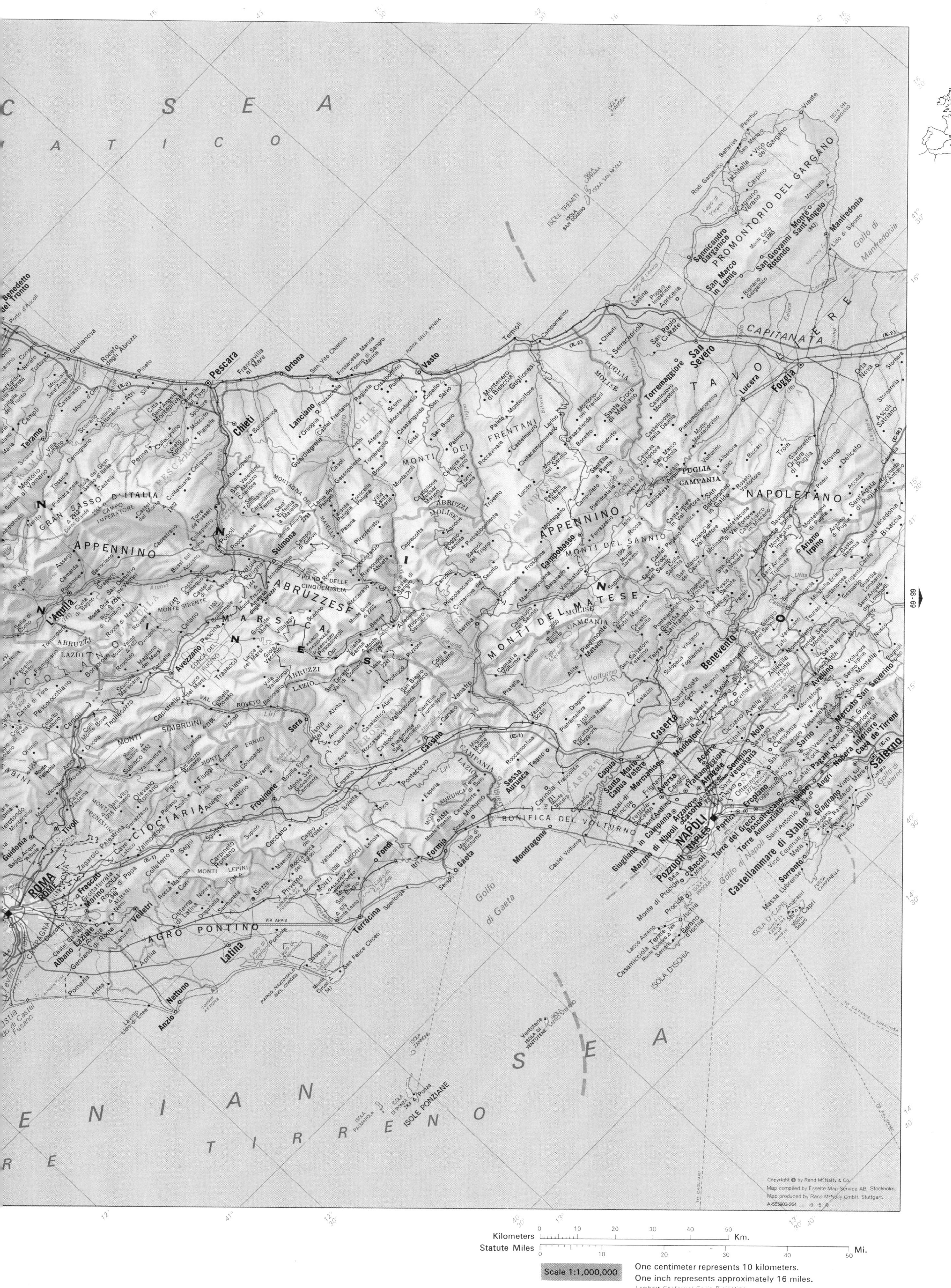
SEA
ADRIATICO
TIRRENIAN SEA
MARE TIRRENO
ISOLE TREMITI
PROMONTORIO DEL GARGANO
Golfo di Manfredonia
CAPITANATA
TAVOLIERE
APPENNINO NAPOLETANO
APPENNINO ABRUZZESE
GRAN SASSO D'ITALIA
MONTI DEI FRENTANI
MONTI DEL SANNIO
MONTI DEL MATESE
MARSICA
MONTI SIMBRUINI
MONTI ERNICI
CIOCIARIA
MONTI LEPINI
AGRO PONTINO
BONIFICA DEL VOLTURNO
Golfo di Gaeta
Golfo di Napoli
ISOLE PONZIANE
ISOLA D'ISCHIA
ISOLA DI CAPRI
Pescara
Chieti
Lanciano
Ortona
Vasto
Termoli
Teramo
L'Aquila
Sulmona
Avezzano
Campobasso
Foggia
Lucera
San Severo
Manfredonia
Vieste
Benevento
Avellino
Caserta
NAPOLI NAPLES
Salerno
Sorrento
Castellammare di Stabia
Torre del Greco
Pozzuoli
Gaeta
Formia
Terracina
Latina
Anzio
Nettuno
Frosinone
Cassino
Sora
Tivoli
Velletri
ROMA ROME
Kilometers 0 10 20 30 40 50 Km.
Statute Miles 0 10 20 30 40 50 Mi.
Scale 1:1,000,000
One centimeter represents 10 kilometers.
One inch represents approximately 16 miles.
Lambert Conformal Conic Projection
69 · 68
A-555900-264

MAP FORM	capo	golfo	isola	lago	monte	monti	punta
ENGLISH	cape	gulf	island	lake	mountain	mountains	point
DEUTSCH	Kap	Golf	Insel	See	Berg	Berge	Landspitze
ESPAÑOL	cabo	golfo	isla	lago	montaña	montañas	punta
FRANÇAIS	cap	golfe	île	lac	montagne	montagnes	pointe
PORTUGUÊS	cabo	golfo	ilha	lago	montanha	montanhas	ponta

For complete glossary see page *I • 1*.

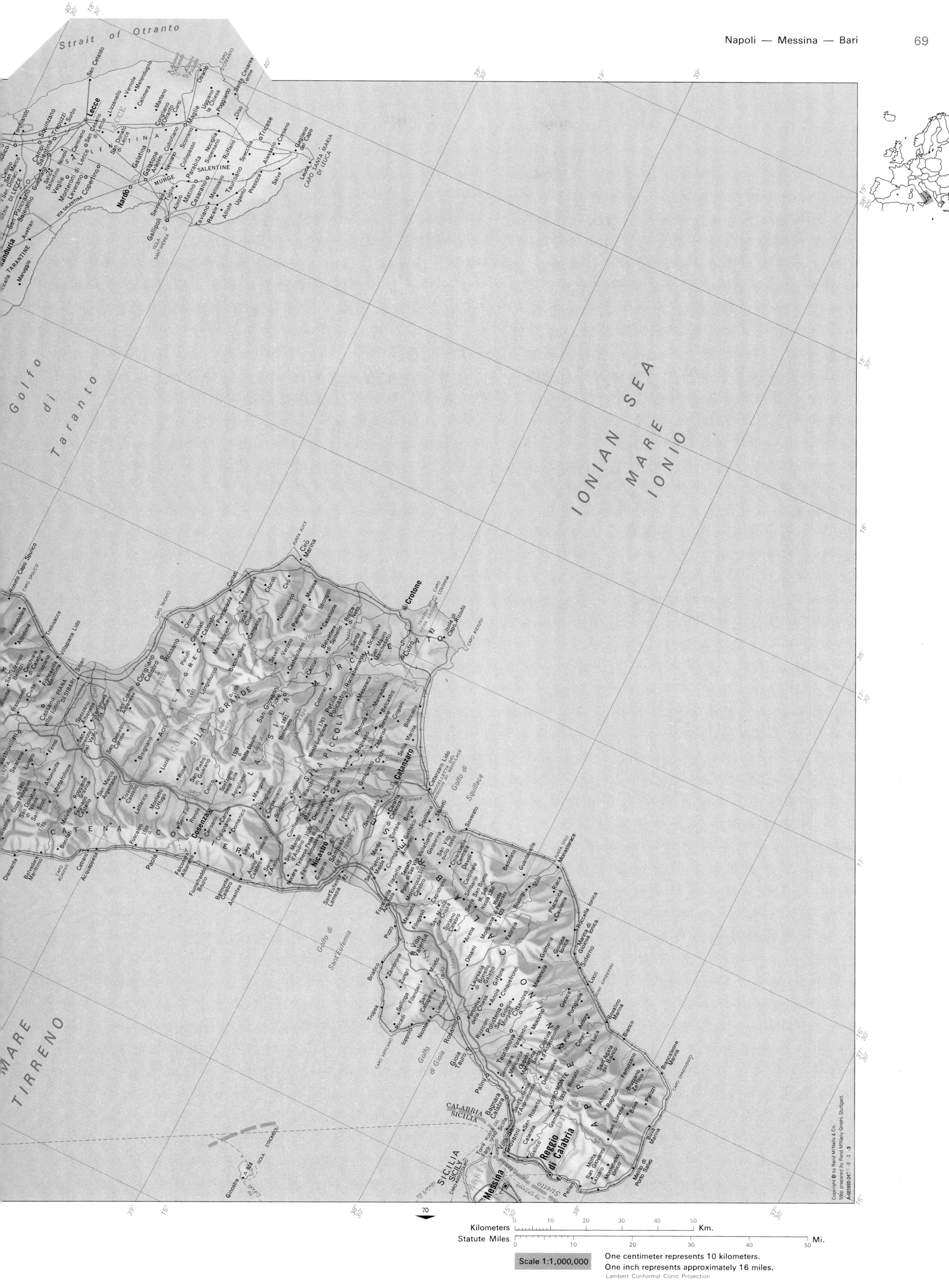

Strait of Otranto
Lecce
Gallipoli
Golfo di Taranto
IONIAN SEA
MARE IONIO
MARE TIRRENO
Crotone
Catanzaro
Cosenza
Nicastro
Reggio di Calabria
Messina
SILA GRANDE
SILA PICCOLA
CATENA COSTIERA
ASPROMONTE
Golfo di Squillace
Golfo di Sant'Eufemia
Golfo di Gioia
CALABRIA
SICILIA
70
Kilometers
Km.
Statute Miles
Mi.
Scale 1:1,000,000
One centimeter represents 10 kilometers.
One inch represents approximately 16 miles.
Lambert Conformal Conic Projection

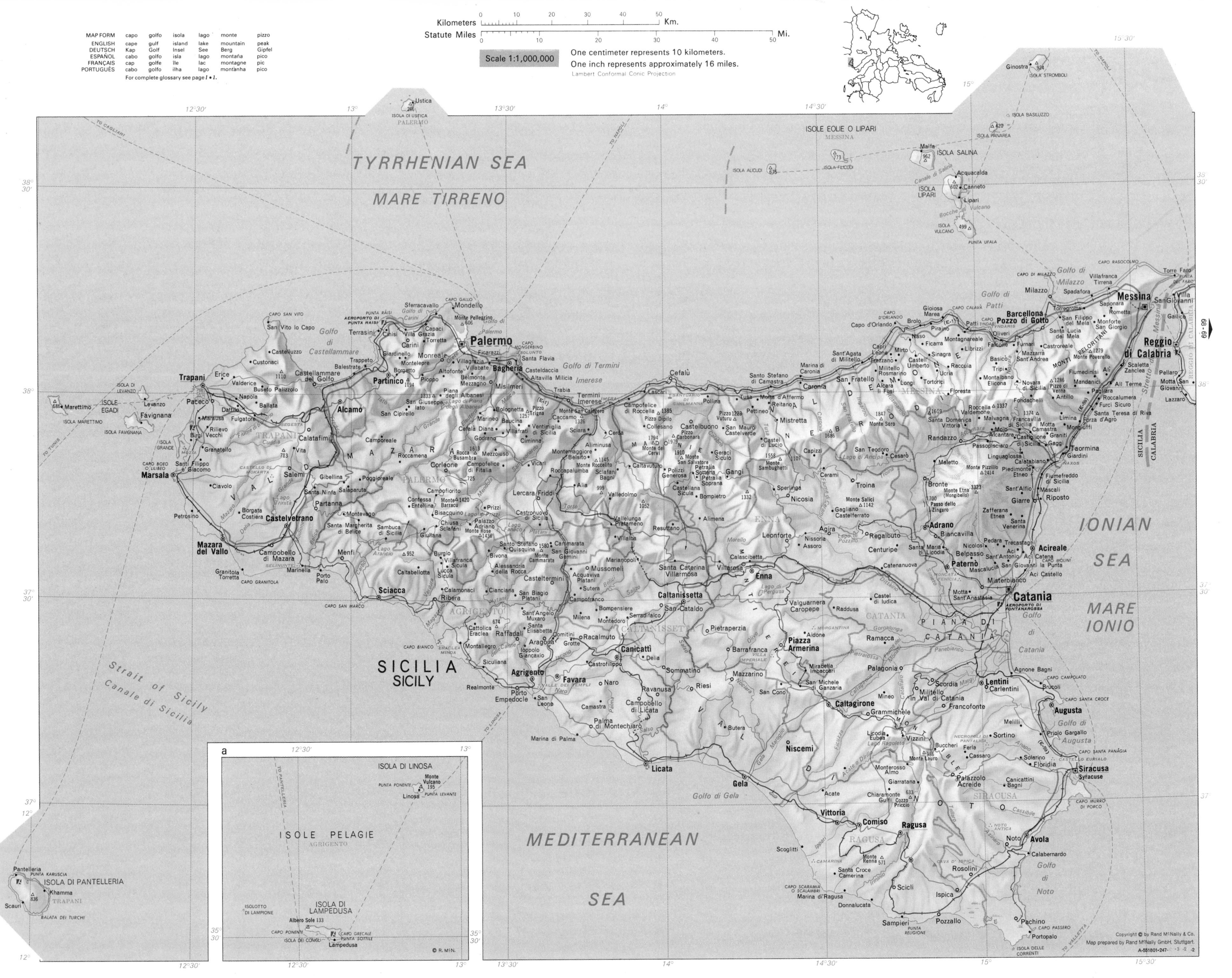

68 - 69
Kilometers
Statute Miles
Km.
Mi.
Scale 1:1,000,000
One centimeter represents 10 kilometers.
One inch represents approximately 16 miles.
Lambert Conformal Conic Projection
MAP FORM capo golfo isola lago monte pizzo
ENGLISH cape gulf island lake mountain peak
DEUTSCH Kap Golf Insel See Berg Gipfel
ESPAÑOL cabo golfo isla lago montaña pico
FRANÇAIS cap golfe île lac montagne pic
PORTUGUÊS cabo golfo ilha lago montanha pico
For complete glossary see page I • I.
TYRRHENIAN SEA
MARE TIRRENO
IONIAN SEA
MARE IONIO
MEDITERRANEAN SEA
SICILIA
SICILY
Strait of Sicily
Canale di Sicilia
ISOLE EOLIE O LIPARI
ISOLA SALINA
ISOLA LIPARI
ISOLE EGADI
Favignana
ISOLE PELAGIE
ISOLA DI LINOSA
ISOLA DI LAMPEDUSA
ISOLA DI PANTELLERIA
Ustica
Palermo
Bagheria
Catania
Messina
Reggio di Calabria
Siracusa
Augusta
Trapani
Marsala
Mazara del Vallo
Castelvetrano
Alcamo
Sciacca
Agrigento
Caltanissetta
Enna
Ragusa
Gela
Licata
Vittoria
Caltagirone
Acireale
Taormina
Cefalù
Golfo di Gela
Golfo di Termini Imerese
Golfo di Castellammare
Golfo di Patti
Golfo di Noto
Copyright © by Rand McNally & Co.
Map prepared by Rand McNally GmbH, Stuttgart.

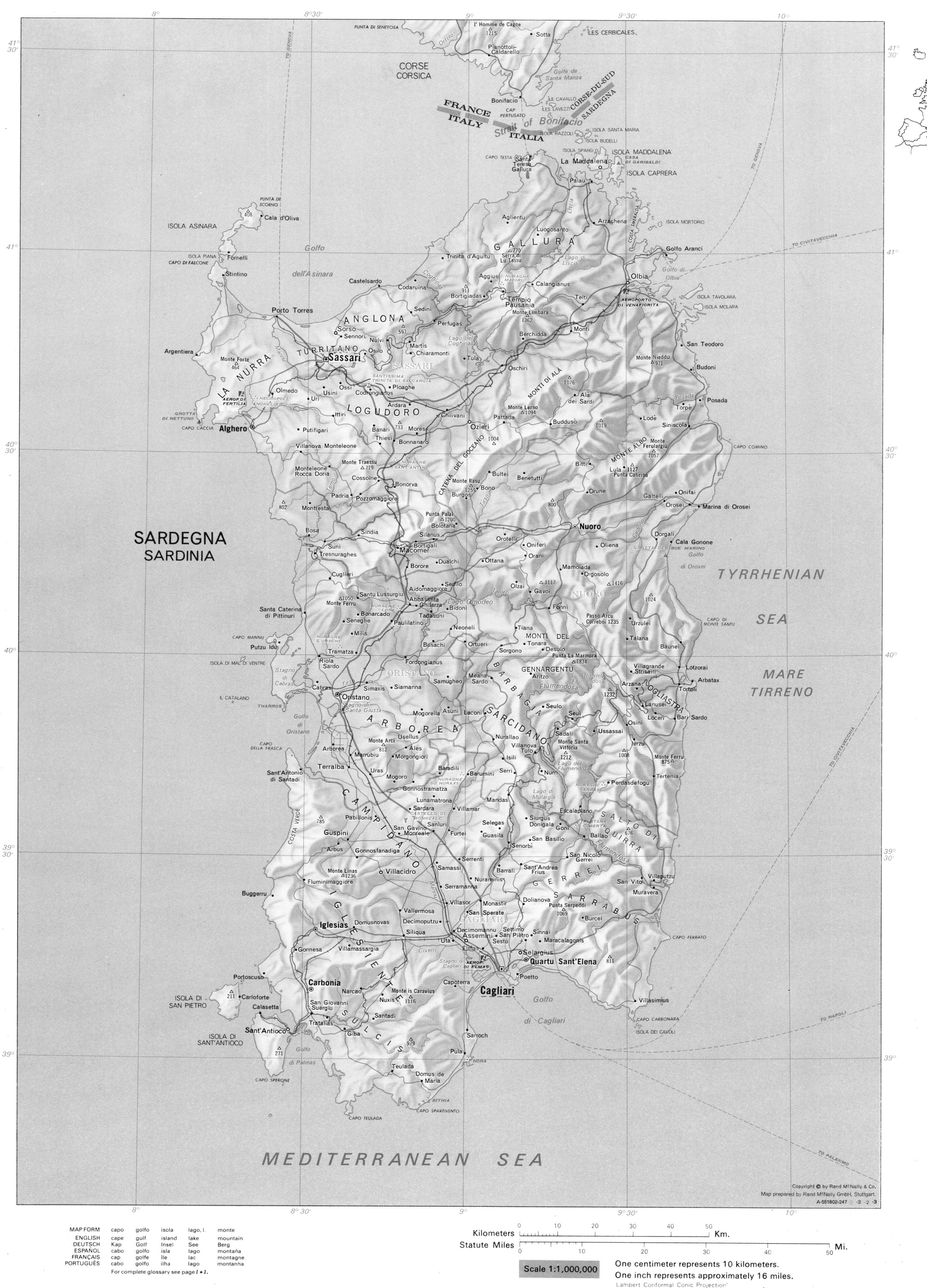

MAP FORM	capo	golfo	isola	lago, l.	monte
ENGLISH	cape	gulf	island	lake	mountain
DEUTSCH	Kap	Golf	Insel	See	Berg
ESPAÑOL	cabo	golfo	isla	lago	montaña
FRANÇAIS	cap	golfe	île	lac	montagne
PORTUGUÊS	cabo	golfo	ilha	lago	montanha

For complete glossary see page I • 1.

Kilometers 0 10 20 30 40 50 Km.
Statute Miles 0 10 20 30 40 50 Mi.

Scale 1:1,000,000

One centimeter represents 10 kilometers.
One inch represents approximately 16 miles.
Lambert Conformal Conic Projection

22 · 23
118 · 119

MAP FORM	chrebet	gora	guba	mys	ostrov	ozero	poluostrov	proliv	vodochranilišče
ENGLISH	range	mountain	bay	cape	island	lake	peninsula	strait	reservoir
DEUTSCH	Gebirge	Berg	Bucht	Kap	Insel	See	Halbinsel	Meeresstrasse	Stausee
ESPAÑOL	sierra	montaña	bahía	cabo	isla	lago	península	estrecho	embalse
FRANÇAIS	chaîne	montagne	baïe	cap	île	lac	péninsule	détroit	réservoir
PORTUGUÊS	serra	montanha	baía	cabo	ilha	lago	península	estreito	reservatório

For complete glossary see page *I • 1*.

Kilometers 0 200 400 600 Km.

Statute Miles 0 200 400 600 Mi.

Scale 1:12,000,000

One centimeter represents 120 kilometers.
One inch represents approximately 190 miles.
Lambert Conformal Conic Projection

MAP FORM	chrebet	gora	guba	mys	ostrov	ozero	poluostrov	proliv	vodochranilišče
ENGLISH	range	mountain	bay	cape	island	lake	peninsula	strait	reservoir
DEUTSCH	Gebirge	Berg	Bucht	Kap	Insel	See	Halbinsel	Meeresstrasse	Stausee
ESPAÑOL	sierra	montaña	bahía	cabo	isla	lago	península	estrecho	embalse
FRANÇAIS	chaîne	montagne	baie	cap	île	lac	péninsule	détroit	réservoir
PORTUGUÊS	serra	montanha	baía	cabo	ilha	lago	península	estreito	reservatório

For complete glossary see page 1 • 1.

Kilometers 0 200 400 600 Km.
Statute Miles 0 200 400 600 Mi.

Scale 1:12,000,000

One centimeter represents 120 kilometers.
One inch represents approximately 190 miles.
Lambert Conformal Conic Projection

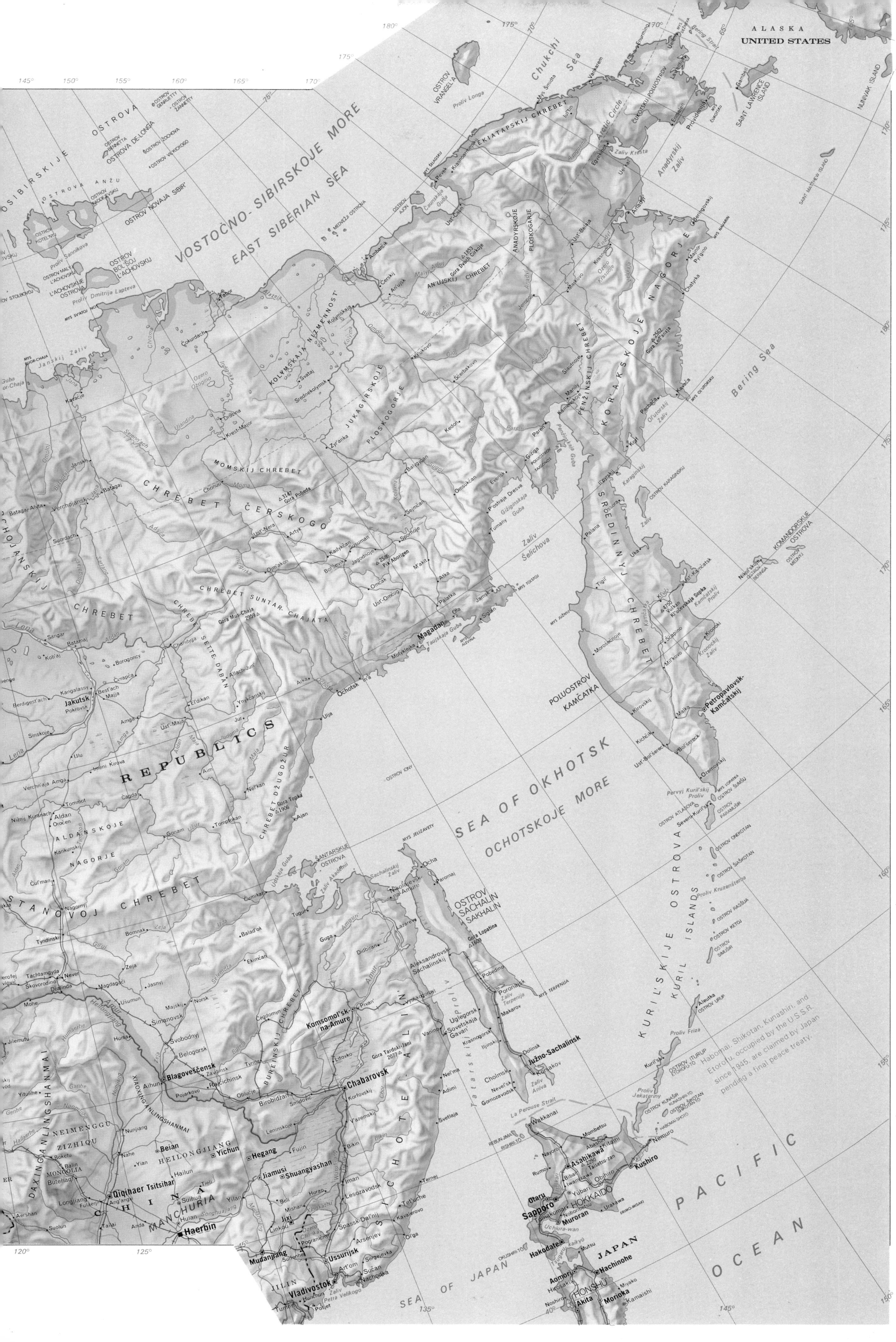

ALASKA
UNITED STATES
Chukchi Sea
OSTROV VRANGEL'A
Proliv Longa
Bering Strait
Arctic Circle
ČUKOTSKIJ POLUOSTROV
SAINT LAWRENCE ISLAND
NUNIVAK ISLAND
SAINT MATTHEW ISLAND
Anadyrskij Zaliv
Zaliv Kresta
VOSTOČNO-SIBIRSKOJE MORE
EAST SIBERIAN SEA
NOVOSIBIRSKIJE OSTROVA
OSTROVA DE-LONGA
OSTROVA ANŽU
OSTROV NOVAJA SIBIR'
OSTROV KOTEL'NYJ
MEDVEŽ'A OSTROVA
ANADYRSKOJE PLOSKOGORJE
AN'UJSKIJ CHREBET
EKIATAPSKIJ CHREBET
KOLYMSKAJA NIZMENNOST'
JUKAGIRSKOJE PLOSKOGORJE
KOR'AKSKOJE NAGORJE
PENŽINSKIJ CHREBET
Bering Sea
KOMANDORSKIJE OSTROVA
MOMSKIJ CHREBET
CHREBET ČERSKOGO
CHREBET SUNTAR-CHAJATA
CHREBET SETTE-DABAN
CHREBET DŽUGDŽUR
Zaliv Šelichova
Penžinskaja Guba
Gižiginskaja Guba
SREDINNYJ CHREBET
POLUOSTROV KAMČATKA
Petropavlovsk-Kamčatskij
Magadan
Ochotsk
Jakutsk
REPUBLICS
ALDANSKOJE NAGORJE
STANOVOJ CHREBET
SEA OF OKHOTSK
OCHOTSKOJE MORE
OSTROV SACHALIN
SAKHALIN
Južno-Sachalinsk
KURIL'SKIJE OSTROVA
KURIL ISLANDS
Habomai, Shikotan, Kunashiri, and Etorofu, occupied by the U.S.S.R. since 1945, are claimed by Japan pending a final peace treaty.
La Perouse Strait
Tatarskij Proliv
SICHOTE-ALIN'
BUREINSKIJ CHREBET
Komsomol'sk-na-Amure
Chabarovsk
Blagoveščensk
Vladivostok
Ussurijsk
DAXINGANLINGSHANMAI
XIAOXINGANLINGSHANMAI
NEIMENGGU ZIZHIQU
HEILONGJIANG
CHINA
MANCHURIA
Qiqihaer Tsitsihar
Haerbin
Mudanjiang
Jiamusi
Hegang
Yichun
Beian
HOKKAIDO
Sapporo
Asahikawa
Kushiro
Hakodate
Aomori
Hachinohe
Morioka
Akita
HONSHU
JAPAN
SEA OF JAPAN
PACIFIC OCEAN

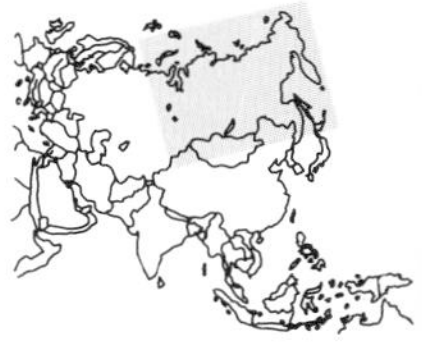

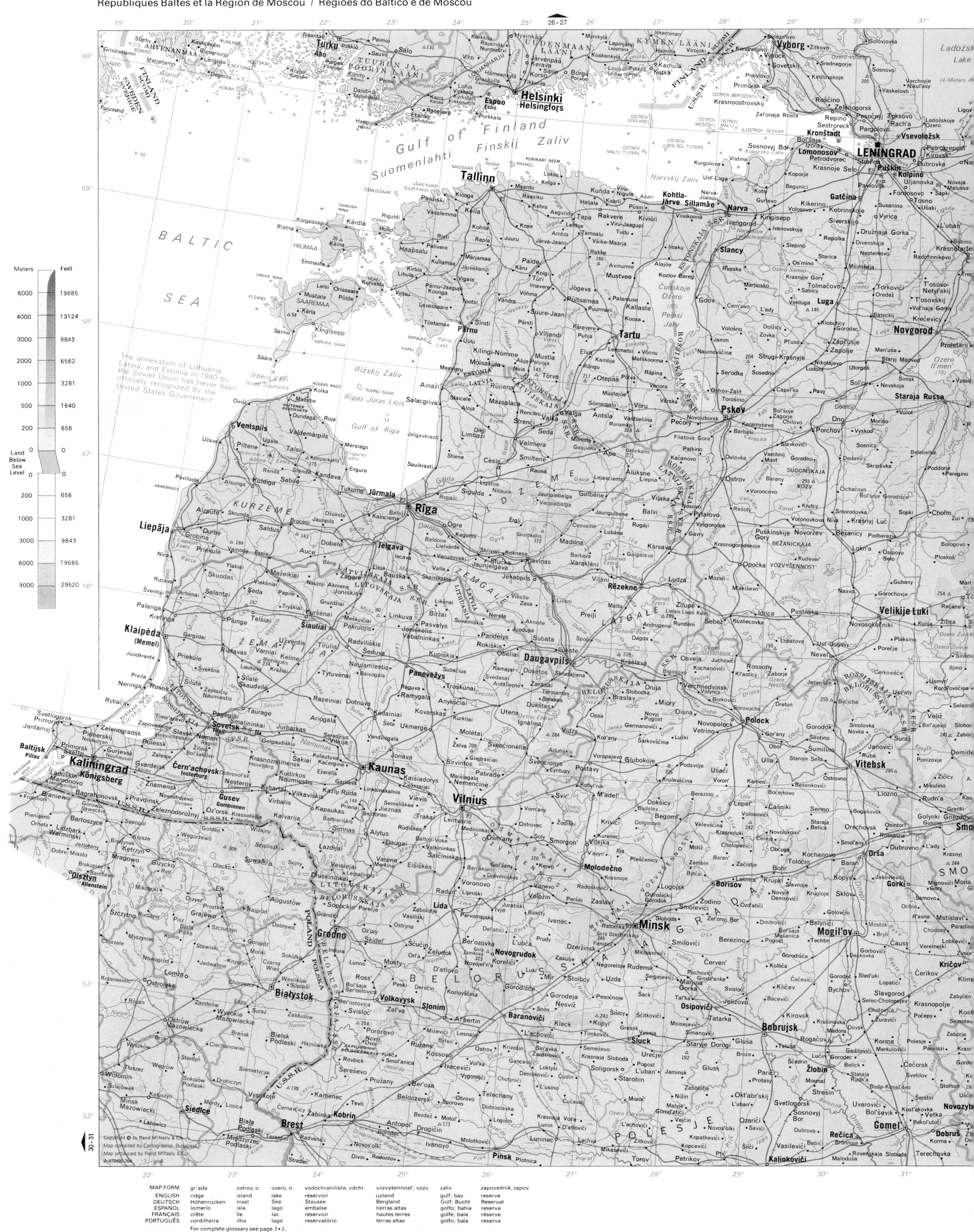

MAP FORM	gr'ada	ostrov, o.	ozero, o.	vodochranilišče, vdchr.	vozvyšennost', vozv.	zaliv	zapovednik, zapov.
ENGLISH	ridge	island	lake	reservoir	upland	gulf; bay	reserve
DEUTSCH	Höhenrücken	Insel	See	Stausee	Bergland	Golf; Bucht	Reservat
ESPAÑOL	lomerío	isla	lago	embalse	tierras altas	golfo; bahía	reserva
FRANÇAIS	crête	île	lac	réservoir	hautes terres	golfe; baie	réserve
PORTUGUÊS	cordilheira	ilha	lago	reservatório	terras altas	golfo; baía	reserva

For complete glossary see page I • 1.
For Leningrad metropolitan map see page 265.

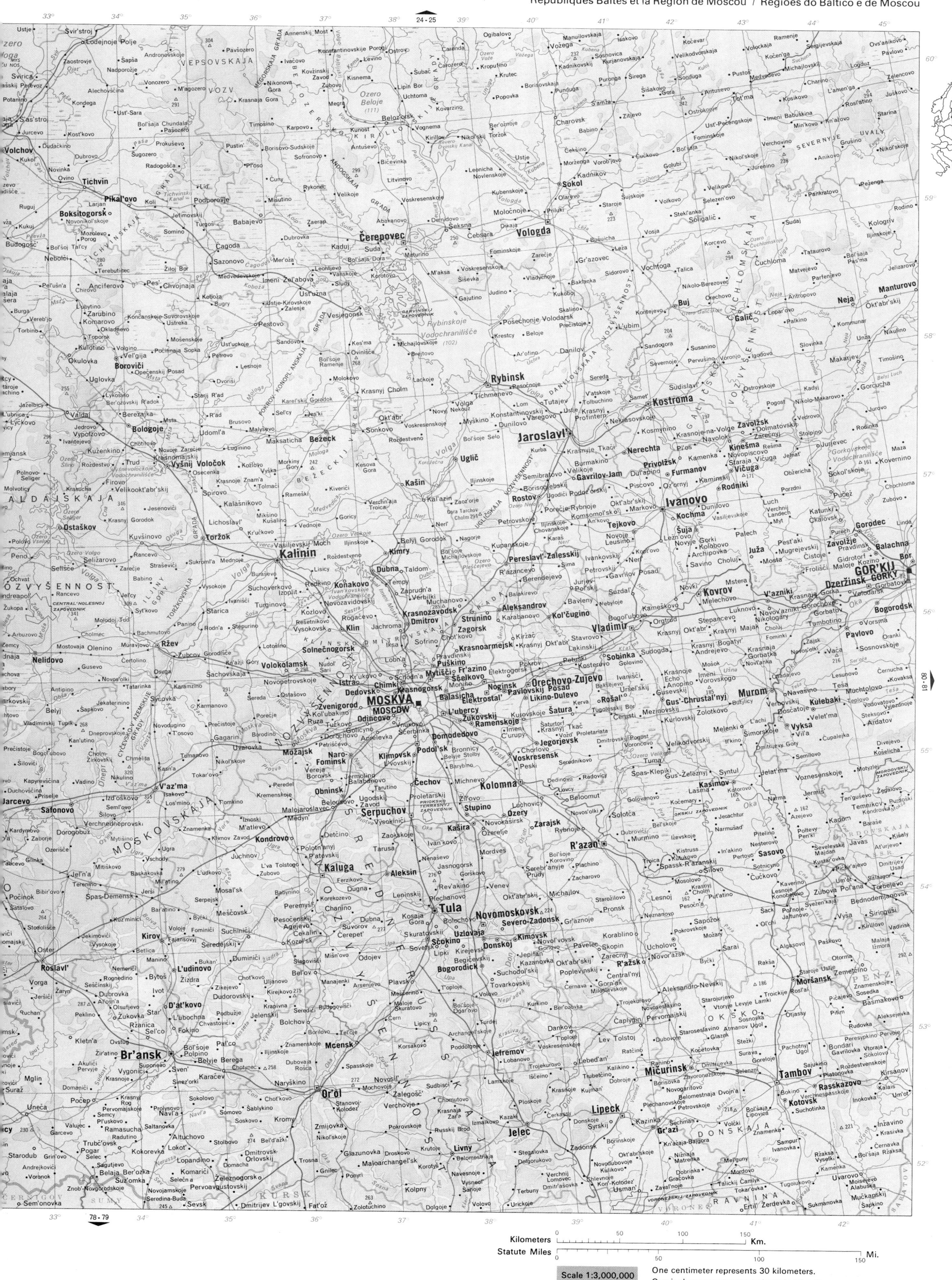
24-25
80-81
78-79
MOSKVA
MOSCOW
Jaroslavl'
Rybinsk
Vologda
Čerepovec
Kalinin
Ivanovo
Kostroma
Vladimir
GOR'KIJ
Tula
Kaluga
Br'ansk
Or'ol
Lipeck
Tambov
R'azan'
Kilometers 0 50 100 150 Km.
Statute Miles 0 50 100 150 Mi.
Scale 1:3,000,000
One centimeter represents 30 kilometers.
One inch represents approximately 47 miles.
Lambert Conformal Conic Projection

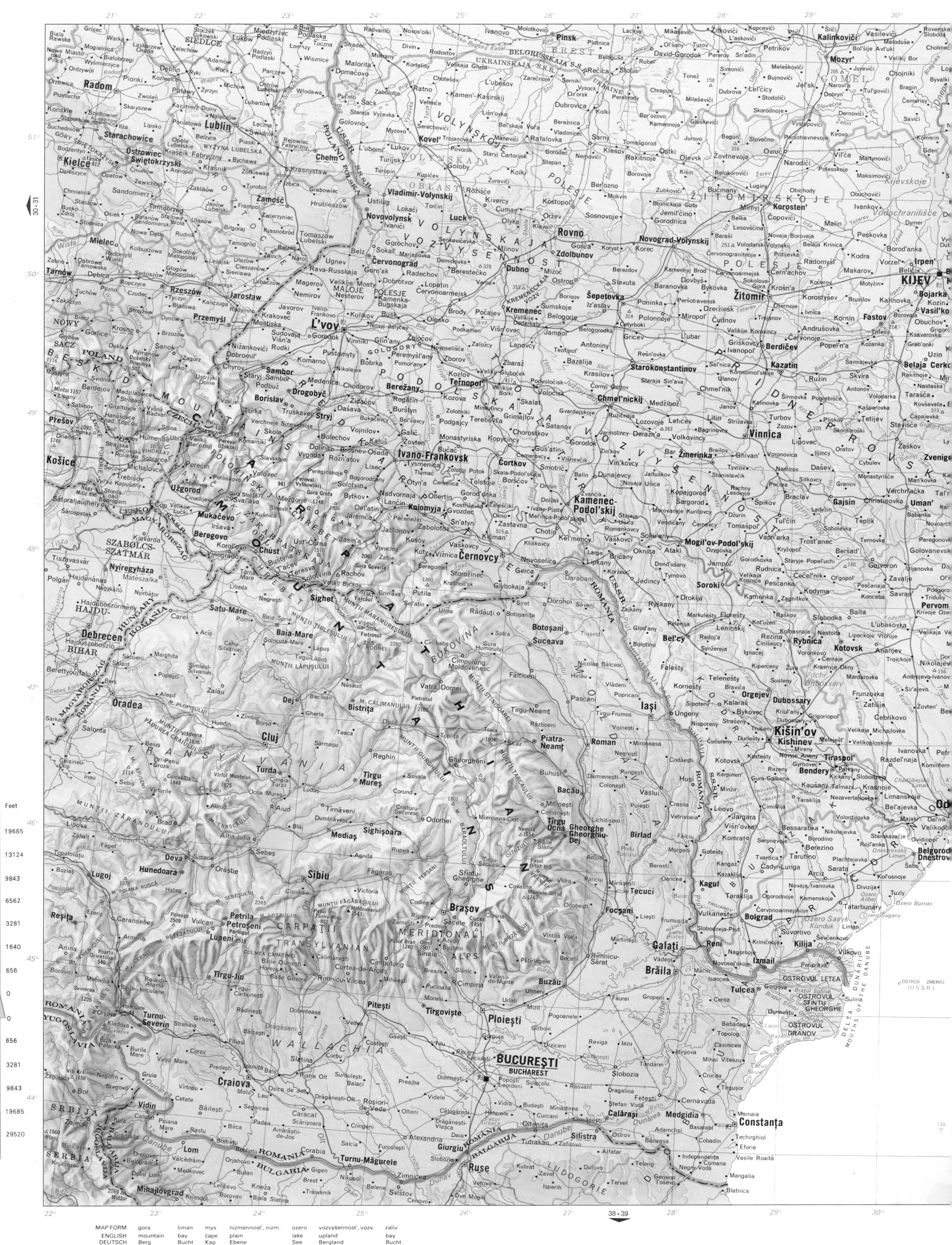

MAP FORM	gora	liman	mys	nizmennost', nizm.	ozero	vozvyšennost', vozv.	zaliv
ENGLISH	mountain	bay	cape	plain	lake	upland	bay
DEUTSCH	Berg	Bucht	Kap	Ebene	See	Bergland	Bucht
ESPAÑOL	montaña	bahía	cabo	llanno	lago	tierras altas	bahía
FRANÇAIS	montagne	baie	cap	plaine	lac	hautes terres	baie
PORTUGUÊS	montanha	baía	cabo	planície	lago	terras altas	baía

For complete glossary see page 1•2

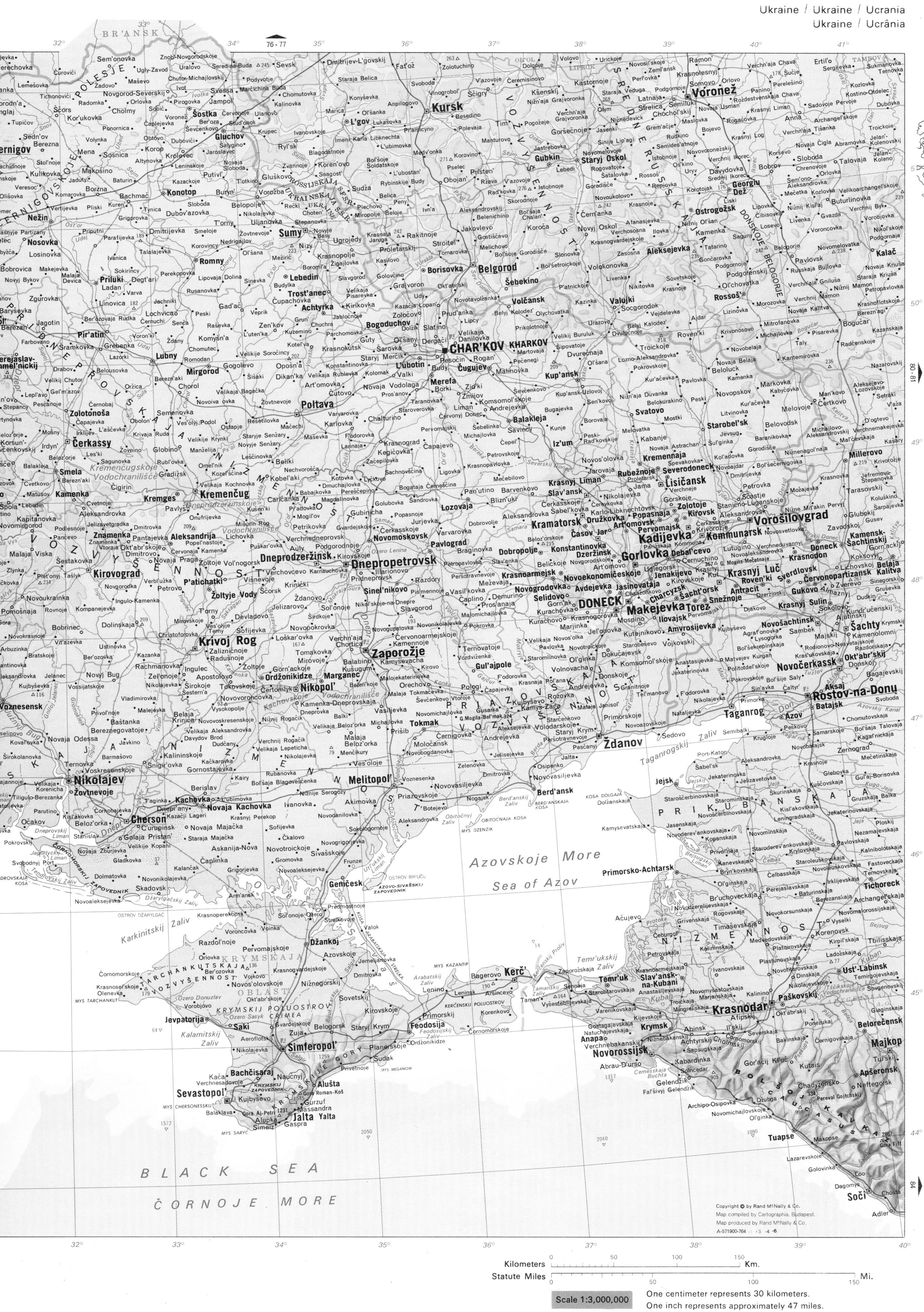

Kilometers 0 50 100 150 Km.
Statute Miles 0 50 100 150 Mi.

Scale 1:3,000,000

One centimeter represents 30 kilometers.
One inch represents approximately 47 miles.
Lambert Conformal Conic Projection

24 · 25

76 · 77

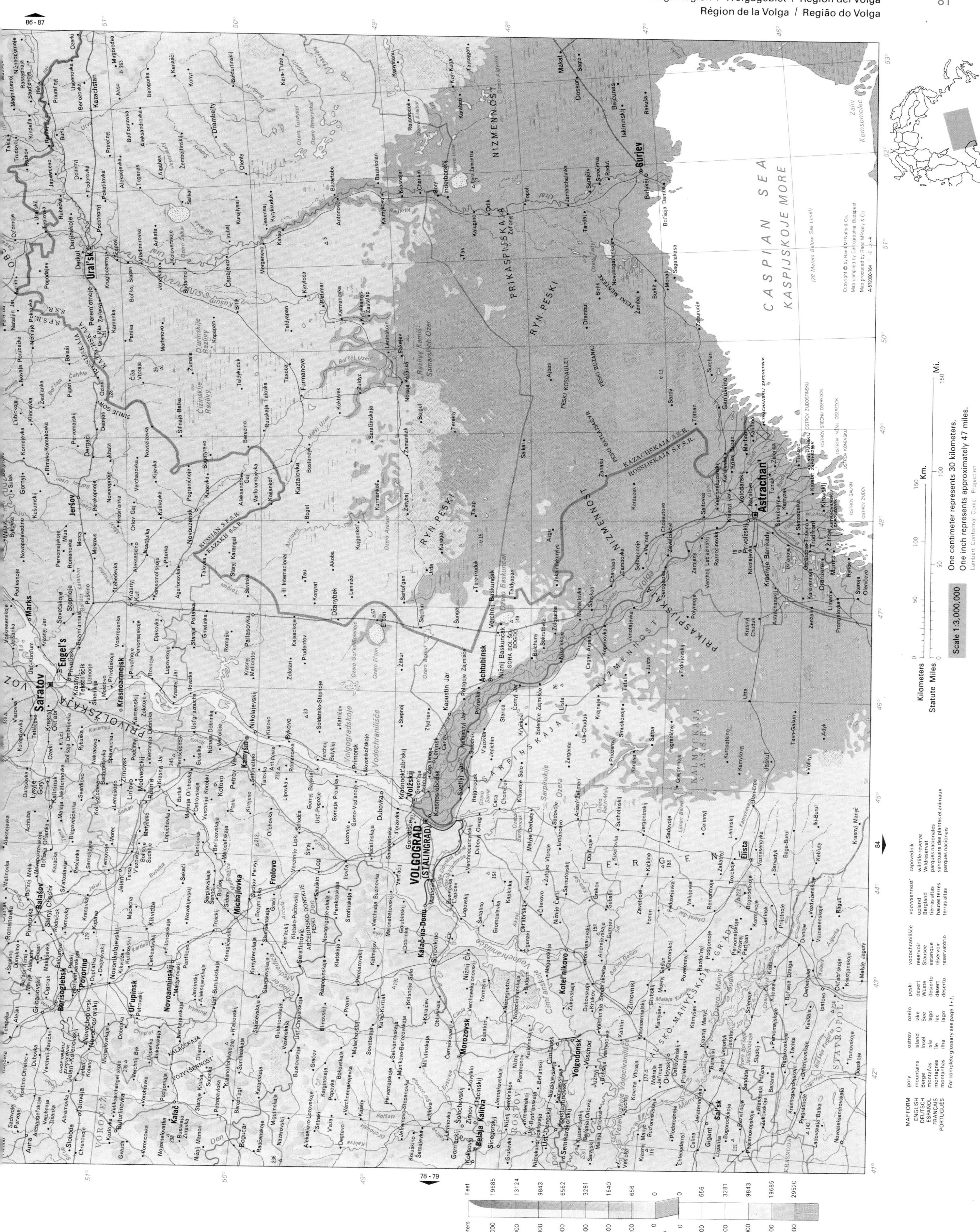
86 - 87
78 - 79
84
CASPIAN SEA
KASPIJSKOJE MORE
PRIKASPIJSKAJA NIZMENNOST'
RYN-PESKI
NIZMENNOST'
PRIVOLŽSKAJA VOZ
Saratov
Engel's
Marks
Volgograd (Stalingrad)
Volžskij
Astrachan'
Ural'sk
Gurjev
Elista
Kamyšin
Balašov
Borisoglebsk
Uralsk
Achtubinsk
Kalač-na-Donu
Volgodonsk
Zaliv Komsomolec
Vodochranilišče
KAZACHSKAJA S.S.R.
ROSSIJSKAJA S.F.S.R.
RUSSIAN S.F.S.R.
KAZAKH S.S.R.
Scale 1:3,000,000
One centimeter represents 30 kilometers.
One inch represents approximately 47 miles.
Lambert Conformal Conic Projection
Kilometers
Statute Miles
Km.
Mi.
Copyright © by Rand McNally & Co.
Map compiled by Cartographia, Budapest.
Map produced by Rand McNally & Co.
A-572000-764 -4 -3 -4
(28 Meters Below Sea Level)
MAP FORM | gory | ostrov | ozero | peski | vodochranilišče | vozvyšennost' | zapovednik
ENGLISH | mountains | island | lake | desert | reservoir | upland | wildlife reserve
DEUTSCH | Berge | Insel | See | Wüste | Stausee | Bergland | Wildreservat
ESPAÑOL | montañas | isla | lago | desierto | estanque | tierras altas | parques nacionales
FRANÇAIS | montagnes | île | lac | désert | réservoir | hautes terres | sanctuaire des plantes et animaux
PORTUGUÊS | montanhas | ilha | lago | deserto | reservatório | terras altas | parques nacionais
For complete glossary see page I • I.
Feet
Meters
Land Below Sea Level
19685
13124
9843
6562
3281
1640
656
0
6000
4000
3000
2000
1000
500
200
0
656
3281
9843
19685
29520
200
1000
3000
6000
9000

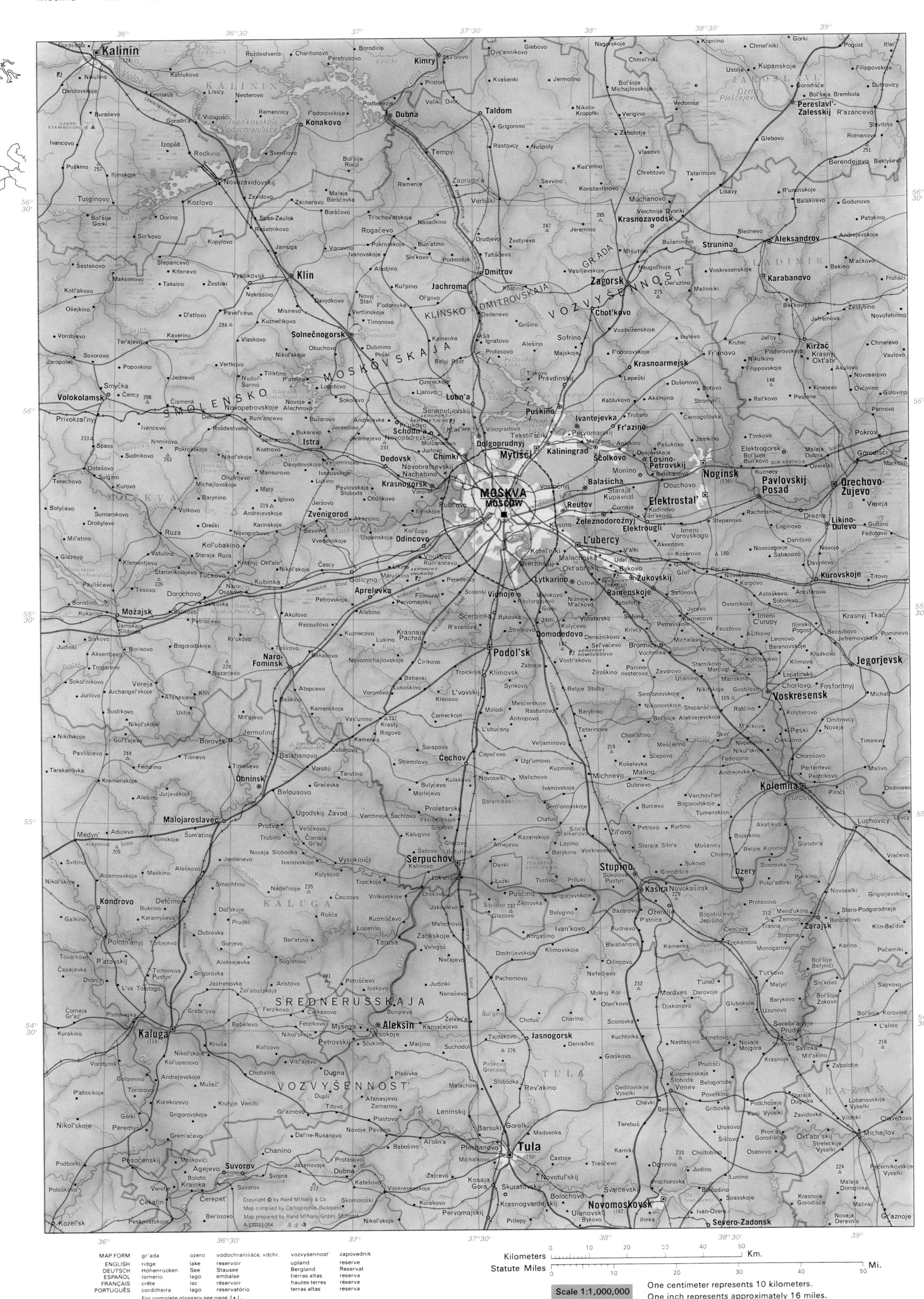

MAP FORM	gr'ada	ozero	vodochranilišće, vdchr.	vozvyšennost'	zapovednik
ENGLISH	ridge	lake	reservoir	upland	reserve
DEUTSCH	Höhenrücken	See	Stausee	Bergland	Reservat
ESPAÑOL	lomerío	lago	embalse	tierras altas	reserva
FRANÇAIS	crête	lac	réservoir	hautes terres	réserve
PORTUGUÊS	cordilheira	lago	reservatório	terras altas	reserva

For complete glossary see page *I • 1*.
For Moskva metropolitan map see page 265

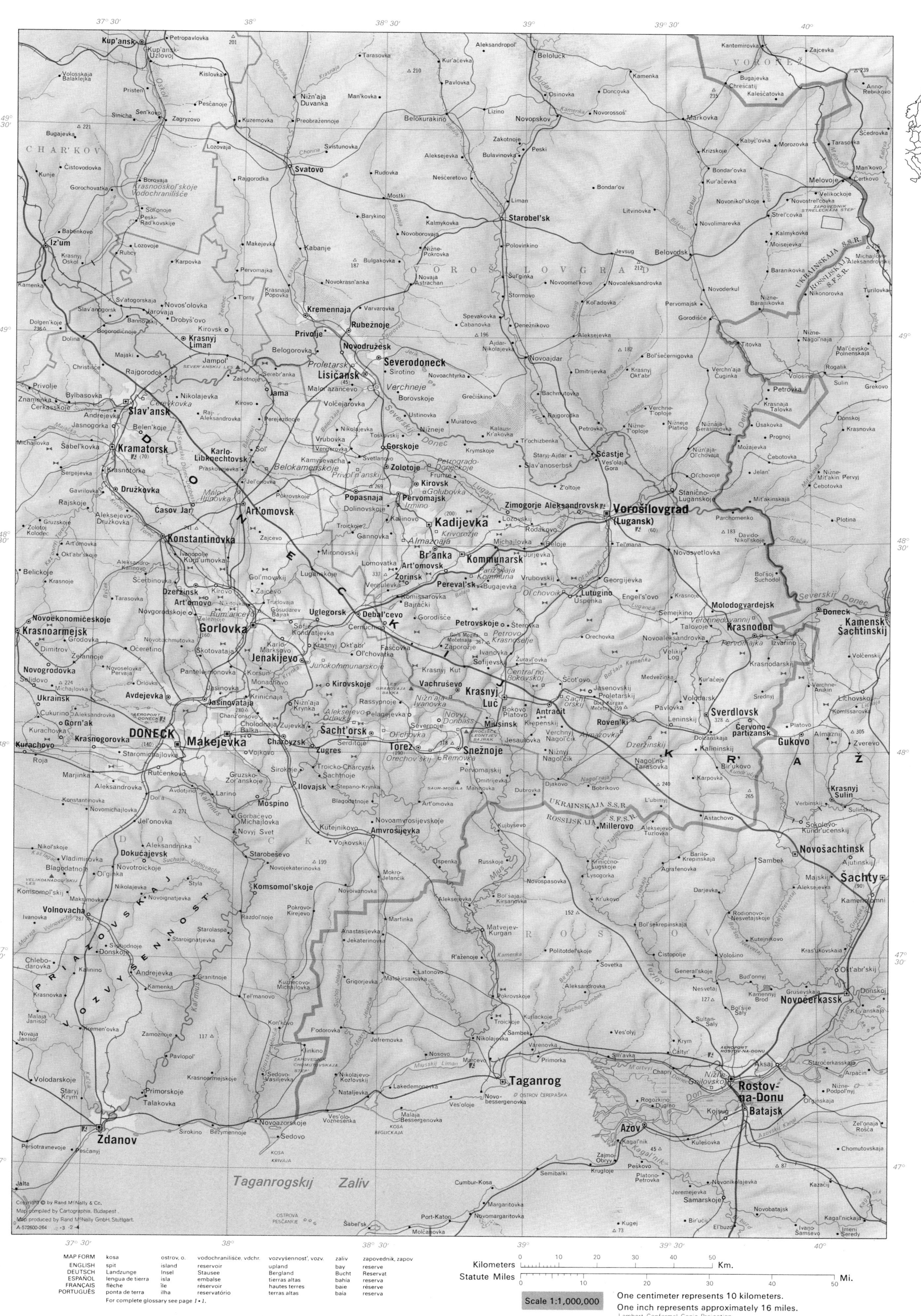

Kup'ansk
Svatovo
Starobel'sk
Iz'um
Krasnyj Liman
Slav'ansk
Kramatorsk
Družkovka
Konstantinovka
Art'omovsk
Severodoneck
Lisičansk
Rubežnoje
Kremennaja
Popasnaja
Pervomajsk
Kadijevka
Br'anka
Kommunarsk
Vorošilovgrad (Lugansk)
Ščastje
Krasnodon
Sverdlovsk
Rovenʼki
Antracit
Krasnyj Luč
Gorlovka
Jenakijevo
Debal'cevo
Šacht'orsk
Torez
Snežnoje
Makejevka
DONECK
Krasnoarmejsk
Dzeržinsk
Avdejevka
Jasinovataja
Charcyzsk
Zugres
Ilovajsk
Amvrosijevka
Volnovacha
Ždanov
Taganrog
Rostov-na-Donu
Batajsk
Azov
Novočerkassk
Šachty
Novošachtinsk
Gukovo
Krasnyj Sulin
Millerovo
Kamensk Šachtinskij
Doneck
Taganrogskij Zaliv
Severskij Donec
VOROŠILOVGRAD
DONECKIJ
CHAR'KOV
ROSTOV
VORONEŽ
UKRAINSKAJA S.S.R.
ROSSIJSKAJA S.F.S.R.
PRIAZOVSKAJA VOZVYŠENNOST'
DONECKIJ KR'AŽ
MAP FORM | kosa | ostrov, o. | vodochranilišče, vdchr. | vozvyšennost', vozv. | zaliv | zapovednik, zapov.
ENGLISH | spit | island | reservoir | upland | bay | reserve
DEUTSCH | Landzunge | Insel | Stausee | Bergland | Bucht | Reservat
ESPAÑOL | lengua de tierra | isla | embalse | tierras altas | bahia | reserva
FRANÇAIS | flèche | île | réservoir | hautes terres | baie | réserve
PORTUGUÊS | ponta de terra | ilha | reservatório | terras altas | baia | reserva
For complete glossary see page I·1.
Kilometers 0 10 20 30 40 50 Km.
Statute Miles 0 10 20 30 40 50 Mi.
Scale 1:1,000,000
One centimeter represents 10 kilometers.
One inch represents approximately 16 miles.
Lambert Conformal Conic Projection
Copyright © by Rand McNally & Co.
Map compiled by Cartographia, Budapest.
Map produced by Rand McNally GmbH, Stuttgart.
A-572600-264 -3 -2 -4

MAP FORM
ENGLISH
DEUTSCH
ESPAÑOL
FRANÇAIS
PORTUGUÊS
chrebet, chr. mountain range Gebirge sierra chaîne serra
dağ, dağı mountain Berg montaña montagne montanha
dağları mountains Berge montañas montagnes montanhas
geçidi pass Pass paso col passo
gölü lake See lago lac lago
gora, g. mountain Berg montaña montagne montanha
mys cape Kap cabo cap cabo
ostrov, o. island Insel isla île ilha
For complete glossary see page I·1.
Kilometers
Statute Miles
Scale 1:3,000,000
One centimeter represents 30 kilometers.
One inch represents approximately 47 miles.
Lambert Conformal Conic Projection
Meters
Feet
Land Below Sea Level
CASPIAN SEA
KASPIJSKOJE MORE
(28 Meters Below Sea Level)
BLACK SEA
TBILISI
BAKU
Jerevan
Groznyj
Machačkala
Batumi
Suchumi
Trabzon
Erzurum
78-79
80-81
128-129
130-131
Copyright © by Rand McNally & Co.
Map compiled by Cartographia, Budapest.
Map produced by Rand McNally & Co.
A-572700-764

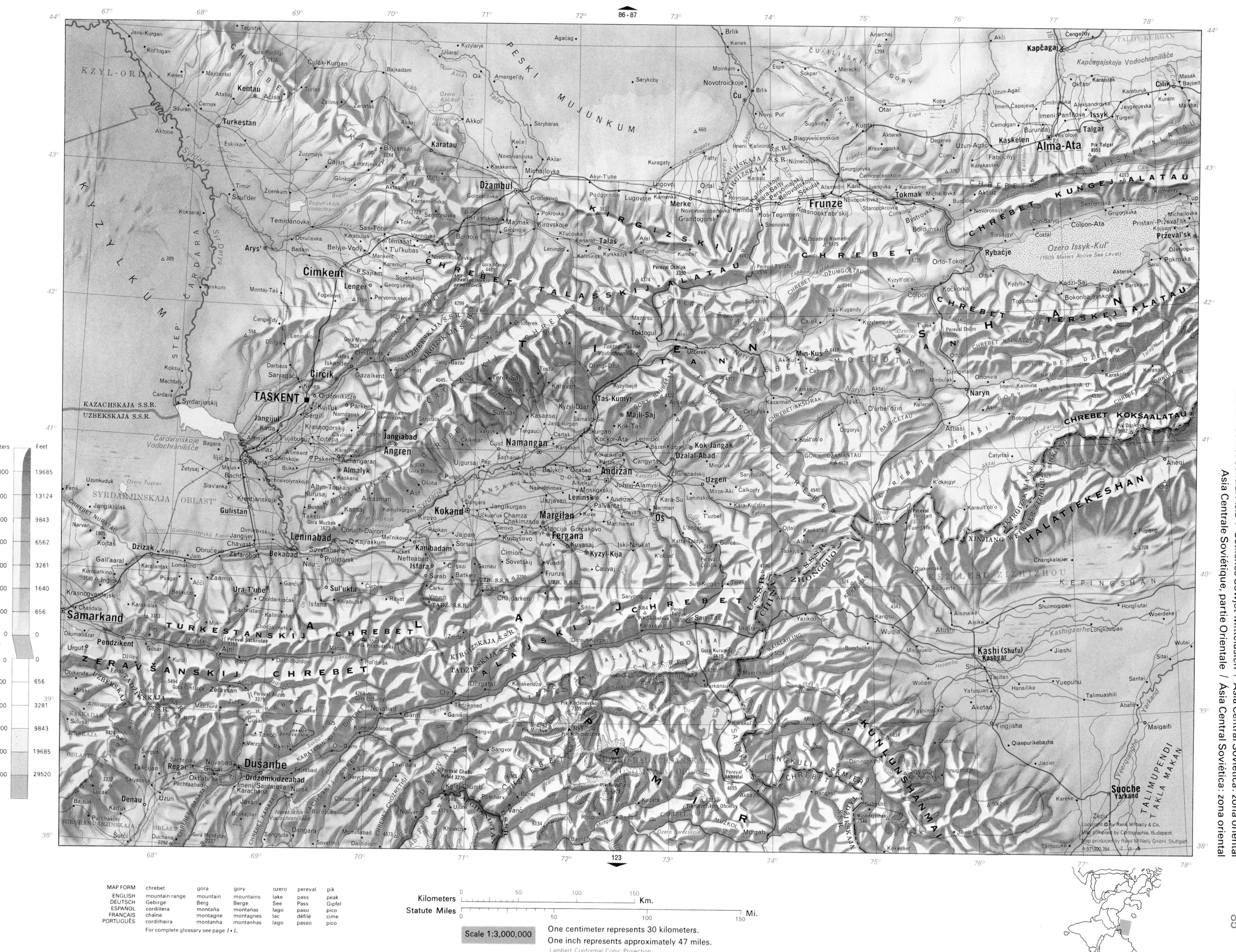
86·87
Alma-Ata
Frunze
Taškent
Dušanbe
Samarkand
Kokand
Andižan
Namangan
Leninabad
Džambul
Čimkent
Fergana
Oš
Naryn
Prževal'sk
Kashi (Shufu)
Kashgar
Suoche
Yarkand
Ozero Issyk-Kul'
KIRGIZSKIJ CHREBET
TALASSKIJ ALATAU
TURKESTANSKIJ CHREBET
ZERAVŠANSKIJ CHREBET
ALAJSKIJ CHREBET
TIAN SHAN
KUNLUNSHANMAI
PAMIR
KYZYLKUM
PESKI MUJUNKUM
Syr Darya
KAZACHSKAJA S.S.R.
UZBEKSKAJA S.S.R.
123
Meters 6000 4000 3000 2000 1000 500 200 0
Feet 19685 13124 9843 6562 3281 1640 656 0
Land Below Sea Level
0 200 1000 3000 6000 9000
0 656 3281 9843 19685 29520
MAP FORM chrebet gora gory ozero pereval pik
ENGLISH mountain range mountain mountains lake pass peak
DEUTSCH Gebirge Berg Berge See Pass Gipfel
ESPAÑOL cordillera montaña montañas lago paso pico
FRANÇAIS chaîne montagne montagnes lac défilé cime
PORTUGUÊS cordilheira montanha montanhas lago passo pico
For complete glossary see page I·1.
Kilometers
Statute Miles
Scale 1:3,000,000
One centimeter represents 30 kilometers.
One inch represents approximately 47 miles.
Lambert Conformal Conic Projection

Meters	Feet
6000	19685
4000	13124
3000	9843
2000	6562
1000	3281
500	1640
200	656
0	0
Land Below Sea Level	
0	0
200	656
1000	3281
3000	9843
6000	19685
9000	29520

MAP FORM	chrebet	gora	-he	-hu	ozero	plato	porog
ENGLISH	mountain range	mountain	river	lake	lake	plateau	waterfall
DEUTSCH	Gebirge	Berg	Fluss	See	See	Hochebene	Wasserfall
ESPAÑOL	cordillera	montaña	río	lago	lago	meseta	cascada
FRANÇAIS	chaîne	montagne	rivière	lac	lac	plateau	chute d'eau
PORTUGUÊS	cordilheira	montanha	rio	lago	lago	meseta	cascata

For complete glossary see page I • 1.

Kilometers 0 100 200 300 Km.
Statute Miles 0 100 200 300 Mi.

Scale 1:6,000,000

One centimeter represents 60 kilometers.
One inch represents approximately 95 miles.
Lambert Conformal Conic Projection

Lake Baikal Region / Baikalseegebiet / Región del Lago Baikal
Région du Lac Baïkal / Região do Lago Baikal

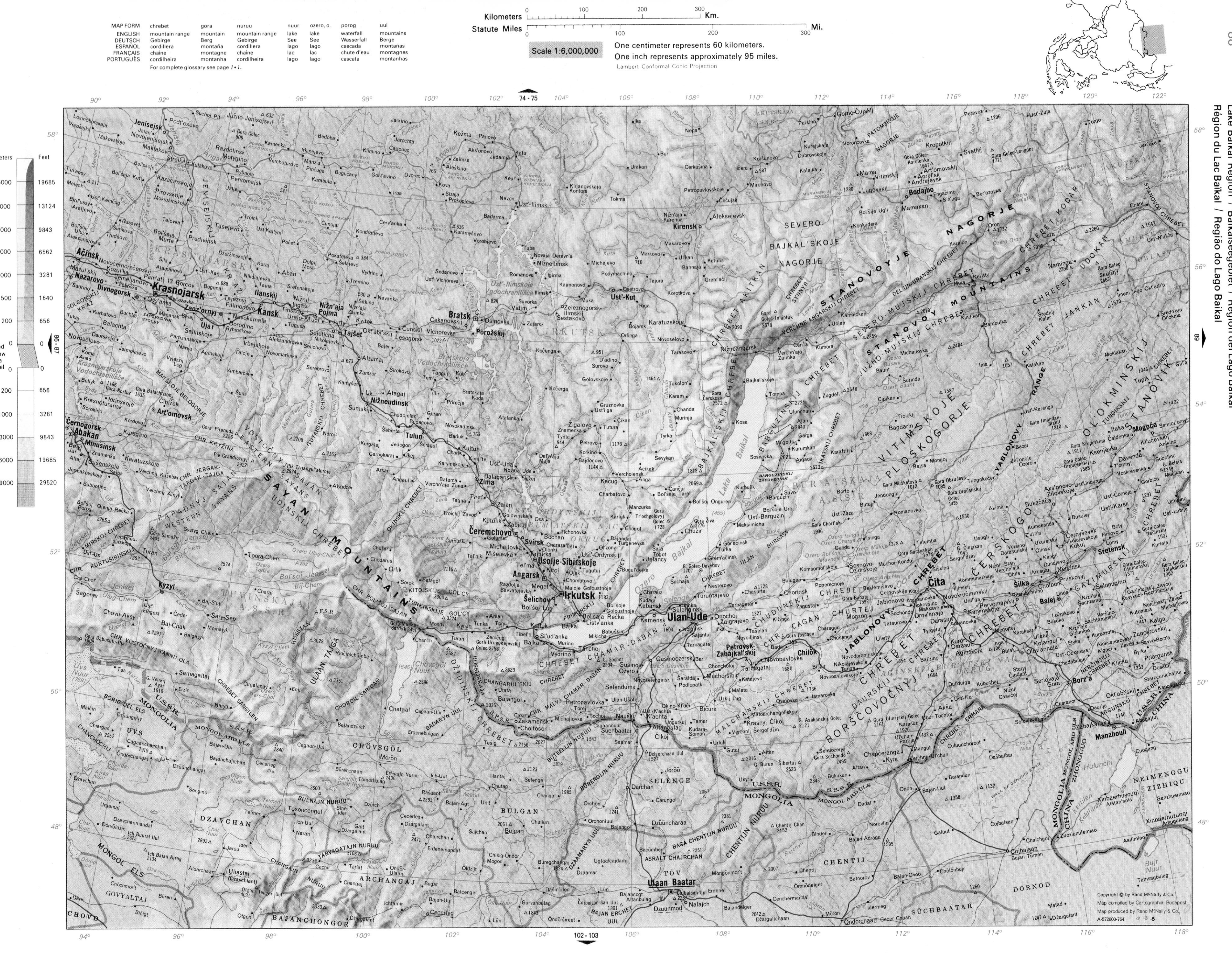

74-75
88
92-93
98-99
SEA OF OKHOTSK
OCHOTSKOJE MORE
OSTROV SACHALIN
SAKHALIN
SEA OF JAPAN
La Perouse Strait
Tatarskij Proliv
Tatar Strait
SICHOTE-ALIN'
CHREBET DŽAGDY
CHREBET TUKURINGRA
BUREINSKIJ CHREBET
DAXINGANLINGSHANMAI
GREATER KHINGAN MOUNTAINS
XIAOXING'ANLINGSHANMAI
LESSER KHINGAN MTS.
HEILONGJIANG
JILIN
MANCHURIA
NEIMENGGU ZIZHIQU
INNER MONGOLIA
Chabarovsk
Komsomol'sk-na-Amure
Blagoveščensk
Vladivostok
HAERBIN
CHANGCHUN
Qiqihaer
Južno-Sachalinsk
Sapporo
Meters
Feet
Land Below Sea Level
Kilometers
Statute Miles
Km.
Mi.
Scale 1:6,000,000
One centimeter represents 60 kilometers.
One inch represents approximately 95 miles.
Lambert Conformal Conic Projection
MAP FORM
ENGLISH
DEUTSCH
ESPAÑOL
FRANÇAIS
PORTUGUÊS
chrebet mountain range Gebirge cordillera chaîne cordilheira
-he river Fluss rio rivière rio
mys cape Kap cabo cap cabo
ostrov island Insel isla île ilha
ozero, o. lake See lago lac lago
-shan mountains Berge montañas montagnes montanhas
zaliv gulf; bay Golf; Bucht golfo; bahía golfe; baie golfo; baía
For complete glossary see page I·1.
Copyright © by Rand McNally & Co.
Map compiled by Cartographia, Budapest.
Map produced by Rand McNally & Co.

74 • 75

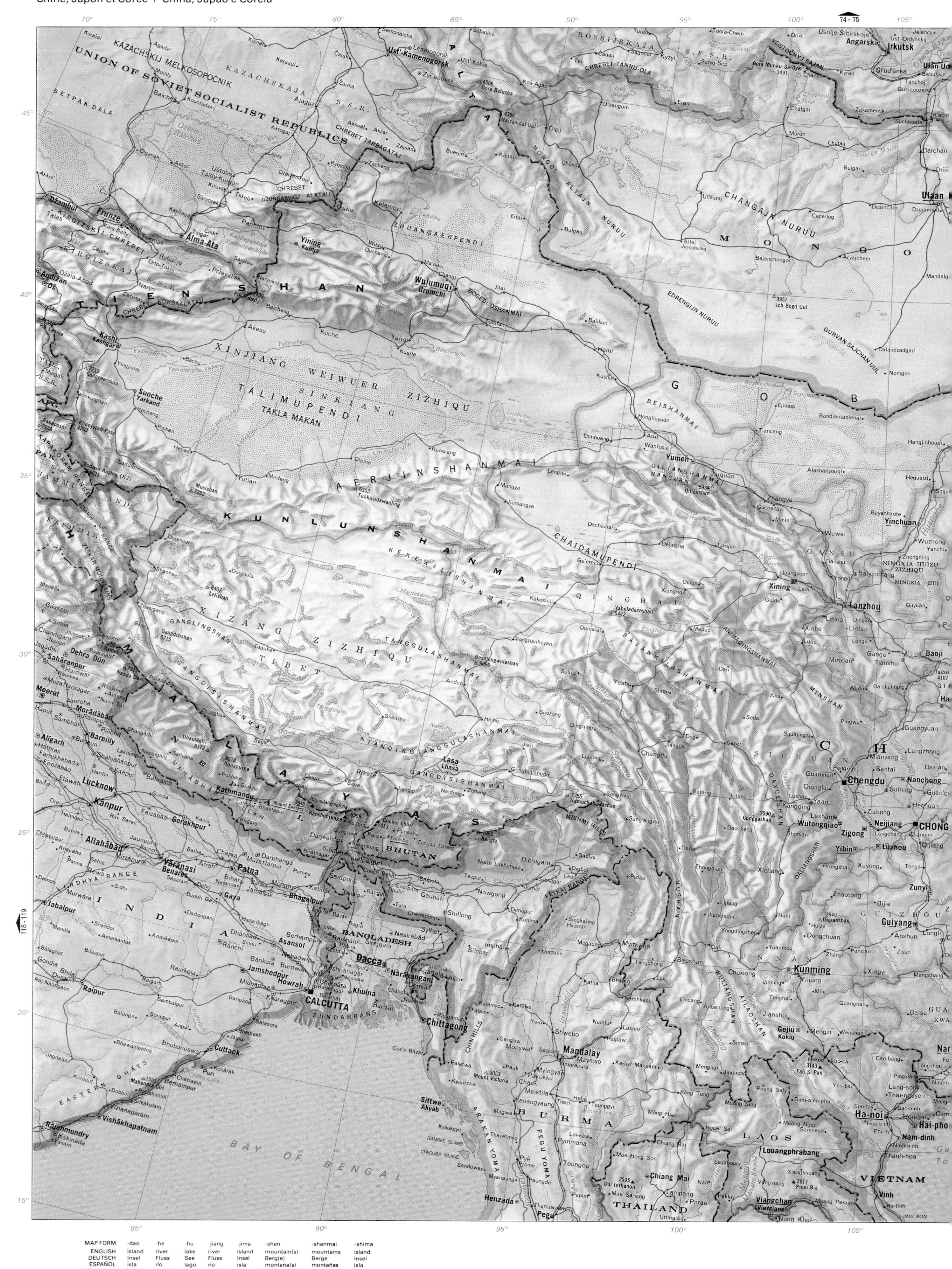

118 • 119

MAP FORM	-dao	-he	-hu	-jiang	-jima	-shan	-shanmai	-shima
ENGLISH	island	river	lake	river	island	mountain(s)	mountains	island
DEUTSCH	Insel	Fluss	See	Fluss	Insel	Berg(e)	Berge	Insel
ESPAÑOL	isla	río	lago	río	isla	montaña(s)	montañas	isla
FRANÇAIS	île	rivière	lac	rivière	île	montagne(s)	montagnes	île
PORTUGUÊS	ilha	rio	lago	rio	ilha	montanha(s)	montanhas	ilha

For complete glossary see page *1 • 1*.

Map prepared by Esselte Map Service AB, Stockholm.
A-569700-264 -4 -2 -8

108 - 109

Kilometers 0 200 400 600 Km.

Statute Miles 0 200 400 600 Mi.

Scale 1:12,000,000

One centimeter represents 120 kilometers.
One inch represents approximately 190 miles.

Lambert Conformal Conic Projection

a
OSTROV SACHALIN
SAKHALIN
R.S.F.S.R.
La Perouse Strait
Sōya-kaikyō
U.S.S.R.
JAPAN
S.S.S.R.
NIHON
SEA OF OKHOTSK
KURIL'SKIJE OSTROVA
CHISHIMA RETTŌ
KURIL ISLANDS
Habomai, Shikotan, Kunashiri, and Etorofu, occupied by the U.S.S.R. since 1945, are claimed by Japan pending a final peace treaty.
OSTROV KUNAŠIR
KUNASHIRI-TŌ
Nemuro Strait
SEA OF JAPAN
NIHON-KAI
HOKKAIDŌ
PACIFIC OCEAN
HONSHŪ
Wakkanai
Asahikawa
Kitami
Kushiro
Nemuro
Obihiro
Otaru
Sapporo
Tomakomai
Muroran
Hakodate
Aomori
Hachinohe
Hirosaki
Noshiro
Morioka
Akita
Kamaishi
Sakata
Tsuruoka
Ishinomaki
Shiogama
Sendai
Yamagata
Fukushima
Yonezawa
Niigata
Aizu-wakamatsu
Koriyama
Iwaki (Taira)
Nagaoka
Hitachi
Mito
Utsunomiya
Takada
Nagano
Maebashi
Takasaki
Toyama
Kanazawa
Matsumoto
Kōfu
TŌKYŌ
Yokohama
Kawasaki
Chiba
Funabashi
Chōshi
KITAKAMI-SANCHI
HIDAKA-SAMMYAKU
KITAMI-SANCHI
TESHIO-SANCHI
OSHIMA-HANTŌ
SHIMOKITA-HANTŌ
TSUGARU HEIYA
SENDAI HEIYA
SADO
Sado-kaikyō
Tsugaru-kaikyō
© R.M.N.

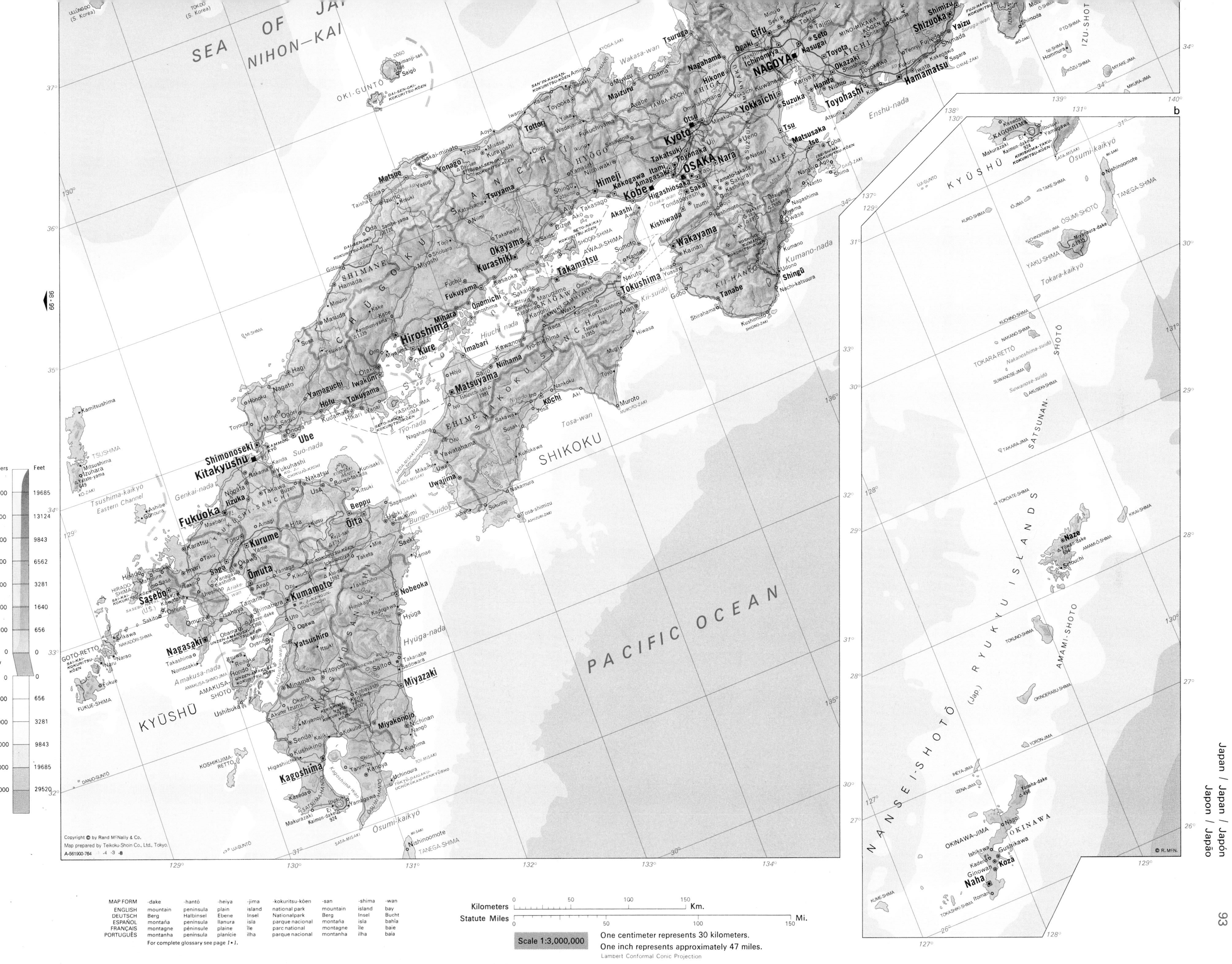
SEA OF JAPAN
NIHON-KAI
PACIFIC OCEAN
SHIKOKU
KYŪSHŪ
RYUKYU ISLANDS
NANSEI-SHOTŌ (Jap.)
OKINAWA
AMAMI-SHOTŌ
ŌSUMI-SHOTŌ
IZU-SHOTŌ
OKI-GUNTŌ
NAGOYA
OSAKA
Kyōto
Kōbe
Hiroshima
Fukuoka
Kitakyūshū
Nagasaki
Kagoshima
Kumamoto
Naha
Kilometers
Statute Miles
Scale 1:3,000,000
One centimeter represents 30 kilometers.
One inch represents approximately 47 miles.
Lambert Conformal Conic Projection
MAP FORM -dake -hantō -heiya -jima -kokuritsu-kōen -san -shima -wan
ENGLISH mountain peninsula plain island national park mountain island bay
DEUTSCH Berg Halbinsel Ebene Insel Nationalpark Berg Insel Bucht
ESPAÑOL montaña península llanura isla parque nacional montaña isla bahía
FRANÇAIS montagne péninsule plaine île parc national montagne île baie
PORTUGUÊS montanha península planície ilha parque nacional montanha ilha baía
For complete glossary see page I • I.
Copyright © by Rand McNally & Co.
Map prepared by Teikoku-Shoin Co., Ltd., Tokyo.
A-561900-764 -4 -3 -8
98 - 99
Meters Feet
6000 19685
4000 13124
3000 9843
2000 6562
1000 3281
500 1640
200 656
0 0
Land Below Sea Level
0 0
200 656
1000 3281
3000 9843
6000 19685
9000 29520

MAP FORM	-dake	-hantō	-kokuteikōen	-misaki	-san	-tōge	-wan	-yama	-zaki
ENGLISH	mountain	peninsula	national park	cape	mountain	pass	bay	mountain	point
DEUTSCH	Berg	Halbinsel	Nationalpark	Kap	Berg	Pass	Bucht	Berg	Landspitze
ESPAÑOL	montaña	península	parque nacional	cabo	montaña	paso	bahía	montaña	punta
FRANÇAIS	montagne	péninsule	parc national	cap	montagne	défilé	baie	montagne	pointe
PORTUGUÊS	montanha	península	parque nacional	cabo	montanha	passo	baía	montanha	ponta

For complete glossary see page I•1.
For Tōkyō-Yokohama metropolitan map see page 268.

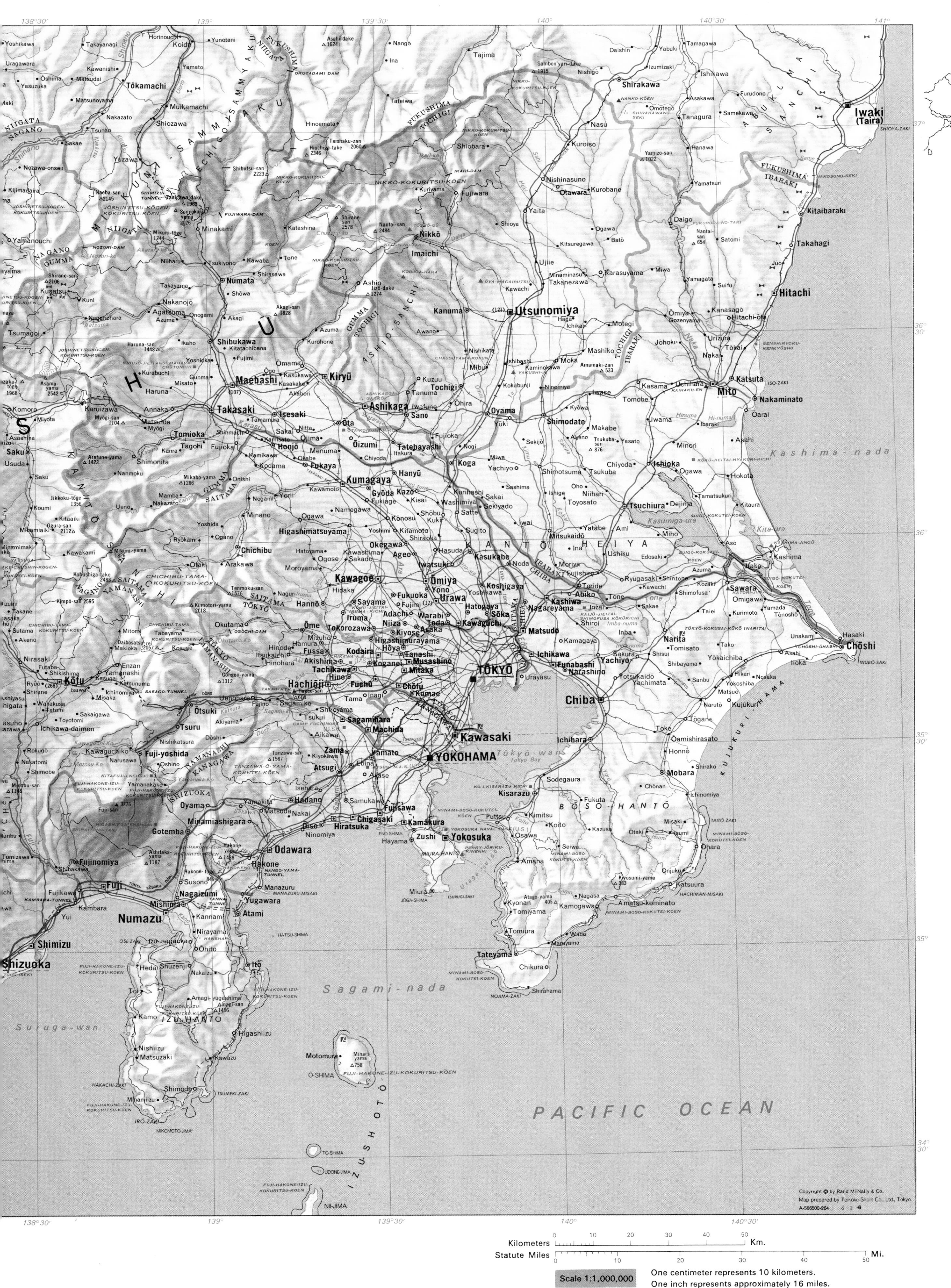

Kilometers 0 10 20 30 40 50 Km.
Statute Miles 0 10 20 30 40 50 Mi.

Scale 1:1,000,000
One centimeter represents 10 kilometers.
One inch represents approximately 16 miles.
Lambert Conformal Conic Projection

MAP FORM	-jima	-misaki	-san	-sen	-shima	-tōge	-yama	-zen
ENGLISH	island	cape	mountain	mountain	island	pass	mountain	mountain
DEUTSCH	Insel	Kap	Berg	Berg	Insel	Pass	Berg	Berg
ESPAÑOL	isla	cabo	montaña	montaña	isla	paso	montaña	montaña
FRANÇAIS	île	cap	montagne	montagne	île	défilé	montagne	montagne
PORTUGUÊS	ilha	cabo	montanha	montanha	ilha	passo	montanha	montanha

For complete glossary see page *I • 1*.
For Ōsaka-Kōbe-Kyōto metropolitan map, see page 270.

HONSHU
SHIKOKU
PACIFIC OCEAN
Tosa-wan
Harima-nada
Ōsaka-wan
Hiuchi-nada
Mizushima-nada
Wakasa-wan
Kii-suidō
Inland Sea
KYŌTO
ŌSAKA
KOBE
Okayama
Kurashiki
Himeji
Tottori
Matsue
Yonago
Takamatsu
Tokushima
Kōchi
Wakayama
Fukuyama
Onomichi
Mihara
Niihama
Nara
Sakai
Kishiwada
Higashiōsaka
Amagasaki
Nishinomiya
Akashi
Kakogawa
Maizuru
Fukuchiyama
Tsuyama
Naruto
Muroto
AWAJI-SHIMA
SHŌDO-SHIMA
IESHIMA-SHOTŌ
SETO-NAIKAI-KOKURITSU-KŌEN
SAN'IN-KAIGAN-KOKURITSU-KŌEN
KII-HANTŌ
SHIKOKU-SANCHI
CHŪGOKU-SANCHI
PACIFIC OCEAN
Copyright © by Rand McNally & Co.
Map prepared by Teikoku-Shoin Co., Ltd., Tokyo.
Kilometers
Km.
Statute Miles
Mi.
Scale 1:1,000,000
One centimeter represents 10 kilometers.
One inch represents approximately 16 miles.
Lambert Conformal Conic Projection

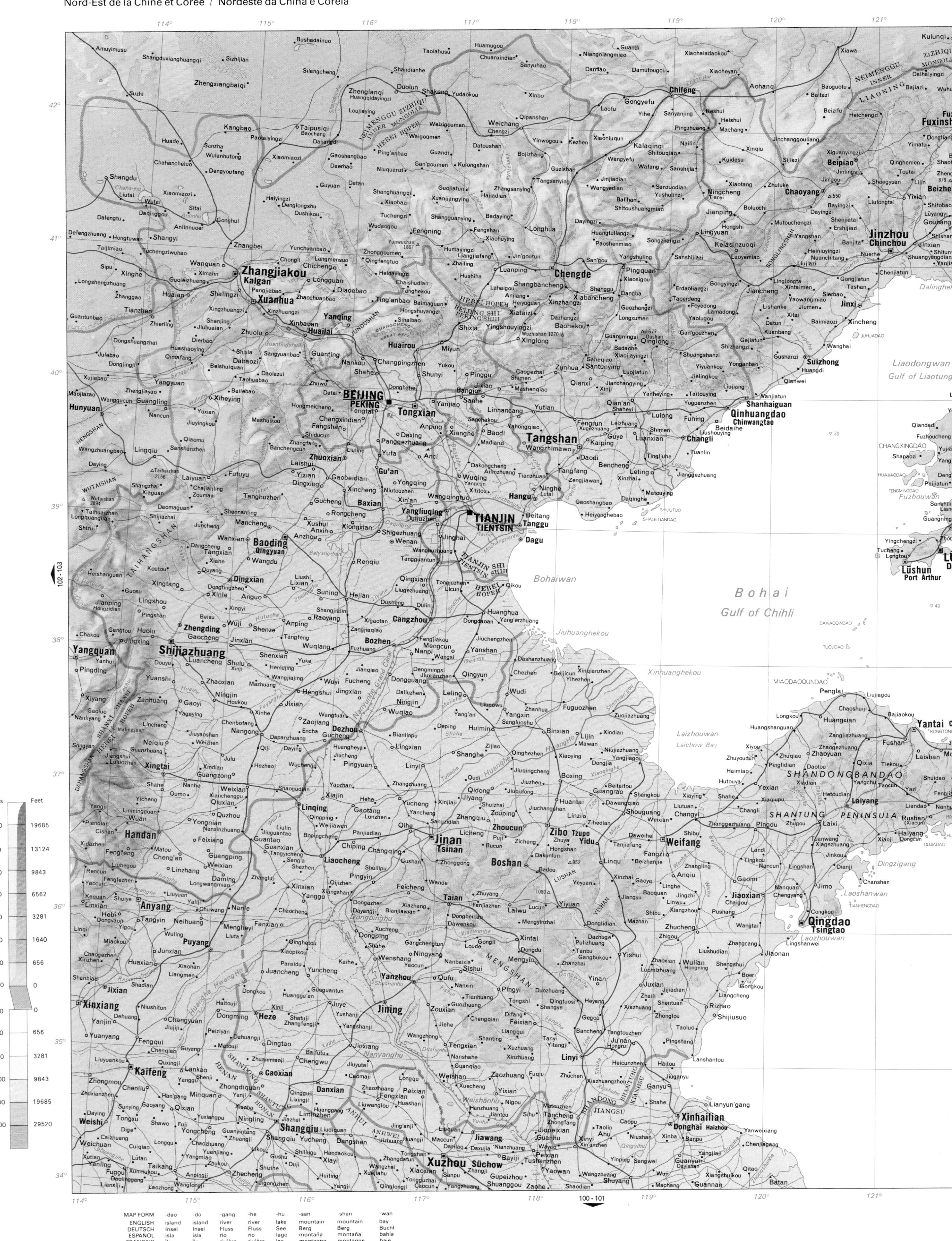

MAP FORM	-dao	-do	-gang	-he	-hu	-san	-shan	-wan
ENGLISH	island	island	river	river	lake	mountain	mountain	bay
DEUTSCH	Insel	Insel	Fluss	Fluss	See	Berg	Berg	Bucht
ESPAÑOL	isla	isla	rio	rio	lago	montaña	montaña	bahia
FRANÇAIS	île	île	rivière	rivière	lac	montagne	montagne	baie
PORTUGUÊS	ilha	ilha	rio	rio	lago	montanha	montanha	baia

For complete glossary see page *I•1*.
For Sŏul metropolitan map, see page 271.

SEA OF JAPAN

Korea Bay

YELLOW SEA

Western Channel

Korea Strait

Kilometers 0 50 100 150 Km.

Statute Miles 0 50 100 150 Mi.

Scale 1:3,000,000

One centimeter represents 30 kilometers.

One inch represents approximately 47 miles.

Lambert Conformal Conic Projection

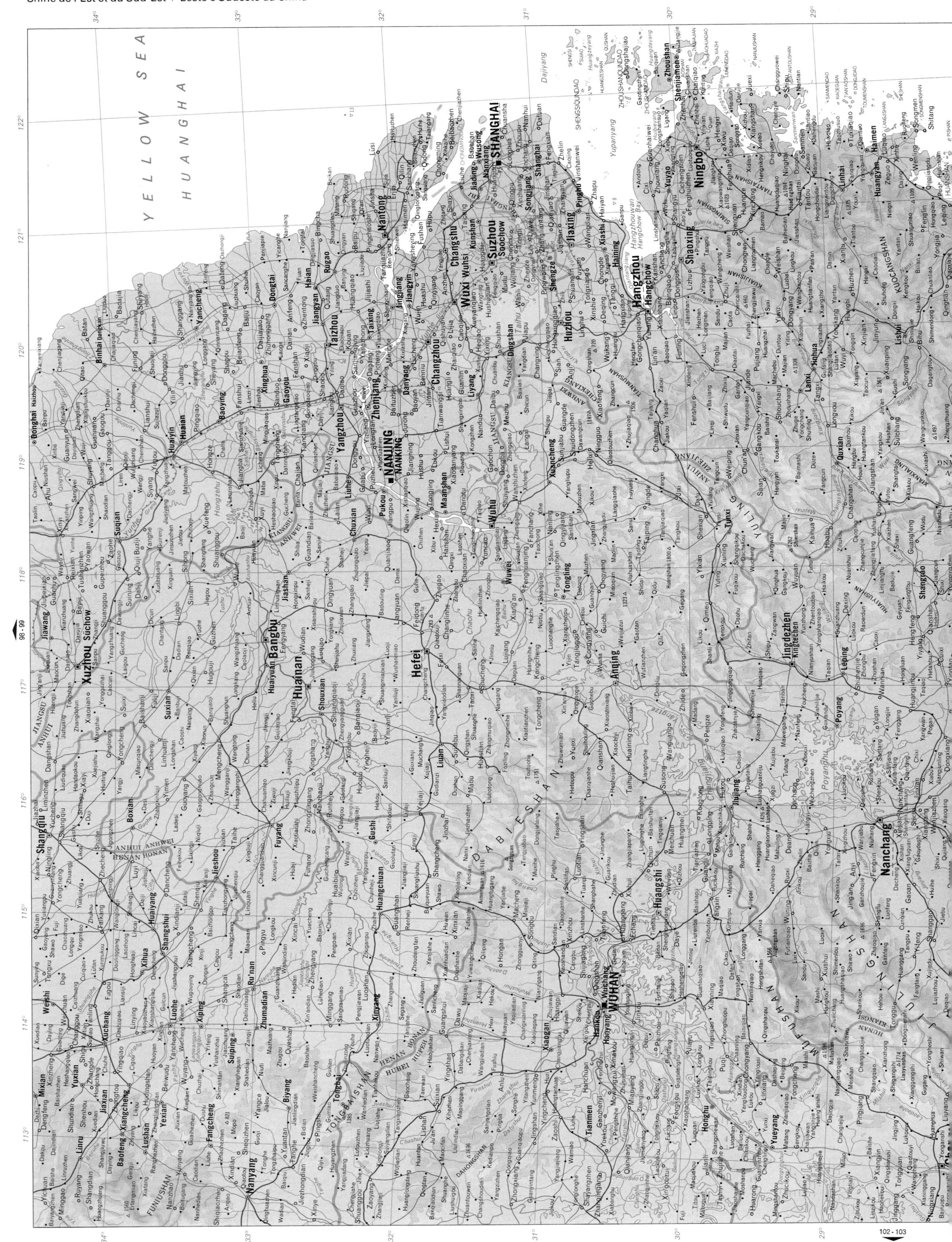
YELLOW SEA
HUANGHAI
SHANGHAI
Nanjing
NANKING
Hangzhou
Hangchow
Suzhou
Soochow
Wuxi
Ningbo
Hefei
Wuhan
Nanchang
Xuzhou
Suchow
Bangbu
Huainan
Anqing
Jingdezhen
Kingtechen
Huangshi
Nanyang
DABIESHAN

98 · 99
102 · 103

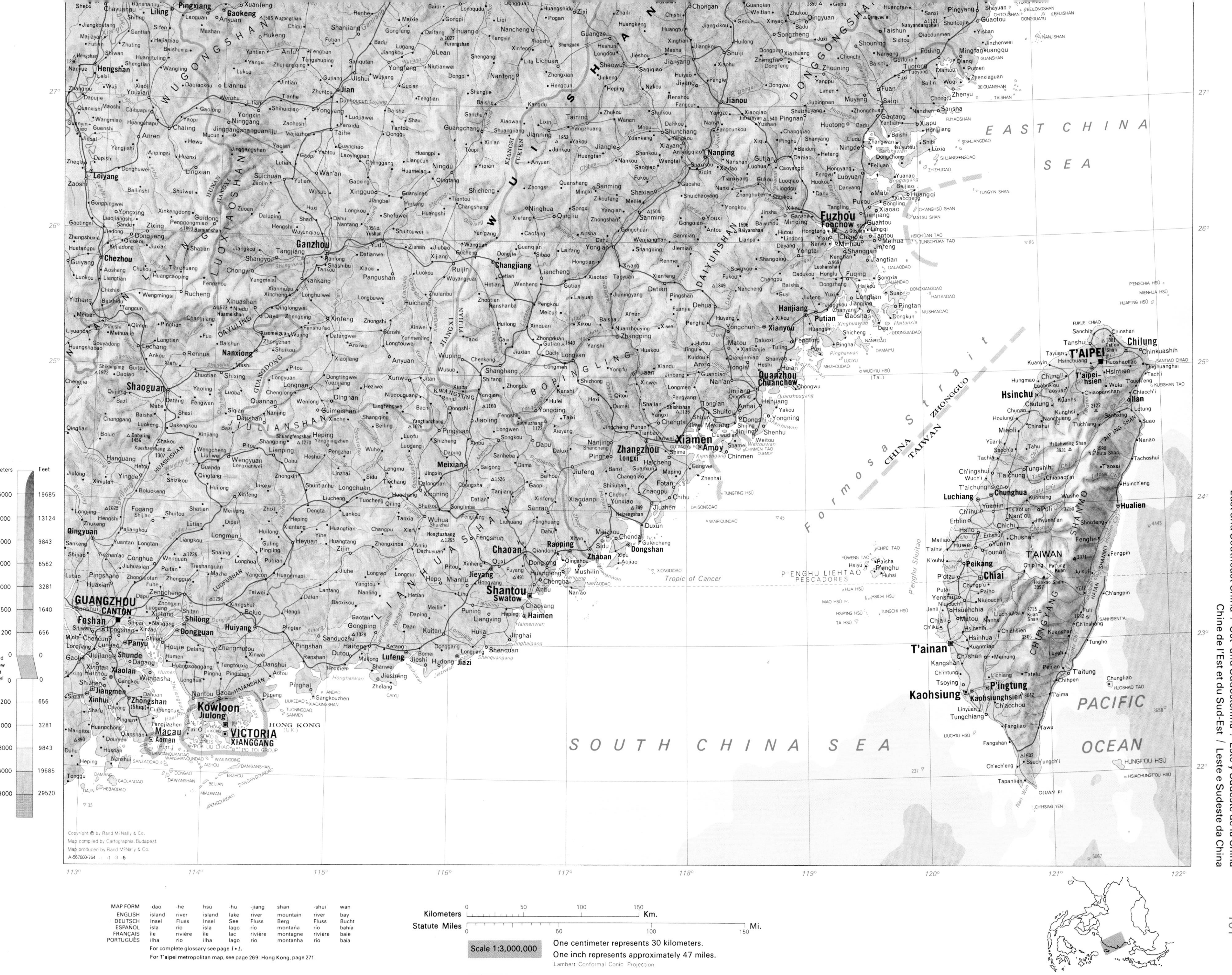
EAST CHINA SEA
SOUTH CHINA SEA
PACIFIC OCEAN
Formosa Strait
CHINA TAIWAN ZHONGGUO
T'AIWAN
GUANGZHOU CANTON
Kowloon Jiulong
VICTORIA XIANGGANG
HONG KONG (U.K.)
Macau Aomen
T'AIPEI
Fuzhou Foochow
Xiamen Amoy
Shantou Swatow
Kaohsiung
T'ainan
Tropic of Cancer
Meters
Feet
Land Below Sea Level
Copyright © by Rand M°Nally & Co.
Map compiled by Cartographia, Budapest.
Map produced by Rand M°Nally & Co.
A-567600-764
MAP FORM -dao -he hsü -hu -jiang shan -shui wan
ENGLISH island river island lake river mountain river bay
DEUTSCH Insel Fluss Insel See Fluss Berg Fluss Bucht
ESPAÑOL isla rio isla lago rio montaña rio bahia
FRANÇAIS île rivière île lac rivière montagne rivière baie
PORTUGUÊS ilha rio ilha lago rio montanha rio baía
For complete glossary see page I • 1.
For T'aipei metropolitan map, see page 269; Hong Kong, page 271.
Kilometers
Statute Miles
Scale 1:3,000,000
One centimeter represents 30 kilometers.
One inch represents approximately 47 miles.
Lambert Conformal Conic Projection

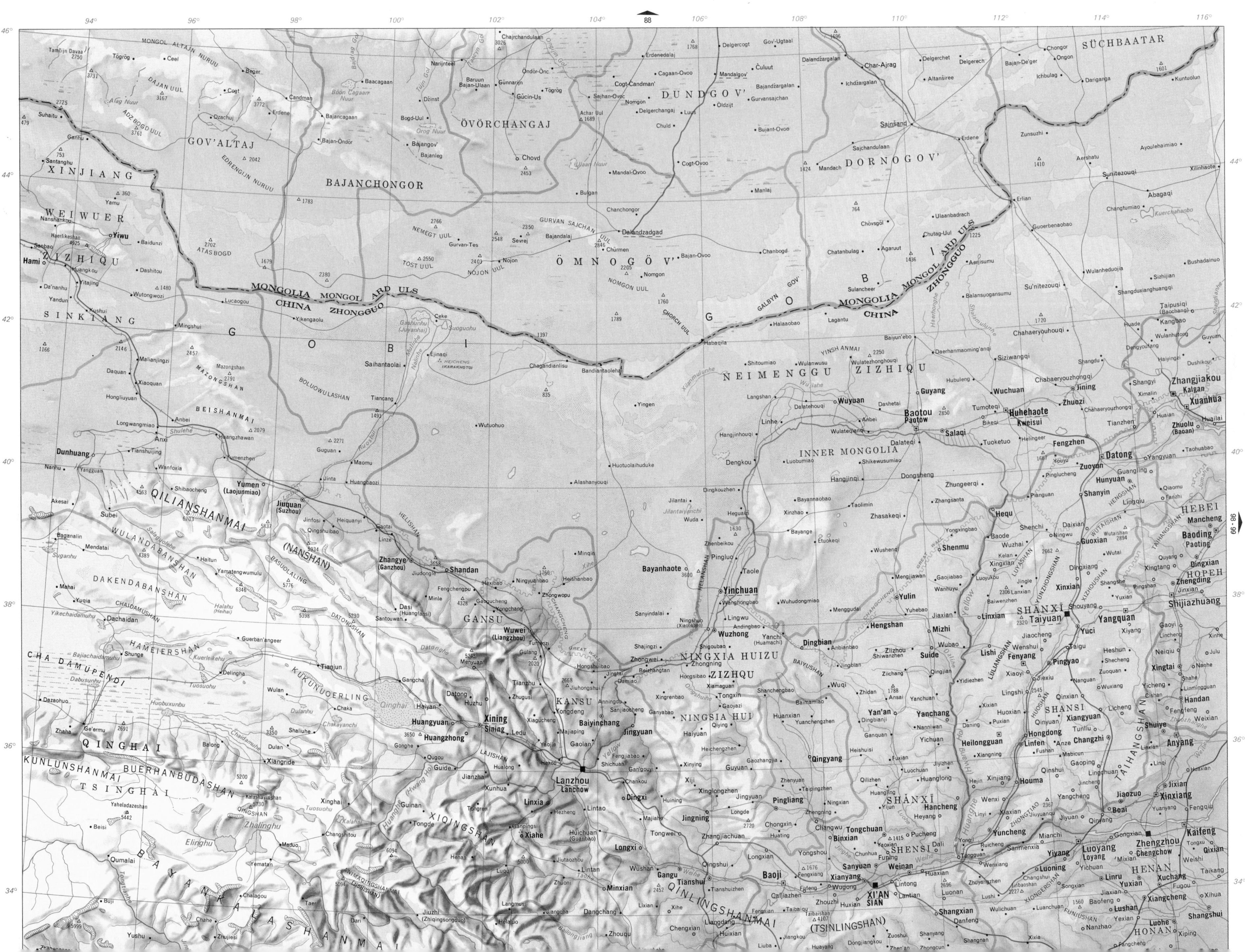
88
98 - 99
SÜCHBAATAR
DUNDGOV'
DORNOGOV'
ÖVÖRCHANGAJ
GOV'ALTAJ
BAJANCHONGOR
ÖMNOGÖV'
XINJIANG
WEIWUER
ZIZHIQU
SINKIANG
MONGOLIA MONGOL ARD ULS
CHINA ZHONGGUO
GOBI
NEIMENGGU ZIZHIQU
INNER MONGOLIA
NINGXIA HUIZU ZIZHIQU
NINGSIA HUI
GANSU
KANSU
QINGHAI
TSINGHAI
QILIANSHANMAI
(NANSHAN)
QINLINGSHANMAI
(TSINLINGSHAN)
KUNLUNSHANMAI
SHANXI
SHANSI
SHÂNXI
SHENSI
HEBEI
HOPEH
HENAN
HONAN
Hami
Dunhuang
Jiuquan
(Suzhou)
Zhangye
(Ganzhou)
Wuwei
(Liangzhou)
Xining
Sining
Lanzhou
Lanchow
Yinchuan
Baotou
Paotow
Huhehaote
Kweisui
Zhangjiakou
Kalgan
Datong
Taiyuan
Shijiazhuang
Baoding
Paoting
Zhengzhou
Chengchow
Kaifeng
Luoyang
Loyang
Xi'AN
SIAN
Baoji
Tianshui
Yumen
(Laojunmiao)

Scale 1:6,000,000
One centimeter represents 60 kilometers.
One inch represents approximately 95 miles.
Lambert Conformal Conic Projection
Kilometers
Km.
Statute Miles
Mi.
MAP FORM -he -hu -jiang -ling -shan -shanmai -shui uul
ENGLISH river lake river mountains mountain mountains river mountain
DEUTSCH Fluss See Fluss Berge Berg Berge Fluss Berg
ESPAÑOL río lago río montañas montaña montañas río montaña
FRANÇAIS rivière lac rivière montagnes montagne montagnes rivière montagne
PORTUGUÊS rio lago rio montanhas montanha montanhas rio montanha
For complete glossary see page I • 1.
Meters
Feet
Land Below Sea Level
SOUTH CHINA SEA
Gulf of Tonkin
Copyright © by Rand McNally & Co.
Map compiled by Cartographia, Budapest.
Map produced by Rand McNally GmbH, Stuttgart.
100-101
110-111
120-121

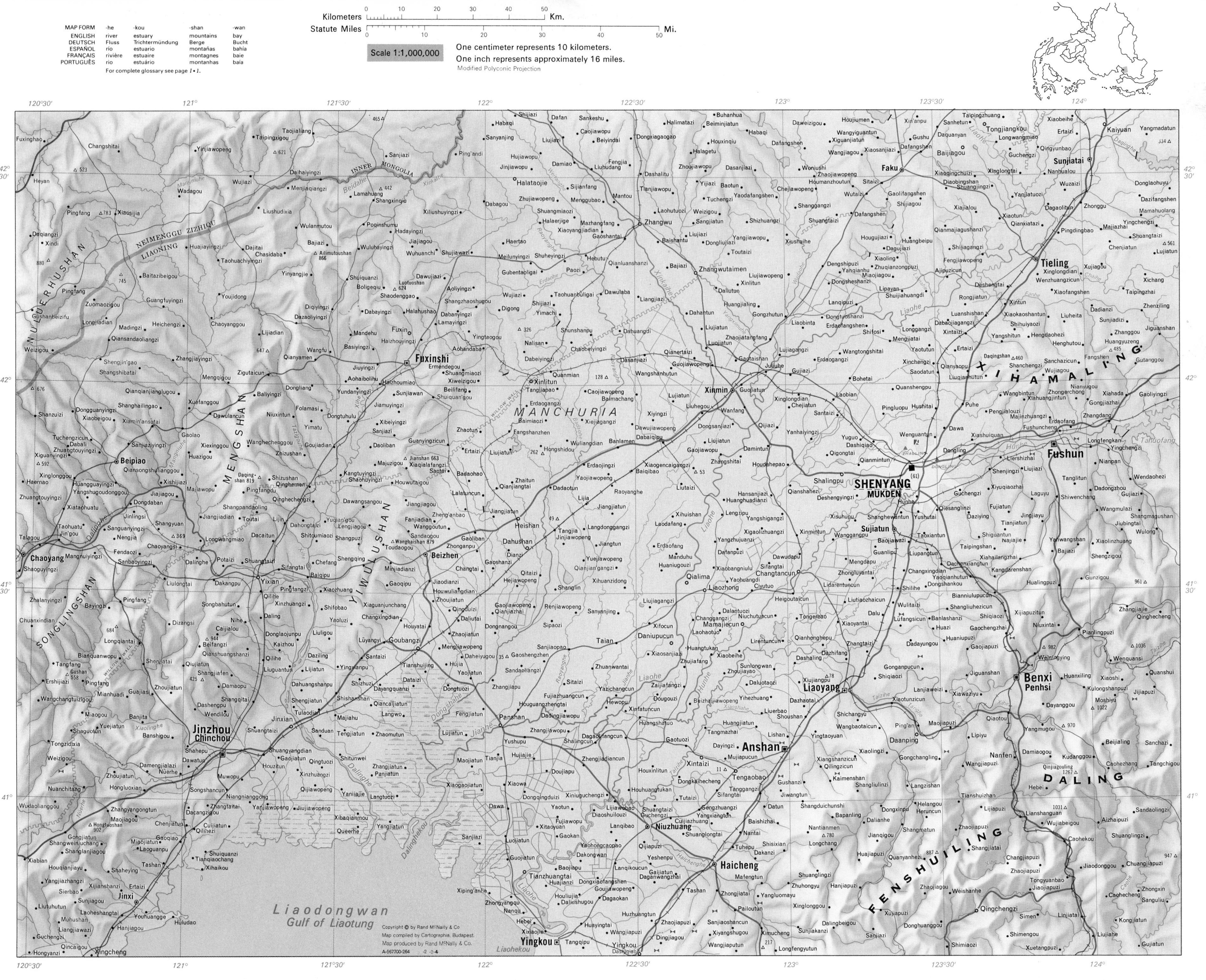
MAP FORM -he -kou -shan -wan
ENGLISH river estuary mountains bay
DEUTSCH Fluss Trichtermündung Berge Bucht
ESPAÑOL río estuario montañas bahía
FRANÇAIS rivière estuaire montagnes baie
PORTUGUÊS rio estuário montanhas baía
For complete glossary see page I • I.
Kilometers 0 10 20 30 40 50 Km.
Statute Miles 0 10 20 30 40 50 Mi.
Scale 1:1,000,000
One centimeter represents 10 kilometers.
One inch represents approximately 16 miles.
Modified Polyconic Projection
SHENYANG
MUKDEN
Fushun
Benxi
Penhsi
Liaoyang
Anshan
Haicheng
Yingkou
Jinzhou
Chinchou
Fuxinshi
Tieling
Faku
Beipiao
Chaoyang
Jinxi
MANCHURIA
XIHAMALING
DALING
FENSHUILING
YIWULUSHAN
MENGSHAN
SONGLINGSHAN
NULUERHUSHAN
INNER MONGOLIA
NEIMENGGU ZIZHIQU
LIAONING
Liaodongwan
Gulf of Liaotung
Copyright © by Rand McNally & Co.
Map compiled by Cartographia, Budapest.
Map produced by Rand McNally & Co.

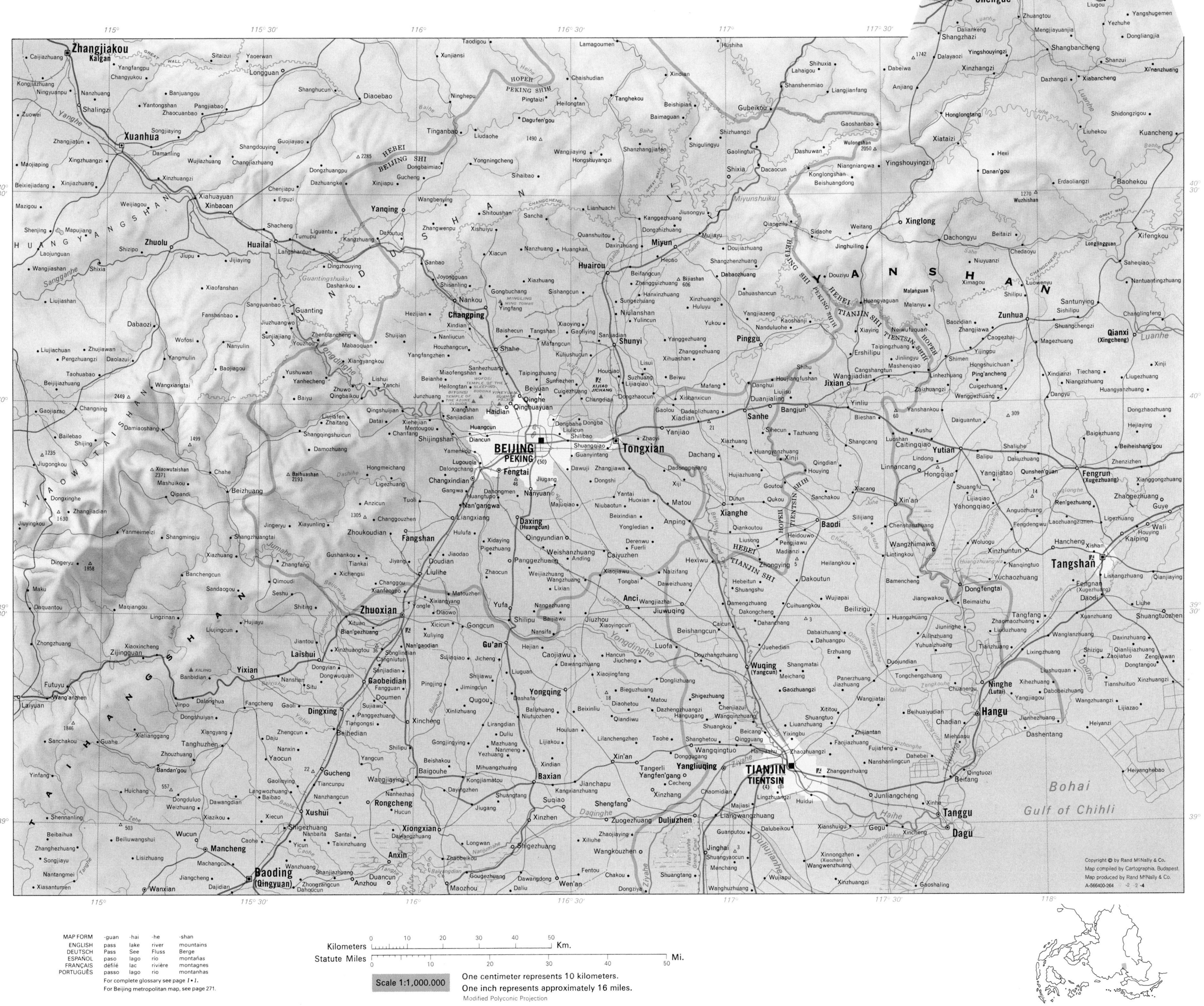

BEIJING
PEKING
TIANJIN
TIENTSIN
Bohai
Gulf of Chihli
Tangshan
Baoding (Qingyuan)
Zhangjiakou Kalgan
Scale 1:1,000,000
Kilometers
Statute Miles
One centimeter represents 10 kilometers.
One inch represents approximately 16 miles.
Modified Polyconic Projection
MAP FORM -guan -hai -he -shan
ENGLISH pass lake river mountains
DEUTSCH Pass See Fluss Berge
ESPAÑOL paso lago río montañas
FRANÇAIS défilé lac rivière montagnes
PORTUGUÊS passo lago rio montanhas
For complete glossary see page [•].
For Beijing metropolitan map, see page 271.
Copyright © by Rand McNally & Co.
Map compiled by Cartographia, Budapest.
Map produced by Rand McNally & Co.

MAP FORM -he -hu -jiang -kou -shan -wan
ENGLISH river lake river river mouth mountains bay
DEUTSCH Fluss See Fluss Flussmündung Berge Bucht
ESPAÑOL río lago río desembocadura montañas bahía
FRANÇAIS rivière lac rivière embouchure montagnes baie
PORTUGUÊS rio lago rio desembocadura montanhas baía
For complete glossary see page I • I.
For Shanghai metropolitan map see page 269.
Kilometers
Km.
Statute Miles
Mi.
Scale 1:1,000,000
One centimeter represents 10 kilometers.
One inch represents approximately 16 miles.
Lambert Conformal Conic Projection
EAST CHINA SEA
DONGHAI
NANJING
NANKING
Pukou
Zhenjiang
Chinkiang
Taixing
Danyang
Nantong
Nantung
Changzhou
Changchow
Jiangyin
Wuxi
Wuhsi
Changshu
Liyang
Yixing
Dingshan
Taihu
(3 Meters Above Sea Level)
Suzhou
Soochow
Kunshan
Jiading
Nanxiang
Wusong
SHANGHAI
Songjiang
Huzhou
Shengze
Jiaxing
Pinghu
Xiashi
Haining
Hangzhou
Hangchow
Xuancheng
CHONGMINGDAO
Changjiang
Yangtze
Hangzhouwan
Hangchow Bay
JIANGSU
ANHUI
ZHEJIANG
TIANMUSHAN
Copyright © by Rand McNally & Co.
Map compiled by Cartographia, Budapest.
Map produced by Rand McNally & Co.

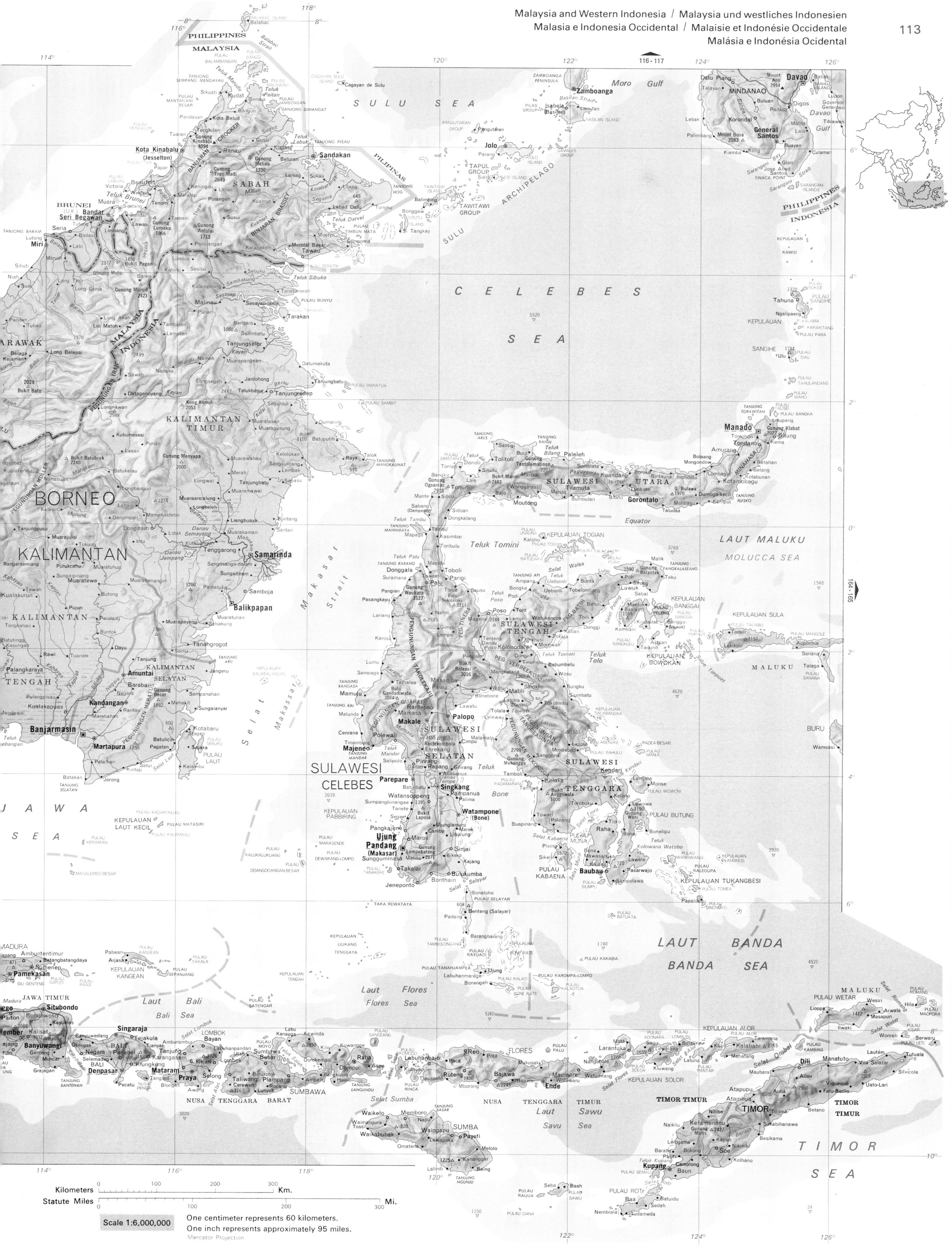

116 - 117

164 - 165

PHILIPPINES
MALAYSIA
SULU SEA
Moro Gulf
MINDANAO
Davao Gulf
SABAH
BRUNEI
SARAWAK
CELEBES SEA
PHILIPPINES
INDONESIA
BORNEO
KALIMANTAN
KALIMANTAN TIMUR
KALIMANTAN TENGAH
KALIMANTAN SELATAN
Makasar Strait
Selat Makassar
SULAWESI
CELEBES
SULAWESI UTARA
SULAWESI TENGAH
SULAWESI SELATAN
SULAWESI TENGGARA
Teluk Tomini
Teluk Bone
LAUT MALUKU
MOLUCCA SEA
MALUKU
LAUT BANDA
BANDA SEA
JAWA SEA
JAWA TIMUR
MADURA
BALI
LOMBOK
SUMBAWA
FLORES
SUMBA
TIMOR
NUSA TENGGARA BARAT
NUSA TENGGARA TIMUR
Laut Flores
Flores Sea
Laut Bali
Bali Sea
Laut Sawu
Savu Sea
TIMOR SEA
Equator

Kilometers 0 100 200 300 Km.
Statute Miles 0 100 200 300 Mi.

Scale 1:6,000,000
One centimeter represents 60 kilometers.
One inch represents approximately 95 miles.
Mercator Projection

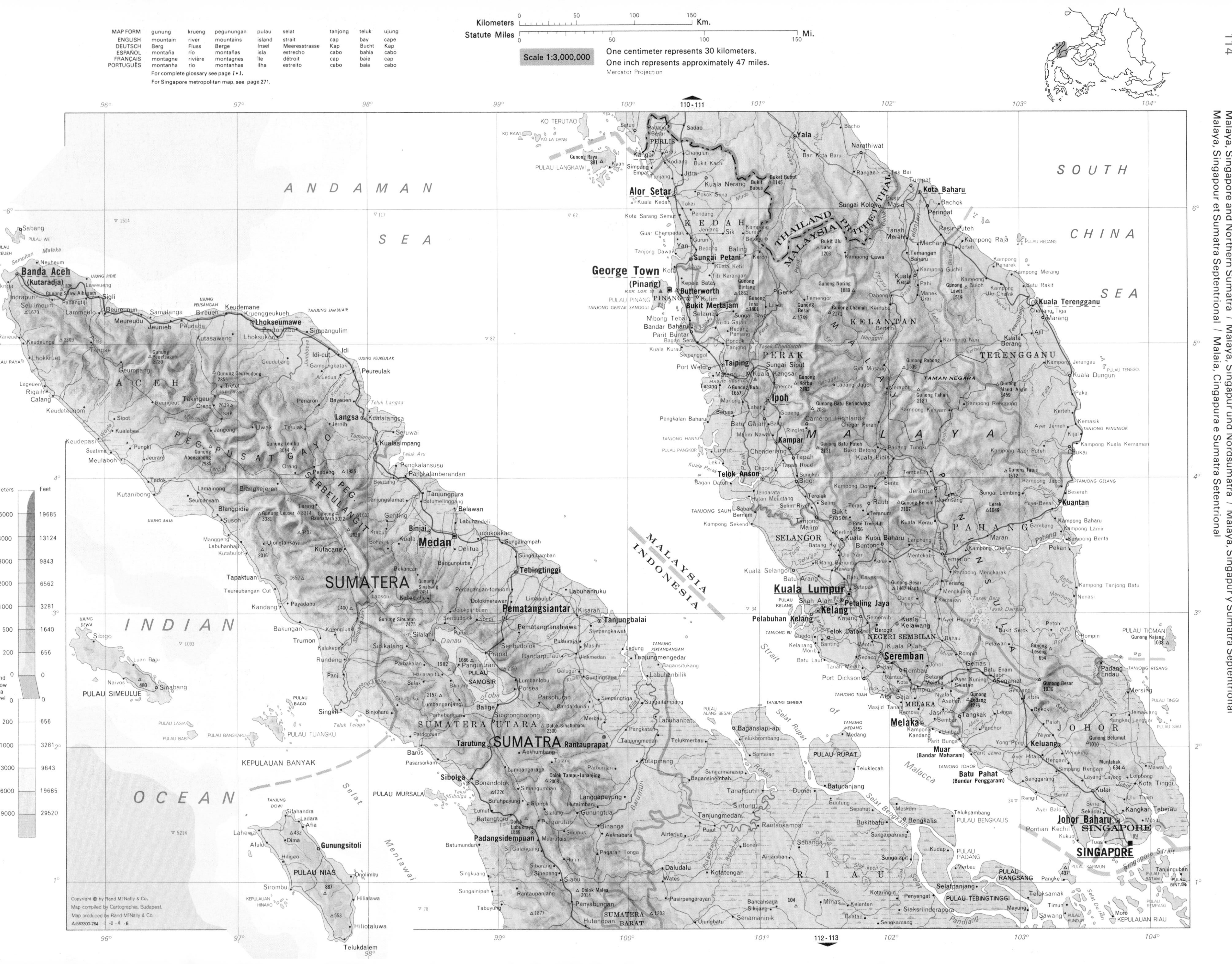
MAP FORM gunung krueng pegunungan pulau selat tanjong teluk ujung
ENGLISH mountain river mountains island strait cap bay cape
DEUTSCH Berg Fluss Berge Insel Meeresstrasse Kap Bucht Kap
ESPAÑOL montaña río montañas isla estrecho cabo bahía cabo
FRANÇAIS montagne rivière montagnes île détroit cap baie cap
PORTUGUÊS montanha rio montanhas ilha estreito cabo baía cabo
For complete glossary see page I•1.
For Singapore metropolitan map, see page 271.
Kilometers
Statute Miles
Scale 1:3,000,000
One centimeter represents 30 kilometers.
One inch represents approximately 47 miles.
Mercator Projection
110-111
112-113
SOUTH CHINA SEA
ANDAMAN SEA
INDIAN OCEAN
MALAYSIA
INDONESIA
THAILAND
SUMATERA
SUMATRA
SINGAPORE
Kuala Lumpur
George Town (Pinang)
Medan
Banda Aceh (Kutaradja)
Johor Baharu
Melaka
Seremban
Ipoh
Kuantan
Kota Baharu
Kuala Terengganu
Alor Setar
Pematangsiantar
Tebingtinggi
Tanjungbalai
Sibolga
Padangsidempuan
Lhokseumawe
Langsa
Strait of Malacca
Meters
Feet
Land Below Sea Level
Copyright © by Rand McNally & Co.
Map compiled by Cartographia, Budapest.
Map produced by Rand McNally & Co.

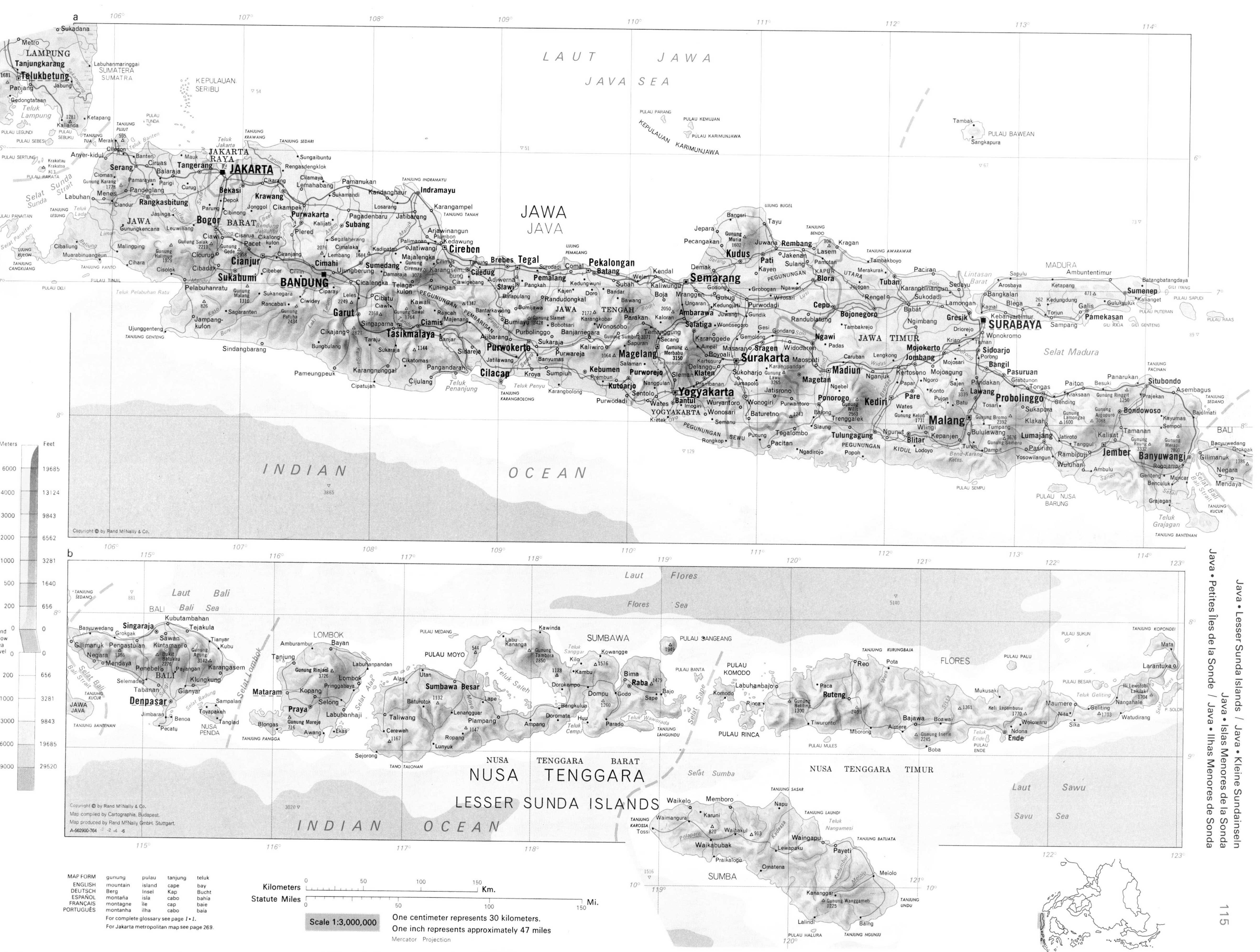
LAUT JAWA
JAVA SEA
JAWA
JAVA
INDIAN OCEAN
NUSA TENGGARA
LESSER SUNDA ISLANDS
Scale 1:3,000,000
One centimeter represents 30 kilometers.
One inch represents approximately 47 miles
Mercator Projection
Kilometers
Statute Miles
Meters
Feet
Land Below Sea Level
MAP FORM gunung pulau tanjung teluk
ENGLISH mountain island cape bay
DEUTSCH Berg Insel Kap Bucht
ESPAÑOL montaña isla cabo bahía
FRANÇAIS montagne île cap baie
PORTUGUÊS montanha ilha cabo baía
For complete glossary see page I • I.
For Jakarta metropolitan map see page 269.

Scale 1:3,000,000

One centimeter represents 30 kilometers.
One inch represents approximately 47 miles.
Lambert Conformal Conic Projection

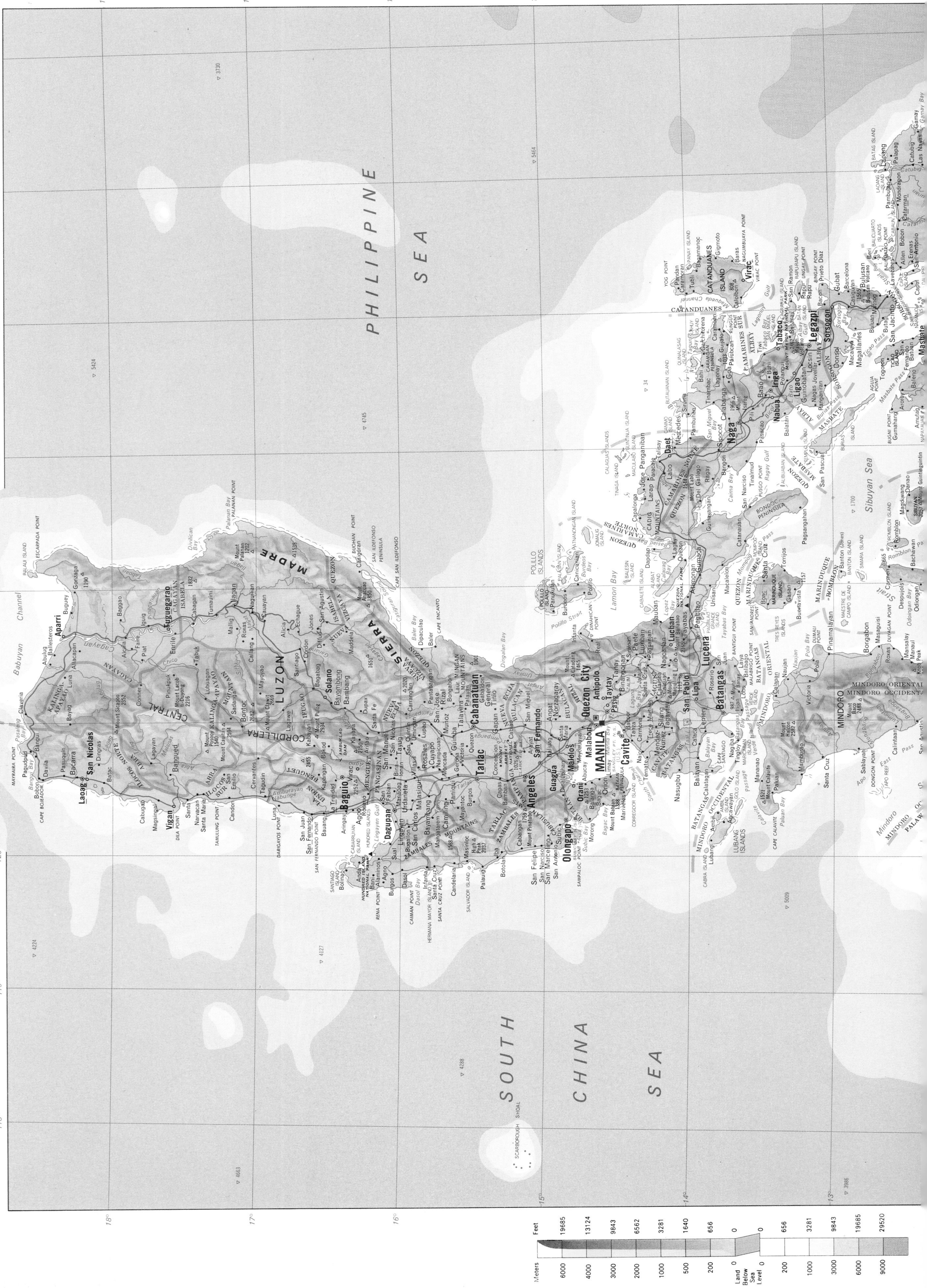

Kilometers 0 50 100 150 Km.
Statute Miles 0 50 100 150 Mi.

MAP FORM	bay	channel	island, i.	mount, mt.	passage	peak, pk.	point	strait
ENGLISH	bay	channel	island	mount	passage	peak	point	strait
DEUTSCH	Bucht	Kanal	Insel	Berg	Durchfahrt	Gipfel	Landspitze	Meeresstrasse
ESPAÑOL	bahía	canal	isla	montaña	pasaje	pico	punta	estrecho
FRANÇAIS	baie	détroit	île	mont	passage	cime	pointe	détroit
PORTUGUÊS	baía	canal	ilha	montanha	passagem	pico	ponta	estreito

For complete glossary see page I • 1.
For Manila metropolitan map see page 269.

Meters	Feet
6000	19685
4000	13124
3000	9843
2000	6562
1000	3281
500	1640
200	656
0	0
Land Below Sea Level 0	0
200	656
1000	3281
3000	9843
6000	19685
9000	29520

PHILIPPINE SEA
SOUTH CHINA SEA
LUZON
MANILA
Quezon City
Sibuyan Sea
MINDORO
CATANDUANES
BABUYAN ISLANDS
POLILLO ISLANDS
LUBANG ISLANDS
SCARBOROUGH SHOAL

SULU SEA
CELEBES SEA
Mindanao Sea
Moro Gulf
Davao Gulf
Illana Bay
Iligan Bay
Camotes Sea
Visayan Sea
Panay Gulf
Cuyo East Pass
West Cuyo Pass
Palawan Passage
Balabac Strait
MINDANAO
PALAWAN
NEGROS
CEBU
BOHOL
PANAY
LEYTE
SAMAR
SULU ARCHIPELAGO
CAGAYAN ISLANDS
CUYO ISLANDS
Zamboanga
Davao
Cebu
Iloilo
Bacolod
Cagayan de Oro
Butuan
Surigao
Tacloban
Ormoc
Dumaguete
Dipolog
Ozamiz
Pagadian
Cotabato
General Santos
Puerto Princesa
Roxas
Jolo
Isabela
Sandakan
BORNEO
KALIMANTAN
PHILIPPINES
PILIPINAS
MALAYSIA
SABAH
NORTH BORNEO
Copyright © by Rand McNally & Co.
Map prepared by Rand McNally & Co.
A-563100-764

112·113

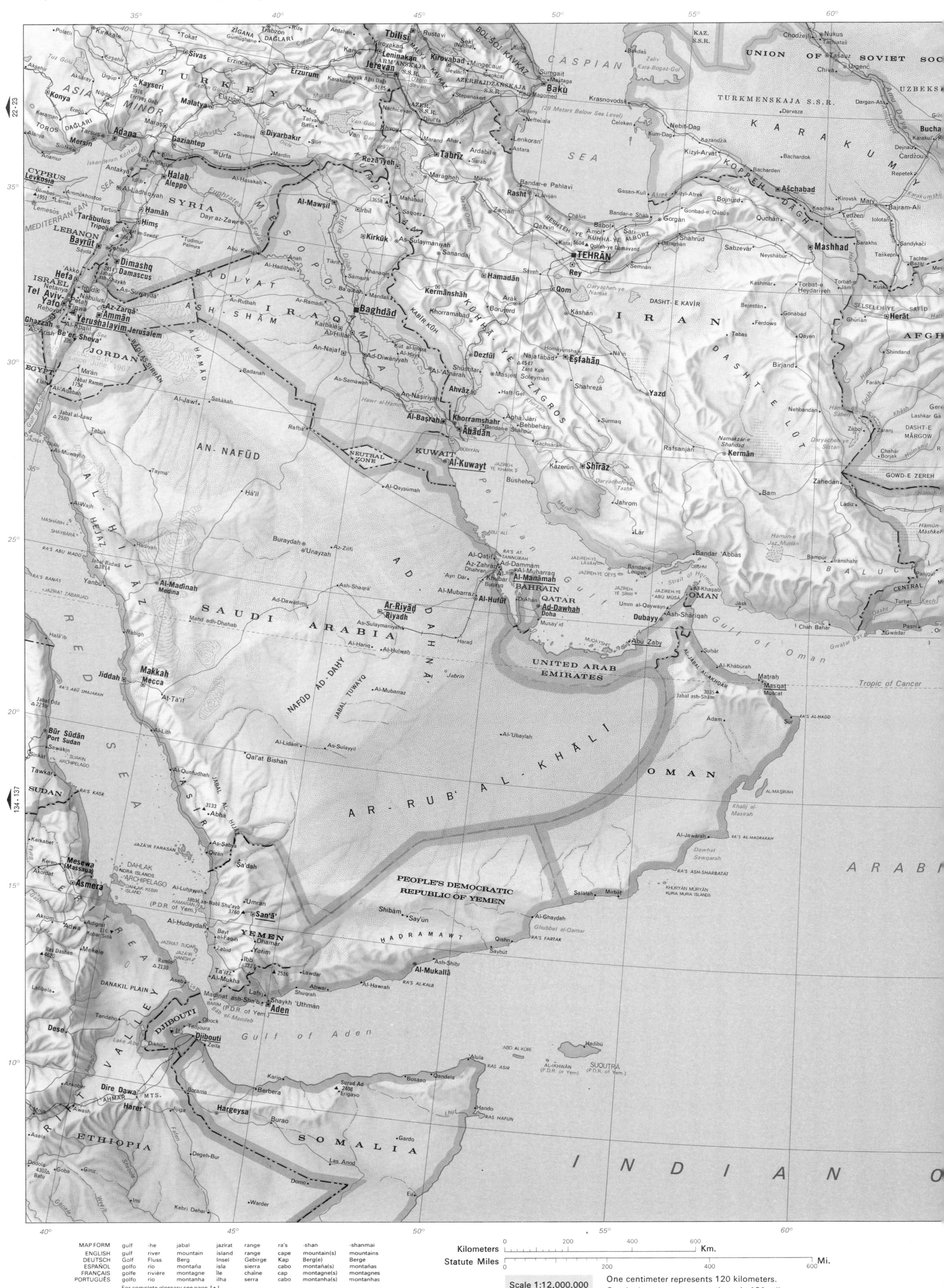
TURKEY
SYRIA
IRAQ
IRAN
JORDAN
LEBANON
ISRAEL
CYPRUS
KUWAIT
NEUTRAL ZONE
BAHRAIN
QATAR
UNITED ARAB EMIRATES
OMAN
SAUDI ARABIA
YEMEN
PEOPLE'S DEMOCRATIC REPUBLIC OF YEMEN
DJIBOUTI
ETHIOPIA
SOMALIA
SUDAN
EGYPT
UNION OF SOVIET SOC
TURKMENSKAJA S.S.R.
CASPIAN SEA
MEDITERRANEAN SEA
RED SEA
Persian Gulf
Gulf of Oman
Gulf of Aden
ARABI
INDIAN O
AN NAFŪD
AR RUB' AL KHĀLĪ
Tropic of Cancer
TEHRĀN
Baghdād
Ar-Riyāḍ Riyadh
Dimashq Damascus
Makkah Mecca
Al-Madīnah Medina
Ṣan'ā'
Aden
Masqaṭ Muscat
Al-Kuwayt
Ad-Dawḥah Doha
Abū Ẓaby
Yerushalayim Jerusalem
'Ammān
Bayrūt
Djibouti
MAP FORM | gulf | -he | jabal | jazirat | range | ra's | -shan | -shanmai
ENGLISH | gulf | river | mountain | island | range | cape | mountain(s) | mountains
DEUTSCH | Golf | Fluss | Berg | Insel | Gebirge | Kap | Berg(e) | Berge
ESPAÑOL | golfo | río | montaña | isla | sierra | cabo | montaña(s) | montañas
FRANÇAIS | golfe | rivière | montagne | île | chaîne | cap | montagne(s) | montagnes
PORTUGUÊS | golfo | rio | montanha | ilha | serra | cabo | montanha(s) | montanhas
For complete glossary see page I • 1.
Kilometers 0 200 400 600 Km.
Statute Miles 0 200 400 600 Mi.
Scale 1:12,000,000
One centimeter represents 120 kilometers.
One inch represents approximately 190 miles.
Lambert Conformal Conic Projection

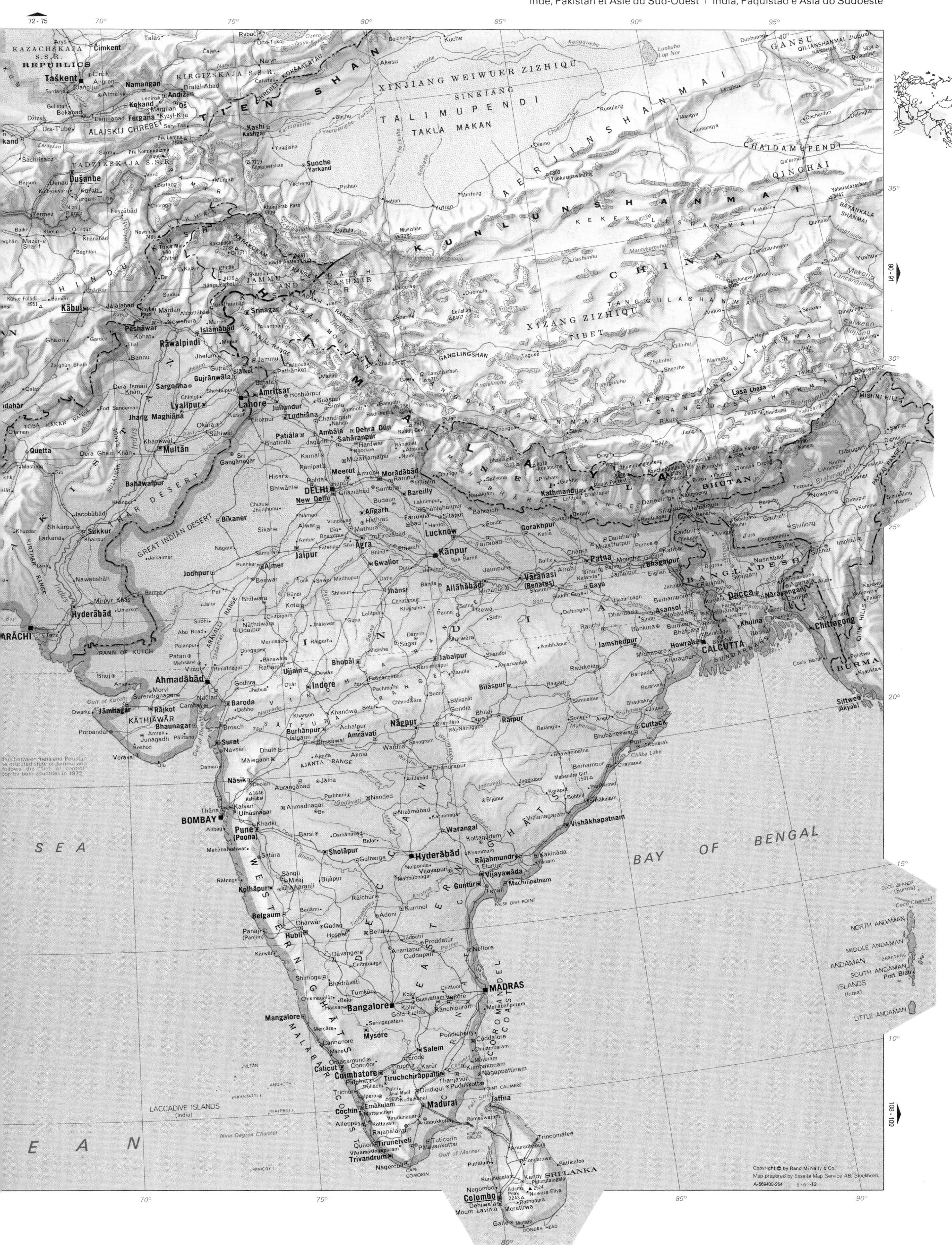
72 - 75
70°
75°
80°
85°
90°
95°
KAZACHSKAJA S.S.R.
REPUBLICS
Taškent
KIRGIZSKAJA S.S.R.
TADŽIKSKAJA S.S.R.
Dušanbe
XINJIANG WEIWUER ZIZHIQU
SINKIANG
TALIMUPENDI
TAKLA MAKAN
KUNLUN SHANMAI
ALTUN SHAN
QINGHAI
CHAIDAMUPENDI
GANSU
TIEN SHAN
HINDU KUSH
KARAKORAM
JAMMU AND KASHMIR
Kābul
Peshāwar
Islāmābād
Rāwalpindi
Srīnagar
Lahore
Amritsar
Multān
Quetta
CHINA
XIZANG ZIZHIQU
TIBET
HIMALAYA
NEPAL
Kathmandu
Mount Everest
BHUTAN
Lasa Lhasa
DELHI
New Delhi
Āgra
Jaipur
Kānpur
Lucknow
Vārānasi (Benares)
Patna
GREAT INDIAN DESERT
THAR DESERT
Hyderābād
KARĀCHI
Ahmadābād
RANN OF KUTCH
Gulf of Kutch
KĀTHIĀWĀR
Baroda
Surat
Bhopāl
Indore
Jabalpur
Nāgpur
BANGLADESH
Dacca
CALCUTTA
Chittagong
BURMA
INDIA
BOMBAY
Pune (Poona)
Hyderābād
WESTERN GHĀTS
EASTERN GHĀTS
DECCAN
BAY OF BENGAL
SEA
Bangalore
MADRAS
COROMANDEL COAST
MALABAR COAST
Mangalore
Madurai
Cochin
Trivandrum
LACCADIVE ISLANDS (India)
Nine Degree Channel
Gulf of Mannar
Jaffna
SRI LANKA
Colombo
Kandy
ANDAMAN ISLANDS (India)
NORTH ANDAMAN
MIDDLE ANDAMAN
SOUTH ANDAMAN
LITTLE ANDAMAN
Port Blair
COCO ISLANDS (Burma)
EAN
Copyright © by Rand McNally & Co.
Map prepared by Esselte Map Service AB, Stockholm.
90 - 91
108 - 109

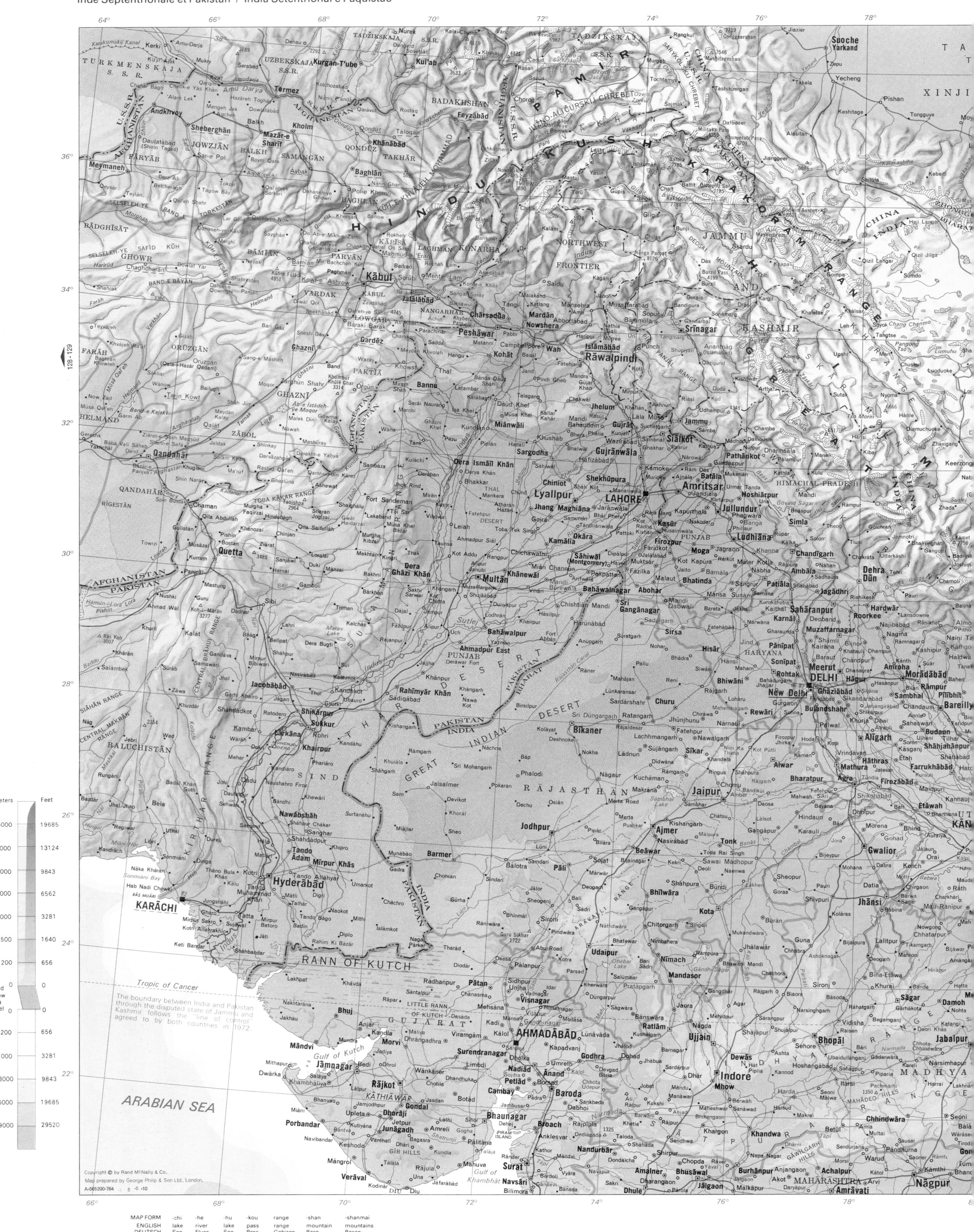

MAP FORM	-chi	-he	-hu	-kou	range	-shan	-shanmai
ENGLISH	lake	river	lake	pass	range	mountain	mountains
DEUTSCH	See	Fluss	See	Pass	Gebirge	Berg	Berge
ESPAÑOL	lago	río	lago	paso	sierra	montaña	montañas
FRANÇAIS	lac	rivière	lac	col	chaîne	montagne	montagnes
PORTUGUÊS	lago	rio	lago	passo	serra	montanha	montanhas

For complete glossary see page I·1.

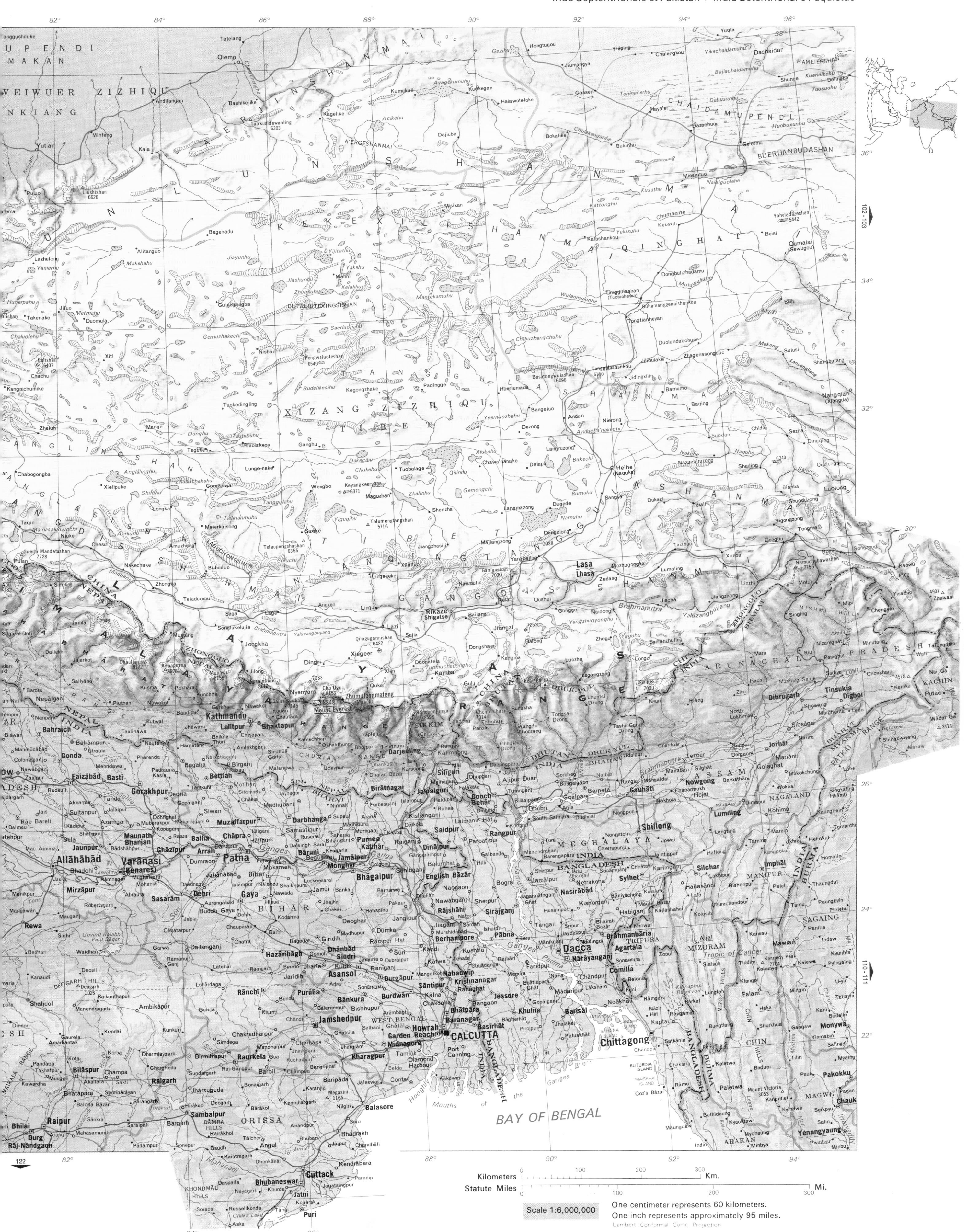
BAY OF BENGAL
Kilometers 0 100 200 300 Km.
Statute Miles 0 100 200 300 Mi.
Scale 1:6,000,000
One centimeter represents 60 kilometers.
One inch represents approximately 95 miles.
Lambert Conformal Conic Projection
102-103
110-111
122

120 - 121
ARABIAN SEA
BAY OF BENGAL
INDIAN OCEAN
Laccadive Sea
Gulf of Khambhāt
Gulf of Mannar
Palk Strait
Palk Bay
Nine Degree Channel
Eight Degree Channel
INDIA BHĀRAT
MALDIVES
INDIA BHARAT
SRI LANKA
SRI LANKA
LAKSHADWEEP
LACCADIVE ISLANDS
AMĪNDĪVI ISLANDS
MALDIVE ISLANDS
MALABAR COAST
COROMANDEL COAST
NORTHERN CIRCARS
EASTERN GHATS
WESTERN GHATS
SATPURA RANGE
VINDHYA RANGE
MADHYA PRADESH
MAHARASHTRA
ANDHRA PRADESH
KARNATAKA
ORISSA
BOMBAY
Pune (Poona)
Surat
Nāsik
Aurangābād
Indore
Nāgpur
Raipur
HYDERĀBĀD
Warangal
Vijayawāda
Guntūr
Vishākhapatnam
Rājahmundry
Kākināda
Sholāpur
Kolhāpur
Belgaum
Hubli
Gulbarga
Kurnool
Nellore
MADRAS
BANGALORE
Mysore
Mangalore
Calicut
Coimbatore
Salem
Tiruchchirāppalli
Madurai
Cochin
Ernākulam
Alleppey
Quilon
Trivandrum
Tirunelveli
Tuticorin
Nāgercoil
CAPE COMORIN
Pondicherry
Cuddalore
Thanjāvūr
Nāgappattinam
Jaffna
Trincomalee
Anuradhapura
Batticaloa
Kandy
Colombo
Kotte
Dehiwala-Mount Lavinia
Moratuwa
Negombo
Galle
Matara
DONDRA HEAD
Meters
Feet
6000 19685
4000 13124
3000 9843
2000 6562
1000 3281
500 1640
200 656
0 0
Land Below Sea Level
0 0
200 656
1000 3281
3000 9843
6000 19685
9000 29520
Copyright © by Rand McNally & Co.
Map prepared by George Philip & Son Ltd., London
ENGLISH atoll hills island lagoon lake range reservoir
DEUTSCH Atoll Hügel Insel Haff See Gebirge Stausee
ESPAÑOL atolón colinas isla laguna lago sierra embalse
FRANÇAIS atoll collines île lagune lac chaîne réservoir
PORTUGUÊS atol colinas ilha laguna lago serra reservatório
For complete glossary see page I·1.
For Bombay metropolitan map, see page 272.
Kilometers 0 100 200 300 Km.
Statute Miles 0 100 200 300 Mi.
Scale 1:6,000,000
One centimeter represents 60 kilometers.
One inch represents approximately 95 miles.
Lambert Conformal Conic Projection

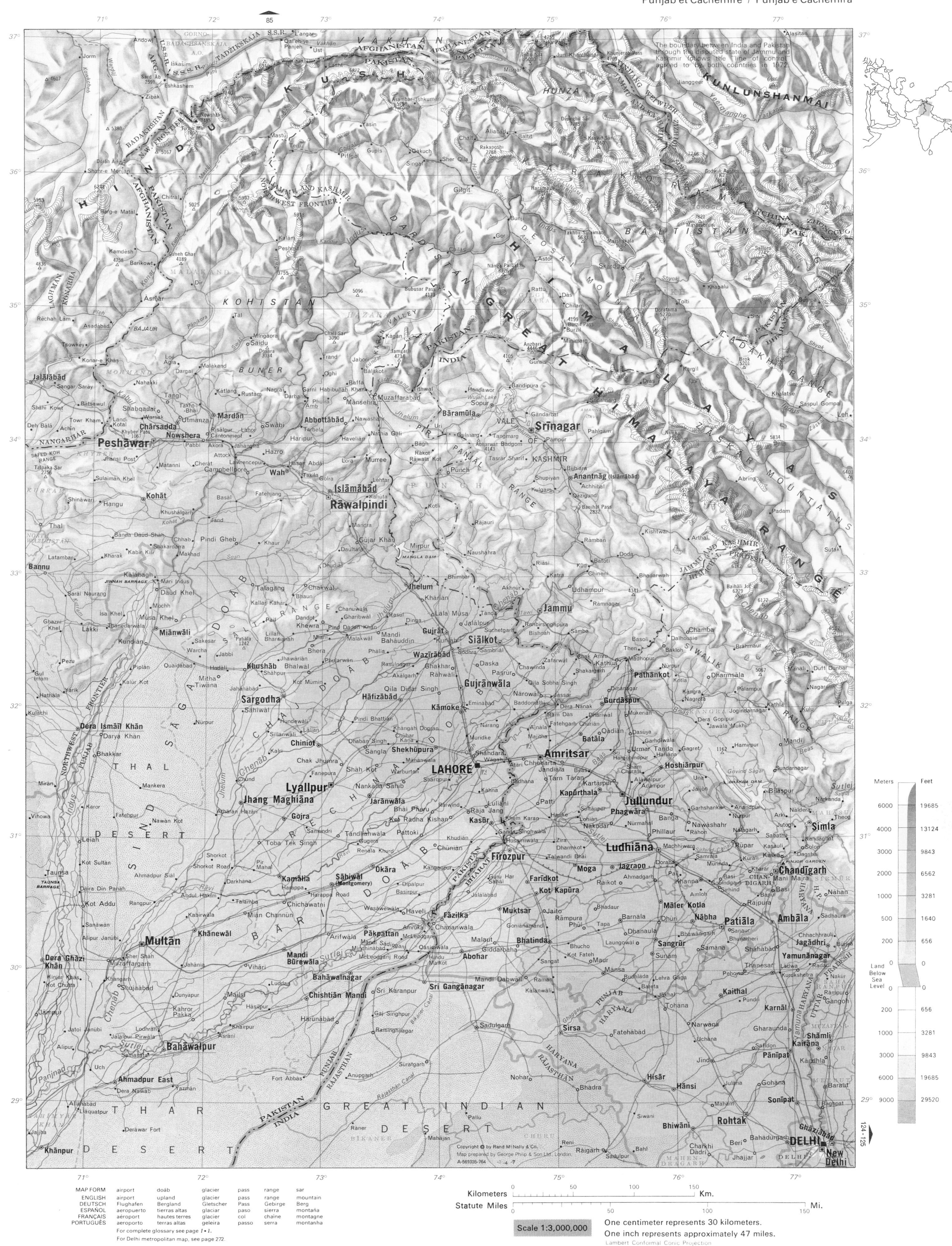
The boundary between India and Pakistan through the disputed state of Jammu and Kashmir follows the "line of control" agreed to by both countries in 1972.
KUNLUNSHANMAI
HINDU KUSH
KARAKORAM RANGE
GREAT HIMALAYA
ZASKAR MOUNTAINS
LADAKH RANGE
PIR PANJAL RANGE
SIWALIK RANGE
SALT RANGE
HUNZA
BALTISTAN
DEOSAI MOUNTAINS
KOHISTAN
BUNER
MALAKAND
BAJAUR
MOHMAND
KASHMIR
VALE OF KASHMIR
KAGAN VALLEY
PUNCH
SIND SAGAR DOAB
CHAJ DOAB
RECHNA DOAB
BARI DOAB
THAL DESERT
THAR DESERT
GREAT INDIAN DESERT
AFGHANISTAN
PAKISTAN
INDIA
CHINA
JAMMU AND KASHMIR
NORTHWEST FRONTIER
PUNJAB
HARYANA
RAJASTHAN
HIMACHAL PRADESH
UTTAR PRADESH
Peshāwar
Islāmābād
Rāwalpindi
Srīnagar
Jammu
Lahore
Amritsar
Lyallpur
Jhang Maghiāna
Multān
Bahāwalpur
Sargodha
Gujrānwāla
Siālkot
Jullundur
Ludhiāna
Patiāla
Ambāla
Chandīgarh
Simla
Firozpur
Bhatinda
Sirsa
Hisār
Rohtak
Delhi
New Delhi
Gilgit
Skardu
Mardān
Nowshera
Kohāt
Bannu
Dera Ismāīl Khān
Dera Ghāzi Khān
Mīānwāli
Jhelum
Gujrāt
Sāhīwal (Montgomery)
Okāra
Kasūr
Pathānkot
Gurdāspur
Hoshiārpur
Kapūrthala
Batāla
Karnāl
Pānīpat
Sonīpat
Bhiwāni
Hānsi
Sri Gangānagar
Meters
Feet
6000 19685
4000 13124
3000 9843
2000 6562
1000 3281
500 1640
200 656
0 0
Land Below Sea Level
200 656
1000 3281
3000 9843
6000 19685
9000 29520
Copyright © by Rand McNally & Co.
Map prepared by George Philip & Son Ltd, London.
85
124-125
MAP FORM airport doāb glacier pass range sar
ENGLISH airport upland glacier pass range mountain
DEUTSCH Flughafen Bergland Gletscher Pass Gebirge Berg
ESPAÑOL aeropuerto tierras altas glaciar paso sierra montaña
FRANÇAIS aéroport hautes terres glacier col chaîne montagne
PORTUGUÊS aeroporto terras altas geleira passo serra montanha
For complete glossary see page I·1.
For Delhi metropolitan map, see page 272.
Kilometers 0 50 100 150 Km.
Statute Miles 0 50 100 150 Mi.
Scale 1:3,000,000
One centimeter represents 30 kilometers.
One inch represents approximately 47 miles.
Lambert Conformal Conic Projection

Ganges Lowland and Nepal / Gangestiefland und Nepal / Llanuras del Ganges y Nepal
Plaine du Gange et Népal / Planicie do Ganges e Nepal

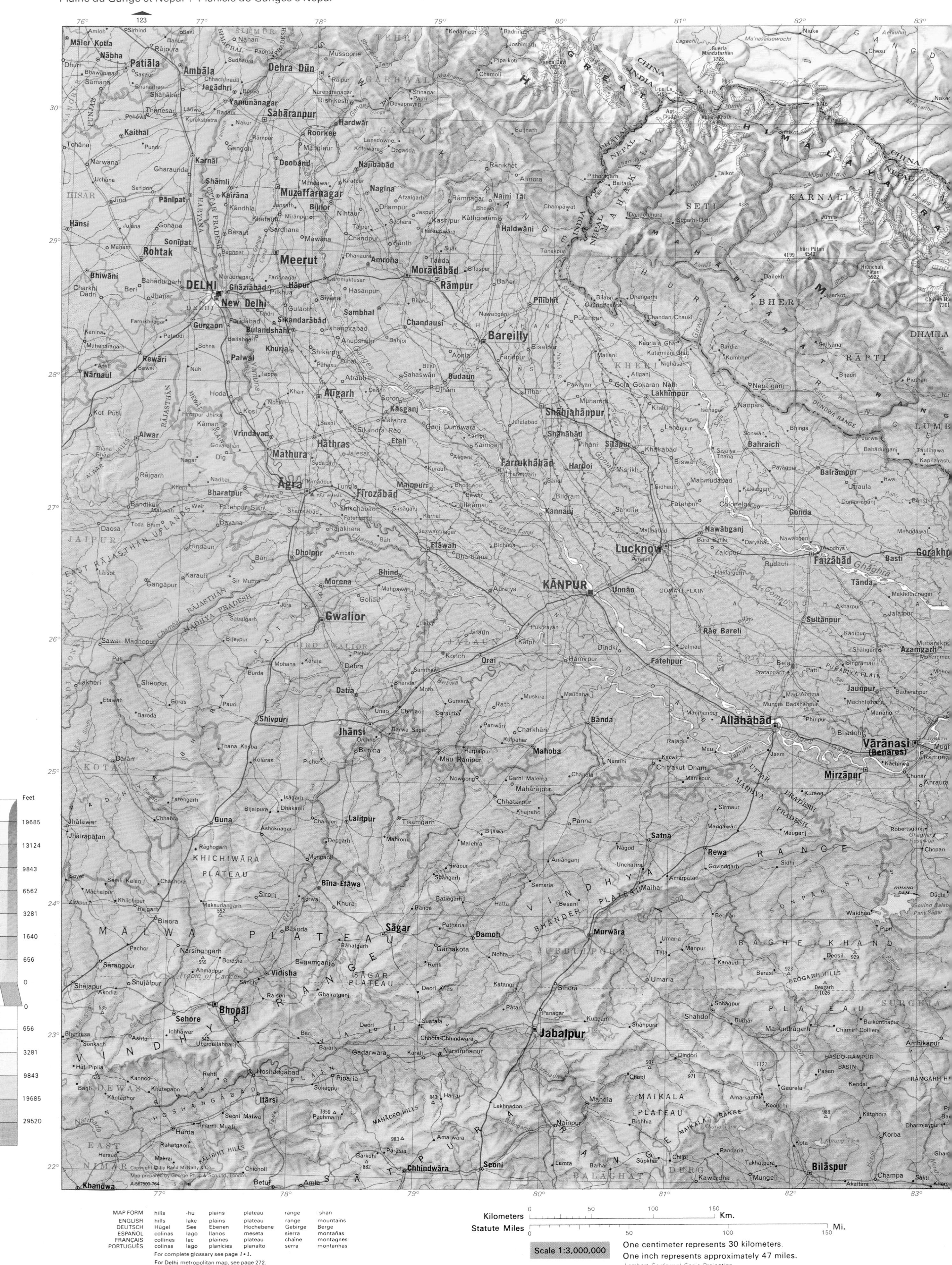

Kathmandu
Patna
Calcutta
Howrah
Dacca
Lasa
Lhasa
Thimbu
Darjeeling
Siliguri
Muzaffarpur
Darbhanga
Gaya
Jamshedpur
Ranchi
Asansol
Burdwan
Khulna
Jessore
Bhagalpur
Monghyr
Raurkela
Kharagpur
Midnapore
BAY OF BENGAL
Mouths of the Ganges
GANGES DELTA
NEPAL
INDIA
BHUTAN
SIKKIM
BANGLADESH
BIHAR
WEST BENGAL
ORISSA
ASSAM
MEGHALAYA
HIMALAYA RANGE
GREAT HIMALAYA
XIZANG ZIZHIQU
TIBET
Brahmaputra
Ganges
Padma
Meghna
Hooghly
Tropic of Cancer
HAZARIBAGH PLATEAU
RANCHI PLATEAU
CHOTA NAGPUR PLATEAU

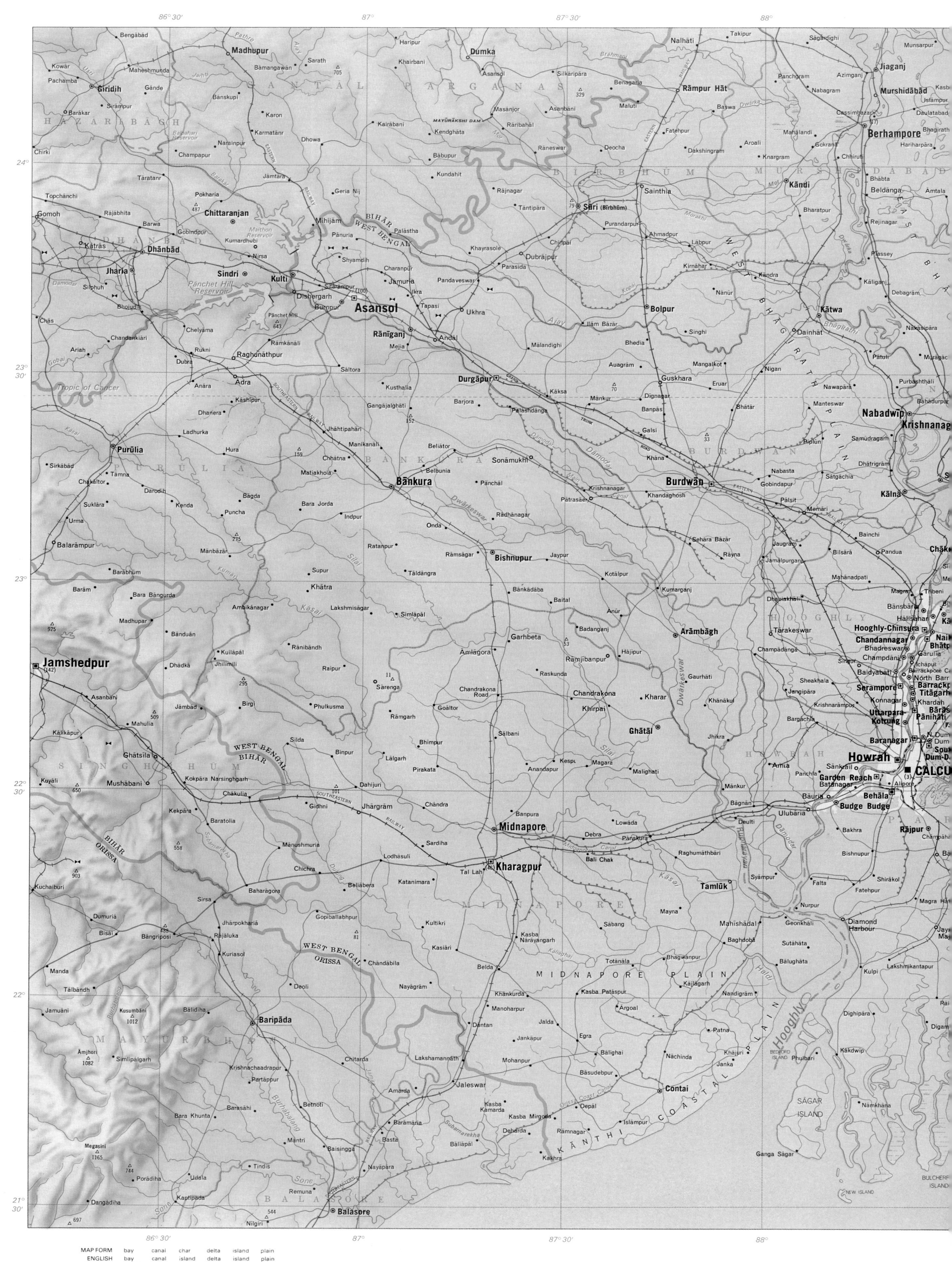

MAP FORM	bay	canal	char	delta	island	plain
ENGLISH	bay	canal	island	delta	island	plain
DEUTSCH	Bucht	Kanal	Insel	Delta	Insel	Ebene
ESPAÑOL	bahía	canal	isla	delta	isla	llanura
FRANÇAIS	baie	canal	île	delta	île	plaine
PORTUGUÊS	baía	canal	ilha	delta	ilha	planície

For complete glossary see page *I* • *1*.
For Calcutta metropolitan map, see page 272.

89°
89° 30′
90°
90° 30′
24°
23° 30′
23°
22° 30′
22°
21° 30′
Tropic of Cancer
BAY OF BENGAL
Ganges
Padma
Ganga
Jamuna
Meghna
Dhaleswari
Madhumati
Tetulia
Shāhbāzpur
Hātia
HĀTIA ISLAND
DAKHIN SHĀHBĀZPUR ISLAND
DONMĀNICK ISLANDS
RABNĀBĀD ISLANDS
KUKURI MUKURI CHAR
PUTNEY ISLAND
DALHOUSIE ISLAND
PANGADUNI ISLAND
SUNDARBANS
BENGAL
WEST BENGAL
INDIA
BANGLADESH
BHARAT
DACCA
Nārāyanganj
Narsingdi
Tangail
Pābna
Kushtia
Rājbāri
Farīdpur
Mānikganj
Munshiganj
Chāndpur
Mādārīpur
Barisāl
Patuākhāli
Bhola
Jessore
Khulna
Bāgherhāt
Sātkhira
Basīrhāt
Bangaon
Chuādānga
Jhenida
Māgura
Gopālganj
Pirojpur
Jhālakāti
Kurmitala Airport
Ayubnagar
Tungi
Meherpur
Dārsana
Kotchāndpur
Mahespur
Hābra
Bāduria
Canning
Tāki
Debhāta
Scale 1:1,000,000
Kilometers
Km.
Statute Miles
Mi.
0 10 20 30 40 50
One centimeter represents 10 kilometers.
One inch represents approximately 16 miles.
Lambert Conformal Conic Projection

MAP FORM	harrat	jabal	jazireh	kūh	ra's	sabkhat	wādī
ENGLISH	lava flow	mountain	island	mountain	cape	salt marsh	wadi
DEUTSCH	Lavastrom	Berg	Insel	Berg	Kap	Salzmarsch	Wadi
ESPAÑOL	corriente de lava	montaña	isla	montaña	cabo	pantano salado	uadi
FRANÇAIS	coulée de lave	montagne	île	montagne	cap	marais salé	wadi
PORTUGUÊS	corrente de lava	montanha	ilha	montanha	cabo	pântano salgado	uádi

For complete glossary see page *I* • *1*.
For Tehrān metropolitan map see page 267.

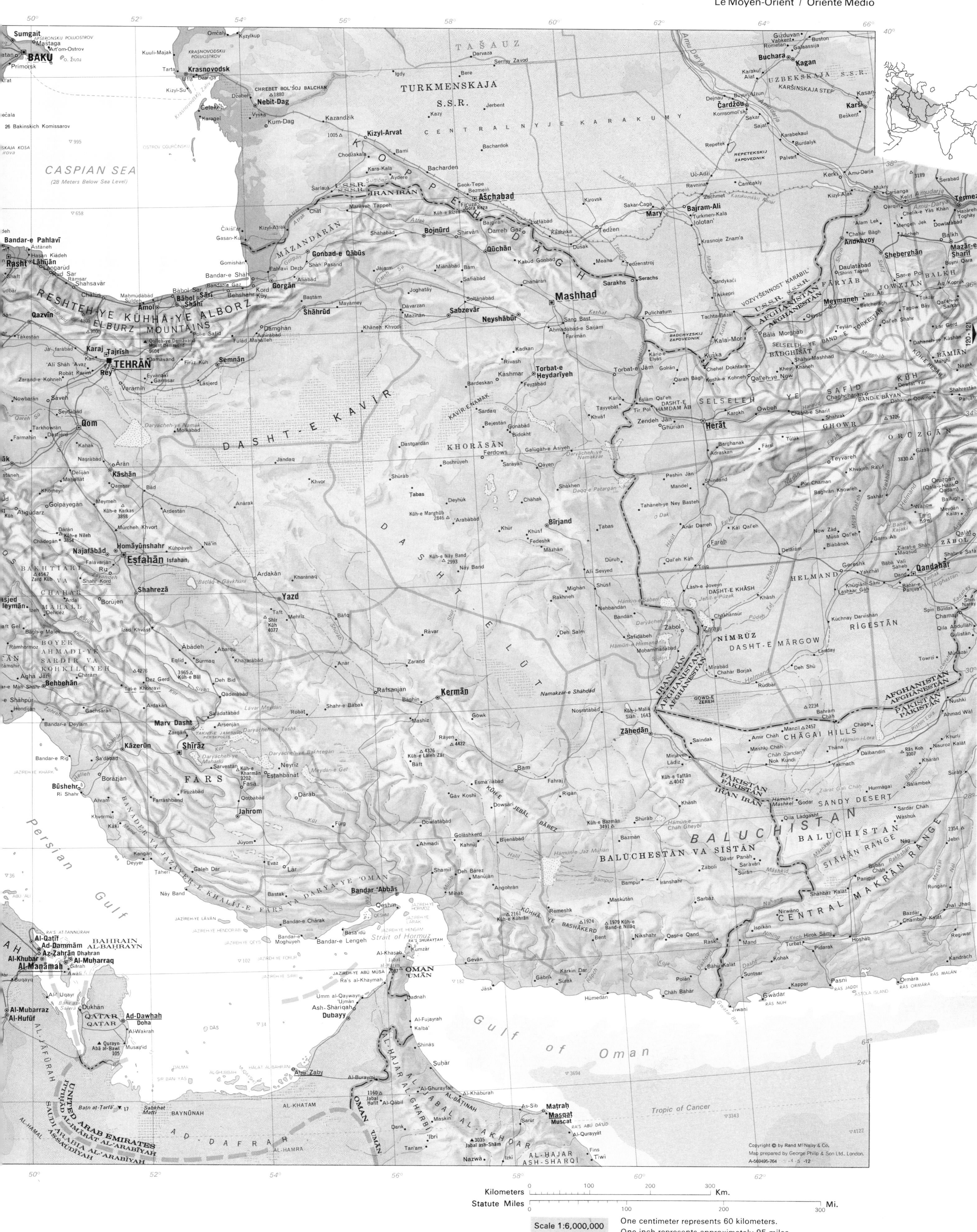
CASPIAN SEA
(28 Meters Below Sea Level)
TURKMENSKAJA
S.S.R.
TAŠAUZ
CENTRAL'NYJE KARAKUMY
UZBEKSKAJA S.S.R.
KOPPEH DĀGH
Sumgait
BAKU
Krasnovodsk
Nebit-Dag
Kizyl-Arvat
Aşchabad
Mary
Bajram-Ali
Čardžou
Buchara
Kagan
Karši
Termez
Bandar-e Pahlavī
Rasht
Qazvīn
Karaj
TEHRĀN
Qom
Kāshān
Eşfahān
Yazd
Kermān
Shīrāz
Bandar 'Abbās
Zāhedān
Mashhad
Herāt
Qandahār
Bīrjand
Semnān
Gorgān
Sabzevār
Neyshābūr
RESHTEH-YE KŪHHĀ-YE ALBORZ
ELBURZ MOUNTAINS
DASHT-E KAVĪR
DASHT-E LŪT
KHORĀSĀN
FARS
BALUCHISTAN
BALUCHESTĀN VA SĪSTĀN
AFGHANISTAN
PAKISTAN
IRAN
DASHT-E MĀRGOW
CHĀGAI HILLS
SIĀHĀN RANGE
CENTRAL MAKRĀN RANGE
Persian Gulf
Strait of Hormuz
Gulf of Oman
Tropic of Cancer
BAHRAIN
QATAR
Ad-Dawhah
Doha
Al-Manāmah
UNITED ARAB EMIRATES
Abū Zaby
Dubayy
OMAN
Masqat
Muscat
Maţraḩ
SAUDI ARABIA
Copyright © by Rand McNally & Co.
Map prepared by George Philip & Son Ltd., London.
Kilometers 0 100 200 300 Km.
Statute Miles 0 100 200 300 Mi.
Scale 1:6,000,000
One centimeter represents 60 kilometers.
One inch represents approximately 95 miles.
Lambert Conformal Conic Projection

MAP FORM	burnu	dag, dağı	dağları	gölü	jabal	körfezi	sabkhat
ENGLISH	cape	mountain	mountains	lake	mountains	bay, gulf	salt marsh
DEUTSCH	Kap	Berg	Berge	See	Berge	Bucht, Golf	Salzmarsch
ESPAÑOL	cabo	montaña	montañas	lago	montañas	bahía, golfo	pantano salado
FRANÇAIS	cap	montagne	montagnes	lac	montagnes	baie, golfe	marais salé
PORTUGUÊS	cabo	montanha	montanhas	lago	montanhas	baía, gôlfo	pântano salgado

For complete glossary see page I • 1.
For İstanbul metropolitan map see page 267.

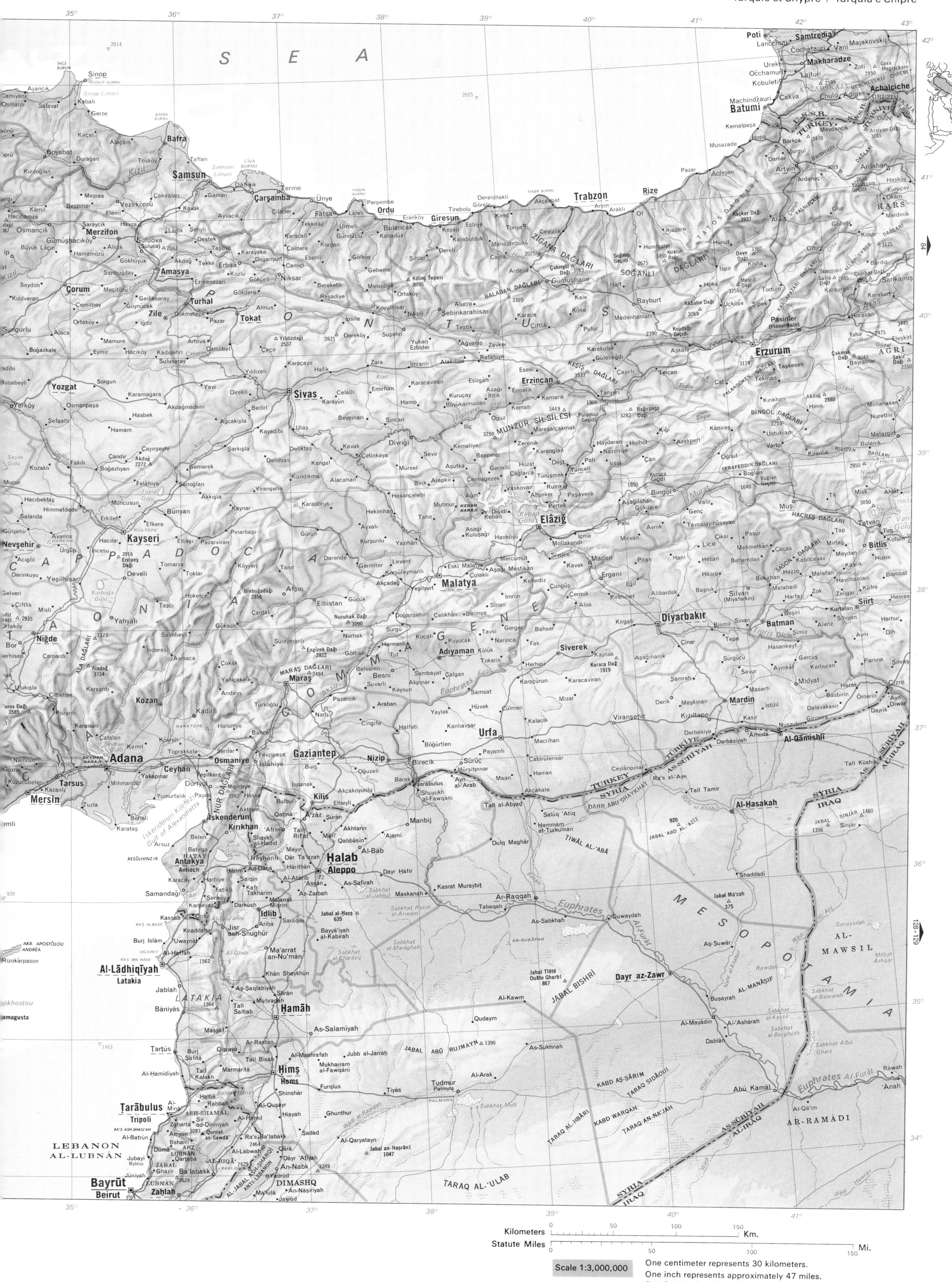
S E A
Sinop
Samsun
Bafra
Çarşamba
Ünye
Ordu
Giresun
Trabzon
Rize
Batumi
Poti
Samtredia
Makharadze
Achalciche
Artvin
Ardahan
KARS
Amasya
Merzifon
Çorum
Tokat
Turhal
Zile
Sivas
Yozgat
Erzincan
Erzurum
Bayburt
Gümüşhane
Kayseri
Nevşehir
Niğde
Malatya
Elâzığ
Bingöl
Muş
Bitlis
Siirt
Batman
Diyarbakır
Mardin
Adıyaman
Urfa
Gaziantep
Maraş
Osmaniye
Adana
Tarsus
Mersin
Kozan
Ceyhan
İskenderun
Antakya
Kilis
Halab
Aleppo
Idlib
Al-Lādhiqīyah
Latakia
Ḥamāh
Ḥimṣ
Homs
Ṭarābulus
Tripoli
Bayrūt
Beirut
Zaḥlah
DIMASHQ
Tudmur
Palmyra
Ar-Raqqah
Dayr az-Zawr
Al-Ḥasakah
Al-Qāmishlī
Abū Kamāl
Euphrates
MESOPOTAMIA
AL-MAWSIL
AR-RAMĀDI
LEBANON
AL-LUBNĀN
TURKEY
SYRIA
IRAQ
U.S.S.R.
C A P P A D O C I A
C O M M A G E N E
P O N T U S
SOĞANLI DAĞLARI
MUNZUR SILSILESI
NUR DAĞLARI
JABAL BISHRI
Kilometers 0 50 100 150 Km.
Statute Miles 0 50 100 150 Mi.
Scale 1:3,000,000
One centimeter represents 30 kilometers.
One inch represents approximately 47 miles.
Conic Projection, Two Standard Parallels

MEDITERRANEAN
SEA
Dimashq Damascus
Bayrūt Beirut
Şaydā Sidon
Şūr Tyre
Hefa Haifa
TEL AVIV-YAFO
Yerushalayim
'Ammān
Irbid
Nābulus
Dar'ā
As-Suwaydā'
Az-Zarqā'

SAUDI ARABIA
JORDAN AL-URDUNN
AL-QURAYYĀT
AL-'ARABĪYAH AS-SA'ŪDĪYAH
ARD AṢ-ṢAWWĀN
JIBĀL WAQF AṢ-ṢIWWĀN
JABAL AT TUBAYQ
AL-KARAK
QĀ' AL-ḤAFĪRA
QĀ' AL-JINZ
MA'ĀN
QĀ' AL-JAFR
ASH-SHARĀH
ISRAEL YISRA'EL
JORDAN AL-URDUNN
EGYPT MIṢR
WILDERNESS OF JUDAEA
MIDBAR YEHUDA
AL-KHALĪL
HADAROM
HAMAKHTESH HAQATAN
HAMAKHTESH HAGADOL
HANEGEV
MAKHTESH RAMON
BIQ'AT 'UVDA
JABAL AL-'AMR
JABAL HILĀL
SĪNĀ'
SHIBH JAZĪRAT SĪNĀ'
SINAI PENINSULA
Yam HaMelah
Dead Sea
Al-Baḥr al-Mayyit
Ghazzah Gaza
Al-Khalīl Hebron
Qiryat Gat
Be'er Sheva' Beersheba
Dimona
Khān Yūnus
Rafaḥ
Al-'Arīsh
Al-Karak
At-Tafīlah
Ma'ān
Al-Jafr
Elat
Al-'Aqabah
Area occupied by Israel since June, 1967
Copyright © by Rand McNally & Co.
Map prepared by George Philip & Son Ltd. London
A-567800-264
MAP FORM | har | jabal | nahr | ra's | sede-te'ufa | tall | wādī
ENGLISH | mountain | mountain(s) | river | cape | airport | mountain | wadi
DEUTSCH | Berg | Berg(e) | Fluss | Kap | Flughafen | Berg | Wadi
ESPAÑOL | montaña | montaña(s) | río | cabo | aeropuerto | montaña | uadi
FRANÇAIS | montagne | montagne(s) | rivière | cap | aéroport | montagne | wadi
PORTUGUÊS | montanha | montanha(s) | rio | cabo | aeroporto | montanha | uádi
For complete glossary see page I·1.
Kilometers
Statute Miles
Km.
Mi.
Scale 1:1,000,000
One centimeter represents 10 kilometers.
One inch represents approximately 16 miles.
Lambert Conformal Conic Projection

MAP FORM	bahr, baḥr	chott	jabal	lake	mountains	oued	wahāt
ENGLISH	river, sea	salt marsh	mountain(s)	lake	mountains	wadi	oasis
DEUTSCH	Fluss, Meer	Salzmarsch	Berg(e)	See	Berge	Wadi	Oase
ESPAÑOL	río, mar	pantano salado	montaña(s)	lago	montañas	uadi	oasis
FRANÇAIS	rivière, mer	marais salé	montagne(s)	lac	montagnes	wadi	oasis
PORTUGUÊS	rio, mar	pântano salgado	montanha(s)	lago	montanhas	uádi	oásis

For complete glossary see page *I • 1*.

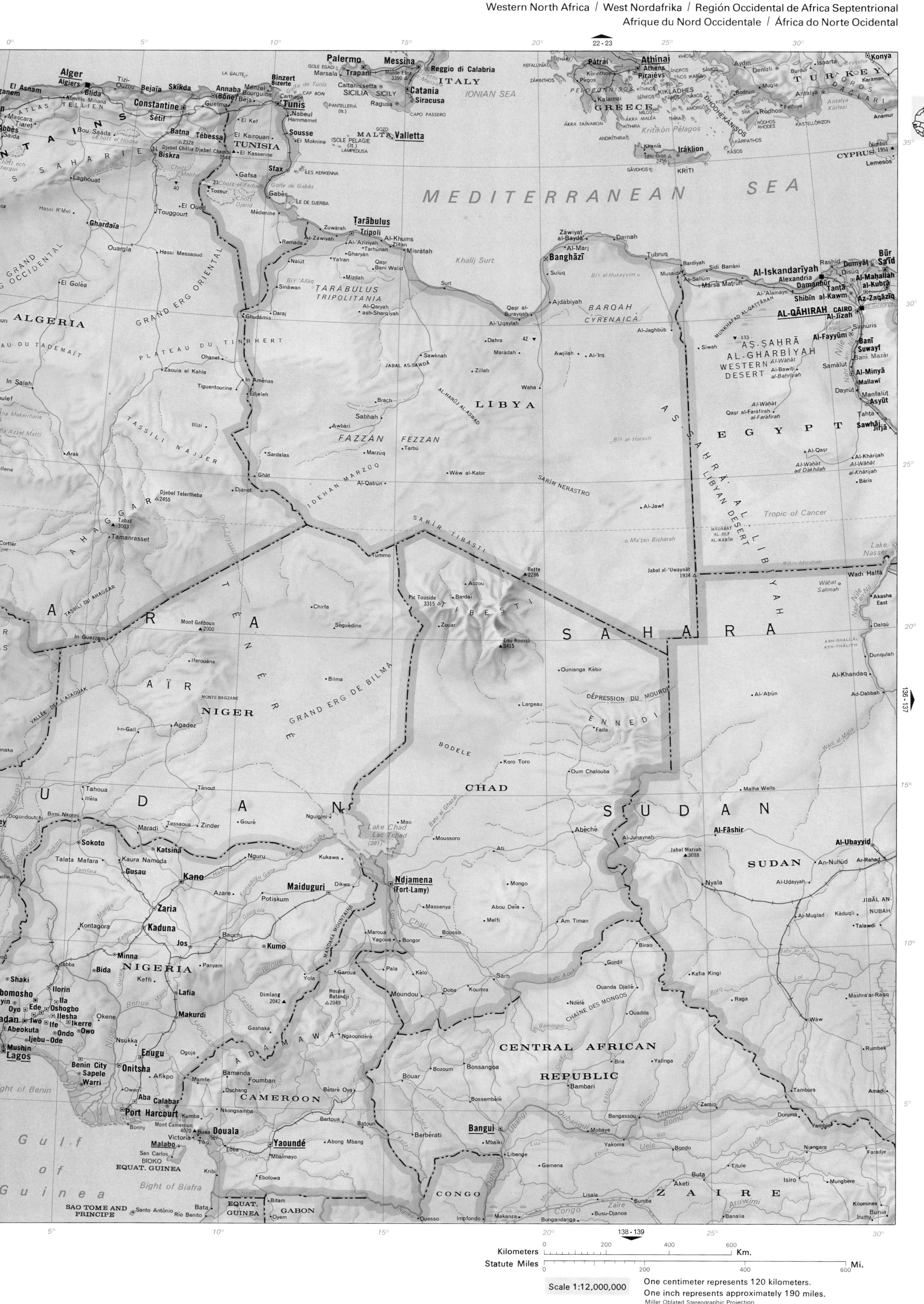
22 - 23
MEDITERRANEAN SEA
IONIAN SEA
ITALY
GREECE
TURKEY
CYPRUS
TUNISIA
ALGERIA
LIBYA
EGYPT
NIGER
CHAD
SUDAN
NIGERIA
CAMEROON
CENTRAL AFRICAN REPUBLIC
CONGO
ZAIRE
GABON
EQUAT. GUINEA
SAO TOME AND PRINCIPE
S A H A R A
S U D A N
Palermo
Messina
Reggio di Calabria
Catania
Siracusa
Trapani
Marsala
Caltanissetta
Ragusa
Malta
Valletta
Alger
Algiers
Blida
Constantine
Sétif
Annaba
(Bône)
Skikda
Bejaïa
Batna
Tébessa
Biskra
Tunis
Bizerte
Sousse
Sfax
Gabès
Gafsa
Kairouan
Ṭarābulus
Tripoli
Miṣrātah
Banghāzī
Darnah
Tubruq
Al-Marj
Ajdābiyah
Khalij Surt
Surt
Sabhah
Marzūq
Ghāt
Ghudāmis
BARQAH
CYRENAICA
FAZZĀN
FEZZAN
ṬARĀBULUS
TRIPOLITANIA
Al-Iskandarīyah
Alexandria
AL-QĀHIRAH
CAIRO
Al-Jīzah
Al-Fayyūm
Al-Minyā
Asyūṭ
Sīwah
AṢ-ṢAḤRĀ AL-GHARBĪYAH
WESTERN DESERT
AṢ-ṢAḤRĀ AL-LĪBIYAH
LIBYAN DESERT
Tropic of Cancer
Lake Nasser
Wādī Halfā
Athínai
Athens
Pátrai
Iráklion
Kríti
Ghardaïa
Ouargla
Touggourt
Laghouat
El Goléa
In Salah
Tamanrasset
AHAGGAR
TASSILI N'AJJER
GRAND ERG ORIENTAL
GRAND ERG OCCIDENTAL
PLATEAU DU TINRHERT
In Amenas
Djanet
TÉNÉRÉ
AÏR
Agadez
Bilma
GRAND ERG DE BILMA
TIBESTI
Emi Koussi
3415
Pic Toussidé
3315
Bardaï
Faya-Largeau
Largeau
BODELE
ENNEDI
Ouadai
Abéché
Al-Fāshir
Al-Ubayyid
Tahoua
Zinder
Maradi
Sokoto
Katsina
Kano
Kaduna
Zaria
Jos
Maiduguri
Ndjamena
(Fort-Lamy)
Lake Chad
Lac Tchad
Moundou
Sarh
Ilorin
Oshogbo
Ibadan
Abeokuta
Lagos
Benin City
Onitsha
Enugu
Port Harcourt
Calabar
Douala
Yaoundé
Malabo
Bight of Biafra
Bight of Benin
Gulf of Guinea
Bangui
Bambari
Bouar
Berbérati
Ngaoundéré
Garoua
ADAMAWA
CHAÎNE DES MONGOS
Nyala
Wāw
Juba
Gulf of Guinea
138 - 139
136 - 137
Kilometers 0 200 400 600 Km.
Statute Miles 0 200 400 600 Mi.
Scale 1:12,000,000
One centimeter represents 120 kilometers.
One inch represents approximately 190 miles.
Miller Oblated Stereographic Projection

MAP FORM	bahr, baḩr	chott	jabal	lake	mountains	oued	ra's; ras	wāhāt
ENGLISH	river, sea	salt marsh	mountain(s)	lake	mountains	wadi	cape	oasis
DEUTSCH	Fluss, Meer	Salzmarsch	Berg(e)	See	Berge	Wadi	Kap	Oase
ESPAÑOL	río, mar	pantano salado	montaña(s)	lago	montañas	uadi	cabo	oasis
FRANÇAIS	rivière, mer	marais salé	montagne(s)	lac	montagnes	wadi	cap	oasis
PORTUGUÊS	rio, mar	pântano salgado	montanha(s)	lago	montanhas	uádi	cabo	oásis

For complete glossary see page *I • 1*.

Kilometers 0 200 400 600 Km.
Statute Miles 0 200 400 600 Mi.

Scale 1:12,000,000

One centimeter represents 120 kilometers.
One inch represents approximately 190 miles.
Miller Oblated Stereographic Projection

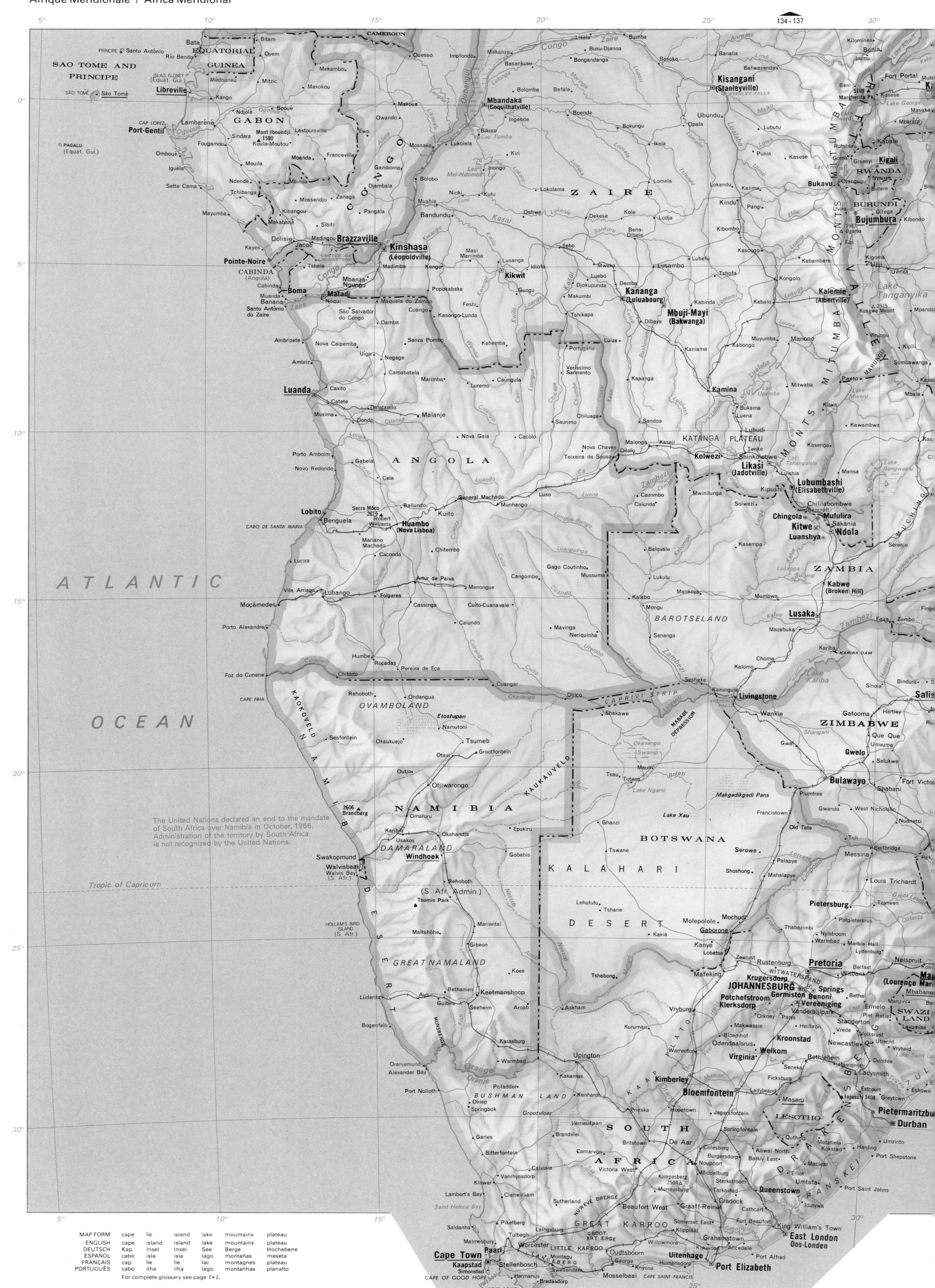

MAP FORM	cape	île	island	lake	mountains	plateau
ENGLISH	cape	island	island	lake	mountains	plateau
DEUTSCH	Kap	Insel	Insel	See	Berge	Hochebene
ESPAÑOL	cabo	isla	isla	lago	montañas	meseta
FRANÇAIS	cap	île	île	lac	montagnes	plateau
PORTUGUÊS	cabo	ilha	ilha	lago	montanhas	planalto

For complete glossary see page *I* • *1*.

Kilometers 0 200 400 600 Km.
Statute Miles 0 200 400 600 Mi.

Scale 1:12,000,000
One centimeter represents 120 kilometers.
One inch represents approximately 190 miles.
Miller Oblated Stereographic Projection

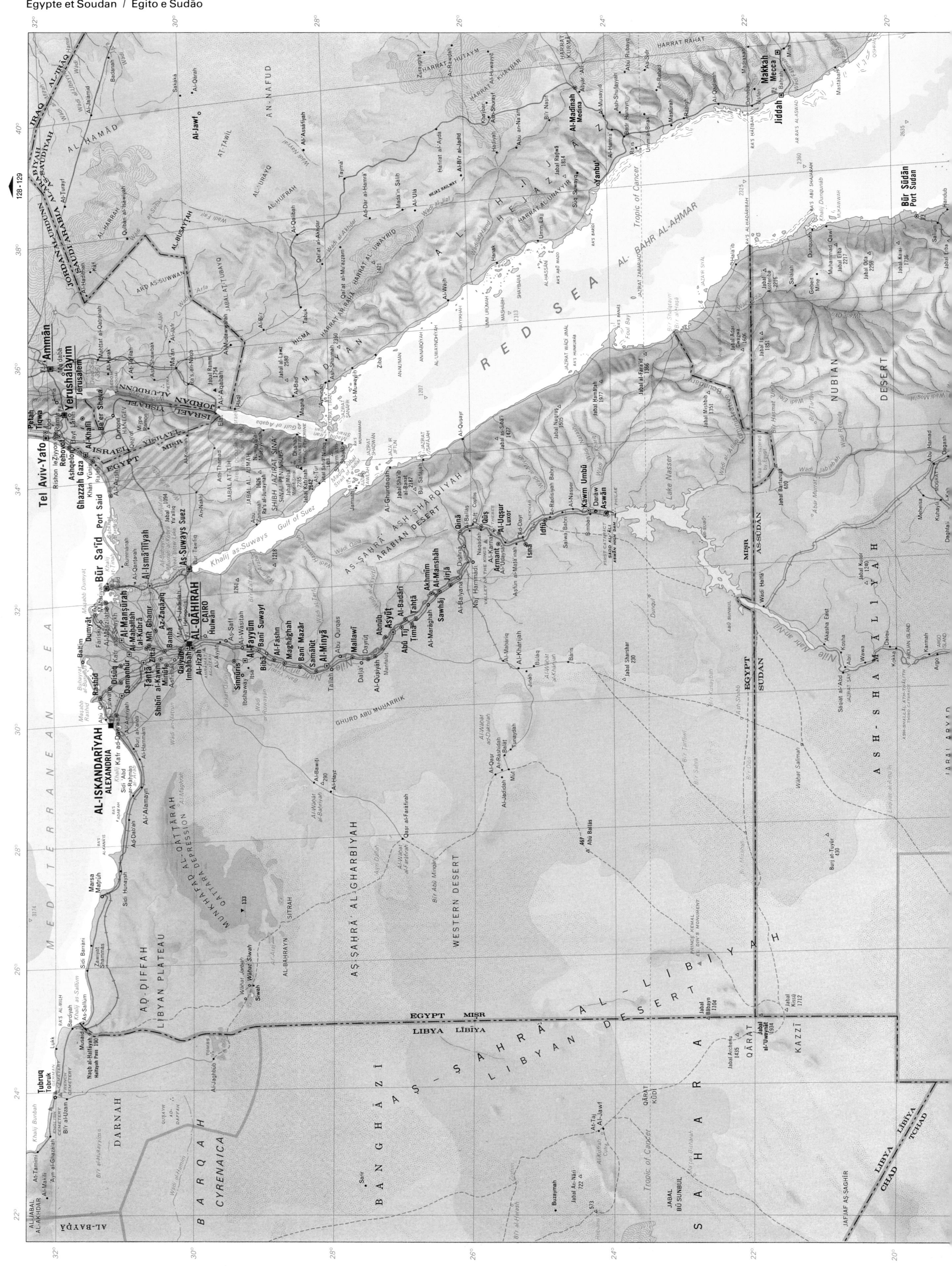
MEDITERRANEAN SEA
RED SEA
AL-BAHR AL-AHMAR
AL-QAHIRAH
CAIRO
AL-ISKANDARIYAH
ALEXANDRIA
Bur Sa'id
Port Said
As-Suways Suez
Aswan
Luxor
Tel Aviv-Yafo
Yerushalayim
Jerusalem
Amman
Makkah
Mecca
Jiddah
Al-Madinah
Medina
Bur Sudan
Port Sudan
Tubruq
Tobruk
WESTERN DESERT
LIBYAN DESERT
ARABIAN DESERT
NUBIAN DESERT
LIBYAN PLATEAU
QATTARA DEPRESSION
CYRENAICA
EGYPT
MISR
LIBYA
SUDAN
AS-SUDAN
ISRAEL
JORDAN
SAUDI ARABIA
Lake Nasser
Nile
Gulf of Suez
Gulf of Aqaba
Tropic of Cancer
LIBYA
TCHAD
CHAD

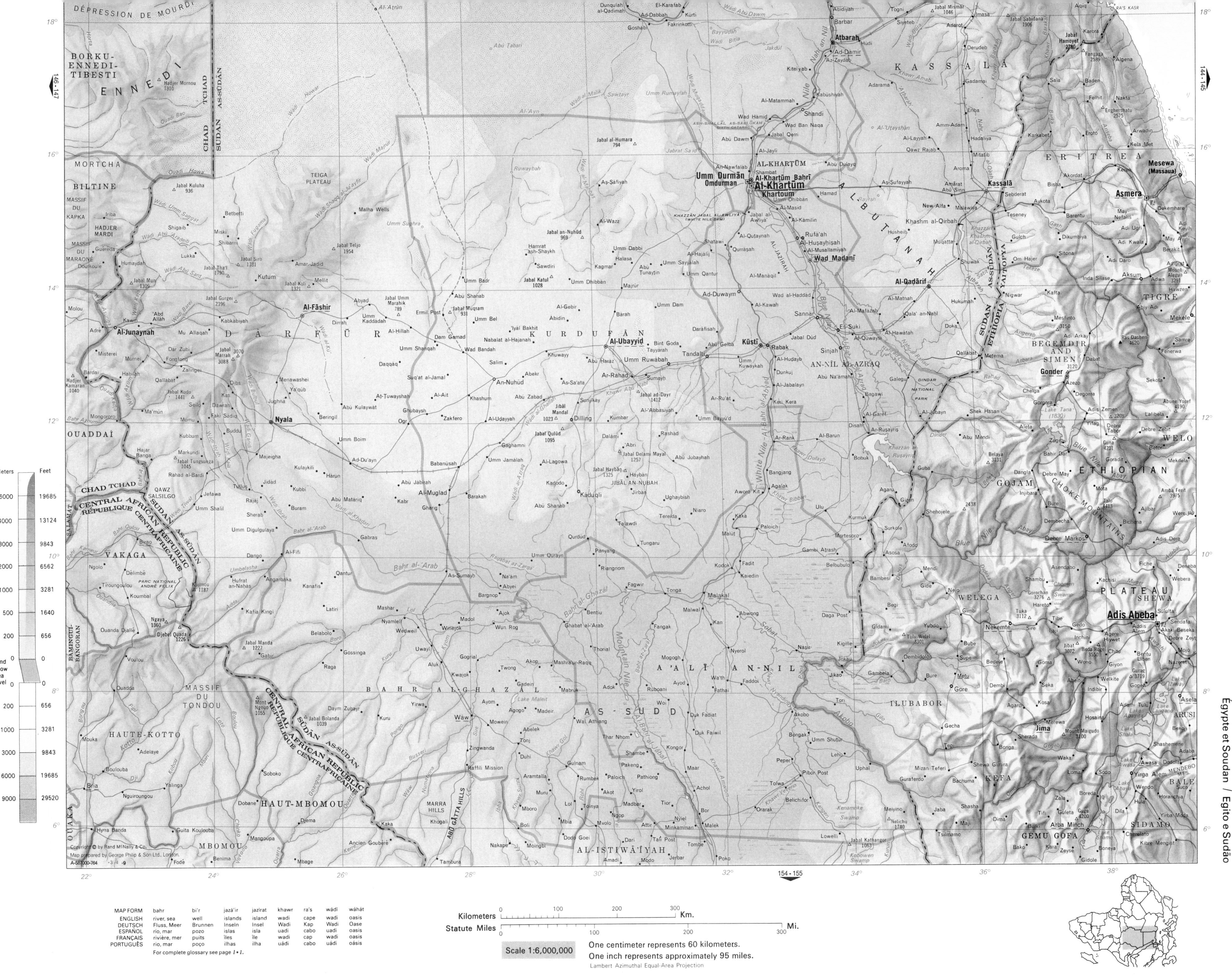

MAP FORM	bahr	bi'r	jazā'ir	jazīrat	khawr	ra's	wādī	wāhāt
ENGLISH	river, sea	well	islands	island	wadi	cape	wadi	oasis
DEUTSCH	Fluss, Meer	Brunnen	Inseln	Insel	Wadi	Kap	Wadi	Oase
ESPAÑOL	río, mar	pozo	islas	isla	uadi	cabo	uadi	oasis
FRANÇAIS	rivière, mer	puits	îles	île	wadi	cap	wadi	oasis
PORTUGUÊS	rio, mar	poço	ilhas	ilha	uádi	cabo	uádi	oásis

For complete glossary see page I • 1.

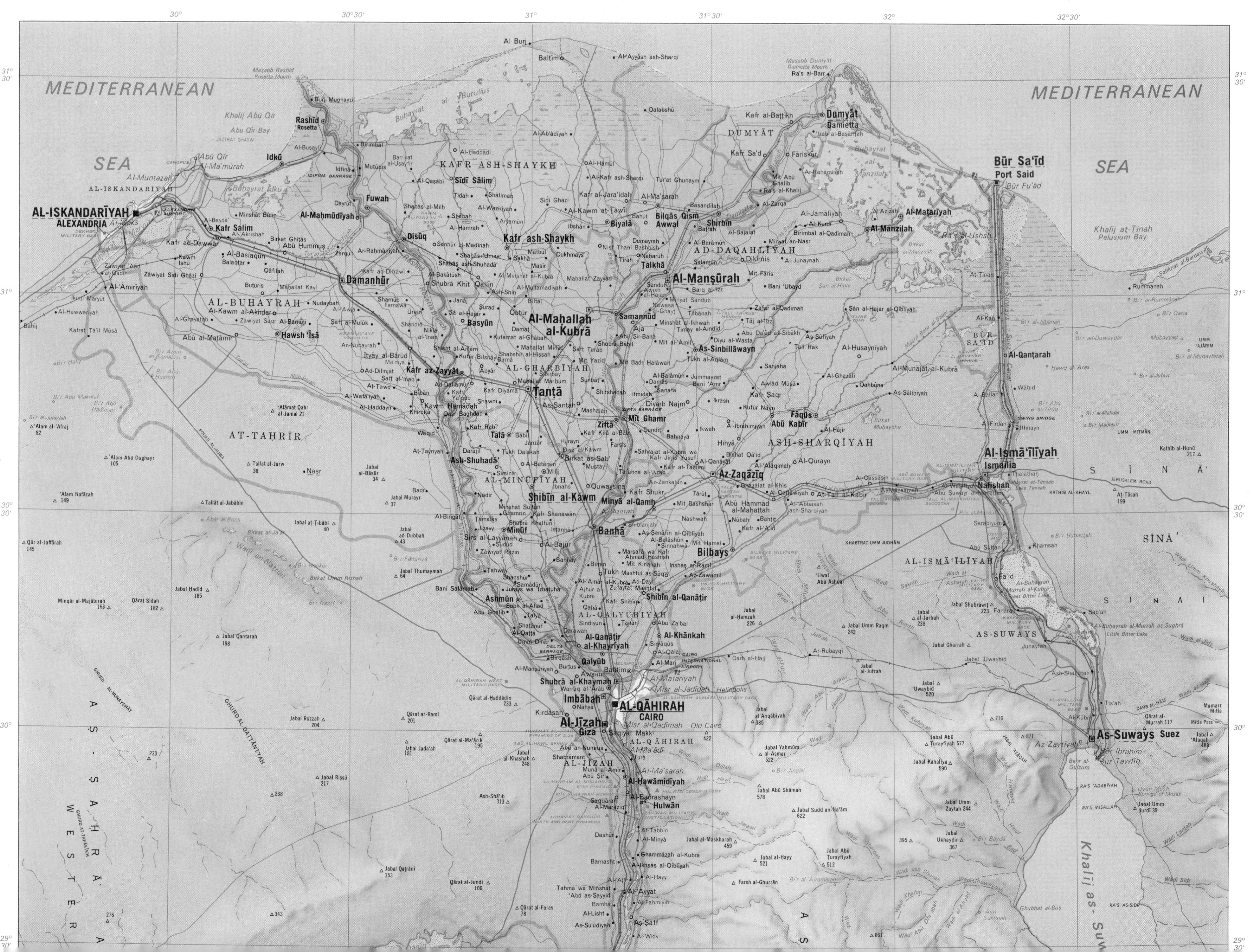
MEDITERRANEAN
SEA
MEDITERRANEAN
SEA
Khalīj at-Tīnah
Pelusium Bay
Būr Sa'īd
Port Said
Būr Fu'ād
Al-Ismā'īlīyah
Ismailia
As-Suways Suez
Khalīj as-Suw
SĪNĀ'
S Ī N Ā'
S I N A I
AS-SUWAYS
AL-ISMĀ'ĪLĪYAH
Dumyāt
Damietta
DUMYĀT
Al-Manṣūrah
AD-DAQAHLĪYAH
Az-Zaqāzīq
ASH-SHARQĪYAH
Al-Maḥallah al-Kubrā
Ṭanṭā
AL-GHARBĪYAH
Kafr ash-Shaykh
KAFR ASH-SHAYKH
Shibīn al-Kawm
AL-MINŪFĪYAH
Banhā
AL-QALYŪBĪYAH
AL-QĀHIRAH
CAIRO
AL-QĀHIRAH
Al-Jīzah
Giza
AL-JĪZAH
Ḥulwān
Damanhūr
AL-BUḤAYRAH
Rashīd
Rosetta
AL-ISKANDARĪYAH
ALEXANDRIA
AL-ISKANDARĪYAH
AT-TAḤRĪR
AṢ-ṢAḤRĀ'
WESTER

Gulf of Suez
JABAL AL-JALĀLAT AL-QIBLĪYAH
JABAL AL-JALĀLAT AL-BAḤRĪYAH
ARABIAN DESERT
AṢ-ṢAḤRĀ' ASH-SHARQĪYAH
AL-BAḤR AL-AḤMAR
MARSĀ MAṬRŪḤ
BANĪ SUWAYF
AL-MINYĀ
ASYŪṬ
GHURD ABŪ MUḤARRIK
Al-Fayyūm
Banī Suwayf
Bibā
Al-Fashn
Maghāghah
Banī Mazār
Samālūṭ
Al-Minyā
Al-Madīnah al-Fikrīyah
Mallawī
Dayr Mawās
Dayrūṭ
Al-Qūṣīyah
Manfalūṭ
Abnūb
Asyūṭ
Nile
Kilometers
Statute Miles
Km.
Mi.
Scale 1:1,000,000
One centimeter represents 10 kilometers.
One inch represents approximately 16 miles.
Lambert Conformal Conic Projection
MAP FORM bi'r birkat buḥayrat ghurd jabal ra's wādī
ENGLISH well lake lake dunes mountain cape wadi
DEUTSCH Brunnen See See Dünen Berg Kap Wadi
ESPAÑOL pozo lago lago dunas montaña cabo uadi
FRANÇAIS puits lac lac dunes montagne cap wadi
PORTUGUÊS poço lago lago dunas montanha cabo uádi
For complete glossary see page I·1.
For Al-Qāhirah (Cairo) metropolitan map, see page 273.
Copyright © by Rand McNally & Co.
Map prepared by George Philip & Son Ltd., London.

128-129

140-141

INDIAN OCEAN
Equator
Muqdisho
Mogadishu
Kismayu
Hargeysa
Harer
Adis Abeba
Nairobi
ETHIOPIA
SOMALIA
KENYA
UGANDA
TANZANIA
MUDUGH
HARERGE
BALE
SIDAMO
SHEWA
WELEGA
KEFA
GEMU GOFA
ILUBABOR
HIRAN
UPPER JUBA
LOWER JUBA
BENADIR
NORTH EASTERN
COAST
RIFT VALLEY
WESTERN
NYANZA
CENTRAL
EASTERN
Kilometers
Statute Miles
Km.
Mi.
Scale 1:6,000,000
One centimeter represents 60 kilometers.
One inch represents approximately 95 miles.
Lambert Azimuthal Equal-Area Projection
Copyright © by Rand McNally & Co.
Map prepared by George Philip & Son Ltd, London.
A-587100-764
154 - 155
MAP FORM / ENGLISH / DEUTSCH / ESPAÑOL / FRANÇAIS / PORTUGUÊS
bi'r / well / Brunnen / pozo / puits / poço
hills / hills / Hügel / colinas / collines / colinas
jabal / mountain / Berg / montaña / montagne / montanha
lake / lake / See / lago / lac / lago
mount / mount / Berg / monte / mont / montanha
plain / plain / Ebene / llano / plaine / planície
ras, ra's / cape / Kap / cabo / cap / cabo
wādi / wadi / Wadi / uadi / wadi / uádi
For complete glossary see page I • 1.
Feet
Meters
Land Below Sea Level

MEDITERRANEAN SEA
Tarābulus
Tripoli
Banghāzī
Ajdābiyah
Darnah
Tubruq
Tobruk
Misrātah
Surt
Sabhah
Ghudāmis
Khalīj Surt
Gulf of Sidra
BARQAH
CYRENAICA
TARĀBULUS
TRIPOLITANIA
FEZZAN
AL-HARŪJ AL-ASWAD
SARĪR CALANSCIO
SARĪR NERASTRO
REBIANA SAND SEA
AS-SAHRĀ' AL-LĪBĪYAH
LIBYAN DESERT
TIBESTI
TÉNÉRÉ DU TAFASSASSET
PLATEAU DU DJADO
PLATEAU DE MANGUENI
TASSILI N'AJJER
TAMANRASSET
GRAND ERG ORIENTAL
AL-HAMMĀDAH AL-HAMRĀ'
EGYPT MISR
LIBYA LĪBIYĀ
SUDAN
LIBYA LĪBIYĀ
CHAD TCHAD
LIBYA LĪBIYĀ
NIGER
LIBYA LĪBIYĀ
ALGERIA ALGÉRIE
TUNISIA TUNISIE
ALGERIA ALGÉRIE
NIGER
Tropic of Cancer
Al-Jaghbūb
Al-Kufrah
As-Sallūm
Ghāt
Murzuq
Awbārī
Hūn
Waddān
Zarzis
Djanet

148 · 149

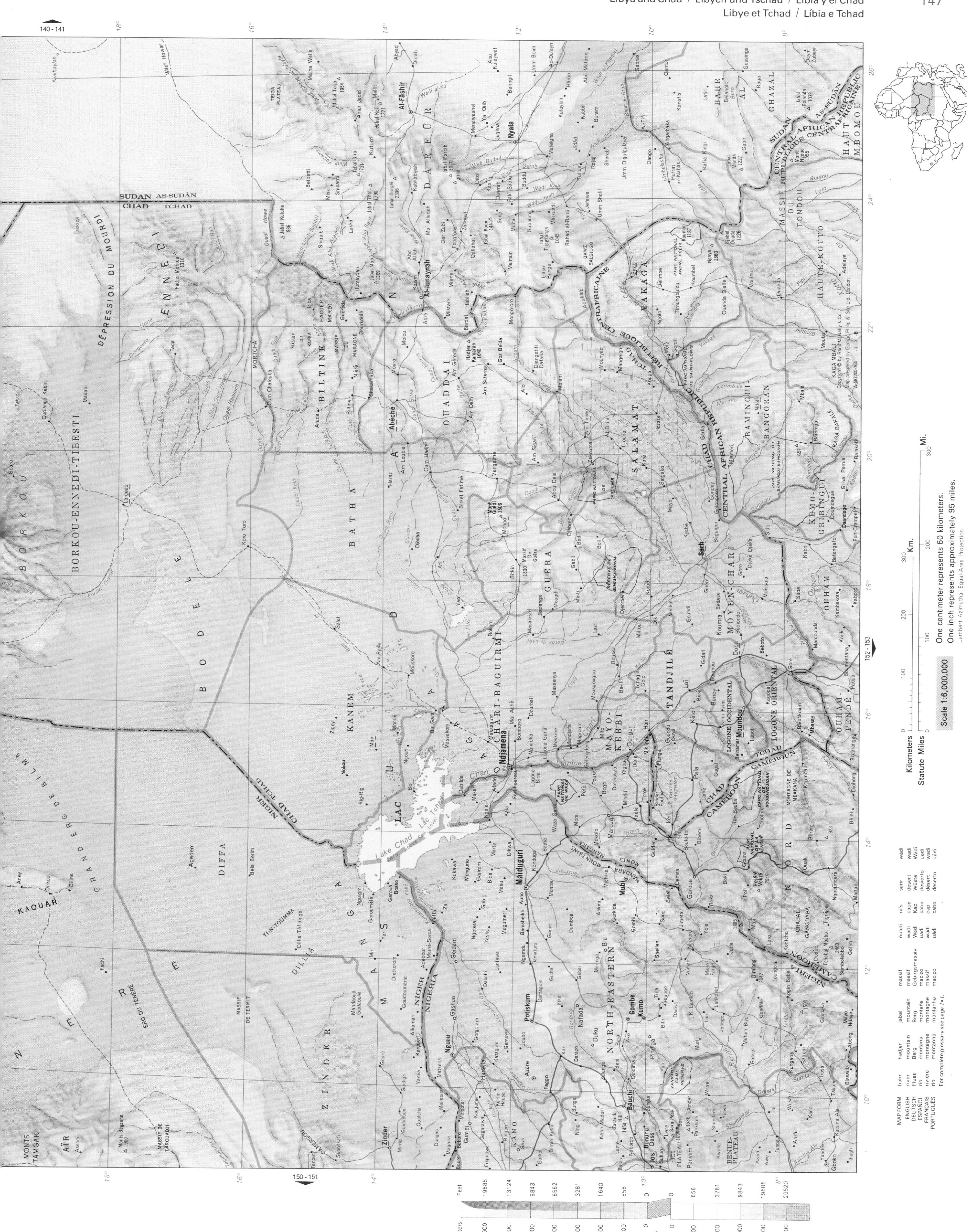
Scale 1:6,000,000
One centimeter represents 60 kilometers.
One inch represents approximately 95 miles.
Lambert Azimuthal Equal-Area Projection
Kilometers
Statute Miles
Meters
Feet
Land Below Sea Level
MAP FORM ENGLISH DEUTSCH ESPAÑOL FRANÇAIS PORTUGUÊS
bahr river Fluss rio rivière rio
hadjer mountain Berg montaña montagne montanha
jabal mountain Berg montaña montagne montanha
massif massif Gebirgsmassiv macizo massif maciço
ouadi wadi Wadi uadi wadi uádi
ra's cape Kap cabo cap cabo
sarir desert Wüste desierto désert deserto
wādi wadi Wadi uadi wadi uádi
For complete glossary see page I • 1.
140 - 141
150 - 151
152 - 153

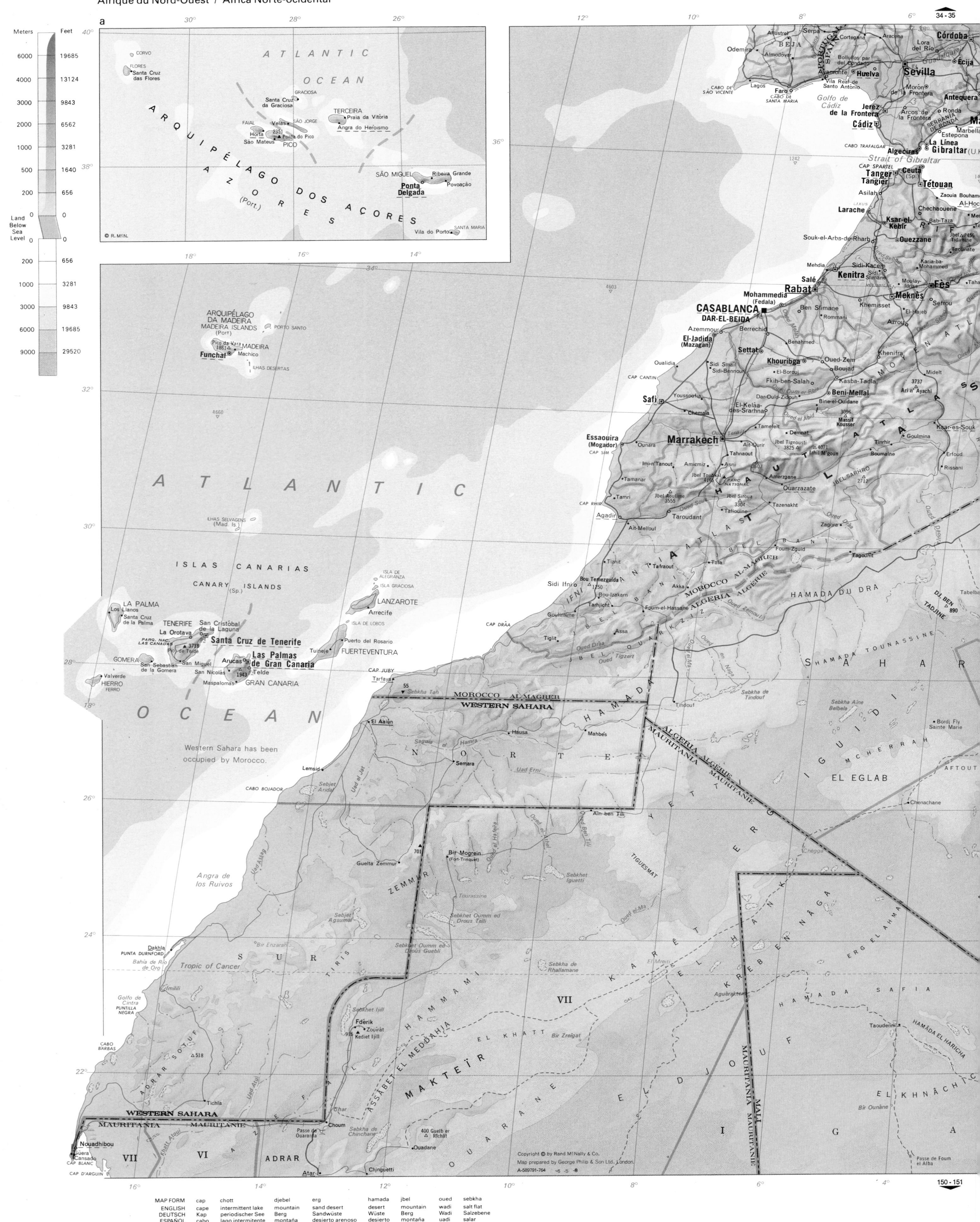

MAP FORM	cap	chott	djebel	erg	hamada	jbel	oued	sebkha
ENGLISH	cape	intermittent lake	mountain	sand desert	desert	mountain	wadi	salt flat
DEUTSCH	Kap	periodischer See	Berg	Sandwüste	Wüste	Berg	Wadi	Salzebene
ESPAÑOL	cabo	lago intermitente	montaña	desierto arenoso	desierto	montaña	uadi	salar
FRANÇAIS	cap	lac périodique	montagne	désert de sable	désert	montagne	wadi	saline
PORTUGUÊS	cabo	lago intermitente	montanha	deserto arenoso	deserto	montanha	uádi	salina

For complete glossary see page 1•1.

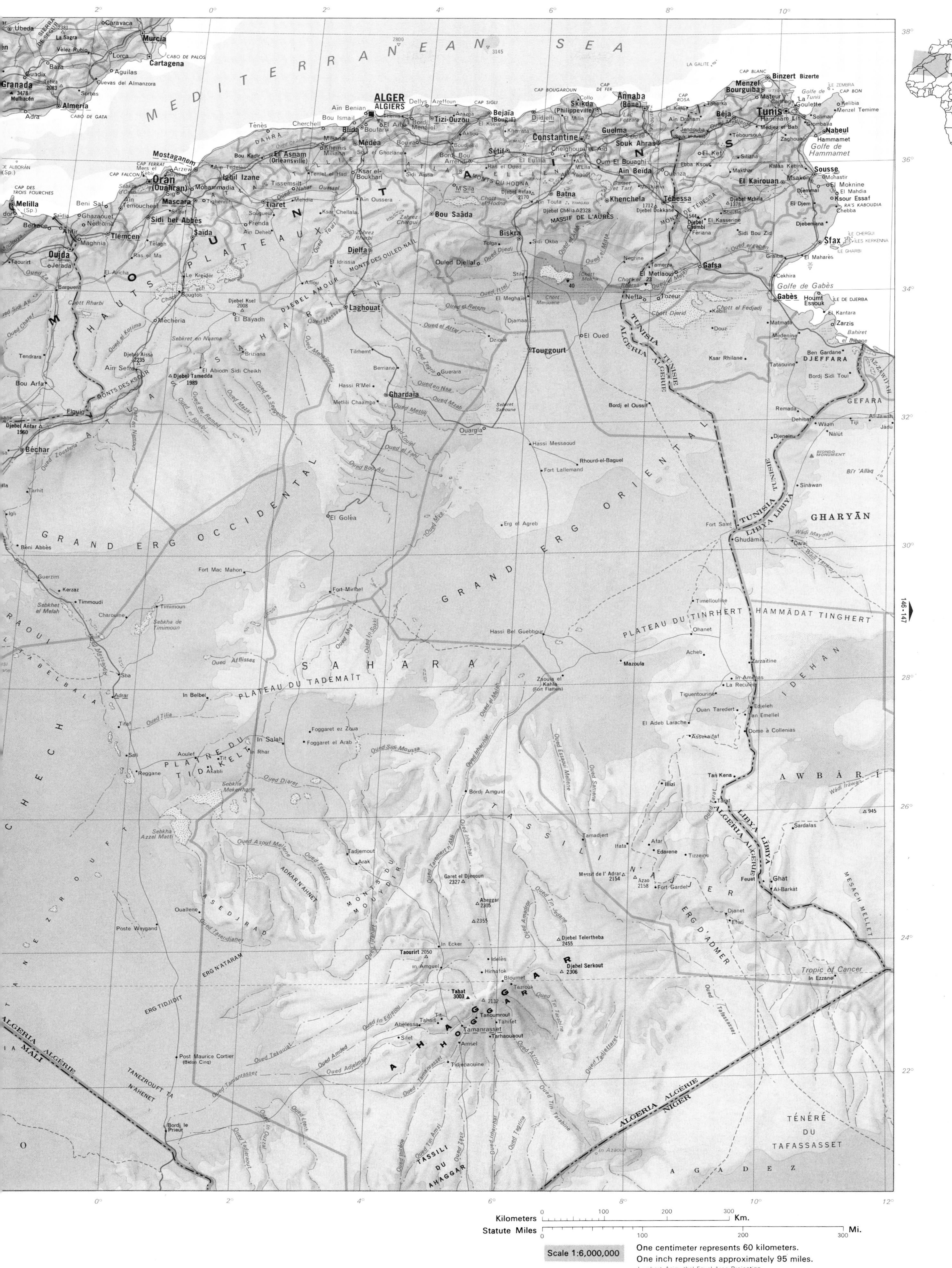
MEDITERRANEAN SEA
ALGER
ALGIERS
Oran
(Ouahran)
Constantine
Tunis
Sfax
Sousse
Gabès
Biskra
Touggourt
Ghardaïa
Ouargla
Laghouat
Djelfa
Tlemcen
Oujda
Béchar
Murcia
Cartagena
Granada
Almería
Melilla
HAUTS PLATEAUX
ATLAS SAHARIEN
GRAND ERG OCCIDENTAL
GRAND ERG ORIENTAL
PLATEAU DU TINRHERT
HAMMĀDAT TINGHERT
PLATEAU DU TADEMAÏT
SAHARA
TASSILI N'AJJER
AHAGGAR
Tamanrasset
In Salah
TANEZROUFT
ERG D'ADMER
TÉNÉRÉ DU TAFASSASSET
GHARYĀN
AWBĀRĪ
Tropic of Cancer
ALGERIA ALGÉRIE
TUNISIA TUNISIE
LIBYA LIBYE
ALGERIA ALGÉRIE MALI
ALGERIA ALGÉRIE NIGER
146-147
Kilometers
Km.
Statute Miles
Mi.
Scale 1:6,000,000
One centimeter represents 60 kilometers.
One inch represents approximately 95 miles.
Lambert Azimuthal Equal-Area Projection

MAP FORM	coast	dhar	game reserve	ilha	lac	monts	mountains	vallée
ENGLISH	coast	escarpment	game reserve	island	lake	mountains	mountains	valley
DEUTSCH	Küste	Landstufe	Wildpark	Insel	See	Berge	Berge	Tal
ESPAÑOL	costa	escarpa	vedado de caza	isla	lago	montes	montañas	valle
FRANÇAIS	côte	escarpement	réserve à gibier	île	lac	monts	montagnes	vallée
PORTUGUÊS	costa	escarpa	reserva de caça	ilha	lago	montes	montanhas	vale

For complete glossary see page I • 1.
For Lagos metropolitan map, see page 273

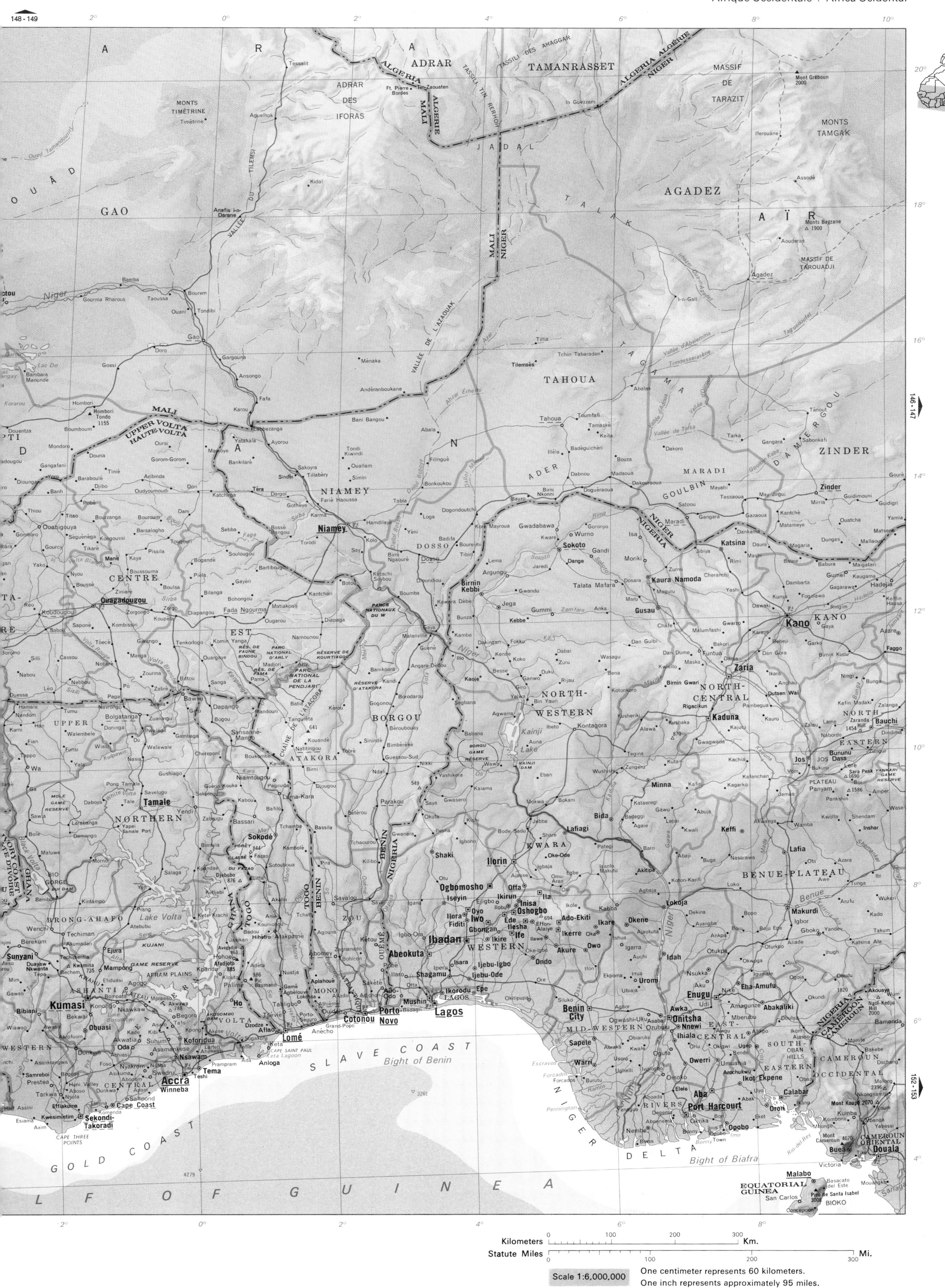
148 - 149
146 - 147
152 - 153
ADRAR
TAMANRASSET
ALGERIA
ALGÉRIE
MALI
NIGER
ADRAR DES IFORAS
MONTS TIMÉTRINE
MASSIF DE TARAZIT
MONTS TAMGAK
Mont Gréboun 2000
AGADEZ
A Ï R
Monts Bagzane 1900
MASSIF DE TAROUADJI
Agadez
GAO
Gao
Tessalit
Kidal
Bourem
Tombouctou
Niger
VALLÉE DE L'AZAOUAK
TAHOUA
Tahoua
ZINDER
Zinder
MARADI
Maradi
NIAMEY
Niamey
DOSSO
Dosso
UPPER VOLTA
HAUTE-VOLTA
CENTRE
Ouagadougou
EST
Fada Ngourma
Sokoto
Kaura Namoda
Gusau
Katsina
KANO
Kano
Zaria
NORTH-CENTRAL
Kaduna
NORTH-WESTERN
NORTH EASTERN
Bauchi
Jos
BORGOU
Kainji Lake
KWARA
Ilorin
BENUE-PLATEAU
Makurdi
Lokoja
Minna
Bida
Lafiagi
Ogbomosho
Oshogbo
Ibadan
WESTERN
Abeokuta
Lagos
Porto-Novo
Cotonou
Lomé
Accra
Tema
Kumasi
ASHANTI
BRONG-AHAFO
Sunyani
NORTHERN
Tamale
UPPER
VOLTA
Lake Volta
Koforidua
Ho
Sekondi-Takoradi
Cape Coast
Winneba
CAPE THREE POINTS
GHANA
TOGO
BENIN
NIGERIA
IVORY COAST
CÔTE D'IVOIRE
Benin City
MID-WESTERN
Sapele
Warri
Onitsha
Enugu
EAST-CENTRAL
Owerri
Aba
Port Harcourt
RIVERS
SOUTH-EASTERN
Calabar
Abakaliki
CAMEROUN
CAMEROON
Mont Koupé 2070
Mont Cameroun 4070
Buea
Douala
Victoria
Malabo
EQUATORIAL GUINEA
BIOKO
Pico de Santa Isabel 3008
San Carlos
NIGER DELTA
Bight of Biafra
SLAVE COAST
Bight of Benin
GOLD COAST
GULF OF GUINEA
Kilometers 0 100 200 300 Km.
Statute Miles 0 100 200 300 Mi.
Scale 1:6,000,000
One centimeter represents 60 kilometers.
One inch represents approximately 95 miles.
Lambert Azimuthal Equal-Area Projection

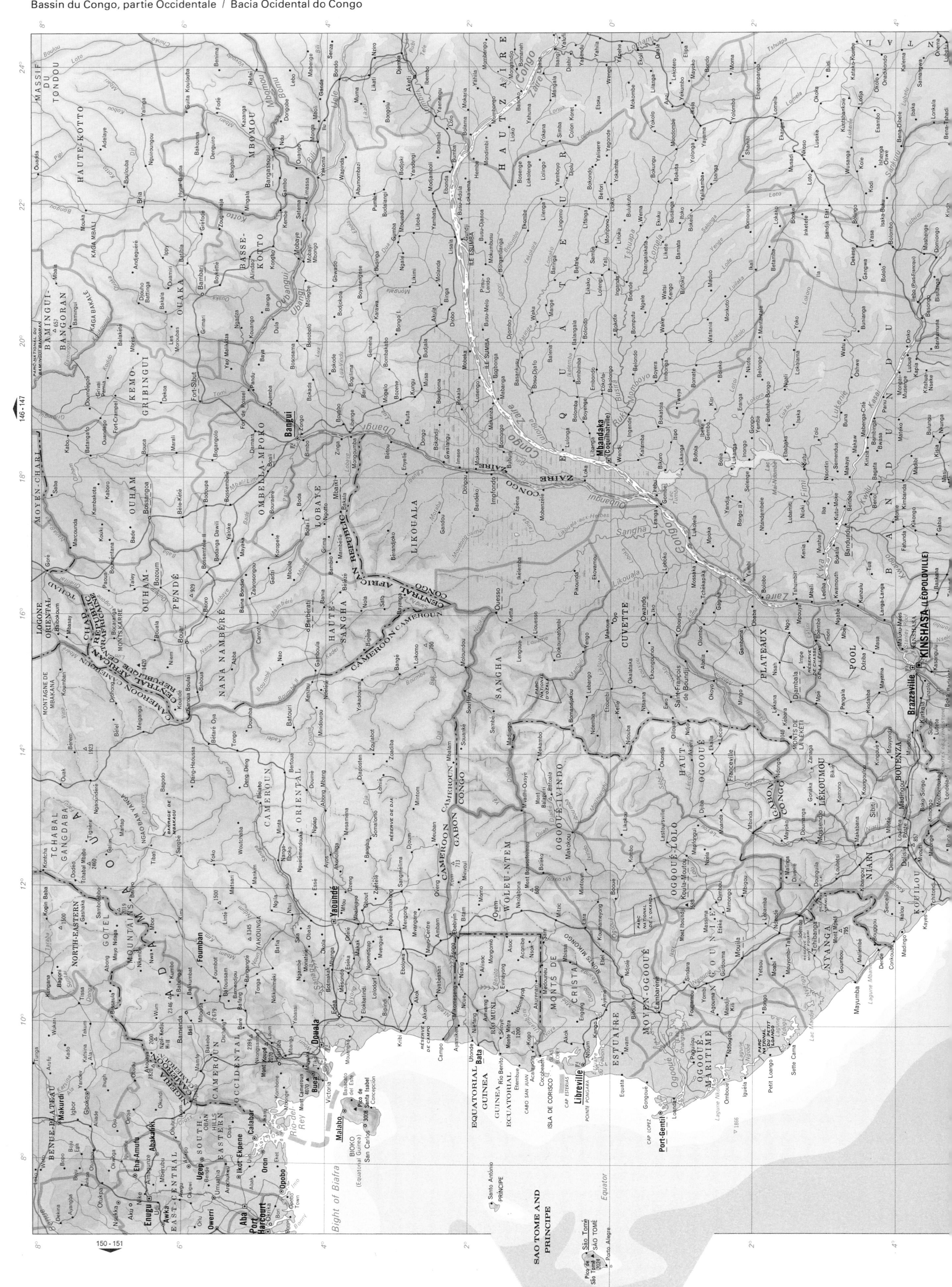
146-147
150-151
KINSHASA (LÉOPOLDVILLE)
Brazzaville
Bangui
Yaoundé
Douala
Libreville
Malabo
Port-Gentil
Mbandaka (Coquilhatville)
Bight of Biafra
Equator
SAO TOME AND PRINCIPE
EQUATORIAL GUINEA
CENTRAL AFRICAN REPUBLIC
CAMEROON
CONGO
ZAIRE
GABON

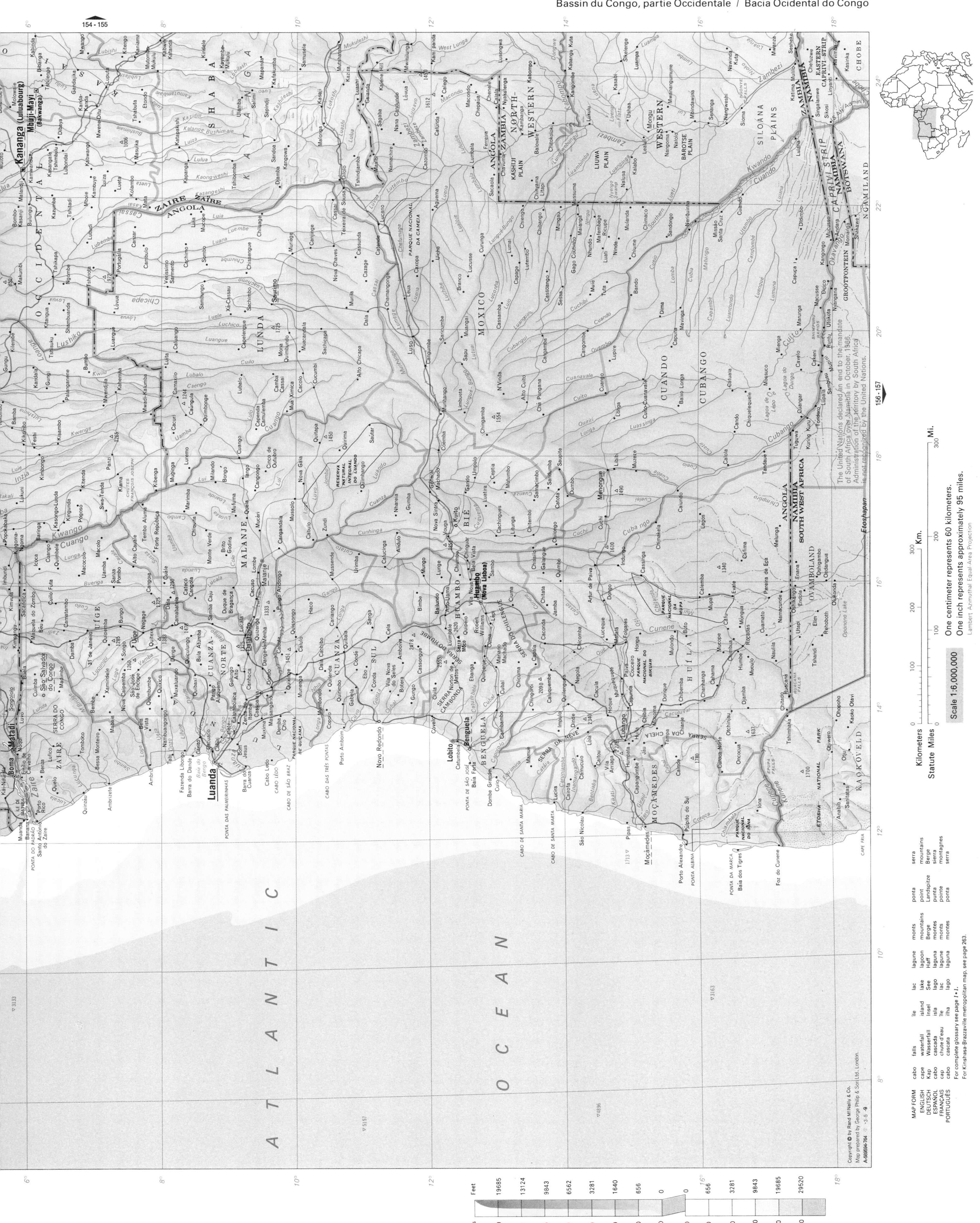
154 - 155
156 - 157
ATLANTIC OCEAN
ANGOLA
ZAIRE
ZAMBIA
NAMIBIA
SOUTH WEST AFRICA
BOTSWANA
CAPRIVI STRIP
Luanda
Lobito
Benguela
Huambo (Nova Lisboa)
Moçâmedes
Matadi
Boma
Kananga (Luluabourg)
Mbuji-Mayi (Bakwanga)
The United Nations declared an end to the mandate of South Africa over Namibia in October, 1966. Administration of the territory by South Africa is not recognized by the United Nations.
Scale 1:6,000,000
One centimeter represents 60 kilometers.
One inch represents approximately 95 miles.
Lambert Azimuthal Equal-Area Projection
Kilometers
Statute Miles
MAP FORM cabo falls île lac lagune monts ponta serra
ENGLISH cape waterfall island lake lagoon mountains point mountains
DEUTSCH Kap Wasserfall Insel See Haff Berge Landspitze Berge
ESPAÑOL cabo cascada isla lago laguna montes punta sierra
FRANÇAIS cap chute d'eau île lac lagune monts pointe montagnes
PORTUGUÊS cabo cascata ilha lago laguna montes ponta serra
For complete glossary see page I•1.
For Kinshasa-Brazzaville metropolitan map, see page 263.
Copyright © by Rand McNally & Co.
Map prepared by George Philip & Son Ltd. London.
Meters
Feet
Land Below Sea Level

ENGLISH falls game reserve island lake mountains national park plain swamp
DEUTSCH Wasserfall Wildreservat Insel See Berge Nationalpark Ebene Sumpf
ESPAÑOL cascada vedado de caza isla lago montañas parque nacional llano pantano
FRANÇAIS chute d'eau réserve à gibier île lac montagnes parc national plaine marais
PORTUGUÊS cascata reserva de caça ilha lago montanhas parque nacional planície pântano
For complete glossary see page I•1.
Kilometers 0 100 200 300 Km.
Statute Miles 0 100 200 300 Mi.
Scale 1:6,000,000
One centimeter represents 60 kilometers.
One inch represents approximately 95 miles.
Lambert Azimuthal Equal-Area Projection
140-141
144-145
152-153
INDIAN OCEAN
SOMALIA
KENYA
UGANDA
TANZANIA
SUDAN
ETHIOPIA
RWANDA
BURUNDI
CENTRAL AFRICAN REP.
ZAIRE
HAUT-ZAÏRE
KASAI-ORIENTAL
Nairobi
Mombasa
Dar-es-Salaam
Zanzibar
Kampala
Kigali
Bujumbura
Kisangani (Stanleyville)
Kalemie (Albertville)
Dodoma
Tabora
Mwanza
Arusha
Moshi
Lake Victoria
Lake Tanganyika
Lake Rudolf
Lake Albert
Lake Edward
KILIMANJARO
SERENGETI PLAIN
MASAI STEPPE
CHALBI DESERT
Equator

MOZAMBIQUE
CHANNEL
CABO DELGADO
NIASSA
ZAMBÉZIA
MANICA
MASHONALAND NORTH
MASHONALAND SOUTH
MIDLANDS
MATABELELAND NORTH
MATABELELAND SOUTH
VICTORIA
COPPERBELT
KATANGA
CENTRAL
SOUTHERN
WESTERN
NORTH WESTERN
NORTHERN
EASTERN
ZAMBIA
TANZANIA
MOZAMBIQUE
MALAWI
ZIMBABWE
BOTSWANA
NAMIBIA
SOUTH AFRICA
ZAÏRE
Lake Malawi
Lake Kariba
Zambezi
Lubumbashi (Élisabethville)
Likasi (Jadotville)
Kolwezi
Kamina
Lusaka
Ndola
Kitwe
Livingstone
Salisbury
Bulawayo
Gwelo
Que Que
Umtali
Beira
Blantyre
Zomba
Lilongwe
Tete
Quelimane
Moçambique
Nampula
Mtwara
Lindi
Francistown
Wankie
156-157
Feet
Meters
Land Below Sea Level
Copyright © by Rand McNally & Co.
Map prepared by George Philip & Son Ltd, London.

152 - 153
ATLANTIC
OCEAN
KAOKOVELD
OVAMBOLAND
ETOSHA NATIONAL PARK
TSUMEB
GROOTFONTEIN
CUANDO-CUBANGO
ANGOLA
NAMIBIA
CAPRIVI STRIP
CHOBE NATIONAL PARK
Livingstone
OUTJO
OTJIWARONGO
OMARURU
OKAHANDJA
GOBABIS
DAMARLAND
WINDHOEK
Windhoek
Swakopmund
Walvisbaai
WALVIS BAY
REHOBOTH
GIBEON
MALTAHOHE
GREAT NAMALAND
BETHANIEN
KEETMANSHOOP
Keetmanshoop
LÜDERITZ
Lüderitz
WARMBAD
LITTLE NAMALAND
NAMIB DESERT
SOUTH WEST AFRICA
BOTSWANA
NGAMILAND
Okavango Swamp
Makgadikgadi Pans
GHANZI
KALAHARI DESERT
KGALAGADI
KWENENG
NGWAKETS
CENTRAL
Serowe
Molepolole
Gaborone
Kanye
Mafeking
Tropic of Capricorn
BECHUANALAND
GRIQUALAND WEST
Upington
Kimberley
Bloemfontein
ORANGE FREE STATE
ORANJE-VRYSTAAT
Welkom
Klerksdorp
Potchefstroom
BUSHMAN LAND
Port Nolloth
Springbok
CAPE
KAAP
GREAT KARROO
Beaufort West
Cape Town
Kaapstad
Worcester
Paarl
Stellenbosch
Oudtshoorn
George
Mosselbaai
Uitenhage
Port Elizabeth
Grahamstown
CAPE OF GOOD HOPE
CAPE AGULHAS
The United Nations declared an end to the mandate of South Africa over Namibia in October, 1966. Administration of the territory by South Africa is not recognized by the United Nations.
Meters
Feet
Land Below Sea Level
Copyright © by Rand McNally & Co.
Map prepared by George Philip & Son Ltd., London.
MAP FORM | bay | berg, berge | cape | game reserve | ilha | lake | national park
ENGLISH | bay | mountain, mountains | cape | game reserve | island | lake | national park
DEUTSCH | Bucht | Berg, Berge | Kap | Wildpark | Insel | See | Nationalpark
ESPAÑOL | bahía | montaña, montañas | cabo | vedado de caza | isla | lago | parque nacional
FRANÇAIS | baie | montagne, montagnes | cap | réserve à gibier | île | lac | parc national
PORTUGUÊS | baía | montanha, montanhas | cabo | reserva de caça | ilha | lago | parque nacional
For complete glossary see page I • 1.
Kilometers 0 100 200 300 Km.
Statute Miles 0 100 200 300 Mi.
Scale 1:6,000,000
One centimeter represents 60 kilometers.
One inch represents approximately 95 miles.
Lambert Azimuthal Equal-Area Projection

154 - 155
a
INDIAN OCEAN
GRANDE COMORE
Moroni
COMOROS
COMORES
MAYOTTE (Fr.)
Dzaoudzi
MOZAMBIQUE CHANNEL
b
MOZAMBIQUE CHANNEL
Salisbury
MASHONALAND SOUTH
Que Que
MIDLANDS
Gwelo
Bulawayo
MATABELELAND SOUTH
VICTORIA
Umtali
MANICALAND
MANICA E SOFALA
Beira
Quelimane
ZAMBEZIA
Chinde
ZIMBABWE
MOZAMBIQUE
INHAMBANE
GAZA
Inhambane
Pietersburg
TRANSVAAL
Pretoria
Maputo
(Lourenço Marques)
Mbabane
SWAZILAND
ZULULAND
NATAL
Ladysmith
Pietermaritzburg
Durban
Bethlehem
TRANSKEI
Umtata
London
Londen
INDIAN
OCEAN
Diégo-Suarez
MASSIF DU TSARATANANA
Majunga
Tamatave
Antananarivo
Antsirabe
Fianarantsoa
Tuléar
Fort-Dauphin
MADAGASCAR
MADAGASIKARA
INDIAN
OCEAN
Tropic of Capricorn
c
INDIAN
MAURITIUS
Port Louis
Rose Hill
Curepipe
Mahébourg
Saint-Denis
RÉUNION
MASCARENE ISLANDS
OCEAN
© R. McN.

MAP FORM	bay	berge	cape	dam	game reserve	national park	pass	point
ENGLISH	bay	mountains	cape	dam	game reserve	national park	pass	point
DEUTSCH	Bucht	Berge	Kap	Damm	Wildpark	Nationalpark	Pass	Landspitze
ESPAÑOL	bahía	montañas	cabo	presa	vedado de caza	parque nacional	paso	punta
FRANÇAIS	baie	montagnes	cap	barrage	réserve à gibier	parc national	col	pointe
PORTUGUÊS	baía	montanhas	cabo	represa	reserva de caça	parque nacional	passo	ponta

For complete glossary see page *I* • *1*.
For Johannesburg metropolitan map, see page 273

INDIAN OCEAN

LESOTHO

SWAZILAND

MOZAMBIQUE

Kilometers 0 50 100 150 Km.

Statute Miles 0 50 100 150 Mi.

Scale 1:3,000,000

One centimeter represents 30 kilometers.
One inch represents approximately 47 miles.
Lambert Conformal Conic Projection

ENGLISH	bay	cape	island	lake	mount	point	range	reef
DEUTSCH	Bucht	Kap	Insel	See	Berg	Landspitze	Gebirge	Riff
ESPAÑOL	bahía	cabo	isla	lago	montaña	punta	cordillera	arrecife
FRANÇAIS	baie	cap	île	lac	mont	pointe	chaîne	récif
PORTUGUÊS	baía	cabo	ilha	lago	montanha	ponta	cordilheira	recife

For complete glossary see page *I • 1*.

Coral Sea
PACIFIC OCEAN
Tasman Sea
Solomon Sea
Gulf of Carpentaria
Arafura Sea
Torres Strait
Bass Strait
NEW GUINEA
PAPUA NEW GUINEA
Port Moresby
SOLOMON ISLANDS
GREAT BARRIER REEF
GREAT DIVIDING RANGE
CAPE YORK PENINSULA
QUEENSLAND
GREAT ARTESIAN BASIN
SIMPSON DESERT
NEW SOUTH WALES
VICTORIA
SOUTH AUSTRALIA
TASMANIA
A.C.T.
Canberra
SYDNEY
MELBOURNE
Brisbane
Adelaide
Hobart
Newcastle
Wollongong
Geelong
Ballarat
Bendigo
Albury
Broken Hill
Mount Isa
Townsville
Cairns
Mackay
Rockhampton
Bundaberg
Toowoomba
Ipswich
Southport
Launceston
Devonport
Burnie
Tropic of Capricorn
Kilometers
Statute Miles
Km.
Mi.
Scale 1:12,000,000
One centimeter represents 120 kilometers.
One inch represents approximately 190 miles.
Lambert Conformal Conic Projection

ENGLISH	bay	cape	creek, cr.	island, i.	lake, l.	mount	point	range
DEUTSCH	Bucht	Kap	Bach	Insel	See	Berg	Landspitze	Gebirge
ESPAÑOL	bahía	cabo	riachuelo	isla	lago	montaña	punta	cordillera
FRANÇAIS	baie	cap	crique	île	lac	mont	pointe	chaîne
PORTUGUÊS	baía	cabo	riacho	ilha	lago	montanha	ponta	cordilheira

For complete glossary see page I • 1.

Scale 1:6,000,000 One centimeter represents 60 kilometers.
One inch represents approximately 95 miles.
Lambert Conformal Conic Projection

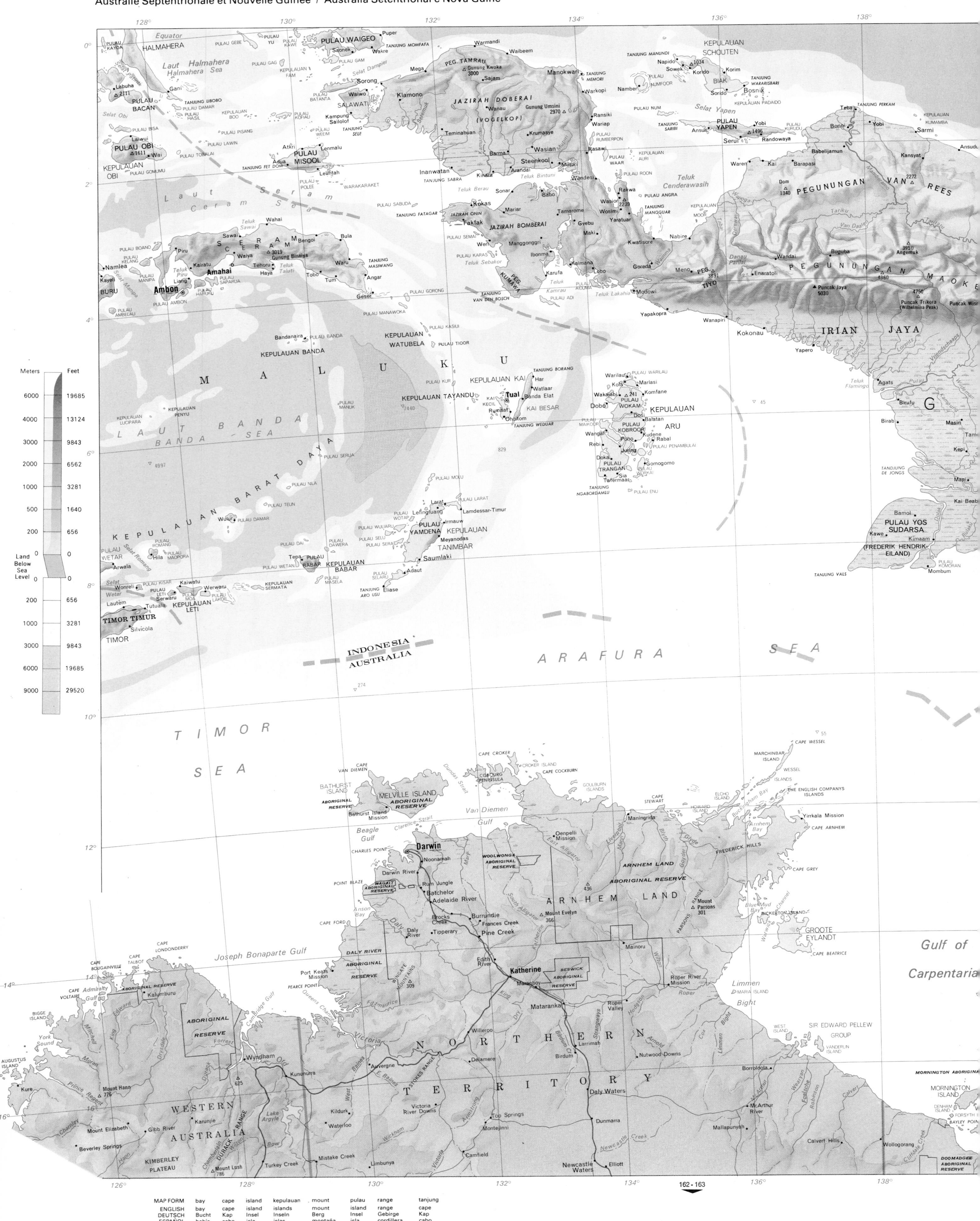

MAP FORM	bay	cape	island	kepulauan	mount	pulau	range	tanjung
ENGLISH	bay	cape	island	islands	mount	island	range	cape
DEUTSCH	Bucht	Kap	Insel	Inseln	Berg	Insel	Gebirge	Kap
ESPAÑOL	bahía	cabo	isla	islas	montaña	isla	cordillera	cabo
FRANÇAIS	baie	cap	île	îles	mont	île	chaîne	cap
PORTUGUÊS	baía	cabo	ilha	ilhas	montanha	ilha	cordilheira	cabo

For complete glossary see page *I • 1*.

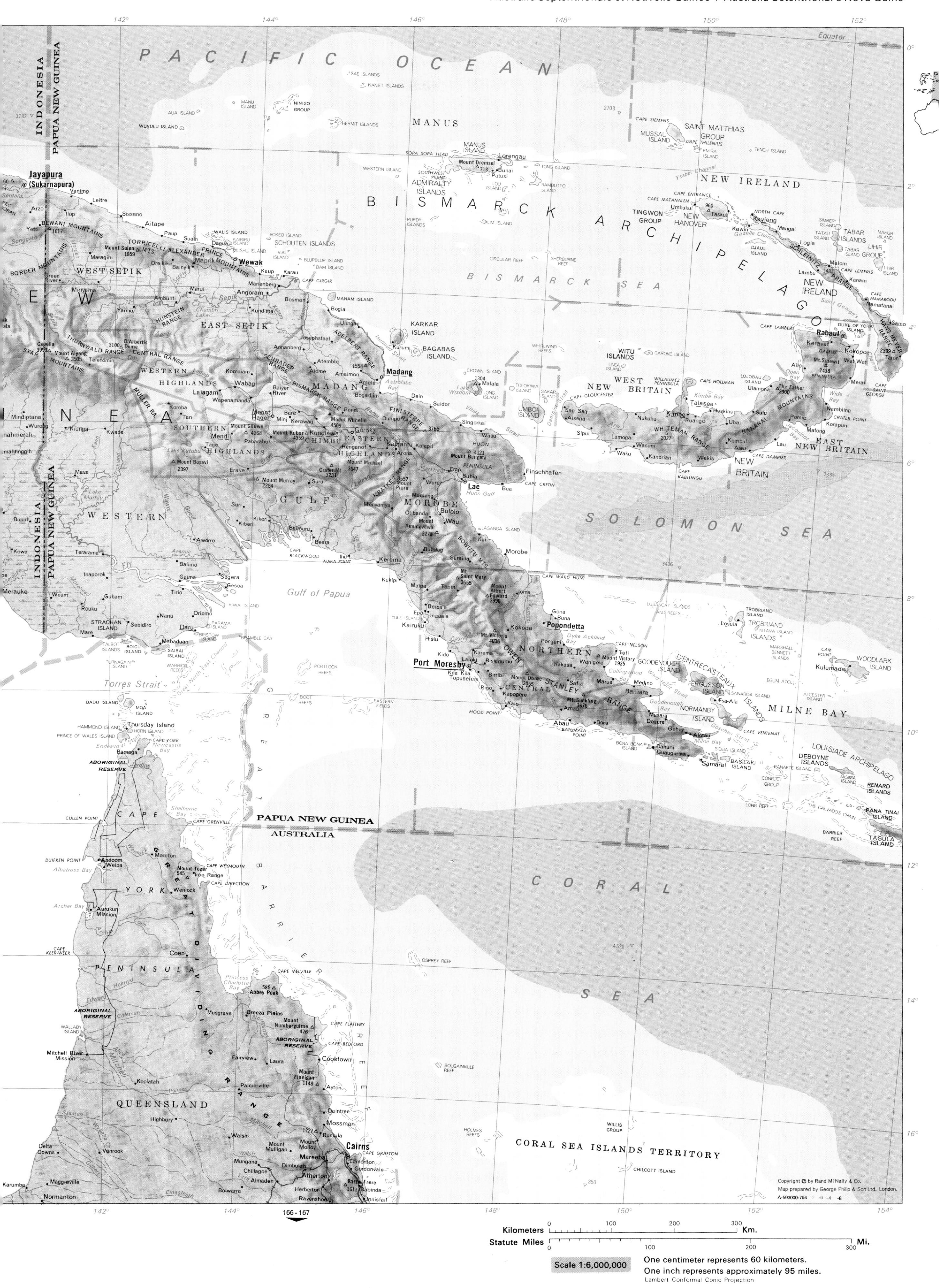

Kilometers 0 100 200 300 Km.
Statute Miles 0 100 200 300 Mi.

Scale 1:6,000,000
One centimeter represents 60 kilometers.
One inch represents approximately 95 miles.
Lambert Conformal Conic Projection

164-165
162-163

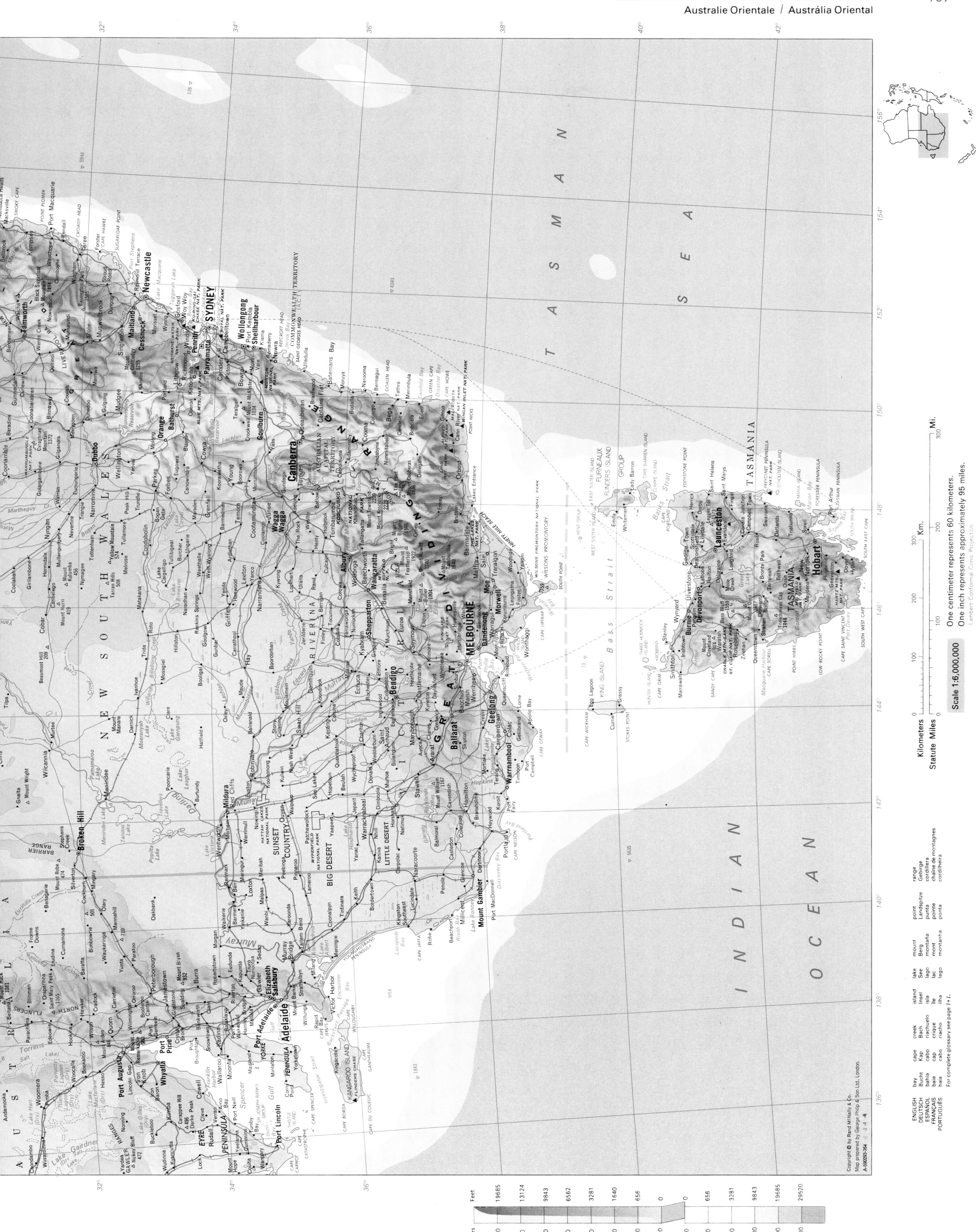
Scale 1:6,000,000
One centimeter represents 60 kilometers.
One inch represents approximately 95 miles.
Lambert Conformal Conic Projection
Kilometers
Statute Miles
TASMAN SEA
INDIAN OCEAN
NEW SOUTH WALES
VICTORIA
TASMANIA
GREAT DIVIDING RANGE
Bass Strait
SYDNEY
MELBOURNE
Canberra
Adelaide
Hobart
Newcastle
Broken Hill
Launceston
Geelong
Ballarat
Bendigo
Wollongong
KANGAROO ISLAND
KING ISLAND
FLINDERS ISLAND
AUSTRALIAN CAPITAL TERRITORY
For complete glossary see page I • I.
Copyright © by Rand McNally & Co.
Map prepared by George Philip & Son Ltd., London.

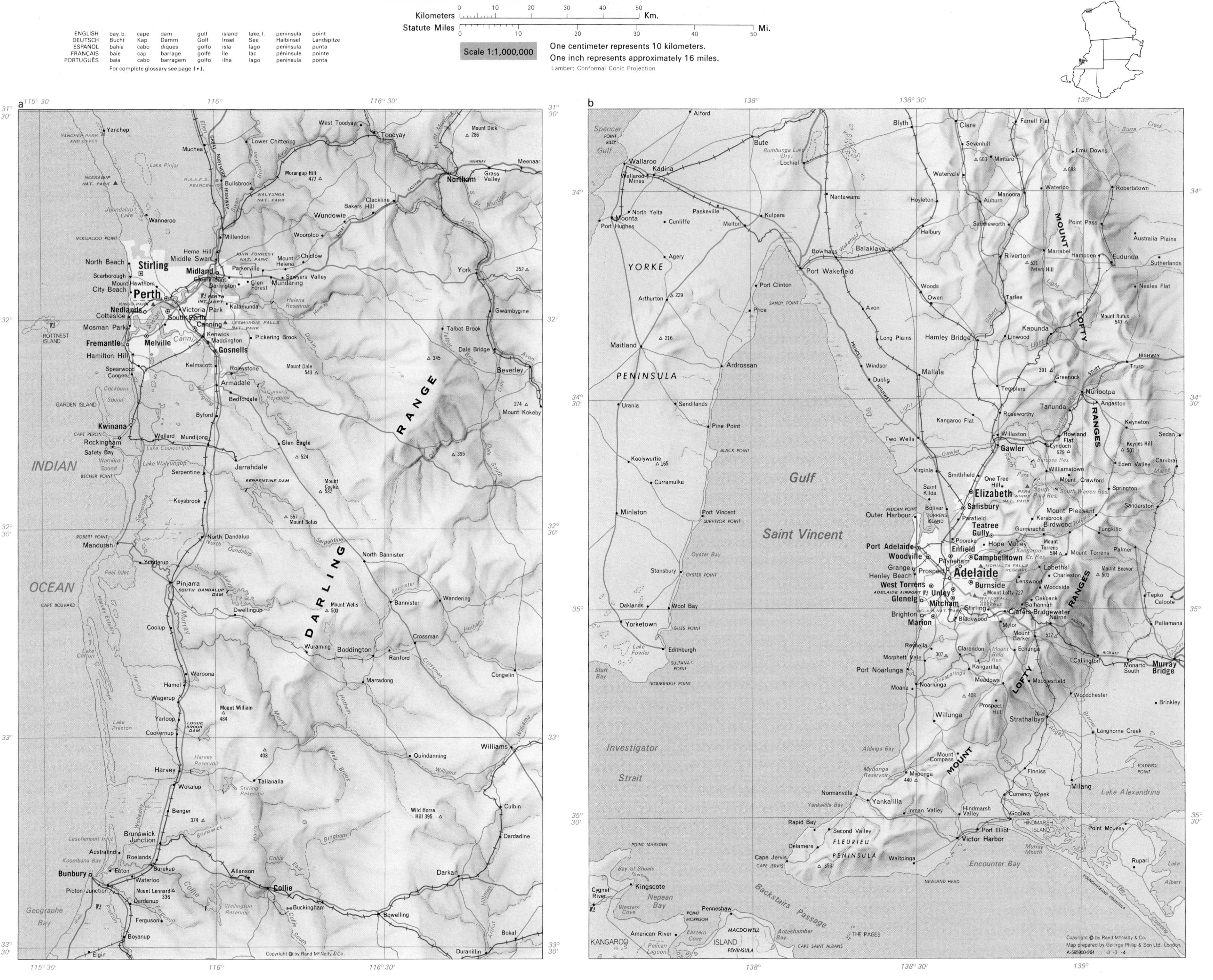
ENGLISH bay, b. cape dam gulf island lake, l. peninsula point
DEUTSCH Bucht Kap Damm Golf Insel See Halbinsel Landspitze
ESPAÑOL bahía cabo dique golfo isla lago península punta
FRANÇAIS baie cap barrage golfe île lac péninsule pointe
PORTUGUÊS baía cabo barragem golfo ilha lago península ponta
For complete glossary see page I•1.
Kilometers 0 10 20 30 40 50 Km.
Statute Miles 0 10 20 30 Mi.
Scale 1:1,000,000
One centimeter represents 10 kilometers.
One inch represents approximately 16 miles.
Lambert Conformal Conic Projection
a
Perth
Fremantle
Stirling
Melville
Gosnells
Nedlands
Cottesloe
Midland
Kwinana
Rockingham
Mandurah
Pinjarra
Harvey
Bunbury
Collie
Northam
York
Toodyay
Beverley
Williams
Darkan
DARLING RANGE
INDIAN OCEAN
Geographe Bay
Copyright © by Rand McNally & Co.
b
Adelaide
Elizabeth
Salisbury
Port Adelaide
Gawler
Murray Bridge
Victor Harbor
Kingscote
MOUNT LOFTY RANGES
Gulf Saint Vincent
YORKE PENINSULA
FLEURIEU PENINSULA
Investigator Strait
KANGAROO ISLAND
Backstairs Passage
Encounter Bay
Lake Alexandrina
Copyright © by Rand McNally & Co.
Map prepared by George Philip & Son Ltd., London.

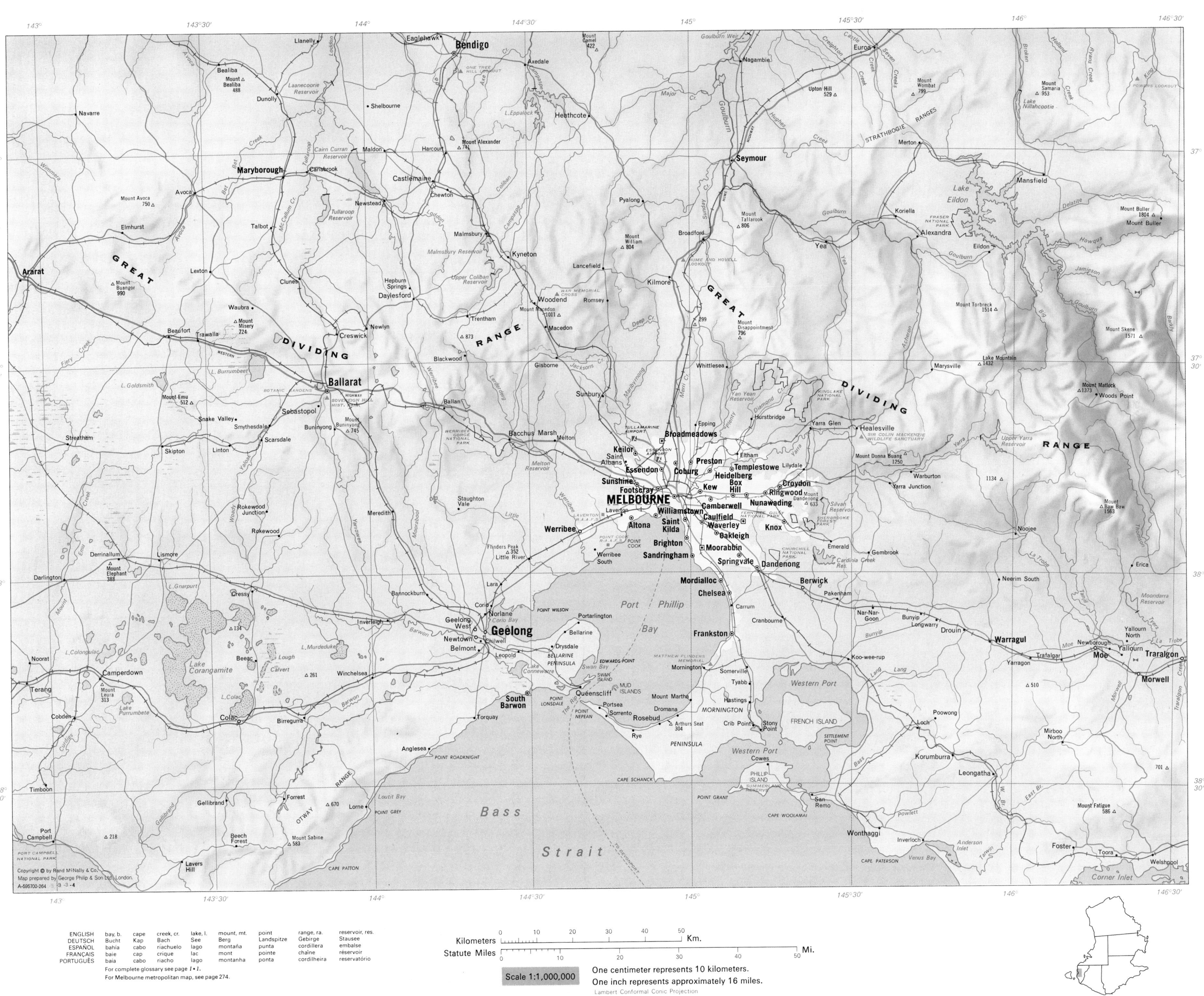
MELBOURNE
Geelong
Ballarat
Bendigo
Port Phillip Bay
Western Port
Bass Strait
GREAT DIVIDING RANGE
Copyright © by Rand McNally & Co.
Map prepared by George Philip & Son Ltd., London.
Kilometers
Statute Miles
Scale 1:1,000,000
One centimeter represents 10 kilometers.
One inch represents approximately 16 miles.
Lambert Conformal Conic Projection
ENGLISH bay, b. cape creek, cr. lake, l. mount, mt. point range, ra. reservoir, res.
DEUTSCH Bucht Kap Bach See Berg Landspitze Gebirge Stausee
ESPAÑOL bahía cabo riachuelo lago montaña punta cordillera embalse
FRANÇAIS baie cap crique lac mont pointe chaîne réservoir
PORTUGUÊS baía cabo riacho lago montanha ponta cordilheira reservatório
For complete glossary see page I • I.
For Melbourne metropolitan map, see page 274.

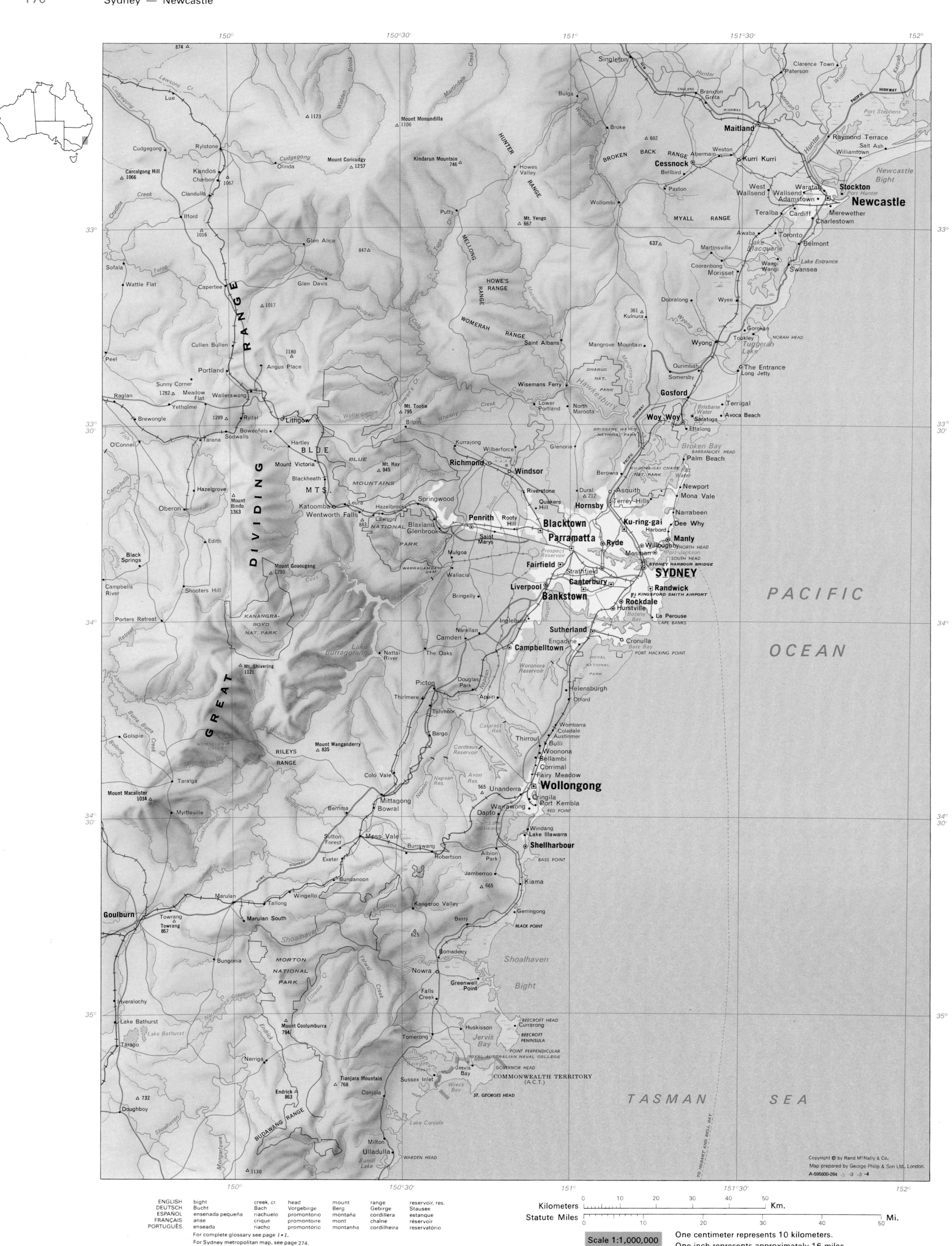
150°
150°30'
151°
151°30'
152°
33°
33° 30'
34°
34° 30'
35°
Singleton
Clarence Town
Paterson
Branxton
Greta
Bulga
Broke
Maitland
Raymond Terrace
Salt Ash
Williamtown
Port Stephens
Cessnock
Kurri Kurri
Abermain
Weston
Bellbird
Paxton
BROKEN BACK RANGE
Newcastle Bight
Stockton
Port Hunter
Newcastle
Waratah
Wallsend
West Wallsend
Adamstown
Merewether
Charlestown
Cardiff
Teralba
MYALL RANGE
Wollombi
Howes Valley
HUNTER RANGE
Mt. Yengo 667
Putty
Kindarun Mountain 746
Mount Monundilla 1106
Mount Coricudgy 1257
Olinda
Rylstone
Cudgegong
Kandos
Charbon
Clandulla
Ilford
Carcalgong Hill 1066
Lue
Awaba
Toronto
Belmont
Lake Macquarie
Lake Entrance
Swansea
Martinsville
Cooranbong
Morisset
Wangi Wangi
Dooralong
Wyee
Kulnura
Gorokan
Toukley
NORAH HEAD
Tuggerah Lake
Wyong
Mangrove Mountain
Ourimbah
Somersby
The Entrance
Long Jetty
Gosford
Terrigal
Avoca Beach
Woy Woy
Saratoga
Ettalong
Glen Alice
Glen Davis
Capertee
Sofala
Wattle Flat
MELLONG RANGE
HOWE'S RANGE
WOMERAH RANGE
Saint Albans
Wisemans Ferry
Lower Portland
North Maroota
Hawkesbury
DHARUG NAT. PARK
BRISBANE WATER NATIONAL PARK
Cullen Bullen
Portland
Angus Place
Peel
Sunny Corner
Meadow Flat
Wallerawang
Raglan
Yetholme
Brewongle
Rydal
Lithgow
Bowenfels
Sodwalls
Tarana
O'Connell
Hartley
Mt. Tootie 795
Bilpin
Kurrajong
Wilberforce
Glenorie
Richmond
Windsor
Broken Bay
BARRANJOEY HEAD
Palm Beach
Newport
Mona Vale
Narrabeen
Dee Why
Manly
NORTH HEAD
Port Jackson
SOUTH HEAD
SYDNEY HARBOUR BRIDGE
SYDNEY
Berowra
KU-RING-GAI CHASE NAT. PARK
Asquith
Terrey Hills
Hornsby
Ku-ring-gai
Harbord
Dural
Riverstone
Quakers Hill
BLUE MTS.
BLUE MOUNTAINS
Mt. Hay 945
Mount Victoria
Blackheath
Hazelgrove
Oberon
Mount Bindo 1363
Katoomba
Leura
Wentworth Falls
Hazelbrook
Lawson
Springwood
Blaxland
Glenbrook
NATIONAL PARK
Penrith
Rooty Hill
Blacktown
Parramatta
Ryde
Willoughby
Mosman
Saint Marys
Prospect Reservoir
Mulgoa
Fairfield
Strathfield
Canterbury
Randwick
KINGSFORD SMITH AIRPORT
Wallacia
WARRAGAMBA DAM
Liverpool
Bankstown
Rockdale
Hurstville
Botany Bay
La Perouse
CAPE BANKS
Bringelly
Ingleburn
Sutherland
Engadine
Cronulla
Bate Bay
PORT HACKING POINT
ROYAL NATIONAL PARK
Narellan
Camden
Campbelltown
Woronora Reservoir
The Oaks
Nattai River
Lake Burragorang
Edith
Black Springs
DIVIDING
GREAT
RANGE
Mount Gouougang 1290
KANANGRA-BOYD NAT. PARK
Campbells River
Shooters Hill
Porters Retreat
Mt. Shivering 1121
PACIFIC
OCEAN
Picton
Douglas Park
Appin
Helensburgh
Otford
Thirlmere
Tahmoor
Bargo
Wombarra
Coledale
Austinmer
Thirroul
Bulli
Woonona
Bellambi
Corrimal
Fairy Meadow
Wollongong
Cataract Res.
Cordeaux Reservoir
Avon Res.
Nepean Res.
Unanderra
Cringila
Port Kembla
RED POINT
Warrawong
Dapto
Lake Illawarra
Windang
Shellharbour
BASS POINT
Albion Park
Golspie
RILEYS RANGE
Mount Wanganderry 835
Colo Vale
Taralga
Mount Macalister 1034
Myrtleville
Mittagong
Bowral
Berrima
Sutton Forest
Moss Vale
Burrawang
Robertson
Exeter
Bundanoon
Jamberoo
665
Kiama
Wingello
Tallong
Marulan
Marulan South
Kangaroo Valley
Gerringong
BLACK POINT
Goulburn
Towrang
Towrang 867
Berry
625
Shoalhaven
Bungonia
MORTON NATIONAL PARK
Bomaderry
Nowra
Shoalhaven Bight
Greenwell Point
Falls Creek
Inveralochy
Lake Bathurst
Tarago
Mount Coolumburra 794
BEECROFT HEAD
Currarong
BEECROFT PENINSULA
Huskisson
Jervis Bay
Tomerong
POINT PERPENDICULAR
ROYAL AUSTRALIAN NAVAL COLLEGE
GOVERNOR HEAD
COMMONWEALTH TERRITORY (A.C.T.)
Jervis Bay
Sussex Inlet
Wreck Bay
ST. GEORGES HEAD
Nerriga
Tianjara Mountain 768
Endrick 863
Conjola
BUDAWANG RANGE
Lake Conjola
Doughboy
732
Milton
Ulladulla
WARDEN HEAD
Burrill Lake
1130
TASMAN
SEA
TO HOBART AND BELL BAY
Copyright © by Rand McNally & Co.
Map prepared by George Philip & Son Ltd., London.
A-595800-264
ENGLISH bight creek, cr. head mount range reservoir, res.
DEUTSCH Bucht Bach Vorgebirge Berg Gebirge Stausee
ESPAÑOL ensenada pequeña riachuelo promontorio montaña cordillera estanque
FRANÇAIS anse crique promontoire mont chaîne réservoir
PORTUGUÊS enseada riacho promontório montanha cordilheira reservatório
For complete glossary see page 1 • 1.
For Sydney metropolitan map, see page 274.
Kilometers 0 10 20 30 40 50 Km.
Statute Miles 0 10 20 30 40 50 Mi.
Scale 1:1,000,000
One centimeter represents 10 kilometers.
One inch represents approximately 16 miles.
Lambert Conformal Conic Projection

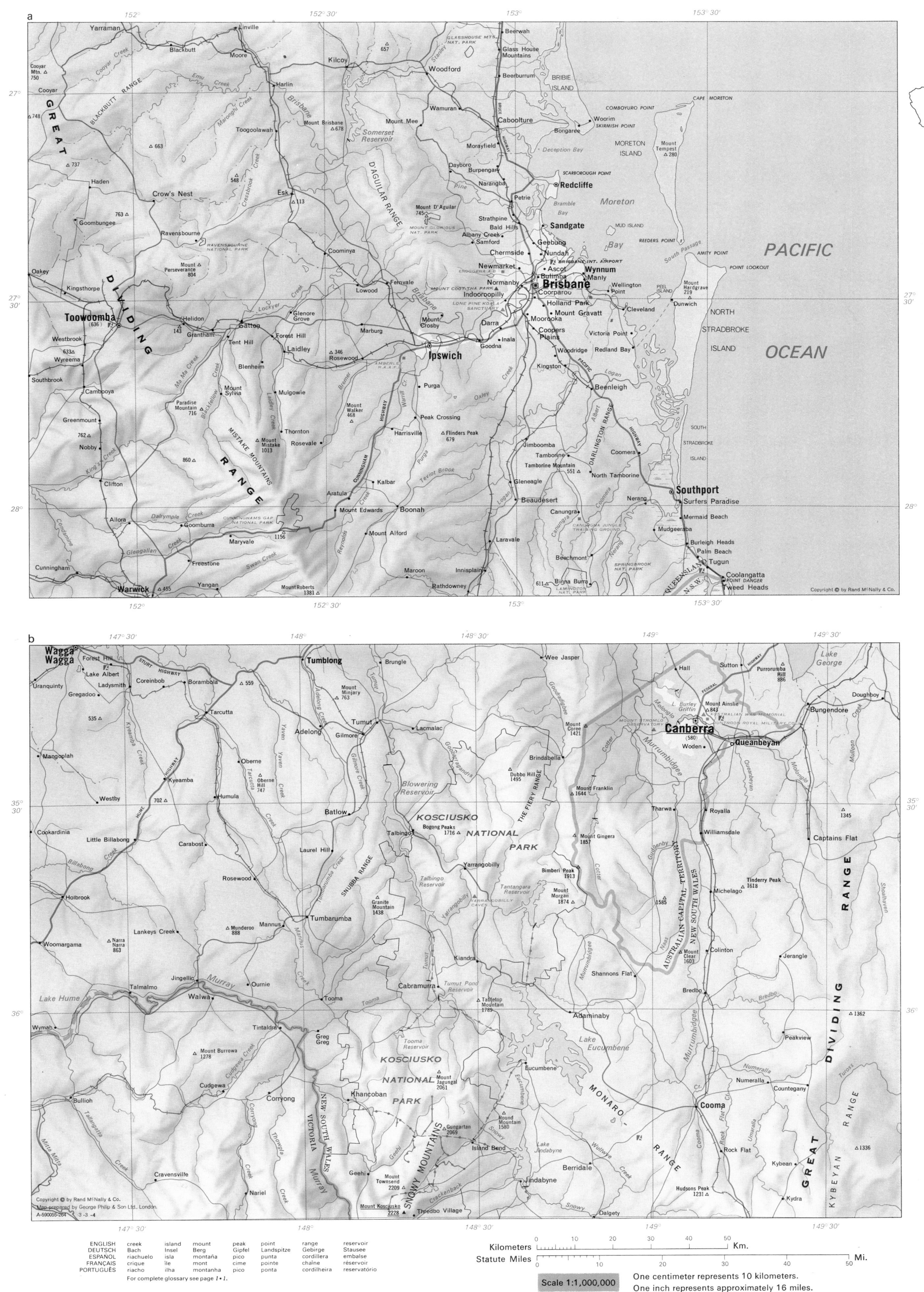

ENGLISH	creek	island	mount	peak	point	range	reservoir
DEUTSCH	Bach	Insel	Berg	Gipfel	Landspitze	Gebirge	Stausee
ESPAÑOL	riachuelo	isla	montaña	pico	punta	cordillera	embalse
FRANÇAIS	crique	île	mont	cime	pointe	chaîne	réservoir
PORTUGUÊS	riacho	ilha	montanha	pico	ponta	cordilheira	reservatório

For complete glossary see page I • 1.

Kilometers 0 10 20 30 40 50 Km.
Statute Miles 0 10 20 30 40 50 Mi.

Scale 1:1,000,000
One centimeter represents 10 kilometers.
One inch represents approximately 16 miles.
Lambert Conformal Conic Projection

New Zealand / Neuseeland / Nueva Zelanda
Nouvelle Zélande / Nova Zelândia

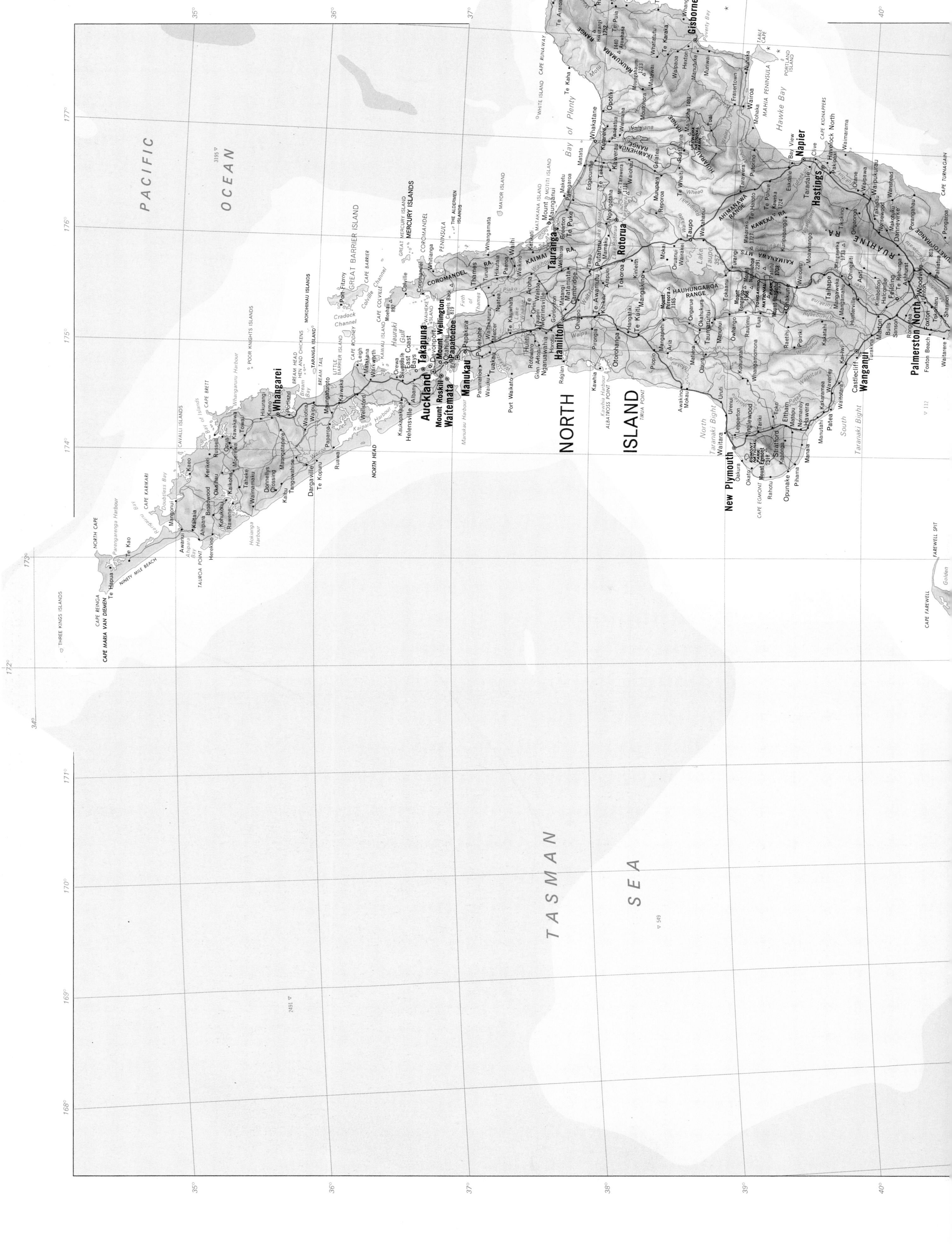

PACIFIC OCEAN
SOUTH ISLAND
SOUTHERN ALPS
CANTERBURY PLAINS
Canterbury Bight
Pegasus Bay
BANKS PENINSULA
Palliser Bay
Karamea Bight
Foveaux Strait
STEWART ISLAND
Wellington
Lower Hutt
Upper Hutt
Porirua
Nelson
Blenheim
Kaikoura
Westport
Greymouth
Hokitika
Christchurch
Ashburton
Timaru
Oamaru
Dunedin
Invercargill
Bluff
Mosgiel
Milton
Balclutha
Gore
Queenstown
Alexandra
Cromwell
Roxburgh
Waimate
Meters
Feet
Land Below Sea Level
ENGLISH bay bight cape harbour mount pass point range
DEUTSCH Bucht Bucht Kap Hafen Berg Pass Landspitze Gebirge
ESPAÑOL bahia ensenada pequeña cabo puerto montaña paso punta cordillera
FRANÇAIS baie anse cap port mont col pointe chaîne
PORTUGUÊS baía enseada cabo porto montanha passo ponta cordilheira
For complete glossary see page I•I.
Kilometers
Statute Miles
Km.
Mi.
Scale 1:3,000,000
One centimeter represents 30 kilometers.
One inch represents approximately 47 miles.
Lambert Conformal Conic Projection
Copyright © by Rand McNally & Co.
Map compiled by George Philip & Son Ltd., London.
Map produced by Rand McNally & Co.

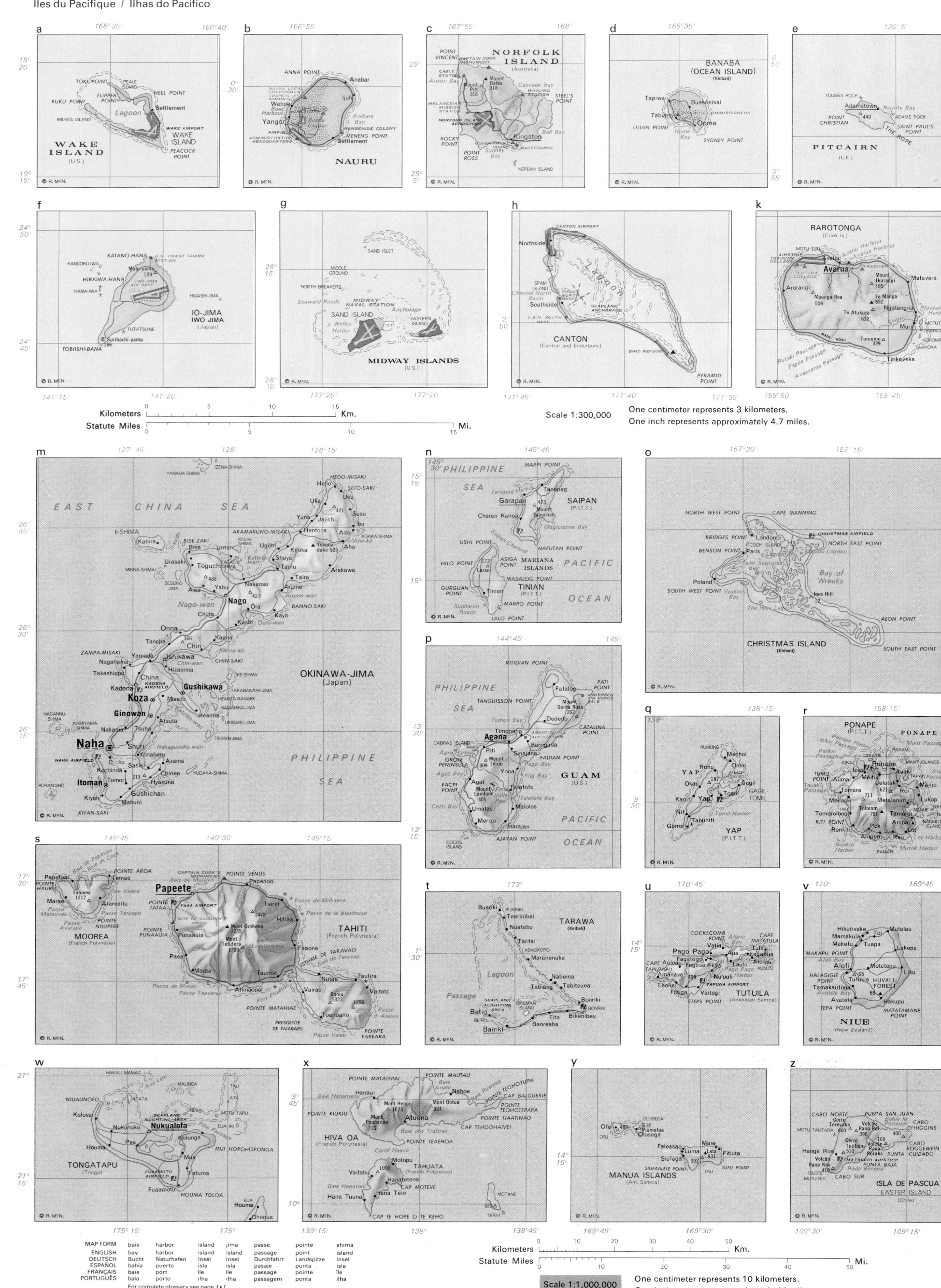

MAP FORM	baie	harbor	island	jima	passe	pointe	shima
ENGLISH	bay	harbor	island	island	passage	point	island
DEUTSCH	Bucht	Naturhafen	Insel	Insel	Durchfahrt	Landspitze	Insel
ESPAÑOL	bahía	puerto	isla	isla	pasaje	punta	isla
FRANÇAIS	baie	port	île	île	passage	pointe	île
PORTUGUÊS	baía	porto	ilha	ilha	passagem	ponta	ilha

For complete glossary see page I • 1.

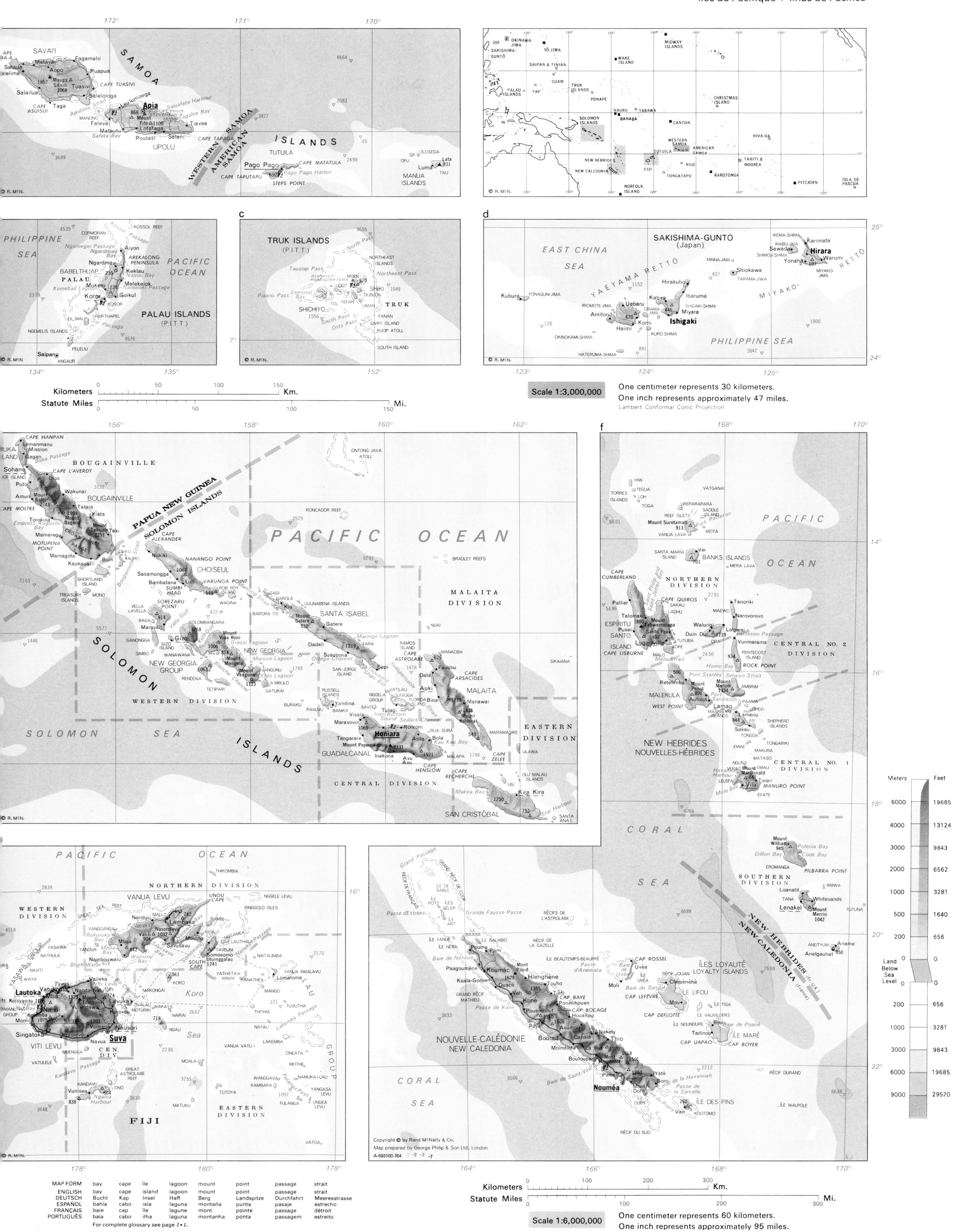

MAP FORM	bay	cape	île	lagoon	mount	point	passage	strait
ENGLISH	bay	cape	island	lagoon	mount	point	passage	strait
DEUTSCH	Bucht	Kap	Insel	Haff	Berg	Landspitze	Durchfahrt	Meeresstrasse
ESPAÑOL	bahía	cabo	isla	laguna	montaña	punta	pasaje	estrecho
FRANÇAIS	baie	cap	île	lagune	mont	pointe	passage	détroit
PORTUGUÊS	baía	cabo	ilha	laguna	montanha	ponta	passagem	estreito

For complete glossary see page I • 1.

ENGLISH	bay	cape	island	lake, l.	mountains, mts.	point	range	strait
DEUTSCH	Bucht	Kap	Insel	See	Berge	Landspitze	Gebirge	Meeresstrasse
ESPAÑOL	bahía	cabo	isla	lago	montañas	punta	sierra	estrecho
FRANÇAIS	baie	cap	île	lac	montagnes	pointe	chaîne	détroit
PORTUGUÊS	baía	cabo	ilha	lago	montanhas	ponta	serra	estreito

For complete glossary see page *I • 1*.

178 - 179

Kilometers 0 200 400 600 Km.
Statute Miles 0 200 400 600 Mi.

Scale 1:12,000 000

One centimeter represents 120 kilometers.
One inch represents approximately 190 miles.
Lambert Conformal Conic Projection

230 - 231

ENGLISH	bay	cape	desert	island	lake	mountains	peak	range
DEUTSCH	Bucht	Kap	Wüste	Insel	See	Berge	Gipfel	Gebirge
ESPAÑOL	bahía	cabo	desierto	isla	lago	montañas	pico	sierra
FRANÇAIS	baie	cap	désert	île	lac	montagnes	cime	chaîne
PORTUGUÊS	baía	cabo	deserto	ilha	lago	montanhas	pico	serra

For complete glossary see page *I* • *1*.

176 - 177
95°
90°
85°
80°
75°
70°
65°
60°
50°
45°
40°
35°
30°
25°
20°
ONTARIO
QUÉBEC
James Bay
Gulf of Saint Lawrence
NEW BRUNSWICK
PRINCE EDWARD ISLAND
NOVA SCOTIA
CAPE BRETON ISLAND
NOTRE DAME
MINNESOTA
WISCONSIN
MICHIGAN
IOWA
ILLINOIS
INDIANA
OHIO
PENNSYLVANIA
NEW YORK
MAINE
KENTUCKY
MISSOURI
TENNESSEE
ARKANSAS
MISSISSIPPI
ALABAMA
GEORGIA
LOUISIANA
FLORIDA
VIRGINIA
NORTH CAROLINA
SOUTH CAROLINA
APPALACHIAN MOUNTAINS
ADIRONDACK MTS.
OZARK PLATEAU
BOSTON MTS.
Lake Superior
Lake Michigan
Lake Huron
Lake Erie
Lake Ontario
Thunder Bay
Duluth
Minneapolis
St. Paul
Milwaukee
CHICAGO
DETROIT
Toledo
Cleveland
Pittsburgh
Buffalo
Rochester
Syracuse
Albany
TORONTO
Hamilton
Ottawa
MONTRÉAL
Québec
Sherbrooke
Halifax
Saint John
Bangor
Portland
BOSTON
Providence
Hartford
NEW YORK
PHILADELPHIA
Baltimore
WASHINGTON
Richmond
Norfolk
Atlantic City
Des Moines
Kansas City
St. Louis
Indianapolis
Columbus
Dayton
Cincinnati
Louisville
Lexington
Nashville
Knoxville
Memphis
Little Rock
Springfield
Charleston
Charlotte
Raleigh
Greensboro
Columbia
Atlanta
Birmingham
Huntsville
Chattanooga
Montgomery
Jackson
Shreveport
Baton Rouge
New Orleans
Mobile
Pensacola
Tallahassee
Jacksonville
Savannah
Daytona Beach
Orlando
Tampa
St. Petersburg
West Palm Beach
Fort Lauderdale
Miami
Key West
Straits of Florida
FLORIDA KEYS
Tropic of Cancer
BAHAMAS
Nassau
ANDROS ISLAND
BERMUDA (U.K.)
Hamilton
ATLANTIC OCEAN
GULF OF MEXICO
La Habana Havana
Matanzas
Santa Clara
Cienfuegos
Camagüey
Holguín
Santiago de Cuba
Guantánamo
Mérida
YUCATAN PENINSULA
Yucatan Channel
CARIBBEAN SEA
CAYMAN IS. (U.K.)
WEST INDIES
TURKS AND CAICOS ISLANDS (U.K.)
HISPANIOLA
HAITI
Port-au-Prince
DOMINICAN REPUBLIC
Santo Domingo
Windward Passage
Kilometers 0 200 400 600 Km.
Statute Miles 0 200 400 600 Mi.
Scale 1:12,000,000
One centimeter represents 120 kilometers.
One inch represents approximately 190 miles.
Albers Conical Equal-Area Projection

Chukchi Sea
BERING SEA
ARCTIC
PACIFI
Anadyrskij Zaliv
Norton Sound
Kotzebue Sound
Kuskokwim Bay
Bristol Bay
Bering Strait
Arctic Circle
International Date Line
UNION OF SOVIET SOCIALIST REPUBLICS
UNITED STATES
ANADYRSKOJE PLOSKOGORJE
EKITYKSKIJ CHREBET
PEGTYMEL'SKIJ CHREBET
CHREBET PEKUL'NEJ
OSINOVSKIJ CHREBET
CHREBET ISKATEN
ČUKOTSKIJ POLUOSTROV
BROOKS
DE LONG MOUNTAINS
BAIRD MOUNTAINS
SCHWATKA MOUNTAINS
WARING MOUNTAINS
LOOKOUT RIDGE
ZANE HILLS
SEWARD PENINSULA
KUSKOKWIM
TAYLOR MOUNTAINS
KILBUCK MOUNTAINS
AHKLUN MOUNTAINS
BEAVER MOUNTAINS
KAIYUH MOUNTAINS
ALASKA PENINSULA
ALEUTIAN ISLANDS
FOX ISLANDS
ISLANDS OF THE FOUR MOUNTAINS
ANDREANOF ISLANDS
SHUMAGIN ISLANDS
PRIBILOF ISLANDS
SAINT LAWRENCE ISLAND
SAINT MATTHEW ISLAND
NUNIVAK ISLAND
NELSON ISLAND
UNIMAK ISLAND
UMNAK ISLAND
UNALASKA ISLAND
KRENITZIN ISLANDS
ATKA ISLAND
ADAK ISLAND
Anadyr'
Providenija
Barrow
Wainwright
Point Hope
Kivalina
Noatak
Kotzebue
Kiana
Ambler
Kobuk
Shungnak
Selawik
Shishmaref
Wales
Teller
Nome
Golovin
Koyuk
Candle
Buckland
Deering
Unalakleet
Saint Michael
Stebbins
Kaltag
Nulato
Galena
Ruby
Kokrines
McGrath
Takotna
Ophir
Holy Cross
Anvik
Grayling
Shageluk
Flat
Russian Mission
Pilot Station
Saint Marys
Mountain Village
Hooper Bay
Chevak
Bethel
Akiak
Kwethluk
Napaskiak
Oscarville
Quinhagak
Goodnews Bay
Platinum
Togiak
Dillingham
Aleknagik
Naknek
King Salmon
Egegik
Pilot Point
Ugashik
Port Heiden
Chignik
Port Moller
Perryville
Cold Bay
King Cove
Sand Point
False Pass
Akutan
Unalaska
Dutch Harbor
Nikolski
Saint Paul Island
Saint George
Gambell
Savoonga
Northeast Cape
Uelen
Lavrentija
Lorino
Enmelen
Nunligran
Sireniki
Egvekinot
Amguema
Vankarem
Mys Šmidta
Pil'gyn
Nutepel'men
Neškan
Enurmino
Inčoun
Naukan
Beringovskij
Krasneno
Velikaja
Tumanskij
Mount Katmai
Iliamna Lake
Meters
Feet
6000 19685
4000 13124
3000 9843
2000 6562
1000 3281
500 1640
200 656
0 0
Land Below Sea Level
0 0
200 656
1000 3281
3000 9843
6000 19685
9000 29520
ENGLISH bay cape island, i. lake, l. mount, mt. peak, pk. point volca
DEUTSCH Bucht Kap Insel See Berg Gipfel Landspitze Vulka
ESPAÑOL bahía cabo isla lago monte pico punta volcá
FRANÇAIS baie cap île lac mont cime pointe volca
PORTUGUÊS baía cabo ilha lago monte pico ponta vulcã
For complete glossary see page I • 1.

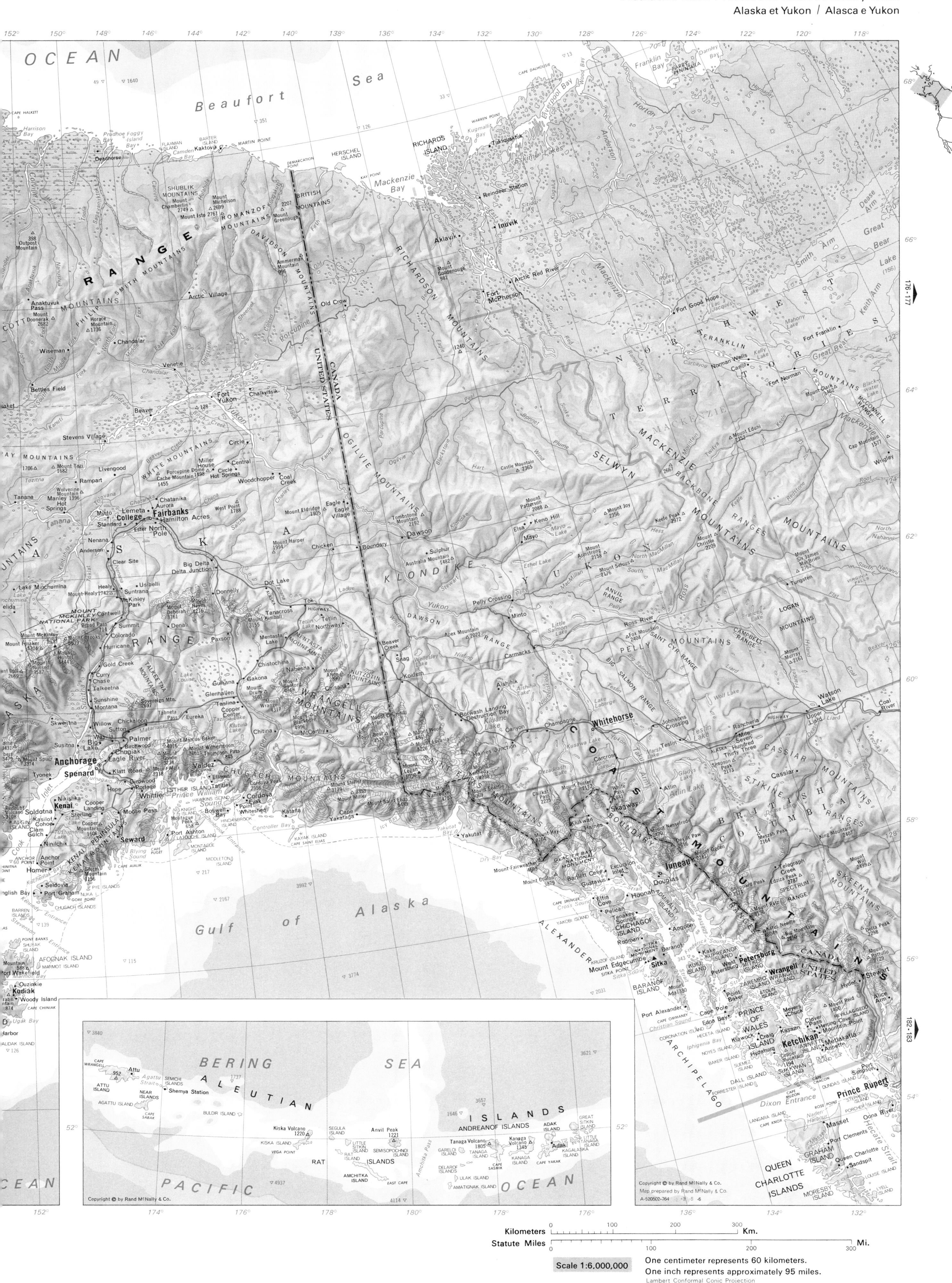

Kilometers 0 100 200 300 Km.
Statute Miles 0 100 200 300 Mi.

Scale 1:6,000,000
One centimeter represents 60 kilometers.
One inch represents approximately 95 miles.
Lambert Conformal Conic Projection

ENGLISH	creek	Indian reserve	inlet	island	lake, l.	mountain	peak	provincial park	sound
DEUTSCH	Bach	Indianerreservation	Einfahrt	Insel	See	Berg	Gipfel	Provinz-Park	Sund
ESPAÑOL	riachuelo	reserva de Indios	abra	isla	lago	montaña	pico	parque de provincia	sonda
FRANÇAIS	crique	réserve indienne	bras de mer	île	lac	montagne	cime	parc provincial	détroit
PORTUGUÊS	riacho	reserva indígena	braço de mar	ilha	lago	montanha	pico	parque provincial	estreito

For complete glossary see page *I • 1*.

ROCKY MOUNTAINS
COLUMBIA MOUNTAINS
MONASHEE MOUNTAINS
SELKIRK MOUNTAINS
PURCELL MOUNTAINS
CASCADE RANGE
BRITISH COLUMBIA
ALBERTA
CANADA
UNITED STATES
WASHINGTON
IDAHO
MONTANA
Edmonton
Calgary
Red Deer
Lethbridge
Grande-Prairie
Dawson Creek
Kamloops
Kelowna
Penticton
Vernon
Cranbrook
Kalispell
Peace River
Fort St. John
Medicine Hat
Lesser Slave Lake
JASPER NATIONAL PARK
BANFF NATIONAL PARK
GLACIER NATIONAL PARK
WATERTON-GLACIER INTERNATIONAL PEACE PARK
202 - 203
184 - 185
Kilometers 0 50 100 150 Km.
Statute Miles 0 50 100 150 Mi.
Scale 1:3,000,000
One centimeter represents 30 kilometers.
One inch represents approximately 47 miles.
Lambert Conformal Conic Projection

182 - 183
202 - 203
198 - 199

ENGLISH	creek, cr.	hills	Indian reserve	island, i.	lake, l.	provincial park
DEUTSCH	Bach	Hügel	Indianerreservation	Insel	See	Provinz-Park
ESPAÑOL	riachuelo	colinas	reserva de Indios	isla	lago	parque de provincia
FRANÇAIS	crique	collines	réserve indienne	île	lac	parc provincial
PORTUGUÊS	riacho	colinas	reserva indígena	ilha	lago	parque provincial

For complete glossary see page *I* • *1*.

Kilometers 0 50 100 150 Km.
Statute Miles 0 50 100 150 Mi.

Scale 1:3,000,000
One centimeter represents 30 kilometers.
One inch represents approximately 47 miles.
Lambert Conformal Conic Projection

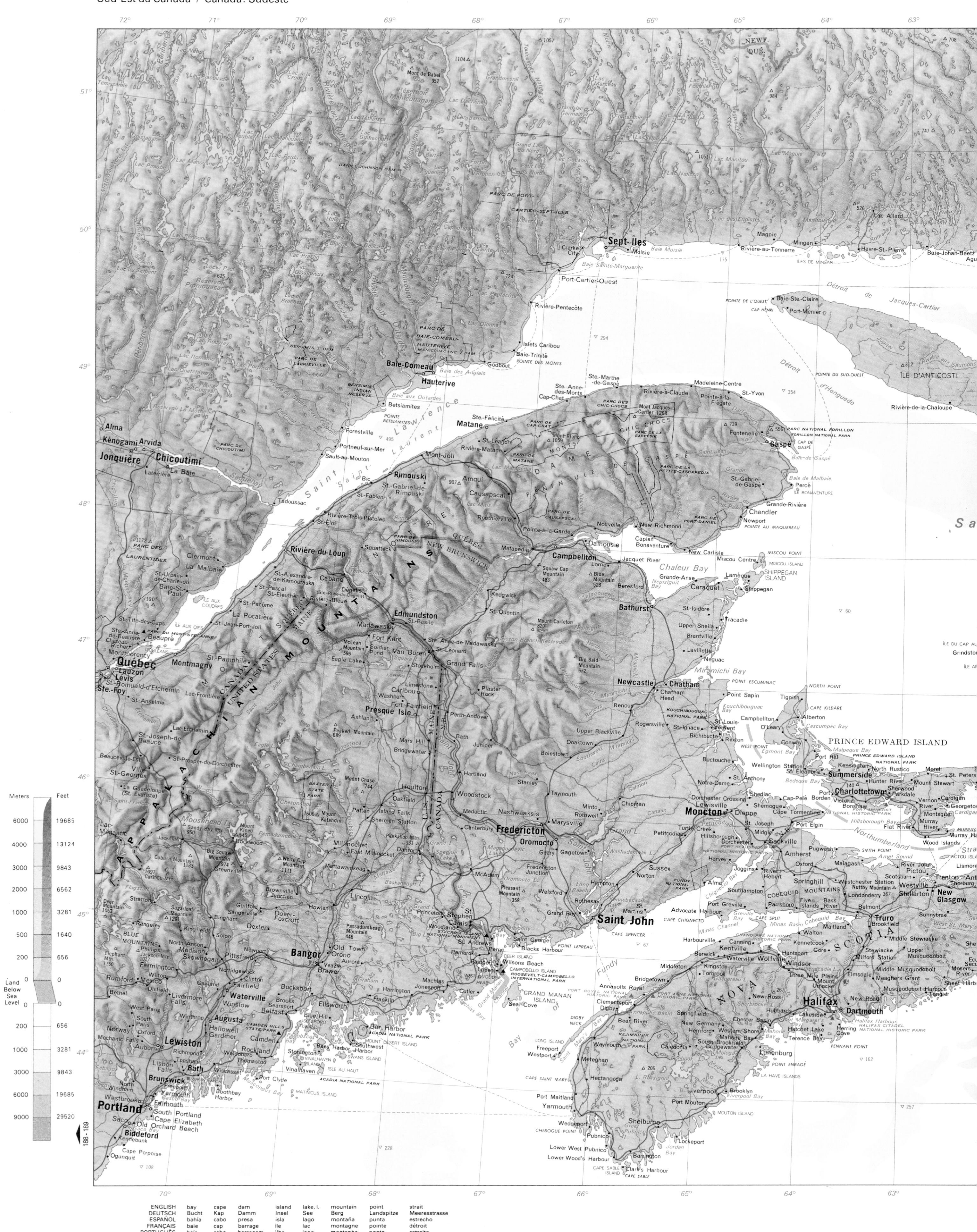

ENGLISH	bay	cape	dam	island	lake, l.	mountain	point	strait
DEUTSCH	Bucht	Kap	Damm	Insel	See	Berg	Landspitze	Meeresstrasse
ESPAÑOL	bahía	cabo	presa	isla	lago	montaña	punta	estrecho
FRANÇAIS	baie	cap	barrage	île	lac	montagne	pointe	détroit
PORTUGUÊS	baía	cabo	barragem	ilha	lago	montanha	ponta	estreito

For complete glossary see page *I • 1*.

LABRADOR SEA
ATLANTIC OCEAN
NEWFOUNDLAND
LONG RANGE MOUNTAINS
Gulf of Saint Lawrence
Cabot Strait
SAINT PIERRE AND MIQUELON (France)
SAINT-PIERRE-ET-MIQUELON
MIQUELON
Saint-Pierre
CANADA
QUEBEC
NEWF.
Red Bay
West St. Modeste
Cook's Harbour
CAPE BAULD
Raleigh
St. Anthony
Middle Bay
Forteau
Old Fort Bay
Bradore Bay
Blanc Sablon
Salmon Bay
Port-St-Servan
Flower's Cove
St-Augustin-Saguenay
Shekatika Bay
Brig Bay
Bartletts Harbour
Conche
GREY ISLANDS
Roddickton
Englee
Baie des Hal Hal
La Tabatière
Mutton Bay
Tête-à-la-Baleine
Port Saunders
River of Ponds
Hooping Harbour
Williamsport
Harbour Deep
Little Harbour Deep
Pointe-à-Maurier
Washicoutai
Wolf Bay
Kegaska
Gethsemani
Daniel's Harbour
Fleur-de-Lys
White Bay
Parson's Pond
Cow Head
Pacquet
Baie Verte
La Scie
Shoe Cove
Round Harbour
Seal Cove
Jackson's Arm
Westport
Nippers Harbour
Burlington
Notre Dame Bay
Fogo
Joe Batt's Arm
Change Islands
Durrell
Twillingate
GROS MORNE NATIONAL PARK
Gros Morne 806
Rocky Harbour
Norris Point
Bonne Bay
Trout River
Mount Saint Gregory 686
Hampden
Rattling Brook
King's Point
Springdale
Robert's Arm
Little Bay Islands
Beaumont
Port Anson
Pilley's Island
Fortune Harbour
Summerford
Boyd's Cove
Carmanville
Doting Cove
Lumsden
Newtown
Wesleyville
Valleyfield
Greenspond
Point Leamington
Campbellton
Lewisporte
Northern Arm
Botwood
Birchy Bay
Gander Bay
Old Man Mountain 496
Howley
Deer Lake
Pasadena
Cox's Cove
Lark Harbour
Main Topsail 555
Hodges Hill 570
Bishop's Falls
Badger
Norris Arm
Glenwood
Gander
Hare Bay
Trinity
Middle Brook
St. Brendan's
Millertown Junction
Windsor
Grand Falls
Corner Brook 814
Buchans
Millertown
EXPLOITS DAM
Gambo
Glovertown
Salvage
Eastport
Keels
Bonavista Bay
CAPE BONAVISTA
Bonavista
Elliston
Little Catalina
Catalina
Port Union
TERRA NOVA NATIONAL PARK
Musgravetown
Princeton
Port Rexton
Lethbridge
Spruce Brook
Lourdes
Piccadilly
Port au Port
Stephenville
Stephenville Crossing
St. George's
St. George's Bay
Flat Bay
Mount Howley 450
BARACHOIS POND PROVINCIAL PARK
ANNIEOPSQUOTCH MOUNTAINS
Red Indian L.
Port Blandford
Clarenville
Shoal Harbour
Hickman's Harbour
Old Perlican
Bay de Verde
Hant's Harbour
Robinson
St. David's
Mount Sylvester 376
Winterton
Heart's Content
Trinity Bay
Conception Bay
Codroy Pond
South Branch
Codroy
CAPE ANGUILLE
Doyles
Tompkins
Table Mountain 587
Channel-Port-aux-Basques
Isle-aux-Morts
Burnt Island
Rose Blanche
BLUE HILLS OF COUTEAU
Grand Bruit
Burgeo
Ramea
François
Cape la Hune
Head Bay d'Espoir
St. Alban's
Sunnyside
Come by Chance
Carbonear
Harbour Grace
Upper Island Cove
Spaniard's Bay
Bay Roberts
Torbay
Pouch Cove
Wabana
St. John's
Petty Harbour
Richard's Harbour
Pushthrough
McCallum
Hermitage
Rencontre East
Belleoram
Bay L'Argent
Terrenceville
Davis Cove
Harbour Buffett
Long Harbour
Whitbourne
Brigus
Pass Island
Harbour Breton
English Harbour West
Fortune Bay
Garnish
Grand Bank
Fortune
Marystown
Creston
Burin
BURIN PENINSULA
Lawn
St. Lawrence
Lamaline
Merasheen
Fox Harbour
Argentia
Placentia
Placentia Bay
Dunville
Colinet
Sawyers Hill
AVALON PENINSULA
Mount Carmel
Bay Bulls
Witless Bay
Tors Cove
Cape Broyle
Ferryland
Renews
Ship Cove
St. Bride's
Branch
St. Mary's
St. Vincent's
Trepassey
Portugal Cove South
St. Shotts
CAPE RACE
LA MADELEINE (Qué.)
Grand-Entrée
CAPE SAINT LAWRENCE
CAPE NORTH
Dingwall
Pleasant Bay
CAPE BRETON HIGHLANDS NATIONAL PARK
Ingonish
Chéticamp
Grand-Étang
Margaree Harbour
Margaree
Inverness
Indian Brook
Sydney Mines
North Sydney
New Waterford
Dominion
Glace Bay
Sydney
Port Morien
Mabou
Baddeck
CAPE BRETON ISLAND
Whycocomagh
Iona
Louisbourg
FORTRESS OF LOUISBOURG NATIONAL HISTORIC PARK
Judique
Bras d'Or L.
Gabarus
West Bay
Fourchu
St. Peters
Louisdale
L'Ardoise
Port Hawkesbury
Arichat
Guysborough
Queensport
Canso
Larrys River
SABLE ISLAND (N.S.)
Copyright © by Rand McNally & Co.
Map prepared by Rand McNally & Co.
A-520219-764
Kilometers 0 50 100 150 Km.
Statute Miles 0 50 100 150 Mi.
Scale 1:3,000,000
One centimeter represents 30 kilometers.
One inch represents approximately 47 miles.
Lambert Conformal Conic Projection

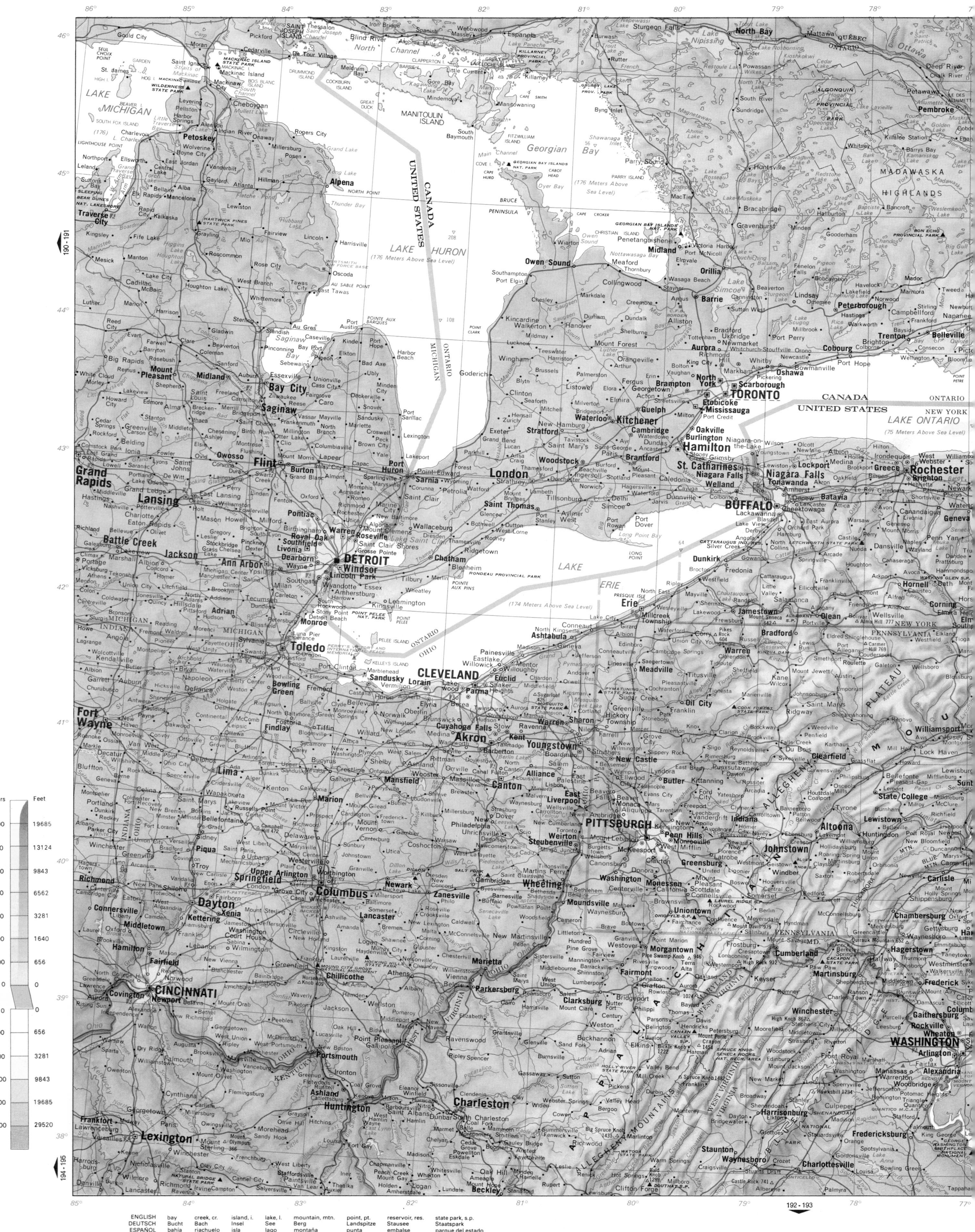

ENGLISH	bay	creek, cr.	island, i.	lake, l.	mountain, mtn.	point, pt.	reservoir, res.	state park, s.p.
DEUTSCH	Bucht	Bach	Insel	See	Berg	Landspitze	Stausee	Staatspark
ESPAÑOL	bahía	riachuelo	isla	lago	montaña	punta	embalse	parque del estado
FRANÇAIS	baie	crique	île	lac	montagne	pointe	réservoir	parc régional
PORTUGUÊS	baía	riacho	ilha	lago	montanha	ponta	reservatório	parque estadual

For complete glossary see page *1 • 1*.

186 - 187
ATLANTIC
OCEAN
MONTRÉAL
Ottawa
Trois-Rivières
Sherbrooke
Portland
Bangor
Augusta
Lewiston
Concord
Manchester
BOSTON
Worcester
Springfield
Providence
Hartford
New Haven
Bridgeport
Albany
Schenectady
Syracuse
Utica
Binghamton
Scranton
Wilkes-Barre
Allentown
Reading
Lancaster
Trenton
Newark
NEW YORK
PHILADELPHIA
Camden
Wilmington
Atlantic City
Burlington
Montpelier
Plattsburgh
Watertown
Massachusetts Bay
Cape Cod Bay
Long Island Sound
Rhode Island Sound
Nantucket Sound
Delaware Bay
Chesapeake Bay
Copyright © by Rand McNally & Co.
Map prepared by Rand McNally & Co.
A-520596-764
Kilometers
Km.
Statute Miles
Mi.
Scale 1:3,000,000
One centimeter represents 30 kilometers.
One inch represents approximately 47 miles.
Albers Conical Equal-Area Projection

ENGLISH	bay	creek, cr.	Indian reservation	island, i.	lake, l.	point	reservoir, res.	state park, s.p.
DEUTSCH	Bucht	Bach	Indianerreservation	Insel	See	Landspitze	Stausee	Staatspark
ESPAÑOL	bahía	riachuelo	reserva de Indios	isla	lago	punta	embalse	parque del estado
FRANÇAIS	baie	crique	réserve indienne	île	lac	pointe	réservoir	parc régional
PORTUGUÊS	baía	riacho	reserva indígena	ilha	lago	ponta	reservatório	parque estadual

For complete glossary see page *I* • *1*.

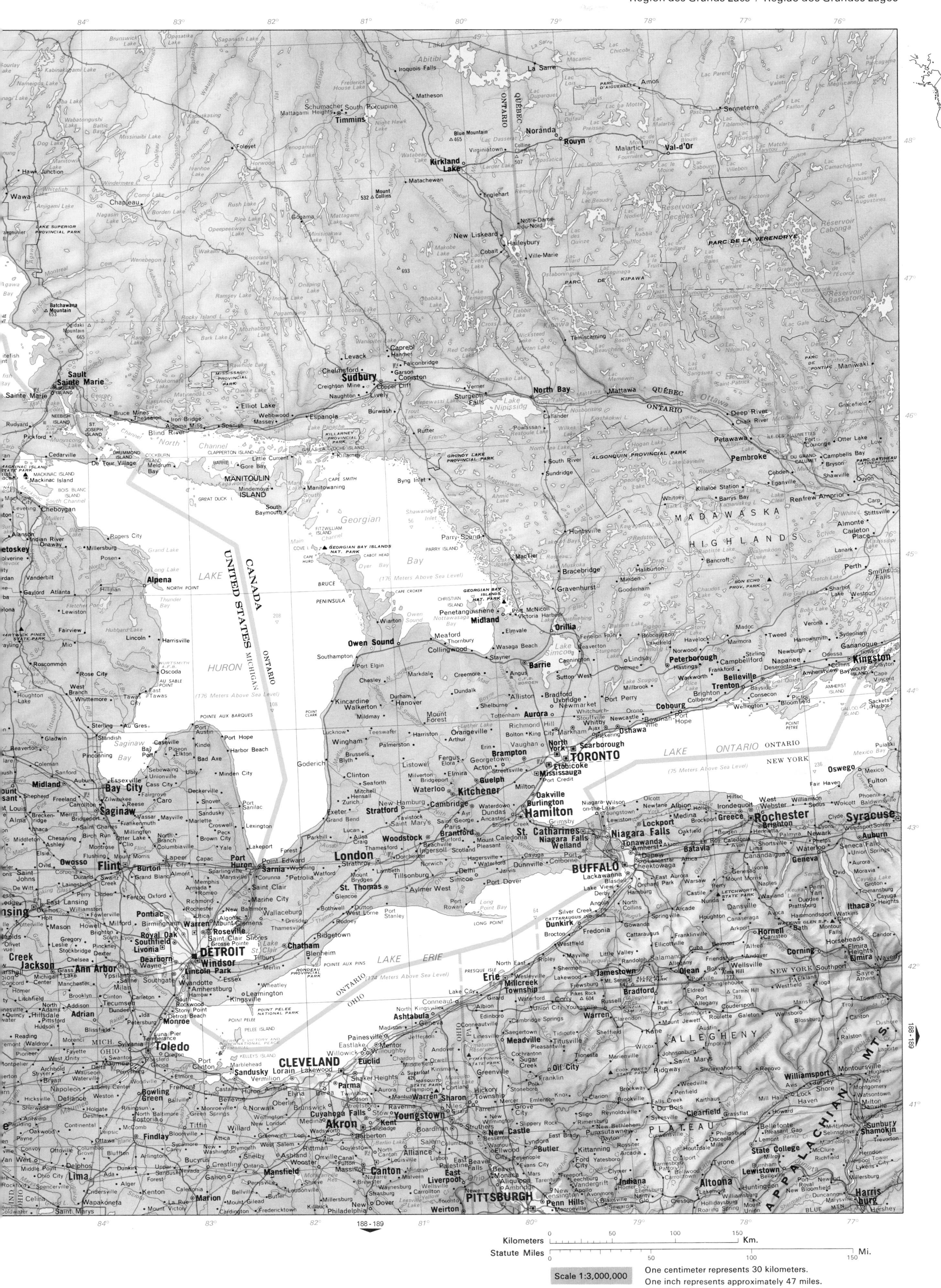

Kilometers 0 50 100 150 Km.
Statute Miles 0 50 100 150 Mi.

Scale 1:3,000,000
One centimeter represents 30 kilometers.
One inch represents approximately 47 miles.
Albers Conical Equal Area Projection

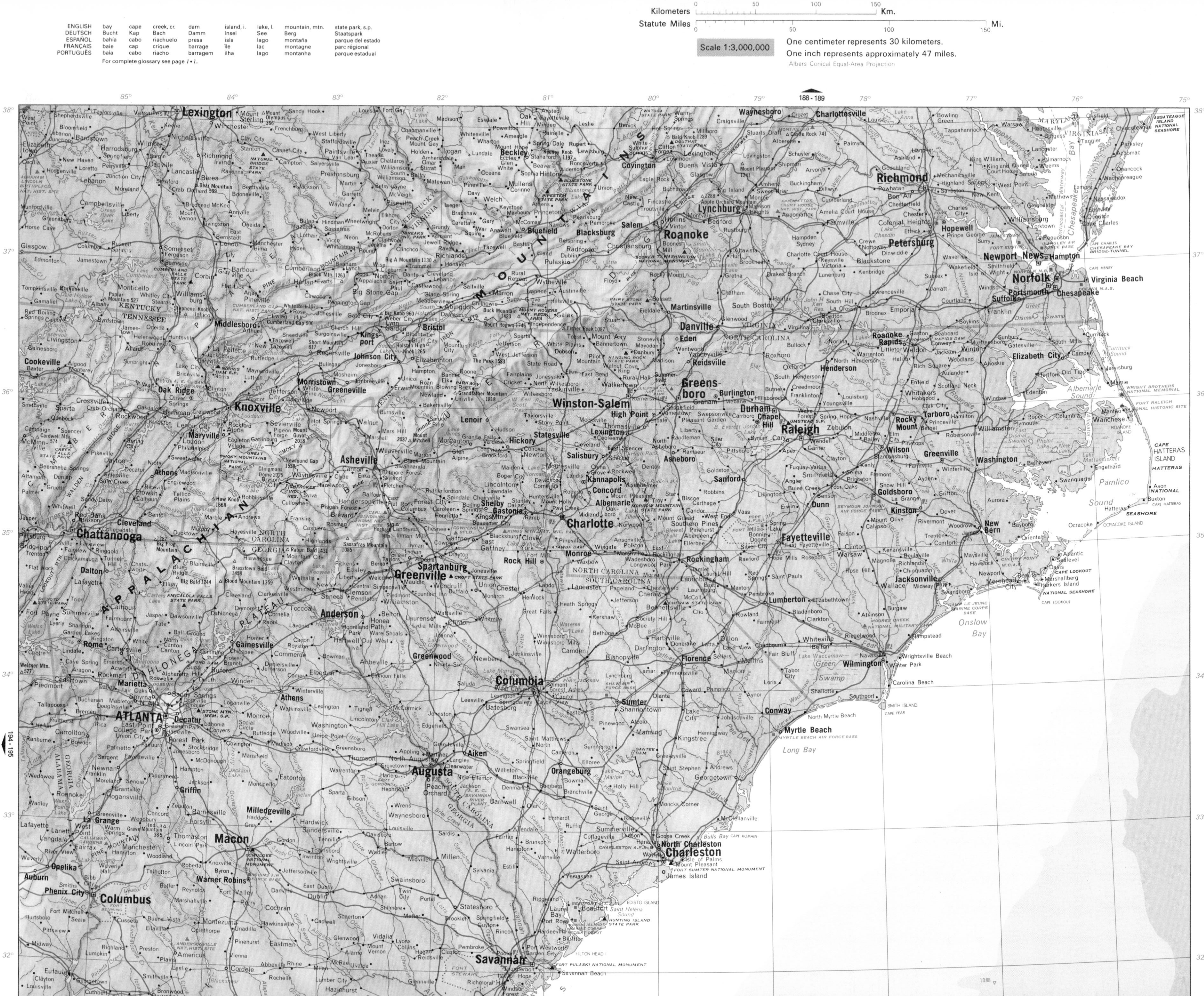
Kilometers 0 50 100 150 Km.
Statute Miles 0 50 100 150 Mi.
Scale 1:3,000,000
One centimeter represents 30 kilometers.
One inch represents approximately 47 miles.
Albers Conical Equal-Area Projection
ENGLISH bay cape creek, cr. dam island, i. lake, l. mountain, mtn. state park, s.p.
DEUTSCH Bucht Kap Bach Damm Insel See Berg Staatspark
ESPAÑOL bahía cabo riachuelo presa isla lago montaña parque del estado
FRANÇAIS baie cap crique barrage île lac montagne parc régional
PORTUGUÊS baía cabo riacho barragem ilha lago montanha parque estadual
For complete glossary see page I•1.
188-189
194-195

ATLANTIC
OCEAN
GULF OF
MEXICO
Jacksonville
St. Augustine
Daytona Beach
Orlando
Tampa
St. Petersburg
Sarasota
Fort Myers
West Palm Beach
Fort Lauderdale
MIAMI
Miami Beach
Key West
Tallahassee
Gainesville
Ocala
Valdosta
Waycross
Brunswick
Thomasville
Dothan
Freeport
Nassau
Okeechobee
GEORGIA
FLORIDA
UNITED STATES
BAHAMAS
Northwest Providence Channel
Northeast Providence Channel
GRAND BAHAMA
GREAT ABACO
ANDROS ISLAND
BERRY ISLANDS
BIMINI ISLANDS
ELEUTHERA
NEW PROVIDENCE
Straits of Florida
238 - 239
Meters
Feet
Land Below Sea Level
Copyright © by Rand McNally & Co.

188 - 189

190 - 191

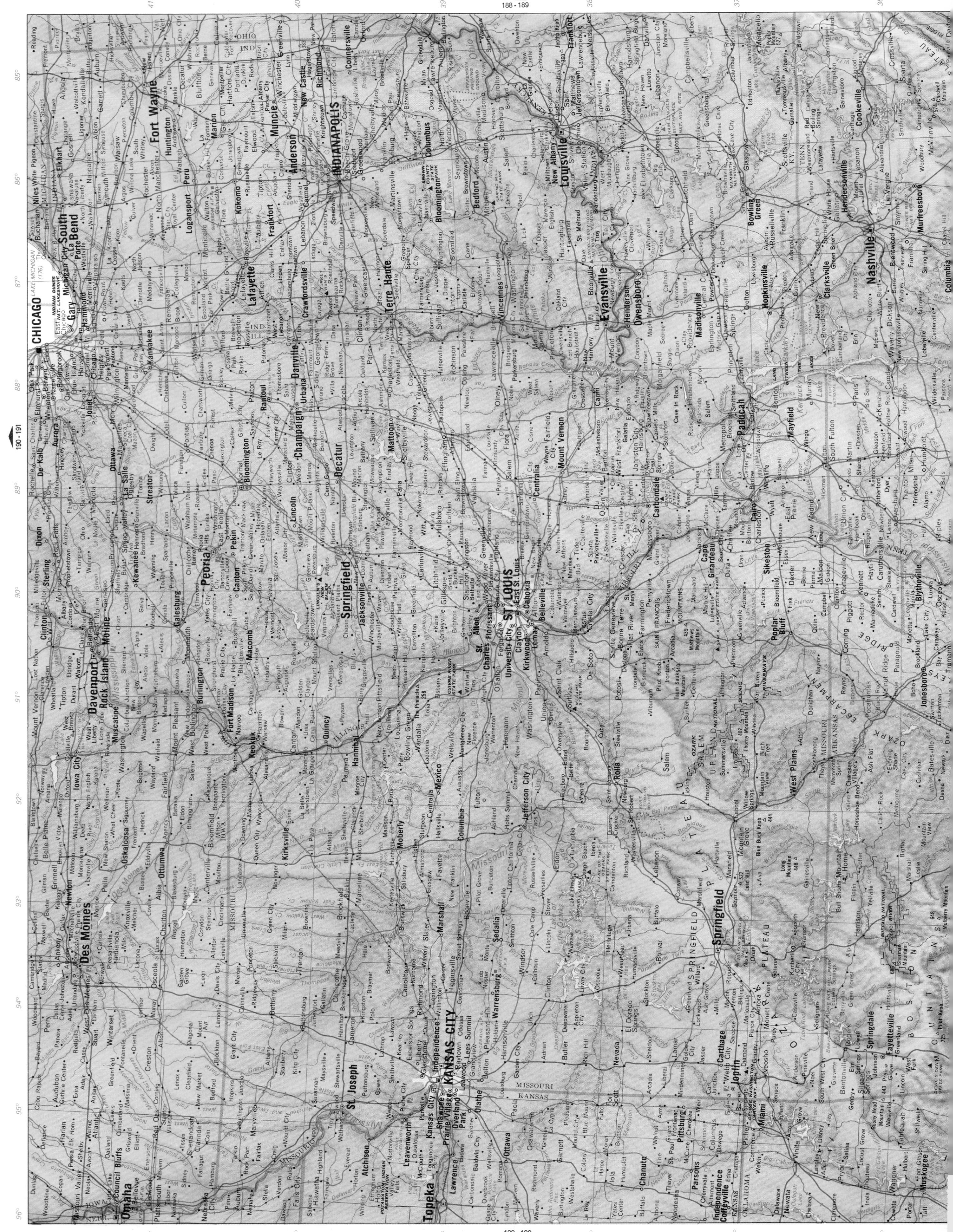

198 - 199

192 - 193
196 - 197
GULF OF MEXICO
Copyright © by Rand McNally & Co.
Map prepared by Rand McNally & Co.
Meters
Feet
Land Below Sea Level
ENGLISH bay / bayou, bay / creek, cr. / dam / lake / mountain, mtn. / reservoir, res. / state park, s.p.
DEUTSCH Bucht / Altwasser / Bach / Damm / See / Berg / Stausee / Staatspark
ESPAÑOL bahía / ensenada / riachuelo / presa / lago / montaña / embalse / parque del estado
FRANÇAIS baie / bayou / crique / barrage / lac / montagne / réservoir / parc régional
PORTUGUÊS baía / enseada / riacho / barragem / lago / montanha / reservatório / parque estadual
For complete glossary see page I·I.
Kilometers
Statute Miles
Scale 1:3,000,000
One centimeter represents 30 kilometers.
One inch represents approximately 47 miles.
Albers Conical Equal-Area Projection

194 - 195

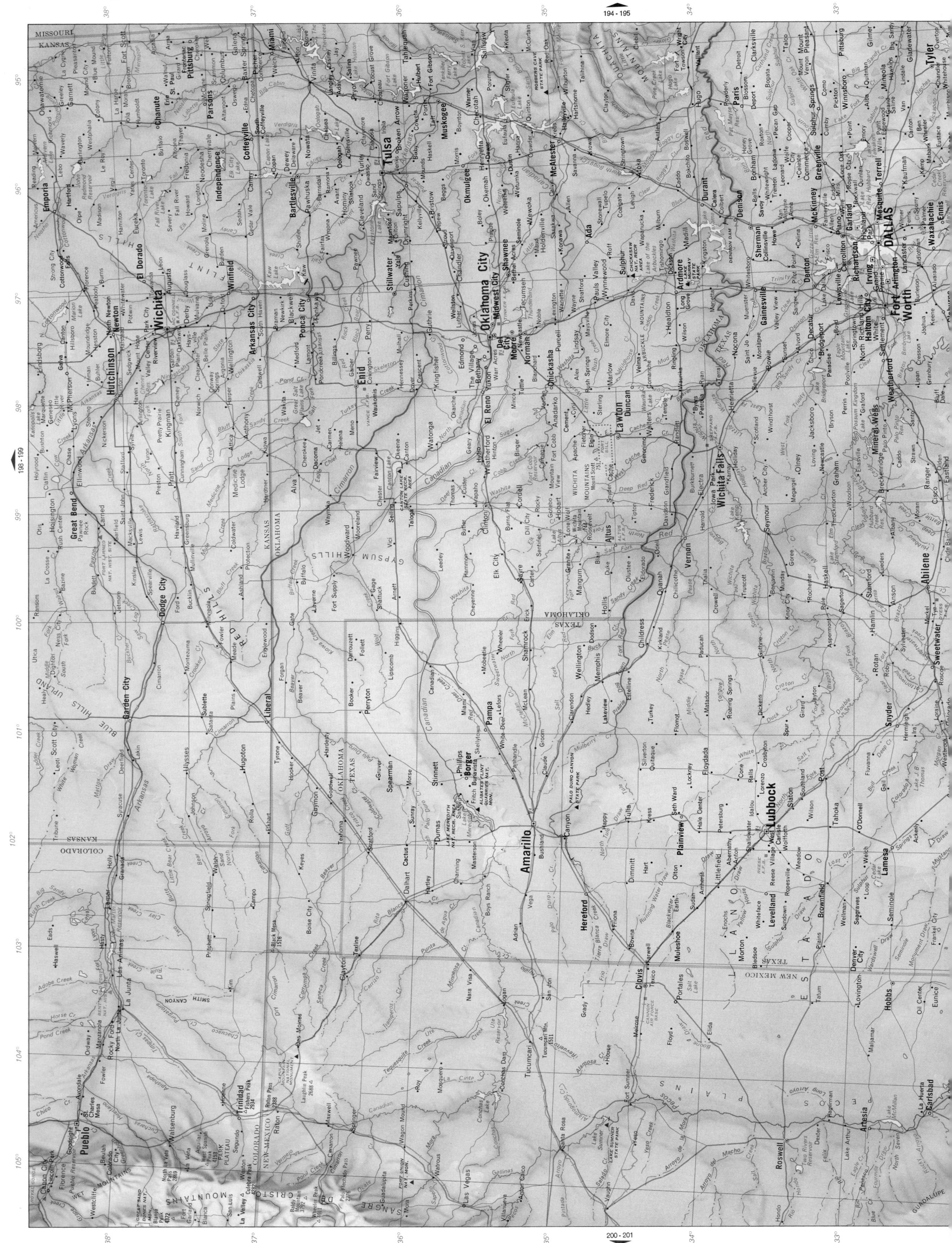

198 - 199

200 - 201

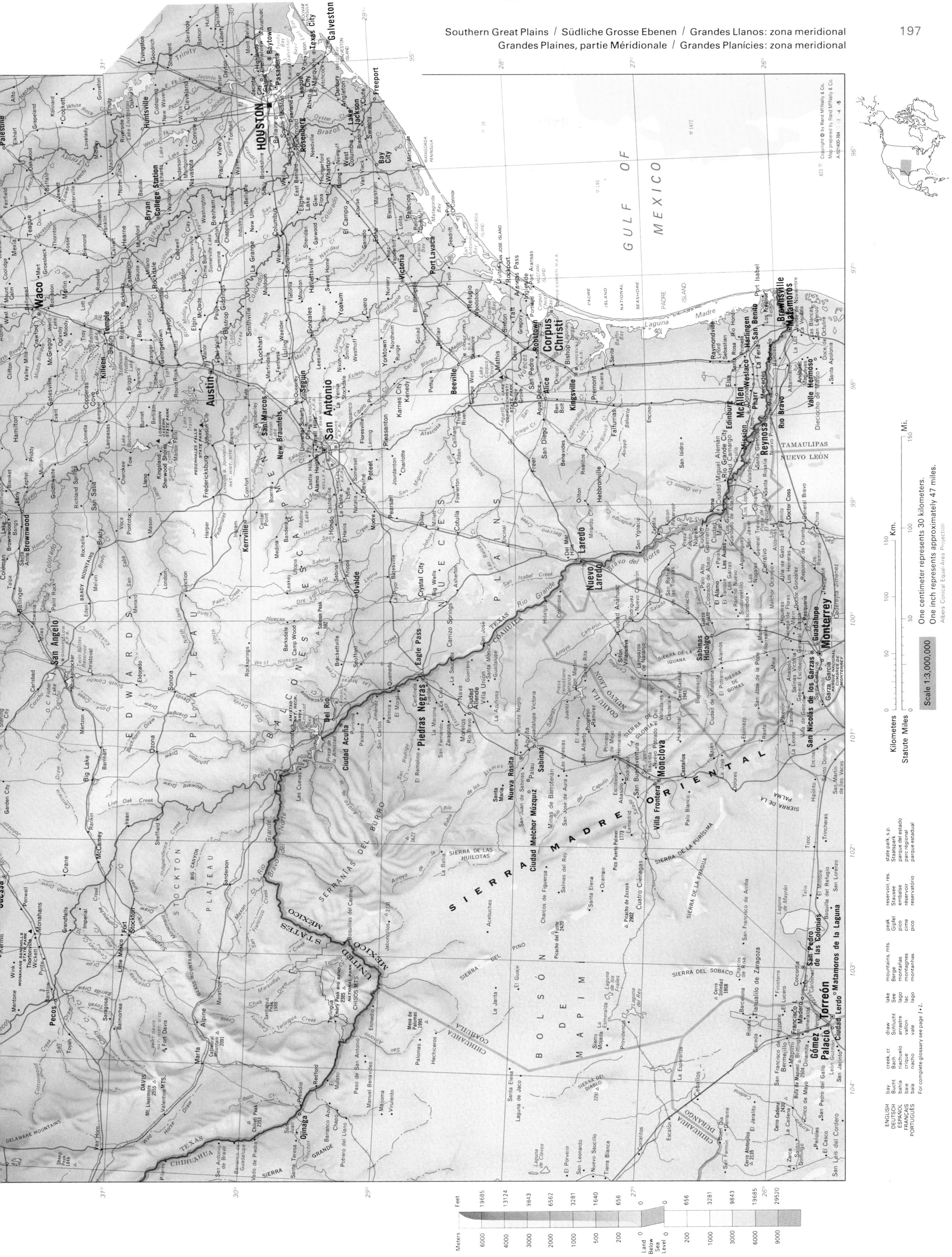
GULF OF MEXICO
SIERRA MADRE ORIENTAL
EDWARDS PLATEAU
NUECES PLAINS
BALCONES ESCARPMENT
STOCKTON PLATEAU
BOLSÓN DE MAPIMÍ
SERRANÍAS DEL BURRO
TAMAULIPAS
NUEVO LEÓN
COAHUILA
CHIHUAHUA
DURANGO
TEXAS
UNITED STATES
MEXICO
HOUSTON
San Antonio
Austin
Corpus Christi
Monterrey
Torreón
Scale 1:3,000,000
One centimeter represents 30 kilometers.
One inch represents approximately 47 miles.
Albers Conical Equal-Area Projection
Kilometers
Statute Miles
Feet
Meters
Land Below Sea Level

190 - 191

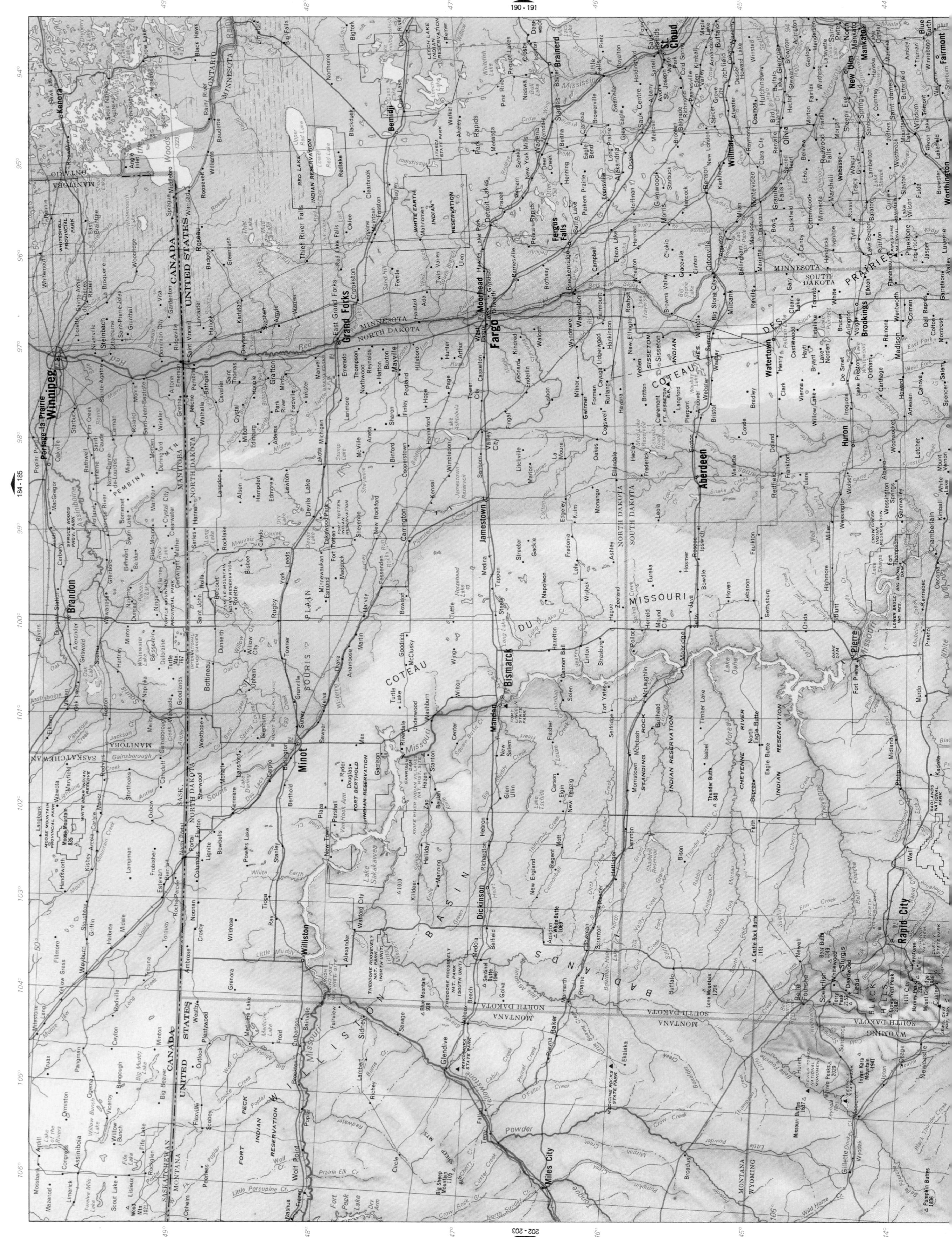

184 - 185

202 - 203

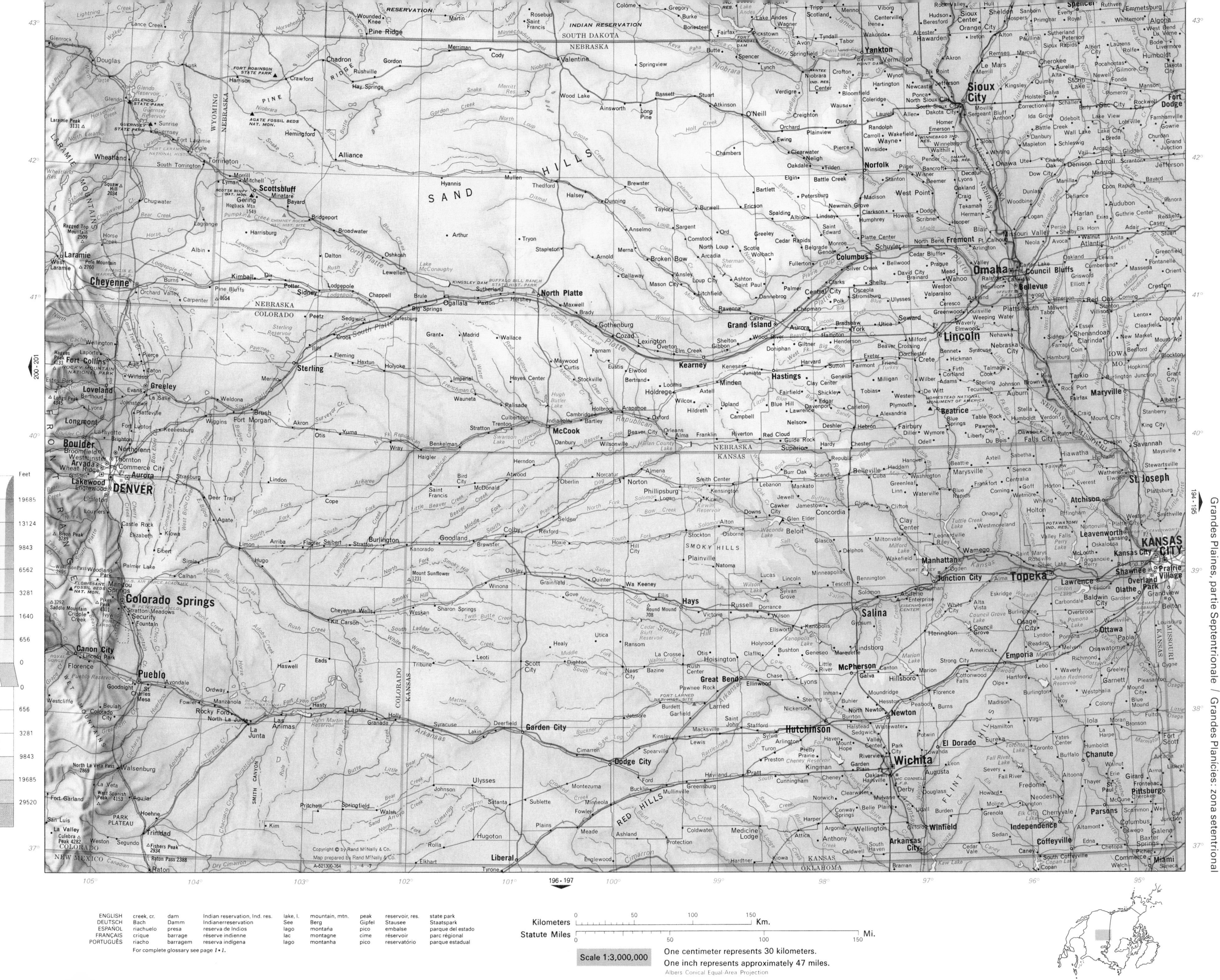
ENGLISH creek, cr. dam Indian reservation, Ind. res. lake, l. mountain, mtn. peak reservoir, res. state park
DEUTSCH Bach Damm Indianerreservation See Berg Gipfel Stausee Staatspark
ESPAÑOL riachuelo presa reserva de Indios lago montaña pico embalse parque del estado
FRANÇAIS crique barrage réserve indienne lac montagne cime réservoir parc régional
PORTUGUÊS riacho barragem reserva indígena lago montanha pico reservatório parque estadual
For complete glossary see page I•1.
Kilometers
Statute Miles
Scale 1:3,000,000
One centimeter represents 30 kilometers.
One inch represents approximately 47 miles.
Albers Conical Equal Area Projection
Copyright © by Rand McNally & Co.
Map prepared by Rand McNally & Co.

198 - 199

202 - 203

204 - 205

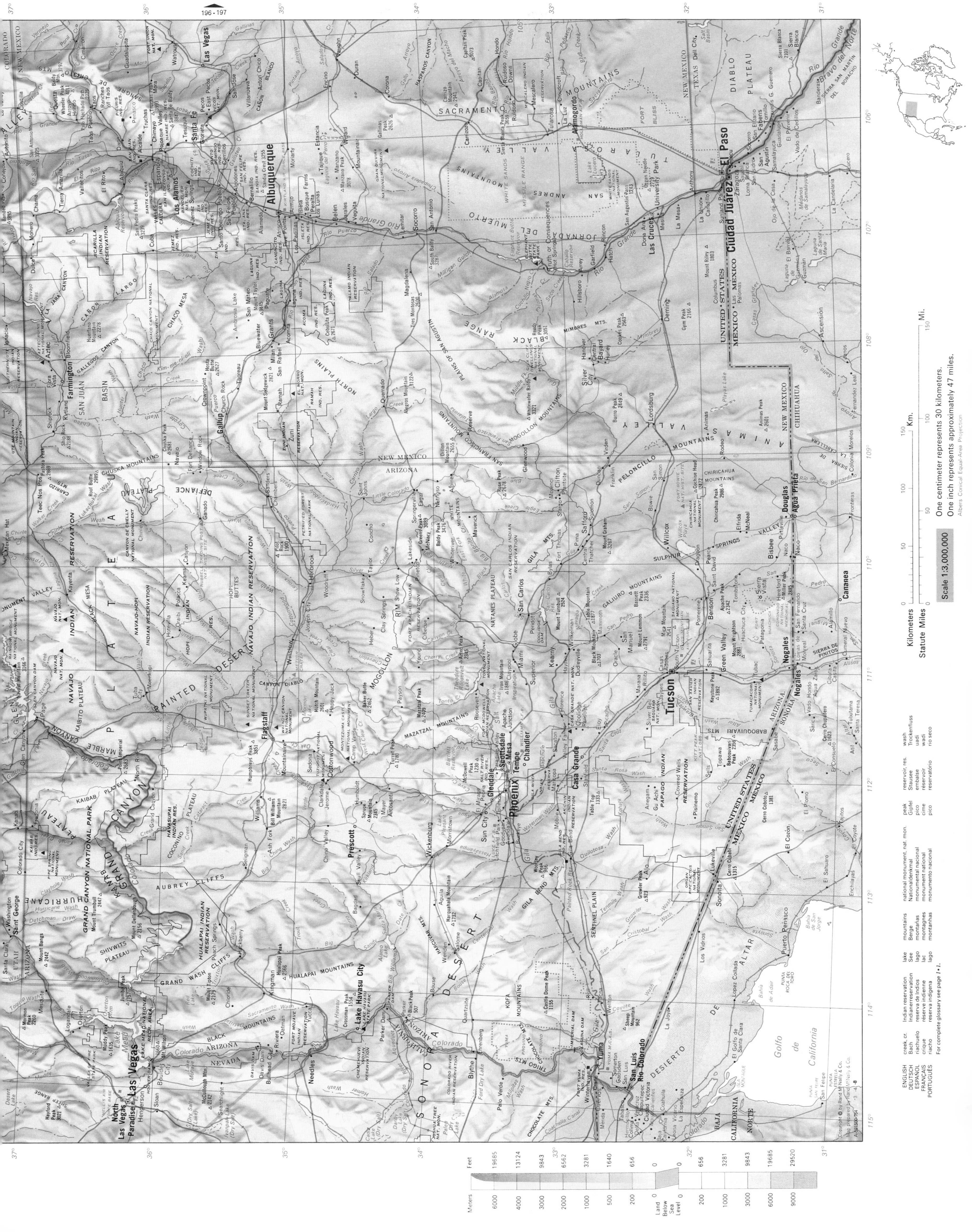

196 - 197

Scale 1:3,000,000

One centimeter represents 30 kilometers.
One inch represents approximately 47 miles.
Albers Conical Equal-Area Projection

Kilometers 0 50 100 150 Km.
Statute Miles 0 50 100 150 Mi.

ENGLISH	creek, cr.	Indian reservation	lake	mountains	national monument, nat. mon.	peak	reservoir, res.	wash
DEUTSCH	Bach	Indianerreservation	See	Berge	Nationaldenkmal	Gipfel	Stausee	Trockenfluss
ESPAÑOL	riachuelo	reserva de indios	lago	montañas	monumento nacional	pico	embalse	uadi
FRANÇAIS	crique	reserve indienne	lac	montagnes	monument national	cime	réservoir	wadi
PORTUGUÊS	riacho	reserva indígena	lago	montanhas	monumento nacional	pico	reservatório	rio seco

For complete glossary see page I • I.

Meters	Feet
6000	19685
4000	13124
3000	9843
2000	6562
1000	3281
500	1640
200	656
0	0
Land Below Sea Level 0	0
200	656
1000	3281
3000	9843
6000	19685
9000	29520

ENGLISH	creek, cr.	Indian reservation	lake, l.	mountain, mtn.	pass	peak	range	reservoir, res.
DEUTSCH	Bach	Indianerreservation	See	Berg	Pass	Gipfel	Gebirge	Stausee
ESPAÑOL	riachuelo	reserva de indios	lago	montaña	paso	pico	sierra	embalse
FRANÇAIS	crique	réserve indienne	lac	montagne	col	cime	chaîne	réservoir
PORTUGUÊS	riacho	reserva indígena	lago	montanha	passo	pico	serra	reservatório

For complete glossary see page I • 1.

184 - 185
CANADA
UNITED STATES
ALBERTA
SASKATCHEWAN
MONTANA
BRITISH COLUMBIA
MONTANA
WYOMING
IDAHO
UTAH
WYOMING
COLORADO
Great Falls
Havre
Helena
Missoula
Kalispell
Butte
Anaconda
Bozeman
Billings
Lewistown
Miles City
Sheridan
Casper
Rock Springs
Idaho Falls
Pocatello
Twin Falls
Logan
Ogden
Brigham City
Riverton
Lander
Cody
ROCKY MOUNTAINS
BIG HORN BASIN
GREAT DIVIDE BASIN
GREAT SALT LAKE DESERT
Great Salt Lake
SNAKE RIVER PLAIN
YELLOWSTONE NATIONAL PARK
GLACIER NATIONAL PARK
Missouri
Yellowstone
Fort Peck Lake
198 - 199
200 - 201
Copyright © by Rand McNally & Co.
Map prepared by Rand McNally & Co.
A-520597-764
Kilometers
0 50 100 150 Km.
Statute Miles
0 50 100 150 Mi.
Scale 1:3,000,000
One centimeter represents 30 kilometers.
One inch represents approximately 47 miles.
Albers Conical Equal-Area Projection

200 - 201
202 - 203
GREAT SALT LAKE DESERT
SAN FRANCISCO
Oakland
San Jose
Sacramento
Stockton
Reno
Sparks
Carson City
Eureka
Redding
Klamath Falls
Medford
Coos Bay
Twin Falls
Elko
Winnemucca
OREGON
NEVADA
CALIFORNIA
IDAHO
UTAH
CASCADE RANGE
KLAMATH MOUNTAINS
COAST RANGES
SIERRA NEVADA
GREAT BASIN
COLUMBIA PLATEAU
SNAKE RIVER PLAIN
BLACK ROCK DESERT
RUBY MOUNTAINS
SACRAMENTO VALLEY
TOIYABE RANGE

PACIFIC OCEAN
MOJAVE DESERT
LOS ANGELES
SAN DIEGO
Las Vegas
Bakersfield
Fresno
Tijuana
Mexicali
Ensenada
Scale 1:3,000,000
One centimeter represents 30 kilometers.
One inch represents approximately 47 miles.
Albers Conical Equal-Area Projection
Kilometers
Statute Miles
Km.
Mi.
ENGLISH creek, cr. lake mountain, mtn. peak, pk. range reservoir, res. state park valley
DEUTSCH Bach See Berg Gipfel Gebirge Stausee Staatspark Tal
ESPAÑOL riachuelo lago montaña pico sierra embalse parque del estado valle
FRANÇAIS crique lac montagne cime chaîne réservoir parc régional vallée
PORTUGUÊS riacho lago montanha pico serra reservatório parque estadual vale
For complete glossary see page I • 1.
Copyright © by Rand McNally & Co.
Map prepared by Rand McNally & Co.
Meters
Feet
Land Below Sea Level

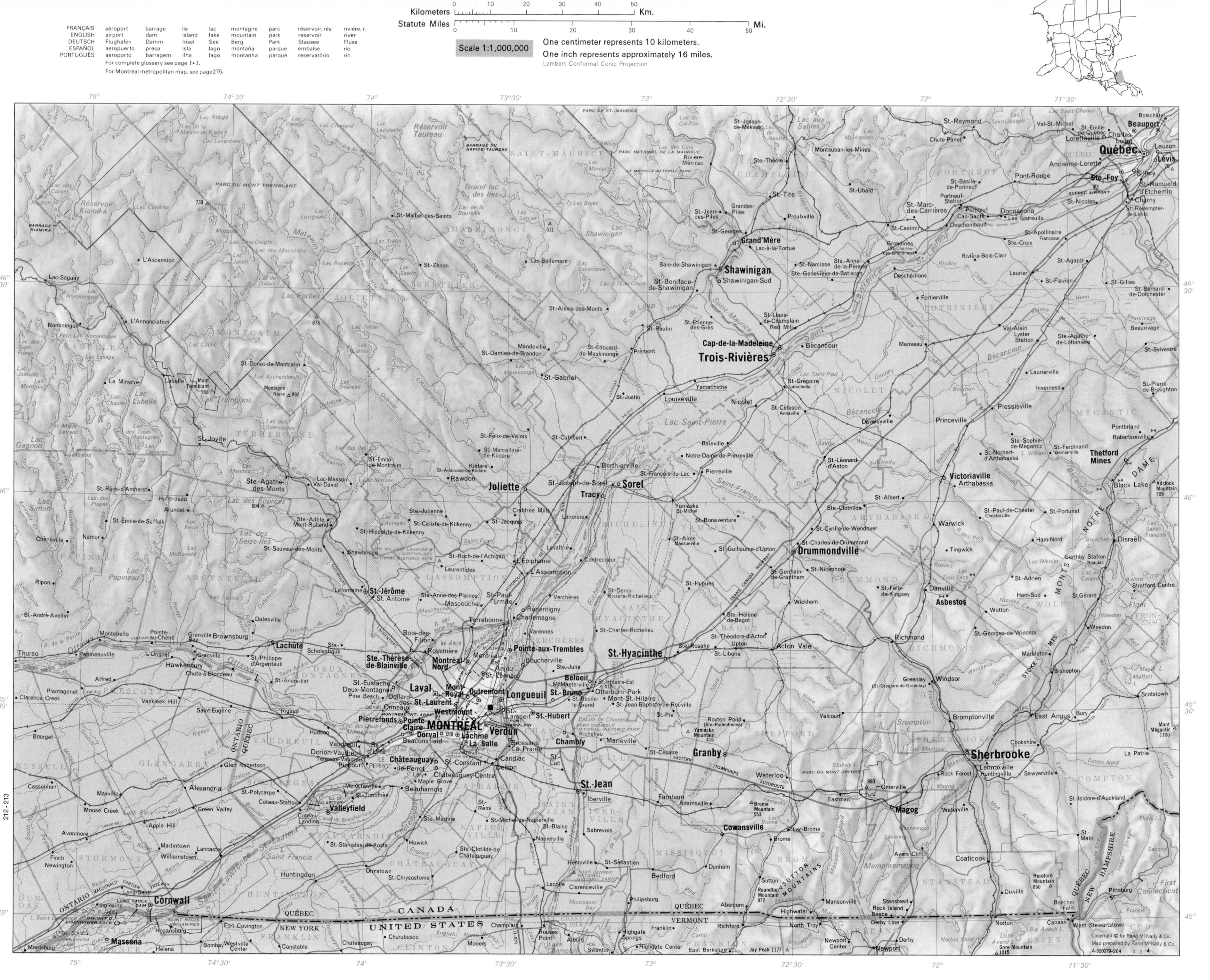
FRANÇAIS aéroport barrage île lac montagne parc réservoir, rés. rivière, r.
ENGLISH airport dam island lake mountain park reservoir river
DEUTSCH Flughafen Damm Insel See Berg Park Stausee Fluss
ESPAÑOL aeropuerto presa isla lago montaña parque embalse río
PORTUGUÊS aeroporto barragem ilha lago montanha parque reservatório rio
For complete glossary see page I • 1.
For Montréal metropolitan map, see page 275.
Kilometers 0 10 20 30 40 50 Km.
Statute Miles 0 10 20 30 40 50 Mi.
Scale 1:1,000,000
One centimeter represents 10 kilometers.
One inch represents approximately 16 miles.
Lambert Conformal Conic Projection
212-213
Copyright © by Rand McNally & Co.
Map prepared by Rand McNally & Co.
A-520079-264

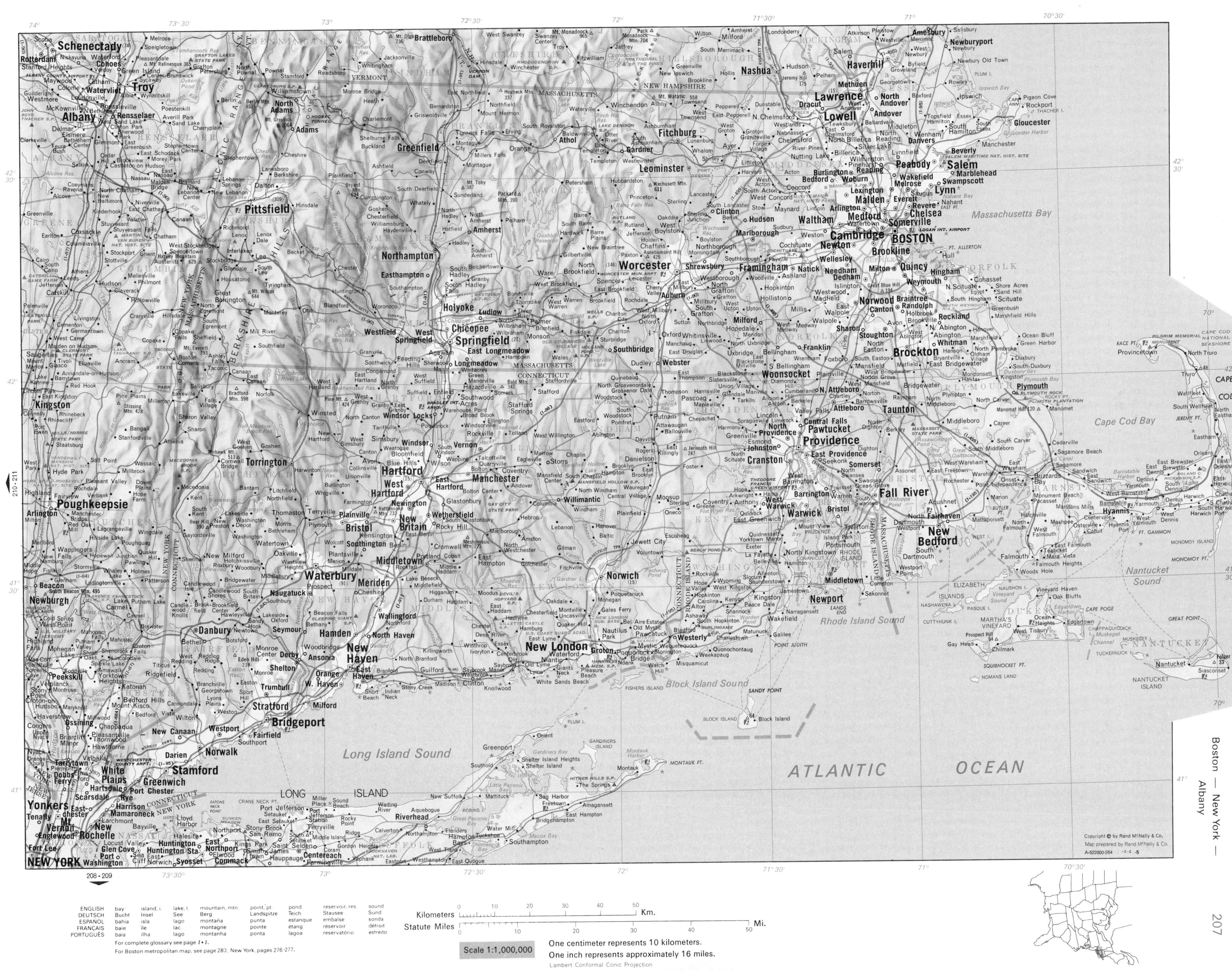

ENGLISH	bay	island, i.	lake, l.	mountain, mtn.	point, pt.	pond	reservoir, res.	sound
DEUTSCH	Bucht	Insel	See	Berg	Landspitze	Teich	Stausee	Sund
ESPAÑOL	bahía	isla	lago	montaña	punta	estanque	embalse	sonda
FRANÇAIS	baie	île	lac	montagne	pointe	étang	réservoir	détroit
PORTUGUÊS	baía	ilha	lago	montanha	ponta	lagoa	reservatório	estreito

For complete glossary see page I • 1.
For Boston metropolitan map, see page 283. New York, pages 276-277.

NEW YORK
Jersey City
Bayonne
NEWARK
East Orange
Elizabeth
Perth Amboy
New Brunswick
Red Bank
Long Branch
Asbury Park
Freehold
Lakewood
Princeton
Trenton
Levittown
PHILADELPHIA
Camden
Norristown
Chester
Wilmington
Atlantic City
Vineland
Millville
Dover
Delaware Bay
Allentown
Bethlehem
Easton
Reading
Pottstown
Lancaster
West Chester
York
Harrisburg
Carlisle
Hanover
Chambersburg
Frederick
BALTIMORE
Towson
Dundalk
Catonsville
Annapolis
Silver Spring
Rockville
Bethesda
WASHINGTON
Arlington
Alexandria
APPALACHIAN
210-211

ATLANTIC
OCEAN
Chesapeake
Bay
Richmond
Petersburg
Fredericksburg
Williamsburg
Newport News
Hampton
Norfolk
Portsmouth
Chesapeake
Virginia Beach
Suffolk
Salisbury
Ocean City
Chincoteague
Cape Charles
MARYLAND
VIRGINIA
NORTH CAROLINA
ENGLISH airport, arpt. bay creek, cr. inlet island, i. mountain point, pt. reservoir, res. state park
DEUTSCH Flughafen Bucht Bach Einfahrt Insel Berg Landspitze Stausee Naturpark
ESPAÑOL aeropuerto bahía riachuelo abra isla montaña punta embalse parque provincial
FRANÇAIS aéroport baie crique bras de mer île montagne pointe réservoir parc régional
PORTUGUÊS aeroporto baía riacho braço de mar ilha montanha ponta reservatório parque estadual
For complete glossary see page I·1.
For New York metropolitan map, see pages 276-277; Philadelphia, page 285; Baltimore and Washington, D.C., page 284.
Kilometers
Statute Miles
Scale 1:1,000,000
One centimeter represents 10 kilometers.
One inch represents approximately 16 miles.
Lambert Conformal Conic Projection
Copyright © by Rand McNally & Co.
Map prepared by Rand McNally & Co.
A-523100-264

212-213

214-215

ENGLISH	airport, arpt.	bay	creek, cr.	hill	island	lake	mountain	reservoir	state park, s.p.
DEUTSCH	Flughafen	Bucht	Bach	Hügel	Insel	See	Berg	Stausee	Naturpark
ESPAÑOL	aeropuerto	bahía	riachuelo	colina	isla	lago	montaña	embalse	parque provincial
FRANÇAIS	aéroport	baie	crique	colline	île	lac	montagne	réservoir	parc régional
PORTUGUÊS	aeroporto	baía	riacho	colina	ilha	lago	montanha	reservatório	parque estadual

For complete glossary see page I • 1.
For Buffalo metropolitan map, see page 284; New York, pages 276-277.

Scale 1:1,000,000

One centimeter represents 10 kilometers.
One inch represents approximately 16 miles.
Lambert Conformal Conic Projection

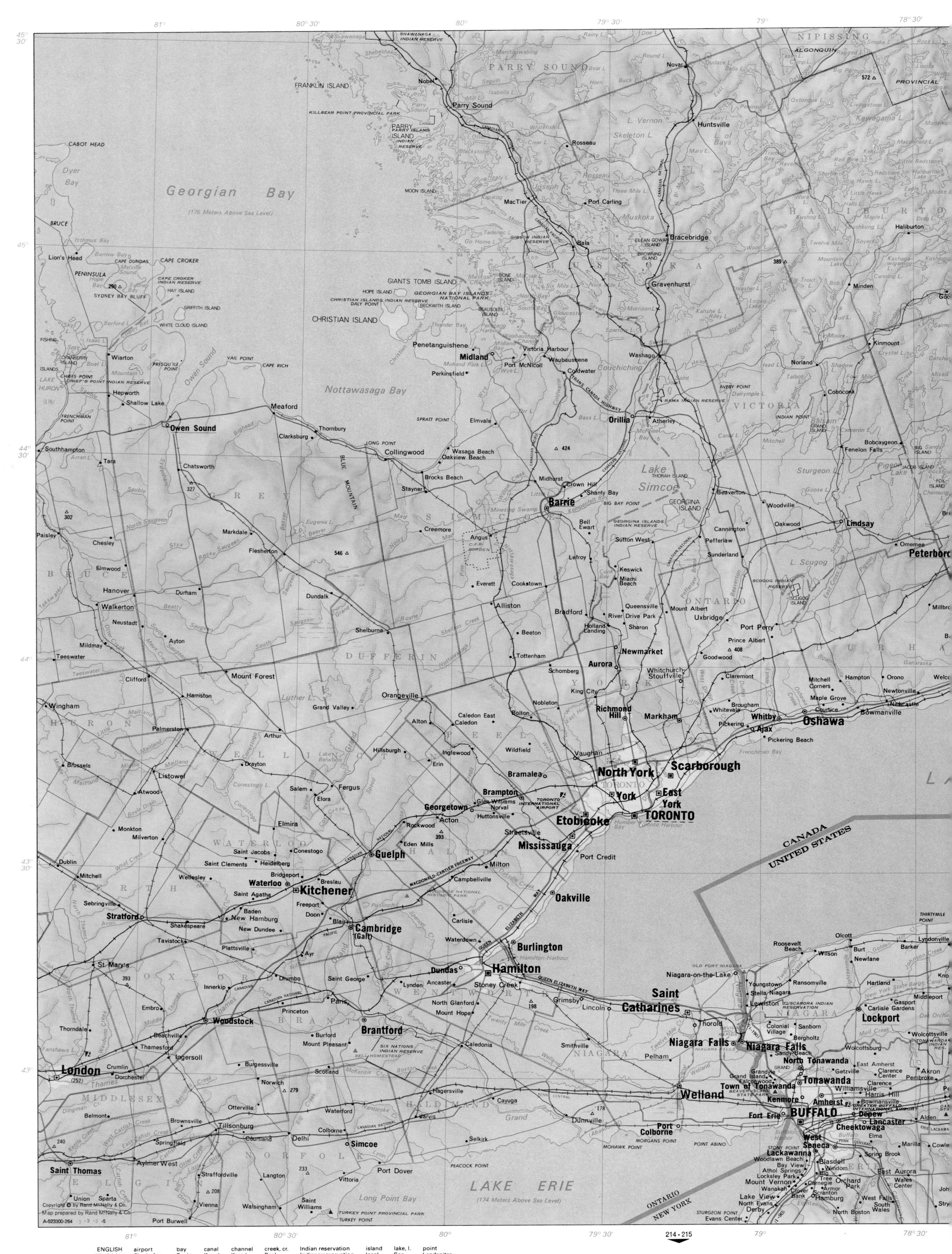

214-215

ENGLISH	airport	bay	canal	channel	creek, cr.	Indian reservation	island	lake, l.	point
DEUTSCH	Flughafen	Bucht	Kanal	Kanal	Bach	Indianerreservation	Insel	See	Landspitze
ESPAÑOL	aeropuerto	bahía	canal	canal	riachuelo	reserva de Indios	isla	lago	punta
FRANÇAIS	aéroport	baie	canal	canal	crique	réserve indienne	île	lac	pointe
PORTUGUÊS	aeroporto	baía	canal	canal	riacho	reserva indígena	ilha	lago	ponta

For complete glossary see page *I • 1*.
For Toronto metropolitan map, see page 275; Buffalo, page 284.

206
Ottawa
Hull
Pointe-Gatineau
Gatineau
Vanier
Rockcliffe Park
Aylmer East
Templeton
Orléans
Cardinal Heights
Sarsfield
Limoges
Embrun
Russell
RUSSELL
Metcalfe
Vernon
Osgoode
Manotick
Richmond
Stittsville
Carp
Almonte
Carleton Place
North Gower
Kemptville
Winchester
Chesterville
Williamsburg
DUNDAS
Morrisburg
Iroquois
Cardinal
Spencerville
Prescott
Ogdensburg
Merrickville
Smiths Falls
Perth
Lanark
LANARK
GRENVILLE
LEEDS
Athens
Westport
Newboro
Delta
Elgin
Brockville
Maitland
Morristown
Heuvelton
Rensselaer Falls
De Kalb Junction
Hermon
Richville
Gouverneur
Hailesboro
Edwards
Antwerp
Philadelphia
Theresa
Redwood
Alexandria Bay
Clayton
LaFargeville
Depauville
Cape Vincent
Three Mile Bay
Chaumont
Dexter
Brownville
Glen Park
Watertown
Sackets Harbor
Black River
Felts Mills
Great Bend
Deferiet
Evans Mills
Natural Bridge
Carthage
West Carthage
Deer River
Castorland
Croghan
Beaver Falls
Copenhagen
Barnes Corners
Lowville
Martinsburg
Glenfield
Turin
Lyons Falls
Port Leyden
Constableville
Boonville
West Leyden
LEWIS
JEFFERSON
ST. LAWRENCE
Adams Center
Henderson
Adams
Belleville
Ellisburg
Pierrepont Manor
Mannsville
Sandy Creek
Lacona
Rainbow Shores
Pulaski
Richland
Orwell
Altmar
Redfield
Mexico Bay
New Haven
Mexico
Oswego
Parish
Williamstown
Westdale
Hastings
Camden
Fulton
Minetto
Hannibal
Fair Haven
Red Creek
Phoenix
Brewerton
Central Square
Constantia
Cleveland
Bernhards Bay
North Bay
McConnellsville
Taberg
Lee Center
North Western
Westernville
Rome
Stittville
Oriskany
Whitesboro
Yorkville
New York Mills
Utica
Clark Mills
New Hartford
Clinton
Westmoreland
Vernon
Oneida
Sherrill
Oneida Castle
Canastota
Wampsville
Chittenango Falls
Munnsville
Morrisville
Peterboro
Cazenovia
Madison
Hamilton
Eaton
West Eaton
Earlville
Lebanon
Georgetown
De Ruyter
Sherburne
Smyrna
New Berlin
Kingston
Barriefield
Wolfe Island
WOLFE ISLAND
AMHERST ISLAND
Amherstview
Bath
Collins Bay
Odessa
Westbrook
Cataraqui
Kingston Mills
Gananoque
Lansdowne
Seeleys Bay
Sydenham
Harrowsmith
Yarker
Newburgh
Napanee
Deseronto
Shannonville
Belleville
Trenton
Frankford
Batawa
Stirling
Campbellford
Glen Ross
Foxboro
Cannifton
Tweed
Madoc
Marmora
Deloro
Havelock
Norwood
Hastings
Warkworth
Brighton
Colborne
Grafton
Cobourg
Wellington
Bloomfield
Picton
Consecon
PRINCE EDWARD
Smithfield
FALSE DUCKS ISLANDS
Tamworth
Verona
Kaladar
Northbrook
Sharbot Lake
Denbigh
Bancroft
Apsley
Calabogie
Renfrew
Douglas
Barrys Bay
Madawaska
Arnprior
Braeside
Pakenham
MADAWASKA
HIGHLANDS
RENFREW
HASTINGS
FRONTENAC
ADDINGTON
LENNOX
PRINCE EDWARD
NORTHUMBERLAND
ONTARIO
(75 Meters Above Sea Level)
ONTARIO
NEW YORK
Rochester
Irondequoit
Greece
Gates
Brighton
Penfield
East Rochester
Fairport
Pittsford
Henrietta
West Henrietta
Webster
West Webster
Ontario
Williamson
Sodus
Sodus Point
Pultneyville
Alton
Wolcott
North Rose
Rose
Lyons
Clyde
Newark
Palmyra
Macedon
Marion
Walworth
Savannah
Montezuma
Port Byron
Weedsport
Jordan
Elbridge
Baldwinsville
Cicero
Liverpool
North Syracuse
Syracuse
De Witt
Fayetteville
Manlius
East Syracuse
Camillus
Solvay
Marcellus
Skaneateles
Auburn
Cayuga
Seneca Falls
Waterloo
Geneva
Phelps
Clifton Springs
Shortsville
Manchester
Canandaigua
Victor
Honeoye Falls
Mendon
Rush
Avon
Lima
Geneseo
Livonia
Mount Morris
Perry
Warsaw
Le Roy
Batavia
Caledonia
Stafford
Bergen
Churchville
Spencerport
Brockport
Holley
Albion
Hamlin
Kendall
Hilton
Penn Yan
Dresden
Ovid
Romulus
Union Springs
Aurora
King Ferry
Genoa
Moravia
Homer
Tully
Cortland
Preble
Truxton
Fabius
Pompey
Jamesville
Nedrow
LIVINGSTON
ONTARIO
WAYNE
MONROE
SENECA
CAYUGA
ONONDAGA
YATES
78°
77°30'
77°
76°30'
76°
75°30'
45°
44°30'
44°
43°30'
43°
210-211
Kilometers 0 10 20 30 40 50 Km.
Statute Miles 0 10 20 30 40 50 Mi.
Scale 1:1,000,000
One centimeter represents 10 kilometers.
One inch represents approximately 16 miles.
Lambert Conformal Conic Projection

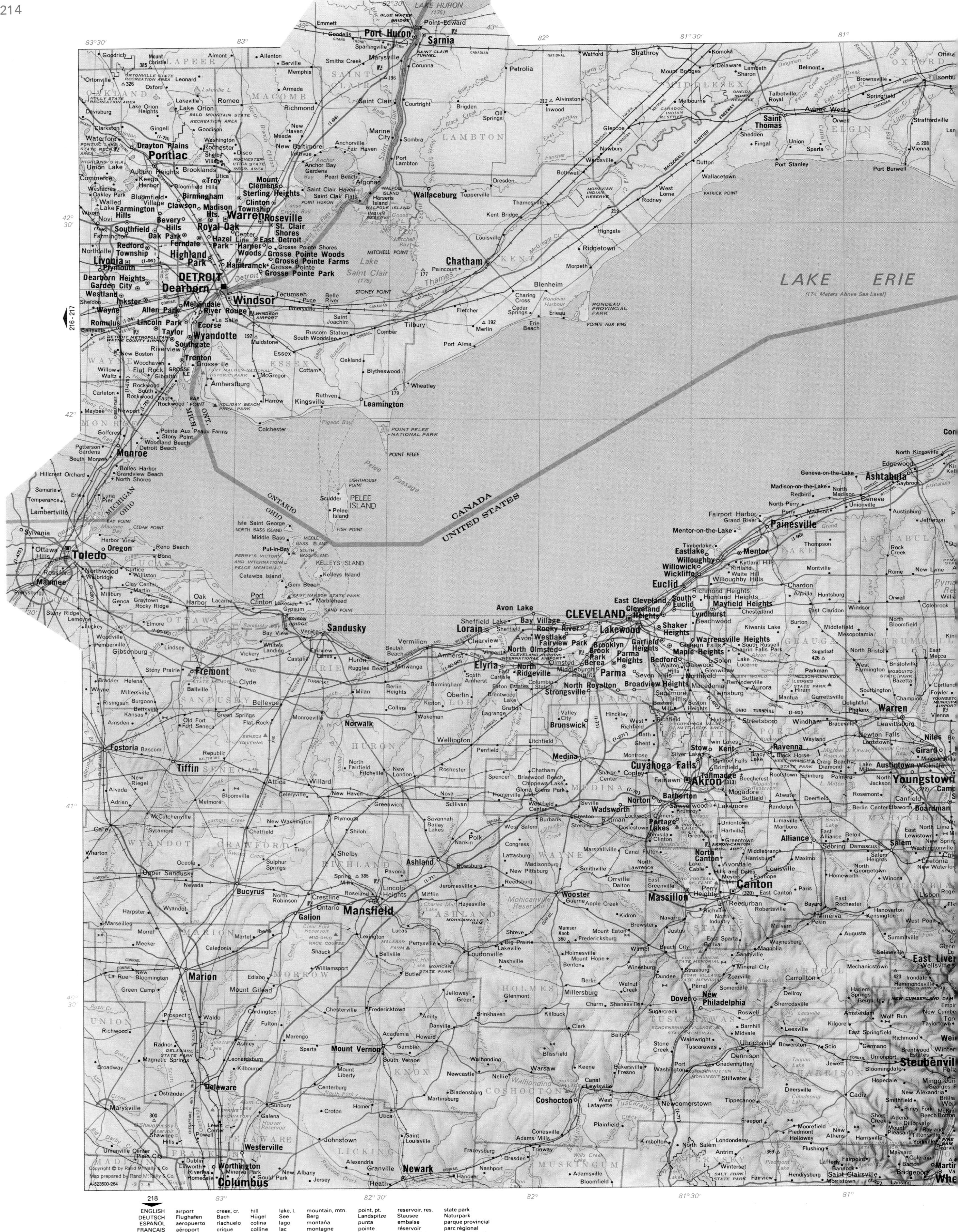

ENGLISH	airport	creek, cr.	hill	lake, l.	mountain, mtn.	point, pt.	reservoir, res.	state park
DEUTSCH	Flughafen	Bach	Hügel	See	Berg	Landspitze	Stausee	Naturpark
ESPAÑOL	aeropuerto	riachuelo	colina	lago	montaña	punta	embalse	parque provincial
FRANÇAIS	aéroport	crique	colline	lac	montagne	pointe	réservoir	parc régional
PORTUGUÊS	aeroporto	riacho	colina	lago	montanha	ponta	reservatório	parque estadual

For complete glossary see page *I* • *1*.
For Pittsburgh and Cleveland metropolitan maps, see page 279; Detroit, page 281; Buffalo, page 284.

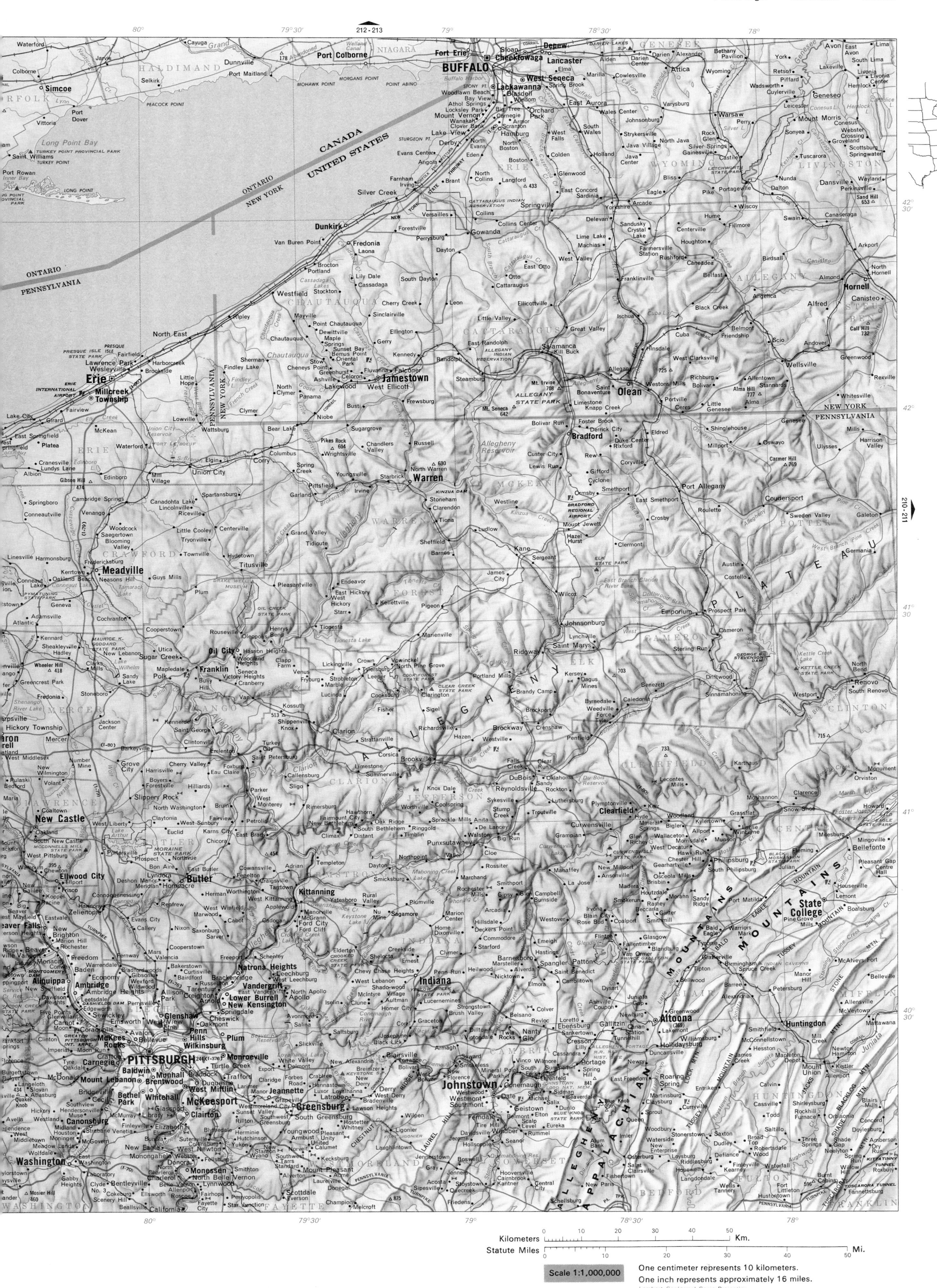
212-213
210-211
ONTARIO
NEW YORK
PENNSYLVANIA
CANADA
UNITED STATES
Long Point Bay
BUFFALO
Erie
PITTSBURGH
Jamestown
Warren
Olean
Bradford
Meadville
Oil City
Franklin
New Castle
Butler
Kittanning
Indiana
Johnstown
Altoona
Greensburg
Washington
McKeesport
State College
Hornell
Wellsville
Dunkirk
Lackawanna
West Seneca
Cheektowaga
Depew
Lancaster
ALLEGHENY
PLATEAU
APPALACHIAN
MOUNTAINS
ALLEGHENY MOUNTAIN
BALD EAGLE MOUNTAIN
CHAUTAUQUA
CATTARAUGUS
ALLEGANY
ERIE
WYOMING
LIVINGSTON
McKEAN
WARREN
POTTER
CAMERON
ELK
FOREST
VENANGO
CRAWFORD
MERCER
LAWRENCE
BUTLER
CLARION
JEFFERSON
CLEARFIELD
CENTRE
ARMSTRONG
INDIANA
CAMBRIA
BLAIR
HUNTINGDON
WESTMORELAND
SOMERSET
BEDFORD
FULTON
FAYETTE
WASHINGTON
CLINTON
MIFFLIN
FRANKLIN
80°
79°30′
79°
78°30′
78°
42°
41°30′
41°
40°30′
Kilometers 0 10 20 30 40 50 Km.
Statute Miles 0 10 20 30 40 50 Mi.
Scale 1:1,000,000
One centimeter represents 10 kilometers.
One inch represents approximately 16 miles.
Lambert Conformal Conic Projection

219

ENGLISH	airport	creek, cr.	ditch	lake, l.	reservoir	state park, s.p.
DEUTSCH	Flughafen	Bach	Graben	See	Stausee	Naturpark
ESPAÑOL	aeropuerto	riachuelo	acequia	lago	embalse	parque provincial
FRANÇAIS	aéroport	crique	fossé	lac	réservoir	parc régional
PORTUGUÊS	aeroporto	riacho	fosso	lago	reservatório	parque estadual

For complete glossary see page *I • 1*.
For Chicago metropolitan map, see page 278; Detroit, page 281.

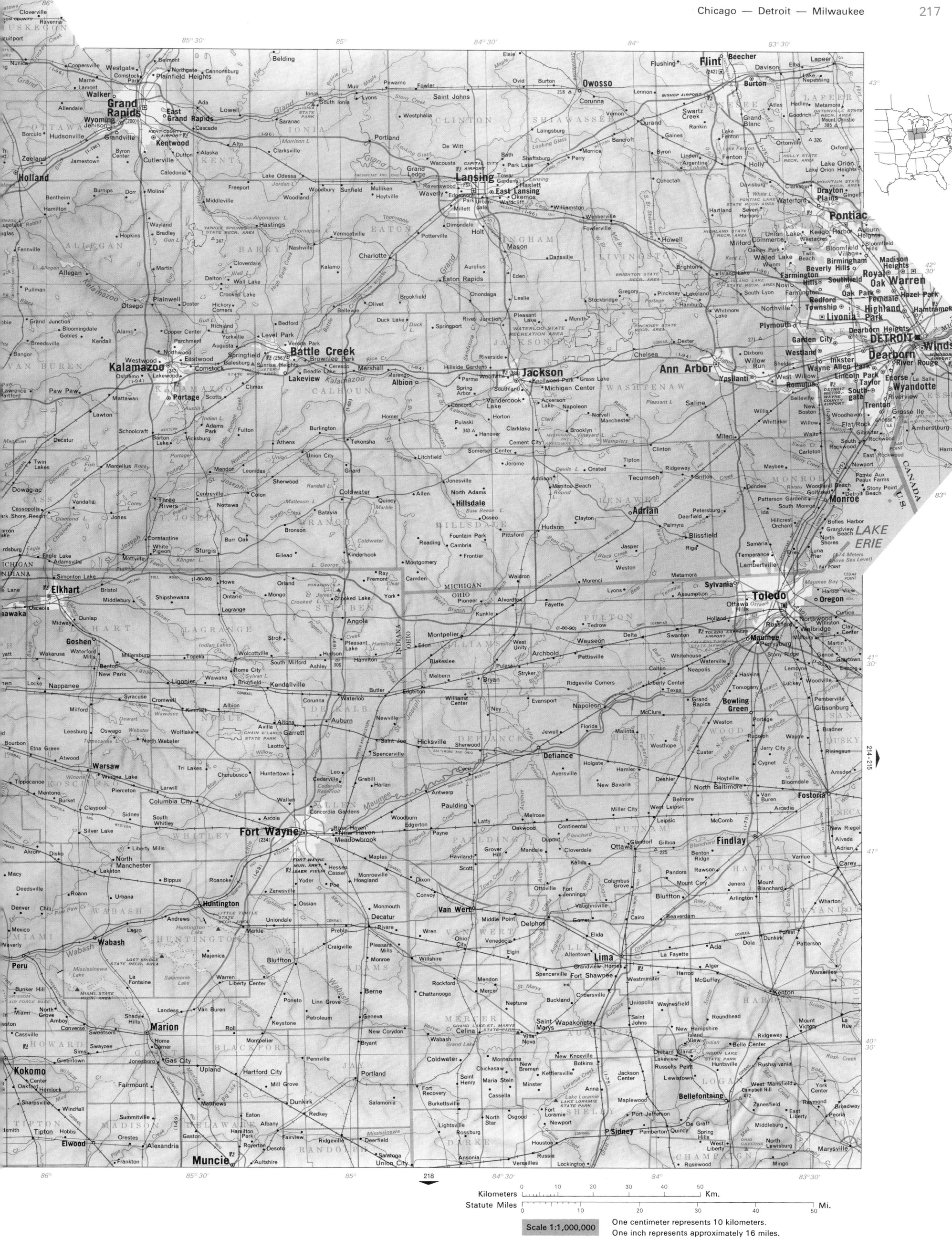

214 · 215

218

Kilometers 0 10 20 30 40 50 Km.

Statute Miles 0 10 20 30 40 50 Mi.

Scale 1:1,000,000

One centimeter represents 10 kilometers.
One inch represents approximately 16 miles.
Lambert Conformal Conic Projection

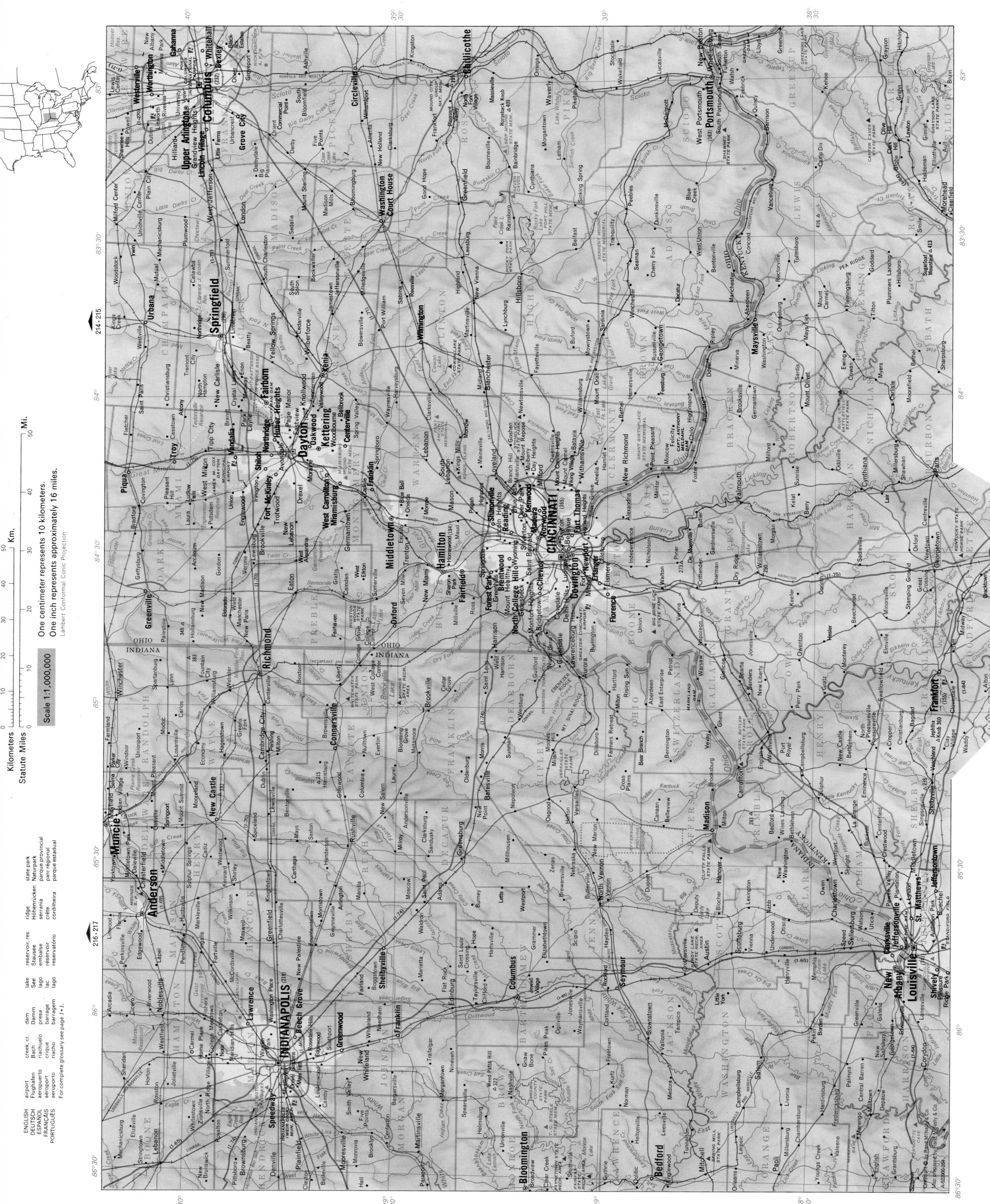

Scale 1:1,000,000
One centimeter represents 10 kilometers.
One inch represents approximately 16 miles.
Lambert Conformal Conic Projection
Kilometers
Statute Miles
Km.
Mi.
ENGLISH airport creek, cr. dam lake reservoir, res. ridge state park
DEUTSCH Flughafen Bach Damm See Stausee Höhenrücken Naturpark
ESPAÑOL aeropuerto riachuelo presa lago embalse serranía parque provincial
FRANÇAIS aéroport crique barrage lac réservoir crête parc régional
PORTUGUÊS aeroporto riacho barragem lago reservatório cordilheira parque estadual
For complete glossary see page I • 1.
214-215
216-217
INDIANAPOLIS
CINCINNATI
Louisville
Dayton
Columbus
Springfield
Richmond
Hamilton
Middletown
Frankfort
OHIO
INDIANA
KENTUCKY

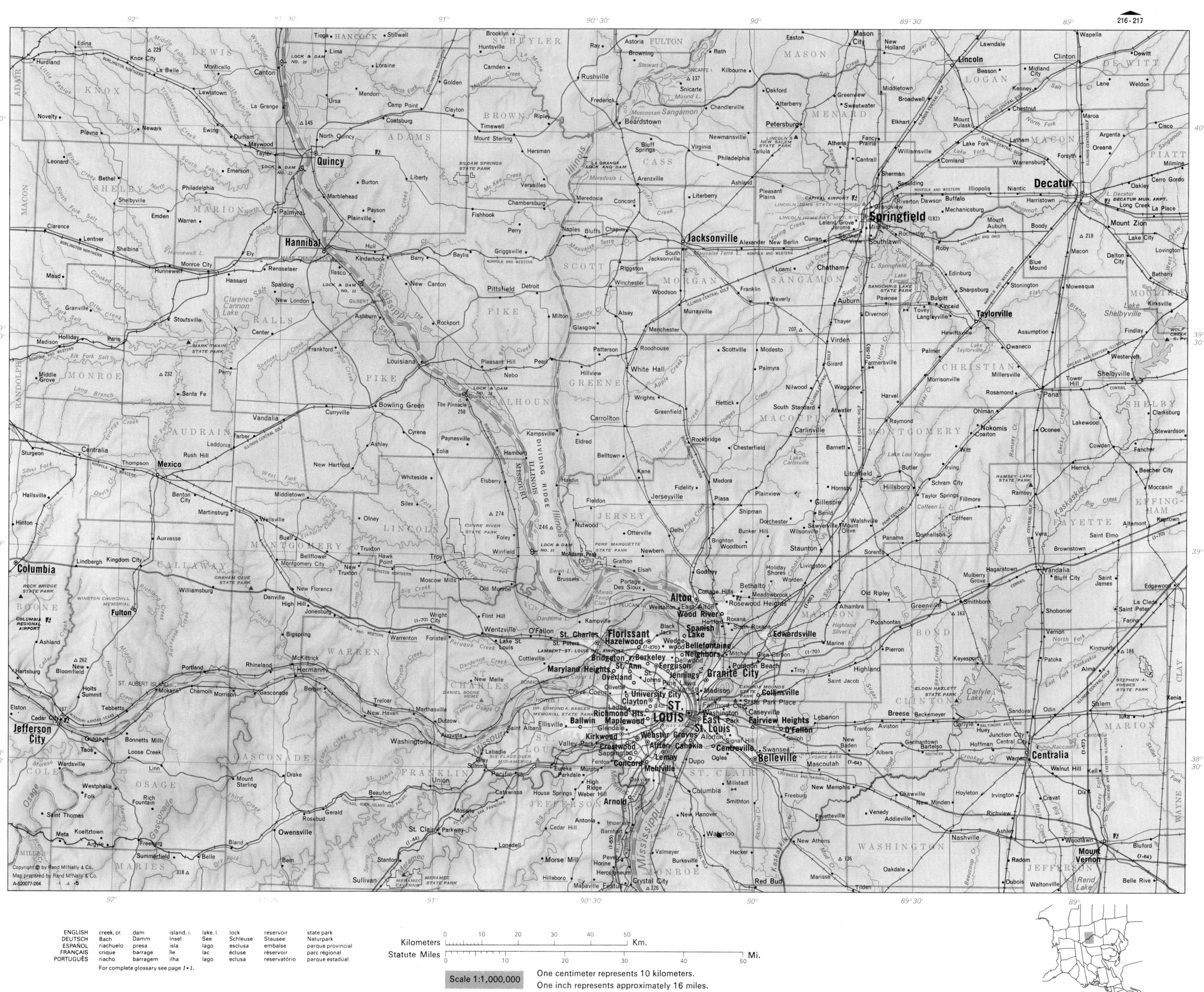

216 · 217
Scale 1:1,000,000
One centimeter represents 10 kilometers.
One inch represents approximately 16 miles.
Lambert Conformal Conic Projection
Kilometers
Statute Miles
Km.
Mi.
ENGLISH creek, cr. dam island, i. lake, l. lock reservoir state park
DEUTSCH Bach Damm Insel See Schleuse Stausee Naturpark
ESPAÑOL riachuelo presa isla lago esclusa embalse parque provincial
FRANÇAIS crique barrage île lac écluse réservoir parc régional
PORTUGUÊS riacho barragem ilha lago eclusa reservatório parque estadual
For complete glossary see page I·1.
Copyright © by Rand McNally & Co.
Map prepared by Rand McNally & Co.
A-520077-264
Mississippi
Illinois
Missouri
ST. LOUIS
Springfield
Decatur
Jefferson City
Columbia
Quincy
Hannibal
Jacksonville
Taylorville
Centralia
Belleville
Mount Vernon

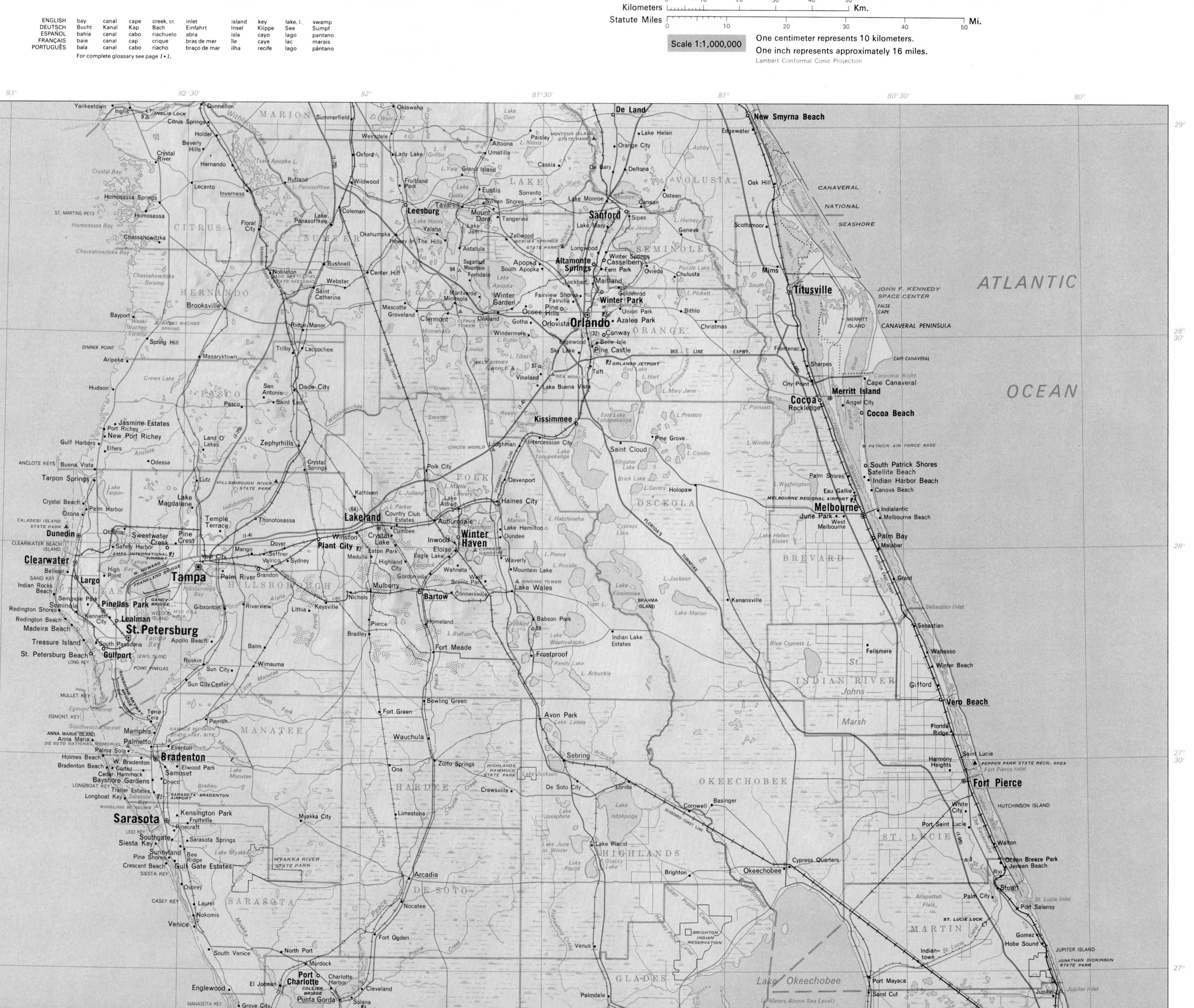

ENGLISH bay canal cape creek, cr. inlet island key lake, l. swamp
DEUTSCH Bucht Kanal Kap Bach Einfahrt Insel Klippe See Sumpf
ESPAÑOL bahia canal cabo riachuelo abra isla cayo lago pantano
FRANÇAIS baie canal cap crique bras de mer île caye lac marais
PORTUGUÊS baía canal cabo riacho braço de mar ilha recife lago pântano
For complete glossary see page I • 1.
Kilometers 0 10 20 30 40 50 Km.
Statute Miles 0 10 20 30 40 50 Mi.
Scale 1:1,000,000
One centimeter represents 10 kilometers.
One inch represents approximately 16 miles.
Lambert Conformal Conic Projection
ATLANTIC OCEAN
CANAVERAL NATIONAL SEASHORE
JOHN F. KENNEDY SPACE CENTER
CANAVERAL PENINSULA
New Smyrna Beach
Titusville
Merritt Island
Cape Canaveral
Cocoa Beach
Cocoa
Melbourne
Vero Beach
Fort Pierce
Stuart
Jupiter
Lake Okeechobee
Okeechobee
De Land
Sanford
Orlando
Winter Park
Kissimmee
Leesburg
Lakeland
Winter Haven
Bartow
Plant City
Tampa
St. Petersburg
Clearwater
Dunedin
Largo
Bradenton
Sarasota
Port Charlotte
Punta Gorda
Arcadia
Sebring
VOLUSIA
SEMINOLE
ORANGE
OSCEOLA
BREVARD
INDIAN RIVER
ST. LUCIE
MARTIN
OKEECHOBEE
HIGHLANDS
GLADES
DE SOTO
HARDEE
POLK
LAKE
SUMTER
MARION
CITRUS
HERNANDO
PASCO
HILLSBOROUGH
PINELLAS
MANATEE
SARASOTA

Riviera Beach
Palm Beach
West Palm Beach
Lake Worth
Lantana
Boynton Beach
Delray Beach
Highland Beach
Boca Raton
Deerfield Beach
Hillsboro Beach
Lighthouse Point
Pompano Beach
Lauderdale-by-the-Sea
Oakland Park
Wilton Manors
Fort Lauderdale
Dania
Hollywood
Hallandale
Golden Beach
North Miami Beach
North Miami
Bay Harbor Islands
Surfside
North Bay Village
MIAMI
Miami Beach
Key Biscayne
Coral Gables
South Miami
Hialeah
Miami Springs
Opa Locka
Carol City
Miramar
Pembroke Pines
West Hollywood
Davie
Plantation
Sunrise
Lauderdale Lakes
North Andrews Gardens
Margate
Coral Springs
Pompano Beach Highlands
Kendall
Perrine
Cutler Ridge
Goulds
Princeton
Naranja
Leisure City
Florida City
Homestead
Richmond Heights
South Miami Heights
Westwood Lakes
Olympia Heights
Belle Glade
South Bay
Clewiston
Harlem
La Belle
Felda
Immokalee
Corkscrew
Alva
Lehigh Acres
Fort Myers Shores
Fort Myers
Tice
North Fort Myers
Fort Myers Villas
Estero
Fort Myers Beach
Bonita Springs
Cape Coral
Sanibel
Captiva
Bokeelia
Boca Grande
Naples
Naples Park
North Naples
East Naples
Golden Gate
Marco
Goodland
Everglades City
Chokoloskee
Copeland
Ochopee
Monroe
Flamingo
Key Largo
Tavernier
Plantation
Islamorada
Marathon
Big Pine Key
Stock Island
Key West
PALM BEACH
BROWARD
DADE
HENDRY
COLLIER
MONROE
LEE
The Everglades
EVERGLADES NATIONAL PARK
BIG CYPRESS NATIONAL PRESERVE
BISCAYNE NATIONAL MONUMENT
JOHN PENNEKAMP CORAL REEF STATE PARK
FLORIDA STATE INDIAN RESERVATION
Biscayne Bay
Florida Bay
FLORIDA KEYS
TEN THOUSAND ISLANDS
CAPE SABLE
GULF OF MEXICO
TAMIAMI TRAIL
North New River Canal
Miami Canal
Big Cypress Swamp
DRY TORTUGAS
FORT JEFFERSON NATIONAL MONUMENT
MARQUESAS KEYS
Copyright © by Rand McNally & Co.
Map prepared by Rand McNally & Co.
A-522200-264

Dallas
Fort Worth
Arlington
Irving
Garland
Mesquite
Waco
Temple
Tyler
Longview
Kilgore
Lufkin
Nacogdoches
Palestine
Jacksonville
Corsicana
Ennis
Waxahachie
Cleburne
Denton
McKinney
Greenville
Sulphur Springs
Mount Pleasant
Terrell
Athens
Crockett
Henderson
Mexia
Killeen
Weatherford
HARRISON
SMITH
RUSK
CHEROKEE
ANDERSON
HENDERSON
NAVARRO
ELLIS
JOHNSON
HILL
MCLENNAN
LIMESTONE
FREESTONE
LEON
HOUSTON
ANGELINA
NACOGDOCHES
KAUFMAN
VAN ZANDT
WOOD
RAINS
HUNT
HOPKINS
FRANKLIN
TITUS
CAMP
UPSHUR
MARION
CASS
MORRIS
GREGG
PANOLA
COLLIN
DENTON
TARRANT
PARKER
WISE
ROCKWALL
DALLAS
BOSQUE
CORYELL
FALLS
TRINITY
HOOD
SOMERVELL

ENGLISH	airport	bay	bayou	creek, cr.	island	lake, l.	reservoir	state park
DEUTSCH	Flughafen	Bucht	Altwasser	Bach	Insel	See	Stausee	Naturpark
ESPAÑOL	aeropuerto	bahía	ensenada pantanosa	riachuelo	isla	lago	embalse	parque provincial
FRANÇAIS	aéroport	baie	bayou	crique	île	lac	réservoir	parc régional
PORTUGUÊS	aeroporto	baía	enseada pantanosa	riacho	ilha	lago	reservatório	parque estadual

For complete glossary see page I • 1.

Kilometers 0 10 20 30 40 50 Km.

Statute Miles 0 10 20 30 40 50 Mi.

Scale 1:1,000,000

One centimeter represents 10 kilometers.
One inch represents approximately 16 miles.
Lambert Conformal Conic Projection

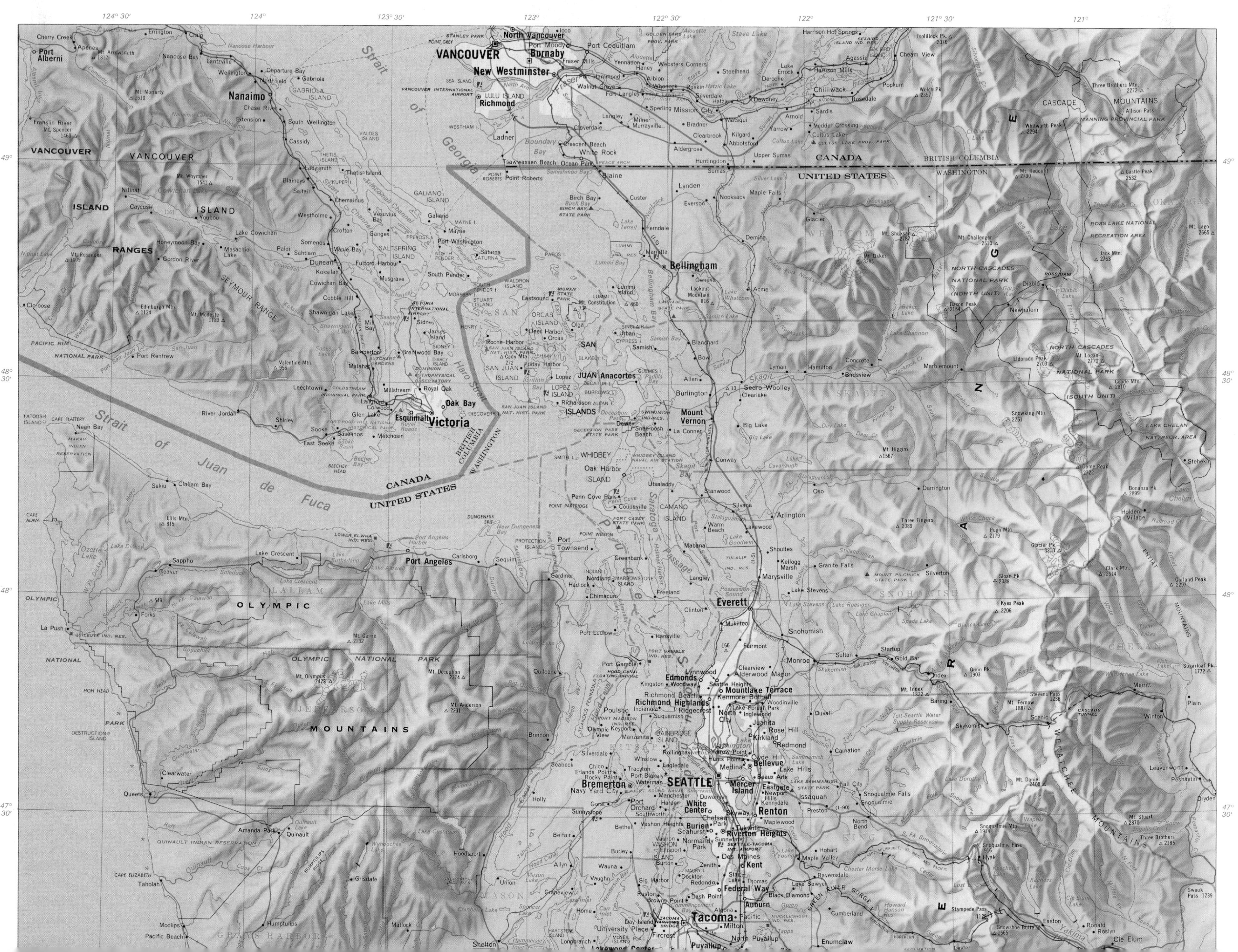
VANCOUVER
North Vancouver
Burnaby
New Westminster
Richmond
Strait of Georgia
Nanaimo
VANCOUVER ISLAND
Victoria
Oak Bay
Esquimalt
Haro Strait
Strait of Juan de Fuca
CANADA
UNITED STATES
BRITISH COLUMBIA
WASHINGTON
Port Angeles
OLYMPIC MOUNTAINS
OLYMPIC NATIONAL PARK
Bellingham
Mount Vernon
Anacortes
Everett
Edmonds
SEATTLE
Bellevue
Renton
Kent
Auburn
Tacoma
Puyallup
Bremerton
CASCADE MOUNTAINS
NORTH CASCADES NATIONAL PARK
WENATCHEE MOUNTAINS

ENGLISH	bay	cape	channel	creek, cr.	island, i.	lake, l.	mount	peak	strait
DEUTSCH	Bucht	Kap	Kanal	Bach	Insel	See	Berg	Gipfel	Meeresstrasse
ESPAÑOL	bahia	cabo	canal	riachuelo	isla	lago	monte	pico	estrecho
FRANÇAIS	baie	cap	canal	crique	île	lac	mont	cime	détroit
PORTUGUÊS	baia	cabo	canal	riacho	ilha	lago	monte	pico	estreito

For complete glossary see page I•1.

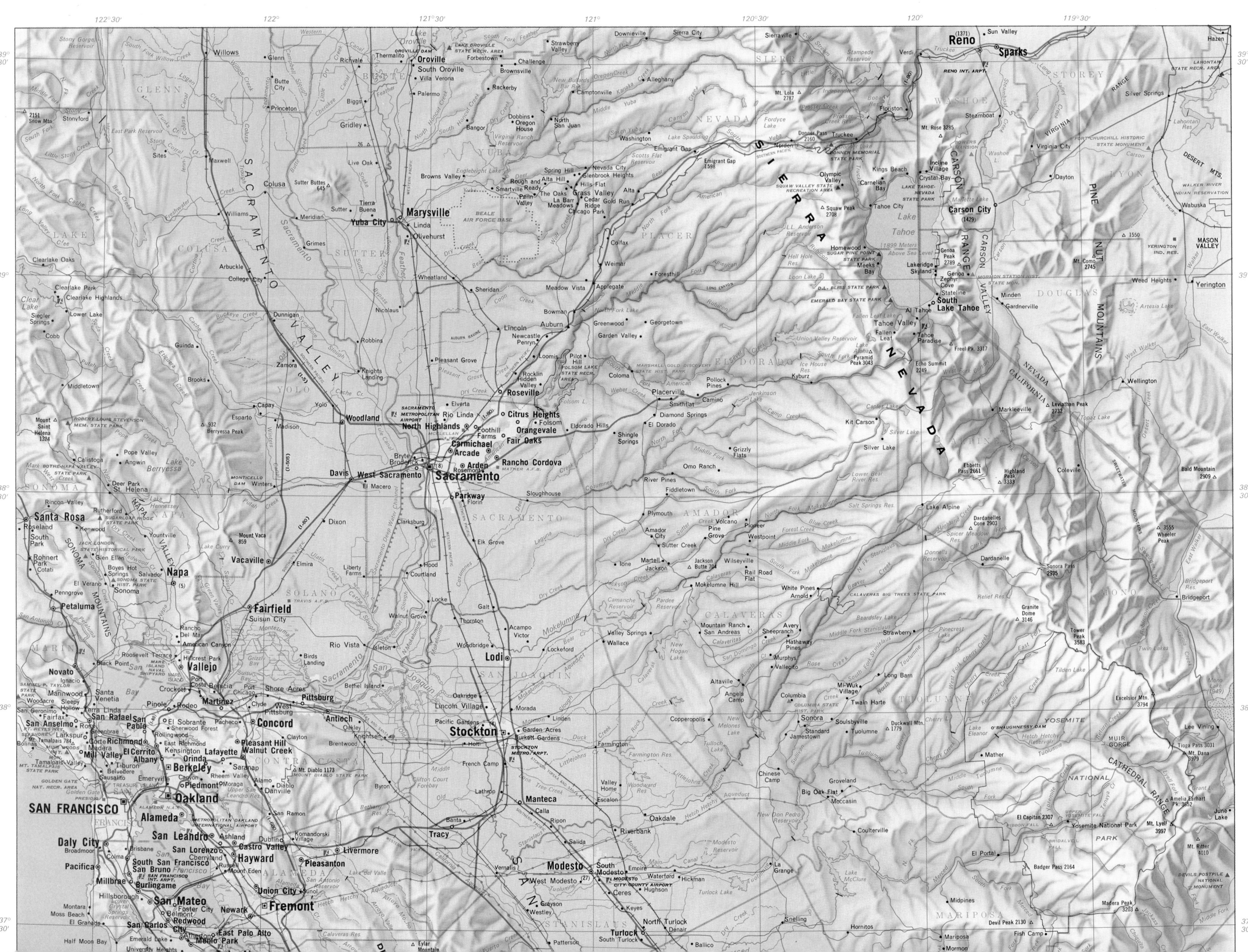

SIERRA NEVADA
SACRAMENTO VALLEY
CARSON VALLEY
PINE NUT MOUNTAINS
Reno
Sparks
Carson City
South Lake Tahoe
Lake Tahoe
Sacramento
Stockton
Modesto
Lodi
Tracy
Manteca
Oroville
Marysville
Yuba City
Roseville
Davis
Woodland
Vacaville
Fairfield
Napa
Vallejo
Santa Rosa
Petaluma
Concord
Berkeley
Oakland
Alameda
Hayward
Fremont
San Mateo
Daly City
SAN FRANCISCO

ENGLISH	bay	canal	creek, cr.	lake, l.	mountain, mtn.	pass	range	reservoir	slough
DEUTSCH	Bucht	Kanal	Bach	See	Berg	Pass	Gebirge	Stausee	verlandene Wasserfläche
ESPAÑOL	bahía	canal	riachuelo	lago	montaña	paso	sierra	embalse	pantano
FRANÇAIS	baie	canal	crique	lac	montagne	col	chaîne	réservoir	fondrière
PORTUGUÊS	baía	canal	riacho	lago	montanha	passo	serra	reservatório	pântano

For complete glossary see page *I* • *1*.

For San Francisco metropolitan map, see page 282.

Kilometers 0 10 20 30 40 50 Km.

Statute Miles 0 10 20 30 40 50 Mi.

Scale 1:1,000,000

One centimeter represents 10 kilometers.
One inch represents approximately 16 miles.

Lambert Conformal Conic Projection

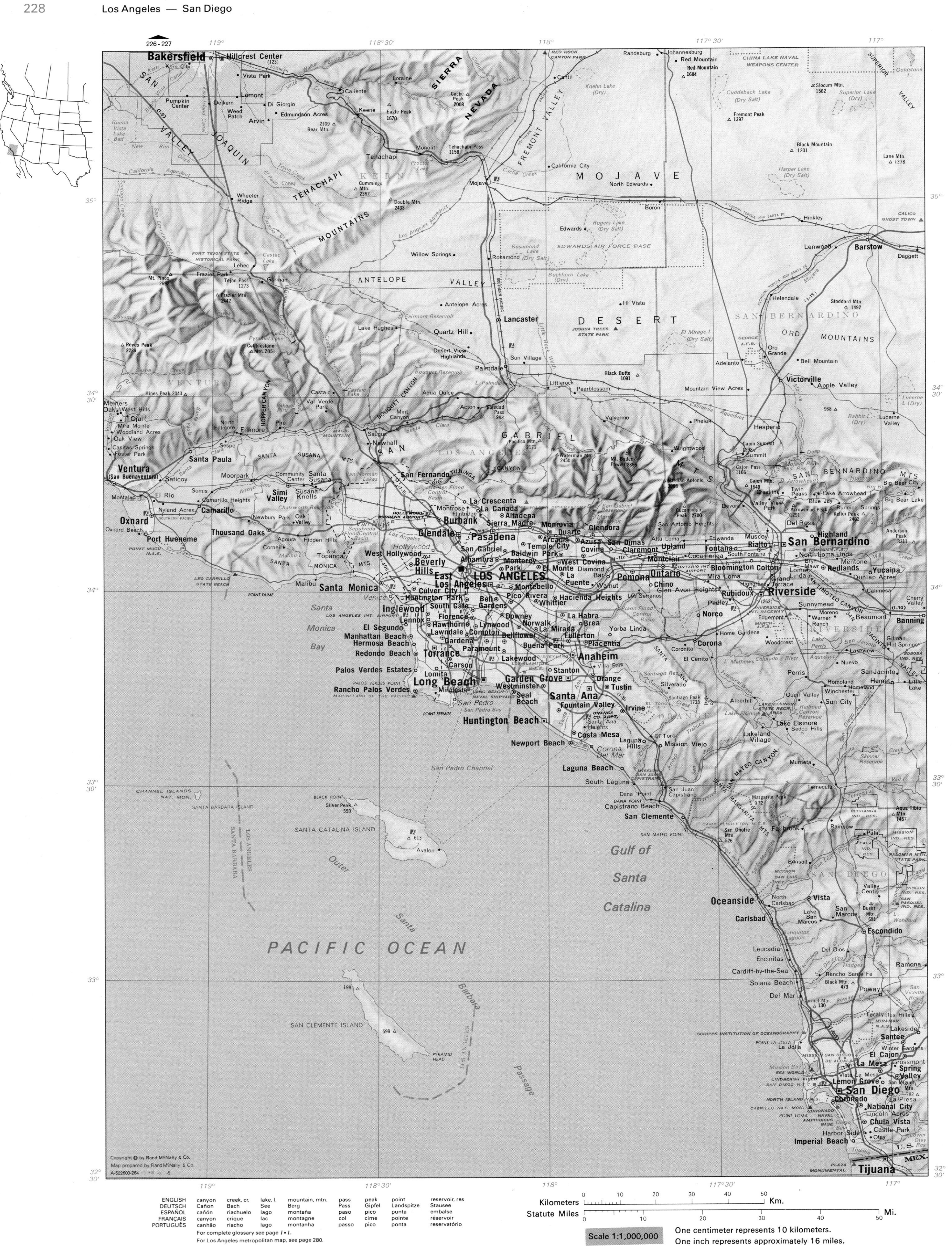

ENGLISH	canyon	creek, cr.	lake, l.	mountain, mtn.	pass	peak	point	reservoir, res
DEUTSCH	Cañon	Bach	See	Berg	Pass	Gipfel	Landspitze	Stausee
ESPAÑOL	cañón	riachuelo	lago	montaña	paso	pico	punta	embalse
FRANÇAIS	canyon	crique	lac	montagne	col	cime	pointe	réservoir
PORTUGUÊS	canhão	riacho	lago	montanha	passo	pico	ponta	reservatório

For complete glossary see page *I • 1*.
For Los Angeles metropolitan map, see page 280.

Kilometers 0 10 20 30 40 50 Km.
Statute Miles 0 10 20 30 40 50 Mi.

Scale 1:1,000,000
One centimeter represents 10 kilometers.
One inch represents approximately 16 miles.
Lambert Conformal Conic Projection

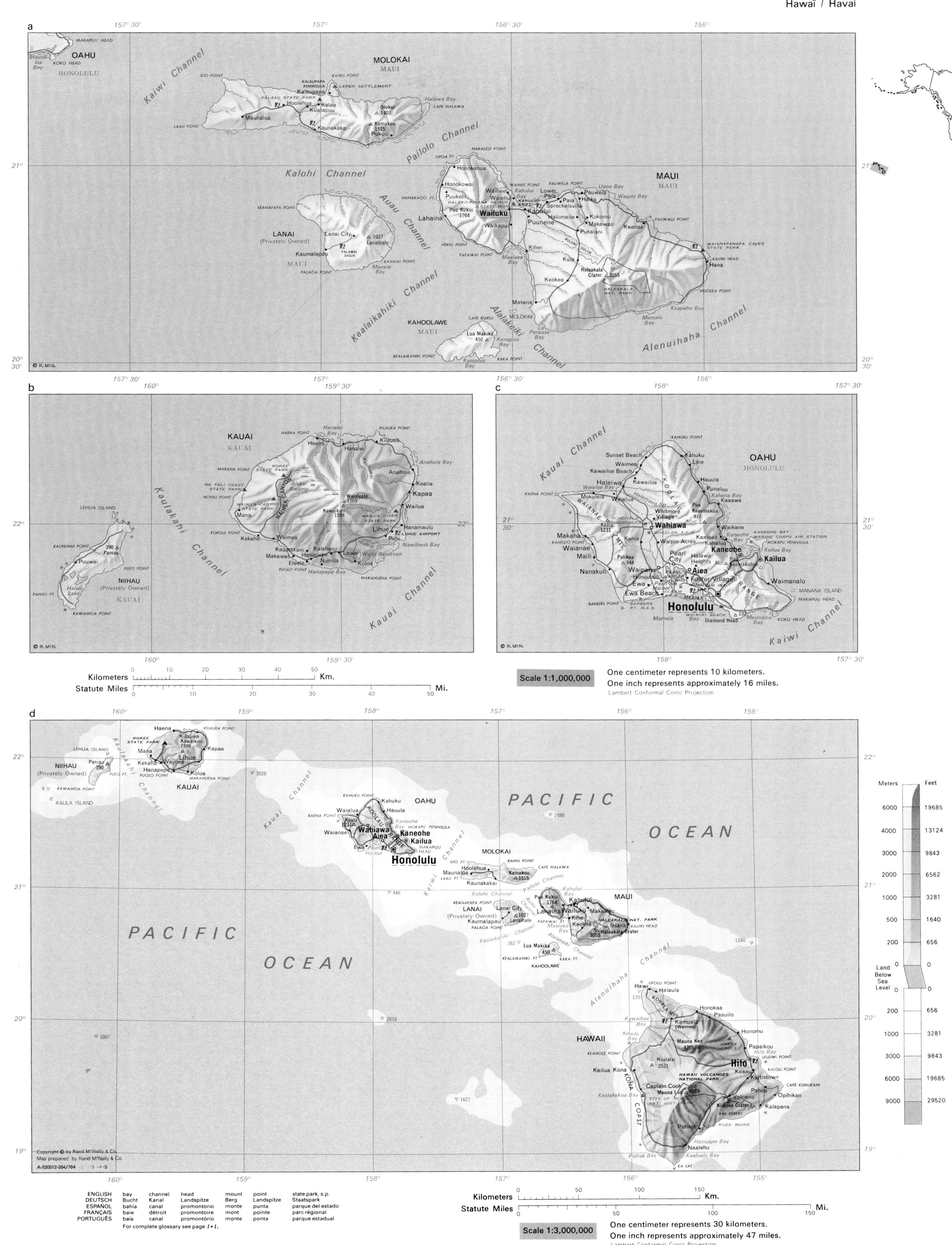
a
OAHU
HONOLULU
MAKAPUU HEAD
KOKO HEAD
Kaiwi Channel
MOLOKAI
MAUI
KALAUPAPA PENINSULA
LEPER SETTLEMENT
Kalaupapa
Hoolehua
Kalae
Kualapuu
Maunaloa
Kaunakakai
Olokui 1403
Kamakou 1515
Pukoo
Halawa Bay
CAPE HALAWA
LAAU POINT
ILIO POINT
Pailolo Channel
NAKALELE POINT
Kalohi Channel
Auau Channel
LANAI
(Privately Owned)
Lanai City
1027 Lanaihale
Kaumalapau
PALAWAI BASIN
KAMAIKI POINT
Manele Bay
PALAOA POINT
KEANAPAPA POINT
Honokahua
Honokowai
Puukolii
Lahaina
Puu Kukui 1764
Wailuku
Waikapu
Waihee
Waiehu
Kahului Bay
Kahului
Lower Paia
Paia
Spreckelsville
Haiku
Pauwela
Uaoa Bay
Waipio Bay
Halimaile
Kokomo
Makawao
Pukalani
Puunene
Keanae
Kihei
Kula
Maalaea Bay
Haleakala Crater 3055
HALEAKALA NAT. PARK
WAIANAPANAPA CAVES STATE PARK
Hana
KAUIKI HEAD
Keokea
Makena
MOLOKINI
La Perouse Bay
Kaapahu Bay
Mamalu Bay
MUOLEA POINT
Kealaikahiki Channel
Alalakeiki Channel
Alenuihaha Channel
KAHOOLAWE
MAUI
CAPE KUIKUI
Lua Makika 450
Kanapou Bay
KEALAIKAHIKI POINT
Kamohio Bay
KAKA POINT
© R. McN.
b
KAUAI
Hanalei Bay
Hanalei
Haena
Kilauea
KILAUEA POINT
Anahola Bay
Anahola
Kealia
Kapaa
Wailua
Waialeale 1569
Kawaikini 1598
Alakai Swamp
KOKEE STATE PARK
NA PALI COAST STATE PARK
WAIMEA CANYON STATE PARK
Mana
Kekaha
Waimea
Kaumakani
Hanapepe
Makaweli
Eleele
Numila
Kalaheo
Lawai
Koloa
Lihue
Hanamaulu
LIHUE AIRPORT
Nawiliwili Bay
Hanapepe Bay
MAKAHUENA POINT
Kaulakahi Channel
Kauai Channel
LEHUA ISLAND
KAUNUNUI POINT
390 Paniau
Puuwai
PUEO POINT
NIIHAU
(Privately Owned)
KAUAI
Halalii Lake
KAWAIHOA POINT
© R. McN.
c
Kauai Channel
KAHUKU POINT
Kahuku
Laie
Sunset Beach
Waimea
Kawailoa Beach
Haleiwa
Waialua Bay
Waialua
Mokuleia
KAENA POINT
Hauula
Punaluu
Kahana Bay
Kaaawa
Puu Kaaumakua 817
Whitmore Village
Wahiawa
Kaala 1231
Makaha
Waianae
Maili
Nanakuli
Kunia
Waipio Acres
Palikea 944
Waipahu
Pearl City
Aiea
Ewa
Ewa Beach
Kaalaea
Kahaluu
Kaneohe
Kailua
Halawa Heights
Foster Village
Honolulu
Waimanalo
MANANA ISLAND
MAKAPUU HEAD
KOKO HEAD
Diamond Head
Maunalua Bay
Mamala Bay
BARBERS POINT
OAHU
HONOLULU
Kaiwi Channel
© R. McN.
Kilometers
Statute Miles
Km.
Mi.
Scale 1:1,000,000
One centimeter represents 10 kilometers.
One inch represents approximately 16 miles.
Lambert Conformal Conic Projection
d
PACIFIC OCEAN
PACIFIC OCEAN
KAUAI
NIIHAU (Privately Owned)
KAULA ISLAND
OAHU
Honolulu
MOLOKAI
LANAI
MAUI
KAHOOLAWE
HAWAII
Hawi
Halaula
Honokaa
Paauilo
Kamuela (Waimea)
Mauna Kea 4205
Honomu
Papaikou
Hilo
Hilo Bay
Hualalai 2521
Kailua Kona
KONA COAST
Keaau
Kurtistown
Captain Cook
Mauna Loa 4169
HAWAII VOLCANOES NATIONAL PARK
Kilauea Crater
Volcano
Pahoa
Kalapana
Opihikao
CAPE KUMUKAHI
Pahala
Naalehu
Honuapo Bay
Kaalualu Bay
KA LAE
Pohue Bay
Kealakekua Bay
Kawaihae Bay
Meters
Feet
Land Below Sea Level
Copyright © by Rand McNally & Co.
Map prepared by Rand McNally & Co.
ENGLISH bay channel head mount point state park, s.p.
DEUTSCH Bucht Kanal Landspitze Berg Landspitze Staatspark
ESPAÑOL bahia canal promontorio monte punta parque del estado
FRANÇAIS baie détroit promontoire mont pointe parc régional
PORTUGUÊS baia canal promontório monte ponta parque estadual
For complete glossary see page I•1.
Kilometers
Statute Miles
Km.
Mi.
Scale 1:3,000,000
One centimeter represents 30 kilometers.
One inch represents approximately 47 miles.
Lambert Conformal Conic Projection

ESPAÑOL	cabo	cordillera	golfo	isla, i.	lago, l.	punta	sierra	volcán, vol.
ENGLISH	cape	mountains	gulf	island	lake	point	mountains	volcano
DEUTSCH	Kap	Berge	Golf	Insel	See	Landspitze	Berge	Vulkan
FRANÇAIS	cap	montagnes	golfe	île	lac	pointe	montagnes	volcan
PORTUGUÊS	cabo	cordilheira	golfo	ilha	lago	ponta	serra	vulcão

For complete glossary see page *I* • *1*.

242 - 243

Kilometers 0 200 400 600 Km.
Statute Miles 0 200 400 600 Mi.

Scale 1:12,000,000

One centimeter represents 120 kilometers.
One inch represents approximately 190 miles.
Oblique Conic Conformal Projection

116° 114° 112° 110° 108° 106° 104°
32° 30° 28° 26° 24° 22° 20° 18° 16°
San Diego
Tijuana
Tecate
Mexicali
Yuma
San Luis Rio Colorado
Ensenada
ARIZONA
Tucson
NEW MEXICO
Las Cruces
Carlsbad
Hobbs
El Paso
Ciudad Juárez
UNITED STATES
MEXICO
Heroica Nogales
Nogales
Agua Prieta
Golfo de California
SIERRA SAN PEDRO MARTIR
BAJA CALIFORNIA NORTE
BAJA CALIFORNIA SUR
SIERRA DE LA GIGANTA
SONORA
Hermosillo
Guaymas
Ciudad Obregón
Navojoa
Los Mochis
Guamuchil
Culiacán
SINALOA
Mazatlán
Chihuahua
Delicias
Hidalgo del Parral
Ciudad Jiménez
Torreón
Durango
SIERRA MADRE OCCIDENTAL
NAYARIT
Tepic
Guadalajara
JALISCO
Colima
Tecoman
Puerto Vallarta
La Paz
Bahía Sebastián Vizcaíno
Tropic of Cancer
ISLAS MARÍAS
ISLAS REVILLAGIGEDO (Mex.)
ISLA CLARIÓN (Mex.)
PACIFIC OCEAN
Meters Feet
6000 19685
4000 13124
3000 9843
2000 6562
1000 3281
500 1640
200 656
0 0
Land Below Sea Level
0 0
200 656
1000 3281
3000 9843
6000 19685
9000 29520
ESPAÑOL bahia cerro isla laguna presa punta rio sierra
ENGLISH bay mountain island lagoon reservoir point river mountains
DEUTSCH Bucht Berg Insel Haff Stausee Landspitze Fluss Berge
FRANÇAIS baie montagne île lagune réservoir pointe rivière montagnes
PORTUGUÊS baia montanha ilha laguna reservatório ponta rio serra
For complete glossary see page I • 1.
Kilometers 0 100 200 300 Km.
Statute Miles 0 100 200 300 Mi.
Scale 1:6,000,000
One centimeter represents 60 kilometers.
One inch represents approximately 95 miles.
Lambert Conformal Conic Projection

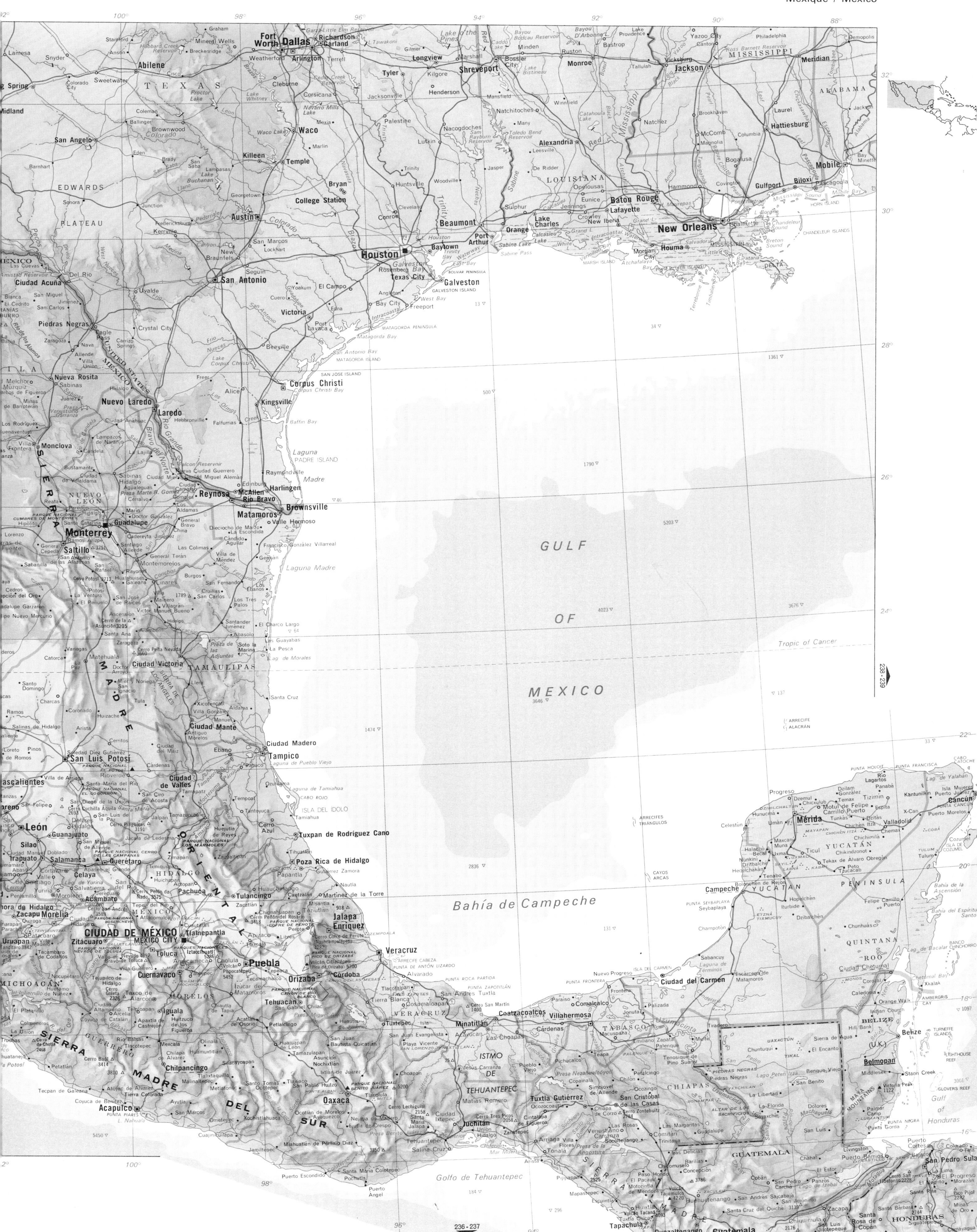
GULF
OF
MEXICO
Bahía de Campeche
Golfo de Tehuantepec
Gulf of Honduras
Tropic of Cancer
TEXAS
LOUISIANA
MISSISSIPPI
ALABAMA
EDWARDS
PLATEAU
SIERRA MADRE
SIERRA MADRE ORIENTAL
SIERRA MADRE DEL SUR
TAMAULIPAS
NUEVO LEÓN
YUCATÁN
PENINSULA
QUINTANA ROO
CHIAPAS
TABASCO
VERACRUZ
ISTMO DE TEHUANTEPEC
GUATEMALA
BELIZE (U.K.)
HONDURAS
Fort Worth
Dallas
Abilene
Shreveport
Jackson
Waco
San Angelo
Austin
Houston
San Antonio
Galveston
Beaumont
Baton Rouge
New Orleans
Mobile
Corpus Christi
Laredo
Nuevo Laredo
Monterrey
Saltillo
Matamoros
Brownsville
Reynosa
Ciudad Victoria
Tampico
San Luis Potosí
León
Querétaro
Pachuca
CIUDAD DE MÉXICO
MEXICO CITY
Toluca
Puebla
Jalapa Enríquez
Veracruz
Orizaba
Cuernavaco
Chilpancingo
Acapulco
Oaxaca
Coatzacoalcos
Villahermosa
Tuxtla Gutiérrez
Campeche
Mérida
Cancún
Ciudad del Carmen
Belize
Belmopan
Guatemala
San Pedro Sula
236-237
238-239

ESPAÑOL	arroyo	boca	cerro	lago	laguna	punta	río	sierra	volcán
ENGLISH	brook	entrance	butte	lake	lagoon	point	river	ranges	volcano
DEUTSCH	Bach	Einfahrt	Restberg	See	Haff	Landspitze	Fluss	Bergketten	Vulkan
FRANÇAIS	ruisseau	entrée	butte	lac	lagune	pointe	rivière	chaîne	volcan
PORTUGUÊS	arroio	entrada	cerro	lago	laguna	ponta	rio	serra	vulcão

For complete glossary see page *I* • *1*.
For Ciudad de México metropolitan map, see page 286.

Tropic of Cancer
GULF OF MEXICO
Bahía de Campeche
Golfo de Tehuantepec
Ciudad Victoria
Ciudad Mante
Ciudad Madero
Tampico
Ciudad Valles
Túxpan de Rodríguez Cano
Poza Rica de Hidalgo
Papantla
Martínez de la Torre
Pachuca
Tulancingo
Teziutlán
Jalapa Enríquez
Veracruz
CIUDAD DE MÉXICO
MEXICO CITY
Tlalnepantla
Puebla
Atlixco
Orizaba
Córdoba
Ciudad Mendoza
Izúcar de Matamoros
Tehuacán
Tierra Blanca
San Andrés Tuxtla
Cosamaloapan
Coatzacoalcos
Minatitlán
Villahermosa
Oaxaca
Juchitán
Tuxtla Gutiérrez
San Cristóbal de las Casas
Tehuantepec
Salina Cruz
Puerto Ángel
Alvarado
Acayucan
Matías Romero
Ciudad Ixtepec
Frontera
Comalcalco
Cárdenas
Tonalá
Arriaga
SIERRA MADRE ORIENTAL
SIERRA MADRE DEL SUR
SIERRA AZUL
TAMAULIPAS
VERACRUZ
SAN LUIS POTOSÍ
HIDALGO
PUEBLA
TLAXCALA
MORELOS
GUERRERO
OAXACA
TABASCO
CHIAPAS
ISTMO DE TEHUANTEPEC
Bahía Coatzacoalcos
Laguna Madre
Laguna de Tamiahua
Kilometers 0 50 100 150 Km.
Statute Miles 0 50 100 150 Mi.
Scale 1:3,000,000
One centimeter represents 30 kilometers.
One inch represents approximately 47 miles.
Lambert Conformal Conic Projection

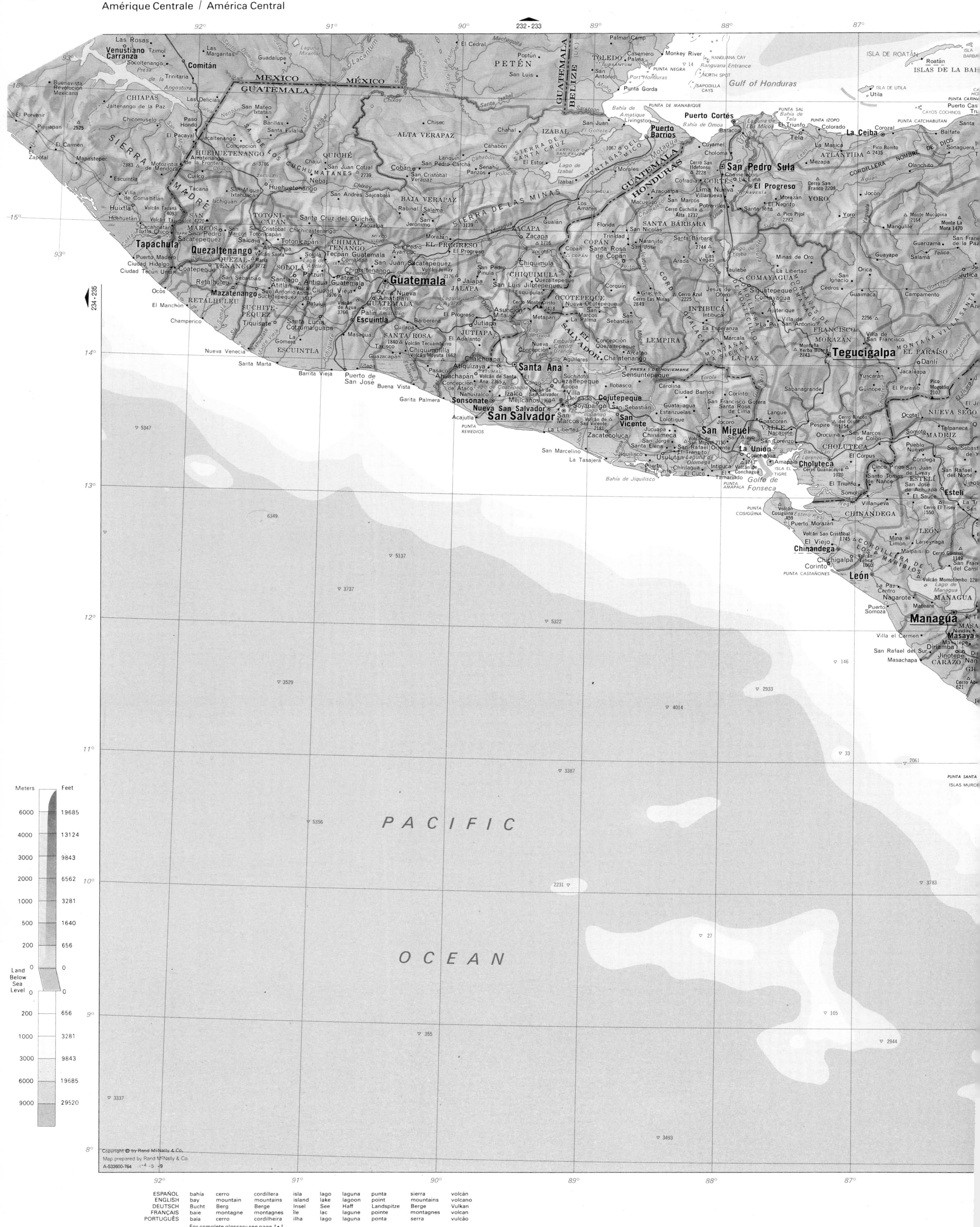
232-233
234-235
MEXICO
MÉXICO
GUATEMALA
BELIZE
HONDURAS
EL SALVADOR
PETÉN
ALTA VERAPAZ
BAJA VERAPAZ
IZABAL
QUICHÉ
HUEHUETENANGO
SAN MARCOS
QUEZALTENANGO
TOTONICAPÁN
SOLOLÁ
CHIMALTENANGO
SUCHITEPÉQUEZ
RETALHULEU
ESCUINTLA
SANTA ROSA
JUTIAPA
JALAPA
CHIQUIMULA
ZACAPA
EL PROGRESO
CHIAPAS
SIERRA MADRE
SIERRA DE LOS CUCHUMATANES
SIERRA DE LAS MINAS
SANTA BÁRBARA
COPÁN
OCOTEPEQUE
LEMPIRA
INTIBUCÁ
LA PAZ
COMAYAGUA
FRANCISCO MORAZÁN
ATLÁNTIDA
YORO
CORTÉS
VALLE
CHOLUTECA
EL PARAÍSO
NUEVA SEGOVIA
MADRIZ
ESTELÍ
CHINANDEGA
LEÓN
MANAGUA
MASAYA
CARAZO
Comitán
Tapachula
Quezaltenango
Mazatenango
Escuintla
Guatemala
Cobán
Huehuetenango
Puerto Barrios
Puerto Cortés
San Pedro Sula
El Progreso
La Ceiba
Tela
Tegucigalpa
Santa Ana
San Salvador
Sonsonate
San Miguel
San Vicente
Cojutepeque
La Unión
Choluteca
Chinandega
León
Managua
Masaya
Estelí
Puerto de San José
Gulf of Honduras
Golfo de Fonseca
ISLA DE ROATÁN
ISLAS DE LA BAHÍA
P A C I F I C
O C E A N
Meters Feet
6000 19685
4000 13124
3000 9843
2000 6562
1000 3281
500 1640
200 656
0 0
Land Below Sea Level
0 0
200 656
1000 3281
3000 9843
6000 19685
9000 29520
Copyright © by Rand McNally & Co.
Map prepared by Rand McNally & Co.
ESPAÑOL bahía cerro cordillera isla lago laguna punta sierra volcán
ENGLISH bay mountain mountains island lake lagoon point mountains volcano
DEUTSCH Bucht Berg Berge Insel See Haff Landspitze Berge Vulkan
FRANÇAIS baie montagne montagnes île lac lagune pointe montagnes volcan
PORTUGUÊS baía cerro cordilheira ilha lago laguna ponta serra vulcão
For complete glossary see page I • 1.

Scale 1:3,000,000

One centimeter represents 30 kilometers.
One inch represents approximately 47 miles.
Lambert Conformal Conic Projection

246-247

MAP FORM	bahía	cabo	cerro	channel	golfo	isla	passage	pico	punta
ENGLISH	bay	cape	mountain	channel	gulf	isle	passage	peak	point
DEUTSCH	Bucht	Kap	Berg	Kanal	Golf	Insel	Durchfahrt	Gipfel	Landspitze
ESPAÑOL	bahía	cabo	cerro	canal	golfo	isla	pasaje	pico	punta
FRANÇAIS	baie	cap	montagne	détroit	golfe	île	passage	cime	pointe
PORTUGUÊS	baía	cabo	cerro	canal	golfo	ilha	passagem	pico	ponta

For complete glossary see page I • 1.
For Caracas metropolitan map, see page 286.

ATLANTIC
OCEAN
Tropic of Cancer
INDIES
TURKS AND CAICOS ISLANDS
(U.K.)
CAICOS ISLANDS
GREAT INAGUA
SILVER BANK
HAITI
HAÏTI
Cap-Haïtien
Port-au-Prince
HISPANIOLA
Santiago
San Francisco de Macorís
Santo Domingo
San Pedro de Macorís
La Romana
DOMINICAN REPUBLIC
REPÚBLICA DOMINICANA
PUERTO RICO
(U.S.)
SAN JUAN
Arecibo
Mayagüez
Ponce
Caguas
Bayamón
VIRGIN ISLANDS
Charlotte Amalie
Road Town
Christiansted
Frederiksted
SAINT CROIX
ANGUILLA
The Valley
Marigot
Philipsburg
SAINT KITTS-NEVIS
Basseterre
Charlestown
ANTIGUA
(U.K.)
Saint Johns
MONTSERRAT
(U.K.)
Plymouth
LESSER
ANTILLES
LEEWARD ISLANDS
Pointe-à-Pitre
GUADELOUPE
(Fr.)
Basse-Terre
GRANDE-TERRE
DOMINICA
Roseau
Marigot
Dominica Channel
MARTINIQUE
(Fr.)
Fort-de-France
Saint Lucia Channel
SAINT LUCIA
Castries
Saint Vincent Passage
SAINT VINCENT
Kingstown
BARBADOS
Bridgetown
WINDWARD ISLANDS
GRENADA
Saint George's
SEA
NETHERLANDS ANTILLES
NEDERLANDSE ANTILLEN
ARUBA
Oranjestad
CURAÇAO
Willemstad
BONAIRE
Kralendijk
LESSER ANTILLES
LA GUAJIRA
Golfo de Venezuela
Maracaibo
Lago de Maracaibo
Cabimas
Punto Fijo
Coro
FALCÓN
Barquisimeto
Valencia
Maracay
CARACAS
La Guaira
Puerto Cabello
Barcelona
Cumaná
Carúpano
ISLA DE MARGARITA
NUEVA ESPARTA
Maturín
MONAGAS
ANZOÁTEGUI
SUCRE
DELTA AMACURO
ORINOCO
TRINIDAD AND TOBAGO
Port of Spain
San Fernando
TOBAGO
Scarborough
Gulf of Paria
COLOMBIA
VENEZUELA
ZULIA
LARA
PORTUGUESA
COJEDES
GUÁRICO
ARAGUA
Valle de la Pascua
Guanare
Acarigua
El Tigre
Valera
Kilometers
Statute Miles
Km.
Mi.
Scale 1:6,000,000
One centimeter represents 60 kilometers.
One inch represents approximately 95 miles.
Lambert Conformal Conic Projection
246-247

Islands of the West Indies / Westindische Inseln / Islas de las Antillas
Îles des Antilles / Ilhas do Caribe

a

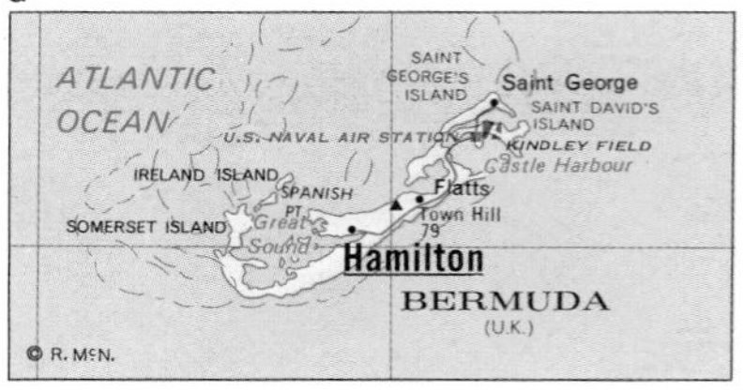

b

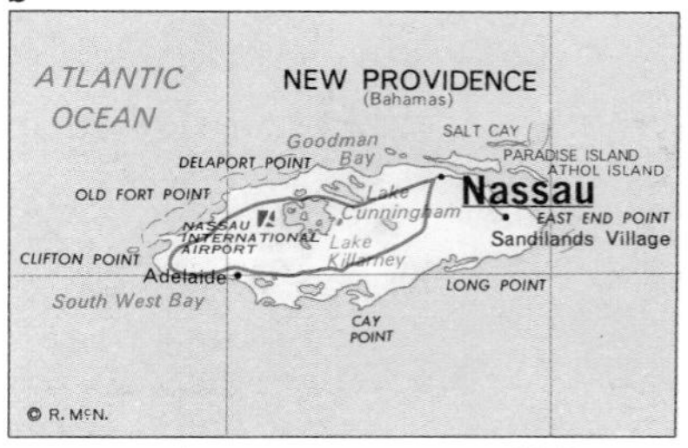

c

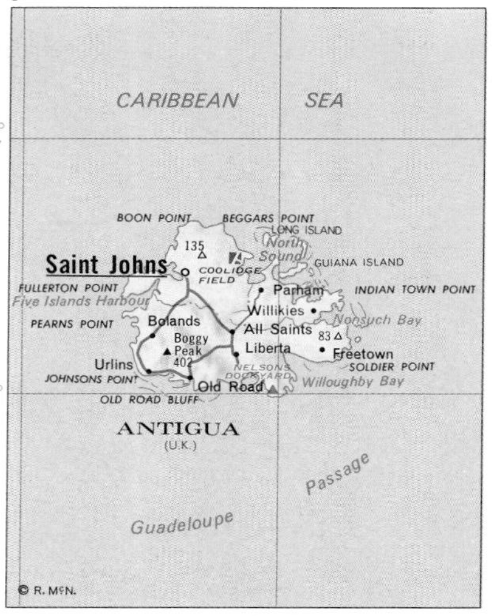

d

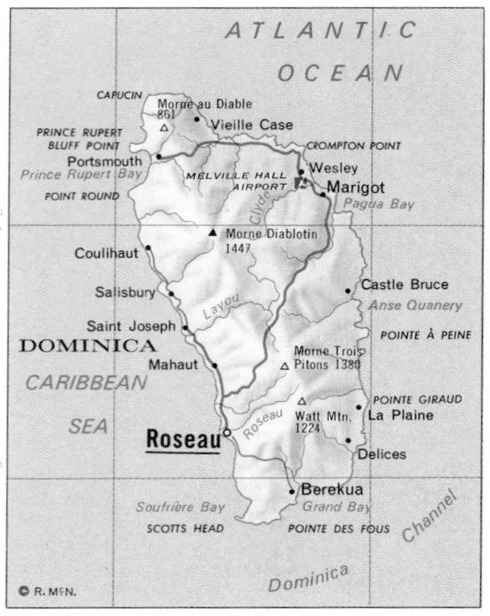

e

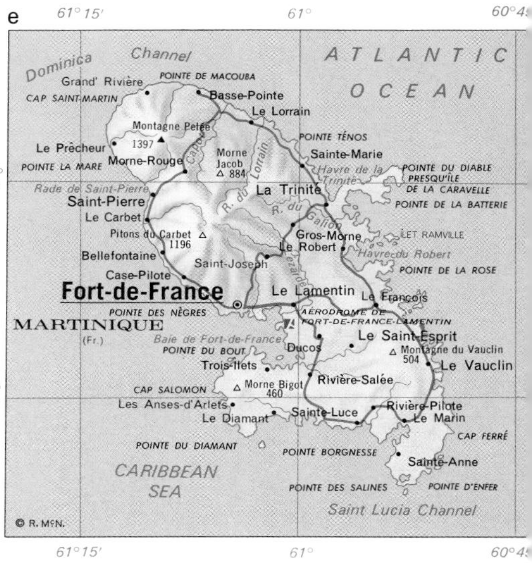

m

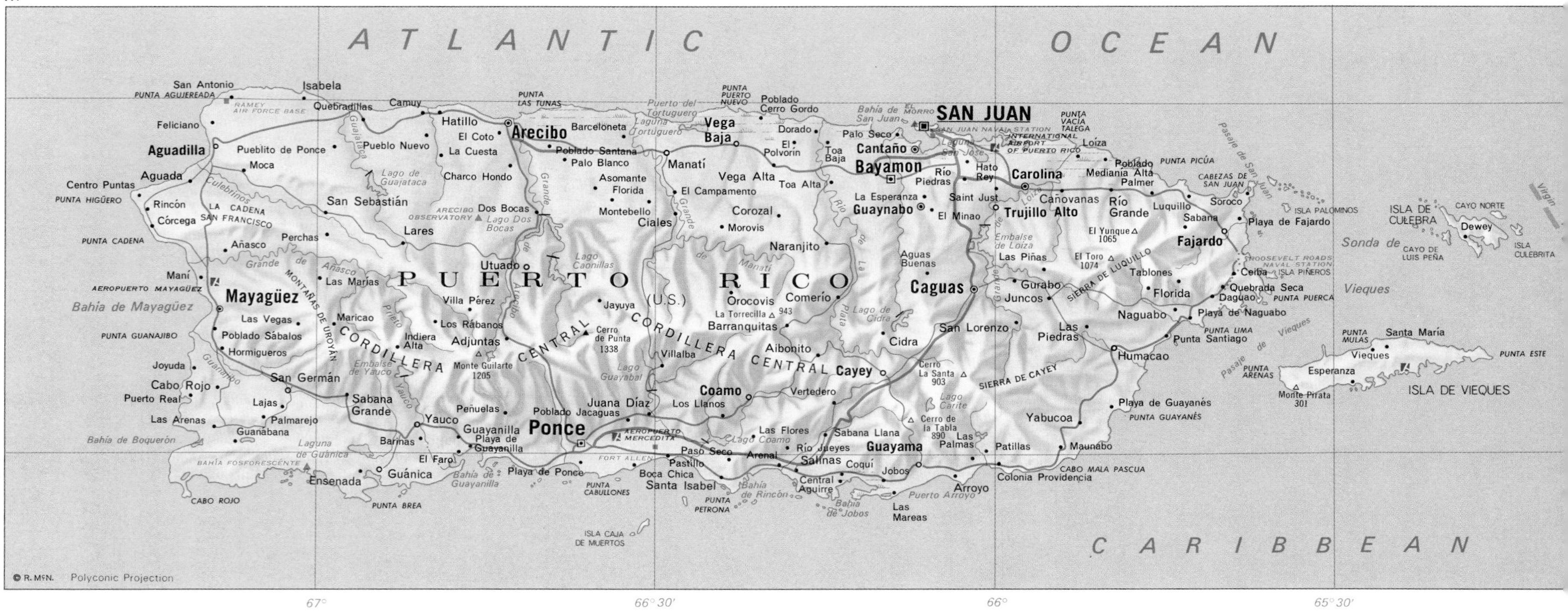

p

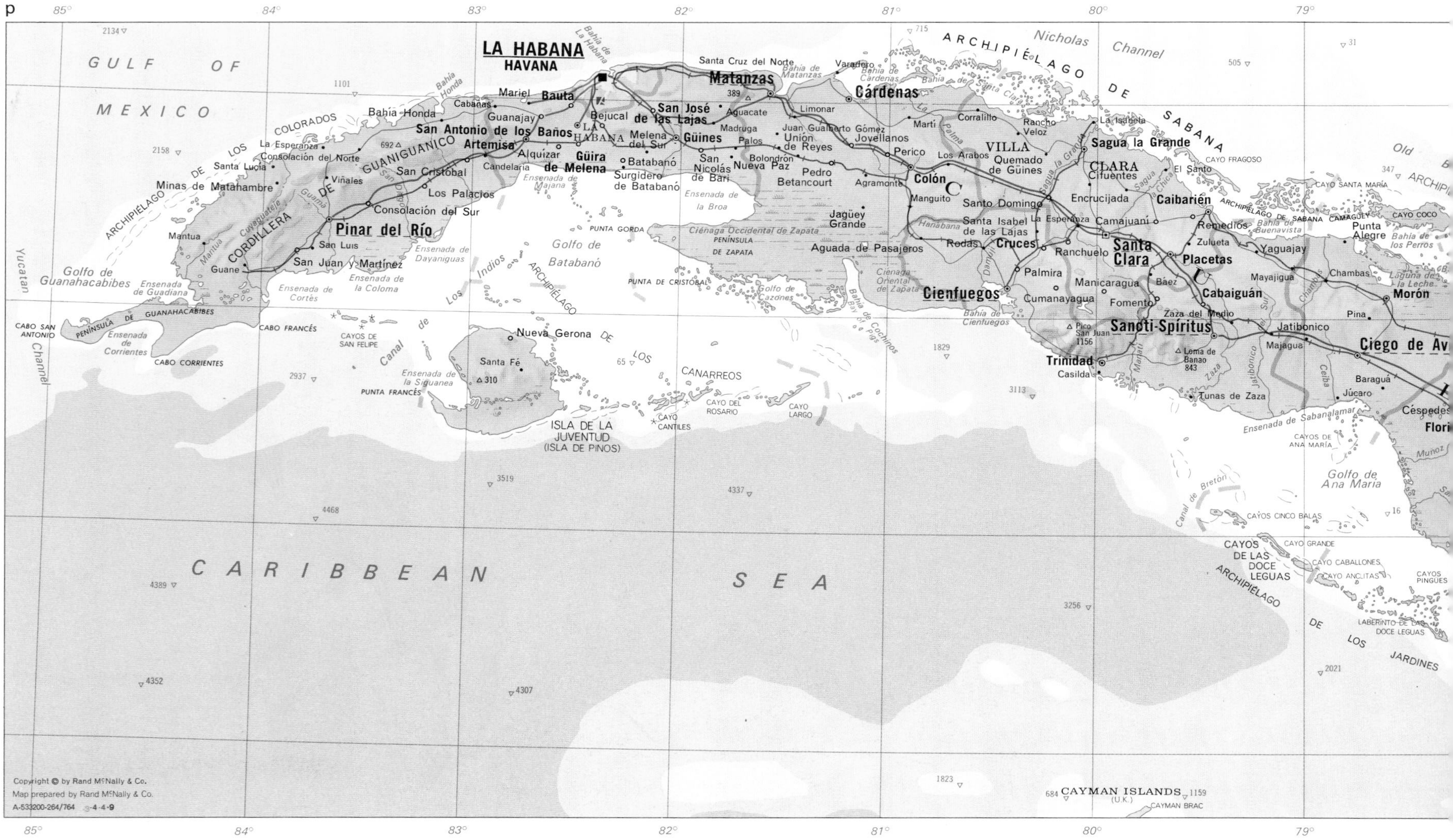

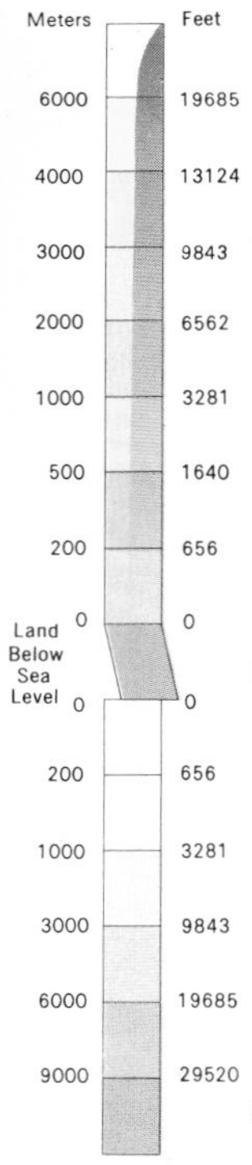

MAP FORM	bahía	cayo	channel	ensenada	golfo	island	mount	passage	point
ENGLISH	bay	cay	channel	bayou	gulf	island	mount	passage	point
DEUTSCH	Bucht	Klippe	Kanal	Altwasser	Golf	Insel	Berg	Durchfahrt	Landspitze
ESPAÑOL	bahía	cayo	canal	ensenada	golfo	isla	montaña	pasaje	punta
FRANÇAIS	baie	caye	détroit	bayou	golfe	île	mont	passage	pointe
PORTUGUÊS	baía	recife	canal	enseada	golfo	ilha	montanha	passagem	ponta

For complete glossary see page I • 1.
For La Habana metropolitan map, see page 286.

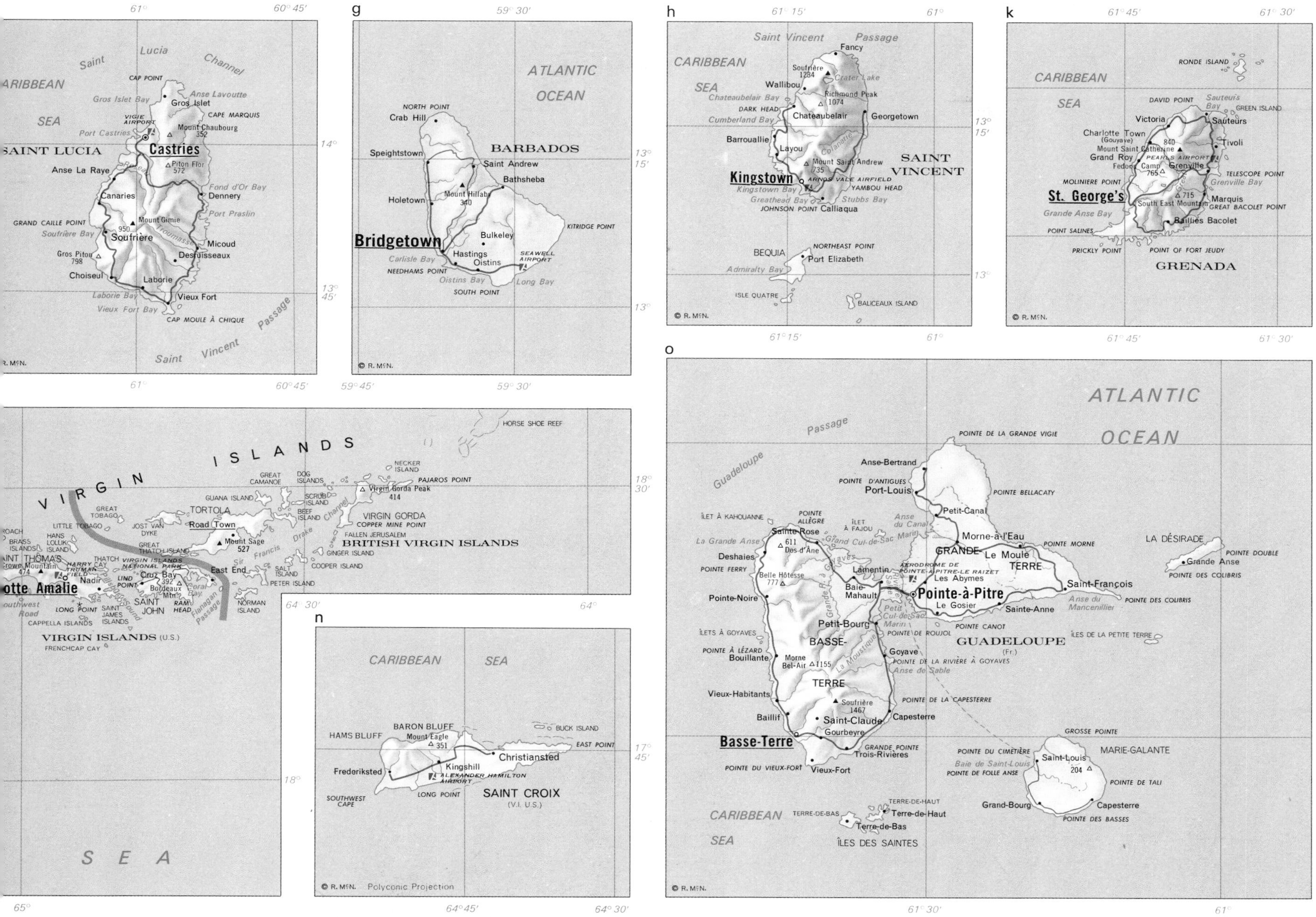

Kilometers 0 10 20 30 40 50 Km.
Statute Miles 0 10 20 30 40 50 Mi.

Scale 1:1,000,000

One centimeter represents 10 kilometers.
One inch represents approximately 16 miles.
Transverse Mercator Projection (except as noted)

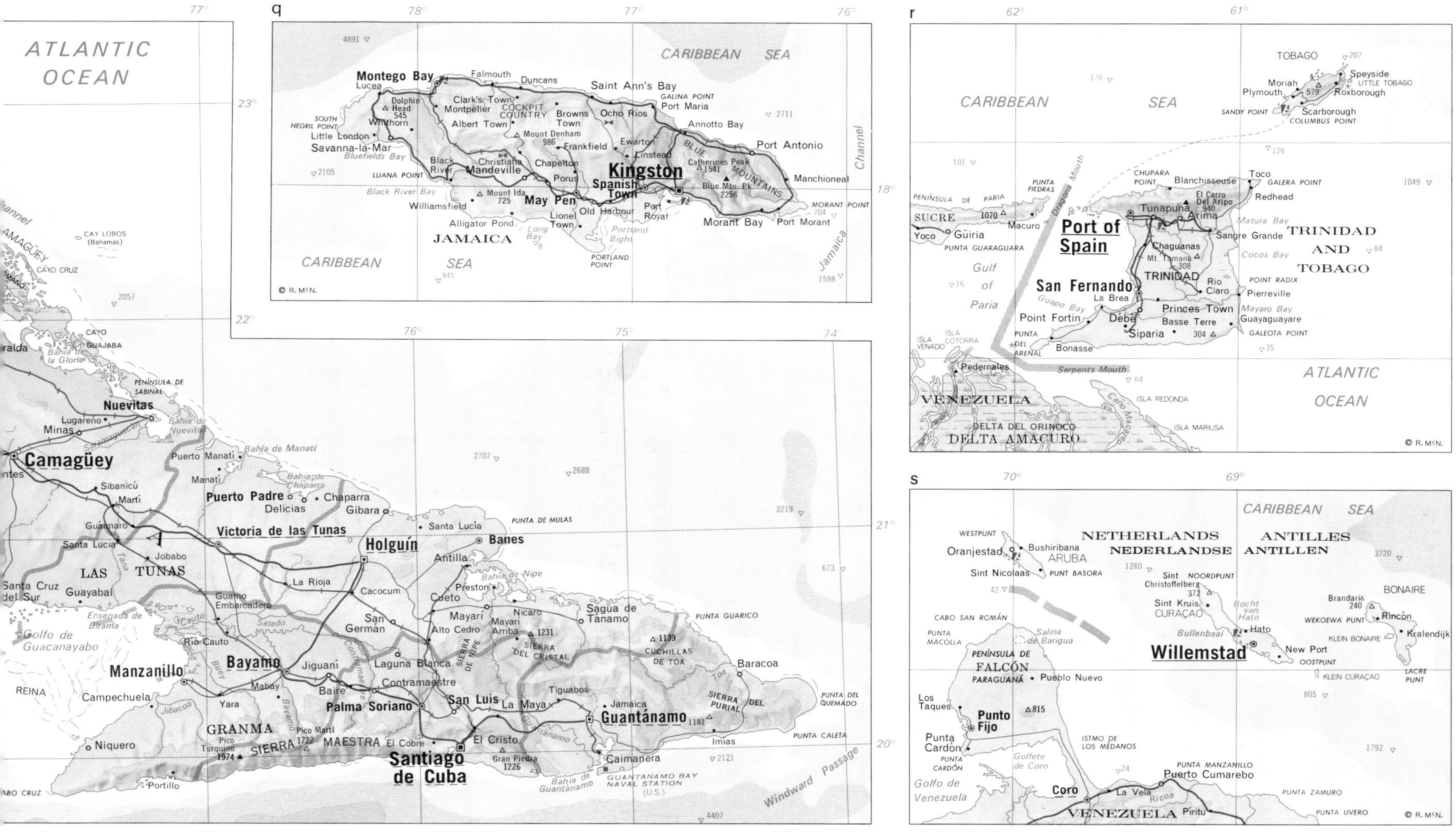

Kilometers 0 50 100 150 Km.
Statute Miles 0 50 100 150 Mi.

Scale 1:3,000,000

One centimeter represents 30 kilometers.
One inch represents approximately 47 miles.
Lambert Conformal Conic Projection

Kilometers 0 200 400 600 Km.

Statute Miles 0 200 400 600 Mi.

Scale 1:12,000,000

One centimeter represents 120 kilometers.
One inch represents approximately 190 miles.
Oblique Conic Conformal Projection

MAP FORM	cerro	cordillera	ilha	lago	nevado	peninsula	serra
ENGLISH	mountain	range	island	lake	mountain	peninsula	mountains
DEUTSCH	Berg	Gebirge	Insel	See	Berg	Halbinsel	Berge
ESPAÑOL	montaña	cordillera	isla	lago	montaña	península	montañas
FRANÇAIS	montagne	chaîne	île	lac	montagne	péninsule	montagnes
PORTUGUÊS	montanha	cordilheira	ilha	lago	montanha	península	montanhas

For complete glossary see page *I • 1*.

MAP FORM	cerro, co.	golfo	ilha	isla	lago	lagoa	monte	salar
ENGLISH	butte	gulf	island	isle	lake	lake	mountain	saltflat
DEUTSCH	Restberg	Golf	Insel	Insel	See	See	Berg	Salzebene
ESPAÑOL	cerro	golfo	isla	isla	lago	lago	montaña	salobral
FRANÇAIS	butte	golfe	île	île	lac	lac	montagne	salina
PORTUGUÊS	cerro	golfo	ilha	ilha	lago	lago	montanha	salina

For complete glossary see page I • 1.

Kilometers 0 200 400 600 Km.
Statute Miles 0 200 400 600 Mi.

Scale 1:12,000,000

One centimeter represents 120 kilometers.
One inch represents approximately 190 miles.
Oblique Conic Conformal Projection

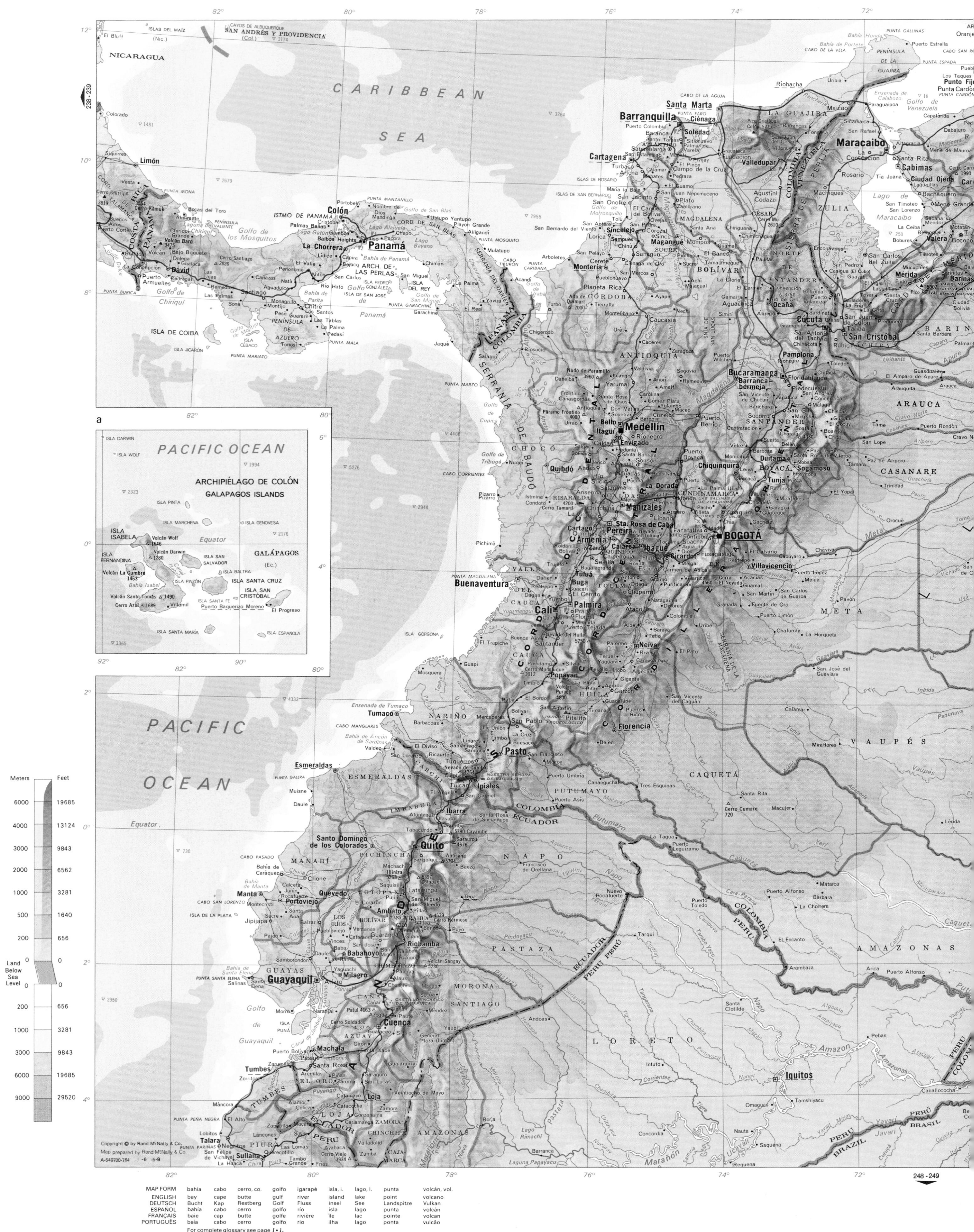

MAP FORM	bahia	cabo	cerro, co.	golfo	igarapé	isla, i.	lago, l.	punta	volcán, vol.
ENGLISH	bay	cape	butte	gulf	river	island	lake	point	volcano
DEUTSCH	Bucht	Kap	Restberg	Golf	Fluss	Insel	See	Landspitze	Vulkan
ESPAÑOL	bahía	cabo	cerro	golfo	río	isla	lago	punta	volcán
FRANÇAIS	baie	cap	butte	golfe	rivière	île	lac	pointe	volcan
PORTUGUÊS	baía	cabo	cerro	golfo	rio	ilha	lago	ponta	vulcão

For complete glossary see page I • 1.
For Caracas metropolitan map, see page 286.

238 - 239
250 - 251
LESSER ANTILLES
ATLANTIC OCEAN
GRENADA
Saint George's
TRINIDAD AND TOBAGO
Port of Spain
TOBAGO
ISLA DE MARGARITA
NUEVA ESPARTA
DISTRITO FEDERAL
CARACAS
La Guaira
Maiquetía
Puerto Cabello
Valencia
Maracay
Barquisimeto
San Juan de los Morros
Barcelona
Puerto la Cruz
Cumaná
Carúpano
Maturín
SUCRE
MONAGAS
ANZOÁTEGUI
GUÁRICO
Calabozo
Valle de la Pascua
El Tigre
Anaco
Ciudad Guayana
Ciudad Bolívar
DELTA AMACURO
Tucupita
San Fernando de Apure
APURE
BOLÍVAR
Puerto Carreño
Puerto Páez
Puerto Ayacucho
AMAZONAS
LA GRAN SABANA
Mount Roraima 2772
Santa Elena de Uairén
PAKARAIMA MOUNTAINS
SIERRA PARIMA
SIERRA DE CURUPIRA
Pico da Neblina 3014
VENEZUELA
COLOMBIA
BRAZIL
GUYANA
SURINAME
Georgetown
New Amsterdam
NORTH WEST
MAZARUNI-POTARO
WEST DEMERARA-ESSEQUIBO COAST
EAST DEMERARA-WEST COAST BERBICE
EAST BERBICE-CORENTYNE
RUPUNUNI
KANUKU MOUNTAINS
KAMOA MOUNTAINS
NICKERIE
SARAMACCA
CORONIE
WILHELMINA GEB.
RORAIMA
Boa Vista
Caracaraí
AMAZONAS
PARÁ
Manaus
Amazon
Negro
Orinoco
Solimões
Equator
Kilometers 0 100 200 300 Km.
Statute Miles 0 100 200 300 Mi.
Scale 1:6,000,000
One centimeter represents 60 kilometers.
One inch represents approximately 95 miles.
Oblique Conic Conformal Projection

MAP FORM	cerro	cordillera	isla, i.	lago, l.	nevado	punta	rio	serra
ENGLISH	mountain	mountains	island	lake	mountain	point	river	mountains
DEUTSCH	Berg	Berge	Insel	See	Berg	Landspitze	Fluss	Berge
ESPAÑOL	montaña	montañas	isla	lago	nevado	punta	rio	sierra
FRANÇAIS	montagne	montagnes	île	lac	montagne	pointe	rivière	montagnes
PORTUGUÊS	montanha	montanhas	ilha	lago	pico nevado	ponta	rio	serra

For complete glossary see page I • 1.
For Lima metropolitan map, see page 286.

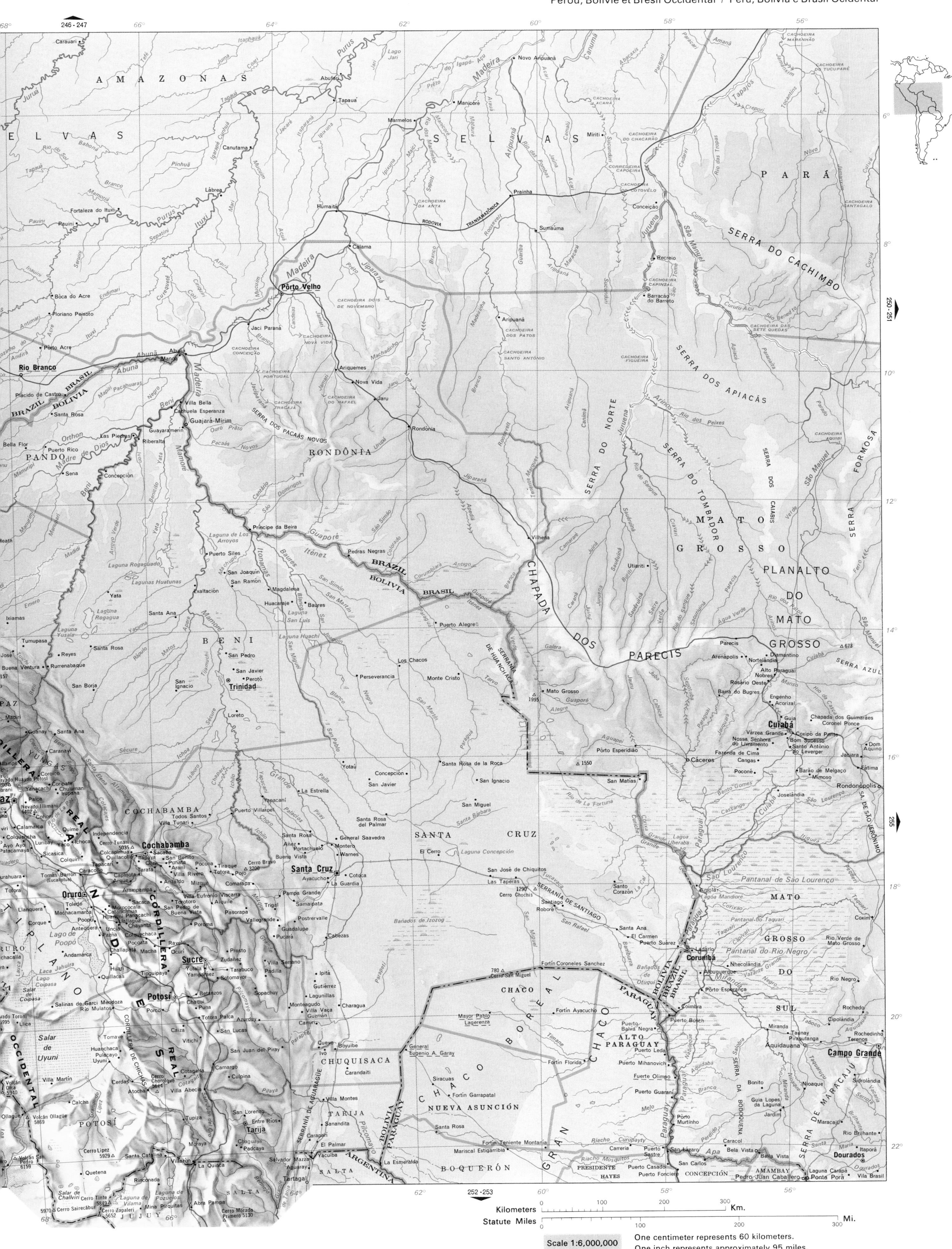
246 - 247
250 - 251
255
252 - 253
AMAZONAS
SELVAS
PARÁ
RONDÔNIA
SERRA DO CACHIMBO
SERRA DOS APIACÁS
SERRA DO NORTE
SERRA DO TOMBADOR
SERRA DOS CAIABIS
SERRA FORMOSA
SERRA AZUL
MATO GROSSO
PLANALTO DO MATO GROSSO
CHAPADA DOS PARECIS
SERRA DOS PACAÁS NOVOS
SERRANIA DE HUANCHACA
PANDO
BENI
COCHABAMBA
SANTA CRUZ
CHUQUISACA
TARIJA
POTOSÍ
CHACO BOREAL
ALTO PARAGUAY
NUEVA ASUNCIÓN
BOQUERÓN
GRAN CHACO
PRESIDENTE HAYES
CONCEPCIÓN
AMAMBAY
SALTA
JUJUY
ARGENTINA
BRAZIL
BOLIVIA
BRASIL
PARAGUAY
MATO GROSSO DO SUL
SERRA DE MARACAJU
SERRA DA BODOQUENA
SERRANIA DE SANTIAGO
SERRANÍA DE AGUARAGÜE
CORDILLERA REAL
CORDILLERA DE CHICHAS
ALTIPLANO
CORDILLERA OCCIDENTAL
Salar de Uyuni
Salar de Coipasa
Lago de Poopó
Pantanal de São Lourenço
Pantanal do Taquari
Pantanal do Rio Negro
Madeira
Purus
Juruá
Guaporé
Itenez
Mamoré
Beni
Madre de Dios
Jiparaná
Aripuanã
Juruena
Teles Pires
Paraguai
Porto Velho
Rio Branco
Humaitá
Guajará-Mirim
Riberalta
Trinidad
Cochabamba
Oruro
Sucre
Potosí
Tarija
Santa Cruz
Cuiabá
Corumbá
Cáceres
Campo Grande
Dourados
Rondonópolis
Vilhena
Rondônia
Aquidauana
Ponta Porã
Pedro Juan Caballero
Puerto Suárez
Concepción
Camiri
Villazón
La Quiaca
Tartagal
Kilometers
Statute Miles
0
100
200
300
Km.
Mi.
Scale 1:6,000,000
One centimeter represents 60 kilometers.
One inch represents approximately 95 miles.
Oblique Conic Conformal Projection

MAP FORM	cabo	cachoeira, cach.	ilha, i.	lago, l.	riacho	ribeirão, rão.	rio, r.	serra, sa.
ENGLISH	cape	waterfall	island	lake	creek	creek	river	mountains
DEUTSCH	Kap	Wasserfall	Insel	See	Bach	Bach	Fluss	Berge
ESPAÑOL	cabo	cascada	isla	lago	riachuelo	riachuelo	río	montañas
FRANÇAIS	cap	chute d'eau	île	lac	crique	crique	rivière	montagnes
PORTUGUÊS	cabo	cascata	ilha	lago	riacho	riacho	rio	montanhas

For complete glossary see page *I*•*1*.

Kilometers 0 100 200 300 Km.
Statute Miles 0 100 200 300 Mi.

Scale 1:6,000,000
One centimeter represents 60 kilometers.
One inch represents approximately 95 miles.
Oblique Conic Conformal Projection

MAP FORM	cabo	cerro	cuchilla	ilha	laguna	punta	salar	sierra	volcán
ENGLISH	cape	mountain	hills	island	lagoon; lake	point	saltflat	mountains	volcano
DEUTSCH	Kap	Berg	Hügel	Insel	Haff; See	Landspitze	Salzebene	Berge	Vulkan
ESPAÑOL	cabo	cerro	cuchilla	isla	laguna	punta	salobral	sierra	volcán
FRANÇAIS	cap	montagne	collines	île	lagune; lac	pointe	salina	montagnes	volcan
PORTUGUÊS	cabo	cerro	colina	ilha	laguna	ponta	salina	serra	vulcão

For complete glossary see page I • 1.
For Santiago metropolitan map, see page 286.

255
ATLANTIC
OCEAN
BUENOS AIRES
MONTEVIDEO
PORTO ALEGRE
SÃO PAULO
Asunción
Curitiba
Santos
Florianópolis
La Plata
Mar del Plata
Rio Grande
Pelotas
Posadas
Corrientes
Concordia
Paysandú
Kilometers
0 100 200 300 Km.
Statute Miles
0 100 200 300 Mi.
Scale 1:6,000,000
One centimeter represents 60 kilometers.
One inch represents approximately 95 miles.
Oblique Conic Conformal Projection

Southern Argentina and Chile / Südliches Argentinien und südliches Chile / Argentina y Chile: zonas meridionales / Argentine et Chili, parties Méridionales / Argentina e Chile: zonas meridionais

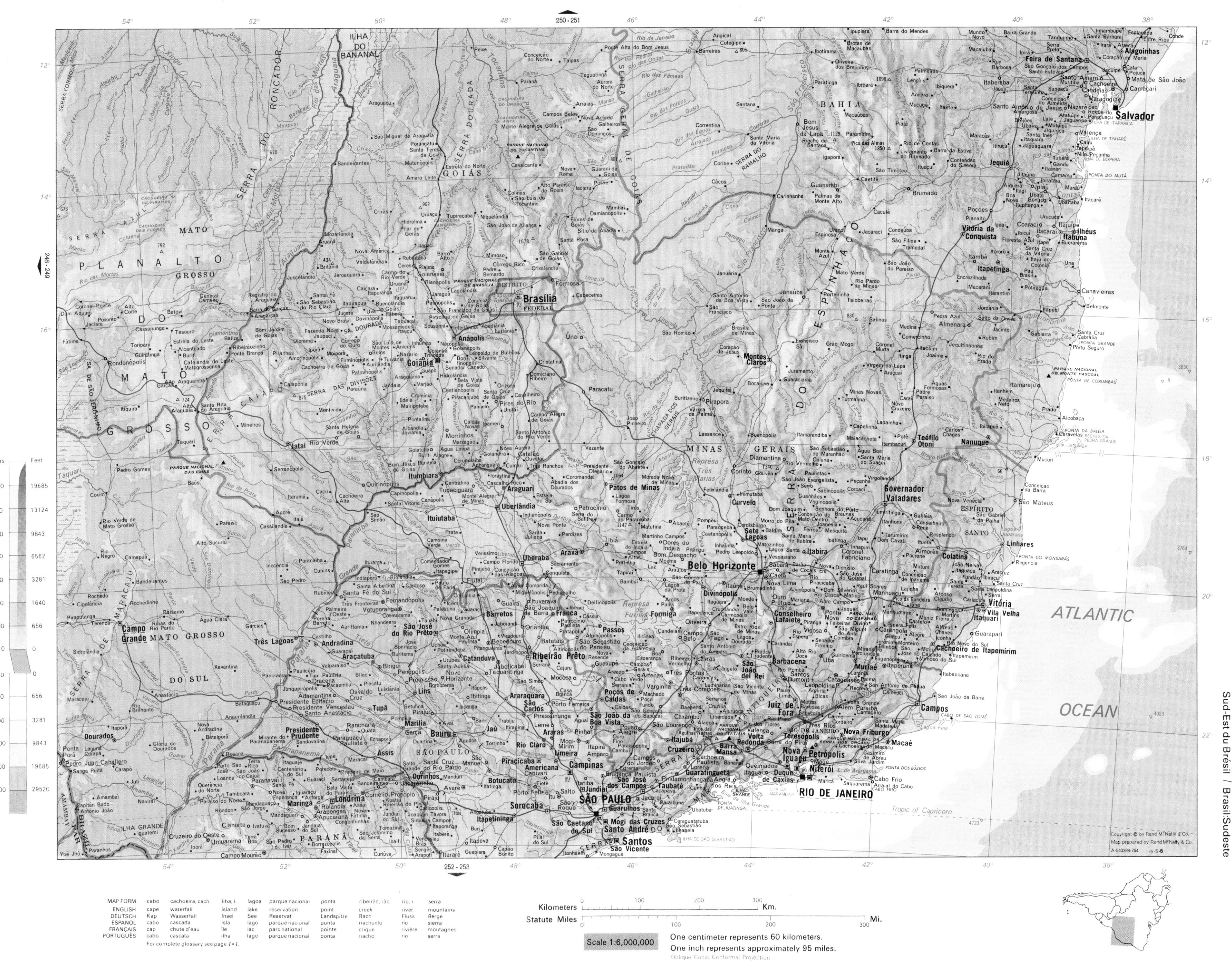

MAP FORM	cabo	cachoeira, cach.	ilha, I.	lagoa	parque nacional	ponta	ribeirão, rão	rio, r.	serra
ENGLISH	cape	waterfall	island	lake	reservation	point	creek	river	mountains
DEUTSCH	Kap	Wasserfall	Insel	See	Reservat	Landspitze	Bach	Fluss	Berge
ESPAÑOL	cabo	cascada	isla	lago	parque nacional	punta	riachuelo	rio	sierra
FRANÇAIS	cap	chute d'eau	île	lac	parc national	pointe	crique	rivière	montagnes
PORTUGUÊS	cabo	cascata	ilha	lago	parque nacional	ponta	riacho	rio	serra

For complete glossary see page I • I.

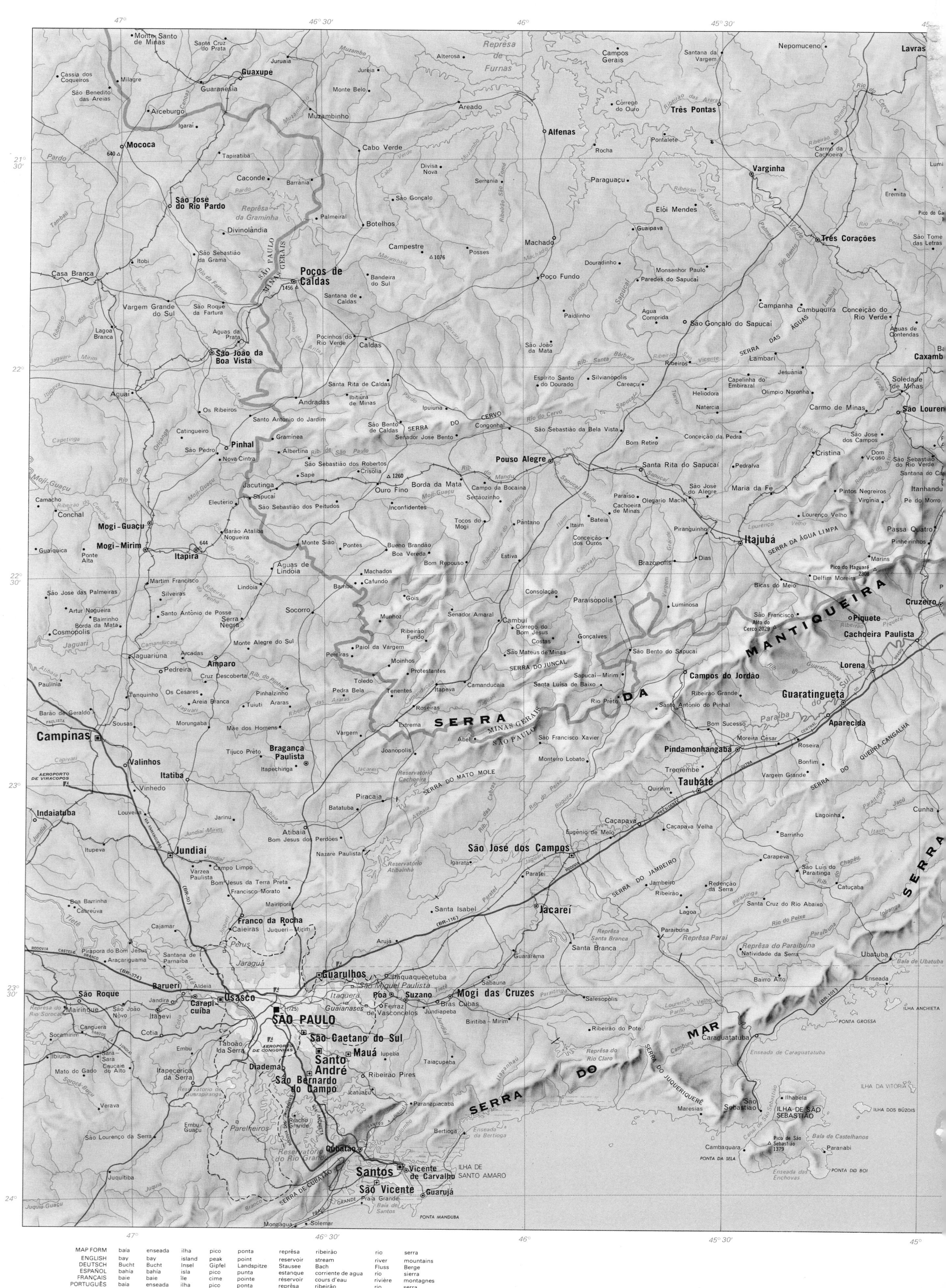

MAP FORM	baia	enseada	ilha	pico	ponta	represa	ribeirão	rio	serra
ENGLISH	bay	bay	island	peak	point	reservoir	stream	river	mountains
DEUTSCH	Bucht	Bucht	Insel	Gipfel	Landspitze	Stausee	Bach	Fluss	Berge
ESPAÑOL	bahía	bahía	isla	pico	punta	estanque	corriente de agua	río	sierra
FRANÇAIS	baie	baie	île	cime	pointe	réservoir	cours d'eau	rivière	montagnes
PORTUGUÊS	baía	enseada	ilha	pico	ponta	represa	ribeirão	rio	serra

For complete glossary see page I • 1.
For Rio de Janeiro and São Paulo metropolitan maps, see page 287.

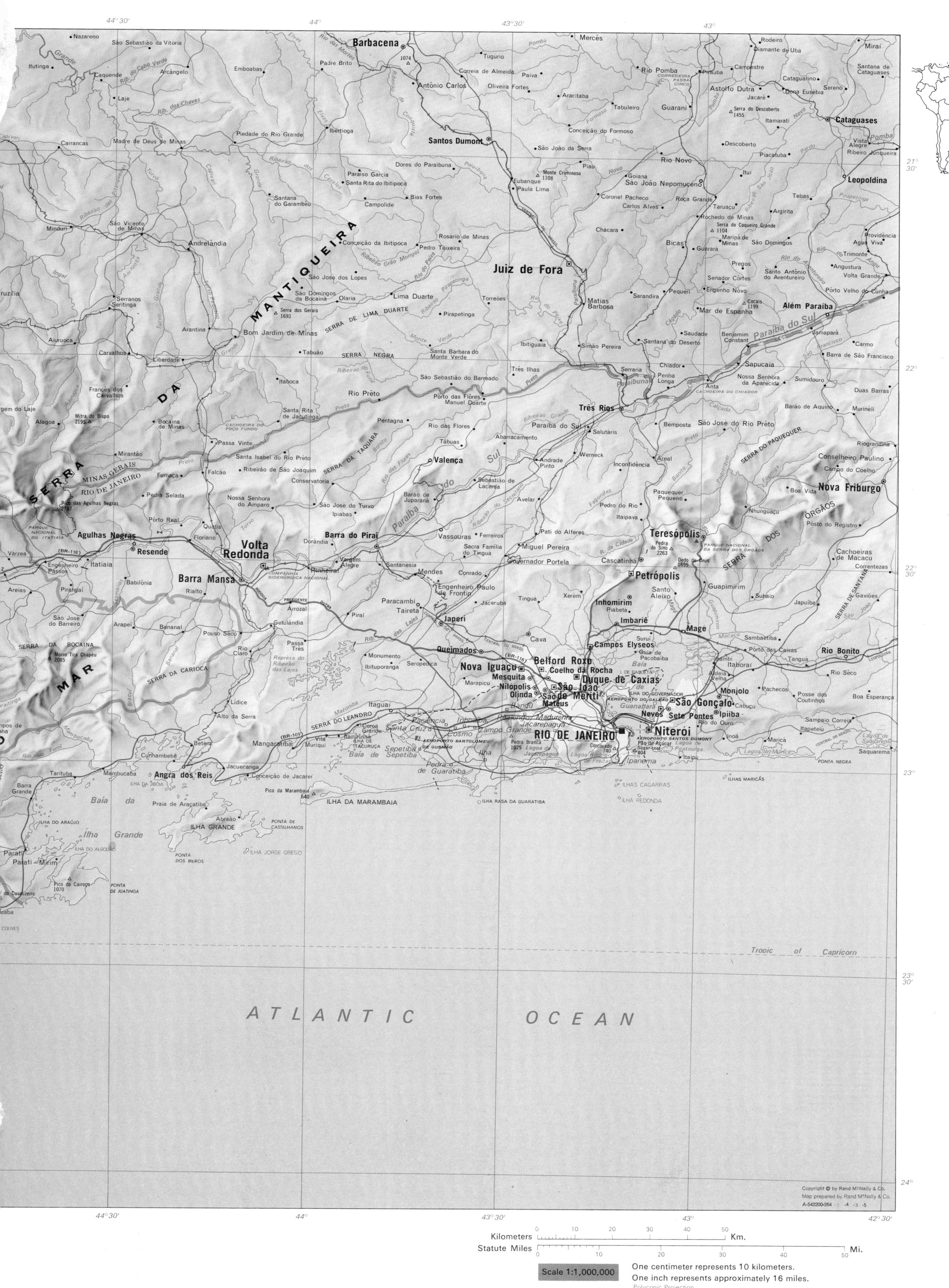
ATLANTIC OCEAN
RIO DE JANEIRO
Niterói
Juiz de Fora
Barbacena
Santos Dumont
Cataguases
Leopoldina
Além Paraíba
Nova Friburgo
Teresópolis
Petrópolis
Volta Redonda
Barra Mansa
Barra do Piraí
Três Rios
Valença
Resende
Agulhas Negras
Angra dos Reis
Nova Iguaçu
Duque de Caxias
São Gonçalo
São João de Meriti
Belford Roxo
Nilópolis
Mesquita
Queimados
Japeri
Campos Elyseos
Magé
Rio Bonito
Paraíba do Sul
SERRA DA MANTIQUEIRA
SERRA DO MAR
SERRA DOS ÓRGÃOS
MINAS GERAIS
RIO DE JANEIRO
Baía de Guanabara
Baía de Sepetiba
Baía da Ilha Grande
ILHA GRANDE
ILHA DA MARAMBAIA
Tropic of Capricorn
44° 30′
44°
43° 30′
43°
42° 30′
21° 30′
22°
22° 30′
23°
23° 30′
24°
Copyright © by Rand McNally & Co.
Map prepared by Rand McNally & Co.
A-542200-264
Kilometers 0 10 20 30 40 50 Km.
Statute Miles 0 10 20 30 40 50 Mi.
Scale 1:1,000,000
One centimeter represents 10 kilometers.
One inch represents approximately 16 miles.
Polyconic Projection

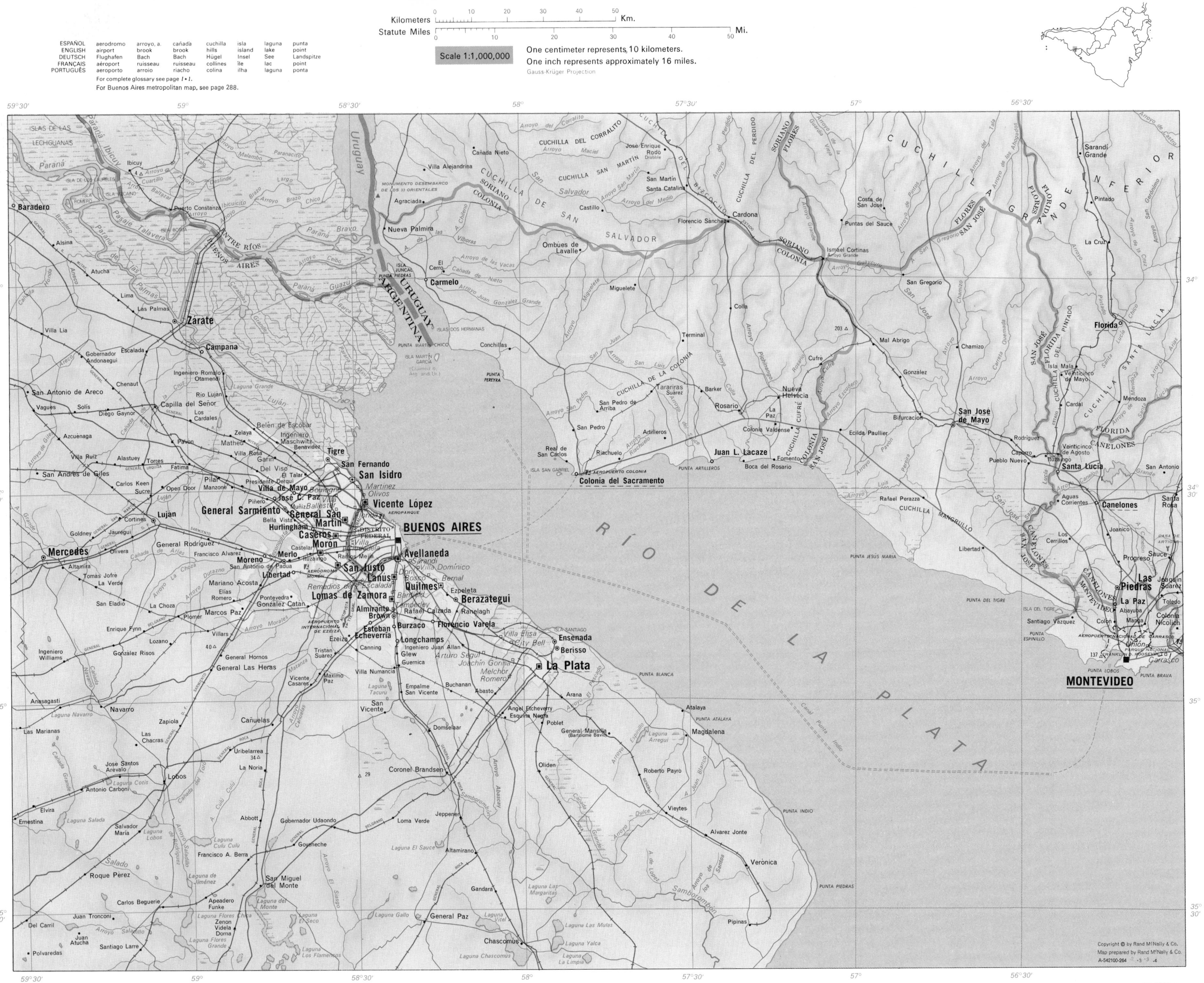
Kilometers 0 10 20 30 40 50 Km.
Statute Miles 0 10 20 30 40 50 Mi.
Scale 1:1,000,000
One centimeter represents 10 kilometers.
One inch represents approximately 16 miles.
Gauss-Krüger Projection
ESPAÑOL aerodromo arroyo, a. cañada cuchilla isla laguna punta
ENGLISH airport brook brook hills island lake point
DEUTSCH Flughafen Bach Bach Hügel Insel See Landspitze
FRANÇAIS aéroport ruisseau ruisseau collines île lac point
PORTUGUÊS aeroporto arroio riacho colina ilha laguna ponta
For complete glossary see page I·1.
For Buenos Aires metropolitan map, see page 288.
BUENOS AIRES
MONTEVIDEO
RÍO DE LA PLATA
URUGUAY
ARGENTINA
Uruguay
CUCHILLA GRANDE INFERIOR
CUCHILLA DE SAN SALVADOR
La Plata
Colonia del Sacramento
San José de Mayo
Florida
Canelones
Santa Lucía
Las Piedras
Quilmes
Avellaneda
Lanús
Lomas de Zamora
Berazategui
Ensenada
Berisso
Vicente López
San Isidro
San Fernando
Tigre
Zarate
Campana
Luján
Mercedes
Cardona
Carmelo
Nueva Palmira
Rosario
Juan L. Lacaze
Chascomús
Lobos
Cañuelas
San Miguel del Monte
Magdalena
Verónica
Pipinas
Baradero
Copyright © by Rand McNally & Co.
Map prepared by Rand McNally & Co.

THIS SECTION CONSISTS of 60 maps of the world's major metropolitan areas, at the scale of 1:300,000. The maps show the generalized land-use patterns in and around each city—the total urban extent, major industrial areas, parks and preserves, and wooded areas. Airports are shown, as are many details of the highway and rail transportation networks. Selected points of interest appear, such as Fisherman's Wharf and Chinatown in San Francisco, the Welcome monument in Jakarta, the Temple of the Jade Buddha in Shanghai, and the Cristo Redentor statue in Rio de Janeiro.

The maps name and locate a great number of towns, villages, and suburbs, and also sections or neighborhoods within limits of the larger cities. Prominent physical features, including elevations, named and unnamed, have been indicated to give a general impression of the local topography. Shaded relief has been omitted, however, to permit display of such details as streams, parks, airport runways, important public buildings and monuments, and the names of major streets. The corporate limits of major cities are also outlined. For the symbols used on these maps see the Legend to Maps, pages x-xii.

Maps of major world cities usually vary widely in scale, and heretofore have not been consistent in design and coverage. For this section, a special effort has been made to portray these varied metropolitan areas in as standard and comparable a fashion as possible. However, for a few cities (notably several in Asia) there has not been adequate source material to include certain information, such as major industrial areas and corporate limits.

The order of presentation is generally regional, with some exceptions where for ease of comparison major capitals or industrial centers or cities located in similar physical surroundings have been juxtaposed. Many American cities and some European cities, with their lower densities and more extensive areas, require larger maps than do Asiatic cities of comparable population. The total land area and population within the confines of each map are stated in the margin as a further aid to comparison. Additional data for these and other metropolitan areas with 1,000,000 or more inhabitants are listed in a table on page ***I* • 14.**

DIESER KARTENTEIL UMFASST 60 Karten der bedeutendsten Stadtregionen der Erde im Massstab 1:300 000. Die Karten zeigen in generalisierter Form die Landnutzung in und um jede Stadt: die gesamte Ausdehnung des verstädterten Gebietes, wichtige Industriegebiete, Parks, Landflächen in Gemeinbesitz und Wald. Flughäfen werden ebenso dargestellt wie viele Einzelheiten des Strassen- und Eisenbahnnetzes. Bekannte Sehenswürdigkeiten sind eingetragen wie die "Fisherman's Wharf" und "Chinatown" in San Francisco, das Willkomm-Denkmal in Jakarta, der Tempel des Jade-Buddhas in Shanghai und die "Cristo Redentor"-Statue in Rio de Janeiro.

Die Karten verzeichnen Name and Lage einer grossen Zahl von Städten, Dörfern, Vororten ebenso wie eingemeindete Ortsteile bei grösseren Städten. Hervortretende physische Formen wie benannte und unbenannte Erhebungen sind aufgenommen, um eine allgemeine Vorstellung des lokalen Reliefs zu geben. Auf die Schummerung wurde jedoch verzichtet, um klar solche Einzelheiten wie Flüsse, Parks, Start- und Landebahnen der Flughäfen, bedeutende öffentliche Gebäude und Denkmäler sowie die Namen der wichtigsten Strassen herausstellen zu können. Eingetragen sind ferner die Gemeindegrenzen der wichtigsten Städte. Zu den auf diesen Karten verwendeten Signaturen siehe "Zeichenerklärung" Seite x-xii.

Karten der bedeutendsten Weltstädte differieren normalerweise sehr stark in ihren Massstäben und sind daher uneinheitlich in ihrer Gestaltung und Begrenzung. Deshalb wurde in diesem Kartenteil besonderer Wert darauf gelegt, die verschiedenen städtischen Ballungsgebiete in möglichst einheitlicher und vergleichbarer Form darzustellen. Für einige Städte, vor allem mehrere asiatische, war das Quellenmaterial jedoch nicht ausreichend genug, um gewisse Informationen wie Hauptindustriegebiete oder Stadtgrenzen einzutragen.

Im allgemeinen sind diese Karten nach regionalen Gesichtspunkten geordnet. Um Vergleiche zu erleichtern wurden einige Ausnahmen gemacht, indem wichtige Hauptstädte, Industriezentren oder Städte in vergleichbarer landschaftlicher Lage einander gegenübergestellt wurden. Viele americkanische und einige europäische Städte mit ihrer geringen Bevölkerungsdichte, aber ausgedehnteren Fläche erfordern eine grössere Kartenfläche als asiatische Städte von vergleichbarer Bevölkerungszahl. Die gesamte Landfläche und die Bevölkerung innerhalb des dargestellten Gebietes ist am Kartenrand verzeichnet als ein weiteres Hilfsmittel für Vergleiche. Weitere Angaben über die dargestellten und andere Stadtregionen mit 1 000 000 oder mehr Bewohnern sind in einer Tabelle auf Seite ***I* • 14.**

INTEGRAN ESTA SECCION 60 mapas de las áreas metropolitanas más importantes del mundo, a la escala de 1:300 000. Los mapas muestran los patrones de uso del suelo dentro de cada ciudad y en sus alrededores—la extensión total del conglomerado urbano, las principales áreas industriales, parques y reservas, y zonas boscosas. Aparecen los aeropuertos, así como muchos otros detalles de las redes de carreteras y ferrocarriles. Se seleccionaron también puntos de interés, como el Muelle de los Pescadores y el Barrio Chino de San Francisco, el monumento de Bienvenida de Jakarta, el Templo del Buda de Jade de Shanghai y la estatua del Cristo Redentor de Rio de Janeiro.

Los mapas incluyen los nombres y la ubicación de gran número de ciudades, poblaciones menores, suburbios, e inclusive barrios y distritos de algunas de las ciudades más importantes. Las características físicas sobresalientes, e incluso algunas elevaciones con o sin nombre, están indicados para dar una impresión general de la topografía local. Se omitió sin embargo el relieve sombreado, lo cual permite mostrar detalles como ríos y arroyos, parques, pistas de aterrizaje, edificios y monumentos públicos notables y los nombres de las calles principales. También están marcados los límites territoriales de las ciudades más grandes. Para la interpretación de los símbolos usados en estos mapas, véanse Leyendas para Mapas en las páginas x-xii.

Los mapas de las ciudades más importantes del mundo varían generalmente en escala, y hasta ahora no han sido consistentes ni en diseño ni en contenido. En esta sección hemos hecho un esfuerzo de presentar las distintas áreas metropolitanas en la forma más uniforme posible, para facilitar sus comparaciones. Para algunas ciudades (la mayoría de ellas en Asia), no fué posible obtener de las propias fuentes material adecuado para la inclusión de ciertos datos, tales como las mayores áreas industriales y los límites municipales.

Los mapas de áreas metropolitanas se presentan por regiones, a excepción de unos cuantos que aparecen yuxtapuestos para facilitar la comparación entre grandes capitales, o centros comerciales, o ciudades ubicadas en contextos físicos similares. Muchas ciudades de América y algunas ciudades de Europa, por su baja densidad de población y su área extensa, requieren mapas más grandes que los ocupados por ciudades asiáticas con poblaciones comparables. Al margen de cada mapa se anotaron el área total y la población de territorio representado, lo cual facilita también las comparaciones. Datos adicionales acerca de éstas y otras áreas metropolitanas con un millón o más de habitantes, figuran en la tabla de la página ***I* • 14.**

CETTE PARTIE COMPREND 60 cartes des principales zones métropolitaines à l'échelle du 1:300 000. Les cartes représentent les principaux types d'occupation du sol des villes et de leurs environs, c'est-à-dire de toute la zone urbanisée, les principales zones industrielles, les parcs et réserves naturelles, et les régions boisées. Les aéroports sont aussi représentés ainsi que de nombreux éléments des réseaux routier et ferroviaire. Certains lieux particulièrement intéressants sont indiqués, tels que le quai des pêcheurs et la ville chinoise à San Francisco, le monument de la Bienvenue à Jakarta, le temple du Bouddha de Jade à Shanghai et la statue du Christ Rédempteur à Rio de Janeiro.

Les cartes permettent de localiser un grand nombre de villes, villages et banlieues, ainsi que des quartiers de grandes villes. Les caractéristiques topographiques notables, comme les hauteurs sont indiquées même si elles ne portent pas de nom, pour donner une idée du site de l'aire métropolitaine. L'estompage du relief est omis cependant pour permettre de représenter cours d'eau, parcs, pistes d'envol des aéroports, monuments et bâtiments publics importants, noms des principales rues, ainsi que les limites municipales des grandes villes. (Pour la signification des symboles voir légende, pages x-xii.)

En général, les échelles des cartes des grandes villes du monde varient considérablement, et jusqu'ici la présentation et le contenu de ces cartes n'étaient pas comparables. Dans cette partie de l'Atlas, un effort spécial a été fait pour représenter les diverses zones métropolitaines de manière aussi homogène que possible. Cependant, dans certains cas (en Asie notamment), les documents de base n'étaient pas assez complets pour qu'il fût possible d'inclure avec précision des données comme les zones industrielles et les limites municipales.

L'ordre de présentation est régional, avec des exceptions quand, pour faciliter les comparaisons, de grandes capitales de grands centres industriels ou encore des villes possédant un même environnement naturel, sont juxtaposés. Beaucoup de villes américaines et quelques villes européennes ont une faible densité de population et une étendue considérable; elles requièrent, par conséquent, des cartes plus grandes que des villes asiatiques de population similaire. La superficie et la population de chaque carte sont indiquées dans la marge. Des informations supplémentaires concernant ces zones métropolitaines ou celles dont la population est au moins égale à un million d'habitants sont rassemblées dans la table, page ***I* • 14.**

INTEGRAM ESTA SEÇÃO 60 mapas das áreas metropolitanas mais importantes do mundo, em escala de 1:300 000. Os mapas mostram os principais tipos de uso do solo em cada cidade e seus arredores, seja, a extensão total da zona urbanizada, as principais áreas industriais, os parques e reservas, e as áreas florestais. Mostram os aeroportos, e muitos detalhes das redes rodo e ferroviária. Indicam também pontos de interesse, selecionados, tais como o Cais dos Pescadores e o Bairro Chinês de San Francisco, o monumento de Boasvindas, em Jakarta, o templo do Buda de Jade, em Shanghai, e a Estátua do Cristo Redentor, no Rio de Janeiro.

Os mapas apresentam o nome e a localização de grande número de cidades, vilas e subúrbios, e incluem bairros das cidades mais importantes. Foram indicadas as características físicas principais, inclusive elevações, com ou sem nome, com o objetivo de proporcionar uma idéia geral da topografia local. No entanto, omitiu-se o sombreado do relevo, para permitir a indicação de detalhes tais como cursos d'água, parques, pistas de aeroportos, edifícios públicos e monumentos notáveis, e os nomes das principais ruas, bem como os limites municipais das grandes cidades. Para a interpretação dos símbolos usados nesses mapas, ver as *Legendas dos mapas*, nas pág. x-xii.

Os mapas das cidades mais importantes do mundo variam consideravelmente, de modo geral, quanto à escala, e até o presente não são comparáveis nem na forma de apresentação nem no conteúdo. Nesta seção, fez-se um esforço especial para representar as diversas áreas metropolitanas do modo mais uniforme e comparável possível. No entanto, para algumas cidades, a maioria das quais da Ásia, não foi possível obter fontes fidedignas de informações, tais como áreas industriais principais e limites municipais.

A ordem de apresentação dos mapas das áreas metropolitanas é geralmente regional, exceto em certos casos em que, para facilidade de comparação, capitais ou centros industriais e cidades importantes localizadas em meio físico semelhante foram justapostos. Muitas cidades da América e algumas da Europa, por sua baixa densidade demográfica e áreas mais extensas, exigem mapas maiores que as cidades asiáticas de população comparável. À margem de cada mapa indicam-se a área terrestre e a população total do território representado, também para maior facilidade de comparação. Dados suplementares relativos a essas e outras áreas metropolitanas de um milhão de habitantes ou mais figuram na tabela de pág. ***I* • 14.**

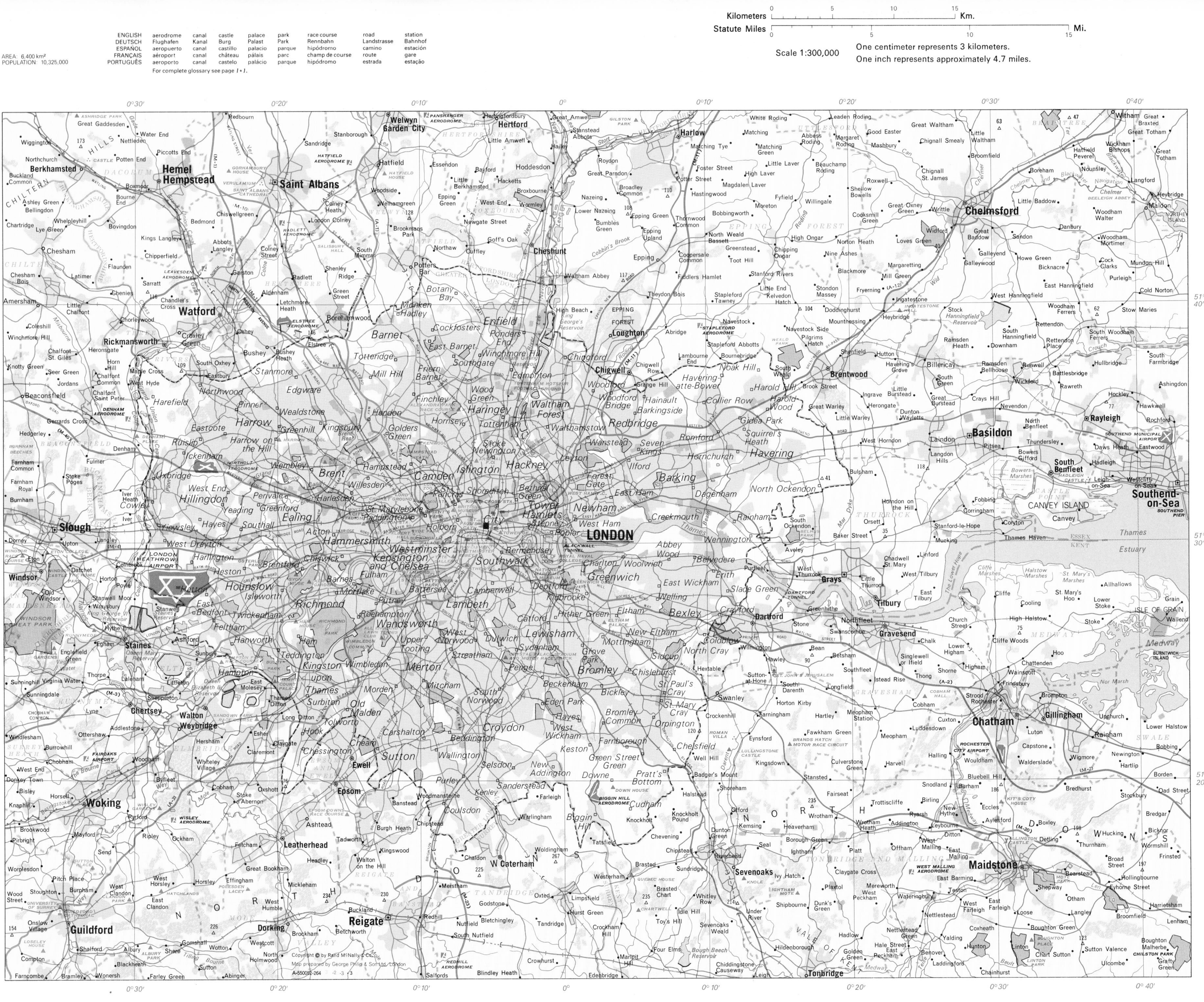
Kilometers 0 5 10 15 Km.
Statute Miles 0 5 10 15 Mi.
Scale 1:300,000
One centimeter represents 3 kilometers.
One inch represents approximately 4.7 miles.
ENGLISH DEUTSCH ESPAÑOL FRANÇAIS PORTUGUÊS
aerodrome Flughafen aeropuerto aéroport aeroporto
canal Kanal canal canal canal
castle Burg castillo château castelo
palace Palast palacio palais palácio
park Park parque parc parque
race course Rennbahn hipódromo champ de course hipódromo
road Landstrasse camino route estrada
station Bahnhof estación gare estação
For complete glossary see page I•1.
AREA 6,400 km²
POPULATION 10,325,000
LONDON
Copyright © by Rand McNally & Co.
Map prepared by George Philip & Son Ltd. London

PARIS
Versailles
Saint-Denis
Meaux
Melun
Rambouillet
Pontoise
Mantes-la-Jolie
AREA 6 500 km²
POPULATION 9 800 000
FRANÇAIS aérodrome bois château étang forêt ruisseau
ENGLISH airport woods castle pond forest brook
DEUTSCH Flughafen Gehölz Burg Teich Wald Bach
ESPAÑOL aeropuerto bosques castillo charca bosque arroyo
PORTUGUÊS aeroporto bosques castelo lagoa bosque arroio
For complete glossary see page [•].
Kilometers
Statute Miles
Scale 1:300,000
One centimeter represents 3 kilometers.
One inch represents approximately 4.7 miles.
Copyright © by Rand McNally & Co.
Map prepared by Rand McNally GmbH, Stuttgart.

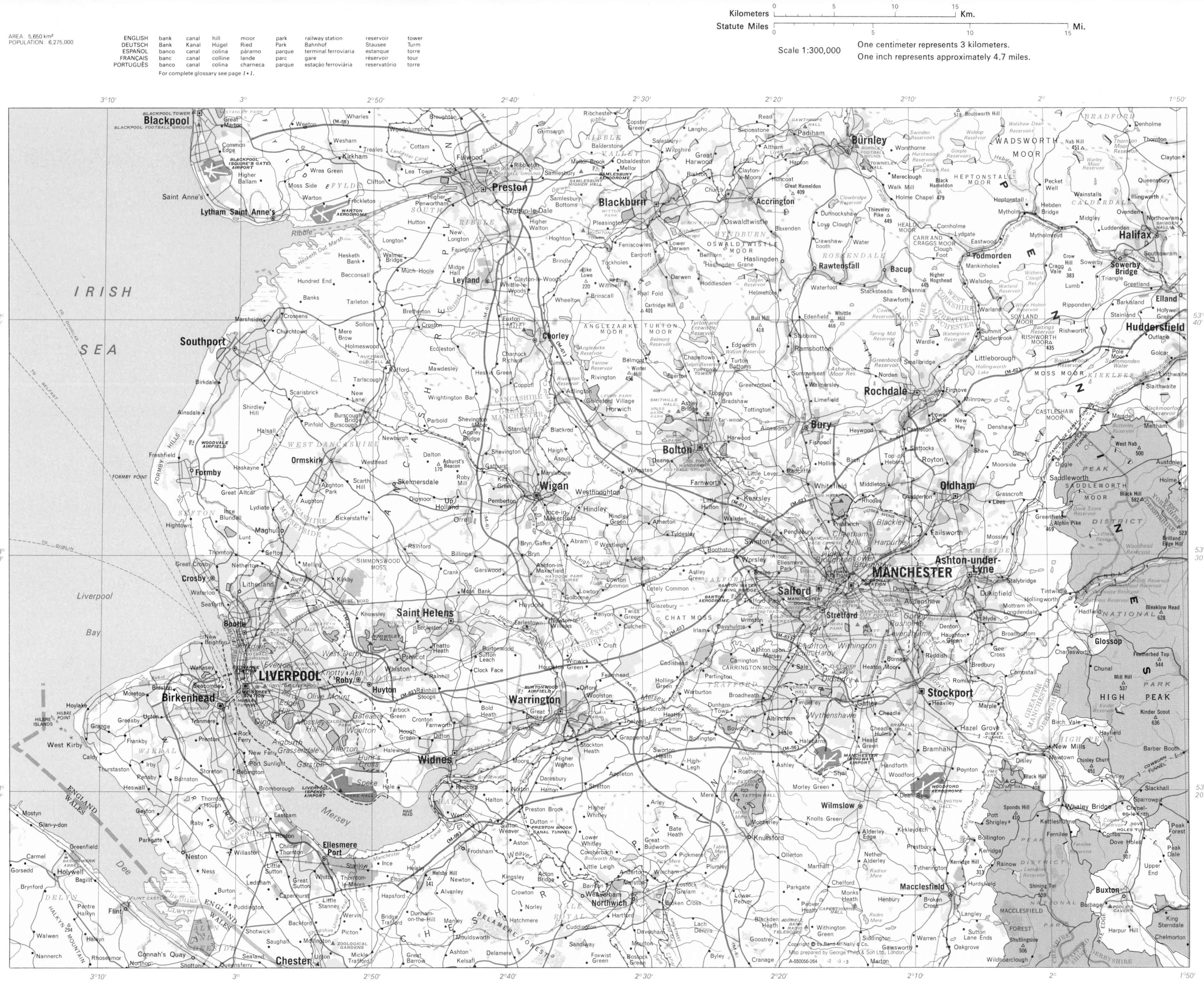
AREA 5,650 km²
POPULATION 6,275,000
ENGLISH bank canal hill moor park railway station reservoir tower
DEUTSCH Bank Kanal Hügel Ried Park Bahnhof Stausee Turm
ESPAÑOL banco canal colina páramo parque terminal ferroviaria estanque torre
FRANÇAIS banc canal colline lande parc gare réservoir tour
PORTUGUÊS banco canal colina charneca parque estação ferroviária reservatório torre
For complete glossary see page I • I.
Kilometers 0 5 10 15 Km.
Statute Miles 0 5 10 15 Mi.
Scale 1:300,000
One centimeter represents 3 kilometers.
One inch represents approximately 4.7 miles.
MANCHESTER
LIVERPOOL
Blackpool
Preston
Blackburn
Burnley
Halifax
Huddersfield
Rochdale
Bolton
Bury
Oldham
Stockport
Wigan
Warrington
Saint Helens
Widnes
Birkenhead
Chester
Southport
Salford
Ashton-under-Lyne
Macclesfield
IRISH SEA
Liverpool Bay
Mersey
Dee
ENGLAND
WALES

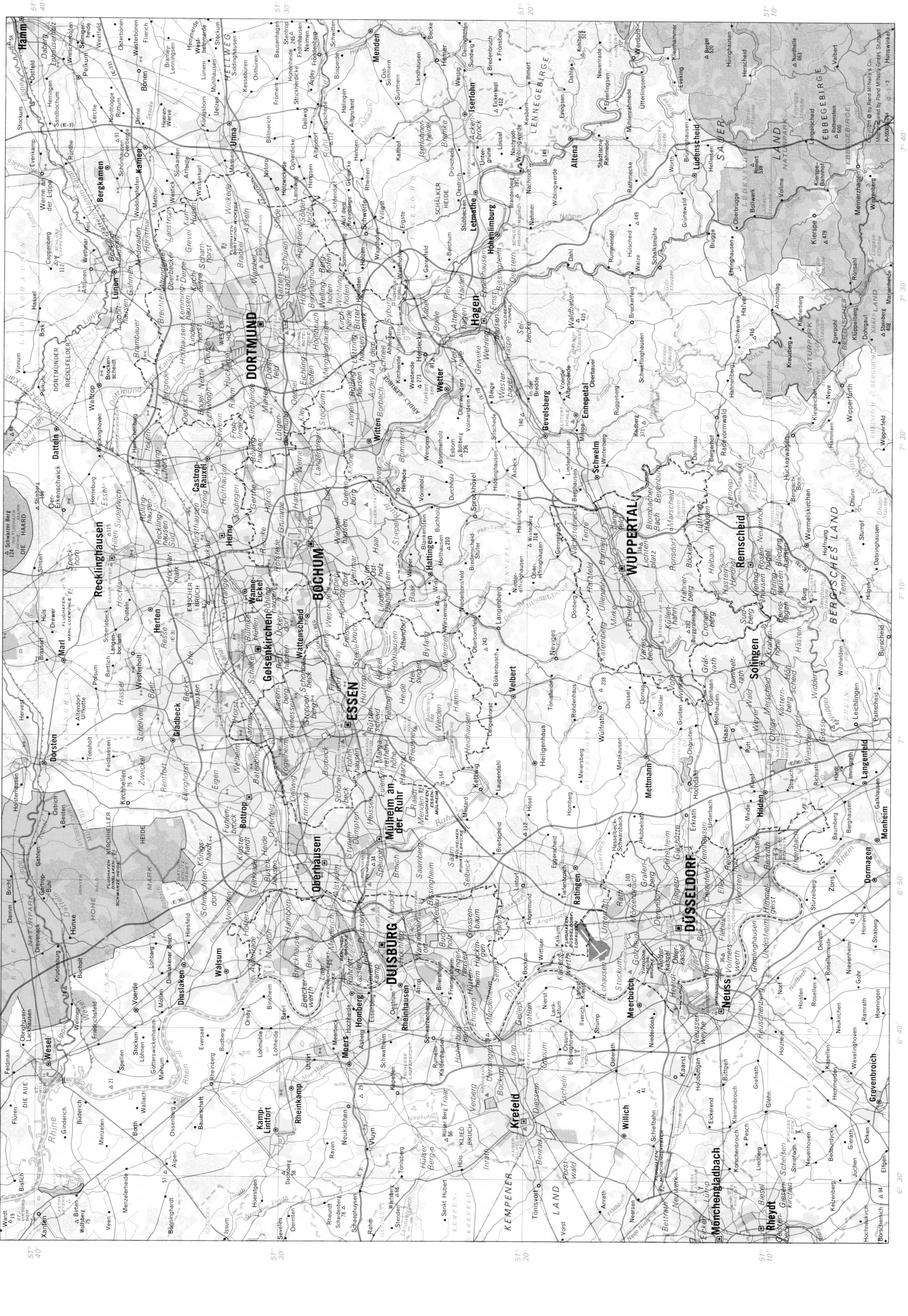

Kilometers 0 5 10 15 Km.

Statute Miles 0 5 10 15 Mi.

Scale 1:300,000

One centimeter represents 3 kilometers.

One inch represents approximately 4.7 miles.

DEUTSCH	Bach	Berg	Flughafen	Heide	Kanal	Schloss	Stausee
ENGLISH	creek	mountain	airport	heath	canal	castle	reservoir
ESPAÑOL	riachuelo	montaña	aeropuerto	matorral	canal	castillo	estanque
FRANÇAIS	crique	montagne	aéroport	lande	canal	château	réservoir
PORTUGUÊS	riacho	montanha	aeroporto	charneca	canal	castelo	reservatório

For complete glossary see page *I • 1*.

AREA: 6,500 km²
POPULATION: 8,450,000

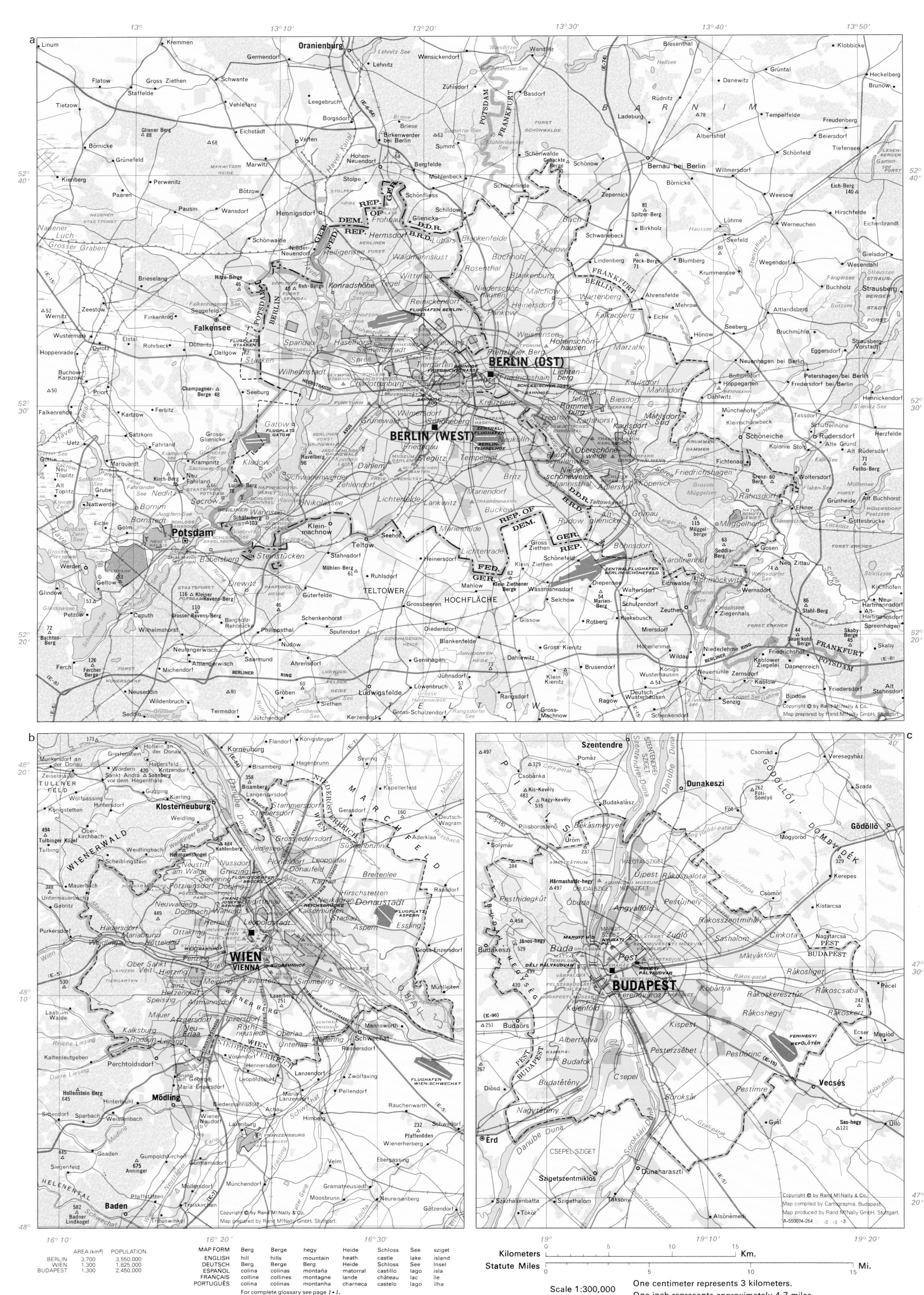
a
b
c
BERLIN (OST)
BERLIN (WEST)
Potsdam
Oranienburg
WIEN
VIENNA
Klosterneuburg
Mödling
Baden
BUDAPEST
Szentendre
Dunakeszi
Gödöllő
Vecsés
Érd
Copyright © by Rand McNally & Co.
Map prepared by Rand McNally GmbH, Stuttgart.
Map compiled by Cartographia, Budapest.
Map produced by Rand McNally GmbH, Stuttgart.
AREA (km²) POPULATION
BERLIN 3,700 3,550,000
WIEN 1,300 1,825,000
BUDAPEST 1,300 2,450,000
MAP FORM Berg Berge hegy Heide Schloss See sziget
ENGLISH hill hills mountain heath castle lake island
DEUTSCH Berg Berge Berg Heide Schloss See Insel
ESPAÑOL colina colinas montaña matorral castillo lago isla
FRANÇAIS colline collines montagne lande château lac île
PORTUGUÊS colina colinas montanha charneca castelo lago ilha
For complete glossary see page I • 1.
Kilometers 0 5 10 15 Km.
Statute Miles 0 5 10 15 Mi.
Scale 1:300,000
One centimeter represents 3 kilometers.
One inch represents approximately 4.7 miles.

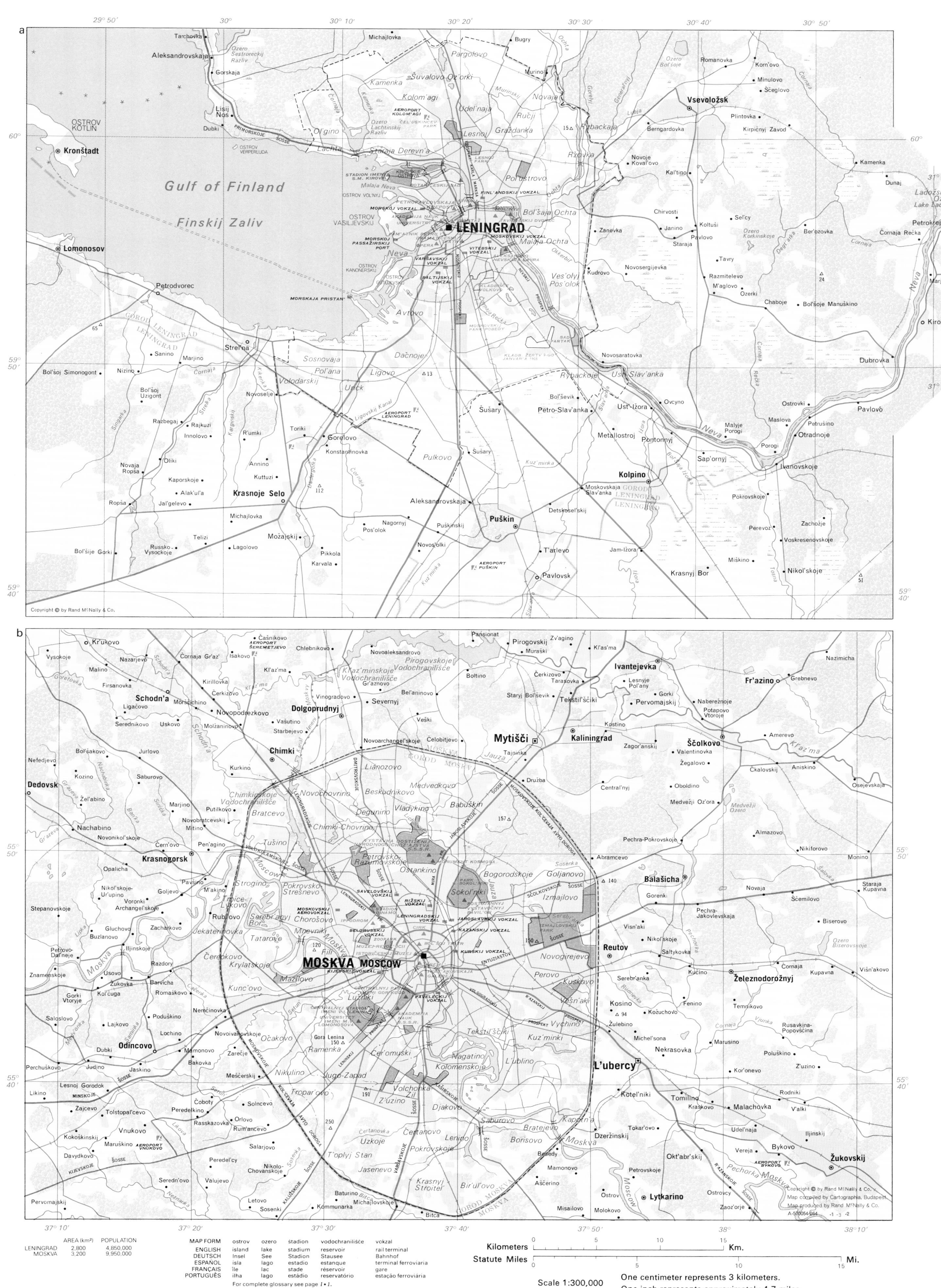
a
Gulf of Finland
Finskij Zaliv
OSTROV KOTLIN
Kronštadt
Lomonosov
Petrodvorec
Strel'na
LENINGRAD
Neva
Sestroreckij Razliv
Aleksandrovskaja
Gorskaja
Tarchovka
Lisij Nos
Dubki
Pargolovo
Murino
Bugry
Kamenka
Kolom'agi
Ol'gino
Lachta
Staraja Derevn'a
Udel'naja
Lesnoj
Graždanka
Ručji
Novaja
Šuvalovo
Oz'orki
Michajlovka
Vsevoložsk
Romanovka
Korn'ovo
Minulovo
Ščeglovo
Plintovka
Berngardovka
Kirpičnyj Zavod
Rybackaja
Novoje Koval'ovo
Kal'tino
Kamenka
Dunaj
Ladožskoje Ozero
Lake Ladoga
Petrokrepost'
Polustrovo
Bol'šaja Ochta
Malaja Ochta
Chirvosti
Janino
Koltuši
Pavlovo
Staraja
Sel'cy
Čornaja Rečka
Ber'ozovka
Zanevka
Kudrovo
Novosergijevka
Tavry
Razmitelevo
M'aglovo
Ozerki
Chaboje
Bol'šoje Manuškino
Marjino
Kirovsk
Ves'olyj Pos'olok
Avtovo
Dačnoje
Ligovo
Sosnovaja Pol'ana
Volodarskij
Urick
Novosaratovka
Rybackoje
Ust'-Slav'anka
Dubrovka
Bol'ševik
Petro-Slav'anka
Ust'-Ižora
Ovcyno
Ostrovki
Pavlovo
Maslova
Petrušino
Otradnoje
Porogi
Malyje Porogi
Metallostroj
Pontonnyj
Sap'ornyj
Ivanovskoje
Kolpino
Šušary
Pulkovo
Gorelovo
Konstantinovka
Toriki
R'umki
Annino
Kuttuzi
Krasnoje Selo
Aleksandrovskaja
Puškin
Moskovskaja Slav'anka
Detskosel'skij
Pokrovskoje
Perevoz
Zachožje
Voskresenovskoje
Miškino
Nikol'skoje
Krasnyj Bor
Jam-Ižora
T'arlevo
Pavlovsk
Puškinskij
Novos'olki
Nagornyj Pos'olok
Možajskij
Pikkola
Karvala
Michajlovka
Telizi
Lagolovo
Russko-Vysockoje
Bol'šije Gorki
Ropša
Jal'gelevo
Alak'ul'a
Kaporskoje
Novaja Ropša
Oliki
Razbegaj
Rajkuzi
Innolovo
Bol'šoj Uzigont
Nizino
Bol'šoj Simonogont
Sanino
Marjino
Novosel'je
GOROD LENINGRAD
Copyright © by Rand McNally & Co.
b
Kr'ukovo
Vysokoje
Nazarjevo
Malino
Firsanovka
Schodn'a
Ligačovo
Serednikovo
Uskovo
Čornaja Gr'az'
Isakovo
Kirillovka
Čerkizovo
Novopodrezkovo
Molžaninovo
Dolgoprudnyj
Vinogradovo
Severnyj
Chlebnikovo
Novoaleksandrovo
Pirogovskoje Vodochranilišče
Gr'aznovo
Bel'aninovo
Pansionat
Pirogovskij
Zv'agino
Muraški
Kl'as'ma
Ivantejevka
Tarasovka
Čerkizovo
Lesnyje Pol'any
Gorki
Pervomajskij
Tekstil'ščiki
Fr'azino
Grebnevo
Nazimicha
Naberežnoje
Potapovo
Vtoroje
Mytišči
Kalinigrad
Kostino
Zagor'anskij
Ščolkovo
Valentinovka
Žegalovo
Amerevo
Čkalovskij
Aniskino
Osejevskaja
Chimki
Kurkino
Nefedjevo
Bol'šakovo
Jurlovo
Kozino
Saburovo
Dedovsk
Žel'abino
Marjino
Putilkovo
Novobratcevskij
Mitino
Nachabino
Novonikol'skoje
Cern'ovo
Pen'agino
Krasnogorsk
Opalicha
Nikol'skoje-Ur'upino
Voronki
Archangel'skoje
Stepanovskoje
Gluchovo
Buzlanovo
Petrovo-Dal'neje
Znamenskoje
Gorki Vtoryje
Kol'cuga
Žukovka
Barvicha
Usovo
Razdory
Romaškovo
Saloslovo
Lajkovo
Poduškino
Lochino
Odincovo
Dubki
Mamonovo
Perchuškovo
Judino
Jaskino
Likino
Lesnoj Gorodok
Zajcevo
Tolstopal'cevo
Peredelkino
Rasskazovka
Vnukovo
Kokoškinskij
Maruškino
Davydkovo
Peredel'cy
Valujevo
Seredn'ovo
Pervomajskij
Letovo
Sosenki
Kommunarka
Baturino
Michajlovskoje
Bitca
Lianozovo
Medvedkovo
Babuškin
Beskudnikovo
Novochovrino
Degunino
Vladykino
Chimkinskoje Vodochranilišče
Bratcevo
Tušino
Strogino
Pokrovsko Strešnevo
Ostankino
Bogorodskoje
Goljanovo
Sokol'niki
Izmajlovo
Trojce-Lykovo
Serebr'anyj Bor
Chorošovo
Mnevniki
Tatarovo
Krylatskoje
MOSKVA MOSCOW
Mazilovo
Kunc'ovo
Nemčinovka
Novoivanovskoje
Zarečje
Očakovo
Nikulino
Tropar'ovo
Jugo-Zapad
Ramenka
Čer'omuški
Volchonka-Zil
Z'uzino
Djakovo
Nagatino
Kolomenskoje
L'ublino
Tekstil'ščiki
Kuz'minki
Vychino
Perovo
Novogirejevo
Kuskovo
Vešn'aki
Reutov
Balašicha
Abramcevo
Pechra-Pokrovskoje
Almazovo
Nikiforovo
Monino
Čcentral'nyj
Družba
Oboldino
Medvežji Oz'ora
Staraja Kupavna
Novaja
Ščemilovo
Pechra-Jakovlevskaja
Biserovo
Vişn'aki
Nikol'skoje
Saltykovka
Kučino
Železnodorožnyj
Cornaja
Kupavna
Višn'akovo
Serebr'anka
Fenino
Temnikovo
Kosino
Kožuchovo
Žulebino
Michel'sona
Nekrasovka
Marusino
Rusavkina-Popovščina
Polučkino
Z'uzino
Kor'onevo
L'ubercy
Kotel'niki
Tomilino
Kraskovo
Malachovka
Rodniki
V'alki
Il'jinskij
Bykovo
Žukovskij
Udel'naja
Tokar'ovo
Dzeržinskij
Okt'abr'skij
Vereja
Kapotn'a
Bratejevo
Borisovo
Saburovo
Lenino
Čertanovo
Uzkoje
Pokrovskoje
T'oplyj Stan
Jasenevo
Krasnyj Stroitel
Bir'ul'ovo
Besedy
Mamonovo
Aščerino
Ostrov
Lytkarino
Petrovskoje
Ostrovcy
Zaoz'orje
Misailovo
Molokovo
Solncevo
Čoboty
Orlovo
Rum'ancevo
Salarjevo
Nikolo-Chovanskoje
GOROD MOSKVA
Copyright © by Rand McNally & Co.
Map compiled by Cartographia, Budapest
Map produced by Rand McNally & Co.
LENINGRAD AREA (km²) 2,800 POPULATION 4,850,000
MOSKVA AREA (km²) 3,200 POPULATION 9,950,000
MAP FORM: ostrov, ozero, stadion, vodochranilišče, vokzal
ENGLISH: island, lake, stadium, reservoir, rail terminal
DEUTSCH: Insel, See, Stadion, Stausee, Bahnhof
ESPAÑOL: isla, lago, estadio, estanque, terminal ferroviaria
FRANÇAIS: île, lac, stade, réservoir, gare
PORTUGUÊS: ilha, lago, estádio, reservatório, estação ferroviária
For complete glossary see page I • 1.
Kilometers 0 5 10 15 Km.
Statute Miles 0 5 10 15 Mi.
Scale 1:300,000
One centimeter represents 3 kilometers.
One inch represents approximately 4.7 miles.

	AREA (km²)	POPULATION
MADRID	1,250	3,875,000
MILANO	1,900	3,975,000
LISBOA	1,150	2,150,000
BARCELONA	950	3,825,000

MAP FORM	aeroporto	arroyo	estación	ponta	ribeira	riera
ENGLISH	airport	brook	station	point	creek	creek
DEUTSCH	Flughafen	Bach	Bahnhof	Landspitze	Bach	Bach
ESPAÑOL	aeropuerto	arroyo	estación	punta	riachuelo	riera
FRANÇAIS	aéroport	ruisseau	gare	pointe	crique	crique
PORTUGUÊS	aeroporto	arroio	estação	ponta	riacho	arroio

For complete glossary see page I • 1.

Kilometers 0 5 10 15 Km.
Statute Miles 0 5 10 15 Mi.
Scale 1:300,000
One centimeter represents 3 kilometers.
One inch represents approximately 4.7 miles.

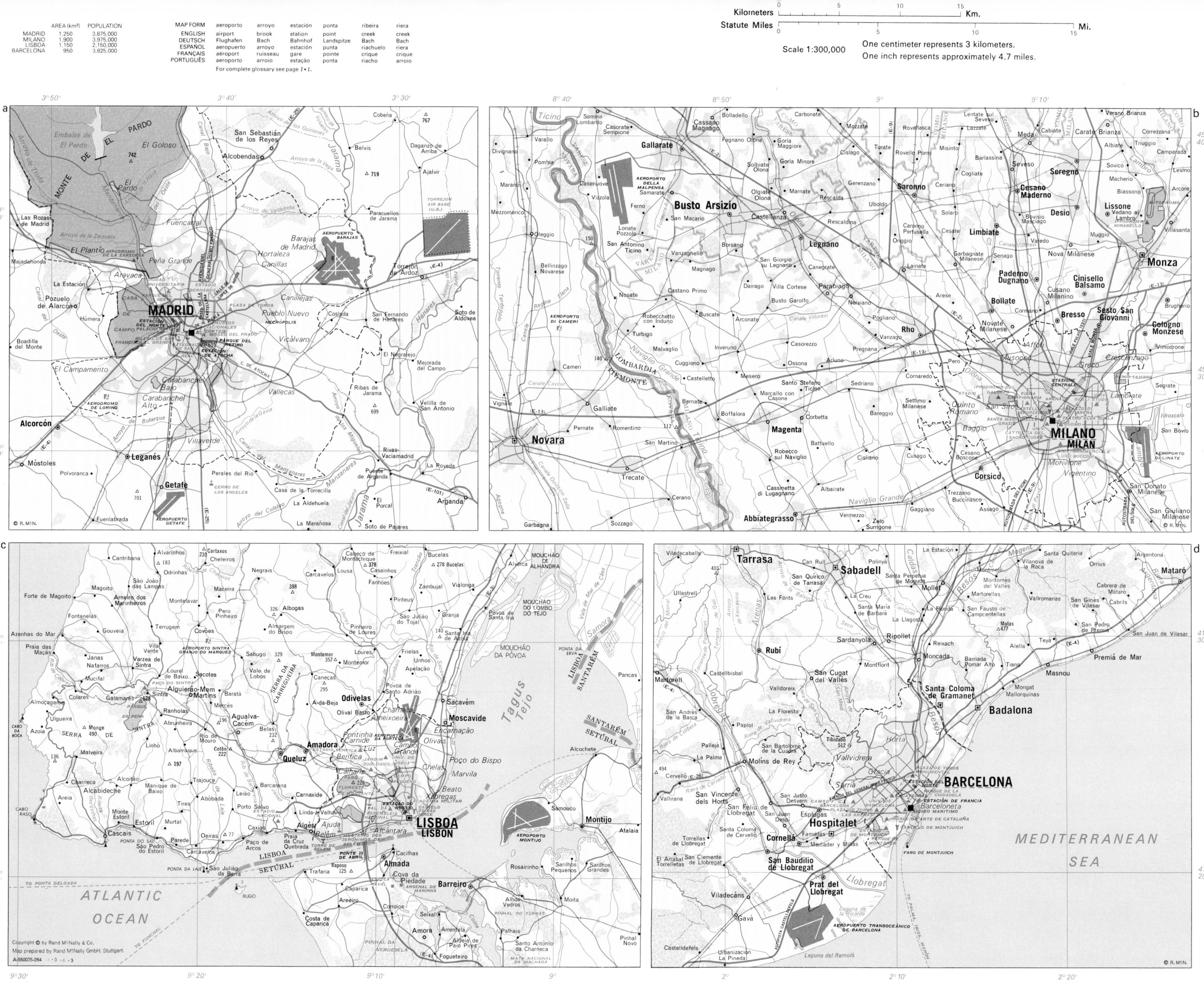

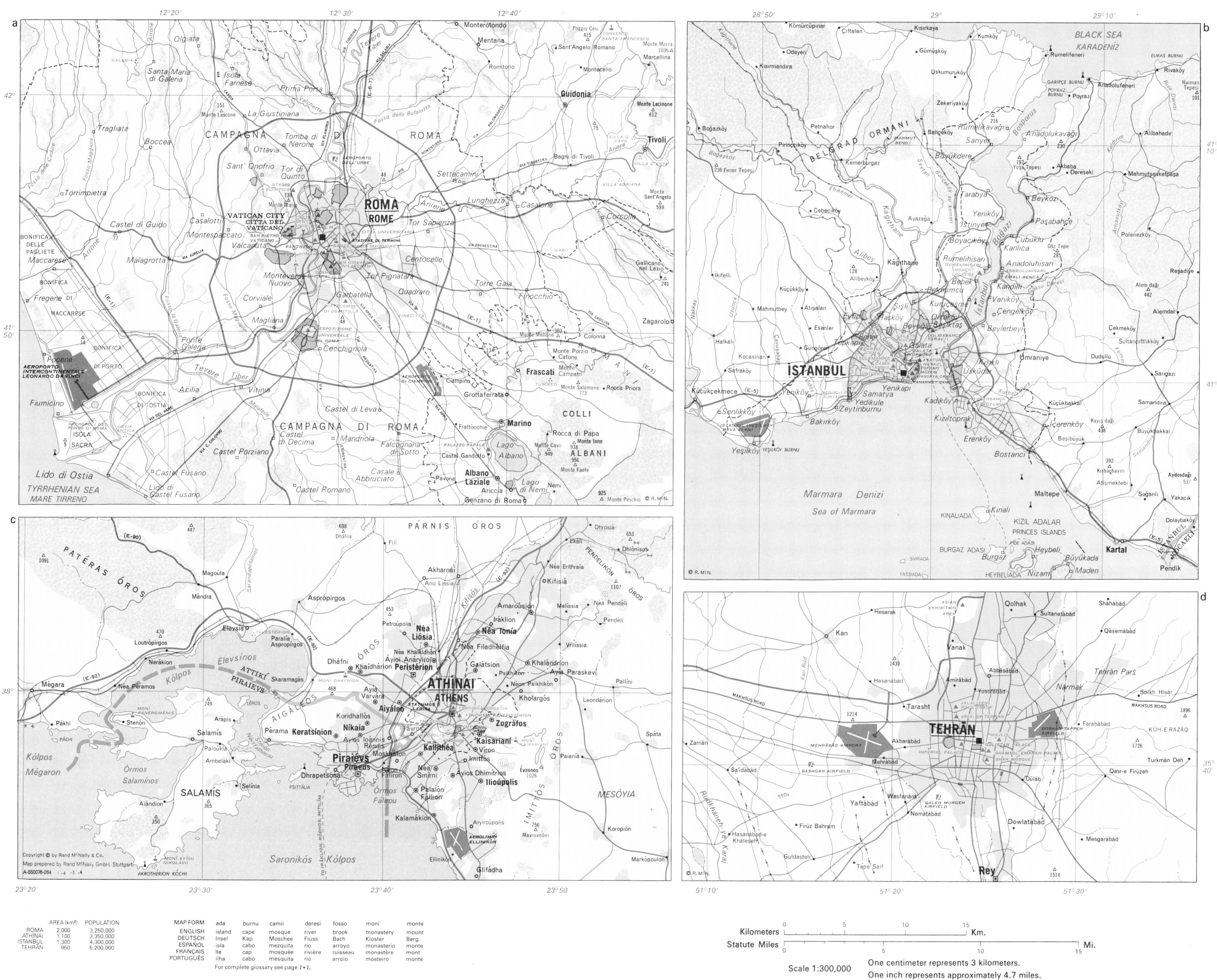
a
ROMA
ROME
VATICAN CITY
CITTÀ DEL VATICANO
TYRRHENIAN SEA
MARE TIRRENO
Lido di Ostia
Fiumicino
AEROPORTO INTERCONTINENTALE LEONARDO DA VINCI
Tivoli
Guidonia
Frascati
Marino
COLLI ALBANI
CAMPAGNA DI ROMA
Lago Albano
b
BLACK SEA
KARADENİZ
İSTANBUL
Marmara Denizi
Sea of Marmara
BELGRAD ORMANI
KIZIL ADALAR
PRINCES ISLANDS
Üsküdar
Kadıköy
Kartal
Pendik
c
ATHÍNAI
ATHENS
Piraiévs
Piraeus
SALAMÍS
Saronikós Kólpos
PÁRNIS ÓROS
PATÉRAS ÓROS
MESÓYIA
Elevsís
Mégara
d
TEHRĀN
Rey
Mehrābād Airport
Tehrān Pārs
Karaj

	AREA (km²)	POPULATION
ROMA	2,000	3,250,000
ATHÍNAI	1,100	3,350,000
İSTANBUL	1,300	4,300,000
TEHRĀN	950	5,200,000

MAP FORM	ada	burnu	camii	deresi	fosso	moni	monte
ENGLISH	island	cape	mosque	river	brook	monastery	mount
DEUTSCH	Insel	Kap	Moschee	Fluss	Bach	Kloster	Berg
ESPAÑOL	isla	cabo	mezquita	rio	arroyo	monasterio	monte
FRANÇAIS	île	cap	mosquée	rivière	ruisseau	monastère	mont
PORTUGUÊS	ilha	cabo	mesquita	rio	arroio	mosteiro	monte

For complete glossary see page I • I.
Kilometers 0 5 10 15 Km.
Statute Miles 0 5 10 15 Mi.
Scale 1:300,000
One centimeter represents 3 kilometers.
One inch represents approximately 4.7 miles.
Copyright © by Rand McNally & Co.
Map prepared by Rand McNally GmbH, Stuttgart.
A-550076-264

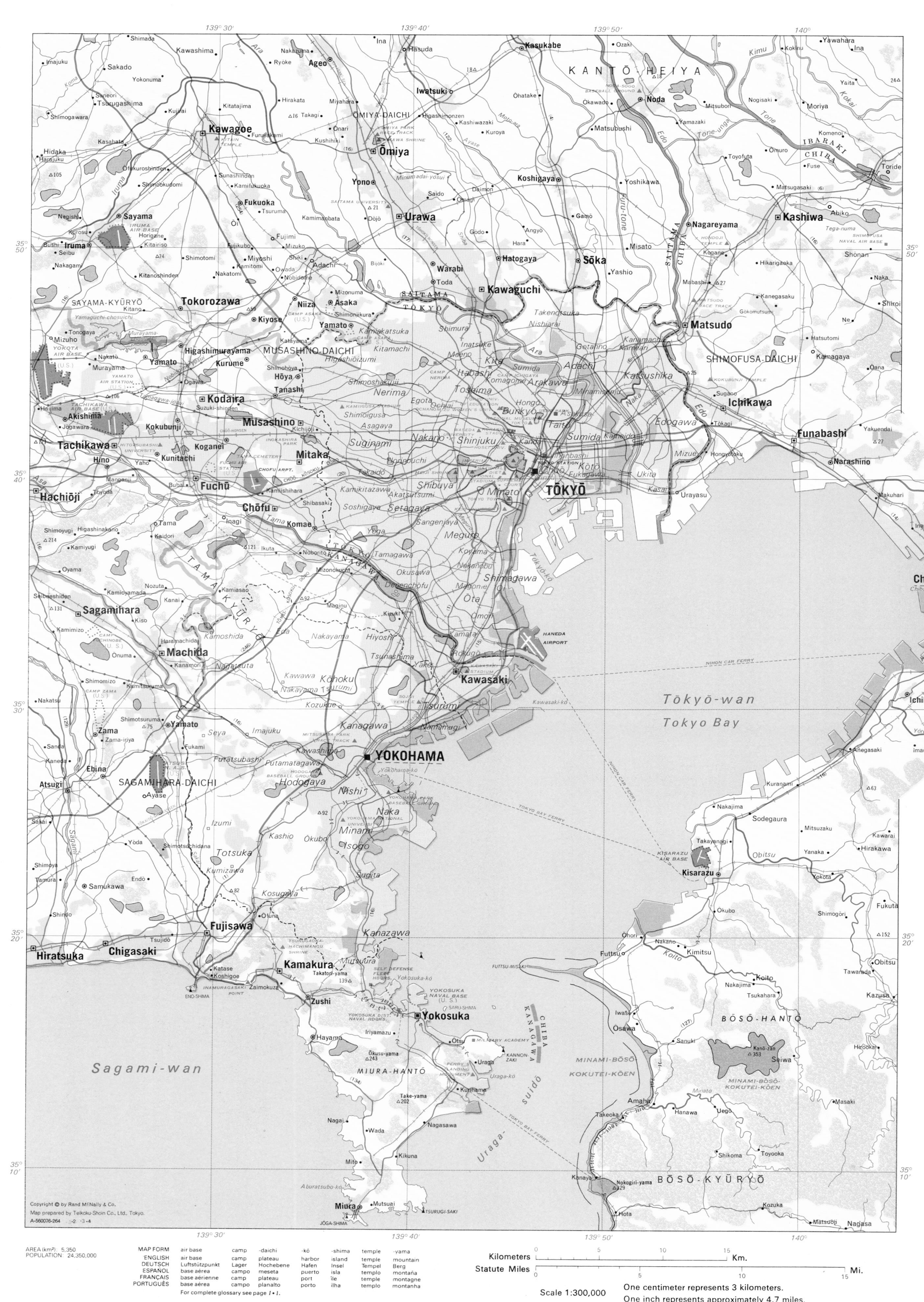

AREA (km²) 5,350
POPULATION 24,350,000

MAP FORM	air base	camp	-daichi	-kō	-shima	temple	-yama
ENGLISH	air base	camp	plateau	harbor	island	temple	mountain
DEUTSCH	Luftstützpunkt	Lager	Hochebene	Hafen	Insel	Tempel	Berg
ESPAÑOL	base aérea	campo	meseta	puerto	isla	templo	montaña
FRANÇAIS	base aérienne	camp	plateau	port	île	temple	montagne
PORTUGUÊS	base aérea	campo	planalto	porto	ilha	templo	montanha

For complete glossary see page *I* • *1*.

Kilometers 0 5 10 15 Km.
Statute Miles 0 5 10 15 Mi.

Scale 1:300,000
One centimeter represents 3 kilometers.
One inch represents approximately 4.7 miles.

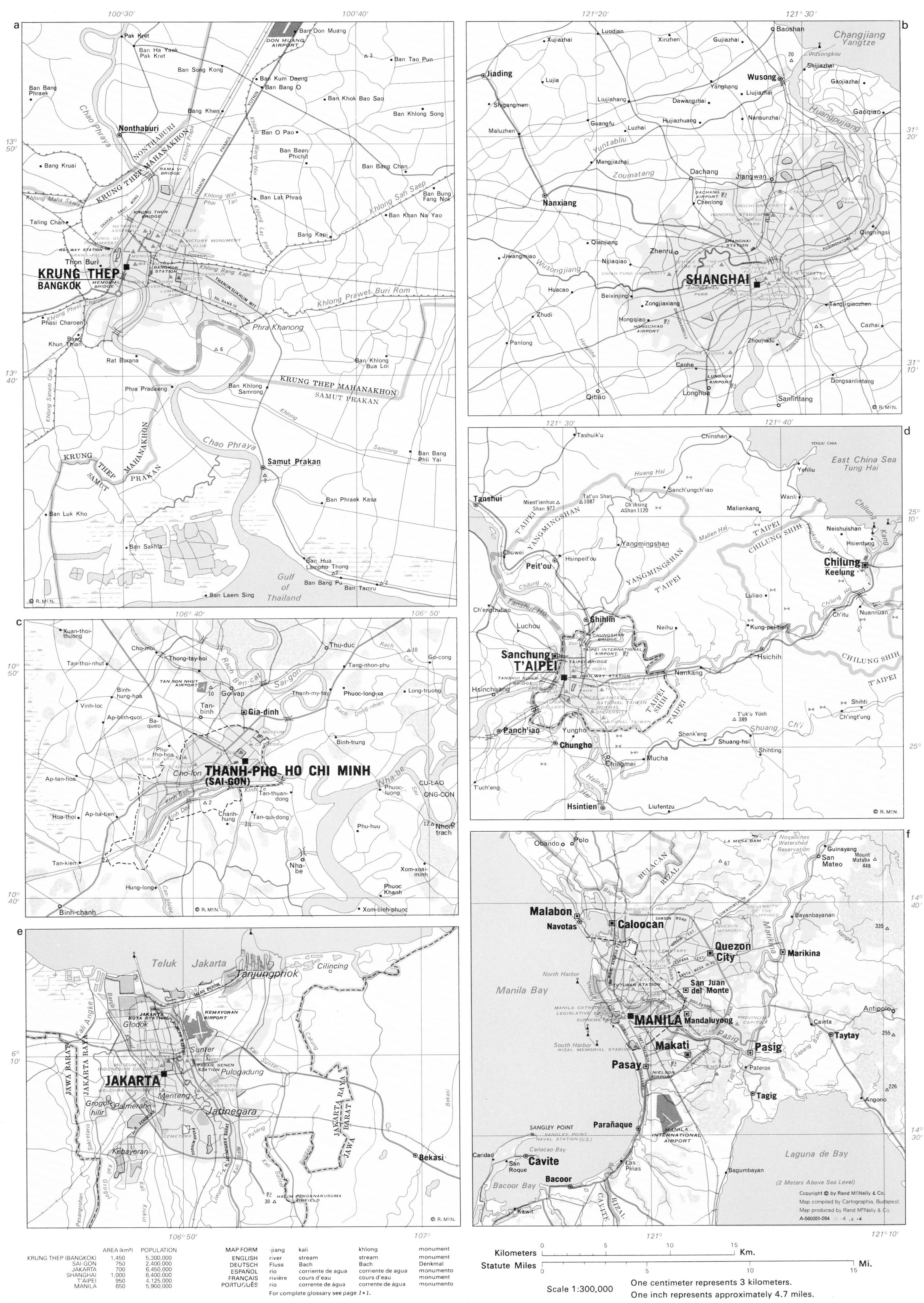

	AREA (km²)	POPULATION
KRUNG THEP (BANGKOK)	1,450	5,300,000
SAI-GON	750	2,400,000
JAKARTA	700	6,450,000
SHANGHAI	1,000	8,400,000
T'AIPEI	950	4,125,000
MANILA	650	5,900,000

MAP FORM	-jiang	kali	khlong	monument
ENGLISH	river	stream	stream	monument
DEUTSCH	Fluss	Bach	Bach	Denkmal
ESPAÑOL	río	corriente de agua	corriente de agua	monumento
FRANÇAIS	rivière	cours d'eau	cours d'eau	monument
PORTUGUÊS	rio	corrente de água	corrente de água	monumento

For complete glossary see page *I • 1*.

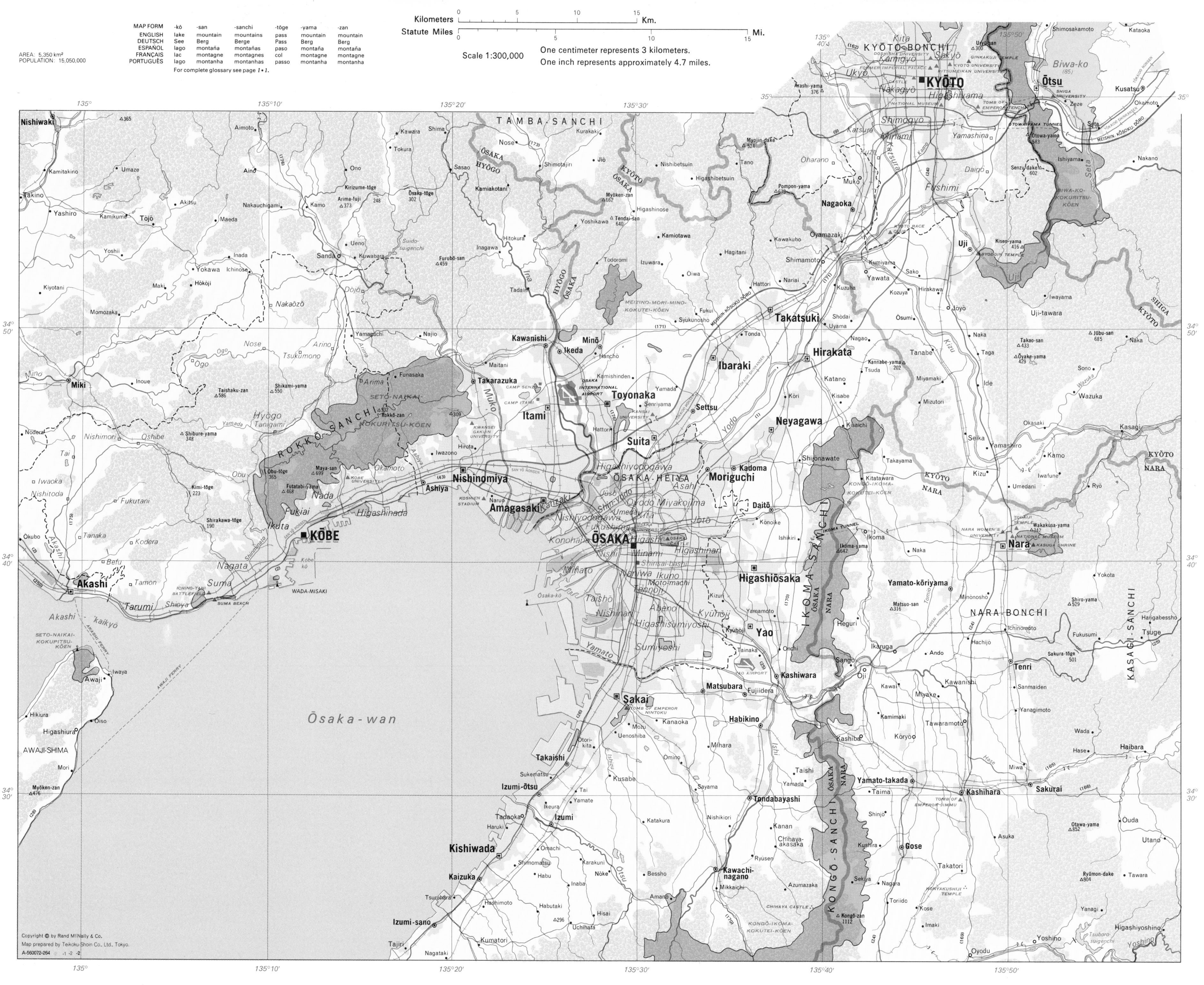

Kilometers 0 5 10 15 Km.
Statute Miles 0 5 10 15 Mi.
Scale 1:300,000
One centimeter represents 3 kilometers.
One inch represents approximately 4.7 miles.
MAP FORM -kō -san -sanchi -tōge -yama -zan
ENGLISH lake mountain mountains pass mountain mountain
DEUTSCH See Berg Berge Pass Berg Berg
ESPAÑOL lago montaña montañas paso montaña montaña
FRANÇAIS lac montagne montagnes col montagne montagne
PORTUGUÊS lago montanha montanhas passo montanha montanha
For complete glossary see page I·1.
AREA 5,350 km²
POPULATION 15,050,000
ŌSAKA
KŌBE
KYŌTO
Nara
Ōtsu
Sakai
Ōsaka-wan
Biwa-ko
Awaji
Akashi-kaikyō
TAMBA-SANCHI
ROKKŌ-SANCHI
IKOMA-SANCHI
KONGŌ-SANCHI
KASAGI-SANCHI
NARA-BONCHI
KYŌTO-BONCHI
Copyright © by Rand McNally & Co.
Map prepared by Teikoku-Shoin Co., Ltd., Tokyo.
A-560072-264 -1 -2 -2

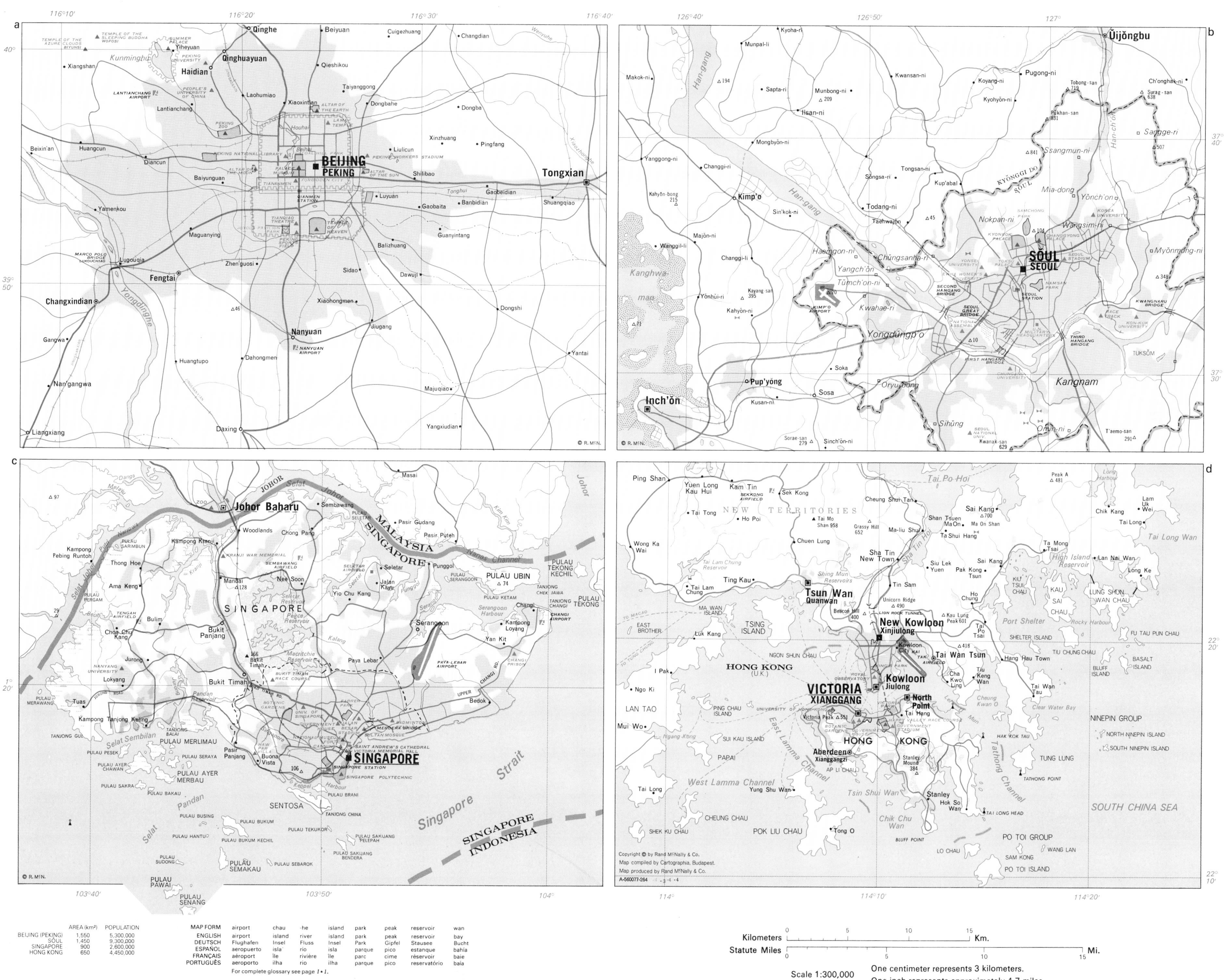

	AREA (km²)	POPULATION
BEIJING (PEKING)	1,550	5,300,000
SŎUL	1,450	9,300,000
SINGAPORE	900	2,600,000
HONG KONG	650	4,450,000

MAP FORM	airport	chau	-he	island	park	peak	reservoir	wan
ENGLISH	airport	island	river	island	park	peak	reservoir	bay
DEUTSCH	Flughafen	Insel	Fluss	Insel	Park	Gipfel	Stausee	Bucht
ESPAÑOL	aeropuerto	isla	río	isla	parque	pico	estanque	bahía
FRANÇAIS	aéroport	île	rivière	île	parc	cime	réservoir	baie
PORTUGUÊS	aeroporto	ilha	rio	ilha	parque	pico	reservatório	baía

For complete glossary see page *I • 1*.

Kilometers 0 5 10 15 Km.
Statute Miles 0 5 10 15 Mi.

Scale 1:300,000
One centimeter represents 3 kilometers.
One inch represents approximately 4.7 miles.

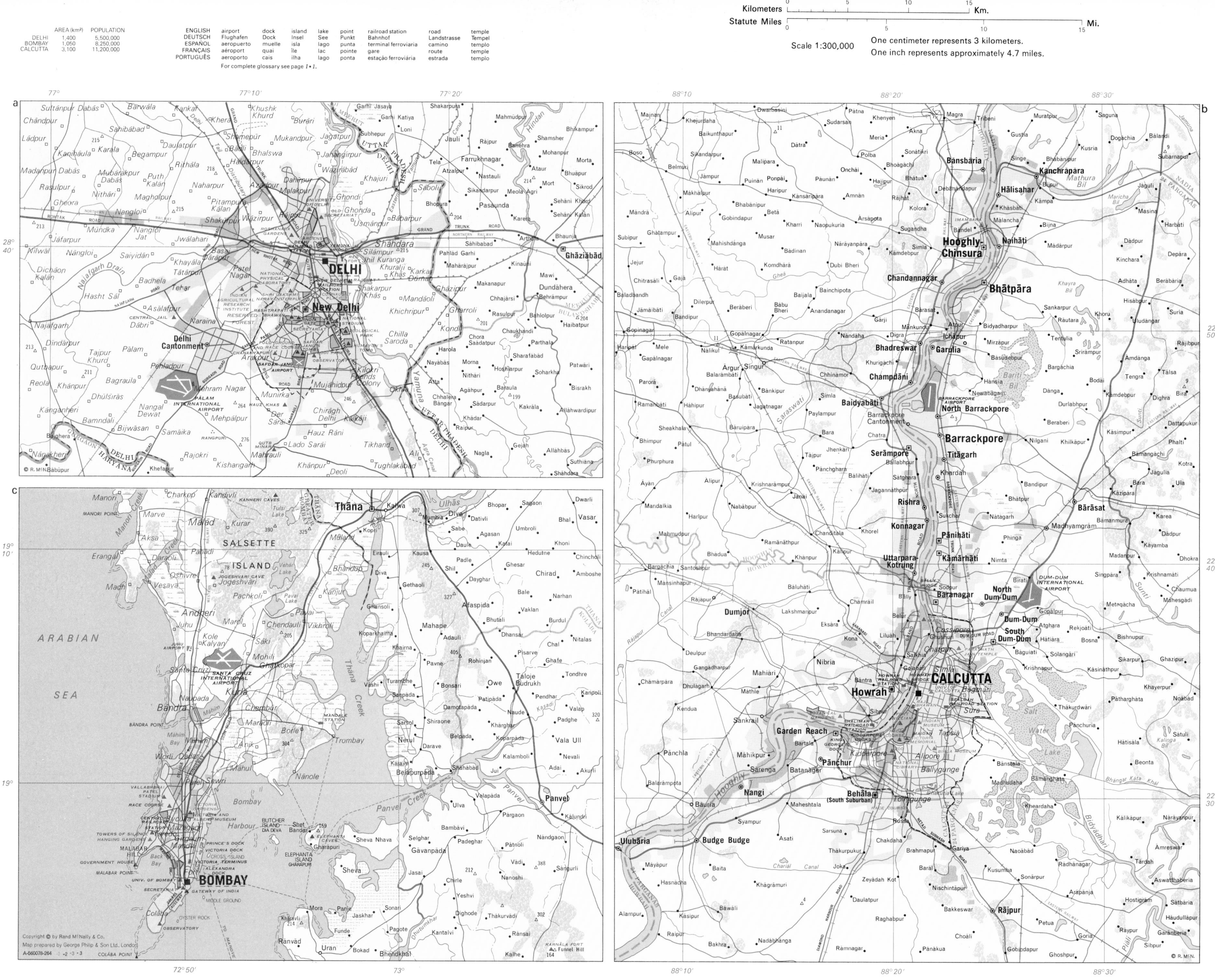
AREA (km²) POPULATION
DELHI 1,400 5,500,000
BOMBAY 1,050 8,250,000
CALCUTTA 3,100 11,200,000
ENGLISH airport dock island lake point railroad station road temple
DEUTSCH Flughafen Dock Insel See Punkt Bahnhof Landstrasse Tempel
ESPAÑOL aeropuerto muelle isla lago punta terminal ferroviaria camino templo
FRANÇAIS aéroport quai île lac pointe gare route temple
PORTUGUÊS aeroporto cais ilha lago ponta estação ferroviária estrada templo
For complete glossary see page I•1.
Kilometers 0 5 10 15 Km.
Statute Miles 0 5 10 15 Mi.
Scale 1:300,000
One centimeter represents 3 kilometers.
One inch represents approximately 4.7 miles.
a
b
c
DELHI
New Delhi
Delhi Cantonment
Ghāziābād
Shāhdara
PĀLAM INTERNATIONAL AIRPORT
UTTAR PRADESH
HARYANA
Yamuna
Thāna
SALSETTE ISLAND
ARABIAN SEA
Thāna Creek
Trombay
Panvel
SANTA CRUZ INTERNATIONAL AIRPORT
Bāndra
BOMBAY
ELEPHANTA ISLAND
Hooghly-Chinsura
Bhātpāra
Chandannagar
Barrackpore
North Barrackpore
Rishra
Konnagar
Bārāsat
DUM-DUM INTERNATIONAL AIRPORT
North Dum-Dum
South Dum-Dum
CALCUTTA
Howrah
Garden Reach
Nangi
Behāla (South Suburban)
Budge Budge
Ulubāria
Rājpur
Hooghly
Copyright © by Rand McNally & Co.
Map prepared by George Philip & Son Ltd. London
© R. M©N.

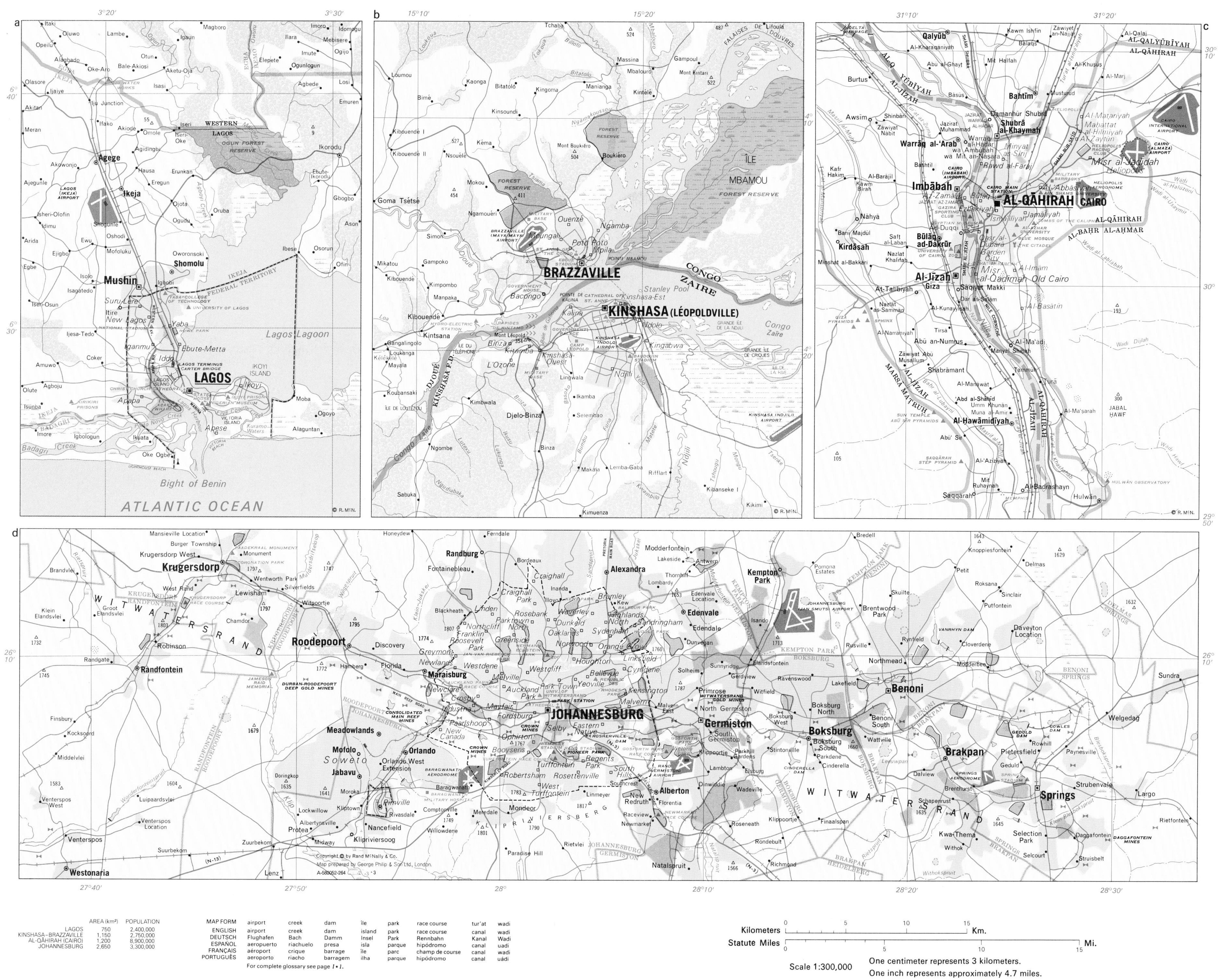

	AREA (km²)	POPULATION
LAGOS	750	2,400,000
KINSHASA–BRAZZAVILLE	1,150	2,750,000
AL-QĀHIRAH (CAIRO)	1,200	8,900,000
JOHANNESBURG	2,650	3,300,000

MAP FORM	airport	creek	dam	île	park	race course	tur'at	wadi
ENGLISH	airport	creek	dam	island	park	race course	canal	wadi
DEUTSCH	Flughafen	Bach	Damm	Insel	Park	Rennbahn	Kanal	Wadi
ESPAÑOL	aeropuerto	riachuelo	presa	isla	parque	hipódromo	canal	uadi
FRANÇAIS	aéroport	crique	barrage	île	parc	champ de course	canal	wadi
PORTUGUÊS	aeroporto	riacho	barragem	ilha	parque	hipódromo	canal	uádi

For complete glossary see page *I • 1*.

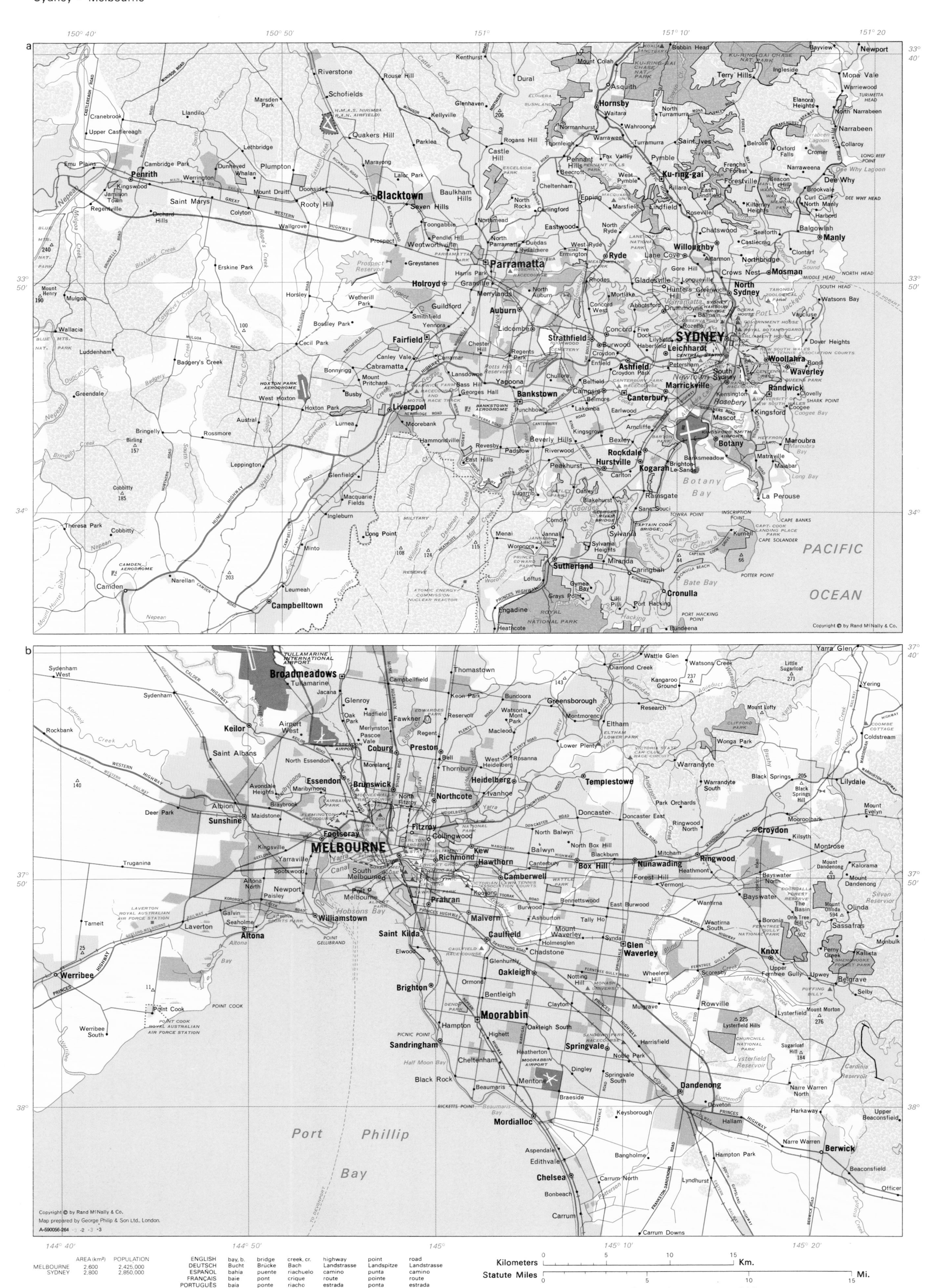

	AREA (km²)	POPULATION
MELBOURNE	2,600	2,425,000
SYDNEY	2,800	2,850,000

ENGLISH	bay, b.	bridge	creek, cr.	highway	point	road
DEUTSCH	Bucht	Brücke	Bach	Landstrasse	Landspitze	Landstrasse
ESPAÑOL	bahia	puente	riachuelo	camino	punta	camino
FRANÇAIS	baie	pont	crique	route	pointe	route
PORTUGUÊS	baia	ponte	riacho	estrada	ponta	estrada

For complete glossary see page *I* • *1*.

Kilometers 0 5 10 15 Km.
Statute Miles 0 5 10 15 Mi.

Scale 1:300,000

One centimeter represents 3 kilometers.
One inch represents approximately 4.7 miles.

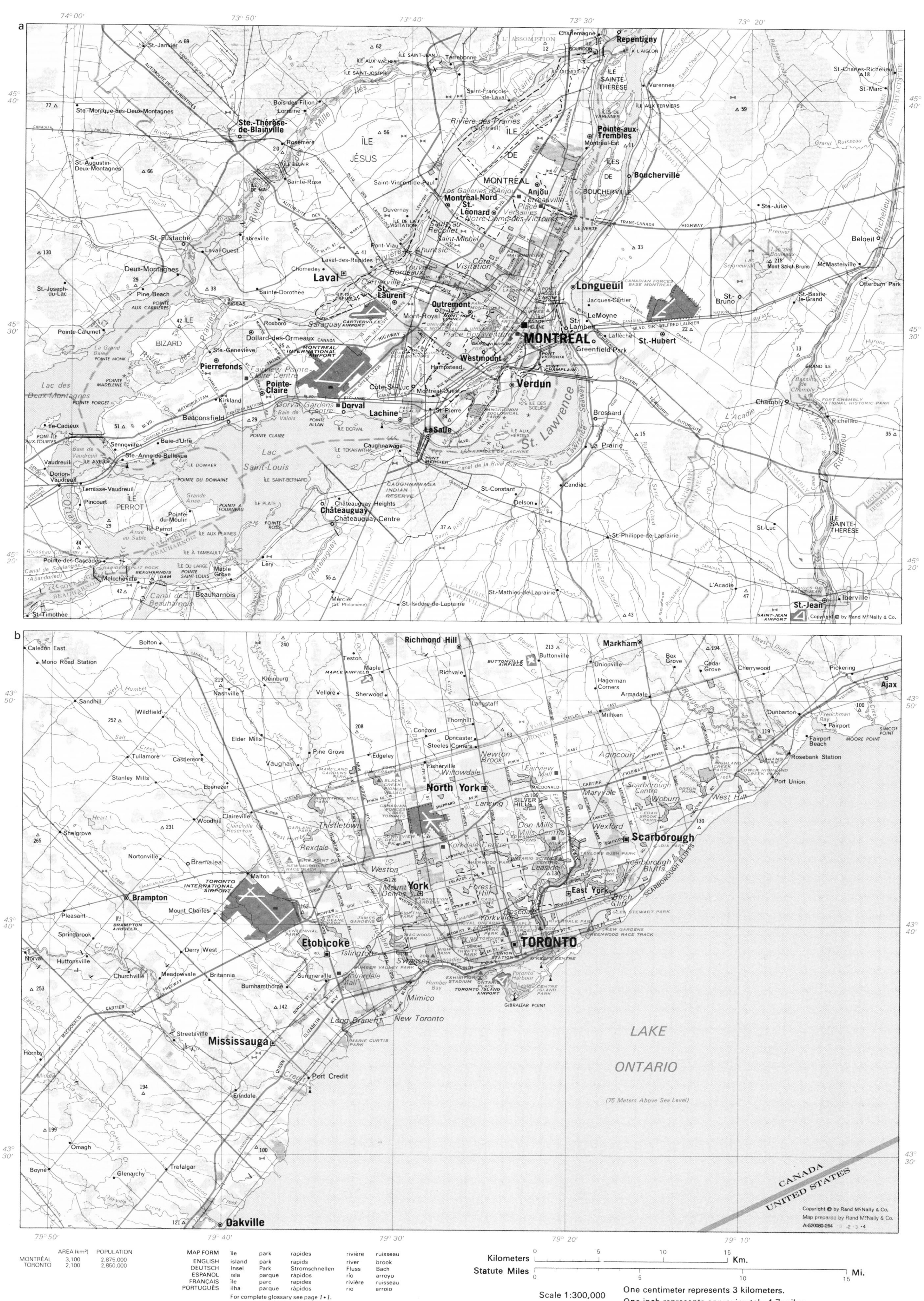

	AREA (km²)	POPULATION
MONTRÉAL	3,100	2,875,000
TORONTO	2,100	2,850,000

MAP FORM	île	park	rapides	rivière	ruisseau
ENGLISH	island	park	rapids	river	brook
DEUTSCH	Insel	Park	Stromschnellen	Fluss	Bach
ESPAÑOL	isla	parque	rápidos	río	arroyo
FRANÇAIS	île	parc	rapides	rivière	ruisseau
PORTUGUÊS	ilha	parque	rápidos	rio	arroio

For complete glossary see page *I • 1*.

Kilometers 0 5 10 15 Km.
Statute Miles 0 5 10 15 Mi.

Scale 1:300,000 One centimeter represents 3 kilometers. One inch represents approximately 4.7 miles.

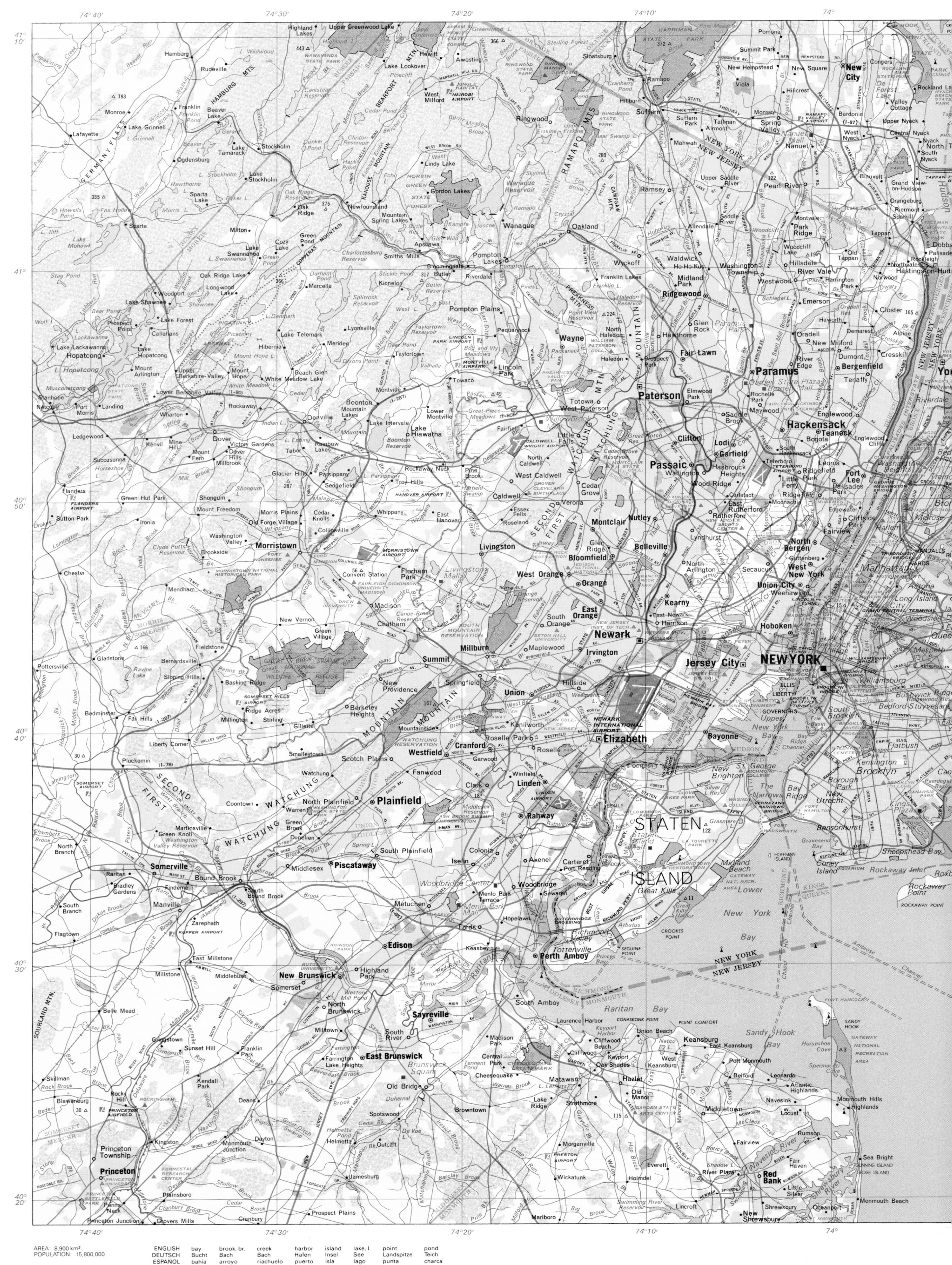

AREA: 8,900 km²
POPULATION: 15,800,000

ENGLISH	bay	brook, br.	creek	harbor	island	lake, l.	point	pond
DEUTSCH	Bucht	Bach	Bach	Hafen	Insel	See	Landspitze	Teich
ESPAÑOL	bahía	arroyo	riachuelo	puerto	isla	lago	punta	charca
FRANÇAIS	baie	ruisseau	crique	port	île	lac	pointe	étang
PORTUGUÊS	baía	arroio	riacho	porto	ilha	lago	ponta	lagoa

For complete glossary see page *I* • *1*.

73°40'
73°30'
73°20'
73°10'
41° 10'
41°
40° 50'
40° 40'
40° 30'
40° 20'
NEW YORK
CONNECTICUT
Bridgeport
Fairfield
Westport
Norwalk
New Canaan
Darien
Stamford
Greenwich
Port Chester
Rye
White Plains
Scarsdale
Harrison
Mamaroneck
New Rochelle
Pelham
Chappaqua
Pleasantville
Thornwood
Armonk
Hawthorne
Valhalla
Elmsford
Hartsdale
Eastchester
Tuckahoe
Bronxville
Larchmont
Riverside
Cos Cob
Old Greenwich
Southport
Saugatuck
Greens Farms
BRIDGEPORT MUNICIPAL AIRPORT
STRATFORD POINT
NORWALK ISLANDS
Long Island Sound
WESTCHESTER COUNTY AIRPORT
Kensico Reservoir
Glen Cove
Sea Cliff
Glen Head
Locust Valley
Lattingtown
Mill Neck
Oyster Bay
Bayville
Centre Island
Cove Neck
Lloyd Harbor
Lloyd Neck
Huntington Bay
Huntington
Huntington Station
Cold Spring Harbor
Centerport
Northport
East Northport
Greenlawn
Asharoken
Eatons Neck
Fort Salonga
Kings Park
San Remo
Smithtown
Smithtown Bay
Nissequogue
St. James
Stony Brook
Setauket
East Setauket
Port Jefferson
Port Jefferson Station
Poquott
Belle Terre
Old Field
Mount Sinai
Miller Place
Terryville
Centereach
Selden
Coram
Lake Grove
Nesconset
Hauppauge
Ronkonkoma
Lake Ronkonkoma
Holbrook
Holtsville
Farmingville
Medford
ISLIP-MACARTHUR AIRPORT
North Patchogue
Patchogue
Bohemia
Central Islip
Brentwood
Commack
Elwood
Dix Hills
Half Hollow Hills
East Half Hollow Hills
Melville
LONG ISLAND
Deer Park
Wyandanch
Plainview
Hicksville
Jericho
Syosset
Woodbury
Bethpage
Farmingdale
Levittown
East Meadow
Hempstead
Garden City
Mineola
New Hyde Park
Great Neck
Kings Point
Port Washington
Manhasset
Roslyn
Westbury
Franklin Square
West Hempstead
Elmont
Valley Stream
Rockville Centre
Freeport
Baldwin
Oceanside
Lynbrook
Merrick
Wantagh
Seaford
Massapequa
Massapequa Park
Amityville
Copiague
Lindenhurst
Babylon
West Babylon
North Babylon
West Islip
Bay Shore
Brightwaters
Islip
East Islip
Oakdale
Sayville
West Sayville
Bayport
Blue Point
North Great River
Long Beach
Lido Beach
Point Lookout
Atlantic Beach
East Atlantic Beach
Far Rockaway
Rockaway Park
Lawrence
Cedarhurst
Woodmere
Hewlett
Inwood
JOHN F. KENNEDY INTERNATIONAL AIRPORT
Jamaica
Flushing
Bayside
Hollis
St. Albans
Great South Bay
South Oyster Bay
Jones Beach State Park
Gilgo State Park
West Gilgo Beach
Oak Beach
Fire Island Inlet
Robert Moses State Park
FIRE ISLAND
FIRE ISLAND NATIONAL SEASHORE
Saltaire
Kismet
Fair Harbor
Ocean Beach
Ocean Bay Park
Point O'Woods
Cherry Grove
Fire Island Pines
Water Island
Davis Park
ATLANTIC OCEAN
Copyright © by Rand McNally & Co.
Map prepared by Rand McNally & Co.
A-520060-264
Kilometers 0 5 10 15 Km.
Statute Miles 0 5 10 15 Mi.
Scale 1:300,000
One centimeter represents 3 kilometers.
One inch represents approximately 4.7 miles.

88°
87° 50′
87° 40′
87° 30′
87° 20′
42° 20′
42° 10′
42°
41° 50′
41° 40′
41° 30′
LAKE
MICHIGAN
(176 Meters Above Sea Level).
ILLINOIS
INDIANA
Waukegan
North Chicago
GREAT LAKES NAVAL TRAINING CENTER
Round Lake Park
Round Lake
Highland Lake
Grayslake
Gages Lake
Wildwood
Wilson
Park City
CAMPBELL AIRPORT
Countryside Manor
Green Oaks
North Hills
Libertyville
Mundelein
Ivanhoe
Rondout
Knollwood
Lake Bluff
Wauconda
Lake Forest
Diamond Lake
Sylvan Lake
Timber Lake
Gilmer
Indian Creek
Mettawa
Hawthorn Woods
Vernon Hills
FORT SHERIDAN
Forest Lake
Lake Zurich
Prairie View
Half Day
Del Mar Woods
Highwood
Bannockburn
Highland Park
CHICAGOLAND AIRPORT
Aptakisic
Lincolnshire
Kildeer
Long Grove
Deerfield Manor
Deerfield
Horatio Gardens
Deer Park
Barrington
Barrington Woods
Riverwoods
RAVINIA PARK
Buffalo Grove
Glencoe
Wheeling
Northern Aire Estates
Inverness
Palatine
Northbrook
PAL-WAUKEE AIRPORT
Winnetka
Northfield
South Barrington
Arlington Heights
Prospect Heights
GLENVIEW N.A.S.
Sunset Trailer Park
Kenilworth
Wilmette
Prospect Meadows
Forest River
Northfield Woods
ARLINGTON PARK RACE TRACK
Plum Grove Estates
Rolling Meadows
Mount Prospect
Glenview Countryside
Glenview
BAHA'I TEMPLE
DYCHE STADIUM
NORTHWESTERN UNIVERSITY
Golf
Golf Park Terrace
Old Orchard
Golf Mill
The Greens
Hoffman Estates
Woodfield Mall
Schaumburg
Des Plaines
Park Ridge Manor
Morton Grove
Skokie
Evanston
Niles
Elk Grove Village
CHICAGO-O'HARE INTERNATIONAL AIRPORT
Park Ridge
Edison Park
Lincolnwood
Rogers Park
LOYOLA UNIVERSITY
SCHAUMBURG AIRPORT
Roselle
Medinah
Rosemont
Norwood Park
NORTHEASTERN ILLINOIS UNIVERSITY
Keeneyville
Itasca
Harwood Heights
Jefferson Park
Albany Park
Uptown
Crib
Bloomingdale
Wood Dale
Bensenville
Norridge
Portage Park
Irving Park
Montrose Harbor
Nordic Park
Schiller Park
Dunning
Avondale
Belmont Harbor
Cloverdale
Oakdale Woods
White Pines
Churchville
Franklin Park
Lakeview
Glendale Heights
Addison
River Grove
Elmwood Park
Belmont-Cragin
Logan Square
Carol Stream
Glen Ellyn Countryside
Westdale
Northlake
Stone Park
Melrose Park
MAYWOOD PARK RACE TRACK
North Glen Ellyn
Lombard
Elmhurst
Villa Park
River Forest
Oak Park
Austin
Near North Side
NORTHWESTERN UNIVERSITY (CHICAGO CAMPUS)
NAVY PIER
CHICAGO
Glen Ellyn
Glen Oak
Berkeley
Hillside
Bellwood
Maywood
Forest Park
Wheaton
Brandywine
Yorkfield
York Center
Oakbrook Terrace
Timber Trails
Broadview
Westchester
North Riverside
Berwyn
Cicero
Lawndale
FIELD MUSEUM
ADLER PLANETARIUM
SOLDIER FIELD
MEIGS FIELD
McCORMICK PLACE
Highland Hills
Yorktown
Butterfield
Oakbrook Center
Oak Brook
LaGrange Park
Riverside
Bridgeport
ILLINOIS INSTITUTE OF TECHNOLOGY
Valley View
MORTON ARBORETUM
Brookfield
Stickney
HAWTHORNE RACE TRACK
Brighton Park
Downers Grove
Westmont
Hinsdale
Western Springs
LaGrange
Lyons
Forest View
Kenwood
Lisle
Clarendon Hills
LaGrange Highlands
McCook
CHICAGO MIDWAY AIRPORT
Gage Park
Hyde Park
MUSEUM OF SCIENCE AND INDUSTRY
UNIVERSITY OF CHICAGO
Golfview Hills
Countryside
Summit
Clearing
Chicago Lawn
Englewood
Woodlawn
Indian Head Park
Hodgkins
Bedford Park
Woodridge
Willowbrook
Nottingham Park
South Shore
Darien
Burr Ridge
Justice
Bridgeview
Ford City
Burbank
Ashburn
Chatham
South Chicago
U.S. STEEL CORP. (SOUTH WORKS)
Calumet Harbor
Tristate Village
Willow Springs
Roberts Park
Hickory Hills
Hometown
Oak Lawn
ARGONNE NATIONAL LABORATORY
Evergreen Park
Beverly
Roseland
Pullman
Bolingbrook
Palos Hills
Chicago Ridge
Worth
Mount Greenwood
Morgan Park
Lake Calumet
Indiana Harbor
Hastings
Lemont
Alsip
Merrionette Park
West Pullman
Whiting
YOUNGSTOWN SHEET AND TUBE CO. (INDIANA HARBOR WORKS)
INLAND STEEL COMPANY (INDIANA HARBOR WORKS)
Palos Park
Palos Heights
Worth
Calumet Park
Riverdale
Hegewisch
Romeoville
JOHN J. DUFFY PRESERVE
Creekwood
Blue Island
HOWELL AIRPORT
MacArthur Crestwood
Robbins
Posen
Dolton
Burnham
East Chicago
Buffington Harbor
Orland Park
Midlothian
Dixmoor
Riverdale
GARY MUNICIPAL AIRPORT
UNITED STATES STEEL CORP. (GARY WORKS)
Gary Harbor
LEWIS-LOCKPORT AIRPORT
Oak Forest
Phoenix
Calumet City
Harvey
Hammond
South Holland
Gary
Markham
PURDUE UNIVERSITY (CALUMET CAMPUS)
STATEVILLE STATE PENITENTIARY
Lockport
Westhaven
Hazel Crest
Black Oak
Tinley Park
East Hazel Crest
Thornton
Lansing
Munster
Highland
Crest Hill
Dellwood Highlands
Homewood
Homewood Acres
GLEASON PARK
Fairmont
JOLIET STATE PENITENTIARY
Country Club Hills
Flossmoor
CHICAGO-HAMMOND AIRPORT
Marley
Joliet
Ridgewood
Arbury Hills
Sunny Crest
Glenwood
Ross
Mokena
Crawford Countryside
Olympia Fields
Lynwood
Griffith
GRIFFITH AIRPORT
Ingalls Park
Cherry Hill
Chicago Heights
East Chicago Heights
New Lenox
Lincolnwood Hills
Frankfort
Lincoln Estates
Lincoln Mall
Matteson
Dyer
Merrillville
Copyright © by Rand McNally & Co.
Map prepared by Rand McNally & Co.
AREA: 4,500 km²
POPULATION: 6,700,000
ENGLISH airport creek, cr. harbor lake, l. park woods
DEUTSCH Flughafen Bach Hafen See Park Gehölz
ESPAÑOL aeropuerto riachuelo puerto lago parque bosques
FRANÇAIS aéroport crique port lac parc bois
PORTUGUÊS aeroporto riacho porto lago parque bosques
For complete glossary see page I • I.
Kilometers 0 5 10 15 Km.
Statute Miles 0 5 10 15 Mi.
Scale 1:300,000
One centimeter represents 3 kilometers.
One inch represents approximately 4.7 miles.

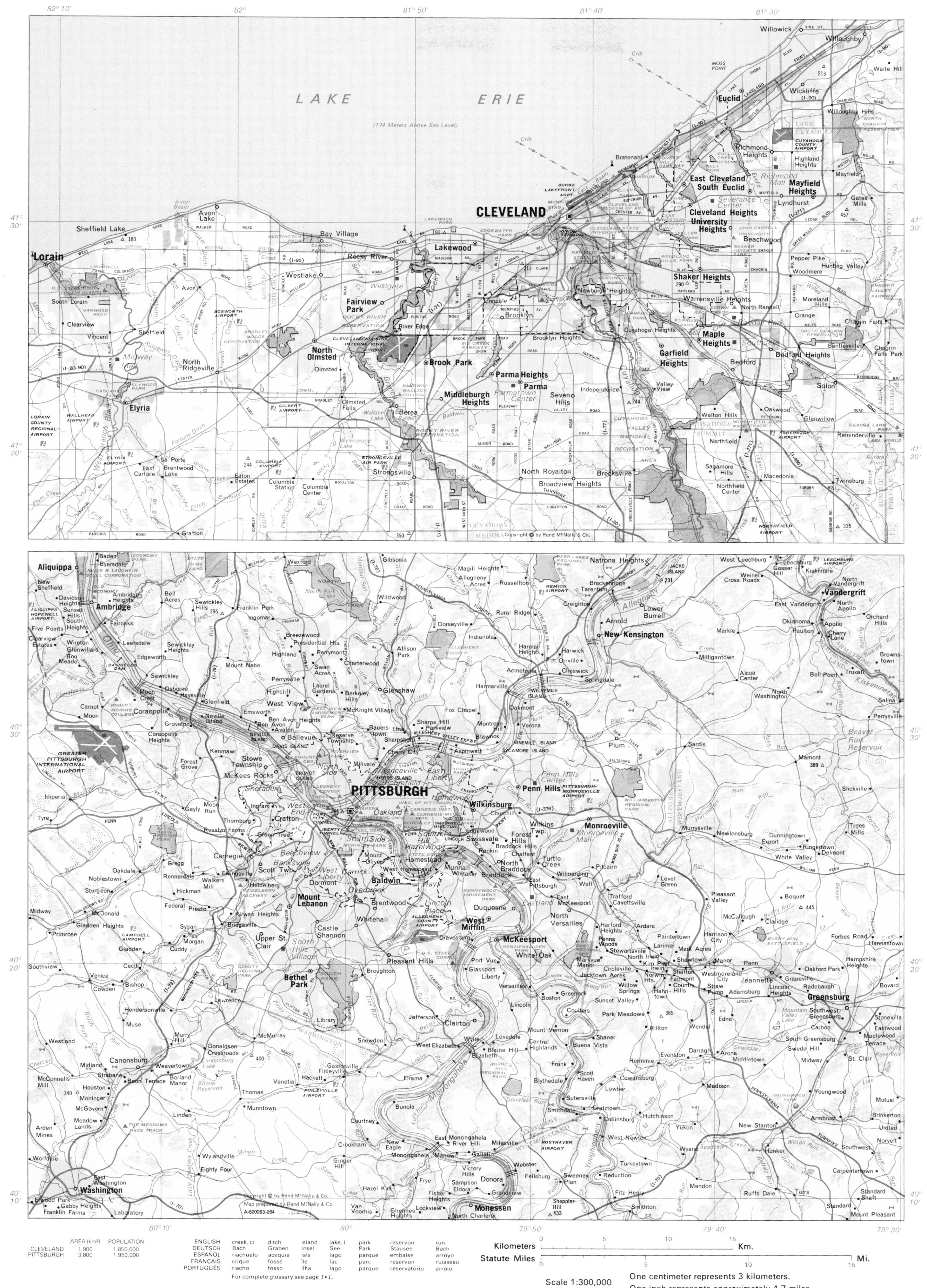

	AREA (km²)	POPULATION
CLEVELAND	1,900	1,850,000
PITTSBURGH	3,800	1,950,000

ENGLISH	creek, cr.	ditch	island	lake, l.	park	reservoir	run
DEUTSCH	Bach	Graben	Insel	See	Park	Stausee	Bach
ESPAÑOL	riachuelo	acequia	isla	lago	parque	embalse	arroyo
FRANÇAIS	crique	fossé	île	lac	parc	reservoir	ruisseau
PORTUGUÊS	riacho	fosso	ilha	lago	parque	reservatório	arroio

For complete glossary see page I•1.

Kilometers 0 5 10 15 Km.

Statute Miles 0 5 10 15 Mi.

Scale 1:300,000

One centimeter represents 3 kilometers.

One inch represents approximately 4.7 miles.

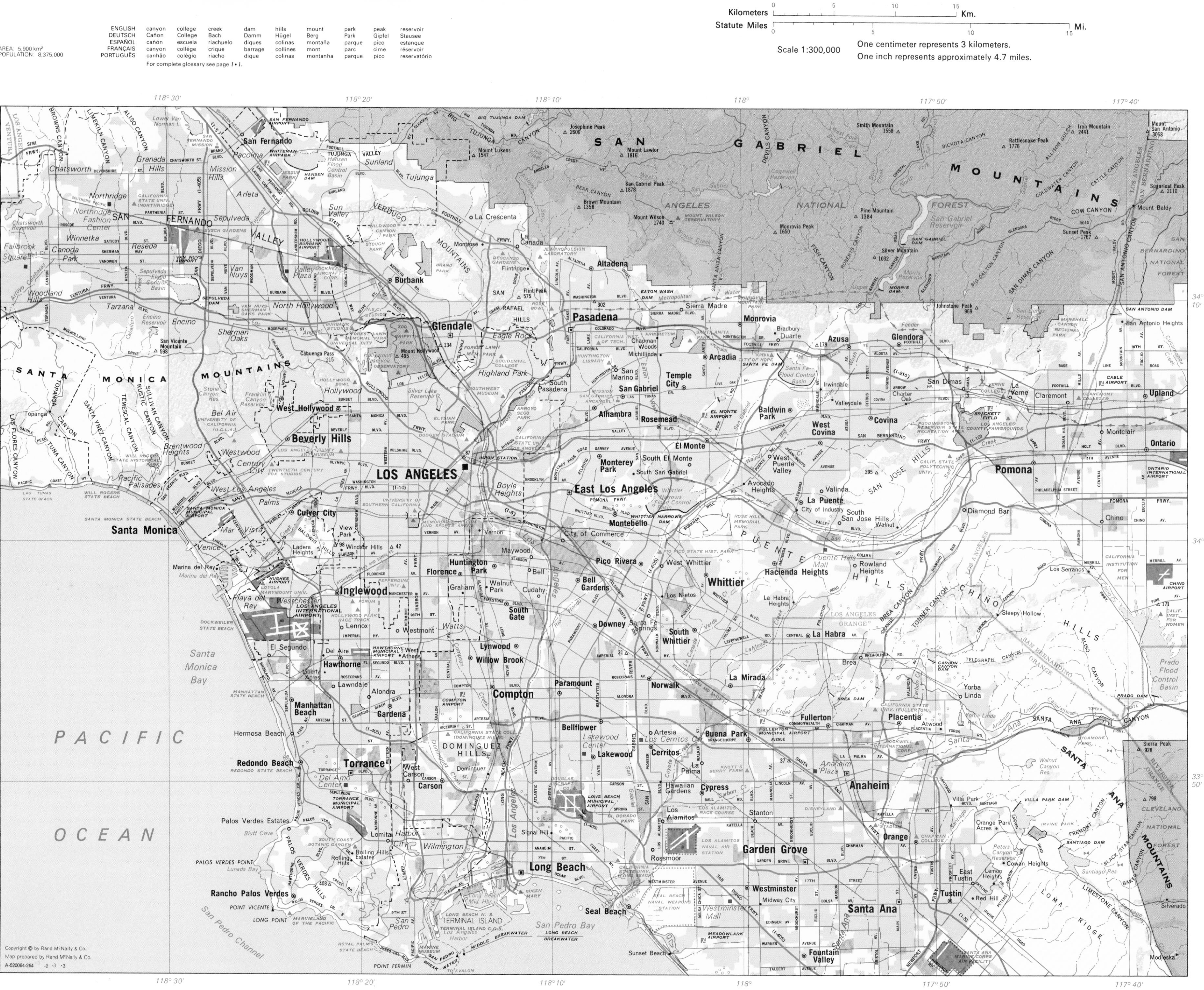

Kilometers 0 5 10 15 Km.
Statute Miles 0 5 10 15 Mi.
Scale 1:300,000
One centimeter represents 3 kilometers.
One inch represents approximately 4.7 miles.
ENGLISH canyon college creek dam hills mount park peak reservoir
DEUTSCH Cañon College Bach Damm Hügel Berg Park Gipfel Stausee
ESPAÑOL cañon escuela riachuelo diques colinas montaña parque pico estanque
FRANÇAIS canyon collège crique barrage collines mont parc cime réservoir
PORTUGUÊS canhão colégio riacho dique colinas montanha parque pico reservatório
For complete glossary see page I • I.
AREA 5,900 km²
POPULATION 8,375,000
PACIFIC OCEAN
SAN GABRIEL MOUNTAINS
SANTA MONICA MOUNTAINS
SANTA ANA MOUNTAINS
LOS ANGELES
Long Beach
Pasadena
Santa Monica
Glendale
Burbank
Pomona
Anaheim
Santa Ana
Torrance
Inglewood
Compton
Whittier
Beverly Hills
San Pedro Bay
Santa Monica Bay
Copyright © by Rand McNally & Co.
Map prepared by Rand McNally & Co.

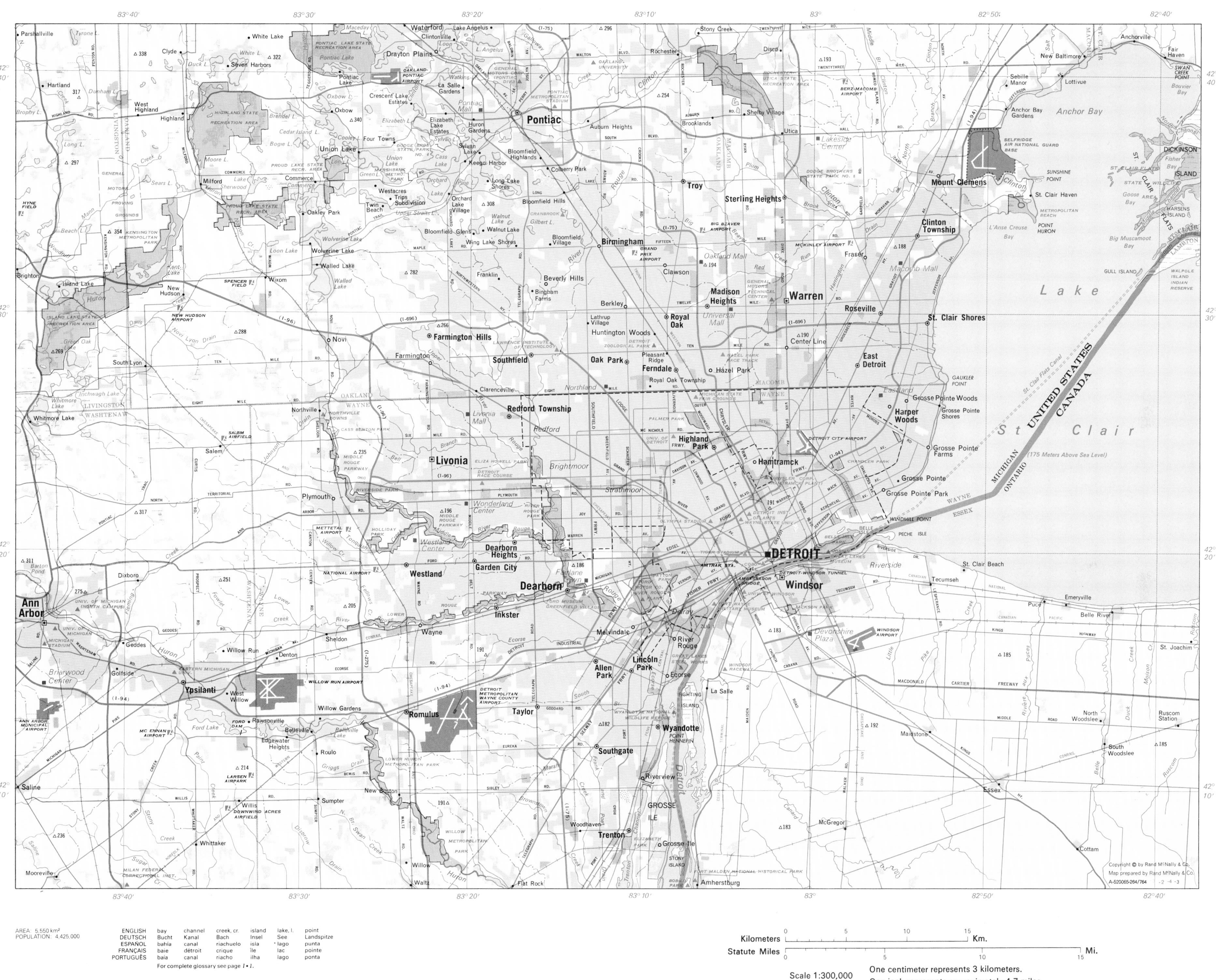

DETROIT
Windsor
Lake St. Clair
UNITED STATES
CANADA
MICHIGAN
ONTARIO
(175 Meters Above Sea Level)
Anchor Bay
Mount Clemens
Clinton Township
St. Clair Shores
Grosse Pointe Woods
Harper Woods
Grosse Pointe Shores
Grosse Pointe Farms
Grosse Pointe
Grosse Pointe Park
Roseville
East Detroit
Warren
Center Line
Hamtramck
Highland Park
Sterling Heights
Madison Heights
Hazel Park
Royal Oak
Ferndale
Oak Park
Berkley
Troy
Birmingham
Pontiac
Southfield
Farmington Hills
Redford Township
Livonia
Dearborn
Dearborn Heights
Garden City
Inkster
Westland
Wayne
Romulus
Taylor
Lincoln Park
Allen Park
Southgate
Wyandotte
Trenton
Grosse Ile
Amherstburg
Ann Arbor
Ypsilanti
Plymouth
Northville
Novi
Utica
Rochester
Tecumseh
Belle River
Essex
Maidstone
McGregor
River Rouge
Ecorse
Melvindale
Riverview
Flat Rock
Belleville
Saline
Detroit Metropolitan Wayne County Airport
Willow Run Airport
Windsor Airport
Detroit City Airport
Selfridge Air National Guard Base
Kilometers 0 5 10 15 Km.
Statute Miles 0 5 10 15 Mi.
Scale 1:300,000
One centimeter represents 3 kilometers.
One inch represents approximately 4.7 miles.
Copyright © by Rand McNally & Co.
Map prepared by Rand McNally & Co.
AREA 5,550 km²
POPULATION 4,425,000
ENGLISH bay channel creek, cr. island lake, l. point
DEUTSCH Bucht Kanal Bach Insel See Landspitze
ESPAÑOL bahía canal riachuelo isla lago punta
FRANÇAIS baie détroit crique île lac pointe
PORTUGUÊS baía canal riacho ilha lago ponta
For complete glossary see page I·I.

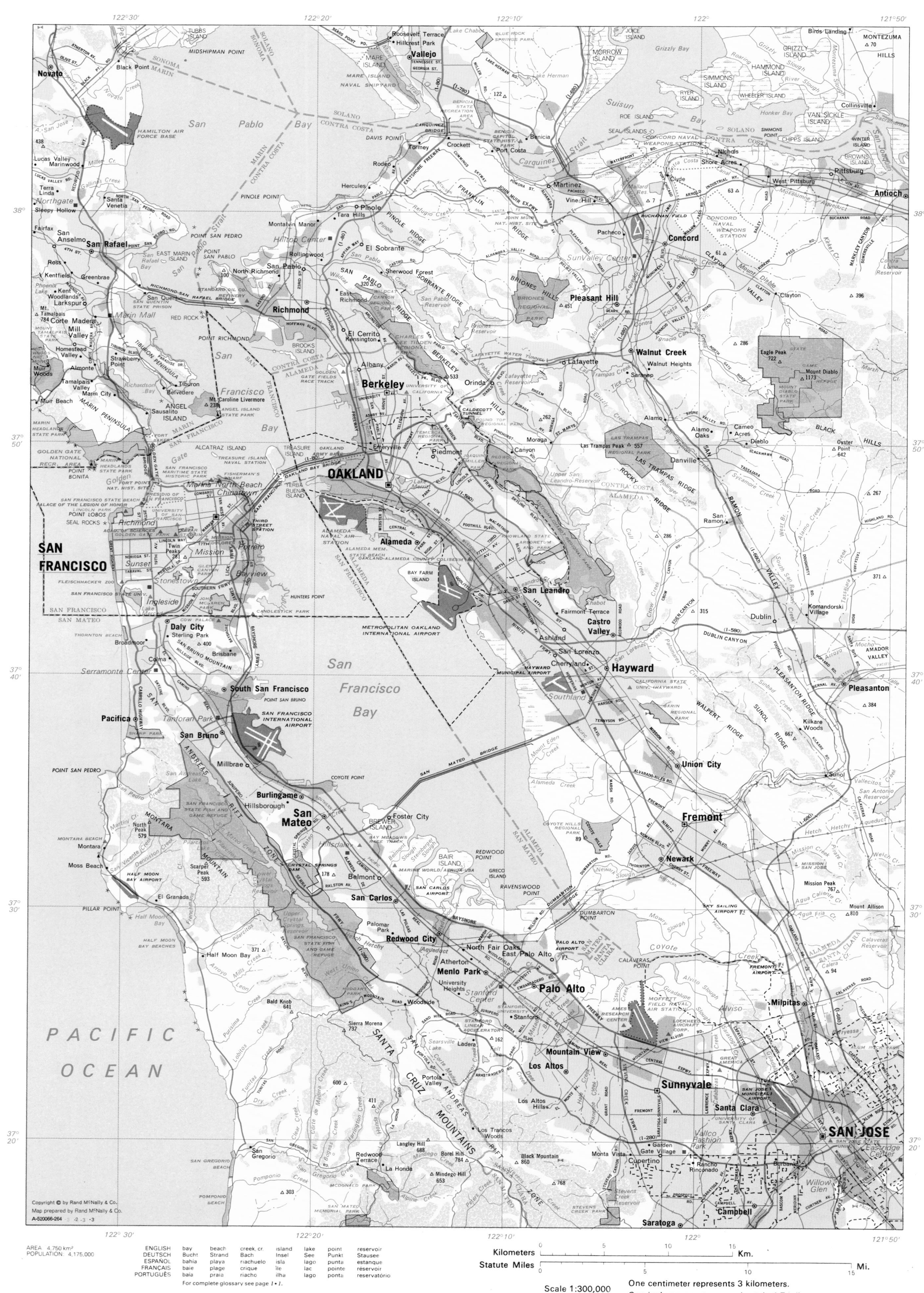

AREA 4,750 km²
POPULATION 4,175,000

ENGLISH	bay	beach	creek, cr.	island	lake	point	reservoir
DEUTSCH	Bucht	Strand	Bach	Insel	See	Punkt	Stausee
ESPAÑOL	bahía	playa	riachuelo	isla	lago	punta	estanque
FRANÇAIS	baie	plage	crique	île	lac	pointe	réservoir
PORTUGUÊS	baía	praia	riacho	ilha	lago	ponta	reservatório

For complete glossary see page I • 1.

Kilometers 0 5 10 15 Km.
Statute Miles 0 5 10 15 Mi.

Scale 1:300,000
One centimeter represents 3 kilometers.
One inch represents approximately 4.7 miles.

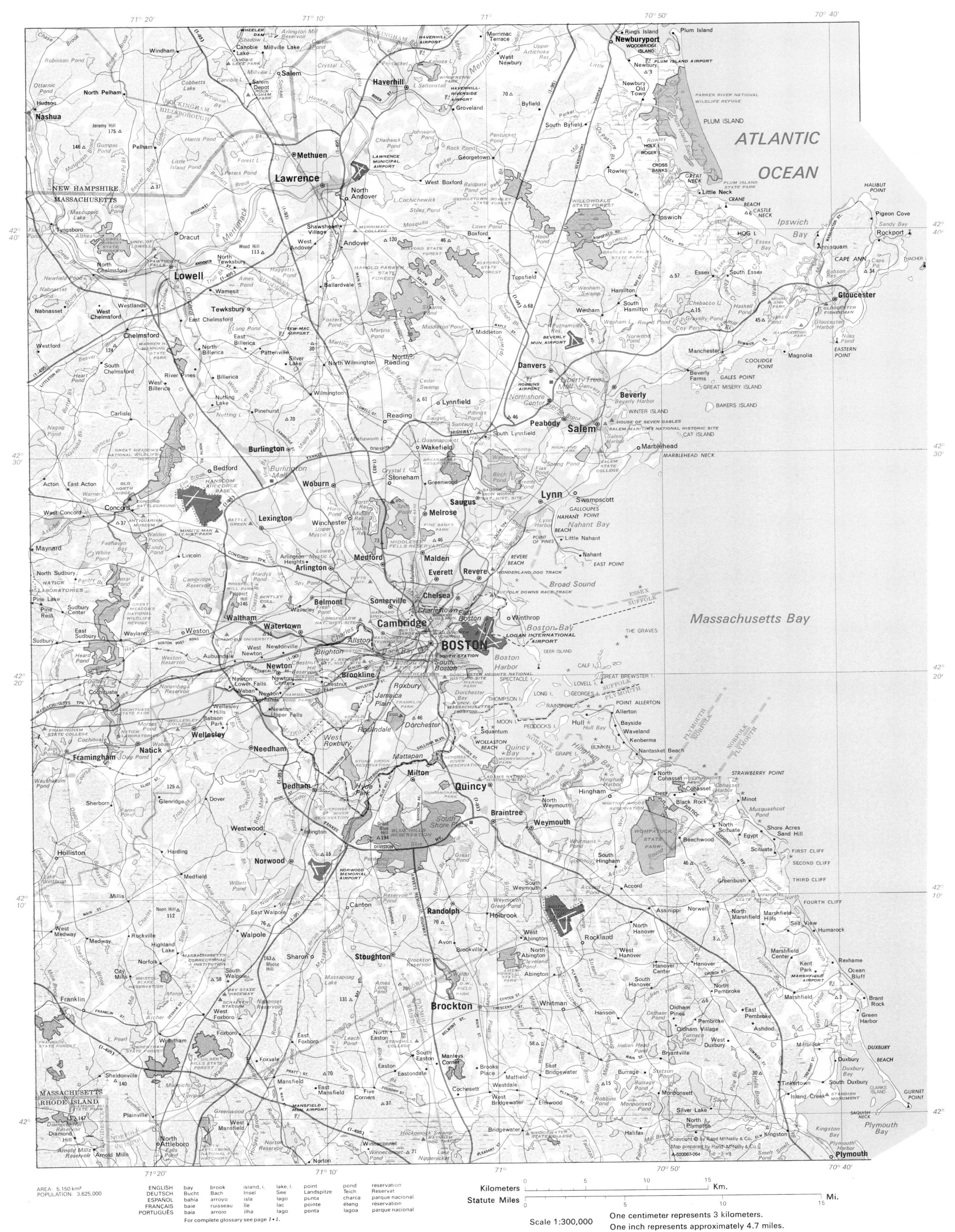
ATLANTIC OCEAN
Massachusetts Bay
BOSTON
Cambridge
Lowell
Lawrence
Haverhill
Newburyport
Nashua
Methuen
North Andover
Andover
Salem
Lynn
Peabody
Beverly
Danvers
Gloucester
Rockport
Ipswich
Marblehead
Swampscott
Chelsea
Revere
Winthrop
Somerville
Medford
Malden
Everett
Melrose
Saugus
Woburn
Burlington
Lexington
Arlington
Belmont
Waltham
Watertown
Newton
Brookline
Wellesley
Needham
Natick
Framingham
Dedham
Milton
Quincy
Braintree
Weymouth
Hingham
Norwood
Randolph
Stoughton
Brockton
Walpole
Concord
Chelmsford
Tewksbury
Wilmington
Reading
Wakefield
Lynnfield
Topsfield
Hamilton
Wenham
Manchester
Essex
Scituate
Cohasset
Hull
Marshfield
Duxbury
Kingston
Plymouth
Franklin
Foxboro
Mansfield
North Attleboro
Wrentham
Sharon
Canton
Whitman
Hanover
Rockland
Abington
Pembroke
Bridgewater
East Bridgewater
West Bridgewater
NEW HAMPSHIRE
MASSACHUSETTS
RHODE ISLAND
ESSEX
SUFFOLK
NORFOLK
PLYMOUTH
Boston Harbor
Broad Sound
Ipswich Bay
Plymouth Bay
CAPE ANN
PLUM ISLAND
LOGAN INTERNATIONAL AIRPORT
BLUE HILLS RESERVATION
MIDDLESEX FELLS RESERVATION
HANSCOM AIR FORCE BASE
71° 20′
71° 10′
71°
70° 50′
70° 40′
42° 40′
42° 30′
42° 20′
42° 10′
42°
Copyright © by Rand McNally & Co.
Map prepared by Rand McNally & Co.
AREA: 5,150 km²
POPULATION: 3,625,000
ENGLISH bay brook island, i. lake, l. point pond reservation
DEUTSCH Bucht Bach Insel See Landspitze Teich Reservat
ESPAÑOL bahía arroyo isla lago punta charca parque nacional
FRANÇAIS baie ruisseau île lac pointe étang réservation
PORTUGUÊS baía arroio ilha lago ponta lagoa parque nacional
For complete glossary see page I • 1.
Kilometers 0 5 10 15 Km.
Statute Miles 0 5 10 15 Mi.
Scale 1:300,000
One centimeter represents 3 kilometers.
One inch represents approximately 4.7 miles.

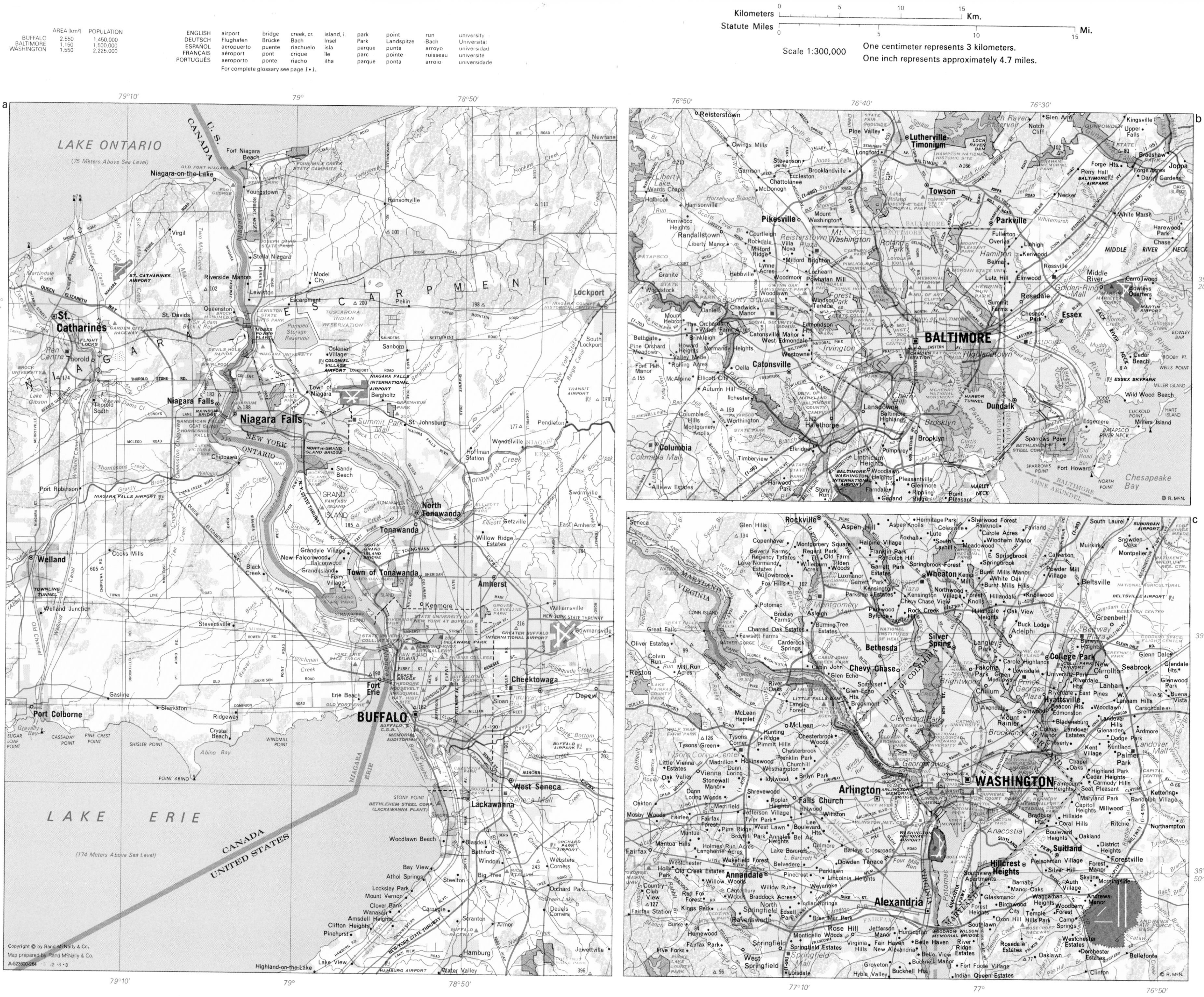

AREA (km²) POPULATION
BUFFALO 2,550 1,450,000
BALTIMORE 1,150 1,500,000
WASHINGTON 1,550 2,225,000
ENGLISH airport bridge creek, cr. island, i. park point run university
DEUTSCH Flughafen Brücke Bach Insel Park Landspitze Bach Universität
ESPAÑOL aeropuerto puente riachuelo isla parque punta arroyo universidad
FRANÇAIS aéroport pont crique île parc pointe ruisseau université
PORTUGUÊS aeroporto ponte riacho ilha parque ponta arroio universidade
For complete glossary see page I•1.
Kilometers 0 5 10 15 Km.
Statute Miles 0 5 10 15 Mi.
Scale 1:300,000
One centimeter represents 3 kilometers.
One inch represents approximately 4.7 miles.
LAKE ONTARIO
(75 Meters Above Sea Level)
LAKE ERIE
(174 Meters Above Sea Level)
CANADA
UNITED STATES
NIAGARA ESCARPMENT
St. Catharines
Niagara Falls
Lockport
North Tonawanda
Tonawanda
Amherst
Cheektowaga
BUFFALO
West Seneca
Lackawanna
Welland
Port Colborne
Hamburg
BALTIMORE
Towson
Parkville
Essex
Dundalk
Catonsville
Pikesville
Columbia
Chesapeake Bay
Rockville
Bethesda
Silver Spring
College Park
WASHINGTON
Arlington
Alexandria
Falls Church
Annandale
Copyright © by Rand McNally & Co.
Map prepared by Rand McNally & Co.

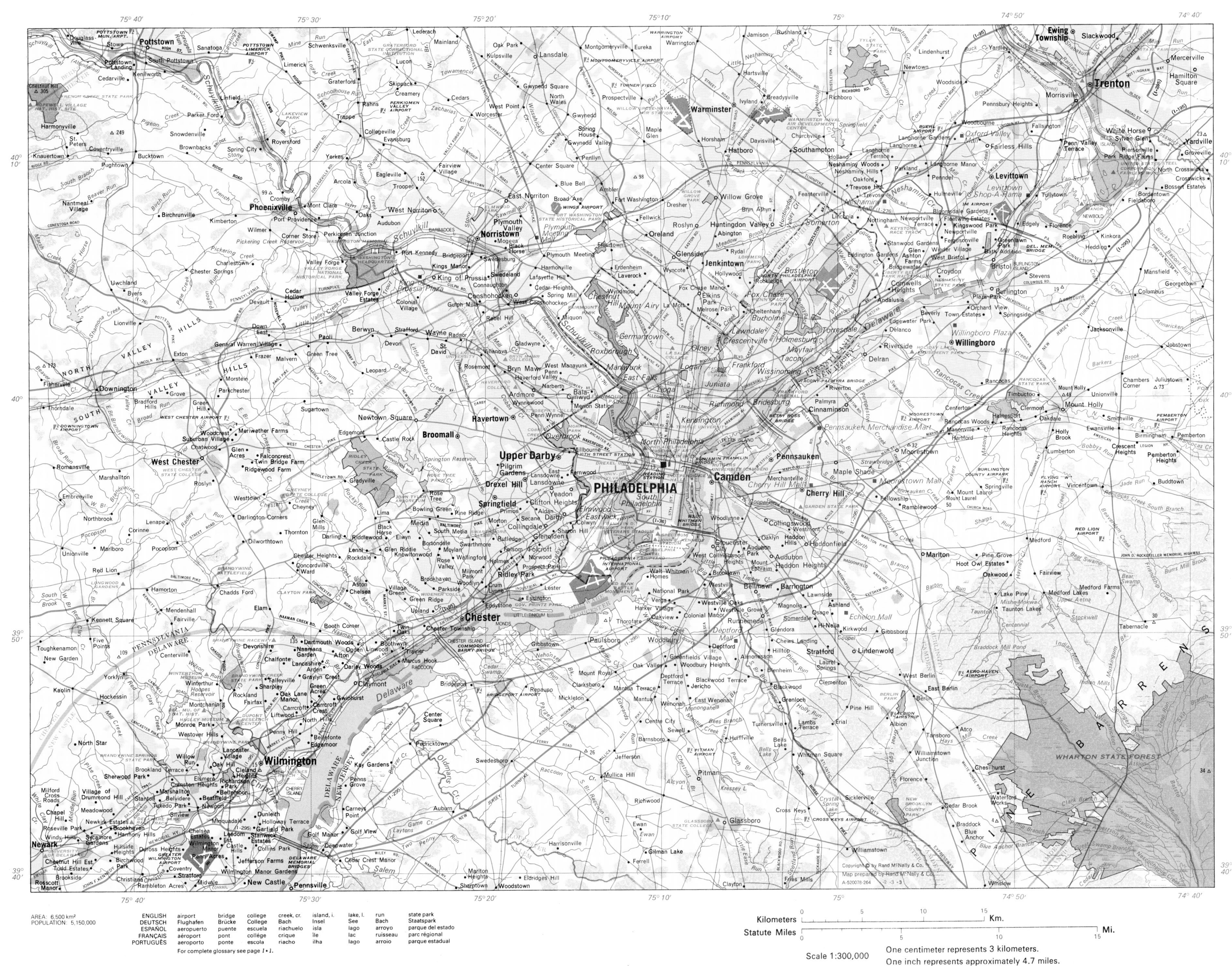
AREA: 6,500 km²
POPULATION: 5,150,000
ENGLISH airport bridge college creek, cr. island, i. lake, l. run state park
DEUTSCH Flughafen Brücke College Bach Insel See Bach Staatspark
ESPAÑOL aeropuerto puente escuela riachuelo isla lago arroyo parque del estado
FRANÇAIS aéroport pont collége crique île lac ruisseau parc régional
PORTUGUÊS aeroporto ponte escola riacho ilha lago arroio parque estadual
For complete glossary see page I • 1.
Kilometers
Km.
Statute Miles
Mi.
Scale 1:300,000
One centimeter represents 3 kilometers.
One inch represents approximately 4.7 miles.
Copyright © by Rand McNally & Co.
Map prepared by Rand McNally & Co.
A-520078-264
PHILADELPHIA
Trenton
Camden
Chester
Wilmington
Norristown
Phoenixville
Pottstown
West Chester
Newark
Upper Darby
Willingboro
PINE BARRENS
WHARTON STATE FOREST

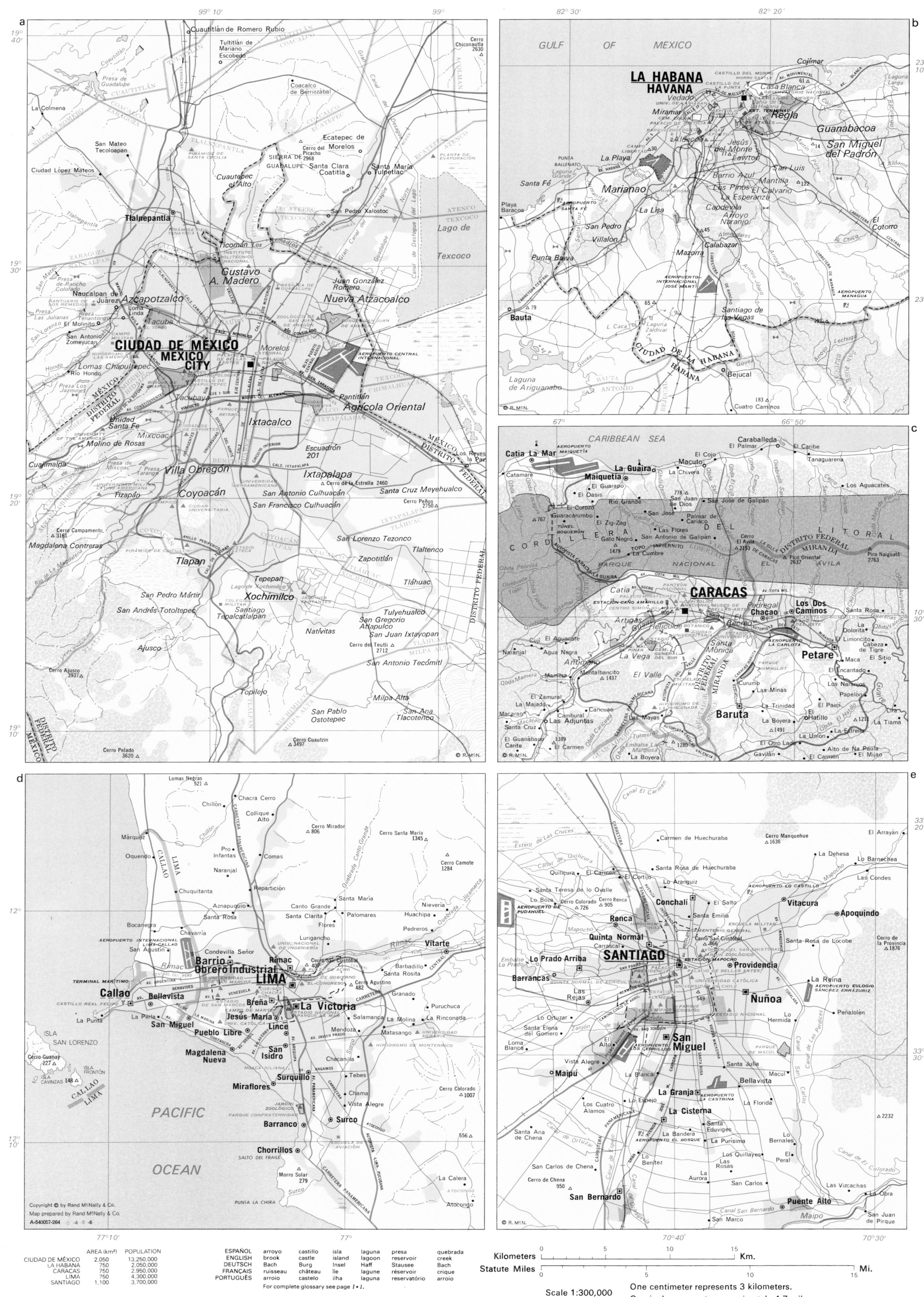

	AREA (km²)	POPULATION
CIUDAD DE MÉXICO	2,050	13,250,000
LA HABANA	750	2,050,000
CARACAS	750	2,950,000
LIMA	750	4,300,000
SANTIAGO	1,100	3,700,000

ESPAÑOL	arroyo	castillo	isla	laguna	presa	quebrada
ENGLISH	brook	castle	island	lagoon	reservoir	creek
DEUTSCH	Bach	Burg	Insel	Haff	Stausee	Bach
FRANÇAIS	ruisseau	château	île	lagune	réservoir	crique
PORTUGUÊS	arroio	castelo	ilha	laguna	reservatório	arroio

For complete glossary see page I • 1.

Kilometers 0 5 10 15 Km.
Statute Miles 0 5 10 15 Mi.

Scale 1:300,000

One centimeter represents 3 kilometers.
One inch represents approximately 4.7 miles.

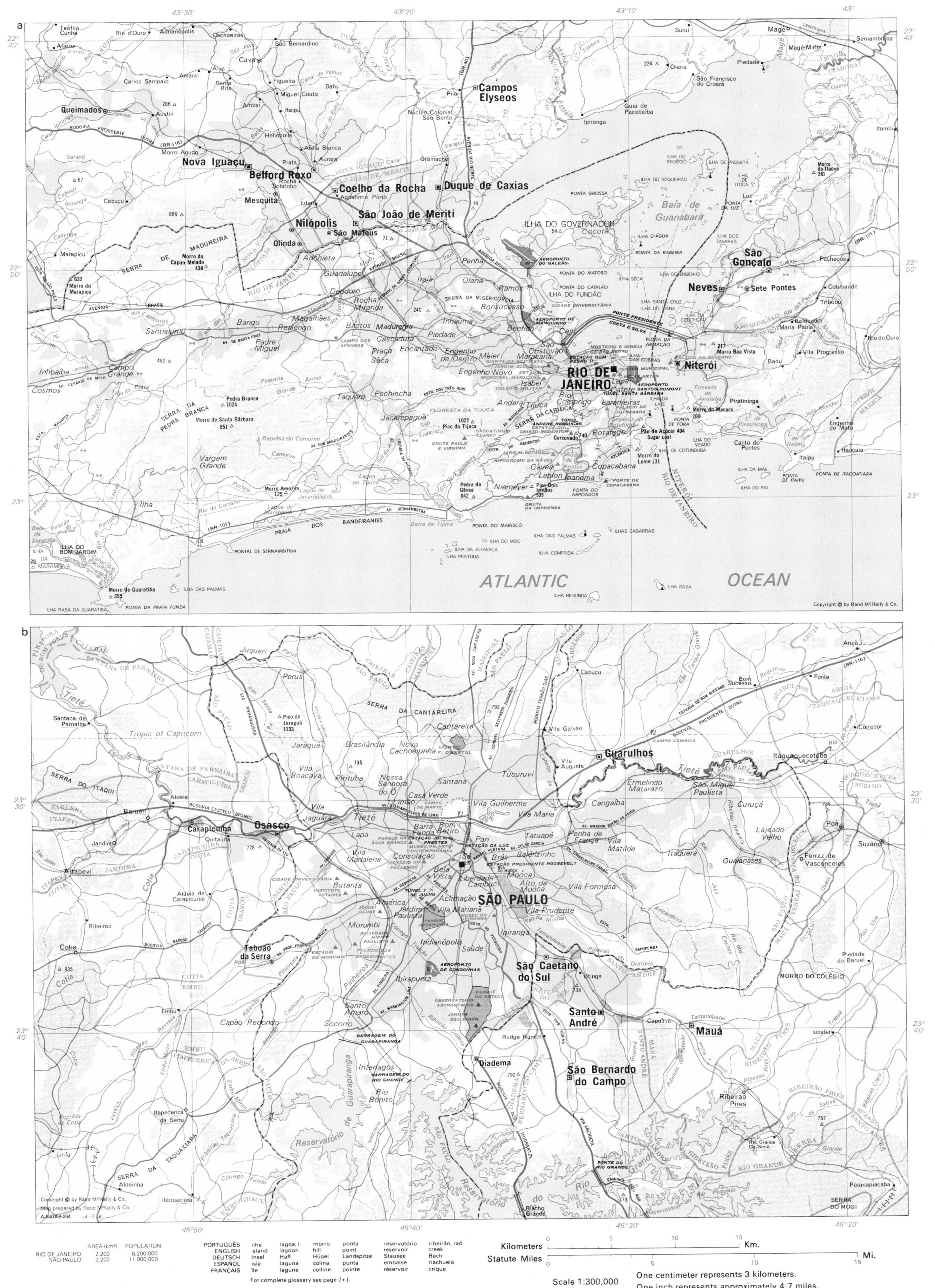

	AREA (km²)	POPULATION
RIO DE JANEIRO	2,200	8,200,000
SÃO PAULO	3,200	11,000,000

PORTUGUÊS	ilha	lagoa, l.	morro	ponta	reservatório	ribeirão, raó.
ENGLISH	island	lagoon	hill	point	reservoir	creek
DEUTSCH	Insel	Haff	Hügel	Landspitze	Stausee	Bach
ESPAÑOL	isla	laguna	colina	punta	embalse	riachuelo
FRANÇAIS	île	lagune	colline	pointe	réservoir	crique

For complete glossary see page *I•1*.

Kilometers 0 5 10 15 Km.
Statute Miles 0 5 10 15 Mi.

Scale 1:300,000
One centimeter represents 3 kilometers.
One inch represents approximately 4.7 miles.

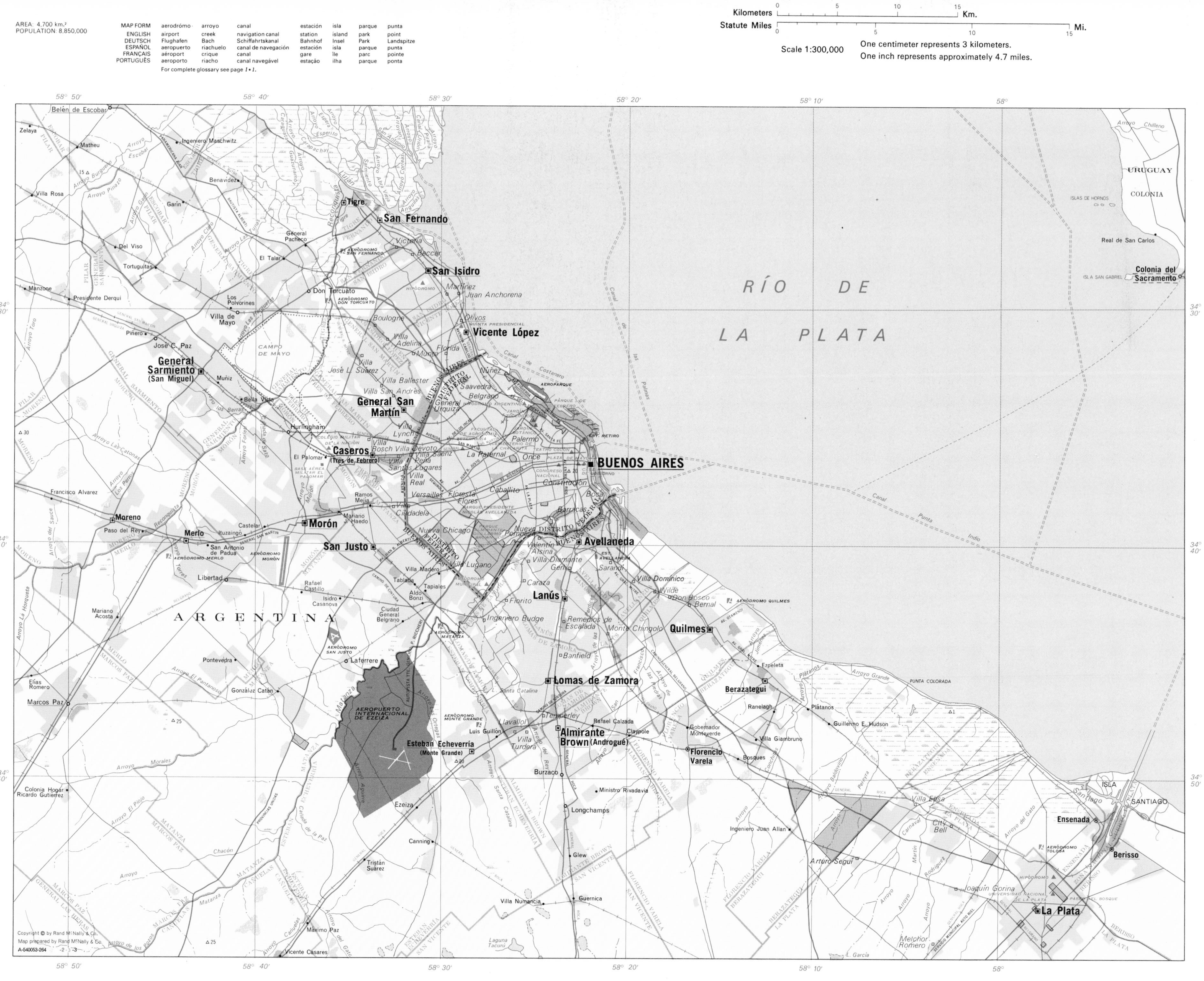

AREA 4,700 km.²
POPULATION 8,850,000
MAP FORM aerodrómo arroyo canal estación isla parque punta
ENGLISH airport creek navigation canal station island park point
DEUTSCH Flughafen Bach Schiffahrtskanal Bahnhof Insel Park Landspitze
ESPAÑOL aeropuerto riachuelo canal de navegación estación isla parque punta
FRANÇAIS aéroport crique canal gare île parc pointe
PORTUGUÊS aeroporto riacho canal navegável estação ilha parque ponta
For complete glossary see page I • I.
Kilometers 0 5 10 15 Km.
Statute Miles 0 5 10 15 Mi.
Scale 1:300,000
One centimeter represents 3 kilometers.
One inch represents approximately 4.7 miles.
RÍO DE LA PLATA
BUENOS AIRES
URUGUAY
COLONIA
Colonia del Sacramento
Real de San Carlos
ARGENTINA
San Fernando
Tigre
San Isidro
Vicente López
General Sarmiento (San Miguel)
General San Martín
Caseros (Tres de Febrero)
Morón
San Justo
Avellaneda
Lanús
Lomas de Zamora
Quilmes
Berazategui
Florencio Varela
Almirante Brown (Androgué)
Esteban Echeverría (Monte Grande)
AEROPUERTO INTERNACIONAL DE EZEIZA
Ezeiza
Moreno
Merlo
Marcos Paz
Belén de Escobar
Ensenada
Berisso
La Plata
Canal Punta Indio
Copyright © by Rand McNally & Co.
Map prepared by Rand McNally & Co.
A-540053-264

World Scene

World Scene

Table of Contents

The World, May 1, 1980 292–293
Politically Related Areas 292–293
(United Kingdom, United States, and others)
Seaward Claims 294–295
(to seas, continental shelf, and fishing rights)
The World, January 1, 1914 296–297
The World, January 1, 1937 296–297
Population 298–299
(urbanization, distribution, metropolitan areas, age and sex composition for selected countries)
Religions 300–301
Languages 300–301
Agricultural Regions 302–303
Forests and Fisheries 302–303
Minerals 304–305
Energy Production and Consumption 306–307
(coal, petroleum, gas, and electricity)
Gross National Product 308–309
International Trade 308–309
Intercontinental Air Connections 310–311
Great Circle Distances 311
(between selected cities)
Continental Transport Routes 312
(railroads, roads, and inland waterways)
Time Zones 313
Climate 314–315
(regions, temperature, precipitation, and graphs of selected weather stations)
Surface Configuration 316–317
Earth Structure and Tectonics 316–317
Natural Vegetation 318–319
Soils 318–319
Drainage Regions and Ocean Currents 320

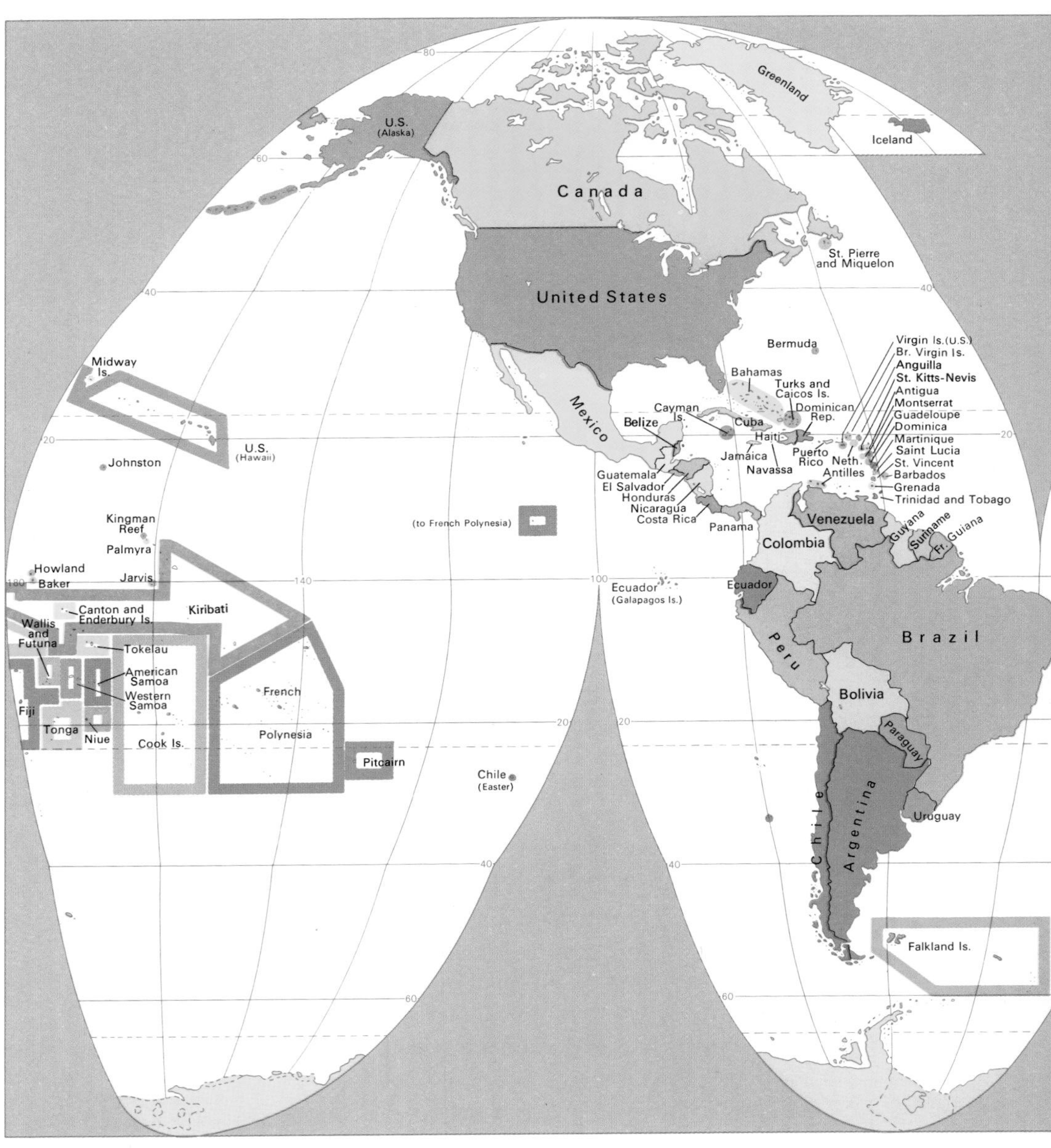

The World May 1, 1980

Every political entity that has a separate administration, whether it is independent or dependent, is named here and is distinguished from adjacent units by color. In all, over 200 political units are named. A noncontiguous part of a country has the same color as the country. If it lies at any distance, it is identified (for example, Alaska, a state of the United States), but if it lies close by, it is not (for example, the island of Corsica, which comprises two departments of France).

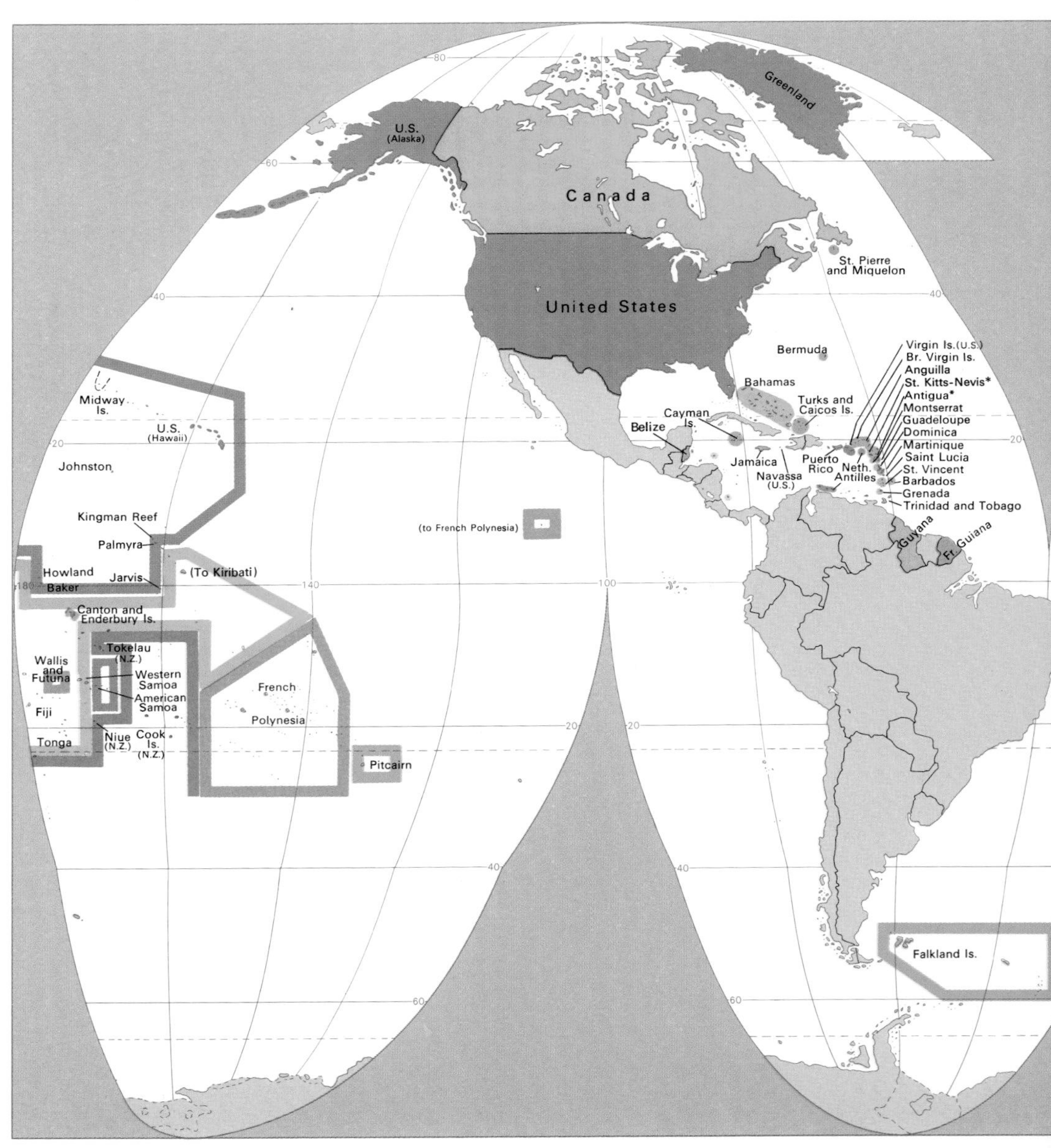

Politically Related Areas

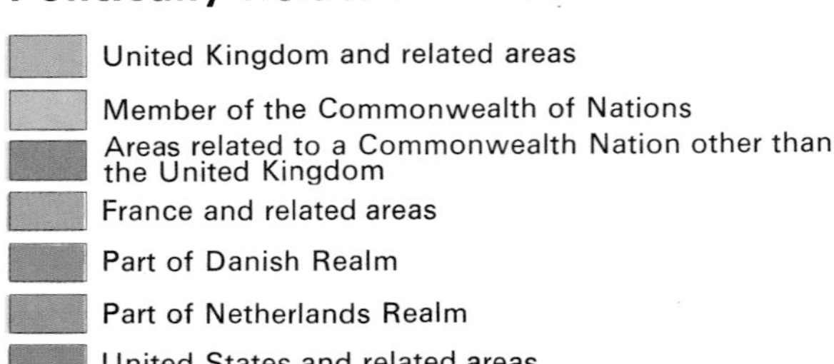

*Virtually independent: major country primarily responsible for foreign relations and defense.

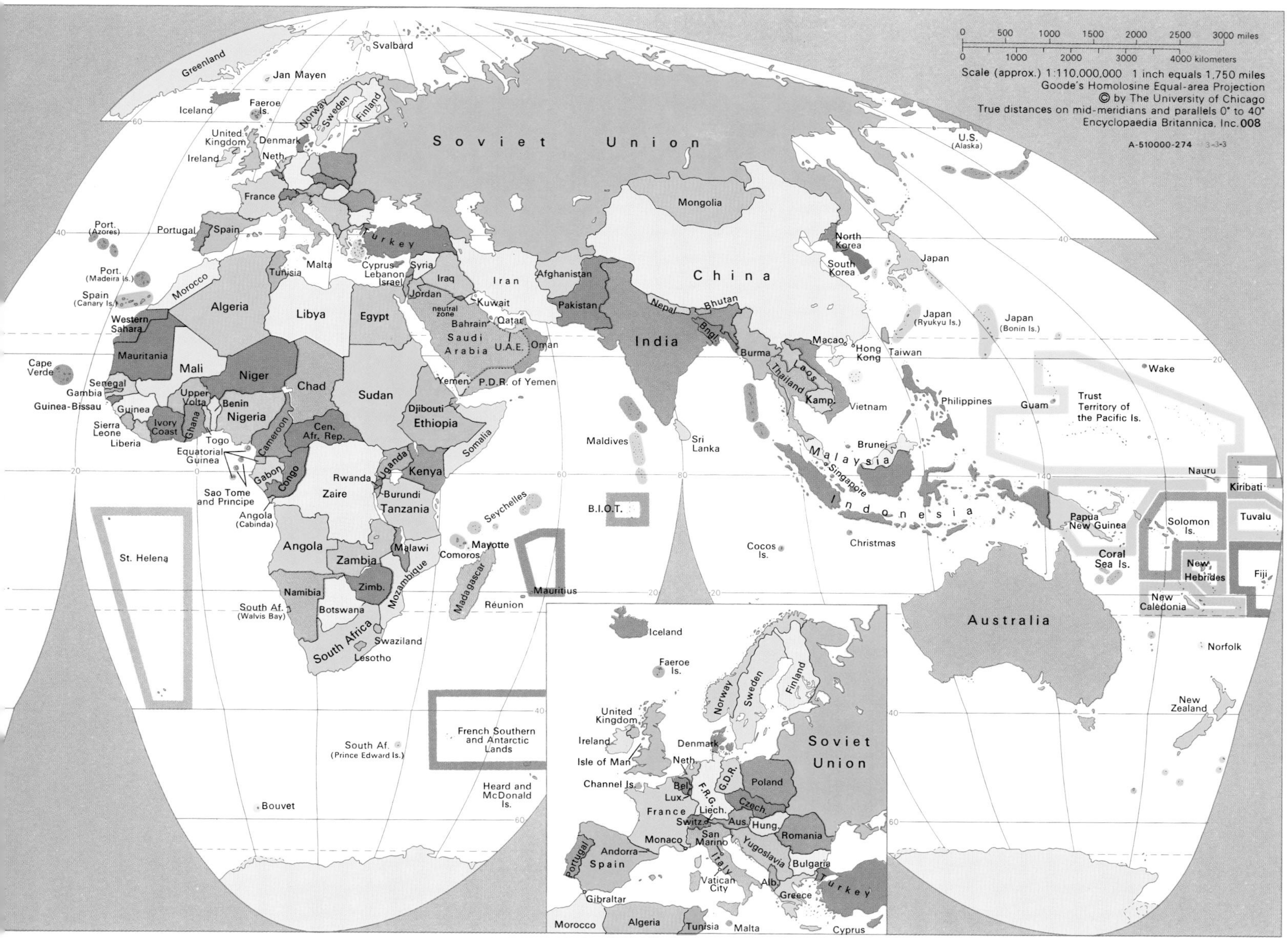

0 500 1000 1500 2000 2500 3000 miles
0 1000 2000 3000 4000 kilometers
Scale (approx.) 1:110,000,000 1 inch equals 1,750 miles
Goode's Homolosine Equal-area Projection
© by The University of Chicago
True distances on mid-meridians and parallels 0° to 40°
Encyclopaedia Britannica, Inc. 008
A-510000-274
Greenland
Svalbard
Jan Mayen
Iceland
Faeroe Is.
Norway
Sweden
Finland
United Kingdom
Denmark
Ireland
Neth.
France
Soviet Union
Mongolia
North Korea
South Korea
Japan
Port. (Azores)
Portugal
Spain
Turkey
Port. (Madeira Is.)
Malta
Tunisia
Cyprus
Lebanon
Israel
Syria
Iraq
Iran
Afghanistan
China
Spain (Canary Is.)
Morocco
Jordan
Kuwait
neutral zone
Bahrain
Qatar
Pakistan
Nepal
Bhutan
Bngl.
Algeria
Libya
Egypt
Saudi Arabia
U.A.E.
Oman
India
Japan (Ryukyu Is.)
Japan (Bonin Is.)
Western Sahara
Mauritania
Macao
Hong Kong
Taiwan
Burma
Laos
Thailand
Cape Verde
Mali
Niger
Chad
Sudan
Yemen
P.D.R. of Yemen
Kamp.
Vietnam
Philippines
Guam
Trust Territory of the Pacific Is.
Wake
Senegal
Gambia
Guinea-Bissau
Guinea
Upper Volta
Benin
Nigeria
Djibouti
Ethiopia
Sierra Leone
Liberia
Ivory Coast
Ghana
Togo
Cameroon
Cen. Afr. Rep.
Somalia
Maldives
Sri Lanka
Brunei
Malaysia
Singapore
Equatorial Guinea
Gabon
Congo
Uganda
Kenya
Rwanda
Burundi
Zaire
Tanzania
Nauru
Kiribati
Sao Tome and Principe
Angola (Cabinda)
Seychelles
B.I.O.T.
Indonesia
Papua New Guinea
Solomon Is.
Tuvalu
Angola
Zambia
Malawi
Mayotte
Comoros
Cocos Is.
Christmas
Coral Sea Is.
New Hebrides
Fiji
St. Helena
Namibia
Zimb.
Mozambique
Madagascar
Mauritius
Réunion
New Caledonia
South Af. (Walvis Bay)
Botswana
South Africa
Swaziland
Lesotho
Australia
Norfolk
New Zealand
South Af. (Prince Edward Is.)
French Southern and Antarctic Lands
Heard and McDonald Is.
Bouvet
Iceland
Faeroe Is.
United Kingdom
Ireland
Isle of Man
Channel Is.
Denmark
Neth.
Bel.
Lux.
France
F.R.G.
G.D.R.
Poland
Czech.
Liech.
Switz.
Aus.
Hung.
Romania
Soviet Union
Monaco
San Marino
Yugoslavia
Bulgaria
Andorra
Spain
Portugal
Italy
Vatican City
Alb.
Greece
Turkey
Gibraltar
Morocco
Algeria
Tunisia
Malta
Cyprus

0 500 1000 1500 2000 2500 3000 miles
0 1000 2000 3000 4000 kilometers
Scale (approx.) 1:110,000,000 1 inch equals 1,750 miles
Goode's Homolosine Equal-area Projection
© by The University of Chicago
True distances on mid-meridians and parallels 0° to 40°
Encyclopaedia Britannica, Inc. 008
Greenland
Faeroe Is.
United Kingdom
Isle of Man
Denmark
Neth.
Channel Is.
France
U.S. (Alaska)
Gibraltar (U.K.)
Malta
Cyprus
Bhutan (India)
Bngl.
India
Hong Kong (U.K.)
Wake
Gambia
Sierra Leone
Ghana
Nigeria
India (Andaman and Nicobar Is.)
Sri Lanka
Guam
Trust Territory of the Pacific Is.
Brunei
Malaysia
Singapore
Nauru
Kiribati
Uganda
Kenya
Tanzania
Malawi
Seychelles
B.I.O.T.
Papua New Guinea
Solomon Is.
Tuvalu
St. Helena
Mayotte
Zambia
Zimb.
Cocos Is. (Austr.)
Christmas (Austr.)
New Hebrides
Fiji
Mauritius
Réunion
New Caledonia
Botswana
Swaziland
Australia
Norfolk (Austr.)
Lesotho
New Zealand
French Southern and Antarctic Lands
Heard and McDonald Is. (Austr.)

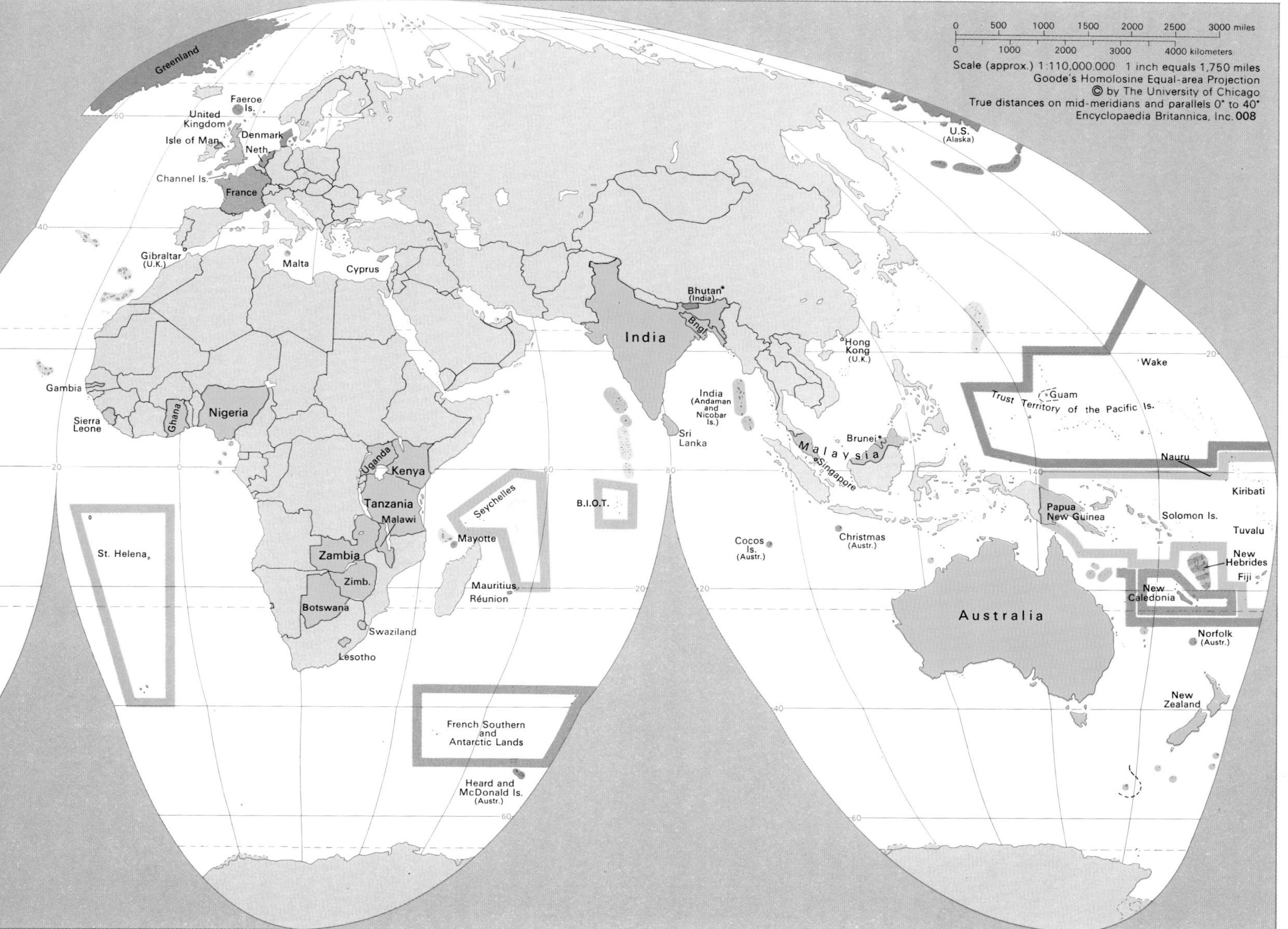

Seaward Claims

Common territorial sea claims

- 3 nautical miles
- 6 nautical miles
- 12 nautical miles

Less common claims

- 4 nautical miles
- 10 nautical miles
- Over 12 nautical miles
- Unusual claim

Other features

- Landlocked countries
- Continental shelf

Note: Territorial claims of outlying islands to their offshore waters are the same as those of the administering country.

Coastal states have long claimed jurisdiction over adjacent waters as a measure of defense from attack, in order to exploit offshore resources, and to control such matters as customs, sanitation, immigration, and criminal acts. Recently most states have become more aware of offshore fishing rights and of the resources on and under the floor of the sea.

Traditionally, the breadth of the territorial sea was generally three nautical miles, but in recent years greater claims have become more and more common. Today, the breadth varies sharply from place to place, for each state unilaterally establishes a limit according to its own political and economic objectives. The world map and table show the variety of claims.

Within the last few years a number of states have laid claim to offshore fishing zones for exclusive rights in waters previously accessible to fishermen from all states.

Numerous disputes involving conflicting claims prompted the United Nations to convene the several Law of the Sea conferences, the First in 1958, the Second in 1960, and the Third, sessions 1974-78. The diagrams *Offshore zones* illustrate the division of the waters adjacent to a coastal state into four zones as defined by the Law of the Sea Conventions: territorial sea, contiguous zone, high seas, and continental shelf. The low-water line along the coast has been defined as the baseline from which the limits of these various zones are measured. Each state has determined the breadth of its territorial sea where it may exercise sovereign control over the water, the seabed, and the airspace. Seaward of this zone a state may also establish a contiguous zone where it has limited jurisdictional rights. The high seas encompass all waters beyond the territorial sea; these are open to all states for navigation and other activities not precluded by convention or agreement.

The physical continental shelf may be very narrow or may extend seaward for hundreds of miles. The Law of the Sea Convention has therefore defined the limits of the continental shelf where a coastal state has the exclusive right to exploit seabed resources. This legal version of the shelf, as illustrated in the diagram, extends from the outer limit of the territorial sea to where the depth is 200 meters, or to greater depths if they will admit exploitation of the resources of the seabed and subsoil.

The thirty landlocked states must negotiate with coastal states for rights of transit to the sea, as well as for any rights within offshore jurisdictional zones.

Extended claims tend to decrease the area of the high seas and restrict or completely close narrow straits and channels that provide access to seas and gulfs. These broader claims could interfere seriously with established shipping lanes through which food and fuel resources pass. In addition, they could disrupt international air routes and impede military operations.

At the Law of the Sea conferences, many complex problems were faced in an effort to arrive at a territorial sea of uniform breadth and to promote international cooperation. Although the conferences were successful in resolving many legal maritime matters they failed to standardize the breadth of the territorial sea in a manner agreeable to all states. The small maps on this page illustrate the solutions for two types of claims. Conferences in the future may achieve international accord on jurisdictional issues.

Offshore zones

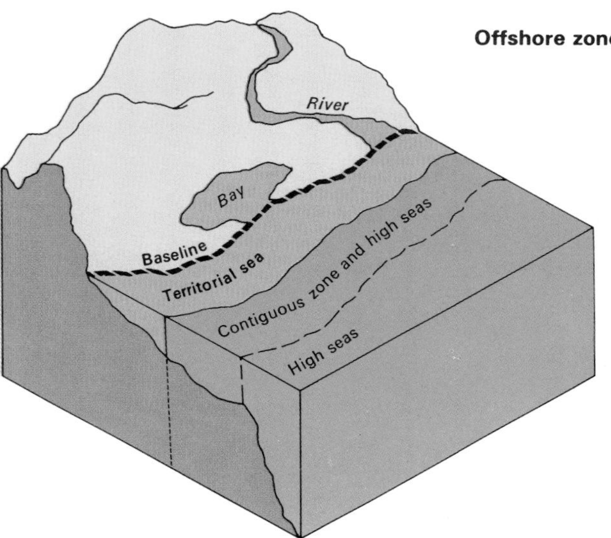

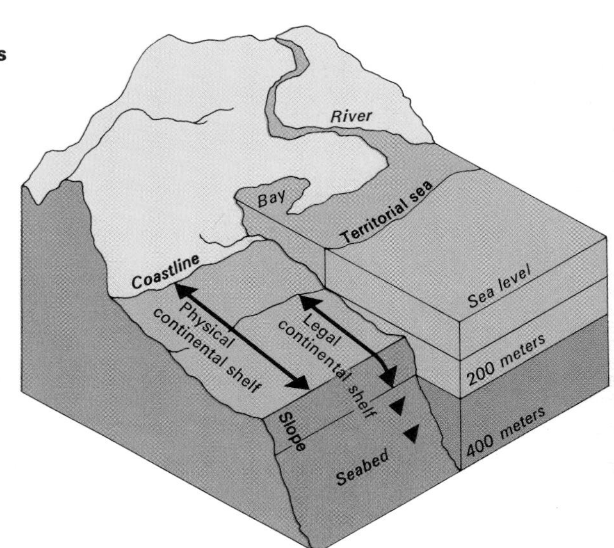

Irregular coastline of Norway

Norway measures its territorial sea from a straight baseline, which in general runs along the outer fringe of offshore islands and coastal promontories. The Law of the Sea Convention permits this type of claim in the case of highly irregular coastlines fringed with islands. In other cases the coastal features do not justify such claims to additional waters, and the claims may not be recognized.

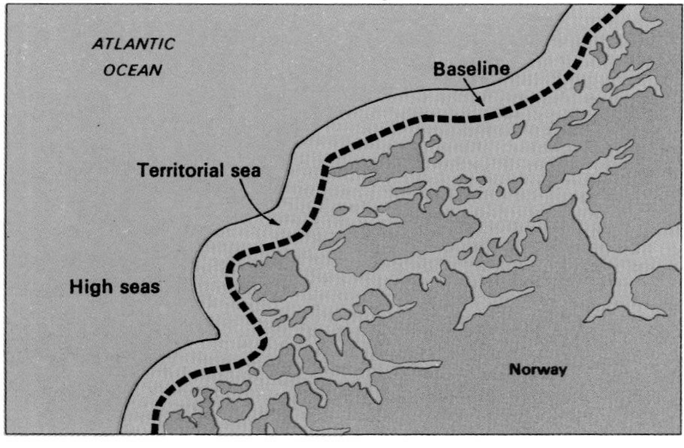

Overlapping claims in the Persian Gulf

The waters of the Persian Gulf are less than 200 meters in depth and the entire seabed is continental shelf. To determine the extent of jurisdiction that each state has over the resources of the seabed beyond its territorial sea, the Law of the Sea Convention provides for median lines, measured from the same baseline as the territorial sea. The median lines divide the continental shelf between opposite and adjacent states.

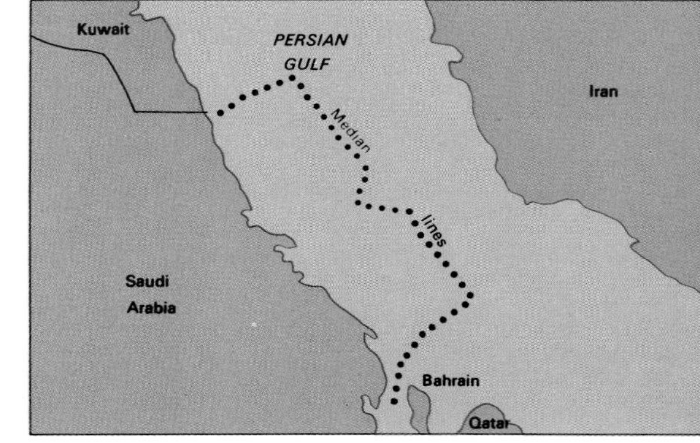

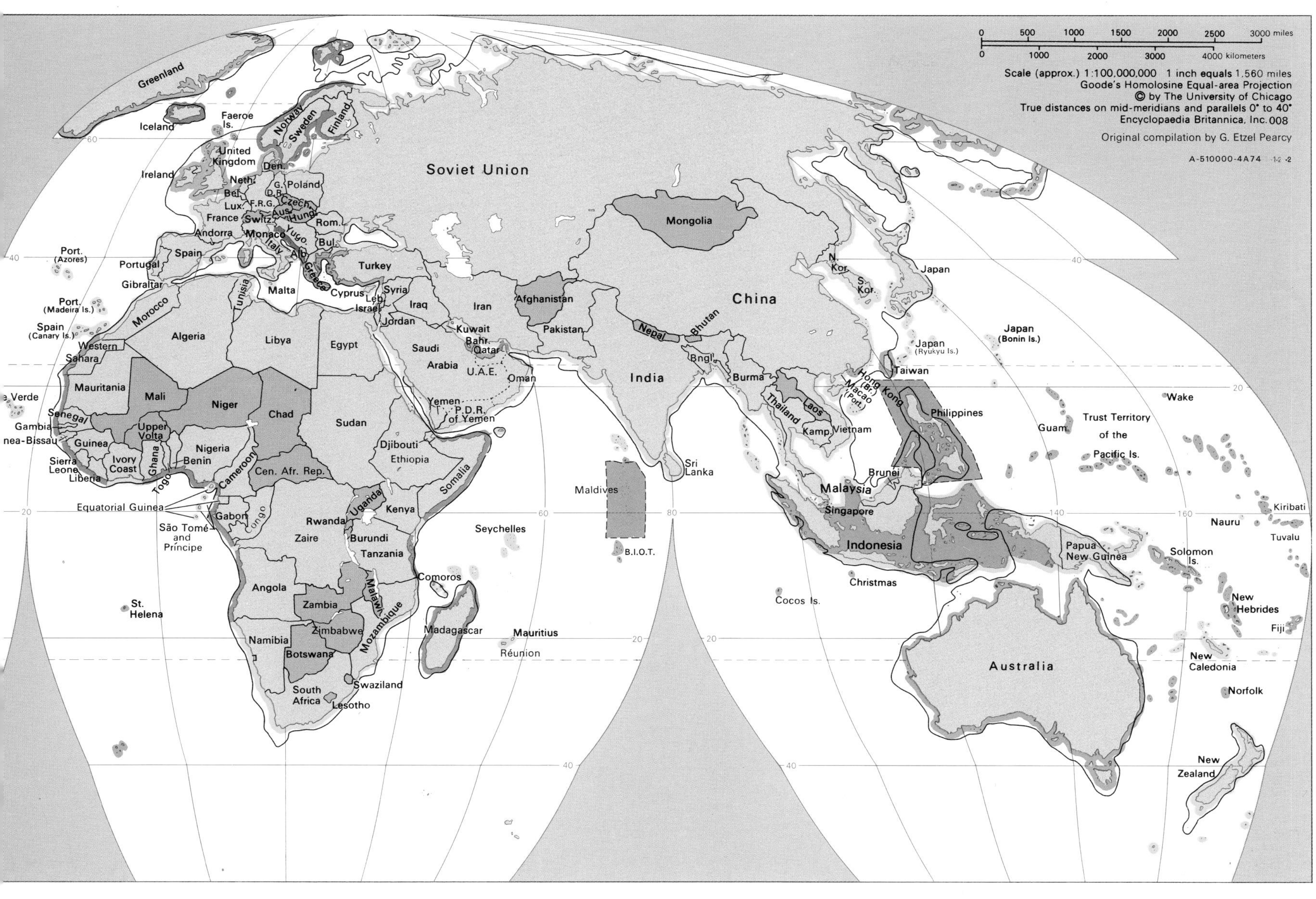

Political unit	Territorial sea claim*	Fishing claim*†
Albania	15 A	
Algeria	12	
Angola	20	200
Argentina	200 A	
Australia	3 A	12
Bahamas	3	200
Bahrain	3	
Bangladesh	12 A	200
Barbados	12	200
Belgium	3	6
Belize	3 B	
Benin	200	
Brazil	200 A	
Brunei	3 B	
Bulgaria	12	
Burma	12 A	200
Cambodia (Kampuchea)	12 A	200
Cameroon	50 A	
Canada	12 A	200
Cape Verde	12	200
Chile	3	200
China	12 A	
Colombia	12	200
Comoros	12	200
Congo	200	
Costa Rica	12	200
Cuba	12 A	200
Cyprus	12	
Denmark	3 A	200
Djibouti	12	
Dominican Republic	6 A	200
Ecuador	200 A	
Egypt	12 A	
El Salvador	200	
Equatorial Guinea	12	
Ethiopia	12 A	
Fiji	12 C	
Finland	4 A	12
France	12 A	200
French Guiana	12 B	80
Gabon	100 A	150
Gambia, The	50	
German Dem. Rep.	3 A	200
Germany, Fed. Rep. of	3 A	200
Ghana	200	
Gibraltar	3 B	
Greece	6	
Greenland	3 B	12
Grenada	12	200
Guatemala	12 A	200
Guinea	200 A	
Guinea-Bissau	12	200
Guyana	12	200
Haiti	12 A	200
Honduras	12	
Hong Kong	3 B	
Iceland	4 A	200
India	12	200
Indonesia	12 C	
Iran	12 A	50
Iraq	12	
Ireland	3 A	200
Israel	6	
Italy	12	
Ivory Coast	12	200
Jamaica	12	
Japan	12	200
Jordan	3	
Kenya	12 A	
Korea, North	12	200
Korea, South	12 A	200
Kuwait	12	
Lebanon	‡	6
Liberia	200	
Libya	12 A	
Madagascar	50 A	150
Malaysia	12 A	
Maldives		35–300
Malta	12 A	25
Mauritania	70 A	200
Mauritius	12 A	200
Mexico	12 A	200
Monaco	12	
Morocco	12	70
Mozambique	12 A	200
Namibia	6 B	12
Nauru	12	
Netherlands	3	200
New Caledonia	12 B	
New Zealand	12	200
Nicaragua	3	200
Nigeria	30	
Norway	4 A	200
Oman	12 A	200
Pakistan	12	200
Panama	200 A	
Papua New Guinea	12	200
Peru	200	
Philippines	C	
Poland	12 A	200
Portugal	12 A	200
Qatar	3	
Romania	12	
São Tomé and Príncipe	12	200
Saudi Arabia	12 A	
Senegal	150 A	200
Seychelles	12 D	200
Sierra Leone	200	
Singapore	3	
Solomon Islands	3 D	200
Somalia	200 A	
South Africa	12	200
Soviet Union	12 A	200
Spain	12	200
Sri Lanka	12 A	200
Sudan	12 A	
Suriname	12	200
Sweden	4 A	200
Syria	12 A	
Taiwan	3	12
Tanzania	50 A	
Thailand	12 A	
Togo	30	200
Tonga	C	
Trinidad and Tobago	12	
Tunisia	12 E	
Turkey	6–12 A	
United Arab Emirates	3 or 12	
United Kingdom	3 A	200
United States	3	200
Uruguay	200	
Venezuela	12 A	200
Vietnam	12	200
Western Sahara	6 D	
Western Samoa	12	
Yemen	12	
Yemen, P.D.R.	12	200
Yugoslavia	10 A	12
Zaire	12	

* Nautical miles.
† When claim is beyond the territorial sea.
‡ No specific claim.

A. Measured from a straight (or extended) baseline.
B. Same as that of administering country.
C. Extends beyond a perimeter drawn around archipelago.
D. Newly independent; assumed to be same as former metropole.
E. For part of the coast, the territorial sea follows the 50-meter isobath (max. breadth 65 mi.).

Dissolution of the Ottoman Empire

Ottoman Empire 1913

Administrative boundaries (1923) as a result of WW I settlements; dotted are indefinite

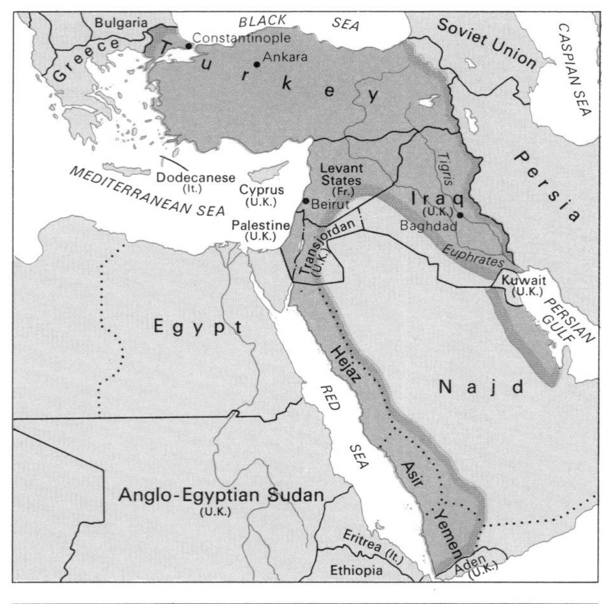

Dissolution of Austria-Hungary

Austria-Hungary 1913

Administrative boundaries (1923) as a result of WW I settlements

Japanese Expansion World War II

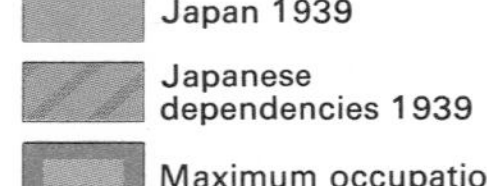

Japan 1939

Japanese dependencies 1939

Maximum occupation

Neutral states

States joining Allies 1945

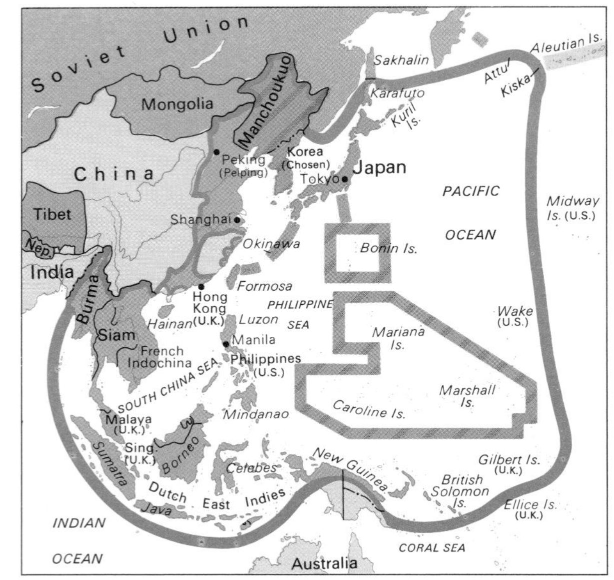

Axis Expansion World War II

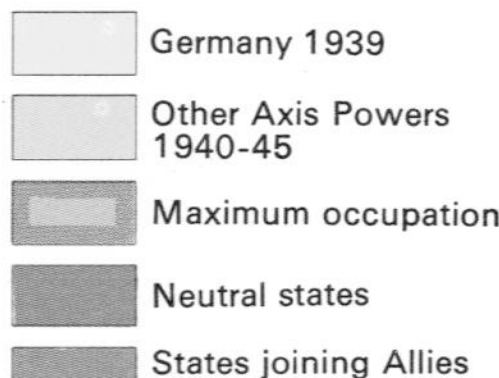

Germany 1939

Other Axis Powers 1940-45

Maximum occupation

Neutral states

States joining Allies 1943-45

*Occupied by Allies

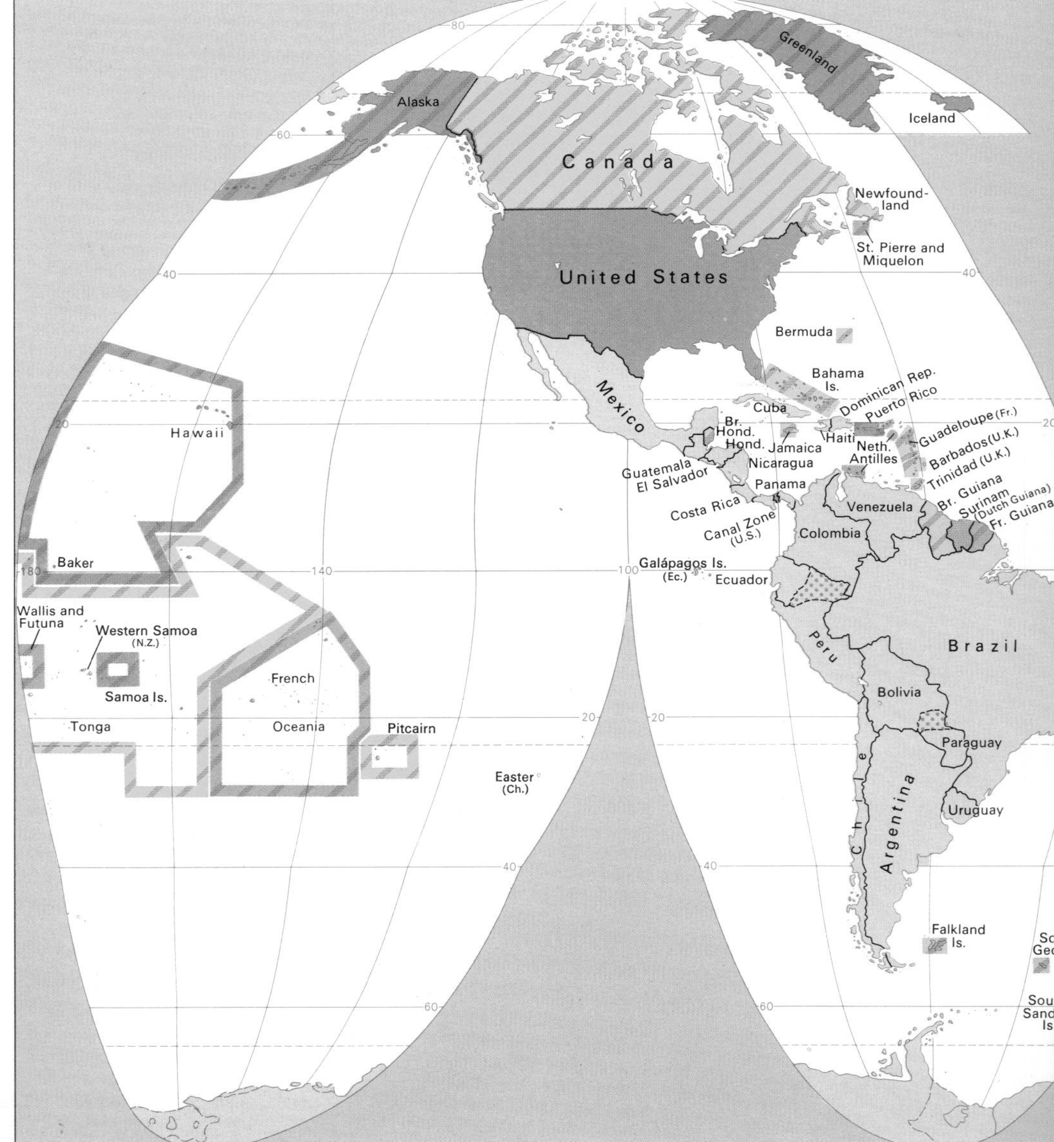

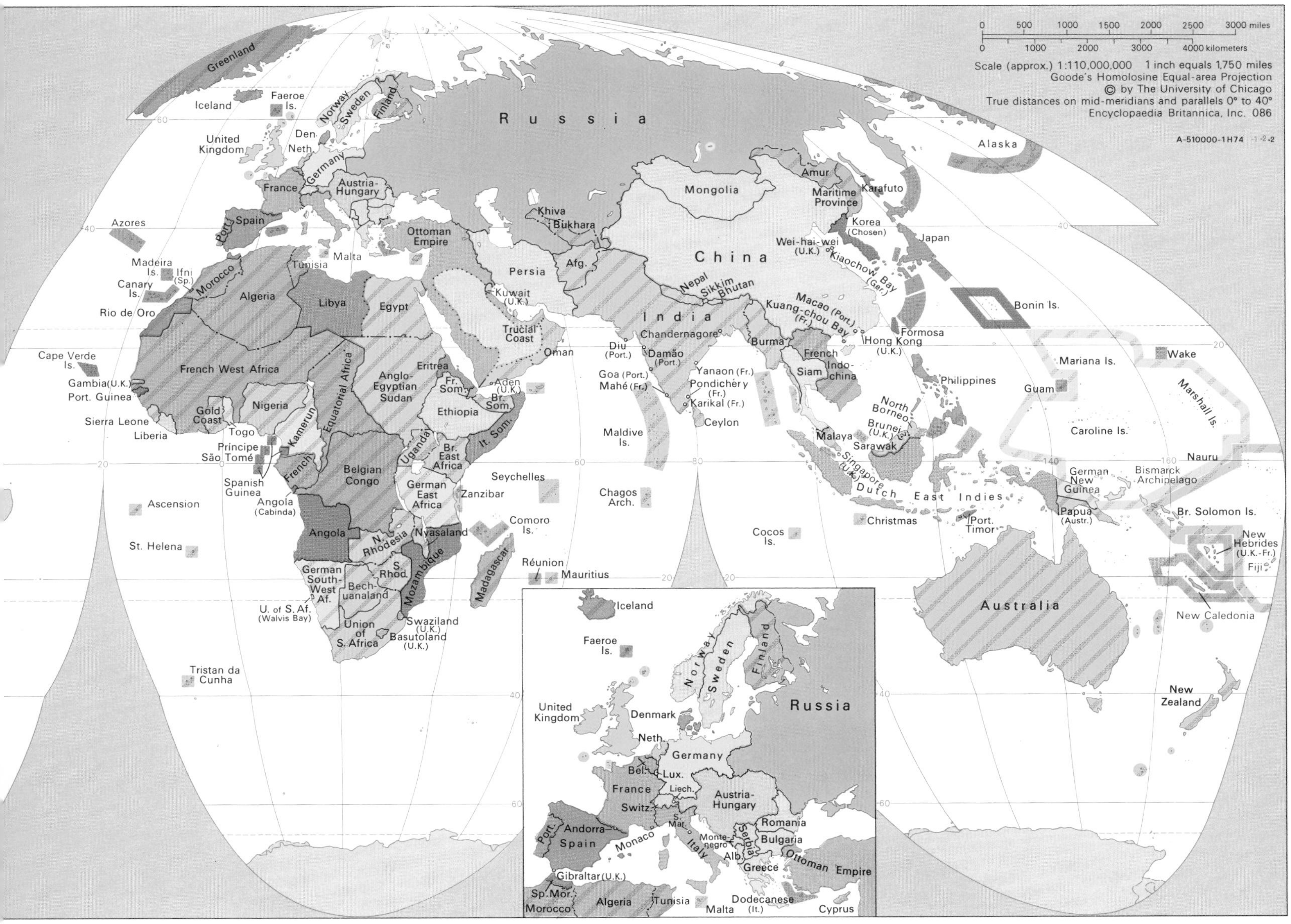

The World January 1, 1914

0 500 1000 1500 2000 2500 3000 miles
0 1000 2000 3000 4000 kilometers
Scale (approx.) 1:110,000,000 1 inch equals 1,750 miles
Goode's Homolosine Equal-area Projection

True distances on mid-meridians and parallels 0° to 40°
Encyclopaedia Britannica, Inc. 086
A-510000-1H74

- United Kingdom
  - Related areas
- France
  - Related areas
- Portugal
  - Related areas
- Spain
  - Related areas
- Netherlands
  - Related areas
- Belgium
  - Related areas
- Germany
  - Related areas
- Denmark
  - Related areas
- Japan
  - Related areas
- Italy
  - Related areas
- United States
  - Related areas
- Ottoman Empire
- Russia
  - Related areas
- Austria-Hungary
- Countries without related areas
- Disputed areas
- Intercolonial boundary

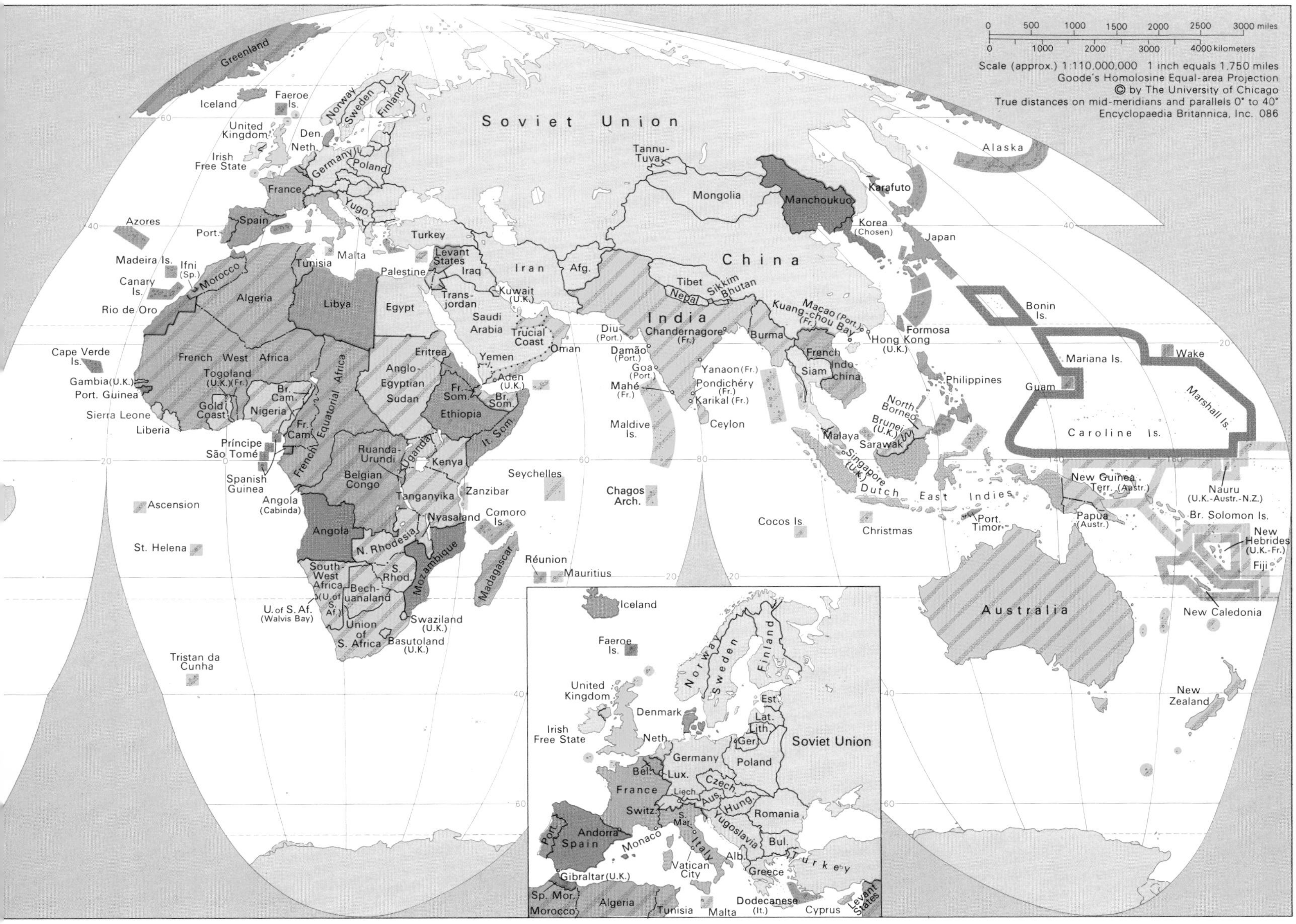

0 500 1000 1500 2000 2500 3000 miles
0 1000 2000 3000 4000 kilometers
Scale (approx.) 1:110,000,000 1 inch equals 1,750 miles
Goode's Homolosine Equal-area Projection

True distances on mid-meridians and parallels 0° to 40°
Encyclopaedia Britannica, Inc. 086

The World January 1, 1937

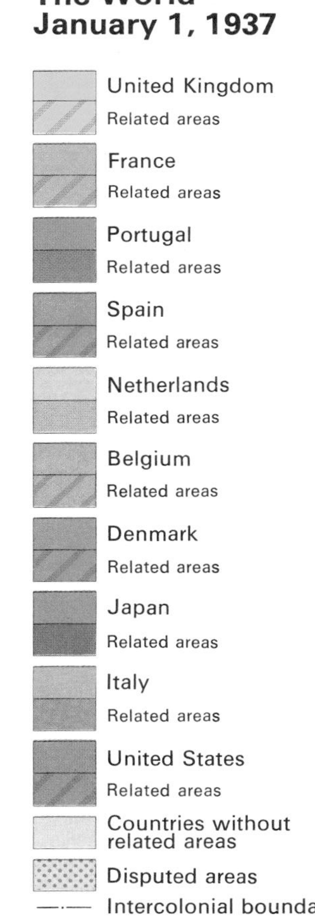

Population

Extent of urbanization
Percent of total population urban

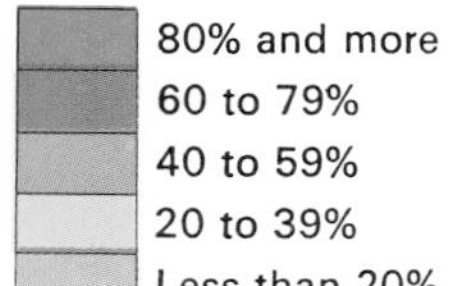

Major metropolitan areas

- 5,000,000 and more persons
- 3,000,000 to 4,999,999
- 2,000,000 to 2,999,999

The increase in the proportion of urban to total population reflects the change from a dispersed pattern of human settlement to a concentrated one. In industrialized countries the proportion of people living in cities increases mainly through movement from country to city, due to the attraction of higher wages and greater opportunities, a process which in most cases started about 100 years ago. In the underdeveloped countries, where in recent years the number of people living in cities has risen sharply, the proportion of urban population has not increased appreciably; here the urban growth is generally due not so much to rural-urban migration as it is to the natural population increase in both urban and rural areas, and to the decline in the urban mortality rate.

In population studies the definitions of "urban" differ from country to country, but generally take into account the total number of people in a settlement and the percent of the population engaged in nonagricultural activities. The map shows the degree of urbanization (the proportion of urban to total population), considering as urban those communities having no fewer than 2,000 inhabitants, more than half of them dependent on nonfarm occupations. Also indicated are selected metropolitan areas where cities have expanded beyond their boundaries into the surrounding regions in patterns of continuous settlement oriented toward the central cities.

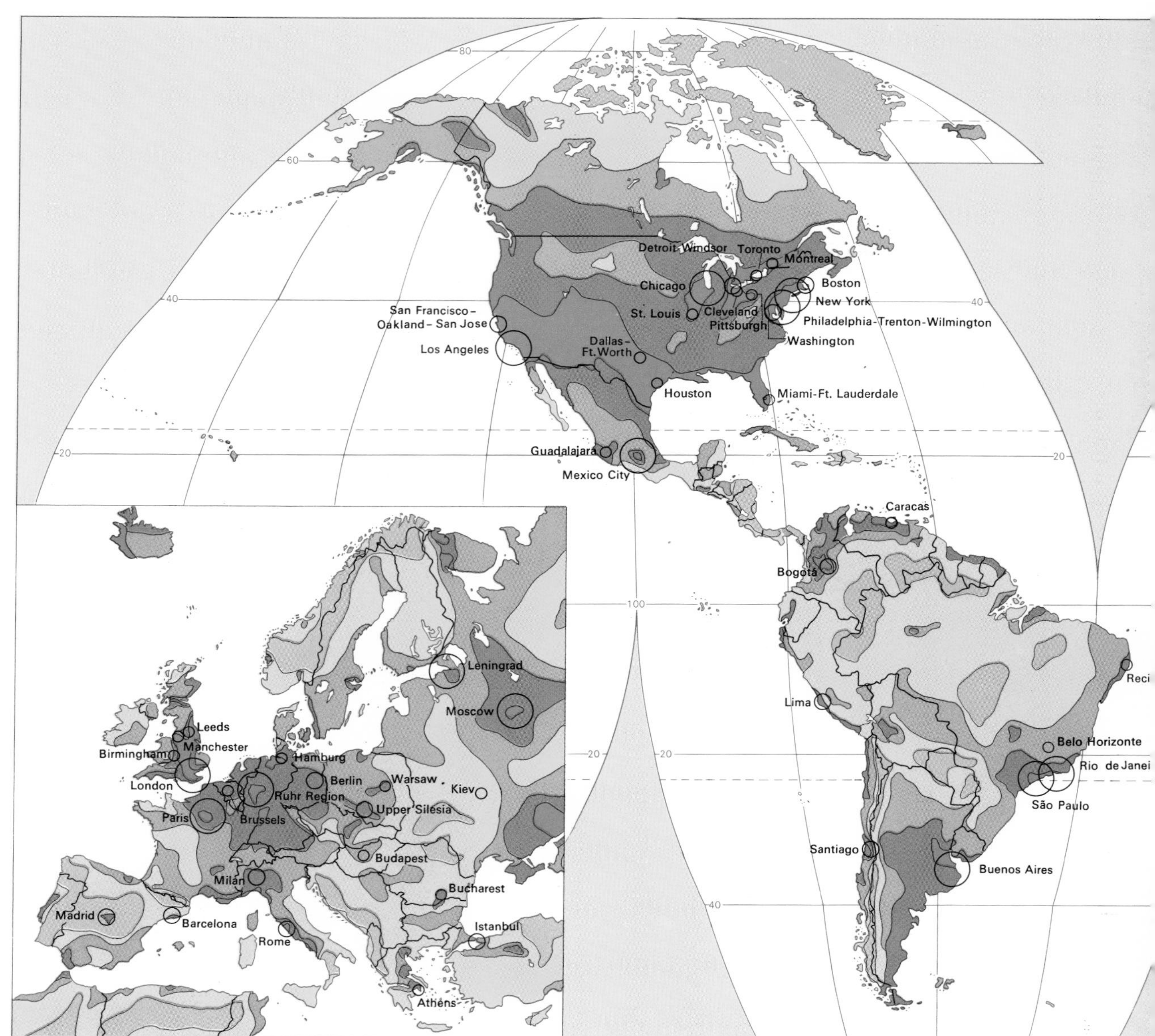

Age and sex composition

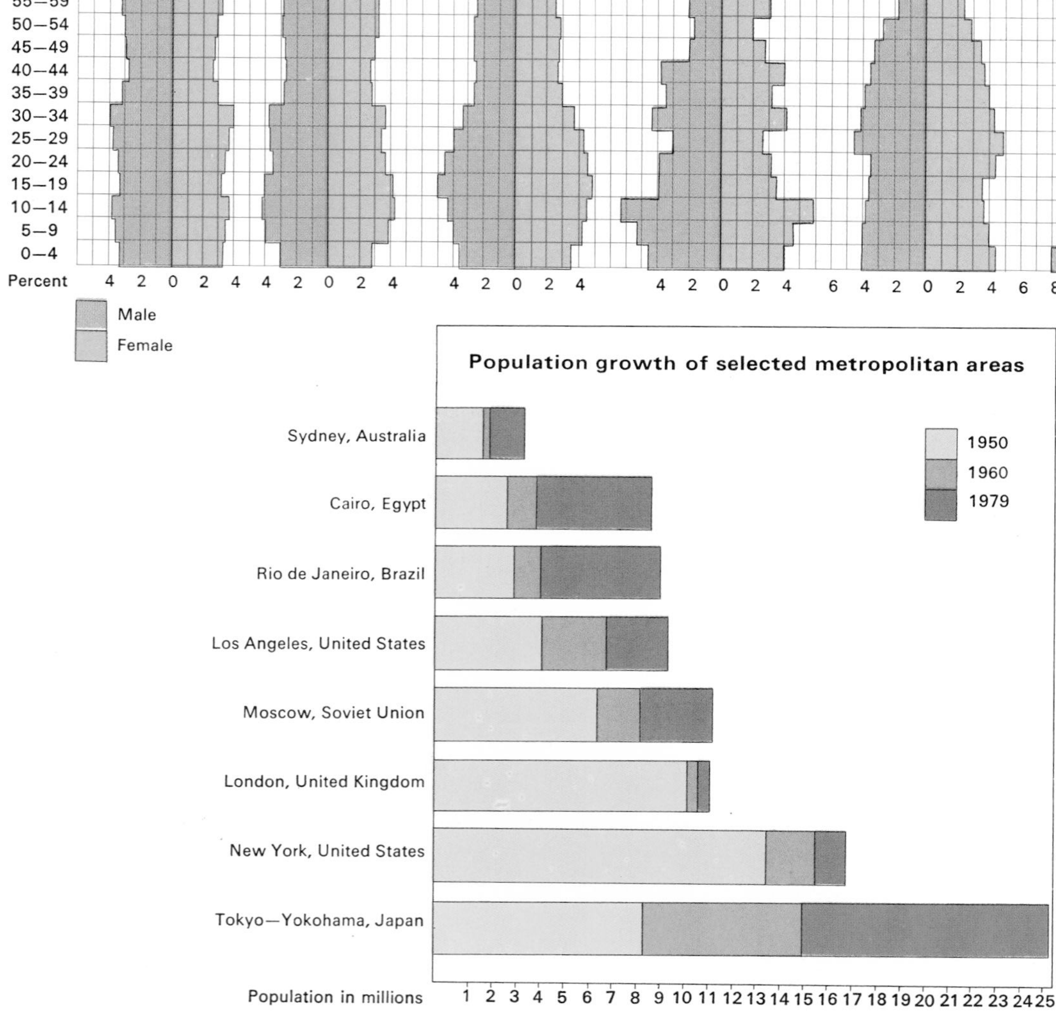

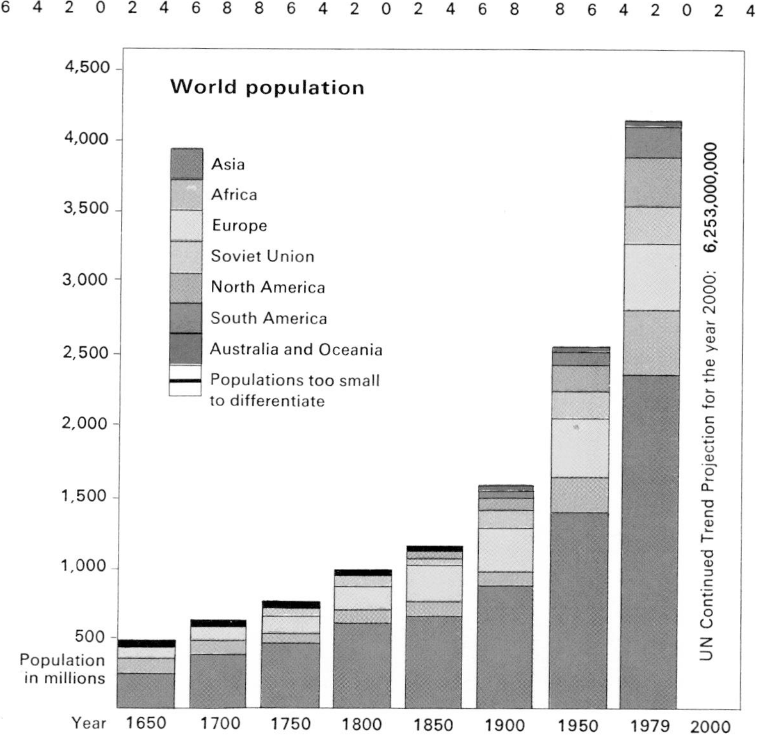

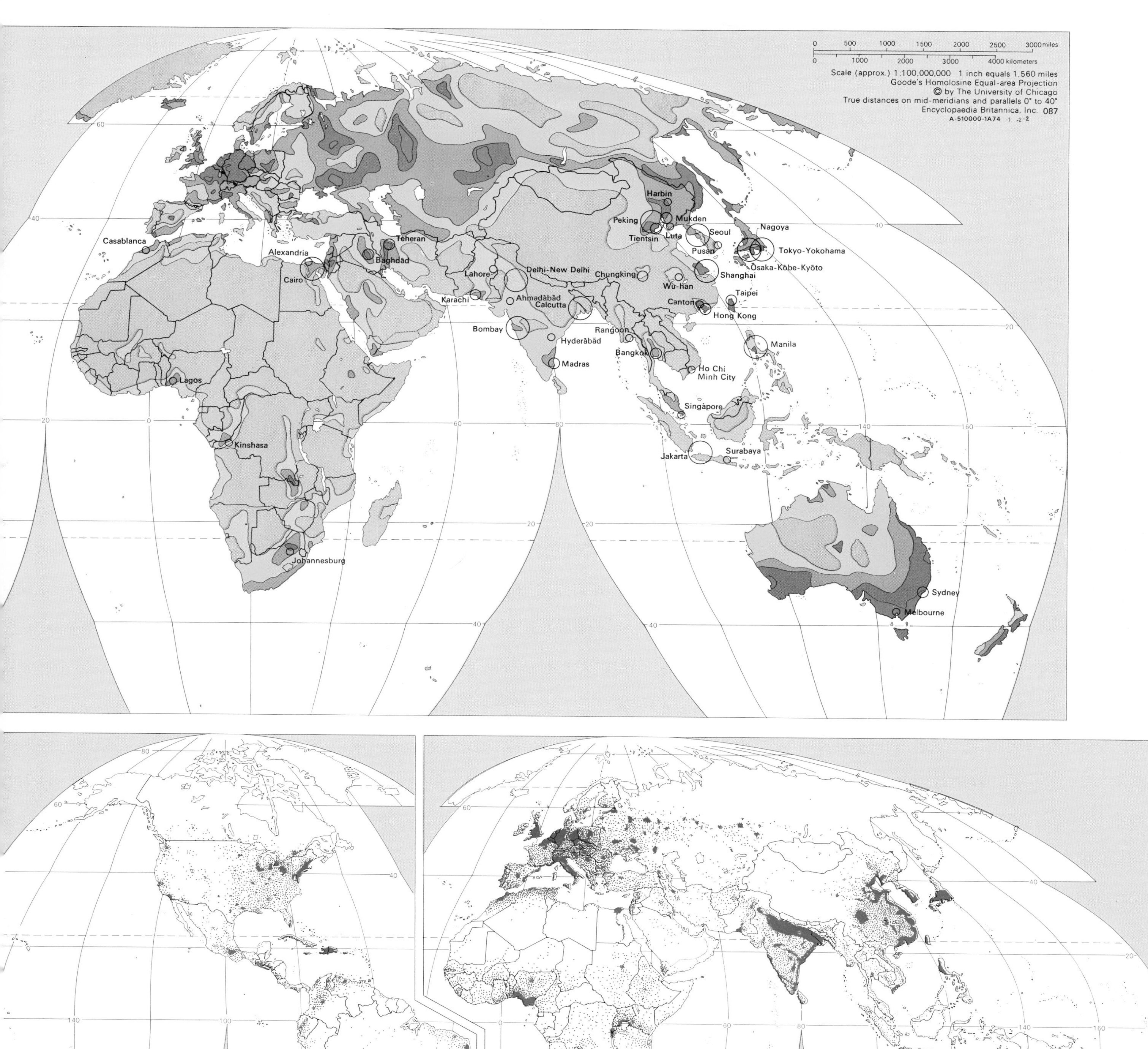

Encyclopaedia Britannica, Inc. 086

Distribution

Each dot represents 100,000 persons. The dots show the location of concentrated areas of population rather than the location of cities.

Religions

The majority of the inhabitants in each of the areas colored on the map share the religious tradition indicated. Letter symbols show religious traditions shared by at least 25% of the inhabitants within areal units no smaller than one thousand square miles. Therefore minority religions of city-dwellers have generally not been represented.

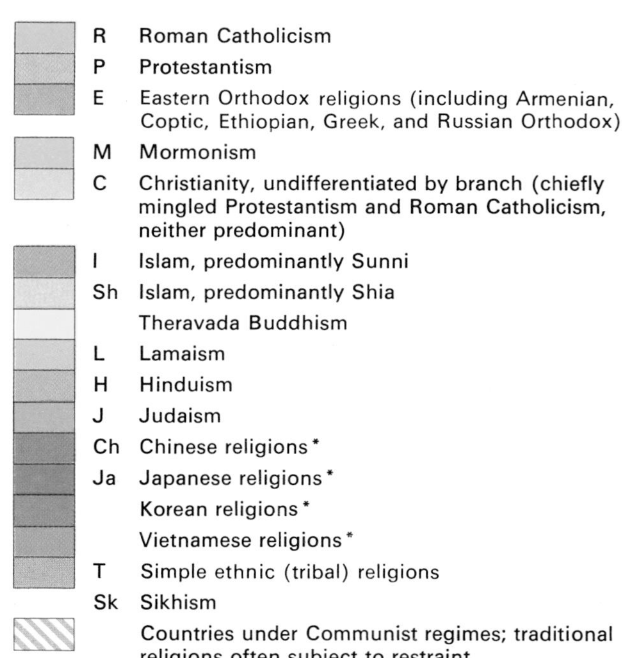

*In certain Eastern Asian areas, most of the people have plural religious affiliations. Chinese, Korean, and Vietnamese religions include Mahayana Buddhism, Taoism, Confucianism, and folk cults. The Japanese religions include Shinto and Mahayana Buddhism.

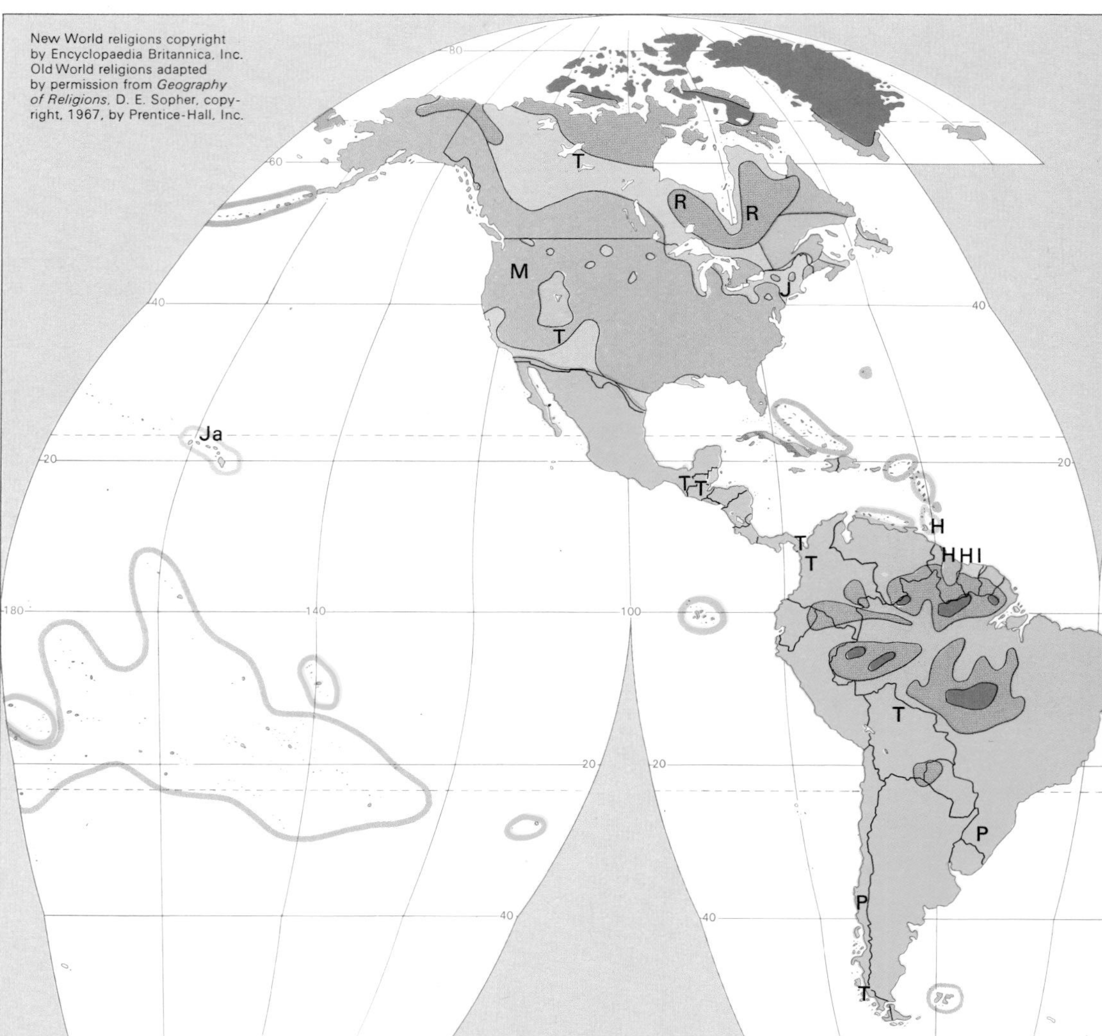

Languages

Languages of Europe

The following languages are ranked in descending order by number of speakers. Languages spoken by more than 4 million persons are indicated by color. Others listed, spoken by fewer than 4 million persons, are named on the map.

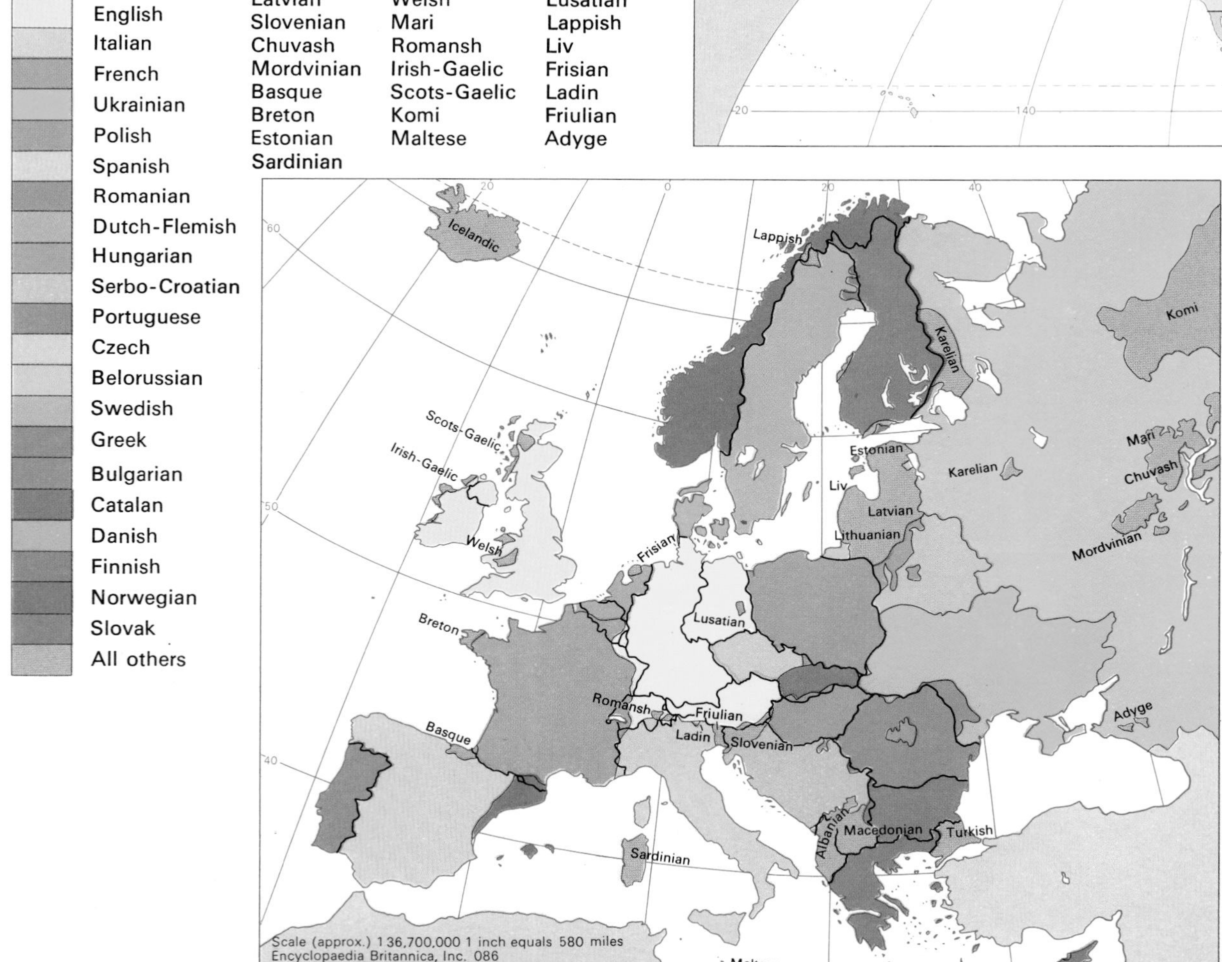

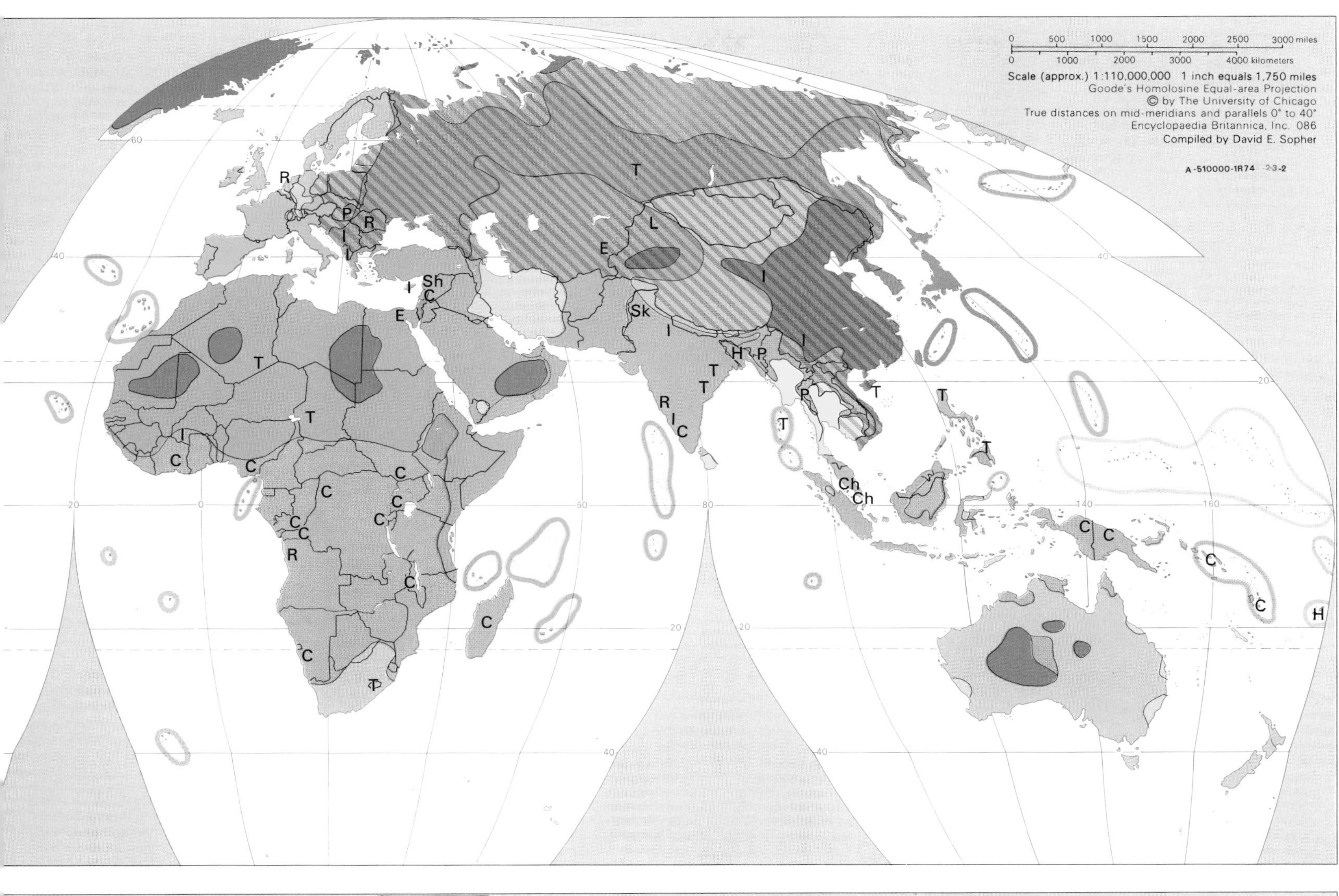

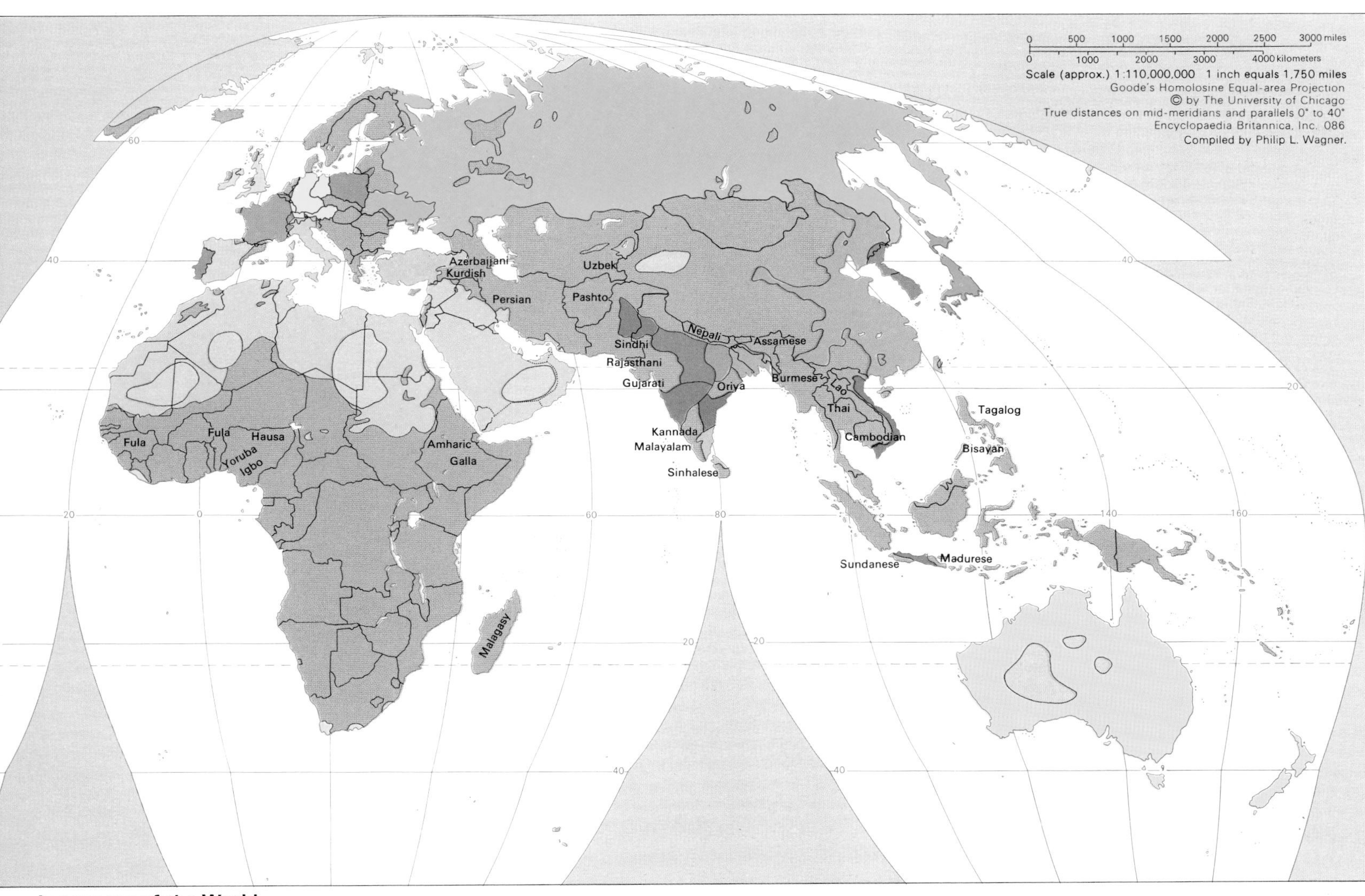

Languages of the World

The following languages are ranked in descending order by number of speakers. Languages spoken by more than 25 million persons are indicated by color. Others listed, spoken by 5–25 million persons, are named on the map.

Chinese
English
Spanish
Russian
Hindi
German
Japanese
Bengali
Portuguese
Arabic
French
Italian
Bihari
Javanese
Telugu
Ukrainian
Korean
Marathi
Tamil
Polish
Punjabi
Vietnamese
Turkish
All others
Uninhabited

Gujarati
Rajasthani
Kannada
Malayalam
Oriya
Burmese
Pashto
Thai
Sundanese
Bisayan
Amharic
Persian
Hausa
Quechua
Uzbek
Fula
Lao
Sinhalese
Yoruba
Azerbaijani
Sindhi
Igbo
Kurdish
Madurese
Assamese
Tagalog
Malagasy
Nepali
Cambodian
Galla

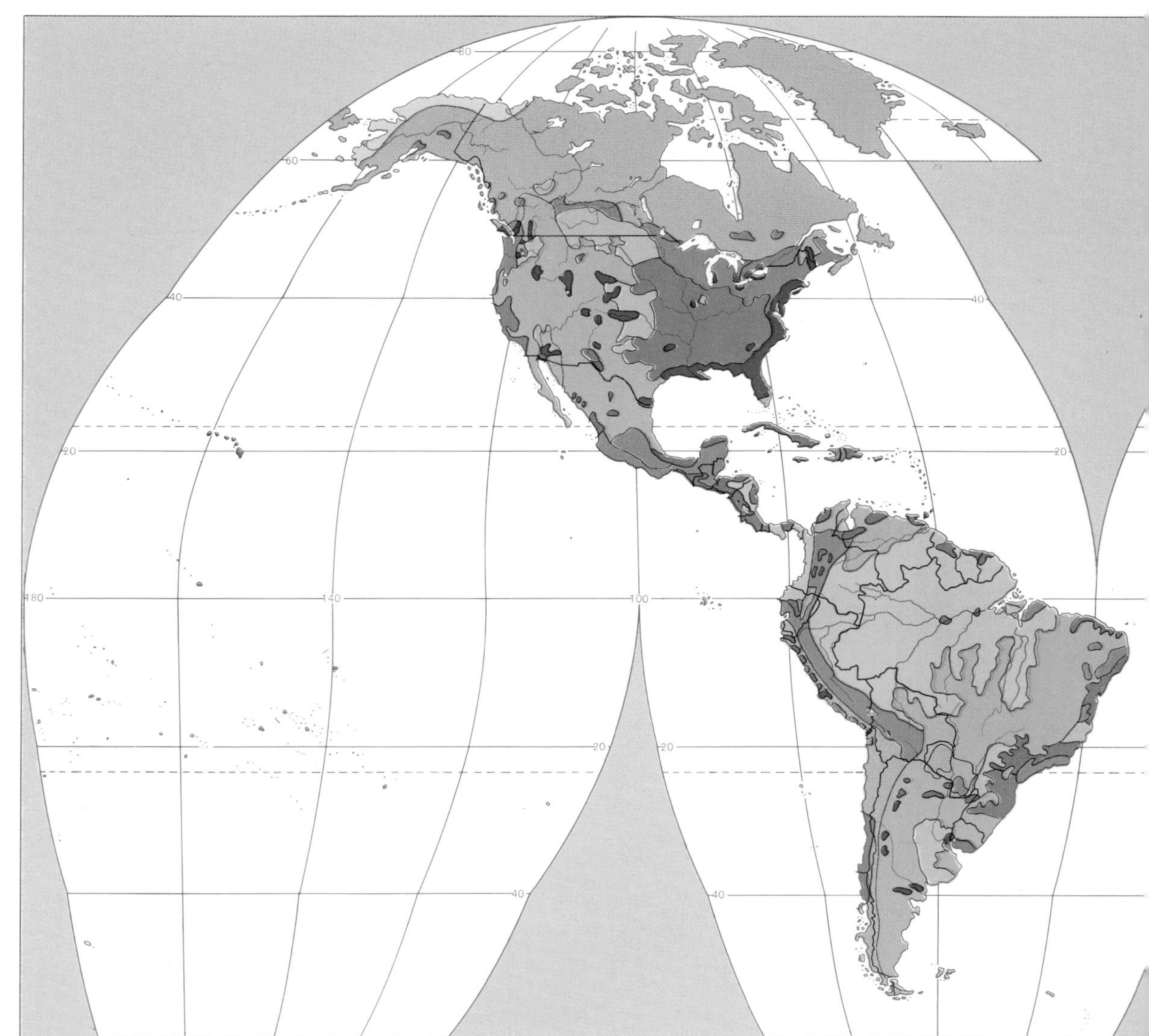

Agricultural Regions

- Cash crop and livestock farming
- Cash crop farming, grain or cotton dominant
- Crop and livestock farming with cash products minor
- Livestock ranching
- Dairying
- Mediterranean agriculture
- Specialized horticulture
- Plantation agriculture
- Intensive subsistence tillage, rice dominant
- Intensive subsistence tillage, with no dominant crop
- Rudimental sedentary farming
- Shifting cultivation
- Nomadic herding
- No agriculture

Forests and Fisheries

Forests

- Conifers: cedar, fir, hemlock, pine, redwood, spruce
- Regions of exploitation
- Tropical hardwoods: ebony, mahogany, rosewood, teak
- Regions of exploitation
- Temperate hardwoods: hickory, maple, oak, poplar, walnut, and some mixed hardwoods and conifers
- Regions of exploitation

Fisheries

- Pelagic fishing regions: anchoveta, anchovy, herring, menhaden, pilchard, sardine, sprat, tuna
- Ground fishing regions: cod, haddock, hake, horse mackerel, mackerel, pollack, redfish
- Mixed ground and pelagic fishing regions
- Shellfish: clam, crab, lobster, mussel, oyster, scallop, shrimp, squid
- Whales: blue, fin, minke, pilot, sei, sperm
  Each ⟝ represents an average annual catch of about 300 whales; Each ⟝ represents an average annual catch of less than 200 whales
- Fishing regions showing percentage of world catch (excluding whales)

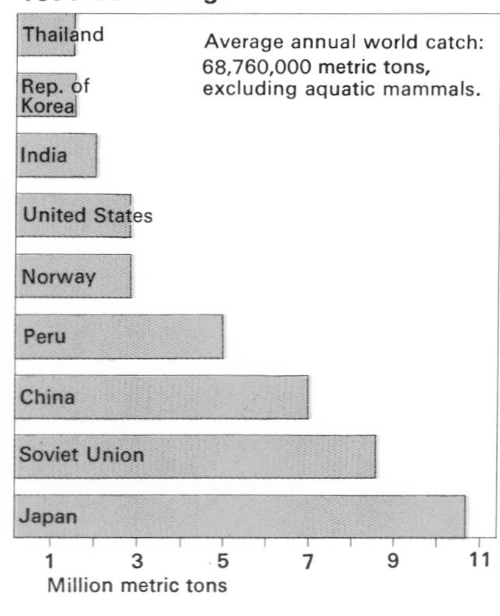

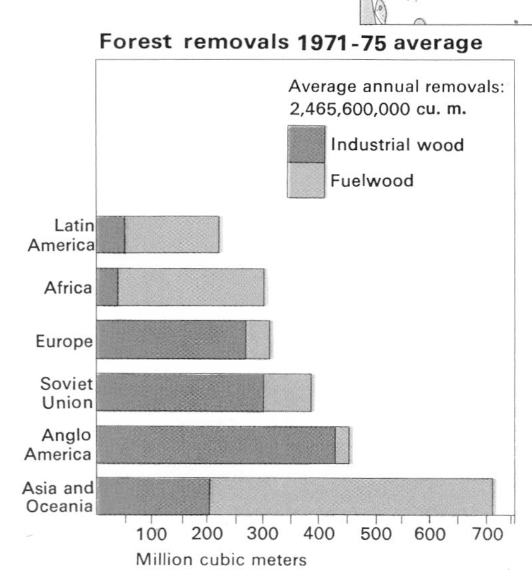

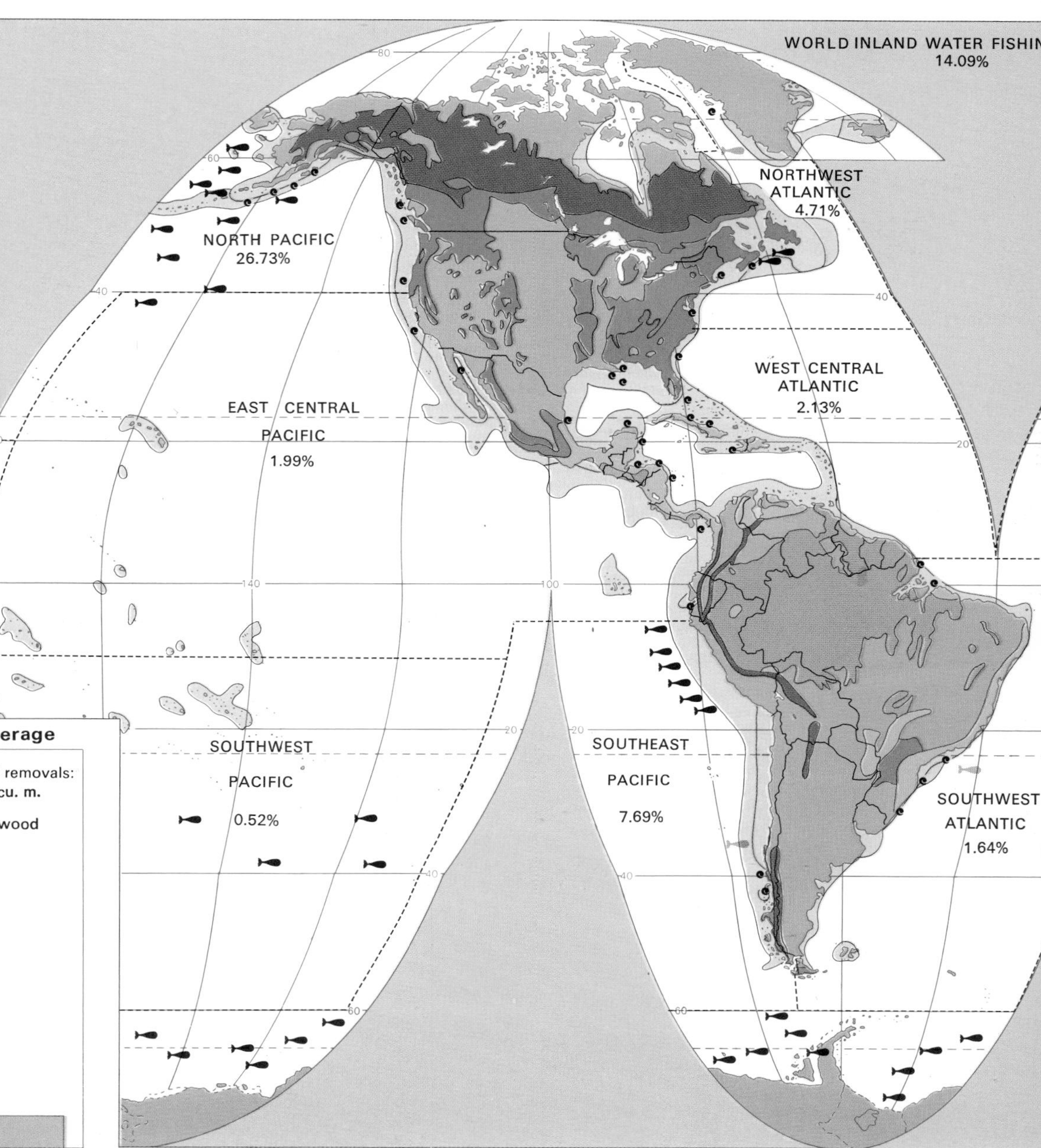

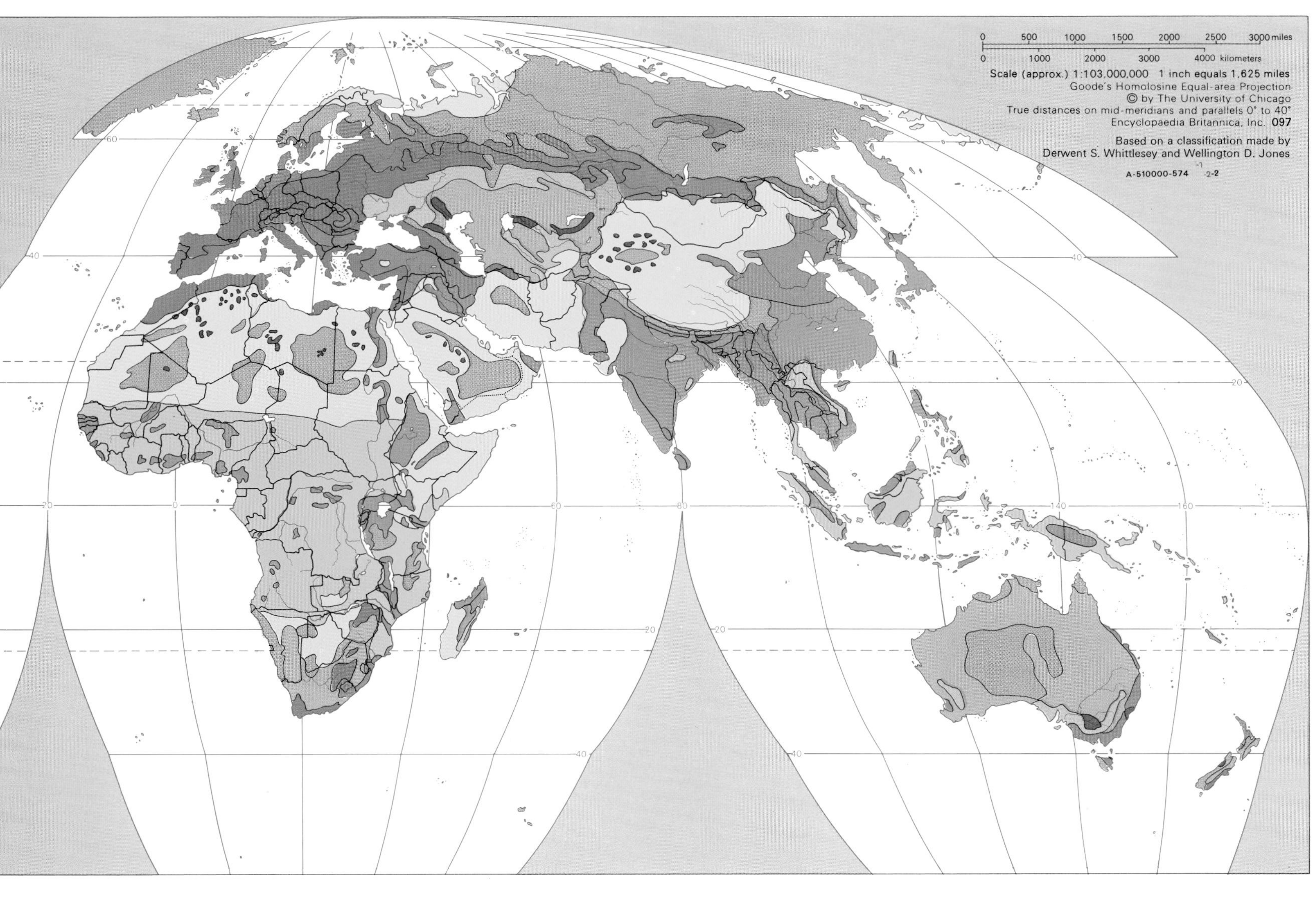

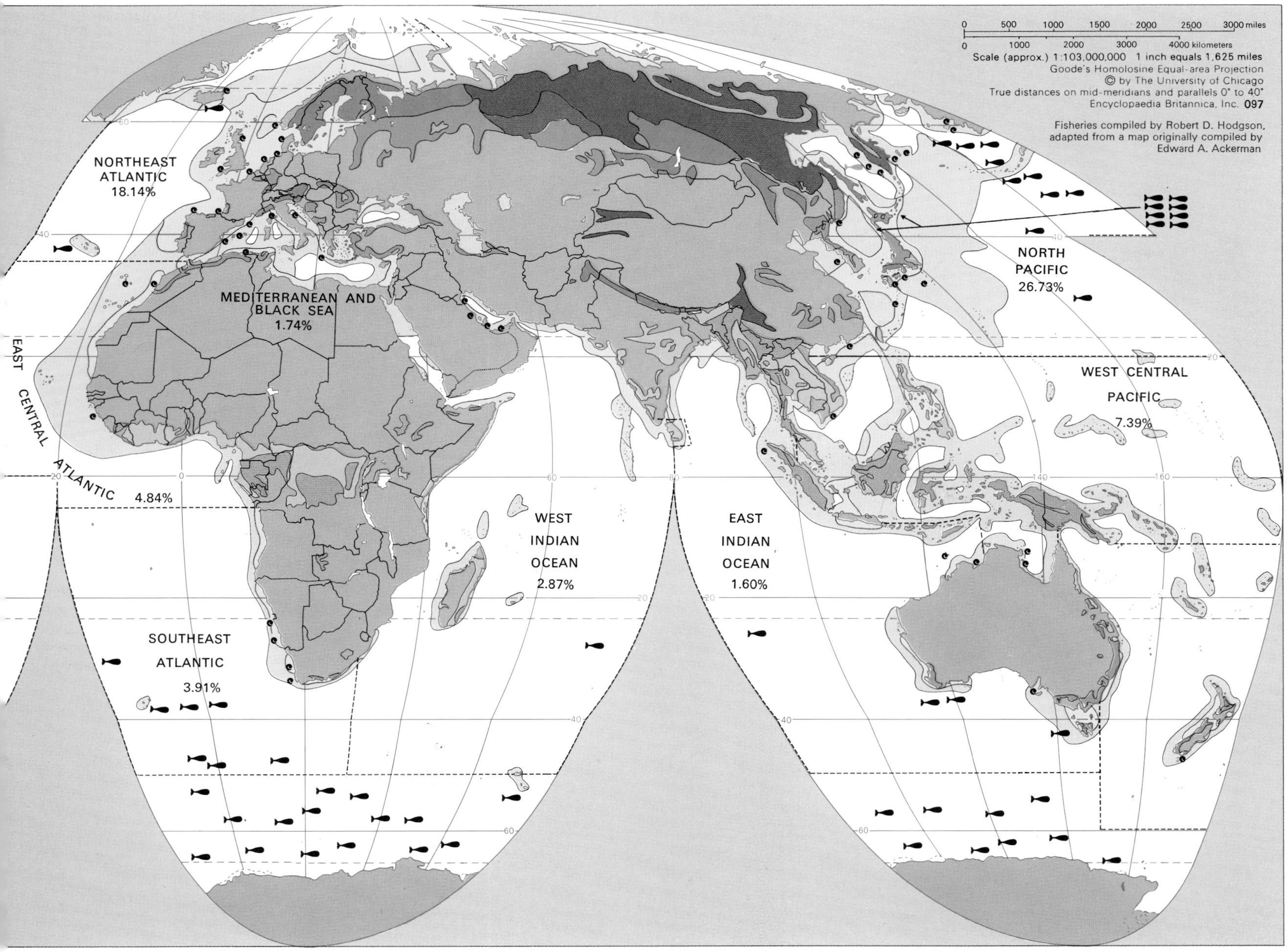

0 500 1000 1500 2000 2500 3000 miles
0 1000 2000 3000 4000 kilometers
Scale (approx.) 1:103,000,000 1 inch equals 1,625 miles
Goode's Homolosine Equal-area Projection
© by The University of Chicago
True distances on mid-meridians and parallels 0° to 40°
Encyclopaedia Britannica, Inc. 097
Based on a classification made by
Derwent S. Whittlesey and Wellington D. Jones
A-510000-574

0 500 1000 1500 2000 2500 3000 miles
0 1000 2000 3000 4000 kilometers
Scale (approx.) 1:103,000,000 1 inch equals 1,625 miles
Goode's Homolosine Equal-area Projection
© by The University of Chicago
True distances on mid-meridians and parallels 0° to 40°
Encyclopaedia Britannica, Inc. 097
Fisheries compiled by Robert D. Hodgson,
adapted from a map originally compiled by
Edward A. Ackerman
NORTHEAST ATLANTIC 18.14%
MEDITERRANEAN AND BLACK SEA 1.74%
EAST CENTRAL ATLANTIC 4.84%
SOUTHEAST ATLANTIC 3.91%
WEST INDIAN OCEAN 2.87%
EAST INDIAN OCEAN 1.60%
NORTH PACIFIC 26.73%
WEST CENTRAL PACIFIC 7.39%

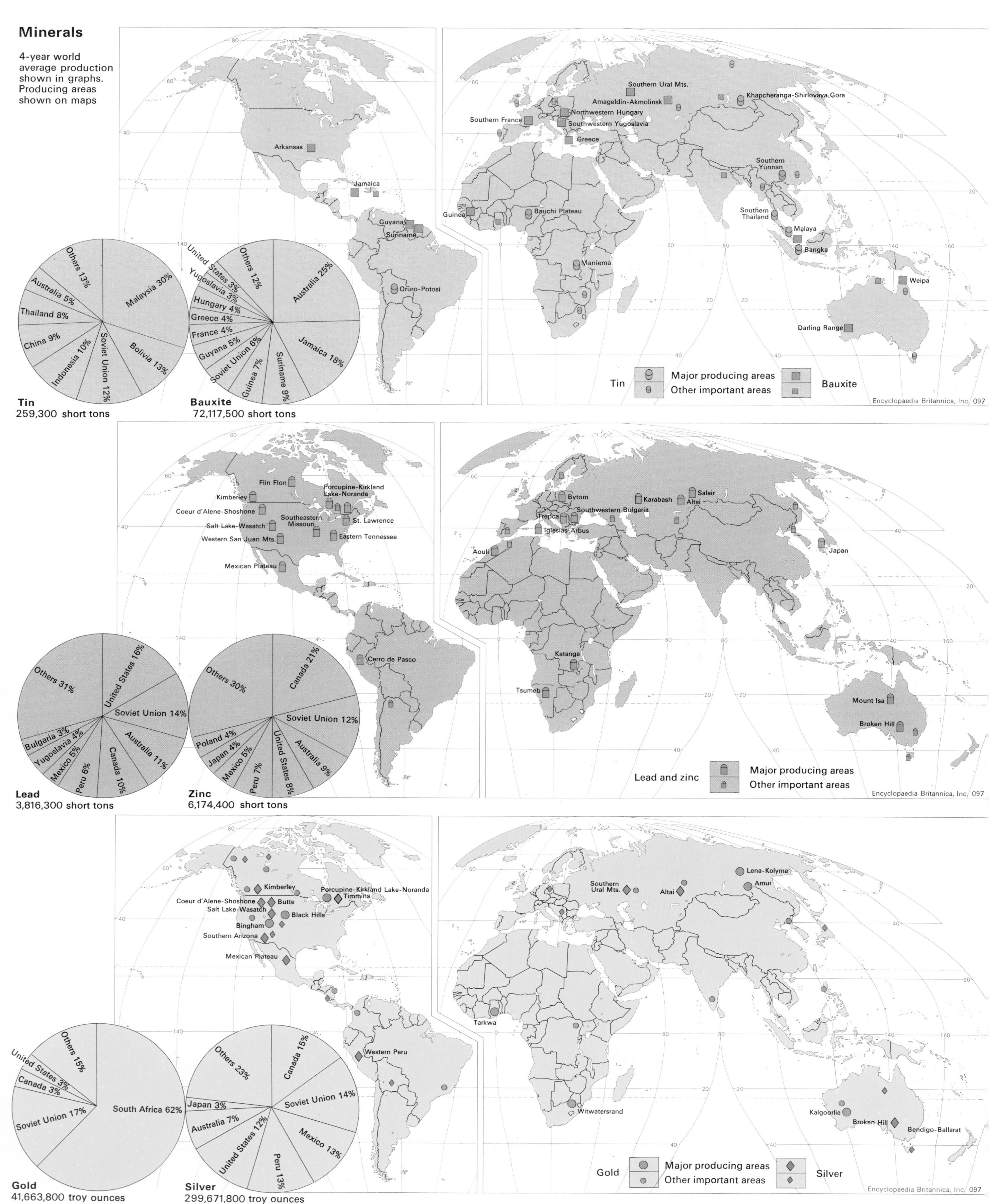
Minerals
4-year world average production shown in graphs. Producing areas shown on maps
Arkansas
Jamaica
Guyana
Suriname
Oruro-Potosí
Southern Ural Mts.
Amageldin-Akmolinsk
Khapcheranga-Shirlovaya Gora
Northwestern Hungary
Southern France
Southwestern Yugoslavia
Greece
Southern Yünnan
Guinea
Bauchi Plateau
Southern Thailand
Malaya
Bangka
Maniema
Weipa
Darling Range
Malaysia 30%
Bolivia 13%
Soviet Union 12%
Indonesia 10%
China 9%
Thailand 8%
Australia 5%
Others 13%
Tin
259,300 short tons
Australia 25%
Jamaica 18%
Suriname 9%
Guinea 7%
Soviet Union 6%
Guyana 5%
France 4%
Greece 4%
Hungary 4%
Yugoslavia 3%
United States 3%
Others 12%
Bauxite
72,117,500 short tons
Tin
Major producing areas
Other important areas
Bauxite
Encyclopaedia Britannica, Inc. 097
Flin Flon
Porcupine-Kirkland Lake-Noranda
Kimberley
Coeur d'Alene-Shoshone
Southeastern Missouri
St. Lawrence
Salt Lake-Wasatch
Eastern Tennessee
Western San Juan Mts.
Mexican Plateau
Cerro de Pasco
Bytom
Karabash
Salair
Altai
Southwestern Bulgaria
Trepca
Iglesias-Arbus
Aouli
Japan
Katanga
Tsumeb
Mount Isa
Broken Hill
United States 16%
Soviet Union 14%
Australia 11%
Canada 10%
Peru 6%
Mexico 5%
Yugoslavia 4%
Bulgaria 3%
Others 31%
Lead
3,816,300 short tons
Canada 21%
Soviet Union 12%
Australia 9%
United States 8%
Peru 7%
Mexico 5%
Japan 4%
Poland 4%
Others 30%
Zinc
6,174,400 short tons
Lead and zinc
Major producing areas
Other important areas
Encyclopaedia Britannica, Inc. 097
Kimberley
Porcupine-Kirkland Lake-Noranda
Timmins
Coeur d'Alene-Shoshone
Butte
Salt Lake-Wasatch
Black Hills
Bingham
Southern Arizona
Mexican Plateau
Western Peru
Southern Ural Mts.
Altai
Lena-Kolyma
Amur
Tarkwa
Witwatersrand
Kalgoorlie
Broken Hill
Bendigo-Ballarat
South Africa 62%
Soviet Union 17%
Canada 3%
United States 3%
Others 15%
Gold
41,663,800 troy ounces
Canada 15%
Soviet Union 14%
Mexico 13%
Peru 13%
United States 12%
Australia 7%
Japan 3%
Others 23%
Silver
299,671,800 troy ounces
Gold
Major producing areas
Other important areas
Silver
Encyclopaedia Britannica, Inc. 097

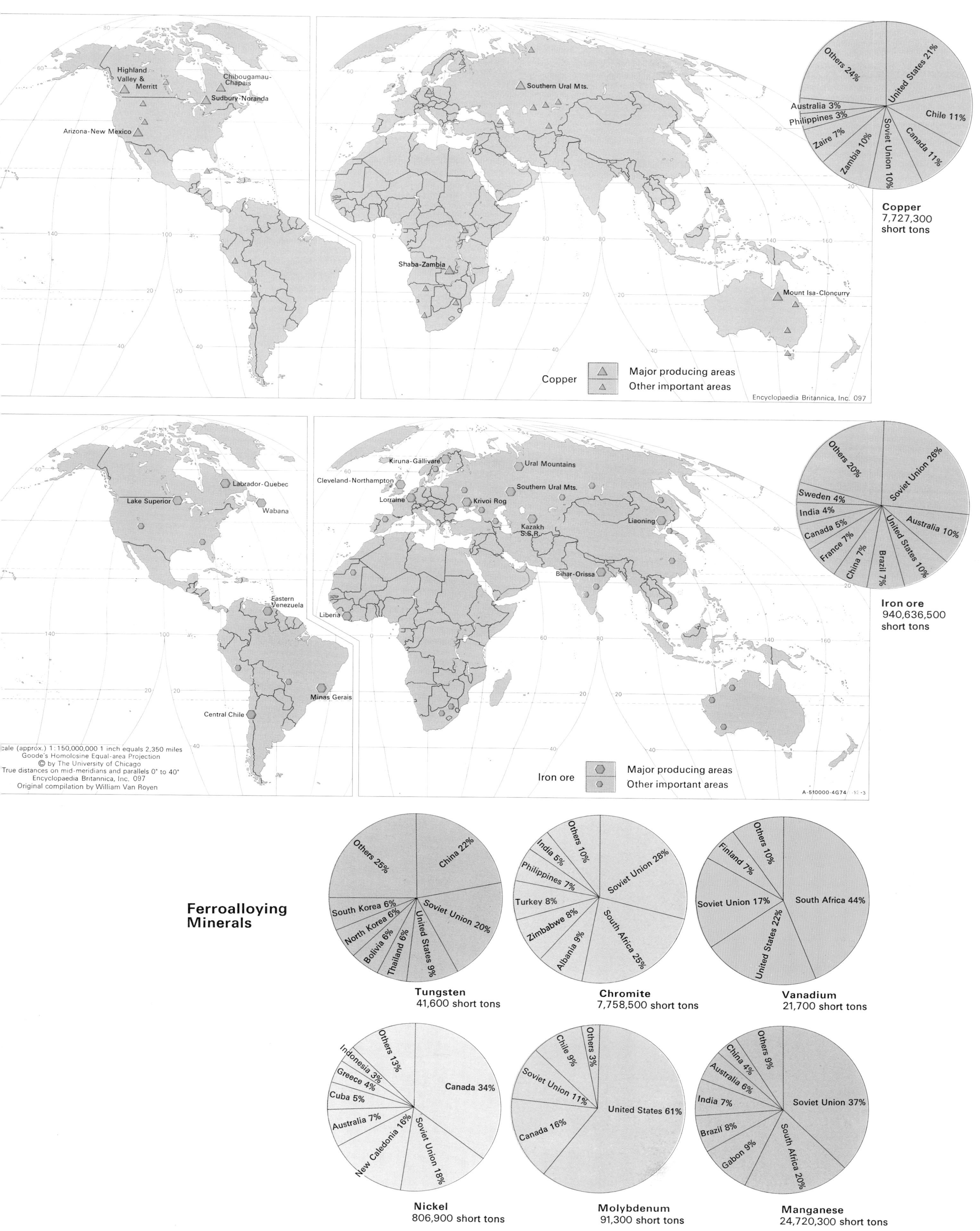
Highland Valley & Merritt
Chibougamau-Chapais
Sudbury-Noranda
Arizona-New Mexico
Southern Ural Mts.
Shaba-Zambia
Mount Isa-Cloncurry
Copper
Major producing areas
Other important areas
Encyclopaedia Britannica, Inc. 097
Others 24%
United States 21%
Chile 11%
Canada 11%
Soviet Union 10%
Zambia 10%
Zaire 7%
Philippines 3%
Australia 3%
Copper
7,727,300
short tons
Labrador-Quebec
Wabana
Lake Superior
Kiruna-Gällivare
Cleveland-Northampton
Lorraine
Krivoi Rog
Ural Mountains
Southern Ural Mts.
Kazakh S.S.R.
Liaoning
Bihar-Orissa
Eastern Venezuela
Liberia
Minas Gerais
Central Chile
Scale (approx.) 1:150,000,000 1 inch equals 2,350 miles
Goode's Homolosine Equal-area Projection
© by The University of Chicago
True distances on mid-meridians and parallels 0° to 40°
Encyclopaedia Britannica, Inc. 097
Original compilation by William Van Royen
Iron ore
Major producing areas
Other important areas
Others 20%
Soviet Union 26%
Australia 10%
United States 10%
Brazil 7%
China 7%
France 7%
Canada 5%
India 4%
Sweden 4%
Iron ore
940,636,500
short tons
Ferroalloying Minerals
Others 25%
China 22%
Soviet Union 20%
United States 9%
Thailand 6%
Bolivia 6%
North Korea 6%
South Korea 6%
Tungsten
41,600 short tons
Others 10%
Soviet Union 28%
South Africa 25%
Albania 9%
Zimbabwe 8%
Turkey 8%
Philippines 7%
India 5%
Chromite
7,758,500 short tons
Others 10%
South Africa 44%
United States 22%
Soviet Union 17%
Finland 7%
Vanadium
21,700 short tons
Others 13%
Canada 34%
Soviet Union 18%
New Caledonia 16%
Australia 7%
Cuba 5%
Greece 4%
Indonesia 3%
Nickel
806,900 short tons
Others 3%
United States 61%
Canada 16%
Soviet Union 11%
Chile 9%
Molybdenum
91,300 short tons
Others 9%
Soviet Union 37%
South Africa 20%
Gabon 9%
Brazil 8%
India 7%
Australia 6%
China 4%
Manganese
24,720,300 short tons

Energy Production and Consumption

Unit of measure is metric tons coal equivalent (m.t.c.e.)

Production

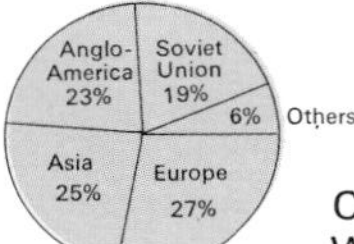

Coal and lignite
World total: 2,640,000,000

Soviet Union 18% · Africa 9% · Latin America 8% · Anglo-America 20% · Others 3% · Asia 42%

Crude petroleum
World total: 4,035,000,000

Europe 17% · Soviet Union 24% · Asia 6% · Others 4% · Anglo-America 49%

Natural gas
World total: 1,658,000,000

Asia 13% · Soviet Union 8% · Latin America 8% · Others 4% · Europe 29% · Anglo-America 38%

Primary electricity (hydro-, geothermal, and nuclear)
World total: 221,000,000

Table of equivalents

Coal, anthracite and bituminous	1 metric ton = 1.0 m.t.c.e.
Lignite	1 metric ton = 0.3 – 0.6 m.t.c.e.
Petroleum	1 metric ton = 1.5 m.t.c.e.
Natural gas	1,000 cubic meters = 1.33 m.t.c.e.
Hydro-, geothermal, and nuclear electricity	1.0 megawatt-hour = 0.125 m.t.c.e.

Potential energy of 1 metric ton of coal equals 28,000,000 B.T.U.

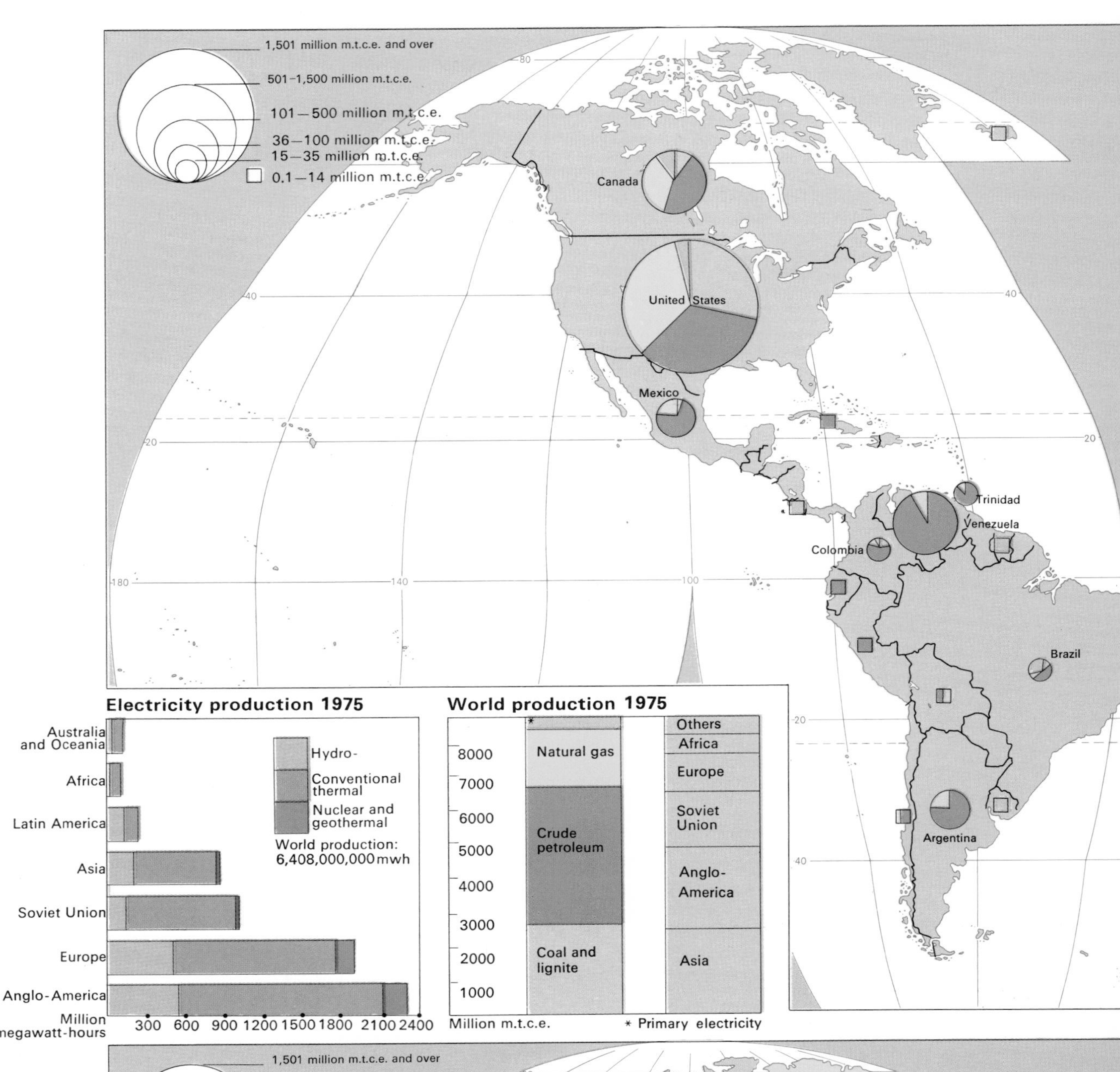

Consumption

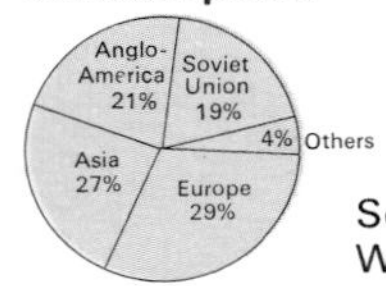

Solid fuels
World total: 2,626,000,000

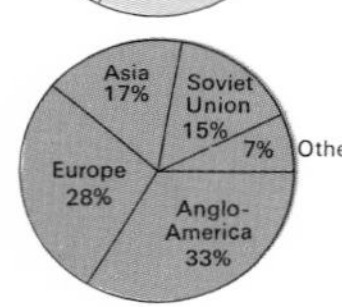

Liquid fuels
World total: 3,525,000,000

Europe 19% · Soviet Union 24% · 9% Others · Anglo-America 48%

Natural and manufactured gas
World total: 1,633,000,000

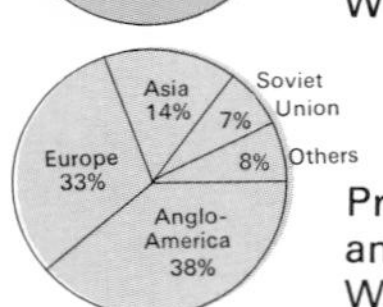

Primary electricity (hydro-, geothermal, and nuclear)
World total: 221,000,000

Consumption totals exclude noncommercial fuels, fuels consumed by vessels engaged in international trade, and nonfuel petroleum products.

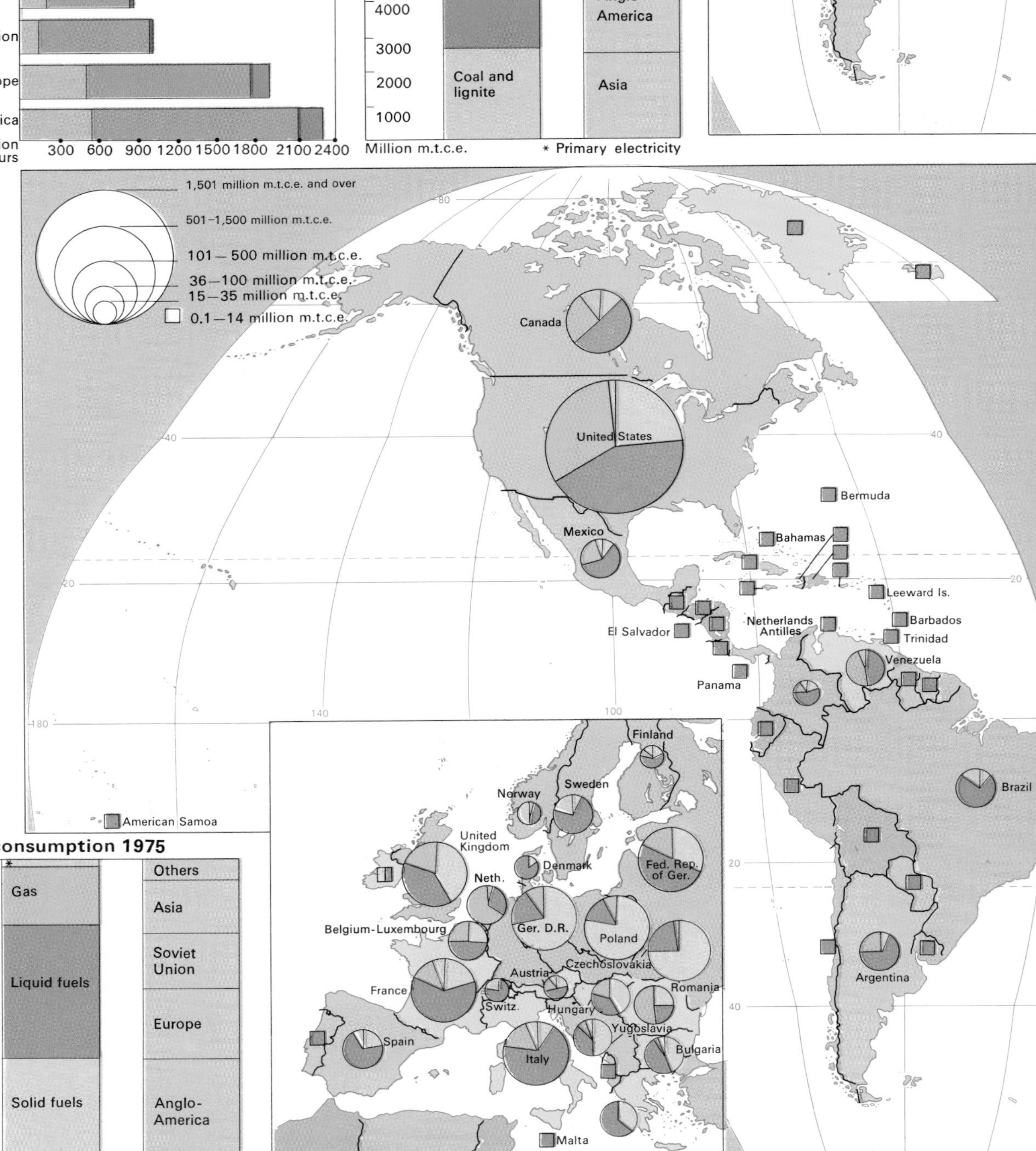

Per capita consumption

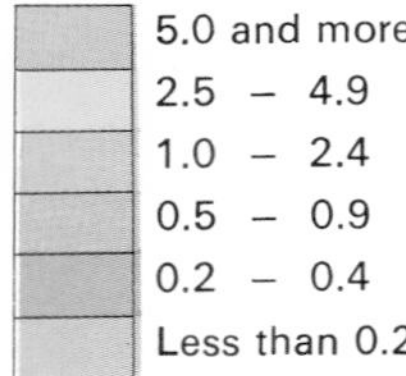

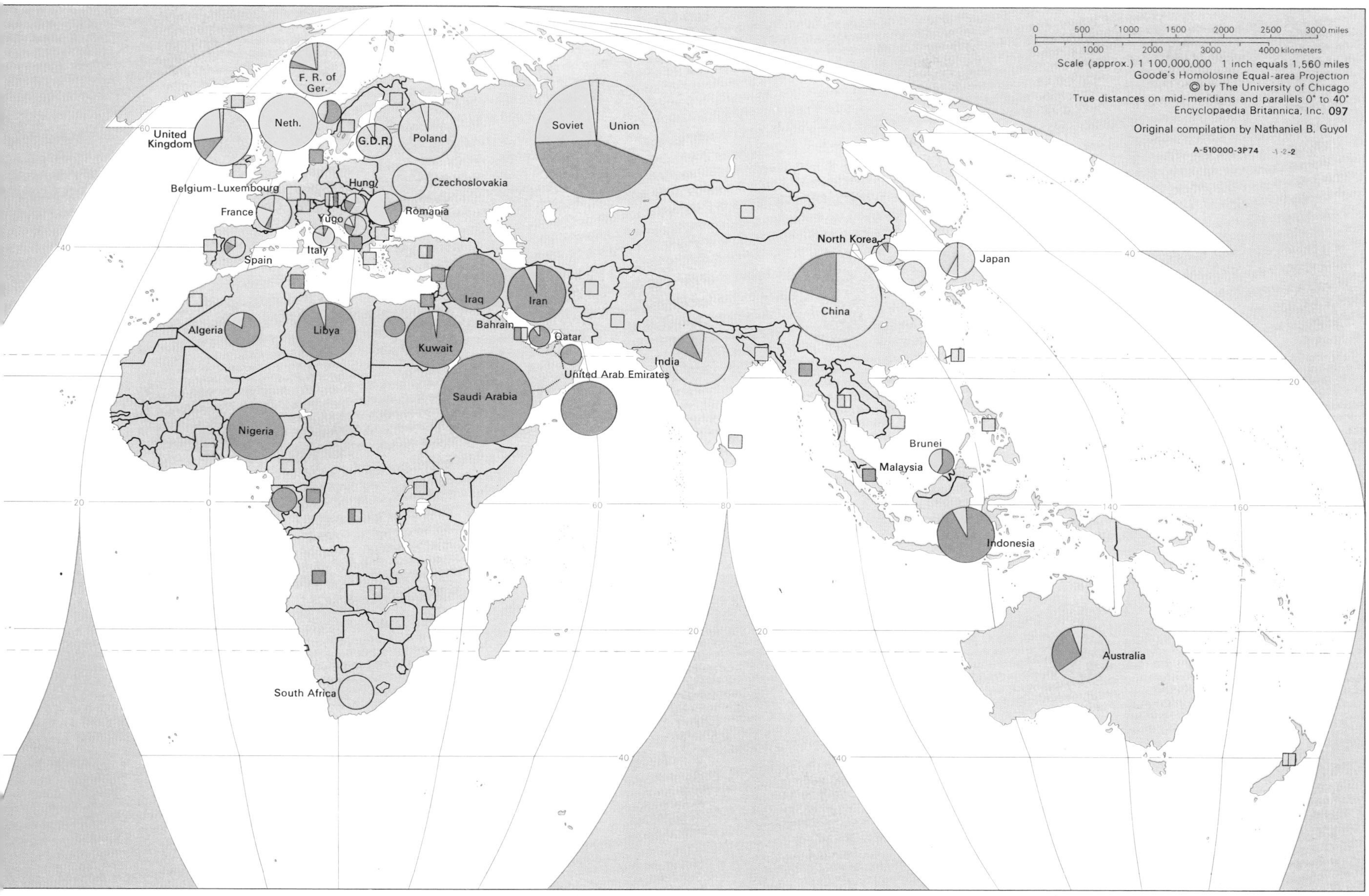

0 500 1000 1500 2000 2500 3000 miles
0 1000 2000 3000 4000 kilometers
Scale (approx.) 1:100,000,000 1 inch equals 1,560 miles
Goode's Homolosine Equal-area Projection
© by The University of Chicago
True distances on mid-meridians and parallels 0° to 40°
Encyclopaedia Britannica, Inc. 097
Original compilation by Nathaniel B. Guyol
A-510000-3P74

F. R. of Ger.
Neth.
United Kingdom
G.D.R.
Poland
Soviet Union
Belgium-Luxembourg
Hung.
Czechoslovakia
France
Yugo.
Romania
Italy
Spain
North Korea
Japan
Iraq
Iran
Algeria
Libya
Bahrain
Qatar
Kuwait
China
India
United Arab Emirates
Saudi Arabia
Nigeria
Brunei
Malaysia
Indonesia
Australia
South Africa

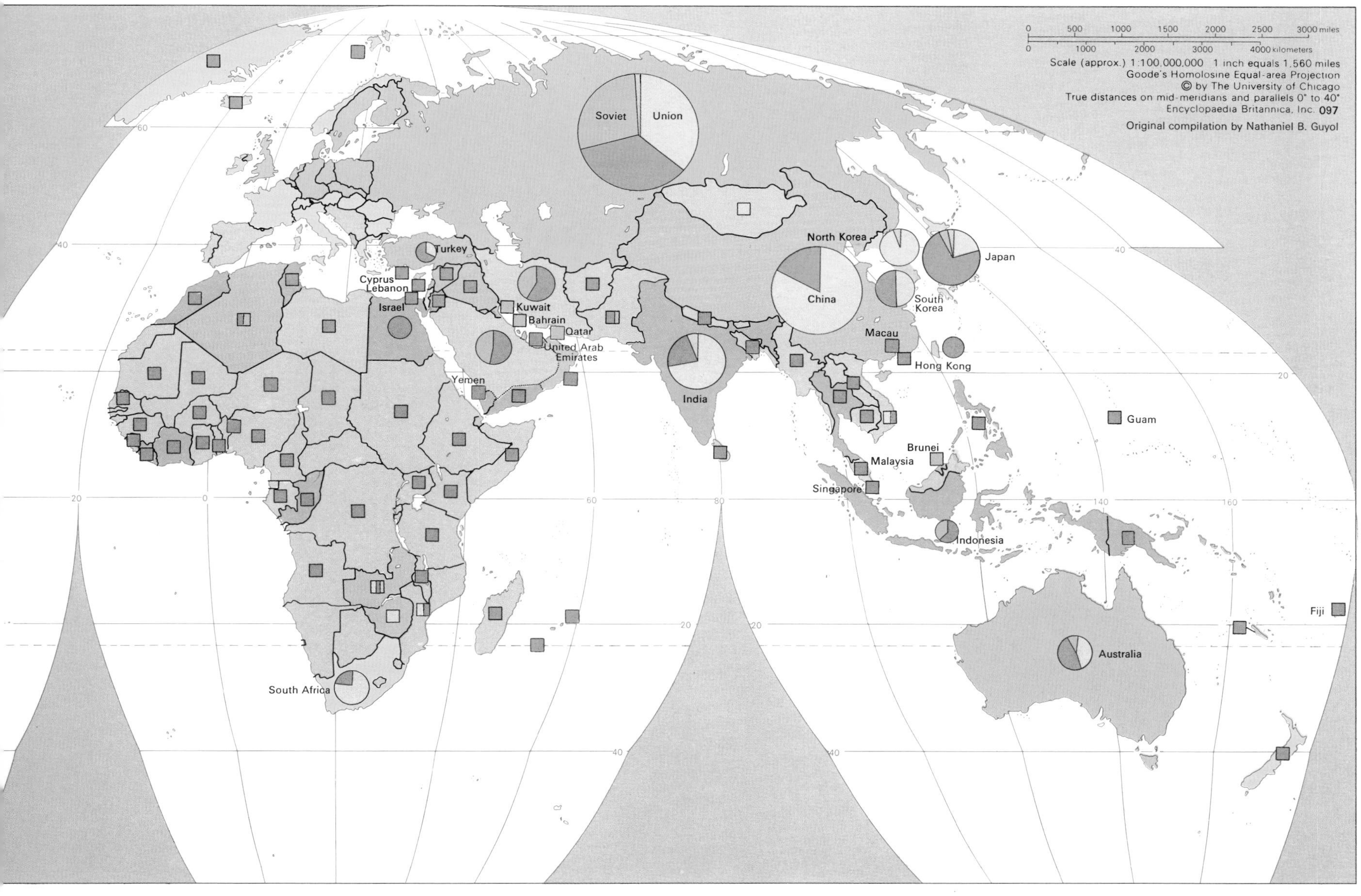

0 500 1000 1500 2000 2500 3000 miles
0 1000 2000 3000 4000 kilometers
Scale (approx.) 1:100,000,000 1 inch equals 1,560 miles
Goode's Homolosine Equal-area Projection
© by The University of Chicago
True distances on mid-meridians and parallels 0° to 40°
Encyclopaedia Britannica, Inc. 097
Original compilation by Nathaniel B. Guyol

Soviet Union
North Korea
Japan
Turkey
Cyprus
Lebanon
Israel
Kuwait
Bahrain
Qatar
United Arab Emirates
China
South Korea
Macau
Hong Kong
Yemen
India
Guam
Brunei
Malaysia
Singapore
Indonesia
Fiji
Australia
South Africa

Gross National Product

Total per country at market price In U.S. $000,000	Number of countries
84,000 and more	13
42,000–83,999	9
14,000–41,999	21
4,667–13,999	23
2,334–4,666	16
Less than 2,334	101
No data available	

Per capita In U.S. dollars	
■ 3,720 and more	34
▮▮ 1,860–3,719	24
◗ 620–1,859	42
▲ 207–619	51
❤ 104–206	26
● Less than 104	6

International Trade

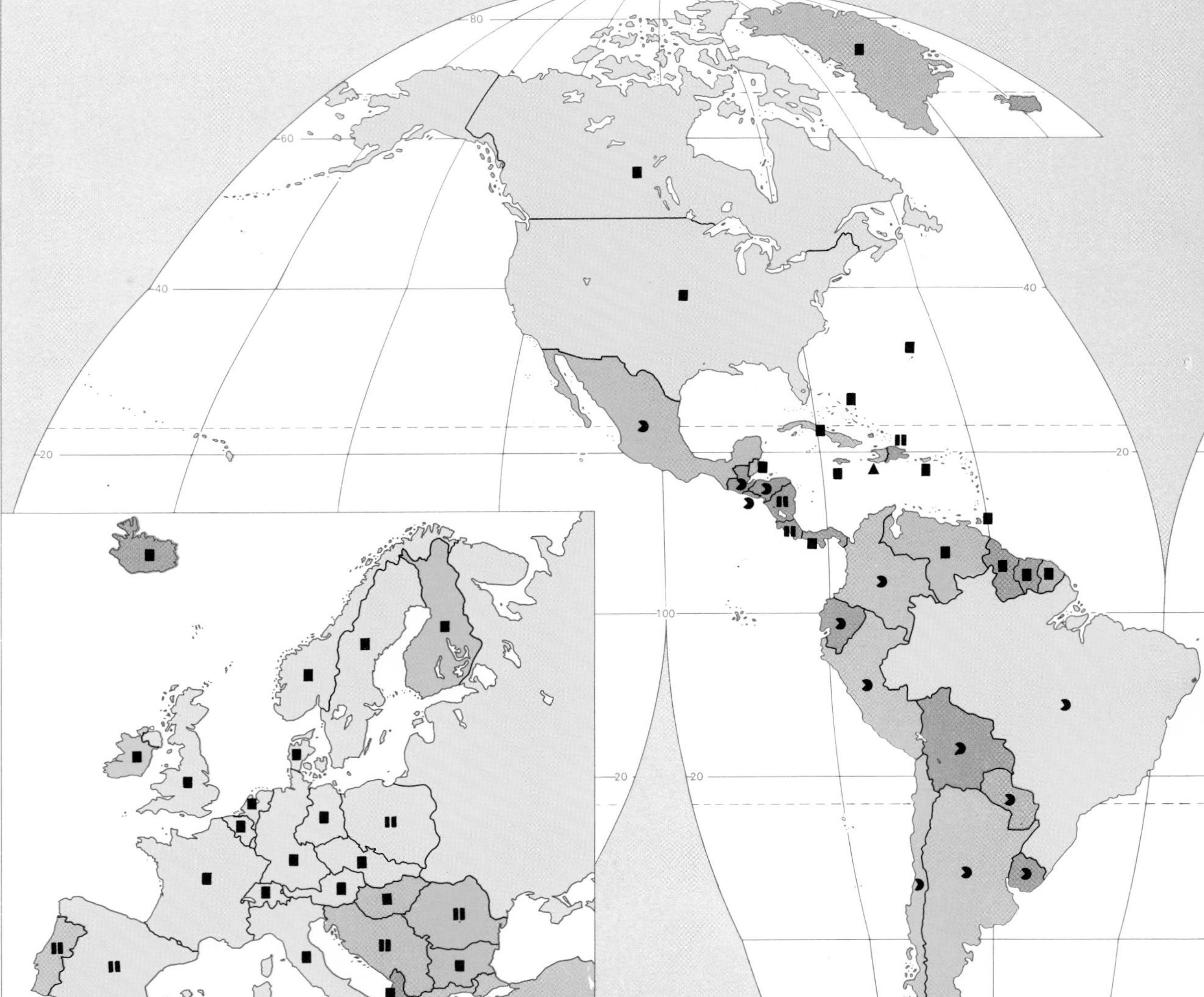

Total per country In U.S. $000,000	Number of countries
15,174 and more	25
7,587–15,173	19
2,529–7,586	22
844–2,528	31
423–843	19
Less than 423	41
No data available	

Per capita In U.S. dollars	
■ 702 and more	60
▮▮ 351–701	18
◗ 117–350	39
▲ 40–116	24
❤ 22–39	8
● Less than 22	9

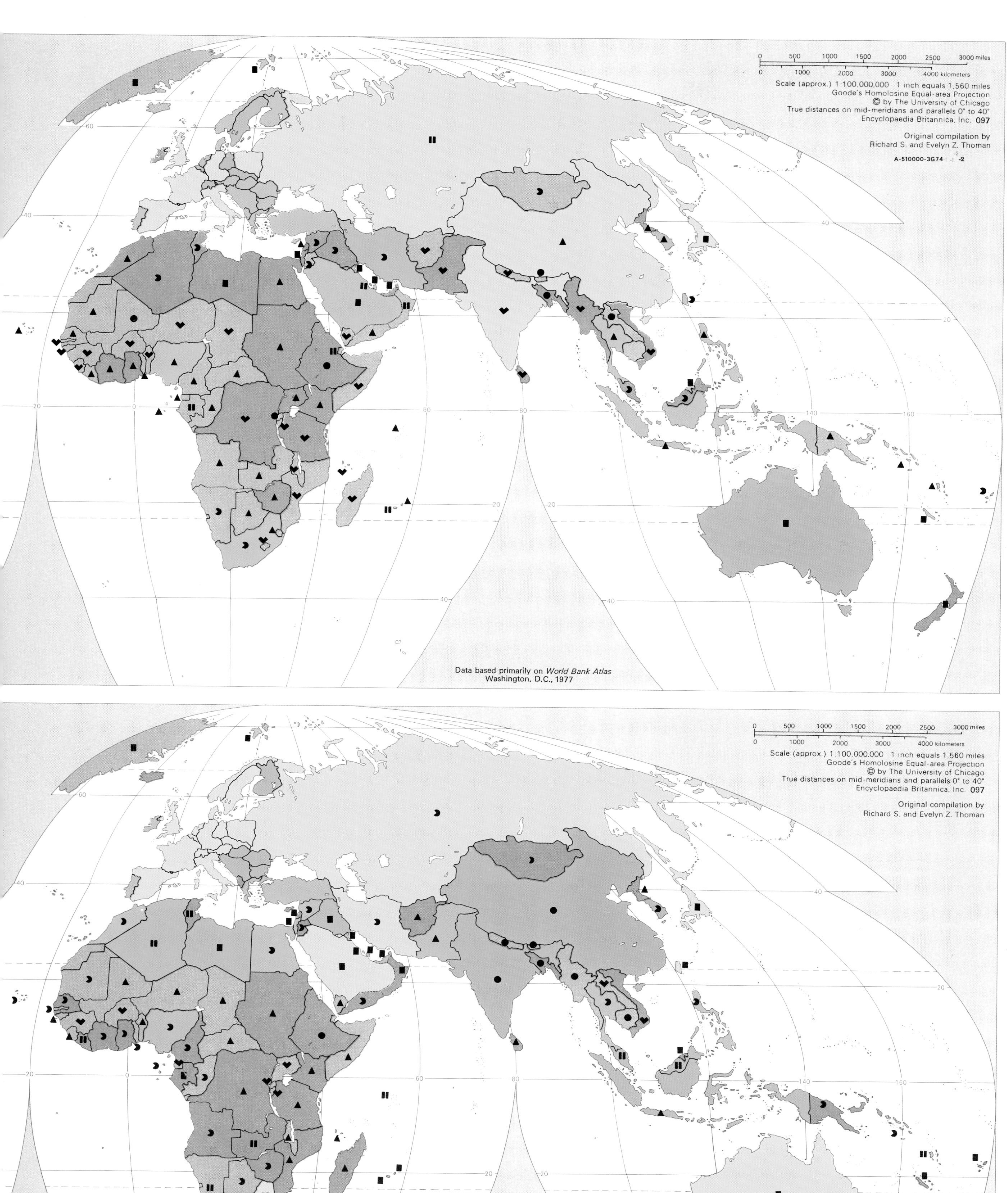

0 500 1000 1500 2000 2500 3000 miles
0 1000 2000 3000 4000 kilometers
Scale (approx.) 1:100,000,000 1 inch equals 1,560 miles
Goode's Homolosine Equal-area Projection
© by The University of Chicago
True distances on mid-meridians and parallels 0° to 40°
Encyclopaedia Britannica, Inc. 097
Original compilation by
Richard S. and Evelyn Z. Thoman
A-510000-3G74 -2
Data based primarily on World Bank Atlas
Washington, D.C., 1977
0 500 1000 1500 2000 2500 3000 miles
0 1000 2000 3000 4000 kilometers
Scale (approx.) 1:100,000,000 1 inch equals 1,560 miles
Goode's Homolosine Equal-area Projection
© by The University of Chicago
True distances on mid-meridians and parallels 0° to 40°
Encyclopaedia Britannica, Inc. 097
Original compilation by
Richard S. and Evelyn Z. Thoman
Data based primarily on 1977 Statistical Yearbook
United Nations, New York, 1978

Intercontinental Air Connections

Scale (approx.) 1:70,000,000 1 inch equals 1100 miles
Center: 45° North Latitude, 10° East Longitude
Briesemeister Elliptical Equal-area Projection
Adapted by permission from the American Geographical Society
Encyclopaedia Britannica, Inc. 087
A-510000-4D74 -1-2-1

Great Circle Distances

	Statute miles	Kilo-meters
Beirut to Belgrade	1,107	1,782
Lagos	2,784	4,481
Paris	1,980	3,186
Rome	1,377	2,216
Cairo to Colombo	3,524	5,671
London	2,192	3,528
Moscow	1,808	2,910
Teheran	1,214	1,954
Caracas to Guatemala City	1,609	2,590
Las Palmas	3,540	5,696
Madrid	4,349	6,999
Miami	1,361	2,190
Copenhagen to Anchorage	4,310	6,935
Montreal	3,604	5,799
Sondre Stromfjord	2,129	3,427
Tel Aviv-Yafo	1,953	3,143
Dakar to Geneva	2,567	4,132
Madrid	1,964	3,161
New York	3,800	6,115
Recife	1,980	3,186
Honolulu to Brisbane	4,694	7,554
Los Angeles	2,551	4,106
Manila	5,292	8,515
Tokyo	3,846	6,189
Karachi to Addis Ababa	2,167	3,486
Athens	2,684	4,320
Cairo	2,210	3,556
Nairobi	2,713	4,367
Lima to Kingston	2,069	3,330
Miami	2,619	4,215
New York	3,642	5,861
Panama City	1,465	2,357
Lisbon to Luanda	3,588	5,774
Montreal	3,261	5,248
Paramaribo	3,679	5,920
Rio de Janeiro	4,791	7,710
London to Bermuda	3,428	5,514
Chicago	3,941	6,343
Los Angeles	5,439	8,753
Tunis	1,137	1,830
Los Angeles to Panama City	3,007	4,840
Papeete	4,105	6,607
Paris	5,659	9,108
Tokyo	5,473	8,808
Mexico City to Chicago	1,689	2,718
Lima	2,635	4,241
Vancouver	2,448	3,940
Washington, D.C.	1,879	3,024
Moscow to Amsterdam	1,330	2,142
Delhi	2,709	4,360
Peking	3,606	5,802
Teheran	1,545	2,486
New York to Bogotá	2,481	3,993
Brasília	4,238	6,821
London	3,440	5,536
Rome	4,263	6,861
Panama City to Brasília	2,754	4,433
Houston	1,772	2,852
Los Angeles	3,007	4,840
Quito	640	1,029
Paris to Colombo	5,292	8,516
Fort-de-France	4,255	6,848
Kano	2,559	4,115
Moscow	1,541	2,479
Rio de Janeiro to London	5,746	9,248
Monrovia	2,994	4,818
New York	4,800	7,725
Panama City	3,289	5,293
Rome to Delhi	3,685	5,929
Lagos	2,490	4,007
Nairobi	3,353	5,396
Tel Aviv-Yafo	1,416	2,280
Sydney to Auckland	1,341	2,159
Manila	3,888	6,258
Pago Pago	2,733	4,399
Singapore	3,912	6,296
Tokyo to Anchorage	3,457	5,563
San Francisco	5,145	8,280
Seattle	4,790	7,708
Wake	1,983	3,192

The routes shown represent the generalized pattern of principal world air flights between continents showing points of departure and arrival. Connecting flights between points on the same continent are not shown. The data are taken primarily from the *Official Airline Guide*, Worldwide edition (R. H. Donnelley Corp.), and *Air Distances Manual* (International Air Transport Association).

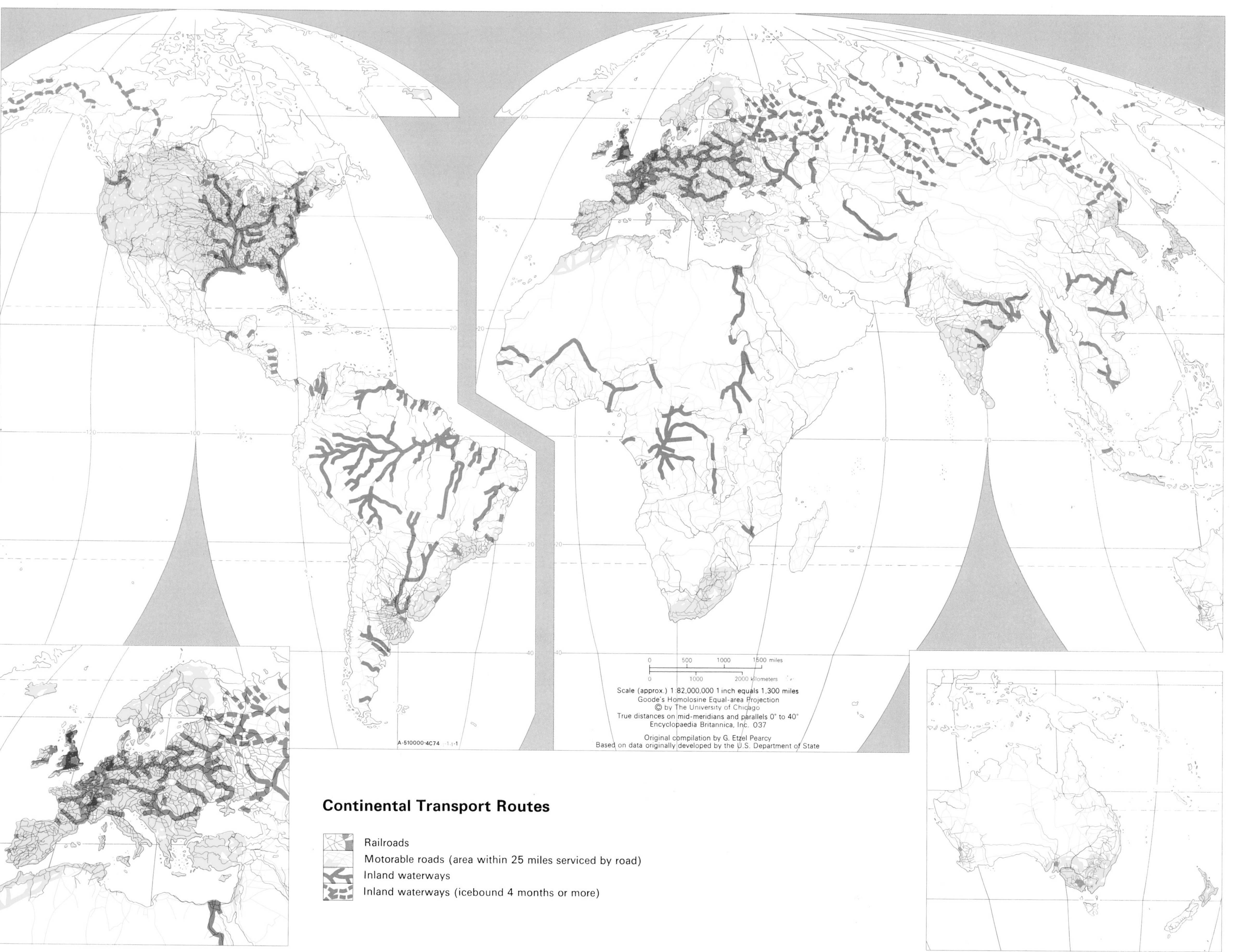
0 500 1000 1500 miles
0 1000 2000 kilometers
Scale (approx.) 1:82,000,000 1 inch equals 1,300 miles
Goode's Homolosine Equal-area Projection
© by The University of Chicago
True distances on mid-meridians and parallels 0° to 40°
Encyclopaedia Britannica, Inc. 037
Original compilation by G. Etzel Pearcy
Based on data originally developed by the U.S. Department of State
Continental Transport Routes
Railroads
Motorable roads (area within 25 miles serviced by road)
Inland waterways
Inland waterways (icebound 4 months or more)

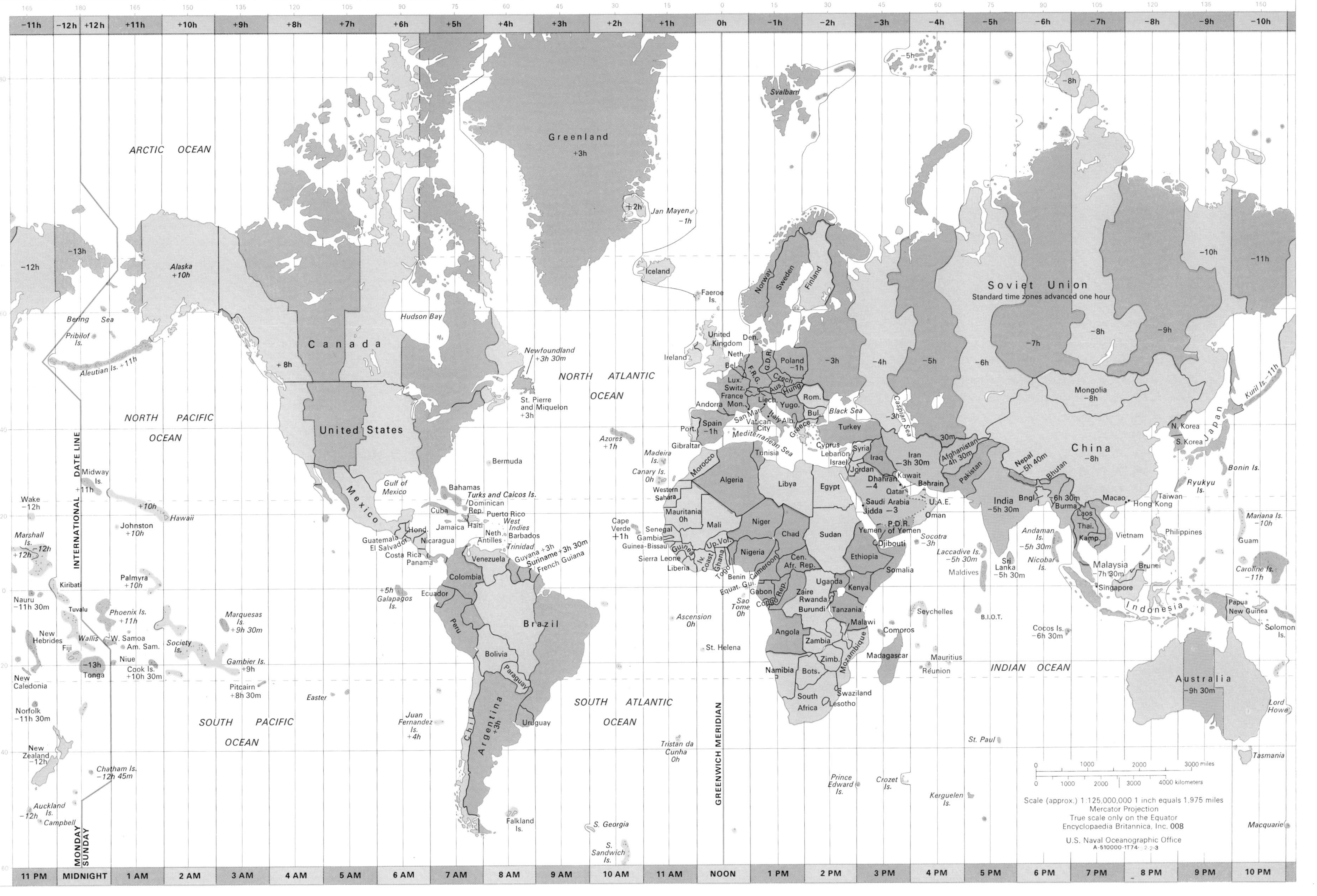

Time Zones

- Standard time zone of even-numbered hours from Greenwich time
- Standard time zone of odd-numbered hours from Greenwich time
- Time varies from the standard time zone by half an hour
- Time varies from the standard time zone by other than half an hour
- "Solar time", all watches set daily to midnight at sundown.

h m — hours, minutes

The standard time zone system, fixed by international agreement and by law in each country, is based on a theoretical division of the globe into 24 zones of 15° longitude each. The mid-meridian of each zone fixes the hour for the entire zone. The zero time zone extends 7½° east and 7½° west of the Greenwich meridian, 0° longitude. Since the earth rotates toward the east, time zones to the west of Greenwich are earlier, to the east, later.

Plus and minus hours at the top of the map are added to or subtracted from local time to find Greenwich time. Local standard time can be determined for any area in the world by adding one hour for each time zone counted in an easterly direction from one's own, or by subtracting one hour for each zone counted in a westerly direction. To separate one day from the next, the 180th meridian has been designated as the international date line. On both sides of the line the time of day is the same, but west of the line it is one day later than it is to the east.

Countries that adhere to the international zone system adopt the zone applicable to their location. Some countries, however, establish time zones based on political boundaries, or adopt the time zone of a neighboring unit. For all or part of the year some countries also advance their time by one hour, thereby utilizing more daylight hours each day.

Climate Graphs

Each graph below shows temperature and rainfall at a weather station that was selected to illustrate one of the climate regions described in the legend at the right. The weather stations are keyed by number to the maps. The elements of the graphs are identified in the sample graph at the top, with a temperature scale in degrees Fahrenheit and Celsius (Centigrade), and a precipitation scale in inches and millimeters.

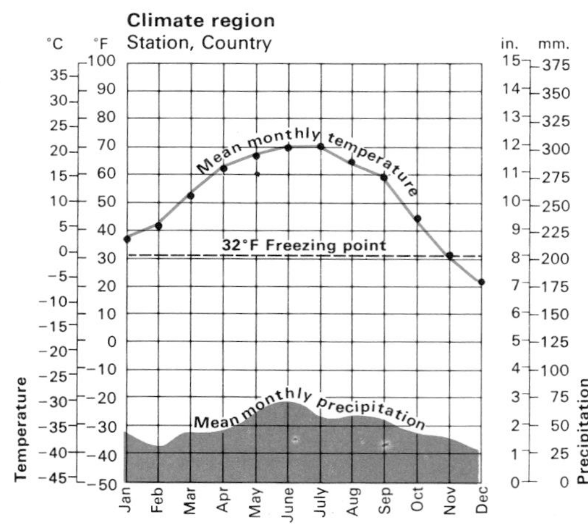

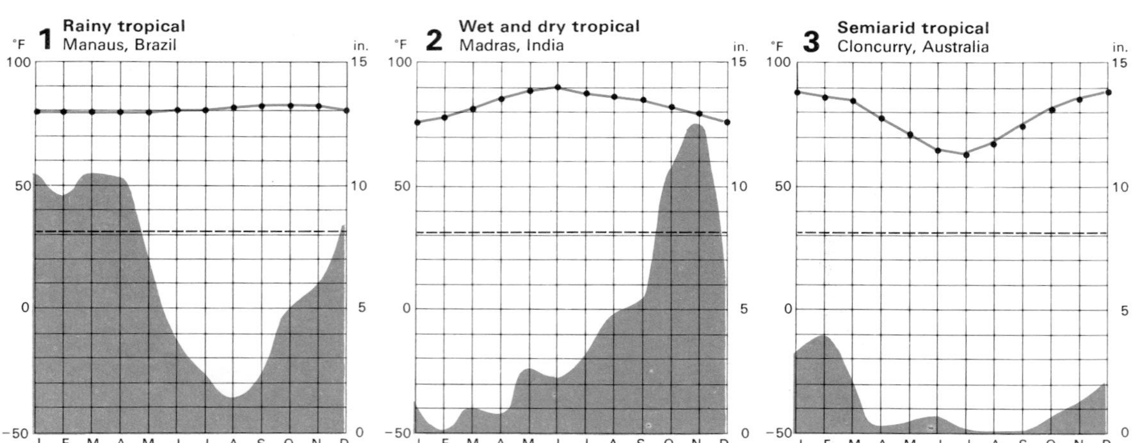

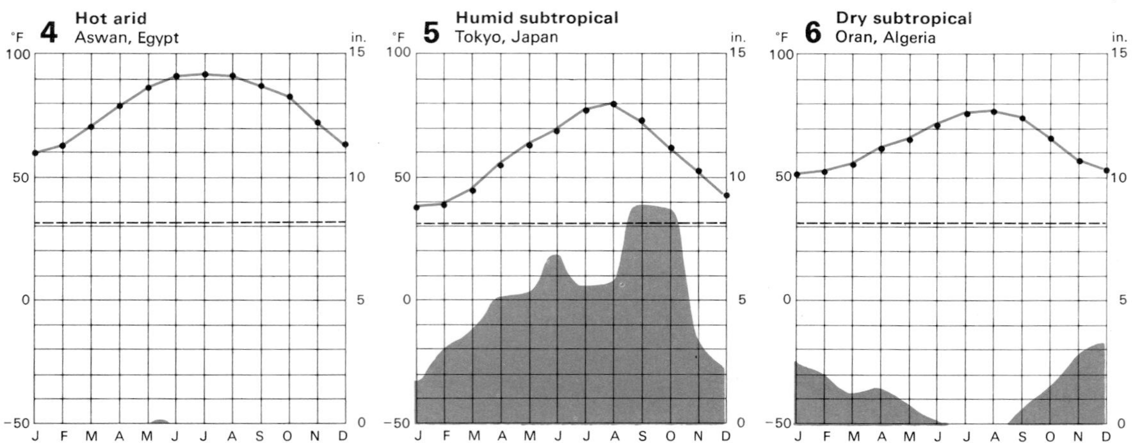

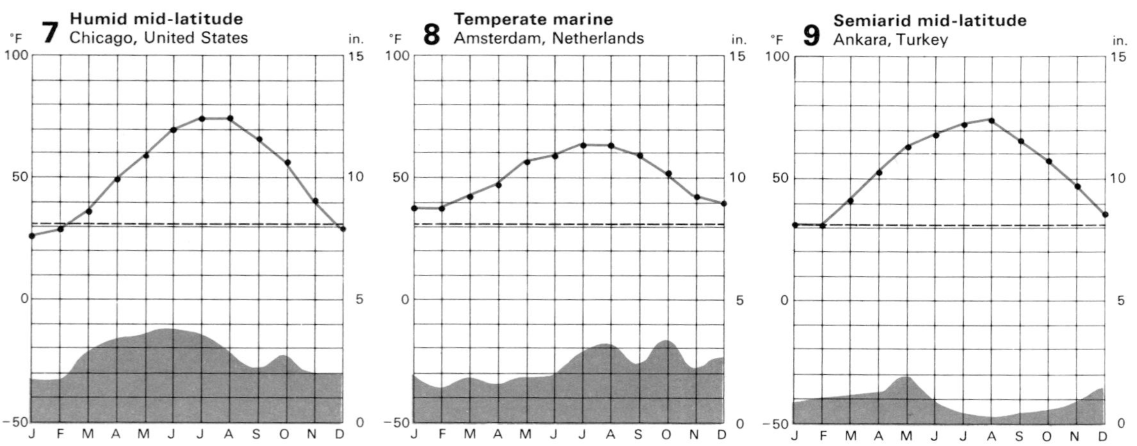

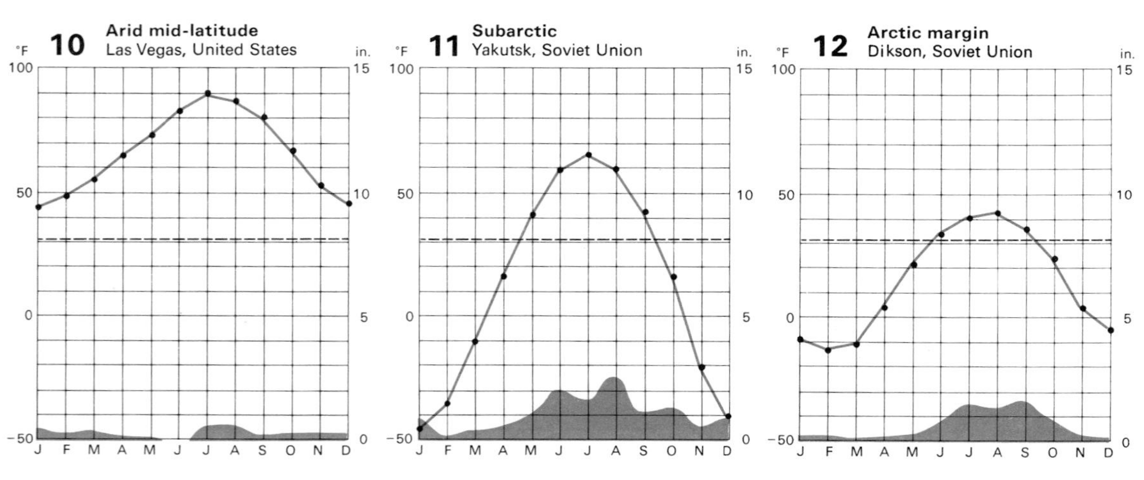

Climate Regions

- **Rainy tropical** At most, one or two dry months; all months warm or hot
- **Wet and dry tropical** A well-developed dry season with one or two rainy seasons; all months warm or hot
- **Semiarid tropical** Light precipitation, rapid evaporation; all months warm or hot
- **Hot arid** Negligible precipitation, rapid evaporation; all months warm or hot
- **Humid subtropical** Precipitation in all seasons with maximum in summer; long warm summers, cool winters
- **Dry subtropical** Hot dry summers; cool, moderately rainy winters
- **Humid mid-latitude** Precipitation in all seasons with maximum in summer; warm or hot summers, cold winters
- **Temperate marine** Numerous rainy days in all seasons with moderate total precipitation, higher precipitation in highland areas; warm summers, cool winters
- **Semiarid mid-latitude** Light precipitation; warm or hot summers, cool or cold winters
- **Arid mid-latitude** Extremely light precipitation; warm or hot summers, cool or cold winters
- **Subarctic** Light precipitation; short cool summers, long very cold winters
- **Arctic margin** Extremely light precipitation; very short cold summers, extremely long cold winters
- **High altitude** Climate varies with elevation, latitude, and exposure

Mean Annual Temperature

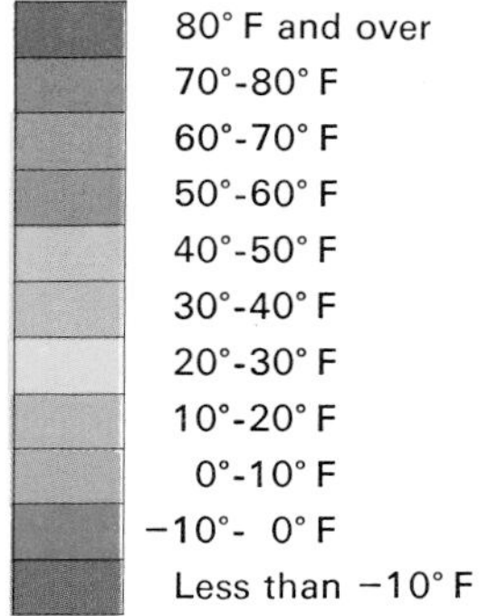

Mean Annual Precipitation

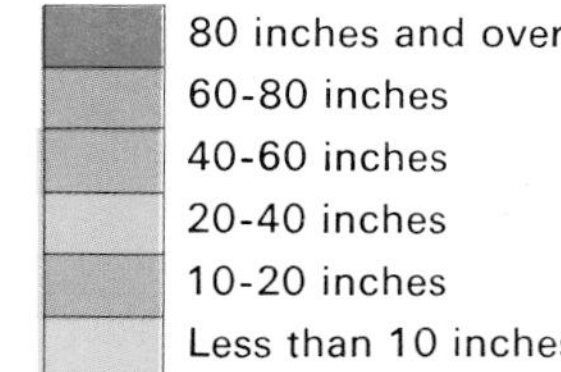

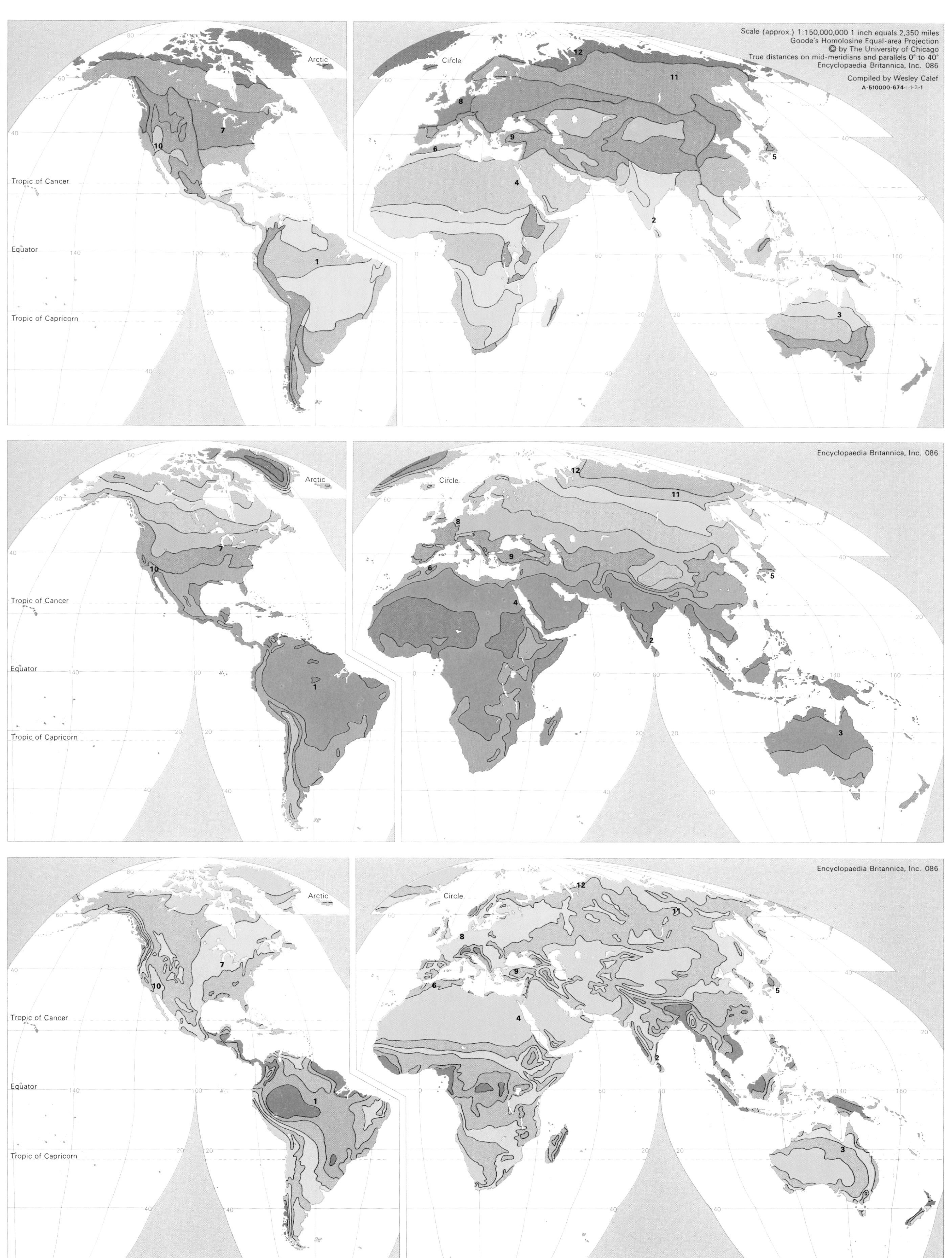

Scale (approx.) 1:150,000,000 1 inch equals 2,350 miles
Goode's Homolosine Equal-area Projection
© by The University of Chicago
True distances on mid-meridians and parallels 0° to 40°
Encyclopaedia Britannica, Inc. 086
Compiled by Wesley Calef
A-510000-674-1-2-1
Arctic
Circle
Tropic of Cancer
Equator
Tropic of Capricorn
Encyclopaedia Britannica, Inc. 086
Encyclopaedia Britannica, Inc. 086

Surface Configuration

Smooth lands

- Level plains: nearly all slopes gentle; local relief less than 100 ft. (30 m.)
- Irregular plains: majority of slopes gentle; local relief 100-300 ft. (30-90 m.)

Broken lands

- Tablelands and plateaus: majority of slopes gentle, with the gentler slopes on the uplands; local relief more than 300 ft. (90 m.)
- Hill-studded plains: majority of slopes gentle, with the gentler slopes in the lowlands; local relief 300-1,000 ft. (90-300 m.)
- Mountain-studded plains: majority of slopes gentle, with the gentler slopes in the lowlands; local relief more than 1,000 ft. (300 m.)

Rough lands

- Hill lands: steeper slopes predominate; local relief less than 1,000 ft. (300 m.)
- Mountains: steeper slopes predominate; local relief 1,000-5,000 ft. (300-1,500 m.)
- Mountains of great relief: steeper slopes predominate; local relief more than 5,000 ft. (1,500 m.)

Other surfaces

- Ice caps: permanent ice
- Maximum extent of glaciation

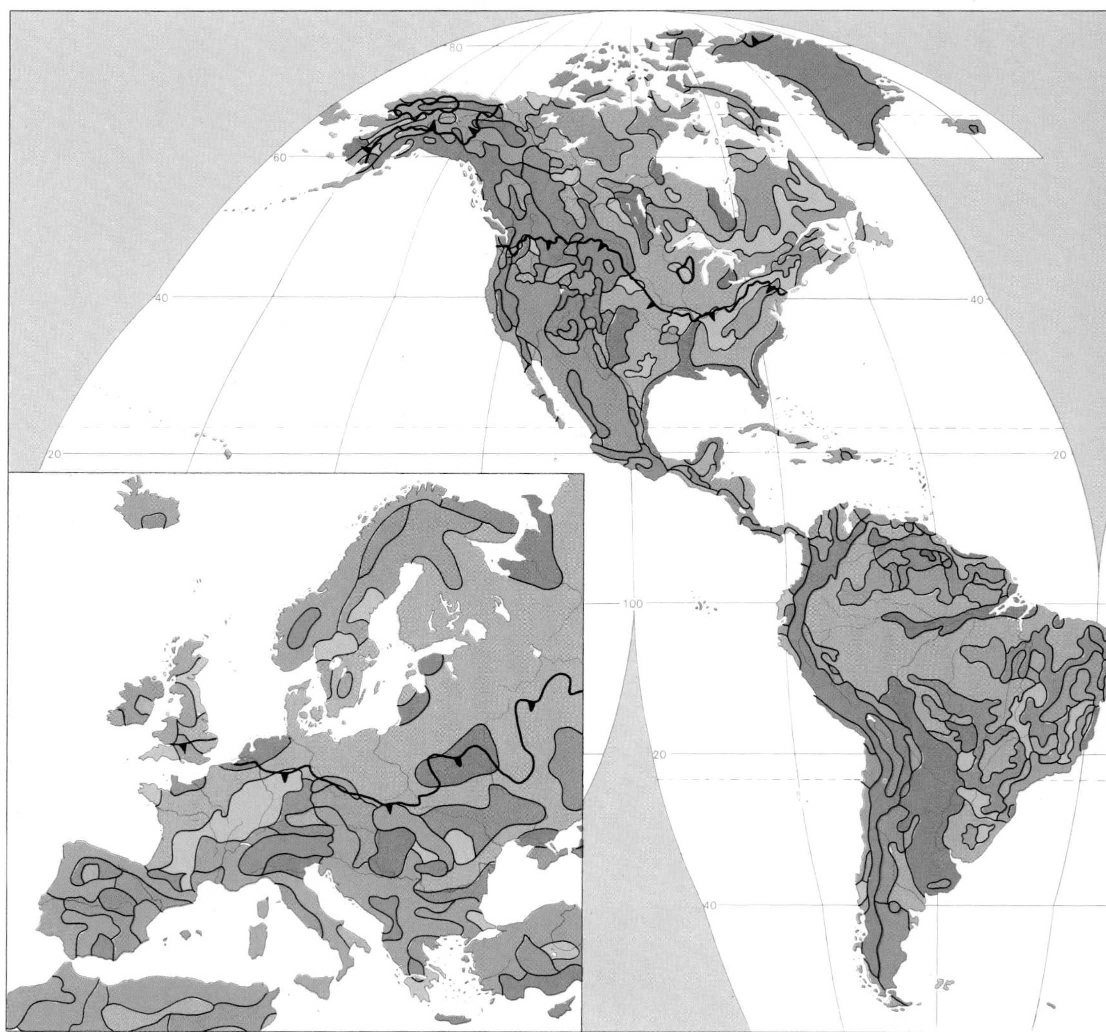

Earth Structure and Tectonics

- Precambrian stable shield areas
- Exposed Precambrian rock
- Paleozoic and Mesozoic flat-lying sedimentary rocks
- Principal Paleozoic and Mesozoic folded areas
- Cenozoic sedimentary rocks
- Principal Cenozoic folded areas
- Lava plateaus
- Major trends of folding

Geologic time chart

Precambrian—from formation of the earth (at least 4 billion years ago) to 600 million years ago

Paleozoic—from 600 million to 200 million years ago

Mesozoic—from 200 million to 70 million years ago

Cenozoic—from 70 million years ago to present time

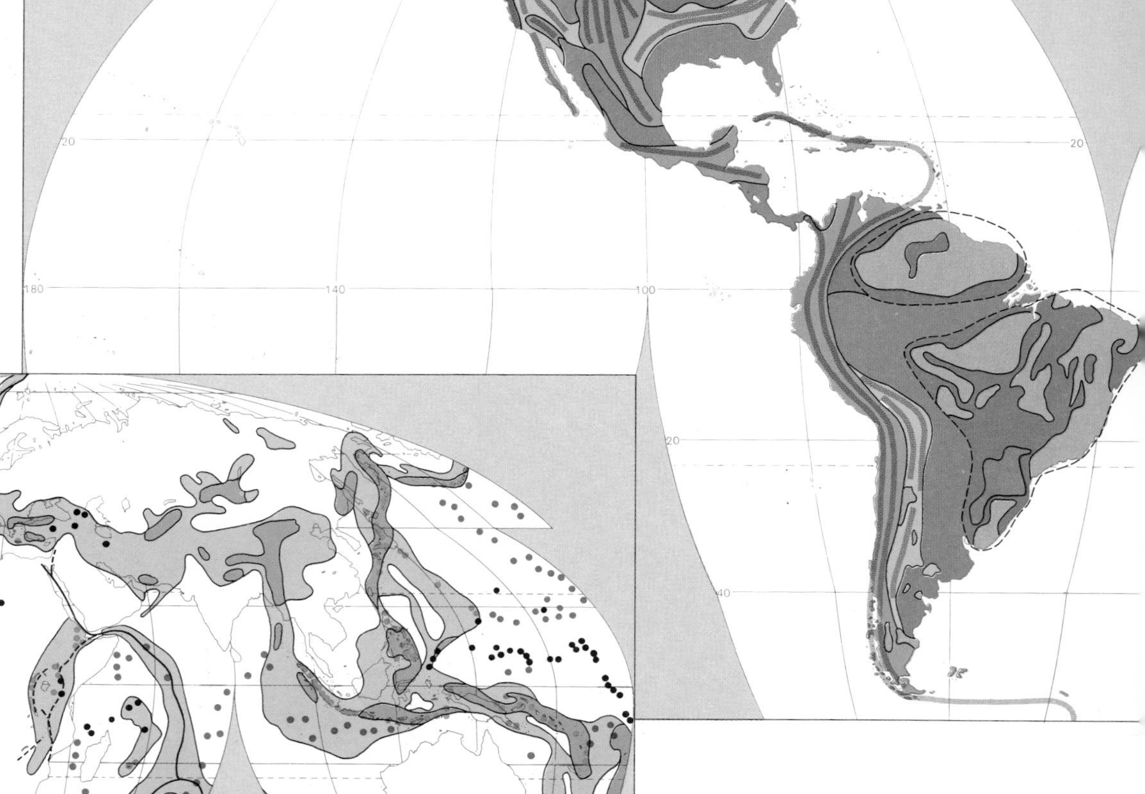

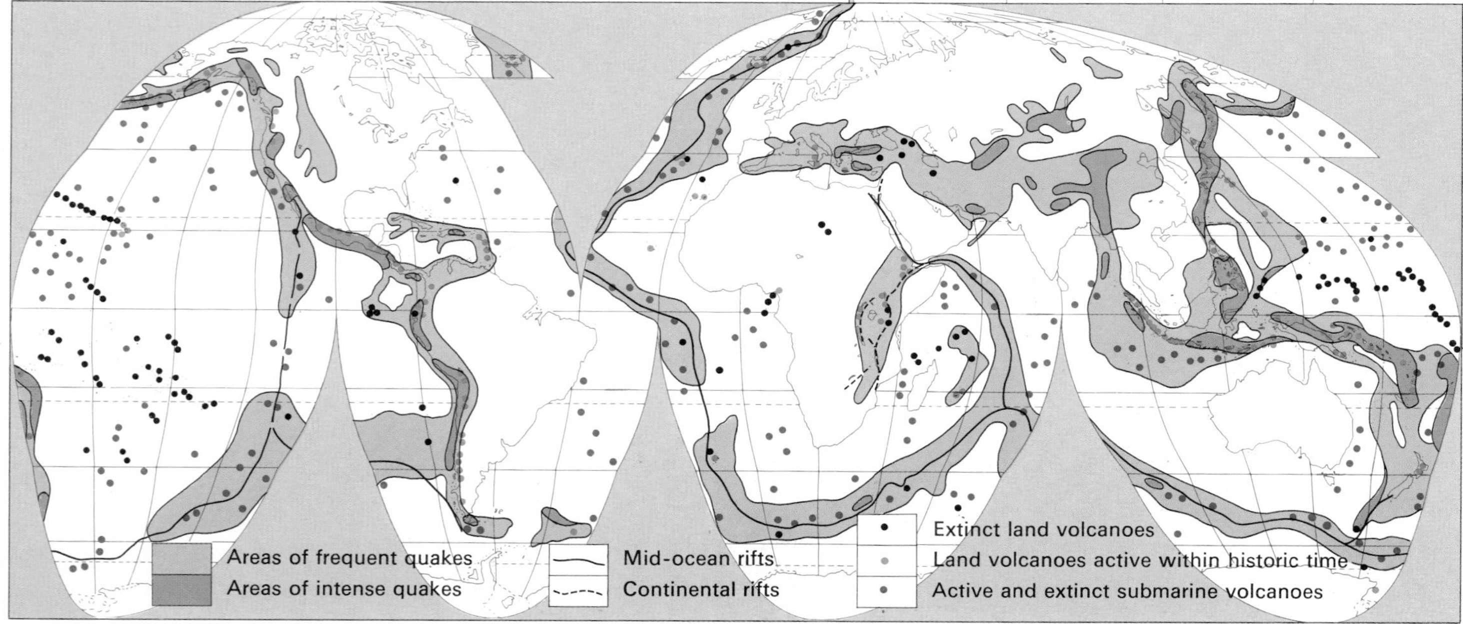

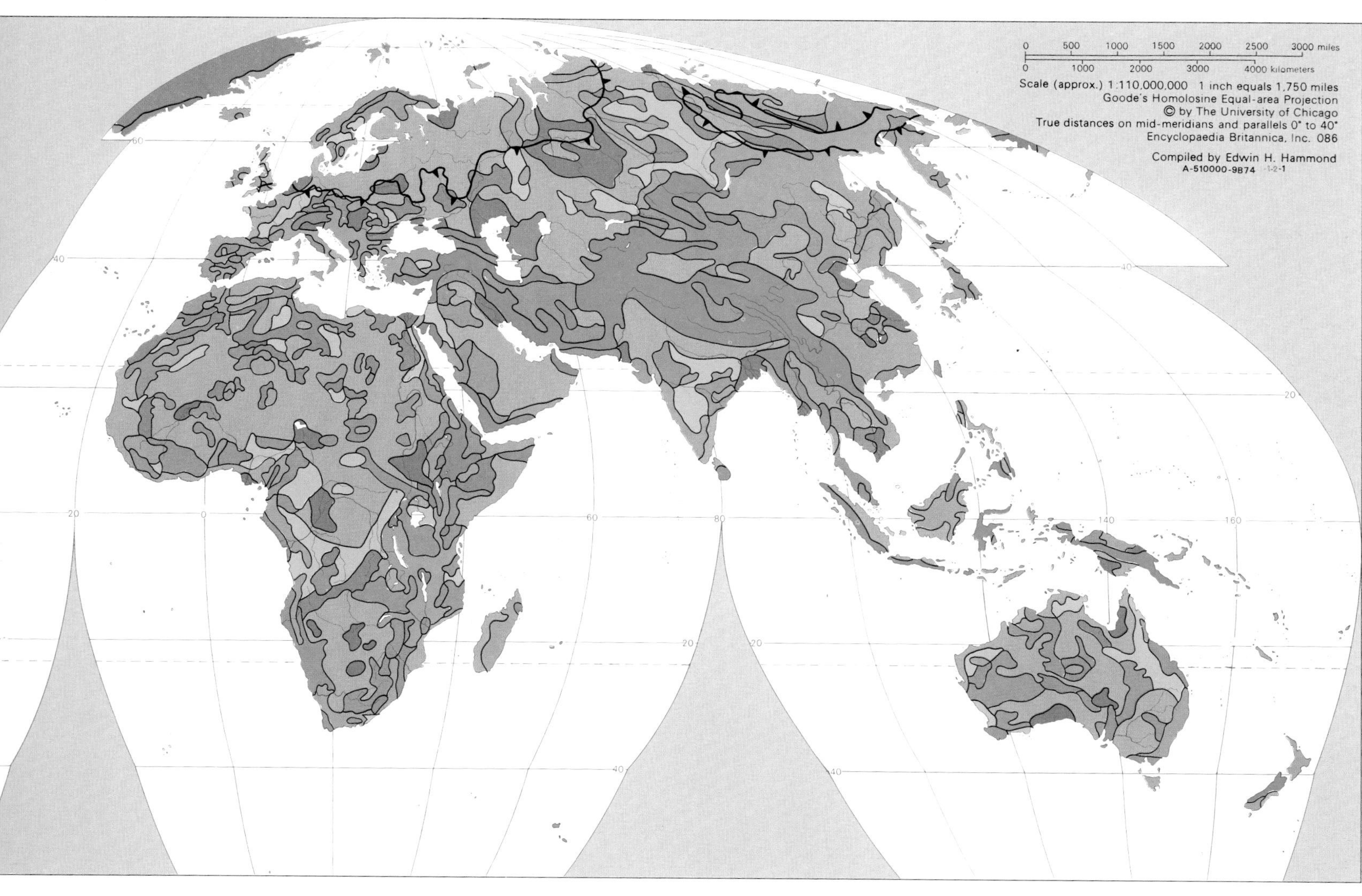

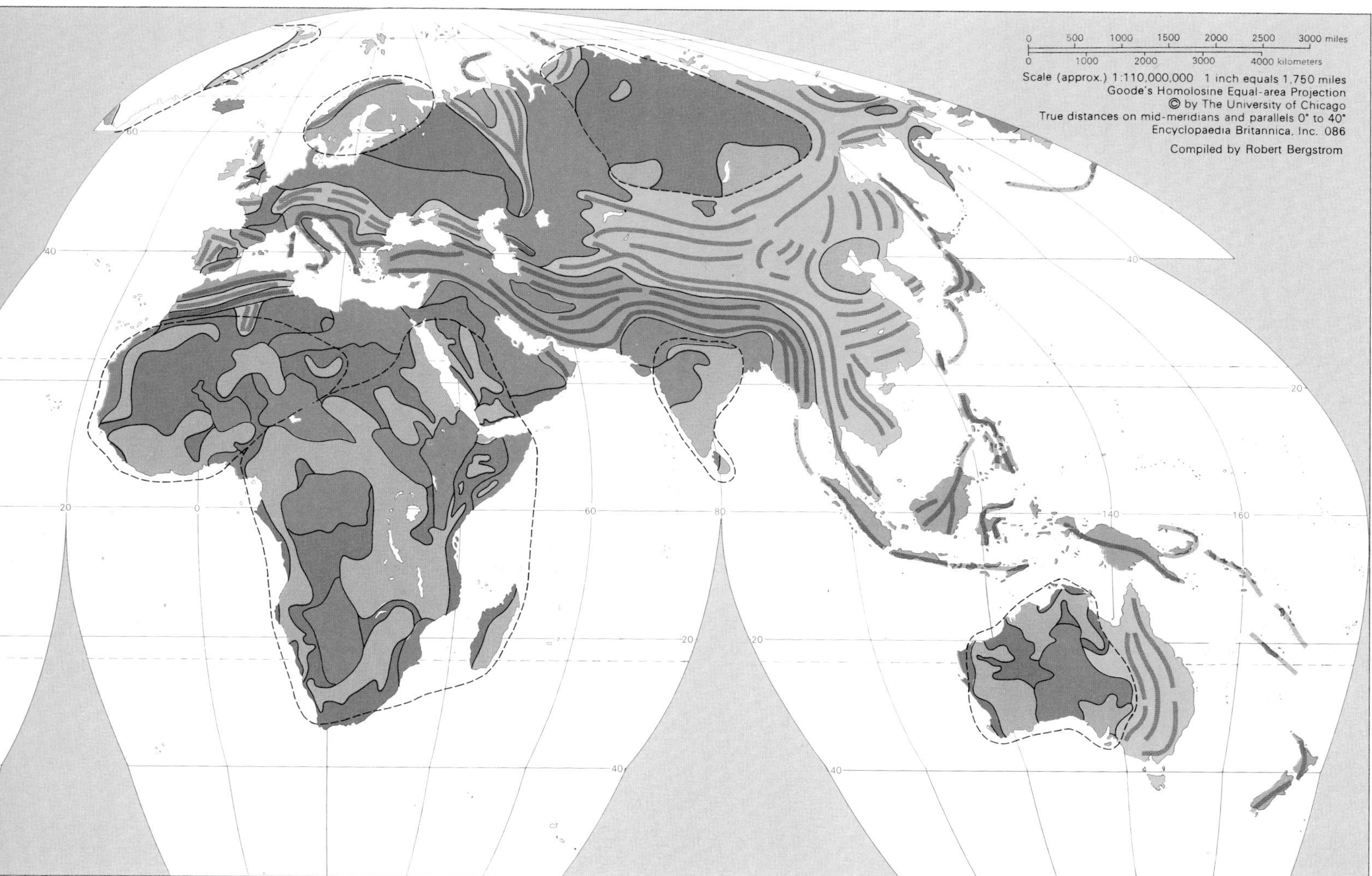

Development of the earth's structure

The earth is in process of constant transformation. Movements in the hot, dense interior of the earth result in folding and fracture of the crust and transfer of molten material to the surface. As a result, large structures such as mountain ranges, volcanoes, lava plateaus, and rift valleys are created. The forces that bring about these structural changes are called *tectonic forces*.

The present continents have developed from stable nuclei, or *shields*, of ancient (Precambrian) rock. Erosive forces such as water, wind, and ice have worn away particles of the rock, depositing them at the edges of the shields, where they have accumulated and ultimately become sedimentary rock. Subsequently, in plaees, these extensive areas of flat-lying rock have been elevated, folded, or warped, by the action of tectonic forces, to form mountains. The shape of these mountains has been altered by later erosion. Where the forces of erosion have been at work for a long time, the mountains tend to have a low relief and rounded contours, like the Appalachians. Mountains more recently formed are high and rugged, like the Himalayas.

The map above depicts some of the major geologic structures of the earth and identifies them according to the period of their formation. A geologic time chart is included in the legend. The inset map shows the most important areas of earthquakes, rifts, and volcanic activity. Comparison of all the maps will show the close correlation between present-day mountain systems, recent (Cenozoic) mountain-building, and the areas of frequent earthquakes and active volcanoes.

Natural Vegetation

Broad-leaved evergreen vegetation
- Broad-leaved evergreen forest
- Broad-leaved evergreen shrub formation
- Scattered broad-leaved evergreen shrubs
- Scattered broad-leaved evergreen dwarf shrubs

Broad-leaved deciduous vegetation
- Broad-leaved deciduous forest
- Broad-leaved deciduous shrub formation
- Scattered broad-leaved deciduous shrubs
- Scattered broad-leaved deciduous dwarf shrubs

Coniferous vegetation
- Needle-leaved evergreen forest
- Scattered needle-leaved evergreen trees
- Needle-leaved deciduous forest

Mixed vegetation without grass
- Forest of broad-leaved evergreen and deciduous trees
- Forest of broad-leaved and needle-leaved evergreen trees
- Broad-leaved deciduous forests with broad-leaved evergreen shrubs
- Forest of broad-leaved deciduous and needle-leaved evergreen trees

Mixed vegetation with grass
- Grassland with scattered broad-leaved evergreen trees
- Grassland with broad-leaved evergreen shrubs
- Grassland with scattered broad-leaved deciduous trees
- Grassland with broad-leaved deciduous shrubs

Grassland, tundra, barren

- Grassland
- Patches of grass
- Lichens and grasses
- Lichens and mosses
- Barren

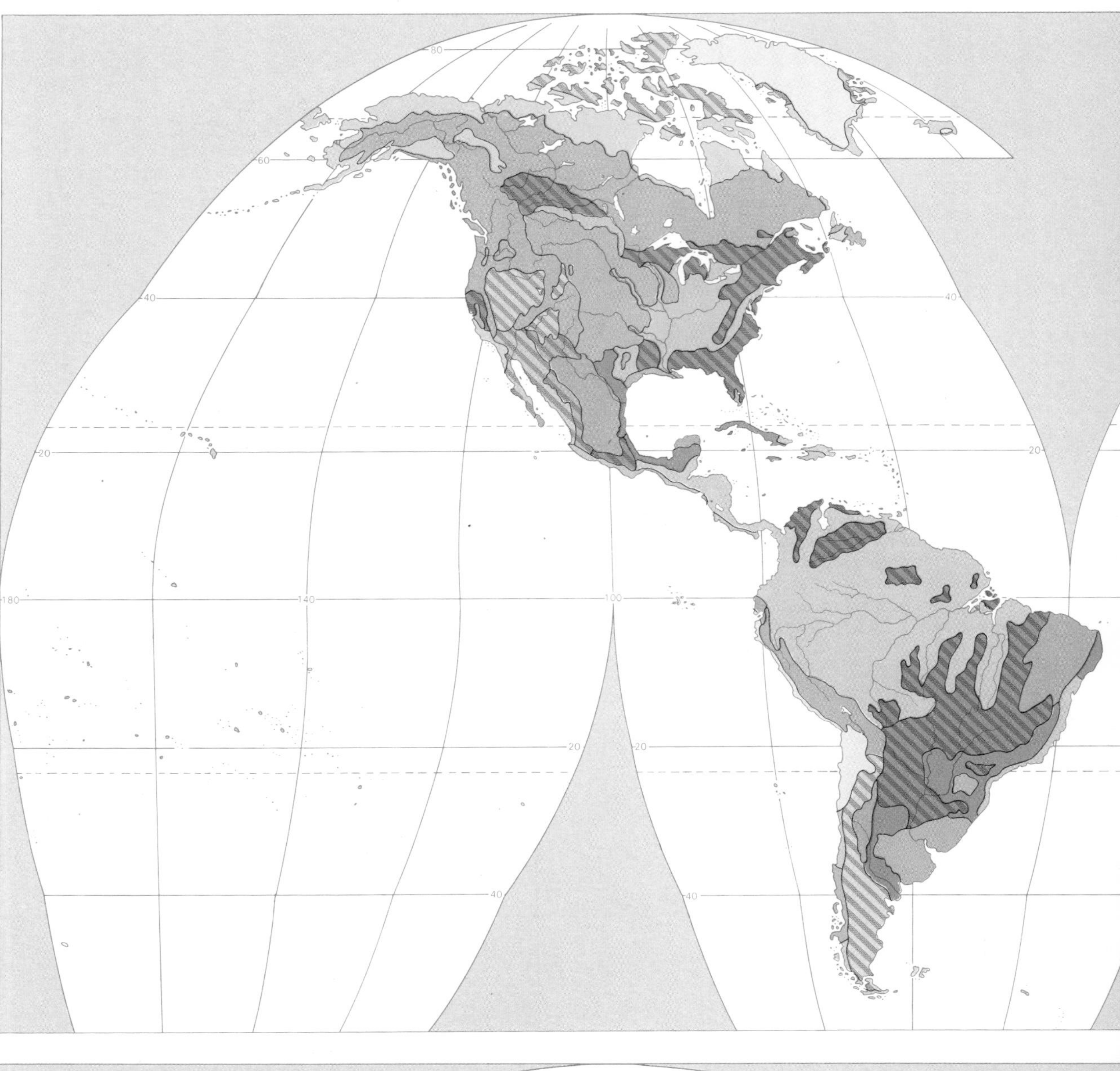

Soils

- Tundra soils of frigid climates; commonly with permanently frozen subsoil; supports dwarf shrubs, mosses, and lichens; some used for reindeer pasture
- Podzolic soils of humid, cool climates; covered with predominantly coniferous forest; some farming, mainly subsistence
- Podzolic soils of humid, temperate climates; originally covered with predominantly deciduous forest, much of it removed to accommodate extensive general farming, industry, and cities
- Podzolic soils of humid, warm climates; covered with coniferous or mixed forest; general farming
- Chernozemic soils of subhumid and semiarid, cool to tropical climates; supports mainly grasslands; extensive grain and livestock farming
- Latosolic soils of humid or wet-dry tropical and subtropical climates; supports forest or savanna; shifting cultivation with some plantation agriculture
- Grumusolic soils of humid to semiarid and temperate to tropical climates, with distinct wet and dry seasons; mainly grass-covered; livestock and grain farming
- Desertic soils of arid climates; includes many areas of shallow, stony soils; sparse cover of shrubs and grass, some suitable for grazing; fertile if irrigated; dry farming possible in some areas
- Mountain soils of all climates; shallow, stony; barren, grass-covered, or forested, depending on climate; includes many areas of other soils
- Alluvial soils of all climates; deposited by water in flood plains and deltas of rivers; intensive farming in most temperate and some tropical regions (many smaller areas not shown)
- Ice cap of polar regions

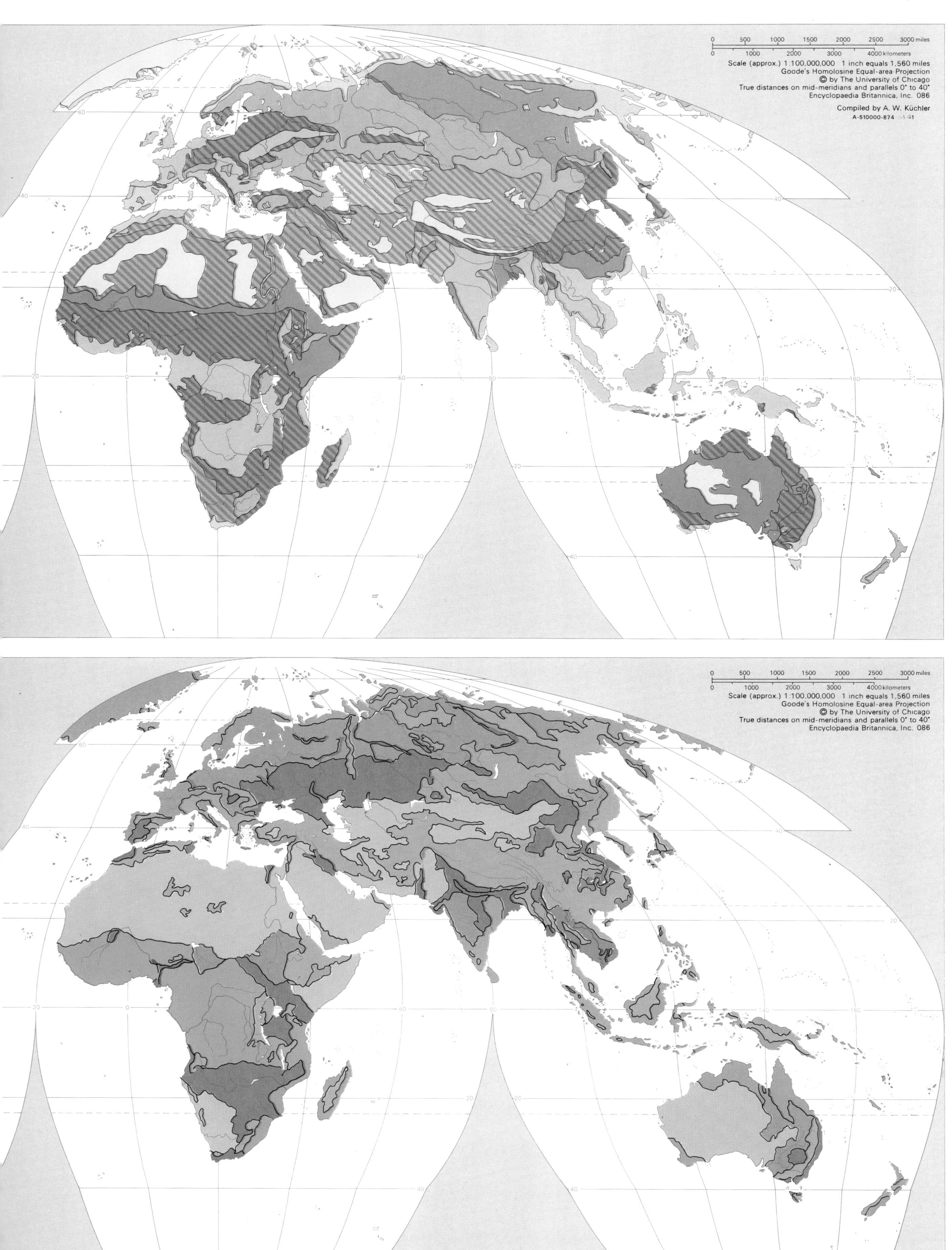
0 500 1000 1500 2000 2500 3000 miles
0 1000 2000 3000 4000 kilometers
Scale (approx.) 1:100,000,000 1 inch equals 1,560 miles
Goode's Homolosine Equal-area Projection
© by The University of Chicago
True distances on mid-meridians and parallels 0° to 40°
Encyclopaedia Britannica, Inc. 086
Compiled by A. W. Küchler
0 500 1000 1500 2000 2500 3000 miles
0 1000 2000 3000 4000 kilometers
Scale (approx.) 1:100,000,000 1 inch equals 1,560 miles
Goode's Homolosine Equal-area Projection
© by The University of Chicago
True distances on mid-meridians and parallels 0° to 40°
Encyclopaedia Britannica, Inc. 086

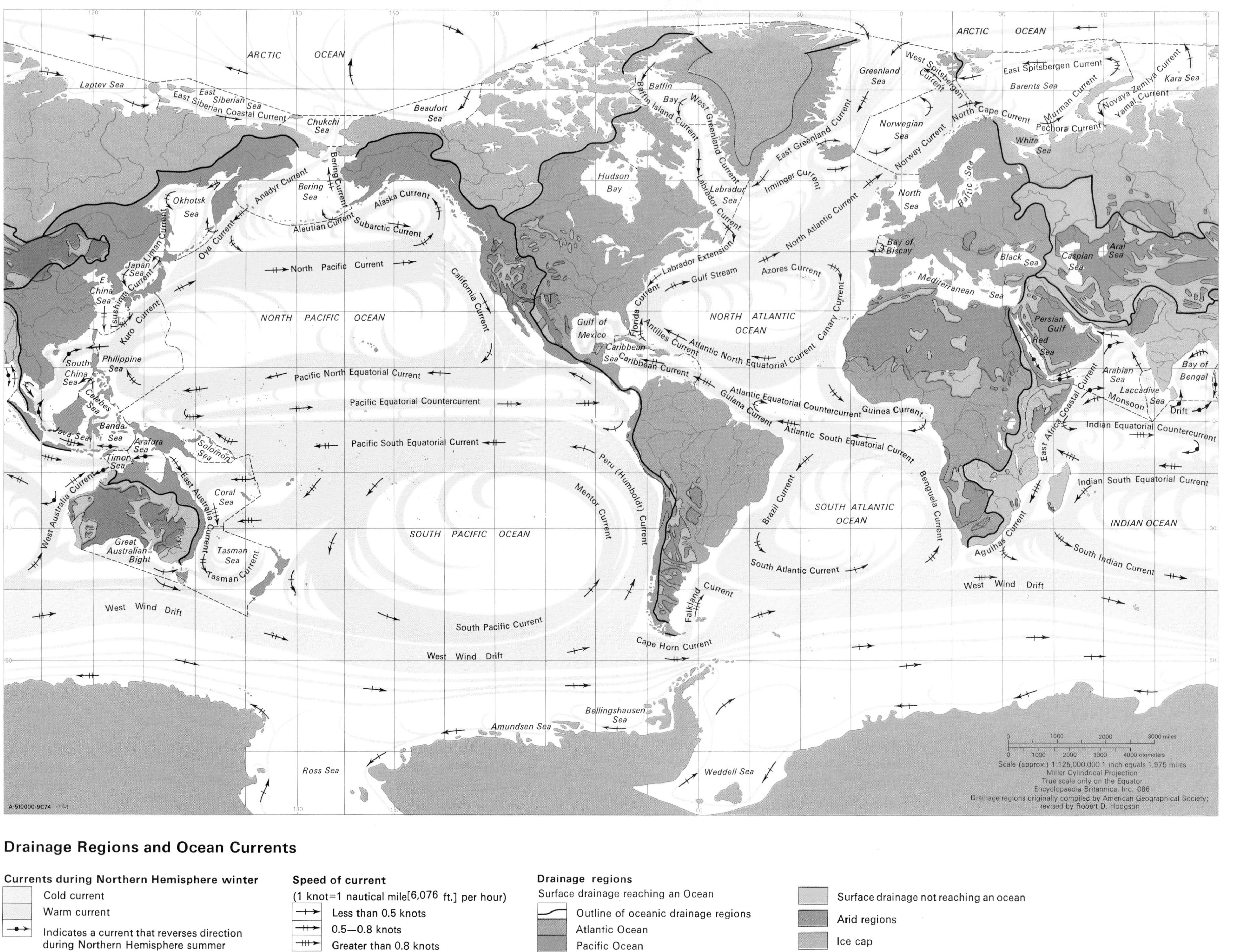

Drainage Regions and Ocean Currents

Currents during Northern Hemisphere winter

- Cold current
- Warm current
- Indicates a current that reverses direction during Northern Hemisphere summer

Speed of current
(1 knot=1 nautical mile[6,076 ft.] per hour)

- Less than 0.5 knots
- 0.5—0.8 knots
- Greater than 0.8 knots
- Limits of seas

Drainage regions
Surface drainage reaching an Ocean

- Outline of oceanic drainage regions
- Atlantic Ocean
- Pacific Ocean
- Indian Ocean
- Arctic Ocean
- Surface drainage not reaching an ocean
- Arid regions
- Ice cap

THE MAP FORM column of the Glossary lists in alphabetical order the geographical terms, including any abbreviations, that appear on the maps. Terms preceded by a hyphen are those which commonly appear as endings in map names (for example, -san in Fuji-san, -älven in Dalälven). The languages of the terms are identified by abbreviations in *italics* (see Abbreviations of Language Names below). The Glossary provides the English, German, Spanish, French, and Portuguese equivalent for each term.

As a rule, the translations were made from the map form to English, then from English into the other four languages. Since the glossary terms and translations refer to specific map features, some may vary from the customary dictionary definitions of the terms.

IN DER SPALTE "Geographische Begriffe" werden alle Begriffe und Abkürzungen in alphabetischer Ordnung aufgeführt, die in den Karten erscheinen. Begriffe mit vorgesetztem Bindestrich erscheinen normalerweise als Wortendungen in Kartennamen (z.B. -san in Fuji-san, -älven in Dalälven). In *Kursivschrift* sind die jeweiligen Abkürzungen angegeben für die Sprachen, in denen der Begriff wiedergegeben ist (siehe unten: Abkürzungen der Sprachen). Das Verzeichnis gibt für jeden Begriff den entsprechenden Ausdruck in englisch, deutsch, spanisch, französisch, und portugiesisch.

In der Regel wurde der Begriff in der Karte ins Englische übersetzt und dann vom Englischen in die vier anderen Sprachen. Da die Begriffe und Übersetzungen sich auf bestimmte Objekte in der Karte beziehen, können einige von ihnen von den in den üblichen Wörterbüchern aufgeführten Begriffsbestimmungen abweichen.

LOS TÉRMINOS GEOGRÁFICOS que aparecen en los mapas, incluyendo abreviaciones, son presentados en la columna de Términos Geográficas del Glosario, en orden alfabético. Los términos que están precedidos por un guión aparecen frecuentemente como terminaciones de los nombres en los mapas (por ejemplo, -san en Fuji-san, -älven en Dalälven). Los idiomas que representan los términos están identificados por medio de abreviaciones en *cursiva* (véase abajo, Abreviaciones de los Idiomas Extranjeros). El Glosario provee el equivalente para cada término en inglés, alemán, español, francés y portugués.

Generalmente las traducciones están hechas de las formas originales de la terminología de los mapas que aparecen primero en inglés, y luego se traducen a las otras cuatro lenguas. Algunos términos y traducciones pueden aparecer distintas a las usadas en los diccionarios generales porque se refieren a los rasgos particulares de los mapas.

LE GLOSSAIRE cite par ordre alphabétique les termes géographiques et les abréviations utilisées. Les mots précédés d'un tiret sont des suffixes (par exemple -san dans Fuji-san, -älven dans Dalälven). La langue d'origine du nom cité est indiquée par une abréviation en *italique* (voir Abréviations des noms de langues, ci-dessous). Le Glossaire donne chaque nom en anglais, allemand, espagnol, français, et portugais.

En général, les termes géographiques des cartes ont d'abord été traduits en anglais, puis de l'anglais dans les quatre autres langues. Les définitions de certains termes sont adaptées aux particularités de l'Atlas. Il peut arriver qu'elles diffèrent des définitions habituelles données par les dictionnaires.

A COLUNA 'TERMINOLOGIA', do *Glossário*, contém todos os termos geográficos que figuram nos mapas, em ordem alfabética e com as respectivas abreviações. Os termos precedidos por um hífen são os que freqüentemente aparecem nos mapas como sufixos de nomes tais como *-san* (em Fuji-san), *-älven* (em Dalälven). As línguas em que os termos são expressos estão identificadas por abreviações em *grifo* (ver abaixo, 'Abreviações das línguas estrangeiras'). O Glossário fornece o equivalente de cada termo em inglês, alemão, espanhol, português e francês.

De modo geral, as traduções foram feitas das formas originais da terminologia usada nos mapas para o inglês, e, em seguida, do inglês para as outras quatro línguas. Uma vez que os termos geográficos e traduções do *Glossário* referem-se a acidentes específicos de cada mapa, é possível que algumas definições sejam diferentes das consignadas nos dicionários gerais das línguas.

Abbreviations of Language Names / Abkürzungen der Nationalsprachen / Abreviaciones de los Idiomas Extranjeros / Abréviations des Noms de Langues / Abreviações dos Idiomas Estrangeiros

	ENGLISH	DEUTSCH	ESPAÑOL	FRANÇAIS	PORTUGUÊS
Afk.	Afrikaans	Afrikaans	Africano	Afrikaans	Afrikaans
Alb.	Albanian	Albanisch	Albanesa	Albanais	Albanês
Ara.	Arabic	Arabisch	Árabe	Arabe	Árabe
Ber.	Berber	Berberisch	Bereber	Berbère	Berbere
Ben.	Bengali	Bengali	Bengali	Bengali	Bengali
Blg.	Bulgarian	Bulgarisch	Búlgaro	Bulgare	Búlgaro
Bur.	Burmese	Burmanisch	Birmano	Birman	Birmanês
Cat.	Catalan	Katalanisch	Catalán	Catalan	Catalão
Cbd.	Cambodian	Kambodschanisch	Camboyano	Cambodgien	Cambojano
Ch.	Chinese	Chinesisch	Chino	Chinois	Chinês
Czech	Czech	Tschechisch	Checo	Tchèque	Tcheco
Dan.	Danish	Dänisch	Danés	Danois	Dinamarquês
Du.	Dutch	Niederländisch	Holandés	Néerlandais	Holandês
Eng.	English	Englisch	Inglés	Anglais	Inglês
Est.	Estonian	Estnisch	Estonio	Esthonien	Estoniano
Finn.	Finnish	Finnisch	Finés	Finnois	Finlandês
Flm.	Flemish	Flämisch	Flamenco	Flamand	Flamengo
Fr.	French	Französisch	Francés	Français	Francês
Gae.	Gaelic	Gälisch	Gaélico	Gaélique	Gaélico
Ger.	German	Deutsch	Alemán	Allemand	Alemão
Gr.	Greek	Griechisch	Griego	Grec	Grego
Hau.	Hausa	Haussa	Hausa	Haoussa	Haussa
Heb.	Hebrew	Hebräisch	Hebreo	Hébreu	Hebreu
Hung.	Hungarian	Ungarisch	Húngaro	Hongrois	Húngaro
Ice.	Icelandic	Isländisch	Islandés	Islandais	Islandês
Indon.	Indonesian	Indonesisch	Indonesio	Indonésien	Indonésio

	ENGLISH	DEUTSCH	ESPAÑOL	FRANÇAIS	PORTUGUÊS
It.	Italian	Italienisch	Italiano	Italien	Italiano
Jap.	Japanese	Japanisch	Japonés	Japonais	Japonês
Kor.	Korean	Koreanisch	Coreano	Coréen	Coreano
Lao.	Laotian	Laotisch	Laosiano	Laotien	Laosiano
Lapp.	Lappish	Lappisch	Lapón	Lapon	Lapão
Latv.	Latvian	Lettisch	Letón	Letton	Letão
Lith.	Lithuanian	Litauisch	Lituano	Lithuanien	Lituano
Mal.	Malay	Malaiisch	Malayo	Malais	Malaio
Mong.	Mongolian	Mongolisch	Mogol	Mongol	Mongol
Nor.	Norwegian	Norwegisch	Norvego	Norvégien	Norueguês
Pas.	Pashto	Paschtu	Pushtu	Pachtou	Pachtu
Per.	Persian	Persisch	Persa	Persan	Persa
Pol.	Polish	Polnisch	Polaco	Polonais	Polonês
Poly.	Polynesian	Polynesisch	Polinesio	Polynésien	Polinésio
Port.	Portuguese	Portugiesisch	Portugués	Portugais	Português
Rom.	Romanian	Rumänisch	Rumano	Roumain	Romeno
Rus.	Russian	Russisch	Ruso	Russe	Russo
S./C.	Serbo-Croatian	Serbokroatisch	Servio-croata	Serbo-croate	Servo-croata
Sin.	Sinhalese	Singhalesisch	Cingalés	Cinghalais	Cingalês
Slo.	Slovak	Slowakisch	Eslovaco	Slovaque	Eslovaco
Sp.	Spanish	Spanisch	Español	Espagnol	Espanhol
Swe.	Swedish	Schwedisch	Sueco	Suédois	Sueco
Thai	Thai	Thai	Tai	Thaï	Tailandês
Tib.	Tibetan	Tibetisch	Tibetano	Tibétain	Tibetano
Tur.	Turkish	Türkisch	Turco	Turc	Turco
Viet.	Vietnamese	Vietnamesisch	Vietnamita	Vietnamien	Vietnamita
Welsh	Welsh	Walisisch	Galés	Gallois	Galês

A

ENGLISH	DEUTSCH	Map Form / Geographische Begriffe / Términos Geográficos / Termes Géographiques / Termos Geográficos	ESPAÑOL	FRANÇAIS	PORTUGUÊS
river	Fluss	**-å** *Dan., Nor., Swe.*	río	rivière	rio
brook	Bach	**a., arroyo** *Sp.*	arroyo	ruisseau	córrego
river	Fluss	**āb** *Per.*	río	rivière	rio
army base	Heeresstützpunkt	**a.b., army base** *Eng.*	base del ejército	base d'armée	base militar
well	Brunnen	**ābār** *Ara.*	pozo	puits	poço
abbey	Abtei	**abb., abbazia** *It.*	abadía	abbaye	abadia
abbey	Abtei	**abbaye** *Fr.*	abadía	abbaye	abadia
abbey	Abtei	**abbazia** *It.*	abadía	abbaye	abadia
abbey	Abtei	**abbey** *Eng.*	abadía	abbaye	abadia
aboriginal reserve	Eingeborenenschutzgebiet	**aboriginal reserve** *Eng.*	zona de aborígenes	réserve des indigènes	reserva indígena
abbey	Abtei	**Abtei** *Ger.*	abadía	abbaye	abadia
ditch	Graben	**acequia** *Sp.*	acequia	fossé	fosso
reservoir	Stausee	**açude** *Port.*	embalse	réservoir	açude
island(s)	Insel(n)	**ada(lar)** *Tur.*	isla(s)	île(s)	ilha(s)
island	Insel	**adası** *Tur.*	isla	île	ilha
mountains	Berge	**adrar** *Ber.*	montañas	montagnes	montanhas
Atomic Energy Commission	Atomenergiekommission	**A.E.C., Atomic Energy Commission** *Eng.*	Comisión de Energía Atomica	Commission de l'Énergie Atomique	Comissão de Energia Atômica
airport	Flughafen	**aérd., aérodrome** *Fr.*	aeródromo	aérodrome	aeródromo
airport	Flughafen	**aeródromo** *Port., Sp.*	aeródromo	aérodrome	aeródromo
airport	Flughafen	**aeroparque** *Sp.*	aeroparque	aéroport	aeroporto
airport	Flughafen	**aéroport** *Fr.*	aeropuerto	aéroport	aeroporto
airport	Flughafen	**aeroporto** *It., Port.*	aeropuerto	aéroport	aeroporto
airport	Flughafen	**aeropuerto** *Sp.*	aeropuerto	aéroport	aeroporto
air force base	Luftwaffenstützpunkt	**a.f.b., air force base** *Eng.*	base aeronáutica	base aérienne	base aérea
wadi	Wadi	**ahzar** *Ara.*	uadi	wadi	uádi
peak	Gipfel	**aiguille** *Fr.*	pico	aiguille	pico
air base	Luftstützpunkt	**air base** *Eng.*	base aérea	base aérienne	base aérea
airfield	Flugplatz	**airfield** *Eng.*	camp de aviación	aérodrome	campo de pouso
air force base	Luftwaffenstützpunkt	**air force base** *Eng.*	base aeronáutica	base aérienne	base aérea
airport	Flughafen	**airport** *Eng.*	aeropuerto	aéroport	aeroporto
cape	Kap	**ákra, akrotírion** *Gr.*	cabo	cap	cabo
hill	Hügel	**'alam, 'alāmat** *Ara.*	colina	colline	colina
avenue	Allee	**alameda** *Sp.*	alameda	avenue	avenida
alps	Alpen	**alpes** *Fr.*	alpes	alpes	alpes
alps	Alpen	**alpi** *It.*	alpes	alpes	alpes
mountains, hills	Berge, Hügel	**altos** *Sp.*	altos	montagnes, collines	montanhas, colinas
river	Fluss	**-älv, -älven** *Swe.*	río	rivière	rio
amusement park	Vergnügungspark	**amusement park** *Eng.*	parque de diversiones	parc récréatif	parque de diversões
river	Fluss	**-ån** *Swe.*	río	rivière	rio
anchorage	Ankerplatz	**anchorage** *Eng.*	ancladero	ancrage	ancoradouro
bay	Bucht	**angra** *Sp.*	angra	baie	baía
cove	kleine Bucht	**anse** *Fr.*	ensenada	anse	enseada
bay	Bucht	**ao** *Thai*	bahía	baie	baía
aqueduct	Aquädukt	**aqueduc** *Fr.*	acueducto	aqueduc	aqueduto
aqueduct	Aquädukt	**aqueduct** *Eng.*	acueducto	aqueduc	aqueduto
archipelago	Archipel	**archipel** *Fr.*	archipiélago	archipel	arquipélago
archipelago	Archipel	**archipelag** *Rus.*	archipiélago	archipel	arquipélago
archipelago	Archipel	**archipelago** *Eng.*	archipiélago	archipel	arquipélago
archipelago	Archipel	**archipiélago** *Sp.*	archipiélago	archipel	arquipélago
arm	Arm	**arm** *Eng.*	brazo	bras	braço de rio
army base	Heeresstützpunkt	**army base** *Eng.*	base del ejército	base d'armée	base militar
airport	Flughafen	**arpt., aéroport** *Fr.* **aeroporto** *It., Port.* **aeropuerto** *Sp.* **airport** *Eng.*	aeropuerto	aéroport	aeroporto
archipelago	Archipel	**arquipélago** *Port.*	archipiélago	archipel	arquipélago
reef	Riff	**arrecife** *Sp.*	arrecife	récif	recife
brook	Bach	**arroyo** *Sp.*	arroyo	ruisseau	córrego
hills	Hügel	**-ås,-åsen** *Swe.*	colinas	collines	colinas
ridge	Höhenrücken	**'assâbet** *Ara.*	sierra	crête	serra
atoll	Atoll	**atol** *Port.*	atolón	atoll	atol
atoll	Atoll	**atoll** *Eng., Fr.*	atolón	atoll	atol
auditorium	Auditorium	**aud., auditorium** *Eng.*	auditorio	auditorium	auditório
race course	Rennbahn	**autodrome** *Fr.*	autódromo	autodrome	autódromo
race course	Rennbahn	**autodromo** *It.*	autódromo	autodrome	autódromo
expressway	Autobahn	**autopista** *Sp.*	autopista	autoroute	via expressa
avenue	Allee	**av., avenida** *Port., Sp.* **avenue** *Eng., Fr.*	avenida	avenue	avenida
channel	Kanal	**ava** *Poly.*	canal, estrecho	canal, détroit	canal, estreito
avenue	Allee	**avenida** *Port., Sp.*	avenida	avenue	avenida
avenue	Allee	**avenue** *Eng., Fr.*	avenida	avenue	avenida
spring	Quelle	**'ayn** *Ara.*	manantial	source	manancial, fonte

Glossary and Abbreviations of Geographical Terms / Verzeichnis und Abkürzungen Geographischer Begriffe
Glosario y Abreviaciones de Términos Geográficos / Glossaire et Abréviations de Termes Géographiques
Glossário e Abreviações de Termos Geográficos

B

ENGLISH	DEUTSCH	Map Form Geographische Begriffe Términos Geográficos Termes Géographiques Termos Geográficos	ESPAÑOL	FRANÇAIS	PORTUGUÊS
bay	Bucht	**baai** *Du.*	bahía	baie	baía
strait	Meeresstrasse	**bab** *Ara.*	estrecho	détroit	estreito
brook, creek	Bach	**Bach** *Ger.*	arroyo, riachuelo	ruisseau, crique	córrego, arroio
hill	Hügel	**-backen** *Swe.*	colina	colline	colina
desert	Wüste	**bādiyat** *Ara.*	desierto	désert	deserto
strait	Meeresstrasse	**bælt** *Dan.*	estrecho	détroit	estreito
bay	Bucht	**bahía** *Sp.*	bahía	baie	baía
inlet	Einfahrt	**bahiret** *Ara.*	abra	bras de mer	enseada, estuário
railroad station	Bahnhof	**Bahnhof** *Ger.*	estación de ferrocarril	gare	estação ferroviária
river; sea	Fluss; Meer	**bahr, baḥr** *Ara.*	río; mar	rivière; mer	rio; mar
reservoir	Stausee	**baḥrat** *Ara.*	embalse	réservoir	reservatório
bay	Bucht	**baía** *Port.*	bahía	baie	baía
bay	Bucht	**baie** *Fr.*	bahía	baie	baía
reef, sand bar	Riff, Sandbarre	**bajo** *Sp.*	bajo	récif, banc de sable	recife, banco de areia
gorge	Schlucht	**balka** *Rus.*	garganta	gorge	garganta
dome	Kuppe	**ballon** *Fr.*	domo	ballon	domo
marsh	Marsch	**balta** *Rom.*	pantano	marais	pântano
cape	Kap	**-bana** *Jap.*	cabo	cap	cabo
marsh	Marsch	**bañados** *Sp.*	bañados	marais	pântano
island	Insel	**-banare** *Jap.*	isla	île	ilha
bank	Bank	**banco** *Sp.*	banco	banc	banco
peninsula	Halbinsel	**-bandao** *Ch.*	península	péninsule	península
bank	Bank	**bank** *Eng.*	banco	banc	banco
shoal	Untiefe	**-banken** *Swe.*	bajo	haut-fond	escolho
sand bar	Sandbarre	**barra** *Sp.*	barra	banc de sable	banco de areia
dam	Damm	**barrage** *Fr.*	presa	barrage	represa
ravine	Tobel	**barranca** *Sp.*	barranca	ravin	ravina
air base	Luftstützpunkt	**base aérea** *Sp.*	base aérea	base aérienne	base aérea
basilica	Basilika	**basílica** *Sp.*	basílica	basilique	basílica
basilica	Basilika	**basilique** *Fr.*	basílica	basilique	basílica
basin	Becken	**basin** *Eng.*	cuenca	bassin	bacia
basin	Becken	**bassin** *Fr.*	cuenca	bassin	bacia
marsh	Marsch	**batakliği** *Tur.*	pantano	marais	pântano
river	Fluss	**batang** *Indon.*	río	rivière	rio
river	Fluss	**batha** *Ara.*	río	rivière	rio
marsh	Marsch	**bāṭlāq** *Per.*	pantano	marais	pântano
battlefield	Schlachtfeld	**battlefield** *Eng.*	campo de batalla	champ de bataille	campo de batalha
mountain	Berg	**batu** *Mal.*	montaña	montagne	montanha
bay	Bucht	**bay** *Eng.*	bahía	baie	baía
bayou	Altwasser	**bayou** *Fr., Eng.*	ensenada pantanosa	bayou	enseada pantanosa
beach	Strand	**beach** *Eng.*	playa	plage	praia
mountain	Berg	**bein, beinn** *Gae.*	montaña	montagne	montanha
snowcapped mountains	Schneegipfel	**belogorje** *Rus.*	nevados	montagnes neigeuses	picos nevados
mountain	Berg	**ben** *Gae.*	montaña	montagne	montanha
mountain, hill	Berg	**Berg** *Ger.*	montaña, colina	montagne, colline	montanha, colina
mountains	Berge	**berg** *Afk.*	montañas	montagnes	montanhas
hill(s), mountain(s)	Hügel, Berg(e)	**-berg** *Swe.*	colina(s), montaña(s)	colline(s), montagne(s)	colina(s), montanha(s)
mountains	Berge	**Berge** *Ger.*	montañas	montagnes	montanhas
mountains	Berge	**berge** *Afk.*	montañas	montagnes	montanhas
hills, mountains	Hügel, Berge	**-bergen** *Swe.*	colinas, montañas	collines, montagnes	colinas, montanhas
hill, mountain	Hügel, Berg	**-berget** *Swe.*	colina, montaña	colline, montagne	colina, montanha
upland	Bergland	**Bergland** *Ger.*	tierras altas	hautes terres	terras altas
battlefield	Schlachtfeld	**bfld., battlefield** *Eng.*	campo de batalla	champ de bataille	campo de batalha
mountain, hill	Berg	**Bg., Berg** *Ger.*	montaña, colina	montagne, colline	montanha, colina
bridge	Brücke	**bge., bridge** *Eng.*	puente	pont	ponte
bight	Bucht	**bight** *Eng.*	bahía	baie	baía, enseada
bill (point)	Landspitze	**bill** *Eng.*	punta	pointe	ponta
valley	Tal	**biq'at** *Heb.*	valle	vallée	vale
well	Brunnen	**bi'r** *Ara.*	pozo	puits	poço
lake	See	**birkat** *Ara.*	lago	lac	lago
mountains	Berge	**bjeshkët** *Alb.*	montañas	montagnes	montanhas
brook	Bach	**bk., brook** *Eng.*	arroyo	ruisseau	córrego
upland	Bergland	**blaenau** *Welsh*	tierras altas	hautes terres	terras altas
bluff(s)	Steilufer	**bluff(s)** *Eng.*	acantilado(s)	falaise(s)	falésia(s)
boulevard	Boulevard	**blvd., boulevard** *Fr., Eng.*	bulevar	boulevard	bulevar
mountain	Berg	**b'nom** *Viet.*	montaña	montagne	montanha
lake	See	**-bo** *Ch.*	lago	lac	lago
river mouth	Flussmündung	**boca** *Sp.*	boca	embouchure	foz
river mouth; pass	Flussmündung; Pass	**bocca** *It.*	boca; paso	embouchure; col	foz; passo
bay	Bucht	**bocht** *Du.*	bahía	baie	baía
bay	Bodden	**Bodden** *Ger.*	bahía	baie	baía
bog	Moor	**bog** *Eng.*	pantano	fondrière	pântano
strait	Meeresstrasse	**boğazı** *Tur.*	estrecho	détroit	estreito
range	Gebirge	**bogd** *Mong.*	sierra	chaîne	cordilheira
woods	Gehölz	**bois** *Fr.*	bosque	bois	bosque
enclosed basin	Becken	**bolsón** *Sp.*	bolsón	bassin fermée	bacia fechada
forest	Wald	**bory** *Pol.*	bosque	forêt	floresta
forest	Wald	**bosque** *Sp.*	bosque	forêt	floresta
boulevard	Boulevard	**boulevard** *Fr., Eng.*	bulevar	boulevard	bulevar
branch	Arm	**br., branch** *Eng.*	brazo	bras	braço
stream distributary	Flussarm	**braţul** *Rom.*	brazo de río	bras	braço de rio
breakwater	Wellenbrecher	**breakwater** *Eng.*	rompeolas	brise-lames	quebra-mar
glacier	Gletscher	**-breen** *Nor.*	glaciar	glacier	geleira
bridge	Brücke	**bridge** *Eng.*	puente	pont	ponte
brook	Bach	**brook** *Eng.*	arroyo	ruisseau	córrego
marsh	Bruch	**Bruch** *Ger.*	pantano	marais	pântano
bridge	Brücke	**Brücke** *Ger.*	puente	pont	ponte
bridge	Brücke	**brug** *Du.*	puente	pont	ponte
bay	Bucht	**Bucht** *Ger.*	bahía	baie	baía
bay	Bucht	**buchta** *Rus.*	bahía	baie	baía
mountain	Berg	**bufa** *Sp.*	bufa	montagne	montanha
bay	Bucht	**bugt** *Dan.*	bahía	baie	baía
lake	See	**buḥayrah** *Ara.*	lago	lac	lago
lake, lagoon	See, Lagune, Haff	**buḥayrat** *Ara.*	lago, laguna	lac, lagune	lago, laguna
mountain, hill	Berg, Hügel	**bukit** *Indon., Mal.*	montaña, colina	montagne, colline	montanha, colina
bay	Bucht	**-bukten** *Swe.*	bahía	baie	baía
mountain	Berg	**bulu** *Indon.*	montaña	montagne	montanha
castle	Burg	**Burg** *Ger.*	castillo	château	castelo
hill	Hügel	**burj** *Ara.*	colina	colline	colina
creek	Bach	**burn** *Ger.*	riachuelo	crique	riacho
cape	Kap	**burnu, burun** *Tur.*	cabo	cap	cabo
bay	Busen	**Busen** *Ger.*	bahía	baie	baía
butte(s)	Restberg(e)	**butte(s)** *Eng., Fr.*	butte(s)	butte(s)	colina, outeiro

C

ENGLISH	DEUTSCH	Map Form Geographische Begriffe Términos Geográficos Termes Géographiques Termos Geográficos	ESPAÑOL	FRANÇAIS	PORTUGUÊS
cape	Kap	**c., cabo** *Sp.* **cap** *Fr.* **cape** *Eng.*	cabo	cap	cabo
street	Strasse	**c., calle** *Sp.*	calle	rue	rua
peaks	Gipfel	**cabezas** *Sp.*	cabezas	cimes	picos
cape	Kap	**cabo** *Port., Sp.*	cabo	cap	cabo
waterfall	Wasserfall	**cachoeira** *Port.*	cascada	chute d'eau	cachoeira
street	Strasse	**calle** *Sp.*	calle	rue	rua
parkway	Ferienstrasse	**calzada** *Sp.*	calzada	allée de parc	alameda de parque
mosque	Moschee	**camii** *Tur.*	mezquita	mosquée	mesquita
road	Weg	**camino** *Sp.*	camino	route	rodovia
camp	Lager	**camp** *Eng., Fr.*	campo	camp	campo
plain	Ebene	**campo** *It.*	llanura	plaine	planície
brook; ravine	Bach; Tobel	**cañada** *Sp.*	cañada	ruisseau; ravin	ravina
canal	Kanal	**canal** *Eng.*	canal	canal	canal
canal, channel	Kanal	**canal** *Fr., Port., Sp.*	canal	canal	canal
canal, channel	Kanal	**canale** *It.*	canal	canal	canal
stream distributary	Flussarm	**caño** *Sp.*	caño	bras	braço de rio, igarapé
canyon	Cañon	**cañón** *Sp.*	cañón	canyon	canhão
canyon	Cañon	**canyon** *Eng.*	cañón	canyon	canhão
plateau	Hochebene	**cao nguyen** *Viet.*	meseta	plateau	planalto
cape	Kap	**cap** *Fr.*	cabo	cap	cabo
cape	Kap	**cape** *Eng.*	cabo	cap	cabo
capitol	Kapitol	**capitolio** *Sp.*	capitolio	capitole	capitólio
cape	Kap	**capo** *It.*	cabo	cap	cabo
captain	Kapitän	**capt., captain** *Eng.*	capitán	capitaine	capitão
highway	Strasse	**carretera** *Sp.*	carretera	route	rodovia
valley	Tal	**carse** *Gae.*	valle	vallée	vale
waterfall	Wasserfall	**cascada** *Sp.*	cascada	chute d'eau	queda d'água
waterfall	Wasserfall	**cascata** *It.*	cascada	chute d'eau	queda d'água
castle	Burg, Schloss	**castel, castello** *It.*	castillo	château	castelo
castle	Burg, Schloss	**castelo** *Port.*	castillo	château	castelo
castle	Burg, Schloss	**castillo** *Sp.*	castillo	château	castelo
castle	Burg, Schloss	**castle** *Eng.*	castillo	château	castelo
cataracts	Katarakten	**cataratas** *Port., Sp.*	cataratas	cataractes	cataratas
cathedral	Kathedrale	**catedral** *Sp.*	catedral	cathédrale	catedral
range	Gebirge	**catena** *Sp.*	catena	chaîne	cordilheira
cathedral	Kathedrale	**cathedral** *Eng.*	catedral	cathédrale	catedral
causeway	Dammweg	**causeway** *Eng.*	calzada	chaussée	estrada elevada
upland	Bergland	**causse** *Fr.*	tierras altas	causse	terras altas
cave(s)	Höhle(n)	**cave(s)** *Eng.*	cueva(s)	caverne(s)	caverna(s)
cay	Klippe	**cay** *Eng.*	cayo	caye	baixio
cay(s)	Klippe(n)	**cayo(s)** *Sp.*	cayo(s)	cave(s)	baixio(s)
cemetery	Friedhof	**cementerio** *Sp.*	cementerio	cimetière	cemitério
cemetery	Friedhof	**cemetery** *Eng.*	cementerio	cimetière	cemitério
mountain(s), hill(s)	Berg(e), Hügel	**cerro(s)** *Sp.*	cerro(s)	montagne(s), colline(s)	montanha(s), colina(s)
range	Gebirge	**chaîne** *Fr.*	sierra	chaîne	cordilheira
channel	Kanal	**channel** *Eng.*	canal, estrecho	canal, détroit	canal, estreito
hills	Hügel	**chapada** *Port.*	colinas	collines	chapada
island	Insel	**char** *Ben.*	isla	île	ilha
castle	Burg, Schloss	**château** *Fr.*	castillo	château	castelo
island	Insel	**chau** *Ch.*	isla	île	ilha
road	Landstrasse	**chemin** *Fr.*	camino	chemin	rodovia
bay	Bucht	**chhăk** *Cbd.*	bahía	baie	baía
river	Fluss	**ch'i** *Ch.*	río	rivière	rio
lake	See	**-chi** *Ch.*	lago	lac	lago
cape	Kap	**chia** *Ch.*	cabo	cap	cabo
harbor	Hafen	**chiang** *Ch.*	puerto	port	porto
cape	Kap	**chiao** *Ch.*	cabo	cap	cabo
road	Landstrasse	**chin., chemin** *Fr.*	camino	chemin	rodovia
river	Fluss	**-ch'ŏn** *Kor.*	río	rivière	rio
reservoir	Stausse	**-chŏsuji** *Kor.*	embalse	réservoir	reservatório
intermittent lake, salt marsh	periodischer See, Salzmarsch	**chott** *Ara.*	lago intermitente, pantano salado	lac périodique, marais salé	lago intermitente, pântano salgado
range	Gebirge	**chr., chrebet** *Rus.*	sierra	chaîne	cordilheira
river	Fluss	**ch'uan** *Ch.*	río	rivière	rio
mountains	Berge	**chuŏr phnum** *Cbd.*	montañas	montagnes	montanhas
church	Kirche	**church** *Eng.*	iglesia	église	igreja
waterfalls	Wasserfälle	**chutes** *Fr.*	cascadas	chutes d'eau	quedas d'água
marsh	Marsch	**ciénaga** *Sp.*	ciénaga	marais	pântano
peak	Gipfel	**cima** *It., Sp.*	cima	cime	pico
peak	Gipfel	**cime** *Fr.*	cima	cime	pico
cemetery	Friedhof	**cimetière** *Fr.*	cementerio	cimetière	cemitério
city	Stadt	**città** *It.*	ciudad	ville	cidade
city	Stadt	**city** *Eng.*	ciudad	ville	cidade
city	Stadt	**ciudad** *Sp.*	ciudad	ville	cidade
claypan	Tonpfanne	**claypan** *Eng.*	capa de arcilla	couche argilleuse	camada de argila
cliff(s)	Kliff(e)	**cliff(s)** *Eng.*	risco(s)	falaise(s)	falésia(s)
mountain	Berg	**co** *Viet.*	montaña	montagne	montanha
mountain, hill	Berg, Hügel	**co., cerro** *Sp.*	cerro	montagne, colline	montanha, colina
coast	Küste	**coast** *Eng.*	costa	côte	costa
coast guard station	Küstenwachtstation	**coast guard station** *Eng.*	estación de los guardacostas	station des gardes de la côte	estação de guarda costeira
pass	Pass	**col** *Fr.*	paso	col	passo
college	Hochschule	**colegio** *Sp.*	colegio	collège	colégio
hill(s)	Hügel	**colina(s)** *Sp.*	colina(s)	colline(s)	colina(s)
college	Hochschule	**coll., college** *Eng.*	colegio	collège	colégio
hills	Hügel	**colli** *It.*	colinas	collines	colinas
hills	Hügel	**colline** *It.*	colinas	collines	colinas
hills	Hügel	**collines** *Fr.*	colinas	collines	colinas
common	Gemeindeland	**common** *Eng.*	campo común	commune	terra comum
islands	Inseln	**con** *Viet.*	islas	îles	ilhas
plain	Ebene	**conca** *It.*	llanura	plaine	planície
convent	Nonnenkloster	**convent** *Eng.*	convento	couvent	convento
convent	Nonnenkloster	**convento** *It., Port., Sp.*	convento	couvent	convento
range	Gebirge	**cord., cordillera** *Sp.*	cordillera	chaîne	cordilheira
mountain	Berg	**corno** *It.*	montaña	montagne	montanha
brook	Bach	**córrego** *Port.*	arroyo	ruisseau	córrego
coast	Küste	**costa** *Sp.*	costa	côte	costa
coast, hills	Küste, Hügel	**côte** *Fr.*	costa, colinas	côte	costa, colinas
hills	Hügel	**coteau** *Fr.*	colinas	coteau	colinas
coulee	breite Schlucht	**coulee** *Eng.*	rambla	coulée	barranco
coulee	breite Schlucht	**coulée** *Fr.*	rambla	coulée	barranco
county park	Park	**county park** *Eng.*	parque del condado	parc de comté	parque de condado
convent	Nonnenkloster	**couvent** *Fr.*	convento	couvent	convento
cove	kleine Bucht	**cove** *Eng.*	ensenada	anse	enseada
creek	Bach	**cr., creek** *Eng.*	riachuelo	crique	riacho
crag	Felsspitze	**crag** *Eng.*	despeñadero	pointe de rocher	despenhadeiro
crater	Krater	**crater** *Eng.*	cráter	cratère	cratera
crater	Krater	**cratère** *Fr.*	cráter	cratère	cratera
creek	Bach	**creek** *Eng.*	riachuelo	crique	riacho
peak	Gipfel	**croda** *It.*	pico	cime	pico
canal	Kanal	**csatorna** *Hung.*	canal	canal	canal
bay	Bucht	**cua** *Viet.*	bahía	baie	baía
hills, ridge	Hügel, Höhenrücken	**cuchilla** *Sp.*	cuchilla	collines, crête	coxilha
caves	Höhen	**cuevas** *Sp.*	cuevas	cavernes	cavernas
cove	kleine Bucht	**cul-de-sac** *Fr.*	ensenada	cul-de-sac	enseada
mountains	Berge	**culmea** *Rom.*	montañas	montagnes	montanhas
summit	Gipfel	**cumbre** *Sp.*	cumbre	sommet	cume

D

ENGLISH	DEUTSCH	Map Form Geographische Begriffe Términos Geográficos Termes Géographiques Termos Geográficos	ESPAÑOL	FRANÇAIS	PORTUGUÊS
mountain	Berg	**dağ, dağı** *Tur.*	montaña	montagne	montanha
mountains	Berge	**dāgh** *Per.*	montañas	montagnes	montanhas
mountains	Berge	**dağlar, dağları** *Tur.*	montañas	montagnes	montanhas
hill	Hügel	**ḍahr** *Ara.*	colina	colline	colina
plateau	Hochebene	**-dai, -daichi** *Jap.*	meseta	plateau	planalto

ENGLISH	DEUTSCH	Map Form / Geographische Begriffe / Términos Geográficos / Termes Géographiques / Termos Geográficos	ESPAÑOL	FRANÇAIS	PORTUGUÊS
mountain	Berg	**-dake** *Jap.*	montaña	montagne	montanha
valley	Tal	**-dal, -dalen** *Nor., Swe.*	valle	vallée	vale
dale	weites Tal	**dale** *Eng.*	valle ancho	vallée large	vale aberto
dam	Damm	**dam** *Eng.*	presa	barrage	represa
lake	See	**danau** *Indon.*	lago	lac	lago
island	Insel	**-dao** *Ch., Viet.*	isla	île	ilha
marsh	Marsch	**daqq** *Per.*	pantano	marais	pântano
lake	See	**daryācheh** *Per.*	lago	lac	lago
desert	Wüste	**dasht** *Per.*	desierto	désert	deserto
monastery	Kloster	**dayr** *Ara.*	monasterio	monastère	mosteiro
deep	Tiefe	**deep** *Eng.*	fosa marina	fossé marin	fossa submarina
delta	Delta	**delta** *Eng., Fr., Sp.*	delta	delta	delta
sea	Meer	**deniz, denizi,** *Tur.*	mar	mer	mar
monument	Denkmal	**Denkmal** *Ger.*	monumento	monument	monumento
pass	Pass	**deo** *Viet.*	paso	col	passo
depression	Senke	**depression** *Eng.*	depresión	dépression	depressão
river	Fluss	**deresi** *Tur.*	río	rivière	rio
desert	Wüste	**desert** *Eng.*	desierto	désert	deserto
desert	Wüste	**desierto** *Sp.*	desierto	désert	deserto
strait	Meeresstrasse	**détroit** *Fr.*	estrecho	détroit	estreito
escarpment	Landstufe	**dhar** *Ara.*	escarpa	escarpement	escarpa
canal	Kanal	**dhiórix** *Gr.*	canal	canal	canal
lake	See	**-dian** *Ch.*	lago	lac	lago
channel	Kanal	**diep** *Du.*	canal, estrecho	canal, détroit	canal, estreito
dike	Deich	**dijk** *Du.*	dique	digue	dique
district	Distrikt	**district** *Eng.*	distrito	district	distrito
district	Distrikt	**distrito** *Sp.*	distrito	district	distrito
ditch	Graben	**ditch** *Eng.*	acequia	fossé	fosso
peninsula	Halbinsel	**djazirah** *Indon.*	península	péninsule	península
mountain(s)	Berg(e)	**djebel** *Ara.*	montaña(s)	montagne(s)	montanha(s)
fjord	Fjord	**-djúp** *Ice.*	fiordo	fjord	fiorde
channel, sound	Kanal, Sund	**-djupet** *Swe.*	canal, sonda	canal, détroit	canal, estreito
zoo	Zoo	**djurpark** *Swe.*	parque zoológico	zoo	jardim zoológico
island	Insel	**-do** *Kor.*	isla	île	ilha
interfluve	Erhebung	**doāb** *Per.*	interfluvio	interfluve	interflúvio
dock	Dock	**dock** *Eng.*	muelle	quai	doca
mountain	Berg	**doi** *Thai*	montaña	montagne	montanha
valley	Tal	**dolina** *Rus.*	valle	vallée	vale
mountain	Berg	**dolok** *Indo.*	montaña	montagne	montanha
hills	Hügel	**dombrovidék** *Hung.*	colinas	collines	colinas
hills	Hügel	**dombvidék** *Hung.*	colinas	collines	colinas
peak	Gipfel	**dos** *Fr.*	pico	dos	pico
downs (hills)	Hügelland	**downs** *Eng.*	colinas	collines	terras baixas (colinas)
drive	Fahrweg	**dr., drive** *Eng.*	calzada	avenue	avenida
drain	Abzugsgraben	**drain** *Eng.*	desaguadero	drainage	escoadouro
draw	kleines Tal	**draw** *Eng.*	valle pequeño	ravine	bacia, vale
drive	Fahrweg	**drive** *Eng.*	calzada	avenue	avenida
dry lake	Trockensee	**dry lake** *Eng.*	lago seco	lac asséché	lago seco
dunes	Dünen	**dunes** *Eng., Fr.*	dunas	dunes	dunas

E

ENGLISH	DEUTSCH	Map Form	ESPAÑOL	FRANÇAIS	PORTUGUÊS
east	Ost	**e., east** *Eng.*	este	est	leste
school	Schule	**école** *Fr.*	escuela	école	escola
mountain	Berg	**-egga** *Nor.*	montaña	montagne	montanha
memorial	Ehrenmal	**Ehrenmal** *Ger.*	monumento	memorial	monumento
river	Fluss	**-elv, -elva** *Nor.*	río	rivière	rio
reservoir	Stausee	**embalse** *Sp.*	embalse	réservoir	reservatório
pier	Landungsbrücke	**embarcadero** *Sp.*	embarcadero	jetée	cais
valley	Tal	**'emeq** *Heb.*	valle	vallée	vale
monument	Denkmal	**emlékmü** *Hung.*	monumento	monument	monumento
spring	Quelle	**'en** *Heb.*	manantial	source	fonte, manancial
cove	kleine Bucht	**enseada** *Port.*	ensenada	anse	enseada
cove	kleine Bucht	**ensenada** *Sp.*	ensenada	anse	enseada
entrance	Einfahrt	**entrance** *Eng.*	entrada	entrée	entrada
forest	Wald	**erdő** *Hung.*	bosque	forêt	floresta
sand desert	Sandwüste	**erg** *Ara.*	desierto arenoso	désert de sable	deserto arenoso
escarpment	Landstufe	**escarpment** *Eng.*	escarpa	escarpement	escarpa
school	Schule	**escuela** *Sp.*	escuela	école	escola
highland	Hochland	**espigão** *Port.*	región montañosa	pays montagneux	espigão
station	Bahnhof, Stützpunkt	**est., estação** *Port.* **estación** *Sp.*	estación	station	estação
stadium	Stadion	**estadio** *Sp.*	estadio	stade	estádio
reservoir	Stausee	**estanque** *Sp.*	estanque	réservoir	reservatório
estuary	Trichtermündung	**estero** *Sp.*	estero	estuaire	estuário
road	Landstrasse	**estr., estrada** *Port.*	camino	route	estrada
strait	Meeresstrasse	**estrecho** *Sp.*	estrecho	détroit	estreito
estuary	Trichtermündung	**estuary** *Eng.*	estuario	estuaire	estuário
pond	Teich	**étang** *Fr.*	charca	étang	lagoa, açude
expressway	Autobahn	**expy., expressway** *Eng.*	autopista	autoroute	via expressa
island	Insel	**-ey** *Ice.*	isla	île	ilha
lake	See	**ežeras** *Lith.*	lago	lac	lago
lake	See	**ezers** *Latv.*	lago	lac	lago

F

ENGLISH	DEUTSCH	Map Form	ESPAÑOL	FRANÇAIS	PORTUGUÊS
faculty (school)	Fakultät	**faculté** *Fr.*	facultad	faculté	faculdade
fairground	Ausstellungsgelände	**fairground** *Eng.*	campo para ferias	champ de foire	terreno para feiras
cliff	Kliff	**falaise** *Fr.*	risco	falaise	falésia
waterfall	Wasserfall	**fall(s)** *Eng.*	cascada	chute d'eau	queda d'água
waterfall	Wasserfall	**Fall** *Ger.*	cascada	chute d'eau	queda d'água
waterfall	Wasserfall	**-fallet** *Swe.*	cascada	chute d'eau	queda d'água
river	Fluss	**far'** *Ara.*	río	rivière	rio
lighthouse	Leuchtturm	**faro** *Sp.*	faro	phare	farol
upland	Bergland	**farsh** *Ara.*	tierras altas	hautes terres	terras altas
fell (mountain, hill)	ödes Hügelland	**fell** *Eng.*	colina rocosa	colline rocheuse	colina rochosa
mountain	Berg	**-fell** *Ice.*	montaña	montagne	montanha
mountain	Berg	**-feng** *Ch.*	montaña	montagne	montanha
upland	Bergland	**fennsík** *Hung.*	tierras altas	hautes terres	terras altas
ferry	Fähre	**ferry** *Eng.*	balsadera	bac	balsa
lake	See	**fertő** *Hung.*	lago	lac	lago
fortress	Feste	**Feste** *Ger.*	fortaleza	fort	fortaleza
estuary, strait	Trichtermündung, Meeresstrasse	**firth** *Gae.*	estuario, estrecho	estuaire, détroit	estuário, estreito
mountain(s)	Berg(e)	**fjäll(en)** *Swe.*	montaña(s)	montagne(s)	montanha(s)
mountain	Berg	**fjället** *Swe.*	montaña	montagne	montanha
fjord	Fjord	**fjärden** *Swe.*	fiordo	fjord	fiorde
mountain	Berg	**-fjell, -fjellet** *Nor.*	montaña	montagne	montanha
mountain	Berg	**fjöll** *Ice.*	montaña	montagne	montanha
fjord	Fjord	**-fjord** *Nor.*	fiordo	fjord	fiorde
fjord, lake	Fjord, See	**-fjorden** *Nor., Swe.*	fiordo, lago	fjord, lac	fiorde, lago
fjord, bay	Fjord, Bucht	**fjördur** *Ice.*	fiordo, bahía	fjord, baie	fiorde, baía
fork	Arm	**fk., fork** *Eng.*	brazo	bras	braço de rio
flat	Flachland	**flat** *Eng.*	llano	plat	planície
river	Fluss	**-fljót** *Ice.*	río	rivière	rio
bay	Bucht	**-flói** *Ice.*	bahía	baie	baía
flood control basin	Hochwasserrückhaltebecken	**flood control basin** *Eng.*	cuenca para controlar la inundación	bassin de contrôle d'inondation	bacia de controle de inundações
airport	Flughafen	**Flughafen** *Ger.*	aeropuerto	aéroport	aeroporto
airport	Flugplatz	**Flugplatz** *Ger.*	aeropuerto	aéroport	aeroporto
airport	Flugplatz	**flygplats** *Swe.*	aeropuerto	aéroport	aeroporto
river mouth; pass	Flussmündung; Pass	**foce** *It.*	desembocadura; paso	embouchure; col	desembocadura; foz; passo
canal	Kanal	**főcsatorna** *Hung.*	canal	canal	canal
glacier	Gletscher	**-fonn** *Nor.*	glaciar	glacier	geleira
spring	Quelle	**fontaine** *Fr.*	manantial	fontaine	manancial
pass	Pass	**forca** *It.*	paso	col	passo
inlet	Förde	**Förde** *Ger.*	abra	bras de mer	enseada
foreland	Vorland	**foreland** *Eng.*	promontorio	promontoire	promontório
forest	Wald	**forest** *Eng.*	bosque	forêt	floresta
forest reserve	Waldreservat	**forest reserve** *Eng.*	reserva de bosque	réserve forestière	reserva florestal
forest	Wald	**forêt** *Fr.*	bosque	forêt	floresta
waterfall	Wasserfall	**-forsen** *Swe.*	cascada	chute d'eau	queda d'água
forest	Forst	**Forst** *Ger.*	bosque	forêt	floresta
fort	Fort	**fort** *Eng., Fr.*	fuerte	fort	forte
waterfall	Wasserfall	**-foss** *Ice.*	cascada	chute d'eau	queda d'água
waterfall	Wasserfall	**-fossen** *Nor.*	cascada	chute d'eau	queda d'água
brook	Bach	**fosso** *It.*	arroyo	ruisseau	córrego
pass	Pass	**foum** *Ara.*	paso	col	passo
fracture zone	Bruchzone	**fracture zone** *Eng.*	zona de fractura	zone de faille	zona de fratura
freeway	Autobahn	**frwy., freeway** *Eng.*	autopista	autoroute	via expressa
fort	Fort	**ft., fort** *Eng., Fr.*	fuerte	fort	forte
stream distributary	Flussarm	**furo** *Port.*	brazo de río	bras	furo

G

ENGLISH	DEUTSCH	Map Form	ESPAÑOL	FRANÇAIS	PORTUGUÊS
mountain, hill	Berg, Hügel	**g., gora** *Rus.*	montaña, colina	montagne, colline	montanha, colina
mountain	Berg	**g., gunong** *Mal.* **gunung** *Indon.*	montaña	montagne	montanha
mountain	Berg	**-gai'sa** *Lapp.*	montaña	montagne	montanha
tunnel	Tunnel	**galleria** *It.*	túnel	tunnel	túnel
gallery	Galerie	**gallery** *Eng.*	galería	galerie	galeria
game farm	Wildfarm	**game farm** *Eng.*	criadero de caza	ferme de gibier	fazenda de caça
game park	Wildpark	**game park** *Eng.*	vedado de caza	parc à gibier	parque de caça
game refuge	Wildgehege	**game refuge** *Eng.*	refugio de caza	refuge de gibier	refúgio de caça
game reserve	Wildreservat	**game reserve** *Eng.*	vedado de caza	réserve à gibier	reserva de caça
game sanctuary	Wildschutzgebiet	**game sanctuary** *Eng.*	vedado de caza	réserve à gibier	santuário de caça
bay	Bucht	**-gang** *Ch.*	bahía	baie	baía
river	Fluss	**-gang** *Kor.*	río	rivière	rio
gap	Pass	**gap** *Eng.*	paso	col	passo
intermittent lake	periodischer See	**garaet** *Ara.*	lago intermitente	lac périodique	lago intermitente
garden	Garten	**gard., garden** *Eng.*	jardín	jardin	jardim
gardens	Gärten	**gardens** *Eng.*	jardines	jardins	jardins
mountain	Berg	**garet** *Ara.*	montaña	montagne	montanha
station	Bahnhof, Stützpunkt	**garı** *Tur.*	estación	station	estação
lake	See	**-gata** *Jap.*	lago	lac	lago
gate	Tor	**gate** *Eng.*	puerta	porte	portão
mountain torrent	Wildbach	**gave** *Fr.*	torrente	gave	torrente
range	Gebirge	**gebergte** *Du.*	sierra	chaîne	cordilheira
range	Gebirge	**Gebirge** *Ger.*	sierra	chaîne	cordilheira
pass	Pass	**geçidi** *Tur.*	paso	col	passo
oasis, well	Oase, Brunnen	**ghadīr** *Ara.*	oasis, pozo	oasis, puits	oásis, poço
mountains	Berge	**ghar** *Pas.*	montañas	montagnes	montanhas
spring	Quelle	**ghayl** *Ara.*	manantial	source	manancial
bay	Bucht	**ghubbat** *Ara.*	bahía	baie	baía
dunes	Dünen	**ghurd** *Ara.*	dunas	dunes	dunas
island	Insel	**gili** *Indon.*	isla	île	ilha
peak	Gipfel	**Gipfel** *Ger.*	pico	cime	pico
hill	Hügel	**giva't** *Heb.*	colina	colline	colina
bay	Bucht	**gji** *Alb.*	bahía	baie	baía
glacier	Gletscher	**glacier** *Eng., Fr.*	glaciar	glacier	geleira
river	Fluss	**gol** *Mong.*	río	rivière	rio
lake	See	**göl** *Tur.*	lago	lac	lago
bald mountains	kahle Berge	**gol'cy** *Rus.*	montañas calvas	monts chauves	montanhas calvas
golf course	Golfplatz	**golf course** *Eng.*	campo de golf	champ de golf	campo de golfe
gulf	Golf	**golfe** *Fr.*	golfo	golfe	golfo
bay	Bucht	**golfete** *Sp.*	golfete	baie	baía
gulf	Golf	**golfo** *It., Sp.*	golfo	golfe	golfo
lake	See	**gölü** *Tur.*	lago	lac	lago
mountain, hill	Berg, Hügel	**gora** *Rus.*	montaña, colina	montagne, colline	montanha, colina
mountains	Berge	**gora** *S./C.*	montañas	montagnes	montanhas
mountain	Berg	**góra** *Pol.*	montaña	montagne	montanha
gorge	Schlucht	**gorge** *Eng., Fr.*	garganta	gorge	garganta
mountains, hills	Berge, Hügel	**gorje** *S./C.*	montañas, colinas	montagnes, collines	montanhas, colinas
ruins	Ruinen	**gorodišče** *Rus.*	ruinas	ruines	ruínas
mountains, hills	Berge, Hügel	**gory** *Rus.*	montañas, colinas	montagnes, collines	montanhas, colinas
mountains	Berge	**góry** *Pol.*	montañas	montagnes	montanhas
river	Fluss	**-gou** *Ch.*	río	rivière	rio
sinkhole	Schluckloch	**gouffre** *Fr.*	sumidero	gouffre	sumidouro
wadi	Wadi	**goulbin** *Hau.*	uadi	wadi	uádi
ditch	Graben	**Graben** *Ger.*	acequia	fossé	fosso
ridge	Höhenrücken	**gr'ada** *Rus.*	sierra	crête	cordilheira
mountain	Berg	**gradište** *Blg.*	montaña	montagne	montanha
ridges	Höhenrücken	**gr'ady** *Rus.*	sierras	crêtes	cordilheira
general	General	**gral., general** *Eng., Sp.*	general	général	geral
ridge	Grat	**Grat** *Ger.*	sierra	crête	cordilheira
grotto	Grotte	**grotta** *It.*	gruta	grotte	gruta
grotto	Grotte	**grotte** *Fr.*	gruta	grotte	gruta
group	Gruppe	**group** *Eng.*	grupo	groupe	grupo
island	Insel	**-grund** *Swe.*	isla	île	ilha
group	Gruppe	**grupo** *Sp.*	grupo	groupe	grupo
group	Gruppe	**gruppo** *It.*	grupo	groupe	grupo
pass	Pass	**-guan** *Ch.*	paso	col	passo
bay	Bucht	**guba** *Rus.*	bahía	baie	baía
mountain	Berg	**guelb** *Ara.*	montaña	montagne	montanha
gulch	Wildbachschlucht	**gulch** *Eng.*	quebrada	ravin	quebrada
gulf	Golf	**gulf** *Eng.*	golfo	golfe	golfo
mountain	Berg	**gunong** *Mal.*	montaña	montagne	montanha
mountain	Berg	**gunung** *Indon.*	montaña	montagne	montanha
islands	Inseln	**-guntō** *Jap.*	islas	îles	ilhas

H

ENGLISH	DEUTSCH	Map Form	ESPAÑOL	FRANÇAIS	PORTUGUÊS
upland	Bergland	**haḍabat** *Ara.*	tierras altas	hautes terres	terras altas
mountain	Berg	**hadjer** *Ara.*	montaña	montagne	montanha
lagoon	Haff	**Haff** *Ger.*	laguna	lagune	laguna
sea, lake	Meer, See	**-hai** *Ch.*	mar, lago	mer, lac	mar, lago
strait	Meeresstrasse	**-haixia** *Ch.*	estrecho	détroit	estreito
reef	Riff	**hakau** *Poly.*	arrecife	récif	recife
peninsula	Halbinsel	**Halbinsel** *Ger.*	península	péninsule	península
hall	Halle	**hall** *Eng., Fr.*	salón	hall	hall
peninsula	Halbinsel	**-halvøya** *Nor.*	península	péninsule	península
beach	Strand	**-hama** *Jap.*	playa	plage	praia
desert	Wüste	**hamada** *Ara.*	desierto	désert	deserto
plateau	Hochebene	**ḥammādat** *Ara.*	meseta	plateau	planalto
lake, marsh	See, Marsch	**hāmūn** *Per.*	lago, pantano	lac, marais	lago, pântano
point	Landspitze	**-hana** *Jap.*	punta	pointe	ponta
peninsula	Halbinsel	**-hantō** *Jap.*	península	péninsule	península
mountain, hill	Berg, Hügel	**har** *Heb.*	montaña, colina	montagne, colline	montanha, colina
harbor, harbour	Hafen	**harbor, harbour** *Eng.*	puerto	port	porto
mountains, hills	Berge, Hügel	**hare** *Heb.*	montañas, colinas	montagnes, collines	montanhas, colinas
ridge	Höhenrücken	**-harju** *Finn.*	sierra	crête	cordilheira
lava flow	Lavastrom	**ḥarrat** *Ara.*	corriente de lava	coulée de lave	corrente de lava
hills	Hügel	**hauteurs** *Fr.*	colinas	hauteurs	colinas

Glossary and Abbreviations of Geographical Terms / Verzeichnis und Abkürzungen Geographischer Begriffe
Glosario y Abreviaciones de Términos Geográficos / Glossaire et Abréviations de Termes Géographiques
Glossário e Abreviações de Termos Geográficos

ENGLISH	DEUTSCH	Map Form / Geographische Begriffe / Términos Geográficos / Termes Géographiques / Termos Geográficos	ESPAÑOL	FRANÇAIS	PORTUGUÊS
sea, bay	Meer, Bucht	**-hav** *Swe.*	mar, bahía	mer, baie	mar, baía
harbor	Hafen	**havre** *Fr.*	puerto	havre	porto
oasis	Oase	**ḥawḍ** *Ara.*	oasis	oasis	oásis
lake	See	**hawr** *Ara.*	lago	lac	lago
harbor, harbour	Hafen	**hbr., harbor, harbour** *Eng.*	puerto	port	porto
headquarters	Hauptquartier	**hdqrs., headquarters** *Eng.*	cuartel general	guartier général	quartel-general
river	Fluss	**-he** *Ch.*	río	rivière	rio
head (headland)	Landspitze	**head** *Eng.*	promontorio	promontoire	promontório
heath	Heide	**heath** *Eng.*	matorral	lande	charneca
mountain(s)	Berg(e)	**hegy(ség)** *Hung.*	montaña(s)	montagne(s)	montanha(s)
heath	Heide	**Heide** *Ger.*	matorral	lande	charneca
plain	Ebene	**-heiya** *Jap.*	llanura	plaine	planície
river mouth	Flussmündung	**-hekou** *Ch.*	desembocadura	embouchure	desembocadura
hills	Hügel	**heuwells** *Afk.*	colinas	collines	colinas
highland	Hochland	**highland** *Eng.*	región montañosa	pays montagneux	terras altas
highway	Strasse	**highway** *Eng.*	carretera	route	rodovia
hill(s)	Hügel	**hill(s)** *Eng.*	colina(s)	colline(s)	colina(s)
race course	Rennbahn	**hipódromo** *Sp.*	hipódromo	hippodrome	hipódromo
race course	Rennbahn	**hippodrome** *Fr.*	hipódromo	hippodrome	hipódromo
historical	historisch	**hist., historical** *Eng.*	histórico	historique	histórico
historical park	historischer Park	**historical park** *Eng.*	parque histórico	parc historique	parque histórico
historic(al) site	historische Stätte	**historic(al) site** *Eng.*	sitio histórico	site historique	sítio histórico
river	Fluss	**hka** *Bur.*	río	rivière	rio
Her Majesty's Air Station (U.K.)	Luftwaffenstützpunkt (U.K.)	**H.M.A.S., Her Majesty's Air Station** *Eng.*	Real Estación Aeronáutica (U.K.)	Station Aérienne Royale (U.K.)	Real Estação Aeronáutica (U.K.)
river	Fluss	**ho** *Ch.*	río	rivière	rio
reservoir	Stausee	**-ho** *Kor.*	embalse	réservoir	reservatório
mountain	Berg	**-hó** *Nor.*	montaña	montagne	montanha
plateau	Hochebene	**Hochebene** *Ger.*	meseta	plateau	planalto
forest	Hochwald	**Hochwald** *Ger.*	bosque	forêt	floresta
mountain	Berg	**-högarna** *Swe.*	montaña	montagne	montanha
height	Höhe	**Höhe** *Ger.*	altura	hauteur	elevação
cave(s)	Höhle(n)	**Höhle(n)** *Ger.*	cueva(s)	caverne(s)	caverna(s)
bay	Bucht	**hoi** *Ch.*	bahía	baie	baía
island	Insel	**-holm** *Dan.*	isla	île	ilha
hook	Haken	**hook** *Eng.*	gancho	crochet	cabo, promontório
mountain	Berg	**hora** *Czech., Slo.*	montaña	montagne	montanha
point; peak	Horn	**Horn** *Ger.*	punta; pico	pointe; cime	ponta; pico
ruin	Ruine	**horva** *Heb.*	ruina	ruine	ruína
mountains	Berge	**hory** *Czech., Slo.*	montañas	montagnes	montanhas
hospital	Krankenhaus	**hospital** *Eng., Sp.*	hospital	hôpital	hospital
point	Landspitze	**houma** *Poly.*	punta	pointe	ponta
house	Haus	**house** *Eng.*	casa	maison	casa
island	Insel	**hsü** *Ch.*	isla	île	ilha
lake	See	**-hu** *Ch.*	lago	lac	lago
hill	Hügel	**Hügel** *Ger.*	colina	colline	colina
cape	Huk	**Huk** *Ger.*	cabo	cap	cabo
cape	Huk	**-huk** *Swe.*	cabo	cap	cabo
highway	Strasse	**hy., highway** *Eng.*	carretera	route	rodovia

I

ENGLISH	DEUTSCH	Map Form	ESPAÑOL	FRANÇAIS	PORTUGUÊS
island	Insel	**i., isla** *Sp.* **island** *Eng.*	isla	île	ilha
icefield	Eisdecke	**icefield** *Eng.*	helero	champ de glace	geleira
ice shelf	Schelfeis	**ice shelf** *Eng.*	corniza glacial	barrière de glace	banco de gelo
ice tongue	Eiszunge	**ice tongue** *Eng.*	lengua de glaciar	langue glaciaire	língua de geleira
dunes	Dünen	**idehan** *Ber.*	dunas	dunes	dunas
river	Fluss	**ig., igarapé** *Port.*	río	rivière	igarapé
church	Kirche	**iglesia** *Sp.*	iglesia	église	igreja
lake	See	**-ike** *Jap.*	lago	lac	lago
island(s)	Insel(n)	**île(s)** *Fr.*	isla(s)	île(s)	ilha(s)
islet(s)	kleine Insel(n)	**îlet(s)** *Fr.*	isleta(s)	îlet(s)	ilhota(s)
island(s)	Insel(n)	**ilha(s)** *Port.*	isla(s)	île(s)	ilha(s)
islet(s)	kleine Insel(n)	**ilhéu(s)** *Port.*	isleta(s)	îlot(s)	ilhéu(s)
hill, upland	Hügel, Bergland	**'ilw** *Ara.*	colina, tierras altas	colline, hautes terres	colina, terras altas
hill	Hügel	**'ilwat** *Ara.*	colina	colline	colina
lake	See	**in** *Bur.*	lago	lac	lago
Indian reservation	Indianerreservation	**Ind. res., Indian reservation, Indian reserve** *Eng.*	reserva de Indios	réserve Indienne	reserva indígena
inlet	Einfahrt	**inlet** *Eng.*	abra	bras de mer	enseada
island(s)	Insel(n)	**Insel(n)** *Ger.*	isla(s)	île(s)	ilha(s)
institute	Institut	**inst., institute** *Eng.*	instituto	institut	instituto
international	international	**int., international** *Eng.*	internacional	international	internacional
race course	Rennbahn	**ippodromo** *It.*	hipódromo	hippodrome	hipódromo
wadi	Wadi	**irhazer** *Ber.*	uadi	wadi	uádi
dunes	Dünen	**'irq** *Ara.*	dunas	dunes	dunas
islands	Inseln	**is., islands** *Eng.* **islas** *Sp.*	islas	îles	ilhas
island	Insel	**isla** *Sp.*	isla	île	ilha
island(s)	Insel(n)	**island(s)** *Eng.*	isla(s)	île(s)	ilha(s)
islands	Inseln	**islas** *Sp.*	islas	îles	ilhas
isle(s)	Insel(n)	**isle(s)** *Eng.*	isla(s)	île(s)	ilha(s)
islet(s)	kleine Insel(n)	**islet(s)** *Eng.*	isleta(s)	îlot(s)	ilhota(s)
islet	kleine Insel	**islote** *Sp.*	islote	îlot	ilhota
island	Insel	**isola** *It.*	isla	île	ilha
islands	Inseln	**isole** *It.*	islas	îles	ilhas
islet	kleine Insel	**isolotto** *It.*	isleta	îlot	ilhota
isthmus	Landenge	**isthme** *Fr.*	istmo	isthme	istmo
isthmus	Landenge	**isthmus** *Eng.*	istmo	isthme	istmo
isthmus	Landenge	**istmo** *Sp.*	istmo	isthme	istmo
island	Insel	**-iwa** *Jap.*	isla	île	ilha

J

ENGLISH	DEUTSCH	Map Form	ESPAÑOL	FRANÇAIS	PORTUGUÊS
mountain(s)	Berg(e)	**jabal** *Ara.*	montaña(s)	montagne(s)	montanha(s)
garden	Garten	**jardin** *Fr.*	jardín	jardin	jardim
garden	Garten	**jardín** *Sp.*	jardín	jardin	jardim
gardens	Gärten	**jardines** *Sp.*	jardines	jardins	jardins
lake	See	**järv** *Est.*	lago	lac	lago
lake	See	**-järvi** *Finn.*	lago	lac	lago
mountains	Berge	**jary** *Rus.*	montañas	montagnes	montanhas
cave	Höhle	**jaskyně** *Slo.*	cueva	caverne	caverna
lake	See	**-jaur** *Lapp.*	lago	lac	lago
islands	Inseln	**jazā'ir** *Ara.*	islas	îles	ilhas
island	Insel	**jazīrat** *Ara.*	isla	île	ilha
island	Insel	**jazīreh** *Per.*	isla	île	ilha
reservoir	Stausee	**jazovir** *Blg.*	embalse	réservoir	reservatório
mountain(s)	Berg(e)	**jbel** *Ara.*	montaña(s)	montagne(s)	montanha(s)
lake	See	**jezero** *S./C.*	lago	lac	lago
lake, lagoon	See, Lagune, Haff	**jezioro** *Pol.*	lago, laguna	lac, lagune	lago, laguna
river	Fluss	**-jiang** *Ch.*	río	rivière	rio
cape	Kap	**-jiao** *Ch.*	cabo	cap	cabo
mountains	Berge	**jibāl** *Ara.*	montañas	montagnes	montanhas
island	Insel	**-jima** *Jap.*	isla	île	ilha
saddle	Joch	**Joch** *Ger.*	paso	col	passo
river	Fluss	**-joki** *Finn.*	río	rivière	rio
glacier	Gletscher	**-jøkulen** *Nor.*	glaciar	glacier	geleira
glacier	Gletscher	**-jökull** *Ice.*	glaciar	glacier	geleira
gulf	Golf	**jūras līcis** *Latv.*	golfo	golfe	golfo
islands	Inseln	**juzur** *Ara.*	islas	îles	ilhas

K

ENGLISH	DEUTSCH	Map Form	ESPAÑOL	FRANÇAIS	PORTUGUÊS
mountains	Berge	**kabīr** *Per.*	montañas	montagnes	montanhas
dunes	Dünen	**kahal** *Ara.*	dunas	dunes	dunas
sea	Meer	**-kai** *Jap.*	mar	mer	mar
strait	Meeresstrasse	**-kaikyō** *Jap.*	estrecho	détroit	estreito
mountain	Berg	**-kaise** *Lapp.*	montaña	montagne	montanha
navy installation	Anlage der Marine	**ka.j., kaijō-jieitai** *Jap.*	estación de la marina	installation navale	instalação naval
creek	Bach	**kali** *Indon.*	riachuelo	crique	riacho
mountain	Berg	**kalns** *Latv.*	montaña	montagne	montanha
ridge	Kamm	**Kamm** *Ger.*	sierra	crête	serra
canal	Kanal	**kanaal** *Du.*	canal	canal	canal
canal, channel	Kanal	**Kanal** *Ger.*	canal	canal	canal
canal, channel	Kanal	**kanal** *Rus., S./C., Swe.*	canal	canal	canal
canal, channel	Kanal	**kanał** *Pol.*	canal	canal	canal
canal, channel	Kanal	**Kanalen** *Swe.*	canal	canal	canal
canal, channel	Kanal	**kanava** *Finn.*	canal	canal	canal
pass	Pass	**kandao** *Pas.*	paso	col	passo
river	Fluss	**-kang** *Kor.*	río	rivière	rio
moor	Moor	**-kangas** *Finn.*	páramo	lande	charneca
national park	Nationalpark	**kansallis-puisto** *Finn.*	parque nacional	parc national	parque nacional
island	Insel	**kaôh** *Cbd.*	isla	île	ilha
cape	Kap	**Kap** *Ger.*	cabo	cap	cabo
gorge	Schlucht	**kapija** *S./C.*	garganta	gorge	garganta
cape	Kap	**-kapp** *Nor.*	cabo	cap	cabo
dunes	Dünen	**kathīb** *Ara.*	dunas	dunes	dunas
desert	Wüste	**kavīr** *Per.*	desierto	désert	deserto
mountain	Berg	**kawlat** *Ara.*	montaña	montagne	montanha
hill	Hügel	**kawm** *Ara.*	colina	colline	colina
mountain	Berg	**kedīet** *Ara.*	montaña	montagne	montanha
lake	See	**kenohan** *Indon.*	lago	lac	lago
cape	Kap	**kep** *Alb.*	cabo	cap	cabo
islands	Inseln	**kepulauan** *Indon.*	islas	îles	ilhas
key(s), cay(s)	Klippe(n)	**key(s)** *Eng.*	cayo(s)	caye(s)	baixio(s)
intermittent lake	periodischer See	**khabrat** *Ara.*	lago intermitente	lac périodique	lago intermitente
gulf	Golf	**khalīj** *Ara.*	golfo	golfe	golfo
mountain	Berg	**khao** *Bur., Thai*	montaña	montagne	montanha
mountain	Berg	**khashm** *Ara.*	montaña	montagne	montanha
wadi	Wadi	**khatt** *Ara.*	uadi	wadi	uádi
wadi, river	Wadi, Fluss	**khawr** *Ara.*	uadi, río	wadi, rivière	uádi, rio
dam	Damm	**khazzān** *Ara.*	presa	barrage	represa
river, canal	Fluss, Kanal	**khlong** *Thai*	río, canal	rivière, canal	rio, canal
dunes	Dünen	**khubb** *Ara.*	dunas	dunes	dunas
kill (river, channel)	Fluss, Kanal	**kill** *Eng.*	río, canal	rivière, canal	rio, canal
cemetery	Friedhof	**kladb., kladbišče** *Rus.*	cementerio	cimetière	cemitério
cloister	Kloster	**klasztory** *Pol.*	claustro	cloître	claustro, convento
cloister, monastery	Kloster	**Kloster** *Ger.*	claustro, monasterio	cloître, monastère	claustro, mosteiro
knob	Kuppe	**knob** *Eng.*	protuberancia	bosse	cerro, colina
island	Insel	**ko** *Thai*	isla	île	ilha
lake, lagoon	See, Lagune, Haff	**-ko** *Jap.*	lago, laguna	lac, lagune	lago, laguna
harbor	Hafen	**-kō** *Jap.*	puerto	port	porto
highland	Hochland	**-kōchi** *Jap.*	región montañosa	pays montagneux	terras altas
mountain	Kogel	**Kogel** *Ger.*	montaña	montagne	montanha
plateau	Hochebene	**-kogen** *Jap.*	meseta	plateau	planalto
mountains	Berge	**koh** *Per.*	montañas	montagnes	montanhas
air force installation	Anlage der Luftwaffe	**ko.j., kōkū-jieitai** *Jap.*	estación aeronáutica	installation aérienne	instalação da força aérea
national park	Nationalpark	**-kokuritsu-kōen** *Jap.*	parque nacional	parc national	parque nacional
national park	Nationalpark	**-kokutei-kōen** *Jap.*	parque nacional	parc national	parque nacional
bay	Bucht	**kólpos** *Gr.*	bahía	baie	baía
bay	Bucht	**kong** *Ch.*	bahía	baie	baía
mountain	Berg	**kong** *Indon.*	montaña	montagne	montanha
peak	Kopf	**Kopf** *Ger.*	pico	cime	pico
bridge	Brücke	**köprüsü** *Tur.*	puente	pont	ponte
gulf, bay	Golf, Bucht	**körfezi** *Tur.*	golfo, bahía	golfe, baie	golfo, baía
spit	Landzunge	**kosa** *Rus.*	lengua de tierra	flèche	ponta de terra
rapids	Stromschnellen	**-koski** *Finn.*	rápidos	rapides	rápidos
pass	Pass	**kotal** *Per.*	paso	col	passo
basin	Becken	**kotlina** *Pol.*	cuenca	bassin	bacia
bay; pass	Bucht; Pass	**-kou** *Ch.*	bahía; paso	baie; col	baía; passo
mountains	Berge	**kras** *Slo.*	montañas	montagnes	montanhas
ridge	Höhenrücken	**kr'až** *Rus.*	sierra	crête	serra
escarpment	Landstufe	**kreb** *Ara.*	escarpa	escarpement	escarpa
fort	Fort	**krepost'** *Rus.*	fuerte	fort	forte
national park	Nationalpark	**krk., kokuritsu-kōen** *Jap.*	parque nacional	parc national	parque nacional
river	Fluss	**krueng** *Indon.*	río	rivière	rio
national park	Nationalpark	**ktk., kokutei-kōen** *Jap.*	parque nacional	parc national	parque nacional
river mouth	Flussmündung	**-ku** *Ch.*	desembocadura	embouchure	desembocadura
bay	Bucht	**kuala** *Mal.*	bahía	baie	baía
mountain(s)	Berg(e)	**kūh(ha)** *Per.*	montaña(s)	montagne(s)	montanha(s)
hill	Hügel	**-kulle** *Swe.*	colina	colline	colina
dome	Kuppe	**Kuppe** *Ger.*	domo	dôme	domo
strait	Meeresstrasse	**-kurkku** *Finn.*	estrecho	détroit	estreito
channel	Kanal	**kyle** *Gae.*	canal, estrecho	canal, détroit	canal, estreito
island	Insel	**kyun** *Bur.*	isla	île	ilha
hills	Hügel	**-kyūryū** *Jap.*	colinas	collines	colinas

L

ENGLISH	DEUTSCH	Map Form	ESPAÑOL	FRANÇAIS	PORTUGUÊS
lake	See	**l., lac** *Fr.* **lago** *It., Sp.* **lagoa** *Port.* **lake** *Eng.*	lago	lac	lago, lagoa
pass	Pass	**la** *Tib.*	paso	col	passo
province	Provinz	**lääni** *Finn.*	provincia	province	província
lake(s)	See(n)	**lac(s)** *Fr.*	lago(s)	lac(s)	lago(s)
lake	See	**lacul** *Rom.*	lago	lac	lago
river	Fluss	**lae** *Indon.*	río	rivière	rio
cape	Kap	**laem** *Thai*	cabo	cap	cabo
lagoon, lake	Lagune, Haff, See	**lag., laguna** *Sp.*	laguna	lagune, lac	laguna
lake	See	**lago** *It., Port., Sp.*	lago	lac	lago
lake, lagoon	See, Lagune, Haff	**lagoa** *Port.*	lago, laguna,	lac, lagune	lagoa
lagoon	Lagune, Haff	**lagoon** *Eng.*	laguna	lagune	laguna
lakes	Seen	**lagos** *Port., Sp.*	lagos	lacs	lagos
lagoon, lake	Lagune, Haff, See	**laguna** *Sp.*	laguna	lagune, lac	laguna, lago
lagoon	Lagune, Haff	**lagune** *Fr.*	laguna	lagune	laguna
bay	Bucht	**laht** *Est.*	bahía	baie	baía
gulf	Golf	**-lahti** *Finn.*	golfo	golfe	golfo
lake(s)	See(n)	**lake(s)** *Eng.*	lago(s)	lac(s)	lago(s)
county	Grafschaft	**län** *Swe.*	condado	comté	condado
lake	Lanke (See)	**Lanke** *Ger.*	lago	lac	lago
sea	Meer	**laut** *Indon.*	mar	mer	mar
lava flow	Lavastrom	**lava flow** *Eng.*	corriente de lava	coulée de lave	corrente de lava
hill, mountain	Hügel, Berg	**law** *Gae.*	colina, montaña	colline, montagne	colina montanha
mountains; forest	Berge; Wald	**les** *Czech*	montañas; bosque	montagnes; forêt	montanhas; floresta
forest	Wald	**les** *Rus.*	bosque	forêt	floresta
level (plain)	Niveau (Ebene)	**level** *Eng.*	nivel (llano)	niveau (plaine)	planície
islands	Inseln	**liehtao** *Ch.*	islas	îles	ilhas
lighthouse	Leuchtturm	**lighthouse** *Eng.*	faro	phare	farol
estuary	Trichtermündung	**liman** *Rus.*	estuario	estuaire	estuário

ENGLISH	DEUTSCH	Map Form Geographische Begriffe Términos Geográficos Termes Géographiques Termos Geográficos	ESPAÑOL	FRANÇAIS	PORTUGUÊS
bay	Bucht	**limanı** *Tur.*	bahía	baie	baía
lake	See	**limni** *Gr.*	lago	lac	lago
peak	Gipfel	**-ling** *Ch.*	pico	cime	pico
plain	Ebene	**llano** *Sp.*	llano	plaine	planície
plains	Ebenen	**llanos** *Sp.*	llanos	plaines	planícies
lake, inlet	See, Einfahrt	**loch** *Gae.*	lago, abra	lac, bras de mer	lago, angra
lock	Schleuse	**lock** *Eng.*	esclusa	écluse	eclusa
lock and dam	Damm mit Schleuse	**lock and dam** *Eng.*	presa y esclusa	écluse et barrage	represa e eclusa
gorge	Schlucht	**log** *Rus.*	garganta	gorge	garganta
mountain	Berg	**loi** *Bur.*	montaña	montagne	montanha
hills	Hügel	**lomas** *Sp.*	lomas	collines	colinas
lake	See	**lough** *Gae.*	lago	lac	lago
lowland	Tiefland	**lowland** *Eng.*	tierra baja	terrain bas	terras baixas
marsh	Luch (Bruch)	**Luch** *Ger.*	pantano	marais	pântano
airport	Flughafen	**luchthaven** *Du.*	aeropuerto	aéroport	aeroporto
island	Insel	**-luoto** *Finn.*	isla	île	ilha

M

ENGLISH	DEUTSCH	Map Form	ESPAÑOL	FRANÇAIS	PORTUGUÊS
mountains	Berge	**m., munții** *Rom.*	montañas	montagnes	montanhas
island	Insel	**-maa** *Est.*	isla	île	ilha
river	Fluss	**mae** *Thai*	río	rivière	rio
strait	Meeresstrasse	**maḍiq** *Ara.*	estrecho	détroit	estreito
depression	Senke	**makhtesh** *Heb.*	depresión	dépression	depressão
bay	Bucht	**-man** *Kor.*	bahía	baie	baía
monastery	Kloster	**manastir** *S./C.*	monasterio	monastère	mosteiro
sea	Meer	**mar** *Sp.*	mar	mer	mar
marsh	Marsch	**marais** *Fr.*	pantano	marais	pântano
sea	Meer	**mare** *It.*	mar	mer	mar
Marine Corps Air Station	Flugstützpunkt des Marine-Corps	**Marine Corps Air Station** *Eng.*	estación aeronáutica de la infantería de marina	station aérienne des fusiliers marins	estação aérea de fuzileiros navais
Marine Corps Base	Marine-Corps-Stützpunkt	**Marine Corps Base** *Eng.*	base de la infantería de marina	base des fusiliers marins	base de fuzileiros navais
bay	Bucht	**marsā** *Ara.*	bahía	baie	baía
marsh	Marsch	**Marsch** *Ger.*	pantano	marais	pântano
marsh(es)	Marsch(en)	**marsh(es)** *Eng.*	pantano(s)	marais	pântano(s)
river mouth	Flussmündung	**maṣabb** *Ara.*	desembocadura	embouchure	desembocadura
canal	Kanal	**maṣrif** *Ara.*	canal	canal	canal
massif	Gebirgsmassiv	**massif** *Eng., Fr.*	macizo	massif	maciço
Marine Corps Air Station	Flugstützpunkt des Marine-Corps	**M.C.A.S., Marine Corps Air Station** *Eng.*	estación aeronáutica de la infantería de marina	station aérienne des fusiliers marins	estação aérea de fuzileiros navais
Marine Corps Base	Marine-Corps-Stützpunkt	**M.C.B., Marine Corps Base** *Eng.*	base de la infantería de marina	base des fusiliers marins	base de fuzileiros navais
meadow	Wiese	**meadow** *Eng.*	prado	prairie	pradaria
dunes	Dünen	**médanos** *Sp.*	médanos	dunes	dunas
sea, lake	Meer	**Meer** *Ger.*	mar, lago	mer, lac	mar, lago
sea, lake	Meer	**meer** *Afk., Du.*	mar, lago	mer, lac	mar, lago
hills	Hügel	**melkosopočnik** *Rus.*	colinas	collines	colinas
memorial	Gedenkstätte	**mem., memorial** *Eng., Fr.*	monumento	memorial	monumento
peninsula	Halbinsel	**menandjung** *Indon.*	península	péninsule	península
sea	Meer	**mer** *Fr.*	mar	mer	mar
mesa	Tafelberg	**mesa** *Sp.*	mesa	mesa	mesa
plateau	Hochebene	**meseta** *Sp.*	meseta	plateau	planalto
middle	Mittel-	**mid., middle** *Eng.*	medio	moyen	médio, central
spit	Landzunge	**mierzeja** *Pol.*	lengua de tierra	flèche	ponta de terra
bay	Bucht	**mifraz** *Heb.*	bahía	baie	baía
mines	Bergwerke	**mikhrot** *Heb.*	minas	mines	minas
military	militärisch	**mil., military** *Eng.*	militar	militaire	militar
harbor	Hafen	**-minato** *Jap.*	puerto	port	porto
mine	Bergwerk	**mine** *Eng., Fr.*	mina	mine	mina
mountain	Berg	**-mine** *Jap.*	montaña	montagne	montanha
cliff	Kliff	**minqār** *Ara.*	risco	falaise	falésia
cape	Kap	**-misaki** *Jap.*	cabo	cap	cabo
mission	Mission	**mission** *Eng., Fr.*	misión	mission	missão
monument	Denkmal	**mon., monument** *Eng. Fr.*	monumento	monument	monumento
monastery	Kloster	**monasterio** *Sp.*	monasterio	monastère	mosteiro
monastery	Kloster	**monastero** *It.*	monasterio	monastère	mosteiro
monastery	Kloster	**monastery** *Eng.*	monasterio	monastère	mosteiro
monastery	Kloster	**moní** *Gr.*	monasterio	monastère	mosteiro
mount	Berg	**mont** *Fr.*	monte	mont	monte
mountain	Berg	**montagna** *It.*	montaña	montagne	montanha
mountain(s)	Berg(e)	**montagne(s)** *Fr.*	montaña(s)	montagne(s)	montanha(s)
mountain(s)	Berg(e)	**montaña(s)** *Sp.*	montaña(s)	montagne(s)	montanha(s)
mount	Berg	**monte** *It., Port., Sp.*	monte	mont	monte
mountains	Berge	**montes** *Port., Sp.*	montes	monts	montes
mountains	Berge	**monti** *It.*	montes	monts	montes
mountains	Berge	**monts** *Fr.*	montes	monts	montes
monument	Denkmal	**monument** *Eng., Fr.*	monumento	monument	monumento
moor	Moor	**moor** *Eng.*	páramo	lande	charneca
moor	Moos	**Moos** *Ger.*	páramo	lande	charneca
sea	Meer	**more** *Rus.*	mar	mer	mar
mountain	Berg	**-mori** *Jap.*	montaña	montagne	montanha
mountain	Berg	**morne** *Fr.*	montaña	morne	montanha
hill, mountain	Hügel, Berg	**morro** *Port., Sp.*	morro	colline, montagne	morro
mosque	Moschee	**mosque** *Eng.*	mezquita	mosquée	mesquita
island, rock	Insel, Fels	**motu** *Poly.*	isla, roca	île, rocher	ilha, rochedo
island	Insel	**mouchão** *Port.*	isla	île	mouchão
mound	Erdhügel	**mound** *Eng.*	montículo	tertre	montículo
mount	Berg	**mount** *Eng.*	monte	mont	monte
mountain(s)	Berg(e)	**mountain(s)** *Eng.*	montaña(s)	montagne(s)	montanha(s)
mouth	Mündung	**mouth** *Eng.*	desembocadura	embouchure	desembocadura
mount	Berg	**mt., mount** *Eng.*	monte	mont	monte
mountain	Berg	**mtn., mountain** *Eng.*	montaña	montagne	montanha
mountains	Berge	**mts., mountains** *Eng.*	montañas	montagnes	montanhas
point	Landspitze	**mui** *Viet.*	punta	pointe	ponta
headland	Landspitze	**mull** *Gae.*	promontorio	promontoire	promontório
channel	Kanal	**mun** *Ch.*	canal,estrecho	canal, détroit	canal, estreito
depression	Senke	**munkhafaḍ** *Ara.*	depresión	dépression	depressão
mountain	Berg	**muntele** *Rom.*	montaña	montagne	montanha
mountains	Berge	**munții** *Rom.*	montañas	montagnes	montanhas
museum	Museum	**museo** *It., Sp.*	museo	musée	museu
museum	Museum	**Museum** *Ger.*	museo	musée	museu
museum	Museum	**museum** *Eng.*	museo	musée	museu
museum	Museum	**múzeum** *Hung.*	museo	musée	museu
museum	Museum	**muzej** *Rus.*	museo	musée	museu
cape	Kap	**mys** *Rus.*	cabo	cap	cabo

N

ENGLISH	DEUTSCH	Map Form	ESPAÑOL	FRANÇAIS	PORTUGUÊS
north	Nord	**n., north** *Eng.*	norte	nord	norte
sea, gulf	Meer, Golf	**-nada** *Jap.*	mar, golfo	mer, golfe	mar, golfo
desert	Wüste	**nafūd** *Ara.*	desierto	désert	deserto
plateau, mountains	Hochebene, Berge	**nagorje** *Rus.*	meseta, montañas	plateau, montagnes	planalto, montanhas
river	Fluss	**nahr** *Ara.*	río	rivière	rio
sea	Meer	**-naikai** *Jap.*	mar	mer	mar
salt flat	Salzebene	**namakzār** *Per.*	salar	saline	salina
narrows	Meeresenge	**narrows** *Eng.*	angostura	goulet	estreito
peninsula	Halbinsel	**-näs** *Swe.*	península	péninsule	península
naval air station	Flugstützpunkt der Marine	**n.a.s., naval air station** *Eng.*	estación aeronáutica de la marina	station des forces aériennes navales	estação aérea da marinha

ENGLISH	DEUTSCH	Map Form Geographische Begriffe Términos Geográficos Termes Géographiques Termos Geográficos	ESPAÑOL	FRANÇAIS	PORTUGUÊS
National Aeronautics and Space Administration	Nationale Aeronautik- und Weltraum-Behörde	**N.A.S.A., National Aeronautics and Space Administration** *Eng.*	Administración Nacional Aeronáutica y Espacial	Administration Nationale de l'Espace et Aéronautique	Administração Nacional do Espaço e Aeronáutica
national park	Nationalpark	**nasjonal park** *Nor.*	parque nacional	parc national	parque nacional
national	national	**nat., national** *Eng., Fr.*	nacional	national	nacional
national battlefield site	Schlachtfeld	**national battlefield site** *Eng.*	campo de batalla nacional	champ de bataille national	campo de batalha nacional
national cemetery	National-friedhof	**national cemetery** *Eng.*	cementerio nacional	cimetière national	cemitério nacional
national forest	Wald in Gemeinbesitz	**national forest** *Eng.*	bosque nacional	forêt nationale	floresta nacional
national historical park	Park an historischer Stätte	**national historical park** *Eng.*	parque histórico nacional	parc historique national	parque histórico nacional
national historical site	historische Stätte	**national historical site** *Eng.*	lugar histórico nacional	site historique national	sítio histórico nacional
national laboratory	staatliche Forschungsanstalt	**national laboratory** *Eng.*	laboratorio nacional	laboratoire national	laboratório nacional
national memorial	nationale Gedenkstätte	**national memorial** *Eng.*	monumento nacional	memorial national	monumento nacional
national military park	Park bei einem Schlachtfeld	**national military park** *Eng.*	parque militar nacional	parc militaire national	parque militar nacional
national monument	Nationaldenkmal	**national monument** *Eng.*	monumento nacional	monument national	monumento nacional
national park	Nationalpark	**national park** *Eng.*	parque nacional	parc national	parque nacional
natioanal recreation area	Ausflugsgebiet	**national recreation area** *Eng.*	campo nacional de recreo	région de récréation nationale	área de lazer nacional
national seashore	öffentlicher Badestrand	**national seashore** *Eng.*	playa nacional	plage nationale	praia nacional
reserve	Naturpark	**Naturpark** *Ger.*	reserva natural	réserve naturelle	reserva natural
nature reserve	Naturschutzgebiet	**Naturschutzgebiet** *Ger.*	reserva natural	réserve naturelle	reserva natural
naval air station	Flugstützpunkt der Marine	**naval air station** *Eng.*	estación aeronáutica de la marina	station des forces aériennes navales	estação aérea da marinha
naval base	Flottenstützpunkt	**naval base** *Eng.*	base naval	base navale	base naval
naval station	Marinestation	**naval station** *Eng.*	estación naval	station navale	estação naval
naval base	Flottenstützpunkt	**n.b., naval base** *Eng.*	base naval	base navale	base naval
rock	Fels	**-ne** *Jap.*	roca	rocher	rochedo
neck	Landenge	**neck** *Eng.*	istmo	isthme	istmo
necropolis	Friedhof	**necrópolis** *Sp.*	necrópolis	nécropole	necrópole
cape	Kap	**neem** *Est.*	cabo	cap	cabo
peninsula, point	Halbinsel, Landspitze	**-nes** *Ice., Nor.*	península, punta	péninsule, pointe	península, ponta
promontory	Vorgebirge	**ness** *Gae.*	promontorio	promontoire	promontório
snowcapped mountain(s)	Schneegipfel	**nev(s)., nevado(s)** *Sp.*	nevado(s)	montagne(s) neigeuse(s)	pico(s) nevado(s)
mountain	Berg	**ngoc** *Viet.*	montaña	montagne	montanha
cape	Kap	**nina** *Est.*	cabo	cap	cabo
islands	Inseln	**nísoi** *Gr.*	islas	îles	ilhas
island	Insel	**nísos** *Gr.*	isla	île	ilha
lowland	Tiefland	**nizina** *Rus.*	tierra baja	terrain bas	terras baixas
lowland	Tiefland	**nižina** *Slo.*	tierra baja	terrain bas	terras baixas
lowland	Tiefland	**nizmennost'** *Rus.*	tierra baja	terrain bas	terras baixas
cape	Kap	**nos** *Blg.*	cabo	cap	cabo
naval station	Marinestation	**n.s., naval station** *Eng.*	estación naval	station navale	estação naval
nature reserve	Naturschutzgebiet	**Nsg., Naturschutzgebiet** *Ger.*	reserva natural	réserve naturelle	reserva natural
mountain	Berg	**nui** *Viet.*	montaña	montagne	montanha
lake	See	**-numa** *Jap.*	lago	lac	lago
mountains	Berge	**nuruu** *Mong.*	montañas	montagnes	montanhas
island	Insel	**nusa** *Indon.*	isla	île	ilha
lake	See	**nuur** *Mong.*	lago	lac	lago

O

ENGLISH	DEUTSCH	Map Form	ESPAÑOL	FRANÇAIS	PORTUGUÊS
bay	Bucht	**o** *Ch.*	bahía	baie	baía
island	Insel	**-ø** *Dan., Nor.*	isla	île	ilha
island	Insel	**-ö** *Swe.*	isla	île	ilha
island	Insel	**o., ostrov** *Rus.*	isla	île	ilha
islands	Inseln	**-öarna** *Swe.*	islas	îles	ilhas
oasis	Oase	**oasis** *Eng., Fr., Sp.*	oasis	oasis	oásis
observatory	Observatorium	**observatorio** *Sp.*	observatorio	observatoire	observatório
observatory	Observatorium	**observatory** *Eng.*	observatorio	observatoire	observatório
ocean	Ozean	**ocean** *Eng.*	océano	océan	oceano
island	Insel	**-ön** *Swe.*	isla	île	ilha
mountains	Berge	**óri** *Gr.*	montañas	montagnes	montanhas
bay	Bucht	**órmos** *Gr.*	bahía	baie	baía
mountain(s)	Berg(e)	**óros** *Gr.*	montaña(s)	montagne(s)	montanha(s)
island(s)	Insel(n)	**ostrov(a)** *Rus.*	isla(s)	île(s)	ilha(s)
island	Insel	**ostrovul** *Rom.*	isla	île	ilha
islands	Inseln	**otoci** *S./C.*	islas	îles	ilhas
island	Insel	**otok** *S./C.*	isla	île	ilha
wadi	Wadi	**ouadi** *Ara.*	uadi	wadi	uádi
wadi	Wadi	**oued** *Ara.*	uadi	wadi	uádi
outlet	Abfluss	**outlet** *Eng.*	desagüe	débouché	escoadouro
island	Insel	**-øy, -øya** *Nor.*	isla	île	ilha
lake	See	**oz., ozero** *Rus.*	lago	lac	lago
lakes	Seen	**ozera** *Rus.*	lagos	lacs	lagos

P

ENGLISH	DEUTSCH	Map Form	ESPAÑOL	FRANÇAIS	PORTUGUÊS
hills	Hügel	**pahorkatina** *Czech.*	colinas	collines	colinas
palace	Palast	**pal., palace** *Eng.*	palacio	palais	palácio
palace	Palast	**palacio** *Sp.*	palacio	palais	palácio
palace	Palast	**palais** *Fr.*	palacio	palais	palácio
palace	Palast	**palazzo** *It.*	palacio	palais	palácio
palace	Palast	**paleis** *Du.*	palacio	palais	palácio
railroad station	Bahnhof	**pályaudvar** *Hung.*	estación ferrocarril	gare	estação ferroviária
monument	Denkmal	**pam'atnik** *Rus.*	monumento	monument	monumento
plain	Ebene	**pampa** *Sp.*	pampa	plaine	pampa
basin	Becken	**pánev** *Czech*	cuenca	bassin	bacia
swamp	Sumpf	**pantanal** *Port., Sp.*	pantanal	marais	pantanal
marsh, swamp; reservoir	Marsch, Sumpf; Stausee	**pantano** *Sp.*	pantano	marais; réservoir	pântano
moor	Moor	**páramo** *Sp.*	páramo	lande	charneca
park	Park	**parc** *Fr.*	parque	parc	parque
national park	National park	**parc national** *Fr.*	parque nacional	parc national	parque nacional
park	Park	**parco** *It.*	parque	parc	parque
national park	Nationalpark	**parco nazionale** *It.*	parque nacional	parc national	parque nacional
provincial park	Naturpark	**parc provincial** *Fr.*	parque de la provincia	parc provincial	parque provincial
park	Park	**Park** *Ger.*	parque	parc	parque
park	Park	**park** *Eng.*	parque	parc	parque
national park	Nationalpark	**park narodowy** *Pol.*	parque nacional	parc national	parque nacional
parkway	Ferienstrasse	**parkway** *Eng.*	calzada	allée de parc	alameda de parque
park	Park	**parque** *Port., Sp.*	parque	parc	parque
national park	Nationalpark	**parq. nac., parque nacional** *Port., Sp.*	parque nacional	parc national	parque nacional
beach	Strand	**part** *Hung.*	playa	plage	praia
strait	Meeresstrasse	**pas** *Fr.*	estrecho	détroit	estreito
passage	Durchfahrt	**pasaje** *Sp.*	pasaje	passage	passagem
pass	Pass	**paso** *Sp.*	paso	col	passo
pass	Pass	**Pass** *Ger.*	paso	col	passo
pass	Pass	**pass** *Eng.*	paso	col	passo
passage	Durchfahrt	**passage** *Eng., Fr.*	pasaje	passage	passagem
passage	Durchfahrt	**passe** *Fr.*	pasaje	passe	passagem

Glossary and Abbreviations of Geographical Terms / Verzeichnis und Abkürzungen Geographischer Begriffe
Glosario y Abreviaciones de Términos Geográficos / Glossaire et Abréviations de Termes Géographiques
Glossário e Abreviações de Termos Geográficos

ENGLISH	DEUTSCH	Map Form / Geographische Begriffe / Términos Geográficos / Termes Géographiques / Termos Geográficos	ESPAÑOL	FRANÇAIS	PORTUGUÊS
pass	Pass	**passo** *It.*	paso	col	passo
pass	Pass	**pasul** *Rom.*	paso	col	passo
creek	Bach	**patak** *Hung.*	riachuelo	crique	riacho
peak(s)	Gipfel	**peak(s)** *Eng.*	pico(s)	pic(s)	pico(s)
cave	Höhle	**pećina** *S./C.*	cueva	caverne	caverna
mountains	Berge	**peg., pegunungan** *Indon.*	montañas	montagnes	montanhas
sea	Meer	**pélagos** *Gr.*	mar	mer	mar
bay	Bucht	**pellg** *Alb.*	bahía	baie	baía
peninsula	Halbinsel	**pen., peninsula** *Eng.*	península	péninsule	península
peak; rock	Gipfel; Fels	**peña** *Sp.*	peña	pic; rocher	penha
peak; large rock	Gipfel; grosser Fels	**peñasco** *Sp.*	peñasco	pic; rocher	penhasco
basin	Becken	**-pendi** *Ch.*	cuenca	bassin	bacia
peninsula	Halbinsel	**peninsula** *Eng.*	península	péninsule	península
peninsula	Halbinsel	**península** *Sp.*	península	péninsule	península
peninsula	Halbinsel	**péninsule** *Fr.*	península	péninsule	península
rock	Fels	**peñón** *Sp.*	peñón	rocher	rochedo
pass	Pass	**pereval** *Rus.*	paso	col	passo
strait	Meeresstrasse	**pertuis** *Fr.*	estrecho	pertuis	estreito
sand desert	Sandwüste	**peski** *Rus.*	desierto arenoso	désert de sable	deserto arenoso
mountain	Berg	**phnum** *Cbd.*	montaña	montagne	montanha
mountain	Berg	**phou** *Lao.*	montaña	montagne	montanha
mountain	Berg	**phu** *Thai*	montaña	montagne	montanha
cape	Kap	**pi** *Ch.*	cabo	cap	cabo
plain	Ebene	**piano** *It.*	llanura	plaine	planície
peak	Gipfel	**pic** *Fr.*	pico	pic	pico
peak	Gipfel	**picacho** *Sp.*	picacho	pic	pico
peak	Gipfel	**picco** *It.*	pico	pic	pico
peak(s)	Gipfel	**pico(s)** *Port., Sp.*	pico(s)	pic(s)	pico(s)
pier	Landungsbrücke	**pier** *Eng.*	embarcadero	jetée	cais
mountain	Berg	**-piggen** *Nor.*	montaña	montagne	montanha
peak	Gipfel	**pik** *Rus.*	pico	pic	pico
forest	Wald	**pinhal** *Port.*	bosque	forêt	pinhal
peak	Gipfel	**pique** *Fr.*	pico	pique	pico
pyramid	Pyramide	**pirámide** *Sp.*	pirámide	pyramide	pirâmide
peak(s)	Gipfel	**piton(s)** *Fr.*	pico(s)	piton(s)	pico(s)
peak	Gipfel	**piz, pizzo** *It.*	pico	pic	pico
peak	Gipfel	**pk., peak** *Eng.*	pico	pic	pico
parkway	Ferienstrasse	**pkwy., parkway** *Eng.*	calzada	allée de parc	alameda de parque
plain	Ebene	**plain** *Eng.*	llanura	plaine	planície
plain	Ebene	**plaine** *Fr.*	llanura	plaine	planície
plains	Ebenen	**plains** *Eng.*	llanura	plaines	planícies
plateau	Hochebene	**planalto** *Port.*	meseta	plateau	planalto
planetarium	Planetarium	**planetario** *Sp.*	planetario	planétarium	planetário
planetarium	Planetarium	**planetarium** *Eng.*	planetario	planétarium	planetário
mountain, range	Berg, Gebirge	**planina** *S./C.*	montaña, sierra	montagne, chaîne	montanha, cordilheira
plateau	Hochebene	**plateau** *Eng., Fr.*	meseta	plateau	planalto
plateau	Hochebene	**plato** *Afk., Blg., Rus.*	meseta	plateau	planalto
beach	Strand	**playa** *Sp.*	playa	plage	praia
square	Platz	**plaza** *Sp.*	plaza	place	praça
plateau	Hochebene	**plošina** *Czech*	meseta	plateau	planalto
plateau	Hochebene	**ploskogorje** *Rus.*	meseta	plateau	planalto
pass	Pass	**poarta** *Rom.*	paso	col	passo
hill	Hügel	**poggio** *It.*	colina	colline	colina
mountains	Berge	**pohorie** *Slo.*	montañas	montanges	montanhas
point	Landspitze	**point** *Eng.*	punta	pointe	ponta
point	Landspitze	**pointe** *Fr.*	punta	pointe	ponta
island	Insel	**pol** *Du.*	isla	île	ilha
plain, basin	Ebene, Becken	**polje** *S./C.*	llanura, cuenca	plaine, bassin	planície, bacia
peninsula	Halbinsel	**poluostrov** *Rus.*	península	péninsule	península
peninsula	Halbinsel	**poluotok** *S./C.*	península	péninsule	península
pond	Teich	**pond** *Eng.*	charca	étang	lago
peak	Gipfel	**-pong** *Kor.*	pico	cime	pico
bridge	Brücke	**pont** *Fr.*	puente	pont	ponte
point	Landspitze	**ponta, pontal** *Port.*	punta	pointe	ponta, pontal
bridge	Brücke	**ponte** *Port.*	puente	pont	ponte
pool	Tümpel	**pool** *Eng.*	charco	étang	charco
rapids	Stromschnellen	**porog** *Rus.*	rápidos	rapides	rápidos
port	Hafen	**port** *Eng., Fr.*	puerto	port	porto
port	Hafen	**porto** *It.*	puerto	port	porto
strait	Meeresstrasse	**porthmós** *Gr.*	estrecho	détroit	estreito
provincial park	Naturpark	**p.p., provincial park** *Eng.*	parque de la provincia	parc provincial	parque provincial
beach	Strand	**praia** *Port.*	playa	plage	praia
reservoir	Stausee	**přehr., přehradová nádrž** *Czech*	embalse	réservoir	reservatório
reservoir, dam	Stausee, Damm	**presa** *Sp.*	presa	réservoir, barrage	represa
peninsula	Halbinsel	**presqu'île** *Fr.*	península	presqu'île	península
pass	Pass	**priesmyk** *Slo.*	paso	col	passo
reservoir	Stausee	**priehradová nádrž** *Slo.*	embalse	réservoir	reservatório
prison	Gefängnis	**prison** *Eng.*	prisión	prison	prisão
pass	Pass	**prohod** *Blg.*	paso	col	passo
strait	Meeresstrasse	**proliv** *Rus.*	estrecho	détroit	estreito
promontory	Vorgebirge	**promontorio** *It., Sp.*	promontorio	promontoire	promontório
promontory	Vorgebirge	**promontory** *Eng.*	promontorio	promontoire	promontório
provincial park	Naturpark	**prov. park, provincial park** *Eng.*	parque de la provincia	parc provincial	parque provincial
reservoir	Stausee	**prudy** *Rus.*	embalse	réservoir	reservatório
pass	Pass	**průsmyk** *Czech*	paso	col	passo
pass	Pass	**przełęcz** *Pol.*	paso	col	passo
cape	Kap	**przylądek** *Pol.*	cabo	cap	cabo
point	Landspitze	**pt., point** *Eng.*	punta	pointe	ponta
railroad station	Bahnhof	**pu., pályaudvar** *Hung.*	estación de ferrocarril	gare	estação ferroviária
port	Hafen	**puerto** *Sp.*	puerto	port	porto
peak	Gipfel	**puig** *Cat.*	pico	cime	pico
island	Insel	**pulau** *Indon., Mal.*	isla	île	ilha
islands	Inseln	**pulau-pulau** *Indon.*	islas	îles	ilhas
upland	Bergland	**puna** *Sp.*	puna	hautes terres	terras altas
point	Landspitze	**punt** *Du.*	punta	pointe	ponta
point, peak	Landspitze, Gipfel	**punta** *It., Sp.*	punta	pointe, cime	ponta
point	Landspitze	**puntilla** *Sp.*	puntilla	pointe	ponta pequena
peak	Gipfel	**puntjak** *Indon.*	pico	cime	pico
forest	Wald	**puszcza** *Pol.*	bosque	forêt	floresta
pyramid	Pyramide	**pyramid** *Eng.*	pirámide	pyramide	pirâmide
		Q			
salt flat	Salzebene	**qā'** *Ara.*	salar	saline	salina
pass	Pass	**qaf'** *Alb.*	paso	col	passo
canal	Kanal	**qanāt** *Ara.*	canal	canal	canal
hill	Hügel	**qārat** *Ara.*	colina	colline	colina
hills	Hügel	**qārāt** *Ara.*	colinas	collines	colinas
dunes	Dünen	**qawz** *Ara.*	dunas	dunes	dunas
creek	Bach	**qbda, quebrada** *Sp.*	quebrada	crique	arroio
mountain	Berg	**qolleh** *Per.*	montaña	montagne	montanha
canal	Kanal	**-qu** *Ch.*	canal	canal	canal
quarry	Steinbruch	**quarry** *Eng.*	cantera	carrière	pedreira
creek	Bach	**quebrada** *Sp.*	quebrada	crique	arroio
rapids	Stromschnellen	**quedas** *Port.*	rápidos	rapides	quedas
islands	Inseln	**-qundao** *Ch.*	islas	îles	ilhas
hill	Hügel	**qūr** *Ara.*	colina	colline	colina
mountain	Berg	**qurnat** *Ara.*	montaña	montagne	montanha
		R			
river	Fluss	**r., rio** *Port.* **río** *Sp.*	río	rivière	rio

ENGLISH	DEUTSCH	Map Form / Geographische Begriffe / Términos Geográficos / Termes Géographiques / Termos Geográficos	ESPAÑOL	FRANÇAIS	PORTUGUÊS
		river *Eng.* **rivière** *Fr.*			
range	Gebirge	**ra., range** *Eng.*	sierra	chaîne	cordilheira
Royal Australian Air Force Station	Luftwaffenstützpunkt (Austl.)	**R.A.A.F.S., Royal Australian Air Station** *Eng.*	Real Estación Aeronáutica (Austl.)	Station Aérienne Royale (Austl.)	Real Estação da Força Aérea Australiana
race course	Rennbahn	**race course** *Eng.*	hipódromo	champ de course	hipódromo
race track	Rennbahn	**race track** *Eng.*	hipódromo	champ de course	hipódromo
raceway	Rennbahn	**raceway** *Eng.*	hipódromo	champ de course	hipódromo
river	Fluss	**rach** *Viet.*	río	rivière	rio
anchorage	Ankerplatz	**rada** *Sp.*	rada	ancrage	ancoradouro
cape	Kap	**rags** *Latv.*	cabo	cap	cabo
railroad	Eisenbahn	**railroad** *Eng.*	ferrocarril	chemin de fer	ferrovia
railway	Eisenbahn	**railway** *Eng.*	ferrocarril	chemin de fer	ferrovia
railway station	Bahnhof	**railway station** *Eng.*	estación de ferrocarril	gare	estação ferroviária
dunes	Dünen	**ramlat** *Ara.*	dunas	dunes	dunas
range(s)	Gebirge	**range(s)** *Eng.*	sierra(s)	chaîne(s)	cordilheira(s)
river	Fluss	**ráo., ribeirão** *Port.*	río	rivière	rio, ribeirão
rapids	Stromschnellen	**rapides** *Fr.*	rápidos	rapides	rápidos
rapids	Stromschnellen	**rapids** *Eng.*	rápidos	rapides	rápidos
wadi	Wadi	**raqabat** *Ara.*	uadi	wadi	uádi
cape	Kap	**ras, ra's** *Ara.*	cabo	cap	cabo
cape	Kap	**rās** *Per.*	cabo	cap	cabo
ravine	Tobel	**ravine** *Eng.*	barranca	ravin	ravina
plain	Ebene	**ravnina** *Rus.*	llanura	plaine	planície
canal	Kanal	**rayyāḥ** *Ara.*	canal	canal	canal
flood plain	Überschwemmungsebene	**razlivy** *Rus.*	llanura de inundación	lit d'inondation	planície de inundação
road	Landstrasse	**rd., road** *Eng.*	camino	route	rodovia
reef	Riff	**récif** *Fr.*	arrecife	récif	recife
reefs	Riffe	**recifes** *Port.*	arrecifes	récifs	recifes
reefs	Riffe	**récifs** *Fr.*	arrecifes	récifs	recifes
reef(s)	Riff(e)	**reef(s)** *Eng.*	arrecife(s)	récif(s)	recife(s)
regional park	Regionalpark	**regional park** *Eng.*	parque regional	parc régional	parque regional
mountain	Berg	**-rei** *Jap.*	montaña	montagne	montanha
race course	Rennbahn	**Rennbahn** *Ger.*	hipódromo	champ de course	hipódromo
dam; reservoir	Damm; Stausee	**represa** *Port.*	presa; embalse	barrage; réservoir	represa
airport	Flughafen	**repülőtér** *Hung.*	aeropuerto	aéroport	aeroporto
reservoir	Stausee	**res., reservoir** *Eng.*	embalse	réservoir	reservatório
reservation	Reservat	**reservation** *Eng.*	reservación	réservation	reserva
reservoir	Stausee	**reservatório** *Port.*	embalse	rèservoir	reservatório
reserve	Reservat	**reserve** *Eng.*	reserva	réserve	reserva
reserve	Reservat	**rèserve** *Fr.*	reserva	rèserve	reserva
game reserve	Wildreservat	**rèserve de chasse** *Fr.*	vedado de caza	réserve de chasse	reserva de caça
reservoir	Stausee	**reservoir** *Eng.*	embalse	réservoir	reservatório
reservoir	Stausee	**réservoir** *Fr.*	embalse	réservoir	reservatório
islands	Inseln	**-retto** *Jap.*	islas	îles	ilhas
ria	Ria	**ría** *Sp.*	ría	ria	ria
creek	Bach	**riacho** *Port., Sp.*	riacho	crique	riacho
creek	Bach	**riachuelo** *Sp.*	riachuelo	crique	riacho
creek	Bach	**rib., ribeira** *Port.*	riachuelo	crique	ribeira
river	Fluss	**ribeirão** *Port.*	río	rivière	ribeirão
ridge	Höhenrücken	**ridge** *Eng.*	sierra	crête	serra
moor	Ried	**Ried** *Ger.*	páramo	lande	charneca
creek	Bach	**riera** *Sp.*	riera	crique	riacho
national museum	Reichsmuseum	**rijksmuseum** *Du.*	museo nacional	musée national	museu nacional
army installation	Anlage des Heeres	**rikujō-jieitai** *Jap.*	estación del ejército	installation militaire	instalação militar
river	Fluss	**rio** *Port.*	río	rivière	rio
river	Fluss	**río** *Sp.*	río	rivière	rio
river	Fluss	**riozinho** *Port.*	río	rivière	riozinho
rise (submarine)	Schwelle (untermeerische)	**rise** *Eng.*	elevación (submarina)	élévation (sous-marine)	elevação (submarina)
river	Fluss	**river** *Eng.*	río	rivière	rio
brook	Bach	**rivera** *Sp.*	rivera	ruisseau	córrego
coast	Küste	**riviera** *It.*	costa	côte	costa
river	Fluss	**rivière** *Fr.*	río	rivière	rio
army installation	Anlage des Heeres	**r.j., rikujō-jieitai** *Jap.*	estación del ejército	installation militaire	instalação do exército
road	Landstrasse	**road** *Eng.*	camino	route	rodovia
roads (anchorage)	Ankerplatz	**roads** *Eng.*	ancladero	ancrage	ancoradouro
rock	Fels	**roca** *Sp.*	roca	rocher	rochedo
rock, mountain	Fels, Berg	**rocca** *It.*	roca, montaña	rocher, montagne	rochedo, montanha
rock(s)	Fels(en)	**rock(s)** *Eng.*	roca(s)	rocher(s)	rochedo(s)
cape	Kap	**rt** *S./C.*	cabo	cap	cabo
brook	Bach	**rû** *Fr.*	arroyo	rû	córrego
mountains	Berge	**rudohorie** *Slo.*	montañas	montagnes	montanhas
brook	Bach	**ruisseau** *Fr.*	arroyo	ruisseau	córrego
mountain	Berg	**rujm** *Ara.*	montaña	montagne	montanha
run	Bach	**run** *Eng.*	arroyo	ruisseau	córrego
		S			
south	süd	**s., south** *Eng.*	sur	sud	sul
range	Gebirge	**sa., serra** *Port.*	sierra	chaîne	cordilheira
island	Insel	**saar** *Est.*	isla	île	ilha
savanna	Savanne	**sabana** *Sp.*	sabana	savane	savana
salt marsh; lagoon	Salzmarsch; Lagune, Haff	**sabkhat** *Ara.*	pantano salado; laguna	marais salé; lagune	pântano salgado; laguna
dam	Damm	**sadd** *Ara.*	presa	barrage	represa
wadi	Wadi	**saguia** *Ara.*	uadi	wadi	uádi
desert	Wüste	**ṣaḥrā'** *Ara.*	desierto	désert	deserto
cape	Kap	**-saki** *Jap.*	cabo	cap	cabo
salt flat	Salzebene	**salar** *Sp.*	salar	saline	salina
salt marsh, salt flat	Salzmarsch, Salzebene	**salina(s)** *Sp.*	salina(s)	marais salé, saline	salina(s)
salt marsh, salt flat	Salzmarsch, Salzebene	**salines** *Fr.*	pantano salado, salinas, salar	salines	pântano salgado, salinas
salt flat	Salzebene	**salt flat** *Eng.*	salar	saline	salina
salt lake	Salzsee	**salt lake** *Eng.*	lago salado	lac salé	lago salgado
salt marsh	Salzmarsch	**salt marsh** *Eng.*	pantano salado	marais salé	pântano salgado
waterfall	Wasserfall	**salto(s)** *Port., Sp.*	salto(s)	chute d'eau	salto(s)
reservoir	Stausee	**samudra** *Sin.*	embalse	réservoir	reservatório
range	Gebirge	**-sammyaku** *Jap.*	sierra	chaîne	cordilheira
mountain	Berg	**-san** *Jap., Kor.*	montaña	montagne	montanha
mountains	Berge	**-sanchi** *Jap.*	montañas	montagnes	montanhas
mountains	Berge	**-sanmaek** *Kor.*	montañas	montagnes	montanhas
shrine	Schrein	**santuario** *It., Sp.*	santuario	châsse	santuário
mountain	berg	**sar** *Pas.*	montaña	montagne	montanha
island	Insel	**sari** *Est.*	isla	île	ilha
desert	Wüste	**sarir** *Ara.*	desierto	désert	deserto
saddle	Sattel	**Sattel** *Ger.*	paso	col	passo
strait	Meeresstrasse	**šaurums** *Latv.*	estrecho	détroit	estreito
waterfall	Wasserfall	**saut** *Fr.*	cascada	saut	queda d'água
castle	Schloss	**Schloss** *Ger.*	castillo	château	castelo
gorge	Schlucht	**Schlucht** *Ger.*	garganta	gorge	garganta
school	Schule	**school** *Eng.*	escuela	école	escola
sea	Meer	**sea** *Eng.*	mar	mer	mar
seamount	untermeerische Kuppe	**seamount** *Eng.*	montaña submarina	montagne sous-marine	montanha submarina
sea scarp	Abbruch	**sea scarp** *Eng.*	cantil	escarpement sous-marine	escarpa submarina
dry lake	Trockensee	**sebjet** *Ara.*	lago seco	lac asséché	lago seco
salt flat	Salzebene	**sebkha** *Ara.*	salar	saline	salina
intermittent lake	periodischer See	**sebkra** *Ara.*	lago intermitente	lac périodique	lago intermitente
salt marsh	Salzmarsch	**sebkret** *Ara.*	pantano salado	marais salé	pântano salgado
airport	Flughafen	**sede-te'ufa** *Heb.*	aeropuerto	aéroport	aeroporto
saddle	Sattel	**sedlo** *Czech*	paso	col	passo
lake(s)	See(n)	**See(n)** *Ger.*	lago(s)	lac(s)	lago(s)

ENGLISH	DEUTSCH	Map Form Geographische Begriffe Términos Geográficos Termes Géographiques Termos Geográficos	ESPAÑOL	FRANÇAIS	PORTUGUÊS
strait	Meeresstrasse	**selat** *Indon.*	estrecho	détroit	estreito
peninsula	Halbinsel	**semenandjung** *Indon.*	península	péninsule	península
seminary	Seminar	**seminary** *Eng.*	seminario	séminaire	seminário
mountain	Berg	**-sen** *Jap.*	montaña	montagne	montanha
sound	Sund	**seno** *Sp.*	seno	détroit	estreito
range, mountain	Gebirge, Berg	**serra** *Port.*	sierra	chaîne, montagne	serra
ridge(s)	Höhenrücken	**serranía(s)** *Sp.*	serranía(s)	crête(s)	serrania(s)
rapids	Stromschnellen	**shallāl** *Ara.*	rápidos	rapides	rápidos
mountain(s); island	Berg(e); Insel	**-shan** *Ch.*	montaña(s); isla	montagne(s); île	montanha(s) ilha
pass	Pass	**-shankou** *Ch.*	paso	col	passo
mountains	Berge	**-shanling, -shanmai, -shanmo** *Ch.*	montañas	montagnes	montanhas
bay	Bucht	**sharm** *Ara.*	bahía	baie	baía
peninsula	Halbinsel	**shibh jazīrat** *Ara.*	península	péninsule	península
island	Insel	**-shima** *Jap.*	isla	île	ilha
reef	Riff	**-shō** *Jap.*	arrecife	récif	recife
shoal(s)	Untiefe(n)	**shoal(s)** *Eng.*	bajo(s)	haut-fond(s)	baixio(s)
islands	Inseln	**-shotō** *Jap.*	islas	îles	ilhas
shrine	Schrein	**shrine** *Eng.*	santuario	châsse	santuário
river	Fluss	**-shui** *Ch.*	río	rivière	rio
reservoir	Stausee	**-shuiku** *Ch.*	embalse	réservoir	reservatório
strait	Meeresstrasse	**shuitao** *Ch.*	estrecho	détroit	estreito
temple	Tempel	**-si** *Ch.*	templo	temple	templo
range, ridge	Gebirge, Höhenrücken	**sierra** *Sp.*	sierra	chaîne, crête	serra
range	Gebirge	**silsilesi** *Tur.*	sierra	chaîne	cordilheira
rapids	Stromschnellen	**šivera** *Rus.*	rápidos	rapides	rápidos
lake	See	**-sjö** *Nor.*	lago	lac	lago
lakes	Seen	**-sjöarna** *Swe.*	lagos	lacs	lagos
lake	See	**-sjøen** *Nor.*	lago	lac	lago
lake, bay	See, Bucht	**-sjön** *Swe.*	lago, bahía	lac, baie	lago, baía
island	Insel	**-skär** *Swe.*	isla	île	ilha
forest	Wald	**-skog, -skogen** *Swe.*	basque	forêt	floresta
mountain	Berg	**slieve** *Gae.*	montaña	montagne	montanha
castle	Schloss	**slot** *Du.*	castillo	château	castelo
castle	Schloss	**slott** *Swe.*	castillo	château	castelo
slough	verlandende Wasserfläche	**slough** *Eng.*	pantano	fondrière	pântano, brejo
ridge	Höhenrücken	**snía., serranía** *Sp.*	serranía	crête	serrania
snowfield	Schneefeld	**snowfield** *Eng.*	ventisquero	champ de neige	campo de neve
lake	See	**-sø** *Dan.*	lago	lac	lago
sound	Sund	**sonda** *Sp.*	sonda	détroit	estreito
sound	Sund	**sound** *Eng.*	sonda	détroit	estreito
cave, tunnel	Höhle, Tunnel	**souterrain** *Fr.*	cueva, túnel	souterrain	caverna, túnel
state park	Naturpark	**s.p., state park** *Eng.*	parque provincial	parc régional	parque estadual
cave	Höhle	**špilja** *S./C.*	cueva	caverne	caverna
spit	Landzunge	**spit** *Eng.*	lengua de tierra	flèche	ponta de terra
peak	Spitze	**Spitze** *Ger.*	pico	cime	pico
spring	Quelle	**spr., spring** *Eng.*	manantial	source	manancial
square	Platz	**sq., square** *Eng.*	plaza	place	praça
range, ridge	Gebirge Höhenrücken	**srra., sierra** *Sp.*	sierra	chaîne, crête	serra
saint	Sankt	**st., saint** *Eng., Fr.*	san, santa, santo	saint	são, santa, santo
street	Strasse	**st., street** *Eng.*	calle	rue	rua
saint	Sankt	**sta., santa** *Port., Sp.*	santa	sainte	santa
station	Bahnhof, Stützpunkt	**sta., station** *Eng., Fr.*	estación	station	estação
stadium	Stadion	**stad., stadium** *Eng.*	estadio	stade	estádio
stadium	Stadion	**stadio** *It.*	estadio	stade	estádio
stadium	Stadion	**Stadion** *Ger.*	estadio	stade	estádio
stadium	Stadion	**stadion** *Rus.*	estadio	stade	estádio
stadium	Stadion	**stadium** *Eng.*	estadio	stade	estádio
state beach	öffentlicher Badestrand	**state beach** *Eng.*	playa provincial	plage régionale	praia estadual
state forest	Wald in Gemeinbesitz	**state forest** *Eng.*	bosque provincial	forêt régionale	floresta estadual
state historical park	Park an historischer Stätte	**state historical park** *Eng.*	parque histórico provincial	parc historique régional	parque histórico estadual
state park	Naturpark	**state park** *Eng.*	parque provincial	parc régional	parque estadual
state recreation area	Ausflugsgebiet	**state recreation area** *Eng.*	zona de recreo provincial	zone récréative regional	área de lazer estadual
station	Bahnhof, Stützpunkt	**station** *Eng., Fr.*	estación	station	estação
reservoir	Stausee	**Stausee** *Ger.*	embalse	réservoir	reservatório
station	Bahnhof, Stützpunkt	**stazione** *It.*	estación	station	estação
saint	Sankt	**ste., sainte** *Fr.*	santa	sainte	santa
mountains	Berge	**stěny** *Czech*	montañas	montagnes	montanhas
steppe	Steppe	**step'** *Rus.*	estepa	steppe	estepe
peak	Gipfel	**štít** *Slo.*	pico	cime	pico
saint	Sankt	**sto., santo** *Port., Sp.*	santo	saint	santo
strait(s)	Meeresstrasse	**strait(s)** *Eng.*	estrecho	détroit	estreito
stream	Strom	**stream eng.**	corriente de agua	cours d'eau	curso d'água
street	Strasse	**street** *Eng.*	calle	rue	rua
strait	Meeresstrasse	**stretto** *It.*	estrecho	détroit	estreito
stream	Strom	**Strom** *Ger.*	corriente de agua	cours d'eau	curso d'água
stream	Strom	**-ström, -strömmen** *Swe.*	corriente de agua	cours d'eau	curso d'água
river	Fluss	**-su** *Kor.*	río	rivière	rio
channel	Kanal	**-suidō** *Jap.*	canal, estrecho	canal, détroit	canal, estreito
sound	Sund	**Sund** *Ger.*	sonda	détroit	estreito
sound	Sund	**-sund** *Swe.*	sonda	détroit	estreito
river	Fluss	**suyu** *Tur.*	río	rivière	rio
swamp	Sumpf	**swamp** *Eng.*	pantano	marais	pântano
ridge	Höhenrücken	**syrt** *Tur.*	sierra	crête	serra
island	Insel	**sziget** *Hung.*	isla	île	ilha

T

ENGLISH	DEUTSCH	Map Form	ESPAÑOL	FRANÇAIS	PORTUGUÊS
tableland	Tafelland	**tableland** *Eng.*	mesa, altiplano	plateau	planalto
woods	Gehölz	**tailis** *Fr.*	bosque	taillis	bosque
reef	Riff	**taka** *Indon.*	arrecife	récif	recife
mountain	Berg	**-take** *Jap.*	montaña	montagne	montanha
waterfall	Wasserfall	**-taki** *Jap.*	cascada	chute d'eau	queda d'água
valley	Tal	**Tal** *Ger.*	valle	vallée	vale
mountain	Berg	**tall** *Ara.*	montaña	montagne	montanha
mountain, hill	Berg, Hügel	**tallat** *Ara.*	montaña, colina	montagne, colline	montanha, colina
hills	Hügel	**tallāt** *Ara.*	colinas	collines	colinas
dam	Talsperre	**Talsperre** *Ger.*	presa	barrage	represa
cape	Kap	**tandjung** *Indon.*	cabo	cap	cabo
point	Landspitze	**-tangar, -tangi** *Ice.*	punta	pointe	ponta
cape	Kap	**tanjong** *Mal.*	cabo	cap	cabo
island	Insel	**tao** *Ch.*	isla	île	ilha
hills	Hügel	**ṭaraq** *Ara.*	colinas	collines	colinas
lake	See	**tasek** *Mal.*	lago	lac	lago
lake	See	**tasik** *Indon.*	lago	lac	lago
plateau	Hochebene	**tassili** *Ber.*	meseta	plateau	planalto
mountain	Berg	**taung** *Bur.*	montaña	montagne	montanha
range	Gebirge	**taungdan** *Bur.*	sierra	chaîne	cordilheira
theatre	Theater	**teatro** *It., Sp.*	teatro	théâtre	teatro
bay	Bucht	**teluk** *Indon.*	bahía	baie	baía
temple	Tempel	**temple** *Eng., Fr.*	templo	temple	templo
church	Kirche	**templom** *Hung.*	iglesia	église	igreja
desert	Wüste	**ténéré** *Ber.*	desierto	désert	deserto
peak, hill	Gipfel, Hügel	**tepe, tepesi** *Tur.*	pico, colina	cime, colline	pico, colina
territory	Territorium	**territory** *Eng.*	territorio	territoire	território
lagoon	Lagune, Haff	**thale** *Thai*	laguna	lagune	laguna
mountains	Berge	**thiu khao** *Thai*	montañas	montagnes	montanhas
mountain	Berg	**-tind, -tinderne** *Nor.*	montaña	montagne	montanha
ridge	Höhenrücken	**ṭiwāl** *Ara.*	sierra	crête	serra
mountain	Berg	**-tjåkko, -tjõure** *Lapp.*	montaña	montagne	montanha
island	Insel	**-to** *Kor.*	isla	île	ilha
island	Insel	**-tō** *Jap.*	isla	île	ilha
lake	See	**tó** *Hung.*	lago	lac	lago
pass	Pass	**-tōge** *Jap.*	paso	col	passo
island	Insel	**tokong** *Mal.*	isla	île	ilha
lake	See	**tônlé** *Cbd.*	lago	lac	lago
mountain torrent	Wildbach	**torrente** *It., Sp.*	torrente	torrent	torrente
tower	Turm	**tower** *Eng.*	torre	tour	torre
turnpike	gebührenpflichtige Autobahn	**tpk., turnpike** *Eng.*	camino con peaje	grande route à péage	rodovia com pedágio
lake	See	**-träsk** *Swe.*	lago	lac	lago
trench	Tiefseegraben	**trench** *Eng.*	trinchera	tranchée	fossa submarina
trough	Tiefseegraben	**trough** *Eng.*	trinchera	tranchée	fossa submarina
volcano	Vulkan	**tulūl** *Ara.*	volcán	volcan	vulcão
tunnel	Tunnel	**túnel** *Sp.*	túnel	tunnel	túnel
tunnel	Tunnel	**tunnel** *Eng., Fr.*	túnel	tunnel	túnel
hill, mountain	Hügel, Berg	**-tunturi** *Finn.*	colina, montaña	colline, montagne	colina, montanha
island	Insel	**-tuo** *Ch.*	isla	île	ilha
canal	Kanal	**tur'at** *Ara.*	canal	canal	canal
turnpike	gebührenpflichtige Autobahn	**turnpike** *Eng.*	camino con peaje	grande route à péage	rodovia com pedágio

U-V

ENGLISH	DEUTSCH	Map Form	ESPAÑOL	FRANÇAIS	PORTUGUÊS
cape	Kap	**udjung** *Indon.*	cabo	cap	cabo
lagoon	Lagune, Haff	**-umi** *Jap.*	laguna	lagune	laguna
United Nations	Vereinte Nationen	**U.N., United Nations** *Eng.*	Naciones Unidas	Nations Unies	Nações Unidas
canal	Kanal	**-unga** *Jap.*	canal	canal	canal
university	Universität	**univ., universidad** *Sp.* **universidade** *Port.* **università** *It.* **university** *Eng.*	universidad	université	universidade
university	Universität	**Universität** *Ger.*	universidad	université	universidade
university	Universität	**université** *Fr.*	universidad	université	universidade
university	Universität	**universitet** *Rus.*	universidad	université	universidade
upland	Bergland	**upland** *Eng.*	tierras altas	hautes terres	terras altas
lake	See	**-ura** *Jap.*	lago	lac	lago
mountain(s)	Berg(e)	**uul** *Mong.*	montaña(s)	montagne(s)	montanha(s)
elevation(s)	Höhe(n)	**uval(y)** *Rus.*	altura(s)	élévation(s)	elevação(ões)
spring	Quelle	**'uyūn** *Ara.*	manantial	source	manancial
hill	Hügel	**-vaara** *Finn.*	colina	colline	colina
strait	Meeresstrasse	**väin** *Est.*	estrecho	détroit	estreito
valley	Tal	**val** *Fr., It.*	valle	val	vale
valley	Tal	**valle** *It., Sp.*	valle	vallée	vale
valley	Tal	**vallée** *Fr.*	valle	vallée	vale
waterfall	Wasserfall	**vallen** *Du.*	cascada	chute d'eau	queda d'água
valley	Tal	**valley** *Eng.*	valle	vallée	vale
valley	Tal	**vallon** *Fr.*	valle	vallon	vale
lake	See	**-vatn** *Ice., Nor.*	lago	lac	lago
lake	See	**-vatnet** *Nor.*	lago	lac	lago
lake	See	**-vattnett** *Swe.*	lago	lac	lago
reservoir	Stausee	**vdchr., vodochranilišče** *Rus.*	embalse	réservoir	reservatório
hills	Hügel	**-veden** *Swe.*	colinas	collines	colinas
upland	Bergland	**verch** *Rus.*	tierras altas	hautes terres	terras altas
lake	See	**-vesi** *Finn.*	lago	lac	lago
viaduct	Viadukt	**viaducto** *Sp.*	viaducto	viaduc	viaduto
plateau	Hochebene	**-vidda** *Nor.*	meseta	plateau	planalto
gulf	Golf	**-viken** *Swe.*	golfo	golfe	golfo
bay	Bucht	**vinh** *Viet.*	bahía	baie	baía
mountain	Berg	**vîrful** *Rom.*	montaña	montagne	montanha
airport	Flughafen	**vliegveld** *Du.*	aeropuerto	aéroport	aeroporto
channel	Kanal	**vliet** *Du.*	canal, estrecho	canal, détroit	canal, estreito
canal	Kanal	**vodnyj put'** *Rus.*	canal	canal	canal
reservoir	Stausee	**vodochranilišče** *Rus.*	embalse	réservoir	reservatório
railroad station	Bahnhof	**vokzal** *Rus.*	estación de ferrocarril	gare	estação ferroviária
volcano	Vulkan	**vol., volcán** *Sp.* **volcano** *Eng.*	volcán	volcan	vulcão
pass	Pass	**vorota** *Rus.*	paso	col	passo
upland	Bergland	**vozvyšennost'** *Rus.*	tierras altas	hautes terres	terras altas
mountain	Berg	**vrăh** *Blg.*	montaña	montagne	montanha
mountains	Berge	**vrchovina** *Czech, Slo.*	montañas	montagnes	montanhas
peak	Gipfel	**vrh** *S./C.*	pico	cime	pico
volcano	Vulkan	**vulkan** *Rus.*	volcán	volcan	vulcão
bay	Bucht	**vung** *Viet.*	bahía	baie	baía
mountain, hill	Berg, Hügel	**-vuori** *Finn.*	montaña, colina	montagne, colline	montanha, colina

W-Z

ENGLISH	DEUTSCH	Map Form	ESPAÑOL	FRANÇAIS	PORTUGUÊS
west	West	**w., west** *Eng.*	oeste	ouest	oeste
wadi	Wadi	**wādī** *Ara.*	uadi	wadi	uádi
oasis	Oase	**wāḥat, wāḥāt** *Ara.*	oasis	oasis	oásis
forest; mountains	Wald	**Wald** *Ger.*	bosque; montañas	forêt; montagnes	floresta; montanhas
bay	Bucht	**-wan** *Ch., Jap.*	bahía	baie	baía
wash	Wadi	**wash** *Eng.*	uadi	wadi	uádi
waterfalls	Wasserfälle	**Wasserfälle** *Ger.*	cascadas	chutes d'eau	quedas d'água
water (lake; river)	Wasser (See; Fluss)	**water** *Eng.*	agua (lago;rio)	eau (lac; rivière)	água (lago, rio)
waterway	Wasserstrasse	**waterway** *Eng.*	canal	canal	canal
pond	Weiher	**Weiher** *Ger.*	charca	étang	charco
well	Brunnen	**well** *Eng.*	pozo	puits	poço
bay	Wiek	**Wiek** *Ger.*	bahía	baie	baía
woods	Gehölz	**woods** *Eng.*	bosque	bois	bosque
water (lake; river)	Wasser (See; Fluss)	**wr., water** *Eng.*	agua (lago; rio)	eau (lac; rivière)	água (lago, rio)
river	Fluss	**-xi** *Ch.*	río	rivière	rio
strait	Meeresstrasse	**-xia** *Ch.*	estrecho	détroit	estreito
lake, sea	See, Meer	**yam** *Heb.*	lago, mar	lac, mer	lago, mar
mountain	Berg	**-yama** *Jap.*	montaña	montagne	montanha
sea, bay, lake	Meer, Bucht, See	**-yang** *Ch.*	mar, bahía, lago	mer, baie, lac	mar, baía, lago
peninsula	Halbinsel	**yarımadası** *Tur.*	península	péninsule	península
mountain	Berg	**yebel** *Ara.*	montaña	montagne	montanha
rock, island	Fels, Insel	**yen** *Ch.*	roca, isla	rocher,île	rochedo, ilha
mountains	Berge	**yoma** *Bur.*	montañas	montagnes	montanhas
island	Insel	**-yu** *Ch.*	isla	île	ilha
intermittent lake	periodischer See	**zahrez** *Ara.*	lago intermitente	lac périodique	lago intermitente
point	Landspitze	**-zaki** *Jap.*	punta	pointe	ponta
lagoon	Lagune, Haff	**zalew** *Pol.*	laguna	lagune	laguna
gulf, bay	Golf, Bucht	**zaliv** *Rus.*	golfo, bahía	golfe, baie	golfo, baía
reserve	Reservat	**zapov., zapovednik** *Rus.*	reserva	réserve	reserva
sea, lake	Meer, See	**zee** *Du.*	mar, lago	mer, lac	mar, lago
autonomous province	autonome Provinz	**zizhiqu** *Ch.*	provincia autónoma	province autonome	província autônoma
autonomous district	autonomer Distrikt	**zizhizhou** *Ch.*	distrito autónomo	district autonome	distrito autônomo
zoo	Zoo	**zoo** *Eng.*	parque zoológico	zoo	jardim zoológico

THE FOLLOWING FIVE TABLES show a selection of the large number of geographic changes which have occurred since the first edition of this atlas.

Table 1 lists country name changes and newly independent countries. If the country gained independence, a star appears after the year. Abbreviations indicate the former administration and are defined on pages *I•30–I•32*. Table 2 lists territories transferred from one administration to another. Tables 3 and 4 show name changes (other than country names) and major construction projects. Table 5 lists countries which moved their capital cities or changed their internal boundaries. The heading "Number of Units" refers to a change in the number of provinces, departments or other political divisions within a nation.

Information in tables 1, 2, and 5 is arranged in chronological order. In tables 3 and 4 the information is arranged alphabetically by country name. Symbols used are defined at the end of each table. Dots (.....) in any column indicate no change.

DIE FOLGENDEN TABELLEN führen eine große Anzahl geographischer Veränderungen auf, die sich seit der ersten Ausgabe dieses Atlas ergeben haben.

Tabelle 1 listet Veränderungen bei Ländernamen und seit kurzem unabhängige Länder. Wenn das Land die Unabhängigkeit erhielt, erscheint die Jahreszahl mit einem Stern. Die frühere Verwaltung ist durch Abkürzungen angegeben, die auf den Seiten *I•30–I•32* erläutert sind. Tabelle 2 listet Territorien, die einer neuen Verwaltungszuständigkeit zugeordnet wurden. Tabellen 3 und 4 zeigen Namensänderungen (außer Ländernamen) und wichtige neu angelegte Projekte. Tabelle 5 listet Länder, deren Hauptstädte verlegt worden sind oder die ihre internen Grenzen verändert haben. Die Überschrift "Anzahl der Bezirke" bezieht sich auf eine Veränderung in der Anzahl der Provinzen, der Departements oder anderer politischer Unterteilungen innerhalb der Grenzen einer Nation.

Die Angaben in Tabellen 1, 2 und 5 sind chronologisch geordnet. In Tabellen 3 und 4 sind die Angaben alphabetisch nach Ländernamen geordnet. Die verwendeten Zeichen sind am Fuß jeder Tabelle erläutert. Pünktchen (.....) in einer Spalte bedeuten "keine Veränderung."

LAS CINCO TABLAS que se presentan a continuación muestran una selección de la gran cantidad de cambios geográficos registrados desde la primera edición de este atlas.

La tabla 1 menciona los cambios de nombres de países y las naciones recientemente independizadas. Cuando se trata de un país que ha obtenido su independencia, aparece una estrella después del año. Las abreviaturas, explicadas en las páginas *I•30–I•32* indican el nombre del país del que dependía la antigua colonia. La tabla 2 menciona los territorios que han pasado de una administración a otra. Las tablas 3 y 4 incluyen cambios de nombres geográficos (excepto los que corresponden a países) y obras de construcción importantes. La tabla 5 menciona los países que han trasladado sus capitales o modificado sus fronteras internas. El encabezado "Número de unidades" se refiere a cambios en el número de provincias, departamentos u otras divisiones políticas dentro de la nación.

La información de las tablas 1, 2 y 5 aparece en orden cronológico. Los datos de las tablas 3 y 4 se presentan en orden alfabético por país. La explicación de los símbolos utilizados aparece al pie de cada tabla. Los puntos suspensivos (.....) indican que no ha habido ningún cambio.

LES TABLEAUX suivants donnent une sélection des modifications intervenues depuis la 1e édition de l'Atlas.

Le tableau 1 donne la liste des pays qui ont récemment changé de nom ou qui sont récemment devenus indépendants. Si le pays est devenu indépendant, la date est suivie d'une étoile. Les abréviations indiquent l'ancienne désignation administrative et leurs définitions se trouvent aux pages *I•30–I•32*. Le tableau 2 donne la liste des territoires qui ont changé de régime administratif. Les tableaux 3 et 4 indiquent les autres modifications de nom (sauf les noms de pays) et les principaux projets de construction. Le tableau 5 donne la liste des pays dont les capitaux ont changé ou dont les divisions internes ont été modifiées. Le titre "Nombre d'unités" a rapport a un changement dans le nombre de provinces, départements, ou autres divisions politiques internes du même pays.

Dans les tableaux 1, 2, et 5, l'ordre chronologique a été adopté. Dans les tableaux 3 et 4, les noms de pays sont données par ordre alphabétique. Les points de suspension (.....) dans une colonne indiquent "sans changement."

AS CINCO TABELAS a seguir mostram as principais mudanças geográficas ocorridas desde a primeira edição deste atlas.

A tabela 1 registra as mudanças nos nomes de países e os países recentemente independentes. Se o país se tornou independente, aparece uma estrela depois do ano. As abreviações indicam a antiga administração e estão explicadas nas páginas *I•30–I•32*. A tabela 2 enumera os territórios transferidos de uma administração para outra. As tabelas 3 e 4 mostram as mudanças de nomes (não de países) e os principais projetos de construção. A tabela 5 enumera os países que mudaram suas capitais ou suas fronteiras interiores. O título "Número de unidades" refere-se a mudança no número de províncias, departamentos ou outras divisões políticas dentro de uma nação.

A informação nas tabelas 1, 2 e 5 é disposta em ordem cronológica. Nas tabelas 3 e 4 a informação se apresenta em ordem alfabética, pelo nome do país. Os símbolos utilizados são explicados no pé de cada tabela. Pontos (.....) em qualquer coluna significam que não houve mudança.

Table 1 • Country Independence and Name Changes / **Tabelle 1** • Unabhängigkeit und Namensänderungen
Tabla 1 • Cambios de Nombres de Países y Naciones Independizadas / **Tableau 1** • Independance d'États et Modifications des Toponymes
Tabela 1 • Independência e Mudança de Nome de Países

Year / Jahr / Año / Année / Ano	COUNTRY NAME / LÄNDERNAME / NOMBRE DEL PAÍS / NOM DE PAYS / NOME DO PAÍS — FORMER / FRÜHER / ANTIGUO / ANCIEN / ANTIGO: English / Englisch / Inglés / Anglais / Inglês	FORMER: Local / Einheimisch / Local / Local / Local	NEW / NEU / NUEVO / NOUVELLE / NOVO: English / Englisch / Inglés / Anglais / Inglês	NEW: Local / Einheimisch / Local / Local / Local	P	Location / Lage / Ubicación / Emplacement / Localização	Page / Seite / Página / Page / Página
1970★	**Fiji**	Fiji	.....	.....	U.K.	18.00 S 175.00 E	**14**
1970	**Muscat and Oman**	Masqaṭ wa 'Umān	Oman	'Umān	. . .	22.00 N 58.00 E	**118**
1970	**Southern Yemen**	Al-Yaman al-Janūbī	People's Democratic Republic of Yemen	Al-Yamin ash-Sha'bīyah	. . .	15.00 N 48.00 E	**144**
1970★	**Tonga**	Tonga	.....	.....	U.K.	20.00 S 175.00 W	**14**
1971★	**Bahrain**	Al-Baḩrayn	.....	.....	U.K.	26.00 N 50.30 E	**118**
1971	**Democratic Republic of the Congo**	République Démocratique du Congo	Zaire	Zaïre	. . .	0.00 25.00 E	**10**
1971★	**East Pakistan**	East Pākistān	Bangladesh	Bangladesh	Pāk.	24.00 N 90.00 E	**110**
1971★	**Qatar**	Qaṭar	.....	.....	U.K.	25.00 N 51.10 E	**110**
1971	**Trucial States**	Imārāt Saḩil as-Sulh al-Baḩrī	United Arab Emirates	Ittihād al-Imārāt al-Arabīyah	. . .	24.00 N 54.00 E	**110**
1971	**United Arab Republic**	Al-Jumhūriyāh al-Arabīyah al-Muttaḩidah	Egypt	Miṣr	. . .	27.00 N 30.00 E	**140**
1972	**Ceylon**	Sihala (Ilam)	Sri Lanka	Sri Lanka	. . .	7.00 N 81.00 E	**118**
1973★	**Bahamas**	Bahamas	.....	.....	U.K.	24.15 N 76.00 W	**230**
1973	**British Honduras**	British Honduras	Belize	Belize	. . .	17.15 N 88.45 W	**230**
1974★	**Grenada**	Grenada	.....	.....	U.K.	12.07 N 61.40 W	**230**
1974★	**Portuguese Guinea**	Guiné	Guinea-Bissau	Guinea-Bissau	Port.	12.00 N 15.00 W	**150**
1975★	**Angola**	Angola	.....	.....	Port.	12.30 S 18.30 E	**138**
1975	**British Solomon Islands**	British Solomon Islands	Solomon Islands	Solomon Islands	. . .	8.00 S 159.00 E	**14**
1975★	**Cape Verde Islands**	Cabo Verde	.....	.....	Port.	16.00 N 24.00 W	**134**
1975★	**Comoro Islands**	Comores	.....	.....	Fr.	12.10 S 44.10 E	**138**
1975	**Dahomey**	Dahomey	Benin	Bénin	. . .	9.30 N 2.15 E	**134**
1975	**Ellice Islands**	Ellice Islands	Tuvalu	Tuvalu	. . .	8.00 S 178.00 E	**14**
1975	**Malagasy Republic**	République malgache	Madagascar	Madigasikara	. . .	19.00 S 46.00 E	**138**
1975★	**Mozambique**	Moçambique	.....	.....	Port.	18.15 S 35.00 E	**138**
1975★	**Sao Tome and Principe**	São Tomé e Príncipe	.....	.....	Port.	1.00 N 7.00 E	**138**
1975★	**Surinam**	Suriname	.....	.....	Ned.	4.00 N 56.00 W	**242**
1975★	**New Guinea, Papua**	Territory of New Guinea, Papua	Papua New Guinea	Papua New Guinea	Austl.	6.00 S 150.00 E	**14**
1976	**North Vietnam, South Vietnam**	Viet-nam Dan-chu Cong-hoa, Viet-nam Cong-hoa	Vietnam	Viet-nam	. . .	16.00 N 108.00 E	**110**
1976★	**Seychelles**	Seychelles	.....	.....	U.K.	4.35 S 55.40 E	**138**
1977★	**Afars and Issas**	Afars et Issas	Djibouti	Djibouti	Fr.	11.30 N 43.00 E	**136**
1977	**Central African Republic**	République centrafricaine	Central African Empire	Empire centrafricaine	. . .	7.00 N 21.00 E	**136**
1977	**South West Africa**	South West Africa	Namibia	Namibia	. . .	22.00 S 17.00 E	**156**
1978★	**Dominica**	Dominica	.....	.....	U.K.	15.30 N 61.20 W	**230**
1978★	**Solomon Islands**	Solomon Islands	.....	.....	U.K.	8.00 S 159.00 E	**14**
1978★	**Tuvalu**	Tuvalu	.....	.....	U.K.	8.00 S 178.00 E	**14**
1979	**Central African Empire**	Empire centrafricaine	Central African Republic	République centrafricaine	. . .	7.00 N 21.00 E	**136**
1979★	**Gilbert Islands**	Gilbert Islands	Kiribati	Kiribati	U.K.	4.00 S 175.00 E	**14**
1979★	**Saint Lucia**	Saint Lucia	.....	.....	U.K.	13.53 N 60.58 W	**230**
1979★	**Saint Vincent**	Saint Vincent	.....	.....	U.K.	13.15 N 61.12 W	**230**
1980★	**Rhodesia**	Rhodesia	Zimbabwe	Zimbabwe	. . .	20.00 S 30.00 E	**138**

★ Newly independent country
P Former administration (for list of abbreviations see pp. *I•30–I•32*)

★ Seit kurzem unabhängiges Land
P Frühere Verwaltung (Verzeichnis der Abkürzungen s. Seiten *I•30–I•32*)

★ País recientemente independizado
P Antigua adminstración (vease la lista de abreviaturas en las pp. *I•30–I•32*)

★ Pays récemment indépendants
P Administration anterieure (por une liste d'abbréviations, voir pp. *I•30–I•32*)

★ País recentemente independente
P Antiga administração (para abreviações ver pp. *I•30–I•32*)

Table 2 • Territorial Transfers / **Tabelle 2** • Territoriale Übertragungen / **Tabla 2** • Transferencias Territoriales
Tableau 2 • Transferts Territoriaux / **Tabela 2** • Mudanças Territoriais

Year / Jahr / Año / Année / Ano	TERRITORY / TERRITORIUM / TERRITORIO / TERRITOIRE / TERRITÓRIO: English / Englisch / Inglés / Anglais / Inglês	TERRITORY: Local / Einheimisch / Local / Local / Local	FORMER ADMINISTRATION / FRÜHERE VERWALTUNG / ANTIGUA ADMINISTRACIÓN / ADMINISTRATION ANTERIEURE / ANTIGA ADMINISTRAÇÃO: English / Englisch / Inglés / Anglais / Inglês	FORMER ADMINISTRATION: Local / Einheimisch / Local / Local / Local	NEW ADMINISTRATION / NEUE VERWALTUNG / NUEVA ADMINSTRACIÓN / NOUVEL ADMINISTRATION / NOVA ADMINISTRAÇÃO: English / Englisch / Inglés / Anglais / Inglês	NEW ADMINISTRATION: Local / Einheimisch / Local / Local / Local	Location / Lage / Ubicación / Emplacement / Localização	Page / Seite / Página / Page / Página
1969	**Ifni**	Ifni	Spain	España	Morocco	Al-Magreb	29.20 N 10.00 W	**138**
1971	**Corn Islands**	Corn Islands	United States	United States	Nicaragua	Nicaragua	12.15 N 83.00 W	**236**
1972	**Southern Ryukyu Islands**	Southern Ryukyu Islands	United States	United States	Japan	Nihon	25.00 N 126.00 E	**90**
1976	**Mayotte**	Mayotte	Comoros	Comores	France	France	12.50 S 45.10 E	**157a**
1976	**Aldabra Islands**	Aldabra Islands	British Indian Ocean Territory	British Indian Ocean Territory	Seychelles	Seychelles	9.25 S 46.22 E	**138**
1976	**Desroches Island**	Île Desroches	British Indian Ocean Territory	British Indian Ocean Territory	Seychelles	Seychelles	5.41 S 53.41 E	**138**
1976	**Farquhar Group**	Farquhar Group	British Indian Ocean Territory	British Indian Ocean Territory	Seychelles	Seychelles	10.10 S 51.10 E	**138**
1976	**Portuguese Timor**	Timor	Portugal	Portugal	Indonesia	Indonesia	8.35 S 126.00 E	**112**
1976	**Spanish Sahara**	Sahara Español	Spain	España	Mauritania, Morocco	Mauritanie, Al-Magreb	24.30 N 13.00 W	**134**
1979	**Canal Zone**	Canal Zone	United States	United States	Panama	Panamá	9.10 N 79.48 W	**236**
1979	**Line Islands**	Line Islands	United Kingdom, United States	United Kingdom, United States	Kiribati	Kiribati	0.05 N 157.00 W	**14**
1979	**Phoenix Islands**	Phoenix Islands	United Kingdom, United States	United Kingdom, United States	Kiribati	Kiribati	4.00 S 172.00 W	**14**
1979	**Western Sahara (Spanish Sahara)**	—	Mauritania, Morocco	Mauritanie, Al-Magreb	Morocco	Al-Magreb	24.30 N 13.00 W	**134**

Table 3 • Place Name Changes / **Tabelle 3** • Veränderungen von Ortsnamen / **Tabla 3** • Cambios de Nombres Geográficos
Tableau 3 • Modifications des Toponymes / **Tabela 3** • Mudanças de Nome de Lugares e Acidentes

COUNTRY NAME / LÄNDERNAME / NOMBRE DEL PAÍS NOM DE PAYS / NOME DO PAÍS		FEATURE NAME / ORTSNAME / NOMBRE GEOGRÁFICO NOM D'ÉLÉMENT / NOME DO LUGAR OU ACIDENTE		Type of Feature Art Descripción Sorte d'Elément Tippo de Lugar ou Acidente	Loacation Lage Ubicación Emplacement Localização	Page Seite Página Page Página
English / Englisch Inglés / Anglais / Inglês	Local / Einheimisch Local / Local / Local	Former / Früher / Antiguo Ancien / Antigo	New / Neu / Nuevo Nouvelle / Novo			
Afghanistan	Afghānestān	Paropamisus	Selseleh-ye Safīd Kūh	∧∧	34.30 N 63.30 E	**128**
Algeria	Algérie	Assekrem	Tahat	∧	23.18 N 5.47 E	**148**
Brazil	Brasil	Teles Pires	São Manuel	≃	7.21 S 58.07 W	**248**
Brunei	Brunei	Brunei	Bandar Seri Begawan	⊙[1]	4.56 N 114.55 E	**112**
Canada	Canada	Grand Rapids Forebay	Cedar Lake	◎[1]	53.15 N 100.10 W	**184**
Canada	Canada	Peace River Reservoir	Williston Lake	◎[1]	56.00 N 124.00 W	**182**
Canada	Canada	Port Arthur/Fort William	Thunder Bay	⊙	48.23 N 89.15 W	**190**
Chad	Tchad	Fort-Lamy	Ndjamena	⊙[1]	12.07 N 15.03 E	**146**
Cuba	Cuba	Isla de Pinos	Isla de la Juventud	I	21.40 N 82.50 W	**240p**
Ecuador	Ecuador	Archipiélago de Colón	Galapagos	□[4]	0.30 S 90.30 W	**246a**
Equatorial Guinea	Guinea Ecuatorial	Fernando Poo	Macías Nguema Biyogo	I	3.30 N 8.42 E	**152**
Equatorial Guinea	Guinea Ecuatorial	Macías Nguema Biyogo	Bioko	I	3.30 N 8.42 E	**152**
Equatorial Guinea	Guinea Ecuatorial	Santa Isabel	Malabo	⊙[1]	3.45 N 8.47 E	**152**
France	France	Basses-Alpes	Alpes-de-Haute	□[5]	44.10 N 6.00 E	**62**
France	France	Basses-Pyrénées	Pyrénées-Atlantiques	□[5]	43.15 N 0.50 W	**32**
Gambia	Gambia	Bathurst	Banjul	⊙[1]	13.28 N 16.39 W	**150**
Greece	Ellás	Kastellórizon	Meyísti	I	36.08 N 29.34 E	**130**
India	Bhārat	Laccadive, Minicoy, and Amīndīvi	Lakshadweep	□[3]	10.00 N 73.00 E	**122**
India	Bhārat	Mysore	Karnataka	□[3]	14.00 N 76.00 E	**122**
Indonesia	Indonesia	Lesser Sunda Islands	Nusa Tenggara Barat	II	8.50 S 117.30 E	**115b**
Indonesia	Indonesia	Makasar	Ujung Pandang	⊙	5.07 S 119.24 E	**112**
Indonesia	Indonesia	Pegunungan Sukarno	Puncak Jaya	∧	11.13 N 79.22 E	**122**
Indonesia	Indonesia	Sukarnapura	Jayapura	⊙	2.32 S 140.42 E	**164**
Indonesia	Indonesia	Teluk Sarera	Teluk Cenderawasih	C	2.30 S 135.20 E	**164**
Laos	Lao	Vientiane	Viangchan	⊙[1]	17.58 N 102.36 E	**110**
Mexico	México	Islas Tres Marías	Islas Marías	II	21.25 N 106.28 W	**234**
Mexico	México	Ixtacihuatl	Iztaccíhuatl	∧[1]	19.11 N 106.28 W	**234**
Mozambique	Moçambique	Lourenço Marques	Maputo	⊙[1]	25.58 S 32.35 E	**156**
Nigeria	Nigeria	Vogel Peak	Dimlang	∧	8.24 N 11.47 E	**146**
Panama	Panamá	Volcán de Chiriquí	Volcán Barú	∧[1]	8.48 N 82.33 W	**236**
Vietnam	Viet-nam	Saigon	Thanh-pho Ho Chi Minh	⊙	10.45 N 106.40 E	**110**
Yemen	Al-Yaman	Ḥaḍūr Shu 'ayb	Jābāl an-Nabī Shu 'ayb	∧	15.20 N 43.55 E	**144**
Zaire	Zaïre	Lac Léopold II	Lac Mai-Ndombe	◎	2.00 S 18.20 E	**152**
Zaire	Zaïre	Luluabourg	Kananga	⊙	5.54 S 22.25 E	**152**
—	—	Gulf of Siam	Gulf of Thailand	C	10.00 N 101.00 E	**110**

- ⊙ City / Stadt / Ciudad / Ville / Cidade
- ⊙[1] Capital / Hauptstadt / Capital / Capitale / Capital
- ∧ Mountain / Berg / Montaña / Montagne / Montanha
- ∧[1] Volcano / Vulkan / Volcán / Volcan / Vulcão
- ∧∧ Mountains / Berge / Montañas / Montagnes / Montanhas
- I Island / Insel / Isla / Île / Ilha
- II Islands / Inseln / Islas / Îles / Ilhas
- ≃ River / Fluß / Río / Rivière, Fleuve / Rio
- C Bay, gulf / Bucht, Golf / Bahía, golfo / Baie, golfe / Baía, golfo
- ◎ Lake, lakes / See, Seen / Lago, lagos / Lac, lacs / Lago, lagos
- ◎[1] Reservoir / Stausee / Embalse / Réservoir, retenue / Reservatório, represa
- □[3] State, canton, republic / Land, Kanton, Republik / Estado, cantón, república / État, canton, république / Estado, cantão, república
- □[4] Province, region, oblast / Provinz, Landschaft, Oblast / Provincia, región, oblest / Province, région, oblast / Província, região, oblast
- □[5] Department, district, prefecture / Departement, Distrikt, Präfektur / Departamento, distrito, prefectura / Département, district, préfecture / Departamento, distrito, prefeitura

Table 4 • New Man Made Features / **Tabelle 4** • Neu Angelegte Projekte / **Tabla 4** • Nuevas Obras de Construcción
Tableau 4 • Nouvelles Éléments Culturels / **Tabela 4** • Obras Recém-Construídas

COUNTRY NAME / LÄNDERNAME / NOMBRE DEL PAÍS NOM DE PAYS / NOME DO PAÍS		FEATURE NAME / BEZEICHNUNG NOMBRE DE LA OBRA NOM D'ÉLÉMENT / NOME DA OBRA	Type of Feature Art Descripción Sorte d'Élément Tippo de Obra	Location Lage Ubicación Emplacement Localização	Page Seite Página Page Página
English / Englisch / Inglés Anglais / Inglês	Local / Einheimisch / Local Local / Local				
Argentina	Argentina	Embalse El Chocón	◎[1]	39.30 S 69.00 W	**254**
Argentina	Argentina	Embalse Florentino Ameghino	◎[1]	43.55 S 66.20 W	**254**
Argentina	Argentina	Zarate-Brazo Largo	⋈	34.06 S 59.02 W	**258**
Australia	Australia	Lake Argyle	◎[1]	16.30 S 128.45 E	**162**
Brazil	Brasil	Reprêsa Boa Esperança	◎[1]	6.50 S 44.00 W	**250**
Brazil	Brasil	Ponte Presidente Costa e. Silva	⋈	22.53 S 43.10 W	**287a**
Brazil	Brasil	Rodovia Transamazônica	//	7.30 S 60.00 W	**242**
Canada	Canada	Exploits Dam	◎[1]	48.45 N 56.35 W	**186**
Canada	Canada	Pudops Dam	◎[1]	48.15 N 56.50 W	**186**
China, Pakistan	Zhongguo, Pākistān	Karakoram Highway	//	36.52 N 75.27 E	**123**
France	France	Aéroport Charles De Gaulle	⊠	49.01 N 2.33 E	**261**
Iran, Turkey	Īrān, Türkiye	—	⊣	38.28 N 44.25 E	**119**
Mexico	México	Presa de las Adjuntas	◎[1]	24.00 N 98.50 W	**234**
Mexico	México	Presa de la Angostura	◎[1]	16.10 N 92.40 W	**234**
Mozambique	Moçambique	Cabora Bassa Dam	◎[1]	15.30 S 32.20 W	**154**
Portugal	Portugal	Barragem de Alqueva	◎[1]	38.14 N 7.29 W	**34**
Portugal	Portugal	Ponte 25 de Abril	⋈	38.41 N 9.11 W	**266c**
Romania, Yugoslavia	România, Jugoslavija	Iron Gate Reservoir	◎[1]	44.30 N 22.00 E	**38**
South Africa	South Africa (English) Suid-Afrika (Afrikaans)	Verwoerd Reservoir	◎[1]	30.40 S 25.40 E	**158**
Spain	España	Embalse de Alcántara	◎[1]	39.45 N 6.25 W	**34**
Spain	España	Embalse de Almendra	◎[1]	41.15 N 6.10 W	**34**
Tanzania, Zambia	Tanzania, Zambia	Tazara (Tanzania Zambia Railroad)	⊣	9.20 S 32.42 E	**154**
Turkey	Türkiye	Bosporus (Boğaziçi Köprüsü)	⋈	41.02 N 29.02 E	**267b**
Turkey	Türkiye	Keban Gölü	◎[1]	38.50 N 39.15 E	**130**
Union of Soviet Socialist Republics	Sojuz Sovetskich Socialističeskich Respublik	Kapčagajskoje vodochranilišče	◎[1]	44.00 N 78.00 E	**85**
Union of Soviet Socialist Republics	Sojuz Sovetskich Socialističeskich Respublik	Krasnojarskoje vodochranilišče	◎[1]	55.00 N 92.00 E	**86**
Union of Soviet Socialist Republics	Sojuz Sovetskich Socialističeskich Respublik	Nurekskoje vodochranilišče	◎[1]	38.30 N 69.30 E	**85**
Union of Soviet Socialist Republics	Sojuz Sovetskich Socialističeskich Respublik	Saratovskoje vodochranilišče	◎[1]	53.00 N 49.00 E	**80**
Union of Soviet Socialist Republics	Sojuz Sovetskich Socialističeskich Respublik	Ust'-Ilimskoje vodochranilišče	◎[1]	57.00 N 102.00 E	**88**
United States	United States	California Aqueduct	≡	33.52 N. 117.12 W	**204**
United States	United States	Dallas-Fort Worth Regional Airport	⊠	32.54 N 97.01 W	**222**
United States	United States	Harry S. Truman Reservoir	◎[1]	38.15 N 93.30 W	**194**
United States	United States	Lake Livingston	◎[1]	30.45 N 95.10 W	**196**
United States	United States	Sears Tower	⌂	41.54 N 87.37 W	**278**
Venezuela	Venezuela	Embalse Guri	◎[1]	7.30 N 62.50 W	**246**

- ◎[1] Reservoir/dam / Stausee/Damm / Embalse/presa / Réservoir/barrage / Represa/barragem
- ≡ Canal / Kanal / Canal / Canal / Canal
- ⊠ Airport / Flughafen / Aeropuerto / Aéroport / Aeroporto
- ⋈ Bridge / Brücke / Puente / Pont / Ponte
- // Road / Straße / Carretera / Route / Rodovia
- ⊣ Railroad / Eisenbahn / Via ferroviaria / Voie ferrée / Ferrovia
- ⌂ Building / Gebäude / Edificio / Bâtiment / Edifício

Table 5 • Internal Administrative Changes / **Tabelle 5** • Interne Administrative Veränderungen / **Tabla 5** • Cambios Administrativos Internos
Tableau 5 • Modifications Administratives Internes / **Tabela 5** • Mudanças Administrativas Internas

Year Jahr Año Année Ano	COUNTRY NAME / LÄNDERNAME / NOMBRE DEL PAÍS NOM DE PAYS / NOME DO PAÍS		Number of Units / Anzahl der Bezirke Número de Unidades / Nombre d'Unités Número de Unidades		CAPITAL / HAUPTSTADT / CAPITAL CAPITALE / CAPITAL		Location Lage Ubicación Emplacement Localização	Page Seite Página Page Página
	English / Englisch / Inglés Anglais / Inglês	Local / Einheimisch / Local Local / Local	Former / Früher / Antiguo Ancien / Antigo	New / Neu / Nuevo Nouvelle / Novo	Former / Früher / Antiguo Ancien / Antigo	New / Neu / Nuevo Nouvelle / Novo		
1970	**Belize**	Belize	…	…	Belize	Belmopan	17.15 N 88.46 W	**232**
1970	**Tonga**	Tonga	…	…		Nukualofa	20.00 S 175.00 W	**14**
1971	**United Arab Emirates**	Ittiḥad al-Imārāt al-'Arabīyah	…	…	—	Abū Ẓaby	24.28 N 54.22 E	**128**
1973	**China**	Zhongguo	29	30	— …	…	39.15 N 117.15 W	**98**
1974	**Algeria**	Algérie	15	31	…	…	28.00 N 3.00 E	**148**
1974	**Guyana**	Guyana	9	6	…	…	5.00 N 59.00 W	**246**
1974	**Paraguay**	Paraguay	16	19	…	…	23.00 S 58.00 W	**242**
1974	**United Kingdom (England and Wales)**	United Kingdom (England and Wales)	61	48	…	…	52.30 N 2.30 W	**28**
1975	**Malawi**	Malawi	…	…	Zomba	Lilongwe	13.59 S 33.44 E	**154**
1975	**Poland**	Polska	17	49	…	…	52.00 N 19.00 E	**30**
1975	**Tuvalu**	Tuvalu	…	…	Tarawa	Funafuti	8.00 S 178.00 E	**14**
1975	**United Kingdom (Scotland)**	United Kingdom (Scotland)	32	12	…	…	57.00 N 4.00 W	**28**
1976	**Cuba**	Cuba	6	14	…	…	21.30 N 80.00 W	**240p**
1976	**Philippines**	Pilipinas	…	…	Quezon City	Manila	14.35 N 121.00 E	**116**
1977	**Chile**	Chile	0	13	…	…	30.00 S 71.00 W	**252**

THIS TABLE gives the area, population, population density, capital, and political status for every country in the world. The political units listed are categorized by political status in the last column of the table, as follows: A—independent countries; B—internally independent political entities which are under the protection of another country in matters of defense and foreign affairs; C—colonies and other dependent political units; and D—the major administrative subdivisions of Australia, Canada, China, the Soviet Union, the United Kingdom, and the United States. For comparison, the table also includes the continents and the world. For units categorized B, the names of protecting countries are specified in the political-status column. For units categorized C, the names of administering countries are given in parentheses in the first column. A key to abbreviations of country names appears on page I·30. All footnotes to this table appear on page I·13.

The populations are estimates for January 1, 1980, made by Rand McNally & Company on the basis of official data, United Nations estimates, and other available information.

IN DIESER ÜBERSICHT sind Fläche, Bevölkerung, Bevölkerungsdichte, Hauptstadt und politischer Status für jedes Land der Erde aufgeführt. Die politischen Einheiten sind in der letzten Spalte der Tabelle nach ihrem politischen Status wie folgt gegliedert: A—souveräne Staaten; B—innenpolitisch unabhängige Länder unter der Protektion eines anderen Landes in Angelegenheiten der Aussenpolitik und Verteidigung; C—Kolonien oder anderweitig abhängige Gebiete; D—die wichtigsten Verwaltungseinheiten von Australien, Kanada, China, der Sowjetunion, dem Vereinigten Königreich und den Vereinigten Staaten. Für Vergleiche enthält die Übersicht auch Angaben über die Kontinente und die Welt. Für die unter B eingestuften Einheiten ist der Name des Schutzstaates in der Spalte Politischer Status aufgeführt. Für die unter C eingestuften Gebiete steht der Name des die Verwaltung ausübenden Landes in Klammern in der ersten Spalte. Ein Verzeichnis der Abkürzungen der Ländernamen findet sich auf Seite I·30. Alle Fussnoten zu dieser Übersicht erscheinen auf Seite I·13.

Die Bevölkerungsangaben sind Schätzungen zum 1. Januar 1980, die Rand McNally & Company auf der Grundlage amtlicher Zahlen, Schätzungen der Vereinten Nationen und anderer zugänglicher Informationen berechnet hat.

EL CUADRO ABAJO incluye la extensión, población y densidad de población, la capital y el estado político de todos los países del mundo. Las entidades políticas nombradas están clasificadas de acuerdo a su estado político en la última columna de la tabla, de esta manera: A—países independientes; B—entidades políticas internamente independientes las cuales se encuentran bajo la protección de otro país en cuanto a asuntos de defensa nacional y relaciones con el extranjero; C—colonias y otras entidades políticas dependientes; y D—las mayores subdivisiones administrativas de Australia, Canadá, China, la Unión Soviética, el Reino Unido, y los Estados Unidos. Para servir de medida comparativa, el cuadro también incluye los continentes y el mundo. Para las entidades de la clasificación B, los nombres de los países protectores están especificados en la columna de estado político. Para las unidades bajo la categoría C, los nombres de los países administradores se encuentran entre paréntesis en la primera columna. El código de las abreviaciones de los nombres de los países aparece en la página I·30. Todas las notas para este cuadro se encuentran en la página I·13.

Las poblaciones son los estimados de Rand McNally & Company, tomados el lo. de Enero de 1980, en base a datos oficiales, estimados de las Naciones Unidas y varias otras informaciones disponibles.

CETTE TABLE donne, pour chaque pays du monde, les renseignements suivants: superficie, population, densité de population, capitale, statut politique. Les entités politiques sont classées, selon leur statut, dans la dernière colonne du tableau: A—pays indépendants; B—entités politiques indépendants intérieurement, mais qui se trouvent sous la protection d'un autre pays pour leur défense et leurs relations extérieures; C—colonies et autres entités politiques dépendantes; D—principales subdivisions administratives de l'Australie, du Canada, de la Chine, de l'U.R.S.S., du Royaume-Uni, des États-Unis. Pour permettre les comparaisons, la table comprend aussi les continents et le monde. Pour les entités politiques de la catégorie B, les noms des pays protecteurs sont spécifiés dans la colonne "statut politique". Pour celles de la catégorie C, les noms des pays administrateurs sont mis entre parenthèses dans la première colonne. Un index des abréviations des noms de pays se trouve à la page I·30. Toutes les notes et renvois relatifs à cette table se trouvent à la page I·13.

Les chiffres concernant la population sont des estimations au 1er janvier 1980, établies par Rand McNally & Company, d'après les sources officielles, les estimations des Nations Unies et autres informations disponibles.

A TABELA que se segue apresenta a área, a população, a densidade demográfica, a capital e o estatuto político de todos os países do mundo. As unidades políticas relacionadas na tabela estão classificadas de acordo com o respectivo estatuto político na última coluna, do seguinte modo; A—países independentes; B—unidades políticas internamente independentes mas que se encontram sob a proteção de outro país no tocante a assuntos de defesa nacional e negócios estrangeiros; C—colônias e outras unidades políticas dependentes; e D—subdivisões administrativas principais da Austrália, Canadá, China, União Soviética, Reino Unido e Estados Unidos. Para fins de comparabilidade, a tabela também inclui os continentes e o mundo. No tocante às unidades classificadas em B, os nomes dos países protetores estão especificados na coluna relativa ao estatuto político. Para as unidades da categoria C, os nomes dos países administradores figuram entre parênteses na primeira coluna. Uma lista das abreviaturas dos nomes dos países aparece à pág. I·30. Todas as chamadas de pé-de-página da tabela encontram-se à pág. I·13.

Os dados relativos à população são estimativas de Rand McNally & Company para 1 de janeiro de 1980, com base em dados oficiais, estimativas das Nações Unidas e outras informações disponíveis.

NAME / NAME / NOMBRE / NOM / NOME English / Englisch Inglés / Anglais / Inglês	Local / Einheimisch Local / Local / Local	AREA / FLÄCHE AREA / SUPERFICIE / ÁREA km²	sq. mi.	POPULATION BEVÖLKERUNG POBLACIÓN POPULATION POPULAÇÃO	DENSITY PER BEVÖLKERUNGSDICHTE PRO / DENSIDAD POR DENSITÉ / DENSIDÀDE POR km²	sq. mi.	CAPITAL HAUPTSTADT CAPITAL CAPITALE CAPITAL	POLITICAL STATUS POLITISCHER STATUS ESTADO POLÍTICO STATUT POLITIQUE ESTATUTO POLÍTICO
†Afghanistan	Afghānestān	647,500	250,000	15,670,000	24	63	Kābul	A
Africa	...	30,264,000	11,685,000	463,800,000	15	40	...	...
Alabama, U.S.	Alabama	133,667	51,609	3,813,200	29	74	Montgomery	D
Alaska, U.S.	Alaska	1,518,800	586,412	406,100	0.3	0.7	Juneau	D
†Albania	Shqipëri	28,748	11,100	2,785,000	97	251	Tiranë	A
Alberta, Can.	Alberta	661,185	255,285	1,905,000	2.9	7.5	Edmonton	D
†Algeria	Algérie	2,381,741	919,595	19,415,000	8.2	21	Alger (Algiers)	A
American Samoa (U.S.)	American Samoa	197	76	34,000	173	447	Pago Pago	C
Andorra	Andorra	453	175	36,000	79	206	Andorra	A
†Angola	Angola	1,246,700	481,353	7,875,000	6.3	16	Luanda	A
Anguilla (U.K.)	Anguilla	91	35	7,500	82	214	The Valley	C
Anhwei, China	Anhui	139,900	54,000	45,905,000	328	850	Hefei (Hofei)	D
Antarctica	...	13,209,000	5,100,000	(1)	...	...	...	...
Antigua (incl. Barbuda)	Antigua	442	171	74,000	167	433	Saint Johns	B (U.K.)
†Argentina	Argentina	2,776,889	1,072,162	26,885,000	9.7	25	Buenos Aires	A
Arizona, U.S.	Arizona	295,023	113,909	2,451,400	8.3	22	Phoenix	D
Arkansas, U.S.	Arkansas	137,539	53,104	2,232,300	16	42	Little Rock	D
Armenia, U.S.S.R.	Arm'anskaja S.S.R.	29,800	11,500	3,050,000	102	265	Jerevan	D
Asia	...	44,250,000	17,085,000	2,581,000,000	58	151	...	...
†Australia	Australia	7,686,849	2,967,909	14,510,000	1.9	4.9	Canberra	A
Australian Capital Territory, Austl.	Australian Capital Territory	2,432	939	220,000	90	234	Canberra	D
†Austria	Österreich	83,849	32,374	7,505,000	90	232	Wien (Vienna)	A
Azerbaidzhan, U.S.S.R.	Azerbajdžanskaja S.S.R.	86,600	33,450	6,105,000	70	183	Baku	D
†Bahamas	Bahamas	13,935	5,380	235,000	17	44	Nassau	A
†Bahrain	Al-Baḥrayn	598	231	305,000	510	1,320	Al-Manāmah	A
†Bangladesh	Bangladesh	142,775	55,126	87,560,000	613	1,588	Dacca	A
†Barbados	Barbados	430	166	260,000	605	1,566	Bridgetown	A
†Belgium	Belgique (French) België (Dutch)	30,513	11,781	9,890,000	324	839	Bruxelles (Brussels)	A
Belize (U.K.)	Belize	22,965	8,867	155,000	6.7	17	Belmopan	C
†Benin	Benin	112,622	43,484	3,510,000	31	81	Porto Novo	A
Bermuda (U.K.)	Bermuda	54	21	60,000	1,111	2,857	Hamilton	C
†Bhutan	Druk-Yul	47,000	18,200	1,450,000	31	80	Paro and Thimbu	B (India)
†Bolivia	Bolivia	1,098,581	424,164	7,370,000	6.7	17	Sucre and La Paz	A
†Botswana	Botswana	600,372	231,805	750,000	1.2	3.2	Gaborone	A
†Brazil	Brasil	8,511,965	3,286,487	120,400,000	14	37	Brasília	A
British Antarctic Territory (excl. Antarctic mainland) (U.K.)	British Antarctic Territory	5,284	2,040	(1)	...	...	Stanley, Falkland Islands	C
British Columbia, Can.	British Columbia	948,596	366,255	2,575,000	2.7	7.0	Victoria	D
British Indian Ocean Territory (U.K.)	British Indian Ocean Territory	47	18	(1)	...	...	Victoria, Seychelles	C
British Virgin Islands (U.K.)	British Virgin Islands	153	59	10,000	65	169	Road Town	C
Brunei	Brunei	5,765	2,226	220,000	38	99	Bandar Seri Begawan	B (U.K.)
†Bulgaria	Bâlgarija	110,912	42,823	8,865,000	80	207	Sofija (Sofia)	A
†Burma	Myanma	678,033	261,790	33,255,000	49	127	Rangoon	A
†Burundi	Burundi	27,834	10,747	4,435,000	159	413	Bujumbura	A
†Byelorussia, U.S.S.R.	Belorusskaja S.S.R.	207,600	80,150	9,660,000	47	121	Minsk	D
California, U.S.	California	411,013	158,693	22,848,000	56	144	Sacramento	D
†Cameroon	Cameroun	475,442	183,569	8,310,000	17	45	Yaoundé	A
†Canada	Canada	9,976,139	3,851,809	23,845,000	2.4	6.2	Ottawa	A
Canton and Enderbury (U.K.-U.S.)	Canton and Enderbury	70	27	...	...	...	...	C
†Cape Verde	Cabo Verde	4,033	1,557	320,000	79	206	Praia	A
Cayman Islands (U.K.)	Cayman Islands	260	100	16,000	62	160	Georgetown	C
†Central African Republic	République centrafricaine	622,984	240,535	2,010,000	3.2	8.4	Bangui	A
†Chad	Tchad	1,284,000	495,800	4,455,000	3.5	9.0	Ndjamena	A
Chekiang, China	Zhejiang	101,800	39,300	40,590,000	399	1,033	Hangzhou (Hangchow)	D
†Chile	Chile	756,945	292,258	11,170,000	15	38	Santiago	A
†China (excl. Taiwan)	Zhongguo	9,561,000	3,691,500	933,070,000	98	253	Beijing (Peking)	A
Christmas Island (Austl.)	Christmas Island	135	52	3,600	27	69	The Settlement	C
Cocos (Keeling) Islands (Austl.)	Cocos (Keeling) Islands	14	5	700	50	140	...	C
†Colombia	Colombia	1,138,914	439,737	26,710,000	23	61	Bogotá	A
Colorado, U.S.	Colorado	269,998	104,247	2,755,300	10	26	Denver	D
†Comoros	Comores	2,079	803	390,000	188	486	Moroni	A
†Congo	Congo	342,000	132,000	1,505,000	4.4	11	Brazzaville	A
Connecticut, U.S.	Connecticut	12,973	5,009	3,099,400	239	619	Hartford	D
Cook Islands (N.Z.)	Cook Islands	241	93	16,000	66	172	Avarua	C
Coral Sea Islands (Austl.)	Coral Sea Islands	2.6	1	(1)	...	...	Canberra, Australia	C

NAME / NAME / NOMBRE / NOM / NOME — English / Englisch / Inglés / Anglais / Inglês	Local / Einheimisch / Local / Local / Local	AREA / FLÄCHE / AREA / SUPERFICIE / ÁREA km²	sq. mi.	POPULATION / BEVÖLKERUNG / POBLACIÓN / POPULATION / POPULAÇÃO	DENSITY PER / BEVÖLKERUNGSDICHTE / PRO / DENSIDAD POR / DENSITÉ / DENSIDADE POR km²	sq. mi.	CAPITAL / HAUPTSTADT / CAPITAL / CAPITALE / CAPITAL	POLITICAL STATUS / POLITISCHER STATUS / ESTADO POLÍTICO / STATUT POLITIQUE / ESTATUTO POLÍTICO
†Costa Rica	Costa Rica	50,900	19,650	2,185,000	43	111	San José	A
†Cuba	Cuba	114,524	44,218	9,930,000	87	225	La Habana (Havana)	A
†Cyprus	Kípros (Greek) Kıbrıs (Turkish)	9,251	3,572	620,000	67	174	Levkósia (Nicosia)	A
†Czechoslovakia	Československo	127,876	49,373	15,310,000	120	310	Praha (Prague)	A
Delaware, U.S.	Delaware	5,328	2,057	583,500	110	284	Dover	D
†Denmark	Danmark	43,069	16,629	5,120,000	119	308	København (Copenhagen)	A
District of Columbia, U.S.	District of Columbia	174	67	652,000	3,747	9,731	Washington	D
†Djibouti	Djibouti	23,000	8,900	143,000	6.2	16	Djibouti	A
†Dominica	Dominica	751	290	83,000	111	286	Roseau	A
†Dominican Republic	República Dominicana	48,734	18,816	5,330,000	109	283	Santo Domingo	A
†Ecuador	Ecuador	283,561	109,483	8,190,000	29	75	Quito	A
†Egypt(2)	Mișr	1,002,000	386,900	40,980,000	41	106	Al-Qāhirah (Cairo)	A
†El Salvador	El Salvador	21,393	8,260	4,505,000	211	545	San Salvador	A
England, U.K.	England	130,359	50,332	46,330,000	355	920	London	D
†Equatorial Guinea	Guinea Ecuatorial	28,051	10,830	335,000	12	31	Malabo	A
Estonia, U.S.S.R.	Estonskaja S.S.R.	45,100	17,400	1,515,000	34	87	Tallinn	D
†Ethiopia	Yaitopya	1,221,900	471,778	30,415,000	25	64	Addis Abeba	A
Europe	...	9,907,000	3,825,000	660,300,000	67	173	...	...
Faeroe Islands (Den.)	Føroyar	1,399	540	42,000	30	78	Tórshavn	C
Falkland Islands (Islas Malvinas) (excl. Dependencies) (U.K.)(3)	Falkland Islands	11,961	4,618	2,000	0.2	0.4	Stanley (Port Stanley)	C
†Fiji	Fiji	18,272	7,055	635,000	35	90	Suva	A
†Finland	Suomi	337,032	130,129	4,780,000	14	37	Helsinki (Helsingfors)	A
Florida, U.S.	Florida	151,670	58,560	8,917,600	59	152	Tallahassee	D
†France	France	543,998	210,039	53,580,000	98	255	Paris	A
French Guiana (Fr.)	Guyane française	91,000	35,100	62,000	0.7	1.8	Cayenne	C
French Polynesia (Fr.)	Polynésie française	4,000	1,550	146,000	37	94	Papeete	C
French Southern and Antarctic Territories (excl. Adelie Coast) (Fr.)	Terres australes et antarctiques françaises	7,557	2,918	200	0.03	0.07	...	C
Fukien, China	Fujian	123,000	47,500	22,300,000	181	469	Fuzhou (Foochow)	D
†Gabon	Gabon	267,667	103,347	545,000	2.0	5.3	Libreville	A
†Gambia	Gambia	11,295	4,361	595,000	53	136	Banjul	A
Georgia, U.S.S.R.	Gruzinskaja S.S.R.	69,700	26,900	5,070,000	73	188	Tbilisi	D
Georgia, U.S.	Georgia	152,488	58,876	5,163,400	34	88	Atlanta	D
†German Democratic Republic	Deutsche Demokratische Republik	108,178	41,768	16,740,000	155	401	Berlin (Ost) (East Berlin)	A
†Germany, Federal Republic of (incl. West Berlin)	Bundesrepublik Deutschland	248,533	95,959	61,170,000	246	637	Bonn	A
†Ghana	Ghana	238,537	92,100	11,475,000	48	125	Accra	A
Gibraltar (U.K.)	Gibraltar	6	2	29,000	4,833	14,500	Gibraltar	C
†Greece	Ellás	131,944	50,944	9,490,000	72	186	Athínai (Athens)	A
Greenland (Den.)	Grønland	2,175,600	840,000	52,000	0.02	0.06	Godthåb	C
†Grenada	Grenada	344	133	115,000	334	865	Saint George's	A
Guadeloupe (incl. Dependencies) (Fr.)	Guadeloupe	1,780	687	310,000	174	451	Basse-Terre	C
Guam (U.S.)	Guam	549	212	97,000	177	458	Agana	C
†Guatemala	Guatemala	108,889	42,042	6,890,000	63	164	Guatemala	A
Guernsey (incl. Dependencies) (U.K.)	Guernsey	78	30	54,000	692	1,800	St. Peter Port	C
†Guinea	Guinée	245,857	94,926	4,935,000	20	52	Conakry	A
†Guinea-Bissau	Guinea-Bissau	36,125	13,948	570,000	16	41	Bissau	A
†Guyana	Guyana	214,969	83,000	840,000	3.9	10	Georgetown	A
†Haiti	Haïti	27,750	10,714	4,950,000	178	462	Port-au-Prince	A
Hawaii, U.S.	Hawaii	16,705	6,450	922,200	55	143	Honolulu	D
Heilungkiang, China	Heilongjiang	705,300	272,300	27,525,000	39	1,011	Haerbin (Harbin)	D
Honan, China	Henan	166,800	64,400	65,500,000	393	1,017	Zhengzhou (Chengchow)	D
†Honduras	Honduras	112,088	43,277	3,100,000	28	72	Tegucigalpa	A
Hong Kong (U.K.)	Hong Kong	1,034	399	4,750,000	4,594	11,905	Victoria (Hong Kong)	C
Hopeh (incl. Peking and Tientsin), China	Hebei	214,200	82,700	70,725,000	330	855	Tianjin (Tientsin)	D
Hunan, China	Hunan	210,600	81,300	49,825,000	237	613	Changsha	D
†Hungary	Magyarország	93,032	35,920	10,775,000	116	300	Budapest	A
Hupeh, China	Hubei	187,500	72,400	41,895,000	223	579	Wuhan	D
†Iceland	Ísland	103,000	39,800	225,000	2.2	5.7	Reykjavík	A
Idaho, U.S.	Idaho	216,412	83,557	912,000	4.2	11	Boise	D
Illinois, U.S.	Illinois	146,075	56,400	11,281,400	77	200	Springfield	D
†India (incl. part of Kashmir)	Bhārat	3,183,643	1,229,210	657,240,000	206	535	New Delhi	A
Indiana, U.S.	Indiana	93,993	36,291	5,414,200	58	149	Indianapolis	D
†Indonesia	Indonesia	1,919,270	741,034	150,070,000	78	203	Jakarta	A
Inner Mongolia, China	Neimenggu Zizhiqu	424,500	163,900	17,075,000	40	104	Huhehaote	D
Iowa, U.S.	Iowa	145,790	56,290	2,909,800	20	52	Des Moines	D
†Iran	Īrān	1,648,000	636,300	36,525,000	22	57	Tehrān	A
†Iraq	Al-'Irāq	434,924	167,925	12,955,000	30	77	Baghdād	A
†Ireland	Eire	70,285	27,137	3,325,000	47	123	Dublin (Baile Átha Cliath)	A
Isle of Man (U.K.)	Isle of Man	588	227	62,000	105	273	Douglas	C
†Israel(2)	Yisra'el	20,770	8,019	3,810,000	183	475	Yerushalayim (Jerusalem)	A
†Italy	Italia	301,250	116,313	57,080,000	189	491	Roma (Rome)	A
†Ivory Coast	Côte d'Ivoire	322,463	124,504	8,135,000	25	65	Abidjan	A
†Jamaica	Jamaica	10,962	4,232	2,190,000	200	517	Kingston	A
†Japan	Nihon	372,197	143,706	116,480,000	313	811	Tōkyō	A
Jersey (U.K.)	Jersey	116	45	76,000	655	1,689	St. Helier	C
†Jordan(2)	Al-Urdunn	97,740	37,738	3,130,000	32	83	'Ammān	A
†Kampuchea	Kampuchea	181,035	69,898	6,785,000	37	97	Phnum Pénh	A
Kansas, U.S.	Kansas	213,063	82,264	2,388,200	11	29	Topeka	D
Kansu, China	Gansu	720,300	278,100	17,075,000	24	61	Lanzhou (Lanchow)	D
Kazakh S.S.R., U.S.S.R.	Kazachskaja S.S.R.	2,715,000	1,048,300	14,860,000	5.5	14	Alma-Ata	D
Kentucky, U.S.	Kentucky	104,623	40,395	3,554,700	34	88	Frankfort	D
†Kenya	Kenya	582,644	224,960	15,625,000	27	69	Nairobi	A
Kiangsi, China	Jiangxi	164,700	63,600	28,830,000	175	453	Nanchang	D
Kiangsu (incl. Shanghai), China	Jiangsu	108,000	41,700	75,581,000	700	1,812	Nanjing (Nanking)	D
Kirghiz S.S.R., U.S.S.R.	Kirgizskaja S.S.R.	198,500	76,650	3,555,000	18	46	Frunze	D
Kiribati	Kiribati	886	342	62,000	70	181	Bairiki	A
Kirin, China	Jilin	271,700	104,900	22,300,000	82	213	Changchun	D
Korea, North	Chosŏn Minjujuŭi In'min Konghwaguk	120,538(4)	46,540(4)	17,635,000	146	379	P'yŏngyang	A
Korea, South	Taehan-Min'guk	98,477(4)	38,022(4)	37,890,000	385	997	Sŏul (Seoul)	A
†Kuwait	Al-Kuwayt	16,000	6,200	1,300,000	81	210	Al-Kuwayt	A
Kwangsi Chuang, China	Guangxi Zhuang Zizhiqu	240,100	92,700	31,445,000	131	339	Nanning	D
Kwangtung, China	Guangdong	211,600	81,700	52,440,000	248	642	Guangzhou (Canton)	D
Kweichow, China	Guizhou	174,000	67,200	22,300,000	128	332	Guiyang (Kweiyang)	D
†Laos	Lao	236,800	91,400	3,680,000	16	40	Viangchan (Vientiane)	A
Latvia, U.S.S.R.	Latvijskaja S.S.R.	63,700	24,600	2,550,000	40	104	Rīga	D
†Lebanon	Al-Lubnān	10,230	3,950	3,115,000	304	789	Bayrūt (Beirut)	A
†Lesotho	Lesotho	30,355	11,720	1,330,000	44	113	Maseru	A
Liaoning, China	Liaoning	229,500	88,600	36,670,000	160	414	Shenyang (Mukden)	D
†Liberia	Liberia	111,369	43,000	1,825,000	16	42	Monrovia	A
†Libya	Lībiyā	1,759,540	679,362	2,930,000	1.7	4.3	Ṭarābulus (Tripoli)	A
Liechtenstein	Liechtenstein	160	62	26,000	163	419	Vaduz	A
Lithuania, U.S.S.R.	Litovskaja S.S.R.	65,200	25,150	3,450,000	53	137	Vilnius	D
Louisiana, U.S.	Louisiana	125,674	48,523	4,025,400	32	83	Baton Rouge	D
†Luxembourg	Luxembourg	2,586	998	350,000	135	351	Luxembourg	A
Macau (Port.)	Macau	16	6	285,000	17,813	47,500	Macau	C
†Madagascar	Madagasikara	587,041	226,658	8,610,000	15	38	Antananarivo	A
Maine, U.S.	Maine	86,026	33,215	1,106,800	13	33	Augusta	D
†Malawi	Malawi	118,484	45,747	5,820,000	49	127	Lilongwe	A
†Malaysia	Malaysia	332,633	128,430	13,480,000	41	105	Kuala Lumpur	A
†Maldives	Maldives	298	115	150,000	503	1,304	Male	A
†Mali	Mali	1,239,710	478,655	6,545,000	5.3	14	Bamako	A
†Malta	Malta	316	122	340,000	1,076	2,787	Valletta	A
Manitoba, Can.	Manitoba	650,087	251,000	1,050,000	1.6	4.2	Winnipeg	D
Martinique (Fr.)	Martinique	1,100	425	310,000	282	729	Fort-de-France	C
Maryland, U.S.	Maryland	27,394	10,577	4,170,900	152	394	Annapolis	D
Massachusetts, U.S.	Massachusetts	21,386	8,257	5,783,700	270	700	Boston	D
†Mauritania	Mauritanie	1,030,700	397,950	1,600,000	1.6	4.0	Nouakchott	A
†Mauritius (incl. Dependencies)	Mauritius	2,045	789	940,000	460	1,191	Port Louis	A
Mayotte (Fr.)	Mayotte	373	144	46,000	123	319	Dzaoudzi	C
†Mexico	México	1,972,546	761,604	70,435,000	36	92	Ciudad de México (Mexico City)	A

NAME / NAME / NOMBRE / NOM / NOME English / Englisch Inglés / Anglais / Inglês	Local / Einheimisch Local / Local / Local	AREA / FLÄCHE AREA / SUPERFICIE / ÁREA km²	sq. mi.	POPULATION BEVÖLKERUNG POBLACIÓN POPULATION POPULAÇÃO	DENSITY PER BEVÖLKERUNGSDICHTE PRO / DENSIDAD POR DENSITÉ / DENSIDADE POR km²	sq. mi.	CAPITAL HAUPTSTADT CAPITAL CAPITALE CAPITAL	POLITICAL STATUS POLITISCHER STATUS ESTADO POLÍTICO STATUT POLITIQUE ESTATUTO POLÍTICO
Michigan, U.S.	Michigan	150,779	58,216	9,262,900	61	159	Lansing	D
Midway Islands (U.S.)	Midway Islands	5	2	1,500	300	750	...	C
Minnesota, U.S.	Minnesota	217,735	84,068	4,052,100	19	48	St. Paul	D
Mississippi, U.S.	Mississippi	123,584	47,716	2,437,800	20	51	Jackson	D
Missouri, U.S.	Missouri	180,486	69,686	4,905,800	27	70	Jefferson City	D
Moldavia, U.S.S.R.	Moldavskaja S.S.R.	33,700	13,000	3,980,000	118	306	Kišin'ov (Kishinev)	D
Monaco	Monaco	1.5	0.6	26,000	17,333	43,333	Monaco	A
†Mongolia	Mongol Ard Uls	1,565,000	604,200	1,650,000	1.1	2.7	Ulaanbaatar (Ulan Bator)	A
Montana, U.S.	Montana	381,086	147,138	808,100	2.1	5.5	Helena	D
Montserrat (U.K.)	Montserrat	101	39	12,000	119	308	Plymouth	C
†Morocco	Al-Magreb	446,550	172,415	19,815,000	44	115	Rabat	A
†Mozambique	Moçambique	783,763	303,771	10,325,000	13	34	Maputo	A
Namibia (excl. Walvis Bay) (S. Afr.)[5]	Namibia	823,168	317,827	950,000	1.2	3.0	Windhoek	C
Nauru	Nauru	21	8	10,000	476	1,250	...	A
Nebraska, U.S.	Nebraska	200,017	77,227	1,583,200	7.9	21	Lincoln	D
†Nepal	Nepāl	140,797	54,362	13,840,000	98	255	Kāthmāndu	A
†Netherlands	Nederland	40,844	15,770	14,075,000	345	893	Amsterdam and 's-Gravenhage (The Hague)	A
Netherlands Antilles (Neth.)	Nederlandse Antillen	961	371	255,000	265	687	Willemstad	C
Nevada, U.S.	Nevada	286,297	110,540	709,300	2.5	6.4	Carson City	D
New Brunswick, Can.	New Brunswick	73,437	28,354	715,000	9.7	25	Fredericton	D
New Caledonia (incl. Dependencies) (Fr.)	Nouvelle-Calédonie	19,058	7,358	144,000	7.6	20	Nouméa	C
Newfoundland, Can.	Newfoundland	404,517	156,185	570,000	1.4	3.6	St. John's	D
New Hampshire, U.S.	New Hampshire	24,097	9,304	901,700	37	97	Concord	D
New Hebrides (Fr.-U.K.)	New Hebrides (English) Nouvelles-Hébrides (French)	14,760	5,700	106,000	7.2	19	Vila	C
New Jersey, U.S.	New Jersey	20,295	7,836	7,347,000	362	938	Trenton	D
New Mexico, U.S.	New Mexico	315,113	121,666	1,250,000	4.0	10	Santa Fe	D
New South Wales, Austl.	New South Wales	801,428	309,433	5,105,000	6.4	16	Sydney	D
New York, U.S.	New York	128,401	49,576	17,584,400	137	355	Albany	D
†New Zealand	New Zealand	268,675	103,736	3,155,000	12	30	Wellington	A
†Nicaragua	Nicaragua	130,000	50,200	2,535,000	20	50	Managua	A
†Niger	Niger	1,267,000	489,200	5,190,000	4.1	11	Niamey	A
†Nigeria	Nigeria	923,768	356,669	75,600,000	82	212	Lagos	A
Ningsia Hui, China	Ningxia Huizu Zizhiqu	66,300	25,600	2,615,000	39	102	Yinchuan (Yinchwan)	D
Niue (N.Z.)	Niue	259	100	3,400	13	34	Alofi	C
Norfolk Island (Austl.)	Norfolk Island	36	14	1,800	50	129	Kingston	C
North America	...	24,398,000	9,420,000	365,000,000	15	39	...	...
North Carolina, U.S.	North Carolina	136,197	52,586	5,677,700	42	108	Raleigh	D
North Dakota, U.S.	North Dakota	183,022	70,665	658,300	3.6	9.3	Bismarck	D
Northern Ireland, U.K.	Northern Ireland	14,120	5,452	1,540,000	109	282	Belfast	D
Northern Territory, Austl.	Northern Territory	1,347,519	520,280	115,000	0.09	0.2	Darwin	D
Northwest Territories, Can.	Northwest Territories	3,379,683	1,304,903	45,000	0.01	0.03	Yellowknife	D
†Norway	Norge	323,878	125,050	4,085,000	13	33	Oslo	A
Nova Scotia, Can.	Nova Scotia	55,491	21,425	860,000	15	40	Halifax	D
Oceania (incl. Australia)	...	8,534,000	3,295,000	22,700,000	2.7	6.9	...	...
Ohio, U.S.	Ohio	106,764	41,222	10,806,300	101	262	Columbus	D
Oklahoma, U.S.	Oklahoma	181,089	69,919	2,964,500	16	42	Oklahoma City	D
†Oman	'Umān	212,457	82,030	880,000	4.1	11	Masqaṭ (Muscat)	A
Ontario, Can.	Ontario	1,068,582	412,582	8,585,000	8.0	21	Toronto	D
Oregon, U.S.	Oregon	251,180	96,981	2,543,600	10	26	Salem	D
Pacific Islands Trust Territory (U.S.)	Pacific Islands Trust Territory	1,857	717	133,000	72	185	Saipan	C
†Pakistan (incl. part of Kashmir)	Pākistān	895,496	345,753	82,570,000	92	239	Islāmābād	A
†Panama	Panamá	77,096	29,767	1,960,000	25	66	Panamá	A
†Papua New Guinea	Papua New Guinea	461,691	178,260	3,110,000	6.7	17	Port Moresby	A
†Paraguay	Paraguay	406,752	157,048	2,990,000	7.4	19	Asunción	A
Pennsylvania, U.S.	Pennsylvania	117,412	45,333	11,719,600	100	259	Harrisburg	D
†Peru	Perú	1,285,216	496,224	17,505,000	14	35	Lima	A
†Philippines	Pilipinas	300,000	115,831	48,315,000	161	417	Manila	A
Pitcairn (excl. Dependencies) (U.K.)	Pitcairn	5	2	65	13	33	Adamstown	C
†Poland	Polska	312,677	120,725	35,490,000	114	294	Warszawa (Warsaw)	A
†Portugal	Portugal	92,082	35,553	9,900,000	108	278	Lisboa (Lisbon)	A
Prince Edward Island, Can.	Prince Edward Island	5,657	2,184	120,000	21	55	Charlottetown	D
Puerto Rico (U.S.)	Puerto Rico	8,897	3,435	3,570,000	401	1,039	San Juan	C
†Qatar	Qaṭar	11,000	4,247	215,000	20	51	Ad-Dawḥah (Doha)	A
Quebec, Can.	Québec	1,540,680	594,860	6,440,000	4.2	11	Québec	D
Queensland, Austl.	Queensland	1,727,522	667,000	2,205,000	1.3	3.3	Brisbane	D
Reunion (Fr.)	Réunion	2,510	969	505,000	201	521	Saint-Denis	C
Rhode Island, U.S.	Rhode Island	3,144	1,214	933,600	297	769	Providence	D
†Romania	România	237,500	91,699	22,145,000	93	241	București (Bucharest)	A
Russian Soviet Federated Socialist Republic, U.S.S.R.	Rossijskaja S.F.S.R.	17,075,400	6,592,850	139,090,000	8.1	21	Moskva (Moscow)	D
†Rwanda	Rwanda	26,338	10,169	4,700,000	178	462	Kigali	A
St. Helena (incl. Dependencies) (U.K.)	St. Helena	419	162	7,000	17	43	Jamestown	C
St. Kitts-Nevis	St. Kitts-Nevis	267	103	50,000	187	485	Basseterre	B (U.K.)
†Saint Lucia	Saint Lucia	616	238	121,000	196	508	Castries	A
St. Pierre and Miquelon (Fr.)	St.-Pierre-et-Miquelon	242	93	6,000	25	65	Saint-Pierre	C
St. Vincent	St. Vincent	388	150	121,000	312	807	Kingstown	A
San Marino	San Marino	61	24	21,000	344	875	San Marino	A
†Sao Tome and Principe	São Tome e Príncipe	964	372	86,000	89	231	São Tomé	A
Saskatchewan, Can.	Saskatchewan	651,900	251,700	955,000	1.5	3.8	Regina	D
†Saudi Arabia	Al-'Arabīyah as-Sa'ūdīyah	2,149,690	830,000	8,225,000	3.8	9.9	Ar-Riyāḍ (Riyadh)	A
Scotland, U.K.	Scotland	78,772	30,414	5,170,000	66	170	Edinburgh	D
†Senegal	Sénégal	196,722	75,955	5,575,000	28	73	Dakar	A
†Seychelles	Seychelles	404	156	66,000	163	423	Victoria	A
Shansi, China	Shānxī	157,200	60,700	23,605,000	150	389	Taiyuan (Taiyüan)	D
Shantung, China	Shandong	153,600	59,300	74,740,000	487	1,260	Jinan (Tsinan)	D
Shensi, China	Shānxī	195,800	75,600	27,525,000	141	364	Xi'an (Sian)	D
†Sierra Leone	Sierra Leone	71,740	27,699	3,940,000	55	142	Freetown	A
†Singapore	Singapore	581	224	2,375,000	4,088	10,603	Singapore	A
Sinkiang Uighur, China	Xinjiang Weiwuer Zizhiqu	1,646,700	635,800	10,450,000	6.3	16	Wulumuqi (Urumchi)	D
†Solomon Islands	Solomon Islands	29,785	11,500	225,000	7.6	20	Honiara	A
†Somalia	Somaliya	637,657	246,201	3,930,000	6.2	16	Mogadisho	A
†South Africa (incl. Walvis Bay)	South Africa (English) Suid-Afrika (Afrikaans)	1,222,161	471,879	28,860,000	24	61	Pretoria and Cape Town	A
South America	...	17,793,000	6,870,000	239,200,000	13	35	...	...
South Australia, Austl.	South Australia	984,377	380,070	1,305,000	1.3	3.4	Adelaide	D
South Carolina, U.S.	South Carolina	80,432	31,055	2,983,600	37	96	Columbia	D
South Dakota, U.S.	South Dakota	199,551	77,047	694,600	3.5	9.0	Pierre	D
†Spain	España	504,750	194,885	37,410,000	74	192	Madrid	A
Spanish North Africa (Sp.)[6]	Plazas de Soberanía en el Norte de África	32	12	127,000	3,969	10,583	...	C
†Sri Lanka	Sri Lanka	65,610	25,332	14,870,000	227	587	Colombo	A
†Sudan	As-Sūdān	2,505,813	967,500	18,175,000	7.3	19	Al-Khurṭūm (Khartoum)	A
†Suriname	Suriname	163,265	63,037	430,000	2.6	6.8	Paramaribo	A
Svalbard and Jan Mayen (Nor.)	Svalbard og Jan Mayen	62,423	24,102	(1)	...	...	Longyearbyen	C
†Swaziland	Swaziland	17,366	6,705	525,000	30	78	Mbabane	A
†Sweden	Sverige	449,750	173,649	8,325,000	19	48	Stockholm	A
Switzerland	Schweiz (German); Suisse (French); Svizzera (Italian)	41,288	15,941	6,250,000	151	392	Bern	A
†Syria[2]	As-Sūriyah	185,180	71,498	8,460,000	46	118	Dimashq (Damascus)	A
Szechwan, China	Sichuan	569,000	219,700	91,720,000	161	417	Chengdu (Chengtu)	D
Tadzhik S.S.R., U.S.S.R.	Tadžikskaja S.S.R.	143,100	55,250	3,850,000	27	70	Dušanbe	D
Taiwan	T'aiwan	35,961	13,885	18,410,000	512	1,326	T'aipei	A
†Tanzania	Tanzania	945,087	364,900	17,250,000	18	47	Dar-es-Salaam	A
Tasmania, Austl.	Tasmania	68,332	26,383	420,000	6.1	16	Hobart	D
Tennessee, U.S.	Tennessee	109,411	42,244	4,454,800	41	105	Nashville	D
Texas, U.S.	Texas	692,405	267,339	13,427,800	19	50	Austin	D
†Thailand	Prathet Thai	514,000	198,500	46,695,000	91	235	Krung Thep (Bangkok)	A
Tibet, China	Xizang Zizhiqu	1,221,700	471,700	1,680,000	1.4	3.6	Lasa (Lhasa)	D
†Togo	Togo	56,000	21,600	2,500,000	45	116	Lomé	A
Tokelau Islands (N.Z.)	Tokelau Islands	10	4	2,300	230	575	...	C
Tonga	Tonga	699	270	94,000	134	348	Nukualofa	A
†Trinidad and Tobago	Trinidad and Tobago	5,128	1,980	1,160,000	226	586	Port of Spain	A
Tsinghai, China	Qinghai	721,000	278,400	2,615,000	3.6	9.3	Xining (Sining)	D

NAME / NAME / NOMBRE / NOM / NOME English / Englisch Inglés / Anglais / Inglês	Local / Einheimisch Local / Local / Local	AREA / FLÄCHE AREA / SUPERFICIE / ÁREA km²	sq. mi.	POPULATION BEVÖLKERUNG POBLACIÓN POPULATION POPULAÇÃO	DENSITY PER BEVÖLKERUNGSDICHTE PRO / DENSIDAD POR DENSITÉ / DENSIDADE POR km²	sq. mi.	CAPITAL HAUPTSTADT CAPITAL CAPITALE CAPITAL	POLITICAL STATUS POLITISCHER STATUS ESTADO POLÍTICO STATUT POLITIQUE ESTATUTO POLÍTICO
†Tunisia	Tunisie	164,150	63,379	6,360,000	39	100	Tunis	A
†Turkey	Türkiye	780,576	301,382	44,815,000	57	149	Ankara	A
Turkmen S.S.R., U.S.S.R.	Turkmenskaja S.S.R.	488,100	188,450	2,785,000	5.7	15	Ašchabad	D
Turks and Caicos Islands (U.K.)	Turks and Caicos Islands	430	166	6,000	14	36	Grand Turk	C
Tuvalu	Tuvalu	23	9.1	10,000	434	1,099	Funafuti	A
†Uganda	Uganda	235,886	91,076	13,420,000	57	147	Kampala	A
†Ukraine, U.S.S.R.	Ukrainskaja S.S.R.	603,700	233,100	50,320,000	83	216	Kijev (Kiev)	D
†Union of Soviet Socialist Republics	Sojuz Sovetskich Socialističeskich Respublik	22,274,900	8,600,350	265,390,000	12	31	Moskva (Moscow)	A
†United Arab Emirates	Ittiḥād al-Imārāt al-'Arabīyah	83,600	32,300	775,000	9.3	24	Abū Ẓaby	A
†United Kingdom	United Kingdom	244,013	94,214	55,810,000	229	592	London	A
†United States	United States	9,519,617(7)	3,675,545(7)	220,090,000	23	60	Washington, D.C.	A
†Upper Volta	Haute-Volta	274,200	105,800	6,790,000	25	64	Ouagadougou	A
†Uruguay	Uruguay	177,508	68,536	2,890,000	16	42	Montevideo	A
Utah, U.S.	Utah	219,931	84,916	1,367,200	6.2	16	Salt Lake City	D
Uzbek S.S.R., U.S.S.R.	Uzbekskaja S.S.R.	449,600	173,600	15,550,000	35	90	Taškent	D
Vatican City	Città del Vaticano	0.4	0.2	1,000	2,500	5,000	Città del Vaticano (Vatican City)	A
†Venezuela	Venezuela	912,050	352,144	13,730,000	15	39	Caracas	A
Vermont, U.S.	Vermont	24,887	9,609	495,000	20	52	Montpelier	D
Victoria, Austl.	Victoria	227,618	87,884	3,890,000	17	44	Melbourne	D
†Vietnam	Viet-nam	332,559	128,402	51,620,000	155	402	Ha-noi	A
Virginia, U.S.	Virginia	105,716	40,817	5,242,600	50	128	Richmond	D
Virgin Islands (U.S.)	Virgin Islands	344	133	113,000	328	850	Charlotte Amalie	C
Wake Island (U.S.)	Wake Island	8	3	200	25	67	...	C
Wales, U.K.	Wales	20,761	8,016	2,770,000	133	346	Cardiff	D
Wallis and Futuna (Fr.)	Wallis et Futuna	255	98	9,500	37	97	Mata-Utu	C
Washington, U.S.	Washington	176,616	68,192	3,922,000	22	58	Olympia	D
Western Australia, Austl.	Western Australia	2,527,621	975,920	1,250,000	0.5	1.3	Perth	D
Western Sahara	...	266,000	102,700	165,000	0.6	1.6	El Aaiún	C
†Western Samoa	Western Samoa	2,842	1,097	156,000	55	142	Apia	A
West Virginia, U.S.	West Virginia	62,628	24,181	1,876,800	30	78	Charleston	D
Wisconsin, U.S.	Wisconsin	145,438	56,154	4,731,600	33	84	Madison	D
Wyoming, U.S.	Wyoming	253,596	97,914	452,300	1.8	4.6	Cheyenne	D
†Yemen	Al-Yaman	195,000	75,300	5,840,000	30	78	Ṣan'ā'	A
†Yemen, People's Democratic Republic of	Al-Yamin ash-Sha'bīyah	287,683	111,075	1,935,000	6.7	17	Aden	A
†Yugoslavia	Jugoslavija	255,804	98,766	22,145,000	87	224	Beograd (Belgrade)	A
Yukon, Can.	Yukon	536,324	207,076	25,000	0.05	0.1	Whitehorse	D
Yunnan, China	Yunnan	436,100	168,400	30,140,000	69	179	Kunming	D
†Zaire	Zaïre	2,345,409	905,567	29,650,000	13	33	Kinshasa (Léopoldville)	A
†Zambia	Zambia	752,614	290,586	5,730,000	7.6	20	Lusaka	A
Zimbabwe	Zimbabwe	390,580	150,804	7,255,000	19	48	Salisbury	A
WORLD	**...**	**148,354,000**	**57,280,000**	**4,332,000,000**	**29**	**76**	**...**	**...**

† Member of the United Nations (1979).
... None, or not applicable.
(1) No permanent population.
(2) Data do not reflect de facto changes during 1967.
(3) Claimed by Argentina.
(4) The 1,262 km² or 487 sq. mi. of the demilitarized zone are not included in either North or South Korea.
(5) In October 1966 the United Nations terminated the South African mandate over Namibia, a decision which South Africa did not accept.
(6) Comprises Ceuta, Melilla, and several small islands.
(7) Total area of the United States includes 156,492 km² or 60,422 sq. mi. of Great Lakes area, not included in any State.

† Membre des Nations Unies (1979).
... Pas d'information, ou pas applicable.
(1) Pas de population permanente.
(2) Ces données ne reflètent pas les changements de facto depuis 1967.
(3) Revendiqué par l'Argentine.
(4) Les 1 262 km² ou 487 sq. mi. de la zone démilitarisée ne sont inclus ni dans la Corée du Nord ni dans celle du Sud.
(5) En octobre 1966, les Nations Unies ont mis fin au mandat de l'Afrique du Sud sur le Namibie; l'Afrique du Sud n'a pas accepté cetta décision.
(6) Inclus Ceuta, Melilla et plusieurs petites îles.
(7) La superficie totale des États-Unis comprend les 156 492 km² ou 60 422 sq. mi. des Grands Lacs qui ne sont inclus dans aucun des États.

† Mitglied der Vereinten Nationen (1979).
... Kein(e), oder nicht anwendbar.
(1) Bevölkerungszahl schwankend.
(2) Die Angaben zeigen nicht die de facto Veränderungen des Jahres 1967.
(3) Von Argentinien beansprucht.
(4) Die 1 262 km² oder 487 sq. mi. entmilitarisierter Zone sind weder in Nord-noch in Südkorea eingetragen.
(5) Im Oktober 1966 setzten die Vereinten Nationen dem Mandat Südafrikas über Namibia ein Ende; Südafrika erkannte diese Entscheidung nicht an.
(6) Umfasst Ceuta, Melilla und mehrere kleine Inseln.
(7) Die Gesamtfläche der Vereinigten Staaten schliesst die 156 492 km² oder 60 422 sq. mi. der grossen Seen ein, die jedoch in der Flächenangabe keines Einzelstaates enthalten sind.

Membro das Nações Unidas (1979).
... Inexistente ou não aplicável.
(1) Sem população permanente.
(2) Os dados não refletem as mudanças de fato durante 1967.
(3) Reivindicado pela Argentina.
(4) Exclusive 1 262 km² (487 milhas quadradas) da zona desmilitarizada.
(5) Em outubro de 1966, as Nações Unidas terminaram o mandato da África do Sul sobre o Sudoeste Africano [Namíbia], decisão não acatada pela África do Sul.
(6) Compreende Ceuta, Melilla e várias ilhas pequenas.
(7) A área total dos Estados Unidos inclui 156 492 km² (60 422 milhas quadradas) referentes à área dos Grandes Lagos, não incluída em nenhum Estado.

† Miembro de las Naciones Unidas (1979).
... Ninguno, o no se aplica.
(1) Sin población permanente.
(2) Los datos no indican ningunos cambios de facto durante 1967.
(3) Reclamado por la Argentina.
(4) Los 1 262 km² o 487 sq. mi. de la zona desmilitarizada, no están incluídos para Corea del Norte o del Sur.
(5) En octubre de 1966, las Naciones Unidas terminaron el mandato asignado sobre Namibia, dicha decisión no fue aceptada por Sudáfrica.
(6) Comprende Ceuta, Melilla y varias islas pequeñas.
(7) Área total de los Estados Unidos que encluye 156 492 km² o 60 422 sq. mi. del área de los Grandes Lagos que no se encluye en el total de ninguno de los estados.

THIS TABLE lists the major metropolitan areas of the world according to their estimated population on January 1, 1980. For convenience in reference, the areas are grouped by major region with the total for each region given. The number of areas by population classification is given in parentheses with each size group.

For ease of comparison, each metropolitan area has been defined by Rand McNally & Company according to consistent rules. A metropolitan area includes a central city, neighboring communities linked to it by continuous built-up areas, and more distant communities if the bulk of their population is supported by commuters to the central city. Some metropolitan areas have more than one central city; in such cases each central city is listed.

IN DIESER TABELLE sind die Hauptmetropolen der Welt verzeichnet, gemessen nach ihrer Bevölkerung, die nach dem Stand vom 1. Januar 1980 geschätzt wurde. Zur besseren Übersicht sind die Zonen nach grösseren Regionen gruppiert, wobei die Gesamtzahl für jede Region angegeben ist. Die Anzahl der Zonen ist nach Bevölkerung klassifiziert und in Klammern hinter denen nach Grössen sortierten Gruppen angegeben.

Zum einfacheren Vergleich ist jede Metropole von Rand McNally & Company nach übereinstimmenden Massstäben definiert worden. Eine Metropole schliesst eine zentrale Stadt mit benachbarten Gemeinden, die mit ihr durch ununterbrochen bebaute Gebiete verbunden sind ein, sowie weiter entfernte Gemeinden, wenn der grösste Teil ihrer Bevölkerung von den Pendlern unterhalten wird. Einige Metropolen haben mehr als eine zentrale Stadt; in solchen Fällen ist jede dieser zentralen Städte angeführt.

ESTA TABLA indica las principales áreas metropolitanas del mundo, de acuerdo con su población calculada al 1 de enero de 1980. Para facilitar las referencias, las áreas se han agrupado por regiones principales, indicándose el total para cada región. El número de áreas, clasificadas por población, se indica entre paréntesis en los grupos de cada tamaño.

Para facilitar las comparaciones, Rand McNally y Compañía ha definido cada área metropolitana de acuerdo con reglas consistentes. Un área metropolitana incluye una ciudad central, localidades vecinas vinculadas con ella mediante sectores construídos y contínuos, y localidades más distantes, si el grueso de su población lo constituye un núcleo que diariamente viaja a la ciudad central. Algunas áreas metropolitanas incluyen más de una ciudad central; en tales casos se indica cada una dichas ciudades.

CETTE TABLE contient la liste des aires métropolitaines les plus considérables dans le monde pour ce qui est du peuplement a la date du 1 er janvier 1980. Afin de faciliter la consultation, on a groupé les aires par grandes régions en indiquant la population totale pour chaque région, et, entre parenthèses, le nombre d'aires comprises dans celle-ci.

Afin de rendre plus faciles les comparaisons, Rand McNally & Co. a défini chaque aire métropolitaine selon des règles cohérentes: une aire métropolitaine englobe une cité centrale ou métropole et l'environnement urbain continu qui s'y rattache; elle inclut également des agglomérations éloignées de la métropole lorsque la population de ces dernières est pour sa májorité constituée d'habitants se rendant quotidiennement dans la cité ou est situé le lieu de travail de ceux-ci. On trouvera quelques aires métropolitaines pourvues de plus d'une métropole. Dans ce cas, chaque métropole est mentionnée.

A TABELA que se segúe relaciona as principais áreas metropolitanas do mundo, de acordo com as respectivas populações, estimadas para 1 de janeiro de 1980. Para facilidade de referência, as áreas metropolitanas foram agrupadas dentro das regiões maiores, indicando-se, entre parênteses, os totais de cada região maior e o número de áreas metropolitanas, classificadas segundo a população, compreendidas em cada uma.

Para fins de comparabilidade, Rand McNally & Company definiu cada área metropolitana de acordo com regras uniformes. Uma área metropolitana inclui uma cidade central, as localidades vizinhas ligadas a ela por áreas construídas contínuas, e as localidades mais distantes, desde que a maior parte de suas respectivas populações dependa economicamente da cidade central e que para ela viaje diariamente. Algumas áreas metropolitanas incluem mais de uma cidade central; em tais casos, indicam-se ambas as cidades.

CLASSIFICATION KLASSIFIZIERT CLASIFICADAS CLASSIFICATION CLASSIFICAÇÃO	ANGLO-AMERICA ANGLO-AMERIKA AMÉRICA ANGLOSAJONA AMÉRIQUE ANGLO-SAXONNE AMÉRICA ANGLO-SAXÔNICA	LATIN AMERICA LATEIN-AMERIKA AMÉRICA LATINA AMÉRIQUE LATINE AMÉRICA LATINA	EUROPE EUROPA EUROPA EUROPE EUROPA	U.S.S.R. U.S.S.R. U.R.S.S. U.R.S.S. U.R.S.S.	ASIA ASIEN ASIA ASIE ÁSIA	AFRICA-OCEANIA AFRIKA-OZEANIEN AFRICA-OCEANÍA AFRIQUE-OCÉANIE ÁFRICA-OCEANIA
OVER–15,000,000 (3)	New York				Ōsaka-Kōbe-Kyōto Tōkyō-Yokohama	
10,000,000–15,000,000 (7)		Buenos Aires Ciudad de México (Mexico City) São Paulo	London	Moskva (Moscow)	Calcutta Sŏul (Seoul)	
5,000,000–10,000,000 (17)	Chicago Los Angeles Philadelphia-Trenton-Wilmington	Rio de Janeiro	Essen-Dortmund-Duisburg (The Ruhr) Paris	Leningrad	Beijing (Peking) Bombay Delhi Jakarta Karāchi Krung Thep (Bangkok) Manila Shanghai Tehrān	Al-Qāhirah (Cairo)
3,000,000–5,000,000 (27)	Boston Detroit-Windsor San Francisco-Oakland-San Jose Washington	Bogotá Caracas Lima Santiago	Athínai (Athens) Barcelona Berlin İstanbul Madrid Milano (Milan) Roma (Rome)		Baghdād Chongqing (Chungking) Dacca Madras Nagoya Shenyang (Mukden) T'aipei Tianjin (Tientsin) Victoria Wuhan	Sydney Johannesburg
2,000,000–3,000,000 (46)	Cleveland Dallas-Fort Worth Houston Miami-Fort Lauderdale Montréal Pittsburgh St. Louis San Diego-Tijuana Toronto	Belo Horizonte Guadalajara La Habana (Havana) Monterrey Pôrto Alegre Recife	Birmingham Bruxelles (Brussels) Bucureşti (Bucharest) Budapest Hamburg Katowice-Bytom-Gliwice Lisboa (Lisbon) Manchester Napoli (Naples) Warszawa (Warsaw)	Doneck-Makejevka Kijev (Kiev) Taškent	Ahmadābād Ankara Bangalore Guangzhou (Canton) Haerbin (Harbin) Hyderābād Lahore Pusan Rangoon Singapore Thanh-pho Ho Chi Minh (Sai-gon) Xi'an (Sian)	Alger (Algiers) Al-Iskandarīyah (Alexandria) Casablanca Kinshasa Lagos Melbourne
1,500,000–2,000,000 (33)	Atlanta Baltimore Buffalo-Niagara Falls-Saint Catharines-Niagara Falls Minneapolis-St. Paul Seattle-Tacoma	Medellín Salvador San Juan	Amsterdam Frankfurt am Main Glasgow København (Copenhagen) Köln (Cologne) Leeds-Bradford Liverpool München (Munich) Stuttgart Torino (Turin) Wien (Vienna)	Baku Char'kov (Kharkov) Gor'kij (Gorky)	Chengdu (Chengtu) Colombo Dimashq (Damascus) Fukuoka Kānpur Kitakyūshū-Shimonoseki Nanjing (Nanking) Pune (Poona) Surabaya Taegu Taiyuan	
1,000,000–1,500,000 (85)	Cincinnati Denver El Paso-Ciudad Juárez Hartford-New Britain Indianapolis Kansas City Milwaukee New Orleans Phoenix Portland San Antonio Vancouver	Cali Córdoba Curitiba Fortaleza Guatemala Guayaquil Montevideo Rosario Santo Domingo	Antwerpen (Anvers) Beograd (Belgrade) Bilbao Düsseldorf Hannover Lille Łódź Lyon Mannheim Marseille Newcastle-Sunderland Nürnberg Porto Praha (Prague) Rotterdam Sofija (Sofia) Stockholm Valencia	Čel'abinsk (Chelyabinsk) Dnepropetrovsk Jerevan Kazan' Kujbyšev (Kuybyshev) Minsk Novosibirsk Odessa Omsk Perm Rostov-na-Donu Saratov Sverdlovsk Tbilisi Ufa Volgograd	Al-Kuwayt Anshan Bandung Bayrūt (Beirut) Changchun (Hsinking) Chittagong Dimashq (Damascus) Fushun Ha-noi Hiroshima-Kure İzmir Jinan (Tsinan) Kaohsiung Kuala Lumpur Kunming Lanzhou (Lanchow) Lucknow Lüda (Dairen) Lyallpur Nāgpur P'yongyang Qingdao (Tsingtao) Sapporo Shijiazhuang (Shihchiachuang) Tel Aviv-Yafo Zhengzhou (Chengchow)	Ādīs Ābeba Brisbane Cape Town Durban Tunis
TOTAL/GESAMTZAHL TOTAL/TOTAL/TOTAL (218)	34	26	49	24	71	14

ALL URBAN CENTERS of 50,000 or more population and many other important or well-known cities and towns are listed in the following table. The populations are from recent censuses (designated C) or official estimates (designated E) for the dates specified. For a few cities, only unofficial estimates are available (designated UE). For comparison, the total population of each country is also given. For each country, the date stated for the total population also applies to the cities, except those for which another date is specified.

Population estimates for 1980 for countries may be found in the World Information Table (pages *I•10–I•13*).

A population figure in parentheses and preceded by a star (★) is the population of a city's entire metropolitan area. To permit meaningful comparisons of metropolitan areas, these have been defined by Rand McNally according to consistent rules (see introduction to Metropolitan Areas Table, page *I•14*), and in some cases may differ somewhat from the officially recognized metropolitan areas. Where a town is located within the metropolitan area of another city, that city's name is given in parentheses preceded by a star (★). The capital of a country is denoted by CAPITAL letters.

ALLE STÄDTISCHEN ZENTREN mit 50 000 oder mehr Einwohnern und zahlreiche andere bedeutende oder bekannte Städte sind in der folgenden Tabelle zusammengestellt. Die Bevölkerungszahlen stammen von neuesten Zählungen (mit C gekennzeichnet) oder amtlichen Schätzungen (E) zu den angegebenen Zeitpunkten. Für einige wenige Städte waren lediglich inoffizielle Schätzungen erhältlich (UE). Zu Vergleichszwecken ist ferner die Gesamtbevölkerung jedes Landes angegeben. Das Bezugsjahr für die Einwohnerzahl eines Landes betrifft auch die Städte mit Ausnahme jener, bei denen ein anderes Datum angegeben ist.

Schätzungen der Bevölkerungszahlen der Länder für 1980 finden sich in der Welt-Informationstabelle (Seite *I•10–I•13*).

Bevölkerungszahlen in Klammern mit vorangestelltem Stern (★) beziehen sich auf die gesamte Stadtregion einer Stadt. Um sinnvolle Vergleiche von Stadtregionen zu ermöglichen, wurden diese von Rand McNally nach einheitlichen Regeln festgelegt (siehe Einleitung: Tabelle der Stadtregionen, Seite *I•14*), weshalb sie in einigen Fällen etwas von der offiziellen Abgrenzung von Stadtregionen abweichen können. Ist eine Stadt in die Stadtregion einer anderen Grossstadt einbezogen, so wird der Name der Stadtregion mit vorangestelltem Stern (★) in Klammern aufgeführt. Die Hauptstadt eines Landes wird durch GROSSBUCHSTABEN hervorgehoben.

TODAS LOS CENTROS URBANOS de 50 000 habitantes o más y muchos otros de importancia así como bien conocidas ciudades y pueblos están incluídos en la tabla que se presenta a continuación. El número de habitantes indicados está tomado del censo más reciente (cifras identificadas con la letra C) o estimados oficiales (E) para las fechas especificadas. Para algunas ciudades, sólo existen informes no oficiales (UE). Para medida de comparación, la población total de cada país se encuentra incluída también.

Para permitir una comparación, se da la población total de cada país, referente al mismo año que se usa para las ciudades principles, excepto para aquellas en las que se especifica otra fecha. El número de habitantes para 1980 para los países, se encuentra en la Tabla de Información Mundial (páginas *I•10–I•13*).

La segunda cifra para la población que aparece en paréntesis y está precedida por una estrella (★) constituye la población de un área metropolitana entera. Para permitir comparaciones validas de áreas metropolitanas, éstas fueron definidas por Rand McNally siguiendo las reglas establecidas para estos propósitos (véase la Introducción a la Tabla de las Áreas Metropolitanas, página *I•14*), y en algunas ocasiones pueden ser un poco distintas de las áreas metropolitanas oficialmente reconocidas. Cuando una población se encuentra dentro de los límites de un área metropolitana de otra ciudad, el nombre de ésta se da entre paréntesis precedido por una (★). La capital de un país se indica con letras MAYÚSCULAS.

TOUTES LES VILLES de plus de 50 000 habitants et des villes moins peuplées, mais célèbres ou importantes, sont mentionnées dans la table ci-dessous. Les chiffres donnant la population proviennent de recensements récents (référence C), ou d'estimations officielles (référence E), aux dates indiquées. Pour quelques villes, on dispose seulement d'estimations non officielles (référence UE). La population totale de chaque pays est également donnée, ce qui permet des comparaisons. Dans chaque pays, la date des renseignements est identique pour les villes et le pays, sauf indication contraire.

On trouvera dans la table d'informations mondiales (pages *I•10* à *I•13*) les estimations de la population en 1980 pour chaque pays.

Les chiffres entre parenthèses, précédés d'une étoile (★), indiquent la population de l'ensemble de la zone métropolitaine. Pour permettre d'établir des comparaisons significatives entre les zones métropolitaines, ces dernières ont été définies selon des critères uniformes par Rand McNally & Company (voir l'introduction à la table des zones métropolitaines, page *I•14*). Parfois, les limites des zones métropolitaines ainsi définies diffèrent des limites officielles. Quand une ville fait partie de la zone métropolitaine d'une autre ville, le nom de celle-ci, précédé d'une étoile (★), est mis entre parenthèses. Le nom des capitales de pays est écrit en lettres MAJUSCULES.

TODOS OS CENTROS URBANOS de 50 000 habitantes e mais, bem como muitas outras cidades e vilas importantes ou muito conhecidas figuram na tabela que se apresenta em seguida. Os dados relativos à população referem-se a censos recentes (identificadas com a letra C), ou a estimativas oficiais (E) nas datas indicadas. Para algumas cidades só existem estimativas não oficiais (UE). Para fins de comparabilidade, apresenta-se também a população total de cada país.

Para cada país, a data de referência da população total aplica-se também às cidades exceto quando especificado em contrário. As estimativas da população dos países para 1980 encontra-se na *Tabela de informaçoes mundiais* (páginas *I•10–I•13*).

Um dado de população apresentado entre parênteses e precedido por uma estrela (★), refere-se à população de toda a área metropolitana. Para fins de comparabilidade, as áreas metropolitanas foram definidas por Rand McNally segundo regras coerentes (ver a 'Introdução' à *Tabela das áreas metropolitanas*, página *I•14*), e em certos casos podem ser um pouco diferentes das áreas metropolitanas oficialmente reconhecidas. Quando um centro urbano esta localizado dentro dos limites da área metropolitana de outro, seu nome figura entre parênteses precedido por uma estrela (★). A capital de um país é indicada por letras MAIÚSCULAS.

AFGHANISTAN / Afghānestān	
1975 E	19,280,000
Andkhvoy	46,000
Herāt	157,000
Jalālābād	58,000
•KĀBUL	749,000
Mazār-e Sharīf	97,000
Qandahār	209,000
Qondūz	46,000

ALBANIA / Shqipëri	
1971 E	2,188,000
Durrës	55,000
Korçë	47,900
Shkodër	56,500
•TIRANË	174,800
Vlorë (Valona)	51,400

ALGERIA / Algérie	
1974 E	16,275,000
Aïn Témouchent	47,977
•ALGER (ALGIERS) (★1,800,000)	1,503,720
Annaba (Bône)	313,174
Batna (115,138▲)	91,500
Béchar (Colomb-Béchar)	71,081
Bejaïa (Bougie) (103,996▲)	80,000
Biskra	84,971
Blida	158,947
Bordj Bou Arreridj (85,545▲)	66,400
Bordj Ménaïel (87,736▲)	38,700
Boufarik (109,234▲)	77,700
Constantine	350,183
Djidjelli (61,545▲)	43,500
Douéra	55,993
El Affroun (67,566▲)	47,500
El Asnam (Orléansville) (114,327▲)	80,500
Ghardaïa (85,230▲)	55,200
Ighil Izane (Relizane)	65,918
Khemis Miliana (63,370▲)	41,400
Laghouat (60,249▲)	41,900
Mascara (82,468▲)	70,600
Médéa (102,336▲)	70,700
Mostaganem	101,780
Oran (Ouahran)	485,139
Saïda (59,344▲)	51,800
Sétif	157,065
Sidi bel Abbès	151,148
Skikda (Philippeville)	127,968
Souk Ahras (60,551▲)	48,800
Tébessa	58,008
Tiaret	63,039
Tizi-Ouzou (223,702▲)	108,000
Tlemcen	115,054
Touggourt (65,935▲)	34,800

AMERICAN SAMOA	
1970 C	27,159
•PAGO PAGO	2,451

ANDORRA	
1971 C	20,550
•ANDORRA	2,000

ANGOLA	
1970 C	5,673,046
Cabinda	21,124
Huambo (Nova Lisboa)	61,885
Lobito	59,528
•LUANDA	475,328

ANGUILLA	
1974 C	6,519
•South Hill	774
THE VALLEY	760

ANTIGUA	
1970 C	65,525
•SAINT JOHNS	21,814

ARGENTINA	
1970 C	23,362,204
Almirante Brown (★Buenos Aires)	245,017
Avellaneda (★Buenos Aires)	337,538
Bahía Blanca	182,158
Berazategui (★Buenos Aires)	127,740
Berisso (★La Plata)	58,833
•BUENOS AIRES (1974 E) (★9,300,000)	2,976,000
Caseros (Tres de Febrero) (★Buenos Aires)	313,460
Catamarca (★64,410)	57,228
Comodoro Rivadavia	72,906
Concordia	72,136
Córdoba (★825,000)	798,663
Corrientes	136,924
Esteban Echeverría (★Buenos Aires)	111,150
Florencio Varela (★Buenos Aires)	98,446
Formosa	61,071
General San Martín (★Buenos Aires)	360,573
General Sarmiento (San Miguel) (★Buenos Aires)	315,457
Godoy Cruz (★Mendoza)	112,481
Guaymallén (★Mendoza)	112,081
Junín	59,020
Lanús (★Buenos Aires)	449,824
La Plata (★510,000)	408,300
La Rioja	46,090
Las Heras (★Mendoza)	67,789
Lomas de Zamora (★Buenos Aires)	410,806
Mar del Plata	302,282
Mendoza (★500,000)	118,568
Merlo (★Buenos Aires)	188,868
Moreno (★Buenos Aires)	114,041
Morón (★Buenos Aires)	485,983
Olavarría	52,453
Paraná	127,635
Pergamino	56,078
Posadas	97,514
Quilmes (★Buenos Aires)	355,265
Resistencia	142,848
Río Cuarto	88,852
Rosario (★875,000)	750,455
Salta	176,216
San Fernando (★Buenos Aires)	119,565
San Francisco	45,023
San Isidro (★Buenos Aires)	250,008
San Juan (★225,000)	112,500
San Justo (★Buenos Aires)	659,193
San Lorenzo (★Rosario)	56,487
San Luis	50,771
San Miguel de Tucumán (★380,000)	321,567
San Nicolás de los Arroyos	64,730
San Rafael	58,237
San Salvador de Jujuy	82,637
Santa Fe	244,655
Santiago del Estero (★140,000)	105,127
Tandil	65,876
Tigre (★Buenos Aires)	152,335
Vicente López (★Buenos Aires)	285,178
Villa Krause (★San Juan)	47,794
Villa María	56,087
Zárate	54,772

AUSTRALIA	
1978 E	14,248,600
Adelaide (★930,500)	13,500
Auburn (★Sydney)	48,400
Ballarat (★72,100)	38,600
Bankstown (★Sydney)	159,300
Blacktown (★Sydney)	173,700
Blue Mountains (★Sydney)	49,300
Box Hill (★Melbourne)	49,300
Brisbane (1976 C) (★957,745)	696,740
Brisbane Water (★Sydney) (1976 C)	54,819
Broadmeadows (★Melbourne)	111,300
Brunswick (★Melbourne)	45,200
Camberwell (★Melbourne)	88,200
Campbelltown (★Sydney)	68,200
CANBERRA (★234,700)	214,450
Canning (★Perth)	46,400
Canterbury (★Sydney)	133,200
Caulfield (★Melbourne)	75,000
Coburg (★Melbourne)	57,600
Dandenong (★Melbourne)	53,500
Darwin (1976 C) (★46,655)	39,193
Doncaster and Templestowe (★Melbourne)	87,300
Enfield (★Adelaide)	71,200
Essendon (★Melbourne)	49,800
Fairfield (★Sydney)	118,500
Footscray (★Melbourne)	52,200
Frankston (★Melbourne)	78,700
Geelong (★139,800)	15,400
Heidelberg (★Melbourne)	67,200
Hobart (1977 E) (★164,500)	50,100
Holroyd (★Sydney)	82,400
Hurstville (★Sydney)	67,200
Ipswich (★Brisbane) (1976 C)	69,242

▲ Population of an entire municipality, commune, or district, including rural area.
• Largest city in country.
★ Population or designation of the metropolitan area, including suburbs.
C Census. E Official estimate. UE Unofficial estimate.
L Population within municipal limits of year specified.

▲ Bevölkerung eines ganzen städtischen Verwaltungsgebietes, eines Kommunalbezirkes oder eines Distrikts, einschliesslich ländlicher Gebiete.
• Grösste Stadt des Landes.
★ Bevölkerung oder Bezeichnung der Stadtregion einschliess lich Vororte.
C Volkszählung. E Offizielle Schätzung. UE Inoffizielle Schätzung.
L Bevölkerung innerhalb der städtischen Verwaltungseinheit des angegebenen Jahres.

▲ Población de un municipio, comuna o distrito entero, incluyendo sus áreas rurales.
• Ciudad más grande de un país.
★ Población o designación de un área metropolitana, incluyendo los suburbios.
C Censo. E Estimado oficial. UE Estimado no oficial.
L Población dentro de los límites municipales de un año especifico.

▲ Population d'une municipalité, d'une commune ou d'un district, zone rurale incluse.
• Ville la plus peuplée du pays.
★ Population de l'agglomération (ou nom de la zone métropolitaine englobante).
C Recensement. E Estimation officielle. UE Estimation non officielle.
L Population comprise dans les limites municipales de l'année indiquée.

▲ População de um município, comuna ou distrito, inclusive as respectivas áreas rurais.
• Maior cidade de um país.
★ População ou indicação de uma área metropolitana, inclusive subúrbios.
C Censo. E Estimativa oficial. UE Estimativa não oficial.
L População dentro dos limites municipais no ano indicado.

AUSTRALIA *continued*

Keilor (★Melbourne)	74,900
Knox (★Melbourne)	80,600
Kogarah (★Sydney)	47,800
Ku-ring-gai (★Sydney)	102,800
Lake Macquarie (★Newcastle)	138,000
Launceston (1977 E) (★83,000)	32,900
Leichhardt (★Sydney)	63,100
Liverpool (★Sydney)	95,200
Malvern (★Melbourne)	47,200
Marion (★Adelaide)	69,800
Marrickville (★Sydney)	90,800
Melbourne (★2,717,600)	66,800
Melville (★Perth)	56,300
Mitcham (★Adelaide)	59,900
Moorabbin (★Melbourne)	103,300
Newcastle (★375,300)	139,900
Northcote (★Melbourne)	52,600
North Sydney (★Sydney)	48,400
Nunawading (★Melbourne)	95,900
Oakleigh (★Melbourne)	54,800
Parramatta (★Sydney)	134,200
Penrith (★Sydney)	88,900
Perth (★864,900)	89,400
Prahran (★Melbourne)	48,300
Preston (★Melbourne)	88,400
Randwick (★Sydney)	123,900
Rockdale (★Sydney)	86,600
Rockhampton (1976 C) (★51,669)	51,133
Ryde (★Sydney)	91,700
St. Kilda (★Melbourne)	52,600
Salisbury (★Adelaide)	83,500
Southport (Gold Coast) (1976 C) (★116,195)	87,510
Springvale (★Melbourne)	77,700
Stirling (★Perth)	168,900
Sunshine (★Melbourne)	94,400
•Sydney (★3,155,200)	50,700
Tea Tree Gully (★Adelaide)	62,000
Toowoomba (1976 C)	66,436
Townsville (1976 C) (★88,401)	80,365
Waverley (★Melbourne)	121,600
Waverley (★Sydney)	63,900
West Torrens (★Adelaide)	46,800
Willoughby (★Sydney)	52,400
Wollongong (★222,000)	171,700
Woodville (★Adelaide)	76,600
Woollahra (★Sydney)	54,700

AUSTRIA / Österreich

1977 E	7,518,342
Bruck an der Mur (★50,000)	16,359
Graz (1976 E) (★275,000)	250,900
Innsbruck (1976 E) (★150,000)	120,400
Klagenfurt (1973 L)	82,512
Leoben (1971 C) (★48,000)	35,153
Linz (1976 E) (★290,000)	208,000
Salzburg (1976 E) (★165,000)	139,000
Sankt Pölten (1973 L)	50,144
Steyr (1971 C) (★54,000)	40,578
Villach (1973 L)	50,993
Wels (1971 C) (★59,000)	47,279
•WIEN (VIENNA) (★1,935,000)	1,590,100

BAHAMAS

1970 C	168,812
Freeport	15,286
•NASSAU (★101,503)	3,233

BAHRAIN / Al-Baḥrayn

1971 C	216,078
•AL-MANĀMAH (★145,000)	89,112
Al-Muḥarraq (★Al-Manāmah)	37,577

BANGLADESH

1974 C	71,479,071
Barisāl	98,127
Bogra	47,154
Brāhmanbāria	62,407
Chāndpur	51,668
Chittagong (★1,050,000)	416,733
Comilla	86,446
•DACCA (★2,400,000)	1,310,976
Dinājpur	61,866
Doublemooring (★Chittagong)	125,453
Farīdpur	46,232
Harirāmpur (★Dacca)	71,429
Jamālpur	60,261
Jessore (★82,817)	76,168
Khulna	437,304
Mīrpur (★Dacca)	91,525
Nārāyanganj (★Dacca)	176,459
Nasirābād (Mymensingh) (★182,153)	76,036
Nawābganj	46,059
Pābna	62,254
Pānchlāish (★Chittagong)	127,839
Rājshāhi (Rampur Boalia) (★132,909)	96,645
Rangpur	72,829
Saidpur	90,132
Sirājganj	74,457
Sītākunda (★Chittagong)	99,929
Sylhet	59,546
Tangail	51,863
Tongi (★Dacca)	67,420

BARBADOS

1970 C	238,141
•BRIDGETOWN (★115,000)	8,789

BELGIUM / Belgique / België

1977 E	9,837,413
Aalst (Alost) (★Bruxelles)	80,556
Anderlecht (★Bruxelles)	98,300
Antwerpen (Anvers) (★1,105,000)	201,806
Bastogne	10,972
Berchem (★Antwerpen)	47,227
Borgerhout (★Antwerpen)	45,624
Brugge (Bruges) (★215,000)	118,333
•BRUXELLES (BRUSSEL) (BRUSSELS) (★2,400,000)	150,005
Charleroi (★500,000)	227,115
Deurne (★Antwerpen)	80,021
Etterbeek (★Bruxelles)	47,356
Forest (Vorst) (★Bruxelles)	51,547
Genk (★Hasselt)	61,313
Gent (Gand) (★470,000)	246,171
Hasselt (★270,000)	63,681
Ixelles (Elsene) (★Bruxelles)	79,657
Kortrijk (Courtrai) (★200,000)	77,173
La Louvière (★150,000)	77,859
Leuven (Louvain) (★165,000)	87,125
Liège (Luik) (★770,000)	227,974
Mechelen (Malines) (★120,000)	78,462
Molenbeek-St.-Jean (Sint-Jans-Molenbeek) (★Bruxelles)	71,176
Mons (Bergen) (★255,000)	97,445
Mouscron (Moeskroen) (★Lille, France)	54,551
Namur (★140,000)	100,296
Oostende (Ostende) (★120,000)	71,319
Roeselare (Roulers)	51,518
Saint-Gilles (Sint-Gillis) (★Bruxelles)	50,032
Schaerbeek (Schaarbeek) (★Bruxelles)	100,558
Seraing (★Liège)	66,713
Sint-Niklaas (Saint-Nicolas)	67,323
Spa	9,629
Tournai (Doornik)	70,346
Uccle (Ukkel) (★Bruxelles)	76,854
Verviers (★105,000)	56,861
Waterloo (★Bruxelles)	24,019

BELIZE

1972 E	127,200
•Belize City	41,500
BELMOPAN (1971 E)	5,000

BENIN

1975 E	3,112,000
•Cotonou	178,000
PORTO-NOVO	104,000

BERMUDA

1970 C	52,330
•HAMILTON (★13,757)	2,060

BHUTAN / Druk-Yul

1977 E	1,232,000
•THIMBU	8,982

BOLIVIA

1976 C	4,647,816
Cochabamba	205,002
•LA PAZ	654,713
Oruro	124,121
Potosí	77,334
Santa Cruz	256,946
SUCRE	62,207

BOTSWANA

1971 C	574,094
Francistown	18,613
•GABORONE (GABERONES)	18,799

BRAZIL / Brasil

1970 C	93,215,301
Alagoinhas	53,891
Americana	62,387
Anápolis	89,405
Aracaju	179,512
Araçatuba	85,660
Araguari	48,702
Araraquara	82,607
Bagé	57,036
Barbacena	57,766
Barra Mansa (★Volta Redonda)	75,006
Barretos	53,050
Bauru	120,178
Belém (★660,000)	565,097
Belford Roxo (★Rio de Janeiro)	173,427
Belo Horizonte (1975 E) (★1,945,000)	1,557,464
Blumenau	85,942
BRASÍLIA (1975 UE) (★750,000)	350,000
Cachoeira do Sul	50,001
Cachoeiro de Itapemirim	58,968
Campina Grande	163,206
Campinas	328,629
Campo Grande	130,792
Campos	153,310
Campos Elyseos (★Rio de Janeiro)	104,636
Canoas (★Pôrto Alegre)	148,798
Carapicuíba (★São Paulo)	54,907
Caruaru	101,006
Catanduva	48,446
Cavaleiro (★Recife)	58,811
Caxias do Sul	107,487
Coelho da Rocha (★Rio de Janeiro)	100,781
Colatina	46,012
Corumbá	48,607
Criciúma	50,430
Cuiabá	83,621
Curitiba (★680,000)	483,038
Diadema (★São Paulo)	68,552
Divinópolis	69,872
Duque de Caxias (★Rio de Janeiro)	256,582
Feira de Santana	127,105
Florianópolis	115,665
Fortaleza (1975 E) (★1,175,000)	1,109,837
Franca	86,852
Garanhuns	49,579
Goiânia	362,152
Governador Valadares	125,174
Guaratinguetá	55,069
Guarulhos (★São Paulo)	221,639
Ilhéus	58,529
Ipiíba (★Rio de Janeiro)	55,486
Itabuna	89,928
Itajaí	54,135
Itaquari (★Vitória)	64,559
Ituiutaba	46,784
Jaboatão (★Recife)	52,537
Jacareí	48,684
Jequié	62,341
João Pessoa (★310,000)	197,398
Joinvile	77,760
Juàzeiro do Norte	79,796
Juiz de Fora	218,832
Jundiaí	145,785
Lajes	82,325
Limeira	77,243
Londrina	156,670
Macapá	51,563
Maceió	242,867
Manaus	284,118
Marília	73,165
Maringá	51,620
Mauá (★São Paulo)	101,569
Mesquita (★Rio de Janeiro)	93,926
Mogi das Cruzes (★São Paulo)	90,330
Monjolo (★Rio de Janeiro)	46,793
Montes Claros	81,572
Mossoró	77,251
Muribeca dos Guararapes (★Recife)	74,963
Natal	250,787
Neves (★Rio de Janeiro)	112,912
Nilópolis (★Rio de Janeiro)	86,720
Niterói (★Rio de Janeiro) (1975 E)	376,033
Nova Friburgo	65,732
Nova Iguaçu (★Rio de Janeiro)	331,457
Nôvo Hamburgo (★Pôrto Alegre)	81,248
Olinda (★Recife)	187,553
Osasco (★São Paulo)	283,303
Paranaguá	51,510
Parnaíba	57,031
Parque Industrial (★Belo Horizonte)	80,572
Passo Fundo	69,135
Pelotas	150,278
Petrópolis (★Rio de Janeiro)	116,080
Pinheirinho (★Curitiba)	50,302
Piracicaba	125,490
Poços de Caldas	51,844
Ponta Grossa	92,344
Pôrto Alegre (1975 E) (★1,760,000)	1,043,964
Presidente Prudente	91,188
Queimados (★Rio de Janeiro)	62,560
Recife (1975 E) (★2,100,000)	1,249,821
Ribeirão Prêto	190,897
Rio Claro	69,240
Rio de Janeiro (1975 E) (★8,235,000)	4,857,716
Rio Grande	98,863
Salvador (1975 E) (★1,270,000)	1,237,373
Santa Maria	120,667
Santana do Livramento	48,448
Santarém	51,123
Santo André (★São Paulo)	415,025
Santos (★610,000)	341,317
São Bernardo do Campo (★São Paulo)	187,368
São Caetano do Sul (★São Paulo)	150,171
São Carlos	74,835
São Gonçalo (★Rio de Janeiro)	161,392
São João del Rei	45,019
São João de Meriti (★Rio de Janeiro)	163,934
São José do Rio Prêto	108,319
São José dos Campos	130,118
São Leopoldo (★Pôrto Alegre)	62,861
São Luís	167,529
•São Paulo (1975 E) (★9,900,000)	7,198,608
São Vicente (★Santos)	116,075
Sete Lagoas	61,063
Sete Pontes (★Rio de Janeiro)	53,766
Sobral	51,864
Sorocaba	165,990
Taubaté	98,933
Teófilo Otoni	64,568
Teresina	181,071
Teresópolis	53,462
Tubarão	51,121
Uberaba	108,576
Uberlândia	110,463
Uruguaiana	60,667
Vicente de Carvalho (★Santos)	59,767
Vitória (★345,000)	121,978
Vitória da Conquista	82,477
Volta Redonda (★205,000)	120,645

BRUNEI

1971 C	136,256
•BANDAR SERI BEGAWAN (BRUNEI) (★37,000)	17,410
Seria	20,824

BULGARIA / Bâlgarija

1976 E	8,761,000
Burgas	146,700
Gabrovo (1969 E)	71,800
Haskovo (Khaskovo) (1969 E)	66,900
Jambol (Yambol) (1969 E)	70,300
Kazanlâk (1969 E)	50,300
Pazardžik (1969 E)	61,400
Pernik (Dimitrovo) (1969 E)	79,900
Pleven	109,500
Plovdiv	307,400
Ruse	161,600
Sliven (1969 E)	81,100
•SOFIJA (SOFIA) (1977 E) (★1,099,269)	1,020,704
Stara Zagora	123,900
Šumen (Shumen) (Kolarovgrad) (1969 E)	69,600
Tolbuhin (Dobrich) (1969 E)	64,100
Varna	257,700
Veliko Târnovo (1969 E)	43,700
Vidin (1969 E)	42,600
Vraca (1969 E)	47,600

BURMA / Myanma

1977 E	31,512,000
Bassein	138,000
Henzada (1970 E)	85,000
Mandalay	458,000
Moulmein	188,000
Myingyan (1970 E)	65,000
Pegu	135,000
Pyè (Prome) (1970 E)	65,000
•RANGOON	2,276,000
Sittwe (Akyab) (1970 E)	82,000
Tavoy (1970 E)	53,000

BURUNDI

1976 E	3,864,000
•BUJUMBURA	157,000

CAMEROON / Cameroun

1976 C	7,663,246
Bafoussam	62,239
•Douala	458,246
Garoua	63,900
Maroua	67,187
Nkongsamba	71,298
YAOUNDÉ	313,706

CANADA

1976 C	22,992,604
Beauport, Québec (★Québec)	55,339
Brampton, Ontario (★Toronto)	103,459
Brantford, Ontario (★82,800)	66,950
Burlington, Ontario (★Hamilton)	104,314
Burnaby, British Columbia (★Vancouver)	131,599
Calgary, Alberta	469,917
Cambridge (Galt), Ontario (★Kitchener)	72,383
Charlesbourg, Québec (★Québec)	63,147
Charlottetown, Prince Edward Island (★24,837)	17,063
Chicoutimi, Québec (★128,643)	57,737
Dartmouth, Nova Scotia (★Halifax)	65,341
East York, Ontario (★Toronto)	106,950
Edmonton, Alberta (★554,228)	461,361
Etobicoke, Ontario (★Toronto)	297,109
Gatineau, Québec (★Ottawa)	73,479
Guelph, Ontario (★70,388)	67,538
Halifax, Nova Scotia (★267,991)	117,882
Hamilton, Ontario (★529,371)	312,003
Hull, Québec (★Ottawa)	61,039
Jonquière, Québec (★Chicoutimi)	60,691
Kamloops, British Columbia	58,311
Kelowna, British Columbia	51,955
Kingston, Ontario (★90,741)	56,032
Kitchener, Ontario (★272,158)	131,870
LaSalle, Québec (★Montréal)	76,713
Laval, Québec (★Montréal)	246,243
London, Ontario (★270,383)	240,392
Longueuil, Québec (★Montréal)	122,429
Markham, Ontario (★Toronto)	56,206
Mississauga, Ontario (★Toronto)	250,017
Moncton, New Brunswick (★77,571)	55,934
•Montréal, Québec (★2,802,485)	1,080,546
Montréal-Nord, Québec (★Montréal)	97,250
Niagara Falls, Ontario (★Saint Catharines)	69,423
North Bay, Ontario (★53,961)	51,639
North York, Ontario (★Toronto)	558,398
Oakville, Ontario (★Toronto)	68,950
Oshawa, Ontario (★135,196)	107,023
OTTAWA, Ontario (★693,288)	304,462
Peterborough, Ontario (★65,293)	59,683
Prince George, British Columbia	59,929
Québec, Québec (★542,158)	177,082
Regina, Saskatchewan (★151,191)	149,593
Richmond, British Columbia (★Vancouver)	80,034
Saint Catharines, Ontario (★301,921)	123,351
Sainte-Foy, Québec (★Québec)	71,237
Saint John, New Brunswick (★112,974)	85,956
Saint John's, Newfoundland (★143,390)	86,576
Saint-Laurent, Québec, (★Montréal)	64,404
Saint-Léonard, Québec (★Montréal)	78,452
Sarnia, Ontario (★81,342)	55,576
Saskatoon, Saskatchewan	133,750
Sault Sainte Marie, Ontario (★81,992)	81,048
Scarborough, Ontario (★Toronto)	387,149
Shawinigan, Québec (★55,414)	24,921
Sherbrooke, Québec (★104,505)	76,804
Sudbury, Ontario (★157,030)	97,604
Sydney, Nova Scotia (★88,614)	30,645
Thunder Bay, Ontario (★119,253)	111,476
Toronto, Ontario (★2,803,101)	633,318
Trois-Rivières, Québec (★98,583)	52,518
Vancouver, British Columbia (★1,166,348)	410,188
Verdun, Québec (★Montréal)	68,013
Victoria, British Columbia (★218,250)	62,551
Whitehorse, Yukon	13,311
Windsor, Ontario (★247,582)	196,526
Winnipeg, Manitoba (★578,217)	560,874
Yellowknife, N.W. Ter.	8,256
York, Ontario (★Toronto)	141,367

▲ Population of an entire municipality, commune, or district, including rural area.
• Largest city in country.
★ Population or designation of the metropolitan area, including suburbs.
C Census. E Official estimate. UE Unofficial estimate.
L Population within municipal limits of year specified.

▲ Bevölkerung eines ganzen städtischen Verwaltungsgebietes, eines Kommunalbezirkes oder eines Distrikts, einschliesslich ländlicher Gebiete.
• Grösste Stadt des Landes.
★ Bevölkerung oder Bezeichnung der Stadtregion einschliess lich Vororte.
C Volkszählung. E Offizielle Schätzung.
UE Inoffizielle Schätzung.
L Bevölkerung innerhalb der städtischen Verwaltungseinheit des angegebenen Jahres.

CAPE VERDE / Cabo Verde
1970 C ... 272,071
•Mindelo ... 28,797
PRAIA ... 21,494

CAYMAN IS.
1970 C ... 10,652
•GEORGETOWN ... 3,975

CENTRAL AFRICAN REPUBLIC / République centrafricaine
1971 E ... 1,637,000
Bambari (1968 E) ... 35,300
•BANGUI ... 187,000

CHAD / Tchad
1975 E ... 4,030,000
Moundou ... 45,000
•NDJAMENA ... 224,000
Sarh ... 50,000

CHILE
1970 C ... 8,880,889
Antofagasta ... 138,821
Apoquindo (★Santiago) ... 90,722
Arica ... 87,726
Calama ... 45,863
Chillán ... 87,555
Concepción (★395,000) ... 175,853
Conchalí (★Santiago) ... 246,046
Copiapó ... 45,194
Coquimbo ... 50,405
Iquique ... 65,040
La Cisterna (★Santiago) ... 246,537
La Granja (★Santiago) ... 163,882
La Serena ... 61,897
Lo Prado Arriba (★Santiago) ... 112,548
Los Angeles ... 49,175
Lota ... 48,166
Ñuñoa (★Santiago) ... 280,733
Osorno ... 68,815
Providencia (★Santiago) ... 85,678
Puente Alto (★Santiago) ... 61,077
Puerto Montt ... 62,726
Punta Arenas ... 61,813
Quinta Normal (★Santiago) ... 138,007
Rancagua ... 86,404
Renca (★Santiago) ... 68,440
San Antonio ... 46,744
San Bernardo (★Santiago) ... 100,225
San Miguel (★Santiago) ... 320,883
•SANTIAGO (★2,925,000) ... 517,473
Talca ... 94,449
Talcahuano (★Concepción) ... 152,755
Temuco ... 110,335
Valdivia ... 82,362
Valparaíso (★530,000) ... 250,358
Viña del Mar (★Valparaíso) ... 188,811

CHINA / Zhongguo
1958 UE ... 650,000,000
Andong (Antung) ... 370,000
Anqing (Anking) (1953 C) ... 105,300
Anshan ... 833,000
Anyang (1953 C) ... 124,900
Baiyinchang (Paiyin) ... 50,000
Bangbu (Pengpu) ... 330,000
Baoding (Paoting) (1957 E) ... 265,000
Baoji (Paoki) ... 180,000
Baotou (Paotow) ... 490,000
Belan (Peian) (1953 UE) ... 70,000
Beihai (Pakhoi) (1953 C) ... 80,000
BEIJING (PEKING) (1970 E) (7,570,000▲) ... 4,800,000
Benxi (Penki) (1953 C) ... 449,000
Boshan (Tzupo) ... 250,000
Boxian (Pohsien) (1953 UE) ... 90,000
Cangzhou (1953 UE) ... 60,000
Changchun (Hsinking) ... 988,000
Changde (Changte) (1953 C) ... 94,800
Changsha ... 709,000
Changshu (1953 C) ... 101,400
Changzhi (Changchih) ... 180,000
Changzhou (Changchow) ... 300,000
Chaoan ... 101,300
Chengde (Chengteh) ... 120,000
Chengdu (Chengtu) ... 1,135,000
Chifeng (Chihfeng) (1953 C) ... 49,000
Chongqing (Chungking) ... 2,165,000
Datong (Tatung) (1953 C) ... 228,500
Duyun (Tuyün) ... 60,000
Foshan (Fatshan) ... 120,000
Fuling (Fowling) (1953 UE) ... 60,000
Fushun ... 1,019,000
Fuxian (Fuhsien) (1953 UE) ... 70,000
Fuxinshi (Fusin) ... 290,000
Fuyang (Fowyang) (1953 UE) ... 65,000
Fuzhou (Foochow) ... 623,000
Ganzhou (Kanchow) (1953 C) ... 98,600
Gejiu (Kokiu) ... 180,000
Guangzhou (Canton) ... 1,867,000
Guilin (Kweilin) ... 170,000
Guiyang (Kweiyang) ... 530,000
Haerbin (Harbin) (1959 E) ... 1,814,000
Haicheng (1953 UE) ... 80,000
Haikou (Hoihow) ... 402,000
Hailaer (Hailar) ... 60,000
Handan (Hantan) ... 380,000
Hangu (Hanku) (1953 UE) ... 50,000
Hangzhou (Hangchow) ... 794,000
Hanzhong (Hanchung) (1953 C) ... 70,000
Hechuan (Hochwan) (1953 UE) ... 50,000
Hefei (Hofei) ... 360,000
Hegang (Hokang) ... 200,000
Hengyang ... 240,000
Hepu (Lianzhou) (1953 UE) ... 45,000
Huaian (Hwaian) (1953 UE) ... 55,000
Huaide (Hwaite) ... 60,000
Huainan (Hwainan) ... 280,000
Huaiyin (Hwaiyin) (1953 C) ... 77,000
Huangshi (Hwangshih) (1953 C) ... 110,500
Huhehaote (Kweisui) ... 320,000
Huiyang (Waiyeung) ... 73,000
Hulan (1953 UE) ... 60,000
Huzhou (Huchow) ... 120,000
Jiamusi (Kiamusze) ... 232,000
Ji'an (Kian) (1953 C) ... 52,800
Jiangmen (Kongmoon) ... 110,000
Jiaozuo (Tsiaotso) ... 250,000
Jiaxing (Kashing) ... 132,000
Jieyang (Kityang) (1953 UE) ... 55,000
Jilin (Kirin) ... 583,000
Jinan (Tsinan) ... 882,000
Jingdezhen (Kingtechen) ... 266,000
Jinhua (Kinhwa) (1953 C) ... 46,200
Jining ... 100,000
Jining (Tsining) (1953 C) ... 86,200
Jinshi (Tsingshih) (1953 UE) ... 50,000
Jinxian (Chinhsien) (1953 UE) ... 60,000
Jinzhou (Chinchow) ... 400,000
Jiujiang (Kiukiang) (1953 C) ... 64,600
Jixi (Chihsi) ... 253,000
Kaifeng (1953 C) ... 299,100
Kashi (Kashgar) ... 100,000
Kelamayi (Karamai) ... 43,000
Kunming ... 900,000
Lanzhou (Lanchow) ... 732,000
Lasa (Lhasa) (1953 C) ... 70,000
Leshan (Loshan) (1953 UE) ... 60,000
Liaoyang ... 169,000
Liaoyuan (Shwangliao) ... 177,000
Linxia (Linsia) (1953 UE) ... 50,000
Liuzhou (Liuchow) ... 190,000
Luda (Dairen) (1,590,000▲) ... 1,000,000
Luohe (Loho) (1953 UE) ... 50,000
Luoyang (Loyang) ... 500,000
Lüshun (Port Arthur) (1953 C) ... 126,000
Luzhou (Luchow) ... 130,000
Meixian (Meihsien) (1953 UE) ... 45,000
Mudanjiang (Mutankiang) ... 251,000
Nanchang ... 520,000
Nanchong (Nanchung) (1953 C) ... 164,700
Nanjing (Nanking) ... 1,455,000
Nanning (1957 E) ... 264,000
Nantong (Nantung) ... 240,000
Nanyang (1953 UE) ... 50,000
Neijiang (Neikiang) ... 180,000
Ningbo (Ningpo) ... 280,000
Pingdingshan ... 70,000
Pingliang (1953 C) ... 60,000
Qingdao (Tsingtao) ... 1,144,000
Qinhuangdao (Chinwangtao) ... 210,000
Qiqihaer (Tsitsihar) ... 704,000
Quanzhou (Chüanchow) ... 110,000
Rugao (Jukao) (1953 UE) ... 40,000
•Shanghai (1970 E) (10,820,000▲) ... 7,900,000
Shangqiu (Shangkiu) (1953 C) ... 134,400
Shangrao (Shangjao) (1953 UE) ... 50,000
Shangshui (Chowkiakow) (1953 C) ... 85,500
Shantou (Swatow) ... 250,000
Shaoguan (Kükong) (1953 C) ... 81,700
Shaoxing (Shaohing) (1953 C) ... 130,600
Shaoyang ... 170,000
Shashi (Shasi) (1953 C) ... 85,800
Shenyang (Mukden) ... 2,423,000
Shijiazhuang (Shihkiachwang) ... 623,000
Shuangcheng (1953 UE) ... 80,000
Shuangyashan ... 110,000
Siping (Szeping) ... 130,000
Suihua (Suihwa) (1953 UE) ... 55,000
Suining (1953 UE) ... 50,000
Suouche (Yarkand) (1953 C) ... 80,000
Suzhou (Soochow) ... 651,000
Taiyuan (Taiyüan) ... 1,053,000
Taizhou (Taichow) (1953 C) ... 159,800
Tangshan ... 812,000
Taoan (1953 UE) ... 65,000
Tianjin (Tientsin) (1970 E) (4,280,000▲) ... 3,800,000
Tianshui (Tienshui) (1953 C) ... 63,000
Tieling (Tiehling) (1953 UE) ... 65,000
Tonghua (Tunghwa) (1953 C) ... 129,100
Tongxian (1953 UE) ... 55,000
Tunxi (Tunki) (1953 UE) ... 50,000
Wanxian (Wanhsien) (1953 UE) ... 90,000
Weifang ... 190,000
Weihai (1953 UE) ... 45,000
Wenzhou (Wenchow) ... 210,000
Wuhan (Hankow) ... 2,226,000
Wuhu ... 240,000
Wulanhaote (Ulanhot) (1953 C) ... 51,400
Wulumuqi (Urumchi) ... 320,000
Wutongqiao (Wutungkiao) ... 40,000
Wuxi (Wusih) ... 616,000
Wuzhou (Wuchow) ... 120,000
Xiamen (Amoy) ... 308,000
Xi'an (Sian) ... 1,368,000
Xiangfan (Siangfan) (1953 C) ... 73,300
Xiangtan (Siangtan) ... 247,000
Xianyang (Sienyang) (1953 C) ... 70,000
Xinghua (Hinghwa) (1953 UE) ... 85,000
Xingtai (Singtai) (1953 UE) ... 70,000
Xinhailian (Sinhailien) ... 210,000
Xining (Sining) (1957 E) ... 300,000
Xinxiang (Sinsiang) ... 203,000
Xinyang (Sinyang) (1953 UE) ... 50,000
Xuanhua (Süanhwa) (1953 C) ... 114,100
Xuchang (Hsüchang) (1953 C) ... 58,000
Xuzhou (Süchow) ... 710,000
Yaan (1953 C) ... 55,200
Yancheng (1953 UE) ... 50,000
Yangjiang (Yeungkong) (1953 UE) ... 50,000
Yangquan (Yangchüan) ... 200,000
Yangzhou (Yangchow) ... 160,000
Yanji (Yenki) ... 80,000
Yantai (Chefoo) ... 140,000
Yibin (Ipin) ... 190,000
Yichang (Ichang) (1953 UE) ... 85,000
Yichun (Ichun) ... 200,000
Yinchuan (Yinchwan) ... 91,000
Yingkou (Yingkow) (1953 C) ... 131,400
Yining (Kuldja) ... 85,000
Yiyang (Iyang) (1953 UE) ... 80,000
Yuci (Yütze) ... 100,000
Yumen (Yümen) ... 200,000
Zhangjiakou (Kalgan) (480,000▲) ... 350,000
Zhangzhou (1953 C) ... 81,200
Zhanjiang (Tsamkong) ... 170,000
Zhaoqing (Kaoyao) ... 70,000
Zhengzhou (Chengchow) ... 785,000
Zhenjiang (Chinkiang) ... 190,000
Zhongshan (Shekki) (1953 C) ... 93,000
Zhuzhou (Chuchow) ... 190,000
Zibo (Tzupo) (875,000▲) ... 30,000
Zigong (Tzekung) ... 280,000
Zunyi (Tsunyi) ... 200,000

COLOMBIA
1973 C ... 21,070,115
Armenia (★180,000) ... 135,615
Barrancabermeja (99,155▲) ... 87,191
Barranquilla (★730,000) ... 661,920
Bello (★Medellín) ... 121,204
•BOGOTÁ (★2,925,000) ... 2,855,065
Bucaramanga (★350,000) ... 298,051
Buenaventura (139,839▲) ... 115,770
Buga (84,057▲) ... 71,016
Cali (★955,000) ... 923,446
Cartagena ... 313,305
Cartago (77,890▲) ... 69,154
Ciénaga (89,723▲) ... 42,546
Cúcuta ... 269,565
Envigado (★Medellín) ... 69,921
Girardot (★78,000) ... 61,829
Ibagué (204,810▲) ... 176,223
Itagüí (★Medellín) ... 96,972
Manizales ... 231,066
Medellín (★1,500,000) ... 1,100,082
Montería (149,442▲) ... 89,583
Neiva (121,432▲) ... 105,476
Palmira (180,801▲) ... 140,481
Pasto (149,620▲) ... 119,339
Pereira (★270,000) ... 210,543
Popayán (94,120▲) ... 77,669
Santa Marta ... 128,577
Sincelejo (76,701▲) ... 68,797
Sogamoso (67,738▲) ... 48,891
Soledad (★Barranquilla) ... 64,469
Tuluá (109,437▲) ... 86,736
Tunja (77,473▲) ... 51,620
Valledupar (110,038▲) ... 87,425
Villavicencio (92,814▲) ... 82,869

COMOROS / Comores
1974 E ... 292,000
•MORONI ... 12,000

CONGO
1970 C ... 1,089,300
•BRAZZAVILLE ... 175,000
Pointe-Noire ... 135,000

COOK IS.
1971 C ... 21,227
•AVARUA (1961 E) ... 4,000

COSTA RICA
1976 E ... 1,993,800
Alajuela ... 35,000
Desamparados (★San José) ... 32,700
Limón (43,800▲) ... 31,900
Puntarenas ... 29,000
•SAN JOSÉ (1978 E) (★519,400) ... 239,800

CUBA
1970 C ... 8,553,400
Bayamo (92,700▲) ... 71,700
Camagüey (1975 E) ... 221,800
Cárdenas ... 55,700
Chaparra (51,000▲) ... 8,400
Ciego de Avila (70,200▲) ... 60,900
Cienfuegos (90,700▲) ... 85,200
Guanabacoa (★La Habana) ... 69,700
Guantánamo (1975 E) ... 148,800
Holguín (1975 E) (151,900▲) ... 122,500
•LA HABANA (HAVANA) (1975 E) (★1,935,000) ... 1,861,400
Manzanillo (88,900▲) ... 77,900
Matanzas ... 85,400
Palma Soriano (59,600▲) ... 41,200
Pinar del Río ... 73,200
Sancti-Spíritus (66,500▲) ... 57,700
Santa Clara (1975 E) ... 146,700
Santiago de Cuba (1975 E) ... 315,800
Victoria de las Tunas (65,000▲) ... 53,700

CYPRUS / Kípros / Kıbrıs
1974 E ... 639,000
Lemesós (Limassol) (★80,600) ... 55,000
•LEVKOSÍA (NICOSIA) (★117,100) ... 51,000

CZECHOSLOVAKIA / Československo
1977 E ... 15,081,747
Banská Bystrica ... 59,330
Bratislava ... 357,574
Brno ... 365,837
České Budějovice (Budweis) ... 86,170
Gottwaldov (Zlín) ... 81,129
Havířov (★Ostrava) ... 93,516
Hradec Králové ... 90,882
Karlovy Vary (Karlsbad) ... 61,495
Karviná (★Ostrava) ... 81,864
Kladno (★83,000) ... 63,827
Košice ... 191,015
Liberec (★94,000) ... 83,859
Martin ... 53,511
Most ... 61,185
Nitra ... 69,340
Olomouc ... 99,013
Opava ... 57,937
Ostrava (★735,000) ... 319,688
Pardubice ... 90,230
Plzeň (Pilsen) ... 165,351
•PRAHA (PRAGUE) (★1,265,000) ... 1,182,853
Prešov ... 65,858
Prostějov ... 47,712
Teplice ... 53,209
Trenčín ... 45,077
Trnava ... 57,125
Ústí nad Labem (★99,000) ... 77,431
Žilina ... 63,647

DENMARK / Danmark
1977 E ... 5,079,879
Ålborg ... 154,563
Århus ... 245,866
Ballerup-Måløv (★København) ... 50,397
Esbjerg ... 79,354
Fredericia ... 45,226
Frederiksberg (★København) ... 91,278
Gentofte (★København) ... 68,873
Gladsakse (★København) ... 67,435
Helsingør (Elsinore) ... 56,439
Herning (55,313▲) ... 47,200
Horsens ... 54,018
Hvidovre (★København) ... 50,620
•KØBENHAVN (COPENHAGEN) (1979 E) (★1,480,000) ... 505,982
Kolding ... 54,617
Lyngby (Kongens Lyngby)-Tårbæk (★København) ... 54,520
Odense ... 167,616
Randers ... 63,662
Rødovre (★København) ... 40,311
Rønne ... 15,313
Roskilde ... 49,397
Tårnby (★København) ... 43,121
Vejle ... 49,013

DJIBOUTI
1971 E ... 125,000
•DJIBOUTI ... 40,000

DOMINICA
1970 C ... 70,302
•ROSEAU ... 10,157

DOMINICAN REPUBLIC / República Dominicana
1970 C ... 4,009,458
San Francisco de Macorís ... 44,271
Santiago [de los Caballeros] ... 155,240
•SANTO DOMINGO ... 668,507

ECUADOR
1974 C ... 6,500,845
Ambato ... 77,052
Cuenca (1978 E) ... 128,788
Esmeraldas ... 60,132
•Guayaquil (1978 E) ... 1,022,010
Loja ... 47,268
Machala ... 68,379
Manta ... 63,514
Milagro ... 53,058
Portoviejo ... 59,404
QUITO (1978 E) ... 742,858
Riobamba ... 58,029

EGYPT / Miṣr
1976 C ... 36,656,180
Al-Fayyūm ... 167,081
Al-Iskandarīyah (Alexandria) (★2,700,000) ... 2,318,655
Al-Ismā'īlīyah (★185,000) ... 145,478
Al-Jīzah (Giza) (★Al-Qāhirah) ... 1,246,713
Al-Maḥallah al-Kubrā ... 292,853
Al-Manṣūrah (★290,000) ... 257,866
Al-Minyā ... 146,423
•AL-QĀHIRAH (CAIRO) (★8,000,133) ... 5,084,463
Al-Uqṣur (Luxor) (1966 C) ... 77,578
As-Suways (Suez) ... 194,001
Aswān ... 144,377
Asyūṭ ... 213,983
Az-Zaqāzīq ... 202,637
Banhā (1966 C) ... 63,849
Banī Suwayf ... 118,148
Bilbays (1966 C) ... 58,070
Būlāq ad-Dakrūr (★Al-Qāhirah) (1966 C) ... 75,130
Būr Sa 'īd (Port Said) ... 262,620
Damanhūr ... 188,927
Dumyāṭ (Damietta) (1975 E) ... 113,200
Kafr ad-Dawwār (★Al-Iskandarīyah) ... 160,554
Kafr ash-Shaykh (1966 C) ... 51,544
Mallawī (1966 C) ... 59,938
Minūf (1966 C) ... 48,256
Mīt Ghamr (1966 C) (★82,000) ... 43,665
Qalyūb (1966 C) ... 49,303
Qinā (1966 C) ... 68,536
Sawhāj ... 101,758
Shibīn al-Kawm ... 102,844
Shubrā al-Khaymah (★Al-Qāhirah) ... 393,700
Ṭanṭā ... 284,636

EL SALVADOR
1976 E ... 4,123,000
Mejicanos (★San Salvador) (82,200▲) ... 67,900
San Miguel (140,100▲) ... 70,500
•SAN SALVADOR (★700,000) ... 386,600
Santa Ana (183,800▲) ... 109,300
Villa Delgado (★San Salvador) (74,800▲) ... 51,800

EQUATORIAL GUINEA / Guinea Ecuatorial
1965 C ... 254,684
•MALABO (37,152▲) ... 17,500

ETHIOPIA / Yaitopya
1977 E ... 28,925,000
•ĀDĪS ĀBEBA (1978 E) ... 1,196,300
Asmera (1978 E) ... 343,800
Dese ... 57,493
Dire Dawa ... 79,973
Gonder ... 68,364
Harer ... 59,122
Jima ... 63,390
Mitsiwa (Massaua) ... 27,486
Nazeret ... 69,491

FAEROE ISLANDS / Føroyar
1977 E ... 41,575
•TÓRSHAVN ... 11,586

▲ Población de un municipio, comuna o distrito entero, incluyendo sus áreas rurales.
• Ciudad más grande de un país.
★ Población o designación de un área metropolitana, incluyendo los suburbios.
C Censo. E Estimado oficial.
UE Estimado no oficial.
L Población dentro de los límites municipales de un año específico.

▲ Population d'une municipalité, d'une commune ou d'un district, zone rurale incluse.
• Ville la plus peuplée du pays.
★ Population de l'agglomération (ou nom de la zone métropolitaine englobante).
C Recensement. E Estimation officielle.
UE Estimation non officielle.
L Population comprise dans les limites municipales de l'année indiquée.

▲ População de um município, comuna ou distrito, inclusive as respectivas áreas rurais.
• Maior cidade de um país.
★ População ou indicação de uma área metropolitana, inclusive subúrbios.
C Censo. E Estimativa oficial.
UE Estimativa não oficial.
L População dentro dos limites municipais no ano indicado.

FALKLAND ISLANDS
1972 C 1,957
•STANLEY 1,081

FIJI
1976 C 588,068
Lautoka (★28,847) 22,672
•SUVA (★117,827) 63,628

FINLAND / Suomi
1977 E 4,737,969
Espoo (Esbo) (★Helsinki) 124,064
Hämeenlinna 40,978
•HELSINKI (HELSINGFORS) (★876,000) 492,413
Jyväskylä (★86,000) 62,209
Kotka (★62,000) 61,869
Kouvola (★53,000) 30,104
Kuopio 72,765
Lahti (★108,000) 95,024
Lappeenranta 53,459
Oulu (★111,000) 93,166
Pori 80,261
Tampere (★240,000) 166,400
Turku (Åbo) (★219,000) 164,945
Vaasa (Vasa) 53,989
Vantaa (Vanda) (★Helsinki) 122,724

FRANCE
1975 C 52,655,802
Aix-en-Provence 110,659
Ajaccio 50,726
Albi 46,162
Alès (★67,513) 44,245
Amiens (★512,997) 131,476
Angers (★188,695) 137,587
Angoulême (★100,528) 47,221
Annecy (★103,543) 53,262
Antibes (★Cannes) 55,960
Antony (★Paris) 57,540
Argenteuil (★Paris) 102,530
Arles (50,059▲) 37,340
Armentières (★58,000) 26,346
Arras (★79,783) 46,446
Asnières [-sur-Seine] (★Paris) 75,431
Aubervilliers (★Paris) 72,976
Aulnay-sous-Bois (★Paris) 78,137
Avignon (★162,562) 90,786
Bastia (★56,984) 50,718
Bayonne (★121,474) 42,938
Beauvais 54,089
Belfort (★75,795) 54,615
Besançon (★126,349) 120,315
Béthune (★145,155) 26,982
Béziers (★88,619) 84,029
Blois 49,778
Bondy (★Paris) 48,333
Bordeaux (★612,456) 223,131
Boulogne-Billancourt (★Paris) 103,578
Boulogne-sur-Mer (★100,581) 48,440
Bourg-en-Bresse 42,181
Bourges (★86,041) 77,300
Brest (★190,812) 166,826
Brive-la-Gaillarde 51,864
Bruay-en-Artois (★116,340) 25,714
Caen (★181,390) 119,474
Calais (★100,327) 78,820
Cambrai (★51,357) 39,049
Cannes (★210,000) 70,527
Carcassonne 42,154
Castres 45,978
Châlons-sur-Marne (★63,407) 52,275
Chalon-sur-Saône (★72,407) 58,187
Chambéry (★88,081) 54,415
Champigny-sur-Marne (★Paris) 80,291
Charleville-Mézières (★69,124) 60,176
Chartres (★72,246) 38,928
Châteauroux (★66,836) 53,429
Châttellerault (★66,836) 37,080
Cherbourg (★82,539) 32,536
Cholet 52,976
Clamart (★Paris) 52,952
Clermont-Ferrand (★253,244) 156,900
Clichy (★Paris) 47,764
Cognac 22,237
Colmar (★83,435) 64,771
Colombes (★Paris) 83,390
Compiègne (★57,210) 37,699
Courbevoie (★Paris) 54,488
Creil (★77,225) 32,509
Créteil (★Paris) 59,023
Denain (★Valenciennes) 26,204
Dieppe (★40,000) 25,822
Dijon (★208,432) 151,705
Douai (★210,508) 45,239
Drancy (★Paris) 64,430
Dunkerque (★186,314) 83,163
Elbeuf (★48,000) 19,116
Épinal (★53,522) 39,525
Épinay-sur-Seine (★Paris) 46,578
Évreux 47,412
Fontainebleau (★36,000) 16,778
Fontenay-sous-Bois (★Paris) 46,475
Forbach (★62,000) 25,244
Fréjus (★50,000) 28,851
Gennevilliers (★Paris) 50,290
Grenoble (★389,088) 166,037
Hayange (★75,000) 20,426
Issy-les-Moulineaux (★Paris) 47,561
Ivry-sur-Seine (★Paris) 62,856
La Rochelle (★100,649) 75,367
La Seyne-sur-Mer (★Toulon) 51,155
Laval 51,544
Le Blanc-Mesnil (★Paris) 49,107
Le Havre (★264,422) 217,881
Le Mans (★192,057) 152,285
Lens (★328,741) 40,199
Le Puy [-en-Velay] (★41,000) 26,594
Levallois-Perret (★Paris) 52,523
Lille (★1,015,000) 172,280
Limoges (★167,664) 143,689
Longwy (★83,000) 20,131
Lorient (★105,797) 69,769
Lourdes 17,870
Lyon (★1,170,660) 456,716
Mâcon 39,344
Maisons-Alfort (★Paris) 54,146
Mantes [-la-Jolie] 42,465
Marseille (★1,070,912) 908,600
Maubeuge (★105,000) 35,399
Melun (★77,272) 37,705
Menton (★34,000) 25,129
Mérignac (★Bordeaux) 50,652
Metz (★181,191) 111,869
Meudon (★Paris) 52,806
Montargis (★50,200) 18,380
Montbéliard (★132,343) 30,425
Montceau-les-Mines (★51,385) 28,177
Montluçon (★71,988) 56,468
Montpellier (★211,430) 191,354
Montreuil-sous-Bois (★Paris) 96,587
Moulins (★42,000) 26,067
Moyeuvre [-Grande] (★77,000) 12,523
Mulhouse (★218,743) 117,013
Nancy (★280,569) 107,902
Nanterre (★Paris) 95,032
Nantes (★453,500) 256,693
Neuilly-sur-Seine (★Paris) 65,983
Nevers (★59,424) 45,480
Nice (★437,566) 344,481
Nîmes (★131,638) 127,933
Niort (★64,128) 62,267
Noisy-le-Sec (★Paris) 37,734
Orléans (★209,234) 106,246
Orly (★Paris) 26,109
Pantin (★Paris) 42,739
•PARIS (1978 E) (★9,350,000) 2,155,200
Pau (★126,859) 83,498
Périgueux (★57,830) 35,120
Perpignan (★117,689) 106,426
Pessac (★Bordeaux) 51,360
Poissy (★Paris) 37,431
Poitiers (★98,554) 81,313
Quimper 55,977
Reims (★197,021) 178,381
Rennes (★229,310) 198,305
Roanne (★83,561) 55,195
Romans-sur-Isère (★46,000) 33,030
Roubaix (★Lille) 109,553
Rouen (★388,711) 114,927
Rueil-Malmaison (★Paris) 62,727
Saint-Brieuc (★82,148) 52,559
Saint-Chamond 40,250
Saint-Denis (★Paris) 96,132
Saint-Dizier 37,266
Saint-Étienne (★334,846) 220,070
Saint-Lô 23,221
Saint-Malo 45,030
Saint-Maur-des-Fossés (★Paris) 80,920
Saint-Nazaire (★119,418) 69,251
Saint-Ouen (★Paris) 43,588
Saint-Quentin (★75,056) 67,243
Sarcelles (★Paris) 55,007
Soissons (★49,000) 30,009
Strasbourg (★390,000) 253,384
Suresnes (★Paris) 37,537
Tarbes (★78,645) 54,897
Thionville (★141,881) 43,020
Toulon (★378,430) 181,801
Toulouse (★509,939) 373,796
Tourcoing (★Lille) 102,239
Tours (★245,631) 140,686
Troyes (★126,611) 72,167
Valence (★104,330) 68,604
Valenciennes (★350,599) 42,473
Vénissieux (★Lyon) 74,347
Verdun 23,621
Versailles (★Paris) 94,145
Vichy (★59,062) 32,117
Villefranche-sur-Saône (★42,000) 30,341
Villejuif (★Paris) 55,606
Villeurbanne (★Lyon) 116,535
Vitry-sur-Seine (★Paris) 87,316
Wattrelos (★Lille) 45,440

FRENCH GUIANA / Guyane française
1974 C 55,125
•CAYENNE 30,461

FRENCH POLYNESIA / Polynésie française
1977 C 137,382
•PAPEETE (★42,000) 23,453

GABON
1970 E 500,000
•LIBREVILLE (1969 C) 73,000
Port-Gentil (1970 C) 31,000

GAMBIA
1978 E 569,000
•BANJUL (BATHURST) (★88,000) 45,600

GAZA STRIP
1967 C 356,261
•GHAZZAH (GAZA) 118,272
Jabālyah 43,604
Khān Yūnus 52,997
Rafaḥ 49,812

GERMAN DEMOCRATIC REPUBLIC (EAST GERMANY) / Deutsche Demokratische Republik
1977 E 16,757,857
Altenburg 53,814
Bautzen 46,976
•BERLIN, OST-(EAST BERLIN) (★Berlin) 1,118,142
Bitterfeld (★105,000) 24,509
Brandenburg 93,890
Cottbus 105,182
Dessau (★135,000) 101,064
Dresden (★640,000) 512,490
Eberswald 49,606
Eisenach 49,819
Eisenhüttenstadt 48,199
Erfurt 206,963
Frankfurt an der Oder 75,328
Freiberg 50,661
Freital (★Dresden) 46,651
Gera 119,280
Görlitz 82,474
Gotha 58,658
Greifswald 59,398
Halberstadt 47,491
Halle (★480,000) 231,480
Halle-Neustadt (★Halle) 89,268
Hoyerswerda 69,111
Jena 100,979
Karl-Marx-Stadt (Chemnitz) (★460,000) 310,770
Leipzig (★710,000) 564,306
Magdeburg (★395,000) 281,578
Merseburg (★Halle) 52,051
Neubrandenburg 71,479
Nordhausen 46,102
Pirna 48,556
Plauen 79,500
Potsdam (★Berlin) 124,583
Riesa 50,411
Rostock 220,875
Schwedt [Oder] 50,738
Schwerin 113,038
Stralsund 73,188
Weimar 62,787
Wismar 57,060
Wittenberg 52,471
Zwickau (★170,000) 122,640

GERMANY, FEDERAL REPUBLIC OF (WEST GERMANY) / Bundesrepublik Deutschland
1977 E 61,352,500
Aachen (★540,000) 243,282
Aalen (★80,000) 63,194
Ahlen 53,600
Albstadt 49,321
Alsdorf (★Aachen) 46,527
Amberg 45,607
Ansbach 38,635
Arnsberg 79,320
Aschaffenburg (★140,000) 55,268
Augsburg (★385,000) 244,432
Baden-Baden 48,959
Bad Homburg (★Frankfurt am Main) 51,063
Bad Kreuznach 41,984
Bad Oeynhausen 44,281
Bad Salzuflen (★Herford) 50,891
Bamberg (★120,000) 72,860
Bayreuth (★88,000) 69,240
Berchtesgaden 8,399
Bergheim (★Köln) 51,386
Bergisch Gladbach (★Köln) 100,134
Bergkamen (★Essen) 46,825
Berlin, West- (★3,775,000) 1,926,826
Bielefeld (★525,000) 313,230
Bocholt 65,394
Bochum (★Essen) 409,242
BONN (★540,000) 284,003
Bottrop (★Essen) 115,293
Braunschweig (Brunswick) (★335,000) 264,918
Bremen (★800,000) 562,664
Bremerhaven (★190,000) 140,505
Brühl (★Köln) 43,813
Castrop-Rauxel (★Essen) 80,359
Celle 73,511
Coburg 46,463
Cuxhaven 60,083
Dachau (★München) 33,330
Darmstadt (★305,000) 138,593
Delmenhorst (★Bremen) 71,645
Detmold 65,881
Dinslaken (★Essen) 57,257
Dormagen (★Köln) 54,802
Dorsten (★Essen) 66,783
Dortmund (★Essen) 617,590
Duisburg (★Essen) 572,101
Düren (★109,000) 86,947
Düsseldorf (★1,135,000) 607,560
Emden 53,042
Erlangen (★Nürnberg) 100,603
Eschweiler (★Aachen) 52,890
•Essen (★5,175,000) 664,408
Esslingen (★Stuttgart) 93,562
Euskirchen 43,641
Flensburg (★104,000) 90,036
Frankfurt am Main (★1,865,000) 632,565
Freiburg (★215,000) 174,928
Friedrichshafen 50,994
Fulda (★78,000) 57,865
Fürth (★Nürnberg) 98,699
Garbsen (★Hannover) 56,282
Garmisch-Partenkirchen 27,114
Gelsenkirchen (★Essen) 313,439
Gladbeck 81,040
Göppingen (★150,000) 52,805
Goslar (★83,000) 53,745
Göttingen 124,982
Grevenbroich (★Düsseldorf) 57,282
Gummersbach 48,357
Gütersloh (★Bielefeld) 77,254
Hagen (★Essen) 224,345
Hamburg (★2,265,000) 1,680,340
Hameln (★72,000) 60,042
Hamm 171,489
Hanau (★Frankfurt am Main) 85,848
Hannover (★1,005,000) 542,134
Hettingen (★Essen) 57,799
Heidelberg (★Mannheim) 129,179
Heidenheim (★87,000) 48,927
Heilbronn (★225,000) 111,699
Herford (★120,000) 63,509
Herne (★Essen) 186,440
Herten (★Essen) 69,945
Hilden (★Düsseldorf) 52,336
Hildesheim (★138,000) 103,503
Hof 53,794
Hürth (★Köln) 50,910
Ingolstadt (★132,000) 88,550
Iserlohn 95,484
Kaiserslautern (★137,000) 100,106
Karlsruhe (★485,000) 275,828
Kassel (★370,000) 199,450
Kempten 57,009
Kerpen (★Köln) 52,125
Kiel (★340,000) 256,512
Koblenz (★175,000) 115,729
Köln (Cologne) (★1,710,000) 976,761
Konstanz 69,079
Krefeld (★Essen) 224,525
Lahn (Giessen) 154,089
Landshut 55,548
Langenfeld (★Wuppertal) 46,632
Langenhagen (★Hannover) 46,703
Leverkusen (★Köln) 163,398
Lippstadt 61,903
Lübeck (★265,000) 227,184
Lüdenscheid 74,733
Ludwigsburg (★Stuttgart) 82,111
Ludwigshafen (★Mannheim) 163,671
Lüneburg 63,199
Lünen (★Essen) 85,802
Mainz (★Wiesbaden) 183,858
Mannheim (★1,390,000) 305,741
Marburg an der Lahn 73,313
Marl (★Essen) 90,889
Meerbusch (★Düsseldorf) 50,417
Menden [Sauerland] 53,115
Minden (★120,000) 78,281
Moers (★Essen) 100,538
Mönchengladbach (★385,000) 258,854
Mülheim an der Ruhr (★Essen) 185,888
München (Munich) (★1,930,000) 1,313,939
Münster 267,182
Neumünster 82,823
Neunkirchen (★135,000) 53,606
Neuss (★Düsseldorf) 148,884
Neustadt [an der Weinstrasse] 50,544
Neu-Ulm (★Ulm) 46,310
Neuwied (★145,000) 61,247
Norderstedt (★Hamburg) 62,211
Nordhorn 48,940
Nürnberg (★1,020,000) 488,755
Oberammergau 4,827
Oberhausen (★Essen) 232,558
Offenbach (★Frankfurt am Main) 112,303
Offenburg 50,748
Oldenburg 134,832
Osnabrück (★265,000) 159,492
Paderborn 107,020
Passau 50,489
Peine 48,229
Pforzheim (★220,000) 107,002
Pirmasens 51,844
Ratingen (★Düsseldorf) 88,977
Ravensburg (★72,000) 42,265
Recklinghausen (★Essen) 120,664
Regensburg (★195,000) 133,533
Remscheid (★Wuppertal) 130,714
Reutlingen (★150,000) 94,275
Rheine 71,276
Rüsselsheim (★Wiesbaden) 63,239
Saarbrücken (★395,000) 198,885
Saarlouis (★115,000) 39,751
Salzgitter 114,831
Schwäbisch Gmünd 56,451
Schweinfurt (★110,000) 54,108
Schwerte (★Essen) 46,550
Siegen (★205,000) 114,516
Sindelfingen (★Stuttgart) 53,999
Singen 44,295
Solingen (★Wuppertal) 168,332
Speyer 43,857
Stade 42,346
Stolberg (★Aachen) 57,163
Stuttgart (★1,915,000) 584,554
Trier (★125,000) 97,822
Troisdorf (★Bonn) 57,028
Tübingen 71,820
Ulm (★205,000) 98,815
Unna (★Essen) 55,245
Velbert (★Essen) 94,510
Viersen (★Mönchengladbach) 82,361
Villingen-Schwenningen 78,588
Völklingen (★Saarbrücken) 45,983
Waiblingen (★Stuttgart) 44,726
Wesel 56,691
Wiesbaden (★785,000) 270,298
Wilhelmshaven (★135,000) 101,516
Witten (★Essen) 107,036
Wolfenbüttel (★Braunschweig) 50,892
Wolfsburg 127,510
Worms (★Mannheim) 74,345
Wuppertal (★910,000) 398,729
Würzburg (★200,000) 115,746
Zweibrücken (★105,000) 35,530

GHANA
1970 C 8,559,313
•ACCRA (★738,498) 633,880
Cape Coast 71,594
Koforidua 46,235
Kumasi 345,117
Sekondi-Takoradi 160,868
Tamale 83,653
Tema 60,767

GIBRALTAR
1977 E 30,100
•GIBRALTAR 30,100

GREECE / Ellás
1971 C 8,768,641
Agrínion (★41,794) 30,973
Aiyáleo (★Athínai) 79,961
Árgos 18,890
•ATHÍNAI (ATHENS) (★2,540,241) 867,023
Áyios Dhimítrios (★Athínai) 40,968
Ilioúpolis (★Athínai) 49,215
Ioánnina (Yanina) 40,130
Iráklion (Candia) (★84,710) 77,506
Kalámai (★40,402) 39,133

▲ Population of an entire municipality, commune, or district, including rural area.
• Largest city in country.
★ Population or designation of the metropolitan area, including suburbs.
C Census. E Official estimate. UE Unofficial estimate.
L Population within municipal limits of year specified.

▲ Bevölkerung eines ganzen städtischen Verwaltungsgebietes, eines Kommunalbezirkes oder eines Distrikts, einschliesslich ländlicher Gebiete.
• Grösste Stadt des Landes.
★ Bevölkerung oder Bezeichnung der Stadtregion einschliess lich Vororte.
C Volkszählung. E Offizielle Schätzung. UE Inoffizielle Schätzung.
L Bevölkerung innerhalb der städtischen Verwaltungseinheit des angegebenen Jahres.

Kallithéa (★Athínai) 82,438
Kavála 46,234
Keratsínion (★Athínai) 67,672
Khalkís (Chalcis) 36,300
Khaniá (Canea) (★53,026) 40,564
Khíos (Chios) (★30,021) 24,084
Koridhallós (★Athínai) 47,335
Kórinthos (Corinth) 20,773
Lárisa 72,336
Mégara 17,294
Néa Ionía (★Athínai) 54,906
Néa Liósia (★Athínai) 56,217
Néa Smírni (★Athínai) 42,512
Níkaia (★Athínai) 86,269
Pátrai (Patras) (★120,847) 111,607
Peristérion (★Athínai) 118,413
Piraiévs (Piraeus) (★Athínai) 187,362
Ródhos (Rhodes) 32,092
Spárti (Sparta) (★13,432) 10,549
Thessaloníki (Salonika) (★557,360) 345,799
Thívai (Thebes) 15,971
Tríkkala 34,794
Víron (★Athínai) 44,021
Vólos (★88,096) 51,290
Zografós (★Athínai) 56,722

GREENLAND / Grønland

1977 E 49,719
Egedesminde 3,347
•GODTHÅB 8,545

GRENADA

1970 C 93,858
•SAINT GEORGE'S (★23,000) 7,303

GUADELOUPE

1974 C 324,530
BASSE-TERRE (★25,202) 15,457
•Pointe-à-Pitre (★59,000) 23,889

GUAM

1970 C 84,996
•AGANA (★29,000) 2,119

GUATEMALA

1973 C 5,211,929
Escuintla 37,180
•GUATEMALA (★945,000) 717,322
Quezaltenango 45,977

GUERNSEY

1971 C 53,734
•ST. PETER PORT (★36,000) 16,303

GUINEA / Guinée

1967 E 3,702,000
•CONAKRY (1967 C) 197,267
Kankan 50,000
Kindia 45,000

GUINEA-BISSAU

1970 C 487,448
•BISSAU 71,169

GUYANA

1976 E 783,000
•GEORGETOWN (★187,056) 72,049

HAITI / Haïti

1975 E 4,583,785
Cap-Haïtien 52,220
Gonaïves 33,837
•PORT-AU-PRINCE (1978 E) (★800,000) 745,700

HONDURAS

1974 C 2,656,948
El Progreso 28,105
La Ceiba 38,788
San Pedro Sula 150,991
•TEGUCIGALPA 273,894

HONG KONG

1976 C 4,402,990
Kowloon (★Victoria) 749,600
New Kowloon (★Victoria) 1,628,880
Tai Wan Tsun (Ngau Tau Kok) (★Victoria) (1961 C) 53,836
Tsun Wan (★Victoria) 455,270
•VICTORIA (HONG KONG) (★3,975,000) 1,026,870

HUNGARY / Magyarország

1979 E 10,698,800
Békéscsaba (66,485▲) 57,800
•BUDAPEST (★2,565,000) 2,093,200
Debrecen 199,700
Dunaújváros 60,288
Eger 61,149
Érd (★Budapest) 42,098
Györ 126,400
Hódmezövásárhely (54,317▲) 45,400
Kaposvár 74,101
Kecskemét (96,194▲) 76,700
Miskolc 210,900
Nagykanizsa 48,195
Nyíregyháza (108,914▲) 86,100
Ózd 46,807
Pécs 170,900
Salgótarján 49,116
Sopron 55,658
Szeged 177,700
Székesfehérvár 105,224
Szolnok 77,017
Szombathely 82,664
Tatabánya 75,555
Vác 35,942
Veszprém 55,382
Zalaegerszeg 55,313

ICELAND / Ísland

1978 E 224,384
Akureyri 12,889
•REYKJAVÍK (★118,570) 83,376

INDIA / Bhārat

1971 C 547,949,809
Abohar 58,925
Achalpur (Ellichpur) (★66,451) 42,326
Ādoni 85,311
Agartala (★100,264) 59,625
Āgra (★634,622) 591,917
Ahmadābād (★1,950,000) 1,585,544
Ahmadnagar (★148,405) 118,236
Ajmer (★264,291) 262,851
Akola 168,438
Alandur (★Madras) 65,039
Alīgarh 252,314
Alīpur Duār (★54,454) 36,667
Allahābād (★513,036) 490,622
Alleppey 160,166
Alwar 100,378
Amalner 55,544
Ambāla (★186,126) 83,633
Ambāla Cantonment (★Ambāla) 102,493
Ambarnāth (★Bombay) 56,276
Āmbūr 54,011
Amrāvati (Amraoti) (★221,277) 193,800
Amritsar (★458,029) 407,628
Amroha 82,702
Anakapalle 57,273
Ānand 59,155
Anantapur 80,069
Arcot (★75,911) 30,230
Arrah 92,919
Aruppukkottai 62,223
Asansol (★925,000) 155,968
Aurangābād (★165,253) 150,483
Avadi (★Madras) 77,413
Badagara 53,938
Bāgalkot 51,746
Bahraich 73,931
Baidyabāti (★Calcutta) 54,130
Balasore 46,239
Ballia 47,101
Bālurghāt 67,088
Bānda 50,575
Bangalore (★1,750,000) 1,540,741
Bangaon 50,538
Bānkura 79,129
Bansbāria (★Calcutta) 61,748
Baranagar (★Calcutta) 136,842
Bareilly (★326,106) 296,248
Baroda (Vadodara) (★467,487) 466,696
Barrackpore (★Calcutta) 96,889
Bārsi 62,374
Basīrhāt 63,816
Basti 49,635
Batāla (★76,488) 58,200
Beāwar 66,114
Behāla (South Suburban) (★Calcutta) 272,600
Belgaum (★213,872) 192,427
Bellary 125,183
Berhampore *(West Bengal St.)* (★78,909) 72,605
Berhampur *(Orissa St.)* 117,662
Bettiah 51,018
Bhadrāvati (★101,358) 40,203
Bhāgalpur 172,202
Bharatpur (★69,902) 68,036
Bhatinda (★65,318) 53,684
Bhātpāra (★Calcutta) 204,750
Bhaunagar (★225,974) 225,358
Bhavāni (★56,696) 23,114
Bhilai (Bhilainagar) (★245,124) 157,173
Bhīlwāra 82,155
Bhīmavaram 63,762
Bhiwandi (★Bombay) 79,576
Bhiwāni 73,086
Bhopāl (★384,859) 298,022
Bhubaneswar 105,491
Bhuj (★52,861) 52,177
Bhusāwal (★104,708) 96,800
Bīdar 50,670
Bihar 100,046
Bijāpur 103,931
Bīkaner (★208,894) 188,518
Bilāspur (★130,740) 98,410
Bīr (Bhir) 49,965
Bodināyakkanūr 54,176
Bokāro Steel City (★107,159) 94,007
Bombay (★6,750,000) 5,970,575
Broach (Bharuch) (★92,251) 91,589
Budaun 72,204
Budge Budge (★Calcutta) 51,039
Bulandshahr 59,505
Bulsār (Valsad) (★54,966) 43,254
Burdwān 143,318
Burhānpur (★105,335) 105,246
•Calcutta (★9,100,000) 3,148,746
Calicut (Kozhikode) 333,979
Cambay 62,097
Cannanore (★59,912) 55,162
Chākdaha 46,345
Champdāni (★Calcutta) 58,596
Chandannagar (Chandernagore) (★Calcutta) 75,238
Chandausi 53,393
Chandīgarh (★232,940) 218,743
Chandrapur 75,134
Changanācheri 48,545
Chāpra (★98,401) 83,101
Chhindwāra (★53,508) 53,492
Chidambaram (★57,658) 48,811
Chīrāla 54,487
Chitradurga 50,254
Chittoor 63,035
Churu (★53,185) 52,502
Cochin 439,066
Coimbatore (★750,000) 356,368
Cooch Behār (★62,664) 53,684
Coonoor (★70,813) 38,007
Cuddalore 101,335
Cuddapah 66,195
Cuttack (★205,759) 194,068
Damoh (★59,983) 59,489
Darbhanga 132,059
Darjeeling 42,873
Dāvangere 121,110
Dehra Dūn (★203,464) 166,073
Dehri 46,037
Delhi (★4,500,000) 3,706,558
Delhi Cantonment (★Delhi) 57,339
Deolāli (★Nāsik) 55,436
Dewās (★51,866) 51,545
Dhānbād (★600,000) 79,838
Dhorāji (★60,080) 59,773
Dhule (Dhulia) 137,129
Dibrugarh 80,348
Dindigul 128,429
Dohad (★51,406) 44,506
Dombivli (★Bombay) 51,108
Durg (★Bhilai) 67,892
Durgapur 206,638
Elūru (Ellore) 127,023
English Bāzār (★68,026) 61,335
Erode (★169,613) 105,111
Etāwah 85,894
Faizābād (★109,806) 102,835
Farīdābād New Township (★Delhi) 85,762
Farrukhābād (★110,835) 102,768
Fatehpur 54,665
Fīrozābād 133,863
Fīrozpur (Ferozepore) (★97,709) 49,545
Gadag 95,426
Garden Reach (★Calcutta) 154,913
Gauhāti (★200,377) 123,783
Gaya 179,884
Ghāziābād (★Delhi) 118,836
Ghāzīpur 45,635
Godhra (★66,853) 66,403
Gonda 52,662
Gondal (★55,329) 54,928
Gondia 77,992
Gorakhpur 230,911
Govindpura (★Bhopāl) 53,922
Gudivāda 61,068
Gudiyāttam (★67,966) 63,007
Gulbarga 145,588
Guntakal 66,320
Guntūr 269,991
Gurgaon 57,151
Gwalior (★406,140) 384,772
Hābra (★93,351) 51,435
Haldwāni 52,205
Hālisahar (★Calcutta) 68,906
Hāpur 71,266
Hardoi 46,639
Hardwār (★79,277) 77,864
Hassan 51,325
Hāthras 74,349
Hazāribāgh 54,818
Hisār 89,437
Hooghly-Chinsura (★Calcutta) 105,241
Hoshiārpur 57,691
Hospet 65,196
Howrah (★Calcutta) 737,877
Hubli-Dhārwār 379,166
Hyderābād (★2,000,000) 1,607,396
Ichalkaranji 87,731
Imphāl 100,366
Indore (★560,936) 543,381
Jabalpur (★534,845) 426,224
Jabalpur Cantonment (★Jabalpur) 50,195
Jagādhri (★115,020) 35,094
Jagannāthnagar (★Rānchī) 55,663
Jaipur (★636,768) 615,258
Jālgaon 106,711
Jālna 91,099
Jalpaiguri 55,159
Jamālpur (★Monghyr) 61,731
Jammu (★164,207) 155,338
Jāmnagar (★227,640) 199,709
Jamshedpur (★456,146) 341,576
Jaunpur 80,737
Jhānsi (★198,135) 173,292
Jharia (★Dhānbād) 45,236
Jodhpur 317,612
Jorhāt (★70,674) 30,247
Jullundur (★329,830) 296,106
Junāgadh (★95,900) 95,485
Kadaiyanallūr 50,295
Kaithal 45,199
Kākināda 164,200
Kālol (★Ahmadābād) 50,321
Kalyān (★Bombay) 99,547
Kamarhati (★Calcutta) 169,404
Kāmthi (★Nāgpur) 53,412
Kānchipuram (Conjeeveram) (★119,693) 110,657
Kānchrāpāra (★Calcutta) 78,768
Kānpur (★1,320,000) 1,154,388
Kānpur Cantonment (★Kānpur) 69,452
Kāraikkudi (★88,371) 55,449
Karīmnagar 48,918
Karnāl 92,784
Karūr 65,706
Kāsganj 46,467
Katihār (★80,121) 67,014
Kayankulam (Kayamkulam) 54,102
Kerkend (★Dhānbād) 51,314
Khadki (Kirkee) (★Pune) 65,497
Khāmgaon 53,692
Khammam 56,919
Khandwa (★85,403) 84,517
Kharagpur (★161,257) 61,783
Khurja 50,245
Kolār Gold Fields (★118,861) 76,112
Kolhāpur (★267,513) 259,050
Kota 212,991
Kottagūdem 75,542
Kottayam 59,714
Kovilpatti 48,509
Krishnanagar 85,923
Kumbakonam (★119,655) 113,130
Kurnool 136,710
Lātūr 70,156
Lucknow (★840,000) 749,239
Ludhiāna (★401,176) 397,850
Machilīpatnam (Bandar) 112,612
Madakulam (★Madurai) 46,317
Madras (★3,200,000) 2,469,449
Madurai (★725,000) 549,114
Mahbūbnagar 51,756
Mālegaon 191,847
Māler Kotla (★48,859) 48,536
Mandasor (★56,988) 52,347
Mandya 72,132
Mangalore (★215,122) 165,174
Mathura (★140,150) 132,028
Maunath Bhanjan 64,058
Māyūram 60,195
Meerut (★367,754) 270,993
Meerut Cantonment (★Meerut) 85,415
Mehsāna (Mahesāna) (★51,713) 51,598
Mettupālaiyam 48,365
Mhow (★63,739) 59,037
Midnapore 71,326
Miraj (★Sāngli) 77,606
Mirzāpur 105,939
Moga (★61,625) 55,270
Monghyr (★164,205) 102,474
Morādābād (★272,652) 258,590
Morvi 60,976
Murwāra (Katni) (★86,535) 54,864
Muzaffarnagar 114,783
Muzaffarpur 126,379
Mysore 355,685
Nabadwīp 94,204
Nadiād 108,269
Nāgappattinam (★74,019) 68,026
Nāgercoil 141,288
Nāgpur (★950,000) 866,076
Naihāti (★Calcutta) 82,080
Nānded 126,538
Nandurbār 54,070
Nandyāl 63,193
Nangi (★Calcutta) 47,555
Nāsik (★271,681) 176,091
Navsāri (★80,101) 72,979
Neemuch (★49,748) 47,113
Nellore 133,590
NEW DELHI (★Delhi) 301,801
Neyveli 58,285
Nizāmābād 115,640
North Barrackpore (★Calcutta) 76,335
North Dum-Dum (★Calcutta) 63,873
Nowgong 56,537
Ongole 53,330
Ootacamund 63,310
Outer Burnpur (★Asansol) 56,900
Pālayankottai (★Tirunelveli) 70,070
Pālghāt 95,788
Pāli 49,834
Pallavaram (★Madras) 51,374
Palni (★51,664) 49,575
Panaji (Panjim) (Nova Goa) (★59,258) 34,953
Pānchur (★Calcutta) 59,021
Pandharpur 53,638
Pānihāti (★Calcutta) 148,046
Pānīpat 87,981
Paramagudi 48,880
Parbhani 61,570
Pātan 64,519
Pathānkot (★78,192) 76,355
Patiāla (★151,041) 148,686
Patna (★625,000) 473,001
Phagwāra (★55,012) 50,863
Pīlībhīt 68,273
Pimpri-Chinchwad (★Pune) 83,542
Pollāchi (★93,838) 68,655
Pondicherry (★153,325) 90,637
Porbandar (★106,727) 96,881
Proddatūr 70,822
Pudukkottai 66,384
Pune (Poona) (★1,175,000) 856,105
Pune Cantonment (★Pune) 77,774
Puri 72,674
Purnea (★71,311) 56,484
Purūlia 57,708
Quilon 124,208
Rāichūr 79,831
Raigarh (★48,049) 46,745
Raipur (★205,986) 174,518
Rājahmundry (★188,805) 165,912
Rājapālaiyam 86,952
Rājkot 300,612
Rāj-Nāndgaon (★55,827) 41,183
Rāmpur 161,417
Rānāghāt 47,815
Rānchī (★255,551) 175,934
Ratlām (★119,247) 106,666
Raurkela (★172,502) 125,426
Rewa 69,182
Rishra (★Calcutta) 63,486
Rohtak 124,755
Roorkee (★62,456) 47,561
Sāgar (★154,785) 118,574
Sahāranpur 225,396
Salem (★416,440) 308,716
Sambalpur (★105,085) 64,675
Sambhal 86,323
Sāngli (★201,597) 115,138
Sāntipur 61,166
Sāsarām 48,282
Sātāra 66,433
Satna (★62,162) 57,531
Secunderābād Cantonment (★Hyderābād) 94,416
Serampore (★Calcutta) 102,023
Shāhjahānpur (★144,065) 135,604
Shillong (★122,752) 87,659
Shimoga 102,709
Shivpuri (★50,858) 42,120
Sholāpur 398,361
Sīkar 70,987
Silchar 52,596
Silīguri (★136,343) 97,484
Simla 55,368
Singānallūr (★Coimbatore) 112,206
Sirsa 48,808
Sītāpur 66,715
Sivakāsi (★60,753) 44,883

▲ Población de un municipio, comuna o distrito entero, incluyendo sus áreas rurales.
● Ciudad más grande de un país.
★ Población o designación de un área metropolitana, incluyendo los suburbios.
C Censo. **E** Estimado oficial.
UE Estimado no oficial.
L Población dentro de los límites municipales de un año específico.

▲ Population d'une municipalité, d'une commune ou d'un district, zone rurale incluse.
● Ville la plus peuplée du pays.
★ Population de l'agglomération (ou nom de la zone métropolitaine englobante).
C Recensement. **E** Estimation officielle.
UE Estimation non officielle.
L Population comprise dans les limites municipales de l'année indiquée.

▲ População de um município, comuna ou distrito, inclusive as respectivas áreas rurais.
● Maior cidade de um país.
★ População ou indicação de uma área metropolitana, inclusive subúrbios.
C Censo. **E** Estimativa oficial.
UE Estimativa não oficial.
L População dentro dos limites municipais no ano indicado.

INDIA *continued*
Sonīpat........................ 62,393
South Dum-Dum (★Calcutta)...174,342
Sri Gangānagar (Gangānagar).. 90,042
Srīnagar (★423,253)............403,413
Srīrangam (★Tiruchchirāppalli) .51,069
Srīvilliputtūr..................... 53,855
Surat (★493,001)................471,656
Surendranagar (★97,251)........ 66,667
Tāmbaram (★Madras).......... 58,805
Tellicherry....................... 68,759
Tenāli...........................102,937
Thāna (★Bombay)..............170,675
Thanjāvūr (Tanjore)............140,547
Tinsukia......................... 54,911
Tiruchchirāppalli (Trichinopoly)
(★475,000).......................307,400
Tiruchendūr (★55,636).......... 18,126
Tirunelveli (★266,688)...........108,498
Tirupati (★71,984)............... 65,843
Tiruppur (★151,127).............113,302
Tiruvannāmalai................. 61,370
Tiruvottiyūr (★Madras)......... 82,853
Titāgarh (★Calcutta)............ 88,218
Tonk............................ 55,866
Trichūr......................... 76,241
Trivandrum.....................409,627
Tumkūr......................... 70,476
Tuticorin (★181,913).............155,310
Udaipur.........................161,278
Ujjain (★208,561)................203,278
Ulhāsnagar (★Bombay).........168,462
Uttarpara-Kotrung (★Calcutta). 67,568
Valparai........................ 95,175
Vāniyambādi (★57,686).......... 51,810
Vārānasi (Benares) (★606,271)..583,856
Vellore (★178,554)...............139,082
Verāval (★75,520)................. 58,771
Vijayawāda (★344,607)...........317,258
Villupuram...................... 60,242
Virudunagar..................... 61,902
Vishākhapatnam (★363,467).....352,504
Vizianagaram.................... 86,608
Warangal.......................207,520
Wardha......................... 69,037
Yamunānagar (★Jagādhri)..... 72,594
Yavatmāl........................ 64,836

INDONESIA
1971 C.......................119,232,499
Ambon (Amboina).............. 79,636
Balikpapan.....................137,340
Banda Aceh (Kutaradja)........ 53,668
Bandung (★1,250,000).........1,201,730
Banjarmasin....................281,673
Banyuwangi..................... 89,303
Bekasi.......................... 45,694
Binjai........................... 59,882
Blitar............................ 67,856
Blora............................ 53,504
Bogor...........................195,882
Bojonegoro...................... 52,597
Bukittinggi...................... 63,132
Cianjur (Tjiandjur)............. 62,546
Cilacap (Tjilatjap).............. 82,043
Cimahi (Tjimahi)................ 72,367
Cirebon (Tjirebon)..............178,529
Denpasar........................ 88,142
Garut............................ 81,234
Gresik........................... 48,561
Gorontalo....................... 82,328
•JAKARTA (DJAKARTA)
(1975 E) (★4,900,000).........4,810,531
Jambi (Telanaipura)............158,559
Jayapura (Sukarnapure)....... 45,786
Jember.........................122,712
Jombang........................ 45,450
Kediri...........................178,865
Krawang........................ 61,361
Kudus........................... 87,767
Kupang.......................... 52,698
Langsa.......................... 55,016
Lumajang........................ 48,995
Madiun..........................136,147
Magelang........................110,308
Malang..........................422,428
Manado.........................169,684
Martapura........................ 69,729
Medan..........................635,562
Mojokerto....................... 60,013
Padang..........................196,339
Padangsidempuan.............. 49,090
Pakanbaru......................145,030
Palembang......................582,961
Pangkalpinang................... 74,733
Parepare........................ 72,538
Pasuruan........................ 75,266
Pati............................. 46,037
Payakumbuh.................... 63,388
Pekalongan.....................111,537
Pemalang........................ 77,672
Pematangsiantar...............129,232
Ponorogo........................ 67,711
Pontianak.......................217,555
Probolinggo..................... 82,008
Purwakarta...................... 49,703
Purwokerto...................... 94,023
Purworejo....................... 52,956
Salatiga......................... 69,831
Samarinda......................137,521
Semarang.......................646,590
Serang.......................... 56,263
Situbondo....................... 55,348
Solok............................ 24,771
Sukabumi....................... 96,242
Surabaya (★1,400,000).........1,332,249
Surakarta.......................414,285
Tangerang....................... 50,893
Tanjungkarang-Telukbetung...198,986
Tasikmalaya....................136,004
Tegal...........................105,752
Tulungagung.................... 68,899
Ujung Pandang (Makasar).....434,766
Watampone (Bone)............. 54,720
Yogyakarta (Jogjakarta)........342,267

IRAN / Īrān
1976 C.......................33,591,875
Ābādān.........................296,081
Ahvāz..........................329,006
Āmol............................ 68,782
Arāk............................114,507
Ardabīl.........................147,404
Bābol........................... 67,790
Bandar 'Abbās.................. 89,103
Bandar-e Pahlavī............... 55,978
Borūjerd........................100,103
Dezfūl..........................110,287
Eşfahān (Isfahan)..............671,825
Gonbad-e Qābūs............... 59,868
Gorgān......................... 88,348
Hamadān.......................155,846
Homāyunshahr (1966 C)........ 46,836
Karaj...........................138,774
Kāshān......................... 84,545
Kāzerūn........................ 51,309
Kermān........................140,309
Kermānshāh....................290,861
Khorramābād...................104,928
Khorramshahr..................146,709
Khvoy.......................... 70,040
Marāgheh....................... 60,820
Mashhad (Meshed)............670,180
Masjed Soleymān............... 77,161
Najafābād...................... 76,236
Neyshābūr...................... 59,101
Qazvīn.........................138,527
Qom............................246,831
Rasht..........................187,203
Rezā'īyeh......................163,991
Sabzevār....................... 69,174
Sanandaj....................... 95,834
Sārī............................ 70,936
Shāhī........................... 63,289
Shīrāz..........................416,408
Tabrīz..........................598,576
•TEHRĀN (★4,700,000).........4,496,159
Yazd...........................135,978
Zāhedān........................ 92,628
Zanjān......................... 99,967

IRAQ / Al-'Irāq
1970 E........................9,465,800
Ad-Dīwānīyah.................. 62,300
Al-'Amārah..................... 80,100
Al-Başrah (Basra)..............370,900
Al-Ḩillah (Hilla)...............128,800
Al-Mawşil (Mosul)..............293,100
An-Najaf.......................179,200
An-Nāşirīyah.................. 62,400
As-Sulaymānīyah............... 98,100
•BAGHDĀD (★2,183,800)........1,300,000
Irbīl............................107,400
Karbalā'........................107,500
Kirkūk.........................207,900

IRELAND / Eire
1971 C........................2,978,248
Cork (Corcaigh) (★134,430).......128,645
•DUBLIN (BAILE ÁTHA CLIATH)
(★835,000).....................567,866
Dún Laoghaire (★Dublin)...... 53,171
Limerick (Luimneach) (★63,002). 57,161
Waterford (Port Láirge)
(★33,676)....................... 31,968

ISLE OF MAN
1976 C......................... 61,723
•DOUGLAS (★28,500)............ 20,262
Ramsey.......................... 5,458

ISRAEL / Yisra'el
1977 E........................3,653,200
Ashdod......................... 56,400
Ashqelon....................... 49,700
Bat Yam (★Tel Aviv-Yafo)......124,100
Be'er Sheva' (Beersheba)......101,000
Bene Beraq (★Tel Aviv-Yafo)... 85,900
Elat............................ 17,300
Giv'atayim (★Tel Aviv-Yafo).... 49,600
Ḩefa (Haifa) (★410,000)........227,800
Herzliyya (★Tel Aviv-Yafo)..... 52,000
Ḩolon (★Tel Aviv-Yafo).........121,200
Nazerat (Nazareth) (★59,000)... 38,600
Netanya........................ 89,100
Petaḩ Tiqwa (★Tel Aviv-Yafo)..112,000
Ramat Gan (★Tel Aviv-Yafo)...120,900
Reḩovot........................ 57,600
Rishon leZiyyon
(★Tel Aviv-Yafo)................ 79,100
•Tel Aviv-Yafo (Tel Aviv-Jaffa)
(★1,305,000)....................343,300
YERUSHALAYIM (AL-QUDS)
(JERUSALEM) (incl. Old City)
(★395,000)......................376,000

ITALY / Italia
1978 E.......................56,828,511
Afragola (★Napoli)............. 58,434
Agrigento....................... 51,058
Alessandria....................102,024
Altamura........................ 49,360
Ancona.........................108,466
Andria.......................... 83,150
Arezzo.......................... 92,087
Ascoli Piceno................... 56,420
Asti............................. 79,644
Avellino......................... 59,178
Aversa (★Napoli)............... 51,608
Bari (★460,000)................388,336
Barletta........................ 80,489
Benevento (62,358▲)........... 52,700
Bergamo (★340,000)............126,479
Biella........................... 56,070
Bologna (★555,000)............476,471
Bolzano (Bozen)................106,464
Brescia........................213,939
Brindisi......................... 88,795
Busto Arsizio (★Milano)........ 81,453
Cagliari (★300,000)............241,720
Caltanissetta (61,114▲)........ 54,400
Campobasso..................... 46,552
Carpi (59,524▲)................. 51,500
Carrara (★Massa)............... 70,213
Caserta......................... 66,898
Casoria (★Napoli)............... 66,822
Castellammare di Stabia
(★Napoli)........................ 74,299
Catania (★510,000).............400,130
Catanzaro....................... 93,538
Cerignola (51,004▲)............ 44,900
Cesena (90,046▲)............... 67,900
Chieti........................... 56,459
Chioggia (53,534▲)............. 38,100
Cinisello Balsamo (★Milano)... 80,091
Civitavecchia................... 47,988
Cologno Monzese (★Milano)... 51,341
Como (★160,000)............... 96,733
Cosenza (★128,000)............102,629
Cremona........................ 82,169
Crotone......................... 56,427
Cuneo.......................... 55,808
Empoli.......................... 45,802
Ercolano (Resina) (★Napoli).... 56,468
Faenza (55,630▲)............... 40,200
Fano (53,027▲)................. 43,800
Ferrara (153,767▲).............126,000
Firenze (Florence) (★660,000)...463,826
Foggia..........................156,459
Foligno (52,393▲)............... 46,100
Forlì (110,275▲)................. 92,300
Gela............................ 74,570
Genova (Genoa) (★860,000).....789,057
Grosseto (69,301▲)............. 61,200
Imola (60,125▲)................ 47,900
Imperia......................... 42,103
L'Aquila........................ 66,215
La Spezia (★192,000)...........118,740
Latina (93,380▲)................ 81,900
Lecce........................... 89,661
Lecco........................... 53,264
Legnano (★Milano).............. 49,252
Livorno (Leghorn)..............177,101
Lucca........................... 91,184
Manfredonia (52,333▲).......... 45,200
Mantova........................ 64,329
Marsala (85,466▲).............. 50,100
Massa (★145,000).............. 65,814
Matera.......................... 49,954
Messina........................269,414
•Milano (Milan) (★3,800,000)...1,693,351
Modena.........................180,557
Molfetta........................ 66,384
Moncalieri (★Torino)........... 63,981
Monza (★Milano)...............123,184
Napoli (Naples) (★2,720,000)..1,225,377
Nicastro (Lamezia Terme)
(61,490▲)........................ 29,500
Nocera Inferiore (51,520▲)...... 43,300
Novara.........................102,132
Padova (★280,000).............242,816
Palermo........................687,587
Parma..........................178,064
Pavia........................... 87,222
Paterno......................... 48,773
Perugia........................138,766
Pesaro.......................... 90,413
Pescara........................136,921
Piacenza.......................109,095
Pisa...........................103,849
Pistoia (94,637▲)............... 84,600
Pordenone...................... 52,284
Portici (★Napoli)............... 83,448
Potenza......................... 63,797
Pozzuoli (★Napoli) (69,451▲).... 60,500
Prato (★199,000)...............156,955
Ragusa (65,998▲)............... 54,700
Ravenna (139,226▲)............102,200
Reggio di Calabria.............180,298
Reggio nell'Emilia.............130,031
Rho (★Milano).................. 49,179
Rimini..........................127,352
Rivoli (★Torino)................ 50,392
ROMA (ROME) (★3,190,000)...2,914,640
Rovigo.......................... 52,300
Salerno (★240,000).............162,780
San Benedetto del Tronto...... 46,037
San Giorgio a Cremano
(★Napoli)........................ 63,847
San Remo (63,867▲)............ 52,800
San Severo...................... 54,504
Sassari.........................118,384
Savona (★120,000).............. 78,606
Scandicci (★Firenze)........... 53,897
Sesto Fiorentino (★Firenze).... 44,458
Sesto San Giovanni
(★Milano)........................ 98,300
Siena........................... 64,251
Siracusa.......................124,111
Taranto........................246,828
Teramo (51,397▲)............... 40,700
Terni...........................113,147
Tivoli (★Roma).................. 45,705
Torino (Turin) (★1,675,000)....1,172,482
Torre Annunziata (★Napoli)..... 57,778
Torre del Greco (★Napoli)......100,868
Trapani (70,308▲)............... 60,900
Trento.......................... 98,680
Treviso......................... 89,991
Trieste.........................262,929
Udine (★128,000)...............103,051
Varese.......................... 91,130
Venezia (Venice) (★445,000)....358,266
Vercelli......................... 54,543
Verona.........................270,858
Viareggio....................... 59,460
Vicenza........................118,178
Vigevano........................ 67,378
Viterbo (58,013▲)............... 49,600
Vittoria......................... 50,293

IVORY COAST / Côte d'Ivoire
1975 C........................6,709,600
•ABIDJAN.......................555,000
Bouaké.........................173,248
Daloa........................... 60,958
Korhogo........................ 47,657
Man............................ 50,315

JAMAICA
1976 E........................2,084,000
•KINGSTON......................635,100
Montego Bay (1970 C).......... 43,754

JAPAN / Nihon
1978 E......................115,171,000
Abiko (★Tōkyō) (1975 C)........ 76,218
Ageo (★Tōkyō)..................158,841
Aizu-wakamatsu................112,237
Akashi (★Ōsaka)...............248,422
Akishima (★Tōkyō) (1975 C).... 83,864
Akita...........................275,839
Akō (1975 C).................... 49,583
Amagaski (★Ōsaka).............536,543
Anan (1975 C) (60,439▲)......... 37,200
Anjō...........................119,063
Aomori.........................279,104
Arao (★Ōmuta) (1975 C)
(58,296▲)........................ 47,300
Asahikawa......................336,909
Asaka (★Tōkyō) (1975 C)....... 81,755
Ashikaga.......................164,352
Ashiya (★Ōsaka) (1975 C)...... 76,211
Atami (1975 C).................. 51,437
Atsugi (★Tōkyō)................126,903
Ayase (★Tōkyō) (1975 C)....... 50,365
Beppu..........................136,995
Bisai (1975 C).................. 54,247
Chiba (★Tōkyō).................720,999
Chichibu (1975 C)............... 61,798
Chigasaki (★Tōkyō)............165,182
Chita (★Nagoya) (1975 C)...... 56,560
Chitose (1975 C)................ 61,031
Chōfu (★Tōkyō)................180,089
Chōshi (1975 C)................. 90,374
Daitō (★Ōsaka).................114,364
Ebetsu (1975 C)................. 77,624
Ebina (Tōkyō) (1975 C)......... 59,783
Fuchū (★Tōkyō)................187,105
Fuchū (1975 C).................. 50,217
Fuji (★325,000)................204,096
Fujieda (1975 C) (90,358▲)...... 64,300
Fujiidera (★Ōsaka) (1975 C).... 59,515
Fujimi (★Tōkyō) (1975 C)....... 70,391
Fujinomiya (★Fuji) (105,408▲)... 81,900
Fujisawa (★Tōkyō).............286,663
Fuji-yoshida (1975 C)........... 51,976
Fukaya (1975 C) (75,748▲)...... 53,100
Fukuchiyama (1975 C) (60,003▲). 43,000
Fukui...........................237,659
Fukuoka (★1,515,000)..........1,055,454
Fukushima......................256,772
Fukuyama......................339,945
Funabashi (★Tōkyō)............459,939
Futtsu (1975 C)................. 56,653
Gamagōri (1975 C).............. 85,282
Gifu............................409,232
Ginowan (1975 C)............... 53,835
Gotemba (1975 C) (62,722▲)..... 49,300
Gyōda (1975 C).................. 66,069
Habikino (★Ōsaka)..............101,538
Hachinohe......................233,024
Hachiōji (★Tōkyō)..............365,348
Hadano (★Tōkyō)...............114,722
Hakodate.......................313,189
Hamada (1975 C)................ 50,316
Hamakita (1975 C) (67,180▲)..... 49,600
Hamamatsu.....................481,054
Handa (1975 C).................. 85,824
Hannō (★Tōkyō) (1975 C)....... 55,926
Hatogaya (★Tōkyō) (1975 C)..... 56,693
Hekinan (1975 C)................ 60,680
Higashihiroshima (★Hiroshima)
(1975 C)......................... 66,231
Higashikurume (★Tōkyō)........105,783
Higashimatsuyama (1975 C).... 57,684
Higashimurayama (★Tōkyō)....118,815
Higashiōsaka (★Ōsaka).........524,380
Higashiyamato (★Tōkyō)
(1975 C)......................... 58,464
Hikari (★Tokuyama) (1975 C)... 48,794
Hikone (1975 C)................. 85,066
Himeji..........................444,335
Hino (★Tōkyō).................141,277
Hirakata (★Ōsaka)..............333,112
Hiratsuka (★Tōkyō).............206,632
Hirosaki (172,032▲).............111,300
Hiroshima (★1,465,000).........883,265
Hita (1975 C) (63,969▲)......... 47,300
Hitachi.........................203,381
Hōfu (109,305▲)................. 85,700
Honjō (1975 C).................. 51,090
Hōya (★Tōkyō) (1975 C)......... 91,546
Ibaraki (★Ōsaka)...............224,155
Ichihara (★Tōkyō)..............206,605
Ichikawa (★Tōkyō).............351,618
Ichinomiya.....................247,682
Iida (1975 C) (77,112▲)......... 51,900
Iizuka (1975 C) (★103,000)...... 75,417
Ikeda (★Ōsaka).................102,115
Ikoma (★Ōsaka) (1975 C)........ 48,848
Imabari........................123,325
Inazawa (★Nagoya) (1975 C).... 88,606
Inuyama (★Nagoya) (1975 C)... 58,731
Iruma (★Tōkyō) (1975 C)........ 83,997
Isahaya (1975 C) (73,341▲)...... 49,400
Ise (Uji-yamada)................105,174
Isehara (★Tōkyō) (1975 C)...... 61,616
Isesaki........................102,598
Ishinomaki.....................118,654
Itami (★Ōsaka).................177,289
Itō (1975 C).................... 68,072
Itsukaichi (★Hiroshima)
(1975 C)......................... 64,885
Iwaki (Taira) (337,206▲)........265,500
Iwakuni........................111,526
Iwamizawa (1975 C) (72,305▲).... 56,800
Iwata (1975 C).................. 67,665
Iwatsuki (★Tōkyō) (1975 C)
(83,825▲)........................ 60,900
Izumi (★Ōsaka).................121,729
Izumi (★Sendai) (1975 C)....... 70,087
Izumi-ōtsu (★Ōsaka) (1975 C)... 66,250
Izumi-sano (★Ōsaka) (1975 C)... 86,139
Izumo (1975 C) (71,568▲)........ 47,700

▲ Population of an entire municipality, commune, or district, including rural area.
• Largest city in country.
★ Population or designation of the metropolitan area, including suburbs.
C Census. E Official estimate. UE Unofficial estimate.
L Population within municipal limits of year specified.

▲ Bevölkerung eines ganzen städtischen Verwaltungsgebietes, eines Kommunalbezirkes oder eines Distrikts, einschliesslich ländlicher Gebiete.
• Grösste Stadt des Landes.
★ Bevölkerung oder Bezeichnung der Stadtregion einschliess lich Vororte.
C Volkszählung. E Offizielle Schätzung. UE Inoffizielle Schätzung.
L Bevölkerung innerhalb der städtischen Verwaltungseinheit des angegebenen Jahres.

Joetsu (Takada) ... 125,722
Jōyō (★Ōsaka) (1975 C) ... 58,923
Kadoma (★Ōsaka) ... 142,226
Kaga (1975 C) (61,599▲) ... 47,400
Kagamigahara ... 108,897
Kagoshima ... 486,495
Kainan (1975 C) ... 53,250
Kaizuka (★Ōsaka) (1975 C) ... 79,506
Kakogawa (★Ōsaka) ... 190,095
Kamagaya (★Tōkyō) (1975 C) ... 63,288
Kamaishi (1975 C) ... 68,981
Kamakura (★Tōkyō) ... 172,981
Kamifukuoka (★Tōkyō)
(1975 C) ... 58,332
Kanazawa ... 407,318
Kanoya (1975 C) (67,951▲) ... 38,500
Kanuma (1975 C) (81,799▲) ... 55,800
Karatsu (1975 C) ... 75,224
Kariya (★Nagoya) ... 102,221
Kasaoka (1975 C) (63,413▲) ... 42,700
Kashihara (★Ōsaka) ... 103,987
Kashiwa (★Tōkyō) ... 229,179
Kashiwara (★Ōsaka) (1975 C) ... 63,586
Kashiwazaki (1975 C)
(80,351▲) ... 53,500
Kasuga (★Fukuoka) (1975 C) ... 55,160
Kasugai (★Nagoya) ... 236,690
Kasukabe (★Tōkyō) ... 146,485
Katano (★Ōsaka) (1975 C) ... 52,732
Katsuta (1975 C) ... 79,996
Kawachi-nagano (★Ōsaka)
(1975 C) ... 66,936
Kawagoe (★Tōkyō) ... 247,671
Kawaguchi (★Tōkyō) ... 365,536
Kawanishi (★Ōsaka) ... 126,057
Kawasaki (★Tōkyō) ... 1,040,716
Kesennuma (1975 C) ... 66,616
Kimitsu (1975 C) ... 76,016
Kiryū ... 133,485
Kisarazu ... 104,620
Kishiwada (★Ōsaka) ... 176,575
Kitakyūshū (★1,515,000) ... 1,067,612
Kitami (1975 C) (91,519▲) ... 73,000
Kiyose (★Tōkyō) (1975 C) ... 60,574
Kōbe (★Ōsaka) ... 1,370,509
Kōchi ... 294,650
Kodaira (★Tōkyō) ... 158,647
Kōfu ... 197,019
Koga (★Tōkyō) (1975 C) ... 55,973
Koganei (★Tōkyō) ... 103,838
Kokubunji (★Tōkyō)
(1975 C) ... 88,159
Komae (★Tōkyō) (1975 C) ... 70,043
Komaki (★Nagoya) (1975 C) ... 97,445
Komatsu ... 102,982
Kōnan (1975 C) ... 90,426
Kōnosu (★Tōkyō) (1975 C) ... 51,632
Kōriyama (277,616▲) ... 189,600
Koshigaya (★Tōkyō) ... 212,569
Kudamatsu (★Tokuyama)
(1975 C) ... 55,825
Kumagaya ... 133,384
Kumamoto ... 510,086
Kunitachi (★Tōkyō) (1975 C) ... 64,495
Kurashiki ... 400,294
Kure (★Hiroshima) ... 238,529
Kurume ... 212,553
Kusatsu (★Ōsaka) (1975 C) ... 64,873
Kushiro ... 213,059
Kuwana (1975 C) ... 83,440
Kyōto (★Ōsaka) ... 1,466,958
Machida (★Tōkyō) ... 279,155
Maebashi ... 260,279
Maizuru (1975 C) (97,780▲) ... 82,600
Marugame (1975 C) ... 65,662
Matsubara (★Ōsaka) ... 135,929
Matsudo (★Tōkyō) ... 380,282
Matsue ... 132,694
Matsumoto ... 189,807
Matsuyama ... 385,599
Matsuzaka (112,138▲) ... 81,300
Mihara (1975 C) ... 83,679
Minō (★Ōsaka) (1975 C) ... 79,621
Misato (★Tōkyō) (1975 C) ... 79,355
Mishima (★Numazu) (1975 C) ... 89,248
Mitaka (★Tōkyō) ... 166,651
Mito ... 209,380
Miura (1975 C) ... 47,888
Miyako (1975 C) ... 61,912
Miyakonojō (125,662▲) ... 80,900
Miyazaki ... 252,578
Mobara (1975 C) ... 64,942
Moriguchi (★Ōsaka) ... 168,125
Morioka ... 225,240
Muroran (★220,000) ... 164,628
Musashi-murayama (★Tōkyō)
(1975 C) ... 50,842
Musashino (★Tōkyō) ... 139,732
Nagahama (1975 C) ... 54,064
Nagano (317,663▲) ... 239,300
Nagaoka ... 176,834
Nagaokakyo (★Ōsaka)
(1975 C) ... 65,557
Nagareyama (★Tōkyō) ... 100,160
Nagasaki ... 447,865
Nagoya (★3,635,000) ... 2,086,118
Naha ... 291,225
Nara (★Ōsaka) ... 282,381
Narashino (★Tōkyō) ... 120,137
Naruto (1975 C) (61,959▲) ... 50,600
Neyagawa (★Ōsaka) ... 259,354
Niigata ... 441,766
Niihama ... 133,634
Niiza (★Tōkyō) ... 118,376
Nishinomiya (★Ōsaka) ... 409,805
Nishio (1975 C) (82,524▲) ... 62,600
Nobeoka ... 136,130
Noboribetsu (★Muroran)
(1975 C) ... 50,885
Noda (★Tōkyō) (1975 C) ... 78,193
Nōgata (1975 C) ... 58,551
Numazu (★430,000) ... 202,172
Obihiro ... 148,086
Ōbu (★Nagoya) (1975 C) ... 56,211
Ōdate (1975 C) (71,828▲) ... 50,200

Odawara ... 176,791
Ōgaki ... 141,396
Ōita ... 344,847
Ōkawa (1975 C) ... 50,395
Okaya (1975 C) ... 61,776
Okayama ... 533,263
Okazaki ... 250,890
Okegawa (★Tōkyō) (1975 C) ... 48,034
Okinawa (1975 C) ... 91,347
Ōme (★Tōkyō) (1975 C) ... 86,152
Ōmiya (★Tōkyō) ... 342,621
Ōmuta (★225,000) ... 164,170
Onojo (★Fukuoka) (1975 C) ... 52,169
Onomichi ... 102,489
Ōsaka (★15,000,000) ... 2,700,303
Ōta ... 118,578
Otaru ... 186,603
Ōtsu (★Ōsaka) ... 204,223
Oyama (123,731▲) ... 79,800
Saga ... 159,792
Sagamihara (★Tōkyō) ... 415,905
Sakado (★Tōkyō) (1975 C) ... 51,230
Sakai (★Ōsaka) ... 794,638
Sakaide (1975 C) ... 67,624
Sakata (100,853▲) ... 73,500
Sakura (★Tōkyō) (1975 C)
(80,804▲) ... 61,500
Sanjō (1975 C) ... 81,806
Sano (1975 C) ... 75,844
Sapporo (★1,380,000) ... 1,336,702
Sasebo ... 251,586
Sayama (★Tōkyō) ... 118,421
Seki (1975 C) ... 53,881
Sendai (*Kagoshima-ken*)
(1975 C) (61,788▲) ... 34,700
Sendai (*Miyagi-ken*) (★850,000) ... 616,664
Seto ... 118,575
Settsu (★Ōsaka) (1975 C) ... 76,704
Shibata (1975 C) (74,025▲) ... 48,700
Shijōnawate (★Ōsaka) (1975 C) ... 52,368
Shimada (1975 C) ... 68,820
Shimizu (★Shizuoka) ... 242,275
Shimonoseki (★Kitakyūshū) ... 269,697
Shiogama (★Sendai) (1975 C) ... 59,235
Shizuoka (★730,000) ... 454,002
Sōka (★Tōkyō) ... 182,642
Suita (★Ōsaka) ... 319,101
Suwa (1975 C) ... 49,594
Suzaka (1975 C) ... 49,513
Suzuka (150,452▲) ... 105,500
Tachikawa (★Tōkyō) ... 142,267
Tajimi (1975 C) ... 68,901
Takaishi (★Ōsaka) (1975 C) ... 66,824
Takamatsu ... 309,610
Takaoka (★220,000) ... 173,228
Takarazuka (★Ōsaka) ... 175,666
Takasago (★Ōsaka) (1975 C) ... 77,080
Takasaki ... 218,557
Takatsuki (★Ōsaka) ... 342,109
Takawa (1975 C) ... 61,464
Takayama (1975 C) ... 60,504
Takefu (1975 C) (65,012▲) ... 48,700
Takikawa (1975 C) ... 50,090
Tama (★Tōkyō) (1975 C) ... 65,466
Tamano (1975 C) ... 78,516
Tanabe (1975 C) (66,999▲) ... 51,800
Tanashi (★Tōkyō) (1975 C) ... 67,433
Tatebayashi (1975 C) ... 66,410
Tochigi (1975 C) ... 83,189
Toda (★Tōkyō) (1975 C) ... 77,137
Tokai (★Nagoya) (1975 C) ... 95,457
Toki (1975 C) ... 63,324
Tokoname (1975 C) ... 54,865
Tokorozawa (★Tōkyō) ... 222,377
Tokushima ... 244,149
Tokuyama (★255,000) ... 110,596
•TŌKYŌ (★25,200,000) ... 8,493,804
Tomakomai ... 141,783
Tondabayashi (★Ōsaka)
(1975 C) ... 91,393
Toride (★Tōkyō) (1975 C) ... 52,816
Tosu (1975 C) ... 50,733
Tottori ... 127,132
Toyama ... 299,589
Toyohashi ... 295,910
Toyokawa ... 101,548
Toyonaka (★Ōsaka) ... 409,511
Toyota ... 270,559
Tsu ... 143,497
Tsuchiura ... 109,060
Tsuruga (1975 C) ... 60,205
Tsuruoka (1975 C) (95,932▲) ... 74,600
Tsushima (1975 C) ... 58,241
Tsuyama (1975 C) (79,907▲) ... 56,500
Ube (★222,000) ... 166,392
Ueda ... 109,261
Uji (★Ōsaka) ... 146,396
Urawa (★Tōkyō) ... 347,870
Utsunomiya ... 365,023
Uwajima (1975 C) ... 70,428
Wakayama ... 396,675
Wakkanai (1975 C) ... 55,464
Warabi (★Tōkyō) (1975 C) ... 76,311
Yachiyo (★Tōkyō) ... 129,781
Yaizu ... 101,762
Yamagata ... 230,316
Yamaguchi (110,275▲) ... 79,700
Yamato (★Tōkyō) ... 161,600
Yamato-kōriyama (★Ōsaka)
(1975 C) ... 71,001
Yamato-takada (★Ōsaka)
(1975 C) ... 58,637
Yao (★Ōsaka) ... 271,491
Yashio (★Tōkyō) (1975 C) ... 56,127
Yatsushiro (106,193▲) ... 79,300
Yawata (★Ōsaka) (1975 C) ... 50,131
Yokkaichi ... 252,768
Yokohama (★Tōkyō) ... 2,729,433
Yokosuka (★Tōkyō) ... 412,270
Yonago ... 123,071
Yonezawa (1975 C) (91,974▲) ... 71,400
Yono (★Tōkyō) (1975 C) ... 71,044
Yūbari (1975 C) ... 50,131
Zama (★Tōkyō) (1975 C) ... 80,562
Zushi (★Tōkyō) (1975 C) ... 56,298

JERSEY
1976 C ... 74,470
•ST. HELIER (★45,000) ... 26,343

JORDAN / Al-Urdunn
1977 E ... 2,890,000
Al-Quds (Jerusalem, Old City)
(1973 E) ... 90,000
•'AMMĀN ... 711,900
Az-Zarqā' ... 263,400
Bayt Lahm (Bethlehem)
(1971 E) ... 25,000
Irbid ... 136,800
Nābulus (1971 E) ... 64,000

KAMPUCHEA
1962 C ... 5,728,771
•PHNUM PÉNH ... 393,995

KENYA
1978 E ... 14,856,000
Mombasa ... 391,000
•NAIROBI ... 818,000
Nakuru (1971 E) ... 45,000

KOREA, NORTH / Chosŏn Minjujuŭi In'min Konghwaguk
1967 E ... 12,780,000
Ch'ŏngjin ... 265,000
Haeju ... 115,000
Hamhŭng (1944 C) ... 112,184
Hŭngnam (1944 C) ... 143,600
Kaesŏng ... 140,000
Kimch'aek (Sŏngjin) ... 265,000
Namp'o (Chinnamp'o) ... 130,000
•P'YŎNGYANG ... 840,000
Sariwŏn (1944 C) ... 42,957
Sinŭiju ... 165,000
Songnim (1944 C) ... 53,035
Wŏnsan ... 215,000

KOREA, SOUTH / Taehan-Min'guk
1975 C ... 34,708,542
Andong (95,449▲) ... 79,900
Anyang (★Sŏul) ... 134,862
Bucheon (★Sŏul) ... 109,236
Chech'ŏn (74,239▲) ... 51,300
Cheju (135,189▲) ... 73,700
Chinhae ... 103,657
Chinju (154,676▲) ... 121,400
Ch'ŏnan (96,789▲) ... 68,000
Ch'ŏngju ... 192,734
Chŏnju ... 311,432
Ch'unch'ŏn ... 140,521
Ch'ungju (105,143▲) ... 73,100
Chungmu (66,817▲) ... 55,900
Inch'ŏn (★Sŏul) ... 799,982
Iri (117,111▲) ... 97,200
Kangnŭng (85,040▲) ... 55,900
Kimch'ŏn (67,066▲) ... 50,700
Kunsan ... 154,485
Kwangju ... 607,058
Kyŏngju (108,447▲) ... 64,800
Masan ... 371,937
Mokp'o ... 192,927
P'ohang (134,404▲) ... 110,000
Pusan ... 2,454,051
Seongnam (★Sŏul) ... 272,329
Sŏkch'o ... 71,475
•SŎUL (SEOUL) (★8,625,000) ... 6,889,470
Sunch'ŏn (108,034▲) ... 72,500
Suwŏn ... 224,177
Taegu ... 1,311,078
Taejŏn ... 506,703
Ŭijŏngbu (★Sŏul) ... 108,365
Ulsan (252,639▲) ... 171,200
Wŏnju ... 120,335
Yŏngju (70,793▲) ... 50,800
Yŏsu ... 130,641

KUWAIT / Al-Kuwayt
1975 C ... 994,837
Abraq Khīṭān (★Al-Kuwayt) ... 59,443
Al-Farwānīyah (★Al-Kuwayt) ... 44,875
Al-Jahrah (★Al-Kuwayt) ... 52,302
•AL-KUWAYT (★780,000) ... 78,116
As-Sālimīyah (★Al-Kuwayt) ... 113,943
Ḥawallī (★Al-Kuwayt) ... 130,565

LAOS / Lao
1973 E ... 3,181,000
Louangphrabang ... 43,000
Pakxé ... 44,860
Savannakhet ... 50,691
•VIANGCHAN (VIENTIANE) ... 174,229

LEBANON / Al-Lubnān
1970 E ... 2,126,355
•BAYRŪT (BEIRUT) (★1,010,000) ... 474,870
Ṣaydā (Sidon) ... 34,000
Ṭarābulus (Tripoli) ... 157,320

LESOTHO
1972 E ... 972,000
•MASERU ... 17,000

LIBERIA
1974 C ... 1,503,368
•MONROVIA ... 204,210

LIBYA / Lībiyā
1970 E ... 1,938,000
Banghāzī (Bengasi) ... 170,000
Misrātah ... 44,000
•ṬARĀBULUS (TRIPOLI) ... 264,000
Ṭubruq (Tobruk) (1964 C) ... 15,900

LIECHTENSTEIN
1977 E ... 24,715
•VADUZ ... 4,704

LUXEMBOURG
1976 E ... 358,000
Esch-sur-Alzette (★98,000) ... 27,600
•LUXEMBOURG (★110,000) ... 79,300

MACAU
1970 C ... 248,636
•MACAU (★248,636) ... 241,413

MADAGASCAR / Madagasikara
1972 E ... 7,928,868
•ANTANANARIVO ... 366,530
Antsirabe (70,003▲) ... 33,287
Diégo-Suarez ... 45,487
Fianarantsoa ... 58,818
Majunga ... 67,456
Tamatave ... 59,503
Tuléar ... 39,183

MALAWI
1976 E ... 5,175,000
•Blantyre ... 219,000
LILONGWE ... 75,000

MALAYSIA
1970 C ... 10,452,309
Alor Setar (★85,748) ... 66,179
Batu Pahat (Bandar
Penggaram) ... 53,291
Butterworth (★Pinang) ... 61,187
George Town (Pinang)
(★450,000) ... 270,019
Ipoh (★257,309) ... 247,689
Johor Baharu (★Singapore) ... 136,229
Kelang ... 113,607
Keluang ... 43,272
Kota Baharu (★69,756) ... 55,052
•KUALA LUMPUR (★750,000) ... 451,728
Kuala Terengganu (★59,494) ... 53,353
Kuantan ... 43,358
Kuching ... 63,535
Melaka (Malacca) (★99,782) ... 86,357
Muar (Bandar Maharani) ... 61,218
Petaling Jaya (★Kuala
Lumpur) ... 93,447
Sandakan ... 42,413
Seremban (★90,062) ... 79,915
Sibu ... 50,635
Taiping ... 54,645
Telok Anson ... 44,524

MALDIVES
1978 C ... 143,046
•MALE ... 29,555

MALI
1972 E ... 5,257,000
•BAMAKO (1976 C) ... 404,022
Kayes ... 37,000
Mopti ... 43,000
Ségou ... 40,000
Tombouctou (Timbuktu)
(1971 E) ... 11,900

MALTA
1972 E ... 318,500
•VALLETTA (★202,000) ... 15,200

MARTINIQUE
1974 C ... 324,832
•FORT-DE-FRANCE (★113,556) ... 98,807

MAURITANIA / Mauritanie
1971 E ... 1,190,000
•NOUAKCHOTT ... 35,000

MAURITIUS
1978 E ... 924,663
Beau Bassin (★Port Louis) ... 83,714
Curepipe (★Port Louis) ... 54,356
•PORT LOUIS (★405,000) ... 142,853
Quatre Bornes (★Port Louis) ... 53,835
Vacoas-Phoenix (★Port Louis) ... 51,793

MEXICO / México
1976 E ... 62,329,000
Acapulco [de Juárez] ... 402,200
Aguascalientes ... 230,000
Campeche (1970 C) ... 69,506
Celaya (1970 C) ... 79,977
Chihuahua ... 365,800
•CIUDAD DE MÉXICO (MEXICO
CITY) (★12,450,000) ... 8,628,000
Ciudad de Valles (1970 C) ... 47,587
Ciudad Guzmán (1970 C) ... 48,166
Ciudad Juárez
(★El Paso, Tex.) ... 544,900
Ciudad Madero (★Tampico) ... 128,600
Ciudad Mante (1970 C) ... 51,247
Ciudad Obregón ... 161,300
Ciudad Victoria ... 116,800
Coatzacoalcos ... 105,400
Colima (1970 C) ... 58,450
Córdoba ... 109,400
Cuernavaca ... 313,000
Culiacán ... 262,500
Delicias (1970 C) ... 52,446
Durango ... 199,800
Ensenada (1970 C) ... 77,687
Gómez Palacio (★Torreón)
(1970 C) ... 79,650
Guadalajara (★2,150,000) ... 1,640,900
Guadalupe (★Monterrey)
(1970 C) ... 51,899
Guaymas (1970 C) ... 57,492
Hermosillo ... 264,100
Hidalgo del Parral (1970 C) ... 57,619
Irapuato ... 145,300
Jalapa Enríquez ... 183,200
León [de los Aldamas] ... 525,900
Los Mochis (1970 C) ... 67,953
Matamoros
(★Brownsville, Tex.) ... 179,400
Mazatlán ... 161,600
Mérida ... 244,700
Mesa de Tijuana
(★San Diego, Calif.) (1970 C) ... 50,094
Mexicali (★360,000) ... 345,900
Minatitlán ... 105,800
Monclova ... 115,700

▲ Población de un municipio, comuna o distrito entero, incluyendo sus áreas rurales.
• Ciudad más grande de un país.
★ Población o designación de un área metropolitana, incluyendo los suburbios.
C Censo. E Estimado oficial.
UE Estimado no oficial.
L Población dentro de los límites municipales de un año específico.

▲ Population d'une municipalité, d'une commune ou d'un district, zone rurale incluse.
• Ville la plus peuplée du pays.
★ Population de l'agglomération (ou nom de la zone métropolitaine englobante).
C Recensement. E Estimation officielle.
UE Estimation non officielle.
L Population comprise dans les limites municipales de l'année indiquée.

▲ População de um município, comuna ou distrito, inclusive as respectivas áreas rurais.
• Maior cidade de um país.
★ População ou indicação de uma área metropolitana, inclusive subúrbios.
C Censo. E Estimativa oficial.
UE Estimativa não oficial.
L População dentro dos limites municipais no ano indicado.

MEXICO *continued*
Monterrey (★1,725,000)........1,090,200
Morelia........................219,400
Netzahualcóyotl (★Ciudad de México) (1970 C)............ 580,438
Nogales (1970 C)............... 52,108
Nuevo Laredo (★Laredo, Tex.).............203,700
Oaxaca [de Juárez].............122,800
Orizaba (★250,000)..............111,500
Pachuca [de Soto] (1970 C)..... 83,892
Poza Rica de Hidalgo...........169,600
Puebla [de Zaragoza]..........498,900
Querétaro.....................158,400
Reynosa.......................206,500
Salamanca (1970 C)............ 61,039
Saltillo.......................222,100
San Luis Potosí................292,300
San Luis Rio Colorado (1970 C)..................... 49,990
Tampico (★400,000)............231,200
Tapachula (1970 C)............ 60,620
Tehuacán (1970 C)............. 47,497
Tepic..........................120,300
Tijuana (★San Diego, Calif.)....411,600
Tlaquepaque (★Guadalajara) (1970 C)..................... 59,760
Toluca [de Lerdo]..............147,600
Torreón (★420,000).............257,000
Tuxtla Gutiérrez (1970 C)....... 66,851
Uruapan [del Progreso]........122,300
Veracruz [Llave] (★345,000).....277,300
Villahermosa...................152,200
Zacatecas (1970 C)............. 50,251
Zamora de Hidalgo (1970 C)..... 57,775

MONACO
1975 E.......................... 25,000
•MONACO (★50,000)............. 25,000

MONGOLIA / Mongol Ard Uls
1970 E........................1,285,000
Darchan (1969 C).............. 22,800
•ULAAN BAATAR (ULAN BATOR)......................287,000

MONTSERRAT
1970 C......................... 11,458
•PLYMOUTH...................... 1,267

MOROCCO / Al-Magreb
1971 C.....................15,379,259
Agadir......................... 61,192
Beni-Mellal.................... 53,826
•Casablanca (Dar-el-Beida) (★1,575,000)................1,506,373
El-Jadida (Mazagan)........... 55,501
Fès (Fez).......................325,327
Kenitra........................139,206
Khouribga...................... 73,667
Ksar-el-Kebir.................. 48,262
Larache........................ 45,710
Marrakech......................332,741
Meknès.........................248,369
Mohammedia (Fedala)......... 70,392
Oujda..........................175,532
RABAT (★540,000)..............367,620
Safi...........................129,113
Salé (★Rabat)..................155,557
Tanger (Tangier)..............187,894
Taza........................... 55,157
Tétouan........................139,105

MOZAMBIQUE / Moçambique
1970 C........................8,168,933
Beira..........................110,752
João Belo...................... 63,494
•MAPUTO (LOURENÇO MARQUES)..................341,922
Nampula........................120,188
Quelimane...................... 71,289
Tete........................... 51,453

NAMIBIA
1970 C.........................722,867
•WINDHOEK...................... 61,260

NEPAL / Nepāl
1971 C.......................11,555,983
Bhaktapur...................... 40,112
Birātnagar..................... 45,100
•KATHMANDU (★215,000).......150,402
Lalitpur (★Kathmandu)........ 59,049

NETHERLANDS / Nederland
1979 E.....................13,985,523
Alkmaar (★105,000)............ 69,067
Almelo......................... 63,230
Alphen aan den Rijn........... 50,347
Amersfoort (★127,588)......... 87,225
Amstelveen (★Amsterdam)...... 69,770
•AMSTERDAM (★1,810,000)......718,577
Apeldoorn......................137,244
Arnhem (★286,000).............126,998
Bergen op Zoom................ 43,270
Breda (★151,000)...............117,521
Delft (★'s-Gravenhage)......... 83,674
Den Helder..................... 61,317
Deventer....................... 64,268
Dordrecht (★195,000)..........106,109
Ede (82,095▲).................. 43,100
Eindhoven (★366,000)...........192,687
Emmen (88,969▲)............... 35,200
Enschede (★284,000)...........141,917
Geleen (★180,000)............. 35,367
Gouda.......................... 58,559
Groningen (★201,000)..........160,615
Haarlem (★Amsterdam).........159,747
Haarlemmermeer (75,984▲)..... 10,400
Heerlen (★268,000)............ 71,080
Helmond........................ 58,602
Hengelo (★Enschede)........... 74,589
Hilversum (★Amsterdam)...... 93,393
IJmuiden (Velsen) (★Amsterdam)............... 61,733
Kerkrade (★Heerlen)........... 47,157
Leeuwarden..................... 84,457
Leiden (★171,000)..............102,747
Maastricht (★145,000)..........109,313
Nijmegen (★217,000)...........147,670
Oss............................ 46,159
Ridderkerk (★Rotterdam)...... 45,474
Rijswijk (★'s-Gravenhage)...... 52,765
Roosendaal..................... 54,208
Rotterdam (★1,075,000).........582,396
Schiedam (★Rotterdam)....... 75,257
's-GRAVENHAGE (THE HAGUE) (★770,000)...................458,242
's-Hertogenbosch (★183,000).... 87,409
Soest (★Amersfoort)........... 40,363
Tilburg (★215,000)..............150,751
Utrecht (★476,000).............236,053
Venlo (★86,000)................ 62,444
Vlaardingen (★Rotterdam)..... 79,347
Vlissingen (Flushing) (44,937▲).. 25,700
Zaanstad (Zaandam) (★Amsterdam)..............127,698
Zeist (★Utrecht)................ 61,406
Zoetermeer (★'s-Gravenhage).. 59,079
Zwolle......................... 81,302

NETHERLANDS ANTILLES / Nederlandse Antillen
1977 E.........................245,000
•WILLEMSTAD (1960 C) (★94,133). 43,547

NEW CALEDONIA / Nouvelle-Calédonie
1976 C.........................133,233
•NOUMÉA (★70,600).............. 56,100

NEW HEBRIDES / Nouvelles-Hébrides
1979 C.........................112,596
•VILA (★14,801)................. 10,158

NEW ZEALAND
1978 E........................3,145,900
•Auckland (★775,000)...........149,000
Christchurch (★309,000)........172,400
Dunedin (★114,000)............. 82,300
Hamilton (★96,800)............. 90,300
Invercargill (★54,000).......... 50,000
Lower Hutt (★Wellington)...... 65,000
Manukau (★Auckland)..........142,200
Napier (★102,200).............. 47,700
Palmerston North (★64,600).... 58,600
Rotorua (★47,200).............. 37,700
Takapuna (★Auckland).......... 63,200
Tauranga (★48,700)............ 34,100
Waitemata (★Auckland)........ 81,300
WELLINGTON (★351,000).......139,200

NICARAGUA
1971 C........................1,877,952
León........................... 54,841
•MANAGUA......................375,278

NIGER
1975 E........................4,600,000
•NIAMEY........................130,300
Zinder (1972 E)................. 39,500

NIGERIA
1975 E.......................62,925,000
Aba............................177,000
Abeokuta.......................253,000
Ado-Ekiti......................213,000
Akure (1963 C).................. 71,106
Awka (1963 C)................... 48,725
Benin City.....................136,000
Bida (1963 C)................... 55,007
Calabar........................103,000
Deba (1963 C)................... 60,679
Ede............................182,000
Effon Alaiye (1963 C)........... 67,090
Enugu..........................187,000
Epe (1963 C).................... 44,268
Gombe (1963 C).................. 47,265
Gusau (1963 C).................. 69,231
Ibadan.........................847,000
Ife............................176,000
Igboho (1963 C)................. 46,776
Ijebu-Ode (1963 C).............. 68,543
Ikare (1963 C).................. 61,696
Ikerre.........................145,000
Ikire (1963 C).................. 54,022
Ikirun (1963 C)................. 79,516
Ikorodu (1963 C)................ 81,024
Ila.............................155,000
Ilawe (1963 C).................. 80,833
Ilesha.........................224,000
Ilobu (1963 C).................. 87,223
Ilorin.........................282,000
Inisa (1963 C).................. 52,482
Iseyin (1971 E).................115,000
Iwo............................214,000
Jos (1963 C).................... 90,402
Kaduna.........................202,000
Kano...........................399,000
Katsina (1971 E)................109,000
Kumo (1963 C)................... 64,878
Lafia (1963 C).................. 53,667
•LAGOS (★1,450,000)...........1,060,800
Maiduguri......................189,000
Makurdi (1963 C)................ 53,967
Minna (1963 C).................. 59,988
Mushin (★Lagos)................197,000
Offa (1963 C)................... 86,425
Ogbomosho......................432,000
Oka (1963 C).................... 62,761
Ondo (1963 C)................... 74,343
Onitsha........................220,000
Oshogbo........................282,000
Owo (1963 C).................... 89,693
Oyo............................152,000
Port Harcourt..................242,000
Sapele (1963 C)................. 61,007
Shagamu (1963 C)................ 51,371
Shaki (1963 C).................. 76,290
Shomolu (★Lagos) (1963 C)...... 64,731
Sokoto (1963 C)................. 89,817
Warri (1963 C).................. 55,254
Zaria..........................224,000

NORWAY / Norge
1979 E........................4,066,134
Bergen (★240,000)..............210,405
Drammen (★71,000)............. 50,167
Fredrikstad (★48,500).......... 28,265
Hammerfest...................... 7,457
Kristiansand.................... 60,722
•OSLO (★725,000)...............457,446
Skien (★79,114)................ 47,530
Stavanger (★127,000)........... 89,597
Tromsø.......................... 45,360
Trondheim......................134,683

OMAN / 'Umān
1962 E.........................565,000
MASQAṬ (MUSCAT)............ 6,000
•Maṭraḥ......................... 14,000

PAKISTAN / Pākistān
1972 C.......................64,979,732
Abbottābād (★47,122)........... 27,963
Ahmadpur East.................. 43,312
Bahāwalnagar................... 50,991
Bahāwalpur (★133,782).........115,660
Baldia (★Karāchi).............. 79,529
Bannu (★43,795)................ 33,000
Burewala....................... 57,741
Chārsadda...................... 45,555
Chiniot........................ 70,108
Dera Ghāzi Khān................ 72,343
Dera Ismāīl Khān (★58,778)..... 57,296
Gujrānwāla (★360,478)..........323,880
Gujrāt.........................100,333
Hāfizābād...................... 61,597
Hyderābād (★660,000)...........600,796
ISLĀMĀBĀD (★Rāwalpindi).... 77,000
Jacobābād...................... 57,596
Jhang Maghiāna.................131,843
Jhelum (★70,157)............... 63,676
Kamālia........................ 50,934
Kāmoke......................... 50,257
•Karāchi (1975 E) (★4,500,000)..2,800,000
Karāchi Cantonment (★Karāchi)..................133,176
Kasūr..........................102,531
Khānewāl....................... 67,746
Khānpur........................ 49,235
Kohāt (★65,202)................ 48,096
Lahore (★2,200,000)...........2,022,577
Lahore Cantonment (★Lahore).147,165
Landhi Korangi (★Karāchi).....551,236
Lārkāna........................ 71,893
Lyallpur.......................823,343
Mardān (★115,194)..............105,157
Miānwāli....................... 48,304
Mīrpur Khās.................... 81,965
Multān (★538,949)..............504,365
Nawābshāh...................... 81,045
New Karāchi No. 1 (★Karāchi). 85,398
New Karāchi No. 2 (★Karāchi). 67,682
Nowshera (★55,916)............. 31,101
Okāra (★101,052)............... 84,334
Orangi (★Karāchi)..............109,979
Peshāwar (★284,833)...........219,562
Quetta (★158,026)..............137,659
Rahīmyār Khān (★85,699)....... 74,262
Rāwalpindi (★725,000)..........372,919
Rāwalpindi Cantonment (★Rāwalpindi)..............241,890
Sāhiwāl (Montgomery).........106,648
Sargodha (★200,460)...........166,391
Shekhūpura..................... 80,560
Shikārpur...................... 70,924
Siālkot (★203,650).............183,685
Sukkur.........................158,781
Wah Cantonment.................107,510

PANAMA / Panamá
1970 C........................1,472,280
Balboa (★Panamá).............. 2,569
Colón (1976 E) (★82,000)................ 73,600
•PANAMÁ (1978 E) (★645,000)....................439,800
San Miguelito (★Panamá) (1977 E)....................135,100

PAPUA NEW GUINEA
1977 E........................2,905,000
Lae............................ 45,100
•PORT MORESBY..................106,600
Rabaul......................... 13,400

PARAGUAY
1974 E........................2,572,000
•ASUNCIÓN (★600,000)..........434,900
Fernando de la Mora (★Asunción)............... 36,834

PERU / Perú
1972 C.......................13,572,052
Arequipa (★304,653)............ 98,605
Ayacucho (★43,304)............. 34,593
Barranco (★Lima)............... 46,449
Barrio Obrero Industrial (★Lima)......................238,402
Breña (★Lima)..................123,345
Callao (★Lima).................196,919
Cerro de Pasco (★47,178)....... 35,975
Chiclayo (★189,685)............148,932
Chimbote.......................159,045
Chorrillos (★Lima)............. 87,021
Cuzco (★120,881)............... 67,658
Huancayo (★115,693)............ 64,777
Huánuco........................ 41,123
Ica............................ 73,883
Iquitos........................111,327
Jesús María (★Lima)............ 82,988
La Victoria (★Lima)............265,157
•LIMA (★3,250,000).............340,339
Lince (★Lima).................. 82,749
Magdalena del Mar (★Lima).... 54,855
Miraflores (★Lima)............. 93,926
Pisco.......................... 41,429
Piura (★126,702)............... 81,683
Pucallpa....................... 57,525
Pueblo Libre (★Lima)........... 76,279
Puno........................... 41,166
Rímac (★Lima)..................165,340
San Isidro (★Lima)............. 61,682
Sullana........................ 60,112
Surco (★Lima).................. 70,949
Surquillo (★Lima).............. 89,201
Tacna.......................... 55,752
Trujillo (★241,882)............127,535
Vitarte (★Lima)................ 54,417

PHILIPPINES / Pilipinas
1975 C.......................42,070,660
Angeles........................151,164
Bacolod........................223,392
Bacoor (★Manila)............... 62,225
Baguio......................... 97,449
Baliuag........................ 61,624
Batangas (125,363▲)............ 18,592
Biñan (★Manila)................ 67,444
Bocaue......................... 40,577
Butuan (132,682▲).............. 53,578
Cabanatuan (115,258▲).......... 32,003
Cadiz (127,653▲)............... 26,581
Cagayan de Oro (165,220▲)...... 37,272
Calbayog (102,619▲)............ 10,795
Caloocan (★Manila).............397,201
Cavite (★160,000).............. 82,456
Cebu (★500,000)................413,025
Cotabato (67,097▲)............. 49,134
Dagupan........................ 90,092
Davao (484,678▲)...............214,849
Iligan (118,778▲).............. 10,367
Iloilo.........................227,027
Isabela (Basilan) (27,261▲)..... 7,204
Laoag (66,259▲)................ 31,336
Lapu-Lapu...................... 79,484
Las Piñas (★Manila)............ 81,610
Legazpi (88,378▲).............. 37,724
Lipa (106,094▲)................ 18,330
Lucena......................... 92,336
Makati (★Manila)...............334,448
Malabon (★Manila)..............174,878
Malolos........................ 83,491
Mandaluyong (★Manila).........182,267
Mandaue (★Cebu)................ 75,904
•MANILA (★5,500,000)..........1,479,116
Marawi......................... 63,332
Marikina (★Manila).............168,453
Mecauayan (★Manila)............ 60,225
Muntinglupa (★Manila)......... 94,563
Naga........................... 83,337
Navotas (★Manila).............. 97,098
Olongapo.......................147,109
Ormoc (89,466▲)................ 13,075
Parañaque (★Manila)...........158,974
Pasay (★Manila)................254,999
Pasig (★Manila)................209,915
Quezon City (★Manila).........956,864
San Carlos (90,982▲)........... 23,950
San Fernando................... 98,382
San Juan del Monte (★Manila)...................122,492
San Pablo (116,607▲)........... 42,489
San Pedro...................... 43,439
Santa Cruz..................... 52,672
Santa Rosa (★Manila)........... 47,639
Tacloban (80,707▲)............. 63,693
Tagig (★Manila)................ 73,702
Tarlac (160,895▲).............. 28,216
Valenzuela (★Manila)...........150,605
Zamboanga (265,023▲)........... 53,678

POLAND / Polska
1977 E.......................34,850,000
Będzin (★Katowice)............. 71,400
Biała Podlaska................. 34,900
Białystok......................207,400
Bielsko-Biała..................148,700
Bydgoszcz......................339,200
Bytom (Beuthen) (★Katowice)..236,500
Chełm.......................... 49,000
Chorzów (★Katowice)...........156,600
Częstochowa....................226,900
Dąbrowa Górnicza (★Katowice)..............105,200
Dzierżoniów (Reichenbach) (★87,000).................... 35,800
Elbląg (Elbing)................102,700
Gdańsk (Danzig) (★810,000).....443,800
Gdynia (★Gdańsk)...............229,800
Gliwice (Gleiwitz) (★Katowice)..200,100
Głogów......................... 41,100
Gniezno........................ 59,200
Gorzów Wielkopolski............ 95,300
Grudziądz...................... 88,000
Inowrocław..................... 62,300
Jastrzębie Zdrój............... 99,800
Jaworzno (★Katowice)........... 87,700
Jelenia Góra................... 82,700
Kalisz......................... 95,100
•Katowice (★2,505,000).........350,400
Kędzierzyn-Koźle (Heydebreck)................ 70,900
Kielce.........................162,100
Konin.......................... 60,200
Koszalin (Köslin).............. 82,500
Kraków (★785,000)..............712,600
Legnica (Liegnitz)............. 85,400
Łódź (★1,005,000)..............818,400
Lubin.......................... 56,300
Lublin (★335,000)..............291,900
Mysłowice (★Katowice)........ 77,200
Nowy Sącz...................... 60,300
Olsztyn (Allenstein)...........129,100
Opole (Oppeln).................111,100
Ostrowiec Świętokrzyski........ 59,500
Ostrów Wielkopolski............ 56,000
Pabianice (★Łódź).............. 67,800
Piekary Śląskie (★Katowice)... 63,300
Piła (Schneidemühl)............ 54,100
Piotrków Trybunalski........... 68,100
Płock.......................... 93,600
Poznań (★595,000)..............534,400
Przemyśl....................... 60,600

▲ Population of an entire municipality, commune, or district, including rural area.
• Largest city in country.
★ Population or designation of the metropolitan area, including suburbs.
C Census. E Official estimate. UE Unofficial estimate.
L Population within municipal limits of year specified.

▲ Bevölkerung eines ganzen städtischen Verwaltungsgebietes, eines Kommunalbezirkes oder eines Distrikts, einschliesslich ländlicher Gebiete.
• Grösste Stadt des Landes.
★ Bevölkerung oder Bezeichnung der Stadtregion einschliess lich Vororte.
C Volkszählung. E Offizielle Schätzung. UE Inoffizielle Schätzung.
L Bevölkerung innerhalb der städtischen Verwaltungseinheit des angegebenen Jahres.

Racibórz (Ratibor) 50,800
Radom 183,600
Ruda Śląska (★Katowice) 155,900
Rybnik 111,900
Rzeszów 109,600
Siedlce 48,800
Siemianowice Śląskie
(★Katowice) 73,400
Skarżysko-Kamienna 43,300
Słupsk (Stolp) 82,400
Sopot (Zoppot) (★Gdańsk) 54,500
Sosnowiec (★Katowice) 204,600
Stalowa Wola 46,900
Starachowice 47,600
Stargard Szczeciński 54,800
Świdnica (Schweidnitz) 54,300
Świętochłowice (★Katowice) 57,600
Świnoujście (Swinemünde) 45,400
Szczecin (Stettin) (★415,000) ... 381,400
Tarnów 102,500
Tarnowskie Góry
(★Katowice) 62,900
Tczew 49,000
Tomaszów Mazowiecki 63,400
Toruń 164,000
Tychy (★Katowice) 142,400
Wałbrzych (★195,000) 129,800
WARSZAWA (WARSAW)
(★2,025,000) 1,532,100
Wejherowo 41,000
Włocławek 95,000
Wodzisław Śląski 105,500
Wrocław (Breslau) 592,500
Zabrze (Hindenburg)
(★Katowice) 204,000
Zamość 42,200
Zawiercie 59,300
Zgierz (★Łódź) 49,900
Zielona Góra (Grünberg) 89,600

PORTUGAL

1970 C 8,663,252
Amadora (★Lisboa) 65,870
Barreiro (★Lisboa) 53,690
Brega 48,735
Çoimbra 55,985
•LISBOA (LISBON) (1975 E)
(★1,950,000) 829,900
Ponta Delgada (*Açores*) 20,190
Porto (1975 E) (★1,150,000) 335,700
Setúbal 49,670
Vila Nova de Gaia (★Porto) 50,805

PUERTO RICO

1970 C 2,712,033
Bayamón (★San Juan) 147,552
Caguas (★San Juan) (95,661▲) ... 63,215
Carolina (★San Juan) 94,271
Guaynabo (★San Juan) 55,310
Mayagüez (★116,100) 68,872
Ponce (★213,984) 128,233
•SAN JUAN (★1,185,000) 452,749

QATAR / Qaṭar

1971 E 160,000
•AD-DAWḤAH (DOHA) 95,000

REUNION / Réunion

1974 C 476,675
•SAINT-DENIS (103,512▲) 80,082

ROMANIA / România

1977 C 21,559,416
Alba-Iulia 41,474
Arad 171,110
Bacău 126,654
Baia-Mare 100,992
Bîrlad 55,937
Bistriṭa 44,477
Botoşani 63,182
Brăila 194,633
Braşov 257,150
•BUCUREŞTI (BUCHAREST)
(★2,000,000) 1,807,044
Buzău 97,787
Călăraşi 49,581
Cluj 262,421
Constanṭa (★290,226) 256,875
Craiova 222,399
Deva 60,538
Drobeta-Turnu-Severin 76,955
Focşani 56,490
Galaṭi 239,306
Giurgiu 51,440
Hunedoara 79,630
Iaşi 264,947
Mediaş 64,861
Oradea 171,258
Petroşani (★73,000) 40,684
Piatra-Neamṭ 78,100
Piteşti 123,943
Ploieşti (★254,592) 199,269
Reşiṭa 84,998
Rîmnicu-Vîlcea 66,103
Roman 51,019
Satu-Mare 103,612
Sfîntu-Gheorghe 40,718
Sibiu 151,120
Slatina 44,988
Suceava 62,869
Timişoara 268,785
Tîrgovişte 61,663
Tîrgu-Jiu 63,651
Tîrgu-Mureş 130,051
Tulcea 61,752
Turda 55,256

RWANDA

1970 E 3,736,000
•KIGALI 59,100

ST. HELENA

1966 C 4,649
•JAMESTOWN 1,475

ST. KITTS-NEVIS

1970 C 47,457
•BASSETERRE (*St. Kitts*) 13,055
Charlestown (*Nevis*) 1,880

ST. LUCIA

1970 C 101,064
•CASTRIES 39,132

ST. PIERRE AND MIQUELON / Saint-Pierre-et-Miquelon

1974 C 5,840
•SAINT-PIERRE 5,232

ST. VINCENT

1970 C 89,129
•KINGSTOWN (★23,782) 17,258

SAN MARINO

1977 E 20,000
•SAN MARINO 4,628

SAO TOME AND PRINCIPE / São Tomé e Príncipe

1970 C 73,631
•SÃO TOMÉ 17,380

SAUDI ARABIA / Al-'Arabiyah as-Sa'ūdiyah

1974 C 7,012,642
Abhā 30,150
Ad-Dammām 127,844
Al-Hufūf (Hofuf) 101,271
Al-Khubar 48,817
Al-Madīnah (Medina) 198,186
Al-Mubarraz 54,325
•AR-RIYĀD (RIYADH) 666,840
Aṭ-Ṭā'if 204,857
Buraydah 69,940
Hā'il 40,502
Jiddah 561,104
Khamīs Mushayt 49,581
Makkah (Mecca) 366,801
Najran 47,501
Tabūk 74,825

SENEGAL / Sénégal

1976 C 5,085,388
•DAKAR 798,792
Diourbel (1973 E) 44,000
Kaolack 106,899
Rufisque (★Dakar) (1973 E) 54,000
Saint-Louis (1973 E) 99,000
Thiès 117,333
Ziguinchor (1973 E) 58,000

SEYCHELLES

1971 C 52,437
•VICTORIA 13,622

SIERRA LEONE

1974 C 2,730,000
Bo 30,000
•FREETOWN (★335,000) 274,000

SINGAPORE

1978 E 2,334,400
•SINGAPORE (★2,535,000) 2,334,400

SOLOMON IS.

1970 C 160,998
•HONIARA 11,911

SOMALIA / Somaliya

1972 E 2,941,000
Hargeysa (1966 E) 42,000
•MUQDISHO (MOGADISHU) 230,000

SOUTH AFRICA / Suid-Afrika

1970 C 21,794,328
Alexandra (★Johannesburg) 57,040
Bellville (★Cape Town) 49,026
Benoni (★Johannesburg) 151,294
Bloemfontein (★182,329) 149,836
Boksburg (★Johannesburg) 106,126
Brakpan (★Johannesburg) 73,210
CAPE TOWN (KAAPSTAD)
(★1,125,000) 697,514
Carletonville 93,096
Durban (★1,040,000) 736,852
East London (Oos-Londen)
(★190,000) 119,727
Edendale (★Pietermaritzburg) . 41,194
Elsies River (★Cape Town) 64,539
Ga-Rankuwa 45,631
Germiston (★Johannesburg) ... 221,972
Grahamstown 41,302
•Johannesburg (★2,550,000) 654,232
Kimberley 105,258
Klerksdorp (★175,000) 63,558
Kroonstad 51,988
Krugersdorp (★Johannesburg) . 92,725
Mdantsane (★East London) 67,501
Nigel 41,179
Paarl 49,244
Parow (★Cape Town) 60,768
Pietermaritzburg (★160,855) 114,822
Port Elizabeth (★475,869) 392,231
Potchefstroom 57,443
PRETORIA (★575,000) 545,450
Randburg (★Johannesburg) 46,011
Randfontein (★Johannesburg) . 50,481
Roodepoort-Maraisburg
(★Johannesburg) 115,366
Sandton (★Johannesburg) 49,022
Soweto (★Johannesburg) 602,043
Springs (★Johannesburg) 142,812
Stilfontein (★Klerksdorp) 70,661
Tembisa (★Johannesburg) 83,637
Uitenhage (★Port Elizabeth) ... 70,517
Umlazi (★Durban) 123,495
Vanderbijlpark (★Vereeniging) . 80,375
Vereeniging (★310,188) 172,549
Virginia 46,138
Welkom (★132,880) 67,472
Worcester 41,198

SPAIN / España

1976 E 36,856,302
Albacete 102,618
Alcalá de Henares (★Madrid)
(1975 C) 101,416
Alcobendas (★Madrid)
(1975 C) 50,015
Alcorcón (★Madrid) (1975 C) 112,493
Alcoy (1975 C) 60,336
Algeciras (1975 C) 88,006
Alicante 226,582
Almería 127,587
Avilés (1977 E) (★127,000) 89,285
Badajoz (106,571▲) 84,700
Badalona (★Barcelona)
(1975 C) 201,867
Baracaldo (★Bilbao) (1975 C) .. 118,136
Barcelona (1977 E)
(★3,915,000) 1,886,921
Bilbao (1977 E) (★985,000) 450,661
Burgos 139,968
Cáceres 61,177
Cádiz (1977 E) (★225,000) 153,327
Cartagena (1975 C) (158,180▲) .. 129,200
Castellón de la Plana 112,399
Córdoba 258,313
Cornellá (★Barcelona) (1975 C). 91,110
Elche (1975 C) (147,614▲) 121,900
Elda (1975 C) 48,259
El Ferrol del Caudillo (1977 E)
(★123,000) 88,161
El Puerto de Santa María
(1975 C) 51,600
Gerona 81,656
Getafe (★Madrid) (1975 C) 116,523
Gijón (1975 C) 237,187
Granada 218,647
Guadalajara 46,273
Hospitalet (★Barcelona)
(1975 C) 280,640
Huelva 116,666
Irún (1975 C) 51,098
Jaén 86,057
Jerez de la Frontera (1975 C)
(167,720▲) 125,800
La Coruña 212,536
La Línea (1975 C) 54,158
Las Palmas de Gran Canaria
(*Is. Canarias*) 334,885
Leganés (★Madrid) (1975 C) 136,990
León (1977 E) (★141,000) 120,761
Lérida (103,675▲) 83,500
Logroño 100,169
Lorca (1975 C) (60,513▲) 25,200
Lugo (70,290▲) 58,900
•MADRID (1977 E)
(★4,340,000) 3,355,720
Málaga 443,823
Manresa (1975 C) 65,469
Mataró (1975 C) 91,587
Mieres (1975 C) (59,136▲) 20,900
Móstoles (★Madrid) (1975 C) ... 76,250
Murcia (272,223▲) 178,700
Orense (85,366▲) 74,000
Oviedo 175,398
Palencia 63,945
Palma [de Mallorca] 276,655
Pamplona 167,762
Pontevedra (62,439▲) 32,300
Portugalete (★Bilbao)
(1975 C) 54,014
Prat de Llobregat (★Barcelona)
(1975 C) 51,017
Puertollano (1975 C) 49,209
Reus (1975 C) 72,331
Sabadell (★Barcelona) (1975 C). 182,012
Sagunto (1975 C) 52,424
Salamanca 137,425
San Baudilio de Llobregat
(★Barcelona) (1975 C) 65,595
San Cristóbal de la Laguna
(*Is. Canarias*) (1975 C)
(109,061▲) 23,800
San Fernando (★Cádiz)
(1975 C) 68,051
San Sebastián (1977 E)
(★285,000) 174,818
Santa Coloma de Gramanet
(★Barcelona) (1975 C) 137,579
Santa Cruz de Tenerife
(Is. Canarias) 179,613
Santander 170,768
Santiago de Compostela
(1975 C) (84,138▲) 61,300
Santurce-Antiguo (★Bilbao)
(1975 C) 52,924
Segovia 47,924
Sevilla (Seville) (1977 E)
(★725,000) 622,532
Talavera de la Reina
(1975 C) 55,350
Tarragona 103,241
Tarrasa (★Barcelona) (1975 C) .. 161,679
Toledo 53,673
Valencia (1977 E) (★1,115,000) ... 737,129
Valladolid 297,255
Vigo (1975 C) 230,611
Vitoria 175,564
Zamora 53,866
Zaragoza (Saragossa) 539,021

SPANISH NORTH AFRICA / Plazas de Soberanía en el Norte de África

1976 E 116,848
•Ceuta 62,470
Melilla 54,378

SRI LANKA

1977 E 13,940,000
•COLOMBO (★1,540,000) 616,000
Dehiwala-Mount Lavinia
(★Colombo) 169,000
Galle 79,000
Jaffna 118,000
Kandy 103,000
Kotte (★Colombo) 102,000

Moratuwa (★Colombo) 104,000
Negombo 63,000

SUDAN / As-Sūdān

1973 C 12,427,795
Al-Fāshir 51,932
•AL-KHARṬŪM (KHARTOUM)
(★790,000) 333,921
Al-Kharṭūm Baḥrī (Khartoum
North) (★Al-Kharṭūm) 150,991
Al-Qaḍārif 66,465
Al-Ubayyiḍ (El Obeid) 90,060
'Aṭbarah 66,116
Būr Sūdān (Port Sudan) 132,631
Jūbā 56,737
Kassalā 98,751
Kūstī 65,257
Nyala 59,852
Umm Durmān (Omdurman)
(★Al-Kharṭūm) 299,401
Wad Madanī 106,776
Wāw 52,752

SURINAME

1971 C 384,900
•PARAMARIBO (★175,000) 102,300

SWAZILAND

1976 C 496,800
•Manzini (★26,000) 10,000
MBABANE 22,000

SWEDEN / Sverige

1977 E 8,267,116
Borås 104,151
Eskilstuna 91,548
Gävle 87,463
Göteborg (Gothenburg)
(1978 E) (★665,000) 436,985
Halmstad (74,990▲) 50,000
Helsingborg 101,105
Huddinge (★Stockholm) 64,784
Järfälla (★Stockholm) 52,227
Jönköping 108,568
Karlskrona (60,297▲) 33,400
Karlstad 72,975
Linköping 110,779
Luleå 67,405
Lund 76,970
Malmö (1978 E) (★305,000) 236,716
Nacka (★Stockholm) 55,681
Norrköping 120,647
Örebro 117,036
Södertälje (★Stockholm) 77,829
Solna (★Stockholm) 52,365
•STOCKHOLM (1978 E)
(★1,380,426) 653,929
Sundsvall (94,336▲) 52,500
Trollhättan 50,311
Umeå (77,458▲) 51,200
Uppsala 141,444
Västerås 118,141

SWITZERLAND / Schweiz / Suisse

1977 E 6,297,600
Baden (★66,800) 13,700
Basel (Bâle) (★555,000) 188,800
BERN (BERNE) (★283,500) 146,800
Biel (Bienne) (★88,600) 59,200
Fribourg (Freiburg) (★53,600) ... 39,800
Genève (Geneva) (★400,000) 152,600
Lausanne (★227,300) 132,800
Lugano (★68,100) 28,400
Luzern (Lucerne) (★156,200) 64,200
Neuchâtel (Neuenburg)
(★59,900) 35,800
Sankt Gallen (St. Gall)
(★113,000) 76,300
Schaffhausen (Schaffhouse)
(★52,400) 32,900
Thun (Thoune) (★64,700) 36,900
Winterthur (★107,300) 87,900
•Zürich (★775,000) 383,000

SYRIA / As-Sūrīyah

1978 E 8,103,000
Al-Lādhiqīyah (Latakia) 204,000
Dayr az-Zawr (1970 C) 66,164
•DIMASHQ (DAMASCUS)
(★1,520,000) 1,142,000
Ḥalab (Aleppo) 878,000
Ḥamāh 180,000
Ḥimṣ (Homs) 306,000
Mukhayyam al-Yarmūk
(★Dimashq) (1970 C) 64,273

TAIWAN / T'aiwan

1977 E 16,813,127
Changhua (166,612▲) 129,000
Chiai 252,972
Chilung (Keelung) 342,168
Chungho (★T'aipei) 175,778
Chungli (Chunli) (180,689▲) 151,000
Chutung 52,000
Hsichih 51,000
Hsinchu 233,459
Hsinchuang (★T'aipei) 124,609
Hsintien (★T'aipei) 145,809
Hualien 101,010
Ilan (78,983▲) 66,000
Kangshan 58,000
Kaohsiung (★1,380,000) 1,041,364
Kaohsiunghsien (Fengshan)
(★Kaohsiung) 177,982
Miaoli 66,000
Nant'ou 60,000
P'ingtung 182,114
Sanch'ung (★T'aipei) 292,909
Shulin (★T'aipei) 54,000
T'aichung 570,661
T'aichunghsien (Fengyüan)
(121,491▲) 94,000
T'ainan 546,990
•T'AIPEI (★3,515,000) 2,127,625
T'aipeihsien (Panch'iao)
(★T'aipei) 314,848

▲ Población de un municipio, comuna o distrito entero, incluyendo sus áreas rurales.
• Ciudad más grande de un país.
★ Población o designación de un área metropolitana, incluyendo los suburbios.
C Censo. E Estimado oficial.
UE Estimado no oficial.
L Población dentro de los límites municipales de un año específico.

▲ Population d'une municipalité, d'une commune ou d'un district, zone rurale incluse.
• Ville la plus peuplée du pays.
★ Population de l'agglomération (ou nom de la zone métropolitaine englobante).
C Recensement. E Estimation officielle.
UE Estimation non officielle.
L Population comprise dans les limites municipales de l'année indiquée.

▲ População de um município, comuna ou distrito, inclusive as respectivas áreas rurais.
• Maior cidade de um país.
★ População ou indicação de uma área metropolitana, inclusive subúrbios.
C Censo. E Estimativa oficial.
UE Estimativa não oficial.
L População dentro dos limites municipais no ano indicado.

TAIWAN / T'aiwan *continued*
T'aitung (111,647▲) 78,000
T'aoyüan 163,404
Yungho (★T'aipei) 162,731

TANZANIA
1967 C 12,313,469
•DAR-ES-SALAAM (1975 E) 517,000
Dodoma 23,559
Mwanza 34,861
Tanga 61,058
Zanzibar 68,490

THAILAND / Prathet Thai
1972 E 36,286,000
Ayutthaya 46,664
Chiang Mai 93,353
Chon Buri 46,368
Hat Yai 57,255
•KRUNG THEP (BANGKOK) (★3,375,000) 3,133,834
Lampang 42,007
Nakhon Ratchasima 77,397
Nakhon Sawan 51,378
Nakhon Si Thammarat 50,761
Phitsanulok 70,649
Samut Prakan (★Krung Thep) 44,916
Songkhla 50,687
Ubon Ratchathani 52,171
Udon Thani 70,110

TOGO
1977 E 2,348,000
•LOMÉ 229,400
Sokodé 33,500

TONGA
1966 C 77,429
•NUKUALOFA 15,545

TRINIDAD AND TOBAGO
1973 E 1,061,850
•PORT OF SPAIN (★350,000) 60,450
San Fernando (★73,000) 36,650

TUNISIA / Tunisie
1975 C 5,588,209
Ariana (★Tunis) 47,833
Binzert (Bizerte) 62,856
Kairouan 54,546
Le Bardo (★Tunis) 49,367
Menzel Bourguiba 42,111
Sfax (★260,000) 171,297
Sousse 69,530
•TUNIS (★915,000) 550,404

TURKEY / Türkiye
1975 C 40,347,719
Adana 475,384
Adapazarı 114,130
Afyon 60,150
Akhisar 53,357
ANKARA (★1,750,000) 1,701,004
Antakya (Antioch) 77,518
Antalya 130,774
Aydın 59,579
Balıkesir 99,443
Batman 64,384
Bayrampaşa (★İstanbul) 157,367
Bornova (İzmir) 45,096
Buca (★İzmir) 70,715
Bursa 346,103
Ceyhan 62,909
Çorum 64,852
Denizli 106,902
Diyarbakır 169,535
Edirne 63,001
Elâzığ 131,415
Ereğli 50,354
Erzincan 60,351
Erzurum 162,973
Esenler (★İstanbul) 49,379
Eskişehir 259,952
Gaziantep 300,882
Gelibolu (Gallipoli) 13,466
İskenderun (Alexandretta) 107,437
İsparta 62,870
•İstanbul (★3,700,000) 2,547,364
İzmir (Smyrna) (★955,000) 636,834
İzmit (Kocaeli) 165,483
Kâğithane (★İstanbul) 164,448
Karabük 69,182
Kars 54,892
Kartal (★İstanbul) 53,073
Kayseri 207,037
Kilis 54,055
Kırıkkale 137,874
Konya 246,727
Küçükçekmece (★İstanbul) 58,709
Kütahya 82,442
Malatya 154,505
Manisa 78,114
Maraş 135,782
Mersin 152,236
Nazilli 52,176
Ordu 47,481
Osmaniye 61,581
Samsun 168,478
Sivas 149,201
Tarsus 102,186
Tokat 48,588
Trabzon 97,210
Urfa 132,934
Uşak 58,578
Van 63,663
Zile 32,157
Zonguldak (★160,000) 90,221

TURKS AND CAICOS IS.
1970 C 5,607
•GRAND TURK 2,287

UGANDA
1969 C 9,548,847
Bugembe 46,884
Jinja 52,509
•KAMPALA 330,700

UNION OF SOVIET SOCIALIST REPUBLICS / Sojuz Sovetskich Socialističeskich Respublik
1979 C 262,442,000
Abakan 128,000
Abay (1974 E) 41,000
Achtubinsk (1974 E) 44,000
Achtyrka (1974 E) 43,000
Ačinsk (Achinsk) 117,000
Ajaguz (1974 E) 40,000
Akt'ubinsk (Aktyubinsk) 191,000
Alapajevsk (1977 E) 52,000
Alatyr' (1974 E) 46,000
Aleksandrija (1977 E) 79,000
Aleksandrov (1977 E) 58,000
Aleksin (1977 E) 66,000
Alma-Ata (★950,000) 910,000
Almalyk 101,000
Al'metjevsk 110,000
Alytus (1977 E) 51,000
Andižan (Andizhan) 230,000
Angarsk 239,000
Angren 106,000
Antracit (★Krasnyj Luč) (1977 E) 60,000
Anžero-Sudžensk 105,000
Apatity (1977 E) 58,000
Archangel'sk (Archangel) 385,000
Armavir 162,000
Arsenjev (1977 E) 60,000
Art'om (Artem) (1977 E) 70,000
Art'omovsk (Artemovsk) (1977 E) 91,000
Arzamas (1977 E) 89,000
Asbest (1977 E) 80,000
Aščhabad (Ashkhabad) 312,000
Astrachan' (Astrakhan') 461,000
Azov (1977 E) 75,000
Baku (★1,760,000) 1,022,000
Balakovo 152,000
Balašicha (★Moskva) 118,000
Balašov (Balashov) (1977 E) 91,000
Balchaš (Balkhash) (1977 E) 79,000
Baranoviči (Baranovichi) 131,000
Barnaul (★600,000) 533,000
Batajsk (★Rostov-na-Donu) (1977 E) 102,000
Batumi 124,000
Bekabad (1977 E) 63,000
Belaja Cerkov' 151,000
Bel'cy (Bel'tsy) 125,000
Belgorod 240,000
Belogorsk (1977 E) 65,000
Beloreck (Beloretsk) (1977 E) 72,000
Belovo 112,000
Bendery 101,000
Berd'ansk (Berdyansk) 122,000
Berdičev (Berdichev) (1977 E) 80,000
Berdsk (★Novosibirsk) (1977 E) 64,000
Berezniki 185,000
Bijsk (Biysk) 212,000
Birobidžan (Birobidzhan) (1977 E) 67,000
Blagoveščensk 172,000
Bobrujsk (Bobruysk) 192,000
Bor (★Gor'kij) (1977 E) 62,000
Borisoglebsk (1977 E) 69,000
Borisov 112,000
Boroviči (Borovichi) (1977 E) 59,000
Br'anka (★Stachanov) (1977 E) 67,000
Br'ansk (Bryansk) 394,000
Bratsk 214,000
Brest 177,000
Brovary (★Kijev) (1977 E) 50,000
Buchara (Bukhara) 185,000
Bugul'ma (1977 E) 82,000
Buguruslan (1977 E) 53,000
Bujnaksk (1974 E) 42,000
Buzuluk (1977 E) 76,000
Čajkovskij (Chaykovskij) (1977 E) 64,000
Čapajevsk (Chapayevsk) (1977 E) 87,000
Čardžou (Chardzhou) 140,000
Čeboksary (Cheboksary) 308,000
Čel'abinsk (★1,205,000) 1,031,000
Celinograd (Tselinograd) 234,000
Čeremchovo (Cheremkhovo) (1977 E) 87,000
Čerepovec (Cherepovets) 266,000
Čerkassy (Cherkassy) 228,000
Čerkessk (Cherkessk) (1977 E) 85,000
Černigov (Chernigov) 238,000
Černogorsk (Chernogorsk) (1977 E) 70,000
Černovcy (Chernovtsy) 218,000
Červonograd (Chervonograd) (1977 E) 53,000
Chabarovsk (Khabarovsk) 528,000
Charcyzsk (Khartsyzsk) (★Doneck) (1977 E) 60,000
Char'kov (Kharkov) (★1,730,000) 1,444,000
Chasavjurt (Khasavyurt) (1977 E) 66,000
Cherson (Kherson) 319,000
Chimki (Khimki) (★Moskva) 118,000
Chmel'nickij (Khmel'nitskiy) 172,000
Chodžejli (1974 E) 40,000
Cholmsk (1974 E) 43,000
Čimkent (Chimkent) 321,000
Čirčik (Chirchik) (★Taškent) 132,000
Čistopol' (Chistopol') (1977 E) 67,000
Čita (Chita) 302,000
Čusovoj (Chusovoy) (1977 E) 59,000
Daugavpils 116,000
Derbent (1977 E) 69,000
Dimitrov (★Krasnoarmejsk) (1977 E) 58,000
Dimitrovgrad (Melekess) 106,000
Dmitrov (1977 E) 50,000
Dneprodzeržinsk (★Dnepropetrovsk) 250,000
Dnepropetrovsk (★1,440,000) 1,066,000
Dolgoprudnyj (★Moskva) (1977 E) 64,000
Doneck (Donetsk) (★2,050,000) 1,021,000
Drogobyč (Drogobych) (1977 E) 68,000
Družkovka (★Kramatorsk) (1977 E) 61,000
Dubna (1977 E) 51,000
Dušanbe (Dushanbe) 493,000
Džalal-Abad (1977 E) 54,000
Džambul (Dzhambul) 264,000
Džankoj (1974 E) 46,000
Dzeržinsk (★Gor'kij) 257,000
Džezkazgan (Dzhezkazgan) (1977 E) 85,000
Džizak (1977 E) 59,000
Ečmiadzin (★Jerevan) (1974 E) 37,000
Ekibastuz (1977 E) 55,000
Elektrostal' 139,000
Elista (1977 E) 63,000
Engel's (★Saratov) 161,000
Fastov (1974 E) 44,000
Feodosija (1977 E) 77,000
Fergana 176,000
Frunze 533,000
Fryazino (★Moskva) (1974 E) 39,000
Furmanov (1974 E) 41,000
Gatčina (★Leningrad) (1977 E) 74,000
Georgijevsk (1977 E) 51,000
Georgiu-Dež (Liski) (1977 E) 52,000
Glazov (1977 E) 82,000
Gomel' 383,000
Gori (1977 E) 54,000
Gor'kij (Gorky) (★1,875,000) 1,344,000
Gorlovka (★695,000) 337,000
Gorno-Altajsk (1975 E) 39,000
Gr'azi (1974 E) 42,000
Grodno 195,000
Groznyj (Groznyy) 375,000
Gubkin (1977 E) 68,000
Gulistan (1975 E) 39,000
Gukovo (1977 E) 71,000
Gurjev (Gur'yev) 130,000
Gus'-Chrustal'nyj (1977 E) 70,000
Igarka (1974 E) 16,000
Ilichevsk (1974 E) 43,000
Ingulets (1974 E) 35,000
Inta (1977 E) 52,000
Irbit (1977 E) 52,000
Irkutsk 550,000
Išim (Ishim) (1977 E) 63,000
Išimbaj (Ishimbay) (1977 E) 58,000
Iskitim (1977 E) 59,000
Ivano-Frankovsk 150,000
Ivanovo 465,000
Ivanteyevka (★Moskva) (1974 E) 41,000
Iževsk (Izhevsk) 549,000
Izmail (1977 E) 79,000
Iz'um (1977 E) 58,000
Jakutsk (Yakutsk) 152,000
Jalta (Yalta) (1977 E) 77,000
Jangijul' (Yangiyul') (1977 E) 62,000
Jaroslavl' (Yaroslavl') 597,000
Jefremov (Yefremov) (1977 E) 53,000
Jegorjevsk (Yegor'yevsk) (1977 E) 71,000
Jejsk (Yeysk) (1977 E) 71,000
Jelec (Yelets) 112,000
Jelgava (1977 E) 65,000
Jenakijevo (★Gorlovka) 114,000
Jerevan (Yerevan) (★1,135,000) 1,019,000
Jessentuki (Yessentuki) (1977 E) 74,000
Jevpatorija (Yevpatoriya) (1977 E) 94,000
Joškar-Ola (Yoshkar-Ola) 201,000
Jurga (Yurga) (1977 E) 75,000
Jūrmala (★Rīga) (1977 E) 59,000
Južno-Sachalinsk 140,000
Kachovka (1974 E) 35,000
Kagan (1974 E) 38,000
Kalinin 412,000
Kaliningrad (★Moskva) 133,000
Kaliningrad (Königsberg) 355,000
Kaluga 265,000
Kaluš (1977 E) 57,000
Kamenec-Podol'skij (1977 E) 79,000
Kamensk-Šachtinskij (1977 E) 76,000
Kamensk-Ural'skij 187,000
Kamyšin (Kamyshin) 112,000
Kanaš (1974 E) 46,000
Kansk 101,000
Karaganda 572,000
Karpinsk (1974 E) 37,000
Karši (Karshi) 107,000
Kaspijsk (1974 E) 42,000
Kašira (1974 E) 42,000
Kattakurgan (1977 E) 51,000
Kaunas 370,000
Kazan' (★1,040,000) 993,000
Kemerovo 471,000
Kentau (1977 E) 61,000
Kerč (Kerch') 157,000
Kijev (Kiev) (★2,375,000) 2,144,000
Kimovsk (1974 E) 44,000
Kimry (1977 E) 59,000
Kinel' (1974 E) 40,000
Kinešma (Kineshma) 101,000
Kirov 390,000
Kirovabad 232,000
Kirovakan 146,000
Kirovo-Čepeck (1977 E) 64,000
Kirovograd 237,000
Kirovsk (1974 E) 40,000
Kisel'ovsk (★Prokopjevsk) 122,000
Kišin'ov (Kishinev) 503,000
Kislovodsk 101,000
Kizel (1974 E) 42,000
Klaipėda (Memel) 176,000
Klimovsk (★Moskva) (1977 E) 52,000
Klin (1977 E) 89,000
Klincy (Klintsy) (1977 E) 66,000
Kohtla-Järve (1977 E) 72,000
Kokand 153,000
Kokčetav (Kokchetav) 103,000
Kol'čugino (1974 E) 43,000
Kolomna 147,000
Kolomyja (1977 E) 51,000
Kolpino (★Leningrad) 114,000
Kommunarsk (★Stachanov) 120,000
Komsomol'sk-na-Amure 264,000
Konotop (1977 E) 77,000
Konstantinovka 112,000
Kopejsk (★Čel'abinsk) 146,000
Korkino (1977 E) 66,000
Korosten' (1977 E) 62,000
Korsakov (1974 E) 40,000
Kostroma 255,000
Kotlas (1977 E) 63,000
Kovel' (1974 E) 40,000
Kovrov 143,000
Kramatorsk (★435,000) 178,000
Krasnoarmejsk (1977 E) (★150,000) 59,000
Krasnodar 560,000
Krasnodon (1974 E) 46,000
Krasnogorsk (★Moskva) (1977 E) 72,000
Krasnojarsk (Krasnoyarsk) 796,000
Krasnokamsk (1977 E) 58,000
Krasnoturjinsk (1977 E) 60,000
Krasnoufimsk (1974 E) 40,000
Krasnoural'sk (1974 E) 40,000
Krasnovodsk (1977 E) 55,000
Krasnyj Luč (★225,000) 106,000
Krasnyj Sulin (1974 E) 43,000
Kremenčug (Kremenchug) 210,000
Krivoj Rog (Krivoy Rog) 650,000
Kropotkin (1977 E) 74,000
Krymsk (Krymskaja) (1974 E) 43,000
Kstovo (★Gor'kij) (1977 E) 56,000
Kujbyšev (Kuybyshev) (★1,430,000) 1,216,000
Kul'ab (1977 E) 51,000
Kumertau (1977 E) 54,000
Kungur (1977 E) 83,000
Kurgan 310,000
Kursk 375,000
Kustanaj (Kustanay) 164,000
Kutaisi 194,000
Kuzneck (Kuznetsk) (1977 E) 96,000
Kyzyl (1977 E) 59,000
Kzyl-Orda 156,000
Labinsk (1977 E) 57,000
Leninabad 130,000
Leninakan 207,000
Leningrad (★5,300,000) 4,073,000
Leninogorsk (*Tatarsk obl.*) (1977 E) 52,000
Leninogorsk (*Vostochno-Kazakh obl.*) (1977 E) 69,000
Leninsk-Kuzneckij 132,000
Lida (1977 E) 56,000
Liepāja 108,000
Lipeck (Lipetsk) 396,000
Lisičansk (★365,000) 120,000
L'ubercy (★Moskva) 160,000
Lubny (1977 E) 51,000
Luck (Lutsk) 137,000
L'vov 667,000
Lys'va (1977 E) 76,000
Machačkala (Makhachkala) 250,000
Magadan 122,000
Magnitogorsk 406,000
Majkop (Maykop) 128,000
Makejevka (★Doneck) 436,000
Margilan 111,000
Mary (1977 E) 72,000
Melitopol' 161,000
Meždurečensk (1977 E) 91,000
Miass 150,000
Michajlovka (Mikhaylovka) (1977 E) 58,000
Mičurinsk (Michurinsk) 102,000
Mineral'nyje Vody (1977 E) 64,000
Mingečaur (1977 E) 54,000
Minsk (★1,295,000) 1,262,000
Minusinsk (1977 E) 51,000
Mogil'ov (Mogilev) 290,000
Molodečno (Molodechno) (1977 E) 66,000
Moršansk (1977 E) 50,000
•MOSKVA (MOSCOW) (★11,600,000) 7,831,000
Mozhga (1974 E) 41,000
Mozyr' (1977 E) 72,000
Mukačevo (Mukachevo) (1977 E) 71,000
Murmansk 381,000
Murom 114,000
Mytišči (Mytishchi) (★Moskva) 141,000
Naberežnyje Čelny (Naberezhnyye Chelny) 301,000
Nachodka (Nakhodka) 133,000
Nal'čik (Nal'chik) 207,000
Namangan 227,000
Naro-Fominsk (1977 E) 54,000
Narva (1977 E) 72,000
Navoi (1977 E) 87,000
Nebit-Dag (1977 E) 67,000
Neftekamsk (1977 E) 63,000
Nevinnomyssk 104,000
Nežin (Nezhin) (1977 E) 70,000
Nikolajev (Nikolayev) 441,000
Nikopol' 146,000
Nižnekamskij (Nizhnekamsk) 134,000
Nižneudinsk (1974 E) 42,000
Nižnevartovsk 109,000
Nižnij Tagil (Nizhniy Tagil) 398,000
Noginsk 119,000
Noril'sk 180,000
Novgorod 186,000
Novoaltajsk (★Barnaul) (1977 E) 53,000
Novočeboksarsk (1977 E) 74,000
Novočerkassk 183,000
Novokujbyševsk (★Kujbyšev) 109,000
Novokuzneck (Novokuznetsk) 541,000
Novomoskovsk (*Dnepropetrovsk obl.*) (1977 E) 70,000
Novomoskovsk (*Tula obl.*) (★365,000) 147,000
Novopolock (1977 E) 65,000
Novorossijsk (Novorossiysk) 159,000
Novošachtinsk 104,000

¹ For abbreviations of state names, see Index, page *I • 30*.
² Rand McNally & Company estimates.
• Largest city in country.
★ Population or designation of the metropolitan area, including suburbs.
C Census. E Official estimate. UE Unofficial estimate.

¹ Für die Abkürzungen der Namen der Staaten siehe Register, S. *I • 30*.
² Schätzungen der Rand McNally & Company.
• Grösste Stadt des Landes.
★ Bevölkerung oder Bezeichnung der Stadtregion einschliesslich Vororte.
C Volkszählung. E Offizielle Schätzung. UE Inoffizielle Schätzung.

Novosibirsk (★1,445,000)......1,312,000
Novotroick (Novotroitsk) (1977 E)........ 96,000
Novovolynsk (1974 E)........... 44,000
Nukus........................109,000
Obninsk (1977 E)............... 69,000
Odessa (★1,110,000)..........1,046,000
Odincovo (★Moskva)...........101,000
Okt'abr'skij (Oktyabr'skiy) (1977 E)........ 88,000
Omsk (★1,025,000)............1,014,000
Ordžonikidze (Ordzhonikidze).279,000
Orechovo-Zujevo (★200,000).....132,000
Orenburg......................459,000
Or'ol (Orel)...................305,000
Orša (Orsha)...................112,000
Orsk..........................247,000
Oš (Osh).......................169,000
Osinniki (1977 E).............. 60,000
Panevėžys.....................102,000
Pärnu (1977 E)................. 50,000
P'atigorsk (Pyatigorsk).........110,000
Pavlodar......................273,000
Pavlograd.....................107,000
Pavlovo (1977 E)............... 68,000
Pavlovskij Posad (1977 E)....... 69,000
Penza.........................483,000
Perm' (★1,075,000)............999,000
Pervomajsk (1977 E)............. 75,000
Pervoural'sk..................129,000
Petrodvorec (Petrodvorets) (★Leningrad) (1977 E)........ 65,000
Petropavlovsk.................207,000
Petropavlovsk-Kamčatskij.......215,000
Petrozavodsk..................234,000
Pinsk (1977 E)................. 87,000
Podol'sk (★Moskva)............202,000
Polevskoj (Polevskoy) (1977 E).. 64,000
Polock (Polotsk) (1977 E)....... 76,000
Poltava.......................279,000
Poti (1977 E).................. 54,000
Priluki (1977 E)................ 66,000
Prokopjevsk (Prokop'yevsk) (★395,000)................266,000
Prževal'sk (1977 E)............ 51,000
Pskov.........................176,000
Puškin (★Leningrad) (1977 E)... 86,000
Puškino (Pushkino) (1977 E).... 65,000
Ramenskoje (★Moskva) (1977 E)........................ 73,000
R'azan' (Ryazan').............453,000
Rečica (Rechitsa) (1977 E)...... 60,000
Reutov (★Moskva) (1977 E)...... 59,000
Revda (1977 E)................. 61,000
Rīga (★915,000)................835,000
Romny (1977 E)................. 51,000
Roslavl' (1977 E).............. 55,000
Rostov-na-Donu (★1,070,000)....934,000
Roven'ki (1977 E).............. 62,000
Rovno.........................179,000
Rubcovsk (Rubtsovsk)..........157,000
Rubežnoje (★Lisičansk) (1977 E)........................ 68,000
Rudnyj (Rudnyy)...............109,000
Rustavi (★Tbilisi)..............129,000
Rybinsk.......................239,000
Ržev (Rzhev) (1977 E).......... 69,000
Šachtinsk (1977 E)............. 52,000
Šach'torsk (★Torez) (1977 E)... 73,000
Šachty (Shakhty)...............210,000
Šadrinsk (Shadrinsk) (1977 E).. 82,000
Safonovo (1977 E).............. 53,000
Salavat.......................137,000
Salsk (1977 E)................. 57,000
Samarkand.....................476,000
Saran' (1977 E)................ 55,000
Saransk.......................263,000
Sarapul.......................107,000
Saratov (★1,075,000)..........856,000
Ščelkovo (★Moskva)............100,000
Ščokino (Shchekino) (1977 E)... 72,000
Semipalatinsk.................283,000
Serov.........................101,000
Serpuchov (Serpukhov).........140,000
Sevastopol'...................301,000
Ševčenko (Shevchenko).........110,000
Severodoneck (★Lisičansk).....113,000
Severodvinsk..................197,000
Šiauliai......................118,000
Simferopol'...................302,000
Slav'ansk (★Kramatorsk)........140,000
Slav'ansk-na-Kubani (1977 E)... 57,000
Smela (1977 E)................. 60,000
Smolensk......................276,000
Snežnoje (★Torez) (1977 E)...... 63,000
Soči (Sochi)...................287,000
Sokol (1974 E)................. 48,000
Soligorsk (1977 E)............. 57,000
Solikamsk.....................101,000
Solncevo (★Moskva) (1977 E).... 51,000
Šostka (Shostka) (1977 E)...... 64,000
Spassk-Dal'nij (1977 E)......... 52,000
Stachanov (Kadijevka) (★590,000)...................108,000
Staryj Oskol..................115,000
Stavropol'....................258,000
Sterlitamak...................220,000
Stryj (1977 E)................. 57,000
Stupino (1977 E)............... 64,000
Suchumi (Sukhumi).............114,000
Šuja (Shuya) (1977 E).......... 72,000
Sumgait (★Baku)................190,000
Sumy..........................228,000
Surgut........................107,000
Sverdlovsk (*Sverdlovsk obl.*) (★1,435,000)...............1,211,000
Sverdlovsk (*Vorosilovgrad obl.*) (1977 E)........................ 72,000
Svetlogorsk (1977 E)........... 57,000
Svobodnyj (1977 E)............. 72,000
Syktyvkar.....................171,000
Syzran'.......................179,000
Taganrog......................277,000
Taldy-Kurgan (1977 E).......... 84,000
Tallinn.......................430,000
Tambov........................270,000
Tartu.........................104,000
Tašauz (Tashauz) (1977 E)...... 84,000

Taškent (Tashkent) (★1,975,000)...............1,779,000
Tbilisi (★1,225,000)...........1,066,000
Temirtau......................213,000
Termez (1977 E)................ 57,000
Ternopol'.....................144,000
Tichoreck (Tikhoretsk) (1977 E)........................ 63,000
Tichvin (1977 E)............... 54,000
Tiraspol'.....................139,000
Tobol'sk (1977 E).............. 53,000
Tokmak (1977 E)................ 56,000
Toljatti (Togliatti)............502,000
Tomsk.........................421,000
Torez (Thorez) (1977 E) (★290,000)........................ 96,000
Toržok (1977 E)................ 50,000
Troick (Troitsk) (1977 E)....... 92,000
Tuapse (1977 E)................ 63,000
Tula (★610,000)................514,000
Tulun (1977 E)................. 51,000
T'umen' (Tyumen').............359,000
Turkestan (1977 E)............. 61,000
Uchta (Ukhta) (1977 E)......... 77,000
Ufa (★980,000).................969,000
Uglič (Uglich) (1974 E)......... 37,000
Ulan-Ude......................300,000
Uljanovsk (Ul'yanovsk).........464,000
Uman' (1977 E)................. 81,000
Ural'sk.......................167,000
Urgenč (Urgench)..............100,000
Usolje-Sibirskoje..............103,000
Ussurijsk.....................147,000
Ust'-Ilimsk (1977 E)........... 53,000
Ust'-Kamenogorsk..............274,000
Užgorod (Uzhgorod) (1977 E)... 85,000
Uzlovaja (★Novomoskovsk) (1977 E)........................ 64,000
V'az'ma (Vyaz'ma) (1977 E)..... 51,000
Velikije Luki.................102,000
Ventspils (1974 E)............. 44,000
Verchn'aja Salda (1977 E)...... 52,000
Vičuga (Vichuga) (1977 E)...... 52,000
Vilnius.......................481,000
Vinnica (Vinnitsa)............313,000
Vitebsk.......................297,000
Vladimir......................296,000
Vladivostok...................550,000
Volchov (1974 E)............... 48,000
Volgodonsk (1977 E)............ 54,000
Volgograd (Stalingrad) (★1,210,000)..................929,000
Vologda.......................237,000
Vol'sk (1977 E)................ 72,000
Volžsk (1977 E)................ 54,000
Volžskij (★Volgograd)..........209,000
Vorkuta (1977 E)............... 96,000
Voronež (Voronezh)............783,000
Vorošilovgrad (Lugansk)........463,000
Voskresensk (1977 E)........... 74,000
Votkinsk (1977 E).............. 88,000
Vyborg (1977 E)................ 72,000
Vyksa (1974 E)................. 47,000
Vyšnij Voločok (1977 E)......... 75,000
Zagorsk.......................107,000
Zaporožje (Zaporozh'ye)........781,000
Ždanov (Zhdanov)..............503,000
Zelenograd (★Moskva)..........130,000
Železnodorožnyj (★Moskva) (1977 E)........................ 72,000
Železnogorsk (1977 E).......... 60,000
Zel'onodol'sk (Zelenodol'sk) (1977 E)........................ 86,000
Žigulevsk (Zhigulevsk) (1977 E). 50,000
Zima (1977 E).................. 51,000
Žitomir (Zhitomir).............244,000
Zlatoust......................198,000
Žoltyje Vody (1977 E).......... 52,000
Žukovskij (Zhukovskiy) (1977 E)........................ 87,000
Zyr'anovsk (Zyryanovsk) (1977 E)........................ 55,000

UNITED ARAB EMIRATES / Ittiḥād al-Imārāt al-'Arabīyah

1973 E.........................208,000
ABŪ ZABY.......................50,000
•Dubayy (1970 E)................ 60,000

UNITED KINGDOM

1978 E......................55,835,500
Aberdeen, Scot.................208,569
Accrington (Hyndburn) (★Blackburn)................ 79,700
Adur (★Brighton)............... 57,700
Aldershot (Rushmoor) (★London).................... 80,500
Ashton-under-Lyne (Tameside) (★Manchester)...............219,100
Aylesbury (1973 E)............. 41,420
Ayr, Scot. (1974 E) (★97,000)..... 47,991
Barnsley......................222,100
Barrow-in-Furness.............. 72,200
Basildon (★London).............145,900
Basingstoke (1973 E)........... 60,910
Bath........................... 83,900
Bedford (1973 E)............... 74,390
Beeston and Stapleford (★Nottingham) (1973 E)....... 65,360
Belfast, N. Ire. (★710,000).......354,400
Benfleet (Castle Point) (★London).................... 83,900
Birkenhead (Wirral) (★Liverpool)..................344,500
Birmingham (★2,665,000)......1,041,000
Blackburn (★222,600)............142,900
Blackpool (★280,000)............147,300
Blyth (Blyth Valley)............ 74,200
Bolton (★Manchester)...........260,000
Bootle (★Liverpool) (1973 E).... 71,160
Bournemouth (★310,000)........144,200
Bradford (★Leeds)..............463,100
Brentwood (★London) (1973 E).. 58,690
Brighton (★425,000).............153,700
Bristol (★635,000)..............411,500
Burnley (★160,000)............. 92,700
Burton upon Trent (1973 E)..... 49,480
Bury (★Manchester).............177,500

Bury St. Edmunds (1973 E)...... 26,800
Camborne-Redruth (1973 E)..... 43,970
Cambridge.....................102,300
Cannock (Cannock Chase) (★Birmingham)............. 83,200
Cardiff, Wales (★620,000).......278,400
Carlisle (1973 E)............... 70,930
Carlton (Gedling) (★Nottingham)................102,500
Castlereagh, N. Ire. (★Belfast). 63,900
Chatham (Medway) (★London).144,300
Chelmsford (★London) (1973 E)........................ 58,320
Cheltenham..................... 86,000
Chertsey (Runnymede) (★London).................... 72,600
Cheshunt (Broxbourne) (★London).................... 78,800
Chester (1973 E)............... 61,370
Chesterfield (★128,000)......... 97,100
Chigwell (★London) (1973 E)... 54,220
Clacton-on-Sea (1973 E)......... 39,380
Clydebank, Scot. (★Glasgow)... 54,225
Colchester (1973 E)............ 79,600
Corby.......................... 54,200
Coventry (★655,000)............340,100
Crawley (★London).............. 71,500
Crewe (1973 E)................. 50,450
Crosby (★Liverpool) (1973 E).... 56,750
Darlington (1973 E)............. 85,120
Dartford (★London) (1973 E).... 44,130
Derby (★270,000)................215,400
Dewsbury (★Leeds) (1973 E)..... 50,560
Doncaster (1973 E) (★160,000)... 81,530
Dover (1973 E)................. 34,160
Dudley (★Birmingham)..........296,500
Dundee, Scot...................191,517
Dunfermline, Scot. (1974 E) (★124,893)..................... 53,418
Durham (1973 E)................ 29,490
Eastbourne..................... 71,900
East Kilbride, Scot. (★Glasgow) (1977 E)........................ 75,800
Edinburgh, Scot. (★640,000).....456,512
Ellesmere Port (★Liverpool) (1973 E)........................ 63,870
Epsom and Ewell (★London)... 70,700
Exeter......................... 95,300
Falkirk, Scot. (1974 E) (★142,058)..................... 36,589
Fareham (★Portsmouth)........ 84,600
Folkestone (1973 E)............ 45,610
Gateshead (★Newcastle).........214,200
Gillingham (★London)........... 92,200
Glasgow, Scot. (★1,845,000).....809,679
Gloucester (★113,000)........... 90,600
Gosport (★Portsmouth)......... 79,300
Gravesend (Gravesham) (★London).................... 95,500
Great Yarmouth (1973 E)........ 49,410
Grimsby (★150,000).............. 91,900
Guildford (★London) (1973 E).... 58,470
Halifax (1973 E) (★173,000)...... 88,580
Haltemprice (★Hull) (1973 E)... 54,850
Hamilton, Scot. (★Glasgow)....107,183
Harlow (★London)............... 79,100
Harrogate (1973 E)............. 64,620
Hartlepool (★Middlesbrough).. 95,400
Hastings....................... 73,200
Havant (★Portsmouth)..........115,900
Hemel Hempstead (★London) (1973 E)........................ 71,150
Hereford....................... 46,700
Hertford (★London) (1973 E).... 20,760
Hertsmere (★London)........... 87,600
High Wycombe (1973 E)......... 61,190
Hove (★Brighton)............... 88,300
Huddersfield (1973 E) (★209,000)..................... 130,060
Huyton-with-Roby (Knowsley) (★Liverpool)................182,200
Iverclyde (Greenock), Scot....102,839
Ipswich.......................120,300
Irvine, Scot. (1977 E) (★92,000).. 54,800
Islwyn, Wales (★Newport)..... 64,100
Kidderminster (1973 E)......... 49,960
Kilmarnock, Scot. (1974 E) (★82,000).................... 50,318
Kingston upon Hull (Hull) (★350,000)...................272,400
Kingswood (★Bristol)........... 81,100
Kirkcaldy, Scot. (1974 E) (★148,028)................... 50,063
Lancaster (1973 E) (★100,000) ... 50,570
Leeds (★1,545,000)..............728,500
Leicester (★480,000)............277,500
Leyland (South Ribble) (★Preston).................... 94,200
Lincoln........................ 71,900
Liverpool (★1,550,000).........528,000
•LONDON (★11,065,000).........6,918,000
Londonderry, N. Ire. (1973 E) (★87,000)............. 51,200
Loughborough (1973 E).......... 49,010
Lowestoft (1973 E)............. 53,260
Lurgan, N. Ire. (1971 C) (★59,000)..................... 25,431
Luton (★215,000)...............161,500
Macclesfield (1973 E)........... 45,420
Maidenhead (★London) (1973 E).48,210
Maidstone (1973 E)............. 72,110
Manchester (★2,815,000)........489,300
Mansfield (1973 E) (★198,000)... 58,450
Margate (1973 E)............... 50,290
Merthyr Tydfil, Wales (1973 E).. 53,680
Middlesbrough (Teesside) (★580,000)...................152,900
Monklands (Coatbridge), Scot..........................110,094
Motherwell, Scot. (★Glasgow)..152,561
Newcastle-under-Lyme (★Stoke-on-Trent) (1973 E).... 75,940
Newcastle-upon-Tyne (★1,305,000)..................291,600
Newport (Wales) (★305,000).....133,100
Newtownabbey, N. Ire. (★Belfast).................... 75,000
Northampton...................151,300

North Down (Bangor), N. Ire. (★Belfast)..................... 61,500
Norwich (★203,000).............119,800
Nottingham (★645,000)..........280,900
Nuneaton (★Coventry)..........110,000
Oadby and Wigston (★Leicester).................. 52,200
Oldham (★Manchester)..........224,300
Oxford (★220,000)...............123,700
Penzance (1973 E).............. 19,360
Perth, Scot. (1974 E)............ 44,066
Peterborough (1973 E).......... 72,270
Plymouth (★295,000)............256,400
Pontypool (Torfaen), Wales (★Newport)................... 90,300
Poole (★Bournemouth).........114,200
Portsmouth (★490,000)..........191,400
Port Talbot, Wales (1973 E) (★132,000).................... 50,200
Preston (★245,000)..............127,500
Ramsgate (1973 E).............. 40,090
Reading (★205,000)..............138,700
Redditch (★Birmingham)...... 60,900
Reigate and Banstead (★London)...................113,700
Renfrew, Scot. (★Glasgow).....213,188
Rhondda, Wales (★Cardiff)..... 82,900
Rochdale (★Manchester).......209,100
Rotherham (★Sheffield)........248,100
Rugby (1973 E)................. 60,380
Saint Albans (★London)........123,400
Saint Helens...................189,500
Salford (★Manchester).........256,000
Salisbury (1973 E)............. 35,460
Scarborough (1973 E)........... 43,300
Scunthorpe..................... 67,400
Sheffield (★715,000)............547,900
Shrewsbury (1973 E)............ 56,120
Slough (★London)............... 98,000
Smethwick (Sandwell) (★Birmingham)...............309,500
Solihull (★Birmingham)........198,300
Southampton (★405,000).........210,300
Southend-on-Sea (★London)....154,700
Southport (★Liverpool) (1973 E)........................ 86,030
South Shields (South Tyneside) (★Newcastle)..................164,200
Stafford (1973 E)............... 54,860
Staines (Spelthorne) (★London).................... 94,000
Stanley (★Newcastle) (1973 E).. 42,280
Stevenage...................... 72,900
Stirling, Scot. (1974 E) (★58,000). 29,818
Stockport (★Manchester).......291,100
Stockton-on-Tees (★Middlesbrough)............170,800
Stoke-on-Trent (★445,000).......257,200
Stratford-upon-Avon (1973 E).... 20,080
Stretford (Trafford) (★Manchester)...............225,800
Sunderland (★Newcastle)......300,200
Swansea, Wales (★270,000)......187,700
Swindon (Thamesdown).........144,100
Tamworth....................... 57,200
Taunton (1973 E)............... 37,570
Thurrock (★London)............127,500
Torquay (Torbay)...............108,900
Tunbridge Wells (1973 E)....... 44,800
Tynemouth (North Tyneside) (★Newcastle)..................194,900
Wakefield (★Leeds) (1973 E).... 58,490
Walsall (★Birmingham).........265,600
Walton and Weybridge (Elmbridge) (★London).......110,800
Wansbeck....................... 61,000
Warrington....................166,100
Watford (★London).............. 76,500
Weston-super-Mare (1973 E).... 51,960
Weymouth and Portland......... 57,200
Widnes (Halton)................118,100
Wigan (★Manchester)...........311,300
Woking (★London).............. 79,500
Wolverhampton (★Birmingham)................260,600
Worcester...................... 74,100
Worthing (★Brighton).......... 89,900
Wrexham, Wales (1973 E)........ 39,530
York (★140,000).................101,000

UNITED STATES[1]

1980 UE[2]....................221,185,700
Abilene, Tex. (★100,500)........ 97,000
Akron, Ohio (★608,300)..........232,900
Alameda, Calif. (★San Francisco)............ 69,600
Albany, Ga. (★95,300)........... 76,900
Albany, N.Y. (★748,100).........104,200
Albuquerque, N. Mex. (★415,900)..................306,300
Alexandria, La. (★101,200)...... 49,200
Alexandria, Va. (★Washington).104,600
Alhambra, Calif. (★Los Angeles)............. 62,700
Allentown, Pa. (★529,500)....... 99,100
Alliance, Ohio (★51,600)........ 25,600
Altoona, Pa. (★119,300)......... 57,400
Amarillo, Tex. (★148,800).......144,800
Ames, Iowa (★60,200)............ 45,600
Amherst, N.Y. (★Buffalo)...... 68,100
Anaheim, Calif. (★Los Angeles)...............209,400
Anchorage, Alaska (★193,000)...182,800
Anderson, Ind. (★148,200)...... 67,800
Anderson, S.C. (★67,100)........ 31,200
Annapolis, Md. (★71,400)........ 33,500
Ann Arbor, Mich. (★Detroit)....108,600
Anniston, Ala. (★105,300)....... 33,100
Antioch, Calif. (★105,200)....... 41,700
Appleton, Wis. (★167,900)....... 62,300
Arcadia, Calif. (★Los Angeles).. 46,800
Arden, Calif. (★Sacramento).... 54,800
Arlington, Mass. (★Boston)..... 47,800
Arlington, Tex. (★Dallas).......139,600
Arlington, Va. (★Washington)..144,700
Arlington Heights, Ill. (★Chicago).................. 74,000
Arvada, Colo. (★Denver)........ 91,500

[1] Para las abreviaciones de los nombres de estado véase el Índice, página *I • 30*.
[2] Cifras de Rand McNally y Compañía.
• Ciudad más grande de un país.
★ Población o designación de un área metropolitana, incluyendo los suburbios.
C Censo. **E** Estimado oficial. **UE** Estimado no oficial.

[1] Pour les abréviations des noms des États, voir Index page *I • 30*.
[2] Estimations de Rand McNally & Company.
• Ville la plus peuplée du pays.
★ Population de l'agglomération (ou nom de la zone métropolitaine englobante).
C Recensement. **E** Estimation officielle.
UE Estimation non officielle.

[1] Para as abreviaturas dos nomes dos Estados, ver o Índice, pág. *I • 30*.
[2] Estimativas de Rand McNally & Company.
• Maior cidade do país.
★ População ou indicação de uma área metropolitana, inclusive subúrbios.
C Censo. **E** Estimativa oficial.
UE Estimativa não oficial.

UNITED STATES *continued*

Asheville, N.C. (★134,800) 58,800
Ashtabula, Ohio (★44,700) 23,700
Athens, Ga. (★85,400) 48,700
Atlanta, Ga. (★1,840,000) 392,900
Atlantic City, N.J. (★169,500) 41,900
Auburn, N.Y. (★47,600) 31,400
Augusta, Ga. (★221,700) 51,700
Augusta, Maine (★52,000) 20,700
Aurora, Colo. (★Denver) 147,000
Aurora, Ill. (★Chicago) 82,000
Austin, Tex. (★399,000) 327,200
Bakersfield, Calif. (★223,600) 95,900
Baltimore, Md. (★1,880,500) 766,000
Bangor, Maine (★87,900) 30,900
Baton Rouge, La. (★407,000) 223,000
Battle Creek, Mich. (★105,000) 38,500
Bay City, Mich. (★189,400) 45,400
Bayonne, N.J. (★New York) 68,400
Baytown, Tex. (★Houston) 56,000
Beaumont, Tex. (★330,500) 116,400
Beckley, W.Va. (★65,300) 21,300
Belleville, Ill. (★St. Louis) 45,200
Bellevue, Wash. (★Seattle) 73,200
Bellflower, Calif. (★Los Angeles) 52,500
Bellingham, Wash. (★66,900) 45,600
Beloit, Wis. (★60,500) 33,200
Benton Harbor, Mich. (★102,300) 15,000
Berkeley, Calif. (★San Francisco) 111,500
Berwyn, Ill. (★Chicago) 45,900
Bethesda, Md. (★Washington) 78,000
Bethlehem, Pa. (★Allentown) 72,100
Billings, Mont. (★96,700) 75,100
Biloxi, Miss. (★Gulfport) 42,400
Binghamton, N.Y. (★250,300) 58,100
Birmingham, Ala. (★698,200) 274,400
Bismarck, N.Dak. (★61,100) 43,300
Bloomfield, N.J. (★New York) 49,400
Bloomington, Ill. (★90,800) 42,900
Bloomington, Ind. (★91,800) 50,600
Bloomington, Minn. (★Minneapolis) 77,600
Boca Raton, Fla. (★Miami) 48,800
Boise, Idaho (★151,000) 120,700
Bossier City, La. (★Shreveport) 48,400
Boston, Mass. (★3,804,000) 585,000
Boulder, Colo. (★101,300) 77,400
Bowling Green, Ky. (★52,000) 38,100
Bremerton, Wash. (★118,000) 40,700
Bridgeport, Conn. (★443,800) 134,400
Bristol, Conn. (★Hartford) 57,500
Bristol, Tenn. (★73,900) 30,000
Brockton, Mass. (★Boston) 95,600
Brookline, Mass. (★Boston) 47,600
Brownsville, Tex. (★285,000) 74,600
Brunswick, Ga. (★45,500) 18,600
Bryan, Tex. (★76,000) 37,300
Buena Park, Calif. (★Los Angeles) 64,000
Buffalo, N.Y. (★1,545,000) 361,400
Burbank, Calif. (★Los Angeles) 84,500
Burlington, N.C. (★92,600) 36,600
Burlington, Vt. (★109,700) 37,800
Butler, Pa. (★79,100) 19,600
Butte-Silver Bow, Mont. (★39,300) 38,100
Calumet City, Ill. (★Chicago) 41,200
Cambridge, Mass. (★Boston) 98,400
Camden, N.J. (★Philadelphia) 84,800
Canton, Ohio (★308,400) 94,300
Cape Girardeau, Mo. (★50,500) 34,600
Carson, Calif. (★Los Angeles) 79,600
Carson City, Nev. 32,800
Casper, Wyo. (★62,800) 49,200
Catonsville, Md. (★Baltimore) 47,000
Cedar Rapids, Iowa (★155,400) 105,900
Cerritos, Calif. (★Los Angeles) 51,900
Champaign, Ill. (★127,600) 57,700
Charleston, S.C. (★337,700) 56,400
Charleston, W.Va. (★243,000) 65,600
Charlotte, N.C. (★460,400) 314,000
Charlottesville, Va. (★71,200) 38,200
Chattanooga, Tenn. (★348,500) 160,900
Cheektowaga, N.Y. (★Buffalo) 102,300
Cherry Hill, N.J. (★Philadelphia) 68,100
Chesapeake (South Norfolk), Va. (★Norfolk) 116,000
Chester, Pa. (★Philadelphia) 42,500
Cheyenne, Wyo. (★62,300) 49,500
Chicago, Ill. (★7,775,000) 2,950,000
Chico, Calif. (★63,700) 26,200
Chicopee, Mass. (★Springfield) 54,600
Chula Vista, Calif. (★San Diego) 82,400
Cicero, Ill. (★Chicago) 57,900
Cincinnati, Ohio (★1,445,000) 391,900
Clarksburg, W.Va. (★56,400) 21,400
Clarksville, Tenn. (★86,200) 60,100
Clearwater, Fla. (★St. Petersburg) 81,700
Cleveland, Ohio (★2,237,700) 567,000
Cleveland Heights, Ohio (★Cleveland) 53,300
Clifton, N.J. (★New York) 72,500
Clinton, Iowa (★45,500) 33,100
Clinton Township, Mich. (★Detroit) 71,200
Coatesville, Pa. (★77,800) 12,000
Cocoa, Fla. (★92,300) 15,300
Colorado Springs, Colo. (★281,000) 210,000
Columbia, Md. (★Washington) 60,500
Columbia, Mo. (★75,400) 67,700
Columbia, S.C. (★351,600) 109,300
Columbus, Ga. (★223,800) 164,300
Columbus, Ind. (★67,700) 29,600
Columbus, Ohio (★945,000) 526,800
Compton, Calif. (★Los Angeles) 76,600
Concord, Calif. (★San Francisco) 100,600
Concord, N.H. (★55,200) 29,500
Coral Gables, Fla. (★Miami) 40,900
Corpus Christi, Tex. (★262,000) 215,300
Corvallis, Oreg. (★51,700) 38,500
Costa Mesa, Calif. (★Los Angeles) 81,200
Council Bluffs, Iowa (★Omaha) 56,800
Covington, Ky. (★Cincinnati) 45,700
Cranston, R.I. (★Providence) 73,300
Cumberland, Md. (★80,900) 24,800
Cuyahoga Falls, Ohio (★Akron) 43,500
Dallas, Tex. (★2,665,000) 844,600
Daly City, Calif. (★San Francisco) 73,100
Danbury, Conn. (★134,300) 57,600
Danville, Ill. (★80,900) 40,700
Danville, Va. (★72,500) 43,700
Davenport, Iowa (★323,100) 102,200
Dayton, Ohio (★897,300) 184,000
Daytona Beach, Fla. (★138,000) 49,000
Dearborn, Mich. (★Detroit) 89,100
Dearborn Heights, Mich. (★Detroit) 69,500
Decatur, Ala. (★60,400) 41,200
Decatur, Ill. (★117,600) 90,000
De Kalb, Ill. (★47,600) 30,900
Denver, Colo. (★1,375,000) 457,700
Des Moines, Iowa (★328,600) 188,800
Des Plaines, Ill. (★Chicago) 56,300
Detroit, Mich. (★4,635,000) 1,198,000
Dothan, Ala. (★62,900) 47,900
Dover, Del. (★76,300) 24,000
Dover, N.H. (★71,100) 22,200
Downey, Calif. (★Los Angeles) 87,400
Dubuque, Iowa (★83,500) 60,800
Duluth, Minn. (★144,800) 92,100
Dundalk, Md. (★Baltimore) 89,500
Durham, N.C. (★199,800) 108,000
East Chicago, Ind. (★Chicago) 40,500
East Detroit, Mich. (★Detroit) 39,600
East Hartford, Conn. (★Hartford) 52,500
East Lansing, Mich. (★Lansing) 51,600
East Liverpool, Ohio (★64,500) 20,400
East Los Angeles, Calif. (★Los Angeles) 100,900
East Orange, N.J. (★New York) 69,000
East Providence, R.I. (★Providence) 49,200
East St. Louis, Ill. (★St. Louis) 50,700
Eau Claire, Wis. (★88,400) 50,300
Edina, Minn. (★Minneapolis) 50,700
Edison, N.J. (★New York) 65,300
El Cajon, Calif. (★San Diego) 73,600
Elgin, Ill. (★Chicago) 65,200
Elizabeth, N.J. (★New York) 100,800
Elkhart, Ind. (★South Bend) 49,500
Elmhurst, Ill. (★Chicago) 44,600
Elmira, N.Y. (★129,100) 34,400
El Monte, Calif. (★Los Angeles) 69,100
El Paso, Tex. (★1,095,000) 415,800
Elyria, Ohio (★Cleveland) 52,100
Englewood, Colo. (★Denver) 41,800
Enid, Okla. (★56,600) 53,300
Erie, Pa. (★242,300) 118,300
Escondido, Calif. (★San Diego) 62,300
Essex, Md. (★Baltimore) 43,700
Euclid, Ohio (★Cleveland) 58,100
Eugene, Oreg. (★213,200) 104,900
Eureka, Calif. (★73,400) 24,400
Evanston, Ill. (★Chicago) 69,300
Evansville, Ind. (★213,800) 134,000
Everett, Wash. (★Seattle) 53,800
Fairbanks, Alaska (★41,500) 29,500
Fairfield, Calif. (105,600) 56,600
Fairfield, Conn. (★Bridgeport) 59,000
Fairmont, W.Va. (★54,300) 26,100
Fall River, Mass. (★170,300) 99,600
Fargo, N.Dak. (★103,400) 59,500
Farmington Hills, Mich. (★Detroit) 61,900
Fayetteville, Ark. (★81,100) 35,900
Fayetteville, N.C. (★230,600) 70,400
Fitchburg, Mass. (★101,500) 35,600
Flint, Mich. (★544,100) 155,200
Florence, Ala. (★94,700) 37,700
Florence, S.C. (★59,900) 34,000
Florissant, Mo. (★St. Louis) 72,000
Fond du Lac, Wis. (★51,300) 36,500
Fort Collins, Colo. (★76,900) 64,000
Fort Lauderdale, Fla. (★Miami) 144,800
Fort Myers, Fla. (★108,700) 36,900
Fort Pierce, Fla. (★74,200) 30,600
Fort Smith, Ark. (★103,000) 70,700
Fort Walton Beach, Fla. (★87,000) 22,100
Fort Wayne, Ind. (★303,200) 185,500
Fort Worth, Tex. (★Dallas) 362,800
Fountain Valley, Calif. (★Los Angeles) 54,500
Framingham, Mass. (★Boston) 63,700
Frankfort, Ky. 25,200
Freeport, Tex. (★72,100) 12,500
Fremont, Calif. (★San Francisco) 125,500
Fresno, Calif. (★366,000) 200,700
Fullerton, Calif. (★Los Angeles) 102,500
Gadsden, Ala. (★84,200) 48,500
Gainesville, Fla. (★112,000) 71,900
Galesburg, Ill. (★42,500) 32,300
Galveston, Tex. (★152,300) 59,200
Garden Grove, Calif. (★Los Angeles) 119,000
Garland, Tex. (★Dallas) 141,300
Gary, Ind. (★Chicago) 152,300
Gastonia, N.C. (★117,300) 49,100
Glendale, Ariz. (★Phoenix) 81,700
Glendale, Calif. (★Los Angeles) 135,100
Glens Falls, N.Y. (★63,800) 16,600
Goldsboro, N.C. (★65,300) 35,700
Grand Forks, N.Dak. (★55,100) 42,700
Grand Island, Nebr. (★40,300) 35,000
Grand Junction, Colo. (★57,000) 25,600
Grand Prairie, Tex. (★Dallas) 65,100
Grand Rapids, Mich. (★484,000) 181,900
Great Falls, Mont. (★76,500) 61,600
Greece, N.Y. (★Rochester) 59,100
Greeley, Colo. (★67,800) 51,600
Green Bay, Wis. (★166,400) 91,900
Greensboro, N.C. (★364,700) 158,100
Greenville, Miss. (★52,300) 42,300
Greenville, S.C. (★313,100) 55,200
Greenwich, Conn. (★New York) 60,000
Gulfport, Miss. (★180,400) 45,200
Hackensack, N.J. (★New York) 36,300
Hagerstown, Md. (★143,900) 37,400
Hamden, Conn. (★New Haven) 49,900
Hamilton, Ohio (★Cincinnati) 67,400
Hammond, Ind. (★Chicago) 99,000
Hampton, Va. (★Newport News) 123,200
Hanover, Pa. (★52,700) 14,200
Harlingen, Tex. (★77,000) 41,500
Harrisburg, Pa. (★404,600) 53,400
Hartford, Conn. (★1,072,300) 124,700
Hattiesburg, Miss. (★62,700) 41,500
Haverhill, Mass. (★Boston) 43,700
Hawthorne, Calif. (★Los Angeles) 54,100
Hayward, Calif. (★San Francisco) 94,500
Hazleton, Pa. (★72,100) 27,800
Helena, Mont. 30,100
Hialeah, Fla. (★Miami) 128,200
Hickory, N.C. (★77,900) 19,600
Hicksville, N.Y. (★New York) 50,000
High Point, N.C. (★Greensboro) 66,700
Hilo, Haw. (★40,400) 30,100
Hoboken, N.J. (★New York) 39,300
Holland, Mich. (★63,200) 29,300
Hollywood, Fla. (★Miami) 112,000
Honolulu, Haw. (★738,900) 318,000
Hot Springs National Park, Ark. (★59,800) 41,800
Houma, La. (★59,400) 30,700
Houston, Tex. (★2,600,000) 1,665,000
Huntington, W.Va. (★256,200) 67,000
Huntington Beach, Calif. (★Los Angeles) 169,600
Huntsville, Ala. (★193,800) 146,400
Hutchinson, Kans. (★50,000) 42,000
Idaho Falls, Idaho (★65,300) 40,200
Independence, Mo. (★Kansas City) 117,600
Indianapolis, Ind. (★1,085,200) 694,600
Inglewood, Calif. (★Los Angeles) 92,200
Iowa City, Iowa (★68,200) 49,400
Irondequoit, N.Y. (★Rochester) 56,600
Irvine, Calif. (★Los Angeles) 60,800
Irving, Tex. (★Dallas) 108,300
Irvington, N.J. (★New York) 53,500
Ithaca, N.Y. (★79,900) 28,800
Jackson, Mich. (★134,900) 42,700
Jackson, Miss. (★287,900) 192,200
Jackson, Tenn. (★57,400) 49,200
Jacksonville, Fla. (★621,300) 533,000
Jacksonville, N.C. (★96,000) 20,500
Jamestown, N.Y. (★67,900) 34,500
Janesville, Wis. (★72,700) 50,900
Jefferson City, Mo. (★46,100) 38,900
Jersey City, N.J. (★New York) 220,000
Johnson City, Tenn. (★106,700) 40,300
Johnstown, Pa. (★174,400) 36,700
Joliet, Ill. (★Chicago) 70,200
Joplin, Mo. (★71,600) 41,200
Juneau, Alaska 18,500
Kailua, Haw. (★Honolulu) 39,800
Kalamazoo, Mich. (★214,000) 77,900
Kankakee, Ill. (★76,900) 28,100
Kannapolis, N.C. (★90,200) 39,500
Kansas City, Kans. (★Kansas City) 163,200
Kansas City, Mo. (★1,236,400) 459,000
Kenner, La. (★New Orleans) 55,400
Kenosha, Wis. (★Chicago) 79,700
Kettering, Ohio (★Dayton) 68,300
Key West, Fla. 20,000
Killeen, Tex. (★123,000) 55,300
Kingsport, Tenn. (★118,100) 33,700
Kingston, N.Y. (★91,700) 22,200
Knoxville, Tenn. (★477,600) 188,700
Kokomo, Ind. (★94,000) 54,200
La Crosse, Wis. (★89,200) 48,900
Lafayette, Ind. (★109,100) 49,300
Lafayette, La. (★154,100) 82,400
Lake Charles, La. (★135,600) 78,200
Lakeland, Fla. (★122,900) 48,000
Lakewood, Calif. (★Los Angeles) 80,900
Lakewood, Colo. (★Denver) 134,500
Lakewood, Ohio (★Cleveland) 61,700
Lakewood Center, Wash. (★Seattle) 52,000
La Mesa, Calif. (★San Diego) 50,800
Lancaster, Calif. (★83,800) 47,800
Lancaster, Ohio (★56,400) 39,200
Lancaster, Pa. (★204,500) 56,400
Lansing, Mich. (★324,900) 124,700
Laredo, Tex. (★330,000) 83,500
Largo, Fla. (★St. Petersburg) 54,900
Las Cruces, N.Mex. (★69,500) 44,500
Las Vegas, Nev. (★388,000) 176,600
Lawrence, Kans. (★54,400) 53,200
Lawrence, Mass. (★Boston) 63,400
Lawton, Okla. (★108,600) 89,000
Lebanon, Pa. (★78,700) 28,300
Levittown, N.Y. (★New York) 65,300
Levittown, Pa. (★Philadelphia) 78,700
Lewiston, Maine (★87,400) 39,800
Lexington, Ky. (★250,200) 194,500
Lima, Ohio (★98,200) 50,300
Lincoln, Nebr. (★177,400) 170,300
Lincoln Park, Mich. (★Detroit) 45,100
Little Rock, Ark. (★370,000) 160,400
Livermore, Calif. (★San Francisco) 47,900
Livonia, Mich. (★Detroit) 105,700
Lockport, N.Y. (★66,700) 26,400
Lompoc, Calif. (★48,600) 27,000
Long Beach, Calif. (★Los Angeles) 352,600
Longview, Tex. (★82,600) 58,200
Longview, Wash. (★60,900) 30,500
Lorain, Ohio (★Cleveland) 82,000
Los Angeles, Calif. (★9,415,000) 2,815,000
Louisville, Ky. (★863,500) 306,500
Lowell, Mass. (★Boston) 86,200
Lubbock, Tex. (★191,000) 167,200
Lufkin, Tex. (★46,800) 31,000
Lynchburg, Va. (★118,700) 65,600
Lynn, Mass. (★Boston) 77,300
Lynwood, Calif. (★Los Angeles) 41,200
McAllen, Tex. (★121,000) 55,600
Macon, Ga. (★227,000) 120,600
Madison, Wis. (★278,900) 169,500
Malden, Mass. (★Boston) 54,500
Manchester, Conn. (★Hartford) 50,100
Manchester, N.H. (★127,900) 83,300
Manitowoc, Wis. (★62,400) 33,600
Mankato, Minn. (★46,100) 26,200
Mansfield, Ohio (★111,300) 57,100
Marion, Ind. (★75,600) 39,900
Marion, Ohio (★55,900) 38,700
Marrero, La. (★New Orleans) 48,500
Martinsville, Va. (★68,200) 17,400
Marysville, Calif. (★78,100) 10,100
Mason City, Iowa (★40,100) 30,000
Medford, Mass. (★Boston) 58,800
Medford, Oreg. (★85,700) 38,900
Melbourne, Fla. (★99,000) 42,700
Memphis, Tenn. (★849,700) 678,500
Mentor, Ohio (★Cleveland) 43,200
Merced, Calif. (★77,800) 34,400
Meriden, Conn. (★New Haven) 56,800
Meridian, Miss. (★60,400) 42,700
Mesa, Ariz. (★Phoenix) 122,300
Mesquite, Tex. (★Dallas) 66,100
Metairie, La. (★New Orleans) 176,300
Miami, Fla. (★2,509,500) 343,000
Miami Beach, Fla. (★Miami) 86,300
Michigan City, Ind. (★64,600) 42,000
Middletown, N.Y. (★81,900) 26,600
Middletown, Ohio (★110,000) 48,400
Midland, Tex. (★74,900) 68,700
Midwest City, Okla. (★Oklahoma City) 52,000
Milford, Conn. (★Bridgeport) 50,100
Millcreek Township, Pa. (★Erie) 42,300
Milwaukee, Wis. (★1,382,700) 616,300
Minneapolis, Minn. (★1,970,300) 340,300
Minnetonka, Minn. (★Minneapolis) 47,300
Minot, N.Dak. (★37,000) 32,600
Mishawaka, Ind. (★South Bend) 41,100
Mission Viejo, Calif. (★Los Angeles) 48,000
Missoula, Mont. (★60,800) 30,000
Mobile, Ala. (★358,600) 214,400
Modesto, Calif. (★188,100) 102,600
Moline, Ill. (★Davenport) 42,700
Monroe, La. (★122,600) 64,700
Monroe, Mich. (★60,200) 25,100
Montebello, Calif. (★Los Angeles) 50,200
Monterey, Calif. (★123,100) 27,200
Monterey Park, Calif. (★Los Angeles) 52,000
Montgomery, Ala. (★218,500) 166,400
Montpelier, Vt. (★36,400) 8,000
Morgantown, W.Va. (★63,200) 31,700
Mountain View, Calif. (★San Francisco) 56,700
Mount Prospect, Ill. (★Chicago) 52,800
Mount Vernon, N.Y. (★New York) 74,200
Muncie, Ind. (★126,400) 80,000
Muskegon, Mich. (★178,700) 43,400
Muskogee, Okla. (★51,600) 42,900
Napa, Calif. (★San Francisco) 48,800
Nashua, N.H. (★124,900) 67,200
Nashville, Tenn. (★581,100) 454,200
Natchez, Miss. (★43,100) 24,000
National City, Calif. (★San Diego) 48,500
Newark, N.J. (★New York) 298,700
Newark, Ohio (★78,100) 39,000
New Bedford, Mass. (164,100) 97,700
New Britain, Conn. (★Hartford) 74,400
Newburgh, N.Y. (★116,500) 25,800
New Castle, Pa. (★66,800) 34,400
New Haven, Conn. (★499,000) 119,000
New London, Conn. (★253,900) 28,200
New Orleans, La. (★1,154,200) 555,400
Newport, R.I. (★64,100) 31,500
Newport Beach, Calif. (★Los Angeles) 65,600
Newport News, Va. (★327,000) 144,800
New Rochelle, N.Y. (★New York) 69,000
Newton, Mass. (★Boston) 85,500
•New York, N.Y. (★16,625,000) 7,001,000
Niagara Falls, N.Y. (★Buffalo) 76,000
Nogales, Ariz. (★85,000) 13,100
Norfolk, Va. (★801,400) 275,900
Norman, Okla. (★Oklahoma City) 67,600
Northampton, Mass. (★36,200) 28,300
North Bergen, N.J. (★New York) 45,200
North Charleston, S.C. (★Charleston) 62,300
North Las Vegas, Nev. (★Las Vegas) 41,700
North Little Rock, Ark. (★Little Rock) 63,400
North Miami, Fla. (★Miami) 44,400

[1] For abbreviations of state names, see Index, page *I* • *30*.
[2] Rand McNally & Company estimates.
• Largest city in country.
★ Population or designation of the metropolitan area, including suburbs.
C Census. **E** Official estimate. **UE** Unofficial estimate.

[1] Für die Abkürzungen der Namen der Staaten siehe Register, S. *I* • *30*.
[2] Schätzungen der Rand McNally & Company.
• Grösste Stadt des Landes.
★ Bevölkerung oder Bezeichnung der Stadtregion einschliesslich Vororte.
C Volkszählung. **E** Offizielle Schätzung.
UE Inoffizielle Schätzung.

Norwalk, Calif. (★Los Angeles)	84,800
Norwalk, Conn. (★New York)	75,300
Oakland, Calif. (★San Francisco)	328,100
Oak Lawn, Ill. (★Chicago)	62,000
Oak Park, Ill. (★Chicago)	54,700
Oceanside, Calif. (★189,900)	78,000
Odessa, Tex. (★106,200)	93,300
Ogden, Utah (★204,900)	67,200
Oklahoma City, Okla. (★705,900)	379,400
Olympia, Wash. (★92,900)	32,000
Omaha, Nebr. (★582,700)	372,100
Ontario, Calif. (★Los Angeles)	78,500
Opelika, Ala. (★55,700)	23,000
Orange, Calif. (★Los Angeles)	88,900
Orem, Utah (★Provo)	50,200
Orlando, Fla. (★508,100)	119,500
Oshkosh, Wis. (★69,300)	49,400
Overland Park, Kans. (★Kansas City)	87,000
Owensboro, Ky. (★63,500)	50,900
Oxnard, Calif. (★Ventura)	99,400
Paducah, Ky. (★68,700)	33,700
Palo Alto, Calif. (★San Francisco)	54,600
Panama City, Fla. (★90,700)	41,200
Paradise, Nev. (★Las Vegas)	41,600
Parkersburg, W.Va. (★90,500)	38,400
Park Ridge, Ill. (★Chicago)	40,700
Parma, Ohio (★Cleveland)	96,800
Pasadena, Calif. (★Los Angeles)	107,400
Pasadena, Tex. (★Houston)	110,200
Pascagoula, Miss. (★74,500)	33,000
Pasco, Wash. (★115,000)	16,700
Passaic, N.J. (★New York)	48,400
Paterson, N.J. (★New York)	144,000
Pawtucket, R.I. (★Providence)	67,600
Peabody, Mass. (★Boston)	44,300
Penn Hills, Pa. (★Pittsburgh)	61,000
Pensacola, Fla. (★218,000)	66,200
Peoria, Ill. (★323,800)	123,400
Petersburg, Va. (★120,400)	42,600
Philadelphia, Pa. (★5,230,000)	1,731,000
Phoenix, Ariz. (★1,336,600)	682,900
Pico Rivera, Calif. (★Los Angeles)	50,500
Pierre, S.Dak.	12,800
Pine Bluff, Ark. (★69,900)	56,600
Piscataway, N.J. (★New York)	39,600
Pittsburgh, Pa. (★2,160,000)	416,200
Pittsfield, Mass. (★93,300)	51,100
Plainfield, N.J. (★New York)	42,900
Plano, Tex. (★Dallas)	55,800
Plantation, Fla. (★Miami)	46,100
Pocatello, Idaho (★57,700)	48,700
Pomona, Calif. (★Los Angeles)	87,900
Pompano Beach, Fla. (★Miami)	55,100
Pontiac, Mich. (★Detroit)	78,000
Port Arthur, Tex. (★Beaumont)	62,300
Port Huron, Mich. (★153,500)	34,100
Portland, Maine (★216,300)	60,800
Portland, Oreg. (★1,161,300)	344,000
Portsmouth, N.H. (★55,800)	26,300
Portsmouth, Ohio (★68,700)	23,400
Portsmouth, Va. (★Norfolk)	107,500
Pottstown, Pa. (★81,200)	25,700
Pottsville, Pa. (★58,700)	17,700
Poughkeepsie, N.Y. (★223,900)	30,300
Providence, R.I. (★868,800)	154,900
Provo, Utah (★184,900)	56,300
Pueblo, Colo. (★120,200)	99,600
Quincy, Ill. (★53,400)	40,900
Quincy, Mass. (★Boston)	91,100
Racine, Wis. (★147,900)	92,600
Raleigh, N.C. (★278,100)	142,900
Rancho Cordova, Calif. (★Sacramento)	40,000
Rapid City, S.Dak. (★74,800)	53,000
Reading, Pa. (★211,000)	75,600
Redding, Calif. (★88,900)	44,400
Redford Township, Mich. (★Detroit)	59,400
Redlands, Calif. (★San Bernardino)	40,000
Redondo Beach, Calif. (★Los Angeles)	63,300
Redwood City, Calif. (★San Francisco)	55,500
Reno, Nev. (★166,000)	86,000
Revere, Mass. (★Boston)	40,300
Richardson, Tex. (★Dallas)	71,600
Richfield, Minn. (★Minneapolis)	39,600
Richmond, Calif. (★San Francisco)	67,300
Richmond, Ind. (★62,600)	42,900
Richmond, Va. (★557,000)	214,200
Riverside, Calif. (★San Bernardino)	169,500
Roanoke, Va. (★203,300)	99,600
Rochester, Minn. (★82,200)	58,100
Rochester, N.Y. (★808,300)	241,700
Rockford, Ill. (★242,600)	139,900
Rock Hill, S.C. (★63,100)	38,800
Rock Island, Ill. (★Davenport)	45,600
Rockville, Md. (★Washington)	43,200
Rocky Mount, N.C. (★67,400)	41,500
Rome, Ga. (★72,500)	28,200
Rome, N.Y. (★Utica)	46,200
Rosemead, Calif. (★Los Angeles)	41,100
Roseville, Mich. (★Detroit)	55,200
Roseville, Minn. (★Minneapolis)	41,100
Royal Oak, Mich. (★Detroit)	73,500
Sacramento, Calif. (★840,000)	265,200
Saginaw, Mich. (★183,400)	78,100
St. Charles, Mo. (★St. Louis)	42,200
St. Clair Shores, Mich. (★Detroit)	84,000
St. Cloud, Minn. (★72,900)	40,700
St. Joseph, Mo. (★88,900)	76,600
St. Louis, Mo. (★2,250,500)	479,000
St. Louis Park, Minn. (★Minneapolis)	44,900
St. Paul, Minn. (★Minneapolis)	251,900
St. Petersburg, Fla. (★671,200)	235,000
Salem, Oreg. (★156,100)	89,200
Salina, Kans. (★46,000)	41,200
Salinas, Calif. (★107,200)	78,800
Salisbury, Md. (★52,500)	17,000
Salisbury, N.C. (★55,600)	26,400
Salt Lake City, Utah (★630,700)	163,700
San Angelo, Tex. (★72,900)	69,000
San Antonio, Tex. (★1,020,000)	838,900
San Bernardino, Calif. (★710,300)	109,500
San Diego, Calif. (★2,200,000)	844,000
Sandusky, Ohio (★62,100)	30,400
San Francisco, Calif. (★4,550,000)	655,000
San Jose, Calif. (★San Francisco)	609,600
San Leandro, Calif. (★San Francisco)	67,000
San Mateo, Calif. (★San Francisco)	79,700
San Rafael, Calif. (★San Francisco)	44,100
Santa Ana, Calif. (★Los Angeles)	188,900
Santa Barbara, Calif. (★166,300)	73,600
Santa Clara, Calif. (★San Francisco)	83,400
Santa Cruz, Calif. (★137,600)	40,300
Santa Fe, N.Mex. (★51,800)	46,400
Santa Maria, Calif. (★61,600)	38,400
Santa Monica, Calif. (★Los Angeles)	89,700
Santa Rosa, Calif. (★170,200)	77,400
Sarasota, Fla. (★266,900)	49,100
Savannah, Ga. (★199,200)	138,000
Schaumburg, Ill. (★Chicago)	56,300
Schenectady, N.Y. (★Albany)	70,700
Scottsdale, Ariz. (★Phoenix)	82,300
Scranton, Pa. (★476,600)	88,400
Seattle, Wash. (★1,965,000)	481,000
Sharon, Pa. (★90,200)	20,800
Sheboygan, Wis. (★76,200)	49,200
Sherman, Tex. (★63,500)	27,400
Shreveport, La. (★279,600)	199,000
Silver Spring, Md. (★Washington)	84,000
Simi (Simi Valley), Calif. (★Los Angeles)	77,100
Sioux City, Iowa (★104,400)	83,400
Sioux Falls, S.Dak. (★86,800)	75,400
Skokie, Ill. (★Chicago)	64,700
Somerville, Mass. (★Boston)	72,400
South Bend, Ind. (★430,100)	112,700
Southfield, Mich. (★Detroit)	79,100
South Gate, Calif. (★Los Angeles)	61,900
South San Francisco, Calif. (★San Francisco)	49,100
South Whittier, Calif. (★Los Angeles)	45,700
Spartanburg, S.C. (★144,400)	47,400
Spokane, Wash. (★295,600)	180,500
Springfield, Ill. (★153,700)	83,900
Springfield, Mass. (★500,200)	163,700
Springfield, Mo. (★182,200)	153,400
Springfield, Ohio (★Dayton)	72,700
Springfield, Oreg. (★Eugene)	42,200
Stamford, Conn. (★New York)	104,000
State College, Pa. (★80,800)	37,800
Sterling Heights, Mich. (★Detroit)	109,900
Steubenville, Ohio (★141,300)	26,400
Stockton, Calif. (★264,200)	135,000
Stratford, Conn. (★Bridgeport)	51,300
Suffolk, Va. (★Norfolk)	47,200
Sumter, S.C. (★70,800)	25,400
Sunnyvale, Calif. (★San Francisco)	107,100
Syracuse, N.Y. (★555,900)	170,200
Tacoma, Wash. (★Seattle)	160,500
Tallahassee, Fla. (★123,500)	87,800
Tampa, Fla. (★540,000)	247,800
Taunton, Mass. (★57,300)	41,000
Taylor, Mich. (★Detroit)	80,500
Tempe, Ariz. (★Phoenix)	108,000
Temple, Tex. (★59,900)	41,000
Terre Haute, Ind. (★125,500)	61,900
Texarkana, Tex. (★78,100)	37,200
Texas City, Tex. (★Galveston)	43,600
Thousand Oaks, Calif. (★Los Angeles)	71,300
Toledo, Ohio (★564,800)	347,600
Topeka, Kans. (★154,900)	124,500
Torrance, Calif. (★Los Angeles)	126,300
Town of Tonawanda, N.Y. (★Buffalo)	77,500
Towson, Md. (★Baltimore)	84,500
Trenton, N.J. (★Philadelphia)	93,300
Troy, Mich. (★Detroit)	72,400
Troy, N.Y. (★Albany)	56,500
Tucson, Ariz. (★448,400)	302,000
Tulsa, Okla. (★516,600)	342,100
Tuscaloosa, Ala. (★107,700)	70,800
Tyler, Tex. (★91,200)	66,600
Union, N.J. (★New York)	48,900
Union City, N.J. (★New York)	49,900
Uniontown, Pa. (★53,600)	14,900
University City, Mo. (★St. Louis)	43,600
Upland, Calif. (★Los Angeles)	44,500
Upper Darby, Pa. (★Philadelphia)	49,500
Utica, N.Y. (★262,800)	75,900
Vacaville, Calif. (★Fairfield)	42,500
Valdosta, Ga. (★57,500)	35,500
Vallejo, Calif. (★San Francisco)	75,100
Vancouver, Wash. (★Portland)	49,900
Ventura (San Buenaventura), Calif. (★298,700)	71,300
Vicksburg, Miss. (★46,300)	30,400
Victoria, Tex. (★53,400)	50,200
Vineland, N.J. (★102,600)	53,000
Virginia Beach, Va. (★Norfolk)	254,800
Visalia, Calif. (★82,700)	47,200
Waco, Tex. (★137,200)	100,200
Walnut Creek, Calif. (★San Francisco)	51,200
Waltham, Mass. (★Boston)	53,400
Warner Robins, Ga. (★Macon)	43,300
Warren, Mich. (★Detroit)	165,500
Warren, Ohio (★Youngstown)	59,600
Warwick, R.I. (★Providence)	85,900
WASHINGTON, D.C. (★3,185,000)	652,000
Washington, Pa. (★55,100)	19,600
Waterbury, Conn. (★216,100)	103,500
Waterloo, Iowa (★134,500)	81,700
Waukegan, Ill. (★Chicago)	64,600
Waukesha, Wis. (★Milwaukee)	47,500
Wausau, Wis. (★70,200)	32,600
Wauwatosa, Wis. (★Milwaukee)	54,400
Wayne, N.J. (★New York)	47,100
West Allis, Wis. (★Milwaukee)	66,800
West Covina, Calif. (★Los Angeles)	78,200
West Hartford, Conn. (★Hartford)	65,300
West Haven, Conn. (★New Haven)	51,300
Westland, Mich. (★Detroit)	87,700
Westminster, Calif. (★Los Angeles)	70,500
West Orange, N.J. (★New York)	40,300
West Palm Beach, Fla. (★348,200)	57,600
West Seneca, N.Y. (★Buffalo)	55,300
Weymouth, Mass. (★Boston)	56,600
Wheaton, Ill. (★Chicago)	42,500
Wheaton, Md. (★Washington)	73,800
Wheeling, W.Va. (★153,700)	42,200
White Plains, N.Y. (★New York)	46,000
Whittier, Calif. (★Los Angeles)	69,700
Wichita, Kans. (★361,200)	274,000
Wichita Falls, Tex. (★114,800)	95,100
Wilkes-Barre, Pa. (★Scranton)	52,700
Williamsport, Pa. (★89,700)	32,800
Willingboro (Levittown), N.J. (★Philadelphia)	42,600
Wilmington, Del. (★Philadelphia)	69,100
Wilmington, N.C. (★101,100)	56,100
Winston-Salem, N.C. (★259,600)	141,100
Winter Haven, Fla. (★77,800)	19,200
Woonsocket, R.I. (★Providence)	46,400
Worcester, Mass. (★368,000)	162,600
Wyoming, Mich. (★Grand Rapids)	59,500
Yakima, Wash. (★100,300)	54,000
Yonkers, N.Y. (★New York)	184,900
York, Pa. (★209,000)	45,300
Youngstown, Ohio (★504,300)	126,500
Yuma, Ariz. (★50,700)	31,500
Zanesville, Ohio (★59,600)	35,500

UPPER VOLTA / Haute-Volta

1975 C	6,144,013
Bobo Dioulasso	115,063
Koudougou	36,838
•OUAGADOUGOU	172,661

URUGUAY

1975 C	2,763,964
Las Piedras (★Montevideo)	53,983
Melo	38,260
Mercedes	34,667
Minas	35,433
•MONTEVIDEO (★1,350,000)	1,229,748
Paysandú	62,412
Rivera	49,013
Salto	71,881

VATICAN CITY

1977 E	723

VENEZUELA

1971 C	10,721,522
Acarigua	56,743
Barcelona	78,201
Barinas	56,329
Barquisimeto	330,815
Baruta (★Caracas)	121,066
Cabimas	118,037
Calabozo	38,360
•CARACAS (★2,475,000)	1,658,500
Carora	36,115
Carúpano	50,935
Catia La Mar (★Caracas)	62,200
Chacao (★Caracas)	78,528
Ciudad Bolívar	103,728
Ciudad Guayana (Santo Tomé de Guayana)	143,540
Ciudad Ojeda (Lagunillas)	83,083
Coro	68,701
Cumaná	119,751
El Tigre	49,801
Guacara	38,793
La Victoria	40,731
Los Dos Caminos (★Caracas)	59,211
Los Teques (★Caracas)	63,106
Maiquetía (★Caracas)	59,238
Maracaibo	651,574
Maracay	255,134
Maturín	98,188
Mérida	74,214
Petare (★Caracas)	227,727
Pozuelos	44,011
Puerto Cabello	72,103
Puerto la Cruz	63,276
Punto Fijo	55,483
San Cristóbal	151,717
San Felipe	42,905
Valencia	367,171
Valera	76,740

VIETNAM / Viet-nam Dan-chu Cong-hoa

1967 E	37,073,000
Bien-hoa	52,200
Can-tho	61,100
Da-lat (1971 E)	86,600
Da-nang (1971 E)	437,700
Gia-dinh (★Sai-gon) (1968 E)	151,100
Hai-phong (1960 C) (369,248*)	182,496
HA-NOI (1960 C) (★643,576)	414,620
Hue (1971 E)	199,900
My-tho	62,700
Nam-dinh (1960 C)	86,132
Nha-trang	59,600
Phan-thiet	58,300
Phu-vinh (1971 E)	51,500
Qui-nhon	50,000
Rach-gia	56,000
•Thanh-pho Ho Chi Minh (Sai-gon) (1971 E) (★2,750,000)	1,804,900
Vung-tau (Cap-St.-Jacques)	54,200

VIRGIN ISLANDS, BRITISH

1970 C	10,484
•ROAD TOWN	2,183

VIRGIN ISLANDS OF THE U.S.

1970 C	62,468
•CHARLOTTE AMALIE	12,220

WALLIS AND FUTUNA / Wallis et Futuna

1976 C	9,192
MATA-UTU	558
•Ono	624

WESTERN SAHARA

1974 E	108,000
•EL AAIÚN (AIÚN)	20,000

WESTERN SAMOA

1976 C	151,983
•APIA	32,099

YEMEN / Al-Yaman

1975 C	5,237,893
Al-Ḥudaydah (Hodeida)	80,000
•SAN'Ā'	134,588
Ta'izz	79,000

YEMEN, PEOPLE'S DEMOCRATIC REPUBLIC OF / Al-Yaman ash-Sha'biyah

1977 E	1,797,000
•ADEN	271,600
Al-Mukallā (1970 E)	65,000

YUGOSLAVIA / Jugoslavija

1971 C	20,504,516
Banja Luka	89,866
•BEOGRAD (BELGRADE) (★1,150,000)	770,140
Bitola	65,851
Kragujevac	71,180
Ljubljana	173,662
Maribor	97,167
Niš	127,178
Novi Sad	141,712
Osijek	93,912
Pančevo (★Beograd)	54,269
Priština	69,524
Rijeka	132,933
Sarajevo	244,045
Skopje	312,092
Split	151,875
Subotica	88,787
Titograd	54,509
Tuzla	53,825
Zagreb	566,084
Zenica	51,279
Zrenjanin	59,580

ZAIRE / Zaïre

1974 E	24,222,000
Bandundu (1970 C)	74,467
Boma (1970 E)	61,100
Bukavu	182,000
Gandajika (1970 E)	60,100
Kabinda (1970 E)	60,500
Kalemie (Albertville) (1970 E)	62,300
Kamina (1970 E)	56,300
Kananga (Luluabourg)	601,000
Kikwit	150,000
•KINSHASA (LÉOPOLDVILLE) (1975 E)	2,202,000
Kisangani (Stanleyville)	311,000
Kolwezi (1970 E)	81,600
Likasi (Jadotville) (1970 C)	146,394
Lubumbashi (Élisabethville)	404,000
Matadi	144,000
Mbandaka (Coquilhatville)	134,000
Mbanza Ngungu (1970 E)	55,800
Mbuji-Mayi (Bakwanga)	337,000
Mwene-Ditu (1970 E)	71,100

ZAMBIA

1978 E	5,472,000
Chililabombwe (Bancroft)	70,000
Chingola	173,000
Kabwe (Broken Hill)	131,000
Kalulushi	54,000
Kitwe	310,000
Livingstone	72,000
Luanshya	149,000
•LUSAKA	559,000
Mufulira	170,000
Ndola	291,000

ZIMBABWE

1978 E	7,040,000
Bulawayo (★358,000)	84,500
Harari (★Salisbury) (1969 C)	58,007
Highfield (★Salisbury) (1969 C)	52,560
•SALISBURY (★610,000)	115,300

[1] Para las abreviaciones de los nombres de estado véase el Índice, página *I* • *30*.
[2] Cifras de Rand McNally y Compañia.
• Ciudad más grande de un país.
★ Población o designación de un área metropolitana, incluyendo los suburbios.
C Censo. **E** Estimado oficial. **UE** Estimado no oficial.

[1] Pour les abréviations des noms des États, voir Index page *I* • *30*.
[2] Estimations de Rand McNally & Company.
• Ville la plus peuplée du pays.
★ Population de l'agglomération (ou nom de la zone métropolitaine englobante).
C Recensement. **E** Estimation officielle. **UE** Estimation non officielle.

[1] Para as abreviaturas dos nomes dos Estados, ver o Índice, pág. *I* • *30*.
[2] Estimativas de Rand McNally & Company.
• Maior cidade do país.
★ População ou indicação de uma área metropolitana, inclusive subúrbios.
C Censo. **E** Estimativa oficial. **UE** Estimativa não oficial.

The Index includes in a single alphabetical list some 160,000 names appearing on the maps. Each name is followed by a page reference to one or more maps and by the location of the feature on the map, in coordinates of latitude and longitude. If a page contains several maps, a lowercase letter identifies the particular map. The page reference for two-page maps is always to the left-hand page.

Most map features are indexed to the largest-scale map on which they appear. However, a feature usually is not indexed to a Metropolitan Area map if it is also shown on another map where it can be seen in a broader setting. Countries, mountain ranges, and other extensive features are generally indexed to the largest-scale map that shows them in their entirety.

The order in which index information is presented is shown in the English, German, Spanish, French, and Portuguese headings at the center of each two-page spread.

For example:

ENGLISH

Name	Page	Lat.°'	Long.°'

The features indexed are of three types: *point, areal,* and *linear.* For *point* features (for example, cities, mountain peaks, dams), latitude and longitude coordinates give the location of the point on the map. For *areal* features (countries, mountain ranges, etc.), the coordinates generally indicate the approximate center of the feature. For *linear* features (rivers, canals, aqueducts), the coordinates locate a terminating point—for example, the mouth of a river, or the point at which a feature reaches the map margin.

Name Forms Names in the Index, as on the maps, are generally in the local language and insofar as possible are spelled according to official practice. Diacritical marks are included, except that those used to indicate tone, as in Vietnamese, are usually not shown. Most features that extend beyond the boundaries of one country have no single official name, and these are usually named in English. Many English, German, Spanish, French, and Portuguese names, which may not be shown on the maps, appear in the Index as cross references. All cross references are indicated by the symbol →. A name that appears in a shortened version on the map due to space limitations is given in full in the Index, with the portion that is omitted on the map enclosed in brackets, for example, Acapulco [de Juárez].

Transliteration For names in languages not written in the Roman alphabet, the locally official transliteration system has been used where one exists. Thus, names in the Soviet Union and Bulgaria have been transliterated according to the systems adopted by the academies of science of these countries. Similarly, the transliteration for mainland Chinese names follows the Pinyin system, which has been officially adopted in mainland China. For languages with no one locally accepted transliteration system, notably Arabic, transliteration in general follows closely a system adopted by the United States Board on Geographic Names.

Alphabetization Names are alphabetized in the order of the letters of the English alphabet. Spanish *ll* and *ch*, for example, are not treated as distinct letters. Furthermore, diacritical marks are disregarded in alphabetization—German or Scandinavian *ä* or *ö* are treated as *a* or *o*.

The names of physical features may appear inverted, since they are always alphabetized under the proper, not the generic, part of the name, thus: "Gibralter, Strait of ʉ." Otherwise every entry, whether consisting of one word or more, is alphabetized as a single continuous entity. "Lakeland," for example, appears after "La Crosse" and before "La Salle." Names beginning with articles (Le Havre, Den Helder, A-Qāhirah, As-Suways) are not inverted. Names beginning "Mc" are alphabetized as though spelled "Mac," and names beginning "St." and "Sainte" as though spelled "Saint."

In the case of identical names, towns are listed first, then political divisions, then physical features. Entries that are completely identical (including symbols, discussed below) are distinguished by abbreviations of their official country names and are sequenced alphabetically by country name. The many duplicate names in Canada, the United Kingdom, and the United States are further distinguished by abbreviations of the names of their primary subdivisions. (See list of abbreviations on pages *I* · *30* through *I* · *32*.)

Abbreviation and Capitalization Abbreviation and styling have been standardized for all languages. A period is used after every abbreviation even when this may not be the local practice. The abbreviation "St." is used only for "Saint." "Sankt" and other forms of the term are spelled out.

All names are written with an initial capital letter except for a few Dutch names, such as 's-Gravenhage. Capitalization of noninitial words in a name generally follows local practice.

Symbol The symbols that appear in the Index represent graphically the broad categories of the features named, for example, ʌ for mountain (Everest, Mount ʌ). An abbreviated key to the symbols, in the five Atlas languages, appears at the foot of each pair of Index pages. Superior numbers following some symbols in the Index indicate finer distinctions, for example, ʌ[1] for volcano (Fuji-san ʌ[1]). A complete list of the symbols and superior numbers is given on page *I* · *30*.

Das Register umfasst in alphabetischer Anordnung etwa 160 000 in den Karten erscheinende Namen. Nach jedem Namen folgt die Seitenangabe zu einer oder mehreren Karten und die Lageangabe des Objektes in der Karte mit geographischer Länge und Breite. Enthält eine Seite mehrere Karten, so wird die betreffende Karte durch einen Kleinbuchstaben gekennzeichnet. Die Seitenangabe für Doppelseiten bezieht sich immer auf die linke Seite.

Die Verweise für die meisten Objekte in den Karten beziehen sich auf die Karte mit dem grössten Massstab. Normalerweise werden jedoch Verweise auf Objekte in den Karten der Stadtregionen nicht gegeben, wenn sie auf einer anderen Karte in grösserem Zusammenhang dargestellt sind. Die Lageangaben für Länder, Gebirgszüge und andere ausgedehnte Objekte beziehen sich allgemein auf die Karte grössten Massstabes, die sie in ihrer ganzen Ausdehnung zeigt.

Die Anordnung, in welcher die Lageangabe erfolgt, geht aus den englischen, deutschen, spanischen, französischen und portugiesischen Überschriften in der Mitte jeder Doppelseite hervor.

Zum Beispiel:

DEUTSCH

Name	Seite	Breite°'	Länge°' E=Öst

Die aufgeführten Objekte gliedern sich in drei Gruppen: *punkt-, flächen-* und *linienförmige* Objekte. Bei *punktförmigen* Objekten (z.B. Städte, Berge, Dämme) beziehen sich die Angaben nach Länge und Breite auf die Signatur in der Karte. Bei *flächenhaften* Objekten (Länder, Gebirgszüge usw.) verweisen die Koordinaten im allgemeinen auf das ungefähre Zentrum des Objektes. Bei *linienhaften* Objekten (Flüsse, Kanäle, Wasserleitungen) beziehen sich die Koordinaten auf einen bestimmten Punkt, z.B. die Mündung eines Flusses oder den Punkt, an dem das Objekt den Kartenrand schneidet.

Namengebung Wie in den karten so sind auch im Register die Namen im allgemeinen in der örtlichen Namensform wiedergegeben und soweit als möglich in der amtlichen Schreibweise. Diakritische Zeichen wurden gesetzt; sie wurden nur dort weggelassen, wo sie, wie im Vietnamesischen, Tonhöhen kennzeichnen. Meist haben Objekte, die sich über die Grenzen eines Landes hinaus erstrecken, keinen einzelnen offiziellen Namen; normalerweise sind sie daher englisch beschriftet. Viele englische, deutsche, spanische, französische und portugiesische Namensformen, die nicht in den Karten enthalten sind, erscheinen im Register als Kreuzverweis. Alle Kreuzverweise werden durch das Symbol → gekennzeichnet. Namen, die aus Platzgründen in abgekürzter Form in der Karte erscheinen, werden im Register voll ausgeschrieben, wobei der auf der Karte weggelassene Teil in Klammern gesetzt ist, z.B. Acapulco [de Juárez].

Transkription Für die Transkription von Namen aus Sprachen, die nicht im lateinischen Alphabet geschrieben werden, wurde das offizielle Transkriptionssystem benutzt, sofern ein solches vorhanden ist. So wurden die Namen in der Sowjetunion und in Bulgarien nach dem von den wissenschaftlichen Akademien dieser Länder angewandten System transkribiert. Entsprechend wurden die Namen auf dem chinesischen Festland nach dem Pinyin-System übertragen, das offiziell in der Volksrepublik China eingeführt wurde. Bei Sprachen, für die ein allgemein anerkanntes Transkriptionssystem nicht vorliegt, vor allem für Arabisch, erfolgte die Transkription in enger Anlehnung an das vom United States Board on Geographic Names angewandte System.

Alphabetische Ordnung Die alphabetische Ordnung der Namen entspricht der Reihenfolge der Buchstaben im englischen Alphabet. So werden z.B. das spanische *ll* und *ch* nicht als besondere Buchstaben behandelt. Ferner wurden diakritische Zeichen beim Alphabetisieren nicht berücksichtigt, das deutsche oder skandinavische *ä* oder *ö* als *a* oder *o* behandelt.

Physische Objekte können umgestellt erscheinen, da sie immer nach dem Eigennamen und nicht nach dem Gattungsbegriff eingeordnet wurden, z.B. "Gibraltar, Strait of ʉ". Ansonsten wurde jeder Eintrag, ob er aus einem Wort oder aus mehreren besteht, als eine einzige Einheit behandelt. So ist z.B. "Lakeland" nach "La Crosse," aber vor "La Salle" aufgeführt. Namen, die mit einem Artikel beginnen, wirden nicht umgestellt (Le Havre, Den Helder, Al-Qāhirah, As-Suways). Namen, die mit "Mc" beginnen, sind der Schreibweise "Mac" nach eingeordnet und Namen, die mit "St." und "Sainte" beginnen, entsprechend der Schreibweise "Saint".

Wo Namensgleichheit besteht, werden zunächst die Städte aufgeführt, dann politische Einheiten und schliesslich physische Objekte. Eintragungen, die vollkommen identisch sind (einschliesslich der weiter unten erläuterten Symbole), werden durch Hinzufügung der Abkürzung des offiziellen Ländernamens unterschieden und sind den Ländernamen nach alphabetisch geordnet. Die zahlreichen identischen Namen in Kanada, dem Vereinigten Königreich und den Vereinigten Staaten sind darüber hinaus noch durch Abkürzungen der obersten Verwaltungseinheit unterschieden. (Siehe Verzeichnis der Abkürzungen, Seite *I* · *30*—*I* · *32*.)

Abkürzungen und Grossschreibung Abkürzung und Schreibweise wurden für alle Sprachen vereinheitlicht. Nach jeder Abkürzung steht ein Punkt, auch wenn dies nicht der jeweiligen Gepflogenheit entspricht. Die Abkürzung "St." wird ausschliesslich für "Saint" gebraucht. "Sankt" und andere Formen dieses Begriffes werden ausgeschrieben.

Der erste Buchstabe eines Namens wird gross geschrieben, ausgenommen einige holländische Namen wie 's-Gravenhage. Die Grossschriebung der weiteren Worte eines zusammengesetzten Namens folgt im allgemeinen der landesüblichen Schreibweise.

Symbole Die im Register verwendeten Symbole veranschaulichen graphisch die zahlreichen Kategorien der benannten Objekte, z.B. ʌ = Berg (Everest, Mount ʌ). Eine Kurzgefasste Erläuterung der Symbole erscheint in jeder die fünf Sprachen des Atlas am Fusse jeder Doppelseite des Registers. Hochgestellte Ziffern hinter Symbolen im Register bezeichnen feinere Unterscheidungen, z.B. ʌ[1]= Vulkan (Fuji-san ʌ[1]). Eine vollständige Übersicht der Symbole und hochgestellten Ziffern findet sich auf Seite *I* · *30*.

El Índice contiene en una sola lista alfabética, alrededor de 160 000 nombres que aparecen en los mapas. Después de cada nombre está indicada la página o las páginas de referencia, en los cuales se encuentran los mismos, y las coordinadas de la latitud y la longitud del lugar del rasgo. Si una página contiene various mapas, letras minúsculas identifican el mapa correspondiente. Para mapas que ocupan dos páginas, la página de referencia siempre es la de la izquierda.

La mayoría de los nombres que figuran en el Índice, se efiere a los mapas en la escala más grande. Sin embargo, un nombre no se refiere en un mapa metropolitano si ya aparece en otro mapa, donde se muestra en un marco de mayor proporción. Los países, sierras y otros rasgos extensivos se refieren generalmente en el Índice en los mapas de escalas mayores en que se muestran completos.

El orden en que la información del Índice se presenta, aparece en un encabezamiento al centro de cada par de páginas, en inglés, alemán, español, francés y portugués.

Por ejemplo:

ESPAÑOL

Nombre	Página	Lat.°'	Long.°' W=Oeste

Los rasgos anotados en el Índice son de tres tipos: *el punto, el área y la extensión linear.* Para rasgos que indican *el punto* (como por ejemplo, las ciudades, picos de montañas, presas), las coordinadas de latitud y longitud indican la posición exacta del punto sobre el mapa. Respecto a *las áreas* (como países, sierras, etc.), las coordinadas indican usualmente el centro aproximado del rasgo particular. En cuanto a *los rasgos lineares* (ríos, canales, acueductos) las coordinadas indican los puntos terminales, por ejemplo, la boca de un río, o el punto en que un rasgo físico alcanza el margen del mapa.

Las Formas de los Nombres Los nombres que aparecen en el Índice, así como también en los mapas, se dan en general en el idioma local, y en tanto que es posible siguen la ortografía oficialmente aceptada. Incluímos también marcas diacríticas, excepto las que se usan para indicar tono, como en la lengua vietnamita. A causa de que la mayoría de los rasgos que se extienden más allá de las fronteras de un país no tienen un solo nombre oficial, éstos se denominan usualmente en inglés. Muchos nombres, en inglés, alemán, español, francés y portugués, que pueden no figurar en el mapa, se dan como referencia de una página a otra en el Índice. Todas las referencias que pasan a otras páginas se indican con el símbolo →. Un nombre que aparece en el mapa en forma abreviada, debido a la limitación de espacio, en el Índice figura en su forma completa, poniendo entre paréntesis angulares la parte omitida en el mapa, por ejemplo Acapulco [de Juárez].

"Trasliteración" Para los nombres escritos en los idiomas que no usan el alfabeto latino, el sistema oficial de trasliteración ha sido utilizado donde localmente existe. Así, los nombres de la Unión Soviética y de Bulgaria se trasliteran conforme a los sistemas aceptados por las academias de las ciencias de sus respectivos países. De la misma manera, la trasliteración de los nombres en chino continental siguen el sistema Pinyin que ha sido oficialmente adoptado en este país. Para idiomas sin ningún sistema localmente aceptado de trasliteración, particularmente para el árabe, éstos se trasliteran usando por lo general un sistema adoptado por el United States Board on Geographic Names.

Alfabetización Los nombres se han ordenado de acuerdo con el alfabeto inglés. Las letras del alfabeto en español *ll* y *ch* por ejemplo, no se han considerado letras separadas. Además, los signos diacríticos no se toman en cuenta en la alfabetización—en alemán o escadinavo letras *ä u ö* se tratan como *a u o*.

Los nombres de los rasgos físicos algunas veces se invierten, ya que se ordenan alfabéticamente según la parte propia y no genérica del nombre. Así por ejemplo, en el caso del Estrecho de Gibraltar aparece: Gibraltar, Strait of ʉ. Por lo demás, cada renglón, sea una palabra o una frase, se alfabetiza como una unidad. Por ejemplo, "Lakeland" aparece después de "La Crosse" y antes de "La Salle". Los nombres que comienzan con artículos (Le Havre, Den Helder, Al-Qāhirah, As-Suways) no están invertidos. Nombres que empiezan con "Mc" se tratan como si fueran del grupo de "Mac", y los que comienzan con "St." y "Sainte" se incluyen con "Saint".

En los casos de nombres idénticos, las poblaciones aparecen primero, las divisiones políticas después y finalmente los rasgos físicos. En caso de ser completamente idénticos (incluyendo los símbolos, discutidos más abajo) se distinguen por medio de abreviaciones de los nombres oficiales de los países a que pertenecen y son puestos en orden alfabético, de acuerdo al nombre de cada país. Hay muchos nombres duplicados en Canadá, el Reino Unido y los Estados Unidos de América, y éstos se distinguen además, por sus subdivisiones primarias. (Vease abajo, la lista de abreviaciones en las páginas *I • 30-I • 32*.)

Abreviaciones y Mayúsculas Las abreviaciones y el uso de las mayúsculas se han hecho uniformes para todos los idiomas. Se usa un punto al final de la abreviación, aun cuando en algunos casos no sea ésta la práctica local. La abreviación "St." se usa sólo para "Saint". Las otras formas del mismo término, como "Sankt", se escriben completas.

La mayúscula se usa al comienzo de todos los nombres a excepción de algunos holandeses, como 's-Gravenhage. Las palabras que no son iniciales, se dan con mayúscula o minúscula, según la práctica local.

Símbolos Los símbolos que aparecen en el Índice representan gráficamente las grandes categorías de los rasgos que se han ido nombrando, por ejemplo, ∧ para montaña (Everest, Mount ∧). Una clave abreviada para los símbolos aparece en los cinco idiomas del Atlas al pie de cada par de páginas del Índice. Los números que siguen más arriba del símbolo indican alguna diferencia más precisa, por ejemplo, $\wedge^1$ para un volcán (Fuji-san $\wedge^1$). Una lista completa de símbolos y números superiores aparece en la página *I • 30*.

L'index rassemble en une seule liste alphabétique, quelque 160 000 noms qui figurent sur les cartes. Chaque nom est suivi d'un renvoi à une ou plusieurs pages de cartes et de coordonnées géographiques qui permettent de localiser ce qu'il désigne. Si une page contient plusieurs cartes, une lettre minuscule permet d'identifier chaque carte. Pour les cartes en double page, la référence indiquée est toujours celle de la page de gauche.

En général, l'index renvoie aux cartes où l'information recherchée est reproduite à la plus grande échelle; cependant, les cartes de zones métropolitaines ne sont pas utilisées si le terme géographique figure sur une autre carte dans un contexte plus large. Pour les éléments de grande dimension comme les pays et les chaînes de montagnes, l'index renvoie généralement à la carte à grande échelle qui les représente en entier.

L'ordre des informations de l'index est rappelé en tête de chaque double page dans les cinq langues: anglais, allemand, espagnol, français et portugais.

Par exemple:

FRANÇAIS

Nom	Page	Lat.°′	Long.°′ W=Ouest

Les termes de l'index désignent des réalités géographiques de type *ponctuel, spatial* ou *linéaire*. Leur position est déterminée par les coordonnées géographiques du lieu quand les données sont de type *ponctuel* (villes, sommets, barrages, etc.), quand elles sont de type *spatial* (pays, chaînes de montagnes, etc.) par les coordonnées du centre approximatif de la zone considérée, et, quand elles sont du type *linéaire* (aqueducs, canaux, etc.) par les coordonnées soit d'un point terminal comme l'embouchure d'un cours d'eau, soit du point où les limites de la carte les interrompent.

Forme des Toponymes Les noms de l'index comme ceux des cartes sont généralement reproduits dans la langue locale et, dans la mesure du possible, selon leur orthographe officielle. Les signes diacritiques sont conservés, à l'exclusion de ceux qui servent à indiquer le ton, comme en vietnamien. La plupart des données géographiques qui s'étendent au-delà des frontières d'un pays sont nommées souvent en anglais, car elles n'ont pas de nom officiel unique. Beaucoup de noms anglais, allemands, espagnols, français et portugais, qui ne se trouvent pas sur les cartes, sont cités dans l'index sous forme de renvois. Tous les renvois sont signalés par le symbole (→). Un nom écrit sur la carte sous forme abrégée, par manque de place, figure en entier dans l'index; la partie omise est entre crochets, par exemple: Acapulco [de Juárez].

Transcription des Noms Pour les noms qui viennent de langues n'utilisant pas l'alphabet romain, le système local et officiel de transcription a été utilisé là où il existait. Ainsi, les noms russes et bulgares ont été transcrits selon les systèmes adoptés par les académies des sciences de ces pays. De même, pour la transcription des noms de la Chine continentale, on a employé le système Pinyin, officiellement adopté en Chine continentale. Pour les langues qui n'ont pas de système officiel de transcription en alphabet romain, notamment l'arabe, la transcription suit généralement de près le système adopté par le United States Board on Geographic Names (Comité américain pour les noms géographiques).

Orde Alphabétique Les noms sont classés dans l'ordre de l'alphabet anglais. Les *ll* et *ch* espagnols, par exemple, ne sont pas traités comme des lettres séparées. De plus, on ne tient pas compte des signes diacritiques: le *ä* et le *ö* allemand ou scandinave correspondent au *a* et *o* sans tréma.

Les noms des données physiques peuvent se trouver inversés car ils sont toujours classés suivant le nom propre. Exemple: "Gibraltar, Strait of ʉ". Par ailleurs, les noms composés d'un ou plusieurs mots sont considérés comme une seule entité. Exemple: "Lakeland" est inscrit après "La Crosse" et avant "La Salle". Les noms qui commencent par un article (Le Havre, Den Helder, Al-Qāhirah, As-Suways) ne sont pas inversés. Les noms qui commencent par "Mc" sont classés comme s'ils s'écrivaient "Mac" et les noms qui commencent par "St." ou "Sainte" sont classés comme s'ils s'écrivaient "Saint".

Dans le cas de noms identiques, les villes sont inscrites d'abord, puis les divisions politiques, et ensuite les données physiques. Les noms qui sont tout à fait identiques (y compris les symboles qui s'y rapportent) se distinguent par leur pays d'origine, noté en abrégé dans l'ordre alphabétique. Les noms que l'on rencontre plusieurs fois, au Canada, au Royaume-Uni et aux Etats-Unis se distinguent grâce à l'abréviation de la première subdivision administrative de ce pays (voir la liste des abréviations de la page *I • 30* à la page *I • 32*.)

Abréviations et Majuscules L'usage des abréviations a été standardisé pour toutes les langues. Un point suit chaque abréviation, même quand ce n'est pas l'usage dans certaines langues. L'abréviation "St." sert uniquement pour le mot "Saint". "Sankt" et les autres formes du mot "Saint" sont écrites en entier.

Tous les noms commencent par une majuscule, sauf quelques noms des Pays-Bas comme 's-Gravenhage. Certains noms prennent une majuscule, même s'ils ne se trouvent pas au début du terme; on a adopté, en général, l'orthographe locale.

Symboles Les symboles utilisés dans l'index donnent une représentation graphique des réalités géographiques mentionnées. Par exemple, ∧ pour une montagne (Everest, Mount ∧). Une explication abrégée des symboles dans les cinq langues de l'Atlas se trouve au bas de chaque double page de l'index. Les indices qui accompagnent certains symboles permettent une distinction plus précise. Par exemple, $\wedge^1$ pour volcan (Fujisan $\wedge^1$). Une liste complète des symboles et indices est donnée à la page *I • 30*.

O Índice contém, numa só lista alfabética, cerca de 160 000 nomes que figuram nos mapas. Segue-se a cada nome a referência a um ou mais mapas e a localização do acidente geográfico no mapa pelas respectivas coordenadas de latitude e longitude. A referência a mapas que ocupam duas páginas fica sempre na página da esquerda. A maior parte dos acidentes geográficos estão indexados no mapa em que aparecem em escala maior. No entanto, um acidente geográfico não é geralmente indexado num mapa de Área Metropolitana se também figura em outro mapa em que aparece em contexto mais amplo. Os países, cordilheiras e outros acidentes geográficos de maior extensão estão geralmente indexados no mapa em escala maior que os apresente em seu todo.

A ordem em que as informações são apresentadas no Índice figura no cabeçalho, a cada duas páginas, em inglês, alemão, espanhol, francês e PORTUGUÊS.

Por exemplo:

PORTUGUÊS

Nome	Página	Lat.°′	Long.°′ W=Oeste

Os acidentes indexados são de três tipos: *ponto, espacial* (área) e *linear* (extensão). Para acidentes que indicam *pontos* (como, por exemplo, cidades, picos de montanhas, represas), as coordenadas de latitude e longitude indicam a posição exata do ponto no mapa. No que se refere aos acidentes espaciais (como países, cordilheiras etc.), as coordenadas geralmente indicam o centro aproximado do acidente específico. Quanto aos *acidentes lineares* (rios, canais, aquedutos), as coordenadas localizam os pontos terminais, como, por exemplo, a foz de um rio, ou o ponto em que um acidente físico atinge a margem do mapa.

Formas dos nomes Os nomes que aparecem no Índice, assim como também nos mapas, são geralmente apresentados na língua local, e tanto quanto possível, seguem a ortografia oficial. Usam-se, também, os sinais diacríticos, exceto os que indicam tom, como na língua vietnamita. A maioria dos acidentes geográficos que se estendem além das fronteiras de um só país não possuem um nome oficial único; nesses casos, estão geralmente indicados em inglês. Muitos nomes em inglês, alemão, espanhol, português e francês podem não figurar nos mapas, mas aparecem no Índice como referências remissivas. Todas essas referências são indicadas pelo símbolo (→). Um nome que aparece no mapa em forma abreviada devido a limitações de espaço, figura no Índice em sua forma completa, com a parte omitida no mapa entre chaves (por exemplo, Acapulco [de Juárex]).

Transliteração Para os nomes escritos em línguas que não usam o alfabeto latino, foi utilizado o sistema oficial de transliteração, sempre que este existia. Assim, os nomes da União Soviética e da Bulgária foram transliterados de acordo com os sistemas adotados pelas academias de ciências desses países. Do mesmo modo, a transliteração dos nomes da China continental seguem o sistema Pinyin, que foi oficialmente adotado nesse país. Para as línguas que não possuem um sistema de transliteração adotado oficialmente, em especial o árabe, a transliteração geralmente segue de perto o sistema adotado pelo Conselho de Nomes Geográficos dos Estados Unidos (United States Board on Geographic Names).

Alfabetação Os nomes foram ordenados de acordo com o alfabeto inglês. Por exemplo, o espanhol *ll* e *ch* não foram considerados como letras separadas. Ademais, os sinais diacríticos não foram considerados na alfabetação. Por exemplo, em alemão ou escandinavo as letras *ä* ou *ö* foram tratradas como *a* ou *o*.

Os nomes dos acidentes físicos podem aparecer, às vezes, invertidos, já que foram sempre alfabetados pela parte específica e não genérica do nome, como, por exemplo, *Gibraltar, estreito de* ʉ. Por outro lado, cada entrada do Índice, quer constituída por uma só palavra ou mais de uma, foi alfabetada como uma unidade contínua. Por exemplo, "Lakeland" aparece depois de "La Grosse" e antes de "La Salle". Os nomes que começam por artigo (Le Havre, Den Helder, Al-Qāhirah, As-Suways) não são invertidos. Os nomes que começam por "Mc" são alfabetados como se fossem soletrados "Mac", e os que começam por "St." e "Sainte" como se fossem soletrados "Saint".

Nos casos de nomes idênticos, as cidades estão relacionadas em primeiro lugar; depois as divisões políticas e em seguida os acidentes físicos. As entradas completamente idênticas (inclusive símbolos, mencionados mais abaixo), distinguem-se pelas abreviaturas dos nomes oficiais dos países a que pertencem e são arrolados na ordem alfabética do nome do país. Os muitos nomes repetidos no Canadá, no Reino Unido e nos Estados Unidos, são ainda diferenciados pelas abreviaturas dos nomes das respectivas subdivisões primárias (Ver a lista de abreviaturas, das páginas *I • 30* a *I • 32*.)

Abreviações e uso de maiúsculas As abreviaturas e o estilo foram normalizados em todas as línguas. Usa-se um ponto depois de cada abreviatura, mesmo que não seja essa a prática local. A abreviatura "St." só é usada para "Saint". As outras formas do termo, tal como "Sankt", são escritas por extenso.

Todos os nomes são escritos com a inicial maiúscula exceto em alguns nomes holandeses, como 's-Gravenhage. O uso de maiúsculas em palavras não iniciais de um nome segue geralmente a prática local.

Símbolos Os símbolos que aparecem no Índice representam graficamente as grandes categorias dos acidentes indicados, por exemplo, ∧ para montanha (Everest, Mount ∧). Uma chave abreviada dos símbolos nas cinco línguas do Atlas figura no pé de cada par de páginas do Índice. Os números altos que acompanham certos símbolos do Índice indicam diferenças mais precisas, como, por exemplo, $\wedge^1$ para vulcão (Fuji-san $\wedge^1$). Uma lista completa de símbolos e números altos aparece à pág. *I • 30*.

Key to Index Symbols

The symbols below represent the categories into which the physical and cultural features are classified in the Index. Broad categories appear in **boldface** type. Symbols with superior numbers identify subcategories.

Schlüssel zu den Symbolen des Registers

Die folgenden Symbole veranschaulichen die Kategorien, nach denen physische und kulturgeographische Objekte im Register geordnet sind. Die Oberbegriffe sind in **Fettdruck** hervorgehoben. Symbole mit hochgestellten Nummern kennzeichnen Unterbegriffe.

Clave de los Símbolos del Índice

Los símbolos abajo representan las categorías dentro de las cuales están clasificados los rasgos físicos y culturales que están incluídos en el Índice. Las grandes categorías aparecen en **negrilla.** Los símbolos que tienen números en su parte superior identifican las subcategorías.

Signification des Symboles de l'Index

Les symboles ci-dessous représentent les catégories sous lesquelles les données physiques et culturelles sont classées dans l'index. Les symboles en caractères **gras** correspondent aux catégories principales. Ceux suivis d'un indice désignent les subdivisions d'une même catégorie.

Chave dos Símbolos do Índice

Os símbolos abaixo representam as categorias em que estão classificados os acidentes físicos e culturais no Índice. As grandes categorias aparecem em **negrito.** Os símbolos acompanhados de números altos identificam as subcategorias.

ENGLISH	DEUTSCH	ESPAÑOL	FRANÇAIS	PORTUGUÊS
Mountain	**Berg**	**Montaña**	**Montagne**	**Montanha**
^{1} Volcano	^{1} Vulkan	^{1} Volcán	^{1} Volcan	^{1} Vulcão
^{2} Hill	^{2} Hügel	^{2} Colina	^{2} Colline	^{2} Colina
Mountains	**Berge**	**Montañas**	**Montagnes**	**Montanhas**
^{1} Plateau	^{1} Hochebene	^{1} Meseta	^{1} Plateau	^{1} Planalto
^{2} Hills	^{2} Hügel	^{2} Colinas	^{2} Collines	^{2} Colinas
Pass	**Pass**	**Paso**	**Col**	**Passo**
Valley, Canyon	**Tal, Cañon**	**Valle, Cañón**	**Vallée, Canyon**	**Vale, Canhão**
Plain	**Ebene**	**Llano**	**Plaine**	**Planície**
^{1} Basin	^{1} Becken	^{1} Cuenca	^{1} Bassin	^{1} Bacia
^{2} Delta	^{2} Delta	^{2} Delta	^{2} Delta	^{2} Delta
Cape	**Kap**	**Cabo**	**Cap**	**Cabo**
^{1} Peninsula	^{1} Halbinsel	^{1} Península	^{1} Péninsule	^{1} Península
^{2} Spit, Sand Bar	^{2} Landzunge, Sandbarre	^{2} Lengua de Tierra, Bajo	^{2} Flèche, Banc de sable	^{2} Ponta de Terra, Banco de Areia
Island	**Insel**	**Isla**	**Île**	**Ilha**
^{1} Atoll	^{1} Atoll	^{1} Atolón	^{1} Atoll	^{1} Atol
^{2} Rock	^{2} Fels	^{2} Roca	^{2} Rocher	^{2} Rochedo
Islands	**Inseln**	**Islas**	**Îles**	**Ilhas**
^{1} Rocks	^{1} Felsen	^{1} Rocas	^{1} Rochers	^{1} Rochedos
Other Topographic Features	**Andere Topographische Objekte**	**Otros Elementos Topográficos**	**Autres données topographiques**	**Outros Acidentes Topográficos**
^{1} Continent	^{1} Erdteil	^{1} Continente	^{1} Continent	^{1} Continente
^{2} Coast, Beach	^{2} Küste, Strand	^{2} Costa, Playa	^{2} Côte, Plage	^{2} Costa, Praia
^{3} Isthmus	^{3} Landenge	^{3} Istmo	^{3} Isthme	^{3} Istmo
^{4} Cliff	^{4} Kliff	^{4} Risco	^{4} Falaise	^{4} Falésia
^{5} Cave, Caves	^{5} Höhle, Höhlen	^{5} Cueva, Cuevas	^{5} Caverne, Cavernes	^{5} Caverna, Cavernas
^{6} Crater	^{6} Krater	^{6} Cráter	^{6} Cratère	^{6} Cratera
^{7} Depression	^{7} Senke	^{7} Depresión	^{7} Dépression	^{7} Depressão
^{8} Dunes	^{8} Dünen	^{8} Dunas	^{8} Dunes	^{8} Dunas
^{9} Lava Flow	^{9} Lavastrom	^{9} Corriente de Lava	^{9} Coulée de lave	^{9} Corrente de Lava
River	**Fluss**	**Río**	**Rivière, Fleuve**	**Rio**
^{1} River Channel	^{1} Flussarm	^{1} Brazo de Río	^{1} Bras de rivière	^{1} Canal de Rio
Canal	**Kanal**	**Canal**	**Canal**	**Canal**
^{1} Aqueduct	^{1} Aquädukt	^{1} Acueducto	^{1} Aqueduc	^{1} Aqueduto
Waterfall, Rapids	**Wasserfall, Stromschnellen**	**Cascada, Rápidos**	**Chute d'eau, Rapides**	**Quedas d'água, Rápidos**
Strait	**Meeresstrasse**	**Estrecho**	**Détroit**	**Estreito**
Bay, Gulf	**Bucht, Golf**	**Bahía, Golfo**	**Baie, Golfe**	**Baía, Golfo**
^{1} Estuary	^{1} Trichtermündung	^{1} Estuario	^{1} Estuaire	^{1} Estuário
^{2} Fjord	^{2} Fjord	^{2} Fiordo	^{2} Fjord	^{2} Fiorde
^{3} Bight	^{3} Bucht	^{3} Bahía	^{3} Baie	^{3} Enseada
Lake, Lakes	**See, Seen**	**Lago, Lagos**	**Lac, Lacs**	**Lago, Lagos**
^{1} Reservoir	^{1} Stausee	^{1} Embalse	^{1} Réservoir, Retenue	^{1} Reservatório
Swamp	**Sumpf**	**Pantano**	**Marais**	**Pântano**
Ice Features, Glacier	**Eis- und Gletscherformen**	**Accidentes Glaciales, Glaciar**	**Formes glaciaires, Glacier**	**Acidentes Glaciares, Geleira**
Other Hydrographic Features	**Andere Hydrographische Objekte**	**Otros Elementos Hidrográficos**	**Autres données hydrographiques**	**Outros Acidentes Hidrográficos**
^{1} Ocean	^{1} Ozean	^{1} Océano	^{1} Océan	^{1} Oceano
^{2} Sea	^{2} Meer	^{2} Mar	^{2} Mer	^{2} Mar

ENGLISH	DEUTSCH	ESPAÑOL	FRANÇAIS	PORTUGUÊS
Other Hydrographic Features	**Andere Hydrographische Objekte**	**Otros Elementos Hidrográficos**	**Autres données hydrographiques**	**Outros Acidentes Hidrográficos**
^{3} Anchorage	^{3} Ankerplatz	^{3} Ancladero	^{3} Ancrage	^{3} Ancoradouro
^{4} Oasis, Well, Spring	^{4} Oase, Brunnen, Quelle	^{4} Oasis, Pozo, Manantial	^{4} Oasis, Puits, Source	^{4} Oásis, Poço, Fonte, Manancial
Submarine Features	**Untermeerische Objekte**	**Accidentes Submarinos**	**Formes de relief sous-marin**	**Acidentes Submarinos**
^{1} Depression	^{1} Senke	^{1} Depresión	^{1} Dépression	^{1} Depressão
^{2} Reef, Shoal	^{2} Riff, Untiefe	^{2} Arrecife, Bajo	^{2} Récif, Haut-fond	^{2} Recife, Baixio
^{3} Mountain, Mountains	^{3} Berg, Berge	^{3} Montaña, Montañas	^{3} Montagne, Montagnes	^{3} Montanha, Montanhas
^{4} Slope, Shelf	^{4} Abhang, Schelf	^{4} Talud, Plataforma	^{4} Talus, Plateau continental	^{4} Talude, Plataforma
Political Unit	**Politische Einheit**	**Unidad Política**	**Entité politique**	**Unidade Política**
^{1} Independent Nation	^{1} Unabhängiger Staat	^{1} Nación Independiente	^{1} État indépendant	^{1} País Independente
^{2} Dependency	^{2} Abhängiges Gebiet	^{2} Dependencia	^{2} Dépendance	^{2} Dependência
^{3} State, Canton, Republic	^{3} Land, Kanton, Republik	^{3} Estado, Cantón, República	^{3} État, Canton, République	^{3} Estado, Cantão, República
^{4} Province, Region, Oblast	^{4} Provinz, Landschaft, Oblast	^{4} Provincia, Región, Oblast	^{4} Province, Région, Oblast	^{4} Província, Região, Oblast
^{5} Department, District, Prefecture	^{5} Département, Distrikt, Präfektur	^{5} Departamento, Distrito, Prefectura	^{5} Département, District, Préfecture	^{5} Departamento, Distrito, Prefeitura
^{6} County	^{6} Grafschaft	^{6} Condado	^{6} Comté	^{6} Condado
^{7} City, Municipality	^{7} Stadt, Stadtkreis	^{7} Ciudad, Municipalidad	^{7} Ville, Municipalité	^{7} Cidade, Municipalidade
^{8} Miscellaneous	^{8} Verschiedenes	^{8} Misceláneo	^{8} Divers	^{8} Diversos
^{9} Historical	^{9} Historisch	^{9} Histórico	^{9} Historique	^{9} Sítio Histórico
Cultural Institution	**Kulturelle Institution**	**Institución Cultural**	**Institution culturelle**	**Instituição Cultural**
^{1} Religious Institution	^{1} Religiöse Institution	^{1} Institución Religiosa	^{1} Institution religieuse	^{1} Instituição Religiosa
^{2} Educational Institution	^{2} Erziehungs-institution	^{2} Institución Educacional	^{2} Établissement d'éducation	^{2} Estabelecimento de Ensino
^{3} Scientific, Industrial Facility	^{3} Wissenschaftliche, Industrielle Anlage	^{3} Institución Científica o Industrial	^{3} Établissement scientifique ou industriel	^{3} Estabelecimento Científico ou Industrial
Historical Site	**Historische Stätte**	**Sitio Histórico**	**Site historique**	**Sítio Histórico**
Recreational Site	**Erholungs- und Ferienort**	**Sitio de Recreo**	**Centre de loisirs**	**Área de Lazer**
Airport	**Flughafen**	**Aeropuerto**	**Aéroport**	**Aeroporto**
Military Installation	**Militäranlage**	**Instalación Militar**	**Installation militaire**	**Instalação Militar**
Miscellaneous	**Verschiedenes**	**Misceláneo**	**Divers**	**Diversos**
^{1} Region	^{1} Region	^{1} Región	^{1} Région	^{1} Região
^{2} Desert	^{2} Wüste	^{2} Desierto	^{2} Désert	^{2} Deserto
^{3} Forest, Moor	^{3} Wald, Moor	^{3} Bosque, Páramo	^{3} Forêt, Lande	^{3} Floresta, Pântano
^{4} Reserve, Reservation	^{4} Reservat	^{4} Reserva, Reservación	^{4} Réserve	^{4} Reserva
^{5} Transportation	^{5} Verkehr	^{5} Transporte	^{5} Transport	^{5} Transporte
^{6} Dam	^{6} Damm	^{6} Presa	^{6} Barrage	^{6} Represa
^{7} Mine, Quarry	^{7} Bergwerk, Steinbruch	^{7} Mina, Cantera	^{7} Mine, Carrière	^{7} Mina, Pedreira
^{8} Neighborhood	^{8} Nachbarschaft	^{8} Barrio	^{8} Quartier	^{8} Arredores, Vizinhança
^{9} Shopping Center	^{9} Einkaufszentrum	^{9} Mercado	^{9} Centre commercial	^{9} Shopping Center

List of Abbreviations / Verzeichnis der Abkürzungen
Lista de Abreviaciones / Liste des Abréviations / Lista de Abreviaturas

	LOCAL NAME	ENGLISH	DEUTSCH	ESPAÑOL	FRANÇAIS	PORTUGUÊS
Afg.	Afghānestān	Afghanistan	Afghanistan	Afganistán	Afghanistan	Afeganistão
Afr.	—	Africa	Afrika	Africa	Afrique	África
Ala., U.S.	Alabama	Alabama	Alabama	Alabama	Alabama	Alabama
Alaska, U.S.	Alaska	Alaska	Alaska	Alaska	Alaska	Alasca
Alg.	Algérie	Algeria	Algerien	Argelia	Algérie	Argélia
Alta., Can.	Alberta	Alberta	Alberta	Alberta	Alberta	Alberta
Am. Sam.	American Samoa	American Samoa	Amerikanisch-Samoa	Samoa Americana	Samoa américaines	Samoa Americana
And.	Andorra	Andorra	Andorra	Andorra	Andorre	Andorra
Ang.	Angola	Angola	Angola	Angola	Angola	Angola
Anguilla	Anguilla	Anguilla	Anguilla	Anguilla	Anguilla	Anguilla
Ant.	—	Antarctica	Antarktis	Antártida	Antarctique	Antártida
Antig.	Antigua	Antigua	Antigua	Antigua	Antigua	Antígua
Arc. O.	—	Arctic Ocean	Nördliches Eismeer	Océano Artico	Océan Glacial arctique	Ártico, Oceano
Arg.	Argentina	Argentina	Argentinien	Argentina	Argentine	Argentina
Ariz., U.S.	Arizona	Arizona	Arizona	Arizona	Arizona	Arizona
Ark., U.S.	Arkansas	Arkansas	Arkansas	Arkansas	Arkansas	Arkansas
Ar. Sa.	Al-'Arabīyah as-Sa'ūdīyah	Saudi Arabia	Saudi-Arabien	Arabia Saudita	Arabie Saoudite	Arábia Saudita
As.	—	Asia	Asien	Asia	Asie	Ásia
Atl. O.	—	Atlantic Ocean	Atlantischer Ozean	Océano Atlántico	Océan Atlantique	Atlântico, Oceano
Austl.	Australia	Australia	Australien	Australia	Australie	Austrália
Ba.	Bahamas	Bahamas	Bahama-Inseln	Bahamas	Bahama	Bahamas
Bahr.	Al-Baḥrayn	Bahrain	Bahrain	Bahrein	Bahreïn	Bahrein
Barb.	Barbados	Barbados	Barbados	Barbados	Barbade	Barbados
B.A.T.	British Antarctic Territory	British Antarctic Territory	Britisches Antarktis-Territorium	Territorio Antártico Británico	Terre antarctique britannique	Território Antártico Britânico
B.C., Can.	British Columbia	British Columbia	Britisch Kolumbien	Columbia Británica	Colombie-Britannique	Colúmbia Britânica
Bdi.	Burundi	Burundi	Burundi	Burundi	Burundi	Burundi
Bel.	Belgique België	Belgium	Belgien	Bélgica	Belgique	Bélgica
Belize	Belize	Belize	Belize	Belize	Belize	Belize

	LOCAL NAME	ENGLISH	DEUTSCH	ESPAÑOL	FRANÇAIS	PORTUGUÊS
Benin	Benin	Benin	Benin	Benin	Benin	Benin
Ber.	Bermuda	Bermuda	Bermuda	Bermudas	Bermudes	Bermudas
Ber. S.	—	Bering Sea	Beringmeer	Mar de Bering	Mer de Bering	Bering, Mar de
Bhārat	Bhārat	India	Indien	India	Inde	Índia
B.I.O.T.	British Indian Ocean Territory	British Indian Ocean Territory	Britisches Indischer Ozean-Territorium	Territorio Británico del Océano Indico	Territoire britannique de l'océan Indien	Território Britânico do Oceano Índico
Blg.	Bâlgarija	Bulgaria	Bulgarien	Bulgaria	Bulgarie	Bulgária
Bngl.	Bangladesh	Bangladesh	Bangladesch	Bangladesh	Bangla Desh	Bangladesh
Bol.	Bolivia	Bolivia	Bolivien	Bolivia	Bolivie	Bolívia
Bots.	Botswana	Botswana	Botswana	Botswana	Botswana	Botsuana
Bra.	Brasil	Brazil	Brasilien	Brasil	Brésil	Brasil
B.R.D.	Bundesrepublik Deutschland	Federal Republic of Germany	Bundesrepublik Deutschland	República Federal de Alemania	République fédérale d' Allemagne	Alemanha, República Federal da
Bru.	Brunei	Brunei	Brunei	Brunei	Brunéi	Brunei
Br. Vir. Is.	British Virgin Islands	British Virgin Islands	Britischen Jungferninseln	Islas Vírgenes Británicas	Îles Vierges britanniques	Virgens Britânicas, Ilhas
Calif., U.S.	California	California	Kalifornien	California	Californie	Califórnia
Cam.	Cameroun	Cameroon	Kamerun	Camerún	Cameroun	Camarão
Can.	Canada	Canada	Kanada	Canadá	Canada	Canadá
Can./End.	Canton and Enderbury	Canton and Enderbury	Canton und Enderbury	Islas Canton y Enderbury	Îles Canton et Enderbury	Cantão e Enderbury
Carib. S.	—	Caribbean Sea	Karibisches Meer	Mar Caribe	Mer des Caraïbes	Caribe, Mar do
Cay. Is.	Cayman Islands	Cayman Islands	Kaiman-Inseln	Islas Caimán	Îles Caïmanes	Cayman, Ilhas
Centraf.	République centrafricaine	Central African Republic	Zentralafrika-nische-Republik	República Centroafricana	République centrafricaine	Centro-Africana, República
Česko.	Československo	Czechoslovakia	Tschechoslo-wakei	Checoslovaquia	Tchécoslovaquie	Tchecoslováquia
Chile	Chile	Chile	Chile	Chile	Chili	Chile
Christ. I.	Christmas Island	Christmas Island	Weihnachtsinsel	Isla Christmas	Île Christmas	Christmas, Ilha
C.Iv.	Côte d'Ivoire	Ivory Coast	Elfenbeinküste	Costa de Marfil	Côte d'Ivoire	Costa do Marfim
C.M.I.K.	Chosŏn Minjujuŭi In'min Konghwaguk	North Korea	Nordkorea	Corea del Norte	Corée du Nord	Coréia do Norte

	LOCAL NAME	ENGLISH	DEUTSCH	ESPAÑOL	FRANÇAIS	PORTUGUÊS
Cocos Is.	Cocos (Keeling) Islands	Cocos (Keeling) Islands	Kokos-Inseln	Islas Cocos (Keeling)	Îles des Cocos (Keeling)	Cocos (Keeling), Ilhas
Col.	Colombia	Colombia	Kolumbien	Colombia	Colombie	Colômbia
Colo., U.S.	Colorado	Colorado	Colorado	Colorado	Colorado	Colorado
Comores	Comores	Comoros	Komoren	Comoras	Comores	Comores
Congo	Congo	Congo	Kongo	Congo	Congo	Congo
Conn., U.S.	Connecticut	Connecticut	Connecticut	Connecticut	Connecticut	Connecticut
Cook Is.	Cook Islands	Cook Islands	Cook-Inseln	Islas Cook	Îles Cook	Cook, Ilhas
C.R.	Costa Rica	Costa Rica	Costa Rica	Costa Rica	Costa Rica	Costa Rica
Cuba	Cuba	Cuba	Kuba	Cuba	Cuba	Cuba
C.V.	Cabo Verde	Cape Verde	Kap Verde	Cabo Verde	Cap-Vert	Cabo Verde
C.Z.	Canal Zone	Canal Zone	Panama-kanal-Zone	Zona del Canal de Panamá	Zone du Canal de Panama	Zona do Canal
Dan.	Danmark	Denmark	Dänemark	Dinamarca	Danemark	Dinamarca
D.C., U.S.	District of Columbia	District of Columbia	District of Columbia	District of Columbia	District of Columbia	Distrito de Columbia
D.D.R.	Deutsche Demokratische Republik	German Democratic Republic	Deutsche Demokratische Republik	República Democrática Alemana	Republique démocratique allemande	Alemã, República Democrática
Del., U.S.	Delaware	Delaware	Delaware	Delaware	Delaware	Delaware
Den.	Danmark	Denmark	Dänemark	Dinamarca	Danemark	Dinamarca
Dji.	Djibouti	Djibouti	Djibouti	Djibouti	Djibouti	Djibouti
Dom.	Dominica	Dominica	Dominica	Dominica	Dominique	Dominica
D.Y.	Druk-Yul	Bhutan	Bhutan	Bhután	Bhoutan	Butã
Ec.	Ecuador	Ecuador	Ecuador	Ecuador	Équateur	Equador
Eire	Eire	Ireland	Irland	Irlanda	Irlande	Irlanda
Ellás	Ellás	Greece	Griechenland	Grecia	Grèce	Grécia
El Sal.	El Salvador	El Salvador	El Salvador	El Salvador	El Salvador	El Salvador
Eng., U.K.	England	England	England	Inglaterra	Angleterre	Inglaterra
Esp.	España	Spain	Spanien	España	Espagne	Espanha
Eur.	—	Europe	Europa	Europa	Europe	Europa
Falk. Is.	Falkland Islands	Falkland Islands (Islas Malvinas)	Falkland-Inseln	Islas Malvinas	Îles Falkland	Falkland (Malvinas), Ilhas
Fiji	Fiji	Fiji	Fidschi	Fiji	Fidji	Fiji (Fidji)
Fla., U.S.	Florida	Florida	Florida	Florida	Floride	Flórida
Før.	Føroyar	Faeroe Islands	Färöer	Islas Feroe	Îles Féroé	Faeroe, Ilhas
Fr.	France	France	Frankreich	Francia	France	França
Ga., U.S.	Georgia	Georgia	Georgia	Georgia	Georgie	Geórgia
Gabon	Gabon	Gabon	Gabun	Gabón	Gabon	Gabão
Gam.	Gambia	Gambia	Gambia	Gambia	Gambie	Gâmbia
Gaza	—	Gaza Strip	Ghaza	Área de Gaza	Zone de Gaza	Gaza
Ghana	Ghana	Ghana	Ghana	Ghana	Ghana	Gana
Gib.	Gibraltar	Gibraltar	Gibraltar	Gibraltar	Gibraltar	Gibraltar
Gren.	Grenada	Grenada	Grenada	Granada	Grenade	Grenada
Grn.	Grønland	Greenland	Grönland	Groenlandia	Groenland	Groenlândia
Guad.	Guadeloupe	Guadeloupe	Guadeloupe	Guadalupe	Guadeloupe	Guadalupe
Guam	Guam	Guam	Guam	Guam	Guam	Guam
Guat.	Guatemala	Guatemala	Guatemala	Guatemala	Guatemala	Guatemala
Guer.	Guernsey	Guernsey	Guernsey	Guernesey	Guernesey	Guernsey
Gui.-B	Guinea-Bissau	Guinea-Bissau	Guina-Bissau	Guinea-Bissau	Guinée-Bissau	Guiné-Bissau
Gui. Ecu.	Guinea Ecuatorial	Equatorial Guinea	Äquatorial-Guinea	Guinea Ecuatorial	Guinée équatoriale	Guiné Equatorial
Guinée	Guinée	Guinea	Guinea	Guinea	Guinée	Guiné
Guy.	Guyana	Guyana	Guayana	Guyana	Guyane	Guiana
Guy. fr.	Guyane française	French Guiana	Französisch-Guayana	Guayana Francesa	Guyane française	Guiana Francesa
Haï.	Haïti	Haiti	Haiti	Haití	Haïti	Haiti
Haw., U.S.	Hawaii	Hawaii	Hawaii	Hawaii	Hawaii	Havaí
H.K.	Hong Kong	Hong Kong	Hongkong	Hong Kong	Hong-kong	Hong Kong
Hond.	Honduras	Honduras	Honduras	Honduras	Honduras	Honduras
H. Vol.	Haute-Volta	Upper Volta	Obervolta	Alto Volta	Haute-Volta	Alto Volta
Idaho, U.S.	Idaho	Idaho	Idaho	Idaho	Idaho	Idaho
I.I.A.	Ittihād al-Imārāt al-'Arabīyah	United Arab Emirates	Vereinigte Arabische Emirate	Emiratos Arabes Unidos	Union des Émirats Arabes	Emirados Árabes Unidos
Ill., U.S.	Illinois	Illinois	Illinois	Illinois	Illinois	Illinois
Ind., U.S.	Indiana	Indiana	Indiana	Indiana	Indiana	Indiana
Ind. O.	—	Indian Ocean	Indischer Ozean	Océano Índico	Océan Indien	Índico, Oceano
Indon.	Indonesia	Indonesia	Indonesien	Indonésia	Indonésie	Indonésia
I. of Man	Isle of Man	Isle of Man	Insel Man	Isla de Man	Île de Man	Man, Ilha de
Iowa, U.S.	Iowa	Iowa	Iowa	Iowa	Iowa	Iowa
Īrān	Īrān	Iran	Iran	Irán	Iran	Irã
'Irāq	Al-'Irāq	Iraq	Irak	Irak	Irak	Iraque
Ísland	Ísland	Iceland	Island	Islandia	Islande	Islândia
It.	Italia	Italy	Italien	Italia	Italie	Itália
Jam.	Jamaica	Jamaica	Jamaika	Jamaica	Jamaïque	Jamaica
Jersey	Jersey	Jersey	Jersey	Jersey	Jersey	Jersey
Jugo.	Jugoslavija	Yugoslavia	Jugoslawien	Yugoslavia	Yougoslavie	Iugoslávia
Kam.	Kâmpŭchea	Cambodia	Kambodscha	Camboya	Cambodge	Camboja
Kans., U.S.	Kansas	Kansas	Kansas	Kansas	Kansas	Kansas
Kenya	Kenya	Kenya	Kenia	Kenia	Kenya	Quênia
Kípros	Kípros Kıbrıs	Cyprus	Zypern	Chipre	Chypre	Chipre
Kiribati	Kiribati	Kiribati	Kiribati	Kiribati	Kiribati	Kiribati
Kuwayt	Al-Kuwayt	Kuwait	Kuwait	Kuwait	Koweït	Kuwait
Ky., U.S.	Kentucky	Kentucky	Kentucky	Kentucky	Kentucky	Kentucky
La., U.S.	Louisiana	Louisiana	Louisiana	Luisiana	Louisiane	Louisiana
Lao	Lao	Laos	Laos	Laos	Laos	Lao
Leso.	Lesotho	Lesotho	Lesotho	Lesotho	Lesotho	Lesoto
Liber.	Liberia	Liberia	Liberia	Liberia	Libéria	Libéria
Lībiyā	Lībiyā	Libya	Libyen	Libia	Libye	Líbia
Liech.	Liechtenstein	Liechtenstein	Liechtenstein	Liechtenstein	Liechtenstein	Liechtenstein
Lubnān	Al-Lubnān	Lebanon	Libanon	Líbano	Liban	Líbano
Lux.	Luxembourg	Luxembourg	Luxemburg	Luxemburgo	Luxembourg	Luxemburgo
Macau	Macau	Macau	Macau	Macao	Macao	Macau
Madag.	Madagasikara	Madagascar	Madagaskar	Madagascar	Madagascar	Madagascar
Magreb	Al-Magreb	Morocco	Marokko	Marruecos	Maroc	Marrocos
Magy.	Magyarország	Hungary	Ungarn	Hungría	Hongrie	Hungria
Maine, U.S.	Maine	Maine	Maine	Maine	Maine	Maine
Malawi	Malawi	Malawi	Malawi	Malawi	Malawi	Malaui
Malay.	Malaysia	Malaysia	Malaysia	Malasia	Malaisie	Malásia
Mald.	Maldives	Maldives	Malediven	Maldivas	Maldives	Maldivas
Mali	Mali	Mali	Mali	Malí	Mali	Mali
Malta	Malta	Malta	Malta	Malta	Malte	Malta
Man., Can.	Manitoba	Manitoba	Manitoba	Manitoba	Manitoba	Manitoba
Mart.	Martinique	Martinique	Martinique	Martinica	Martinique	Martinica
Mass., U.S.	Massachusetts	Massachusetts	Massachusetts	Massachusetts	Massachusetts	Massachusetts
Maur.	Mauritanie	Mauritania	Mauretanien	Mauritania	Mauritanie	Mauritânia
Maus.	Mauritius	Mauritius	Mauritius	Mauricio	Maurice	Maurício
Mayotte	Mayotte	Mayotte	Mayotte	Mayotte	Mayotte	Mayotte
Md., U.S.	Maryland	Maryland	Maryland	Maryland	Maryland	Maryland
Medit. S.	—	Mediterranean Sea	Mittelmeer	Mar Mediterráneo	Méditerranée, Mer	Mediterrâneo, Mar
Méx.	México	Mexico	Mexiko	México	Mexique	México
Mich., U.S.	Michigan	Michigan	Michigan	Michigan	Michigan	Michigan
Mid. Is.	Midway Islands	Midway Islands	Midway-Inseln	Islas Midway	Îles Midway	Midway, Ilhas
Minn., U.S.	Minnesota	Minnesota	Minnesota	Minnesota	Minnesota	Minnesota
Miṣr	Miṣr	Egypt	Ägypten	Egipto	Égypte	Egito
Miss., U.S.	Mississippi	Mississippi	Mississippi	Misisipi	Mississippi	Mississippi
Mo., U.S.	Missouri	Missouri	Missouri	Misuri	Missouri	Missouri
Moç.	Moçambique	Mozambique	Mosambik	Mozambique	Mozambique	Moçambique
Monaco	Monaco	Monaco	Monaco	Mónaco	Monaco	Mônaco
Mong.	Mongol Ard Uls	Mongolia	Mongolei	Mongolia	Mongolie	Mongólia
Mont., U.S.	Montana	Montana	Montana	Montana	Montana	Montana
Monts.	Montserrat	Montserrat	Montserrat	Montserrat	Montserrat	Montserrat
Mya.	Myanma	Burma	Birma	Birmania	Birmanie	Birmânia
N.A.	—	North America	Nordamerika	América del Norte	Amérique du Nord	América do Norte
Namibia	Namibia	Namibia	Namibia	Namibia	Namibie	Namíbia
Nauru	Nauru	Nauru	Nauru	Nauru	Nauru	Nauru

	LOCAL NAME	ENGLISH	DEUTSCH	ESPAÑOL	FRANÇAIS	PORTUGUÊS
N.B., Can.	New Brunswick	New Brunswick	Neubraun-schweig	Nueva Brunswick	Nouveau-Brunswick	Nova Brunswick
N.C., U.S.	North Carolina	North Carolina	Nord Karolina	Carolina del Norte	Caroline du Nord	Carolina do Norte
N. Cal.	Nouvelle-Calédonie	New Caledonia	Neukaledonien	Nueva Caledonia	Nouvelle-Calédonie	Nova Caledônia
N. Dak., U.S.	North Dakota	North Dakota	Nord Dakota	Dakota del Norte	Dakota du Nord	Dakota do Norte
Nebr., U.S.	Nebraska	Nebraska	Nebraska	Nebraska	Nebraska	Nebraska
Ned.	Nederland	Netherlands	Niederlande	Países Bajos	Pays-Bas	Países Baixos
Ned. Ant.	Nederlandse Antillen	Netherlands Antilles	Niederländische Antillen	Antillas Neerlandesas	Antilles néerlandaises	Antilhas Holandesas
Nepāl	Nepāl	Nepal	Nepal	Nepal	Népal	Nepal
Nev., U.S.	Nevada	Nevada	Nevada	Nevada	Nevada	Nevada
Newf., Can.	Newfoundland	Newfoundland	Neufundland	Terranova	Terre-Neuve	Terra Nova
N.H., U.S.	New Hampshire	New Hampshire	New Hampshire	Nuevo Hampshire	New Hampshire	Nova Hampshire
N. Heb.	New Hebrides Nouvelles-Hébrides	New Hebrides	Neuen Hebriden	Nuevas Hébridas	Nouvelles-Hébrides	Novas Hébridas
Nic.	Nicaragua	Nicaragua	Nicaragua	Nicaragua	Nicaragua	Nicarágua
Nig.	Nigeria	Nigeria	Nigeria	Nigeria	Nigéria	Nigéria
Niger	Niger	Niger	Niger	Niger	Niger	Níger
Nihon	Nihon	Japan	Japan	Japón	Japon	Japão
N. Ire., U.K.	Northern Ireland	Northern Ireland	Nord Irland	Irlanda del Norte	Irlande du Nord	Irlanda do Norte
Niue	Niue	Niue	Niue	Niue	Niue	Niue
N.J., U.S.	New Jersey	New Jersey	New Jersey	Nueva Jersey	New Jersey	Nova Jersey
N. Mex., U.S.	New Mexico	New Mexico	New Mexico	Nueva Mexico	Nouveau Mexique	Nova México
Nor.	Norge	Norway	Norwegen	Noruega	Norvège	Noruega
Norf. I.	Norfolk Island	Norfolk Island	Norfolk-Insel	Islas Norfolk	Îles Norfolk	Norfolk, Ilha
N.S., Can.	Nova Scotia	Nova Scotia	Neu Schottland	Nueva Escocia	Nouvelle-Écosse	Nova Scotia
N.W. Ter., Can.	Northwest Territories	Northwest Territories	Nord-West Territorien	Territorios del Noroeste	Territoires du Nord-Ouest	Territórios do Noroeste
N.Y., U.S.	New York	New York	New York	Nueva York	New York	Nova York
N.Z.	New Zealand	New Zealand	Neuseeland	Nueva Zelanda	Nouvelle-Zélande	Nova Zelândia
Oc.	—	Oceania	Ozeanien	Oceanía	Océanie	Oceania
Ohio, U.S.	Ohio	Ohio	Ohio	Ohio	Ohio	Ohio
Okla., U.S.	Oklahoma	Oklahoma	Oklahoma	Oklahoma	Oklahoma	Oklahoma
Ont., Can.	Ontario	Ontario	Ontario	Ontario	Ontario	Ontário
Oreg., U.S.	Oregon	Oregon	Oregon	Oregón	Oregon	Oregon
Öst.	Österreich	Austria	Österreich	Austria	Autriche	Áustria
Pa., U.S.	Pennsylvania	Pennsylvania	Pennsylvanien	Pensilvania	Pennsylvanie	Pennsylvania
Pac. O.	—	Pacific Ocean	Pazifischer Ozean	Océano Pacífico	Océan Pacifique	Pacífico, Oceano
Pāk.	Pākistān	Pakistan	Pakistan	Paquistán	Pakistan	Paquistão
Pan.	Panamá	Panama	Panama	Panamá	Panama	Panamá
Pap. N. Gui.	Papua New Guinea	Papua New Guinea	Papua Neuguinea	Papua Nueva Guinea	Papua Nouvelle-Guinée	Papua-Nova Guiné
Para.	Paraguay	Paraguay	Paraguay	Paraguay	Paraguay	Paraguai
P.E.I., Can.	Prince Edward Island	Prince Edward Island	Prinz Edward-Insel	Isla Príncipe Eduardo	Île-du-Prince-Édouard	Príncipe Eduardo, Ilha do
Perú	Perú	Peru	Peru	Perú	Pérou	Peru
Pil.	Pilipinas	Philippines	Philippinen	Filipinas	Philippines	Filipinas
Pit.	Pitcairn	Pitcairn	Pitcairn	Pitcairn	Pitcairn	Pitcairn
P.I.T.T.	Pacific Islands Trust Territory	Pacific Islands Trust Territory	Treuhandgebiet Pazifische Inseln	Territorio Fidei-cometido de las Islas Pacificas	Îles du Pacifique (Territoire sous tutelle)	Pacífico, Ilhas do (Território sob Tutela)
Pol.	Polska	Poland	Polen	Polonia	Pologne	Polônia
Poly. fr.	Polynésie française	French Polynesia	Französisch-Polynesien	Polinesia Francesa	Polynésie française	Polinésia Francesa
Port.	Portugal	Portugal	Portugal	Portugal	Portugal	Portugal
P.R.	Puerto Rico	Puerto Rico	Puerto Rico	Puerto Rico	Porto Rico	Porto Rico
P.S.N.Á.	Plazas de Soberanía en el Norte de Africa	Spanish North Africa	Spanisch-Nordafrika	Plazas de Soberanía en el Norte de África	Afrique du Nord espagnole	África do Norte Espanhola
Qaṭar	Qaṭar	Qatar	Katar	Qatar	Qatar	Qatar
Que., Can.	Québec	Quebec	Quebec	Quebec	Québec	Québec
Rep. Dom.	República Dominicana	Dominican Republic	Dominikanische Republik	República Dominicana	République Dominicaine	Dominicana, República
Réu.	Réunion	Reunion	Réunion	Reunión	Réunion	Reunião
Rh.	Rhodesia	Rhodesia	Rhodesien	Rhodesia	Rhodésie	Rodésia
R.I., U.S.	Rhode Island	Rhode Island	Rhode Island	Rhode Island	Rhode Island	Rhode Island
Rom.	România	Romania	Rumänien	Rumania	Roumanie	Romênia
Rw.	Rwanda	Rwanda	Ruanda	Rwanda	Rwanda	Ruanda
S.A.	—	South America	Südamerika	América del Sur	Amérique du Sud	América do Sul
S. Afr.	South Africa Suid-Afrika	South Africa	Südafrika	Sudáfrica	Afrique du Sud	África do Sul
Sah. Occ.	Sahara Occidentale	Western Sahara	Westliche Sahara	Sahara Occidental	Sahara Occidentale	Saara Ocidental
Sask., Can.	Saskatchewan	Saskatchewan	Saskatchewan	Saskatchewan	Saskatchewan	Saskatchewan
S.C., U.S.	South Carolina	South Carolina	Süd Karolina	Carolina del Sur	Caroline du Sud	Carolina do Sul
S. Ch. S.	—	South China Sea	Südchinesisches Meer	Mar de China Meridional	Mer de Chine Méridionale	China do Sul, Mar da
Schw.	Schweiz Suisse Svizzera	Switzerland	Schweiz	Suiza	Suisse	Suíça
Scot., U.K.	Scotland	Scotland	Schottland	Escocia	Écosse	Escócia
S., Dak., U.S.	South Dakota	South Dakota	Süd Dakota	Dakota del Sur	Dakota du Sud	Dakota do Sul
Sén.	Sénégal	Senegal	Senegal	Senegal	Sénégal	Senegal
Sey.	Seychelles	Seychelles	Seychellen	Seychelles	Seychelles	Seychelles
Shq.	Shqipëri	Albania	Albanien	Albania	Albanie	Albânia
Sing.	Singapore	Singapore	Singapur	Singapur	Singapour	Cingapura
S.L.	Sierra Leone	Sierra Leone	Sierra Leone	Sierra Leone	Sierra Leone	Serra Leoa
S. Lan.	Sri Lanka	Sri Lanka	Sri Lanka	Sri Lanka	Sri Lanka	Sri Lanka
S. Mar.	San Marino	San Marino	San Marino	San Marino	Saint-Marin	San Marino
Sol. Is.	Solomon Islands	Solomon Islands	Salomon-Inseln	Islas Salomón	Îles Salomon	Salomão, Ilhas
Som.	Somaliya	Somalia	Somaliland	Somalia	Somalie	Somália
Sp.	España	Spain	Spanien	España	Espagne	Espanha
S.S.R.	Sovetskaja Socialističeskaja Respublika	Soviet Socialist Republic	Sowjetische Sozialistische Republik	República Socialista Soviética	République socialiste soviétique	República Socialista Soviética
S.S.S.R.	Sojuz Sovetskich Socialističeskich Respublik	Union of Soviet Socialist Republics	Union der Sozialistischen Sowjet-republiken	Unión de Repúblicas Socialistas Soviéticas	Union des Républiques socialistes soviétiques	União das Repúblicas Socialistas Soviéticas
St. Hel.	St. Helena	St. Helena	Sankt Helena	Santa Elena	Sainte-Hélène	Santa Helena
St. K.-N.	St. Kitts-Nevis	St. Kitts-Nevis	Sankt Christo-pher-Nevis	San Cristóbal-Nevis	Saint-Christo-phe-Nevis	São Cristóvão-Neves
St. Luc.	St. Lucia	St. Lucia	Santa Lucia	Santa Lucía	Sainte-Lucie	Santa Lúcia
S. Tom./P.	São Tomé e Príncipe	Sao Tome and Principe	São Tomé und Principe	São Tomé y Príncipe	São Tomé et Principe	São Tomé e Príncipe
St. P./M.	St.-Pierre-et-Miquelon	St. Pierre and Miquelon	Saint-Pierre und Miquelon	San Pedro y Miquelón	Saint-Pierre-et-Miquelon	São Pedro e Miquelon
St. Vin.	St. Vincent	St. Vincent	Sankt Vincent	San Vicente	Saint-Vincent	São Vicente
Sūd.	As-Sūdān	Sudan	Sudan	Sudán	Soudan	Sudão
Suomi	Suomi	Finland	Finnland	Finlandia	Finlande	Finlândia
Sur.	Suriname	Suriname	Suriname	Suriname	Suriname	Suriname
Sūriy.	As-Sūrīyah	Syria	Syrien	Siria	Syrie	Síria
Sval.	Svalbard og Jan Mayen	Svalbard and Jan Mayen	Svalbard und Jan Mayen	Svalbard e Isla de Jan Mayen	Svalbard et Île Jan Mayen	Svalbard e Jan Mayen, Ilhas
Sve.	Sverige	Sweden	Schweden	Suecia	Suède	Suécia
Swaz.	Swaziland	Swaziland	Swasiland	Swazilandia	Swaziland	Suazilândia
T.a.a.f.	Terres australes et antarctiques françaises	French Southern and Antarctic Territories	Französische Süd- und Antarktis-Gebiete	Tierras Australes y Antárticas Francesas	Terres australes antarctiques françaises	Terras Austrais e Antárticas Francesas

	LOCAL NAME	ENGLISH	DEUTSCH	ESPAÑOL	FRANÇAIS	PORTUGUÊS
Taehan	Taehan-Min'guk	South Korea	Südkorea	Corea del Sur	Corée du Sud	Coréia do Sul
T'aiwan	T'aiwan	Taiwan	Taiwan	Taiwán	Taïwan	Taiwan (Formosa)
Tan.	Tanzania	Tanzania	Tansania	Tanzania	Tanzanie	Tanzania
Tchad	Tchad	Chad	Tschad	Chad	Tchad	Tchad
T./C. Is.	Turks and Caicos Islands	Turks and Caicos Islands	Turks- und Caicos-Inseln	Islas Turcas y Caicos	Îles Turques et Caïques	Turcas e Caicos, Ilhas
Tenn., U.S.	Tennessee	Tennessee	Tennessee	Tennessee	Tennessee	Tennessee
Tex., U.S.	Texas	Texas	Texas	Texas	Texas	Texas
Thai.	Prathet Thai	Thailand	Thailand	Tailandia	Thaïlande	Tailândia
Togo	Togo	Togo	Togo	Togo	Togo	Togo
Tok. Is.	Tokelau Islands	Tokelau Islands	Tokelau-Inseln	Islas Tokelau	Îles Tokelaou	Tokelau, Ilhas
Tonga	Tonga	Tonga	Tonga	Tonga	Tonga	Tonga
Trin.	Trinidad and Tobago	Trinidad and Tobago	Trinidad und Tobago	Trinidad y Tabago	Trinité-et-Tobago	Trinidad e Tobago
Tun.	Tunisie	Tunisia	Tunesien	Túnez	Tunisie	Tunísia
Tür.	Türkiye	Turkey	Türkei	Turquía	Turquie	Turquia
Tuvalu	Tuvalu	Tuvalu	Tuvalu	Tuvalu	Tuvalu	Tuvalu
Ug.	Uganda	Uganda	Uganda	Uganda	Ouganda	Uganda
U.K.	United Kingdom	United Kingdom	Vereinigtes Königreich	Reino Unido	Royaume-Uni	Reino Unido
'Uman	'Umān	Oman	Oman	Omán	Oman	Omã
Ur.	Uruguay	Uruguay	Uruguay	Uruguay	Uruguay	Uruguai
Urd.	Al-Urdunn	Jordan	Jordanien	Jordania	Jordania	Jordânia
U.S.	United States	United States	Vereinigte Staaten	Estados Unidos	États-Unis	Estados Unidos
U.S.S.R.	Sojuz Sovetskich Socialist-ičeskich Respublik	Union of Soviet Socialist Republics	Union der Sozialistischen Sowjet-republiken	Unión de Repúblicas Socialistas Soviéticas	Union des Républiques socialistes soviétiques	União das Repúblicas Socialistas Soviéticas
Utah, U.S.	Utah	Utah	Utah	Utah	Utah	Utah
Va., U.S.	Virginia	Virginia	Virginia	Virginia	Virginie	Virgínia
Vat.	Città del Vaticano	Vatican City	Vatikanstadt	Ciudad del Vaticano	Cité du Vatican	Vaticano
Ven.	Venezuela	Venezuela	Venezuela	Venezuela	Venezuela	Venezuela
Viet.	Viet-nam	Vietnam	Vietnam	Viet-Nam	Viet-Nam	Vietnam
Vir. Is., U.S.	Virgin Islands	Virgin Islands (U.S.)	Amerikanische Jungferninseln	Islas Vírgenes (americanas)	Îles Vierges (américaines)	Virgens Americanas, Ilhas
Vt., U.S.	Vermont	Vermont	Vermont	Vermont	Vermont	Vermont
Wake I.	Wake Island	Wake Island	Wake	Isla Wake	Île de Wake	Wake
Wales, U.K.	Wales	Wales	Wales	Gales	Galles	Gales
Wal./F.	Wallis et Futuna	Wallis and Futuna	Wallis und Futuna	Wallis y Futuna	Wallis et Futuna	Wallis e Futuna
Wash., U.S.	Washington	Washington	Washington	Washington	Washington	Washington
Wis., U.S.	Wisconsin	Wisconsin	Wisconsin	Wisconsin	Wisconsin	Wisconsin
W. Sam.	Western Samoa	Western Samoa	Westsamoa	Samoa Occidental	Samoa-Occidentale	Samoa Ocidental
W. Va., U.S.	West Virginia	West Virginia	West Virginia	Virginia Occidental	Virginie Occidentale	Virgínia Ocidental
Wyo., U.S.	Wyoming	Wyoming	Wyoming	Wyoming	Wyoming	Wyoming
Yai.	Yaitopya	Ethiopia	Äthiopien	Etiopía	Ethiopie	Etiópia
Yaman	Al-Yaman	Yemen	Jemen	Yemen	Yémen	Iêmen
Yam. S.	Al-Yaman ash-Sha'bīyah	People's Democratic Republic of Yemen	Volksrepublik Jemen	República Popular Democrática del Yemen	République démocratique populaire du Yémen	Iêmen, República Popular Democrática do
Yis.	Yisra'el	Israel	Israel	Israel	Israël	Israel
Yukon, Can.	Yukon	Yukon	Yukon	Yukón	Yukon	Yukon
Zaïre	Zaïre	Zaire	Zaire	Zaire	Zaïre	Zaire
Zam.	Zambia	Zambia	Sambia	Zambia	Zambie	Zâmbia
Zimb.	Zimbabwe	Zimbabwe	Zimbabwe	Zimbabwe	Zimbabwe	Zimbabwe

Index / Register / Índice / Index / Indice

A

Name	Page	Lat.	Long.
A, Peak ∧	271d	22.27 N	114.18 E
Aa ≃	50	51.01 N	2.06 E
Aach, B.R.D.	58	47.31 N	9.58 E
Aach, B.R.D.	58	47.50 N	8.51 E
Aachen	56	50.47 N	6.05 E
Aach im Allgäu	58	47.31 N	9.58 E
Aach-Linz	58	47.54 N	9.11 E
Aadorf	58	47.30 N	8.54 E
Aaiun → El Aaiún	148	27.09 N	13.12 W
Aalen	56	48.50 N	10.05 E
A'alī an-Nīl □[4]	140	9.00 N	32.00 E
Aalsmeer	52	52.16 N	4.45 E
Aalst (Alost), Bel.	50	50.56 N	4.02 E
Aalst, Ned.	52	51.23 N	5.29 E
Aalten	52	51.56 N	6.35 E
Aalter	50	51.05 N	3.27 E
Äänekoski	26	62.36 N	25.44 E
Aarau	58	47.23 N	8.03 E
Aarberg	58	47.03 N	7.16 E
Aarburg	58	47.19 N	7.54 E
Aardenburg	52	51.16 N	3.27 E
Aare ≃	58	47.37 N	8.13 E
Aareschlucht ♠	58	46.44 N	8.12 E
Aargau □[3]	58	47.30 N	8.10 E
Aarle-Rixtel	52	51.31 N	5.38 E
Aaronsburg	210	40.54 N	77.27 W
Aarschot	56	50.59 N	4.50 E
Aarwangen	58	47.15 N	7.46 E
Aazanèn	34	35.13 N	3.10 W
Aba, Nig.	150	5.06 N	7.21 E
Aba, Zaïre	154	3.52 N	30.14 E
Abā al-Bawl, Qurayn ∧[2]	128	24.57 N	51.13 E
Abacaxis ≃	242	3.54 S	58.47 W
Ābādān	128	30.20 N	48.16 E
Ābādeh	128	31.10 N	52.37 E
Abagaqi (Hanbumiao)	102	43.41 N	114.40 E
Abai, Malay.	116	5.41 N	118.23 E
Abaí, Para.	252	26.01 S	55.57 W
Abaj, S.S.S.R.	86	50.27 N	85.05 E
Abaj, S.S.S.R.	86	49.38 N	72.52 E
Abaji	150	8.28 N	6.57 E
Abajo Mountains ∧∧	200	37.50 N	109.25 W
Abajo Peak ∧	200	37.51 N	109.28 W
Abakaliki	150	6.21 N	8.06 E
Abakan	86	53.43 N	91.26 E
Abakanovo	76	59.18 N	37.39 E
Abakanskij Chrebet ∧∧	86	52.20 N	88.50 E
Abala, Congo	152	1.21 S	15.30 E
Abala, Niger	150	14.56 N	3.26 E
Abalak, Niger	150	15.27 N	6.17 E
Abalak, S.S.S.R.	86	58.08 N	68.36 E
Abalemma, Vallée d' ∨	150	15.34 N	6.23 E
Aban	88	56.41 N	96.04 E
Abancay	248	13.35 S	72.55 W
Abanga ≃	152	0.20 S	10.30 E
Abano Terme	64	45.21 N	11.47 E
Abar Irir	144	4.54 N	46.18 E
Abarqū	128	31.08 N	53.17 E
Abarracamento	256	22.12 S	43.30 W
Abaša	84	42.12 N	42.13 E
Abashiri	92a	44.01 N	144.17 E
Abasolo, Méx.	196	25.57 N	100.24 W
Abasolo, Méx.	196	27.12 N	101.24 W
Abasolo, Méx.	204	32.39 N	115.21 W
Abasolo, Méx.	232	24.04 N	98.22 W
Abasolo, Méx.	232	25.18 N	104.40 W
Abasolo, Méx.	234	20.27 N	101.32 W
Abasolo del Valle	234	17.44 N	95.29 W
Abastumani	84	41.46 N	42.50 E
Abate	85	39.03 N	77.36 E
Abate Alonia, Lago di ⊜	68	41.01 N	15.45 E
Abatiá	255	23.19 S	50.18 W
Abatskij	86	56.18 N	70.28 E
Abau	164	10.11 S	148.42 E
Abava ≃	76	57.06 N	21.54 E
Abay → Blue Nile ≃	140	15.38 N	32.31 E
Abaya, Lake ⊜	144	6.20 N	37.55 E
Abayuba	258	34.51 S	56.14 W
Abaza	86	52.39 N	90.06 E
Abba	152	5.20 N	15.11 E
Abbabach ≃	263	51.28 N	7.41 E
'Abbādah	132	33.30 N	36.33 E
Abbadia San Salvatore	66	42.53 N	11.41 E
'Abbāsābād	267d	35.44 N	51.25 E
Abbasanta	71	40.08 N	8.49 E
Abbaye, Étang de l' ⊜	261	48.41 N	1.56 E
Abbaynagar	126	23.01 N	89.28 E
Abbé, Lac (Lake Abe) ⊜	144	11.09 N	41.47 E
Abbehausen	52	53.29 N	8.26 E
Abbekås	41	55.24 N	13.36 E
Abbensen	52	52.23 N	10.11 E
Abbert ≃	48	53.26 N	9.54 W
Abbess Roding	260	51.47 N	0.17 E
Abbeville, Fr.	50	50.06 N	1.50 E
Abbeville, Ga., U.S.	192	31.59 N	83.18 W
Abbeville, La., U.S.	194	29.58 N	92.08 W
Abbeville, Miss., U.S.	194	34.25 N	89.37 W
Abbeville, S.C., U.S.	192	34.11 N	82.23 W
Abbey	184	50.43 N	108.45 W
Abbeydorney	48	52.19 N	9.41 W
Abbeyfeale	48	52.24 N	9.18 W
Abbey Head ≻	44	54.46 N	3.58 W
Abbeyleix	48	52.55 N	7.20 W
Abbey Peak ∧	164	14.18 S	144.29 E
Abbey Town	44	54.50 N	3.17 W
Abbey Wood ⇀[8]	260	51.29 N	0.08 E
Abbiategrasso	62	45.24 N	8.54 E
Abbot, Mount ∧	166	20.03 S	147.45 E
Abbotsbury	42	50.40 N	2.36 W
Abbotsford, Austl.	274a	33.51 S	151.08 E
Abbotsford, B.C., Can.	182	49.03 N	122.17 W
Abbotsford, Wis., U.S.	190	44.57 N	90.19 W
Abbots Langley	260	51.43 N	0.25 W
Abbott	222	31.53 N	97.04 W
Abbottābād	123	34.09 N	73.13 E
Abbott Butte ∧	202	42.57 N	122.33 W
Abbottstown	208	39.53 N	76.59 W
Abchazskaja Avtonomnaja Sovetskaja Socialističeskaja Respublika □[3]	84	43.10 N	41.00 E
Abcoude	52	52.16 N	4.58 E
'Abd al-'Azīz, Jabal ∧∧	130	36.25 N	40.20 E
'Abd al-Ḥafiẓ, Qārat ∧[2]	142	28.53 N	30.08 E
'Abd al-Kūrī I	118	12.12 N	52.15 E
'Abd Allāh	140	13.30 N	23.02 E
'Abd Allāh, Khawr ⩌	128	29.50 N	48.20 E
'abd al-Shāhīd	273c	29.55 N	31.13 E
Ābdānān	128	32.58 N	47.26 E
Abdrachmanovo	80	54.46 N	52.30 E
Abdul Ghadir	144	10.32 N	42.52 E
Abdul Hakīm	123	30.33 N	72.07 E
Abdulino	80	53.42 N	53.40 E
Abdulovo	80	54.16 N	53.27 E
Abe ≃	94	34.56 N	138.24 E
Abe, Lake (Lac Abbé) ⊜	144	11.06 N	41.50 E
Abéché	146	13.49 N	20.49 E
Abéjar	34	41.48 N	2.47 W
Abejorral	246	5.47 N	75.26 W
Abekr	140	12.43 N	28.55 E
Abel	256	22.54 S	46.08 W
Abelek	140	7.23 N	28.46 E
Abêlessa	148	22.54 N	4.50 E
Abel Tasman National Park ♠	172	40.55 S	173.00 E
Abelti	144	8.10 N	37.37 E
Abemama I[1]	14	0.21 N	173.51 E
Abenberg	56	49.14 N	10.57 E
Abengourou	150	6.44 N	3.29 W
Abengourou □[5]	150	6.30 N	3.30 W
Abeno ⇀[8]	270	34.38 N	135.30 E
Abenójar	34	38.53 N	4.21 W
Åbenrå	41	55.02 N	9.26 E
Åbenrå Fjord C	41	55.03 N	9.34 E
Abens ≃	60	48.51 N	11.46 E
Abensberg	60	48.49 N	11.51 E
Abeokuta	150	7.10 N	3.26 E
Aber	154	2.12 N	32.21 E
Aberaman	42	51.42 N	3.25 W
Aberavon → Port Talbot	42	51.36 N	3.47 W
Aberayron	42	52.15 N	4.15 W
Abercarn	42	51.39 N	3.08 W
Aberchirder	46	57.33 N	2.38 W
Abercorn, Qué., Can.	206	45.02 N	72.40 W
Abercorn → Mbala, Zam.	154	8.50 S	31.22 E
Abercrombie ≃	170	34.09 S	149.40 E
Aberdare	42	51.43 N	3.27 W
Aberdare National Park ♠	154	0.30 S	36.45 E
Aberdare Range ∧∧	154	0.25 S	36.38 E
Aberdaron	42	52.49 N	4.43 W
Aberdeen, Sask., Can.	184	52.19 N	106.17 W
Aberdeen (Xianggangzi), H.K.	271d	22.15 N	114.09 E
Aberdeen, S. Afr.	158	32.29 S	24.03 E
Aberdeen, Scot., U.K.	46	57.10 N	2.04 W
Aberdeen, Idaho, U.S.	202	42.57 N	112.50 W
Aberdeen, Md., U.S.	208	39.30 N	76.10 W
Aberdeen, Miss., U.S.	194	33.49 N	88.33 W
Aberdeen, N.C., U.S.	192	35.08 N	79.26 W
Aberdeen, Ohio, U.S.	218	38.39 N	83.46 W
Aberdeen, S. Dak., U.S.	198	45.28 N	98.29 W
Aberdeen, Wash., U.S.	224	46.59 N	123.50 W
Aberdeen Lake ⊜	176	64.27 N	99.00 W
Aberdeen Proving Ground ■	208	39.25 N	76.10 W
Aberdour	46	56.03 N	3.19 W
Aberdovey	42	52.33 N	4.02 W
Aberdulais	42	51.41 N	3.48 W
Aberfeldy	46	56.37 N	3.54 W
Aberfoyle	46	56.11 N	4.23 W
Abergavenny	42	51.50 N	3.00 W
Abergele	44	53.17 N	3.34 W
Abergwynfi	42	51.40 N	3.35 W
Abergynolwyn	42	52.40 N	3.58 W
Aberjona ≃	283	42.27 N	71.08 W
Aberlour	46	57.28 N	3.14 W
Abermain	170	32.49 S	151.25 E
Abernathy	196	33.50 N	101.51 W
Abernethy, Sask., Can.	184	50.45 N	103.25 W
Abernethy, Scot., U.K.	46	56.20 N	3.19 W
Aberporth	42	52.09 N	4.33 W
Abersee ⊜	64	47.44 N	13.26 E
Abersoch	42	52.50 N	4.29 W
Abersychan	42	51.44 N	3.04 W
Abert, Lake ⊜	202	42.38 N	120.13 W
Abertillery	42	51.45 N	3.09 W
Aberuthven	46	56.19 N	3.39 W
Aberystwyth	42	52.25 N	4.05 W
Abessinien, Hochland von → Amhara Plateau ∧∧[1]	144	9.00 N	38.00 E
Abetone	66	44.08 N	10.40 E
Abez'	24	66.32 N	61.42 E
Abhā	144	18.13 N	42.30 E
Abhar	128	36.09 N	49.13 E
Abhayāpuri	124	26.20 N	90.40 E
Abiaca Creek ≃	194	33.20 N	90.15 W
'Ābidīn	140	13.33 N	29.38 E
'Abīdīyah	140	18.14 N	33.57 E
Abidjan	150	5.19 N	4.02 W
Abidjan □[5]	150	5.30 N	4.30 W
Abiengama	154	2.35 N	27.46 E
Abiko	94	35.52 N	140.03 E
Abilene, Kans., U.S.	198	38.55 N	97.13 W
Abilene, Tex., U.S.	196	32.27 N	99.44 W
Abingdon, Eng., U.K.	42	51.41 N	1.17 W
Abingdon, Va., U.S.	192	36.43 N	81.59 W
Abinger	260	51.12 N	0.24 W
Abington, Conn., U.S.	207	41.52 N	72.01 W
Abington, Mass., U.S.	207	42.07 N	70.57 W
Abington, Pa., U.S.	208	40.07 N	75.08 W
Abington Reefs ⊹[2]	166	18.00 S	149.36 E
Abino, Point ≻	212	42.50 N	79.05 W
Abino Bay C	284a	42.51 N	79.05 W
Abinsk	78	44.52 N	38.09 E
Āb-i-Panja (P'andž) ≃	72	37.06 N	68.20 E
Abiquiu	200	36.12 N	106.19 W
Abiquiu Reservoir ⊜[1]	200	36.18 N	106.32 W
Abisko	24	68.20 N	18.51 E
Abisko Nationalpark ♠	24	68.20 N	18.30 E
Abita Springs	194	30.29 N	90.02 W
Abitau ≃	176	59.53 N	109.03 W
Abitibi ≃	176	51.03 N	80.55 W
Abitibi, Lake ⊜	190	48.42 N	79.45 W
Abiy Adi	144	13.36 N	39.00 E
Abja-Paluoja	76	58.08 N	25.21 E
Ableiges	261	49.05 N	1.59 E
Ablis	50	48.31 N	1.50 E
Ablon-sur-Seine	261	48.43 N	2.25 E
Abminga	162	26.07 S	134.52 E
Abnūb	142	27.16 N	31.09 E
Åbo → Turku	26	60.27 N	22.17 E
Abóbada	266c	38.43 N	9.20 W
Abodom	150	5.32 N	0.49 W
Abohar	123	30.09 N	74.11 E
Aboisso	150	5.28 N	3.12 W
Aboisso □[5]	150	5.30 N	3.15 W
Abomey	150	7.11 N	1.59 E
Abondance	58	46.17 N	6.44 E
Abong Mbang	152	3.59 N	13.10 E
Abony	30	47.11 N	20.01 E
Aborigen, Pik ∧	74	61.59 N	149.19 E
Aborrebjerg ∧[2]	41	54.59 N	12.32 E
Aboso	150	5.22 N	1.56 W
Abou	144	4.27 N	43.05 E
Abou Deïa	146	11.27 N	19.17 E
Aboyne	46	57.05 N	2.50 W
Abra □[4]	116	17.35 N	120.50 E
Abra ≃	116	17.31 N	120.23 E
Abraão	256	23.08 S	44.10 W
Abrahamsdam	158	29.08 S	22.39 E
Abram	262	53.31 N	2.35 W
Abramcevo	265b	55.50 N	37.50 E
Abramovka	78	51.12 N	41.01 E
Abramovskaja	24	65.11 N	51.43 E
Abram S. Hewitt State Forest ♠	276	41.11 N	74.22 W
Abrantes	34	39.28 N	8.12 W
Abra Pampa	252	22.43 S	65.42 W
Abraq, Wādī al- ∨	146	26.27 N	18.48 E
Abrau-D'urso	78	44.43 N	37.37 E
Abra Vieja, Arroyo ≃	288	34.26 S	58.34 W
Abre Campo	255	20.18 S	42.29 W
Ábrego	246	8.05 N	73.13 W
Abreojos, Punta ≻	232	26.42 N	113.35 W
Abreschviller	58	48.38 N	7.06 E
Abreu e Lima	250	7.54 S	34.53 W
'Abrī, Sūd.	140	11.40 N	30.28 E
'Abrī, Sūd.	140	20.48 N	30.20 E
Abriachan	46	57.22 N	4.24 W
Abridge	260	51.39 N	0.07 E
Abriès	62	44.47 N	6.56 E
Abring	123	33.42 N	76.35 E
Abriola	68	40.30 N	15.49 E
Abrud	38	46.17 N	23.04 E
Abruka Saar I	76	58.10 N	22.30 E
Abrunheira	266c	38.46 N	9.21 W
Abruzzi □[4]	66	42.20 N	13.45 E
Abruzzo, Parco Nazionale d' ♠	66	41.45 N	13.45 E
Absam	64	47.18 N	11.30 E
Absaroka Range ∧∧	202	44.45 N	109.50 W
Absarokee	202	45.31 N	109.27 W
Abscon	50	50.20 N	3.18 E
Absdorf	61	48.24 N	15.59 E
Absecon	208	39.26 N	74.30 W
Absecon Bay C	208	39.24 N	74.28 W
Abşeker	130	38.55 N	39.11 E
Abtenau	64	47.33 N	13.21 E
Abtsgmünd	56	48.54 N	10.00 E
Abu	96	34.30 N	131.28 E
Abu ≃	96	34.25 N	131.24 E
Abū Ahl ⊤[4]	128	34.06 N	43.45 E
Abū 'Alāwī, Wādī ∨	142	30.07 N	31.51 E
Abū al-Ghayṭ	273c	30.09 N	31.11 E
Abū al-Ḥamām, Jabal ∧	132	30.27 N	35.38 E
Abū al-Hawl (Sphinx) ⊥	142	29.59 N	31.08 E
Abū al-Khaṣīb	128	30.27 N	47.59 E
Abū al-Maṭāmīr	142	30.55 N	30.11 E
Abū al-'Urūq, Bi'r ⊤[4]	142	30.45 N	32.23 E
Abū an-Na'am	128	25.15 N	38.51 E
Abū 'Aradeib, Wādī ∨	140	14.12 N	23.06 E
Abū 'Arīsh	144	16.57 N	42.50 E
Abū Ashqar, 'Ilwat ∧[2]	142	30.22 N	31.46 E
Abū Ballās ∧[2]	140	24.26 N	27.39 E
Abucay	116	14.45 N	120.30 E
Abū Daraj, Ra's ≻	142	29.23 N	32.34 E
Abū Dā'ūd, Ra's ≻	128	23.20 N	58.55 E
Abū Dawm	140	16.16 N	32.36 E
Abū Dawm, Wādī ∨	140	18.28 N	31.49 E
Abū Dhi'ābah, Wādī ∨	142	29.37 N	32.06 E
Abū Dīs	140	19.08 N	33.34 E
Abū Dughayr, 'Alam ∧[2]	142	30.36 N	29.46 E
Abū Dulayq	140	15.54 N	33.49 E
Abufari	248	5.25 S	62.59 W
Abū Gatta Hills ∧∧[2]	140	6.06 N	27.44 E
Abū Ghaush	132	31.48 N	35.06 E
Abū Ḥabl, Khawr ∨	140	12.49 N	31.15 E
Abū Ḥād, Wādī ∨	142	28.20 N	32.49 E
Abū Ḥadīmah, Bi'r ⊤[4]	142	30.44 N	29.51 E
Abū Ḥammād al-Maḥaṭṭah	142	30.32 N	31.40 E
Abū Ḥarāz, Sūd.	140	19.04 N	32.07 E
Abū Ḥarāz, Sūd.	140	12.58 N	29.52 E
Abū Ḥasan, Jabal ∧	144	17.42 N	42.54 E
Abū Ḥummuṣ	142	31.06 N	30.19 E
Abū Ḥushsh, Bi'r ⊤[4]	142	30.49 N	29.57 E
Abū Jābirah	140	11.04 N	26.51 E
Abū Jandīr	142	29.14 N	30.41 E
Abū Jirj	142	28.32 N	30.47 E
Abū Jubayhah	140	11.27 N	31.14 E
Abū Kabīr	142	30.44 N	31.40 E
Abū Kamāl	130	34.27 N	40.55 E
Abū Kharjah, Wādī ∨	142	28.38 N	31.44 E
Abūksāh	142	29.23 N	30.42 E
Abū Kulaywāt	140	12.20 N	26.00 E
Abukuma ≃	92	38.02 N	140.56 E
Abukuma-sanchi ∧∧	94	37.30 N	140.45 E
Abū Latt I	144	19.58 N	40.08 E
Abulug ≃	116	18.29 N	121.25 E
Abū Madd, Ra's ≻	128	24.50 N	37.07 E
Abū Makhlūf, Bi'r ⊤[4]	142	30.45 N	29.42 E
Abū Maṭāriq	140	10.58 N	26.17 E
Abu Mendi	144	11.47 N	35.43 E
Abū Minqār, Bi'r ⊤[4]	140	26.30 N	27.35 E
Abumombazi	152	3.42 N	22.10 E
Abū Muḥammad, Bi'r ⊤[4]	132	29.43 N	34.13 E
Abū Muḥarrik, Ghurd ⊥[8]	140	27.50 N	29.40 E
Abū Mūsā, Jazīreh-ye I	128	25.52 N	55.03 E
Abunã	248	9.42 S	65.23 W
Abuná (Abunã) ≃	248	9.41 S	65.23 W
Abū Na'āmah	140	12.44 N	34.08 E
Abune Yosef ∧	144	12.10 N	39.12 E
Abū Qardī, Qā' ≍	132	32.08 N	37.11 E
Abū Qashash	132	31.57 N	35.11 E
Abū Qīr	142	31.19 N	30.04 E
Abū Qīr, Khalīj C	142	31.23 N	30.13 E
Abū Qurqāṣ	142	27.56 N	30.50 E
Aburatsubo-kō C	268	35.09 N	135.38 E
Abū Rimth, Wādī ∨	142	28.45 N	31.27 E
Abū Rīshat, Wādī ∨	142	28.54 N	31.37 E
Abu Road	120	24.29 N	72.47 E
Abū Rubayq	128	23.44 N	39.42 E
Abū Rūḥ, Qārat ∧[2]	142	28.21 N	30.25 E
Abū Rujmayn, Jabal ∧∧	130	34.52 N	38.20 E
Abū Sanṭ, Wādī ∨	140	14.11 N	23.06 E
Abū Shajarah, Ra's ≻	140	21.04 N	37.14 E
Abū Shanab, Sūd.	140	13.57 N	27.47 E
Abū Shanab, Sūd.	140	10.47 N	29.32 E
Abū Shaykhāt, Ḍahr ∧[2]	130	36.36 N	39.40 E
Abu Simbel → Abū Sunbul ⊥	140	22.22 N	31.38 E
Abū Ṣīr	273c	29.53 N	31.13 E
Abu Ṣīr al-Malaq	142	29.15 N	31.05 E
Abū Ṣīr-Banā	142	30.55 N	31.15 E
Abū Ṣīr Pyramids ⊥	273c	29.54 N	31.12 E
Abū Sulṭan	142	30.25 N	32.19 E
Abū Sunbul ⊥	140	22.22 N	31.38 E
Abū Ṣuwayr al-Maḥaṭṭah	142	30.34 N	32.07 E
Abū Ṣuwayr Military Base ■	142	30.34 N	32.06 E
Abuta	92a	42.33 N	140.46 E
Abū Ṭabarī ⊤[4]	140	17.35 N	28.31 E
Abut Head ≻	172	43.07 N	170.15 E
Abū Tīj	140	27.02 N	31.19 E
Abū Ṭunayṭin	140	14.24 N	31.01 E
Abū Ṭurayfīyah, Jabal ∧, Miṣr	142	29.58 N	32.06 E
Abū Ṭurayfīyah, Jabal ∧, Miṣr	142	29.42 N	31.49 E
Abū 'Uwayjilah ⊤[4]	132	30.50 N	34.07 E
Abuye Meda ∧	144	10.28 N	39.44 E
Abū Zabad	140	12.21 N	29.15 E
Abū Za'bal	142	30.15 N	31.21 E
Abū Ẓaby	128	24.28 N	54.22 E
Abū Zanīmah	140	29.03 N	33.06 E
Abwong	140	9.07 N	32.12 E
Åby	40	58.40 N	16.11 E
Åby ⇀[8]	41	56.09 N	10.10 E
Aby, Lagune C	150	5.15 N	3.14 W
Abyaḍ	140	13.46 N	26.28 E
Abyaḍ, Wādī al- ∨	142	29.38 N	32.13 E
Åbyälven ≃	26	65.01 N	21.24 E
Abyār	142	30.50 N	30.52 E
Abyār 'Alī	128	24.25 N	39.32 E
Åbybro	26	57.09 N	9.45 E
Abydos	162	21.25 S	118.54 E
Abyei	140	9.36 N	28.26 E
Åbyggeby	40	60.44 N	17.07 E
Åbytorp	40	59.07 N	15.04 E
Abzanovo, S.S.S.R.	86	51.51 N	56.46 E
Abzanovo, S.S.S.R.	86	53.50 N	58.36 E
Acacías	246	3.59 N	73.46 W
Acacio	232	24.50 N	102.44 W
Academia	214	40.25 N	82.28 W
Academy Corners	208	41.57 N	77.23 W
Academy of Sciences ⊍[3]	282	37.46 N	122.28 W
Acadia National Park ♠	188	44.18 N	68.15 W
Acadia Valley	184	51.08 N	110.13 W
Acahay	252	25.55 S	57.09 W
Acajete	234	19.06 N	97.57 W
Acajutiba	250	11.40 S	38.01 W
Acajutla	236	13.36 N	89.50 W
Acala	234	16.34 N	92.48 W
Acalayong	152	1.05 N	9.40 E
Acámbaro	234	20.02 N	100.44 W
Acampo	226	38.10 N	121.13 W
Acandí	246	8.32 N	77.14 W
Acaponeta	234	22.30 N	105.22 W
Acaponeta, Río de ≃	234	22.20 N	105.37 W
Acapulco [de Juárez]	234	16.51 N	99.55 W
Acará	250	1.57 S	48.11 W
Acará ≃	250	1.40 S	48.25 W
Acará, Cachoeira ⌊	248	5.47 S	59.12 W
Acará, Lago ⊜	246	3.39 S	62.40 W
Acaraí ≃	250	2.02 S	52.15 W
Acarai Mountains ∧∧	246	1.50 N	57.40 W
Acará-Mirim ≃	250	1.58 S	48.12 W
Acaraú	250	2.53 S	40.07 W
Acaraú ≃	250	2.51 S	40.08 W
Acaray ≃	252	25.29 S	54.42 W
Acari, Bra.	250	6.31 S	36.38 W
Acarí, Perú	248	15.26 S	74.37 W
Acari ≃, Bra.	248	5.18 S	59.42 W
Acari ≃, Bra.	255	16.00 S	45.03 W
Acarí ≃, Perú	248	15.39 S	74.39 W
Acarigua	246	9.33 N	69.12 W
Acate	70	37.02 N	14.28 E
Acatic	234	20.47 N	102.53 W
Acatlán	234	20.09 N	98.27 W
Acatlán ≃	234	18.04 N	98.19 W
Acatlán de Juárez	234	20.26 N	103.38 W
Acatlán de Osorio	234	18.12 N	98.03 W
Acatlán [de Pérez Figueroa]	234	18.32 N	96.37 W
Acatzingo [de Hidalgo]	234	18.59 N	97.47 W
Acay, Nevado de ∧	252	24.21 S	66.12 W
Acayucan	234	17.57 N	94.55 W
Accadia	68	41.10 N	15.10 E
Acceglio	62	44.28 N	7.00 E
Aččen, Mys ≻	180	64.45 N	175.30 W
Accettura	68	40.29 N	16.09 E
Aččhoj-Martan	84	43.11 N	45.18 E
Ačči	85	39.57 N	68.14 E
Acciano	66	42.10 N	13.43 E
Accokeek	208	38.40 N	77.02 W
Accomac	208	37.43 N	75.40 W
Accomack □[6]	208	37.45 N	75.40 W
Accord, Mass., U.S.	283	42.10 N	70.53 W
Accord, N.Y., U.S.	210	41.48 N	74.13 W
Accord Brook ≃	283	42.10 N	70.53 W
Accord Pond ⊜	283	42.10 N	70.53 W
Accotink Creek ≃	284c	38.46 N	77.13 W
Accotink Creek, Bear Branch ≃	284c	38.52 N	77.15 W
Accotink Creek, Long Branch ≃	284c	38.48 N	77.13 W
Accoville	192	37.46 N	81.50 W
Accra	150	5.33 N	0.13 W
Accrington	262	53.46 N	2.21 W
Accumoli	66	42.42 N	13.15 E

Symbols in the index entries represent the broad categories identified in the key at the right. Symbols with superior numbers (∧∧[2]) identify subcategories (see complete key on page I · 30).

Kartensymbole in dem Registerverzeichnis stellen die rechts in Schlüssel erklärten Kategorien dar. Symbole mit hochgestellten Ziffern (∧∧[2]) bezeichnen Unterabteilungen einer Kategorie (vgl. vollständiger Schlüssel auf Seite I · 30).

Los símbolos incluídos en el texto del índice representan las grandes categorias identificadas con la clave a la derecha. Los símbolos con numeros en su parte superior (∧∧[2]) identifican las subcategorías (véase la clave completa en la página I · 30).

Les symboles de l'index représentent les catégories indiquées dans la légende à droite. Les symboles suivis d'un indice (∧∧[2]) représentent des sous-catégories (voir légende complète à la page I · 30).

Os símbolos incluídos no texto do índice representam as grandes categorias identificadas com a chave à direita. Os símbolos com números em sua parte superior (∧∧[2]) identificam as subcategorias (veja-se a chave completa à página I · 30).

∧	Mountain	Berg	Montaña	Montagne	Montanha
∧∧	Mountains	Berge	Montañas	Montagnes	Montanhas
)(	Pass	Pass	Paso	Col	Passo
∨	Valley, Canyon	Tal, Cañon	Valle, Cañón	Vallée, Canyon	Vale, Canhão
≍	Plain	Ebene	Llano	Plaine	Planície
≻	Cape	Kap	Cabo	Cap	Cabo
I	Island	Insel	Isla	Île	Ilha
II	Islands	Inseln	Islas	Îles	Ilhas
⊥	Other Topographic Features	Andere Topographische Objekte	Otros Elementos Topográficos	Autres données topographiques	Outros Elementos Topográficos

ESPAÑOL

Nombre	Página	Lat.°′	Long.°′ W=Oeste
Acebal	252	33.14 S	60.50 W
Acebuches	232	28.15 N	102.43 W
Aceh □4	114	4.00 N	97.00 E
Aceh ≃	114	5.36 N	95.20 E
Acerentia ⊥	68	39.16 N	16.49 E
Acerenza	68	40.48 N	15.57 E
Acerno	68	40.44 N	15.03 E
Acerra	68	40.57 N	14.22 E
Acevedo	252	33.45 S	60.27 W
Ach	60	48.09 N	12.50 E
Achacachi	248	16.03 S	68.43 W
Achaguas	246	7.46 N	68.14 W
Achalciche	84	41.38 N	42.59 E
Achali-Kindgi	84	42.48 N	41.16 E
Achalkalaki	84	41.25 N	43.29 E
Achalpur	120	21.16 N	77.31 E
Achangaran	85	40.54 N	69.37 E
Achao	254	42.28 S	73.30 W
Achar	252	32.25 S	56.10 W
Acharacle	46	56.44 N	5.47 W
Achau	264b	48.05 N	16.23 E
Achavanich	46	58.22 N	3.24 W
Acheb	148	28.23 N	9.05 E
Achen ≃	60	47.51 N	12.30 E
Achêne	56	50.16 N	5.03 E
Acheng	89	45.32 N	126.59 E
Achenkirch	64	47.31 N	11.42 E
Achen Pass)(	64	47.35 N	11.38 E
Achen See ⊜	64	47.28 N	11.42 E
Achères	261	48.58 N	2.04 E
Achern	56	48.37 N	8.04 E
Acheron ≃	169	37.14 S	145.42 E
Acheux-en-Amiénois	50	50.04 N	2.32 E
Achhībal	123	33.41 N	75.14 E
Achhnera	124	27.11 N	77.46 E
Achí, Col.	246	8.34 N	74.33 W
Achi, Nihon	94	35.27 N	137.45 E
Achiasi	150	5.52 N	1.00 W
Achicourt	50	50.16 N	2.46 E
Achigan, Lac de l' ⊜	206	45.56 N	73.58 W
Achiguate ≃	236	13.55 N	90.55 W
Achill	28	53.56 N	9.54 W
Achilles	208	37.17 N	76.27 W
Achill Head ≻	48	53.59 N	10.13 W
Achill Island I	48	54.00 N	10.00 W
Achill Sound	48	53.55 N	9.58 W
Achim	52	53.00 N	9.02 E
Āchīn	120	34.08 N	70.42 E
Achiras	252	33.10 S	65.00 W
Achmeta	84	42.02 N	45.13 E
Achnasaul	46	56.58 N	4.59 W
Achnasheen	46	57.35 N	5.06 W
Acho, Plaza de ♠	286d	12.02 S	77.02 W
Achol	140	6.34 N	31.31 E
Acholi □5	154	3.00 N	32.30 E
Achosnich	46	56.45 N	6.06 W
Achsu	84	40.34 N	48.24 E
Achterwasser C	54	54.00 N	13.57 E
Achterwehr	41	54.19 N	9.57 E
Achthuizen	52	51.42 N	4.16 E
Achtuba	80	51.37 N	44.22 E
Achtuba ≃	80	46.42 N	48.00 E
Achtubinsk	80	48.17 N	46.10 E
Achty	84	41.28 N	47.43 E
Achtyrka	78	50.19 N	34.55 E
Achtyrskij	78	44.52 N	38.20 E
Achur'an (Arpa) ≃	84	40.06 N	43.39 E
Ači	85	41.17 N	73.02 E
Aci Castello	70	37.33 N	15.08 E
Aci Catena	70	37.36 N	15.08 E
Acıgöl	130	38.35 N	34.31 E
Acı Göl ⊜	130	37.50 N	29.54 E
Acikak	88	54.11 N	106.18 E
Acikehu ⊜	120	37.05 N	88.05 E
Ačikulak	84	44.34 N	44.50 E
Acilia ◆8	267a	41.47 N	12.22 E
Ačimovy Vtoryje	86	60.04 N	75.12 E
Ačinsk	86	56.17 N	90.30 E
Acıpayam	130	37.25 N	29.22 E
Acireale	70	37.37 N	15.10 E
Aciş	38	47.33 N	22.47 E
Ačisaj	85	43.35 N	68.53 E
Aci Sant'Antonio	70	37.36 N	15.07 E
Ačisu	84	42.38 N	47.40 E
Ačit	86	56.48 N	57.54 E
Ačit Nuur ⊜	86	49.28 N	90.33 E
Ackenbrock ◆8	263	51.21 N	7.40 E
Ackerly	196	32.32 N	101.43 W
Ackerman	194	33.19 N	89.10 W
Ackermanville	210	40.49 N	75.17 W
Ackerson Lake	216	42.11 N	84.20 W
Ackley	190	42.33 N	93.03 W
Acklins, The Bight of C3	238	22.30 N	74.15 W
Acklins Island I	238	22.26 N	73.58 W
Acland, Mount ∧	166	24.55 S	148.05 E
Aclan Point ≻	116	11.44 N	122.22 E
Acle	42	52.38 N	1.33 E
Aclimação ◆8	287b	23.34 S	46.37 W
Acme, Alta., Can.	182	51.30 N	113.30 W
Acme, Pa., U.S.	214	40.08 N	79.26 W
Acme, Wash., U.S.	224	48.43 N	122.12 W
Acmetonia	279b	40.32 N	79.49 W
Acobamba	248	12.48 S	74.34 W
Acolla	248	11.44 S	75.34 W
Acolman □7	286a	19.37 N	98.58 W
Acoma Indian Reservation ◆4	200	34.52 N	107.40 W
Acomayo, Perú	248	9.46 S	76.05 W
Acomayo, Perú	248	13.55 S	71.41 W
Acomita	200	35.03 N	107.35 W
Aconcagua, Cerro ∧	252	32.39 S	70.01 W
Aconchi	232	29.50 N	110.12 W
Aconibe	152	1.18 N	10.56 E
Acopiara	250	6.06 S	39.27 W
Açores, Arquipélago dos II	148a	38.30 N	28.00 W
Acoria	248	12.37 S	74.53 W
Acorizal	248	15.12 S	56.22 W
Acornhoek	156	24.37 S	31.02 E
Acosta	214	40.07 N	79.04 W
Acoyapa	236	11.58 N	85.10 W
Acoyapa ≃	236	11.48 N	85.16 W
Acquabona, Passo di)(	68	39.02 N	16.20 E
Acquacalda	70	38.31 N	14.57 E
Acqualagna	66	43.37 N	12.40 E
Acquanegra sul Chiese	64	45.10 N	10.26 E
Acquapendente	66	42.44 N	11.52 E
Acquappesa	68	39.29 N	15.57 E
Acquarossa	58	46.28 N	8.57 E
Acquasanta Terme	66	42.46 N	13.24 E
Acquasparta	66	42.41 N	12.33 E
Acquavina	66	43.57 N	12.25 E
Acquaviva delle Fonti	68	40.54 N	16.50 E
Acquaviva Platani	70	37.34 N	13.42 E
Acqui Terme	62	44.41 N	8.28 E
Acra	210	42.19 N	74.03 W
Acraman, Lake ⊜	162	32.02 S	135.26 E
Acre → 'Akko	132	32.55 N	35.05 E
Acre □3	248	9.00 S	70.00 W
Acre ≃	248	8.45 S	67.22 W
Acre Homes	222	29.53 N	95.27 W
Acri	68	39.29 N	16.23 E
Acropolis → Akrópolis ⊥	267c	37.58 N	23.43 E
Acton, Ont., Can.	212	43.37 N	80.02 W
Acton, Calif., U.S.	228	34.26 N	118.09 W
Acton, Mass., U.S.	207	42.29 N	71.26 W
Acton, Tex., U.S.	222	32.27 N	97.41 W
Acton ◆8	260	51.30 N	0.16 W
Acton Bridge	262	53.16 N	2.36 W
Acton Homes	158	28.36 S	29.26 E
Acton Lake ⊜	218	39.34 N	84.45 W
Acton Turville	42	51.32 N	2.17 W
Acton Vale	206	45.39 N	72.34 W
Actopan	234	20.16 N	98.56 W

FRANÇAIS

Nom	Page	Lat.°′	Long.°′ W=Ouest
Actopan ≃	234	19.25 N	96.20 W
Açu	250	5.34 S	36.54 W
Açu, Igarapé ≃	250	3.44 S	55.31 W
Açuã ≃	248	7.12 S	64.11 W
Açucena	255	19.04 S	42.32 W
Acuitzio del Canje	234	19.29 N	101.20 W
Ačujevo	78	45.43 N	37.45 E
Acuña	252	29.55 S	57.58 W
Acuracay	248	5.35 S	74.10 W
Acuraúa ≃	248	7.37 S	70.48 W
Acushnet	207	41.41 N	70.55 W
Acuto	66	41.47 N	13.10 E
Acvež	80	58.21 N	47.46 E
Acworth	192	34.04 N	84.41 W
Ada, Ghana	150	5.47 N	0.24 E
Ada, Jugo.	38	45.48 N	20.08 E
Ada, Nihon	174m	26.44 N	128.19 E
Ada, Mich., U.S.	216	42.57 N	85.29 W
Ada, Minn., U.S.	198	47.18 N	96.31 W
Ada, Ohio, U.S.	216	40.46 N	83.49 W
Ada, Okla., U.S.	196	34.46 N	96.41 W
Ada, Mount ∧	180	56.41 N	134.41 W
Adab ⊥	128	31.59 N	45.45 E
Adaba	144	7.07 N	39.20 E
Adabai ≃	144	10.10 N	38.21 E
A-da-Beja	266c	38.47 N	9.14 W
'Adabīyah, Ra's ≻	142	29.52 N	32.30 E
Adachi	94	35.49 N	139.35 E
Adachi ◆8	268	35.45 N	139.48 E
Adachi-yama ∧	96	33.51 N	130.55 E
Adado, Ras ≻	144	11.20 N	48.45 E
Adâfer el Abiod ◆1	150	19.30 N	10.00 W
Adagide	130	38.06 N	28.02 E
Adai	272c	19.01 N	73.08 E
Adainville	261	48.43 N	1.39 E
Adair, Iowa, U.S.	198	41.30 N	94.39 W
Adair, Okla., U.S.	196	36.26 N	95.16 W
Adair □6	219	40.08 N	92.22 W
Adair, Bahía de C	232	31.30 N	113.48 W
Adair, Cape ≻	176	71.24 N	71.13 W
Adairsville	192	34.22 N	84.56 W
Adairville	194	36.40 N	86.51 W
Adaja ≃	34	41.32 N	4.52 W
Adak, S.S.S.R.	24	66.30 N	59.38 E
Adak, Alaska, U.S.	180	51.54 N	176.35 W
Adaka-shima I	174m	26.45 N	128.20 E
Adak Island I	180	51.45 N	176.40 W
Adala	130	38.34 N	28.17 E
Adale	144	2.47 N	46.27 E
Ådalen ∨	26	63.10 N	17.16 E
Ādam	118	22.24 N	57.32 E
Adam, Mount ∧	254	51.36 S	59.55 W
Adamantina	255	21.42 S	51.04 W
Adamaoua ⋀⋀	152	7.00 N	12.00 E
Adamawa ⋀⋀	134	7.00 N	12.00 E
Adamclisi	38	44.05 N	27.57 E
Adamello ⋀⋀	64	46.10 N	10.35 E
Adamello, Monte ∧	64	46.09 N	10.30 E
Adaminaby	171b	36.03 S	148.43 E
Adami Tulu	144	7.52 N	38.40 E
Adamovskoje	82	54.52 N	35.57 E
Adamów	30	51.45 N	22.17 E
Ādampur	123	31.26 N	75.43 E
Adams, Ind., U.S.	218	39.23 N	85.34 W
Adams, Mass., U.S.	207	42.37 N	73.07 W
Adams, Minn., U.S.	190	43.34 N	92.43 W
Adams, Nebr., U.S.	198	40.28 N	96.31 W
Adams, N. Dak., U.S.	198	48.25 N	98.05 W
Adams, N.Y., U.S.	212	43.49 N	76.01 W
Adams, Tenn., U.S.	194	36.35 N	87.04 W
Adams, Wis., U.S.	190	43.58 N	89.49 W
Adams □6, Ill., U.S.	219	39.56 N	91.23 W
Adams □6, Ind., U.S.	216	40.50 N	84.56 W
Adams □6, Ohio, U.S.	218	38.48 N	83.32 W
Adams □6, Pa., U.S.	208	39.48 N	77.15 W
Adams ≃	182	50.52 N	119.35 W
Adams, Mount ∧, N.Z.	172	41.19 S	175.46 E
Adams, Mount ∧, Wash., U.S.	224	46.12 N	121.28 W
Adams Bridge ✢2	122	9.04 N	79.37 E
Adamsburg	279b	40.19 N	79.40 W
Adams Center	212	43.52 N	76.00 W
Adams Creek ≃	224	46.18 N	121.40 W
Adams Lake ⊜	182	51.13 N	119.33 W
Adams Mills	214	40.09 N	81.57 W
Adams National Historic Site ⊥	283	42.15 N	71.01 W
Adams Park	216	42.08 N	85.29 W
Adams Park ♠	275b	43.48 N	79.09 W
Adams Peak ∧	122	6.48 N	80.30 E
Adams Rock I2	174e	25.04 S	130.05 W
Adamston	208	40.03 N	74.04 W
Adamstown, Austl.	170	32.56 S	151.44 E
Adamstown, Pit.	174e	25.04 S	130.05 W
Adamstown, Md., U.S.	208	39.19 N	77.29 W
Adamstown, Pa., U.S.	208	40.15 N	76.03 W
Adamsville, Qué., Can.	206	45.17 N	72.47 W
Adamsville, Mich., U.S.	216	41.47 N	86.00 W
Adamsville, Ohio, U.S.	214	40.04 N	81.53 W
Adamsville, Pa., U.S.	214	41.31 N	80.22 W
Adamsville, Tenn., U.S.	194	35.14 N	88.23 W
Adana	130	37.01 N	35.18 E
Adana □4	130	37.20 N	35.45 E
Adanero	34	40.56 N	4.36 W
Adapazarı	130	40.46 N	30.24 E
Adarama	140	17.05 N	34.54 E
Adare	48	52.34 N	8.48 W
Adare, Cape ≻	9	71.17 S	170.14 E
Adar Gwagwa, Jabal ∧	144	22.15 N	35.20 E
Adarot	140	17.50 N	36.07 E
Adaševo	80	53.56 N	44.19 E
Adauli	272c	19.06 N	73.02 E
Adaut	164	8.08 S	131.07 E
Adavale	166	25.55 S	144.36 E
Adayto	144	14.25 N	40.53 E
Adda ≃, It.	36	45.08 N	9.53 E
Aḍ-Ḍab'ah	140	31.02 N	28.26 E
Ad-Dabbah	140	18.03 N	30.57 E
Ad-Dafīnah	128	23.18 N	41.58 E
Aḍ-Ḍafrah ◆1	128	23.25 N	53.25 E
Ad-Dahnā' ◆2	128	24.30 N	48.10 E
Ad-Daljamūn	142	30.48 N	30.50 E
Ad-Dāmir	144	17.35 N	33.58 E
Ad-Dammām	128	26.26 N	50.07 E
Ad-Dāmūr	132	33.44 N	35.27 E
Ad-Dānā	130	36.13 N	36.46 E
Ad-Daqahlīyah □4	142	30.55 N	31.30 E
Ad-Dār al-Ḥamrā'	128	27.19 N	37.44 E
Ad-Darb	144	17.43 N	42.15 E
Ad-Dawādimī	128	24.28 N	44.18 E
Ad-Dawḥah (Doha)	128	25.17 N	51.32 E
Ad-Dayr, Miṣr	140	25.20 N	32.35 E
Ad-Dayr, Miṣr	142	30.20 N	31.16 E
Ad-Dayr, Sūrīy.	132	32.28 N	36.27 E
Adderbury	42	52.00 N	1.17 W
Ad-Dibdibah ◆1	128	28.00 N	46.30 E
Addicks	222	29.47 N	95.39 W
Addicks Reservoir ⊜1	222	29.49 N	95.40 W
Addieville	219	38.23 N	89.29 W
Aḍ-Ḍiffah (Libyan Plateau) ⋀⋀1	140	30.30 N	25.30 E
Ad-Dilam	128	23.59 N	47.12 E
Ad-Dilinjāt	142	30.50 N	30.30 E
Ad-Dīmās	132	33.35 N	36.05 E
Addingham	44	53.57 N	1.53 W
Addington	260	51.18 N	0.23 E
Addis	194	30.21 N	91.16 W
Addis Ababa → Addis Abeba	144	9.00 N	38.50 E
Addis Abeba	144	9.00 N	38.50 E
Addis Alem	144	9.02 N	38.23 E
Addison, Ill., U.S.	216	41.55 N	88.00 W
Addison, Mich., U.S.	216	41.59 N	84.21 W

PORTUGUÊS

Nome	Página	Lat.°′	Long.°′ W=Oeste
Addison, N.Y., U.S.	210	42.06 N	77.14 W
Addison, Tex., U.S.	222	32.58 N	96.50 W
Addison Creek ≃	278	41.51 N	87.51 W
Ad-Dīwānīyah	128	31.59 N	44.56 E
Addlestone	260	51.22 N	0.30 W
Addo	158	33.32 S	25.45 E
Addo Elephant National Park ♠	158	33.29 S	25.46 E
Ad-Du'ayn	140	11.26 N	26.09 E
Aḍ-Ḍuhayr	132	31.10 N	32.00 E
Ad-Dūqah	144	19.36 N	40.54 E
Ad-Duqqī	273c	30.04 N	31.15 E
Ad-Duwayd	128	30.15 N	42.17 E
Ad-Duwaym	140	14.00 N	32.19 E
Ad-Duwayr	132	33.23 N	35.25 E
Adébour	146	13.20 N	11.54 E
Adegem	50	51.12 N	3.29 E
Adego	144	8.57 N	49.35 E
Adel, Ga., U.S.	192	31.08 N	83.25 W
Adel, Iowa, U.S.	190	41.37 N	94.01 W
Adelaida → Adelaide	168b	34.55 S	138.35 E
Adelaide, Austl.	168b	34.55 S	138.35 E
Adelaide, Ba.	240b	25.00 N	77.31 W
Adelaide, S. Afr.	158	32.42 S	26.20 E
Adelaide Airport ⊠	168b	34.58 S	138.32 E
Adelaide Island I	9	67.15 S	68.30 W
Adelaide Peninsula ≻1	176	68.09 N	97.45 W
Adelaide River	164	13.15 S	131.06 E
Adelanto	228	34.35 N	117.24 W
Adelaye	152	7.07 N	22.49 E
Adelbert Range ⋀⋀	164	4.35 S	145.10 E
Adelboden	58	46.30 N	7.33 E
Adelebsen	52	51.34 N	9.45 E
Adèle Island I	160	15.32 S	123.09 E
Adelfia	68	41.00 N	16.52 E
Adélie Coast ◆2	9	67.00 S	139.00 E
Adelong Creek ≃	171b	35.06 S	148.02 E
Adelphi	284c	39.00 N	76.58 W
Adelphia	208	40.13 N	74.15 W
Adelphi University ♥2	276	40.43 N	73.36 W
Adelsheim	56	49.24 N	9.23 E
Adelsö I	40	59.23 N	17.30 E
Adelzhausen	60	48.21 N	11.08 E
Aden	144	12.45 N	45.12 E
Aden, Gulf of C	144	12.30 N	48.00 E
Adena	214	40.13 N	80.53 W
Adenau	56	50.23 N	6.55 E
Adendorf	52	53.17 N	10.26 E
Adendorp	158	32.20 S	24.33 E
Adenstedt	52	52.15 N	10.10 E
Ader ⋀⋀1	150	14.10 N	5.05 E
Aderklaa	264b	48.17 N	16.32 E
Adéta	150	7.08 N	0.44 E
Adhāta	272b	22.52 N	88.32 E
'Adhrā'	132	33.37 N	36.30 E
Adi	154	3.24 N	30.48 E
Adiaké	150	5.16 N	3.17 W
Adi Arkay	144	13.17 N	13.17 E
Adi Daro	144	14.27 N	38.16 E
Adieu, Cape ≻	162	31.59 S	132.09 E
Adigala	144	10.25 N	42.17 E
Adige (Etsch) ≃	64	45.10 N	12.20 E
Adigeni	84	41.42 N	42.42 E
Adigrat	144	14.18 N	39.31 E
Adi Keyih	144	14.49 N	39.23 E
Adi Kwala	144	14.39 N	38.53 E
Ādilābād	122	19.40 N	78.32 E
Adilang	154	2.44 N	33.29 E
Adilcevaz	84	38.44 N	42.44 E
Adimi	89	47.20 N	138.56 E
Adin	204	41.12 N	120.57 W
Adirondack Mountains ⋀⋀	188	44.00 N	74.00 W
Adirondack Park ♠	188	44.00 N	74.20 W
Adis Dera	144	10.15 N	38.50 E
Adis Zemen	144	12.07 N	37.47 E
Adi Ugri	144	14.55 N	38.53 E
Adiwerna	115a	6.56 S	109.07 E
Adıyaman	130	37.46 N	38.17 E
Adıyaman □4	130	37.45 N	38.30 E
Adjan	112	2.11 N	113.12 E
Adjelman, Oued ∨	148	22.09 N	3.47 E
Adjohon	150	6.42 N	2.28 E
Adjud	38	46.04 N	27.11 E
Adjumani	154	3.22 N	31.47 E
Adjuntas	240m	18.10 N	66.43 W
Adjuntas, Presa de las ⊜1	234	24.00 N	98.50 W
Adler	78	43.27 N	39.55 E
Adler Planetarium ♥	278	41.52 N	87.37 W
Adlershof ◆8	264a	52.26 N	13.33 E
Adlington	262	53.37 N	2.36 W
Adlington Hall ⊥	262	53.19 N	2.09 W
Adliswil	58	47.19 N	8.32 E
Admer, Erg d' ◆2	148	24.00 N	9.15 E
Admiral	184	49.43 N	108.01 W
Admiralitäts-Inseln → Admiralty Islands II	164	2.10 S	147.00 E
Admiralty Bay C, St. Vin.	241h	13.00 N	61.16 W
Admiralty Bay C, Alaska, U.S.	180	70.53 N	155.45 W
Admiralty Gulf C	160	14.20 S	125.50 E
Admiralty Inlet C, N.W. Ter., Can.	176	73.00 N	86.00 W
Admiralty Inlet C, Wash., U.S.	224	48.05 N	122.39 W
Admiralty Island I, N.W. Ter., Can.	176	69.30 N	101.00 W
Admiralty Island I, Alaska, U.S.	180	57.50 N	134.30 W
Admiralty Islands II	164	2.10 S	147.00 E
Admiralty Mountains ⋀⋀	9	71.45 S	168.30 E
Admont	61	47.34 N	14.27 E
Adna	224	46.38 N	123.04 W
Ado ≃	94	35.19 N	136.05 E
Adobe Creek ≃, Calif., U.S.	282	37.26 N	122.06 W
Adobe Creek ≃, Colo., U.S.	198	38.05 N	103.18 W
Ado-Ekiti	150	7.38 N	5.12 E
Adogawa	94	35.20 N	136.02 E
Adok	140	8.11 N	30.19 E
Adolfo López Mateos, Presa ⊜1	232	25.13 N	107.25 W
Adolfo Ruíz Cortines	232	25.40 N	108.40 W
Adolfsberg	40	59.15 N	15.10 E
Adolphus Reach ⋓	212	44.05 N	76.55 W
Adonara, Pulau I	112	8.20 S	123.10 E
Ādoni	122	15.38 N	77.17 E
Ado-Odo	150	6.36 N	2.56 E
Adorf	54	50.19 N	12.15 E
Adoua, Vallée d' ∨	150	14.37 N	6.40 E
Adour ≃	32	43.32 N	1.32 E
Adowa → Adwa	144	14.10 N	38.55 E
Ādra, Bhārat	126	23.30 N	86.40 E
Adra, Esp.	34	36.44 N	3.01 W
Adranga	154	2.55 N	29.58 E
Adrano	70	37.40 N	14.50 E
Adrar	148	27.54 N	0.17 W
Adrar ◆1	134	20.30 N	13.30 W
Adrar, Massif de l' ∧	148	25.03 N	7.55 W
Adraskan	128	33.39 N	62.16 E
Adrasman	85	40.38 N	69.58 E
Adré	146	13.28 N	22.12 E
Adrī	146	27.32 N	13.14 E
Adria	64	45.03 N	12.03 E
Adrian, Ga., U.S.	192	32.32 N	82.35 W
Adrian, Mich., U.S.	216	41.54 N	84.02 W
Adrian, Minn., U.S.	198	43.38 N	95.56 W
Adrian, Mo., U.S.	194	38.24 N	94.21 W
Adrian, Ohio, U.S.	214	41.03 N	83.20 W
Adrian, Oreg., U.S.	202	43.44 N	117.04 W
Adrian, Pa., U.S.	214	40.53 N	79.32 W
Adrian, Tex., U.S.	196	35.16 N	102.40 W
Adrian, W. Va., U.S.	188	38.54 N	80.17 W
Adrianople → Edirne	130	41.40 N	26.34 E
Adrianópolis	287a	22.39 S	43.30 W
Adrianovka	88	51.34 N	114.30 E
Adriatico Mar → Adriatic Sea ⊤2	22	42.30 N	16.00 E
Adriatic Sea ⊤2	22	42.30 N	16.00 E
Adriatique, Mer → Adriatic Sea ⊤2	22	42.30 N	16.00 E
Adriatisches Meer → Adriatic Sea ⊤2	22	42.30 N	16.00 E
Adrigole	48	51.40 N	9.42 W
Adro	64	45.37 N	9.57 E
Adrogué → Almirante Brown	258	34.48 S	58.23 W
Adstock Mountain ∧	206	46.02 N	71.12 W
Adua	164	1.55 S	129.50 E
Aduard	52	53.15 N	6.26 E
Adujevo	82	54.59 N	35.59 E
Aduku	154	2.01 N	32.43 E
Adur ≃	42	50.49 N	0.16 W
Adusa	154	1.23 N	28.01 E
Adutiškis	76	55.09 N	26.36 E
Advance	194	37.06 N	89.55 W
Adventure, Bahía ⋓	254	44.50 S	74.45 W
Advie	46	57.23 N	3.27 W
Advocate Harbour	186	45.20 N	64.47 W
Adwa	144	14.10 N	38.55 E
'Adwān, Wādī ∨	146	31.35 N	21.13 E
Adwick le Street	44	53.34 N	1.11 W
Adyča ≃	74	68.13 N	134.41 E
Adyge	84	44.19 N	41.57 E
Adygejskaja Avtonomnaja Oblast' □8	78	45.00 N	40.00 E
Adyk	80	45.48 N	45.38 E
Adžarskaja Avtonomnaja Sovetskaja Socialističeskaja Respublika □3	84	41.40 N	42.00 E
Adžikend	84	40.31 N	46.21 E
Adžima	89	48.08 N	139.40 E
Adzopé	150	6.06 N	3.52 W
Adzopé □5	150	6.00 N	3.30 W
Adzragyn ≃	88	49.54 N	104.09 E
Adz'va ≃	24	66.36 N	59.28 E
Adz'vavom	24	66.36 N	59.12 E
Ae, Water of ≃	44	55.08 N	3.27 W
Æbelø I	41	55.38 N	10.12 E
Aegean Sea ⊤2	38	38.30 N	25.00 E
Aegerisee ⊜	58	47.07 N	8.38 E
Aegina → Aíyina I	38	37.46 N	23.26 E
Aegna I	76	59.35 N	24.48 E
Aegviidu	76	59.17 N	25.37 E
Aekhumbang	114	1.59 N	99.11 E
Aeon Point ≻	174o	1.46 N	157.11 W
A'ergeshanmai ⋀⋀	120	36.40 N	88.00 E
Aerhuola	89	51.01 N	120.10 E
A'erjinshanmai ⋀⋀	90	37.30 N	86.30 E
Aerjisumu	102	42.58 N	111.08 E
Aerkuhu ⊜	120	30.43 N	82.55 E
Ærø I	41	54.53 N	10.20 E
Aeroflotskij	78	45.03 N	34.01 E
Aero-Haven Airport ⊠	285	39.49 N	74.54 W
Aeron ≃	42	52.14 N	4.16 W
Aeroparque ⊠	288	34.35 S	58.24 W
Ærøskøbing	41	54.53 N	10.25 E
Aerqishan ∧	89	48.35 N	121.07 E
Aershan	89	47.11 N	119.57 E
Aershatu	102	44.11 N	113.36 E
Aerzen	52	52.03 N	9.16 E
Aesch	58	47.28 N	7.36 E
Aeschi	58	46.40 N	7.42 E
Aetna	182	49.08 N	113.15 W
Afade	146	12.14 N	14.38 E
Afadjoto ∧2	150	7.05 N	0.35 E
'Afak	128	32.04 N	45.15 E
Afanasjevka	78	50.47 N	38.36 E
Afanasjevo, S.S.S.R.	82	54.20 N	37.01 E
Afanasjevo, S.S.S.R.	82	55.18 N	36.12 E
Afanasjevskoje	86	56.49 N	58.17 E
Afándou	38	36.17 N	28.10 E
Afar	148	25.30 N	8.22 E
Afareaitu	174s	17.33 S	149.47 W
Afars and Issas → Djibouti □1	144	11.30 N	43.00 E
Afaspida	272c	19.08 N	73.04 E
Afdem	144	9.26 N	41.02 E
Afferde, B.R.D.	52	52.06 N	9.25 E
Afferde, B.R.D.	263	51.34 N	7.39 E
Affi	64	45.33 N	10.46 E
Affing	58	48.27 N	10.58 E
Afflisses, Oued ∨	148	28.29 N	1.09 E
Affollé ⋀⋀2	150	16.55 N	10.25 W
Affoltern am Albis	58	47.17 N	8.27 E
Affori ◆8	266b	45.31 N	9.10 E
Affric ≃	46	57.19 N	4.50 W
Affric, Glen ∨	46	57.17 N	4.56 W
Affton	219	38.33 N	90.20 W
Afghānestān → Afghanistan □1	118	33.00 N	65.00 E
Afghanistan □1	118	33.00 N	65.00 E
Afgoi	144	2.10 N	45.09 E
'Afīf	128	23.55 N	42.56 E
Afikpo	150	5.53 N	7.56 E
Afipskij	78	44.55 N	38.50 E
Afiqim	132	32.40 N	35.35 E
Åfjord	26	63.58 N	10.12 E
Aflao	150	6.05 N	1.08 E
Aflenz Kurort	61	47.32 N	15.14 E
Aflou	148	34.07 N	2.06 E
Afmadu	144	0.32 N	42.10 E
Afodo	144	10.17 N	34.50 E
Afogados da Ingàzeira	250	7.45 S	37.39 W
Afognak Island I	180	58.15 N	152.30 W
Afonicha	24	68.13 N	53.17 E
Afono Bay C	174u	14.15 S	170.39 W
Afonso Bezerra	250	5.30 S	36.30 W
Afonso Cláudio	255	20.05 S	41.08 W
Afonsos, Campo dos ■	287a	22.53 S	43.23 W
Afonsos, Rio dos ≃	287a	22.51 S	43.23 W
'Afrā', Wādī ∨	128	30.59 N	35.38 E
Afragola	68	40.55 N	14.18 E
'Afraj, 'Alam al- ∧2	142	30.40 N	29.37 E
Afram ≃	150	7.00 N	0.52 E
Afram Plains ☷	150	6.50 N	0.10 W
Africa ◆1	10	10.00 N	22.00 E
Africa del Sur → South Africa □1	156	30.00 S	26.00 E
Africo	68	38.04 N	15.59 E
Afrika → Africa ◆1	10	10.00 N	22.00 E
Afrikanda	24	67.25 N	32.43 E
'Afrīn	130	36.31 N	36.52 E
Afrique → Africa ◆1	10	10.00 N	22.00 E
Afrique du Sud (République d') → South Africa □1	156	30.00 S	26.00 E
Afritz	64	46.43 N	13.48 E
Afşin	130	38.15 N	36.55 E
Afsluitdijk ◆5	52	53.00 N	5.15 E
Afton, Iowa, U.S.	194	41.02 N	94.12 W
Afton, N.Y., U.S.	210	42.14 N	75.32 W
Afton, Okla., U.S.	196	36.42 N	94.58 W
Afton, Wis., U.S.	216	42.36 N	89.04 W
Afton, Wyo., U.S.	200	42.44 N	110.56 W
Aftout ◆1	148	26.40 N	3.48 W
Afuá	250	0.10 S	50.23 W
'Afula	132	32.36 N	35.17 E
'Afula 'Illit	132	32.38 N	35.20 E
Afyon	130	38.45 N	30.33 E
Afyon □4	130	38.40 N	30.30 E
Afyonkarahisar → Afyon	130	38.45 N	30.33 E
Afzalgarh	124	29.24 N	78.41 E
Aga, Nor.	26	60.18 N	6.36 E
Aga, S.S.S.R.	88	51.12 N	115.10 E
Aga ≃	88	51.30 N	115.50 E
Agačag	85	44.03 N	71.58 E
Agadem	146	16.50 N	13.17 E
Agadez	150	16.58 N	7.59 E
Agadez □5	146	19.45 N	12.00 E
Agadir	148	30.26 N	9.36 W
Agadyr'	86	48.17 N	72.53 E
Agafonovka	80	50.36 N	47.26 E
Agāhpur	272a	28.34 N	77.22 E
Ägäisches Meer → Aegean Sea ⊤2	38	38.30 N	25.00 E
Agalak	140	11.01 N	32.42 E
Agalega Islands II	138	10.24 S	56.37 E
Agan ≃	72	61.23 N	74.35 E
Agana	174p	13.28 N	144.45 E
Agana Naval Air Station ■	174p	13.29 N	144.48 E
Agano ≃	92	37.57 N	139.08 E
Agapa	74	71.27 N	89.15 E
Agapovka	86	53.18 N	59.28 E
Agar	120	23.42 N	76.01 E
Agara	84	42.03 N	43.49 E
Ågård	41	55.35 N	9.26 E
Agaro	144	7.50 N	36.40 E
Agartala	120	23.49 N	91.16 E
Agaru	140	10.59 N	34.44 E
Agaruut	102	43.11 N	109.28 E
Agasan	272c	19.11 N	73.04 E
Agassiz	182	49.14 N	121.46 W
Agassiz, Cape ≻	9	68.29 S	62.56 W
Agat	174p	13.24 N	144.39 E
Agat Bay C	174p	13.24 N	144.39 E
Agate	198	39.28 N	103.56 W
Agate Beach	202	44.41 N	124.04 W
Agats	164	5.33 S	138.08 E
Agatsuma	94	36.34 N	138.50 E
Agatsuma ≃	94	36.30 N	139.01 E
Agatti Island I	122	10.50 N	72.12 E
Agattu Island I	181a	52.25 N	173.35 E
Agattu Strait ⋓	181a	52.35 N	173.25 E
Agawa	96	33.34 N	133.10 E
Agawa ≃	190	47.21 N	84.38 W
Agawa Bay C	190	47.20 N	84.42 W
Agawam, Mass., U.S.	207	42.05 N	72.37 W
Agawam, Mont., U.S.	182	48.00 N	112.10 W
Agay	62	43.26 N	6.51 E
Agazzano	62	44.57 N	9.31 E
Agbélouvé	150	6.40 N	1.10 E
Agboju	273a	6.28 N	3.17 E
Agbor	150	6.18 N	6.11 E
Agboville	150	5.56 N	4.13 W
Agboville □5	150	5.45 N	4.10 W
Agboyi Creek ≃	273a	6.34 N	3.25 E
Ağcakışla	130	39.33 N	36.22 E
Agcawayan	116	13.46 N	120.16 E
Agdam	84	39.59 N	46.57 E
Agdaš	84	40.38 N	47.28 E
Agde	32	43.19 N	3.28 E
Agde, Cap d' ≻	32	43.16 N	3.30 E
Agdžabedi	84	40.03 N	47.28 E
Agege	150	6.37 N	3.20 E
Agejevo	82	54.10 N	36.29 E
Agematsu	94	35.47 N	137.42 E
Agen	32	44.12 N	0.37 E
Agency	190	41.00 N	92.18 W
Agency Lake ⊜	202	42.32 N	121.58 W
Ageo	94	35.58 N	139.36 E
Agepsta, Gora ∧	84	43.32 N	40.30 E
Ager ≃	60	48.05 N	13.51 E
Ageraro	144	4.08 N	42.40 E
Agerbæk	41	55.36 N	8.48 E
Agere Hiywet	144	8.56 N	37.56 E
Agerskov	41	55.07 N	9.08 E
Agersø I	41	55.12 N	11.12 E
Ager Tay ◆4	146	20.15 N	17.31 E
Agery	168b	34.10 S	137.44 E
Aggeneis	158	29.03 S	18.51 E
Agger ≃	56	50.48 N	7.11 E
Aggius	71	40.46 N	9.04 E
Aggstein ⊥	61	48.18 N	15.25 E
Aggteleki Barlang ◆5	30	48.30 N	20.32 E
Āghā Jārī	128	30.42 N	49.50 E
Aghleam	48	54.08 N	10.07 W
Agia	124	26.05 N	90.32 E
Agimont	56	50.10 N	4.48 E
Ağın	130	38.57 N	38.43 E
Agincourt ◆8	275b	43.48 N	79.17 W
Aginskij Bur'atskij Nacional'nyj Okrug □8	88	51.00 N	114.00 E
Aginskoje, S.S.S.R.	86	55.15 N	94.55 E
Aginskoje, S.S.S.R.	88	51.06 N	114.32 E
Agira	70	37.39 N	14.31 E
Aglasterhausen	56	49.21 N	8.59 E
Ağlasun	130	37.40 N	30.32 E
Agliana	66	43.54 N	11.00 E
Agliano	62	44.47 N	8.15 E
Aglientu	71	41.05 N	9.07 E
Agly ≃	32	42.47 N	3.02 E
Agna	64	45.10 N	11.58 E
Agnadello	62	45.26 N	9.33 E
Agnes, Mount ∧	162	26.51 S	128.59 E
Agnes Lake ⊜	190	48.13 N	91.21 W
Agnew	162	28.01 S	120.30 E
Agnews Hill ∧2, N. Ire., U.K.	48	54.50 N	6.54 W
Agnibilékrou	150	7.08 N	3.12 W
Agnije-Afanasjevskij	89	51.57 N	138.45 E
Agnita	38	45.59 N	24.38 E
Agno, Pil.	116	16.07 N	119.48 E
Agno, Schw.	58	46.00 N	8.54 E
Agno ≃, It.	64	45.15 N	11.28 E
Agno ≃, Pil.	116	16.02 N	120.08 E
Agnone	66	41.48 N	14.22 E
Agnone Bagni ◆8	70	37.18 N	15.06 E
Ago	92	34.20 N	136.51 E
Agogna ≃	62	45.04 N	8.54 E
Agogo, Ghana	150	6.47 N	1.04 W
Agogo, Sūd.	140	7.49 N	28.52 E
Agoo	116	16.20 N	120.22 E
Agordat → Akordat	144	15.35 N	37.54 E
Agordo	64	46.17 N	12.02 E
Agostinho Pôrto	287a	22.47 S	43.23 W
Agostitlán	234	19.33 N	100.41 W
Agouma	152	1.32 S	10.11 E
Agouna	150	7.34 N	1.42 E
Agoura	228	34.08 N	118.45 W
Agout ≃	32	43.47 N	1.41 E
Agoza ⊥	146	18.30 N	23.45 E
Āgra	124	27.11 N	78.01 E
Āgra □5	124	27.10 N	78.00 E
Āgra Canal ⩧	272a	28.34 N	77.18 E
Agrachanskij Poluostrov ≻1	84	43.42 N	47.36 E
Agraciada	258	33.48 S	58.15 W
Agrado	246	2.15 N	75.46 W
Agrafenovka	83	47.45 N	39.29 E
Agram → Zagreb	36	45.48 N	15.58 E
Agramonte	240p	22.41 N	81.07 W
Agrate Brianza	62	45.34 N	9.21 E
Ágreda	34	41.51 N	1.56 W
Agrestina	250	8.27 S	35.57 W
Agri → Karaköse	84	39.44 N	43.03 E
Ağrı □4	84	39.30 N	43.15 E
Agri ≃	68	40.13 N	16.44 E
Agri Bavnehøj ∧2	41	56.14 N	10.33 E
Agrícola Oriental ◆8	286a	19.24 N	99.05 W
Agrigento □4	70	37.27 N	13.30 E
Agrihan I	108	18.46 N	145.40 E
Agrínion	38	38.37 N	21.24 E
Agrio ≃	252	38.21 S	69.43 W
Agripoli	68	40.21 N	15.00 E
Agro Pontino ◆1	66	41.25 N	12.55 E
Agryz	80	56.33 N	53.00 E
Agsumal, Sebjet ⊜	148	24.21 N	12.52 W
Agtuuganon, Mount ∧	116	7.48 N	126.12 E
Agua, Cayo I	236	9.09 N	82.02 W
Agua, Ilha d' I	287a	22.49 S	43.10 W
Agua, Volcán de ∧1	236	14.28 N	90.45 W
Água Boa	255	17.59 S	42.24 W
Água Branca, Bra.	250	7.31 S	37.40 W
Água Branca, Bra.	250	9.17 S	37.55 W
Água Branca, Bra.	250	5.53 S	42.38 W
Água Branca, Parque da ♠	287b	23.32 S	46.40 W
Agua Brava, Laguna de C	234	22.10 N	105.32 W
Agua Caliente	234	23.20 N	105.20 W
Agua Caliente, Cerro ∧	232	26.27 N	106.12 W
Agua Caliente Creek ≃	282	37.29 N	121.56 W
Agua Caliente de Chínipas	232	27.27 N	108.32 W
Agua Caliente Grande de Gastelum	232	26.31 N	108.22 W
Aguacate	240p	22.59 N	81.49 W
Aguachica	246	8.19 N	73.38 W
Água Clara	255	20.27 S	52.52 W
Água Comprida, Bra.	255	20.04 S	48.08 W
Água Comprida, Bra.	256	21.54 S	45.40 W
Aguada	240m	18.23 N	67.11 W
Aguada Cecilio	254	40.51 S	65.51 W
Aguada de Guerra	254	41.04 S	68.25 W
Aguada de Pasajeros	240p	22.23 N	80.51 W
Aguadas	246	5.37 N	75.27 W
Agua de Afuera, Sierra del ⋀⋀	234	23.53 N	99.45 W
Agua de Dios	246	4.23 N	74.40 W
Aguadilla	240m	18.26 N	67.09 W
Água Doce	252	27.00 S	51.33 W
Agua Dulce, Méx.	234	18.08 N	94.08 W
Aguadulce, Pan.	236	8.15 N	80.33 W
Agua Dulce, Calif., U.S.	228	34.30 N	118.23 W
Agua Escondida	234	19.08 N	103.27 W
Agua Fria ≃	200	33.23 N	112.21 W
Agua Fria Creek ≃	282	37.28 N	121.56 W
Aguaí	256	22.04 S	46.58 W
Aguaje Copal, Cerro ∧	234	16.33 N	95.15 W
Agualeguas	232	26.18 N	99.34 W
Água Limpa	255	18.06 S	48.46 W
Água Limpa, Serra da ⋀⋀	256	22.30 S	45.25 W
Agualva-Cacém	266c	38.46 N	9.18 W
Aguán ≃	236	15.57 N	85.44 W
Aguanaval ≃, Méx.	232	25.28 N	102.53 W
Aguanaval ≃, Méx.	234	23.39 N	103.08 W
Agua Negra	286c	10.28 N	67.01 W
Aguanish	186	50.13 N	62.05 W
Aguanus ≃	186	50.13 N	62.05 W
Aguapeí ≃	248	15.53 S	58.25 W
Aguapepito	232	24.33 N	107.39 W
Aguapey ≃	252	29.07 S	56.36 W
Água Preta, Igarapé ≃	246	1.41 S	63.48 W
Agua Prieta	232	31.18 N	109.34 W
Aguaragüe, Serranía de ⋀⋀	248	21.30 S	63.40 W
Aguaray	252	22.16 S	63.44 W
Aguaray-Guazú ≃, Para.	252	24.05 S	56.40 W
Aguaray-Guazú ≃, Para.	252	24.47 S	57.19 W
Aguarico ≃	246	0.59 S	75.11 W
Aguaruto	232	24.47 N	107.29 W
Aguas ≃	34	37.09 N	1.49 W
Águas, Serra das ∧	256	21.55 S	45.25 W
Aguasabon ≃	190	48.46 N	87.07 W
Águas Belas	250	9.07 S	37.07 W
Aguas Buenas	240m	18.15 N	66.06 W
Aguascalientes, Méx.	200	32.18 N	115.10 W
Aguascalientes, Méx.	234	21.53 N	102.18 W
Aguascalientes □3	234	22.00 N	102.30 W
Aguascalientes, Río de ≃	234	21.23 N	102.28 W
Aguas Corrientes	258	34.31 S	56.24 W
Águas Formosas	255	17.05 S	40.57 W
Aguasvivas ≃	34	41.20 N	0.25 W
Agua Tibia ∧	228	33.24 N	116.59 W
Água Verde ≃	248	13.42 S	56.43 W
Água Viva	256	21.41 S	42.33 W
Aguayo	252	31.40 S	65.54 W
Aguaytía ≃	248	8.08 S	74.37 W
Agua Zarca, Méx.	200	31.10 N	110.59 W
Agua Zarca, Méx.	234	23.10 N	104.28 W
Agu Bay C	176	70.18 N	86.30 W
Agudo	252	29.38 S	53.15 W
Agudos	255	22.28 S	49.00 W
Águeda	34	40.34 N	8.27 W
Águeda ≃	34	41.02 N	6.56 W
Aguelhok	150	19.28 N	0.52 E
Aguema	152	12.03 S	21.49 E
Aguenier, Lac ⊜	186	50.43 N	68.13 W
Agugliano	66	43.32 N	13.23 E
Agui	94	34.55 N	136.55 E
Aguijan I	108	14.51 N	145.34 E
Aguila	200	33.56 N	113.11 W
Águila, Cerro del ∧	232	26.58 N	112.28 W
Aguilar, Esp.	34	37.31 N	4.39 W
Aguilar, Colo., U.S.	198	37.24 N	104.46 W
Aguilares, Arg.	252	27.26 S	65.37 W
Aguilares, El Sal.	236	13.58 N	89.12 W
Águilas	34	37.24 N	1.35 W
Aguililla	234	18.44 N	102.44 W
Aguirre ≃	246	8.28 N	61.02 W
Aguirre, Arroyo ≃	288	34.46 S	58.35 W
Aguirre, Bahía C	254	54.57 S	65.50 W
Aguja, Cerro ∧	254	42.11 S	71.51 W
Aguja, Punta ≻	248	5.48 S	81.06 W
Aguja Point ≻	116	12.42 N	123.23 E
Agujas, Cabo de las → Agulhas, Cape ≻	158	34.52 S	20.00 E
Agujereada, Punta ≻	240m	18.31 N	67.08 W
Agujita	196	27.53 N	101.09 W
Agul ≃	88	55.44 N	95.41 E
Agulaa	144	13.42 N	39.35 E
Agulhas	158	34.50 S	20.00 E
Agulhas, Cape ≻	158	34.52 S	20.00 E
Agulhas Basin ✢1	8	45.00 S	25.00 E
Agulhas Negras	256	22.28 S	44.27 W
Agulhas Negras, Pico das ∧	256	22.23 S	44.38 W
Agung, Gunung ∧	115b	8.21 S	115.30 E
Agusan □4	116	8.35 N	125.35 E
Agusan ≃	116	9.00 N	125.31 E
Agustín Codazzi	246	10.02 N	73.14 W
Agustino, Cerro ∧	286d	12.04 S	77.00 W
Agutaya	116	11.09 N	120.56 E
Agutaya Island I	116	11.09 N	120.58 E
Ağva	130	41.09 N	29.50 E
Agvali	84	42.33 N	46.06 E
Ağvaniş	130	40.04 N	38.37 E
Agwarra	150	10.42 N	4.35 E
Ägypten → Egypt □1	140	27.00 N	30.00 E
Aha	174m	26.43 N	128.17 E
Ahaggar (Hoggar) ⋀⋀	148	23.00 N	6.30 E
Ahaggar, Tassili des ⋀⋀	150	20.20 N	4.40 E
Ahaggar, Tassili du ⋀⋀1	148	21.00 N	6.00 E
Aha Hills ⋀⋀2	156	19.45 S	21.10 E
Aha-kō C	174m	26.43 N	128.18 E
Ahalt	130	40.50 N	41.33 E
Aham	60	48.32 N	12.28 E

≃	River	Fluss	Río	Rivière	Rio
⩧	Canal	Kanal	Canal	Canal	Canal
ʟ	Waterfall, Rapids	Wasserfall, Stromschnellen	Cascada, Rápidos	Chute d'eau, Rapides	Cascata, Rápidos
⋓	Strait	Meeresstrasse	Estrecho	Détroit	Estreito
C	Bay, Gulf	Bucht, Golf	Bahía, Golfo	Baie, Golfe	Baía, Golfo
⊜	Lake, Lakes	See, Seen	Lago, Lagos	Lac, Lacs	Lago, Lagos
☷	Swamp	Sumpf	Pantano	Marais	Pântano
⩒	Ice Features, Glacier	Eis- und Gletscherformen	Accidentes Glaciales	Formes glaciaires	Acidentes Glaciares
⊤	Other Hydrographic Features	Andere Hydrographische Objekte	Otros Elementos Hidrográficos	Autres données hydrographiques	Outros Elementos Hidrográficos
✢	Submarine Features	Untermeerische Objekte	Accidentes Submarinos	Formes de relief sous-marin	Acidentes Submarinos
□	Political Unit	Politische Einheit	Unidad Politica	Entité politique	Unidade Política
♥	Cultural Institution	Kulturelle Institution	Institución Cultural	Institution culturelle	Instituição Cultural
⊥	Historical Site	Historische Stätte	Sitio Histórico	Site historique	Sitio Histórico
♠	Recreational Site	Erholungs- und Ferienort	Sitio de Recreo	Centre de loisirs	Sítio de Lazer
⊠	Airport	Flughafen	Aeropuerto	Aéroport	Aeroporto
■	Military Installation	Militäranlage	Instalación Militar	Installation militaire	Instalação Militar
◆	Miscellaneous	Verschiedenes	Misceláneo	Divers	Miscelânea

ENGLISH — Name / Page / Lat.°′ / Long.°′
DEUTSCH — Name / Seite / Breite°′ / Länge°′ E=Ost

Ahar 128 38.28 N 47.04 E
Ahar ≃ 128 38.32 N 47.31 E
Ahascragh 48 53.24 N 8.20 W
Ahaura 172 42.21 S 171.32 E
Ahaus 52 52.04 N 7.00 E
Ahe ≃ 263 51.13 N 7.43 E
Aheggar ∧ 148 24.43 N 5.39 E
Aheqi 85 40.52 N 77.58 E
Ahfir 148 34.57 N 2.17 W
Ahipara 172 35.10 S 173.10 E
Ahipara Bay ⊂ 172 35.10 S 173.07 E
'Āhirah 132 32.53 N 36.28 E
Ahırlı, Tür. 130 37.14 N 32.08 E
Ahırlı, Tür. 130 38.37 N 26.31 E
Ahklun Mountains ∧∧ 180 59.15 N 161.00 W
Ahlât 130 38.45 N 42.29 E
Ahlbeck 54 53.40 N 14.11 E
Ahlem 52 52.23 N 9.40 E
Ahlen 52 51.46 N 7.53 E
Ahlenberg 263 51.25 N 7.28 E
Ahlenmoor ◆[3] 52 53.40 N 8.45 E
Ahlhorn 52 52.54 N 8.14 E
Ahlsdorf 54 51.32 N 11.28 E
Ahmadābād 120 23.02 N 72.37 E
Aḥmadābād-e Sarjām 128 35.51 N 59.36 E
Aḥmad al-Bāqirī, Jabal ∧ 132 29.36 N 35.08 E
Ahmadgarh 123 30.41 N 75.50 E
Aḥmadī 128 27.56 N 56.42 E
Ahmadnagar 122 19.05 N 74.44 E
Ahmadpur, Bhārat 124 23.31 N 77.13 E
Ahmadpur, Bhārat 126 23.50 N 87.42 E
Ahmadpur East 123 29.09 N 71.16 E
Ahmadpur Siāl 123 30.41 N 71.46 E
Ahmad Wāl 120 29.25 N 65.56 E
Ahmar, 'egr el ◆[2] 148 23.30 N 4.54 W
Aḥmar, Jabal al- ∧ 132 29.40 N 35.09 E
Ahmar Mountains ∧∧ 144 9.15 N 41.00 E
Ahmedabad → Ahmadābād 120 23.02 N 72.37 E
Ahmetli 130 38.31 N 27.57 E
Ahmic Lake ⊜ 190 45.37 N 79.42 W
Ahnet, Adrar n' ∧∧ 148 24.58 N 2.57 E
Ahogados, Arroyo de los ≃ 258 33.37 S 56.31 W
Ahon, Tarso ∧ 146 20.23 N 18.18 E
Ahornspitz ∧ 64 47.08 N 11.56 E
Ahoskie 192 36.17 N 76.59 W
Ahr ≃ 56 50.33 N 7.17 E
Ahram 128 28.52 N 51.16 E
Ahrāmāt Dahshūr (North and Bent Pyramids) ⊥ 142 29.48 N 31.13 E
Ahrāmāt Maydūm (Maydūm Pyramid) ⊥ 142 29.23 N 31.10 E
Ahraura 124 25.01 N 83.01 E
Ahrensbök 54 54.00 N 10.34 E
Ahrensburg 52 53.40 N 10.14 E
Ahrensdorf, D.D.R. 54 52.10 N 14.05 E
Ahrensdorf, D.D.R. 264a 52.19 N 13.12 E
Ahrensfelde 264a 52.35 N 13.35 E
Ahrgebirge ∧∧ 56 50.30 N 6.50 E
Ahtanum 224 46.34 N 120.37 W
Ahtanum Creek ≃ 202 46.32 N 120.31 W
Ahtanum Ridge ∧ 224 46.30 N 120.50 W
Ähtäri 26 62.34 N 24.06 E
Ähtärinjärvi ⊜ 26 62.40 N 24.03 E
Ähtävänjoki ≃ 26 63.38 N 22.48 E
Ahtopol 38 42.06 N 27.57 E
Ahu 98 34.27 N 118.39 E
Ahuacatlán, Méx. 234 21.03 N 104.29 W
Ahuacatlán, Méx. 234 20.00 N 97.52 W
Ahuachapán 236 13.55 N 89.51 W
Ahuacuotzingo 234 17.42 N 98.56 W
Ahualulco de Mercado 234 20.42 N 103.59 W
Ahuijullo 234 19.05 N 103.05 W
Ahuijullo ≃ 234 18.49 N 103.37 W
Ahumada 204 32.30 N 115.30 W
Ahun 32 46.05 N 2.05 E
Ahuntsic ◆[8] 275a 45.33 N 73.39 W
Ahunui I[1] 14 19.39 S 140.25 W
Ahuriri ≃ 172 44.33 S 170.11 E
Åhus 26 55.55 N 14.17 E
Ahvāz 128 31.19 N 48.42 E
Ahvenanmaa □[4] 26 60.15 N 20.00 E
Ahvenanmaa (Åland) II 26 60.15 N 20.00 E
Ahwahnee 226 37.23 N 119.44 W
Aḥwar 144 13.31 N 46.42 E
Ahwa-ri 98 35.54 N 129.02 E
Aialik, Cape ≻ 180 59.42 N 149.31 W
Aiándion 267c 37.55 N 23.28 E
Aiapuá 246 4.29 S 62.04 W
Aiapuá, Lago ⊜ 246 4.27 S 62.08 W
Aibihu ⊜ 86 44.55 N 82.55 E
Aibonito 240m 18.08 N 66.16 W
Aich, B.R.D. 60 48.25 N 12.24 E
Aich, Öst. 64 47.25 N 13.49 E
Aichach 60 48.28 N 11.08 E
Aicha vorm Wald 60 48.41 N 13.18 E
Aichi □[5] 94 35.00 N 137.15 E
Aichi-yōsui ≍ 94 34.42 N 136.57 E
Aichstetten 58 47.54 N 10.04 E
Aide ≃ 42 52.10 N 1.27 E
Aidenbach 60 48.34 N 13.06 E
Aidomaggiore 71 40.10 N 8.51 E
Aidone 70 37.25 N 14.27 E
Aidong 102 24.46 N 107.21 E
Aiduma, Pulau I 164 3.58 S 134.06 E
Aiea 229c 21.23 N 157.56 W
Aiello Calabro 68 39.07 N 16.10 E
Aigáleos Óros ∧[2] 267c 38.00 N 23.37 E
Aigburth ◆[8] 262 53.22 N 2.55 W
Aigen im Mühlkreis 60 48.39 N 13.58 E
Aigenmiao 89 44.36 N 120.50 E
Aigle 58 46.19 N 6.58 E
Aigle, Lac à l' ⊜ 186 51.12 N 65.25 W
Aiglon, Île à l' I 275a 45.42 N 73.28 W
Aignay-le-Duc 58 47.40 N 4.44 E
Aigre 32 45.54 N 0.01 E
Aiguá 252 34.12 S 54.45 W
Aiguebelette, Lac d' ⊜ 62 45.33 N 5.48 E
Aiguebelette-le-Lac 62 45.32 N 5.49 E
Aiguebelle 62 45.32 N 6.18 E
Aiguebelle, Réserve (Aiguebelle Reserve) ♠ 190 48.33 N 78.45 W
Aigueperse 32 46.01 N 3.12 E
Aigues ≃ 62 44.07 N 4.43 E
Aigues-Mortes 62 43.34 N 4.11 E
Aigues-Mortes, Golfe d' ⊂ 62 43.31 N 4.03 E
Aigues-Vives 62 43.44 N 4.10 E
Aiguilles 62 44.47 N 6.52 E
Aiguines 62 43.46 N 6.15 E
Aigurande 32 46.26 N 1.50 E
Aihun (Heihe) 89 50.13 N 127.33 E
Aija 248 9.46 S 77.38 W
Aijal 120 23.44 N 92.43 E
Aikawa, Nihon 92 38.02 N 138.15 E
Aikawa, Nihon 94 35.32 N 139.17 E
Aiken 192 33.34 N 81.43 W
Aikens Lake ⊜ 184 51.12 N 95.20 W
Ailaoshan ∧∧ 102 24.08 N 101.25 E
Ailefroide 62 44.53 N 6.27 E
Aileron 162 22.39 S 133.20 E
Ailigandí 246 9.14 N 78.01 W
Ailingen 58 47.41 N 9.29 E
Ailinglapalap I[1] 14 7.23 N 168.46 E
Ailinzhuang 105 39.27 N 117.36 E
Aillant-sur-Tholon 50 47.52 N 3.21 E
Aille ≃ 62 43.26 N 6.30 E
Ailly-le-Haut-Clocher 50 50.05 N 2.00 E
Ailly-sur-Noye 50 49.45 N 2.22 E
Ailly-sur-Somme 50 49.55 N 2.12 E
Ailo 164 4.50 S 151.40 E
Ailsa Craig 190 43.08 N 81.33 W
Ailsa Craig I 44 55.16 N 5.07 W
Aim 74 58.50 N 134.12 E
Aimargues 62 43.41 N 4.12 E
Aime 62 45.33 N 6.39 E
Aimenguan)(100 31.24 N 115.22 E
Aimere 115b 8.50 S 120.52 E
Aimi 96 35.22 N 133.22 E
Aimogasta 252 28.33 S 66.49 W
Aimorés 255 19.30 S 41.04 W
Aimoto 270 34.59 N 135.10 E
Ain ≃ 62 45.48 N 5.10 E
Ainabo 144 8.57 N 46.30 E
Aïn Arnat 34 36.11 N 5.19 E
Aïn Azel 34 35.49 N 5.31 E
Ainaži 76 57.52 N 24.21 E
Aïn Beïda 148 35.48 N 7.24 E
Aïn Benian 148 36.48 N 2.55 E
Aïn ben Tili 148 26.00 N 9.32 W
Aïn Berda 36 36.39 N 7.35 E
Aïn Bessem 34 36.18 N 3.40 E
Aincourt 261 49.04 N 1.47 E
Aïn Defla 34 36.16 N 1.58 E
Aïn Deheb 148 34.51 N 1.33 E
Aïn Djelloula 36 35.48 N 9.51 E
Aïn Draham 148 36.47 N 8.42 E
Aine ≃ 56 50.23 N 5.31 E
Aïne Belbela, Sebkha ⌣ 148 27.30 N 5.20 W
Aïn el Hadjel 34 35.40 N 3.53 E
Aïn el Kebira 34 36.22 N 5.30 E
Aïn M'Lila 148 36.02 N 6.34 E
Aino-shima I, Nihon 96 33.59 N 130.50 E
Aïn Oulmène 34 35.55 N 5.18 E
Aïn Oussera 148 35.27 N 2.54 E
Ainring 64 47.48 N 12.56 E
Ainsdale 262 53.36 N 3.02 W
Aïn Sefra 148 32.45 N 0.35 W
Ain Shams University ⊌[2] 273c 30.05 N 31.18 E
Ainslie, Mount ∧ 171b 35.16 S 149.10 E
Ainslie Lake ⊜ 186 46.08 N 61.12 W
Ainsworth, Eng., U.K. 262 53.35 N 2.22 W
Ainsworth, Nebr., U.S. 198 42.33 N 99.52 W
Aïn Taghrout 34 36.08 N 5.05 E
Aïn Tedelès 148 36.00 N 0.18 E
Aïn Témouchent 148 35.18 N 1.08 W
Aïn Touta 148 35.23 N 5.54 E
Aintree 262 53.29 N 2.56 W
Aintree Race Course ♠ 262 53.28 N 2.56 W
Aïn Yagout 148 35.47 N 6.25 E
Aio 96 34.00 N 131.28 E
Aioi 96 34.48 N 134.28 E
Aiome 164 5.10 S 144.45 E
Aipe 246 3.13 N 75.15 W
Aiquara 255 14.07 S 39.52 W
Aiquile 248 18.10 S 65.10 W
Aïr ∧∧ 150 18.00 N 8.30 E
Airabu, Pulau I 112 2.46 N 106.14 E
Airaines 50 49.58 N 1.57 E
Airão 246 1.56 S 61.22 W
Airasca 62 44.55 N 7.29 E
Airbangis 110 0.12 N 99.23 E
Airdikit 112 2.40 S 101.15 E
Airdrie, Alta., Can. 182 51.18 N 114.02 W
Airdrie, Scot., U.K. 46 55.52 N 3.59 W
Aire ≃, Fr. 56 49.19 N 4.49 E
Aire ≃, Eng., U.K. 44 53.44 N 0.54 W
Aire-sur-l'Adour 32 43.42 N 0.16 W
Aire-sur-la-Lys 50 50.38 N 2.24 E
Air Force Island I 176 67.55 N 74.10 W
Airgegas 112 2.42 S 106.25 E
Airhaji 112 1.57 S 100.53 E
Airjamban 114 1.13 N 101.14 E
Airmolek 112 0.22 S 102.17 E
Airmont 276 41.06 N 74.06 W
Airola 68 41.04 N 14.33 E
Airole 62 43.52 N 7.33 E
Airolo 58 46.32 N 8.37 E
Airor 46 57.04 N 5.46 W
Airport West 274b 37.44 S 144.53 E
Airtenang 112 3.08 S 101.43 E
Airterjun 114 1.20 N 100.27 E
Airuno 62 45.45 N 9.25 E
Airvault 32 46.50 N 0.08 W
Aisch ≃ 60 49.46 N 11.01 E
Aisega 164 5.44 S 148.21 E
Aisey-sur-Seine 58 47.45 N 4.35 E
Aishihik 180 61.35 N 137.30 W
Aishihik Lake ⊜ 180 61.25 N 137.06 W
Aisike 85 39.43 N 76.08 E
Aisinaike 85 39.47 N 75.47 E
Aising 64 47.49 N 12.06 E
Aislingen 56 48.30 N 10.27 E
Aisne □[5] 50 49.30 N 3.30 E
Aisne ≃ 50 49.26 N 2.50 E
Aisne à la Marne, Canal de l' ≍ 50 49.24 N 3.55 E
Aïssa, Djebel ∧ 148 32.51 N 0.30 W
Aïssey 58 47.16 N 6.20 E
Aist ≃ 61 48.14 N 14.35 E
Aisy-sur-Armançon 50 47.39 N 4.13 E
Aitana ∧ 34 38.44 N 0.16 W
Aitape 164 3.08 S 142.21 E
Aiterach ≃ 60 48.54 N 12.38 E
Aiterhofen 60 48.51 N 12.37 E
Aith 46 60.16 N 1.23 W
Aitkin 190 46.32 N 93.43 W
Aït-Melloul 148 30.21 N 9.31 W
Aitolikón 38 38.27 N 21.22 E
Aït-Ourir 148 31.38 N 7.42 W
Aitrach 58 47.56 N 10.05 E
Aitutaki I[1] 14 18.52 S 159.45 W
Ait Youssef ou Ali 34 35.13 N 3.55 W
Aiuaba 250 6.38 S 40.07 W
Aiud 38 46.19 N 23.44 E
Aiún → El Aaiún 148 27.09 N 13.12 W
Aiurua, Passe d' ʮ 174s 17.49 S 149.07 W
Aiuruoca 256 21.58 S 44.36 W
Aiuruoca ≃ 256 21.42 S 44.22 W
Aiva 287a 22.42 S 43.28 W
Aiviekste ≃ 76 56.37 N 25.45 E
Aix, Mount ∧ 224 46.47 N 121.15 W
Aix-en-Othe 50 48.13 N 3.44 E
Aix-en-Provence 62 43.32 N 5.26 E
Aix-la-Chapelle → Aachen 56 50.47 N 6.05 E
Aix-les-Bains 62 45.42 N 5.55 E
Aiyáleo 267c 37.59 N 23.41 E
Aiyang, Mount ∧ 164 5.05 S 141.19 E
Aiyansh 182 55.17 N 129.03 W
Aiyialoúsa 130 35.32 N 34.11 E
Aíyina 38 37.44 N 23.27 E
Aíyina I 38 37.46 N 23.26 E
Aiyínion 38 40.30 N 22.33 E
Aíyion 38 38.15 N 22.05 E
Aiyon 175b 7.43 N 134.37 E
Aizhaipuzi 104 40.57 N 124.01 E
Aizpute 76 56.43 N 21.38 E
Aizu-bange 92 37.34 N 139.49 E
Aizu-wakamatsu 92 37.30 N 139.56 E
Ajā 142 30.57 N 31.17 E
'Ajab Shīr 128 37.28 N 45.54 E
Ajaccio 36 41.55 N 8.44 E
Ajaguz 86 47.56 N 80.23 E
Ajaguz ≃ 86 46.42 N 79.15 E
Ajaijú ≃ 246 0.59 N 72.20 W
Ajalpan 234 18.22 N 97.15 W
'Ajaltūn 132 33.58 N 35.41 E
Ajalvir 266a 40.32 N 3.29 W
'Ajamī 130 36.28 N 37.42 E
Ajan, S.S.S.R. 74 56.27 N 138.10 E
Ajan, S.S.S.R. 88 54.43 N 110.55 E
Ajan ≃ 74 70.10 N 95.50 E
Ajana 162 27.57 S 114.38 E
Ajanta 122 20.32 N 75.45 E
Ajaokuta 150 7.28 N 6.39 E
Ajarani ≃ 246 1.33 N 61.16 W
Ajasse 150 8.17 N 4.48 E
Ajasso 150 5.52 N 8.52 E
Ajat ≃ 86 52.54 N 63.02 E
Ajax 212 43.51 N 79.02 W
Ajay ≃ 126 23.39 N 88.08 E
Ajayan Point ≻ 174p 13.15 N 144.43 E
Ajbas 80 47.51 N 49.37 E
Ajdābiyah 146 30.48 N 20.14 E
Ajdabul' 86 52.42 N 68.59 E
Ajdar 78 50.03 N 38.56 E
Ajdar ≃ 83 48.42 N 39.13 E
Ajdarly 86 44.32 N 65.50 E
Ajdar-Nikolajevka 83 48.58 N 38.58 E
Ajdovščina 64 45.53 N 13.53 E
Ajdyrlinskij 86 52.03 N 59.50 E
Ajgurka ≃ 80 45.46 N 43.12 E
Ajgyrkol', Ozero ⊜ 80 48.15 N 52.50 E
Aji 96 34.23 N 134.08 E
Ajibar 144 10.41 N 38.37 E
Ajibarang 115a 7.25 S 109.04 E
Ajigasawa 92 40.47 N 140.12 E
Ajijic 234 20.18 N 103.17 W
Ajil 114 5.05 N 103.05 E
Ajimu 96 33.26 N 131.21 E
Ajipuzicun 104 42.16 N 123.33 E
Ajisu 96 34.00 N 131.22 E
Ajjer, Tassili n' ∧∧[1] 148 25.10 N 8.00 E
Ajka 30 47.07 N 17.34 E
Ajke, Ozero ⊜ 86 50.57 N 61.36 E
Ajkino 24 62.15 N 49.56 E
'Ajlūn 132 32.20 N 35.45 E
Ajlune 224 46.31 N 122.26 W
'Ajmah, Jabal al- ∧∧ 140 29.12 N 34.02 E
Ajmer 120 26.27 N 74.38 E
Ajnāla 123 31.51 N 74.48 E
Ajni 85 39.23 N 68.32 E
Ajo 200 32.22 N 112.52 W
Ajo, Cabo de ≻ 34 43.31 N 3.35 W
Ajok 140 9.15 N 28.27 E
Ajon, Ostrov I 74 69.50 N 168.40 E
Ajoya 232 24.04 N 106.22 W
Ajrag Nuur ⊜ 88 48.54 N 93.28 E
'Ajramīyah, Bi'r al- ▾[4] 142 29.39 N 31.50 E
Ajrum 84 41.13 N 44.53 E
Ajryk 86 50.30 N 76.48 E
Ajsary 86 53.18 N 71.52 E
Ajtos 38 42.42 N 27.15 E
Ajuchitlán del Progreso 234 18.09 N 100.29 W
Ajuda ◆[8] 266c 38.43 N 9.12 W
Ajusco 204 31.35 N 116.25 W
Ajusco ◆[8] 286a 19.14 N 99.12 W
Ajusco, Cerro ∧ 286a 19.12 N 99.15 W
Ajuta ≃ 83 47.34 N 40.07 E
Ajuterique 236 14.20 N 87.43 W
Ajutinskij 83 47.46 N 40.08 E
Ajuy 116 11.10 N 123.01 E
Ajuy Bay ⊂ 116 11.10 N 123.02 E
Ak ≃ 130 37.50 N 28.15 E
Aka ≃ 92 38.54 N 139.50 E
Akaba 150 7.57 N 1.03 E
Akaba Dağı ∧ 130 40.12 N 40.51 E
Akabane 94 34.37 N 137.12 E
Akabira 92a 43.34 N 142.03 E
Akabli 148 26.42 N 1.22 E
Akabori 94 36.22 N 139.14 E
Akademii, Zaliv ⊂ 89 54.15 N 138.05 E
Akademija Nauk ⊌[3] 265a 59.56 N 30.18 E
Akagi, Nihon 94 36.33 N 139.03 E
Akagi, Nihon 96 35.00 N 132.43 E
Akagi-san ∧ 94 36.33 N 139.11 E
Akaishi-dake ∧ 94 35.27 N 138.09 E
Akaishi-sammyaku ∧∧ 92 35.18 N 138.07 E
Akaka Falls ♠ 229d 19.52 N 155.09 W
Akáki 130 35.08 N 33.08 E
Akaki Beseka 144 8.56 N 38.50 E
Akālgarh 123 32.16 N 73.49 E
Akalkot 122 17.32 N 76.13 E
Akaltara 124 22.01 N 82.26 E
Akámas, Akrotírion ≻ 130 35.06 N 32.17 E
Akan 92a 43.06 N 144.10 E
Akana-tōge)(96 34.57 N 132.44 E
Akan-kokuritsu-kōen ♠ 92a 43.30 N 144.15 E
Akaoka 96 33.32 N 133.43 E
Ak-Aral 86 49.10 N 90.57 E
Akaroa 172 43.48 S 172.58 E
Akaroa Harbour ⊂ 172 43.50 S 172.56 E
Åkarp 41 55.39 N 13.07 E
Akasaki 96 35.31 N 133.38 E
'Akasha East 140 21.05 N 30.43 E
Akashi 96 34.38 N 134.59 E
Akashi ≃ 270 34.38 N 134.59 E
Akashi-kaikyō ʮ 96 34.37 N 135.02 E
Akashina 94 36.21 N 137.56 E
Akashi-sammyaku ∧∧ 94 35.18 N 138.07 E
Akatani-ko ⊜[1] 94 36.43 N 138.54 E
Akatjevo 82 54.59 N 38.45 E
Akatova 76 55.09 N 31.48 E
Akatsutsumi ◆[8] 268 35.39 N 139.39 E
Akbaba 267b 41.09 N 29.06 E
Akbajtal 85 38.20 N 73.51 E
Akbarābād 267d 35.41 N 51.21 E
Akbarpur, Bhārat 124 26.25 N 82.33 E
Akbarpur, Bhārat 124 24.39 N 83.58 E
Akbeit 86 51.38 N 70.02 E
Akbou 148 36.28 N 4.32 E
Akbulak, S.S.S.R. 86 49.26 N 80.28 E
Akbulak, S.S.S.R. 86 51.01 N 55.37 E
Akbura ≃ 85 40.39 N 72.36 E
Akçaabat 130 41.02 N 39.34 E
Akçadağ 130 38.21 N 37.59 E
Akçakale 130 36.41 N 38.56 E
Akçakoca 130 41.05 N 31.09 E
Akçakoyunlu 130 36.46 N 37.38 E
Akçaova, Tür. 130 37.30 N 28.02 E
Akçaova, Tür. 130 41.03 N 29.57 E
Akčatau 86 47.59 N 74.02 E
Akçay ≃ 130 37.20 N 30.50 E
Ak-Chin Indian Reservation ◆[4] 200 33.02 N 112.05 W
Akči 85 44.00 N 76.20 E
Akdağ 130 40.43 N 36.00 E
Akdağ ∧, Tür. 130 39.29 N 41.54 E
Akdağ ∧, Tür. 130 36.32 N 29.34 E
Akdağ ∧∧ 84 40.35 N 41.46 E
Akdağmadeni 130 39.40 N 35.54 E
Akdala 86 45.02 N 74.35 E
Ak-Dovurak 86 51.16 N 90.31 E
Akechi 94 35.18 N 137.23 E
Akehama 96 33.19 N 132.26 E
Akeley 190 47.00 N 94.44 W
Aken 54 51.51 N 12.02 E
Akeno, Nihon 94 35.46 N 138.26 E
Akeno, Nihon 94 36.15 N 140.02 E
Åker 40 59.15 N 17.05 E
Åkera ≃ 84 39.09 N 46.51 E
Åkerby 40 60.25 N 17.46 E
Åkersberga 40 59.29 N 18.18 E
Akershus □[6] 26 60.00 N 11.10 E
Akersloot 52 52.34 N 4.44 E
Akesai 102 39.28 N 94.26 E
Akespe 86 46.48 N 60.31 E
Akesu 90 41.10 N 80.20 E
Aketao 85 39.08 N 75.57 E
Aketi 152 2.44 N 23.46 E
Åketilepa 85 39.57 N 74.03 E
Åkforsån ≃ 40 58.54 N 16.28 E
Ak Göl ⊜ 130 38.58 N 31.48 E
Akharnaí 38 38.05 N 23.44 E
Akhḍar, Wādī al- ∨ 128 27.59 N 36.36 E
Akhelóös ≃ 38 38.36 N 21.14 E
Akh Gol ⊜ 84 39.33 N 44.47 E
Akhiok 180 56.57 N 154.10 W
Akhisar 130 38.55 N 27.51 E
Akhmīm 140 26.34 N 31.44 E
Akhnūr 123 32.54 N 74.44 E
Akhtarīn 130 36.31 N 37.20 E
Aki, Nihon 96 33.28 N 131.43 E
Aki, Nihon 96 33.30 N 133.54 E
Aki ≃, Nihon 94 35.41 N 139.21 E
Aki ≃, Nihon 96 33.30 N 133.55 E
Akiachak 180 60.55 N 161.27 W
Akiak 180 60.55 N 161.12 W
Akiéni 152 1.11 S 13.53 E
Akigami-chosuichi ⊜[1] 94 36.04 N 137.24 E
Akima 88 53.06 N 115.44 E
Akimiski Island I 176 53.00 N 81.20 W
Akimovka 78 46.42 N 35.09 E
Åki-nada ▾[2] 96 34.05 N 132.48 E
Åkirkeby 26 55.04 N 14.56 E
Akishima 94 35.41 N 139.22 E
Akišma ≃ 89 52.08 N 132.40 E
Akita 92 39.43 N 140.07 E
Akita-heiya ⌣ 92 39.45 N 140.10 E
Akitkan, Chrebet ∧∧ 88 57.05 N 109.05 E
Akitsu, Nihon 96 34.14 N 132.50 E
Akitsu, Nihon 270 34.56 N 135.06 E
Akiyama 94 35.34 N 139.05 E
Akiyoshi-dai ∧∧[1] 96 34.15 N 131.15 E
Akiyoshi-do ⊥[5] 96 34.14 N 131.19 E
Akjar 86 51.50 N 58.14 E
Akjoujt 150 19.45 N 14.23 W
Akka 148 29.22 N 8.14 W
Akkala 86 43.43 N 59.31 E
Akkani 180 65.30 N 171.10 W
Akkerman → Belgorod-Dnestrovskij 78 46.12 N 30.20 E
Akkermanovka 86 51.11 N 58.12 E
Akkerwoude 52 53.17 N 5.58 E
Akkeshi 92a 43.02 N 144.51 E
Akkışla 130 39.00 N 36.11 E
'Akko (Acre) 132 32.55 N 35.05 E
Akkol', S.S.S.R. 85 43.25 N 70.47 E
Akkol', S.S.S.R. 86 45.02 N 75.40 E
Akkol'skij 86 52.12 N 75.05 E
Akköy 130 37.29 N 27.15 E
Akkra → Accra 150 5.33 N 0.13 W
Akkrum 52 53.03 N 5.50 E
Ak-Kul' 85 41.41 N 74.16 E
Aklan □[4] 116 11.40 N 122.20 E
Aklan ≃ 116 11.44 N 122.20 E
Aklavik 180 68.12 N 135.00 W
'Aklé 'Âduâna ◆[1] 150 18.00 N 5.30 W
Akmeņrags ≻ 76 56.51 N 21.03 E
Akmeşe 130 40.51 N 30.12 E
Akmuz 85 41.16 N 76.09 E
Ākna 272b 22.59 N 88.21 E
Aknīste 76 56.10 N 25.45 E
Aknoul 148 34.43 N 3.49 W
Akō 96 34.45 N 134.24 E
Akoba 80 49.28 N 47.25 E
Akobo 140 7.47 N 33.01 E
Akobo ≃ 140 7.48 N 33.03 E
Akodia 124 23.23 N 76.36 E
Akok, Cam. 152 2.46 N 10.18 E
Akok, Gabon 152 0.31 N 9.45 E
Akola 122 20.44 N 77.00 E
Akom 152 2.37 N 10.04 E
Akonolinga 152 3.47 N 12.15 E
Akop 140 8.21 N 29.05 E
Akor 150 14.53 N 6.58 W
Akora 123 34.00 N 72.08 E
Akordat 144 15.35 N 37.54 E
Akosombo Dam ◆[6] 150 6.16 N 0.03 E
Akot, Bhārat 120 21.11 N 77.04 E
Akot, Sūd. 140 6.33 N 30.03 E
Akouaya 152 6.30 N 9.40 E
Akoupé 150 6.23 N 3.54 W
Akpatok Island I 176 60.25 N 68.00 W
Akpınar, Tür. 130 39.17 N 33.40 E
Akpınar, Tür. 130 37.34 N 38.13 E
Åkrafjorden ⊂[2] 26 59.46 N 6.06 E
Akranes 24a 64.18 N 22.02 W
Åkrehamn 26 59.16 N 5.11 E
Akrítas, Ákra ≻ 38 36.43 N 21.54 E
Akrofuom 150 6.07 N 1.39 W
Akron, Colo., U.S. 198 40.10 N 103.13 W
Akron, Ind., U.S. 216 41.02 N 86.01 W
Akron, Iowa, U.S. 198 42.49 N 96.33 W
Akron, N.Y., U.S. 210 43.01 N 78.30 W
Akron, Ohio, U.S. 214 41.05 N 81.31 W
Akron, Pa., U.S. 208 40.09 N 76.12 W
Akron-Canton Regional Airport ⊠ 214 40.55 N 81.27 W
Akron City Reservoir ⊜[1] 214 41.20 N 81.17 W
Akrópolis ⊥ 267c 37.58 N 23.43 E
Akrothérion Kóchi ≻ 267c 37.53 N 23.27 E
Akrotíri 130 34.36 N 32.57 E
Akša 88 50.16 N 113.17 E
Aksa ◆[8] 272c 19.10 N 72.48 E
Aksaj, S.S.S.R. 83 47.15 N 39.52 E
Aksaj, S.S.S.R. 85 43.22 N 70.12 E
Aksaj (Tuoshihanhe) ≃, As. 85 40.55 N 78.16 E
Aksaj ≃, S.S.S.R. 80 48.01 N 43.13 E
Aksaj ≃, S.S.S.R. 83 47.15 N 39.53 E
Aksaj ≃, S.S.S.R. 84 43.32 N 46.51 E
Aksakovo, S.S.S.R. 80 54.02 N 54.09 E
Aksakovo, S.S.S.R. 86 53.58 N 54.36 E
Aksaray 130 38.23 N 34.03 E
Aksarka 74 66.36 N 67.46 E
Aksatau 86 49.23 N 54.36 E
Akşehir 130 38.21 N 31.25 E
Akşehir Gölü ⊜ 130 38.30 N 31.28 E
Akseki 130 37.02 N 31.48 E
Aksengir ≃ 85 43.40 N 76.14 E
Aksenkino 80 53.59 N 53.06 E
Aksenovo 82 55.40 N 38.15 E
Aksenovo-Zilovskoje 89 53.07 N 117.32 E
Aksentjevo 82 55.25 N 35.54 E
Akšij 86 47.37 N 55.56 E
Akšijrak, Chrebet ∧∧ 85 41.20 N 74.15 E
Aksinjino, S.S.S.R. 82 56.02 N 38.12 E
Aksinjino, S.S.S.R. 82 55.44 N 36.59 E
Aks'onovo 88 58.51 N 101.43 E
Aks'onovo-Zilovskoje 88 53.04 N 117.32 E
Akstafa 84 41.08 N 45.28 E
Akstafa ≃ 84 41.15 N 45.26 E
Aksu, S.S.S.R. 80 50.56 N 53.06 E
Aksu, S.S.S.R. 86 52.28 N 71.59 E
Aksu, S.S.S.R. 86 45.37 N 79.30 E
Aksu ≃, S.S.S.R. 85 43.22 N 73.54 E
Aksu ≃, S.S.S.R. 86 46.20 N 78.15 E
Aksu ≃, Tür. 130 37.36 N 36.46 E
Aksuat, S.S.S.R. 86 47.48 N 82.50 E
Aksuat, S.S.S.R. 86 51.32 N 64.34 E
Aksuat, S.S.S.R. 86 48.16 N 83.50 E
Aksuat, Ozero ⊜ 86 51.24 N 64.28 E
Aksubajevo 80 54.52 N 50.50 E
Aksum 144 14.08 N 38.48 E
Aktal 85 41.25 N 75.03 E
Aktanyš 80 55.43 N 54.05 E
Aktas, S.S.S.R. 85 42.57 N 70.04 E
Aktas, S.S.S.R. 86 49.47 N 72.59 E
Aktas, S.S.S.R. 86 48.02 N 66.21 E
Aktaš, S.S.S.R. 86 50.18 N 87.44 E
Aktasty 86 50.44 N 61.43 E
Aktau 86 50.16 N 73.02 E
Aktepe 130 36.44 N 36.27 E
Akterek, S.S.S.R. 85 42.14 N 77.45 E
Akterek, S.S.S.R. 85 43.22 N 75.18 E
Aktobe 85 43.13 N 67.46 E
Aktogaj, S.S.S.R. 86 48.18 N 74.58 E
Aktogaj, S.S.S.R. 86 46.57 N 79.40 E
Aktogaj, S.S.S.R. 86 44.27 N 76.42 E
Aktubek 86 48.37 N 71.06 E
Akt'ubinsk 86 50.17 N 57.10 E
Akt'ubinskij 80 54.49 N 52.47 E
Aktumsyk 86 46.40 N 57.19 E
Akt'uz 85 42.54 N 76.07 E
Aku 150 6.42 N 7.20 E
Akula 152 2.22 N 20.11 E
Akuliči Pervyje 76 53.11 N 33.13 E
Akulovo, S.S.S.R. 82 55.31 N 36.42 E
Akulovo, S.S.S.R. 82 56.05 N 38.59 E
Akumadan 150 7.24 N 1.57 W
Akune 92 32.01 N 130.11 E
Akun Island I 180 54.12 N 165.35 W
Akure 150 7.15 N 5.12 E
Akurenan 152 1.02 N 10.40 E
Akureyri 24a 65.44 N 18.08 W
Akurli 272c 19.01 N 73.08 E
Akuša 84 42.17 N 47.21 E
Akuse 150 6.06 N 0.08 E
Akuseki-shima I 93b 29.27 N 129.37 E
Akutan 180 54.08 N 165.46 W
Akutan Island I 180 54.10 N 165.55 W
Akutan Pass ʮ 180 54.00 N 166.10 W
Akuticha 86 52.27 N 84.29 E
Akviran, Tür. 130 37.27 N 32.23 E
Akviran, Tür. 130 40.54 N 29.30 E
Akwanga 150 8.55 N 8.23 E
Akwatia 150 6.04 N 0.49 W
Akwawa ∧[2] 150 6.27 N 0.25 W
Akyab → Sittwe 110 20.09 N 92.54 E
Akyazı 130 40.41 N 30.37 E
Akyr-T'ube 85 42.59 N 72.07 E
Akžajkyn, Ozero ⊜ 86 44.55 N 67.46 E
Akžal, S.S.S.R. 86 47.47 N 74.02 E
Akžal, S.S.S.R. 86 49.13 N 81.25 E
Akžar, S.S.S.R. 85 43.08 N 71.38 E
Akžar, S.S.S.R. 86 47.35 N 83.42 E
Akžaryk 86 48.34 N 75.30 E
Ål 26 60.38 N 8.34 E
Ala 64 45.45 N 11.00 E
Alà, Monti di ∧∧ 71 40.40 N 9.14 E
Alabama 210 43.06 N 78.23 W
Alabama □[3] 178
194 32.50 N 87.00 W
Alabama ≃ 194 31.08 N 87.57 W
Alabama and Coushatta Indian Reservation ◆[4] 222 30.13 N 94.42 W
Alabaster 194 33.15 N 86.49 W
Alabat Island I 116 14.07 N 122.03 E
Al-'Abbāsīyah 140 12.10 N 31.18 E
Al-'Abbāsīyah ◆[8] 273c 30.04 N 31.17 E
Alabino 82 55.31 N 37.01 E
Āl-'Ābis 144 18.04 N 43.10 E
Alabuga ≃ 85 41.26 N 74.41 E
Ala-Buka 85 41.23 N 71.30 E
Al-Abyār 146 32.11 N 20.36 E
Alaca 130 40.10 N 34.51 E
Alaca Dağı ∧ 84 40.30 N 43.26 E
Alacahan 130 39.07 N 37.37 E
Alaçalı 130 41.11 N 29.27 E
Alaçam 130 41.37 N 35.37 E
Alaçatı 130 38.16 N 26.23 E
Alachadzy 84 43.14 N 40.18 E
Alachua 192 29.47 N 82.30 W
Alacrán, Arrecife ⌖[2] 232 22.24 N 89.42 W
Aladağ ∧, Tür. 84 40.11 N 42.49 E
Aladağ ∧, Tür. 84 39.20 N 43.35 E
Aladağ ∧, Tür. 130 37.44 N 35.09 E
Ala Dağları ∧∧ 130 37.55 N 35.13 E
Al-'Adasīyah 132 32.40 N 35.37 E
Alà dei Sardi 71 40.39 N 9.20 E
Aladino 82 54.49 N 38.12 E
Aladinskij, Porog ⌊ 86 58.24 N 95.29 E
Ala di Stura 62 45.19 N 7.19 E
Aladjino 82 56.21 N 37.04 E
Aladža-Džamija ⊌[1] 38 43.31 N 18.47 E
Aladža manastir ⊌[1] 38 43.17 N 28.01 E
Alafia ≃ 220 27.52 N 82.23 W
Alafia, South Prong ≃ 220 27.51 N 82.08 W
Al-Aflāj 144 22.15 N 46.50 E
Alagir 72 43.03 N 44.14 E
Alagna Valsesia 62 45.51 N 7.56 E
Alag Nuur ⊜ 102 45.09 N 94.28 E
Alagoa 256 22.10 S 44.38 W
Alagoa Grande 250 7.03 S 35.38 W
Alagoa Nova 250 7.04 S 35.46 W
Alagoas □[3] 250 9.00 S 36.00 W
Alagoinhas 255 12.07 S 38.26 W
Alagón 34 41.46 N 1.07 W
Alagón ≃ 34 39.44 N 6.53 W
Alah ≃ 116 6.53 N 124.33 E
Alahanpanjang 112 1.05 S 100.47 E
Alahärmä 26 63.14 N 22.51 E
Al-Ait 140 12.22 N 27.27 E
Alaj ∧∧ 85 39.45 N 72.00 E
Al-'Ajamīyīn 142 29.20 N 30.43 E
Alajärvi 26 63.00 N 23.49 E
Alajku 85 40.18 N 74.25 E
Alajõe 76 59.01 N 27.26 E
Alajskaja Dolina ∨ 85 39.30 N 73.00 E
Alajskij Chrebet ∧∧ 85 39.45 N 72.00 E
Alajuela 236 10.01 N 84.13 W
Alajuela □[4] 236 10.30 N 84.30 W
Alajuela, Lago ⊜[1] 236 9.15 N 79.35 W
Ālājūjeh 84 38.57 N 46.41 E
Alakai Swamp ≡ 229b 22.08 N 159.35 W
Alakamisy 157b 21.19 S 47.14 E
Alakanuk 180 62.41 N 164.37 W
Alakilise 130 39.56 N 38.38 E
Alaknanda ≃ 124 30.08 N 78.36 E
Alakol', Ozero ⊜ 86 46.10 N 81.45 E
Alak'ul'a 265a 59.44 N 29.56 E
Alakurtti 24 66.57 N 30.18 E
Al-'Āl 132 32.48 N 35.44 E
Alalakeiki Channel ʮ 229a 20.35 N 156.30 W
Al-'Alamayn 140 30.49 N 28.57 E
Al-'Alāqimah 142 30.37 N 31.38 E
Alalaú ≃ 246 0.30 S 61.09 W
Al-'Amādīyah 128 37.06 N 43.29 E
Al-'Amārah 128 31.50 N 47.09 E
Al-'Amārah □[4] 128 32.00 N 47.00 E
Alamata 144 12.21 N 39.30 E
Alamdānga 124 23.46 N 88.57 E
Alameda, Esp. 34 37.12 N 4.39 W
Alameda, Calif., U.S. 226 37.46 N 122.16 W
Alameda, N. Mex., U.S. 200 35.11 N 106.37 W
Alameda □[6] 226 37.35 N 121.55 W
Alameda, Estación ◆[5] 286e 33.27 S 70.41 W
Alameda Creek ≃ 226 37.35 N 122.09 W
Alameda Memorial State Beach ♠ 282 37.46 N 122.16 W
Alameda Naval Air Station ■ 226 37.47 N 122.18 W
Alamedin 85 42.54 N 74.37 E
Alamein → Al-'Alamayn 140 30.49 N 28.57 E
Alamillo 200 31.02 N 110.35 W
Alaminos 116 16.10 N 119.59 E
Al-'Āmirīyah 142 31.01 N 29.48 E
'Alam Lek 128 37.02 N 65.57 E
Alamo, Méx. 234 20.55 N 97.41 W
Alamo, Calif., U.S. 226 37.51 N 122.02 W
Alamo, Ga., U.S. 192 32.09 N 82.47 W
Alamo, Mich., U.S. 216 42.22 N 85.43 W
Alamo, Nev., U.S. 204 37.22 N 115.10 W
Alamo, Tenn., U.S. 194 35.47 N 89.07 W
Alamo ≃ 204 33.14 N 115.39 W
Alamo Creek ≃ 282 37.42 N 121.55 W
Alamo Creek, West Branch ≃ 282 37.45 N 121.55 W
Álamo de San Felipe, Cerro ∧ 232 30.41 N 112.35 W
Alamogordo 200 32.54 N 105.57 W
Alamogordo Creek ≃ 196 34.40 N 104.23 W
Alamo Heights 196 29.28 N 98.28 W
Alamo Indian Reservation ◆[4] 200 34.30 N 107.30 W
Alamo Oaks 282 37.51 N 121.59 W
Alamor 246 4.02 S 80.02 W
Alamos, Méx. 196 26.25 N 100.25 W
Alamos, Méx. 232 27.01 N 108.56 W
Álamos, Río de los ≃ 232 27.53 N 101.12 W
Alamosa 200 37.28 N 105.52 W
Alamosa ≃, Colo., U.S. 200 37.22 N 105.46 W
Alamosa ≃, N. Mex., U.S. 200 33.20 N 107.21 W
Alamosa Creek ≃ 196 34.26 N 103.58 W
Alampur, Bhārat 272b 22.25 N 88.08 E
Alampur, Bngl. 126 23.49 N 89.06 E
Alanäs 26 64.10 N 15.42 E
Al-'Ānāt 132 32.21 N 36.48 E
Aland 122 17.34 N 76.34 E
Åland-Inseln → Ahvenanmaa II 26 60.15 N 20.00 E
Aland Sea ▾[2] 26 60.00 N 19.30 E
Alandur 122 13.02 N 80.15 E
Alanga Arba 154 0.07 N 40.25 E
Alangalang 116 11.12 N 124.51 E
Alang-besar, Pulau I 114 2.12 N 100.39 E
Alanje 236 8.24 N 82.33 W
Alano di Piave 64 45.55 N 11.52 E
Alanson 190 45.27 N 84.47 W
Alanya 130 36.33 N 32.01 E
Al-'Anz 132 32.23 N 36.38 E
Alaotra, Lac ⊜ 157b 17.30 S 48.30 E
Alapaha 192 31.23 N 83.13 W
Alapaha ≃ 192 30.26 N 83.06 W
Alapajevsk 86 57.52 N 61.42 E
Alaplı 130 41.11 N 31.24 E
Al-'Aqabah 132 29.31 N 35.00 E
Al-'Aqabah Landing Ground ⊠ 132 29.32 N 34.59 E
'Alaqah, Jabal ∧ 142 29.59 N 32.53 E
Alaquines 234 22.08 N 99.36 W
Al-'Arabīyah as-Sa'ūdīyah → Saudi Arabia □[1] 118 25.00 N 45.00 E
Al-Arak 130 34.38 N 38.35 E
Alarcón 34 39.33 N 2.05 W
Alarcón, Embalse de ⊜[1] 34 39.36 N 2.10 W
Al-'Arīsh 132 31.08 N 33.48 E
Al-'Arīsh Airfield ⊠ 132 31.04 N 33.50 E
Al-'Armah ∧∧[1] 128 25.30 N 46.30 E
Alarobia Vohiposa 157b 20.59 S 47.09 E
Alas 115b 8.32 S 117.00 E
Alas ≃ 114 3.05 N 97.55 E
Alas, Selat ʮ 115b 8.40 S 116.40 E
Alasan 112 1.45 S 123.19 E
Alasdair, Sgurr ∧ 46 57.12 N 6.14 W
Alaşehir 130 38.21 N 28.32 E
Alashanyouqi 102 40.02 N 103.33 E
Al-'Ashārah 130 34.55 N 40.34 E
Al-'Āṣimah □[8] 132 31.45 N 36.30 E
Alasitan 120 37.01 N 76.59 E
Alaska 216 42.50 N 85.29 W
Alaska □[3] 180 65.00 N 153.00 W
Alaska, Gulf of ⊂ 180 58.00 N 146.00 W
Alaska Peninsula ≻[1] 180 57.00 N 158.00 W
Alaska Range ∧∧ 180 62.30 N 150.00 W
Al-'Assāfīyah ▾[4] 128 28.21 N 39.08 E
Alassio 62 44.00 N 8.10 E
Alastaro 26 60.56 N 22.55 E
Al'at, S.S.S.R. 84 39.57 N 49.25 E
Alat, S.S.S.R. 128 39.26 N 63.48 E
Alatan'aola → Xinbaerhuyouqi 88 48.41 N 116.53 E
Al-Atārib 130 36.08 N 36.49 E
Al-'Athāmīn ∧∧ 128 30.22 N 43.40 E
Al-'Atīqah 132 33.42 N 35.27 E
Alatna ≃ 180 66.34 N 152.34 W
Alatri 66 41.43 N 13.21 E
Al-'Aṭrūn 140 18.11 N 26.36 E
Alatyr' 80 54.51 N 46.36 E
Alatyr' ≃ 80 54.52 N 46.36 E
Alausí 246 2.12 S 78.50 W
Alava □[4] 34 42.50 N 2.45 W
Alava, Cape ≻ 224 48.10 N 124.43 W
Alaverdi 84 41.08 N 44.39 E
Alavieska 26 64.10 N 24.18 E
Alavus 26 62.35 N 23.37 E
Alaw ≃ 44 53.18 N 4.32 W
Alaw, Llyn ⊜[1] 44 53.20 N 4.22 W
Alāwalpur 123 31.26 N 75.39 E
Al-'Awsajīyah 128 26.49 N 41.41 E
'Ālayh 132 33.48 N 35.36 E
Al-'Ayn ▾[4] 140 16.36 N 29.19 E
Alayor 34 39.56 N 4.08 E
Al-'Ayyāṭ 142 29.37 N 31.15 E
Al-'Ayyināt ∧∧[1] 140 22.08 N 32.45 E
Alazani ≃ 84 41.05 N 46.40 E
Alazeja ≃ 74 70.51 N 153.34 E
Al-Azhar University ⊌[2] 273c 30.03 N 31.16 E
Al-Azraq ◆[1] 132 31.52 N 36.50 E
Alb ≃ 58 47.35 N 8.08 E
Alba, It. 62 44.42 N 8.02 E
Alba, Mich., U.S. 190 44.59 N 84.58 W
Alba, Pa., U.S. 210 41.42 N 76.50 W
Alba, Tex., U.S. 222 32.48 N 95.38 W
Alba □[4] 38 46.15 N 23.30 E
Al-Bāb 130 36.22 N 37.31 E
Albacete 34 38.59 N 1.51 W
Albachten 52 51.55 N 7.31 E
Albacina 66 43.21 N 13.01 E
Al-Badārī 140 26.59 N 31.25 E
Alba de Tormes 34 40.49 N 5.31 W
Al-Badrashayn 142 29.51 N 31.16 E
Ålbæk 26 57.36 N 10.25 E
Al-Baḥr al-Abyaḍ → White Nile ≃ 140 15.38 N 32.31 E
Al-Baḥr al-Aḥmar □[5] 142 28.45 N 32.00 E
Al-Baḥr al-Aḥmar → Red Sea ▾[2] 136 20.00 N 38.00 E
Al-Baḥr al-Azraq → Blue Nile ≃ 140 15.38 N 32.31 E
Al-Baḥr al-Mayyit → Dead Sea ⊜ 132 31.30 N 35.30 E
Al-Baḥr aṣ-Ṣaghīr ≍ 142 31.09 N 31.56 E
Al-Baḥrayn → Bahrain □[1] 128 26.00 N 50.30 E
Al-Baḥrayn ◆[1] 140 28.40 N 26.32 E
Albaida 34 38.51 N 0.31 W
Albairate 266b 45.25 N 8.56 E
Alba-Iulia 38 46.04 N 23.35 E
Al-Bājūr 142 30.26 N 31.02 E
Al-Ballaḥ 142 30.46 N 32.19 E
Al-Ballāṣ 140 26.01 N 32.46 E
Al-Balqā' □[8] 132 31.50 N 35.40 E
Al-Bālū'ah ⊜ 130 35.55 N 36.28 E
Al-Balyanā 140 26.14 N 32.00 E
Alban 32 43.54 N 2.28 E
Albanel, Lac ⊜ 176 50.55 N 73.12 W
Albanella 68 40.30 N 15.08 E
Albani, Colli ∧∧[2] 66 41.45 N 12.45 E
Albania □[1] 22
38 41.00 N 20.00 E
Albanie → Albania □[1] 38 41.00 N 20.00 E
Albanien → Albania □[1] 38 41.00 N 20.00 E
Albano, Lago ⊜ 66 41.45 N 12.40 E
Albano, Monte ∧ 66 43.50 N 10.58 E
Albano di Lucania 68 40.35 N 16.02 E
Albano Laziale 66 41.44 N 12.39 E
Albany, Austl. 162 35.02 S 117.53 E
Albany, N.Z. 172 36.43 S 174.42 E
Albany, Calif., U.S. 226 37.53 N 122.18 W
Albany, Ga., U.S. 192 31.35 N 84.10 W
Albany, Ill., U.S. 190 41.47 N 90.13 W
Albany, Ind., U.S. 216 40.18 N 85.14 W
Albany, Ky., U.S. 194 36.42 N 85.08 W
Albany, Minn., U.S. 190 45.38 N 94.34 W
Albany, Mo., U.S. 194 40.15 N 94.20 W
Albany, N.Y., U.S. 210 42.39 N 73.45 W
Albany, Ohio, U.S. 188 39.14 N 82.12 W

Symbols in the index entries represent the broad categories identified in the key at the right. Symbols with superior numbers (∧∧[2]) identify subcategories (see complete key on page I · 30).

Kartensymbole in dem Registerverzeichnis stellen die rechts in Schlüssel erklärten Kategorien dar. Symbole mit hochgestellten Ziffern (∧∧[2]) bezeichnen Unterabteilungen einer Kategorie (vgl. vollständiger Schlüssel auf Seite I · 30).

Los símbolos incluídos en el texto del índice representan las grandes categorias identificadas con la clave a la derecha. Los símbolos con numeros en su parte superior (∧∧[2]) identifican las subcategorías (véase la clave completa en la página I · 30).

Les symboles de l'index représentent les catégories indiquées dans la légende à droite. Les symboles suivis d'un indice (∧∧[2]) représentent des sous-catégories (voir légende complète à la page I · 30).

Os símbolos incluídos no texto do índice representam as grandes categorias identificadas com a chave à direita. Os símbolos com números em sua parte superior (∧∧[2]) identificam as subcategorias (veja-se a chave completa à página I · 30).

Symbol	English	Deutsch	Español	Français	Português
∧	Mountain	Berg	Montaña	Montagne	Montanha
∧∧	Mountains	Berge	Montañas	Montagnes	Montanhas
)(	Pass	Pass	Paso	Col	Passo
∨	Valley, Canyon	Tal, Cañon	Valle, Cañón	Vallée, Canyon	Vale, Canhão
⌣	Plain	Ebene	Llano	Plaine	Planície
≻	Cape	Kap	Cabo	Cap	Cabo
I	Island	Insel	Isla	Île	Ilha
II	Islands	Inseln	Islas	Îles	Ilhas
⊥	Other Topographic Features	Andere Topographische Objekte	Otros Elementos Topográficos	Autres données topographiques	Outros Elementos Topográficos

ESPAÑOL / FRANÇAIS / PORTUGUÊS

Nombre / Nom / Nome	Página / Page	Lat.°′	Long.°′ W=Oeste / W=Ouest
Albany, Oreg., U.S.	202	44.38 N	123.06 W
Albany, Tex., U.S.	196	32.44 N	99.18 W
Albany, Wis., U.S.	190	42.43 N	89.26 W
Albany □[6]	210	42.39 N	73.45 W
Albany ≃	176	52.17 N	81.31 W
Albany County Airport ⊠	210	42.45 N	73.48 W
Albany Park ⬥[8]	278	41.58 N	87.43 W
Al-Barājīl	273c	30.04 N	31.09 E
Albardón	252	31.26 S	68.32 W
Albaredo d'Adige	64	45.19 N	11.16 E
Al-Bāriḥah	132	32.34 N	35.50 E
Albaron	62	43.37 N	4.28 E
Albaron Λ	62	45.20 N	7.07 E
Albarracín	34	40.25 N	1.26 W
Albarradas	234	16.50 N	96.15 W
Al-Barrah	128	24.55 N	45.52 E
Albarraque	266c	38.46 N	9.21 W
Al-Barun	140	11.44 N	33.30 E
Al-Basātīn ⬥[8]	273c	29.59 N	31.16 E
Al-Baṣrah (Basra)	128	30.30 N	47.47 E
Al-Baṣrah □[4]	128	30.30 N	47.47 E
Al-Batānūn	142	30.37 N	30.59 E
Al-Baṭḥā'	128	31.06 N	45.53 E
Al-Bāṭinah ⬥[1]	128	23.45 N	57.20 E
Albatross Bay C	164	12.45 S	141.43 E
Albatross Cordillera ✣[3]	9	62.00 S	155.00 W
Albatross Point ≻	172	38.06 S	174.41 E
Al-Batrūn	130	34.15 N	35.39 E
Al-Baṭrūnah	132	33.39 N	36.02 E
Al-Bauga	140	18.16 N	33.55 E
Al-Bawīṭī	140	28.21 N	28.52 E
Albay □[4]	116	13.00 N	123.40 E
Al-Bayḍā (Beida), Lībīya	146	28.22 N	18.55 E
Al-Bayḍā', Miṣr	142	31.10 N	30.05 E
Al-Bayḍā' □[4]	146	32.30 N	21.30 E
Albay Gulf C	116	13.10 N	124.00 E
Albazino	89	53.23 N	124.05 E
Albbruck	58	47.35 N	8.07 E
Albegna ≃	66	42.30 N	11.11 E
Albemarle	192	35.21 N	80.12 W
Albemarle and Chesapeake Canal ≖	208	36.43 N	76.15 W
Albemarle Sound ⩌	192	36.03 N	76.12 W
Albenga	62	44.03 N	8.13 E
Albens	62	45.47 N	5.57 E
Alberche ≃	34	39.58 N	4.46 W
Alberdi	252	26.10 S	58.09 W
Alberene	192	37.53 N	78.37 W
Ålberga, Austl.	162	27.12 S	135.28 E
Ålberga, Sve.	40	58.44 N	16.34 E
Alberga Creek ≃	162	27.06 S	135.33 E
Albergaria-a-Velha	34	40.42 N	8.29 W
Alberhill	228	33.44 N	117.23 W
Alberique	34	39.07 N	0.31 W
Alberni Inlet C	224	49.07 N	124.50 W
Alberobello	68	40.47 N	17.15 E
Alberona	68	41.26 N	15.07 E
Albero Sole Λ	71a	35.31 N	12.32 E
Albers	219	38.33 N	89.37 W
Alberschwende	58	47.27 N	9.49 E
Albersloh	52	51.52 N	7.43 E
Albert	50	50.00 N	2.39 E
Albert ≃	171a	27.42 S	153.15 E
Albert, Lake ⊛, Afr.	154	1.40 N	31.00 E
Albert, Lake ⊛, Austl.	166	35.38 S	139.17 E
Albert, Parc National ♠	154	1.00 S	29.15 E
Alberta	194	32.14 N	87.25 W
Alberta □[4]	176	54.00 N	113.00 W
Alberta, Mount Λ	182	52.18 N	117.28 W
Albert Canyon	182	51.08 N	117.52 W
Albert City	198	42.47 N	94.57 W
Albert Edward, Mount Λ	164	8.23 S	147.24 E
Albert Edward Bay C	176	69.32 N	103.00 W
Albert Falls	158	29.27 S	30.25 E
Albertfalva ⬥[8]	264c	47.27 N	19.02 E
Alberti	252	35.02 S	60.16 W
Al'bertin	76	53.05 N	25.23 E
Albertina	256	22.12 S	46.37 W
Albertinia	158	34.13 S	21.36 E
Albertirsa	30	47.15 N	19.38 E
Albert Kanaal ≖	56	50.39 N	5.37 E
Albert Lea	190	43.39 N	93.22 W
Albert Markham, Mount Λ	9	81.23 S	158.12 E
Albert Nile ≃	154	3.36 N	32.02 E
Alberto, Lago → Albert, Lake ⊛	154	1.40 N	31.00 E
Alberto Eduardo → Albert Edward, Mount Λ	164	8.23 S	147.24 E
Alberton, P.E.I., Can.	186	46.49 N	64.04 W
Alberton, S. Afr.	273d	26.16 S	28.08 E
Alberton, Mont., U.S.	202	47.00 N	114.29 W
Albert Park ♠	274b	37.51 S	144.57 E
Albertshof	264a	52.42 N	13.40 E
Albertson	276	40.46 N	73.39 W
Albertson Brook ≃	285	39.41 N	74.43 W
Albertson Brook, Blue Anchor Branch ≃	285	39.42 N	74.49 W
Albertson Brook, Pump Branch ≃	285	39.42 N	74.49 W
Albert Town	241q	18.17 N	77.33 W
Albertville, Fr.	62	45.41 N	6.23 E
Albertville, Ala., U.S.	194	34.16 N	86.12 W
Albertville → Kalemie, Zaïre	154	5.56 S	29.12 E
Albertville ⬥[8]	273d	26.10 S	27.59 E
Albertynsville	273d	26.17 S	27.52 E
Albestroff	56	48.56 N	6.51 E
Albettone	64	45.21 N	11.35 E
Albi	32	43.56 N	2.09 E
Albia, Iowa, U.S.	190	41.02 N	92.48 W
Albia, N.Y., U.S.	210	42.43 N	73.39 W
Albiate	266b	45.39 N	9.15 E
Al-Bid'	128	28.25 N	35.04 E
Al Bidia	146	10.33 N	20.13 E
Albidona	68	39.55 N	16.28 E
Albignasego	64	45.21 N	11.52 E
Albin	198	41.25 N	104.06 W
Albina	250	5.30 N	54.03 W
Albina, Ponta ≻	152	15.51 S	11.44 E
Albinea	64	44.37 N	10.36 E
Albino	62	45.46 N	9.47 E
Albion, Austl.	274b	37.47 S	144.49 E
Albion, B.C., Can.	224	49.11 N	122.33 W
Albion, Calif., U.S.	204	39.13 N	123.46 W
Albion, Idaho, U.S.	202	42.25 N	113.35 W
Albion, Ill., U.S.	194	38.23 N	88.04 W
Albion, Ind., U.S.	216	41.24 N	85.25 W
Albion, Iowa, U.S.	190	42.07 N	92.59 W
Albion, Mich., U.S.	216	42.15 N	84.45 W
Albion, Nebr., U.S.	198	41.42 N	98.00 W
Albion, N.J., U.S.	285	39.47 N	74.56 W
Albion, N.Y., U.S.	210	43.15 N	78.12 W
Albion, Pa., U.S.	214	41.53 N	80.22 W
Albion, R.I., U.S.	207	41.57 N	71.27 W
Albion, Wash., U.S.	202	46.48 N	117.15 W
Albion, Wis., U.S.	216	42.53 N	89.04 W
Albion Airstrip ⊠	285	39.46 N	74.58 W
Albion Park	170	34.34 S	150.47 E
Al-Biqā' □[4]	130	34.00 N	36.00 E
Al-Bi'r	128	28.50 N	36.19 E
Al-Bīrah	132	31.54 N	35.13 E
Al-Bi'r al-Jadīd	128	26.01 N	38.29 E
Al-Birīgāt	142	30.30 N	30.49 E
Al-Birk	144	18.13 N	41.33 E
Al-Birkah ⊤[4]	144	22.12 N	40.43 E
Albisola Marina	62	44.19 N	8.30 E
Albisola Superiore	62	44.20 N	8.31 E
Albizzate	62	45.43 N	8.44 E
Alblasserdam	52	51.52 N	4.40 E
Albo, Monte Λ	71	40.32 N	9.35 E
Albocácer	34	40.21 N	0.02 E
Albogas	266c	38.51 N	9.15 W
Alborán, Isla de I	34	35.58 N	3.02 W
Ålborg	26	57.03 N	9.56 E
Ålborg Bugt C	26	56.45 N	10.30 E
Alborz, Reshteh-ye Kūhhā-ye ΛΛ	128	36.00 N	53.00 E
Albreda	182	52.38 N	119.09 W
Albrighton	42	52.38 N	2.16 W
Al-Bu'ayrāt	146	31.24 N	15.44 E
Albuch ΛΛ	56	48.15 N	9.50 E
Albuera	116	10.55 N	124.42 E
Albufeira	34	37.05 N	8.15 W
Ālbū Gharz, Sabkhat ⊛	130	34.45 N	41.15 E
Al-Buḥayrah □[4]	142	30.59 N	30.12 E
Albula ≃	58	46.42 N	9.27 E
Al-Bunbah	146	32.24 N	23.08 E
Albuñol	34	36.47 N	3.12 W
Albuquerque	200	35.05 N	106.40 W
Albuquerque, Cayos de II	236	12.10 N	81.50 W
Al-Buraymī	128	24.15 N	55.45 E
Alburg, B.R.D.	60	48.52 N	12.32 E
Alburg, Vt., U.S.	188	44.59 N	73.18 W
Alburno, Monte Λ	68	40.33 N	15.17 E
Alburquerque,esp.	34	39.13 N	7.00 W
Albuquerque, N.M.,u.S	200	35.05 N	106.40 W
Alburtis	208	40.31 N	75.36 W
Albury, Austl.	166	36.05 S	146.55 E
Albury, N.Z.	172	44.14 S	170.52 E
Albury, Eng., U.K.	260	51.13 N	0.30 W
Albury Park ♠	260	51.13 N	0.29 W
Al-Buṣaylī	142	31.20 N	30.24 E
Al-Buṭanah ⬥[1]	140	15.00 N	34.40 E
Al-Buṭaynah	132	32.57 N	36.42 E
Al-Buwayḍah	132	32.28 N	36.04 E
Albuzzano	62	45.11 N	9.16 E
Alby, Fr.	62	45.49 N	6.01 E
Alby, Sve.	26	62.30 N	15.28 E
Alca	248	15.08 S	72.46 W
Alcabideche	266c	38.44 N	9.24 W
Alcácer do Sal	34	38.22 N	8.30 W
Alcains	34	39.55 N	7.27 W
Alcala	116	17.54 N	121.39 E
Alcalá de Guadaira	34	37.20 N	5.50 W
Alcalá de Henares	34	40.29 N	3.22 W
Alcalá la Real	34	37.28 N	3.56 W
Alcalde	200	36.05 N	106.03 W
Alcamo	70	37.59 N	12.58 E
Alčan ≃	89	46.38 N	134.22 E
Alcanadre ≃	34	41.37 N	0.12 W
Alcanar	34	40.33 N	0.29 E
Alcañices	34	41.42 N	6.21 W
Alcañiz	34	41.03 N	0.08 W
Alcântara, Bra.	250	2.24 S	44.24 W
Alcántara, Esp.	34	39.43 N	6.53 W
Alcantara, Pil.	116	12.16 N	122.03 E
Alcântara ⬥[8]	266c	38.42 N	9.10 W
Alcantara ≃	70	37.49 N	15.16 E
Alcántara, Embalse de ⊛[1]	34	39.45 N	6.25 W
Alcantarilla	34	37.58 N	1.13 W
Alcantilado	255	16.23 S	53.31 W
Alcara li Fusi	70	38.01 N	14.42 E
Alcaraz	34	38.40 N	2.29 W
Alcarrache ≃	34	38.16 N	7.24 W
Alcatraz Island I	282	37.49 N	122.26 W
Alcaudete	34	37.36 N	4.05 W
Alcázar de San Juan	34	39.24 N	3.12 W
Alcazarquivir → Ksar-el-Kebir	148	35.01 N	5.54 W
Alcester, Eng., U.K.	42	52.13 N	1.52 W
Alcester, S. Dak., U.S.	198	43.01 N	96.38 W
Alcester Island I	164	9.35 S	152.25 E
Alcihuatl	234	19.55 N	104.34 W
Alcira (Gigena), Arg.	252	32.45 S	64.20 W
Alcira, Esp.	34	39.09 N	0.26 W
Alcoa	192	35.48 N	83.59 W
Alcoa Center	279b	40.33 N	79.39 W
Alcoa Lake ⊛[1]	222	30.34 N	97.03 W
Alcobaça, Bra.	255	17.30 S	39.13 W
Alcobaça, Port.	34	39.33 N	8.59 W
Alcobendas	34	40.32 N	3.38 W
Alcochete	266c	38.45 N	8.58 W
Alcockspruit	158	27.55 S	30.01 E
Alcoitão	266c	38.44 N	9.24 W
Alcolea del Piuar	34	41.02 N	2.28 W
Alcomunga	234	18.25 N	97.02 W
Alconbury Brook ≃	42	52.19 N	0.12 W
Alconchel	34	38.31 N	7.04 W
Alcony	218	40.01 N	84.04 W
Alcorcón	266a	40.21 N	3.50 W
Alcorn College	194	31.52 N	91.09 W
Alcorta	252	33.32 S	61.07 W
Alcoutim	34	37.28 N	7.28 W
Alcova Reservoir ⊛[1]	200	42.32 N	106.45 W
Alcove	210	42.28 N	73.55 W
Alcove Reservoir ⊛[1]	210	42.29 N	73.57 W
Alcovy ≃	192	33.26 N	83.50 W
Alcoy	34	38.42 N	0.28 W
Alcoy, Nevado Λ	248	11.17 S	76.30 W
Alcubierre	34	41.48 N	0.27 W
Alcudia	34	39.52 N	3.07 E
Alcudia, Bahía de C	34	39.48 N	3.13 E
Alcyon Lake ⊛	285	39.44 N	75.08 W
Aldabra Islands I[1]	138	9.25 S	46.22 E
Aldama, Méx.	232	28.51 N	105.54 W
Aldama, Méx.	234	22.55 N	98.04 W
Aldama, Arroyo ≃	286b	23.05 N	82.15 W
Aldan, S.S.S.R.	74	58.37 N	125.24 E
Aldan, Pa., U.S.	285	39.55 N	75.17 W
Aldan ≃	74	63.28 N	129.35 E
Aldanskoje Nagorje ΛΛ[1]	74	57.00 N	127.00 E
Aldbourne	42	51.31 N	1.37 W
Aldbrough	44	53.50 N	0.07 W
Aldbury	42	51.48 N	0.36 W
Alde ≃	42	52.03 N	1.28 E
Aldea Apeleg	254	44.41 S	70.51 W
Aldeburgh	42	52.09 N	1.35 E
Aldecoa ⬥[8]	286b	23.07 N	82.24 W
Aldeia	256	23.30 S	46.51 W
Aldeia de Carapicuiba	287b	23.35 S	46.48 W
Aldeia de Paio Pires	266c	38.38 N	9.05 W
Aldeia Nova de Santo Bento	34	37.55 N	7.25 W
Aldeia Velha	256	22.47 S	42.55 W
Aldeinha	287b	23.45 S	46.53 W
Alden, Ill., U.S.	216	42.27 N	88.31 W
Alden, Iowa, U.S.	190	42.31 N	93.23 W
Alden, Mich., U.S.	190	44.53 N	85.17 W
Alden, Minn., U.S.	190	43.40 N	93.34 W
Alden, N.Y., U.S.	210	42.54 N	78.30 W
Alden, Pa., U.S.	210	41.11 N	75.59 W
Alden Center	212	42.55 N	78.32 W
Aldenham	260	51.40 N	0.21 W
Aldenhoven	56	50.53 N	6.16 E
Aldenrade ⬥[8]	263	51.31 N	6.44 E
Alder, Ben Λ	46	56.48 N	4.28 W
Alder Creek ≃	202	45.50 N	119.56 W
Aldergrove	224	49.04 N	122.28 W
Alder Lake ⊛[1]	224	46.45 N	122.15 W
Alderley	166	22.39 S	139.44 E
Alderley Edge	262	53.18 N	2.15 W
Aldermaston	42	51.23 N	1.09 W
Alderney I	43b	49.43 N	2.12 W
Alder Peak Λ	226	35.53 N	121.22 W
Aldersbach	60	48.36 N	13.05 E
Aldershot	42	51.15 N	0.47 W
Alderson	192	37.43 N	80.39 W
Alderton	224	47.10 N	122.14 W
Alderwood Manor	224	47.49 N	122.17 W
Aldine	222	29.54 N	95.24 W
Aldinga Bay C	168b	35.20 S	138.25 E
Aldingen	58	48.05 N	8.41 E
Aldino	64	46.23 N	11.20 E
Aldo Bonzi	288	34.42 S	58.31 W
Aldridge	42	52.36 N	1.55 W
Aldwell, Lake ⊛[1]	224	48.05 N	123.34 W
Alechovščina	76	60.25 N	33.52 E
Aled ≃	44	53.14 N	3.34 W
Aledo, Ill., U.S.	190	41.12 N	90.45 W
Aledo, Tex., U.S.	222	32.42 N	97.36 W
Aleg	150	17.03 N	13.55 W
Alegranza, Isla de I	148	29.23 N	13.30 W
Alegre	255	20.46 S	41.32 W
Alegre ≃	248	15.01 S	59.57 W
Alegrete	252	29.46 S	55.46 W
Alegros Mountain Λ	200	34.09 N	108.11 W
Alegua, Mount Λ	144	14.12 N	39.40 E
Alejandría → Al-Iskandarīyah	142	31.12 N	29.54 E
Alejandro, Isla → Alexander Island I	9	71.00 S	70.00 W
Alejandro Roca	252	33.21 S	63.43 W
Alejandro Selkirk, Isla (Isla Más Afuera) I	244	33.45 S	80.46 W
Alejo Ledesma	252	33.37 S	62.37 W
Alejsk	86	52.28 N	82.45 E
Aleknagik	180	59.17 N	158.38 W
Aleknagik, Lake ⊛	180	59.20 N	158.45 W
Aleksandrija	78	48.40 N	33.07 E
Aleksandrijskaja	84	43.54 N	47.08 E
Aleksandrinka	83	47.47 N	37.41 E
Aleksandro-Kalinovo	83	48.25 N	37.40 E
Aleksandro-Nevskaja	84	43.55 N	46.35 E
Aleksandro Nevskaja Lavra ⊎[1]	265a	59.55 N	30.24 E
Aleksandro-Nevskij	80	53.28 N	40.13 E
Aleksandropol'	83	49.42 N	38.50 E
Aleksandrov	82	56.24 N	38.43 E
Aleksandrov Gaj	80	50.09 N	48.34 E
Aleksandrovka, S.S.S.R.	78	47.42 N	31.16 E
Aleksandrovka, S.S.S.R.	78	46.47 N	39.01 E
Aleksandrovka, S.S.S.R.	78	48.57 N	32.14 E
Aleksandrovka, S.S.S.R.	78	46.32 N	35.29 E
Aleksandrovka, S.S.S.R.	78	48.43 N	36.55 E
Aleksandrovka, S.S.S.R.	80	52.36 N	50.37 E
Aleksandrovka, S.S.S.R.	80	50.47 N	52.59 E
Aleksandrovka, S.S.S.R.	83	47.26 N	39.13 E
Aleksandrovka, S.S.S.R.	83	48.05 N	37.27 E
Aleksandrovka, S.S.S.R.	83	47.55 N	37.35 E
Aleksandrovka, S.S.S.R.	85	43.27 N	77.20 E
Aleksandrovka, S.S.S.R.	86	53.07 N	69.50 E
Aleksandrovka, S.S.S.R.	86	56.32 N	90.47 E
Aleksandrovka, S.S.S.R.	86	52.43 N	54.17 E
Aleksandrovsk	83	48.35 N	39.12 E
Aleksandrovskaja, S.S.S.R.	265a	59.44 N	30.21 E
Aleksandrovskaja, S.S.S.R.	265a	50.03 N	29.59 E
Aleksandrovskij	78	51.03 N	36.44 E
Aleksandrovskij Šl'uz	86	59.26 N	89.20 E
Aleksandrovskij Zavod	88	50.55 N	117.57 E
Aleksandrovskoje, S.S.S.R.	84	44.42 N	43.00 E
Aleksandrovskoje, S.S.S.R.	86	60.26 N	77.50 E
Aleksandrovskoje, S.S.S.R.	86	56.44 N	85.23 E
Aleksandrovsk-Sachalinskij	89	50.54 N	142.10 E
Aleksandrów Kujawski	30	52.52 N	18.42 E
Aleksandrów Łódzki	30	51.49 N	19.19 E
Aleksaškino	80	50.57 N	47.42 E
Aleksejevka, S.S.S.R.	78	50.37 N	38.42 E
Aleksejevka, S.S.S.R.	78	47.14 N	36.32 E
Aleksejevka, S.S.S.R.	80	53.15 N	50.30 E
Aleksejevka, S.S.S.R.	80	53.02 N	42.46 E
Aleksejevka, S.S.S.R.	80	52.18 N	48.01 E
Aleksejevka, S.S.S.R.	80	51.49 N	43.56 E
Aleksejevka, S.S.S.R.	80	52.35 N	51.17 E
Aleksejevka, S.S.S.R.	80	50.58 N	52.25 E
Aleksejevka, S.S.S.R.	82	54.41 N	36.34 E
Aleksejevka, S.S.S.R.	83	49.25 N	38.46 E
Aleksejevka, S.S.S.R.	83	47.38 N	38.49 E
Aleksejevka, S.S.S.R.	83	49.01 N	39.11 E
Aleksejevka, S.S.S.R.	83	47.41 N	39.54 E
Aleksejevka, S.S.S.R.	86	51.59 N	70.59 E
Aleksejevka, S.S.S.R.	86	55.22 N	72.03 E
Aleksejevka, S.S.S.R.	86	53.31 N	69.30 E
Aleksejevka, S.S.S.R.	86	48.25 N	85.40 E
Aleksejevka, S.S.S.R.	86	54.31 N	81.08 E
Aleksejevka, S.S.S.R.	86	52.30 N	79.33 E
Aleksejevka, S.S.S.R.	86	47.16 N	81.34 E
Aleksejevo-Družkovka	83	48.34 N	37.36 E
Aleksejevo-Lozovskoje	78	49.24 N	40.39 E
Aleksejevo-Orlovka ⬥[8]	83	48.04 N	38.25 E
Aleksejevo-Tuzlovka	83	47.50 N	39.24 E
Aleksejevsk	88	57.50 N	108.23 E
Aleksejevskaja	80	50.17 N	42.11 E
Aleksejevskoje	80	55.18 N	50.06 E
Aleksin	82	54.31 N	37.05 E
Aleksinac	38	43.32 N	21.43 E
Alella	266d	41.30 N	2.18 E
Alemana, República Democrática → German Democratic Republic □[1]	30	52.00 N	12.30 E
Alemania, Arg.	252	25.36 S	65.38 W
Alemania, Chile	252	25.10 S	69.55 W
Alemania, República Federal de → Germany, Federal Republic of □[1]	30	51.00 N	9.00 E
Alemdar	267b	41.03 N	29.14 E
Além Paraíba	256	21.52 S	42.41 W
Alençon	50	48.26 N	0.05 E
Alenquer	250	1.56 S	54.46 W
Alentejo □[9]	34	38.00 N	8.00 W
Alenuihaha Channel ⩌	229a	20.26 N	156.00 W
Alenz	130	37.51 N	41.36 E
Aléoutiennes, Îles → Aleutian Islands II	180	52.00 N	176.00 W
Alep → Ḥalab	130	36.12 N	37.10 E
Aleppo → Ḥalab	130	36.12 N	37.10 E
Alerces, Parque Nacional ♠	254	42.50 S	71.52 W
Aléria	36	42.05 N	9.30 E
Alert Bay	182	50.35 N	126.55 W
Alès, Fr.	62	44.08 N	4.05 E
Ales, It.	71	39.46 N	8.49 E
Aleșd	38	47.04 N	22.24 E
Alešino, S.S.S.R.	82	55.04 N	36.05 E
Alešino, S.S.S.R.	82	56.09 N	37.45 E
Aleški	80	51.38 N	41.46 E
Aleškino	88	58.35 N	100.32 E
Aleškovo	82	54.53 N	36.23 E
Alessandria	62	44.54 N	8.37 E
Alessandria □[4]	62	44.49 N	8.42 E
Alessandria del Carretto	68	39.57 N	16.23 E
Alessandria della Rocca	70	37.34 N	13.27 E
Alessano	68	39.53 N	18.20 E
Ålesund	26	62.28 N	6.09 E
Aleta	144	11.53 N	36.56 E
Aletai	86	47.52 N	88.07 E
Aletschhorn Λ	58	46.28 N	8.00 E
Alëuten → Aleutian Islands II	180	52.00 N	176.00 W
Aleutianas, Islas → Aleutian Islands II	180	52.00 N	176.00 W
Aleutian Basin ✣[1]	16	57.00 N	179.00 E
Aleutian Islands II	180	52.00 N	176.00 W
Aleutian Range ΛΛ	180	59.00 N	155.00 W
Aleutian Trench ✣[1]	16	52.00 N	170.00 W
Ale Water ≃	46	55.31 N	2.35 W
Alex	196	34.55 N	97.47 W
Alexander, Man., Can.	184	49.50 N	100.17 W
Alexander, Ill., U.S.	219	39.43 N	90.02 W
Alexander, N. Dak., U.S.	198	47.51 N	103.39 W
Alexander, N.Y., U.S.	210	42.54 N	78.16 W
Alexander ≃	132	32.24 N	34.52 E
Alexander, Cape ≻	175e	6.35 S	156.30 E
Alexander, Mount Λ	162	22.39 S	115.32 E
Alexander Archipelago II	180	56.30 N	134.00 W
Alexander Bay	156	28.40 S	16.30 E
Alexander City	194	32.56 N	85.57 W
Alexander Ditch ≖	279a	41.20 N	82.05 W
Alexander Hamilton Airport ⊠	241n	17.42 N	64.48 W
Alexander Indian Reserve ⬥[4]	182	53.09 N	113.58 W
Alexander Island I	9	71.00 S	70.00 W
Alexandra, Austl.	169	37.12 S	145.43 E
Alexandra, N.Z.	172	45.15 S	169.24 E
Alexandra, S. Afr.	273d	26.06 S	28.05 E
Alexandra ≃	166	18.14 S	139.54 E
Alexandra Canal ≖	274a	33.56 S	151.10 E
Alexandra Falls ⅃	176	60.29 N	116.18 W
Alexandra Park ♠	262	53.27 N	2.15 W
Alexandra Park Race Course ♠	260	51.36 N	0.08 W
Alexandretta → İskenderun	130	36.37 N	36.07 E
Alexandretta, Gulf of → İskenderun Körfezi C	130	36.30 N	35.40 E
Alexandria, Austl.	166	19.05 S	136.40 E
Alexandria, Bra.	250	6.25 S	38.01 W
Alexandria, B.C., Can.	182	52.38 N	122.27 W
Alexandria, Ont., Can.	206	45.19 N	74.38 W
Alexandria → Al-Iskandarīyah, Miṣr	142	31.12 N	29.54 E
Alexandria, Rom.	38	43.58 N	25.20 E
Alexandria, S. Afr.	158	33.39 S	26.24 E
Alexandria, Scot., U.K.	46	55.59 N	4.36 W
Alexandria, Ind., U.S.	216	40.16 N	85.41 W
Alexandria, Ky., U.S.	218	38.58 N	84.23 W
Alexandria, La., U.S.	194	31.18 N	92.27 W
Alexandria, Minn., U.S.	198	45.53 N	95.22 W
Alexandria, Mo., U.S.	194	40.27 N	91.28 W
Alexandria, Nebr., U.S.	198	40.15 N	97.23 W
Alexandria, Ohio, U.S.	214	40.05 N	82.37 W
Alexandria, Pa., U.S.	214	40.34 N	78.06 W
Alexandria, S. Dak., U.S.	198	43.39 N	97.47 W
Alexandria, Tenn., U.S.	194	36.05 N	86.02 W
Alexandria, Va., U.S.	208	38.48 N	77.03 W
Alexandria Airport ⊠	142	31.11 N	29.57 E
Alexandria Bay	212	44.20 N	75.55 W
Alexandrie → Al-Iskandarīyah	142	31.12 N	29.54 E
Alexandrina, Lake ⊛	168b	35.26 S	139.10 E
Alexandroúpolis	38	40.50 N	25.52 E
Alexis	190	41.04 N	90.33 W
Alexis Creek	182	52.05 N	123.17 W
Alexis Indian Reserve ⬥[4]	182	53.46 N	114.30 W
Alezio	68	40.04 N	18.03 E
Alf	56	50.03 N	7.07 E
Ālfādānga	126	23.18 N	89.42 E
Al-Fahmīyīn	142	29.36 N	31.17 E
Al-Fallūjah	128	33.20 N	43.46 E
Alfambra	34	40.33 N	1.02 W
Alfambra ≃	34	40.21 N	1.07 W
Al-Fant	142	28.46 N	30.53 E
Alfarata	208	40.39 N	77.27 W
Al-Farḍah	144	14.51 N	48.27 E
Alfaro, Ec.	246	2.12 S	79.50 W
Alfaro, Esp.	34	42.11 N	1.45 W
Alfarrás	34	41.49 N	0.35 E
Al-Fāshir	140	13.38 N	25.21 E
Al-Fashn	142	28.49 N	30.54 E
Alfatar	38	43.57 N	27.17 E
Alfavaca, Ilha da I	287a	23.02 S	43.18 W
Al-Fāw	128	29.58 N	48.29 E
Al-Fayyūm	142	29.19 N	30.50 E
Al-Fayyūm □[4]	142	29.19 N	30.48 E
Alfbach ≃	56	50.03 N	7.08 E
Alfedena	66	41.44 N	14.02 E
Alfeld, B.R.D.	52	51.59 N	9.50 E
Alfeld, B.R.D.	60	49.26 N	11.33 E
Alfenas	256	21.25 S	45.57 W
Alfianello	64	45.16 N	10.10 E
Al-Fifi	140	10.03 N	25.01 E
Alfiós ≃	38	37.40 N	21.33 E
Al-Firdān	142	30.41 N	32.20 E
Alfonsine	66	44.30 N	12.03 E
Alford, Austl.	168b	33.49 S	137.49 E
Alford, Eng., U.K.	44	53.16 N	0.10 E
Alford, Scot., U.K.	46	57.13 N	2.42 W
Alfortville	261	48.49 N	2.25 E
Ålfotbreen I	26	61.45 N	5.40 E
Alfred, Ont., Can.	206	45.34 N	74.53 W
Alfred, Maine, U.S.	188	43.29 N	70.43 W
Alfred, N.Y., U.S.	210	42.15 N	77.47 W
Alfred National Park ♠	166	37.35 S	149.20 E
Alfredo Chaves	255	20.38 S	40.45 W
Alfredo M. Terrazas	234	21.28 N	98.51 W
Alfriston	42	50.48 N	0.10 E
Alfta	26	61.21 N	16.05 E
Al-Fujayrah	128	25.06 N	56.21 E
Al-Fuqahā'	146	27.50 N	16.22 E
Al-Furāt → Euphrates ≃	128	31.00 N	47.25 E
Al-Furzul	132	33.52 N	35.56 E
Alga	86	49.46 N	57.20 E
Algabas, S.S.S.R.	80	50.39 N	52.07 E
Algabas, S.S.S.R.	86	48.21 N	81.39 E
Algabas, S.S.S.R.	86	44.41 N	78.06 E
Algači	88	50.43 N	117.47 E
Älgarås	40	58.48 N	14.14 E
Ålgård	26	58.46 N	5.51 E
Al-Garef	144	12.03 N	34.19 E
Algarrobal	252	28.08 S	70.39 W
Algarrobo, Arg.	252	38.53 S	63.08 W
Algarrobo, Chile	252	33.22 S	71.40 W
Algarrobo del Águila	252	36.26 S	67.09 W
Algarrobo Verde	252	31.44 S	68.18 W
Algarve □[9]	34	37.10 N	8.15 W
Algasovo	76	53.41 N	41.40 E
Al-Gebir	140	13.43 N	29.49 E
Algeciras, Col.	246	2.35 N	75.18 W
Algeciras, Esp.	34	36.08 N	5.30 W
Algemesí	34	39.11 N	0.26 W
Algena	144	16.20 N	38.34 E
Alger (Algiers), Alg.	148	36.47 N	3.03 E
Alger, Ohio, U.S.	216	40.42 N	83.51 W
Alger, Baie d' C	34	36.50 N	3.15 E
Algeria □[1]	134		
	148	28.00 N	3.00 E
Algérie → Algeria □[1]	148	28.00 N	3.00 E
Algerien → Algeria □[1]	148	28.00 N	3.00 E
Algermissen	52	52.15 N	9.58 E
Algés	266c	38.42 N	9.13 W
Al-Ghāb ⊛	130	35.30 N	36.18 E
Al-Gharaq as-Sulṭānī	142	29.08 N	30.42 E
Al-Gharbīyah □[4]	142	31.08 N	31.00 E
Al-Gharbīyah, Aṣ-Ṣaḥrā' (Western Desert) ⬥[2]	140	27.00 N	27.00 E
Al-Ghārīyah	132	32.23 N	36.39 E
Al-Ghāṭ	128	26.00 N	45.03 E
Al-Ghawr V	132	31.50 N	35.30 E
Al-Ghayatah	142	30.57 N	30.06 E
Al-Ghayḍah	118	16.12 N	52.15 E
Al-Ghazālah	128	26.48 N	41.19 E
Al-Ghazālī	142	30.49 N	31.49 E
Al-Ghāzīyah	132	33.31 N	35.22 E
Alghero	71	40.33 N	8.19 E
Al-Ghizlānīyah	132	33.23 N	36.27 E
Al-Ghubbah I	128	24.18 N	53.18 E
Al-Ghulayfiqah	144	14.27 N	43.02 E
Al-Ghurayfah	128	24.00 N	56.29 E
Al-Ghurdaqah	140	27.14 N	33.50 E
Algier → Alger	148	36.47 N	3.03 E
Algiers → Alger	148	36.47 N	3.03 E
Alginet	34	39.16 N	0.28 W
Algoa	222	29.24 N	95.11 W
Algoabaai C	158	33.50 S	25.65 E
Algodão, Ilha do I	256	23.13 S	44.36 W
Algodón ≃	246	2.23 S	71.56 W
Algodones	200	35.23 N	106.29 W
Algodor ≃	34	39.55 N	3.53 W
Algoma	190	44.36 N	87.27 W
Algoma Mills	190	46.10 N	82.50 W
Algona, Iowa, U.S.	190	43.04 N	94.14 W
Algona, Wash., U.S.	224	47.17 N	122.15 W
Algonac	214	42.37 N	82.32 W
Algonquin	216	42.10 N	88.18 W
Algonquin Lake ⊛	216	42.40 N	85.20 W
Algonquin Provincial Park ♠	190	45.27 N	78.26 W
Algood	194	36.12 N	85.27 W
Algorta, Esp.	34	43.22 N	3.01 W
Algorta, Ur.	252	32.25 S	57.23 W
Algoy ≃	86	42.50 N	88.40 E
Alguierão-Mem Martins	266c	38.48 N	9.20 W
Al-Ḥaddādī	142	31.20 N	30.47 E
Al-Ḥaddayn	142	30.44 N	30.38 E
Al-Ḥadīthah, Ar. Sa.	128	31.30 N	37.09 E
Al-Ḥadīthah, 'Irāq	128	34.07 N	42.23 E
Al-Ḥaḍr	128	35.35 N	42.44 E
Al-Ḥaffah	130	35.35 N	36.02 E
Al-Ḥafīr al-Fawqānī	132	33.42 N	36.28 E
Al-Ḥajālīj	140	14.36 N	31.54 E
Al-Ḥajarah ⬥[1]	128	30.00 N	44.00 E
Al-Ḥajar al-Gharbī ΛΛ	128	24.22 N	56.17 E
Al-Ḥajar ash-Sharqī ΛΛ	128	23.00 N	59.00 E
Al-Ḥājir	142	30.41 N	31.49 E
Al-Ḥalfāyah	128	31.49 N	47.26 E
Al-Ḥamād ≚	128	32.00 N	39.30 E
Alhama de Granada	34	37.00 N	3.59 W
Alhama de Murcia	34	37.51 N	1.25 W
Al-Hamal ⬥[1]	128	23.30 N	49.45 E
Alhambra, Calif., U.S.	228	34.06 N	118.08 W
Alhambra, Ill., U.S.	219	38.53 N	89.44 W
Al-Ḥamīdīyah	130	34.43 N	35.56 E
Al-Ḥammām	140	30.50 N	29.23 E
Al-Ḥamrā'	128	23.57 N	38.52 E
Al-Ḥamrā' ⬥[1]	128	22.40 N	55.05 E
Al-Ḥamrah	142	31.10 N	30.52 E
Al-Ḥāmūl	142	31.19 N	31.10 E
Alhandra	250	7.26 S	34.54 W
Alhandra, Mouchão de I	266c	38.54 N	9.00 W
Al-Ḥanīsh al-Kabīr I	144	13.43 N	42.45 E
Al-Ḥarāk	132	32.44 N	36.18 E
Al-Ḥarīq	128	23.37 N	46.31 E
Al-Ḥārrah	132	33.03 N	36.00 E
Al-Ḥarrah ⬥[9]	128	31.00 N	38.30 E
Al-Ḥasakah	130	36.29 N	40.45 E
Al-Ḥasakah □[8]	130	36.30 N	41.00 E
Al-Ḥassānī I	128	24.58 N	37.05 E
Alhaurín el Grande	34	36.38 N	4.41 W
Al-Ḥawāmidīyah	273c	29.54 N	31.15 E
Al-Ḥawātah	144	13.25 N	34.38 E
Al-Ḥawātikah	142	27.16 N	31.01 E
Al-Ḥawrah	144	13.49 N	47.37 E
Al-Ḥawṭah, Ar. Sa.	128	23.27 N	46.46 E
Al-Ḥawṭah, Yam. S.	144	15.50 N	48.27 E
Al-Ḥawwārīyah	142	30.58 N	29.41 E
Al-Ḥayy, 'Irāq	128	32.10 N	46.03 E
Al-Ḥayy, Miṣr	142	29.39 N	31.18 E
Al-Ḥayyānīyah	128	28.38 N	42.45 E
Al-Ḥayz	140	28.02 N	28.39 E
Al-Ḥībah	142	28.45 N	30.55 E
Al-Ḥījānah	132	33.21 N	36.33 E
Al-Ḥijāz ⬥[1]	118	24.30 N	38.30 E
Al-Ḥillah, 'Irāq	128	32.29 N	44.25 E
Al-Ḥillah, Sūd.	140	13.27 N	27.08 E
Al-Ḥillah □[4]	128	32.40 N	44.35 E
Al-Ḥilmīyah ⬥[8]	273c	30.07 N	31.19 E
Al-Hindīyah	128	32.33 N	44.13 E
Al-Ḥiṣn	132	32.29 N	35.52 E
Al-Hoceima	148	35.15 N	3.55 W
Al Hoceima, Baie d' C	34	35.20 N	3.50 W
Alhos Vedros	266c	38.39 N	9.02 W
Alhucemas, Islas de II	34	35.13 N	3.53 W
Al-Ḥuḍayb	140	13.00 N	32.50 E
Al-Ḥudaydah	144	14.48 N	42.57 E
Al-Ḥufrah	146	29.10 N	18.02 E
Al-Ḥufrah ⬥[1]	128	28.40 N	38.30 E
Al-Hufūf	128	25.22 N	49.34 E
Al-Ḥulwah	128	23.27 N	46.47 E
Al-Ḥumayshī	144	13.41 N	45.52 E
Al-Ḥuṣayḥiṣah	140	14.44 N	33.18 E
Al-Ḥusaynīyah	142	30.52 N	31.55 E
Al-Ḥuṣaynīyah ⊤[4]	144	17.48 N	44.27 E
Al-Ḥuwaymī	144	14.05 N	47.44 E
Al-Ḥuwayyiṭ	128	25.36 N	40.23 E
Alì	70	38.02 N	15.25 E
Ali ⬥[8]	272a	28.31 N	77.18 E
'Ālī, Sadd al- (Aswān High Dam) ⬥[6]	140	23.58 N	32.52 E
Alía, Esp.	34	39.27 N	5.13 W
Alia, It.	70	37.47 N	13.43 E
'Alīābād, Īrān	128	36.57 N	54.59 E
Aliabād, Pāk.	123	36.18 N	74.37 E
Aliabad, S.S.S.R.	84	41.29 N	46.37 E
Aliaga	34	40.40 N	0.42 W
Aliağaçiftliği	130	38.48 N	26.59 E
Aliákmon ≃	38	40.30 N	22.36 E
Aliaksin, Cape ≻	180	55.30 N	160.43 W
'Alī al-Gharbī	128	32.27 N	46.41 E
Aliança	250	7.35 S	35.13 W
'Alī an-Nahrī	132	33.51 N	36.01 E
Aliano	68	40.19 N	16.14 E
Alībāg	122	18.39 N	72.54 E
Alibahadır	267b	41.11 N	29.12 E
Ali-Bajramly	84	39.56 N	48.56 E
Alibardak	130	38.06 N	40.25 E
Alibejli	84	41.23 N	46.49 E
Alibey ≃	267b	41.03 N	28.56 E
Alibey Adası I	130	39.20 N	26.38 E
Alibeyköy	267b	41.04 N	28.56 E
Alibijaban Island I	116	13.20 N	122.43 E
Alibori ≃	150	11.56 N	3.17 E
Al-Ibrāhīmīyah	142	30.57 N	30.35 E
Alibunar	38	45.05 N	20.58 E
Alicante	34	38.21 N	0.29 W
Alice, S. Afr.	158	32.47 S	26.50 E
Alice, Tex., U.S.	196	27.45 N	98.04 W
Alice ≃	166	24.02 S	144.50 E
Alice, Punta ≻	68	39.24 N	17.10 E
Alice Arm	182	55.29 N	129.29 W
Alicedale	158	33.18 S	26.05 E
Alice Downs	162	17.45 S	127.56 E
Alice Springs	162	23.42 S	133.53 E
Alice Superiore	62	45.28 N	7.47 E
Alice Town	238	25.44 N	79.17 W
Aliceville	194	33.08 N	88.09 W
Alicia, Pil.	116	16.45 N	121.42 E
Alicia, Pil.	116	7.30 N	122.55 E
Alıcık	130	40.49 N	35.21 E
Alick Creek ≃	166	20.25 S	142.00 E
Alicudi, Isola I	70	38.32 N	14.21 E
Al-'Idwah	142	29.21 N	30.55 E
Alief	222	29.43 N	95.35 W
Alife	68	41.20 N	14.20 E
Al-Ifranj	132	31.11 N	35.41 E
Alīganj, Bhārat	124	28.07 N	80.36 E
Alīganj, Bhārat	124	27.30 N	79.11 E
Alīgarh	124	27.53 N	78.05 E
Alignements de Carnac ⊥	32	47.35 N	3.05 W
Alīgūdarz	128	33.24 N	49.41 E
Alijos, Escollos II[1]	232	24.57 N	115.44 W
'Alī Khēl	120	33.57 N	69.43 E
Al-Ikhṣāṣ al-Qiblīyah	142	29.42 N	31.17 E
Al-Ikhwān II	118	12.09 N	53.12 E
Alikovo	80	55.45 N	46.45 E
Alima ≃	152	1.36 S	16.36 E
Al-'Imārīyah	142	27.37 N	30.53 E
Alimena	70	37.42 N	14.07 E
Alimini Grande ⊛	68	40.12 N	18.27 E
Alimini Piccolo ⊛	68	40.10 N	18.27 E
Aliminusa	70	37.52 N	13.47 E
Alim Island I	164	2.55 S	147.05 E
Alimkent	85	40.58 N	69.11 E
Alimodian	116	10.49 N	122.26 E
Alindao	152	5.02 N	21.13 E
Alingsås	26	57.56 N	12.31 E
Alip Mountains ΛΛ	116	6.44 N	125.05 E
Alipore	126	22.31 N	88.20 E
Alipur, Bhārat	272b	22.55 N	88.11 E
Ālipur, Bhārat	272b	22.43 N	88.12 E
Alīpur, Pāk.	123	29.23 N	70.55 E
Alīpur Duār	124	26.29 N	89.44 E
Alīpur Janūbi	123	30.13 N	71.18 E
Aliquippa	214	40.37 N	80.15 W
Aliquippa-Hopewell Airport ⊠	279b	40.35 N	80.17 W
Āli Rājpur	120	22.19 N	74.21 E
Al-'Irāq	132	31.05 N	35.39 E
Al-'Irāq → Iraq □[1]	128	33.00 N	44.00 E
Al-'Irq	146	29.02 N	21.33 E
Al-'Irqah	144	13.30 N	47.22 E
Ali-Sabieh	144	11.09 N	42.42 E
Aliseda	34	39.26 N	6.41 W
Alise-Sainte-Reine	58	47.32 N	4.29 E
Alī Seyyed	128	32.09 N	59.52 E
'Alī Shāh 'Avaz	128	35.39 N	51.04 E
Alīshārī	84	39.02 N	47.15 E
Al-Iskandarīyah (Alexandria)	142	31.12 N	29.54 E
Al-Iskandarīyah □[4]	142	31.10 N	29.53 E
Al-Ismā'īlīyah (Ismailia)	142	30.35 N	32.16 E
Al-Ismā'īlīyah □[4]	142	30.30 N	32.15 E
Aliso Canyon V, Calif., U.S.	280	33.53 N	117.40 W
Aliso Canyon V, Calif., U.S.	280	34.18 N	118.33 W
Aliso Creek ≃	228	33.31 N	117.45 W
Alisos ≃	200	30.51 N	110.52 W
Al-Istiwā'īyah □[4]	140	5.00 N	31.00 E
Alistráti	38	41.04 N	23.57 E
Alitak, Cape ≻	180	56.51 N	154.21 W
Alitak Bay C	180	57.00 N	154.05 W
Alitanguo	120	35.10 N	83.30 E
Alì Terme	70	38.01 N	15.26 E
Alivérion	38	38.24 N	24.02 E
Aliwal North	158	30.45 S	26.45 E
Alix	182	52.24 N	113.11 W
Al-'Izzīyah	142	27.13 N	30.59 E
Al-Jabal al-Abyaḍ Λ[2]	142	28.46 N	31.00 E
Al-Jabal al-Aḥmar Λ[2]	142	28.19 N	31.07 E
Al-Jabal al-Akhḍar ΛΛ, Lībīya	146	32.30 N	21.30 E
Al-Jabal al-Akhḍar ΛΛ, 'Umān	128	23.15 N	57.20 E
Al-Jabal ash-Sharqī (Anti-Lebanon) ΛΛ	132	33.35 N	36.00 E
Al-Jabalayn	140	12.36 N	32.48 E
Al-Jadīdah	140	25.34 N	28.51 E
Al-Jafādūn	142	28.50 N	30.48 E
Al-Jafr	132	30.18 N	36.13 E
Al-Jāfūrah ⬥[2]	128	24.14 N	50.00 E
Al-Jaghbūb	146	29.45 N	24.31 E
Al-Jahrah	128	29.20 N	47.40 E
Al-Jalāmīd	128	31.20 N	39.56 E
Al-Jamālīyah	142	31.11 N	31.51 E
Al-Janūb □[4]	132	33.20 N	35.30 E
Al-Jarnūs	142	28.36 N	30.43 E
Al-Jawārah	118	18.55 N	57.17 E
Al-Jawf, Ar. Sa.	128	29.50 N	39.52 E
Al-Jawf, Lībīya	146	24.11 N	23.19 E
Al-Jawsh	146	32.00 N	11.40 E
Al-Jaylī	140	16.01 N	32.36 E
Al-Jazīrah ⊤[4]	146	25.42 N	21.07 E
Al-Jazīrah ⬥[1]	140	14.25 N	33.00 E
Aljezur, Bra.	287a	22.40 S	43.36 W
Aljezur, Port.	34	37.19 N	8.48 W
Al-Jibāb	132	33.06 N	36.15 E
Al-Jīzah (Giza)	142		
	273c	30.01 N	31.13 E
Al-Jīzah □[4]	142	29.46 N	31.18 E
Al-Jubayn	140	12.07 N	35.10 E
Aljucén ≃	34	38.56 N	6.25 W
Al-Judayyidah, Urd.	132	31.32 N	35.39 E
Al-Judayyidah, Urd.	132	31.15 N	35.49 E
Al-Julaydah ⊤[4]	128	29.03 N	45.38 E
Al-Junaynah, Miṣr	142	31.06 N	31.41 E
Al-Junaynah, Sūd.	140	13.27 N	22.27 E
Al-Junaynah, Sūrīy.	132	32.54 N	36.44 E
Al-Jundīyah	142	28.34 N	30.50 E
Aljustrel	34	37.52 N	8.10 W
Al-Kafr	132	32.38 N	36.38 E
Al-Kafr ash-Sharqī	142	37.17 N	31.10 E
Al-Kahfah	128	27.04 N	43.02 E
Alkali Creek ≃, Alta., Can.	184	50.52 N	110.30 W
Alkali Creek ≃, Wyo., U.S.	202	43.16 N	107.40 W
Alkali Lake	182	51.47 N	122.14 W
Alkali Lake ⊛, Nev., U.S.	204	41.42 N	119.50 W
Alkali Lake ⊛, Oreg., U.S.	202	43.10 N	120.02 W
Alkamari	146	13.24 N	11.07 E
Al-Kāmilīn	140	15.05 N	33.11 E
Al-Karabah	140	18.33 N	33.42 E
Al-Karak	132	31.11 N	35.42 E
Al-Karak □[8]	132	31.03 N	35.44 E
Al-Karnak	140	25.43 N	32.39 E
Al-Kawah	140	13.44 N	32.30 E
Al-Kawd	144	13.05 N	45.22 E
Al-Kawm	130	35.11 N	38.52 E
Al-Kawm al-Akhḍar	142	30.58 N	30.17 E
Al-Kawm aṭ-Ṭawīl	142	31.12 N	31.05 E
Al-Kāẓimīyah	128	33.22 N	44.20 E
Alken	56	50.15 N	7.26 E

≃	River	Fluss	Río	Rivière	Rio
≖	Canal	Kanal	Canal	Canal	Canal
⅃	Waterfall, Rapids	Wasserfall, Stromschnellen	Cascada, Rápidos	Chute d'eau, Rapides	Cascata, Rápidos
⩌	Strait	Meeresstrasse	Estrecho	Détroit	Estreito
C	Bay, Gulf	Bucht, Golf	Bahía, Golfo	Baie, Golfe	Baía, Golfo
⊛	Lake, Lakes	See, Seen	Lago, Lagos	Lac, Lacs	Lago, Lagos
⩸	Swamp	Sumpf	Pantano	Marais	Pântano
⊼	Ice Features, Glacier	Eis- und Gletscherformen	Accidentes Glaciales	Formes glaciaires	Acidentes Glaciares
⊤	Other Hydrographic Features	Andere Hydrographische Objekte	Otros Elementos Hidrográficos	Autres données hydrographiques	Outros Elementos Hidrográficos
✣	Submarine Features	Untermeerische Objekte	Accidentes Submarinos	Formes de relief sous-marin	Acidentes Submarinos
□	Political Unit	Politische Einheit	Unidad Politica	Entité politique	Unidade Política
⊎	Cultural Institution	Kulturelle Institution	Institución Cultural	Institution culturelle	Instituição Cultural
⊥	Historical Site	Historische Stätte	Sitio Histórico	Site historique	Sitio Histórico
♠	Recreational Site	Erholungs- und Ferienort	Sitio de Recreo	Centre de loisirs	Sítio de Lazer
⊠	Airport	Flughafen	Aeropuerto	Aéroport	Aeroporto
■	Military Installation	Militäranlage	Instalación Militar	Installation militaire	Instalação Militar
⬥	Miscellaneous	Verschiedenes	Misceláneo	Divers	Miscelânea

ENGLISH — Name | Page | Lat.°′ | Long.°′

DEUTSCH — Name | Seite | Breite°′ | Länge°′ E=Ost

Name	Page	Lat.°′	Long.°′
Al-Khabrā'	128	25.59 N	43.39 E
Al-Khābūrah	128	23.59 N	57.08 E
Al-Khalīl (Hebron)	132	31.32 N	35.06 E
Al-Khalīl □[8]	132	31.32 N	35.06 E
Al-Khālis	128	33.49 N	44.32 E
Al-Khāmis, Ash-Shallāl (Fifth Cararact) ⌊	140	18.23 N	33.47 E
Al-Khandaq	140	18.36 N	30.34 E
Al-Khānkah	142	30.13 N	31.21 E
Al-Kharaqānīyah	273c	30.10 N	31.10 E
Al-Khārijah	140	25.26 N	30.33 E
Al-Khaṣab	128	26.12 N	56.15 E
Al-Khatam ◆[1]	128	24.16 N	55.10 E
Al-Khirbah as-Samrā'	132	32.11 N	36.10 E
Al-Khiyām	132	33.19 N	35.36 E
Al-Khubar	128	26.17 N	50.12 E
Al-Khums (Homs)	146	32.39 N	14.16 E
Al-Khums □[4]	146	32.00 N	14.00 E
Al-Khuraybah, Urd.	132	32.40 N	35.52 E
Al-Khuraybah, Yam. S.	144	15.06 N	48.19 E
Al-Khurmah	144	21.54 N	42.03 E
Al-Khurṭūm (Khartoum)	140	15.36 N	32.32 E
Al-Khurṭūm □[4]	140	15.45 N	32.30 E
Al-Khurṭūm Baḥrī	140	15.38 N	32.33 E
Al-Khushnīyah	132	33.00 N	35.48 E
Al-Khuṣūṣ	273c	30.09 N	31.19 E
Al-Kifl	128	32.14 N	44.22 E
Al-Kiswah	132	33.21 N	36.14 E
Alkmaar	52	52.37 N	4.44 E
Al-Kūfah	128	32.02 N	44.24 E
Al-Kufayr	132	33.26 N	35.44 E
Al-Kufrah (Cufra) ◆[1]	146	24.20 N	23.15 E
Al-Kunayyisah	273c	29.59 N	31.11 E
Al-Kuntillah	140	30.00 N	34.41 E
Al-Kūt	128	32.25 N	45.49 E
Al-Kūt □[4]	128	32.45 N	45.25 E
Al-Kuwayt	128	29.20 N	47.59 E
Al-Kuwayt → Kuwait □[1]	128	29.30 N	47.45 E
Alkvettern ◎	40	59.25 N	14.21 E
Allaben	210	42.07 N	74.22 W
Al-Labwah	130	34.12 N	36.21 E
Allacapan	116	18.15 N	121.35 E
Allach-Jun'	74	61.08 N	138.03 E
Allada	150	6.39 N	2.09 E
Al-Lādhiqīyah (Latakia)	130	35.31 N	35.47 E
Al-Lādhiqīyah □[8]	130	35.10 N	36.10 E
Allagash ≃	186	47.05 N	69.02 W
Allagen	56	51.28 N	8.14 E
Al-Lagowa	140	11.24 N	29.08 E
Allāhābād, Bhārat	124	25.27 N	81.51 E
Allāhābād, Pāk.	123	28.57 N	70.53 E
Allahābād □[5]	124	25.20 N	82.00 E
Allāhbās	272a	28.31 N	77.25 E
Allāhwardipur	272a	28.33 N	77.26 E
Allaines	50	48.12 N	1.50 E
Allaire State Park ♠	208	40.08 N	74.08 W
Allakaket	180	66.34 N	152.41 W
Allaman	58	46.28 N	6.24 E
Allamuchy	210	40.55 N	74.49 W
Allan	184	51.53 N	106.04 W
Allan, Pointe ≻	275a	45.26 N	73.45 W
Allanche	32	45.14 N	2.56 E
Alland	61	48.03 N	16.05 E
Allandale	220	29.07 N	80.58 W
Allan Island ▮	224	48.28 N	122.42 W
Allanmyo	110	19.22 N	95.13 E
Allanridge	158	27.55 S	26.44 E
Allanson	168a	33.20 S	116.06 E
Allan Water ≃	46	56.08 N	3.56 W
Allapattah Flats ≚	220	27.29 N	82.34 W
'Allāq, Bi'r ⊤[4]	146	31.05 N	11.42 E
'Allāqī, Wādī al- ∨	140	23.07 N	32.47 E
Allard, Lac ◎, Qué., Can.	186	50.32 N	63.31 W
Allard, Lac ◎, Qué., Can.	190	47.20 N	78.51 W
Allardt	194	36.23 N	84.53 W
Allariz	34	42.11 N	7.48 W
Állatkert ♠	264c	47.31 N	19.05 E
Allatoona Lake ◎[1]	192	34.08 N	84.38 W
Allauch	62	43.20 N	5.29 E
Al-Layyah	140	16.16 N	35.25 E
Alldays	156	22.44 S	29.04 E
Alle, Bel.	56	49.51 N	4.58 E
Alle, Schw.	58	47.26 N	7.08 E
Åleberg ∧[2]	26	58.08 N	13.36 E
Allegan	216	42.32 N	85.51 W
Allegan □[6]	216	42.35 N	85.53 W
Allegan, Lake ◎	216	42.33 N	85.55 W
Allegany	210	42.06 N	78.30 W
Allegany □[6]	210	42.13 N	78.02 W
Allegany Indian Reservation ◆[4]	210	42.10 N	78.47 W
Allegany State Park ♠	210	42.04 N	78.44 W
Alleghany	226	39.28 N	120.51 W
Alleghe	64	46.24 N	12.01 E
Allegheny □[6]	214	40.26 N	79.59 W
Allegheny ≃	214	40.27 N	80.00 W
Allegheny Acres	279b	40.37 N	79.53 W
Allegheny Center ⊍	279b	40.27 N	80.01 W
Allegheny County Airport ⊠	279b	40.21 N	79.56 W
Allegheny County Park ♠	279b	40.34 N	79.55 W
Allegheny Mountains ⋀	188	38.30 N	80.00 W
Allegheny Observatory ⊍[3]	279b	40.29 N	80.01 W
Allegheny Plateau ⋀[1]	188	41.30 N	78.00 W
Allegheny Portage Railroad National Historic Site ⊥	214	40.28 N	78.32 W
Allegheny Reservoir ◎[1]	214	42.00 N	78.56 W
Allègre	62	45.12 N	3.42 E
Allègre, Pointe ≻	241o	16.22 N	61.45 W
Allemagne, République fédérale d' → Germany, Federal Republic Of □[1]	30	51.00 N	9.00 E
Allemande, République démocratique → German Democratic Republic □[1]	30	52.00 N	12.30 E
Allemanskraaldam ◆[6]	158	28.16 S	27.07 E
Allemant	261	48.45 N	1.37 E
Allemont	62	45.08 N	6.02 E
Allen, Arg.	252	38.58 S	67.50 W
Allen, Pil.	116	12.30 N	124.17 E
Allen, Md., U.S.	208	38.17 N	75.42 W
Allen, Mich., U.S.	216	41.57 N	84.46 W
Allen, Nebr., U.S.	198	42.25 N	96.51 W
Allen, Okla., U.S.	196	34.53 N	96.25 W
Allen, Pa., U.S.	208	40.10 N	77.05 W
Allen, S. Dak., U.S.	198	43.17 N	101.55 W
Allen, Tex., U.S.	222	33.06 N	96.40 W
Allen, Wash., U.S.	224	48.31 N	122.23 W
Allen □[6], Ind., U.S.	216	41.04 N	85.09 W
Allen □[6], Ohio, U.S.	216	40.46 N	84.06 W
Allen ≃	44	54.58 N	2.19 W
Allen, Lough ◎	48	54.08 N	8.08 W
Allen, Mount ∧, N.Z.	172	47.05 S	167.48 E
Allen, Mount ∧, Alaska, U.S.	180	62.14 N	142.13 W
Allenby Bridge ◆[5]	132	31.52 N	35.52 E
Allendale, Ill., U.S.	194	38.32 N	87.43 W
Allendale, Mich., U.S.	216	42.58 N	85.57 W
Allendale, N.J., U.S.	276	41.02 N	74.08 W
Allendale, S.C., U.S.	192	33.06 N	81.18 W
Allendale Town	44	54.54 N	2.15 W
Allende, Méx.	232	25.17 N	100.01 W
Allende, Méx.	232	28.20 N	100.51 W
Allende, Méx.	234	18.09 N	94.16 W
Allendorf, B.R.D.	56	51.02 N	8.38 E
Allendorf, B.R.D.	56	51.16 N	9.58 E
Allenfarm	222	30.24 N	96.14 W
All England Lawn Tennis Club ♠	260	51.26 N	0.13 W
Allen Grove	216	42.35 N	88.41 W
Allen Park	216	42.15 N	83.13 W
Allenport, Pa., U.S.	214	40.06 N	79.51 W
Allenport, Pa., U.S.	214	40.20 N	77.53 W
Allensbach	58	47.43 N	9.03 E
Allenstein → Olsztyn	30	53.48 N	20.29 E
Allensville	214	40.32 N	77.49 W
Allenton, Mich., U.S.	214	42.55 N	82.57 W
Allenton, R.I., U.S.	207	41.32 N	71.29 W
Allentown, N.J., U.S.	208	40.11 N	74.35 W
Allentown, N.Y., U.S.	210	42.05 N	78.04 W
Allentown, Ohio, U.S.	216	40.46 N	84.12 W
Allentown, Pa., U.S.	208	40.36 N	75.29 W
Allentsteig	61	48.42 N	15.20 E
Allenwood, N.J., U.S.	208	40.09 N	74.06 W
Allenwood, N.Y., U.S.	276	40.48 N	73.44 W
Allenwood, Pa., U.S.	210	41.07 N	76.54 W
Alleppey	122	9.29 N	76.19 E
Aller ≃	30	52.57 N	9.11 E
Allerona	66	42.49 N	11.58 E
Allersberg	60	49.15 N	11.15 E
Allershausen	60	48.26 N	11.36 E
Allerslev	41	55.05 N	12.03 E
Allerton, Iowa, U.S.	190	40.42 N	93.22 W
Allerton, Mass., U.S.	283	42.18 N	70.53 W
Allerton ◆[8]	262	53.22 N	2.53 W
Allerton, Point ≻	207	42.18 N	70.53 W
Allestree	42	52.57 N	1.29 W
Allevard	62	45.24 N	6.04 E
Alley Park ♠	276	40.45 N	73.44 W
Alleyton	222	29.43 N	96.29 W
Allgäu ◆[1]	58	47.35 N	10.10 E
Allgäuer Alpen ⋀	58	47.20 N	10.25 E
Allhallows	260	51.28 N	0.39 E
Alli ≃	68	38.51 N	16.40 E
Alliance, Alta., Can.	182	52.26 N	111.47 W
Alliance, Nebr., U.S.	198	42.06 N	102.52 W
Alliance, Ohio, U.S.	214	40.55 N	81.06 W
Allibaudières	50	48.35 N	4.07 E
Al-Lidām	144	20.29 N	44.50 E
Allier □[5]	32	46.25 N	3.00 E
Allier ≃	62	45.05 N	3.35 E
Alligator ≃	192	35.58 N	75.58 W
Alligator Creek ≃, Ga., U.S.	192	31.58 N	82.22 W
Alligator Creek ≃, Tex., U.S.	222	30.42 N	97.07 W
Alligator Lake ◎	220	28.13 N	81.13 W
Alligator Pond	241q	17.52 N	77.34 W
Alligny-en-Morvan	50	47.12 N	4.10 E
Allihies	48	51.38 N	10.03 W
Allinagaram	122	10.02 N	77.30 E
Allinge	26	55.16 N	14.49 E
Allington Castle ⊥	260	51.17 N	0.31 E
Al-Lisān ≻[1]	132	31.17 N	35.28 E
Al-Lisht	142	29.34 N	31.14 E
Allison	190	42.45 N	92.48 W
Allison, Mount ∧	282	37.30 N	121.52 W
Allison Gulch ∨	280	34.16 N	117.44 W
Allison Harbour	182	51.03 N	127.30 W
Allison Park	214	40.34 N	79.57 W
Alliste	68	39.57 N	18.05 E
Alliston	212	44.09 N	79.52 W
Al-Līth	144	20.09 N	40.16 E
Al-Imām ◆[8]	273c	30.01 N	31.10 E
Allmendingen	58	48.20 N	9.43 E
Alloa	46	56.07 N	3.49 W
Allochio, Galleria degli ◆[5]	66	44.03 N	11.30 E
Allogny	50	47.13 N	2.19 E
Allonby	44	54.46 N	3.25 W
Allone Abba	132	32.44 N	35.10 E
Allonnes	50	48.20 N	1.40 E
Allora	171a	28.02 S	151.59 E
Allos	62	44.14 N	6.38 E
Allott, Mount ∧[2]	162	26.06 S	124.46 E
Allouez	190	44.29 N	88.01 W
Alloway	208	39.34 N	75.22 W
Alloway Creek ≃	208	39.27 N	75.30 W
Allport	214	40.58 N	78.12 W
All Saints	240c	17.03 N	61.48 W
Allschwil	58	47.33 N	7.33 E
Allstedt	54	51.24 N	11.23 E
Allston ◆[8]	283	42.22 N	71.08 W
Al-Lubnān → Lebanon □[1]	128	33.50 N	35.50 E
Alluets, Forêt des ♠	261	48.55 N	1.55 E
Al-Luḥayyah	144	15.42 N	42.42 E
Allumette Lake ◎	190	45.53 N	77.13 W
Allumettes, Île des ▮	190	45.50 N	77.05 W
Allumiere	66	42.09 N	11.54 E
Allview Estates	208	39.12 N	76.51 W
Allyn	224	47.23 N	122.50 W
Alm	64	47.24 N	12.54 E
Alm ≃	60	48.05 N	13.55 E
Alma, Qué., Can.	186	48.33 N	71.39 W
Alma, Ark., U.S.	194	35.29 N	94.13 W
Alma, Ga., U.S.	192	31.33 N	82.28 W
Alma, Ill., U.S.	219	38.43 N	88.55 W
Alma, Kans., U.S.	198	39.01 N	96.17 W
Alma, Mich., U.S.	190	43.23 N	84.39 W
Alma, Nebr., U.S.	198	40.06 N	99.22 W
Alma, N.Y., U.S.	210	42.01 N	78.03 W
Alma, Wis., U.S.	190	44.20 N	91.55 W
Al-Ma'ābidah	142	27.20 N	31.01 E
Al-Ma'ādī ◆[8]	142	29.58 N	31.15 E
Al-Ma'ānīyah	128	30.44 N	43.00 E
Alma-Ata	85	43.15 N	76.57 E
Alma-Ata □[4]	85	44.00 N	76.00 E
Alma Center	190	44.26 N	90.55 W
Almada	34	38.41 N	9.09 W
Almaden, Austl.	166	17.20 S	144.41 E
Almadén, Esp.	34	38.46 N	4.50 W
Almadén de la Plata	34	37.52 N	6.04 W
Al-Madīnah (Medina)	128	24.28 N	39.36 E
Al-Madīnah al-Fikrīyah	142	27.56 N	30.49 E
Al-Madwar	132	32.17 N	36.00 E
Al-Mafāzah	140	13.36 N	34.33 E
Al-Mafraq	132	32.21 N	36.12 E
Almafuerte	252	32.12 S	64.15 W
Al-Maghārīm	144	15.01 N	47.51 E
Al-Maghrah ◎	140	30.15 N	28.56 E
Almagor	132	32.55 N	35.36 E
Almagre, Laguna ⊂	234	23.48 N	97.48 W
Al-Magreb → Morocco □[1]	148	32.00 N	5.00 W
Almagro	34	38.53 N	3.43 W
Almagro Island ▮	116	11.56 N	124.18 E
Al-Maḥallah al-Kubrā	142	30.58 N	31.10 E
Al-Maḥārīq	140	25.37 N	30.39 E
Alma Hill ∧[2]	210	42.03 N	78.01 W
Al-Maḥmūdīyah	142	31.11 N	30.32 E
Al-Maḥraṣ	142	27.49 N	30.48 E
Al-Maḥsamah	142	30.34 N	32.01 E
Al-Majdal	132	32.47 N	36.30 E
Almăjului, Munții ⋀	38	44.43 N	22.12 E
Al-Makīlī	146	32.09 N	22.17 E
Al-Maks	142	31.09 N	29.51 E
Almalyk	85	40.50 N	69.35 E
Al-Ma'mūrah	142	31.18 N	30.03 E
Al-Manāmah	128	26.13 N	50.35 E
Al-Manāqil	140	14.15 N	32.59 E
Al-Manāṣif ◆[1]	130	35.13 N	40.54 E
Al-Manāwāt	273c	29.55 N	31.14 E
Almanor, Lake ◎	204	40.15 N	121.08 W
Almansa	34	38.52 N	1.05 W
Al-Manshāh	140	26.28 N	31.48 E
Almansor ≃	34	38.56 N	8.54 W
Al-Manṣūrah	142	31.03 N	31.23 E
Al-Manṣūrīyah	142	30.08 N	31.05 E
Almanza	34	42.39 N	5.02 W
Al-Manzilah	142	31.09 N	31.56 E
Almanzor, Pico de ∧	34	40.15 N	5.18 W
Almanzora ≃	34	37.14 N	1.46 W
Al-Maqnāh	128	28.24 N	34.45 E
Almar ≃	34	40.54 N	5.29 W
Al-Marāghah	140	26.42 N	31.36 E
Al-Marāzīq	142	29.49 N	31.16 E
Almargem do Bispo	266c	38.51 N	9.16 W
Al-Marj	146	32.30 N	20.54 E
Al-Marj ◆[8]	273c	30.09 N	31.20 E
Almas	250	11.33 S	47.09 W
Almaș ≃	38	47.14 N	23.19 E
Almas, Pico das ∧	255	13.33 S	41.56 W
Al-Ma'ṣarah, Miṣr	142	27.42 N	30.52 E
Al-Ma'ṣarah, Miṣr	142	29.54 N	31.17 E
Al-Ma'ṣarah, Miṣr	142	31.13 N	31.19 E
Al-Mashqūq	132	32.24 N	36.43 E
Al-Mashrafah	130	34.50 N	36.52 E
Al-Masīd	140	15.15 N	32.57 E
Al-Maṣīrah ▮	118	20.25 N	58.50 E
Al-Matammah	140	16.43 N	33.22 E
Al-Maṭarīyah	142	31.11 N	32.02 E
Al-Maṭarīyah ◆[8]	142	30.07 N	31.19 E
Al-Matnah	140	13.47 N	35.03 E
Al-Mawṣil (Mosul)	128	36.20 N	43.08 E
Al-Mawṣil □[4]	128	36.10 N	42.35 E
Al-Mayādīn	130	35.01 N	40.27 E
Al-Maymūn	142	29.14 N	31.12 E
Almazán	34	41.29 N	2.32 W
Almazar, S.S.S.R.	85	40.59 N	68.54 E
Al-Mazār, Urd.	132	31.04 N	35.42 E
Almaznaja ◆[8]	83	48.31 N	38.35 E
Almaznij	83	48.02 N	40.03 E
Almazora	34	39.57 N	0.03 W
Almazovka ◆[8]	83	48.04 N	39.18 E
Almazovo	265b	55.51 N	38.02 E
Al-Mazzah	132	33.30 N	36.15 E
Alme	56	51.28 N	8.37 E
Almeida	34	40.43 N	6.54 W
Almeirim, Bra.	250	1.32 S	52.34 W
Almeirim, Port.	34	39.12 N	8.38 W
Almejas, Bahía ⊂	232	24.29 N	111.44 W
Almelo	52	52.21 N	6.39 E
Almelo-Nordhorn, Kanaal ≡	52	52.20 N	6.40 E
Almena	198	39.54 N	99.43 W
Almenar	34	41.48 N	2.34 W
Almenara	255	16.11 S	40.42 W
Almenar de Soria	34	41.41 N	2.12 W
Almendares ≃	286b	23.08 N	82.25 W
Almendra, Embalse de ◎[1]	34	41.15 N	6.10 W
Almendralejo	34	38.41 N	6.24 W
Almenêches	50	48.42 N	0.07 E
Al'menevo	86	54.57 N	63.34 E
Almenno San Salvatore	62	45.45 N	9.35 E
Almería	34	36.50 N	2.27 W
Almería, Golfo de ⊂	34	36.46 N	2.30 W
Al'metjevsk	80	54.53 N	52.20 E
Al'mež	24	60.03 N	48.03 E
Älmhult	26	56.33 N	14.08 E
Al-Midhnab	128	25.54 N	44.14 E
Al-Mīnā'	130	34.27 N	35.49 E
Almina, Punta ≻	34	35.53 N	5.15 W
Almino Afonso	250	6.09 S	37.46 W
Al-Minshāt al-Kubrā	142	31.03 N	30.54 E
Al-Minūfīyah □[4]	142	30.30 N	31.00 E
Al-Minyā, Miṣr	142	28.06 N	30.45 E
Al-Minyā, Miṣr	142	29.14 N	30.45 E
Al-Minyā, Miṣr	142	29.45 N	31.18 E
Al-Minyā □[4]	142	28.26 N	30.42 E
Almira	202	47.43 N	118.56 W
Almirantazgo → Admiralty Mountains ⋀	9	71.45 S	168.30 E
Almirantazgo, Islas → Admiralty Islands ▮▮	164	2.10 S	147.00 E
Almirante	236	9.18 N	82.24 W
Almirante, Bahía ⊂	236	9.20 N	82.18 W
Almirante Brown	258	34.48 S	58.23 W
Almirante Brown □[5]	288	34.50 S	58.20 W
Almirante Guillermo Brown, Parque ♠	288	34.40 S	58.28 W
Almirante Latorre	252	29.38 S	70.58 W
Almirante Montt, Golfo ⋃	254	51.55 S	72.45 W
Almirós	38	39.11 N	22.46 E
Almiroú, Kólpos ⊂	38	35.23 N	24.20 E
Al-Mismīyah	132	33.08 N	36.23 E
Almo	202	42.06 N	113.38 W
Almoçageme	266c	38.48 N	9.28 W
Almodôvar	34	37.31 N	8.04 W
Almodóvar del Campo	34	38.43 N	4.10 W
Almolonga	236	14.49 N	91.30 W
Almond, N.Y., U.S.	210	42.19 N	77.44 W
Almond, Wis., U.S.	190	44.16 N	89.24 W
Almond ≃, Scot., U.K.	46	56.25 N	3.27 W
Almond ≃, Scot., U.K.	46	55.58 N	3.18 W
Almondsbury	42	51.34 N	2.34 W
Almonesson	208	39.49 N	75.06 W
Almont	214	42.55 N	83.03 W
Almont ≃	261	48.32 N	2.40 E
Almonte, Ont., Can.	212	45.14 N	76.12 W
Almonte, Esp.	34	37.15 N	6.31 W
Almonte, Calif., U.S.	282	37.53 N	122.32 W
Almonte ≃	34	39.42 N	6.28 W
Almora	124	29.37 N	79.40 E
Almōra □[5]	124	29.45 N	79.35 E
Almsee ◎	64	47.45 N	13.57 E
Älmsta	40	59.58 N	18.48 E
Al-Mu'allaqah	132	33.50 N	35.54 E
Al-Mu'aẓẓamīyah	132	33.45 N	36.39 E
Al-Mubarraz, Ar. Sa.	128	25.55 N	49.36 E
Al-Mubarraz, Ar. Sa.	144	22.17 N	46.44 E
Al-Mudawwarah	128	29.19 N	36.01 E
Al-Mudawwarah ∧[2]	142	29.11 N	30.21 E
Almudébar	34	42.03 N	0.35 W
Al-Muglad	140	11.02 N	27.44 E
Al-Muḥarraq	128	26.16 N	50.37 E
Al-Mukallā	144	14.32 N	49.08 E
Al-Mukhā (Mocha)	144	13.19 N	43.15 E
Al-Munājāt al-Kubrā	142	30.50 N	32.01 E
Almuñécar	34	36.43 N	3.41 W
Almunge	40	59.53 N	18.03 E
Al-Muntazah	142	31.17 N	30.01 E
Al-Murrah al-Kubrā, Al-Buḥayrah (Great Bitter Lake) ◎	142	30.20 N	32.23 E
Al-Murrah aṣ-Ṣughrā, Al-Buḥayrah (Little Bitter Lake ◎	142	30.13 N	32.33 E
Almus	130	40.23 N	36.55 E
Al-Musallamīyah	140	14.34 N	33.21 E
Al-Musayfirah	132	32.37 N	36.20 E
Al-Musayjid	128	24.05 N	39.06 E
Al-Musayyib	128	32.47 N	44.18 E
Al-Mushannaf	132	32.44 N	36.46 E
Al-Musharrak Qiblī	142	29.23 N	30.34 E
Al-Mutā'iyah	132	32.29 N	36.17 E
Al-Mu'tamadīyah	142	31.02 N	31.05 E
Al-Mutayn	132	33.54 N	35.44 E
Al-Muṭī'ah	142	27.08 N	31.18 E
Al-Muwassam	144	16.25 N	42.20 E
Al-Muwayh	144	22.45 N	41.36 E
Al-Muwayliḥ	128	27.41 N	35.27 E
Aln ≃	44	55.23 N	1.37 W
Alnarp	41	55.39 N	13.05 E
Al'n'aš	80	56.44 N	54.43 E
Alnaši	80	56.11 N	52.28 E
Al-Nasser	140	24.32 N	32.55 E
Alne ≃	42	52.13 N	1.52 W
Alness	46	57.41 N	4.15 W
Alnmouth	44	55.23 N	1.36 W
Alnön ▮	26	62.25 N	17.26 E
Alnor	41	54.55 N	9.36 E
Alnwick	44	55.25 N	1.42 W
Alnwick Indian Reserve ◆[4]	212	44.10 N	78.06 W
Alo	146	11.47 N	20.53 E
Aloândia	255	17.43 S	49.29 W
Alofau	174u	14.16 S	170.36 W
Alofi	174v	19.01 S	169.55 W
Alofi Bay ⊂	174v	19.01 S	169.56 W
Aloha	224	45.29 N	122.52 W
Aloha, Lake ◎	226	38.52 N	120.09 W
Aloi	154	2.17 N	33.10 E
Aloja	76	57.46 N	24.53 E
Alondra	280	33.54 N	118.19 W
Alónnisos	38	39.08 N	23.50 E
Alónnisos ▮	38	39.13 N	23.55 E
Alor, Kepulauan ▮▮	112	8.15 S	124.30 E
Alor, Pulau ▮	112	8.15 S	124.45 E
Alor, Selat ⋃	112	8.20 S	123.48 E
Álora	34	36.48 N	4.42 W
Alor Gajah	114	2.23 N	102.13 E
Alor Setar	114	6.07 N	100.22 E
Alor Star → Alor Setar	114	6.07 N	100.22 E
Alorton	219	38.36 N	96.08 W
Alos	130	38.07 N	39.32 E
Al'ošn'a, S.S.S.R.	76	53.38 N	33.29 E
Al'ošn'a, S.S.S.R.	82	54.14 N	37.16 E
Alosno	34	37.33 N	7.07 W
Alost → Aalst	50	50.56 N	4.02 E
Alouette ≃	224	49.16 N	122.42 W
Alouette Lake ◎	224	49.19 N	122.28 W
Alovo	80	54.38 N	46.27 E
Aloxe-Corton	58	47.04 N	4.52 E
Aloysius, Mount ∧	162	26.01 S	128.34 E
Alpachiri	252	37.22 S	63.46 W
Alpaugh	226	35.53 N	119.29 W
Alpen	52	51.35 N	6.30 E
Alpen → Alps ⋀	32	46.25 N	10.00 E
Alpena, Ark., U.S.	194	36.17 N	93.18 W
Alpena, Mich., U.S.	190	45.04 N	83.26 W
Alpena, S. Dak., U.S.	198	44.11 N	98.22 W
Alpercatas ≃	250	6.02 S	44.19 W
Alpes → Alps ⋀	32	46.25 N	10.00 E
Alpes Dináricos → Dinara ⋀	36	43.50 N	16.35 E
Alpes Maritimes □[5]	62	44.00 N	7.10 E
Alpes Marítimos → Maritime Alps ⋀	62	44.15 N	7.10 E
Alpes Transilvanos → Carpații Meridionali ⋀	38	45.30 N	24.15 E
Alpha, Austl.	166	23.39 S	146.38 E
Alpha, Ill., U.S.	190	41.12 N	90.23 W
Alpha, Mich., U.S.	190	46.02 N	88.22 W
Alpha, N.J., U.S.	210	40.40 N	75.09 W
Alpharetta	192	34.04 N	84.18 W
Alphen aan den Rijn	52	52.07 N	4.40 E
Alphington	42	50.42 N	3.31 W
Alphin Pike ∧[2]	262	53.31 N	2.00 W
Alphonse Island ▮	138	7.00 S	52.45 E
Alpi → Alps ⋀	32	46.25 N	10.00 E
Alpiarça	34	39.15 N	8.35 W
Alpi Dinariche → Dinara ⋀	36	43.50 N	16.35 E
Alpignano	62	45.06 N	7.31 E
Alpilles, Chaîne des ⋀[2]	62	43.45 N	4.50 E
Alpine, Ariz., U.S.	200	33.51 N	109.09 W
Alpine, Calif., U.S.	204	32.50 N	116.47 W
Alpine, N.J., U.S.	276	40.56 N	73.56 W
Alpine, N.Y., U.S.	210	42.19 N	76.44 W
Alpine, Tex., U.S.	196	30.22 N	103.40 W
Alpine □[6]	226	38.41 N	119.47 W
Alpine Creek ≃	282	37.19 N	122.17 W
Alpinópolis	255	20.52 S	46.23 W
Alpi Retiche → Rhaetian Alps ⋀	58	46.30 N	10.00 E
Alpirsbach	58	48.21 N	8.23 E
Alplaus Kill ≃	210	42.51 N	73.54 W
Alpnachstad	58	46.57 N	8.17 E
Alps ⋀	22	46.25 N	10.00 E
Alpsee ◎	58	47.34 N	10.10 E
Alpu	130	39.47 N	30.58 E
Al-Qābil	128	23.57 N	55.48 E
Al-Qābūn	132	33.33 N	36.20 E
Al-Qadam	132	33.28 N	36.17 E
Al-Qaḍārif	140	14.02 N	35.24 E
Al-Qaddāḥīyah	146	31.22 N	15.14 E
Al-Qadīmah	144	22.21 N	39.09 E
Al-Qāhirah (Cairo), Miṣr	142		
	273c	30.03 N	31.15 E
Al-Qāhirah □[4]	142	30.02 N	31.13 E
Al-Qaḥmah	144	18.00 N	41.41 E
Al-Qā'im	128	34.21 N	41.07 E
Al-Qā'īyah ⊤[4]	128	26.27 N	45.35 E
Al-Qāiyāt	142	28.40 N	30.41 E
Al-Qalaj	273c	30.11 N	31.21 E
Al-Qalībah	128	28.32 N	37.42 E
Al-Qalyūbīyah □[4]	142	30.18 N	31.18 E
Al-Qāmishlī	130	37.02 N	41.14 E
Al-Qanāṭir al-Khayrīyah	142	30.12 N	31.08 E
Al-Qanāyāt	142	30.37 N	31.28 E
Al-Qanṭarah	142	30.52 N	32.19 E
Al-Qārah	128	29.52 N	40.15 E
Al-Qaryah ash-Sharqīyah	146	30.24 N	13.36 E
Al-Qaryatayn	130	34.14 N	37.14 E
Al-Qaṣabāt	146	32.35 N	14.03 E
Al-Qaṣābī	142	31.16 N	30.41 E
Al-Qaṣr, Miṣr	140	25.42 N	28.53 E
Al-Qaṣr, Urd.	132	31.19 N	35.45 E
Al-Qaṣṣāṣīn	142	30.34 N	31.56 E
Al-Qaṭīf	128	26.33 N	50.00 E
Al-Qaṭrūn	146	24.56 N	14.38 E
Al-Qaṭṭā	142	30.13 N	30.58 E
Al-Qaṭṭāwīyah	142	30.33 N	31.40 E
Al-Qays	142	28.29 N	30.47 E
Al-Qayṣūmah	128	28.16 N	46.03 E
Al-Qir'awn	132	33.34 N	35.43 E
Al-Qiṣfah	132	32.38 N	35.52 E
Al-Quds → Yerushalayim	132	31.46 N	35.14 E
Al-Quds □[8]	132	31.45 N	35.20 E
Alqueva, Barragem de ◆[6]	34	38.14 N	7.29 W
Alquízar	240p	22.48 N	82.35 W
Al-Qunayṭirah	132	33.07 N	35.49 E
Al-Qunayṭirah □[8]	132	33.00 N	35.50 E
Al-Qunfudhah	144	19.08 N	41.05 E
Al-Qurayn	142	30.37 N	31.44 E
Al-Qurayyah	132	32.32 N	36.36 E
Al-Qurayyāt	128	23.17 N	58.55 E
Al-Qurnah	128	31.00 N	47.26 E
Al-Quṣaymah	132	30.40 N	34.22 E
Al-Quṣayr, Miṣr	128	26.06 N	34.17 E
Al-Quṣayr, Miṣr	142	27.27 N	30.52 E
Al-Quṣayr, Sūrīy.	130	34.31 N	36.35 E
Al-Qūṣīyah	142	27.26 N	30.49 E
Al-Quṭayfah	132	33.44 N	36.36 E
Al-Quṭaynah	140	14.52 N	32.21 E
Al-Quway'īyah	128	24.03 N	45.15 E
Al-Quwaysī	140	13.20 N	34.05 E
Alright, Île ▮	186	47.25 N	61.47 W
Alrø ▮	41	55.51 N	10.05 E
Alroy Downs	162	19.18 S	136.04 E
Als ▮	41	54.59 N	9.55 E
Alsace □[9]	58	48.30 N	7.30 E
Alsace, Ballon d' ∧	58	47.50 N	6.51 E
Alsask	184	51.23 N	109.59 W
Alsasua	34	42.54 N	2.10 W
Alsdorf	56	50.53 N	6.10 E
Alsea	202	44.23 N	123.36 W
Alsea ≃	202	44.26 N	124.05 W
Alsek ≃	180	59.10 N	138.10 W
Alsen	198	48.38 N	98.42 W
Alseno	64	44.54 N	9.59 E
Alsenz	56	49.43 N	7.49 E
Alsenz ≃	56	49.49 N	7.51 E
Alsey	219	39.34 N	90.25 W
Alsfeld	56	50.45 N	9.16 E
Als Fjord ⊂[2]	41	55.02 N	9.38 E
Alsh, Loch ⊂	46	57.15 N	5.39 W
Alsike	40	59.45 N	17.45 E
Alsina	252	33.54 S	59.23 W
Alsip	216	41.40 N	87.44 W
Alsleben	54	51.42 N	11.41 E
Alsónémedi	264c	47.19 N	19.10 E
Alstaden ◆[8]	263	51.28 N	6.50 E
Ålstäket	40	59.20 N	18.28 E
Alstätte	52	52.08 N	6.55 E
Alstead ≃	184	55.50 N	107.26 W
Alster	40	59.24 N	13.36 E
Alster ≃	52	53.36 N	9.59 E
Alsterbro	26	56.57 N	15.55 E
Alstern ◎	40	59.40 N	13.55 E
Alston	44	54.49 N	2.26 W
Alsunga	76	56.59 N	21.34 E
Alswede	52	52.20 N	8.33 E
Alt ≃	262	53.32 N	3.03 W
Alta, Nor.	24	69.55 N	23.12 E
Älta, Sve.	40	59.16 N	18.11 E
Alta, Calif., U.S.	226	39.12 N	120.49 W
Alta, Iowa, U.S.	198	42.40 N	95.18 W
Alta, Cachoeira ⌊	250	5.46 S	54.28 W
Alta, Mount ∧	172	44.30 S	168.58 E
Altadena	228	34.12 N	118.08 W
Alta Gracia, Arg.	252	31.40 S	64.26 W
Alta Gracia, Nic.	236	11.34 N	85.35 W
Altagracia de Orituco	246	9.52 N	66.23 W
Alta Hill	226	39.14 N	121.04 W
Al Tahoe	226	38.57 N	119.59 W
Altai ⋀	90	48.00 N	90.00 E
Altair	222	29.34 N	96.28 W
Altaj, Mong.	86	48.18 N	89.35 E
Altaj (Jesönbulag), Mong.	90	46.25 N	96.20 E
Altaj, S.S.S.R.	86	53.27 N	91.48 E
Altajskij	86	51.58 N	85.22 E
Alta Loma, Calif., U.S.	228	34.07 N	117.36 W
Alta Loma, Tex., U.S.	222	29.22 N	95.04 W
Altamachi ≃	248	16.08 S	66.50 W
Altamaha ≃	192	31.19 N	81.17 W
Altamira, Bra.	250	3.12 S	52.12 W
Altamira, Chile	252	25.47 S	69.51 W
Altamira, C.R.	236	10.30 N	84.23 W
Altamira, Méx.	234	22.24 N	97.55 W
Altamira, Las Cuevas de ≗[5]	34	43.18 N	4.08 W
Altamirano	196	25.55 N	97.47 W
Altamont, Ill., U.S.	219	39.04 N	88.46 W
Altamont, Kans., U.S.	198	37.12 N	95.18 W
Altamont, N.Y., U.S.	210	42.42 N	74.02 W
Altamont, Oreg., U.S.	202	42.12 N	121.44 W
Altamont, Tenn., U.S.	194	35.26 N	85.43 W
Altamonte Springs	220	28.40 N	81.22 W
Altamura	68	40.50 N	16.33 E
Altamura, Isla ▮	232	25.00 N	108.10 W
Altan, S.S.S.R.	88	49.31 N	111.32 E
Altan, S.S.S.R.	88	49.53 N	109.04 E
Altanbulag, Mong.	88	50.19 N	106.30 E
Altanbulag, Mong.	88	47.41 N	106.22 E
Altancögc	86	49.03 N	90.27 E
Altanširee	102	45.31 N	110.29 E
Altar	232	30.43 N	111.44 W
Altar ≃	232	30.39 N	111.53 W
Altar, Desierto de ◆[2]	232	31.50 N	114.15 W
Altar de los Sacrificios ⊥	232	16.28 N	90.32 W
Altare	62	44.20 N	8.20 E
Altario	184	51.55 N	110.09 W
Altarnun	42	50.37 N	4.30 W
Altar of the Earth ⊍[1]	271a	39.57 N	116.24 E
Altar of the Moon ⊍[1]	271a	39.55 N	116.20 E
Altar of the Sun ⊍[1]	271a	39.54 N	116.27 E
Altar Wash ∨	200	32.05 N	111.19 W
Altaskij Kraj □[8]	86	52.30 N	83.00 E
Altastenberg	56	51.11 N	8.28 E
Altata, Méx.	232	24.38 N	107.55 W
Altata, S.S.S.R.	80	51.07 N	48.44 E
Alta Verapaz □[5]	236	15.40 N	90.00 W
Altavilla Irpina	68	41.00 N	14.47 E
Altavilla Milicia	70	38.02 N	13.32 E
Altavilla Silentina	68	40.32 N	15.08 E
Altaville	226	38.05 N	120.33 W
Alta Vista, Kans., U.S.	198	38.52 N	96.29 W
Altavista, Va., U.S.	192	37.06 N	79.17 W
Altay	86	60.20 N	68.58 E
Alt Buchhorst	264a	52.26 N	13.51 E
Altdamm → Dąbie ◆[8]	54	53.24 N	14.40 E
Altdöbern	54	51.39 N	14.02 E
Altdorf, B.R.D.	60	48.34 N	12.07 E
Altdorf, Schw.	58	46.53 N	8.39 E
Altdorf bei Nürnberg	60	49.23 N	11.21 E
Alte Donau ◎	264b	48.14 N	16.26 E
Alteelva ≃	24	69.58 N	23.23 E
Altefähr	54	54.20 N	13.07 E
Alteglofsheim	60	48.55 N	12.12 E
Alte Grund	264a	52.28 N	13.47 E
Altena	56	51.17 N	7.40 E
Altenahr	56	50.31 N	6.59 E
Altenau	52	51.48 N	10.26 E
Altenbeken	52	51.46 N	8.56 E
Altenberg	54	50.46 N	13.45 E
Altenberge	52	52.03 N	7.27 E
Altenbruch	52	53.49 N	8.46 E
Altenbüren	56	51.23 N	8.30 E
Altenburg, D.D.R.	54	50.59 N	12.26 E
Altenburg, Öst.	61	48.38 N	15.35 E
Altenderne Oberbecker ◆[8]	263	51.35 N	7.33 E
Altendorf	263	51.29 N	7.40 E
Altendorf ◆[8]	263	51.25 N	7.06 E
Altendorf-Ulfkotte	263	51.38 N	7.00 E
Altenerding	60	48.18 N	11.55 E
Altenesch	52	53.08 N	8.37 E
Altenessen ◆[8]	263	51.29 N	7.00 E
Altenfelden	60	48.29 N	13.58 E
Altengamme ◆[8]	52	53.25 N	10.16 E
Altenhagen, B.R.D.	52	52.03 N	8.38 E
Altenhagen, D.D.R.	54	53.45 N	13.06 E
Altenhagen ◆[8]	263	51.22 N	7.28 E
Altenhof	54	52.55 N	13.43 E
Altenholz	41	54.24 N	10.07 E
Altenkirchen (Westerwald), B.R.D.	56	50.41 N	7.38 E
Altenkirchen, D.D.R.	54	54.38 N	13.20 E
Altenkrempe	54	54.08 N	10.49 E
Altenkunstadt	54	50.07 N	11.14 E
Altenmarkt	60	48.00 N	12.32 E
Altenmarkt an der Alz	64	48.00 N	12.32 E
Altenoythe	52	53.02 N	7.52 E
Altenpleen	54	54.21 N	12.57 E
Altenstadt an der Waldnaab	60	49.48 N	12.10 E
Altensteig	56	48.35 N	8.37 E
Altentreptow	54	53.42 N	13.14 E
Altenvoerde	263	51.18 N	7.22 E
Altenwalde	52	53.49 N	8.40 E
Altenweddingen	54	52.00 N	11.31 E
Alte Oder ≃	54	52.52 N	14.09 E
Alter do Chão	34	39.12 N	7.40 W
Alterosa	256	21.15 S	46.08 W
Alter Rhein ≃	263	51.35 N	6.36 E
Altes Land ◆[1]	52	53.33 N	9.38 E
Altfraunhofen	60	48.27 N	12.10 E
Altfriedland	54	52.38 N	14.12 E
Altglashütten	58	47.51 N	8.06 E
Alt-glienicke ◆[8]	264a	52.25 N	13.32 E
Altgruland	263	51.27 N	7.41 E
Altha	192	30.34 N	85.08 W
Altham	262	53.47 N	2.21 W
Alt-Hartmannsdorf	264a	52.21 N	13.50 E
Althea Lake ◎	283	42.40 N	71.23 W
Altheim	60	48.15 N	13.13 E
Altheimer	194	34.19 N	91.51 W
Althofen	61	46.54 N	14.27 E
Altinho	250	8.29 S	36.04 W
Altinópolis	255	21.02 S	47.23 W
Altıntaş	130	39.04 N	30.07 E
Altiplano ⋀[1]	248	18.00 S	68.00 W
Alt Käbelich	54	53.29 N	13.29 E
Altkirch	58	47.37 N	7.15 E
Altlandsberg	54	52.33 N	13.43 E
Altlangerwisch	264a	52.19 N	13.04 E
Altlewin	54	52.42 N	14.16 E
Altlüdersdorf	54	53.02 N	13.11 E
Altlünen	52	51.38 N	7.31 E
Altmannsdorf ◆[8]	264b	48.10 N	16.20 E
Altmannstein	60	48.54 N	11.39 E
Altmar	212	43.31 N	76.00 W
Altmark □[9]	54	52.40 N	11.20 E
Altmittweida	54	50.58 N	12.57 E
Altmühl ≃	60	48.55 N	11.58 E
Altmünster	64	47.54 N	13.45 E
Altnaharra	46	58.16 N	4.27 W
Alto, Mich., U.S.	216	42.51 N	85.23 W
Alto, Tex., U.S.	222	31.39 N	95.04 W
Alto, Cerro ∧, Méx.	234	20.50 N	100.22 W
Alto, Cerro ∧, Calif., U.S.	226	35.25 N	120.43 W
Alto Anapu ≃	250	2.15 S	51.27 W
Alto Araguaia	255	17.19 S	53.12 W
Alto Cauale	152	7.34 S	16.16 E
Alto Cedro	240p	20.31 N	75.58 W
Alto Chicapa	152	10.53 S	19.14 E
Alto Coité	255	15.47 S	54.20 W
Alto Cuito	152	13.27 S	18.49 E
Alto da Moóca ◆[8]	287b	23.34 S	46.35 W
Alto da Serra	256	22.53 S	44.14 W
Alto del Carmen	252	28.46 S	70.30 W
Alto de Ña Paula	286c	10.24 N	66.48 W
Altofonte	70	38.03 N	13.18 E
Alto Garças	255	16.56 S	53.32 W
Alto Ligonha	154	15.30 S	38.20 E
Alto Longá	250	5.15 S	42.12 W
Alto Lucero	234	19.37 N	96.43 W
Alto Madre de Dios ≃	248	12.17 S	70.52 W
Alto Molócuè	154	15.38 S	37.42 E
Altomonte	68	39.42 N	16.08 E
Altomünster	60	48.23 N	11.15 E
Alton, Ont., Can.	212	43.52 N	80.04 W
Alton, Eng., U.K.	42	51.09 N	0.59 W
Alton, Ill., U.S.	219	38.54 N	90.10 W
Alton, Iowa, U.S.	198	42.59 N	96.01 W
Alton, Kans., U.S.	198	39.28 N	98.57 W
Alton, Ky., U.S.	218	38.04 N	84.55 W
Alton, Mo., U.S.	194	36.42 N	91.24 W
Alton, N.H., U.S.	188	43.27 N	71.13 W
Alton, N.Y., U.S.	210	43.13 N	76.59 W
Alton, R.I., U.S.	207	41.26 N	71.43 W
Altona, Austl.	162	27.34 S	120.00 E
Altona, Austl.	169	37.52 S	144.50 E
Altona, Man., Can.	184	49.06 N	97.33 W
Altona, Ind., U.S.	216	41.21 N	85.10 W
Altona ◆[8]	52	53.32 N	9.56 E
Altona Bay ⊂	274b	37.53 S	144.50 E
Altona North	274b	37.50 S	144.51 E
Altona Sports Park ♠	274b	37.52 S	144.52 E
Altoona, Ala., U.S.	194	34.02 N	86.20 W
Altoona, Fla., U.S.	220	28.58 N	81.39 W
Altoona, Iowa, U.S.	190	41.39 N	93.28 W
Altoona, Kans., U.S.	198	37.32 N	95.40 W
Altoona, Pa., U.S.	214	40.30 N	78.24 W
Altoona, Wash., U.S.	224	46.16 N	123.39 W
Altoona, Wis., U.S.	190	44.48 N	91.26 W
Alto Pacajá ≃	250	3.07 S	50.20 W
Alto Paraguai	248	14.30 S	56.31 W
Alto Paraguay □[5]	248	21.00 S	58.45 W
Alto Paraíso de Goiás	255	14.07 S	47.31 W
Alto Paraná □[5]	252	25.00 S	54.50 W
Alto Parnaíba	250	9.06 S	45.57 W
Alto Purús ≃	248	9.34 S	70.36 W
Alto Rio Doce	255	21.02 S	43.25 W
Alto Río Senguerr	254	45.02 S	70.50 W
Altos	250	5.03 S	42.28 W
Alto Santo	250	5.31 S	38.15 W
Alto Sucuriú	255	19.19 S	52.47 W
Altotonga	234	19.46 N	97.14 W
Altötting	60	48.13 N	12.40 E
Alto-Uama	152	12.14 S	15.33 E
Alto Volta → Upper Volta □[1]	150	13.00 N	2.00 W
Alto Yurua ≃	248	9.24 S	72.43 W
Altrincham	262	53.24 N	2.21 W
Altruppin	54	52.56 N	12.50 E
Altshausen	58	47.56 N	9.32 E
Alt Stahnsdorf	264a	52.17 N	13.53 E
Altstätten, Öst.	36	47.28 N	9.30 E
Altstätten, Schw.	58	47.23 N	9.33 E
Alt Töplitz	264a	52.26 N	12.55 E
Altuchovo	76	52.40 N	34.20 E
Āltūn Kūprī	128	35.45 N	44.09 E
Altunoluk	130	39.34 N	26.44 E
Altunova	130	39.13 N	26.47 E
Alturas	204	41.29 N	120.32 W
Altus, Ark., U.S.	194	35.27 N	93.46 W
Altus, Okla., U.S.	196	34.38 N	99.20 W
Altus, Lake ◎[1]	196	34.56 N	99.18 W
Altus Air Force Base ■	196	34.40 N	99.16 W
Altusried	58	47.48 N	10.13 E
Altyagač	84	40.50 N	48.54 E
Altyaryk	85	40.23 N	71.30 E
Altykarasu	86	49.12 N	55.52 E
Altynaj	86	57.04 N	62.00 E
Altynasar ⊥	86	45.10 N	63.07 E
Altynkul'	85	40.48 N	72.10 E
Altynovka	78	51.27 N	33.10 E
Altyntau	86	44.08 N	68.03 E
Altyn-Topkan	85	40.38 N	69.35 E
Al-'Ubaylah	144	21.59 N	50.57 E
Al-Ubayyiḍ	140	13.11 N	30.13 E
Alubijid	116	8.35 N	124.29 E
Alucra	130	40.20 N	38.46 E
Al-'Udaysāt	140	25.35 N	32.29 E
Al-Uḍayyah	140	12.03 N	28.17 E
Aluedua	114	4.47 N	97.47 E
Aluk	140	8.26 N	27.27 E
Alūksne	76	57.25 N	27.03 E
Al-'Ulā, Ar. Sa.	128	26.37 N	37.52 E
'Alula, Som.	144	11.58 N	50.48 E
Alum Bank	214	40.14 N	78.34 W
Alum Creek Lake ◎[1]	214	40.15 N	82.58 W
Aluminé	254	39.13 S	70.57 W
Aluminé ≃	254	39.50 S	70.53 W
Aluminé, Lago ◎	252	38.55 S	71.09 W
Alum Rock	226	37.23 N	121.50 W
Alum Rock Park ♠	282	37.24 N	121.49 W
Alunda	40	60.04 N	18.05 E
Alunitdag	84	40.32 N	46.03 E
Alupka	78	44.26 N	34.03 E
Al-'Uqaylah	146	30.16 N	19.12 E
Al-'Uqayr	128	25.39 N	50.12 E
Al-Uqṣur (Luxor)	140	25.41 N	32.39 E
Al-'Urayq ≗[8]	128	29.10 N	39.15 E
Al-'Urayq ◆[1]	128	24.47 N	42.55 E
Al-Urdunn → Jordan □[1]	128	31.00 N	36.00 E
Al-Urdunn → Jordan ≃	132	31.46 N	35.33 E
Alušta	78	44.42 N	34.24 E
Al-'Uṭayshān ⊤[4]	140	16.25 N	34.30 E
Al-'Uwayjāt ∧[2]	142	28.25 N	30.08 E
Al-'Uyaynah	128	24.54 N	46.23 E
Alva, Scot., U.K.	46	56.09 N	3.48 W
Alva, Fla., U.S.	220	26.43 N	81.37 W
Alva, Okla., U.S.	196	36.48 N	98.40 W
Alva ≃	34	40.18 N	8.15 W
Alvada	214	41.03 N	83.24 W
Alvaiázere	34	39.49 N	8.23 W

Symbols in the index entries represent the broad categories identified in the key at the right. Symbols with superior numbers (⋀[2]) identify subcategories (see complete key on page *I · 30*).

Kartensymbole in dem Registerverzeichnis stellen die rechts in Schlüssel erklärten Kategorien dar. Symbole mit hochgestellten Ziffern (⋀[2]) bezeichnen Unterabteilungen einer Kategorie (vgl. vollständiger Schlüssel auf Seite *I · 30*).

Los símbolos incluídos en el texto del índice representan las grandes categorias identificadas con la clave a la derecha. Los símbolos con numeros en su parte superior (⋀[2]) identifican las subcategorías (véase la clave completa en la página *I · 30*).

Les symboles de l'index représentent les catégories indiquées dans la légende à droite. Les symboles suivis d'un indice (⋀[2]) représentent des sous-catégories (voir légende complète à la page *I · 30*).

Os símbolos incluídos no texto do índice representam as grandes categorias identificadas com a chave à direita. Os símbolos com números em sua parte superior (⋀[2]) identificam as subcategorias (veja-se a chave completa à página *I · 30*).

	English	Deutsch	Español	Français	Português
∧	Mountain	Berg	Montaña	Montagne	Montanha
⋀	Mountains	Berge	Montañas	Montagnes	Montanhas
)(	Pass	Pass	Paso	Col	Passo
∨	Valley, Canyon	Tal, Cañon	Valle, Cañón	Vallée, Canyon	Vale, Canhão
≚	Plain	Ebene	Llano	Plaine	Planície
≻	Cape	Kap	Cabo	Cap	Cabo
▮	Island	Insel	Isla	Île	Ilha
▮▮	Islands	Inseln	Islas	Îles	Ilhas
≗	Other Topographic Features	Andere Topographische Objekte	Otros Elementos Topográficos	Autres données topographiques	Outros Elementos Topográficos

ESPAÑOL
Nombre Página Lat.°′ Long.°′ W=Oeste

Alvaneu-bad 58 46.40 N 9.39 E
Älvängen 26 57.58 N 12.07 E
Alvanley 262 53.16 N 2.45 W
Alvarado, Méx. 234 18.46 N 95.46 W
Alvarado, Tex., U.S. 222 32.24 N 97.13 W
Alvarães 246 3.12 S 64.50 W
Alvarinhos 266c 38.54 N 9.22 W
Álvaro Obregón 234 19.50 N 101.05 W
Alvaro Obregon □7 286a 19.22 N 99.16 W
Álvaro Obregón, Presa ⊜1 232 27.55 N 109.52 W
Alvastra ⊥ 26 58.18 N 14.39 E
Alvdal 26 62.07 N 10.39 E
Älvdalen 26 61.14 N 14.02 E
Alvear 252 29.06 S 56.33 W
Alvechurch 42 52.21 N 1.57 W
Alverca 34 38.54 N 9.02 W
Alverda 214 40.38 N 78.52 W
Alverton 214 40.08 N 79.35 W
Alvesta 26 56.54 N 14.33 E
Alveston 42 51.36 N 2.32 W
Ålvik, Nor. 26 60.26 N 6.26 E
Alvik, Sve. 26 62.25 N 17.24 E
Alvin, Ill., U.S. 216 40.19 N 87.37 W
Alvin, Tex., U.S. 222 29.25 N 95.15 W
Alvinópolis 255 20.06 S 43.03 W
Alvinston 214 42.49 N 81.52 W
Alviso ◆8 282 37.26 N 121.58 W
Alviso Slough ≐ 282 37.27 N 122.02 W
Alvito, It. 66 41.41 N 13.45 E
Alvito, Port. 34 38.15 N 7.59 W
Älvkarleby 40 60.34 N 17.27 E
Älvkarleö bruk 40 60.32 N 17.24 E
Alvord 196 33.22 N 97.42 W
Alvord Desert ◆2 202 42.30 N 118.25 W
Alvord Lake ⊜ 202 42.23 N 118.36 W
Alvordton 216 41.40 N 84.26 W
Alvra, Pass d')(58 46.35 N 9.50 E
Älvros 26 62.03 N 14.39 E
Älvsborgs Län □6 26 58.00 N 12.30 E
Älvsbyn 24 65.39 N 20.59 E
Älvsnabben ⊥ 40 58.59 N 18.10 E
Al-Wafā'īyah 142 30.46 N 30.36 E
Al-Wāḥāt ad-Dākhilah ▾4 140 25.30 N 29.05 E
Al-Wāḥāt al-Baḥrīyah ▾4 140 28.15 N 28.57 E
Al-Wāḥat al-Farāfirah ▾4 140 27.15 N 28.10 E
Al-Wāḥāt al-Khārijah ▾4 140 25.20 N 30.35 E
Al-Wajh 128 26.15 N 36.26 E
Al-Wakrah 128 25.10 N 51.36 E
Al-Walīdīyah 142 27.12 N 31.10 E
Alwar 124 27.34 N 76.36 E
Alwar □5 124 27.40 N 76.35 E
Alwar Hills ⋀2 124 27.20 N 76.15 E
Al-Wāṣifīyah 142 30.35 N 32.10 E
Al-Wāsiṭah 142 29.20 N 31.12 E
Alwaye 122 10.07 N 76.21 E
Al-Wazīrīyah 142 31.11 N 30.57 E
Al-Wazz 140 15.01 N 30.10 E
Alwen ≐ 42 52.58 N 3.24 W
Al-Widy 142 29.31 N 31.16 E
Al-Yamāmah → As-Sulaymānīyah 128 24.09 N 47.19 E
Al-Yaman → Yemen □1 144 15.00 N 44.00 E
Al-Ayaman ash-Sha'bīyah → Yemen, People's Democratic Republic of □1 144 15.00 N 48.00 E
Al Yāmūn 132 32.29 N 35.14 E
Alygdžer 88 53.38 N 98.16 E
Alyn and Deeside □8 262 53.16 N 3.02 W
Alypsatar 86 48.03 N 80.21 E
Alyth 46 56.37 N 3.13 W
Alytus 76 54.24 N 24.03 E
Alz ≐ 60 48.16 N 12.49 E
Alzamaj 88 55.33 N 98.39 E
Alzano Lombardo 62 45.44 N 9.43 E
Al-Zarqa 142 31.13 N 31.38 E
Alzenau 56 50.05 N 9.04 E
Alzette ≐ 56 49.22 N 6.09 E
Alzey 56 49.45 N 8.07 E
Amab, Khawr ∨ 140 17.08 N 34.51 E
Amacuro ≐ 246 8.32 N 60.28 W
Amacuzac ≐ 234 17.53 N 99.12 W
Amadeus, Lake ⊜ 162 24.50 S 130.45 E
Āmādi, Bngl. 126 22.28 N 89.19 E
Amadi, Sūd. 140 5.31 N 30.20 E
Amadi, Zaïre 154 3.35 N 26.47 E
Amadjuak Lake ⊜ 176 65.00 N 71.00 W
Amador □6 226 38.21 N 120.46 W
Amadora 266c 38.45 N 9.14 W
Amador City 226 38.25 N 120.56 W
Amadores 234 22.51 N 99.43 W
Amador Valley ∨ 282 37.41 N 121.51 W
Amagansett 207 40.58 N 72.08 W
Amagasaki 96 34.43 N 135.25 E
Amagase 96 33.15 N 131.02 E
Amager I 41 55.37 N 12.37 E
Amagi 96 33.25 N 130.39 E
Amagi-san ∧ 94 34.51 N 139.00 E
Amagi-yugashima 94 34.53 N 138.56 E
Amagunze 150 6.20 N 7.40 E
Amaha 94 35.13 N 139.52 E
Amahai 164 3.20 S 128.55 E
Amaichá del Valle 252 26.36 S 65.55 W
Amaimon 164 5.10 S 145.25 E
Amajac ≐ 234 21.15 N 98.46 W
Amaka ≐ 236 14.14 N 85.07 W
Ama Keng 271c 1.24 N 103.42 E
Amak Island I 180 55.25 N 163.07 W
Amakusa-nada ▾2 92 32.35 N 130.05 E
Amakusa-shotō II 92 32.20 N 130.15 E
Amal, Lībīya 146 29.25 N 21.10 E
Åmål, Sve. 26 59.03 N 12.42 E
Amalāpuram 122 16.35 N 82.01 E
Amalat ≐ 88 54.49 N 115.12 E
Amalfi, Col. 246 6.55 N 75.04 W
Amalfi, It. 68 40.38 N 14.36 E
Amalia 158 27.16 S 25.03 E
Amaliás 38 37.49 N 21.23 E
Amalner 120 21.03 N 75.04 E
Amambahag Point > 116 11.41 N 124.32 E
Amambaí 255 23.05 S 55.13 W
Amambaí ≐ 255 23.22 S 53.56 W
Amambay □5 252 23.00 S 56.00 W
Amambay, Cordillera de ⋀ 252 23.10 S 55.30 W
Amami-Ō-shima I 93b 28.15 N 129.20 E
Amami-shotō II 93b 28.16 N 129.21 E
Amamula 154 0.18 S 27.50 E
Amana 190 41.48 N 91.52 W
Amanã ≐, Bra. 250 4.25 S 57.34 W
Amana ≐, Ven. 238 9.45 N 62.39 W
Amaná, Lago ⊜ 246 2.35 S 64.40 W
Amanave 174u 14.19 S 170.49 W
Amance 58 47.48 N 6.04 E
Amancey 58 47.02 N 6.05 E
Amanda 188 39.39 N 82.45 W
Amanda Park 224 47.28 N 123.54 W
Amandola 66 42.59 N 13.21 E
Amānganj 124 24.26 N 80.02 E
Amāngarh 123 34.00 N 71.55 E
Amangel'dy, S.S.S.R. 85 43.43 N 71.07 E
Amangel'dy, S.S.S.R. 86 50.10 N 65.13 E
Amangel'dy, S.S.S.R. 86 49.52 N 59.00 E
Åmänningen ⊜ 40 59.57 N 15.56 E
Amano 270 34.26 N 135.33 E
Amanotkel' 86 46.07 N 61.34 E
Amantea 68 39.08 N 16.05 E
Amantogaj 86 50.22 N 65.33 E
Amapá 250 2.03 N 50.48 W
Amapá □8 250 1.00 N 52.00 W
Amapala 236 13.17 N 87.40 W
Amapala, Punta > 236 13.10 N 87.54 W

FRANÇAIS
Nom Page Lat.°′ Long.°′ W=Ouest

Amapari ≐ 250 0.43 N 51.32 W
Amaraji 250 8.24 S 35.27 W
Amaral 287a 22.42 S 43.29 W
Amarante 250 6.14 S 42.50 W
Amarante do Maranhão 250 5.36 S 46.45 W
Amaranth 184 50.36 N 98.43 W
Amarapura 110 21.54 N 96.03 E
Amărăștii-de-Jos 38 43.59 N 24.10 E
'Amārat Abū Sinn 140 15.21 N 35.45 E
Amarāvati ≐ 122 10.51 N 78.11 E
Amarda 126 21.47 N 87.08 E
Amareleja 34 38.12 N 7.14 W
Amares 34 41.38 N 8.21 W
Amarete (Charazani) 248 15.14 S 68.58 W
Amargosa 255 13.02 S 39.36 W
Amargosa ≐ 204 36.13 N 116.48 W
Amargosa Range ⋀ 204 36.30 N 116.45 W
Amarillo 196 35.13 N 101.49 W
Amarillo, Mar → Yellow Sea ▾2 90 36.00 N 123.00 E
Amar Jadīd 140 14.28 N 25.14 E
Amarkantak 124 22.40 N 81.45 E
Amarnāth Cave •5 123 34.13 N 75.31 E
Amaro, Monte ∧ 66 42.05 N 14.05 E
Amaro Leite 255 13.58 S 49.09 W
Amaroúsion 267c 38.03 N 23.49 E
Amarpātan 124 24.19 N 80.59 E
Amarti 144 14.16 N 41.10 E
Amarume 92 38.50 N 139.55 E
Amarwāra 124 22.18 N 79.10 E
Amasa 190 46.14 N 88.27 W
Amaseno ≐ 66 41.34 N 13.13 E
Amasija 84 40.58 N 43.46 E
Amasra 130 41.45 N 32.24 E
Amasya 130 40.39 N 35.51 E
Amasya □4 130 40.45 N 35.30 E
Amataurá 246 3.29 S 68.06 W
Amatenango de la Frontera 236 15.26 N 92.07 W
Amatignak Island I 181a 51.15 N 179.08 W
Amatikulu 158 29.06 S 31.27 E
Amatique, Bahía de C 236 15.55 N 88.45 W
Amatitán 234 20.50 N 103.43 W
Amatitlán 236 14.29 N 90.37 W
Amatitlán, Lago de ⊜ 236 14.27 N 90.34 W
Amatlán de Cañas 234 20.52 N 104.27 W
Amatlán de los Reyes 234 18.50 N 96.55 W
Amatrice 66 42.38 N 13.17 E
Amatsu-kominato 94 35.07 N 140.10 E
Amau 164 10.02 S 148.34 E
Amausi 124 26.46 N 80.51 E
Amawalk 210 41.17 N 73.46 W
Amay 56 50.33 N 5.19 E
Ama-zaki > 94 37.08 N 136.40 E
Amazar 89 53.54 N 120.53 E
Amazhaer 89 53.25 N 122.03 E
Amazon (Solimões) (Amazonas) ≐ 242 0.05 S 50.00 W
Amazonas □3 246 2.00 S 64.00 W
Amazonas □5, Col. 246 1.00 S 72.00 W
Amazonas □5, Perú 248 5.30 S 78.00 W
Amazonas □8 246 3.30 S 66.00 W
Amazonas → Amazon ≐ 242 0.05 S 50.00 W
Amb 123 34.19 N 72.51 E
Ambāh 124 26.43 N 78.14 E
Ambahikily 157b 21.36 S 43.41 E
Ambahita 157b 24.01 S 45.16 E
Ambaí 287a 22.43 S 43.28 W
Ambājogāi 122 18.44 N 76.23 E
Ambakaka 157b 24.10 S 46.17 E
Ambāla 124 30.21 N 76.50 E
Ambāla □5 124 30.20 N 77.05 E
Ambāla Airport ⊠ 123 30.22 N 76.50 E
Ambalabe 157b 18.24 S 49.10 E
Ambalangoda 122 6.14 N 80.03 E
Ambalanjanakomby 157b 16.42 S 47.05 E
Ambalavao 157b 21.50 S 46.56 E
Ambalema 246 4.47 N 74.46 W
Ambam 152 2.23 N 11.17 E
Ambanja 157b 13.41 S 48.27 E
Ambar 248 10.44 S 77.16 W
Ambararata 157b 15.03 S 48.33 E
Ambarawa 115a 7.15 S 110.24 E
Ambarčik, S.S.S.R. 74 69.39 N 162.20 E
Ambarčik, S.S.S.R. 88 55.09 N 95.46 E
Ambarijeby 157b 14.56 S 47.41 E
Ambarnāth 122 19.11 N 73.10 E
Ambarnyj 24 65.56 N 33.43 E
Ambaro, Baie d' C 157b 13.23 S 48.38 E
Ambāsamudram 122 8.42 N 77.28 E
Ambassador Bridge ◆5 281 42.20 N 83.05 W
Ambato, Ec. 246 1.15 S 78.37 W
Ambato, Madag. 157b 13.24 S 48.29 E
Ambato Boeni 157b 16.28 S 46.43 E
Ambatofinandrahana 157b 20.33 S 46.48 E
Ambatolampy 157b 19.23 S 47.25 E
Ambatomainty 157b 17.41 S 45.40 E
Ambatomanoina 157b 18.18 S 47.37 E
Ambatondrazaka 157b 17.50 S 48.25 E
Ambatosoratra 157b 17.34 S 48.32 E
Ambeláki 267c 37.57 N 23.32 E
Ambelau, Pulau I 164 3.51 S 127.12 E
Ámbelos, Ákra > 38 39.56 N 23.55 E
Ambenja 157b 15.17 S 46.58 E
Amber 120 26.59 N 75.52 E
Amber ≐ 44 53.08 N 1.29 W
Amberes → Antwerpen 50 51.13 N 4.25 E
Amberg, B.R.D. 60 49.27 N 11.52 E
Amberg, Wis., U.S. 190 45.30 N 88.00 W
Ambergris Cay I 232 18.03 N 87.56 W
Ambérieu-en-Bugey 58 45.57 N 5.21 E
Amberley 172 43.10 S 172.44 E
Amberley Royal Australian Air Force Base ■ 171a 27.37 S 152.41 E
Amberson 214 40.10 N 77.41 W
Ambert 62 45.33 N 3.45 E
Ambevongo 157b 15.27 S 47.27 E
Ambia 216 40.30 N 87.31 W
Ambidédi 150 14.35 N 11.47 W
Ambikānagar 126 22.57 N 86.46 E
Ambikāpur 124 23.07 N 83.12 E
Ambil 116 13.49 N 120.20 E
Ambil Island I 116 13.48 N 120.18 E
Ambilobe 157b 13.12 S 49.04 E
Ambinanyndrano 157b 20.20 S 48.19 E
Ambinanytelo 157b 15.21 S 49.35 E
Ambinda 157b 16.25 S 45.52 E
Ambivy 157b 21.31 S 44.02 E
Ambjörby 26 60.30 N 13.10 E
Ambla 76 59.11 N 25.51 E
Amble 44 55.20 N 1.34 W
Amblecote 42 52.28 N 2.09 W
Ambler, Alaska, U.S. 180 67.05 N 157.52 W
Ambler, Pa., U.S. 208 40.09 N 75.13 W
Ambleside 44 54.26 N 2.58 W
Ambleteuse 50 50.49 N 1.36 E
Amblève ≐ 56 50.28 N 5.36 E
Ambo 248 10.07 S 76.10 W
Amboahangy 157b 24.15 S 46.22 E
Amboasary, Madag 157b 25.02 S 46.23 E
Amboasary, Madag 157b 18.26 S 48.16 E
Ambodifototra 157b 16.59 S 49.52 E
Ambodilazana 157b 18.06 S 49.10 E
Ambodiriana 157b 17.55 S 49.18 E
Ambohibary 157b 19.20 S 46.17 E
Ambohidratrimo 157b 18.50 S 47.26 E
Ambohidray 157b 18.36 S 48.18 E
Ambohimahamasina 157b 21.56 S 47.11 E
Ambohimahasoa 157b 21.07 S 47.13 E
Ambohimanga du Sud 157b 20.52 S 47.36 E
Ambohimitombo 157b 20.43 S 47.26 E
Amboina → Ambon 164 3.43 S 128.12 E

PORTUGUÊS
Nome Página Lat.°′ Long.°′ W=Oeste

Amboise 50 47.25 N 0.59 E
Amboiva 152 11.32 S 14.44 E
Ambon 164 3.43 S 128.12 E
Ambon, Pulau I 164 3.40 S 128.10 E
Ambondro 157b 25.13 S 45.44 E
Ambonnay 50 49.04 N 4.10 E
Amboseli, Lake ⊜ 154 2.37 S 37.08 E
Amboshe 272c 19.09 N 73.08 E
Ambositra 157b 20.31 S 47.15 E
Ambovombe 157b 25.11 S 46.05 E
Amboy, Ill., U.S. 190 41.44 N 89.20 W
Amboy, Ind., U.S. 216 40.36 N 85.56 W
Amboy, Minn., U.S. 190 43.59 N 94.10 W
Amboy, Wash., U.S. 224 45.55 N 122.27 W
Ambre, Cap d' > 157b 11.57 S 49.17 E
Ambre, Montagne d' ∧ 157b 12.30 S 49.10 E
Ambridge 214 40.36 N 80.14 W
Ambridge Heights 214 40.36 N 80.13 W
Ambrières 32 48.24 N 0.38 W
Ambrim I 175f 16.15 S 168.10 E
Ambriz 152 7.50 S 13.06 E
Ambrizete 152 7.14 S 12.52 E
Ambrolauri 84 42.31 N 43.09 E
Ambronay 58 46.00 N 5.21 E
Ambrose 198 48.57 N 103.29 W
Ambrose Brook ≐ 276 40.33 N 74.32 W
Ambrosia Lake 200 35.26 N 107.54 W
Ambuklao Dam ◆6 116 16.28 N 120.45 E
Ambulong Island I 116 12.12 N 121.01 E
Ambulu 115a 8.21 S 113.36 E
Ambuntentimur 115a 6.54 S 113.45 E
Ambunti 164 4.14 S 142.50 E
Āmbūr 122 12.47 N 78.42 E
Amburambur 115b 8.15 S 116.18 E
Amby 56 50.53 N 5.44 E
Amchitka Island I 181a 51.30 N 179.00 E
Amchitka Pass U 181a 51.30 N 179.30 W
'Amd 144 15.18 N 48.00 E
Am Dam 146 12.46 N 20.29 E
Āmdānga 272b 22.49 N 88.31 E
Amded, Oued ∨ 148 22.09 N 3.15 E
Amden 58 47.09 N 9.11 E
Amderma 72 69.45 N 61.39 E
Ameagle 188 37.57 N 81.25 W
Ameca 234 20.33 N 104.02 W
Ameca ≐ 234 20.41 N 105.18 W
Amecameca [de Juárez] 234 19.07 N 98.46 W
Ameghino 252 34.50 S 62.27 W
Ameglia 64 44.04 N 9.57 E
Ameis Berg ∧ 60 48.33 N 13.50 E
Ameixoeira ◆8 266c 38.47 N 9.10 W
Ameland I 52 53.25 N 5.45 E
Amele 164 5.16 S 145.42 E
Amelia, It. 66 42.33 N 12.25 E
Amelia, Ohio, U.S. 218 39.02 N 84.13 W
Amelia, Passo d')(66 42.36 N 12.32 E
Amelia Court House 192 37.21 N 77.59 W
Amelia Earhart Peak ∧ 226 37.47 N 119.17 W
Amelia Island I 192 30.37 N 81.27 W
Amelinghausen 52 53.08 N 10.13 E
Amelsbüren 52 51.53 N 7.37 E
Amendolara 68 39.57 N 16.35 E
Ameng 102 23.50 N 104.32 E
Amenia 210 41.51 N 73.33 W
Amenucourt 261 49.06 N 1.39 E
Amerang 60 48.00 N 12.18 E
Amerevo 265b 55.55 N 38.03 E
America 52 51.26 N 5.59 E
América del Norte → North America •1 16 45.00 N 100.00 W
América del Sur → South America •1 18 15.00 S 60.00 W
American ≐, Calif., U.S. 226 38.36 N 121.30 W
American ≐, Wash., U.S. 224 46.58 N 121.08 W
American, Middle Fork ≐ 226 38.55 N 121.02 W
American, North Fork ≐ 226 38.43 N 121.09 W
American, South Fork ≐ 226 38.43 N 121.09 W
Americana 255 22.45 S 47.20 W
American Canyon 226 38.10 N 122.15 W
American Falls 202 42.47 N 112.51 W
American Falls L 284a 43.05 N 79.04 W
American Falls Reservoir ⊜1 202 43.00 N 113.00 W
American Fork 200 40.23 N 111.48 W
American Highland ⋀1 9 72.30 S 78.00 E
American Lake ⊜ 224 47.07 N 122.34 W
American Museum of Natural History ʋ 276 40.47 N 73.59 W
Americano 250 1.19 S 48.04 W
American River 168b 35.47 S 137.47 E
American Samoa □2 14
175a 14.20 S 170.00 W
American University ʋ2 284c 38.56 N 77.05 W
Américas, Hipódromo de las ♠ 286a 19.26 N 99.13 W
Americas, University of the ʋ2 286a 19.23 N 99.15 W
Americus, Ga., U.S. 192 32.04 N 84.14 W
Americus, Kans., U.S. 198 38.30 N 96.16 W
Amerikanisches Hochland → American Highland ⋀1 9 72.30 S 78.00 E
Ameringkogel ∧ 61 47.04 N 14.48 E
Amérique du Nord → North America •1 16 45.00 N 100.00 W
Amern 56 51.14 N 6.15 E
Amerongen 52 52.00 N 5.27 E
Amersfoort, Ned. 52 52.09 N 5.24 E
Amersfoort, S. Afr. 158 26.59 S 29.53 E
Amersham 260 51.40 N 0.38 W
Amery, Austl. 162 31.09 S 117.05 E
Amery, Man., Can. 184 56.34 N 94.03 W
Amery, Wis., U.S. 190 45.19 N 92.22 W
Amery Ice Shelf ⚑ 9 69.30 S 72.00 E
Amerzgane 148 31.00 N 7.10 W
Ames, Iowa, U.S. 190 42.02 N 93.37 W
Ames, N.Y., U.S. 210 42.50 N 74.36 W
Ames, Tex., U.S. 222 30.03 N 94.46 W
Amesbury, Eng., U.K. 42 51.10 N 1.45 W
Amesbury, Mass., U.S. 207 42.51 N 70.56 W
Ames Long Pond ⊜ 283 42.05 N 71.07 W
Ames Nowell State Park ♠ 283 42.07 N 70.59 W
Ames Pond ⊜ 283 42.38 N 71.13 W
Ames Research Center ʋ3 282 37.25 N 122.04 W
Amet Sound U 186 45.47 N 63.13 W
Amfíklia 38 38.38 N 22.35 E
Amfilokhía 38 38.51 N 21.10 E
Ámfissa 38 38.31 N 22.24 E
Amfiteátrum ⊥ 264c 47.35 N 19.03 E
Amfreville-la-Campagne 50 49.13 N 0.57 E
Amfreville-les-Champs 50 49.42 N 0.49 E
Amga 74 60.53 N 132.00 E
Amga ≐ 74 62.38 N 134.32 E
Am Géréda 146 12.52 N 21.10 E
Amguema 180 66.58 N 179.16 W
Amguema ≐ 180 68.10 N 177.40 W
Amgun' ≐ 89 52.56 N 139.40 E
Amhara Plateau ⋀1 144 9.00 N 38.00 E
Amherst, N.S., Can. 186 45.49 N 64.14 W
Amherst, Mass., U.S. 207 42.23 N 72.31 W
Amherst, N.H., U.S. 207 42.52 N 71.38 W
Amherst, N.Y., U.S. 210 42.58 N 78.48 W
Amherst, Ohio, U.S. 214 41.24 N 82.14 W
Amherst, Tex., U.S. 196 34.01 N 102.25 W
Amherst, Va., U.S. 192 37.35 N 79.03 W
Amherst, Wis., U.S. 190 44.27 N 89.17 W
Amherst, Île I 186 47.13 N 62.57 W
Amherst, Mount ∧ 162 18.11 S 126.59 E
Amherstburg 214 42.06 N 83.06 W
Amherstdale 188 37.47 N 81.49 W
Amherst Island I 212 44.08 N 76.45 W
Amherstview 212 44.13 N 76.38 W
Ami 94 36.02 N 140.14 E
Amiata, Monte ∧ 66 42.53 N 11.37 E
Amidon 198 46.29 N 103.19 W
Amiens, Austl. 166 28.35 S 151.49 E
Amiens, Fr. 50 49.54 N 2.18 E
Amik Gölü ⊜ 130 36.22 N 36.17 E
Amili, Bhārat 120 28.26 N 95.52 E
Amili, Zhg. 120 28.25 N 95.52 E
Amīn as-Samālūsī, Bi'r ▾4 142 29.52 N 30.02 E
Amīndīvi I 122 11.07 N 72.44 E
Amīndīvi Islands II 122 11.23 N 72.23 E
Aminga 252 28.50 S 66.54 W
Amino, Nihon 96 35.41 N 135.02 E
Amino, Yai. 144 4.22 N 41.56 E
Aminuis 156 23.43 S 19.21 E
Amirābād 128 36.04 N 54.10 E
Amirante Islands II 138 6.00 S 53.10 E
Amirauté, Îles de l' → Admiralty Islands II 164 2.10 S 147.00 E
Amīr Chāh 128 29.13 N 62.28 E
Amisk 182 52.33 N 111.04 W
Amisk Lake ⊜ 184 54.35 N 102.13 W
Amistad National Recreation Area ♠ 196 29.32 N 101.12 W
Amistad Reservoir (Presa de la Amistad) ⊜1 196 29.34 N 101.15 W
Amite 194 30.44 N 90.30 W
Amite ≐ 194 30.12 N 90.35 W
Amite, East Fork ≐ 194 30.58 N 90.51 W
Amiterno ⊥ 66 42.21 N 13.42 E
Amitori 175d 24.18 N 123.41 E
Amity, Ark., U.S. 194 34.16 N 93.28 W
Amity, Ohio, U.S. 214 40.03 N 83.17 W
Amity, Oreg., U.S. 224 45.07 N 123.12 W
Amity Point > 171a 27.24 S 153.27 E
Amityville 276 40.40 N 73.25 W
Amixtlán 234 20.03 N 97.48 W
Amizmiz 148 31.14 N 8.14 W
Āmjhori ∧ 126 21.51 N 86.19 E
Āmjhupi 126 23.45 N 88.42 E
Amla, Bhārat 124 21.56 N 78.07 E
Āmla, Bngl. 126 23.54 N 88.56 E
Āmlāgora 126 22.50 N 87.20 E
Amlekhganj 124 27.17 N 84.59 E
Åmli 26 58.47 N 8.30 E
Amlia Island I 180 52.06 N 173.30 W
Amloh 124 30.37 N 76.14 E
Am Loubia 146 13.39 N 20.08 E
Amlwch 44 53.25 N 4.20 W
Amm-Adām 140 16.22 N 36.06 E
Ammagan 85 38.56 N 67.15 E
Ammān 132 31.57 N 35.56 E
Amman Airport ⊠ 132 35.57 N 35.58 E
Ammanford 42 51.45 N 0.35 W
Ämmänsaari 26 64.53 N 28.55 E
Ammansville 222 29.47 N 96.51 W
'Ammār, Tall ∧2 132 32.53 N 36.29 E
Ammarnäs 24 65.56 N 16.09 E
Ammaroo 162 21.45 S 135.15 E
Åmmeberg 40 58.52 N 15.00 E
Ammeloe 52 52.05 N 6.47 E
Ammendorf ◆8 54 51.25 N 11.59 E
Ammer ≐ 64 47.57 N 11.08 E
Ammerån ≐ 26 63.09 N 16.13 E
Ammerland ◆1 52 53.15 N 8.00 E
Ammerman Mountain ∧ 180 68.21 N 141.03 W
Ammerschwihr 58 48.07 N 7.17 E
Ammersee ⊜ 60 48.00 N 11.08 E
Ammerthal 60 49.26 N 11.45 E
Ammókhostos (Famagusta) 130 35.07 N 33.57 E
Ammókhostou, Kólpos C 130 35.15 N 34.10 E
Ammon 202 43.30 N 111.57 W
Ammonoosuc ≐ 188 44.10 N 72.02 W
Amnān 272b 22.56 N 88.18 E
Amnat Charoen 110 15.51 N 104.38 E
Amnay ≐ 116 12.58 N 120.46 E
Amne Machin Shan → Animaqingshanmai ⋀ 102 34.24 N 100.10 E
Amnicon ≐ 190 46.41 N 91.52 W
Amnok-kang (Yalujiang) ≐ 98 39.55 N 124.22 E
Amo ≐ 124 26.16 N 89.36 E
Amohe ≐ 102 22.58 N 101.44 E
Āmol 128 36.23 N 52.20 E
Amolar 248 18.01 S 57.30 W
Amöneburg 56 50.48 N 8.55 E
Amora 266c 38.37 N 9.07 W
Amorbach 56 49.39 N 9.13 E
Amorgós 38 36.50 N 25.54 E
Amorgós I 38 36.50 N 25.59 E
Amorim, Morro ∧2 287a 23.00 S 43.26 W
Amorinópolis 255 16.36 S 51.08 W
Amorosi 68 41.12 N 14.28 E
Amory 194 33.59 N 88.29 W
Amos 190 48.35 N 78.07 W
Åmose Å ≐ 41 55.35 N 11.18 E
Åmot, Nor. 26 59.54 N 9.54 E
Åmot, Nor. 26 59.35 N 8.00 E
Åmotfors 26 59.46 N 12.22 E
Amour → Amur ≐ 74 52.56 N 141.10 E
Amour, Djebel ⋀ 148 34.00 N 2.15 E
Amoy → Xiamen 100 24.28 N 118.07 E
Amozoc 234 19.02 N 98.03 W
Ampana 112 0.51 S 121.32 E
Ampanavoana 157b 15.41 S 50.22 E
Ampang 115b 8.47 S 118.00 E
Ampanihy 157b 24.42 S 44.45 E
Ampaoid, Mount ∧ 116 7.57 N 125.41 E
Amparafaravola 157b 17.35 S 48.13 E
Amparihy, Madag. 157b 16.40 S 44.49 E
Amparihy, Madag. 157b 23.57 S 47.20 E
Amparo 256 22.42 S 46.45 W
Ampasibe 157b 22.56 S 46.58 E
Ampasilava, Baie d' C 157b 21.16 S 43.43 E
Ampasinambo 157b 20.31 S 48.00 E
Ampasindava, Baie d' C 157b 13.16 S 48.43 E
Ampel 115a 7.27 S 110.32 E
Amper 150 9.20 N 9.43 E
Amper ≐, B.R.D. 60 48.01 N 11.50 E
Amper ≐, B.R.D. 64 48.10 N 11.50 E
Ampermoching 60 48.18 N 11.29 E
Ampezzo 64 46.25 N 12.48 E
Ampezzo, Valle d' ∨ 64 46.30 N 12.10 E
Ampfing 60 48.16 N 12.25 E
Ampflwang 64 48.05 N 13.34 E
Amphion-les-Bains 58 46.23 N 6.32 E
Amphitrite Group II 108 17.00 N 112.25 E
Ampitsikinana 157b 12.57 S 49.49 E
Ampiyacu ≐ 246 3.19 S 71.51 W
Ampleforth 44 54.12 N 1.06 W
Ampollino, Lago ⊜ 68 39.12 N 16.37 E
Ampombiantambo 157b 12.42 S 48.57 E
Amposta 34 40.43 N 0.35 E
Ampotaka 157b 25.03 S 44.41 E
Ampoza 157b 22.20 S 44.44 E
Ampthill 42 52.02 N 0.30 W
Ampuis 62 45.29 N 4.49 E
Ampus 62 43.36 N 6.23 E
Amqui 186 49.28 N 67.26 W
'Amr, Jabal al- ⋀ 132 30.45 N 34.20 E
Amraoti → Amrāvati 120 20.56 N 77.45 E
Amrāvati 120 20.56 N 77.45 E
Am-Raya 146 14.00 N 16.35 E
Amreli 120 21.37 N 71.14 E
Āmreswar 272b 22.28 N 88.34 E
Amriswil 58 47.33 N 9.18 E
Amritsar 123 31.35 N 74.53 E
Amroha 124 28.55 N 78.28 E
Amrūka 123 30.19 N 73.53 E
Amrum I 30 54.39 N 8.21 E
Am Saterna 146 12.26 N 21.25 E
Amsden 214 41.13 N 83.20 W
Amsel 148 22.37 N 5.26 E
Åmsele 26 64.32 N 19.20 E
Am Sigan 146 11.41 N 19.51 E
Amsoldingen 58 46.43 N 7.35 E
Amsteg 58 46.46 N 8.41 E
Amstel ≐ 52 52.22 N 4.54 E
Amstelmeer ⊜ 52 52.52 N 4.45 E
Amstelveen 52 52.18 N 4.51 E
Amsterdam, Ned. 52 52.22 N 4.54 E
Amsterdam, S. Afr. 158 26.35 S 30.45 E
Amsterdam, N.Y., U.S. 210 42.57 N 74.11 W
Amsterdam, Ohio, U.S. 214 40.28 N 80.55 W
Amsterdam-Rijn-Kanaal Ξ 52 51.57 N 5.20 E
Amstetten 61 48.07 N 14.53 E
Amston 207 41.38 N 72.21 W
Amta 126 22.35 N 88.01 E
Āmtala 126 23.55 N 88.27 E
Āmtāli 126 22.08 N 90.14 E
Am Timan 146 11.02 N 20.17 E
Amtrak Station ◆5 281 42.19 N 83.04 W
Amubri 236 9.31 N 82.56 W
Āmūdā 130 37.05 N 40.54 E
Amu-Darja 128 37.56 N 65.15 E
Amu Darya (Amudarja) ≐ 72 43.40 N 59.01 E
Amugulang → Xinbaerhuzuoqi 88 48.14 N 118.18 E
Amukta Island I 180 52.29 N 171.15 W
Amukta Pass U 180 52.25 N 172.00 W
Amulree 46 56.30 N 3.47 W
Amun 175e 5.57 S 154.45 E
Amundsen Bay C 9 66.55 S 50.00 E
Amundsen Gulf C 176 71.00 N 124.00 W
Amundsen Sea ▾2 9 72.30 S 112.00 W
Amungen ⊜ 26 61.09 N 15.39 E
Amuntai 112 2.26 S 115.15 E
Amur (Heilongjiang) ≐ 74 52.56 N 141.10 E
Amūr, Wādī ∨ 140 18.56 N 33.34 E
Amurang 112 1.11 N 124.35 E
Amurd 85 38.12 N 71.21 E
Amuria 154 2.01 N 33.38 E
Amurrio 34 43.04 N 3.00 W
Amursk 89 50.13 N 136.52 E
Amurskaja Oblast' □4 89 53.00 N 129.00 E
Amurskij Liman C 89 52.45 N 141.40 E
Amurzet 89 47.43 N 131.06 E
Amusgos 234 16.39 N 98.06 W
Amutag 116 12.23 N 123.16 E
Amuwo 273a 6.28 N 3.18 E
Amuyimusu 98 42.25 N 113.21 E
Amuzhong 120 30.33 N 84.28 E
Amvamg 152 1.45 N 10.29 E
Amvrakikós Kólpos C 38 39.00 N 21.00 E
Amvrosijevka 83 47.47 N 38.29 E
Amyl ≐ 86 53.47 N 92.54 E
Amyūn 130 34.18 N 35.49 E
Amz'a 80 56.13 N 54.23 E
An 110 19.47 N 94.02 E
Anaa I1 14 17.25 S 145.30 W
Anabanua 112 3.57 S 120.04 E
Anabar 174b 0.30 S 166.57 E
Anabib 152 18.08 S 12.30 E
Anabtā 132 32.19 N 35.07 E
Anabuki 96 34.02 N 134.11 E
Anacapri 68 40.33 N 14.13 E
Anaco 246 9.27 N 64.28 W
Anacoco 194 31.15 N 93.20 W
Anacoco, Bayou ≐ 194 30.52 N 93.34 W
Anaconda 202 46.08 N 112.57 W
Anaconda Range ⋀ 202 45.55 N 113.30 W
Anacortes 224 48.30 N 122.37 W
Anacostia ◆8 284c 38.52 N 76.59 W
Anacostia ≐ 284c 38.52 N 77.01 W
Anacostia, Little Paint Branch ≐ 284c 39.01 N 76.56 W
Anacostia, Northeast Branch ≐ 284c 38.57 N 76.57 W
Anacostia, Paint Branch ≐ 284c 38.58 N 76.55 W
Anacuao, Mount ∧ 116 16.16 N 121.53 E
Anadarko 196 35.04 N 98.15 W
Anadia 250 9.42 S 36.18 W
Anadolufeneri 267b 41.12 N 29.09 E
Anadoluhisarı ⊥ 267b 41.04 N 29.03 E
Anadolukavağı ◆8 267b 41.10 N 29.05 E
Anadyr' 180 64.45 N 177.29 E
Anadyr' ≐ 74 64.55 N 176.05 E
Anadyrskaja Nizmennost' ≚ 180 65.30 N 176.00 E
Anadyrskij Liman C 180 64.30 N 177.45 E
Anadyrskij Zaliv C 180 64.00 N 179.00 W
Anadyrskoje Ploskogorje ⋀1 180 67.00 N 174.00 E
Anáfi I 38 36.21 N 25.50 E
Anagni 66 41.44 N 13.09 E
'Ānah 128 34.28 N 41.56 E
Anaheim 228
280 33.51 N 117.57 W
Anaheim Plaza ◆9 280 33.51 N 117.56 W
Anaheim Stadium ♠ 280 33.51 N 117.57 W
Anaheim Union Canal Ξ 280 33.54 N 117.52 W
Anahi, Baie C 174x 9.45 S 138.56 W
Anahim Lake 182 52.28 N 125.18 W
Anahola 229b 22.09 N 159.19 W
Anahola Bay C 229b 22.09 N 159.18 W
Anáhuac, Méx. 196 25.48 N 97.45 W
Anáhuac, Méx. 232 28.25 N 106.40 W
Anahuac, Tex., U.S. 222 29.46 N 94.41 W
Anahuac, Lake ⊜ 222 29.48 N 94.41 W
Ānai Mudi ∧ 122 10.10 N 77.04 E
Anajás 250 0.59 S 49.57 W
Anajás, Ilha I 250 0.20 S 50.30 W
Anajatuba 250 3.16 S 44.37 W
Anakāpalle 122 17.41 N 83.01 E
Anaklia 84 42.24 N 41.34 E
Anaktuvuk ≐ 180 69.32 N 151.30 W
Anaktuvuk Pass 180 68.10 N 151.50 W
Analalava 157b 14.38 S 47.45 E
Analamaitso, Plateau d' ⋀1 157b 16.15 S 48.15 E
Analapetsa 157b 25.10 S 46.42 E
Analavoka 157b 22.33 S 46.30 E
Analomink 210 41.03 N 75.13 W
Anamã 246 3.35 S 61.22 W
Anamã, Lago ⊜ 246 3.32 S 61.35 W
Anama Bay 184 51.56 N 98.05 W
Anamalai 122 10.35 N 76.56 E
Ana María, Cayos de II 240p 21.29 N 78.46 W
Ana María, Golfo de C 240p 21.25 N 78.40 W
Anamas Dağı ∧ 130 37.47 N 31.13 E
Anambas, Kepulauan II 112 3.00 N 106.00 E
Aname 175f 20.08 S 169.47 E
Anamizu 94 37.14 N 136.54 E
Anamoose 198 47.53 N 100.15 W
Anamosa 190 42.07 N 91.17 W
Anamur 130 36.06 N 32.50 E
Anamur Burnu > 130 36.03 N 32.48 E
Anan, Nihon 94 35.19 N 137.49 E
Anan, Nihon 96 33.55 N 134.39 E
Ānand 120 22.34 N 72.56 E
Ananda 150 7.17 N 4.16 W
Anandanagar 272b 22.51 N 88.16 E
Anandapur 126 22.34 N 87.25 E
Anandpur 123 31.15 N 76.30 E
Ananea 248 14.42 S 69.33 W
Ananindeua 250 1.22 S 48.23 W
Ananjev 78 47.40 N 29.55 E
Ananjevo 85 42.45 N 77.40 E
Anantapur 122 14.41 N 77.36 E
Anantnāg (Islāmābād) 123 33.44 N 75.09 E
Anao-aon 116 9.47 N 125.25 E
Anapa 78 44.53 N 37.19 E
Ana Pink, Bahía C 254 45.50 S 74.50 W
Anapo ≐ 70 47.03 N 15.16 E
Anápolis 255 16.20 S 48.58 W
Anapu ≐ 250 1.53 S 50.53 W
Anapurus 250 3.40 S 43.06 W
Anār, Īrān 128 30.53 N 55.18 E
Anar, S.S.S.R. 86 50.38 N 72.27 E
Anāra 126 23.28 N 86.33 E
Anārak 128 33.20 N 53.42 E
Anarchaj 85 44.02 N 75.15 E
Anār Darreh 128 32.46 N 61.39 E
Anaš 86 54.52 N 91.00 E
Anasagasti 258 35.01 S 59.24 W
Añasco 240m 18.17 N 67.08 W
Anäset 26 64.16 N 21.03 E
Anasofya Camii ʋ1 267b 41.00 N 28.58 E
Anastácio 255 21.31 S 54.08 W
Anastasia Island I 192 29.48 N 81.16 W
Anastasijevka 83 47.34 N 38.31 E
Anastasijevskaja 78 45.13 N 37.53 E
Anātā 132 31.49 N 35.16 E
Anatahan I 108 16.22 N 145.40 E
Anatoljevka 78 46.48 N 31.13 E
Añatuya 252 28.28 S 62.50 W
Anauá ≐ 246 0.58 N 61.21 W
Anaurilândia 255 22.03 S 52.45 W
Anavelona ∧ 157b 22.37 S 44.10 E
Anavilhanas, Arquipélago das II 246 2.42 S 60.45 W
Anawalt 192 37.15 N 81.26 W
'Anazah, Jabal ∧ 128 32.12 N 39.18 E
Anbanjing 102 23.57 N 100.55 E
Anbei, Zhg. 102 40.45 N 96.06 E
Anbei, Zhg. 102 40.49 N 108.56 E
Anbianbao 102 37.39 N 108.11 E
Anbo 98 39.51 N 122.19 E
Anbu 100 23.28 N 116.44 E
Anbyŏn 98 39.03 N 127.32 E
Ancarano 66 42.50 N 13.44 E
Ancash □5 248 9.30 S 77.45 W
Ancaster, Ont., Can. 212 43.12 N 80.00 W
Ancaster, Eng., U.K. 42 52.59 N 0.32 W
Ancasti 252 28.49 S 65.30 W
Ancasti, Sierra de ⋀ 252 28.50 S 65.39 W
Ance ≐, Fr. 62 45.17 N 4.08 E
Ance ≐, Fr. 62 44.58 N 3.40 E
Ancenis 32 47.22 N 1.11 W
Ancerville 58 48.38 N 5.02 E
Anchang 100 30.09 N 120.30 E
Anchau 150 10.59 N 8.23 E
Anchieta ◆8 287a 22.49 S 43.24 W
Anchieta, Ilha I 256 23.33 S 45.04 W
Anch'ing → Anqing 100 30.31 N 117.02 E
Ancholme ≐ 44 53.41 N 0.32 W
Anchor 216 40.34 N 88.32 W
Anchorage 180 61.13 N 149.53 W
Anchor Bay C 214 42.38 N 82.45 W
Anchor Bay Gardens 214 42.39 N 82.46 W
Anchorena 252 35.41 S 65.27 W
Anchor Point 180 59.46 N 151.52 W
Anchor Point > 180 59.47 N 151.52 W
Anchorville 214 42.42 N 82.41 W
Anchuras 34 39.29 N 4.50 W
Anci (Langfang) 105 39.31 N 116.41 E
Ancien Goubéré 140 5.51 N 26.46 E
Ancienne-Lorette 206 46.48 N 71.21 W
Anciferovo, S.S.S.R. 76 58.58 N 34.01 E
Anciferovo, S.S.S.R. 82 55.33 N 38.49 E
Ancipa, Lago di ⊜ 70 37.50 N 14.34 E
Anclitas, Cayo I 240p 20.48 N 78.54 W
Anclote ≐ 220 39.59 N 88.49 W
Anclote Keys II 220 28.12 N 82.51 W
Ancón, Méx. 234 22.35 N 101.11 W
Ancón, Perú 248 11.47 S 77.11 W
Ancona, It. 66 43.38 N 13.30 E
Ancona, S. Afr. 158 27.40 S 26.32 E
Ancona □4 66 43.33 N 13.10 E
Ancón de Sardinas, Bahía de C 246 1.30 N 79.00 W
Ancoraimes 248 15.54 S 68.58 W
Ancram 210 42.03 N 73.38 W
Ancre ≐ 50 49.54 N 2.28 E
Ancrum 46 55.31 N 2.35 W
Ancuabe 154 12.58 S 39.54 E
Ancud 254 41.52 S 73.50 W
Ancud, Golfo de C 254 42.05 S 73.00 W
Ancy-le-Franc 50 47.46 N 4.10 E
Ancy-sur-Moselle 56 49.03 N 6.04 E
Anda, Pil. 116 16.17 N 119.57 E
Anda, Zhg. 89 46.24 N 125.19 E
Andacollo, Arg. 252 37.11 S 70.41 W
Andacollo, Chile 252 30.14 S 71.06 W
Andahuaylas 248 13.39 S 73.23 W
Andaingo 157b 18.12 S 48.17 E
Andāl 124 23.36 N 87.12 E
Andalgalá 252 27.36 S 66.19 W
Andalo 64 46.10 N 11.00 E
Åndalsnes 26 62.34 N 7.42 E
Andalucía □9 34 37.36 N 4.30 W
Andalusia 194 31.19 N 86.29 W
Andaman Basin ◆1 12 10.00 N 95.00 E
Andamanen → Andaman Islands II 110 12.00 N 92.45 E
Andaman Islands II 110 12.00 N 92.45 E
Andaman Sea ▾2 110 10.00 N 95.00 E
Andamarca, Bol. 248 18.49 S 67.31 W
Andamarca, Perú 248 11.46 S 74.44 W
Andamooka 166 30.27 S 137.12 E
Andance 62 45.14 N 4.47 E
Andao I 100 22.37 N 114.57 E
Andapa 157b 14.39 S 49.39 E
Andara 152 18.03 S 21.27 E
Andaraí 255 12.48 S 41.20 W
Andaraí ◆8 287a 22.56 S 43.15 W
Andarax ≐ 34 36.48 N 2.26 W
Andaray 248 15.49 S 72.50 W
Andechs, Kloster ʋ1 64 47.58 N 11.10 E
Andeer 58 46.36 N 9.26 E
Andelfingen 58 47.36 N 8.41 E
Andelle ≐ 50 49.19 N 1.44 E
Andelot 58 48.15 N 5.18 E
Andelot-en-Montagne 58 46.51 N 5.56 E
Andelu 261 48.53 N 1.50 E
Anden → Andes ⋀ 18 20.00 S 68.00 W
Andenes 24 69.16 N 16.08 E
Andenne 56 50.29 N 5.06 E
Andéranboukane 150 15.26 N 3.02 E
Ånderdalen Nasjonalpark ♠ 24 69.14 N 17.17 E
Andere Reboucas, Túnel ◆5 287a 22.56 S 43.14 W
Anderlecht 50 50.50 N 4.18 E
Anderlues 50 50.24 N 4.16 E
Andermatt 58 46.38 N 8.36 E
Andernach 56 50.26 N 7.24 E

≐ River	Fluss	Río	Rivière	Rio
Ξ Canal	Kanal	Canal	Canal	Canal
L Waterfall, Rapids	Wasserfall, Stromschnellen	Cascada, Rápidos	Chute d'eau, Rapides	Cascata, Rápidos
U Strait	Meeresstrasse	Estrecho	Détroit	Estreito
C Bay, Gulf	Bucht, Golf	Bahía, Golfo	Baie, Golfe	Baía, Golfo
⊜ Lake, Lakes	See, Seen	Lago, Lagos	Lac, Lacs	Lago, Lagos
≚ Swamp	Sumpf	Pantano	Marais	Pântano
⚑ Ice Features, Glacier	Eis- und Gletscherformen	Accidentes Glaciales	Formes glaciaires	Acidentes Glaciares
▾ Other Hydrographic Features	Andere Hydrographische Objekte	Otros Elementos Hidrográficos	Autres données hydrographiques	Outros Elementos Hidrográficos

◆ Submarine Features	Untermeerische Objekte	Accidentes Submarinos	Formes de relief sous-marin	Acidentes Submarinos
□ Political Unit	Politische Einheit	Unidad Política	Entité politique	Unidade Política
ʋ Cultural Institution	Kulturelle Institution	Institución Cultural	Institution culturelle	Instituição Cultural
⊥ Historical Site	Historische Stätte	Sitio Histórico	Site historique	Sítio Histórico
♠ Recreational Site	Erholungs- und Ferienort	Sitio de Recreo	Centre de loisirs	Sítio de Lazer
⊠ Airport	Flughafen	Aeropuerto	Aéroport	Aeroporto
■ Military Installation	Militäranlage	Instalación Militar	Installation militaire	Instalação Militar
◆ Miscellaneous	Verschiedenes	Misceláneo	Divers	Miscelânea

Name	Page	Lat. °′	Long. °′
Andersen Air Force Base ■	174p	13.35 N	144.56 E
Anderslöv	41	55.26 N	13.22 E
Anderson, Ala., U.S.	194	34.50 N	87.16 W
Anderson, Alaska, U.S.	180	64.21 N	149.10 W
Anderson, Calif., U.S.	204	40.27 N	122.18 W
Anderson, Ind., U.S.	218	40.10 N	85.41 W
Anderson, Mo., U.S.	194	36.39 N	94.27 W
Anderson, S.C., U.S.	192	34.31 N	82.39 W
Anderson, Tex., U.S.	222	30.29 N	95.59 W
Anderson □[6], Ky., U.S.	218	38.05 N	84.55 W
Anderson □[6], Tex., U.S.	222	31.47 N	95.40 W
Anderson ≃	180	69.43 N	128.58 W
Anderson, Mount ∧	224	47.43 N	123.20 W
Anderson Creek ≃	194	33.18 N	94.26 W
Anderson Dam	202	43.30 N	115.30 W
Anderson Inlet C	169	38.39 S	145.48 E
Anderson Island I	224	47.10 N	122.42 W
Anderson Lake ⊜	182	50.41 N	122.07 W
Anderson Lake ⊜[1]	226	37.11 N	121.37 W
Anderson Peak ∧	228	34.08 N	116.53 W
Anderson Ranch Reservoir ⊜[1]	202	43.25 N	115.20 W
Andersonville	218	39.30 N	85.17 W
Anderstorp	26	57.17 N	13.38 E
Anderten	52	52.21 N	9.51 E
Anderton	262	53.17 N	2.32 W
Andes, Col.	246	5.40 N	75.53 W
Andes, N.Y., U.S.	210	42.12 N	74.47 W
Andes ∧∧	18	20.00 S	68.00 W
Andes, Lake ⊜	198	43.11 N	98.27 W
Andeville	50	49.15 N	2.10 E
Andevoranto	157b	18.57 S	49.06 E
Andfjorden ⊔	24	69.10 N	16.20 E
Andheri ◆[8]	272c	19.07 N	72.51 E
Andhra Lake ⊜	122	18.54 N	73.32 E
Andhra Pradesh □[3]	122	16.00 N	79.00 E
Andijk	52	52.45 N	5.12 E
Andijskij Chrebet ∧∧	84	42.50 N	46.25 E
Andikíthira I	38	35.52 N	23.18 E
Andilamena	157b	17.01 S	48.35 E
Andilangan	120	37.36 N	83.50 E
Andimákhia	38	36.48 N	27.07 E
Andīmeshk	128	32.27 N	48.21 E
Anding	105	39.38 N	116.29 E
Andingbao	102	37.58 N	107.02 E
Andinkerke	50	51.04 N	2.36 E
Andirá ≃	250	2.45 S	56.49 W
Andirá, Riozinho do ≃	248	9.21 S	67.31 W
Andırın	130	37.34 N	36.20 E
Andisleben	54	51.04 N	10.56 E
Ándissa	38	39.14 N	25.59 E
Andižan	85	40.45 N	72.22 E
Andižan □[4]	85	40.45 N	72.00 E
Andjeguéré	152	6.41 N	21.03 E
Andkhvoy	120	36.56 N	65.08 E
Andlau-au-Val	58	48.23 N	7.25 E
Ando	270	34.37 N	135.46 E
Andoas	246	2.50 S	76.30 W
Andoga ≃	76	59.10 N	37.27 E
Andolsheim	58	48.04 N	7.25 E
Andomskij Pogost	24	61.14 N	36.36 E
Andong, Taehan	98	36.35 N	128.44 E
Andong, Zhg.	98	39.54 N	124.09 E
Andong (Antung), Zhg.	98	40.08 N	124.20 E
Andong, Zhg.	100	30.16 N	121.13 E
Andong-ni	98	39.28 N	127.27 E
Andora	62	43.59 N	8.08 E
Andorf	60	48.23 N	13.35 E
Andorno Micca	62	45.37 N	8.03 E
Andorra	34	42.30 N	1.31 E
Andorra □[1]	22		
	34	42.30 N	1.30 E
Andorre → Andorra □[1]	34	42.30 N	1.30 E
Andover, Eng., U.K.	42	51.13 N	1.28 W
Andover, Conn., U.S.	207	41.44 N	72.23 W
Andover, Maine, U.S.	188	44.38 N	70.45 W
Andover, Mass., U.S.	207	42.39 N	71.08 W
Andover, N.J., U.S.	210	40.59 N	74.45 W
Andover, N.Y., U.S.	210	42.09 N	77.48 W
Andover, Ohio, U.S.	214	41.36 N	80.34 W
Andover, S. Dak., U.S.	198	45.25 N	97.54 W
Andowj	123	37.02 N	71.27 E
Andøya I	24	69.08 N	15.54 E
Andradas	256	22.04 S	46.34 W
Andrade Araújo	287a	22.45 S	43.26 W
Andrade Pinto	256	22.14 S	43.22 W
Andradina	255	20.54 S	51.23 W
Andramaimba, Baie C	157b	12.15 S	48.50 E
Andramasina	157b	19.11 S	47.35 E
Andranopasy	157b	21.17 S	43.44 E
Andranovory	157b	23.08 S	44.10 E
Andrate	62	45.32 N	7.53 E
Andreafsky ≃	180	52.02 N	163.16 W
Andreafsky, East Fork ≃	180	62.03 N	163.07 W
Andreanof Islands II	180	52.00 N	176.00 W
Andreapol'	76	56.39 N	32.15 E
Andreas	208	40.45 N	75.48 W
Andreashütte → Zawadzkie	30	50.37 N	18.29 E
André Félix, Parc National ♠	146	9.25 N	23.20 E
Andrejevka, S.S.S.R.	78	47.06 N	36.35 E
Andrejevka, S.S.S.R.	78	49.32 N	36.38 E
Andrejevka, S.S.S.R.	80	52.19 N	51.55 E
Andrejevka, S.S.S.R.	80	55.42 N	54.23 E
Andrejevka, S.S.S.R.	82	55.07 N	38.37 E
Andrejevka, S.S.S.R.	82	55.59 N	37.08 E
Andrejevka, S.S.S.R.	83	47.28 N	37.39 E
Andrejevka, S.S.S.R.	83	48.49 N	37.33 E
Andrejevka, S.S.S.R.	86	52.59 N	67.23 E
Andrejevka, S.S.S.R.	86	45.50 N	80.35 E
Andrejevo	80	55.56 N	41.08 E
Andrejevo-Ivanovka	78	47.28 N	30.28 E
Andrejevsk	88	58.06 N	114.08 E
Andrejevskaja	80	47.21 N	43.02 E
Andrejevskoje, S.S.S.R.	82	56.24 N	39.01 E
Andrejevskoje, S.S.S.R.	82	54.23 N	36.12 E
Andrejevskoje, S.S.S.R.	82	55.46 N	36.35 E
Andrejkoviči	76	52.25 N	33.00 E
Andrelândia	256	21.44 S	44.18 W
Andrésy	261	48.59 N	2.04 E
Andretta	68	40.56 N	15.19 E
Andrew	182	53.53 N	112.21 W
Andrew, Mount ∧	162	32.52 S	122.56 E
Andrew Gordon Bay C	176	64.23 N	75.30 W
Andrews, Ind., U.S.	216	40.52 N	85.36 W
Andrews, Mich., U.S.	216	41.57 N	86.22 W
Andrews, N.C., U.S.	192	35.12 N	83.49 W
Andrews, S.C., U.S.	192	33.27 N	79.34 W
Andrews, Tex., U.S.	196	32.19 N	102.33 W
Andrews Air Force Base ■	208	38.48 N	76.52 W
Andrezel	261	48.37 N	2.49 E
Andrézieux Bouthéon	62	45.32 N	4.16 E
Andria	68	41.13 N	16.18 E
Andriamena	157b	17.26 S	47.30 E
Andriandampy	157b	22.45 S	45.41 E
Andriba	157b	17.36 S	46.55 E
Andrija, Otok I	36	43.02 N	15.45 E
Andrijevica	38	42.44 N	19.46 E
Androka	157b	25.02 S	44.05 E
Andronovskoje	76	60.39 N	34.46 E
Ándros	38	37.50 N	24.57 E
Ándros I	38	37.45 N	24.42 E
Androscoggin ≃	188	43.55 N	69.55 W
Andros Island I	238	24.26 N	77.57 W
Androsovka	80	52.41 N	49.35 E
Andros Town	238	24.43 N	77.47 W
Androth Island I	122	10.50 N	73.41 E
Andrupene	76	56.11 N	27.23 E
Andr'ušino	86	59.12 N	62.59 E
Andrušovka	78	50.01 N	29.01 E
Andrychów	30	49.52 N	19.21 E
Anducha'nakechi ⊜	120	32.00 N	91.15 E
Andudu	154	2.29 N	28.41 E
Andújar	34	38.03 N	4.04 W
Andulo	152	11.30 S	16.45 E
Anduo	120	32.18 N	91.04 E
Anduze	62	44.03 N	3.59 E
Andžijevskij	84	44.14 N	43.05 E
Âne, Dos d' ∧	241o	16.19 N	61.46 W
Aneby	26	57.50 N	14.48 E
Anécho	150	6.14 N	1.36 E
Anecón Grande, Cerro ∧	254	41.25 S	70.16 W
Anefis I-n-Darane	150	18.03 N	0.36 E
Anegada I	238	18.45 N	64.20 W
Anegada, Bahía C	254	40.15 S	62.15 W
Anegada Passage ⊔	238	18.30 N	63.40 W
Anegam	200	32.23 N	112.02 W
Anegasaki	268	35.28 N	140.02 E
Aneityum I	175f	20.12 S	169.45 E
Anelgauhat	175f	20.14 S	169.44 E
Añelo	252	38.21 S	68.47 W
Anémata, Passe d' ⊔	175f	20.31 S	166.12 E
Anepahan Peak ∧	116	9.40 N	118.25 E
Aneroid	184	49.43 N	107.20 W
Anet	50	48.51 N	1.26 E
Aneta	198	47.41 N	97.59 W
Aneto, Pico de ∧	34	42.38 N	0.40 E
Aney	146	19.24 N	12.56 E
Añez	248	17.19 S	63.43 W
Anfeng	100	32.44 N	120.24 E
Anfengqiao	100	26.41 N	118.08 E
Anfengying	102	24.59 N	102.18 E
Anfo	64	45.46 N	10.29 E
Anfu	100	27.23 N	114.37 E
Anfuzhen	107	29.21 N	105.28 E
Anga	88	53.58 N	106.12 E
Angamacutiro [de la Unión]	234	20.10 N	101.41 W
Angamos, Punta ≻	252	23.01 S	70.32 W
Angangueo	234	19.37 N	100.18 W
Ang'angxi	89	47.09 N	123.48 E
An'ganka	89	52.18 N	126.17 E
Angao	100	33.08 N	112.22 E
Angar	164	3.39 S	130.50 E
Angara ≃	88	58.06 N	93.00 E
Angara-Débou	150	11.19 N	3.03 E
Angarbaka	140	9.44 N	24.44 E
Āngāria	126	22.29 N	90.22 E
Angarsk	88	52.34 N	103.54 E
Angas ≃	168b	35.23 S	138.59 E
Angas Downs	162	24.49 S	132.14 E
Angas Hills ∧∧[2]	162	22.55 S	128.00 E
Angastaco	252	25.38 S	66.11 W
Angaston	168b	34.30 S	139.02 E
Angat	116	14.56 N	121.02 E
Angat ≃	116	14.53 N	120.46 E
Angathonísi I	38	37.28 N	27.00 E
Angatuba	255	23.29 S	48.25 W
Angaul	88	53.49 N	100.18 E
Angden Pass)(	124	29.43 N	86.17 E
Angduo	102	32.20 N	98.55 E
Ånge	26	62.31 N	15.37 E
Ángel, Cerro ∧	234	22.49 N	102.34 W
Ángel, Salto (Angel Falls) ⌊	246	5.57 N	62.30 W
Angel Albino Corzo	234	16.10 N	93.15 W
Angel City	220	28.20 N	80.10 W
Ángel de la Guarda, Isla I	232	29.20 N	113.25 W
Angeles	116	15.09 N	120.35 E
Angeles, Sierra de los ∧∧	234	23.30 N	99.33 W
Angeles National Forest ♠	280	34.15 N	117.56 W
Angel Etcheverry	258	35.02 S	58.04 W
Angel Falls → Ángel, Salto ⌊	246	5.57 N	62.30 W
Ängelholm	41	56.15 N	12.51 E
Angelica	210	42.18 N	78.01 W
Angelim	250	8.53 S	36.17 W
Angelina □[6]	222	31.17 N	94.42 W
Angelina ≃	194	30.53 N	94.12 W
Angelina, East Fork ≃	222	31.50 N	94.56 W
Angel Island I	282	37.52 N	122.26 W
Angellala Creek ≃	166	26.40 S	146.08 E
Angeln ◆[1]	41	54.39 N	9.44 E
Angelo ≃	162	23.43 S	117.45 E
Angel R. Cabada	234	18.35 N	95.26 W
Ängelsberg	40	59.58 N	16.00 E
Angels Camp	226	38.04 N	120.32 W
Angels Creek ≃	226	38.01 N	120.33 W
Angelus, Lake ⊜	281	42.41 N	83.20 W
Angemuk ∧	164	3.30 S	138.34 E
Anger ≃	144	9.37 N	36.06 E
Angera	62	45.46 N	8.35 E
Angerbach ≃	263	51.23 N	6.44 E
Angerburg → Węgorzewo	30	54.14 N	21.44 E
Angereb ≃	144	13.45 N	36.40 E
Angeren	52	51.55 N	5.58 E
Angerhausen ◆[8]	263	51.23 N	6.44 E
Ångermanälven ≃	26	62.48 N	17.56 E
Ångermanland □[9]	26	63.30 N	18.05 E
Angermund	263	51.20 N	6.47 E
Angermünde	54	53.01 N	14.00 E
Angern, D.D.R.	54	52.21 N	11.44 E
Angern, Öst.	61	48.22 N	16.50 E
Angers	32	47.28 N	0.33 W
Angerville	50	48.19 N	2.00 E
Angervilliers	261	48.36 N	2.04 E
Ängesön I	26	63.43 N	20.55 E
Angevillers	56	49.23 N	6.02 E
Anghiari	66	43.32 N	12.03 E
Angical	255	12.00 S	44.42 W
Angical do Piauí	250	6.05 S	42.44 W
Angicos	250	5.40 S	36.36 W
Angier	192	35.31 N	78.44 W
Angijak Island I	176	65.40 N	62.15 W
Angikuni Lake ⊜	176	62.13 N	99.50 W
Angke, Kali ≃	269e	6.06 S	106.46 E
Angkor, Ruines d' ⊥	110	13.26 N	103.52 E
Ângk Tasaôm	110	11.01 N	104.41 E
Anglais, Baie des C	186	49.15 N	68.07 W
Anglais, Jardin ♠	261	48.38 N	1.49 E
Anglalinghu ⊜	120	31.40 N	83.00 E
Angle	42	51.41 N	5.06 W
Angle Inlet	198	49.21 N	95.04 W
Anglem, Mount ∧	172	46.44 S	167.56 E
Anglesea	169	38.25 S	144.11 E
Anglesey I	44	53.17 N	4.22 W
Angleterre → England □[8]	28	52.30 N	1.30 W
Angleton	222	29.10 N	95.26 W
Anglezarke Moor ◆[3]	262	53.40 N	2.33 W
Anglezarke Reservoir ⊜[1]	262	53.39 N	2.35 W
Angling ≃	184	56.45 N	93.36 W
Angling Lake ⊜	184	53.55 N	93.52 W
Anglona ◆[1]	71	40.48 N	8.45 E
Anglo-Normandes, Îles → Channel Islands II	28	49.20 N	2.20 W
Anglure	50	48.35 N	3.49 E
Angmagssalik	176	65.36 N	37.41 W
Angmering	42	50.48 N	0.28 W
Ango	154	4.02 N	25.52 E
Angoche, Ilha I	154	16.20 S	39.50 E
Angohrān	128	26.35 N	57.54 E
Angol	252	37.48 S	72.43 W
Angola, Ind., U.S.	216	41.38 N	85.00 W
Angola, N.Y., U.S.	210	42.38 N	79.02 W
Angola □[1]	138		
	152	12.30 S	18.30 E
Angola Basin ✦[1]	10	15.00 S	2.00 E
Angola Lake Shore	214	42.37 N	79.05 W
Angono	269f	14.31 N	121.09 E
Angoon	180	57.30 N	134.35 W
Angora → Ankara	130	39.56 N	32.52 E
Angoram	164	4.04 S	144.04 E
Angostura, Méx.	232	25.22 N	108.11 W
Angostura → Ciudad Bolívar, Ven.	246	8.08 N	63.33 W
Angostura, Presa de la ⊜[1]	234	16.10 N	92.40 W
Angostura Reservoir ⊜[1]	198	43.18 N	103.27 W
Angoulême	32	45.39 N	0.09 E
Angoumois □[9]	32	45.30 N	0.05 W
Angra, Pulau I	164	2.42 S	134.50 E
Angra do Heroísmo	148a	38.39 N	27.13 W
Angra dos Reis	256	23.00 S	44.18 W
Angren, S.S.S.R.	85	41.01 N	70.12 E
Angren, Zhg.	120	29.25 N	86.40 E
Angri	68	40.44 N	14.34 E
Angrignon Zoological Park ♠	275a	45.26 N	73.36 W
Angrogna	62	44.50 N	7.13 E
Ängsö	40	59.32 N	16.51 E
Ängsö Nationalpark ♠	40	59.39 N	18.44 E
Ang Thong	110	14.35 N	100.27 E
Angu	154	3.33 N	24.28 E
Angu, Rio do ≃	256	21.48 S	42.30 W
Angualasto	252	30.03 S	69.09 W
Anguang	89	45.31 N	123.45 E
Anguchang	107	29.30 N	103.39 E
Anguilas, Arroyo ≃	288	34.26 S	58.31 W
Anguilla	194	32.58 N	90.50 W
Anguilla □[2]	230		
	238	18.15 N	63.05 W
Anguilla Cays II	238	23.31 N	79.33 W
Anguillara Sabazia	66	42.05 N	12.16 E
Anguillara Veneta	64	45.08 N	11.53 E
Anguille, Cape ≻	186	47.55 N	59.25 W
Angul	120	20.51 N	85.06 E
Angumu	154	0.07 S	27.42 E
Anguo	98	38.25 N	115.19 E
Anguozhuang	105	39.44 N	117.59 E
Angus	212	44.19 N	79.53 W
Angus Place	170	33.20 S	150.06 E
Angustura	256	21.45 S	42.41 W
Angusville	184	50.44 N	101.01 W
Angwa ≃	154	15.51 S	30.35 E
Angwin	226	38.34 N	122.26 W
Angyalföld ◆[8]	264c	47.33 N	19.05 E
Angyō	268	35.51 N	139.46 E
An-hai, Viet.	110	15.13 N	108.56 E
Anhai, Zhg.	100	24.45 N	118.27 E
Anhanduí ≃	255	21.37 S	52.59 W
Anhanguera	255	18.19 S	48.14 W
Anholt	52	51.52 N	6.27 E
Anholt I	26	56.42 N	11.34 E
Anhovo	64	46.03 N	13.37 E
Anhua	102	28.18 N	111.14 E
Anhuai	100	33.04 N	117.50 E
Anhui □[4]	100	32.00 N	117.00 E
Anhŭng	98	36.41 N	126.10 E
Anhwei → Anhui □[4]	100	32.00 N	117.00 E
Aniak	180	61.35 N	159.33 W
Aniak ≃	180	61.34 N	159.30 W
Anibare Bay C	174b	0.32 S	166.57 E
Aniche	50	50.20 N	3.15 E
Anichovka	86	51.29 N	60.15 E
Anicuns	255	16.28 S	49.58 W
Anié	150	7.45 N	1.12 E
Anié ≃	150	7.40 N	1.18 E
Anie, Pic d' ∧	32	42.57 N	0.43 W
Aniene ≃	66	41.56 N	12.30 E
Anif	64	47.45 N	13.04 E
Anik ◆[8]	272c	19.02 N	72.53 E
Anikino, S.S.S.R.	86	56.32 N	73.56 E
Anikino, S.S.S.R.	88	53.26 N	120.20 E
Anikovo	76	59.23 N	43.45 E
Anil	250	2.32 S	44.14 W
Anil, Rio do ≃	287a	22.59 S	43.21 W
Animaqingshanmai (Jishishan) ∧∧	102	34.24 N	100.10 E
Animas	200	31.57 N	108.48 W
Animas ≃	200	36.43 N	108.13 W
Ánimas, Cerro de las ∧	252	34.46 S	55.19 W
Animas Peak ∧	200	31.35 N	108.47 W
Animas Valley ∨	200	32.05 N	108.50 W
Anin	110	15.40 N	97.46 E
Anina	38	45.05 N	21.51 E
Anipaj	174r	6.50 N	158.19 E
Anipemza	84	40.27 N	43.37 E
Anipen	174r	6.49 N	158.14 E
Aniskino	82	55.54 N	38.06 E
Añisoc	152	1.51 N	10.46 E
Anita, Iowa, U.S.	198	41.27 N	94.46 W
Anita, Pa., U.S.	214	41.00 N	78.58 W
Aniva	89	46.43 N	142.32 E
Aniva, Mys ≻	89	46.01 N	143.25 E
Aniva, Zaliv C	89	46.16 N	142.48 E
Anivorano	157b	18.44 S	48.58 E
Anivorano Nord	157b	12.44 S	49.13 E
Anizy-le-Château	50	49.30 N	3.27 E
Anjad	120	22.02 N	75.03 E
Anjan	26	63.41 N	12.49 E
Anjangaon	120	21.10 N	77.18 E
Anjār	120	23.08 N	70.01 E
'Anjarah	132	32.18 N	35.45 E
Anjavimihavana	157b	12.32 S	49.16 E
Anji	106	30.45 N	119.41 E
Anjiabe	157b	12.07 S	49.20 E
Anjiang, Zhg.	102	27.11 N	110.04 E
Anjiang, Zhg.	105	40.45 N	117.38 E
Anjigami Lake ⊜	190	47.51 N	84.34 W
Anjō	94	34.57 N	137.05 E
Anjou	206	45.36 N	73.33 W
Anjou □[9]	32	47.20 N	0.30 W
Anjozorobe	157b	18.24 S	47.52 E
Anju	98	39.36 N	125.40 E
Anjuba	107	30.21 N	105.27 E
Anjudin	24	62.33 N	58.12 E
Anjuzhen	107	29.59 N	106.02 E
Anka	150	12.07 N	5.55 E
Ankang	102	32.31 N	109.19 E
Ankara	130	39.56 N	32.52 E
Ankara □[4]	130	39.50 N	32.50 E
Ankara ≃	130	39.51 N	31.55 E
Ankaramena	157b	21.57 S	46.39 E
Ankaratra ∧∧	157b	19.25 S	47.12 E
Ankarimbelo	157b	22.08 S	47.20 E
Ankarsrum	26	57.42 N	16.19 E
Ankasakasa	157b	16.21 S	44.52 E
Ankata	80	50.44 N	51.34 E
Ankavandra	157b	18.46 S	45.18 E
Ankazoabo	157b	22.18 S	44.31 E
Ankazobe	157b	18.21 S	47.07 E
Ankazomiriotra	157b	19.38 S	46.32 E
Ankeny	190	41.44 N	93.36 W
Ankhor	144	10.47 N	46.17 E
Ankiabe	157b	13.13 S	48.56 E
Ankilimalinika	157b	22.58 S	43.45 E
Ankilizato	157b	20.25 S	45.01 E
Anking → Anqing	100	30.31 N	117.02 E
Ankisabe	157b	19.17 S	46.29 E
Anklam	54	53.51 N	13.41 E
Anklesvar	120	21.36 N	73.00 E
Ankober	144	9.30 N	39.44 E
Ankole □[5]	154	0.30 S	30.30 E
Ankoro	154	6.45 S	26.57 E
Ankororoka	157b	25.30 S	45.11 E
Ankou	100	25.03 N	113.24 E
An'kovo	80	56.57 N	39.57 E
Ankpa	150	7.23 N	7.37 E
Ankum	52	52.32 N	7.52 E
Anlaby	44	53.45 N	0.27 W
Anlinnuoer	98	41.11 N	114.31 E
Anliu	100	23.42 N	115.42 E
An-loc	110	11.39 N	106.36 E
Anloga	150	5.47 N	0.50 E
Anlong	102	25.02 N	105.31 E
Ânlóng Vêng	110	14.14 N	104.05 E
Anlu	100	31.17 N	113.40 E
Ånn ⊜	26	63.16 N	12.34 E
Ann, Cape ≻, Ant.	9	66.10 S	51.22 E
Ann, Cape ≻, Mass., U.S.	283	42.39 N	70.38 W
Anna, S.S.S.R.	78	51.29 N	40.25 E
Anna, Ill., U.S.	194	37.28 N	89.15 W
Anna, Ohio, U.S.	216	40.24 N	84.10 W
Anna, Tex., U.S.	196	33.21 N	96.33 W
Anna, Lake ⊜[1]	188	38.04 N	77.45 W
Annaba (Bône)	148	36.54 N	7.46 E
Annaba □[5]	148	35.35 N	8.00 E
An-Nabaṭīyah at-Taḥtā	132	33.23 N	35.29 E
Annaberg, Öst.	61	47.52 N	15.22 E
Annaberg, Öst.	64	47.31 N	13.26 E
Annaberg-Buchholz	54	50.35 N	13.00 E
An-Nabī Shīt	132	33.52 N	36.07 E
An-Nabk	130	34.01 N	36.44 E
An-Nabqīyah I	128	26.44 N	36.01 E
Annaburg	54	51.44 N	13.03 E
Annaburger Heide ◆[3]	54	51.40 N	13.05 E
Anna Creek	166	28.51 S	136.08 E
An-Nafī	128	24.57 N	43.42 E
An-Nafūd ◆[2]	128	28.30 N	41.00 E
Annagassan	48	53.53 N	6.20 W
Annahütte	54	51.34 N	13.53 E
An-Najaf	128	31.59 N	44.20 E
Annaka	94	36.19 N	138.54 E
An-Nakhl, Miṣr	140	29.55 N	33.45 E
An-Nakhl, Sūrīy.	132	33.00 N	36.07 E
Annalee ≃	48	54.03 N	7.24 W
Annalee Heights	208	38.52 N	77.11 W
Anna Maria	220	27.32 N	82.44 W
Anna Maria Island I	220	27.30 N	82.43 W
An-Nāmir	132	32.47 N	36.13 E
Annan	44	54.59 N	3.16 W
Annan ≃	44	54.59 N	3.16 W
Annanberg	164	4.55 S	144.40 E
Annandale, Austl.	166	21.57 S	148.22 E
Annandale, Minn., U.S.	190	45.16 N	94.08 W
Annandale, N.J., U.S.	210	40.39 N	74.53 W
Annandale, Va., U.S.	208	38.50 N	77.12 W
Annandale ∨	44	55.10 N	3.25 W
Annandale-on-Hudson	210	42.01 N	73.54 W
Anna Plains	162	19.17 S	121.37 E
Anna Point ≻	174b	0.30 S	166.56 E
Annapolis	208	38.59 N	76.30 W
Annapolis Basin C	186	44.39 N	65.42 W
Annapolis Royal	186	44.45 N	65.31 W
Annapurna ∧	124	28.34 N	83.50 E
An-Naqīrah ⊤[4]	128	27.53 N	48.15 E
An-Nāqūrah	132	33.07 N	35.08 E
Ann Arbor	216	42.18 N	83.45 W
Ann Arbor Municipal Airport ⊠	281	42.14 N	83.45 W
Anna Regina	246	7.16 N	58.30 W
Annaricken Brook ≃	285	40.03 N	74.42 W
An-Narrānīyah	273c	29.58 N	31.10 E
An-Nāṣirīyah, 'Irāq	128	31.02 N	46.16 E
An-Nāṣirīyah, Sūrīy.	130	33.52 N	36.49 E
An-Nāṣirīyah □[4]	128	31.00 N	46.15 E
An-Nawfalāb	140	15.52 N	32.32 E
An-Nawfalīyah	146	30.47 N	17.50 E
An-Nazlah	132	31.32 N	34.29 E
An-Nazlat	142	29.19 N	30.39 E
Annean, Lake ⊜	162	26.54 S	118.14 E
Anne Arundel □[6]	208	38.59 N	76.30 W
Annebault	50	49.15 N	0.04 E
Annecy	58	45.54 N	6.07 E
Annecy, Lac d' ⊜	58	45.51 N	6.11 E
Annecy-le-Vieux	58	45.55 N	6.09 E
Annemasse	58	46.12 N	6.15 E
Annen ◆[8]	263	51.27 N	7.22 E
Annenkov Island I	244	54.29 S	37.05 W
Annenskij Most	76	60.45 N	37.10 E
Annenskoje	86	53.08 N	60.26 E
Anner ≃	48	52.22 N	7.39 W
Annestown	48	52.07 N	7.16 W
Annet I	42a	49.54 N	6.21 W
Annet-sur-Marne	261	48.56 N	2.43 E
Annette	180	55.03 N	131.34 W
Annette Island I	180	55.10 N	131.28 W
Annevoie-Rouillon	56	50.21 N	4.50 E
Annezin	50	50.32 N	2.37 E
Annfield Plain	44	54.51 N	1.45 W
An-nhon	110	13.53 N	109.06 E
Anniangniang	89	51.33 N	125.49 E
Annicco	62	45.14 N	9.52 E
Annieopsquotch Mountains ∧∧	186	48.20 N	57.30 W
An-Nīl al-Azraq □[4]	140	13.00 N	33.00 E
Anningdu	102	36.56 N	104.31 E
Anninger ∧	264b	48.03 N	16.15 E
Annino	265a	59.46 N	30.03 E
Anninskije Mineral'nyje Vody	89	52.44 N	140.12 E
Annisquam	283	42.39 N	70.41 W
Annisquam ≃	283	42.39 N	70.41 W
Anniston	194	33.40 N	85.50 W
Annobón → Pagalu I	138	1.25 S	5.36 E
Annonay	62	45.14 N	4.40 E
Annopol	30	50.54 N	21.52 E
Anno-Rebrikovo	83	49.36 N	40.12 E
Annot	62	43.58 N	6.40 E
Annotto Bay	241q	18.16 N	76.46 W
Annsjön ⊜	40	58.48 N	15.26 E
An-Nubayrah	142	30.54 N	30.35 E
An-Nuhūd	140	12.42 N	28.26 E
An-Nuwayrah	142	29.06 N	30.59 E
Ann'val'kal', Mys ≻	180	65.36 N	180.40 E
Annville, Ky., U.S.	192	37.19 N	83.58 W
Annville, Pa., U.S.	208	40.19 N	76.31 W
Annweiler am Trifels	56	49.12 N	7.58 E
Anō	94	34.46 N	136.27 E
Anoia	68	38.27 N	16.05 E
Anoka	190	45.11 N	93.23 W
Anole	144	2.01 N	42.20 E
Áno Liósia	267c	38.05 N	23.42 E
Año Nuevo Bay C	226	37.07 N	122.19 W
Anopino	80	55.42 N	40.40 E
Anori, Bra.	246	3.47 S	61.38 W
Anorí, Col.	246	7.05 N	75.08 W
Anorotsangana	157b	13.56 S	47.55 E
Anosibe	157b	19.26 S	48.13 E
Anotaie ≃	250	3.29 N	52.04 W
Anpilogovo	78	51.47 N	36.01 E
Anping, Zhg.	98	38.16 N	115.30 E
Anping, Zhg.	105	39.43 N	116.53 E
Anpingji	98	34.01 N	115.07 E
Anpingsi	100	26.33 N	113.22 E
Anpu	102	21.27 N	110.00 E
'Anqābīyah, Jabal al- ∧[2]	142	30.01 N	31.37 E
Anqing	100	30.31 N	117.02 E
Anqiu	98	36.25 N	119.10 E
Anrath	56	51.17 N	6.28 E
Anren, Zhg.	100	26.42 N	113.16 E
Anren, Zhg.	100	28.04 N	119.20 E
Anren, Zhg.	107	30.31 N	103.38 E
Anrenzhen	89	43.04 N	125.03 E
Anröchte	52	51.33 N	8.19 E
Ans, Bel.	56	50.39 N	5.32 E
Ans, Dan.	41	56.19 N	9.36 E
Anṣāb, Ar. Sa.	128	29.11 N	44.43 E
Anṣāb, Yam. S.	144	14.31 N	46.30 E
Ansager	41	55.42 N	8.45 E
Ansai	102	36.54 N	109.10 E
Anṣār	132	33.23 N	35.21 E
Ansbach	56	49.17 N	10.34 E
Anschan → Anshan	104	41.08 N	122.59 E
Anschlag	263	51.10 N	7.29 E
Anse	58	45.56 N	4.43 E
Anseba ≃	144	16.00 N	38.30 E
Anse-Bertrand	241o	16.29 N	61.31 W
Anse-d'Hainault	238	18.30 N	74.27 W
Anse La Raye	241f	13.57 N	61.03 W
Anselmo	198	41.37 N	99.52 W
Anseremme	56	50.15 N	4.54 E
Anserma	246	5.13 N	75.48 W
Ansha	100	26.04 N	117.04 E
Anshan	104	41.08 N	122.59 E
Anshun	102	26.19 N	105.50 E
Ansina	252	31.54 S	55.28 W
Ansley	198	41.18 N	99.23 W
Anson	196	32.45 N	99.54 W
Anson Bay C, Austl.	164	13.20 S	130.06 E
Anson Bay C, Norf. I.	174c	29.01 S	167.55 E
Anson Creek ≃	212	44.53 N	79.03 W
Ansŏng	98	37.02 N	127.16 E
Ansongo	150	15.40 N	0.30 E
Ansonia, Conn., U.S.	207	41.20 N	73.05 W
Ansonia, Ohio, U.S.	216	40.13 N	84.38 W
Anson Lake ⊜	184	56.45 N	100.47 W
Ansonville, N.C., U.S.	192	35.06 N	80.07 W
Ansonville, Pa., U.S.	214	40.51 N	78.34 W
Ansouis	62	43.44 N	5.28 E
Anspach	56	50.17 N	8.29 E
Ansted	188	38.08 N	81.06 W
Anstey	42	52.40 N	1.11 W
Anstruther	46	56.13 N	2.42 W
Anstruther Lake ⊜	212	44.45 N	78.12 W
Ansudu	164	2.08 S	139.20 E
Ansus	164	1.44 S	135.49 E
Anta, Bra.	256	22.03 S	42.59 W
Anta, Perú	248	13.29 S	72.09 W
Anta, Cachoeira ⌊	255	13.06 S	48.09 W
Anta, Cachoeira da ⌊	248	7.29 S	61.51 W
Antabamba	248	14.19 S	72.55 W
Antakya (Antioch)	130	36.14 N	36.07 E
Antalaha	157b	14.53 S	50.16 E
Antalieptė	76	55.40 N	25.51 E
Antalovcy	78	48.38 N	22.31 E
Antalya	130	36.53 N	30.42 E
Antalya □[4]	130	37.00 N	31.00 E
Antalya, Gulf of → Antalya Körfezi C	130	36.30 N	31.00 E
Antalya Körfezi C	130	36.30 N	31.00 E
Antambohobe	157b	22.20 S	46.47 E
An-tan	110	15.26 N	108.39 E
Antanambao Manampotsy	157b	19.29 S	48.34 E
Antanambe	157b	16.26 S	49.52 E
Antananarivo	157b	18.55 S	47.31 E
Antanetibe	157b	18.27 S	46.42 E
Antanifotsy	157b	19.39 S	47.19 E
Antanimora	157b	24.49 S	45.40 E
Antar, Djebel ∧	148	31.57 N	1.56 W
Antarctica ⚫[1]	9	90.00 S	0.00
Antarctic Peninsula ≻[1]	9	69.30 S	65.00 W
Antarctique, Péninsule → Antarctic Peninsula ≻[1]	9	69.30 S	65.00 W
Antarctiques territoires britanniques → British Antarctic Territory □[2]	9	60.00 S	45.00 W
Antarktis → Antarctica ⚫[1]	9	90.00 S	0.00
Antártica, Península → Antarctic Peninsula ≻[1]	9	69.30 S	65.00 W
Antas	250	10.23 S	38.20 W
Antas, Rio das ≃	252	29.04 S	51.21 W
An Teallach ∧	46	57.48 N	5.14 W
Antegnate	62	45.29 N	9.47 E
Antela, Laguna de ⊜	34	42.07 N	7.41 W
Antelope Acres	228	34.44 N	118.19 W
Antelope Creek ≃, Nev., U.S.	204	40.00 N	117.24 W
Antelope Creek ≃, Oreg., U.S.	202	42.28 N	117.13 W
Antelope Creek ≃, S. Dak., U.S.	198	45.19 N	102.27 W
Antelope Creek ≃, Wyo., U.S.	198	43.29 N	105.23 W
Antelope Island I	202	40.57 N	112.12 W
Antelope Mine	154	21.02 S	28.27 E
Antelope Peak ∧	204	41.19 N	114.58 W
Antelope Reservoir ⊜[1]	202	42.54 N	117.13 W
Antelope Valley ∨	228	34.45 N	118.20 W
Antelope Wash ∨	204	39.33 N	116.17 W
Antenor Navarro	250	6.44 S	38.27 W
Antequera, Bol.	248	18.29 S	66.53 W
Antequera, Esp.	34	37.01 N	4.33 W
Antequera, Para.	252	24.08 S	57.07 W
Antero Reservoir ⊜[1]	200	39.00 N	105.55 W
Anterselva, Lago d' ⊜	64	46.53 N	12.10 E
Anterselva di Sopra	64	46.52 N	12.08 E
Antes Fort	210	41.12 N	77.14 W
Antetikireja	157b	14.42 S	47.29 E
Antevamena	157b	21.02 S	44.08 E
Antey-Saint-André	62	45.48 N	7.36 E
Anthéor	62	43.26 N	6.53 E
Anthon	198	42.23 N	95.52 W
Anthony, Fla., U.S.	192	29.18 N	82.07 W
Anthony, Kans., U.S.	198	37.09 N	98.02 W
Anthony, R.I., U.S.	207	41.42 N	71.32 W
Anthony Chabot Regional Park ♠	282	37.45 N	122.06 W
Anthony Creek ≃	188	37.54 N	80.20 W
Anthony Lagoon	162	17.59 S	135.32 E
Anthony Peak ∧	204	39.51 N	122.58 W
Anti Atlas ∧∧	148	30.00 N	8.30 W
Antibes	62	43.35 N	7.07 E
Antibes, Cap d' ≻	62	43.32 N	7.07 E
Anticosti, Île d' I	186	49.30 N	63.00 W
Antiesen ≃	60	48.22 N	13.24 E
Antietam Creek, West Branch ≃	208	39.41 N	77.37 W
Antietam National Battlefield Site ⊥	188	39.24 N	77.47 W
Antifer, Cap d' ≻	50	49.41 N	0.10 E
Antignano	66	43.30 N	10.19 E
Antigo	190	45.09 N	89.09 W
Antigonish	186	45.35 N	61.55 W
Antigorio, Valle ∨	58	46.18 N	8.20 E
Antigua □[1]	230		
	240c	17.03 N	61.48 W
Antigua Guatemala	236	14.34 N	90.44 W
Antigues, Pointe d' ≻	241o	16.26 N	61.33 W
Antiguo Morelos	234	22.33 N	99.05 W
Anti-Lebanon → Al-Jabal ash-Sharqī ∧∧	132	33.35 N	36.00 E
Antilla, Arg.	252	26.07 S	64.36 W
Antilla, Cuba	240p	20.50 N	75.45 W
Antillas Holandesas → Netherlands Antilles □[2]	241s	12.15 N	69.00 W
Antilles hollandaise → Netherlands Antilles □[2]	241s	12.15 N	69.00 W
Antillo	70	37.58 N	15.15 E
Anṭilyās	132	33.55 N	35.35 E
Antímano ◆[8]	286c	10.28 N	66.59 W
Antimari ≃	248	9.04 S	67.23 W
Antimony	200	38.07 N	111.55 W

Name	Seite	Breite °′	Länge °′ E=Ost
Anting	106	31.18 N	121.09 E
Antioch → Antakya, Tür.	130	36.14 N	36.07 E
Antioch, Calif., U.S.	226	38.01 N	121.49 W
Antioch, Ill., U.S.	216	42.29 N	88.06 W
Antioquia	246	6.33 N	75.50 W
Antioquia □[5]	246	7.00 N	75.30 W
Antipino, S.S.S.R.	76	55.55 N	33.16 E
Antipino, S.S.S.R.	86	57.49 N	66.34 E
Antipino, S.S.S.R.	86	59.01 N	55.10 E
Antipodes Islands II	9	49.40 S	178.47 E
Antipolo	116	14.35 N	121.10 E
Antipovka	80	49.50 N	45.20 E
Antique □[4]	116	11.00 N	121.45 E
Antler ≃	184	49.08 N	101.00 W
Antlers	196	34.14 N	95.37 W
Antoetra	157b	20.46 S	47.20 E
Antofagasta	252	23.39 S	70.24 W
Antofagasta □[4]	248	23.30 S	69.00 W
Antofagasta de la Sierra	252	26.04 S	67.25 W
Antofalla, Salar de ≚	252	25.44 S	67.45 W
Antofalla, Volcán ∧[1]	252	25.34 S	67.55 W
Antoing	50	50.34 N	3.27 E
Antón, Pan.	236	8.24 N	80.16 W
Anton, Tex., U.S.	196	33.49 N	102.10 W
Anton Chico	200	35.12 N	105.09 W
Antongil, Baie d' C	157b	15.45 S	49.50 E
Antonia	219	38.20 N	90.29 W
Antonibe	157b	15.07 S	47.24 E
Antonina	252	25.27 S	48.43 W
Antonina do Norte	250	6.43 S	39.58 W
Antoniny	78	49.49 N	26.52 E
Antonio Amaro	232	24.16 N	104.01 W
Antônio Carlos	256	21.19 S	43.45 W
Antonio de Biedma	254	47.29 S	66.30 W
Antônio Diogo	250	4.18 S	38.45 W
António Enes	154	16.14 S	39.58 E
Antonio Escobedo	234	20.46 N	103.57 W
Antônio João	255	23.15 S	55.31 W
Antônio Lemos	250	1.22 S	50.50 W
Antônio Prado	252	28.51 S	51.17 W
Antonito	200	37.05 N	106.00 W
Antón Lizardo, Punta de ≻	234	19.03 N	95.58 W
Antonov	78	49.37 N	29.47 E
Antonovka, S.S.S.R.	80	54.55 N	49.30 E
Antonovka, S.S.S.R.	86	53.19 N	68.26 E
Antonovka, S.S.S.R.	86	45.38 N	80.15 E
Antonovo	80	49.23 N	51.47 E
Antony	50	48.45 N	2.18 E
Antopol'	76	52.12 N	24.47 E
Antou	100	26.07 N	118.11 E
Antracit	83	48.06 N	39.06 E
Antraigues	62	44.43 N	4.21 E
Antrain	32	48.27 N	1.29 W
Antratsit → Antracit	83	48.06 N	39.06 E
Antrift ≃	56	50.54 N	9.15 E
Antrim, N. Ire., U.K.	48	54.43 N	6.13 W
Antrim, Ohio, U.S.	214	40.06 N	81.23 W
Antrim, Pa., U.S.	210	41.37 N	77.18 W
Antrodoco	66	42.25 N	13.05 E
Antronapiana	58	46.03 N	8.07 E
Antropovo, S.S.S.R.	80	58.26 N	43.00 E
Antropovo, S.S.S.R.	82	55.15 N	37.39 E
Antsahe	157a	12.21 S	44.32 E
Antsakabary	157b	15.03 S	48.56 E
Antsalova	157b	18.40 S	44.37 E
Antsenavolo	157b	21.24 S	48.03 E
Antsiafabositra	157b	17.18 S	46.57 E
Antsirabe, Madag.	157b	15.57 S	48.58 E
Antsirabe, Madag.	157b	19.51 S	47.02 E
Antsirabe, Madag.	157b	14.00 S	49.59 E
Antsirane → Diégo-Suarez	157b	12.16 S	49.17 E
Antsla	76	57.50 N	26.32 E
Antsohihy	157b	14.52 S	47.59 E
Anttis	24	67.16 N	22.52 E
Antu	89	43.07 N	128.54 E
An-tuc (An-khe)	110	13.57 N	108.39 E
Antun'	89	47.36 N	135.46 E
Antung → Andong	98	40.08 N	124.20 E
Antuševo, S.S.S.R.	76	59.54 N	37.40 E
Antuševo, S.S.S.R.	76	59.59 N	42.18 E
Antwerp → Antwerpen, Bel.	50	51.13 N	4.25 E
Antwerp, S. Afr.	273d	26.06 S	28.10 E
Antwerp, N.Y., U.S.	212	44.12 N	75.37 W
Antwerp, Ohio, U.S.	216	41.11 N	84.45 W
Antwerpen (Anvers)	50	51.13 N	4.25 E
Antwerpen □[4]	56	51.10 N	4.50 E
Antykan	89	54.55 N	135.12 E
An Uaimh → Navan	48	53.39 N	6.41 W
Anučino, S.S.S.R.	80	52.58 N	43.52 E
Anučino, S.S.S.R.	89	43.58 N	133.02 E
Anŭi	98	35.38 N	127.48 E
An'uj ≃	89	49.18 N	136.27 E
An'ujsk	74	68.18 N	161.38 E
Anujskij Chrebet ∧∧	86	51.30 N	84.55 E
Anundshögen ⊥	40	59.25 N	16.32 E
Anūpgarh	123	29.11 N	73.13 E
Anūpshahr	124	28.22 N	78.16 E
Ānūr	126	22.55 N	87.39 E
Anuradhapura	122	8.21 N	80.23 E
Anvers → Antwerpen	50	51.13 N	4.25 E
Anversa degli Abruzzi	66	41.59 N	13.48 E
Anvers Island I	9	64.33 S	63.35 W
Anvik	180	62.40 N	160.12 W
Anvik ≃	180	62.39 N	160.14 W
Anvil Peak ∧	181a	52.00 N	179.35 E
Anvil Range ∧∧	180	62.30 N	133.50 W
Anvin	50	50.27 N	2.15 E
Anxi, Zhg.	100	25.06 N	118.12 E
Anxi, Zhg.	102	40.32 N	95.51 E
Anxi, Zhg.	106	30.25 N	120.01 E
Anxian	102	31.40 N	104.32 E
Anxiang	102	29.23 N	112.09 E
Anxin	105	38.55 N	115.55 E
Anxing	106	31.24 N	119.06 E
Anxious Bay C	162	33.25 S	134.35 E
Anxiwei	100	25.15 N	115.06 E
Anyama	150	5.30 N	4.03 W
Anyang	98	36.06 N	114.21 E
Anyanghe ≃	98	36.01 N	114.46 E
Anyeke	154	2.24 N	32.31 E
Anyer-kidul	115a	6.04 S	105.53 E
Anyi	100	28.50 N	115.31 E
Anykščiai	76	55.32 N	25.06 E
Anysberg	158	33.31 S	20.46 E
Anyuan, Zhg.	100	27.37 N	113.54 E
Anyuan, Zhg.	100	25.08 N	115.28 E
Anyuan, Zhg.	100	26.36 N	116.38 E
Anyuanyi → Tianzhu	102	37.14 N	102.59 E
Anyue	107	30.06 N	105.21 E
Anza ≃	58	46.00 N	8.17 E
Anza-Borrego Desert State Park ♠	204	33.00 N	116.26 W
Anzac	184	56.27 N	111.02 W
Anzaldo	248	17.50 S	65.55 W
Anzano di Puglia	68	41.07 N	15.17 E
Anze	102	36.10 N	112.10 E
Anžero-Sudžensk	86	56.07 N	86.00 E
Anzhen	106	31.36 N	120.28 E
Anzhou	105	38.52 N	115.49 E
Anzhuang	106	31.04 N	121.01 E
Anzi, It.	68	40.31 N	15.55 E
Anzi, Zaïre	152	0.52 S	23.24 E
Anzicun	105	39.46 N	115.50 E
Anzin	50	50.22 N	3.30 E
Anzio	66	41.27 N	12.37 E
Anzoátegui □[3]	246	9.00 N	64.30 W
Anzob	85	39.10 N	68.48 E
Anzob, Pereval)(	85	39.07 N	68.52 E
Anzola dell'Emilia	64	44.33 N	11.11 E

Symbols in the index entries represent the broad categories identified in the key at the right. Symbols with superior numbers (∧∧[2]) identify subcategories (see complete key on page I · 30).

Kartensymbole in dem Registerverzeichnis stellen die rechts in Schlüssel erklärten Kategorien dar. Symbole mit hochgestellten Ziffern (∧∧[2]) bezeichnen Unterabteilungen einer Kategorie (vgl. vollständiger Schlüssel auf Seite I · 30).

Los símbolos incluidos en el texto del índice representan las grandes categorías identificadas con la clave a la derecha. Los símbolos con numeros en su parte superior (∧∧[2]) identifican las subcategorías (véase la clave completa en la página I · 30).

Les symboles de l'index représentent les catégories indiquées dans la légende à droite. Les symboles suivis d'un indice (∧∧[2]) représentent des sous-catégories (voir légende complète à la page I · 30).

Os símbolos incluídos no texto do índice representam as grandes categorias identificadas com a chave à direita. Os símbolos com números em sua parte superior (∧∧[2]) identificam as subcategorias (veja-se a chave completa à página I · 30).

	English	Deutsch	Español	Français	Português
∧	Mountain	Berg	Montaña	Montagne	Montanha
∧∧	Mountains	Berge	Montañas	Montagnes	Montanhas
)(	Pass	Pass	Paso	Col	Passo
∨	Valley, Canyon	Tal, Cañon	Valle, Cañón	Vallée, Canyon	Vale, Canhão
≚	Plain	Ebene	Llano	Plaine	Planície
≻	Cape	Kap	Cabo	Cap	Cabo
I	Island	Insel	Isla	Île	Ilha
II	Islands	Inseln	Islas	Îles	Ilhas
⊥	Other Topographic Features	Andere Topographische Objekte	Otros Elementos Topográficos	Autres données topographiques	Outros Elementos Topográficos

ESPAÑOL

Nombre | Página | Lat. °′ | Long. °′ W=Oeste

Anzon 62 45.45 N 3.57 E
Anžu, Ostrova 74 75.30 N 143.00 E
Aogaki 96 35.14 N 135.00 E
Aohaibolihu 104 42.01 N 121.32 E
Aohandaba 104 42.05 N 121.59 E
Aohanqi 98 42.19 N 119.59 E
Aoíz 34 42.47 N 1.22 W
Aoji 98 42.31 N 130.23 E
Aojiao 100 23.37 N 117.26 E
Aola 175e 9.32 S 160.29 E
Aoliyingzi 104 42.14 N 121.58 E
Aoloau 174u 14.18 S 170.46 W
Ao Luk 110 8.23 N 98.43 E
Aomar 34 36.30 N 3.47 E
Aomen → Macau 100 22.14 N 113.35 E
Aomori 92 40.49 N 140.45 E
Aonla 124 28.17 N 79.09 E
Aono-yama 96 34.27 N 131.48 E
Aóös (Vijosë) 38 40.37 N 19.20 E
Aopo 175a 13.29 S 172.30 W
Aôral, Phnum 110 12.02 N 104.10 E
Aorangi Mountains 172 41.26 S 175.20 E
Aore 175f 15.35 S 167.10 E
Aorere 172 40.41 S 172.40 E
Aoshan 100 29.56 N 122.14 E
Aoshang 100 25.42 N 113.00 E
Ao-shima, Nihon 96 33.44 N 132.29 E
Aosta 62 45.44 N 7.20 E
Aosta 58 45.45 N 7.20 E
Aosta, Valle d' 62 45.46 N 7.25 E
Aoste 62 45.35 N 5.36 E
Aotou 100 22.44 N 114.33 E
Aoudaghost 150 17.25 N 10.40 W
Aouderas 150 17.37 N 8.26 E
Aoudour, Oued 34 35.02 N 5.02 W
Aouis, Ouadi 146 11.03 N 19.47 E
Aouk, Bahr 146 8.51 N 18.53 E
Aoukalé 146 9.17 N 22.42 E
Aoukâr 150 18.00 N 9.30 W
Aoulef 148 26.58 N 1.05 E
Aoumou 175f 21.24 S 165.50 E
Aourou 150 14.57 N 11.35 W
Aoya 96 35.31 N 133.59 E
Aoyama 94 34.40 N 136.11 E
Aozi 146 21.04 N 18.41 E
Aozou 146 21.49 N 17.25 E
Apa 252 22.06 S 58.00 W
Apache 196 34.54 N 98.22 W
Apache Lake 200 33.36 N 111.16 W
Apache Peak 200 31.49 N 110.25 W
Apalachee 192 33.32 N 83.17 W
Apalachee Bay 192 30.00 N 84.13 W
Apalaches → Appalachian Mountains 178 41.00 N 77.00 W
Apalachicola 192 29.44 N 84.59 W
Apalachicola 192 29.44 N 84.59 W
Apalachicola Bay 192 29.40 N 85.00 W
Apalachin 210 42.04 N 76.09 W
Apam, Ghana 150 5.17 N 0.44 W
Apam, Méx. 234 19.43 N 98.25 W
Apanás, Lago de 236 13.11 N 85.59 W
Apango 234 17.44 N 99.20 W
Apapa 273a 6.27 N 3.22 E
Apapa Wharf 273a 6.23 N 3.23 E
Apaporis 246 1.23 S 69.25 W
Aparados da Serra, Parque Nacional dos 252 29.30 S 50.32 W
Aparan 84 40.36 N 44.23 E
Aparecida 256 22.50 S 45.14 W
Aparima 172 46.20 S 168.01 E
Aparri 116 18.22 N 121.39 E
Apaseo el Grande 234 20.33 N 100.41 W
Apastovo 80 55.11 N 48.30 E
Apatin 38 45.40 N 18.59 E
Apatity 24 67.34 N 33.18 E
Apatzingán [de la Constitución] 232 19.05 N 102.21 W
Apaxtla de Castrejón 234 18.09 N 99.52 W
Ap-ba-tien 269c 10.44 N 106.36 E
Ap-binh-quoi 269c 10.48 N 106.36 E
Ap-binh-thanh 110 11.11 N 108.42 E
Apcheron, Péninsule de l' → Apšeronskij Poluostrov 84 40.30 N 50.00 E
Ape 76 57.32 N 26.40 E
Apeadero Funke 258 35.28 S 58.59 W
Apecchio 66 43.33 N 12.25 E
Ape Dale 42 52.30 N 2.45 W
Apediá 248 11.39 S 61.11 W
Apeganau Lake 184 55.35 N 99.35 W
Apelacão 266c 38.49 N 9.08 W
Apeldoorn 52 52.13 N 5.58 E
Apeleg, Arroyo 254 44.58 S 70.07 W
Apen 52 53.13 N 7.48 E
Apenes 224 49.16 N 124.41 W
Apeninos → Appennino 36 43.00 N 13.00 E
Apenninen → Appennino 36 43.00 N 13.00 E
Apennines → Appennino 36 43.00 N 13.00 E
Apennins → Appennino 36 43.00 N 13.00 E
Apensen 52 53.26 N 9.37 E
Apese 273a 6.25 N 3.25 E
Apetlon 61 47.45 N 16.50 E
Apeú 250 1.18 S 47.59 W
Apex 192 35.44 N 78.51 W
Apex Mountain 180 62.28 N 138.04 W
Api 154 3.40 N 25.26 E
Api 124 30.00 N 80.57 E
Api, Tanjung 112 0.48 S 121.39 E
Apía, Col. 246 5.05 N 75.58 W
Apia, W. Sam. 175a 13.50 S 171.44 W
Apiacá 255 21.08 S 41.34 W
Apiacá 250 9.16 S 57.03 W
Apiacás, Serra dos 248 10.15 S 57.15 W
Apiaí 252 24.31 S 48.50 W
Apiaú 246 2.39 N 61.12 W
Apice 68 41.07 N 14.56 E
Apinajé 250 11.31 S 48.18 W
Apipilulco 234 18.11 N 99.41 W
Apisancho 248 7.18 S 76.50 W
Apishapa 198 38.08 N 103.57 W
Apiti 172 39.58 S 175.53 E
Apizaco 234 19.25 N 98.09 W
Apizolaya 232 24.50 N 102.15 W
Aplao 248 16.05 S 72.31 W
Aplerbeck 263 51.29 N 7.33 E
Aplinskij, Porog 88 58.28 N 100.32 E
Apo 234 19.25 N 102.25 W
Apo, Mount 116 6.59 N 125.16 E
Apodi 250 5.39 S 37.48 W
Apodi 250 4.56 S 37.10 W
Apo East Pass 116 12.40 N 120.40 E
Apolakkiá 38 36.06 N 27.50 E
Apolda 54 51.01 N 11.31 E
Apolima Strait 175a 14.50 S 172.10 W
Apolinario Saravia 252 24.25 S 64.02 W
Apollo 214 40.35 N 79.34 W
Apollo Bay 166 38.45 S 143.40 E
Apollo Beach 220 27.45 N 82.25 W
Apollonia 146 32.54 N 21.58 E
Apolo 248 14.43 S 68.31 W
Apón 246 10.06 N 72.23 W
Aponguao 246 4.48 N 61.36 W
Apopa 236 13.48 N 89.11 W
Apopka 220 28.40 N 81.30 W
Apopka, Lake 220 28.37 N 81.38 W
Apoquindo 286e 33.24 S 70.32 W
Aporá 250 11.39 S 38.05 W
Aporé 255 18.58 S 52.01 W
Aporé 255 19.27 S 50.57 W
Apo Reef 116 12.40 N 120.29 E
Aporema 250 1.14 N 50.49 W
Aporo 234 19.41 N 100.25 W

FRANÇAIS

Nom | Page | Lat. °′ | Long. °′ W=Ouest

Apostle Islands 190 46.50 N 90.30 W
Apostle Islands National Lakeshore 190 46.55 N 91.00 W
Apóstoles 252 27.55 S 55.46 W
Apostólou Andréa, Akrotírion 130 35.42 N 34.35 E
Apostolovo 78 47.39 N 33.44 E
Apozolco 234 21.22 N 104.00 W
Appalachen → Appalachian Mountains 178 41.00 N 77.00 W
Appalaches, Monts → Appalachian Mountains 178 41.00 N 77.00 W
Appalachia 192 36.54 N 82.47 W
Appalachian Mountains 178 41.00 N 77.00 W
Äppelbo 40 60.30 N 14.00 E
Appelhülsen 52 51.54 N 7.25 E
Appen 52 53.40 N 9.44 E
Appennino (Appennines) 36 43.00 N 13.00 E
Appennino, Galleria dell 66 44.10 N 11.10 E
Appennino Abruzzese 66 42.00 N 14.00 E
Appennino Calabrese 68 38.30 N 16.15 E
Appennino Ligure 62 44.30 N 9.00 E
Appennino Lucano 68 40.30 N 16.00 E
Appennino Napoletano 66 41.30 N 15.00 E
Appennino Tosco-Emiliano 36 44.00 N 11.30 E
Appennino Umbro-Marchigiano 66 43.00 N 13.00 E
Appenweier 58 48.32 N 7.58 E
Appenzell 58 47.20 N 9.25 E
Appenzell-Ausser Rhoden 58 47.22 N 9.28 E
Appiano (Eppan) 64 46.28 N 11.15 E
Appiano Gentile 62 45.44 N 8.59 E
Appin 170 34.12 S 150.47 E
Appingedam 52 53.18 N 6.52 E
Apple, U.S. 190 42.11 N 90.14 W
Apple, Wis., U.S. 190 45.09 N 92.45 W
Appleby, S. Afr. 158 27.39 S 22.36 E
Appleby, Eng., U.K. 44 54.36 N 2.29 W
Appleby, Tex., U.S. 222 31.43 N 94.36 W
Apple Creek 214 40.45 N 81.50 W
Apple Creek, Ill., U.S. 219 39.22 N 90.37 W
Apple Creek, Mo., U.S. 194 37.35 N 89.32 W
Apple Creek, N. Dak., U.S. 198 46.40 N 100.46 W
Applecross 46 57.25 N 5.49 W
Appledore 42 51.03 N 4.10 W
Applegate 226 39.06 N 120.59 W
Applegate 202 42.26 N 123.27 W
Apple Hill 206 45.13 N 74.46 W
Apple Orchard Mountain 192 37.31 N 79.31 W
Apples 58 46.34 N 6.25 E
Apple Springs 222 31.13 N 94.58 W
Appleton, Eng., U.K. 262 53.21 N 2.33 W
Appleton, Minn., U.S. 198 45.12 N 96.01 W
Appleton, Wash., U.S. 224 45.49 N 121.16 W
Appleton, Wis., U.S. 190 44.16 N 88.25 W
Appleton City 194 38.11 N 94.02 W
Apple Valley 228 34.32 N 117.14 W
Applewold 214 40.47 N 79.36 W
Appley Bridge 262 53.35 N 2.43 W
Appling 192 33.33 N 82.19 W
Appoigny 50 47.53 N 3.32 E
Appomattox 192 37.21 N 78.50 W
Appomattox 192 37.18 N 77.18 W
Appomattox Court House National Historical Park 192 37.23 N 78.48 W
Approuague 250 4.38 N 51.58 W
Apra Harbor 174p 13.27 N 144.38 E
Aprelevka 82 55.33 N 37.04 E
Aprel'sk 88 58.10 N 114.34 E
Aprel'skij 89 53.30 N 126.16 E
Apremont 58 46.13 N 5.40 E
Apremont-la-Forêt 56 48.51 N 5.38 E
Aprica, Passo d' 64 46.09 N 10.09 E
Apricena 68 41.47 N 15.27 E
Aprigliano 68 39.14 N 16.20 E
April 164 4.18 S 142.26 E
Aprilia 66 41.36 N 12.39 E
Apscheron → Apšeronskij Poluostrov 84 40.30 N 50.00 E
Apšeronsk 84 44.28 N 39.44 E
Apšeronskij Poluostrov 84 40.30 N 50.00 E
Apshawa 276 41.01 N 74.22 W
Apsley 212 44.45 N 78.06 W
Apt 62 43.53 N 5.24 E
Aptakisic 278 42.12 N 87.56 W
Ap-talai 110 11.24 N 107.23 E
Ap-tan-hoa 269c 10.45 N 106.35 E
Ap-tan-my 110 11.43 N 108.49 E
Aptos 226 36.59 N 121.54 W
Apuane, Alpi 64 44.09 N 10.15 E
Apucarana 255 23.33 S 51.29 W
Apuiarés 250 3.56 S 39.24 W
Apulia Station 210 42.49 N 76.05 W
Apure 246 7.10 N 68.50 W
Apure 246 7.37 N 66.25 W
Apurímac 248 14.00 S 73.00 W
Apurímac 248 11.48 S 74.03 W
Apurito 246 7.56 N 68.27 W
Aqaba, Gulf of 128 29.00 N 34.40 E
Aqabah, Wādī al- 132 30.14 N 33.53 E
Āqbolāgh 84 38.54 N 44.32 E
Āqcheh 120 36.56 N 66.11 E
'Aqīq 140 18.14 N 38.12 E
'Aqīq, Khalīj 140 18.20 N 38.10 E
'Aqīq, Wādī al- 128 24.17 N 40.10 E
Āq Koprūk 120 36.05 N 66.51 E
'Aqrabā 132 33.06 N 36.00 E
'Aqrah 128 36.45 N 43.54 E
Aquasco 208 38.35 N 76.43 W
Aquashicola 210 40.49 N 75.35 W
Aquashicola Creek 210 40.47 N 75.37 W
Äquatorial-Guinea → Equatorial Guinea 152 2.00 N 9.00 E
Aquebogue 207 40.57 N 72.37 W
Aqueduct Race Track 276 40.40 N 73.50 W
Aquia Creek 208 38.23 N 77.18 W
Aquiaulne 50 47.37 N 2.30 E
Aquibi, Cachoeira 250 11.08 S 55.22 W
Aquidabã 250 10.17 S 37.02 W
Aquidabã 248 20.58 S 57.50 W
Aquidabán 252 23.11 S 57.32 W
Aquidauana 248 20.28 S 55.48 W
Aquidauana 248 19.44 S 56.50 W
Aquila, Méx. 234 18.36 N 103.30 W
Aquila, Schw. 58 46.31 N 8.57 E
Aquileia 64 45.46 N 13.22 E
Aquiles Serdán 232 28.36 N 105.53 W
Aquilla, Ohio, U.S. 214 41.34 N 81.09 W
Aquilla, Tex., U.S. 222 31.51 N 97.13 W
Aquilla Creek 222 31.40 N 97.10 W
Aquilonia (S.M.) 68 41.00 N 15.29 E
Aquin 238 18.17 N 73.24 W
Aquincumi Múzeum 264c 47.34 N 19.03 E
Aquino 66 41.30 N 13.42 E
Aquio 246 2.42 N 67.34 W
Ara, Eire 48 52.24 N 7.56 W

PORTUGUÊS

Nome | Página | Lat. °′ | Long. °′ W=Oeste

Ara, Esp. 34 42.25 N 0.09 E
Ara, Nihon 94 35.39 N 139.51 E
Arab 194 34.19 N 86.29 W
'Arab, Baḥr al- 140 9.02 N 29.28 E
'Arab, Khalīj al- 140 30.55 N 29.05 E
Arab, Oued el 148 34.41 N 6.31 E
Arab, Shatt al- 128 29.57 N 48.34 E
'Arab, Wādī al- 132 32.35 N 35.35 E
'Arabābād 128 33.02 N 57.41 E
'Arabah, Wādī 142 29.07 N 32.40 E
Araban 130 37.26 N 37.41 E
Arabatskij Zaliv 78 45.20 N 35.30 E
Arabba 64 46.30 N 11.52 E
Arabei Dalon 144 3.34 N 46.30 E
Arabelo 246 4.55 N 64.13 W
Arabi 194 29.57 N 90.02 W
Arabian Basin 12 10.00 N 65.00 E
Arabian Desert → Ash-Sharqīyah, Aṣ-Ṣaḥrā' 140 28.00 N 32.00 E
Arabian Peninsula 12 25.00 N 45.00 E
Arabian Sea 118 15.00 N 65.00 E
Arabia Saudita → Saudi Arabia 118 25.00 N 45.00 E
Arabie, Mer d' → Arabian Sea 118 15.00 N 65.00 E
Arabie Saoudite → Saudi Arabia 118 25.00 N 45.00 E
Arabique, Péninsule → Arabian Peninsula 12 25.00 N 45.00 E
Arabisches Meer → Arabian Sea 118 15.00 N 65.00 E
Arab-Jengidža 84 39.29 N 44.58 E
'Arab Muṭayr 142 27.16 N 31.14 E
Araç 130 41.15 N 33.21 E
Araçá 246 0.25 S 62.55 W
Aracaju 250 10.55 S 37.04 W
Araçariguama 256 23.26 S 47.04 W
Aracataca 246 10.36 N 74.12 W
Aracati 250 4.34 S 37.46 W
Aracatiaçu, Açude 250 3.56 S 39.59 W
Araçatuba 255 21.12 S 50.25 W
Araceli 116 10.33 N 119.59 E
Aracena 34 37.53 N 6.33 W
Arâches-les-Carroz 58 46.02 N 6.39 E
Arachlej, Ozero 88 52.12 N 112.52 E
Araci 250 11.20 S 38.57 W
Aracitaba 256 21.20 S 43.23 W
Aracoiaba 250 4.23 S 38.49 W
Aracruz 255 19.49 S 40.16 W
Aracu 246 4.20 S 59.15 W
Araçuaí 255 16.52 S 42.04 W
Araçuaí 255 16.46 S 42.02 W
Arad, Rom. 38 46.11 N 21.20 E
'Arad, Yis. 132 31.15 N 35.13 E
Arad 38 46.20 N 21.40 E
Arada, Hond. 236 14.48 N 88.18 W
Arada, Tchad 146 15.01 N 20.40 E
Aradeo 68 40.08 N 18.08 E
Aradhíppou 130 34.57 N 33.35 E
Arafune-yama 94 36.12 N 138.38 E
Arafura Sea 164 9.00 S 133.00 E
Aragarças 255 15.55 S 52.15 W
Arago, Cape 202 43.18 N 124.25 W
Aragoiânia 255 16.57 S 49.30 W
Aragon 192 34.03 N 85.03 W
Aragón 34 41.00 N 1.00 W
Aragón 34 42.13 N 1.44 W
Aragona 70 37.24 N 13.37 E
Aragua 246 10.00 N 67.10 W
Araguacema 250 8.50 S 49.34 W
Araguaçu 255 12.49 S 49.51 W
Aragua de Barcelona 246 9.28 N 64.49 W
Aragua de Maturín 246 9.58 N 63.29 W
Araguaia 242 5.21 S 48.41 W
Araguaia, Parque Nacional do 250 12.00 S 50.20 W
Araguaína 250 7.12 S 48.12 W
Araguainha 255 16.49 S 53.05 W
Araguari 255 18.38 S 48.11 W
Araguari, Bra. 250 1.15 N 49.55 W
Araguari, Bra. 255 18.21 S 48.40 W
Araguatins 250 5.38 S 48.07 W
Aragvi 84 41.50 N 44.43 E
Arai, Nihon 94 37.01 N 138.15 E
Arai, Nihon 94 34.41 N 137.34 E
Arāihāzār 126 23.47 N 90.40 E
Araioses 250 2.53 S 41.55 W
Arak, Alg. 148 25.18 N 3.45 E
Arāk, Īrān 128 34.05 N 49.41 E
Araka 154 4.20 N 30.23 E
Arakan 110 19.00 N 94.15 E
Arakan, Porog 88 57.35 N 96.36 E
Arakan Yoma 110 19.00 N 94.40 E
Arakawa, Nihon 94 35.57 N 139.02 E
Arakawa, Nihon 174m 26.39 N 128.15 E
Arakawa 268 35.47 N 139.44 E
Arakawa-dake 94 35.30 N 138.10 E
Arákhova 38 38.29 N 22.35 E
Árakhthos 38 39.01 N 21.03 E
Araklı 130 40.57 N 40.03 E
Arakpur 272a 28.35 N 77.10 E
Araks (Aras) 84 40.01 N 48.28 E
Aral, S.S.S.R. 85 42.32 N 72.40 E
Aral, S.S.S.R. 85 41.50 N 73.03 E
Araldy 84 44.18 N 50.24 E
Aral Sea → Aral'skoje More 86 45.00 N 60.00 E
Aral'sk 86 46.48 N 61.40 E
Aral'skoje More 86 45.00 N 60.00 E
Aralsor, Ozero, S.S.S.R. 80 48.42 N 52.24 E
Aralsor, Ozero, S.S.S.R. 80 49.05 N 48.12 E
Aralsul'fat 86 46.50 N 61.58 E
Aramá 250 1.06 S 50.40 W
Aramac 166 22.59 S 145.14 E
Aramac 166 23.02 S 144.31 E
Aramari 255 12.04 S 38.30 W
Arāmbāgh 126 22.53 N 87.47 E
Arambaza 246 2.04 S 73.06 W
Aramberri 232 24.06 N 99.49 W
Aramil' 86 56.46 N 60.50 E
Aramon 62 43.53 N 4.41 E
Arampampa 248 17.55 S 66.04 W
Aramtalla 140 6.47 N 29.13 E
Ārān 128 34.04 N 51.29 E
Arana 258 35.00 S 57.54 W
Arana, Sierra 34 37.20 N 3.30 W
Arancio, Lago 70 37.38 N 13.05 E
Aranda de Duero 34 41.41 N 3.41 W
Arandai 164 2.10 S 133.01 E
Arandas 234 20.42 N 102.21 W
Aranđelovac 38 44.18 N 20.35 E
Arandis 156 22.24 S 15.00 E
Aran Fawddwy 42 52.47 N 3.41 W
Arang 120 21.12 N 81.58 E
Ārani, Bhārat 122 12.40 N 79.17 E
Ārāni, Bngl. 126 24.17 N 88.52 E
Arani, Bol. 248 17.34 S 65.46 W
Aran Island 48 54.58 N 8.33 W
Aran Islands 48 53.07 N 9.43 W
Aranjuez 34 40.02 N 3.36 W
Aranos 156 24.09 S 19.09 E
Aransas 196 28.04 N 97.14 W
Aransas Pass 196 27.54 N 97.09 W
Arantāngi 122 10.10 N 78.59 E
Arantina 256 21.56 S 44.15 W
Aranyaprathet 110 13.41 N 102.30 E
Arany-hegyi-patak 264c 47.34 N 19.04 E
Arao 96 33.00 N 130.28 E
Araouane 150 18.54 N 3.33 W
Arapa, Laguna 248 15.10 S 70.01 W
Arapaho 196 35.34 N 98.57 W
Arapahoe 198 40.18 N 99.54 W
Arāpānja 272b 22.26 N 88.28 E
Arapawa Island 172 41.11 S 174.19 E
Arapeí 256 22.41 S 44.27 W
Arapey 252 30.58 S 57.32 W
Arapey Chico 252 30.57 S 57.30 W
Arapey Grande 252 30.55 S 57.49 W
Arapiraca 250 9.45 S 36.39 W
Arapiri, Ilha 250 2.04 S 54.56 W
Arápis 267c 37.59 N 23.32 E
Arapiuns 250 2.18 S 55.00 W
Arapkir 130 39.03 N 38.30 E
Arapongas 255 23.23 S 51.27 W
Arapoti 255 24.08 S 49.50 W
Arapuni 172 38.04 S 175.39 E
Araquari 252 26.23 S 48.43 W
Araquil 34 42.48 N 1.45 W
'Ar'ar 128 13.53 N 44.50 E
'Ar'ar, Wādī 128 31.23 N 42.26 E
Araranguá 252 28.56 S 49.29 W
Araraquara 255 21.47 S 48.10 W
Araras, Bra. 255 22.22 S 47.23 W
Araras, Bra. 256 22.49 S 46.36 W
Araras, Açude 250 4.20 S 40.28 W
Araras, Ribeirão das, Bra. 256 22.52 S 46.37 W
Araras, Ribeirão das, Bra. 256 21.18 S 45.45 W
Ararat, Austl. 169 37.17 S 142.56 E
Ararat, S.S.S.R. 84 39.50 N 44.42 E
Ararat, Mount → Büyük Ağrı Dağı 84 39.42 N 44.18 E
Arari 250 3.28 S 44.47 W
Arāria 124 26.08 N 87.24 E
Araripe 250 7.12 S 40.08 W
Araripe, Chapada do 250 7.20 S 40.00 W
Araripina 250 7.33 S 40.34 W
Ararirá 246 0.30 S 63.33 W
Arar Lugole 144 3.17 N 45.28 E
Araruna 250 6.32 S 35.44 W
Aras (Araks) 84 40.01 N 48.28 E
'Aras, Ḥawḍ al- 142 30.51 N 32.32 E
Aråsviken 40 59.02 N 14.01 E
Arataú 250 2.35 S 50.41 W
Aratiba 252 27.24 S 52.19 W
Araticu 250 1.55 S 49.51 W
Áratos 38 41.05 N 25.33 E
Aratuípe 255 13.05 S 39.00 W
Aratula 171a 27.59 S 152.32 E
Arau 114 6.26 N 100.16 E
Arauá 250 11.16 S 37.37 W
Arauá, Bra. 246 4.06 S 63.36 W
Arauã, Bra. 248 7.59 S 65.14 W
Arauá, Bra. 248 5.40 S 60.48 W
Arauca 246 7.05 N 70.45 W
Arauca 246 6.40 N 71.00 W
Arauca 246 7.24 N 66.35 W
Araucária 252 25.35 S 49.25 W
Arauco 252 37.15 S 73.19 W
Arauco, Golfo de 252 37.11 S 73.25 W
Araújo, Ilha do 256 23.09 S 44.42 W
Araújos 255 19.56 S 45.04 W
Arauquita 246 7.02 N 71.25 W
Araure 246 9.34 N 69.13 W
Aravaca 266a 40.28 N 3.46 W
Aravaipa Creek 200 32.50 N 110.43 W
Arāvalli Range 120 25.00 N 73.30 E
Aravan 85 40.32 N 72.30 E
Araviana 34 41.41 N 2.07 W
Arawa 144 9.55 N 41.59 E
Arawata 172 44.00 S 168.41 E
Araxá 255 19.35 S 46.55 W
Araya 246 10.34 N 64.15 W
Araya, Punta de 246 10.38 N 64.18 W
Arayat 116 15.10 N 120.46 E
Arba 144 9.00 N 40.26 E
Arba 34 41.52 N 1.18 W
Arbagar 88 51.56 N 116.15 E
Arbagia 36 40.00 N 9.10 E
'Arbah, Wādī 144 17.30 N 51.25 E
Ārbālia 126 22.41 N 88.47 E
Arba Minch 144 6.02 N 37.40 E
Arbaoua 34 34.54 N 5.56 W
Arbatax 71 39.56 N 9.42 E
Arbaž 80 57.41 N 48.18 E
Arbedo 58 46.12 N 9.03 E
Arbel 132 32.49 N 35.29 E
Arbesbach 61 48.29 N 14.57 E
Arbia 66 43.08 N 11.28 E
Arboga 40 59.24 N 15.50 E
Arbogaån 40 59.26 N 16.04 E
Arbois 58 46.54 N 5.46 E
Arboledas 252 36.53 S 61.29 W
Arboletes 246 8.51 N 76.26 W
Arbon 58 47.31 N 9.26 E
Arbonne 50 48.25 N 2.34 E
Arborea 71 39.46 N 8.35 E
Arborea 71 39.50 N 8.50 E
Arborfield 184 53.06 N 103.39 W
Arborg 184 50.55 N 97.15 W
Arbrå 26 61.29 N 16.23 E
Arbroath 46 56.34 N 2.35 W
Arbuckle 226 39.01 N 122.03 W
Arbuckle, Lake 220 27.41 N 81.24 W
Arbuckle Creek 220 27.26 N 81.17 W
Arbuckle Mountains 196 34.25 N 97.20 W
Arbury Hills 216 41.33 N 87.51 W
Arbus 71 39.32 N 8.36 E
Arbutus Lake 276 40.31 N 74.10 W
Arbuzinka 78 47.53 N 31.19 E
Arbuzovo 76 56.21 N 32.27 E
Arc, Fr. 62 45.34 N 6.12 E
Arc, Fr. 62 43.31 N 5.07 E
Arc, Bayou des 194 35.00 N 91.30 W
Arcachon 32 44.37 N 1.12 W
Arcachon, Bassin d' 32 44.40 N 1.10 W
Arcadas 256 22.42 S 46.52 W
Arcade, It. 64 45.47 N 12.13 E
Arcade, Calif., U.S. 226 34.02 N 118.15 W
Arcade, N.Y., U.S. 210 42.32 N 78.25 W
Arcadia, Calif., U.S. 228 34.08 N 118.01 W
Arcadia, Fla., U.S. 220 27.14 N 81.52 W
Arcadia, Ind., U.S. 218 40.11 N 86.01 W
Arcadia, Iowa, U.S. 198 42.05 N 95.03 W
Arcadia, Kans., U.S. 198 37.38 N 94.37 W
Arcadia, La., U.S. 194 32.33 N 92.55 W
Arcadia, Mich., U.S. 190 44.30 N 86.14 W
Arcadia, Nebr., U.S. 198 41.25 N 99.07 W
Arcadia, Ohio, U.S. 216 41.07 N 83.31 W
Arcadia, Pa., U.S. 214 40.47 N 78.51 W
Arcadia, S.C., U.S. 192 34.57 N 82.00 W
Arcadia, Tex., U.S. 222 29.23 N 95.07 W
Arcadia, Wis., U.S. 190 44.15 N 91.30 W
Arcângelo 256 21.18 S 44.19 W
Arcanum 218 39.59 N 84.33 W
Arcata 204 40.52 N 124.05 W
Arcatao 236 14.05 N 88.45 W
Arc de Triomphe 261 48.53 N 2.17 E
Arc Dome 204 38.51 N 117.22 W
Arce 66 41.35 N 13.34 E
Arceburgo 256 21.22 S 46.56 W
Arčedinsko-Donskije Peski 80 49.33 N 43.15 E
Arcelia 234 18.17 N 100.16 W
Arcen 52 51.29 N 6.11 E
Arc-en-Barrois 58 47.57 N 5.00 E
Arces 50 48.05 N 3.36 E
Arc-et-Senans 58 47.02 N 5.46 E
Arcevia 66 43.30 N 12.56 E
Archambault, Lac 206 46.18 N 74.15 W
Archangaj 88 48.00 N 101.30 E
Archangel → Archangel'sk 24 64.34 N 40.32 E
Archangel'sk 24 64.34 N 40.32 E
Archangel'skaja 78 45.41 N 40.15 E
Archangel'skoje, S.S.S.R. 76 53.16 N 37.42 E
Archangel'skoje, S.S.S.R. 78 51.27 N 40.55 E
Archangel'skoje, S.S.S.R. 80 55.13 N 44.05 E
Archangel'skoje, S.S.S.R. 80 54.26 N 48.40 E
Archangel'skoje, S.S.S.R. 82 55.19 N 35.58 E
Archangel'skoje, S.S.S.R. 84 44.37 N 44.05 E
Archangel'skoje, S.S.S.R. 265b 55.47 N 37.18 E
Archara 89 49.27 N 130.07 E
Archara 89 49.13 N 129.53 E
Archbald 210 41.30 N 75.32 W
Archbold 216 41.31 N 84.18 W
Archdale 192 35.56 N 79.57 W
Archer 192 29.32 N 82.31 W
Archer 164 13.28 S 141.41 E
Archer, Lake 283 42.04 N 71.20 W
Archer Bay 164 13.25 S 141.43 E
Archer City 196 33.36 N 98.38 W
Archer's Post 154 0.39 N 37.41 E
Arches 58 48.07 N 6.32 E
Arches National Park 200 38.42 N 109.45 W
Archi 66 42.05 N 14.23 E
Archiac 32 45.31 N 0.18 W
Archibald Makin National Park 166 35.50 S 140.25 E
Archidona 34 37.05 N 4.23 W
Archipo-Osipovka 78 44.22 N 38.33 E
Archipovka 80 56.38 N 41.14 E
Archipovo 24 66.26 N 45.52 E
Archonskaja 84 43.07 N 44.30 E
Archshofen 56 49.27 N 10.04 E
Archville 276 41.07 N 73.52 W
Arci, Monte 71 39.47 N 8.44 E
Arcidosso 66 42.52 N 11.33 E
Arcille 66 42.48 N 11.15 E
Arcinazzo Romano 66 41.48 N 13.12 E
Arcisate 62 45.54 N 8.52 E
Arcis-sur-Aube 50 48.32 N 4.08 E
Arciz 78 46.00 N 29.26 E
Arckaringa 162 27.56 S 134.45 E
Arckaringa Creek 162 28.10 S 135.22 E
Arc-les-Gray 58 47.27 N 5.35 E
Arco, It. 64 45.55 N 10.53 E
Arco, Idaho, U.S. 202 43.38 N 113.18 W
Arco de Baúlhe 34 41.29 N 7.58 W
Arcola, Sask., Can. 184 49.37 N 102.30 W
Arcola, It. 64 44.07 N 9.54 E
Arcola, Ill., U.S. 194 39.41 N 88.19 W
Arcola, Ind., U.S. 216 41.06 N 85.18 W
Arcola, Miss., U.S. 194 33.16 N 90.53 W
Arcola, Pa., U.S. 285 40.09 N 75.27 W
Arcola, Tex., U.S. 222 29.31 N 95.27 W
Arconate 266b 45.32 N 8.51 E
Arcore 266b 45.38 N 9.19 E
Arcos 255 20.17 S 45.32 W
Arcos, Cayos 232 20.12 N 91.58 W
Arcos de la Frontera 34 36.45 N 5.48 W
Arcot 122 12.54 N 79.20 E
Arcoverde 250 8.25 S 37.04 W
Arctic Bay 176 73.02 N 85.11 W
Arctic Ocean 16 85.00 N 170.00 E
Arctic Red 180 67.27 N 133.46 W
Arctic Red River 180 67.27 N 133.46 W
Arctic Village 180 68.08 N 145.19 W
Arctique, Océan Glacial → Arctic Ocean 16 85.00 N 170.00 E
Arcturus 154 17.47 S 31.20 E
Arcu Correboi, Passo 71 40.05 N 9.21 E
Arcueil 261 48.48 N 2.20 E
Arcy-sur-Cure 50 47.36 N 3.45 E
Ard, Loch 46 56.11 N 4.28 W
Arḍ, Ra's al- 128 29.21 N 48.05 E
Arda, Eur. 38 41.39 N 26.29 E
Arda, It. 64 45.02 N 10.02 E
Ardabīl 128 38.15 N 48.18 E
Ardagh 48 52.28 N 9.04 W
Ardahan 130 41.07 N 42.41 E
Ardakān, Īrān 128 30.16 N 52.01 E
Ardakān, Īrān 128 32.19 N 53.59 E
Ardal 128 31.59 N 50.39 E
Ardalanish, Rubh' 46 56.17 N 6.18 W
Årdalsfjorden 26 61.12 N 7.30 E
Årdalstangen 26 61.14 N 7.43 E
Ardanuç 130 41.08 N 42.04 E
Ardara, Eire 48 54.46 N 8.25 E
Árdara, It. 71 40.37 N 8.48 E
Ardara, Pa., U.S. 279b 40.22 N 79.44 W
Ardarroch 46 57.25 N 5.38 W
Ardasa 130 40.35 N 39.18 E
Ardatov, S.S.S.R. 80 54.51 N 46.13 E
Ardatov, S.S.S.R. 80 55.15 N 43.06 E
Ardbeg 46 55.39 N 6.05 W
Ardcharnich 46 57.51 N 5.05 W
Ardea 66 41.36 N 12.33 E
Ardèche 62 44.40 N 4.20 E
Ardèche 62 44.16 N 4.39 E
Ardee 48 53.52 N 6.33 W
Arden, Man., Can. 184 50.17 N 99.14 W
Arden, Calif., U.S. 226 38.36 N 121.23 W
Arden, Del., U.S. 208 39.48 N 75.29 W
Arden, Forest of 42 52.23 N 1.42 W
Arden, Mount 166 32.09 S 137.59 E
Ardenay-sur-Mérize 50 48.00 N 0.25 E
Arden Mines 279b 40.12 N 80.17 W
Ardennes 50 49.40 N 4.40 E
Ardennes 56 50.10 N 5.45 E
Ardennes, Canal des 50 49.26 N 4.02 E
Ardenno 58 46.10 N 9.39 E
Ardentinny 46 56.03 N 4.55 W
Ardenza 66 43.31 N 10.19 E
Arderin 48 53.02 N 7.40 W
Ardeşen 130 41.12 N 41.00 E
Ardestān 128 33.22 N 52.23 E
Ardey 263 51.28 N 7.43 E
Ardey 263 51.26 N 7.23 E
Ardeygebirge 263 51.25 N 7.20 E
Ardez 58 46.46 N 10.11 E
Ardfern 46 56.10 N 5.32 W
Ardglass 48 54.16 N 5.36 W
Ardgroom 48 51.42 N 9.52 W
Ardila 34 38.12 N 7.28 W
Ardill 184 49.53 N 105.49 W
Ardino 38 41.35 N 25.08 E
Ardlethan 166 34.21 S 146.54 E
Ardlui 46 56.18 N 4.43 W
Ardlussa 46 56.02 N 5.47 W
Ardmolich 46 56.49 N 5.41 W
Ardmore, Eire 48 51.57 N 7.43 W
Ardmore, Ala., U.S. 194 34.59 N 86.52 W
Ardmore, Ind., U.S. 216 41.42 N 86.19 W
Ardmore, Md., U.S. 284c 38.56 N 76.52 W
Ardmore, Okla., U.S. 196 34.10 N 97.08 W
Ardmore, Pa., U.S. 208 40.01 N 75.18 W
Ardmore Point, Scot., U.K. 46 55.42 N 6.01 W
Ardmore Point, Scot., U.K. 46 56.39 N 6.07 W
Ardnamurchan 46 56.43 N 6.00 W
Ardnamurchan, Point of 46 56.44 N 6.13 W
Ardnaree 48 54.06 N 9.08 W
Ardnave Point 46 55.44 N 6.20 W
Ardoch 166 27.26 S 144.08 E
Ardon, Schw. 58 46.13 N 7.15 E
Ardon, S.S.S.R. 84 43.12 N 44.18 E
Ardon 84 43.17 N 44.18 E
Ardooie 50 50.59 N 3.12 E
Ardore 68 38.11 N 16.10 E
Ardoux 50 47.42 N 1.35 E
Ardoz, Arroyo de 266a 40.26 N 3.27 W
Ardres 50 50.51 N 1.59 E
Ardres 50 49.18 N 3.40 E
Ardrishaig 46 56.01 N 5.27 W
Ardrossan, Austl. 168b 34.25 S 137.55 E
Ardrossan, Scot., U.K. 46 55.39 N 4.49 W
Ardsley, Eng., U.K. 44 53.32 N 1.28 W
Ardsley, N.Y., U.S. 276 41.01 N 73.51 W
Ardtalnaig 46 56.31 N 4.06 W
Arduan Island 140 19.55 N 30.22 E
Ardusson 50 48.30 N 3.32 E
Åre 26 63.24 N 13.04 E
Areado 256 21.21 S 46.09 W
Areal 256 22.14 S 43.07 W
Arèches 62 45.41 N 6.34 E
Arecibo 240m 18.28 N 66.43 W
Areco 258 33.56 S 59.16 W
Areeiro 266c 38.39 N 9.12 W
Arefjevo 86 57.01 N 90.40 E
Areguá 252 25.18 S 57.25 W
Areia, Bra. 250 6.58 S 35.42 W
Areia, Port. 266c 38.43 N 9.08 W
Areia, Ribeirão da 255 16.07 S 45.52 W
Areia Branca, Bra. 250 4.56 S 37.07 W
Areia Branca, Bra. 256 22.48 S 46.51 W
Areia Branca, Bra. 287a 22.44 S 43.25 W
Areias 256 22.35 S 44.42 W
Arekalong Peninsula 175b 7.40 N 134.38 E
Arena 68 38.34 N 16.13 E
Arena, Point 204 38.57 N 123.44 W
Arena, Punta 232 23.33 N 109.28 W
Arena de la Ventana, Punta 232 24.04 N 109.52 W
Arena Island 116 9.14 N 120.46 E
Arenal, C.R. 236 10.29 N 84.53 W
Arenal, P.R. 240m 17.59 N 66.19 W
Arenal, Laguna de 236 10.32 N 84.56 W
Arenal, Punta del 241r 10.03 N 61.56 W
Arenal, Volcán 236 10.28 N 84.44 W
Arenápolis 248 14.26 S 56.49 W
Arenas 266d 41.26 N 2.00 E
Arenas, Punta, Chile 248 21.39 S 70.10 W
Arenas, Punta, P.R. 240m 18.07 N 65.35 W
Arenas, Punta de 254 53.09 S 68.13 W
Arenas de San Pedro 34 40.12 N 5.05 W
Arenberg 56 50.22 N 7.39 E
Arendal 26 58.27 N 8.48 E
Arendonk 56 51.19 N 5.05 E
Arendsee 54 52.53 N 11.30 E
Arendsee 54 52.53 N 11.30 E
Arendtsville 208 39.55 N 77.18 W
Arenillas 246 3.33 S 80.04 W
Arennig Fawr 42 52.55 N 3.45 W
Arenosa Creek 196 28.52 N 96.44 W
Arenys de Mar 34 41.35 N 2.33 E
Arenzano 62 44.24 N 8.41 E
Arenzville 219 39.53 N 90.22 W
Areq, Sebkha Bou 34 35.10 N 2.45 W
Arequipa 248 16.24 S 71.33 W
Arequipa 248 16.00 S 72.15 W
Arequito 252 33.09 S 61.28 W
Arero 144 4.42 N 38.47 E
Arês, Bra. 250 6.11 S 35.09 W
Arès, Fr. 32 44.46 N 1.08 W
Arese 266b 45.33 N 9.05 E
Åresing 60 48.32 N 11.18 E
Åreskutan 26 63.26 N 13.06 E
Areuse 58 46.56 N 6.53 E
Arévalo 34 41.04 N 4.43 W
Arezzo 66 43.25 N 11.53 E
Arezzo 66 43.32 N 11.50 E
Arfa', Jabal 132 29.51 N 35.27 E
'Arfā', Wādī al- 132 30.16 N 36.34 E
Arga 34 42.18 N 1.47 W
Argada 88 54.14 N 110.41 E
Argadargada 166 21.40 S 136.40 E
Argajaš 86 55.29 N 60.52 E
Argamasilla de Alba 34 39.07 N 3.06 W
Arganda 34 40.18 N 3.26 W
Argao 116 9.52 N 123.36 E
Arga-Sala 74 68.30 N 112.12 E
Argedeb 144 6.10 N 41.10 E
Argegno 58 45.56 N 9.08 E
Argel → Alger 148 36.47 N 3.03 E
Argelès-Gazost 32 43.01 N 0.06 E
Argelès-sur-Mer 32 42.33 N 3.01 E
Argelia → Algeria 148 28.00 N 3.00 E
Argen 58 47.35 N 9.33 E
Argens 62 43.24 N 6.44 E
Argent 158 26.04 S 28.50 E
Argenta, It. 66 44.37 N 11.50 E
Argenta, Ill., U.S. 219 39.59 N 88.49 W
Argentan 32 48.45 N 0.01 W
Argentario, Monte 66 42.24 N 11.09 E
Argentat 32 45.06 N 1.56 E
Argentera 62 44.24 N 6.57 E
Argentera 62 44.10 N 7.18 E
Argenteuil 50 48.57 N 2.15 E
Argenteuil 206 45.45 N 74.30 W
Argentia 186 47.18 N 53.59 W
Argentiera 71 40.44 N 8.09 E
Argentière 58 45.59 N 6.56 E
Argentières 261 48.39 N 2.52 E
Argentina 244 34.00 S 64.00 W
Argentina 62 43.50 N 7.51 E
Argentine 216 42.47 N 83.51 W
Argentine → Argentina 244 34.00 S 64.00 W
Argentine Basin 18 45.00 S 45.00 W
Argentinien → Argentina 244 34.00 S 64.00 W
Argentino, Hipódromo 288 34.34 S 58.26 W
Argentino, Lago 254 50.13 S 72.25 W
Argentona 266d 41.33 N 2.24 E
Argentona, Riera 266d 41.31 N 2.26 E
Argenton-Château 32 46.59 N 0.27 W
Argenton-sur-Creuse 32 46.35 N 1.31 E
Argentré 32 48.05 N 0.39 W
Argent-sur-Sauldre 50 47.33 N 2.27 E
Argeș 38 45.00 N 24.45 E
Argeș 38 44.04 N 26.37 E
Arghandāb 128 31.27 N 64.23 E
Arghastān 120 31.23 N 65.45 E
Argirita 256 21.37 S 42.50 W
Argıthanı 130 38.17 N 31.43 E
Argo 140 19.31 N 30.25 E
Ārgoal 126 21.58 N 87.38 E
Argo Island 140 19.25 N 30.27 E
Argolikós Kólpos 38 37.33 N 22.45 E
Argolís 38 37.40 N 22.50 E
Argonia 198 37.16 N 97.46 W
Argonne 190 45.40 N 88.53 W
Argonne 56 49.30 N 5.00 E
Argonne National Laboratory 216 41.43 N 87.58 W
Árgos, Ellás 38 37.39 N 22.44 E
Argos, Ind., U.S. 216 41.14 N 86.15 W
Árgos Orestikón 38 40.28 N 21.16 E
Argostólion 38 38.10 N 20.30 E
Argoules 50 50.21 N 1.50 E
Argueil 50 49.32 N 1.31 E
Arguello, Point 204 34.35 N 120.39 W
Arguin, Cap d' 148 20.34 N 16.32 W
Argun 84 43.16 N 45.52 E
Argun 84 43.22 N 45.55 E
Argungu 150 12.45 N 4.31 E
Argunskij Chrebet 88 50.05 N 118.20 E
Ārgur 272b 22.48 N 88.13 E
Argut 86 49.51 N 87.03 E
Argut 86 50.16 N 86.43 E
Argyle, Minn., U.S. 198 48.20 N 96.49 W
Argyle, Mo., U.S. 219 38.18 N 92.02 W
Argyle, N.Y., U.S. 210 43.14 N 73.30 W
Argyle, Tex., U.S. 222 33.07 N 97.11 W

English	Deutsch	Español	Français	Português
River	Fluss	Río	Rivière	Rio
Canal	Kanal	Canal	Canal	Canal
Waterfall, Rapids	Wasserfall, Stromschnellen	Cascada, Rápidos	Chute d'eau, Rapides	Cascata, Rápidos
Strait	Meeresstrasse	Estrecho	Détroit	Estreito
Bay, Gulf	Bucht, Golf	Bahía, Golfo	Baie, Golfe	Baía, Golfo
Lake, Lakes	See, Seen	Lago, Lagos	Lac, Lacs	Lago, Lagos
Swamp	Sumpf	Pantano	Marais	Pântano
Ice Features, Glacier	Eis- und Gletscherformen	Accidentes Glaciales	Formes glaciaires	Acidentes Glaciares
Other Hydrographic Features	Andere Hydrographische Objekte	Otros Elementos Hidrográficos	Autres données hydrographiques	Outros Elementos Hidrográficos
Submarine Features	Untermeerische Objekte	Accidentes Submarinos	Formes de relief sous-marin	Acidentes Submarinos
Political Unit	Politische Einheit	Unidad Politica	Entité politique	Unidade Política
Cultural Institution	Kulturelle Institution	Institución Cultural	Institution culturelle	Instituição Cultural
Historical Site	Historische Stätte	Sitio Histórico	Site historique	Sitio Histórico
Recreational Site	Erholungs- und Ferienort	Sitio de Recreo	Centre de loisirs	Sítio de Lazer
Airport	Flughafen	Aeropuerto	Aéroport	Aeroporto
Military Installation	Militäranlage	Instalación Militar	Installation militaire	Instalação Militar
Miscellaneous	Verschiedenes	Misceláneo	Divers	Miscelânea

Name	Page	Lat.°′	Long.°′
'Arhāb, Wādī ∨	142	28.55 N	31.09 E
Arhrījit	150	18.24 N	9.15 W
Århus	41	56.09 N	10.13 E
Århus □[6]	41	56.15 N	10.05 E
Århus Bugt ⊂	41	56.09 N	10.18 E
Aria	172	38.33 S	174.59 E
Aria ≃	164	5.45 S	149.15 E
Ariadnoje	89	45.08 N	134.25 E
Ariah	126	23.33 N	86.20 E
Ariāl Khān ≃	126	23.56 N	90.46 E
Ariāl Khān ≃[1]	126	22.38 N	90.32 E
Ariamsvlei	156	28.08 S	19.50 E
Ariana	36	36.52 N	10.12 E
Ariano, Isola d' I	64	45.10 N	12.10 E
Ariano Irpino	68	41.09 N	15.05 E
Ariano nel Polesine	64	44.56 N	12.07 E
Ariari ≃	246	2.35 N	72.47 W
Arias	252	33.38 S	62.25 W
Arias, Arroyo de ≃	258	34.17 S	56.06 W
Arias, Cañada de ≃	258	34.39 S	58.59 W
Ariaú	250	3.11 S	57.14 W
Aribinda	150	14.14 N	0.52 W
Arica, Chile	248	18.29 S	70.20 W
Arica, Col.	246	2.08 S	71.47 W
Aricanduva, Ribeirão ≃	287b	23.32 S	46.33 W
Ariccia	66	41.43 N	12.40 E
Arichat	186	45.31 N	61.01 W
Arichuna	246	7.42 N	67.08 W
Arid, Cape ≻	162	34.00 S	123.09 E
Arida, Nig.	273a	6.34 N	3.16 E
Arida, Nihon	96	34.05 N	135.07 E
Aridal, Sebjet ⊜	148	26.12 N	14.05 W
Aridhaía	38	40.59 N	22.03 E
Ariège □[5]	32	43.00 N	1.30 E
Ariège ≃	32	43.31 N	1.25 E
Ariel	224	45.57 N	122.34 W
Arienzo	68	41.01 N	14.30 E
Arieș ≃	38	46.26 N	23.59 E
'Arif, Har Λ	132	30.26 N	34.44 E
Ārifwāla	123	30.17 N	73.04 E
Ariguanabo, Laguna de ⊜	286b	22.56 N	82.33 W
Ariguaní ≃	246	9.35 N	73.46 W
Arīḥā, Sūrīy.	130	35.48 N	35.36 E
Arīḥā, Urd.	132	31.25 N	35.47 E
Arīḥā (Jericho), Urd.	132	31.52 N	35.27 E
Arikaree ≃	198	40.01 N	101.56 W
Arikaree, North Fork ≃	198	39.39 N	102.57 W
Arikaree, South Fork ≃	198	39.39 N	102.57 W
Arikawa	92	32.59 N	129.07 E
Arild	41	56.16 N	12.34 E
Arima	241r	10.38 N	61.17 W
Arima ↞[8]	270	34.48 N	135.15 E
Arima ≃	270	34.52 N	135.15 E
Arima-fuji Λ[2]	270	34.55 N	135.14 E
Arimine-dam ↞[6]	94	36.29 N	137.27 E
Arinagour	46	56.37 N	6.31 W
Aringay	116	16.26 N	120.21 E
Arino ↞[8]	270	34.50 N	135.14 E
Arinos ≃	248	10.25 S	58.20 W
Arinthod	58	46.23 N	5.34 E
Ario de Rosales	234	19.12 N	101.43 W
Ariogala	76	55.16 N	23.30 E
Aripeka	220	28.26 N	82.40 W
Ariporo ≃	246	6.03 N	69.54 W
Aripuanã	248	9.10 S	60.38 W
Aripuanã ≃	248	5.07 S	60.24 W
Ariquemes	248	9.56 S	63.04 W
Arisa ≃	246	7.32 N	64.00 W
Arisaig	46	56.51 N	5.51 W
Arisaig, Sound of ⊂	46	56.51 N	5.51 W
'Arīsh, Wādī al- ∨	140	31.09 N	33.49 E
Arismendi	246	8.29 N	68.22 W
Arista, Méx.	234	22.39 N	100.50 W
Arista, Méx.	234	15.56 N	93.48 W
Aristazabal Island I	182	52.30 N	129.05 W
Aristes	210	40.49 N	76.20 W
Aristizábal, Cabo ≻	254	45.13 S	66.31 W
Aristovo	82	54.37 N	36.40 E
Aritao	116	16.18 N	121.02 E
Ariton	194	31.36 N	85.43 W
Aritzo	71	39.57 N	9.12 E
Arivonimamo	157b	19.01 S	47.15 E
Ariyalūr	122	11.08 N	79.05 E
Arizaro, Salar de ≚	252	24.42 S	67.45 W
Arizgoiti	34	43.01 N	2.24 W
Arizona	252	35.43 S	65.18 W
Arizona □[3]	178		
	200	34.00 N	112.00 W
Arizpe	232	30.20 N	110.10 W
Arja	80	57.31 N	45.59 E
Årjäng	26	59.23 N	12.08 E
Arjasa	112	6.51 S	115.16 E
Arjawinangun	115a	6.39 S	108.24 E
Arjeplog	24	66.00 N	17.58 E
Arjona, Col.	246	10.15 N	75.21 W
Arjona, Esp.	34	37.56 N	4.03 W
Arka	74	60.03 N	142.12 E
Arkadak	80	51.58 N	43.28 E
Arkadelphia	194	34.07 N	93.04 W
Arkaig, Loch ⊜	46	56.58 N	5.08 W
Arkalyk	86	50.13 N	66.50 E
Arkansas □[3]	178	34.50 N	93.40 W
Arkansas ≃	178	33.48 N	91.04 W
Arkansas, Salt Fork ≃	196	36.36 N	97.03 W
Arkansas City, Ark., U.S.	194	33.36 N	91.12 W
Arkansas City, Kans., U.S.	198	37.04 N	97.02 W
Arkansas Post National Memorial ⊥	194	33.55 N	91.26 W
Arken-Ahon Λ	146	20.05 N	18.25 E
Arkhangélos	38	36.12 N	28.08 E
Arkhangel'sk → Archangel'sk	24	64.34 N	40.32 E
Arki	123	31.09 N	76.58 E
Árki I	38	37.22 N	26.45 E
Arkit	85	41.47 N	71.58 E
Arklow	48	52.48 N	6.09 W
Arkona, Kap ≻	54	54.41 N	13.26 E
Arkonam	122	13.06 N	79.40 E
Arkösund	26	58.30 N	16.56 E
Arkport	210	42.24 N	77.42 W
Arktičeskij, Mys ≻	74	81.15 N	95.45 E
Arktičeskogo Instituta, Ostrova II	74	75.20 N	81.55 E
Arkul'	80	57.17 N	50.03 E
Arkville	210	42.09 N	74.37 W
Arkwright	207	41.43 N	71.33 W
Ärla	40	59.17 N	16.40 E
Arlan	80	55.58 N	54.15 E
Arlanc	62	45.25 N	3.44 E
Arlanda flygplats ⊠	40	59.37 N	17.55 E
Arlanza ≃	34	42.06 N	4.09 W
Arlanzón ≃	34	42.03 N	4.17 W
Arlbergpass)(	64	47.08 N	10.12 E
Arlberg-Tunnel ↞[5]	58	47.08 N	10.12 E
Arlee	202	47.10 N	114.05 W
Arles	62	43.40 N	4.38 E
Arles à Port de Bouc, Canal d ≅	62	43.40 N	4.37 E
Arlesheim	58	47.30 N	7.37 E
Arleta ↞[8]	280	34.15 N	118.26 W
Arleux	50	50.17 N	3.06 E
Arley	262	53.19 N	2.30 W
Arlington, S. Afr.	158	28.06 S	27.54 E
Arlington, Ga., U.S.	192	31.27 N	84.44 W
Arlington, Ind., U.S.	218	39.39 N	85.35 W
Arlington, Iowa, U.S.	190	42.45 N	91.40 W
Arlington, Kans., U.S.	198	37.54 N	98.11 W
Arlington, Ky., U.S.	194	36.47 N	89.01 W
Arlington, Mass., U.S.	207	42.25 N	71.09 W
Arlington, Minn., U.S.	190	44.36 N	94.05 W
Arlington, Nebr., U.S.	198	41.27 N	96.21 W
Arlington, N.Y., U.S.	210	41.42 N	73.54 W
Arlington, Ohio, U.S.	216	40.54 N	83.39 W
Arlington, Oreg., U.S.	202	45.16 N	120.13 W
Arlington, S. Dak., U.S.	198	44.22 N	97.08 W
Arlington, Tenn., U.S.	194	35.18 N	89.40 W
Arlington, Tex., U.S.	222	32.44 N	97.07 W
Arlington, Vt., U.S.	188	43.05 N	73.09 W
Arlington, Va., U.S.	208	38.52 N	77.05 W
Arlington, Wash., U.S.	224	48.12 N	122.08 W
Arlington □[6]	284c	38.50 N	77.10 W
Arlington, Lake ⊜[1]	222	32.42 N	97.13 W
Arlington Heights, Ill., U.S.	216	42.05 N	87.59 W
Arlington Heights, Mass., U.S.	283	42.25 N	71.11 W
Arlington Memorial Bridge ↞[5]	284c	38.53 N	77.03 W
Arlington Mill Reservoir ⊜[1]	283	42.48 N	71.13 W
Arlington National Cemetery ↞	284c	38.53 N	77.04 W
Arlington Park Race Track ♠	278	42.05 N	88.01 W
Arlod	58	46.06 N	5.49 E
Arlon	56	49.41 N	5.49 E
Arlöv	41	55.39 N	13.05 E
Arltunga	162	23.26 S	134.41 E
Arl'uk	86	55.26 N	84.50 E
Arluno	62	45.30 N	8.56 E
Arly	150	11.35 N	1.28 E
Arly ≃	62	45.40 N	6.23 E
Arly, Parc National d' ♠	150	11.35 N	1.15 E
Arlyn Oaks	276	40.40 N	73.27 W
Arm ≃	184	50.46 N	105.00 W
Arma	198	37.33 N	94.42 W
Armação, Ponta da ≻	287a	22.53 S	43.08 W
Armada	214	42.51 N	82.53 W
Armadale, Austl.	168a	32.09 S	116.00 E
Armadale, Ont., Can.	275b	43.50 N	79.15 W
Armadale, Scot., U.K.	46	55.54 N	3.42 W
Arma di Taggia	62	43.50 N	7.51 E
Armagh, N. Ire., U.K.	48	54.21 N	6.39 W
Armagh, Pa., U.S.	214	40.27 N	79.02 W
Armagnac □[9]	32	43.45 N	0.10 E
Armāh, Wādī ∨	144	18.15 N	51.00 E
Armainvilliers, Étang d' ⊜	261	48.45 N	2.44 E
Armainvilliers, Forêt d' ♠	261	48.45 N	2.45 E
Armance ≃	50	47.26 N	3.33 E
Armançon ≃, Fr.	50	47.57 N	3.30 E
Armançon ≃, Fr.	58	47.33 N	4.17 E
Arm'ansk	78	46.07 N	33.41 E
Arm'anskaja Sovetskaja Socialističeskaja Respublika □[3]	84	40.00 N	45.00 E
Armant	140	25.37 N	32.32 E
Armavir	72	45.00 N	41.08 E
Armazém	252	28.16 S	49.01 W
Armbrust	214	40.13 N	79.33 W
Armells Creek ≃	202	47.37 N	108.40 W
Armenia	246	4.31 N	75.41 W
Armenia □[9]	84	40.00 N	45.00 E
Armenian Soviet Socialist Republic → Arm'anskaja Sovetskaja Socialističeskaja Respublika □[3]	84	40.00 N	45.00 E
Armeniș	38	45.12 N	22.19 E
Armenistís	38	37.36 N	26.08 E
Armeno	62	45.49 N	8.26 E
Armenonville-les-Gâtineaux	261	48.33 N	1.39 E
Armentières	50	50.41 N	2.53 E
Armento	68	40.18 N	16.04 E
Armería	234	18.56 N	103.58 W
Armería ≃	234	18.52 N	103.59 W
Armero	246	4.58 N	74.54 W
Armidale	166	30.31 S	151.39 E
Armijo	200	35.03 N	106.41 W
Armil Island I	144	16.25 N	40.12 E
Armit Lake ⊜	176	64.10 N	91.32 W
Armizonskoje	86	55.57 N	67.42 E
Armona	226	36.19 N	119.42 W
Armonk	276	41.08 N	73.43 W
Armor	210	42.44 N	78.48 W
Armori	122	20.28 N	79.59 E
Armour	198	43.19 N	98.21 W
Armoy	58	46.21 N	6.31 E
Armstrong, Arg.	252	32.47 S	61.36 W
Armstrong, B.C., Can.	182	50.27 N	119.12 W
Armstrong, Ill., U.S.	216	40.18 N	87.53 W
Armstrong, Iowa, U.S.	198	43.24 N	94.29 W
Armstrong, Mo., U.S.	194	39.16 N	92.42 W
Armstrong □[6]	214	40.49 N	79.32 W
Armstrong ≃	164	16.46 S	131.12 E
Armstrong, Mount Λ	180	63.12 N	133.16 W
Armstrong Station	176	50.18 N	89.02 W
Armthorpe	44	53.32 N	1.03 W
Ārmūr	122	18.48 N	78.17 E
Armutlu	130	40.31 N	28.50 E
Arnå ≃	41	54.57 N	8.53 E
Arnaccio	66	43.40 N	10.17 E
Arnaía	38	40.29 N	23.35 E
Arnarfjördur ⊂[2]	24a	65.45 N	23.40 W
Arnäs	40	58.41 N	13.35 E
Arnaud ≃	176	59.59 N	69.46 W
Arnaudville	194	30.24 N	91.56 W
Arnay-le-Duc	58	47.08 N	4.29 E
Arnaz	62	45.38 N	7.43 E
Arnbach	60	48.20 N	11.21 E
Arnborg	41	56.01 N	8.59 E
Arnbruck	60	49.08 N	13.00 E
Arncliffe	274a	33.56 S	151.09 E
Arneburg	54	52.40 N	12.00 E
Arnedo	34	42.13 N	2.06 W
Arneiro dos Marinheiros	266c	38.51 N	9.25 W
Arneiroz	250	6.20 S	40.08 W
Arnejevo	82	54.58 N	37.35 E
Arnemuiden	52	51.30 N	3.41 E
Årnes	26	60.09 N	11.28 E
Arnett	196	36.08 N	99.46 W
Arney ≃	48	54.16 N	7.37 W
Arnhem	52	51.59 N	5.55 E
Arnhem, Cape ≻	164	12.21 S	136.21 E
Arnhem Bay ⊂	164	12.20 S	136.12 E
Arnhem Land ↞[1]	164	13.10 S	134.30 E
Arnhem Land Aboriginal Reserve ↞[4]	164	13.10 S	134.30 E
Arni	64	44.04 N	10.15 E
Arnis	41	54.38 N	9.56 E
Árnissa	38	40.48 N	21.50 E
Arno I[1]	14	7.05 N	171.41 E
Arno ≃	66	43.41 N	10.17 E
Arno Bay	166	33.54 S	136.34 E
Arnold, B.C., Can.	224	49.08 N	122.03 W
Arnold, Eng., U.K.	44	53.00 N	1.08 W
Arnold, Calif., U.S.	204	38.15 N	120.21 W
Arnold, Minn., U.S.	190	46.53 N	92.05 W
Arnold, Mo., U.S.	219	38.26 N	90.23 W
Arnold, Nebr., U.S.	198	41.26 N	100.12 W
Arnold, Pa., U.S.	214	40.35 N	79.45 W
Arnold Mills	283	41.59 N	71.24 W
Arnolds Park	198	43.22 N	95.08 W
Arnoldstein	64	46.33 N	13.43 E
Arnon ≃	50	48.16 N	0.38 E
Arnos Vale Airfield ⊠	241h	13.09 N	61.13 W
Arnot	210	41.40 N	77.07 W
Arnouville-lès-Gonesse	261	49.00 N	2.25 E
Arnouville-lès-Mantes	261	48.55 N	1.44 E
Arnoya ≃	34	42.15 N	8.09 W
Arnprior	212	45.26 N	76.21 W
Arnsberg, B.R.D.	56	51.24 N	8.03 E
Arnsberg, B.R.D.	60	48.56 N	11.23 E
Arnsberg □[5]	52	51.20 N	7.15 E
Arnsberger Wald, Naturpark ♠	56	51.25 N	8.20 E
Arnschwang	60	49.16 N	12.49 E
Arnsdorf	54	51.05 N	13.59 E
Arnstadt	54	50.50 N	10.57 E
Arnstein	56	49.58 N	9.58 E
Arnstorf	60	48.34 N	12.49 E
Arnum	41	55.15 N	8.59 E
Ærø I	41	55.15 N	9.45 E
Aro ≃	246	8.01 N	64.11 W
Aroa	246	10.26 N	68.54 W
Aroa ≃	246	10.40 N	68.19 W
Aroa, Pointe ≻	174s	17.28 S	149.46 W
Aroab	156	26.47 S	19.40 E
Aroali	126	24.03 N	87.56 E
Arochukwu	150	5.23 N	7.55 E
Aroeiras	250	7.31 S	35.41 W
Ar'ofino	80	58.16 N	39.15 E
Arolla	58	46.02 N	7.29 E
Arolsen	56	51.23 N	9.01 E
Aroma	140	15.49 N	36.08 E
Aroma Park	216	41.05 N	87.48 W
Aromas	226	36.53 N	121.39 W
Aromaševo	86	56.52 N	68.39 E
Aron ≃	50	47.15 N	2.02 E
Arona, It.	62	45.46 N	8.34 E
Arona, Pap. N. Gui.	164	6.20 S	146.00 E
Arona, Pa., U.S.	279b	40.16 N	79.39 W
Arongqi (Najitun)	89	48.07 N	123.28 E
Aroostook ≃	186	46.48 N	67.45 W
Aropuk Lake ⊜	180	61.12 N	163.50 W
Arorae I	14	2.38 S	176.49 E
Arorangi	174k	21.13 S	159.49 W
Aroroy	116	12.31 N	123.24 E
Arosa	58	46.47 N	9.41 E
Arosa, Ría de ⊂[1]	34	42.28 N	8.57 W
Arosbaya	115a	6.56 S	112.51 E
Årøsund	41	55.16 N	9.45 E
Arotali	144	15.02 N	39.43 E
Aro Usu, Tanjung ≻	164	8.20 S	130.45 E
Arowhana Λ	172	38.07 S	177.52 E
Arp	222	32.13 N	95.04 W
Arpa (Achur'an) ≃, As.	84	40.06 N	43.39 E
Arpa ≃, S.S.S.R.	84	39.28 N	44.57 E
Arpaçay	84	40.52 N	43.20 E
Arpačin	83	47.14 N	40.11 E
Arpaia	68	41.02 N	14.33 E
Arpajon	50	48.35 N	2.15 E
Ārpāra	126	23.23 N	89.23 E
Arpino	66	41.39 N	13.36 E
Arpoador, Ponta do ≻, Bra.	252	24.25 S	47.00 W
Arpoador, Ponta do ≻, Bra.	287a	22.59 S	43.12 W
Arquà Petrarca	64	45.16 N	11.43 E
Arquà Polesine	64	45.01 N	11.45 E
Arquata del Tronto	66	42.46 N	13.18 E
Arquata Scrivia	62	44.41 N	8.53 E
Arque	248	17.48 S	66.23 W
Arques	50	50.44 N	2.17 E
Arques-la-Bataille	50	49.53 N	1.08 E
Arra	150	6.40 N	3.58 W
Ar-Rabad	128	23.11 N	39.32 E
Ar-Rabbah	132	31.16 N	35.44 E
Ar-Rābi', Ash-Shallāl (Fourth Cataract) ᒪ	140	18.47 N	32.03 E
Arracourt	58	48.44 N	6.32 E
Ar-Radīsīyah Baḥrī	140	24.57 N	32.53 E
Ar-Rafīd	132	32.57 N	35.53 E
Arraga	252	28.04 S	64.14 W
Arrah	124	25.34 N	84.40 E
Ar-Rahad	140	12.43 N	30.39 E
Ar-Raḥāminah	142	31.18 N	31.45 E
Ar-Raḥmānīyah	142	31.06 N	30.38 E
Arraial do Cabo	255	22.58 S	42.01 W
Arraias	255	12.56 S	46.57 W
Arraias ≃, Bra.	250	11.10 S	53.35 W
Arraias ≃, Bra.	255	12.28 S	47.18 W
Ar-Ramādī	128	33.25 N	43.17 E
Ar-Ramādī □[4]	128	33.30 N	43.00 E
Ar-Ramthā	132	32.34 N	36.00 E
Arran, Island of I	46	55.36 N	5.15 W
Ar-Rank	140	11.45 N	32.48 E
Arran Lake ⊜	212	44.29 N	81.16 W
Ar-Raqqah	130	35.56 N	39.01 E
Ar-Raqqah □[8]	130	36.00 N	39.00 E
Arras	50	50.17 N	2.47 E
Arras, Nuraghe ⊥	71	39.40 N	9.25 E
Ar-Rāshidah	140	25.35 N	28.56 E
Ar-Rass	128	25.52 N	43.28 E
Ar-Rastān	130	34.55 N	36.44 E
Arrats ≃	32	44.06 N	0.52 E
Ar-Rawḍah, Ar. Sa.	128	26.05 N	40.37 E
Ar-Rawḍah, Miṣr	142	29.27 N	31.00 E
Ar-Rawḍah, Miṣr	142	27.48 N	30.52 E
Ar-Rawḍah, Yam. S.	144	14.28 N	47.17 E
Ar-Rāwuk	144	15.45 N	48.54 E
Ar-Rayramūn	142	27.45 N	30.52 E
Ar-Rayyāḥ ar-Minūfīya ≅	142	30.20 N	31.00 E
Ar-Rayyāḥ at-Tawfīqī ≅	142	30.11 N	31.07 E
Arrecife	148	28.57 N	13.32 W
Arrecifes	252	34.03 S	60.07 W
Arrée, Montagnes d' ΛΛ	32	48.26 N	3.55 W
Arregui, Laguna ⊜	258	35.05 S	57.33 W
Arrentela	266c	38.38 N	9.06 W
Arresø ⊜	41	55.58 N	12.08 E
Arrey	200	32.51 N	107.19 W
Arriaga	234	16.14 N	93.54 W
Arriba	198	39.17 N	103.17 W
Arrild	41	55.09 N	8.58 E
Ar-Rimāh	128	25.34 N	47.09 E
Ar-Riyāḍ (Riyadh)	128	24.38 N	46.43 E
Arrochar	46	56.12 N	4.44 W
Arroio Grande	252	32.14 S	53.05 W
Arrojado ≃	255	13.24 S	44.20 W
Arronches	34	39.07 N	7.17 W
Arrone ≃, It.	66	41.52 N	12.11 E
Arrone ≃, It.	66	42.18 N	11.38 E
Arros ≃	32	43.40 N	0.02 W
Arroscia ≃	62	44.03 N	8.11 E
Arroux ≃	32	46.29 N	3.58 E
Arrow ≃, Eng., U.K.	42	52.12 N	2.43 W
Arrow ≃, Eng., U.K.	42	52.09 N	1.53 W
Arrow, Lough ⊜	48	54.04 N	8.21 W
Arrow Creek ≃	202	47.43 N	109.50 W
Arrow Dam ↞[6]	182	49.20 N	117.49 W
Arrowhead, Lake ⊜[1]	228	34.15 N	117.11 W
Arrowhead Peak Λ	228	34.13 N	117.16 W
Arrowhead Village	208	40.04 N	74.07 W
Arrow Lake ⊜	190	48.08 N	90.18 W
Arrowrock Reservoir ⊜[1]	202	43.36 N	115.51 W
Arrowsmith	216	40.27 N	88.38 W
Arrowsmith, Mount Λ, Austl.	166	30.09 S	141.50 E
Arrowsmith, Mount Λ, N.Z.	172	43.21 S	170.59 E
Arrowsmith Bay ⊂	176	68.00 N	95.15 W
Arrowsmith Range ΛΛ	172	43.18 S	171.00 E
Arrowtown	172	44.56 S	168.50 E
Arrowwood	182	50.44 N	113.09 W
Arroyan, Arroyo ≃[1]	288	34.24 S	58.32 W
Arroyito	252	31.25 S	63.03 W
Arroyo	240m	17.58 N	66.04 W
Arroyo, Puerto ⊂	240m	17.58 N	66.05 W
Arroyo de la Luz	34	39.29 N	6.35 W
Arroyo Frío	234	17.26 N	100.35 W
Arroyo Grande, Calif., U.S.	204	35.07 N	120.34 W
Arroyo Grande → Ismael Cortinas, Ur.	258	33.58 S	57.06 W
Arroyo Hondo	200	36.32 N	105.40 W
Arroyo Naranjo ↞[8]	286b	23.02 N	82.23 W
Arroyo Seco Park ♠	280	34.06 N	118.12 W
Arroyos y Esteros	252	25.04 S	57.06 W
Arrozal	256	22.37 S	44.03 W
Ar-Ru'at	140	12.21 N	32.17 E
Ar-Rub' al-Khālī ↞[2]	136	20.00 N	51.00 E
Ar-Rubayqī	142	30.10 N	31.46 E
Ar-Ruḥaybah	132	33.45 N	36.42 E
Ar-Rukhaymīyah ⊤[4]	128	29.14 N	45.35 E
Ar-Rumaythah	128	31.32 N	45.12 E
Ar-Rummān	132	32.10 N	35.50 E
Ar-Ruqayyah ⊥	132	32.47 N	37.05 E
Ar-Ruṣāfah ⊥	130	35.37 N	38.45 E
Ar-Ruṣayriṣ	144	11.51 N	34.23 E
Ar-Rushaydah	132	32.40 N	36.50 E
Ar-Ruṭbah	128	33.02 N	40.17 E
Ar-Ru'ūs	142	29.21 N	31.04 E
Års	26	56.48 N	9.32 E
Arsacides, Cape ≻	175e	8.39 S	161.01 E
Aršan, S.S.S.R.	88	51.54 N	102.27 E
Aršan, S.S.S.R.	88	53.54 N	99.54 E
Aršan'-Zel'men'	80	47.36 N	44.36 E
Ārsāpota	272b	22.55 N	88.18 E
Arsbeck	56	51.08 N	6.12 E
Arsenal de Marinha ▪	266c	38.39 N	9.09 W
Arsenal Football Club ♠	260	51.33 N	0.06 W
Arsenault Lake ⊜	184	55.06 N	108.30 W
Arsenjān	128	29.56 N	53.18 E
Arsenjev	89	44.10 N	133.15 E
Arsenjevo	76	53.44 N	36.40 E
Arsiè	64	45.59 N	11.45 E
Arsiero	64	45.48 N	11.21 E
Arsikere	122	13.20 N	76.15 E
Arsin	130	40.58 N	39.56 E
Aršincevo	78	45.17 N	36.25 E
Arsıyan Dağı Λ	130	41.24 N	42.30 E
Arsk	80	56.06 N	49.54 E
Arslanbob	85	41.21 N	72.56 E
Årslev	41	55.18 N	10.29 E
Arsoli	66	42.02 N	13.01 E
Ars-on-Ré	32	46.12 N	1.31 W
Ársos	130	34.50 N	32.46 E
Ars-sur-Formans	58	45.59 N	4.49 E
Ars-sur-Moselle	56	49.05 N	6.04 E
Årsta havsbad	40	59.05 N	18.10 E
Arsufhsa ≃	84	39.08 N	46.50 E
Årsunda	40	60.32 N	16.44 E
Arsuz	130	36.27 N	35.51 E
Art, Île I	175f	19.43 S	163.38 E
Árta, Ellás	38	39.09 N	20.59 E
Artá, Esp.	34	39.42 N	3.21 E
Artarmon	274a	33.49 S	151.11 E
Artašat	84	39.59 N	44.33 E
Arta Terme	64	46.28 N	13.01 E
Arteaga	234	18.28 N	102.25 W
Arteche	116	12.17 N	125.22 E
Artegna	64	46.14 N	13.09 E
Artemare	62	45.52 N	5.42 E
Artemisa	240p	22.49 N	82.46 W
Artemón	38	36.59 N	24.43 E
Artémou	150	15.31 N	12.16 W
Artemovsk → Art'omovsk	83	48.35 N	38.00 E
Artèn	64	46.00 N	11.50 E
Artenay	50	48.05 N	1.53 E
Artern	54	51.22 N	11.17 E
Artesia → Mosomane, Bots.	156	24.04 S	26.15 E
Artesia, Calif., U.S.	280	33.52 N	118.05 W
Artesia, Miss., U.S.	194	33.25 N	88.39 W
Artesia, N. Mex., U.S.	196	32.51 N	104.24 W
Artesia Lake ⊜	226	38.57 N	119.22 W
Artesian	198	44.00 N	97.55 W
Arth, B.R.D.	60	48.35 N	12.04 E
Arth, Schw.	58	47.04 N	8.31 E
Arthabaska	206	46.02 N	71.55 W
Arthabaska □[6]	206	46.05 N	72.00 W
Arthal	123	33.16 N	76.11 E
Arthala	272a	28.40 N	77.24 E
Arthies	261	49.06 N	1.48 E
Arthonnay	50	47.56 N	4.13 E
Arthur, Ont., Can.	212	43.50 N	80.32 W
Arthur, Ill., U.S.	194	39.43 N	88.28 W
Arthur, Nebr., U.S.	198	41.35 N	101.41 W
Arthur, N. Dak., U.S.	198	47.06 N	97.13 W
Arthur, Tenn., U.S.	192	36.33 N	83.40 W
Arthur ≃	168a	33.31 S	116.50 E
Arthur, Lake ⊜[1]	214	40.57 N	80.05 W
Arthur Fiord ⊂[2]	176	76.33 N	93.11 W
Arthur Kill ⋓	276	40.30 N	74.15 W
Arthur's Pass	172	42.57 S	171.34 E
Arthur's Pass)(	172	42.54 S	171.34 E
Arthur's Pass National Park ♠	172	42.50 S	171.40 E
Arthurs Seat Λ[2]	169	38.21 S	144.57 E
Arthurs Town	238	24.38 N	75.42 W
Arthurton	168b	34.16 S	137.45 E
Arti	86	56.26 N	58.32 E
Artibonite ≃	238	19.15 N	72.47 W
Artico, Océano → Arctic Ocean ⊤[1]	16	85.00 N	170.00 E
Artigas	252	30.24 S	56.28 W
Artigas ↞[8]	286c	10.30 N	66.56 W
Artigas, Casa de ⊥	258	34.39 S	56.03 W
Artik	84	40.37 N	43.59 E
Artilleros	258	34.22 S	57.34 W
Artilleros, Punta ≻	258	34.28 S	57.32 W
Artillery Lake ⊜	176	63.09 N	107.52 W
Artlenburg	52	53.22 N	10.29 E
Artney, Glen ∨	46	56.20 N	4.04 W
Artois □[9]	50	50.30 N	2.30 E
Art'om	89	43.22 N	132.13 E
Art'om-Ostrov	84	40.28 N	50.20 E
Art'omovka, S.S.S.R.	78	49.46 N	35.04 E
Art'omovka, S.S.S.R.	83	48.29 N	37.23 E
Art'omovka, S.S.S.R.	83	47.53 N	38.38 E
Art'omovo	83	48.22 N	37.53 E
Art'omovsk, S.S.S.R.	83	48.27 N	38.42 E
Art'omovsk, S.S.S.R.	83	48.35 N	38.00 E
Art'omovsk, S.S.S.R.	86	54.21 N	93.26 E
Art'omovskij, S.S.S.R.	86	57.21 N	61.54 E
Art'omovskij, S.S.S.R.	88	58.12 N	114.45 E
Art'omovskij, S.S.S.R.	89	43.27 N	132.22 E
Artova	130	40.03 N	36.19 E
Artuby ≃	62	43.44 N	6.22 E
Artur de Paiva	152	14.28 S	16.20 E
Artur Nogueira	256	22.35 S	47.09 W
Arturo Seguí ↞[8]	258	34.51 S	58.09 W
Artvin	130	41.11 N	41.49 E
Artvin □[4]	130	41.05 N	42.00 E
Artybaš	86	51.48 N	87.16 E
Artyk	74	64.12 N	145.06 E
Aru, Kepulauan II	164	6.00 S	134.30 E
Aru, Tanjung ≻	112	2.10 S	116.34 E
Aru, Teluk ⊂	114	4.09 N	98.12 E
Arua	154	3.01 N	30.55 E
Aruã ≃	250	2.39 S	55.38 W
Aruanã	255	14.54 S	51.05 W
Aruângua (Luangwa) ≃	154	15.36 S	30.25 E
Aruba I	241s	12.30 N	69.58 W
Aru Basin ⊹[1]	14	5.30 S	133.30 E
Arufu	150	7.50 N	9.14 E
Arujá	256	23.24 S	46.20 W
Arujá □[7]	287b	23.24 S	46.20 W
Arumanduba	250	1.29 S	52.29 W
Arume	174m	26.36 N	128.07 E
Arume-wan ⊂	174m	26.35 N	128.08 E

ENGLISH

Name	Page	Lat.°′	Long.°′
Arumuganeri	122	8.34 N	78.07 E
Arun ≃, As.	124	26.49 N	87.09 E
Arun ≃, Eng., U.K.	42	50.48 N	0.33 W
Arunachal Pradesh □[8]	120	28.30 N	95.00 E
Arundel, Qué., Can.	206	45.58 N	74.37 W
Arundel, Eng., U.K.	42	50.51 N	0.34 W
Årup	41	55.23 N	10.04 E
Aru Passage ⋓	174r	6.57 N	158.20 E
Aruppukkottai	122	9.31 N	78.06 E
Arurandéua ≃	250	3.43 S	48.50 W
Arus, Tanjung ≻	112	1.20 N	120.48 E
Arusha	154	3.22 S	36.41 E
Arusha □[4]	154	4.00 S	36.15 E
Arusha Chini	154	3.35 S	37.20 E
Arusha National Park ♠	154	3.17 S	36.56 E
Arusi □[4]	144	8.00 N	39.40 E
Aruvi ≃	122	8.49 N	79.55 E
Aruwimi ≃	138	1.13 N	23.36 E
Arvada	200	39.50 N	105.05 W
Arvagh	48	53.55 N	7.34 W
Arvajcheer	90	46.15 N	102.45 E
Arve ≃	58	46.12 N	6.08 E
Arverne ↞[8]	276	40.35 N	73.48 W
Arves, Les Aiguilles d' Λ	62	45.08 N	6.21 E
Arvi	120	20.59 N	78.14 E
Arvida	186	48.25 N	71.11 W
Arvidsjaur	24	65.35 N	19.07 E
Arvier	62	45.42 N	7.11 E
Arvieux	62	44.46 N	6.44 E
Arvika	26	59.39 N	12.36 E
Arvillard	62	45.27 N	6.07 E
Arvin	228	35.12 N	118.50 W
Arvo, Lago ⊜	68	39.14 N	16.29 E
Arvonia	192	37.41 N	78.20 W
Arvorezinha	252	28.53 S	52.10 W
Arwadin	144	16.16 N	38.46 E
Arwal	124	25.15 N	84.41 E
Arwala	112	7.41 S	126.49 E
Aryamūn	142	31.11 N	30.54 E
Aryiroúpolis	267c	37.54 N	23.45 E
Arys → Orzysz, Pol.	30	53.49 N	21.56 E
Arys', S.S.S.R.	85	42.26 N	68.48 E
Arys, Ozero ⊜	86	45.50 N	66.20 E
Arzachena	71	41.05 N	9.23 E
Arzamas	80	55.23 N	43.50 E
Arzana	71	39.55 N	9.31 E
Arzano	68	40.55 N	14.16 E
Arzew	148	35.51 N	0.19 W
Arzew, Golfe d' ⊂	34	35.50 N	0.10 W
Arzew, Salines d' ⊜	34	35.40 N	0.15 W
Arzfeld	56	50.05 N	6.16 E
Arzignano	64	45.31 N	11.20 E
Arz Lubnān ↞[3]	130	34.14 N	36.03 E
Arzni	84	40.19 N	44.36 E
Arzo	164	2.56 S	140.47 E
Arzon ≃	62	45.11 N	3.54 E
Arzúa	34	42.56 N	8.09 W
As, Bel.	56	51.01 N	5.35 E
Aš, Česko.	54	50.10 N	12.10 E
Ås, Nor.	26	59.40 N	10.48 E
Asa, Nihon	96	34.33 N	132.26 E
Aša, S.S.S.R.	86	55.00 N	57.16 E
Asa ≃, Nihon	94	35.39 N	139.26 E
Asa ≃, Nihon	96	34.01 N	131.09 E
Asab	156	25.29 S	17.59 E
Asaba, Nig.	150	6.12 N	6.44 E
Asaba, Nihon	94	34.42 N	137.56 E
Asadābād, Afg.	120	34.52 N	71.09 E
Asadābād, Īrān	128	34.47 N	48.07 E
Asafo	150	6.11 N	0.28 W
Asagaya ↞[8]	268	35.42 N	139.38 E
Aşağıçığıl	130	38.03 N	31.52 E
Aşağı Dağ Λ	84	40.01 N	43.11 E
Aşağıhanik	130	37.43 N	39.59 E
Asağı İhtik	130	39.38 N	38.49 E
Asagı Kuluşağı	130	38.39 N	38.39 E
Aşağılahan	130	38.50 N	39.59 E
Aşağı Mestikân	130	38.25 N	38.46 E
Ašagy-G'ojn'uk	84	41.18 N	47.00 E
Asahan	114	2.23 N	102.33 E
Asahan ≃	114	3.02 N	99.52 E
Asahi, Nihon	94	36.57 N	137.34 E
Asahi, Nihon	94	36.07 N	137.52 E
Asahi, Nihon	94	35.12 N	137.02 E
Asahi, Nihon	94	36.05 N	137.21 E
Asahi, Nihon	94	35.59 N	136.07 E
Asahi, Nihon	94	35.02 N	136.40 E
Asahi, Nihon	94	35.43 N	140.39 E
Asahi, Nihon	94	36.14 N	140.31 E
Asahi, Nihon	94	35.14 N	137.22 E
Asahi, Nihon	96	34.59 N	133.50 E
Asahi, Nihon	96	34.17 N	131.28 E
Asahi, Nihon	96	34.51 N	132.16 E
Asahi ↞[8]	270	34.44 N	135.34 E
Asahi ≃	96	34.36 N	133.58 E
Asahi-chosuichi ⊜[1]	94	36.04 N	137.25 E
Asahi-dake Λ, Nihon	92a	43.40 N	142.51 E
Asahi-dake Λ, Nihon	94	37.14 N	139.21 E
Asahigawa → Asahikawa	92a	43.46 N	142.22 E
Asahi-gawa-daiichi-dam ↞[6]	96	34.53 N	133.22 E
Asahikawa	92a	43.46 N	142.22 E
Asahi-ko ⊜[1]	96	34.56 N	133.51 E
Ašt	85	40.41 N	70.20 E
Asaka	94	35.48 N	139.36 E
Asaka, Camp (United States) ▪	268	35.47 N	139.36 E
Asakanskij Golec, Gora Λ	88	50.18 N	109.55 E
Asakawa	94	37.05 N	140.25 E
Asake ≃	94	35.00 N	136.41 E
Asako	96	35.14 N	134.48 E
Asakura	96	33.23 N	130.44 E
Asālafpur ↞[8]	272a	28.38 N	77.05 E
Asale	144	14.22 N	40.32 E
Asale, Lake ⊜	144	14.19 N	40.18 E
Asamankese	150	5.52 N	0.42 W
Asama-yama Λ	94	36.24 N	138.31 E
Asambar Λ	123	36.29 N	73.38 E
Asanbani, Bhārat	126	22.43 N	86.20 E
Asanbāni, Bhārat	126	24.07 N	87.27 E
Asani	154	4.25 S	29.05 E
Asankrangwa	150	5.48 N	2.26 W
Asan-man ⊂	98	36.56 N	126.51 E
Asanovo	80	52.19 N	47.24 E
Asansol, Bhārat	126	23.41 N	86.59 E
Asansol, Bhārat	126	24.14 N	87.17 E
Ašap	86	57.07 N	56.30 E
Åsarna	26	62.39 N	14.21 E
Asarum	26	56.12 N	14.50 E
Asashina	94	36.16 N	138.25 E
Āsāsuni	126	22.32 N	89.10 E
Asati	272b	22.29 N	88.14 E
Asa-yama Λ	96	34.47 N	132.23 E
Asayita	144	11.33 N	41.30 E
Asbeck	263	51.21 N	7.18 E
Asberg	263	51.26 N	6.40 E
Asbesberge ΛΛ	158	28.55 S	23.15 E
Asbest	86	57.00 N	61.30 E
Asbestos	206	45.46 N	71.57 W
Asbe Teferi	144	9.02 N	40.58 E
Åsbro	40	59.00 N	15.03 E
Asbury	210	40.42 N	75.01 W
Asbury Park	208	40.13 N	74.01 W
Ascea	68	40.08 N	15.11 E
Ascensión, Méx.	232	31.06 N	107.59 W
Ascensión, Méx.	232	24.20 N	99.55 W
Ascension I	10	7.57 S	14.22 W
Ascensión, Bahía de la ⊂	232	19.40 N	87.30 W
Ascent	158	27.12 S	29.03 E
Aščerino	265b	55.36 N	37.46 E
Asch	58	47.57 N	10.49 E
Aschabad	128	37.57 N	58.23 E
Aschach an der Donau	61	48.22 N	14.02 E

DEUTSCH

Name	Seite	Breite°′	Länge°′ E=Ost
Aschaffenburg	56	49.59 N	9.09 E
Ascheberg, B.R.D.	52	51.47 N	7.37 E
Ascheberg, B.R.D.	54	54.08 N	10.20 E
Aschendorf	52	53.04 N	7.22 E
Aschersleben	54	51.45 N	11.27 E
Asciano	66	43.14 N	11.33 E
Aščikol', Ozero ⊜, S.S.S.R.	85	43.32 N	70.35 E
Aščikol', Ozero ⊜, S.S.S.R.	86	45.05 N	67.15 E
Aščiozek ≃	80	49.12 N	48.06 E
Aščitastysor, Ozero ⊜	86	49.19 N	63.59 E
Ascoli Piceno	66	42.51 N	13.34 E
Ascoli Piceno □[4]	66	43.01 N	13.34 E
Ascoli Satriano	68	41.12 N	15.34 E
Ascona	58	46.09 N	8.46 E
Ascope	248	7.43 S	79.07 W
Ascot, Austl.	171a	27.26 S	153.04 E
Ascot, Eng., U.K.	42	51.25 N	0.41 W
Ascot ≃	206	45.21 N	71.51 W
Ascotán	252	21.44 S	68.18 W
Ascros	62	43.55 N	7.01 E
Aseb	144	13.00 N	42.45 E
Åseda	26	57.10 N	15.20 E
Asekejevo	80	53.36 N	52.49 E
Asela	144	7.59 N	39.08 E
Åsele	26	64.10 N	17.20 E
Asem ≃	115a	6.14 S	107.42 E
Asembagus	115a	7.45 S	114.14 E
Asembourg	56	49.43 N	6.02 E
Åsen	26	63.36 N	11.03 E
Asendabo	144	9.50 N	37.33 E
Asendorf	52	52.46 N	9.00 E
Asenovgrad	38	42.01 N	24.52 E
Åsensbruk	26	58.48 N	12.25 E
Aseri	76	59.27 N	26.52 E
Aṣfar, Jabal al- Λ	132	32.12 N	36.54 E
Aṣfar al-Maḥaṭṭah	132	30.11 N	35.46 E
Aṣfūn al-Maṭā'inah	140	25.23 N	32.32 E
Åsgårdstrand	26	59.21 N	10.28 E
Ash, Eng., U.K.	42	51.15 N	0.44 W
Ash, Eng., U.K.	42	51.17 N	1.16 E
Ash ≃	42	51.48 N	0.02 W
Åshammar	40	60.39 N	16.32 E
Ashanti □[4]	150	6.45 N	1.30 W
'Asharah, Wādī al- ∨	142	30.21 N	32.15 E
Asharoken	276	40.56 N	73.22 W
Ashaway	207	41.25 N	71.47 W
Ashbourne, Eire	48	53.31 N	6.24 W
Ashbourne, Eng., U.K.	44	53.02 N	1.44 W
Ash Brook Swamp Reservation ♠	276	40.37 N	74.21 W
Ashburn, Ga., U.S.	192	31.43 N	83.39 W
Ashburn, Mo., U.S.	219	39.33 N	91.10 W
Ashburn, Va., U.S.	208	39.03 N	77.29 W
Ashburnham	207	42.38 N	71.55 W
Ashburton, Austl.	274b	37.52 S	145.05 E
Ashburton, N.Z.	172	43.55 S	171.45 E
Ashburton, Eng., U.K.	42	50.31 N	3.45 W
Ashburton ≃, Austl.	162	21.40 S	114.56 E
Ashburton ≃, N.Z.	172	44.04 S	171.48 E
Ashburton, North Branch ≃	172	43.54 S	171.44 E
Ashburton, South Branch ≃	172	43.44 S	171.32 E
Ashburton Downs	162	23.24 S	117.04 E
Ashby	207	42.41 N	71.49 W
Ashby, Lake ⊜	220	28.56 N	81.07 W
Ashby-de-la-Zouch	42	52.46 N	1.28 W
Ash Creek ≃, Calif., U.S.	204	41.05 N	121.08 W
Ash Creek ≃, Conn., U.S.	276	41.08 N	73.14 W
Ashcroft	182	50.43 N	121.17 W
Ashdod, Mass., U.S.	283	42.04 N	70.45 W
Ashdod, Yis.	132	31.49 N	34.40 E
Ashdod ⊥	132	31.45 N	34.40 E
Ashdot Ya'aqov	132	32.40 N	35.35 E
Ashdown	194	33.41 N	94.08 W
Ashdown Forest ↞[3]	42	51.04 N	0.03 E
Asheboro	192	35.42 N	79.49 W
Ashern	184	51.11 N	98.21 W
Asherton	196	28.27 N	99.46 W
Asheville	192	35.34 N	82.33 W
Ashewat	120	31.22 N	68.32 E
Asheweig ≃	176	54.17 N	87.12 W
Ashfield, Austl.	274a	33.53 S	151.08 E
Ashfield, Mass., U.S.	207	42.32 N	72.48 W
Ashford, Austl.	166	29.20 S	151.06 E
Ashford, Eng., U.K.	42	51.08 N	0.53 E
Ashford, Eng., U.K.	260	51.26 N	0.27 W
Ashford, Ala., U.S.	194	31.11 N	85.14 W
Ashford, Wash., U.S.	224	46.46 N	122.02 W
Ashford Airport ⊠	42	51.04 N	1.01 E
Ash Fork	200	35.13 N	112.29 W
Ash Grove	194	37.19 N	93.35 W
Ashhurst	172	40.18 S	175.45 E
Ashibe	92	33.48 N	129.46 E
Ashibetsu	92a	43.31 N	142.11 E
Ashida	96	34.31 N	133.16 E
Ashida ≃	96	34.26 N	133.25 E
Ashikaga	94	36.20 N	139.27 E
Ashikagga-gakkō ⊥	94	36.22 N	139.30 E
Ashimori	96	34.43 N	133.48 E
Ashingdon	260	51.36 N	0.42 E
Ashington	44	55.12 N	1.35 W
Ashino-ko ⊜	94	35.13 N	139.00 E
Ashio	94	36.38 N	139.27 E
Ashio-sanchi ΛΛ	94	36.35 N	139.30 E
Ashippun	216	43.14 N	88.31 W
Ashippun ≃	216	43.10 N	88.33 W
Ashitaka-yama Λ	94	35.12 N	138.49 E
Ashiya, Nihon	96	34.43 N	135.17 E
Ashiya, Nihon	96	33.53 N	130.40 E
Ashiya ≃	270	34.43 N	135.18 E
Ashiyasu	94	35.38 N	138.23 E
Ashiyoro	92a	43.15 N	143.30 E
Ashizuri-kokutei-kōen ♠	96	33.07 N	132.27 E
Ashizuri-zaki ≻	92	32.44 N	133.01 E
Ashkhabad → Aschabad	128	37.57 N	58.23 E
Ashkum	216	40.53 N	87.57 W
Ashland, Ala., U.S.	194	33.16 N	85.50 W
Ashland, Calif., U.S.	226	37.42 N	122.07 W
Ashland, Ill., U.S.	219	39.53 N	90.01 W
Ashland, Kans., U.S.	198	37.11 N	99.46 W
Ashland, Ky., U.S.	188	38.28 N	82.38 W
Ashland, Maine, U.S.	186	46.38 N	68.24 W
Ashland, Mass., U.S.	207	42.16 N	71.28 W
Ashland, Miss., U.S.	194	34.50 N	89.11 W
Ashland, Mo., U.S.	219	38.47 N	92.16 W
Ashland, Mont., U.S.	202	45.35 N	106.16 W
Ashland, Nebr., U.S.	198	41.03 N	96.22 W
Ashland, N.H., U.S.	188	43.42 N	71.38 W
Ashland, N.Y., U.S.	210	42.18 N	74.20 W
Ashland, Ohio, U.S.	214	40.52 N	82.19 W
Ashland, Oreg., U.S.	202	42.12 N	122.42 W
Ashland, Pa., U.S.	210	40.47 N	76.21 W
Ashland, Va., U.S.	208	37.45 N	77.29 W
Ashland, Wis., U.S.	190	46.35 N	90.53 W
Ashland □[6]	214	40.52 N	82.19 W
Ashland, Mount Λ	202	42.05 N	122.43 W
Ashland City	194	36.16 N	87.04 W
Ashley, Austl.	166	29.19 S	149.49 E
Ashley, Eng., U.K.	262	53.21 N	2.20 W
Ashley, Ill., U.S.	219	38.20 N	89.11 W
Ashley, Ind., U.S.	216	41.32 N	85.04 W
Ashley, Mich., U.S.	190	43.11 N	84.29 W
Ashley, Mo., U.S.	219	39.15 N	91.14 W
Ashley, N. Dak., U.S.	198	46.02 N	99.22 W
Ashley, Ohio, U.S.	214	40.25 N	82.57 W
Ashley ≃	172	43.16 S	172.43 E
Ashley Creek ≃	200	40.21 N	109.22 W
Ashley Falls	207	42.03 N	73.20 W
Ashley Green	260	51.44 N	0.35 W
Ashmore	194	39.32 N	88.01 W
Ashmore Islands II	160	12.14 S	123.05 E

Symbols in the index entries represent the broad categories identified in the key at the right. Symbols with superior numbers (ΛΛ[2]) identify subcategories (see complete key on page *I · 30*).

Kartensymbole in dem Registerverzeichnis stellen die rechts in Schlüssel erklärten Kategorien dar. Symbole mit hochgestellten Ziffern (ΛΛ[2]) bezeichnen Unterabteilungen einer Kategorie (vgl. vollständiger Schlüssel auf Seite *I · 30*).

Los símbolos incluídos en el texto del índice representan las grandes categorías identificadas con la clave a la derecha. Los símbolos con numeros en su parte superior (ΛΛ[2]) identifican las subcategorías (véase la clave completa en la página *I · 30*).

Les symboles de l'index représentent les catégories indiquées dans la légende à droite. Les symboles suivis d'un indice (ΛΛ[2]) représentent des sous-catégories (voir légende complète à la page *I · 30*).

Os símbolos incluídos no texto do índice representam as grandes categorias identificadas com a chave à direita. Os símbolos com números em sua parte superior (ΛΛ[2]) identificam as subcategorias (veja-se a chave completa à página *I · 30*).

	English	Deutsch	Español	Français	Português
Λ	Mountain	Berg	Montaña	Montagne	Montanha
ΛΛ	Mountains	Berge	Montañas	Montagnes	Montanhas
)(	Pass	Pass	Paso	Col	Passo
∨	Valley, Canyon	Tal, Cañon	Valle, Cañón	Vallée, Canyon	Vale, Canhão
≚	Plain	Ebene	Llano	Plaine	Planície
≻	Cape	Kap	Cabo	Cap	Cabo
I	Island	Insel	Isla	Île	Ilha
II	Islands	Inseln	Islas	Îles	Ilhas
⊥	Other Topographic Features	Andere Topographische Objekte	Otros Elementos Topográficos	Autres données topographiques	Outros Elementos Topográficos

ESPAÑOL

Nombre	Página	Lat.°′	Long.°′ W=Oeste
Ashmūn	142	30.18 N	30.58 E
Ashmura	132	33.03 N	35.39 E
Ashokan Reservoir ⊚[1]	210	41.58 N	74.10 W
Ashoknagar	120	24.34 N	77.43 E
Ashqelon	132	31.40 N	34.35 E
Ashridge Park ♠	260	51.48 N	0.34 W
Ash-Shabakah	128	30.49 N	43.39 E
Ash-Shabb ⊤[4]	140	22.19 N	29.46 E
Ash-Shāgūr	132	31.50 N	35.39 E
Ash-Shā'ib ∧[2]	142	29.50 N	30.56 E
Ash-Shajarah	132	32.39 N	35.56 E
Ash-Shallūfah	142	30.07 N	32.34 E
Ash-Shamāl □[4]	130	34.30 N	36.00 E
Ash-Shamālīyah □[4]	140	19.00 N	30.00 E
Ash-Shanāwīyah	142	29.08 N	31.08 E
Ash-Shaqrā'	128	25.15 N	45.15 E
Ash-Sharāh ◆[1]	132	30.20 N	35.30 E
Ash-Shāriqah	128	25.22 N	55.23 E
Ash-Sharmah	128	28.01 N	35.18 E
Ash-Sharqāṭ	128	35.27 N	43.16 E
Ash-Sharqīyah □[4]	142	30.48 N	31.48 E
Ash-Sharqīyah ◆[1]	128	27.00 N	49.00 E
Ash-Sharqīyah, Aṣ-Ṣaḥrā' (Eastern Desert) ◆[2]	140	28.00 N	32.00 E
Ash-Shaṭrah	128	31.25 N	46.10 E
Ash-Shawāshinah	142	29.22 N	30.36 E
Ash-Shawbak	132	30.32 N	35.34 E
Ash-Shaykh Faḍl	142	28.29 N	30.50 E
Ash-Shaykh 'Ibādah	142	27.48 N	30.52 E
Ash-Shaykh Miskīn	132	32.49 N	36.09 E
Ash-Shaykh Sa'd	132	32.50 N	36.02 E
Ash-Shaykh Timay	142	27.53 N	30.51 E
Ash-Shiḥr	144	14.44 N	49.35 E
Ash-Shīn	142	31.01 N	30.53 E
Ash-Shināfīyah	128	31.35 N	44.39 E
Ash-Shīyāḥ	132	33.51 N	35.30 E
Ash-Shufayyah	128	23.50 N	39.08 E
Ash-Shuhadā'	142	30.36 N	30.54 E
Ash-Shuqayq	144	17.43 N	42.01 E
Ash-Shurayf	128	25.43 N	39.14 E
Ash-Shurayk	140	18.48 N	33.34 E
Ash-Shuwayfāt	132	33.49 N	35.31 E
Ash-Shuwayr	132	33.55 N	35.43 E
Ash Slough ≃	226	37.02 N	120.32 W
Ashta, Bhārat	122	16.57 N	74.24 E
Ashta, Bhārat	124	23.01 N	76.43 E
Ashtabula	214	41.52 N	80.48 W
Ashtabula □[6]	214	41.44 N	80.46 W
Ashtabula ≃	214	41.55 N	80.47 W
Ashtabula, East Branch ≃	214	41.48 N	80.37 W
Ashtabula, Lake ⊚[1]	198	47.11 N	97.58 W
Ashtabula, West Branch ≃	214	41.48 N	80.37 W
Ashtead	260	51.19 N	0.18 W
Ashton, S. Afr.	158	33.50 S	20.05 E
Ashton, Eng., U.K.	262	53.13 N	2.45 W
Ashton, Idaho, U.S.	202	44.04 N	111.27 W
Ashton, Ill., U.S.	190	41.52 N	89.13 W
Ashton, Iowa, U.S.	198	43.19 N	95.47 W
Ashton, Md., U.S.	208	39.09 N	77.00 W
Ashton, Nebr., U.S.	198	41.15 N	98.48 W
Ashton, R.I., U.S.	207	41.56 N	71.26 W
Ashton-in-Makerfield	262	53.29 N	2.39 W
Ashton-under-Lyne	262	53.29 N	2.06 W
Ashton upon Mersey	262	53.26 N	2.19 W
Ashuanipi Lake ⊚	176	52.35 N	66.10 W
Ashuelot ≃	188	42.46 N	72.29 W
Ashurst's Beacon ∧[2]	262	53.34 N	2.45 W
Ashville, Ala., U.S.	194	33.50 N	86.15 W
Ashville, N.Y., U.S.	214	42.06 N	79.23 W
Ashville, Ohio, U.S.	218	39.43 N	82.57 W
Ashville, Pa., U.S.	214	40.34 N	78.33 W
Ashwater	42	50.44 N	4.16 W
Ashwaubenon	190	44.29 N	88.03 W
Ashworth Moor Reservoir ⊚[1]	262	53.38 N	2.16 W
Asi (Nahr al-'Āṣī) ≃	130	36.02 N	35.58 E
Asia ⦁[1]	12	50.00 N	100.00 E
Asia, Kepulauan II	108	1.03 N	131.18 E
Asiago	64	45.52 N	11.30 E
Asia Menor → Asia Minor ◆[1]	22	39.00 N	32.00 E
Asia Minor ◆[1]	22	39.00 N	32.00 E
Asian Exhibition Area ♠	267d	35.47 N	51.24 E
Asid Gulf C	116	12.07 N	123.30 E
Asie → Asia ⦁[1]	12	50.00 N	100.00 E
Asie Mineure → Asia Minor ◆[1]	22	39.00 N	32.00 E
Asien → Asia ⦁[1]	12	50.00 N	100.00 E
Asiga Point ≻	174n	15.03 N	145.40 E
Asikuma	150	5.35 N	1.00 W
Asilah	148	35.32 N	6.00 W
Asilimiao	88	47.56 N	117.37 E
Asinara, Golfo dell' C	71	41.00 N	8.32 E
Asinara, Isola I	71	41.04 N	8.16 E
Asinaro ≃	70	36.53 N	15.08 E
Asino	86	57.00 N	86.09 E
Asipoquobah Lake ⊚	184	53.40 N	91.15 W
'Asīr ◆[1]	144	19.00 N	42.00 E
Asir, Ras (Cape Guardafui) ≻	144	11.48 N	51.22 E
Ašitkovo	82	55.26 N	38.36 E
Aska	120	19.36 N	84.39 E
Aşkale	130	39.55 N	40.42 E
Askanija-Nova	78	46.27 N	33.52 E
Askarovo	86	53.21 N	58.30 E
Askeaton	48	52.36 N	8.58 W
Asker	26	59.50 N	10.26 E
Askern	44	53.37 N	1.09 W
Askersund	40	58.53 N	14.54 E
Askham	158	26.59 S	20.47 E
Askim	26	59.35 N	11.10 E
Askino	86	56.05 N	56.34 E
Askira	146	10.39 N	12.55 E
Askival ∧	46	56.59 N	6.17 W
Askiz	86	53.08 N	90.32 E
Askja ∧[1]	24a	65.00 N	16.48 W
Askø I	41	54.54 N	11.30 E
Äsköping	40	59.09 N	16.04 E
Askov	41	55.28 N	9.06 E
Askraal	158	34.09 S	20.52 E
Askrigg	44	54.19 N	2.04 W
Askvoll	26	61.21 N	5.04 E
Aslanapa	130	39.13 N	29.52 E
Aslan-Sara	84	39.02 N	48.16 E
Åsljunga	41	56.19 N	13.22 E
Ašlyk	86	57.33 N	68.40 E
Asmaca	130	37.53 N	35.58 E
Āsmār	120	35.02 N	71.22 E
Asmara → Asmera	144	15.20 N	38.53 E
Asmera	144	15.20 N	38.53 E
Asmundtorp	41	55.53 N	12.56 E
Asnæs	41	55.49 N	11.31 E
Asnæs ≻[1]	41	55.40 N	11.00 E
Asnebumskit Hill ∧[2]	207	42.18 N	71.54 W
Åsnen ⊚	26	56.38 N	14.42 E
Asni	148	31.14 N	7.55 W
Asnières [-sur-Seine]	50	48.55 N	2.17 E
Asō, Nihon	94	35.59 N	140.29 E
Aso, Nihon	96	32.58 N	131.02 E
Aso ≃	66	43.06 N	13.51 E
Asoc	152	1.26 N	11.18 E
Aso-kokuritsu-kōen ♠	92	33.00 N	131.07 E
Asola	64	45.13 N	10.24 E
Asolo	64	45.48 N	11.54 E
Asomante	240m	18.23 N	66.36 W
Ason	273a	6.34 N	3.31 E
Asosa	144	10.03 N	34.32 E
Aso-san ∧	92	32.53 N	131.06 E
Asotin	202	46.20 N	117.03 W

FRANÇAIS

Nom	Page	Lat.°′	Long.°′ W=Ouest
Asouf Mellene, Oued ∨	148	25.51 N	1.33 E
Asowsches Meer → Azovskoje More ⊤[2]	78	46.00 N	36.00 E
Aspach	60	48.11 N	13.18 E
Aspach-le-Bas	58	47.46 N	7.09 E
Aspang Markt	61	47.33 N	16.06 E
Aspatria	44	54.46 N	3.20 W
Aspe	34	38.21 N	0.46 W
Aspeas	208	39.59 N	77.13 W
Aspen	200	39.11 N	106.49 W
Aspen Butte ∧	202	42.19 N	122.05 W
Aspendale	274b	38.02 S	145.07 E
Aspendus ⊥	130	37.08 N	31.12 E
Aspen Knolls	284c	39.05 N	77.05 W
Aspen Lake ⊚	202	42.18 N	122.00 W
Asperg	56	48.54 N	9.07 E
Aspermont	196	33.08 N	100.14 W
Aspern ◆[8]	264b	48.13 N	16.29 E
Aspern, Flugplatz ⊠	264b	48.13 N	16.30 E
Asperup	41	55.29 N	9.55 E
Aspid, Mount ∧	180	53.30 N	167.33 W
Aspindza	84	41.36 N	43.15 E
Aspinwall → Colón, Pan.	236	9.22 N	79.54 W
Aspinwall, Pa., U.S.	279b	40.30 N	79.55 W
Aspiring, Mount ∧	172	44.23 S	168.44 E
Aspö	40	59.29 N	17.02 E
Aspres-sur-Buëch	62	44.31 N	5.45 E
Aspromonte ⛰	68	38.10 N	15.55 E
Aspróπirgos	267c	38.04 N	23.35 E
Aspropótamos ≃	38	40.52 N	21.41 E
Aspull	262	53.34 N	2.35 W
Aspy Bay C	186	46.55 N	60.25 W
Asquins	50	47.29 N	3.45 E
Asquith, Austl.	274a	33.41 S	151.06 E
Asquith, Sask., Can.	184	52.08 N	107.13 W
Asralt Chajrchan ⛰	88	48.29 N	107.24 E
Asrāni	123	29.31 N	72.07 E
Assa	148	28.34 N	9.27 W
As-Sa'ata	140	13.37 N	29.59 E
Assab → Aseb	144	13.00 N	42.45 E
'Assâba ⛰[1]	150	16.00 N	12.00 W
Assabet ≃	283	42.28 N	71.21 W
As-Sabkhah	130	35.48 N	39.15 E
As-Sablūkah, Ash-Shallāl (Sixth Cataract) ⌞	140	16.20 N	32.42 E
Aṣ-Ṣabyā	144	17.09 N	42.37 E
Aṣ-Ṣadārah	144	14.30 N	48.04 E
As-Sa'dīyah	128	34.11 N	45.07 E
Aṣ-Ṣaff	140	29.34 N	31.17 E
Aṣ-Ṣāfī	132	31.02 N	35.28 E
As-Safīrah	130	36.04 N	37.22 E
Aṣ-Ṣāfiyah	140	15.31 N	30.07 E
Assag, Uad ∨	148	25.41 N	14.40 W
Assago	266b	45.24 N	9.08 E
Aṣ-Ṣaḥrā' al-Lībīyah (Libyan Desert) ◆[2]	136	24.00 N	25.00 E
Assai	255	23.22 S	50.49 W
Assaikwatamo ≃	184	56.52 N	95.50 W
Assal, Lac ⊚	144	11.41 N	42.25 E
'Assāl al-Ward	132	33.52 N	36.24 E
As-Salamīyah	130	35.01 N	37.03 E
As-Salīf	144	15.18 N	42.40 E
Aṣ-Ṣāliḥīyah	142	30.47 N	31.59 E
As-Salīmah	144	14.02 N	45.46 E
As-Sallūm	140	31.34 N	25.09 E
As-Salmān	128	30.30 N	44.32 E
As-Salṭ	132	32.03 N	35.44 E
Assam □[3]	120	26.00 N	92.00 E
As-Samāwah	128	31.18 N	45.17 E
As-Samū'	132	31.24 N	35.04 E
Assam Valley ∨	124	26.30 N	90.30 E
'Assān	130	36.05 N	37.14 E
Aṣ-Ṣanāfīn al-Qiblīyah	142	30.27 N	31.18 E
Aṣ-Ṣanamayn	132	33.05 N	36.10 E
As-Santah	142	30.45 N	31.08 E
Aṣ-Ṣaqlabīyah	130	35.22 N	36.23 E
Aṣ-Ṣarafand	132	33.27 N	35.18 E
Assaré	250	6.52 S	39.52 W
Aṣ-Ṣarīḥ	132	32.30 N	35.54 E
As-Sarīrīyah	142	28.20 N	30.45 E
Assateague Island I	208	38.05 N	75.10 W
Assawoman Bay C	208	38.25 N	75.05 W
Assawoman Canal ≅	208	38.31 N	75.04 W
Assawompset Pond ⊚	207	41.50 N	70.55 W
Asse	50	50.55 N	4.12 E
Asse ≃	62	43.53 N	5.53 E
Assean Lake ⊚	184	56.13 N	96.30 W
Assebroek	50	51.12 N	3.16 E
Assekaifaf	148	27.08 N	8.50 E
Assel	52	53.41 N	9.25 E
Asseln ◆[8]	263	51.32 N	7.35 E
Assembleia Nacional, Palacio da ♉	266c	38.43 N	9.09 W
Assemini	71	39.17 N	9.00 E
Assen	52	52.59 N	6.34 E
Assendelft	52	52.27 N	4.45 E
Assenede	50	51.14 N	3.45 E
Assens	41	55.16 N	9.55 E
Asserbo	41	56.01 N	12.01 E
Assergi	66	42.25 N	13.30 E
Asseria ⊥	36	44.02 N	15.39 E
Àssia	130	35.09 N	33.36 E
As-Sīb	128	23.41 N	58.11 E
As-Sidr	128	23.27 N	39.45 E
As-Sijn	132	32.47 N	36.28 E
As-Simākīyah	132	31.18 N	35.48 E
As-Sinbillāwayn	142	30.53 N	31.27 E
Assiniboia	184	49.38 N	105.59 W
Assiniboine ≃	184	49.53 N	97.08 W
Assiniboine, Mount ∧	182	50.52 N	115.39 W
Assiniboine Indian Reserve ◆[4]	184	50.21 N	103.28 W
Assinika ≃	184	52.37 N	96.10 W
Assinippi	283	42.09 N	70.51 W
Assis	255	22.40 S	50.25 W
Assiscunk Creek ≃	208	40.05 N	74.51 W
Assisi	66	43.04 N	12.37 E
Asslar	56	50.35 N	8.28 E
Assling	60	48.00 N	12.00 E
Assmannshausen	56	49.59 N	7.52 E
Asso	62	45.52 N	9.16 E
Assodé	150	18.26 N	8.28 E
Assomada	150a	15.06 N	23.41 W
Assonet	207	41.48 N	71.04 W
Assoro	70	37.37 N	14.25 E
As-Subū' ⊥	140	22.45 N	32.34 E
As-Sūdān → Sudan □[1]	140	15.00 N	30.00 E
As-Sufāl	144	14.06 N	48.42 E
Aṣ-Ṣufayyah	140	15.30 N	34.42 E
Aṣ-Ṣūfīyah	142	30.55 N	31.46 E
As-Sukhnah, Sūrīy.	130	34.52 N	38.52 E
As-Sukhnah, Urd.	132	32.08 N	36.04 E
As-Sulaymānīyah, Ar. Sa.	128	24.09 N	47.19 E
As-Sulaymānīyah, 'Irāq	128	35.33 N	45.26 E
As-Sulaymānīyah □[4]	128	35.40 N	45.30 E
As-Sulaymī	128	26.17 N	41.21 E
As-Sulayyil	144	20.27 N	45.34 E
As-Sulṭān	146	31.07 N	17.10 E
As-Sumayḥ	140	9.49 N	27.39 E
Aṣ-Ṣummān ◆[1]	128	25.00 N	47.00 E
As-Summāqīyāt	132	32.26 N	36.24 E
Assumption, Ill., U.S.	219	39.31 N	89.03 W
Assumption, Ohio, U.S.	216	41.40 N	83.54 W
Assumption Island I	138	9.45 S	46.30 E
Assunpink Creek ≃	285	40.13 N	74.46 W

PORTUGUÊS

Nome	Página	Lat.°′	Long.°′ W=Oeste
As-Sūrīyah → Syria □[1]	128	35.00 N	38.00 E
As-Su'ūdīyah	142	29.33 N	31.14 E
Aṣ-Ṣuwār	130	35.30 N	40.39 E
As-Suwaydā'	132	32.42 N	36.34 E
As-Suwaydā' □[8]	132	32.45 N	36.45 E
As-Suways (Suez)	142	29.58 N	32.33 E
As-Suways □[4]	142	29.59 N	32.33 E
Assynt, Loch ⊚	46	58.11 N	5.06 W
Asta, Cima d' ∧	64	46.10 N	11.36 E
Astachovo	83	47.52 N	39.37 E
Astaffort	32	44.04 N	0.40 E
Astakós	38	38.32 N	21.05 E
Āstāneh, Īrān	128	33.53 N	49.22 E
Āstāneh, Īrān	128	37.17 N	49.59 E
Āstārā, Īrān	128	38.26 N	48.52 E
Astara, S.S.S.R.	84	38.28 N	48.52 E
Aštarak	84	40.18 N	44.22 E
Astaškovo	82	55.32 N	38.38 E
Astatula	220	28.43 N	81.44 W
Asten	52	51.24 N	5.45 E
Asti	62	44.54 N	8.12 E
Asti □[4]	62	44.55 N	8.10 E
Astica	252	30.56 S	67.23 W
Astico ≃	64	45.37 N	11.37 E
Astillero	34	43.24 N	3.49 W
Astipálaia	38	36.30 N	26.30 E
Astipálaia I	38	36.35 N	26.25 E
Astley Bridge	262	53.36 N	2.26 W
Astley Green	262	53.29 N	2.27 W
Astley Hall ⊥	262	53.39 N	2.38 W
Astola Island I	120	25.07 N	63.51 E
Astolfo Dutra	256	21.19 S	42.52 W
Aston, Eng., U.K.	262	53.18 N	2.40 W
Aston, Pa., U.S.	285	39.52 N	75.27 W
Aston Clinton	42	51.48 N	0.44 W
Astor	123	35.22 N	74.51 E
Astor ≃	123	35.35 N	74.38 E
Astorga, Bra.	255	23.13 S	51.40 W
Astorga, Esp.	34	42.27 N	6.03 W
Astorga, Pil.	116	6.54 N	125.27 E
Astoria, Ill., U.S.	194	40.14 N	90.21 W
Astoria, Oreg., U.S.	224	46.11 N	123.50 W
Astoria ◆[8]	276	40.46 N	73.55 W
Astoria Column ⊥	224	46.11 N	123.50 W
Åstorp	41	56.08 N	12.57 E
Astove Island I	138	10.06 S	47.45 E
Astra	254	45.44 S	67.30 W
Astrachan'	80	46.21 N	48.03 E
Astrachan Bazar	84	39.14 N	48.31 E
Astrachanka	86	51.33 N	69.47 E
Astrachanskij	80	46.12 N	47.16 E
Astrachanskij Zapovednik ◆[4]	80	46.00 N	48.32 E
Astrakhan → Astrachan'	80	46.21 N	48.03 E
Astrodome ♠	222	29.41 N	95.25 W
Astrolabe, Cape ≻	175e	8.20 S	160.34 E
Astrolabe, Récifs de l' ✢[2]	175f	19.48 S	165.37 E
Astrolabe Bay C	164	5.20 S	145.50 E
Astudillo	34	42.12 N	4.18 W
Asturias	116	10.34 N	123.43 E
Asturias □[9]	34	43.20 N	6.00 W
Asubulak	86	49.31 N	83.03 E
Asuisui, Cape ≻	175a	13.47 S	172.29 W
Asuka	96	34.28 N	135.50 E
Asuke	94	35.08 N	137.19 E
Asunción	252	25.16 S	57.40 W
Asunción, Bahía C	232	27.06 N	114.11 W
Asunción, Cerro de la ∧	232	24.15 N	99.56 W
Asuncion Island I	108	19.40 N	145.24 E
Asunción Mita	236	14.20 N	89.43 W
Asunción Nochixtlán	234	17.28 N	97.14 W
Åsunden ⊚, Sve.	26	57.58 N	15.50 E
Åsunden ⊚, Sve.	26	57.44 N	13.22 E
Asunga, Wādī ∨	146	13.21 N	22.17 E
Asuni	71	39.52 N	8.56
Aşutka	130	39.09 N	38.37 E
Asuwa	94	36.01 N	136.16 E
Asuwa ≃	94	36.04 N	136.11 E
Aswa ≃	154	3.43 N	31.55 E
Aswān	140	24.05 N	32.53 E
Aswatthaberia	272b	22.26 N	88.32 E
Asyūṭ	142	27.11 N	31.11 E
Asyūṭ □[4]	142	27.20 N	30.50 E
Asyūṭī, Wādī al- ∨	142	27.11 N	31.16 E
Aszód	30	47.39 N	19.31 E
Ata I, Tonga	14	22.20 S	176.12 W
Ata I, Tonga	174w	21.03 S	175.00 W
Atabaj	85	43.30 N	68.20 E
Atabasca → Athabasca ≃	176	58.40 N	110.50 W
Atabasca, Lago → Athabasca, Lake ⊚	176	59.07 N	110.00 W
Atabey	130	37.57 N	30.39 E
Atacama □[4]	252	27.30 S	70.00 W
Atacama, Desierto de ◆[2]	18	24.30 S	69.15 W
Atacama, Puna de ⛰[1]	252	25.00 S	68.00 W
Atacama, Salar de ≋	252	23.30 S	68.15 W
Ataco	246	3.35 N	75.23 W
Atacora, Chaîne de l' ⛰	150	10.45 N	1.30 E
Atacuari ≃	246	3.47 S	70.44 W
Atagaj	88	55.06 N	99.23 E
Atago-san ∧	96	35.03 N	135.37 E
Atago-yama ∧	94	35.18 N	140.03 E
Ātāi ≃[1]	126	22.51 N	89.33 E
'Aṭā'iṭah, Jabal al- ∧	132	30.40 N	35.39 E
Atakakup Indian Reserve ◆[4]	184	53.24 N	106.55 W
Atakano-seki ⊥	94	36.24 N	136.25 E
Ataki	78	48.25 N	27.47 E
Atakora □[5]	150	10.00 N	1.35 E
Atakora, Réserve d' ◆[4]	150	11.30 N	2.10 E
Atakpamé	150	7.32 N	1.08 E
Atalaia, Bra.	250	9.31 S	36.02 W
Atalaia, Port.	266c	38.42 N	8.55 W
Atalándi	38	38.39 N	23.00 E
Atalanka	88	54.50 N	103.05 E
Atalaya, Arg.	258	35.02 S	57.32 W
Atalaya, Pan.	236	8.03 N	80.56 W
Atalaya, Perú	248	10.44 S	73.45 W
Atalaya, Cerro ∧, Chile	254	52.45 S	72.42 W
Atalaya, Cerro ∧, Perú	248	12.38 S	71.56 W
Atalaya, Punta ≻	258	35.01 S	57.31 W
Atamanovka	88	51.56 N	113.37 E
Atamanovo	86	56.24 N	93.36 E
Atambua	112	9.07 S	124.54 E
Atami	94	35.05 N	139.04 E
Atapupu	112	9.00 S	124.51 E
'Atāq	144	14.33 N	46.48 E
Atar	150	20.31 N	13.03 W
Ataram, Erg n' ◆[2]	148	23.46 N	1.44 E
Atarés, Castillo de ⊥	286b	23.08 N	82.21 W
Atāri	123	31.36 N	74.35 E
Atary	80	57.32 N	49.18 E
Atascadero	226	35.29 N	120.40 W
At'aševo	80	54.36 N	46.06 E
Atasu	86	48.42 N	71.38 E
Atatžurk Heykeli ⊥	267b	41.00 N	28.59 E
Ataur	272a	28.43 N	77.24 E
Atbara ('Aṭbarah) ≃	140	17.40 N	33.56 E
'Aṭbarah	140	17.42 N	33.59 E
'Aṭbarah (Atbara) ≃	140	17.40 N	33.56 E
Atbasar	86	51.48 N	68.20 E
Atbaši	85	41.10 N	75.48 E
Atchafalaya ≃	194	29.53 N	91.28 W
Atchafalaya Bay C	194	29.25 N	91.20 W
Atchison	198	39.34 N	95.07 W
Atco	208	39.46 N	74.53 W
Atebubu	150	7.45 N	0.59 W
Ateca	34	41.20 N	1.47 W
Atelchu ≃	255	12.05 S	53.46 W
Ateleta	66	41.51 N	14.12 E
Ateli	124	28.06 N	76.17 E
Atella	68	40.52 N	15.39 E
Atemajac de Brizuela	234	20.11 N	103.42 W
Atemajac del Valle	234	20.45 N	103.22 W
Atemar	80	54.11 N	45.24 E
Atemble	164	5.05 S	144.45 E
Atena Lucana	68	40.27 N	15.33 E
Atenango del Río	234	18.05 N	99.06 W
Atenas, C.R.	236	9.58 N	84.23 W
Atenas → Athínai, Ellás	38	37.58 N	23.43 E
Atencingo	234	18.30 N	98.36 W
Atenco □[7]	286a	19.34 N	99.00 W
Atengo ≃	234	21.50 N	104.43 W
Atenguillo	234	20.25 N	104.31 W
Atenguillo ≃	234	20.55 N	104.38 W
Atenquique	234	19.31 N	103.30 W
Atepcevo	82	55.20 N	36.46 E
Aterno ≃	66	42.11 N	13.51 E
Aterrado, Ribeirão do ≃	256	22.09 S	45.03 W
Atessa	66	42.04 N	14.27 E
Aṭfīḥ	142	29.24 N	31.15 E
Aṭfīḥī, Wādī al- ∨	142	29.23 N	31.16 E
Atghara	272b	22.37 N	88.27 E
Ātgharia	126	24.06 N	89.14 E
Atglen	208	39.57 N	75.58 W
Ath	50	50.38 N	3.47 E
Athabasca	182	54.43 N	113.17 W
Athabasca ≃	176	58.40 N	110.50 W
Athabasca, Lake ⊚	176	59.07 N	110.00 W
Athalmer	182	50.32 N	116.02 W
Athapapuskow Lake ⊚	184	54.33 N	101.40 W
Athārān Hazāri	123	31.11 N	72.06 E
Athboy	48	53.37 N	6.55 W
Athea	48	52.28 N	9.17 W
Athel, Oued el- ∨	148	25.09 N	9.53 W
Athen → Athínai	38	37.58 N	23.43 E
Athena	202	45.49 N	118.30 W
Athènes → Athínai	38	37.58 N	23.43 E
Athenry	48	53.18 N	8.45 W
Athens, Ont., Can.	212	44.38 N	75.57 W
Athens → Athínai, Ellás	38	37.58 N	23.43 E
Athens, Ala., U.S.	194	34.48 N	86.58 W
Athens, Ga., U.S.	192	33.57 N	83.23 W
Athens, Ill., U.S.	219	39.58 N	89.44 W
Athens, La., U.S.	194	32.39 N	93.01 W
Athens, Maine, U.S.	188	44.55 N	69.41 W
Athens, Mich., U.S.	216	42.05 N	85.14 W
Athens, N.Y., U.S.	210	42.16 N	73.49 W
Athens, Ohio, U.S.	188	39.20 N	82.06 W
Athens, Pa., U.S.	210	41.57 N	76.31 W
Athens, Tenn., U.S.	192	35.27 N	84.36 W
Athens, Tex., U.S.	222	32.12 N	95.51 W
Athens, W. Va., U.S.	192	37.25 N	81.01 W
Athens, Wis., U.S.	190	45.02 N	90.05 W
Athenstedt	54	51.56 N	10.55 E
Atherley	212	44.36 N	79.22 W
Atherstone	42	52.35 N	1.31 W
Atherton, Austl.	166	17.16 S	145.29 E
Atherton, Eng., U.K.	262	53.31 N	2.31 W
Atherton, Calif., U.S.	226	37.28 N	122.12 W
Athiaínou	130	35.04 N	33.32 E
Athiémé	150	6.35 N	1.40 E
Athies-sur-Laon	50	49.34 N	3.41 E
Athínai (Athens)	38		
	267c	37.58 N	23.43 E
Athinisin Panepistimion ♉[2]	267c	37.59 N	23.44 E
Äthiopien → Ethiopia □[1]	144	9.00 N	39.00 E
Athi River	154	1.27 S	36.59 E
Athis-Mons	261	48.43 N	2.24 E
Athleague	48	53.34 N	8.15 W
Athlone	48	53.25 N	7.56 W
Áth Luain → Athlone	48	53.25 N	7.56 W
Athni	122	16.44 N	75.04 E
Athok	110	17.12 N	95.05 E
Athol, N.Z.	172	45.31 S	168.35 E
Athol, Mass., U.S.	207	42.36 N	72.14 W
Athol Bay C	212	43.53 N	77.15 W
Athol Island I	240b	25.05 N	77.16 W
Atholl, Forest of ◆[3]	46	56.50 N	4.00 W
Athol Springs	210	42.46 N	78.52 W
Áthos ∧	38	40.09 N	24.19 E
Ath-Tha'lah	132	32.42 N	36.26 E
Ath-Thālith, Ash-Shallāl (Third Cataract) ⌞	140	19.49 N	30.19 E
Ath-Thamad	140	29.41 N	34.18 E
Ath-Thanīyah	132	31.10 N	35.43 E
Athus	56	49.34 N	5.50 E
Athy	48	53.00 N	7.00 W
Ati	146	13.13 N	18.20 E
Atiak	154	3.15 N	32.07 E
Atibaia	256	23.07 S	46.33 W
Atico	248	16.14 S	73.39 W
Aticonipi, Lac ⊚	186	51.52 N	59.22 W
Atienza	34	41.12 N	2.52 W
Atikokan	190	48.45 N	91.37 W
Atikonak Lake ⊚	176	52.40 N	64.30 W
Atil	200	30.50 N	111.35 W
Atimaono	174s	17.46 S	149.28 W
Atimonan	116	14.00 N	121.55 E
Atina	66	41.37 N	13.48 E
Atiquizaya	236	13.58 N	89.46 W
Atirāmpattinam	122	10.21 N	79.24 E
Atışalan	267b	41.03 N	28.52 E
Atışmektebi	267b	40.55 N	29.11 E
Atitlán, Lago de ⊚	236	14.42 N	91.12 W
Atitlán, Volcán ∧[1]	236	14.35 N	91.11 W
Atka, S.S.S.R.	74	60.50 N	151.48 E
Atka, Alaska, U.S.	180	52.12 N	174.12 W
Atka Island I	180	52.15 N	174.30 W
Atkaracalar	130	40.50 N	33.04 E
Atkarsk	80	51.52 N	45.00 E
Atkins	194	35.14 N	92.56 W
Atkinson, Ill., U.S.	190	41.25 N	90.01 W
Atkinson, Nebr., U.S.	198	42.32 N	98.59 W
Atkinson, N.H., U.S.	207	42.51 N	71.10 W
Atkinson, N.C., U.S.	192	34.28 N	78.06 W
Atkinson Island I	222	29.40 N	94.58 W
Atkinson Lake ⊚	184	55.59 N	94.48 W
Atkri	164	1.44 S	130.04 E
Atlacomulco de Fabela	234	19.48 N	99.53 W
Atlanta, Ga., U.S.	192	33.45 N	84.23 W
Atlanta, Ill., U.S.	194	40.16 N	89.14 W
Atlanta, Mich., U.S.	190	45.00 N	84.09 W
Atlanta, Mo., U.S.	194	39.54 N	92.29 W
Atlanta, N.Y., U.S.	210	42.33 N	77.28 W
Atlanta, Ohio, U.S.	218	39.34 N	83.11 W
Atlanta, Tex., U.S.	194	33.07 N	94.10 W
Atlantic, Iowa, U.S.	198	41.24 N	95.01 W
Atlantic, N.C., U.S.	192	34.54 N	76.20 W
Atlantic, Pa., U.S.	214	41.30 N	80.21 W
Atlantic, Va., U.S.	208	37.54 N	75.30 W
Atlantic □[6]	208	39.27 N	74.44 W
Atlantic Beach	276	40.35 N	73.44 W
Atlantic City	208	39.22 N	74.26 W
Atlantic Highlands	208	40.25 N	74.03 W
Atlantic-Indian Basin ✢[1]	9	60.00 S	15.00 E
Atlantic Indian Ridge ✢[3]	4	54.00 S	20.00 E
Atlántico □[5]	246	10.45 N	75.00 W
Atlántico, Océano → Atlantic Ocean ⊤[1]	8	0.00	25.00 W
Atlantic Ocean ⊤[1]	4		
	8	0.00	25.00 W
Atlantic Peak ∧	200	42.37 N	109.00 W
Atlántida	252	34.46 S	55.45 W
Atlántida □[5]	236	15.40 N	87.00 W
Atlantique	276	40.39 N	73.10 W
Atlantique □[5]	150	6.35 N	2.15 E
Atlantique, Océan → Atlantic Ocean ⊤[1]	8	0.00	25.00 W
Atlantischer Ozean → Atlantic Ocean ⊤[1]	8	0.00	25.00 W
Atlas, Mich., U.S.	216	42.56 N	83.32 W
Atlas, Pa., U.S.	208	40.48 N	76.26 W
Atlasburg	214	40.20 N	80.23 W
Atlas Mountains ⛰	148	33.00 N	2.00 W
Atlasova, Ostrov I	74	50.53 N	155.27 E
Atlas Saharien ⛰	148	33.25 N	1.20 E
Atlas Tellien ⛰	148	36.00 N	3.00 E
Atlin	180	59.35 N	133.42 W
Atlin Lake ⊚	180	59.20 N	133.45 W
'Atlit	132	32.41 N	34.56 E
Atlixco	234	18.54 N	98.26 W
Atmakūr	122	15.53 N	78.35 E
Atmanov Ugol	80	53.07 N	41.23 E
Atmis	80	53.28 N	43.57 E
Atmore	194	31.02 N	87.29 W
Ätna → Etna, Monte ∧[1]	70	37.46 N	14.55 E
Atna ≃	26	61.44 N	10.49 E
Atna Peak ∧	182	53.57 N	128.03 W
Atna Range ⛰	182	55.25 N	127.00 W
Atnis	86	58.48 N	69.38 E
Atnosen	26	61.44 N	10.49 E
Atō	96	34.24 N	131.43 E
Atocha	248	20.56 S	66.14 W
Atocongo	286d	12.08 S	76.56 W
Atocongo ⊥	286d	12.12 S	76.55 W
Atoka	196	34.23 N	96.08 W
Atomic Energy Commission Nevada Test Site ♉[3]	204	37.00 N	116.10 W
Atomic Energy Commission Oak Ridge Area ♉[3]	192	35.56 N	85.15 W
Atotonilco	234	23.35 N	104.20 W
Atotonilco, Cerro ⛰	196	26.08 N	104.43 W
Atotonilco, Lago de ⊚	234	20.22 N	103.39 W
Atotonilco de los Martínez	232	24.15 N	102.45 W
Atotonilco de Tula	234	20.00 N	99.13 W
Atotonilco el Alto	234	20.33 N	102.31 W
Atoui, Khatt (Uad Atui) ∨	148	20.30 N	15.35 W
Atoyac	234	20.01 N	103.32 W
Atoyac ≃, Méx.	234	16.30 N	97.31 W
Atoyac ≃, Méx.	234	18.10 N	98.31 W
Atoyac ≃, Méx.	234	17.05 N	100.29 W
Atoyac de Alvarez	234	17.12 N	100.26 W
Atpur	272b	22.50 N	88.23 E
Atrå	26	59.59 N	8.45 E
'Aṭrah, Jabal ∧	132	29.40 N	35.34 E
Atrai ≃	124	24.29 N	89.03 E
Atrak (Atrek) ≃	128	37.28 N	53.57 E
Ätran ≃	26	56.53 N	12.30 E
Atrato ≃	246	8.17 N	76.58 W
Atrauli	124	28.02 N	78.17 E
Atrek (Atrak) ≃	128	37.28 N	53.57 E
Atri	66	42.35 N	13.58 E
Atripalda	68	40.55 N	14.50 E
Atrisco	200	34.59 N	106.41 W
Atrop	263	51.24 N	6.43 E
Atsion Lake ⊚	285	39.44 N	74.44 W
Atsugi	94	35.27 N	139.22 E
Atsugi Naval Air Station (United States) ■	94	35.28 N	139.27 E
Atsumi, Nihon	92	38.37 N	139.35 E
Atsumi, Nihon	94	34.37 N	137.07 E
Atsumi-hantō ≻[1]	94	34.39 N	137.15 E
Atsumi-wan C	94	34.43 N	137.10 E
Atsuta	174m	26.17 N	127.49 E
Atta	272a	28.34 N	77.20 E
At-Tabbīn	142	29.47 N	31.18 E
Attaching	60	48.23 N	11.46 E
Aṭ-Ṭafīlah	132	30.50 N	35.36 E
At-Taḥrīr □[4]	142	30.40 N	30.15 E
Aṭ-Ṭā'if	144	21.16 N	40.24 E
Attainville	261	49.03 N	2.21 E
At-Tāj	146	24.13 N	23.18 E
Aṭ-Ṭalibīyah	273c	30.00 N	31.11 E
At-Tall	132	33.36 N	36.18 E
Attalla	194	34.01 N	86.05 W
At-Tall al-Kabīr	142	30.34 N	31.47 E
At-Tamīmī	146	32.20 N	23.04 E
Attapu	110	14.48 N	106.50 E
Attar, Oued el ∨	148	33.27 N	5.26 E
Aṭ-Ṭāsah ∧[2]	142	30.34 N	32.37 E
At-Taṭālīyah	142	27.20 N	30.50 E
Attáviros ∧, Ellás	38	36.12 N	27.52 E
Attawapiskat	176	52.55 N	82.26 W
Attawapiskat ≃	176	52.57 N	82.18 W
Attawapiskat Lake ⊚	176	52.18 N	87.54 W
Attawaugan	207	41.52 N	71.53 W
Aṭ-Ṭawd	142	30.47 N	30.37 E
Aṭ-Ṭawīl ⛰	128	29.20 N	39.35 E
Aṭ-Ṭayrīyah	142	30.39 N	30.46 E
Aṭ-Ṭayyibah, Miṣr	142	28.16 N	30.39 E
Aṭ-Ṭayyibah, Sūrīy.	132	32.48 N	36.46 E
Aṭ-Ṭayyibah, Sūrīy.	132	32.33 N	36.14 E
Aṭ-Ṭayyibah, Urd.	132	32.33 N	35.43 E
Attel	60	48.01 N	12.01 E
Attel ≃	64	48.01 N	12.11 E
Attendorn	56	51.07 N	7.54 E
Attenhausen	58	47.59 N	10.20 E
Attenkirchen	60	48.30 N	11.46 E
Atterberry	219	40.04 N	89.55 W
Attersee	64	47.55 N	13.33 E
Attersee ⊚	64	47.52 N	13.33 E
Attert ≃	56	49.52 N	6.05 E
Attica, Ind., U.S.	216	40.17 N	87.15 W
Attica, Kans., U.S.	198	37.15 N	98.13 W
Attica, N.Y., U.S.	210	42.52 N	78.17 W
Attica, Ohio, U.S.	214	41.04 N	82.53 W
Attichy	50	49.25 N	3.03 E
Attigliano	66	42.31 N	12.17 E
Attigny	56	49.29 N	4.35 E
Attikí ◆[1]	38	38.00 N	23.30 E
'Attīl	132	32.22 N	35.04 E
Attimis	64	46.11 N	13.16 E
Aṭ-Ṭīnah	142	31.03 N	32.18 E
Attingal	122	8.41 N	76.50 E
Attir	140	6.04 N	30.50 E
Attleboro	207	41.56 N	71.17 W
Attleborough	42	52.31 N	1.01 E
Attnang	60	48.01 N	13.43 E
Attock	123	33.54 N	72.15 E
Attow, Ben ∧	46	57.13 N	5.18 W
Attoyac Bayou ≃	194	31.29 N	94.18 W
Attu	181a	52.56 N	174.45 E
Attu Island I	181a	52.55 N	173.00 E
At-Tulaymāt ∧[2]	142	29.04 N	32.20 E
Aṭ-Ṭunayb	132	31.48 N	35.57 E
Āttūr, Bhārat	122	11.36 N	78.37 E
Aṭ-Ṭūr, Miṣr	140	28.14 N	33.37 E
Aṭ-Ṭurayf	128	31.44 N	38.33 E
Aṭ-Ṭuwayshah	140	12.21 N	26.32 E
Aṭ-Ṭuwayyah	128	27.36 N	41.13 E
Attymon	48	53.19 N	8.35 W
Atucatiquini ≃	248	7.44 S	67.57 W
Atucha	258	33.58 S	59.18 W
Atuel ≃	252	36.17 S	66.50 W
Atui, Uad (Khatt Atoui) ∨	148	2.03 N	15.35 W
Atuntaqui	246	0.20 N	78.13 W
Atuona	174x	9.48 S	139.02 W
At'urjevo	80	54.21 N	43.19 E
Atushi	85	39.42 N	75.48 E
Åtvidaberg	26	58.12 N	16.00 E
Atwater, Sask., Can.	184	50.47 N	102.10 W
Atwater, Calif., U.S.	226	37.21 N	120.36 W
Atwater, Ill., U.S.	219	39.20 N	89.44 W
Atwater, Minn., U.S.	198	45.08 N	94.47 W
Atwater, Ohio, U.S.	214	41.01 N	81.10 W
Atwood, Ont., Can.	212	43.40 N	81.01 W
Atwood, Calif., U.S.	280	33.52 N	117.50 W
Atwood, Ill., U.S.	194	39.48 N	88.28 W
Atwood, Ind., U.S.	216	41.16 N	85.59 W
Atwood, Kans., U.S.	198	39.48 N	101.03 W
Atwood, Tenn., U.S.	194	35.59 N	88.41 W
Atwood Lake ⊚[1]	214	40.33 N	81.13 W
Atzacán	234	18.54 N	97.05 W
Atzalpur	272a	28.43 N	77.21 E
Atzendorf	54	51.55 N	11.35 E
Atzgersdorf ◆[8]	264b	48.09 N	16.18 E
Au	58	47.19 N	9.59 E
Aua	174u	14.16 S	170.40 W
Auagrām	126	23.31 N	87.41 E
Auaiá-Miçu ≃	250	10.51 S	53.08 W
Aua Island I	164	1.27 S	143.04 E
Auak	174r	6.58 N	158.16 E
Auari ≃	246	3.33 N	63.48 W
Auasberge ⛰	156	22.45 S	17.22 E
Auau Channel Ц	229a	20.51 N	156.45 W
Aub, B.R.D.	56	49.33 N	10.04 E
Aub, Namibia	158	26.33 S	19.08 E
Aubagne	62	43.17 N	5.34 E
Aubange	56	49.35 N	5.48 E
Aube □[5]	50	48.15 N	4.05 E
Aube ≃	50	48.34 N	3.43 E
Aubenas	62	44.37 N	4.23 E
Aubenton	50	49.50 N	4.12 E
Aubepierre	261	48.38 N	2.53 E
Aubergenville	261	48.58 N	1.51 E
Auberive	58	47.47 N	5.03 E
Auberry	226	37.05 N	119.29 W
Aubervilliers	50	48.55 N	2.23 E
Aubetin ≃	50	48.49 N	3.01 E
Aubette ≃	261	49.00 N	1.54 E
Aubigny-en-Artois	50	50.21 N	2.35 E
Aubigny-sur-Nère	50	47.29 N	2.26 E
Aubin	32	44.32 N	2.14 E
Aubinadong ≃	190	46.51 N	83.22 W
Auboué	56	49.13 N	5.59 E
Aubrac ⛰	32	44.40 N	3.00 E
Aubrives	56	50.06 N	4.46 E
Aubry Lake ⊚	180	67.23 N	126.30 W
Auburn, Austl.	168b	34.01 S	138.41 E
Auburn, Austl.	274a	33.51 S	151.02 E
Auburn, Ala., U.S.	194	32.36 N	85.29 W
Auburn, Calif., U.S.	226	38.54 N	121.04 W
Auburn, Ill., U.S.	219	39.36 N	89.45 W
Auburn, Ind., U.S.	216	41.22 N	85.04 W
Auburn, Ky., U.S.	194	36.52 N	86.43 W
Auburn, Maine, U.S.	188	44.06 N	70.14 W
Auburn, Mass., U.S.	207	42.12 N	71.50 W
Auburn, Mich., U.S.	190	43.36 N	84.04 W
Auburn, Nebr., U.S.	198	40.23 N	95.51 W
Auburn, N.J., U.S.	285	39.43 N	75.22 W
Auburn, N.Y., U.S.	210	42.56 N	76.34 W
Auburn, Pa., U.S.	208	40.36 N	76.06 W
Auburn, Wash., U.S.	224	47.18 N	122.13 W
Auburn ≃	166	25.38 S	151.12 E
Auburndale, Fla., U.S.	220	28.04 N	81.48 W
Auburndale, Mass., U.S.	283	42.21 N	71.22 W
Auburn Heights	216	42.41 N	83.15 W
Auburn Range ⛰	166	25.10 S	150.30 E
Auburn Ravine ∨	226	38.51 N	121.31 W
Auburn Southeast	210	42.54 N	76.32 W
Aubusson	32	45.57 N	2.11 E
Auby-sur-Semois	56	49.49 N	5.10 E
Auca Mahuida	252	37.53 S	68.31 W
Aucará	248	14.15 S	74.05 W
Auce	76	56.28 N	22.53 E
Auch	32	43.39 N	0.35 E
Auchel	50	50.30 N	2.28 E
Auchenblae	46	56.54 N	2.26 W
Auchencairn	44	54.51 N	3.53 W
Auchi	150	7.02 N	6.14 E
Auchinleck	44	55.28 N	4.17 W
Auchterarder	46	56.18 N	3.43 W
Auchterderran	46	56.09 N	3.16 W
Auchtermuchty	46	56.17 N	3.15 W
Aucilla ≃	192	30.05 N	83.59 W
Auckland	172	36.52 S	174.46 E
Auckland Islands II	9	50.40 S	166.30 E
Auckland Park ◆[8]	273d	26.11 S	28.00 E
Auckland Park Race Course ♠	273d	26.11 S	28.00 E
Aude □[5]	32	43.05 N	2.30 E
Aude ≃	32	43.13 N	3.14 E
Audenge	32	44.41 N	1.31 W
Audenshaw	262	53.28 N	2.08 W
Audenshaw Reservoirs ⊚[1]	262	53.28 N	2.08 W
Auderghem	50	50.49 N	4.26 E
Audeux	58	47.16 N	5.53 E
Audierne	32	48.01 N	4.32 W
Audincourt	58	47.29 N	6.50 E
Audo Range ⛰	144	6.30 N	41.30 E
Audrain □[6]	219	39.12 N	91.50 W
Audresselles	50	50.49 N	1.36 E
Audruicq	50	50.53 N	2.05 E
Audubon, Iowa, U.S.	198	41.43 N	94.55 W
Audubon, N.J., U.S.	208	39.54 N	75.04 W
Audubon, Pa., U.S.	285	40.07 N	75.27 W
Audubon Park	218	38.12 N	85.43 W
Audun-le-Roman	56	49.22 N	5.53 E
Aue	54	50.35 N	12.42 E
Aue ≃	52	53.05 N	8.04 E
Auer → Ora	64	46.21 N	11.18 E
Auerbach, B.R.D.	60	48.48 N	13.06 E
Auerbach, D.D.R.	54	50.41 N	12.54 E
Auerbach, D.D.R.	54	50.30 N	12.23 E
Auerbach in der Oberpfalz	60	49.42 N	11.38 E
Auersberg ∧	54	50.27 N	12.39 E
Auerswalde	54	50.54 N	12.55 E
Auf dem Kreinberge	263	51.27 N	7.36 E
Auf dem Schnee ◆[8]	263	51.26 N	7.25 E
Auffargis	261	48.42 N	1.53 E
Auffay	50	49.43 N	1.06 E
Aufham	60	48.28 N	11.37 E
Aufsess	60	49.54 N	11.13 E
Augarten ♠	264b	48.14 N	16.23 E
Augathella	166	25.48 S	146.35 E
Augher	48	54.26 N	7.09 W
Aughnacloy	48	54.25 N	6.58 W
Aughrim	48	52.51 N	6.17 W
Aughton	262	53.32 N	2.56 W
Aughton Park	262	53.33 N	2.53 W
Aughty, Slieve ⛰	48	53.05 N	8.35 W
Aughwick Creek ≃	214	40.22 N	77.50 W
Auglaize □[6]	216	40.34 N	84.12 W
Auglaize ≃	188	41.17 N	84.21 W
Augrabies	158	28.37 S	20.20 E
Augrabies Falls National Park ♠	158	28.35 S	20.19 E
Augrabiesvalle ⌞	158	28.35 S	20.19 E
Au Gres	190	44.03 N	83.42 W
Au Gres ≃	190	44.02 N	83.40 W
Au Gres, East Branch ≃	190	44.05 N	83.41 W
Augsburg	58	48.23 N	10.53 E
Augusta, Austl.	162	34.19 S	115.10 E
Augusta, It.	70	37.13 N	15.13 E
Augusta, Ark., U.S.	194	35.17 N	91.22 W
Augusta, Ga., U.S.	192	33.29 N	81.57 W
Augusta, Ill., U.S.	194	40.14 N	90.57 W
Augusta, Kans., U.S.	198	37.41 N	96.58 W
Augusta, Ky., U.S.	218	38.46 N	84.00 W
Augusta, Maine, U.S.	188	44.19 N	69.47 W
Augusta, Mich., U.S.	216	42.20 N	85.21 W
Augusta, Mo., U.S.	219	38.34 N	90.53 W
Augusta, Mont., U.S.	202	47.30 N	112.24 W
Augusta, N.J., U.S.	210	41.08 N	74.44 W
Augusta, Ohio, U.S.	214	40.41 N	81.01 W
Augusta, Wis., U.S.	190	44.41 N	91.07 W
Augusta, Golfo di C	70	37.12 N	15.13 E

Symbol	English	Deutsch	Español	Français	Português
≃	River	Fluss	Río	Rivière	Rio
≅	Canal	Kanal	Canal	Canal	Canal
⌞	Waterfall, Rapids	Wasserfall, Stromschnellen	Cascada, Rápidos	Chute d'eau, Rapides	Cascata, Rápidos
Ц	Strait	Meeresstrasse	Estrecho	Détroit	Estreito
C	Bay, Gulf	Bucht, Golf	Bahía, Golfo	Baie, Golfe	Baía, Golfo
⊚	Lake, Lakes	See, Seen	Lago, Lagos	Lac, Lacs	Lago, Lagos
≋	Swamp	Sumpf	Pantano	Marais	Pântano
⌂	Ice Features, Glacier	Eis- und Gletscherformen	Accidentes Glaciales	Formes glaciaires	Acidentes Glaciares
⊤	Other Hydrographic Features	Andere Hydrographische Objekte	Otros Elementos Hidrográficos	Autres données hydrographiques	Outros Elementos Hidrográficos
✢	Submarine Features	Untermeerische Objekte	Accidentes Submarinos	Formes de relief sous-marin	Acidentes Submarinos
□	Political Unit	Politische Einheit	Unidad Politica	Entité politique	Unidade Política
♉	Cultural Institution	Kulturelle Institution	Institución Cultural	Institution culturelle	Instituição Cultural
⊥	Historical Site	Historische Stätte	Sitio Histórico	Site historique	Sitio Histórico
♠	Recreational Site	Erholungs- und Ferienort	Sitio de Recreo	Centre de loisirs	Sítio de Lazer
⊠	Airport	Flughafen	Aeropuerto	Aéroport	Aeroporto
■	Military Installation	Militäranlage	Instalación Militar	Installation militaire	Instalação Militar
◆	Miscellaneous	Verschiedenes	Misceláneo	Divers	Miscelânea

ENGLISH: Name · Page · Lat.°′ · Long.°′
DEUTSCH: Name · Seite · Breite°′ · Länge°′ E=Ost

Name	Page	Lat.°′	Long.°′
Augustdorf	52	51.53 N	8.43 E
Augustenborg	41	54.57 N	9.53 E
Augustine Island I	180	59.22 N	153.28 W
Augustines, Lac des ⊜	190	47.37 N	76.05 W
Augusto Cardoso	154	12.44 S	34.50 E
Augusto Severo	250	5.52 S	37.19 W
Augustów	30	53.51 N	22.59 E
Augustowski, Kanał ≅	76	53.54 N	23.26 E
Augustus, Mount ∧	162	24.20 S	116.50 E
Augustusburg	54	50.49 N	13.06 E
Augustus Downs	166	18.33 S	139.52 E
Au in der Hallertau	60	48.33 N	11.45 E
Aujon ≃	58	48.09 N	4.48 E
Auki	175e	8.46 S	160.42 E
Aulander	192	36.14 N	77.06 W
Aulanko	26	61.02 N	24.27 E
Auld, Lake ⊜	162	22.32 S	123.44 E
Auldearn	46	57.34 N	3.49 W
Aulendorf	58	47.57 N	9.38 E
Aulestad	26	61.13 N	10.17 E
Auletta	68	40.34 N	15.25 E
Aulís ⊥	38	38.27 N	23.35 E
Aulitivik Island I	176	69.32 N	67.50 W
Aulla	64	44.12 N	9.58 E
Aulnay	32	46.01 N	0.21 W
Aulnay-sous-Bois	50	48.57 N	2.31 E
Aulnay-sur-Mauldre	261	48.56 N	1.51 E
Aulne ≃	32	48.17 N	4.16 W
Aulneau Peninsula ≻[1]	184	49.23 N	94.29 W
Aulnois-sur-Seille	56	48.52 N	6.19 E
Aulnoye-Aymeries	50	50.12 N	3.50 E
Ault, Fr.	50	50.06 N	1.27 E
Ault, Ky., U.S.	218	38.12 N	83.14 W
Aultbea	46	57.50 N	5.35 W
Aultman	214	40.34 N	79.16 W
Aultshire	216	40.13 N	85.19 W
Auly	78	48.33 N	34.28 E
Auma	54	50.42 N	11.54 E
Aumale	50	49.46 N	1.45 E
Auma Point ≻	164	7.55 S	145.25 E
Aumar	174r	6.57 N	158.10 E
Aumetz	56	49.25 N	5.56 E
Aumont-Aubrac	32	44.43 N	3.17 E
Aumühle	52	53.31 N	10.19 E
Auna	150	10.12 N	4.45 E
Auneau	50	48.27 N	1.46 E
Auneuil	50	49.22 N	2.00 E
Auning	26	56.26 N	10.23 E
Aunkirchen	60	48.36 N	13.08 E
Auno	146	11.50 N	12.53 E
Auob ≃	156	26.25 S	20.35 E
Auponhia	112	1.56 S	125.29 E
Aups	62	43.37 N	6.14 E
Aura	26	60.36 N	22.34 E
Aurach	56	49.15 N	10.25 E
Aurach ≃	56	49.34 N	10.59 E
Aurachmat	85	41.34 N	70.07 E
Auraiya	124	26.28 N	79.31 E
Aurangābād, Bhārat	122	19.53 N	75.20 E
Aurangābād, Bhārat	124	24.45 N	84.22 E
Auray	32	47.40 N	2.59 W
Aurdal	26	60.56 N	9.24 E
Aure	26	63.16 N	8.32 E
Aure ≃	164	7.05 S	145.19 E
Aurelius	216	42.31 N	84.31 W
Aurès, Massif de l' ⋀	148	35.08 N	6.30 E
Auri, Kepulauan II	164	1.59 S	134.42 E
Aurich	52	53.28 N	7.29 E
Aurich □[6]	52	53.20 N	7.20 E
Auriesville Shrine ʊ[1]	210	42.54 N	74.19 W
Auriflama	255	20.41 S	50.34 W
Aurigny → Alderney I	43b	49.43 N	2.12 W
Aurilândia	255	16.44 S	50.28 W
Aurillac	32	44.56 N	2.26 E
Aurina, Valle ∨	64	47.00 N	12.00 E
Aurine, Alpi (Zillertaler Alpen) ⋀	64	47.00 N	11.55 E
Aurino ≃	64	46.48 N	11.55 E
Auriol	62	43.23 N	5.38 E
Aurisina	64	45.45 N	13.41 E
Aurizona	250	1.17 S	45.46 W
Aurlandsfjorden C[2]	26	61.05 N	7.02 E
Aurlandsvangen	26	60.54 N	7.11 E
Aurolzmünster	60	48.15 N	13.27 E
Auron	62	44.14 N	6.56 E
Auronzo di Cadore	64	46.33 N	12.26 E
Aurora, Bra.	250	6.57 S	38.58 W
Aurora, Bra.	287a	22.46 S	43.24 W
Aurora, Ont., Can.	212	44.00 N	79.28 W
Aurora, S. Afr.	158	32.42 S	18.29 E
Aurora, Alaska, U.S.	180	64.51 N	147.46 W
Aurora, Colo., U.S.	200	39.44 N	104.52 W
Aurora, Ill., U.S.	216	42.46 N	88.19 W
Aurora, Ind., U.S.	218	39.04 N	84.54 W
Aurora, Maine, U.S.	186	44.51 N	68.20 W
Aurora, Minn., U.S.	190	47.31 N	92.14 W
Aurora, Mo., U.S.	194	36.58 N	93.43 W
Aurora, Nebr., U.S.	198	40.52 N	98.00 W
Aurora, N.C., U.S.	192	35.18 N	76.47 W
Aurora, N.Y., U.S.	210	42.46 N	76.42 W
Aurora, Ohio, U.S.	214	41.19 N	81.21 W
Aurora, Oreg., U.S.	224	45.14 N	122.45 W
Aurora, Utah, U.S.	200	38.55 N	111.56 W
Aurora, W. Va., U.S.	188	39.19 N	79.33 W
Aurora do Norte	255	12.43 S	46.24 W
Aurora Pond ⊜	279a	41.20 N	81.23 W
Auroux	62	44.45 N	3.44 E
Aursunden ⊜	26	62.40 N	11.40 E
Aurukun Mission	164	13.19 S	141.45 E
Aurunci, Monti ⋀	66	41.22 N	13.40 E
Aus	156	26.40 S	16.15 E
Ausable ≃, Ont., Can.	190	43.19 N	81.46 W
Au Sable ≃, Mich., U.S.	190	44.25 N	83.20 W
Au Sable, North Branch ≃	190	44.40 N	84.23 W
Au Sable, South Branch ≃	190	44.40 N	84.23 W
Au Sable Forks	188	44.27 N	73.41 W
Au Sable Point ≻	190	44.20 N	83.20 W
Auschwitz → Oświęcim	30	50.03 N	19.12 E
Ausevik ⊥	26	61.32 N	5.16 E
Auskerry I	46	59.02 N	2.34 W
Ausoni, Monti ⋀	66	41.25 N	13.20 E
Ausserferrera	58	46.33 N	9.26 E
Ausserfragant	64	46.56 N	13.06 E
Aussig → Ústí nad Labem	54	50.40 N	14.02 E
Aussois	62	45.14 N	6.45 E
Aust-Agder □[6]	26	58.50 N	8.00 E
Austerlitz, Ned.	52	52.05 N	5.19 E
Austerlitz, N.Y., U.S.	210	42.19 N	73.28 W
Austerlitz ✦[5]	261	48.50 N	2.22 E
Austin, Bra.	287a	22.43 S	43.32 W
Austin, Man., Can.	184	49.57 N	98.56 W
Austin, Ind., U.S.	218	38.45 N	85.48 W
Austin, Minn., U.S.	190	43.40 N	92.59 W
Austin, Nev., U.S.	204	39.30 N	117.04 W
Austin, Pa., U.S.	214	41.38 N	78.05 W
Austin, Tex., U.S.	222	30.16 N	97.45 W
Austin □[6]	222	29.53 N	96.15 W
Austin ✦[8]	278	41.54 N	87.45 W
Austin, Lake ⊜	162	27.40 S	118.00 E
Austin, Lake ⊜[1]	222	30.19 N	97.46 W
Austin Bayou ≃	222	29.07 N	95.18 W
Austinburg	214	41.46 N	80.51 W
Austin Channel ⋃	176	75.35 N	103.25 W
Austin Lake ⊜	216	42.11 N	85.33 W
Austinmer	170	34.18 S	150.56 E
Austin's Post	158	29.32 S	25.49 E
Austintown	214	41.06 N	80.46 W
Austinville	192	36.51 N	80.55 W
Austnes	26	62.38 N	6.16 E
Austonio	222	31.11 N	95.38 W
Austonley	262	53.34 N	1.50 W
Australes, Îles II	14	23.00 S	150.00 W
Australia □[1]	160	25.00 S	135.00 E
Australia Mountain ∧	180	63.36 N	138.08 W
Australian-Antarctic Rise ⊹[3]	9	50.00 S	130.00 E
Australian Capital Territory □[8]	171b	35.30 S	149.00 E
Australian War Memorial ⊥	171b	35.17 S	149.09 E
Australia Plains	168b	34.06 S	139.09 E
Australie → Australia □[1]	160	25.00 S	135.00 E
Australien → Australia □[1]	160	25.00 S	135.00 E
Australind	168a	33.16 S	115.44 E
Austral Seamount Chain ⊹[3]	14	24.00 S	150.00 W
Austråt	26	63.43 N	9.45 E
Austria □[1]	22		
	30	47.20 N	13.20 E
Austvågøya I	24	68.20 N	14.36 E
Autazes	246	3.35 S	59.08 W
Auteuil, Fr.	50	49.21 N	2.05 E
Auteuil, Fr.	261	48.50 N	1.49 E
Auteuil, Lac d' ⊜	186	50.38 N	61.17 W
Autheuil	50	49.06 N	1.17 E
Authie ≃	50	50.21 N	1.38 E
Authon	62	44.14 N	6.08 E
Authon-du-Perche	50	48.12 N	0.55 E
Authon-la-Plaine	50	48.27 N	1.57 E
Autlán de Navarro	234	19.46 N	104.22 W
Autore, Monte ∧	66	41.58 N	13.12 E
Autoua	175f	16.21 S	167.45 E
Autrey-lès-Gray	58	47.29 N	5.30 E
Autriche → Austria □[1]	30	47.20 N	13.20 E
Autumn Hill	284b	39.16 N	76.48 W
Autun	32	46.57 N	4.18 E
Auve	56	49.02 N	4.42 E
Auvergne	164	15.41 S	130.01 E
Auvergne □[9]	32	45.25 N	2.30 E
Auvernaux	261	48.32 N	2.30 E
Auvers-sur-Oise	50	49.04 N	2.10 E
Auvézère ≃	32	45.12 N	0.51 E
Aux Barques, Pointe ≻	190	44.04 N	82.58 W
Aux Cayes → Les Cayes	238	18.12 N	73.45 W
Auxerre	50	47.48 N	3.34 E
Auxier	192	37.44 N	82.46 W
Auxi-le-Château	50	50.14 N	2.07 E
Auxon	50	48.06 N	3.55 E
Auxonne	58	47.12 N	5.23 E
Aux Sable Creek ≃	216	41.23 N	88.20 W
Auxvasse	219	39.01 N	91.54 W
Auxvasse Creek ≃	219	38.41 N	91.49 W
Auxy	58	46.57 N	4.24 E
Auyamita, Quebrada ≃	286c	10.30 N	66.46 W
Auyán Tepuy ∧	246	5.55 N	62.32 W
Auzances	32	46.02 N	2.30 E
Auzangate, Nevado ∧	248	13.48 S	71.14 W
Auzon ≃	62	44.02 N	4.54 E
Ava, Ill., U.S.	194	37.53 N	89.30 W
Ava, Mo., U.S.	194	36.57 N	92.40 W
Avadchara	84	43.31 N	40.39 E
Avaí	255	22.08 S	49.22 W
Avakubi	154	1.20 N	27.34 E
Aval'	85	40.19 N	71.50 E
Avala ⊥	38	44.45 N	20.35 E
Avaldsnes	26	59.21 N	5.16 E
Avallon	50	47.29 N	3.54 E
Avaloirs, Les ∧[2]	32	48.28 N	0.07 W
Avalon, Calif., U.S.	228	33.49 N	118.16 W
Avalon, N.J., U.S.	208	39.06 N	74.43 W
Avalon, Pa., U.S.	214	40.30 N	80.04 W
Avalon, Tex., U.S.	222	32.12 N	96.48 W
Avalon, Wis., U.S.	216	42.38 N	88.52 W
Avalon Peninsula ≻[1]	186	47.30 N	53.30 W
Avan ≃	42	51.35 N	3.48 W
Avana ≃	174k	21.14 S	159.43 W
Avanley	262	53.16 N	2.45 W
Avanos	130	38.43 N	34.51 E
Avant	196	36.29 N	96.04 W
Avarapa, Passe ⋃	174s	17.35 S	149.50 W
Avaray, Château d' ⊥	50	47.43 N	1.34 E
Avaré	255	23.05 S	48.55 W
Avarua	174k	21.12 S	159.46 W
Avarua Harbour C	174k	21.11 S	159.46 W
Avatanak Island I	180	54.03 N	165.19 W
Avatele	174v	19.06 S	169.55 W
Avatele Bay C	174v	19.05 S	169.56 W
Avatiu	174k	21.12 S	159.47 W
Avatiu Harbour C	174k	21.11 S	159.47 W
Avčala	84	41.48 N	44.48 E
'Avdat ⊥	132	30.48 N	34.46 E
Avdejevka	83	48.08 N	37.46 E
Avdotjino	83	47.55 N	37.51 E
Ave ≃	34	41.20 N	8.45 W
Avebury	42	51.27 N	1.51 W
Avebury Stone Circle ⊥	42	51.28 N	1.51 W
Avegadje ∧	150	7.14 N	0.38 E
Aveiro, Bra.	250	3.15 S	55.10 W
Aveiro, Port.	34	40.38 N	8.39 W
Aveiro, Ria de ≃[1]	34	40.38 N	8.44 W
Āvej	128	35.34 N	49.13 E
Avelar	256	22.20 S	43.25 W
Avelengo	64	46.38 N	11.13 E
Aveley	260	51.30 N	0.16 E
Avelgem	50	50.46 N	3.26 E
Avella, It.	68	40.58 N	14.36 E
Avella, Pa., U.S.	214	40.17 N	80.28 W
Avellaneda, Arg.	252	29.07 S	59.40 W
Avellaneda, Arg.	258	34.39 S	58.23 W
Avellaneda □[5]	288	34.40 S	58.20 W
Avellaneda, Estacion ✦[5]	288	34.41 S	58.22 W
Avelle, Île I	275a	45.24 N	74.00 W
Avellino	68	40.54 N	14.47 E
Avellino □[4], It.	68	40.57 N	15.00 E
Avellino □[4], It.	68	41.00 N	15.10 E
Avenal	226	36.00 N	120.08 W
Avenal Creek ≃	226	35.47 N	120.04 W
Aven Armand •[5]	32	44.15 N	3.22 E
Avenas	58	46.12 N	4.37 E
Avenches	58	46.53 N	7.02 E
Avenel	276	40.35 N	74.17 W
Aventureiro, Rio do ≃	256	21.52 S	42.39 W
Avenue	208	38.17 N	76.45 W
Avenwedde	52	51.55 N	8.27 E
Averbode	56	51.02 N	4.59 E
Averbode, Abbaye d' ʊ[1]	56	51.02 N	4.59 E
Averill Park	210	42.38 N	73.33 W
Avern ⊜	40	58.54 N	15.32 E
Avernakø I	41	55.01 N	10.17 E
Avernes	261	49.05 N	1.52 E
Avernes, Rû des ≃	261	49.04 N	2.51 E
Averøya I	26	63.01 N	7.34 E
Aversa	68	40.58 N	14.12 E
Avery, Calif., U.S.	226	38.13 N	120.22 W
Avery, Idaho, U.S.	202	47.15 N	115.49 W
Avery, Tex., U.S.	194	33.33 N	94.47 W
Avery Island	194	29.55 N	91.55 W
Avery Point ≻	212	44.40 N	79.07 W
Aves, Islas de II	246	12.00 N	67.30 W
Avesnelles	50	50.07 N	3.57 E
Avesnes	32	50.07 N	3.56 E
Avesnes-le-Comte	50	50.17 N	2.32 E
Avesnes-lès-Aubert	50	50.12 N	3.23 E
Avesnes-sur-Helpe	50	50.07 N	3.56 E
Avesta	40	60.09 N	16.12 E
Aveto ≃	62	44.42 N	9.23 E
Avetrana	68	40.21 N	17.43 E
Aveyron □[5]	32	44.15 N	2.40 E
Aveyron ≃	32	44.05 N	1.16 E
Avezzano	66	42.02 N	13.25 E
Avgustovka	80	52.16 N	50.44 E
Aviano	64	46.04 N	12.36 E
Avich, Loch ⊜	46	56.16 N	5.20 W
Aviemore	46	57.12 N	3.50 W
Avigliana	62	45.05 N	7.23 E
Avigliano	68	40.44 N	15.44 E
Avignon	62	43.57 N	4.49 E
Ávila	34	40.39 N	4.42 W
Avila, Parque Nacional el ♦	246	10.35 N	66.48 W
Ávila, Sierra de ⋀	34	40.35 N	5.08 W
Avila Beach	226	35.11 N	120.44 W
Avilés	34	43.33 N	5.55 W
Avilla	216	41.22 N	85.14 W
Avilley	58	47.26 N	6.16 E
Avinger	222	32.54 N	94.33 W
Avinurme	76	58.59 N	26.51 E
Avio	64	45.44 N	10.56 E
Avion	50	50.24 N	2.50 E
Avioth	56	49.34 N	5.24 E
Avis	210	41.11 N	77.19 W
Avisio ≃	64	46.07 N	11.05 E
Aviston	219	38.36 N	89.36 W
Aviz	34	39.03 N	7.53 W
Avize	50	48.58 N	4.01 E
Avlan Gölü ⊜	130	36.34 N	29.57 E
Avlum	41	56.16 N	8.48 E
Avnbøl	41	54.58 N	9.39 E
Avnik	130	39.50 N	41.59 E
Avoca, Austl.	169	37.05 S	143.28 E
Avoca, Iowa, U.S.	198	41.29 N	95.20 W
Avoca, N.Y., U.S.	210	42.25 N	77.25 W
Avoca, Pa., U.S.	210	41.20 N	75.45 W
Avoca ≃, Austl.	169	36.41 S	143.28 E
Avoca ≃, Eire	48	52.48 N	6.09 W
Avoca, Mount ∧	169	37.07 S	143.21 E
Avoca Beach	170	33.29 S	151.29 E
Avocado Heights	280	34.03 N	118.00 W
Avola, B.C., Can.	182	51.47 N	119.19 W
Avola, It.	70	36.54 N	15.08 E
Avon, Austl.	168b	34.17 S	138.20 E
Avon, Fr.	50	48.24 N	2.43 E
Avon, Conn., U.S.	207	41.49 N	72.50 W
Avon, Ill., U.S.	190	40.40 N	90.26 W
Avon, Mass., U.S.	207	42.08 N	71.02 W
Avon, Minn., U.S.	190	45.37 N	94.27 W
Avon, Mont., U.S.	202	46.36 N	112.36 W
Avon, N.C., U.S.	192	35.21 N	75.30 W
Avon, N.Y., U.S.	210	42.55 N	77.45 W
Avon, Ohio, U.S.	214	41.27 N	82.01 W
Avon, Pa., U.S.	208	40.22 N	76.23 W
Avon, S. Dak., U.S.	198	43.00 N	98.04 W
Avon □[6]	42	51.30 N	2.40 W
Avon ≃, Austl.	168a	31.40 S	116.07 E
Avon ≃, N.S., Can.	186	45.10 N	64.15 W
Avon ≃, Ont., Can.	212	43.18 N	81.11 W
Avon ≃, Eng., U.K.	42	50.43 N	1.46 W
Avon ≃, Eng., U.K.	42	52.25 N	1.31 W
Avon ≃, Eng., U.K.	42	51.59 N	2.10 W
Avon ≃, Eng., U.K.	42	50.17 N	3.52 W
Avon ≃, Eng., U.K.	42	51.30 N	2.43 W
Avon ≃, Scot., U.K.	46	56.00 N	3.40 W
Avon ≃, Scot., U.K.	46	57.25 N	3.23 W
Avon, Ben ∧	46	57.05 N	3.27 W
Avon, Rû d' ≃	261	48.39 N	2.46 E
Avon Basin C	279a	41.30 N	82.03 W
Avon by the Sea	208	40.12 N	74.01 W
Avondale, Ariz., U.S.	200	33.26 N	112.21 W
Avondale, Colo., U.S.	198	38.14 N	104.21 W
Avondale, Md., U.S.	284c	38.56 N	76.59 W
Avondale, Ohio, U.S.	214	40.53 N	81.26 W
Avondale, Zimb.	154	17.43 S	30.58 E
Avondale Heights	274b	37.46 S	144.51 E
Avon Downs	166	20.05 S	137.30 E
Avondrust	158	34.21 S	21.51 E
Avon Lake	214	41.30 N	82.01 W
Avonlea	184	50.00 N	105.04 W
Avonmore, Ont., Can.	206	45.10 N	74.58 W
Avonmore, Pa., U.S.	214	40.32 N	79.28 W
Avonmore ≃	48	52.50 N	6.13 W
Avonmouth	42	51.31 N	2.42 W
Avon Park	220	27.36 N	81.31 W
Avon Reservoir ⊜[1]	170	34.24 S	150.40 E
Avontuur	158	33.44 S	23.11 E
Avon Water ≃	46	55.47 N	4.01 W
Avoudrey	58	47.08 N	6.26 E
Avrainville	261	48.34 N	2.15 E
Avranches	32	48.41 N	1.22 W
Avranlo	84	41.39 N	43.52 E
Avre ≃, Fr.	50	48.47 N	1.22 E
Avre ≃, Fr.	50	49.53 N	2.20 E
Avrieux	62	45.13 N	6.43 E
Avrora ʊ	265a	59.57 N	30.21 E
Avroult	50	50.38 N	2.09 E
Avtatkujul ≃	180	64.06 N	178.10 E
Avtovo ✦[8]	265a	59.52 N	30.15 E
Avu Avu	175e	9.50 S	160.23 E
Awa, Nihon	96	34.04 N	134.12 E
Awa, Nihon	174m	26.36 N	127.56 E
Awaba	170	33.01 S	151.33 E
A'waj, Nahr al- ≃	132	33.20 N	36.34 E
Awaji	96	34.35 N	135.01 E
Awaji-shima I	96	34.21 N	134.51 E
Awakino	172	38.39 S	174.38 E
Awal Aw Ballou	144	1.29 N	43.02 E
Awal Edo	144	4.14 N	40.39 E
'Awālī	128	26.05 N	50.33 E
Awang	115b	8.54 S	116.24 E
Awano	94	36.31 N	139.41 E
Awanui	172	35.03 S	173.15 E
Awara, Nihon	94	36.13 N	136.12 E
Awara, Yai.	144	5.30 N	40.00 E
Awarawar, Tanjung ≻	115a	6.45 S	111.56 E
Aware	144	8.15 N	44.10 E
Awarua Point ≻	172	44.15 S	168.03 E
Awasa	144	6.45 N	38.15 E
Awasa, Lake ⊜	144	7.05 N	38.25 E
Awasan Bay C	116	9.56 N	125.36 E
Awash	144	8.59 N	40.10 E
Awash ≃	144	11.45 N	41.05 E
Awa-shima I, Nihon	92	38.27 N	139.14 E
Awa-shima I, Nihon	96	34.16 N	133.38 E
Awaso	150	6.14 N	2.16 W
Awatere ≃	172	41.37 S	174.10 E
Awbārī	146	26.35 N	12.46 E
Awbārī □[4]	146	25.30 N	13.00 E
Awdeyle	144	2.00 N	44.51 E
Awe	150	8.09 N	9.07 E
Awe, Loch ⊜	46	56.15 N	5.17 W
Awegyun	110	12.44 N	98.44 E
Awīn	267d	35.48 N	51.24 E
Awīsh al-Ḥajar	142	31.01 N	31.19 E
Awjilah	146	29.09 N	21.15 E
Awka	150	6.12 N	7.05 E
Awlād Mūsā	142	30.48 N	31.44 E
Aworo Kit	140	10.59 N	32.38 E
Aworro	164	7.45 S	143.10 E
Awosting	276	41.09 N	74.20 W
Awsīm	142	30.07 N	31.08 E
Awul	164	6.00 S	151.00 E
Awuna ≃	180	69.04 N	155.30 W
Axams	64	47.14 N	11.18 E
Axarfjördur C	24a	66.15 N	16.45 W
Axat	32	42.48 N	2.14 E
Axbridge	42	51.18 N	2.49 W
Axe ≃, Eng., U.K.	42	50.42 N	3.03 W
Axe ≃, Eng., U.K.	42	51.19 N	2.59 W
Axedale	169	36.47 S	144.30 E
Axe Edge ⋀[2]	262	53.14 N	1.57 W
Axel	52	51.16 N	3.55 E
Axel Heiberg Island I	16	80.30 N	92.00 W
Axim	150	4.52 N	2.14 W
Axinim	246	4.02 S	59.22 W
Axiós (Vardar) ≃	38	40.31 N	22.43 E
Axixá	250	2.51 S	44.04 W
Ax-les-Thermes	32	42.43 N	1.50 E
Axminster	42	50.47 N	3.00 W
Axmouth	42	50.42 N	3.02 W
Axochiapan	234	18.30 N	98.46 W
Axtell, Kans., U.S.	198	39.52 N	96.15 W
Axtell, Nebr., U.S.	198	40.29 N	99.08 W
Axtell, Tex., U.S.	222	31.39 N	96.58 W
Aÿ	50	49.03 N	4.00 E
Ayabaca	246	4.38 S	79.43 W
Ayabe	96	35.18 N	135.15 E
Ayacucho, Arg.	252	37.09 S	58.29 W
Ayacucho, Bol.	248	17.51 S	63.20 W
Ayacucho, Perú	248	13.07 S	74.13 W
Ayacucho □[5]	248	14.00 S	74.00 W
Ayamé	150	5.37 N	3.11 W
Ayamiken	152	2.07 N	10.01 E
Ayamonte	34	37.13 N	7.24 W
Āyān	272b	22.43 N	88.09 E
Ayancık	130	41.57 N	34.36 E
Ayangba	150	7.30 N	7.08 E
Ayapel	246	8.19 N	75.09 W
Ayarza, Laguna de ⊜	236	14.25 N	90.08 W
Ayas, It.	62	45.50 N	7.41 E
Ayaş, Tür.	130	40.01 N	32.21 E
Ayase	94	35.26 N	139.26 E
Ayase ≃	268	35.45 N	139.49 E
Ayauta	96	33.14 N	133.53 E
Ayaviri	248	14.52 S	70.35 W
Ayaviri ≃	248	15.01 S	70.22 W
Ayazağa	267b	41.06 N	28.59 E
Āybak	120	36.16 N	68.01 E
Ayden	192	35.25 N	77.20 W
Aydere	128	38.24 N	56.45 E
Aydın	130	37.51 N	27.51 E
Aydın □[4]	130	37.45 N	28.00 E
Aydıncık	130	36.08 N	33.19 E
Aydın Dağları ⋀	130	38.00 N	28.00 E
Aydos Dağı ∧	267b	40.56 N	29.15 E
Ayelu ∧	144	10.04 N	40.46 E
Ayémé	152	0.02 N	10.17 E
Ayer, Schw.	58	46.11 N	7.36 E
Ayer, Mass., U.S.	207	42.34 N	71.35 W
Ayer Baloi	114	1.35 N	103.20 E
Ayer Hitam, Malay.	114	1.55 N	103.11 E
Ayer Hitam, Malay.	114	2.56 N	102.24 E
Ayer Jerneh	114	4.24 N	103.24 E
Ayer Kuning Selatan	114	2.30 N	102.28 E
Ayer Merbau, Pulau I	271c	1.16 N	103.43 E
Ayers Cliff	206	45.10 N	72.03 W
Ayers Rock ∧	162	25.23 S	131.05 E
Ayersville	216	41.14 N	84.17 W
Ayía Marína	38	37.09 N	26.52 E
Ayía Paraskeví	38	39.15 N	26.16 E
Ayiássos	38	39.05 N	26.23 E
Ayía Varvára	267c	37.59 N	23.39 E
Aying	64	47.58 N	11.46 E
Ayınkâf	130	37.34 N	41.10 E
Áyioi Anáryiroi	267c	38.02 N	23.43 E
Áyion Óros ≻[1]	38	40.15 N	24.15 E
Áyios Dhimítrios	267c	37.56 N	23.44 E
Áyios Ioánnis Réndis	267c	37.58 N	23.40 E
Áyios Kírikos	38	37.37 N	26.14 E
Áyios Nikólaos	38	35.11 N	25.42 E
Ayíou Nikoláou, Moní ʊ[1]	267c	37.53 N	23.27 E
Ayíou Órous, Kólpos C	38	40.12 N	24.03 E
Aykota	144	15.12 N	37.05 E
Ayl	132	30.13 N	35.32 E
Aylesbury	42	51.50 N	0.50 W
Aylesford	260	51.18 N	0.29 E
Aylesham	42	51.13 N	1.13 E
Aylmer, Lake ⊜	206	45.50 N	71.22 W
Aylmer, Mount ∧	182	51.19 N	115.26 W
Aylmer, Passage ⋃	186	50.33 N	59.23 W
Aylmer East	188	45.24 N	75.51 W
Aylmer Lake ⊜	176	64.05 N	108.30 W
Aylmer West	212	42.46 N	80.59 W
Aylsham, Sask., Can.	184	53.11 N	103.49 W
Aylsham, Eng., U.K.	42	52.49 N	1.15 E
'Ayn, Jabal al- ∧[2]	132	30.49 N	34.26 E
'Ayn al-'Arab	130	36.54 N	38.21 E
'Ayn al-Ghazālah	146	32.10 N	23.20 E
'Ayn Dār	128	25.59 N	49.23 E
'Ayn Dīwār	130	37.17 N	42.11 E
Aynı	130	37.43 N	41.55 E
'Aynīn ⊤[4]	144	20.48 N	41.39 E
Aynor	192	34.00 N	79.12 W
'Aynūnah	128	28.05 N	35.08 E
Ayo	248	15.41 S	72.16 W
Ayo Ayo	248	17.05 S	68.00 W
Ayod	140	8.07 N	31.26 E
Ayodhya	124	26.48 N	82.12 E
Ayo el Chico	234	20.32 N	102.21 W
Ayom	140	7.52 N	28.23 E
Ayoquezco	234	16.41 N	96.50 W
Ayora	34	39.04 N	1.03 W
Ayorou	150	14.44 N	0.55 E
Ayos	152	3.54 N	12.31 E
Ayoulehaimiao	102	44.19 N	115.22 E
'Ayoûn el 'Atroûs	150	16.40 N	9.37 W
Ayr, Austl.	166	19.35 S	147.24 E
Ayr, Ont., Can.	212	43.17 N	80.27 W
Ayr, Scot., U.K.	44	55.28 N	4.38 W
Ayr ≃	44	55.29 N	4.28 W
'Ayrah	132	32.37 N	36.32 E
Ayrancı	130	37.22 N	33.42 E
Ayre, Point of ≻	44	54.26 N	4.22 W
Ayrolle, Étang de l' ⊜	32	43.05 N	3.03 E
Aysgarth	44	54.17 N	2.00 W
Aysha	144	10.46 N	42.37 E
'Aytā al-Fakhkhār	132	33.38 N	35.54 E
'Aytanīt	132	33.34 N	35.40 E
Ayton, Austl.	164	15.56 S	145.22 E
Ayton, Ont., Can.	212	44.03 N	80.56 W
Ayu, Kepulauan II	108	0.28 N	131.03 E
Ayun ≃	110	13.24 N	108.28 E
Ayuñgon	116	9.51 N	123.08 E
Ayuquila ≃	234	19.23 N	103.51 W
Ayutla	234	20.07 N	104.22 W
Ayutla [de los Libres]	234	16.54 N	99.13 W
Ayvacık, Tür.	130	41.00 N	36.39 E
Ayvacık, Tür.	130	39.36 N	26.24 E
Ayvalı	130	38.44 N	37.38 E
Ayvalık	130	39.18 N	26.41 E
Aywaille	56	50.28 N	5.40 E
Azacualpa, Hond.	236	14.27 N	86.09 W
Azacualpa, Hond.	236	15.19 N	88.33 W
Azādpur ✦[8]	272a	28.43 N	77.11 E
Azai	94	35.26 N	136.18 E
Azaila	34	41.17 N	0.29 W
Azakpert	130	39.14 N	40.30 E
Azalea Park	220	28.32 N	81.15 W
Azama	174m	26.11 N	127.49 E
Azamatovo	80	53.18 N	53.28 E
Azambuja	34	39.04 N	8.52 W
Azamgarh	124	26.04 N	83.11 E
Azamgarh □[5]	124	26.00 N	83.00 E
Azamiga-dake ∧	96	34.20 N	131.47 E
Azángaro	248	14.55 S	70.13 W
Azángaro ≃	248	15.17 S	70.10 W
Azanka	86	58.02 N	64.48 E
Azanovo	80	56.43 N	48.13 E
Azao ∧	148	25.12 N	8.08 E
Azaouâd ✦[1]	150	19.00 N	3.00 W
Azaouak, Vallée de l' ∨	150	15.30 N	3.18 E
Azapa, Quebrada de ≃	248	18.30 S	70.17 W
Azar ∨	150	16.02 N	4.04 E
Azara	150	8.21 N	9.12 E
Āzarbāījān-e Bākhtarī □[4]	84	38.00 N	45.00 E
Āzarbāījān-e Khāvarī □[4]	84	38.00 N	47.00 E
Azare	150	11.40 N	10.11 E
Āzar Shahr	128	37.45 N	45.59 E
Azas ≃	88	52.26 N	96.15 E
Azay-le-Rideau	50	47.16 N	0.28 E
Azay-sur-Cher	50	47.21 N	0.51 E
Azay-sur-Indre	50	47.12 N	0.57 E
A'zāz	130	36.35 N	37.03 E
Azazga	148	36.44 N	4.22 E
Azcapotzalco □[7]	286a	19.24 N	99.12 W
Azcuénaga	258	34.23 S	59.21 W
Azdavay	130	41.39 N	33.18 E
Azefal •[8]	148	21.00 N	14.45 W
Azeffoun	148	36.53 N	4.25 E
Azejevo	80	54.41 N	42.02 E
Azemmour	148	33.20 N	8.25 W
Azenhas do Mar	266c	38.50 N	9.28 W
Azerbaidzhan Soviet Socialist Republic → Azerbajdžanskaja Sovetskaja Socialističeskaja Respublika □[3]	84	40.30 N	47.30 E
Azerbajdžanskaja Sovetskaja Socialističeskaja Respublika □[3]	84	40.30 N	47.30 E
Azergues ≃	58	45.56 N	4.44 E
Azezo	144	12.35 N	37.28 E
Azgir	80	47.50 N	47.54 E
Azhikode	122	11.59 N	75.21 E
Azile	154	3.32 N	29.52 E
Azimganj	126	24.14 N	88.15 E
Azincourt	50	50.28 N	2.08 E
Azizbekov	84	39.40 N	45.30 E
Azle	222	32.54 N	97.33 W
Aznakajevo	80	54.53 N	53.04 E
Aznapuquio	286d	11.59 S	77.04 W
Azogues	246	2.44 S	78.50 W
Azoia	266c	38.46 N	9.29 W
Azor	132	32.01 N	34.48 E
Azores → Açores, Arquipélago dos II	148a	38.30 N	28.00 W
Azores Plateau ⊹[3]	10	39.00 N	29.00 W
Azoum, Bahr (Wādī 'Azūm) ∨	146	10.53 N	20.15 E
Azov	83	47.07 N	39.25 E
Azov, Sea of → Azovskoje More ⊤[2]	78	46.00 N	36.00 E
Azovskij Kanal ≅	83	47.07 N	39.27 E
Azovskoje	78	45.34 N	34.34 E
Azovskoje More ⊤[2]	78	46.00 N	36.00 E
Azoyú	234	16.43 N	98.44 W
Azpeitia	34	43.11 N	2.16 W
Azraq, Bahr ≃	146	10.52 N	20.35 E
Azraq, Wādī al- ∨	140	10.33 N	28.40 E
Azrou	148	33.27 N	5.14 W
Azrou, Oued ∨	148	22.15 N	6.39 E
Aztalan State Park ♦	216	43.04 N	88.51 W
Aztec	200	36.49 N	107.59 W
Azteca, Estadio ♦	286a	19.18 N	99.09 W
Aztec Peak ∧	200	33.48 N	110.55 W
Aztec Ruins National Monument ♦	200	36.51 N	108.10 W
Azua	238	18.27 N	70.44 W
Azuaga	34	38.16 N	5.41 W
Azuay □[4]	246	3.00 S	79.00 W
Azucena	252	37.29 S	59.18 W
Azuchi	94	35.09 N	136.08 E
Azuchi-jō ⊥	94	35.10 N	136.08 E
Azuer ≃	34	39.08 N	3.36 W
Azuero, Península de ≻[1]	246	7.40 N	80.35 W
Azuga	38	45.27 N	25.33 E
Azul	252	36.47 S	59.51 W
Azul, Cerro ∧, C.R.	236	9.54 N	85.14 W
Azul, Cerro ∧, Ec.	246a	0.54 S	91.21 W
Azul, Cerro ∧, Hond.	236	14.32 N	88.23 W
Azul, Serra ⋀[1]	248	14.50 S	54.50 W
Azul, Sierra ⋀	234	23.15 N	98.20 W
'Azūm, Wādī (Bahr Azoum) ∨	146	10.53 N	20.15 E
Azuma, Nihon	94	36.36 N	138.20 E
Azuma, Nihon	94	35.56 N	140.30 E
Azumazaka	270	34.26 N	135.39 E
Azumi	94	36.11 N	137.47 E
Azur, Côte D' •[2]	62	43.30 N	7.00 E
Azurduy	248	19.59 S	64.29 W
Azure Lake ⊜	182	52.23 N	120.00 W
Azusa	228	34.08 N	117.55 W
Azusa ≃	94	36.17 N	137.56 E
Az-Zabābidah	132	32.23 N	35.20 E
Az-Zāb al-Kabīr → Great Zab ≃	128	36.00 N	43.21 E
Az-Zāb as-Şaghīr → Little Zab ≃	128	35.12 N	43.25 E
Az-Zabdānī	132	33.43 N	36.05 E
Aẓ-Ẓāhirīyah	132	31.25 N	34.58 E
Aẓ-Ẓahrān (Dhahran)	128	26.18 N	50.08 E
Az-Zamālik ✦[8]	273c	30.04 N	31.13 E
Azzanello	64	45.18 N	9.55 E
Az-Zankalūn	142	30.33 N	31.27 E
Azzano Decimo	64	45.53 N	12.43 E
Az-Zaqāzīq	142	30.35 N	31.31 E
Az-Zarbah	130	36.04 N	36.59 E
Az-Zarqā'	132	32.05 N	36.06 E
Az-Zawāmil	142	30.21 N	31.26 E
Az-Zāwiyah	146	32.45 N	12.44 E
Az-Zāwiyah □[4]	146	32.50 N	12.15 E
Az-Zaydāb	140	17.26 N	33.53 E
Az-Zaydīyah	144	15.18 N	43.04 E
Az-Zaytīyah ✦[8]	142	29.58 N	32.31 E
Az-Zaytūn ✦[8]	273c	30.06 N	31.19 E
Azzel Matti, Sebkha ≚	148	25.55 N	0.56 E
Az-Zilfī	128	26.18 N	44.48 E
Az-Zrārīyah	132	33.21 N	35.20 E
Az-Zubayr	128	30.23 N	47.43 E
'Azzūn	132	32.11 N	35.03 E
Azzurra, Grotta (Blue Grotto) •[5]	68	40.35 N	14.14 E
Az-Zuwaytīnah	146	30.58 N	20.07 E
B			
Ba ≃	110	13.02 N	109.03 E
Ba, Loch ⊜	46	56.36 N	4.44 W
Baa	112	10.43 S	123.03 E
Baaba, Île I	175f	20.03 S	163.59 E
Baacagaan	102	45.35 N	99.27 E
Baad	58	47.19 N	10.07 E
Ba'adweyn	144	7.12 N	47.24 E
Baah	112	10.28 S	121.59 E
Baak	263	51.25 N	7.10 E
Baal	56	51.02 N	6.17 E
Baao	116	13.27 N	123.22 E
Baar	58	47.12 N	8.32 E
Baar ✦[1]	58	48.00 N	8.30 E
Baarbach ≃	263	51.27 N	7.39 E
Baardskeerdersbos	158	34.34 S	19.35 E
Baarle-Hertog	56	51.27 N	4.56 E
Baarle-Nassau	52	51.27 N	4.53 E
Baarlo	52	51.20 N	6.05 E
Baarn	52	52.13 N	5.16 E
Baasrode	50	51.02 N	4.10 E
Baba	246	1.47 S	79.40 W
Baba ≃	152	6.25 N	17.07 E
Baba Burnu ≻	130	39.29 N	26.04 E
Babaçulândia	250	7.13 S	47.46 W
Babadag, Rom.	38	44.54 N	28.43 E
Babadağ, Tür.	130	37.48 N	28.52 E
Babaeski	130	41.26 N	27.06 E
Babahoyo	246	1.49 S	79.31 W
Babaiqiao	100	32.26 N	118.57 E
Babajevo	76	59.23 N	35.56 E
Babajkovka	78	49.01 N	34.32 E
Babajurt	84	43.36 N	46.47 E
Babak	112	7.08 N	125.41 E
Babakin	162	32.07 S	118.01 E
Babana	150	10.26 N	3.50 E
Babanango	158	28.30 S	31.00 E
Babanka	78	48.43 N	30.26 E
Babanūsah	140	11.20 N	27.48 E
Babar, Kepulauan II	164	7.50 S	129.45 E
Babar, Pulau I	164	7.55 S	129.45 E
Bābarpur ✦[8]	272a	28.41 N	77.17 E
Babat, Indon.	112	2.45 S	103.38 E
Babat, Indon.	115a	7.06 S	112.10 E
Babatag, Chrebet ⋀	85	38.15 N	68.20 E
Babati	154	4.13 S	35.45 E
Bābā Valī Şāḥeb	120	31.40 N	65.40 E
Bābayn, Jabal ∧	140	22.38 N	25.00 E
Babb	182	48.51 N	113.26 W
Babbacombe Bay C	42	50.30 N	3.25 W
Babb Creek ≃	210	41.33 N	77.23 W
Babbitt, Minn., U.S.	190	47.43 N	91.57 W
Babbitt, Nev., U.S.	204	38.39 N	118.37 W
B'abdā	132	33.50 N	35.32 E
B'abdāt	132	33.53 N	35.40 E
Babel, Mont de ∧	186	51.27 N	68.42 W
Babelijamun	164	2.04 S	137.43 E
Babelsberg ✦[8]	264a	52.24 N	13.05 E
Babelsberg, Schloss ⊥	264a	52.24 N	13.05 E
Babelthuap I	175b	7.30 N	134.36 E
Babenhausen, B.R.D.	56	49.57 N	8.56 E
Babenhausen, B.R.D.	58	48.09 N	10.15 E
Babenki	82	55.21 N	37.11 E
Babenkovo	83	49.15 N	37.21 E
Babeyru	154	1.52 N	27.27 E
Babi, Pulau I	114	2.05 N	96.39 E
Babia, Arroyo de la ≃	196	28.25 N	101.45 W
Babiči	76	52.17 N	30.00 E
Bābil	142	30.41 N	31.00 E
Babile	144	9.15 N	42.19 E
Babilônia	256	22.33 S	44.28 W
Babilônia ≃	255	17.10 S	53.05 W
Babimost	30	52.10 N	15.51 E
Babīna	124	25.15 N	78.28 E
Babina Greda	38	45.07 N	18.33 E
Babinda	166	17.20 S	145.55 E
Babine	182	55.19 N	126.37 W
Babine ≃	182	55.42 N	127.40 W
Babine Lake ⊜	182	54.45 N	126.00 W
Babine Range ⋀	182	55.00 N	126.25 W
Babino, S.S.S.R.	76	59.14 N	31.26 E
Babino, S.S.S.R.	76	59.50 N	40.49 E
Babino, S.S.S.R.	76	56.44 N	34.17 E
Babino, S.S.S.R.	80	57.22 N	48.45 E
Babiogórski Park Narodowy ♦	30	49.35 N	19.30 E
Babo	164	2.33 S	133.25 E
Bābol	128	36.34 N	52.42 E
Bābol Sar	128	36.43 N	52.39 E
Babonã ≃	248	6.35 S	66.27 W
Baboon Point ≻	158	32.19 S	18.20 E
Baboquivari Mountains ⋀	200	31.45 N	111.35 W
Baboquivari Peak ∧	200	31.46 N	111.35 W
Babor, Djebel ∧	34	36.30 N	5.28 E
Baborów	30	50.09 N	17.59 E
Babošino	82	54.13 N	37.08 E
Baboua	152	5.48 N	14.49 E
Babrongan Tower ∧[2]	162	18.36 S	123.33 E
Babson Park, Fla., U.S.	220	27.50 N	81.32 W
Babson Park, Mass., U.S.	283	42.18 N	71.23 W
Babson Reservoir ⊜[1]	283	42.38 N	70.40 W
Babstovo	89	48.07 N	132.27 E
Bab-Taza	148	35.03 N	5.14 W
Bābu Bheri	272b	22.51 N	88.14 E
Babungo	152	6.04 N	10.26 E
Bābupur, Bhārat	126	24.01 N	87.10 E
Bābūpur, Bhārat	272a	28.30 N	76.59 E
Babura	150	12.46 N	9.01 E
Babuškin	88	51.41 N	105.54 E
Babuškin ✦[8]	265b	55.52 N	37.42 E
Babuyan	116	10.00 N	118.54 E
Babuyan Channel ⋃	116	18.44 N	121.40 E
Babuyan Island I	108	19.32 N	121.57 E
Babuyan Islands II	108	19.10 N	121.40 E
Baby	287a	22.42 S	43.23 W
Baby, Canal do ≅	287a	22.42 S	43.21 W
Babylon	210	40.42 N	73.20 W
Babylon ⊥	128	32.33 N	44.24 E
Babynino	76	54.23 N	35.43 E
Babyšmola ⊥	86	44.23 N	63.10 E
Bača ≃	64	46.09 N	13.48 E
Bacaba, Igarapé ≃	246	3.35 S	68.45 W
Bacabal	250	4.14 S	44.47 W
Bacacay	116	13.18 N	123.47 E
Bacajá ≃	250	3.25 S	51.50 W
Bacajaí ≃	250	3.27 S	51.53 W
Bacalar, Laguna de ⊜	232	18.43 N	88.22 W
Bacalhau, Canal do ≅	287a	23.03 S	43.35 W
Bacaligo	84	42.33 N	44.57 E
Bačalino	86	57.46 N	67.17 E
Bacan, Pulau I	164	0.35 S	127.30 E
Bacao	116	10.27 N	119.48 E
Bacarra	116	18.15 N	120.35 E
Bacatuba	250	5.40 S	43.42 W
Bacău	38	46.34 N	26.55 E
Bacău □[4]	38	46.30 N	26.45 E
Baccalieu Island I	186	48.08 N	52.48 W
Baccarat	58	48.27 N	6.45 E
Bacchiglione ≃	64	45.11 N	12.14 E
Bacchus Marsh	169	37.41 S	144.27 E
Baceno	58	46.16 N	8.19 E
Bacerac	232	30.18 N	108.50 W
Bacevići	76	53.24 N	29.14 E
Bac-giang	110	21.16 N	106.12 E
Bach	58	47.16 N	10.24 E
Bac-ha	102	22.32 N	104.17 E
Bachagou	98	40.36 N	122.54 E
Bachaquero	246	9.56 N	71.08 W
Bacharach	56	50.04 N	7.46 E
Bacharden	128	38.26 N	57.25 E
Bachardok	128	38.46 N	58.30 E
Bachawan	116	12.28 N	122.06 E
Bachčisaraj	78	44.45 N	33.51 E
Bacheli	122	18.40 N	81.16 E
Bacheng	106	31.27 N	120.52 E
Bachi, Zhg.	100	24.48 N	115.49 E
Bachi, Zhg.	106	31.04 N	120.39 E
Bachíniva	232	28.45 N	107.15 W
Bachl	60	48.49 N	11.57 E
Bach-ma	110	16.12 N	107.52 E
Bachmač	78	51.13 N	32.46 E
Bachmetjevka	80	51.06 N	44.46 E
Bachmut ≃	83	48.56 N	38.03 E
Bachmutovka	83	48.52 N	39.03 E
Bachmutovo	76	56.22 N	34.03 E
Bacho	114	6.37 N	101.39 E
Bachok	114	6.04 N	102.24 E
Bacht	85	40.43 N	68.42 E
Bachta, S.S.S.R.	74	62.28 N	89.00 E
Bachta, S.S.S.R.	86	55.45 N	92.26 E
Bachtemir ≃	80	45.43 N	47.38 E
Bachten-Berg ∧[2]	264a	52.20 N	12.54 E
Bachty	86	46.39 N	82.42 E
Bachu	90	39.50 N	78.20 E
Bachuma	144	6.48 N	35.53 E
Back ≃, N.W. Ter., Can.	176	67.15 N	95.15 W
Back ≃, Va., U.S.	208	37.06 N	76.17 W
Bačka ✦[1]	38	45.50 N	19.30 E
Bac-kan	110	22.08 N	105.50 E
Bačka Palanka	38	45.15 N	19.24 E
Bačka Topola	38	45.49 N	19.38 E
Back Bay ✦[8]	283	42.21 N	71.05 W

Symbols in the index entries represent the broad categories identified in the key at the right. Symbols with superior numbers (⋀[2]) identify subcategories (see complete key on page I · 30).

Kartensymbole in dem Registerverzeichnis stellen die rechts in Schlüssel erklärten Kategorien dar. Symbole mit hochgestellten Ziffern (⋀[2]) bezeichnen Unterabteilungen einer Kategorie (vgl. vollständiger Schlüssel auf Seite I · 30).

Los símbolos incluídos en el texto del índice representan las grandes categorias identificadas con la clave a la derecha. Los símbolos con numeros en su parte superior (⋀[2]) identifican las subcategorías (véase la clave completa en la página I · 30).

Les symboles de l'index représentent les catégories indiquées dans la légende à droite. Les symboles suivis d'un indice (⋀[2]) représentent des sous-catégories (voir légende complète à la page I · 30).

Os símbolos incluídos no texto do índice representam as grandes categorias identificadas com a chave à direita. Os símbolos com números em sua parte superior (⋀[2]) identificam as subcategorias (veja-se a chave completa à página I · 30).

Symbol	English	Deutsch	Español	Français	Português
∧	Mountain	Berg	Montaña	Montagne	Montanha
⋀	Mountains	Berge	Montañas	Montagnes	Montanhas
)(	Pass	Pass	Paso	Col	Passo
∨	Valley, Canyon	Tal, Cañon	Valle, Cañón	Vallée, Canyon	Vale, Canhão
≚	Plain	Ebene	Llano	Plaine	Planície
≻	Cape	Kap	Cabo	Cap	Cabo
I	Island	Insel	Isla	Île	Ilha
II	Islands	Inseln	Islas	Îles	Ilhas
•	Other Topographic Features	Andere Topographische Objekte	Otros Elementos Topográficos	Autres données topographiques	Outros Elementos Topográficos

ESPAÑOL Nombre	Página	Lat. °′	Long. °′ W=Oeste

FRANÇAIS Nom	Page	Lat. °′	Long. °′ W=Ouest

PORTUGUÊS Nome	Página	Lat. °′	Long. °′ W=Oeste

Back Bay C, Bhārat 272c 18.56 N 72.49 E
Back Bay C, Va., U.S. 208 36.35 N 75.57 W
Backberg 40 60.37 N 16.37 E
Backbone Ranges ⛰ 180 63.30 N 129.00 W
Back Branch ≃ 284c 38.50 N 76.48 W
Back Brook ≃ 276 40.26 N 74.39 W
Back Channel ≃[1] 279b 40.30 N 80.05 W
Back Creek ≃ 188 38.02 N 79.54 W
Backe 26 63.49 N 16.24 E
Bäckefors 26 58.48 N 12.10 E
Bäckehagen 40 60.39 N 15.34 E
Backford 262 53.15 N 2.54 W
Bäckhammar 40 59.10 N 14.11 E
Bački Petrovac 38 45.22 N 19.35 E
Backnang 56 48.56 N 9.25 E
Back River C 208 39.16 N 76.27 W
Backstairs Passage ㄩ 168b 35.42 S 138.05 E
Bac-lieu (Vinh-loi) 110 9.17 N 105.44 E
Bacliff 222 29.31 N 94.59 W
Bac-ninh 110 21.11 N 106.03 E
Baco, Mount ⋀ 116 12.49 N 121.10 E
Bacoachi 232 30.38 N 109.56 W
Bacoli 68 40.48 N 14.05 E
Bacolod 116 10.40 N 122.57 E
Bacon 116 13.03 N 124.03 E
Baconga ◆[8] 273b 4.18 S 15.16 E
Bacon Peak ⋀ 224 48.39 N 121.31 W
Bacons Run ≃ 285 40.06 N 74.41 W
Baconton 192 31.23 N 84.10 W
Bacoor 116 14.28 N 120.56 E
Bacoor Bay C 269f 14.28 N 120.54 E
Bac-quang 110 22.29 N 104.52 E
Bacqueville-en-Caux 50 49.47 N 1.00 E
Bácsalmás 38 46.08 N 19.20 E
Bács-Kiskun □[6] 30 46.30 N 19.25 E
Bacton 42 52.52 N 1.28 E
Bacuag 116 9.37 N 125.38 E
Bacuit Bay C 116 11.07 N 119.23 E
Bácum 232 27.33 N 110.05 W
Bacümber 88 48.29 N 106.42 E
Bacungan 116 9.56 N 118.42 E
Bacup 262 53.43 N 2.12 W
Bacuranao ≃ 286b 23.10 N 82.14 W
Bacuri, Cachoeira ㄴ 250 5.29 S 54.18 W
Bacuri, Ilha do I 250 2.55 S 49.43 W
Bacurituba 250 2.43 S 44.43 W
Bačurka 24 68.32 N 56.57 E
Bacuyangan 116 9.39 N 122.27 E
Bād 128 33.41 N 52.01 E
Bad ≃, S. Dak., U.S. 198 44.22 N 100.22 W
Bad ≃, Wis., U.S. 190 46.38 N 90.40 W
Bad, South Fork ≃ 198 44.02 N 101.40 W
Bada 88 51.23 N 109.54 E
Bad Abbach 60 48.56 N 12.03 E
Badagara 122 11.36 N 75.35 E
Badagri 150 6.27 N 2.55 E
Badagri □[8] 273a 6.27 N 3.18 E
Badagri Creek C 273a 6.25 N 3.18 E
Badahl 142 28.56 N 30.54 E
Bad Aibling 64 47.52 N 12.00 E
Badajia 100 33.57 N 120.17 E
Badajós ≃ 246 3.15 S 63.02 W
Badajós, Lago ⊜ 246 3.15 S 62.47 W
Badajoz 34 38.53 N 6.58 W
Badakani 152 4.46 S 14.52 E
Badakhshan □[4] 120 36.45 N 72.00 E
Badal Khān Goth 120 26.31 N 67.06 E
Badalona 34 41.27 N 2.15 E
Badalucco 62 43.55 N 7.51 E
Badam 85 42.23 N 69.15 E
Bādāmi 122 15.55 N 75.41 E
Bādāmpahār 124 22.06 N 86.06 E
Badana, Lac ≃ 144 0.52 S 42.05 E
Badanah 128 30.59 N 41.02 E
Badanga 146 11.36 N 17.26 E
Badanganj 126 22.54 N 87.33 E
Badaohao 104 41.47 N 121.57 E
Badaohe, Zhg. 98 40.24 N 118.42 E
Badaohe, Zhg. 98 40.02 N 122.17 E
Badaojiang 98 41.56 N 126.24 E
Badarma 88 57.46 N 102.36 E
Badas 112 4.36 N 114.27 E
Badas, Kepulauan II 112 0.35 N 107.06 E
Bad Aussee 64 47.36 N 13.47 E
Bad Axe 190 43.48 N 83.00 W
Badaying 98 41.22 N 117.28 E
Badazhou 102 24.36 N 105.04 E
Bad Bentheim 52 52.19 N 7.10 E
Bad Bergzabern 56 49.07 N 8.00 E
Bad Berka 54 50.54 N 11.17 E
Bad Bertrich 56 50.04 N 7.02 E
Bad Bibra 54 51.12 N 11.35 E
Bad Blankenburg 54 50.41 N 11.16 E
Bad Bramstedt 52 53.55 N 9.53 E
Bad Breisig 56 50.31 N 7.18 E
Bad Buchau 58 48.03 N 9.36 E
Bad Cannstatt ◆[8] 56 48.48 N 9.12 E
Bad Creek ≃ 216 41.25 N 83.57 W
Baddā 132 33.41 N 36.26 E
Baddeck 186 46.07 N 60.45 W
Bad Ditzenbach 56 48.35 N 9.41 E
Baddo ≃ 120 27.59 N 64.21 E
Bad Doberan 54 54.06 N 11.53 E
Baddomalhi 123 31.59 N 74.40 E
Bad Dreibergen 52 53.12 N 8.01 E
Bad Driburg 52 51.44 N 9.01 E
Bad Düben 54 51.36 N 12.34 E
Bad Dürkheim 56 49.28 N 8.10 E
Bad Dürrenberg 54 51.18 N 12.04 E
Bad Dürrheim 58 48.01 N 8.32 E
Bade, Centraf. 152 6.41 N 17.07 E
Bade, Indon. 164 7.10 S 139.35 E
Badé ≃ 152 4.26 N 18.16 E
Badeggi 150 9.05 N 6.08 E
Badéguichéri 150 14.31 N 5.22 E
Bad Eilsen 52 52.14 N 9.06 E
Badel 54 52.44 N 11.19 E
Bad Elster 54 50.17 N 12.14 E
Bademli 130 37.02 N 32.41 E
Bad Ems 56 50.20 N 7.43 E
Baden, B.R.D. 52 53.00 N 9.04 E
Baden, Ont., Can. 212 43.24 N 80.39 W
Baden, Öst. 264b 48.00 N 16.14 E
Baden, Schw. 58 47.29 N 8.18 E
Baden, Pa., U.S. 214 40.38 N 80.14 W
Baden, Yai. 144 17.00 N 38.00 E
Baden-Baden 56 48.46 N 8.14 E
Badenoch ◆[1] 46 56.57 N 4.19 W
Baden-Powell, Mount ⋀ 228 34.21 N 117.46 W
Badenweiler 58 47.48 N 7.40 E
Baden-Württemberg □[3] 30 48.30 N 9.00 E
Badenyon 46 57.15 N 3.05 W
Baderna 64 45.12 N 13.46 E
Badersleben 54 51.59 N 10.53 E
Bad Essen 52 52.19 N 8.20 E
Badfish Creek ≃ 216 42.50 N 89.10 W
Bad Frankenhausen 54 51.21 N 11.06 E
Bad Freienwalde 54 52.47 N 14.01 E
Bad Friedrichshall 56 49.14 N 9.11 E
Bad Fusch 64 47.12 N 12.51 E
Bad Gandersheim 52 51.52 N 10.01 E
Badgastein 64 47.07 N 13.08 E
Badger, Newf., Can. 186 48.59 N 56.02 W
Badger, Minn., U.S. 198 48.47 N 96.01 W
Badger Creek ≃, Colo., U.S. 198 40.17 N 103.42 W
Badger Creek ≃, Colo., U.S. 200 38.28 N 105.52 W
Badger Creek ≃, Oreg., U.S. 224 45.16 N 121.11 W
Badger Pass)(226 37.40 N 119.39 W
Badger's Mount 260 51.20 N 0.09 E
Badgery Creek ≃ 274a 33.51 S 150.46 E
Badgery's Creek 274a 33.53 S 150.44 E
Bādghīsāt □[4] 128 35.00 N 63.45 E
Bad Gleichenberg 61 46.52 N 15.54 E
Bad Godesberg 56 50.41 N 7.10 E
Bad Goisern 64 47.38 N 13.37 E
Badgom 123 34.01 N 74.43 E
Bad Gottleuba 54 50.51 N 13.56 E
Bad Griesbach 58 48.27 N 8.14 E
Bad Grund 52 51.48 N 10.14 E
Bad Hall 61 48.02 N 14.13 E
Badhāna 123 31.28 N 74.37 E
Bad Harzburg 54 51.53 N 10.33 E
Bad Heilbrunn 64 47.45 N 11.28 E
Badhela ◆[8] 272a 28.38 N 77.04 E
Bad Helmstedt 54 52.14 N 11.03 E
Bad Hersfeld 56 50.52 N 9.42 E
Badhoevedorp 52 52.21 N 4.46 E
Bad Hofgastein 64 47.10 N 13.06 E
Bad Homburg vor der Höhe 56 50.13 N 8.37 E
Bad Honnef am Rhein 56 50.39 N 7.13 E
Bad Hönningen 56 50.31 N 7.19 E
Badia (Abtei) 64 46.37 N 11.54 E
Badia, Val ∨ 64 46.40 N 11.53 E
Badia a Prataglia 66 43.47 N 11.52 E
Badia Calavena 64 45.34 N 11.09 E
Badia Polesine 64 45.05 N 11.29 E
Badia Tedalda 66 43.42 N 12.11 E
Badifa 150 13.12 N 3.47 E
Badile Camuno, Pizzo ⋀ 58 46.01 N 10.25 E
Badīn 120 24.39 N 68.50 E
Bādinan 272b 22.54 N 88.14 E
Badinko ≃ 150 13.42 N 9.35 W
Badin Lake ⊜[1] 192 35.27 N 80.06 W
Badiraguato 232 25.22 N 107.31 W
Bad Ischl 64 47.43 N 13.37 E
Bad Kissingen 56 50.12 N 10.04 E
Bad Kleinen 54 53.46 N 11.28 E
Bad Kleinkirchheim 64 46.49 N 13.49 E
Bad Klosterlausnitz 54 50.55 N 11.52 E
Bad Kohlgrub 64 47.40 N 11.03 E
Bad König 56 49.45 N 9.01 E
Bad Kösen 54 51.08 N 11.43 E
Bad Köstritz 54 50.56 N 12.01 E
Bad Kreuznach 56 49.52 N 7.51 E
Bad Krozingen 58 47.55 N 7.43 E
Bādkulla 126 23.17 N 88.32 E
Badlands ⛰ 198 46.45 N 103.30 W
Badlands ⛰[2] 198 43.30 N 102.20 W
Badlands National Park ♠ 198 43.47 N 102.15 W
Bad Langensalza 56 51.06 N 10.38 E
Bad Lauchstädt 54 51.23 N 11.52 E
Bad Lausick 54 51.08 N 12.38 E
Bad Lauterberg [im Harz] 52 51.38 N 10.28 E
Bad Leonfelden 61 48.33 N 14.19 E
Bādli 272a 28.45 N 77.09 E
Bad Liebenstein 54 50.49 N 10.21 E
Bad Liebenwerda 54 51.31 N 13.23 E
Bad Liebenzell 56 48.46 N 8.44 E
Bad Lippspringe 52 51.46 N 8.49 E
Bad Meinberg 52 51.53 N 8.58 E
Bad Mergentheim 56 49.30 N 9.46 E
Bad Mingolsheim 56 49.14 N 8.39 E
Badminton Stadium ♠ 271c 1.18 N 103.53 E
Bad Mukran 54 54.26 N 13.35 E
Bad Münder 52 52.12 N 9.27 E
Bad Münster am Stein 56 49.49 N 7.51 E
Bad Münstereifel 56 50.33 N 6.46 E
Bad Muskau 54 51.32 N 14.43 E
Bad Nauheim 56 50.22 N 8.44 E
Bad Nenndorf 52 52.20 N 9.22 E
Badnera 122 20.52 N 77.44 E
Badner Lindkogel ⋀ 264b 48.01 N 16.11 E
Bad Neuenahr-Ahrweiler 56 50.33 N 7.08 E
Bad Neustadt an der Saale 56 50.19 N 10.13 E
Bad Niedernau 58 48.27 N 8.53 E
Bad Oeynhausen 52 52.12 N 8.48 E
Badogo 150 11.02 N 8.13 W
Badolato 68 38.34 N 16.31 E
Bad Oldesloe 52 53.48 N 10.22 E
Ba-don 110 17.45 N 106.27 E
Ba-dong, Viet. 110 9.40 N 106.34 E
Badong, Zhg. 102 31.02 N 110.20 E
Badonviller 58 48.30 N 6.54 E
Bad Orb 56 50.14 N 9.20 E
Badou, Togo 150 7.35 N 0.36 E
Badou, Zhg. 98 36.27 N 117.55 E
Badouling 100 32.10 N 117.36 E
Badoumbé 150 13.38 N 10.13 W
Bad Peterstal 58 48.26 N 8.12 E
Badplaas 158 25.57 S 30.35 E
Bad Polzin → Połczyn Zdrój 30 53.46 N 16.06 E
Bad Pyrmont 52 51.59 N 9.15 E
Badr 142 30.33 N 30.43 E
Bad Ragaz 58 47.00 N 9.30 E
Bādrāh 120 27.20 N 68.01 E
Badrao 120 34.46 N 69.40 E
Bad Rappenau 56 49.14 N 9.06 E
Bad Rehburg 52 52.26 N 9.13 E
Bad Reichenhall 64 47.43 N 12.52 E
Badreïna ⊤[4] 150 17.44 N 11.05 W
Badr Ḥunayn 128 23.44 N 38.46 E
Badrīnāth 124 30.44 N 79.29 E
Bad Rippoldsau 58 48.26 N 8.19 E
Bad River Indian Reservation ◆[4] 190 46.33 N 90.40 W
Bad Rothenfelde 52 52.06 N 8.09 E
Bad Saarow-Pieskow 54 52.17 N 14.03 E
Bad Sachsa 54 51.36 N 10.32 E
Bad Salzdetfurth 52 52.03 N 10.01 E
Bad Salzig 56 50.12 N 7.38 E
Bad Salzschlierf 56 50.37 N 9.29 E
Bad Salzuflen 52 52.05 N 8.44 E
Bad Salzungen 56 50.48 N 10.13 E
Bad Sankt Leonhard im Lavanttal 61 46.58 N 14.48
Bad Sassendorf 52 51.35 N 8.10 E
Bad Schallerbach 61 48.14 N 13.55 E
Bad Schandau 54 50.55 N 14.10 E
Bad Schmiedeberg 54 51.41 N 12.44 E
Bad Schwalbach 56 50.08 N 8.04 E
Bad Schwartau 54 53.55 N 10.40 E
Bad Segeberg 52 53.56 N 10.17 E
Bādshāhpur 124 25.47 N 82.49 E
Bad Soden, B.R.D. 56 50.08 N 8.30 E
Bad Soden, B.R.D. 56 50.17 N 9.22 E
Bad Sooden-Allendorf 56 51.16 N 9.58 E
Bad Steben 54 50.22 N 11.38 E
Bad Stuer 54 53.22 N 12.19 E
Bad Suderode 54 51.44 N 11.07 E
Bad Sulza 54 51.05 N 11.37 E
Bad Sülze 54 54.06 N 12.38 E
Bad Tatzmannsdorf 61 47.20 N 16.13 E
Bad Teinach 56 48.41 N 8.41 E
Bad Tennstedt 54 51.09 N 10.50 E
Bad Tölz 64 47.46 N 11.34 E
Badu, Bra. 287a 22.54 S 43.04 W
Badu, Zhg. 100 27.38 N 118.57 E
Badu, Zhg. 100 26.51 N 119.35 E
Badu, Zhg. 102 24.15 N 105.41 E
Badu Island I 164 10.07 S 142.08 E
Badujie 100 28.32 N 117.57 E
Badulla 122 6.59 N 81.03 E
Badung, Selat ㄩ 115b 8.40 S 115.22 E
Badupi 120 21.36 N 93.25 E
Bādura 126 22.16 N 90.21 E
Bāduria 126 22.44 N 88.47 E
Badvel 122 14.45 N 79.03 E
Bad Vilbel 56 50.12 N 8.42 E
Bad Vöslau 61 47.57 N 16.16 E
Bad Waldsee 58 47.55 N 9.45 E
Bad Warmbrunn → Cieplice Śląskie-Zdrój 30 50.52 N 15.41 E
Badwater Creek ≃ 202 43.17 N 108.08 W
Bad Westernkotten 52 51.38 N 8.21 E
Bad Wiessee 64 47.43 N 11.43 E
Bad Wildungen 56 51.07 N 9.07 E
Bad Wilsnack 54 52.57 N 11.57 E
Bad Wimpfen 56 49.14 N 9.09 E
Bad Wimsbach-Neydharting 64 48.04 N 13.54 E
Bad Windsheim 56 49.31 N 10.25 E
Bad Wörishofen 58 48.00 N 10.36 E
Bad Wurzach 58 47.54 N 9.54 E
Badžalskij Chrebet ⛰ 89 50.40 N 134.50 E
Baediam 150 15.03 N 11.51 W
Bække 41 55.34 N 9.09 E
Baena 34 37.37 N 4.19 W
Baependi 256 21.57 S 44.53 W
Baependi ≃ 256 21.52 S 45.04 W
Baerl 263 51.29 N 6.41 E
Baesweiler 56 50.54 N 6.11 E
Báez 240p 22.13 N 79.45 W
Baeza, Ec. 246 0.27 S 77.53 W
Baeza, Esp. 34 37.59 N 3.28 W
Baezaeko ≃ 182 53.09 N 123.48 W
Bafang 152 5.09 N 10.11 E
Bafatá 150 12.10 N 14.40 W
Bafelé 150 10.09 N 10.08 W
Baffa 123 34.26 N 73.13 E
Baffin Bay C, N.A. 16 73.00 N 66.00 W
Baffin Bay C, Tex., U.S. 196 27.15 N 97.33 W
Baffin Island I 176 68.00 N 70.00 W
Bafia 152 4.44 N 11.16 E
Bafilo 150 9.21 N 1.16 E
Bafing ≃ 150 13.49 N 10.50 W
Bafing Makana 150 12.33 N 10.15 W
Bafoulabé 150 13.48 N 10.50 W
Bafoussam 152 5.29 N 10.24 E
Bāfq 128 31.35 N 55.24 E
Bafra 130 41.34 N 35.56 E
Bafra Burnu ⟩ 130 41.44 N 35.58 E
Bāft 128 29.14 N 56.38 E
Bafuku 154 4.15 N 27.54 E
Bafwabaka 154 2.07 N 27.40 E
Bafwabalinga 154 0.51 N 27.04 E
Bafwaboli 154 0.39 N 26.10 E
Bafwangbe 154 1.39 N 26.51 E
Bafwapada 154 0.56 N 26.57 E
Bafwasende 154 1.05 N 27.16 E
Bafwasomboli 154 1.27 N 27.01 E
Baga 126 22.26 N 90.28 E
Baga I 175e 7.49 S 156.33 E
Bagabag 116 16.37 N 121.15 E
Bagabag Island I 164 4.50 S 146.15 E
Baga-Burul 80 46.00 N 44.36 E
Bagac 116 14.36 N 120.23 E
Bagacay Point ⟩ 116 8.58 N 124.48 E
Bagac Bay C 116 14.36 N 120.22 E
Bagaces 236 10.31 N 85.15 W
Baga Chentijn Nuruu ⛰ 88 48.30 N 107.30 E
Bagage ⋀ 154 3.23 N 40.12 E
Bagagem ≃, Bra. 250 11.37 S 48.12 W
Bagagem ≃, Bra. 255 13.58 S 48.21 W
Bagaha 124 27.06 N 84.05 E
Bagahu ⊜ 86 46.57 N 87.27 E
Bagajevskij 78 47.19 N 40.23 E
Bāgalkot 122 16.11 N 75.42 E
Bagamanoc 116 13.57 N 124.17 E
Bagamoyo 154 6.26 S 38.54 E
Bagan 86 54.06 N 77.40 E
Bagana 80 54.22 N 51.25 E
Bagana, Mount ⋀ 175e 6.09 S 155.12 E
Baganalin 102 38.57 N 94.08 E
Bagan Datoh 114 3.59 N 100.47 E
Bagañga 116 7.35 N 126.34 E
Bagan Serai 114 5.01 N 100.32 E
Bagansiapi-api 114 2.09 N 100.49 E
Bagansinembah 114 1.46 N 100.29 E
Bagansitukang 114 2.38 N 100.15 E
Baganza ≃ 64 44.47 N 10.19 E
Bagara 85 40.55 N 68.26 E
Bağarası 130 37.42 N 27.33 E
Bagasra 120 21.29 N 70.57 E
Bagata 152 3.44 S 17.57 E
Bāgātipāra 126 24.18 N 88.57 E
Bagawi 140 12.19 N 34.21 E
Bagbag Creek ≃ 269f 14.39 N 120.57 E
Bagband 52 53.21 N 7.36 E
Bagbe ≃ 150 8.42 N 11.15 W
Bagbele 154 4.21 N 29.17 E
Bāgda 126 23.13 N 86.41 E
Bagdad → Baghdād, 'Irāq 128 33.21 N 44.25 E
Bagdad, Ariz., U.S. 200 34.34 N 113.11 W
Bagdad, Fla., U.S. 194 30.36 N 87.02 W
Bagdad, Ky., U.S. 218 38.16 N 85.04 W
Bagdaha 126 23.13 N 88.53 E
Bagdanga 126 24.02 N 88.32 E
Bagdarin 88 54.26 N 113.36 E
Bagé 252 31.20 S 54.06 W
Bagehadu 120 35.25 N 85.50 E
Bâgé-le-Châtel 58 46.18 N 4.56 E
Bagenkop 41 54.45 N 10.41 E
Bagerovo 78 45.23 N 36.17 E
Bāgevādi 122 16.35 N 75.58 E
Baggao 116 17.56 N 121.46 E
Baggeryd 24 57.30 N 14.07 E
Baggetorp 40 59.01 N 16.04 E
Baggio ◆[8] 266b 45.27 N 9.06 E
Baggs 200 41.02 N 107.39 W
Baggy Point ⟩ 42 51.09 N 4.16 W
Bāgh 123 33.59 N 73.47 E
Baghdād 128 33.21 N 44.25 E
Baghdād □[4] 128 34.00 N 43.46 E
Baghdobā 126 22.08 N 87.54 E
Baghelkhand Plateau ⛰[1] 124 23.45 N 82.20 E
Bāgh-e Malek 128 31.32 N 49.55 E
Bāgherhāt 124 22.40 N 89.48 E
Bagheria 70 38.05 N 13.30 E
Bāgherpāra 126 23.14 N 89.21 E
Bāghia 126 23.27 N 90.29 E
Baghia Bīl ☵ 126 23.07 N 90.03 E
Bāghīn 128 30.12 N 36.48 E
Baghlān 120 36.13 N 68.46 E
Baghlān □[4] 120 35.45 N 69.00 E
Baghlīn 120 36.14 N 65.55 E
Bāghmati ≃ 124 25.46 N 85.58 E
Bāghmundi 124 23.12 N 86.03 E
Bāghpat 124 28.57 N 77.13 E
Baghrān Khowleh 120 33.01 N 64.58 E
Bagillt 262 53.16 N 3.10 W
Bağırpaşa Dağı ⋀ 130 39.30 N 40.06 E
Bagley 198 47.31 N 95.24 W
Bāgli 124 22.39 N 76.21 E
Bağlum 130 40.03 N 32.51 E
Bāglung 124 28.16 N 83.36 E
Bagmanl'ar 84 40.38 N 46.18 E
Bāgmāri ◆[8] 272b 22.34 N 88.25 E
Bagn 26 60.49 N 9.34 E
Bagnacavallo 66 44.25 N 12.00 E
Bagnaia 66 42.25 N 12.09 E
Bāgnān 126 22.28 N 87.59 E
Bagnara Calabra 68 38.18 N 15.49 E
Bagnara di Romagna 66 44.23 N 11.49 E
Bagnasco 62 44.18 N 8.02 E
Bagnell Dam ◆[6] 194 38.11 N 92.39 W
Bagnères-de-Bigorre 32 43.04 N 0.09 E
Bagnères-de-Luchon 32 42.47 N 0.36 E
Bagnes, Vallée de ∨ 58 46.03 N 7.18 E
Bagneux 261 48.48 N 2.18 E
Bagni Acque Albule 66 41.57 N 12.43 E
Bagni del Masino 58 46.15 N 9.36 E
Bagni di Lucca 66 44.01 N 10.35 E
Bagni di Rabbi 64 46.24 N 10.48 E
Bagno a Ripoli 66 43.45 N 11.19 E
Bagno di Romagna 66 43.50 N 11.57 E
Bagnolet 261 48.52 N 2.25 E
Bagnoli del Trigno 66 41.42 N 14.27 E
Bagnoli di Sopra 64 45.11 N 11.53 E
Bagnoli Irpino 68 40.50 N 15.04 E
Bagnolo in Piano 64 44.46 N 10.40 E
Bagnolo Mella 64 45.26 N 10.10 E
Bagnols-en-Forêt 62 43.32 N 6.42 E
Bagnols-les-Bains 62 44.30 N 3.40 E
Bagnols-sur-Cèze 62 44.10 N 4.37 E
Bagnone 64 44.19 N 10.00 E
Bagnoregio 66 42.37 N 12.05 E
Bagno Vignoni 66 43.02 N 11.39 E
Bågø I 41 55.18 N 9.49 E
Bago ≃ 116 10.33 N 122.50 E
Bagodar 124 24.05 N 85.52 E
Bagodo 152 6.25 N 13.23 E
Bagoé ≃ 150 12.36 N 6.34 W
Bagolino 64 45.49 N 10.28 E
Bagoni 146 7.53 N 10.43 E
Bagot □[6] 206 45.40 N 72.45 W
Bagrationovsk 76 54.23 N 20.39 E
Bagraula ◆[8] 272a 28.34 N 77.04 E
Bagre 250 1.54 S 50.12 W
Bagrinovcy 78 49.17 N 27.56 E
Bagshot 42 51.22 N 0.42 W
Bagua 248 5.40 S 78.31 W
Baguazhou 106 32.11 N 118.46 E
Bāguiati 272b 22.36 N 88.26 E
Baguio 116 16.25 N 120.36 E
Bagula 126 23.19 N 88.39 E
Bagumbayan 269f 14.28 N 121.03 E
Bagur, Cabo ⟩ 34 41.57 N 3.14 E
Bagyrlaj ≃ 80 48.08 N 51.14 E
Bagzane, Monts ⛰ 150 17.43 N 8.45 E
Bāh 124 26.53 N 78.36 E
Bahado 144 5.48 N 47.11 E
Bāhādurābād Ghāt 124 25.09 N 89.42 E
Bahādurganj 124 27.32 N 82.50 E
Bahādurgarh 124 28.41 N 76.56 E
Bāhādurpur 126 23.25 N 88.28 E
Bahaia, Mount ⋀ 144 11.13 N 49.43 E
Bahamas □[1] 230
238 24.15 N 76.00 W
Bahār 128 34.54 N 48.26 E
Baharāgora 126 22.17 N 86.43 E
Baharpur 126 23.41 N 89.34 E
Bahau 114 2.49 N 102.25 E
Bahau ≃ 112 2.34 N 116.20 E
Bahāwalnagar 123 29.59 N 73.16 E
Bahāwalpur 123 29.24 N 71.41 E
Bahce 130 37.14 N 36.34 E
Bahçeköy 267b 41.11 N 28.59 E
Bahçeköy su kemeri ☲[1] 267b 41.03 N 28.59 E
Bahechuan 98 40.59 N 124.49 E
Bahemdan 130 38.19 N 41.09 E
Baheri 124 28.47 N 79.30 E
Bahi, Pil. 116 13.53 N 123.38 E
Bahi, Tan. 154 5.59 S 35.19 E
Bahía → Salvador 255 12.59 S 38.31 W
Bahia □[3] 250 11.00 S 42.00 W
Bahía Blanca 252 38.43 S 62.17 W
Bahía Bustamante 254 45.08 S 66.32 W
Bahía de Caráquez 246 0.36 S 80.25 W
Bahía Honda 240p 22.54 N 83.10 W
Bahia Honda Key I 220 24.40 N 81.16 W
Bahia Honda Point ⟩ 116 9.24 N 118.07 E
Bahía Kino 232 28.50 N 111.55 W
Bahía Laura 254 48.24 S 66.29 W
Bahīj 142 30.56 N 29.35 E
Bahir Dar 144 11.35 N 37.28 E
Bah'i Temple ⚑[1] 278 42.05 N 87.41 W
Bahjoi 124 28.24 N 78.37 E
Bahl 123 28.38 N 75.38 E
Bahlolpur 272a 28.37 N 77.24 E
Bahn 150 7.05 N 8.45 W
Bahnāy 142 30.23 N 31.04 E
Bahnayā 142 30.41 N 31.23 E
Baḥrah 144 21.24 N 39.29 E
Bahraich 124 27.35 N 81.36 E
Bahraich □[5] 124 27.50 N 81.40 E
Bahrain □[1] 118
128 26.00 N 50.30 E
Bahrām Chāh 128 29.26 N 64.03 E
Baḥrānī, Ḥālat al- I 128 24.22 N 54.15 E
Bahrdorf 54 52.23 N 11.00 E
Bahrein → Bahrain □[1] 128 26.00 N 50.30 E
Bahser 130 37.57 N 39.18 E
Bahtīm 142 30.08 N 31.17 E
Baḥṭīṭ 142 30.29 N 31.38 E
Bāhū Kalāt 128 25.43 N 61.25 E
Bahulu, Pulau I 112 3.33 S 122.18 E
Bahumbelu 112 2.13 S 121.41 E
Bahūt 142 31.10 N 31.19 E
Bahuta 89 43.20 N 122.16 E
Baï 150 13.38 N 3.22 W
Baia 68 40.49 N 14.04 E
Baia-de-Aramă 38 45.00 N 22.49 E
Baía dos Tigres 152 16.36 S 11.43 E
Baía Farta 152 12.40 S 13.11 E
Baía Formosa 250 6.22 S 35.00 W
Baia-Mare 38 47.40 N 23.35 E
Baiano 68 40.57 N 14.37 E
Baião 250 2.41 S 49.41 W
Baiardo 62 43.54 N 7.43 E
Baia Sprie 38 47.40 N 23.42 E
Baibao 105 39.04 N 115.31 E
Baibaoying 89 46.34 N 128.05 E
Baïbokoum 146 7.46 N 15.43 E
Baibuting 106 30.33 N 120.46 E
Baicaochang 102 32.08 N 103.59 E
Baicheng 89 45.38 N 122.46 E
Baidian 106 30.47 N 119.14 E
Baidiao 102 28.07 N 101.28 E
Baidoa 144 3.04 N 43.48 E
Baidunzi 102 43.11 N 95.19 E
Baidyabāti 126 22.47 N 88.20 E
Baidya Bāzār 126 23.39 N 90.37 E
Baidyanāth 124 24.29 N 86.42 E
Baie-Comeau 186 49.13 N 68.10 W
Baie-Comeau-Hauterive, Parc de ♠ 186 49.30 N 68.05 W
Baie-des-ha! Ha! 186 50.56 N 58.56 W
Baie-de-Shawinigan 206 46.34 N 72.45 W
Baie-du-Renard 186 49.17 N 61.50 W
Baie-d'Urfé 206 45.25 N 73.55 W
Baie-Johan-Beetz 186 50.17 N 62.48 W
Baie-Mahault 241o 16.16 N 61.35 W
Baienfurt 64 47.49 N 9.38 E
Baiersbronn 58 48.30 N 8.22 E
Baiersdorf 60 49.39 N 11.01 E
Baies, Lac des ⊜ 190 47.18 N 77.40 W
Baie-Saint-Claire 186 49.54 N 64.30 W
Baie-Saint-Paul 186 47.27 N 70.30 W
Baie-Trinité 186 49.25 N 67.18 W
Baie Verte 186 49.56 N 56.11 W
Baieville 206 46.08 N 72.43 W
Baifutu 98 35.01 N 116.07 E
Baigezhuang 105 39.54 N 118.09 E
Baigneux-les-Juifs 58 47.36 N 4.38 E
Baigong 100 24.18 N 116.14 E
Baigouhe, Zhg. 105 39.07 N 116.01 E
Baigouhe, Zhg. 105 39.42 N 115.58 E
Baiguoshu 106 30.45 N 119.07 E
Baigusi 102 33.10 N 103.52 E
Baihaojiang 106 31.16 N 121.08 E
Baihar 124 22.06 N 80.33 E
Baihe ≃ 105 40.22 N 116.19 E
Baihedian 100 29.12 N 120.55 E
Baihekou 102 31.46 N 110.13 E
Baihou 100 24.18 N 116.48 E
Baihu ⊜, Zhg. 100 31.16 N 117.30 E
Baihu ⊜, Zhg. 100 30.17 N 113.15 E
Baihuachang 107 29.07 N 104.37 E
Baihuashan ⋀ 105 39.50 N 115.35 E
Baijala 272b 22.51 N 88.16 E
Baijiagou 104 42.34 N 123.36 E
Baijiang 100 29.51 N 119.20 E
Baijiawu 105 39.30 N 116.28 E
Baijiechang 107 29.17 N 106.31 E
Baijietan 107 28.44 N 105.30 E
Baijnāth 124 29.55 N 79.37 E
Baiju 100 33.04 N 120.20 E
Baikal, Lago → Bajkal, Ozero ⊜ 88 53.00 N 107.40 E
Baikal Lake → Bajkal, Ozero ⊜ 88 53.00 N 107.40 E
Baikal-See → Bajkal, Ozero ⊜ 88 53.00 N 107.40 E
Baikeshu 106 30.26 N 118.55 E
Baikonur → Bajkonyr 86 47.50 N 66.03 E
Baikuerte 85 39.58 N 75.33 E
Baikunthapur, Bhārat 124 23.15 N 82.33 E
Baikunthapur, Bhārat 272b 22.59 N 88.13 E
Bailadores 246 8.15 N 71.50 W
Bailaiqiao 100 32.40 N 118.23 E
Bailang, Zhg. 89 46.57 N 120.05 E
Bailang, Zhg. 120 29.11 N 89.12 E
Baildon 44 53.52 N 1.46 W
Baile Átha Cliath → Dublin 28 53.20 N 6.15 W
Bailebao 105 39.55 N 114.51 E
Băile Govora 38 45.05 N 24.11 E
Băile Herculane 38 44.54 N 22.25 E
Bailén 34 38.06 N 3.46 W
Băile Olănești 38 45.11 N 24.16 E
Băilești 38 44.02 N 23.21 E
Bailey 192 35.47 N 78.07 W
Bailey Lakes 214 40.57 N 82.21 W
Bailey Run ≃ 279b 40.35 N 79.47 W
Baileys Crossroads 284c 38.51 N 77.08 W
Bail Hongal 122 15.49 N 74.52 E
Baili 102 25.45 N 110.33 E
Bailian 102 24.09 N 112.22 E
Bailieborough 48 53.54 N 6.59 W
Bailin, Zhg. 100 27.12 N 120.10 E
Bailin, Zhg. 107 29.11 N 105.57 E
Bailinchang 107 28.45 N 106.26 E
Bailingmiao → Daerhanmao-ming'anqi 102 41.42 N 110.23 E
Bailinshi 100 26.20 N 113.18 E
Bailique 250 0.58 N 50.04 W
Bailique, Ilha I 250 1.02 N 49.58 W
Bailleau-sous-Gallardon 261 48.32 N 1.39 E
Bailleul 50 50.44 N 2.44 E
Ba-Illi 146 10.30 N 16.34 E
Baillie ≃ 176 65.10 N 104.24 W
Baillie-Hamilton Island I 176 75.53 N 94.35 W
Baillie Islands II 176 70.33 N 128.10 W
Baillies Bacolet 241k 12.02 N 61.41 W
Baillif 241o 16.01 N 61.45 W
Bailly-Romainvilliers 261 48.50 N 2.49 E
Bailonggang 106 31.15 N 121.44 E
Bailongjiang ≃ 102 32.18 N 105.42 E
Bailuchang 107 28.56 N 105.57 E
Bailugh 120 32.41 N 66.46 E
Bailuhu ⊜ 100 30.03 N 113.06 E
Bailundo 152 12.12 S 15.52 E
Bailuo 100 29.37 N 113.15 E
Baima 107 30.03 N 103.44 E
Baimachang, Zhg. 102 29.18 N 107.30 E
Baimachang, Zhg. 104 41.59 N 122.30 E
Baimachang, Zhg. 107 29.39 N 103.57 E
Baimachang, Zhg. 107 29.11 N 104.37 E
Baimachang, Zhg. 107 29.09 N 104.16 E
Baimaguan 105 40.41 N 116.52 E
Baimahe ≃ 98 35.14 N 116.14 E
Baimakou 102 25.55 N 102.06 E
Baimamiao, Zhg. 102 36.58 N 108.08 E
Baimamiao, Zhg. 107 29.33 N 104.59 E
Baimao 106 31.39 N 120.52 E
Baimaokou C[1] 106 31.44 N 121.04 E
Baimaosha I 106 31.43 N 121.14 E
Baimaotang ≃ 106 31.44 N 121.04 E
Baimaoxinshi 106 31.35 N 120.54 E
Baimaqiao 106 31.35 N 119.10 E
Baimashan ⋀ 102 27.12 N 110.32 E
Baimashi 100 29.15 N 118.42 E
Baimazhai 100 28.06 N 115.50 E
Baimiaozi, Zhg. 89 46.18 N 123.35 E
Baimiaozi, Zhg. 98 40.34 N 120.36 E
Baimiaozi, Zhg. 104 41.55 N 122.12 E
Baimiaozi, Zhg. 107 29.47 N 106.29 E
Baimuqiao 106 32.01 N 120.19 E
Baimuru 164 7.30 S 144.49 E
Bain ≃ 44 53.05 N 0.12 W
Baïna Bondio 152 5.10 N 16.33 E
Bainbridge, Ga., U.S. 192 30.54 N 84.34 W
Bainbridge, N.Y., U.S. 210 42.18 N 75.29 W
Bainbridge, Ohio, U.S. 218 39.14 N 83.16 W
Bainbridge, Pa., U.S. 208 40.05 N 76.40 W
Bainbridge Island I 224 47.37 N 122.33 W
Bainchi 126 23.07 N 88.14 E
Bainchipota 272b 22.52 N 88.16 E
Bain-de-Bretagne 32 47.50 N 1.41 W
Baing 115b 10.14 S 120.34 E
Bainiqiao 100 29.35 N 114.09 E
Bains-les-Bains 58 48.00 N 6.16 E
Bainville 198 48.08 N 104.13 W
Bainyik 164 3.40 S 143.00 E
Baipeng 102 24.09 N 109.25 E
Baipi 100 27.45 N 115.52 E
Baipu 106 32.15 N 120.46 E
Baiqibao 104 41.48 N 122.30 E
Baiqipu 104 41.32 N 121.24 E
Baiqitun 89 44.23 N 126.32 E
Baiqiu 100 32.44 N 112.38 E
Baiquan, Zhg. 89 47.36 N 126.07 E
Baiquan, Zhg. 100 30.06 N 122.08 E
Baiqueyuan 100 31.48 N 115.05 E
Bair, Pa., U.S. 208 39.54 N 76.50 W
Bā'ir, Urd. 132 30.46 N 36.41 E
Bā'ir, Wādī ∨ 132 30.58 N 37.09 E
Baird 196 32.24 N 99.24 W
Bairdford 214 40.38 N 79.53 W
Baird Inlet C 180 60.45 N 164.00 W
Baird Mountains ⛰ 180 67.35 N 161.30 W
Baird Peninsula ⟩[1] 176 69.00 N 75.15 W
Baire 240p 20.19 N 76.20 W
Bairia 124 27.00 N 85.23 E
Bairiki 174t 1.20 N 173.01 E
Bair Island I 282 37.32 N 122.13 W
Bairkum 85 42.05 N 68.11 E
Bairnsdale 166 37.50 S 147.38 E
Bairoil 200 42.15 N 107.33 W
Bairrinho 256 22.36 S 47.06 W
Bairro Alto 256 23.29 S 45.21 W
Bairuopu 100 28.12 N 112.46 E
Bais, Fr. 32 48.15 N 0.22 W
Bais, Pil. 116 9.35 N 123.07 E
Baise 102 23.57 N 106.26 E
Baïse ≃ 32 44.07 N 0.17 E
Baisha, Zhg. 100 25.24 N 117.16 E
Baisha, Zhg. 100 29.26 N 119.16 E
Baisha, Zhg. 100 25.40 N 118.59 E
Baisha, Zhg. 100 34.22 N 112.32 E
Baisha, Zhg. 100 24.39 N 113.31 E
Baisha, Zhg. 100 26.58 N 115.22 E
Baisha, Zhg. 102 21.51 N 112.09 E
Baisha, Zhg. 107 28.47 N 104.41 E
Baisha, Zhg. 110 19.17 N 109.27 E
Baishaba 107 30.03 N 106.21 E
Baishachang 107 28.55 N 105.45 E
Baishanji 100 33.48 N 116.40 E
Baishantu 104 42.21 N 122.35 E
Baishapu 100 29.58 N 115.04 E
Baishatan 98 36.52 N 121.43 E
Baishazhen, Zhg. 100 34.20 N 113.14 E
Baishazhen, Zhg. 107 29.04 N 106.07 E
Baishe 100 27.02 N 116.20 E
Baishecun 105 40.10 N 116.18 E
Baishi, Zhg. 100 27.18 N 119.45 E
Baishi, Zhg. 100 26.48 N 119.46 E
Baishi, Zhg. 102 22.36 N 110.55 E
Baishidu 100 25.26 N 113.01 E
Baishilashan ⋀ 89 46.38 N 128.27 E
Baishiyi 107 29.29 N 106.22 E
Baishizhai 104 40.57 N 122.58 E
Baishui, Zhg. 100 28.42 N 113.04 E
Baishui, Zhg. 107 30.06 N 105.38 E
Baishuifan 100 30.17 N 115.43 E
Baishuijiang 102 33.29 N 106.01 E
Baishuijie 102 32.39 N 105.32 E
Baishuiwan 106 30.34 N 119.39 E
Baishun 100 25.12 N 114.01 E
Baishuxia 100 27.22 N 113.41 E
Baisingga 126 21.39 N 86.54 E
Baisley Pond ⊜ 276 40.41 N 73.47 W
Baisogala 76 55.38 N 23.43 E
Bāisrasi 126 23.27 N 90.02 E
Baita, Bhārat 272b 22.27 N 88.11 E
Baita, Zhg. 106 31.48 N 119.35 E
Baitadi 124 29.32 N 80.26 E
Baital 126 22.57 N 87.28 E
Baitazi 98 42.19 N 120.19 E
Baitazibeigou 104 42.17 N 120.48 E
Bai-thuong 110 19.54 N 105.23 E
Baitings Reservoir ⊜[1] 262 53.40 N 1.59 W
Baitoutan 102 32.30 N 106.56 E
Baitugang 100 33.28 N 112.22 E
Baituzhen 106 31.59 N 119.21 E
Baiwang 102 24.14 N 108.32 E
Baiwenzhen 102 38.15 N 111.06 E
Baixa Grande 255 11.57 S 40.11 W
Baixi, Zhg. 100 28.21 N 121.07 E
Baixi, Zhg. 107 29.39 N 106.28 E
Baixian 106 31.09 N 119.39 E
Baixio 250 6.44 S 38.43 W
Baixo Longa 152 15.42 S 18.50 E
Baiyan 100 28.04 N 120.02 E
Baiyangdian ⊜ 98 38.51 N 116.01 E
Baiyanghe 86 43.13 N 88.28 E
Baiyangzhen 100 34.25 N 112.12 E
Baiyer River 164 5.35 S 144.10 E
Baiyinchang 102 36.47 N 104.07 E
Baiyinheshuo 89 44.31 N 119.51 E
Baiyinnuoletun 89 46.45 N 124.16 E
Baiyintaohai 89 43.12 N 120.23 E
Baiyu, Zhg. 102 31.18 N 98.49 E
Baiyu, Zhg. 105 40.01 N 115.37 E
Baiyunding 102 29.00 N 98.34 E
Baiyundu 100 26.10 N 118.47 E
Baiyunebo 102 41.58 N 110.02 E
Baiyunguan 271a 39.54 N 116.19 E
Baiyushan ⛰ 102 37.21 N 107.50 E
Baizha 100 29.11 N 115.37 E
Baizhongpu 100 33.22 N 114.50 E
Baizizhen 107 30.06 N 105.43 E
Baja 30 46.11 N 18.57 E
Baja, Punta ⟩, Chile 174z 27.10 S 109.22 W
Baja, Punta ⟩, Méx. 232 29.58 N 115.49 W
Baja, Punta ⟩, Méx. 232 28.28 N 111.45 W
Baja California 200 32.18 N 115.12 W
Baja California ⟩[1] 232 28.00 N 113.30 W
Baja California Norte □[3] 232 30.00 N 115.00 W
Baja California Seamount Province ✦ 16 26.00 N 124.00 W
Baja California Sur □[3] 232 26.00 N 112.00 W
Bajada del Agrio 252 38.23 S 70.02 W
Baján, Méx. 196 26.32 N 101.15 W
Bajan, S.S.S.R. 84 40.34 N 46.09 E
Bajan-Adraga 88 48.37 N 111.05 E
Bajan-Agt 88 49.02 N 102.05 E
Bajanaul 86 50.47 N 75.42 E
Bajancagaan 102 45.06 N 98.40 E
Bajanchajrchan 88 49.18 N 96.20 E
Bajanchongor 90 46.10 N 100.45 E
Bajanchongor □[4] 102 45.00 N 99.30 E
Bajancogt 88 45.54 N 106.10 E
Bajandaj 88 53.04 N 105.30 E
Bajandalaj 102 43.28 N 103.31 E
Bajande'ger 102 45.45 N 112.24 E
Bajandelger 88 47.44 N 108.07 E
Bajandun 88 49.15 N 113.20 E
Bajandžargalan 102 45.31 N 108.01 E
Bajandzürch 88 50.12 N 98.58 E
Bajan-Enger 86 48.25 N 90.50 E
Bajan Erchet Uul ⛰ 88 47.30 N 105.30 E
Bajango 88 48.55 N 106.06 E
Bajangol 88 50.44 N 103.27 E
Bajangov' 102 44.44 N 100.24 E
Bajanleg 102 44.33 N 100.35 E
Bajannuur 86 48.54 N 91.14 E
Bajanölgij □[4] 86 48.20 N 89.50 E
Bajan-Öndör 102 44.47 N 98.39 E
Bajan-Ovoo, Mong. 88 47.47 N 112.05 E
Bajan-Ovoo, Mong. 102 43.11 N 105.37 E
Bajánsenye 61 46.48 N 16.23 E
Bajan Tümen → Čojbalsan 88 48.04 N 114.30 E
Bajan-Uul, Mong. 88 49.41 N 96.20 E
Bajan-Uul, Mong. 88 49.07 N 112.45 E
Bajan-Uul, Mong. 88 47.40 N 101.30 E
Bājaur □[9] 123 34.50 N 71.25 E
Baja Verapaz □[5] 236 15.05 N 90.20 W
Bajawa 115b 8.47 S 120.59 E
Bajbičetau ⛰ 85 41.12 N 75.15 E
Baj-Chak 88 51.13 N 94.34 E
Bajčunas 80 47.14 N 52.55 E
Bajčurovo 80 51.20 N 42.41 E
Bajdonovo 88 54.17 N 104.38 E
Bajdrag Gol ≃ 102 45.38 N 99.15 E
Bājengdoba 124 25.54 N 90.31 E
Baje Phukura 126 23.09 N 89.45 E
Bajer 88 55.44 N 99.30 E
Bajevo 86 53.17 N 80.46 E
Bajgakum 86 44.18 N 66.28 E
Bajghera 272a 28.32 N 77.01 E
Bājgīrān 128 37.36 N 58.24 E
Bajgul 80 48.49 N 49.08 E
Bajiachaidamuhu ⊜ 102 37.30 N 95.12 E
Bajiaokou 98 37.38 N 121.05 E
Bajiazi, Zhg. 104 42.17 N 122.37 E
Bajiazi, Zhg. 104 41.36 N 123.53 E
Bajiazi, Zhg. 104 42.21 N 121.27 E
Bājil 144 15.04 N 43.16 E
Bajimba, Mount ⋀ 166 29.18 S 152.07 E
Bajina Bašta 38 43.58 N 19.34 E
Bajinghe ≃ 102 23.02 N 100.39 E
Bajkadam 85 43.44 N 69.55 E
Bajkal 88 51.53 N 104.47 E
Bajkal, Ozero (Lake Baikal) ⊜ 88 53.00 N 107.40 E
Bajkalovo, S.S.S.R. 86 57.45 N 67.40 E
Bajkalovo, S.S.S.R. 86 57.24 N 63.46 E
Bajkal'sk 88 51.33 N 104.05 E
Bajkal'skij Chrebet ⛰ 88 55.00 N 108.40 E
Bajkal'skoje 88 55.21 N 109.12 E
Bajkit 74 61.41 N 96.25 E
Bajkonyr 86 47.50 N 66.03 E
Bajkovo 80 54.47 N 44.51 E
Bajmak 86 52.36 N 58.19 E
Bajmok 38 45.58 N 19.25 E
Bajnazar 86 48.32 N 73.42 E
Bajo, Indon. 112 0.27 N 120.48 E
Bajo, Indon. 115b 8.35 S 119.01 E
Bajo, Canal ☲ 266a 40.27 N 3.43 W
Bajo Boquete 236 8.47 N 82.26 W
Bajool 166 23.39 S 150.39 E
Bajos de Haina 238 18.25 N 70.02 W
Bajos del Balsamar 234 17.34 N 100.48 W
Bajrački 83 48.22 N 38.32 E
Bajr'aki 80 54.43 N 53.24 E
Bajram-Ali 128 37.37 N 62.10 E

Symbol	English	Deutsch	Español	Français	Português
≃	River	Fluss	Río	Rivière	Rio
☲	Canal	Kanal	Canal	Canal	Canal
ㄴ	Waterfall, Rapids	Wasserfall, Stromschnellen	Cascada, Rápidos	Chute d'eau, Rapides	Cascata, Rápidos
ㄩ	Strait	Meeresstrasse	Estrecho	Détroit	Estreito
C	Bay, Gulf	Bucht, Golf	Bahía, Golfo	Baie, Golfe	Baía, Golfo
⊜	Lake, Lakes	See, Seen	Lago, Lagos	Lac, Lacs	Lago, Lagos
☵	Swamp	Sumpf	Pantano	Marais	Pântano
⊼	Ice Features, Glacier	Eis- und Gletscherformen	Accidentes Glaciales	Formes glaciaires	Acidentes Glaciares
⊤	Other Hydrographic Features	Andere Hydrographische Objekte	Otros Elementos Hidrográficos	Autres données hydrographiques	Outros Elementos Hidrográficos
✦	Submarine Features	Untermeerische Objekte	Accidentes Submarinos	Formes de relief sous-marin	Acidentes Submarinos
□	Political Unit	Politische Einheit	Unidad Política	Entité politique	Unidade Política
⚑	Cultural Institution	Kulturelle Institution	Institución Cultural	Institution culturelle	Instituição Cultural
⊥	Historical Site	Historische Stätte	Sitio Histórico	Site historique	Sitio Histórico
♠	Recreational Site	Erholungs- und Ferienort	Sitio de Recreo	Centre de loisirs	Sítio de Lazer
⊠	Airport	Flughafen	Aeropuerto	Aéroport	Aeroporto
■	Military Installation	Militäranlage	Instalación Militar	Installation militaire	Instalação Militar
◆	Miscellaneous	Verschiedenes	Misceláneo	Divers	Miscelânea

ENGLISH — Name, Page, Lat.°′, Long.°′ · DEUTSCH — Name, Seite, Breite°′, Länge°′ E=Ost

Name	Page	Lat.°′	Long.°′
Bajsa	88	53.58 N	113.33 E
Bajseit	85	43.35 N	78.20 E
Bajsun	85	38.14 N	67.12 E
Bajsuntau, Gory ⛰	85	38.35 N	67.28 E
Baj-S'ut	88	51.42 N	95.22 E
Bajtajlak	86	45.15 N	75.00 E
Bajtas	86	45.24 N	64.51 E
Bajulmati	115a	7.56 S	114.23 E
Bajžansaj	85	43.13 N	69.56 E
Bak	61	46.43 N	16.51 E
Bakal	86	54.56 N	58.48 E
Bakala, Centraf.	152	6.11 N	20.22 E
Bakala, Centraf.	152	3.46 N	17.33 E
Bakaldy	80	55.39 N	44.44 E
Bakalé, Kaga ⛰	152	7.21 N	20.29 E
Bakali ≃	152	4.34 S	17.06 E
Bakaly	80	55.10 N	53.48 E
Bakambe	152	5.39 S	23.37 E
Bakanas	86	44.50 N	76.15 E
Bakanas ≃	86	47.05 N	79.18 E
Bakap	114	4.26 N	101.04 E
Bākarganj	124	22.33 N	90.21 E
Bakaruma	124	22.32 N	83.25 E
Bakbakty	86	44.35 N	76.40 E
Bakčar	86	57.01 N	82.05 E
Bakčar ≃	86	57.37 N	82.18 E
Bake	112	3.03 S	100.16 E
Bakel	150	14.54 N	12.27 W
Bakem	112	1.58 S	105.54 E
Bakenberg ∧[2]	54	54.35 N	13.07 E
Bakenkop	158	28.01 S	23.02 E
Bakeoven Creek ≃	224	45.12 N	121.05 W
Baker, Calif., U.S.	204	35.16 N	116.04 W
Baker, Fla., U.S.	194	30.48 N	86.40 W
Baker, La., U.S.	194	30.35 N	91.10 W
Baker, Mont., U.S.	198	46.22 N	104.17 W
Baker, Oreg., U.S.	202	44.47 N	117.50 W
Baker ≃	224	48.38 N	121.41 W
Baker, Canal ⊔	254	48.00 S	74.00 W
Baker, Mount ∧	224	48.47 N	121.49 W
Baker Butte ∧	200	34.27 N	111.22 W
Baker Canyon ∨	280	33.47 N	117.38 W
Baker Creek ≃, B.C., Can.	182	52.59 N	122.30 W
Baker Creek ≃, Ohio, U.S.	279a	41.21 N	81.54 W
Baker Creek ≃, Oreg., U.S.	224	45.15 N	123.14 W
Baker Island ❙, Oc.	14	0.15 N	176.27 W
Baker Island ❙, Alaska, U.S.	180	55.20 N	133.36 W
Baker Lake	176	64.15 N	96.00 W
Baker Lake ⊜, Austl.	162	26.54 S	126.05 E
Baker Lake ⊜, N.W. Ter., Can.	176	64.10 N	95.30 W
Baker Lake ⊜, Ill., U.S.	278	42.08 N	88.07 W
Baker Lake ⊜[1]	224	48.43 N	121.37 W
Bakersfield	226		
	228	35.23 N	119.01 W
Bakersfield South	228	35.20 N	119.03 W
Bakers Hill	168a	31.45 S	116.27 E
Bakers Island ❙	283	42.32 N	70.47 W
Bakerstown	214	40.39 N	79.56 W
Baker Street	260	51.30 N	0.21 E
Bakersville, N.C., U.S.	192	36.01 N	82.09 W
Bakersville, Ohio, U.S.	214	40.21 N	81.39 W
Bakerville	158	26.00 S	26.06 E
Bakeshu	98	42.26 N	124.37 E
Bâ Kêv	110	13.42 N	107.12 E
Bakewell	44	53.13 N	1.40 W
Bakhra	126	22.24 N	88.11 E
Bākhrābād	126	23.43 N	90.53 E
Bakhri	124	25.35 N	86.16 E
Bakhtegān, Daryācheh-ye ⊜	128	29.20 N	54.05 E
Bakhtīarī va Chahār Maḥāll □[8]	128	32.00 N	51.00 E
Bakhtiyārpur	124	25.28 N	85.31 E
Bakile	154	13.58 S	35.15 E
Bakino	82	56.20 N	38.59 E
Bakinskaja	78	44.46 N	39.18 E
Bakinskij Archipelag ❙❙	84	39.30 N	49.45 E
Bakır ≃	130	38.55 N	27.00 E
Bakırköy	38	40.59 N	28.52 E
Bakkafjörður	24a	66.04 N	14.45 W
Bakkaflói C	24a	66.10 N	14.45 W
Bakkagerði	24a	65.32 N	13.48 W
Bakkeswar	272b	22.25 N	88.22 E
Bakkeveen	52	53.05 N	6.15 E
Baklanka	76	58.43 N	40.06 E
Bakloh	123	32.28 N	75.55 E
Bakluši	80	52.07 N	43.22 E
Bako, C. Iv.	150	9.09 N	7.37 W
Bako, Yai.	144	5.50 N	36.40 E
Bakony ⛰	30	46.55 N	17.40 E
Bakoondfontein	158	32.43 S	22.30 E
Bakori	150	11.34 N	7.27 E
Bakou → Baku	84	40.23 N	49.51 E
Bakouma	152	5.42 N	22.47 E
Bakovka	265b	55.41 N	37.20 E
Bakoye ≃	150	13.49 N	10.50 W
Bakruz'ak	86	52.59 N	58.42 E
Baksan	84	43.40 N	43.32 E
Bakšejevo, S.S.S.R.	80	55.44 N	39.53 E
Bakšejevo, S.S.S.R.	86	57.26 N	73.00 E
Baksir Chāndpur	126	23.30 N	89.44 E
Bakšty	76	53.56 N	26.11 E
Baksuk ≃	86	51.50 N	69.30 E
Baku	84	40.23 N	49.51 E
Bakulin Point ≻	116	8.33 N	126.22 E
Bakum	52	52.45 N	8.11 E
Bakumpai	112	1.26 S	113.05 E
Bakun	120	32.32 N	80.26 E
Bakung, Pulau ❙	112	0.04 N	104.27 E
Bakungan	114	2.56 N	97.30 E
Bakuriani	84	41.46 N	43.32 E
Bakury	80	52.22 N	44.42 E
Bakwa-Kenge	152	4.51 S	22.04 E
Bakwanga → Mbuji-Mayi	152	6.09 S	23.38 E
Bakyrčik	86	49.46 N	81.38 E
Bakyrly	86	44.21 N	67.48 E
Bala, Ont., Can.	212	45.01 N	79.37 W
Bala, Sén.	150	14.02 N	13.10 W
Bâlâ, Tür.	130	39.34 N	33.08 E
Bala, Wales, U.K.	42	52.54 N	3.35 W
Balabac	116	7.59 N	117.04 E
Balabac Island ❙	116	7.57 N	117.01 E
Balabac Strait ⊔	108	7.35 N	117.00 E
Bālā Bāgh	120	34.24 N	70.14 E
Ba'labakk	130	34.00 N	36.12 E
Balabalangan, Kepulauan ❙❙	112	2.20 S	117.25 E
Balaban Dağları ⛰	130	40.28 N	39.15 E
Balabanovo	82	55.11 N	36.40 E
Balabino	78	47.44 N	35.13 E
Balabio, Île ❙	175f	20.07 S	164.11 E
Balachany	84	40.29 N	49.54 E
Balachčin	86	54.09 N	89.23 E
Balachna	80	56.30 N	43.36 E
Balachta	86	55.24 N	91.37 E
Balaci	38	44.21 N	24.55 E
Bala-Cynwyd	285	40.00 N	75.14 W
Balad, 'Irāq	128	34.01 N	44.09 E
Balad, Som.	144	2.22 N	45.25 E
Baladbandh	272b	22.52 N	88.07 E
Baladeh	128	36.12 N	51.48 E
Balad'ok	89	53.41 N	133.07 E
Balagansk	88	53.57 N	103.02 E
Bālāghāt	120	21.48 N	80.11 E
Bālāghāt □[5]	124	22.10 N	80.25 E
Bālāghāt Range ⛰	122	18.45 N	76.30 E
Balagne ◆[1]	36	42.30 N	8.50 E
Balagny-sur-Thérain	50	49.18 N	2.20 E
Balaguer	34	41.47 N	0.49 E
Balaguiri, Mont ∧	152	0.55 N	13.12 E
Balaikarangan	112	0.50 N	110.26 E
Balaiselasa	112	1.48 S	100.50 E
Balaisepuah	112	0.27 N	111.13 E
Balaj	86	55.52 N	93.59 E
Balaka, Malawi	154	14.59 S	34.57 E
Balaka, Zaïre	152	4.51 S	19.57 E
Balakété	152	6.56 N	19.54 E
Balakirevo	82	56.30 N	38.51 E
Balaklava	168b	34.09 S	138.25 E
Balakleja, S.S.S.R.	78	49.14 N	31.44 E
Balakleja, S.S.S.R.	78	49.27 N	36.52 E
Bālākot	123	34.33 N	73.21 E
Balakovo	80	52.02 N	47.47 E
Balallan	46	58.05 N	6.35 W
Balama, Moç.	154	13.20 S	38.30 E
Bal'amā, Urd.	132	32.14 N	36.05 E
Balamban	116	10.30 N	123.42 E
Balambangan, Pulau ❙	112	7.15 N	116.55 E
Bālā Morghāb	128	35.35 N	63.20 E
Bālandi	272b	22.58 N	88.32 E
Balanga	116	14.41 N	120.32 E
Balangala	152	0.24 N	19.45 E
Balangero	62	45.16 N	7.31 E
Balangiga	116	11.07 N	125.23 E
Balāngīr	122	20.43 N	83.29 E
Balanguingui Island ❙	116	6.01 N	121.41 E
Balansuogansumu	102	42.27 N	111.01 E
Balanşūrah	142	27.55 N	30.41 E
Balao ≃	246	2.54 S	79.50 W
Balapulang	115a	7.03 S	109.05 E
Bālāpur	122	20.40 N	76.46 E
Balaqs	273c	30.10 N	31.17 E
Balaqṭar	142	31.05 N	30.13 E
Balaraja	115a	6.12 S	106.27 E
Balarāmbāti	272b	22.48 N	88.13 E
Balarāmpota	272b	22.31 N	88.08 E
Balarāmpur	126	23.07 N	86.13 E
Bālārampuram	122	8.26 N	77.03 E
Balaruc-le-Vieux	62	43.27 N	3.41 E
Balaši	80	51.24 N	49.55 E
Balašicha	82	55.49 N	37.58 E
Balasore	126	21.30 N	86.56 E
Balasore □[5]	126	21.35 N	87.05 E
Balašov	80	51.32 N	43.08 E
Balassagyarmat	30	48.05 N	19.18 E
Balāṭ	140	25.33 N	29.16 E
Balatan, Indon.	164	6.05 S	134.45 E
Balatan, Pil.	116	13.20 N	123.10 E
Balaton	198	44.14 N	95.52 W
Balaton ⊜	30	46.50 N	17.45 E
Balaurin	112	8.15 S	123.43 E
Balavé	150	12.23 N	4.09 W
Balayan	116	13.57 N	120.44 E
Balayan Bay C	116	13.51 N	120.47 E
Balazote	34	38.53 N	2.08 W
Balazote ≃	34	38.59 N	2.05 W
Balbi, Mount ∧[1]	175e	5.55 S	154.59 E
Balbieriškis	76	54.32 N	23.52 E
Balbigny	62	45.49 N	4.11 E
Balbini	60	49.18 N	12.26 E
Balboa	236	8.57 N	79.34 W
Balboa Heights	236	8.57 N	79.33 W
Balbriggan	48	53.37 N	6.11 W
Balcanoona	166	30.31 S	139.18 E
Balcarce	252	37.50 S	58.15 W
Balcarres	184	50.48 N	103.33 W
Bălceşti	38	44.37 N	23.56 E
Balchaš	86	46.49 N	74.59 E
Balchaš, Ozero ⊜	86	46.00 N	74.00 E
Balchen Glacier ◸	9	76.46 S	145.30 W
Balch Springs	222	32.44 N	96.40 W
Balcı	130	38.43 N	34.06 E
Balčik	38	43.25 N	28.10 E
Balclutha	172	46.14 S	169.44 E
Balcombe	42	51.04 N	0.08 W
Balcones Escarpment ⦁[4]	196	29.30 N	99.15 W
Balcosna	252	27.53 S	65.43 W
Balde	252	33.20 S	66.38 W
Baldeador	287a	22.53 S	43.02 W
Bald Eagle	214	40.42 N	78.12 W
Bald Eagle Creek ≃	210	41.08 N	77.24 W
Bald Eagle Mountain ∧	214	41.00 N	77.45 W
Bald Eagle State Park ♠	214	41.00 N	77.40 W
Baldegger See ⊜	58	47.12 N	8.16 E
Baldenburg → Biały Bór	30	53.54 N	16.51 E
Baldeneysee ⊜	263	51.24 N	7.03 E
Balderschwang	58	47.28 N	10.06 E
Balderstone	262	53.47 N	2.34 W
Balderton	42	53.03 N	0.47 W
Bald Head ≻	162	35.07 S	118.01 E
Bald Hill Branch ≃	284c	18.55 N	76.49 W
Baldhill Creek ≃	198	47.09 N	98.03 W
Bald Hills	171a	27.19 S	153.01 E
Baldichieri d'asti	62	44.54 N	8.07 E
Baldim	255	19.17 S	43.57 W
Bald Island ❙	162	34.55 S	118.27 E
Bald Knob	194	35.19 N	91.34 W
Bald Knob ∧, Calif., U.S.	282	37.25 N	122.21 W
Bald Knob ∧, Va., U.S.	192	37.56 N	79.51 W
Bald Knoll ∧	200	42.24 N	110.29 W
Bald Mountain ∧, Conn., U.S.	207	41.59 N	72.25 W
Bald Mountain ∧, Nev., U.S.	226	38.33 N	119.07 W
Bald Mountain ∧, N.J., U.S.	188	41.07 N	74.12 W
Bald Mountain ∧, Oreg., U.S.	202	44.36 N	117.53 W
Bald Mountain ∧, Oreg., U.S.	202	43.16 N	121.21 W
Bald Mountain ∧, Vt., U.S.	210	42.55 N	73.09 W
Bald Mountain State Recreation Area ♠	216	42.46 N	83.14 W
Baldo, Monte ∧	64	45.47 N	10.48 E
Baldock	42	51.59 N	0.12 W
Baldock Lake ⊜	184	56.33 N	97.57 W
Baldone	76	56.45 N	24.24 E
Baldovino, Arroyo ≃	288	34.46 S	58.07 W
Baldoyle	48	53.24 N	6.08 W
Baldpate Pond ⊜	283	42.42 N	71.00 W
Balduinstein	56	50.20 N	7.58 E
Baldur	184	49.23 N	99.15 W
Baldwin, Fla., U.S.	192	30.18 N	81.59 W
Baldwin, La., U.S.	194	29.51 N	91.33 W
Baldwin, Mich., U.S.	190	43.54 N	85.51 W
Baldwin, N.Y., U.S.	210	40.39 N	73.37 W
Baldwin, Pa., U.S.	214	40.23 N	79.58 W
Baldwin, Wis., U.S.	190	44.58 N	92.22 W
Baldwin Bay C	276	40.38 N	73.35 W
Baldwin City	198	38.47 N	95.11 W
Baldwin Creek ≃	279a	41.22 N	81.51 W
Baldwin Hills ⛰[2]	280	34.00 N	118.22 W
Baldwin Lake ⊜	279a	41.21 N	81.51 W
Baldwin Park	228	34.06 N	117.58 W
Baldwin Peninsula ≻[1]	180	66.44 N	162.15 W
Baldwinsville	210	43.09 N	76.20 W
Baldwinville	207	42.36 N	72.05 W
Baldwin-Wallace College ♉[2]	279a	41.23 N	81.51 W
Baldwyn	194	34.31 N	88.38 W
Baldy Mountain ∧, B.C., Can.	182	51.28 N	120.02 W
Baldy Mountain ∧, Man., Can.	184	51.28 N	100.44 W
Baldy Mountain ∧, Mont., U.S.	202	48.09 N	109.39 W
Baldy Mountain ∧, N. Mex., U.S.	200	36.38 N	105.13 W
Baldy Peak ∧	200	33.55 N	109.35 W
Bal'dzuan	120	38.15 N	69.31 E
Bale, Bhārat	272c	19.08 N	73.06 E
Bale, Jugo.	64	45.02 N	13.48 E
Bâle → Basel, Schw.	58	47.33 N	7.35 E
Bale □[4]	144	6.20 N	41.30 E
Bale ∧	144	7.00 N	40.10 E
Bale-Akiosi	273a	6.41 N	3.21 E
Balearen → Baleares, Islas ❙❙	34	39.30 N	3.00 E
Baleares □[4]	34	39.30 N	3.00 E
Baléares, Îles → Baleares, Islas ❙❙	34	39.30 N	3.00 E
Baleares, Islas (Balearic Islands) ❙❙	34	39.30 N	3.00 E
Balearic Islands → Baleares, Islas ❙❙	34	39.30 N	3.00 E
Balegane	158	26.04 S	31.34 E
Baleia, Ponta da ≻	255	17.40 S	39.07 W
Baleine, Rivière à la ≃	176	58.15 N	67.40 W
Balej	88	51.36 N	116.38 E
Balelasberg ⛰	158	27.30 S	30.07 E
Bâle-Mulhouse, Aéroport ⊠	58	47.35 N	7.32 E
Balen	56	51.10 N	5.09 E
Balena	152	0.55 N	20.00 E
Baleno	116	12.28 N	123.30 E
Baler	116	15.46 N	121.34 E
Baler Bay C	116	15.50 N	121.35 E
Baleshare ❙	46	57.31 N	7.22 W
Balesin Island ❙	116	14.26 N	122.02 E
Balestrand	26	61.12 N	6.32 E
Balestrate	70	38.03 N	13.00 E
Baléya	150	9.15 N	10.29 W
Balezino	80	57.58 N	53.00 E
Balfate	236	15.48 N	86.25 W
Balfes Creek	166	20.13 S	145.55 E
Balfour, N.Z.	172	45.50 S	168.35 E
Balfour, S. Afr.	158	26.44 S	28.31 E
Balfour, Scot., U.K.	46	59.01 N	2.55 W
Balfour, N.C., U.S.	192	35.21 N	82.28 W
Balfour Downs	162	22.50 S	120.50 E
Balfour Park ♠	273d	26.08 S	28.06 E
Balfron	46	56.04 N	4.20 W
Balgach	58	47.25 N	9.35 E
Balgarčaj ≃	84	39.27 N	48.33 E
Bâlgarija → Bulgaria □[1]	38	43.00 N	25.00 E
Balgazyn	88	51.08 N	95.00 E
Balgo Hill Mission	162	20.09 S	127.48 E
Balgowlah	274a	33.48 S	151.16 E
Balguerie, Cap ≻	174x	9.45 S	138.47 W
Balhannah	168b	35.00 S	138.50 E
Bali, Bhārat	120	25.50 N	74.05 E
Bali, Cam.	152	5.53 N	10.01 E
Bali □[4]	115b	8.30 S	115.00 E
Bali ❙	115b	8.20 S	115.00 E
Bali, Laut (Bali Sea) ⊤[2]	112	7.45 S	115.30 E
Bali, Selat ⊔	112	8.18 S	114.25 E
Balia	150	9.20 N	10.57 W
Bāliākāndi	126	23.38 N	89.33 E
Baliangao	116	8.40 N	123.36 E
Bāliāpāl	126	21.40 N	87.17 E
Bāliāti	126	23.59 N	90.03 E
Balibago	116	13.37 N	121.18 E
Baliceaux Island ❙	241h	12.57 N	61.08 W
Bāli Chak	126	22.22 N	87.33 E
Balicuatro Islands ❙❙	116	12.39 N	124.24 E
Balicuatro Point ≻	116	12.35 N	124.16 E
Balidianzi	98	41.13 N	124.49 E
Bālidiha	126	21.58 N	86.38 E
Balige	114	2.20 N	99.04 E
Bālighai	126	21.52 N	87.35 E
Balihan	98	41.29 N	118.41 E
Bālihāti	272b	22.44 N	88.19 E
Balıkesir	130	39.39 N	27.53 E
Balıkesir □[4]	130	39.45 N	27.50 E
Balīkh ≃	130	35.53 N	39.10 E
Balikpapan	112	1.17 S	116.50 E
Balikumbat	152	5.54 N	10.23 E
Balikun	90	43.50 N	93.30 E
Balimbing, Indon.	112	5.55 S	104.34 E
Balimbing, Pil.	116	5.05 N	119.58 E
Balimo	164	8.03 S	142.56 E
Balin, S.S.S.R.	78	48.52 N	26.40 E
Balin, Zhg.	89	48.19 N	122.19 E
Balindong (Watu)	116	7.55 N	124.12 E
Baling	114	5.40 N	100.55 E
Balingasag	116	8.45 N	124.47 E
Balingen	58	48.16 N	8.51 E
Balingian	112	2.55 N	112.32 E
Balingup	162	33.48 S	115.58 E
Balintang Channel ⊔	108	19.49 N	121.40 E
Balinzuoqi	90	44.00 N	119.00 E
Balipu	105	39.53 N	117.48 E
Balışıh	130	39.56 N	33.43 E
Baliuag	116	14.57 N	120.54 E
Baliung ≃	115a	6.50 S	105.52 E
Baliungan Island ❙	116	5.09 N	120.12 E
Baliyingzi	104	41.59 N	121.14 E
Baliza	255	16.15 S	52.25 W
Balizhuang, Zhg.	105	39.16 N	116.28 E
Balizhuang, Zhg.	271a	39.52 N	116.28 E
Balk	52	52.54 N	5.34 E
Balkach, Lago → Balchaš, Ozero ⊜	86	46.00 N	74.00 E
Balkan Mountains → Stara Planina ⛰	38	43.15 N	25.00 E
Balkašino	86	52.31 N	68.46 E
Balkbrug	52	52.36 N	6.24 E
Balkh	120	36.46 N	66.54 E
Balkh □[4]	120	36.30 N	67.00 E
Balkhash → Balchaš	86	46.49 N	74.59 E
Balkhash, Lake → Balchaš, Ozero ⊜	86	46.00 N	74.00 E
Balki	78	47.23 N	34.57 E
Balla	48	53.48 N	9.09 W
Balla Balla	154	20.26 S	29.02 E
Ballabgarh	124	28.21 N	77.19 E
Ballabhpur	272b	22.44 N	88.21 E
Ballachulish	46	56.40 N	5.10 W
Balladonia	162	32.27 S	123.51 E
Ballagh	48	52.35 N	7.59 W
Ballaghaderreen	48	53.55 N	8.36 W
Ballālpur	122	19.50 N	79.22 E
Ballan	169	37.36 S	144.14 E
Ballancourt	50	48.31 N	2.23 E
Ballangen	24	68.20 N	16.50 E
Ballantine	202	45.57 N	108.09 W
Ballantrae	44	55.06 N	5.00 W
Ballao	71	39.33 N	9.22 E
Ballarat	169	37.34 S	143.52 E
Ballard, Lake ⊜	162	29.27 S	120.55 E
Ballardvale	207	42.38 N	71.10 W
Ballata	70	37.58 N	12.41 E
Ballater	46	57.03 N	3.03 W
Ballaugh	44	54.20 N	4.32 W
Ball Bay C	174c	29.03 S	167.59 E
Ballé	150	15.20 N	8.35 W
Ballen	41	55.49 N	10.39 E
Ballenas, Bahía de C	232	26.45 N	113.26 W
Ballenas, Canal de ⊔	232	29.10 N	113.29 W
Ballenato, Punta ≻	286b	23.06 N	82.30 W
Ballengeich	158	27.52 S	29.59 E
Ballenita, Punta ≻	252	25.46 S	70.44 W
Ballenstedt	54	51.43 N	11.14 E
Balleny Islands ❙❙	9	66.35 S	162.50 E
Balleroy	32	49.11 N	0.50 W
Ballerup	41	55.44 N	12.22 E
Ballesteros, Arg.	252	32.33 S	62.59 W
Ballesteros, Pil.	116	18.25 N	121.31 E
Ball Ground	192	34.21 N	84.23 W
Ballı	130	40.50 N	27.03 E
Ballia	124	25.45 N	84.10 E
Ballia □[5]	124	26.00 N	84.00 E
Ballico	226	37.27 N	120.42 W
Ballidu	162	30.36 S	116.46 E
Ballina, Austl.	166	28.52 S	153.33 E
Ballina, Eire	28	54.07 N	9.09 W
Ballina, Eire	48	52.49 N	8.26 W
Ballinakill	48	52.53 N	7.18 W
Ballinalack	48	53.37 N	7.28 W
Ballinascarty	48	51.40 N	8.51 W
Ballinasloe	48	53.20 N	8.13 W
Ballinderry ≃	44	54.40 N	6.31 W
Ballindine	48	53.39 N	8.59 W
Ballineen	48	51.44 N	8.56 W
Ballingarry	48	52.29 N	8.52 W
Ballingeary	48	51.49 N	9.13 W
Ballinger	196	31.44 N	99.57 W
Ballingslöv	41	56.13 N	13.51 E
Ballinluig	46	56.38 N	3.39 W
Ballino	64	45.58 N	10.48 E
Ballinrobe	48	53.37 N	9.13 W
Ballinskelligs Bay C	48	51.50 N	10.15 W
Ballintoy	48	55.14 N	6.21 W
Ballintra	48	54.35 N	8.08 W
Balloch	46	57.29 N	4.07 W
Ballon	50	48.10 N	0.14 E
Ballona Creek ≃	280	33.58 N	118.27 W
Ballos, Col d')(	62	44.18 N	6.36 E
Ballouville	207	41.52 N	71.52 W
Balls Pyramid ❙	160	31.45 S	159.15 E
Ballston	224	45.04 N	123.15 W
Ballston Lake	210	42.54 N	73.52 W
Ballston Spa	210	43.00 N	73.51 W
Ballville	214	41.20 N	83.09 W
Ballwin	219	38.35 N	90.33 W
Bālly, Bhārat	272b	22.38 N	88.21 E
Bally, Pa., U.S.	208	40.24 N	75.35 W
Bālly ◆[8]	272b	22.39 N	88.21 E
Ballybay	48	54.08 N	6.54 W
Ballybofey	48	54.57 N	7.47 W
Ballybogey	48	55.07 N	6.34 W
Bālly Bridge ◆[5]	272b	22.39 N	88.21 E
Ballybunion	48	52.31 N	9.40 W
Ballycanew	48	52.36 N	6.19 W
Ballycastle, Eire	48	54.16 N	9.23 W
Ballycastle, N. Ire., U.K.	48	55.12 N	6.15 W
Ballycastle Bay C	44	55.13 N	6.15 W
Ballyclare	48	54.46 N	6.01 W
Ballyconneely	48	53.26 N	10.02 W
Ballyconnell	48	54.07 N	7.35 W
Ballycotton	48	51.50 N	8.01 W
Ballycroy	48	54.01 N	9.51 W
Ballyduff, Eire	48	52.27 N	9.40 W
Ballyduff, Eire	48	52.09 N	8.03 W
Ballyferriter	48	52.09 N	10.26 W
Ballyfinboy ≃	48	53.02 N	8.15 W
Ballygar	48	53.32 N	8.20 W
Ballygawley	48	54.28 N	7.02 W
Ballygorman	48	55.22 N	7.21 W
Ballygunge ◆[8]	272b	22.31 N	88.21 E
Ballyhaise	48	54.03 N	7.19 W
Ballyhalbert	48	54.30 N	5.28 W
Ballyhaunis	48	53.46 N	8.46 W
Ballyhoura Hills ⛰[2]	48	52.20 N	8.35 W
Ballyjamesduff	48	53.52 N	7.12 W
Ballylongford	48	52.33 N	9.28 W
Ballymacoda	48	51.57 N	7.54 W
Ballymahon	48	53.34 N	7.45 W
Ballymakeery (Ballyvourney)	48	51.55 N	9.09 W
Ballymena	48	54.52 N	6.17 W
Ballymoe	48	53.42 N	8.29 W
Ballymoney	48	55.04 N	6.31 W
Ballymurray	48	53.35 N	8.08 W
Ballyneety	48	52.35 N	8.33 W
Ballynoe	48	52.03 N	8.05 W
Ballyquintin Point ≻	48	54.20 N	5.29 W
Ballyragget	48	52.47 N	7.20 W
Ballysadare	48	54.13 N	8.31 W
Ballyshannon	48	54.30 N	8.11 W
Ballyvaughan	48	53.07 N	9.07 W
Ballyvoy	48	55.12 N	6.11 W
Ballywalter	48	54.33 N	5.30 W
Balm	220	27.46 N	82.16 W
Balmaceda	254	45.55 S	71.41 W
Balmaceda, Cerro ∧	254	51.25 S	73.11 W
Balmain	274a	33.51 S	151.11 E
Balme	62	45.18 N	7.13 E
Balmerino	46	56.24 N	3.02 W
Balmertown	184	51.04 N	93.44 W
Balmoral, Austl.	166	37.15 S	141.51 E
Balmoral, S. Afr.	158	25.52 S	28.59 E
Balmoral Castle	46	57.20 N	3.15 W
Balmoral Castle ⊥	46	57.02 N	3.14 W
Balmorhea	196	30.59 N	103.45 W
Balmumcu ◆[8]	267b	41.04 N	29.01 E
Balmville	210	41.32 N	74.01 W
Balnacra	46	57.28 N	5.23 W
Balnearia	252	31.00 S	62.40 W
Balobanovo	82	55.51 N	38.14 E
Balobe	154	0.05 N	28.00 E
Baloda Bāzār	120	21.40 N	82.10 E
Balogoje	24	57.54 N	34.02 E
Balong, Indon.	115a	7.57 S	111.26 E
Balong, Zhg.	102	36.17 N	97.20 E
Balonne ≃	166	28.47 S	147.56 E
Bālotra	120	25.50 N	72.14 E
Balovale	152	13.33 S	23.06 E
Baloži	76	56.53 N	24.06 E
Balpahari Reservoir ⊜[1]	126	24.04 N	86.28 E
Balrāmpur	124	27.26 N	82.11 E
Balranald	166	34.38 S	143.33 E
Balş	38	44.21 N	24.06 E
Balsam Lake	190	45.27 N	92.27 W
Balsam Lake ⊜	212	44.35 N	78.50 W
Bálsamo	255	20.27 S	53.57 W
Balsas	250	7.31 S	46.02 W
Balsas ≃, Méx.	234	17.55 N	102.10 W
Balsas ≃, Pan.	246	8.15 N	77.59 W
Balsas, Rio das ≃, Bra.	250	7.14 S	44.33 W
Balsas, Rio das ≃, Bra.	250	9.58 S	47.52 W
Balseiros ≃	250	5.51 S	43.44 W
Balsham	42	52.08 N	0.20 E
Balsorano	66	41.49 N	13.34 E
Bålsta	40	59.35 N	17.30 E
Balsthal	58	47.19 N	7.42 E
Balta	78	47.55 N	29.37 E
Baltaj	80	52.28 N	46.38 E
Baltanás	34	41.56 N	4.15 W
Baltasar Brum	252	30.44 S	57.19 W
Baltasi	80	56.21 N	50.12 E
Baltasound	46a	60.45 N	0.52 W
Baltazar, Arroyo ≃	258	33.47 S	58.58 W
Bălţi → Bel'cy	78	47.46 N	27.56 E
Baltic, Conn., U.S.	207	41.37 N	72.05 W
Baltic, Ohio, U.S.	214	40.27 N	81.42 W
Baltic Bay C	190	48.22 N	83.43 W
Baltico, Mar → Baltic Sea ⊤[2]	24	57.00 N	19.00 E
Baltic Sea ⊤[2]	24	57.00 N	19.00 E
Baltijsk	76	54.39 N	19.55 E
Baltijskaja Kosa ≻[2]	30	54.25 N	19.35 E
Baltijskij Vokzal ◆[5]	265a	59.55 N	30.18 E
Balṭīm	142	31.33 N	31.05 E
Baltimore, Eire	48	51.29 N	9.22 W
Baltimore, S. Afr.	156	23.15 S	28.20 E
Baltimore, Md., U.S.	208		
	284b	39.17 N	76.37 W
Baltimore, Ohio, U.S.	188	39.51 N	82.36 W
Baltimore □[6]	208	39.24 N	76.36 W
Baltimore, University of ♉[2]	284b	39.21 N	76.40 W
Baltimore Airpark ⊠	284b	39.24 N	76.25 W
Baltimore Highlands	284b	39.14 N	76.38 W
Baltimore-Washington International Airport ⊠	208	39.11 N	76.40 W
Baltinglass	48	52.55 N	6.41 W
Baltique, Mer → Baltic Sea ⊤[2]	24	57.00 N	19.00 E
Baltistān ◆[1]	123	35.30 N	76.05 E
Baltit	123	36.20 N	74.40 E
Baltoji-Vokė	76	54.28 N	25.06 E
Baltoro Glacier ◸	123	35.45 N	76.25 E
Baltra, Isla ❙	246a	0.26 S	90.16 W
Baltrum ❙	52	53.44 N	7.23 E
Baluarte, Arroyo ∨	196	27.09 N	98.07 W
Baluarte, Boca del ≃[1]	234	22.48 N	106.02 W
Baluarte, Río del ≃	234	22.49 N	106.02 W
Balucas, Barranca ≃	234	18.36 N	100.40 W
Balūchestān va Sīstān □[4]	128	28.30 N	60.30 E
Baluchistān □[4]	120	29.00 N	67.00 E
Baluchistan □[9]	128	28.00 N	63.00 E
Balud	116	12.02 N	123.12 E
Bālughāta	126	22.05 N	88.01 E
Bāluhāti	272b	22.39 N	88.16 E
Balui ≃	112	2.42 N	113.47 E
Balukbaluk Island ❙	116	6.40 N	121.43 E
Balum	144	8.38 N	46.48 E
Bālurghāt	124	25.13 N	88.46 E
Balut Island ❙	116	5.24 N	125.23 E
Balvano	68	40.39 N	15.31 E
Balve	56	51.20 N	7.51 E
Balvi	76	57.08 N	27.17 E
Balvicar	46	56.14 N	5.38 W
Balvupe ≃	76	56.57 N	26.55 E
Balwyn	274b	37.49 S	145.05 E
Balxuca, Arroyo de la ≃	266d	41.31 N	2.06 E
Balya	130	39.45 N	27.35 E
Balygyčan	74	63.56 N	154.12 E
Balykči	85	40.54 N	71.50 E
Balyksa	86	53.25 N	89.05 E
Balykši	80	47.05 N	51.54 E
Balzac	182	51.10 N	114.01 W
Balzar	246	1.22 S	79.54 W
Balzers	58	47.04 N	9.30 E
Bal'zino	88	51.03 N	113.35 E
Balzola	62	45.11 N	8.24 E
Bam, Īrān	128	29.06 N	58.21 E
Bām, Īrān	128	36.58 N	57.59 E
Bama, Nig.	146	11.30 N	13.41 E
Bama, Zhg.	102	24.21 N	107.08 E
Bamaga	164	10.52 S	142.24 E
Bamaji Lake ⊜	184	51.09 N	91.25 W
Bamako	150	12.39 N	8.00 W
Bamako □[4]	150	13.00 N	8.00 W
Bāmangāchi	272b	22.46 N	88.31 E
Bāmangawān	126	24.14 N	86.49 E
Bāmanghāra	272b	22.31 N	88.28 E
Bāmanmura	272b	22.42 N	88.31 E
Bamao	100	29.26 N	120.59 E
Bamata	152	1.00 S	21.06 E
Bamba, Mali	150	17.02 N	1.24 W
Bamba, Zaïre	152	5.45 S	18.23 E
Bambamarca	248	6.41 S	78.32 W
Bamban	116	15.17 N	120.34 E
Bambana ≃	236	13.27 N	83.50 W
Bambang	116	16.23 N	121.06 E
Bambannan Island ❙	116	5.37 N	120.17 E
Bambara Maoundé	150	15.51 N	2.47 W
Bambari	152	5.45 N	20.40 E
Bambaroo	166	18.52 S	146.12 E
Bambatana	175e	7.02 S	156.48 E
Bambāvi	272c	18.58 N	73.03 E
Bamberg, B.R.D.	56	49.53 N	10.53 E
Bamberg, S.C., U.S.	192	33.17 N	81.02 W
Bamber Lake	208	39.54 N	74.19 W
Bamberton	224	48.35 N	123.31 W
Bambesa	154	3.28 N	25.43 E
Bambesi	144	9.45 N	34.38 E
Bambetoka, Baie de C	157b	15.50 S	46.17 E
Bambili	154	3.39 N	26.07 E
Bambinga	152	3.42 S	18.54 E
Bambio	152	3.54 N	16.59 E
Bamboesberg ⛰	158	31.30 S	26.10 E
Bamboi	150	8.10 N	2.02 W
Bamboo Creek	162	20.56 S	120.13 E
Bamboo Springs	162	22.04 S	119.38 E
Bambu	256	22.31 S	46.26 W
Bambuí	255	20.01 S	45.58 W
Bambujka	88	55.47 N	115.48 E
Bambula	154	1.17 S	25.38 E
Bamburgh	44	55.36 N	1.42 W
Bamencheng	105	39.35 N	117.37 E
Bamenda	152	5.56 N	10.10 E
Bamendjou	152	5.24 N	10.19 E
Bamfield	182	48.50 N	125.08 W
Bamhā	142	29.35 N	31.14 E
Bami	128	38.44 N	56.48 E
Bāmīān	120	34.50 N	67.50 E
Bāmīān □[4]	120	34.45 N	67.15 E
Bamiancheng	89	43.13 N	124.02 E
Bamianshan ∧	100	26.02 N	113.40 E
Bamingui	152	7.34 N	20.11 E
Bamingui ≃	146	8.33 N	19.05 E
Bamingui-Bangoran □[5]	146	7.50 N	20.15 E
Bamingui-Bangoran, Parc National du ♠	146	8.00 N	19.40 E
Bam Island ❙	164	3.35 S	144.50 E
Bāmna	126	22.19 N	90.06 E
Bamndali ◆[8]	272a	28.33 N	77.03 E
Bamol	164	7.38 S	138.37 E
Bampton, Eng., U.K.	42	51.00 N	3.29 W
Bampton, Eng., U.K.	42	51.44 N	1.33 W
Bampūr	128	27.12 N	60.27 E
Bampūr ≃	128	27.18 N	59.06 E
Bāmra Hills ⛰[2]	120	21.30 N	84.30 E
Bamumo	120	32.30 N	93.15 E
Bana, Malawi	154	12.25 S	34.08 E
Ba-na, Viet.	110	15.59 N	107.59 E
Baña, Punta de la ≻	34	40.34 N	0.38 E
Banā, Wādī ∨	144	13.03 N	45.24 E
Banāder va Jazāyer-e Khalīj-e Fārs □[4]	128	28.00 N	52.00 E
Banāder va Jazāyer-e 'Ommān □[4]	128	27.00 N	56.00 E
Ban Aen	110	18.02 N	98.37 E
Banagher	48	53.11 N	7.59 W
Banagher, Lake ⊜	158	26.20 S	30.19 E
Banagi	154	2.16 S	34.51 E
Banago	116	7.30 N	124.07 E
Banagrām	126	22.35 N	89.55 E
Banahao, Mount ∧	116	14.04 N	121.29 E
Banalia	154	1.33 N	25.20 E
Banamba	150	13.33 N	7.27 W
Banana, Austl.	166	24.28 S	150.07 E
Banana, Zaïre	152	6.01 S	12.24 E
Banana Creek ≃	220	28.36 N	80.38 W
Banana Islands ❙❙	150	8.07 N	13.13 W
Bananal	256	22.41 S	44.19 W
Bananal ≃, Bra.	250	8.33 S	49.26 W
Bananal ≃, Bra.	256	22.32 S	44.11 W
Bananal, Ilha do ❙	250	11.30 S	50.15 W
Banana River C	220	28.25 N	80.38 W
Bananeiras	250	6.45 S	35.37 W
Bananga	110	6.56 N	93.54 E
Bānār ≃	126	24.04 N	90.38 E
Banaras → Vārānasi	124	25.20 N	83.00 E
Banari	71	40.34 N	8.42 E
Bānaripāra	126	22.47 N	90.10 E
Banarlı	130	41.04 N	27.20 E
Banās ≃	120	25.54 N	76.45 E
Banās, Ra's ≻	140	23.54 N	35.48 E
Banat ◆[1]	38	45.20 N	20.40 E
Banate Bay C	116	10.58 N	122.48 E
Banay, Mount ∧	116	13.42 N	121.10 E
Banaz	130	38.46 N	29.46 E
Ban Baen Phichit	269a	13.50 N	100.40 E
Ban Ban	110	19.38 N	103.34 E
Ban Bang Chan	269a	13.49 N	100.42 E
Ban Bang O	269a	13.53 N	100.36 E
Ban Bang Phli Yai	269a	13.36 N	100.42 E
Ban Bang Phraek	269a	13.53 N	100.26 E
Ban Bang Pu	269a	13.31 N	100.39 E
Ban-bat	110	13.13 N	108.39 E
Banbidian, Zhg.	105	39.21 N	115.21 E
Banbidian, Zhg.	271a	39.54 N	116.32 E
Ban-blech	110	13.12 N	108.13 E
Ban Bonèng	110	17.58 N	104.35 E
Ban Bouang-nom	110	15.47 N	106.47 E
Banbridge	48	54.21 N	6.16 W
Ban Bua Chum	110	15.15 N	101.12 E
Banbuji	100	33.34 N	116.44 E
Ban Bung Fang Nok	269a	13.48 N	100.43 E
Ban Bung Na Rang	110	16.11 N	100.09 E
Ban Bungxai	110	15.42 N	106.14 E
Banbury	42	52.04 N	1.20 W
Bancahsaga	114	0.49 N	101.07 E
Bancalan Island ❙	116	8.14 N	117.06 E
Ban Chak	110	14.17 N	105.25 E
Ban Cha La	110	17.11 N	106.05 E
Bancheng	98	35.17 N	118.18 E
Banchengcun	105	39.36 N	115.16 E
Bānchhārāmpur	126	23.46 N	90.48 E
Banchory	46	57.30 N	2.30 W
Banco, Punta ≻	236	8.23 N	83.09 W
Bancos, Isla → Banks Island ❙	176	73.15 N	121.30 W
Bancroft, Ont., Can.	212	45.03 N	77.51 W
Bancroft, Idaho, U.S.	202	42.43 N	111.53 W
Bancroft, Iowa, U.S.	190	43.18 N	94.13 W
Bancroft, Mich., U.S.	216	42.53 N	84.04 W
Bancroft, Nebr., U.S.	198	42.00 N	96.34 W
Bancroft → Chililabombwe, Zam.	154	12.18 S	27.43 E
Bancun	106	30.53 N	118.48 E
Band	120	33.17 N	68.39 E
Bānda, Bhārat	124	25.29 N	80.20 E
Banda, Bhārat	124	24.03 N	78.57 E
Banda, Zaïre	154	4.11 N	27.04 E
Banda, Kepulauan ❙❙	164	4.35 S	129.55 E
Banda, Laut (Banda Sea) ⊤[2]	108	5.00 S	128.00 E
Banda, Pulau ❙	164	4.34 S	129.55 E
Banda Aceh (Kuturaja)	114	5.34 N	95.20 E
Bandabe	157b	15.31 S	49.04 E
Bānda Dāūd Shāh	123	33.16 N	71.11 E
Banda del Río Salí	252	26.50 S	65.10 W
Banda Elat	164	5.39 S	132.59 E
Bandahara, Gunung ∧	114	3.45 N	97.47 E
Bandai-asahi-kokuritsu-kōen ♠	92	38.16 N	139.57 E
Bandai-san ∧	92	37.36 N	140.04 E
Bandak ⊜	26	59.24 N	8.15 E
Bandama ≃	150	5.10 N	5.00 W
Bandama Blanc ≃	150	6.54 N	5.31 W
Bandama Rouge ≃	150	6.54 N	5.31 W
Bandān, Īrān	128	31.23 N	60.44 E
Ban Dan, Thai	110	15.19 N	105.30 E
Bandanaira	164	4.32 S	129.54 E
Bandan'gou	105	39.08 N	115.11 E
Ban Dangtai	110	17.06 N	104.57 E
Ban Dan Lan Hoi	110	17.00 N	99.35 E
Bandar → Machilīpatnam, Bhārat	122	16.10 N	81.08 E
Bandar, Indon.	115a	7.02 S	109.47 E
Bandar 'Abbās	128	27.11 N	56.17 E
Bandar Baharu	114	5.08 N	100.30 E
Bandardurian	114	2.21 N	99.44 E
Bandar-e Chārak	128	26.43 N	54.16 E
Bandar-e Deylam	128	30.04 N	50.10 E
Bandar-e Gaz	128	36.47 N	53.59 E
Bandar-e Lengeh	128	26.33 N	54.53 E
Bandar-e Māh Shahr	128	30.33 N	49.12 E
Bandar-e Moghūyeh	128	26.35 N	54.31 E
Bandar-e Pahlavī	128	37.28 N	49.27 E
Bandar-e Rīg	128	29.29 N	50.38 E
Bandar-e Shāh	128	36.56 N	54.06 E
Bandar-e Shāhpūr	128	30.25 N	49.05 E
Bandar Penggaram → Batu Pahat	114	1.51 N	102.56 E
Bandarpulau	114	2.41 N	99.31 E
Bandar Seri Begawan	112	4.56 N	114.55 E
Bandawe	154	11.57 S	34.10 E
Bande	34	42.02 N	7.58 W
Banded Peak ∧	200	37.06 N	106.38 W
Bandeira, Pico da ∧	255	20.26 S	41.47 W
Bandeira do Sul	256	21.47 S	46.23 W
Bandeirantes, Bra.	255	23.06 S	50.21 W
Bandeirantes, Bra.	255	13.41 S	50.48 W
Bandeirantes, Bra.	255	19.53 S	54.23 W
Bandeirantes, Palácio dos ♉	287b	23.36 S	46.43 W
Bandeirantes, Praia dos ⦁[2]	287a	23.01 S	43.25 W
Bandéko	152	1.56 N	17.28 E
Bāndel	272b	22.56 N	88.22 E
Bandeli	157a	12.55 S	45.13 E
Bandelier National Monument ♠	200	35.45 N	106.20 W
Band-e Nīlāq, Kūh-e ∧	128	26.37 N	59.49 E
Bandera, Arg.	252	28.54 S	62.16 W
Bandera, Tex., U.S.	196	29.44 N	99.04 W
Bandera, Alto ∧	238	18.49 N	70.37 W
Bandera Bajada	252	27.14 S	63.31 W
Banderas	200	31.01 N	105.35 W
Banderas, Bahía de C	234	20.40 N	105.25 W
Banderilla	234	19.36 N	96.56 W
Bāndhi	120	26.35 N	68.18 E
Bandholm	41	54.50 N	11.29 E
Bandiagara	150	14.21 N	3.37 W
Bandiantaolehai	102	41.41 N	104.06 E
Bāndikūi	124	27.03 N	76.34 E
Bandipur, Bhārat	272b	22.44 N	88.26 E
Bandipur, Bhārat	272b	22.51 N	88.10 E
Bandīpur, Nepāl	124	27.56 N	84.25 E
Bandipura	123	34.25 N	74.39 E
Bandırma	130	40.20 N	27.58 E
Bandırma Körfezi C	130	40.25 N	28.00 E
Bando	152	15.00 S	20.30 E
Bandol	62	43.08 N	5.45 E
Bandon, Eire	48	51.45 N	8.45 W
Ban Don → Surat Thani, Thai	110	9.08 N	99.19 E
Bandon, Oreg., U.S.	202	43.07 N	124.25 W
Ban-don, Viet.	110	12.53 N	107.48 E
Bandon ≃	48	51.42 N	8.30 W
Ban Donhiang	110	18.05 N	101.48 E
Ban Dônko	110	16.12 N	106.17 E
Ban Don Muang	269a	13.55 N	100.36 E
B'andovan	84	39.46 N	49.23 E
Bāndra ◆[8]	272c	19.03 N	72.49 E
Bāndra Point ≻	272c	19.03 N	72.49 E
Bānduān	126	22.53 N	86.31 E
Bandula	156	19.02 S	33.07 E
Bandundu	152	3.18 S	17.20 E
Bandundu □[4]	152	4.30 S	18.30 E

Symbols in the index entries represent the broad categories identified in the key at the right. Symbols with superior numbers (⛰[2]) identify subcategories (see complete key on page *I · 30*).

Kartensymbole in dem Registerverzeichnis stellen die rechts in Schlüssel erklärten Kategorien dar. Symbole mit hochgestellten Ziffern (⛰[2]) bezeichnen Unterabteilungen einer Kategorie (vgl. vollständiger Schlüssel auf Seite *I · 30*).

Los símbolos incluídos en el texto del índice representan las grandes categorias identificadas con la clave a la derecha. Los símbolos con numeros en su parte superior (⛰[2]) identifican las subcategorías (véase la clave completa en la página *I · 30*).

Les symboles de l'index représentent les catégories indiquées dans la légende à droite. Les symboles suivis d'un indice (⛰[2]) représentent des sous-catégories (voir légende complète à la page *I · 30*).

Os símbolos incluídos no texto do índice representam as grandes categorias identificadas com a chave à direita. Os símbolos com números em sua parte superior (⛰[2]) identificam as subcategorias (veja-se a chave completa à página *I · 30*).

	English	Deutsch	Español	Français	Português
∧	Mountain	Berg	Montaña	Montagne	Montanha
⛰	Mountains	Berge	Montañas	Montagnes	Montanhas
)(	Pass	Pass	Paso	Col	Passo
∨	Valley, Canyon	Tal, Cañon	Valle, Cañón	Vallée, Canyon	Vale, Canhão
⌣	Plain	Ebene	Llano	Plaine	Planície
≻	Cape	Kap	Cabo	Cap	Cabo
❙	Island	Insel	Isla	Île	Ilha
❙❙	Islands	Inseln	Islas	Îles	Ilhas
⦁	Other Topographic Features	Andere Topographische Objekte	Otros Elementos Topográficos	Autres données topographiques	Outros Elementos Topográficos

ESPAÑOL · FRANÇAIS · PORTUGUÊS

Nombre / Nom / Nome	Página / Page	Lat.°′	Long.°′ W=Oeste / W=Ouest
Bandung	115a	6.54 S	107.36 E
Băneasa	38	44.04 N	27.42 E
Bāneh	128	35.59 N	45.53 E
Banehra	272a	28.44 N	77.23 E
Banes	240p	20.58 N	75.43 W
Banff, Alta., Can.	182	51.10 N	115.34 W
Banff, Scot., U.K.	46	57.40 N	2.33 W
Banff National Park ♠	182	51.38 N	116.22 W
Banfield ◆[8]	258	34.44 S	58.23 W
Banfora	150	10.38 N	4.46 W
Banga, Bhārat	123	31.11 N	75.59 E
Banga, Pil.	116	11.38 N	122.20 E
Banga, Zaïre	152	5.27 S	20.28 E
Bañgad	116	12.10 N	123.24 E
Bangaduni Island I	126	21.34 N	88.52 E
Bangala Dam ◆[6]	154	20.40 S	31.15 E
Bangall	210	41.53 N	73.42 W
Bangalore	122	12.59 N	77.35 E
Bangalur → Bangalore	122	12.59 N	77.35 E
Bangangté	152	5.09 N	10.31 E
Bangaon	126	23.04 N	88.49 E
Bangārapet	122	12.58 N	78.12 E
Bangassou	152	4.50 N	23.07 E
Bangbari	152	5.12 N	22.21 E
Bangbu	100	32.58 N	117.24 E
Bangda	102	27.59 N	98.40 E
Bangé	152	3.01 N	15.07 E
Bangeluo	120	32.27 N	90.35 E
Bangeswardi	126	23.29 N	89.44 E
Bangeta, Mount ∧	164	6.15 S	147.04 E
Banggai (Luwuk)	112	1.34 S	123.30 E
Banggai, Kepulauan II	112	1.30 S	123.15 E
Banggai, Pulau I	112	1.37 S	123.33 E
Banggi, Pulau I	112	7.17 N	117.12 E
Banghāzī	146	32.07 N	20.04 E
Banghāzī ◻[4]	146	26.00 N	22.00 E
Banghāzī ◆[1]	146	31.00 N	22.30 E
Banghiang ≃	110	16.03 N	105.15 E
Bangholme	274b	38.02 S	145.11 E
Bangi → Bangui	152	4.22 N	18.35 E
Bangil	115a	7.36 S	112.47 E
Bangjang	140	11.23 N	32.42 E
Bangjun	105	39.59 N	117.16 E
Bangka I	112	2.15 S	106.00 E
Bangka, Pulau I	112	1.48 N	125.09 E
Bangka, Selat Ʊ	112	2.20 S	105.45 E
Bangkalan	115a	7.02 S	112.44 E
Bang Kapi	269a	13.46 N	100.39 E
Bang Kapi, Khlong ⊼	269a	13.45 N	100.36 E
Bangkaru, Pulau I	114	2.04 N	97.07 E
Bang Khen	269a	13.52 N	100.36 E
Bang Khun Thian	269a	13.42 N	100.28 E
Bangkinang	112	0.21 N	101.02 E
Bangkir	112	0.48 N	120.14 E
Bangko	112	2.05 S	102.17 E
Bangkok → Krung Thep	110	13.45 N	100.31 E
Bangkou	106	31.40 N	121.26 E
Bang Krathum	110	16.34 N	100.18 E
Bang Kruai	269a	13.48 N	100.29 E
Bangkulu, Pulau I	112	1.50 S	123.06 E
Bangkulua	115b	8.41 S	118.13 E
Bangladesch → Bangladesh ◻[1]	120	24.00 N	90.00 E
Bangladesh ◻[1]	118		
	120	24.00 N	90.00 E
Bangla Desh → Bangladesh ◻[1], As.	120	24.00 N	90.00 E
Bang Lamung	110	12.58 N	100.54 E
Bang Mun Nak	110	16.02 N	100.23 E
Ban Gnômmarat Kèo	110	17.36 N	105.10 E
Bangolo	150	7.01 N	7.29 W
Bangon	116	13.44 N	122.50 E
Bangor, N. Ire., U.K.	44	54.40 N	5.40 W
Bangor, Wales, U.K.	44	53.13 N	4.08 W
Bangor, Calif., U.S.	226	39.23 N	121.24 W
Bangor, Maine, U.S.	188	44.49 N	68.47 W
Bangor, Mich., U.S.	216	42.18 N	86.07 W
Bangor, Pa., U.S.	210	40.52 N	75.13 W
Bangoran ≃	146	8.42 N	19.06 E
Bangor Erris	48	54.09 N	9.45 W
Bang Pa In	110	14.14 N	100.35 E
Bāngriposi	126	22.10 N	86.32 E
Bangs	196	31.43 N	99.08 W
Bangs, Mount ∧	200	36.48 N	113.51 W
Bang Saphan	110	11.12 N	99.31 E
Bangshi	98	40.23 N	122.46 E
Bangs Lake ◍	278	42.16 N	88.08 W
Bangsri	115a	6.30 S	110.45 E
Bangu ◆[8]	256	22.52 S	43.27 W
Bangued	116	17.36 N	120.37 E
Bangui, Centraf.	152	4.22 N	18.35 E
Bangui, Pil.	116	18.32 N	120.46 E
Bangui Bay C	116	18.34 N	120.44 E
Bangunpurba	114	3.23 N	98.50 E
Banguru	154	0.27 N	27.17 E
Bangwei	102	23.46 N	107.34 E
Bangweulu, Lake ◍	154	11.05 S	29.45 E
Bangweulu Swamp ☷	154	11.30 S	30.15 E
Bangzhen	106	31.39 N	121.29 E
Banh	150	14.05 N	2.27 W
Banhā	142	30.28 N	31.11 E
Ban Hatgnao	110	14.40 N	106.35 E
Ban Hatkiang	110	18.11 N	102.40 E
Ban Hat Yai → Hat Yai	110	7.01 N	100.28 E
Ban Ha Yaek Pak Kret	269a	13.54 N	100.31 E
Ban Hèt	110	14.44 N	107.29 E
Ban Hin Heup	110	18.38 N	102.20 E
Ban Hom	110	15.33 N	98.46 E
Ban Hong	110	18.18 N	98.50 E
Ban Hong Muang	110	17.04 N	105.12 E
Ban Houayxay	110	20.18 N	100.26 E
Ban Huai Yang	110	11.36 N	99.40 E
Ban Hua Lamphu Thong	269a	13.32 N	100.38 E
Bani, Pil.	116	16.11 N	119.52 E
Baní, Rep. Dom.	238	18.17 N	70.20 W
Bani ≃	150	14.30 N	4.12 W
Bani, Jbel ⛰	148	29.30 N	8.00 W
Bania	152	4.00 N	16.07 E
Banī 'Adī al-Baḥrīyah	142	27.15 N	30.55 E
Banī 'Adī al-Qiblīyah	142	27.15 N	30.56 E
Banī Aḥmad	142	28.03 N	30.46 E
Banī 'Alī	142	28.29 N	30.43 E
Baniara, Indon.	114	2.31 N	98.39 E
Baniara, Pap. N. Gui.	164	9.46 S	149.53 E
Bānibaha	126	23.42 N	89.37 E
Bani Bangou	150	15.03 N	2.42 E
Banie	30	53.08 N	14.38 E
Banifing ≃	150	12.27 N	7.07 W
Banihāl Pass)(	123	33.31 N	75.13 E
Banī Ḥasan ash-Shurūq	142	27.54 N	30.51 E
Banika I	175e	9.05 S	159.12 E
Banī Khālid	142	27.50 N	30.44 E
Banikoara	150	11.18 N	2.26 E
Banī Majdūl	273c	30.02 N	31.07 E
Banī Mazār	142	28.30 N	30.48 E
Banī Muḥammadīyāt	142	27.17 N	31.05 E
Banī Mūsā	142	29.08 N	31.03 E
Banīnah	146	32.05 N	20.16 E
Baniou	34	35.25 N	4.21 E
Banī Rāfi'	142	27.22 N	30.53 E
Banī Salāmah	142	30.19 N	30.51 E
Banī Sha'rān	142	27.19 N	30.51 E
Banī Shuqayr	142	27.23 N	30.59 E
Banister ≃	192	36.42 N	78.48 W
Banī Suhaylah	132	31.20 N	34.20 E
Banī Suwayf	142	29.05 N	31.05 E
Banī Suwayf ◻[4]	142	29.03 N	31.02 E
Banī 'Ubayd, Miṣr	142	31.01 N	31.39 E
Banī 'Ubayd, Miṣr	142	27.57 N	30.46 E
Bāniyāchung	120	24.31 N	91.22 E
Bāniyās, Sūrīy.	130	35.11 N	35.57 E
Bāniyās, Sūrīy.	132	33.15 N	35.41 E
Banī Zayd	142	27.13 N	31.09 E
Banja Luka	36	44.46 N	17.11 E
Banjar	115a	7.22 S	108.32 E
Banjarmasin	112	3.20 S	114.35 E
Banjarnegara	115a	7.23 S	109.41 E
Banjing	106	32.19 N	120.24 E
Banjir Kanal ⊼	269e	6.11 S	106.49 E
Banjita	104	41.11 N	120.52 E
Banjšcice ⛰[1]	64	46.04 N	13.42 E
Banjuangou	105	40.44 N	115.11 E
Banjul	150	13.28 N	16.39 W
Bank	84	39.25 N	49.15 E
Bānka	124	24.53 N	86.55 E
Ban'ka ≃	265b	55.49 N	37.22 E
Banka Banka	162	18.48 S	134.01 E
Bānkādāba	126	22.58 N	87.21 E
Ban Kaeng Khoi	110	14.35 N	101.01 E
Ban Kai Kiang	110	14.57 N	99.12 E
Bankana	152	4.25 S	16.11 E
Bankas	150	14.04 N	3.31 W
Ban Katèp	110	16.48 N	105.52 E
Ban Kavak	110	17.18 N	105.37 E
Bankberg ⛰	158	32.22 S	25.26 E
Ban Kèngkabao	110	16.48 N	104.45 E
Ban Kèngkok	110	16.26 N	105.12 E
Ban Kèngtangan	110	16.05 N	105.22 E
Bankeryd	26	57.51 N	14.07 E
Bankfoot	46	56.30 N	3.30 W
Ban Khamphô	110	14.38 N	106.17 E
Ban Khan Na Yao	269a	13.47 N	100.41 E
Bankhari	126	23.44 N	90.03 E
Ban Kheun	110	20.13 N	101.07 E
Ban Khlong Bua Loi	269a	13.41 N	100.41 E
Ban Khlong Kua	110	6.57 N	100.08 E
Ban Khlong Samrong	269a	13.39 N	100.36 E
Ban Khlong Song	269a	13.51 N	100.43 E
Ban Khok Bao Sao	269a	13.52 N	100.39 E
Ban Khuan Mao	110	7.58 N	99.37 E
Bankilaré	150	14.35 N	0.44 E
Bānkipur	272b	22.48 N	88.14 E
Ban Kota Baru	114	6.27 N	101.21 E
Ban Krang	110	12.52 N	99.18 E
Ban Kruat	110	14.25 N	103.07 E
Banks, Eng., U.K.	262	53.41 N	2.56 W
Banks, Ala., U.S.	194	31.44 N	85.50 W
Banks, Oreg., U.S.	224	45.37 N	123.07 W
Banks, Cape ≻	274a	34.00 S	151.15 E
Banks, Point ≻	180	58.36 N	152.18 W
Banksian ≃	184	53.41 N	94.10 W
Banks Island I, B.C., Can.	182	53.25 N	130.10 W
Banks Island I, N.W. Ter., Can.	176	73.15 N	121.30 W
Banks Islands II	175f	13.50 S	167.30 E
Banks Lake ◍[1]	202	47.45 N	119.15 W
Banksmeadow	274a	33.58 S	151.13 E
Banks Peninsula ≻[1]	172	43.45 S	173.00 E
Banks Sands ⊹[4]	262	53.43 N	2.59 W
Banks Strait Ʊ	166	40.40 S	148.07 E
Bankstown	170	33.55 S	151.02 E
Bankstown Aerodrome ⊠	274a	33.55 S	150.59 E
Banksville	276	41.09 N	73.38 W
Banksville ◆[8]	279b	40.24 N	80.03 W
Ban Kum Daeng	269a	13.53 N	100.36 E
Bankumuna	152	4.28 S	19.57 E
Bānkura	126	23.15 N	87.04 E
Bānkura ◻[5]	126	23.15 N	87.15 E
Ban Laem Sing	269a	13.30 N	100.34 E
Banlamen	104	41.51 N	122.27 E
Banlashanzi	104	41.26 N	123.28 E
Ban Lat Phrao	269a	13.47 N	100.36 E
Ban Le Kathe	110	15.49 N	98.53 E
Banliyuan	106	30.50 N	118.58 E
Ban Luk Kho	269a	13.34 N	100.27 E
Ban Mae La Luang	110	18.32 N	97.56 E
Ban Mae Mo	110	18.15 N	99.42 E
Bānmankhi Bazar	124	25.53 N	87.11 E
Banmauk	110	24.24 N	95.51 E
Ban-m'diap	110	12.56 N	108.43 E
Ban-m'drack	110	12.42 N	108.47 E
Banmian	100	26.02 N	118.06 E
Ban Mit	110	18.51 N	101.55 E
Ban Muangngat	110	19.05 N	104.04 E
Ban Muang Yot	110	19.22 N	100.34 E
Bann ≃	48	55.10 N	6.45 W
Banna ≃	62	45.11 N	7.51 E
Ban Nadou	110	15.51 N	105.38 E
Ban Nagnom	110	17.02 N	105.44 E
Ban Nahin	110	18.14 N	104.13 E
Bannaja	88	57.05 N	108.12 E
Ban Nakala	110	16.17 N	105.11 E
Ban Na Kha	110	9.26 N	98.28 E
Ban Nalan	110	15.50 N	106.04 E
Ban Nalè	110	18.42 N	101.34 E
Ban Namcha	110	19.09 N	102.53 E
Ban Nam Chan	110	18.01 N	103.53 E
Ban Namnga	110	20.22 N	102.19 E
Ban Nam Tao	110	17.50 N	101.15 E
Ban Nam Thaeng	110	15.34 N	105.30 E
Ban Na San	110	8.48 N	99.22 E
Ban Naxon	110	18.12 N	103.05 E
Ban Naxouang	110	18.25 N	104.29 E
Bannay	50	47.23 N	2.53 E
Bannerman, Mount ∧[2]	162	19.26 S	127.10 E
Bannesdorf	54	54.28 N	11.13 E
Bannewitz	54	51.00 N	13.43 E
Ban Ngam	110	20.11 N	104.53 E
Bannikovo	86	56.07 N	70.17 E
Banning	228	33.56 N	116.52 W
Banningville → Bandundu	152	3.18 S	17.20 E
Bannister	168a	32.40 S	116.33 E
Bannister ≃	168a	32.49 S	116.29 E
Bannister Ditch ⊼	279a	41.18 N	82.01 W
Bannock	214	40.06 N	80.59 W
Bannockburn, Austl.	169	38.03 S	144.10 E
Bannockburn, Scot., U.K.	46	56.06 N	3.55 W
Bannockburn, Ill., U.S.	278	42.12 N	87.52 W
Bannockburn, Zimb.	154	20.16 S	29.51 E
Bannockburn Battlesite (1314) ⊥	46	56.06 N	3.54 W
Bannock Creek ≃	202	42.53 N	112.40 W
Bannock Peak ∧	202	42.36 N	112.42 W
Ban Nong Lumphuk	110	14.40 N	102.43 E
Ban Nong Takhian	110	13.08 N	101.24 E
Banno-saki ≻	174m	26.33 N	128.09 E
Bannovka	86	53.45 N	62.57 E
Bannovskij	83	49.02 N	37.35 E
Bannu	123	32.59 N	70.36 E
Bañolas	34	42.07 N	2.46 E
Banon, Fr.	62	44.02 N	5.38 E
Bañón, Méx.	234	23.11 N	102.29 W
Ban O Pao	269a	13.50 N	100.38 E
Baños, Ec.	246	1.24 S	78.25 W
Baños, Perú	248	10.05 S	76.45 W
Baños de Cerrato	34	41.55 N	4.28 W
Bánovce nad Bebravou	30	48.43 N	18.14 E
Banow	120	35.38 N	69.15 E
Ban Pak Bong	110	18.32 N	98.56 E
Ban Pak Chan	110	10.32 N	98.51 E
Ban Pakha	110	14.38 N	107.24 E
Ban Pakkhop	110	19.49 N	100.36 E
Ban Pak Nam	110	10.26 N	99.15 E
Ban Pakneun	110	19.14 N	101.50 E
Ban Pak Phraek	110	8.13 N	100.12 E
Banpās	126	23.24 N	87.45 E
Ban Phai, Thai	110	17.33 N	103.00 E
Ban Phai, Thai	110	16.04 N	102.44 E
Ban Phe	110	12.38 N	101.26 E
Ban Pho	110	13.36 N	101.05 E
Ban Phon	110	15.25 N	106.42 E
Ban Phông Pho	110	14.36 N	105.52 E
Banphot Phisai	110	15.56 N	99.59 E
Ban Phraek Kasa	269a	13.34 N	100.38 E
Ban Phya	110	21.35 N	102.55 E
Ban Pong	110	13.49 N	99.53 E
Banpu	98	34.28 N	119.18 E
Banpura	126	22.27 N	87.22 E
Banqiao, Zhg.	100	30.06 N	120.27 E
Banqiao, Zhg.	106	31.55 N	118.39 E
Banqiao, Zhg.	107	29.31 N	105.59 E
Banqiaochang	107	29.54 N	104.21 E
Banqiaodian	100	31.46 N	112.31 E
Banqiaoji	100	32.19 N	116.37 E
Banqiaoxi	107	29.41 N	103.47 E
Ban Rai	110	15.05 N	99.31 E
Banreaba	174t	1.20 N	173.02 E
Ban Ron Phibun	110	8.09 N	99.51 E
Ban Sa-ang	110	17.26 N	105.44 E
Ban Saen To	110	16.05 N	99.51 E
Ban Sakhla	269a	13.32 N	100.30 E
Ban Salik	110	18.30 N	100.45 E
Ban Samang	110	19.43 N	102.36 E
Ban Sam Phan	110	8.33 N	99.09 E
Ban Sam Pong	110	18.32 N	102.47 E
Ban Samrong	110	14.23 N	102.50 E
Bansang	150	13.26 N	14.39 W
Ban San Xieng La	110	19.27 N	102.26 E
Bānsbāria	126	22.58 N	88.24 E
Bānsda	120	20.45 N	73.22 E
Bansha	48	52.28 N	8.04 W
Banshanpu	100	27.42 N	113.24 E
Banshi	100	25.20 N	115.23 E
Banshigou	104	41.09 N	120.58 E
Bānsi	124	27.11 N	82.56 E
Ban Signo	110	17.51 N	105.04 E
Banská Bystrica	30	48.44 N	19.07 E
Banská Štiavnica	30	48.28 N	18.56 E
Bansko	38	41.50 N	23.29 E
Bānskupi	126	24.10 N	86.41 E
Ban Songkhon	110	17.58 N	105.10 E
Ban Song Kong	269a	13.53 N	100.34 E
Ban Sop Huai Hai	110	19.33 N	98.05 E
Ban Sôppheung	110	18.33 N	104.17 E
Banstala	272b	22.32 N	88.25 E
Banstead	260	51.19 N	0.12 W
Ban Sum Sui	110	14.28 N	99.05 E
Bānswāra	120	23.33 N	74.27 E
Banta, Calif., U.S.	226	37.45 N	121.22 W
Banta, Zhg.	100	32.41 N	118.35 E
Banta, Pulau I	115b	8.25 S	119.14 E
Bantaian	114	1.56 N	100.54 E
Ban Takhlo	110	15.27 N	100.44 E
Bantam	207	41.44 N	73.14 W
Bantam Lake ◍	207	41.42 N	73.13 W
Ban Tamru	269a	13.31 N	100.41 E
Bantan	107	29.52 N	105.52 E
Ban Tao Pun	269a	13.53 N	100.41 E
Bantarkawung	115a	7.13 S	108.55 E
Bantayan	116	11.10 N	123.43 E
Bantayan Island I	116	11.13 N	123.44 E
Banteer	48	52.07 N	8.54 W
Banteln	52	52.04 N	9.44 E
Banten	115a	6.03 S	106.09 E
Banten, Teluk C	115a	6.00 S	106.10 E
Bantenan, Tanjung ≻	115a	8.47 S	114.32 E
Ban Teung	110	17.54 N	105.29 E
Ban Thabôk	110	18.22 N	103.12 E
Ban Thanoun	110	19.50 N	101.29 E
Ban Thapayi	110	16.19 N	105.41 E
Bantheville	56	49.21 N	5.05 E
Ban Thieng	110	19.08 N	102.12 E
Ban Tian Sa	110	18.43 N	103.14 E
Bantigui Point ≻	116	13.41 N	121.28 E
Banting	114	2.49 N	101.30 E
Banton (Jones)	116	12.57 N	122.05 E
Ban Tong Khop	110	17.04 N	104.16 E
Banton Island I	116	12.56 N	122.04 E
Bāntra	272b	22.35 N	88.19 E
Bantry	48	51.41 N	9.27 W
Bantry Bay C	48	51.38 N	9.48 W
Bantul	115a	7.54 S	110.20 E
Bāntva	120	21.29 N	70.05 E
Banūr	124	30.34 N	76.43 E
Ban Van Hom	110	18.44 N	104.01 E
Ban Vat	110	16.54 N	106.25 E
Banwell	42	51.20 N	2.52 W
Banwy ≃	42	52.42 N	3.16 W
Ban Xènkhalôk	110	19.42 N	101.54 E
Banxiancun	106	30.33 N	119.42 E
Ban Xot	110	18.11 N	104.05 E
Banyak, Kepulauan II	114	2.10 N	97.15 E
Ban Ya Plong	110	8.53 N	98.35 E
Banyo	152	6.45 N	11.49 E
Banyumas	115a	7.31 S	109.17 E
Banyuwangi	115a	8.12 S	114.21 E
Banyuwedang	115b	8.08 S	114.36 E
Banz	164	5.47 S	144.37 E
Banzare Coast •[2]	9	67.00 S	126.00 E
Banzhuyuan	107	28.44 N	106.18 E
Banzi, It.	68	40.52 N	16.01 E
Banzi, Zhg.	100	24.18 N	117.19 E
Bao, Ouadi ∨	146	16.36 N	23.55 E
Baoan, Zhg.	100	22.34 N	114.07 E
Baoan, Zhg.	100	30.11 N	114.43 E
Baoan, Zhg.	106	31.46 N	121.21 E
Baoancun	89	48.13 N	125.52 E
Baochang → Taipusiqi, Zhg.	98	41.56 N	115.22 E
Baochang, Zhg.	106	32.04 N	121.25 E
Baocheng	102	33.08 N	107.09 E
Baode	102	39.06 N	111.11 E
Baodi	105	39.44 N	117.17 E
Baoding (Qingyuan)	105	38.52 N	115.29 E
Baofeng	100	33.55 N	113.02 E
Baofutan	106	30.31 N	119.29 E
Baoguosi	107	29.35 N	103.31 E
Baoguotu	98	42.20 N	120.43 E
Bao-ha	110	22.11 N	104.21 E
Baohe ≃	105	39.02 N	115.39 E
Baohekou	105	40.32 N	118.15 E
Baoji, Zhg.	100	33.08 N	118.19 E
Baoji, Zhg.	102	34.22 N	107.14 E
Baojiagou	105	40.05 N	115.22 E
Baojiapu	104	40.51 N	122.14 E
Baojiatou	106	30.11 N	119.48 E
Baojiawazi	104	41.38 N	123.24 E
Baojing	102	28.43 N	109.25 E
Baokang → Keerqinzuozhongqi	89	44.07 N	123.18 E
Bao-lac	110	22.57 N	105.40 E
Baolinchang	107	30.24 N	105.02 E
Baolizhen	89	42.56 N	123.46 E
Bao-loc	110	11.32 N	107.48 E
Baolunyuan	102	32.22 N	105.40 E
Baoma	150	7.58 N	11.37 W
Baomachang	107	29.58 N	104.12 E
Baon	116	6.47 N	126.05 E
Baoning	102	23.31 N	106.24 E
Baoqing	89	46.21 N	132.14 E
Baoquan	98	36.16 N	119.04 E
Baoro	152	5.40 N	15.58 E
Baoshan, Zhg.	100	32.39 N	113.54 E
Baoshan, Zhg.	102	25.09 N	99.09 E
Baoshan, Zhg.	102	26.19 N	104.27 E
Baoshan, Zhg.	106	31.25 N	121.29 E
Baoting	110	18.42 N	109.45 E
Baotou (Paotow)	102	40.40 N	109.59 E
Baotun	104	42.29 N	122.52 E
Baoulé ≃, Afr.	150	12.36 N	6.34 W
Baoulé ≃, Mali	150	13.33 N	9.54 W
Baowei	102	22.39 N	106.50 E
Baoxikou	100	23.16 N	115.14 E
Baoxingchang	107	29.38 N	105.41 E
Baoxinji	100	32.35 N	115.00 E
Baoyan	106	31.55 N	119.21 E
Baoyiji	100	32.13 N	116.42 E
Baoying	100	33.16 N	119.20 E
Baoyinghu ◍	100	33.05 N	119.10 E
Baozhuchang	107	29.48 N	104.15 E
Baozidian	105	40.11 N	117.48 E
Baozixie	100	30.28 N	114.34 E
Bāp	120	27.23 N	72.21 E
Bapanling	104	40.58 N	123.08 E
Bāpatla	122	15.54 N	80.28 E
Bapaume	50	50.06 N	2.51 E
Bapchule	200	33.12 N	111.50 W
Bapsfontein	158	26.08 S	28.25 E
Baptiste Lake ◍	212	45.07 N	78.02 W
Baptistown	208	40.31 N	75.00 W
Bāqa el Gharbiyya	132	32.25 N	35.03 E
Baqar, Maṣrif Baḥr al- ⊼	142	31.05 N	32.08 E
Baqar, Wādī al- ∨	146	27.49 N	18.37 E
Baqing	120	32.15 N	93.30 E
B'aqlīn	132	33.41 N	35.33 E
Ba'qūbah	128	33.45 N	44.38 E
Baquedano	252	23.20 S	69.51 W
Ba-queo	269c	10.48 N	106.38 E
Bar, Jugo.	38	42.05 N	19.05 E
Bar, S.S.S.R.	78	49.04 N	27.40 E
Bar, S.S.S.R.	88	51.17 N	107.33 E
Bar ≃	56	49.42 N	4.50 E
Bāra, Bhārat	124	25.13 N	87.22 E
Bara, Bhārat	272b	22.43 N	88.31 E
Bara, Bhārat	272b	22.46 N	88.17 E
Barabai	112	2.35 S	115.23 E
Bara Bāngurda	126	22.57 N	86.24 E
Bāra Banki	124	26.55 N	81.12 E
Bāra Banki ◻[5]	124	27.00 N	81.20 E
Barabanovo	82	54.43 N	38.10 E
Barābhūm	126	23.02 N	86.22 E
Barabinsk	86	55.21 N	78.21 E
Barabinskaja Step' ⌣	86	55.00 N	79.00 E
Baraboo	190	43.28 N	89.45 W
Baraboo Range ⛰[2]	190	43.25 N	89.40 W
Baraboulé	150	14.12 N	1.51 W
Baracaju ≃	255	12.21 S	51.00 W
Barachois Pond Provincial Park ♠	186	48.26 N	58.14 W
Baracoa, Cuba	240p	20.21 N	74.30 W
Baracoa, Hond.	236	15.43 N	87.52 W
Baradā ≃	132	33.30 N	36.28 E
Baradero	258	33.48 S	59.30 W
Baradero ≃	258	33.55 S	59.16 W
Baradili	71	39.43 N	8.54 E
Baradine	166	30.56 S	149.04 E
Bara Doāni	126	22.06 N	89.59 E
Baraga	190	46.47 N	88.30 W
Baragaon → Nālanda	124	25.07 N	85.25 E
Baragiano	68	40.41 N	15.35 E
Baragoi	154	1.47 N	36.47 E
Baraguá	240p	21.41 N	78.38 W
Baragwanath	273d	26.16 S	27.59 E
Baragwanath Aerodrome ⊠	273d	26.15 S	27.59 E
Baragwanath Military Hospital ⊽	273d	26.16 S	27.56 E
Bārah	140	13.42 N	30.22 E
Barahānuddin	126	22.30 N	90.43 E
Barāigrām	126	24.19 N	89.10 E
Baraily	124	23.00 N	78.14 E
Bara Issa ≃	150	16.09 N	3.28 W
Bāra Jamda	124	22.09 N	85.23 E
Barajas, Aeropuerto ⊠	266a	40.28 N	3.34 W
Barajas de Madrid ◆[8]	266a	40.28 N	3.35 E
Bara Jorda	126	23.10 N	86.50 E
Barak	130	36.51 N	37.59 E
Baraka	154	4.06 S	29.06 E
Baraka, Khawr (Barka) ∨	144	18.13 N	37.35 E
Barakah	140	10.58 N	27.59 E
Barākar	126	24.07 N	86.14 E
Barakār ≃	126	23.42 N	86.48 E
Bara Khunta	126	21.43 N	86.38 E
Barakī Barak	120	33.56 N	68.55 E
Barakkol'skij	86	52.12 N	67.49 E
Bārākot	120	21.33 N	85.01 E
Bārākpur	126	22.55 N	89.32 E
Barakula	166	26.26 S	150.31 E
Barāl	272b	22.27 N	88.22 E
Baralaba	166	24.11 S	149.49 E
Barām	126	22.57 N	86.18 E
Baram ≃	112	4.36 N	113.59 E
Baram, Tanjong ≻	112	4.35 N	113.59 E
Barama ≃	246	7.40 N	59.15 W
Barāmāria	126	21.42 N	87.04 E
Bārāmati	122	18.09 N	74.35 E
Bārāmūla	123	34.12 N	74.21 E
Bārān, Bhārat	124	25.06 N	76.31 E
Baran', S.S.S.R.	76	54.29 N	30.18 E
Baran', S.S.S.R.	76	54.30 N	28.40 E
Baranagar	126	22.38 N	88.22 E
Baranakovo	86	58.08 N	82.58 E
Barancevo	82	55.04 N	37.38 E
Baranello	66	41.32 N	14.34 E
Barangbarang	112	6.24 S	120.28 E
Barangeon ≃	50	47.12 N	2.10 E
Barani	150	13.10 N	3.53 W
Barania Góra ∧	30	49.37 N	19.00 E
Baraniki	80	46.31 N	41.50 E
Baranikovka	83	49.10 N	39.50 E
Baranoa	246	10.48 N	74.55 W
Barano d'Ischia	61	40.42 N	13.55 E
Baranof	180	57.05 N	134.50 W
Baranof Island I	180	57.00 N	135.00 W
Baranoviči	76	53.08 N	26.02 E
Baranovka	78	50.18 N	27.40 E
Baranovskoje	82	55.25 N	38.45 E
Baranów Sandomierski	30	50.30 N	21.33 E
Barany, S.S.S.R.	76	57.20 N	29.09 E
Barany, S.S.S.R.	80	57.38 N	52.16 E
Baranya ◻[6]	30	46.05 N	18.15 E
Barão Ataliba Nogueira	256	22.24 S	46.45 W
Barão de Aquino	256	22.07 S	42.39 W
Barão de Cocais	255	19.56 S	43.28 W
Barão de Geraldo	256	22.49 S	47.06 W
Barão de Grajaú	250	6.45 S	43.01 W
Barão de Juparanã	256	22.21 S	43.41 W
Barão de Melgaço	248	16.13 S	55.58 W
Barão de Tromai	250	1.29 S	45.36 W
Baraolt	38	46.05 N	25.36 E
Baraoltului, Munții ⛰	38	46.15 N	25.45 E
Barapasi	164	2.07 S	137.00 E
Baras	116	13.40 N	124.22 E
Barasāhi	126	21.43 N	86.44 E
Bārāsat, Bhārat	126	22.43 N	88.29 E
Bārāsat, Bhārat	272b	22.51 N	88.22 E
Baraševo	80	54.32 N	42.53 E
Baraši	78	50.43 N	28.01 E
Baraški	24	65.40 N	52.10 E
Barat, Lintasan Ʊ	115a	7.08 S	112.40 E
Baratā	266c	38.48 N	9.19 W
Baratang Island I	110	12.13 N	92.45 E
Barataria	194	29.44 N	90.08 W
Barataria Bay C	194	29.22 N	89.57 W
Barat Daya, Kepulauan II	108	7.25 S	128.00 E
Barate	112	9.54 S	123.38 E
Bar'atino, S.S.S.R.	76	54.19 N	34.31 E
Bar'atino, S.S.S.R.	82	54.43 N	36.49 E
Baratolia	126	22.25 N	86.37 E
Baratta	166	31.59 S	139.06 E
Baraula	272a	28.34 N	77.22 E
Baraut	124	29.06 N	77.16 E
Baraya	246	3.10 N	75.04 W
Barbacena	256	21.14 S	43.46 W
Barbacoas	246	1.41 N	78.09 W
Barbades → Barbados ◻[1]	241g	13.10 N	59.32 W
Barbadillo	286d	12.02 S	76.56 W
Barbadillo del Mercado	34	42.02 N	3.21 W
Barbadoes Island I	285	40.07 N	75.22 W
Barbados ◻[1]	230		
	241g	13.10 N	59.32 W
Barbagia ◆[1]	71	39.55 N	9.12 E
Barbalha	250	7.19 S	39.17 W
Barbar	140	18.01 N	33.59 E
Bárbara	246	0.53 S	72.30 W
Barbarano Vicentino	64	45.24 N	11.32 E
Barbarasco	64	44.14 N	9.56 E
Barbareta, Isla I	236	16.26 N	86.09 W
Barbaros	130	40.54 N	27.27 E
Barbas, Cabo ≻	148	22.18 N	16.41 W
Barbaši	76	57.42 N	28.24 E
Barbastro	34	42.02 N	0.08 E
Barbate ≃	34	36.11 N	5.55 W
Barbate de Franco	34	36.12 N	5.55 W
Barbeau Peak ∧	16	81.54 N	75.01 W
Barbentane	62	43.54 N	4.45 E
Barber Booth	262	53.22 N	1.50 W
Barberena	236	14.18 N	90.22 W
Barberena, Río de ≃	234	22.34 N	97.52 W
Barberino di Mugello	66	44.00 N	11.15 E
Barberino Val d'Elsa	66	43.32 N	11.10 E
Barbers Point ≻	229c	21.18 N	158.07 W
Barbers Point Naval Air Station ■	229c	21.19 N	158.04 W
Barberton, S. Afr.	156	25.48 S	31.03 E
Barberton, Ohio, U.S.	214	41.01 N	81.36 W
Barbezieux	32	45.28 N	0.09 W
Bar Bigha	124	25.13 N	85.44 E
Barbil	124	22.06 N	85.20 E
Barbis	54	51.37 N	10.25 E
Barbizon	50	48.27 N	2.36 E
Barbosa, Col.	246	5.57 N	73.37 W
Barbosa, Col.	246	6.26 N	75.20 W
Barboursville	188	38.24 N	82.18 W
Barbourville	192	36.52 N	83.53 W
Barbuda I	238	17.38 N	61.48 W
Barbuise ≃	50	48.33 N	3.35 E
Barby	54	51.58 N	11.53 E
Barca	30	48.41 N	21.16 E
Barčadiv	85	38.19 N	72.29 E
Barcaldine	166	23.33 S	145.17 E
Barcarena	266c	38.44 N	9.17 W
Barcarena, Ribeira de ≃	266c	38.42 N	9.27 W
Barcarrota	34	38.31 N	6.51 W
Barce → Al-Marj	146	32.30 N	20.54 E
Barcellona Pozzo di Gotto	70	38.09 N	15.13 E
Barcelona, Esp.	34		
	266d	41.23 N	2.11 E
Barcelona, Méx.	232	26.12 N	103.25 W
Barcelona, Pil.	116	12.52 N	124.09 E
Barcelona, Ven.	246	10.08 N	64.42 W
Barcelona ◆[8]	266a	40.22 N	3.34 E
Barcelona, Aeropuerto Transoceánico de ⊠	266d	41.18 N	2.05 E
Barcelona, Campo Fútbol Club ♠	266d	41.23 N	2.08 E
Barcelona, Universidad de ⊽[2]	266d	41.23 N	2.10 E
Barcelone → Barcelona	34	41.23 N	2.11 E
Barceloneta	240m	18.27 N	66.32 W
Barcelonnette	62	44.23 N	6.39 E
Barcelos, Bra.	246	0.58 S	62.57 W
Barcelos, Port.	34	41.32 N	8.37 W
Barchaticha	80	57.34 N	45.13 E
Barchyn ≃	88	48.43 N	110.17 E
Barcillonnette	62	44.26 N	5.55 E
Barcin	30	52.52 N	17.57 E
Barcis	64	46.11 N	12.33 E
Barclay	208	39.08 N	75.51 W
Barclay Brook ≃	276	40.19 N	74.22 W
Barcoo ≃	166	25.30 S	142.50 E
Barcroft, Lake ◍[1]	284c	38.51 N	77.09 W
Barcs	30	45.58 N	17.28 E
Barcy	261	49.01 N	2.53 E
Barczewo	30	53.50 N	20.42 E
Bard	62	45.36 N	7.45 E
Barda, S.S.S.R.	84	40.23 N	47.08 E
Barda, S.S.S.R.	86	56.54 N	55.38 E
Barda del Medio	252	38.43 S	68.10 W
Bardai, Sūd.	140	12.43 N	21.53 E
Bardaï, Tchad	146	21.22 N	16.59 E
Bardawīl, Sabkhat al- ☷	140	31.10 N	33.10 E
Bardejov	30	49.18 N	21.16 E
Bárdenas Reales ⛰[1]	34	42.10 N	1.25 W
Bardera	144	2.21 N	42.20 E
Bardeskan	128	35.12 N	57.58 E
Bardi	62	44.38 N	9.44 E
Bardīa	124	28.18 N	81.22 E
Bardīyah	146	31.46 N	25.06 E
Bardız	130	40.26 N	42.20 E
Bardney	44	53.12 N	0.21 W
Bardoc	162	30.20 S	121.17 E
Bardoli	120	21.07 N	73.07 E
Bardolino	64	45.33 N	10.43 E
Bardonecchia	62	45.05 N	6.42 E
Bardonia	276	41.07 N	74.00 W
Bardoux, Lac ◍	186	51.09 N	67.50 W
Bardowick	52	53.18 N	10.23 E
Bardsey Island I	42	52.45 N	4.45 W
Bardsey Sound Ʊ	42	52.47 N	4.45 W
Bardstown	194	37.49 N	85.28 W
Bardswell Group II	182	52.10 N	128.20 W
Bardu	24	68.52 N	18.21 E
Bardufoss	24	69.04 N	18.30 E
Bardwell, Ky., U.S.	194	36.52 N	89.01 W
Bardwell, Tex., U.S.	222	32.16 N	96.42 W
Bardwell Lake ◍[1]	222	32.16 N	96.39 W
Bare	144	4.42 N	42.47 E
Bareggio	266b	45.29 N	9.00 E
Barei, Wādī ∨	140	13.27 N	23.57 E
Bareilly	124	28.21 N	79.25 E
Barenburg	52	52.37 N	8.47 E
Barenc'ovo More → Barents Sea ⊤[2]	12	74.00 N	36.00 E
Barendrecht	52	51.51 N	4.32 E
Barengapāra	124	25.14 N	90.14 E
Bärenklau	54	51.56 N	14.34 E
Bärenstein, D.D.R.	54	50.48 N	13.47 E
Bärenstein, D.D.R.	54	50.30 N	13.02 E
Barentin	50	49.33 N	0.57 E
Barentsøya I	10	78.27 N	21.15 E
Barents Sea ⊤[2]	12	74.00 N	36.00 E
Barentu	144	15.04 N	37.37 E
Bareo	112	3.45 N	115.27 E
Baresville	208	39.48 N	76.57 W
Bareta	123	29.52 N	75.42 E
Barfleur	32	49.40 N	1.15 W
Barfleur, Pointe de ≻	32	49.42 N	1.16 W
Barga	64	44.04 N	10.29 E
Bargāchia, Bhārat	126	22.39 N	88.07 E
Bargāchia, Bhārat	272b	22.48 N	88.27 E
Bargagli	62	44.27 N	9.05 E
Bargaintown	208	39.22 N	70.35 W
Bargal	144	11.18 N	51.07 E
Bargara	166	24.49 S	152.27 E
Bargarh	120	21.20 N	83.37 E
Bargas	34	39.56 N	4.03 W
Barge	62	44.43 N	7.20 E
Barg-e Maṯāl	120	35.40 N	71.21 E
Bargemon	62	43.37 N	6.32 E
Bargen	58	47.48 N	8.37 E
Bargersville	218	39.31 N	86.10 W
Barghanak	128	33.56 N	62.26 E
Barghe	64	45.41 N	10.24 E
Bargnop	140	9.30 N	28.28 E
Bargo	170	34.18 S	150.35 E
Bargoed	42	51.43 N	3.15 W
Bargteheide	52	53.44 N	10.16 E
Bārguna	126	22.09 N	90.07 E
Barguzin	88	53.37 N	109.37 E
Barguzinskij Chrebet ⛰	88	54.30 N	110.20 E
Barguzinskij Zaliv C	88	53.26 N	108.48 E
Bārh	124	25.29 N	85.43 E
Bar Harbor	188	44.23 N	68.13 W
Barharwa	124	24.52 N	87.47 E
Barhau	112	5.19 S	102.10 E
Barhi	124	24.18 N	85.25 E
Barhiya	124	25.17 N	86.02 E
Bāri, Bhārat	124	26.39 N	77.36 E
Bāri, Bhārat	124	23.03 N	78.05 E
Bari, It.	68	41.07 N	16.52 E
Bari, Zaïre	152	3.19 N	19.23 E
Bari ◻[4]	68	40.56 N	16.40 E
Bari ≃	124	27.55 N	83.27 E
Baria ≃	246	1.56 N	66.35 W
Baricella	64	44.39 N	11.32 E
Barichara	246	6.38 N	73.14 W
Barīdī, Ra's ≻	128	24.17 N	37.31 E
Bāri Doāb ⛰[1]	123	30.25 N	73.00 E
Barī Gāv	120	33.52 N	67.49 E
Barigazzo	64	44.16 N	10.39 E
Barigua, Salina de ⌣	241s	12.08 N	69.59 W
Barika	34	35.23 N	5.22 E
Barika, Oued ≃	34	35.22 N	5.18 E
Barikiwa	154	9.28 S	37.54 E
Barīkowṯ	120	35.18 N	71.32 E
Barile	68	40.57 N	15.40 E
Barillas	236	15.48 N	91.18 W
Bariloche → San Carlos de Bariloche	254	41.09 S	71.18 W
Barilo-Krepinskaja	83	47.45 N	39.32 E
Barīm I	144	12.40 N	43.25 E
Barima ≃	246	8.33 N	60.25 W
Barin	84	39.13 N	44.28 E
Barinas, P.R.	240m	18.01 N	66.51 W
Barinas, Ven.	246	8.38 N	70.12 W
Barinas ◻[3]	246	8.10 N	69.50 W
Baring	224	47.46 N	121.29 W
Baring, Cape ≻	176	70.05 N	117.20 W
Baringa, Zaïre	152	6.17 S	16.55 E
Baringa, Zaïre	152	0.45 N	20.52 E
Baring Channel Ʊ	176	73.48 N	98.50 W
Baringo	154	0.28 N	35.58 E
Baringo, Lake ◍	154	0.38 N	36.05 E
Båring Vig C	41	55.32 N	9.56 E
Barinitas	246	8.45 N	70.25 W
Baripāda	126	21.56 N	86.43 E
Bariri	255	22.04 S	48.44 W
Bārīs	140	24.40 N	30.36 E
Barisacho	84	42.28 N	44.54 E
Bari Sādri	120	24.25 N	74.28 E
Barisāl	124	22.42 N	90.22 E
Barisan, Pegunungan ⛰	112	3.00 S	102.15 E
Bari Sardo	71	39.50 N	9.38 E
Barisciano	66	42.19 N	13.35 E
Barit Island I	116	18.52 N	121.15 E
Barito ≃	112	3.32 S	114.29 E
Barjā	132	33.39 N	35.26 E
Barjac	62	44.18 N	4.21 E
Barjols	62	43.33 N	6.00 E
Barjora	126	23.26 N	87.17 E
Barjūj, Wādī ∨	146	25.57 N	13.12 E
Bark ≃	216	42.55 N	88.50 W
Barka (Khawr Baraka) ≃	144	18.13 N	37.35 E
Barka Kāna	124	23.37 N	85.29 E
Barkal	120	22.44 N	92.23 E
Barkava	76	56.43 N	26.36 E
Barkelsby	41	54.30 N	9.50 E
Barken ◍	40	60.07 N	15.31 E
Barker, N.Y., U.S.	210	43.20 N	78.33 W
Barker, Ur.	258	34.16 S	57.27 W
Barker Point ≻	276	40.51 N	73.44 W
Barker Reservoir ◍[1]	222	29.44 N	95.44 W
Barkers Brook ≃	285	40.03 N	74.45 W
Barkerville	182	53.04 N	121.31 W
Barkerville Historical Park ⊥	182	53.04 N	121.30 W
Barkeyville	214	41.12 N	79.58 W
Barkhamsted Reservoir ◍[1]	207	41.57 N	72.57 W
Bārkhān	120	29.54 N	69.31 E
Barkhanpur	126	23.50 N	89.33 E
Barking ◆[8]	260	51.33 N	0.06 E
Barkingside ◆[8]	260	51.36 N	0.05 E
Barki Saraiya	124	24.10 N	85.53 E
Barkisland	262	53.41 N	1.55 W
Bark Lake ◍, Ont., Can.	190	46.54 N	82.28 W
Bark Lake ◍, Ont., Can.	212	45.27 N	77.51 W
Barkley, Lake ◍[1]	194	36.40 N	87.55 W
Barkley Sound Ʊ	182	48.53 N	125.20 W
Barkly, Mount ∧[2]	162	21.34 S	132.28 E
Barkly East	158	30.58 S	27.33 E
Barkly Tableland ⛰[1]	162	18.00 S	136.00 E
Barkly West	158	28.05 S	24.31 E
Barksdale	196	29.44 N	100.02 W
Barkuhi	124	22.13 N	78.42 E
Barla	130	38.01 N	30.47 E
Bârlad → Bîrlad	38	46.14 N	27.40 E
Barlassina	266b	45.39 N	9.08 E
Barlby	44	53.48 N	1.03 W
Barleben	54	52.12 N	11.37 E
Bar-le-Duc	56	48.47 N	5.10 E
Barlee, Lake ◍	162	29.10 S	119.30 E
Barlee, Mount ∧[2]	162	24.37 S	128.06 E
Barlee Range ⛰	162	23.35 S	116.00 E
Barles	62	44.16 N	6.16 E
Barletta	68	41.19 N	16.17 E
Barlin	50	50.27 N	2.37 E
Barlinek	30	53.00 N	15.12 E
Barlow	194	37.03 N	89.03 W
Barluk	88	54.32 N	101.43 E
Barma	164	1.54 S	133.00 E
Barmancak, Ozero ◍	80	48.02 N	44.40 E
Barmašovo	78	47.07 N	32.26 E
Barmedman	166	34.09 S	147.23 E
Barmen ◆[8]	263	51.17 N	7.13 E
Barmer	120	25.45 N	71.23 E
Barmera	166	34.15 S	140.28 E
Barmer-Stausee ◍[1]	263	51.14 N	7.16 E
Barmouth	42	52.43 N	4.03 W
Barmouth Bay C	42	52.42 N	4.08 W
Barmstedt	52	53.47 N	9.46 E
Barnaby Manor Oaks	284c	38.50 N	76.58 W
Barnagar	120	23.03 N	75.22 E
Barnāla	123	30.23 N	75.33 E
Barnard Castle	44	54.33 N	1.55 W
Barnasht	142	29.41 N	31.15 E
Bärnau	60	49.49 N	12.26 E
Barnaul	86	53.22 N	83.45 E
Barn Bluff ∧	166	41.43 S	145.56 E
Barneberg	54	52.08 N	11.03 E
Barnegat	208	39.45 N	74.13 W
Barnegat Bay C	208	39.52 N	74.07 W
Barnegat Light	208	39.46 N	74.06 W
Barne Inlet C	9	80.15 S	160.15 E
Barnes	214	41.40 N	79.01 W
Barnes ◆[8]	260	51.28 N	0.15 W
Barnesboro	214	40.40 N	78.47 W
Barnes Corners	212	43.49 N	75.49 W
Barnes Lake ◍	184	56.23 N	98.06 W
Barnes Sound Ʊ	220	25.14 N	80.23 W
Barnesville, Ga., U.S.	192	33.04 N	84.09 W
Barnesville, Minn., U.S.	198	46.39 N	96.25 W
Barnesville, Ohio, U.S.	188	39.59 N	81.11 W
Barnet ◆[8]	260	51.40 N	0.13 W
Barnetby le Wold	44	53.35 N	0.25 W
Barnett	219	39.16 N	89.42 W
Barnetts	208	37.22 N	77.09 W
Barneveld, Ned.	52	52.08 N	5.35 E

	English	Deutsch	Español	Français	Português
≃	River	Fluss	Río	Rivière	Rio
⊼	Canal	Kanal	Canal	Canal	Canal
⌊	Waterfall, Rapids	Wasserfall, Stromschnellen	Cascada, Rápidos	Chute d'eau, Rapides	Cascata, Rápidos
Ʊ	Strait	Meeresstrasse	Estrecho	Détroit	Estreito
C	Bay, Gulf	Bucht, Golf	Bahía, Golfo	Baie, Golfe	Baía, Golfo
◍	Lake, Lakes	See, Seen	Lago, Lagos	Lac, Lacs	Lago, Lagos
☷	Swamp	Sumpf	Pantano	Marais	Pântano
⧍	Ice Features, Glacier	Eis- und Gletscherformen	Accidentes Glaciales	Formes glaciaires	Acidentes Glaciares
⊤	Other Hydrographic Features	Andere Hydrographische Objekte	Otros Elementos Hidrográficos	Autres données hydrographiques	Outros Elementos Hidrográficos
⊹	Submarine Features	Untermeerische Objekte	Accidentes Submarinos	Formes de relief sous-marin	Acidentes Submarinos
◻	Political Unit	Politische Einheit	Unidad Política	Entité politique	Unidade Política
⊽	Cultural Institution	Kulturelle Institution	Institución Cultural	Institution culturelle	Instituição Cultural
⊥	Historical Site	Historische Stätte	Sitio Histórico	Site historique	Sitio Histórico
♠	Recreational Site	Erholungs- und Ferienort	Sitio de Recreo	Centre de loisirs	Sítio de Lazer
⊠	Airport	Flughafen	Aeropuerto	Aéroport	Aeroporto
■	Military Installation	Militäranlage	Instalación Militar	Installation militaire	Instalação Militar
◆	Miscellaneous	Verschiedenes	Misceláneo	Divers	Miscelânea

Name (ENGLISH) / Name (DEUTSCH)	Page / Seite	Lat.°' / Breite°'	Long.°' / Länge°' E=Ost
Barneveld, N.Y., U.S.	210	43.16 N	75.12 W
Barneville-Carteret	32	49.23 N	1.47 W
Barnhart, Mo., U.S.	219	38.23 N	92.40 W
Barnhart, Tex., U.S.	196	31.08 N	101.10 W
Barnhill	214	40.27 N	81.21 W
Barnim □[9]	54	52.40 N	13.45 E
Barnoldswick	44	53.55 N	2.11 W
Barnówko	54	52.48 N	14.45 E
Barnsboro	285	39.46 N	75.09 W
Barnsdall	196	36.34 N	96.10 W
Barnsley	44	53.34 N	1.28 W
Barnstable	207	41.42 N	70.18 W
Barnstable □[6]	207	41.42 N	70.18 W
Barnstable Harbor C	207	41.43 N	70.18 W
Barnstaple	42	51.05 N	4.04 W
Barnstaple Bay C	42	51.05 N	4.20 W
Barnston	262	53.21 N	3.05 W
Barnstorf	52	52.42 N	8.30 E
Barnt Green	42	52.22 N	1.59 W
Barnton	262	53.16 N	2.33 W
Barntrup	52	51.59 N	9.06 E
Barnum Island	276	40.36 N	73.39 W
Barnwell, Alta., Can.	182	49.46 N	112.15 W
Barnwell, S.C., U.S.	192	33.15 N	81.23 W
Baro	150	8.37 N	6.25 E
Baro ≃	144	8.26 N	33.13 E
Barobo	116	8.33 N	126.07 E
Baroda, Bhārat	122	22.18 N	73.12 E
Baroda, Bhārat	124	25.30 N	76.39 E
Baroda, Mich., U.S.	216	41.57 N	86.29 W
Baroe	158	33.13 S	24.33 E
Barola I	175e	7.30 S	158.20 E
Barometer ∧	172	41.50 S	173.39 E
Baron Bluff •[4]	241n	17.47 N	64.47 W
Baronissi	68	40.44 N	14.45 E
Barons	182	50.00 N	113.05 W
Barora Ite I	175e	7.35 S	158.24 E
Barossa Reservoir @[1]	168b	34.39 S	138.51 E
Barotac Nuevo	116	10.54 N	122.42 E
Barotac Viejo	116	11.03 N	122.51 E
Barotseland □[9]	138	16.00 S	24.00 E
Barotse Plain ≚	152	15.40 S	23.10 E
Barouéli	150	13.04 N	6.50 W
Barpathār	120	26.17 N	93.53 E
Barpeta	120	26.19 N	91.00 E
Bar Point ≻	214	42.03 N	83.07 W
Barqah (Cyrenaica) ⇠[1]	146	31.00 N	22.30 E
Barqah, Jabal al- ∧	132	30.25 N	34.18 E
Barq al-'Izz	142	31.01 N	31.26 E
Barquisimeto	246	10.04 N	69.19 W
Barr	58	48.24 N	7.27 E
Barra, Bra.	250	11.05 S	43.10 W
Barra, Gam.	150	13.20 N	16.36 W
Barra I	46	56.58 N	7.29 W
Barra, Ponta da ≻	156	23.45 S	35.30 E
Barra, Sound of Ʉ	46	57.05 N	7.25 W
Barraba	166	30.22 S	150.36 E
Barracão	252	26.15 S	53.38 W
Barracão do Barreto	248	8.48 S	58.24 W
Barracas ⇠[8]	288	34.38 S	58.22 W
Barrackpore	126	22.46 N	88.21 E
Barrackpore Airport ⊠	272b	22.47 N	88.22 E
Barrackpore Cantonment	272b	22.46 N	88.22 E
Barrackville	188	39.30 N	80.10 W
Barracouta, Cape ≻	158	34.26 S	21.22 E
Barracu, Monte ∧	70	37.43 N	13.20 E
Barra da Estiva	255	13.38 S	41.19 W
Barra de Río Grande	236	12.54 N	83.32 W
Barra de Santa Rosa	250	6.43 S	36.04 W
Barra de Santo Antônio	250	9.24 S	35.30 W
Barra de São Francisco	256	21.58 S	42.42 W
Barra do Bugres	248	15.05 S	57.11 W
Barra do Corda	250	5.30 S	45.15 W
Barra do Cuanza	152	9.09 S	13.00 E
Barra do Dande	152	8.28 S	13.22 E
Barra do Garças	255	15.53 S	52.15 W
Barra do Mendes	255	11.43 S	42.04 W
Barra do Piraí	256	22.28 S	43.49 W
Barra do Ribeiro	252	30.18 S	51.18 W
Barra dos Coqueiros	250	10.54 S	37.03 W
Barra Falsa, Ponta da ≻	156	22.55 S	35.37 E
Barrafranca	70	37.22 N	14.12 E
Barra Funda ⇠[8]	287b	23.31 S	46.39 W
Barra Head ≻	46	56.46 N	7.38 W
Barrali	71	39.28 N	9.06 E
Barra Mansa	256	22.32 S	44.11 W
Barranca, Perú	248	10.45 S	77.46 W
Barranca, Perú	248	4.50 S	76.42 W
Barrancabermeja	246	7.03 N	73.52 W
Barranca del Cobre, Parque Nacional ♠	232	27.15 N	107.41 W
Barrancas, Chile	252	33.27 S	70.46 W
Barrancas, Col.	246	10.57 N	72.50 W
Barrancas, Ven.	246	8.42 N	62.11 W
Barrancas, Ven.	246	8.46 N	70.06 W
Barrancas ≃	252	36.52 S	69.45 W
Barranco	286d	12.09 S	77.02 W
Barranco Azul	196	29.21 N	104.17 W
Barranco de Guadalupe	196	30.02 N	104.44 W
Barranco do Velho	34	37.14 N	7.56 W
Barrancos	34	38.08 N	6.59 W
Barrânia	256	21.33 S	46.32 W
Barranjoey Head ≻	170	33.34 S	151.20 E
Barranqueras	252	27.29 S	58.56 W
Barranquilla	246	10.59 N	74.48 W
Barranquitas	240m	18.11 N	66.18 W
Barra Punta Gorda	236	11.31 N	83.47 W
Barras	250	4.15 S	42.18 W
Barrax	34	39.03 N	2.12 W
Barre, Mass., U.S.	207	42.26 N	72.06 W
Barre, Vt., U.S.	188	44.12 N	72.30 W
Barrea	66	41.45 N	13.59 E
Barreal	252	31.38 S	69.28 W
Barre-des-Cévennes	62	44.15 N	3.39 E
Barre des Écrins ∧	62	44.55 N	6.22 E
Barree	214	40.35 N	78.06 W
Barre Falls Reservoir @[1]	207	42.24 N	72.00 W
Barreiras	255	12.08 S	45.00 W
Barreirinha	250	2.47 S	57.03 W
Barreirinhas	250	2.45 S	42.50 W
Barreiro	34	38.40 N	9.04 W
Barreiro ≃	255	15.43 S	52.45 W
Barreiros	250	8.49 S	35.12 W
Barrême	62	43.57 N	6.22 E
Barren ≃	194	37.11 N	86.37 W
Barren, Îles II	157b	18.25 S	43.40 E
Barren Islands II	180	58.55 N	152.15 W
Barren River Lake @[1]	194	36.45 N	86.02 W
Barren Run ≃	279b	40.09 N	79.42 W
Barre Plains	207	42.23 N	72.07 W
Barret-le-Bas	62	44.16 N	5.44 E
Barretos	255	20.33 S	48.33 W
Barrett	222	29.53 N	95.04 W
Barrett, Mount ∧	162	18.10 S	127.33 E
Barrhead, Alta., Can.	182	54.08 N	114.24 W
Barrhead, Scot., U.K.	46	55.48 N	4.24 W
Barrhill	44	55.07 N	4.46 W
Barriada Pomar Alto	266d	41.29 N	2.14 E
Barrie	212	44.24 N	79.40 W
Barriefield	212	44.14 N	76.28 W
Barrie Island I	190	45.55 N	82.40 W
Barrien	52	52.56 N	8.49 E
Barrier, Cape ≻	172	36.21 S	175.31 E
Barrier Bay C	9	67.45 S	81.10 E
Barrier Range ⩓	166	31.25 S	141.25 E
Barrigada	174p	13.28 N	144.48 E
Barrilla Draw ∨	196	31.21 N	103.23 W
Barr Ilyās	132	33.46 N	35.54 E
Barrington, N.S., Can.	186	43.34 N	65.34 W
Barrington, Ill., U.S.	216	42.09 N	88.08 W
Barrington, N.J., U.S.	285	39.52 N	75.04 W
Barrington, R.I., U.S.	207	41.44 N	71.18 W
Barrington Hills	216	42.07 N	88.09 W
Barrington Lake @	184	56.55 N	100.15 W
Barrington Tops ∧	166	32.00 S	151.28 E
Barrington Woods	278	42.09 N	88.04 W
Barringun	166	29.01 S	145.43 E
Barrinho	256	23.07 S	45.22 W
Barrio Azul ⇠[8]	286b	23.04 N	82.23 W
Barrio Obrero Industrial	286d	12.04 S	77.04 W
Barrita Vieja	236	13.55 N	90.54 W
Barrīyat al-Uşayfir	142	31.18 N	30.40 E
Barro, Bra.	250	7.11 S	38.47 W
Barro, Gui.-B.	150	12.24 N	15.30 W
Barro Alto	255	15.04 S	48.58 W
Barro Duro	250	2.52 S	42.17 W
Barrois □[9]	56	48.40 N	5.15 E
Barron	190	45.24 N	91.51 W
Barron Creek ≃	282	37.27 N	122.05 W
Barron Lake	216	41.51 N	86.11 W
Barrouallie	241h	13.14 N	61.17 W
Barrow, Arg.	252	38.18 S	60.14 W
Barrow, Alaska, U.S.	180	71.17 N	156.47 W
Barrow ≃	48	52.15 N	7.00 W
Barrow, Point ≻	180	71.23 N	156.30 W
Barrow Bay C	212	44.58 N	81.13 W
Barrow Creek	162	21.33 S	133.53 E
Barrowford	44	53.52 N	2.13 W
Barrow-in-Furness	44	54.07 N	3.14 W
Barrow Island I	162	20.48 S	115.23 E
Barrow Range ⩓	162	26.04 S	127.28 E
Barrows	184	52.49 N	101.27 W
Barrow Strait Ʉ	176	74.21 N	94.10 W
Barrowsville	207	41.57 N	71.12 W
Barry, Wales, U.K.	42	51.24 N	3.18 W
Barry, Ill., U.S.	219	39.42 N	91.02 W
Barry, Tex., U.S.	222	32.06 N	96.38 W
Barry □[6]	216	42.35 N	85.18 W
Barrydale	158	33.55 S	20.43 E
Barrys Bay	212	45.29 N	77.41 W
Barrys Bay C	212	45.28 N	77.42 W
Barryton	190	43.45 N	85.09 W
Barrytown	210	42.00 N	73.56 W
Barryville	210	41.29 N	74.55 W
Barsakel'mes, Ostrov I	86	45.40 N	59.58 E
Barsalogho	150	13.25 N	1.03 W
Baršatas	86	48.13 N	78.21 E
Bårse	41	55.07 N	11.58 E
Bārsi	122	18.14 N	75.42 E
Baršin	86	49.45 N	69.36 E
Barsinghausen	52	52.18 N	9.27 E
Barskaun	85	42.10 N	77.37 E
Barsø I	41	55.07 N	9.34 E
Barssel	52	53.10 N	7.44 E
Barst	56	49.04 N	6.50 E
Barstow, Calif., U.S.	228	34.54 N	117.01 W
Barstow, Tex., U.S.	196	31.28 N	103.24 W
Barsuki	82	54.15 N	37.30 E
Bar-sur-Aube	58	48.14 N	4.43 E
Bar-sur-Seine	50	48.07 N	4.22 E
Bart	208	39.56 N	76.05 W
Bartala	272b	22.33 N	88.16 E
Bartang	120	38.05 N	71.51 E
Bartazuga, Jabal ∧	140	21.44 N	33.33 E
Bartelso	219	38.32 N	89.28 W
Bartenheim	58	47.38 N	7.28 E
Bartenstein	56	49.21 N	9.53 E
Barter Island I	180	70.08 N	143.35 W
Barth	54	54.22 N	12.43 E
Barthe ≃	54	54.22 N	12.41 E
Barthélemy, Deo)(	110	19.26 N	104.06 E
Bārthi	126	23.02 N	90.12 E
Bartholomew □[6]	218	39.13 N	85.55 W
Bartholomew, Bayou ≃	194	32.43 N	92.04 W
Bartibougou	150	12.52 N	0.48 E
Bartica	246	6.24 N	58.37 W
Bartın	130	41.38 N	32.21 E
Bartle Frere ∧	166	17.23 S	145.49 E
Bartlesville	196	36.45 N	95.59 W
Bartlett, Ill., U.S.	216	41.59 N	88.11 W
Bartlett, Nebr., U.S.	198	41.53 N	98.33 W
Bartlett, N.H., U.S.	188	44.05 N	71.17 W
Bartlett, Tenn., U.S.	194	35.12 N	89.52 W
Bartlett, Tex., U.S.	222	30.48 N	97.26 W
Bartlett Brook ≃	283	42.42 N	71.13 W
Bartlett Cove	180	58.27 N	135.55 W
Bartlett Reservoir @[1]	200	33.52 N	111.37 W
Bartletts Harbour	186	50.57 N	57.00 W
Bartley	198	40.15 N	100.18 W
Bartolomé Bavio → General Mansilla	258	35.05 S	57.45 W
Bartolomé de las Casas	252	25.24 S	59.34 W
Bartolomeu de Gusmão, Aeroporto ⊠	256	22.56 S	43.43 W
Bartolomeu Dias	156	21.10 S	35.09 E
Barton, Austl.	162	30.31 S	132.39 E
Barton, N.Y., U.S.	210	42.03 N	76.27 W
Barton, Ohio, U.S.	214	40.06 N	80.51 W
Barton, Vt., U.S.	188	44.45 N	72.11 W
Barton Aerodrome ⊠	262	53.28 N	2.23 W
Barton Lake	216	42.06 N	85.35 W
Barton Mills	42	52.20 N	0.31 E
Barton Park ♠	274a	33.57 S	151.09 E
Barton Run ≃	285	39.53 N	74.51 W
Barton-under-Needwood	42	52.45 N	1.43 W
Barton-upon-Humber	44	53.41 N	0.27 W
Bartonville	190	40.39 N	89.39 W
Barton Water Swing Bridge ⇠[5]	262	53.28 N	2.21 W
Bartoszyce	30	54.16 N	20.49 E
Bartow, Fla., U.S.	220	27.54 N	81.50 W
Bartow, Ga., U.S.	192	32.53 N	82.29 W
Baru, Kali ≍	269e	6.10 S	106.51 E
Barú, Volcán ∧[1]	236	8.48 N	82.33 W
Barueri	256	23.31 S	46.53 W
Barugo	116	11.20 N	124.44 E
Bāruipāra	272b	22.46 N	88.14 E
Bāruipur	126	22.21 N	88.27 E
Bārūk, Jabal al- ∧	132	33.43 N	35.45 E
Barumini	71	39.42 N	9.00 E
Barumun ≃	114	2.30 N	100.09 E
Bāruni	124	25.29 N	85.59 E
Barun-Šibertuj, Gora ∧	74	49.42 N	109.59 E
Barus	114	2.00 N	98.24 E
Baruta	286c	10.26 N	66.53 W
Baruth	54	52.03 N	13.30 E
Baruun Bajan-Ulaan	102	45.32 N	101.40 E
Baruun Urt	90	46.40 N	113.12 E
Barva, Volcán ∧[1]	236	10.08 N	84.06 W
Barvas	46	58.22 N	6.32 W
Barvenkovo	78	48.54 N	37.02 E
Barver	52	52.37 N	8.35 E
Barvicha	265b	55.44 N	37.16 E
Barview	202	43.21 N	124.18 W
Barwa	126	23.51 N	86.26 E
Barwāh	120	22.16 N	76.03 E
Barwāla ⇠[8]	272a	28.46 N	77.04 E
Bärwalde → Mieszkowice	30	52.46 N	14.30 E
Barwāni	120	22.02 N	74.54 E
Barwa Sāgar	124	25.23 N	78.44 E
Barwell	42	52.32 N	1.21 W
Barwice	30	53.45 N	16.22 E
Barwick	192	30.54 N	83.44 W
Barwidgee	162	27.02 S	120.54 E
Barwon ≃, Austl.	166	30.00 S	148.05 E
Barwon ≃, Austl.	169	38.13 S	144.25 E
Barybino, S.S.S.R.	82	55.16 N	37.54 E
Barybino, S.S.S.R.	82	54.56 N	37.47 E
Barycz ≃	30	51.42 N	16.15 E
Barykino	83	49.17 N	38.24 E
Barykova, Mys ≻	180	63.02 N	179.29 E
Barykovo	82	54.38 N	38.48 E
Barynino	82	55.47 N	36.21 E
Baryš	80	53.39 N	47.08 E
Baryš ≃	80	54.35 N	46.48 E
Baryševka	78	50.22 N	31.19 E
Baryševo	86	54.58 N	83.11 E
Baryśniki	80	56.57 N	46.33 E
Barzah	132	33.34 N	36.19 E
Barzas	86	55.43 N	86.19 E
Barzio	58	45.57 N	9.27 E
Basa	150	4.55 N	7.30 W
Bas'a ≃	76	53.46 N	31.01 E
Basacato del Este	152	3.37 N	8.54 E
Basai Dārāpur ⇠[8]	272a	28.40 N	77.08 E
Bāsa'īdū	128	26.39 N	55.17 E
Basail, Arg.	252	27.52 S	59.18 W
Bāsāil, Bngl.	126	24.14 N	90.04 E
Basakin	80	48.11 N	42.18 E
Basāl	123	33.33 N	72.15 E
Basalt ≃	166	19.38 S	145.52 E
Basalt Island I	271d	22.19 N	114.22 E
Basaluzzo	62	44.46 N	8.42 E
Basandīlah	142	31.12 N	31.26 E
Basankusu	152	1.14 N	19.48 E
Bašanta	80	46.05 N	41.56 E
Basanti	126	22.12 N	88.42 E
Basarabi	38	44.10 N	28.24 E
Basargečar	84	40.11 N	45.43 E
Basavakalyān	122	17.52 N	76.57 E
Basavilbaso	252	32.22 S	58.53 W
Basbirin	130	37.19 N	41.38 E
Baščelakskij Chrebet ⩓	86	51.15 N	84.30 E
Baschi	66	42.40 N	12.13 E
Basco	108	20.27 N	121.58 E
Bascom	214	41.08 N	83.17 W
Bascuñán, Cabo ≻	252	28.51 S	71.30 W
Basdahl	52	53.26 N	8.59 E
Basdorf, B.R.D.	56	51.12 N	8.58 E
Basdorf, D.D.R.	54	52.44 N	13.26 E
Basekpio	154	4.44 N	24.40 E
Basel (Bâle)	58	47.33 N	7.35 E
Baselga di Pinè	64	46.08 N	11.14 E
Baselice	68	41.24 N	14.58 E
Basella	34	42.01 N	1.18 E
Basel-Land □[3]	58	47.30 N	7.50 E
Basel-Stadt □[3]	58	47.38 N	7.40 E
Basen ≃	96	34.48 N	132.51 E
Bas-en-Basset	62	45.18 N	4.06 E
Basentello ≃	68	40.40 N	16.23 E
Basento ≃	68	40.21 N	16.50 E
Başeu ≃	38	47.44 N	27.15 E
Basey	116	11.17 N	125.04 E
Bashākerd, Kūhhā-ye ⩓	128	26.42 N	59.00 E
Bashaw	182	52.35 N	112.58 W
Bashee ≃	158	32.15 S	28.53 E
Basher Kill ≃	210	41.27 N	74.35 W
Bashgah Airfield ⊠	267d	35.40 N	51.16 E
Bashi Channel Ʉ	108	22.00 N	121.00 E
Bashikejike	120	37.30 N	85.50 E
Bashiqiao	106	31.40 N	120.22 E
Bashtīl	273c	30.05 N	31.11 E
Basi, Bhārat	123	30.36 N	76.50 E
Basi, Bhārat	123	30.41 N	76.24 E
Basiad Bay C	116	14.16 N	122.19 E
Basiano	112	1.16 S	122.50 E
Basibasy	157b	22.10 S	43.40 E
Başıbüyük	267b	40.57 N	29.08 E
Basicò	70	38.04 N	15.04 E
Basid	85	38.07 N	72.09 E
Basilaki Island I	164	10.35 S	151.00 E
Basilan → Isabela	116	6.42 N	121.58 E
Basilan Island I	116	6.34 N	122.03 E
Basilan Peak ∧	116	6.33 N	122.04 E
Basilan Strait Ʉ	116	6.49 N	122.05 E
Basildon	260	51.35 N	0.25 E
Basildon □[8]	260	51.35 N	0.29 E
Basile	194	30.29 N	92.36 W
Basiliano	64	46.01 N	13.06 E
Basilicata □[4]	68	40.30 N	16.10 E
Basílio	252	31.53 S	53.01 W
Basiluzzo, Isola I	70	38.39 N	15.07 E
Basin, Mont., U.S.	202	46.16 N	112.16 W
Basin, Wyo., U.S.	202	44.23 N	108.02 W
Bäsingen @	40	60.09 N	16.20 E
Basinger	220	27.23 N	81.02 W
Basingstoke	42	51.15 N	1.05 W
Basingstoke Canal ≍	260	51.21 N	0.29 W
Basingwerk Abbey ʊ[1]	262	53.17 N	3.12 W
Basin Lake @	184	52.38 N	105.18 W
Basīrhāt	126	22.40 N	88.53 E
Basīrpur	123	30.35 N	73.50 E
Basīt, Ra's al- ≻	130	35.51 N	35.48 E
Basiyingzi	104	42.05 N	121.37 E
Basjanovskij	86	58.19 N	60.44 E
Baška	36	44.58 N	14.46 E
Baskahegan Lake @	188	45.30 N	67.48 W
Baskakovka	76	54.36 N	34.19 E
Başkale	128	38.02 N	44.00 E
Baskatong, Réservoir @[1]	190	46.48 N	75.50 W
Baškaus ≃	86	51.09 N	87.43 E
Baškend	84	40.38 N	45.32 E
Basket Lake @	184	49.43 N	92.00 W
Basking Ridge	276	40.42 N	74.33 W
Baškino	82	55.18 N	36.41 E
Baškirskaja Avtonomnaja Sovetskaja Socialističeskaja Respublika □[3]	86	54.00 N	56.00 E
Başköy	84	39.53 N	44.32 E
Baskuduk	86	49.43 N	61.32 E
Baš-Kugandy	85	42.00 N	74.39 E
Baskunčak, Ozero @	80	48.12 N	46.54 E
Baslow	44	53.15 N	1.38 W
Başmakcı	130	37.54 N	30.01 E
Basmakovo	80	53.12 N	43.02 E
Basmat	122	19.19 N	77.10 E
Bäsna	40	60.32 N	15.12 E
Başnık	130	38.07 N	40.44 E
Bāsoda	124	23.51 N	77.56 E
Basoko	152	1.14 N	23.36 E
Basoko ≃	273b	4.19 S	15.16 E
Basoli	123	32.30 N	75.49 E
Basom	210	43.04 N	78.24 W
Basongo	152	4.20 S	20.24 E
Basora, Punt ≻	241s	12.25 N	69.52 W
Basovizza	64	45.38 N	13.52 E
Başpınar	130	39.12 N	38.42 E
Basque Provinces → Vascongadas □[9]	34	43.00 N	2.45 W
Basra → Al-Başrah	128	30.30 N	47.47 E
Bas-Rhin □[5]	32	48.35 N	7.40 E
Bass, Îlots de II	14	27.55 S	143.26 W
Bassano	182	50.47 N	112.28 W
Bassano del Grappa	64	45.46 N	11.44 E
Bassari	150	9.15 N	0.47 E
Bassas da India ⇠[2]	138	21.25 S	39.42 E
Bass Creek ≃	216	42.37 N	89.04 W
Basse-Californie → Baja California ≻[1]	232	28.00 N	113.30 W
Bassecourt	58	47.20 N	7.15 E
Bassein	110	16.47 N	94.44 E
Bassein ≃[1]	110	15.56 N	94.18 E
Basse-Kotto □[5]	152	5.00 N	21.30 E
Bassen	52	53.04 N	9.04 E
Bassenheim	56	50.21 N	7.27 E
Bassenthwaite	44	54.41 N	3.12 W
Bassenthwaite Lake @	44	54.38 N	3.13 W
Basse-Pointe	240e	14.52 N	61.07 W
Basses, Pointe des ≻	241o	15.52 N	61.17 W
Basses-Alpes □[5]	62	44.10 N	6.00 E
Basse Santa Su	150	13.19 N	14.13 W
Basses-Pyrénées □[5]	32	43.15 N	0.50 W
Basse-Terre, Guad.	241o	16.00 N	61.44 W
Basseterre, St. K.-N.	238	17.18 N	62.43 W
Basse Terre, Trin.	241r	10.08 N	61.18 W
Basse-Terre I	241o	16.10 N	61.40 W
Bassett, Nebr., U.S.	198	42.35 N	99.32 W
Bassett, Va., U.S.	192	36.46 N	79.59 W
Bassett Creek ≃	194	31.25 N	87.56 W
Bassetts Creek ≃	194	31.27 N	87.55 W
Basse-Yutz	56	49.21 N	6.11 E
Bassfield	194	31.30 N	89.44 W
Bass Harbor	188	44.16 N	68.19 W
Bass Hill	274a	33.54 S	151.00 E
Bassignana	62	45.00 N	8.44 E
Bassikounou	150	15.52 N	5.57 W
Bassila	150	9.01 N	1.40 E
Bassin Des Aghlabites ⊥	36	35.43 N	10.10 E
Bass Lake, Calif., U.S.	226	37.19 N	119.33 W
Bass Lake, Ind., U.S.	216	41.12 N	86.36 W
Bass Lake @, Ont., Can.	212	44.49 N	76.08 W
Bass Lake @, Ind., U.S.	216	41.13 N	86.36 W
Bass Lake @[1]	226	37.19 N	119.34 W
Bass Point ≻	170	34.36 S	150.54 E
Bass River	186	45.25 N	63.47 W
Bass Strait Ʉ	166	39.20 S	145.30 E
Bassum	52	52.51 N	8.43 E
Basswood Lake @, Ont., Can.	190	46.20 N	83.23 W
Basswood Lake @, N.A.	190	48.06 N	91.40 W
Basta	126	21.41 N	87.03 E
Båstad	26	56.26 N	12.51 E
Baştah	132	30.14 N	35.32 E
Bastak	128	27.14 N	54.22 E
Baştām	128	36.29 N	55.04 E
Baštanka	78	47.24 N	32.25 E
Bastei ♠	54	50.58 N	14.04 E
Bastelica	36	42.00 N	9.02 E
Basti	124	26.48 N	82.43 E
Bastia, Fr.	32	42.42 N	9.27 E
Bastia, It.	66	43.04 N	12.33 E
Bastian	192	37.09 N	81.09 W
Bastiglia	64	44.43 N	11.00 E
Bastimentos	236	9.21 N	82.12 W
Bastimentos, Isla I	236	9.18 N	82.08 W
Bastogne	56	50.00 N	5.43 E
Bastrop, La., U.S.	194	32.47 N	91.55 W
Bastrop, Tex., U.S.	222	30.07 N	97.19 W
Bastrop □[6]	222	33.00 N	97.18 W
Bastrop Bay C	222	29.06 N	95.11 W
Bastrop State Park ♠	222	30.07 N	97.17 W
Bastuträsk	26	64.47 N	20.02 E
Basubāti	272b	22.47 N	88.12 E
Bāsudebpur, Bhārat	126	21.49 N	87.38 E
Bāsudebpur, Bhārat	272b	22.49 N	88.25 E
Basuo → Dongfang	110	19.05 N	108.39 E
Basuolaling ⩓	102	38.44 N	98.20 E
Bāsūr, Jabal al- ∧[2]	142	30.34 N	30.35 E
Bāsūs	273c	30.08 N	31.13 E
Baswa	126	24.08 N	87.52 E
Basyūn	142	30.57 N	30.49 E
Bas-Zaïre □[4]	152	5.30 S	14.30 E
Bata	152	1.51 N	9.45 E
Bataan □[4]	116	14.40 N	120.25 E
Bataan, Mount ∧	116	14.31 N	120.28 E
Bataan Peninsula ≻[1]	116	14.40 N	120.25 E
Batabanó	240p	22.43 N	82.17 W
Batabanó, Golfo de C	240p	22.15 N	82.30 W
Batac	116	18.05 N	120.35 E
Batad	116	11.25 N	123.06 E
Batagaj	74	67.38 N	134.38 E
Batagaj-Alyta	74	67.48 N	130.25 E
Batag Island I	116	12.38 N	125.04 E
Batagol	88	52.22 N	100.45 E
Bataguaçu	255	21.42 S	52.22 W
Bataiporã	255	22.20 S	53.17 W
Batajsk	83	47.10 N	39.44 E
Batak	38	41.57 N	24.13 E
Batak, Jazovir @[1]	38	41.59 N	24.11 E
Batakan	112	4.05 S	114.38 E
Batāla	123	31.48 N	75.12 E
Batalha, Bra.	250	9.41 S	37.08 W
Batalha, Bra.	250	4.01 S	42.05 W
Batalha, Port.	34	39.39 N	8.50 W
Bataly	86	52.52 N	62.00 E
Batam, Pulau I	112	1.05 N	104.03 E
Batama, S.S.S.R.	88	53.53 N	101.36 E
Batama, Zaïre	154	0.56 N	26.39 E
Batamaj	74	63.31 N	129.27 E
Batamšinskij	86	50.36 N	58.16 E
Batan, Pil.	116	11.35 N	122.30 E
Batan, Zhg.	98	34.10 N	120.04 E
Batanagar	126	22.31 N	88.15 E
Batanes □[4]	116	20.30 N	121.50 E
Batang, Indon.	115a	6.55 S	109.45 E
Batang, Zhg.	102	30.02 N	99.02 E
Batangafo	152	7.18 N	18.18 E
Batangas	116	13.45 N	121.03 E
Batangas □[4]	116	13.50 N	121.00 E
Batangas Bay C	116	13.43 N	121.00 E
Batangbatangdaya	115a	6.56 S	113.59 E
Batang Berjuntai	114	3.23 N	101.25 E
Batang Kali	114	3.28 N	101.38 E
Batangtoru	114	1.29 N	99.03 E
Batan Island I, Pil.	108	20.26 N	121.58 E
Batan Island I, Pil.	116	13.15 N	124.00 E
Batan Islands II	108	20.30 N	121.50 E
Batas ≃	287a	22.44 S	43.24 W
Batas Island I	116	11.10 N	119.36 E
Bátaszék	30	46.12 N	18.44 E
Batatais	255	20.53 S	47.37 W
Batatuba	256	23.04 S	46.25 W
Batavia, Arg.	252	34.47 S	65.41 W
Batavia, Ill., U.S.	216	41.51 N	88.19 W
Batavia, Iowa, U.S.	190	41.00 N	92.10 W
Batavia, Mich., U.S.	216	41.55 N	85.06 W
Batavia, N.Y., U.S.	210	43.00 N	78.11 W
Batavia, Ohio, U.S.	218	39.05 N	84.11 W
Batawa	212	44.10 N	77.36 W
Batbatan Island I	116	11.28 N	121.55 E
Batcengel	88	47.47 N	101.58 E
Batchawana ≃	190	46.55 N	84.32 W
Batchawana Mountain ∧	190	47.04 N	84.24 W
Batchelor	164	13.04 S	131.01 E
Bătdâmbâng	110	13.06 N	103.12 E
Bateau Channel Ʉ	212	44.10 N	76.31 W
Bate Bay C	274a	34.04 S	151.12 E
Bateckij	76	58.39 N	30.19 E
Bate Heath	262	53.19 N	2.28 W
Bateia	256	22.20 S	45.49 W
Batemans Bay	166	35.43 S	150.11 E
Batenbrock ⇠[8]	263	51.31 N	6.57 E
Bates, Mount ∧	174c	29.01 S	167.56 E
Batesburg	192	33.54 N	81.33 W
Bates Creek ≃	200	42.41 N	106.37 W
Bates Range ⩓	162	27.25 S	121.13 E
Batesville, Ark., U.S.	194	35.46 N	91.39 W
Batesville, Ind., U.S.	218	39.18 N	85.13 W
Batesville, Miss., U.S.	194	34.18 N	90.00 W
Batesville, Tex., U.S.	196	28.57 N	99.37 W
Bath, Ont., Can.	212	44.11 N	76.47 W
Bath, Eng., U.K.	42	51.23 N	2.22 W
Bath, Ill., U.S.	219	40.11 N	90.08 W
Bath, Maine, U.S.	188	43.55 N	69.49 W
Bath, Mich., U.S.	216	42.49 N	84.27 W
Bath, N.Y., U.S.	210	42.20 N	77.19 W
Bath, Ohio, U.S.	214	41.11 N	81.38 W
Bath, Pa., U.S.	208	40.44 N	75.24 W
Bath □[6]	218	38.14 N	83.48 W
Batha □[5]	146	14.00 N	19.00 E
Bath Addition	285	40.06 N	74.52 W
Bathgate, Scot., U.K.	46	55.55 N	3.39 W
Bathgate, N. Dak., U.S.	198	48.53 N	97.29 W
Bathsheba	241g	13.13 N	59.31 W
Bathurst, Austl.	166	33.25 S	149.35 E
Bathurst, N.B., Can.	186	47.36 N	65.39 W
Bathurst → Banjul, Gam.	150	13.28 N	16.39 W
Bathurst, S. Afr.	158	33.30 S	26.50 E
Bathurst, Cape ≻	176	70.35 N	128.00 W
Bathurst, Lake @	170	35.04 S	149.44 E
Bathurst Inlet	176	66.50 N	108.01 W
Bathurst Inlet C	176	68.10 N	108.50 W
Bathurst Island I, Austl.	164	11.37 S	130.23 E
Bathurst Island I, N.W. Ter., Can.	16	76.00 N	100.30 W
Bathurst Island Mission	164	11.45 S	130.38 E
Bati	144	11.10 N	40.02 E
Batia	150	10.54 N	1.29 E
Batiāgarh	124	24.07 N	79.21 E
Batibla	152	5.56 N	21.09 E
Batié	150	9.53 N	2.55 W
Bāţin, Wādī al- ∨	128	29.35 N	47.00 E
Batina	38	45.51 N	18.51 E
Batiquitos Lagoon C	228	33.05 N	117.18 W
Batīr	132	31.16 N	35.42 E
Batırga	130	36.24 N	36.11 E
Batiscan ≃	206	46.31 N	72.15 W
Batiste Creek ≃	222	30.04 N	94.28 W
Batkanu	150	9.05 N	12.25 W
Batken	85	40.03 N	70.50 E
Batlajsagyr, Peski ⇠[2]	80	47.20 N	48.40 E
Batley	44	53.44 N	1.37 W
Batlow	171b	35.31 S	148.09 E
Batman	130	37.52 N	41.07 E
Batna	148	35.34 N	6.11 E
Batna □[5]	148	35.00 N	6.00 E
Batnorov	88	47.57 N	111.27 E
Batō, Nihon	94	36.44 N	140.10 E
Bato, Pil.	116	10.20 N	124.47 E
Ba-to, Viet.	110	14.46 N	108.44 E
Bato, Lake @	116	13.19 N	123.21 E
Batoala	152	0.48 N	13.27 E
Batoche Rectory National Historic Site ⊥	184	52.41 N	106.02 W
Batoka	154	16.47 S	27.15 E
Baton Rouge	194	30.23 N	91.11 W
Batorampon Point ≻	116	7.07 N	121.54 E
Batoti	123	33.06 N	75.19 E
Batouri	152	4.26 N	14.22 E
Batovi	255	15.53 S	53.24 W
Baţrah	142	31.10 N	31.27 E
Ba-tri	110	10.02 N	106.36 E
Bātsawul	120	34.15 N	70.52 E
Batson	222	30.15 N	94.37 W
Batsto ≃	285	39.39 N	74.39 W
Batsto, Skit Branch ≃	285	39.46 N	74.41 W
Batsto Village ⊥	208	39.39 N	74.39 W
Battaglia Terme	64	45.17 N	11.47 E
Battambang → Bătdâmbâng	110	13.06 N	103.12 E
Battenberg	56	51.01 N	8.38 E
Batten Kill ≃	210	43.06 N	73.35 W
Batterie, Pointe de la ≻	240e	14.44 N	60.54 W
Bätterkinden	58	47.08 N	7.32 E
Battersea ⇠[8]	260	51.28 N	0.10 W
Battersea Park ♠	260	51.29 N	0.09 W
Batticaloa	122	7.43 N	81.42 E
Battice	56	50.39 N	5.49 E
Battin	224	45.29 N	122.34 W
Battipaglia	68	40.37 N	14.58 E
Battle	42	50.55 N	0.29 E
Battle ≃	184	52.43 N	108.15 W
Battle Creek, Iowa, U.S.	198	42.19 N	95.36 W
Battle Creek, Mich., U.S.	216	42.19 N	85.11 W
Battle Creek, Nebr., U.S.	198	42.00 N	97.36 W
Battle Creek ≃, N.A.	202	48.36 N	109.11 W
Battle Creek ≃, Calif., U.S.	204	40.21 N	122.11 W
Battle Creek ≃, Idaho, U.S.	202	42.14 N	116.32 W
Battle Creek ≃, Mich., U.S.	216	42.19 N	85.12 W
Battle Creek ≃, Tex., U.S.	196	32.50 N	98.58 W
Battle Creek, North Fork ≃	204	40.26 N	122.00 W
Battle Creek, South Fork ≃	204	40.26 N	122.00 W
Battlefields	154	18.31 S	29.52 E
Battle Green ⊥	283	42.27 N	71.14 W
Battle Ground, Ind., U.S.	216	40.31 N	86.50 W
Battle Ground, Wash., U.S.	224	45.47 N	122.32 W
Battle Harbour	176	52.16 N	55.35 W
Battle Lake	198	46.17 N	95.43 W
Battlement Mesa ∧	200	39.20 N	108.00 W
Battlemount	158	26.57 S	23.46 E
Battle Mountain	204	40.38 N	116.56 W
Battle Mountain ∧	200	41.02 N	107.16 W
Battlesbridge	260	51.37 N	0.34 E
Battonya	30	46.17 N	21.01 E
Battuello	266b	45.27 N	8.56 E
Batu	115a	7.52 S	112.31 E
Batu, Kepulauan II	110	0.18 S	98.28 E
Batuan	116	12.25 N	123.47 E
Batu Arang	114	3.19 N	101.28 E
Batuata, Pulau I	112	6.12 S	122.42 E
Batuata, Tanjung ≻	115b	9.37 S	120.29 E
Batu-batu	112	4.09 S	119.52 E
Batu Berinchang, Gunong ∧	114	4.31 N	101.23 E
Batubetumpang	112	2.53 S	106.09 E
Batuc	232	29.15 N	109.44 W
Batu Caves	114	3.14 N	101.40 E
Batudaka, Pulau I	112	0.28 S	121.48 E
Batu Enam	114	2.35 N	102.43 E
Batu Gajah	114	4.28 N	101.03 E
Batui	112	1.17 S	122.33 E
Batui, Pegunungan ⩓	112	1.15 S	122.10 E
Batuidu	112	10.38 S	123.25 E
Batukau, Bukit ∧	115b	8.20 S	115.05 E
Batukelau	112	0.48 N	115.01 E
Batu Laut	114	2.41 N	101.31 E
Batulicin	112	3.27 S	116.00 E
Batumata Point ≻	164	10.17 S	148.57 E
Batumelinggang	114	3.50 N	98.25 E
Batumi	84	41.38 N	41.38 E
Batu Pahat (Bandar Penggaram)	114	1.51 N	102.56 E
Batupanjang	114	1.43 N	101.31 E
Batu Puteh, Gunong ∧	114	4.13 N	101.27 E
Batuputih	112	1.24 N	118.29 E
Batura ∧	123	36.31 N	74.30 E
Baturaja	112	4.08 S	104.10 E
Batu Rakit	114	5.27 N	103.03 E
Baturetno	115a	7.59 S	110.56 E
Baturin	78	51.21 N	32.51 E
Baturino, S.S.S.R.	86	57.48 N	85.12 E
Baturino, S.S.S.R.	265b	55.35 N	37.31 E
Baturinskaja	78	45.47 N	39.22 E
Baturité	250	4.20 S	38.53 W
Baturotok	115b	8.42 S	117.10 E
Baturusa	112	2.02 S	106.07 E
Batusangkar	112	0.27 S	100.35 E
Batutinggi	112	1.55 S	113.19 E
Bat Yam	132	32.01 N	34.45 E
Batyrevo	80	55.04 N	47.38 E
Batyr-Mala, Ozero @	80	47.35 N	44.45 E
Bau	112	1.25 N	110.08 E
Bauang	116	16.31 N	120.20 E
Baubašata, Gory ⩓	85	41.20 N	72.45 E
Baubau	112	5.28 S	122.38 E
Bauchi	150	10.19 N	9.50 E
Baucina	70	37.55 N	13.32 E
Baud	32	47.52 N	3.01 W
Baudette	190	48.43 N	94.36 W
Baudh	120	20.50 N	84.19 E
Baudó ≃	246	4.57 N	77.22 W
Baudó, Serranía de ⩓	246	6.00 N	77.05 W
Baudouin Stadium ♠	273b	4.20 S	15.20 E
Baudour	50	50.29 N	3.49 E
Bauernschaft	263	51.34 N	6.33 E
Bauerstown	279b	40.30 N	79.59 W
Baugé	32	47.33 N	0.06 W
Baugo Creek ≃	216	41.40 N	86.04 W
Baukau ⇠[8]	263	51.33 N	7.12 E
Baúl, Cerro ∧	234	17.38 N	100.19 W
Bauld, Cape ≻	186	51.38 N	55.25 W
Baulkham Hills	274a	33.46 S	151.00 E
Baulmes	58	46.48 N	6.32 E
Bauma	58	47.23 N	8.53 E
Baumann, Pic ∧	150	6.52 N	0.46 E
Baumberg	263	51.07 N	6.54 E
Baume ≃	62	44.26 N	4.20 E
Baume-les-Dames	58	47.21 N	6.22 E
Baumholder	56	49.37 N	7.20 E
Baumschulenweg ⇠[8]	264a	52.28 N	13.29 E
Baun	112	10.18 S	123.43 E
Baunach	56	49.59 N	10.50 E
Baunach ≃	56	50.14 N	10.28 E
Baunatal	56	51.16 N	9.25 E
Baunei	71	40.02 N	9.40 E
Baunt	88	55.16 N	113.08 E
Baunt, Ozero @	88	55.12 N	113.00 E
Bāuphal	126	22.25 N	90.33 E
Baure	150	12.50 N	8.45 E
Baures	248	13.35 S	63.35 W
Baures ≃	248	12.30 S	64.18 W
Bāuria	126	22.29 N	88.10 E
Bauru	255	22.19 S	49.04 W
Baús	255	18.19 S	53.10 W
Bausendorf	56	50.01 N	6.59 E
Bausenhagen	263	51.31 N	7.48 E
Bauska	76	56.24 N	24.14 E
Bauta	240p	22.59 N	82.33 W
Bauta □[7]	286b	22.59 N	82.33 W
Bautino	84	44.33 N	50.15 E
Bautzen	54	51.11 N	14.26 E
Bauxite	194	34.33 N	92.30 W
Bauya	150	8.11 N	12.34 W
Bavans	58	47.29 N	6.44 E
Bavari	62	44.26 N	9.01 E
Bavaria → Bayern □[9]	30	49.00 N	11.30 E
Bavarian Alps → Bayerische Alpen ⩓	64	47.30 N	11.00 E
Bavay	50	50.18 N	3.47 E
Båven @	40	59.01 N	16.56 E
Baveno	58	45.55 N	8.30 E
Baviaanskloofberge ⩓	158	33.35 S	24.10 E
Bavilliers	58	47.37 N	6.50 E
Bavispe	232	30.24 N	108.50 W
Bavispe, Río de ≃	232	29.15 N	109.11 W
Bavleny	80	56.24 N	39.34 E
Bavly	80	54.25 N	53.17 E
Bavnhöj ∧[2]	41	55.55 N	10.07 E
Bavtugaj	84	43.11 N	46.49 E
Baw	110	23.19 N	95.50 E
Bāwal	124	28.05 N	76.35 E
Bāwāli	272b	22.25 N	88.12 E
Bawang	115a	7.06 S	109.55 E
Baw Baw, Mount ∧	169	37.50 S	146.17 E
Baw Beese Lake @	216	41.54 N	84.36 W
Bawdeswell	42	52.45 N	1.01 E
Bawdwin	110	23.06 N	97.18 E
Bawean, Pulau I	115a	5.46 S	112.40 E
Baweigang	106	31.57 N	120.14 E
Bawku	150	11.05 N	0.14 W
Bawlake	110	19.11 N	97.21 E
Bawmi	110	17.19 N	94.35 E
Bawn	144	10.12 N	43.02 E
Bawtry	44	53.26 N	1.01 W
Baxenden	262	53.44 N	2.20 W
Baxian, Zhg.	105	39.06 N	116.23 E
Baxian, Zhg.	107	29.23 N	106.32 E
Baxiantong	89	43.08 N	121.03 E
Baxley	192	31.47 N	82.21 W
Baxter, Iowa, U.S.	190	41.49 N	93.09 W
Baxter, Minn., U.S.	190	46.20 N	94.16 W
Baxter, Tenn., U.S.	194	36.09 N	85.38 W
Baxter Estates	276	40.50 N	73.42 W
Baxter Springs	198	37.02 N	94.44 W
Baxter State Park ♠	188	46.00 N	68.58 W
Baxterville	194	31.06 N	89.36 W
Bay	194	35.45 N	90.34 W
Bay, Laguna de @	269f	14.28 N	121.07 E
Baya, Zaïre	152	4.57 N	19.43 E
Baya, Zaïre	154	11.52 S	27.27 E
Bayāḑah, Wādī al- ∨	146	26.08 N	18.35 E
Bayāḑ an-Naşārā	142	29.04 N	31.08 E
Bayag	116	18.16 N	121.02 E
Bay al-Kabīr, Wādī ∨	146	31.15 N	15.57 E
Bayambang	116	15.49 N	120.27 E
Bayamo	240p	20.23 N	76.39 W
Bayamo ≃	240p	20.34 N	76.44 W
Bayamón	240m	18.24 N	66.09 W
Bayan, Indon.	115b	8.16 S	116.26 E
Bayan, Zhg.	89	46.05 N	127.24 E
Bayāna	124	26.54 N	77.17 E
Bayanbayanan	269f	14.39 N	121.06 E
Bayanchagan	89	47.19 N	124.03 E
Bayanchaganmiao	89	48.35 N	119.49 E
Bayang	116	7.48 N	124.12 E
Bayanga	152	2.53 N	16.19 E
Bayange	102	39.19 N	107.31 E
Bayanhaote	102	38.50 N	105.41 E
Bayanheshuomiao	89	48.51 N	119.46 E
Bayanjie	89	49.36 N	124.37 E
Bayankalashanmai ⩓	102	33.48 N	98.10 E
Bayanluke	89	50.52 N	119.33 E
Bayannaobao	102	39.44 N	107.40 E
Bayantala	89	43.44 N	123.16 E
Bayard, Fla., U.S.	192	30.09 N	81.31 W
Bayard, Iowa, U.S.	198	41.51 N	94.33 W
Bayard, Nebr., U.S.	198	41.45 N	103.20 W
Bayard, N. Mex., U.S.	200	32.46 N	108.08 W
Bayard, Ohio, U.S.	214	40.46 N	81.04 W
Bayard, W. Va., U.S.	188	39.16 N	79.22 W
Bayard, Col)(	62	44.37 N	6.05 E
Bayard Cutting Arboretum ♠	276	40.45 N	73.10 W
Bayat, Indon.	112	2.06 S	103.38 E
Bayat, Tür.	130	40.39 N	34.15 E
Bayat, Tür.	130	38.59 N	30.56 E
Bayawan	116	9.22 N	122.48 E
Baybay	116	10.41 N	124.48 E
Bayberry	210	43.08 N	76.13 W
Bayble	46	58.12 N	6.13 W
Bayboro	192	35.09 N	76.46 W
Bay Bulls	186	47.19 N	52.49 W
Bayburt	130	40.16 N	40.15 E
Bay Center	224	46.38 N	123.57 W

Symbols in the index entries represent the broad categories identified in the key at the right. Symbols with superior numbers (⩓[2]) identify subcategories (see complete key on page *I* · *30*).

Kartensymbole in dem Registerverzeichnis stellen die rechts in Schlüssel erklärten Kategorien dar. Symbole mit hochgestellten Ziffern (⩓[2]) bezeichnen Unterabteilungen einer Kategorie (vgl. vollständiger Schlüssel auf Seite *I* · *30*).

Los símbolos incluídos en el texto del índice representan las grandes categorias identificadas con la clave a la derecha. Los símbolos con numeros en su parte superior (⩓[2]) identifican las subcategorías (véase la clave completa en la página *I* · *30*).

Les symboles de l'index représentent les catégories indiquées dans la légende à droite. Les symboles suivis d'un indice (⩓[2]) représentent des sous-catégories (voir légende complète à la page *I* · *30*).

Os símbolos incluídos no texto do índice representam as grandes categorias identificadas com a chave à direita. Os símbolos com números em sua parte superior (⩓[2]) identificam as subcategorias (veja-se a chave completa à página *I* · *30*).

Symbol	English	Deutsch	Español	Français	Português
∧	Mountain	Berg	Montaña	Montagne	Montanha
⩓	Mountains	Berge	Montañas	Montagnes	Montanhas
)(	Pass	Pass	Paso	Col	Passo
∨	Valley, Canyon	Tal, Cañon	Valle, Cañón	Vallée, Canyon	Vale, Canhão
≚	Plain	Ebene	Llano	Plaine	Planície
≻	Cape	Kap	Cabo	Cap	Cabo
I	Island	Insel	Isla	Île	Ilha
II	Islands	Inseln	Islas	Îles	Ilhas
•	Other Topographic Features	Andere Topographische Objekte	Otros Elementos Topográficos	Autres données topographiques	Outros Elementos Topográficos

ESPAÑOL

Nombre	Página	Lat.°′	Long.°′ W=Oeste
Bay City, Mich., U.S.	190	43.36 N	83.53 W
Bay City, Oreg., U.S.	224	45.31 N	123.53 W
Bay City, Tex., U.S.	222	28.59 N	95.58 W
Bay Creek ≃, Ill., U.S.	194	37.16 N	88.31 W
Bay Creek ≃, Ill., U.S.	219	39.20 N	90.46 W
Bayḍā', Bi'r ╤[4]	142	29.45 N	32.13 E
Bay de Verde	186	48.05 N	52.54 W
Bay du Nord ≃	186	47.44 N	55.25 W
Baye, Cap ≻	175f	20.57 S	165.25 E
Bayel	58	48.12 N	4.47 E
Bayerische Alpen ⛰	64	47.30 N	11.00 E
Bayerisch Eisenstein	60	49.07 N	13.12 E
Bayerischer Wald ⛰	60	49.00 N	12.40 E
Bayerischer Wald, Naturpark ♠	60	49.20 N	12.30 E
Bayern □[3]	30	49.00 N	11.30 E
Bayern □[9]	30	49.00 N	11.30 E
Bayers Creek ≃	284a	43.00 N	79.02 W
Bayeuen	114	4.36 N	97.53 E
Bayeux, Bra.	250	7.08 S	34.56 W
Bayeux, Fr.	32	49.16 N	0.42 W
Bay Farm Island I	282	37.43 N	122.14 W
Bayfield, Colo., U.S.	200	37.14 N	107.36 W
Bayfield, Wis., U.S.	190	46.49 N	90.49 W
Bayfield, Île I	186	51.13 N	58.23 W
Bayfield Ridge ∧	190	46.45 N	91.25 W
Bayford	260	51.46 N	0.06 W
'Bayh	132	33.44 N	35.31 E
Bayḥā al-Qiṣād	144	14.48 N	45.43 E
Bay Harbor Islands	220	25.53 N	80.08 W
Bayhead, Scot., U.K.	46	57.33 N	7.24 W
Bay Head, N.J., U.S.	208	40.04 N	74.03 W
Bayiji	98	34.18 N	117.41 E
Bayındır	130	38.13 N	27.40 E
Bayinguoleng Zizhiziou □[4]	86	42.30 N	85.00 E
Bayingzi	104	41.28 N	120.46 E
Baykonur → Bajkonyr	86	47.50 N	66.03 E
Bay L'Argent	186	47.33 N	54.54 W
Bayley Point ≻	164	16.56 S	139.02 E
Baylis	219	39.44 N	90.54 W
Bay Meadows Race Track ♠	282	37.32 N	122.18 W
Bay Minette	194	30.53 N	87.47 W
Baynūnah ◆[1]	128	23.50 N	52.45 E
Bayo	34	43.09 N	8.58 W
Bayombong	116	16.29 N	121.09 E
Bayon	58	48.29 N	6.19 E
Bayona	34	42.07 N	8.51 W
Bayonne, Fr.	32	43.29 N	1.29 W
Bayonne, N.J., U.S.	210	40.41 N	74.07 W
Bayonne ≃	206	46.05 N	73.10 W
Bayonne Bridge ◆[5]	276	40.38 N	74.09 W
Bayons	62	44.20 N	6.10 E
Bayou La Batre	194	30.24 N	88.15 W
Bayóvar	248	5.50 S	81.03 W
Bay Park	276	40.38 N	73.40 W
Bay Point ≻	216	41.44 N	83.25 W
Bayport, Fla., U.S.	220	28.33 N	83.39 W
Bay Port, Mich., U.S.	190	43.51 N	83.23 W
Bayport, Minn., U.S.	190	45.01 N	92.47 W
Bayport, N.Y., U.S.	210	40.44 N	73.03 W
Bayraktar	84	39.41 N	42.08 E
Bayramıç	130	39.48 N	26.37 E
Bayramören	130	40.57 N	33.12 E
Bayreuth	60	49.57 N	11.35 E
Bay Ridge	208	38.56 N	76.28 W
Bay Ridge ◆[8]	276	40.37 N	74.02 W
Bay Ridge Channel ⋓	276	40.39 N	74.02 W
Bayrischzell	64	47.40 N	12.00 E
Bay Roberts	186	47.36 N	53.16 W
Bayrūt (Beirut)	130	33.53 N	35.30 E
Bayrūt □[4]	132	33.56 N	35.30 E
Bays, Lake of @	212	45.15 N	79.04 W
Bay Saint Louis	194	30.19 N	89.20 W
Bay Shore	210	40.44 N	73.15 W
Bayshore Gardens	220	27.26 N	82.35 W
Bayside, Ont., Can.	212	44.07 N	77.30 W
Bayside, Mass., U.S.	283	42.18 N	70.53 W
Bayside, Wis., U.S.	216	43.11 N	87.54 W
Bayside ◆[8]	276	40.46 N	73.46 W
Bay Springs	194	31.53 N	89.17 W
Bayswater	274b	37.51 S	145.16 E
Bayswater North	274b	37.49 S	145.17 E
Bayt ad-Dīn	132	33.42 N	35.35 E
Bayt ad-Din ⊥	132	33.41 N	35.34 E
Bayt al-Faqīh	144	14.32 N	43.20 E
Bayt Ḥānūm	132	31.32 N	34.33 E
Bayt Jālā	132	31.43 N	35.11 E
Bayt Jinn	132	33.19 N	35.53 E
Bayt Laḥm (Bethlehem)	132	31.43 N	35.12 E
Bayt Mirī	132	33.52 N	35.36 E
Baytown	222	29.44 N	94.58 W
Bayt Sāḥūr	132	31.42 N	35.13 E
Bayt Sīrā	132	31.53 N	35.03 E
Bayuan ≃	116	9.22 N	122.48 E
Bayunglencir	112	2.03 S	103.41 E
Bayview, Austl.	274a	33.40 S	151.18 E
Bay View, N.Z.	172	39.25 S	176.53 E
Bay View, N.Y., U.S.	210	42.47 N	78.51 W
Bay View, Ohio, U.S.	214	41.28 N	82.50 W
Bayview ◆[8]	282	37.44 N	122.23 W
Bay Village	214	41.29 N	81.55 W
Bayville, N.J., U.S.	208	39.55 N	74.09 W
Bayville, N.Y., U.S.	210	40.54 N	73.33 W
Baywood Park	226	35.20 N	120.50 W
Bayyāḍah, Ra's al- ≻	132	33.10 N	35.10 E
Bayyā'īyah al-Kabīrah	130	35.42 N	37.09 E
Bayyūḍah ╤[4]	140	17.32 N	32.07 E
Bayzo	150	13.52 N	4.45 E
Baza	34	37.29 N	2.46 W
Baza, Sierra de ⛰	34	37.15 N	2.45 W
Bazainville	261	48.48 N	1.40 E
Bazalija	78	49.43 N	26.27 E
Bazar	88	53.58 N	116.05 E
Bazarčaj	84	39.40 N	45.48 E
Bāzār-e Panjvā'ī	120	31.32 N	65.28 E
Bazargic → Tolbuhin	38	43.34 N	27.50 E
Bazar-Kurgan	85	41.02 N	72.45 E
Bazarnyje Mataki	80	54.56 N	49.56 E
Bazarnyj Karabulak	80	52.16 N	46.25 E
Bazarnyj Syzgan	80	53.45 N	45.46 E
Bazarovo	82	54.47 N	38.10 E
Bazaršolan	80	49.04 N	51.56 E
Bazartobe	80	49.23 N	51.50 E
Bazaruto, Ilha do I	156	21.40 S	35.28 E
Bazas	32	44.26 N	0.13 W
Bazdār	120	26.21 N	65.03 E
Bazeilles	56	49.40 N	4.59 E
Bazemont	261	48.56 N	1.52 E
Bazetta	214	41.20 N	80.47 W
Bazhong	102	31.51 N	106.39 E
Bazi, Zhg.	100	24.32 N	114.10 E
Bazi, Zhg.	100	24.46 N	113.10 E
Baziège	32	43.27 N	1.37 E
Bažigan	84	44.33 N	45.41 E
Bazine	198	38.27 N	99.42 W
Baziqiao	106	32.07 N	119.52 E
Bazkovskaja	80	49.36 N	41.43 E
Bazmān	128	27.49 N	60.12 E
Bazmān, Kūh-e ∧	128	28.04 N	60.01 E
Bazoches-les-Gallerandes	50	48.10 N	2.03 E
Bazoches-sur-Hoëne	50	48.33 N	0.28 E
Bazoj	86	55.45 N	83.22 E
Bazzano	64	44.30 N	11.05 E
Beach, Ill., U.S.	216	42.26 N	87.50 W
Beach, N. Dak., U.S.	198	46.55 N	103.52 W
Beach, Tex., U.S.	222	30.20 N	95.29 W
Beach Channel ⋓	276	40.35 N	73.50 W
Beach City	214	40.39 N	81.35 W
Beach City Lake @[1]	214	40.41 N	81.36 W
Beach Glen	276	40.56 N	74.29 W

FRANÇAIS

Nom	Page	Lat.°′	Long.°′ W=Ouest
Beach Haven, N.J., U.S.	208	39.34 N	74.14 W
Beach Haven, Pa., U.S.	210	41.04 N	76.11 W
Beach Haven Terrace	208	39.36 N	74.14 W
Beach Lake	210	41.36 N	75.09 W
Beach Lake @	281	42.33 N	83.43 W
Beach Pond State Park ♠	207	41.35 N	71.45 W
Beachport	166	37.30 S	140.01 E
Beachville	212	43.05 N	80.49 W
Beachwood, N.J., U.S.	208	39.56 N	74.12 W
Beachwood, Ohio, U.S.	214	41.34 N	81.28 W
Beachy Head ≻	42	50.44 N	0.16 E
Beacon, Austl.	162	30.26 S	117.51 E
Beacon, N.Y., U.S.	210	41.30 N	73.58 W
Beacon Falls	207	41.27 N	73.04 W
Beacon Hill, Austl.	274a	33.45 S	151.15 E
Beacon Hill, Wash., U.S.	224	46.08 N	122.57 W
Beacon Hill ∧[2], H.K.	271d	22.21 N	114.09 E
Beacon Hill ∧[2], Wales, U.K.	42	52.23 N	3.12 W
Beacon Rock State Park ♠	224	45.38 N	122.03 W
Beaconsfield, Austl.	166	41.12 S	146.48 E
Beaconsfield, Austl.	274b	38.03 S	145.22 E
Beaconsfield, Qué., Can.	206	45.26 N	73.50 W
Beaconsfield, Eng., U.K.	260	51.37 N	0.39 W
Beaconsfield □[8]	260	51.34 N	0.35 W
Beadle Lake	216	42.18 N	85.12 W
Beagle, Canal ⋓	254	54.53 S	68.10 W
Beagle Bay Mission	162	16.58 S	122.40 E
Beagle Gulf C	164	12.00 S	130.20 E
Beagle Reef +[2]	160	15.20 S	123.29 E
Bealanana	157b	14.33 S	48.44 E
Beale, Cape ≻	182	48.44 N	125.20 W
Beale, Lake @	122	19.45 N	73.44 E
Beale Air Force Base ■	226	39.08 N	121.20 W
Bealiba	169	36.48 S	143.33 E
Beallsville	214	40.04 N	80.01 W
Beals Creek ≃	196	32.10 N	100.51 W
Beam ≃	260	51.31 N	0.10 E
Beaminster	42	50.49 N	2.45 W
Beampingaratra ⛰	157b	24.30 S	46.50 E
Bean	260	51.25 N	0.17 E
Beanblossom Creek ≃	194	39.20 N	86.39 W
Bean Creek ≃	216	41.35 N	84.19 W
Bear ≃, Sask., Can.	184	54.33 N	103.58 W
Bear ≃, U.S.	200	41.30 N	112.08 W
Bear ≃, Calif., U.S.	226	38.57 N	121.35 W
Bear, Mount ∧	180	61.17 N	141.09 W
Beara	164	7.30 S	144.50 E
Bear Bay C	176	75.47 N	87.00 W
Bear Branch	218	38.55 N	85.05 W
Bear Brook ≃, Ont., Can.	212	45.25 N	75.10 W
Bear Brook ≃, N.J., U.S.	276	41.02 N	74.03 W
Bear Brook State Park ♠	188	43.05 N	71.26 W
Bear Canyon V	280	34.14 N	118.07 W
Bear Creek	210	41.11 N	75.45 W
Bear Creek ≃, Ont., Can.	214	42.44 N	82.23 W
Bear Creek ≃, U.S.	196	37.45 N	101.23 W
Bear Creek ≃, U.S.	216	41.17 N	83.57 W
Bear Creek ≃, Ala., U.S.	194	33.11 N	88.05 W
Bear Creek ≃, Calif., U.S.	226	37.17 N	120.50 W
Bear Creek ≃, Calif., U.S.	226	38.56 N	122.20 W
Bear Creek ≃, Calif., U.S.	226	38.02 N	121.18 W
Bear Creek ≃, Calif., U.S.	228	34.10 N	117.01 W
Bear Creek ≃, Calif., U.S.	280	34.14 N	117.53 W
Bear Creek ≃, Colo., U.S.	200	39.40 N	105.00 W
Bear Creek ≃, Ill., U.S.	219	39.33 N	89.23 W
Bear Creek ≃, Ill., U.S.	219	40.07 N	91.29 W
Bear Creek ≃, Md., U.S.	284b	39.13 N	76.30 W
Bear Creek ≃, Mo., U.S.	219	39.03 N	91.14 W
Bear Creek ≃, N. Dak., U.S.	198	46.10 N	98.06 W
Bear Creek ≃, Ohio, U.S.	218	39.39 N	84.17 W
Bear Creek ≃, Oreg., U.S.	202	42.26 N	122.58 W
Bear Creek ≃, Pa., U.S.	214	41.23 N	78.50 W
Bear Creek ≃, Wyo., U.S.	198	41.41 N	104.13 W
Bear Creek, South Fork ≃	219	40.09 N	91.18 W
Bear Creek, West Fork ≃	280	34.16 N	117.53 W
Bearden	194	33.43 N	92.37 W
Beardmore	176	49.36 N	87.57 W
Beardmore Glacier ᗅ	9	83.45 S	171.00 E
Beardsley Lake @[1]	226	38.13 N	120.03 W
Beardstown, Ill., U.S.	219	40.01 N	90.26 W
Beardstown, Ind., U.S.	216	41.08 N	86.36 W
Bearfort Mountain ∧	276	41.09 N	74.23 W
Bear Head Creek ≃	194	30.18 N	93.35 W
Bear Head Lake @	184	55.33 N	96.10 W
Bear Head Lake State Park ♠	190	47.49 N	92.04 W
Bearhead Mountain ∧	224	47.02 N	121.53 W
Bear Hill ∧[2], Conn., U.S.	207	41.39 N	73.24 W
Bear Hill ∧[2], N.Y., U.S.	210	41.18 N	74.00 W
Bear-in-the-Lodge Creek ≃	198	43.41 N	101.50 W
Bear Island I, Ant.	9	74.30 S	110.45 W
Bear Island I, Eire	48	51.40 N	9.48 W
Bear Island I, Va., U.S.	284c	38.59 N	77.14 W
Bear Lake, B.C., Can.	182	56.11 N	126.51 W
Bear Lake, Pa., U.S.	214	42.00 N	79.30 W
Bear Lake @, Alta., Can.	182	55.16 N	119.00 W
Bear Lake @, B.C., Can.	182	56.06 N	126.45 W
Bear Lake @, Man., Can.	184	55.08 N	96.00 W
Bear Lake @, Ont., Can.	212	45.26 N	79.35 W
Bear Lake @, U.S.	200	42.00 N	111.20 W
Bear Meadow Brook ≃	283	42.33 N	71.06 W
Bear Mountain ∧, Calif., U.S.	228	35.12 N	118.38 W
Bear Mountain ∧, Ky., U.S.	192	37.32 N	84.16 W
Bear Mountain ∧, Oreg., U.S.	202	43.51 N	122.53 W
Bear Mountain State Park ♠	210	41.17 N	74.00 W
Béarn ◆[1]	32	43.20 N	0.45 W
Bearpaw Mountains ⛰	202	48.15 N	109.30 W
Bear Pond @	276	40.58 N	74.40 W
Bear River	186	44.34 N	65.39 W

PORTUGUÊS

Nome	Página	Lat.°′	Long.°′ W=Oeste
Bear Run ≃	279b	40.33 N	80.04 W
Bearsden	46	55.56 N	4.20 W
Bearstead	260	51.16 N	0.35 E
Bearsville	210	42.02 N	74.09 W
Bear Swamp ≃	285	39.54 N	74.47 W
Bear Swamp ≣	285	39.53 N	74.45 W
Bear Swamp Brook ≃	276	41.04 N	74.13 W
Bear Swamp Lake @	276	41.06 N	74.13 W
Bear Tooth Pass)(	202	44.58 N	109.28 W
Beartooth Range ⛰	202	45.00 N	109.30 W
Beās	123	31.31 N	75.17 E
Beās ≃	123	31.10 N	74.59 E
Beasain	34	43.03 N	2.11 W
Beas de Segura	34	38.15 N	2.53 W
Beasley	222	29.30 N	95.55 W
Beasley Bay C	208	37.51 N	75.44 W
Beason	219	40.09 N	89.12 W
Beata, Cabo ≻	238	17.36 N	71.25 W
Beata, Isla I	238	17.35 N	71.31 W
Beatenberg	58	46.42 N	7.48 E
Beato ◆[8]	266c	38.44 N	9.06 W
Beaton	182	50.44 N	117.44 W
Beatrice, Ala., U.S.	194	31.38 N	87.19 W
Beatrice, Nebr., U.S.	198	40.16 N	96.44 W
Beatrice, Zimb.	154	18.15 S	30.55 E
Beatrice, Cape ≻	164	14.15 S	136.59 E
Beattie	198	39.52 N	96.25 W
Beattock	44	55.18 N	3.28 W
Beatton ≃	176	56.10 N	120.25 W
Beatty, Nev., U.S.	204	36.54 N	116.46 W
Beatty, Ohio, U.S.	218	39.53 N	83.50 W
Beatty Saugeen ≃	212	44.08 N	81.02 W
Beattyville	192	37.35 N	83.42 W
Beaubru	56	49.46 N	5.05 E
Beaucaire	62	43.48 N	4.38 E
Beauce ◆[1]	50	48.22 N	1.50 E
Beauceville-Est	188	46.12 N	70.46 W
Beauchamp	261	49.01 N	2.12 E
Beauchamp Roding	260	51.46 N	0.18 E
Beauchêne, Lac @	190	46.39 N	78.55 W
Beaucoup Creek ≃	194	37.47 N	89.17 W
Beaucourt	58	47.29 N	6.55 E
Beaudesert	171a	27.59 S	153.00 E
Beaudet ≃	206	45.12 N	74.19 W
Beaudry, Lac @	190	47.44 N	78.55 W
Beauduc, Pointe de ≻	62	43.22 N	4.34 E
Beaufays	56	50.34 N	5.38 E
Beaufort, Austl.	169	37.26 S	143.23 E
Beaufort, Fr.	58	46.34 N	5.26 E
Beaufort, Fr.	62	45.43 N	6.35 E
Beaufort, Lux.	56	49.51 N	6.18 E
Beaufort, Malay.	112	5.20 N	115.45 E
Beaufort, Mo., U.S.	219	38.26 N	91.12 W
Beaufort, N.C., U.S.	192	34.43 N	76.40 W
Beaufort, S.C., U.S.	192	32.26 N	80.40 W
Beaufort ⊥	132	33.19 N	35.32 E
Beaufort, Cape ≻	162	34.26 S	115.32 E
Beaufort, Massif de ⛰[1]	62	45.44 N	6.35 E
Beaufort Sea ╤[2]	16	73.00 N	140.00 W
Beaufort West	158	32.18 S	22.36 E
Beaugency	50	47.47 N	1.38 E
Beauharnois	206	45.19 N	73.52 W
Beauharnois □[6]	206	45.15 N	74.00 W
Beauharnois, Canal de Ξ	206	45.19 N	73.54 W
Beauharnois Dam ◆[6]	275a	45.19 N	73.55 W
Beaujeu	58	46.09 N	4.36 E
Beaujolais, Monts du ⛰	32	46.00 N	4.30 E
Beaulieu	42	50.49 N	1.27 W
Beaulieu-lès-Loches	50	47.07 N	1.01 E
Beaulieu-sur-Mer	62	43.42 N	7.20 E
Beauly	46	57.29 N	4.29 W
Beauly ≃	46	57.28 N	4.28 W
Beauly Firth C[1]	46	57.30 N	4.23 W
Beaumaris, Austl.	274b	37.59 S	145.02 E
Beaumaris, Wales, U.K.	44	53.16 N	4.05 W
Beaumaris Bay C	274b	38.00 S	145.03 E
Beaumes-de-Venise	62	44.07 N	5.02 E
Beaumesnil	50	49.01 N	0.43 E
Beaumetz-lès-Loges	50	50.14 N	2.39 E
Beaumont, Bel.	50	50.14 N	4.14 E
Beaumont, Newf., Can.	186	49.34 N	55.36 W
Beaumont, Fr.	32	48.13 N	0.08 E
Beaumont, Fr.	32	49.40 N	1.51 W
Beaumont, N.Z.	172	45.49 S	169.32 E
Beaumont, Calif., U.S.	228	33.56 N	116.58 W
Beaumont, Miss., U.S.	194	31.11 N	88.55 W
Beaumont, Tex., U.S.	194	30.05 N	94.06 W
Beaumont-du-Gâtinais	50	48.08 N	2.29 E
Beaumont-en-Argonne	56	49.32 N	5.03 E
Beaumont Hill ∧[2]	166	31.33 S	145.13 E
Beaumont-la-Ronce	50	47.34 N	0.40 E
Beaumont-le-Roger	50	49.05 N	0.47 E
Beaumont Place	222	29.50 N	95.14 W
Beaumont-sur-Oise	50	49.08 N	2.17 E
Beaumont-sur-Sarthe	50	48.13 N	0.08 E
Beaune	58	47.02 N	4.50 E
Beaune-la-Rolande	50	48.04 N	2.26 E
Beauport	206	46.52 N	71.11 W
Beaupré	186	47.03 N	70.54 W
Beaupréau	32	47.12 N	1.00 W
Beaupre Island I	212	44.26 N	76.29 W
Beauraing	56	50.07 N	4.58 E
Beaurepaire	62	45.20 N	5.03 E
Beaurepaire-en-Bresse	58	46.40 N	5.23 E
Beaurières	62	44.35 N	5.33 E
Beaurivage	206	46.25 N	71.14 W
Beaurivage ≃	206	46.42 N	71.16 W
Beauséjour	184	50.04 N	96.33 W
Beausoleil	62	43.45 N	7.26 E
Beausoleil Island I	212	44.51 N	79.52 W
Beautemps-Beaupré, Île I	175f	20.24 S	166.09 E
Beautor	50	49.39 N	3.20 E
Beauvais, Fr.	50	49.26 N	2.05 E
Beauvais, Fr.	261	48.32 N	2.03 E
Beauvais Creek ≃	202	45.29 N	107.45 W
Beauval	50	50.06 N	2.20 E
Beauvezer	62	44.09 N	6.36 E
Beauville	32	44.17 N	0.52 E
Beauvoir	261	48.39 N	2.52 E
Beauvoir-sur-Mer	32	46.55 N	2.02 W
Beauvoir-sur-Niort	32	46.11 N	0.28 W
Beaux Arts	224	47.35 N	122.11 W
Beaver, Alaska, U.S.	180	66.22 N	147.24 W
Beaver, Okla., U.S.	196	36.49 N	100.31 W
Beaver, Oreg., U.S.	224	45.17 N	123.49 W
Beaver, Pa., U.S.	214	40.42 N	80.18 W
Beaver, Utah, U.S.	200	38.17 N	112.38 W
Beaver, Wash., U.S.	224	48.03 N	124.19 W
Beaver, W. Va., U.S.	192	37.45 N	81.09 W
Beaver □[6]	214	40.40 N	80.25 W
Beaver ≃, Can.	176	59.43 N	124.16 W
Beaver ≃, Ont., Can.	212	44.34 N	80.27 W
Beaver ≃, N.Y., U.S.	212	43.54 N	75.30 W
Beaver ≃, Pa., U.S.	214	40.40 N	80.18 W
Beaver ≃, Utah, U.S.	200	39.10 N	112.57 W
Beaver Brook	210	40.55 N	75.59 W
Beaver Brook ≃, U.S.	207	42.40 N	71.19 W
Beaver Brook ≃, Mass., U.S.	283	42.23 N	71.14 W
Beaver Brook ≃, Mass., U.S.	283	42.03 N	70.58 W
Beaver Brook ≃, Mass., U.S.	283	42.36 N	71.21 W
Beaver Brook ≃, N.J., U.S.	276	40.58 N	74.35 W
Beaver Brook ≃, N.J., U.S.	276	40.54 N	74.30 W
Beaver City	198	40.08 N	99.50 W
Beaver Creek, Yukon, Can.	180	62.22 N	140.52 W
Beavercreek, Oreg., U.S.	224	45.17 N	122.32 W
Beaver Creek ≃, Ont., Can.	212	44.44 N	76.58 W
Beaver Creek ≃, Ont., Can.	212	44.30 N	77.42 W
Beaver Creek ≃, Ont., Can.	275b	43.51 N	79.20 W
Beaver Creek ≃, Ont., Can.	284a	42.58 N	79.01 W
Beaver Creek ≃, U.S.	198	40.04 N	99.20 W
Beaver Creek ≃, U.S.	198	47.20 N	103.39 W
Beaver Creek ≃, U.S.	198	43.25 N	103.59 W
Beaver Creek ≃, Alaska, U.S.	180	66.15 N	147.32 W
Beaver Creek ≃, Calif., U.S.	226	38.12 N	120.19 W
Beaver Creek ≃, Colo., U.S.	198	40.20 N	103.33 W
Beaver Creek ≃, Idaho, U.S.	202	44.02 N	112.14 W
Beaver Creek ≃, Ill., U.S.	216	42.16 N	88.56 W
Beaver Creek ≃, Ill., U.S.	219	38.33 N	89.30 W
Beaver Creek ≃, Ky., U.S.	218	38.31 N	84.11 W
Beaver Creek ≃, Md., U.S.	208	39.32 N	77.42 W
Beaver Creek ≃, Mo., U.S.	194	36.38 N	93.02 W
Beaver Creek ≃, Mont., U.S.	202	48.29 N	107.24 W
Beaver Creek ≃, Nebr., U.S.	198	41.26 N	97.42 W
Beaver Creek ≃, Nebr., U.S.	198	40.42 N	97.20 W
Beaver Creek ≃, N.J., U.S.	285	39.45 N	75.23 W
Beaver Creek ≃, N. Dak., U.S.	198	46.15 N	100.29 W
Beaver Creek ≃, N.Y., U.S.	212	44.36 N	75.22 W
Beaver Creek ≃, Ohio, U.S.	216	41.25 N	83.51 W
Beaver Creek ≃, Ohio, U.S.	216	40.34 N	84.45 W
Beaver Creek ≃, Ohio, U.S.	218	39.57 N	83.46 W
Beaver Creek ≃, Oreg., U.S.	224	44.56 N	121.22 W
Beaver Creek ≃, Pa., U.S.	285	40.00 N	75.42 W
Beaver Creek ≃, Tex., U.S.	196	33.53 N	98.49 W
Beaver Creek ≃, Wyo., U.S.	202	42.58 N	108.26 W
Beaver Creek State Park ♠	214	40.44 N	80.35 W
Beaver Crossing	198	40.47 N	97.17 W
Beaverdale	214	40.19 N	78.42 W
Beaver Dam, Ky., U.S.	194	37.24 N	86.52 W
Beaverdam, Ohio, U.S.	216	40.50 N	83.59 W
Beaver Dam, Wis., U.S.	190	43.28 N	88.50 W
Beaverdam Brook ≃	276	40.26 N	74.28 W
Beaverdam Creek ≃, U.S.	284c	38.55 N	76.57 W
Beaverdam Creek ≃, Md., U.S.	284c	39.01 N	76.54 W
Beaverdam Creek ≃, N.J., U.S.	285	39.56 N	74.45 W
Beaver Dams	210	42.17 N	76.58 W
Beaver Dams Creek ≃	284a	43.06 N	79.11 W
Beaver Dam Wash V	200	36.54 N	114.55 W
Beaverdell	182	49.26 N	119.05 W
Beaver Falls, N.Y., U.S.	212	43.53 N	75.26 W
Beaver Falls, Pa., U.S.	214	40.46 N	80.19 W
Beaverhead ≃	202	45.31 N	112.21 W
Beaverhead Mountains ⛰	202	45.00 N	113.20 W
Beaverhill Lake @, Alta., Can.	182	53.27 N	112.32 W
Beaver Hill Lake @, Man., Can.	184	54.16 N	94.53 W
Beaverhouse Lake @	190	48.32 N	92.05 W
Beaver Island I	190	45.40 N	85.31 W
Beaver Island State Park ♠	210	42.58 N	78.57 W
Beaver Kill ≃	210	41.59 N	75.08 W
Beaver Lake	210	41.07 N	74.33 W
Beaver Lake @, Alta., Can.	182	54.43 N	111.50 W
Beaver Lake @, Ont., Can.	212	44.44 N	78.17 W
Beaver Lake @, Ont., Can.	212	44.30 N	77.02 W
Beaver Lake @, N.Y., U.S.	276	40.53 N	73.34 W
Beaver Lake @[1]	194	36.20 N	93.55 W
Beaver Lake Indian Reserve ◆[4]	182	54.39 N	111.54 W
Beaverlodge	182	55.13 N	119.26 W
Beaver Meadow	210	42.40 N	75.41 W
Beaver Meadows	210	40.56 N	75.55 W
Beaver Mountains ⛰	180	62.54 N	156.58 W
Beaver Run ≃, N.J., U.S.	276	41.11 N	74.36 W
Beaver Run ≃, Pa., U.S.	279b	40.34 N	79.33 W
Beaver Run ≃, Pa., U.S.	285	40.10 N	75.40 W
Beaver Run Reservoir @[1]	214	40.29 N	79.33 W
Beaver Springs	208	40.45 N	77.13 W
Beaver Swamp Brook ≃	276	40.57 N	73.43 W
Beaverton, Ont., Can.	212	44.26 N	79.09 W
Beaverton, Mich., U.S.	190	43.53 N	84.29 W
Beaverton, Oreg., U.S.	224	45.29 N	122.48 W
Beaverton ≃	212	44.26 N	79.10 W
Beavertown	210	40.45 N	77.10 W
Beaverville	216	40.57 N	87.39 W
Beāwar	120	26.06 N	74.19 E
Beazley	252	33.45 S	66.39 W
Bebao	157b	17.22 S	44.33 E
Bebar ≃	114	3.07 N	103.27 E
Bebedouro	255	20.56 S	48.28 W
Bebeji	150	11.40 N	8.19 E
Bebek ◆[8]	267b	41.04 N	29.02 E
Bebekler	130	37.21 N	30.04 E
Bebelevo	82	54.32 N	36.30 E
Bebeli	130	36.41 N	35.27 E
Bebenhausen	56	48.33 N	9.03 E
Beberibe	250	4.11 S	38.08 W
Bebertal	54	52.15 N	11.18 E
Béboto	146	8.16 N	16.56 E
Bebra	56	50.58 N	9.47 E
Becal	232	20.27 N	90.02 W
Bécancour	206	46.20 N	72.26 W
Bécancour ≃	206	46.22 N	72.27 W
Beccar ◆[8]	288	34.28 S	58.31 W
Beccaria	214	40.46 N	78.27 W
Beccero Creek ≃	196	28.05 N	98.55 W
Beccles	42	52.28 N	1.34 E
Becconsall	262	53.42 N	2.50 W
Bečej	38	45.37 N	20.03 E
Beceni	38	45.23 N	26.46 E
Becerreá	34	42.51 N	7.10 W
Becerro, Cayos II	236	15.57 N	83.17 W
Béchar	148	31.37 N	2.13 W
Becharof Lake @	180	58.00 N	156.30 W
Bechater	36	37.18 N	9.45 E
Bechem	150	7.05 N	2.02 W
Becher Bay C	224	48.19 N	123.37 W
Becher Point ≻	168a	32.23 S	115.44 E
Bechet	38	43.46 N	23.58 E
Bechevin Bay C	180	55.00 N	163.27 W
Bechhofen	56	49.09 N	10.33 E
Bechtelsville	208	40.22 N	75.38 W
Bechuanaland ◆[1]	158	27.10 S	22.10 E
Bechyně	30	49.18 N	14.29 E
Becke	263	51.24 N	7.47 E
Beckemeyer	219	38.36 N	89.26 W
Beckenham ◆[8]	260	51.24 N	0.02 W
Beckenried	58	46.58 N	8.29 E
Becket	207	42.20 N	73.05 W
Beckhausen ◆[8]	263	51.34 N	7.02 E
Beckinghausen ◆[8]	263	51.37 N	7.34 E
Beckington	42	51.16 N	2.18 W
Beck Lake @	278	42.04 N	87.52 W
Beckler ≃	224	47.43 N	121.21 W
Beckley	188	37.46 N	81.13 W
Beck Pond @	283	42.36 N	70.49 W
Becks Creek ≃	219	39.08 N	88.56 W
Beckum	52	51.45 N	8.02 E
Beckville	222	32.14 N	94.27 W
Beckwith Island I	212	44.52 N	80.08 W
Becky Peak ∧	204	39.58 N	114.36 W
Beclean	38	47.11 N	24.10 E
Bečov nad Teplou	54	50.02 N	12.19 E
Becsehely	61	46.27 N	16.48 E
Bedale	44	54.17 N	1.35 W
Bédarieux	32	43.37 N	3.09 E
Beda Roge ∧	144	8.42 N	37.50 E
Bédarrides	62	44.02 N	4.54 E
Bédaya	146	8.55 N	17.52 E
Bedburdyck	56	51.07 N	6.34 E
Bedburg, B.R.D.	56	50.59 N	6.35 E
Bedburg, B.R.D.	56	51.03 N	8.23 E
Bedburg-Hau	52	51.45 N	6.10 E
Beddgelert	44	53.01 N	4.06 W
Beddinge läge	41	55.21 N	13.29 E
Beddington ◆[8]	260	51.22 N	0.08 W
Beddome, Mount ∧	162	25.50 S	134.22 E
Bedele	144	8.33 N	36.23 E
Beden Brook ≃	276	40.25 N	74.38 W
Bedeque Bay C	186	46.22 N	63.53 W
Beder	41	56.04 N	10.13 E
Bederkesa	52	53.38 N	8.50 E
Bederwanak	144	9.34 N	44.25 E
Bedeso	144	8.55 N	40.50 E
Bedford, Qué., Can.	206	45.07 N	72.59 W
Bedford, S. Afr.	158	32.41 S	26.05 E
Bedford, Eng., U.K.	42	52.08 N	0.29 W
Bedford, Ind., U.S.	218	38.52 N	86.29 W
Bedford, Iowa, U.S.	198	40.40 N	94.44 W
Bedford, Ky., U.S.	218	38.36 N	85.19 W
Bedford, Mass., U.S.	207	42.29 N	71.17 W
Bedford, Mich., U.S.	216	42.23 N	85.14 W
Bedford, N.Y., U.S.	210	41.12 N	73.39 W
Bedford, Ohio, U.S.	214	41.23 N	81.32 W
Bedford, Pa., U.S.	188	40.01 N	78.30 W
Bedford, Tex., U.S.	222	32.51 N	97.08 W
Bedford, Va., U.S.	192	37.20 N	79.31 W
Bedford □[6]	214	40.09 N	78.30 W
Bedford, Cape ≻	164	15.14 S	145.21 E
Bedfordale	168a	32.10 S	116.03 E
Bedford Harbour C	162	33.35 S	120.35 E
Bedford Heights	279a	41.22 N	81.30 W
Bedford Hills	210	41.14 N	73.42 W
Bedford Island I	126	21.51 N	88.05 E
Bedford Level ≚	42	52.27 N	0.02 W
Bedford Park	278	41.46 N	87.49 W
Bedford Park ◆[8]	276	40.52 N	73.53 W
Bedfordshire □[6]	42	52.05 N	0.30 W
Bedford-Stuyvesant ◆[8]	276	40.41 N	73.55 W
Bedi, Bhārat	120	22.30 N	70.02 E
Bédi, Tchad	146	11.06 N	18.33 E
Bedias	222	30.46 N	95.57 W
Bedias Creek ≃	222	30.54 N	95.37 W
Bedinggong	112	2.42 S	106.13 E
Bédiondo	146	8.39 N	17.12 E
Bedirli	130	39.35 N	36.38 E
Bedminster, N.J., U.S.	276	40.41 N	74.39 W
Bedminster, Pa., U.S.	208	40.26 N	75.11 W
Bedmond	260	51.43 N	0.25 W
Bednodemjanovsk	80	53.56 N	43.10 E
Bedoba	88	58.48 N	97.12 E
Bédoin	62	44.07 N	5.10 E
Bedok	271c	1.19 N	103.57 E
Bedong	114	5.44 N	100.31 E
Bedonia	62	44.30 N	9.38 E
Bedourie	166	24.21 S	139.28 E
Bedum	52	53.17 N	6.36 E
Bedwas	42	51.35 N	3.13 W
Bedworth	42	52.28 N	1.29 W
Beeac	169	38.12 S	143.38 E
Beebe, Qué., Can.	206	45.01 N	72.09 W
Beebe, Ark., U.S.	194	35.04 N	91.53 W
Beech ≃	194	35.37 N	88.10 W
Beechal Creek ≃	166	27.24 S	145.13 E
Beech Bottom	214	40.14 N	80.39 W
Beech Brook ≃	276	41.08 N	74.18 W
Beech Creek, Ky., U.S.	194	37.11 N	87.03 W
Beech Creek, Pa., U.S.	210	41.05 N	77.35 W
Beech Creek ≃	210	41.04 N	77.34 W
Beechcrest	214	41.05 N	81.20 W
Beecher, Ill., U.S.	216	41.21 N	87.38 W
Beecher, Mich., U.S.	216	43.05 N	83.42 W
Beecher City	219	39.11 N	88.47 W
Beecher Falls	206	45.01 N	71.31 W
Beechey Head ≻	224	48.19 N	123.39 W
Beech Forest	169	38.38 S	143.34 E
Beech Fork ≃	194	37.46 N	85.41 W
Beech Grove	218	39.43 N	86.03 W
Beechmont	171a	28.07 S	153.11 E
Beechview ◆[8]	279b	40.25 N	80.02 W
Beechwood, Ky., U.S.	218	38.24 N	84.44 W
Beechwood, Mass., U.S.	283	42.13 N	70.49 W
Beechwood, Mich., U.S.	216	46.09 N	88.46 W
Beechworth	166	36.22 S	146.41 E
Beechy	184	50.51 N	107.25 W
Beeck ◆[8]	263	51.29 N	6.44 E
Beeckerwerth ◆[8]	263	51.29 N	6.41 E
Beecroft	274a	33.45 S	151.04 E
Beecroft Head ≻	170	35.01 S	150.50 E
Beecroft Peninsula ≻[1]	170	35.02 S	150.50 E
Beedenbostel	52	52.38 N	10.16 E
Beef Island I	240m	18.27 N	64.31 W
Beek, Ned.	52	51.51 N	5.54 E
Beek, Ned.	52	51.32 N	5.38 E
Beek, Ned.	56	50.56 N	5.49 E
Beela ≃	44	54.13 N	2.47 W
Beeleigh Abbey ♥[1]	260	51.44 N	0.40 E
Beelen	52	51.55 N	8.07 E
Beelitz	54	52.14 N	12.58 E
Beemer	198	41.56 N	96.48 W
Beemster ◆[1]	52	52.35 N	4.55 E
Beendorf	54	52.14 N	11.05 E
Beenleigh	171a	27.43 S	153.12 E
Beerburrum	171a	26.58 S	152.58 E
Beerfelden	56	49.34 N	8.58 E
Bee Ridge	220	27.16 N	82.31 W
Be'er Menuḥa	132	30.19 N	35.08 E
Beernem	50	51.09 N	3.20 E
Be'er Ora	132	29.43 N	34.59 E
Beerse	56	51.19 N	4.52 E
Beersheba → Be'er Sheva'	132	31.14 N	34.47 E
Beersheba Springs	194	35.28 N	85.39 W
Be'er Sheva' (Beersheba)	132	31.14 N	34.47 E
Be'er Sheva', Naḥal V	132	31.11 N	34.35 E
Be'er Sheva', Sede-Tek'ufa ⊠	132	31.16 N	34.43 E
Beerta	52	53.10 N	7.05 E
Be'er Toviyya	132	31.44 N	34.44 E
Beervlei Brak ≃	158	29.58 S	23.12 E
Beerwah	171a	26.51 S	152.58 E
Beerwah National Park ♠	171a	26.56 S	152.52 E
Be'er Ya'agov	132	31.56 N	34.50 E
Beesenlaublingen	54	51.42 N	11.41 E
Beeskow	54	52.10 N	14.14 E
Beestekraal	156	25.23 S	27.38 E
Beesten	52	52.26 N	7.30 E
Beeston	42	52.56 N	1.12 W
Beet ≃	115a	6.16 S	107.15 E
Beethoven Peninsula ≻[1]	9	71.40 S	73.45 W
Beeton	212	44.05 N	79.47 W
Beetsterzwaag	52	53.03 N	6.05 E
Beetz, Lac @	186	50.34 N	62.42 W
Beetzendorf	54	52.42 N	11.05 E
Beeville	196	28.24 N	97.45 W
Befale	152	0.28 N	20.58 E
Befandriana, Madag.	157b	15.16 S	48.32 E
Befandriana, Madag.	157b	22.06 S	43.54 E
Befasy	157b	20.33 S	44.23 E
Befori	152	0.06 N	22.17 E
Befotaka, Madag.	157b	21.29 S	44.44 E
Befotaka, Madag.	157b	14.32 S	48.01 E
Befotaka, Madag.	157b	23.49 S	46.59 E
Befotaka, Madag.	157b	13.15 S	48.16 E
Befu ◆[8]	270	34.40 N	135.02 E
Beg, Lough @	44	54.47 N	6.28 W
Bega	166	36.40 S	149.50 E
Bega (Begej) ≃	38	45.13 N	20.19 E
Begamganj	124	23.36 N	78.20 E
Begampur ◆[8]	272a	28.44 N	77.04 E
Begej (Bega) ≃	38	45.13 N	20.19 E
Begemdir and Simen □[4]	144	13.10 N	37.00 E
Beger	102	45.42 N	97.05 E
Beggars Point ≻	240c	17.10 N	61.48 W
Beggs	196	35.45 N	96.04 W
Begi	144	9.16 N	34.33 E
Begičevskij	76	53.47 N	38.15 E
Beginsel	158	26.57 S	20.39 E
Beglés	32	44.47 N	0.34 W
Begoml'	76	54.44 N	28.04 E
Begonias, Presa @[1]	234	20.55 N	100.50 W
Begoro	150	6.23 N	0.23 W
Begovat → Bekabad	85	40.13 N	69.14 E
Béguigui	146	9.00 N	18.56 E
Begun'	78	51.24 N	28.17 E
Begunici	76	59.35 N	29.19 E
Begusarai	124	25.25 N	86.08 E
Béhague, Pointe ≻	250	4.40 N	51.54 W
Behāla	126	22.31 N	88.19 E
Behbehān	128	30.35 N	50.14 E
Behm Canal ⋓	180	55.41 N	131.35 W
Beho	56	50.13 N	6.00 E
Béhoust	261	48.50 N	1.43 E
Behrāmpur	272a	28.38 N	77.24 E
Behren-lès-Forbach	56	49.10 N	6.57 E
Behring, Détroit de → Bering Strait ⋓	180	65.30 N	169.00 W
Behringen, B.R.D.	52	53.07 N	9.58 E
Behringen, D.D.R.	54	51.01 N	10.31 E
Behshahr	128	36.43 N	53.34 E
Beian	89	48.15 N	126.30 E
Beianfeng	100	33.06 N	120.08 E
Beianhe	105	40.04 N	116.06 E
Beibaihua	105	38.57 N	114.51 E
Beibaozhen	106	31.33 N	121.38 E
Beibei	107	29.49 N	106.26 E
Beicang	105	39.13 N	117.07 E
Beichi	106	31.05 N	120.40 E
Beida → Zāwiyat al-Bayḍā'	146	32.46 N	21.43 E
Beïda, Chott @	34	35.56 N	5.49 E
Beidahe ≃	104	42.29 N	121.44 E
Beidaihe	98	39.54 N	119.29 E
Beidaoqiao	86	44.12 N	89.38 E
Beidian	98	41.23 N	124.18 E
Beidouzhen	107	30.02 N	104.26 E
Beidun	100	26.42 N	118.57 E
Beidunshui ≃	100	24.18 N	115.10 E
Beierfeld	54	50.33 N	12.47 E
Beiersdorf	264a	52.42 N	13.47 E
Beifangcun	105	40.20 N	116.42 E
Beifangzi	104	41.22 N	121.03 E
Beigang	100	29.20 N	113.41 E
Beigou	106	31.45 N	120.40 E
Beiguanshan I	100	27.10 N	120.32 E
Beihai (Pakhoi)	102	21.29 N	109.05 E
Beihai @	271a	39.56 N	116.22 E
Beihedian	105	39.13 N	115.45 E
Beiheishang'gou	105	39.53 N	118.15 E
Beihuaiyudian	105	39.16 N	117.33 E
Beijialing	104	41.08 N	124.02 E
Beijian I	100	21.53 N	114.02 E
Beijiang ≃	90	23.09 N	112.48 E
Beijiao	100	26.22 N	119.58 E
Beijiaohe ≃	98	37.05 N	119.33 E
Beijicun	98	37.57 N	118.01 E
Beijiean	106	32.15 N	121.12 E
Beijijiazhuang	105	40.01 N	114.51 E
Beijing (Peking)	105		
	271a	39.55 N	116.25 E
Beijing Shih □[7]	105	40.15 N	116.30 E
Beijumahe ≃	105	39.30 N	115.56 E
Beikan	100	32.23 N	121.21 E
Beilen	52	52.52 N	6.31 E
Beilifang	104	41.59 N	121.57 E
Beiling	100	24.36 N	115.20 E
Beiliu	102	22.42 N	110.22 E
Beiliuqiao	106	32.11 N	120.51 E
Beiliuwangshui	105	38.57 N	115.03 E
Beilizhen	110	19.10 N	108.43 E
Beilizigu	105	39.30 N	117.28 E
Beilngries	60	49.02 N	11.29 E
Beilrode	54	51.35 N	13.03 E
Beilstein, B.R.D.	56	49.02 N	9.18 E
Beilstein, B.R.D.	56	50.36 N	8.14 E
Beilstein, B.R.D.	56	50.06 N	7.14 E
Beiluxu	106	31.01 N	120.50 E
Beimaizhu	105	39.31 N	117.44 E
Beimayang @	106	30.56 N	120.33 E
Beiminjiatun	104	42.38 N	122.43 E
Beimuzhen	107	29.31 N	105.05 E
Beinamar	146	8.40 N	15.23 E
Beine-Nauroy	50	49.15 N	4.13 E
Beinette	62	44.22 N	7.39 E
Beinwil	58	47.22 N	7.35 E
Beinwil am See	58	47.16 N	8.13 E
Beipa'a	164	8.30 S	146.35 E
Beipanjiang ≃	102	25.05 N	106.00 E
Beipanxiaozhen	106	31.44 N	121.26 E
Beipiao	104	41.49 N	120.46 E
Beiqi	98	40.27 N	122.20 E
Beiqiao	106	31.03 N	121.24 E
Beira, Moç.	156	19.49 S	34.52 E
Beira, Som.	144	6.59 N	47.20 E
Beira Baixa □[9]	34	39.45 N	7.30 W
Beira Litoral □[9]	34	40.15 N	8.25 W
Beirut → Bayrūt	130	33.53 N	35.30 E
Beirut International Airport ⊠	132	33.49 N	35.30 E
Beisanjia	98	42.04 N	124.42 E
Beiseker	182	51.23 N	113.32 W
Beishakou	105	39.08 N	116.07 E
Beishan	102	24.28 N	108.35 E
Beishan ⛰	106	31.12 N	118.53 E
Beishangcun	105	39.28 N	116.58 E

≃ River	Fluss	Río	Rivière	Rio	
Ξ Canal	Kanal	Canal	Canal	Canal	
ᒪ Waterfall, Rapids	Wasserfall, Stromschnellen	Cascada, Rápidos	Chute d'eau, Rapides	Cascata, Rápidos	
⋓ Strait	Meeresstrasse	Estrecho	Détroit	Estreito	
C Bay, Gulf	Bucht, Golf	Bahía, Golfo	Baie, Golfe	Baía, Golfo	
@ Lake, Lakes	See, Seen	Lago, Lagos	Lac, Lacs	Lago, Lagos	
≣ Swamp	Sumpf	Pantano	Marais	Pântano	
ᗅ Ice Features, Glacier	Eis- und Gletscherformen	Accidentes Glaciales	Formes glaciaires	Acidentes Glaciares	
╤ Other Hydrographic Features	Andere Hydrographische Objekte	Otros Elementos Hidrográficos	Autres données hydrographiques	Outros Elementos Hidrográficos	
+ Submarine Features	Untermeerische Objekte	Accidentes Submarinos	Formes de relief sous-marin	Acidentes Submarinos	
□ Political Unit	Politische Einheit	Unidad Politica	Entité politique	Unidade Política	
♥ Cultural Institution	Kulturelle Institution	Institución Cultural	Institution culturelle	Instituição Cultural	
⊥ Historical Site	Historische Stätte	Sitio Histórico	Site historique	Sitio Histórico	
♠ Recreational Site	Erholungs- und Ferienort	Sitio de Recreo	Centre de loisirs	Sítio de Lazer	
⊠ Airport	Flughafen	Aeropuerto	Aéroport	Aeroporto	
■ Military Installation	Militäranlage	Instalación Militar	Installation militaire	Instalação Militar	
◆ Miscellaneous	Verschiedenes	Misceláneo	Divers	Miscelânea	

ENGLISH / DEUTSCH

Name	Page / Seite	Lat. / Breite	Long. / Länge E=Ost
Beishanmai ⩓	102	41.12 N	97.05 E
Beishipian	105	40.43 N	116.55 E
Beishuangdong	105	40.32 N	117.24 E
Beishuiquan	98	40.05 N	114.40 E
Beisi	102	34.59 N	95.07 E
Beisu	98	38.13 N	114.46 E
Beitaitou	98	37.06 N	118.31 E
Beitaizi	105	40.24 N	117.56 E
Beitang	105	39.07 N	117.42 E
Beitanshiqiao	106	31.05 N	121.38 E
Beitbridge	154	22.13 S	30.00 E
Beith	46	55.45 N	4.38 W
Beitstadfjorden C[2]	26	63.53 N	11.00 E
Beiuș	38	46.40 N	22.21 E
Beiwei	106	32.05 N	121.12 E
Beiwenguan	107	29.51 N	106.24 E
Beiwu	105	40.04 N	116.48 E
Beiwudu	100	33.39 N	113.39 E
Beixiadai	106	32.12 N	120.08 E
Beixiejiadang	105	40.30 N	114.50 E
Beixili	89	51.47 N	125.45 E
Beixin'an	271a	39.55 N	116.08 E
Beixindian	105	39.44 N	116.44 E
Beixing	89	48.29 N	125.40 E
Beixinjing	106	31.13 N	121.22 E
Beixinliu	105	39.16 N	116.31 E
Beixinzhen	106	31.49 N	121.31 E
Beiyin	106	31.07 N	120.47 E
Beiyindai	104	42.35 N	122.22 E
Beiyishui ≃	105	39.19 N	115.39 E
Beiyuan	105	40.01 N	116.24 E
Beiyunhe ≃	105	39.15 N	117.05 E
Beizangzong	124	30.14 N	90.44 E
Beizhaijiawopeng	104	41.14 N	122.41 E
Beizhanjie	98	36.33 N	118.42 E
Beizhen	104	41.36 N	121.47 E
Beizhouzhuang	106	31.52 N	120.24 E
Beizhuang	105	39.47 N	115.24 E
Beizifu	98	42.09 N	120.29 E
Beja, Bra.	250	1.36 S	48.47 W
Beja, Port.	34	38.01 N	7.52 W
Beja, S.S.S.R.	86	53.03 N	90.54 E
Béja, Tun.	148	36.44 N	9.11 E
Béja □[8]	36	36.35 N	9.20 E
Bejaïa (Bougie)	148	36.45 N	5.05 E
Bejaïa, Golfe de C	34	36.45 N	5.25 E
Béjar	34	40.23 N	5.46 W
Bejestān	128	34.31 N	58.10 E
Beji ≃	120	29.47 N	67.58 E
Bejneu	86	45.15 N	55.07 E
Bejsug ≃	78	45.54 N	38.56 E
Bejsugskij Liman C	78	46.07 N	38.25 E
Bejtonovo	89	53.14 N	124.27 E
Bejucal	240p	22.56 N	82.23 W
Bejucal □[7]	286b	22.56 N	82.23 W
Bejuco	236	8.36 N	79.53 W
Bejuma	246	10.11 N	68.16 W
Bek ≃	152	2.29 N	15.15 E
Béka	146	9.04 N	12.53 E
Bekabad	85	40.13 N	69.14 E
Bekancan	114	3.18 N	98.24 E
Bekasi	115a	6.14 S	106.59 E
Bekasi ≃	269e	6.10 S	107.02 E
Békásmegyer ⌖[8]	264c	47.36 N	19.03 E
Bekasovo	82	55.26 N	36.49 E
Bekdaš	72	41.34 N	52.32 E
Békés	30	46.46 N	21.08 E
Békés □[6]	30	46.46 N	21.08 E
Békéscsaba	30	46.41 N	21.06 E
Beketovo	89	53.13 N	125.01 E
Bekilli	130	38.14 N	29.26 E
Bekily	157b	24.13 S	45.19 E
Bekirhan	130	38.10 N	41.19 E
Bekisopa	157b	21.40 S	45.54 E
Bekitro	157b	24.33 S	45.18 E
Bekkai	92a	43.23 N	145.17 E
Bekkaria	36	35.22 N	8.15 E
Bekkevoort	56	50.57 N	4.58 E
Beklemiševo, S.S.S.R.	80	53.52 N	47.25 E
Beklemiševo, S.S.S.R.	88	52.07 N	112.40 E
Bekodoka	157b	16.58 S	45.07 E
Bekoji	144	7.34 N	39.17 E
Bekok	114	2.18 N	103.08 E
Bekopaka	157b	19.09 S	44.48 E
Bekovo	80	52.28 N	43.43 E
Bektyševo	82	56.34 N	39.14 E
Bekwai	150	6.27 N	1.35 W
Bela, Bhārat	124	25.56 N	81.59 E
Bela, Pāk.	120	26.14 N	66.19 E
Bela, Zaïre	154	0.38 N	29.14 E
Béla Bérim	146	15.59 N	13.12 E
Bélabo	152	5.00 N	13.20 E
Belabolo	140	8.57 N	25.51 E
Bélâbre	32	46.33 N	1.09 E
Bela Crkva	38	44.54 N	21.26 E
Bela Cruz	250	3.03 S	40.11 W
Belaga	108	2.42 N	113.47 E
Bel'agaš	86	50.48 N	80.44 E
Bel-Air, Fr.	261	48.37 N	2.10 E
Bel Air, Md., U.S.	208	39.32 N	76.21 W
Bel Air, Va., U.S.	284c	38.52 N	77.10 W
Bel Air ⌖[8]	280	34.05 N	118.27 W
Bélair, Île I	275a	45.37 N	73.48 W
Bel-Air, Morne ∧	241o	16.06 N	61.44 W
Bel Aire Estates	207	41.23 N	72.00 W
Belair National Park ♠	168b	35.01 S	138.39 E
Belaja	80	57.59 N	51.42 E
Belaja ≃, S.S.S.R.	72	56.00 N	54.32 E
Belaja ≃, S.S.S.R.	78	45.04 N	39.23 E
Belaja ≃, S.S.S.R.	83	48.35 N	39.10 E
Belaja, Gora ∧, S.S.S.R.	88	53.10 N	119.50 E
Belaja, Gora ∧, S.S.S.R.	180	65.50 N	174.40 E
Belaja Ber'ozka	76	52.23 N	33.29 E
Belaja Cerkov'	78	49.49 N	30.07 E
Belaja Cholunica	86	58.50 N	50.48 E
Belaja Gora	76	58.31 N	31.45 E
Belaja Kalitva	78	48.11 N	40.46 E
Belaja Krinica, S.S.S.R.	78	47.21 N	33.10 E
Belaja Krinica, S.S.S.R.	78	50.38 N	29.29 E
Bel'ajevka, S.S.S.R.	78	46.29 N	30.12 E
Bel'ajevka, S.S.S.R.	86	57.28 N	55.28 E
Bel'ajevka, S.S.S.R.	86	51.24 N	56.26 E
Bel'ajevo	76	55.31 N	31.06 E
Belalcázar	34	38.34 N	5.10 W
Bel Alton	208	38.28 N	76.59 W
Belambanganumpu	112	4.54 S	105.03 E
Belampalli	122	19.02 N	79.30 E
Bělá nad Radbuzou	60	49.36 N	12.44 E
Belang	112	0.57 N	124.47 E
Bélanger ≃	184	53.26 N	97.40 W
Bel'aninovo	265b	55.57 N	37.39 E
Bel'anskij	80	47.45 N	41.33 E
Bela Palanka	38	43.13 N	22.19 E
Bělá pod Bezdězem	54	50.30 N	14.50 E
Belapurpāda	272c	19.01 N	73.02 E
Belas	266c	38.47 N	9.16 W
Bela Slatina	78	43.28 N	23.56 E
Belavenona	157b	24.50 S	47.04 E
Bela Vista, Ang.	152	7.50 S	13.40 E
Bela Vista, Ang.	152	12.35 S	16.13 E
Bela Vista, Bra.	252	22.06 S	56.31 W
Bela Vista, Moç.	156	26.20 S	32.40 E
Bela Vista ⌖[8]	287b	23.33 S	46.38 W
Bela Vista de Goiás	255	16.58 S	48.57 W
Bela Vista do Paraíso	255	23.00 S	51.12 W
Belawan	114	3.47 N	98.41 E
Belaya ∧	144	11.25 N	36.12 E
Belayan ≃	112	0.14 S	116.36 E
Belaya Tserkov' → Belaja Cerkov'	78	49.49 N	30.07 E
Belbo ≃	62	44.54 N	8.31 E
Belbubulo	140	9.57 N	34.04 E
Belbunia	126	23.17 N	87.09 E
Belcamp	208	39.28 N	76.14 W
Belcastro	68	39.02 N	16.47 E
Bełchatów	30	51.22 N	19.21 E
Belchen ∧	58	47.49 N	7.50 E
Belcher	194	32.45 N	93.50 W
Belcherāgh	120	35.50 N	65.14 E
Belcher Creek ≃	276	41.08 N	74.23 W
Belcher Islands II	176	56.20 N	79.30 W
Belchertown	207	42.17 N	72.24 W
Belchite	34	41.18 N	0.45 W
Bělčice	60	49.30 N	13.53 E
Belcobos	158	27.10 S	24.00 E
Belcoo	48	54.17 N	7.52 W
Belcourt	198	48.50 N	99.45 W
Bel'cy	78	47.46 N	27.56 E
Belda	126	22.05 N	87.21 E
Beldānga	126	23.56 N	88.15 E
Bel'd'ažki	76	52.39 N	35.42 E
Belding	216	43.06 N	85.14 W
Belebej	80	54.07 N	54.07 E
Belebelka	76	57.34 N	30.56 E
Belecke	52	51.29 N	8.20 E
Beled Weyne	144	4.47 N	45.12 E
Béle-Kété	152	6.01 N	17.26 E
Bélel, Cam.	152	7.03 N	14.26 E
Belel, Nig.	146	9.38 N	13.12 E
Belém, Bra.	250	1.27 S	48.29 W
Belém, Moç.	154	14.13 S	35.58 E
Belém ⌖[8]	266c	38.42 N	9.12 W
Belém, Torre de ⊥	266c	38.42 N	9.13 W
Belém de São Francisco	250	8.46 S	38.58 W
Belén, Arg.	252	27.39 S	67.02 W
Belén, Chile	248	18.29 S	69.31 W
Belén, Col.	246	1.26 N	75.56 W
Belén, Col.	246	6.00 N	72.55 W
Belén, Nic.	236	11.30 N	85.53 W
Belén, Para.	252	23.30 S	57.06 W
Belen, Tür.	130	36.32 N	36.10 E
Belen, N. Mex., U.S.	200	34.40 N	106.46 W
Belén, Ur.	252	30.47 S	57.47 W
Belén de Escobar	258	34.21 S	58.47 W
Belén del Refugio	234	21.31 N	102.25 W
Belene	38	43.39 N	25.07 E
Belenichino	78	50.56 N	36.37 E
Belen'koje, S.S.S.R.	78	47.37 N	35.03 E
Belen'koje, S.S.S.R.	83	48.46 N	37.38 E
Belènzinho ⌖[8]	287b	23.32 S	46.35 W
Bélep, Îles II	175f	19.45 S	163.40 E
Beles ≃	144	11.10 N	36.10 E
Belesar, Embalse de ◎[1]	34	42.45 N	7.40 W
Belet Uen → Beled Weyne	144	4.47 N	45.12 E
Beleuli ⊥	86	44.30 N	57.05 E
Bélézé	152	3.51 N	16.19 E
Belfair	224	47.27 N	122.50 W
Belfast, N.Z.	172	43.27 S	172.38 E
Belfast, S. Afr.	156	25.43 S	30.03 E
Belfast, N. Ire., U.K.	48	54.35 N	5.55 W
Belfast, Maine, U.S.	188	44.27 N	69.01 W
Belfast, N.Y., U.S.	210	42.21 N	78.07 W
Belfast, Ohio, U.S.	218	39.03 N	83.32 W
Belfast (Aldergrove) Airport ⊠	44	54.38 N	6.12 W
Belfast Lough C	48	54.40 N	5.36 W
Belfeld	52	51.19 N	6.06 E
Belfield, Austl.	274a	33.54 S	151.05 E
Belfield, N. Dak., U.S.	198	46.53 N	103.12 W
Belfiore	64	45.23 N	11.12 E
Belford, Eng., U.K.	44	55.36 N	1.49 W
Belford, N.J., U.S.	276	40.25 N	74.06 W
Belford Roxo	256	22.46 S	43.24 W
Belfort	58	47.38 N	6.52 E
Belfort □[8]	58	47.38 N	6.55 E
Belforte del Chienti	66	43.10 N	13.14 E
Belfry, Ky., U.S.	192	37.37 N	82.16 W
Belfry, Mont., U.S.	202	45.09 N	109.01 W
Belgard → Białogard	30	54.01 N	16.00 E
Belgaum	122	15.52 N	74.30 E
Belgern	54	51.29 N	13.07 E
Bélgica → Belgium □[1]	30	50.50 N	4.00 E
Belgica Mountains ⩓	9	72.35 S	31.10 E
België → Belgium □[1]	30	50.50 N	4.00 E
Belgien → Belgium □[1]	30	50.50 N	4.00 E
Belgioioso	62	45.10 N	9.19 E
Belgique → Belgium □[1]	30	50.50 N	4.00 E
Belgium □[1]	22		
	30	50.50 N	4.00 E
Belgodere	36	42.35 N	9.01 E
Belgorod	78	50.36 N	36.35 E
Belgorod-Dnestrovskij	78	46.12 N	30.20 E
Belgrad → Beograd	38	44.50 N	20.30 E
Belgrade → Beograd, Jugo.	38	44.50 N	20.30 E
Belgrade, Minn., U.S.	198	45.27 N	95.00 W
Belgrade, Mont., U.S.	202	45.47 N	111.11 W
Belgrade, Nebr., U.S.	198	41.28 N	98.04 W
Belgrado → Beograd	38	44.50 N	20.30 E
Belgrad Ormanı ⌖[3]	267b	41.10 N	28.55 E
Belgrano ⌖[8]	288	34.34 S	58.28 W
Belgrano ≃	254	48.15 S	71.14 W
Belgrano, Lago ◎	254	47.50 S	72.09 W
Belgrave	274b	37.55 S	145.21 E
Belhar	124	24.55 N	86.36 E
Belhaven	192	35.33 N	76.37 W
Belhus Park ♠	260	51.31 N	0.17 E
Beliābera	126	22.17 N	86.57 E
Beliātor	126	23.20 N	87.13 E
Belica	78	51.07 N	35.34 E
Belice → Belize	232	17.30 N	88.12 W
Belice → Belize □[2]	232	17.15 N	88.45 W
Belice ≃	70	37.35 N	12.52 E
Belichifor	140	6.33 N	33.16 E
Beliči	78	50.29 N	30.19 E
Belici ≃	70	37.31 N	13.50 E
Beličij, Ostrov I	89	54.26 N	137.51 E
Belick	76	52.55 N	30.27 E
Belickoje	83	48.25 N	37.13 E
Beli Drim ≃	38	42.06 N	20.25 E
Beliki	78	49.15 N	34.16 E
Beliling, Gunung ∧	115b	8.37 S	119.59 E
Beli Manastir	38	45.46 N	18.36 E
Belin	32	44.30 N	0.47 W
Belington	188	39.01 N	79.56 W
Belingwe	154	20.30 S	29.53 E
Belinskij	80	52.58 N	43.26 E
Belinyu	112	1.38 S	105.46 E
Belitung I	112	2.50 S	107.55 E
Belize	232	17.30 N	88.12 W
Belize □[2]	230		
	232	17.15 N	88.45 W
Belize ≃	232	17.32 N	88.14 W
Belize Inlet C	182	51.08 N	127.15 W
Belka	78	50.49 N	28.11 E
Belknap Crater ⊥[6]	202	44.17 N	121.50 W
Belkofski	180	55.05 N	162.02 W
Bel'kovo	82	56.15 N	38.48 E
Bel'kovskij, Ostrov ≃	74	75.32 N	135.44 E
Bell, S. Afr.	158	33.15 S	27.23 E
Bell, Calif., U.S.	280	33.58 N	118.11 W
Bell □[6]	222	31.03 N	97.27 W
Bell ≃, Qué., Can.	176	49.48 N	77.38 W
Bell ≃, Yukon, Can.	180	67.17 N	137.46 W
Bella	68	40.45 N	15.32 E
Bella Bella	182	52.09 N	128.07 W
Bellac	32	46.07 N	1.02 E
Bellacaty, Pointe ≻	241o	16.25 N	61.24 W
Bella Coola	182	52.22 N	126.46 W
Bella Coola ≃	182	52.22 N	126.43 W
Bell Acres	279b	40.36 N	80.10 W
Bella Flor	248	11.09 S	67.49 W
Bellagio	58	45.59 N	9.15 E
Bellahy	48	53.58 N	8.48 W
Bellaire, Mich., U.S.	190	44.59 N	85.13 W
Bellaire, Ohio, U.S.	188	40.02 N	80.45 W
Bellaire, Tex., U.S.	222	29.43 N	95.03 W
Bella Isla, Estrecho de → Belle Isle, Strait of ⩌	176	51.35 N	56.30 W
Bella Lake ◎	212	45.27 N	79.02 W
Bellambi	170	34.21 S	150.55 E
Bellamy, Ala., U.S.	194	32.22 N	88.08 W
Bellamy, Va., U.S.	208	37.24 N	76.34 W
Bellano	58	46.03 N	9.18 E
Bellaria	66	44.09 N	12.28 E
Bellarine	169	38.08 S	144.37 E
Bellarine Peninsula ≻[1]	169	38.13 S	144.35 E
Bellariva	68	41.55 N	15.58 E
Bellary	122	15.09 N	76.56 E
Bellas Artes, Palacio de ⚲	286a	19.26 N	99.08 W
Bellata	166	29.55 S	149.47 E
Bella Tola ∧	58	46.15 N	7.39 E
Bella Unión	252	30.15 S	57.35 W
Bella Vista, Arg.	252	27.02 S	65.18 W
Bella Vista, Arg.	252	28.30 S	59.03 W
Bella Vista, Arg.	258	34.33 S	58.41 W
Bellavista, Chile	286e	33.31 S	70.37 W
Bella Vista, Para.	252	22.08 S	56.31 W
Bellavista, Perú	248	7.04 S	76.35 W
Bellavista, Perú	248	4.54 S	80.42 W
Bellavista, Perú	286d	12.04 S	77.08 W
Bell Bay C	212	45.30 N	77.51 W
Bellbird	170	32.51 S	151.21 E
Bellbrook, Austl.	166	30.49 S	152.31 E
Bellbrook, Ohio, U.S.	218	39.38 N	84.04 W
Bell Crags ∧[2]	44	55.03 N	2.22 W
Bell Creek ≃, Calif., U.S.	280	34.12 N	118.36 W
Bell Creek ≃, Ind., U.S.	218	40.09 N	85.27 W
Belle, Mo., U.S.	219	38.17 N	91.43 W
Belle, W. Va., U.S.	188	38.14 N	81.32 W
Belle ≃, Ont., Can.	214	42.17 N	82.43 W
Belle ≃, Mich., U.S.	214	42.43 N	82.30 W
Belleair	220	27.56 N	82.19 W
Belleau	50	49.06 N	3.18 E
Belle Bay C	186	47.36 N	55.18 W
Belle Center	216	40.31 N	83.45 W
Belledonne, Chaîne de ⩓	62	45.18 N	6.08 E
Belle-Église	50	49.12 N	2.13 E
Belleek	48	54.28 N	8.06 W
Belle Farm Estates	208	39.23 N	76.45 W
Bellefontaine, Fr.	58	46.33 N	6.04 E
Bellefontaine, Fr.	261	49.06 N	2.28 E
Bellefontaine, Mart.	240e	14.40 N	61.10 W
Bellefontaine, Ohio, U.S.	216	40.22 N	83.46 W
Bellefontaine Neighbors	219	38.44 N	90.14 W
Bellefonte, Del., U.S.	208	39.46 N	75.30 W
Bellefonte, Pa., U.S.	214	40.55 N	77.46 W
Belle Fourche	198	44.40 N	103.51 W
Belle Fourche ≃	198	44.26 N	102.19 W
Belle Fourche Reservoir ◎[1]	198	44.44 N	103.42 W
Bellegarde, Fr.	58	46.06 N	5.49 E
Bellegarde, Fr.	62	43.45 N	4.31 E
Bellegarde-du-Loiret	50	47.59 N	2.26 E
Bellegem	50	50.47 N	3.16 E
Belle Glade	220	26.41 N	80.40 W
Belle Glade Camp	220	26.40 N	80.41 W
Bellegrove	208	40.22 N	76.33 W
Belle Haven, Va., U.S.	208	37.33 N	75.49 W
Belle Haven, Va., U.S.	284c	38.47 N	77.04 W
Belleherbe	58	47.16 N	6.40 E
Belle Hôtesse ∧	241o	16.16 N	61.46 W
Belle-Île I	32	47.20 N	3.10 W
Belle Isle	220	28.27 N	81.21 W
Belle Isle I, Newf., Can.	176	51.55 N	55.20 W
Belle Isle I, Mich., U.S.	281	42.20 N	82.58 W
Belle Isle, Strait of ⩌	176	51.35 N	56.30 W
Belle Isle Park ♠	281	42.20 N	82.59 W
Bellelay	58	47.16 N	7.10 E
Bellême	50	48.22 N	0.34 E
Belle Mead	208	40.28 N	74.40 W
Bellencombre	50	49.42 N	1.14 E
Belleplain	208	39.11 N	74.46 W
Belle-Plaine, Sask., Can.	184	50.24 N	105.09 W
Belle Plaine, Iowa, U.S.	190	41.54 N	92.17 W
Belle Plaine, Kans., U.S.	198	37.24 N	97.17 W
Belle Plaine, Minn., U.S.	190	44.37 N	93.46 W
Belle Rive	219	38.14 N	88.45 W
Belle River	214	42.18 N	82.43 W
Bellerose	276	40.44 N	73.43 W
Bellerose ⌖[8]	276	40.45 N	73.43 W
Bellerose Terrace	276	40.43 N	73.43 W
Belle Terre	276	40.58 N	73.04 W
Bellevaux-Ligneuville	56	50.24 N	6.00 E
Belle Vernon	214	40.07 N	79.50 W
Bellevesvre	58	46.50 N	5.22 E
Belleview, Fla., U.S.	192	29.04 N	82.03 W
Belleview, Ind., U.S.	218	38.53 N	85.23 W
Belle View, Va., U.S.	208	38.47 N	77.03 W
Belleville, Ont., Can.	212	44.10 N	77.23 W
Belleville, Fr.	56	48.49 N	6.06 E
Belleville, Ill., U.S.	219	38.31 N	90.00 W
Belleville, Ind., U.S.	218	39.41 N	86.29 W
Belleville, Kans., U.S.	198	39.49 N	97.38 W
Belleville, Mich., U.S.	216	42.12 N	83.29 W
Belleville, N.J., U.S.	210	40.48 N	74.09 W
Belleville, N.Y., U.S.	212	43.47 N	76.07 W
Belleville, Pa., U.S.	214	40.36 N	77.43 W
Belleville, R.I., U.S.	207	41.34 N	71.29 W
Belleville, Wis., U.S.	216	42.52 N	89.32 W
Belleville Lake ◎	281	42.12 N	83.29 W
Belleville-sur-Meuse	56	49.11 N	5.23 E
Belleville-sur-Saône	58	46.06 N	4.45 E
Bellevue, Alta., Can.	182	49.35 N	114.22 W
Bellevue, Fr.	50	49.53 N	4.12 E
Bellevue, Idaho, U.S.	202	43.28 N	114.16 W
Bellevue, Iowa, U.S.	190	42.16 N	90.26 W
Bellevue, Ky., U.S.	218	39.06 N	84.29 W
Bellevue, Md., U.S.	208	38.42 N	76.11 W
Bellevue, Mich., U.S.	216	42.27 N	85.01 W
Bellevue, Nebr., U.S.	198	41.09 N	95.54 W
Bellevue, Ohio, U.S.	214	41.17 N	82.50 W
Bellevue, Pa., U.S.	214	40.30 N	80.03 W
Bellevue, Tex., U.S.	196	33.38 N	98.01 W
Bellevue, Wash., U.S.	224	47.37 N	122.12 W
Bellevue ⌖[8]	273d	26.11 S	28.05 E
Belle Vue Zoological Gardens ♠	262	53.28 N	2.11 W
Bell Ewart	212	44.16 N	79.33 W
Belley	62	45.46 N	5.41 E
Belleydoux	58	46.15 N	5.46 E
Belle Yella	150	7.22 N	10.00 W
Bellflower, Calif., U.S.	228	33.53 N	118.07 W
Bellflower, Ill., U.S.	216	40.20 N	88.32 W
Bellflower, Mo., U.S.	219	39.00 N	91.21 W
Bell Gardens	228	33.58 N	118.09 W
Bellheim	56	49.11 N	8.16 E
Bell Hill ∧[2]	210	43.09 N	75.07 W
Bell Homestead ⊥	212	43.04 N	80.18 W
Bellicourt	50	49.57 N	3.14 E
Bellin	176	60.01 N	70.01 W
Bellingdon	260	51.44 N	0.38 W
Bellinge	41	55.20 N	10.20 E
Bellingen	166	30.27 S	152.54 E
Bellingham, Eng., U.K.	44	55.09 N	2.16 W
Bellingham, Mass., U.S.	207	42.05 N	71.28 W
Bellingham, Minn., U.S.	198	45.08 N	96.17 W
Bellingham, Wash., U.S.	224	48.46 N	122.29 W
Bellingham Bay C	224	48.45 N	122.35 W
Bellingshausen I[1]	14	15.48 S	154.33 W
Bellingshausen Sea ⊤[2]	9	71.00 S	85.00 W
Bellingwolde	52	53.07 N	7.09 E
Bellinzago Novarese	62	45.34 N	8.38 E
Bellinzona	58	46.11 N	9.02 E
Bell Island I, Newf., Can.	186	50.44 N	55.35 W
Bell Island I, Newf., Can.	186	47.36 N	52.58 W
Bell Island Hot Springs	182	55.56 N	131.34 W
Bellmans Creek ≃	276	40.48 N	74.02 W
Bellmawr	208	39.51 N	75.06 W
Bellmead	222	31.35 N	97.06 W
Bellmore	276	40.40 N	73.32 W
Bellmore Creek ≃	276	40.38 N	73.31 W
Bell Mountain	228	34.35 N	117.15 W
Bellnhausen	56	50.42 N	8.43 E
Bello, Col.	246	6.20 N	75.33 W
Bello, Cuba	286b	23.07 N	82.24 W
Bello Horizonte → Belo Horizonte	255	19.55 S	43.56 W
Bellona	210	42.46 N	77.01 W
Bellona Plateau ⊹[3]	14	21.00 S	160.00 E
Bellona Reefs ⊹[2]	160	21.30 S	159.00 E
Bellone, Cap ≻	157b	16.14 S	49.51 E
Bellosguardo	68	40.25 N	15.19 E
Bellot Strait ⩌	176	71.58 N	94.45 W
Bellows Falls	188	43.08 N	72.27 W
Belloy-en-France	261	49.05 N	2.22 E
Bellpat	120	29.00 N	68.01 E
Bell Peninsula ≻[1]	176	63.50 N	82.00 W
Bell Point	279b	40.33 N	79.33 W
Bells, Tenn., U.S.	194	35.43 N	89.05 W
Bells, Tex., U.S.	196	33.37 N	96.25 W
Bells Corners	212	45.19 N	75.50 W
Bells Lake	285	39.44 N	75.02 W
Bells Lake ◎	285	39.45 N	75.04 W
Belltown, Del., U.S.	208	38.45 N	75.11 W
Belltown, Ill., U.S.	219	39.23 N	90.25 W
Belluno	64	46.09 N	12.13 E
Belluno □[4]	64	46.15 N	12.08 E
Bellvale	210	41.15 N	74.18 W
Bell Ville, Arg.	252	32.37 S	62.42 W
Bellville, S. Afr.	158	33.53 S	18.36 E
Bellville, Ohio, U.S.	214	40.37 N	82.31 W
Bellville, Tex., U.S.	222	29.57 N	96.16 W
Bellwood, Ill., U.S.	278	41.53 N	87.52 W
Bellwood, Nebr., U.S.	198	41.21 N	97.14 W
Bellwood, Pa., U.S.	214	40.36 N	78.20 W
Bellwood, Lake ◎	212	43.46 N	80.20 W
Belly ≃	182	49.46 N	113.02 W
Bellyk	86	54.32 N	91.17 E
Belmar	208	40.11 N	74.01 W
Bélmez	34	38.16 N	5.12 W
Belmond	190	42.51 N	93.37 W
Belmont, Austl.	169	38.10 S	144.21 E
Belmont, Austl.	170	33.02 S	151.40 E
Belmont, Man., Can.	184	49.24 N	99.27 W
Belmont, Ont., Can.	212	42.53 N	81.05 W
Belmont, S. Afr.	158	29.28 S	24.22 E
Belmont, Eng., U.K.	262	53.38 N	2.30 W
Belmont, Calif., U.S.	226	37.31 N	122.17 W
Belmont, Mass., U.S.	283	42.24 N	71.10 W
Belmont, Mich., U.S.	216	43.05 N	85.37 W
Belmont, Miss., U.S.	194	34.31 N	88.13 W
Belmont, N.H., U.S.	188	43.27 N	71.29 W
Belmont, N.Y., U.S.	210	42.13 N	78.02 W
Belmont, Pa., U.S.	214	40.17 N	78.53 W
Belmont, Tex., U.S.	222	29.31 N	97.41 W
Belmont, Wis., U.S.	190	42.44 N	90.20 W
Belmont □[6]	214	40.05 N	80.54 W
Belmonte, Bra.	255	15.51 S	38.54 W
Belmonte, Esp.	34	43.10 N	6.05 W
Belmonte, Esp.	34	39.34 N	2.42 W
Belmonte, Port.	34	40.21 N	7.21 W
Belmonte Calabro	68	39.09 N	16.05 E
Belmonte Mezzagno	70	38.02 N	13.23 E
Belmont Harbor C	278	41.57 N	87.38 W
Belmont Lake ◎, Ont., Can.	212	44.30 N	77.50 W
Belmont Lake ◎, N.Y., U.S.	276	40.44 N	73.20 W
Belmont Lake State Park ♠	276	40.43 N	73.20 W
Belmont Park	214	41.10 N	80.39 W
Belmont Park Race Track ♠	276	40.43 N	73.43 W
Belmont Reservoir ◎[1]	262	53.39 N	2.30 W
Belmont Slough ≃	282	37.33 N	122.14 W
Belmopan	232	17.15 N	88.46 W
Belmore, Austl.	274a	33.55 S	151.05 E
Belmore, Ohio, U.S.	216	41.09 N	83.56 W
Belmullet	48	54.14 N	10.00 W
Belmuri	272b	22.57 N	88.09 E
Belo	157b	19.42 S	44.33 E
Beloeil, Bel.	50	50.33 N	3.43 E
Beloeil, Qué., Can.	206	45.34 N	73.12 W
Belœil, Château de ⚲	50	50.35 N	3.44 E
Beloglazovo	86	56.05 N	72.40 E
Belogorje, S.S.S.R.	78	50.01 N	26.25 E
Belogorje, S.S.S.R.	78	50.30 N	40.01 E
Belogorka	80	50.42 N	53.27 E
Belogornoje	80	52.25 N	47.35 E
Belogorode	82	54.23 N	38.31 E
Belogorodka	78	50.00 N	26.39 E
Belogorovka	83	48.55 N	38.15 E
Belogorsk, S.S.S.R.	78	45.03 N	34.36 E
Belogorsk, S.S.S.R.	86	55.05 N	88.28 E
Belogorsk, S.S.S.R.	89	50.57 N	128.25 E
Belogorskij	86	49.27 N	83.10 E
Belogorskoje	80	53.35 N	48.12 E
Belogradčik	38	43.38 N	22.41 E
Beloguša	78	51.57 N	26.56 E
Beloha	157b	25.10 S	45.03 E
Belo Horizonte	255	19.55 S	43.56 W
Beloit, Kans., U.S.	198	39.28 N	98.06 W
Beloit, Ohio, U.S.	214	40.56 N	81.00 W
Beloit, Wis., U.S.	216	42.31 N	89.02 W
Belo Jardim	250	8.20 S	36.26 W
Belojarsk	86	53.26 N	83.58 E
Belojarskij	86	56.45 N	61.24 E
Beloje, S.S.S.R.	78	51.03 N	35.43 E
Beloje, S.S.S.R.	80	58.23 N	39.24 E
Beloje, S.S.S.R.	83	48.31 N	39.04 E
Beloje, S.S.S.R.	86	48.55 N	82.58 E
Beloje, Ozero ◎	76	60.11 N	37.37 E
Beloje More (White Sea) ⊤[2]	24	65.30 N	38.00 E
Belokamenskoje ⌖[8]	83	48.41 N	38.06 E
Belokany	84	41.43 N	46.26 E
Belokoroviči	78	51.07 N	28.02 E
Belokurakino	83	49.33 N	38.44 E
Belokuricha	86	51.59 N	84.59 E
Beloluck	83	49.41 N	39.02 E
Belomestnaja	76	52.24 N	37.37 E
Belomestnaja Dvojn'a	80	52.42 N	41.03 E
Belomorsk	24	64.32 N	34.48 E
Belomorsko-Baltijskij Kanal ⌅	24	62.48 N	34.48 E
Belondo	152	0.16 S	19.31 E
Belonge	152	2.06 S	19.32 E
Belonia	124	23.15 N	91.27 E
Beloomut	76	54.57 N	39.20 E
Beloozersk	76	52.28 N	25.11 E
Belopolje	78	51.09 N	34.18 E
Belorado	34	42.25 N	3.11 W
Belorečensk	78	44.46 N	39.52 E
Beloreck	86	53.58 N	58.24 E
Belören	130	40.51 N	33.30 E
Belorusskaja Gr'ada ∧	76	53.40 N	27.00 E
Belorusskaja Sovetskaja Socialističeskaja Respublika □[3]	76	53.50 N	28.00 E
Belorusskij Vokzal ⌖[5]	265b	55.47 N	37.35 E
Belosarajskaja Kosa ≻[2]	83	46.52 N	37.20 E
Beloščelje	24	64.52 N	46.56 E
Belo-sur-mer	157b	20.44 S	44.00 E
Belot, Lac ◎	180	66.55 N	126.18 W
Belousovka, S.S.S.R.	78	49.57 N	32.20 E
Belousovka, S.S.S.R.	86	50.08 N	82.33 E
Belousovo	82	55.05 N	36.40 E
Bel'ov	76	53.48 N	36.08 E
Belo Vale	255	20.25 S	44.01 W
Belovo, S.S.S.R.	86	52.57 N	82.16 E
Belovo, S.S.S.R.	86	54.25 N	86.18 E
Belovodsk	83	49.12 N	39.35 E
Belovodskoje	85	42.50 N	74.06 E
Beloz'orje, S.S.S.R.	78	49.29 N	31.35 E
Beloz'orje, S.S.S.R.	78	49.18 N	31.54 E
Beloz'orka	78	46.37 N	32.27 E
Beloz'orsk	76	60.02 N	37.48 E
Beloz'orskoje	78	48.33 N	37.04 E
Belp	58	46.53 N	7.30 E
Belpāda	272c	19.02 N	73.03 E
Belpasso	70	37.35 N	14.58 E
Belper	42	53.01 N	1.29 W
Belpre	188	39.17 N	81.34 W
Belrose	274a	33.44 S	151.13 E
Belsano	214	40.31 N	78.52 W
Belsele	50	51.09 N	4.05 E
Bel'skaja Vol'a	78	51.27 N	25.49 E
Bel'skoje, S.S.S.R.	80	54.44 N	40.22 E
Bel'skoje, S.S.S.R.	86	57.49 N	92.09 E
Belson Run ≃	279b	40.12 N	79.37 W
Belspring	192	37.11 N	80.36 W
Belt	202	47.23 N	110.55 W
Beltana	166	30.48 S	138.25 E
Belt Creek ≃	202	47.36 N	111.02 W
Belted Range ⩓	204	37.25 N	116.10 W
Belterra	250	2.38 S	54.57 W
Belthorn	262	53.43 N	2.26 W
Beltinci	61	46.36 N	16.15 E
Belton, Mo., U.S.	194	38.49 N	94.32 W
Belton, S.C., U.S.	192	34.31 N	82.30 W
Belton, Tex., U.S.	222	31.04 N	97.28 W
Belton Lake ◎[1]	222	31.08 N	97.32 W
Beltra	48	54.13 N	8.37 W
Beltrán	252	27.50 S	64.04 W
Beltsville	284c	39.02 N	76.54 W
Beltsville Airport ⊠	284c	39.02 N	76.50 W
Bel'tsy → Bel'cy	78	47.46 N	27.56 E
Belturbet	48	54.06 N	7.28 W
Bel'tyrskij	86	53.02 N	90.16 E
Beltzville State Park ♠	210	40.52 N	75.36 W
Belucha, Gora ∧	86	49.48 N	86.40 E
Belugino	82	54.47 N	37.54 E
Belumut, Gunung ∧	114	2.02 N	103.34 E
Belūr, Bhārat	122	13.10 N	75.52 E
Belur, Bhārat	272b	22.38 N	88.18 E
Beluran	112	5.54 N	117.33 E
Belur Math ⚲[1]	272b	22.38 N	88.22 E
Belušje	24	66.54 N	47.31 E
Belvedere, It.	64	45.44 N	13.23 E
Belvedere, Calif., U.S.	226	37.52 N	122.28 W
Belvedere, Va., U.S.	284c	38.50 N	77.10 W
Belvedere ⌖[8]	260	51.29 N	0.09 E
Belvedere ⚲	264b	48.11 N	16.23 E
Belvedere di Spinello	68	39.12 N	16.53 E
Belvedere Homes	220	26.26 N	80.06 W
Belvedere Marittimo	68	39.37 N	15.52 E
Belvedere Ostrense	66	43.34 N	13.09 E
Belveren	130	37.39 N	37.34 E
Belvès	32	44.47 N	1.00 E
Belvidere, Del., U.S.	208	39.43 N	75.37 W
Belvidere, Ill., U.S.	216	42.15 N	88.50 W
Belvidere, N.J., U.S.	210	40.49 N	75.05 W
Belview	198	44.36 N	95.20 W
Belvis	266a	40.33 N	3.33 W
Belvís de la Jara	34	39.45 N	4.57 W
Belvoir ⊥	132	32.36 N	35.31 E
Belvoir, Vale of ∨	42	52.57 N	0.53 W
Belyando ≃	166	21.38 S	146.50 E
Belyj	76	55.50 N	32.56 E
Belyj, Ostrov I	74	73.10 N	70.45 E
Belyje Berega	76	53.12 N	34.40 E
Belyje Gory ⩓	80	53.45 N	48.15 E
Belyje Kolodezi	82	54.55 N	38.42 E
Belyje Stolby	82	55.20 N	37.52 E
Belyje-Vody	85	42.25 N	69.50 E
Belyj Gorodok	76	56.58 N	37.30 E
Belyj Jar, S.S.S.R.	80	53.57 N	48.58 E
Belyj Jar, S.S.S.R.	86	58.26 N	85.01 E
Belyj Jar, S.S.S.R.	86	53.36 N	91.24 E
Belyj Kalodez'	78	50.02 N	38.40 E
Belyj Kolodez'	78	50.12 N	37.08 E
Belyj Luch ≃	80	57.43 N	43.42 E
Belyj Rast	82	56.08 N	37.26 E
Belyniči	76	53.59 N	29.42 E
Belynkoviči	76	53.15 N	32.08 E
Belz, Fr.	32	47.41 N	3.10 W
Belz, S.S.S.R.	78	50.23 N	24.01 E
Bełżec	30	50.24 N	23.26 E
Belzig	54	52.08 N	12.35 E
Belzoni	194	33.11 N	90.29 W
Bełżyce	30	51.11 N	22.18 E
Bem	219	38.15 N	91.28 W
Bemaraha, Plateau du ⩓[1]	157b	20.00 S	45.15 E
Bemarivo, Madag.	157b	16.56 S	44.21 E
Bemarivo, Madag.	157b	21.45 S	44.45 E
Bemarivo ≃, Madag.	157b	14.09 S	50.09 E
Bemarivo ≃, Madag.	157b	15.27 S	47.40 E
Bemavo	157b	21.37 S	45.24 E
Bemban	114	2.16 N	102.23 E
Bembe	152	7.02 S	14.18 E
Bembesi	154	20.00 S	28.56 E
Bembézar ≃	34	37.45 N	5.13 W
Bembezi ≃	154	18.57 S	27.47 E
Bembou Sambayabé	150	10.55 N	13.44 W
Bembridge	42	50.41 N	1.05 W
Bement	194	39.55 N	88.34 W
Bemidji	190	47.29 N	94.53 W
Bemis	194	35.35 N	88.49 W
Bemmel	52	51.54 N	5.54 E
Bemolanga	157b	17.44 S	45.06 E
Bemposta	256	22.09 S	43.07 W
Bemus Point	214	42.09 N	79.24 W
Bemyž	80	56.08 N	51.44 E
Ben, Kinh ⌅	269c	10.43 N	106.37 E
Bena	150	11.18 N	5.55 E
Benāb	128	37.20 N	46.04 E
Benabarre	34	42.07 N	0.29 E
Bena-Dibele	152	4.07 S	22.50 E
Benadir □[4]	144	2.20 N	45.00 E
Benagaria	126	24.11 N	87.37 E
Benagerie	166	31.25 S	140.24 E
Benahmed	148	33.07 N	7.17 W
Benain ≃	112	9.39 S	124.59 E
Ben'akoni	76	54.15 N	25.22 E
Bena-Leka	152	5.08 S	22.10 E
Benalla	166	36.33 S	145.59 E
Benamejí	34	37.16 N	4.32 W
Benares → Vārānasi	124	25.20 N	83.00 E
Bénat, Cap ≻	62	43.05 N	6.22 E
Benátky nad Jizerou	54	50.17 N	14.51 E
Bena-Tshadi	152	4.40 S	22.49 E
Benavente, Esp.	34	42.00 N	5.41 W
Benavente, Port.	34	38.59 N	8.48 W
Benavides	196	27.36 N	98.25 W
Benavidez	258	34.25 S	58.42 W
Ben Avon Heights	279b	40.31 N	80.04 W
Ben Badis	34	34.57 N	0.55 W
Benbane Head ≻	48	55.15 N	6.28 W
Benbecula I	46	57.26 N	7.21 W
Ben Bolt	196	27.39 N	98.05 W
Benbonyathe Hill ∧	166	30.24 S	139.11 E
Benbrook	222	32.41 N	97.28 W
Benbrook Lake ◎[1]	222	32.38 N	97.27 W
Ben-cat	110	11.09 N	106.36 E
Ben-cat, Rach ≃	269c	10.50 N	106.42 E
Bencha, Khao Phanom ∧	110	8.17 N	98.56 E
Bencheng	98	39.32 N	118.39 E
Ben-Chicao, Col de)(	34	36.12 N	2.45 E
Bencubbin	162	30.48 S	117.52 E
Benculuk	115a	8.26 S	114.13 E
Bend	202	44.03 N	121.19 W
Bendaja	150	7.10 N	11.15 W
Bende	150	5.36 N	7.39 E
Bendela	152	3.18 S	17.36 E
Bendeleben, Mount ∧	180	65.10 N	164.03 W
Bendemeer	166	30.53 S	151.10 E
Bender Beila	144	9.30 N	50.30 E
Benderge ∧	158	31.06 S	27.58 E
Bender Merhagno	144	11.39 N	50.25 E
Bendersville	208	39.59 N	77.15 W
Bendery	78	46.48 N	29.29 E
Bendigo	169	36.46 S	144.17 E
Bendorf	56	50.25 N	7.34 E
Bēne	76	56.29 N	23.04 E
Bene Beraq	132	32.05 N	34.50 E
Bene Berit	132	32.35 N	35.26 E
Benedict	208	38.31 N	76.41 W
Benediktbeuern	64	47.42 N	11.25 E
Benediktenwand ⊥[4]	64	47.39 N	11.28 E
Beneditinos	250	5.27 S	42.22 W
Benedito Leite	250	7.13 S	44.34 W
Benemérita de San Cristóbal	238	18.25 N	70.06 W
Bénéna	150	13.07 N	4.22 W
Benenitra	157b	23.27 S	45.05 E
Beneraird ∧[2]	44	55.04 N	4.57 W
Bene Re'em	132	31.46 N	34.47 E
Benešov nad Ploučnicí	54	50.45 N	14.22 E
Bénestroff	56	48.55 N	6.45 E
Benetovka	80	48.35 N	44.25 E
Benetutti	71	40.27 N	9.10 E
Beneuvre	58	47.42 N	4.57 E
Bene Vagienna	62	44.33 N	7.50 E
Bénévent-l'Abbaye	32	46.07 N	1.38 E
Benevento	68	41.08 N	14.45 E
Benevento □[4]	68	41.15 N	14.17 E
Benezett	214	41.19 N	78.23 W
Benfeld	58	48.22 N	7.36 E
Benfica ⌖[8], Bra.	287a	22.53 S	43.15 W
Benfica ⌖[8], Port.	266c	38.45 N	9.12 W
Benfica, Estádio ♠	266c	38.45 N	9.11 W
Bèng ≃	110	19.53 N	101.08 E
Benga	154	13.19 S	34.16 E
Bengābād	126	24.18 N	86.21 E
Bengal, Bay of C	12	15.00 N	90.00 E
Bengala, Golfo del → Bengal, Bay of C	12	15.00 N	90.00 E
Bengalen, Golf von → Bengal, Bay of C	12	15.00 N	90.00 E
Bengamisa	154	0.57 N	25.10 E
Bengara	112	3.11 N	117.12 E
Bengasi → Banghāzī	146	32.07 N	20.04 E
Bengbis	152	3.27 N	12.27 E
Benger	168a	33.11 S	115.52 E
Ben Ghardane	148	33.08 N	11.13 E
Benghazi → Banghāzī	146	32.07 N	20.04 E
Ben-giang	110	15.41 N	107.47 E
Bengkalis	114	1.28 N	102.07 E
Bengkalis, Pulau I	114	1.30 N	102.15 E
Bengkalis, Selat ⩌	114	1.30 N	102.00 E
Bengkayang	112	0.50 N	109.29 E
Bengkoka ≃	116	6.50 N	117.03 E
Bengkulu	112	3.48 S	102.16 E
Bengo ≃	152	8.45 S	13.24 E
Bengo, Baía do C	152	8.43 S	13.21 E
Bengoi	164	3.01 S	130.12 E
Bengough	184	49.24 N	105.08 W
Bengtsfors	26	59.02 N	12.13 E
Benguela	152	12.35 S	13.25 E
Benguela □[5]	152	12.00 S	15.00 E
Benguérua, Ilha I	156	21.58 S	35.28 E
Benguet □[4]	116	16.30 N	120.40 E
Bengut, Cap ≻	34	36.55 N	3.54 E
Benha → Banhā	142	30.28 N	31.11 E
Benham	192	36.58 N	82.57 W
Ben Hur	222	31.30 N	96.44 W
Beni	154	0.30 N	29.28 E
Beni □[5]	248	14.00 S	65.30 W
Beni ≃	248	10.23 S	65.24 W
Béni Abbès	148	30.08 N	2.10 W
Benicarló	34	40.25 N	0.26 E
Benicia	226	38.03 N	122.09 W
Benicia Capitol State Historic Park ♠	282	38.03 N	122.09 W
Benicia State Recreation Area ♠	282	38.05 N	122.13 W
Benicito ≃	248	11.32 S	65.47 W
Benidorm	34	38.32 N	0.08 W
Benima	152	5.26 N	23.54 E
Beni-Mellal	148	32.22 N	6.29 W
Benin □[1]	134		
	150	9.30 N	2.15 E
Benin ≃	150	5.45 N	5.04 E
Benin, Bight of C[3]	150	5.30 N	3.00 E
Benin City	150	6.19 N	5.41 E
Benisa	34	38.34 N	0.03 E
Beni Saf	148	35.19 N	1.23 W
Benisheikh	146	11.49 N	12.29 E
Beni Suef → Banī Suwayf	142	29.05 N	31.05 E
Benito	184	51.55 N	101.31 W
Benito ≃	152	1.35 N	9.37 E
Benito Juárez, Méx.	234	19.14 N	100.28 W
Benito Juárez, Méx.	234	17.50 N	92.32 W
Benito Juárez □[7]	286a	19.22 N	99.10 W
Benito Juárez, Parque Nacional ♠	234	17.07 N	96.43 W
Benito Juárez, Presa ◎[1]	234	16.27 N	95.30 W
Benjamin	196	33.35 N	99.48 W
Benjamín, Isla I	254	44.40 S	74.08 W
Benjamín Aceval	252	24.58 S	57.34 W
Benjamin Constant	246	4.22 S	70.02 W
Benjamín Hill	232	30.10 N	111.10 W
Benjamín Zorrilla	252	39.06 S	65.29 W
Benkelman	198	40.03 N	101.32 W
Benken	54	52.10 N	12.28 E
Benkovac	36	44.02 N	15.37 E
Benld	219	39.06 N	89.48 W
Benlidi	166	24.34 S	144.52 E
Benllech	44	53.19 N	4.13 W
Ben Lomond	226	37.05 N	122.05 W
Ben Mehidi	36	36.46 N	7.54 E
Ben Morrow, Lake ◎[1]	224	45.30 N	122.04 W
Benndale	194	30.52 N	88.48 W
Benndorf	54	51.34 N	11.29 E
Benneckenstein	54	51.40 N	10.45 E
Bennekom	52	52.00 N	5.40 E
Bennet	198	40.41 N	96.30 W
Bennett, Lake ◎	162	22.55 S	130.57 E
Bennetta, Ostrov I	74	76.21 N	148.56 E
Bennett Lake ◎, Man., Can.	184	53.28 N	96.05 W
Bennett Lake ◎, Ont., Can.	212	44.55 N	76.27 W

Symbols in the index entries represent the broad categories identified in the key at the right. Symbols with superior numbers (⩓[2]) identify subcategories (see complete key on page *I · 30*).

Kartensymbole in dem Registerverzeichnis stellen die rechts in Schlüssel erklärten Kategorien dar. Symbole mit hochgestellten Ziffern (⩓[2]) bezeichnen Unterabteilungen einer Kategorie (vgl. vollständiger Schlüssel auf Seite *I · 30*).

Los símbolos incluídos en el texto del índice representan las grandes categorias identificadas con la clave a la derecha. Los símbolos con numeros en su parte superior (⩓[2]) identifican las subcategorías (véase la clave completa en la página *I · 30*).

Les symboles de l'index représentent les catégories indiquées dans la légende à droite. Les symboles suivis d'un indice (⩓[2]) représentent des sous-catégories (voir légende complète à la page *I · 30*).

Os símbolos incluídos no texto do índice representam as grandes categorias identificadas com a chave à direita. Os símbolos com números em sua parte superior (⩓[2]) identificam as subcategorias (veja-se a chave completa à página *I · 30*).

	English	Deutsch	Español	Français	Português
∧	Mountain	Berg	Montaña	Montagne	Montanha
⩓	Mountains	Berge	Montañas	Montagnes	Montanhas
)(	Pass	Pass	Paso	Col	Passo
∨	Valley, Canyon	Tal, Cañon	Valle, Cañón	Vallée, Canyon	Vale, Canhão
⩦	Plain	Ebene	Llano	Plaine	Planície
≻	Cape	Kap	Cabo	Cap	Cabo
I	Island	Insel	Isla	Île	Ilha
II	Islands	Inseln	Islas	Îles	Ilhas
⊥	Other Topographic Features	Andere Topographische Objekte	Otros Elementos Topográficos	Autres données topographiques	Outros Elementos Topográficos

ESPAÑOL

Nombre	Página	Lat.°′	Long.°′ W=Oeste
Bennett Pass)(	224	45.18 N	121.39 W
Bennettsbridge	48	52.36 N	7.12 W
Bennetts Creek ≃	210	42.16 N	77.35 W
Bennettsville	192	34.37 N	79.41 W
Bennettswood	274b	37.51 S	145.07 E
Bennigsen	52	52.14 N	9.40 E
Benninghofen ⤚[8]	263	51.29 N	7.31 E
Bennington, Ind., U.S.	218	38.52 N	85.08 W
Bennington, Kans., U.S.	198	39.02 N	97.36 W
Bennington, Vt., U.S.	188	42.53 N	73.12 W
Bennington □[6]	207	42.50 N	73.08 W
Bennington Battle Monument ⊥	210	42.53 N	73.13 W
Benniu	106	31.52 N	119.48 E
Bennstedt	54	51.29 N	11.49 E
Beno	152	3.37 S	17.48 E
Benoa	115b	8.46 S	115.13 E
Ben Ohau Range ⩘	172	44.00 S	170.00 E
Benoit	194	33.39 N	91.01 W
Benom, Gunong ∧	114	3.49 N	102.04 E
Benoni	158	26.19 S	28.27 E
Benoni South	273d	26.13 S	28.18 E
Bénoué (Benue) ≃	134	7.48 N	6.46 E
Bénoué, Parc National de la ♠	146	8.20 N	13.50 E
Benover	260	51.13 N	0.26 E
Benoy	146	8.59 N	16.19 E
Benque Viejo	232	17.05 N	89.08 W
Benrad ⤚[8]	263	51.20 N	6.30 E
Benrath ⤚[8]	56	51.10 N	6.51 E
Benrath, Schloss ⊥	263	51.10 N	6.52 E
Bensbach ≃	164	9.08 S	141.00 E
Bensberg	56	50.58 N	7.09 E
Bensdorf	54	52.24 N	12.20 E
Bensenville	278	41.57 N	87.57 W
Bensersiel	52	53.40 N	7.34 E
Benshausen	54	50.38 N	10.35 E
Bensheim	56	49.41 N	8.37 E
Bensley	208	37.26 N	77.26 W
Ben-Slimane	148	33.41 N	7.10 W
Ben Smih	36	36.23 N	7.31 E
Benson, Eng., U.K.	42	51.38 N	1.05 W
Benson, Ariz., U.S.	200	31.58 N	110.18 W
Benson, Md., U.S.	208	39.31 N	76.23 W
Benson, Minn., U.S.	198	45.19 N	95.36 W
Benson, N.C., U.S.	192	35.23 N	78.33 W
Bensonhurst ⤚[8]	276	40.35 N	73.59 W
Benson Point >	174o	1.56 N	157.29 W
Bens Run ≃	284b	39.19 N	76.48 W
Bent	128	26.17 N	59.31 E
Benta	114	4.01 N	101.58 E
Ben Tadjine, Djebel ⩘	148	29.20 N	4.00 W
Benteng (Salayar)	112	6.08 S	120.27 E
Bentheim, B.R.D.	52	52.17 N	7.10 E
Bentheim, Mich., U.S.	216	42.42 N	85.55 W
Ben-thuy	110	18.39 N	105.42 E
Ben Tili, Oued ∨	148	25.48 N	9.32 W
Bentinck Island I, Austl.	164	17.04 S	139.30 E
Bentiu	140	9.14 N	29.50 E
Bentleigh	274b	37.55 S	145.02 E
Bentley, Alta., Can.	182	52.28 N	114.04 W
Bentley, Eng., U.K.	44	53.33 N	1.09 W
Bentleyville, Ohio, U.S.	279a	41.25 N	81.26 W
Bentleyville, Pa., U.S.	214	40.07 N	80.01 W
Bento Gomes ≃	248	16.40 S	57.12 W
Bento Gonçalves	252	29.10 S	51.31 W
Benton, Ark., U.S.	194	34.34 N	92.35 W
Benton, Ill., U.S.	194	38.00 N	88.55 W
Benton, Ind., U.S.	216	41.31 N	85.46 W
Benton, La., U.S.	194	32.42 N	93.44 W
Benton, Miss., U.S.	194	32.50 N	90.15 W
Benton, Mo., U.S.	194	37.06 N	89.34 W
Benton, Ohio, U.S.	214	40.36 N	81.51 W
Benton, Pa., U.S.	210	41.12 N	76.23 W
Benton, Tenn., U.S.	192	35.10 N	84.39 W
Benton, Wis., U.S.	190	42.34 N	90.23 W
Benton □[6]	216	40.37 N	87.19 W
Benton City, Mo., U.S.	219	39.08 N	91.46 W
Benton City, Wash., U.S.	202	46.16 N	119.29 W
Bentong	114	3.32 N	101.55 E
Benton Harbor	216	42.06 N	86.27 W
Benton Heights	216	42.07 N	86.24 W
Bentonia	194	32.38 N	90.22 W
Benton Lake ⊜	202	47.40 N	111.20 W
Benton Ridge	216	41.00 N	83.48 W
Bentonville, Ark., U.S.	194	36.22 N	94.13 W
Bentonville, Ind., U.S.	218	39.45 N	85.15 W
Bentonville, Ohio, U.S.	218	38.45 N	83.37 W
Bent's Old Fort National Historic Site ⊥	198	38.05 N	103.28 W
Bentu Liben	144	8.40 N	38.28 E
Benua, Pulau I	112	0.56 N	107.27 E
Benue (Bénoué) ≃	134	7.48 N	6.46 E
Benue-Plateau □[3]	150	8.00 N	9.00 E
Benut	114	1.38 N	103.16 E
Benwee ∧	48	53.35 N	9.31 W
Benwee Head >	48	54.20 N	9.50 W
Ben Wheeler	222	32.27 N	95.42 W
Benxi (Penhsi)	104	41.18 N	123.45 E
Benza	152	6.16 S	12.57 E
Beograd (Belgrade)	38	44.50 N	20.30 E
Beohāri	124	24.03 N	81.23 E
Beonta	272b	22.31 N	88.31 E
Béoumi	150	7.40 N	5.34 W
Beowawe	204	40.35 N	116.29 W
Beppu	96	33.17 N	131.30 E
Beppu-wan C	96	33.18 N	131.35 E
Bequia I	241h	13.01 N	61.13 W
Bequimão	250	2.26 S	44.47 W
Bera, Bngl.	126	23.59 N	89.40 E
Bera, Bngl.	126	24.05 N	89.37 E
Berābāria	272b	22.52 N	88.34 E
Berāberi, Bhārat	272b	22.51 N	88.12 E
Beraberi, Bhārat	272b	22.46 N	88.27 E
Beraketa, Madag.	157b	23.07 S	44.25 E
Beraketa, Madag.	157b	24.11 S	45.42 E
Berakit	144	14.35 N	39.28 E
Bérandjoko	152	3.06 N	17.17 E
Berāsi	124	23.36 N	81.51 E
Berasia	124	23.38 N	77.26 E
Berat	38	40.42 N	19.57 E
Beratzhausen	60	49.06 N	11.48 E
Berau	58	47.42 N	8.15 E
Berau ≃	112	2.10 N	117.42 E
Berau, Teluk C	164	2.30 S	132.30 E
Beravina	157b	18.10 S	45.14 E
Berazategui	258	34.46 S	58.13 W
Berazategui □[5]	288	34.50 S	58.10 W
Berbenno di Valtellina	64	46.10 N	9.44 E
Berbera	144	10.25 N	45.02 E
Berbérati	152	4.16 N	15.47 E
Berbería, Cabo >	34	38.38 N	1.23 E
Berbice ≃	246	6.17 N	57.32 W
Berceto	64	44.31 N	9.59 E
Berchem, Bel.	50	51.12 N	4.26 E
Berchem, Bel.	50	50.47 N	3.30 E
Berchem-Sainte-Agathe	50	50.52 N	4.17 E
Berchidda	71	40.47 N	9.10 E
Berching	60	49.07 N	11.27 E
Berchtesgaden	64	47.38 N	13.01 E
Berchum	263	51.23 N	7.32 E
Berck	50	50.24 N	1.34 E
Berck-sur-Mer	50	50.24 N	1.36 E
Berclair	196	28.32 N	97.36 W
Berčogur	86	48.25 N	58.44 E
Bercu	50	50.31 N	3.17 E
Berd	84	40.53 N	45.23 E
Berda ≃	78	46.48 N	36.52 E
Berd'ansk	78	46.45 N	36.49 E

FRANÇAIS

Nom	Page	Lat.°′	Long.°′ W=Ouest
Berd'anskij Zaliv C	78	46.42 N	36.35 E
Berd'auš	86	55.09 N	59.09 E
Berdičev	78	49.54 N	28.36 E
Berdigest'ach	74	62.06 N	126.40 E
Berdniki	82	56.03 N	36.46 E
Berdorf	56	49.50 N	6.21 E
Berdsk	86	54.47 N	83.02 E
Berd'užje	86	55.48 N	68.19 E
Berdyansk → Berd'ansk	78	46.45 N	36.49 E
Bere, S.S.S.R.	128	39.47 N	58.06 E
Béré, Tchad	146	9.20 N	16.09 E
Berea, Ky., U.S.	192	37.34 N	84.17 W
Berea, Ohio, U.S.	214	41.22 N	81.52 W
Bere Alston	42	50.29 N	4.11 W
Beregajevo	86	57.10 N	87.32 E
Beregomet	78	48.12 N	25.21 E
Beregovo	78	48.13 N	22.39 E
Beregovoj	86	55.12 N	73.12 E
Bereguardo	62	45.15 N	9.01 E
Bereka ≃	78	49.12 N	36.59 E
Bereketli	130	40.31 N	37.18 E
Bereku	154	4.27 S	35.44 E
Berekua	240d	15.14 N	61.19 W
Berekum	150	7.27 N	2.37 W
Bérem	152	7.33 N	13.55 E
Berenda Slough ≃	226	37.00 N	120.29 W
Berendejevo	82	56.36 N	39.01 E
Berendža	89	54.35 N	136.18 E
Berens ≃	184	52.21 N	97.02 W
Berens Island I	184	52.18 N	97.17 W
Berens River	184	52.22 N	97.02 W
Bere Regis	42	50.46 N	2.14 W
Beresford, Austl.	166	29.14 S	136.40 E
Beresford, N.B., Can.	186	47.42 N	65.42 W
Beresford, S. Dak., U.S.	198	43.05 N	96.47 W
Beresina → Berezina ≃	76	52.33 N	30.14 E
Berestečko	78	50.23 N	25.07 E
Bereşti	38	46.06 N	27.53 E
Beretău (Berettyó) ≃	38	46.59 N	21.07 E
Berettyó (Beretău) ≃	38	46.59 N	21.07 E
Berettyóújfalu	30	47.14 N	21.32 E
Berevo, Madag.	157b	19.44 S	44.58 E
Berevo, Madag.	157b	17.14 S	44.17 E
Berezajka	76	57.59 N	33.54 E
Berezan'	78	50.19 N	31.30 E
Berezanskaja	78	45.43 N	39.34 E
Berežany	78	49.27 N	24.56 E
Berezdov	78	50.27 N	27.05 E
Berezina ≃, S.S.S.R.	76	53.48 N	25.59 E
Berezina ≃, S.S.S.R.	76	52.33 N	30.14 E
Berezino, S.S.S.R.	76	54.54 N	28.12 E
Berezino, S.S.S.R.	76	53.49 N	28.59 E
Berezino, S.S.S.R.	78	46.14 N	29.12 E
Berezino, S.S.S.R.	80	50.06 N	48.52 E
Berezna	78	51.34 N	31.47 E
Berezn'agi	78	49.59 N	41.06 E
Berezn'aki, S.S.S.R.	78	49.51 N	33.01 E
Berezn'aki, S.S.S.R.	78	49.09 N	31.57 E
Bereznegovatoje	78	47.20 N	32.49 E
Berežnica	78	51.27 N	26.27 E
Bereznik	78	62.51 N	42.40 E
Berezniki	86	59.24 N	56.46 E
Berford Lake ⊜	212	44.48 N	81.14 W
Berg, B.R.D.	64	47.58 N	11.21 E
Berg, Lux.	56	49.49 N	6.05 E
Berg, Nor.	28	69.26 N	17.15 E
Berg, Öst.	64	46.45 N	13.09 E
Berga, D.D.R.	54	51.27 N	11.00 E
Berga, D.D.R.	54	50.45 N	12.10 E
Berga, Esp.	34	42.06 N	1.51 E
Berga, Sve.	40	59.21 N	16.26 E
Bergama	130	39.07 N	27.11 E
Bergambacht	52	51.56 N	4.46 E
Bergamo	62	45.41 N	9.43 E
Bergamo □[4]	64	45.50 N	9.48 E
Bergantín	246	10.01 N	64.22 W
Bergantino	64	45.05 N	11.15 E
Bergbaumuseum ɤ	263	51.29 N	7.13 E
Bergby	26	60.56 N	17.02 E
Berge, B.R.D.	52	52.37 N	7.44 E
Berge, B.R.D.	263	51.21 N	7.22 E
Berge, D.D.R.	54	53.15 N	11.50 E
Bergedorf ⤚[8]	52	53.29 N	10.13 E
Bergei ∧[2]	263	51.13 N	7.46 E
Bergeijk	52	51.19 N	5.22 E
Bergen → Mons, Bel.	50	50.27 N	3.56 E
Bergen, B.R.D.	52	52.48 N	9.58 E
Bergen, B.R.D.	54	52.53 N	10.58 E
Bergen, B.R.D.	64	47.48 N	12.35 E
Bergen, Ned.	52	52.40 N	4.41 E
Bergen, Nor.	26	60.23 N	5.20 E
Bergen, N.Y., U.S.	210	43.05 N	77.57 W
Bergen □[6]	210	40.53 N	74.03 W
Bergen aan Zee	52	52.38 N	4.37 E
Bergen [auf Rügen]	54	54.25 N	13.26 E
Bergen Basin C	276	40.39 N	73.49 W
Bergen-Belsen-Denkmal ⊥	52	52.46 N	9.55 E
Berg en Dal	250	5.09 N	55.04 W
Bergenfield	210	40.55 N	74.00 W
Bergen Mall ⤚[9]	276	40.55 N	74.04 W
Bergen op Zoom	52	51.30 N	4.17 E
Berger	219	38.40 N	91.21 W
Bergerac	32	44.51 N	0.29 E
Bergères-Lès-Vertus	50	48.53 N	4.00 E
Bergerhof	263	51.12 N	7.21 E
Bergfelde	54	52.40 N	13.19 E
Berggiesshübel	54	50.52 N	13.57 E
Bergham	60	49.12 N	12.17 E
Berghausen, B.R.D.	263	51.07 N	6.55 E
Berghausen, B.R.D.	263	51.18 N	7.17 E
Bergheim, B.R.D.	56	50.55 N	6.38 E
Bergheim, Fr.	58	48.12 N	7.22 E
Bergheim, Öst.	64	47.50 N	13.02 E
Berghem	52	51.46 N	5.34 E
Berghofen ⤚[8]	263	51.29 N	7.32 E
Bergholtz	210	43.06 N	78.53 W
Bergholtz Creek ≃	284a	43.05 N	78.57 W
Bergholz	214	40.31 N	80.53 W
Bergholz-Rehbrücke	54	52.20 N	13.05 E
Bergisch-Born	263	51.09 N	7.15 E
Bergisches Land ⤚[1]	263	51.07 N	7.10 E
Bergisches Land, Naturpark ♠	263	51.07 N	7.29 E
Bergisch Gladbach	56	50.59 N	7.07 E
Bergkamen	52	51.38 N	7.38 E
Bergkvara	26	56.23 N	16.05 E
Bergland	190	46.35 N	89.34 W
Bergneustadt	56	51.01 N	7.39 E
Bergnicourt	50	49.25 N	4.15 E
Bergö I	26	62.58 N	21.11 E
Bergoo	188	38.29 N	80.18 W
Bergos	130	40.14 N	26.36 E
Bergplaas	158	33.54 S	22.40 E
Bergrheinfeld	56	50.00 N	10.10 E
Bergsäng	40	60.06 N	13.33 E
Bergsbrunna	40	59.49 N	17.43 E
Bergse Maas ≃	52	51.45 N	5.08 E
Bergshamra	40	59.38 N	18.37 E
Bergsjö	26	61.59 N	17.04 E
Bergslagen ⤚[1]	40	59.55 N	15.00 E
Bergstrasse-Odenwald, Naturpark ♠	56	49.40 N	9.00 E
Bergstrom Air Force Base ■	222	30.12 N	97.40 W
Bergtheim	56	49.54 N	10.04 E
Berguent	148	34.03 N	2.02 W
Bergues	50	50.58 N	2.26 E
Bergum	52	53.11 N	5.59 E
Bergün	58	46.38 N	9.45 E
Bergville	158	28.52 S	29.18 E
Bergvreten	40	60.31 N	16.26 E
Bergwitz	54	51.47 N	12.35 E
Berhala, Selat ʊ	112	0.48 S	104.25 E

PORTUGUÊS

Nome	Página	Lat.°′	Long.°′ W=Oeste
Berhampore	126	24.06 N	88.15 E
Berhampur	122	19.19 N	84.47 E
Beri, Bhārat	124	28.42 N	76.35 E
Beri, Pil.	116	12.41 N	124.22 E
Berici, Monti ⩘	64	45.26 N	11.31 E
Berih ≃	271c	1.23 N	103.40 E
Berikul'skij	86	55.32 N	88.08 E
Beringa, Ostrov I	74	55.00 N	165.15 E
Beringen	56	51.03 N	5.13 E
Bering Glacier ⍓	180	60.15 N	143.30 W
Beringhausen	56	51.24 N	8.46 E
Beringil	140	12.10 N	25.41 E
Beringin	112	3.41 S	104.18 E
Beringovskij	180	63.03 N	179.19 E
Bering Sea ⍑[2]	16	60.00 N	175.00 W
Bering Strait ʊ	180	65.30 N	169.00 W
Berislav	78	46.51 N	33.26 E
Berisso	258	34.52 S	57.53 W
Berisso □[5]	288	34.55 S	57.53 W
Berja	34	36.51 N	2.57 W
Berkåk	26	62.50 N	10.00 E
Berkane	148	34.59 N	2.20 W
Berkel ≃	52	52.09 N	6.12 E
Berkeley, Eng., U.K.	42	51.42 N	2.27 W
Berkeley, Calif., U.S.	226	37.57 N	122.18 W
Berkeley, Ill., U.S.	278	41.53 N	87.55 W
Berkeley, Mo., U.S.	219	38.45 N	90.20 W
Berkeley, R.I., U.S.	207	41.56 N	71.25 W
Berkeley, Vale of ∨	42	51.43 N	2.25 W
Berkeley Heights	210	40.41 N	74.27 W
Berkeley Hills	279b	40.32 N	80.00 W
Berkeley Hills ⩘[2]	282	37.54 N	122.16 W
Berkeley Springs	188	39.38 N	78.14 W
Berkhamsted	260	51.46 N	0.35 W
Berkheim	58	48.02 N	10.04 E
Berkley	207	41.51 N	71.05 W
Berkley Plantation ⊥	208	37.19 N	77.10 W
Berkner Island I	9	79.30 S	49.30 W
Berks □[6]	208	40.20 N	75.50 W
Berkshire, Mass., U.S.	207	42.30 N	73.12 W
Berkshire, N.Y., U.S.	210	42.18 N	76.11 W
Berkshire □[6], Eng., U.K.	42	51.30 N	1.20 W
Berkshire □[6], Mass., U.S.	207	42.27 N	73.15 W
Berkshire Downs ⩘[1]	42	51.33 N	1.24 W
Berkshire Hills ⩘[2]	207	42.20 N	73.10 W
Berlaar	56	51.07 N	4.39 E
Berlaimont	50	50.12 N	3.49 E
Berland ≃	182	54.01 N	116.50 W
Berlanga de Duero	34	41.28 N	2.51 W
Berlenga I	34	39.25 N	9.30 W
Berlengas ≃	250	5.39 S	42.19 W
Berlevåg	24	70.51 N	29.06 E
Berlicum	52	51.42 N	5.23 E
Berlikum	52	53.15 N	5.39 E
Berlin (West), B.R.D.	54 264a	52.31 N	13.24 E
Berlin (Ost), D.D.R.	54 264a	52.30 N	13.25 E
Berlin, S. Afr.	158	32.54 S	27.35 E
Berlin, Conn., U.S.	207	41.37 N	72.45 W
Berlin, Md., U.S.	208	38.20 N	75.13 W
Berlin, Mass., U.S.	207	42.23 N	71.38 W
Berlin, N.H., U.S.	188	44.29 N	71.10 W
Berlin, N.J., U.S.	208	39.48 N	74.57 W
Berlin, N.Y., U.S.	210	42.42 N	73.23 W
Berlin, Ohio, U.S.	214	40.34 N	81.48 W
Berlin, Pa., U.S.	188	39.55 N	78.57 W
Berlin, Wis., U.S.	190	43.58 N	88.55 W
Berlin □[5]	264a	52.33 N	13.30 E
Berlin, Mount ∧	9	76.03 S	135.52 W
Berlin Center	214	41.01 N	80.57 W
Berlinchen	54	53.13 N	12.34 E
Berliner Brücke ⤚[5]	263	51.27 N	6.47 E
Berliner Forst Düppel ♠	264a	52.25 N	13.07 E
Berliner Forst Grunewald ♠	264a	52.28 N	13.13 E
Berliner Mauer (Berlin Wall) ⊥	264a	52.35 N	13.22 E
Berliner Stadtforst Spandau ♠	264a	52.35 N	13.10 E
Berlinguet Inlet C	176	71.10 N	85.35 W
Berlin Heights	214	41.20 N	82.30 W
Berlin-ichthyosaur State Park ♠	204	38.51 N	117.35 W
Berlin Lake ⊜[1]	214	41.00 N	81.00 W
Berlin Mountain ∧	210	42.42 N	73.17 W
Berlinsville	210	40.47 N	75.35 W
Berlin-Tegel, Flughafen ⊠	264a	52.34 N	13.18 E
Berlin-Tempelhof, Zentralflughafen ⊠	264a	52.29 N	13.25 E
Bermagui	166	36.25 S	150.04 E
Bermejillo	232	25.53 N	103.37 W
Bermejo	252	31.37 S	67.39 W
Bermejo ≃	252	26.51 S	58.23 W
Bermejo, Paso de)(	252	32.50 S	70.05 W
Bermen, Lac ⊜	176	53.35 N	68.55 W
Bermeo	34	43.26 N	2.43 W
Bermillo de Sayago	34	41.22 N	6.06 W
Bermo	124	23.47 N	85.57 E
Bermondsey ⤚[8]	260	51.30 N	0.04 W
Bermuda □[2]	230 240a	32.20 N	64.45 W
Bermudes → Bermuda □[2]	240a	32.20 N	64.45 W
Bermudian Creek ≃	208	40.01 N	76.55 W
Bern (Berne)	58	46.57 N	7.26 E
Bern (Berne) □[3]	58	46.55 N	7.35 E
Berna → Bern	58	46.57 N	7.26 E
Bernabéu, Estadio ♠	266a	40.27 N	3.41 W
Bernal ⤚[8]	258	34.42 S	58.17 W
Bernalda	68	40.24 N	16.41 E
Bernam ≃	114	3.48 N	100.57 E
Bernardston	207	42.40 N	72.33 W
Bernardsville	210	40.43 N	74.34 W
Bernasconi	252	37.54 S	63.43 W
Bernate	266b	45.29 N	8.49 E
Bernau am Chiemsee	64	47.48 N	12.22 E
Bernau bei Berlin	54	52.40 N	13.35 E
Bernaville	50	50.08 N	2.10 E
Bernay	50	49.06 N	0.36 E
Bern-Belp, Flughafen ⊠	58	46.55 N	7.30 E
Bernbeuren	58	47.44 N	10.46 E
Bernburg	54	51.48 N	11.44 E
Berndorf	61	47.57 N	16.08 E
Berne, B.R.D.	52	53.11 N	8.29 E
Berne → Bern, Schw.	58	46.57 N	7.26 E
Berne, Ind., U.S.	216	40.39 N	84.57 W
Berne, N.Y., U.S.	210	42.38 N	74.08 W
Berneburg	56	51.04 N	9.53 E
Berner Alpen ⩘	58	46.30 N	7.30 E
Berneray I	46	57.43 N	7.12 W
Berneval-le-Grand	50	49.57 N	1.12 E
Berngardovka	265a	60.01 N	30.36 E
Bernhardina	158	27.53 S	28.40 E
Bernhards Bay	210	43.15 N	75.56 W
Bernice	194	32.49 N	92.39 W
Bernie	194	36.40 N	89.58 W
Bernier Bay C	176	71.00 N	87.30 W
Bernier Island I	162	24.52 S	113.08 E
Bernina ⩘	58	46.22 N	9.50 E
Bernina, Passo del)(	58	46.24 N	10.03 E
Bernina, Piz ∧	58	46.21 N	9.51 E
Bernisdale	46	57.27 N	6.24 W
Bernkastel-Kues	56	49.55 N	7.04 E
Bernried, B.R.D.	60	49.19 N	12.33 E
Bernried, B.R.D.	64	47.52 N	11.17 E
Bernrieth	60	49.34 N	12.17 E
Bernsbach	54	50.34 N	12.46 E
Bernsdorf	54	51.22 N	14.04 E
Bernsfelden	56	49.34 N	9.53 E
Bernstadt, D.D.R.	54	51.03 N	14.50 E
Bernstadt → Bierutów, Pol.	30	51.08 N	17.32 E
Bernstein, B.R.D.	60	49.50 N	12.09 E
Bernstein → Pełczyce, Pol.	30	53.03 N	15.18 E
Bernville	208	40.26 N	76.07 W
Bero ≃	152	15.10 S	12.09 E
Beroga	114	2.56 N	101.55 E
Beroldingen ⊥	58	46.55 N	8.36 E
Berolzheim	56	49.28 N	9.32 E
Beromünster	58	47.12 N	8.11 E
Berón de Astrada	252	27.33 S	57.32 W
Beror H̱ayil	132	31.33 N	34.38 E
Beroroha	157b	21.41 S	45.10 E
Ber'ostovica	76	53.07 N	23.58 E
Béroubouay	150	10.32 N	2.44 E
Beroun	30	49.58 N	14.04 E
Berounka ≃	30	50.00 N	14.24 E
Berovo	38	41.42 N	22.51 E
Berowra	170	33.37 S	151.09 E
Ber'oza, S.S.S.R.	76	52.32 N	24.59 E
Ber'oza, S.S.S.R.	78	51.44 N	33.52 E
Ber'ozno	78	51.00 N	26.45 E
Ber'ožnoje	76	59.55 N	39.17 E
Ber'ozovaja ≃	80	48.31 N	41.03 E
Ber'ozovaja Rudka	78	50.19 N	32.14 E
Ber'ozovka, S.S.S.R.	24	65.00 N	56.26 E
Ber'ozovka, S.S.S.R.	76	53.43 N	25.30 E
Ber'ozovka, S.S.S.R.	76	53.26 N	38.53 E
Ber'ozovka, S.S.S.R.	78	45.35 N	33.20 E
Ber'ozovka, S.S.S.R.	78	47.12 N	30.55 E
Ber'ozovka, S.S.S.R.	78	47.49 N	32.28 E
Ber'ozovka, S.S.S.R.	80	52.06 N	45.07 E
Ber'ozovka, S.S.S.R.	80	51.11 N	53.16 E
Ber'ozovka, S.S.S.R.	86	57.37 N	57.18 E
Ber'ozovka, S.S.S.R.	86	54.02 N	76.35 E
Ber'ozovka, S.S.S.R.	86	51.51 N	82.58 E
Ber'ozovka, S.S.S.R.	86	59.24 N	82.38 E
Ber'ozovka, S.S.S.R.	86	59.35 N	56.02 E
Ber'ozovka, S.S.S.R.	88	57.46 N	116.09 E
Ber'ozovka, S.S.S.R.	88	56.03 N	93.07 E
Ber'ozovka, S.S.S.R.	89	50.35 N	127.52 E
Ber'ozovka, S.S.S.R.	265a	59.56 N	30.49 E
Ber'ozovo, S.S.S.R.	74	63.56 N	65.02 E
Ber'ozovo, S.S.S.R.	78	51.35 N	27.20 E
Ber'ozovo, S.S.S.R.	80	51.56 N	48.28 E
Ber'ozovo, S.S.S.R.	82	54.19 N	41.01 E
Ber'ozovo, S.S.S.R.	82	54.03 N	36.24 E
Ber'ozovskaja	80	50.16 N	43.59 E
Ber'ozovskij	86	55.39 N	86.16 E
Ber'ozovskij R'adok	76	58.06 N	34.29 E
Ber'ozovskoje	86	55.50 N	89.36 E
Ber'ozovyj, Ostrov I	76	60.18 N	28.38 E
Berra	64	44.59 N	11.58 E
Berras, Arroyo los ≃	288	34.34 S	58.40 W
Berre ≃	62	44.24 N	4.40 E
Berre, Étang de C	62	43.28 N	5.11 E
Berrechid	148	33.17 N	7.35 W
Berre-des-Alpes	62	43.50 N	7.19 E
Berre-l'Étang	62	43.28 N	5.11 E
Ber Remad, Oued ∨	148	31.45 N	1.10 E
Berri	166	34.17 S	140.36 E
Berriane	148	32.50 N	3.46 E
Berridale	171b	36.22 S	148.50 E
Berriedale	46	58.11 N	3.29 W
Berrien □[6]	216	41.59 N	86.30 W
Berrien Springs	216	41.57 N	86.20 W
Berrigan	166	35.40 S	145.49 E
Berrima	170	34.30 S	150.20 E
Berriozábal	234	16.48 N	93.16 W
Berrouaghia	34	36.08 N	2.55 E
Berrugosa Point >	116	10.23 N	125.33 E
Berry, Austl.	170	34.47 S	150.42 E
Berry, Ala., U.S.	194	33.39 N	87.36 W
Berry, Ky., U.S.	218	38.31 N	84.23 W
Berry □[9]	50	47.20 N	2.10 E
Berry, Canal du ≍	50	47.17 N	1.25 E
Berry-au-Bac	50	49.24 N	3.54 E
Berry Creek ≃, Alta., Can.	182	50.50 N	111.36 W
Berry Creek ≃, Tex., U.S.	222	30.40 N	97.36 W
Berryessa, Lake ⊜[1]	226	38.35 N	122.14 W
Berryessa Creek ≃	282	37.24 N	121.53 W
Berryessa Peak ∧	226	38.40 N	122.11 W
Berry Head >	42	50.24 N	3.29 W
Berry Islands II	238	25.34 S	77.45 W
Berry Mountain ∧	208	40.31 N	77.02 W
Berrysburg	208	40.36 N	76.49 W
Berrys Creek ≃	276	40.47 N	74.05 W
Berryville, Ark., U.S.	194	36.22 N	93.34 W
Berryville, Va., U.S.	188	39.09 N	77.59 W
Beršad'	78	48.23 N	29.30 E
Berseba	156	26.00 S	17.46 E
Bersenbrück	52	52.33 N	7.56 E
Bersimis 2 Dam ⤚[6]	186	49.22 N	69.47 W
Bersimis Indian Reserve ⤚[4]	186	49.05 N	68.37 W
Bersut	80	55.32 N	50.54 E
Bertam	114	5.09 N	102.03 E
Bertasuyu ≃	84	41.09 N	41.53 E
Berté, Lac ⊜	186	50.48 N	68.30 W
Bertha	198	46.16 N	95.04 W
Berthåga	40	59.52 N	17.35 E
Berthelsdorf	54	51.05 N	14.13 E
Berthier □[6]	206	46.30 N	73.45 W
Berthierville	206	46.05 N	73.10 W
Berthold	198	48.19 N	101.44 W
Berthoud	200	40.18 N	105.05 W
Berthoud Pass)(	200	39.45 N	105.45 W
Bertincourt	50	50.05 N	2.59 E
Bertinoro	66	44.09 N	12.08 E
Bertioga	256	23.51 S	46.09 W
Bertioga, Enseada da C	256	23.50 S	46.08 W
Bertkow	54	52.43 N	11.54 E
Bertlich	263	51.37 N	7.04 E
Bertogne	56	50.05 N	5.40 E
Bertolínia	250	7.38 S	43.57 W
Bertoua	152	4.35 N	13.41 E
Bertraghboy Bay C	48	52.12 N	6.50 W
Bertram	196	30.45 N	98.03 W
Bertrand, Mich., U.S.	216	41.46 N	86.16 W
Bertrand, Nebr., U.S.	198	40.32 N	99.38 W
Bertrix	56	49.51 N	5.15 E
Bertry	50	50.05 N	3.27 E
Beruas	114	4.30 N	100.47 E
Beruri	246	3.54 S	61.22 W
Berville	214	42.55 N	82.53 W
Berville-sur-Mer	50	49.26 N	0.22 E
Berwang	58	47.24 N	10.45 E
Berwick, Austl.	169	38.02 S	145.21 E
Berwick, N.S., Can.	186	45.03 N	64.44 W
Berwick, La., U.S.	194	29.42 N	91.13 W
Berwick, Maine, U.S.	188	43.16 N	70.51 W
Berwick, Pa., U.S.	210	41.03 N	76.15 W
Berwick-upon-Tweed	44	55.46 N	2.00 W
Berwyn, Ill., U.S.	216	41.50 N	87.47 W
Berwyn, Pa., U.S.	208	40.03 N	75.27 W
Berwyn ⩘	42	52.53 N	3.24 W
Berwyn Heights	284c	38.59 N	76.54 W
Bērze ≃	76	56.41 N	23.37 E
Berzé-la-Ville	58	46.22 N	4.42 E
Berz-Macomb Airport ⊠	281	42.40 N	82.58 W
Bès ≃	62	44.08 N	6.14 E
Besalampy	157b	16.45 S	44.30 E
Besana in Brianza	62	45.42 N	9.17 E
Besançon	58	47.15 N	6.02 E
Besani	124	24.08 N	80.17 E
Besar, Gunong ∧, Malay.	114	5.10 N	101.18 E
Besar, Gunong ∧, Malay.	114	2.30 N	103.10 E
Besar, Pulau I	115b	8.28 S	122.22 E
Besar Hantu, Gunong ∧	114	3.12 N	102.02 E
Besaya ≃	34	43.21 N	4.04 W
Besbes	36	36.42 N	7.51 E
Besed' ≃	76	52.38 N	31.09 E
Besedino	78	51.42 N	36.28 E
Besedy	265b	55.37 N	37.47 E
Besenfeld	56	48.35 N	8.25 E
Bešenkoviči	76	55.03 N	29.27 E
Beserah	114	3.52 N	103.22 E
Besigheim	56	49.00 N	9.08 E
Besikama	112	9.36 S	124.57 E
Beşiktaş ⤚[8]	267b	41.03 N	29.01 E
Beşiri	130	37.55 N	41.18 E
Besitang	114	4.02 N	98.12 E
Beškent	128	38.49 N	65.39 E
Beskid Mountains ⩘	30	49.40 N	20.00 E
Beškube	85	39.50 N	68.18 E
Beskudnikovo ⤚[8]	265b	55.52 N	37.34 E
Beslan	84	43.12 N	44.33 E
Beslenej	84	44.14 N	41.44 E
Besnard Lake ⊜	184	55.24 N	106.05 W
Besni	130	37.41 N	37.52 E
Besor, Naẖal ∨	132	31.28 N	34.22 E
Besós ≃	266d	41.25 N	2.04 E
Besozzo	62	45.51 N	8.39 E
Besp'atovo	82	54.45 N	38.54 E
Beşpınar	130	41.09 N	35.14 E
Besputa ≃	82	54.50 N	37.58 E
Bessa Monteiro	152	7.07 S	13.44 E
Bessancourt	261	49.02 N	2.13 E
Bessans	62	45.19 N	7.00 E
Bessarabia □[9]	38	47.00 N	28.30 E
Bessarabka, S.S.S.R.	78	46.20 N	28.58 E
Bessarabka, S.S.S.R.	86	53.37 N	73.17 E
Besse, B.R.D.	56	51.13 N	9.23 E
Besse, Nig.	150	11.15 N	4.30 E
Bessèges	62	44.17 N	4.06 E
Bessemer, Ala., U.S.	194	33.25 N	86.57 W
Bessemer, Mich., U.S.	190	46.27 N	89.24 W
Bessemer, Pa., U.S.	214	40.59 N	80.30 W
Bessemer City	192	35.17 N	81.17 W
Besser	41	55.52 N	10.39 E
Bessé-sur-Braye	50	47.50 N	0.45 E
Bessheim	26	61.31 N	8.51 E
Besshiyama	96	33.50 N	133.23 E
Bessho	270	34.27 N	135.31 E
Bessonovka	80	53.18 N	45.03 E
Best	52	51.31 N	5.24 E
Best'ach	74	61.52 N	129.55 E
Bestamak, S.S.S.R.	86	49.43 N	55.07 E
Bestamak, S.S.S.R.	86	49.13 N	78.21 E
Beštau, Gora ∧	84	44.06 N	43.01 E
Besten	263	51.39 N	6.54 E
Bestensee	54	52.15 N	13.37 E
Bestobe	86	52.30 N	73.05 E
Beštor, Gora ∧	85	42.03 N	70.50 E
Bestuževo	24	61.37 N	43.58 E
Besuki	115a	7.45 S	113.41 E
Besut ≃	114	5.48 N	102.35 E
Beswick Aboriginal Reserve ⤚[4]	164	14.30 S	133.10 E
Betā	272b	22.55 N	88.14 E
Betafo	157b	19.50 S	46.51 E
Betāgi	126	22.25 N	90.11 E
Bet Alfa	132	32.31 N	35.26 E
Beta Main Canal ≍	226	36.34 N	120.11 W
Betamba	152	2.13 S	21.23 E
Betang Melaka	114	2.28 N	102.25 E
Betano	112	9.10 S	125.43 E
Betanzos, Bol.	248	19.34 S	65.27 W
Betanzos, Esp.	34	43.17 N	8.12 W
Betanzos, Ría de C[1]	34	43.23 N	8.15 W
Bétaré Oya	152	5.36 N	14.05 E
Betarsjön ⊜	26	63.44 N	16.52 E
Bet Bet Creek ≃	169	36.52 S	143.52 E
Betbetti	140	15.06 N	24.12 E
Betchworth	260	51.14 N	0.16 W
Bet Dagan	132	32.00 N	34.50 E
Betém	256	22.52 S	44.17 W
Bétera	34	39.35 N	0.27 W
Bétérou	150	9.12 N	2.16 E
Bet Guvrin	132	31.36 N	34.54 E
Bet Ha'arava	132	31.48 N	35.32 E
Bethal	158	26.27 S	29.28 E
Bethalto	219	38.55 N	90.03 W
Bethanien	156	26.32 S	17.11 E
Bethanien □[5]	156	26.30 S	17.00 E
Bethany, Conn., U.S.	207	41.26 N	73.01 W
Bethany, Ill., U.S.	219	39.39 N	88.44 W
Bethany, Mo., U.S.	194	40.16 N	94.02 W
Bethany, N.Y., U.S.	210	42.55 N	78.08 W
Bethany, Okla., U.S.	196	35.31 N	97.38 W
Bethany, Pa., U.S.	210	41.37 N	75.21 W
Bethany, W. Va., U.S.	214	40.12 N	80.33 W
Bethany Reservoir ⊜[1]	226	37.47 N	121.37 W
Bet HaShitta	132	32.33 N	35.26 E
Bethel, Alaska, U.S.	180	60.48 N	161.46 W
Bethel, Conn., U.S.	207	41.22 N	73.25 W
Bethel, Del., U.S.	208	38.34 N	75.37 W
Bethel, Ky., U.S.	218	38.15 N	83.52 W
Bethel, Maine, U.S.	188	44.25 N	70.48 W
Bethel, Mo., U.S.	219	39.53 N	92.02 W
Bethel, N.C., U.S.	192	35.48 N	77.22 W
Bethel, N.Y., U.S.	210	41.41 N	74.52 W
Bethel, Ohio, U.S.	218	38.58 N	84.05 W
Bethel, Pa., U.S.	208	40.28 N	76.18 W
Bethel, Wash., U.S.	224	47.32 N	122.38 W
Bethel Island	226	38.01 N	121.39 W
Bethel Manor	208	37.06 N	76.25 W
Bethel Park	214	40.18 N	80.02 W
Bethelsdorp	158	33.52 S	25.34 E
Bethel Springs	194	35.14 N	88.36 W
Béthencourt-sur-Mer	50	50.05 N	1.30 E
Bethersden	42	51.08 N	0.48 E
Bethesda, Wales, U.K.	44	53.11 N	4.03 W
Bethesda, Md., U.S.	208	38.59 N	77.06 W
Bethesda, Ohio, U.S.	188	40.01 N	81.04 W
Bethesdaweg	158	31.55 S	24.45 E
Béthisy-Saint-Pierre	50	49.18 N	2.49 E
Bethlehem, S. Afr.	158	28.15 S	28.15 E
Bethlehem, Conn., U.S.	207	41.38 N	73.13 W
Bethlehem, Ind., U.S.	218	38.32 N	85.25 W
Bethlehem, Ky., U.S.	218	38.24 N	85.04 W
Bethlehem, Pa., U.S.	210	40.37 N	75.25 W
Bethlehem, W. Va., U.S.	188	40.02 N	80.40 W
Bethlehem → Bayt Laẖm, Urd.	132	31.43 N	35.12 E
Bethlehem Center	210	42.40 N	73.42 W
Bethlehem Steel Corporation ɤ[3], Md., U.S.	284b	39.13 N	76.29 W
Bethlehem Steel Corporation (Lackawanna Plant) ɤ[3], N.Y., U.S.	284a	42.49 N	78.52 W
Bethnal Green ⤚[8]	260	51.32 N	0.03 W
Bethoncourt	58	47.32 N	6.48 E
Bethpage	210	40.45 N	73.29 W
Bethpage State Park ♠	210	40.45 N	73.27 W
Bethulie	158	30.32 S	25.59 E
Bethune, Sask., Can.	184	50.43 N	105.08 W
Béthune, Fr.	50	50.32 N	2.38 E
Bethune, S.C., U.S.	192	34.25 N	80.21 W
Béthune ≃	50	49.53 N	1.09 E
Beticos, Sistemas ⩘	34	37.00 N	4.00 W
Betijoque	246	9.23 N	70.44 W
Betil	126	24.14 N	89.43 E
Betio	174t	1.21 N	172.56 E
Betioky, Madag.	157b	23.42 S	44.22 E
Betioky, Madag.	157b	22.27 S	43.44 E
Betis ≃	114	4.53 N	101.48 E
Betlica	76	54.01 N	33.57 E
Bet Netofa, Biq'at ≋	132	32.49 N	35.19 E
Betnoti	126	21.44 N	86.51 E
Beton-Bazoches	50	48.42 N	3.15 E
Betong, Malay.	112	1.24 N	111.31 E
Betong, Thai	110	5.45 N	101.05 E
Betoota	166	25.42 S	140.44 E
Betor	144	11.40 N	39.00 E
Bétou	152	3.03 N	18.31 E
Betpak-Dala ⤚[2]	86	46.00 N	70.00 E
Betroka	157b	23.16 S	46.06 E
Betsham	260	51.25 N	0.19 E
Bet Sh'ean	132	32.30 N	35.30 E
Bet She'arim, H̱orbat ⊥	132	32.42 N	35.08 E
Bet Shemesh	132	31.45 N	35.00 E
Betsiamites	186	48.56 N	68.38 W
Betsiamites ≃	186	48.56 N	68.38 W
Betsiamites, Pointe >	186	48.55 N	68.37 W
Betsiboka ≃	157b	16.03 S	46.36 E
Betsie, Point >	190	44.42 N	86.16 W
Betsioky	157b	21.31 S	44.28 E
Betsy Layne	192	37.33 N	82.38 W
Bette ∧	146	22.00 N	19.12 E
Bettembourg	56	49.32 N	6.02 E
Bettendorf	190	41.32 N	90.30 W
Betterton	208	39.52 N	76.04 W
Bettiah	124	26.48 N	84.30 E
Bettie	222	32.48 N	94.58 W
Bettles Field	180	66.55 N	151.30 W
Bettola	62	44.47 N	9.36 E
Bettona	66	43.01 N	12.29 E
Bettrath ⤚[8]	263	51.13 N	6.26 E
Bettsville	214	41.15 N	83.14 W
Bettyhill	46	58.32 N	4.14 W
Betty's Bay	158	34.22 S	18.52 E
Betūl	124	21.55 N	77.54 E
Betūl □[5]	124	22.00 N	78.00 E
Betumbe-Bongo	152	2.11 S	18.46 E
Betung, Indon.	112	1.52 S	103.16 E
Betung, Indon.	112	2.50 S	104.14 E
Betuwe ⤚[1]	52	51.55 N	5.30 E
Betwa ≃	124	25.55 N	80.12 E
Betws-y-Coed	44	53.05 N	3.48 W
Betz	50	49.09 N	2.57 E
Betz ≃	50	48.09 N	2.45 E
Betzdorf	56	50.47 N	7.53 E
Betzenstein	60	49.41 N	11.25 E
Béu	152	6.14 S	15.28 E
Beucha	54	51.19 N	12.34 E
Beuel	56	50.38 N	7.14 E
Beugneux	50	49.14 N	3.25 E
Beuil	62	44.06 N	6.59 E
Beulah, Austl.	166	35.56 S	142.26 E
Beulah, Colo., U.S.	200	38.05 N	104.59 W
Beulah, Mich., U.S.	190	44.38 N	86.06 W
Beulah, Miss., U.S.	194	33.42 N	90.59 W
Beulah, N. Dak., U.S.	198	47.16 N	101.47 W
Beulah, Lake ⊜	216	42.49 N	88.23 W
Beulah Beach	214	41.25 N	82.22 W
Beulah Reservoir ⊜[1]	202	43.56 N	118.09 W
Beulaville	192	34.55 N	77.46 W
Beult ≃	260	51.14 N	0.25 E
Beure	58	47.12 N	6.00 E
Beuron	58	48.03 N	8.58 E
Beuthen → Bytom	30	50.22 N	18.54 E
Beuvron ≃, Fr.	50	47.28 N	3.31 E
Beuvron ≃, Fr.	50	47.29 N	1.15 E
Beuvronne ≃	261	48.56 N	2.44 E
Beuvry	50	50.31 N	2.41 E
Beuzeville	50	49.20 N	0.21 E
Bevagna	66	42.56 N	12.36 E
Bevensen	52	53.05 N	10.34 E
Bever ≃	52	52.01 N	7.46 E
Bevera ≃	62	43.49 N	7.34 E
Beveren	50	51.13 N	4.15 E
Beverino	62	44.14 N	9.47 E
Beverley, Austl.	168a	32.06 S	116.56 E
Beverley, Eng., U.K.	44	53.52 N	0.26 W
Beverley Minster ɤ[1]	44	53.50 N	0.27 W
Beverlo	56	51.05 N	5.12 E
Beverly, Mass., U.S.	207	42.33 N	70.53 W
Beverly, N.J., U.S.	208	40.04 N	74.55 W
Beverly, Ohio, U.S.	188	39.33 N	81.38 W
Beverly, Tex., U.S.	222	31.30 N	97.10 W
Beverly ⤚[8]	278	41.43 N	87.41 W
Beverly Farms, Md., U.S.	284c	39.04 N	77.11 W
Beverly Farms, Mass., U.S.	283	42.34 N	70.49 W
Beverly Harbor C	283	42.32 N	70.53 W
Beverly Hills, Austl.	274a	33.57 S	151.05 E
Beverly Hills, Calif., U.S.	228	34.03 N	118.26 W
Beverly Hills, Fla., U.S.	220	28.56 N	82.28 W
Beverly Hills, Mich., U.S.	216	42.32 N	83.15 W
Beverly Lake ⊜	176	64.36 N	100.30 W
Beverly Municipal Airport ⊠	283	42.35 N	70.55 W
Beverly Run ≃	208	37.55 N	77.11 W
Beverly Shores	216	41.41 N	87.00 W
Bevern	52	51.51 N	9.29 E
Beverstausee ⊜[1]	263	51.09 N	7.23 E
Beverstedt	52	53.26 N	8.49 E
Beverungen	52	51.39 N	9.22 E
Beverwijk	52	52.28 N	4.40 E
Bevier	194	39.45 N	92.34 W
Bevin, Lac ⊜	206	45.57 N	74.35 W
Bevoalavo	157b	25.13 S	45.26 E
Bewār	124	27.13 N	79.18 E
Bewdley, Ont., Can.	212	44.05 N	78.19 W
Bewdley, Eng., U.K.	42	52.22 N	2.19 W
Bex	58	46.15 N	7.01 E
Bexhill on Sea	42	50.50 N	0.29 E
Bexley, Austl.	274a	33.57 S	151.08 E
Bexley, Ohio, U.S.	218	39.58 N	82.56 W
Bexley ⤚[8]	260	51.26 N	0.10 E
Beyazköy	130	41.21 N	27.42 E
Beybach ≃	56	50.13 N	7.23 E
Beyçayırı	130	40.15 N	26.55 E
Beyce	130	39.54 N	29.00 E
Beycuma	130	41.19 N	31.59 E
Bey Dağları ⩘	130	36.40 N	30.15 E
Beydili	130	40.10 N	31.01 E
Beyenburg ⤚[8]	263	51.15 N	7.18 E
Beykoz	130	41.08 N	29.05 E
Beyla	150	8.41 N	8.37 W
Beyla □[4]	150	8.55 N	8.25 W
Beylerbeyi ⤚[8]	267b	41.03 N	29.03 E
Beylikahır	130	39.42 N	31.13 E
Beylul	144	13.10 N	42.26 E
Beynes	261	48.51 N	1.53 E
Beynes-Thiverval, Aérodrome de ⊠	261	48.51 N	1.54 E
Beyoğlu ⤚[8]	267b	41.02 N	28.59 E
Beypazarı	130	40.10 N	31.56 E
Beypınarı	130	39.31 N	37.44 E
Beypore	122	11.11 N	75.49 E
Beyrouth → Bayrūt	130	33.53 N	35.30 E
Beyşehir	130	37.41 N	31.43 E
Beyşehir Gölü ⊜	130	37.40 N	31.30 E
Bezaha	157b	23.30 S	44.31 E
Bežanicy	76	56.58 N	29.53 E
Bezau	58	47.23 N	9.54 E
Bezavona ∧	157b	15.02 S	49.52 E
Bezdež	76	52.19 N	25.18 E
Bezděz ∧	54	50.32 N	14.43 E
Bezděz ⊥	54	50.32 N	14.46 E
Bezdružice	60	49.55 N	12.59 E
Bèze	58	47.28 N	5.16 E
Bežeck	76	57.47 N	36.39 E
Bežeckij Verch ⩘[1]	76	57.36 N	36.54 E
Bezenčuk	80	52.59 N	49.26 E
Bezerra ≃	255	13.16 S	47.31 W
Bezerros	250	8.14 S	35.45 W
Bezet	132	33.05 N	35.08 E

≃ River	Fluss	Río	Rivière	Rio
≍ Canal	Kanal	Canal	Canal	Canal
ᒐ Waterfall, Rapids	Wasserfall, Stromschnellen	Cascada, Rápidos	Chute d'eau, Rapides	Cascata, Rápidos
ʊ Strait	Meeresstrasse	Estrecho	Détroit	Estreito
C Bay, Gulf	Bucht, Golf	Bahía, Golfo	Baie, Golfe	Baía, Golfo
⊜ Lake, Lakes	See, Seen	Lago, Lagos	Lac, Lacs	Lago, Lagos
≋ Swamp	Sumpf	Pantano	Marais	Pântano
⍓ Ice Features, Glacier	Eis- und Gletscherformen	Accidentes Glaciales	Formes glaciaires	Acidentes Glaciares
⍑ Other Hydrographic Features	Andere Hydrographische Objekte	Otros Elementos Hidrográficos	Autres données hydrographiques	Outros Elementos Hidrográficos

⤙ Submarine Features	Untermeerische Objekte	Accidentes Submarinos	Formes de relief sous-marin	Acidentes Submarinos
□ Political Unit	Politische Einheit	Unidad Politica	Entité politique	Unidade Política
ɤ Cultural Institution	Kulturelle Institution	Institución Cultural	Institution culturelle	Instituição Cultural
⊥ Historical Site	Historische Stätte	Sitio Histórico	Site historique	Sitio Histórico
♠ Recreational Site	Erholungs- und Ferienort	Sitio de Recreo	Centre de loisirs	Sítio de Lazer
⊠ Airport	Flughafen	Aeropuerto	Aéroport	Aeroporto
■ Military Installation	Militäranlage	Instalación Militar	Installation militaire	Instalação Militar
⤚ Miscellaneous	Verschiedenes	Misceláneo	Divers	Miscelânea

ENGLISH — Name, Page, Lat.°′, Long.°′ / DEUTSCH — Name, Seite, Breite°′, Länge°′ E=Ost

Name	Page	Lat.°′	Long.°′
Béziers	32	43.21 N	3.15 E
Bezmein	128	38.05 N	58.12 E
Bezmenšur	80	56.29 N	51.17 E
Bezons	261	48.56 N	2.13 E
Bežta	84	42.08 N	46.08 E
Bezwada → Vijayawāda	122	16.31 N	80.37 E
Bezym'anka	80	49.56 N	43.15 E
Bezym'annaja	80	51.20 N	46.26 E
Bezymennoje	83	47.06 N	37.56 E
Bezzecca	64	45.55 N	10.43 E
Bezzubovo	82	55.27 N	38.55 E
Bhabānipur, Bhārat	272b	22.57 N	88.27 E
Bhabānipur, Bhārat	272b	22.56 N	88.13 E
Bhābta	126	23.59 N	88.15 E
Bhabua	124	25.03 N	83.37 E
Bhadarwah	123	32.59 N	75.43 E
Bhadaur	123	30.29 N	75.19 E
Bhādgāon → Bhaktapur	124	27.42 N	85.27 E
Bhadohi	124	25.25 N	82.34 E
Bhādra	123	29.07 N	75.10 E
Bhadra ⊜[1]	122	13.42 N	75.35 E
Bhadrāchalam	122	17.40 N	80.53 E
Bhadrakh	120	21.04 N	86.30 E
Bhadrāvati	122	13.52 N	75.43 E
Bhadreswar	126	22.50 N	88.21 E
Bhādua	272b	22.41 N	88.12 E
Bhāg	120	29.02 N	67.49 E
Bhagaiya	124	25.12 N	87.29 E
Bhāgalpur	124	25.15 N	87.00 E
Bhāgalpur □[5]	124	25.00 N	87.00 E
Bhāgīrathi ≃, Bhārat	126	23.25 N	88.23 E
Bhagirathpur	126	24.05 N	88.29 E
Bhagwānpur	126	22.07 N	87.45 E
Bhāi Pheru	123	31.12 N	73.57 E
Bhairab ≃[1]	126	22.51 N	89.34 E
Bhairab Bāzār	120	24.04 N	90.58 E
Bhairawa	124	27.31 N	83.24 E
Bhaironghāti	120	31.01 N	78.53 E
Bhaisa	122	19.06 N	77.58 E
Bhakkar	123	31.38 N	71.04 E
Bhākra Dam ◆[6]	123	31.24 N	76.30 E
Bhaktapur	124	27.42 N	85.27 E
Bhal	272c	19.11 N	73.08 E
Bhālki	122	18.02 N	77.13 E
Bhalswa ◆[8]	272a	28.44 N	77.10 E
Bhalwāl	123	32.16 N	72.54 E
Bhamo	110	24.16 N	97.14 E
Bhandāra	120	21.10 N	79.39 E
Bhandārdaha	272b	22.37 N	88.13 E
Bhandāria	126	22.29 N	90.04 E
Bhānder	124	25.44 N	78.45 E
Bhander Plateau ⩕[1]	124	24.10 N	80.20 E
Bhāndup ◆[8]	272c	19.09 N	72.57 E
Bhānga	126	23.22 N	89.59 E
Bhāngar	126	22.31 N	88.37 E
Bhānvad	120	21.56 N	69.47 E
Bhārat → India □[1]	118	20.00 N	77.00 E
Bharatpur, Bhārat	124	27.13 N	77.29 E
Bharatpur, Bhārat	126	23.53 N	88.05 E
Bharatpur □[5]	124	27.00 N	77.15 E
Bharthana	124	26.45 N	79.14 E
Bhātai	126	23.36 N	89.11 E
Bhātāpāra	120	21.44 N	81.56 E
Bhātār	126	23.25 N	87.54 E
Bhatewar	120	24.38 N	74.00 E
Bhatgaon → Bhaktapur	124	27.42 N	85.27 E
Bhātghar Lake ⊜[1]	122	18.12 N	73.49 E
Bhātiāpāra Ghāt	124	23.13 N	89.42 E
Bhatinda	123	30.12 N	74.57 E
Bhatkal	122	13.58 N	74.34 E
Bhātpāra	126	22.52 N	88.24 E
Bhātpur	272b	22.43 N	88.25 E
Bhātsāla	126	22.33 N	90.30 E
Bhattapratāp	126	22.45 N	89.48 E
Bhattiprolu	122	16.06 N	80.47 E
Bhātua	272b	22.57 N	88.22 E
Bhaun	123	32.52 N	72.45 E
Bhaunagar	122	21.46 N	72.09 E
Bhaunja	272a	28.40 N	77.25 E
Bhavāni	122	11.27 N	77.41 E
Bhawānīgarh	124	30.16 N	76.02 E
Bhawāni Mandi	120	24.25 N	75.50 E
Bhawānipatna	122	19.54 N	83.10 E
Bhedia	126	23.36 N	87.42 E
Bheigeir, Beinn ∧[2]	46	55.44 N	6.05 W
Bhendkhal	272c	18.53 N	72.59 E
Bhera	123	32.29 N	72.55 E
Bheramara	126	24.02 N	88.58 E
Bheri ≃	124	28.44 N	81.16 E
Bheula, Beinn ∧	46	56.08 N	4.58 W
Bhīkampur	272a	28.45 N	77.27 E
Bhikangaon	120	21.52 N	75.57 E
Bhilai	120	21.13 N	81.26 E
Bhilainagar → Bhilai	120	21.13 N	81.26 E
Bhīlsa □[5]	124	24.00 N	77.50 E
Bhīlwāra	120	25.21 N	74.38 E
Bhīmavaram	122	16.32 N	81.32 E
Bhimbar	123	32.59 N	74.04 E
Bhīmphedi	124	27.32 N	85.07 E
Bhīmpur, Bhārat	126	22.37 N	87.08 E
Bhimpur, Bhārat	272b	22.46 N	88.08 E
Bhind	124	26.34 N	78.48 E
Bhind □[5]	124	26.30 N	78.35 E
Bhinga	124	27.43 N	81.56 E
Bhīnmāl	120	25.00 N	72.15 E
Bhiwandi	122	19.18 N	73.04 E
Bhiwāni	124	28.47 N	76.08 E
Bhoāgāchi	272b	22.57 N	88.20 E
Bhojpur	124	27.10 N	87.03 E
Bhojudih	126	23.38 N	86.27 E
Bhokardan	122	20.16 N	75.46 E
Bhola	124	22.41 N	90.39 E
Bhola ≃[1]	126	22.04 N	89.49 E
Bhongaon	124	27.15 N	79.11 E
Bhongīr	122	17.31 N	78.53 E
Bhonrāsa	124	22.59 N	76.12 E
Bhopāl	124	23.16 N	77.24 E
Bhopar	272c	19.12 N	73.05 E
Bhopura	272a	28.42 N	77.20 E
Bhoutan → Bhutan □[1]	120	27.30 N	90.30 E
Bhowali	124	29.23 N	79.31 E
Bhuāpur	272a	28.43 N	77.26 E
Bhuban	120	20.53 N	85.50 E
Bhubaneswar	120	20.14 N	85.50 E
Bhucho	123	30.13 N	75.06 E
Bhuj	120	23.16 N	69.40 E
Bhunarheri	124	30.13 N	76.27 E
Bhusāwal	120	21.03 N	75.46 E
Bhūshana	126	23.24 N	89.40 E
Bhutali	272c	19.07 N	73.04 E
Bhutan □[1]	118		
	120	27.30 N	90.30 E
Biá ≃	246	3.28 S	67.23 W
Bia, Phou ∧	110	18.59 N	103.09 E
Bīābānak	128	32.11 N	64.11 E
Biabo ≃	248	6.58 S	76.23 W
Biacesa	64	45.56 N	10.47 E
Biache-Saint-Vaast	50	50.18 N	2.57 E
Biadene	64	45.47 N	12.04 E
Biafra, Bight of C[3]	134	4.00 N	8.00 E
Biak I	164	1.00 S	136.00 E
Biała	30	50.23 N	17.40 E
Biała ≃	30	50.03 N	20.55 E
Biała Piska	30	53.37 N	22.04 E
Biała Podlaska	30	52.02 N	23.06 E
Biała Rawska	30	51.49 N	20.29 E
Białobrzegi	30	51.40 N	20.57 E
Białogard	30	54.01 N	16.00 E
Białowieski Park Narodowy ♠	30	52.40 N	23.50 E
Biały Bór	30	53.54 N	16.51 E
Białystok	30	53.09 N	23.09 E
Bian ≃	164	8.07 S	139.56 E
Bian, Bidean nam ∧	46	56.38 N	5.02 W
Bianba	120	30.49 N	94.59 E
Biancavilla	70	37.38 N	14.52 E
Bianchi	68	39.06 N	16.24 E
Bianco	68	38.05 N	16.09 E
Bianco, Canale ≋	64	45.02 N	11.30 E
Bianco, Capo ≻	70	37.23 N	13.16 E
Bianco, Monte (Mont Blanc) ∧	62	45.50 N	6.52 E
Bian'er	102	31.14 N	101.28 E
Bianga	152	4.51 N	20.25 E
Bian'gezhuang	105	39.28 N	115.53 E
Bianjiayuan	98	36.02 N	116.53 E
Biankouma	150	7.44 N	7.37 W
Biankouma □[5]	150	7.45 N	7.30 W
Bianlinpu	98	37.26 N	116.32 E
Bianminchang	107	29.41 N	105.04 E
Bianniulupucun	104	41.30 N	123.42 E
Bianquanwopu	104	41.21 N	120.48 E
Bianzè	62	45.18 N	8.07 E
Biaora	124	23.55 N	76.54 E
Biaro, Pulau I	112	2.05 N	125.20 E
Biarritz	32	43.29 N	1.34 W
Biasca	58	46.22 N	8.58 E
Bias Fortes	256	21.36 S	43.46 W
Biassono	62	45.37 N	9.16 E
Biaza	86	56.38 N	78.18 E
Bibā	142	28.55 N	30.59 E
Bibai	92a	43.19 N	141.52 E
Bībān	142	30.47 N	30.40 E
Bibane, Bahiret el C	148	33.16 N	11.19 E
Bibanga	152	6.15 S	23.56 E
Bibban, Khawr ∨	140	11.00 N	32.41 E
Bibb City	192	32.30 N	84.59 W
Bibbiano	64	44.40 N	10.28 E
Bibbiena	66	43.42 N	11.49 E
Bibbona	66	43.16 N	10.35 E
Bibémi	146	9.19 N	13.53 E
Biberach	58	48.20 N	8.02 E
Biberach an der Riss	58	48.06 N	9.47 E
Biberbach	56	48.31 N	10.48 E
Bibert ≃	56	49.27 N	10.59 E
Bibey ≃	34	42.24 N	7.13 W
Bibiani	150	6.28 N	2.20 W
Bībi Chīni	126	22.28 N	90.12 E
Bībi Nāni	120	29.42 N	67.23 E
Bibione	64	45.38 N	13.00 E
Bibir'ovo	76	54.28 N	33.08 E
Biblián	246	2.42 S	78.52 W
Biblis	56	49.41 N	8.27 E
Bibo	102	29.02 N	99.20 E
Bic	186	48.22 N	68.42 W
Biča	86	57.53 N	70.37 E
Bicas	256	21.43 S	43.04 W
Bicas do Meio	256	22.31 S	45.21 W
Bicaz	38	46.54 N	26.05 E
Bicaz, Lacul ⊜[1]	38	47.00 N	26.00 E
Biccari	68	41.24 N	15.11 E
Bicester	42	51.54 N	1.09 W
Bičevinka	76	59.44 N	37.40 E
Biche, Lac la ⊜	182	54.50 N	112.03 W
Bichhia	124	22.27 N	80.42 E
Bichl	64	47.43 N	11.24 E
Bichlbach	58	47.25 N	10.47 E
Bichota Canyon ∨	280	34.16 N	117.48 W
Biči ≃	89	52.10 N	139.50 E
Bičigt	88	47.06 N	95.05 E
Bickenbach	56	49.45 N	8.37 E
Bickerstaffe	262	53.32 N	2.50 W
Bickerton, Cape ≻	9	66.20 S	136.56 E
Bickerton Island I	164	13.45 S	136.12 E
Bickle Knob ∧	188	38.56 N	79.44 W
Bickley ◆[8]	260	51.24 N	0.03 E
Bicknacre	260	51.42 N	0.35 E
Bicknell, Ind., U.S.	194	38.47 N	87.19 W
Bicknell, Utah, U.S.	200	38.20 N	111.33 W
Bicknor	260	51.18 N	0.40 E
Bicol ≃	116	13.44 N	123.07 E
Bicske	30	47.29 N	18.37 E
Bicudo ≃	255	18.04 S	44.33 W
Bičura	88	50.36 N	107.35 E
Bičurina	86	56.51 N	55.25 E
Bida, Nig.	146	12.20 N	13.25 E
Bida, Nig.	150	9.05 N	6.01 E
Bīdar	122	17.54 N	77.33 E
Biddeford	188	43.30 N	70.26 W
Biddenden	42	51.07 N	0.39 E
Biddiyā	132	32.07 N	35.05 E
Biddulph	44	53.08 N	2.10 W
Bideford	42	51.01 N	4.13 W
Bidente ≃	66	44.24 N	12.12 E
Bidford-on-Avon	42	52.10 N	1.51 W
Bidhūna	124	26.49 N	79.31 E
Bidi	144	1.00 N	42.40 E
Bidian	100	32.38 N	113.03 E
Bīdokht	128	34.21 N	58.46 E
Bidon Cinq → Post Maurice Cortier	148	22.18 N	1.05 E
Bidoni	71	40.07 N	8.56 E
Bidor	114	4.07 N	101.17 E
Bidston	262	53.24 N	3.05 W
Bidwell	188	38.55 N	82.18 W
Bidwell, Mount ∧	204	41.58 N	120.10 W
Bidyādhari ≃	272b	22.23 N	88.35 E
Bidyādharpur	272b	22.50 N	88.24 E
Bidžan	89	47.58 N	131.58 E
Bie	40	59.05 N	16.12 E
Bié □[5]	152	16.00 S	19.30 E
Biebelried	56	49.46 N	10.04 E
Bieber, B.R.D.	56	50.09 N	9.19 E
Bieber, Calif., U.S.	204	41.07 N	121.08 W
Biebrza ≃	30	53.37 N	22.56 E
Biecz	30	49.44 N	21.14 E
Biedenkopf	56	50.55 N	8.32 E
Biederitz	54	52.09 N	11.43 E
Biedermannsdorf	264b	48.05 N	16.21 E
Bieguzhuang	105	39.19 N	116.39 E
Biei	92a	43.35 N	142.28 E
Biel (Bienne)	58	47.10 N	7.12 E
Bielawa	30	50.41 N	16.38 E
Bielawski, Mount ∧	226	37.13 N	122.06 W
Bielefeld	52	52.01 N	8.31 E
Bieler Lake ⊜	176	70.20 N	73.00 W
Bielersee ⊜	58	47.05 N	7.10 E
Bielin	54	52.47 N	14.28 E
Biella	62	45.34 N	8.03 E
Bielsk	30	52.40 N	19.49 E
Bielsko-Biała	30	49.49 N	19.02 E
Bielsk Podlaski	30	52.47 N	23.12 E
Biemenhorst	52	51.49 N	6.36 E
Bienenbüttel	52	53.08 N	10.29 E
Bienfait	184	49.08 N	102.47 W
Bien-hoa	110	10.57 N	106.49 E
Bienne → Biel	58	47.10 N	7.12 E
Bienne ≃, Fr.	50	48.15 N	0.04 E
Bienne ≃, Fr.	58	46.20 N	5.38 E
Bienno	64	45.56 N	10.18 E
Bientina	66	43.42 N	10.37 E
Bienville	194	32.21 N	92.59 W
Bienville, Lac ⊜	176	55.05 N	72.40 W
Biere, D.D.R.	54	51.58 N	11.39 E
Bière, Schw.	58	46.33 N	6.20 E
Bierné	28	47.49 N	0.32 W
Bieruń Stary	30	50.06 N	19.06 E
Bierutów	30	51.08 N	17.32 E
Bierwart	56	50.34 N	5.01 E
Biesbos ◆[1]	52	51.45 N	4.50 E
Biesdorf ◆[8]	264a	52.31 N	13.33 E
Biese ≃	54	52.45 N	11.37 E
Biesel ◆[8]	263	51.10 N	6.29 E
Biesenthal	54	52.46 N	13.37 E
Bieshan	105	39.58 N	117.29 E
Biesiesvlei	158	26.22 S	25.55 E
Biesles	58	48.05 N	5.18 E
Bieszczadzki Park Narodowy ♠	30	49.05 N	22.45 E
Bieteluobaoluosika	89	48.35 N	119.56 E
Bietigheim, B.R.D.	56	48.58 N	9.07 E
Bietigheim, B.R.D.	56	48.54 N	8.14 E
Bietschhorn ∧	58	46.24 N	7.51 E
Bièvre	56	49.56 N	5.01 E
Bièvre ≃	261	48.47 N	2.20 E
Bièvres	261	48.45 N	2.13 E
Biferno ≃	66	41.59 N	15.02 E
Bifoum	152	0.22 S	10.23 E
Bifuka	92a	44.29 N	142.21 E
Bifurcación	258	34.19 S	56.48 W
Big ≃, Austl.	169	37.18 S	146.02 E
Big ≃, Alaska, U.S.	180	63.00 N	154.56 W
Big ≃, Mo., U.S.	219	38.28 N	90.37 W
Biga	130	40.13 N	27.14 E
Bigadiç	130	39.23 N	28.08 E
Big A Mountain ∧	192	37.03 N	82.02 W
Big Annemessex River C	208	38.03 N	75.50 W
Big Averill Lake ⊜	206	44.59 N	71.44 W
Big Bald ∧	192	34.45 N	84.19 W
Big Bald Mountain ∧	186	47.12 N	66.25 W
Big Baldy ∧	202	44.47 N	115.13 W
Big Baldy Mountain ∧	202	46.58 N	110.37 W
Big Bar Creek	182	51.12 N	122.06 W
Big Basin Redwoods State Park ♠	226	37.09 N	122.17 W
Big Bay	190	46.49 N	87.44 W
Big Bay C	172	44.18 S	168.05 E
Big Bay De Noc C	190	45.46 N	86.43 W
Big Bay Point ≻	212	44.24 N	79.31 W
Big Bear City	228	34.16 N	116.51 W
Big Bear Lake	228	34.15 N	116.53 W
Big Bear Lake ⊜	228	34.15 N	116.55 W
Big Beaver, Sask., Can.	184	49.08 N	105.10 W
Big Beaver, Pa., U.S.	214	40.50 N	80.20 W
Big Beaver Airport ⊠	281	42.33 N	83.06 W
Big Beaver Creek ≃, Mich., U.S.	281	42.32 N	83.01 W
Big Beaver Creek ≃, Ohio, U.S.	218	39.01 N	83.03 W
Big Beaver Creek ≃, Wash., U.S.	224	48.40 N	121.08 W
Big Bell	162	27.21 S	117.40 E
Big Belt Mountains ⩕	202	46.40 N	111.25 W
Big Bend, Swaz.	158	26.50 S	31.57 E
Big Bend, Wis., U.S.	216	42.53 N	88.12 W
Big Bend National Park ♠	196	29.12 N	103.12 W
Big Bend Reservoir ⊜[1]	182	52.57 N	115.37 W
Big Black ≃	194	32.00 N	91.05 W
Big Blue ≃, U.S.	198	39.11 N	96.32 W
Big Blue ≃, Ind., U.S.	218	39.20 N	85.59 W
Big Blue, West Fork ≃	198	40.42 N	96.59 W
Big Bone Lick State Park ♠	218	38.53 N	84.45 W
Big Bonito Creek ≃	200	33.34 N	109.56 W
Big Brady Creek ≃	196	31.07 N	98.59 W
Big Brook ≃	276	40.19 N	74.10 W
Big Brushy Creek ≃, Tex., U.S.	222	29.12 N	96.55 W
Big Brushy Creek ≃, Tex., U.S.	222	32.32 N	96.20 W
Big Bureau Creek ≃	194	41.17 N	89.21 W
Bigbury Bay C	42	50.16 N	3.48 W
Big Cabin Creek ≃	194	36.26 N	95.08 W
Big Canoe Creek ≃	194	33.52 N	86.04 W
Big Canyon ∨	196	30.05 N	101.55 W
Big Carlos Pass C	220	26.24 N	81.52 W
Big Cedar Lake ⊜	212	44.37 N	78.10 W
Big Chino Wash ∨	200	34.52 N	112.28 W
Big Clear Lake ⊜	212	44.43 N	76.55 W
Big Clifty	194	37.33 N	86.09 W
Big Coulee Creek ≃	202	46.17 N	108.56 W
Big Cow Creek ≃	194	30.34 N	93.44 W
Big Creek, B.C., Can.	182	51.44 N	123.03 W
Big Creek, Calif., U.S.	226	37.12 N	119.09 W
Big Creek ≃, B.C., Can.	182	51.40 N	122.50 W
Big Creek ≃, Ont., Can.	214	42.19 N	82.27 W
Big Creek ≃, Ont., Can.	214	42.36 N	80.27 W
Big Creek ≃, U.S.	194	40.16 N	94.03 W
Big Creek ≃, Ark., U.S.	194	34.21 N	91.03 W
Big Creek ≃, Calif., U.S.	226	36.53 N	119.15 W
Big Creek ≃, Calif., U.S.	226	37.12 N	119.19 W
Big Creek ≃, Idaho, U.S.	202	45.06 N	114.44 W
Big Creek ≃, Ill., U.S.	219	39.07 N	88.52 W
Big Creek ≃, Ind., U.S.	216	40.38 N	86.46 W
Big Creek ≃, Ind., U.S.	218	38.48 N	85.39 W
Big Creek ≃, Kans., U.S.	198	38.47 N	98.55 W
Big Creek ≃, La., U.S.	194	32.10 N	91.53 W
Big Creek ≃, Mo., U.S.	219	38.52 N	90.50 W
Big Creek ≃, Ohio, U.S.	279a	41.27 N	81.41 W
Big Creek ≃, Oreg., U.S.	224	46.11 N	123.35 W
Big Creek ≃, Tex., U.S.	222	31.09 N	96.52 W
Big Creek ≃, Tex., U.S.	222	29.22 N	95.34 W
Big Creek ≃, Wash., U.S.	224	47.15 N	121.10 W
Big Creek, East Fork ≃	194	40.16 N	94.03 W
Big Creek Parkway ♠	279a	41.24 N	81.45 W
Big Creek Peak ∧	202	44.28 N	113.32 W
Big Crow Island I	276	40.37 N	73.33 W
Big Cypress Creek ≃	222	33.00 N	94.51 W
Big Cypress Indian Reservation ◆[4]	220	26.14 N	80.49 W
Big Cypress National Preserve ♠	220	25.55 N	81.10 W
Big Cypress Swamp ≣	220	26.10 N	81.38 W
Big Dalton Canyon ∨	280	34.10 N	117.48 W
Big Dalton Wash ∨	280	34.04 N	117.58 W
Big Darby Creek ≃	218	39.37 N	82.58 W
Big Delta	180	64.09 N	145.50 W
Big Diomede Island → Ratmanova, Ostrov I	180	65.46 N	169.02 W
Big Ditch ≋	216	40.13 N	88.22 W
Big Dry Creek ≃	202	47.30 N	106.19 W
Big Eau Pleine ≃	190	44.48 N	90.00 W
Big Elk Creek ≃	208	39.35 N	75.52 W
Big Elkhart Creek ≃	222	31.22 N	95.41 W
Big Elm Creek ≃	222	30.53 N	96.56 W
Bigelow Bight C[3]	188	43.15 N	70.30 W
Bigéné	152	3.25 N	15.38 E
Big Escambia Creek ≃	194	30.58 N	87.14 W
Big Falls	190	48.12 N	93.48 W
Bigflat	194	36.00 N	92.24 W
Big Flat Creek ≃	194	31.33 N	87.31 W
Big Flats	210	42.08 N	76.56 W
Bigfork, Minn., U.S.	190	47.45 N	93.39 W
Bigfork, Mont., U.S.	202	48.04 N	114.04 W
Big Fork ≃	190	48.31 N	93.43 W
Big Four Ditch ≋	216	40.27 N	88.10 W
Big Frog Mountain ∧	192	35.00 N	84.32 W
Biggar, Sask., Can.	184	52.04 N	108.00 W
Biggar, Scot., U.K.	46	55.38 N	3.32 W
Biggarsberg ∧	158	28.12 S	29.48 E
Bigge	56	51.21 N	8.28 E
Biggers	194	36.20 N	90.48 W
Biggestausee ⊜[1]	56	51.05 N	7.55 E
Biggin Hill ◆[8]	260	51.18 N	0.04 E
Biggin Hill Aerodrome ⊠	260	51.19 N	0.03 E
Biggleswade	42	52.05 N	0.17 W
Biggs, Calif., U.S.	226	39.25 N	121.43 W
Biggs, Oreg., U.S.	224	45.40 N	120.50 W
Big Gull Lake ⊜	212	44.50 N	76.58 W
Big Gully Creek ≃	184	53.13 N	109.03 W
Bighāi ≃[1]	126	22.10 N	90.13 E
Big Hawk Lake ⊜	212	45.10 N	78.44 W
Bighead ≃	212	44.36 N	80.35 W
Big Hole ≃	202	45.34 N	112.20 W
Big Hole National Battlefield ⊥	202	45.35 N	113.35 W
Bighorn ≃	202	46.09 N	107.28 W
Big Horn Basin ⩡[1]	202	44.15 N	108.10 W
Bighorn Canyon National Recreation Area ♠	202	45.00 N	108.15 W
Big Horn Lake ⊜[1]	202	45.06 N	108.08 W
Bighorn Mountains ⩕	202	44.00 N	107.30 W
Bight, Head of ≻	162	31.30 S	131.10 E
Big Huckleberry Mountain ∧	224	45.51 N	121.47 W
Big Island	192	37.32 N	79.22 W
Big Island I, N.W. Ter., Can.	176	62.43 N	70.43 W
Big Island I, Ont., Can.	184	49.10 N	94.40 W
Big Island I, Ont., Can.	212	44.33 N	78.30 W
Big Knob ∧	192	36.40 N	82.31 W
Big Koniuji Island I	180	55.06 N	159.33 W
Big Lake, Alaska, U.S.	180	61.33 N	149.52 W
Big Lake, Minn., U.S.	190	45.20 N	93.45 W
Big Lake, Tex., U.S.	196	31.12 N	101.28 W
Big Lake, Wash., U.S.	224	48.24 N	122.14 W
Big Lake ⊜, Maine, U.S.	186	45.10 N	67.40 W
Big Lake ⊜, Wash., U.S.	224	48.23 N	122.12 W
Bigler	214	40.59 N	78.19 W
Biglerville	208	39.56 N	77.15 W
Big Lick Creek ≃	216	40.22 N	85.27 W
Big Lookout Mountain ∧	202	44.37 N	117.17 W
Big Lost ≃	202	43.50 N	112.44 W
Big Monon Ditch ≋	216	40.52 N	86.46 W
Big Mossy Point ≻	184	53.42 N	98.03 W
Big Mountain ∧, B.C., Can.	180	56.53 N	131.31 W
Big Mountain ∧, Nev., U.S.	204	41.17 N	119.04 W
Big Mountain Creek ≃	182	55.04 N	118.39 W
Big Muddy ≃	194	37.35 N	89.31 W
Big Muddy, Casey Fork ≃	194	38.06 N	88.57 W
Big Muddy Creek ≃, Mont., U.S.	198	48.08 N	104.36 W
Big Muddy Creek ≃, N. Dak., U.S.	198	46.37 N	101.24 W
Big Muddy Lake ⊜	184	49.08 N	104.54 W
Big Muscamoot Bay C	281	42.33 N	82.40 W
Bignasco	58	46.20 N	8.36 E
Big Nasty Creek ≃	198	45.41 N	102.51 W
Bignona	150	12.49 N	16.14 W
Big Oak Flat	226	37.49 N	120.16 W
Bigosovo	76	55.49 N	27.43 E
Bigot, Morne ∧[2]	240e	14.31 N	61.04 W
Big Otter ≃	192	37.07 N	79.23 W
Big Otter Creek ≃	212	42.38 N	80.48 W
Big Ox Creek ≃	218	38.44 N	85.52 W
Big Pine	204	37.10 N	118.17 W
Big Pine Creek ≃	216	40.18 N	87.15 W
Big Pine Key	220	24.40 N	81.21 W
Big Pine Key I	220	24.42 N	81.23 W
Big Pine Mountain ∧	204	34.42 N	119.39 W
Big Piney	200	42.32 N	110.07 W
Big Piney ≃	194	37.53 N	92.04 W
Big Piney Creek ≃	194	35.20 N	93.20 W
Big Pipe Creek ≃	208	39.36 N	77.17 W
Big Plain	218	39.50 N	83.17 W
Big Pocono State Park ♠	210	41.03 N	75.19 W
Bigpoint	194	30.35 N	88.29 W
Big Pond	210	41.53 N	76.43 W
Big Porcupine Creek ≃	202	46.16 N	106.43 W
Big Porcupine Lake ⊜	212	45.27 N	78.36 W
Big Prairie	214	40.40 N	82.06 W
Big Prairie Creek ≃	194	32.35 N	87.45 W
Big Quilcene ≃	224	47.49 N	122.52 W
Big Quill Lake ⊜	184	51.55 N	104.22 W
Big Raccoon Creek ≃	194	39.46 N	87.22 W
Big Rapids	190	43.42 N	85.29 W
Bigras, Île I	275a	45.31 N	73.51 W
Big Rib ≃	190	44.56 N	89.41 W
Big Rideau Lake ⊜	212	44.45 N	76.14 W
Big River	184	53.50 N	107.01 W
Big River Indian Reserve ◆[4]	184	53.33 N	107.10 W
Big Rock	216	41.46 N	88.33 W
Big Rock Creek ≃	216	41.38 N	88.32 W
Big Rocky Creek ≃	222	29.34 N	96.50 W
Big Run	214	40.58 N	78.53 W
Big Sable ≃	190	44.02 N	86.31 W
Big Sable Point ≻	190	44.03 N	86.31 W
Big Salmon ≃	180	61.52 N	134.56 W
Big Salmon Range ⩕	180	60.20 N	132.40 W
Big Sand Lake ⊜	176	57.45 N	99.42 W
Big Sandy, Mont., U.S.	202	48.11 N	110.07 W
Big Sandy, Tenn., U.S.	194	36.15 N	88.05 W
Big Sandy, Tex., U.S.	222	32.35 N	95.07 W
Big Sandy ≃, U.S.	188	31.20 N	81.20 W
Big Sandy ≃, Ariz., U.S.	200	34.19 N	113.31 W
Big Sandy ≃, Tenn., U.S.	194	36.15 N	88.06 W
Big Sandy ≃, Wyo., U.S.	202	41.51 N	109.47 W
Big Sandy, Levisa Fork ≃	192	38.06 N	82.36 W
Big Sandy, Rolling Fork ≃	192	37.24 N	82.26 W
Big Sandy, Tug Fork ≃	192	38.06 N	82.36 W
Big Sandy Creek ≃, Calif., U.S.	226	35.47 N	120.43 W
Big Sandy Creek ≃, Colo., U.S.	198	38.06 N	102.29 W
Big Sandy Creek ≃, Ga., U.S.	192	32.42 N	82.57 W
Big Sandy Creek ≃, Mont., U.S.	202	48.34 N	109.48 W
Big Sandy Creek ≃, Nebr., U.S.	198	40.13 N	97.18 W
Big Sandy Creek ≃, Tex., U.S.	196	33.11 N	97.40 W
Big Sandy Creek ≃, Tex., U.S.	222	32.33 N	95.05 W
Big Sandy Creek ≃, Tex., U.S.	222	30.31 N	94.28 W
Big Sandy Lake ⊜, Sask., Can.	184	54.26 N	104.04 W
Big Sandy Lake ⊜, Minn., U.S.	190	46.45 N	93.17 W
Big Sandy Reservoir ⊜[1]	200	42.16 N	109.26 W
Big Satilla Creek ≃	192	31.27 N	82.03 W
Bigsby Island I	198	49.04 N	94.35 W
Big Sewickley Creek ≃	279b	40.35 N	80.13 W
Big Shawnee Creek ≃	216	40.15 N	87.18 W
Big Sheep Mountain ∧	202	47.03 N	105.43 W
Big Signal Peak ∧	204	39.31 N	123.06 W
Big Sioux ≃	198	42.30 N	96.25 W
Big Sky	202	45.17 N	111.17 W
Big Slough ≃	192	30.56 N	84.33 W
Big Smoky Valley ∨	204	38.30 N	117.15 W
Big Snowy Mountains ⩕	202	46.50 N	109.30 W
Big Southern Butte ∧	202	43.23 N	113.01 W
Big Spanish Channel ⋃	220	24.44 N	81.20 W
Bigspring, Mo., U.S.	219	38.38 N	91.28 W
Big Spring, Tex., U.S.	196	32.15 N	101.28 W
Big Springs	198	41.04 N	102.05 W
Big Spruce Knob ∧	188	38.16 N	80.12 W
Big Squaw Mountain ∧	188	45.30 N	69.45 W
Bigstick Lake ⊜	184	50.16 N	109.20 W
Bigstone ≃	184	55.55 N	94.36 W
Big Stone City	198	45.18 N	96.28 W
Big Stone Gap	192	36.52 N	82.47 W
Bigstone Lake ⊜, Man., Can.	184	53.42 N	95.44 W
Big Stone Lake ⊜, U.S.	198	45.25 N	96.40 W
Big Sur	226	36.15 N	121.48 W
Big Sur ≃	226	36.17 N	121.51 W
Big Swamp Creek ≃	194	32.19 N	86.49 W
Big Swan Creek ≃	194	35.46 N	87.24 W
Big Thicket National Preserve ♠	222	32.35 N	94.40 W
Big Thompson ≃	200	40.21 N	104.45 W
Big Timber	202	45.50 N	109.57 W
Big Timber Creek ≃	285	39.53 N	75.08 W
Big Timber Creek, South Branch ≃	285	39.50 N	75.05 W
Big Torch Key I	220	24.43 N	81.26 W
Big Tree	210	42.46 N	78.49 W
Big Trout Lake ⊜, Ont., Can.	176	53.45 N	90.00 W
Big Trout Lake ⊜, Ont., Can.	212	44.56 N	78.56 W
Big Tujunga Canyon ∨	228	34.16 N	118.18 W
Big Tujunga Dam ◆[6]	280	34.18 N	118.12 W
Biguaçu	252	27.30 S	48.40 W
Big Valley	182	52.02 N	112.46 W
Bigwa	154	7.13 S	39.09 E
Big Walnut Creek ≃, Ind., U.S.	194	39.30 N	86.57 W
Big Walnut Creek ≃, Ohio, U.S.	214	40.02 N	82.54 W
Big Warrambool ≃	166	30.05 S	147.33 E
Big Wells	196	28.34 N	99.34 W
Big White Mountain ∧	182	49.42 N	118.58 W
Big Wood ≃	202	42.52 N	114.54 W
Bihać	36	44.49 N	15.52 E
Bīhar	124	25.11 N	85.31 E
Bihār □[3]	124	25.00 N	86.00 E
Biharamulo	154	2.38 S	31.20 E
Bihārīganj	124	25.44 N	86.59 E
Bihen	144	10.38 N	48.24 E
Bihor □[5]	38	47.00 N	22.15 E
Bihoro	92a	43.49 N	144.07 E
Bihta	124	25.33 N	84.52 E
Bihu	100	28.21 N	119.48 E
Bija ≃	86	52.25 N	85.05 E
Bijagós, Arquipélago dos II	150	11.25 N	16.20 W
Bijainagar	120	25.56 N	74.38 E
Bījaipura	124	24.46 N	77.48 E
Bījāpur, Bhārat	122	18.48 N	80.49 E
Bijāpur, Bhārat	122	16.50 N	75.42 E
Bījār	128	35.52 N	47.36 E
Bijauri	124	28.06 N	82.20 E
Bijāwar	124	24.38 N	79.30 E
Bijbān Chāh	128	26.54 N	64.42 E
Bījbiāra	123	33.48 N	75.06 E
Bijeljina	38	44.45 N	19.13 E
Bijelo Polje	38	43.02 N	19.44 E
Bījenābād	128	27.55 N	58.03 E
Bijeypur	124	26.03 N	77.22 E
Bijiang	110	26.30 N	98.55 E
Bijianqiao	107	30.14 N	106.09 E
Bijiaqiao	106	31.02 N	119.02 E
Bijie	102	27.18 N	105.20 E
Bijna	272b	22.55 N	88.27 E
Bijni	124	26.31 N	90.40 E
Bijnor	124	29.22 N	78.08 E
Bijnor □[5]	124	29.30 N	78.25 E
Bijōki	268	35.49 N	139.39 E
Bijou	204	38.57 N	119.58 W
Bijou Creek ≃	198	40.17 N	103.52 W
Bijpur	126	22.56 N	88.26 E
Bijsk	86	52.34 N	85.15 E
Bijwāsan ◆[8]	272a	28.32 N	77.03 E
Bīkaner	120	28.01 N	73.18 E
Bīkaner □[5]	123	28.42 N	73.25 E
Bīkaner Canal ≋	123	30.08 N	73.57 E
Bikar I[1]	14	12.15 N	170.06 E
Bikbulovo	80	55.39 N	53.26 E
Bike	144	9.30 N	41.18 E
Bikeman Island I	174t	1.22 N	173.00 E
Bikenibeu	174t	1.21 N	173.07 E
Bikeqi	102	40.49 N	111.13 E
Bikeru	112	5.15 S	120.07 E
Bikfayyā	132	33.55 N	35.41 E
Bikié	152	3.06 S	13.52 E
Bikin	89	46.48 N	134.16 E
Bikin ≃	89	46.51 N	134.02 E
Bikini I[1]	14	11.35 N	165.23 E
Bikita	154	20.06 S	31.41 E
Bikl'an'	80	55.37 N	52.10 E
Bikoro	152	0.45 S	18.07 E
Bikova	76	56.45 N	27.04 E
Bikuar, Parque Nacional do ♠	152	15.12 S	14.42 W
Bila ≃	114	2.30 N	100.08 E
Bilaa Point ≻	116	9.49 N	125.26 E
Bilac	255	21.24 S	50.28 W
Bilād Ghāmid ◆[1]	144	20.00 N	41.30 E
Bilād Zahrān ◆[1]	144	20.16 N	41.14 E
Bílá hora ⊥	54	50.10 N	14.10 E
Bilanga	150	12.32 N	0.02 W
Bilāra	120	26.10 N	73.42 E
Bilāri	124	28.38 N	78.48 E
Bil'arsk	80	54.58 N	50.22 E
Bilāsipāra	124	26.14 N	90.14 E
Bilāspur, Bhārat	123	31.20 N	76.45 E
Bilaspur, Bhārat	124	28.53 N	79.16 E
Bilāspur, Bhārat	124	22.05 N	82.09 E
Bilāspur □[5]	124	22.30 N	82.10 E
Bil'asuvar	84	39.24 N	48.24 E
Bilatan Island I	116	4.59 N	120.00 E
Bilato	112	0.32 N	122.38 E
Bilauktaung Range ⩕	110	13.00 N	99.00 E
Bilauri	124	28.41 N	80.21 E
Bilbao	34	43.15 N	2.58 W
Bilbays	142	30.25 N	31.34 E
Bilbilis ⊥	34	41.25 N	1.39 W
Bil'čir	88	51.02 N	110.34 E
Bileća	38	42.53 N	18.26 E
Bilecik	130	40.09 N	29.59 E
Bilecik □[4]	130	40.10 N	30.10 E
Biles Island I	285	40.10 N	74.45 W
Biłgoraj	30	50.34 N	22.43 E
Bilgrām	124	27.11 N	80.02 E
Bili	154	4.09 N	25.10 E
Bili ≃	136	4.50 N	22.29 E
Bilian	100	28.21 N	120.33 E
Bilican Dağları ⩕	130	38.58 N	42.10 E
Bilifyā	142	29.07 N	31.03 E
Bilimora	120	20.45 N	72.57 E
Bilin	110	17.14 N	97.15 E
Bilin ≃	110	17.05 N	97.08 E
Bílina	54	50.35 N	13.45 E
Bílina ≃	54	50.40 N	14.02 E
Bilioso ≃	68	40.39 N	16.24 E
Biliran Island I	116	11.35 N	124.28 E
Biliran Strait ⋃	116	11.30 N	124.28 E
Biliuhe ≃	98	39.30 N	122.36 E
Bilk ◆[8]	263	51.12 N	6.47 E
Bilkfontein	158	27.50 S	23.56 E
Billabong Creek ≃	166	35.06 S	144.02 E
Billeberga	41	55.53 N	13.00 E
Billerbeck	52	51.59 N	7.17 E
Billerica	207	42.34 N	71.16 W
Billericay	260	51.38 N	0.25 E
Billesdon	42	52.37 N	0.55 W
Billesholm	41	56.03 N	13.00 E
Billiat	58	46.04 N	5.47 E
Billiatt National Park ♠	166	35.00 S	140.30 E
Billigheim	56	49.21 N	9.15 E
Billiluna	162	19.37 S	127.41 E
Billinge, Sve.	41	55.58 N	13.21 E
Billinge, Eng., U.K.	262	53.30 N	2.42 W
Billingen ⩕[2]	26	58.24 N	13.45 E
Billingham	44	54.36 N	1.17 W
Billings, Mo., U.S.	194	37.04 N	93.33 W
Billings, Mont., U.S.	202	45.47 N	118.27 W
Billings, Okla., U.S.	196	36.32 N	97.27 W
Billingsfors	26	58.59 N	12.15 E
Billings Heights	202	45.50 N	108.33 W
Billingshurst	42	51.01 N	0.28 W
Billmerich	263	51.30 N	7.47 E
Billolo ≃	273b	4.07 S	15.19 E
Billom	32	45.44 N	3.21 E
Billund	41	55.44 N	9.07 E
Bill Williams ≃	200	34.17 N	114.03 W
Bill Williams Mountain ∧	200	35.17 N	112.12 W
Billy Chinook, Lake ⊜[1]	202	44.33 N	121.20 W
Billy-Montigny	50	50.25 N	2.52 E
Bilma	146	18.41 N	12.56 E
Biloela	166	24.24 S	150.30 E
Bilo Gora ⩕	36	46.06 N	16.46 E
Biloxi	194	30.24 N	88.53 W
Biloxi ≃	194	30.26 N	89.00 W
Biloxi Creek ≃	222	31.05 N	94.37 W
Bilpa Morea Claypan ⩡	166	25.00 S	140.00 E
Bilpin	170	33.30 S	150.31 E
Bilqās Qism Awwal	142	31.13 N	31.21 E
Bilsārā	126	23.05 N	88.10 E
Bilshausen	52	51.37 N	10.10 E
Bilsi	124	28.08 N	78.55 E
Bilston	42	52.34 N	2.04 W
Biltāj	142	31.00 N	30.59 E
Biltān	142	30.23 N	31.10 E
Bilthoven	52	52.07 N	5.17 E
Biltine	146	14.32 N	20.55 E
Biltine □[5]	146	15.00 N	21.00 E
Biltmore Forest	192	35.32 N	82.32 W
Bilugyun Island I	110	16.24 N	97.32 E
Bilwaskarma	236	14.45 N	83.53 W
Bilzen	56	50.52 N	5.31 E
Bima	115b	8.28 S	118.43 E
Bimbān	140	24.26 N	32.53 E
Bimbe	152	11.49 S	15.49 E
Bimbéréké	150	10.13 N	2.40 E
Bimberi Peak ∧	171b	35.40 S	148.47 E
Bimbila	150	8.51 N	0.04 E
Bimbo	152	4.18 N	18.33 E
Bimbowrie	166	32.03 S	140.09 E
Bimé	273b	4.09 S	15.11 E
Bimini Islands II	238	25.44 N	79.15 W
Bina	175e	8.55 S	160.46 E
Bīna-Etāwa	124	24.11 N	78.11 E
Binagadi	84	40.28 N	49.49 E
Binaiya, Gunung ∧	164	3.11 S	129.26 E
Binalbagan	116	10.12 N	122.50 E
Binalbagan ≃	116	10.12 N	122.51 E
Binalonan	116	16.03 N	120.36 E
Binanga	114	1.24 N	99.46 E
Binangonan	116	14.28 N	121.11 E
Bin'anzhen	89	45.50 N	127.45 E
Binas	50	47.54 N	1.28 E
Binasco	62	45.20 N	9.06 E
Binau	56	49.22 N	9.04 E
Binche	50	50.24 N	4.10 E
Bindal	24	65.06 N	12.30 E
Bindebango	166	27.45 S	147.24 E
Binder	88	48.35 N	110.36 E
Binder Foulbé	146	9.58 N	14.28 E
Bindki	124	26.02 N	80.36 E
Bindlach	60	49.59 N	11.37 E
Bindloss	184	50.52 N	110.16 W
Bindow	264a	52.17 N	13.45 E
Bindura	154	17.19 S	31.20 E
Bine-el-Ouidane	148	32.07 N	6.26 W
Binéfar	34	41.51 N	0.18 E
Binford	198	47.34 N	98.21 W
Binga, Pil.	116	10.45 N	119.19 E
Binga, Zaïre	152	2.23 N	20.30 E
Binga, Monte ∧	156	19.45 S	33.04 E
Bingara	166	29.52 S	150.34 E
Bingaram Island I	122	10.56 N	72.17 E
Bingay Point ≻	116	13.04 N	124.11 E
Bingcha	100	32.30 N	120.52 E
Bingen, B.R.D.	56	49.57 N	7.54 E
Bingen, Wash., U.S.	224	45.43 N	121.28 W
Binger	196	35.18 N	98.21 W
Bingerbrück	56	49.58 N	7.53 E
Bingerville	150	5.21 N	3.54 W
Bingham, Eng., U.K.	42	52.57 N	0.57 W
Bingham, Maine, U.S.	188	45.03 N	69.53 W
Bingham Creek ≃	224	47.09 N	123.24 W
Bingham Farms	281	42.32 N	83.16 W
Binghamton	210	42.08 N	75.54 W
Bingi	154	0.24 S	29.05 E
Bingley	44	53.51 N	1.50 W
Bingöl	130	38.53 N	40.29 E
Bingöl □[4]	130	39.00 N	40.40 E
Bingöl Dağları ⩕	130	39.20 N	41.20 E
Binhai (Dongkan)	100	34.03 N	119.51 E
Binh-ca	110	21.48 N	105.18 E
Binh-chanh	269c	10.40 N	106.34 E
Binh-gia	110	21.59 N	106.21 E
Binh-hung-hoa	269c	10.49 N	106.37 E
Binh-khe	110	13.57 N	108.51 E
Binh-kieu	110	15.35 N	108.04 E
Binh-son	110	15.18 N	108.46 E
Binh-trung	269c	10.47 N	106.46 E
Binigsian Point ≻	116	9.50 N	122.23 E
Bining-lès-Rohrbach	56	49.02 N	7.15 E
Binit Point ≻	116	9.54 N	125.17 E
Binjai	114	3.36 N	98.30 E
Binjiang ≃	100	23.40 N	112.58 E
Binjohara	114	2.12 N	98.12 E
Binna Burra	171a	28.13 S	153.14 E
Binnah, Ras ≻	144	11.06 N	51.13 E
Binnaway	166	31.33 S	149.23 E
Binnian, Slieve ∧	44	54.08 N	5.58 W
Binningen	58	47.32 N	7.34 E
Binodepur	126	23.26 N	89.30 E
Binpur	126	22.36 N	86.55 E
Binscarth	184	50.37 N	101.16 W
Binsheim	263	51.31 N	6.42 E
Bintan, Pulau I	112	1.05 N	104.30 E
Bintang	150	13.10 N	16.08 W
Bintauna	112	0.53 N	123.33 E
Bint Goda	140	13.17 N	31.33 E

Symbols in the index entries represent the broad categories identified in the key at the right. Symbols with superior numbers (⩕[2]) identify subcategories (see complete key on page *I · 30*).

Kartensymbole in dem Registerverzeichnis stellen die rechts in Schlüssel erklärten Kategorien dar. Symbole mit hochgestellten Ziffern (⩕[2]) bezeichnen Unterabteilungen einer Kategorie (vgl. vollständiger Schlüssel auf Seite *I · 30*).

Los símbolos incluídos en el texto del índice representan las grandes categorias identificadas con la clave a la derecha. Los símbolos con numeros en su parte superior (⩕[2]) identifican las subcategorías (véase la clave completa en la página *I · 30*).

Les symboles de l'index représentent les catégories indiquées dans la légende à droite. Les symboles suivis d'un indice (⩕[2]) représentent des sous-catégories (voir légende complète à la page *I · 30*).

Os símbolos incluídos no texto do índice representam as grandes categorias identificadas com a chave à direita. Os símbolos com números em sua parte superior (⩕[2]) identificam as subcategorias (veja-se a chave completa à página *I · 30*).

Symbol	English	Deutsch	Español	Français	Português
∧	Mountain	Berg	Montaña	Montagne	Montanha
⩕	Mountains	Berge	Montañas	Montagnes	Montanhas
)(	Pass	Pass	Paso	Col	Passo
∨	Valley, Canyon	Tal, Cañon	Valle, Cañón	Vallée, Canyon	Vale, Canhão
⩡	Plain	Ebene	Llano	Plaine	Planície
≻	Cape	Kap	Cabo	Cap	Cabo
I	Island	Insel	Isla	Île	Ilha
II	Islands	Inseln	Islas	Îles	Ilhas
⊥	Other Topographic Features	Andere Topographische Objekte	Otros Elementos Topográficos	Autres données topographiques	Outros Elementos Topográficos

ESPAÑOL Nombre	Página	Lat.°′	Long.°′ W=Oeste
Bintimani ∧	150	9.13 N	11.07 W
Bint Jubayl	132	33.07 N	35.26 E
Bintuhan	112	4.48 S	103.22 E
Bintulu	112	3.10 N	113.02 E
Bintuni, Teluk C	164	2.20 S	133.30 E
Binxian, Zhg.	89	45.44 N	127.29 E
Binxian, Zhg.	98	37.28 N	117.56 E
Binxian, Zhg.	102	35.00 N	108.08 E
Binyamina	132	32.31 N	34.57 E
Binyang	102	23.18 N	108.46 E
Bin Yauri	150	10.47 N	4.50 E
Bin Yumayn, Ghayl ⊤[4]	144	15.35 N	49.20 E
Binz	54	54.24 N	13.36 E
Binza	273b	4.21 S	15.14 E
Binza ≃	273b	4.21 S	15.14 E
Binzert (Bizerte)	148	37.17 N	9.52 E
Bio Addo	144	8.16 N	49.52 E
Bio-Bio □[4]	252	37.00 S	72.00 W
Biobío ≃	252	36.49 S	73.10 W
Biodi	154	3.19 N	28.35 E
Bio Gorge V	150	8.20 N	2.20 W
Biograd	36	43.56 N	15.27 E
Bioko I	152	3.30 N	8.40 E
Biola	226	36.48 N	120.01 W
Bionaz	62	45.52 N	7.25 E
Biondo	154	0.23 S	25.13 E
Biondo Monument ⊥	146	31.25 N	10.15 E
Biot	62	43.38 N	7.06 E
Bipindi	152	3.05 N	10.25 E
Bippus	216	40.57 N	85.37 W
Bīr	122	18.59 N	75.46 E
Bir, Ras ≻	144	11.59 N	43.22 E
Bira, Bhārat	272b	22.47 N	88.34 E
Bira, S.S.S.R.	89	49.15 N	137.16 E
Bira, S.S.S.R.	89	49.02 N	132.30 E
Birab	164	6.12 S	138.25 E
Bīraba	126	23.51 N	90.34 E
Birakan	89	49.01 N	131.42 E
Bi'r 'Alī	144	14.01 N	48.19 E
Bi'r al-Uzam	146	31.54 N	23.58 E
Birama, Ensenada de C	240p	20.38 N	77.15 W
Birao	146	10.17 N	22.47 E
Birati	272b	22.39 N	88.27 E
Birātnagar	124	26.29 N	87.17 E
Birava	154	2.21 S	28.54 E
Bīrbhūm □[5]	124	24.00 N	87.40 E
Bîrca	38	43.58 N	23.37 E
Bircao → Bur Gavo	144	1.10 S	41.50 E
Birch	262	53.34 N	2.13 W
Birch ≃, Alta., Can.	176	58.30 N	112.15 W
Birch ≃, W. Va., U.S.	188	38.35 N	80.53 W
Birch Bay	224	48.55 N	122.45 W
Birch Bay C	224	48.53 N	122.47 W
Birch Bay State Park ♠	224	49.54 N	123.47 W
Birch Cliff ⊸[8]	275b	43.41 N	79.17 W
Birch Creek ≃, Alaska, U.S.	180	66.30 N	146.30 W
Birch Creek ≃, Idaho, U.S.	202	43.51 N	112.43 W
Birch Creek ≃, Mont., U.S.	202	47.45 N	109.34 W
Birch Hill Reservoir @[1]	207	42.40 N	72.07 W
Birch Hills	184	52.59 N	105.25 W
Birchington	42	51.23 N	1.19 E
Birch Island	182	51.36 N	119.55 W
Birch Island I	184	52.25 N	99.55 W
Birch Lake @, Ont., Can.	184	51.24 N	92.20 W
Birch Lake @, Sask., Can.	184	53.28 N	108.07 W
Birch Mountains ⩕[2]	176	57.30 N	112.30 W
Bir Chouhada	34	35.53 N	6.18 E
Birch Pond @	283	42.28 N	71.00 W
Birch River	184	52.23 N	101.06 W
Birch Run	190	43.15 N	83.48 W
Birch Run ≃	285	40.09 N	75.37 W
Birch Tree	194	37.00 N	91.30 W
Birch Vale	262	53.23 N	1.57 W
Birchwood, N.Z.	172	45.56 S	167.52 E
Birchwood, Alaska, U.S.	180	61.28 N	149.22 W
Birchwood, Wis., U.S.	190	45.40 N	91.33 W
Birchwood Park, Del., U.S.	285	39.40 N	75.41 W
Birchwood Park, N.J., U.S.	208	40.06 N	74.09 W
Birchy Bay	186	49.21 N	54.44 W
Bird City	198	39.45 N	101.32 W
Bird Creek ≃	196	36.13 N	95.44 W
Bird Hills Wildflower Sanctuary ♠	169	38.23 S	144.11 E
Bird Island	198	44.46 N	94.54 W
Bird Islet I	160	22.10 S	155.28 E
Bird River C	284b	39.23 N	76.23 W
Birdsall	210	42.23 N	77.55 W
Birdsboro	208	40.16 N	75.48 W
Birds Landing	282	38.08 N	121.52 W
Birdsview	224	48.32 N	121.52 W
Birdsville	166	25.54 S	139.22 E
Birdtail Creek ≃	184	50.16 N	101.12 W
Birdum	164	15.39 S	133.13 E
Birdum Creek ≃	164	15.14 S	133.00 E
Birdwood	168b	34.49 S	138.57 E
Birecik	130	37.02 N	37.58 E
Bireuen	114	5.12 N	96.41 E
Bīrganj	124	27.00 N	84.52 E
Bir Gara	146	13.11 N	15.58 E
Bir Ghbalou	34	36.16 N	3.35 E
Birgi	126	22.42 N	86.41 E
Birgi Vecchi	70	37.53 N	12.29 E
Birigui	255	21.18 S	50.19 W
Biri Island I	116	12.40 N	124.22 E
Birik	130	39.01 N	38.15 E
Birikčul'	86	53.20 N	89.56 E
Biril'ussy	86	57.07 N	90.32 E
Birimbāl	142	31.21 N	30.30 E
Birimbāl al-Qadīmah	142	31.10 N	31.44 E
Birimşe	130	38.03 N	38.32 E
Biritiba-Mirim	256	23.35 S	46.02 W
Bīrjand	128	32.53 N	59.13 E
Birkat as-Sab'	142	30.38 N	31.05 E
Birkat Ghiţās	142	31.07 N	30.16 E
Birkdale	262	53.37 N	3.02 W
Birkeland	26	58.20 N	8.14 E
Birken	182	50.29 N	122.36 W
Birkenfeld, B.R.D.	56	49.39 N	7.10 E
Birkenfeld, B.R.D.	56	49.51 N	9.42 E
Birkenfeld, B.R.D.	56	48.52 N	8.38 E
Birkenfeld, Oreg., U.S.	224	46.00 N	123.20 W
Birkenhead	262	53.24 N	3.02 W
Birkenhead Park ♠	262	53.24 N	3.02 W
Birkenwerder bei Berlin	54	52.41 N	13.16 E
Birkerød	41	55.50 N	12.26 E
Birkesdorf	56	50.49 N	6.28 E
Birket Fatimé	146	12.54 N	19.05 E
Birkfeld	61	47.21 N	15.42 E
Birkholz	264a	52.38 N	13.34 E
Birkkar-Spitze ∧	64	47.25 N	11.25 E
Birksgate Range ⩕	162	27.10 S	129.45 E
Bîrlad	38	46.14 N	27.40 E
Bîrlad ≃	38	45.36 N	27.31 E
Birla Museum ɤ	272b	22.32 N	88.22 E
Birlik, S.S.S.R.	80	47.28 N	50.32 E
Birlik, S.S.S.R.	86	44.05 N	73.31 E
Birling	260	51.19 N	0.25 E
Birling ∧[2]	274a	33.57 S	150.43 E
Birmā	142	30.51 N	30.54 E
Birmaj	84	39.46 N	47.56 E
Birmania → Burma □[1]	110	22.00 N	98.00 E
Birmanie → Burma □[1]	110	22.00 N	98.00 E

FRANÇAIS Nom	Page	Lat.°′	Long.°′ W=Ouest
Birmingham, Eng., U.K.	42	52.30 N	1.50 W
Birmingham, Ala., U.S.	194	33.31 N	86.49 W
Birmingham, Iowa, U.S.	190	40.53 N	91.57 W
Birmingham, Mich., U.S.	216	42.33 N	83.15 W
Birmingham, N.J., U.S.	285	39.59 N	74.43 W
Birmingham, Ohio, U.S.	214	41.20 N	82.21 W
Birmingham, Pa., U.S.	214	40.38 N	78.13 W
Birmingham Airport ⊠	42	52.27 N	1.45 W
Birmitrapur	124	22.24 N	84.46 E
Bir Mogreïn (Fort-Trinquet)	148	25.14 N	11.35 W
Birnagar	126	23.14 N	88.33 E
Birnamwood	190	44.56 N	89.13 W
Bi'r Naşīf	128	24.51 N	39.11 E
Birnbaum	64	46.41 N	12.54 E
Birni	150	10.00 N	1.31 E
Birnie I[1]	14	3.35 S	171.31 W
Birni Ngaouré	150	13.05 N	2.54 E
Birnin Gwari	150	11.01 N	6.48 E
Birnin Kebbi	150	12.32 N	4.12 E
Birni Nkonni	150	13.48 N	5.15 E
Birnin Kudu	150	11.27 N	9.30 E
Birobidžan	89	48.48 N	132.57 E
Birofel'd	89	48.26 N	132.47 E
Birome	222	31.49 N	96.58 W
Birqāsh	142	30.10 N	31.02 E
Birr	48	53.05 N	7.54 W
Birregurra	169	38.20 S	143.48 E
Birribi	164	9.31 S	147.27 E
Birrie ≃	166	29.43 S	146.37 E
Birrindudu	162	18.22 S	129.27 E
Birs ≃	58	47.22 N	7.22 E
Birsilpur	120	28.10 N	72.15 E
Birsk	86	55.25 N	55.32 E
Birstall	42	52.41 N	1.07 W
Birstein	56	50.21 N	9.19 E
Birštonas	76	54.37 N	24.02 E
Birten	263	51.38 N	6.29 E
Birtle	184	50.25 N	101.03 W
Birtley	44	54.54 N	1.34 W
Bir'učij	83	46.53 N	39.33 E
Bir'učij, Ostrov I	78	46.08 N	35.05 E
Birufu	164	5.52 S	138.24 E
Bir'ukovo	83	47.57 N	39.44 E
Bir'ul'ka	88	53.52 N	106.21 E
Bir'ul'ovo ⊸[8]	265b	55.35 N	37.40 E
Birūr	122	13.37 N	75.58 E
Bir'usa ≃	88	57.43 N	95.24 E
Biržai	76	56.12 N	24.45 E
Bîrzava ≃	38	45.16 N	20.49 E
Birżebbuġa	36	35.49 N	14.32 E
Bisa, Pulau I	164	1.15 S	127.28 E
Bisaccia	68	41.01 N	15.22 E
Bisacquino	70	37.42 N	13.15 E
Bisāi, Bhārat	126	22.10 N	86.24 E
Bisai, Nihon	94	35.16 N	136.44 E
Bīsalpur	124	28.18 N	79.48 E
Bisamberg	264b	48.20 N	16.22 E
Bisamberg ∧[2]	264b	48.19 N	16.22 E
Bisan-shotō II	96	34.24 N	133.50 E
Bisbee, Ariz., U.S.	200	31.27 N	109.55 W
Bisbee, N. Dak., U.S.	198	48.37 N	99.23 W
Biscarosse, Étang de C	32	44.20 N	1.10 E
Biscarrosse	32	44.24 N	1.10 W
Biscay, Bay of C	32	44.00 N	4.00 W
Biscayne Bay C	220	25.33 N	80.15 W
Biscayne National Monument ♠	220	25.25 N	80.12 W
Bisceglie	68	41.14 N	16.31 E
Bischheim	58	48.37 N	7.45 E
Bischofsburg → Biskupiec	30	53.52 N	20.58 E
Bischofsheim, B.R.D.	56	49.59 N	8.22 E
Bischofsheim, B.R.D.	56	50.24 N	10.01 E
Bischofshofen	64	47.25 N	13.13 E
Bischofstal → Ujazd	30	50.24 N	18.22 E
Bischofstein → Bisztynek	30	54.06 N	20.55 E
Bischofswerda	54	51.07 N	14.10 E
Bischofswiesen	64	47.39 N	12.57 E
Bischofszell	58	47.29 N	9.15 E
Bischwald, Étang de @	56	49.00 N	6.42 E
Bischwiller	56	48.46 N	7.52 E
Biscoe, Ark., U.S.	194	34.49 N	91.24 W
Biscoe, N.C., U.S.	192	35.22 N	79.47 W
Biscoe Islands II	9	66.00 S	66.30 W
Biscotasi Lake @	190	47.19 N	82.07 W
Biscucuy	246	9.22 N	69.59 W
Bise	174m	26.42 N	127.54 E
Bisei	96	34.41 N	133.33 E
Bisentina, Isola I	66	42.35 N	11.54 E
Bisenzio ≃	66	43.46 N	11.06 E
Biser	86	58.25 N	58.53 E
Biserovo	265b	55.47 N	38.07 E
Biserovskoje, Ozero @	265b	55.46 N	38.07 E
Bisert'	86	56.52 N	59.03 E
Bisert' ≃	86	56.39 N	57.55 E
Bise-zaki ≻	174m	26.43 N	127.53 E
Bisha	144	15.28 N	37.34 E
Bīshah, Wādī V	144	21.24 N	43.26 E
Bishahari	126	23.10 N	89.01 E
Bishan	107	29.37 N	106.13 E
Bishanga	152	4.31 S	21.02 E
Bishārah, Ma'ţan ⊤[4]	146	22.58 N	22.39 E
Bīshat Qā'id	142	30.38 N	31.32 E
Bishaykhāli	126	23.28 N	89.09 E
Bishenpur	120	24.38 N	93.46 E
Bishnāh	123	32.37 N	74.52 E
Bishnupur, Bhārat	126	23.05 N	87.19 E
Bishnupur, Bhārat	126	22.23 N	88.16 E
Bishnupur, Bhārat	272b	22.37 N	88.31 E
Bishop, Calif., U.S.	204	37.22 N	118.24 W
Bishop, Pa., U.S.	279b	40.19 N	80.12 W
Bishop, Tex., U.S.	196	27.35 N	97.48 W
Bishop Airport ⊠	216	42.58 N	83.44 W
Bishop Auckland	44	54.40 N	1.40 W
Bishop's Castle	42	52.29 N	3.00 W
Bishop's Cleeve	42	51.57 N	2.04 W
Bishop's Falls	186	49.01 N	55.30 W
Bishops Frome	42	52.08 N	2.29 W
Bishops Head	208	38.16 N	76.05 W
Bishops Lydeard	42	51.04 N	3.12 W
Bishop's Stortford	42	51.53 N	0.09 E
Bishopsteignton	42	50.34 N	3.31 W
Bishopstoke	42	50.59 N	1.19 W
Bishop's Waltham	42	50.58 N	1.12 W
Bishopton	206	45.35 N	71.35 W
Bishopville, Md., U.S.	208	38.22 N	75.12 W
Bishopville, S.C., U.S.	192	34.13 N	80.20 W
Bishrī, Jabal ⩕	130	35.26 N	39.32 E
Bisianumu	164	9.25 S	147.25 E
Bisignano	68	39.31 N	16.17 E
Bisina, Lake @	154	1.38 N	33.56 E
Bisingen	58	48.18 N	8.55 E
Biskamža	86	53.30 N	89.30 E
Biskaya, Golf von → Biscay, Bay of C	32	44.00 N	4.00 W
Biskintā	132	33.57 N	35.48 E
Biškon' ≃	83	49.15 N	39.35 E
Biskra	148	34.51 N	5.44 E
Biskupiec	30	53.52 N	20.58 E
Bisley, Eng., U.K.	42	51.45 N	2.08 W
Bisley, Eng., U.K.	260	51.20 N	0.38 W
Bislich	263	51.41 N	6.29 E
Bislig	116	8.13 N	126.19 E
Bislig Bay C	116	8.14 N	126.22 E
Bismarck, Ill., U.S.	216	40.16 N	87.37 W
Bismarck, Mo., U.S.	194	37.46 N	90.38 W

PORTUGUÊS Nome	Página	Lat.°′	Long.°′ W=Oeste
Bismarck, N. Dak., U.S.	198	46.48 N	100.47 W
Bismarck Archipelago II	164	5.00 S	150.00 E
Bismarck Range ⩕	164	5.30 S	144.45 E
Bismarck Sea ⊤[2]	164	4.00 S	148.00 E
Bismark	54	52.39 N	11.32 E
Bismil	130	37.51 N	40.40 E
Bismo	26	61.53 N	8.16 E
Biso	154	1.46 N	31.25 E
Bison	198	45.31 N	102.28 W
Bison Peak ∧	200	39.14 N	105.30 W
Bispberg	40	60.22 N	15.47 E
Bispgården	26	63.02 N	16.37 E
Bispingen	52	53.05 N	10.00 E
Bisrakh	272a	28.34 N	77.26 E
Bisrāmpur	124	24.15 N	83.56 E
Bissa, Djebel ∧	34	36.26 N	1.28 E
Bissau	150	11.51 N	15.35 W
Bissaula	146	7.00 N	10.27 E
Bissegem	50	50.49 N	3.13 E
Bissendorf	52	52.31 N	9.45 E
Bissett	184	51.02 N	95.40 W
Bissigh, Lach ≃	144	0.34 N	42.08 E
Bissikrima	150	10.51 N	10.56 W
Bissingen	56	48.43 N	10.37 E
Bissingheim ⊸[8], B.R.D.	263	51.24 N	6.49 E
Bissingheim ⊸[8], B.R.D.	263	51.21 N	7.31 E
Bissorã	150	12.14 N	15.31 W
Bistcho Lake @	176	59.40 N	118.40 W
Bisten	56	49.15 N	6.42 E
Bistineau, Lake @[1]	194	32.25 N	93.22 W
Bistra ≃	38	45.29 N	22.11 E
Bistreţ	38	43.54 N	23.30 E
Bistriţa	38	47.08 N	24.30 E
Bistriţa ≃	38	46.30 N	26.57 E
Bistriţa-Năsăud □[4]	38	47.15 N	24.30 E
Biswān	124	27.30 N	81.00 E
Bisztynek	30	54.06 N	20.55 E
Bitadton	116	11.30 N	122.05 E
Bitam	152	2.05 N	11.29 E
Bitam, Oued ≃	34	35.15 N	5.11 E
Bitatolo	273b	4.09 S	15.14 E
Bitatolo ≃	273b	4.09 S	15.19 E
Bitburg	56	49.58 N	6.31 E
Bitca	265b	55.34 N	37.37 E
Bitca ≃	265b	55.34 N	37.37 E
Bitche	56	49.03 N	7.26 E
Bitchū	96	34.47 N	133.27 E
Bitéa, Ouadi V	146	13.11 N	20.10 E
Bitetto	68	41.02 N	16.45 E
Bithia ⊥	71	38.53 N	8.52 E
Bithlo	220	28.33 N	81.06 W
Bitia, Wādī V	140	17.34 N	32.15 E
Bitik	80	50.09 N	50.30 E
Bitkin	146	11.59 N	18.13 E
Bitlis	130	38.22 N	42.06 E
Bitlis □[4]	130	38.30 N	42.10 E
Bitola	38	41.01 N	21.20 E
Bitolj → Bitola	38	41.01 N	21.20 E
Bitonto	68	41.06 N	16.42 E
Bitra Island I	122	11.33 N	72.09 E
Bitritto	68	41.03 N	16.50 E
Bitschwiller-lès-Thann	58	47.50 N	7.05 E
Bitter Creek ≃, Utah, U.S.	200	39.58 N	109.25 W
Bitter Creek ≃, Wyo., U.S.	200	41.31 N	109.27 W
Bitterfeld	54	51.37 N	12.20 E
Bitterfontein	158	31.00 S	18.32 E
Bitter Lake @	184	50.08 N	109.48 W
Bittermark ⊸[8]	263	51.27 N	7.28 E
Bitterness, Mount ∧	172	44.45 S	170.18 E
Bittern Lake @	184	53.55 N	105.50 W
Bitterroot ≃	202	46.52 N	114.06 W
Bitterroot, East Fork ≃	202	45.57 N	114.08 W
Bitterroot, West Fork ≃	202	45.57 N	114.08 W
Bitterroot Range ⩕	202	47.06 N	115.10 W
Bitterwater Creek ≃	226	35.41 N	119.58 W
Bitti	71	40.29 N	9.23 E
Bittou	150	11.16 N	0.18 W
Bit'ug ≃	78	50.37 N	39.55 E
Bitung	112	1.27 N	125.11 E
Bitupitá	250	2.54 S	41.16 W
Bituruna	252	26.10 S	51.34 W
Biu	146	10.35 N	12.13 E
Bivalve	208	38.18 N	75.54 W
Bivins	194	33.01 N	94.12 W
Bivio	58	46.28 N	9.38 E
Bivona	70	37.37 N	13.26 E
Bivongi	68	38.28 N	16.27 E
Biwabik	190	47.32 N	92.23 W
Biwa-ko @	94	35.15 N	136.05 E
Biwako ⊸[5]	94	35.07 N	135.56 E
Biwa-ko-kokutei-kōen ♠	94	35.15 N	136.05 E
Bixby	196	35.57 N	95.53 W
Biyalā	142	31.10 N	31.13 E
Biyang	100	32.44 N	113.20 E
Biyela	158	27.47 S	32.08 E
Biyo Keraba	144	10.22 N	42.37 E
Biyo Weraba	144	8.52 N	42.14 E
Biysk → Bijsk	86	52.34 N	85.15 E
Biyunsi (Temple of the Azure Clouds) ɤ[1]	105	40.00 N	116.11 E
Biz'aki	80	55.56 N	52.28 E
Bizana	158	30.58 S	29.52 E
Biz'ar	86	57.31 N	56.09 E
Bizard, Île I	275a	45.29 N	73.54 W
Bižbul'ak	80	53.43 N	54.16 E
Bizcocho, Cuchilla del ⩕[2]	258	33.45 S	57.30 W
Bizen	96	34.44 N	134.09 E
Bizerte □[8]	36	37.10 N	9.50 E
Bizerte, Lac de @	36	37.12 N	9.52 E
Bjæverskov	41	55.27 N	12.02 E
Bjala	38	43.27 N	25.44 E
Bjala Slatina	38	43.28 N	23.56 E
Bjargtangar ≻	24a	65.31 N	24.32 W
Bjärnum	41	56.17 N	13.42 E
Bjärred	41	55.43 N	13.01 E
Bjärsjölagård	41	55.44 N	13.41 E
Bjästa	26	63.12 N	18.30 E
Bjelaja → Belaja ≃	72	56.00 N	54.32 E
Bjelovar	36	45.54 N	16.51 E
Bjernede	41	55.27 N	11.38 E
Bjerrelide ∧[2]	41	55.47 N	9.53 E
Bjerringbro	26	56.23 N	9.40 E
Björbo	40	60.28 N	14.42 E
Bjørkelangen	26	59.53 N	11.34 E
Björklinge	40	60.02 N	17.33 E
Björknäs	40	59.19 N	18.14 E
Björkö I	40	59.53 N	19.00 E
Björköby	26	63.21 N	21.19 E
Björköfjärden C	40	59.53 N	18.56 E
Björkvik	40	58.50 N	16.31 E
Björna	26	63.34 N	18.33 E
Bjørnafjorden C[2]	26	60.06 N	5.22 E
Björndammen	40	59.12 N	16.49 E
Björneborg → Pori, Suomi	26	61.29 N	21.47 E
Björneborg, Sve.	40	59.15 N	14.15 E
Bjornesfjorden @	26	60.10 N	7.41 E
Björnlunda	40	59.04 N	17.09 E
Bjørnøya I	10	74.25 N	19.00 E
Bjurholm	26	63.56 N	19.13 E
Bjuv	41	56.05 N	12.54 E
Bkāsīn	132	33.34 N	35.35 E
Bla	150	12.57 N	5.46 W
Blace	38	43.17 N	21.18 E
Black (Lixianjiang) (Da) ≃, As.	110	21.15 N	105.20 E
Black ≃, Man., Can.	184	50.49 N	96.20 W
Black ≃, Ont., Can.	190	48.36 N	86.16 W
Black ≃, Ont., Can.	190	48.42 N	80.38 W
Black ≃, Ont., Can.	212	44.32 N	77.22 W
Black ≃, Ont., Can.	212	44.42 N	79.19 W
Black ≃, Ont., Can.	212	44.20 N	79.20 W
Black ≃, U.S.	194	35.38 N	91.19 W
Black ≃, Alaska, U.S.	180	66.39 N	144.50 W
Black ≃, Ariz., U.S.	200	33.44 N	110.13 W
Black ≃, La., U.S.	194	31.16 N	91.50 W
Black ≃, Mich., U.S.	190	45.39 N	84.29 W
Black ≃, Mich., U.S.	190	46.40 N	90.03 W
Black ≃, Mich., U.S.	214	43.00 N	82.25 W
Black ≃, Mich., U.S.	216	42.24 N	86.17 W
Black ≃, N. Mex., U.S.	196	32.14 N	104.03 W
Black ≃, N.C., U.S.	192	34.35 N	78.16 W
Black ≃, N.Y., U.S.	212	43.59 N	76.04 W
Black ≃, Ohio, U.S.	214	41.28 N	82.11 W
Black ≃, S.C., U.S.	192	33.24 N	79.15 W
Black ≃, Vt., U.S.	188	43.16 N	72.27 W
Black ≃, Vt., U.S.	188	44.55 N	72.13 W
Black ≃, Wash., U.S.	224	46.49 N	123.13 W
Black ≃, Wis., U.S.	190	43.57 N	91.22 W
Black, East Branch ≃	214	41.22 N	82.07 W
Black, East Fork ≃	190	44.26 N	90.42 W
Black, Middle Fork ≃	216	42.25 N	86.14 W
Black, North Fork ≃	216	42.25 N	86.15 W
Black, West Branch ≃	214	41.22 N	82.07 W
Blackadder Water ≃	46	55.46 N	2.15 W
Blackall	166	24.25 S	145.28 E
Black Bay C	190	48.40 N	88.30 W
Black Bear Creek ≃	196	36.25 N	96.38 W
Blackberry Heights	216	41.45 N	88.23 W
Black Birch Lake @	184	56.54 N	107.45 W
Black Brook ≃, Mass., U.S.	283	42.38 N	71.21 W
Black Brook ≃, Mass., U.S.	283	41.59 N	71.03 W
Black Brook ≃, N.J., U.S.	276	40.42 N	74.31 W
Blackburn, Austl.	274b	37.49 S	145.09 E
Blackburn, Eng., U.K.	262	53.45 N	2.29 W
Blackburn, Scot., U.K.	46	57.12 N	2.18 W
Blackburn □[8]	262	53.42 N	2.28 W
Blackburn, Mount ∧	180	61.44 N	143.26 W
Blackbutt	171a	26.53 S	152.06 E
Black Butte ∧, Calif., U.S.	228	34.33 N	117.43 W
Black Butte ∧, Mont., U.S.	202	46.47 N	110.56 W
Black Butte ∧, Mont., U.S.	202	44.54 N	111.51 W
Black Butte Lake @[1]	204	39.45 N	122.20 W
Blackbutt Range ⩕	171a	27.00 S	152.00 E
Black Canyon of the Gunnison National Monument ♠	200	38.32 N	107.42 W
Blackcraig Hill ∧	44	55.20 N	4.08 W
Black Creek, B.C., Can.	182	49.50 N	125.08 W
Black Creek, Ont., Can.	284a	43.00 N	79.01 W
Black Creek, N.Y., U.S.	210	42.17 N	78.14 W
Black Creek ≃, Ont., Can.	214	42.43 N	82.21 W
Black Creek ≃, Ont., Can.	275b	43.41 N	79.32 W
Black Creek ≃, Ont., Can.	284a	42.59 N	79.01 W
Black Creek ≃, Ariz., U.S.	200	35.16 N	109.14 W
Black Creek ≃, Fla., U.S.	192	30.03 N	81.42 W
Black Creek ≃, Mich., U.S.	216	41.49 N	83.54 W
Black Creek ≃, Mich., U.S.	216	43.11 N	86.14 W
Black Creek ≃, Miss., U.S.	194	33.01 N	90.21 W
Black Creek ≃, Miss., U.S.	194	30.39 N	88.39 W
Black Creek ≃, Mo., U.S.	219	39.41 N	91.55 W
Black Creek ≃, N.Y., U.S.	210	43.06 N	77.41 W
Black Creek ≃, N.Y., U.S.	210	43.19 N	75.04 W
Black Creek ≃, N.Y., U.S.	284a	43.05 N	78.57 W
Black Creek ≃, N.Y., U.S.	284a	43.03 N	78.42 W
Black Creek ≃, Pa., U.S.	210	41.00 N	76.10 W
Black Creek ≃, S.C., U.S.	192	34.18 N	79.37 W
Black Creek, North Fork ≃	192	30.05 N	81.51 W
Black Creek, South Fork ≃	192	30.05 N	81.51 W
Black Creek Park ♠	275b	43.46 N	79.31 W
Black Creek Pioneer Village ⊥	275b	43.47 N	79.32 W
Black Cypress Bayou ≃	194	32.42 N	93.55 W
Black Cypress Creek ≃	222	32.53 N	94.26 W
Blackden Heath	262	53.14 N	2.20 W
Black Devon ≃	46	56.06 N	3.47 W
Black Diamond, Alta., Can.	182	50.42 N	114.14 W
Black Diamond, Wash., U.S.	224	47.18 N	122.00 W
Black Donald Lake @[1]	212	45.13 N	76.55 W
Black Down Hills ⩕[2]	42	50.57 N	3.09 W
Blackduck	190	47.44 N	94.33 W
Black Duck ≃	176	56.51 N	89.02 W
Black Eagle	202	47.31 N	111.17 W
Black Esk ≃	44	55.12 N	5.10 W
Blackfalds	182	52.23 N	113.47 W
Blackfeet Indian Reservation ⊸[4]	202	48.40 N	113.00 W
Blackfellow Creek ≃	171a	27.34 S	152.14 E
Blackfoot, Idaho, U.S.	202	43.11 N	112.20 W
Blackfoot, Mont., U.S.	182	48.34 N	112.52 W
Blackfoot ≃, Idaho, U.S.	202	43.08 N	112.30 W
Blackfoot ≃, Mont., U.S.	202	46.52 N	113.53 W
Blackfoot, North Fork ≃	202	46.59 N	113.07 W
Blackfoot Indian Reserve ⊸[4]	182	50.45 N	113.00 W
Blackfoot Reservoir @[1]	202	42.55 N	111.35 W
Blackford	46	56.15 N	3.46 W
Blackford □[6]	216	40.27 N	85.22 W
Black Forest → Schwarzwald ⩕	58	48.00 N	8.15 E
Blackhall Colliery	44	54.44 N	1.14 W
Blackhall Mountain ∧	200	41.02 N	106.41 W
Black Hameldon ∧[2]	262	53.44 N	2.08 W
Black Hawk	184	48.48 N	93.59 W
Black Hawk Creek ≃	190	42.30 N	92.21 W
Black Head ≻, Eire	48	53.08 N	9.17 W
Black Head ≻, Eng., U.K.	42	50.01 N	5.06 W
Blackhead Bay C	186	48.34 N	53.15 W
Blackheath, Austl.	170	33.38 S	150.17 E
Blackheath, S. Afr.	273d	26.08 S	27.58 E
Blackheath, Eng., U.K.	260	51.12 N	0.31 W
Black Hill ∧[2], Eng., U.K.	262	53.20 N	2.01 W
Black Hill ∧[2], Eng., U.K.	262	53.33 N	1.53 W
Black Hills ⩕	198	44.00 N	104.00 W
Black Hills ⩕[2]	282	37.50 N	121.52 W
Blackhope Star ∧	46	55.44 N	3.05 W
Black Horse, Ohio, U.S.	214	41.09 N	81.18 W
Black Horse, Pa., U.S.	285	39.55 N	75.25 W
Black Horse Creek ≃	285	40.05 N	75.43 W
Black Island I	184	51.10 N	96.30 W
Black Isle ≻[1]	46	57.35 N	4.15 W
Black Jack	219	38.49 N	90.18 W
Black Lake	206	46.03 N	71.21 W
Black Lake @, Ont., Can.	212	44.46 N	76.18 W
Black Lake @, Sask., Can.	176	59.10 N	105.20 W
Black Lake @, Mich., U.S.	190	45.28 N	84.15 W
Black Lake @, N.Y., U.S.	212	44.31 N	75.35 W
Black Lake @, Wash., U.S.	224	47.00 N	122.58 W
Black Lake Bayou ≃	194	32.01 N	93.09 W
Blacklegs Creek ≃	214	40.30 N	79.27 W
Blackley ⊸[8]	262	53.31 N	2.13 W
Black Lick	214	40.28 N	79.12 W
Blacklick Creek ≃	214	40.28 N	79.13 W
Blacklick Creek, North Branch ≃	214	40.29 N	78.55 W
Blacklick Estates	218	39.54 N	83.22 W
Blacklunans	46	56.44 N	3.22 W
Black Mesa ∧, Ariz., U.S.	200	36.35 N	110.20 W
Black Mesa ∧, Okla., U.S.	196	36.57 N	102.59 W
Blackmoor ⩕[1]	42	50.24 N	4.46 W
Blackmoorfoot Reservoir @[1]	262	53.37 N	1.51 W
Blackmoor Vale V	42	50.56 N	2.25 W
Blackmore	260	51.41 N	0.19 E
Blackmore, Mount ∧	202	45.27 N	111.01 W
Black Moshannon State Park ♠	214	40.54 N	78.03 W
Black Mountain	192	35.37 N	82.19 W
Black Mountain ∧, D.Y.	124	27.17 N	90.23 E
Black Mountain ∧, Wales, U.K.	42	51.52 N	3.46 W
Black Mountain ∧, Ariz., U.S.	200	32.46 N	110.57 W
Black Mountain ∧, Calif., U.S.	226	35.24 N	120.21 W
Black Mountain ∧, Calif., U.S.	228	35.08 N	117.14 W
Black Mountain ∧, Calif., U.S.	282	37.19 N	122.09 W
Black Mountain ∧, Idaho, U.S.	202	46.53 N	115.33 W
Black Mountain ∧, Ky., U.S.	192	36.54 N	82.54 W
Black Mountain ∧, Mont., U.S.	202	46.44 N	112.31 W
Black Mountain ∧, Oreg., U.S.	202	45.13 N	119.17 W
Black Mountain ∧, Wyo., U.S.	202	44.45 N	107.22 W
Black Mountain ∧[2], Calif., U.S.	228	32.59 N	117.07 W
Black Mountain ∧[2], Tex., U.S.	222	31.09 N	97.44 W
Black Mountains ⩕, Wales, U.K.	42	51.57 N	3.08 W
Black Mountains ⩕, Ariz., U.S.	200	35.30 N	114.30 W
Black Nossob ≃	156	23.05 S	18.45 E
Black Oak	216	41.35 N	87.25 W
Black Peak ∧	200	34.22 N	114.13 W
Black Pine Peak ∧	202	42.08 N	113.08 W
Black Pipe Creek ≃	198	43.47 N	101.14 W
Black Point	226	38.07 N	122.31 W
Black Point ≻, Austl.	168b	34.37 S	137.54 E
Black Point ≻, Austl.	170	34.47 S	150.50 E
Black Point ≻, Alaska, U.S.	180	57.00 N	153.18 W
Black Point ≻, Calif., U.S.	228	33.28 N	118.36 W
Blackpool	44		
	262	53.50 N	3.03 W
Blackpool □[8]	262	53.47 N	3.02 W
Blackpool (Squire's Gate) Airport ⊠	262	53.47 N	3.02 W
Blackpool Football Ground ♠	262	53.49 N	3.03 W
Blackpool Tower ɤ	262	53.49 N	3.03 W
Black Range ⩕	200	33.20 N	107.50 W
Black River, Jam.	241q	18.01 N	77.51 W
Black River, N.Y., U.S.	212	44.01 N	75.48 W
Black River Bay C, Jam.	241q	18.00 N	77.51 W
Black River Bay C, N.Y., U.S.	212	43.58 N	76.07 W
Black River Falls	190	44.23 N	90.52 W
Black Rock, Austl.	274b	37.59 S	145.01 E
Black Rock, Ark., U.S.	194	36.06 N	91.06 W
Black Rock, Mass., U.S.	283	42.14 N	70.49 W
Blackrock ∧[2]	48	52.18 N	8.32 W
Black Rock I[2]	48	54.05 N	10.22 W
Black Rock II[1]	244	53.39 S	41.48 W
Black Rock Desert ⊸[2]	204	41.10 N	119.00 W
Black Rock Harbor C	276	41.09 N	73.13 W
Blackrod	262	53.35 N	2.35 W
Blacksburg, S.C., U.S.	192	35.07 N	81.31 W
Blacksburg, Va., U.S.	192	37.14 N	80.25 W
Blacks Creek ≃	285	40.08 N	74.43 W
Black Sea ⊤[2]	22	43.00 N	35.00 E
Blacks Fork ≃	200	41.24 N	109.38 W
Blacks Harbour	186	45.03 N	66.47 W
Blackshear	192	31.18 N	82.14 W
Blackshear, Lake @[1]	192	31.56 N	83.56 W
Blacksod Bay C	48	54.08 N	10.00 W
Black Springs	170	33.52 S	149.42 E
Black Springs Hill ∧[2]	274b	37.46 S	145.19 E
Black Star Canyon V	280	33.47 N	117.39 W
Blackstone, Mass., U.S.	207	42.01 N	71.30 W
Blackstone, Va., U.S.	192	37.04 N	78.00 W
Blackstone ≃, Alta., Can.	182	52.50 N	116.07 W
Blackstone ≃, Yukon, Can.	180	65.51 N	137.12 W
Blackstone Lake @	212	45.14 N	79.53 W
Black Sugarloaf Mountain ∧	166	31.20 S	151.33 E
Black Thunder Creek ≃	198	43.33 N	104.41 W
Blacktown	170	33.46 S	150.55 E
Black Umbeluzi ≃	158	26.08 S	31.52 E
Black Umfolozi ≃	158	28.22 S	31.58 E
Blackville	192	33.22 N	81.16 W
Black Volta (Volta Noire) ≃	150	8.41 N	1.33 W
Blackwall Tunnel ⊸[5]	260	51.30 N	0.01 E
Blackwalnut Point ≻	208	38.40 N	76.20 W
Black Warrior ≃	194	32.32 N	87.51 W
Blackwatch Hills	210	43.05 N	77.27 W
Blackwater, Austl.	166	23.35 S	148.53 E
Blackwater, Eire	48	52.26 N	6.21 W
Blackwater ≃, Eire	48	51.51 N	7.50 W
Blackwater ≃, Eur.	44	54.31 N	6.34 W
Blackwater ≃, Eng., U.K.	260	51.45 N	1.00 E
Blackwater ≃, U.S.	194	30.36 N	87.02 W
Blackwater ≃, Md., U.S.	208	38.21 N	76.01 W
Blackwater ≃, Mo., U.S.	194	38.56 N	92.51 W
Blackwater ≃, Va., U.S.	208	36.33 N	76.55 W
Blackwater Creek ≃, Austl.	166	25.56 S	144.20 E
Black Water Creek ≃, Fla., U.S.	220	28.51 N	81.24 W
Blackwater Draw V	196	33.35 N	101.50 W
Blackwaterfoot	46	55.30 N	5.19 W
Blackwater Lake @	180	64.00 N	123.05 W
Blackwater Reservoir @[1]	46	56.41 N	4.46 W
Blackwater Sound ɯ	220	25.10 N	80.25 W
Blackwell, Okla., U.S.	196	36.48 N	97.17 W
Blackwell, Tex., U.S.	196	32.05 N	100.19 W
Blackwood, Austl.	168b	35.02 S	138.37 E
Blackwood, Austl.	169	37.29 S	144.19 E
Blackwood, N.J., U.S.	285	39.48 N	75.04 W
Blackwood, Cape ≻	164	7.50 S	144.30 E
Blackwood Terrace	285	39.48 N	75.05 W
Bladel	52	51.23 N	5.13 E
Bladenboro	192	34.33 N	78.48 W
Bladensburg, Md., U.S.	284c	38.56 N	76.55 W
Bladensburg, Ohio, U.S.	214	40.17 N	82.17 W
Blades	208	38.38 N	75.36 W
Bladgrond	158	28.52 S	19.57 E
Bladnoch ≃	44	54.51 N	4.25 W
Bladworth	184	51.18 N	106.09 W
Blaenau Ffestiniog	42	52.59 N	3.56 W
Blaenavon	42	51.48 N	3.05 W
Bláfell ∧	24a	64.32 N	19.53 W
Blagaj	36	43.15 N	17.50 E
Blagdon	42	51.20 N	2.43 W
Blagodarnoje, S.S.S.R.	72	45.06 N	43.27 E
Blagodarnoje, S.S.S.R.	86	47.03 N	82.10 E
Blagodatnoje, S.S.S.R.	78	51.32 N	34.54 E
Blagodatnoje, S.S.S.R.	83	47.53 N	38.29 E
Blagodatnoje, S.S.S.R.	83	47.42 N	37.25 E
Blagodatnoje, S.S.S.R.	86	51.18 N	72.49 E
Blagodatovka	80	52.14 N	50.27 E
Blagoevgrad	38	42.01 N	23.06 E
Blagoveščenka, S.S.S.R.	80	51.19 N	44.03 E
Blagoveščenka, S.S.S.R.	86	52.50 N	79.52 E
Blagoveščenka, S.S.S.R.	86	54.22 N	66.58 E
Blagoveščensk, S.S.S.R.	86	55.01 N	55.59 E
Blagoveščensk, S.S.S.R.	89	50.17 N	127.32 E
Blagoveščenskoje, S.S.S.R.	85	43.18 N	74.12 E
Blagoveščenskoje, S.S.S.R.	86	58.08 N	62.58 E
Blåhø ∧	26	62.45 N	9.19 E
Blåhøj	41	55.51 N	9.01 E
Blaichach	58	47.34 N	10.15 E
Blain, Fr.	32	47.29 N	1.46 W
Blain, Pa., U.S.	208	40.20 N	77.31 W
Blaina	42	51.46 N	3.10 W
Blain City	214	40.40 N	78.34 W
Blaine, Minn., U.S.	190	45.11 N	93.14 W
Blaine, Wash., U.S.	224	48.59 N	122.44 W
Blaine Creek ≃	188	38.11 N	82.37 W
Blaine Hill	279b	40.16 N	79.53 W
Blaine Lake	184	52.50 N	106.54 W
Blaineys	224	48.53 N	123.47 W
Blainville-sur-l'Eau	58	48.33 N	6.24 E
Blair, Ont., Can.	212	43.23 N	80.23 W
Blair, Nebr., U.S.	198	41.33 N	96.08 W
Blair, Okla., U.S.	196	34.47 N	99.20 W
Blair, Wis., U.S.	190	44.18 N	91.14 W
Blair □[6]	214	40.30 N	78.25 W
Blair Athol	166	22.42 S	147.33 E
Blair Atholl	46	56.46 N	3.51 W
Blairgowrie	46	56.36 N	3.21 W
Blairmore	182	49.36 N	114.26 W
Blairs Mills	214	40.17 N	77.43 W
Blairstown, Iowa, U.S.	190	41.55 N	92.05 W
Blairstown, N.J., U.S.	210	40.59 N	74.57 W
Blairsville, Ga., U.S.	192	34.53 N	83.58 W
Blairsville, Pa., U.S.	214	40.26 N	79.16 W
Blaise ≃, Fr.	50	48.46 N	1.25 E
Blaise ≃, Fr.	58	48.38 N	4.43 E
Blaisy-Bas	58	47.22 N	4.44 E
Blaj	38	46.11 N	23.55 E
Blajkfjället ∧	26	64.33 N	16.12 E
Blakehurst	274a	33.59 S	151.07 E
Blakeley Canal ≚	226	36.09 N	119.48 W
Blakely, Ga., U.S.	192	31.23 N	84.56 W
Blakely, Pa., U.S.	210	41.28 N	75.31 W
Blakely Island I	224	48.33 N	122.50 W
Blakeney, Eng., U.K.	42	52.58 N	1.00 E
Blakeney, Eng., U.K.	42	51.46 N	2.29 W
Blake Point ≻	190	48.12 N	88.25 W
Blakes	208	37.30 N	76.22 W
Blakesburg	190	40.58 N	92.38 W
Blakeslee, Ohio, U.S.	216	41.31 N	84.44 W
Blakeslee, Pa., U.S.	210	41.06 N	75.36 W
Blalock Island I	202	45.53 N	119.41 W
Blamont, Fr.	58	47.23 N	6.51 E
Blâmont, Fr.	58	48.35 N	6.51 E
Blanba	120	30.49 N	94.59 E
Blanc, Cap ≻, Afr.	148	20.46 N	17.03 W
Blanc, Cap ≻, Tun.	148	37.20 N	9.50 E
Blanc, Mont (Monte Bianco) ∧	62	45.50 N	6.52 E
Blanca	200	37.27 N	105.31 W
Blanca, Bahía C	252	38.55 S	62.10 W
Blanca, Isla I	248	9.06 S	78.38 W
Blanca, Laguna @	254	52.25 S	71.10 W
Blanca, Punta ≻	258	34.57 S	57.40 W
Blanca, Sierra ∧	200	31.15 N	105.26 W
Blanca Lake @	224	47.53 N	121.21 W
Blanca Peak ∧	200	37.35 N	105.29 W
Blanc du Cheilon, Mont ∧	58	45.59 N	7.25 E
Blanchard, Okla., U.S.	196	35.08 N	97.39 W
Blanchard, Pa., U.S.	210	41.04 N	77.36 W
Blanchard, Wash., U.S.	224	48.36 N	122.26 W
Blanchard ≃	216	41.02 N	84.18 W
Blanchardville	190	42.49 N	89.52 W
Blanche ≃, Ont., Can.	190	47.34 N	79.32 W
Blanche ≃, Qué., Can.	206	46.40 N	72.08 W
Blanche, Cape ≻	162	33.01 S	134.09 E
Blanche, Dent ∧	58	46.03 N	7.36 E
Blanche, Lake @, Austl.	162	22.25 S	123.17 E
Blanche, Lake @, Austl.	166	29.15 S	139.39 E

	English	Deutsch	Español	Français	Português
≃	River	Fluss	Río	Rivière	Rio
≚	Canal	Kanal	Canal	Canal	Canal
ʟ	Waterfall, Rapids	Wasserfall, Stromschnellen	Cascada, Rápidos	Chute d'eau, Rapides	Cascata, Rápidos
ɯ	Strait	Meeresstrasse	Estrecho	Détroit	Estreito
C	Bay, Gulf	Bucht, Golf	Bahía, Golfo	Baie, Golfe	Baía, Golfo
@	Lake, Lakes	See, Seen	Lago, Lagos	Lac, Lacs	Lago, Lagos
☷	Swamp	Sumpf	Pantano	Marais	Pântano
⩒	Ice Features, Glacier	Eis- und Gletscherformen	Accidentes Glaciales	Formes glaciaires	Acidentes Glaciares
⊤	Other Hydrographic Features	Andere Hydrographische Objekte	Otros Elementos Hidrográficos	Autres données hydrographiques	Outros Elementos Hidrográficos
✣	Submarine Features	Untermeerische Objekte	Accidentes Submarinos	Formes de relief sous-marin	Acidentes Submarinos
□	Political Unit	Politische Einheit	Unidad Politica	Entité politique	Unidade Política
ɤ	Cultural Institution	Kulturelle Institution	Institución Cultural	Institution culturelle	Instituição Cultural
⊥	Historical Site	Historische Stätte	Sitio Histórico	Site historique	Sitio Histórico
♠	Recreational Site	Erholungs- und Ferienort	Sitio de Recreo	Centre de loisirs	Sítio de Lazer
⊠	Airport	Flughafen	Aeropuerto	Aéroport	Aeroporto
▪	Military Installation	Militäranlage	Instalación Militar	Installation militaire	Instalação Militar
⊸	Miscellaneous	Verschiedenes	Misceláneo	Divers	Miscelânea

Blanche, Mer → Beloje More ⌶² 24 65.30 N 38.00 E
Blanche Channel Ψ 175e 8.30 S 157.30 E
Blancheface 261 48.32 N 2.06 E
Blanchester 188 39.17 N 83.55 W
Blanchisseuse 241r 10.47 N 61.18 W
Blanco, S. Afr. 158 33.57 S 22.24 E
Blanco, Tex., U.S. 196 30.06 N 98.25 W
Blanco ≃, Arg. 254 47.22 S 71.12 W
Blanco ≃, Perú 248 5.27 S 73.47 W
Blanco ≃, Tex., U.S. 196 29.51 N 97.55 W
Blanco, Cabo → Blanc, Cap >, Afr. 148 20.46 N 17.03 W
Blanco, Cabo >, C.R. 236 9.34 N 85.07 W
Blanco, Cañon V 200 35.20 N 105.05 W
Blanco, Cape > 202 42.50 N 124.34 W
Blanco, Lago @ 254 54.03 S 69.00 W
Blanco, Mar → Beloje More ⌶² 24 65.30 N 38.00 E
Blanco, Monte → Blanc, Mont ∧ 62 45.50 N 6.52 E
Blanco, Rio ≃ 200 37.07 N 107.03 W
Blanc-Sablon 186 51.25 N 57.07 W
Bland, Mo., U.S. 219 38.18 N 91.38 W
Bland, Va., U.S. 192 37.06 N 81.07 W
Blanda ≃ 24a 65.39 N 20.18 W
Blandburg 214 40.41 N 78.25 W
Blandford 207 42.11 N 72.56 W
Blandford Forum 42 50.52 N 2.11 W
Blanding 200 37.37 N 109.29 W
Blandinsville 190 40.33 N 90.52 W
Blandon 208 40.26 N 75.53 W
Blandy 261 48.34 N 2.47 E
Blanes 34 41.41 N 2.48 E
Blangkejeren 114 3.59 N 97.20 E
Blangpidie 114 3.45 N 96.51 E
Blangy-le-Château 50 49.14 N 0.17 E
Blangy-sur-Bresle 50 49.56 N 1.38 E
Blanice ≃ 61 49.05 N 14.03 E
Blankenberg 56 50.45 N 7.22 E
Blankenberge 50 51.19 N 3.08 E
Blankenburg 54 51.48 N 10.58 E
Blankenburg •⁸ 264a 52.35 N 13.28 E
Blankenese •⁸ 52 53.33 N 9.48 E
Blankenfelde 54 52.20 N 13.23 E
Blankenfelde •⁸ 264a 52.37 N 13.23 E
Blankenhain 54 50.51 N 11.21 E
Blankenheim, B.R.D. 56 50.26 N 6.39 E
Blankenheim, D.D.R. 54 51.31 N 11.25 E
Blankensee 54 52.14 N 13.08 E
Blankenstein 263 51.24 N 7.14 E
Blanket 196 31.49 N 98.47 W
Blanquefort 32 44.53 N 0.39 W
Blanquilla, Isla I 246 11.51 N 64.37 W
Blansko 30 49.22 N 16.39 E
Blanský Les •³ 61 48.52 N 14.16 E
Blantyre 154 15.47 S 35.00 E
Blanzac 62 45.07 N 3.51 E
Blanzy 58 46.42 N 4.23 E
Blaricum 52 52.16 N 5.15 E
Blarney 48 51.56 N 8.34 W
Blarney Castle ⊥ 48 51.56 N 8.34 W
Blasdell 210 42.47 N 78.49 W
Blasheim 52 52.18 N 8.34 E
Błaszki 30 51.39 N 18.27 E
Blatná 60 49.26 N 13.53 E
Blatnica 38 43.42 N 28.31 E
Blatten 58 46.25 N 7.50 E
Blatzheim 56 50.51 N 6.38 E
Blau ≃ 58 48.23 N 9.49 E
Blaubeuren 58 48.24 N 9.47 E
Blauen ∧ 58 47.47 N 7.42 E
Blauer Nil → Blue Nile ≃ 140 15.38 N 32.31 E
Blaufelden 56 49.18 N 9.58 E
Blauvelt 276 41.04 N 73.58 W
Blauvelt State Park ♠ 276 41.04 N 73.56 W
Blåvands Huk > 26 55.33 N 8.05 E
Blawenburg 276 40.24 N 74.42 W
Blawnox 279b 40.29 N 79.52 W
Blaxland 170 33.45 S 150.36 E
Blaxland Creek ≃ 274a 33.48 S 150.46 E
Blaydon 44 54.58 N 1.42 W
Blaye-et-Sainte-Luce 32 45.08 N 0.39 W
Blayney 166 33.32 S 149.15 E
Blaze, Point > 164 12.56 S 130.12 E
Błażowa 30 49.54 N 22.05 E
Bleaklow Head ∧ 262 53.28 N 1.50 W
Blean 42 51.19 N 1.02 E
Bleckede 54 53.17 N 10.44 E
Bled 36 46.22 N 14.06 E
Bledsoe 196 33.38 N 103.01 W
Bleecker 210 43.07 N 74.22 W
Blefjell ∧ 26 59.48 N 9.10 E
Blega 115a 7.08 S 113.03 E
Bleibach 58 48.07 N 8.01 E
Bleiberg ob Villach 64 46.37 N 13.41 E
Bleiburg 61 46.35 N 14.48 E
Bleicherode 54 51.26 N 10.34 E
Bleidenstadt 56 50.08 N 8.08 E
Blekendorf 54 54.16 N 10.38 E
Blekinge □⁹ 26 56.20 N 15.05 E
Blekinge Län □⁶ 26 56.20 N 15.20 E
Blendecques 50 50.43 N 2.16 E
Bléneau 50 47.42 N 2.57 E
Blénestroff 56 48.54 N 6.45 E
Blenheim, Austl. 171a 27.39 S 152.20 E
Blenheim, Ont., Can. 214 42.20 N 82.00 W
Blenheim, N.Z. 172 41.31 S 173.57 E
Blenheim, N.J., U.S. 285 39.48 N 75.05 W
Blenheim Palace ⊍ 42 51.47 N 1.21 W
Blenio, Val V 58 46.27 N 8.58 E
Blénod-lès-Pont-à-Mousson 56 48.53 N 6.03 E
Blénod-lès-Toul 58 48.36 N 5.50 E
Bléone ≃ 62 44.03 N 6.00 E
Blérancourt 50 49.31 N 3.09 E
Bléré 50 47.20 N 1.00 E
Blerick 52 51.23 N 6.10 E
Blériot-Plage 50 50.57 N 1.50 E
Blesbokspruit ≃ 273d 26.14 S 28.29 E
Blessing 222 28.52 N 96.13 W
Blessington 48 53.10 N 6.32 W
Bletchingley 260 51.14 N 0.06 W
Bletchley 42 52.00 N 0.46 W
Bletterans 58 46.45 N 5.27 E
Bleu → Changjiang ≃ 90 31.48 N 121.10 E
Bleury 261 48.31 N 1.45 E
Blevio 62 45.50 N 9.05 E
Blewett Falls Lake @¹ 192 35.03 N 79.54 W
Blexen 52 53.32 N 8.32 E
Blida 148 36.28 N 2.50 E
Blidö I 40 59.37 N 18.54 E
Bliedinghausen •⁸ 263 51.09 N 7.12 E
Bliersheim 263 51.23 N 6.43 E
Blies ≃ 56 49.07 N 7.04 E
Blieskastel 56 49.14 N 7.16 E
Bligh Sound Ψ 172 44.50 S 167.32 E
Bligh Water Ψ 175g 17.00 S 178.00 E
Bligny 50 49.11 N 3.52 E
Bligny-sur-Ouche 58 47.06 N 4.40 E
Blik, Mount ∧ 116 6.58 N 124.15 E
Blind ≃ 276 40.57 N 73.42 W
Blind Creek ≃ 274b 37.54 S 145.12 E
Blindley Heath 260 51.12 N 0.04 W
Blind River 190 46.10 N 82.58 W
Blinman 166 31.06 S 138.41 E
Blinnenhorn ∧ 58 46.26 N 8.19 E
Blinovskij 80 49.23 N 42.19 E
Bliss 210 42.35 N 78.15 W
Blissfield, Mich., U.S. 216 41.50 N 83.52 W
Blissfield, Ohio, U.S. 214 40.24 N 81.58 W
Blitar 115a 8.06 S 112.09 E
Blithe ≃ 42 52.45 N 1.50 W
Blithfield Reservoir @¹ 42 52.48 N 1.53 W
Blitta 150 8.19 N 0.59 E

Blizn'uki 78 48.52 N 36.33 E
Blocher 218 38.43 N 85.39 W
Block Dam •⁶ 212 45.12 N 76.54 W
Block Island 207 41.10 N 71.34 W
Block Island I 207 41.11 N 71.35 W
Block Island Sound Ψ 207 41.10 N 71.45 W
Blockley 42 52.01 N 1.45 W
Blockton 198 40.37 N 94.29 W
Blodgett Mills 210 42.34 N 76.08 W
Bloedel 182 50.07 N 125.23 W
Bloedrivier, S. Afr. 158 28.06 S 30.33 E
Bloedrivier, S. Afr. 158 27.53 S 30.30 E
Bloekomspruit 158 26.45 S 28.21 E
Bloemendaal 52 52.24 N 4.37 E
Bloemfontein 158 29.12 S 26.07 E
Bloemhof 158 27.38 S 25.32 E
Blois 50 47.35 N 1.20 E
Blokhus 26 57.15 N 9.35 E
Blokzijl 52 52.44 N 5.57 E
Blombacher Bach •⁸ 263 51.15 N 7.14 E
Blombacka 40 59.37 N 13.47 E
Blomberg 52 51.56 N 9.05 E
Blomstermåla 26 56.59 N 16.20 E
Blonay 58 46.28 N 6.54 E
Blönduós 24a 65.39 N 20.15 W
Blongas 115b 8.53 S 116.02 E
Blonville-sur-Mer 50 49.19 N 0.02 E
Blood Indian Creek ≃ 184 50.55 N 111.03 W
Blood Indian Reserve •⁴ 182 49.30 N 113.10 W
Blood Mountain ∧ 192 34.44 N 83.56 W
Blood River ⊥ 158 28.20 S 30.35 E
Bloods Creek 162 26.28 S 135.17 E
Bloodsworth Island I 208 38.10 N 76.03 W
Bloodvein ≃ 184 51.45 N 96.44 W
Bloody Foreland > 48 55.09 N 8.17 W
Bloom, Slieve ∧∧ 48 53.05 N 7.35 W
Bloomdale 216 41.10 N 83.33 W
Bloomer 190 45.07 N 91.29 W
Bloomfield, Ont., Can. 212 43.59 N 77.14 W
Bloomfield, Conn., U.S. 207 41.50 N 72.44 W
Bloomfield, Ind., U.S. 194 39.01 N 86.56 W
Bloomfield, Iowa, U.S. 190 40.45 N 92.25 W
Bloomfield, Ky., U.S. 194 37.55 N 85.19 W
Bloomfield, Mo., U.S. 194 36.53 N 89.56 W
Bloomfield, Nebr., U.S. 198 42.36 N 97.39 W
Bloomfield, N.J., U.S. 210 40.48 N 74.12 W
Bloomfield, N. Mex., U.S. 200 36.43 N 107.59 W
Bloomfield, Ohio, U.S. 214 40.03 N 81.44 W
Bloomfield •⁸ 279b 40.27 N 79.56 W
Bloomfield Glens 281 42.33 N 83.20 W
Bloomfield Highlands 281 42.36 N 83.16 W
Bloomfield Hills 216 42.35 N 83.15 W
Bloomfield Village 216 42.33 N 83.15 W
Bloomingburg, N.Y., U.S. 210 41.33 N 74.26 W
Bloomingburg, Ohio, U.S. 218 39.36 N 83.24 W
Bloomingdale, Ill., U.S. 216 41.58 N 88.05 W
Bloomingdale, Mich., U.S. 216 42.23 N 85.57 W
Bloomingdale, N.J., U.S. 210 41.00 N 74.20 W
Bloomingdale, Ohio, U.S. 214 40.21 N 80.49 W
Blooming Glen 208 40.22 N 75.15 W
Blooming Grove, Ind., U.S. 218 39.30 N 85.04 W
Blooming Grove, N.Y., U.S. 210 41.25 N 74.11 W
Blooming Grove, Pa., U.S. 210 41.21 N 75.09 W
Blooming Grove, Tex., U.S. 222 32.06 N 96.43 W
Blooming Prairie 190 43.52 N 93.03 W
Bloomington, Calif., U.S. 228 34.04 N 117.24 W
Bloomington, Ill., U.S. 216 40.29 N 89.00 W
Bloomington, Ind., U.S. 218 39.10 N 86.32 W
Bloomington, Minn., U.S. 190 44.50 N 93.17 W
Bloomington, N.Y., U.S. 210 41.53 N 74.03 W
Bloomington, Tex., U.S. 196 28.39 N 96.54 W
Bloomington, Wis., U.S. 190 42.53 N 90.55 W
Bloomington, Lake @¹ 216 40.37 N 88.55 W
Blooming Valley 214 41.40 N 80.03 W
Bloomsburg 210 41.00 N 76.27 W
Bloomsbury, Austl. 166 20.43 S 148.35 E
Bloomsbury, N.J., U.S. 210 40.39 N 75.05 W
Bloomsdale Gardens 285 40.07 N 74.52 W
Bloomville, N.Y., U.S. 210 42.20 N 74.48 W
Bloomville, Ohio, U.S. 214 41.03 N 83.01 W
Blora 115a 6.57 S 111.25 E
Bloserville 208 40.12 N 77.24 W
Blossburg 210 41.41 N 77.04 W
Blossom 196 33.40 N 95.23 W
Blossom Hill 208 40.05 N 76.19 W
Blötberget 40 60.07 N 15.04 E
Blotzheim 58 47.36 N 7.29 E
Blouberg 156 23.08 S 28.56 E
Blouberg ∧ 156 23.01 S 28.59 E
Bloubergstrand 158 33.47 S 18.28 E
Blouin, Lac @ 190 48.10 N 77.44 W
Bloumet 148 23.27 N 6.06 E
Blountstown 192 30.27 N 85.03 W
Blountsville 194 34.05 N 86.35 W
Blovice 60 49.35 N 13.33 E
Blovstrød 41 55.52 N 12.24 E
Blowering Reservoir @¹ 171b 35.30 S 148.15 E
Blowing Rock 192 36.08 N 81.41 W
Bloxham 42 52.02 N 1.22 W
Bloxom 208 37.50 N 75.38 W
Blšanka ≃ 54 50.10 N 13.34 E
Blšany 54 50.10 N 13.29 E
Bludenz 58 47.09 N 9.49 E
Blue ≃, Ariz., U.S. 200 33.13 N 109.11 W
Blue ≃, Colo., U.S. 200 40.03 N 106.24 W
Blue ≃, Ind., U.S. 216 41.07 N 85.30 W
Blue ≃, Ind., U.S. 218 38.11 N 86.19 W
Blue ≃, Okla., U.S. 196 33.53 N 95.56 W
Blue, Middle Fork ≃ 218 38.33 N 86.07 W
Blue, South Fork ≃ 218 38.26 N 86.11 W
Blue, West Fork ≃ 218 38.33 N 86.07 W
Blue Anchor 285 39.41 N 74.53 W
Blue Ash 218 39.14 N 84.22 W
Blue Ball 218 39.29 N 84.21 W
Blue Bell 208 40.09 N 75.16 W
Bluebell Hill 260 51.20 N 0.30 E
Blue Bonnets, Champ de Course ♠ 275a 45.29 N 73.39 W
Blue Brook ≃ 276 40.40 N 74.25 W
Blue Buck Knob ∧² 194 36.57 N 92.07 W
Blue Creek 218 38.47 N 83.20 W
Blue Creek ≃, Calif., U.S. 226 38.28 N 120.22 W
Blue Creek ≃, Idaho, U.S. 202 42.02 N 116.08 W
Blue Creek ≃, Nebr., U.S. 198 41.19 N 102.10 W

Blue Creek ≃, N. Mex., U.S. 200 32.50 N 105.00 W
Blue Creek ≃, Ohio, U.S. 216 41.07 N 84.26 W
Blue Cypress Lake @ 220 27.44 N 80.45 W
Blue Earth 190 43.38 N 94.06 W
Blue Earth ≃ 190 44.09 N 94.02 W
Bluefield, Va., U.S. 192 37.15 N 81.17 W
Bluefield, W. Va., U.S. 192 37.16 N 81.13 W
Bluefields 236 12.00 N 83.45 W
Bluefields, Bahía de C 236 12.02 N 83.44 W
Bluefields Bay C 241q 18.10 N 78.03 W
Blue Grass Airport ⊠ 218 38.02 N 84.36 W
Blue Grotto → Azzurra, Grott •⁵ 68 40.35 N 14.14 E
Blue Gum Mine 154 18.25 S 29.25 E
Blue Hill, Maine, U.S. 188 44.25 N 68.36 W
Blue Hill, Nebr., U.S. 198 40.20 N 98.27 W
Blue Hill Bay C 188 44.15 N 68.30 W
Blue Hills 207 41.47 N 72.42 W
Blue Hills of Couteau ∧∧² 186 47.59 N 57.43 W
Blue Hills Reservation ♠ 283 42.13 N 71.05 W
Blue Island 216 41.40 N 87.41 W
Blue Jay 228 34.15 N 117.13 W
Bluejoint Lake @ 202 42.35 N 119.40 W
Blue Knob ∧ 214 40.17 N 78.34 W
Blue Knob State Park ♠ 214 40.16 N 78.35 W
Blue Licks Battlefield State Park ♠ 218 38.26 N 84.00 W
Blue Mesa Reservoir @¹ 200 38.27 N 107.10 W
Blue Mosque ⊍¹ 273c 30.02 N 31.15 E
Blue Mound, Ill., U.S. 219 39.42 N 89.07 W
Blue Mound, Kans., U.S. 198 38.05 N 95.00 W
Blue Mound, Tex., U.S. 222 32.51 N 97.19 W
Blue Mountain, Miss., U.S. 194 34.40 N 89.02 W
Blue Mountain, N.Y., U.S. 210 42.07 N 74.01 W
Blue Mountain ∧, N.B., Can. 186 47.49 N 66.19 W
Blue Mountain ∧, Newf., Can. 186 50.24 N 57.10 W
Blue Mountain ∧, Ont., Can. 212 44.28 N 80.22 W
Blue Mountain ∧, Ark., U.S. 194 34.41 N 94.03 W
Blue Mountain ∧, Mont., U.S. 198 47.16 N 104.10 W
Blue Mountain ∧, N.H., U.S. 188 44.47 N 71.28 W
Blue Mountain ∧, Pa., U.S. 188 40.15 N 77.30 W
Blue Mountain ∧², Ont., Can. 190 48.15 N 80.07 W
Blue Mountain ∧², Ont., Can. 212 44.40 N 77.58 W
Blue Mountain Peak ∧ 241q 18.03 N 76.35 W
Blue Mountains ∧∧, Austl. 170 33.37 S 150.17 E
Blue Mountains ∧∧, Jam. 241q 18.06 N 76.40 W
Blue Mountains ∧∧, U.S. 202 45.30 N 118.15 W
Blue Mountains ∧∧, Maine, U.S. 188 44.50 N 70.35 W
Blue Mud Bay C 164 13.26 S 135.56 E
Blue Nile (Al-Baḥr al-Azraq) (Abay) ≃ 140 15.38 N 32.31 E
Bluenose Lake @ 176 68.30 N 119.35 W
Blue Point 276 40.45 N 73.02 W
Blue Point > 276 40.44 N 73.02 W
Blue Rapids 198 39.41 N 96.39 W
Blue Ridge, Alta., Can. 182 54.08 N 115.22 W
Blue Ridge, Ga., U.S. 192 34.52 N 84.20 W
Blue Ridge, Ill., U.S. 216 40.17 N 88.29 W
Blue Ridge ∧∧ 178 37.00 N 82.00 W
Blue Ridge Summit 208 39.43 N 77.28 W
Blue River 182 52.05 N 119.17 W
Blue Rock Springs Park ♠ 282 38.08 N 122.12 W
Bluesky 182 56.04 N 118.14 W
Blue Springs 198 40.09 N 96.40 W
Blue Stack Mountains ∧∧ 48 54.45 N 8.05 W
Bluestone ≃ 192 37.34 N 80.59 W
Bluestone Dam •⁶ 192 37.36 N 80.53 W
Bluestone Lake @¹ 192 37.30 N 80.50 W
Bluewater 200 35.15 N 107.59 W
Blue Water Bridge •⁵ 214 43.00 N 82.25 W
Bluff, N.Z. 172 46.36 S 168.20 E
Bluff, Utah, U.S. 200 37.17 N 109.33 W
Bluff Cape > 110 18.00 N 94.26 E
Bluff City, Ill., U.S. 219 40.11 N 90.14 W
Bluff City, Tenn., U.S. 192 36.28 N 82.16 W
Bluff Cove C 280 33.48 N 118.24 W
Bluff Creek ≃, U.S. 196 36.58 N 97.26 W
Bluff Creek ≃, Kans., U.S. 198 37.02 N 99.29 W
Bluff Dale 196 32.21 N 98.01 W
Bluff Island I 271d 22.19 N 114.21 E
Bluff Knoll ∧ 162 34.23 S 118.20 E
Bluff Park 194 33.27 N 86.47 W
Bluff Point >, Austl. 162 27.50 S 114.06 E
Bluff Point >, H.K. 271d 22.11 N 114.12 E
Bluffs 219 39.45 N 90.32 W
Bluff Springs 219 39.59 N 90.21 W
Bluffton, Ind., U.S. 216 40.44 N 85.11 W
Bluffton, Ohio, U.S. 216 40.54 N 83.54 W
Bluffton, S.C., U.S. 192 32.14 N 80.52 W
Bluffy Lake @ 184 50.47 N 92.55 W
Bluford 219 38.20 N 88.45 W
Blum 222 32.09 N 97.24 W
Blumberg, B.R.D. 58 47.50 N 8.31 E
Blumberg, D.D.R. 54 52.36 N 13.37 E
Blumenau 252 26.56 S 49.03 W
Blumenhof 184 50.01 N 107.41 W
Blümlisalp ∧ 58 46.30 N 7.47 E
Blunt 198 44.31 N 99.59 W
Blupblup Island I 164 3.30 S 144.37 E
Bly 202 42.24 N 121.02 W
Blying Sound Ψ 180 59.50 N 149.15 W
Blyth, Austl. 168b 33.51 S 138.29 E
Blyth, Ont., Can. 190 43.44 N 81.26 W
Blyth, Eng., U.K. 44 55.07 N 1.30 W
Blyth ≃, Austl. 164 12.04 S 134.35 E
Blyth ≃, Eng., U.K. 42 52.18 N 1.40 E
Blyth ≃, Eng., U.K. 44 55.08 N 1.31 W
Blyth Bridge 46 55.42 N 3.24 W
Blythe 204 33.37 N 114.36 W
Blythe ≃ 42 52.31 N 1.42 W
Blythedale 214 40.15 N 79.48 W
Blytheswood 214 42.07 N 82.36 W
Blytheville 194 35.56 N 89.55 W
Blytheville Air Force Base ■ 194 35.57 N 89.57 W
Blyth Range ∧∧ 162 26.50 S 129.00 E
Bnei Braq → Bene Beraq 132 32.05 N 34.50 E
Bø, Nor. 24 68.37 N 14.33 E
Bø, Nor. 26 59.25 N 9.04 E
Bo, S.L. 150 7.56 N 11.21 W
Boa 154 10.32 S 28.06 E
Boa Barrinha 256 23.18 S 47.10 W
Boac 116 13.27 N 121.50 E
Boaco 236 12.28 N 85.40 W
Boaco □⁵ 236 12.30 N 85.30 W
Boadilla del Monte 266a 40.24 N 3.53 W
Boa Esperança, Bra. 255 21.05 S 45.34 W

Boa Esperança, Bra. 256 22.48 S 42.34 W
Boa Esperança, Represa @¹ 250 6.50 S 44.00 W
Boai 102 35.10 N 113.04 E
Boali 152 4.48 N 18.07 E
Boalia 126 23.35 N 88.57 E
Boalsburg 214 40.46 N 77.48 W
Boano, Pulau I 164 2.56 S 127.56 E
Boa Nova 255 14.22 S 40.10 W
Boara Pisani 64 45.08 N 11.47 E
Boara Polesine 64 45.07 N 11.48 E
Board Camp Mountain ∧ 204 40.42 N 123.43 W
Boardman 214 41.02 N 80.40 W
Boardman ≃ 190 44.46 N 85.38 W
Boarhills 46 56.19 N 2.42 W
Boario Terme 64 45.54 N 10.10 E
Boat Basin 182 49.29 N 126.25 W
Boath 46 57.44 N 4.23 W
Boat Lake @ 212 44.44 N 81.13 W
Boatman 166 27.16 S 146.55 E
Boat of Garten 46 57.20 N 3.44 W
Boa Vereda 256 22.27 S 46.14 W
Boa Viagem 250 5.07 S 39.44 W
Boa Vida 256 22.18 S 42.47 W
Boa Vista, Bra. 246 2.49 N 60.40 W
Boa Vista, Bra. 252 26.17 S 48.50 W
Boa Vista I 150a 16.05 N 22.50 W
Boa Vista, Morro ∧² 287a 22.53 S 43.06 W
Boavita 246 6.20 N 72.35 W
Boawai 115b 8.46 S 121.10 E
Boayan Island I 116 10.34 N 119.09 E
Boaz 194 34.12 N 86.10 W
Boba 115b 8.57 S 121.04 E
Bobai 102 22.12 N 109.52 E
Bobbau 54 51.41 N 12.16 E
Bobbili 122 18.34 N 83.22 E
Bobbing 260 51.21 N 0.43 E
Bobbingworth 260 51.44 N 0.13 E
Bobbin Head 274a 33.39 S 151.08 E
Bobbio 62 44.46 N 9.23 E
Bobbio Pellice 62 44.48 N 7.07 E
Bobbys Run ≃ 285 39.58 N 74.48 W
Bobcaygeon 212 44.33 N 78.33 W
Bobigny 50 48.54 N 2.27 E
Böbingen, B.R.D. 56 48.49 N 9.54 E
Bobingen, B.R.D. 58 48.16 N 10.50 E
Bobitz 54 53.47 N 11.20 E
Bob Lake @ 212 44.55 N 78.47 W
Böblingen 56 48.41 N 9.01 E
Bob-Lo Park ♠ 281 42.06 N 83.07 W
Bobo Dioulasso 150 11.12 N 4.18 W
Boboiob, Gora ∧ 85 40.52 N 70.21 E
Bobolice 30 53.57 N 16.36 E
Bobon 116 12.32 N 124.34 E
Bobonaza ≃ 246 2.36 S 76.38 W
Bobonong 156 21.58 S 28.17 E
Bobotsari 115a 7.18 S 109.22 E
Boboye, Dallol V 150 14.00 N 3.00 E
Bobr 76 54.20 N 29.16 E
Bóbr ≃, Pol. 30 52.04 N 15.04 E
Bobr ≃, S.S.S.R. 76 54.03 N 28.51 E
Bobrik ≃ 76 52.08 N 26.46 E
Bobrikovo 83 47.56 N 39.13 E
Bobrinec 78 48.03 N 32.09 E
Bobrka 78 49.38 N 24.18 E
Bobrov 78 51.06 N 40.02 E
Bobrovica 78 50.44 N 31.22 E
Bobrujsk 76 53.09 N 29.14 E
Bobs Creek ≃ 219 38.57 N 90.42 W
Bobs Lake @ 212 44.40 N 76.35 W
Bobtown 188 39.46 N 79.59 W
Bobuk 140 11.30 N 34.05 E
Bobures 246 9.15 N 71.11 W
Boby, Pic ∧ 157b 22.12 S 46.55 E
Boca •⁸ 288 34.38 S 58.21 W
Bôca, Cachoeira da ⌐ 250 5.27 S 54.24 W
Boca Brava, Isla I 236 8.13 N 82.16 W
Boca Chica 240m 17.59 N 66.32 W
Boca Chica Key I 220 24.34 N 81.42 W
Bôca da Mata 250 9.41 S 36.11 W
Boca del Monte 236 8.21 N 82.07 W
Boca del Pozo 246 11.00 N 64.23 W
Boca del Río 234 19.06 N 96.06 W
Boca del Rosario 258 34.26 S 57.17 W
Boca de Quadra Ψ 182 55.08 N 130.50 W
Bôca do Acre 248 8.45 S 67.23 W
Bôca do Jari 250 1.07 S 51.58 W
Bocage, Cap > 175f 21.12 S 165.35 E
Boca Grande 220 26.45 N 82.16 W
Boca Grande Channel Ψ 220 24.34 N 82.03 W
Boca Grande Key I 220 24.32 N 82.00 W
Bocaina ≃ 256 22.40 S 45.00 W
Bocaina, Serra da ∧∧ 256 22.43 S 44.40 W
Bocaina de Minas 256 22.10 S 44.24 W
Bocaiúva 255 17.07 S 43.49 W
Bocanda 150 7.04 N 4.30 W
Bocanegra 286d 12.01 S 77.07 W
Bocaranga 152 6.59 N 15.39 E
Boca Raton 220 26.21 N 80.05 W
Boca Reservoir @¹ 226 39.24 N 120.06 W
Bocas del Toro 236 9.20 N 82.15 W
Bocas del Toro □⁴ 236 8.50 N 82.10 W
Bocas del Toro, Archipiélago de II 236 9.20 N 82.10 W
Bocay 236 14.19 N 85.10 W
Bocay ≃ 236 14.20 N 85.10 W
Boccaleone 66 44.39 N 11.48 E
Boccea •⁸ 267a 41.58 N 12.19 E
Bocchigliero 68 39.25 N 16.45 E
Boccon 64 45.19 N 11.39 E
Bocconi 64 44.01 N 11.46 E
Bočejkovo 76 55.01 N 29.09 E
Bochan 88 53.09 N 103.48 E
Bochil 234 16.59 N 92.55 W
Böchmörön 86 49.40 N 90.20 E
Bochnia 30 49.58 N 20.26 E
Bocholt, Bel. 56 51.10 N 5.35 E
Bocholt, B.R.D. 52 51.50 N 6.36 E
Bocholtz 56 50.49 N 6.00 E
Bochov 54 50.06 N 13.02 E
Bochum, B.R.D. 56
263 51.28 N 7.13 E
Bochum, S. Afr. 156 23.17 S 29.07 E
Bockel 52 53.12 N 9.17 E
Böckel •⁸ 263 51.13 N 7.12 E
Bockenem 52 52.00 N 10.07 E
Bockhorn 52 53,23 N 8.01 E
Böckstein 64 47.05 N 13.07 E
Bockum 263 51.20 N 6.44 E
Bockum •⁸ 263 51.21 N 6.38 E
Bockum-Hövel 52 51.42 N 7.46 E
Bocognano 36 42.05 N 9.03 E
Boconó 246 9.15 N 70.16 W
Bocq ≃ 56 50.20 N 4.53 E
Boczów 54 52.19 N 14.58 E
Boda, Centraf. 152 4.19 N 17.28 E
Boda, Sve. 26 61.01 N 15.13 E
Böda, Sve. 26 57.15 N 17.03 E
Bodafors 26 57.30 N 14.42 E
Boda Glasbruk 26 56.44 N 15.40 E
Bodāi 272b 22.48 N 88.29 E
Bodajbo 88 57.51 N 114.10 E
Bodalangi 152 3.14 N 22.14 E
Bodalla 166 36.05 S 150.03 E
Bodallin 162 31.22 S 118.52 E
Bodanga Dawili 152 5.33 N 16.45 E
Bodåsgruvan 40 60.25 N 16.26 E
Bodcau Creek ≃ 194 33.01 N 93.31 W
Boddam, Scot., U.K. 46 59.55 N 1.17 W
Boddam, Scot., U.K. 46 57.28 N 1.47 W
Boddington 168a 32.48 S 116.28 E
Bode 198 42.52 N 94.17 W
Bode ≃ 54 52.01 N 11.12 E
Bodega Bay C 204 38.15 N 123.00 W
Bodegraven 52 52.05 N 4.45 E
Bodele •¹ 146 16.30 N 16.30 E

Bodelschwingh •⁸ 263 51.33 N 7.22 E
Boden → Fleres, It. 64 46.58 N 11.21 E
Boden, Sve. 26 65.50 N 21.42 E
Bodenburg 52 52.01 N 10.01 E
Bodenfelde 52 51.38 N 9.33 E
Bodenheim 56 49.56 N 8.18 E
Bodenmais 60 49.04 N 13.06 E
Bodensee (Lake Constance) @ 58 47.35 N 9.25 E
Bodenteich 54 52.50 N 10.41 E
Bodenwerder 52 51.59 N 9.31 E
Bodenwies ∧ 61 47.45 N 14.34 E
Bodenwöhr 60 49.16 N 12.19 E
Boderg, Lough @ 48 53.52 N 7.58 W
Bode Sadu 150 9.00 N 4.47 E
Bodhan 122 18.40 N 77.54 E
Bodiam 42 51.00 N 0.33 E
Bodināyakkanūr 122 10.01 N 77.21 E
Bodine, Mount ∧ 182 55.37 N 125.49 W
Bodjoki 152 2.59 N 22.18 E
Bodjokola 152 3.54 N 20.17 E
Bodmin 42 50.29 N 4.43 W
Bodmin Moor •³ 42 50.33 N 4.33 W
Bodø 24 67.17 N 14.23 E
Bodocó 250 7.47 S 39.55 W
Bodoquena, Serra da ∧∧¹ 248 21.00 S 56.50 W
Bodoupa 152 5.43 N 17.36 E
Bodri ≃ 115a 6.52 S 110.10 E
Bodrog ≃ 38 48.07 N 21.25 E
Bodrum 130 37.02 N 27.26 E
Bodstedt 54 54.22 N 12.37 E
Bo-duc (Bu-dop) 110 11.58 N 106.48 E
Bodzentyn 30 50.56 N 20.57 E
Boè, Piz ∧ 64 46.31 N 11.48 E
Boëge 58 46.13 N 6.25 E
Boegoebergdam •⁶ 158 29.02 S 22.12 E
Boekelo 52 52.13 N 6.47 E
Boele •⁸ 263 51.24 N 7.28 E
Boémbé 152 2.54 S 15.39 E
Boende 152 0.13 S 20.52 E
Bœng Lvea 110 12.36 N 105.34 E
Boeni 157a 12.55 S 45.06 E
Boën-sur-Lignon 62 45.44 N 3.59 E
Boer 98 35.42 N 119.45 E
Boerboonfontein 158 33.43 S 20.32 E
Boerne 196 29.47 N 98.44 W
Boertala Zizhizhou □⁴ 86 45.00 N 83.00 E
Boeslunde 41 55.18 N 11.17 E
Boesmansriviermond 158 33.42 S 26.39 E
Boetsap 158 27.59 S 24.30 E
Boeuf Creek ≃ 219 38.36 N 91.09 W
Boffa 150 10.10 N 14.02 W
Boffa □⁴ 150 10.20 N 14.00 W
Boffalora 266b 45.28 N 8.50 E
Boffzen 52 51.45 N 9.23 E
Bofoku 152 0.57 S 20.53 E
Bofors 40 59.20 N 14.32 E
Bofosso 150 8.40 N 9.42 W
Bōfu → Hōfu 96 34.03 N 131.34 E
Boga 154 1.03 N 29.56 E
Bogachiel ≃ 224 47.55 N 124.28 W
Bogadjim 164 5.25 S 145.45 E
Bogale 110 16.17 N 95.24 E
Bogalusa 194 30.47 N 89.52 W
Bogan ≃ 166 32.45 S 148.08 E
Bogandé 150 12.59 N 0.08 W
Bog and Vly Meadows ≡ 276 40.56 N 74.19 W
Bogan Gate 166 33.07 S 147.48 E
Bogangolo 152 5.34 N 18.15 E
Bogantungan 166 23.39 S 147.18 E
Bogastow Brook ≃ 283 42.12 N 71.22 W
Bogata 196 33.28 N 95.13 W
Bogataja Černeščina 78 48.59 N 35.35 E
Bogatiščevo-Jepišino 82 54.47 N 38.25 E
Bogatyje Saby 80 56.01 N 50.27 E
Bogatynia 54 50.53 N 15.00 E
Bogatyr' 80 53.25 N 50.02 E
Bogatyrevo 80 50.22 N 48.46 E
Boğazkale 130 40.02 N 34.37 E
Boğazköy 267b 41.11 N 28.46 E
Boğazlıyan 130 39.12 N 35.15 E
Bogbonga 152 1.35 N 19.25 E
Bogdanovič 86 56.47 N 62.01 E
Bogdanovka, S.S.S.R. 80 52.10 N 52.37 E
Bogdanovka, S.S.S.R. 80 52.42 N 50.46 E
Bogdanovka, S.S.S.R. 84 41.18 N 43.35 E
Bogdo Ula ∧ 86 43.50 N 88.20 E
Bogd-Uul 102 45.09 N 100.43 E
Bogdyn ≃ 88 47.20 N 95.50 E
Bogeduoshanmai ∧∧ 90 43.30 N 89.45 E
Bogel 56 50.11 N 7.48 E
Bogembaj 86 52.29 N 72.20 E
Bogen 60 48.55 N 12.43 E
Bogenfels 156 27.23 S 15.22 E
Bogense 41 55.34 N 10.06 E
Boger City 192 35.29 N 81.13 W
Boges 56 50.11 N 7.48 E
Bogess Creek ≃ 282 37.18 N 122.19 W
Boget 80 49.40 N 47.59 E
Boggabilla 166 28.37 S 150.21 E
Boggabri 166 30.42 S 150.02 E
Boggeragh Mountains ∧∧ 48 52.03 N 8.55 W
Boggola, Mount ∧ 162 23.48 S 117.40 E
Boggs Run ≃ 279b 40.32 N 80.14 W
Boggstown 218 39.34 N 85.55 W
Boggy Creek ≃ 222 31.07 N 95.46 W
Boggy Peak ∧ 240c 17.03 N 61.51 W
Bogia 164 4.15 S 144.55 E
Bogie Lake @ 281 42.37 N 83.31 W
Bogilima 152 3.34 N 19.16 E
Boğlan 130 38.58 N 41.03 E
Bogliasco 62 44.23 N 9.04 E
Bognanco Fonti 58 46.07 N 8.12 E
Bognes 24 68.10 N 16.00 E
Bognor Regis 42 50.47 N 0.41 W
Bogny-sur-Meuse 56 49.51 N 4.46 E
Bogo, Cam. 146 10.44 N 14.36 E
Bogo, Pil. 116 11.03 N 124.00 E
Bogø I 41 54.56 N 12.04 E
Bogo Bay C 116 11.05 N 124.01 E
Bogoduchov 78 50.10 N 35.30 E
Bogol Manya 144 4.32 N 41.32 E
Bogol'ubovo, S.S.S.R. 76 55.32 N 32.57 E
Bogol'ubovo, S.S.S.R. 80 56.13 N 40.31 E
Bogomila 38 41.36 N 21.28 E
Bogon 144 2.56 N 42.00 E
Bogong, Mount ∧ 166 36.45 S 147.18 E
Bogong Peaks ∧∧ 171b 35.34 S 148.28 E
Bogor 115a 6.35 S 106.47 E
Bogoro 154 1.24 N 30.17 E
Bogorodčany 78 48.48 N 24.32 E
Bogorodick 76 53.46 N 38.08 E
Bogorodickoje 80 46.20 N 41.10 E
Bogorodičnoje 83 49.01 N 37.30 E
Bogorodsk, S.S.S.R. 24 62.16 N 52.28 E
Bogorodsk, S.S.S.R. 80 56.06 N 43.31 E
Bogorodskoje, S.S.S.R. 80 57.49 N 50.45 E
Bogorodskoje, S.S.S.R. 80 46.20 N 43.53 E
Bogorodskoje, S.S.S.R. 82 55.26 N 36.14 E
Bogorodskoje, S.S.S.R. 82 55.02 N 38.29 E
Bogorodskoje, S.S.S.R. 89 52.22 N 140.30 E
Bogorodskoje •⁸ 265b 55.49 N 37.44 E
Bogoso 150 5.34 N 2.01 W
Bogotá, Col. 246 4.36 N 74.05 W

Bogota, N.J., U.S. 276 40.53 N 74.02 W
Bogotol 86 56.12 N 89.33 E
Bogou 150 10.39 N 0.11 E
Bogovarovo 24 58.59 N 47.01 E
Bogra 124 24.51 N 89.22 E
Bograd 86 54.13 N 90.51 E
Bogrie Hill ∧² 44 55.08 N 3.55 W
Bogučany 88 58.23 N 97.29 E
Bogučar 78 49.57 N 40.33 E
Bogučar ≃ 78 49.57 N 40.39 E
Bogué 150 16.35 N 14.16 W
Bogue Chitto ≃ 194 30.35 N 89.49 W
Bogue Chitto Creek ≃ 194 32.10 N 87.14 W
Bogues Bay C 208 37.52 N 75.29 W
Bogunaj 86 56.14 N 94.35 E
Böğürtlen 130 37.10 N 38.04 E
Boguslav 78 49.33 N 30.53 E
Bogušovsk 76 54.51 N 30.13 E
Bogustan 85 41.41 N 70.05 E
Bohai C 98 38.30 N 120.00 E
Bohain-en-Vermandois 50 49.59 N 3.27 E
Bohaiwan C 98 38.40 N 118.20 E
Bohan 56 49.52 N 4.53 E
Bohannon 208 37.24 N 76.22 W
Bohemia 210 40.46 N 73.07 W
Bohemia → Čechy □⁹ 30 49.50 N 14.00 E
Bohemia ≃ 208 39.29 N 75.55 W
Bohemia Downs 162 18.53 S 126.14 E
Bohemian Forest ∧∧ 30 49.15 N 12.45 E
Bohetai 104 42.01 N 123.13 E
Bohicon 150 7.12 N 2.04 E
Bohinjska Bistrica 36 46.17 N 13.57 E
Böhlen 54 51.12 N 12.23 E
Böhlitz-Ehrenberg •⁸ 54 51.21 N 12.17 E
Böhme ≃ 52 52.46 N 9.28 E
Böhmen → Čechy □⁹ 30 49.50 N 14.00 E
Böhmenkirch 56 48.41 N 9.55 E
Böhmerwald → Bohemian Forest ∧∧ 30 49.15 N 12.45 E
Bohmte 52 52.22 N 8.19 E
Bohners Lake 216 42.37 N 88.17 W
Böhnsdorf •⁸ 264a 52.24 N 13.33 E
Bohodou 150 9.46 N 9.04 W
Bohol 144 5.43 N 46.10 E
Bohol □⁴ 116 9.50 N 124.10 E
Bohol I 116 9.50 N 124.10 E
Bohol Strait Ψ 116 9.45 N 123.40 E
Bohon 116 18.30 N 120.35 E
Bohongou 150 12.30 N 0.42 E
Bohorok 114 3.30 N 98.12 E
Bohotleh Wein 144 8.16 N 46.24 E
Bohsdorf 54 51.38 N 14.32 E
Bohuslän □⁹ 26 58.15 N 11.50 E
Bohušovice nad Ohří 54 50.29 N 14.07 E
Bohutín 60 49.40 N 13.55 E
Boi 150 9.34 N 9.27 E
Boi, Ponta do > 256 23.58 S 45.15 W
Boiaçu 246 0.27 S 61.46 W
Boiano 66 41.29 N 14.29 E
Boiceville 210 41.59 N 74.15 W
Boiestown 186 46.27 N 66.25 W
Boigu Island I 164 9.16 S 142.12 E
Boila 154 16.10 S 39.50 E
Boiling Springs, N.C., U.S. 192 35.16 N 81.40 W
Boiling Springs, Pa., U.S. 208 40.09 N 77.08 W
Boinville-en-Mantois 261 48.56 N 1.46 E
Boinvilliers 261 48.55 N 1.40 E
Boipeba, Ilha de I 255 13.39 S 38.55 W
Boiro 34 42.39 N 8.54 W
Bois, Lac des @, N.W. Ter., Can. 180 66.40 N 125.15 W
Bois, Lac des → Woods, Lake of the @, N.A. 184 49.15 N 94.45 W
Bois, Rio dos ≃ 255 18.35 S 50.02 W
Bois Blanc Island I 190 45.45 N 84.28 W
Bois Brule ≃ 190 46.45 N 91.37 W
Boischâtel 206 46.54 N 71.08 W
Bois-Colombes 261 48.55 N 2.16 E
Boisdale, Loch C 46 57.08 N 7.19 W
Bois d'Arc Creek ≃ 196 33.50 N 95.50 W
Bois-d'Arcy 261 48.48 N 2.01 E
Bois-des-Filion 206 45.40 N 73.45 W
Bois de Sioux ≃ 198 46.16 N 96.36 W
Bois du Roi ∧ 32 47.00 N 4.02 E
Boise 202 43.37 N 116.13 W
Boise ≃ 202 43.49 N 117.01 W
Boise, Middle Fork ≃ 202 43.42 N 115.38 W
Boise, North Fork ≃ 202 43.42 N 115.38 W
Boise, South Fork ≃ 202 43.36 N 115.51 W
Boise City 196 36.44 N 102.31 W
Boisemont 261 49.01 N 2.00 E
Bois-Guillaume 50 49.28 N 1.08 E
Bois-le-Roi 50 48.28 N 2.42 E
Boissettes 261 48.31 N 2.37 E
Boissevain 184 49.14 N 100.03 W
Boissise-la-Bertrand 261 48.32 N 2.35 E
Boissy-l'Aillerie 261 49.05 N 2.02 E
Boissy-Saint-Léger 50 48.45 N 2.31 E
Boissy-sous-Saint-Yon 261 48.34 N 2.13 E
Boistfort Peak ∧ 224 46.29 N 123.12 W
Boitzenburg 54 53.15 N 13.37 E
Boizenburg 54 53.22 N 10.43 E
Boja 115a 7.06 S 110.16 E
Bojadła 30 51.57 N 15.50 E
Bojador, Cabo > 148 26.08 N 14.30 W
Bojarka 78 50.19 N 30.19 E
Bojarkino 82 54.57 N 38.31 E
Bojarsk 88 56.19 N 106.04 E
Bojayá ≃ 246 6.35 N 76.54 W
Bojeador, Cape > 116 18.30 N 120.34 E
Bojelebung 116 6.31 N 122.11 E
Bojevo 78 51.24 N 39.19 E
Boji Plain = 154 1.30 N 39.45 E
Bojizhang 98 41.49 N 117.46 E
Bojnūrd 128 37.28 N 57.19 E
Bojonegoro 115a 7.09 S 111.52 E
Boju 150 7.25 N 7.52 E
Boju Ega 150 7.24 N 8.04 E
Bojuru 252 31.38 S 51.26 W
Bokad 272c 18.53 N 72.58 E
Bokada 152 4.08 N 19.23 E
Bokal 168a 33.29 S 116.54 E
Bokala, Zaïre 152 3.07 S 17.02 E
Bokala, Zaïre 152 2.03 N 18.59 E
Bokalike 120 36.47 N 91.41 E
Bokani 150 9.26 N 5.13 E
Bokāro 124 23.51 N 86.02 E
Bokatola 152 0.38 S 18.46 E
Bokchito 196 34.01 N 96.09 W
Boké 150 10.56 N 14.18 W
Boké □⁴ 150 11.00 N 14.20 W
Bokeelia 220 26.42 N 82.09 W
Bokel 52 53.23 N 8.46 E
Bokela 152 1.08 S 21.56 E
Bokes Creek ≃ 188 40.19 N 83.10 W
Boketu 89 48.46 N 121.57 E
Bokfontein 158 32.48 S 19.16 E
Bokhara 158 27.57 S 20.30 E
Bokhara ≃ 166 29.55 S 146.42 E
Boki 146 8.48 N 13.32 E
Bokino 80 52.38 N 41.26 E
Bokkeveldberg ∧∧ 158 31.22 S 19.02 E
Böklund 41 54.36 N 9.34 E
Boknafjorden C² 26 59.10 N 5.35 E
Boko, Congo 152 4.47 S 14.38 E
Boko, S.S.S.R. 86 49.05 N 81.38 E
Bokod 116 16.30 N 120.50 E
Bokode 152 3.58 N 19.29 E

Symbols in the index entries represent the broad categories identified in the key at the right. Symbols with superior numbers (∧∧²) identify subcategories (see complete key on page I · 30).

Kartensymbole in dem Registerverzeichnis stellen die rechts in Schlüssel erklärten Kategorien dar. Symbole mit hochgestellten Ziffern (∧∧²) bezeichnen Unterabteilungen einer Kategorie (vgl. vollständiger Schlüssel auf Seite I · 30).

Los símbolos incluidos en el texto del índice representan las grandes categorías identificadas con la clave a la derecha. Los símbolos con números en su parte superior (∧∧²) identifican las subcategorías (véase la clave completa en la página I · 30).

Les symboles de l'index représentent les catégories indiquées dans la légende à droite. Les symboles suivis d'un indice (∧∧²) représentent des sous-catégories (voir légende complète à la page I · 30).

Os símbolos incluídos no texto do índice representam as grandes categorias identificadas com a chave à direita. Os símbolos com números em sua parte superior (∧∧²) identificam as subcategorias (veja-se a chave completa à página I · 30).

	English	Deutsch	Español	Français	Português
∧	Mountain	Berg	Montaña	Montagne	Montanha
∧∧	Mountains	Berge	Montañas	Montagnes	Montanhas
)(	Pass	Pass	Paso	Col	Passo
V	Valley, Canyon	Tal, Cañon	Valle, Cañón	Vallée, Canyon	Vale, Canhão
=	Plain	Ebene	Llano	Plaine	Planície
>	Cape	Kap	Cabo	Cap	Cabo
I	Island	Insel	Isla	Île	Ilha
II	Islands	Inseln	Islas	Îles	Ilhas
•	Other Topographic Features	Andere Topographische Objekte	Otros Elementos Topográficos	Autres données topographiques	Outros Elementos Topográficos

ESPAÑOL — Nombre · Página · Lat.°′ · Long.°′ W=Oeste

Bokolako 150 13.36 N 12.33 W
Bokonbajevskoje 85 42.07 N 77.00 E
Bokondji 152 2.22 N 18.42 E
Bokondo 152 0.15 N 22.32 E
Bokong 112 9.58 S 124.04 E
Bokoro 146 12.23 N 17.03 E
Boko Songo 152 4.26 S 13.37 E
Bokota 152 0.51 S 22.18 E
Bokote 152 0.05 S 20.08 E
Bokovo-Antratsit → Antracit 83 48.06 N 39.06 E
Bokovo Platovo 83 48.07 N 39.01 E
Bokovskaja 80 49.15 N 41.49 E
Bokpunt ≻ 158 33.34 S 18.19 E
Bokpyin 110 11.16 N 98.46 E
Boksburg 158 26.12 S 28.14 E
Boksburg North 273d 26.12 S 28.15 E
Boksburg South 273d 26.14 S 28.15 E
Boksburg West 273d 26.13 S 28.14 E
Boksitogorsk 76 59.28 N 33.51 E
Bokungu 152 0.41 S 22.19 E
Bol, Jugo. 36 43.16 N 16.40 E
Bol, Tchad 146 13.28 N 14.43 E
Bola 175e 9.37 S 160.39 E
Bolaang Mongondow 112 0.56 N 124.10 E
Bolaï I 152 4.20 N 17.21 E
Bolama, Gui.-B. 150 11.35 N 15.28 W
Bolama, Zaïre 152 1.57 N 22.58 E
Bolān ≃ 120 28.38 N 67.42 E
Bolanda, Jabal ∧ 140 7.44 N 25.28 E
Bolands 240c 17.02 N 61.53 W
Bolangum 166 36.46 S 142.53 E
Bolaños 234 21.41 N 103.47 W
Bolaños ≃ 234 21.14 N 104.08 W
Bolaños de Calatrava 34 38.54 N 3.40 W
Bolayır 130 40.31 N 26.45 E
Bolbec 50 49.34 N 0.29 E
Bolčary 86 59.49 N 68.48 E
Bolchov 76 53.27 N 36.01 E
Bolchuny 80 47.59 N 46.25 E
Bolda ≃ 80 46.10 N 48.14 E
Boldasevo 80 54.43 N 45.33 E
Boldekow 54 53.43 N 13.35 E
Bolderslev 41 54.59 N 9.18 E
Bold Heath 262 53.24 N 2.42 W
Boldon 44 54.57 N 1.27 W
Bol'džuan 85 38.19 N 69.40 E
Bole, Ghana 150 9.02 N 2.29 W
Bole, Zhg. 86 44.53 N 82.05 E
Bolechov 78 49.04 N 23.52 E
Boléko, Gabon 152 0.56 N 12.14 E
Boleko, Zaïre 152 1.31 S 19.53 E
Bolero 154 10.59 S 33.45 E
Boles 194 34.47 N 94.03 W
Bolesławiec 30 51.16 N 15.34 E
Boleszkowice 30 52.44 N 14.36 E
Boletice nad Labem 54 50.45 N 14.13 E
Boley 196 35.29 N 96.29 W
Bolgart 162 31.16 S 116.30 E
Bolgatanga 150 10.46 N 0.52 W
Bolgrad 78 45.41 N 28.36 E
Boli, Sūd. 140 6.01 N 28.43 E
Boli, Tchad 146 10.50 N 18.43 E
Boli, Zhg. 89 45.46 N 130.35 E
Bolia 152 1.36 S 18.23 E
Boliden 26 64.52 N 20.23 E
Boligee 194 32.45 N 88.02 W
Boligeqiu 104 42.14 N 121.40 E
Bolíkov 61 49.02 N 15.22 E
Bolinao 116 16.23 N 119.54 E
Bolinas 226 37.54 N 122.42 W
Boling 222 29.16 N 95.57 W
Bolingbrook 216 41.42 N 88.03 W
Bolinger Creek ≃ 282 37.47 N 122.00 W
Bolingo 152 3.30 S 21.43 E
Bolishan 89 43.50 N 123.31 E
Bolívar, Arg. 252 36.15 S 61.06 W
Bolivar, Austl. 168b 34.46 S 138.36 E
Bolívar, Col. 246 4.21 N 76.10 W
Bolívar, Col. 246 5.50 N 76.01 W
Bolívar, Col. 246 1.50 N 76.58 W
Bolívar, Perú 248 7.18 S 77.48 W
Bolivar, Mo., U.S. 194 37.37 N 93.25 W
Bolivar, N.Y., U.S. 210 42.04 N 78.10 W
Bolivar, Ohio, U.S. 214 40.39 N 81.27 W
Bolivar, Pa., U.S. 214 40.23 N 79.10 W
Bolivar, Tenn., U.S. 194 35.16 N 88.59 W
Bolívar □[3] 246 6.20 N 63.30 W
Bolívar □[4] 246 1.35 S 79.00 W
Bolívar □[5] 246 9.00 N 74.40 W
Bolívar, Cerro ∧ 246 7.28 N 63.25 W
Bolívar, Pico ∧ 246 8.30 N 71.02 W
Bolivar Peninsula ≻[1] 196 29.27 N 94.39 W
Bolivar Run 214 41.59 N 78.39 W
Bolivia □[1] 242
248 17.00 S 65.00 W
Bolivie → Bolivia □[1] 248 17.00 S 65.00 W
Bolivien → Bolivia □[1] 248 17.00 S 65.00 W
Boljarovo 38 42.09 N 26.49 E
Boljoon 116 9.38 N 123.29 E
Bolkar Dağları ⩚ 130 37.15 N 34.20 E
Bölkenbusch 263 51.21 N 7.06 E
Boll 56 48.38 N 9.37 E
Bolladello 266b 45.41 N 8.50 E
Bollate 62 45.33 N 9.07 E
Böllberg ∧[2] 263 51.23 N 7.19 E
Bollendorf 56 49.51 N 6.22 E
Bollène 62 44.17 N 4.45 E
Bollensdorf 264a 52.31 N 13.43 E
Bolles Canal ⩶ 220 26.38 N 80.34 W
Bolles Harbor 216 41.51 N 83.24 W
Bollin ≃ 262 53.23 N 2.28 W
Bolling Air Force Base ■ 284c 38.51 N 77.02 W
Bollington, Eng., U.K. 262 53.18 N 2.06 W
Bollington, Eng., U.K. 262 53.22 N 2.25 W
Bollmora 40 59.15 N 18.13 E
Bollnäs 26 61.21 N 16.25 E
Bollon 166 28.05 S 147.15 E
Bollstabruk 26 63.00 N 17.39 E
Bollstanäs 40 59.30 N 17.56 E
Bollullos par del Condado 34 37.20 N 6.32 W
Bollwerk 263 51.10 N 7.35 E
Bolmen ◎ 26 56.55 N 13.40 E
Bolnisi 84 41.28 N 44.33 E
Bolobo 152 2.10 S 16.14 E
Bolochovo 82 54.05 N 37.50 E
Bologna 64 44.29 N 11.20 E
Bologna □[4] 64 44.28 N 11.26 E
Bologne, Fr. 58 48.12 N 5.08 E
Bologne → Bologna, It. 64 44.29 N 11.20 E
Bolognesi 248 6.35 S 73.10 W
Bolognetta 70 37.58 N 13.27 E
Bolognola 66 42.59 N 13.14 E
Bologoje 76 57.54 N 34.02 E
Bologovo 76 56.54 N 31.42 E
Bololo 152 3.50 S 21.08 E
Bolomba 152 0.29 N 19.12 E
Bolombo 152 3.59 S 21.22 E
Bolombo ≃ 152 1.32 N 21.14 E
Bolon' 89 49.55 N 136.07 E
Bolonchén de Rejón 232 20.00 N 89.49 W
Bolondo 152 0.27 N 20.01 E
Bolondrón 240p 22.46 N 81.27 W
Bolonia → Bologna 64 44.29 N 11.20 E
Bolo Silase 144 8.54 N 39.27 E
Bolótana 71 40.20 N 8.57 E
Bolotino 78 47.42 N 27.21 E
Bolotnoje 86 55.41 N 84.23 E
Boloto 82 54.10 N 36.20 E
Bolotovskoje 86 58.33 N 62.28 E
Bolovens, Plateau des ⩚[1] 110 15.20 N 106.20 E
Bolpur 126 23.40 N 87.43 E
Bol'šaja 76 59.36 N 41.48 E

FRANÇAIS — Nom · Page · Lat.°′ · Long.°′ W=Ouest

Bol'šaja ≃ 80 48.36 N 41.00 E
Bol'šaja Atn'a 80 56.15 N 49.27 E
Bol'šaja Balachn'a ≃ 74 73.37 N 107.05 E
Bol'šaja Belaja ≃ 88 52.52 N 103.05 E
Bol'šaja Ber'ostovica 76 53.11 N 24.01 E
Bol'saja Bira ≃ 89 48.07 N 133.21 E
Bol'šaja Blagoveščenka 78 46.52 N 33.04 E
Bol'šaja Brembola 82 56.45 N 38.55 E
Bol'šaja Černigovka 80 52.07 N 50.52 E
Bol'šaja Chalan' 78 50.56 N 37.26 E
Bol'šaja Cheta ≃ 74 69.33 N 84.15 E
Bol'šaja Chobda ≃ 86 50.56 N 54.34 E
Bol'šaja Chundala 76 60.04 N 34.18 E
Bol'šaja Čuja ≃ 88 58.56 N 112.13 E
Bol'šaja Čurakovka 86 53.03 N 64.20 E
Bol'šaja Damba 80 46.57 N 51.47 E
Bol'šaja Dmitrijevka 80 51.21 N 45.15 E
Bol'šaja Dora 76 59.05 N 37.38 E
Bol'saja Džalga 80 45.59 N 42.42 E
Bol'šaja Glušica 80 52.24 N 50.28 E
Bol'šaja Golova, Porog ⌞ 24 62.49 N 41.48 E
Bol'šaja Ižora 76 59.56 N 29.34 E
Bol'šaja Ižorka ≃ 265a 59.48 N 30.36 E
Bol'šaja Kakša ≃ 80 57.53 N 45.28 E
Bol'šaja Kamenka 80 53.39 N 50.31 E
Bol'šaja Kamenka ≃ 83 48.22 N 40.04 E
Bol'šaja Kandala 80 54.32 N 49.22 E
Bol'šaja Karpunicha 80 57.42 N 45.20 E
Bol'šaja Kaskara 86 57.11 N 65.58 E
Bol'šaja Kemčug ≃ 88 56.53 N 91.51 E
Bol'šaja Ket' 86 57.39 N 91.45 E
Bol'šaja Ket' ≃ 88 57.57 N 91.13 E
Bol'šaja Kinel' ≃ 80 53.14 N 50.30 E
Bol'šaja Kirsanovka 83 47.40 N 38.54 E
Bol'šaja Kokšaga ≃ 80 56.08 N 47.47 E
Bol'šaja Konkudera ≃ 88 57.34 N 112.30 E
Bol'šaja Kuberle ≃ 80 47.20 N 42.02 E
Bol'šaja Kugul'ta ≃ 80 45.45 N 41.57 E
Bol'šaja Kuonamka ≃ 74 70.45 N 113.24 E
Bol'šaja Laba ≃ 84 44.16 N 40.53 E
Bol'šaja Lipovica 80 52.33 N 41.20 E
Bol'šaja Log 83 48.12 N 39.06 E
Bol'šaja Martynovka 80 47.17 N 41.40 E
Bol'šaja Mošanica 76 53.58 N 29.37 E
Bol'šaja Murta 86 56.55 N 93.07 E
Bol'šaja Norja 80 56.41 N 52.43 E
Bol'šaja Ochta ⊸[8] 265a 59.57 N 30.25 E
Bol'šaja Ol'šanka 80 51.32 N 44.17 E
Bol'šaja Orlovka 80 47.20 N 41.16 E
Bol'saja Osinovaja ≃ 180 66.30 N 174.00 E
Bol'šaja Pas'ma 80 58.38 N 43.53 E
Bol'šaja Rečka 88 51.57 N 104.44 E
Bol'šaja Ržaksa 80 52.08 N 42.13 E
Bol'šaja Sestra ≃ 82 56.16 N 35.56 E
Bol'šaja Smedva ≃ 82 54.50 N 38.34 E
Bol'šaja Sosnova 80 57.40 N 54.36 E
Bol'šaja Talovaja 78 46.58 N 40.37 E
Bol'šaja Tarel' 88 53.45 N 106.40 E
Bol'šaja Tavolžka 80 52.07 N 49.04 E
Bol'šaja Uča 80 56.37 N 52.05 E
Bol'šaja Usa 86 56.44 N 55.06 E
Bol'šaja Višera 76 58.55 N 32.08 E
Bol'šaja Vladimirovka 86 50.53 N 79.31 E
Bol'šaja Vys' ≃ 78 48.45 N 30.54 E
Bolsa Knolls 226 36.44 N 121.38 W
Bol'šakovo, S.S.S.R. 76 54.53 N 21.40 E
Bol'šakovo, S.S.S.R. 265b 55.54 N 37.17 E
Bol'šečernigovka 83 48.57 N 39.25 E
Bol'šekrepinskaja 83 47.36 N 39.22 E
Bol'šelig 24 62.07 N 52.25 E
Bolsena 66 42.39 N 11.59 E
Bolsena, Lago di ◎ 66 42.36 N 11.56 E
Bol'šenarymskoje 86 49.16 N 84.32 E
Bol'šerečje 86 56.06 N 74.38 E
Bol'šereck 74 52.25 N 156.24 E
Bol'šetroickoje 78 50.33 N 37.17 E
Bol'šeustjikinskoje 86 55.57 N 58.16 E
Bol'ševik, S.S.S.R. 74 62.44 N 147.30 E
Bol'ševik, S.S.S.R. 76 52.34 N 30.53 E
Bol'ševik, S.S.S.R. 265a 59.49 N 30.30 E
Bol'ševik, Ostrov I 74 78.40 N 102.30 E
Bol'šezemel'skaja Tundra ⊸[1] 72 67.30 N 56.00 E
Bol'shaja Ket' ≃ 86 57.57 N 91.13 E
Bol'shije Liachvi ≃ 84 41.58 N 44.06 E
Bol'šije Algaši 80 55.22 N 46.29 E
Bol'šije Avt'uki 78 52.04 N 29.32 E
Bol'šije Belyniči 82 54.38 N 38.50 E
Bol'šije Berezniki 80 54.11 N 45.58 E
Bol'šije Gorki, S.S.S.R. 82 56.28 N 35.51 E
Bol'šije Gorki, S.S.S.R. 265a 59.42 N 29.51 E
Bol'šije Kajbicy 80 55.25 N 48.13 E
Bol'sije Kizi, Ozero ◎ 89 51.38 N 140.20 E
Bol'šije Kl'uči 80 55.59 N 48.47 E
Bol'šije Kl'učišči 80 54.08 N 48.14 E
Bol'šije Michalicyny 80 58.29 N 48.14 E
Bol'šije Ozerki 80 52.36 N 46.33 E
Bol'šije Pom'aly 80 56.42 N 46.40 E
Bol'šije Ručji 82 56.36 N 36.58 E
Bol'šije Saly 83 47.24 N 39.41 E
Bol' Sije Tarchany 80 54.42 N 48.34 E
Bol'šije Ugli 88 57.47 N 112.51 E
Bol'šije Uki 86 56.57 N 72.37 E
Bol'šije Ždanovy 80 58.40 N 49.05 E
Bol'šoj 80 50.13 N 43.26 E
Bol'šoj An'uj ≃ 74 68.30 N 160.49 E
Bol'šoj Ažbulat, Ozero ◎ 86 53.17 N 77.25 E
Bol'šoj Balchan, Chrebet ⩚ 128 39.40 N 54.30 E
Bol'šoj Begičev, Ostrov I 74 74.20 N 112.30 E
Bol'šoj Bogdo, Gora ∧[2] 80 48.08 N 46.52 E
Bol'šoj Bukon' 86 48.53 N 82.43 E
Bol'šoj Čeremšan ≃ 80 54.11 N 49.39 E
Bol'šoj Civil' ≃ 80 55.54 N 47.28 E
Bol'šoje, Ozero ◎ 265a 60.04 N 30.39 E
Bol'šoje Aksu 86 43.20 N 79.35 E
Bol'šoje Aleksejevskoje 82 55.14 N 38.12 E
Bol'šoje Boldino 80 54.59 N 45.19 E
Bol'šoje Bun'kovo 82 55.51 N 38.37 E
Bol'šoje Goloustnoje 88 52.01 N 105.25 E
Bol'šoje Gorodišče, S.S.S.R. 76 57.17 N 30.31 E
Bol'šoje Gorodišče, S.S.S.R. 78 50.37 N 37.06 E
Bol'šoje Ignatovo 80 55.02 N 45.34 E
Bol'šoje Jarovoje, Ozero ◎ 86 52.53 N 78.36 E
Bol'šoje Jasaltinskoje, Ozero ◎ 80 46.17 N 42.27 E
Bol'šoje Jeravnoje, Ozero ◎ 88 52.35 N 111.27 E
Bol'šoje Kibejevo 80 56.55 N 47.05 E
Bol'šoje Korovino 82 54.30 N 39.02 E
Bol'šoje Kozino 80 56.24 N 43.46 E
Bol'šoje Manuškino 265a 59.53 N 30.49 E
Bol'šoje Michajlovskoje 82 56.47 N 38.04 E
Bol'šoje Mikuškino 80 53.56 N 51.42 E
Bol'šoje Muraškino 80 55.47 N 44.46 E
Bol'šoje Nagatkino 80 54.31 N 47.58 E
Bol'šoje Nurkejevo 80 55.22 N 52.40 E
Bol'šoje Nyrsy 80 55.44 N 50.19 E
Bol'šoje Ogar'ovo 76 53.33 N 37.43 E
Bol'šoje Pikino 80 56.25 N 44.22 E
Bol'šoje Polpino 76 53.14 N 34.30 E

PORTUGUÊS — Nome · Página · Lat.°′ · Long.°′ W=Oeste

Bol'šoje Ramenje 76 58.21 N 36.40 E
Bol'šoje Rybuškino 80 55.25 N 45.48 E
Bol'šoje Sazonovo 80 58.06 N 53.21 E
Bol'šoje Šelo 76 57.43 N 38.56 E
Bol'šoje Šem'akino 80 55.03 N 48.38 E
Bol'šoje Soldatskoje 78 51.21 N 35.31 E
Bol'šoje Sudačje 80 50.49 N 44.05 E
Bol'šoje Topol'noje, Ozero ◎ 86 53.20 N 78.00 E
Bol'šoje Uro 88 53.32 N 109.48 E
Bol'soje Vlasjevo 89 53.24 N 140.55 E
Bol'šoje Zagorje 76 57.51 N 28.57 E
Bol'šoje Žokovo 82 54.35 N 38.57 E
Bol'šoj Gašun ≃ 80 47.22 N 42.43 E
Bol'šoj Irgiz ≃ 80 52.01 N 47.24 E
Bol'šoj Jenisej (Bij-Chem) ≃ 88 51.43 N 94.26 E
Bol'šoj Jugan ≃ 86 60.55 N 73.40 E
Bolsoj Kamen' 89 43.06 N 132.21 E
Bol'šoj Kandarat' 80 54.25 N 47.00 E
Bol'šoj Kanym, Gora ∧ 86 54.13 N 88.20 E
Bol'šoj Karagaj 86 57.57 N 70.15 E
Bol'šoj Karaj 80 52.36 N 42.41 E
Bol'šoj Karaman ≃ 80 51.40 N 46.38 E
Bol'šoj Kavkaz ⩚, S.S.S.R. 84 42.30 N 45.00 E
Bol'šoj Kemčug ≃ 86 56.53 N 91.51 E
Bol'šoj Ketmen' 86 43.27 N 80.24 E
Bol'soj Kinel' ≃ 86 53.14 N 50.30 E
Bol'šoj Kiržač ≃ 82 55.52 N 39.04 E
Bol'šoj Kujal'nik ≃ 78 46.46 N 30.36 E
Bol'šoj Kujaš 86 55.50 N 61.06 E
Bol'šoj Kundyš ≃ 80 56.32 N 47.23 E
Bol'šoj Kuvaj 80 54.37 N 47.05 E
Bol'šoj Kymenej ∧ 180 66.34 N 172.32 W
Bol'šoj L'achovskij, Ostrov I 74 73.35 N 142.00 E
Bol'šoj Lug 88 52.07 N 104.10 E
Bol'soj Matacing ∧ 180 66.28 N 179.25 W
Bol'šoj Melik 80 51.38 N 43.18 E
Bol'šoj Nesvetaj ≃ 83 47.27 N 39.54 E
Bol'šoj Onguren 88 53.38 N 107.36 E
Bol'šoj Patom ≃ 88 59.15 N 113.56 E
Bol'soj Pit ≃ 86 59.01 N 91.44 E
Bol'šoj Porog 86 52.35 N 92.18 E
Bol'šoj Šagan 80 50.57 N 51.08 E
Bol'šoj Sajan, Chrebet ⩚ 88 52.00 N 99.30 E
Bol'soj Šalym ≃ 86 60.55 N 70.25 E
Bol'šoj Šantar, Ostrov I 89 55.00 N 137.42 E
Bol'šoj Simonogont 265a 59.50 N 29.49 E
Bol'šoj Sorokino 86 56.38 N 69.53 E
Bol'šoj Suchodol 83 48.25 N 39.53 E
Bol'šoj Sundyr' 80 56.07 N 46.46 E
Bol'šoj Tal'cy 76 59.13 N 33.00 E
Bol'šoj Teatr ʊ 265b 55.46 N 37.37 E
Bol'šoj Tolkaj 80 53.30 N 51.57 E
Bol'šoj T'uters, Ostrov I 76 59.51 N 27.13 E
Bol'šoj Uluj 86 56.39 N 90.36 E
Bol'šoj Uran ≃ 80 52.24 N 53.15 E
Bol'šoj Uvat, Ozero ◎ 86 57.35 N 70.30 E
Bol'šoj Uzen' ≃ 80 48.50 N 49.40 E
Bol'šoj Uzigont 265a 59.48 N 29.53 E
Bol'šoj Vagil'skij Tuman, Ozero ◎ 86 60.04 N 62.06 E
Bol'šoj Vjass 80 53.48 N 45.30 E
Bol'šoj Zelenčuk ≃ 84 44.36 N 41.56 E
Bol'šovcy 78 49.12 N 24.44 E
Bolsover 44 53.14 N 1.18 W
Bolsward 52 53.03 N 5.31 E
Boltaña 34 42.27 N 0.04 E
Boltigen 58 46.38 N 7.24 E
Boltino 265b 55.58 N 37.41 E
Bolton, Ont., Can. 212 43.53 N 79.44 W
Bolton, Eng., U.K. 262 53.35 N 2.26 W
Bolton, Conn., U.S. 207 41.48 N 72.28 W
Bolton, Miss., U.S. 194 32.21 N 90.28 W
Bolton, N.C., U.S. 192 34.20 N 78.25 W
Bolton □[8] 262 53.34 N 2.28 W
Bolton Abbey 44 53.59 N 1.53 W
Bolton Abbey ʊ[1] 44 53.59 N 1.54 W
Bolton Bridge 44 53.58 N 1.57 W
Bolton Center 207 41.45 N 72.25 W
Bolton Creek ≃ 212 44.58 N 76.23 W
Bolton Lake ◎ 184 54.16 N 95.47 W
Bolton-le-Sands 44 54.06 N 2.47 W
Bolton upon Dearne 44 53.31 N 1.19 W
Bolton Wanderers Football Ground ♠ 262 53.34 N 2.25 W
Bolu, Tür. 130 40.44 N 31.37 E
Bolu, Zhg. 106 30.30 N 120.18 E
Bolu □[4] 130 40.40 N 31.30 E
Boluo, Zhg. 100 24.27 N 113.03 E
Boluo, Zhg. 100 23.11 N 114.17 E
Boluochi 98 41.24 N 119.56 E
Boluokeng 100 24.05 N 113.22 E
Boluowulashan ⩚ 102 41.20 N 98.55 E
Bolus Head ≻ 48 51.46 N 10.21 W
Bolva ≃ 76 53.17 N 34.20 E
Bolvadin 130 38.42 N 31.04 E
Bolwarra 166 17.24 S 144.11 E
Bóly 30 45.58 N 18.32 E
Bolyčevo 82 55.46 N 35.43 E
Bolzaneto 62 44.27 N 8.54 E
Bolzano (Bozen) 64 46.31 N 11.22 E
Bolzano □[4] 64 46.43 N 11.30 E
Boma 152 5.51 S 13.03 E
Bomaderry 170 34.51 S 150.37 E
Bomal 56 50.23 N 5.32 E
Bomandjokou 152 0.34 N 14.23 E
Bomaneh 152 1.18 N 23.47 E
Bomarsund 26 60.13 N 20.15 E
Bomate 152 1.10 S 19.41 E
Bomba 66 42.02 N 14.22 E
Bombakabo 152 3.04 N 19.42 E
Bombala 166 36.54 S 149.14 E
Bombarral 34 39.16 N 9.09 W
Bombat 130 38.08 N 42.14 E
Bombay, Bhārat 122
272c 18.58 N 72.50 E
Bombay, N.Y., U.S. 206 44.54 N 74.34 W
Bombay, University of ʊ[2] 272c 18.57 N 72.50 E
Bombay Harbour C 272c 18.57 N 72.53 E
Bomberai, Jazirah ≻[1] 164 3.00 S 133.00 E
Bombimba 152 0.31 N 19.24 E
Bombo 154 0.35 N 32.32 E
Bombo ≃ 152 3.58 S 15.59 E
Bombo-Kasanji 152 5.54 S 21.51 E
Bomboma 152 2.25 N 18.54 E
Bombo-Makuka 152 5.26 S 16.19 E
Bombombwa 154 1.21 N 25.30 E
Bombon 261 48.34 N 2.52 E
Bomboyo 146 12.01 N 15.28 E
Bom Conselho 250 9.10 S 36.41 W
Bom Despacho 255 19.43 S 45.15 W
Bomei 100 22.57 N 115.46 E
Bömenzien 54 52.59 N 11.31 E
Bomhus 40 60.41 N 17.13 E
Bomili 154 1.40 N 27.01 E
Bom Jardim, Ilha do I 287a 23.02 S 43.35 W
Bom Jardim de Goiás 255 16.17 S 52.07 W
Bom Jardim de Minas 256 21.57 S 44.11 W
Bom Jesus, Ang. 152 9.09 S 13.34 E
Bom Jesus, Bra. 250 9.04 S 44.22 W
Bom Jesus da Gurguéia, Serra ⩚ 250 9.00 S 43.00 W
Bom Jesus da Lapa 255 13.15 S 43.25 W
Bom Jesus da Terra Preta 256 23.15 S 46.36 W
Bom Jesus dos Perdões 256 23.08 S 46.28 W
Bømlafjorden C[2] 26 59.39 N 5.20 E

Bomlitz 52 52.54 N 9.37 E
Bømlo I 26 59.46 N 5.12 E
Bommerholz 263 51.23 N 7.18 E
Bommern ⊸[8] 263 51.25 N 7.20 E
Bomnak 89 54.46 N 128.51 E
Bomokandi ≃ 154 3.39 N 26.08 E
Bomongiri 152 1.57 S 21.13 E
Bomongo 152 1.22 N 18.21 E
Bompata 150 6.38 N 1.04 W
Bompensiere 70 37.28 N 13.47 E
Bompietro 70 37.44 N 14.06 E
Bomputu 152 0.20 S 20.06 E
Bom Repouso 256 22.28 S 46.09 W
Bom Retiro, Bra. 252 27.48 S 49.31 W
Bom Retiro, Bra. 256 22.10 S 45.40 W
Bom Retiro ⊸[8] 287b 23.32 S 46.38 W
Bom Retiro do Sul 252 29.37 S 51.56 W
Bom Sucesso, Bra. 248 15.43 S 56.07 W
Bom Sucesso, Bra. 255 23.42 S 51.45 W
Bom Sucesso, Bra. 256 22.52 S 45.33 W
Bom Sucesso, Bra. 287b 23.25 S 46.24 W
Bomu (Mbomou) ≃ 136 4.08 N 22.26 E
Bon, Cap ≻ 148 37.05 N 11.03 E
Bona 40 58.34 N 15.03 E
Boná, Isla I 236 8.34 N 79.36 W
Bona Bona Island I 164 10.30 S 149.50 E
Bon Accord 158 25.38 S 28.11 E
Bonaduz 58 46.49 N 9.25 E
Bonai 114 1.16 N 100.52 E
Bonaigarh 120 21.50 N 84.57 E
Bonair, Ind., U.S. 278 41.31 N 87.22 W
Bon Air, Va., U.S. 208 37.32 N 77.34 W
Bon Aire 214 40.54 N 79.55 W
Bonaire I 241s 12.10 N 68.15 W
Bonampak ⊥ 232 16.44 N 91.05 W
Bönan 40 60.44 N 17.18 E
Bonandolok 114 1.47 N 98.48 E
Bonanza, Nic. 236 14.01 N 84.35 W
Bonanza, Oreg., U.S. 202 42.12 N 121.24 W
Bonanza, Utah, U.S. 200 40.01 N 109.11 W
Bonanza Peak ∧ 224 48.14 N 120.52 W
Bonao 238 18.56 N 70.25 W
Bonaparte 190 40.42 N 91.48 W
Bonaparte ≃ 182 50.46 N 121.17 W
Bonaparte, Lake ◎ 212 44.09 N 75.23 W
Bonaparte, Mount ∧ 202 48.45 N 119.08 W
Bonaparte Archipelago II 160 14.17 S 125.18 E
Bonaparte Lake ◎ 182 51.16 N 120.35 W
Bonarbridge 46 53.33 N 4.21 W
Bonarcardo 71 40.06 N 8.39 E
Bonasila Dome ∧ 180 62.19 N 160.30 W
Bonasse 241r 10.05 N 61.52 W
Bonassola 62 44.11 N 9.35 E
Bonaventure 186 48.03 N 65.29 W
Bonaventure ≃ 186 48.02 N 65.28 W
Bonaventure, Île I 186 48.30 N 64.10 W
Bonavista 186 48.39 N 53.07 W
Bonavista, Cape ≻ 186 48.42 N 53.05 W
Bonavista Bay C 186 48.45 N 53.20 W
Bonawe 46 56.26 N 5.13 W
Bonawon 116 9.08 N 122.55 E
Bonbeach 274b 38.04 S 145.08 E
Bonboillon 58 47.20 N 5.42 E
Bon Bon 162 30.26 S 135.28 E
Bonbonon Point ≻ 116 9.03 N 123.08 E
Bonchester Bridge 44 55.24 N 2.40 W
Boncourt 58 47.30 N 6.56 E
Bond 194 30.54 N 89.10 W
Bond □[6] 219 38.53 N 89.25 W
Bondari 80 52.57 N 42.04 E
Bondar'ov 83 49.22 N 39.10 E
Bondar'ovka 83 49.23 N 39.37 E
Bondeno 64 44.53 N 11.25 E
Bondi 274a 33.53 S 151.17 E
Bondo, Zaïre 152 3.49 N 23.40 E
Bondo, Zaïre 152 1.22 S 23.53 E
Bondoc Peninsula ≻[1] 116 13.30 N 122.30 E
Bondorf 58 48.31 N 8.49 E
Bondoufle 261 48.37 N 2.23 E
Bondoukou 150 8.02 N 2.48 W
Bondoukou □[5] 150 8.45 N 3.30 W
Bondowoso 115a 7.55 S 113.49 E
Bondsville 207 42.13 N 72.21 W
Bonduel 190 44.44 N 88.27 W
Bondues 50 50.42 N 3.06 E
Bond'užskij 80 55.54 N 52.20 E
Bondy 261 48.54 N 2.28 E
Bondy, Forêt de ♠ 261 48.55 N 2.35 E
Bône → Annaba, Alg. 148 36.54 N 7.46 E
Bone, Indon. 112 4.46 S 122.52 E
Bone → Watampone, Indon. 112 4.32 S 120.20 E
Bone, Teluk C 112 4.00 S 120.40 E
Bonebone 112 2.36 S 120.33 E
Bon Echo Provincial Park ♠ 212 44.52 N 77.15 W
Bonefro 66 41.42 N 14.56 E
Bone Island I 212 44.56 N 79.51 W
Bonelipu 112 4.50 S 123.11 E
Bonelohe 112 5.48 S 120.27 E
Bönen 52 51.36 N 7.44 E
Boneogeh 112 7.16 S 120.48 E
Bone Rate, Kepulauan II 112 7.00 S 121.00 E
Bon Espérance, Cap de → Good Hope, Cape of ≻ 158 34.24 S 18.30 E
Bo'ness 46 56.01 N 3.37 W
Bonesteel 198 43.04 N 98.57 W
Bonete, Cerro ∧ 252 27.51 S 68.47 W
Bonětice 60 49.41 N 12.49 E
Boneya 144 5.44 N 37.45 E
Bonfield 216 41.09 N 88.03 W
Bonfim 256 22.58 S 45.15 W
Bonfinópolis 255 16.38 S 48.58 W
Bonfol 58 47.29 N 7.09 E
Bong □[6] 150 7.00 N 9.30 W
Bonga 144 7.17 N 36.15 E
Bongabon, Pil. 116 12.45 N 121.29 E
Bongabon, Pil. 116 15.38 N 121.08 E
Bongabon ≃ 116 12.40 N 121.33 E
Bongaigaon 124 26.28 N 90.34 E
Bongak 140 7.27 N 33.14 E
Bongandanga 152 1.30 N 21.03 E
Bongao Island I 116 5.01 N 119.46 E
Bongaree 171a 27.05 S 153.10 E
Bonggaw 116 5.02 N 119.46 E
Bongka 112 0.58 S 121.27 E
Bongka ≃ 112 0.59 S 121.05 E
Bong-mieu 110 15.25 N 108.24 E
Bongo, Ang. 152 8.48 S 17.49 E
Bongo, Gabon 152 2.10 S 10.12 E
Bongo, Zaïre 152 3.01 N 20.06 E
Bongo, Zaïre 152 1.47 S 17.41 E
Bongo Island I 116 7.20 N 124.02 E
Bongolu 152 2.48 N 22.29 E
Bongon 112 6.35 N 116.52 E
Bongor 146 10.17 N 15.22 E
Bongou ≃ 152 6.42 N 22.04 E
Bongouanou 150 6.39 N 4.12 W
Bong Range ⩚ 150 6.50 N 10.00 W
Bonham 196 33.35 N 96.11 W
Bonheiden 56 51.02 N 4.32 E
Bonhomme, Col du)(58 48.10 N 7.06 E
Bonhomme, Morne ∧ 238 19.05 N 72.18 W
Bonhomme Island I 219 38.42 N 90.36 W
Bonifacio, Fr. 36 41.23 N 9.10 E
Bonifacio, Pil. 116 8.03 N 123.37 E
Bonifacio, Strait of Ц 36 41.20 N 9.15 E

Bonifacio Monument ⊥ 269f 14.39 N 120.59 E
Bonifati 68 39.35 N 15.54 E
Bonifati, Capo ≻ 68 39.35 N 15.52 E
Bonifay 194 30.48 N 85.41 W
Bonifica del Volturno ⩯ 68 41.01 N 14.00 E
Bonilla Island I 182 53.29 N 130.36 W
Bonin Islands → Ogasawara-guntō II 14 27.00 N 142.10 E
Bonita 194 32.55 N 91.40 W
Bonita, Point ≻ 282 37.49 N 122.32 W
Bonita Springs 220 26.21 N 81.47 W
Bonito, Bra. 248 21.08 S 56.28 W
Bonito, Bra. 250 8.29 S 35.44 W
Bonito, It. 68 41.06 N 15.00 E
Bonito ≃, Bra. 255 16.31 S 51.23 W
Bonito ≃, Bra. 256 22.09 S 43.40 W
Bonito ≃, Bra. 256 22.12 S 43.02 W
Bonito, Pico ∧ 236 15.38 N 86.55 W
Bonito de Santa Fé 250 7.19 S 38.31 W
Bonjol 112 0.01 S 100.13 E
Bonkoukou 150 14.01 N 3.13 E
Bon Meade 279b 40.33 N 80.14 W
Bonn 56 50.44 N 7.05 E
Bonnanaro 71 40.32 N 8.45 E
Bonndorf im Schwarzwald 58 47.49 N 8.20 E
Bonneauville 208 39.46 N 77.10 W
Bonne Bay (Woody Point) 186 49.30 N 57.56 W
Bonne Bay C 186 49.33 N 57.55 W
Bonnebosq 50 49.12 N 0.05 E
Bonnechere ≃ 212 45.31 N 76.33 W
Bonnelles 261 48.37 N 2.02 E
Bonner 202 46.52 N 113.52 W
Bonners Ferry 202 48.41 N 116.18 W
Bonne-sur-Ménoge 58 46.10 N 6.20 E
Bonnet, Lac du ◎ 184 50.22 N 95.55 W
Bonnétable 50 48.11 N 0.26 E
Bonne Terre 194 37.55 N 90.33 W
Bonnet Plume ≃ 180 65.55 N 134.58 W
Bonnetts Mills 219 38.34 N 91.58 W
Bonneuil-sur-Marne 261 48.46 N 2.29 E
Bonneval 50 48.11 N 1.24 E
Bonneval-sur-Arc 62 45.22 N 7.03 E
Bonnevaux 58 46.18 N 6.40 E
Bonneville, Fr. 58 46.05 N 6.25 E
Bonneville, Oreg., U.S. 224 45.38 N 121.57 W
Bonneville Dam ⊸[6] 202 45.33 N 121.54 W
Bonneville Peak ∧ 202 42.46 N 112.08 W
Bonneville Salt Flats ⩯ 200 40.45 N 113.52 W
Bonney Lake 224 47.10 N 122.11 W
Bonnières 50 49.02 N 1.35 E
Bonnie Rock 162 30.32 S 118.21 E
Bonnieux 62 43.49 N 5.18 E
Bonnievale 158 33.57 S 20.06 E
Bönninghardt 263 51.35 N 6.28 E
Bönninghardt ⩚[2] 263 51.34 N 6.27 E
Bonny 150 4.27 N 7.10 E
Bonny ≃[1] 150 4.20 N 7.10 E
Bonnyrigg, Austl. 274a 33.54 S 150.54 E
Bonnyrigg, Scot., U.K. 46 55.52 N 3.08 W
Bonny-sur-Loire 50 47.34 N 2.50 E
Bonnyville 182 54.16 N 110.44 W
Bono, It. 71 40.25 N 9.02 E
Bono, Ohio, U.S. 214 41.38 N 83.16 W
Bonoi 164 1.51 S 137.48 E
Bonorva 71 40.25 N 8.46 E
Bonoua 150 5.16 N 3.36 W
Bonpas Creek ≃ 194 38.16 N 87.59 W
Bonriki 174t 1.23 N 173.09 E
Bonriki I 174t 1.22 N 173.10 E
Bons 58 46.16 N 6.23 E
Bonsall 228 33.17 N 117.13 W
Bonsari 272c 19.04 N 73.02 E
Bon Secour 194 30.19 N 87.44 W
Bon-Secours, Bel. 50 50.30 N 3.36 E
Bonsecours, Fr. 50 49.26 N 1.08 E
Bonshaw 186 46.12 N 63.21 W
Bonsucesso ⊸[8] 287a 22.52 S 43.15 W
Bontang 112 0.08 N 117.30 E
Bontebok National Park ♠ 158 34.07 S 20.23 E
Bonthain 112 5.32 S 119.56 E
Bonthe 150 7.32 N 12.30 W
Bontoc 116 17.05 N 120.58 E
Bonvoufoumou, Mont ∧ 152 1.13 N 12.01 E
Bon Wier 194 30.44 N 93.39 W
Bonygutt Brook ≃ 276 40.35 N 74.29 W
Bonyhád 30 46.19 N 18.32 E
Boo, Kepulauan II 164 1.12 S 129.24 E
Booby Point ≻ 284b 39.17 N 76.23 W
Boock 54 53.29 N 14.15 E
Boody 219 39.46 N 89.03 W
Boogardie 162 28.02 S 117.47 E
Booischot 56 51.03 N 4.46 E
Bookabie 162 31.50 S 132.41 E
Bookaloo 166 31.55 S 137.22 E
Book Cliffs ⩚[4] 200 39.20 N 109.00 W
Booke 152 2.33 S 22.00 E
Booker 196 36.27 N 100.32 W
Booker T. Washington National Monument ♠ 192 37.01 N 79.45 W
Bookwalter 218 39.42 N 83.32 W
Boola 150 8.22 N 8.43 W
Boolaloo 162 22.35 S 115.51 E
Booleroo Centre 166 32.53 S 138.21 E
Booligal 166 33.52 S 144.53 E
Boologooro 162 24.21 S 114.02 E
Boom 50 51.05 N 4.22 E
Boomarra 166 19.33 S 140.20 E
Boomer 188 38.09 N 81.17 W
Boomi 166 28.44 S 149.35 E
Boomrivier 158 29.33 S 20.27 E
Boonah 171a 28.00 S 152.41 E
Böön Cagaan Nuur ◎ 102 45.35 N 99.09 E
Boone, Iowa, U.S. 190 42.04 N 93.53 W
Boone, N.C., U.S. 192 36.13 N 81.41 W
Boone □[6], Ill., U.S. 216 42.15 N 88.50 W
Boone □[6], Ind., U.S. 218 40.03 N 86.28 W
Boone □[6], Ky., U.S. 218 38.57 N 84.45 W
Boone □[6], Mo., U.S. 219 38.55 N 92.15 W
Boone ≃ 190 42.19 N 93.56 W
Boone Draw ∨ 196 33.51 N 103.42 W
Boone Grove 216 41.21 N 87.08 W
Boone Lake ◎[1] 192 36.25 N 82.25 W
Boone Reservoir ◎[1] 279b 40.15 N 80.08 W
Boones Mill 192 37.07 N 79.57 W
Booneville, Ark., U.S. 194 35.08 N 93.55 W
Booneville, Ky., U.S. 192 37.29 N 83.40 W
Booneville, Miss., U.S. 194 34.39 N 88.34 W
Boon Point ≻ 240c 17.10 N 61.50 W
Boons 158 25.59 S 27.13 E
Boonsboro 188 39.30 N 77.39 W
Boonsville 222 33.04 N 97.52 W
Boonton 210 40.54 N 74.24 W
Boonton Reservoir ◎[1] 276 40.53 N 74.25 W
Boonville, Calif., U.S. 204 39.00 N 123.22 W
Boonville, Ind., U.S. 194 38.03 N 87.16 W
Boonville, Mo., U.S. 194 38.58 N 92.44 W
Boonville, N.Y., U.S. 212 43.29 N 75.20 W
Boopi ≃ 248 15.41 S 67.15 W
Boorindal 166 30.21 S 146.08 E
Booroorban 166 34.56 S 144.46 E
Boorowa 166 34.26 S 148.43 E
Boorthanna 166 28.38 S 135.54 E
Boos 50 49.23 N 1.12 E
Boossen 54 52.22 N 14.29 E
Boot 44 54.24 N 3.17 W

Bootahnie Indian Reserve ⊸[4] 182 50.24 N 121.31 W
Booth 194 32.30 N 86.41 W
Booth, Lac ◎ 190 46.45 N 78.34 W
Boothbay Harbor 188 43.51 N 69.38 W
Boothby, Cape ≻ 9 66.34 S 57.16 E
Booth Corner 285 39.51 N 75.29 W
Boothia, Gulf of C 176 71.00 N 91.00 W
Boothia Peninsula ≻[1] 176 70.30 N 95.00 W
Boothstown 262 53.30 N 2.25 W
Booth Wood Reservoir ◎[1] 262 53.38 N 1.58 W
Boothwyn 285 39.49 N 75.26 W
Bootle 262 53.28 N 3.00 W
Boot Reefs ⊹[2] 164 10.00 S 144.40 E
Booué 152 0.06 S 11.56 E
Booysens ⊸[8] 273d 26.14 S 28.01 E
Booze Creek ≃ 284c 38.59 N 77.07 W
Bopeechee 166 29.36 S 137.23 E
Bopfingen 56 48.51 N 10.21 E
Bo Phloi 110 14.19 N 99.31 E
Bopingcheng 98 36.36 N 116.07 E
Bopo 150 7.37 N 7.52 E
Bopolu 150 7.03 N 10.32 W
Boppard 56 50.14 N 7.35 E
Boqer, Har ∧ 132 30.52 N 34.43 E
Boqueirão, Ilha do I 287a 22.46 S 43.09 W
Boqueirão, Serra do ⩚[2] 250 11.30 S 43.45 W
Boquerón 236 8.30 N 82.34 W
Boquerón □[5] 252 21.30 S 60.00 W
Boquerón, Bahía de C 240m 18.01 N 67.12 W
Boquerón, Túnel ⊸[5] 286c 10.34 N 67.00 W
Boquet 279b 40.23 N 79.36 W
Boquilla, Presa de la ◎[1] 232 27.30 N 105.30 W
Boquilla del Refugio 196 25.33 N 102.28 W
Boquillas del Carmen 232 29.17 N 102.53 W
Bor, Česko. 60 49.43 N 12.47 E
Bor, Jugo. 38 44.05 N 22.07 E
Bor, S.S.S.R. 24 63.00 N 42.38 E
Bor, S.S.S.R. 80 56.22 N 44.05 E
Bor, Sūd. 140 6.12 N 31.33 E
Bor, Tür. 130 37.54 N 34.34 E
Bora-Bora I 14 16.30 S 151.45 W
Borabu 110 16.02 N 103.07 E
Borah Peak ∧ 202 44.08 N 113.48 W
Borale 144 9.10 N 42.35 E
Borama 144 9.58 N 43.07 E
Borambola 171b 35.12 S 147.41 E
Borang, Tanjung ≻ 164 5.16 S 133.07 E
Borarė ≃ 287b 23.46 S 46.39 W
Borås 26 57.43 N 12.55 E
Borāzjān 128 29.16 N 51.12 E
Borba, Bra. 246 4.24 S 59.35 W
Borba, Port. 34 38.48 N 7.27 W
Borbach ⊸[8] 263 51.26 N 7.22 E
Borbeck ⊸[8] 263 51.29 N 6.57 E
Borbera ≃ 62 44.42 N 8.52 E
Borborema 255 21.37 S 49.04 W
Borca di Cadore 64 46.26 N 12.13 E
Borcea ≃ 38 44.40 N 27.53 E
Borchen 52 51.39 N 8.44 E
Borculo, Ned. 52 52.07 N 6.31 E
Borculo, Mich., U.S. 216 42.53 N 86.01 W
Borda, Cape ≻ 166 35.45 S 136.34 E
Borda da Mata, Bra. 256 22.16 S 46.10 W
Borda da Mata, Bra. 256 22.37 S 47.01 W
Bordeaux, Fr. 32 44.50 N 0.34 W
Bordeaux, S. Afr. 273d 26.06 S 28.01 E
Bordeaux ⊸[8] 275a 45.33 N 73.41 W
Bordeaux Mountain ∧[2] 240m 18.20 N 64.44 W
Borden, Austl. 162 34.05 S 118.16 E
Borden, Sask., Can. 184 52.25 N 107.13 W
Borden, Eng., U.K. 260 51.20 N 0.42 E
Borden, Ind., U.S. 218 38.28 N 85.57 W
Borden Lake ◎ 190 47.50 N 83.18 W
Borden Peninsula ≻[1] 176 73.00 N 83.00 W
Bordentown 208 40.09 N 74.42 W
Borders □[4] 46 55.37 N 3.15 W
Bordertown 166 36.19 S 140.47 E
Bordesholm 30 54.11 N 10.01 E
Borđeyri 24a 65.15 N 21.10 W
Bordighera 62 43.46 N 7.39 E
Bording 41 56.12 N 9.17 E
Bording Kirkeby 41 56.10 N 9.15 E
Bordino, Fiume di ≃ 70 37.53 N 12.37 E
Bordj Amguid 148 26.26 N 5.22 E
Bordj Bou Arreridj 148 36.04 N 4.46 E
Bordj Bounaama 34 35.51 N 1.36 E
Bordj el Oussif 148 32.20 N 8.02 E
Bordj Fly Sainte Marie 148 27.20 N 3.50 W
Bordj Menaïel 148 36.44 N 3.43 E
Bordj Sidi Toui 148 32.44 N 11.22 E
Bordunskij 85 42.40 N 75.37 E
Bore, It. 62 44.43 N 9.47 E
Boré, Mali 150 15.08 N 3.29 W
Bore, Yai. 144 4.40 N 37.40 E
Boreda 144 6.32 N 37.48 E
Boreham 260 51.46 N 0.33 E
Borehamwood 260 51.40 N 0.16 W
Borel Hill ∧ 282 37.19 N 122.12 W
Borello, It. 64 41.55 N 14.18 E
Borello, It. 66 44.03 N 12.11 E
Borensberg 26 58.34 N 15.17 E
Boreray I 46 57.42 N 7.18 W
Boretto 64 44.54 N 10.33 E
Borgå (Porvoo) 26 60.24 N 25.40 E
Borgallo, Galleria del ⊸[5] 62 44.25 N 9.53 E
Borgarnes 24a 64.35 N 21.53 W
Borgata Costiera 70 37.43 N 12.39 E
Børgefjell Nasjonalpark ♠ 24 65.10 N 14.00 E
Borgentreich 52 51.34 N 9.14 E
Börger, B.R.D. 52 52.54 N 7.32 E
Borger, Ned. 52 52.55 N 6.46 E
Borger, Tex., U.S. 196 35.39 N 101.24 W
Borgerhout 50 51.13 N 4.26 E
Borgetto 70 38.03 N 13.08 E
Borggård 40 58.44 N 15.32 E
Borghetto 64 45.41 N 10.56 E
Borghetto di Vara 62 44.13 N 9.43 E
Borghetto Lodigiano 62 45.13 N 9.30 E
Borghetto Santo Spirito 62 44.06 N 8.14 E
Borgholm 26 56.53 N 16.39 E
Borghorst 52 52.07 N 7.23 E
Borgia 68 38.49 N 16.30 E
Borgio-Verezzi 62 44.10 N 8.18 E
Borgloon 56 50.48 N 5.20 E
Borg Mountain ∧ 9 72.42 S 3.30 W
Borgne, Lake C 194 30.05 N 89.40 W
Borgnesse, Pointe ≻ 240e 14.27 N 60.54 W
Borgo 64 46.03 N 11.27 E
Borgo alla Collina 66 43.45 N 11.43 E
Borgo a Mozzano 66 43.59 N 10.33 E
Borgo Cerreto 66 42.49 N 12.54 E
Borgo d'Ale 62 45.21 N 8.03 E
Borgoforte 64 45.03 N 10.45 E
Borgofranco d'Ivrea 62 45.30 N 7.51 E
Borgolavezzaro 62 45.19 N 8.42 E
Borgomanero 62 45.42 N 8.28 E
Borgomaro 62 43.58 N 7.56 E
Borgonovo Val Tidone 62 45.01 N 9.26 E
Borgo Pace 66 43.39 N 12.17 E
Borgoricco 64 45.32 N 11.58 E
Borgorose 66 42.11 N 13.13 E
Borgo San Dalmazzo 62 44.20 N 7.30 E
Borgo San Giacomo 64 45.21 N 9.58 E
Borgo San Lorenzo 66 43.57 N 11.23 E
Borgosatollo 64 45.28 N 10.14 E

Symbol	English	Deutsch	Español	Français	Português
≃	River	Fluss	Río	Rivière	Rio
⩶	Canal	Kanal	Canal	Canal	Canal
⌞	Waterfall, Rapids	Wasserfall, Stromschnellen	Cascada, Rápidos	Chute d'eau, Rapides	Cascata, Rápidos
Ц	Strait	Meeresstrasse	Estrecho	Détroit	Estreito
C	Bay, Gulf	Bucht, Golf	Bahía, Golfo	Baie, Golfe	Baía, Golfo
◎	Lake, Lakes	See, Seen	Lago, Lagos	Lac, Lacs	Lago, Lagos
⩯	Swamp	Sumpf	Pantano	Marais	Pântano
⛉	Ice Features, Glacier	Eis- und Gletscherformen	Accidentes Glaciales	Formes glaciaires	Acidentes Glaciares
⊤	Other Hydrographic Features	Andere Hydrographische Objekte	Otros Elementos Hidrográficos	Autres données hydrographiques	Outros Elementos Hidrográficos
⊹	Submarine Features	Untermeerische Objekte	Accidentes Submarinos	Formes de relief sous-marin	Acidentes Submarinos
□	Political Unit	Politische Einheit	Unidad Politica	Entité politique	Unidade Política
ʊ	Cultural Institution	Kulturelle Institution	Institución Cultural	Institution culturelle	Instituição Cultural
⊥	Historical Site	Historische Stätte	Sitio Histórico	Site historique	Sitio Histórico
♠	Recreational Site	Erholungs- und Ferienort	Sitio de Recreo	Centre de loisirs	Sítio de Lazer
⊠	Airport	Flughafen	Aeropuerto	Aéroport	Aeroporto
■	Military Installation	Militäranlage	Instalación Militar	Installation militaire	Instalação Militar
⊸	Miscellaneous	Verschiedenes	Misceláneo	Divers	Miscelânea

Borgosesia 62 45.43 N 8.16 E
Borgo Ticino 266b 45.41 N 8.36 E
Borgo Tossignano 66 44.16 N 11.35 E
Borgou □[5] 150 10.30 N 2.50 E
Borgo Val di Taro 62 44.29 N 9.46 E
Borgo Vercelli 62 45.21 N 8.28 E
Borgsdorf 54 52.42 N 13.14 E
Borgund ⱱ[1] 26 61.03 N 7.49 E
Bori 150 4.42 N 7.21 E
Borikhan 110 18.33 N 103.43 E
Borilovo 76 53.22 N 35.58 E
Boring, Md., U.S. 208 39.31 N 76.49 W
Boring, Oreg., U.S. 224 45.26 N 122.23 W
Borinskoje 76 52.27 N 39.22 E
Borislav 78 49.16 N 23.27 E
Borisoglebsk 80 51.23 N 42.06 E
Borisoglebskij 80 57.16 N 39.09 E
Borisov, S.S.S.R. 76 54.15 N 28.30 E
Borisov, S.S.S.R. 78 50.11 N 26.31 E
Borisovka, S.S.S.R. 76 52.50 N 39.58 E
Borisovka, S.S.S.R. 78 50.36 N 36.01 E
Borisovo 82 55.25 N 36.03 E
Borisovo ♦[8] 265b 55.38 N 37.45 E
Borisovo-Sudskoje 76 59.54 N 36.01 E
Borisovskaja 76 60.12 N 39.48 E
Borispol' 78 50.21 N 30.57 E
Borja, Esp. 34 41.50 N 1.32 W
Borja, Perú 246 4.26 S 77.33 W
Borjas Blancas 34 41.31 N 0.52 E
Bork 52 51.40 N 7.30 E
Borkça 130 41.22 N 41.40 E
Borken, B.R.D. 52 51.51 N 6.51 E
Borken, B.R.D. 56 51.03 N 9.16 E
Borkenwirthe 52 51.53 N 6.50 E
Borki, S.S.S.R. 78 49.42 N 36.02 E
Borki, S.S.S.R. 86 59.08 N 82.15 E
Børkop 41 55.39 N 9.39 E
Borkou ♦[1] 146 18.15 N 18.50 E
Borkou-Ennedi-Tibesti □[5] 146 18.15 N 18.50 E
Borkoviči 76 55.40 N 28.20 E
Borkum 52 53.35 N 6.40 E
Borkum I 52 53.35 N 6.41 E
Borland Manor 279b 40.15 N 80.09 W
Borlänge 40 60.29 N 15.25 E
Borle ♦[8] 272c 19.02 N 72.55 E
Borlu 130 38.44 N 28.27 E
Bormes-les-Mimosas 62 43.09 N 6.20 E
Bormida ≃ 62 44.23 N 8.13 E
Bormida di Millesimo ≃ 62 44.40 N 8.20 E
Bormida di Spigno ≃ 62 44.40 N 8.20 E
Bormio 64 46.28 N 10.22 E
Born, D.D.R. 41 54.23 N 12.31 E
Born, D.D.R. 54 45.22 N 12.31 E
Born, D.D.R. 54 52.22 N 11.28 E
Borna, D.D.R. 54 51.07 N 12.30 E
Borna, D.D.R. 54 51.19 N 13.11 E
Borndiep C 52 53.25 N 5.35 E
Borne 52 52.18 N 6.45 E
Borne ≃ 62 45.03 N 3.54 E
Borneo (Kalimantan) I 112 0.30 N 114.00 E
Bornheim 56 50.46 N 6.59 E
Bornholm I 26 55.10 N 15.00 E
Bornholte 52 51.52 N 8.29 E
Bornhöved 54 54.04 N 10.16 E
Börnicke, D.D.R. 54 52.41 N 12.56 E
Börnicke, D.D.R. 264a 52.40 N 13.38 E
Börnig ♦[8] 263 51.33 N 7.16 E
Bornim ♦[8] 264a 52.26 N 13.00 E
Borno 64 45.56 N 10.12 E
Bornos, Embalse de @[1] 34 36.50 N 5.30 W
Bornova 130 38.27 N 27.14 E
Bornsdorf 54 51.46 N 13.41 E
Bornstedt ♦[8] 264a 52.25 N 13.02 E
Boro ≃ 140 8.52 N 26.11 E
Borobudur ⊥ 115a 7.36 S 110.12 E
Borocay Island I 116 11.59 N 121.55 E
Borod'anka 78 50.39 N 29.56 E
Borodarou 150 10.59 N 2.53 E
Borodino, S.S.S.R. 78 46.18 N 29.13 E
Borodino, S.S.S.R. 82 56.53 N 37.00 E
Borodino, S.S.S.R. 82 55.32 N 35.50 E
Borodino, S.S.S.R. 88 55.55 N 94.55 E
Borodulicha 86 50.43 N 80.55 E
Borodulino 80 57.59 N 54.20 E
Borogoncy 74 62.42 N 131.08 E
Boroko 112 0.55 N 123.16 E
Boroml'a 78 50.37 N 34.59 E
Boromo 150 11.45 N 2.56 W
Boron, Mali 150 14.01 N 7.30 W
Boron, Calif., U.S. 228 35.00 N 117.39 W
Boronga Islands II 110 19.58 N 93.06 E
Borongan 116 11.37 N 125.26 E
Boronia 274b 37.52 S 145.17 E
Boron'ki 76 53.09 N 32.08 E
Borore 71 40.13 N 8.48 E
Borotou 150 8.44 N 7.30 W
Boroughbridge 44 54.06 N 1.23 W
Borough Green 260 51.17 N 0.19 E
Borough Park ♦[8] 276 40.38 N 74.00 W
Borovaja, S.S.S.R. 78 50.12 N 30.07 E
Borovaja, S.S.S.R. 83 49.24 N 37.40 E
Borovaja ≃ 83 48.28 N 38.24 E
Borová Lada 60 48.59 N 13.40 E
Borovan 38 43.26 N 23.45 E
Borovany 61 48.54 N 14.39 E
Boroviči 76 58.24 N 33.55 E
Borovik ≃ 83 49.11 N 38.33 E
Borovka ≃ 80 52.54 N 52.00 E
Borovl'anka 86 52.38 N 84.29 E
Borovoj 24 59.55 N 51.38 E
Borovoje, S.S.S.R. 78 51.06 N 27.13 E
Borovoje, S.S.S.R. 86 53.04 N 70.19 E
Borovsk 82 55.12 N 36.30 E
Borovskaja 24 60.46 N 41.06 E
Borovskij 86 57.03 N 65.44 E
Borovskoj 86 53.48 N 64.12 E
Borovskoje, S.S.S.R. 83 48.51 N 38.34 E
Borovskoje, S.S.S.R. 86 52.39 N 82.08 E
Borovucha 76 55.36 N 28.37 E
Borovy 60 49.33 N 13.18 E
Borozdino 82 54.07 N 38.22 E
Borrachudo ≃ 255 18.12 S 45.16 W
Borrazópolis 255 23.56 S 51.36 W
Borrby 26 55.27 N 14.10 E
Borre 41 55.00 N 12.28 E
Borre ⊥ 26 59.23 N 10.28 E
Borreby 41 55.14 N 11.19 E
Borriana 62 45.30 N 8.02 E
Borris 48 52.35 N 6.06 W
Borrisokane 48 52.59 N 8.07 W
Borrisoleigh 48 52.45 N 7.57 W
Borroloola 164 16.04 S 136.17 E
Borrowdale 44 54.31 N 3.10 W
Börry 52 52.01 N 9.27 E
Borş 38 47.07 N 21.49 E
Borşa, Rom. 38 46.56 N 23.40 E
Borşa, Rom. 38 47.39 N 24.40 E
Borsad 120 22.25 N 72.54 E
Borsano 266b 45.35 N 8.51 E
Borschemich 263 51.04 N 6.25 E
Borščov 78 48.48 N 26.03 E
Borščovo 82 56.30 N 36.51 E
Borščovočnyj Chrebet ∧∧ 88 52.00 N 117.00 E
Borsdorf 54 51.21 N 12.32 E
Borskoje 80 53.02 N 51.43 E
Borsod-Abaúj-Zemplén □[6] 30 48.15 N 21.00 E
Börssum 54 52.04 N 10.35 E
Borstel 52 53.32 N 9.41 E
Borstendorf 54 50.46 N 13.10 E
Borth, B.R.D. 52 51.36 N 6.33 E
Borth, Wales, U.K. 42 52.29 N 4.03 W
Borthwick Water ≃ 44 55.24 N 2.50 W
Bortigali 71 40.17 N 8.50 E
Bortigiadas 71 40.53 N 9.02 E
Bort-les-Orgues 32 45.24 N 2.30 E
Bortniči 78 50.22 N 30.41 E
Borto 88 53.35 N 111.53 E
Bortondale 285 39.54 N 79.24 W
Boru 164 10.14 S 148.50 E
Boruca 236 9.00 N 83.20 W
Borūjen 128 31.59 N 51.18 E
Borūjerd 128 33.54 N 48.46 E
Borve 46 56.58 N 7.32 W
Borz'a 88 50.24 N 116.31 E
Borzna 78 51.15 N 32.25 E
Boržomi 84 41.50 N 43.21 E
Borzonasca 62 44.25 N 9.23 E
Borzyszkowy 30 54.03 N 17.22 E
Bosa 71 40.18 N 8.30 E
Bosaga 86 47.55 N 72.58 E
Bosambi 152 2.24 N 22.39 E
Bosanska Dubica 36 45.11 N 16.49 E
Bosanska Gradiška 36 45.09 N 17.15 E
Bosanska Krupa 36 44.53 N 16.10 E
Bosanski Novi 36 45.03 N 16.23 E
Bosanski Petrovac 38 44.33 N 16.22 E
Bosanski Šamac 38 45.03 N 18.28 E
Bosansko Grahovo 36 44.11 N 16.22 E
Bosaso 144 11.13 N 49.08 E
Bosau 54 54.06 N 10.25 E
Bosavi, Mount ∧ 164 6.35 S 142.50 E
Boscastle 42 50.41 N 4.42 W
Bosco, It. 66 43.08 N 12.28 E
Bosco, It. 66 44.53 N 12.14 E
Boscobel 190 43.08 N 90.42 W
Bosco Chiesanuova 64 45.37 N 11.02 E
Bosco Marengo 62 44.49 N 8.41 E
Boscotrecase 68 40.46 N 14.28 E
Bösel 52 53.00 N 7.58 E
Bosencheve, Parque Nacional ♠ 234 19.36 N 100.15 W
Bosenge 152 1.18 N 22.19 E
Bósforo, Estrecho del → İstanbul Boğazı ⩌ 130 41.06 N 29.04 E
Boshan 98 36.29 N 117.50 E
Boshkung Lake @ 212 45.04 N 78.44 W
Boshoek 156 25.30 S 27.09 E
Boshof 158 28.34 S 25.04 E
Boshrūyeh 128 33.53 N 57.26 E
Bosilegrad 38 42.29 N 22.28 E
Bösingen 58 48.14 N 8.34 E
Bositenghu @ 90 42.00 N 87.00 E
Bosjökloster 41 55.54 N 13.31 E
Boškajnar 85 38.13 N 68.51 E
Boskoop 52 52.04 N 4.35 E
Boskop 158 26.34 S 27.08 E
Boskovice 30 49.29 N 16.40 E
Boskuil 158 27.23 S 25.51 E
Bosman 164 4.10 S 144.40 E
Bosna 272b 22.37 N 88.30 E
Bosna ≃ 38 45.04 N 18.29 E
Bosna i Hercegovina □[3] 36 44.15 N 17.30 E
Bošn'akovo 89 49.38 N 142.10 E
Bosnik 164 1.10 S 136.14 E
Boso 272b 22.58 N 88.08 E
Bosobolo 152 4.11 N 19.54 E
Boso-Djafo 152 1.06 N 19.14 E
Bosogo 85 41.09 N 76.25 E
Bōsō-hantō ≻[1] 94 35.18 N 140.10 E
Bososama 152 4.18 N 20.00 E
Bösperde 263 51.28 N 7.46 E
Bosphore, Détroit du → İstanbul Boğazı ⩌ 130 41.06 N 29.04 E
Bosporus → İstanbul Boğazı ⩌ 130 41.06 N 29.04 E
Bosque □[6] 222 31.55 N 97.35 W
Bosque, Paseo del ♠ 288 34.55 S 57.56 W
Bosques 288 34.49 S 58.14 W
Bosqueville 222 31.38 N 97.13 W
Bossangoa 152 6.29 N 17.27 E
Bossdorf 54 51.59 N 12.40 E
Bossé Bangou 150 13.21 N 1.18 E
Bossembélé 152 5.16 N 17.39 E
Bossemtele II 152 5.41 N 16.38 E
Bossert Estates 285 40.09 N 74.44 W
Bossier City 194 32.31 N 93.43 W
Bossley Bush Recreation Ground ♠ 274a 33.52 S 150.54 E
Bossley Park 274a 33.52 S 150.54 E
Bosso 146 13.42 N 13.19 E
Bosso, Dallol ∨ 150 12.25 N 2.50 E
Bossolasco 62 44.32 N 8.02 E
Bossut, Cape ≻ 162 18.43 S 121.38 E
Bostān, Īrān 128 31.43 N 47.59 E
Bostān, Pāk. 120 30.26 N 67.02 E
Bostancı ♦[8] 267b 40.57 N 29.05 E
Bostandyk 80 49.38 N 48.54 E
Bostock Green 262 53.13 N 2.30 W
Boston, Pil. 116 7.52 N 126.22 E
Boston, Eng., U.K. 42 52.59 N 0.01 W
Boston, Ga., U.S. 192 30.47 N 83.47 W
Boston, Ind., U.S. 218 39.44 N 84.51 W
Boston, Mass., U.S. 207
 283 42.21 N 71.04 W
Boston, N.Y., U.S. 210 42.38 N 78.44 W
Boston, Pa., U.S. 279b 40.18 N 79.49 W
Boston Bar 182 49.52 N 121.26 W
Boston Bay C 283 42.22 N 70.54 W
Boston Brook ≃ 283 42.37 N 71.00 W
Boston College ⱱ[2] 283 42.20 N 71.10 W
Boston Common ♠ 283 42.21 N 71.05 W
Boston Corners 210 42.03 N 73.31 W
Boston Creek ≃ 212 43.02 N 79.56 W
Boston Garden ♠ 283 42.22 N 71.04 W
Boston Harbor 224 47.08 N 122.54 W
Boston Harbor C 283 42.20 N 70.58 W
Boston Heights 214 41.16 N 81.30 W
Boston Mill 214 41.16 N 81.34 W
Boston Mountains ∧∧ 194 35.50 N 93.20 W
Boston University ⱱ[2] 283 42.21 N 71.07 W
Bosumtwi, Lake @ 150 6.30 N 1.25 W
Bosut ≃ 38 44.57 N 19.22 E
Boswell, Ind., U.S. 216 40.31 N 87.23 W
Boswell, Okla., U.S. 196 34.02 N 95.52 W
Boswell, Pa., U.S. 214 40.10 N 79.02 W
Boswell Bay 180 60.24 N 146.08 W
Bosworth 194 39.28 N 93.20 W
Bosworth Airport ⊠ 279a 41.26 N 82.00 W
Bosworth Field (1485) ⊥ 42 52.36 N 1.25 W
Botād 120 22.10 N 71.40 E
Botafogo ♦[8] 287a 22.57 S 43.11 W
Botafogo, Enseada de C 287a 22.57 S 43.10 W
Botanic Gardens ♠, Austl. 169 37.33 S 143.50 E
Botanic Gardens ♠, Sing. 271c 1.19 N 103.48 E
Botany 274a 33.57 S 151.12 E
Botany Bay ♦[8] 260 51.41 N 0.07 W
Botany Bay C 274a 33.59 S 151.12 E
Botejevo 78 46.41 N 35.52 E
Boteler Point ≻ 158 27.02 S 32.52 E
Botelhos 256 21.39 S 46.24 W
Botera 152 11.37 S 14.17 E
Botersleegte 158 30.35 S 21.22 E
Boteti ≃ 156 20.08 S 23.23 E
Botev ∧ 38 42.43 N 24.55 E
Botevgrad 38 42.54 N 23.47 E
Botha's Hill 158 29.45 S 30.45 E
Bothaville 158 27.27 S 26.36 E
Bothell 224 47.46 N 122.12 W
Bothe-Napa Valley State Park ♠ 226 38.32 N 122.32 W
Bothnia, Gulf of C 26 63.00 N 20.00 E
Bothwell, Austl. 166 42.23 S 147.00 E
Bothwell, Ont., Can. 214 42.38 N 81.52 W
Boticas 34 41.41 N 7.40 W
Botkins 216 40.28 N 84.11 W
Botkul', Ozero @ 80 48.46 N 46.40 E
Botkyrka 40 59.14 N 17.49 E
Botley 42 50.56 N 1.18 W
Botlich 84 42.39 N 46.14 E
Botmakak 152 4.00 N 10.55 E
Botna ≃ 38 46.45 N 29.34 E
Botnia, Golfo de → Bothnia, Gulf of C 26 63.00 N 20.00 E
Botola 152 1.17 S 18.13 E
Botolan 116 15.17 N 120.01 E
Botoşani 38 47.45 N 26.40 E
Botoşani □[4] 38 48.00 N 26.45 E
Botou 150 12.25 N 0.09 E
Botovo 82 56.03 N 38.26 E
Bo-trach 110 17.35 N 106.32 E
Botrange ∧ 56 50.30 N 6.08 E
Botricello 68 38.56 N 16.51 E
Botro 150 7.51 N 5.19 W
Botsford 210 41.22 N 73.15 W
Botswana □[1] 138
 156 22.00 S 24.00 E
Botte Donato ∧ 68 39.17 N 16.26 E
Bottenhavet (Selkämeri) C 26 62.00 N 20.00 E
Bottenviken (Perämeri) C 26 65.00 N 23.00 E
Bottesford 42 52.56 N 0.48 W
Bottineau 198 48.50 N 100.27 W
Bottnischer Meerbusen → Bothnia, Gulf of C 26 63.00 N 20.00 E
Bottoms Reservoir @[1] 262 53.28 N 1.58 W
Bottrop 52 51.31 N 6.55 E
Botucatu 255 22.52 S 48.26 W
Botwood 186 49.09 N 55.21 W
Boty 88 52.22 N 118.34 E
Bötzingen 58 48.04 N 7.44 E
Bötzow 54 52.39 N 13.08 E
Bötzsee @ 264a 52.34 N 13.50 E
Bouaflé, C. Iv. 150 6.59 N 5.45 W
Bouafle, Fr. 261 48.58 N 1.54 E
Bouaflé □[5] 150 7.15 N 5.45 W
Bou Ajam, Oued ∨ 148 33.36 N 1.31 W
Bouaké 150 7.41 N 5.02 W
Bouaké □[5] 150 7.15 N 5.00 W
Bouala 152 6.23 N 15.37 E
Bou Ali, Oued ∨ 148 31.14 N 4.16 E
Bou Anane 148 32.03 N 3.03 W
Bouar 152 5.57 N 15.36 E
Bou Arada 36 36.20 N 9.38 E
Bou Arfa 148 32.30 N 1.59 W
Bouaye 32 47.09 N 1.42 W
Boubandjidah, Parc National de ♠ 146 8.45 N 14.45 E
Boubin ∧ 60 48.59 N 13.51 E
Bouca 152 6.30 N 18.17 E
Bouchain 50 50.17 N 3.19 E
Bouchegouf 36 36.28 N 7.44 E
Boucher ≃ 186 49.10 N 69.06 W
Boucher, Lac @ 186 51.07 N 59.35 W
Boucherville 206 45.36 N 73.27 W
Boucherville, Îles de II 275a 45.37 N 73.28 W
Bouches-du-Rhône □[5] 62 43.30 N 5.00 E
Bouchoir 50 49.45 N 2.41 E
Bouclans 58 47.14 N 6.15 E
Boucle du Baoulé, Parc National de la ♠ 150 13.50 N 9.00 W
Boudenib 148 31.57 N 4.38 W
Boudeuse, Passe de la ⩌ 174s 17.36 S 149.18 W
Boû Djébéh ⊤[4] 150 18.33 N 2.45 W
Boudjellil 148 36.20 N 4.21 E
Boudouaou 34 36.43 N 3.25 E
Boudry 58 46.57 N 6.50 E
Boué 50 50.01 N 3.42 E
Bouenza □[5] 152 4.00 S 13.45 E
Boufarik 148 36.34 N 2.55 E
Bouffémont 261 49.03 N 2.18 E
Bou Ficha 36 36.18 N 10.29 E
Bougaa 34 36.20 N 5.05 E
Bougainville □[5] 175e 6.00 S 155.00 E
Bougainville I 175e 6.00 S 155.00 E
Bougainville Reef ✢[2] 164 15.30 S 147.06 E
Bougainville Strait ⩌ 175e 6.40 S 156.10 E
Bougaroun, Cap ≻ 148 37.06 N 6.28 E
Bouggou 152 3.45 S 11.12 E
Bough Beech Reservoir @[1] 260 51.13 N 0.08 E
Boughton Green 260 51.14 N 0.32 E
Boughton Malherbe 260 51.13 N 0.42 E
Boughton Place ⱱ 260 51.13 N 0.32 E
Boughton Street 42 51.18 N 0.59 E
Bougie → Bejaïa 148 36.45 N 5.05 E
Bougouni 150 11.25 N 7.29 W
Bougouriba ≃ 150 10.42 N 2.56 W
Bougtob 148 34.02 N 0.05 E
Bougzoul 34 35.42 N 2.51 E
Bou Hadjar, Alg. 36 36.30 N 8.06 E
Bou Hadjar, Tun. 36 35.42 N 10.48 E
Bouillante 241o 16.06 N 61.45 W
Bouillon 56 49.48 N 5.04 E
Bouilly 50 48.12 N 4.00 E
Bouïra 148 36.23 N 3.54 E
Bou Ismail 148 36.38 N 2.41 E
Bouisy, Rû de ≃ 261 48.34 N 2.45 E
Bou Izakarn 148 29.09 N 9.44 W
Boujad 148 32.48 N 6.26 W
Boujailles 58 46.53 N 6.05 E
Bouka ≃ 150 11.00 N 10.50 W
Bou Kadir 148 36.04 N 1.07 E
Bou Khadra 36 35.45 N 8.02 E
Boukiéro 273b 4.12 S 15.18 E
Boukiéro, Mont ∧[2] 273b 4.11 S 15.17 E
Boukombé 150 10.11 N 1.06 E
Boula-Ibi 146 9.34 N 13.46 E
Boulaide 56 49.54 N 5.49 E
Boularderie Island I 186 46.15 N 60.30 W
Boulay-Moselle 56 49.11 N 6.30 E
Boulbon 62 43.52 N 4.41 E
Boulder, Austl. 162 30.47 S 121.29 E
Boulder, Colo., U.S. 200 40.01 N 105.17 W
Boulder, Mont., U.S. 202 46.14 N 112.07 W
Boulder ≃ 202 45.52 N 111.57 W
Boulder City 204 35.59 N 114.50 W
Boulder Creek 226 37.07 N 122.07 W
Boulder Creek ≃, Colo., U.S. 200 40.09 N 105.01 W
Boulder Creek ≃, Utah, U.S. 200 37.47 N 111.22 W
Boulder Hill 216 41.42 N 88.21 W
Bouleaux, Lac des @ 275a 45.33 N 73.19 W
Boulia 166 22.54 S 139.54 E
Bouligny 56 49.17 N 5.45 E
Boullay-les-Troux 261 48.41 N 2.03 E
Boulogne ♦[8] 258 34.31 S 58.34 W
Boulogne, Bois de ♠ 261 48.50 N 2.15 E
Boulogne-Billancourt 50 48.50 N 2.15 E
Boulogne-sur-Gesse 32 43.18 N 0.39 E
Boulogne-sur-Mer 50 50.43 N 1.37 E
Boulogue 32 43.18 N 0.39 E
Bouloire 50 47.58 N 0.33 E
Boulou ≃ 152 6.45 N 24.15 E
Boulouba 152 6.49 N 22.15 E
Boulouli 150 15.34 N 9.21 W
Bouloupari 175f 21.52 S 166.04 E
Boulouris-sur-Mer 62 43.25 N 6.48 E
Boulsa 150 12.39 N 0.34 W
Boulsworth Hill ∧ 262 53.48 N 2.06 W
Bouly 150 15.19 N 11.48 W
Boumalne 148 31.32 N 5.27 W
Boû Maya ⊤[4] 150 18.17 N 8.07 W
Boumba 150 12.25 N 2.51 E
Boumba ≃ 152 2.02 N 15.12 E
Boumbé II ≃ 152 4.08 N 15.08 E
Boumboum 150 15.01 N 1.42 W
Boumdeit 150 17.26 N 9.50 W
Bou Medfaa 34 36.22 N 2.28 E
Bouméntana 152 6.59 N 16.56 E
Boumou 146 9.02 N 16.26 E
Bouna 150 9.16 N 3.00 W
Bouna, Park National de ♠ 150 9.00 N 3.30 W
Boundary 180 64.04 N 141.06 W
Boundary Bay C 224 49.00 N 122.58 W
Boundary Peak ∧ 204 37.51 N 118.21 W
Boundary Ranges ∧∧ 180 59.00 N 134.00 W
Bound Brook 210 40.34 N 74.32 W
Bound Brook ≃, Mass., U.S. 283 42.13 N 70.47 W
Bound Brook ≃, N.J., U.S. 276 40.35 N 74.30 W
Boundiali 150 9.31 N 6.29 W
Boundiali □[5] 150 9.50 N 6.30 W
Boun Nua 110 21.38 N 101.54 E
Bountiful 200 40.53 N 111.53 W
Bounty Bay C 174e 25.04 S 130.05 W
Bouquet Canyon ∨ 228 34.26 N 118.32 W
Bouquet Reservoir @[1] 228 34.35 N 118.24 W
Bouqueval 261 49.01 N 2.26 E
Boura 150 12.25 N 4.33 W
Bouradière 62 43.58 N 5.19 E
Bouraéré 152 4.44 N 17.25 E
Bourail 175f 21.34 S 165.30 E
Bouray-sur-Juine 261 48.31 N 2.18 E
Bourbeuse ≃ 194 38.24 N 90.53 W
Bourbeuse, Dry Fork ≃ 194 38.16 N 91.26 W
Bourbon, Ind., U.S. 216 41.18 N 86.07 W
Bourbon, Mo., U.S. 194 38.09 N 91.15 W
Bourbon □[6] 218 38.14 N 84.14 W
Bourbon ≃ 206 46.17 N 71.55 W
Bourbon-Lancy 32 46.38 N 3.46 E
Bourbonnais 216 41.09 N 87.53 W
Bourbonnais □[9] 32 46.20 N 3.00 E
Bourbonne-les-Bains 58 47.57 N 5.45 E
Bourbourg 50 50.57 N 2.12 E
Bourbre ≃ 62 45.47 N 5.11 E
Bourdeaux 62 44.35 N 5.08 E
Bourdon, Île I 275a 45.43 N 73.29 W
Bourdon, Réservoir du @[1] 50 47.36 N 3.07 E
Bourdonné 261 48.45 N 1.40 E
Boureïmi 150 13.10 N 3.44 E
Bourem 150 16.57 N 0.21 W
Bourg 194 29.34 N 90.36 W
Bourg-Achard 50 49.21 N 0.49 E
Bourganeuf 32 45.57 N 1.46 E
Bourg-Argental 62 45.18 N 4.33 E
Bourg-de-Péage 62 45.02 N 5.03 E
Bourg-en-Bresse 58 46.12 N 5.13 E
Bourges 32 47.05 N 2.24 E
Bourget 206 45.26 N 75.09 W
Bourget, Lac du @ 62 45.44 N 5.52 E
Bourg-la-Reine 261 48.47 N 2.19 E
Bourg-Lastic 32 45.39 N 2.33 E
Bourg-lès-Valence 62 44.57 N 4.53 E
Bourgneuf 261 48.36 N 2.00 E
Bourgneuf-en-Retz 32 47.02 N 1.57 W
Bourgogne 50 49.21 N 4.04 E
Bourgogne □[9] 32 47.00 N 4.30 E
Bourgogne, Canal de ≚ 50 47.58 N 3.30 E
Bourgoin-Jallieu 62 45.35 N 5.17 E
Bourg-Saint-Andéol 62 44.22 N 4.39 E
Bourg-Saint-Maurice 62 45.37 N 6.46 E
Bourg-Saint-Pierre 58 45.57 N 7.12 E
Bourgtheroulde 50 49.18 N 0.53 E
Bourgueil 50 47.17 N 0.10 E
Bou Rjeïmat ⊤[4] 150 19.04 N 15.08 W
Bourke 166 30.05 S 145.56 E
Bourmont 58 48.12 N 5.35 E
Bourne 42 52.46 N 0.23 W
Bourne ≃, Fr. 62 45.04 N 5.15 E
Bourne ≃, Eng., U.K. 42 51.02 N 1.47 W
Bournebridge 260 51.38 N 0.11 E
Bourne End 260 51.45 N 0.32 W
Bournemouth 42 50.43 N 1.54 W
Bourneville, Fr. 50 49.23 N 0.37 E
Bourneville, Ohio, U.S. 218 39.17 N 83.09 W
Bourn Vincent Memorial Park ♠ 48 52.01 N 9.30 W
Bouroum 150 13.37 N 0.39 W
Bourron-Marlotte 50 48.20 N 2.42 E
Bourscheid 56 49.55 N 6.04 E
Bourtange 52 53.00 N 7.11 E
Bourtanger Moor ♦[3] 52 53.00 N 7.15 E
Bourton-on-theWater 42 51.53 N 1.45 W
Bourzanga 150 13.41 N 1.33 W
Bou Saâda 148 35.12 N 4.11 E
Bou Salem 36 36.36 N 8.59 E
Bousbecque 50 50.46 N 3.05 E
Bouse 200 33.56 N 114.00 W
Bouse Wash ∨ 200 34.02 N 114.20 W
Boussac 32 46.21 N 2.13 E
Bousse, Fr. 56 49.17 N 6.12 E
Boussé, H. Vol. 150 12.39 N 1.53 W
Boussières 58 47.09 N 5.54 E
Bousso 146 10.29 N 16.43 E
Boussois 50 50.17 N 4.03 E
Boussouma 150 12.55 N 1.05 W
Boussu 50 50.26 N 3.48 E
Boussy-Saint-Antoine 261 48.41 N 2.32 E
Bout, Pointe du ≻ 240e 14.34 N 61.03 W
Bouteille, Lac de la @ 206 46.42 N 73.41 W
Bouteldja 36 36.47 N 8.12 E
Bou Temezguida ∧ 148 29.21 N 9.55 W
Boutilimit 150 17.33 N 14.42 W
Bouttencourt 50 49.56 N 1.38 E
Bouvard, Cape ≻ 168a 32.41 S 115.37 E
Bouvetøya I 9 54.26 S 3.24 E
Bouvier Bay C 281 42.39 N 82.38 W
Bouvières 62 44.30 N 5.13 E
Bouxières-aux-Dames 56 48.45 N 6.10 E
Bouxwiller 56 48.49 N 7.29 E
Bouyon 62 43.50 N 7.07 E
Bouza 150 14.25 N 6.02 E
Bou Zadjar 34 35.35 N 1.09 W
Bouzonville 56 49.18 N 6.32 E
Bov 41 54.50 N 9.23 E
Bova 68 38.00 N 15.56 E
Bøvågen 26 60.40 N 4.58 E
Bovalino Marina 68 38.10 N 16.11 E
Bova Marina 68 37.56 N 15.55 E
Bovard 279b 40.19 N 79.30 W
Bovec 36 46.20 N 13.33 E
Bovegno 64 45.48 N 10.16 E
Bovenden 52 51.35 N 9.55 E
Bovenkarspel 52 52.42 N 5.15 E
Bøverdal 26 61.43 N 8.21 E
Boves, Fr. 50 49.51 N 2.23 E
Boves, It. 62 44.19 N 7.33 E
Bovey 190 47.17 N 93.25 W
Bovey ≃ 42 50.34 N 3.37 W
Bovey Tracey 42 50.36 N 3.40 W
Bovill 202 46.51 N 116.24 W
Boville Ernica 66 41.38 N 13.28 E
Bovina 196 34.31 N 102.53 W
Bovina Center 210 42.16 N 74.47 W
Bovingdon 260 51.44 N 0.32 W
Bövinghausen ♦[8] 263 51.31 N 7.19 E
Bovino 68 41.15 N 15.20 E
Bovisio Masciago 266b 45.37 N 9.09 E

ENGLISH Name	Page	Lat.°′	Long.°′	DEUTSCH Name	Seite	Breite°′	Länge°′ E=Ost

Bovolenta 64 45.16 N 11.56 E
Bovolone 64 45.15 N 11.07 E
Bovril 252 31.21 S 59.26 W
Bovrup 41 54.59 N 9.36 E
Bow 224 48.31 N 122.21 W
Bow ≃, Alta., Can. 182 49.56 N 111.42 W
Bow ≃, Sask., Can. 184 54.56 N 105.13 W
Bo-Wadrif 158 32.26 S 20.07 E
Bowang 106 31.34 N 118.50 E
Bowbells 198 48.48 N 102.15 W
Bow Brook ≃ 42 52.04 N 2.07 W
Bow Creek ≃ 198 39.35 N 99.14 W
Bowden 182 51.55 N 114.02 W
Bowdle 198 45.27 N 99.39 W
Bowdoin, Lake @ 202 48.24 N 108.41 W
Bowdon, Eng., U.K. 262 53.23 N 2.22 W
Bowdon, Ga., U.S. 192 33.32 N 85.15 W
Bowdon, N. Dak., U.S. 198 47.28 N 99.43 W
Bowelling 168a 33.25 S 116.29 E
Bowen, Arg. 252 35.00 S 67.31 W
Bowen, Austl. 166 20.01 S 148.15 E
Bowen, Ill., U.S. 194 40.14 N 91.04 W
Bowen ≃ 166 20.24 S 147.21 E
Bowenfels 170 33.31 S 150.07 E
Bowers 208 39.04 N 75.24 W
Bowers Gifford 260 51.34 N 0.32 E
Bowers Mansion ⊥ 226 39.17 N 119.50 W
Bowers Marshes ≋ 260 51.33 N 0.32 E
Bowers Ridge ✢[3] 12 54.00 N 177.00 E
Bowerston 214 40.26 N 81.11 W
Bowersville 218 39.35 N 83.44 W
Bowgreave 44 53.52 N 2.45 W
Bowie, Ariz., U.S. 200 32.19 N 109.29 W
Bowie, Md., U.S. 208 39.00 N 76.47 W
Bowie, Tex., U.S. 196 33.34 N 97.51 W
Bow Island 184 49.52 N 111.22 W
Bowkān 128 36.31 N 46.12 E
Bowland, Forest of ♦[3] 44 53.58 N 2.32 W
Bowles Creek ≃ 222 32.02 N 94.59 W
Bowley Bar ≻[2] 284b 39.18 N 76.23 W
Bowling Green, Fla., U.S. 220 27.38 N 81.50 W
Bowling Green, Ky., U.S. 194 37.00 N 86.27 W
Bowling Green, Mo., U.S. 219 39.20 N 91.12 W
Bowling Green, Ohio, U.S. 216 41.22 N 83.39 W
Bowling Green, Pa., U.S. 285 39.55 N 75.23 W
Bowling Green, Va., U.S. 208 38.03 N 77.21 W
Bowling Green, Cape ≻ 166 19.19 S 145.25 E
Bowman, Calif., U.S. 226 38.57 N 121.03 W
Bowman, Ga., U.S. 192 34.12 N 83.02 W
Bowman, N. Dak., U.S. 198 46.11 N 103.24 W
Bowman, S.C., U.S. 192 33.21 N 80.41 W
Bowman, Mount ∧ 182 51.10 N 121.55 W
Bowman Bay C 176 65.30 N 73.40 W
Bowman Creek ≃, Pa., U.S. 210 41.31 N 75.58 W
Bowman Creek ≃, Wash., U.S. 224 45.50 N 121.03 W
Bowman-Haley Lake @[1] 198 46.00 N 103.20 W
Bowman Island I 9 65.17 S 103.08 E
Bowman Lake @[1] 226 39.27 N 120.38 W
Bowmans 168b 34.09 S 138.16 E
Bowmansdale 208 40.10 N 76.59 W
Bowmanstown 208 40.48 N 75.40 W
Bowmansville, N.Y., U.S. 212 42.56 N 78.41 W
Bowmansville, Pa., U.S. 208 40.10 N 76.04 W
Bowmanville 212 43.55 N 78.41 W
Bowmanville Creek ≃ 212 43.53 N 78.40 W
Bowmont Water ≃ 44 55.34 N 2.09 W
Bowmore 46 55.45 N 6.17 W
Bowness-on-Windermere 44 54.22 N 2.55 W
Bowokan, Kepulauan II 112 2.10 S 123.10 E
Bowral 170 34.28 S 150.25 E
Bowraville 166 30.39 S 152.51 E
Bowron ≃ 182 54.04 N 121.48 W
Bowron Lake Porvincial Park ♠ 182 53.10 N 121.06 W
Bowsman 184 52.14 N 101.14 W
Bowwood 154 17.07 S 26.17 E
Box 42 51.26 N 2.15 W
Boxberg 56 49.29 N 9.38 E
Box Butte Creek ≃ 198 42.28 N 102.37 W
Box Creek ≃, Tex., U.S. 222 31.33 N 95.43 W
Box Creek ≃, Tex., U.S. 222 31.35 N 95.10 W
Box Elder 202 48.19 N 110.01 W
Boxelder Creek ≃, U.S. 198 45.59 N 103.57 W
Boxelder Creek ≃, Colo., U.S. 198 40.33 N 105.00 W
Box Elder Creek ≃, Colo., U.S. 198 40.23 N 104.28 W
Box Elder Creek ≃, Mont., U.S. 202 46.57 N 108.04 W
Boxelder Creek ≃, S. Dak., U.S. 198 44.01 N 102.27 W
Boxey 186 47.25 N 55.34 W
Boxford 207 42.40 N 71.00 W
Boxford State Forest ♠ 283 42.39 N 71.02 W
Box Grove 275b 43.51 N 79.14 W
Box Hill 169 37.49 S 145.08 E
Boxholm 26 58.12 N 15.03 E
Boxian 100 33.53 N 115.45 E
Boxing 98 37.08 N 118.07 E
Boxley 260 51.18 N 0.33 E
Boxmeer 52 51.39 N 5.57 E
Boxmoor 260 51.45 N 0.29 W
Boxtel 52 51.35 N 5.20 E
Boyabat 130 41.28 N 34.47 E
Boyabo 152 3.43 N 18.46 E
Boyacá □[5] 246 5.30 N 73.30 W
Boyacıköy ♦[8] 267b 41.06 N 29.02 E
Boyadel → Bojadła 30 51.57 N 15.50 E
Boyali 130 41.02 N 33.19 E
Boyalık 130 41.15 N 28.37 E
Boyanup 168a 33.29 S 115.44 E
Boyasengese 152 3.29 N 20.33 E
Boyce 194 31.23 N 92.40 W
Boyceville 190 45.03 N 92.02 W
Boyd, Minn., U.S. 198 44.51 N 95.54 W
Boyd, Tex., U.S. 222 33.05 N 97.34 W
Boyd ≃ 166 29.51 S 152.35 E
Boyd's Cove 186 49.27 N 54.39 W
Boydton 192 36.40 N 78.24 W
Boyenge 152 0.25 N 18.51 E
Boyer ≃ 198 41.28 N 95.55 W
Boyer, Cap ≻ 175f 21.37 S 168.06 E
Boyera 152 0.38 S 19.25 E
Boyer Aḥmadī-ye Sardsīr va Kohkīlūyeh □[4] 128 30.40 N 50.42 E
Boyer Run ≃ 279b 40.13 N 79.32 W
Boyers 214 41.06 N 79.54 W
Boyertown 208 40.20 N 75.38 W
Boyes Hot Springs 226 38.19 N 122.29 W
Boykétté 152 5.28 N 20.50 E
Boykins 208 36.35 N 77.12 W
Boyle, Alta., Can. 182 54.35 N 112.49 W
Boyle, Eire 48 53.58 N 8.18 W
Boyle, Miss., U.S. 194 33.42 N 90.50 W
Boyle Drain ≃ 212 43.42 N 81.06 W
Boyle Heights ♦[8] 280 34.02 N 118.13 W
Boylston, Ala., U.S. 194 32.26 N 86.17 W
Boylston, Mass., U.S. 207 42.21 N 71.44 W
Boyne 275b 43.29 N 79.50 W
Boyne ≃, Austl. 166 23.56 S 151.21 E
Boyne ≃, Man., Can. 184 49.34 N 97.52 W
Boyne ≃, Ont., Can. 212 44.10 N 79.49 W
Boyne ≃, Eire 48 53.43 N 6.15 W
Boyne Battlesite ⊥ 48 53.42 N 6.23 W
Boyne City 190 45.13 N 85.01 W
Boyni Qara 120 36.19 N 66.53 E
Boynton 196 35.39 N 95.39 W
Boynton Beach 220 26.32 N 80.03 W
Boyoali 115a 7.32 S 110.35 E
Boysen Reservoir @[1] 202 43.19 N 108.11 W
Boysen State Park ♠ 202 43.23 N 108.07 W
Boys Ranch 196 35.32 N 102.15 W
Boyuibe 248 20.25 S 63.17 W
Boyup Brook 162 33.50 S 116.24 E
Bozburun 130 36.41 N 28.04 E
Boz Dağ ∧ 130 38.19 N 28.08 E
Bozdağı ∧ 84 39.20 N 43.02 E
Boz Dağları ∧∧ 130 38.20 N 27.45 E
Bozdoğan 130 37.40 N 28.19 E
Bozel 62 45.27 N 6.39 E
Bozeman 202 45.41 N 111.02 W
Bozen → Bolzano 64 46.31 N 11.22 E
Bozene 152 2.56 N 19.12 E
Bozhen 98 38.07 N 116.32 E
Boží Dar 54 50.24 N 12.55 E
Bozkır 130 37.11 N 32.15 E
Bozkurt 130 37.49 N 29.37 E
Bozman 208 38.46 N 76.16 W
Bozoum 152 6.19 N 16.23 E
Bozovici 38 44.55 N 21.59 E
Bozšakol' 86 51.50 N 74.20 E
Bozum 52 53.05 N 5.42 E
Bozüyük 130 39.54 N 30.03 E
Bozyaka 130 37.08 N 31.12 E
Bozzolo 64 45.06 N 10.29 E
Bra 62 44.42 N 7.51 E
Braan ≃ 46 56.33 N 3.35 W
Braås 26 57.04 N 15.03 E
Brabant □[4] 56 50.45 N 4.30 E
Brabante, Isla de → Brabant Island I 9 64.15 S 62.20 W
Brabant Island I 9 64.15 S 62.20 W
Brabant Lake @ 184 56.00 N 103.43 W
Brabrand 41 56.09 N 10.07 E
Brač, Otok I 36 43.20 N 16.40 E
Bracadale, Loch C 46 57.19 N 6.30 W
Bracciano 66 42.06 N 12.10 E
Bracciano, Lago di @ 66 42.07 N 12.14 E
Bracco, Passo del)(62 44.15 N 9.34 E
Bracebridge 212 45.02 N 79.19 W
Bracebridge Heath 44 53.13 N 0.33 W
Braceville, Ill., U.S. 216 41.14 N 88.16 W
Braceville, Ohio, U.S. 214 41.14 N 80.58 W
Brach 146 27.32 N 14.16 E
Brachfield 222 32.03 N 94.39 W
Bracieux 50 47.33 N 1.33 E
Bracigliano 68 40.49 N 14.42 E
Bracigovo 38 42.01 N 24.22 E
Bräcke 26 62.43 N 15.27 E
Brackel ♦[8] 263 51.32 N 7.33 E
Bracken □[6] 218 38.40 N 84.06 W
Brackendale 182 49.46 N 123.09 W
Brackenheim 56 49.05 N 9.03 E
Bracken Lake @ 184 53.37 N 99.50 W
Brackenridge 214 40.37 N 79.44 W
Brackett Field ⊠ 280 34.05 N 117.47 W
Brackettville 196 29.19 N 100.24 W
Brački Kanal ⩌ 36 43.24 N 16.40 E
Brackley 42 52.02 N 1.09 W
Bracknell 42 51.26 N 0.45 W
Brackwede 52 51.59 N 8.31 E
Braclav 78 48.50 N 28.55 E
Braco 46 56.15 N 3.53 W
Braço do Norte 252 28.17 S 49.11 W
Bracuí ≃ 256 22.57 S 44.24 W
Brad 38 46.08 N 22.47 E
Bradano ≃ 68 40.23 N 16.51 E
Bradbury 280 34.08 N 117.59 W
Braddock, N.J., U.S. 285 39.43 N 74.54 W
Braddock, Pa., U.S. 214 40.25 N 79.50 W
Braddock Bay State Park ♠ 210 43.20 N 77.44 W
Braddock Heights, Md., U.S. 208 39.25 N 77.30 W
Braddock Heights, N.Y., U.S. 210 43.19 N 77.42 W
Braddock Hills 279b 40.25 N 79.51 W
Braddock Mill Pond @ 285 39.49 N 74.51 W
Braddock Point ≻ 210 43.19 N 77.43 W
Braden ≃ 220 27.30 N 82.32 W
Bradenton 220 27.29 N 82.34 W
Bradenton Beach 220 27.28 N 82.42 W
Bradenville 214 40.19 N 79.20 W
Braderup 41 54.50 N 8.53 E
Bradford, Ont., Can. 212 44.07 N 79.34 W
Bradford, Eng., U.K. 44 53.48 N 1.45 W
Bradford, Ark., U.S. 194 35.25 N 91.27 W
Bradford, Ill., U.S. 190 41.11 N 89.39 W
Bradford, N.Y., U.S. 210 42.22 N 77.07 W
Bradford, Ohio, U.S. 218 40.08 N 84.26 W
Bradford, Pa., U.S. 214 41.58 N 78.39 W
Bradford, R.I., U.S. 207 41.24 N 71.45 W
Bradford, Tenn., U.S. 194 36.05 N 88.51 W
Bradford, Vt., U.S. 188 43.59 N 72.09 W
Bradford □[6] 210 41.56 N 78.40 W
Bradford □[8] 262 53.47 N 1.52 W
Bradford Hills 285 40.01 N 75.39 W
Bradford Mountain ∧ 207 41.59 N 73.18 W
Bradford-on-Avon 42 51.20 N 2.15 W
Bradford Regional Airport ⊠ 214 41.48 N 78.38 W
Bradfordwoods 214 40.38 N 80.05 W
Brading 42 50.41 N 1.09 W
Bradley, Ark., U.S. 194 33.06 N 93.39 W
Bradley, Calif., U.S. 226 35.52 N 120.48 W
Bradley, Fla., U.S. 220 27.48 N 81.59 W
Bradley, Ill., U.S. 216 41.09 N 87.52 W
Bradley, Mich., U.S. 216 42.38 N 85.39 W
Bradley, S. Dak., U.S. 198 45.05 N 97.39 W
Bradley Beach 208 40.12 N 74.01 W
Bradley Farms 284c 39.00 N 77.11 W
Bradley Gardens 276 40.34 N 74.39 W
Bradley Institute 154 17.02 S 31.27 E
Bradley International Airport ⊠ 207 41.55 N 72.40 W
Bradley Reefs ✢[2] 175e 6.52 S 160.48 E
Bradley Woods Reservation ♠ 279a 41.25 N 81.58 W
Bradner, B.C., Can. 224 49.06 N 122.25 W
Bradner, Ohio, U.S. 214 41.20 N 83.26 W
Bradore Bay 186 51.28 N 57.14 W
Bradshaw, Eng., U.K. 262 53.36 N 2.24 W
Bradshaw, Md., U.S. 208 39.25 N 76.29 W
Bradshaw, Nebr., U.S. 198 40.53 N 97.45 W
Bradshaw, W. Va., U.S. 192 37.21 N 81.49 W
Bradwell-on-Sea 42 51.44 N 0.54 E
Bradworthy 42 50.54 N 4.22 W
Brady, Mont., U.S. 202 48.02 N 111.51 W
Brady, Nebr., U.S. 198 41.01 N 100.22 W
Brady, Tex., U.S. 196 31.08 N 99.20 W
Brady Lake 214 41.09 N 81.19 W
Brady Mountains ∧∧[2] 196 31.20 N 99.40 W
Brae 46a 60.23 N 1.21 W
Brædstrup 41 55.58 N 9.37 E
Braemar 46 57.01 N 3.23 W
Braeside, Austl. 162 21.12 S 121.01 E
Braeside, Austl. 274b 37.59 S 145.07 E
Braeside, Ont., Can. 212 45.28 N 76.24 W
Braga 34 41.33 N 8.26 W

Symbols in the index entries represent the broad categories identified in the key at the right. Symbols with superior numbers (∧∧[2]) identify subcategories (see complete key on page *I · 30*).

Kartensymbole in dem Registerverzeichnis stellen die rechts in Schlüssel erklärten Kategorien dar. Symbole mit hochgestellten Ziffern (∧∧[2]) bezeichnen Unterabteilungen einer Kategorie (vgl. vollständiger Schlüssel auf Seite *I · 30*).

Los símbolos incluídos en el texto del índice representan las grandes categorias identificadas con la clave a la derecha. Los símbolos con numeros en su parte superior (∧∧[2]) identifican las subcategorías (véase la clave completa en la página *I · 30*).

Les symboles de l'index représentent les catégories indiquées dans la légende à droite. Les symboles suivis d'un indice (∧∧[2]) représentent des sous-catégories (voir légende complète à la page *I · 30*).

Os símbolos incluídos no texto do índice representam as grandes categorias identificadas com a chave à direita. Os símbolos com números em sua parte superior (∧∧[2]) identificam as subcategorias (veja-se a chave completa à página *I · 30*).

	English	Deutsch	Español	Français	Português
∧	Mountain	Berg	Montaña	Montagne	Montanha
∧∧	Mountains	Berge	Montañas	Montagnes	Montanhas
)(	Pass	Pass	Paso	Col	Passo
∨	Valley, Canyon	Tal, Cañon	Valle, Cañón	Vallée, Canyon	Vale, Canhão
⩦	Plain	Ebene	Llano	Plaine	Planície
≻	Cape	Kap	Cabo	Cap	Cabo
I	Island	Insel	Isla	Île	Ilha
II	Islands	Inseln	Islas	Îles	Ilhas
♦	Other Topographic Features	Andere Topographische Objekte	Otros Elementos Topográficos	Autres données topographiques	Outros Elementos Topográficos

ESPAÑOL Nombre / FRANÇAIS Nom / PORTUGUÊS Nome	Página / Page / Página	Lat.°′	Long.°′ W=Oeste / W=Ouest / W=Oeste
Bragado	252	35.08 S	60.30 W
Bragança, Bra.	250	1.03 S	46.46 W
Bragança, Port.	34	41.49 N	6.45 W
Bragança Paulista	256	22.57 S	46.34 W
Bragar	46	58.24 N	6.40 W
Bragin	78	51.47 N	30.14 E
Braginka	78	51.22 N	30.24 E
Braginovka	78	48.29 N	36.21 E
Braham	190	45.41 N	93.28 W
Brahetrolleborg	41	55.09 N	10.22 E
Brahma Island	220	27.52 N	81.15 W
Brāhmanbāria	120	23.59 N	91.07 E
Brāhmani	120	20.39 N	86.46 E
Brahmapur	272b	22.28 N	88.22 E
Brahmaputra (Yaluzangbujiang)	120	24.02 N	90.59 E
Brāhmaur	123	32.27 N	76.32 E
Braich-y-Pwll	42	52.48 N	4.36 W
Braidwood, Austl.	166	35.27 S	149.48 E
Braidwood, Ill., U.S.	216	41.16 N	88.13 W
Braies (Prags)	64	46.42 N	12.08 E
Brăila	38	45.16 N	27.58 E
Brăila □[4]	38	45.00 N	27.40 E
Brăilei, Balta	38	45.00 N	28.00 E
Brailov	78	49.06 N	28.09 E
Brain	42	51.48 N	0.39 E
Brainard, Nebr., U.S.	198	41.11 N	97.00 W
Brainard, N.Y., U.S.	210	42.30 N	73.31 W
Braine	50	49.20 N	3.32 E
Braine-l'Alleud	50	50.41 N	4.22 E
Braine-le-Château	50	50.41 N	4.16 E
Braine-le-Comte	50	50.36 N	4.08 E
Brainerd	190	46.21 N	94.12 W
Braint	44	53.08 N	4.19 W
Braintree, Eng., U.K.	42	51.53 N	0.32 E
Braintree, Mass., U.S.	207	42.13 N	71.00 W
Braintree □[8]	260	51.47 N	0.36 E
Brak	158	29.35 S	22.55 E
Brake, B.R.D.	52	52.01 N	8.55 E
Brake, B.R.D.	52	53.19 N	8.28 E
Brake, B.R.D.	52	52.04 N	8.35 E
Brakel	52	51.43 N	9.10 E
Brakpan	158	26.13 S	28.20 E
Brakpoort	158	31.20 S	23.22 E
Brakputs	158	29.29 S	18.24 E
Brakwater	156	22.24 S	17.06 E
Brålanda	26	58.34 N	12.22 E
Bralorne	182	50.47 N	122.49 W
Bramalea	212	43.44 N	79.43 W
Bramall Hall	262	53.23 N	2.09 W
Braman	196	36.55 N	97.20 W
Brambauer [8]	263	51.35 N	7.27 E
Bramberg am Wildkogel	64	47.16 N	12.21 E
Bramble Bay	171a	27.17 S	153.05 E
Bramble Cay	164	9.08 S	143.52 E
Bramdrupdam	41	55.31 N	9.28 E
Bramey-Lenningsen	263	51.34 N	7.46 E
Bramfeld [8]	260	53.37 N	10.04 E
Bramford	42	52.04 N	1.06 E
Bramhall	262	53.22 N	2.10 W
Bramley	260	51.12 N	0.34 W
Bramley [8]	273d	26.08 S	28.05 E
Bramley Mountain	210	42.18 N	74.49 W
Bramming	41	55.28 N	8.42 E
Brampton, Ont., Can.	212	43.41 N	79.46 W
Brampton, Eng., U.K.	42	52.19 N	0.14 W
Brampton, Eng., U.K.	44	54.57 N	2.43 W
Brampton Airfield	275b	43.40 N	79.47 W
Bramsche	52	52.24 N	7.58 E
Bramsöfjärden	40	60.20 N	17.10 E
Bramstedt	52	53.22 N	8.41 E
Bran, Pasul	38	45.26 N	25.17 E
Brancaleone Marina	68	37.58 N	16.06 E
Brancaster	42	52.58 N	0.39 E
Brancaster Roads [3]	42	53.05 N	0.45 W
Branch	186	46.53 N	53.57 W
Branch □[6]	216	41.55 N	85.03 W
Branch Brook Park	276	40.46 N	74.10 W
Branch Dale	208	40.41 N	76.20 W
Branch Hill	218	39.15 N	84.18 W
Branchport	210	42.36 N	77.09 W
Branchville, Conn., U.S.	207	41.16 N	73.27 W
Branchville, N.J., U.S.	210	41.09 N	74.45 W
Branchville, S.C., U.S.	192	33.15 N	80.49 W
Branchville, Va., U.S.	208	36.34 N	77.15 W
Branco	152	12.30 S	20.32 E
Branco, Bra.	246	1.24 S	61.51 W
Branco, Bra.	248	7.44 S	61.46 W
Branco, Bra.	248	10.03 S	67.51 W
Branco, Bra.	248	9.37 S	60.33 W
Branco, Bra.	248	21.00 S	57.48 W
Branco, Bra.	248	6.41 S	66.41 W
Branco, Bra.	248	13.41 S	60.44 W
Branco, Bra.	248	9.12 S	64.22 W
Branco, Bra.	250	7.01 S	51.42 W
Branco, Bra.	256	24.09 S	46.48 W
Branco, Ilhéu	150a	16.39 N	24.41 W
Brand, B.R.D.	56	50.43 N	6.09 E
Brand, Öst.	58	47.06 N	9.44 E
Brandamore	208	40.03 N	75.50 W
Brandaris [2]	241s	12.17 N	68.24 W
Brandberg	156	21.10 S	14.33 E
Brandbu	26	60.28 N	10.30 E
Brande	41	55.57 N	9.07 E
Brandebourg → Brandenburg	54	52.24 N	12.32 E
Brandeis University [2]	283	42.22 N	71.16 W
Brandenberg	64	47.29 N	11.53 E
Brandenberg [2]	263	51.20 N	7.37 E
Brandenburg	54	52.24 N	12.32 E
Brandenburg □[9]	54	52.00 N	13.30 E
Brandenburger Tor	264a	52.31 N	13.23 E
Brand-Erbisdorf	54	50.52 N	13.19 E
Brandfort	158	28.47 S	26.30 E
Br'andino	80	54.23 N	49.23 E
Brandis, D.D.R.	54	51.20 N	12.36 E
Brandis, D.D.R.	54	51.48 N	13.10 E
Brandizzo	62	45.11 N	7.51 E
Brandkop	158	31.13 S	19.13 E
Brandon, Man., Can.	184	49.50 N	99.57 W
Brandon, Eng., U.K.	42	52.27 N	0.37 E
Brandon, Eng., U.K.	44	54.46 N	1.39 W
Brandon, Fla., U.S.	220	27.56 N	82.17 W
Brandon, Miss., U.S.	194	32.16 N	89.59 W
Brandon, Tex., U.S.	222	32.03 N	96.58 W
Brandon, Vt., U.S.	188	43.48 N	73.05 W
Brandon, Wis., U.S.	190	43.44 N	88.47 W
Brandon Bay	48	52.15 N	10.05 W
Brandon Head	48	52.16 N	10.14 W
Brandon Mountain	48	52.14 N	10.15 W
Brandon Road Lock and Dam [5]	278	41.30 N	88.06 W
Brandonville	210	40.52 N	76.10 W
Brand Park	280	34.11 N	118.16 W
Brands Hatch Motor Race Circuit	260	51.22 N	0.16 E
Brandsø	41	55.21 N	9.43 E
Brandt	218	39.54 N	84.05 W
Brandvlei, S. Afr.	158	30.25 S	20.30 E
Brandvlei, S. Afr.	273d	26.07 S	27.39 E
Brandvlei	158	33.43 S	19.26 E
Brandy Camp	214	41.19 N	78.41 W
Brandy Peak	202	42.36 N	123.53 W
Brandýsek	54	50.10 N	14.10 E
Brandýs nad Labem	54	50.10 N	14.41 E
Brandywine Battlefield (1777)	208	39.53 N	75.35 W
Brandywine Creek, U.S.	285	39.44 N	75.32 W
Brandywine Creek, Ind., U.S.	218	39.31 N	85.52 W
Brandywine Creek, Ohio, U.S.	279a	41.17 N	81.34 W
Brandywine Creek, East Branch	208	39.55 N	75.39 W
Brandywine Creek, West Branch	208	39.55 N	75.39 W
Brandywine Creek State Park	285	39.48 N	75.35 W
Brandywine Park	285	39.45 N	75.33 W
Brandywine Raceway	285	39.50 N	75.32 W
Brandywine Springs State Park	285	39.45 N	75.38 W
Branford, Conn., U.S.	207	41.17 N	72.49 W
Branford, Fla., U.S.	192	29.58 N	82.56 W
Brani, Pulau	271c	1.15 N	103.50 E
Braniewo	30	54.24 N	19.50 E
Branka, Česko.	60	49.50 N	12.33 E
Br'anka, S.S.S.R.	83	48.29 N	38.39 E
Br'anka, S.S.S.R.	86	59.08 N	93.27 E
Branlin	50	47.51 N	3.06 E
Brannenburg	64	47.44 N	12.05 E
Branquinho	248	5.45 S	71.27 W
Bransby	166	28.14 S	142.04 E
Bransfield Strait	9	63.00 S	59.00 W
Brańsk, Pol.	30	52.45 N	22.51 E
Br'ansk, S.S.S.R.	76	53.15 N	34.22 E
Br'ansk □[4]	78	53.00 N	33.00 E
Br'anskaja Kosa, Mys	84	44.22 N	47.00 E
Branson	194	36.39 N	93.13 W
Brant	210	42.35 N	79.01 W
Brant □[6]	212	43.10 N	80.20 W
Brantford	212	43.08 N	80.16 W
Brantingham Lake	212	43.42 N	75.17 W
Brant Lake	188	43.41 N	73.45 W
Brantley	194	31.35 N	86.22 W
Brantôme	32	45.22 N	0.39 E
Brant Rock	283	42.05 N	70.39 W
Brantville	186	47.22 N	64.58 W
Branxholme	166	37.51 S	141.47 E
Branxton	170	32.39 S	151.22 E
Branzi	64	46.00 N	9.46 E
Brás [8]	287b	23.32 S	46.36 W
Brás Cubas	256	23.32 S	46.13 W
Bras d'Or Lake	186	45.52 N	60.50 W
Brashear	222	33.07 N	95.44 W
Brasil → Brazil □[1]	18	10.00 S	55.00 W
Brasilândia [8]	287b	23.28 S	46.41 W
Brasiléia	248	11.00 S	68.44 W
Brasília	255	15.47 S	47.55 W
Brasília, Lago de	255	15.48 S	47.50 W
Brasília de Minas	255	16.12 S	44.26 W
Brasilien → Brazil □[1]	18	10.00 S	55.00 W
Braslav	76	55.38 N	27.02 E
Brașov	38	45.39 N	25.37 E
Brașov □[4]	38	45.45 N	25.15 E
Brass	150	4.19 N	6.14 E
Brass Castle	210	40.47 N	74.58 W
Brasschaat	50	51.17 N	4.27 E
Brassert	263	51.40 N	7.05 E
Brassey, Binjaran	112	4.54 N	117.30 E
Brassey, Mount	162	23.05 S	134.38 E
Brass Islands	240m	18.24 N	64.58 W
Brassó → Brașov	38	45.39 N	25.37 E
Brasstown Bald	192	34.52 N	83.48 W
Brastad	26	58.23 N	11.29 E
Brasted	260	51.16 N	0.17 E
Brasted Chart	260	51.16 N	0.06 E
Břasy	60	49.50 N	13.35 E
Bratca	38	46.56 N	22.37 E
Bratcevo [8]	265b	55.51 N	37.24 E
Bratejevo [8]	265b	55.38 N	37.45 E
Bratenahl	279a	41.35 N	81.33 W
Brateș, Lacul	38	45.30 N	28.05 E
Bratislava	30	48.09 N	17.07 E
Bratol'ubovka	86	51.13 N	66.46 E
Bratsk	88	56.05 N	101.48 E
Bratskaja Kada	88	55.02 N	102.06 E
Bratskoje	78	47.52 N	31.34 E
Bratskoje Vodochranilišče [1]	88	56.10 N	102.10 E
Brattfors	40	59.40 N	14.01 E
Brattleboro	188	42.51 N	72.34 W
Bratto	64	45.55 N	10.04 E
Brattvåg	26	62.36 N	6.27 E
Braubach	56	50.16 N	7.40 E
Braúnas	255	19.04 S	42.43 W
Braunau am Inn	60	48.15 N	13.02 E
Braunfels	56	50.31 N	8.23 E
Braunlage	54	51.44 N	10.37 E
Bräunlingen	58	47.55 N	8.26 E
Braunsbedra	54	51.15 N	11.49 E
Braunsberg → Braniewo	30	54.24 N	19.50 E
Braunschweig, B.R.D.	52	52.16 N	10.31 E
Braunschweig, S. Afr.	158	32.48 S	27.22 E
Braunschweig □[6]	54	52.10 N	10.30 E
Braunton	42	51.07 N	4.10 W
Braunwald	58	46.56 N	9.00 E
Brava	144	1.05 N	44.02 E
Brava	150a	14.52 N	24.43 W
Brava, Costa [2]	34	41.45 N	3.04 E
Brava, Punta	258	34.56 S	56.10 W
Brave	188	39.44 N	80.16 W
Bravica	78	47.22 N	28.26 E
Bråviken	40	58.38 N	16.32 E
Bravo, Cerro, Bol.	248	17.40 S	64.35 W
Bravo, Cerro, Perú	248	5.32 S	79.15 W
Bravo del Norte (Rio Grande)	178	25.55 N	97.09 W
Brawley	204	32.59 N	115.31 W
Brawley Peaks	204	38.15 N	118.55 W
Brawley Wash	200	32.34 N	111.26 W
Bray, Bel.	50	50.26 N	4.06 E
Bray, Eire	48	53.12 N	6.06 W
Bray	42	50.59 N	3.53 W
Bray, Pays de	50	49.46 N	1.26 E
Braybrook	274b	37.47 S	144.51 E
Bray-Dunes	50	51.05 N	2.31 E
Braye	50	47.45 N	0.42 E
Bray Head	48	51.53 N	10.26 W
Bray Island	176	69.20 N	76.45 W
Braymer	194	39.35 N	93.48 W
Bray-sur-Seine	50	48.25 N	3.14 E
Bray-sur-Somme	50	49.56 N	2.43 E
Brazeau	182	52.55 N	115.15 W
Brazeau, Mount	182	52.33 N	117.21 W
Brazeau Dam [6]	182	52.45 N	115.30 W
Brazen Head	158	31.43 S	29.25 E
Brazey-en-Plaine	58	47.08 N	5.13 E
Brazil	194	39.32 N	87.08 W
Brazil □[1]	18	10.00 S	55.00 W
Brazil Basin [1]	8	15.00 S	26.00 W
Brazo Chico, Arroyo	258	33.45 S	58.32 W
Brazo Largo, Arroyo	258	33.47 S	58.36 W
Brazópolis	256	22.28 S	45.37 W
Brazoria	222	29.03 N	95.34 W
Brazoria □[6]	222	29.12 N	95.25 W
Brazos □[6]	222	30.40 N	96.18 W
Brazos	196	28.53 N	95.23 W
Brazos, Clear Fork	196	33.01 N	98.40 W
Brazos, Double Mountain Fork	196	33.15 N	100.00 W
Brazos, Salt Fork	196	33.15 N	100.00 W
Brazo Sur [del Rio Coig]	254	51.32 S	70.04 W
Brazzaville	152, 273b	4.16 S	15.17 E
Brazzaville (Maya Maya) Airport	273b	4.15 S	15.15 E
Brčko	38	44.53 N	18.48 E
Brda	30	53.07 N	18.08 E
Brdy	60	49.40 N	13.50 E
Brea	228	33.55 N	117.54 W
Brea, Punta	240m	17.56 N	66.55 W
Brea Canyon	280	33.55 N	117.55 W
Brea Creek	280	33.53 N	117.59 W
Breadalbane	166	23.49 S	139.35 E
Brea Dam [6]	280	33.54 N	117.56 W
Bread and Cheese Creek	284b	39.17 N	76.29 W
Breaden Bluff [2]	162	26.56 S	124.32 E
Breadysville	285	40.13 N	75.04 W
Breakenridge, Mount	182	49.43 N	121.56 W
Breakheart Reservation	283	42.29 N	71.02 W
Breaksea Sound	172	45.35 S	166.40 E
Bream Bay	172	35.55 S	174.30 E
Bream Head	172	35.51 S	174.35 E
Breamish	44	55.31 N	1.56 W
Bream's Eaves	42	51.45 N	2.34 W
Bream Tail	172	36.03 S	174.35 E
Brea Pozo	252	28.15 S	63.57 W
Bréau	261	48.34 N	2.53 E
Breaux Bridge	194	30.16 N	91.54 W
Breaza	38	45.11 N	25.40 E
Brebes	115a	6.53 S	109.03 E
Brécey	32	48.44 N	1.10 W
Brechfa	42	51.54 N	4.36 W
Brechin	46	56.44 N	2.40 W
Brecht	56	51.21 N	4.38 E
Brechten [8]	263	51.35 N	7.28 E
Breckenridge, Colo., U.S.	200	39.29 N	106.03 W
Breckenridge, Mich., U.S.	190	43.24 N	84.29 W
Breckenridge, Minn., U.S.	198	46.16 N	96.35 W
Breckenridge, Tex., U.S.	196	32.45 N	98.54 W
Breckerfeld	56	51.16 N	7.28 E
Breckland [1]	42	52.28 N	0.37 E
Brecknock → Brecon	42	51.57 N	3.24 W
Brecknock, Peninsula [1]	254	54.35 S	71.50 W
Brecksville	279a	41.19 N	81.38 W
Břeclav	30	48.46 N	16.53 E
Brecon	42	51.57 N	3.24 W
Brecon Beacons	42	51.53 N	3.31 W
Brecon Beacons National Park	42	51.52 N	3.25 W
Bred	41	55.22 N	10.07 E
Breda, Ned.	52	51.35 N	4.46 E
Breda, Iowa, U.S.	198	42.11 N	94.59 W
Bredared	26	57.10 N	13.44 E
Bredasdorp	158	34.32 S	20.02 E
Bredbo	171b	35.57 S	149.10 E
Bredbury	262	53.25 N	2.06 W
Bredbyn	26	63.27 N	18.06 E
Bredde	54	52.52 N	12.13 E
Brede Å	41	55.09 N	8.42 E
Bredebro	41	55.03 N	8.49 E
Bredell	273d	26.05 S	28.17 E
Bredenbeck	52	52.15 N	9.37 E
Bredenbruch	263	51.21 N	7.45 E
Bredenbury	184	50.57 N	102.03 W
Bredene	50	51.14 N	2.58 E
Bredeney [8]	263	51.24 N	6.59 E
Bredenscheid-Stüter	263	51.22 N	7.11 E
Bredereiche	54	53.08 N	13.14 E
Bredgar	260	51.18 N	0.42 E
Bredhurst	260	51.20 N	0.35 E
Bredon Hill [2]	42	52.06 N	2.03 W
Bredsjö	40	59.50 N	14.44 E
Bredsjön	40	60.13 N	13.55 E
Bredstedt	41	54.37 N	8.59 E
Bredsten	41	55.42 N	9.24 E
Bredy	86	52.26 N	60.21 E
Bree	56	51.08 N	5.36 E
Breë	158	34.24 S	20.50 E
Breeches Lake	206	45.54 N	71.28 W
Breedoge	48	53.55 N	8.27 W
Breeds Pond	283	42.28 N	70.59 W
Breedsville	216	42.21 N	86.08 W
Breese	219	38.36 N	89.32 W
Breesport	210	42.10 N	76.44 W
Breeza Plains	164	14.50 S	144.07 E
Breezewood	279b	40.34 N	80.03 W
Breg	58	47.57 N	8.31 E
Bregalnica	38	41.43 N	22.09 E
Breganze	64	45.42 N	11.34 E
Bregenz	58	47.30 N	9.46 E
Bregenzer Wald	58	47.20 N	10.00 E
Bregninge, Dan.	41	55.01 N	10.37 E
Bregninge, Dan.	41	55.41 N	11.19 E
Bregovo	38	44.09 N	22.39 E
Breguzzo	64	46.00 N	10.42 E
Brégy	261	49.05 N	2.52 E
Bréhal	32	48.54 N	1.31 W
Brehna	54	51.33 N	12.12 E
Breiðafjörður	24a	65.15 N	23.15 W
Breidbach	158	32.54 S	27.27 E
Breid Bay	9	70.15 S	24.15 E
Breidenbach	56	49.08 N	7.25 E
Breidenbach	56	50.55 N	8.28 E
Breil-sur-Roya	62	43.56 N	7.30 E
Breinizer	214	40.24 N	79.16 W
Breisach	58	48.01 N	7.40 E
Breisgau [1]	58	47.45 N	7.45 E
Breitbrunn	60	48.02 N	11.08 E
Breitenbrunn	54	50.29 N	12.46 E
Breitenfelde	52	53.36 N	10.38 E
Breitengüssbach	56	49.58 N	10.53 E
Breitenlee [8]	264b	48.15 N	16.30 E
Breitenstein	54	51.37 N	10.56 E
Breitenworbis	54	51.24 N	10.25 E
Breithorn	58	45.56 N	7.45 E
Breitlingsee	54	52.23 N	12.28 E
Breitscheid, B.R.D.	56	50.41 N	8.11 E
Breitscheid, B.R.D.	56	51.22 N	6.52 E
Breitsetten	61	48.12 N	16.42 E
Breitungen	54	50.45 N	10.20 E
Brejinho de Nazaré	250	11.01 S	48.34 W
Brejo	250	3.41 S	42.47 W
Brejo, Riacho do	250	8.08 S	42.49 W
Brejo de São Felix	250	5.24 S	43.24 W
Brejões	255	13.06 S	39.48 W
Brejo Grande	250	10.26 S	36.28 W
Brejo Santo	250	7.29 S	39.00 W
Brejtovo	76	58.18 N	37.52 E
Brekken	26	62.39 N	11.53 E
Brekstad	26	63.41 N	9.41 E
Breloh	52	53.01 N	10.04 E
Bremangerlandet	26	61.51 N	5.02 E
Brembio	62	45.13 N	9.34 E
Brembo	62	45.35 N	9.32 E
Brême → Bremen	52	53.04 N	8.49 E
Bremelau	58	48.20 N	9.32 E
Bremen, B.R.D.	52	53.04 N	8.49 E
Bremen, Ga., U.S.	192	33.43 N	85.09 W
Bremen, Ind., U.S.	216	41.27 N	86.09 W
Bremen, Ohio, U.S.	188	39.42 N	82.26 W
Bremen □[3]	52	53.05 N	8.50 E
Bremer, Austl.	171b	35.23 S	139.02 E
Bremer, Austl.	171a	27.39 S	152.45 E
Bremer Bay	162	34.23 S	119.25 E
Bremerhaven	52	53.33 N	8.34 E
Bremerton	224	47.34 N	122.38 W
Bremerton East	224	47.35 N	122.38 W
Bremervörde	52	53.29 N	9.08 E
Bremgarten	58	47.21 N	8.21 E
Bremke, B.R.D.	52	52.07 N	9.06 E
Bremke, B.R.D.	56	51.15 N	8.12 E
Bremke [8]	263	51.23 N	7.41 E
Bremner	190	48.41 N	85.31 W
Bremond	222	31.10 N	96.41 W
Brem River	182	50.26 N	124.39 W
Breña	286d	12.04 S	77.04 W
Brendel Lake	281	42.38 N	83.30 W
Brenderup	41	55.29 N	9.59 E
Brendlorenzen	56	50.20 N	10.13 E
Brendon Hills [2]	42	51.07 N	3.25 W
Brenes	34	37.33 N	5.52 W
Brenham	222	30.10 N	96.24 W
Brenish	46	58.08 N	7.08 W
Brenish, Aird	46	58.08 N	7.08 W
Bren Mar Park	284c	38.48 N	77.09 W
Brenne	50	47.24 N	0.51 E
Brenne [1]	32	46.45 N	1.10 E
Brennero (Brenner)	64	47.00 N	11.30 E
Brennero, Passo del → Brenner Pass	64	47.00 N	11.30 E
Brenner Pass	64	47.00 N	11.30 E
Breno, It.	64	45.57 N	10.18 E
Breno, Schw.	58	46.02 N	8.53 E
Brénod	58	46.04 N	5.36 E
Brent, Ala., U.S.	194	32.56 N	87.10 W
Brent, Fla., U.S.	194	30.27 N	87.15 W
Brent [8]	260	51.34 N	0.17 W
Brent	260	51.28 N	0.18 W
Brenta	64	45.11 N	12.18 E
Brenta, Gruppo di	64	46.11 N	10.54 E
Brentford [8]	260	51.29 N	0.18 W
Brenthurst	273d	26.16 S	28.23 E
Brentino	64	45.40 N	10.55 E
Brentonico	64	45.49 N	10.57 E
Brentwood, Eng., U.K.	260	51.38 N	0.18 E
Brentwood, Calif., U.S.	226	37.56 N	121.42 W
Brentwood, Md., U.S.	208	38.56 N	76.57 W
Brentwood, N.Y., U.S.	210	40.47 N	73.14 W
Brentwood, Ohio, U.S.	218	39.13 N	84.32 W
Brentwood, Pa., U.S.	214	40.22 N	79.59 W
Brentwood □[8]	260	51.37 N	0.20 E
Brentwood Bay	224	48.35 N	123.28 W
Brentwood Estates	214	40.25 N	80.45 W
Brentwood Heights [8]	280	34.04 N	118.30 W
Brentwood Lake	214	41.19 N	82.05 W
Brentwood Park	273d	26.08 S	28.18 E
Brenz	56	48.33 N	10.17 E
Brenz	56	48.34 N	10.24 E
Bréon, Ruisseu du	261	48.40 N	2.49 E
Brera, Palazzo di	266b	45.28 N	9.11 E
Brereton Park	158	26.55 S	30.30 E
Brescello	64	44.54 N	10.31 E
Brescia	64	45.33 N	13.15 E
Brescia □[4]	64	45.38 N	10.18 E
Bresewitz	54	54.24 N	12.40 E
Brésil → Brazil □[1]	18	10.00 S	55.00 W
Breskens	52	51.24 N	3.34 E
Breslau, Ont., Can.	212	43.28 N	80.25 W
Breslau → Wrocław, Pol.	30	51.06 N	17.00 E
Breslau, Tex., U.S.	222	29.31 N	97.00 W
Bresle	50	50.04 N	1.22 E
Bresles	50	49.25 N	2.15 E
Bresnahan, Mount	162	23.50 S	117.55 E
Bressanone (Brixen)	64	46.43 N	11.39 E
Bressay	46a	60.08 N	1.05 W
Bressay Sound	46a	60.07 N	1.09 W
Bresse [1]	58	46.30 N	5.15 E
Bresso	266b	45.32 N	9.11 E
Bressuire	32	46.51 N	0.30 W
Brest, Blg.	38	43.38 N	24.35 E
Brest, Fr.	32	48.24 N	4.29 W
Brest, S.S.S.R.	76	52.06 N	23.42 E
Brestanica	36	45.59 N	15.29 E
Bretagne □[9]	32	48.00 N	3.00 W
Bretenoux	32	44.55 N	1.50 E
Breteuil	50	49.38 N	2.18 E
Breteuil-sur-Iton	50	48.50 N	0.55 E
Bréthencourt	261	48.30 N	1.55 E
Bretherton	262	53.41 N	2.48 W
Brétigny, Aérodrome de	261	48.35 N	2.20 E
Brétigny-sur-Orge	50	48.37 N	2.19 E
Bretnig	54	51.08 N	14.04 E
Breton	182	53.07 N	114.28 W
Bretón, Canal de	240p	21.10 N	79.30 W
Breton, Pertuis	32	46.25 N	1.20 W
Breton Bay	208	38.16 N	76.39 W
Breton Sound	194	29.30 N	89.30 W
Breton Woods	208	40.03 N	74.07 W
Brett	42	51.58 N	0.58 E
Brett, Cape	172	35.10 S	174.20 E
Bretten	56	49.02 N	8.42 E
Breu, Rio do	246	3.29 S	66.20 W
Breueh, Pulau	110	5.41 N	95.05 E
Breuil-Bois-Robert	261	48.57 N	1.43 E
Breuil-Cervinia	58	45.56 N	7.38 E
Breuillet	261	48.34 N	2.10 E
Breuilpont	50	48.58 N	1.26 E
Breukelen	52	52.10 N	5.00 E
Breux	261	48.34 N	2.11 E
Brevard	192	35.09 N	82.44 W
Brevard □[6]	220	28.18 N	80.42 W
Brévenne	62	45.51 N	4.46 E
Brevens bruk	40	59.01 N	15.35 E
Breves	250	1.40 S	50.29 W
Brevig Mission	180	65.20 N	166.29 W
Brevik, Nor.	26	59.04 N	9.42 E
Brevik, Sve.	40	59.21 N	18.12 E
Brevoort Island	176	63.30 N	64.20 W
Brewarrina	166	29.57 S	146.52 E
Brewer	188	44.48 N	68.46 W
Brewer Island	282	37.33 N	122.16 W
Brewersville	218	39.05 N	85.37 W
Brewerton	210	43.14 N	76.08 W
Brewerville	150	6.26 N	10.47 W
Brewongle	170	33.29 S	149.43 E
Brewood	42	52.41 N	2.10 W
Brewster, Kans., U.S.	198	39.22 N	101.23 W
Brewster, Mass., U.S.	207	41.46 N	70.05 W
Brewster, Minn., U.S.	198	43.42 N	95.28 W
Brewster, Nebr., U.S.	198	41.56 N	99.52 W
Brewster, N.Y., U.S.	210	41.24 N	73.37 W
Brewster, Ohio, U.S.	214	40.43 N	81.36 W
Brewster, Wash., U.S.	202	48.06 N	119.47 W
Brewster, Kap	16	70.19 N	22.05 W
Brewster, Lake	166	33.28 S	145.46 E
Brewster, Mount	172	44.04 S	169.27 E
Brewton	194	31.07 N	87.04 W
Breyten	158	26.16 S	30.00 E
Brežice	36	45.54 N	15.36 E
Brézins	62	45.21 N	5.19 E
Březnice	60	49.33 N	13.57 E
Breznik	38	42.44 N	22.54 E
Brezno, Česko.	30	48.50 N	19.39 E
Březno, Česko.	54	50.24 N	13.26 E
Brézolles	50	48.41 N	1.04 E
Brezová	54	50.06 N	12.39 E
Březové Hory	60	49.41 N	13.58 E
Bria	152	6.32 N	21.59 E
Brian Boru Peak	182	55.05 N	127.35 W
Briançon	62	44.54 N	6.39 E
Brian Head	200	37.41 N	112.50 W
Briar	222	33.00 N	97.34 W
Briarcliff Manor	210	41.09 N	73.50 W
Briar Creek	222	32.06 N	96.22 W
Briare	50	47.38 N	2.44 E
Briare, Canal de	50	48.02 N	2.43 E
Briarres-sur-Essonne	50	48.14 N	2.25 E
Briarwood Beach	214	41.06 N	81.54 W
Briarwood Center [9]	281	42.14 N	83.45 W
Briatico	68	38.43 N	16.02 E
Bribano	64	46.06 N	12.05 E
Bribie Island	171a	27.00 S	153.07 E
Bričany	78	48.22 N	27.04 E
Bricelyn	190	43.34 N	93.49 W
Brick Run	284b	39.19 N	76.50 W
Brices Cross Roads National Battlefield Site	194	34.31 N	88.41 W
Briceville	192	36.11 N	84.11 W
Bricherasio	62	44.49 N	7.18 E
Bricht	263	51.41 N	6.51 E
Bri Chualann → Bray	48	53.12 N	6.06 W
Brickaville	157b	18.49 S	49.04 E
Brickebacken	40	59.15 N	15.15 E
Brick Lake	220	28.10 N	81.12 W
Brick Town	208	40.04 N	74.08 W
Briçonnet, Lac	186	51.27 N	60.11 W
Bricquebec	32	49.28 N	1.38 W
Bridal Veil	224	45.33 N	122.11 W
Bridalveil Fall	226	37.43 N	119.39 W
Bride	44	54.22 N	4.22 W
Bride	48	52.04 N	7.52 W
Bridesburg [8]	285	40.00 N	75.04 W
Bridge	182	50.45 N	121.55 W
Bridge City	194	30.01 N	93.51 W
Bridge Creek	224	48.26 N	120.52 W
Bridgehampton	207	40.56 N	72.18 W
Bridge Lake	182	51.29 N	120.43 W
Bridgend, Scot., U.K.	46	55.48 N	6.16 W
Bridgend, Scot., U.K.	46	56.48 N	2.45 W
Bridgend, Wales, U.K.	42	51.31 N	3.35 W
Bridgenorth	212	44.23 N	78.23 W
Bridge of Allan	46	56.09 N	3.57 W
Bridge of Gaur	46	56.41 N	4.27 W
Bridge of Orchy	46	56.30 N	4.46 W
Bridge of Weir	46	55.52 N	4.35 W
Bridgeport, Ont., Can.	212	43.29 N	80.29 W
Bridgeport, Ala., U.S.	194	34.57 N	85.43 W
Bridgeport, Calif., U.S.	226	38.10 N	119.13 W
Bridgeport, Conn., U.S.	207, 276	41.11 N	73.11 W
Bridgeport, Ill., U.S.	194	38.43 N	87.46 W
Bridgeport, Mich., U.S.	190	43.22 N	83.53 W
Bridgeport, Nebr., U.S.	198	41.40 N	103.06 W
Bridgeport, N.J., U.S.	285	39.48 N	75.21 W
Bridgeport, N.Y., U.S.	210	43.09 N	75.58 W
Bridgeport, Ohio, U.S.	214	40.04 N	80.45 W
Bridgeport, Pa., U.S.	285	40.06 N	75.21 W
Bridgeport, Tex., U.S.	222	33.13 N	97.45 W
Bridgeport, Wash., U.S.	202	48.00 N	119.40 W
Bridgeport, W. Va., U.S.	188	39.17 N	80.15 W
Bridgeport, Lake [1]	222	33.13 N	97.48 W
Bridgeport, University of [2]	276	41.10 N	73.12 W
Bridgeport Airport	285	39.47 N	75.20 W
Bridgeport Harbor	276	41.10 N	73.11 W
Bridgeport Municipal Airport	276	41.10 N	73.08 W
Bridgeport Reservoir [1]	226	38.22 N	119.14 W
Bridger	202	45.18 N	108.55 W
Bridge River Indian Reserve [4]	182	50.45 N	122.00 W
Bridger Peak	200	41.12 N	107.02 W
Bridges Point	174o	1.58 N	157.28 W
Bridgeton, Mo., U.S.	219	38.47 N	90.28 W
Bridgeton, N.J., U.S.	208	39.26 N	75.14 W
Bridgetown, Austl.	162	33.57 S	116.08 E
Bridgetown, Barb.	241g	13.06 N	59.37 W
Bridgetown, N.S., Can.	186	44.51 N	65.18 W
Bridgetown, Ohio, U.S.	218	39.10 N	84.39 W
Bridge Trafford	262	53.14 N	2.49 W
Bridgeville, Del., U.S.	208	38.45 N	75.36 W
Bridgeville, Pa., U.S.	214	40.22 N	80.07 W
Bridgewater, N.S., Can.	186	44.23 N	64.31 W
Bridgewater, Conn., U.S.	210	41.32 N	73.22 W
Bridgewater, Maine, U.S.	186	46.25 N	67.51 W
Bridgewater, Mass., U.S.	207	41.59 N	70.58 W
Bridgewater, N.Y., U.S.	210	42.58 N	75.15 W
Bridgewater, Pa., U.S.	285	40.05 N	74.55 W
Bridgewater, S. Dak., U.S.	198	43.33 N	97.30 W
Bridgewater, Va., U.S.	188	38.18 N	78.59 W
Bridgewater Canal	262	53.20 N	2.45 W
Bridgman	216	41.57 N	86.33 W
Bridgnorth	42	52.33 N	2.25 W
Bridgwater	42	51.08 N	3.00 W
Bridgwater Bay	42	51.16 N	3.12 W
Bridlington	44	54.05 N	0.12 W
Bridlington Bay	44	54.04 N	0.08 W
Bridport	42	50.44 N	2.46 W
Brie [1]	50	48.40 N	3.20 E
Briec	32	48.06 N	4.00 W
Brie-Comte-Robert	50	48.41 N	2.37 E
Brie Français [1]	261	48.40 N	2.50 E
Brieg → Brzeg	30	50.52 N	17.27 E
Brielle, Ned.	52	51.54 N	4.10 E
Brielle, N.J., U.S.	208	40.07 N	74.03 W
Brienne-le-Château	50	48.24 N	4.32 E
Brienne-sur-Aisne	50	49.26 N	4.03 E
Brienno	58	45.55 N	9.07 E
Brienon-sur-Armançon	50	48.00 N	3.37 E
Brien Run	284b	39.20 N	76.28 W
Brienz	58	46.46 N	8.03 E
Brienza	68	40.29 N	15.37 E
Brienzer Rothorn	58	46.48 N	8.04 E
Brienzersee	58	46.43 N	7.57 E
Brierfield	44	53.50 N	2.14 W
Brier Hill	212	44.32 N	75.40 W
Brierley Hill	42	52.29 N	2.07 W
Brier Mountain	210	41.37 N	77.02 W
Briese	264a	52.42 N	13.18 E
Briese	264a	52.41 N	13.15 E
Brieselang	54	52.35 N	13.00 E
Briesen	54	52.20 N	14.16 E
Brieske	54	51.29 N	13.57 E
Brieskow-Finkenheerd	54	52.16 N	14.35 E
Briest	54	52.31 N	12.08 E
Briey	56	49.15 N	5.56 E
Brig	58	46.19 N	8.00 E
Brigach	58	47.58 N	8.30 E
Brigantine	208	39.24 N	74.22 W
Brig Bay	186	51.04 N	56.55 W
Brigden	214	42.49 N	82.17 W
Brigg	44	53.34 N	0.30 W
Briggs	196	30.53 N	97.56 W
Brigham City	200	41.31 N	112.01 W
Brighouse	44	53.42 N	1.47 W
Brighstone	42	50.38 N	1.24 W
Bright	166	36.44 S	146.58 E
Brightlingsea	42	51.49 N	1.02 E
Brightmoor [8]	281	42.24 N	83.14 W
Brighton, Austl.	168b	35.01 S	138.31 E
Brighton, Austl.	169	37.55 S	145.00 E
Brighton, Ont., Can.	212	44.02 N	77.44 W
Brighton, N.Z.	172	45.57 S	170.20 E
Brighton, Eng., U.K.	42	50.50 N	0.08 W
Brighton, Colo., U.S.	200	39.59 N	104.49 W
Brighton, Fla., U.S.	220	28.52 N	82.20 W
Brighton, Ill., U.S.	219	39.02 N	90.08 W
Brighton, Iowa, U.S.	190	41.10 N	91.49 W
Brighton, Mich., U.S.	216	42.32 N	83.47 W
Brighton, N.Y., U.S.	210	43.08 N	77.34 W
Brighton [8]	283	42.21 N	71.08 W
Brighton Downs	166	23.22 S	141.34 E
Brighton Indian Reservation [4]	220	27.04 N	81.05 W
Brighton-Le-Sands	274a	33.58 S	151.09 E
Brighton Park [8]	278	41.49 N	87.42 W
Brighton State Recreation Area	216	42.30 N	83.48 W
Brightsand Lake	184	53.36 N	108.52 W
Brightwaters	276	40.43 N	73.16 W
Brightwood	224	45.23 N	122.01 W
Brightwood [8]	284c	38.58 N	77.02 W
Brigittenau [8]	264b	48.14 N	16.22 E
Brignoles	62	43.24 N	6.04 E
Brignoud	62	45.15 N	5.54 E
Brig o' Turk	46	56.13 N	4.22 W
Brigus	186	47.32 N	53.13 W
Brihuega	34	40.45 N	2.52 W
Briis-sous-Forges	261	48.38 N	2.07 E
Brijuni	64	44.55 N	13.46 E
Brikama	150	13.15 N	16.39 W
Brilhante	255	21.58 S	54.18 W
Brill	42	51.49 N	1.03 W
Brilliant, B.C., Can.	182	49.19 N	117.38 W
Brilliant, Ala., U.S.	194	34.01 N	87.46 W
Brilliant, Ohio, U.S.	214	40.16 N	80.38 W
Brillion	190	44.11 N	88.04 W
Brilon	56	51.24 N	8.34 E
Brilyn Park	284c	38.54 N	77.10 W
Brimfield, Eng., U.K.	42	52.18 N	2.42 W
Brimfield, Ind., U.S.	216	41.27 N	85.24 W
Brimfield, Mass., U.S.	207	42.07 N	72.12 W
Brimfield, Ohio, U.S.	214	41.06 N	81.21 W
Brimington	44	53.16 N	1.23 W
Brindabella	171b	35.23 S	148.45 E
Brindisi	68	40.38 N	17.56 E
Brindisi □[4]	68	40.35 N	17.40 E
Brindisi Montagna	68	40.37 N	15.57 E
Brindle	262	53.43 N	2.36 W
Brindley Heath	260	51.12 N	0.03 W
Bringelly	170	33.56 S	150.44 E
Bringelly Creek	274a	33.58 S	150.38 E
Brinje	36	45.00 N	15.08 E
Brinkerton	279b	40.13 N	79.32 W
Brinkhaven	214	40.28 N	82.12 W
Brinkleigh	284b	39.18 N	76.50 W
Brinkley, Austl.	168b	35.14 S	139.13 E
Brinkley, Ark., U.S.	194	34.53 N	91.12 W
Brinkum	52	53.00 N	8.47 E
Brinkworth	166	33.42 S	138.24 E
Brinnon	224	47.41 N	122.54 W
Brinon-sur-Beuvron	50	47.17 N	3.30 E
Brins, Ābār al- [4]	142	30.29 N	30.05 E
Brinscall	262	53.41 N	2.34 W
Brinyan	46	59.07 N	2.59 W
Brion, Île	186	47.48 N	61.28 W
Brione	58	46.18 N	8.47 E
Briones Hills [2]	282	37.56 N	122.08 W
Briones Regional Park	282	37.56 N	122.08 W
Briones Reservoir [1]	282	37.55 N	122.12 W
Brioni	64	44.55 N	13.46 E
Brionne	50	49.12 N	0.43 E
Brion-sur-Ource	58	47.55 N	4.39 E
Brioso	255	20.21 S	52.05 W
Brioude	32	45.18 N	3.23 E
Briouze	32	48.42 N	0.22 W
Brisbane, Austl.	171a	27.28 S	153.02 E
Brisbane, Calif., U.S.	226	37.41 N	122.24 W
Brisbane	171a	27.24 S	153.09 E
Brisbane, Mount	171a	27.05 S	152.32 E
Brisbane Water National Park	170	33.30 S	151.15 E
Brisben	210	42.22 N	75.41 W
Brisbin	214	40.50 N	78.21 W
Briseñas de Matamoros	234	20.16 N	102.33 W
Brisighella	66	44.13 N	11.46 E
Brissac	62	43.52 N	3.42 E
Brissago	58	46.07 N	8.43 E
Bristol, Eng., U.K.	42	51.27 N	2.35 W
Bristol, Conn., U.S.	207	41.41 N	72.57 W
Bristol, Fla., U.S.	192	30.26 N	84.58 W
Bristol, Ill., U.S.	216	41.39 N	88.27 W
Bristol, Ind., U.S.	216	41.43 N	85.49 W
Bristol, N.H., U.S.	188	43.36 N	71.45 W
Bristol, Pa., U.S.	208	40.06 N	74.52 W
Bristol, R.I., U.S.	207	41.40 N	71.16 W
Bristol, S. Dak., U.S.	198	45.21 N	97.45 W
Bristol, Tenn., U.S.	192	36.36 N	82.11 W
Bristol, Vt., U.S.	188	44.08 N	73.05 W
Bristol, Va., U.S.	192	36.36 N	82.11 W
Bristol, Wis., U.S.	216	42.34 N	88.03 W
Bristol □[6], Mass., U.S.	207	41.54 N	71.06 W
Bristol □[6], R.I., U.S.	207	41.42 N	71.18 W
Bristol (Lulsgate) Airport	42	51.23 N	2.43 W
Bristol Bay	180	58.00 N	159.00 W
Bristol Center	210	42.49 N	77.23 W
Bristol Channel	42	51.20 N	4.00 W
Bristol Lake	204	34.28 N	115.41 W
Bristolville	214	41.23 N	80.52 W
Bristow	196	35.50 N	96.23 W
Bristow Island	164	9.08 S	143.14 E
Britânia	255	15.14 S	51.09 W
Britânicas, Ilhas → British Isles	4	54.00 N	4.00 W
Britannia	275b	43.37 N	79.41 W
Britannia Beach	182	49.38 N	123.12 W
Britannia Range	9	80.00 S	158.00 E
Britische Jungfern-Inseln → British Virgin Islands	240m	18.30 N	64.30 W
Britisches Antarktis-Territorium → British Antarctic Territory □[2]	9	60.00 S	45.00 W
British Antarctic Territory □[2]	9	60.00 S	45.00 W
British Columbia □[4]	176, 182	54.00 N	125.00 W
British Honduras → Belize □[2]	232	17.15 N	88.45 W
British Indian Ocean Territory □[2]	12	7.00 S	72.00 E
British Isles	4	54.00 N	4.00 W
British Mountains	180	69.00 N	140.20 W
British Museum	260	51.31 N	0.08 W
British Virgin Islands □[2]	240m	18.30 N	64.30 W
Britland Edge Hill [2]	262	53.31 N	1.50 W
Brito Godins	152	8.57 S	16.32 E
Briton Ferry	42	51.38 N	3.49 W
Brits	158	25.42 S	27.45 E
Britstown	158	30.37 S	23.30 E
Britt	190	43.06 N	93.48 W
Brittany → Bretagne □[9]	32	48.00 N	3.00 W
Brittas	48	53.14 N	6.27 W
Britten	158	27.42 S	25.17 E
Brittingham	196	25.45 N	103.24 W
Britton, Mich., U.S.	216	41.59 N	83.50 W
Britton, S. Dak., U.S.	198	45.48 N	97.45 W
Britton, Tex., U.S.	222	32.33 N	97.04 W
Britton, Mount [2]	162	26.31 S	134.43 E
Britz	54	52.53 N	13.49 E
Britz [8]	264a	52.27 N	13.26 E
Brive-la-Gaillarde	32	45.10 N	1.32 E
Brives-Charensac	62	45.03 N	3.56 E

Symbol	English	Deutsch	Español	Français	Português
≏	River	Fluss	Rio	Rivière	Rio
	Canal	Kanal	Canal	Canal	Canal
	Waterfall, Rapids	Wasserfall, Stromschnellen	Cascada, Rápidos	Chute d'eau, Rapides	Cascata, Rápidos
	Strait	Meeresstrasse	Estrecho	Détroit	Estreito
	Bay, Gulf	Bucht, Golf	Bahía, Golfo	Baie, Golfe	Baia, Golfo
	Lake, Lakes	See, Seen	Lago, Lagos	Lac, Lacs	Lago, Lagos
	Swamp	Sumpf	Pantano	Marais	Pântano
	Ice Features, Glacier	Eis- und Gletscherformen	Accidentes Glaciales	Formes glaciaires	Acidentes Glaciares
	Other Hydrographic Features	Andere Hydrographische Objekte	Otros Elementos Hidrográficos	Autres données hydrographiques	Outros Elementos Hidrográficos
	Submarine Features	Untermeerische Objekte	Accidentes Submarinos	Formes de relief sous-marin	Acidentes Submarinos
□	Political Unit	Politische Einheit	Unidad Política	Entité politique	Unidade Política
	Cultural Institution	Kulturelle Institution	Institución Cultural	Institution culturelle	Instituição Cultural
	Historical Site	Historische Stätte	Sitio Histórico	Site historique	Sitio Histórico
	Recreational Site	Erholungs- und Ferienort	Sitio de Recreo	Centre de loisirs	Sitio de Lazer
	Airport	Flughafen	Aeropuerto	Aéroport	Aeroporto
	Military Installation	Militäranlage	Instalación Militar	Installation militaire	Instalação Militar
	Miscellaneous	Verschiedenes	Misceláneo	Divers	Miscelânea

Briviesca 34 42.33 N 3.19 W
Brivio 62 45.44 N 9.27 E
Brixen im Thale 64 47.27 N 12.15 E
Brixham 42 50.24 N 3.30 W
Brixlegg 64 47.25 N 11.53 E
Brixton 166 23.32 S 144.57 E
Brixworth 42 52.20 N 0.54 W
Briziana 148 33.04 N 1.14 E
Brlik, S.S.S.R. 85 44.05 N 73.31 E
Brlik, S.S.S.R. 85 43.40 N 73.49 E
Brno 30 49.12 N 16.37 E
Bro 40 59.31 N 17.38 E
Broa, Ensenada de la C 240p 22.35 N 82.00 W
Broach 120 21.42 N 72.58 E
Broad ≃, U.S. 192 34.00 N 81.04 W
Broad ≃, Fla., U.S. 220 25.28 N 81.09 W
Broad ≃, Ga., U.S. 192 33.59 N 82.39 W
Broadalbin 210 43.03 N 74.12 W
Broad Arrow 162 30.20 S 121.27 E
Broad Axe 285 40.10 N 75.15 W
Broadback ≃ 176 51.21 N 78.52 W
Broad Bay C 46 58.15 N 6.15 W
Broadbottom 262 53.26 N 2.01 W
Broad Brook 207 41.55 N 72.33 W
Broad Chalke 42 51.02 N 1.57 W
Broad Clyst 42 50.46 N 3.26 W
Broad Creek C 208 38.45 N 76.15 W
Broadford, Austl. 169 37.13 S 145.03 E
Broadford, Scot., U.K. 46 57.14 N 5.54 W
Broad Haven C 48 54.18 N 9.55 W
Broadheath 262 53.24 N 2.21 W
Broadhurst Range ⩓ 162 22.23 S 122.09 E
Broadkill ≃ 208 38.47 N 75.10 W
Broad Law ∧ 46 55.30 N 3.22 W
Broadley Common 260 51.45 N 0.04 E
Broadmeadows 169 37.40 S 144.54 E
Broad Meadow Water ≃ 44 53.28 N 6.12 W
Broadmoor 226 37.41 N 122.29 W
Broad Pass)(180 63.18 N 149.09 W
Broad Run ≃, Pa., U.S. 285 39.56 N 75.41 W
Broad Run ≃, Pa., U.S. 285 39.59 N 75.40 W
Broad Run ≃, Va., U.S. 208 38.41 N 77.29 W
Broad Sound Ц, Austl. 166 22.10 S 149.45 E
Broad Sound Ц, Mass., U.S. 283 42.25 N 70.58 W
Broad Sound Channel Ц 166 22.05 S 150.20 E
Broadstairs 42 51.22 N 1.27 E
Broad Street 260 51.17 N 0.38 E
Broad Top 214 40.12 N 78.08 W
Broadus 198 45.27 N 105.25 W
Broadview, Sask., Can. 184 50.20 N 102.30 W
Broadview, Ill., U.S. 216 41.52 N 87.51 W
Broadview, Ind., U.S. 218 39.10 N 87.33 W
Broadview Heights 214 41.19 N 81.41 W
Broadwater 198 41.36 N 102.51 W
Broadway, Eng., U.K. 42 52.02 N 1.51 W
Broadway, Ohio, U.S. 214 40.21 N 83.25 W
Broadway, Va., U.S. 188 38.38 N 78.46 W
Broadwell 219 40.04 N 89.27 W
Broadwindsor 42 50.49 N 2.48 W
Broadwood 172 35.16 S 173.23 E
Broager 41 54.53 N 9.41 E
Brobo 150 7.43 N 4.42 W
Broby 26 56.15 N 14.05 E
Brobyværk 41 55.14 N 10.15 E
Broc 58 46.36 N 7.06 E
Brocēni 76 56.42 N 22.35 E
Brochel 46 57.26 N 6.01 W
Brochet 176 57.53 N 101.40 W
Brochet, Lac du @ 186 49.40 N 69.37 W
Brochterbeck 52 52.13 N 7.44 E
Brock 184 51.27 N 108.42 W
Brock ≃ 44 53.52 N 2.47 W
Brock Creek ≃ 285 40.15 N 74.50 W
Brocken ∧ 54 51.48 N 10.36 E
Brockenhurst 42 50.49 N 1.34 W
Brockenscheidt 263 51.38 N 7.25 E
Brockhagen 52 51.59 N 8.20 E
Brockham 260 51.14 N 0.17 W
Brockman, Mount ∧ 162 22.28 S 117.18 E
Brock Monument ⊥ 284a 43.09 N 79.04 W
Brockport, N.Y., U.S. 210 43.13 N 77.56 W
Brockport, Pa., U.S. 214 41.16 N 78.44 W
Brocks Beach 212 44.27 N 80.06 W
Brocks Creek 164 13.28 S 131.25 E
Brockton, Mass., U.S. 207
283 42.05 N 71.01 W
Brockton, Mont., U.S. 198 48.09 N 104.55 W
Brockton, Pa., U.S. 208 40.45 N 76.04 W
Brockton Reservoir @[1] 283 42.07 N 71.03 W
Brockville 212 44.35 N 75.41 W
Brockway 214 41.15 N 78.47 W
Brockworth 42 51.51 N 2.09 W
Brocoió, Ilha do I 287a 22.45 S 43.07 W
Brocton 214 42.23 N 79.27 W
Brod, Česko. 60 49.51 N 12.45 E
Brod, Jugo. 38 41.31 N 21.12 E
Broddbo 40 59.59 N 16.28 E
Brodenbach 56 50.14 N 7.26 E
Broderick 226 38.35 N 121.31 W
Brodeslavy 60 49.56 N 13.34 E
Brodeur Peninsula ≻[1] 176 73.00 N 88.00 W
Brodhead, Ky., U.S. 192 37.24 N 84.25 W
Brodhead, Wis., U.S. 190 42.37 N 89.22 W
Brodhead Creek ≃ 210 40.59 N 75.08 W
Brodheadsville 210 40.55 N 75.24 W
Brodick 46 55.35 N 5.09 W
Brodnax 192 36.42 N 78.02 W
Brodnica 30 53.16 N 19.23 E
Brodokalmak 86 55.35 N 62.06 E
Brody, Pol. 30 51.45 N 14.45 E
Brody, S.S.S.R. 78 50.06 N 25.10 E
Broedersput 158 26.49 S 25.08 E
Broek [op Langendijk] 52 52.40 N 4.48 E
Brogan 202 44.15 N 117.31 W
Broglie 50 49.01 N 0.32 E
Brohlbach ≃ 56 50.29 N 7.20 E
Broich ◆[8] 263 51.25 N 6.51 E
Broichweiden 56 50.49 N 6.09 E
Broitzem 52 52.14 N 10.29 E
Brok 30 52.43 N 21.52 E
Brok ∧ 123 34.32 N 76.35 E
Brokdorf 52 53.52 N 9.19 E
Broke 170 32.45 S 151.06 E
Broke Inlet C 162 34.55 S 116.25 E
Broken ≃ 169 36.41 S 146.00 E
Broken Arrow 196 36.03 N 95.48 W
Broken Back Range ⩓ 170 32.47 S 151.13 E
Broken Bay C 170 33.34 S 151.18 E
Broken Bow, Nebr., U.S. 198 41.24 N 99.38 W
Broken Bow, Okla., U.S. 194 34.02 N 94.44 W
Broken Cross, Eng., U.K. 262 53.15 N 2.10 W
Broken Cross, Eng., U.K. 262 53.15 N 2.29 W
Brokenhead ≃ 184 50.25 N 96.40 W
Broken Hill, Austl. 166 31.57 S 141.27 E
Broken Hill → Kabwe, Zam. 154 14.27 S 28.27 E
Brokenstraw Creek ≃ 214 41.51 N 79.09 W
Broken Sword Creek ≃ 214 40.46 N 83.11 W
Brokopondo 250 5.04 N 54.58 W
Brokopondo □[5] 250 4.20 N 55.20 W
Brölbach ≃ 56 50.47 N 7.18 E
Brolo 70 38.09 N 14.50 E
Bromberg → Bydgoszcz 30 53.08 N 18.00 E
Bromborough 262 53.19 N 2.59 W
Brome, B.R.D. 54 52.36 N 10.56 E
Brome, Qué., Can. 206 45.12 N 72.34 W
Brome □[6] 206 45.10 N 72.30 W
Brome, Lac @ 206 45.15 N 72.30 W
Brome Mountain ∧ 206 45.17 N 72.38 W
Bromley ◆[8] 260 51.24 N 0.02 E
Bromley Common ◆[8] 260 51.22 N 0.03 E
Bromley Plateau ⊹[3] 18 31.00 S 32.00 W
Bromma ◆[8] 40 59.21 N 17.55 E
Bromma flygplats ⊠ 40 59.21 N 17.55 E
Brommö I 40 58.50 N 13.41 E
Bromo, Gunung ∧ 115a 7.57 S 112.57 E
Bromölla 26 56.04 N 14.28 E
Brompton, Eng., U.K. 44 54.22 N 1.25 W
Brompton, Eng., U.K. 260 51.23 N 0.33 E
Brompton Lake @ 206 45.27 N 72.09 W
Bromptonville 206 45.28 N 71.57 W
Bromsgrove 42 52.20 N 2.03 W
Bromyard 42 52.11 N 2.30 W
Bron 62 45.44 N 4.55 E
Bron, Aéroport de ⊠ 62 45.43 N 4.56 E
Brønderslev 26 57.16 N 9.58 E
Bronevskaja 24 61.43 N 39.10 E
Brong-Ahafo □[4] 150 7.45 N 1.30 W
Broni 62 45.04 N 9.16 E
Bronickaja Guta 78 50.56 N 27.19 E
Bronkhorstspruit 158 25.50 S 28.43 E
Bronkhorstspruitdam @[1] 158 25.55 S 28.42 E
Bronkow 54 51.40 N 13.55 E
Bronllys 42 52.01 N 3.16 W
Bronlund Peak ∧ 176 57.26 N 126.38 W
Bronn 60 49.44 N 11.28 E
Bronnicy 82 55.25 N 38.16 E
Bronnikovo 86 58.32 N 68.25 E
Bronnoje 76 52.19 N 30.29 E
Brønnøysund 24 65.30 N 12.10 E
Bronnzell 56 50.31 N 9.41 E
Brøns 41 55.11 N 8.44 E
Bronson, Fla., U.S. 192 29.27 N 82.38 W
Bronson, Kans., U.S. 198 37.54 N 95.04 W
Bronson, Mich., U.S. 216 41.52 N 85.12 W
Bronson, Tex., U.S. 194 31.21 N 94.01 W
Bronson Lake @ 184 53.52 N 109.43 W
Bronte, It. 70 37.47 N 14.50 E
Bronte, Tex., U.S. 196 31.53 N 100.18 W
Bronte Creek ≃ 212 43.23 N 79.43 W
Bronte Park 166 42.08 S 146.30 E
Bronwood 192 31.50 N 84.22 W
Bronx 210 40.49 N 73.56 W
Bronx □[6] 210 40.49 N 73.56 W
Bronx ◆[8] 276 40.49 N 73.56 W
Bronx Park ♠ 276 40.52 N 73.53 W
Bronxville 276 40.56 N 73.50 W
Bronx-Whitestone Bridge ◆[5] 276 40.48 N 73.50 W
Bronx Zoo ♠ 276 40.51 N 73.53 W
Bronzolo (Branzoll) 64 46.24 N 11.19 E
Brooch, Lac @ 186 50.44 N 67.58 W
Broodsnyersplaas 158 26.03 S 29.29 E
Brook 216 40.52 N 87.22 W
Brookdale 226 37.06 N 122.06 W
Brooke 208 38.23 N 77.23 W
Brooke □[6] 214 40.18 N 80.33 W
Brookeborough 48 54.19 N 7.24 W
Brookeland 194 31.09 N 94.00 W
Brooker 192 29.53 N 82.20 W
Brooke's Point 116 8.47 N 117.50 E
Brookfield, N.S., Can. 186 45.15 N 63.17 W
Brookfield, Conn., U.S. 207 41.29 N 73.25 W
Brookfield, Ill., U.S. 216 41.49 N 87.51 W
Brookfield, Mass., U.S. 207 42.13 N 72.06 W
Brookfield, Mich., U.S. 216 42.27 N 84.47 W
Brookfield, Mo., U.S. 194 39.47 N 93.04 W
Brookfield, N.Y., U.S. 210 42.49 N 75.19 W
Brookfield, Ohio, U.S. 214 41.14 N 80.34 W
Brookfield, Wis., U.S. 216 43.04 N 88.09 W
Brookfield Center 207 41.28 N 73.23 W
Brookfield Zoo ♠ 278 41.50 N 87.50 W
Brookford 192 35.42 N 81.21 W
Brookhaven, Miss., U.S. 194 31.35 N 90.26 W
Brookhaven, Pa., U.S. 285 39.52 N 75.23 W
Brookhaven Manor 278 41.44 N 87.58 W
Brookhaven National Laboratory ✿[3] 207 40.54 N 72.52 W
Brookings, Oreg., U.S. 202 42.03 N 124.17 W
Brookings, S. Dak., U.S. 198 44.19 N 96.48 W
Brookland 42 50.59 N 0.50 E
Brookland ◆[8] 284c 38.56 N 76.59 W
Brooklands 214 42.38 N 83.06 W
Brookland Terrace 285 39.44 N 75.37 W
Brooklandville 284b 39.26 N 76.41 W
Brooklawn 285 39.53 N 75.08 W
Brooklet 192 32.23 N 81.40 W
Brooklin 212 43.57 N 78.57 W
Brookline, Mass., U.S. 207 42.21 N 71.07 W
Brookline, N.H., U.S. 207 42.44 N 71.40 W
Brooklyn, N.S., Can. 186 44.03 N 64.42 W
Brooklyn, Conn., U.S. 207 41.47 N 71.57 W
Brooklyn, Ill., U.S. 219 40.14 N 90.46 W
Brooklyn, Ind., U.S. 218 39.32 N 86.22 W
Brooklyn, Iowa, U.S. 190 41.44 N 92.27 W
Brooklyn, Mich., U.S. 216 42.06 N 84.15 W
Brooklyn, Miss., U.S. 194 31.03 N 89.11 W
Brooklyn, Ohio, U.S. 214 41.25 N 81.49 W
Brooklyn, Pa., U.S. 210 41.45 N 75.48 W
Brooklyn, Wash., U.S. 224 46.47 N 123.31 W
Brooklyn, Wis., U.S. 216 42.51 N 89.22 W
Brooklyn ◆[8], Md., U.S. 284b 39.14 N 76.36 W
Brooklyn ◆[8], N.Y., U.S. 210 40.42 N 74.00 W
Brooklyn Battery Tunnel ◆[5] 276 40.42 N 74.01 W
Brooklyn Bridge ◆[5] 276 40.42 N 74.00 W
Brooklyn Center 190 45.05 N 93.20 W
Brooklyn College ✿[2] 276 40.38 N 73.57 W
Brooklyn Heights 279a 41.24 N 81.40 W
Brooklyn Marine Park ♠ 276 40.35 N 73.55 W
Brooklyn Museum ✿ 276 40.40 N 73.58 W
Brookmans Park 260 51.43 N 0.12 W
Brookmere 182 49.49 N 120.53 W
Brookmont 284c 38.57 N 77.07 W
Brookneal 192 37.03 N 78.57 W
Brook Park 214 41.24 N 81.48 W
Brookport 194 37.08 N 88.38 W
Brooks, Alta., Can. 182 50.35 N 111.53 W
Brooks, Calif., U.S. 226 38.45 N 122.09 W
Brooks, Maine, U.S. 188 44.33 N 69.07 W
Brooks, Oreg., U.S. 224 45.03 N 122.58 W
Brooks, Mount ∧ 180 63.11 N 150.40 W
Brooks Bay C 182 50.13 N 127.55 W
Brooksburg 218 38.44 N 85.15 W
Brookshire 222 29.47 N 95.57 W
Brookside, Del., U.S. 285 39.40 N 75.44 W
Brookside, Pa., U.S. 214 42.08 N 80.00 W
Brookside, Tex., U.S. 222 29.35 N 95.18 W
Brookside Park ♠ 279a 41.27 N 81.43 W
Brooks Island I 282 37.54 N 122.21 W
Brooks Mountain ∧ 180 65.33 N 167.09 W
Brooks Place 283 42.02 N 71.01 W
Brooks Range ⩓ 180 68.00 N 154.00 W
Brookston 216 40.36 N 86.52 W
Brook Street 260 51.37 N 0.17 E
Brooksville, Fla., U.S. 220 28.33 N 82.23 W
Brooksville, Ky., U.S. 218 38.41 N 84.04 W
Brooksville, Miss., U.S. 194 33.14 N 88.35 W
Brookton 162 32.22 S 117.01 E
Brooktondale 210 42.23 N 76.24 W
Brookvale 274a 33.46 S 151.17 E
Brookview 210 42.32 N 73.43 W
Brookville, Ind., U.S. 218 39.25 N 85.01 W
Brookville, Mass., U.S. 207 42.08 N 71.01 W
Brookville, N.Y., U.S. 276 40.49 N 73.35 W
Brookville, Ohio, U.S. 218 39.50 N 84.25 W
Brookville, Pa., U.S. 214 41.09 N 79.05 W
Brookville Lake @[1] 218 39.30 N 85.00 W
Brookwood, Eng., U.K. 260 51.18 N 0.38 W
Brookwood, Ind., U.S. 278 40.30 N 87.22 W
Brooloo 166 26.29 S 152.42 E
Broom, Little Loch C 46 57.54 N 5.22 W
Broom, Loch C 46 57.52 N 5.08 W
Broomall 285 39.59 N 75.22 W
Broome 162 17.58 S 122.14 E
Broome □[6] 210 42.08 N 75.54 W
Broome County Airport ⊠ 210 42.13 N 75.59 W
Broomes Island 208 38.25 N 76.33 W
Broomfield, Eng., U.K. 260 51.14 N 0.38 E
Broomfield, Eng., U.K. 260 51.46 N 0.28 E
Broomfield, Colo., U.S. 200 39.56 N 105.04 W
Broons 32 48.19 N 2.16 W
Brooten 198 45.30 N 95.07 W
Brophy, Mount ∧[2] 162 19.11 S 128.51 E
Brophy Lake @ 281 42.39 N 83.46 W
Brora 46 58.01 N 3.51 W
Brora ≃ 46 58.01 N 3.52 W
Brørup 41 55.29 N 9.01 E
Broseley 42 52.37 N 2.29 W
Brosewere Bay C 276 40.37 N 73.42 W
Brosna ≃ 48 53.13 N 7.58 W
Brošnev-Osada 78 49.00 N 24.13 E
Brossac 32 45.20 N 0.03 W
Brossard 206 45.26 N 73.29 W
Brossasco 62 44.34 N 7.21 E
Brosso 62 45.30 N 7.48 E
Brotas de Macaúbas 255 12.00 S 42.38 W
Broteni 158 29.38 S 29.42 E
Brothers Brook ≃ 276 41.02 N 73.36 W
Brötjärna 40 60.30 N 15.01 E
Broto 34 42.36 N 0.06 W
Brotterode 54 50.49 N 10.26 E
Brotton 44 54.34 N 0.56 W
Brou 50 48.13 N 1.11 E
Brough, Eng., U.K. 44 54.32 N 2.19 W
Brough, Eng., U.K. 44 53.44 N 0.35 W
Brough, Scot., U.K. 46 58.39 N 3.20 W
Brougham 212 43.55 N 79.06 W
Brough Head ≻ 46 59.08 N 3.17 W
Broughshane 48 54.54 N 6.12 W
Broughton, Eng., U.K. 42 52.23 N 0.46 W
Broughton, Eng., U.K. 262 53.49 N 2.43 W
Broughton, Scot., U.K. 46 55.37 N 3.25 W
Broughton, Pa., U.S. 214 40.21 N 79.59 W
Broughton in Furness 44 54.17 N 3.12 W
Broughton Island I 176 67.35 N 63.50 W
Broughtown 46 59.15 N 2.36 W
Broughty Ferry 46 56.28 N 2.53 W
Broumov, Česko. 30 50.35 N 16.20 E
Broumov, Česko. 60 49.54 N 12.37 E
Brousseval 58 48.29 N 4.58 E
Brou-sur-Chantereine 261 48.53 N 2.38 E
Brouvelieures 58 48.14 N 6.44 E
Brouwershaven 52 51.44 N 3.54 E
Brouwershavensche Gat Ц 52 51.45 N 3.50 E
Brovary 78 50.31 N 30.46 E
Brovst 26 57.06 N 9.32 E
Broward □[6] 220 26.09 N 80.29 W
Browerville 198 46.05 N 94.52 W
Brown □[6], Ill., U.S. 219 39.59 N 90.45 W
Brown □[6], Ind., U.S. 218 39.12 N 86.15 W
Brown □[6], Ohio, U.S. 218 38.52 N 83.54 W
Brown, Mount ∧ 184 48.52 N 111.09 W
Brown, Point ≻ 224 46.56 N 124.10 W
Brownbacks 285 40.11 N 75.37 W
Brown City 190 43.13 N 82.59 W
Brown Clee Hill ∧[2] 42 52.28 N 2.35 W
Brown County State Park ♠ 218 39.09 N 86.14 W
Brown Creek ≃ 276 40.43 N 73.04 W
Browndale 210 41.40 N 75.27 W
Brown Deer 216 43.10 N 87.59 W
Browne Bay C 176 73.08 N 97.30 W
Brownfield 196 33.11 N 102.16 W
Brown Gelly ∧[2] 42 50.32 N 4.32 W
Brownhills 42 52.39 N 1.55 W
Browning, Ill., U.S. 219 40.08 N 90.22 W
Browning, Mo., U.S. 194 40.02 N 93.10 W
Browning, Mont., U.S. 202 48.34 N 113.01 W
Browning Entrance C 182 53.41 N 130.30 W
Browning Island I 212 45.00 N 79.25 W
Brown Lake @ 176 65.55 N 91.15 W
Brownlee Park 216 42.18 N 85.05 W
Brownlee Reservoir @[1] 202 44.40 N 117.05 W
Brown Mountain ∧, Calif., U.S. 204 35.41 N 117.01 W
Brown Mountain ∧, Calif., U.S. 280 34.14 N 118.08 W
Brown Mountain ∧[2] 222 31.51 N 97.39 W
Brown Point ≻ 276 40.43 N 73.04 W
Brownsboro 222 32.18 N 95.37 W
Browns Brook ≃ 276 41.09 N 73.17 W
Brownsburg, Qué., Can. 206 45.41 N 74.25 W
Brownsburg, Ind., U.S. 218 39.51 N 86.24 W
Browns Canyon ∨ 280 34.18 N 118.35 W
Brownsdale 190 43.44 N 92.52 W
Browns Island I 282 38.02 N 121.52 W
Browns Lake 216 42.42 N 88.14 W
Brownsmead 224 46.13 N 123.32 W
Browns Mills 208 39.58 N 74.34 W
Browns Point 224 47.18 N 122.21 W
Browns Town, Jam. 241q 18.24 N 77.22 W
Brownstown, Ill., U.S. 219 39.00 N 88.57 W
Brownstown, Ind., U.S. 218 38.53 N 86.03 W
Brownstown, Pa., U.S. 208 40.08 N 76.13 W
Brownstown Creek ≃ 281 42.06 N 83.13 W
Browns Valley, Calif., U.S. 226 39.15 N 121.23 W
Browns Valley, Minn., U.S. 198 45.36 N 96.50 W
Brownsville, Ont., Can. 212 42.52 N 80.50 W
Brownsville, Calif., U.S. 226 39.28 N 121.16 W
Brownsville, Fla., U.S. 220 25.50 N 80.17 W
Brownsville, Ind., U.S. 218 39.40 N 85.00 W
Brownsville, Ky., U.S. 194 37.12 N 86.16 W
Brownsville, La., U.S. 194 32.30 N 92.10 W
Brownsville, Oreg., U.S. 202 44.24 N 122.59 W
Brownsville, Pa., U.S. 188 40.01 N 79.53 W
Brownsville, Tenn., U.S. 194 35.36 N 89.15 W
Brownsville, Tex., U.S. 196 25.54 N 97.30 W
Brownton 190 44.44 N 94.21 W
Browntown 276 40.24 N 74.19 W
Brownvale 182 56.08 N 117.53 W
Brownville, Ala., U.S. 194 33.24 N 87.52 W
Brownville, Maine, U.S. 188 45.18 N 69.02 W
Brownville, N.Y., U.S. 212 40.40 N 73.55 W
Brownville Junction 188 45.21 N 69.03 W
Brown Willy ∧[2] 42 50.35 N 4.36 W
Brownwood 196 31.43 N 98.59 W
Brownwood, Lake @[1] 196 31.51 N 99.02 W
Browse Island I 160 14.07 S 123.33 E
Broxbourne 260 51.45 N 0.01 W
Broxbourne □[8] 260 51.44 N 0.04 W
Broxton 192 31.38 N 82.53 W
Broye ≃ 58 46.55 N 7.02 E
Broyhill Park 284c 38.52 N 77.12 W
Broža 76 52.57 N 29.07 E
Brozas 34 39.37 N 6.46 W
Brozzo 64 45.43 N 10.14 E
Brtonigla 64 45.23 N 13.38 E
Brû 58 48.21 N 6.41 E
Bruay-en-Artois 50 50.29 N 2.33 E
Bruay-sur-l'Escaut 50 50.23 N 3.32 E
Bruce, Miss., U.S. 194 33.59 N 89.21 W
Bruce, S. Dak., U.S. 198 44.26 N 96.54 W
Bruce, Wis., U.S. 190 45.28 N 91.20 W
Bruce □[6] 212 44.30 N 81.15 W
Bruce, Mount ∧ 162 22.36 S 118.08 E
Bruce Bay 172 43.35 S 169.41 E
Bruce Creek ≃ 275b 43.52 N 79.18 W
Bruce Lake @ 184 50.49 N 93.20 W
Bruce Mines 190 46.18 N 83.48 W
Bruce Museum ✿ 276 41.01 N 73.37 W
Bruce Peninsula ≻[1] 190 44.50 N 81.20 W
Bruce Rock 162 31.53 S 118.09 E
Bruceville 222 31.19 N 97.14 W
Bruchberg ∧ 54 51.47 N 10.29 E
Bruchhausen 56 51.26 N 8.01 E
Bruchhausen-Vilsen 52 52.50 N 9.00 E
Bruchmühle 264a 52.33 N 13.47 E
Br'uchoveckaja 78 45.48 N 38.59 E
Bruchsal 56 49.07 N 8.35 E
Brück, D.D.R. 54 52.12 N 12.46 E
Bruck, Öst. 64 47.17 N 12.49 E
Bruck an Der Leitha 61 47.57 N 16.44 E
Bruck an der Mur 61 47.25 N 15.16 E
Brückenau 56 50.18 N 9.47 E
Bruckhausen ◆[8] 263 51.29 N 6.44 E
Bruck in der Oberpfalz 60 49.15 N 12.18 E
Bruckmühl 64 47.53 N 11.54 E
Brucoli ◆[8] 70 37.17 N 15.11 E
Brudager 41 55.07 N 10.41 E
Bruderheim 182 53.47 N 112.56 W
Brue ≃ 42 51.13 N 3.00 W
Brue-Auriac 62 43.32 N 5.57 E
Brueil-en-Vexin 261 49.02 N 1.49 E
Brüel 54 53.44 N 11.43 E
Bruff 48 52.29 N 8.33 W
Bruges → Brugge 50 51.13 N 3.14 E
Brugg 58 47.29 N 8.12 E
Brugge (Bruges), Bel. 50 51.13 N 3.14 E
Brügge, B.R.D. 263 51.13 N 7.34 E
Brüggen 56 51.14 N 6.11 E
Brugherio 62 45.33 N 9.18 E
Brugnato 62 44.14 N 9.43 E
Brühl 56 50.48 N 6.54 E
Bruin, Ky., U.S. 218 38.11 N 83.01 W
Bruin, Pa., U.S. 214 41.04 N 79.44 W
Bruinisse 52 51.40 N 4.06 E
Bruin Point ∧ 200 39.39 N 110.22 W
Bruja, Cerro ∧ 236 9.29 N 79.34 W
Brule 198 41.06 N 101.53 W
Brule ≃ 190 45.57 N 88.12 W
Brûlé, Lac @ 176 52.17 N 63.52 W
Brule Lake @ 212 45.03 N 77.04 W
Brûly 50 49.58 N 4.31 E
Brumadinho 255 20.08 S 44.13 W
Brumado 255 14.13 S 41.40 W
Brumath 56 48.44 N 7.43 E
Brumby Creek ≃ 162 24.09 S 118.39 E
Brummen 52 52.05 N 6.09 E
Brumunddal 26 60.53 N 10.56 E
Bruna ≃ 66 42.45 N 10.53 E
Brunate 62 45.49 N 9.06 E
Brunau 54 52.45 N 11.28 E
Brundby 41 55.49 N 10.37 E
Brundidge 194 31.43 N 85.49 W
Brune ≃ 50 49.45 N 3.47 E
Bruneau 202 42.53 N 115.48 W
Bruneau ≃ 202 42.57 N 115.58 W
Bruneau, East Fork ≃ 202 42.34 N 115.38 W
Brunei → Bandar Seri Begawan 112 4.56 N 114.55 E
Brunei □[1] 108
112 4.30 N 114.40 E
Brunei, Teluk C 112 5.05 N 115.18 E
Brünen 52 51.43 N 6.39 E
Brunette Creek ≃ 162 18.47 S 135.41 E
Brunette Downs 162 18.38 S 135.57 E
Brunette Island I 186 47.16 N 55.54 W
Brunflo 26 63.05 N 14.49 E
Brungle 171b 35.10 S 148.14 E
Brunico (Bruneck) 64 46.48 N 11.56 E
Brünigpass)(58 46.46 N 8.09 E
Brüninghausen 263 51.13 N 7.41 E
Brunkeberg 26 59.26 N 8.29 E
Brünn → Brno, Česko. 30 49.12 N 16.37 E
Brünn, D.D.R. 54 50.27 N 10.51 E
Brunn, D.D.R. 54 53.40 N 13.22 E
Brunna 40 59.51 N 17.26 E
Brunn am Gebirge 264b 48.07 N 16.17 E
Brunnen, B.R.D. 60 48.38 N 11.18 E
Brunnen, Schw. 58 47.00 N 8.36 E
Brunner 172 42.27 S 171.19 E
Brunner, Lake @ 172 42.37 S 171.27 E
Brunnerville 208 40.11 N 76.17 W
Brunni 58 47.03 N 8.42 E
Brunnsvik 40 60.12 N 15.08 E
Bruno 184 52.15 N 105.30 W
Brunot Island I 279b 40.28 N 80.03 W
Brunow 264a 52.44 N 13.52 E
Brunoy 50 48.42 N 2.30 E
Brunsbüttel 52 53.54 N 9.07 E
Brunsbüttelkoog 52 53.54 N 9.08 E
Brunson 192 32.56 N 81.11 W
Brunssum 56 50.56 N 5.59 E
Brunswick, Austl. 274b 37.46 S 144.58 E
Brunswick → Braunschweig, B.R.D. 52 52.16 N 10.31 E
Brunswick, Ga., U.S. 192 31.10 N 81.29 W
Brunswick, Maine, U.S. 188 43.55 N 69.58 W
Brunswick, Md., U.S. 208 39.19 N 77.37 W
Brunswick, Mo., U.S. 194 39.26 N 93.08 W
Brunswick, Ohio, U.S. 214 41.14 N 81.50 W
Brunswick ≃ 168a 33.15 S 115.45 E
Brunswick, Península ≻[1] 254 53.30 S 71.25 W
Brunswick Junction 168a 33.15 S 115.51 E
Brunswick Lake @ 190 49.00 N 83.23 W
Brunswick Naval Air Station ▪ 188 43.54 N 69.56 W
Brunswick Square ◆[9] 276 40.25 N 74.23 W
Bruntál 30 49.59 N 17.28 E
Bruree 48 52.26 N 8.36 W
Brus, Laguna de C 236 15.50 N 84.35 W
Brus'any 80 53.13 N 49.24 E
Brusasco 62 45.09 N 8.04 E
Bruselas → Bruxelles 50 50.50 N 4.20 E

ENGLISH Name	Page	Lat.°′	Long.°′

DEUTSCH Name	Seite	Breite°′	Länge°′ E=Ost

Brusendorf 264a 52.19 N 13.31 E
Brush 198 40.15 N 103.37 W
Brush Creek ≃, Ohio, U.S. 216 41.26 N 84.24 W
Brush Creek ≃, Pa., U.S. 279b 40.23 N 79.46 W
Brush Creek ≃, Utah, U.S. 200 40.25 N 109.20 W
Brush Run ≃ 279b 40.18 N 80.07 W
Brush Valley 214 40.32 N 79.04 W
Brushy Creek ≃, Okla., U.S. 196 34.55 N 95.34 W
Brushy Creek ≃, Tex., U.S. 222 30.43 N 97.03 W
Brushy Creek ≃, Tex., U.S. 222 31.55 N 95.26 W
Brushy Creek ≃, Tex., U.S. 222 29.04 N 96.34 W
Brushy Creek ≃, Tex., U.S. 222 30.48 N 95.09 W
Brushy Creek ≃, Tex., U.S. 222 32.59 N 96.12 W
Brusilov 78 50.17 N 29.32 E
Brusio 58 46.14 N 10.07 E
Brus Laguna 236 15.47 N 84.35 W
Brusovo 76 57.51 N 35.24 E
Brusque 252 27.06 S 48.56 W
Brussel → Bruxelles 50 50.50 N 4.20 E
Brussels → Bruxelles, Bel. 50 50.50 N 4.20 E
Brussels, Ont., Can. 212 43.44 N 81.15 W
Brussels, Ill., U.S. 219 38.57 N 90.36 W
Brusson 62 45.45 N 7.44 E
Brüssow 54 53.24 N 14.07 E
Brusy 30 53.53 N 17.45 E
Brutelles 50 50.08 N 1.31 E
Bruthen 166 37.43 S 147.48 E
Bruton 42 51.07 N 2.27 W
Brüx → Most 54 50.32 N 13.39 E
Bruxelles (Brussels) (Brussel), Bel. 50 50.50 N 4.20 E
Bruxelles (Brussel) (Brussels), Bel. 56 50.50 N 4.20 E
Bruxelles National, Aéroport ⊠ 50 50.54 N 4.30 E
Bruyères 58 48.12 N 6.43 E
Bruyères-le-Châtel 261 48.36 N 2.11 E
Bruzual 246 8.03 N 69.19 W
Bruzzano Zeffirio 68 38.02 N 16.05 E
Brwinów 30 52.09 N 20.43 E
Bryan, Ohio, U.S. 216 41.28 N 84.33 W
Bryan, Tex., U.S. 222 30.40 N 96.22 W
Bryan Coast ⊥[2] 9 73.45 S 82.00 W
Bryansk → Br'ansk 76 53.15 N 34.22 E
Bryans Road 208 38.38 N 77.04 W
Bryant, Ind., U.S. 216 40.32 N 84.58 W
Bryant, S. Dak., U.S. 198 44.35 N 97.28 W
Bryant Creek ≃ 194 36.36 N 92.17 W
Bryant Mountain ∧ 207 42.28 N 72.58 W
Bryantville 207 42.03 N 70.51 W
Bryas, Lac @ 206 46.44 N 73.05 W
Bryce Canyon National Park ♠ 200 37.29 N 112.12 W
Bryher I 42a 49.57 N 6.20 W
Brykalansk 24 65.30 N 54.12 E
Brykovka 80 52.32 N 48.35 E
Bryli 76 53.54 N 30.33 E
Brymbo 42 53.06 N 3.04 W
Bryn 262 53.30 N 2.39 W
Brynamman 42 51.49 N 3.52 W
Bryn Athyn 285 40.08 N 75.04 W
Bryn Brawd ∧[2] 42 52.09 N 3.54 W
Bryncethin 42 51.33 N 3.34 W
Bryne 26 58.44 N 5.39 E
Brynford 262 53.16 N 3.14 W
Bryn Gates 262 53.30 N 2.37 W
Bryn'kovskaja 78 46.02 N 38.35 E
Brynmawr, Wales, U.K. 42 51.49 N 3.11 W
Bryn Mawr, Calif., U.S. 228 34.03 N 117.14 W
Bryn Mawr, Pa., U.S. 208 40.01 N 75.19 W
Bryn Mawr College ✿[2] 285 40.02 N 75.19 W
Bryrup 41 56.01 N 9.31 E
Bryson, Qué., Can. 188 45.41 N 76.37 W
Bryson, Tex., U.S. 196 33.10 N 98.23 W
Bryson City 192 35.26 N 83.27 W
Bryte 226 38.36 N 121.33 W
Brza Palanka 38 44.28 N 22.27 E
Brzeg 30 50.52 N 17.27 E
Brześć Kujawski 30 52.37 N 18.55 E
Brześć Nad Bugiem → Brest 76 52.06 N 23.42 E
Brzesko 30 49.59 N 20.36 E
Brzeszcze 30 49.59 N 19.08 E
Brzeziny 30 51.48 N 19.46 E
Brzozów 30 49.42 N 22.02 E
Bsharrī 130 34.15 N 36.01 E
Bua 164 6.45 S 147.35 E
Bua ≃ 154 12.42 S 34.13 E
Buada Lagoon C 174b 0.31 S 166.55 E
Buad Island I 116 11.40 N 124.51 E
Buagan ≃ 269e 6.17 S 106.55 E
Buakonikai 174d 0.52 S 169.36 E
Bū al-Ḥīḏān 146 28.10 N 19.18 E
Bū al-Ḥīḏān, Wādī ∨ 146 27.25 N 19.22 E
Buangor, Mount ∧ 169 37.18 S 143.13 E
Buapinang 112 4.46 S 121.34 E
Buariki 174t 1.36 N 172.58 E
Buariki I 174t 1.36 N 172.58 E
Buatan 114 0.44 N 101.51 E
Bua Yai 110 15.35 N 102.25 E
Buayan 116 6.07 N 125.15 E
Buayan ≃ 116 6.06 N 125.14 E
Buba 150 11.36 N 14.55 W
Bubai 268 35.40 N 139.29 E
Bubanza 154 3.06 S 29.23 E
Bubaque 150 11.17 N 15.50 W
Bubendorf 58 47.27 N 7.44 E
Bubenreuth 60 49.38 N 11.01 E
Bubia 164 6.40 S 146.55 E
Būbiyān I 128 29.47 N 48.10 E
Bublitz → Bobolice 30 53.57 N 16.36 E
Bubu ≃ 154 6.03 S 35.19 E
Bubu, Gunong ∧ 114 4.42 N 100.47 E
Bubuan Island I, Pil. 116 6.21 N 121.58 E
Bubuan Island I, Pil. 116 6.11 N 120.58 E
Bubuduo 120 30.06 N 84.38 E
Buburu 152 1.26 N 18.03 E
Bubus, Bukit (Buket Bubut) ∧ 114 6.12 N 101.06 E
Bubusar Pass)(123 35.09 N 74.02 E
Bubye ≃ 154 22.20 S 31.07 E
Buc 261 48.46 N 2.08 E
Bučač 78 49.04 N 25.23 E
Bucak 130 37.28 N 30.36 E
Bucakkışla 130 36.57 N 33.02 E
Bucaramanga 246 7.08 N 73.09 W
Bucarest → București 38 44.26 N 26.06 E
Bucas Grande Island I 116 9.40 N 125.57 E
Buccaneer Archipelago II 160 16.17 S 123.20 E
Buccheri 70 37.08 N 14.51 E
Bucchianico 66 42.18 N 14.11 E
Buccinasco 266b 45.24 N 9.07 E
Buccino 68 40.37 N 15.23 E
Bucelas 266c 38.54 N 9.07 W
Bucelas ∧[2] 266c 38.53 N 9.07 W
Buch ◆[8] 264a 52.38 N 13.30 E
Buchanan, Arg. 258 34.58 S 58.13 W
Buchanan, Sask., Can. 184 51.43 N 102.45 W
Buchanan, Liber. 150 5.57 N 10.02 W
Buchanan, Ga., U.S. 192 33.48 N 85.11 W
Buchanan, Mich., U.S. 216 41.50 N 86.22 W
Buchanan, N.Y., U.S. 210 41.16 N 73.56 W
Buchanan, Va., U.S. 192 37.32 N 79.41 W
Buchanan, Lake @ 166 21.28 S 145.52 E
Buchanan, Lake @[1] 196 30.48 N 98.25 W
Buchanan Creek ≃ 162 19.11 S 136.16 E
Buchanan Field ⊠ 282 37.59 N 122.03 W
Buchanan Hills ⩓[2] 162 18.53 S 131.02 E
Buchan Gulf C 176 71.47 N 74.16 W
Buchan Ness ≻ 46 57.28 N 1.45 W
Buchans 186 48.49 N 56.52 W
Buchara 128 39.48 N 64.25 E
Buchara □[4] 86 43.30 N 64.00 E
Buchardo 252 34.43 S 63.31 W
Bucharest → București 38 44.26 N 26.06 E
Buchau 60 49.47 N 11.32 E
Buchbach 60 48.19 N 12.17 E
Buchelay 261 48.59 N 1.40 E
Büchen, B.R.D. 52 53.29 N 10.36 E
Buchen, B.R.D. 56 49.32 N 9.17 E
Buchenberg 58 47.42 N 10.14 E
Büchenbeuren 56 49.55 N 7.16 E
Buchenwalddenkmal ⊥ 54 51.01 N 11.15 E
Buchholz, B.R.D. 263 51.23 N 7.15 E
Buchholz, D.D.R. 54 52.10 N 12.55 E
Buchholz, D.D.R. 264a 52.35 N 13.47 E
Buchholz ◆[8], B.R.D. 263 51.23 N 6.46 E
Buchholz ◆[8], D.D.R. 264a 52.36 N 13.26 E
Buchholz in der Nordheide 52 53.20 N 9.52 E
Büchlberg 60 48.40 N 13.30 E
Buchloe 58 48.02 N 10.44 E
Bucholt 263 51.39 N 6.43 E
Buchon, Point ≻ 226 35.15 N 120.54 W
Buchow-Karpzow 264a 52.31 N 12.57 E
Buchs, Schw. 58 47.23 N 8.04 E
Buchs, Schw. 58 47.10 N 9.28 E
Buchufontein 158 30.18 S 19.36 E
Buchy 50 49.35 N 1.22 E
Bučina 60 48.58 N 13.36 E
Bucine 66 43.29 N 11.37 E
Buck, Lake @ 162 19.38 S 130.21 E
Buckatunna 194 31.27 N 88.32 W
Buckatunna Creek ≃ 194 31.30 N 88.32 W
Buck Branch ≃ 284b 39.01 N 77.10 W
Buck Creek 216 40.29 N 86.46 W
Buck Creek ≃, Ind., U.S. 218 39.37 N 85.56 W
Buck Creek ≃, Ind., U.S. 218 40.11 N 85.30 W
Buck Creek ≃, Ky., U.S. 192 36.59 N 84.29 W
Buck Creek ≃, Ohio, U.S. 218 39.56 N 83.51 W
Buck Creek ≃, Pa., U.S. 285 40.15 N 74.50 W
Buckden, Eng., U.K. 42 52.17 N 0.16 W
Buckden, Eng., U.K. 44 54.12 N 2.05 W
Bückeburg 52 52.16 N 9.02 E
Bücken 52 52.46 N 9.07 E
Buckeye 200 33.22 N 112.35 W
Buckeye Creek ≃ 226 38.54 N 121.55 W
Buckeye Lake 188 39.56 N 82.29 W
Buckeystown 208 39.20 N 77.26 W
Buckfastleigh 42 50.29 N 3.46 W
Buckhannon 188 38.59 N 80.14 W
Buckhaven 46 56.11 N 3.03 W
Buck Hill Falls 210 41.11 N 75.16 W
Buck Hollow ≃ 224 45.10 N 120.50 W
Buckholts 222 30.52 N 97.08 W
Buckhorn ≃ 180 66.13 N 161.10 W
Buckhorn Island State Park ♠ 284a 43.03 N 78.59 W
Buckhorn Lake @, Ont., Can. 212 44.28 N 78.23 W
Buckhorn Lake @, Calif., U.S. 228 34.50 N 117.59 W
Buckie 46 57.40 N 2.58 W
Buckingham, Austl. 168a 33.24 S 116.19 E
Buckingham, Qué., Can. 188 45.35 N 75.25 W
Buckingham, Eng., U.K. 42 52.00 N 1.00 W
Buckingham, Pa., U.S. 208 40.18 N 75.01 W
Buckingham, Va., U.S. 192 37.32 N 78.37 W
Buckingham Bay C 164 12.10 S 135.46 E
Buckingham Palace ✿ 260 51.30 N 0.08 W
Buckinghamshire □[6] 42 51.45 N 0.48 W
Buck Island I 241n 17.48 N 64.37 W
Buck Lake @, Alta., Can. 182 53.00 N 114.45 W
Buck Lake @, Ont., Can. 212 45.25 N 79.24 W
Buckland, Eng., U.K. 260 51.15 N 0.15 W
Buckland, Alaska, U.S. 180 66.16 N 161.20 W
Buckland, Mass., U.S. 207 42.36 N 72.48 W
Buckland, Ohio, U.S. 216 40.37 N 84.16 W
Buckland Brewer 42 50.57 N 4.14 W
Buckland Common 260 51.45 N 0.39 W
Buckleboo 166 32.55 S 136.12 E
Buckley, Wales, U.K. 44 53.09 N 3.04 W
Buckley, Ill., U.S. 216 40.36 N 88.02 W
Buckley, Wash., U.S. 224 47.10 N 122.02 W
Buckley ≃ 166 20.22 S 137.57 E
Buckley Bay C 9 68.16 S 148.12 E
Bucklin, Kans., U.S. 198 37.33 N 99.38 W
Bucklin, Mo., U.S. 194 39.47 N 92.53 W
Buck Mountain ∧, Va., U.S. 192 36.40 N 81.15 W
Buck Mountain ∧, Wash., U.S. 202 48.26 N 119.50 W
Bucknell Manor 208 38.46 N 77.04 W
Buckner 218 38.23 N 85.26 W
Buckner Creek ≃ 198 38.11 N 99.34 W
Buckners Creek ≃ 222 29.53 N 96.53 W
Buckow 54 52.34 N 14.04 E
Buckow ◆[8] 264a 52.25 N 13.26 E
Bucks □[6] 208 40.19 N 75.08 W
Buckshot Lake @ 212 45.00 N 77.04 W
Buckskin Creek ≃ 218 39.14 N 83.17 W
Bucks Knob ∧ 224 46.41 N 123.20 W
Bucksport 188 44.34 N 68.48 W
Bucktown 285 40.10 N 75.43 W
Bückwitz 54 52.52 N 12.29 E
Buc-Louis-Blériot, Aérodrome de ⊠ 261 48.45 N 2.05 E
Bučmany 78 51.04 N 28.04 E
Bucoda 224 46.48 N 122.52 W
Buco Zau 152 4.46 S 12.33 E
Bucquoy 50 50.08 N 2.42 E
Buctouche 186 46.28 N 64.43 W
Bucun 98 36.37 N 117.27 E
București 38 44.26 N 26.06 E
Bucutua Island I 116 6.09 N 121.49 E
Bucy-lès-Pierrepont 50 49.39 N 3.54 E
Bucyrus 214 40.48 N 82.58 W
Bud 26 62.55 N 6.55 E
Buda 190 41.20 N 89.41 W
Buda ◆[8] 264c 47.30 N 19.02 E
Budafok ◆[8] 264c 47.26 N 19.02 E
Budagovo 88 54.38 N 100.08 E
Budakalász 264c 47.37 N 19.03 E
Budakeszi 264c 47.31 N 18.56 E
Buda-Kosel'ovo 76 52.43 N 30.34 E
Budalin 110 22.22 N 95.08 E
Budaörs 264c 47.27 N 18.58 E
Budapest 30
264c 47.30 N 19.05 E
Budapest □[7] 264c 47.30 N 19.05 E
Budapesti Műszaki Egyetem ✿[2] 264c 47.29 N 19.02 E

Symbols in the index entries represent the broad categories identified in the key at the right. Symbols with superior numbers (⩓[2]) identify subcategories (see complete key on page *I · 30*).

Kartensymbole in dem Registerverzeichnis stellen die rechts in Schlüssel erklärten Kategorien dar. Symbole mit hochgestellten Ziffern (⩓[2]) bezeichnen Unterabteilungen einer Kategorie (vgl. vollständiger Schlüssel auf Seite *I · 30*).

Los símbolos incluídos en el texto del índice representan las grandes categorias identificadas con la clave a la derecha. Los símbolos con numeros en su parte superior (⩓[2]) identifican las subcategorías (véase la clave completa en la página *I · 30*).

Les symboles de l'index représentent les catégories indiquées dans la légende à droite. Les symboles suivis d'un indice (⩓[2]) représentent des sous-catégories (voir légende complète à la page *I · 30*).

Os símbolos incluídos no texto do índice representam as grandes categorias identificadas com a chave à direita. Os símbolos com números em sua parte superior (⩓[2]) identificam as subcategorias (veja-se a chave completa à página *I · 30*).

Symbol	English	Deutsch	Español	Français	Português
∧	Mountain	Berg	Montaña	Montagne	Montanha
⩓	Mountains	Berge	Montañas	Montagnes	Montanhas
)(	Pass	Pass	Paso	Col	Passo
∨	Valley, Canyon	Tal, Cañon	Valle, Cañón	Vallée, Canyon	Vale, Canhão
≚	Plain	Ebene	Llano	Plaine	Planície
≻	Cape	Kap	Cabo	Cap	Cabo
I	Island	Insel	Isla	Île	Ilha
II	Islands	Inseln	Islas	Îles	Ilhas
⊥	Other Topographic Features	Andere Topographische Objekte	Otros Elementos Topográficos	Autres données topographiques	Outros Elementos Topográficos

ESPAÑOL
Nombre — Página — Lat.°′ — Long.°′ W=Oeste

Búđardalur 24a 65.10 N 21.42 W
Budarin 80 47.54 N 42.36 E
Budarino 80 50.31 N 51.04 E
Budatétény ⬥[8] 264c 47.25 N 19.01 E
Budaun 124 28.03 N 79.07 E
Budaun □[5] 124 28.10 N 79.00 E
Budawang Range ⛰ 170 35.16 S 150.10 E
Budayuan 98 40.56 N 125.19 E
Budberg 263 51.32 N 6.38 E
Bud Bud 144 4.15 N 46.30 E
Budd Coast ⦁[2] 9 66.30 S 113.00 E
Buddh Gaya 124 24.42 N 84.59 E
Budd Inlet C 224 47.06 N 122.54 W
Budd Lake 210 40.52 N 74.44 W
Buddtown 285 39.58 N 74.42 W
Buddu 140 11.54 N 24.08 E
Buddusò 71 40.35 N 9.15 E
Bude, Eng., U.K. 42 50.50 N 4.33 W
Bude, Miss., U.S. 194 31.28 N 90.51 W
Bude Bay C 42 50.50 N 4.37 W
Budel 52 51.17 N 5.35 E
Budelikesihu ⊜ 120 33.00 N 86.25 E
Budelli, Isola I 71 41.17 N 9.21 E
Büdelsdorf 41 54.18 N 9.40 E
Büderich 52 51.37 N 6.34 E
Buderus 263 51.33 N 7.38 E
Budești 38 44.14 N 26.28 E
Budge Budge 126 22.27 N 88.10 E
Budhhāta 126 22.36 N 89.10 E
Budhlāda 123 29.56 N 75.34 E
Budi 152 3.04 S 23.56 E
Büdingen 56 50.17 N 9.07 E
Búđir 24a 64.56 N 13.58 W
Budišov nad Budiôvkou 30 49.47 N 17.38 E
Budjala 152 2.39 N 19.42 E
Budleigh Salterton 42 50.38 N 3.20 W
Budogošč' 76 59.17 N 32.27 E
Budogovišči 76 53.36 N 36.18 E
Budoni 71 40.43 N 9.42 E
Bud'onnovka 80 50.52 N 52.48 E
Bud'onnovskaja 80 46.56 N 41.33 E
Bud'onnyj 83 47.27 N 39.46 E
Bud'onnys 85 42.29 N 72.34 E
Budrio 64 44.32 N 11.32 E
Budslav 76 54.47 N 27.27 E
Budweis → České Budějovice 30 48.59 N 14.28 E
Budworth Mere ⊜ 262 53.17 N 2.31 W
Budy 78 49.53 N 36.02 E
Budylka 78 50.30 N 34.26 E
Budyně nad Ohří 54 50.22 N 14.09 E
Budžak ⛰[1] 78 46.10 N 29.00 E
Buea 152 4.09 N 9.14 E
Buëch ≃ 62 44.12 N 5.57 E
Buechel 218 38.12 N 85.39 W
Bueil 50 48.56 N 1.27 E
Buela 152 5.55 S 14.33 E
Buell 219 39.02 N 91.27 W
Bue Marino, Grotta del ⦁[5] 71 40.15 N 9.38 E
Buena 208 39.31 N 74.56 W
Buena Esperanza 252 34.45 S 65.15 W
Buena Esperanza, Cabo de → Good Hope, Cape of › 158 34.24 S 18.30 E
Buena Park, Calif., U.S. 228 33.52 N 118.00 W
Buena Park, Wis., U.S. 216 42.48 N 88.14 W
Buenaventura, Col. 246 3.53 N 77.04 W
Buenaventura, Méx. 232 29.51 N 107.29 W
Buena Vista, Bol. 248 17.27 S 63.40 W
Buena Vista, Guat. 236 13.49 N 90.19 W
Buena Vista, Méx. 204 32.32 N 116.44 W
Buenavista, Méx. 234 22.30 N 103.10 W
Buena Vista, Para. 252 26.08 S 56.03 W
Buenavista, Pil. 116 8.59 N 125.24 E
Buenavista, Pil. 116 13.15 N 121.57 E
Buenavista, Pil. 116 7.15 N 122.16 E
Buenavista, Pil. 116 10.04 N 118.49 E
Buena Vista, Colo., U.S. 200 38.50 N 106.08 W
Buena Vista, Fla., U.S. 220 25.49 N 80.12 W
Buena Vista, Ga., U.S. 192 32.19 N 84.31 W
Buena Vista, Md., U.S. 284c 38.57 N 76.50 W
Buena Vista, Miss., U.S. 194 33.47 N 88.56 W
Buena Vista, Va., U.S. 192 37.44 N 79.21 W
Buenavista, Bahía de C 240p 22.30 N 79.08 W
Buena Vista Canal ☰ 228 35.21 N 119.06 W
Buenavista de Cuéllar 234 18.27 N 99.25 W
Buena Vista Lake Bed ⊜ 204 35.11 N 119.17 W
Buenavista Revolución Mexicana 234 16.03 N 93.04 W
Buenavista Tomatlán 234 19.12 N 102.36 W
Buen Día 196 26.21 N 104.32 W
Buendia, Embalse de ⊜[1] 34 40.25 N 2.43 W
Buenga ≃ 152 6.07 S 15.58 E
Bueno ≃ 254 40.13 S 73.43 W
Bueno Brandão 256 22.27 S 46.21 W
Buenolândia 255 15.48 S 50.17 W
Buenópolis 255 17.54 S 44.11 W
Buenos Aires, Arg. 258
 288 34.36 S 58.27 W
Buenos Aires, Col. 246 3.02 N 76.38 W
Buenos Aires, C.R. 236 9.10 N 83.20 W
Buenos Aires □[4] 252 36.00 S 60.00 W
Buenos Aires, Lago (Lago General Carrera) ⊜ 254 46.35 S 72.00 W
Buen Pasto 254 45.05 S 69.28 W
Buer ⬥[8] 263 51.36 N 7.03 E
Buerarema 255 14.57 S 39.19 W
Buerāt, Bi'r ⫪[4] 142 28.59 N 32.10 E
Buerhanbudashan ⛰ 102 36.00 N 96.00 E
Buerjin 86 47.43 N 86.53 E
Buertuokai 85 39.35 N 74.58 E
Buesaco 246 1.23 N 77.09 W
Buescher State Park ♠ 222 30.02 N 97.09 W
Buet, Le Λ 58 46.02 N 6.52 E
Buey ≃ 240p 20.28 N 77.05 W
Bufalotta, Fosso della ≃ 267a 41.59 N 12.30 E
Buffalo, Ill., U.S. 219 39.51 N 89.25 W
Buffalo, Ind., U.S. 216 40.53 N 86.45 W
Buffalo, Iowa, U.S. 190 41.27 N 90.43 W
Buffalo, Kans., U.S. 198 37.42 N 95.42 W
Buffalo, Minn., U.S. 190 45.10 N 93.53 W
Buffalo, Mo., U.S. 194 37.39 N 93.06 W
Buffalo, N.Y., U.S. 210
 284a 42.54 N 78.53 W
Buffalo, Ohio, U.S. 188 39.55 N 81.31 W
Buffalo, Okla., U.S. 196 36.50 N 99.38 W
Buffalo, S.C., U.S. 192 34.43 N 81.41 W
Buffalo, S. Dak., U.S. 198 45.35 N 103.33 W
Buffalo, Tex., U.S. 222 31.28 N 96.04 W
Buffalo, Wyo., U.S. 202 44.21 N 106.42 W
Buffalo ≃, Can. 176 60.55 N 115.00 W
Buffalo ≃, S. Afr. 158 28.43 S 30.37 E
Buffalo ≃, Ark., U.S. 194 36.10 N 92.26 W
Buffalo ≃, Minn., U.S. 198 47.06 N 96.49 W
Buffalo ≃, Miss., U.S. 194 31.04 N 91.34 W
Buffalo ≃, N.Y., U.S. 214 42.53 N 78.53 W
Buffalo ≃, Tenn., U.S. 194 36.00 N 87.50 W
Buffalo ≃, Wis., U.S. 190 44.22 N 91.55 W

FRANÇAIS
Nom — Page — Lat.°′ — Long.°′ W=Ouest

Buffalo Airpark ⊠ 284a 42.52 N 78.43 W
Buffalo Bayou ≃ 222 29.46 N 95.05 W
Buffalo Bill Reservoir ⊜[1] 202 44.29 N 109.13 W
Buffalo Bill State Park ♠ 202 44.30 N 109.14 W
Buffalo Center 190 43.23 N 93.57 W
Buffalo Coast Guard Base ■ 284a 42.52 N 78.54 W
Buffalo Creek ≃, U.S. 198 45.57 N 102.56 W
Buffalo Creek ≃, U.S. 214 40.16 N 80.37 W
Buffalo Creek ≃, Ill., U.S. 278 42.08 N 87.55 W
Buffalo Creek ≃, Iowa, U.S. 190 42.06 N 91.18 W
Buffalo Creek ≃, Kans., U.S. 198 39.35 N 97.43 W
Buffalo Creek ≃, Ky., U.S. 218 38.28 N 83.03 W
Buffalo Creek ≃, Minn., U.S. 198 44.51 N 94.00 W
Buffalo Creek ≃, N.Y., U.S. 210 42.52 N 78.47 W
Buffalo Creek ≃, Okla., U.S. 196 36.47 N 99.15 W
Buffalo Creek ≃, Pa., U.S. 208 40.29 N 77.08 W
Buffalo Creek ≃, Pa., U.S. 210 40.58 N 76.53 W
Buffalo Grove 216 42.09 N 87.58 W
Buffalo Harbor C 212 42.51 N 78.52 W
Buffalo Lake 198 44.44 N 94.37 W
Buffalo Lake ⊜, Alta., Can. 182 52.27 N 112.54 W
Buffalo Lake ⊜, N.W. Ter., Can. 176 60.10 N 115.30 W
Buffalo Narrows 184 55.51 N 108.30 W
Buffalo Pound Provincial Park ♠ 184 50.36 N 105.30 W
Buffalo Run ≃ 279b 40.12 N 79.37 W
Buffalo Zoo ♠ 284a 42.56 N 78.51 W
Buffels ≃ 158 33.45 S 21.11 E
Buffington Harbor C 278 41.38 N 87.25 W
Buffum, Lake ⊜ 220 27.48 N 81.40 W
Buford, Ga., U.S. 192 34.07 N 84.00 W
Buford, Ohio, U.S. 218 39.04 N 83.50 W
Buford Dam ⬥[6] 192 34.11 N 84.03 W
Bug ≃ 22 52.31 N 21.05 E
Buga, Col. 246 3.54 N 76.17 W
Buga, Nig. 150 8.30 N 7.21 E
Bugajevka, S.S.S.R. 83 49.28 N 37.23 E
Bugajevka, S.S.S.R. 83 49.39 N 39.42 E
Bugajevka, S.S.S.R. 83 48.25 N 38.53 E
Bugalagrande 246 4.11 N 76.09 W
Bugallon 116 15.57 N 120.13 E
Buganga 154 0.03 S 31.59 E
Bugasong 116 11.03 N 122.04 E
Bugat, Mong. 86 48.59 N 90.10 E
Bugat, Mong. 88 47.55 N 101.16 E
Bug Atoti 144 10.41 N 50.45 E
Bugeat 32 45.35 N 1.59 E
Bugel, Ujung › 115a 6.26 S 111.03 E
Bugene 154 1.35 S 31.08 E
Bugey ⬥[1] 58 45.55 N 5.30 E
Buggenhout 50 51.01 N 4.12 E
Buggerru 71 39.24 N 8.24 E
Bugio I 266c 38.39 N 9.18 W
Bugiri 154 0.34 N 33.45 E
Bugisu □[5] 154 1.03 N 34.10 E
Buğlan Geçidi)(130 38.56 N 41.10 E
Bugle 42 50.24 N 4.47 W
Bug Méridional → Južnyj Bug ≃ 78 46.59 N 31.58 E
Bugni Point › 116 12.36 N 123.14 E
Bugojno 36 44.03 N 17.27 E
Bugøynes 24 69.58 N 29.39 E
Bugrino 24 68.48 N 49.09 E
Bugry, S.S.S.R. 76 58.46 N 35.15 E
Bugry, S.S.S.R. 265a 60.04 N 30.24 E
Bugsanga ≃ 116 12.26 N 120.59 E
Bugsuk Island I 116 8.15 N 117.18 E
Buguba 164 3.41 S 137.30 E
Buguey 116 18.17 N 121.50 E
Bugul'dejka 88 52.33 N 106.05 E
Bugul'ma 80 54.33 N 52.48 E
Bugul'minsko-Belebejevskaja Vozvyšennost' ⛰[1] 80 54.54 N 52.42 E
Bugun' ≃ 85 42.58 N 68.35 E
Bugun'skoje Vodochranilišče ⊜[1] 85 42.45 N 69.05 E
Buguruslan 80 53.39 N 52.26 E
Buhamanggenaishankou)(120 34.00 N 92.43 E
Buhanhua 104 42.39 N 122.46 E
Buḥayrah, Rayyāḥ al- ☰ 142 30.43 N 30.45 E
Buḥaythān, Jabal al- Λ 132 30.55 N 35.53 E
Buhera 154 19.18 S 31.29 E
Buhi 116 13.26 N 123.31 E
Buhi, Lake ⊜ 116 13.26 N 123.31 E
Bühl, B.R.D. 56 48.42 N 8.08 E
Buhl, Fr. 58 47.56 N 7.11 E
Buhl, Idaho, U.S. 202 42.36 N 114.46 W
Buhl, Minn., U.S. 190 47.30 N 92.47 W
Buhler 198 38.08 N 97.46 W
Bühler ≃ 56 49.10 N 9.47 E
Bühlertal 56 48.41 N 8.10 E
Buhuai 120 33.22 N 80.36 E
Buhuși 38 46.43 N 26.41 E
Bui Dam ⬥[6] 150 8.22 N 2.10 W
Buie, Loch C 46 56.20 N 5.52 W
Buile Hill Park ♠ 262 53.29 N 2.18 W
Builth Wells 42 52.09 N 3.24 W
Buin, Chile 252 33.44 S 70.45 W
Buin, Pap. N. Gui. 175e 6.50 S 155.44 E
Buin, Piz Λ 58 46.50 N 10.08 E
Buinen 52 52.55 N 6.50 E
Buinsk, S.S.S.R. 80 55.12 N 47.03 E
Buinsk, S.S.S.R. 80 54.57 N 48.17 E
Buíque 250 8.37 S 37.09 W
Buir Nuur ⊜ 88 47.48 N 117.42 E
Buis-les-Baronnies 62 44.16 N 5.16 E
Buitenpost 52 53.15 N 6.09 E
Buitepos 156 22.18 S 19.57 E
Buj 80 58.30 N 41.30 E
Buj ≃ 80 56.13 N 54.12 E
Bujaki 24 59.03 N 48.40 E
Bujalance 34 37.54 N 4.22 W
Bujant, Mong. 86 48.10 N 91.55 E
Bujant, Mong. 86 48.33 N 89.34 E
Bujant ≃ 88 47.08 N 97.38 E
Bujant-Ovoo 102 44.58 N 107.08 E
Bujaraloz 34 41.30 N 0.09 W
Buje 36 45.24 N 13.40 E
Buji 102 33.58 N 95.22 E
Bujiadong 106 30.55 N 119.31 E
Bujnaksk 84 42.49 N 47.07 E
Bujnoviči 78 51.52 N 28.33 E
Bujukly 89 49.30 N 142.47 E
Bujumbura 154 3.23 S 29.22 E
Bük, Magy. 61 47.23 N 16.45 E
Buk, Pol. 30 52.22 N 16.31 E
Buka 85 40.48 N 69.11 E
Bukačača 88 52.59 N 116.55 E
Bukačevcy 78 49.15 N 24.29 E
Buka Island I 175e 5.15 S 154.35 E
Bukama 154 9.12 S 25.51 E
Bukan' 76 53.55 N 34.42 E
Bukanovskaja 80 49.42 N 42.18 E
Buka Passage ⋓ 175e 5.25 S 154.41 E
Bukarest → București 38 44.26 N 26.06 E
Bukarevo 82 55.57 N 36.44 E
Bukavu 154 2.30 S 28.52 E
Bukechi ⊜ 120 31.30 N 91.05 E

PORTUGUÊS
Nome — Página — Lat.°′ — Long.°′ W=Oeste

Bukedi □[5] 154 0.50 N 34.00 E
Bukene 154 4.14 S 32.53 E
Bukhara → Buchara 128 39.48 N 64.25 E
Bukhayt, Bi'r ⫪[4] 142 29.13 N 32.17 E
Bukide, Pulau I 112 3.47 N 125.36 E
Bukidnon □[4] 116 8.00 N 125.00 E
Bukima 154 1.48 S 33.25 E
Bukitbatu 114 1.27 N 102.00 E
Bukit Betong 114 4.15 N 101.56 E
Bukit Fraser 114 3.43 N 101.45 E
Bukit Kachi 114 6.24 N 100.32 E
Bukit Mertajam 114 5.22 N 100.28 E
Bukit Panjang 271c 1.23 N 103.46 E
Bukit Serok 114 2.55 N 102.50 E
Bukit Timah 271c 1.20 N 103.47 E
Bukit Timah Race Course ♠ 271c 1.20 N 103.48 E
Bukittinggi 112 0.19 S 100.22 E
Bükk ⛰ 30 48.05 N 20.30 E
Bukoba 154 1.20 S 31.49 E
Bukombe 154 3.31 S 32.03 E
Bukovica ⬥[1] 36 44.10 N 15.40 E
Bukovina □[9] 78 48.00 N 25.30 E
Bukrale 144 4.30 N 42.03 E
Bukrino 82 54.48 N 36.14 E
Bukuka 88 51.11 N 116.39 E
Bukukun 88 49.27 N 111.08 E
Bukum, Pulau I 271c 1.14 N 103.47 E
Bukumbirwa 154 0.46 S 28.44 E
Bukunga 154 7.41 S 25.56 E
Bukuru 150 9.48 N 8.51 E
Bukuya 154 0.41 N 31.50 E
Būl, Kūh-e Λ 128 30.48 N 52.45 E
Bula 164 3.06 S 130.30 E
Bula ≃ 80 55.12 N 48.23 E
Bula Atumba 152 8.40 S 14.48 E
Bulacan □[4] 116 15.00 N 121.05 E
Bulacaue Point › 116 11.36 N 123.09 E
Bülach 58 47.31 N 8.32 E
Bulajevo 86 54.54 N 70.26 E
Bulak 88 51.02 N 115.21 E
Bulaku ≃ 164 8.06 S 139.12 E
Bulalacao 116 12.20 N 121.20 E
Bulalacao Island I 116 11.45 N 120.10 E
Bulan, Pil. 116 12.40 N 123.52 E
Bulan, Ky., U.S. 192 37.18 N 83.10 W
Bulanaš 86 57.16 N 62.00 E
Bulancak 130 40.57 N 38.14 E
Bulandshahr 124 28.24 N 77.51 E
Bulandshahr □[5] 272a 28.35 N 77.25 E
Bulanicha 86 52.48 N 84.57 E
Bulanık 130 39.05 N 42.15 E
Bulan Island I 116 6.08 N 121.50 E
Bulanovo 86 52.27 N 55.10 E
Būlāq 140 25.12 N 30.32 E
Būlāq ⬥[8] 273c 30.04 N 31.14 E
Būlāq ad-Dakrūr 142 30.02 N 31.11 E
Bulaquit Point › 116 11.17 N 124.03 E
Bulava 89 51.55 N 140.25 E
Bulavinovka 83 49.25 N 38.58 E
Bulawa, Gunung Λ 112 0.30 N 123.34 E
Bulawayo 154 20.09 S 28.36 E
Bulbjerg Λ[2] 26 57.09 N 9.02 E
Bulbul 130 36.46 N 36.49 E
Bulbul, Wādī V 140 10.59 N 24.33 E
Bulcherry Island I 126 21.33 N 88.31 E
Buldan 130 38.03 N 28.51 E
Buldāna 122 20.32 N 76.11 E
Buldern 52 51.52 N 7.22 E
Buldibuyo 248 8.07 S 77.22 W
Buldir Island I 181a 52.21 N 175.54 E
Buldon 116 7.33 N 124.25 E
Buldurtinskij 80 50.05 N 53.11 E
Buldurty ≃ 80 49.48 N 52.34 E
Bulga 170 32.39 S 151.01 E
Bulgakovka 83 49.11 N 38.33 E
Bulgakovo 76 55.14 N 32.08 E
Bulgan, Mong. 86 46.53 N 91.05 E
Bulgan, Mong. 88 48.52 N 103.34 E
Bulgan, Mong. 102 44.05 N 103.39 E
Bulgan □[4] 88 49.00 N 103.30 E
Bulgaria □[1] 22
 38 43.00 N 25.00 E
Bulgarie → Bulgaria □[1] 38 43.00 N 25.00 E
Bulgarien → Bulgaria □[1] 38 43.00 N 25.00 E
Bulger 214 40.23 N 80.20 W
Bulgnéville 58 48.13 N 5.50 E
Bulgroo 166 25.48 S 143.59 E
Bulhale 144 5.27 N 46.33 E
Bulhar 144 10.23 N 44.27 E
Buliluyan 116 8.20 N 117.12 E
Buliluyan, Cape › 116 8.20 N 117.11 E
Bulim 271c 1.23 N 103.43 E
Bulimba 171a 27.25 S 153.04 E
Bulkeley 241g 13.07 N 59.32 W
Bulki 144 6.10 N 36.40 E
Bulkington 42 52.29 N 1.25 W
Bulkley ≃ 182 55.13 N 127.40 W
Bulkley Ranges ⛰ 182 54.30 N 127.30 W
Bull ≃ 182 49.28 N 115.26 W
Bullabulling 162 31.01 S 120.32 E
Bullah Λ 123 35.40 N 75.56 E
Bullaque ≃ 34 38.59 N 4.17 W
Bullara 162 22.40 S 114.03 E
Bullard 222 32.08 N 95.19 W
Bulla Regia ⊥ 36 36.34 N 8.46 E
Bullas 34 38.03 N 1.40 W
Bullay 56 50.03 N 7.08 E
Bull Creek ≃, Nev., U.S. 204 38.40 N 115.40 W
Bull Creek ≃, N.Y., U.S. 284a 43.03 N 78.50 W
Bull Creek ≃, Ohio, U.S. 214 40.42 N 80.32 W
Bull Creek ≃, S. Dak., U.S. 198 43.41 N 99.28 W
Bull Creek ≃, S. Dak., U.S. 198 45.40 N 103.18 W
Bull Creek ≃, Tex., U.S. 196 32.36 N 101.10 W
Bulldog 164 7.45 S 146.25 E
Bulle 58 46.37 N 7.04 E
Bullenbaai C 241s 12.11 N 69.04 W
Buller ≃ 172 41.44 S 171.35 E
Buller, Mount Λ 169 37.09 S 146.26 E
Bullfinch 162 30.59 S 119.06 E
Bullfrog Creek ≃ 200 37.19 N 110.44 W
Bull Harbour 182 50.54 N 127.55 W
Bullhead 198 45.46 N 101.05 W
Bullhead City 204 35.09 N 114.34 W
Bull Hide Creek ≃ 222 31.23 N 97.01 W
Bull Hill Λ[2] 262 53.40 N 2.21 W
Bulli 170 34.20 S 150.55 E
Bullicame ♠ 66 42.22 N 12.04 E
Büllingen 56 50.25 N 6.16 E
Bullioh 171b 36.12 S 147.20 E
Bullion 261 48.37 N 2.00 E
Bull Lake Creek ≃ 202 43.14 N 109.02 W
Bull Lake Reservoir ⊜[1] 202 43.11 N 109.07 W
Bull Mountain Λ 202 46.05 N 112.04 W
Bull Mountains ⛰ 202 46.05 N 109.00 W
Bullock 192 36.30 N 78.33 W
Bullock Creek 166 17.43 S 144.31 E
Bullock Creek ≃ 166 21.40 S 145.09 E
Bulloo ≃ 166 28.43 S 142.30 E
Bulloo Downs 166 28.31 S 142.57 E
Bulloo Lake ⊜ 166 28.43 S 142.25 E
Bulloo River Overflow ⌣ 166 28.50 S 142.40 E
Bullpound Creek ≃ 182 51.05 N 111.58 W
Bull Run ≃ 224 45.26 N 122.15 W
Bull Run Creek ≃ 208 38.43 N 77.23 W
Bull Run Lake ⊜ 224 45.27 N 121.50 W
Bull Run Reservoir ⊜[1] 224 45.28 N 122.10 W
Bullrun Rock Λ 202 44.21 N 118.17 W
Bulls 172 40.10 S 175.23 E

Bulls Bay C 192 32.59 N 79.33 W
Bullsbrook 168a 31.40 S 116.01 E
Bullsgap 192 36.15 N 83.05 W
Bull Shoals Dam ⬥[6] 194 36.20 N 92.33 W
Bull Shoals Lake ⊜[1] 194 36.30 N 92.50 W
Bullskin Creek ≃, Ky., U.S. 218 38.10 N 85.19 W
Bullskin Creek ≃, Ohio, U.S. 218 38.47 N 84.05 W
Bullville 210 41.33 N 74.22 W
Bully Creek ≃ 202 43.58 N 117.15 W
Bully Hill 214 41.22 N 79.50 W
Bully-les-Mines 50 50.26 N 2.43 E
Bulmke-Hüllen ⬥[8] 263 51.31 N 7.06 E
Bulnajn Nuruu ⛰ 88 49.05 N 98.30 E
Bulnes 252 36.44 S 72.18 W
Bulo Burti 144 3.52 N 45.40 E
Bulo Gedudo 144 2.59 N 43.00 E
Bulolo 164 7.10 S 146.40 E
Bulpham 260 51.33 N 0.22 E
Bulpitt 219 39.35 N 89.26 W
Bulsār 122 20.38 N 72.56 E
Bulstrode ≃ 206 46.02 N 72.15 W
Bultei 71 40.27 N 9.03 E
Bultfontein 158 28.20 S 26.05 E
Buluan 116 6.44 N 124.47 E
Buluan ≃ 116 6.47 N 124.47 E
Buluan, Lake ⊜ 116 6.40 N 124.49 E
Buluduku 114 2.20 N 98.14 E
Bulugan 88 52.24 N 110.23 E
Bulukumba 112 5.33 S 120.11 E
Bulukuto 152 0.12 S 21.42 E
Bululawang 115a 8.05 S 112.38 E
Bulungu, Zaïre 152 4.33 S 18.36 E
Bulungu, Zaïre 152 6.04 S 21.54 E
Buluntal 120 36.34 N 92.38 E
Buluntuohai ⊜ 86 47.15 N 87.20 E
Bulupayung 114 1.38 N 99.11 E
Bulusan 116 12.45 N 124.08 E
Bulusan Volcano Λ[1] 116 12.46 N 124.03 E
Bulwater 158 32.29 S 21.48 E
Bulwer 158 29.46 S 29.47 E
Bulyčevo 82 55.06 N 37.15 E
Bulyee 162 32.22 S 117.31 E
Bumba, Zaïre 152 2.11 N 22.28 E
Bumba, Zaïre 152 6.55 S 19.16 E
Bumbire Island I 154 1.40 S 31.53 E
Bumbles Green 260 51.44 N 0.02 E
Bumbo 152 7.04 S 21.57 E
Bumbu ≃ 273b 4.23 S 15.18 E
Bumbulan 112 0.29 N 122.04 E
Bum Bum, Pulau I 112 4.27 N 118.40 E
Bumbuna 150 9.03 N 11.44 W
Bumbunga Lake ⊜ 168b 33.54 S 138.11 E
Bumiayu 115a 7.15 S 109.00 E
Bumijawa 115a 7.10 S 109.07 E
Bumkin Island I 283 42.17 N 70.54 W
Bumping ≃ 224 46.59 N 121.06 W
Bumping Lake ⊜ 224 46.52 N 121.19 W
Bumpus, Mount Λ[2] 176 69.33 N 112.40 W
Bumtang ≃ 124 26.56 N 90.51 E
Bumuhu ⊜ 120 31.15 N 91.10 E
Buna, Kenya 154 2.47 N 39.31 E
Buna, Pap. N. Gui. 164 8.40 S 148.25 E
Buna, Tex., U.S. 194 30.26 N 93.58 W
Buna, Zaïre 152 3.15 S 18.59 E
Bunagāti 126 23.19 N 89.25 E
Bunai 164 2.11 S 147.14 E
Bunaj 85 38.26 N 71.32 E
Bun'atino 82 56.24 N 37.15 E
Bunawan 116 8.12 N 125.57 E
Bunazi 154 1.13 S 31.24 E
Bunbah, Khalīj C 146 32.20 N 23.10 E
Bunbury 168a 33.19 S 115.38 E
Bunceton 194 38.47 N 92.48 W
Bunche Park 220 25.55 N 80.15 W
Bunclody 48 52.38 N 6.40 W
Buncrana 48 55.08 N 7.27 W
Bundaberg 166 24.52 S 152.21 E
Bundanoon 170 34.39 S 150.18 E
Bundarra 166 30.10 S 151.05 E
Bunde, B.R.D. 52 53.11 N 7.16 E
Bünde, B.R.D. 52 52.12 N 8.35 E
Bunde, Ned. 56 50.54 N 5.45 E
Bundeena 274a 34.05 S 151.09 E
Bundenthal 56 49.06 N 7.48 E
Bundesrepublik Deutschland → Germany, Federal Republic of □[1] 30 51.00 N 9.00 E
Bundey ≃ 162 21.46 S 135.37 E
Bündheim 54 51.53 N 10.32 E
Būndi, Bhārat 120 25.27 N 75.39 E
Bundi, Pap. N. Gui. 164 5.40 S 145.15 E
Būndi □[5] 124 25.30 N 76.10 E
Bundick Creek ≃ 194 30.36 N 92.57 W
Bundooma 162 24.54 S 134.16 E
Bundoora 274b 37.42 S 145.04 E
Bundoran 48 54.28 N 8.17 W
Būndu, Bhārat 124 23.11 N 85.35 E
Bundu, S. Afr. 158 29.45 S 22.02 E
Bunduqiyah 154 5.06 N 30.53 E
Bund'ur 86 57.32 N 82.01 E
Buner □[9] 123 34.35 N 72.35 E
Bunessan 46 56.19 N 6.14 W
Bunga 150 11.04 N 9.38 E
Bunga ≃, Nig. 150 11.23 N 9.56 E
Bunga ≃, Pil. 116 6.44 N 124.34 E
Bungamas 112 3.42 S 102.23 E
Bungay 42 52.28 N 1.26 E
Bungbulang 115a 7.27 S 107.35 E
Bunge 26 57.51 N 19.01 E
Bungegep 164 7.48 S 139.52 E
Bungendore 171b 35.15 S 149.27 E
Bunger Hills ⛰[2] 9 66.17 S 100.47 E
Bung Kan 110 18.23 N 103.37 E
Bungku 112 2.33 S 121.58 E
Bungo 152 7.26 S 15.23 E
Bungonia 170 34.51 S 149.57 E
Bungo-suidō ⋓ 92 33.00 N 132.13 E
Bungo-takada 96 33.33 N 131.27 E
Bungsberg Λ[2] 54 54.12 N 10.43 E
Bungtlang 120 22.20 N 92.46 E
Bungu 154 7.38 S 39.03 E
Bunguran Selatan, Kepulauan II 112 2.45 N 109.00 E
Bunguran Utara, Kepulauan II 112 4.40 N 108.00 E
Buni ≃ 115a 7.26 S 106.47 E
Bunia 154 1.34 N 30.15 E
Bunianga 152 3.34 S 20.06 E
Buninyong 169 37.39 S 143.53 E
Buninyong, Mount Λ 169 37.39 S 143.56 E
Bunji 123 35.40 N 74.36 E
Bunkeflo strand 41 55.33 N 12.57 E
Bunker 194 37.27 N 91.13 W
Bunker Group II 166 23.48 S 152.20 E
Bunker Hill, Ill., U.S. 219 39.03 N 89.57 W
Bunker Hill, Ind., U.S. 216 40.40 N 86.06 W
Bunker Hill, Oreg., U.S. 202 43.21 N 124.12 W
Bunker Hill, Tex., U.S. 222 29.46 N 95.32 W
Bunker Hill Λ 204 39.15 N 117.08 W
Bunker Hill Monument ⊥ 283 42.22 N 71.04 W
Bunkeya 154 10.07 S 27.17 E
Bunkie 194 30.57 N 92.11 W
Bunkyō ⬥[8] 268 35.43 N 139.45 E
Bunnahowen 48 54.11 N 9.54 W
Bunnell 192 29.28 N 81.15 W
Bunnik 52 52.04 N 5.12 E
Bünningstedt 52 53.41 N 10.13 E
Buñol 34 39.25 N 0.47 W
Bunola 214 40.14 N 79.56 W
Bun Plains ⌣ 154 0.44 N 40.42 E
Bunratty Castle ⊥ 48 52.42 N 8.48 W
Bunschoten 52 52.14 N 5.22 E
Bunta 112 0.48 S 122.10 E
Buntay Point › 116 11.18 N 123.44 E

Buntine 162 29.59 S 116.34 E
Buntingford 42 51.57 N 0.01 W
Buntok 112 1.42 S 114.48 E
Bununu Dass 150 10.00 N 9.31 E
Bunut 112 0.46 N 112.30 E
Bunya 158 26.32 S 31.01 E
Bünyan 130 38.51 N 35.52 E
Bunyip 169 38.06 S 145.43 E
Bunyip ≃ 169 38.13 S 145.27 E
Bunyoro □[5] 154 1.40 N 31.30 E
Bunyrevo 82 54.34 N 37.09 E
Bunyu, Pulau I 112 3.30 N 117.50 E
Bunza 150 12.08 N 4.00 E
Buochs 58 46.58 N 8.22 E
Buol 112 1.10 N 121.26 E
Buolkalach 74 72.56 N 119.50 E
Buonalbergo 68 41.13 N 14.59 E
Buona Vista 271c 1.16 N 103.47 E
Buon-bu-n'jang 110 12.06 N 107.40 E
Buonconvento 66 43.08 N 11.29 E
Buon-mrong 110 12.48 N 108.28 E
Buon-ngo 110 12.30 N 108.28 E
Buon-thach-hom 110 12.17 N 108.48 E
Buon-ya-soup 110 13.05 N 107.52 E
Buor-Chaja, Guba C 74 71.30 N 131.00 E
Buor-Chaja, Mys › 74 71.56 N 132.40 E
Bupul 164 7.31 S 140.52 E
Buqay'āwīyah, Qā' al- ⌣ 132 32.03 N 37.07 E
Buqayq 128 25.56 N 49.40 E
Buqda 'Aqable 144 4.04 N 45.21 E
Buqda Kosar 144 4.35 N 44.59 E
Buquim 250 11.09 S 37.37 W
Buquira ≃ 256 23.10 S 45.54 W
Buquirivu ≃ 287b 23.28 S 46.28 W
Buqūm, Ḥarrat al- ⦁[9] 144 20.54 N 42.00 E
Bur 88 58.47 N 107.01 E
Bura, Kenya 154 3.30 S 38.18 E
Bura, Kenya 154 1.06 S 39.57 E
Bura Gaurānga ≃[1] 126 22.00 N 90.33 E
Burakin 162 30.31 S 117.10 E
Buraly 80 55.04 N 52.52 E
Buram 140 10.49 N 25.10 E
Buran, Som. 144 10.10 N 48.48 E
Buran, S.S.S.R. 86 48.04 N 85.15 E
Burangulovo 86 53.26 N 58.23 E
Buranhém ≃ 255 16.27 S 39.04 W
Burankol' 86 46.14 N 54.12 E
Burannoje 86 50.59 N 54.28 E
Burano ≃ 66 43.37 N 12.40 E
Burao 144 9.30 N 45.30 E
Burao □[4] 144 9.30 N 47.30 E
Burao Kibir 144 8.42 N 45.23 E
Burāq 132 33.10 N 36.29 E
Burāri ⬥[8] 272a 28.46 N 77.12 E
Buras 194 29.21 N 89.32 W
Buraševo 82 56.44 N 35.52 E
Burāthum 124 28.04 N 84.50 E
Bur'atskaja Avtonomnaja Sovetskaja Socialističeskaja Respublika □[3] 88 53.00 N 109.00 E
Burauen 116 10.58 N 124.53 E
Burayd, Bi'r ⫪[4] 142 29.08 N 32.07 E
Buraydah 128 26.20 N 43.59 E
Burayj, 'Ilw al- ⛰[1] 142 29.00 N 30.44 E
Burayk 146 26.33 N 13.08 E
Buraykah 132 32.50 N 36.34 E
Burbach 56 50.45 N 8.05 E
Burbage, Eng., U.K. 42 52.31 N 1.20 W
Burbage, Eng., U.K. 262 53.15 N 1.56 W
Burbank, Calif., U.S. 226 37.19 N 121.55 W
Burbank, Calif., U.S. 228 34.12 N 118.18 W
Burbank, Ill., U.S. 216 41.44 N 87.45 W
Burbank, Ohio, U.S. 214 40.59 N 81.59 W
Burbank, Wash., U.S. 202 46.12 N 119.01 W
Burbank Studios ⊍[3] 280 34.09 N 118.21 W
Burbure 50 50.32 N 2.28 E
Burç 130 37.02 N 37.10 E
Burcei 71 39.21 N 9.21 E
Burcevo 82 55.02 N 38.09 E
Burcher 166 33.32 S 147.18 E
Burchun ≃ 86 47.40 N 86.55 E
Burcin 62 45.26 N 5.26 E
Burda 124 25.50 N 77.35 E
Burdalyk 128 38.25 N 64.20 E
Burdekin ≃ 166 19.39 S 147.30 E
Burdekin Falls ⌊ 166 20.39 S 147.09 E
Burden 198 37.19 N 96.45 W
Burdeos → Bordeaux, Fr. 32 44.50 N 0.34 W
Burdeos, Pil. 116 14.51 N 121.58 E
Burdeos Bay C 116 14.44 N 122.06 E
Burdett, Alta., Can. 182 49.50 N 111.32 W
Burdett, Kans., U.S. 198 38.12 N 99.32 W
Burdett, N.Y., U.S. 210 42.25 N 76.52 W
Burdu □[4] 130 37.30 N 30.10 E
Burdul 272c 19.07 N 73.07 E
Burdur 130 37.43 N 30.17 E
Burdwān 126 23.15 N 87.51 E
Burdwān □[5] 126 23.25 N 87.50 E
Burdwood Bank ✢[4] 9 54.00 S 60.00 W
Bure 144 8.15 N 35.09 E
Bure ≃ 42 52.37 N 1.43 E
Bure, Pic de Λ 62 44.38 N 5.56 E
Bureå 26 64.37 N 21.12 E
Bureälven ≃ 26 64.37 N 21.13 E
Büregchangaj 88 48.14 N 103.57 E
Bureinskij Chrebet ⛰ 89 50.35 N 133.35 E
Bureja 89 49.52 N 129.48 E
Bureja ≃ 89 49.25 N 129.35 E
Burekup 168a 33.19 S 115.49 E
Büren, B.R.D. 52 51.33 N 8.33 E
Büren, Mong. 88 47.13 N 95.54 E
Büren an der Aare 58 47.08 N 7.23 E
Bürenchaan 88 49.35 N 99.06 E
Bürengijn Nuruu ⛰ 88 49.30 N 105.15 E
Bures 261 48.57 N 1.58 E
Bures-sur-Yvette 261 48.42 N 2.10 E
Burey-en-Vaux 58 48.34 N 5.40 E
Burfjord 24 69.56 N 22.00 E
Burford, Ont., Can. 212 43.06 N 80.26 W
Burford, Eng., U.K. 42 51.49 N 1.38 W
Burg, B.R.D. 56 50.42 N 8.19 E
Burg, B.R.D. 263 51.08 N 7.09 E
Burg, D.D.R. 54 52.16 N 11.51 E
Burg, D.D.R. 54 51.49 N 14.08 E
Burg, Schloss ⊥ 263 51.08 N 7.10 E
Burga 76 58.45 N 32.29 E
Burgas 38 42.30 N 27.28 E
Burgas □[4] 130 42.10 N 27.30 E
Burgaski zaliv C 38 42.30 N 27.33 E
Burgau 58 48.26 N 10.25 E
Burg [auf Fehmarn] 54 54.26 N 11.12 E
Bur Gavo 144 1.10 S 41.50 E
Burgaw 192 34.33 N 77.56 W
Burgaz ⬥[8] 267b 40.53 N 29.03 E
Burgbernheim 56 49.27 N 10.19 E
Burgdorf, B.R.D. 52 52.27 N 10.00 E
Burgdorf, Schw. 58 47.04 N 7.37 E
Burgebrach 56 49.50 N 10.44 E
Bürgel 54 50.56 N 11.45 E
Burgenland □[3] 61 47.30 N 16.20 E
Burgeo 186 47.37 N 57.37 W
Burgersdorp 158 31.00 S 26.20 E
Burger Township 273d 26.05 S 27.46 E
Burgess 208 37.53 N 76.21 W
Burgess Hill 42 50.57 N 0.07 W
Burgessville 212 43.01 N 80.39 W
Burgettstown 214 40.23 N 80.23 W
Burggrafenberg Λ[2] 263 51.13 N 7.07 E
Burghausen 60 48.09 N 12.49 E
Burghead 46 57.42 N 3.30 W
Burgheim 60 48.42 N 11.01 E
Burgh Heath 260 51.18 N 0.13 W
Burghill 214 41.22 N 80.34 W

Burghūth, Sabkhat al- ⊜ 130 34.58 N 41.0
Bur Gibi 144 3.57 N 45.07
Burgin 194 37.45 N 84.46
Burgio 70 37.36 N 13.17 E
Burgjoss 56 50.12 N 9.29 E
Burgkirchen 60 48.12 N 13.06 E
Burgkunstadt 54 50.08 N 11.14 E
Bürglen, Schw. 58 46.53 N 8.40 E
Bürglen, Schw. 58 47.33 N 9.09 E
Burglengenfeld 60 49.13 N 12.03 E
Burgoon 214 41.16 N 83.15 W
Burgos, Esp. 34 42.21 N 3.42 W
Burgos, It. 71 40.23 N 8.59 E
Burgos, Méx. 232 24.57 N 98.47 W
Burgos, Pil. 116 16.04 N 119.52 E
Burgos, Pil. 116 15.30 N 120.24 E
Burgos □[4] 34 42.20 N 3.40 W
Burgsinn 56 50.09 N 9.38 E
Burgstädt 54 50.55 N 12.49 E
Burgstall, D.D.R. 54 52.24 N 11.41 E
Burgstall → Postal, It. 64 46.36 N 11.11 E
Burg Stargard 54 53.29 N 13.18 E
Burgsteinfurt 52 52.08 N 7.20 E
Burgsvik 26 57.03 N 18.16 E
Burgueño, Arroyo ≃ 288 34.24 S 58.47 W
Burgund → Bourgogne □[9] 32 47.00 N 4.30 E
Burgundy → Bourgogne □[9] 32 47.00 N 4.30 E
Burgusio (Burgeis) 64 46.42 N 10.31 E
Burgwindheim 56 49.49 N 10.35 E
Bur Hakkaba 144 2.43 N 44.10 E
Burham 260 51.20 N 0.29 E
Burhaniye, Tür. 130 39.30 N 26.58 E
Burhaniye, Tür. 130 37.57 N 28.45 E
Burhānpur 120 21.18 N 76.14 E
Burhar 124 23.13 N 81.32 E
Burhave 52 53.34 N 8.21 E
Burholme ⬥[8] 285 40.03 N 75.05 W
Buri 255 23.48 S 48.35 W
Burias Island I 116 12.57 N 123.08 E
Burias Pass ⋓ 116 13.00 N 123.15 E
Buribaj 86 51.57 N 58.11 E
Būr Ibrāhīm 142 29.57 N 32.34 E
Burien 224 47.27 N 122.21 W
Buri Gandaki ≃ 124 27.48 N 84.45 E
Burigi, Lake ⊜ 154 2.05 S 31.15 E
Burila Mare 38 44.27 N 22.34 E
Burin 186 47.02 N 55.10 W
Burin Peninsula ›[1] 186 47.00 N 55.40 W
Buriram 110 15.00 N 103.07 E
Burishwar ≃[1] 126 21.58 N 90.02 E
Buritama 255 21.03 S 50.08 W
Buriti, Bra. 250 3.55 S 42.57 W
Buriti, Bra. 255 16.27 S 53.27 W
Buriti ≃ 248 12.50 S 58.28 W
Buriti Alegre 255 18.09 S 49.03 W
Buriti Bravo 250 5.50 S 43.50 W
Buriti Cortado 250 5.11 S 43.06 W
Buriticupu ≃ 250 4.13 S 46.33 W
Buriti dos Lopes 250 3.10 S 41.52 W
Buritizal, Cachoeira do ⌊ 250 0.17 N 54.40 W
Buritizeiro 255 17.21 S 44.58 W
Būriya 124 30.09 N 77.21 E
Burj al-'Arab 140 30.55 N 29.32 E
Burjasot 34 39.31 N 0.25 W
Burji 144 5.20 N 37.57 E
Burj Islām 130 35.41 N 35.48 E
Burj Mughayzil 142 31.27 N 30.23 E
Burj Ṣāfītā 130 34.49 N 36.07 E
Burkan ≃ 85 41.43 N 76.46 E
Burkau 54 51.10 N 14.10 E
Burkburnett 196 34.06 N 98.34 W
Burke, S. Dak., U.S. 198 43.11 N 99.18 W
Burke, Tex., U.S. 222 31.14 N 94.46 W
Burke, Va., U.S. 284c 38.48 N 77.16 W
Burke ≃ 166 23.12 S 139.33 E
Burke Channel ⋓ 182 52.07 N 127.38 W
Burke Island I 9 73.15 S 104.35 W
Burke Lakefront Airport ⊠ 279a 41.31 N 81.41 W
Burkesville 194 36.48 N 85.22 W
Burket 216 41.09 N 85.58 W
Burketown 166 17.43 S 139.34 E
Burkett Gardens 226 37.57 N 121.15 W
Burkettsville 216 40.21 N 84.39 W
Burkhardtsdorf 54 50.44 N 12.55 E
Burkit 80 47.03 N 50.42 E
Burksville 219 38.16 N 90.09 W
Burla 86 53.19 N 78.21 E
Burla ≃ 86 53.20 N 78.02 E
Burladingen 58 48.17 N 9.07 E
Burleigh 208 39.03 N 74.51 W
Burleigh Falls 212 44.34 N 78.13 W
Burleigh Heads 171a 28.06 S 153.27 E
Burleson 222 32.33 N 97.19 W
Burleson □[6] 222 30.30 N 96.43 W
Burley, Idaho, U.S. 202 42.32 N 113.48 W
Burley, Wash., U.S. 224 47.25 N 122.38 W
Burley Griffin, Lake ⊜ 171b 35.13 S 149.05 E
Burli, S.S.S.R. 80 51.25 N 52.44 E
Burli, S.S.S.R. 86 53.36 N 61.55 E
Burlingame, Calif., U.S. 226 37.35 N 122.22 W
Burlingame, Kans., U.S. 198 38.45 N 95.50 W
Burlingame State Park ♠ 207 41.22 N 71.43 W
Burlington, Newf., Can. 186 49.45 N 56.02 W
Burlington, Ont., Can. 212 43.19 N 79.47 W
Burlington, Colo., U.S. 198 39.18 N 102.16 W
Burlington, Conn., U.S. 207 41.46 N 72.58 W
Burlington, Ill., U.S. 216 42.03 N 88.33 W
Burlington, Ind., U.S. 216 40.29 N 86.24 W
Burlington, Iowa, U.S. 190 40.49 N 91.14 W
Burlington, Kans., U.S. 198 38.12 N 95.45 W
Burlington, Ky., U.S. 218 39.02 N 84.43 W
Burlington, Maine, U.S. 188 45.12 N 68.26 W
Burlington, Mass., U.S. 207 42.30 N 71.12 W
Burlington, Mich., U.S. 216 42.06 N 85.05 W
Burlington, N.J., U.S. 208 40.04 N 74.49 W
Burlington, N.C., U.S. 192 36.04 N 79.26 W
Burlington, N. Dak., U.S. 198 48.17 N 101.26 W
Burlington, Pa., U.S. 210 41.47 N 76.37 W
Burlington, Tex., U.S. 222 31.01 N 96.60 W
Burlington, Vt., U.S. 188 44.29 N 73.13 W
Burlington, Wash., U.S. 224 48.28 N 122.20 W
Burlington, Wis., U.S. 216 42.41 N 88.17 W
Burlington, Wyo., U.S. 202 44.27 N 108.26 W
Burlington □[6] 208 39.50 N 74.47 W
Burlington Beach 216 41.30 N 87.03 W
Burlington County Airpark ⊠ 285 39.56 N 74.50 W
Burlington Island I 285 40.05 N 74.51 W
Burlington Junction 194 40.27 N 95.04 W
Burlit 89 46.33 N 134.14 E
Bùrluk 80 50.34 N 44.33 E
Burma □[1] 12
 110 22.00 N 98.00 E
Burmā, Tall Λ 132 30.38 N 35.50 E
Burmakino 80 57.27 N 40.20 E
Burn ≃ 44 54.12 N 1.38 W
Burnaby 182 49.15 N 122.57 W
Burnaby Island I 182 52.24 N 131.20 W

≃ River — Fluss — Río — Rivière — Rio
☰ Canal — Kanal — Canal — Canal — Canal
⌊ Waterfall, Rapids — Wasserfall, Stromschnellen — Cascada, Rápidos — Chute d'eau, Rapides — Cascata, Rápidos
⋓ Strait — Meeresstrasse — Estrecho — Détroit — Estreito
C Bay, Gulf — Bucht, Golf — Bahía, Golfo — Baie, Golfe — Baía, Golfo
⊜ Lake, Lakes — See, Seen — Lago, Lagos — Lac, Lacs — Lago, Lagos
☷ Swamp — Sumpf — Pantano — Marais — Pântano
⊓ Ice Features, Glacier — Eis- und Gletscherformen — Accidentes Glaciales — Formes glaciaires — Acidentes Glaciares
⫪ Other Hydrographic Features — Andere Hydrographische Objekte — Otros Elementos Hidrográficos — Autres données hydrographiques — Outros Elementos Hidrográficos

✢ Submarine Features — Untermeerische Objekte — Accidentes Submarinos — Formes de relief sous-marin — Acidentes Submarinos
□ Political Unit — Politische Einheit — Unidad Politica — Entité politique — Unidade Política
⊍ Cultural Institution — Kulturelle Institution — Institución Cultural — Institution culturelle — Instituição Cultural
⊥ Historical Site — Historische Stätte — Sitio Histórico — Site historique — Sítio Histórico
♠ Recreational Site — Erholungs- und Ferienort — Sitio de Recreo — Centre de loisirs — Sítio de Lazer
⊠ Airport — Flughafen — Aeropuerto — Aéroport — Aeroporto
■ Military Installation — Militäranlage — Instalación Militar — Installation militaire — Instalação Militar
⬥ Miscellaneous — Verschiedenes — Misceláneo — Divers — Miscelânea

Name	Page	Lat.	Long.
Burnage	262	53.26 N	2.12 W
Burnas, Ozero @	78	45.52 N	30.08 E
Burnet	196	30.46 N	98.14 W
Burnett ≃	166	24.46 S	152.25 E
Burnett Bay C	176	73.53 N	124.00 W
Burnett Brook ≃	276	40.46 N	74.38 W
Burnettsville	216	40.46 N	86.36 W
Burney, Calif., U.S.	204	40.53 N	121.40 W
Burney, Ind., U.S.	218	39.19 N	85.38 W
Burnham, Eng., U.K.	260	51.33 N	0.39 W
Burnham, Ill., U.S.	278	41.39 N	87.34 W
Burnham, Pa., U.S.	208	40.38 N	77.34 W
Burnham Beeches ◂[3]	260	51.34 N	0.38 W
Burnham Market	42	52.57 N	0.44 E
Burnham-on-Crouch	42	51.38 N	0.49 E
Burnham-on-Sea	42	51.15 N	3.00 W
Burnhamthorpe	275b	43.37 N	79.36 W
Burnhaven	46	57.29 N	1.47 W
Burnie	166	41.04 S	145.54 E
Burning Tree Estates	284c	39.01 N	77.12 W
Burnips	216	42.44 N	85.50 W
Burnley	44, 262	53.48 N	2.14 W
Burnley □[8]	262	53.46 N	2.15 W
Burnley Creek ≃	212	44.13 N	77.51 W
Burnley Football Ground ♠	262	53.48 N	2.14 W
Burnmouth	46	55.50 N	2.04 W
Burnoje	85	42.37 N	70.46 E
Burno-Okt'abr'skoje	85	42.42 N	70.49 E
Burnpur	126	23.40 N	86.57 E
Burns, Kans., U.S.	198	38.05 N	96.53 W
Burns, Oreg., U.S.	202	43.35 N	119.03 W
Burns, Tenn., U.S.	194	36.03 N	87.19 W
Burns, Wyo., U.S.	198	41.11 N	104.21 W
Burns Flat	196	35.21 N	99.10 W
Burns Harbor	216	41.37 N	87.10 W
Burnside, Austl.	168b	34.57 S	138.40 E
Burnside, Ky., U.S.	192	36.59 N	84.36 W
Burnside, Pa., U.S.	214	40.49 N	78.47 W
Burnside ≃	176	66.51 N	108.04 W
Burns Lake	182	54.14 N	125.46 W
Burnsville, Ala., U.S.	194	32.28 N	86.53 W
Burnsville, Miss., U.S.	194	34.51 N	88.19 W
Burnsville, N.C., U.S.	192	35.55 N	82.18 W
Burnsville, W. Va., U.S.	188	38.51 N	80.40 W
Burnt ≃, Ont., Can.	212	44.35 N	78.46 W
Burnt ≃, Oreg., U.S.	202	44.22 N	117.14 W
Burnt Cabins	214	40.05 N	77.54 W
Burnt Corn Creek ≃	194	31.06 N	87.04 W
Burnt Hills	210	42.55 N	73.54 W
Burnt Island, Newf., Can.	186	47.36 N	58.53 W
Burntisland, Scot., U.K.	46	56.03 N	3.15 W
Burnt Meadow Brook ≃	276	41.05 N	74.18 W
Burnt Mills, Lake @	208	36.50 N	76.38 W
Burnt Mountain ∧	228	33.12 N	117.04 W
Burntop	158	26.49 S	30.54 E
Burntwick Island I	260	51.25 N	0.41 E
Burntwood ≃	184	56.08 N	96.30 W
Burntwood Lake @	184	55.29 N	100.07 W
Buro	144	11.26 N	49.42 E
Buron	84	42.48 N	44.03 E
Buronzo	62	45.29 N	8.16 E
Burow	54	53.46 N	13.16 E
Burpengary	171a	27.10 S	152.57 E
Burpham	260	51.15 N	0.33 W
Burra	166	33.40 S	138.56 E
Burracoppin	162	31.23 S	118.29 E
Burrage	283	42.02 N	70.51 W
Burrage Pond @	283	42.01 N	70.52 W
Burragorang, Lake @	166	33.58 S	150.25 E
Burramurra	166	20.30 S	137.20 E
Burravoe	46a	60.32 N	1.28 W
Burrawang	170	34.36 S	150.31 E
Burray I	46	58.51 N	2.54 W
Burrel, Shq.	38	41.37 N	20.00 E
Burrel, Calif., U.S.	226	36.30 N	119.59 W
Burren Junction	166	30.06 S	148.58 E
Burriana	34	39.53 N	0.05 W
Burrinjuck Reservoir @[1]	166	35.00 S	148.45 E
Burro, Serranías del ⋀	232	28.56 N	101.32 W
Burr Oak, Ind., U.S.	216	41.15 N	86.25 W
Burr Oak, Kans., U.S.	198	39.52 N	98.18 W
Burr Oak, Mich., U.S.	216	41.51 N	85.19 W
Burroburro ≃	246	4.48 N	58.51 W
Burro Creek ≃	200	34.32 N	113.35 W
Burrowa, Mount ∧	171b	36.05 S	147.42 E
Burrow Head ≻	44	54.41 N	4.24 W
Burrowhill	260	51.21 N	0.36 W
Burrows	216	40.41 N	86.30 W
Burrows Island I	224	48.29 N	122.42 W
Burr Ridge	278	41.46 N	87.55 W
Burrs Mill Brook ≃	285	39.53 N	74.42 W
Burrton	198	38.02 N	97.41 W
Burrumbeet, Lake @	169	37.30 S	143.39 E
Burrundie	164	13.32 S	131.42 E
Burruyacú	252	26.30 S	64.45 W
Burrwood	194	28.58 N	89.22 W
Burry Holms I	42	51.37 N	4.18 W
Burry Port	42	51.42 N	4.15 W
Bürs	58	47.09 N	9.48 E
Bursa	130	40.11 N	29.04 E
Bursa □[4]	130	40.10 N	29.00 E
Būr Safājah	140	26.44 N	33.56 E
Būr Sa'īd (Port Said)	142	31.16 N	32.18 E
Būr Sa'īd □[8]	142	30.36 N	32.15 E
Burscheid	56	51.05 N	7.06 E
Burscough	262	53.35 N	2.51 W
Burscough Bridge	262	53.36 N	2.51 W
Bursey, Mount ∧	9	76.00 S	132.40 W
Burslem	42	53.02 N	2.12 W
Bursol'	86	53.11 N	78.27 E
Bürstadt	56	49.38 N	8.27 E
Burstall	184	50.40 N	109.54 W
Burštyn	78	49.17 N	24.37 E
Būr Sūdān (Port Sudan)	140	19.37 N	37.14 E
Burt, Iowa, U.S.	190	43.12 N	94.14 W
Burt, N.Y., U.S.	210	43.19 N	78.43 W
Būr Tawfīq	128	29.57 N	32.34 E
Burtenbach	58	48.20 N	10.26 E
Burt Lake @	190	45.27 N	84.40 W
Burton, B.C., Can.	182	49.59 N	117.54 W
Burton, Eng., U.K.	262	53.16 N	3.01 W
Burton, Ill., U.S.	219	39.55 N	91.15 W
Burton, Mich., U.S.	216	43.01 N	84.16 W
Burton, Mich., U.S.	216	43.02 N	83.36 W
Burton, Ohio, U.S.	214	41.28 N	81.09 W
Burton, Tex., U.S.	222	30.11 N	96.36 W
Burton, Wash., U.S.	224	47.23 N	122.28 W
Burton, Lake @[1]	192	34.50 N	83.33 W
Burton Fleming	44	54.08 N	0.20 W
Burton Latimer	42	52.23 N	0.41 W
Burtons Bridge	216	42.17 N	88.14 W
Burton Seamount ⟡[3]	14	32.00 S	171.55 W
Burtonsville	208	39.07 N	76.56 W
Burton-upon-Trent	42	52.49 N	1.36 W
Burtonwood	262	53.26 N	2.39 W
Burträsk	26	64.31 N	20.39 E
Burtundy	166	33.44 S	142.16 E
Burțus	142	30.09 N	31.08 E
Burtville	162	28.47 S	122.39 E
Buru I	108	3.24 S	126.40 E
Buruanga	116	11.51 N	121.53 E
Burukan	89	53.02 N	136.03 E
Buruldaj	85	42.48 N	75.52 E
Burullus, Buḥayrat al- @	142	31.30 N	30.50 E
Burūm	144	14.22 N	48.57 E
Burundaj	85	43.23 N	76.51 E
Burundi □[1]	138, 154	3.15 S	30.00 E
Burundučicha	80	58.21 N	46.07 E
Burun-Šibertuj, Gora ∧	88	49.43 N	109.59 E
Bururi	154	3.57 S	29.37 E
Burutu	150	5.21 N	5.31 E
Buruz Bāgān	126	23.03 N	89.00 E
Burwash	190	46.19 N	80.48 W
Burwash Landing	180	61.21 N	139.00 W
Burwell, Eng., U.K.	42	52.16 N	0.19 E
Burwell, Nebr., U.S.	198	41.47 N	99.08 W
Burwell Bay C	208	37.04 N	76.38 W
Burwick	46	58.44 N	2.57 W
Burwood, Austl.	274a	33.53 S	151.06 E
Burwood, Austl.	274b	37.51 S	145.06 E
Bury, Qué., Can.	206	45.28 N	71.30 W
Bury, Eng., U.K.	42	50.54 N	0.34 W
Bury, Eng., U.K.	262	53.36 N	2.17 W
Bury □[8]	262	53.35 N	2.19 W
Buryn'	78	51.13 N	33.49 E
Bury Saint Edmunds	42	52.15 N	0.43 E
Burzaco	258	34.49 S	58.24 W
Burzet	62	44.44 N	4.51 E
Burzil	123	34.52 N	75.07 E
Burzil Pass)(	123	34.54 N	75.06 E
Būş, Ghubbat al- C	142	29.36 N	32.22 E
Busa, Mount ∧	116	6.08 N	124.39 E
Busachi	71	40.02 N	8.54 E
Busalla	62	44.34 N	8.57 E
Busambra, Rocca ∧	70	37.51 N	13.24 E
Busan → Pusan	98	35.06 N	129.03 E
Busana	64	44.22 N	10.19 E
Busanga	152	0.51 S	22.04 E
Busanga Swamp ☰	154	14.10 S	25.50 E
Busangu	154	8.32 S	25.31 E
Buşayrah	130	35.09 N	40.26 E
Busby, Austl.	274a	33.54 S	150.53 E
Busby, Mont., U.S.	202	45.32 N	106.58 W
Busca	62	44.31 N	7.29 E
Buscate	266b	45.32 N	8.49 E
Buschberg ∧[2]	61	48.34 N	16.23 E
Busche	64	46.02 N	11.59 E
Busch Gardens ♠	280	34.13 N	118.28 W
Buschhausen ◂[8]	263	51.30 N	6.51 E
Busdorf	41	54.29 N	9.32 E
Buseto Palizzolo	70	38.01 N	12.43 E
Būsh	142	29.09 N	31.08 E
Bush ≃, N. Ire., U.K.	44	55.13 N	6.32 W
Bush ≃, S.C., U.S.	192	34.08 N	81.36 W
Bushadainuo	98	42.34 N	115.18 E
Būshehr	128	28.59 N	50.50 E
Bushenyi	154	0.32 S	30.11 E
Bushey	260	51.39 N	0.22 W
Bushey Heath	260	51.38 N	0.20 W
Bushi	268	35.50 N	139.22 E
Bushimaie ≃	152	6.02 S	23.45 E
Bushiribana	241s	12.33 N	69.58 W
Bushkill	210	41.06 N	75.00 W
Bush Kill ≃	210	41.05 N	74.59 W
Bushkill Falls ᒪ	210	41.09 N	75.01 W
Bushland	196	35.11 N	102.04 W
Bush Lot	246	6.12 N	57.16 W
Bushmills	48	55.12 N	6.32 W
Bushnell, Fla., U.S.	220	28.40 N	82.07 W
Bushnell, Ill., U.S.	190	40.33 N	90.30 W
Bush River ≃	208	39.21 N	76.14 W
Bushton	198	38.31 N	98.24 W
Bū Shubayrim, Wādī ∨	146	27.07 N	19.30 E
Bushwick ◂[8]	276	40.42 N	73.55 W
Bushy Head Mountain ∧	194	36.02 N	94.35 W
Bushy Park	166	21.16 S	139.43 E
Bushy Park ♠	260	51.25 N	0.20 W
Bushy Run ≃	279b	40.20 N	79.40 W
Bushy Run Battlefield ⊥	279b	40.21 N	79.38 W
Busi	144	5.30 N	44.30 E
Busia	154	0.28 N	34.05 E
Busigny	50	50.02 N	3.28 E
Businga	152	3.20 N	20.53 E
Büsingen	58	47.42 N	8.41 E
Busira ≃	152	0.15 S	18.59 E
Busjön @, Sve.	40	60.31 N	13.58 E
Busjön @, Sve.	40	60.06 N	13.28 E
Busk	78	49.58 N	24.37 E
Buskerud □[6]	26	60.25 N	9.12 E
Buskhyttan	40	58.40 N	16.56 E
Busko Zdrój	30	50.28 N	20.44 E
Buskul'	86	53.45 N	61.12 E
Busoga □[5]	154	0.40 N	33.30 E
Busovača	36	44.06 N	17.53 E
Buşrá al-Ḥarīrī (Bosor)	132	32.50 N	36.20 E
Buşrá ash-Shām	132	32.31 N	36.29 E
Bussa	150	10.15 N	4.33 E
Bussana	62	43.49 N	7.51 E
Bussang	58	47.53 N	6.51 E
Bussang, Col de)(	58	47.54 N	6.54 E
Busse	89	51.16 N	126.58 E
Busselton	162	33.39 S	115.20 E
Busseri ≃	140	7.41 N	28.03 E
Busseron Creek ≃	194	38.55 N	87.31 W
Busseto	64	44.59 N	10.02 E
Bussey	190	41.12 N	92.53 W
Bussières	62	45.50 N	4.16 E
Bussi sul Tirino	66	42.12 N	13.49 E
Bussolengo	64	45.28 N	10.51 E
Bussoleno	62	45.08 N	7.09 E
Bussum	52	52.16 N	5.10 E
Bussy-Rabutin, Château De ⊥	58	47.35 N	4.31 E
Bussy-Saint-Georges	261	48.51 N	2.42 E
Bustamante, Méx.	232	26.33 N	100.30 W
Bustamante, Méx.	234	23.26 N	99.47 W
Bustān, Wādī al- ∨	142	28.24 N	30.49 E
Buštěhrad	54	50.09 N	14.10 E
Buşteni	38	45.25 N	25.32 E
Busti	214	42.02 N	79.17 W
Bustleton ◂[8]	285	40.05 N	75.02 W
Busto Arsizio	62	45.37 N	8.51 E
Busto Garolfo	62	45.33 N	8.53 E
Buston, S.S.S.R.	85	40.31 N	69.19 E
Buston, S.S.S.R.	128	40.04 N	64.49 E
Buštyna	78	48.04 N	23.27 E
Busu-Adula	152	2.05 N	21.40 E
Busuanga	116	12.10 N	119.55 E
Busuanga Island I	116	12.05 N	120.05 E
Busu-Djanoa	152	1.43 N	21.23 E
Bušuicha	76	59.02 N	40.26 E
Bušulej	88	52.45 N	117.13 E
Büsum	30	54.08 N	8.51 E
Busu-Melo	152	1.48 N	20.15 E
Bū Sunbul, Jabal ∧[2]	146	23.10 N	22.21 E
Buta, S.S.S.R.	80	55.02 N	51.57 E
Buta, Zaïre	154	2.48 N	24.44 E
Butag	116	12.38 N	123.56 E
Butan	38	43.39 N	23.45 E
Bután → Bhutan □[1]	120	27.30 N	90.30 E
Butand State Park ♠	226	37.13 N	122.20 W
Butantã ◂[8]	287b	23.34 S	46.43 W
Butantã, Instituto ɤ[3]	287b	23.34 S	46.43 W
Buta Ranquil	252	37.03 S	69.50 W
Butare	154	2.36 S	29.44 E
Butarque, Arroyo de ≃	266a	40.19 N	3.39 W
Butauanan Island I	116	14.07 N	123.17 E
Buṭayḥah	132	32.56 N	35.53 E
Butchart Gardens ♠	224	48.33 N	123.28 W
Butcher Island (Dia Deva) I	272c	18.58 N	72.54 E
Bute	168b	33.52 S	138.01 E
Bute, Island of I	46	55.50 N	5.06 W
Bute, Kyles of ⊔	46	55.53 N	5.13 W
Bute, Sound of ⊔	46	55.44 N	5.12 W
Büteelijn Nuruu ⋀	88	50.00 N	104.50 E
Butehaqi (Zhalantun)	89	48.02 N	122.43 E
Bute Inlet C	182	50.37 N	124.53 W
Bute Jarti	144	4.34 N	37.48 E
Butemba	154	1.09 N	31.36 E
Butembo	154	0.09 N	29.17 E
Butendorf ◂[8]	263	51.33 N	6.59 E
Butera	70	37.11 N	14.11 E
Butere	154	0.13 N	34.30 E
Bütgenbach	56	50.26 N	6.12 E
Butha Buthe	158	28.45 S	28.15 E
Buthidaung	110	20.52 N	92.32 E
Buthier ≃	62	45.44 N	7.22 E
Buthroton ⊥	38	39.46 N	20.00 E
Buti	66	43.44 N	10.35 E
Butiá	252	30.07 S	51.58 W
Butiaba	154	1.49 N	31.19 E
Butig Mountains ⋀	116	7.39 N	124.20 E
Butka	86	56.47 N	63.47 E
Butler, Ala., U.S.	194	32.05 N	88.13 W
Butler, Ga., U.S.	192	32.34 N	84.14 W
Butler, Ill., U.S.	219	39.12 N	80.32 W
Butler, Ind., U.S.	216	41.26 N	84.52 W
Butler, Ky., U.S.	218	38.47 N	84.22 W
Butler, Mo., U.S.	194	38.16 N	94.20 W
Butler, N.J., U.S.	210	41.00 N	74.21 W
Butler, Ohio, U.S.	214	40.35 N	82.26 W
Butler, Okla., U.S.	196	35.38 N	99.11 W
Butler, Pa., U.S.	214	40.52 N	79.54 W
Butler, Tex., U.S.	222	30.19 N	97.18 W
Butler, Wis., U.S.	216	43.06 N	88.05 W
Butler □[6], Ohio, U.S.	218	39.26 N	84.30 W
Butler □[6], Pa., U.S.	214	40.52 N	79.54 W
Butler, Lake @	220	28.28 N	81.33 W
Butler Lake @	278	42.17 N	87.58 W
Butler Point ≻	207	41.40 N	70.43 W
Butler Reservoir @[1]	276	40.59 N	74.23 W
Butlers Bridge	48	54.02 N	7.22 W
Butlerville	218	39.02 N	85.31 W
Buto	152	15.46 S	15.09 E
Butong	112	1.06 S	114.50 E
Bütow → Bytów	30	54.11 N	17.30 E
Butru	166	21.30 S	139.43 E
Butsha	154	0.57 N	29.13 E
Buttapietra	64	45.20 N	11.00 E
Butte, Mont., U.S.	202	46.00 N	112.32 W
Butte, Nebr., U.S.	198	42.58 N	98.51 W
Butte □[6]	226	39.27 N	121.30 W
Butte City	226	39.28 N	121.59 W
Butte Creek ≃, Calif., U.S.	226	39.12 N	121.56 W
Butte Creek ≃, Oreg., U.S.	224	45.09 N	122.46 W
Butte du Lion ♠	50	50.40 N	4.24 E
Butte Falls	202	42.33 N	122.34 W
Buttelstedt	54	51.05 N	11.20 E
Butte Mountains ⋀	204	39.50 N	115.05 W
Butten	56	48.58 N	7.13 E
Butter Brook ≃	283	42.31 N	71.24 W
Butter Creek ≃	202	45.52 N	119.19 W
Butterfield, Ill., U.S.	278	41.50 N	88.02 W
Butterfield, Minn., U.S.	198	43.58 N	94.48 W
Butterfield Creek ≃	278	41.33 N	87.37 W
Butterfield Lake @	212	44.19 N	75.46 W
Butterley Reservoir @[1]	262	53.35 N	1.56 W
Buttermere	44	54.33 N	3.17 W
Butternut	190	46.01 N	90.30 W
Butternut Creek ≃, N.Y., U.S.	210	42.25 N	75.22 W
Butternut Creek ≃, N.Y., U.S.	210	43.06 N	76.00 W
Butterwick	42	52.59 N	0.05 E
Butterworth, Malay.	114	5.25 N	100.24 E
Butterworth, S. Afr.	158	32.23 S	28.04 E
Buttevant	48	52.14 N	8.40 W
Büttgen	56	51.12 N	6.36 E
Buttlar	56	50.45 N	9.57 E
Buttle Lake @	182	49.46 N	125.36 W
Button Islands II	176	60.35 N	64.45 W
Buttonville	275b	43.52 N	79.22 W
Buttonville Airfield ⊠	275b	43.52 N	79.23 W
Buttonwillow	226	35.24 N	119.28 W
Buttrio	64	46.01 N	13.20 E
Buttstädt	54	51.07 N	11.25 E
Butty Head ≻	162	33.54 S	121.38 E
Buttzville	210	40.50 N	75.00 W
Butuan	116	8.57 N	125.33 E
Butuan Bay C	116	9.06 N	125.20 E
Butuj	88	53.27 N	112.22 E
Bū Tumayyim, Wādī ∨	146	26.56 N	19.13 E
Butung, Pulau I	112	5.00 S	122.55 E
Buturlino, S.S.S.R.	80	55.34 N	44.55 E
Buturlino, S.S.S.R.	82	54.55 N	37.29 E
Buturlinovka	78	50.50 N	40.36 E
Butwal	124	27.42 N	83.27 E
Butylicy	80	55.32 N	41.31 E
Butzbach	56	50.26 N	8.40 E
Bützfleth	52	53.39 N	9.28 E
Bützow	54	53.50 N	11.59 E
Bützsee @	54	52.49 N	12.53 E
Butztown	208	40.39 N	75.22 W
Buwarah, Sabkhat al- ☰	130	35.09 N	41.12 E
Buwaydān	132	33.12 N	36.26 E
Buxar	124	25.35 N	83.59 E
Buxtehude	52	53.28 N	9.41 E
Buxton, Guy.	246	6.47 N	58.02 W
Buxton, S. Afr.	158	27.38 S	24.42 E
Buxton, Eng., U.K.	262	53.15 N	1.55 W
Buxton, N.C., U.S.	192	35.16 N	75.32 W
Buxton, N. Dak., U.S.	198	47.36 N	97.06 W
Buxton, Oreg., U.S.	224	45.41 N	123.12 W
Buxton, Mount ∧	182	51.35 N	127.55 W
Buxy	58	46.43 N	4.41 E
Buye	154	4.38 N	27.30 E
Buyiqiao	106	31.47 N	119.48 E
Büyükada I	267b	40.52 N	29.07 E
Büyük Ağrı Dağı ∧	84	39.42 N	44.18 E
Büyükarmudan	130	39.35 N	38.26 E
Büyükbakkal	267b	40.59 N	29.11 E
Büyükçekmece	130	41.01 N	28.34 E
Büyükdere ◂[8]	267b	41.09 N	29.02 E
Buyuk Doğanca	130	41.11 N	26.25 E
Büyükkale	130	38.01 N	27.34 E
Büyükkarıştıran	130	41.18 N	27.32 E
Büyük Lâçin	130	40.47 N	34.54 E
Büyükmenderes ≃	130	37.27 N	27.11 E
Büyükzap → Great Zab ≃	128	36.00 N	43.21 E
Buyun Uzun	128	39.13 N	63.19 E
Buzan ≃	80	46.18 N	49.06 E
Buzanaj, Peski ◂[2]	80	47.30 N	49.50 E
Buzançais	32	46.53 N	1.25 E
Buzancy	56	49.25 N	4.57 E
Bužaninovo	82	56.23 N	38.18 E
Bužarovo	82	55.59 N	36.47 E
Buzău	38	45.09 N	26.49 E
Buzău □[4]	38	47.40 N	23.00 E
Buzău ≃	38	45.26 N	27.44 E
Buzăului, Munții ⋀	38	45.35 N	26.10 E
Buzaymah	146	24.55 N	22.02 E
Buzen	96	33.40 N	131.18 E
Búzi ≃	156	19.50 S	34.43 E
Buziaș	38	45.39 N	21.36 E
Buziji	100	33.49 N	118.14 E
Buzinovka	80	48.32 N	43.53 E
Búzios, Ilha dos I	256	23.48 S	45.08 W
Búzios, Ponta dos ≻	255	22.44 S	41.53 W
Buzlanovo	265b	55.46 N	37.13 E
Buzovna	84	40.31 N	50.04 E
Buzu	144	15.35 N	50.55 E
Buzuluk, S.S.S.R.	80	52.47 N	52.15 E
Buzuluk, S.S.S.R.	86	51.55 N	66.16 E
Buzuluk ≃, S.S.S.R.	80	52.47 N	52.16 E
Buzuluk ≃, S.S.S.R.	80	50.13 N	42.12 E
Buzzards Bay	207	41.45 N	70.37 W
Buzzards Bay C	207	41.33 N	70.47 W
Bwana Mkubwa	154	13.01 S	28.42 E
Bwandougou	150	8.13 N	5.40 W
Bwasa	152	3.53 S	18.25 E
Bwendi	154	4.01 N	26.41 E
Bwlch	42	51.54 N	3.15 W
By	40	60.12 N	16.28 E
Byadgi	122	14.41 N	75.29 E
Byam Channel ⊔	176	75.20 N	105.20 W
Byam Martin Channel ⊔	176	75.45 N	104.00 W
Byam Martin Island I	176	75.15 N	104.00 W
Byberry Creek ≃	285	40.04 N	74.59 W
Byblos → Jubayl	130	34.07 N	35.39 E
Byček ≃	83	48.26 N	37.48 E
Bychawa	30	51.01 N	22.32 E
Bychov	76	53.32 N	30.12 E
Byčicha	76	55.41 N	29.58 E
Byčki, S.S.S.R.	76	54.15 N	34.39 E
Byčki, S.S.S.R.	80	53.38 N	40.54 E
Byculla ◂[8]	272c	18.58 N	72.49 E
Byczyna	30	51.07 N	18.11 E
Bydalen	26	63.06 N	13.47 E
Bydgoski, Kanał ☰	30	53.08 N	17.36 E
Bydgoszcz	30	53.08 N	18.00 E
Byelorussian Soviet Socialist Republic → Belorusskaja Sovetskaja Socialističeskaja Respublika □[3]	76	53.50 N	28.00 E
Byers, Pa., U.S.	285	40.05 N	75.41 W
Byers, Tex., U.S.	196	34.04 N	98.11 W
Byersdale	279b	40.37 N	80.13 W
Byers Run ≃	279b	40.24 N	79.42 W
Byesville	188	39.58 N	81.32 W
Byfang ◂[8]	263	51.24 N	7.06 E
Byfield, Eng., U.K.	42	52.11 N	1.14 W
Byfield, Mass., U.S.	207	42.46 N	70.57 W
Byfleet	260	51.20 N	0.29 W
Byford	168a	32.13 S	116.00 E
Bygdeå	26	64.04 N	20.51 E
Bygdeträsket @	26	64.26 N	20.32 E
Bygdin	26	61.20 N	8.48 E
Bygdin @	26	61.21 N	8.36 E
Bygi	80	57.13 N	53.44 E
Byglandsfjord	26	58.41 N	7.48 E
Byglandsfjorden @	26	58.48 N	7.50 E
Byhalia	194	34.52 N	89.41 W
Byk ≃	78	46.55 N	29.28 E
Bykle	26	59.21 N	7.20 E
Bykov	89	47.21 N	142.32 E
Bykovec	78	47.13 N	28.27 E
Bykovka, S.S.S.R.	78	50.17 N	27.58 E
Bykovka, S.S.S.R.	82	55.29 N	37.40 E
Bykovka ≃	265b	55.34 N	38.07 E
Bykovo, S.S.S.R.	80	49.47 N	45.22 E
Bykovo, S.S.S.R.	82	55.37 N	38.04 E
Bykovo, S.S.S.R.	82	54.01 N	37.54 E
Bykovo, Aeroport ⊠	82	55.36 N	38.05 E
Bylas	200	33.08 N	110.07 W
Bylbasovka	83	48.51 N	37.30 E
Bylderup	41	54.57 N	9.07 E
Byley	262	53.13 N	2.25 W
Bylkyldak	86	48.38 N	75.16 E
Bylnice	30	49.04 N	18.01 E
Bylot Island I	176	73.13 N	78.34 W
Byng Inlet	190	45.46 N	80.33 W
Bynum, Mont., U.S.	182	47.59 N	112.19 W
Bynum, N.C., U.S.	192	35.47 N	79.08 W
Bynum, Tex., U.S.	222	31.58 N	97.00 W
Byodoin Temple ɤ[1]	270	34.53 N	135.48 E
Byram ≃	276	40.59 N	73.39 W
Byramgore Reef ⟡[2]	122	11.54 N	71.49 E
Byram Lake Reservoir @[1]	276	41.10 N	73.41 W
Byrd ɤ[3]	9	80.00 S	120.00 W
Byrd, Lac @	190	47.01 N	76.56 W
Byrd Glacier ⧍	9	80.15 S	160.20 E
Byrd International Airport ⊠	208	37.30 N	77.19 W
Byrd Land ◂[1]	9	80.00 S	120.00 W
Byrdstown	194	36.34 N	85.08 W
Byrka	88	50.39 N	118.31 E
Byrnedale	214	41.17 N	78.30 W
Byro	162	26.05 S	116.09 E
Byrock	166	30.40 S	146.24 E
Byron, Calif., U.S.	226	37.52 N	121.38 W
Byron, Ga., U.S.	192	32.39 N	83.46 W
Byron, Ill., U.S.	190	42.08 N	89.15 W
Byron, Mich., U.S.	216	42.49 N	83.57 W
Byron, N.Y., U.S.	210	43.05 N	78.04 W
Byron, Wyo., U.S.	202	44.48 N	108.30 W
Byron, Cape ≻	166	28.39 S	153.38 E
Byron, Isla I	254	47.47 S	75.12 W
Byron Bay	166	28.39 S	153.37 E
Byron Center	216	42.49 N	85.42 W
Byšice-Liblice	54	50.19 N	14.38 E
Bysjön @	40	60.23 N	14.30 E
Byske	26	64.57 N	21.12 E
Byskeälven ≃	26	64.57 N	21.13 E
Bystraja ≃	80	47.58 N	41.00 E
Bystřany	54	50.38 N	13.51 E
Bystrica ≃	80	58.38 N	49.05 E
Bystřice	30	49.45 N	14.41 E
Bystřice pod Hostýnem	30	49.24 N	17.40 E
Bystrovka	85	42.47 N	75.43 E
Bystryj	86	57.50 N	73.58 E
Bystrzyca ≃	30	51.13 N	16.54 E
Bystrzyca Kłodzka	30	50.18 N	16.38 E
Bytantaj ≃	74	68.46 N	134.20 E
Bytča, Česko.	30	49.14 N	18.36 E
Bytča, S.S.S.R.	76	54.18 N	28.24 E
Byten'	76	52.54 N	25.29 E
Bytkov	78	48.38 N	24.26 E
Bytom (Beuthen)	30	50.22 N	18.54 E
Bytoš'	76	53.50 N	34.06 E
Bytów	30	54.11 N	17.30 E
Byumba	154	1.35 S	30.04 E
Byvalki	78	51.51 N	30.37 E
Byxelkrok	26	57.20 N	17.00 E
Bzura ≃	30	52.23 N	20.09 E
Bzybskij Chrebet ⋀	84	41.18 N	40.41 E
C			
Čaa-Chol'	86	51.32 N	92.23 E
Caacupé	252	25.23 S	57.09 W
Čaadajevka	80	53.09 N	45.56 E
Čaadajevo	80	55.40 N	42.02 E
Caaguazú	252	25.26 S	56.02 W
Caaguazú □[5]	252	25.00 S	55.45 W
Caamaño Sound ⊔	182	52.49 N	129.28 W
Caapiranga	246	3.18 S	61.13 W
Caapucú	252	26.13 S	57.12 W
Caazapá	252	26.09 S	56.24 W
Caazapá □[5]	252	26.10 S	56.00 W
Cabaçal ≃	248	16.00 S	57.42 W
Cabaceiras	250	7.30 S	36.17 W
Cabadbaran	116	9.10 N	125.38 E
Cabagan	116	17.26 N	121.46 E
Cabaiguán	240p	22.05 N	79.30 W
Cabalete Island I	116	14.17 N	121.50 E
Cabalian	116	10.16 N	125.10 E
Cabaliana, Lago @	246	3.20 S	60.50 W
Cabalian Bay C	116	10.13 N	125.10 E
Cabalian Point ≻	116	12.06 N	122.01 E
Caballería, Cabo de ≻	34	40.05 N	4.05 E
Caballero Creek ≃	280	34.11 N	118.32 W
Caballito ◂[8]	288	34.37 S	58.27 W
Caballocha	246	3.54 S	70.32 W
Caballones, Cayo I	240p	20.52 N	79.00 W
Caballo Reservoir @[1]	200	32.58 N	107.18 W
Caballos, Cerro de los ∧	234	23.04 N	102.55 W
Cabana	248	8.24 S	78.02 W
Cabanaconde	248	15.37 S	71.59 W
Cabañas	240p	22.58 N	82.55 W
Cabanatuan	116	15.29 N	120.58 E
Cabangan	116	15.10 N	120.03 E
Cabano	186	47.41 N	68.53 W
Čabanovka	83	49.02 N	38.46 E
Cabarruyan Island I	116	16.18 N	119.59 E
Cabaun Island I	116	12.34 N	124.30 E
Cabeceiras	255	15.48 S	46.59 W
Cabecera de Dupí	236	8.22 N	81.54 W
Cabeço de Montachique	266c	38.54 N	9.11 W
Cabedelo	250	6.58 S	34.50 W
Cabellera, Sierra de la ⋀	200	30.55 N	109.07 W
Cabery	216	41.00 N	88.12 W
Cabeza, Arrecife ⟡[2]	234	19.04 N	95.51 W
Cabeza del Buey	34	38.43 N	5.13 W
Cabeza de Tigre	286c	10.28 N	66.46 W
Cabezas	248	18.46 S	63.24 W
Cabiao	116	15.15 N	120.51 E
Cabiate	266b	45.40 N	9.10 E
Cabildo, Arg.	252	38.29 S	61.54 W
Cabildo, Chile	252	32.26 S	71.05 W
Cabimas	246	10.23 N	71.28 W
Cabin Branch ≃, Md., U.S.	284b	39.13 N	76.35 W
Cabin Branch ≃, Md., U.S.	284c	38.51 N	76.48 W
Cabin Creek ≃	198	46.55 N	104.52 W
Cabinda	152	5.33 S	12.12 E
Cabinda □[5]	152	5.00 S	12.30 E
Cabinet Mountains ⋀	202	48.08 N	115.46 W
Cabingaan Island I	116	5.41 N	121.03 E
Cabin John	208	38.58 N	77.09 W
Cabin John Creek ≃	284b	38.58 N	77.09 W
Cabin John Creek Park ♠	284c	38.59 N	77.09 W
Cabin John Regional Park ♠	284c	39.02 N	77.09 W
Cabiri	152	8.52 S	13.39 E
Cabirülensar	130	37.00 N	38.59 E
Cable	190	46.13 N	91.17 W
Cable Airport ⊠	280	34.08 N	117.41 W
Cables	162	27.59 S	123.23 E
Cabo	250	8.17 S	35.02 W
Cabo Blanco	254	47.12 S	65.45 W
Cabo Delgado □[5]	154	12.35 S	39.00 E
Cabo Frio	255	22.53 S	42.01 W
Cabo Gracias a Dios	236	14.59 N	83.10 W
Cabo Ledo	152	9.39 S	13.17 E
Cabonga, Réservoir @[1]	190	47.20 N	76.35 W
Cabool	194	37.07 N	92.06 W
Caboolture	166	27.05 S	152.57 E
Cabo Raso	254	44.21 S	65.14 W
Cabo Rojo	240m	18.05 N	67.09 W
Cabot, Ark., U.S.	194	34.58 N	92.01 W
Cabot, Pa., U.S.	214	40.46 N	79.46 W
Cabot, Mount ∧	188	44.31 N	71.24 W
Cabot Head ≻	212	45.14 N	81.17 W
Cabot Strait ⊔	186	47.20 N	59.30 W
Cabourg	32	49.17 N	0.08 W
Cabo Verde	256	21.28 S	46.24 W
Cabo Verde → Cape Verde □[1]	150a	16.00 N	24.00 W
Cabo Verde ≃	256	21.28 S	46.17 W
Cabo Verde, Ribeirão do ≃	256	21.20 S	44.32 W
Cabra	34	37.28 N	4.27 W
Cabral	238	18.15 N	71.13 W
Cabramatta	274a	33.54 S	150.56 E
Cabramurra	171b	35.58 S	148.23 E
Cabras	71	39.56 N	8.32 E
Cabras, Ribeirão das ≃	256	23.08 S	46.05 W
Cabras, Stagno di @	71	39.57 N	8.29 E
Cabras Island I	174p	13.27 N	144.40 E
Cabrel	234	20.06 N	105.14 W
Cabrera I	34	39.09 N	2.56 E
Cabrera ≃, Col.	246	3.26 N	75.07 W
Cabrera ≃, Esp.	34	42.25 N	6.49 W
Cabrera, Sierra de la ⋀	34	42.12 N	6.40 W
Cabrera de Mataró	266d	41.32 N	2.24 E
Cabreúva	256	23.18 S	47.08 W
Cabri	184	50.37 N	108.28 W
Cabriel ≃	34	39.14 N	1.03 W
Cabrillo National Monument ♠	228	32.41 N	117.15 W
Cabrils	266d	41.32 N	2.22 E
Cabrobó	250	8.31 S	39.19 W
Cabruta	246	7.38 N	66.15 W
Cabucan Island I	116	6.09 N	120.55 E
Cabucgayan	116	11.29 N	124.34 E
Cabuçu, Bra.	256	22.50 S	42.55 W
Cabuçu, Bra.	287a	22.47 S	43.32 W
Cabuçu, Bra.	287b	23.25 S	46.32 W
Cabuçu ≃	287a	22.59 S	43.37 W
Cabugao	116	17.48 N	120.27 E
Cabullones, Punta ≻	240m	17.58 N	66.35 W
Cabulo	152	10.15 S	16.40 E
Cabure	246	11.08 N	69.38 W
Cabusilan Mountains ⋀	116	15.05 N	120.22 E
Cabuta	152	9.50 S	14.48 E
Cabuya	236	9.36 N	85.06 W
Cabuyal	236	10.40 N	85.40 W
Cabuyaro	246	4.18 N	72.49 W
Caca	80	48.11 N	44.11 E
Caca, Laguna @	286b	22.57 N	82.27 W
Caçador	252	26.47 S	51.00 W
Cacahoatán	236	14.59 N	92.10 W
Čačak	38	43.53 N	20.21 E
Cacaluta	234	20.03 N	104.52 W
Cacaoui, Lac @	186	50.53 N	66.58 W
Caçapava	256	23.06 S	45.42 W
Caçapava do Sul	252	30.30 S	53.30 W
Caçapava Velha	256	23.07 S	45.39 W
Cacapon ≃	188	39.37 N	78.16 W
Cacapon State Park ♠	188	39.32 N	78.23 W
Cacas	130	38.23 N	41.17 E
Caccamo	70	37.56 N	13.40 E
Caccia, Capo ≻	71	40.34 N	8.09 E
Caccuri	68	39.14 N	16.47 E
Cacequi	252	29.53 S	54.49 W
Cáceres, Bra.	248	16.04 S	57.41 W
Cáceres, Col.	246	7.35 N	75.20 W
Cáceres, Esp.	34	39.29 N	6.22 W
Cachan	261	48.48 N	2.20 E
Cachán ≃	234	18.11 N	103.08 W
Cacharí	252	36.24 S	59.32 W
Cache	196	34.38 N	98.38 W
Cache ≃, Ark., U.S.	194	34.42 N	91.20 W
Cache ≃, Ill., U.S.	194	37.04 N	89.10 W
Caché, Lac @	206	46.21 N	74.39 W
Cache Creek	182	50.48 N	121.19 W
Cache Creek ≃, Calif., U.S.	226	38.42 N	121.42 W
Cache Creek ≃, Calif., U.S.	228	35.06 N	117.58 W
Cache Creek, North Fork ≃	226	38.59 N	122.30 W
Cache la Poudre ≃	200	40.25 N	104.36 W
Cache Mountain ∧	180	65.31 N	147.20 W
Cache Peak ∧, Calif., U.S.	228	35.13 N	118.15 W
Cache Peak ∧, Idaho, U.S.	202	42.11 N	113.40 W
Cache Slough ≃	226	38.11 N	121.40 W
Cacheu	150	12.16 N	16.10 W
Cacheu C[1]	150	12.10 N	16.21 W
Cachí	252	25.06 S	66.11 W
Cachimbo, Serra do ⋀	250	8.30 S	55.50 W
Cachimo	152	8.21 S	21.20 E
Cachingues	152	13.05 S	16.43 E
Cachir	88	48.06 N	98.52 E
Cáchira ≃	246	7.52 N	73.40 W
Cachkadzor	84	40.33 N	44.43 E
Cachoeira, Ribeirão ≃	287b	23.38 S	46.43 W
Cachoeira, Rio da ≃	287a	23.00 S	43.18 W
Cachoeira do Sul	252	30.02 S	52.54 W
Cachoeira Paulista	256	22.40 S	45.01 W
Cachoeiras	287a	22.39 S	43.28 W
Cachoeiras de Macacu	256	22.28 S	42.39 W
Cachoeirinha	250	8.29 S	36.14 W
Cachoeiro de Itapemirim	255	20.51 S	41.06 W
Cachorros, Rio dos ≃	287a	22.52 S	43.34 W
Cachos, Punta ≻	252	27.39 S	71.02 W
Cachos, Rio dos ≃	287b	23.36 S	46.26 W
Čachrov	60	49.16 N	13.18 E
Cachuela Esperanza	248	10.32 S	65.38 W
Cachuma, Lake @[1]	204	34.35 N	119.55 W
Cacilhas	266c	38.41 N	9.09 W
Cacimbinhas	250	9.24 S	36.59 W
Cacine	150	11.08 N	14.57 W
Caciporé ≃	250	3.51 N	51.08 W
Caciporé, Cabo ≻	250	3.55 N	51.07 W
Căciulați	38	44.38 N	26.10 E
Cacocum	240p	20.44 N	76.23 W
Cacólo	152	10.07 S	19.17 E
Caconda	152	13.43 S	15.06 E
Caconde	256	21.33 S	46.38 W
Cacra	248	12.48 S	75.48 W
Cactus Flat ≡	204	37.45 N	116.45 W
Cactus Peak ∧	204	37.47 N	116.53 W
Caçu	255	18.37 S	51.04 W
Cacuaco	152	8.47 S	13.22 E
Cacula	152	14.29 S	14.10 E
Caculé	255	14.30 S	42.13 W
Caçumba, Ilha I	255	17.46 S	39.17 W
Cacuri	152	8.14 S	18.20 E
Cacuso	152	9.26 S	15.43 E
Čadan	86	51.17 N	91.35 E
Cadaqués	34	42.17 N	3.17 E
Čadca	30	49.26 N	18.48 E
Caddo, Okla., U.S.	196	34.07 N	96.16 W
Caddo, Tex., U.S.	196	32.38 N	98.40 W
Caddo ≃	194	34.10 N	93.03 W
Caddo Creek ≃	196	34.14 N	96.59 W
Caddo Lake @[1]	194	32.42 N	94.01 W
Caddo Mills	222	33.04 N	96.14 W
Caddo Peak ∧	222	32.29 N	97.24 W
Caddy Vista	216	42.50 N	87.54 W
Cadena, Arroyo de la ≃	196	26.17 N	104.00 W
Cadena, Cerro ∧	196	25.50 N	104.04 W
Cadena, Punta ≻	240m	18.18 N	67.14 W
Cadenberge	52	53.46 N	9.04 E
Cadenet	62	43.44 N	5.22 E
Cadeo	62	44.58 N	9.48 E
Cader Bronwyn ∧	42	52.54 N	3.22 W
Cadereyta Jiménez	232	25.36 N	100.00 W
Cader Idris ∧	42	52.42 N	3.54 W
Cadig Mountains ⋀	116	14.05 N	122.35 E
Cadillac, Sask., Can.	184	49.44 N	107.43 W
Cadillac, Fr.	32	44.38 N	0.19 W
Cadillac, Mich., U.S.	190	44.15 N	85.24 W
Cadipietra (Steinhaus)	64	46.59 N	11.59 E
Cadishead	262	53.25 N	2.26 W
Cadix → Cádiz	34	36.32 N	6.18 W
Cádiz, Esp.	34	36.32 N	6.18 W
Cadiz, Pil.	116	10.57 N	123.18 E
Cadiz, Ind., U.S.	218	39.57 N	85.30 W
Cadiz, Ohio, U.S.	214	40.16 N	81.00 W
Cádiz, Bahía de C	34	36.32 N	6.16 W
Cádiz, Golfo de C	34	36.50 N	7.10 W
Cadiz Lake @	204	34.18 N	115.24 W
Cadnam	42	50.55 N	1.35 W
Čadobec	88	58.40 N	98.51 E
Čadobec ≃	88	58.40 N	98.50 E
Cadogan	214	40.45 N	79.35 W
Cadomin	182	53.02 N	117.20 W
Cadoneghe	64	45.26 N	11.55 E
Cadore ◂[1]	64	46.30 N	12.20 E
Cadosia	210	41.58 N	75.16 W
Cadott	190	44.57 N	91.09 W
Cadoux	162	30.47 S	117.08 E
Cadron Creek, North Fork ≃	194	35.17 N	92.29 W
Cadure, Fosso delle ≃	267a	41.56 N	12.12 E
Caduruan Point ≻	116	11.45 N	124.05 E
Cadwell	192	32.20 N	83.03 W
Cady Marsh Ditch ☰	278	41.33 N	87.29 W
Cady Mountain ∧[2]	224	48.33 N	123.07 W
Čadyr-Lunga	78	46.03 N	28.47 E
Cadzand	52	51.22 N	3.25 E
Caen	32	49.11 N	0.21 W
Caengo (Kwenge) ≃	152	4.50 S	18.42 E
Caerano di San Marco	64	45.47 N	12.00 E
Caere ⊥	66	42.02 N	12.07 E
Caergwrle	44	53.07 N	3.03 W
Caerleon	42	51.37 N	2.57 W
Caernarvon	44	53.08 N	4.16 W
Caernarvon Bay C	44	53.05 N	4.30 W
Caernarvon Castle ⊥	44	53.08 N	4.16 W
Caerphilly	42	51.35 N	3.14 W
Caerphilly Castle ⊥	42	51.34 N	3.14 W
Caersws	42	52.31 N	3.25 W
Caesar Creek ≃	218	39.29 N	84.06 W
Caesar Creek, Anderson Fork ≃	218	39.33 N	83.58 W
Caetanópolis	255	19.18 S	44.24 W
Caeté	255	19.54 S	43.40 W
Caeté ≃	248	9.03 S	68.39 W
Caetité	255	14.04 S	42.29 W
Cafayate	252	26.05 S	65.58 W
Cafelândia do Leste Matogrossense	255	16.40 S	53.25 W
Cafima	152	16.39 S	16.27 E
Cafu	152	16.27 S	15.14 E
Cafuini ≃	246	1.17 N	57.11 W
Cafundó	256	22.31 S	46.25 W
Cagaan Nuur @	88	48.10 N	99.42 E
Cágado ≃	256	22.02 S	43.09 W
Čagan ≃	80	51.12 N	51.20 E
Cagan-Aman	80	47.34 N	46.43 E
Cagan-Churtej, Chrebet ⋀	88	51.32 N	110.00 E
Cagarra, Ilhas II	287a	23.02 S	43.12 W
Cagayan □[4]	116	18.00 N	121.50 E
Cagayan ≃	116	18.22 N	121.37 E
Cagayancillo	116	9.34 N	121.12 E
Cagayan de Oro	116	8.29 N	124.39 E
Cagayan de Sulu	116	7.01 N	118.30 E
Cagayan Islands II	116	9.40 N	121.16 E
Cagayan Sulu Island I	116	7.01 N	118.30 E
Čagda	74	58.45 N	130.37 E
Cageri	84	42.39 N	42.45 E
Caggiano	68	40.34 N	15.29 E
Çağış	130	39.30 N	28.01 E
Çağlarca	130	39.05 N	39.10 E
Cagli	66	43.33 N	12.39 E
Cagliari	71	39.13 N	9.07 E
Cagliari □[4]	71	39.30 N	8.45 E
Cagliari, Golfo di C	71	39.08 N	9.11 E

Symbols in the index entries represent the broad categories identified in the key at the right. Symbols with superior numbers (⋀[2]) identify subcategories (see complete key on page I · 30).

Kartensymbole in dem Registerverzeichnis stellen die rechts in Schlüssel erklärten Kategorien dar. Symbole mit hochgestellten Ziffern (⋀[2]) bezeichnen Unterabteilungen einer Kategorie (vgl. vollständiger Schlüssel auf Seite I · 30).

Los símbolos incluidos en el texto del índice representan las grandes categorías identificadas con la clave a la derecha. Los símbolos con numeros en su parte superior (⋀[2]) identifican las subcategorías (véase la clave completa en la página I · 30).

Les symboles de l'index représentent les catégories indiquées dans la légende à droite. Les symboles suivis d'un indice (⋀[2]) représentent des sous-catégories (voir légende complète à la page I · 30).

Os símbolos incluidos no texto do índice representam as grandes categorias identificadas com a chave à direita. Os símbolos com números em sua parte superior (⋀[2]) identificam as subcategorias (veja-se a chave completa à página I · 30).

Symbol	English	Deutsch	Español	Français	Português
∧	Mountain	Berg	Montaña	Montagne	Montanha
⋀	Mountains	Berge	Montañas	Montagnes	Montanhas
)(	Pass	Pass	Paso	Col	Passo
∨	Valley, Canyon	Tal, Cañon	Valle, Cañón	Vallée, Canyon	Vale, Canhão
≡	Plain	Ebene	Llano	Plaine	Planície
≻	Cape	Kap	Cabo	Cap	Cabo
I	Island	Insel	Isla	Île	Ilha
II	Islands	Inseln	Islas	Îles	Ilhas
◂	Other Topographic Features	Andere Topographische Objekte	Otros Elementos Topográficos	Autres données topographiques	Outros Elementos Topográficos

ESPAÑOL — Nombre / Página / Lat.°′ / Long.°′ W=Oeste
FRANÇAIS — Nom / Page / Lat.°′ / Long.°′ W=Ouest
PORTUGUÊS — Nome / Página / Lat.°′ / Long.°′ W=Oeste

Cagliari, Stagno di ◎ 71 39.13 N 9.02 E
Cagnano Varano 68 41.49 N 15.47 E
Çagnes-sur-Mer 62 43.40 N 7.09 E
Çagoda 76 59.10 N 35.17 E
Çagoda ≃ 76 59.05 N 35.18 E
Çagodošča ≃ 76 58.57 N 36.35 E
Çagra ≃ 80 52.37 N 48.15 E
Çagrankaya 84 40.47 N 40.33 E
Cagraray Island I 116 13.18 N 123.52 E
Cagua 246 10.11 N 67.27 W
Caguán ≃ 246 0.08 S 74.18 W
Caguas 240m 18.14 N 66.02 W
Cagveri 84 41.48 N 43.29 E
Cagwait 116 8.55 N 126.18 E
Cahaba ≃ 194 32.20 N 87.05 W
Cahabón 236 15.34 N 89.49 W
Cahabón ≃ 236 15.25 N 89.36 W
Cahama 152 16.17 S 14.19 E
Caha Mountains ⋀ 48 51.45 N 9.45 W
Caher 48 52.21 N 7.56 W
Caherdaniel 48 51.45 N 10.05 W
Cahirciveen 48 51.57 N 10.13 W
Cahokia 219 38.33 N 90.10 W
Cahokia Creek ≃ 219 38.47 N 90.01 W
Cahokia Mounds State Park ♦ 219 38.39 N 90.03 W
Cahoon Creek ≃ 279a 41.29 N 81.55 W
Cahoon Park ♦ 279a 41.29 N 81.56 W
Cahoonzie 210 41.26 N 74.43 W
Cahore Point ≻ 48 52.34 N 6.11 W
Cahors 32 44.27 N 1.26 E
Cahto Peak ⋀ 204 39.41 N 123.35 W
Cahuilla Indian Reservation ⁴ 204 33.30 N 116.43 W
Cahuinari ≃ 246 1.21 S 70.44 W
Cahuita, Punta ≻ 236 9.45 N 82.49 W
Caí ≃ 252 29.56 S 51.16 W
Caia ≃ 34 38.50 N 7.05 W
Caiabis, Serra dos ⋀¹ 248 11.30 S 56.30 W
Caianda 152 11.02 S 23.31 E
Caiapó ≃, Bra. 250 8.52 S 49.36 W
Caiapó ≃, Bra. 255 15.49 S 51.53 W
Caiapó, Serra ⋀ 255 17.00 S 52.00 W
Caiapônia 255 16.57 S 51.49 W
Caiazzo 68 41.11 N 14.22 E
Caibarién 240p 22.31 N 79.28 W
Caibiran 116 11.34 N 124.35 E
Caiçara, Bra. 250 5.04 S 36.03 W
Caiçara, Bra. 250 6.36 S 35.29 W
Caiçara, Bra. 255 15.34 S 50.12 W
Caicara, Ven. 246 7.37 N 66.10 W
Caicara ≃ 246 3.11 S 64.49 W
Caicara, Caño ≃ 246 7.44 N 69.04 W
Caicara de Maturín 246 9.49 N 63.36 W
Caicedonia 246 4.20 N 75.50 W
Caicó 250 6.27 S 37.06 W
Caicos Islands II 238 21.56 N 71.58 W
Caicos Passage 凵 238 22.00 N 72.30 W
Caicun 105 39.28 N 117.01 E
Caieiras 256 23.22 S 46.44 W
Caieiras □⁷ 287b 23.23 S 46.41 W
Caigou 100 33.16 N 114.32 E
Caihuaping 100 26.54 N 113.23 E
Caijiachang, Zhg. 107 29.44 N 106.29 E
Caijiachang, Zhg. 107 29.53 N 105.02 E
Caijiagang 107 28.55 N 106.21 E
Caijialou 104 41.24 N 121.06 E
Caijiazhen 102 34.17 N 107.39 E
Caijiazhuang 105 40.48 N 114.44 E
Caille 62 43.46 N 6.44 E
Cailloma 248 15.12 S 71.46 W
Caillou Bay C 194 29.06 N 90.56 W
Caima Bay C 116 13.42 N 122.48 E
Caimán, Islas → Cayman Islands □² 238 19.30 N 80.40 W
Caimanera 240p 19.59 N 75.09 W
Caïmanes → Cayman Islands □² 238 19.30 N 80.40 W
Caiman Point ≻ 116 15.55 N 119.46 E
Caimbambo 152 12.58 S 14.01 E
Cain ≃ 42 52.46 N 3.08 W
Cain Creek ≃ 198 44.17 N 98.10 W
Cainde 152 15.42 S 13.12 E
Caine ≃ 248 18.23 S 65.21 W
Caino 64 45.38 N 10.18 E
Cains ≃ 186 46.40 N 65.47 W
Cainsdorf 54 50.41 N 12.29 E
Cainsville 194 40.26 N 93.47 W
Cai-nuoc 110 8.56 N 105.01 E
Cairano 68 40.54 N 15.22 E
Cairari 250 2.33 S 49.07 W
Caire, Le → Al-Qāhirah 142 30.03 N 31.15 E
Cairnbrook 214 40.07 N 78.49 W
Cairn Curran Reservoir ◎¹ 169 37.04 S 143.59 E
Cairndow 46 56.15 N 4.56 W
Cairngorm Mountains ⋀ 46 57.04 N 3.50 W
Cairn Mountain ⋀ 180 61.10 N 155.20 W
Cairnryan 44 54.58 N 5.02 W
Cairns 166 16.55 S 145.46 E
Cairns Lake ◎ 184 51.42 N 94.30 W
Cairnsmore of Carsphairn ⋀ 44 55.15 N 4.12 W
Cairnsmore of Fleet ⋀ 44 54.59 N 4.20 W
Cairn Table ⋀ 44 55.29 N 4.02 W
Cairn Water ≃ 44 55.07 N 3.45 W
Cairo → Al-Qāhirah, Miṣr 142 30.03 N 31.15 E
Cairo, Ga., U.S. 192 30.53 N 84.12 W
Cairo, Ill., U.S. 194 37.00 N 89.11 W
Cairo, Nebr., U.S. 198 41.00 N 98.36 W
Cairo, N.Y., U.S. 210 42.18 N 74.00 W
Cairo, Ohio, U.S. 216 40.50 N 84.05 W
Cairo, W. Va., U.S. 188 39.13 N 81.09 W
Cairo (Almaza) Airport ⊠, Miṣr 273c 30.06 N 31.22 E
Cairo (Imbābah) Airport ⊠, Miṣr 273c 30.04 N 31.12 E
Cairo, University of ♥² 273c 30.02 N 31.02 E
Cairoçu, Pico do ⋀ 256 23.18 S 44.36 W
Cairofa 152 14.05 S 12.54 E
Cairo International Airport ⊠ 142 30.08 N 31.24 E
Cairo Montenotte 62 44.24 N 8.16 E
Cairu 255 13.30 S 39.03 W
Caister-on-Sea 42 52.39 N 1.44 E
Caistor 44 53.30 N 0.20 W
Caitingqiao 105 39.54 N 117.39 E
Caitou 152 14.28 S 13.06 E
Caiundo 152 15.46 S 17.28 E
Caiwan 102 25.50 N 110.50 E
Caixi 100 25.15 N 116.28 E
Caiyu I 100 22.39 N 115.30 E
Caiyuzhen 105 39.39 N 116.37 E
Caiza 248 20.02 S 65.40 W
Caizhuang 98 34.17 N 114.08 E
Çaja ≃, S.S.S.R. 86 58.08 N 82.57 E
Çaja ≃, S.S.S.R. 88 58.15 N 109.35 E
Cajabamba, Ec. 246 1.42 S 78.45 W
Cajabamba, Perú 248 7.37 S 78.03 W
Cajacay 248 10.10 S 77.26 W
Caja de Muertos, Isla I 240m 17.54 N 66.32 W
Cajamar 256 23.21 S 46.53 W
Cajamarca 248 7.10 S 78.31 W
Cajamarca □⁵ 248 6.15 S 78.50 W
Cajan 85 43.02 N 69.23 E
Cajapió 250 2.58 S 44.48 W
Cajarc 32 44.29 N 1.50 E
Cajari 250 3.20 S 45.01 W
Cajari ≃ 250 0.48 S 51.43 W
Çajatambo 248 10.29 S 77.02 W
Çajatyn, Chrebet ⋀ 89 52.25 N 138.25 E
Çajázeiras 250 6.54 S 38.34 W
Çajek 85 41.56 N 74.30 E
Çajkovskij 80 56.47 N 54.09 E
Çajniče 38 43.33 N 19.04 E
Cajones ≃ 234 17.45 N 95.55 W
Cajones, Cayos II 236 16.05 N 83.12 W
Cajon Mountain ⋀ 228 34.16 N 117.25 W
Cajon Pass)(228 34.19 N 117.26 W
Cajon Summit)(228 34.21 N 117.27 W
Caju ⁸ 287a 22.53 S 43.13 W
Cajueiro 250 9.25 S 36.08 W
Cajuru 255 21.17 S 47.18 W
Çakeni 152 17.48 S 19.27 E
Çakir 88 50.27 N 103.35 E
Çakıralan 130 41.10 N 35.47 E
Çakmak 130 37.37 N 34.19 E
Çakmak Dağı ⋀ 130 39.46 N 42.12 E
Čakovec 61 46.23 N 16.26 E
Čakovice ⁸ 54 50.08 N 14.31 E
Çakung ≃ 269e 6.11 S 106.55 E
Çakva 84 41.44 N 41.45 E
Çal 130 38.05 N 29.24 E
Cala, S. Afr. 158 31.30 S 27.37 E
Cala, Tür. 84 41.05 N 43.21 E
Cala, Embalse de ◎¹ 34 37.50 N 6.00 W
Calabacillas 234 23.13 N 99.45 W
Calabanga 116 13.42 N 123.12 E
Calabar 150 4.57 N 8.19 E
Calabasas, Arroyo ≃ 280 34.12 N 118.36 W
Calabazar ⁸ 286b 23.01 N 82.22 W
Calabazas Creek ≃ 282 37.25 N 121.58 W
Calabernardo 70 36.52 N 15.08 E
Calabogie 212 45.18 N 76.43 W
Calabogie Lake ◎ 212 45.16 N 76.45 W
Calabozo 246 8.56 N 67.26 W
Calabozo, Ensenada de C 246 11.30 N 71.45 W
Calabria □⁴ 68 39.00 N 16.30 E
Calabritto 68 40.47 N 15.13 E
Calabro ≃ 70 37.53 N 14.11 E
Calaca 116 13.56 N 120.49 E
Calacuccia 36 42.20 N 9.03 E
Caladang, Mount ⋀ 116 14.49 N 121.21 E
Caladesi Island I 220 28.02 N 82.49 W
Caladesi Island State Park ♦ 220 28.02 N 82.48 W
Cala d'Oliva 71 41.05 N 8.20 E
Calafat 38 43.59 N 22.56 E
Calafate 254 50.20 S 72.18 W
Calafquen, Lago ◎ 254 39.31 S 72.10 W
Cala Gonone 71 40.18 N 9.38 E
Calaguas Islands II 116 14.27 N 122.55 E
Calahorra 34 42.18 N 1.58 W
Calais, Fr. 50 50.57 N 1.50 E
Calais, Maine, U.S. 188 45.11 N 67.17 W
Calais, Canal de ☰ 50 50.58 N 1.51 E
Calala 152 12.59 S 23.30 E
Calalaste, Sierra de ⋀ 252 25.30 S 67.30 W
Calalzo di Cadore 64 46.27 N 12.23 E
Calama, Bra. 248 8.03 S 62.53 W
Calama, Chile 252 22.28 S 68.56 W
Calamar, Col. 246 1.58 N 72.41 W
Calamar, Col. 246 10.15 N 74.55 W
Calamarca 248 16.55 S 68.09 W
Calamba, Pil. 116 10.11 N 123.17 E
Calamba, Pil. 116 8.35 N 123.39 E
Calamba, Pil. 116 14.13 N 121.10 E
Calamian Group II 116 12.00 N 120.00 E
Calamity Creek ≃ 196 29.41 N 103.42 W
Calamocha 34 40.55 N 1.18 W
Calamonaci 70 37.31 N 13.17 E
Calamus ≃ 198 41.48 N 99.09 W
Calañas 34 37.39 N 6.53 W
Calanca, Val ∨ 58 46.22 N 9.07 E
Calanda 34 40.56 N 0.14 W
Calang 114 4.38 N 95.34 E
Calangianus 71 40.56 N 9.11 E
Calanna 68 38.11 N 15.43 E
Calapan 116 13.25 N 121.10 E
Calape 116 9.54 N 123.52 E
Calapooia ≃ 202 44.38 N 123.08 W
Calapooya Mountains ⋀ 202 43.30 N 122.50 W
Călărași 38 44.11 N 27.20 E
Cala Ratjada 34 39.42 N 3.25 E
Calarcá 246 4.31 N 75.38 W
Calascibetta 70 37.35 N 14.16 E
Calasetta 71 39.07 N 8.22 E
Calatabiano 70 37.49 N 15.14 E
Calatafimi 70 37.55 N 12.52 E
Calatagan 116 13.50 N 120.38 E
Calatayud 34 41.21 N 1.38 W
Calatrava 54 51.45 N 13.56 E
Calauag Bay ≃ 116 14.02 N 122.13 E
Calauan 116 14.09 N 121.19 E
Calauit Island I 116 12.18 N 119.54 E
Calavà, Capo ≻ 70 38.11 N 14.55 E
Calaveras □⁶ 226 38.12 N 120.41 W
Calaveras ≃ 226 37.58 N 121.22 W
Calaveras, North Fork ≃ 226 38.12 N 120.43 W
Calaveras Big Trees State Park ♦ 226 38.16 N 120.19 W
Calaveras Point ≻ 282 37.28 N 122.03 W
Calaveras Reservoir ◎¹ 226 37.28 N 121.49 W
Calaveritas Creek ≃ 226 38.10 N 120.40 W
Calavino 64 46.03 N 10.59 E
Calavite, Cape ≻ 116 13.27 N 120.18 E
Calavite, Mount ⋀ 116 13.29 N 120.24 E
Calavite Passage 凵 116 13.36 N 120.25 E
Calavon ≃ 62 43.51 N 5.00 E
Calawah ≃ 224 47.56 N 124.27 W
Calawah, North Fork ≃ 224 47.58 N 124.20 W
Calawah, South Fork ≃ 224 47.58 N 124.20 W
Calayan 116 19.16 N 121.28 E
Calayan Island I 116 19.20 N 121.27 E
Calba 89 52.43 N 131.27 E
Calbayog 116 12.04 N 124.36 E
Calbe 54 51.54 N 11.46 E
Calbiga 116 11.38 N 125.01 E
Calbuco 254 41.46 S 73.08 W
Calca 248 13.20 S 71.57 W
Calcado 250 8.45 S 36.20 W
Calcasieu ≃ 194 30.05 N 93.20 W
Calcasieu Lake ◎ 194 29.50 N 93.17 W
Calceta 246 0.51 S 80.10 W
Calcha 248 21.06 S 67.31 W
Calchaquí 252 29.54 S 60.18 W
Calchaquí ≃ 252 26.03 S 65.50 W
Calciano 68 40.35 N 16.11 E
Calcinaia 66 43.41 N 10.37 E
Calcinato 64 45.27 N 10.24 E
Calcio 62 45.30 N 9.50 E
Calcium 212 44.01 N 75.51 W
Calçoene 250 2.30 N 50.57 W
Calcutta, Bhārat 126 (blank)
Calcutta 272b 22.32 N 88.22 E
Calcutta, Ohio, U.S. 214 40.41 N 80.34 W
Calcutta □⁵ 126 22.30 N 88.30 E
Calcutta, University of ♥² 272b 22.35 N 88.22 E
Caldaro (Kaltern) 64 46.25 N 11.14 E
Caldarola 66 43.08 N 13.13 E
Caldas, Bra. 256 21.56 S 46.23 W
Caldas, Col. 246 6.05 N 75.38 W
Caldas □⁵ 246 5.15 N 75.30 W
Caldas ≃ 266d 41.31 N 2.13 E
Caldas da Rainha 34 39.24 N 9.08 W
Caldas de Reyes 34 42.36 N 8.38 W
Caldas Novas 255 17.45 S 48.38 W
Caldé 58 45.57 N 8.38 E
Caldecott Tunnel ⁵ 282 37.52 N 122.12 W
Caldeirão, Serra do ⋀ 34 37.42 N 8.21 W
Calder, Loch ◎ 46 58.31 N 3.36 W
Caldera 252 27.04 S 70.50 W
Calder and Hebble Navigation Canal ☰ 262 53.43 N 1.54 W
Calder Bridge 44 54.27 N 3.29 W
Calderbrook 262 53.39 N 2.05 W
Calderdale □⁸ 262 53.44 N 2.00 W
Caldere 130 40.49 N 37.01 E
Calderstones Park ♦ 262 53.23 N 2.54 W
Caldes 64 46.22 N 10.56 E
Caldew ≃ 44 54.54 N 2.56 W
Caldey Island I 42 51.38 N 4.41 W
Caldicot 42 51.36 N 2.45 W
Caldiero 64 45.22 N 11.11 E
Çaldıran 84 39.09 N 43.55 E
Caldonazzo 64 45.59 N 11.16 E
Caldonazzo, Lago di ◎ 64 46.01 N 11.15 E
Čáldonka 88 53.47 N 119.12 E
Caldwell, Idaho, U.S. 202 43.40 N 116.41 W
Caldwell, Kans., U.S. 198 37.02 N 97.37 W
Caldwell, N.J., U.S. 276 40.51 N 74.17 W
Caldwell, Ohio, U.S. 188 39.45 N 81.31 W
Caldwell, Tex., U.S. 222 30.32 N 96.42 W
Caldwell □⁶ 222 29.50 N 97.40 W
Caldwell Creek ≃ 214 41.37 N 79.37 W
Caldwell-Wright Airport ⊠ 276 40.53 N 74.17 W
Caldy 262 53.21 N 3.10 W
Cale ≃ 42 50.59 N 2.20 W
Caledon, Ont., Can. 212 43.52 N 80.00 W
Caledon, S. Afr. 158 34.12 S 19.23 E
Caledon ≃ 158 30.31 S 26.05 E
Caledon East 212 43.52 N 79.52 W
Caledonia, Belize 232 18.14 N 88.29 W
Caledonia, N.S., Can. 186 44.22 N 65.02 W
Caledonia, Ont., Can. 212 43.04 N 79.56 W
Caledonia, Ill., U.S. 216 42.22 N 88.53 W
Caledonia, Mich., U.S. 216 42.47 N 85.31 W
Caledonia, Minn., U.S. 190 43.38 N 91.29 W
Caledonia, Miss., U.S. 194 33.39 N 88.20 W
Caledonia, N.Y., U.S. 210 42.58 N 77.51 W
Caledonia, Ohio, U.S. 214 40.38 N 82.58 W
Caledonia, Pa., U.S. 214 41.17 N 78.27 W
Caledonian Canal ☰ 46 56.50 N 5.06 W
Caledonia State Park ♦ 208 39.56 N 77.29 W
Calego 152 12.10 S 23.36 E
Calella 34 41.37 N 2.40 E
Calemba 152 16.04 S 15.44 E
Calen 166 20.54 S 148.46 E
Calendžicha 84 42.37 N 42.04 E
Calenzano 66 43.51 N 11.09 E
Calera 194 33.06 N 86.45 W
Calera Creek ≃ 282 37.27 N 121.54 W
Calera Victor Rosales 234 22.57 N 102.42 W
Caleta, Punta ≻ 240p 20.04 N 74.18 W
Caleta Olivia 254 46.26 S 67.32 W
Caleufú 252 35.35 S 64.33 W
Calexico 232 32.40 N 115.30 W
Calf Island I 283 42.20 N 70.54 W
Calf Islands II 276 40.59 N 73.38 W
Calfkiller ≃ 194 35.49 N 85.29 W
Calf of Man I 44 54.03 N 4.48 W
Calfpasture ≃ 188 37.58 N 79.28 W
Calf Pasture Point ≻ 276 41.05 N 73.24 W
Çalgan 130 37.35 N 38.19 E
Calgary 182 51.03 N 114.05 W
Calhan 198 39.02 N 104.18 W
Calhariz ⁸ 266c 38.44 N 9.12 W
Calhoun, Ala., U.S. 194 32.03 N 86.33 W
Calhoun, Ga., U.S. 192 34.30 N 84.57 W
Calhoun, Ky., U.S. 194 37.32 N 87.16 W
Calhoun, Mo., U.S. 194 38.28 N 93.37 W
Calhoun, Tenn., U.S. 192 35.17 N 84.45 W
Calhoun □⁶, Ill., U.S. 219 39.09 N 90.37 W
Calhoun □⁶, Mich., U.S. 216 42.14 N 85.00 W
Calhoun City 194 33.51 N 89.19 W
Calhoun Falls 192 34.06 N 82.36 W
Cali, Col. 246 3.27 N 76.31 W
Çalı, Tür. 130 40.10 N 28.54 E
Calicoan Island I 116 10.59 N 125.48 E
Calico Ghost Town ⊥ 228 34.57 N 116.52 W
Calico Rock 194 36.07 N 92.09 W
Calicut 122 11.15 N 75.46 E
Caliente, Calif., U.S. 228 35.17 N 118.38 W
Caliente, Nev., U.S. 204 37.37 N 114.31 W
Caliente Creek ≃ 228 35.17 N 118.48 W
Califon 210 40.43 N 74.50 W
California, Mo., U.S. 194 38.38 N 92.34 W
California, Pa., U.S. 214 40.04 N 79.53 W
California □³ 178 (blank)
California 204 37.30 N 119.30 W
California, Golfo de C 232 28.00 N 112.00 W
California, University of (U.C.L.A.) ♥², Calif., U.S. 280 34.04 N 118.26 W
California, University of ♥², Calif., U.S. 282 37.52 N 122.15 W
California Aqueduct ☰¹ 204 33.52 N 117.12 W
California City 228 35.08 N 117.58 W
California Creek ≃ 196 33.05 N 99.33 W
California Institute of Technology ♥² 280 34.08 N 118.08 W
California Institution for Men ♥ 280 33.59 N 117.40 W
California Institution for Women ♥ 280 33.57 N 117.38 W
California State College (Dominguez Hills) ♥² 280 33.52 N 118.17 W
California State Polytechnic University ♥² 280 34.04 N 117.49 W
California State University (Northridge) ♥², Calif., U.S. 280 34.14 N 118.32 W
California State University (Long Beach) ♥², Calif., U.S. 280 33.47 N 118.06 W
California State University (Fullerton) ♥², Calif., U.S. 280 33.53 N 117.53 W
California State University (Los Angeles) ♥², Calif., U.S. 280 34.04 N 118.10 W
California State University (Hayward) ♥², Calif., U.S. 282 37.39 N 122.04 W
Calihualá 234 17.35 N 98.10 W
Calilegua 252 23.47 S 64.47 W
Călimănești 38 45.14 N 24.20 E
Călimani, Munții ⋀ 38 47.07 N 25.03 E
Calimera 68 40.15 N 18.17 E
Calimere, Point ≻ 122 10.18 N 79.52 E
Calimesa 228 34.00 N 117.03 W
Calindó ≃ 255 14.26 S 43.51 W
Calingasta 252 31.19 S 69.25 W
Calingiri 162 31.06 S 116.27 E
Calinog 116 11.07 N 122.32 E
Calintaan 116 12.35 N 120.56 E
Calion 194 33.20 N 92.32 W
Calipatria 204 33.08 N 115.31 W
Calispell Peak ⋀ 202 48.26 N 117.30 W
Calistoga 226 38.35 N 122.35 W
Calitri 68 40.54 N 15.27 E
Calitzdorp 158 33.33 S 21.42 E
Calixtlahuaca ⊥ 234 19.20 N 99.42 W
Calizzano 62 44.14 N 8.07 E
Calka 84 41.37 N 44.05 E
Calkinskoje, Vodochranilišče ◎¹ 84 41.38 N 44.03 E
Čalkojdy 85 40.44 N 73.39 E
Calla 226 37.46 N 121.11 W
Callabonna, Lake ◎ 166 29.45 S 140.04 E
Callabonna Creek ≃ 166 29.38 S 140.08 E
Callac 32 48.24 N 3.26 W
Callaghan, Mount ⋀ 204 39.42 N 116.57 W
Callahan 192 30.34 N 81.49 W
Callahans 276 40.58 N 74.37 W
Callan 48 52.33 N 7.23 W
Callander, Ont., Can. 190 46.13 N 79.23 W
Callander, Scot., U.K. 46 56.15 N 4.14 W
Callang 116 17.02 N 121.38 E
Callanish 46 58.12 N 6.43 W
Callanmarca 248 12.52 S 74.38 W
Callanna 166 29.38 S 137.55 E
Callantsoog 52 52.49 N 4.41 E
Callao, Perú 248 (blank)
Callao 286d 12.04 S 77.09 W
Callao, Va., U.S. 208 37.58 N 76.34 W
Callao □⁴ 286d 12.04 S 77.09 W
Callas 62 43.35 N 6.32 E
Callaway 198 41.17 N 99.56 W
Callaway □⁶ 219 38.50 N 91.52 W
Calle 56 51.20 N 8.13 E
Callensburg 214 41.08 N 79.33 W
Callery 214 40.45 N 80.02 W
Call Hill ⋀² 210 42.13 N 77.40 W
Calliano, It. 62 45.00 N 8.15 E
Calliano, It. 64 45.56 N 11.05 E
Calliaqua 241h 13.08 N 61.12 W
Callicoon 210 41.46 N 75.03 W
Callicoon Center 210 41.50 N 74.57 W
Calliham 196 28.29 N 98.21 W
Calling Lake 182 55.15 N 113.12 W
Calling Lake ◎ 182 55.13 N 113.15 W
Callington, Austl. 168b 35.07 S 139.02 E
Callington, Eng., U.K. 42 50.30 N 4.18 W
Calliope 166 24.00 S 151.12 E
Callosa de Ensarriá 34 38.39 N 0.07 W
Callosa de Segura 34 38.08 N 0.52 W
Calloway Canal ☰ 226 35.24 N 119.01 W
Calmar, Alta., Can. 182 53.16 N 113.49 W
Calmar → Kalmar, Sve. 26 56.40 N 16.22 E
Calmar, Iowa, U.S. 190 43.11 N 91.52 W
Călmățui ≃ 38 44.50 N 27.50 E
Calmazzo 66 43.40 N 12.46 E
Calmbach 56 48.46 N 8.35 E
Calm Lake ◎ 190 48.46 N 92.04 W
Čal'mny-Varre 24 67.10 N 37.33 E
Çalna 24 61.55 N 34.01 E
Calnalí 234 20.55 N 98.35 W
Calne 42 51.27 N 2.00 W
Calobre 236 8.19 N 80.51 W
Calola 152 16.30 S 17.51 E
Calolbon 116 13.36 N 124.06 E
Calolziocorte 62 45.48 N 9.26 E
Calonne-Ricouart 50 50.29 N 2.29 E
Caloocan 269f 14.39 N 120.58 E
Caloosahatchee ≃ 220 26.31 N 82.01 W
Caloosahatchee Canal ☰ 220 26.46 N 81.27 W
Caloote 168b 34.58 S 139.16 E
Calore ≃, It. 68 40.31 N 15.01 E
Calore ≃, It. 68 41.11 N 14.28 E
Calotlán ≃ 234 22.06 N 103.42 W
Caloundra 166 26.48 S 153.09 E
Caloveto 68 39.30 N 16.45 E
Calpan 234 19.06 N 98.27 W
Calpe 34 38.39 N 0.03 E
Calpulalpan 234 19.35 N 98.35 W
Çalpy 80 55.05 N 53.06 E
Calshot 42 50.49 N 1.19 W
Calstock 42 50.30 N 4.12 W
Caltabellotta 70 37.34 N 13.13 E
Caltagirone 70 37.14 N 14.31 E
Caltagirone ≃ 70 37.21 N 14.42 E
Caltanissetta 70 37.29 N 14.04 E
Caltanissetta □⁴ 70 37.29 N 14.04 E
Caltavuturo 70 37.49 N 13.53 E
Çaltılıbük 130 39.57 N 28.36 E
Çaltra 48 53.26 N 8.25 W
Çaltyr' 83 47.17 N 39.30 E
Caluango 152 8.21 S 19.40 E
Calubian 116 11.27 N 124.26 E
Calucinga 152 11.18 S 16.12 E
Călugăreni 38 44.07 N 26.01 E
Caluire-et-Cuire 62 45.48 N 4.51 E
Calulo 152 10.00 S 14.53 E
Calumbolaca 152 9.09 S 13.48 E
Calumet, Mich., U.S. 190 47.14 N 88.27 W
Calumet, Minn., U.S. 190 47.19 N 93.17 W
Calumet, Pa., U.S. 214 40.13 N 79.28 W
Calumet ≃ 278 41.44 N 87.32 W
Calumet, Lake ◎ 278 41.41 N 87.35 W
Calumet City 216 41.37 N 87.31 W
Calumet Harbor C 278 41.44 N 87.32 W
Calumet Park 278 41.44 N 87.32 W
Calumet Park ♦ 278 41.43 N 87.32 W
Calumet Sag Channel ☰ 278 41.42 N 87.57 W
Calunda 152 12.06 S 23.23 E
Caluquembe 152 13.47 S 14.44 E
Calusa Island I 116 9.37 N 121.01 E
Caluso 62 45.18 N 7.53 E
Caluya Island I 116 11.55 N 121.34 E
Calvados □⁵ 32 49.10 N 0.30 W
Calvello 68 40.28 N 15.51 E
Calvene 64 45.46 N 11.30 E
Calvert, Ala., U.S. 194 31.09 N 88.01 W
Calvert, Tex., U.S. 222 30.59 N 96.40 W
Calvert □⁶ 208 38.33 N 76.35 W
Calvert ≃ 166 16.17 S 137.44 E
Calvert Hills 166 17.15 S 137.20 E
Calvert Island I 182 51.35 N 128.00 W
Calverton, Md., U.S. 284c 39.03 N 76.56 W
Calverton, N.Y., U.S. 207 40.55 N 72.45 W
Calvi 32 42.34 N 8.45 E
Calvi, Monte ⋀ 66 43.05 N 10.37 E
Calvi dell'Umbria 66 42.24 N 12.34 E
Calvillo 234 21.51 N 102.43 W
Calvin, Okla., U.S. 196 34.58 N 96.15 W
Calvin, Pa., U.S. 214 40.22 N 78.02 W
Calvinia 158 31.25 S 19.45 E
Calvisano 64 45.20 N 10.20 E
Calvo, Monte ⋀ 68 41.44 N 15.46 E
Calvörde 54 52.23 N 11.17 E
Calw 56 48.43 N 8.44 E
Calwa 226 36.42 N 119.46 W
Calypso 192 35.09 N 78.06 W
Calzada 248 6.02 S 77.02 W
Cam ≃ 42 52.21 N 0.15 E
Camabatela 152 8.11 S 15.22 E
Camaçari 255 12.41 S 38.18 W
Camachigama, Lac ◎ 190 47.50 N 76.19 W
Camacho, Bra. 256 22.20 S 47.13 W
Camacho, Méx. 232 24.25 N 102.18 W
Camacosni 236 14.57 N 85.08 W
Camaguán 246 8.06 N 67.36 W
Camagüey 240p 21.23 N 77.55 W
Camagüey □⁴ 240p 21.30 N 78.00 W
Camagüey, Archipiélago de II 240p 22.18 N 78.00 W
Camaiore 64 43.56 N 10.18 E
Camaiú ≃ 248 5.30 S 59.42 W
Camajuaní 240p 22.28 N 79.44 W
Camaldoli, Eremo di ♥¹ 66 43.46 N 11.47 E
Camaldoli ♥¹ 64 43.48 N 11.46 E
Camamu 255 13.57 S 39.07 W
Camaná 248 16.37 S 72.42 W
Camaná ≃ 248 16.39 S 72.46 W
Camananaú ≃ 246 1.51 S 61.14 W
Camanche 190 41.47 N 90.15 W
Camanche Reservoir ◎¹ 226 38.13 N 120.58 W
Camanducaia 256 22.46 S 46.09 W
Camanducaia ≃, Bra. 256 22.55 S 46.25 W
Camanducaia ≃, Bra. 256 22.39 S 46.58 W
Camano Island I 224 48.10 N 122.30 W
Camaoi ≃ 250 3.12 S 48.04 W
Camapuã 255 19.30 S 54.05 W
Camaquã 252 30.51 S 51.49 W
Camaquã ≃ 252 31.17 S 51.47 W
Camará 246 3.55 S 62.44 W
Camarajibe 250 8.01 S 34.58 W
Camararé ≃ 248 12.15 S 58.55 W
Camarat, Cap ≻ 62 43.12 N 6.41 E
Camarda 66 42.23 N 13.29 E
Çamardı 130 37.50 N 35.00 E
Camarès 32 43.49 N 2.53 E
Camargo 248 20.39 S 65.13 W
Camarillo 228 34.13 N 119.02 W
Camarillo Heights 228 34.14 N 119.02 W
Camarina ⊥ 70 36.52 N 14.27 E
Camariñas 34 43.07 N 9.10 W
Camarines Norte □⁴ 116 14.10 N 122.40 E
Camarines Sur □⁴ 116 13.35 N 123.20 E
Camarón, Arroyo ≃ 196 27.08 N 100.00 W
Camarón, Cabo ≻ 236 16.00 N 85.05 W
Camaronero, Laguna C 234 23.00 N 106.07 W
Camarones 254 44.48 S 65.42 W
Camarones, Bahía C 254 44.45 S 65.34 W
Camas, Esp. 34 37.24 N 6.02 W
Camas, Wash., U.S. 224 45.35 N 122.24 W
Camas Creek ≃, Idaho, U.S. 202 44.53 N 114.44 W
Camas Creek ≃, Idaho, U.S. 202 43.53 N 112.21 W
Camas Creek ≃, Idaho, U.S. 202 43.20 N 114.24 W
Camas Creek ≃, Oreg., U.S. 202 45.01 N 118.59 W
Camastra 70 37.15 N 13.47 E
Camatambo 152 6.30 S 15.18 E
Ca-mau → Quan-long 110 9.11 N 105.08 E
Ca-mau, Mui ≻ 110 8.38 N 104.44 E
Camaxilo 152 8.21 S 18.56 E
Camba 112 4.54 S 119.50 E
Camba Cassai 152 9.40 S 19.18 E
Cambados 34 42.30 N 8.48 W
Cambaquara 256 23.54 S 45.27 W
Cambará 255 23.03 S 50.05 W
Cambay 120 22.18 N 72.37 E
Camberg 56 50.18 N 8.16 E
Camberley 42 51.21 N 0.45 W
Camberwell 169 37.50 S 145.04 E
Camberwell ⁸ 260 51.28 N 0.05 W
Cambiano 62 44.58 N 7.47 E
Cambo 44 55.10 N 1.57 W
Cambo ≃ 152 7.40 S 17.17 E
Cambodia → Kâmpŭchéa □¹ 110 13.00 N 105.00 E
Cambois 44 55.10 N 1.31 W
Cambonda, Serra ⋀ 152 12.06 S 14.00 E
Camboon 166 25.03 S 150.26 E
Cambooya 171a 27.42 S 151.52 E
Camboriú 252 27.01 S 48.38 W
Camboriú, Ponta ≻ 252 25.10 S 47.55 W
Camborne 42 50.12 N 5.19 W
Cambra 210 41.12 N 76.18 W
Cambrai, Austl. 168b 34.39 S 139.17 E
Cambrai, Fr. 50 50.10 N 3.14 E
Cambremer 50 49.09 N 0.03 E
Cambria, Calif., U.S. 226 35.34 N 121.05 W
Cambria, Ind., U.S. 216 40.22 N 86.33 W
Cambria, Mich., U.S. 216 41.49 N 84.40 W
Cambria, Wis., U.S. 190 43.33 N 89.06 W
Cambria □⁶ 214 40.29 N 79.16 W
Cambria Ice Field ☐ 182 55.55 N 129.30 W
Cambrian Mountains ⋀ 42 52.35 N 3.35 W
Cambrian Park 226 37.16 N 121.56 W
Cambridge (Galt), Ont., Can. 212 43.22 N 80.19 W
Cambridge, N.Z. 172 37.53 S 175.28 E
Cambridge, Eng., U.K. 42 52.13 N 0.08 E
Cambridge, Idaho, U.S. 202 44.34 N 116.41 W
Cambridge, Ill., U.S. 190 41.18 N 90.12 W
Cambridge, Iowa, U.S. 190 41.54 N 93.32 W
Cambridge, Md., U.S. 208 38.34 N 76.04 W
Cambridge, Mass., U.S. 207 42.22 N 71.06 W
Cambridge, Minn., U.S. 190 45.31 N 93.14 W
Cambridge, Nebr., U.S. 198 40.17 N 100.10 W
Cambridge, N.Y., U.S. 210 43.02 N 73.23 W
Cambridge, Ohio, U.S. 188 40.02 N 81.35 W
Cambridge, Wis., U.S. 216 43.00 N 89.01 W
Cambridge Bay 176 69.03 N 105.05 W
Cambridge City 218 39.49 N 85.10 W
Cambridge Fiord C² 176 71.20 N 74.44 W
Cambridge Gulf C 164 14.55 S 128.15 E
Cambridge Park 274a 33.45 S 150.43 E
Cambridge Reservoir ◎¹ 283 42.24 N 71.16 W
Cambridgeshire □⁶ 42 52.20 N 0.05 E
Cambridge Springs 214 41.48 N 80.04 W
Cambrils 34 41.04 N 1.03 E
Cambuci 255 21.34 S 41.55 W
Cambuci ⁸ 287b 23.34 S 46.37 W
Cambuí 256 22.37 S 46.04 W
Cambulo 152 7.48 S 21.14 E
Cambuquira 256 21.51 S 45.18 W
Cambural 286c 10.26 N 66.59 W
Camburg 54 51.03 N 11.42 E
Camburu ≃ 256 23.41 S 45.28 W
Çamby 218 39.40 N 86.19 W
Camčakly 128 37.56 N 63.06 E
Camden, Austl. 170 34.03 S 150.42 E
Camden, S. Afr. 158 26.36 S 30.07 E
Camden, Ala., U.S. 194 31.59 N 87.17 W
Camden, Ark., U.S. 194 33.35 N 92.50 W
Camden, Del., U.S. 208 39.07 N 75.33 W
Camden, Ill., U.S. 219 40.09 N 90.46 W
Camden, Ind., U.S. 216 40.37 N 86.32 W
Camden, Maine, U.S. 188 44.12 N 69.04 W
Camden, Mich., U.S. 216 41.45 N 84.46 W
Camden, Miss., U.S. 194 32.42 N 89.50 W
Camden, N.J., U.S. 208 39.57 N 75.07 W
Camden, N.Y., U.S. 210 43.20 N 75.45 W
Camden, N.C., U.S. 192 36.20 N 76.10 W
Camden, Ohio, U.S. 218 39.38 N 84.39 W
Camden, S.C., U.S. 192 34.16 N 80.36 W
Camden, Tenn., U.S. 194 36.04 N 88.06 W
Camden, Tex., U.S. 222 30.55 N 94.44 W
Camden □⁶, N.J., U.S. 208 39.57 N 75.07 W
Camden □⁶, N.C., U.S. 208 36.28 N 76.21 W
Camden ⁸ 260 51.33 N 0.10 W
Camden, Groupe II 254 54.40 S 71.58 W
Camden Aerodrome ⊠ 274a 34.03 S 150.41 E
Camden Bay C 180 70.00 N 145.00 W
Camden Hills State Park ♦ 188 44.17 N 69.05 W
Camden Lake ◎ 212 44.25 N 76.52 W
Camden Station ⁵ 284b 39.17 N 76.37 W
Camdenton 194 38.00 N 92.45 W
Camedo 58 46.09 N 8.37 E
Cameia, Parque Nacional da ♦ 152 11.45 S 21.20 E
Camel ≃ 42 50.33 N 4.55 W
Camel, Mount ⋀ 169 36.45 S 144.43 E
Camelback Mountain ⋀, Alaska, U.S. 180 62.33 N 157.20 W
Camelback Mountain ⋀, Pa., U.S. 210 41.03 N 75.21 W
Camelford 42 50.37 N 4.41 W
Camels Back ⋀ 172 36.58 S 175.35 E
Camels Hump ⋀ 188 44.19 N 72.53 W
Cameo Acres 282 37.51 N 121.58 W
Camerano 66 43.32 N 13.33 E
Cameri 62 45.30 N 8.39 E
Cameri, Aeroporto ⊠ 266b 45.32 N 8.40 E
Camerino 66 43.08 N 13.04 E
Cameron, La., U.S. 194 29.48 N 93.19 W
Cameron, Mo., U.S. 194 39.44 N 94.14 W
Cameron, N.Y., U.S. 210 42.12 N 77.24 W
Cameron, Pa., U.S. 214 41.27 N 78.10 W
Cameron, S.C., U.S. 192 33.33 N 80.43 W
Cameron, Tex., U.S. 222 30.51 N 96.59 W
Cameron, W. Va., U.S. 188 39.50 N 80.34 W
Cameron, Wis., U.S. 190 45.25 N 91.44 W
Cameron □⁶ 214 41.31 N 78.14 W
Cameron ≃ 224 49.17 N 124.38 W
Cameron, Lac ◎ 206 46.06 N 74.50 W
Cameron Highlands 114 4.29 N 101.27 E
Cameron Hills ⋀² 176 59.48 N 118.00 W
Cameron Lake ◎, B.C., Can. 224 49.17 N 124.37 W
Cameron Lake ◎, Ont., Can. 212 44.34 N 78.45 W
Cameron Mills 210 42.11 N 77.22 W
Cameron Mountains ⋀ 172 46.00 S 167.00 E
Cameron Run ≃ 284c 38.48 N 77.04 W
Cameroon □¹ 134 6.00 N 12.00 E
Camerota 68 40.02 N 15.23 E
Cameroun → Cameroon □¹ 134 6.00 N 12.00 E
Cameroun, Mont ⋀ 150 4.12 N 9.11 E
Cameroun Occidental □⁴ 152 5.30 N 9.30 E
Cameroun Oriental □⁴ 152 6.00 N 13.00 E
Camerún → Cameroon □¹ 134 6.00 N 12.00 E
Cametá 250 2.15 S 49.30 W
Camfield 164 17.09 S 131.21 E
Camiçi 130 40.40 N 37.00 E
Camiguin □⁴ 116 9.15 N 124.40 E
Camiguin Island I, Pil. 116 9.11 N 124.42 E
Camiguin Island I, Pil. 116 18.56 N 121.55 E
Camiling 116 15.42 N 120.24 E
Camilla 192 31.14 N 84.12 W
Camillus 210 43.02 N 76.19 W
Camin 54 53.27 N 10.58 E
Camiña 248 19.18 S 69.26 W
Caminha 34 41.52 N 8.50 W
Camino 226 38.44 N 120.41 W
Camiranga 250 1.48 S 46.17 W
Camiri 248 20.03 S 63.31 W
Camisano Vicentino 64 45.31 N 11.43 E
Camiyanı 130 40.52 N 38.38 E
Camlad ≃ 42 52.36 N 3.10 W
Çamlıbel 130 40.05 N 36.29 E
Çamlica 130 40.46 N 26.39 E
Çamlıdere 130 40.30 N 32.29 E
Cam-lo 110 16.49 N 106.59 E
Cammal 210 41.24 N 77.28 W
Cammarata 70 37.38 N 13.38 E
Cammin → Kamień Pomorski 30 53.58 N 14.46 E
Camoapa 236 12.23 N 85.31 W
Camocim 250 2.54 S 40.50 W
Camogli 62 44.21 N 9.09 E
Camonica, Val ∨ 64 46.00 N 10.20 E
Camooweal 166 19.55 S 138.07 E
Camopi ≃ 250 3.11 N 52.20 W
Camorim ≃ 287a 22.59 S 43.25 W
Camorim, Represa do ◎¹ 287a 22.58 S 43.27 W
Camorta Island I 110 8.08 N 93.30 E
Camotes Islands II 116 10.40 N 124.24 E
Camotes Sea ⁷² 116 10.30 N 124.15 E
Camotlán ≃ 234 22.01 N 104.15 W
Camowen ≃ 48 54.36 N 7.18 W
Camp □⁶ 222 33.00 N 94.58 W
Campagna 68 40.40 N 15.08 E
Campagna di Roma ∨¹ 66 41.50 N 12.35 E
Campagna Lupia 64 45.21 N 12.06 E
Campagnano di Roma 66 42.08 N 12.23 E
Campagnatico 66 42.53 N 11.16 E
Campagne-lès-Hesdin 50 50.24 N 1.52 E
Campaign 194 35.46 N 85.38 W
Campamento 236 14.33 N 86.42 W
Campamento, Cerro ⋀ 286a 19.18 N 99.17 W
Campana, Arg. 258 34.10 S 58.57 W
Campana, It. 68 39.24 N 16.50 E
Campana, Isla I 254 48.20 S 75.15 W
Campanario 34 38.52 N 5.37 W
Campanario, Cerro de ⋀ 248 5.57 S 77.31 W
Campanella, Punta ≻ 68 40.34 N 14.19 E
Campanha 256 21.50 S 45.24 W
Campania □⁴ 68 40.55 N 14.50 E
Camparadra 266b 45.39 N 9.19 E
Campaspe ≃, Austl. 166 21.00 S 146.24 E
Campaspe ≃, Austl. 169 36.41 S 144.31 E
Campbell, S. Afr. 158 28.48 S 23.44 E
Campbell, Calif., U.S. 226 37.17 N 121.57 W
Campbell, Mo., U.S. 194 36.30 N 90.04 W
Campbell, Nebr., U.S. 198 40.18 N 98.44 W
Campbell, N.Y., U.S. 210 42.14 N 77.12 W
Campbell, Ohio, U.S. 214 41.05 N 80.36 W
Campbell, Tex., U.S. 222 33.09 N 95.57 W
Campbell □⁶ 218 38.55 N 84.20 W
Campbell, Cape ≻ 172 41.44 S 174.17 E
Campbell Airport ⊠, Ill., U.S. 278 42.20 N 88.04 W
Campbell Airport ⊠, Pa., U.S. 279b 40.21 N 80.11 W
Campbellfield 274b 37.41 S 144.57 E
Campbellford 212 44.18 N 77.48 W
Campbell Hall 210 41.27 N 74.16 W
Campbell Hill ⋀² 216 40.22 N 83.43 W
Campbell Island I 182 52.10 N 128.09 W
Campbell Island I 9 52.30 S 169.05 E
Campbell Lake ◎ 182 50.01 N 125.27 W
Campbell Plateau ⁴³ 9 56.00 S 165.00 E
Campbellpore 123 33.46 N 72.22 E
Campbell Range ⋀ 180 61.08 N 129.45 W
Campbell River 182 50.01 N 125.15 W
Campbells Bay 188 45.44 N 76.36 W
Campbellsburg, Ind., U.S. 218 38.39 N 86.16 W
Campbellsburg, Ky., U.S. 218 38.31 N 85.12 W
Campbell Slough ≃ 226 39.22 N 121.51 W
Campbellsport 190 43.36 N 88.17 W
Campbells River 170 33.54 S 149.37 E
Campbells Run ≃ 279b 40.24 N 80.05 W
Campbellsville 194 37.21 N 85.20 W
Campbellton, N.B., Can. 186 48.00 N 66.40 W
Campbellton, Newf., Can. 186 49.17 N 54.56 W

Symbol	English	Deutsch	Español	Français	Português
≃	River	Fluss	Rio	Rivière	Rio
☰	Canal	Kanal	Canal	Canal	Canal
⌊	Waterfall, Rapids	Wasserfall, Stromschnellen	Cascada, Rápidos	Chute d'eau, Rapides	Cascata, Rápidos
凵	Strait	Meeresstrasse	Estrecho	Détroit	Estreito
C	Bay, Gulf	Bucht, Golf	Bahía, Golfo	Baie, Golfe	Baía, Golfo
◎	Lake, Lakes	See, Seen	Lago, Lagos	Lac, Lacs	Lago, Lagos
☷	Swamp	Sumpf	Pantano	Marais	Pântano
☐	Ice Features, Glacier	Eis- und Gletscherformen	Accidentes Glaciales	Formes glaciaires	Acidentes Glaciares
⁷	Other Hydrographic Features	Andere Hydrographische Objekte	Otros Elementos Hidrográficos	Autres données hydrographiques	Outros Elementos Hidrográficos
⁴	Submarine Features	Untermeerische Objekte	Accidentes Submarinos	Formes de relief sous-marin	Acidentes Submarinos
□	Political Unit	Politische Einheit	Unidad Política	Entité politique	Unidade Política
♥	Cultural Institution	Kulturelle Institution	Institución Cultural	Institution culturelle	Instituição Cultural
⊥	Historical Site	Historische Stätte	Sitio Histórico	Site historique	Sitio Histórico
♦	Recreational Site	Erholungs- und Ferienort	Sitio de Recreo	Centre de loisirs	Sitio de Lazer
⊠	Airport	Flughafen	Aeropuerto	Aéroport	Aeroporto
■	Military Installation	Militäranlage	Instalación Militar	Installation militaire	Instalação Militar
⁵	Miscellaneous	Verschiedenes	Misceláneo	Divers	Miscelânea

ENGLISH — Name | Page | Lat.°′ | Long.°′
DEUTSCH — Name | Seite | Breite°′ | Länge°′ E=Ost

Campbellton, P.E.I., Can. 186 46.47 N 64.18 W
Campbellton, Fla., U.S. 192 30.57 N 85.24 W
Campbell Town, Austl. 166 41.56 S 147.29 E
Campbelltown, Austl. 168b 34.53 S 138.40 E
Campbelltown, Austl. 170 34.04 S 150.49 E
Campbelltown, Scot., U.K. 46 57.34 N 4.02 W
Campbelltown, Pa., U.S. 208 40.17 N 76.35 W
Campbellville 212 43.29 N 79.59 W
Campbeltown 44 55.26 N 5.36 W
Camp Creek ≃, Calif., U.S. 226 38.38 N 120.40 W
Camp Creek ≃, Mo., U.S. 219 39.02 N 91.12 W
Camp Creek Lake ⊜[1] 222 31.03 N 96.19 W
Camp David ʊ 208 39.38 N 77.28 W
Camp de Frileuse ■ 261 48.52 N 1.55 E
Camp de Satory ■ 261 48.47 N 2.06 E
Camp Dix 218 38.29 N 83.17 W
Camp Douglas 190 43.55 N 90.16 W
Campeche 232 19.51 N 90.32 W
Campeche, Bahía de C 232 20.00 N 94.00 W
Campechuela 240p 20.14 N 77.17 W
Campegine 64 44.45 N 10.32 E
Campello Monti 58 45.56 N 8.15 E
Camperdown, Austl. 169 38.14 S 143.09 E
Camperdown, S. Afr. 158 29.42 S 30.33 E
Camperville 184 51.59 N 100.09 W
Campestre, Bra. 256 21.43 S 46.15 W
Campestre, Bra. 256 21.16 S 42.56 W
Camp Fuchinobe (United States) ■ 94 35.34 N 139.10 E
Cam-pha 110 21.01 N 107.19 E
Camp Hill, Ala., U.S. 194 32.43 N 85.39 W
Camp Hill, Pa., U.S. 188 40.14 N 76.55 W
Campi Bisenzio 66 43.49 N 11.08 E
Campidano ◆[1] 71 39.30 N 8.47 E
Campiglia dei Fosci 66 43.27 N 11.03 E
Campiglia Marittima 66 43.03 N 10.37 E
Campillo de Llerena 34 38.30 N 5.50 W
Campillos 34 37.03 N 4.51 W
Campina ◆[1] 34 37.45 N 4.45 W
Campina Grande 250 7.13 S 35.53 W
Campinas 256 22.54 S 47.05 W
Campina Verde 255 19.31 S 49.28 W
Campinho, Rio do ≃ 287a 22.52 S 43.37 W
Campione del Garda 64 45.45 N 10.45 E
Campi Salentina 68 40.24 N 18.01 E
Campitello 64 46.28 N 11.44 E
Camp King 150 4.55 N 7.58 W
Camp Lake 216 42.32 N 88.09 W
Camp Lake ⊜ 212 45.27 N 78.54 W
Camp Leger de Melun ■ 261 48.34 N 2.34 E
Camp Lejeune Marine Corps Base ■ 192 34.40 N 77.21 W
Campli 66 42.43 N 13.41 E
Campo, Cam. 152 2.22 N 9.49 E
Campo, Moç. 156 17.44 S 36.21 E
Campo, Colo., U.S. 198 37.06 N 102.35 W
Campo, Réserve de ◆[4] 152 2.35 N 9.57 E
Campoalegre 246 2.41 N 75.20 W
Campo Alegre ≃ 250 9.19 S 50.06 W
Campo Alegre de Goiás 255 17.39 S 47.45 W
Campobasso 66 41.34 N 14.39 E
Campobasso □[4] 66 41.38 N 14.35 E
Campobello di Licata 70 37.15 N 13.55 E
Campobello di Mazara 70 37.38 N 12.45 E
Campobello Island I 186 44.53 N 66.55 W
Campo Belo 255 20.53 S 45.16 W
Campo Blenio 58 46.34 N 8.56 E
Campo Catino 66 41.48 N 13.20 E
Campocologno 58 46.13 N 10.08 E
Campo Cumbica ■ 287b 23.27 S 46.28 W
Campo da Bocaina 256 22.17 S 46.06 W
Campodarsego 64 45.30 N 11.54 E
Campo de Criptana 34 39.24 N 3.07 W
Campo de la Cruz 246 10.23 N 74.53 W
Campo de Marte ♠ 286d 12.04 S 77.03 W
Campo de Marte ■ 287b 23.30 S 46.37 W
Campo de Mayo ■ 288 34.32 S 58.38 W
Campo di Giove 66 42.01 N 14.03 E
Campo di Trens (Trens) 64 46.52 N 11.29 E
Campo do Coelho 256 22.15 S 42.39 W
Campodolcino 58 46.24 N 9.21 E
Campo Erê 252 26.23 S 53.03 W
Campofelice di Fitalia 70 37.50 N 13.29 E
Campofelice di Roccella 70 37.59 N 13.53 E
Campofiorito 70 37.45 N 13.16 E
Campo Florido 255 19.47 S 48.35 W
Campoformido 64 46.01 N 13.09 E
Campo Formoso 250 10.31 S 40.20 W
Campofranco 70 37.30 N 13.43 E
Campogalliano 64 44.41 N 10.50 E
Campo Gallo 252 26.35 S 62.51 W
Campo Grande, Arg. 252 27.13 S 54.58 W
Campo Grande, Bra. 255 20.27 S 54.37 W
Campo Grande ◆[8], Bra. 256 22.54 S 43.34 W
Campo Grande ◆[8], Port. 266c 38.45 N 9.09 W
Campo Indian Reservation ◆[4] 204 32.40 N 116.20 W
Cam Point ≻ 164 8.55 S 152.30 E
Campo Largo, Arg. 252 26.48 S 60.50 W
Campo Largo, Bra. 252 25.26 S 49.32 W
Campolaro 64 45.55 N 10.20 E
Campolasta (Astfeld) 64 46.40 N 11.22 E
Campolato, Capo ≻ 70 37.17 N 15.12 E
Campo Libertad ■ 286b 23.05 N 82.26 W
Campolide 256 21.36 S 43.53 W
Campolieto 66 41.38 N 14.46 E
Campo Ligure 62 44.32 N 8.42 E
Campo Limpo 256 23.12 S 46.48 W
Campo Maior, Bra. 250 4.49 S 42.10 W
Campo Maior, Port. 34 39.01 N 7.04 W
Campomarino 66 41.57 N 15.02 E
Campo Militar Número Uno ■ 286a 19.27 N 99.14 W
Campo Morado 234 17.35 N 100.05 W
Campomorone 62 44.30 N 8.53 E
Campo Mourão 255 24.03 S 52.22 W
Campo Nôvo 252 27.42 S 53.48 W
Campo Pequeno ♠ 266c 38.44 N 9.08 W
Campo Quijano 252 24.55 S 65.39 W
Campora 68 40.19 N 15.17 E
Camporeale 70 37.54 N 13.06 E
Camporgiano 64 44.09 N 10.20 E
Camporredondo 248 6.07 S 78.21 W
Campos 255 21.45 S 41.18 W
Campos Altos 255 19.41 S 46.10 W
Camposampiero 64 45.34 N 11.56 E
Campo Santo, Arg. 252 24.40 S 65.06 W
Camposanto, It. 64 44.47 N 11.08 E
Campos Belos 255 13.03 S 46.53 W
Campos de Cunha 256 22.55 S 44.49 W
Campos do Jordão 256 22.44 S 45.35 W
Campos Elyseos 256 22.42 S 43.17 W
Campos Gerais 256 21.14 S 45.46 W
Campos Novos 252 27.24 S 51.12 W
Campos Sales 250 7.04 S 40.23 W
Campo Tencia, Pizzo ∧ 58 46.26 N 8.43 E
Campotosto 66 42.33 N 13.22 E
Campotosto, Lago di ⊜ 66 42.32 N 13.22 E
Campo Tures (Sand in Taufers) 64 46.55 N 11.57 E
Campovalano 66 42.44 N 13.40 E
Campoyo Point ≻ 116 9.38 N 123.09 E
Camp Pendleton Marine Corps Base ■ 228 33.19 N 117.18 W
Camp Point 219 40.03 N 91.04 W
Camp Ruby 222 30.42 N 94.45 W
Camps-en-Amiénois 28 49.52 N 1.58 E
Campsie 274a 33.55 S 151.06 E
Campsie Fells ∧∧[2] 46 56.02 N 4.12 W
Camp Springs 208 38.48 N 76.55 W
Campti 194 31.54 N 93.07 W
Campton 192 37.44 N 83.33 W
Camptonville 226 39.27 N 121.03 W
Camptown 210 41.44 N 76.14 W
Campus 216 41.01 N 88.18 W
Campuya ≃ 246 1.43 S 73.30 W
Camp Verde 200 34.34 N 111.51 W
Campville 210 42.06 N 76.09 W
Camp Wood 196 29.40 N 100.01 W
Cam-ranh 110 11.54 N 109.09 E
Cam-ranh, Vinh C 110 11.53 N 109.10 E
Camrose, Alta., Can. 182 53.01 N 112.50 W
Camrose, Wales, U.K. 42 51.51 N 5.01 W
Camsell ≃ 176 65.40 N 118.07 W
Camu ≃ 250 1.15 N 57.09 W
Camucia 66 43.16 N 11.58 E
Camucuio 152 14.12 S 13.20 E
Camuy 240m 18.29 N 66.51 W
Cam-xuyen 110 18.15 N 106.00 E
Čamyndy 85 41.37 N 74.20 E
Čamzinka 80 54.24 N 45.47 E
Çan, Tür. 130 39.09 N 40.13 E
Çan, Tür. 130 40.02 N 27.03 E
Čan ≃ 260 51.48 N 0.25 E
Čaňa 30 48.37 N 21.18 E
Canaan, Conn., U.S. 207 42.02 N 73.20 W
Canaan, Fla., U.S. 220 28.48 N 81.14 W
Canaan, Ind., U.S. 218 38.52 N 85.25 W
Canaan, N.Y., U.S. 210 42.25 N 73.27 W
Canaan, Vt., U.S. 188 45.00 N 71.32 W
Canaan ≃ 186 45.55 N 65.47 W
Canaan Lake ⊜ 276 40.47 N 73.01 W
Canaan Valley State Park ♠ 188 39.02 N 79.32 W
Canaçari, Lago ⊜ 250 2.57 S 58.15 W
Canachal 232 24.04 N 107.05 W
Canada □[1] 176 60.00 N 95.00 W
Canada Bay C[6] 186 50.43 N 56.10 W
Canada Dam ◆[6] 126 24.10 N 87.10 E
Cañada de Caracheo 234 20.22 N 100.57 W
Cañada de Gómez 252 32.49 S 61.24 W
Cañada Honda 252 31.59 S 68.33 W
Canada Lake ⊜ 210 43.10 N 74.32 W
Cañada Nieto 258 33.43 S 58.05 W
Canadarago Lake ⊜ 210 42.48 N 75.01 W
Cañada Verde → Villa Huidobro 252 34.50 S 64.35 W
Canadaway Creek ≃ 214 42.28 N 79.22 W
Canadensis 210 41.12 N 75.15 W
Canadian 196 35.55 N 100.23 W
Canadian ≃ 196 35.27 N 95.03 W
Canadian, Deep Fork ≃ 196 35.28 N 95.50 W
Canadian Forces Base Borden ■ 212 44.17 N 79.55 W
Canadian Forces Base Montreal ■ 275a 45.31 N 73.25 W
Canadice Lake ⊜ 210 42.43 N 77.34 W
Cañadón Seco 254 46.33 S 67.35 W
Canaguá ≃ 246 7.57 N 69.36 W
Canahuan Islands II 116 11.49 N 124.43 E
Canaima, Parque Nacional ♠ 246 4.27 N 62.00 W
Canajoharie 188 42.54 N 74.35 W
Çanakkale 130 40.09 N 26.24 E
Çanakkale □[4] 130 40.10 N 26.45 E
Çanakkale Boğazı (Dardanelles) ⋃ 130 40.15 N 26.25 E
Canal, Anse du C 241o 16.23 N 61.30 W
Canal, Islas del → Channel Islands II 28 49.20 N 2.20 W
Canala 175f 21.32 S 165.57 E
Canale 62 44.48 N 8.00 E
Canale, Val ∨ 64 46.29 N 13.30 E
Canale del Ferro ≃ 64 46.21 N 13.07 E
Canalejas 234 19.57 N 99.39 W
Canal Flats 182 50.09 N 115.48 W
Canal Fulton 214 40.54 N 81.36 W
Canal Lake ⊜ 212 44.34 N 79.03 W
Canal Lewisville 214 40.18 N 81.50 W
Canal Point 220 26.52 N 80.38 W
Canals 252 33.33 S 62.53 W
Canal Winchester 188 39.51 N 82.48 W
Canandaigua 210 42.54 N 77.17 W
Canandaigua Lake ⊜ 210 42.49 N 77.16 W
Canandaigua Outlet ≃ 210 43.04 N 77.00 W
Cananea 232 30.57 N 110.18 W
Cananéia 252 25.01 S 47.57 W
Cananguchal 246 0.51 N 75.47 W
Canan Station 214 40.28 N 78.26 W
Canapine, Forca)(66 42.45 N 13.12 E
Canápolis 255 18.44 S 49.13 W
Canapville 50 49.19 N 0.08 E
Cañar 246 2.33 S 78.56 W
Cañar □[4] 246 2.30 S 79.00 W
Canard ≃ 214 42.08 N 83.06 W
Canard, Lac au ⊜ 206 45.48 N 71.31 W
Canarias, Islas (Canary Islands) II 148 28.00 N 15.30 W
Canaries 241f 13.55 N 61.04 W
Canaro 64 44.56 N 11.40 E
Canarreos, Archipiélago de los II 240p 21.50 N 82.30 W
Canarsie ◆[8] 276 40.38 N 73.53 W
Canarsie Park ♠ 276 40.38 N 73.53 W
Canarsie Pol I 276 40.37 N 73.52 W
Canary Basin ✧[1] 8 27.00 N 25.00 W
Canary Islands → Canarias, Islas II 148 28.00 N 15.30 W
Cañas 236 10.25 N 85.07 W
Cañas, Río de las ≃ 234 22.29 N 105.36 W
Canaseraga Creek ≃ 210 42.45 N 77.50 W
Cañasgordas 246 6.45 N 76.01 W
Canastota 210 43.10 N 75.45 W
Canastra ≃ 250 11.23 S 49.41 W
Canatlán 232 24.31 N 104.47 W
Canaveral, Cape ≻ 220 28.27 N 80.32 W
Canaveral Bight C[3] 220 28.26 N 80.33 W
Canaveral National Seashore ♠ 220 28.45 N 80.45 W
Canaveral Peninsula ≻[1] 220 28.28 N 80.34 W
Cañaveras 34 40.22 N 2.24 W
Canavese ◆[1] 62 45.20 N 7.40 E
Canavieiras 255 15.39 S 38.57 W
Cañazas 236 8.19 N 81.13 W
Canazei 64 46.28 N 11.46 E
Canbelego 166 31.33 S 146.19 E
Canberra 171b 35.17 S 149.08 E
Canby, Calif., U.S. 204 41.27 N 120.52 W
Canby, Minn., U.S. 198 44.43 N 96.16 W
Canby, Oreg., U.S. 224 45.16 N 122.42 W
Cancajanang, Mount ∧ 116 11.04 N 124.47 E
Cancale 32 48.41 N 1.51 W
Cancano, Lago di ⊜ 64 46.31 N 10.18 E
Cance ≃ 62 45.12 N 4.48 E
Cancellara 68 40.44 N 15.56 E
Cancello e Arnone 68 41.04 N 14.03 E
Canchaque 248 5.24 S 79.36 W
Canche ≃ 50 50.31 N 1.39 E
Cancon 32 44.32 N 0.38 E
Cancún 232 21.05 N 86.46 W
Cancún, Punta ≻ 232 21.08 N 86.45 W
Čancur 88 53.49 N 106.59 E
Canda 64 45.03 N 11.30 E
Candala → Qandala 144 11.23 N 49.53 E
Candarave 248 17.16 S 70.15 W
Çandarlı 130 38.56 N 26.56 E
Çandarlı Körfezi C 130 38.52 N 26.55 E
Candás 34 43.35 N 5.46 W
Candé 32 47.34 N 1.02 W
Candeias, Bra. 255 20.47 S 45.16 W
Candeias, Bra. 255 12.40 S 38.33 W
Candeias ≃ 248 8.39 S 63.31 W
Candela, It. 68 41.08 N 15.31 E
Candela, Méx. 232 26.50 N 100.40 W
Candela, Río de ≃ 232 27.16 N 100.18 W
Candelaria, Arg. 252 32.04 S 65.49 W
Candelaria, Arg. 252 27.28 S 55.44 W
Candelária, Bra. 252 29.40 S 52.48 W
Candelaria, Col. 246 3.25 N 76.20 W
Candelaria, Cuba 240p 22.44 N 82.58 W
Candelaria, Pil. 116 15.38 N 119.56 E
Candelaria ≃ 232 18.37 N 91.14 W
Candelaria, Cerro ∧ 234 23.25 N 103.43 W
Candelaria Loxicha 234 15.54 N 96.31 W
Candelaro ≃ 68 41.34 N 15.53 E
Candeleda 34 40.09 N 5.14 W
Candelo, Austl. 166 36.46 S 149.42 E
Candelo, It. 62 45.33 N 8.07 E
Candia → Iráklion 38 35.20 N 25.09 E
Candiac 206 45.23 N 73.31 W
Candia Canavese 62 45.20 N 7.53 E
Candia Lomellina 62 45.11 N 8.36 E
Cándido Aguilar 232 25.30 N 98.02 W
Cândido de Abreu 252 24.35 S 51.20 W
Cândido Mendes 250 1.27 S 45.43 W
Candies Creek ≃ 192 35.18 N 84.51 W
Candijay 116 9.49 N 124.30 E
Çandır, Tür. 130 39.15 N 35.32 E
Çandır, Tür. 130 40.16 N 33.29 E
Candle 180 65.55 N 161.56 W
Candle Lake ⊜ 184 53.50 N 105.18 W
Candlemas Islands II 18 57.03 S 26.40 W
Candlestick Park ♠ 282 37.43 N 122.23 W
Candlewood, Lake ⊜ 207 41.32 N 73.27 W
Candlewood Isle 207 41.29 N 73.27 W
Candlewood Knolls 207 41.29 N 73.28 W
Candlewood Shores 207 41.29 N 73.26 W
Candman' 102 45.20 N 97.59 E
Cando, Ang. 152 16.30 S 18.19 E
Cando, Sask., Can. 184 52.23 N 108.14 W
Cando, N. Dak., U.S. 198 48.32 N 99.12 W
Candon 116 17.12 N 120.27 E
Candor, N.C., U.S. 192 35.18 N 79.45 W
Candor, N.Y., U.S. 210 42.14 N 76.21 W
Candover 158 27.28 S 31.57 E
Cane ≃, Austl. 162 21.33 S 115.23 E
Cane ≃, N.C., U.S. 192 36.00 N 82.16 W
Canea → Khaniá 38 35.31 N 24.02 E
Caneadea 210 42.23 N 78.09 W
Caneças 266c 38.49 N 9.14 W
Cane Creek ≃ 194 36.29 N 90.28 W
Canegrate 266b 45.34 N 8.56 E
Canela 252 29.22 S 50.50 W
Canelles, Embalse de ⊜[1] 34 42.10 N 0.30 E
Canelli 62 44.43 N 8.17 E
Canelones 258 34.32 S 56.17 W
Canelones □[5] 258 34.35 S 56.15 W
Canelón Grande, Arroyo ≃ 258 34.30 S 56.24 W
Canendiyu □[5] 252 24.05 S 55.45 W
Cane Run ≃ 218 38.13 N 84.37 W
Cañete, Chile 252 37.48 S 73.24 W
Cañete, Esp. 34 40.03 N 1.35 W
Caneva 64 45.58 N 12.26 E
Caney 198 37.01 N 95.56 W
Caney ≃ 196 36.20 N 95.42 W
Caney Brook ≃ 276 41.07 N 73.50 W
Caney Creek ≃, U.S. 196 36.50 N 95.58 W
Caney Creek ≃, Ark., U.S. 194 33.46 N 93.07 W
Caney Creek ≃, Tex., U.S. 196 28.46 N 95.39 W
Caney Creek ≃, Tex., U.S. 222 31.03 N 94.33 W
Caney Creek ≃, Tex., U.S. 222 30.07 N 95.10 W
Caney Creek ≃, Tex., U.S. 222 30.04 N 96.08 W
Caney Creek ≃, Tex., U.S. 222 32.48 N 95.33 W
Caney Creek ≃, Tex., U.S. 222 30.28 N 95.38 W
Caney Creek ≃, Tex., U.S. 222 31.52 N 96.13 W
Caney Creek ≃, Tex., U.S. 222 30.53 N 95.48 W
Canfield 214 41.06 N 80.46 W
Canfield Island I 276 41.06 N 73.23 W
Canfranc 34 42.43 N 0.31 W
Cangaíba ◆[8] 287b 23.30 S 46.31 W
Cangallo 248 13.33 S 74.12 W
Cangamba 152 13.40 S 19.54 E
Cangandala 152 9.45 S 16.33 E
Cangas, Bra. 248 16.05 S 56.33 W
Cangas, Esp. 34 42.16 N 8.47 W
Cangas de Narcea 34 43.11 N 6.33 W
Cangas de Onís 34 43.21 N 5.07 W
Cangbu 100 30.49 N 114.35 E
Cangkuang, Tanjung ≻ 115a 6.51 S 105.15 E
Cangniutun 105 39.23 N 115.54 E
Cangola 152 7.58 S 15.52 E
Cangombe 152 14.24 S 19.59 E
Cangongo 152 9.24 S 17.30 E
Cangqian, Zhg. 106 30.18 N 120.00 E
Cangqian, Zhg. 106 30.17 N 120.25 E
Cangshangtun 105 40.03 N 117.32 E
Canguaretama 250 6.24 S 35.08 W
Canguçu 252 31.24 S 52.41 W
Cangumbe 152 12.00 S 19.17 E
Cangwu (Longwei) 102 23.22 N 111.13 E
Cangxi 102 31.48 N 105.57 E
Čangyrtas 85 40.53 N 72.50 E
Cangyuan 102 23.12 N 99.16 E
Cangzhou 98 38.19 N 116.51 E
Canhoca 152 9.15 S 14.41 E
Canhotinho 250 8.53 S 36.12 W
Caniapiscau ≃ 176 57.40 N 69.30 W
Caniapiscau, Lac ⊜ 176 54.10 N 69.55 W
Canicanian 116 14.46 N 122.01 E
Canicattì 70 37.21 N 13.51 E
Canicattini Bagni 70 37.02 N 15.04 E
Canigao Channel ⋃ 116 10.15 N 124.42 E
Canillas ◆[8] 266a 40.28 N 3.38 W
Canillejas ◆[8] 266a 40.27 N 3.37 W
Canimã ≃ 248 8.45 S 59.15 W
Canim Lake 182 51.46 N 120.54 W
Canim Lake ⊜ 182 51.52 N 120.45 W
Canim Lake Indian Reserve ◆[4] 182 51.47 N 121.00 W
Canimo Island I 116 14.07 N 123.04 E
Canindé 250 4.22 S 39.19 W
Canindé ≃ 250 6.15 S 42.52 W
Canindé de São Francisco 250 9.39 S 37.48 W
Canino 66 42.28 N 11.45 E
Canipaan 116 8.35 N 117.16 E
Canipo Island I 116 10.59 N 120.57 E
Canisius College ʊ[2] 284a 42.55 N 78.52 W
Canisp ∧ 46 58.07 N 5.03 W
Canistear Reservoir ⊜[1] 276 41.08 N 74.29 W
Canisteo 210 42.16 N 77.36 W
Canisteo ≃ 210 42.07 N 77.08 W
Canistota 198 43.36 N 97.18 W
Cañitas de Felipe Pescador 234 23.36 N 102.43 W
Canjáyar 34 37.00 N 2.44 W
Canjinge 152 10.12 S 21.17 E
Çankırı 130 40.36 N 33.37 E
Çankırı □[4] 130 40.45 N 33.25 E
Canlaon 116 10.22 N 123.12 E
Canlaon Volcano ∧[1] 116 10.25 N 123.08 E
Canley Vale 274a 33.53 S 150.57 E
Canmore 182 51.05 N 115.21 W
Canna 68 40.05 N 16.30 E
Canna I 46 57.04 N 6.34 W
Canna, Sound of ⋃ 46 56.59 N 6.40 W
Cannanore 122 11.51 N 75.22 E
Cannara 66 43.00 N 12.35 E
Canne ⊥ 68 41.18 N 16.09 E
Canne, Fiume delle ≃ 70 37.20 N 13.24 E
Cannel City 192 37.47 N 83.17 W
Cannelton 194 37.55 N 86.45 W
Canner ≃ 56 49.24 N 6.16 E
Cannero-Riviera 58 46.01 N 8.41 E
Cannes 62 43.33 N 7.01 E
Canneto, It. 66 43.12 N 10.44 E
Canneto, It. 70 38.29 N 14.58 E
Canneto sull'Oglio 64 45.09 N 10.25 E
Cannich 46 57.21 N 4.46 W
Cannich ≃ 46 57.21 N 4.44 W
Cannifton 212 44.12 N 77.23 W
Canning, Arg. 288 34.53 S 58.30 W
Canning, N.S., Can. 186 45.09 N 64.25 W
Canning ≃, Austl. 168a 32.01 S 115.51 E
Canning ≃, Alaska, U.S. 180 70.05 N 145.30 W
Canning Hill ∧[2] 162 28.50 S 117.49 E
Canning Lake ⊜ 212 44.57 N 78.48 W
Canning Reservoir ⊜[1] 168a 32.10 S 116.09 E
Cannington, Ont., Can. 212 44.21 N 79.02 W
Cannington, Eng., U.K. 42 51.09 N 3.04 W
Cannobio 58 46.04 N 8.42 E
Cannock 42 52.42 N 2.09 W
Cannock Chase ◆[4] 42 52.43 N 2.00 W
Cannon ≃ 190 44.35 N 92.33 W
Cannon Air Force Base ■ 196 34.23 N 103.18 W
Cannonball ≃ 198 46.26 N 100.38 W
Cannon Beach 224 45.55 N 123.57 W
Cannondale 207 41.08 N 73.16 W
Cannon Falls 190 44.31 N 92.54 W
Cannonsburg 216 43.03 N 85.28 W
Cannonsville Reservoir ⊜[1] 210 42.08 N 75.19 W
Cann River 166 37.34 S 149.10 E
Caño, Isla del I 236 8.44 N 83.53 W
Canoas 252 29.56 S 51.11 W
Canoas ≃, Bra. 252 27.36 S 51.25 W
Canoas ≃, Bra. 256 21.30 S 47.09 W
Canobie Lake 283 42.48 N 71.15 W
Canobie Lake ⊜ 283 42.49 N 71.15 W
Canoe 182 50.45 N 119.13 W
Canoe ≃, B.C., Can. 182 52.09 N 118.27 W
Canoe ≃, Mass., U.S. 283 41.58 N 71.08 W
Canoe Brook ≃ 276 40.45 N 74.22 W
Canoe Brook Reservoirs ⊜[1] 276 40.45 N 74.21 W
Canoe Creek Indian Reserve ◆[4] 182 51.32 N 122.15 W
Canoe Lake ⊜ 184 55.11 N 108.15 W
Canoe Lake Indian Reserve ◆[4] 184 55.08 N 108.12 W
Canoga Park ◆[8] 280 34.12 N 118.35 W
Canoinhas 252 26.10 S 50.24 W
Canol 180 65.14 N 126.56 W
Canon 192 34.21 N 83.07 W
Canon ≃ 224 46.36 N 123.53 W
Canonbie 44 55.05 N 2.57 W
Canon City 200 38.27 N 105.14 W
Cañón de Río Blanco, Parque Nacional ♠ 234 18.38 N 97.06 W
Caño Negro 236 10.54 N 84.44 W
Canonsburg 214 40.16 N 80.11 W
Canonsburg Lake ⊜ 279b 40.16 N 80.07 W
Canoochee ≃ 192 31.59 N 81.18 W
Canopus ⊥ 142 31.18 N 30.03 E
Canora 184 51.37 N 102.26 W
Canosa di Puglia 68 41.13 N 16.04 E
Canossa ⊥ 64 44.35 N 10.27 E
Canot, Pointe ≻ 241o 16.12 N 61.28 W
Canouan I 238 12.43 N 61.20 W
Canova 198 43.53 N 97.30 W
Canova Beach 220 28.08 N 80.34 W
Cañovanas 240m 18.23 N 65.54 W
Cánoves ≃ 266d 41.37 N 2.22 E
Canow 54 53.12 N 12.54 E
Canowindra 166 33.34 S 148.38 E
Can Quer, Torrente de ≃ 266d 41.31 N 2.11 E
Can Rull 266d 41.33 N 2.05 E
Cansado 148 20.51 N 17.02 W
Cansanção 250 10.41 S 39.31 W
Canso 186 45.20 N 61.00 W
Canso, Strait of ⋃ 186 45.37 N 61.25 W
Canta 248 11.25 S 76.38 W
Cantabria 234 19.50 N 101.44 W
Cantábrica, Cordillera ∧∧ 34 43.00 N 5.00 W
Cantabriques → Cantábrica, Cordillera ∧∧ 34 43.00 N 5.00 W
Cantagalo 255 21.58 S 42.22 W
Cantagalo, Cachoeira ↳ 250 7.18 S 54.52 W
Cantal □[5] 32 45.05 N 2.45 E
Cantal ∧∧ 32 45.10 N 2.40 E
Cantalejo 34 41.15 N 3.55 W
Cantalupo in Sabina 66 42.18 N 12.39 E
Cantalupo nel Sannio 66 41.31 N 14.24 E
Čantal'vejergyn ≃ 180 67.38 N 179.22 W
Cantanhede, Bra. 250 3.39 S 44.24 W
Cantanhede, Port. 34 40.21 N 8.36 W
Cantareira ◆[8] 287b 23.27 S 46.37 W
Cantareira, Serra da ∧ 287b 23.25 S 46.39 W
Cantário ≃ 248 12.13 S 64.34 W
Cantaura 246 9.19 N 64.21 W
Cant Clough Reservoir ⊜[1] 262 53.46 N 2.09 W
Canteleu 50 49.27 N 1.02 E
Canterbury, Austl. 274a 33.55 S 151.07 E
Canterbury, Austl. 274b 37.49 S 145.05 E
Canterbury, N.B., Can. 186 45.53 N 67.29 W
Canterbury, Eng., U.K. 42 51.17 N 1.05 E
Canterbury Bight C[3] 172 44.15 S 171.38 E
Canterbury Cathedral ʊ[1] 42 51.17 N 1.05 E
Canterbury Park Racecourse ♠ 274a 33.54 S 151.07 E
Canterbury Plains ≚ 172 44.00 S 171.45 E
Canterbury Woods 284c 38.49 N 77.15 W
Can-tho 110 10.02 N 105.47 E
Cantiano 66 43.28 N 12.38 E
Cantil 228 35.18 N 117.58 W
Cantiles, Cayo I 240p 21.36 N 82.02 W
Cantin, Cap ≻ 148 32.34 N 9.19 W
Cantin Lake ⊜ 184 53.27 N 95.10 W
Canto do Buriti 250 8.07 S 42.58 W
Canto do Pontes 287a 22.58 S 43.04 W
Canto Grande 286d 11.59 S 77.01 W
Cantoira 62 45.21 N 7.23 E
Canton, Conn., U.S. 207 41.49 N 72.54 W
Canton, Ga., U.S. 192 34.14 N 84.29 W
Canton, Ill., U.S. 190 40.33 N 90.02 W
Canton, Kans., U.S. 198 38.23 N 97.26 W
Canton, Maine, U.S. 188 44.28 N 70.19 W
Canton, Mass., U.S. 207 42.09 N 71.09 W
Canton, Minn., U.S. 190 43.32 N 91.56 W
Canton, Miss., U.S. 194 32.37 N 90.02 W
Canton, Mo., U.S. 219 40.08 N 91.32 W
Canton, N.J., U.S. 208 39.28 N 75.25 W
Canton, N.C., U.S. 192 35.32 N 82.50 W
Canton, N.Y., U.S. 188 44.36 N 75.10 W
Canton, Ohio, U.S. 214 40.48 N 81.22 W
Canton, Okla., U.S. 196 36.03 N 98.35 W
Canton, Pa., U.S. 210 41.39 N 76.51 W
Canton, S. Dak., U.S. 198 43.18 N 96.35 W
Canton, Tex., U.S. 222 32.33 N 95.52 W
Canton → Guangzhou, Zhg. 100 23.06 N 113.16 E
Canton I, Can./End. 174h 2.50 S 171.40 W
Canton I, Oc. 14 2.50 S 171.41 W
Canton Airport ⊠ 174h 2.46 S 171.43 W
Canton and Enderbury □[2] 14 2.50 S 171.43 W
Canton Et Ederburg → Canton and Enderbury □[2] 14 2.50 S 171.43 W
Canton Lake ⊜[1] 196 36.08 N 98.36 W
Cantonment 194 30.38 N 87.19 W
Cantorbéry → Canterbury 42 51.17 N 1.05 E
Cantrall 219 39.56 N 89.41 W
Cantribana 266c 38.53 N 9.25 W
Cantù 62 45.44 N 9.08 E
Cantu ≃ 252 24.46 S 52.54 W
Cantua Creek 226 36.30 N 120.19 W
Cantua Creek ≃ 226 36.28 N 120.17 W
Cantwell 180 63.23 N 148.57 W
Cañuelas 258 35.03 S 58.44 W
Cañuelas □[5] 288 34.56 S 58.41 W
Canumã 246 4.02 S 59.04 W
Canumã ≃ 246 3.55 S 59.10 W
Canungra 171a 28.01 S 153.10 E
Canungra ≃ 171a 27.55 S 153.06 E
Canutama 248 6.32 S 64.20 W
Canutillo 200 31.55 N 106.36 W
Canvastown 172 41.18 S 173.40 E
Canvey 260 51.32 N 0.36 E
Canvey Island I 260 51.33 N 0.34 E
Čany 86 55.19 N 76.46 E
Čany, Ozero ⊜ 86 54.50 N 77.30 E
Cany-Barville 50 49.47 N 0.38 E
Canyon, Yukon, Can. 180 60.52 N 137.02 W
Canyon, Calif., U.S. 282 37.49 N 122.09 W
Canyon, Tex., U.S. 196 34.59 N 101.55 W
Canyon City 202 44.23 N 118.57 W
Canyon Creek 182 54.22 N 115.05 W
Canyon Creek ≃, Ariz., U.S. 200 33.49 N 110.40 W
Canyon Creek ≃, Calif., U.S. 226 39.22 N 120.45 W
Canyon Creek ≃, Idaho, U.S. 202 42.59 N 115.59 W
Canyon Creek ≃, Wash., U.S. 224 48.43 N 120.55 W
Canyon Creek ≃, Wash., U.S. 224 45.57 N 122.22 W
Canyon de Chelly National Monument ♠ 200 36.01 N 109.26 W
Canyon Ferry Lake ⊜[1] 202 46.33 N 111.37 W
Canyon Lake ⊜[1] 196 29.52 N 98.16 W
Canyonlands National Park ♠ 200 38.10 N 110.00 W
Canyonville 202 42.56 N 123.17 W
Canzar 152 7.38 S 21.32 E
Canzo 62 45.51 N 9.16 E
Caobanal 234 17.37 N 93.22 W
Cao-bang 110 22.40 N 106.15 E
Caohe ≃ 98 40.29 N 124.08 E
Cao-lanh 110 10.27 N 105.38 E
Caolaoji 100 33.06 N 117.22 E
Caolisport, Loch C 46 55.54 N 5.37 W
Caomaji 98 34.52 N 116.17 E
Caonao ≃ 240p 22.05 N 78.05 W
Caonillas, Lago ⊜ 240m 18.16 N 66.39 W
Caopeng 106 31.44 N 121.17 E
Caoping 100 28.48 N 118.22 E
Caopu 98 34.34 N 118.52 E
Caoqiao 106 31.32 N 119.59 E
Caorle 64 45.36 N 12.53 E
Caorso 62 45.03 N 9.52 E
Caoshi, Zhg. 98 42.17 N 125.16 E
Caoshi, Zhg. 100 33.32 N 116.29 E
Caota 100 29.42 N 120.08 E
Caotang 106 31.16 N 118.59 E
Caoxi 100 28.42 N 117.18 E
Caoxian 98 34.53 N 115.33 E
Caoyan 100 32.56 N 120.20 E
Caoyangxi 100 26.34 N 118.47 E
Cap, Le → Cape Town 158 33.55 S 18.22 E
Capac 190 43.01 N 82.56 W
Capaccio 68 40.25 N 15.05 E
Capaci 70 38.10 N 13.14 E
Capage 152 13.21 S 21.05 E
Čapajevka ≃ 80 53.08 N 49.37 E
Čapajevsk 80 52.58 N 49.41 E
Capala 152 13.37 S 14.45 E
Capalbio 66 42.27 N 11.25 E
Capalonga 116 14.20 N 122.30 E
Capanaparo ≃ 246 7.01 N 67.07 W
Capanema, Bra. 250 1.12 S 47.11 W
Capanema, Bra. 252 25.40 S 53.48 W
Capangombe 152 15.05 S 13.08 E
Capanne, Monte ∧ 66 42.46 N 10.10 E
Capannoli 66 43.35 N 10.41 E
Capannori 66 43.50 N 10.34 E
Capão Bonito 255 24.01 S 48.20 W
Capão Doce, Morro do ∧ 252 26.43 S 51.25 W
Capaotigamau, Lac ⊜ 186 50.18 N 68.14 W
Caparica 266c 38.40 N 9.12 W
Caparo ≃ 246 7.46 N 70.23 W
Capas 116 15.20 N 120.35 E
Capatárida 246 11.11 N 70.37 W
Cap aux Meules, Île du I 186 47.23 N 61.54 W
Capay 226 38.32 N 122.03 W
Cap-Chat 186 49.06 N 66.42 W
Cap-Chat, Parc de ♠ 186 48.55 N 66.50 W
Cap-de-la-Madeleine 206 46.22 N 72.31 W
Capdevila ◆[8] 286b 23.03 N 82.24 W
Cape ≃ 166 20.49 S 146.51 E
Cape Barren Island I 166 40.25 S 148.12 E
Cape Basin ✧[1] 10 35.00 S 5.00 E
Cape Breton Highlands National Park ♠ 186 46.45 N 60.45 W
Cape Breton Island I 186 46.00 N 60.30 W
Cape Broyle 186 47.06 N 52.57 W
Cape Canaveral 220 28.24 N 80.37 W
Cape Charles 208 37.16 N 76.01 W
Cape Coast 150 5.05 N 1.15 W
Cape Cod Bay C 207 41.52 N 70.22 W
Cape Cod Canal ≅ 207 41.47 N 70.30 W
Cape Cod National Seashore ♠ 207 41.56 N 70.06 W
Cape Comorin → Kanniyākumāri 122 8.05 N 77.34 E
Cape Coral 220 26.33 N 81.57 W
Cape Croker Indian Reserve ◆[4] 212 44.55 N 81.01 W
Cape Dorset 176 64.14 N 76.32 W
Cape Elizabeth 188 43.34 N 70.12 W
Cape Fear ≃ 192 33.53 N 78.00 W
Cape Girardeau 194 37.19 N 89.32 W
Cape Hatteras National Seashore ♠ 192 35.30 N 76.35 W
Cape Henlopen State Park ♠ 208 38.45 N 75.06 W
Cape Jervis 168b 35.36 S 138.06 E
Cape Johnson Seamount ✧[3] 14 17.00 N 177.20 W
Capela, Bra. 250 9.25 S 36.04 W
Capela, Bra. 250 10.30 S 37.04 W
Cape la Hune 186 47.33 N 56.52 W
Capel Curig 42 53.06 N 3.54 W
Capelengue 152 9.12 S 19.43 E
Capelinha 255 17.42 S 42.31 W
Cape Lisburne 180 68.52 N 166.05 W
Capel'ka 76 58.03 N 28.59 E
Capella 166 23.05 S 148.02 E
Capella ∧ 164 5.00 S 141.05 E
Capelle [aan de IJssel] 52 51.55 N 4.35 E
Capellen 56 49.38 N 5.59 E
Cape Lookout State Park ♠ 224 45.21 N 123.59 W
Cape May 208 38.56 N 74.55 W
Cape May □[6] 208 38.56 N 74.55 W
Cape May Court House 208 39.05 N 74.50 W
Cape May Point 208 38.56 N 74.58 W
Capembé ≃ 152 16.10 S 21.00 E
Capenda Camulemba 152 9.24 S 18.27 E
Capenga ≃ 287a 22.49 S 43.37 W
Capenhurst 262 53.15 N 2.57 W
Cape of Good Hope (Kaap) □[4] 156 31.00 S 23.00 E
Cape of Good Hope Nature Reserve ◆[4] 158 34.18 S 18.26 E
Cape Pole 180 55.58 N 133.48 W
Cape Pond ⊜ 283 42.38 N 70.38 W
Cape Porpoise 188 43.22 N 70.26 W
Cape Rise ✧[3] 10 41.00 S 13.00 E
Capernaum ⊥ 132 32.53 N 35.34 E
Cape Romanzof 180 61.49 N 165.56 W
Capertee 170 33.09 S 149.59 E
Capertee ≃ 170 33.12 S 150.28 E
Cape Sable Island I 186 43.25 N 65.37 W
Capesterre, Guad. 241o 16.03 N 61.34 W
Capesterre, Guad. 241o 15.54 N 61.13 W
Capesterre, Pointe de la ≻ 241o 16.03 N 61.33 W
Capesthorne Hall ⊥ 262 53.15 N 2.14 W
Capestrano 66 42.16 N 13.46 E
Capetinga ≃ 256 22.04 S 47.14 W
Cape Tormentine 186 46.08 N 63.47 W
Cape Town (Kaapstad) 158 33.55 S 18.22 E
Cape Verde □[1] 134
150a 16.00 N 24.00 W
Cape Verde Basin ✧[1] 8 14.00 N 33.00 W
Cape Verde Islands → Cape Verde □[1] 150a 16.00 N 24.00 W
Capeville 208 37.12 N 75.57 W
Cape Vincent 212 44.08 N 76.20 W
Cape Yakataga 180 60.04 N 142.26 W
Cape York Peninsula ≻[1] 164 14.00 S 142.30 E
Cap-Haïtien 238 19.45 N 72.12 W
Capilla de Farruco 252 32.53 S 55.25 W
Capilla del Monte 252 30.51 S 64.31 W
Capilla del Señor 258 34.18 S 59.06 W
Capim ≃ 250 1.40 S 47.47 W
Capim Melado, Morro do ∧ 287a 22.50 S 43.29 W
Capinas Point ≻ 116 11.05 N 125.14 E
Capinópolis 255 18.41 S 49.35 W
Capinota 248 17.43 S 66.14 W
Capinzal 252 27.20 S 51.36 W
Capinzal, Cachoeira ↳ 250 8.42 S 58.18 W
Capira 236 8.45 N 79.53 W
Cap Island I 116 5.57 N 120.06 E
Capistrano, Bra. 250 4.28 S 38.55 W
Capistrano, It. 68 38.41 N 16.17 E
Capistrano Beach 228 33.27 N 117.40 W
Capistrello 66 41.57 N 13.23 E
Capitachouane ≃ 190 47.36 N 76.54 W
Capital Airport ⊠ 219 39.51 N 89.41 W
Capital City Airport ⊠ 216 42.47 N 84.35 W
Capitan 200 33.35 N 105.35 W
Capitán Aracena, Isla I 254 54.10 S 71.20 W
Capitanata ◆[1] 68 41.25 N 15.30 E
Capitán Bado 255 23.16 S 55.32 W
Capitán Bermúdez 252 32.49 S 60.43 W
Capitán Meza 252 26.55 S 55.15 W
Capitan Peak ∧ 200 33.36 N 105.16 W
Capitán Sarmiento 252 34.10 S 59.48 W
Capitão de Campos 250 4.28 S 41.57 W
Capitari 246 0.51 N 61.24 W
Capitola 226 36.59 N 121.57 W
Capitol Heights 208 38.53 N 76.55 W
Capitol Park 208 39.08 N 75.30 W
Capitol Peak ∧ 204 41.50 N 117.18 W
Capitol Reef National Park ♠ 200 38.11 N 111.20 W
Capitol View 192 33.57 N 80.56 W
Capivari 255 23.00 S 47.31 W
Capivari ≃, Bra. 248 19.16 S 57.10 W
Capivari ≃, Bra. 255 12.30 S 39.55 W
Capivari ≃, Bra. 256 22.14 S 44.57 W
Capivari ≃, Bra. 256 22.56 S 47.16 W
Capivari ≃, Bra. 256 21.30 S 44.20 W
Capivari ≃, Bra. 256 21.53 S 46.15 W
Capivari ≃, Bra. 256 21.12 S 44.52 W
Capivari ≃, Bra. 256 22.26 S 45.47 W
Capiz → Roxas 116 11.35 N 122.45 E
Capiz □[4] 116 11.30 N 122.30 E
Capizzi 70 37.51 N 14.29 E
Caplan 186 48.06 N 65.41 W
Čaplejevka 78 51.43 N 33.12 E
Caplen 222 29.29 N 94.33 W
Caples Lake ⊜[1] 226 38.42 N 120.03 W
Čaplina ≃ 248 18.14 S 70.33 W
Čaplinka 78 46.23 N 33.32 E
Čaplino, S.S.S.R. 78 48.09 N 36.14 E
Čaplino, S.S.S.R. 180 64.25 N 172.15 W
Čapljina 36 43.07 N 17.42 E
Čaplone, Monte ∧ 64 45.48 N 10.38 E
Čaplygin 76 53.14 N 39.58 E
Cap Mountain ∧ 180 63.25 N 123.29 W
Capoche ≃ 154 15.23 S 32.53 E
Capodichino, Aeroporto di ⊠ 68 40.50 N 14.17 E
Capodimonte 66 42.33 N 11.55 E
Capo di Ponte 64 46.02 N 10.21 E
Capo d'Orlando 70 38.10 N 14.53 E
Capoeira, Corredeira ↳ 250 6.48 S 58.21 W
Capolago 58 45.55 N 8.59 E
Capoliveri 66 42.45 N 10.22 E
Caporolo ≃ 152 12.56 S 13.00 E
Caposele 68 40.49 N 15.13 E
Capostrada 66 43.57 N 10.54 E
Capot ≃ 240e 14.51 N 61.05 W
Capoterra 71 39.11 N 8.58 E
Capoti-an, Mount ∧ 116 11.45 N 125.15 E
Capotoan, Mount ∧ 116 12.09 N 124.57 E
Cappamore 48 52.37 N 8.20 W
Cap-Pelé 186 46.13 N 64.18 W
Cappella Islands II 240m 18.17 N 64.54 W
Cappelle 66 42.03 N 13.22 E

Symbols in the index entries represent the broad categories identified in the key at the right. Symbols with superior numbers (∧∧[2]) identify subcategories (see complete key on page *I* · 30).

Kartensymbole in dem Registerverzeichnis stellen die rechts in Schlüssel erklärten Kategorien dar. Symbole mit hochgestellten Ziffern (∧∧[2]) bezeichnen Unterabteilungen einer Kategorie (vgl. vollständiger Schlüssel auf Seite *I* · 30).

Los símbolos incluídos en el texto del índice representan las grandes categorias identificadas con la clave a la derecha. Los símbolos con numeros en su parte superior (∧∧[2]) identifican las subcategorías (véase la clave completa en la página *I* · 30).

Les symboles de l'index représentent les catégories indiquées dans la légende à droite. Les symboles suivis d'un indice (∧∧[2]) représentent des sous-catégories (voir légende complète à la page *I* · 30).

Os símbolos incluídos no texto do índice representam as grandes categorias identificadas com a chave à direita. Os símbolos com números em sua parte superior (∧∧[2]) identificam as subcategorias (veja-se a chave completa à página *I* · 30).

	English	Deutsch	Español	Français	Português
∧	Mountain	Berg	Montaña	Montagne	Montanha
∧∧	Mountains	Berge	Montañas	Montagnes	Montanhas
)(	Pass	Pass	Paso	Col	Passo
∨	Valley, Canyon	Tal, Cañon	Valle, Cañón	Vallée, Canyon	Vale, Canhão
≚	Plain	Ebene	Llano	Plaine	Planície
≻	Cape	Kap	Cabo	Cap	Cabo
I	Island	Insel	Isla	Île	Ilha
II	Islands	Inseln	Islas	Îles	Ilhas
⊥	Other Topographic Features	Andere Topographische Objekte	Otros Elementos Topográficos	Autres données topographiques	Outros Elementos Topográficos

ESPAÑOL

Nombre	Página	Lat.°′	Long.°′ W=Oeste
Cappelle sul Tavo	66	42.28 N	14.06 E
Cappeln	52	52.48 N	8.07 E
Cappenberg	263	51.39 N	7.32 E
Cappenberg, Schloss ⊥	263	51.39 N	7.32 E
Cappercleuch	44	55.29 N	3.12 W
Cap Point >	241f	14.07 N	60.57 W
Cappoquin	48	52.08 N	7.50 W
Capracotta	66	41.50 N	14.16 E
Capraia	66	43.03 N	9.50 E
Capraia, Isola di I	66	43.02 N	9.49 E
Capranica	66	42.15 N	12.11 E
Caprara, Isola I	68	42.08 N	15.31 E
Caprarola	66	42.19 N	12.14 E
Capreol	190	46.43 N	80.56 W
Caprera, Isola I	71	41.12 N	9.28 E
Caprese Michelangelo	66	43.39 N	11.59 E
Capri	68	40.33 N	14.14 E
Capri, Isola di I	68	40.33 N	14.13 E
Capriati a Volturno	68	41.28 N	14.08 E
Capricorn, Cape >	166	23.30 S	151.13 E
Capricorn Group II	166	23.28 S	152.00 E
Capri Leone	70	38.05 N	14.44 E
Caprino Veronese	64	45.36 N	10.47 E
Caprivi Strip (Caprivizipfel) □[9]	156	17.59 S	23.00 E
Caprolace, Lago di @	66	41.21 N	12.58 E
Capron, Ill., U.S.	216	42.24 N	88.44 W
Capron, Va., U.S.	208	36.42 N	77.11 W
Cap-Saint-Jacques → Vung-tau	110	10.21 N	107.04 E
Cap-Santé	206	46.40 N	71.47 W
Capstone	260	51.21 N	0.34 E
Captain Anthony Meldahl Dam ◆[6]	218	38.48 N	84.11 W
Captain Cook	229d	19.30 N	155.55 W
Captain Cook Bridge ◆[5]	274a	34.00 S	151.08 E
Captain Cook Landing Place ⊥	274a	34.00 S	151.14 E
Captain Cook Monument ⊥	174c	29.00 S	167.56 E
Captain Cook's Monument ⊥	174s	17.30 S	149.30 W
Captain Daniel Wright Woods ♠	278	42.13 N	87.56 W
Captain Harbor C	276	41.00 N	73.36 W
Captain Pond @	283	42.48 N	71.10 W
Captains Flat	171b	35.35 S	149.27 E
Captieux	32	44.18 N	0.16 W
Captina Creek ≃	188	39.52 N	80.48 W
Captiva	220	26.31 N	82.11 W
Captiva Island I	220	26.31 N	82.11 W
Captree Island I	276	40.39 N	73.16 W
Captree State Park ♠	276	40.39 N	73.16 W
Capua	68	41.06 N	14.12 E
Capual Island I	116	6.02 N	121.24 E
Capuáva	287b	23.39 S	46.29 W
Capuça I	152	17.22 S	21.18 E
Capucapu ≃	246	1.45 S	58.35 W
Capucin >	240d	15.38 N	61.28 W
Capul	116	12.25 N	124.11 E
Capulín, Río del ≃	196	27.31 N	101.33 W
Capulin Mountain National Monument ♠	196	36.48 N	103.55 W
Capul Island I	116	12.26 N	124.10 E
Capuna	152	15.38 S	19.43 E
Capurro	258	34.25 S	56.28 W
Capurso	68	41.03 N	16.55 E
Caputh	54	52.21 N	13.00 E
Cap-Vert → Cape Verde □[1]	150a	16.00 N	24.00 W
Caquende	256	21.20 S	44.33 W
Caquetá □[8]	246	1.00 N	74.00 W
Caquetá (Japurá) ≃	246	3.08 S	64.46 W
Çaquiaviri	248	17.03 S	68.38 W
Čar ≃	86	50.22 N	80.55 E
Car, Slieve ∧	48	54.03 N	9.40 W
Čara	88	56.54 N	118.12 E
Čara ≃	74	60.22 N	120.50 E
Caraballeda	286c	10.37 N	66.50 W
Carabanchel Alto ◆[8]	266a	40.22 N	3.45 W
Carabanchel Bajo ◆[8]	266a	40.23 N	3.47 W
Carabao Island I	116	12.04 N	121.56 E
Carabaya, Cordillera de ⩕	248	13.50 S	70.45 W
Carabinani ≃	246	1.58 S	61.31 W
Carabobo □[3]	238	10.10 N	68.05 W
Carabost	171b	35.36 S	147.44 E
Caracal	38	44.07 N	24.21 E
Caracalla, Terme di ⊥	267a	41.53 N	12.29 E
Caracaraí	246	1.50 N	61.08 W
Caracas	246		
	286c	10.30 N	66.56 W
Čarach	86	59.03 N	62.15 E
Carache	246	9.38 N	70.14 W
Caracol, Bra.	250	9.17 S	43.20 W
Caracol, Bra.	252	22.01 S	57.02 W
Caracollo	248	17.39 S	67.10 W
Caracorum → Karakoram Range ⩕	120	35.30 N	77.00 E
Carácuaro de Morelos	234	18.46 N	101.02 W
Caradoc Indian Reserve ◆[4]	214	42.48 N	81.29 W
Caraffa di Catanzaro	68	38.53 N	16.29 E
Caraga	116	7.20 N	126.34 E
Caraga ≃	116	7.20 N	126.34 E
Caragh, Lough @	48	52.03 N	9.52 W
Caraghnan Mountain ∧	166	31.20 S	149.03 E
Caraglio	62	44.25 N	7.26 E
Caraguata, Arroyo ≃	288	34.24 S	58.38 W
Caraguatatuba	256	23.37 S	45.25 W
Caraguatatuba, Enseada de C	256	23.40 S	45.20 W
Caraguatay	252	25.14 S	56.52 W
Caraí	255	17.12 S	41.42 W
Caraibamba	248	14.24 S	73.09 W
Caraïbes, Mer des → Caribbean Sea ⊤[2]	238	15.00 S	73.00 W
Caraigres, Cerro ∧	236	9.43 N	84.05 W
Caraíva ≃	255	16.48 S	39.08 W
Carajari ≃	250	4.45 S	54.20 W
Carajás, Serra dos ⩕	250	6.00 S	51.20 W
Caramagna-Piemonte	62	44.46 N	7.44 E
Caramanico Terme	66	42.09 N	14.00 E
Caramay	116	10.11 N	119.14 E
Caramoan	116	13.46 N	123.52 E
Caramoan Peninsula >[1]	116	13.48 N	123.40 E
Caramoran	116	13.59 N	124.08 E
Caramy ≃	62	43.26 N	6.12 E
Caraná ≃	248	13.20 S	59.17 W
Caranavi	248	15.46 S	67.36 W
Carancahua Creek ≃	222	28.51 N	96.19 W
Carandaí	255	20.57 S	43.48 W
Carandaiti	248	20.45 S	63.04 W
Carangola	255	20.44 S	42.02 W
Carano	64	46.16 N	11.27 E
Caransebeș	38	45.25 N	22.13 E
Carapá ≃	252	24.30 S	54.20 W
Carapachay ≃[1]	288	34.25 S	58.35 W
Carapajó	250	2.16 S	49.22 W
Cara-Paraná ≃	246	1.45 S	73.13 W
Carapari	248	21.49 S	63.46 W
Carapeguá	252	25.48 S	57.14 W
Carapelle ≃	68	41.30 N	15.55 E
Carapeva	256	23.12 S	45.24 W

FRANÇAIS

Nom	Page	Lat.°′	Long.°′ W=Ouest
Carapicuíba	256	23.31 S	46.50 W
Carapicuíba □[7]	287b	23.31 S	46.53 W
Carapó	255	22.38 S	54.48 W
Carapo ≃	246	7.30 N	64.02 W
Carappee Hill ∧[2]	166	33.26 S	136.16 E
Caraquet	186	47.48 N	64.57 W
Carare ≃	246	6.48 N	74.06 W
Caras	248	9.03 S	77.45 W
Carás, Ilha I	250	0.01 S	50.50 W
Carasco	62	44.21 N	9.21 E
Caraș-Severin □[4]	38	45.00 N	22.00 E
Caratasca, Laguna de C	236	15.23 N	83.55 W
Carate Brianza	62	45.41 N	9.14 E
Caratinga	255	19.47 S	42.08 W
Carauari	246	4.52 S	66.54 W
Caraúbas, Bra.	250	5.47 S	37.34 W
Caraúbas, Bra.	250	7.43 S	36.31 W
Caravaca	34	38.06 N	1.51 W
Caravaggio	62	45.30 N	9.38 E
Caravela, Ilha I	150	11.30 N	16.20 W
Caravelas	255	17.45 S	39.15 W
Caravelí	248	15.46 S	73.22 W
Caravelle, Presqu'île de la >[1]	240e	14.45 N	60.55 W
Caravius, Monte is ∧	71	39.09 N	8.49 E
Caraway	194	35.46 N	90.19 W
Carayaó	252	25.10 S	56.26 W
Caraza ◆[8]	288	34.42 S	58.26 W
Caràzinho	252	28.18 S	52.48 W
Carazo □[5]	236	11.45 N	86.15 W
Carballino	34	42.26 N	8.04 W
Carballo	34	43.13 N	8.41 W
Carberry	184	49.52 N	99.20 W
Carbet, Pitons du ⩕	240e	14.42 N	61.07 W
Carbó	232	29.42 N	110.58 W
Carbo ≃	70	37.32 N	12.59 E
Carbon, Alta., Can.	182	51.29 N	113.09 W
Carbon, Pa., U.S.	279b	40.17 N	79.34 W
Carbon, Tex., U.S.	196	32.16 N	98.50 W
Carbon □[6]	210	40.52 N	75.45 W
Carbon ≃	224	47.07 N	122.13 W
Carbon, Cap >	34	36.47 N	5.06 E
Carbonado	224	47.05 N	122.03 W
Carbonara, Capo >	71	39.06 N	9.31 E
Carbonara, Pizzo ∧	70	37.54 N	14.02 E
Carbonare	64	45.56 N	11.13 E
Carbon-Blanc	32	44.53 N	0.31 W
Carbon Canyon Dam ◆[6]	280	33.55 N	117.50 W
Carbon Creek ≃	280	33.49 N	118.04 W
Carbondale, Colo., U.S.	200	39.24 N	107.13 W
Carbondale, Ill., U.S.	194	37.44 N	89.13 W
Carbondale, Kans., U.S.	198	38.49 N	95.41 W
Carbondale, Pa., U.S.	210	41.35 N	75.30 W
Carbone	68	40.09 N	16.05 E
Carbonear	186	47.45 N	53.13 W
Carboneras de Guadazaon	34	39.53 N	1.48 W
Carbon Hill	194	33.48 N	87.32 W
Carbonia	71	39.10 N	8.31 E
Carbonin	64	46.37 N	12.13 E
Carbost	46	57.18 N	6.22 W
Carcagente	34	39.08 N	0.27 W
Carcajou ≃	180	65.37 N	128.43 W
Carcans, Étang de C	32	45.08 N	1.08 W
Carcar	116	10.06 N	123.38 E
Carcarañá	252	32.51 S	61.09 W
Carcarañá ≃	252	32.27 S	60.48 W
Carcare	62	44.21 N	8.18 E
Carcar Point >	116	10.05 N	123.41 E
Carcassonne	32	43.13 N	2.21 E
Carcastillo	34	42.23 N	1.26 W
Carcavelos, Port.	266c	38.53 N	9.14 W
Carcavelos, Port.	266c	38.41 N	9.20 W
Carceri, Eremo delle ⊌[1]	66	43.05 N	12.42 E
Carcès	62	43.28 N	6.11 E
Carchi □[4]	246	0.45 N	78.00 W
Carcross	180	60.10 N	134.42 W
Cardabia	162	23.06 S	113.48 E
Çardak	130	38.06 N	36.49 E
Çardal	258	34.18 S	56.24 W
Čardara	85	41.17 N	67.55 E
Čardarinskoje Vodochranilišče @[1]	85	41.10 N	68.15 E
Cardeña	34	38.13 N	4.19 W
Cárdenas, Cuba	240p	23.02 N	81.12 W
Cárdenas, Méx.	234	22.00 N	99.40 W
Cárdenas, Méx.	234	17.59 N	93.22 W
Cárdenas, Nic.	236	11.12 N	85.31 W
Cárdenas, Bahía de C	240p	23.05 N	81.10 W
Çardi	130	39.41 N	29.10 E
Cardiel, Lago @	254	48.55 S	71.15 W
Cardiff, Austl.	170	32.57 S	151.41 E
Cardiff, Wales, U.K.	42	51.29 N	3.13 W
Cardiff, Md., U.S.	208	39.42 N	76.20 W
Cardiff, N.J., U.S.	208	39.25 N	74.36 W
Cardiff-by-the-Sea	228	33.01 N	117.17 W
Cardigan, P.E.I., Can.	186	46.14 N	62.37 W
Cardigan, Wales, U.K.	42	52.06 N	4.40 W
Cardigan Bay C, P.E.I., Can.	186	46.10 N	62.30 W
Cardigan Bay C, Wales, U.K.	42	52.30 N	4.20 W
Cardigan Island I	42	52.08 N	4.41 W
Cardigan State Park ♠	188	43.38 N	71.54 W
Cardinal	212	44.47 N	75.23 W
Cardinale	68	38.38 N	16.23 E
Cardinal Heights	212	45.27 N	75.37 W
Cardinal Lake @	182	56.14 N	117.44 W
Cardington, S. Afr.	158	27.11 S	23.30 E
Cardington, Ohio, U.S.	214	40.30 N	82.53 W
Cardinia Creek ≃	274b	38.12 S	145.23 E
Cardito	68	40.57 N	14.18 E
Cardón, Punta >	246	11.37 N	70.14 W
Cardona	258	33.53 S	57.23 W
Cardoner ≃	34	41.41 N	1.51 E
Cardoso	255	20.04 S	49.54 W
Cardozo	252	32.38 S	56.21 W
Card Sound Џ	220	25.20 N	80.18 W
Cardston	182	49.12 N	113.18 W
Cardwell, Austl.	166	18.16 S	146.02 E
Cardwell, Mo., U.S.	194	36.03 N	90.17 W
Cardwell Mountain ∧	194	35.41 N	85.41 W
Čardžou	128	39.06 N	63.34 E
Čardžou □[4]	128	38.51 N	63.34 E
Careaçu	256	22.02 S	45.42 W
Careen Lake @	184	57.00 N	108.10 W
Carega, Cima ∧	64	45.44 N	11.08 E
Carei	38	47.42 N	22.28 E
Careiro	246	3.12 S	59.45 W
Careiro, Ilha do I	246	3.10 S	59.44 W
Çarén	252	30.51 S	70.47 W
Čarencavan	84	40.24 N	44.38 E
Carencro	194	30.19 N	92.03 W
Carentan	32	49.18 N	1.14 W
Careri	68	38.10 N	16.07 E
Cares ≃	34	43.19 N	4.36 W
Caresana	62	45.13 N	8.30 E
Caretta	192	37.20 N	81.41 W
Careviščina	80	52.27 N	46.43 E
Carey	214	40.57 N	83.23 W
Carey, Lake @	162	29.05 S	122.15 E
Carey Downs	162	25.38 S	115.27 E
Careysburg	150	6.30 N	10.32 W
Cargill	46	56.30 N	3.22 W
Carhaix-Plouguer	32	48.17 N	3.35 W
Carhué	252	37.11 S	62.44 W
Caria □[9]	130	37.30 N	28.00 E
Cariacica	255	20.16 S	40.25 W
Cariaco	246	10.29 N	63.33 W

PORTUGUÊS

Nome	Página	Lat.°′	Long.°′ W=Oeste
Cariaco, Golfo de C	246	10.30 N	64.00 W
Cariamanga	246	4.20 S	79.35 W
Cariango	152	10.37 S	15.20 E
Cariati	68	39.30 N	16.56 E
Caribana, Punta >	246	8.37 N	76.52 W
Caribbean Sea ⊤[2]	230	15.00 N	73.00 W
Caribe, Mar → Caribbean Sea ⊤[2]	238	15.00 S	73.00 W
Cariboo ≃	182	52.40 N	121.40 W
Cariboo Mountains ⩕	182	53.00 N	121.00 W
Caribou	186	46.52 N	68.01 W
Caribou ≃	176	59.20 N	94.44 W
Caribou, Lac du @	206	46.56 N	72.50 W
Caribou Island I	190	47.22 N	85.49 W
Caribou Mountain ∧, Idaho, U.S.	202	43.06 N	111.18 W
Caribou Mountain ∧, Maine, U.S.	188	45.26 N	70.38 W
Caribou Mountains ⩕	176	59.12 N	115.40 W
Caribou Range ⩕	202	43.05 N	111.15 W
Caričanka	78	48.57 N	34.29 E
Carichic	232	27.56 N	107.03 W
Caricuao	286c	10.27 N	66.59 W
Caricyn → Volgograd	80	48.44 N	44.25 E
Caridad, Pil.	116	10.50 N	124.45 E
Caridad, Pil.	269f	14.29 N	120.53 E
Caridade	250	4.13 S	39.12 W
Carife	68	41.01 N	15.12 E
Carigara	116	11.18 N	124.41 E
Carigara Bay C	116	11.24 N	124.40 E
Carignan	56	49.38 N	5.10 E
Carignano, It.	62	44.55 N	7.40 E
Carignano, It.	66	43.49 N	12.56 E
Cari Laufquén, Lago @	254	41.07 S	69.30 W
Carinda	166	30.28 S	147.41 E
Cariñena	34	41.20 N	1.13 W
Caringbah	274a	34.03 S	151.08 E
Carinhanha	255	14.18 S	43.47 W
Carinhanha ≃	255	14.20 S	43.47 W
Carini	70	38.08 N	13.11 E
Carini, Golfo di C	70	38.12 N	13.22 E
Carinish	46	57.31 N	7.18 W
Carinola	68	41.11 N	13.58 E
Carioca, Serra da ∧	256	22.47 S	44.18 W
Carioca, Serra da ⩕	287a	22.57 S	43.14 W
Caripe	246	10.12 N	63.29 W
Caripi ≃	250	3.56 N	51.27 W
Caripito	246	10.08 N	63.06 W
Carira	250	10.21 S	37.42 W
Cariré	250	3.57 S	40.27 W
Caririaçu	250	7.02 S	39.17 W
Carisbrooke	42	50.41 N	1.19 W
Carisolo	64	46.10 N	10.45 E
Carite	286c	10.24 N	67.01 W
Carite, Lago @	240m	18.04 N	66.06 W
Çariús	250	6.32 S	39.30 W
Čarkesar	85	41.02 N	70.53 E
Čarku	85	39.58 N	70.33 E
Carlentini	70	37.16 N	15.01 E
Carle Place	276	40.45 N	73.37 W
Carles	116	11.34 N	123.08 E
Carlet	34	39.14 N	0.31 W
Carleton, Mich., U.S.	216	42.04 N	83.23 W
Carleton, Nebr., U.S.	198	40.18 N	97.41 W
Carleton, Mount ∧	186	47.23 N	66.53 W
Carleton Place	212	45.08 N	76.09 W
Carletonville	158	26.23 S	27.22 E
Carlin	204	40.43 N	116.07 W
Carling	56	49.10 N	6.43 E
Carlingford	274a	33.47 S	151.03 E
Carlingford Lough C	44	54.04 N	6.10 W
Carlinville	219	39.17 N	89.53 W
Carlinville, Lake @[1]	219	39.14 N	89.51 W
Carlisle, Ont., Can.	212	43.23 N	79.59 W
Carlisle, Eng., U.K.	44	54.54 N	2.55 W
Carlisle, Ark., U.S.	194	34.47 N	91.45 W
Carlisle, Iowa, U.S.	190	41.30 N	93.29 W
Carlisle, Ky., U.S.	218	38.19 N	84.02 W
Carlisle, Mass., U.S.	283	42.32 N	71.21 W
Carlisle, N.Y., U.S.	210	42.45 N	74.27 W
Carlisle, Ohio, U.S.	218	39.35 N	84.20 W
Carlisle, Pa., U.S.	208	40.12 N	77.12 W
Carlisle Barracks ■	208	40.13 N	77.11 W
Carlisle Bay C	241g	13.05 N	59.37 W
Carlisle Gardens	210	43.11 N	78.39 W
Carlisle Island I	180	52.52 N	170.02 W
Carlisle Springs	208	40.16 N	77.10 W
Carl Junction	194	37.11 N	94.34 W
Carlls ≃	276	40.41 N	73.20 W
Carloforte	71	39.08 N	8.18 E
Carlopoli	68	39.03 N	16.27 E
Carlópolis	255	23.25 S	49.41 W
Carlos	218	40.02 N	85.02 W
Carlos, Isla I	254	54.03 S	73.20 W
Carlos Alves	256	21.37 S	43.07 W
Carlos Barbosa	252	29.18 S	51.30 W
Carlos Beguerie	258	35.29 S	59.06 W
Carlos Casares	252	35.38 S	61.21 W
Carlos Chagas	255	17.43 S	40.45 W
Carlos Keen	258	34.29 S	59.14 W
Carlos Pellegrini	252	32.03 S	61.48 W
Carlos Reyles	252	33.03 S	56.29 W
Carlos Sampaio	287a	22.42 S	43.31 W
Carlos Tejedor	252	35.23 S	62.25 W
Carlow	48	52.50 N	6.55 W
Carlow □[6]	48	52.50 N	7.00 W
Carloway	46	58.17 N	6.48 W
Carlsbad → Karlovy Vary, Česko.	54	50.11 N	12.52 E
Carlsbad, Calif., U.S.	228	33.10 N	117.21 W
Carlsbad, N. Mex., U.S.	196	32.25 N	104.14 W
Carlsbad, Tex., U.S.	196	31.36 N	100.38 W
Carlsbad Caverns National Park ♠	196	32.08 N	104.35 W
Carlsborg	224	48.05 N	123.10 W
Carlsfeld	54	50.26 N	12.35 E
Carlstadt	276	40.50 N	74.06 W
Carlton, Austl.	274a	33.58 S	151.08 E
Carlton, Eng., U.K.	42	52.58 N	1.05 W
Carlton, Minn., U.S.	190	46.40 N	92.25 W
Carlton, Oreg., U.S.	224	45.18 N	123.11 W
Carlton, Tex., U.S.	196	31.55 N	98.10 W
Carlton Gardens ♠	274b	37.48 S	144.59 E
Carlton Lake @	224	45.18 N	123.11 W
Carluke	46	55.45 N	3.51 W
Carlyle, Sask., Can.	184	49.38 N	102.16 W
Carlyle, Ill., U.S.	219	38.37 N	89.22 W
Carlyle Lake @[1]	219	38.40 N	89.18 W
Carmacks	180	62.05 N	136.18 W
Carmagnola	62	44.51 N	7.43 E
Carman	184	49.32 N	98.00 W
Carmanah Creek ≃	224	48.37 N	124.44 W
Carmangay	182	50.08 N	113.07 W
Carmanville	186	49.24 N	54.17 W
Carmarthen	42	51.52 N	4.19 W
Carmarthen Bay C	42	51.40 N	4.30 W
Carmaux	32	44.03 N	2.09 E
Carmel, Wales, U.K.	262	53.17 N	3.15 W
Carmel, Calif., U.S.	226	36.33 N	121.55 W
Carmel, Ind., U.S.	218	39.59 N	86.08 W
Carmel, N.J., U.S.	208	39.26 N	75.06 W
Carmel, N.Y., U.S.	210	41.26 N	73.41 W
Carmel ≃	226	36.32 N	121.56 W
Carmel, Mount ∧, Calif., U.S.	226	36.23 N	121.47 W
Carmel, Mount → HaKarmel, Har ∧, Yis.	132	32.44 N	35.02 E
Carmel Bay C	226	36.33 N	121.57 W
Carmel Head >	44	53.24 N	4.34 W
Carmel Highlands	226	36.30 N	121.56 W
Carmel Hills	226	36.32 N	121.53 W
Carmel Mountain ∧[2]	228	32.55 N	117.13 W
Carmelo	258	34.00 S	58.17 W
Carmel Point	226	36.31 N	122.55 W
Carmel Valley	226	36.29 N	121.43 W
Carmel Woods	226	36.34 N	121.54 W
Carmen → Ciudad del Carmen, Méx.	232	18.38 N	91.50 W
Carmen, Okla., U.S.	196	36.35 N	98.28 W
Carmen, Ur.	252	33.15 S	56.01 W
Carmen, Isla I	232	25.57 N	111.12 W
Carmen, Isla del I	232	18.42 N	91.40 W
Carmen, Laguna del C	234	18.17 N	93.48 W
Carmen, Río del ≃, Chile	252	28.45 S	70.30 W
Carmen, Río del ≃, Méx.	232	30.42 N	106.29 W
Carmen Alto	252	23.11 S	69.40 W
Carmen de Apicalá	246	4.09 N	74.44 W
Carmen de Areco	252	34.22 S	59.49 W
Carmen de Huechuraba	286e	33.21 S	70.40 W
Carmen de Patagones	254	40.48 S	62.59 W
Carmer Hill ∧[2]	214	41.54 N	77.58 W
Carmi, Lake @	206	44.58 N	72.53 W
Carmiano	68	40.21 N	18.03 E
Carmichael	226	38.38 N	121.19 W
Carmichael Point >	238	21.15 N	73.26 W
Carmignano di Brenta	64	45.38 N	11.42 E
Carmine	222	30.09 N	96.41 W
Carmo	256	21.56 S	42.37 W
Carmo, Monte ∧	62	44.11 N	8.11 E
Carmo, Rio do ≃	250	5.02 S	37.12 W
Carmo da Cachoeira	256	21.28 S	45.13 W
Carmo de Minas	256	22.07 S	45.08 W
Carmo do Paranaíba	255	18.59 S	46.21 W
Carmo do Rio Verde	255	15.21 S	49.42 W
Carmody Hills	284c	38.54 N	76.54 W
Carmona, Esp.	34	37.28 N	5.38 W
Carmona, Pil.	116	14.19 N	121.03 E
Carmópolis de Minas	255	20.33 S	44.38 W
Carmzow	54	53.23 N	14.02 E
Carnaíba	250	7.48 S	37.49 W
Carnarvon, Austl.	162	24.53 S	113.40 E
Carnarvon, S. Afr.	158	30.56 S	22.08 E
Carnarvon → Caernarvon, Wales, U.K.	44	53.08 N	4.16 W
Carnarvon Gorge National Park ♠	166	25.00 S	148.15 E
Carnatic ◆[1]	118	12.30 N	78.15 E
Carnation	224	47.39 N	121.55 W
Carnaxide	266c	38.43 N	9.15 W
Carncastle	48	54.54 N	5.53 W
Carndonagh	48	55.15 N	7.15 W
Carnduff	184	49.10 N	101.50 W
Carnedd Llewelyn ∧	44	53.10 N	3.58 W
Carnedd Wen ∧	42	52.41 N	3.35 W
Carnegie, Austl.	162	25.43 S	122.59 E
Carnegie, N.Y., U.S.	210	42.45 N	78.51 W
Carnegie, Okla., U.S.	196	35.06 N	98.36 W
Carnegie, Pa., U.S.	214	40.24 N	80.06 W
Carnegie, Lake @	162	26.10 S	122.30 E
Carnegie Institute ⊌[2]	279b	40.27 N	79.57 W
Carnegie-Mellon University ⊌[2]	279b	40.27 N	79.57 W
Carnegie Ridge ✢[3]	18	1.30 S	85.00 W
Carnelian Bay	226	39.14 N	120.05 W
Carnetin	261	48.54 N	2.42 E
Carnew	48	52.43 N	6.30 W
Carneys Point	208	39.43 N	75.28 W
Carnforth	44	54.08 N	2.46 W
Carnia	64	46.22 N	13.08 E
Carnia ◆[1]	64	46.25 N	13.00 E
Carniche, Alpi (Karnische Alpen) ⩕	64	46.40 N	13.00 E
Car Nicobar Island I	110	9.10 N	92.47 E
Carnide ◆[8]	266c	38.46 N	9.11 W
Carnières	50	50.10 N	3.21 E
Carniques → Karnische Alpen ⩕	64	46.40 N	13.00 E
Carnlough	48	54.59 N	5.59 W
Carno	42	52.33 N	3.31 W
Carnon-Plage	62	43.32 N	3.59 E
Carnot, Centraf.	152	4.56 N	15.52 E
Carnot, Pa., U.S.	214	40.31 N	80.13 W
Carnot, Cape >	166	34.57 S	135.38 E
Carnoules	62	43.18 N	6.11 E
Carnoustie	46	56.30 N	2.44 W
Carnsore Point >	48	52.10 N	6.22 W
Carnwath	46	55.43 N	3.38 W
Carnwath ≃	180	68.26 N	128.50 W
Caro	190	43.29 N	83.24 W
Caroga Creek ≃	210	42.58 N	74.38 W
Caroga Lake	210	43.08 N	74.29 W
Carol Beach Estates	216	42.31 N	87.49 W
Carol City	220	25.56 N	80.16 W
Caroleen	192	35.17 N	81.48 W
Carole Highlands	284c	38.58 N	76.59 W
Carolei	68	39.15 N	16.13 E
Carolina, Bra.	250	7.20 S	47.28 W
Carolina, Col.	246	6.43 N	75.17 W
Carolina, El Sal.	236	13.51 N	88.19 W
Carolina, P.R.	240m	18.23 N	65.57 W
Carolina, S. Afr.	158	26.05 S	30.06 E
Carolina, R.I., U.S.	207	41.28 N	71.40 W
Carolina Beach	192	34.02 N	77.54 W
Caroline □[6], Md., U.S.	208	38.53 N	75.50 W
Caroline □[6], Va., U.S.	208	38.00 N	77.20 W
Caroline Atoll I[1]	14	9.58 S	150.13 W
Caroline du Nord → North Carolina □[3]	192	35.30 N	80.00 W
Caroline du Sud → South Carolina □[3]	192	34.00 N	81.00 W
Caroline Islands II	14	8.00 N	147.00 E
Caroline Livermore, Mount ∧[2]	282	37.52 N	122.26 W
Caroline Peak ∧	172	45.56 S	167.13 E
Carol Stream	278	41.55 N	88.08 W
Caron	184	50.28 N	105.52 W
Caron, Lac @	190	48.00 N	78.53 W
Çarona	64	46.01 N	9.47 E
Čaronda	76	60.34 N	38.59 E
Caroní ≃	246	8.21 N	62.43 W
Caronia	70	38.01 N	14.26 E
Caronia ≃	70	38.03 N	14.26 E
Caronno Pertusella	266b	45.36 N	9.03 E
Carora	246	10.11 N	70.05 W
Carosino	68	40.27 N	17.23 E
Carouge	58	46.11 N	6.09 E
Car'ov	80	48.40 N	45.22 E
Carovigno	68	40.42 N	17.39 E
Carovilli	66	41.43 N	14.17 E
Čar'ovščina	80	53.37 N	44.45 E
Čarozero	76	60.28 N	38.39 E
Carp	212	45.21 N	76.02 W
Carp ≃, Ont., Can.	212	45.29 N	76.14 W
Carp ≃, Mich., U.S.	190	46.02 N	84.42 W
Carpaneto Piacentino	62	44.55 N	9.47 E
Carpanzano	68	39.09 N	16.18 E
Carpates → Carpathian Mountains ⩕	22	48.00 N	24.00 E
Carpathian Mountains ⩕	22	48.00 N	24.00 E
Carpații Meridionali ⩕	38	45.30 N	24.15 E
Cárpatos → Carpathian Mountains ⩕	22	48.00 N	24.00 E
Carpegna	66	43.47 N	12.20 E
Carpenedolo	64	45.22 N	10.26 E
Carpentaria, Gulf of C	164	14.00 S	139.00 E
Carpenter	198	41.03 N	104.22 W
Carpenter Creek ≃	216	40.54 N	87.12 W
Carpenter Lake @	182	51.00 N	122.55 W
Carpentersville	216	42.07 N	88.17 W
Carpentertown	279b	40.11 N	79.31 W
Carpentras	62	44.03 N	5.03 E
Carpi	64	44.47 N	10.53 E
Carpignano Sesia	62	45.32 N	8.25 E
Carpina	250	7.51 S	35.15 W
Carpineti	64	44.28 N	10.31 E
Carpineto Romano	66	41.36 N	13.05 E
Carpino	68	41.51 N	15.51 E
Carpinone	66	41.35 N	14.19 E
Carpinteria	204	34.24 N	119.31 W
Carpio	198	48.27 N	101.43 W
Carp Lake @	182	54.45 N	123.20 W
Carquefou	32	47.18 N	1.30 W
Carqueiranne	62	43.05 N	6.05 E
Carquinez Bridge ◆[5]	282	38.04 N	122.14 W
Carquinez Strait Џ	282	38.02 N	122.12 W
Carra, Lough @	48	53.42 N	9.16 W
Carrabelle	192	29.51 N	84.40 W
Carradale	46	55.35 N	5.28 W
Carramar	274a	33.53 S	150.58 E
Carrancas	256	21.30 S	44.39 W
Carr and Craggs Moor ◆[3]	262	53.43 N	2.09 W
Carranglan	116	15.58 N	121.04 E
Carrantoohill ∧	48	52.00 N	9.45 W
Carranza, Cabo >	252	35.36 S	72.38 W
Carrao ≃	246	6.17 N	62.51 W
Carrara	64	44.05 N	10.06 E
Carrascal, Chile	286e	33.25 S	70.43 W
Carrascal, Pil.	116	9.22 N	125.56 E
Carrasco, Aeropuerto Nacional de ⊠	258	34.52 S	56.02 W
Carrazedo	250	1.36 S	51.54 W
Carrboro	192	35.54 N	79.04 W
Carrbridge	46	57.17 N	3.49 W
Carrcroft	285	39.47 N	75.30 W
Carrefour Pompadour ♠	261	48.46 N	2.26 E
Carregueira, Serra da ⩕[2]	266c	38.48 N	9.15 W
Carreria	252	21.59 S	58.35 W
Carretas, Punta >	248	14.13 S	76.18 W
Carriacou I	238	12.30 N	61.27 W
Carrick □[9]	44	55.12 N	4.38 W
Carrick ◆[8]	279b	40.23 N	79.59 W
Carrickart	48	55.10 N	7.47 W
Carrickfergus	48	54.43 N	5.49 W
Carrickmacross	48	53.58 N	6.43 W
Carrick-on-Shannon	48	53.57 N	8.05 W
Carrick-on-Suir	48	52.21 N	7.25 W
Carrie, Mount ∧	224	47.53 N	123.39 W
Carriere	194	30.32 N	89.39 W
Carrière, Lac @	190	47.14 N	77.12 W
Carrières, Pointe aux >	275a	45.31 N	73.54 W
Carrières-sous-Bois	261	48.57 N	2.07 E
Carrières-sous-Poissy	261	48.57 N	2.03 E
Carrières-sur-Seine	261	48.55 N	2.11 E
Carriers Mills	194	37.41 N	88.38 W
Carrigahorig	48	53.04 N	8.09 W
Carrigaline	48	51.48 N	8.24 W
Carrigallen	48	53.59 N	7.39 W
Carrillo, C.R.	236	9.52 N	85.30 W
Carrillo, Méx.	232	26.54 N	103.55 W
Carrillo Puerto, Méx.	234	19.08 N	102.42 W
Carrillo Puerto, Méx.	234	21.09 N	104.52 W
Carrington, Eng., U.K.	262	53.26 N	2.24 W
Carrington, N. Dak., U.S.	198	47.27 N	99.08 W
Carrington Island I	202	41.00 N	112.37 W
Carrington Moss ◆[3]	262	53.25 N	2.23 W
Carr Inlet C	224	47.17 N	122.42 W
Carrión ≃	34	41.53 N	4.32 W
Carrión de los Condes	34	42.20 N	4.36 W
Carrizal ≃	234	18.01 N	102.32 W
Carrizal, Cerro ∧	196	26.43 N	100.36 W
Carrizal, Río del ≃	234	23.03 N	97.46 W
Carrizal Bajo	252	28.05 S	71.10 W
Carrizo	34	42.35 N	5.50 W
Carrizo Creek ≃	196	36.05 N	102.36 W
Carrizo Mountains ⩕	200	36.45 N	109.10 W
Carrizo Plain ≚	226	35.25 N	120.00 W
Carrizo Springs	196	28.31 N	99.52 W
Carrizo Wash ∨, U.S.	200	34.36 N	109.26 W
Carrizo Wash ∨, Calif., U.S.	204	33.05 N	115.56 W
Carrizozo	200	33.38 N	105.53 W
Carro	62	43.20 N	5.02 E
Carrodano	62	44.14 N	9.39 E
Carroll, Iowa, U.S.	198	42.04 N	94.52 W
Carroll, Nebr., U.S.	198	42.17 N	97.17 W
Carroll □[6], Ind., U.S.	216	40.36 N	86.41 W
Carroll □[6], Ky., U.S.	218	38.39 N	85.06 W
Carroll □[6], Md., U.S.	208	39.35 N	77.00 W
Carroll □[6], Ohio, U.S.	214	40.34 N	81.05 W
Carroll Lake @	184	51.07 N	95.05 W
Carroll Park ♠	284b	39.17 N	76.39 W
Carrollton, Ala., U.S.	194	33.16 N	88.05 W
Carrollton, Ga., U.S.	192	33.35 N	85.05 W
Carrollton, Ill., U.S.	219	39.18 N	90.24 W
Carrollton, Ky., U.S.	218	38.41 N	85.11 W
Carrollton, Mich., U.S.	190	43.27 N	83.54 W
Carrollton, Miss., U.S.	194	33.30 N	89.55 W
Carrollton, Mo., U.S.	194	39.22 N	93.30 W
Carrollton, Ohio, U.S.	214	40.34 N	81.05 W
Carrollton, Tex., U.S.	222	32.57 N	96.54 W
Carrollton Manor	208	39.05 N	76.35 W
Carrolltown	214	40.36 N	78.43 W
Carrols	224	46.05 N	122.52 W
Carron ≃, Scot., U.K.	46	56.02 N	3.44 W
Carron ≃, Scot., U.K.	46	57.53 N	4.21 W
Carron ≃, Scot., U.K.	46	57.25 N	5.27 W
Carron, Loch C	46	57.22 N	5.31 W
Carronbridge	44	55.16 N	3.48 W
Carron Valley Reservoir @[1]	46	56.02 N	4.05 W
Carros	62	43.48 N	7.11 E
Carrot ≃	184	53.50 N	101.17 W
Carrot River	184	53.17 N	103.35 W
Carrouges	28	48.34 N	0.09 W
Carrowmore Lake @	48	54.12 N	9.47 W
Carrsville	208	36.43 N	76.50 W
Carrù	62	44.29 N	7.52 E
Carrville	194	32.33 N	85.52 W
Carry Falls Reservoir @[1]	188	44.25 N	74.45 W
Carry-le-Rouet	62	43.20 N	5.09 E
Carsaig	46	56.17 N	6.00 W
Çarşamba	130	41.12 N	36.44 E
Čaršanga	128	37.30 N	66.01 E
Carseland	182	50.51 N	113.28 W
Çarshalton ◆[8]	260	51.22 N	0.10 W
Čarsk	86	49.35 N	81.05 E
Carsoli	66	42.06 N	13.05 E
Carson, Calif., U.S.	228	33.50 N	118.16 W
Carson, N. Dak., U.S.	198	46.25 N	101.34 W
Carson, Va., U.S.	208	37.02 N	77.24 W
Carson, Wash., U.S.	224	45.44 N	121.49 W
Carson ≃	204	39.45 N	118.40 W
Carson, East Fork ≃	226	38.59 N	119.49 W
Carson, West Fork ≃	226	38.59 N	119.49 W
Carson City, Mich., U.S.	190	43.11 N	84.51 W
Carson City, Nev., U.S.	226	39.10 N	119.46 W
Carsondale	284c	38.57 N	76.50 W
Carson Lake @, Ont., Can.	212	45.31 N	77.46 W
Carson Lake @, Nev., U.S.	204	39.19 N	118.43 W
Carson Sink @	204	39.45 N	118.30 W
Carson Valley ∨	226	39.00 N	119.48 W
Carstairs, Alta., Can.	182	51.34 N	114.06 W
Carstairs, Scot., U.K.	46	55.42 N	3.42 W
Carstensz-Toppen → Jaya Puncak ∧	164	4.05 S	137.11 E
Carswell Air Force Base ■	222	32.47 N	97.26 W
Cartagena, Chile	252	33.33 S	71.37 W
Cartagena, Col.	246	10.25 N	75.32 W
Cartagena, Esp.	34	37.36 N	0.59 W
Cartago, Col.	246	4.45 N	75.55 W
Cartago, C.R.	236	9.52 N	83.55 W
Çartago □[4]	236	9.50 N	83.45 W
Čartak	85	41.05 N	71.50 E
Cartaxo	34	39.09 N	8.47 W
Cartaxos ∧[2]	266c	38.54 N	9.20 W
Cartaya	34	37.17 N	7.09 W
Carter	196	35.13 N	99.30 W
Carter □[6]	218	38.20 N	83.05 W
Carter Bridge ◆[5]	273a	6.28 N	3.23 E
Carter Caves State Park ♠	218	38.22 N	83.10 W
Carteret	210	40.35 N	74.13 W
Carter Lake	198	41.18 N	95.54 W
Carter Mountain ∧	202	44.12 N	109.25 W
Carters Lake @[1]	192	34.35 N	84.35 W
Cartersville	192	34.10 N	84.48 W
Carterton	172	41.02 S	175.31 E
Carterville	194	37.46 N	89.05 W
Carthage, Tun.	148	36.51 N	10.21 E
Carthage, Ark., U.S.	194	34.04 N	92.33 W
Carthage, Ill., U.S.	190	40.25 N	91.08 W
Carthage, Ind., U.S.	218	39.44 N	85.34 W
Carthage, Miss., U.S.	194	32.46 N	89.32 W
Carthage, Mo., U.S.	194	37.11 N	94.19 W
Carthage, N.C., U.S.	192	35.21 N	79.25 W
Carthage, N.Y., U.S.	212	43.59 N	75.37 W
Carthage, S. Dak., U.S.	198	44.10 N	97.43 W
Carthage, Tenn., U.S.	194	36.15 N	85.57 W
Carthage, Tex., U.S.	194	32.09 N	94.20 W
Carthage ⊥	148	36.52 N	10.20 E
Cartier, Lac @	206	46.22 N	74.00 W
Cartier Island I	160	12.32 S	123.32 E
Cartierville ◆[8]	275a	45.32 N	73.42 W
Cartierville Airport ⊠	275a	45.31 N	73.43 W
Cartridge Hill ∧[2]	262	53.41 N	2.30 W
Cartura	64	45.16 N	11.50 E
Cartwright, Man., Can.	184	49.06 N	99.20 W
Cartwright, Newf., Can.	176	53.42 N	57.01 W
Caruaru	250	8.17 S	35.58 W
Caruban	115a	7.33 S	111.39 E
Çarumas	248	16.49 S	70.43 W
Čarüngol	88	49.14 N	106.29 E
Carunjamba ≃	152	13.57 S	12.25 E
Carúpano	246	10.40 N	63.14 W
Caruray	116	10.20 N	119.00 E
Carutapera	250	1.13 S	46.01 W
Caruthers	226	36.32 N	119.50 W
Caruthersville	194	36.11 N	89.39 W
Carvalhos	256	22.00 S	44.28 W
Carver	207	41.53 N	70.46 W
Carversville	208	40.23 N	75.04 W
Carvin	50	50.29 N	2.58 E
Carvoeiro	246	1.24 S	61.59 W
Carvoeiro, Cabo >	34	39.21 N	9.24 W
Cary, Ill., U.S.	216	42.13 N	88.15 W
Cary, Miss., U.S.	194	32.49 N	90.56 W
Cary, N.C., U.S.	192	35.47 N	78.46 W
Cary ≃	42	51.09 N	2.59 W
Çaryk, Ozero @	80	46.13 N	42.43 E
Çarymovo	86	58.31 N	77.42 E
Çaryn	86	43.46 N	79.24 E
Çaryš ≃	86	52.22 N	83.45 E
Čaryšskoje	86	51.24 N	83.35 E
Caryville, Fla., U.S.	194	30.46 N	85.49 W
Caryville, Tenn., U.S.	192	36.18 N	84.14 W
Casablanca (Dar-el-Beida)	148	33.39 N	7.35 W
Casa Blanca ◆[8]	286b	23.09 N	82.20 W
Casabona	68	39.15 N	16.57 E
Casa Branca	256	21.46 S	47.04 W
Casacalenda	66	41.44 N	14.51 E
Casa de la Torrecilla	266a	40.19 N	3.37 W
Casa Grande	200	32.53 N	111.45 W
Casa Grande National Monument ♠	200	32.50 N	111.32 W
Casainhos	266c	38.53 N	9.10 W
Casalanguida	66	42.03 N	14.30 E
Casalattico	66	41.37 N	13.43 E
Casalbordino	66	42.09 N	14.35 E
Casalbuono	68	40.13 N	15.41 E
Casalbuttano	64	45.15 N	9.58 E
Casal di Principe	68	41.00 N	14.08 E
Casale Abbruciato ◆[8]	267a	41.44 N	12.33 E
Casalecchio di Reno	64	44.28 N	11.16 E
Casale Monferrato	62	45.08 N	8.27 E
Casale sul Sile	64	45.36 N	12.19 E
Casaletto Spartano	68	40.09 N	15.37 E
Casalmaggiore	64	44.59 N	10.26 E
Casalmorano	62	45.17 N	9.54 E
Casalnuovo Monterotaro	68	41.37 N	15.06 E
Casa Loma ⊌	275b	43.41 N	79.25 W
Casalone ◆[8]	267a	41.56 N	12.41 E
Casalotti ◆[8]	267a	41.55 N	12.22 E
Casalpusterlengo	62	45.11 N	9.39 E
Casal Velino	68	40.11 N	15.06 E
Casalvieri	66	41.38 N	13.43 E
Casamance □[4]	150	12.50 N	15.00 W
Casamance ≃	150	12.33 N	16.46 W
Casamari, Abbazia di ⊌[1]	66	41.41 N	13.29 E
Casamassima	68	40.57 N	16.55 E
Casamicciola Terme	68	40.45 N	13.54 E
Casanare □[3]	246	5.45 N	72.00 W
Casanare ≃	246	6.02 N	69.51 W
Casanay	246	10.30 N	63.25 W
Casa Nova	250	9.25 S	41.08 W
Casarano	68	40.00 N	18.10 E
Casar de Cáceres	34	39.34 N	6.25 W
Casarsa della Delizia	64	45.57 N	12.50 E
Casas	234	23.44 N	98.45 W
Casas Adobes	200	32.19 N	110.59 W
Casas Grandes ≃	232	31.22 N	107.31 W
Casas Ibáñez	34	39.17 N	1.28 W
Casasimarro	34	39.22 N	2.02 W
Casauman ≃	116	7.16 N	126.31 E
Casa Verde ◆[8]	287b	23.30 S	46.39 W
Casavieja	34	40.17 N	4.46 W
Casbas	252	36.45 S	62.30 W
Casca	252	28.34 S	51.59 W
Casca, Rio da ≃	248	14.52 S	55.52 W
Cascade, B.C., Can.	182	49.01 N	118.13 W
Cascade, Idaho, U.S.	202	44.31 N	116.02 W
Cascade, Iowa, U.S.	190	42.18 N	91.01 W
Cascade, Mich., U.S.	216	42.55 N	85.30 W
Cascade, Mont., U.S.	202	47.16 N	111.42 W
Cascade, Wis., U.S.	190	43.40 N	88.00 W
Cascade ≃, N.Z.	172	44.02 S	168.22 E
Cascade ≃, Wash., U.S.	224	48.32 N	121.26 W
Cascade Bay C	174c	29.01 S	167.58 E
Cascade Locks	224	45.40 N	121.54 W

	English	Deutsch	Español	Français	Português
≃	River	Fluss	Río	Rivière	Rio
≊	Canal	Kanal	Canal	Canal	Canal
ᒪ	Waterfall, Rapids	Wasserfall, Stromschnellen	Cascada, Rápidos	Chute d'eau, Rapides	Cascata, Rápidos
Џ	Strait	Meeresstrasse	Estrecho	Détroit	Estreito
C	Bay, Gulf	Bucht, Golf	Bahía, Golfo	Baie, Golfe	Baía, Golfo
@	Lake, Lakes	See, Seen	Lago, Lagos	Lac, Lacs	Lago, Lagos
≋	Swamp	Sumpf	Pantano	Marais	Pântano
⊼	Ice Features, Glacier	Eis- und Gletscherformen	Accidentes Glaciales	Formes glaciaires	Acidentes Glaciares
⊤	Other Hydrographic Features	Andere Hydrographische Objekte	Otros Elementos Hidrográficos	Autres données hydrographiques	Outros Elementos Hidrográficos
✢	Submarine Features	Untermeerische Objekte	Accidentes Submarinos	Formes de relief sous-marin	Acidentes Submarinos
□	Political Unit	Politische Einheit	Unidad Politica	Entité politique	Unidade Política
⊌	Cultural Institution	Kulturelle Institution	Institución Cultural	Institution culturelle	Instituição Cultural
⊥	Historical Site	Historische Stätte	Sitio Histórico	Site historique	Sitio Histórico
♠	Recreational Site	Erholungs- und Ferienort	Sitio de Recreo	Centre de loisirs	Sítio de Lazer
⊠	Airport	Flughafen	Aeropuerto	Aéroport	Aeroporto
■	Military Installation	Militäranlage	Instalación Militar	Installation militaire	Instalação Militar
◆	Miscellaneous	Verschiedenes	Misceláneo	Divers	Miscelânea

Name	Page	Lat.	Long.
Cascade Mountains	224	49.20 N	121.00 W
Cascade Park	279a	41.23 N	82.06 W
Cascade Point	172	44.00 S	168.22 E
Cascade Range	202	45.00 N	121.30 W
Cascade Reservoir	202	44.35 N	116.06 W
Cascade Tunnel	224	47.40 N	121.03 W
Cascadura	287a	22.53 S	43.20 W
Cascais	34	38.42 N	9.25 W
Cascalho Rico	255	18.34 S	47.52 W
Cascapédia	186	48.11 N	65.54 W
Cascatinha	256	22.29 S	43.09 W
Cascavel, Bra.	250	4.07 S	38.14 W
Cascavel, Bra.	252	24.57 S	53.28 W
Cascia	66	42.43 N	13.01 E
Casciana Terme	66	43.31 N	10.32 E
Cascina	66	43.41 N	10.33 E
Casco Bay	188	43.40 N	70.00 W
Cascumpec Bay	186	46.45 N	64.03 W
Čascy	82	55.37 N	36.52 E
Casei Gerola	62	45.00 N	8.55 E
Case Inlet	224	47.19 N	122.53 W
Casekow	54	53.12 N	14.12 E
Casella	62	44.32 N	9.00 E
Caselle, Aeroporto di	62	45.13 N	7.40 E
Caselle in Pittari	68	40.10 N	15.33 E
Caselle Torinese	62	45.10 N	7.39 E
Casemero Palma	236	16.20 N	88.47 W
Casenove	66	42.58 N	12.50 E
Casentino	66	43.40 N	11.50 E
Casenuove	266b	45.38 N	8.42 E
Case-Pilote	240e	14.38 N	61.08 W
Caseros	258	34.36 S	58.33 W
Caserta	68	41.04 N	14.20 E
Caserta □[4]	68	41.14 N	14.10 E
Caseville	190	43.56 N	83.16 W
Case Western Reserve University	279a	41.30 N	81.36 W
Casey, Ill., U.S.	194	39.18 N	87.59 W
Casey, Iowa, U.S.	198	41.31 N	94.32 W
Casey, Mount	182	48.26 N	116.42 W
Casey Bay	9	67.20 S	48.00 E
Casey Key	220	27.10 N	82.29 W
Caseyville	219	38.38 N	90.02 W
Cash	222	32.59 N	96.07 W
Cashel, Eire	48	52.31 N	7.53 W
Cashel, Eire	48	53.25 N	9.48 W
Cashie	192	35.53 N	76.49 W
Cashiers	192	35.06 N	83.06 W
Cashmere	202	47.31 N	120.28 W
Cashmere Downs	162	28.58 S	119.35 E
Cashton	190	43.43 N	90.47 W
Cashtown	208	39.53 N	77.22 W
Casigua (El Cubo)	246	8.46 N	72.30 W
Casiguran, Pil.	116	12.52 N	124.00 E
Casiguran, Pil.	116	16.17 N	122.07 E
Casiguran Sound	116	16.06 N	121.58 E
Casilda, Arg.	252	33.03 S	61.10 W
Casilda, Cuba	240p	21.46 N	79.59 W
Casimcea	38	44.43 N	28.23 E
Casimiro Castillo	234	19.38 N	104.28 W
Casimiro de Abreu	255	22.29 S	42.12 W
Casina	64	44.30 N	10.30 E
Casino	166	28.52 S	153.03 E
Casiquiare	246	2.01 N	67.07 W
Casitas Springs	228	34.22 N	119.18 W
Čáslav	30	49.54 N	15.23 E
Casma	248	9.28 S	78.19 W
Čašniki	76	54.52 N	29.08 E
Čašnikovo	265b	55.59 N	37.25 E
Casogoran Bay	116	10.46 N	125.44 E
Casola in Lunigiana	64	44.14 N	10.10 E
Casole d'Elsa	66	43.20 N	11.02 E
Casoli	66	42.07 N	14.18 E
Cason	222	33.02 N	94.49 W
Casorate Primo	62	45.19 N	9.01 E
Casorate Sempione	62	45.40 N	8.44 E
Casorezzo	266b	45.31 N	8.54 E
Casoria	68	40.54 N	14.17 E
Časov Jar	83	48.35 N	37.50 E
Časovo	24	62.01 N	50.36 E
Caspe	34	41.14 N	0.02 W
Casper	200	42.51 N	106.19 W
Casper Creek, Middle Fork	200	43.01 N	106.29 W
Caspian	190	46.03 N	88.38 W
Caspian Sea	72	42.00 N	50.30 E
Caspienne, Mer → Caspian Sea	72	42.00 N	50.30 E
Caspio, Depresión del → Prikaspijskaja Nizmennost'	80	48.00 N	52.00 E
Caspio, Mar → Caspian Sea	72	42.00 N	50.30 E
Caspoggio	64	46.16 N	9.52 E
Cass □[6], Ill., U.S.	219	39.57 N	90.13 W
Cass □[6], Ind., U.S.	216	40.45 N	86.21 W
Cass □[6], Mich., U.S.	216	41.55 N	86.01 W
Cass □[6], Tex., U.S.	222	33.05 N	94.32 W
Cass	190	43.23 N	83.59 W
Cassadaga	214	42.21 N	79.19 W
Cassadaga Creek	214	42.05 N	79.08 W
Cassadaga Lakes	214	42.21 N	79.19 W
Cassaday Point	284a	42.52 N	79.13 W
Cassagnas	62	44.16 N	3.45 E
Cassagnes-Bégonhès	32	44.10 N	2.32 E
Cassai	152	10.33 S	21.59 E
Cassai (Kasai)	152	3.02 S	16.57 E
Cassamba	152	13.06 S	20.18 E
Cassandra	214	40.24 N	78.38 W
Cassange	248	17.06 S	57.23 W
Cassano allo Ionio	68	39.47 N	16.20 E
Cassano d'Adda	62	45.32 N	9.31 E
Cassano delle Murge	68	40.53 N	16.46 E
Cassano Magnago	62	45.41 N	8.50 E
Cassaro	70	37.07 N	14.56 E
Cass Benton Park	281	42.25 N	83.28 W
Cass City	190	43.36 N	83.10 W
Cassel	50	50.48 N	2.29 E
Casselberry	220	28.41 N	81.20 W
Cassella	216	40.25 N	84.34 W
Casselman	206	45.19 N	75.05 W
Casselton	198	46.54 N	97.13 W
Cássia, Bra.	255	20.36 S	46.56 W
Cassia, Fla., U.S.	220	28.53 N	81.28 W
Cássia dos Coqueiros	256	21.17 S	47.10 W
Cassiar	180	59.16 N	129.40 W
Cassiar Mountains	176	59.00 N	129.00 W
Cassibile	70	36.57 N	15.11 E
Cassidy	224	49.04 N	123.53 W
Cassilândia	255	19.09 S	51.45 W
Cassimbazar	126	24.07 N	88.16 E
Cassine	62	44.45 N	8.31 E
Cassinetta di Lugagnano	266b	45.25 N	8.54 E
Cassinga	152	15.08 S	16.05 E
Cassino, Bra.	252	32.11 S	52.10 W
Cassino, It.	66	41.30 N	13.49 E
Cassio	64	44.35 N	10.02 E
Cassipore	272b	22.37 N	88.22 E
Cassis	62	43.13 N	5.32 E
Cass Lake	190	47.23 N	94.36 W
Cass Lake	190	47.25 N	94.32 W
Cassley	46	57.58 N	4.35 W
Cassoalala	152	9.30 S	14.22 E
Cassoango	152	13.42 S	20.56 E
Cassolnovo	62	45.22 N	8.48 E
Cassone	64	45.44 N	10.46 E
Cassongue	152	11.51 S	15.03 E
Cassopolis	216	41.55 N	86.01 W
Cassou	150	11.35 N	2.03 W
Casstown	218	40.03 N	84.08 W
Cassunda	152	10.57 S	21.03 E
Cassununga	255	16.03 S	53.38 W
Cassville, Ind., U.S.	216	40.33 N	86.08 W
Cassville, Mo., U.S.	194	36.41 N	93.52 W
Cassville, N.Y., U.S.	210	42.57 N	75.15 W
Cassville, Pa., U.S.	214	40.18 N	78.02 W
Cassville, Wis., U.S.	190	42.43 N	90.59 W
Castac Lake	228	34.50 N	118.51 W
Castagnaro	64	45.07 N	11.24 E
Castagneto Carducci	66	43.10 N	10.36 E
Castaic	228	34.30 N	118.37 W
Castaic Creek	228	34.25 N	118.37 W
Castaic Lake	228	34.32 N	118.37 W
Castalia	214	41.24 N	82.48 W
Castanea	210	41.07 N	77.26 W
Castanhal	250	1.18 S	47.55 W
Castanheira de Pêra	34	40.00 N	8.13 W
Castañones, Punta	236	12.28 N	87.11 W
Castano Primo	62	45.33 N	8.47 E
Casteggio	62	45.00 N	9.07 E
Castel	43b	49.28 N	2.34 W
Castelar	258	34.40 S	58.40 W
Castel Baronia	68	41.03 N	15.11 E
Castel Bolognese	66	44.19 N	11.48 E
Castelbuono	70	37.56 N	14.05 E
Castelcivita	68	40.30 N	15.15 E
Casteldaccia	70	38.03 N	13.32 E
Castel d'Ario	64	45.11 N	10.58 E
Casteldarne (Ehrenburg)	64	46.48 N	11.50 E
Casteldelfino	62	44.35 N	7.04 E
Castel del Monte	66	42.22 N	13.43 E
Castel del Piano	66	42.53 N	11.32 E
Castel del Rio	66	44.12 N	11.30 E
Castel di Decima	267a	41.45 N	12.26 E
Castel di Guido	267a	41.54 N	12.17 E
Castel di Ieri	66	42.06 N	13.44 E
Castel di Leva	267a	41.47 N	12.32 E
Castel di Lucio	70	37.53 N	14.19 E
Castel di Iudica	70	37.30 N	14.38 E
Castel di Sangro	66	41.47 N	14.06 E
Castel di Tora	66	42.13 N	12.58 E
Castelfidardo	66	43.28 N	13.33 E
Castelfiorentino	66	43.36 N	10.58 E
Castelfondo	64	46.27 N	11.07 E
Castelforte	66	41.18 N	13.49 E
Castelfranco di Sotto	66	43.42 N	10.45 E
Castelfranco Emilia	64	44.37 N	11.03 E
Castelfranco in Miscano	68	41.18 N	15.05 E
Castelfranco Veneto	64	45.40 N	11.55 E
Castel Frentano	66	42.12 N	14.22 E
Castel Fusano	267a	41.44 N	12.19 E
Castel Gandolfo	66	41.45 N	12.39 E
Castel Giorgio	66	42.42 N	11.59 E
Castelgrande	68	40.47 N	15.26 E
Castelhanos, Baía de	256	23.51 S	45.15 W
Castelhanos, Ponta dos	256	23.10 S	44.06 W
Casteljaloux	32	44.19 N	0.05 E
Castellabate	68	40.17 N	14.57 E
Castell'Alfero	62	44.59 N	8.13 E
Castellalto	66	42.40 N	13.49 E
Castellammare, Golfo di	70	38.08 N	12.54 E
Castellammare del Golfo	70	38.01 N	12.53 E
Castellammare di Stabia	68	40.42 N	14.29 E
Castellamonte	62	45.23 N	7.42 E
Castellana, Grotte di	68	40.53 N	17.07 E
Castellana Grotte	68	40.53 N	17.11 E
Castellana Sicula	70	37.47 N	14.02 E
Castellane	62	43.51 N	6.31 E
Castellaneta	68	40.37 N	16.57 E
Castellanza	62	45.37 N	8.54 E
Castellarano	64	44.30 N	10.44 E
Castell'Arquato	62	44.51 N	9.52 E
Castell'Azzara	66	42.46 N	11.42 E
Castellazzo Bormida	62	44.51 N	8.34 E
Castellbisbal	266d	41.29 N	1.59 E
Castelldefels	266d	41.17 N	1.59 E
Castelleone	62	45.18 N	9.46 E
Castelletto	266b	45.30 N	8.48 E
Castelletto di Brenzone	64	45.41 N	10.45 E
Castelli, Arg.	252	36.06 S	57.47 W
Castelli, It.	66	42.29 N	13.43 E
Castellina in Chianti	66	43.28 N	11.17 E
Castellina Marittima	66	43.25 N	10.35 E
Castelli Romani	267a	41.46 N	12.42 E
Castello, Monte	66	43.03 N	9.49 E
Castello d'Annone	62	44.53 N	8.19 E
Castello di Fiemme	64	46.17 N	11.26 E
Castello Lavazzo	64	46.17 N	12.18 E
Castellón □[4]	34	40.10 N	0.10 W
Castellón de la Plana	34	39.59 N	0.02 W
Castellote	34	40.48 N	0.19 W
Castello Tesino	64	46.04 N	11.38 E
Castellucchio	64	45.09 N	10.39 E
Castelluccio	68	40.00 N	15.58 E
Castell'Umberto	70	38.05 N	14.48 E
Castelluzzo	70	38.06 N	12.44 E
Castel Madama	66	41.58 N	12.52 E
Castel Maggiore	64	44.34 N	11.22 E
Castelmagno	62	44.24 N	7.13 E
Castelmassa	64	45.01 N	11.18 E
Castelmauro	66	41.50 N	14.43 E
Castelmezzano	68	40.32 N	16.03 E
Castelmoron-sur-Lot	32	44.24 N	0.30 E
Castelnaudary	32	43.19 N	1.57 E
Castelnau-Montratier	32	44.16 N	1.21 E
Castelnovo di Sotto	64	44.49 N	10.34 E
Castelnovo ne'Monti	64	44.26 N	10.24 E
Castelnuovo	64	45.26 N	10.47 E
Castelnuovo Berardenga	66	43.21 N	11.30 E
Castelnuovo dell'Abate	66	43.00 N	11.31 E
Castelnuovo della Daunia	68	41.35 N	15.07 E
Castelnuovo di Garfagnana	64	44.06 N	10.24 E
Castelnuovo di Porto	66	42.07 N	12.30 E
Castelnuovo di Val di Cecina	66	43.12 N	10.59 E
Castelnuovo Don Bosco	62	45.03 N	7.58 E
Castelnuovo Nigra	62	45.26 N	7.41 E
Castelnuovo Rangone	64	44.33 N	10.56 E
Castelnuovo Scrivia	62	44.59 N	8.53 E
Castelo	255	20.36 S	41.12 W
Castelo Branco	34	39.49 N	7.30 W
Castelo do Piauí	250	5.20 S	41.33 W
Castel Pagano	68	41.24 N	14.48 E
Castel Porziano	267a	41.44 N	12.24 E
Castelraimondo	66	43.12 N	13.04 E
Castel Romano	267a	41.44 N	12.27 E
Castel San Gimignano	66	43.24 N	11.00 E
Castel San Giorgio	68	40.47 N	14.42 E
Castel San Giovanni	62	45.04 N	9.26 E
Castel San Lorenzo	68	40.25 N	15.14 E
Castel San Pietro	66	44.24 N	11.35 E
Castel Sant'Elia	66	42.15 N	12.22 E
Castelsaraceno	68	40.10 N	16.00 E
Castelsardo	71	40.55 N	8.43 E
Castelsarrasin	32	44.02 N	1.06 E
Castelsilano	68	39.16 N	16.46 E
Casteltermini	70	37.32 N	13.39 E
Castelvecchio Subequo	66	42.08 N	13.44 E
Castelvetere in Val Fortore	68	41.27 N	14.56 E
Castelvetrano	70	37.41 N	12.47 E
Castelvetro di Modena	64	44.30 N	10.57 E
Castelvetro Piacentino	64	45.05 N	9.59 E
Castel Viscardo	66	42.45 N	12.00 E
Castel Volturno, It.	66	44.13 N	11.37 E
Castel Volturno, It.	68	41.02 N	13.56 E
Castenaso	64	44.30 N	11.28 E
Castenedolo	64	45.28 N	10.18 E
Casterton	166	37.35 S	141.24 E
Castets	32	43.53 N	1.09 W
Castiglioncello	66	43.24 N	10.24 E
Castiglione Chiavarese	62	44.16 N	9.31 E
Castiglione d'Adda	62	45.13 N	9.41 E
Castiglione dei Pepoli	64	44.08 N	11.09 E
Castiglione del Lago	66	43.07 N	12.03 E
Castiglione della Pescaia	66	42.46 N	10.53 E
Castiglione delle Stiviere	64	45.23 N	10.29 E
Castiglione del Pepoli	66	44.08 N	11.09 E
Castiglione di Sicilia	70	37.53 N	15.07 E
Castiglione d'Orcia	66	43.00 N	11.37 E
Castiglione d'Ossola	58	46.03 N	8.13 E
Castiglione Messer Marino	66	41.52 N	14.27 E
Castiglione Olona	62	45.46 N	8.52 E
Castiglion Fibocchi	66	43.32 N	11.46 E
Castiglion Fiorentino	66	43.20 N	11.55 E
Castile	210	42.38 N	78.03 W
Castilho	255	20.52 S	51.29 W
Castilla	248	5.12 S	80.38 W
Castilla, Playa de	34	37.00 N	6.33 W
Castilla la Nueva □[9]	34	40.00 N	3.45 W
Castilla la Vieja □[9]	34	41.30 N	4.00 W
Castillo	258	33.53 S	57.40 W
Castillo, Cerro	254	43.03 S	71.57 W
Castillo, Pampa del	254	45.58 S	68.24 W
Castillo de San Marcos National Monument	192	29.44 N	81.20 W
Castillo Incasico de Ingapirca	246	2.34 S	78.50 W
Castillon-la-Bataille	32	44.51 N	0.03 W
Castillos	252	34.12 S	53.50 W
Castillos, Laguna de	252	34.20 S	53.54 W
Castillo Velasco	234	16.45 N	96.35 W
Castine	188	44.23 N	68.43 W
Castione della Presolana	64	45.54 N	10.04 E
Castions di Strada	64	45.54 N	13.11 E
Castle Acre	42	52.42 N	0.41 E
Castle Air Force Base	226	37.22 N	120.34 W
Castlebar	48	53.52 N	9.17 W
Castlebay	46	56.57 N	7.28 W
Castlebellingham	48	53.54 N	6.23 W
Castleberry	194	31.17 N	87.02 W
Castleblayney	48	54.07 N	6.44 W
Castle Bruce	240d	15.26 N	61.16 W
Castle Cape	180	56.15 N	158.06 W
Castle Cary	42	51.06 N	2.31 W
Castlecliff	172	39.57 S	174.59 E
Castlecomer	48	52.48 N	7.12 W
Castlecrag	274a	33.48 S	151.13 E
Castle Crags State Park	204	41.10 N	122.20 W
Castle Creek	210	42.14 N	75.55 W
Castle Creek, Austl.	169	36.41 S	145.29 E
Castle Creek, Idaho, U.S.	202	43.06 N	116.16 W
Castle Dale	200	39.13 N	111.01 W
Castledawson	44	54.47 N	6.33 W
Castlederg	48	54.42 N	7.36 W
Castledermot	48	52.55 N	6.50 W
Castle Dome Peak	200	33.05 N	114.08 W
Castle Donington	42	52.51 N	1.19 W
Castle Douglas	44	54.57 N	3.56 W
Castlefin	48	54.47 N	7.35 W
Castleford	44	53.44 N	1.21 W
Castlegar	182	49.19 N	117.40 W
Castle Harbour	240a	32.21 N	64.40 W
Castle Hill	274a	33.44 S	151.00 E
Castle Hills, Del., U.S.	208	39.41 N	75.34 W
Castle Hills, Tex., U.S.	196	29.32 N	98.31 W
Castleisland	48	52.14 N	9.27 W
Castlemaine, Austl.	169	37.04 S	144.13 E
Castlemaine, Eire	48	52.09 N	9.43 W
Castlemartyr	48	51.55 N	8.03 W
Castlemore	275b	43.47 N	79.41 W
Castle Mountain, Yukon, Can.	180	64.32 N	135.25 W
Castle Mountain, Calif., U.S.	226	35.56 N	120.20 W
Castle Neck	283	42.41 N	70.45 W
Castle Neck	283	42.40 N	70.44 W
Castle Park	228	32.37 N	117.04 W
Castle Peak, Colo., U.S.	200	39.00 N	106.55 W
Castle Peak, Idaho, U.S.	202	44.02 N	114.35 W
Castle Peak, Wash., U.S.	224	48.58 N	120.51 W
Castlepoint	172	40.54 S	176.13 E
Castle Point □[8]	260	51.33 N	0.35 E
Castlepollard	48	53.40 N	7.17 W
Castlerea	48	53.46 N	8.29 W
Castlereagh	48	54.33 N	5.48 W
Castlereagh	166	30.12 S	147.32 E
Castle Rock, Colo., U.S.	200	39.22 N	104.51 W
Castle Rock, Pa., U.S.	285	39.58 N	75.26 W
Castle Rock, Wash., U.S.	224	46.17 N	122.54 W
Castle Rock, Oreg., U.S.	202	44.02 N	118.11 W
Castle Rock, Va., U.S.	192	37.57 N	78.44 W
Castle Rock Butte	198	45.00 N	103.27 W
Castle Rock Lake	190	43.56 N	89.58 W
Castle Shannon	279b	40.22 N	80.02 W
Castleshaw Moor	262	53.36 N	2.00 W
Castleside	44	54.50 N	1.52 W
Castleton, Eng., U.K.	44	54.28 N	0.56 W
Castleton, Eng., U.K.	44	53.21 N	1.46 W
Castleton, Eng., U.K.	262	53.35 N	2.11 W
Castleton, Ind., U.S.	218	39.54 N	86.03 W
Castleton, Vt., U.S.	188	43.37 N	73.11 W
Castleton on Hudson	210	42.32 N	73.45 W
Castletown, Eire	48	53.26 N	7.38 W
Castletown, I. of Man	44	54.04 N	4.40 W
Castletown, Scot., U.K.	46	58.35 N	3.23 W
Castletown Bere (Castletown Bearhaven)	48	51.39 N	9.55 W
Castletownroche	48	52.10 N	8.28 W
Castletownshend	48	51.32 N	9.11 W
Castlewellan	48	54.16 N	5.57 W
Castlewood, Ky., U.S.	218	38.04 N	84.27 W
Castlewood, S. Dak., U.S.	198	44.43 N	97.02 W
Castlewood, Va., U.S.	192	36.54 N	82.17 W
Častoje	82	54.11 N	37.47 E
Častooz'ornoje	86	55.34 N	67.53 E
Castor	182	52.13 N	111.53 W
Castor, Ont., Can.	212	45.18 N	75.10 W
Castor, Mo., U.S.	194	36.51 N	89.44 W
Castorano	66	42.54 N	13.43 E
Castor Creek	194	31.47 N	92.22 W
Castorland	212	43.53 N	75.31 W
Castra Vetera	263	51.39 N	6.28 E
Castres	32	43.36 N	2.15 E
Castricum	52	52.33 N	4.39 E
Castries, Fr.	62	43.40 N	3.59 E
Castries, St. Luc.	241f	14.01 N	61.00 W
Castries, Port	241f	14.01 N	61.01 W
Castro, Bra.	252	24.47 S	50.00 W
Castro, Chile	254	42.29 S	73.46 W
Castro, It.	64	45.48 N	10.04 E
Castro, Arroyo de	258	33.37 S	56.10 W
Castro, Punta	254	43.22 S	65.03 W
Castro Barros	252	30.35 S	65.44 W
Castrocaro	66	44.10 N	11.57 E
Castrocielo	66	41.32 N	13.42 E
Castro Daire	34	40.54 N	7.56 W
Castro dei Volsci	66	41.30 N	13.24 E
Castro del Río	34	37.41 N	4.28 W
Castrofilippo	70	37.21 N	13.46 E
Castrojeriz	34	42.17 N	4.08 W
Castro Marim	34	37.13 N	7.26 W
Castronuño	34	41.23 N	5.16 W
Castronuovo di Sant'Andrea	68	40.11 N	16.11 E
Castronuovo di Sicilia	70	37.41 N	13.36 E
Castropignano	66	41.37 N	14.33 E
Castropol	34	43.32 N	7.02 W
Castrop-Rauxel	52	51.34 N	7.18 E
Castroreale	70	38.06 N	15.12 E
Castro-Urdiales	34	43.23 N	3.13 W
Castro Valley	226	37.42 N	122.04 W
Castro Verde	34	37.42 N	8.05 W
Castrovillari	68	39.49 N	16.13 E
Castroville, Calif., U.S.	226	36.46 N	121.45 W
Castroville, Tex., U.S.	196	29.21 N	98.53 W
Castrovirreyna	248	13.16 S	75.19 W
Castuera	34	38.43 N	5.33 W
Čast Uul	86	48.40 N	90.55 E
Častyje	80	57.19 N	54.59 E
Casula	154	15.25 S	33.40 E
Casummit Lake	184	51.28 N	92.24 W
Casupá	252	34.07 S	55.39 W
Caswell Sound	172	45.00 S	167.10 E
Çat	130	39.40 N	41.00 E
Cat	184	51.07 N	91.25 W
Catacamas	236	14.54 N	85.56 W
Catacaos	248	5.16 S	80.41 W
Catacocha	246	4.04 S	79.38 W
Cataguarino	256	21.18 S	42.43 W
Cataguases	256	21.24 S	42.41 W
Catahoula Lake	194	31.30 N	92.06 W
Çatalan	130	37.14 N	35.16 E
Catalão	255	18.10 S	47.57 W
Catalão, Ponta do	287a	22.51 S	43.13 W
Çatalca	130	41.09 N	28.27 E
Catalfaro	70	37.22 N	14.43 E
Catalina, Newf., Can.	186	48.31 N	53.05 W
Catalina, Chile	252	25.13 S	69.43 W
Catalina → Santa Catalina Island	228	33.23 N	118.24 W
Catalina, Punta	254	52.32 S	68.47 W
Catalina Point	174p	13.31 N	144.55 E
Catalonia → Cataluña □[9]	34	42.00 N	2.00 E
Cataluña □[9]	34	42.00 N	2.00 E
Cataluña, Museo de Arte de	266d	41.23 N	2.09 E
Catalzeytin	130	41.57 N	34.13 E
Catamarca	252	28.28 S	65.47 W
Catamarca □[4]	252	27.00 S	67.00 W
Catamare	286c	10.36 N	67.02 W
Catamayo	246	3.59 S	79.21 W
Catamayo	246	4.18 S	80.09 W
Catanauan	116	13.36 N	122.19 E
Catanduanes □[4]	116	13.47 N	124.16 E
Catanduanes Island	116	13.45 N	124.15 E
Catanduva	255	21.08 S	48.58 W
Catane → Catania	70	37.30 N	15.06 E
Catania	70	37.30 N	15.06 E
Catania □[4]	70	37.23 N	14.40 E
Catania, Golfo di	70	37.24 N	15.09 E
Catania, Piana di	70	37.25 N	14.51 E
Cataño	240m	18.27 N	66.07 W
Catanzaro	68	38.54 N	16.26 E
Catanzaro □[4]	68	38.54 N	16.36 E
Catanzaro Lido	68	38.49 N	16.36 E
Catára	152	13.34 S	12.35 E
Cataract Creek	200	36.03 N	112.35 W
Cataract Reservoir	170	34.16 S	150.48 E
Catarama	246	1.35 S	79.28 W
Cataraqui	212	44.16 N	76.32 W
Cataraqui	212	44.13 N	76.28 W
Cataricahua	248	18.14 S	66.49 W
Catarina	250	6.12 S	39.54 W
Catarman, Pil.	116	9.08 N	124.40 E
Catarman, Pil.	116	12.30 N	124.38 E
Catarman	116	12.31 N	124.39 E
Catarroja	34	39.24 N	0.24 W
Catasauqua	208	40.39 N	75.29 W
Catastrophe, Cape	166	34.59 S	136.00 E
Catatumbo	246	9.22 N	71.45 W
Catawba	218	40.00 N	83.37 W
Catawba	192	34.36 N	80.54 W
Catawba Dam	192	34.57 N	81.04 W
Catawba Island	214	41.35 N	82.50 W
Catawissa, Mo., U.S.	219	38.25 N	90.47 W
Catawissa, Pa., U.S.	210	40.57 N	76.28 W
Catawissa Creek	210	40.57 N	76.28 W
Cataxa	154	15.58 S	33.12 E
Catbalogan	116	11.46 N	124.53 E
Catchabutan, Punta	236	15.50 N	86.32 W
Catchacoma Lake	212	44.45 N	78.20 W
Cateco Cangola	152	8.27 S	15.48 E
Cateel	116	7.48 N	126.27 E
Cateel	116	7.47 N	126.27 E
Cateel Bay	116	7.54 N	126.25 E
Catemaco	234	18.25 N	95.07 W
Catemaco, Lago	234	18.25 N	95.05 W
Catembe	156	26.00 S	32.33 E
Catenanuova	70	37.34 N	14.41 E
Catende	152	11.14 S	21.30 E
Caterham	260	51.17 N	0.04 W
Catete	152	9.06 S	13.43 E
Catete	287a	22.55 S	43.10 W
Catete	250	6.04 S	54.09 W
Catfish Creek, Ont., Can.	212	42.39 N	81.01 W
Catfish Creek, Tex., U.S.	222	31.47 N	95.56 W
Catford	260	51.27 N	0.01 W
Catharine Creek	210	42.21 N	76.51 W
Cathcart	158	32.18 S	27.09 E
Cathead Mountain	210	43.17 N	74.17 W
Cathedral City	204	33.47 N	116.28 W
Cathedral Gorge State Park	204	37.50 N	114.30 W
Cathedral Mountain	196	30.10 N	103.40 W
Cathedral of the Pines	207	42.47 N	71.58 W
Cathedral Pass	158	28.55 S	29.01 E
Cathedral Provincial Park	202	49.05 N	120.10 W
Cathedral Range	226	37.47 N	119.21 W
Catherines Peak	241q	18.04 N	76.42 W
Catheys Valley	226	37.25 N	120.06 W
Cathkin Mountain Pass	158	29.08 S	29.20 E
Cathlamet	224	46.12 N	123.23 W
Catholic University	284c	38.56 N	77.00 W
Catia	286c	10.31 N	66.57 W
Catia La Mar	286c	10.36 N	67.02 W
Catignano	66	42.21 N	13.57 E
Catingueira	250	7.08 S	37.37 W
Catingueiro	256	22.10 S	46.52 W
Catió	150	11.13 N	15.10 W
Catirina, Punta	71	40.29 N	9.32 E
Cat Island, Ba.	238	24.27 N	75.30 W
Cat Island, Mass., U.S.	283	42.31 N	70.49 W
Cat Island, Miss., U.S.	194	30.13 N	89.06 W
Čatkal	85	41.38 N	70.01 E
Cat Lake	184	51.40 N	91.50 W
Catlettsburg	188	38.25 N	82.36 W
Catlin	194	40.04 N	87.42 W
Catlins	172	46.29 S	169.43 E
Catlodge	46	57.00 N	4.15 W
Catnip Mountain	204	41.52 N	119.23 W
Cato	210	43.10 N	76.34 W
Catoche, Cabo	232	21.35 N	87.05 W
Catoctin Creek	208	39.18 N	77.33 W
Catoctin Mountain	208	39.26 N	77.31 W
Cato Island	166	23.15 S	155.32 E
Catolé do Rocha	250	6.21 S	37.45 W
Católica, Universidad, Chile	286e	33.27 S	70.39 W
Católica, Universidad, Perú	286d	12.04 S	77.05 W
Catonsville	208	39.16 N	76.44 W
Catoosa	196	36.11 N	95.45 W
Catorce	234	23.42 N	100.54 W
Catorce, Sierra de	234	23.36 N	100.52 W
Catria, Monte	66	43.28 N	12.42 E
Catriló	252	36.26 S	63.24 W
Catrimani	246	0.27 N	61.41 W
Catrimani	246	0.28 N	61.44 W
Catrine	46	55.30 N	4.20 W
Cats, Mont des	50	50.47 N	2.40 E
Catskill	210	42.13 N	73.52 W
Catskill Aqueduct	276	41.11 N	73.48 W
Catskill Creek	210	42.12 N	73.51 W
Catskill Game Farm	210	42.15 N	74.01 W
Catskill Mountains	210	42.10 N	74.30 W
Catskill Park	210	42.00 N	74.30 W
Cat Spring	222	29.51 N	96.20 W
Catt, Mount	182	54.21 N	128.47 W
Cattaraugus	210	42.20 N	78.52 W
Cattaraugus □[6]	214	42.15 N	78.45 W
Cattaraugus Creek	214	42.35 N	79.10 W
Cattaraugus Creek, South Branch	214	42.26 N	78.53 W
Cattaraugus Indian Reservation	210	42.33 N	78.56 W
Cattenom	56	49.25 N	6.15 E
Catterick	44	54.22 N	1.38 W
Catterick Camp	44	54.22 N	1.43 W
Cattle Canyon	280	34.14 N	117.46 W
Cattolica	66	43.58 N	12.44 E
Cattolica del Sacro Cuore, Università	266b	45.27 N	9.11 E
Cattolica Eraclea	70	37.26 N	13.24 E
Catton	44	54.55 N	2.15 W
Catu	255	12.21 S	38.23 W
Catuane	156	26.48 S	32.18 E
Catubig	116	12.24 N	125.03 E
Catuçaba	256	23.15 S	45.12 W
Catumbela	152	12.27 S	13.29 E
Catur	154	13.45 S	35.30 E
Çatus	32	44.34 N	1.20 E
Čatyrtaš	85	40.55 N	76.26 E
Cau	110	21.07 N	106.18 E
Cauaburi	246	0.17 S	65.56 W
Cauale	152	7.18 S	16.39 E
Cauaxi	250	3.50 S	48.10 W
Cauayan, Pil.	116	9.58 N	122.37 E
Cauayan, Pil.	116	16.56 N	121.46 E
Cauca □[5]	246	2.30 N	76.50 W
Cauca	246	8.54 N	74.28 W
Caucaia	250	3.42 S	38.39 W
Caucaia do Alto	256	23.41 S	47.02 W
Caucase, Monts du → Bol'šoj Kavkaz	84	42.30 N	45.00 E
Caucasia	246	8.00 N	75.12 W
Caucaso → Bol'šoj Kavkaz	84	42.30 N	45.00 E
Caucasus → Bol'šoj Kavkaz	84	42.30 N	45.00 E
Cauchon Lake	184	55.25 N	96.30 W
Caudebec-en-Caux	50	49.32 N	0.44 E
Caudebec-lés-Elbeuf	50	49.17 N	1.02 E
Caudry	50	50.08 N	3.25 E
Caughdenoy	210	43.16 N	76.12 W
Caughnawaga	275a	45.25 N	73.41 W
Caughnawaga Indian Reserve	206	45.23 N	73.41 W
Cauitan, Mount	116	17.16 N	121.00 E
Cauit Point	116	12.16 N	122.38 E
Cauldcleuch Head	44	55.18 N	2.51 W
Caulfield	169	37.53 S	145.03 E
Caulfield Racecourse	274b	37.53 S	145.02 E
Caulkerbush	44	54.54 N	3.40 W
Caulonia	68	38.23 N	16.25 E
Caumont-sur-Durance	62	43.54 N	4.57 E
Caumsett State Park	276	40.55 N	73.28 W
Çaúngula	152	8.25 S	18.40 E
Čaunskaja Guba	74	69.20 N	170.00 E
Cauquenes	252	35.58 S	72.21 W
Caura	246	7.38 N	64.53 W
Caurés	246	1.21 S	62.20 W
Caurimare	286c	10.28 N	66.48 W
Causapscal	186	48.22 N	67.14 W
Causapscal, Parc de	186	48.20 N	66.55 W
Čausovo	82	54.49 N	36.55 E
Çaussade	32	44.10 N	1.32 E
Čausy	76	53.48 N	30.58 E
Caution, Cape	182	51.10 N	127.47 W
Çauto	240p	20.33 N	77.14 W
Čauvaj	85	40.08 N	72.13 E
Cauvery	122	11.09 N	79.52 E
Cauvery Falls	122	12.18 N	77.17 E
Caux, Pays de	50	49.40 N	0.40 E
Cava	256	22.41 S	43.26 W
Cava de' Tirreni	68	40.42 N	14.42 E
Cávado	34	41.32 N	8.48 W
Cavaglià	62	45.24 N	8.05 E
Cavaillon	62	43.50 N	5.02 E
Cavalaire-sur-Mer	62	43.10 N	6.32 E
Cavalcante	255	13.48 S	47.30 W
Cavalese	64	46.17 N	11.27 E
Cavalheiro	255	17.15 S	48.02 W
Cavalier	198	48.48 N	97.37 W
Cavalière	62	43.09 N	6.26 E
Cavalla (Cavally)	150	4.22 N	7.32 W
Cavallermaggiore	62	44.43 N	7.41 E
Cavalli Islands	172	34.58 S	173.58 E
Cavallino, Litorale di	64	45.27 N	12.30 E
Cavallo, Monte	64	46.08 N	12.30 E
Cavalos, Ribeirão dos	256	21.29 S	44.13 W
Cava Manara	62	45.08 N	9.07 E
Cavan	48	54.00 N	7.21 W
Cavan □[6]	48	53.55 N	7.30 W
Çavanaugh, Lake	224	48.23 N	122.00 W
Čavan'ga	24	66.06 N	37.47 E
Cavarzere	64	45.08 N	12.05 E
Cavaso del Tomba	64	45.51 N	11.52 E
Çavdır	130	37.09 N	29.42 E
Cave, It.	66	41.49 N	12.56 E
Cave, N.Z.	172	44.19 S	170.57 E
Cave City, Ark., U.S.	194	35.57 N	91.33 W
Cave City, Ky., U.S.	194	37.08 N	85.58 W
Cave Creek	200	33.34 N	112.07 W
Cave del Predil	64	46.26 N	13.34 E
Cavedine	64	45.59 N	10.59 E
Caveiras	252	27.35 S	50.56 W
Cavelo	152	17.33 S	19.21 E
Cavendish	166	37.31 S	142.02 E
Cavernago	62	45.38 N	9.46 E
Cavertitz	54	51.23 N	13.08 E
Cave Spring	192	34.07 N	85.20 W
Cavettsville	279b	40.22 N	79.46 W
Cavezzo	64	44.50 N	11.02 E
Cavi	62	44.17 N	9.22 E
Caviana, Ilha	250	0.10 N	50.10 W
Cavinzas, Isla	286d	12.07 S	77.13 W
Cavite	116		
	269f	14.29 N	120.55 E
Çavite □[4]	116	14.15 N	120.50 E
Čavlisaj	85	41.08 N	69.44 E
Cavo, Monte	267a	41.45 N	12.42 E
Cavoli, Isola dei	71	39.05 N	9.33 E
Cavonne	68	40.17 N	16.47 E
Cavour	62	44.47 N	7.22 E
Cavour, Canale	62	45.11 N	7.54 E
Cavriago	64	44.42 N	10.31 E
Cavriana	64	45.21 N	10.36 E
Cavtat	38	42.35 N	18.13 E
Cawatose, Lac	190	47.20 N	77.07 W
Cawayan	116	11.56 N	123.46 E
Cawdor	46	57.31 N	3.56 W
Cawit Point	116	9.18 N	126.12 E
Cawker City	198	39.30 N	98.26 W
Cawnpore → Kānpur	124	26.28 N	80.21 E
Cawood, Eng., U.K.	44	53.50 N	1.07 W
Cawood, Ky., U.S.	192	36.47 N	83.14 W
Cawston, B.C., Can.	182	49.11 N	119.45 W
Cawston, Eng., U.K.	42	52.46 N	1.10 E
Cawthon	222	30.25 N	96.14 W
Caxambu	256	21.59 S	44.56 W
Caxias, Bra.	250	4.50 S	43.21 W
Caxias, Port.	266c	38.42 N	9.16 W
Caxias do Sul	252	29.10 S	51.11 W
Caxinas, Punta	236	16.01 N	86.02 W
Caxiuana, Baía de	250	1.45 S	51.20 W
Cayambe	246	0.03 N	78.08 W
Cayambe	246	0.02 N	77.59 W
Cayapoñga	116	5.48 N	125.33 E
Cayce	192	33.59 N	81.04 W
Çaycuma	130	41.25 N	32.05 E
Caycuse	224	48.53 N	124.22 W
Caycuse	224	48.48 N	124.41 W
Cay-duong, Vinh	110	10.10 N	104.45 E
Cayenne	250	4.56 N	52.20 W
Cayenne □[8]	250	4.00 N	52.30 W
Cayes → Les Cayes	238	18.12 N	73.45 W
Cayeux-sur-Mer	50	50.11 N	1.29 E
Cayey	240m	18.07 N	66.10 W
Cayey, Sierra de	240m	18.07 N	66.02 W
Caylus	32	44.14 N	1.46 E
Cayman Brac	238	19.43 N	79.49 W
Cayman Islands □[2]	230		
	238	19.30 N	80.40 W
Cayman Trench	16	19.00 N	80.00 W
Cayna	248	10.11 S	76.20 W
Cayra	130	40.41 N	39.06 E
Cayres	62	44.55 N	3.48 E
Cayucos	226	35.27 N	120.54 W
Cayuga, Ont., Can.	212	42.56 N	79.51 W
Cayuga, Ind., U.S.	194	39.57 N	87.28 W
Cayuga, N. Dak., U.S.	198	46.04 N	97.23 W
Cayuga, N.Y., U.S.	210	42.55 N	76.44 W
Cayuga, Tex., U.S.	222	31.57 N	95.57 W
Cayuga □[6]	210	42.56 N	76.34 W
Cayuga Creek	210	42.52 N	78.47 W
Cayuga Heights	210	42.28 N	76.30 W
Cayuga Lake	210	42.45 N	76.45 W
Cayuta	210	42.17 N	76.42 W
Cayuta Creek	210	41.59 N	76.30 W
Cazage	152	11.02 S	20.45 E
Cazalla de la Sierra	34	37.56 N	5.45 W
Căzănești	38	44.37 N	27.01 E
Cazaux, Étang de	32	44.30 N	1.10 W
Cazenovia	210	42.56 N	75.51 W
Cazenovia Creek	210	42.52 N	78.50 W
Cazenovia Creek, East Branch	210	42.46 N	78.38 W
Cazenovia Creek, West Branch	210	42.46 N	78.39 W
Cazenovia Lake	210	42.57 N	75.53 W
Cazenovia Park	284a	42.51 N	78.48 W
Cazères	32	43.13 N	1.05 E
Cazhai	106	31.12 N	121.34 E
Cazin	36	44.58 N	15.57 E
Çazis	58	46.43 N	9.25 E
Čazma	36	45.45 N	16.37 E
Cazombo	152	11.54 S	22.52 E
Cazones	234	20.44 N	97.12 W
Cazones, Golfo de	240p	21.55 N	81.20 W
Cazorla, Esp.	34	37.55 N	3.00 W
Cazorla, Ven.	246	8.01 N	67.00 W
Cazorla, Sierra de	34	37.55 N	2.55 W
Ccapi	248	13.52 S	72.05 W
Cchaltubo	84	42.20 N	42.35 E
Cchenis-Ckali	84	42.07 N	42.18 E
Çchinvali	84	42.13 N	43.56 E
Čchorocku	84	42.32 N	42.07 E
Cchunkuri	84	42.23 N	42.34 E
Cea	34	42.00 N	5.36 W
Ceanannus Mór	48	53.44 N	6.53 W
Ceará → Fortaleza	250	3.43 S	38.30 W
Ceará □[3]	250	5.00 S	40.00 W
Ceará-Mirim	250	5.38 S	35.26 W
Ceará-Mirim	250	5.40 S	35.13 W
Ceatharlach → Carlow	48	52.50 N	6.55 W
Cébaco, Isla	246	7.32 N	81.09 W
Çeballos	234	23.23 N	104.50 W
Čebarkul'	86	54.58 N	60.25 E
Çebeciköy	267b	41.07 N	28.52 E
Čeboksary	80	56.09 N	47.15 E
Cebolla Creek	200	38.29 N	107.13 W
Cebollar	252	29.06 S	66.33 W
Cebollatí	252	33.16 S	53.47 W
Cebollita Peak	200	34.43 N	107.51 W
Céboruco, Volcán	234	21.09 N	104.30 W
Čebotovka, S.S.S.R.	83	48.42 N	39.51 E
Čebotovka, S.S.S.R.	83	48.41 N	40.00 E
Cebreros	34	40.27 N	4.28 W
Çebrikovo	78	47.09 N	30.06 E
Čebsara	76	59.12 N	38.50 E
Cebu	116	10.18 N	123.54 E
Cebu □[4]	116	10.20 N	123.45 E
Çebu	116	10.20 N	123.40 E
Čeburgol'	78	45.34 N	38.07 E
Ceccano	66	41.34 N	13.20 E
Cecchignola	267a	41.49 N	12.29 E
Ceceda	196	26.04 N	103.25 W
Çeceli	130	39.43 N	33.52 E
Čečel'nik	78	48.14 N	29.21 E
Čečeno-Ingušskaja Avtonomnaja Sovetskaja Socialističeskaja Respublika □[3]	84	43.15 N	45.40 E
Cecer Chaan → Öndörchaan	88	47.19 N	110.39 E
Cecerleg, Mong.	88	48.55 N	101.09 E
Cecerleg, Mong.	88	47.30 N	101.27 E
Çecerleg, Mong.	88	49.30 N	97.36 E
Čečeviči	76	53.31 N	29.51 E
Çecheng	105	39.06 N	116.48 E
Čechov, S.S.S.R.	82	55.09 N	37.27 E
Čechov, S.S.S.R.	89	47.28 N	141.59 E

Symbols in the index entries represent the broad categories identified in the key at the right. Symbols with superior numbers (⛰²) identify subcategories (see complete key on page I · 30).

Kartensymbole in dem Registerverzeichnis stellen die rechts in Schlüssel erklärten Kategorien dar. Symbole mit hochgestellten Ziffern (⛰²) bezeichnen Unterabteilungen einer Kategorie (vgl. vollständiger Schlüssel auf Seite I · 30).

Los símbolos incluídos en el texto del índice representan las grandes categorias identificadas con la clave a la derecha. Los símbolos con numeros en su parte superior (⛰²) identifican las subcategorias (véase la clave completa en la página I · 30).

Les symboles de l'index représentent les catégories indiquées dans la légende à droite. Les symboles suivis d'un indice (⛰²) représentent des sous-catégories (voir légende complète à la page I · 30).

Os símbolos incluídos no texto do índice representam as grandes categorias identificadas com a chave à direita. Os símbolos com números em sua parte superior (⛰²) identificam as subcategorias (veja-se a chave completa à página I · 30).

English	Deutsch	Español	Français	Português
Mountain	Berg	Montaña	Montagne	Montanha
Mountains	Berge	Montañas	Montagnes	Montanhas
Pass	Pass	Paso	Col	Passo
Valley, Canyon	Tal, Cañon	Valle, Cañón	Vallée, Canyon	Vale, Canhão
Plain	Ebene	Llano	Plaine	Planície
Cape	Kap	Cabo	Cap	Cabo
Island	Insel	Isla	Île	Ilha
Islands	Inseln	Islas	Îles	Ilhas
Other Topographic Features	Andere Topographische Objekte	Otros Elementos Topográficos	Autres données topographiques	Outros Elementos Topográficos

ESPAÑOL | FRANÇAIS | PORTUGUÊS

Nombre / Nom / Nome	Página / Page	Lat.°′	Long.°′ W=Oeste / W=Ouest
Čechtice	30	49.37 N	15.03 E
Čechy □[9]	30	49.50 N	14.00 E
Cecil, Ga., U.S.	192	31.05 N	83.11 W
Cecil, Ohio, U.S.	216	41.13 N	84.35 W
Cecil, Pa., U.S.	214	40.20 N	80.11 W
Cecil □[6]	208	39.36 N	75.50 W
Cecilia	194	37.40 N	85.57 W
Cecilia, Mount ∧[2]	162	20.45 S	120.55 E
Cecil Rhodes, Mount ∧	162	25.26 S	121.26 E
Cecilton	208	39.24 N	75.52 W
Cecina	66	43.19 N	10.31 E
Cecina ≃	66	43.18 N	10.29 E
Cecita, Lago di ⊜	68	39.24 N	16.30 E
Čečorsk	76	52.55 N	30.55 E
Čečuj ≃	88	58.12 N	109.18 E
Čečujsk	88	58.05 N	108.42 E
Cedar ≃, Mich., U.S.	190	43.53 N	84.29 W
Cedar ≃, Mich., U.S.	190	45.25 N	87.21 W
Cedar ≃, Nebr., U.S.	198	41.22 N	97.57 W
Cedar ≃, N.Y., U.S.	188	43.51 N	74.11 W
Cedar ≃, Wash., U.S.	224	47.30 N	122.12 W
Cedar, Middle Branch ≃	216	42.38 N	84.05 W
Cedar, West Branch ≃	216	42.41 N	84.09 W
Cedar, West Fork ≃	190	42.37 N	92.29 W
Cedar Bayou ≃	222	29.41 N	94.56 W
Cedar Bluff Reservoir ⊜[1]	198	38.47 N	99.47 W
Cedar Bluffs	198	41.24 N	96.37 W
Cedar Breaks National Monument ♠	200	37.29 N	112.53 W
Cedar Brook	208	39.43 N	74.54 W
Cedar Brook ≃, N.J., U.S.	276	40.19 N	74.33 W
Cedar Brook ≃, N.J., U.S.	276	40.23 N	74.23 W
Cedar Brook ≃, N.J., U.S.	285	39.40 N	74.43 W
Cedar Brook Park ♠	275b	43.45 N	79.14 W
Cedarburg	190	43.17 N	87.59 W
Cedar City, Mo., U.S.	219	38.36 N	92.11 W
Cedar City, Utah, U.S.	200	37.41 N	113.04 W
Cedar Creek	222	30.05 N	97.30 W
Cedar Creek ≃, U.S.	190	41.17 N	91.21 W
Cedar Creek ≃, Ala., U.S.	194	32.13 N	87.06 W
Cedar Creek ≃, Ariz., U.S.	200	33.48 N	110.18 W
Cedar Creek ≃, Conn., U.S.	276	41.09 N	73.13 W
Cedar Creek ≃, Del., U.S.	208	38.55 N	75.20 W
Cedar Creek ≃, Ga., U.S.	194	34.08 N	85.19 W
Cedar Creek ≃, Idaho, U.S.	202	42.24 N	114.49 W
Cedar Creek ≃, Ind., U.S.	216	41.12 N	85.02 W
Cedar Creek ≃, Iowa, U.S.	190	40.58 N	91.40 W
Cedar Creek ≃, Iowa, U.S.	198	42.08 N	94.35 W
Cedar Creek ≃, Iowa, U.S.	198	42.24 N	94.59 W
Cedar Creek ≃, Ky., U.S.	218	38.25 N	84.53 W
Cedar Creek ≃, Mo., U.S.	219	38.38 N	92.13 W
Cedar Creek ≃, N. Dak., U.S.	198	46.07 N	101.18 W
Cedar Creek ≃, Ohio, U.S.	214	41.38 N	83.17 W
Cedar Creek ≃, Pa., U.S.	279b	40.10 N	79.47 W
Cedar Creek ≃, Tex., U.S.	196	32.53 N	98.37 W
Cedar Creek ≃, Tex., U.S.	222	30.51 N	96.12 W
Cedar Creek ≃, Tex., U.S.	222	32.04 N	96.05 W
Cedar Creek ≃, Tex., U.S.	222	30.02 N	97.17 W
Cedar Creek ≃, Wash., U.S.	224	45.56 N	122.37 W
Cedar Creek Reservoir ⊜[1]	222	32.20 N	96.10 W
Cedar Crest Manor	285	39.41 N	75.28 W
Cedaredge	200	38.54 N	107.56 W
Cedar Falls	190	42.32 N	92.27 W
Cedar Grove, Ont., Can.	275b	43.52 N	79.12 W
Cedar Grove, Ind., U.S.	218	39.21 N	84.56 W
Cedar Grove, W. Va., U.S.	188	38.13 N	81.26 W
Cedar Grove, Wis., U.S.	190	43.33 N	87.45 W
Cedar Grove Reservoir ⊜[1]	276	40.52 N	74.13 W
Cedar Hammock	220	27.27 N	82.36 W
Cedar Heights	285	40.05 N	75.17 W
Cedar Hill, Mo., U.S.	219	38.21 N	90.39 W
Cedar Hill, N.Y., U.S.	210	42.33 N	73.47 W
Cedar Hill, Tenn., U.S.	194	36.33 N	87.01 W
Cedar Hill, Tex., U.S.	222	32.35 N	96.57 W
Cedar Hills, Fla., U.S.	192	30.16 N	81.45 W
Cedar Hills, Oreg., U.S.	224	45.31 N	122.46 W
Cedarhurst, Md., U.S.	208	39.07 N	76.41 W
Cedarhurst, N.Y., U.S.	276	40.38 N	73.44 W
Cedar Island I, Md., U.S.	208	37.56 N	75.52 W
Cedar Island I, N.Y., U.S.	276	40.38 N	73.21 W
Cedar Island I, Va., U.S.	208	37.39 N	75.36 W
Cedar Island Lake ⊜	281	42.38 N	83.28 W
Cedar Key	192	29.08 N	83.02 W
Cedar Knolls	276	40.49 N	74.27 W
Cedar Lake, Ind., U.S.	216	41.22 N	87.26 W
Cedar Lake, Tex., U.S.	222	28.54 N	95.35 W
Cedar Lake ⊜, Ont., Can.	190	46.02 N	78.30 W
Cedar Lake ⊜, Ind., U.S.	216	41.22 N	87.26 W
Cedar Lake ⊜, N.J., U.S.	276	40.55 N	74.28 W
Cedar Lake ⊜, Tex., U.S.	196	32.49 N	102.17 W
Cedar Lake ⊜[1]	184	53.15 N	100.10 W
Cedar Lake Creek ≃	222	28.50 N	95.35 W
Cedar Lane	222	28.54 N	95.38 W
Cedar Mill	224	45.32 N	122.51 W
Cedarmont	158	26.50 S	29.01 E
Cedar Mountain ∧	204	41.36 N	120.16 W
Cedar Point	216	41.16 N	89.08 W
Cedar Point ≻, Conn., U.S.	276	41.06 N	73.22 W
Cedar Point ≻, Ohio, U.S.	214	41.42 N	83.20 W
Cedar Pond ⊜	276	41.07 N	74.06 W
Cedar Rapids, Iowa, U.S.	190	41.59 N	91.40 W
Cedar Rapids, Nebr., U.S.	198	41.34 N	98.09 W
Cedar Ridge	226	39.12 N	121.01 W
Cedar Run ≃	208	38.41 N	77.29 W
Cedars	285	40.13 N	75.22 W
Cedars of Lebanon → Arz Lubnān ◆[3]	130	34.14 N	36.03 E
Cedar Springs, Ont., Can.	214	42.17 N	82.02 W
Cedar Springs, Mich., U.S.	190	43.13 N	85.33 W
Cedar Swamp ☷, Mass., U.S.	283	42.33 N	71.05 W
Cedar Swamp ☷, N.J., U.S.	285	39.48 N	75.20 W
Cedartown	192	34.01 N	85.15 W
Cedarvale, B.C., Can.	182	55.01 N	128.20 W
Cedar Vale, Kans., U.S.	198	37.06 N	96.30 W
Cedarville, S. Afr.	158	30.23 S	29.03 E
Cedarville, Calif., U.S.	204	41.32 N	120.10 W
Cedarville, Ind., U.S.	216	40.12 N	85.01 W
Cedarville, Mass., U.S.	207	41.49 N	70.32 W
Cedarville, Mich., U.S.	190	46.00 N	84.22 W
Cedarville, N.Y., U.S.	210	42.56 N	75.07 W
Cedarville, Ohio, U.S.	218	39.44 N	83.48 W
Cedarville, Pa., U.S.	285	40.14 N	75.40 W
Cedarville Reservoir ⊜[1]	216	41.12 N	85.01 W
Cedar Wash ∨	200	35.53 N	111.25 W
Cedarwood Park	208	40.03 N	74.08 W
Cedegolo	64	46.05 N	10.21 E
Cedeira	34	43.39 N	8.03 W
Čeder	88	51.25 N	94.45 E
Cedillo, Embalse de ⊜[1]	34	39.40 N	7.25 E
Cedral	234	23.48 N	100.44 W
Cedrino ≃	71	40.23 N	9.44 E
Cedro	250	6.36 S	39.03 W
Cedrón ≃	34	39.48 N	3.33 W
Cedros, Hond.	236	14.35 N	87.08 W
Cedros, Méx.	232	24.41 N	101.47 W
Cedros, Isla I	232	28.12 N	115.15 W
Ceduna	162	32.07 S	133.40 E
Cedynia	30	52.50 N	14.14 E
Ceel	102	45.47 N	95.32 E
Ceepeecee	182	49.52 N	126.43 W
Cefalá Diana	70	37.54 N	13.28 E
Cefalonia → Kefallinía I	38	38.15 N	20.35 E
Cefalù	70	38.02 N	14.01 E
Cefni ≃	44	53.12 N	4.23 W
Cega ≃	34	41.33 N	4.46 W
Čeganly	80	53.54 N	53.34 E
Čegdomyn	89	51.07 N	133.05 E
Čegem ≃	84	43.38 N	43.48 E
Čegem Pervyj	84	43.34 N	43.35 E
Čegitun'	180	66.34 N	171.06 W
Cegléd	30	47.10 N	19.48 E
Ceglie Messapico	68	40.39 N	17.31 E
Cehegín	34	38.06 N	1.48 W
Ceheng	102	25.10 N	105.48 E
Cehu-Silvaniei	38	47.25 N	23.11 E
Ceiba	240m	18.16 N	65.39 W
Ceiba ≃	240p	21.38 N	78.52 W
Ceibo, Arroyo ≃	258	33.57 S	58.27 W
Ceilán → Sri Lanka □[1]	122	7.00 N	81.00 E
Čeil'dag	84	40.17 N	49.18 E
Ceiriog ≃	42	52.57 N	3.02 W
Ceirw ≃	42	52.59 N	3.27 W
Čekalin	82	54.06 N	36.15 E
Čekan	80	54.51 N	53.34 E
Čekanovskij	88	56.13 N	101.25 E
Çekerek ≃	130	40.34 N	35.46 E
Čekhira	148	34.17 N	10.06 E
Čekmaguš	86	55.08 N	54.40 E
Çekmeköy	267b	41.03 N	29.10 E
Čekšino	76	59.39 N	40.33 E
Čekujevo	24	63.34 N	38.56 E
Čekunda	89	50.48 N	132.10 E
Cela	152	11.25 S	15.07 E
Čel'abinsk	86	55.10 N	61.24 E
Čelákovice	54	50.10 N	14.46 E
Celâlli	130	39.42 N	37.26 E
Celano	66	42.05 N	13.33 E
Celanova	34	42.09 N	7.58 W
Celaya	234	20.31 N	100.49 W
Čelbas ≃	78	46.06 N	38.59 E
Čelbasskaja	78	45.59 N	39.22 E
Cele	120	37.00 N	80.47 E
Celebes → Sulawesi I	112	2.00 S	121.00 E
Celebes Basin ✢[1]	12	4.00 N	122.00 E
Celebes Sea ╤[2]	112	3.00 N	122.00 E
Çelebiler	130	41.26 N	32.57 E
Čeleken	128	39.26 N	53.07 E
Celendín	248	6.52 S	78.09 W
Celenza sul Trigno	66	41.52 N	14.35 E
Celenza Valfortore	68	41.34 N	14.58 E
Celerina	58	46.31 N	9.51 E
Celeryville	214	41.02 N	82.45 W
Celeste	196	33.18 N	96.12 W
Celestún	232	20.52 N	90.24 W
Celica	246	4.07 S	79.59 W
Celico	68	39.19 N	16.20 E
Çelikhân	130	38.02 N	38.15 E
Celina, S.S.S.R.	80	46.32 N	41.02 E
Celina, Ohio, U.S.	216	40.33 N	84.34 W
Celina, Tenn., U.S.	194	36.33 N	85.30 W
Celina, Tex., U.S.	196	33.19 N	96.47 W
Celinnoje, S.S.S.R.	86	54.31 N	63.39 E
Celinnoje, S.S.S.R.	86	53.04 N	85.40 E
Celinnyj	80	46.40 N	44.32 E
Celinograd	86	51.10 N	71.30 E
Celje	36	46.14 N	15.16 E
Čelkar	86	47.50 N	59.36 E
Cellar Head ≻	46	58.26 N	6.10 W
Celldömölk	30	47.16 N	17.09 E
Celle	52	52.37 N	10.05 E
Celle, Ruisseau la ≃	261	48.35 N	2.01 E
Celle Ligure	62	44.20 N	8.33 E
Celles	56	50.14 N	5.01 E
Celles-sur-Plaine	58	48.28 N	6.57 E
Cellettes	50	47.32 N	1.23 E
Cellina ≃	64	46.02 N	12.47 E
Cellino Attanasio	66	42.36 N	13.52 E
Cellino San Marco	68	40.28 N	17.58 E
Čelmozero	24	64.18 N	31.48 E
Čelno-Veršiny	80	54.26 N	51.06 E
Čelobitjevo	265b	55.55 N	37.40 E
Celone ≃	68	41.36 N	15.41 E
Celorico da Beira	34	40.38 N	7.23 W
Celoron	214	42.06 N	79.17 W
Çeltik	130	41.11 N	32.19 E
Çeltikçi, Tür.	130	37.32 N	30.29 E
Çeltikçi, Tür.	130	40.20 N	32.28 E
Čel'uš	86	51.32 N	87.46 E
Čel'uskin, Mys ≻	74	77.45 N	104.20 E
Cemaes Head ≻	42	52.07 N	4.44 W
Čemal	86	51.25 N	86.01 E
Čembilej	80	55.19 N	45.43 E
Cembra	64	46.10 N	11.13 E
Cembra, Val di ∨	64	46.10 N	11.13 E
Cement City	216	42.04 N	84.20 W
Cementon, N.Y., U.S.	210	42.09 N	73.55 W
Cementon, Pa., U.S.	208	40.41 N	75.30 W
Čemer	78	51.07 N	31.13 E
Čemerisy	78	51.42 N	30.24 E
Čemerno	36	43.11 N	18.37 E
Čemerno)(	38	43.14 N	18.37 E
Čemerovcy	78	49.01 N	26.21 E
Cemesskaja Buchta C	78	44.40 N	37.50 E
Cemilbey	130	40.21 N	35.04 E
Çemişgezek	130	39.04 N	38.55 E
Cemmaes	42	52.37 N	3.42 W
Čemolgan	85	43.23 N	76.37 E
Čenča	88	55.57 N	110.59 E
Cencenighe	64	46.21 N	11.58 E
Čenchermandal	88	47.40 N	109.05 E
Čency	82	56.03 N	36.01 E
Cenderawasih, Teluk C	164	2.30 S	135.20 E
Cendras	62	44.09 N	4.04 E
Cene	62	45.47 N	9.49 E
Cenepa ≃	246	4.35 S	78.12 W
Ceneri, Monte)(	58	46.08 N	8.55 E
Čengel	86	48.56 N	89.10 E
Čengel'dy, S.S.S.R.	85	43.59 N	77.26 E
Čengel'dy, S.S.S.R.	85	41.51 N	68.59 E
Cengles, Croda di ∧	64	46.34 N	10.38 E
Ceno ≃	36	44.41 N	10.05 E
Cenovo	38	43.32 N	25.39 E
Cenrana	112	3.18 S	118.50 E
Censeau	58	46.49 N	6.04 E
Centallo	62	44.30 N	7.35 E
Centenario	252	38.48 S	68.08 W
Centenário do Sul	255	22.48 S	51.37 W
Centennial Lake ⊜	285	39.50 N	74.51 W
Centennial Lake ⊜[1]	212	45.10 N	72.05 W
Centennial Mountains ⛰	202	44.35 N	111.55 W
Centennial Park ♠, Austl.	274a	33.54 S	151.14 E
Centennial Park ♠, Ont., Can.	275b	43.39 N	79.35 W
Centennial Wash ∨	200	33.14 N	112.46 W
Centeno	66	42.48 N	11.49 E
Center, Colo., U.S.	200	37.45 N	106.06 W
Center, Ind., U.S.	216	40.26 N	86.04 W
Center, Mo., U.S.	219	39.30 N	91.32 W
Center, Nebr., U.S.	198	42.37 N	97.53 W
Center, N. Dak., U.S.	198	47.07 N	101.18 W
Center, Tex., U.S.	194	31.48 N	94.11 W
Centerbrook	207	41.21 N	72.25 W
Center Brunswick	210	42.45 N	73.37 W
Centerburg	214	40.18 N	82.42 W
Center City	190	45.24 N	92.49 W
Center Cross	208	37.48 N	76.47 W
Centereach	210	40.51 N	73.06 W
Centerfield	218	38.21 N	83.24 W
Center Hill	220	28.38 N	82.03 W
Center Hill Lake ⊜[1]	194	36.00 N	85.45 W
Center Line	214	42.29 N	83.03 W
Center Moriches	188	40.48 N	72.48 W
Center Mountain ∧	202	45.06 N	115.13 W
Center Point, Ala., U.S.	194	33.38 N	86.41 W
Center Point, Iowa, U.S.	190	42.11 N	91.46 W
Center Point, Tex., U.S.	196	29.57 N	99.02 W
Centerport, N.Y., U.S.	210	40.54 N	73.22 W
Centerport, Pa., U.S.	208	40.29 N	76.01 W
Center Square, N.J., U.S.	285	39.46 N	75.23 W
Center Square, Pa., U.S.	208	40.10 N	75.18 W
Centerton, Ind., U.S.	218	39.31 N	86.24 W
Centerton, N.J., U.S.	285	40.00 N	74.57 W
Center Valley	208	40.32 N	75.24 W
Centerville, Del., U.S.	285	39.30 N	75.10 W
Centerville, Ind., U.S.	218	39.49 N	85.00 W
Centerville, Iowa, U.S.	190	40.43 N	92.52 W
Centerville, Mass., U.S.	207	41.39 N	70.21 W
Centerville, Mo., U.S.	194	37.26 N	90.58 W
Centerville, N.Y., U.S.	210	42.29 N	78.15 W
Centerville, Ohio, U.S.	218	39.38 N	84.10 W
Centerville, Pa., U.S.	214	41.44 N	79.46 W
Centerville, S. Dak., U.S.	198	43.07 N	96.58 W
Centerville, Tenn., U.S.	194	35.47 N	87.28 W
Centerville, Tex., U.S.	222	31.16 N	95.59 W
Centerville, Utah, U.S.	200	40.55 N	111.52 W
Centerville, Wash., U.S.	224	45.45 N	120.54 W
Centinela	196	28.47 N	100.34 W
Cento	64	44.43 N	11.17 E
Centocelle ◆[8]	267a	41.53 N	12.34 E
Cento Croci, Passo di)(	62	44.25 N	9.37 E
Centola	68	40.04 N	15.19 E
Central, Bra.	250	11.08 S	42.08 W
Central, Alaska, U.S.	180	65.34 N	144.48 W
Central, Ariz., U.S.	200	32.52 N	109.48 W
Central, N. Mex., U.S.	200	32.46 N	108.09 W
Central, S.C., U.S.	192	34.44 N	82.47 W
Central, Tex., U.S.	222	31.26 N	94.49 W
Central □[4], Ghana	150	5.30 N	1.00 W
Central □[4], Kenya	154	0.45 S	37.00 E
Central □[4], Malawi	154	13.00 S	34.00 E
Central □[4], Scot., U.K.	46	56.05 N	4.20 W
Central □[4], Zam.	154	15.00 S	29.00 E
Central □[5], Bots.	156	21.30 S	26.00 E
Central □[5], Pap. N. Gui.	164	9.00 S	147.00 E
Central □[5], Para.	252	25.30 S	57.30 W
Central □[5], S. Lan.	122	7.30 N	80.50 E
Central,african Empire → Central African Republic □[1]	136	7.00 N	21.00 E
Central, Cordillera ⛰, Col.	246	5.00 N	75.00 W
Central, Cordillera ⛰, C.R.	236	10.10 N	84.05 W
Central, Cordillera ⛰, Perú	248	8.00 S	77.00 W
Central, Cordillera ⛰, Pil.	116	17.20 N	120.57 E
Central, Cordillera ⛰, P.R.	240m	18.10 N	66.35 W
Central, Macizo → Central, Massif ⛰	32	45.00 N	3.10 E
Central, Massif ⛰	32	45.00 N	3.10 E
Central, Planalto ⛰[1]	242	18.00 S	47.00 W
Central, Sistema ⛰	34	40.30 N	5.00 W
Central African Republic □[1]	136	7.00 N	21.00 E
Central Aguirre	240m	17.57 N	66.13 W
Central Barren	218	38.22 N	86.06 W
Central Brāhui Range ⛰	120	29.20 N	66.55 E
Central Bridge	210	42.43 N	74.20 W
Central Butte	184	50.47 N	106.30 W
Central City, Ill., U.S.	219	41.14 N	88.16 W
Central City, Iowa, U.S.	190	42.12 N	91.31 W
Central City, Ky., U.S.	194	37.18 N	87.07 W
Central City, Nebr., U.S.	198	41.07 N	98.00 W
Central City, Pa., U.S.	214	40.06 N	78.48 W
Central Division □[5], Fiji	175g	18.05 S	178.30 E
Central Division □[5], Sol.is.	175e	9.30 S	160.00 E
Central Falls	207	41.54 N	71.23 W
Central Heights	200	32.25 N	110.48 W
Central Highlands	279b	40.16 N	79.50 W
Centralia, Ill., U.S.	219	38.31 N	89.08 W
Centralia, Kans., U.S.	198	39.44 N	96.08 W
Centralia, Mo., U.S.	219	39.13 N	92.08 W
Centralia, Tex., U.S.	222	31.16 N	95.02 W
Centralia, Wash., U.S.	224	46.43 N	122.58 W
Centralia, Lake ⊜	219	38.32 N	88.59 W
Centralia Draw ∨	196	31.27 N	101.16 W
Centralina	255	18.34 S	49.13 W
Central Intelligence Agency ♜	284c	38.57 N	77.09 W
Central Internacional, Aeropuerto ⊠	286a	19.26 N	99.04 W
Central Island I	154	3.30 N	36.03 E
Central Islip	210	40.47 N	73.12 W
Central Lake	190	45.04 N	85.16 W
Central Makrān Range ⛰	128	26.40 N	64.30 E
Central Mount Stuart ∧	162	21.54 S	133.27 E
Central Mount Wedge ∧	162	22.51 S	131.50 E
Central No. 2 Division □[5]	175f	16.10 S	168.00 E
Central No. 2 Division □[8]	175f	16.30 S	167.30 E
Central'no-Bokovskoj	265b	55.53 N	37.51 E
Central'no-Bokovskoj ◆[8]	83	48.11 N	39.03 E
Central No. 1 Division □[5]	175f	17.30 S	169.00 E
Central Nyack	276	41.06 N	73.57 W
Central'nyje Karakumy ◆[2]	128	39.00 N	60.00 E
Centralnyj Park Imeni Gor'kogo ♠	265b	55.44 N	37.46 E
Centralnyj Stadion Imeni V.I. Lenina ♠	265b	55.43 N	37.33 E
Central Pacific Basin ✢[1]	14	7.00 N	176.00 W
Central Park, N.J., U.S.	276	40.26 N	74.18 W
Central Park, Wash., U.S.	224	46.58 N	123.41 W
Central Park ♠	276	40.47 N	73.58 W
Central Point	202	42.23 N	122.57 W
Central Railroad Station ◆[5]	272c	18.58 N	72.50 E
Central Range ⛰	164	5.00 S	142.30 E
Central Square	210	43.17 N	76.09 W
Central Utah Canal ≚	200	39.35 N	112.12 W
Central Valley, Calif., U.S.	204	40.41 N	122.22 W
Central Valley, N.Y., U.S.	210	41.20 N	74.07 W
Central Village	207	41.43 N	71.54 W
Centre	194	34.09 N	85.40 W
Centre □[5]	150	13.00 N	1.00 W
Centre □[6]	210	40.55 N	77.47 W
Centre, Canal du ≚	32	46.27 N	4.07 E
Centre Atomique de Marcoule ♜[3]	62	44.08 N	4.42 E
Centre City	285	39.46 N	75.11 W
Centre d'Energie Atomique de Pierrelatte ♜[3]	62	44.21 N	4.44 E
Centre d'Études ♜[3]	261	48.33 N	2.21 E
Centre Hall	214	40.51 N	77.41 W
Centre Island	276	40.54 N	73.32 W
Centre Island I	172	46.28 S	167.51 E
Centre Island Park ♠	275b	43.37 N	79.23 W
Centre Lake ⊜	212	44.36 N	75.51 W
Centre Peak ∧	182	55.41 N	126.26 W
Centreville, Ala., U.S.	194	32.56 N	87.08 W
Centreville, Ill., U.S.	219	38.33 N	90.06 W
Centreville, Ky., U.S.	218	38.13 N	84.24 W
Centreville, Md., U.S.	208	39.03 N	76.04 W
Centreville, Mich., U.S.	216	41.55 N	85.32 W
Centreville, Miss., U.S.	194	31.05 N	91.04 W
Centreville, Va., U.S.	208	38.50 N	77.26 W
Centro Puntas	240m	18.22 N	67.16 W
Centro Río Mayo	254	45.35 S	71.06 W
Centro Simón Bolívar ◆[9]	286c	10.30 N	66.55 W
Centuripe	70	37.37 N	14.44 E
Century, Fla., U.S.	194	30.58 N	87.16 W
Century, W. Va., U.S.	188	39.06 N	80.11 W
Century City ◆[8]	280	34.03 N	118.26 W
Çenxi	102	22.59 N	111.00 E
Čepca ≃	80	58.36 N	50.04 E
Čepel'	78	49.19 N	36.55 E
Cepoy	50	48.03 N	2.44 E
Ceprano	66	41.33 N	13.31 E
Čepřovice	60	49.10 N	13.59 E
Ceptia	152	12.56 S	17.35 E
Cepu	115a	7.09 S	111.35 E
Ceraino	64	45.35 N	10.50 E
Ceram → Seram I	164	3.00 S	129.00 E
Cerami	70	37.49 N	14.30 E
Cerami, Fiume di ≃	70	37.42 N	14.29 E
Ceram Sea → Seram, Laut ╤[2]	108	2.30 S	128.00 E
Cerano, It.	62	45.25 N	8.47 E
Cerano, Méx.	234	20.07 N	101.23 W
Ceraso	68	40.11 N	15.15 E
Čerčany	30	49.51 N	14.43 E
Cerchiara di Calabria	68	39.51 N	16.23 E
Čerchov ∧	60	49.23 N	12.47 E
Cercié	58	46.07 N	4.40 E
Cercola	66	40.51 N	14.21 E
Cerda	70	37.54 N	13.49 E
Čerdakly	80	54.23 N	48.51 E
Cerdas	248	20.48 S	66.29 W
Cerdeña, Isla de → Sardegna I	71	40.00 N	9.00 E
Čerdojak	86	48.48 N	84.00 E
Cerdon, Fr.	50	47.38 N	2.22 E
Cerdon, Fr.	58	46.05 N	5.28 E
Čerdyn'	24	60.23 N	56.24 E
Cère ≃	32	44.55 N	1.53 E
Cerea	64	45.12 N	11.13 E
Cereal	184	51.25 N	110.48 W
Cereales	252	36.49 S	63.51 W
Čerecha ≃	76	57.46 N	28.21 E
Cereglio	64	44.18 N	11.04 E
Čereja	76	54.37 N	29.17 E
Čerek ≃	84	43.42 N	44.03 E
Čeremchovo	88	53.09 N	103.05 E
Čeremisinovo	78	51.54 N	37.15 E
Čeremšan, S.S.S.R.	80	55.15 N	48.07 E
Čeremšan, S.S.S.R.	80	54.40 N	51.30 E
Cerenti	112	0.30 S	101.52 E
Čerepaška, Ostrov I	83	47.11 N	38.59 E
Čerepkovo ◆[8]	265b	55.46 N	37.23 E
Čerepovec	76	59.08 N	37.54 E
Ceres, Arg.	252	29.53 S	61.57 W
Ceres, Bra.	255	15.17 S	49.35 W
Ceres, It.	62	45.19 N	7.23 E
Ceres, S. Afr.	158	33.21 S	19.18 E
Ceres, Calif., U.S.	226	37.35 N	120.57 W
Ceres, N.Y., U.S.	210	42.00 N	78.16 W
Ceresco, Mich., U.S.	216	42.16 N	85.04 W
Ceresco, Nebr., U.S.	198	41.03 N	96.39 W
Ceresole Reale	62	45.26 N	7.15 E
Céreste	62	43.51 N	5.35 E
Céret	32	42.29 N	2.45 E
Cereté	246	8.53 N	75.48 W
Čerevkovka	78	48.50 N	37.40 E
Čerevkovo	24	61.46 N	45.12 E
Cereweh	115b	8.52 S	116.51 E
Čerga	86	51.35 N	85.38 E
Cergy	261	49.02 N	2.04 E
Ceri ≃	42	52.03 N	4.29 W
Ceriale	62	44.06 N	8.14 E
Ceriana	62	43.53 N	7.46 E
Ceriano	266b	45.38 N	9.05 E
Cerignola	68	41.16 N	15.54 E
Čerikov	76	53.34 N	31.23 E
Cérilly	32	46.37 N	2.49 E
Cerisano	68	39.16 N	16.11 E
Cerisiers	50	48.08 N	3.29 E
Čerkašina	88	58.37 N	108.30 E
Čerkasovo	82	54.33 N	36.48 E
Čerkassy, S.S.S.R.	76	52.41 N	38.43 E
Čerkassy, S.S.S.R.	78	49.26 N	32.04 E
Çerkeş	130	40.50 N	32.54 E
Čerkesovskij	80	50.41 N	42.34 E
Čerkessk	84	44.14 N	42.04 E
Çerkezköy	130	41.17 N	28.00 E
Čerkizovo, S.S.S.R.	82	55.12 N	38.45 E
Čerkizovo, S.S.S.R.	265b	55.58 N	37.48 E
Čerkizovo, S.S.S.R.	265b	55.57 N	37.22 E
Cerknica	36	45.48 N	14.22 E
Čerkovišče	76	55.54 N	30.51 E
Čerlak	86	54.09 N	74.48 E
Čerlakskij	86	53.47 N	74.31 E
Cermei	38	46.33 N	21.51 E
Čermen	84	43.11 N	44.42 E
Cermignano	66	42.35 N	13.47 E
Čern'	76	53.27 N	36.55 E
Cerna, Jugo.	38	45.11 N	18.42 E
Cerna, Rom.	38	45.04 N	28.18 E
Čern'achov	78	50.27 N	28.39 E
Čern'achovsk (Insterburg)	76	54.38 N	21.49 E
Černá hora ∧	30	48.58 N	13.48 E
Černaja	78	47.37 N	29.20 E
Čern'ajevo	89	52.45 N	126.00 E
Černak	85	43.24 N	68.02 E
Čern'anka	78	50.55 N	37.49 E
Cernăuți → Černovcy	78	48.18 N	25.56 E
Černavčicy	76	52.13 N	23.44 E
Cernavodă	38	44.21 N	28.01 E
Cernay	58	47.49 N	7.10 E
Cernay-la-Ville	50	48.40 N	1.58 E
Cerne Abbas	42	50.49 N	2.29 W
Černeckoje	82	55.15 N	37.20 E
Cernei, Munții ⛰	38	45.02 N	22.31 E
Černigov	78	51.30 N	31.18 E
Černigov □[4]	76	52.13 N	32.45 E
Černigovka, S.S.S.R.	78	47.13 N	36.14 E
Černigovka, S.S.S.R.	86	50.28 N	71.27 E
Černigovka, S.S.S.R.	89	44.21 N	132.33 E
Černigovka, S.S.S.R.	89	49.37 N	129.57 E
Černigovskaja	78	44.41 N	39.40 E
Černigovskoje Polesje ◆[1]	78	51.30 N	31.20 E
Černi vrâh ∧	38	42.34 N	23.17 E
Černobaj	78	49.41 N	32.19 E
Cernobbio	62	45.50 N	9.04 E
Černogolovka	82	56.00 N	38.22 E
Černogorsk	86	53.49 N	91.18 E
Černokol'skaja	86	56.42 N	72.49 E
Černorečenskoje	85	43.00 N	74.55 E
Černorečje	84	43.15 N	45.41 E
Černošín	60	49.49 N	12.53 E
Černovcy	78	48.18 N	25.56 E
Černovice	60	49.49 N	13.06 E
Černovskije Kopi	88	52.00 N	113.15 E
Černucha	80	55.36 N	43.46 E
Černuchi	78	50.16 N	32.57 E
Černuchino	83	48.19 N	38.30 E
Cernusco sul Naviglio	62	45.31 N	9.19 E
Černuška, S.S.S.R.	86	56.29 N	56.03 E
Černuška, S.S.S.R.	88	52.58 N	101.55 E
Cerny-en-Laonnois	50	49.27 N	3.40 E
Černyševsk	88	52.35 N	117.00 E
Černyševskij	74	63.00 N	112.15 E
Černyškovskij	80	48.27 N	42.14 E
Čer'omošč ≃	78	48.23 N	25.37 E
Čer'omuchova	80	54.57 N	51.09 E
Cerralvo	232	26.06 N	99.37 W
Cerralvo, Isla I	232	24.15 N	109.55 W
Cerreto, Passo del)(	64	44.18 N	10.13 E
Cerreto d'Esi	66	43.19 N	12.59 E
Cerreto Guidi	66	43.45 N	10.53 E
Cerreto Sannita	68	41.17 N	14.33 E
Cerrigydrudion	44	53.02 N	3.33 W
Cërrik	38	41.02 N	19.57 E
Cerrillos, Arg.	252	24.54 S	65.29 W
Cerrillos, N. Mex., U.S.	200	35.26 N	106.08 W
Cerrina	62	45.07 N	8.13 E
Cerritos, Méx.	234	22.26 N	100.17 W
Cerritos, Calif., U.S.	280	33.51 N	118.05 W
Cerro	58	45.54 N	8.36 E
Cerro, Forca di)(	66	42.45 N	12.47 E
Cerro Azul, Arg.	252	27.38 S	55.29 W
Cêrro Azul, Bra.	252	24.50 S	49.15 W
Cerro Azul, Méx.	234	21.12 N	97.44 W
Cerro Azul, Perú	248	13.02 S	76.30 W
Cerro Chato	252	33.06 S	55.08 W
Cerro Colorado	252	33.52 S	55.33 W
Cêrro Corá	250	6.03 S	36.21 W
Cerro de Garnica, Parque Nacional ♠	234	19.35 N	100.47 W
Cerro de las Campanas, Parque Nacional ♠	234	20.40 N	100.30 W
Cerro de las Mesas ⊥	234	18.47 N	96.05 W
Cerro de los Angeles ♜[1]	266a	40.19 N	3.41 W
Cerro de Pasco	248	10.41 S	76.16 W
Cerro Gordo	219	39.53 N	88.44 W
Cerro Grande ≃	286c	10.37 N	66.49 W
Cêrro Largo	252	28.09 S	54.45 W
Cerro Moreno	252	23.28 S	70.25 W
Cerron, Cerro ∧	246	10.19 N	70.39 W
Cerrón, Embalse ⊜[1]	236	14.00 N	89.00 W
Cerro Prieto	204	32.27 N	115.17 W
Cerros Colorados, Embalse ⊜[1]	252	38.35 S	68.40 W
Cerro Vera	252	33.11 S	57.28 W
Čerskij	74	68.45 N	161.45 E
Čerskogo, Chrebet ⛰	88	52.00 N	114.00 E
Čerskogo, Gora ∧	88	55.05 N	108.40 E
Cersosimo	68	40.03 N	16.21 E
Certaldo	66	43.33 N	11.02 E
Čertanovka ≃	265b	55.38 N	37.47 E
Čertkovo	83	49.23 N	40.10 E
Čertolino	76	56.12 N	33.54 E
Čertomlyk	78	47.37 N	34.09 E
Certosa (Karthaus)	64	46.42 N	10.54 E
Certosa di Pavia	62	45.15 N	9.09 E
Čerusti	76	55.33 N	40.01 E
Červ'anka	88	57.41 N	99.33 E
Cervantes	116	16.59 N	120.44 E
Cervarezza	64	44.23 N	10.20 E
Cervaro	66	41.29 N	13.54 E
Cervaro ≃	68	41.30 N	15.52 E
Cervati, Monte ∧	68	40.17 N	15.29 E
Cervelló	266d	41.24 N	1.57 E
Cervelló, Riera de ≃	266d	41.24 N	2.01 E
Červen'	76	53.42 N	28.26 E
Červen Brjag	38	43.16 N	24.06 E
Červený Kostelec	30	50.29 N	16.06 E
Cervera	34	41.40 N	1.17 E
Cervera del Río Alhama	34	42.01 N	1.57 W
Cervera de Pisuerga	34	42.52 N	4.30 W
Cerveteri	66	42.00 N	12.06 E
Cervi, Monte dei ∧	70	37.53 N	13.58 E
Cervia	66	44.15 N	12.22 E
Cervialto, Monte ∧	68	40.47 N	15.08 E
Cervignano del Friuli	64	45.49 N	13.20 E
Cervin, Mont → Matterhorn ∧	58	45.59 N	7.43 E
Cervinara	68	41.01 N	14.37 E
Cervione	36	42.20 N	9.31 E
Červl'onnaja	84	43.30 N	45.54 E
Cervo, Esp.	34	43.40 N	7.25 W
Cervo, It.	62	43.55 N	8.07 E
Cervo ≃	62	45.22 N	8.24 E
Cervo, Capo ≻	62	43.55 N	8.08 E
Cervo, Rio do ≃, Bra.	256	21.12 S	45.10 W
Cervo, Rio do ≃, Bra.	256	22.07 S	45.49 W
Červonaja Kamenka	78	48.38 N	33.26 E
Červonograd	78	50.24 N	24.14 E
Červonogranitnoje	78	50.34 N	28.33 E
Červonoje, S.S.S.R.	78	49.57 N	28.53 E
Červonoje, S.S.S.R.	78	51.46 N	34.04 E
Červonopartizansk	83	48.04 N	39.50 E
Červonyj Donec	78	49.29 N	36.34 E
Cesana Torinese	62	44.57 N	6.47 E
Cesano, It.	66	42.07 N	12.21 E
Cesano, It.	66	43.45 N	13.10 E
Cesano ≃	66	43.45 N	13.10 E
Cesano Boscone	266b	45.27 N	9.06 E
Cesano Maderno	62	45.38 N	9.08 E
César □[5]	246	9.20 N	73.30 W
César ≃	246	9.00 N	73.58 W
Cesaró	70	37.50 N	14.43 E
Cesate	266b	45.36 N	9.05 E
Cesena	66	44.08 N	12.15 E
Cesenatico	66	44.12 N	12.24 E
Cesi, Poggio ∧	267a	42.02 N	12.44 E
Cesiomaggiore	64	46.05 N	11.59 E
Cēsis	76	57.18 N	25.15 E
Česká Kamenice	54	50.47 N	14.26 E
Česká Kublice	60	49.22 N	12.52 E
Česká Lípa	54	50.42 N	14.32 E
Česká Socialistická Republika □[3]	30	49.40 N	15.10 E
Česká Třebová	30	49.54 N	16.27 E
České Budějovice	61	48.59 N	14.28 E
České středohoří ⛰	54	50.35 N	14.09 E
Českomoravská vrchovina ⛰[1]	30	49.20 N	15.30 E
Československo → Czechoslovakia □[1]	30	49.30 N	17.00 E
Český Brod	54	50.02 N	14.58 E
Český Krumlov	61	48.49 N	14.19 E
Český Těšín	30	49.45 N	18.37 E
Česma	86	53.50 N	60.40 E
Çeşme	130	38.18 N	26.19 E
Céspedes	240p	21.35 N	78.17 W
Cessalto	64	45.42 N	12.36 E
Češskaja Guba C	24	67.30 N	46.30 E
Cessnock	170	32.50 S	151.21 E
Cesson	261	48.34 N	2.36 E
Cestos ≃	150	5.40 N	9.10 W
Cesvaine	76	56.58 N	26.19 E
Cetara	68	40.39 N	14.42 E
Cetate	38	44.06 N	23.03 E
Cetatea Albă → Belgorod-Dnestrovskij	78	46.12 N	30.20 E
Četbulak	85	41.17 N	73.58 E
Cetian	100	25.44 N	116.22 E
Cetina ≃	36	43.26 N	16.42 E
Cetinje	38	42.23 N	18.55 E
Çetinkaya	130	39.15 N	37.38 E
Četlasskij Kamen', Gora ∧[2]	24	64.22 N	50.45 E
Cetona	66	42.58 N	11.54 E
Cetona, Monte ∧	66	42.56 N	11.52 E
Cetraro	68	39.31 N	15.56 E
Cetronia	208	40.35 N	75.31 W
Çetti Bay C	174p	13.19 N	144.39 E
Četyrboki	78	50.02 N	27.01 E
Céüse, Montagne de ∧	62	44.31 N	5.57 E
Ceuta	34	35.53 N	5.19 W
Ceva	62	44.23 N	8.02 E
Cevedale, Monte (Zufallspitze) ∧	64	46.27 N	10.37 E
Cevennen → Cévennes ◆[1]	32	44.00 N	3.30 E
Cévennes ◆[1]	32	44.00 N	3.30 E
Cévennes, Parc National des ♠	62	44.20 N	3.45 E
Cevins	62	45.35 N	6.28 E
Cevio	58	46.19 N	8.36 E
Ceyhan	130	37.04 N	35.47 E
Ceyhan ≃	130	36.45 N	35.42 E
Ceylon, Sask., Can.	184	49.28 N	104.36 W
Ceylon, Minn., U.S.	198	43.32 N	94.38 W
Ceylon → Sri Lanka □[1]	122	7.00 N	81.00 E
Ceyzériat	58	46.10 N	5.19 E
Cèze ≃	62	44.06 N	4.42 E
Chaam, Ned.	52	51.31 N	4.52 E
Cha-am, Thai	110	12.48 N	99.58 E
Chaanling	100	29.39 N	113.49 E
Chaatl Island I	182	53.00 N	132.25 W
Chabanais	32	45.52 N	0.43 E
Chabang Tiga	114	5.19 N	103.08 E
Chabaricha	24	65.50 N	52.16 E
Chabařovice	54	50.40 N	13.56 E
Chabarovo	72	69.39 N	60.24 E
Chabarovsk	89	48.27 N	135.06 E
Chabarovsk □[4]	89	54.00 N	136.00 E
Chabarowsk → Chabarovsk	89	48.27 N	135.06 E
Chabary	86	53.37 N	79.33 E
Chabás	252	33.15 S	61.22 W
Chabeuil	62	44.54 N	5.01 E
Chabez	84	44.02 N	41.47 E
Chābi	124	22.49 N	80.41 E
Chabjuwardoo Bay C	162	22.57 S	113.48 E
Chablais ◆[1]	58	46.18 N	6.39 E
Chablis	50	47.49 N	3.48 E
Chabogongba	120	31.47 N	81.14 E
Chaboje	265a	59.53 N	30.46 E
Chabot, Lake ⊜, Calif., U.S.	282	38.08 N	122.14 W
Chabot, Lake ⊜, Calif., U.S.	282	37.43 N	122.07 W
Chabris	50	47.15 N	1.39 E
Chabuchaer, S.S.S.R.	86	43.42 N	81.04 E
Chabuchaer, Zhg.	86	43.42 N	81.04 E
Chabu-Rabot, Pereval)(	85	38.40 N	70.43 E
Chacabuco	252	34.38 S	60.29 W
Chacaito, Quebrada ≃	286c	10.29 N	66.52 W
Chacaltianguis	234	18.20 N	95.50 W
Chacanilla	248	6.13 S	77.51 W
Chacao	286c	10.30 N	66.51 W
Chácara	256	21.41 S	43.13 W
Chacarão, Cachoeira do ʟ	250	6.32 S	58.12 W
Chacarilla	286d	12.02 S	77.01 W
Chacarita, Cementerio de la ◆	288	34.33 S	58.28 W
Chacayán	248	10.24 S	76.25 W
Chacewater	42	50.15 N	5.10 W
Chachalgi, Gora ∧	84	42.48 N	45.09 E
Chachani, Nevado ∧	248	16.12 S	71.33 W
Chachas	248	15.30 S	72.16 W
Chachoengsao	110	13.42 N	101.05 E
Chāchro	120	25.07 N	70.15 E
Chachu	120	33.16 N	81.41 E
Chačinčaj ≃	84	40.13 N	47.18 E
Chačmas	84	41.28 N	48.48 E
Chaco □[4]	252	26.25 S	60.30 W
Chaco □[5]	248	20.00 S	60.30 W
Chaco ≃	200	36.46 N	108.39 W
Chaco Austral ◆[1]	252	26.30 S	61.30 W
Chaco Boreal ◆[1]	252	23.00 S	60.00 W
Chaco Canyon National Monument ♠	200	36.06 N	108.00 W
Chaco Central ◆[1]	252	25.00 S	59.45 W
Chacón, Arroyo ≃	288	34.53 S	58.39 W
Chacon, Cape ≻	180	54.42 N	132.00 W
Chacra Cerro	286d	11.55 S	77.04 W
Chacra Ríos, Coliseo ♠	286d	12.03 S	77.04 W
Chacuaco Creek ≃	196	37.34 N	103.38 W
Chad □[1]	136		
	146	15.00 N	19.00 E
Chad, Lake (Lac Tchad) ⊜	146	13.20 N	14.00 E
Chadabulak	88	50.38 N	116.18 E
Chadbourn	192	34.19 N	78.50 W
Chadderton	262	53.33 N	2.08 W
Chadds Ford	285	39.52 N	75.35 W
Chādegān	128	32.46 N	50.39 E
Chadian, Zhg.	102	26.48 N	105.48 E
Chadian, Zhg.	105	39.14 N	117.45 E
Chadianzi	107	30.31 N	104.22 E
Chadiza	154	14.05 S	32.28 E
Chadron	198	42.50 N	103.02 W

≃ River	Fluss	Río	Rivière	Rio
≚ Canal	Kanal	Canal	Canal	Canal
ʟ Waterfall, Rapids	Wasserfall, Stromschnellen	Cascada, Rápidos	Chute d'eau, Rapides	Cascata, Rápidos
⊔ Strait	Meeresstrasse	Estrecho	Détroit	Estreito
C Bay, Gulf	Bucht, Golf	Bahía, Golfo	Baie, Golfe	Baía, Golfo
⊜ Lake, Lakes	See, Seen	Lago, Lagos	Lac, Lacs	Lago, Lagos
☷ Swamp	Sumpf	Pantano	Marais	Pântano
⍓ Ice Features, Glacier	Eis- und Gletscherformen	Accidentes Glaciales	Formes glaciaires	Acidentes Glaciares
╤ Other Hydrographic Features	Andere Hydrographische Objekte	Otros Elementos Hidrográficos	Autres données hydrographiques	Outros Elementos Hidrográficos

✢ Submarine Features	Untermeerische Objekte	Accidentes Submarinos	Formes de relief sous-marin	Acidentes Submarinos
□ Political Unit	Politische Einheit	Unidad Política	Entité politique	Unidade Política
♜ Cultural Institution	Kulturelle Institution	Institución Cultural	Institution culturelle	Instituição Cultural
⊥ Historical Site	Historische Stätte	Sitio Histórico	Site historique	Sitio Histórico
♠ Recreational Site	Erholungs- und Ferienort	Sitio de Recreo	Centre de loisirs	Sítio de Lazer
⊠ Airport	Flughafen	Aeropuerto	Aéroport	Aeroporto
■ Military Installation	Militäranlage	Instalación Militar	Installation militaire	Instalação Militar
◆ Miscellaneous	Verschiedenes	Misceláneo	Divers	Miscelânea

ENGLISH — Name | Page | Lat.°′ | Long.°′
DEUTSCH — Name | Seite | Breite°′ | Länge°′ E=Ost

Chadstone 274b 37.53 S 145.05 E
Chadwell Saint Mary 260 51.29 N 0.22 E
Chadwick 190 42.01 N 89.53 W
Chadwick Pond ⊜ 283 42.44 N 71.05 W
Chadwicks 210 43.01 N 75.16 W
Chadyžensk 78 44.25 N 39.33 E
Chadžalmachi 84 42.26 N 47.13 E
Chadžibejskij Liman ⊜ 78 46.39 N 30.33 E
Chae Hom 110 18.43 N 99.35 E
Chaem ≃ 110 18.11 N 98.38 E
Chaersen 89 46.19 N 121.54 E
Chaeryŏng 98 38.24 N 125.36 E
Chafarinas, Islas II 34 35.11 N 2.26 W
Chafe 150 11.56 N 6.55 E
Chaffee 194 37.11 N 89.40 W
Chaffins 207 42.21 N 71.51 W
Chafurray 246 3.10 N 73.14 W
Chāgai 128 29.19 N 64.42 E
Chāgai Hills ∧∧[2] 128 29.30 N 64.15 E
Chagandianlisu 102 41.47 N 103.29 E
Chagang Do □[4] 98 40.50 N 126.30 E
'Chaghcharān 120 34.32 N 65.15 E
Chagny 58 46.55 N 4.45 E
Chagos Archipelago II 12 6.00 S 72.00 E
Chagrin ≃ 214 41.40 N 81.27 W
Chagrin, Aurora Branch ≃ 279a 41.25 N 81.25 W
Chagrin Falls 214 41.26 N 81.24 W
Chagrin Falls Park 214 41.21 N 81.32 W
Chagrin Valley Parkway ♠ 279a 41.26 N 81.25 W
Chaguanas 241r 10.31 N 61.25 W
Chaguaramas 246 9.20 N 66.16 W
Chaguaya 248 21.49 S 64.50 W
Chahaeryouhouqi 102 41.52 N 112.56 E
Chahaeryouzhongqi 102 41.09 N 112.38 E
Chahaignes 50 47.44 N 0.31 E
Chāhak 128 33.17 N 58.54 E
Chahal 236 15.45 N 89.34 W
Chahancheluo 98 41.39 N 114.22 E
Chahanhu ⊜ 98 41.23 N 113.55 E
Chahanwusu → Dulan 102 36.16 N 98.28 E
Chahār Bāgh, Afg. 120 35.58 N 69.38 E
Chahār Bāgh, Afg. 128 37.00 N 65.14 E
Chahār Borjak 128 30.17 N 62.03 E
Chahār Deh-ye Ghowrband 120 34.59 N 68.44 E
Chahayang 89 48.24 N 124.15 E
Chāh Bahār 128 25.18 N 60.37 E
Chahe, Zhg. 100 33.16 N 119.02 E
Chahe, Zhg. 102 33.48 N 97.22 E
Chahe, Zhg. 105 39.50 N 115.21 E
Chāh Gheybī, Hāmūn-e ≋ 128 28.06 N 60.50 E
Chahuamiao 100 33.00 N 115.56 E
Chahuites 234 16.17 N 94.11 W
Chai Badan 110 15.04 N 101.05 E
Chaidamuhe ≃ 102 36.39 N 96.20 E
Chaidamupendi ⊻[1] 120 37.00 N 95.00 E
Chaidamushan ∧∧ 102 38.00 N 95.40 E
Chaigou 98 36.15 N 119.36 E
Chaihe 89 44.47 N 129.42 E
Chaihe ≃ 104 42.20 N 123.52 E
Chaijiawan 100 29.10 N 113.06 E
Chaillé-les-Marais 32 46.24 N 1.01 W
Chailley 50 48.05 N 3.42 E
Chailly-en-Bière 50 48.28 N 2.35 E
Chainat 110 15.11 N 100.08 E
Chaîne Annamitique ∧∧ 110 17.00 N 106.00 E
Chainhurst 260 51.12 N 0.29 E
Chain O'Lakes State Park ♠, Ill., U.S. 216 42.27 N 88.11 W
Chain O'Lakes State Park ♠, Ind., U.S. 216 41.20 N 85.26 W
Chaiqiao 100 29.51 N 121.56 E
Chairel, Laguna de C 234 22.17 N 97.57 W
Chaishudian 105 40.46 N 116.30 E
Chaiši 84 42.57 N 42.12 E
Chait 85 39.11 N 70.53 E
Chaiwobao 86 43.33 N 87.59 E
Chaiya 110 9.23 N 99.14 E
Chaiyaphum 110 15.48 N 102.02 E
Chajarí 252 30.46 S 57.59 W
Chajdarken 85 39.57 N 71.21 E
Chaj Doāb ∧∧[1] 123 32.15 N 73.00 E
Chajia 107 29.37 N 104.27 E
Chajian 100 32.40 N 118.46 E
Chajianling 98 39.14 N 114.36 E
Chajiaqiao, Zhg. 100 34.00 N 120.07 E
Chajiaqiao, Zhg. 107 29.39 N 104.48 E
Chajpudyrskaja Guba C 24 68.30 N 59.30 E
Chajrchan 88 48.37 N 101.53 E
Chajrchandulaan 102 45.57 N 102.03 E
Chajul 236 15.30 N 91.02 W
Chaka, Sūd. 154 4.49 N 31.14 E
Chaka, Zhg. 102 36.48 N 99.19 E
Chakachamna Lake ⊜ 180 61.13 N 152.35 W
Chakaer 120 36.32 N 80.43 E
Chak Amru 123 32.22 N 75.11 E
Chakari 154 18.05 S 29.51 E
Chakaria 120 21.45 N 92.05 E
Chakarnaba 146 14.13 N 20.51 E
Chakasskaja Avtonomnaja Oblast' □[8] 86 53.00 N 90.00 E
Chakayanchi ⊜ 102 36.40 N 99.20 E
Chākdaha, Bhārat 126 23.05 N 88.31 E
Chakdaha, Bhārat 272b 22.20 N 88.20 E
Chake Chake 154 5.15 S 39.46 E
Chakhānsūr 128 31.10 N 62.04 E
Chakhānsūr □[4] 128 30.30 N 62.00 E
Chak Jhumra 123 31.34 N 73.11 E
Chakkarat 110 15.00 N 102.16 E
Chakou, Zhg. 98 38.03 N 113.36 E
Chakou, Zhg. 105 38.53 N 116.41 E
Chakwāl 123 32.56 N 72.52 E
Cha Kwo Ling 271d 22.18 N 114.13 E
Chala 248 15.52 S 74.16 W
Chalabesa 154 11.22 S 31.01 E
Chalagou 102 34.10 N 97.44 E
Chalais 32 45.16 N 0.02 E
Chalamont 58 46.00 N 5.10 E
Chalampé 58 47.49 N 7.33 E
Chalatenango 236 14.03 N 88.56 W
Chalaua 154 16.06 S 39.11 E
Chalaux ≃ 50 47.23 N 3.54 E
Chalbi Desert ◆[2] 154 3.00 N 37.20 E
Chalcatongo de Hidalgo 234 17.02 N 97.35 W
Chalchgol 88 48.11 N 114.54 E
Chalchihuites 234 23.29 N 103.53 W
Chalchuapa 236 13.59 N 89.41 W
Chalcis → Khalkís 38 38.28 N 23.36 E
Chalco [de Díaz Covarrubias] 234 19.16 N 98.54 W
Chaldan 84 40.43 N 47.15 E
Chaldon 260 51.17 N 0.07 W
Chaleine 261 48.36 N 1.43 E
Chalengkou 120 37.57 N 93.40 E
Châlette-sur-Loing 50 48.01 N 2.44 E
Chaleur Bay C 186 48.00 N 65.45 W
Chalfant 279b 40.25 N 79.52 W
Chalfant Run ≃ 279b 40.25 N 79.48 W
Chalfont 208 40.17 N 75.13 W
Chalfont Common 260 51.38 N 0.33 W
Chalfont Saint Giles 260 51.38 N 0.34 W
Chalfont Saint Peter 260 51.37 N 0.33 W
Chalford 42 51.45 N 2.09 W
Chalhuanca 248 14.17 S 73.15 W
Chalifert 261 48.53 N 2.46 E
Chaligny 58 48.37 N 6.05 E
Chalihuey 234 22.43 N 104.04 W
Chalilovo 86 51.24 N 58.04 E
Chalindrey 58 47.48 N 5.26 E
Chaling 100 26.47 N 113.33 E
Chalisi 102 32.55 N 102.04 E
Chaliun 88 48.50 N 103.59 E
Chalk 260 51.26 N 0.25 E
Chalkabad 86 42.42 N 59.43 E
Chalk Draw ∨ 196 29.36 N 103.15 W
Chalk River 190 46.01 N 77.27 W
Chalkyitsik 180 66.39 N 143.43 W
Challans 32 46.51 N 1.53 W
Challapata 248 18.54 S 66.47 W
Challenge 226 39.29 N 121.13 W
Challenger, Mount ∧ 224 48.50 N 121.20 W
Challes-les-Eaux 62 45.33 N 5.59 E
Challis 202 44.30 N 114.14 W
Chall Sar ∧ 123 34.46 N 73.04 E
Challviri, Salar de ⊻ 248 22.32 S 67.34 W
Chal'mer-Ju 24 67.58 N 64.50 E
Chalmers 216 40.40 N 86.52 W
Chalmette 194 29.56 N 89.58 W
Chalone Creek ≃ 226 36.21 N 121.14 W
Chalonnes-sur-Loire 32 47.21 N 0.46 W
Châlons-sur-Marne 50 48.57 N 4.22 E
Chalon-sur-Saône 58 46.47 N 4.51 E
Chalosse ◆[1] 32 43.45 N 0.30 W
Chalt 123 36.15 N 74.20 E
Chaltel, Cerro (Monte Fitzroy) ∧ 254 49.17 S 73.05 W
Chalturin 80 58.33 N 48.54 E
Chalturino 78 49.31 N 35.17 E
Chaluhe 89 43.43 N 126.00 E
Chaluolehu ⊜ 120 34.00 N 81.45 E
Châlus, Fr. 32 45.39 N 0.59 E
Chālūs, Īrān 128 36.38 N 51.26 E
Cham, B.R.D. 60 49.13 N 12.41 E
Cham, Schw. 58 47.11 N 8.28 E
Chama, Perú 286d 12.08 S 77.00 W
Chama, N. Mex., U.S. 200 36.54 N 106.35 W
Chama ≃ 246 9.03 N 71.40 W
Chama, Rio ≃ 200 36.03 N 106.05 W
Chamaicó 252 35.03 S 64.58 W
Chamal, Sierra ∧∧ 234 22.45 N 99.15 W
Chamama 154 12.55 S 33.43 E
Chamamatjurt 84 43.36 N 46.30 E
Chaman 120 30.55 N 66.22 E
Chamangonge 152 11.16 S 20.24 E
Chamarande 261 48.31 N 2.13 E
Chamaya ≃ 248 5.44 S 78.39 W
Chamb ≃ 60 49.13 N 12.42 E
Chamba, Moç. 154 12.07 S 36.57 E
Chamba, Tan. 154 11.35 S 36.58 E
Chambal ≃ 124 26.29 N 79.15 E
Chambaran, Plateau de ∧∧[1] 62 45.15 N 5.15 E
Chambas 240p 22.12 N 78.55 W
Chambas ≃ 240p 22.24 N 78.54 W
Chamberlain, Sask., Can. 184 50.50 N 105.34 W
Chamberlain, S. Dak., U.S. 198 43.49 N 99.20 W
Chamberlain ≃ 164 15.08 S 128.06 E
Chamberlain Lake ⊜ 186 46.17 N 69.20 W
Chamberlin, Mount ∧ 180 69.16 N 144.55 W
Chamberry, Ruisseau ≃ 275a 45.20 N 73.58 W
Chambers, Ariz., U.S. 200 35.11 N 109.26 W
Chambers, Nebr., U.S. 198 42.12 N 98.45 W
Chambers, N.Y., U.S. 210 42.16 N 76.57 W
Chambers □[6] 222 29.42 N 94.40 W
Chambers Brook ≃ 276 40.35 N 74.41 W
Chambersburg, Ill., U.S. 219 39.49 N 90.39 W
Chambersburg, Ind., U.S. 218 38.31 N 86.24 W
Chambersburg, Pa., U.S. 208 39.56 N 77.39 W
Chambers Corner 285 40.01 N 74.44 W
Chambers Creek ≃ 222 31.58 N 96.10 W
Chambers Creek, North Fork ≃ 222 32.16 N 96.58 W
Chambers Creek, South Fork ≃ 222 32.16 N 96.58 W
Chambers Island I 190 45.11 N 87.12 W
Chambéry 62 45.34 N 5.56 E
Chambeshi ≃ 154 11.21 S 30.37 E
Chambi, Djebel ∧ 148 35.11 N 8.42 E
Chambira ≃, Perú 246 4.28 S 74.50 W
Chambira ≃, Perú 246 3.55 S 73.45 W
Chambishi 154 12.40 S 28.03 E
Chamblee 192 33.54 N 84.18 W
Chambley-Bussières 56 49.03 N 5.54 E
Chambly, Qué., Can. 275a 45.27 N 73.17 W
Chambly, Fr. 50 49.10 N 2.15 E
Chambly □[6] 206 45.30 N 73.20 W
Chambly, Bassin de ⊜ 206 45.27 N 73.17 W
Chambly, Canal de ⩸ 275a 45.25 N 73.15 W
Chambois 50 48.48 N 0.07 E
Chambon-sur-Dolore 62 45.30 N 3.37 E
Chambon-sur-Voueize 32 46.11 N 2.25 E
Chambord, Château de ⊥ 50 47.37 N 1.31 E
Chambourcy 261 48.54 N 2.03 E
Chambri Lake ⊜ 164 4.16 S 143.08 E
Chambry 261 49.00 N 2.54 E
Chamburi Kalāt 128 26.08 N 64.43 E
Chamdo → Changdu 102 31.11 N 97.15 E
Chamdor 273d 26.08 S 27.48 E
Chame 236 8.35 N 79.53 W
Chame, Punta ≻ 236 8.39 N 79.42 W
Chamela 234 19.32 N 105.05 W
Chamela, Bahía C 234 19.33 N 105.07 W
Chamelecón 236 15.24 N 88.01 W
Chamelecón ≃ 236 15.51 N 87.49 W
Chamical (Gobernador Gordillo) 252 30.21 S 66.19 W
Chamizo 258 34.10 S 56.41 W
Chamkanī 120 33.48 N 69.49 E
Chamlia ≃ 124 29.38 N 80.24 E
Chamois, It. 62 45.50 N 7.37 E
Chamois, Mo., U.S. 219 38.41 N 91.46 W
Chamojie 89 49.25 N 124.45 E
Chamoli 124 30.24 N 79.21 E
Chamonix-Mont-Blanc 58 45.55 N 6.52 E
Chamousset 62 45.33 N 6.12 E
Chamoux-sur-Gelon 62 45.32 N 6.13 E
Champagne, Yukon, Can. 180 60.47 N 136.29 W
Champagne, Fr. 62 45.16 N 4.48 E
Champagne □[9] 32 49.00 N 4.30 E
Champagne Castle ∧ 158 29.06 S 29.20 E
Champagne-en-Valromay 58 45.54 N 5.41 E
Champagner-Berge ∧[2] 264a 52.31 N 13.05 E
Champagne-sur-Seine 50 48.24 N 2.48 E
Champagney 58 47.42 N 6.41 E
Champagnole 58 46.45 N 5.55 E
Champ-agny 62 45.27 N 6.42 E
Champaign 194 40.07 N 88.14 W
Champaign □[6], Ill., U.S. 216 40.07 N 88.12 W
Champaign □[6], Ohio, U.S. 218 40.07 N 83.45 W
Champaquí, Cerro ∧ 252 31.59 S 64.56 W
Champaran □[5] 124 26.50 N 84.40 E
Champasak 110 14.53 N 105.52 E
Champaubert, Réservoir de ⊜[1] 58 48.35 N 4.50 E
Champcueil 261 48.31 N 2.27 E
Champdāni 126 22.48 N 88.21 E
Champdeniers 32 46.29 N 0.24 W
Champdepraz 62 45.41 N 7.39 E
Champdeuil 261 48.37 N 2.44 E
Champdor 58 46.01 N 5.36 E
Champdoré, Lac ⊜ 176 55.55 N 65.49 W
Champeaux 50 48.35 N 2.48 E
Champeix 32 45.36 N 3.08 E
Champerico 236 14.18 N 91.55 W
Champéry 58 46.10 N 6.52 E
Champex 58 46.02 N 7.07 E
Champier 62 45.27 N 5.17 E
Champigneulles 56 48.44 N 6.10 E
Champigny-sur-Marne 261 48.49 N 2.31 E
Champion, Alta., Can. 182 50.14 N 113.09 W
Champion, Mich., U.S. 190 46.31 N 87.58 W
Champion, Ohio, U.S. 214 41.17 N 80.51 W
Champion, Pa., U.S. 214 40.05 N 79.21 W
Champlain 206 44.59 N 73.27 W
Champlain □[6] 206 46.45 N 72.35 W
Champlain ≃ 206 46.27 N 72.17 W
Champlain, Lake ⊜ 188 44.45 N 73.15 W
Champlain, Pont ◆[5] 206 45.28 N 73.32 W
Champlain Canal ⩸ 210 43.20 N 73.34 W
Champlan 261 48.43 N 2.16 E
Champlin Creek ≃ 276 40.43 N 73.12 W
Champlitte-et-le-Prélot 58 47.37 N 5.31 E
Champlon 56 50.07 N 5.28 E
Champoluc 62 45.50 N 7.44 E
Champotón 232 19.21 N 90.43 W
Champrond-en-Gâtine 50 48.24 N 1.05 E
Champs 50 47.44 N 3.36 E
Champs-sur-Marne 261 48.51 N 2.36 E
Champvans 58 47.06 N 5.26 E
Chamrousse 62 45.08 N 5.52 E
Chamusca 34 39.21 N 8.29 W
Chamza Chakimzada 85 40.26 N 71.30 E
Chana 110 6.55 N 100.44 E
Chanabadskij 85 40.49 N 72.58 E
Chanakyapuri □[9] 272a 28.36 N 77.11 E
Chañar 252 30.32 S 65.58 W
Chañaral 252 26.21 S 70.37 W
Chañaral, Isla I 252 29.02 S 71.35 W
Chanas 62 45.18 N 4.49 E
Chancay 248 11.35 S 77.16 W
Chancay ≃ 248 11.37 S 77.15 W
Chance 208 38.11 N 75.56 W
Chanceaux 58 47.31 N 4.42 E
Chanceaux-sur-Choisille 50 47.28 N 0.42 E
Chan Chan ⊥ 248 8.06 S 79.05 W
Chanchelulla Peak ∧ 204 40.28 N 122.59 W
Chanchiang → Zhanjiang 102 21.16 N 110.28 E
Chanchöchij Uul ∧∧ 88 49.30 N 94.30 E
Chanco 252 35.44 S 72.32 W
Chancy 58 46.08 N 6.00 E
Chanda → Chandrapur, Bhārat 122 19.57 N 79.18 E
Chanda, S.S.S.R. 88 55.00 N 107.14 E
Chanda ≃ 88 55.00 N 107.14 E
Chandagajty 86 50.44 N 92.03 E
Chandalar 180 67.30 N 148.30 W
Chandalar ≃ 180 66.36 N 145.48 W
Chandalar, East Fork ≃ 180 67.05 N 147.16 W
Chandalar, Middle Fork ≃ 180 67.10 N 148.19 W
Chandalar, North Fork ≃ 180 67.10 N 148.19 W
Chandanpratap 126 23.33 N 89.24 E
Chandapāra 126 22.46 N 90.16 E
Chandar 126 23.54 N 89.58 E
Chandeleur Islands II 194 29.48 N 88.51 W
Chandeleur Sound U 194 29.55 N 89.10 W
Chandernagore → Chandannagar 126 22.51 N 88.21 E
Chandīgarh □[3] 123 30.45 N 76.45 E
Chandīpur 126 23.59 N 89.01 E
Chandler, Qué., Can. 186 48.21 N 64.41 W
Chandler, Ariz., U.S. 200 33.18 N 111.50 W
Chandler, Ind., U.S. 194 38.03 N 87.22 W
Chandler, Okla., U.S. 196 35.42 N 96.53 W
Chandler, Tex., U.S. 222 32.18 N 95.29 W
Chandler ≃ 180 69.27 N 151.30 W
Chandler, Mount ∧[2] 162 27.00 S 133.20 E
Chandler Lake ⊜ 180 68.15 N 152.43 W
Chandler Park ♠ 281 42.24 N 82.58 W
Chandler's Cross 260 51.40 N 0.27 W
Chandler's Ford 42 50.59 N 1.23 W
Chandlers Valley 214 41.56 N 79.18 W
Chandlerville 219 40.03 N 90.09 W
Chandless ≃ 248 9.08 S 69.51 W
Chandman' 86 50.02 N 92.03 E
Chandos Lake ⊜ 212 44.49 N 78.00 W
Chāndpur, Bngl. 120 22.08 N 91.55 E
Chāndpur, Bngl. 124 23.13 N 90.39 E
Chandra Dighalia 126 23.04 N 89.46 E
Chandrapur 122 19.57 N 79.18 E
Chāndvad 122 20.20 N 74.15 E
Chandyga 74 62.40 N 135.36 E
Chanfang 105 39.56 N 115.55 E
Chang, Ko I 110 12.05 N 102.20 E
Changa 84 44.27 N 50.36 E
Changācha 126 23.16 N 89.01 E
Changajn Nuruu ∧∧ 90 47.30 N 100.00 E
Changalane 156 26.16 S 32.13 E
Chang'an, Zhg. 102 26.00 N 109.34 E
Changan → Xi'an, Zhg. 102 34.15 N 108.52 E
Chang'an, Zhg. 106 30.28 N 120.27 E
Changanācheri 122 9.28 N 76.33 E
Changane ≃ 156 24.43 S 33.32 E
Changara 154 16.54 S 33.14 E
Changbai 98 41.26 N 128.11 E
Changbaishan ∧∧ 98 42.05 N 128.00 E
Changchaoling 106 31.00 N 119.40 E
Changcheng, Zhg. 100 31.49 N 116.54 E
Changcheng, Zhg. 110 19.24 N 108.42 E
Changcheng (Great Wall) ⊥ 98 40.30 N 117.00 E
Chang Chenmo ≃ 120 34.17 N 78.19 E
Changchiak'ou → Zhangjiakou 105 40.50 N 114.53 E
Ch'angchih → Changzhi 102 36.11 N 113.08 E
Changchou → Zhangzhou 100 24.33 N 117.39 E
Changchow → Changzhou 106 31.47 N 119.57 E
Changchun 89 43.53 N 125.19 E
Changchunling 89 45.22 N 125.28 E
Changdan 98 37.56 N 126.45 E
Changde 102 28.55 N 111.38 E
Changdian 105 40.01 N 116.32 E
Ch'angdo 98 38.30 N 127.40 E
Ch'ang-dong 98 39.03 N 126.34 E
Changdu 102 31.11 N 97.15 E
Change Islands 186 49.40 N 54.25 W
Changgang 100 24.38 N 113.05 E
Changgangzi 104 41.26 N 122.41 E
Changgi-li 271b 37.35 N 126.44 E
Changgi-ri 271b 37.38 N 126.41 E
Changgou, Zhg. 100 34.15 N 113.50 E
Changgou, Zhg. 105 39.34 N 115.53 E
Changgouzhen 105 39.44 N 115.52 E
Changguandian 100 32.58 N 115.16 E
Changguowei 100 29.15 N 121.56 E
Changgye-ri 98 34.33 N 126.49 E
Changgyong Palace ⊍ 271b 37.36 N 127.00 E
Chang-hai → Shanghai 106 31.14 N 121.28 E
Changhang 98 36.01 N 126.40 E
Changhe 106 30.11 N 120.11 E
Changhowŏn 98 37.08 N 127.39 E
Ch'anghsü Shan I 100 26.14 N 119.58 E
Changhu ⊜ 100 30.15 N 112.35 E
Changhua, T'aiwan 100 24.05 N 120.32 E
Changhua, Zhg. 100 30.11 N 119.13 E
Changhŭng 98 34.41 N 126.52 E
Changhŭng-ni 98 40.24 N 128.19 E
Changi 271c 1.23 N 103.59 E
Changi, Tanjong ≻ 271c 1.23 N 104.00 E
Changi Airport ⊠ 271c 1.22 N 103.59 E
Changjiang (Yangtze) ≃ 90 31.48 N 121.10 E
Changjin-ŭp 98 40.23 N 127.15 E
Changji Zizhizhou □[4] 86 42.30 N 85.00 E
Changkiakow → Zhangjiakou 105 40.50 N 114.53 E
Changlapod Pass)(124 30.08 N 87.06 E
Changlejie 100 28.52 N 113.19 E
Changlun 114 6.26 N 100.26 E
Changlupu 106 31.04 N 119.17 E
Changmong-ni 98 34.58 N 128.41 E
Changning, Zhg. 102 26.19 N 112.21 E
Changning (Anningqiao), Zhg. 102 28.21 N 104.53 E
Changning, Zhg. 102 24.55 N 99.35 E
Changning, Zhg. 105 39.59 N 114.55 E
Ch'angnyŏng 98 35.33 N 128.29 E
Changnyŏn-ni 98 38.37 N 125.16 E
Changokurt 72 61.58 N 64.18 E
Ch'angpin 100 23.20 N 121.28 E
Changping, Zhg. 102 32.33 N 107.30 E
Changping, Zhg. 105 40.14 N 116.14 E
Changpingzhen 98 40.14 N 116.14 E
Changpu 100 23.48 N 115.26 E
Changputong 102 28.05 N 98.29 E
Ch'angp'yŏng-dong 98 41.27 N 127.31 E
Changqiao, Zhg. 100 24.15 N 117.39 E
Changqiao, Zhg. 100 26.49 N 118.50 E
Changqing 98 36.34 N 116.43 E
Changsa 102 19.51 N 110.53 E
Changsha, Zhg. 100 24.13 N 116.07 E
Changsha, Zhg. 100 28.11 N 113.01 E
Changshanqundao II 98 39.00 N 122.45 E
Changshu 106 31.39 N 120.45 E
Changshui 102 34.21 N 111.29 E
Changsŏng 98 35.20 N 126.49 E
Changsŏn-gang ≃ 98 39.15 N 126.02 E
Changsu 98 35.40 N 127.32 E
Changtai, Zhg. 100 24.40 N 117.46 E
Changtai, Zhg. 104 41.34 N 122.00 E
Changtancun 104 41.33 N 123.02 E
Ch'angte → Changde 102 28.55 N 111.38 E
Changteh → Anyang 98 36.06 N 114.21 E
Changting 89 44.32 N 128.47 E
Changtumiao 102 43.30 N 114.34 E
Changuinola ≃ 236 9.28 N 82.27 W
Changwu, Zhg. 89 46.00 N 125.36 E
Changwu, Zhg. 102 35.09 N 107.42 E
Changxi ≃ 100 26.53 N 119.41 E
Changxindian 105 39.49 N 116.12 E
Changxing 106 31.01 N 119.54 E
Changxingdian, Zhg. 104 41.33 N 123.29 E
Changxingdian, Zhg. 104 41.27 N 121.44 E
Changxingmeikuang 106 31.06 N 119.43 E
Changxuanling 100 31.08 N 114.20 E
Changyi 98 36.51 N 119.23 E
Changyŏn 98 38.15 N 125.06 E
Changyuan 98 35.13 N 114.39 E
Changyukou 105 40.46 N 115.08 E
Changzhi 102 36.11 N 113.08 E
Changzhou (Changchow) 106 31.47 N 119.57 E
Chanhanga 152 16.04 S 14.07 E
Chanh-hung 269c 10.44 N 106.41 E
Chani 88 57.05 N 120.58 E
Chanino 76 54.13 N 36.37 E
Chanka, Ozero (Xingkathu) ⊜ 89 45.00 N 132.24 E
Chankiang → Zhanjiang 102 21.16 N 110.28 E
Chankou 102 35.52 N 104.27 E
Chanlar 84 40.34 N 46.20 E
Channagiri 122 14.02 N 75.56 E
Channahon 216 41.26 N 88.14 W
Channapatna 122 12.39 N 77.13 E
Channel Islands II, Eur. 28 49.20 N 2.20 W
Channel Islands II, Calif., U.S. 204 34.00 N 120.00 W
Channel Islands National Monument ♠ 228 33.28 N 119.02 W
Channel Lake 216 42.29 N 88.08 W
Channel North Basin C 174h 2.49 S 171.43 W
Channel-Port-aux-Basques 186 47.34 N 59.09 W
Channelview 222 29.46 N 95.07 W
Channing, Mich., U.S. 190 46.09 N 88.05 W
Channing, Tex., U.S. 196 35.41 N 102.20 W
Chanshan 98 36.26 N 120.52 E
Chantada 34 42.37 N 7.46 W
Chantajskoje, Ozero ⊜ 74 68.20 N 91.00 E
Chantajskoje Vodochranilišče ⊜[1] 72 68.00 N 88.00 E
Chantang 100 33.41 N 117.37 E
Chantau 86 44.13 N 73.51 E
Chanteloup 261 48.51 N 2.44 E
Chanteloup-les-Vignes 261 48.59 N 2.02 E
Chantengo, Laguna C 234 16.37 N 99.07 W
Chanthaburi 110 12.36 N 102.09 E
Chantilly 50 49.12 N 2.28 E
Chantonnay 32 46.41 N 1.03 W
Chantraine 58 48.10 N 6.26 E
Chantrans 58 47.03 N 6.09 E
Chantrey Inlet C 176 67.48 N 96.20 W
Chanty-Mansijsk 74 61.00 N 69.06 E
Chanuj ≃ 88 49.22 N 102.22 E
Chanumla 110 8.19 N 93.05 E
Chanute 198 37.41 N 95.27 W
Chanute Air Force Base ■ 216 40.18 N 88.09 W
Chanuwāla 123 32.44 N 73.08 E
Chanž'onkovo 83 48.06 N 38.06 E
Chao, Isla I 248 8.45 S 78.47 W
Chaoan 100 23.41 N 116.38 E
Chaobaihe ≃ 105 39.48 N 117.08 E
Chaobeiyingzi 104 42.06 N 122.18 E
Chaocheng 98 36.05 N 115.35 E
Ch'aochou, T'aiwan 100 22.33 N 120.32 E
Ch'aochou → Chaoan, Zhg. 100 23.41 N 116.38 E
Chaogezhen 98 35.38 N 114.11 E
Chaohe ≃ 105 38.52 N 115.46 E
Chaohu ⊜ 100 31.31 N 117.33 E
Chaomidian 105 39.04 N 117.01 E
Chao Phraya ≃ 110 13.32 N 100.36 E
Chaoshui 89 49.44 N 127.21 E
Chaoshuiji 98 37.42 N 120.55 E
Chaource 50 48.04 N 4.08 E
Chapa 110 22.21 N 103.50 E
Chapada dos Guimarães 248 15.26 S 55.45 W
Chapadinha 250 3.44 S 43.21 W
Chapala 234 20.18 N 103.12 W
Chapala, Lago de ⊜ 234 20.15 N 103.00 W
Chaparé ≃ 248 15.58 S 64.42 W
Chapareillan 62 45.28 N 5.58 E
Chāparmukh 120 26.12 N 92.32 E
Chaparra 240p 21.10 N 76.29 W
Chaparra, Bahía de C 240p 21.13 N 76.31 W
Chaparral 246 3.43 N 75.28 W
Chapčeranga 88 49.42 N 112.24 E
Chapeauroux 62 44.50 N 3.44 E
Chapecó 252 27.06 S 52.36 W
Chapel-en-le-Frith 262 53.20 N 1.54 W
Chapelfell Top ∧ 44 54.41 N 2.13 W
Chapel Hill, N.C., U.S. 192 35.55 N 79.04 W
Chapel Hill, Tenn., U.S. 194 35.38 N 86.41 W
Chapel Hill Channel U 276 40.32 N 74.02 W
Chapelle Creek ≃ 198 44.16 N 99.55 W
Chapel Oaks 284c 38.54 N 76.55 W
Chapel Point ≻ 42 50.16 N 4.46 W
Chapelton 241q 18.05 N 77.16 W
Chapeltown 262 53.38 N 2.24 W
Chapet 261 48.58 N 1.56 E
Chapicuy 252 31.39 S 57.54 W
Chapimarca 248 13.58 S 73.04 W
Chapin 219 39.46 N 90.24 W
Chapin, Lake ⊜ 216 41.56 N 86.21 W
Chaplain, Lake ⊜[1] 224 47.57 N 121.51 W
Chapleau 190 47.50 N 83.24 W
Chapleau ≃ 190 48.29 N 82.57 W
Chapleau, Lac ⊜ 206 46.14 N 74.57 W
Chaplin, Sask., Can. 184 50.28 N 106.40 W
Chaplin, Conn., U.S. 207 41.48 N 72.08 W
Chaplin ≃ 194 37.50 N 85.11 W
Chaplin Lake ⊜ 184 50.18 N 106.35 W
Chapman, Kans., U.S. 198 38.58 N 97.01 W
Chapman, Nebr., U.S. 198 41.02 N 98.09 W
Chapman, Pa., U.S. 208 40.46 N 75.24 W
Chapman ≃ 156 22.19 S 20.00 E
Chapman, Cape ≻ 176 69.12 N 88.59 W
Chapman, Mount ∧ 182 51.50 N 118.20 W
Chapman College ⊍[2] 280 33.47 N 117.51 W
Chapman Creek ≃ 198 38.58 N 97.00 W
Chapman Lake ⊜ 184 56.58 N 98.12 W
Chapmanville 188 37.58 N 82.01 W
Chapman Woods 280 34.08 N 118.05 W
Chapo 196 29.17 N 104.20 W
Chaponval 261 49.04 N 2.09 E
Chappaqua 210 41.10 N 73.46 W
Chappel Hill 222 30.09 N 96.16 W
Chappell 198 41.06 N 102.28 W
Chāpra, Bhārat 124 25.46 N 84.45 E
Chāpra, Bhārat 126 23.32 N 88.33 E
Chapry 83 47.14 N 39.31 E
Chaptico Bay C 208 38.21 N 76.49 W
Chapultepec, Méx. 204 32.22 N 115.05 W
Chapultepec, Méx. 204 31.50 N 116.38 W
Chapultepec ∧ 234 23.27 N 103.04 W
Chapultepec, Bosque de ♠ 286a 19.25 N 99.12 W
Chapultepec, Castillo de ⊥ 286a 19.25 N 99.11 W
Chá Pungana 152 13.44 S 18.39 E
Chaqui 248 19.36 S 65.32 W
Chaquiago 252 27.32 S 66.21 W
Char ≃ 42 50.44 N 2.53 W
Chara ≃ 89 49.48 N 130.45 E
Charabali 80 47.24 N 47.16 E
Charadai 252 27.38 S 59.54 W
Charagua 248 19.48 S 63.13 W
Charagun 88 51.36 N 111.05 E
Char-Ajrag 102 45.48 N 109.19 E
Charal 88 51.58 N 96.39 E
Charalá 246 6.17 N 73.10 W
Charām 128 30.45 N 50.44 E
Charaña 248 17.36 S 69.28 W
Charan Kanoa 174n 15.08 N 145.43 E
Charanor 88 50.05 N 116.40 E
Charapán 234 19.41 N 102.06 W
Charapucu, Ilha I 250 0.18 S 50.48 W
Charata 252 27.13 S 61.12 W
Charauz 88 52.16 N 106.17 E
Charavines-les-Bains 62 45.26 N 5.31 E
Charazani → Amarete 248 15.14 S 68.58 W
Charazargaj 88 52.57 N 104.41 E
Charbala 74 64.07 N 120.19 E
Char Bansi 126 22.59 N 90.43 E
Charbatovo 88 53.46 N 106.00 E
Charbon 170 32.54 S 149.58 E
Charbonnières-les-Bains 62 45.47 N 4.44 E
Charcana 248 15.15 S 73.04 W
Charcas 234 23.08 N 101.07 W
Charco Azul, Bahía de C 236 8.15 N 82.45 W
Charco Hondo 240m 18.25 N 66.43 W
Charcos de Figueroa 232 27.45 N 102.11 W
Charcos de Risa 232 26.15 N 103.10 W
Charcot Island I 9 69.45 S 75.15 W
Charcyzsk 83 48.02 N 38.09 E
Chard 42 50.53 N 2.58 W
Chardon 214 41.35 N 81.12 W
Chardzhou → Čardžou 128 39.06 N 63.34 E
Charef, Oued ∨ 148 34.07 N 2.05 W
Charente □[5] 32 45.40 N 0.10 E
Charente ≃ 32 45.57 N 1.05 W
Charente-Maritime □[5] 32 45.30 N 0.45 W
Charenton-du-Cher 32 46.44 N 2.38 E
Charenton-le-Pont 261 48.49 N 2.25 E
Charentonne ≃ 50 49.07 N 0.44 E
Charest ≃ 206 46.36 N 72.14 W
Chārghāt 126 24.17 N 88.45 E
Char Hāim 126 23.04 N 90.38 E
Chari ≃ 146 12.58 N 14.31 E
Chariāl Canal ⩸ 272b 22.28 N 88.11 E
Chari-Baguirmi □[5] 146 11.00 N 17.00 E
Charik 88 54.15 N 101.39 E
Chārīkār 120 35.01 N 69.11 E
Charing 42 51.13 N 0.48 E
Charing Cross 214 42.20 N 82.06 W
Charino, S.S.S.R. 76 59.57 N 43.44 E
Charino, S.S.S.R. 82 54.33 N 37.52 E
Charistvala 84 42.26 N 43.02 E
Chariton 190 41.01 N 93.19 W
Chariton ≃ 194 39.19 N 92.57 W
Chariton, Mussel Fork ≃ 194 39.24 N 92.55 W
Chariton, South Fork ≃ 194 40.52 N 93.00 W
Charitonovo, S.S.S.R. 24 61.27 N 47.28 E
Charitonovo, S.S.S.R. 82 56.52 N 36.44 E
Charity 246 7.24 N 58.36 W
Char'kin 80 48.46 N 51.49 E
Char'kov (Kharkov) 78 50.00 N 36.15 E
Char'kov □[4] 83 49.42 N 37.10 E
Charkow → Char'kov 78 50.00 N 36.15 E
Char Lākhpur 126 24.04 N 90.40 E
Char Lālmohan 126 22.13 N 90.42 E
Charland, Lac ⊜ 206 46.52 N 74.11 W
Charlbury 42 51.53 N 1.29 W
Charl Cilliers 158 26.39 S 29.12 E
Charlemagne 206 45.43 N 73.29 W
Charlemont 207 42.38 N 72.52 W
Charleroi, Bel. 50 50.25 N 4.26 E
Charleroi, Pa., U.S. 214 40.09 N 79.57 W
Charleroi à Bruxelles, Canal de ⩸ 50 50.51 N 4.19 E
Charles □[6] 208 38.32 N 76.59 W
Charles ≃ 207 42.22 N 71.03 W
Charles, Cape ≻ 208 37.08 N 75.58 W
Charles, Lake ⊜ 278 42.15 N 87.58 W
Charles, Peak ∧ 162 32.52 S 121.11 E
Charlesbourg 206 46.51 N 71.16 W
Charles Branch ≃ 284c 38.47 N 76.48 W
Charles City, Iowa, U.S. 190 43.04 N 92.40 W
Charles City, Va., U.S. 208 37.20 N 77.04 W
Charles City □[6] 208 37.20 N 77.02 W
Charles De Gaulle, Aéroport ⊠ 50 49.01 N 2.33 E
Charles Island I 176 62.40 N 74.15 W
Charles Lee Tilden Regional Park ♠ 282 37.54 N 122.15 W
Charles Mill Lake ⊜[1] 214 40.45 N 82.22 W
Charles Mound ∧[2] 190 42.30 N 90.14 W
Charles Point ≻ 164 12.23 S 130.36 E
Charles Sound U 172 45.02 S 167.04 E
Charleston, Austl. 168b 34.55 S 138.54 E
Charleston, N.Z. 172 41.54 S 171.26 E
Charleston, Ark., U.S. 194 35.18 N 94.02 W
Charleston, Ill., U.S. 194 39.30 N 88.10 W
Charleston, Miss., U.S. 194 34.00 N 90.04 W
Charleston, Mo., U.S. 194 36.55 N 89.21 W
Charleston, S.C., U.S. 192 32.48 N 79.57 W
Charleston, W. Va., U.S. 188 38.21 N 81.38 W
Charleston Lake ⊜ 212 44.32 N 76.00 W
Charleston Peak ∧ 204 36.16 N 115.42 W
Charlestown, Austl. 170 32.58 S 151.42 E
Charlestown, Eire 48 53.57 N 8.49 W
Charlestown, St. K.-N. 238 17.08 N 62.37 W
Charlestown, S. Afr. 158 27.30 S 29.55 E
Charlestown, Ind., U.S. 218 38.27 N 85.40 W
Charlestown, N.H., U.S. 188 43.14 N 72.26 W
Charlestown, Pa., U.S. 285 40.06 N 75.33 W
Charlestown, R.I., U.S. 207 41.23 N 71.45 W
Charles Town, W. Va., U.S. 188 39.17 N 77.52 W
Charlestown ◆[8] 283 42.23 N 71.04 W
Charlesworth 262 53.26 N 1.59 W
Charleville 166 26.24 S 146.15 E
Charleville-Mézières 56 49.46 N 4.43 E
Charlevoix 190 45.19 N 85.16 W
Charlevoix, Lake ⊜ 190 45.15 N 85.08 W
Charley ≃ 180 65.20 N 142.49 W
Charlie Bluff 216 42.50 N 88.58 W
Charlie Creek ≃ 220 27.21 N 81.49 W
Charlie Lake 182 56.16 N 120.57 W
Charlieu 32 46.10 N 4.10 E
Charlotte, Mich., U.S. 216 42.36 N 84.50 W
Charlotte, N.C., U.S. 192 35.14 N 80.50 W
Charlotte, Tenn., U.S. 194 36.11 N 87.24 W
Charlotte, Tex., U.S. 196 28.52 N 98.43 W
Charlotte □[6] 220 26.54 N 81.58 W
Charlotte Amalie 240m 18.21 N 64.56 W
Charlotte Court House 192 37.03 N 78.39 W
Charlotte Creek ≃ 210 42.27 N 75.01 W
Charlotte Harbor 220 26.58 N 82.04 W
Charlotte Harbor C 220 26.45 N 82.12 W
Charlotte Lake ⊜ 182 52.11 N 125.20 W
Charlottenberg 26 59.53 N 12.17 E
Charlottenburg 250 5.51 N 54.46 W
Charlottenburg ◆[8] 264a 52.31 N 13.16 E
Charlottenburg, Schloss ⊥ 264a 52.31 N 13.14 E
Charlottesburg Reservoir ⊜[1] 276 41.02 N 74.26 W
Charlottesville, Ind., U.S. 218 39.47 N 85.37 W
Charlottesville, Va., U.S. 192 38.02 N 78.29 W
Charlottetown, P.E.I., Can. 186 46.14 N 63.08 W
Charlotte Town (Gouyave), Gren. 241k 12.10 N 61.44 W
Charlotteville 210 42.33 N 74.40 W
Charlovka 24 68.47 N 37.15 E
Charlton, Austl. 166 36.16 S 143.21 E
Charlton, Mass., U.S. 207 42.08 N 71.58 W
Charlton ◆[8] 260 51.29 N 0.02 E
Charlton City 207 42.09 N 71.58 W
Charlton Island I 176 52.00 N 79.30 W
Charlton Kings 42 51.53 N 2.03 W
Charlu 24 61.48 N 30.52 E
Charly-sur Marne 50 48.58 N 3.17 E
Charm 214 40.30 N 81.47 W
Charmentray 261 48.57 N 2.47 E
Charmes 58 48.22 N 6.17 E
Charmes-sur-Rhône 62 44.52 N 4.50 E
Charmey 58 46.38 N 7.10 E
Charminster 42 50.43 N 2.28 W
Charmois-l'Orgueilleux 58 48.06 N 6.16 E
Charmont-en-Beauce 50 48.14 N 2.06 E
Charmouth 42 50.45 N 2.55 W
Charnay-lès-Mâcon 58 46.18 N 4.47 E
Charneca 266c 38.44 N 9.27 W
Charnock Richard 262 53.38 N 2.41 W
Char Nuur ⊜, Mong. 88 48.20 N 96.05 E
Char Nuur ⊜, Mong. 88 48.06 N 93.12 E
Charnwood Forest ◆[3] 42 52.43 N 1.15 W
Charny, Qué., Can. 206 46.43 N 71.16 W
Charny, Fr. 50 47.53 N 3.06 E
Charny, Fr. 261 48.58 N 2.46 E
Charny-sur-Meuse 56 49.12 N 5.22 E
Charo 234 19.45 N 101.03 W
Charolles 32 46.26 N 4.17 E
Charouine 148 29.01 N 0.16 W
Charovsk 76 59.59 N 40.11 E
Charpi ≃ 89 49.40 N 136.10 E
Charquemont 58 47.13 N 6.49 E
Charrette Creek ≃ 219 38.37 N 91.03 W
Charron Lake ⊜ 184 52.45 N 95.15 W
Charroux 32 46.09 N 0.24 E
Chars 50 49.10 N 1.56 E
Chārsadda 123 34.09 N 71.44 E
Charter Oak, Calif., U.S. 280 34.06 N 117.52 W
Charter Oak, Iowa, U.S. 198 42.04 N 95.35 W
Charters Towers 166 20.05 S 146.16 E
Charterwood 279b 40.33 N 80.00 W
Chartiers Creek ≃ 214 40.28 N 80.03 W
Chartiers Run ≃, Pa., U.S. 279b 40.36 N 79.43 W
Chartiers Run ≃, Pa., U.S. 279b 40.15 N 80.12 W
Chartley 207 41.57 N 71.14 W
Chartres 50 48.27 N 1.30 E
Chartrettes 50 48.29 N 2.42 E
Chartridge 260 51.44 N 0.39 W
Chart Sutton 260 51.13 N 0.35 E
Chartwell ⊥ 260 51.14 N 0.05 E
Char Us Nuur ⊜ 90 48.00 N 92.10 E
Charutajuvom 24 66.49 N 59.30 E
Chās 126 23.38 N 86.10 E
Chasavjurt 84 43.15 N 46.37 E
Chascomús 258 35.34 S 58.01 W
Chašdala 85 39.42 N 67.07 E
Chase, B.C., Can. 182 50.49 N 119.41 W
Chase, Alaska, U.S. 180 62.27 N 150.07 W
Chase, Kans., U.S. 198 38.21 N 98.21 W
Chase, Md., U.S. 208 39.22 N 76.22 W
Chase, Mount ∧ 188 46.07 N 68.29 W
Chase Brook ≃ 283 42.48 N 71.27 W
Chase City 192 36.48 N 78.28 W
Chasefu Mission 154 11.55 S 33.08 E
Chase Lake 212 43.46 N 75.19 W
Chase River 224 49.08 N 123.55 W
Chasetown 42 52.41 N 1.56 W
Chashui ≃ 100 31.44 N 113.11 E
Chasicó 254 40.18 S 68.58 W
Chasidaba 104 42.19 N 121.19 E
Chaska 190 44.47 N 93.35 W
Chaslands Mistake ≻ 172 46.38 S 169.22 E
Chasŏng 98 41.27 N 126.37 E
Chasŏngganggu 98 41.34 N 126.36 E
Chassahowitzka 220 28.43 N 82.34 W

Symbols in the index entries represent the broad categories identified in the key at the right. Symbols with superior numbers (∧∧[2]) identify subcategories (see complete key on page *I* · 30).

Kartensymbole in dem Registerverzeichnis stellen die rechts in Schlüssel erklärten Kategorien dar. Symbole mit hochgestellten Ziffern (∧∧[2]) bezeichnen Unterabteilungen einer Kategorie (vgl. vollständiger Schlüssel auf Seite *I* · 30).

Los símbolos incluídos en el texto del índice representan las grandes categorias identificadas con la clave a la derecha. Los símbolos con numeros en su parte superior (∧∧[2]) identifican las subcategorías (véase la clave completa en la página *I* · 30).

Les symboles de l'index représentent les catégories indiquées dans la légende à droite. Les symboles suivis d'un indice (∧∧[2]) représentent des sous-catégories (voir légende complète à la page *I* · 30).

Os símbolos incluídos no texto do índice representam as grandes categorias identificadas com a chave à direita. Os símbolos com números em sua parte superior (∧∧[2]) identificam as subcategorias (veja-se a chave completa à página *I* · 30).

	English	Deutsch	Español	Français	Português
∧	Mountain	Berg	Montaña	Montagne	Montanha
∧∧	Mountains	Berge	Montañas	Montagnes	Montanhas
)(	Pass	Pass	Paso	Col	Passo
∨	Valley, Canyon	Tal, Cañon	Valle, Cañón	Vallée, Canyon	Vale, Canhão
⊻	Plain	Ebene	Llano	Plaine	Planície
≻	Cape	Kap	Cabo	Cap	Cabo
I	Island	Insel	Isla	Île	Ilha
II	Islands	Inseln	Islas	Îles	Ilhas
◆	Other Topographic Features	Andere Topographische Objekte	Otros Elementos Topográficos	Autres données topographiques	Outros Elementos Topográficos

ESPAÑOL Nombre / FRANÇAIS Nom / PORTUGUÊS Nome	Página / Page	Lat.° ′	Long.° ′ W=Oeste / W=Ouest
Chassahowitzka Bay C	220	28.41 N	82.40 W
Chassahowitzka Swamp ≋	220	28.38 N	82.37 W
Chasseron, Mont ▲	58	46.51 N	6.33 E
Chasse-sur-Rhône	62	45.34 N	4.49 E
Chassezac ≃	62	44.26 N	4.19 E
Chašuri	84	42.00 N	43.36 E
Chasurta	88	52.17 N	108.52 E
Chasuta	248	6.35 S	76.11 W
Chât	128	37.59 N	55.16 E
Chatanbulag	102	43.11 N	109.10 E
Chatanga	74	71.58 N	102.30 E
Chatanga ≃	74	72.55 N	106.00 E
Chatangskij Zaliv C	74	73.30 N	109.00 E
Chatanika	180	65.07 N	147.31 W
Chatanika ≃	180	65.04 N	149.18 W
Château-Arnoux	62	44.06 N	6.00 E
Chateaubelair	241h	13.17 N	61.15 W
Chateaubelair Bay C	241h	13.17 N	61.15 W
Châteaubriant	32	47.43 N	1.23 W
Château-Chinon	32	47.04 N	3.56 E
Château d'Oex	58	46.28 N	7.08 E
Château-du-Loir	50	47.42 N	0.25 E
Châteaudun	50	48.05 N	1.20 E
Châteaufort	261	48.44 N	2.06 E
Châteaugay	206	44.56 N	74.05 W
Château-Gontier	32	47.50 N	0.42 W
Châteauguay	206	45.23 N	73.45 W
Châteauguay □[6]	206	45.15 N	73.45 W
Châteauguay (Chateauguay) ≃	206	45.24 N	73.45 W
Châteauguay-Centre	206	45.21 N	73.45 W
Châteauguay Heights	275a	45.23 N	73.44 W
Château-Landon	50	48.09 N	2.42 E
Château-la-Vallière	50	47.33 N	0.19 E
Châteaulin	32	48.12 N	4.05 W
Châteaumeillant	32	46.34 N	2.12 E
Châteauneuf	62	43.23 N	5.10 E
Châteauneuf-de-Randon	62	44.39 N	3.40 E
Châteauneuf-du-Pape	62	44.03 N	4.50 E
Châteauneuf-du-Rhône	62	44.29 N	4.43 E
Châteauneuf-en-Thymerais	50	48.35 N	1.15 E
Châteauneuf-sur-Charente	32	45.36 N	0.03 W
Châteauneuf-sur-Loire	50	47.52 N	2.14 E
Châteauneuf-sur-Sarthe	32	47.41 N	0.30 W
Châteauneuf-Val-de-Bargis	50	47.17 N	3.14 E
Château-Porcien	50	49.32 N	4.15 E
Château-Queyras	62	44.45 N	6.47 E
Châteauredon	62	44.01 N	6.13 E
Châteaurenard	50	47.56 N	2.56 E
Châteaurenard-Provence	62	43.53 N	4.51 E
Château-Renault	50	47.35 N	0.55 E
Château-Richer	186	46.58 N	71.01 W
Châteauroux	32	46.49 N	1.42 E
Château-Salins	56	48.49 N	6.30 E
Château-Thierry	50	49.03 N	3.24 E
Châteauvillain	58	48.02 N	4.55 E
Châtel	58	46.17 N	6.50 E
Châtel-Censoir	50	47.31 N	3.38 E
Châtelet	50	50.24 N	4.31 E
Châtelineau	56	50.25 N	4.31 E
Châtellerault	32	46.49 N	0.33 E
Châtel-Saint-Denis	58	46.32 N	6.54 E
Châtel-sur-Moselle	58	48.18 N	6.24 E
Châtelus-Malvaleix	32	46.18 N	2.01 E
Châtenay-en-France	261	49.04 N	2.27 E
Châtenay-Malabry	261	48.46 N	2.17 E
Châtenois, Fr.	58	48.16 N	7.24 E
Châtenois, Fr.	58	48.18 N	5.50 E
Châtenois-les-Forges	58	47.34 N	6.51 E
Chatfield, Minn., U.S.	190	43.51 N	92.11 W
Chatfield, Ohio, U.S.	214	40.57 N	82.56 W
Chatgal	88	50.26 N	100.07 E
Chatham, N.B., Can.	186	47.02 N	65.28 W
Chatham, Ont., Can.	214	42.24 N	82.11 W
Chatham, Eng., U.K.	42, 260	51.23 N	0.32 E
Chatham, Ill., U.S.	219	39.40 N	89.42 W
Chatham, La., U.S.	194	32.19 N	92.27 W
Chatham, Mass., U.S.	207	41.41 N	69.58 W
Chatham, N.J., U.S.	210	40.44 N	74.23 W
Chatham, N.Y., U.S.	210	42.22 N	73.36 W
Chatham, Ohio, U.S.	214	41.06 N	82.01 W
Chatham, Pa., U.S.	208	39.51 N	75.49 W
Chatham, Va., U.S.	192	36.50 N	79.24 W
Chatham ✦[8]	278	41.45 N	87.37 W
Chatham ≃	220	25.42 N	81.17 W
Chatham, Isla I	254	50.40 S	74.20 W
Chatham Head	186	47.00 N	65.33 W
Chatham Island I	14	43.55 S	176.30 W
Chatham Islands II	14	44.00 S	176.30 W
Chatham Rise ✦[3]	14	43.30 S	178.00 W
Chatham Sound ⋓	182	54.32 N	130.35 W
Chatham Strait ⋓	180	57.30 N	134.45 W
Chatian	100	27.54 N	118.58 E
Châtillon, Fr.	58	45.53 N	4.37 E
Châtillon, Fr.	261	48.48 N	2.17 E
Châtillon, It.	62	45.45 N	7.37 E
Châtillon-Coligny	50	47.50 N	2.51 E
Châtillon-en-Bazois	32	47.03 N	3.49 E
Châtillon-en-Diois	62	44.41 N	5.28 E
Châtillon-la-Borde	261	48.33 N	2.49 E
Châtillon-sur-Chalaronne	58	46.07 N	4.58 E
Châtillon-sur-Indre	32	46.59 N	1.11 E
Châtillon-sur-Loire	50	47.35 N	2.45 E
Châtillon-sur-Marne	50	49.06 N	3.45 E
Châtillon-sur-Seine	58	47.51 N	4.33 E
Chatmohar	126	24.13 N	89.15 E
Chat Moss ✦[3]	262	53.27 N	2.27 W
Chato, Cerro ▲	254	42.29 S	72.01 W
Chatom	194	31.28 N	88.16 W
Chatonville	261	48.33 N	1.52 E
Chatou	261	48.54 N	2.09 E
Chatra, Bhārat	124	24.13 N	84.52 E
Chatra, Bhārat	272b	22.46 N	88.20 E
Chatrapur	122	19.21 N	84.59 E
Châtres	261	48.43 N	2.49 E
Chats, Lac des ⊜	212	45.28 N	76.23 W
Chatsquot Mountain ▲	182	53.08 N	127.30 W
Chātsu	120	26.36 N	75.57 E
Chatswood	274a	33.48 S	151.11 E
Chatsworth, Austl.	166	21.58 S	140.19 E
Chatsworth, Ont., Can.	212	44.27 N	80.54 W
Chatsworth, Ga., U.S.	192	34.46 N	84.46 W
Chatsworth, Ill., U.S.	216	40.45 N	88.18 W
Chatsworth, N.J., U.S.	208	39.46 N	74.33 W
Chatsworth, Zimb.	154	19.38 S	31.13 E
Chatsworth ✦[8]	280	34.15 N	118.36 W
Chatsworth Reservoir ⊜[1]	228	34.14 N	118.37 W
Chattahoochee	192	30.42 N	84.51 W
Chattahoochee ≃	192	30.52 N	84.57 W
Chattanooga, Ohio, U.S.	216	40.38 N	84.47 W
Chattanooga, Tenn., U.S.	194	35.03 N	85.19 W
Chattenden	260	51.25 N	0.32 E
Chatteris	42	52.27 N	0.03 E
Chattillon-de-Michaille	58	46.08 N	5.47 E
Chatton	44	55.33 N	1.55 W
Chatun'	82	55.00 N	37.50 E
Chaturat	110	15.34 N	101.51 E
Chatwood	208	39.58 N	75.35 W
Chatyrka	74	62.03 N	175.15 E
Chaubaria	126	22.59 N	88.40 E
Chaubourg, Mount ▲[2]	241f	14.02 N	60.57 W
Chauconin	261	48.58 N	2.51 E
Chaudes-Aigues	32	44.51 N	3.00 E
Chaudfontaine	56	50.35 N	5.38 E
Chaudière ≃	186	46.45 N	71.17 W
Chauekuktuli, Lake ⊜	180	60.03 N	158.45 W
Chauffayer	62	44.45 N	6.01 E
Chaugācha	126	23.16 N	89.01 E
Chauk	110	20.54 N	94.50 E
Chaukhandi	272a	28.37 N	77.24 E
Chaullay	248	12.57 S	72.39 W
Chaulnes	50	49.49 N	2.48 E
Chaumergy	58	46.51 N	5.29 E
Chaumes-en-Brie	261	48.40 N	2.51 E
Chaumont, Fr.	58	48.07 N	5.08 E
Chaumont, N.Y., U.S.	212	44.04 N	76.08 W
Chaumont ≃	212	44.04 N	76.08 W
Chaumont, Rû de ≃	261	48.31 N	2.40 E
Chaumont Bay C	212	44.02 N	76.13 W
Chaumont-en-Vexin	50	49.16 N	1.53 E
Chaumont-Porcien	50	49.39 N	4.15 E
Chaumont-sur-Aire	56	48.56 N	5.15 E
Chaumont-sur-Loire	50	47.29 N	1.11 E
Chaumont-sur-Tharonne	50	47.37 N	1.54 E
Chaumuhāni	124	22.56 N	91.07 E
Chauncey	188	39.24 N	82.08 W
Chaungwabyin	110	13.41 N	98.22 E
Chaungzon	110	16.22 N	97.32 E
Chauny	50	49.37 N	3.13 E
Chaupāran	124	24.23 N	85.15 E
Chau-phu	110	10.42 N	105.07 E
Chaussin	58	46.58 N	5.25 E
Chausu-yama ▲	94	35.14 N	137.39 E
Chausuyama-kofun ⊥	94	36.25 N	139.50 E
Chautāra	124	27.46 N	85.42 E
Chautauqua	214	42.14 N	79.28 W
Chautauqua □[6]	214	42.15 N	79.30 W
Chautauqua Creek ≃	214	42.20 N	79.36 W
Chautauqua Lake ⊜	214	42.12 N	79.27 W
Chauvigny	32	46.34 N	0.39 E
Chauvin	184	52.42 N	110.07 W
Chauvirey-le-Châtel	58	47.47 N	5.45 E
Chauvry	261	49.03 N	2.16 E
Chaval	250	3.02 S	41.15 W
Chavanges	58	48.31 N	4.34 E
Chavannes, Lac ⊜	190	46.51 N	77.10 W
Chavarria, Arg.	252	28.57 S	58.35 W
Chavarría, Perú	286d	12.01 S	77.05 W
Chavast	85	40.13 N	68.50 E
Chavenay	261	48.51 N	1.59 E
Chavenay-Villepreux, Aérodrome de ⊠	261	48.51 N	1.58 E
Chavertovo	82	54.17 N	39.12 E
Chaves, Bra.	250	0.10 S	49.55 W
Chaves, Port.	34	41.44 N	7.28 W
Chaville	261	48.48 N	2.10 E
Chaviña	248	14.59 S	73.50 W
Chavinda	234	20.01 N	102.27 W
Cháviva	246	4.22 N	72.20 W
Chavki	82	54.20 N	38.13 E
Chavornay	58	46.43 N	6.34 E
Chavuma	152	13.05 S	22.40 E
Chawa'nanake	120	31.36 N	89.41 E
Chawang	110	8.25 N	99.30 E
Chawinda	123	32.21 N	74.42 E
Chaya, Nihon	96	34.34 N	133.49 E
Chaya, Zhg.	102	30.32 N	98.00 E
Chayanta	248	18.27 S	66.30 W
Chayuan	100	29.20 N	121.34 E
Chayuanpu	100	27.40 N	112.57 E
Chayue	106	30.49 N	119.21 E
Chazay-d'Azergues	62	45.53 N	4.37 E
Chazelles-sur-Lyon	62	45.38 N	4.23 E
Chazumba	234	18.12 N	97.40 W
Chazy	188	44.53 N	73.26 W
Cheadle, Eng., U.K.	42	52.59 N	1.59 W
Cheadle, Eng., U.K.	262	53.24 N	2.13 W
Cheadle Hulme	262	53.22 N	2.12 W
Cheaha Mountain ▲	194	33.30 N	85.47 W
Cheakamus Indian Reserve ✦[4]	182	49.48 N	123.11 W
Cheam ✦[8]	260	51.21 N	0.13 W
Cheam View	224	49.15 N	121.41 W
Cheapside	222	29.17 N	97.24 W
Cheat, Shavers Fork ≃	188	39.06 N	79.33 W
Cheb	54	50.01 N	12.25 E
Chebacco Lake ⊜	283	42.37 N	70.48 W
Chebanse	216	41.00 N	87.54 W
Chebba	148	35.14 N	10.02 E
Chebeigou	89	43.28 N	127.04 E
Chebogue Point >	186	43.45 N	66.07 W
Cheboksary → Čeboksary	80	56.09 N	47.15 E
Cheboygan	190	45.39 N	84.29 W
Chech, Erg ✦[2]	148	25.00 N	2.15 W
Chechaouene	148	35.10 N	5.16 W
Ch'ech'eng	100	22.05 N	120.42 E
Chech'on	98	37.08 N	128.12 E
Checiny	30	50.48 N	20.28 E
Checleset Bay C	182	50.03 N	127.40 W
Checoslovaquia → Czechoslovakia □[1]	30	49.30 N	17.00 E
Checotah	196	35.28 N	95.31 W
Chedabucto Bay C	186	45.23 N	61.10 W
Chedaoyu	105	40.22 N	117.57 E
Cheddar	42	51.17 N	2.46 W
Cheduba Island I	110	18.48 N	93.38 E
Cheduba Strait ⋓	110	18.56 N	93.45 E
Chedun	100	24.09 N	117.19 E
Chée ≃	56	48.45 N	4.39 E
Cheecham Hills ▲[2]	184	56.20 N	111.10 W
Cheektowaga	210	42.55 N	78.46 W
Cheepie	166	26.39 S	145.01 E
Cheesequake	276	40.25 N	74.17 W
Cheesequake Creek ≃	276	40.28 N	74.16 W
Cheesequake State Park ♠	276	40.26 N	74.16 W
Cheetham Hill ✦[8]	262	53.31 N	2.15 W
Chefang, Zhg.	104	41.35 N	121.26 E
Chefang, Zhg.	106	31.15 N	120.45 E
Chef-Boutonne	32	46.07 N	0.04 W
Chefoo → Yantai	98	37.33 N	121.20 E
Chefornak	180	60.13 N	164.12 W
Chefumage ≃	152	12.15 S	22.19 E
Chefuzwe	156	17.38 S	24.30 E
Chegar Perah	114	4.25 N	101.56 E
Chegga ⊤[4]	148	25.30 N	5.46 W
Chehalis	224	46.40 N	122.58 W
Chehalis ≃	224	46.57 N	123.50 W
Chehalis, South Fork ≃	224	46.40 N	123.15 W
Chehalis Indian Reservation ✦[4]	224	46.49 N	123.13 W
Chehe	102	25.00 N	107.38 E
Chehel Dokhtarān	128	35.06 N	62.19 E
Cheil, Ras el- >	144	7.45 N	49.48 E
Cheine	54	52.52 N	11.04 E
Cheiron, Cime du ▲	62	43.49 N	6.58 E
Cheiron, Montagne du ▲	62	43.48 N	6.58 E
Chejiatun	104	41.57 N	123.01 E
Chejiawopeng	104	42.29 N	123.07 E
Cheju	90	33.31 N	126.32 E
Cheju-do I	90	33.20 N	126.30 E
Chekiang → Zhejiang □[4]	100	29.00 N	120.00 E
Chek Jawa, Tanjong >	271c	1.24 N	104.00 E
Chela, Serra da ▲	152	16.00 S	13.10 E
Chelan	202	47.51 N	120.01 W
Chelan □[6]	224	47.56 N	120.52 W
Chelan, Lake ⊜	202	48.05 N	120.30 W
Chelas ✦[8]	266c	38.45 N	9.07 W
Cheleiros	266c	38.53 N	9.20 W
Cheleiros, Ribeira de ≃	266c	38.54 N	9.22 W
Chelford	262	53.16 N	2.16 W
Chelforó	252	39.04 S	66.32 W
Chelga	144	12.30 N	37.04 E
Chelghoum el Aïd	148	36.10 N	6.10 E
Chélia, Djebel ▲	148	35.19 N	6.42 E
Chéliff, Oued ≃	148	36.01 N	0.07 E
Chelīk-e Yās Khān	120	37.05 N	66.14 E
Chellaston	42	52.53 N	1.27 W
Chelles	50	48.53 N	2.36 E
Chelles-le-Pin, Aérodrome de ⊠	261	48.55 N	2.35 E
Chełm	30	51.10 N	23.28 E
Chelmer	260	51.48 N	0.40 E
Chelmer and Blackwater Navigation ≡	260	51.44 N	0.43 E
Chełmno	30	53.22 N	18.26 E
Chelmorton	262	53.13 N	1.50 W
Chelmsford, Ont., Can.	190	46.35 N	81.12 W
Chelmsford, Eng., U.K.	260	51.44 N	0.28 E
Chelmsford, Mass., U.S.	207	42.36 N	71.21 W
Chelmsford □[8]	260	51.44 N	0.30 E
Chełmża	30	53.12 N	18.37 E
Chelsea, Austl.	169	38.03 S	145.07 E
Chelsea, Iowa, U.S.	190	41.55 N	92.24 W
Chelsea, Mass., U.S.	207	42.24 N	71.02 W
Chelsea, Mich., U.S.	216	42.19 N	84.01 W
Chelsea, Okla., U.S.	196	36.32 N	95.26 W
Chelsea, Vt., U.S.	188	43.59 N	72.27 W
Chelsea Estates	208	39.41 N	75.36 W
Chelsea Park	224	47.28 N	122.21 W
Chelsfield ✦[8]	260	51.21 N	0.08 E
Cheltenham, Austl.	274a	33.46 S	151.05 E
Cheltenham, Austl.	274b	37.58 S	145.03 E
Cheltenham, Eng., U.K.	42	51.54 N	2.04 W
Cheltenham, Md., U.S.	208	38.44 N	76.50 W
Cheltenham, Pa., U.S.	208	40.04 N	75.08 W
Chelva	34	39.45 N	0.59 W
Chelvand	128	38.18 N	48.50 E
Chelyabinsk → Čel'abinsk	86	55.10 N	61.24 E
Chelyāma	126	23.37 N	86.33 E
Chelyan	188	38.12 N	81.30 W
Chemagal	154	0.41 S	35.07 E
Chemaïa	148	31.30 N	8.47 W
Chemainus	182	48.55 N	123.43 W
Chemainus ≃	224	48.53 N	123.41 W
Chemaogang	106	31.33 N	121.52 E
Chemax	232	20.39 N	87.56 W
Chemba	154	17.08 S	34.52 E
Chembe	154	11.58 S	28.45 E
Chembūr ✦[8]	272c	19.04 N	72.54 E
Chemehuevi Indian Reservation ✦[4]	204	34.30 N	114.23 W
Chemillé	32	47.13 N	0.44 W
Chemin	58	46.59 N	5.19 E
Cheminis, Colline ▲[2]	190	48.08 N	79.31 W
Chemnitz → Karl-Marx-Stadt	54	50.50 N	12.55 E
Chemnitz ≃	54	50.59 N	12.47 E
Chemor	114	4.43 N	101.07 E
Chemulpo → Inch'ŏn	98	37.28 N	126.38 E
Chemult	202	43.13 N	121.47 W
Chemung, Ill., U.S.	216	42.25 N	88.40 W
Chemung, N.Y., U.S.	210	42.01 N	76.37 W
Chemung □[6]	210	42.06 N	76.49 W
Chemung ≃	210	41.55 N	76.31 W
Chemung County Airport ⊠	210	42.10 N	76.53 W
Chemung Lake ⊜	212	44.25 N	78.22 W
Chena ≃	180	64.48 N	147.55 W
Chena, Cerro de ▲	286e	33.36 S	70.45 W
Chenāb ≃	123	29.23 N	71.02 E
Chenachane	148	26.00 N	4.15 W
Chenango □[6]	210	42.32 N	75.31 W
Chenango ≃	210	42.05 N	75.55 W
Chenango Bridge	210	42.10 N	75.52 W
Chenango Forks	210	42.14 N	75.51 W
Chenango Valley State Park ♠	210	42.14 N	75.50 W
Chenaut	258	34.15 S	59.13 W
Chenbaerhuqi (Bayankuren)	89	49.21 N	119.31 E
Chenbofang	98	37.27 N	115.18 E
Chencaishi	100	29.37 N	120.22 E
Chenchiang → Zhenjiang	106	32.13 N	119.26 E
Chencun	100	22.58 N	113.13 E
Chencuntang	102	23.48 N	110.49 E
Chendai	100	23.48 N	117.24 E
Chendanli ✦[8]	272c	19.07 N	72.54 E
Chenderiang	114	4.16 N	101.14 E
Chenderoh, Tasek ⊜	114	4.58 N	100.57 E
Chêne, Rivière du ≃, Qué., Can.	206	46.34 N	72.00 W
Chêne, Rivière du ≃, Qué., Can.	206	45.33 N	73.54 W
Chêne-Bourg	58	46.12 N	6.12 E
Chenele	152	12.54 S	23.54 E
Chenequa	216	43.07 N	88.23 W
Chenéville	206	45.53 N	75.03 W
Cheney, Kans., U.S.	198	37.38 N	97.47 W
Cheney, Wash., U.S.	202	47.29 N	117.34 W
Cheney Reservoir ⊜[1]	198	37.45 N	97.50 W
Cheneys Point	214	42.08 N	79.24 W
Cheneyville	194	31.01 N	92.17 W
Chenfang	100	28.01 N	117.32 E
Cheng'an	98	36.27 N	114.41 E
Chengannur	122	9.20 N	76.38 E
Chengbu	102	26.18 N	110.13 E
Chengchow → Zhengzhou	102	34.48 N	113.39 E
Chengde	105	40.58 N	117.53 E
Chengdu (Chengtu)	107	30.39 N	104.04 E
Chengele	120	28.47 N	96.16 E
Chenggang	100	26.32 N	115.26 E
Chenghai	100	23.30 N	116.46 E
Chenghuang	102	22.32 N	109.39 E
Chengjia	100	24.50 N	112.50 E
Chengjiachang	107	29.24 N	104.36 E
Chengjiahe	100	32.18 N	112.27 E
Chengjiang	102	24.40 N	102.56 E
Chengjiangzhen	107	29.52 N	106.23 E
Chengkou	102	31.54 N	108.41 E
Chenglingji	100	29.26 N	113.09 E
Chenglong	100	24.51 N	114.41 E
Chengmai	110	19.48 N	110.02 E
Chengpu	100	25.46 N	118.48 E
Chengqian	100	28.13 N	120.36 E
Chengqianwei	100	28.09 N	116.13 E
Chengshanjiao >	90	37.23 N	122.39 E
Chengteh → Chengde	105	40.58 N	117.53 E
Chengtu → Chengdu	107	30.39 N	104.04 E
Ch'engtzuliao	269d	25.06 N	121.27 E
Chengwu	98	34.58 N	115.52 E
Chengxian	102	33.43 N	105.41 E
Chengyang	98	36.18 N	120.22 E
Chengzi	98	41.57 N	117.16 E
Chengzituan	98	39.30 N	122.30 E
Ch'enhsien → Chenzhou	100	25.48 N	112.59 E
Chenhu ⊜	100	30.19 N	113.22 E
Chenies	260	51.41 N	0.32 W
Chenil, Lac ⊜	186	51.51 N	59.41 W
Cheniménil	58	48.08 N	6.36 E
Chenjiachang, Zhg.	107	30.04 N	105.15 E
Chenjiachang, Zhg.	107	29.35 N	104.52 E
Chenjiagang	98	34.25 N	119.49 E
Chenjiahe	102	29.28 N	109.59 E
Chenjiaji	100	30.42 N	114.21 E
Chenjiapang	106	31.14 N	119.42 E
Chenjiapu	105	40.31 N	115.37 E
Chenjiaqiao	106	31.27 N	121.16 E
Chenjiatun, Zhg.	104	42.20 N	124.06 E
Chenjiatun, Zhg.	104	40.57 N	121.01 E
Chenjiawan	106	31.02 N	120.35 E
Chenjiaxiang	106	31.29 N	113.45 E
Chenjiayang	100	33.47 N	120.10 E
Chenjiazhen	106	31.30 N	121.48 E
Chenjiazui	105	39.17 N	116.59 E
Chenkeng	100	25.06 N	116.15 E
Chenlingjiao	106	30.23 N	118.47 E
Chenliu	98	34.43 N	114.31 E
Chenlong	269b	31.17 N	121.25 E
Chenmu	106	31.10 N	120.53 E
Chennevières	261	49.00 N	2.07 E
Chennevières-lès-Louvres	261	49.03 N	2.33 E
Chenoa	216	40.45 N	88.43 W
Chenonceaux	50	47.20 N	1.04 E
Chenôve	58	47.17 N	5.00 E
Chenoweth	224	45.37 N	121.13 W
Chenqiao	98	34.58 N	114.32 E
Chenqing	89	49.08 N	127.16 E
Chenshanzhuang	105	39.43 N	117.30 E
Chenshian	100	33.50 N	119.11 E
Chenshichang	107	29.17 N	106.00 E
Chens-sur-Léman	58	46.20 N	6.16 E
Chentejn Nuur ▲	88	48.30 N	108.30 E
Chentij	88	48.05 N	109.45 E
Chentij □[4]	88	48.00 N	110.30 E
Chenxi	102	27.51 N	109.59 E
Chenyang → Shenyang	104	41.48 N	123.27 E
Cheonan → Ch'ŏnan	98	36.48 N	127.09 E
Cheongju → Ch'ŏngju	98	36.39 N	127.31 E
Chepachet	207	41.55 N	71.40 W
Chepaizi	86	44.55 N	84.30 E
Chepaúa	152	12.58 S	22.43 E
Chepén	248	7.13 S	79.27 W
Chépénéhé	175f	20.47 S	167.09 E
Chepes	252	31.21 S	66.36 W
Chepo	246	9.10 N	79.06 W
Chepstow	42	51.39 N	2.41 W
Cheptainville	261	48.33 N	2.16 E
Cher □[5]	32	47.05 N	2.30 E
Cher ≃	32	47.21 N	0.29 E
Cheradi, Isole II	68	40.27 N	17.10 E
Cherain	56	50.11 N	5.52 E
Cherán	234	19.41 N	101.57 W
Chéran ≃	62	45.53 N	5.56 E
Cheranchi	150	12.40 N	7.42 E
Cherangany Hills ▲[2]	154	1.15 N	35.27 E
Cherasco	62	44.39 N	7.51 E
Cherāt	123	33.49 N	71.53 E
Cheraw	192	34.42 N	79.53 W
Cheraw State Park ♠	192	34.36 N	79.55 W
Cherbourg	32	49.39 N	1.39 W
Cherchell	148	36.36 N	2.12 E
Cherelato	144	6.00 N	38.10 E
Cheremkhovo → Čeremchovo	88	53.09 N	103.05 E
Chérence	261	49.05 N	1.41 E
Chereponi	150	10.09 N	0.17 E
Cherepovets → Čerepovec	76	59.08 N	37.54 E
Chergui, Chott ech ⊜	148	34.21 N	0.30 E
Chergui, Île I	148	34.44 N	11.14 E
Chergui, Zahrez ⊜	148	35.12 N	3.32 E
Cheribon → Cirebon	115a	6.44 S	108.34 E
Cherio ≃	64	45.46 N	9.55 E
Cherita, Sebkret ⊜	36	35.21 N	10.19 E
Cheriton	208	37.17 N	75.58 W
Cheriyam Island I	122	10.09 N	73.40 E
Cherkassy → Čerkassy	78	49.26 N	32.04 E
Cherkessk → Čerkessk	84	44.14 N	42.04 E
Cherlen → Kerulen ≃	90	48.48 N	117.00 E
Chermside	171a	27.23 S	153.02 E
Chernigov → Černigov	78	51.30 N	31.18 E
Chernofski	180	53.24 N	167.33 W
Chernogorsk → Černogorsk	86	53.49 N	91.18 E
Chernovtsy → Černovcy	78	48.18 N	25.56 E
Chero ≃	62	44.58 N	9.51 E
Cherokee, Ala., U.S.	194	34.46 N	87.58 W
Cherokee, Iowa, U.S.	198	42.45 N	95.33 W
Cherokee, Kans., U.S.	198	37.21 N	94.49 W
Cherokee, Okla., U.S.	196	36.45 N	98.21 W
Cherokee, Tex., U.S.	196	30.59 N	98.43 W
Cherokee □[6]	222	31.48 N	95.10 W
Cherokee, Lake ⊜[1]	222	32.21 N	94.39 W
Cherokee Canal ≡	226	39.18 N	121.55 W
Cherokee Indian Reservation ✦[4]	192	35.25 N	83.24 W
Cherokee Lake ⊜[1]	192	36.16 N	83.20 W
Cherokee Point >	192	26.16 N	77.03 W
Cherokee Ranch	208	40.25 N	75.55 W
Cherokees, Lake O' The ⊜[1]	194	36.39 N	94.49 W
Cherokee Sound	238	26.17 N	77.04 W
Chéroy	50	48.12 N	3.00 E
Cherpuči	89	53.51 N	138.52 E
Cherquenco	252	38.41 S	72.00 W
Cherrabun	162	18.29 S	125.19 E
Cherrapunji	120	25.18 N	91.42 E
Cherry Brook ≃, Mass., U.S.	283	42.23 N	71.17 W
Cherry Brook ≃, N.J., U.S.	276	41.01 N	74.00 W
Cherry City	279b	40.29 N	79.58 W
Cherry Creek, B.C., Can.	224	49.17 N	124.47 W
Cherry Creek, N.Y., U.S.	214	42.18 N	79.06 W
Cherry Creek ≃, Ariz., U.S.	200	33.41 N	110.49 W
Cherry Creek ≃, Calif., U.S.	226	37.53 N	119.58 W
Cherry Creek ≃, Colo., U.S.	198	39.45 N	105.01 W
Cherry Creek ≃, Mont., U.S.	198	46.48 N	105.15 W
Cherry Creek ≃, N. Dak., U.S.	198	47.41 N	103.02 W
Cherry Creek ≃, S. Dak., U.S.	198	44.36 N	101.30 W
Cherry Creek, East Fork ≃	226	38.06 N	119.47 W
Cherry Creek, West Fork ≃	226	38.04 N	119.54 W
Cherry Fork	218	38.53 N	83.37 W
Cherry Grove, N.Y., U.S.	210	40.39 N	73.06 W
Cherry Grove, Oreg., U.S.	224	45.27 N	123.15 W
Cherry Hill, Ill., U.S.	278	41.32 N	88.02 W
Cherry Hill, N.J., U.S.	208	39.55 N	75.01 W
Cherry Hill ✦[8]	284b	39.15 N	76.38 W
Cherry Hill Mall ✦[9]	285	39.56 N	75.02 W
Cherry Island I	285	39.43 N	75.31 W
Cherry Lake ⊜[1]	226	38.00 N	119.54 W
Cherryland	226	37.41 N	122.06 W
Cherry Lane	279b	40.34 N	79.33 W
Cherryplain	210	42.38 N	73.22 W
Cherry Point Marine Corps Air Station ■	192	34.54 N	76.54 W
Cherryvale	198	37.16 N	95.33 W
Cherry Valley, Ark., U.S.	194	35.24 N	90.45 W
Cherry Valley, Calif., U.S.	228	33.57 N	116.53 W
Cherry Valley, Ill., U.S.	216	42.13 N	88.59 W
Cherry Valley, Mass., U.S.	207	42.15 N	71.52 W
Cherry Valley, N.Y., U.S.	210	42.48 N	74.45 W
Cherry Valley, Pa., U.S.	214	41.10 N	79.48 W
Cherry Valley Creek ≃	210	42.35 N	74.56 W
Cherryville, N.C., U.S.	192	35.23 N	81.23 W
Cherryville, Pa., U.S.	208	40.45 N	75.33 W
Cherrywood	275b	43.52 N	79.08 W
Cherson	78	46.38 N	32.35 E
Chersonesskij, Mys >	78	44.35 N	33.23 E
Chertsey	260	51.24 N	0.30 W
Cherwell ≃	42	51.44 N	1.15 W
Chesaning	190	43.11 N	84.07 W
Chesapeake	208	36.43 N	76.15 W
Chesapeake and Delaware Canal ≡	208	40.30 N	75.58 W
Chesapeake and Ohio Canal National Historical Park ♠	208	39.03 N	77.16 W
Chesapeake Bay C	208	38.40 N	76.25 W
Chesapeake Bay Bridge-Tunnel ✦[5]	208	37.00 N	76.02 W
Chesapeake Beach	208	38.41 N	76.32 W
Chesapeake City	208	39.32 N	75.49 W
Chesdin, Lake ⊜[1]	208	37.15 N	77.33 W
Cheseaux	58	46.35 N	6.36 E
Chesham	260	51.43 N	0.38 W
Chesham Bois	260	51.41 N	0.37 W
Cheshire, Conn., U.S.	207	41.30 N	72.54 W
Cheshire, Mass., U.S.	207	42.34 N	73.10 W
Cheshire, N.Y., U.S.	210	42.49 N	77.20 W
Cheshire □[6], Eng., U.K.	262	53.15 N	2.30 W
Cheshire □[6], N.H., U.S.	207	42.50 N	72.15 W
Cheshire Plain ⌢	262	53.18 N	2.40 W
Cheshire Reservoir ⊜[1]	207	42.32 N	73.11 W
Chesht-e Sharīf	128	34.21 N	63.44 E
Cheshunt	260	51.43 N	0.02 W
Chesil Beach ✦[2]	42	50.38 N	2.33 W
Cheslatta Lake ⊜	182	53.44 N	125.18 W
Chesley	212	44.17 N	81.05 W
Chesnee	192	35.09 N	81.52 W
Chess ≃	260	51.38 N	0.27 W
Chessington ✦[8]	260	51.21 N	0.18 W
Chessy	261	48.53 N	2.46 E
Chest Creek ≃	214	40.53 N	78.44 W
Chester, Eng., U.K.	262	53.12 N	2.54 W
Chester, Calif., U.S.	204	40.19 N	121.14 W
Chester, Conn., U.S.	207	41.24 N	72.27 W
Chester, Ill., U.S.	194	37.55 N	89.49 W
Chester, Md., U.S.	208	38.58 N	76.17 W
Chester, Mass., U.S.	207	42.17 N	72.59 W
Chester, Mont., U.S.	202	48.31 N	110.58 W
Chester, Nebr., U.S.	198	40.01 N	97.37 W
Chester, N.J., U.S.	210	40.47 N	74.42 W
Chester, Okla., U.S.	196	36.13 N	98.55 W
Chester, Pa., U.S.	208	39.51 N	75.21 W
Chester, S.C., U.S.	192	34.43 N	81.12 W
Chester, Tex., U.S.	222	30.55 N	94.36 W
Chester, Vt., U.S.	188	43.16 N	72.36 W
Chester, Va., U.S.	208	37.21 N	77.27 W
Chester, W. Va., U.S.	214	40.37 N	80.34 W
Chester □[6]	208	39.58 N	75.36 W
Chester □[8]	262	53.16 N	2.52 W
Chester ≃	208	39.00 N	76.10 W
Chester Basin	186	44.34 N	64.19 W
Chesterbrook	284c	38.55 N	77.09 W
Chester Brook ≃	283	42.23 N	71.14 W
Chester Creek ≃	208	39.50 N	75.22 W
Chester Creek, East Branch ≃	285	39.56 N	75.32 W
Chester Creek, West Branch ≃	285	39.54 N	75.27 W
Chesterfield, Eng., U.K.	44	53.15 N	1.25 W
Chesterfield, Conn., U.S.	207	41.24 N	72.11 W
Chesterfield, Ill., U.S.	219	39.15 N	90.04 W
Chesterfield, Ind., U.S.	218	40.07 N	85.36 W
Chesterfield, Mass., U.S.	207	42.24 N	72.50 W
Chesterfield, S.C., U.S.	192	34.44 N	80.05 W
Chesterfield, Va., U.S.	192	37.23 N	77.31 W
Chesterfield □[6]	208	37.20 N	77.25 W
Chesterfield, Île I	138	16.20 S	43.58 E
Chesterfield, Îles II	160	19.30 S	158.00 E
Chesterfield Inlet	176	63.21 N	90.42 W
Chesterfield Inlet C	176	63.25 N	90.45 W
Chester Heights	285	39.53 N	75.28 W
Chester Hill, Austl.	274a	33.53 S	151.00 E
Chesterhill, Ohio, U.S.	188	39.29 N	81.52 W
Chester Hill, Pa., U.S.	214	40.53 N	78.14 W
Chester Island I	285	39.50 N	75.21 W
Chesterland	214	41.31 N	81.21 W
Chester-le-Street	44	54.52 N	1.34 W
Chester Morse Lake ⊜[1]	224	47.23 N	121.42 W
Chester Octoraro Lake ⊜[1]	208	39.48 N	76.02 W
Chester Springs	285	40.06 N	75.37 W
Chesterton	216	41.37 N	87.04 W
Chesterton Range ▲	166	25.30 S	147.27 E
Chestertown	208	39.13 N	76.04 W
Chesterville, Ont., Can.	212	45.06 N	75.14 W
Chesterville, Ohio, U.S.	214	40.29 N	82.41 W
Chestnut	219	40.03 N	89.11 W
Chestnut Hill, Mass., U.S.	283	42.20 N	71.10 W
Chestnut Hill, Pa., U.S.	210	40.04 N	75.12 W
Chestnut Hill ✦[8]	285	40.04 N	75.13 W
Chestnut Hill ▲[2]	285	40.13 N	75.45 W
Chestnut Hill Reservoir ⊜[1]	283	42.20 N	71.10 W
Chestnut Ridge ▲	214	40.09 N	79.24 W
Chestnut Ridge Park ♠	284a	42.43 N	78.46 W
Chest Peak ▲	172	43.06 S	172.01 E
Chesu	120	30.31 N	82.37 E
Chesuncook Lake ⊜	188	46.00 N	69.20 W
Cheswick	214	40.32 N	79.47 W
Cheswold	208	39.13 N	75.35 W
Chet ≃	42	52.33 N	1.32 E
Cheta ≃	74	71.54 N	102.06 E
Chetaibi	36	37.04 N	7.23 E
Chetco ≃	202	42.03 N	124.16 W
Chetek	190	45.19 N	91.39 W
Chéticamp	186	46.38 N	61.01 W
Chetlat Island I	122	11.42 N	72.42 E
Chetopa	198	37.02 N	95.05 W
Chetput	122	12.28 N	79.21 E
Chetumal Bay C	232	18.20 N	88.05 W
Chetwynd	182	55.42 N	121.40 W
Cheung Chau I	271d	22.12 N	114.01 E
Cheung Kwan O C	271d	22.17 N	114.15 E
Cheung Shui Tan	271d	22.26 N	114.12 E
Chevak	180	61.39 N	165.17 W
Cheval-Blanc, Montagne du ▲	62	44.07 N	6.26 E
Cheval Blanc, Pointe du >	238	19.41 N	73.27 W
Chevannes	261	48.32 N	2.27 E
Chevelon Creek ≃	200	34.57 N	110.31 W
Chevening	260	51.18 N	0.08 E
Chevenoz	58	46.20 N	6.39 E
Cheverly	284c	38.55 N	76.55 W
Cheverny	50	47.30 N	1.28 E
Chevillon	58	48.32 N	5.08 E
Chevilly-Larue	261	48.46 N	2.21 E
Chevington Drift	44	55.17 N	1.36 W
Cheviot, N.Z.	172	42.49 S	173.16 E
Cheviot, Ohio, U.S.	218	39.11 N	84.35 W
Cheviot Hills ▲[2]	46	55.22 N	2.22 W
Chevreuse	50	48.42 N	2.03 E
Chèvreville	261	49.07 N	2.51 E
Chevril, Lac du ⊜	62	45.29 N	6.56 E
Chevry-Cossigny	261	48.43 N	2.40 E
Chevy Chase	284c	38.58 N	77.05 W
Chevy Chase Heights	214	40.36 N	79.08 W
Chevy Chase View	284c	39.01 N	77.05 W
Chewaucan ≃	202	42.30 N	120.18 W
Chew Bahir (Lake Stefanie) ⊜	144	4.40 N	36.50 E
Chewelah	202	48.17 N	117.43 W
Chew Magna	42	51.22 N	2.35 W
Chew Reservoir ⊜[1]	262	53.31 N	1.56 W
Chews Landing	285	39.50 N	75.04 W
Chewton, Austl.	169	37.05 S	144.16 E
Chewton, Pa., U.S.	214	40.53 N	80.20 W
Chexbres	58	46.29 N	6.47 E
Cheyenne, Okla., U.S.	196	35.37 N	99.40 W
Cheyenne, Wyo., U.S.	200	41.08 N	104.49 W
Cheyenne ≃	198	44.40 N	101.15 W
Cheyenne, Dry Fork ≃	198	43.25 N	105.23 W
Cheyenne River Indian Reservation ✦[4]	198	45.05 N	101.20 W
Cheyenne Wells	198	38.51 N	102.11 W
Cheyne Bay C	162	34.35 S	118.50 E
Cheyne Point >	162	33.58 S	122.34 E
Cheyney	285	39.56 N	75.31 W
Chezhen	98	37.54 N	117.37 E
Chezhou	100	25.48 N	112.59 E
Chhab	123	33.14 N	71.54 E
Chhabra	124	24.40 N	76.50 E
Chhachhrauli	124	30.15 N	77.22 E
Chhajārsi	272a	28.38 N	77.23 E
Chhalera Bāngar	272a	28.33 N	77.20 E
Chhanka	126	23.59 N	89.55 E
Chhātak	120	25.02 N	91.40 E
Chhatarpur, Bhārat	124	24.23 N	84.11 E
Chhatarpur, Bhārat	124	24.54 N	79.36 E
Chhatarpur □[5]	124	24.55 N	79.35 E
Chhātna	126	23.18 N	86.58 E
Chhēb Kāndal	110	13.45 N	105.24 E
Chheharta	123	31.38 N	74.48 E
Chhibrāmau	124	27.09 N	79.31 E
Chhināmor	272b	22.48 N	88.18 E
Chhindwāra	124	22.04 N	78.56 E
Chhindwāra □[5]	124	22.00 N	78.50 E
Chhlong ≃	110	12.15 N	105.58 E
Chhota Bāisdia	126	22.00 N	90.27 E
Chhukha Dzong	124	27.09 N	89.36 E
Chi ≃	110	15.11 N	104.43 E
Chia	246	4.52 N	74.04 W
Chiador	256	22.01 S	43.03 W
Chiador, Cachoeira do ⌊	256	22.03 S	43.02 W
Chiahsien	100	23.05 N	120.35 E
Chiahsing → Jiaxing	106	30.46 N	120.45 E
Chiai	100	23.29 N	120.27 E
Chialamberto	62	45.22 N	7.21 E
Chiali	100	23.10 N	120.11 E
Chiambala ≃	152	16.22 S	11.49 E
Chiamboni, Ras >	144	1.38 S	41.36 E
Chiampo	64	45.33 N	11.17 E
Chiampo ≃	64	45.20 N	11.16 E
Chiamussu → Jiamusi	89	46.50 N	130.21 E
Chian → Ji'an	100	27.07 N	114.58 E
Chiana, Val di ∨	66	43.15 N	11.50 E
Chianciano Terme	66	43.03 N	11.50 E
Chiang Dao	110	19.22 N	98.58 E
Chiang Kham	110	19.32 N	100.18 E
Chiang Khan	110	17.52 N	101.36 E
Chiang Khian	110	19.37 N	100.00 E
Chiang Mai	110	18.47 N	98.59 E
Chiangmen → Jiangmen	100	22.35 N	113.05 E
Chiang Rai	110	19.54 N	99.50 E
Chiang Saen	110	20.16 N	100.05 E
Chiangtu → Yangzhou	100	32.24 N	119.26 E
Chiangyin → Jiangyin	106	31.55 N	120.16 E
Chiani ≃	66	42.52 N	12.14 E
Chianje	152	15.45 S	13.48 E
Chianni	66	43.29 N	10.38 E
Chianti □[4]	66	43.22 N	11.23 E
Chianti ▲[1]	66	43.25 N	11.20 E
Chianti, Monti del ▲	66	43.32 N	11.25 E
Chiaoch'i	100	24.49 N	121.46 E
Chiaohsien → Jiaoxian	98	36.18 N	119.58 E
Chiaopanshan	100	24.49 N	121.21 E
Chiaotso → Jiaozuo	102	35.15 N	113.18 E
Chiao-tung University ♁[2]	269b	31.14 N	121.24 E
Chiapa	248	19.32 S	69.13 W
Chiapa de Corzo	234	16.42 N	93.00 W
Chiapaot'ai	100	24.11 N	121.01 E
Chiapas □[3]	232	16.30 N	92.30 W
Chiaramonte Gulfi	70	37.02 N	14.42 E
Chiaramonti	71	40.45 N	8.49 E
Chiaravalle	66	43.36 N	13.19 E
Chiaravalle Centrale	68	38.41 N	16.25 E
Chiareggio	64	46.19 N	9.47 E
Chiari	62	45.32 N	9.56 E
Chiaromonte	68	40.07 N	16.13 E
Chiasso	58	45.50 N	9.01 E
Chiautla de Tapia	234	18.17 N	98.36 W
Chiautzingo	234	19.12 N	98.28 W
Chiavari	62	44.19 N	9.19 E
Chiavenna	58	46.19 N	9.24 E
Chiba	94	35.36 N	140.07 E
Chiba □[5]	94	35.30 N	140.20 E
Chibabava	156	20.19 S	33.39 E
Chiba-kō C	268	35.35 N	140.06 E
Chibakou	100	29.36 N	113.01 E
Chibango	152	13.38 S	21.56 E
Chiba University ♁[2]	268	35.36 N	140.07 E
Chibemba	152	15.45 S	14.05 E
Chibi	154	20.19 S	30.30 E
Chibia	152	15.11 S	13.41 E
Chibiribira Falls ⌊	154	21.14 S	32.20 E
Chibouet ≃	206	45.47 N	72.52 W
Chibougamau	176	49.55 N	74.22 W
Chibuto	156	24.40 S	33.33 E
Chibwe	154	14.12 S	28.31 E
Chica, Laguna ⊜	234	20.06 N	96.40 W
Chicago	216, 278	41.53 N	87.38 W
Chicago, North Branch ≃	216	41.53 N	87.38 W
Chicago, North Branch, West Fork ≃	278	42.03 N	87.54 W
Chicago, South Branch ≃	278	41.53 N	87.38 W
Chicago, University of ♁[2]	278	41.47 N	87.36 W

Symbol	English	Deutsch	Español	Français	Português
≃	River	Fluss	Río	Rivière	Rio
≡	Canal	Kanal	Canal	Canal	Canal
⌊	Waterfall, Rapids	Wasserfall, Stromschnellen	Cascada, Rápidos	Chute d'eau, Rapides	Cascata, Rápidos
⋓	Strait	Meeresstrasse	Estrecho	Détroit	Estreito
C	Bay, Gulf	Bucht, Golf	Bahía, Golfo	Baie, Golfe	Baía, Golfo
⊜	Lake, Lakes	See, Seen	Lago, Lagos	Lac, Lacs	Lago, Lagos
≋	Swamp	Sumpf	Pantano	Marais	Pântano
⊼	Ice Features, Glacier	Eis- und Gletscherformen	Accidentes Glaciales	Formes glaciaires	Acidentes Glaciares
⊤	Other Hydrographic Features	Andere Hydrographische Objekte	Otros Elementos Hidrográficos	Autres données hydrographiques	Outros Elementos Hidrográficos
✦	Submarine Features	Untermeerische Objekte	Accidentes Submarinos	Formes de relief sous-marin	Acidentes Submarinos
□	Political Unit	Politische Einheit	Unidad Política	Entité politique	Unidade Política
♁	Cultural Institution	Kulturelle Institution	Institución Cultural	Institution culturelle	Instituição Cultural
⊥	Historical Site	Historische Stätte	Sitio Histórico	Site historique	Sitio Histórico
♠	Recreational Site	Erholungs- und Ferienort	Sitio de Recreo	Centre de loisirs	Sitio de Lazer
⊠	Airport	Flughafen	Aeropuerto	Aéroport	Aeroporto
■	Military Installation	Militäranlage	Instalación Militar	Installation militaire	Instalação Militar
✦	Miscellaneous	Verschiedenes	Misceláneo	Divers	Miscelânea

Chicago-Hammond Airport ⊠ 278 41.32 N 87.32 W
Chicago Harbor C 278 41.53 N 87.37 W
Chicago Heights 216 41.30 N 87.38 W
Chicago-Hinsdale Airport ⊠ 278 41.46 N 87.56 W
Chicagoland Airport ⊠ 278 42.12 N 87.56 W
Chicago Lawn ⊸[8] 278 41.47 N 87.41 W
Chicago-Midway Airport ⊠ 216 41.47 N 87.45 W
Chicago-O'Hare International Airport ⊠ 278 41.59 N 87.54 W
Chicago Park 226 39.09 N 120.58 W
Chicago Portage National Historic Site ⊥ 278 41.48 N 87.49 W
Chicago Ridge 216 41.42 N 87.47 W
Chicago Sanitary and Ship Canal ≡ 216 41.32 N 88.05 W
Chicago Stadium ♠ 278 41.53 N 87.40 W
Chicama ≃ 248 7.56 S 79.17 W
Chicamacomico ≃ 208 38.26 N 75.59 W
Chicapa ≃ 152 6.26 S 20.47 E
Chic-Chocs, Monts ⛰ 186 48.55 N 66.00 W
Chic-Chocs, Parc des ♠ 186 49.05 N 65.42 W
Chichagof Island I 180 57.30 N 135.30 W
Chichas, Cordillera de ⛰ 248 20.30 S 66.30 W
Chichāwatni 123 30.32 N 72.42 E
Chiche ≃ 250 8.15 S 53.30 W
Chicheng 98 40.54 N 115.46 E
Chichén Itzá 232 20.40 N 88.34 W
Chichén Itzá ⊥ 232 20.40 N 88.35 W
Chichester, Eng., U.K. 42 50.50 N 0.48 W
Chichester, N.Y., U.S. 210 42.06 N 74.19 W
Chichester Range ⛰ 162 22.00 S 118.50 E
Chichi 100 23.50 N 120.46 E
Chichibu 94 35.59 N 139.05 E
Chichibu-tama-kokuritsu-kōen ♠ 94 35.52 N 139.00 E
Chichica 236 8.22 N 81.40 W
Chichicastenango 236 14.56 N 91.07 W
Chichigalpa 236 12.34 N 87.02 W
Chichigapa 234 17.47 N 94.25 W
Ch'ich'ihaerh → Qiqihaer 89 47.19 N 123.55 E
Chichihualco 234 17.41 N 99.39 W
Chichimilá 232 20.37 N 88.13 W
Chichiriviche 246 10.56 N 68.16 W
Chichishima-rettō II 14 27.06 N 142.12 E
Chicholi 124 22.01 N 77.40 E
Chichra 126 22.19 N 86.53 E
Chicicatiapa ≃ 234 18.18 N 96.19 W
Chickahominy ≃ 208 37.14 N 76.53 W
Chickaloon 180 61.48 N 148.28 W
Chickamauga 192 34.52 N 85.18 W
Chickamauga Lake ⊜[1] 192 35.22 N 85.02 W
Chickamin ≃ 182 55.47 N 130.58 W
Chickasaw, Ala., U.S. 194 30.46 N 88.05 W
Chickasaw, Ohio, U.S. 216 40.26 N 84.30 W
Chickasaw Bogue ≃ 194 32.17 N 87.55 W
Chickasaw Creek ≃ 194 30.44 N 88.03 W
Chickasawhatchie Creek ≃ 192 31.19 N 84.29 W
Chickasawhay ≃ 194 31.00 N 88.45 W
Chickasaw National Recreation Area ♠ 196 34.25 N 96.59 W
Chickasha 196 35.02 N 97.58 W
Chicken 180 64.04 N 141.56 W
Chicken Brook ≃ 283 42.08 N 71.25 W
Chickerell 42 50.37 N 2.30 W
Chickies Creek ≃ 208 40.03 N 76.32 W
Chiclana de la Frontera 34 36.25 N 6.08 W
Chiclayo 248 6.46 S 79.51 W
Chico, Calif., U.S. 204 39.44 N 121.50 W
Chico, Tex., U.S. 196 33.18 N 97.48 W
Chico, Wash., U.S. 224 47.37 N 122.43 W
Chico ≃, Arg. 254 42.25 S 70.30 W
Chico ≃, Arg. 254 43.48 S 66.25 W
Chico ≃, Arg. 254 49.56 S 68.32 W
Chico ≃, Pan. 236 8.20 N 80.28 W
Chico ≃, Pil. 116 17.58 N 121.36 E
Chico ≃, S.A. 254 51.40 S 69.09 W
Chicoa 154 15.37 S 32.24 E
Chicoasen, Presa ⊜[1] 234 16.55 N 93.05 W
Chicobi, Lac ⊜ 190 48.53 N 78.30 W
Chico Creek ≃ 198 38.15 N 104.20 W
Chicolete Creek ≃ 222 29.05 N 96.49 W
Chicomba 152 14.09 S 14.57 E
Chicomo 156 24.31 S 34.17 E
Chicomuselo 232 15.46 N 92.16 W
Chiconautla, Cerro ∧ 286a 19.39 N 98.58 W
Chicontepec 234 20.58 N 98.10 W
Chicopee, Ga., U.S. 192 34.16 N 83.51 W
Chicopee, Mass., U.S. 207 42.10 N 72.36 W
Chicopee ≃ 207 42.09 N 72.37 W
Chicora 207 41.56 N 79.45 W
Chicorato 232 26.02 N 107.54 W
Chicot ≃ 275a 45.35 N 73.51 W
Chicot State Park ♠ 194 30.47 N 92.19 W
Chicoutimi 186 48.26 N 71.04 W
Chicoutimi ≃ 186 48.26 N 71.05 W
Chicoutimi, Parc de ♠ 186 48.30 N 70.15 W
Chicualoque 234 20.23 N 97.39 W
Chicuma 152 13.23 S 14.51 E
Chicxulub 232 21.08 N 89.31 W
Chidambaram 122 11.24 N 79.42 E
Chiddingstone Causeway 260 51.12 N 0.10 E
Chidenguele 156 24.54 S 34.13 E
Chidley, Cape ≻ 176 60.23 N 64.26 W
Chidlow 168a 31.52 S 116.14 E
Chidu 120 30.35 N 94.50 E
Chief 222 32.33 N 96.10 W
Chief Justice William Cushing Memorial State Park ♠ 283 42.10 N 70.45 W
Chiefland 192 29.29 N 82.52 W
Chiefs Point ≻ 212 44.42 N 81.18 W
Chief's Point Indian Reserve ⊸[4] 212 44.41 N 81.17 W
Chiehyang → Jieyang 100 23.35 N 116.21 E
Chiemgauer Alpen ⛰ 64 47.40 N 12.30 E
Chiemsee ⊜ 64 47.54 N 12.29 E
Chien, Bayou de ≃ 194 36.35 N 89.11 W
Chienchiao Airport ⊠ 106 30.12 N 120.12 E
Chienes (Kiens) 64 46.48 N 11.50 E
Chiengi 154 8.39 S 29.10 E
Chiengo 152 13.20 S 21.55 E
Chiens, Rivière aux ≃ 275a 45.39 N 73.46 W
Chienti ≃ 66 43.18 N 13.45 E
Chieri 62 45.01 N 7.49 E
Chiers ≃ 56 49.39 N 5.00 E
Chiesa in Valmalenco 64 46.16 N 9.51 E
Chiese ≃ 64 45.08 N 10.25 E
Chieti 66 42.21 N 14.10 E
Chieti □[4] 66 42.21 N 14.21 E
Chietla 234 18.31 N 98.35 W
Chieuti 68 41.51 N 15.10 E
Chieveley 42 51.27 N 1.19 W
Chièvres 50 50.35 N 3.48 E
Chifeng 98 42.18 N 119.00 E
Chigasaki 94 35.19 N 139.24 E
Chiginagak, Mount ∧ 180 57.08 N 156.59 W
Chigmit Mountains ⛰ 180 60.00 N 153.00 W
Chignahuapan 234 19.50 N 98.02 W
Chignall Saint James 260 51.46 N 0.25 E
Chignall Smealy 260 51.47 N 0.25 E
Chignecto, Cape ≻ 186 45.20 N 64.57 W
Chignecto Bay C 186 45.35 N 64.45 W
Chignik 180 56.18 N 158.23 W
Chignik Bay C 180 56.22 N 158.15 W
Chignik Lagoon 180 56.14 N 158.44 W
Chignik Lake 180 56.20 N 158.29 W
Chignolo Po 62 45.09 N 9.29 E
Chigorodó 246 7.41 N 76.42 W
Chigu 100 27.34 N 114.40 E
Chigubo 156 22.50 S 33.34 E
Chigwell 260 51.38 N 0.05 E
Chigwell Row 260 51.37 N 0.07 E
Chigyŏng 98 39.51 N 127.26 E
Chihaya Castle ⊥ 270 34.24 N 135.40 E
Chihe 100 32.32 N 117.58 E
Ch'ihfeng → Chifeng 98 42.18 N 119.00 E
Chihli, Gulf of → Bohai C 98 38.30 N 120.00 E
Chihpen 100 22.42 N 121.03 E
Ch'ihshang 100 23.07 N 121.12 E
Chihsi → Jixi 89 45.17 N 130.59 E
Ch'ihtung 100 22.46 N 120.16 E
Ch'ihu, T'aiwan 100 23.58 N 120.28 E
Chihu, Zhg. 100 24.07 N 117.51 E
Chihuahua 232 28.38 N 106.05 W
Chihuxi ≃ 100 26.38 N 117.24 E
Chiitola 24 61.16 N 29.38 E
Chijiantan 105 39.12 N 106.47 E
Chikaskia ≃ 196 36.37 N 97.15 W
Chik Ballāpur 122 13.28 N 77.44 E
Chikhli 120 20.21 N 76.15 E
Chikindzonot 232 20.20 N 88.29 W
Chik Kang 271d 22.26 N 114.21 E
Chikmagalūr 122 13.19 N 75.47 E
Chiknai ≃ 126 24.06 N 89.17 E
Chiknāyakanhalli 122 13.26 N 76.37 E
Chikoa 154 13.24 S 32.07 E
Chikodi 122 16.26 N 74.36 E
Chikote 154 15.52 S 26.54 E
Chikou 100 30.44 N 117.32 E
Chikrĕng ≃ 110 12.51 N 104.14 E
Ch'iku 100 23.08 N 120.07 E
Chikugo 96 33.10 N 130.33 E
Chikugo ≃ 92 33.09 N 130.21 E
Chikuma ≃ 94 36.59 N 138.14 E
Chikuminuk Lake ⊜ 180 60.14 N 159.00 W
Chikusa ≃ 96 34.44 N 134.24 E
Chikwawa 154 16.03 S 34.48 E
Chi-Kyaw 110 20.17 N 93.54 E
Chila, Ang. 152 12.04 S 14.29 E
Chila, Méx. 234 18.55 N 102.28 W
Chilacachapa 234 18.17 N 99.43 W
Chilakalūrupet 122 16.05 N 80.10 E
Chilam 123 35.03 N 75.07 E
Chilanga 154 15.34 S 28.17 E
Chilapa de Alvarez 234 17.36 N 99.10 W
Chilapa de Díaz 234 17.31 N 97.41 W
Chilās 123 35.26 N 74.05 E
Chilaw 122 7.34 N 79.47 E
Chilca 248 12.32 S 76.44 W
Chilca, Cordillera de ⛰ 248 15.30 S 71.50 W
Chilca, Punta ≻ 248 12.27 S 76.48 W
Chilchota 234 19.51 N 102.08 W
Chilco Lake Indian Reserve ⊸[4] 182 51.25 N 124.07 W
Chilcotin ≃ 182 51.45 N 122.24 W
Childcott Island I 166 16.58 S 149.58 E
Childers 166 25.14 S 152.17 E
Childersburg 194 33.16 N 86.21 W
Childer Thornton 262 53.17 N 2.57 W
Childress 196 34.25 N 100.13 W
Childs 210 41.34 N 75.32 W
Chile □[1] 244 30.00 S 71.00 W
Chile, Hipódromo ♠ 286e 33.24 S 70.41 W
Chile, Universidad de ⊍[2] 286e 33.27 S 70.40 W
Chile Chico 254 46.33 S 71.44 W
Chilecito, Arg. 252 33.53 S 69.03 W
Chilecito, Arg. 252 29.10 S 67.30 W
Chilengue, Serra do ⛰ 152 13.10 S 15.18 E
Chilete 248 7.14 S 78.51 W
Chilham 42 51.15 N 0.57 E
Chilhowie 192 36.48 N 81.41 W
Chili 216 40.52 N 86.02 W
Chili → Chile □[1] 244 30.00 S 71.00 W
Chili ≃ 248 16.23 S 71.46 W
Chili, Ouadi ∨ 146 16.44 N 20.53 E
Chilia, Braţul ≃[1] 78 45.18 N 29.40 E
Chili Center 210 43.06 N 77.44 W
Chililabombwe (Bancroft) 154 12.18 S 27.43 E
Chilin → Jilin 89 43.51 N 126.33 E
Chilingchang 107 28.58 N 105.31 E
Chilivani 71 40.36 N 8.56 E
Chilka Lake ⊜ 122 19.46 N 85.20 E
Chilkat Pass)(180 59.43 N 136.35 W
Chilko ≃ 182 52.08 N 123.30 W
Chilko Lake ⊜ 182 51.20 N 124.05 W
Chillagoe 166 17.09 S 144.32 E
Chillán 252 36.36 S 72.07 W
Chillar 252 37.18 S 59.59 W
Chillicothe, Ill., U.S. 190 40.55 N 89.29 W
Chillicothe, Mo., U.S. 194 39.48 N 93.33 W
Chillicothe, Ohio, U.S. 218 39.20 N 82.59 W
Chillicothe, Tex., U.S. 196 34.10 N 99.31 W
Chilliwack 182 49.10 N 121.57 W
Chilliwack ≃ 224 49.05 N 121.57 W
Chilliwack Lake ⊜ 224 49.03 N 121.25 W
Chillón 286d 11.55 S 77.05 W
Chillón ≃ 248 11.57 S 77.09 W
Chillon ⊥ 58 46.25 N 6.56 E
Chillum 208 38.58 N 76.59 W
Chilly 84 39.25 N 49.05 E
Chilly-Mazarin 261 48.42 N 2.19 E
Chilmāri 124 25.33 N 89.43 E
Chilmark 207 41.21 N 70.45 W
Chilo 218 38.48 N 84.08 W
Chiloane, Ilha I 156 20.40 S 34.55 E
Chiloé, Isla de I 254 42.30 S 73.55 W
Chilok 88 51.21 N 110.28 E
Chilok ≃ 88 51.19 N 106.59 E
Chilón 232 17.14 N 92.25 W
Chilonga 154 12.03 S 31.21 E
Chilonghe ≃ 105 39.00 N 117.18 E
Chilongo 152 13.55 S 16.35 E
Chiloquin 202 42.35 N 121.52 W
Chilovo 76 57.46 N 29.23 E
Chilpancingo [de los Bravos] 234 17.33 N 99.30 W
Chilpi 124 22.15 N 81.33 E
Chiltern □[8] 260 51.40 N 0.37 W
Chiltern Hills ⛰[2] 260 51.42 N 0.48 W
Chilton, Tex., U.S. 222 31.17 N 97.04 W
Chilton, Wis., U.S. 190 44.02 N 88.10 W
Chiluage 152 9.30 S 21.47 E
Chilubula Mission 154 10.09 S 31.00 E
Chilumba 154 10.28 S 34.12 E
Chilung 100
269d 25.08 N 121.44 E
Chilung Ho ≃ 269d 25.07 N 121.27 E
Chilung Shih □[7] 269d 25.09 N 121.42 E
Chiluvya 154 12.18 S 34.01 E
Chilwa, Lake ⊜ 154 15.12 S 35.50 E
Chilwell 169 38.10 S 144.21 E
Chimaco 152 15.12 S 21.56 E
Chimacum 224 48.01 N 122.46 W
Chimacum Creek ≃ 224 48.03 N 122.45 W
Chimakela 152 15.24 S 16.58 E
Chimalhuacán □[7] 286a 19.24 N 99.00 W
Chimaltenango 236 14.40 N 90.49 W
Chimaltenango □[5] 236 14.40 N 90.55 W
Chimaltitán 234 21.46 N 103.50 W
Chimán 236 8.42 N 78.37 W
Chimanimani National Park ♠ 154 19.48 S 33.56 E
Chimay 50 50.03 N 4.19 E
Chimayo 200 36.00 N 105.56 W
Chimbarongo 252 34.42 S 71.03 W
Chimbas 252 31.29 S 68.32 W
Chimborazo □[4] 246 2.00 S 78.40 W
Chimborazo ∧[1] 246 1.28 S 78.48 W
Chimbote 248 9.05 S 78.36 W
Chimbu □[5] 164 6.05 S 145.00 E
Chimbua 152 16.32 S 15.08 E
Chimichagua 246 9.15 N 73.49 W
Chimkent → Čimkent 85 42.18 N 69.36 E
Chimki 82 55.54 N 37.26 E
Chimkinskoje Vodochranilišče ⊜[1] 265b 55.51 N 37.28 E
Chimney Rock National Historic Site ♠ 198 41.39 N 103.20 W
Chimon Island I 276 41.04 N 73.23 W
Chimpay 252 39.10 S 66.09 W
Chimpembe 154 9.31 S 29.33 E
Chimpōro ≃ 152 17.20 S 17.17 E
Chin 174m 26.26 N 127.55 E
Chin □[8] 110 22.00 N 93.30 E
China, Méx. 232 25.42 N 99.14 W
Chinā, Nihon 174m 26.24 N 127.46 E
China □[1] 90 35.00 N 105.00 E
China, Tanjong ≻ 271c 1.14 N 103.51 E
Chinácota 246 7.37 N 72.36 W
China Grove 192 35.34 N 80.35 W
China Lake ⊜ 204 35.46 N 117.39 W
China Lake Naval Weapons Center ■ 204 35.35 N 117.10 W
Chinameca 236 13.30 N 88.21 W
China Meridional, Mar de → South China Sea ≂[2] 108 10.00 N 113.00 E
Chinan, Taehan 98 35.48 N 127.25 E
Chinan → Jinan, Zhg. 98 36.40 N 116.57 E
Chinandega 236 12.37 N 87.09 W
Chinandega □[5] 236 12.45 N 87.05 W
China Spring 222 31.39 N 97.18 W
Chinati Peak ∧ 196 29.57 N 104.29 W
Chinatown ⊸[8] 282 37.48 N 122.26 W
Chincha Alta 248 13.27 S 76.08 W
Chinchaga ≃ 176 58.50 N 118.20 W
Chinchane, Sebkha de ⊜ 148 21.05 N 12.05 W
Chincheros 248 13.27 S 73.44 W
Chinchiang → Quanzhou 100 24.54 N 118.35 E
Chinchilla, Austl. 166 26.45 S 150.38 E
Chinchilla, Pa., U.S. 210 41.28 N 75.41 W
Chinchiná 246 4.58 N 75.36 W
Chincholi 272c 19.10 N 73.08 E
Chinchón, Esp. 34 40.08 N 3.25 W
Ch'inch'ŏn, Taehan 98 36.52 N 127.26 E
Chinchou → Jinzhou 104 41.07 N 121.08 E
Chincilla de Monte Aragón 34 38.55 N 1.55 W
Chincolco 252 32.13 S 70.50 W
Chincoteague 208 37.56 N 75.23 W
Chincoteague Bay C 208 38.06 N 75.15 W
Chincoteague Inlet C 208 37.53 N 75.25 W
Chinde 156 18.37 S 36.24 E
Chindo 98 34.28 N 126.15 E
Chindong 98 35.07 N 128.29 E
Chindwin ≃ 110 21.26 N 95.15 E
Chine (la République populaire de) → China □[1], As. 90 35.00 N 105.00 E
Chine (nationaliste) → Taiwan □[1], As. 100 23.30 N 121.00 E
Chinen 174m 26.09 N 127.49 E
Chineni 123 33.02 N 75.17 E
Chine Orientale, Mer de → East China Sea ≂[2] 90 30.00 N 126.00 E
Chinese Camp 226 37.52 N 120.26 W
Chingamba 152 12.49 S 18.20 E
Chingansk 89 49.07 N 131.11 E
Chingarora Creek ≃ 276 40.27 N 74.12 W
Ch'ingchiang → Huaiyin 100 33.35 N 119.02 E
Chingford ⊸[8] 260 51.38 N 0.01 E
Chingleput 122 12.42 N 79.59 E
Chingmei 269d 24.59 N 121.32 E
Chingola 154 12.32 S 27.52 E
Chingoni 157a 12.48 S 45.08 E
Chingoroi 152 13.37 S 14.01 E
Chingshih → Jinshi 102 29.33 N 111.50 E
Ch'ingshui 100 24.15 N 120.35 E
Chingtao → Qingdao 98 36.06 N 120.19 E
Chingtechen → Jingdezhen 100 29.16 N 117.11 E
Ch'ingt'ung 269d 25.01 N 121.43 E
Chinguar 152 12.36 S 16.20 E
Chinguetti 150 20.27 N 12.22 W
Chingune 156 20.38 S 34.55 E
Chinhae 98 35.09 N 128.40 E
Chin Hills ⛰[2] 108 22.30 N 93.30 E
Chinhsien → Jinxian 98 39.04 N 121.40 E
Chinhua → Jinhua 100 29.07 N 119.39 E
Ch'inhuangtao → Qinhuangdao 98 39.56 N 119.36 E
Chīni 120 31.32 N 78.15 E
Chiniak, Cape ≻ 180 57.36 N 152.08 W
Chining → Jining, Zhg. 98 35.25 N 116.36 E
Chining → Jining, Zhg. 102 41.06 N 112.58 E
Chiniot 123 31.43 N 72.59 E
Chinīt ≃ 110 12.55 N 105.35 E
Chinitna Point ≻ 180 59.43 N 153.02 W
Chinitos 232 25.01 N 107.54 W
Chiniziua 156 19.00 S 35.09 E
Chinju 98 35.11 N 128.05 E
Chinkiang → Zhenjiang 106 32.13 N 119.26 E
Chinkuashih 100 25.08 N 121.51 E
Chin Lakes ⊜ 182 49.37 N 112.13 W
Chinle 200 36.09 N 109.33 W
Chinle Creek ≃ 200 37.12 N 109.43 W
Chinley 262 53.20 N 1.56 W
Chinley Churn ∧[2] 262 53.21 N 1.57 W
Chinmen 100 24.27 N 118.21 E
Chinmen Tao I 100 24.27 N 118.25 E
Chinnampo → Namp'o 98 38.45 N 125.23 E
Chinnor 42 51.43 N 0.56 W
Chino, Nihon 94 35.59 N 138.09 E
Chino, Calif., U.S. 228 34.01 N 117.42 W
Chino Airport ⊠ 280 33.59 N 117.38 W
Chino Creek ≃ 280 33.53 N 117.38 W
Chino Hills ⛰[2] 280 33.56 N 117.45 W
Chinon 50 47.10 N 0.15 E
Chinook, Alta., Can. 184 51.27 N 110.56 W
Chinook, Mont., U.S. 202 48.35 N 109.14 W
Chinook, Wash., U.S. 224 46.16 N 123.57 W
Chinook Cove 182 51.14 N 120.10 W
Chino Valley 200 34.45 N 112.27 W
Chinowths Corner 226 36.20 N 119.19 W
Chinpāi 126 23.50 N 87.28 E
Chinquapin 192 34.50 N 77.49 W
Chinquapin Run ≃ 284b 39.21 N 76.35 W
Chinsali 154 10.34 S 32.03 E
Chinshan 100 25.14 N 121.36 E
Chinshui 100 24.36 N 120.52 E
Chintāmani 122 13.24 N 78.04 E
Chinteche 154 11.52 S 34.09 E
Chintembwe 154 13.25 S 33.59 E
Chinú 246 9.06 N 75.24 W
Chinunje 154 11.19 S 37.19 E
Chin-wan C 174m 26.25 N 127.54 E
Chinwangtao → Qinhuangdao 98 39.56 N 119.36 E
Chiny 56 49.44 N 5.20 E
Chinyama Litapi 152 13.31 S 22.21 E
Chioco 154 16.25 S 32.50 E
Chioggia 64 45.13 N 12.17 E
Chiomonte 62 45.07 N 6.59 E
Chios → Khíos 38 38.22 N 26.08 E
Chios → Khíos I 38 38.22 N 26.00 E
Chipao 248 14.15 S 73.57 W
Chipata (Fort Jameson) 154 13.39 S 32.40 E
Chipehua, Bahía C 234 16.03 N 95.23 W
Chipera 154 15.28 S 32.30 E
Chipili 154 10.44 S 29.04 E
Chip'ing, T'aiwan 100 23.31 N 120.49 E
Chiping, Zhg. 98 36.37 N 116.16 E
Chipinga 154 20.12 S 32.38 E
Chip Lake ⊜ 182 53.40 N 115.20 W
Chipley 194 30.47 N 85.32 W
Chiplūn 122 17.32 N 73.31 E
Chipman 186 46.11 N 65.53 W
Chipogolo 154 6.52 S 36.02 E
Chipoka 154 14.00 S 34.31 E
Chipola ≃ 192 30.01 N 85.05 W
Chippawa ⊸[8] 284a 43.04 N 79.03 W
Chippawa Channel ≡[1] 284a 43.04 N 79.01 W
Chippego Lake ⊜ 212 44.42 N 76.49 W
Chippenham 42 51.28 N 2.07 W
Chipperfield 260 51.42 N 0.29 W
Chippewa ≃, Mich., U.S. 190 43.35 N 84.17 W
Chippewa ≃, Minn., U.S. 198 44.56 N 95.44 W
Chippewa ≃, Wis., U.S. 190 44.25 N 92.10 W
Chippewa, East Branch ≃ 198 45.20 N 95.36 W
Chippewa, East Fork ≃ 190 45.53 N 91.05 W
Chippewa, Lake ⊜ 190 45.56 N 91.13 W
Chippewa Bay C 212 44.27 N 75.47 W
Chippewa Creek ≃ 212 44.27 N 75.46 W
Chippewa Falls 190 44.56 N 91.24 W
Chippewa Lake 214 41.04 N 81.54 W
Chippewanuck Creek ≃ 216 41.07 N 86.12 W
Chipping Campden 42 52.03 N 1.46 W
Chipping Norton 42 51.56 N 1.32 W
Chipping Ongar 260 51.43 N 0.15 E
Chipping Sodbury 42 51.33 N 2.24 W
Chippis 58 46.17 N 7.33 E
Chippokes Plantation State Park ♠ 208 37.08 N 76.44 W
Chipps Island I 282 38.03 N 121.55 W
Chipre → Cyprus □[1] 130 35.00 N 33.00 E
Chipstead 260 51.17 N 0.09 E
Chiquelequele 152 16.40 S 19.06 E
Chiquián 248 10.09 S 77.11 W
Chiquihuitlán de Juárez 234 17.59 N 96.48 W
Chiquimula 236 14.48 N 89.33 W
Chiquimula □[5] 236 14.40 N 89.25 W
Chiquimulilla 236 14.05 N 90.23 W
Chiquinata, Bahía C 248 20.20 S 70.10 W
Chiquinquirá 246 5.37 N 73.50 W
Chiquintirca 248 13.09 S 73.41 W
Chiquita 152 8.38 S 17.05 E
Chiquito Creek ≃ 226 37.20 N 119.20 W
Chira ≃ 246 4.54 S 81.08 W
Chira, Isla I 236 10.06 N 85.09 W
Chirad 272c 19.09 N 73.07 E
Chiradzulu 154 15.42 S 35.10 E
Chīrāla 122 15.49 N 80.21 E
Chirape 156 21.18 S 33.33 E
Chirāwa 120 28.15 N 75.38 E
Chirchik → Čirčik 85 41.29 N 69.35 E
Chire (Shire) ≃ 154 17.42 S 35.19 E
Chiredzi 154 21.03 S 31.45 E
Chireno 194 31.30 N 94.21 W
Chirens 62 45.25 N 5.33 E
Chirfa 146 20.57 N 12.21 E
Chīrgaon 124 25.35 N 78.49 E
Chirgis Nuur ⊜ 88 49.12 N 93.24 E
Chiricahua Mountains ⛰ 200 31.50 N 109.15 W
Chiricahua National Monument ♠ 200 32.02 N 109.19 W
Chiricahua Peak ∧ 200 31.52 N 109.20 W
Chiriguaná 246 9.22 N 73.36 W
Chirikof Island I 180 55.50 N 155.35 W
Chirilagua 236 13.13 N 88.08 W
Chirinos 248 5.16 S 78.52 W
Chiriquí 236 8.24 N 82.19 W
Chiriquí □[4] 236 8.30 N 82.00 W
Chiriquí ≃ 236 8.30 N 82.26 W
Chiriquí, Golfo de C 246 8.00 N 82.20 W
Chiriquí, Laguna de C 236 9.03 N 82.00 W
Chiriquí Grande 236 8.57 N 82.07 W
Chiriquí Viejo ≃ 236 8.20 N 82.41 W
Chirk 42 52.56 N 3.03 W
Chirnside 46 55.48 N 2.13 W
Chiromo 154 16.33 S 35.08 E
Chirovo 76 58.56 N 33.24 E
Chirripó ≃ 236 10.41 N 83.41 W
Chirripó, Cerro ∧ 236 9.29 N 83.30 W
Chirsa 84 41.31 N 46.06 E
Chirundu 154 15.59 S 28.54 E
Chirvosti 265a 59.57 N 30.37 E
Chiryū 94 35.00 N 137.02 E
Chisago City 190 45.22 N 92.53 W
Chisamba 154 14.58 S 28.23 E
Chisana 180 62.09 N 142.10 W
Chisapani 124 27.34 N 85.08 E
Chiscas 246 6.33 N 72.29 W
Chisec 236 15.49 N 90.17 W
Chiseldon 42 51.31 N 1.44 W
Chisenga 154 9.56 S 33.26 E
Chisep'o 98 34.50 N 128.42 E
Ch'ishan 100 22.53 N 120.29 E
Chishanhu ⊜ 106 31.51 N 119.07 E
Chishi 100 27.42 N 117.58 E
Chishima-rettō → Kuril'skije Ostrova II 74 46.10 N 152.00 E
Chishisi 100 25.32 N 113.11 E
Chisholm, Ala., U.S. 194 32.25 N 86.15 W
Chisholm, Maine, U.S. 188 44.29 N 70.12 W
Chisholm, Minn., U.S. 190 47.29 N 92.53 W
Chisholm, Tex., U.S. 222 32.51 N 96.22 W
Chisholm Mills 182 54.55 N 114.08 W
Chishtiān Mandi 123 29.48 N 72.52 E
Chishui, Zhg. 102 28.29 N 105.38 E
Chishuihe ≃ 107 28.49 N 105.50 E
Chisimaio → Kismayu 144 0.23 S 42.30 E
Chişinău → Kišin'ov 78 47.00 N 28.50 E
Chişineu-Criş 38 46.31 N 21.31 E
Chislaviči 76 54.11 N 32.10 E
Chislehurst ⊸[8] 260 51.25 N 0.04 E
Chislenghien (Gellingen) 50 50.39 N 3.52 E
Chisone ≃ 62 44.49 N 7.25 E
Chisone, Valle del ∨ 62 45.01 N 7.07 E
Chisos Mountains ⛰ 196 29.15 N 103.20 W
Chisseaux 50 47.20 N 1.05 E
Chissengue 152 9.14 S 20.42 E
Chissilo 152 13.34 S 16.30 E
Chist'akovo → Torez 83 48.01 N 38.37 E
Chistochina 180 62.34 N 144.40 W
Chistopol → Čistopol' 80 55.21 N 50.37 E
Chistyakovo → Torez 83 48.01 N 38.37 E
Chiswellgreen 260 51.44 N 0.22 W
Chiswick ⊸[8] 260 51.29 N 0.16 W
Chita, Col. 246 6.11 N 72.28 W
Chita, Nihon 94 35.00 N 136.51 E
Chita → Čita, S.S.S.R. 88 52.03 N 113.30 E
Chitado 152 17.20 S 13.54 E
Chitagá 246 7.09 N 72.40 W
Chita-hantō ≻[1] 94 34.50 N 136.53 E
Chitambo 154 12.55 S 30.39 E
Chitata 152 13.47 S 15.43 E
Chita-wan C 94 34.47 N 136.58 E
Chitek Lake ⊜, Man., Can. 184 52.26 N 99.25 W
Chitek Lake ⊜, Sask., Can. 184 53.44 N 107.47 W
Chitembo 152 13.34 S 16.40 E
Chitina 180 61.31 N 144.27 W
Chitina ≃ 180 61.30 N 144.28 W
Chitipa 154 9.43 S 33.16 E
Chitokoloki 152 13.50 S 23.13 E
Chitorgarh 120 24.53 N 74.38 E
Chitose 92a 42.49 N 141.39 E
Chitra ≃[1] 126 22.53 N 89.40 E
Chitradurga 122 14.14 N 76.24 E
Chitrāl 123 35.51 N 71.47 E
Chitra Lada Palace ⊍ 269a 13.46 N 100.32 E
Chitrāvati ≃ 122 14.48 N 78.14 E
Chitré 236 7.58 N 80.26 W
Chittagong 120 22.20 N 91.50 E
Chittenango 210 43.03 N 75.52 W
Chittenango Creek ≃ 210 43.11 N 76.00 W
Chittenango Falls 210 42.59 N 75.50 W
Chittering 162 31.29 S 116.06 E
Chittoor 122 13.12 N 79.07 E
Ch'itu, T'aiwan 269d 25.06 N 121.42 E
Chitu, Yai. 144 8.36 N 37.59 E
Chiuchiang → Jiujiang 100 29.44 N 115.59 E
Chiuchiu 252 22.21 S 68.39 W
Chiuduno 62 45.40 N 9.51 E
Chiumbe 152 12.29 S 16.08 E
Chiumbe ≃ 152 7.00 S 21.12 E
Chiume 152 15.03 S 21.14 E
Chiuppano 64 45.46 N 11.28 E
Chiuro 64 46.10 N 9.59 E
Chiusa (Klausen) 64 46.38 N 11.34 E
Chiusa di Pesio 62 44.19 N 7.40 E
Chiusa di San Michele 62 45.06 N 7.19 E
Chiusaforte 64 46.24 N 13.18 E
Chiusa Sclafani 70 37.41 N 13.16 E
Chiusella ≃ 62 45.24 N 7.55 E
Chiusi 66 43.01 N 11.57 E
Chiusi, Lago di ⊜ 66 43.03 N 11.58 E
Chiuta, Lake ⊜ 154 14.55 S 35.50 E
Chiv 84 41.46 N 47.54 E
Chiva, Esp. 34 39.28 N 0.43 W
Chiva, S.S.S.R. 72 41.24 N 60.22 E
Chivacoa 246 10.10 N 68.54 W
Chivapuri ≃ 246 6.25 N 66.23 W
Chivasso 62 45.11 N 7.53 E
Chivato, Punta ≻ 232 27.05 N 111.59 W
Chivay 248 15.40 S 71.35 W
Chivilcoy 252 34.53 S 60.01 W
Chiwanda 154 11.22 S 34.54 E
Chiwawa ≃ 224 47.47 N 120.40 W
Chixi 100 28.22 N 116.22 E
Chixoy ≃ 236 16.03 N 90.27 W
Chiyoda, Nihon 94 36.27 N 139.07 E
Chiyoda, Nihon 94 36.11 N 140.14 E
Chiyoda, Nihon 96 34.41 N 132.32 E
Chizhen 100 31.55 N 118.12 E
Chizizhen 100 32.22 N 115.11 E
Chizu 96 35.16 N 134.14 E
Chjargas 88 49.35 N 93.51 E
Chkalov → Orenburg 86 51.54 N 55.06 E
Chlebnikovo, S.S.S.R. 80 56.38 N 49.56 E
Chlebnikovo, S.S.S.R. 265b 55.58 N 37.31 E
Chlebodarnyj 80 46.41 N 40.50 E
Chlebodarovka 83 47.29 N 37.23 E
Chlevnoje 76 52.12 N 39.05 E
Chloride 200 35.25 N 114.19 W
Chlum 60 48.52 N 13.55 E
Chlum ∧ 61 48.42 N 14.04 E
Chmelevicy 80 57.45 N 46.22 E
Chmelevo 82 56.09 N 39.08 E
Chmelevoje 78 48.36 N 31.24 E
Chmelita 76 55.25 N 33.53 E
Chmel'nickij 78 49.25 N 27.00 E
Chmel'nik 78 49.33 N 27.57 E
Chmel'niki 82 56.52 N 38.13 E
Chmielnik 30 50.37 N 20.46 E
Chmost' ≃ 76 54.45 N 32.34 E
Choa Chu Kang 271c 1.22 N 103.41 E
Choālī 272b 22.24 N 88.24 E
Chŏăm Khsant 110 14.13 N 104.56 E
Choapa ≃ 252 31.38 S 71.34 W
Choapan 234 17.20 N 95.57 W
Choba 154 2.26 N 38.03 E
Chobe □[5] 156 18.30 S 25.00 E
Chobe (Linyanti) ≃ 156 17.50 S 25.05 E
Chobeju 24 64.53 N 60.10 E
Chobe National Park ♠ 156 18.45 S 24.15 E
Chobham 260 51.21 N 0.36 W
Chobham Common ≡ 260 51.23 N 0.37 W
Chobi 84 42.21 N 41.53 E
Chocaman 234 18.59 N 97.01 W
Choccolocco Creek ≃ 194 33.33 N 86.11 W
Choceň 30 50.00 N 16.13 E
Chocenice 60 49.33 N 13.31 E
Chochis, Cerro ∧ 248 18.04 S 60.03 W
Chochiwŏn 98 36.37 N 127.18 E
Chochloma 80 56.58 N 43.54 E
Chochmort' 88 47.26 N 94.25 E
Chŏch Nuur ⊜ 88 49.30 N 115.35 E
Chochol'skij 78 51.34 N 38.45 E
Cho-chu 110 21.54 N 105.39 E
Chocianów 30 51.25 N 15.55 E
Chociwel 30 53.28 N 15.19 E
Chocó □[5] 246 6.00 N 77.00 W
Chocolate Bay C 222 29.11 N 95.09 W
Chocolate Bayou ≃ 222 29.13 N 95.13 W
Chocolate Mountains ⛰ 204 33.20 N 115.15 W
Chocontá 246 5.09 N 73.41 W
Chocope 248 7.47 S 79.13 W
Choctawhatchee, East Fork ≃ 194 31.21 N 85.33 W
Choctawhatchee, West Fork ≃ 194 31.21 N 85.33 W
Choctawhatchee Bay C 194 30.25 N 86.21 W
Choctaw Indian Reservation ⊸[4] 194 32.49 N 89.14 W
Choctaw Lake ⊜[1] 218 39.58 N 83.29 W
Chodaras 88 52.36 N 99.19 E
Chodavaram 122 17.50 N 82.57 E
Chodecz 30 52.24 N 19.01 E
Chodoi 114 2.50 N 101.27 E
Chodorov 78 49.24 N 24.17 E
Chodosy 76 53.56 N 31.29 E
Chodov 54 50.11 N 12.43 E
Chodova Griva 80 57.08 N 50.16 E
Chodovaricha 24 68.57 N 53.40 E
Chodžaimetk 85 39.37 N 69.14 E
Chodžakala 128 38.43 N 56.20 E
Chodžejli 72 42.48 N 59.25 E
Chodzież 30 52.59 N 16.56 E
Chodžikent 85 41.37 N 69.56 E
Choele-Choel 252 39.16 S 65.41 W
Chofombo 154 14.35 S 31.50 E
Chōfu 94 35.39 N 139.33 E
Chofu Airport ⊠ 268 35.39 N 139.32 E
Chogot 88 53.15 N 105.52 E
Choiceland 184 53.27 N 104.25 W
Choiseul 261 48.41 N 2.01 E
Choiseul 241f 13.47 N 61.03 W
Choiseul I 175e 7.05 S 157.00 E
Choiseul Sound ≈ 254 51.57 S 58.35 W
Choisy 58 45.59 N 6.03 E
Choisy-le-Roi 261 48.46 N 2.25 E
Choix 232 26.43 N 108.17 W
Chojna 30 52.58 N 14.26 E
Chojnice 30 53.42 N 17.34 E
Chojniki 78 51.53 N 29.56 E
Chojnów 30 51.17 N 15.56 E
Choke Mountains ⛰ 144 11.00 N 37.30 E
Chokio 198 45.34 N 96.10 W
Chokoloskee 220 25.49 N 81.22 W
Cholame 226 35.43 N 120.18 W
Cholame Creek ≃ 226 35.39 N 120.22 W
Cholame Hills ⛰[2] 226 35.45 N 120.30 W
Cholbon 88 51.53 N 116.15 E
Choldarkipčak 85 39.51 N 68.52 E
Cholet 32 47.04 N 0.53 W
Cholila 254 42.31 S 71.27 W
Chŏlla Namdo □[4] 98 34.45 N 127.00 E
Chŏlla Pukdo □[4] 98 35.45 N 127.15 E
Cholm 76 57.09 N 31.11 E
Cholmeč' 78 52.09 N 30.37 E
Cholmogorovka 86 44.25 N 78.31 E
Cholmogorskaja 24 63.49 N 40.39 E
Cholmogory 24 64.15 N 41.40 E
Cholmsk 89 47.03 N 142.03 E
Cholmskij 78 44.52 N 38.24 E
Cholmy, S.S.S.R. 78 51.52 N 32.36 E
Cholmy, S.S.S.R. 82 54.56 N 38.33 E
Cholm-Žirkovskij 76 55.31 N 33.29 E
Cholo 154 16.10 S 35.10 E
Cholodnaja Balka 83 48.02 N 38.04 E
Choloma 236 15.34 N 87.56 W
Cho-lon ⊸[8] 269c 10.46 N 106.40 E
Chölönbujr 88 47.55 N 112.57 E
Cholopeniči 76 54.31 N 28.58 E
Ch'ŏlsan 98 39.46 N 124.40 E
Cholsey 42 51.34 N 1.10 W
Choltobino 82 54.11 N 38.28 E
Choltoson 88 50.20 N 103.20 E
Choluj, S.S.S.R. 80 56.04 N 42.08 E
Choluj, S.S.S.R. 80 56.34 N 41.53 E
Cholula [de Rivadabia] 234 19.04 N 98.18 W
Choluteca 236 13.18 N 87.12 W
Choluteca □[5] 236 13.20 N 87.10 W
Choma 154 16.48 S 26.59 E
Chomedey ⊸[8] 275a 45.32 N 73.44 W
Chomen Swamp ☷ 144 9.25 N 37.20 E
Chomérac 62 44.42 N 4.39 E
Chomičev 80 48.11 N 45.01 E
Chomiomo ∧ 124 28.01 N 88.31 E
Cho-moi, Viet. 110 10.33 N 105.24 E
Cho-moi, Viet. 269c 10.51 N 106.38 E
Chomo Lhāri ∧ 124 27.50 N 89.15 E
Chom Thong 110 18.25 N 98.41 E
Chomu 120 27.10 N 75.44 E
Chomutec 78 50.06 N 33.44 E
Chomutov 54 50.28 N 13.26 E
Chomutovka 78 51.56 N 34.33 E
Chomutovka ≃ 54 50.11 N 13.37 E
Chomutovo, S.S.S.R. 76 52.51 N 37.27 E
Chomutovo, S.S.S.R. 88 52.28 N 104.25 E
Chomutovskaja 83 47.03 N 40.04 E
Chōnan, Nihon 94 35.24 N 140.14 E
Ch'ŏnan, Taehan 98 36.48 N 127.09 E
Chon'atino 82 55.11 N 38.07 E
Chon Buri 110 13.22 N 100.59 E
Chonchi 254 42.38 S 73.47 W
Choncholoj 88 51.08 N 108.14 E
Chon Daen 110 16.11 N 100.51 E
Chone 246 0.41 S 80.06 W
Chone ≃ 246 0.35 S 80.25 W
Chongan 100 27.45 N 118.02 E
Ch'ŏngdan 98 37.58 N 125.56 E
Chongde 106 30.32 N 120.26 E
Ch'ŏngdo 98 35.38 N 128.43 E
Chongge-gang ≃ 271b 37.33 N 127.04 E
Chonggu 106 31.12 N 121.10 E
Chonghaizhen 106 31.52 N 121.21 E
Chonghe 89 44.43 N 127.45 E
Ch'ŏngjin 98 41.47 N 129.50 E
Chŏngju, C.M.I.K. 98 39.41 N 125.13 E
Ch'ŏngju, Taehan 98 36.39 N 127.31 E
Chŏng Kal 110 13.57 N 103.35 E
Chongkanzhen 107 30.09 N 105.37 E
Chongli 98 40.54 N 115.16 E
Chongming 106 31.37 N 121.24 E
Chongmingdao I 106 31.36 N 121.33 E
Chongoene 156 25.00 S 33.47 E
Chongor 102 45.50 N 112.43 E
Chongos Bajo 248 12.07 S 75.16 W
Chongoyape 248 6.39 S 79.24 W
Chong Pang 271c 1.26 N 103.50 E
Chŏngp'yŏng-chŏsuji ⊜ 98 37.40 N 127.30 E
Chongqing, Zhg. 107 30.39 N 103.41 E
Chongqing (Chungking), Zhg. 107 29.39 N 106.34 E
Chongren, Zhg. 100 29.37 N 120.43 E
Chongren, Zhg. 100 27.46 N 116.01 E
Chongru 100 27.01 N 120.10 E
Ch'ŏngsong 98 41.47 N 129.48 E
Chongwe ≃ 154 15.43 S 29.20 E
Chongwu 100 24.53 N 118.55 E
Chongxi 98 42.07 N 128.59 E
Chongxin 102 35.13 N 107.29 E
Ch'ŏngyang, Taehan 98 36.27 N 126.48 E
Chongyang, Zhg. 100 29.33 N 114.00 E
Chongyi 100 25.44 N 114.18 E
Chongzuo 102 22.21 N 107.26 E
Chŏnju 98 35.49 N 127.08 E
Ch'ŏnma 98 40.03 N 125.01 E
Chonos, Archipiélago de los II 254 45.00 S 74.00 W
Ch'ŏnsu-ri 98 41.43 N 128.45 E
Chontaleña, Cordillera ⛰ 236 12.12 N 85.19 W
Chontales □[5] 236 12.05 N 85.10 W
Chon-thanh 110 11.24 N 106.36 E
Chonuu 74 66.27 N 143.06 E
Chonzie, Ben ∧ 46 56.27 N 3.59 W
Cho Oyu ∧ 124 28.06 N 86.39 E
Chopim ≃ 252 25.35 S 53.05 W
Chopinzinho 252 25.51 S 52.30 W
Chop'or ≃ 80 49.36 N 42.19 E
Choptank ≃ 208 38.38 N 76.13 W
Chor 89 47.53 N 134.58 E
Chor ≃ 89 47.48 N 134.43 E
Chorch Uul ⛰ 102 42.37 N 105.30 E

Symbols in the index entries represent the broad categories identified in the key at the right. Symbols with superior numbers (⛰[2]) identify subcategories (see complete key on page I · 30).

Kartensymbole in dem Registerverzeichnis stellen die rechts in Schlüssel erklärten Kategorien dar. Symbole mit hochgestellten Ziffern (⛰[2]) bezeichnen Unterabteilungen einer Kategorie (vgl. vollständiger Schlüssel auf Seite I · 30).

Los símbolos incluídos en el texto del índice representan las grandes categorias identificadas con la clave a la derecha. Los símbolos con numeros en su parte superior (⛰[2]) identifican las subcategorías (véase la clave completa en la página I · 30).

Les symboles de l'index représentent les catégories indiquées dans la légende à droite. Les symboles suivis d'un indice (⛰[2]) représentent des sous-catégories (voir légende complète à la page I · 30).

Os símbolos incluídos no texto do índice representam as grandes categorias identificadas com a chave à direita. Os símbolos com números em sua parte superior (⛰[2]) identificam as subcategorias (veja-se a chave completa à página I · 30).

Symbol	English	Deutsch	Español	Français	Português
∧	Mountain	Berg	Montaña	Montagne	Montanha
⛰	Mountains	Berge	Montañas	Montagnes	Montanhas
)(	Pass	Pass	Paso	Col	Passo
∨	Valley, Canyon	Tal, Cañon	Valle, Cañón	Vallée, Canyon	Vale, Canhão
≡	Plain	Ebene	Llano	Plaine	Planície
≻	Cape	Kap	Cabo	Cap	Cabo
I	Island	Insel	Isla	Île	Ilha
II	Islands	Inseln	Islas	Îles	Ilhas
⊥	Other Topographic Features	Andere Topographische Objekte	Otros Elementos Topográficos	Autres données topographiques	Outros Elementos Topográficos

ESPAÑOL — Nombre / Página / Lat. / Long. W=Oeste

Chordil Sar'dag ⛰ 88 50.50 N 99.40 E
Chorejver 24 67.25 N 58.03 E
Chorges 62 44.33 N 6.17 E
Chori 84 41.37 N 45.59 E
Chorin ⊥ 54 52.54 N 13.52 E
Chorinsk 88 52.10 N 109.46 E
Chorley 262 53.39 N 2.39 W
Chorley □[8] 262 53.38 N 2.38 W
Chorleywood 260 51.39 N 0.31 W
Chorlovo 82 55.20 N 38.49 E
Chorlton-cum-Hardy ◆[8] 262 53.27 N 2.17 W
Choro ≃ 248 16.25 S 64.35 W
Chorog 120 37.31 N 71.33 E
Chorol, S.S.S.R. 78 49.47 N 33.17 E
Chorol', S.S.S.R. 89 44.25 N 132.04 E
Chorol ≃ 78 49.28 N 33.47 E
Chorolque, Cerro ∧ 248 20.56 S 66.01 W
Choros, Isla ❙ 252 29.16 S 71.33 W
Chorošovo 82 55.08 N 38.47 E
Chorostkov 78 49.13 N 25.55 E
Choroszcz 30 53.09 N 22.59 E
Chorreras, Cerro ∧ 232 26.02 N 106.21 W
Chorrillos 286d 12.10 S 77.02 W
Chorrochó 250 8.59 S 39.06 W
Chorro Creek ≃ 226 35.20 N 120.50 W
Ch'ŏrwŏn 98 38.16 N 127.12 E
Chorzele 30 53.16 N 20.55 E
Ch'osan 98 40.50 N 125.47 E
Chosanch'am 98 40.22 N 126.11 E
Chosedachard 24 67.02 N 59.22 E
Chosen 220 26.42 N 80.41 W
Chošeutovo 80 47.02 N 47.50 E
Chōshi 94 35.44 N 140.50 E
Choshi-ōhashi ◆[5] 94 35.44 N 140.50 E
Choshui Ch'i ≃ 100 24.03 N 120.23 E
Chosica 248 11.54 S 76.42 W
Chos Malal 252 37.23 S 70.16 W
Chosŏn Minjujuŭi In'min Konghwaguk → Korea, North □[1] 98 40.00 N 127.00 E
Chosrech 84 41.59 N 47.18 E
Chosta 84 43.33 N 39.53 E
Choszczno 30 53.10 N 15.26 E
Chota 248 6.33 S 78.39 W
Chotanāgpur Plateau ⛰[1] 124 23.30 N 84.30 E
Chotča ≃ 82 56.54 N 37.30 E
Choteau 202 47.49 N 112.11 W
Choteau Creek ≃ 198 42.51 N 98.09 W
Chotěboř 30 49.43 N 15.40 E
Choten' 78 51.07 N 34.46 E
Chotěšov, Česko. 60 49.39 N 13.12 E
Chotešov, S.S.S.R. 78 51.43 N 24.47 E
Chotilovo 76 57.44 N 34.05 E
Chotimsk 76 53.26 N 32.35 E
Chotin 78 48.29 N 26.30 E
Chotisino 82 54.24 N 36.33 E
Chot'kovo, S.S.S.R. 76 52.56 N 35.23 E
Chot'kovo, S.S.S.R. 76 53.46 N 35.14 E
Chot'kovo, S.S.S.R. 82 56.15 N 38.00 E
Chotla, Cerro de ∧ 234 17.55 N 101.31 W
Chotovn'a 76 53.17 N 30.32 E
Chotuš' 82 54.32 N 37.44 E
Chotynec 76 53.08 N 35.24 E
Chotyniči 76 52.38 N 26.18 E
Chouchiak'ou → Shangshui 100 33.39 N 114.39 E
Chouk'ou → Shangshui 100 33.39 N 114.39 E
Chouteau 196 36.11 N 95.21 W
Chovaling 85 38.21 N 69.58 E
Chovd, Mong. 86 49.16 N 90.30 E
Chovd, Mong. 86 48.07 N 91.22 E
Chovd, Mong. 86 48.01 N 91.39 E
Chovd, Mong. 102 44.38 N 102.30 E
Chovd ≃ 90 48.06 N 92.11 E
Chövsgöl 102 43.38 N 109.39 E
Chövsgöl □[4] 88 50.00 N 100.00 E
Chövsgöl Nuur ◎ 88 51.00 N 100.30 E
Chovu-Aksy 88 51.11 N 93.53 E
Chowan ≃ 192 36.00 N 76.40 W
Chowchilla 226 37.07 N 120.16 W
Chowchilla ≃ 226 37.07 N 120.32 W
Chowchilla, East Fork ≃ 226 37.20 N 119.50 W
Chowchilla, West Fork ≃ 226 37.20 N 119.50 W
Chowchilla Canal ≋ 226 37.05 N 120.28 W
Chown, Mount ∧ 182 53.24 N 119.22 W
Ch'owŏn-ni 98 39.40 N 127.17 E
Choya 252 28.30 S 64.52 W
Chrapun' 78 51.42 N 27.29 E
Chr'aščevka 80 53.48 N 49.06 E
Chrást 60 49.48 N 13.29 E
Chrebtovo 82 56.35 N 38.16 E
Chrenovoje 80 51.07 N 40.17 E
Chreščatij 83 49.37 N 39.42 E
Chřibská 54 50.50 N 14.29 E
Chříč 60 49.57 N 13.39 E
Chriesman 222 30.36 N 96.46 W
Chrisman 194 39.48 N 87.41 W
Chrissiesmeer 158 26.16 S 30.13 E
Chrissiesmeer ◎ 158 26.19 S 30.13 E
Christanshåb 176 68.50 N 51.12 W
Christburg → Dzierzgoń 30 53.56 N 19.21 E
Christchurch, N.Z. 172 43.32 S 172.38 E
Christchurch, Eng., U.K. 42 50.44 N 1.45 W
Christ Church Cathedral ♉[1] 273a 6.27 N 3.23 E
Christian □[6] 219 39.33 N 89.18 W
Christian ≃ 180 66.36 N 145.49 W
Christian, Cape ≻ 176 70.31 N 68.18 W
Christian, Point ≻ 174e 25.04 S 130.07 W
Christiana, Jam. 241q 18.10 N 77.29 W
Christiana, S. Afr. 158 27.52 S 25.08 E
Christiana, Del., U.S. 285 39.40 N 75.40 W
Christiana, Pa., U.S. 208 39.57 N 76.00 W
Christiana Creek ≃ 216 41.41 N 85.59 W
Christianburg 218 38.17 N 85.06 W
Christian Channel ⋓ 212 44.47 N 80.08 W
Christian Island ❙ 212 44.50 N 80.13 W
Christian Islands Indian Reserve ◆[4] 212 44.50 N 80.10 W
Christiansburg, Ohio, U.S. 218 40.03 N 84.02 W
Christiansburg, Va., U.S. 192 37.08 N 80.24 W
Christiansfeld 41 55.21 N 9.29 E
Christiansø ❙ 26 55.19 N 15.12 E
Christian Sound ⋓ 180 55.56 N 134.40 W
Christiansted 241n 17.45 N 64.42 W
Christie, Mount ∧ 180 63.02 N 129.40 W
Christie, Mount ∧[2] 216 42.53 N 83.20 W
Christie Bay ⊂ 176 62.32 N 111.10 W
Christie Lake ◎, Man., Can. 184 56.54 N 96.56 W
Christie Lake ◎, Ont., Can. 212 44.48 N 76.26 W
Christina ≃, Alta., Can. 184 56.40 N 111.03 W
Christina ≃, Del., U.S. 285 39.43 N 75.31 W
Christina Lake ◎, Alta., Can. 182 55.38 N 110.55 W
Christina Lake ◎, B.C., Can. 182 49.05 N 118.14 W
Christinovka 78 48.49 N 29.58 E
Christišče 83 48.55 N 37.30 E
Christmas 220 28.32 N 81.01 W
Christmas Airfield ⊠ 174o 1.57 N 157.18 W
Christmas Bay ⊂ 222 29.03 N 95.11 W
Christmas Creek 162 18.53 S 125.55 E
Christmas Creek ≃ 162 18.29 S 125.23 E

FRANÇAIS — Nom / Page / Lat. / Long. W=Ouest

Christmas Island □[2] 108
112 10.30 S 105.40 E
Christmas Island ❙ 174o 1.52 N 157.20 W
Christmas Lake ◎ 202 43.18 N 120.36 W
Christmas Mountain ∧ 180 64.34 N 160.34 W
Christmas Ridge ✢[3] 14 6.30 N 161.00 W
Christoforovka 78 47.59 N 33.05 E
Christoforovo 24 60.53 N 47.13 E
Christ of the Andes → Cristo Redentor ⊥ 252 32.50 S 70.05 W
Christoph Columbus-Spitze → Cristóbal Colón, Pico ∧ 246 10.50 N 73.41 W
Christopher 194 37.58 N 89.03 W
Christopher Lake ◎ 162 24.49 S 127.42 E
Christoval 196 31.12 N 100.30 W
Chroma ≃ 74 71.36 N 144.49 E
Chromtau, S.S.S.R. 22
86 50.17 N 58.27 E
Chrudim 30 49.57 N 15.48 E
Chrustal'noje 83 48.10 N 38.50 E
Chrustal'nyj 89 44.24 N 135.06 E
Chrysler Corporation (Hamtramck Plant) ♉[3] 281 42.23 N 83.03 W
Chrzanów 30 50.09 N 19.24 E
Chuādānga 124 23.38 N 88.51 E
Chualar 226 36.34 N 121.31 W
Chuanbu 106 31.17 N 119.49 E
Chuanergu 105 39.20 N 117.43 E
Chuan'gang 106 31.57 N 121.04 E
Chuangjiapuzi 104 40.50 N 124.06 E
Chuanhongjiang 106 31.49 N 121.29 E
Chuanliao 100 28.17 N 120.13 E
Chuansha 106 31.12 N 121.42 E
Chuanshan 100 29.53 N 121.57 E
Chuanxindian, Zhg. 98 42.33 N 117.27 E
Chuanxindian, Zhg. 104 41.25 N 120.30 E
Chuanyanghe ≋ 100 33.46 N 119.51 E
Chuathbaluk 180 61.40 N 159.15 W
Chubbuck 202 42.55 N 112.28 W
Chūbu-sangaku-kokuritsu-kōen ♠ 94 36.30 N 137.41 E
Chubut □[4] 254 44.00 S 69.00 W
Chubut ≃ 254 43.20 S 65.03 W
Ch'üchiang → Shaoguan 100 24.50 N 113.37 E
Chuchi Lake ◎ 182 55.10 N 124.33 W
Chuchou → Zhuzhou 100 27.50 N 113.09 E
Chuchra 78 50.13 N 34.49 E
Chu Chua 182 51.21 N 120.10 W
Chuchuwayha Indian Reserve ◆[4] 182 49.21 N 120.06 W
Chuckatuck 208 36.52 N 76.35 W
Chučni 84 41.57 N 47.55 E
Chucuito 248 15.53 S 69.53 W
Chucun 100 33.04 N 116.32 E
Chucunaque ≃ 246 8.09 N 77.44 W
Chudan ≃ 88 52.08 N 109.40 E
Chudat 84 41.38 N 48.42 E
Chudeč 60 49.58 N 13.05 E
Chudenín 60 49.18 N 13.06 E
Chuderhe ≃ 89 46.48 N 123.37 E
Chudleigh 42 50.36 N 3.38 W
Chudojelan 88 54.42 N 99.37 E
Chuen Lung 271d 22.24 N 114.06 E
Chugach Islands ‖ 180 59.06 N 151.42 W
Chugach Mountains ⛰ 180 61.00 N 145.00 W
Chugiak 180 61.25 N 149.30 W
Chuginadak Island ❙ 180 52.49 N 169.50 W
Chūgoku-sanchi ⛰ 96 34.58 N 132.57 E
Chugwater 200 41.46 N 104.49 W
Chugwater Creek ≃ 198 42.07 N 104.51 W
Chugyo-ri 271b 37.39 N 126.50 E
Chūhar Kāna 123 31.45 N 73.48 E
Chuhe 100 34.03 N 113.35 E
Chuhuichupa 232 29.38 N 108.22 W
Chuí 252 33.41 S 53.27 W
Chuius Mountain ∧ 182 54.51 N 124.30 W
Chukai 114 4.15 N 103.25 E
Chukchi Sea ⊤[2] 16 69.00 N 171.00 W
Chukehu ◎ 120 31.40 N 88.00 E
Chukou 100 25.44 N 113.22 E
Chulakeaganhe ≃ 120 36.35 N 92.20 E
Chulalongkorn University ♉[2] 269a 13.44 N 100.33 E
Chula Vista 228 32.39 N 117.05 W
Chuld 102 45.03 N 105.32 E
Chullora 274a 33.54 S 151.04 E
Chulmleigh 42 50.55 N 3.52 W
Chulo 84 41.41 N 42.18 E
Chulp'o 98 35.37 N 126.40 E
Chulucanas 248 5.06 S 80.10 W
Chulumani 248 16.24 S 67.31 W
Chuluota 220 28.38 N 81.10 W
Chuma 248 15.24 S 68.56 W
Chumaerhe ≃ 120 34.39 N 95.00 E
Chumalag 84 43.14 N 44.28 E
Chumbicha 252 28.52 S 66.14 W
Chum Phae 110 16.32 N 102.06 E
Chumphon 110 10.30 N 99.10 E
Chumphon Buri 110 15.21 N 103.24 E
Chumpi 248 15.06 S 73.46 W
Chum Saeng 110 15.54 N 100.19 E
Chumunjin 98 37.54 N 128.49 E
Chunal 262 53.25 N 1.57 W
Chunan, T'aiwan 100 24.41 N 120.52 E
Chun'an, Zhg. 100 29.35 N 118.58 E
Chuncheon → Ch'unch'ŏn 98 37.52 N 127.43 E
Chunchi, Ec. 246 2.17 S 78.55 W
Chunchi, Zhg. 100 27.22 N 119.20 E
Ch'unch'ŏn 98 37.52 N 127.43 E
Chunchula 194 30.55 N 88.12 W
Chūnd 123 31.26 N 72.17 E
Chungang University ♉[2] 271b 37.30 N 126.58 E
Chungari 89 50.21 N 138.12 E
Chungari ≃ 89 50.04 N 136.55 E
Ch'ungch'ŏng Namdo □[4] 98 36.30 N 127.00 E
Ch'ungch'ŏng Pukdo □[4] 98 36.45 N 128.00 E
Chunggang-ni 98 40.52 N 127.20 E
Chungho 269d 25.00 N 121.29 E
Chunghwa 98 38.52 N 125.47 E
Ch'ungju 98 36.58 N 127.58 E
Chungking → Chongqing 107 29.39 N 106.34 E
Chungli 100 24.57 N 121.13 E
Chungliao 100 22.40 N 121.30 E
Ch'ungmu 98 34.51 N 128.25 E
Chungp'u 100 23.25 N 120.31 E
Chungp'yŏngjang 98 41.11 N 128.03 E
Chungsam-ni 98 38.34 N 127.09 E
Chŭngsan 98 39.06 N 125.22 E
Chungshan → Zhongshan 100 22.31 N 113.22 E
Chungshan Bridge ◆[5] 269d 25.05 N 121.31 E
Chunguj ≃ 88 48.51 N 93.32 E
Chungyang Shanmo ⛰ 100 23.30 N 121.00 E
Chunheji 100 32.12 N 115.22 E
Chunhua, Zhg. 102 34.50 N 108.31 E
Chunhua, Zhg. 106 31.56 N 118.56 E
Chunhuás 232 19.12 N 88.55 W
Chūniān 123 30.58 N 73.59 E
Chuntuquí 232 17.31 N 90.09 W
Chünüj ≃ 88 48.48 N 102.00 E
Chunya 154 8.32 S 33.25 E
Ch'unyang, Taehan 98 36.56 N 128.54 E
Chunyang, Zhg. 89 43.24 N 129.24 E
Chunzach 84 42.33 N 46.43 E
Chunze 124 29.51 N 88.41 E
Chūō 96 35.00 N 133.58 E

PORTUGUÊS — Nome / Página / Lat. / Long. W=Oeste

Chuŏr Phnum Krâvanh ⛰ 110 12.00 N 103.15 E
Chuosijia 102 31.55 N 102.08 E
Chupaca 248 12.04 S 75.19 W
Chupadera Arroyo ∨ 200 33.47 N 106.37 W
Chupadero, Cerro ∧ 200 31.01 N 111.37 W
Chupaderos 234 23.50 N 102.20 W
Chupara Point ≻ 241r 10.48 N 61.22 W
Chuquibamba 248 15.50 S 72.39 W
Chuquibambilla 248 14.07 S 72.43 W
Chuquicamata 252 22.19 S 68.56 W
Chuquisaca □[5] 248 20.00 S 64.20 W
Chuquitanta 286d 11.58 S 77.06 W
Chur 58 46.51 N 9.32 E
Churachandpur 120 24.20 N 93.40 E
Churāmankāti 126 23.14 N 89.09 E
Churcampa 248 12.42 S 74.24 W
Church 262 53.45 N 2.24 W
Churchdown 42 51.53 N 2.10 W
Church Hill 208 39.08 N 75.59 W
Churchill, Man., Can. 176 58.46 N 94.10 W
Churchill, Ohio, U.S. 214 41.09 N 80.39 W
Churchill, Pa., U.S. 279b 40.27 N 79.51 W
Churchill, Va., U.S. 284c 38.54 N 77.10 W
Churchill ≃, Can. 176 58.47 N 94.12 W
Churchill ≃, Newf., Can. 176 53.30 N 60.10 W
Churchill, Cape ≻ 176 58.46 N 93.12 W
Churchill, Mount ∧, B.C., Can. 182 49.58 N 123.51 W
Churchill, Mount ∧, Alaska, U.S. 180 61.25 N 141.43 W
Churchill Downs ♠ 218 38.12 N 85.46 W
Churchill Falls ↳ 176 53.35 N 64.27 W
Churchill Lake ◎ 184 55.55 N 108.20 W
Churchill National Park ♠ 169 37.58 S 145.17 E
Church of the Nativity ♉[1] 132 31.43 N 35.12 E
Church Point 194 30.24 N 92.13 W
Church Rock 200 35.46 N 108.35 W
Church Street 260 51.26 N 0.28 E
Church Stretton 42 52.32 N 2.49 W
Churchton 208 38.48 N 76.32 W
Churchtown, Eng., U.K. 262 53.40 N 2.58 W
Churchtown, Pa., U.S. 208 40.08 N 75.58 W
Church View 208 37.41 N 76.41 W
Churchville, Ont., Can. 275b 43.38 N 79.45 W
Churchville, Md., U.S. 208 39.34 N 76.15 W
Churchville, N.Y., U.S. 210 43.06 N 77.53 W
Churchville, Pa., U.S. 285 40.11 N 75.01 W
Churchyn ≃ 88 48.37 N 110.42 E
Churdan 198 42.09 N 94.29 W
Churen Himāl ∧ 124 28.44 N 83.12 E
Churfirsten ∧ 58 47.08 N 9.17 E
Churia Range ⛰ 124 27.40 N 83.40 E
Churintzio 234 20.09 N 102.04 W
Chürmen 102 43.20 N 104.10 E
Churmuli 89 51.00 N 136.50 E
Churn ≃ 42 51.38 N 1.53 W
Churn Creek ≃ 182 51.30 N 122.17 W
Churnet ≃ 42 52.55 N 1.50 W
Churni ≃[1] 126 23.28 N 88.44 E
Chursdorf 54 50.46 N 12.15 E
Churu 120 28.18 N 74.57 E
Churu □[5] 123 28.45 N 74.50 E
Churubusco, Ind., U.S. 216 41.14 N 85.19 W
Churubusco, N.Y., U.S. 206 44.57 N 73.56 W
Churuguara 246 10.49 N 69.32 W
Churumuco 234 18.37 N 101.38 W
Churwalden 58 46.47 N 9.33 E
Chušenga 88 51.27 N 110.55 E
Chushālgarh 123 33.30 N 71.54 E
Chushan 100 23.46 N 120.41 E
Chushui ≃ 100 26.02 N 113.09 E
Chuska Mountains ⛰ 200 36.15 N 108.50 W
Chuska Peak ∧ 200 35.53 N 108.50 W
Chusovoy → Čusovoj 86 58.17 N 57.49 E
Chust 78 48.10 N 23.18 E
Chūta 174m 26.32 N 127.58 E
Chutag 88 49.23 N 102.43 E
Chutag-Uul 102 43.22 N 110.20 E
Chute-à-Blondeau 206 45.35 N 74.29 W
Chute-Panet 206 46.51 N 71.51 W
Chutor-Michajlovskij 78 52.03 N 33.56 E
Chutorskoj 80 46.52 N 42.59 E
Chutu ≃ 89 49.27 N 140.02 E
Chutung 100 24.44 N 121.06 E
Chuwang 98 36.02 N 114.52 E
Chuwei 269d 25.08 N 121.27 E
Chuxian 100 32.19 N 118.17 E
Chuxiong 102 25.02 N 101.30 E
Chuy 252 33.41 S 53.27 W
Chužar 88 52.49 N 99.54 E
Chuzhai 100 33.22 N 113.37 E
Chužir 88 53.11 N 107.20 E
Chūzu 94 35.06 N 136.00 E
Chvalynsk 80 52.30 N 48.07 E
Chvančkara 84 42.34 N 43.01 E
Chvastoviči 76 53.28 N 35.06 E
Chvatovka 80 52.21 N 46.34 E
Chvojnaja 76 58.54 N 34.32 E
Chvorost'anka 80 52.36 N 48.59 E
Chwefru ≃ 42 52.09 N 3.25 W
Ch'wiya-ri 98 38.03 N 125.32 E
Chypre → Cyprus □[1] 130 35.00 N 33.00 E
Chyrov 78 49.33 N 22.49 E
Chyše 60 50.05 N 13.15 E
Ciago 64 46.12 N 12.46 E
Ciales 240m 18.20 N 66.28 W
Ciampino 66 41.48 N 12.36 E
Ciampino, Aeroporto di ⊠ 267a 41.48 N 12.36 E
Cianciana 70 37.31 N 13.26 E
Ciandur 115a 6.24 S 105.59 E
Cianjur 115a 6.49 S 107.08 E
Ciano d'Enza 64 44.36 N 10.24 E
Cianorte 255 23.37 S 52.37 W
Çians, Gorges du ∨ 62 43.57 N 6.59 E
Čiatura 84 42.17 N 43.17 E
Ciavolo 70 37.46 N 12.33 E
Çiba 107 29.07 N 105.55 E
Čibargata 85 41.08 N 69.48 E
Cibecue 200 34.03 N 110.29 W
Cibiana 64 46.23 N 12.17 E
Čibisovka 78 50.47 N 40.05 E
Čibižek 86 54.27 N 93.40 E
Cibolo Creek ≃ 196 29.34 N 104.24 W
Cibuta 200 31.04 N 110.54 W
Cicagna 62 44.25 N 9.14 E
Çicala 68 39.01 N 16.29 E
Čićarija ⛰ 36 45.30 N 13.54 E
Čičatka 89 54.03 N 121.18 E
Cicciano 44 40.58 N 14.32 E
Cicero, Ill., U.S. 216 41.51 N 87.45 W
Cicero, Ind., U.S. 218 40.08 N 86.01 W
Cicero, N.Y., U.S. 210 43.10 N 76.07 W
Cicero Creek ≃ 194 40.01 N 86.01 W
Cícero Dantas 250 10.36 S 38.23 W
Čichačovo, S.S.S.R. 76 57.17 N 29.54 E
Čichačovo, S.S.S.R. 89 51.50 N 141.07 E
Čichareši 84 42.48 N 43.03 E
Ciche, Sgurr na ∧ 46 57.01 N 5.27 W
Çichengzhen 100 30.00 N 121.22 E
Čičikleja ≃ 78 47.23 N 31.34 E
Cicladas, Islas de la → Kikládhes ‖ 38 37.30 N 25.00 E
Cicolano ◆[1] 66 42.12 N 13.12 E
Cidacos ≃ 34 42.21 N 1.38 W
Cidade, Rio da ≃ 256 22.25 S 43.09 W
Cidade Universitária ♉[2], Bra. 287a 22.52 S 43.14 W
Cidade Universitária ♉[2], Bra. 287b 23.33 S 46.43 W
Cide 130 41.54 N 33.00 E
Cidra 240m 18.11 N 66.10 W
Cidra, Lago de ◎[1] 240m 18.12 N 66.08 W
Ciechanów 30 52.53 N 20.38 E
Ciechanowiec 30 52.42 N 22.31 E
Ciechocinek 30 52.52 N 18.49 E
Ciego de Avila 240p 21.51 N 78.46 W
Ciego de Avila □[4] 240p 22.00 N 78.40 W
Ciempozuelos 34 40.10 N 3.37 W
Ciénaga 246 11.01 N 74.15 W
Ciénaga de Oro 246 8.53 N 75.37 W
Ciénega de Flores 196 25.57 N 100.11 W
Cienfuegos 240p 22.09 N 80.27 W
Cienfuegos □[4] 240p 22.10 N 80.25 W
Cienfuegos, Bahía de ⊂ 240p 22.07 N 80.29 W
Cieplice Śląskie-Zdrój 30 50.52 N 15.41 E
Čierna [nad Tisou] 30 48.25 N 22.05 E
Čierny Balog 30 48.45 N 19.40 E
Cíes, Islas ‖ 34 42.13 N 8.54 W
Cieszanów 30 50.16 N 23.08 E
Cieszyn 30 49.45 N 18.38 E
Cieza 34 38.14 N 1.25 W
Çiftalan 267b 41.15 N 28.54 E
Çiftehan 130 37.31 N 34.46 E
Çifteler 130 39.22 N 31.03 E
Çiftlik, Tür. 130 38.11 N 34.30 E
Çiftlik, Tür. 130 40.08 N 39.27 E
Cifuentes, Cuba 240p 22.39 N 80.03 W
Cifuentes, Esp. 34 40.47 N 2.37 W
Čiganak, S.S.S.R. 80 51.47 N 43.18 E
Čiganak, S.S.S.R. 86 45.06 N 73.58 E
Čiganaki 80 47.57 N 43.05 E
Čigirin 78 49.04 N 32.40 E
Cigliano 62 45.18 N 8.01 E
Čigorak 80 51.26 N 42.09 E
Cigou 100 33.51 N 113.35 E
Cigüela ≃ 34 39.08 N 3.44 W
Cihangir 130 40.03 N 29.07 E
Cihara 115a 6.52 S 106.06 E
Cihe ≃ 100 33.27 N 115.31 E
Cihuatlán 234 19.14 N 104.35 W
Čiili 86 44.10 N 66.45 E
Cijara, Embalse de ◎[1] 34 39.18 N 4.52 W
Čijen 85 43.08 N 75.55 E
Čijirčik, Pereval)(85 40.15 N 73.20 E
Čijli ≃ 85 40.17 N 72.38 E
Čik 86 55.01 N 82.27 E
Čikan 88 54.54 N 105.39 E
Čikan ≃ 88 54.54 N 105.40 E
Čikišl'ar 128 37.34 N 53.55 E
Čikoj 88 50.16 N 106.54 E
Čikoj ≃ 88 51.02 N 106.39 E
Čikola 84 43.12 N 43.55 E
Cikou 100 29.42 N 114.46 E
Ciksı 130 38.30 N 40.55 E
Cilacap 115a 7.44 S 109.00 E
Çilader 130 41.02 N 37.06 E
Cilamaya 115a 6.15 S 107.35 E
Cilavegna 62 45.19 N 8.44 E
Çıldır 84 41.08 N 43.07 E
Çıldır Gölü ◎ 84 41.04 N 43.15 E
Čilekovo 80 47.50 N 43.30 E
Cilento ⛰ 68 40.17 N 15.19 E
Çilento ◆[1] 36 40.15 N 15.10 E
Čil'gazi 85 40.10 N 70.39 E
Çili 102 29.17 N 111.00 E
Čilik, S.S.S.R. 85 43.36 N 78.15 E
Čilik, S.S.S.R. 86 51.07 N 54.07 E
Čilik ≃ 85 43.05 N 78.28 E
Cill Áirne → Killarney 48 51.53 N 9.30 W
Cill Choinnigh → Kilkenny 48 52.39 N 7.15 W
Cilleruelo de Bezana 34 42.58 N 3.51 W
Cil'ma ≃ 24 65.27 N 52.06 E
Cimabanche (Schluderbach) 64 46.37 N 12.11 E
Cima Gogna 64 46.31 N 12.28 E
Cimahi 115a 6.53 S 107.32 E
Cimalmotto 58 46.17 N 8.29 E
Cimarron, Kans., U.S. 198 37.48 N 100.21 W
Cimarron, N. Mex., U.S. 200 36.31 N 104.55 W
Cimarron ≃, U.S. 196 36.10 N 96.17 W
Cimarron ≃, N. Mex., U.S. 196 36.20 N 104.31 W
Cimarron, North Fork ≃ 198 37.25 N 101.13 W
Čimbaj 86 42.57 N 59.47 E
Čimčinej, Gora ∧[2] 180 63.37 N 178.04 E
Cimetière, Pointe du ≻ 241o 15.58 N 61.19 W
Cimini, Monti ⛰ 66 42.20 N 12.10 E
Ciminna 70 37.54 N 13.34 E
Çimino, Monte ∧ 66 42.24 N 12.12 E
Čimion 85 40.16 N 71.31 E
Čimišlija 78 46.32 N 28.44 E
Çimitile 68 40.56 N 14.31 E
Čimkent 85 42.18 N 69.36 E
Čimkent □[4] 85 42.30 N 68.00 E
Čimkorgon 85 42.50 N 75.30 E
Cimla ≃ 80 48.01 N 42.24 E
Ciml'ansk 80 47.38 N 42.04 E
Ciml'anskoje Vodochranilišče ◎[1] 80 48.00 N 43.00 E
Cimolais 64 46.17 N 12.26 E
Cimone, Monte ∧ 64 44.12 N 10.42 E
Cîmpeni 38 46.22 N 23.03 E
Cîmpia Turzii 38 46.33 N 23.54 E
Cîmpina 38 45.08 N 25.44 E
Cîmpulung 38 45.16 N 25.03 E
Cîmpulung Moldovenesc 38 47.31 N 25.34 E
Čina ≃ 88 54.20 N 112.24 E
Çina, Tanjung ≻ 112 5.56 S 104.45 E
Činabad 85 40.52 N 71.58 E
Činadijevo 78 48.30 N 22.50 E
Cinandali 84 41.53 N 45.34 E
Çınar 130 37.44 N 40.25 E
Çınarcık 130 40.39 N 29.06 E
Çinaruco ≃ 246 6.41 N 67.07 W
Činaz 85 40.56 N 68.45 E
Cinca ≃ 34 41.26 N 0.21 E
Cincar ∧ 36 43.54 N 17.04 E
Cincinnati, Iowa, U.S. 190 40.38 N 92.56 W
Cincinnati, Ohio, U.S. 218 39.06 N 84.31 W
Cincinnatus 210 42.33 N 75.54 W
Cinco Balas, Cayos ‖ 240p 21.06 N 79.20 W
Cinco de Mayo 196 25.46 N 104.19 W
Cinco de Outubro 152 9.34 S 17.50 E
Cinco Palos, Sierra ⛰ 234 22.40 N 99.36 W
Cinco Pinos 236 13.14 N 86.52 W
Cinco Saltos 252 38.49 S 68.04 W
Cinderella 273d 26.15 S 28.16 E
Cinderella Dam ◆[6] 273d 26.15 S 28.14 E
Cinderford 42 51.50 N 2.29 W
Cinder Island ❙ 276 40.36 N 73.36 W
Çine 130 37.36 N 28.04 E
Cinebar 224 46.36 N 122.32 W
Cinema 182 53.11 N 122.30 W
Ciney 56 50.18 N 5.06 E
Cingaly 86 60.13 N 69.45 E
Cingife 130 37.20 N 37.33 E
Čingikan, Gora ∧ 88 52.32 N 114.27 E
Čingis 86 54.08 N 81.41 E
Čingistaj 86 49.13 N 85.55 E
Cingoli 66 43.22 N 13.13 E
Cinigiano 66 42.53 N 11.24 E
Cinisello Balsamo 266b 45.33 N 9.13 E
Činišeucy 78 47.42 N 28.52 E
Cinisi 70 38.09 N 13.06 E
Činja-Voryk 24 63.13 N 52.38 E
Cinkota ◆[8] 264c 47.31 N 19.14 E
Cínovec 54 50.43 N 13.45 E
Cinq, Lac des ◎ 206 46.51 N 72.59 W
Cinq-Doigts, Lac ◎ 206 46.36 N 74.32 W
Cinquefrondi 68 38.25 N 16.06 E
Cinquemiglia, Piano delle ☷ 66 41.50 N 14.00 E
Cinqueterre □[9] 62 44.10 N 9.45 E
Cintalapa ≃ 234 16.41 N 93.36 W
Cintalapa de Figueroa 234 16.44 N 93.43 W
Cinto, Monte ∧ 36 42.23 N 8.56 E
Cinto Euganeo 64 45.16 N 11.40 E
Cintra → Sintra 34 38.48 N 9.23 W
Cintra, Golfo de ⊂ 148 23.00 N 16.20 W
Cinzas, Rio das ≃ 252 22.56 S 50.32 W
Ciocănești 38 44.12 N 27.04 E
Ciociaria ◆[1] 66 41.45 N 13.15 E
Çiomas 115a 6.12 S 106.01 E
Čiovo, Otok ❙ 36 43.30 N 16.20 E
Cipa ≃ 88 55.23 N 115.55 E
Ciparay 115a 7.03 S 107.43 E
Cipatujah 115a 7.45 S 108.00 E
Cipikan 88 54.55 N 113.21 E
Cipikan ≃ 88 55.14 N 113.05 E
Cipó 250 11.06 S 38.31 W
Cipó ≃ 255 18.40 S 43.59 W
Cipolândia 255 20.08 S 55.24 W
Cipolletti 252 38.56 S 67.59 W
Çiqikou 107 29.35 N 106.26 E
Čir 80 48.29 N 43.10 E
Čir ≃ 80 48.35 N 42.51 E
Čirachčaj ≃ 84 41.40 N 48.11 E
Čiragidzor 84 40.27 N 46.19 E
Circeo, Monte ∧ 66 41.14 N 13.03 E
Circeo, Parco Nazionale del ♠ 66 41.17 N 13.05 E
Čirčik 85 41.29 N 69.35 E
Čirčik ≃ 85 40.54 N 68.41 E
Çırçır 130 40.04 N 36.48 E
Circle, Alaska, U.S. 180 65.50 N 144.04 W
Circle, Mont., U.S. 202 47.25 N 105.35 W
Circle Hot Springs 180 65.28 N 144.39 W
Circleville, N.Y., U.S. 210 41.31 N 75.23 W
Circleville, Ohio, U.S. 218 39.36 N 82.57 W
Circleville, Pa., U.S. 279b 40.20 N 79.44 W
Circleville, Utah, U.S. 200 38.10 N 112.16 W
Circular Reef ✢[2] 164 3.25 S 147.47 E
Circus World ♠ 220 28.14 N 81.38 W
Cirebon 115a 6.44 S 108.34 E
Cireglio 66 43.59 N 10.51 E
Ciremay, Gunung ∧ 115a 6.54 S 108.24 E
Cirencester 42 51.44 N 1.59 W
Çirey-sur-Vezouze 58 48.35 N 6.57 E
Čirgalandy 88 50.36 N 97.20 E
Ciriè 62 45.14 N 7.36 E
Çirigliano 68 40.24 N 16.10 E
Čirikovo 82 55.23 N 37.14 E
Ciriquiri ≃ 248 8.05 S 65.18 W
Cirk, Gora ∧ 180 64.33 N 175.25 E
Cîrlibaba 38 47.35 N 25.07 E
Ciró 68 39.23 N 17.04 E
Çiró Marina 68 39.22 N 17.08 E
Čirpan 38 42.12 N 25.20 E
Ciruas 115a 6.06 S 106.13 E
Cisa, Passo della)(64 44.28 N 9.55 E
Cisano 64 45.32 N 10.43 E
Cisarua 115a 6.40 S 106.59 E
Cisco, Ill., U.S. 219 40.01 N 88.43 W
Cisco, Tex., U.S. 196 32.23 N 98.59 W
Cishan 98 36.37 N 114.07 E
Cislago 62 45.39 N 8.58 E
Cisliano 266b 45.27 N 8.59 E
Çismar 54 54.11 N 10.59 E
Čismena 82 56.02 N 36.13 E
Cismon ≃ 64 46.55 N 11.43 E
Çismon del Grappa 64 45.55 N 11.44 E
Čišmy 86 54.35 N 55.20 E
Cisnădie 38 45.43 N 24.09 E
Cisne 194 38.31 N 88.26 W
Cisneros 246 6.33 N 75.04 W
Cisnes ≃ 254 44.45 S 72.42 W
Cisolok 115a 6.57 S 106.26 E
Cison di Valmarino 64 45.58 N 12.10 E
Cispus ≃ 224 46.25 N 122.10 W
Cisse ≃ 50 47.25 N 0.47 E
Çissna Park 216 40.34 N 87.54 W
Čistá 54 50.03 N 12.42 E
Cisterna di Latina 66 41.35 N 12.49 E
Cisternino 68 40.44 N 17.25 E
Cistern Point ≻ 238 23.43 N 77.35 W
Cistierna 34 42.48 N 5.07 W
Čistoje 80 56.32 N 43.02 E
Čistooz'ornoje 86 54.43 N 76.33 E
Čistopol' 80 55.21 N 50.37 E
Čistopolje, S.S.S.R. 83 47.31 N 39.27 E
Čistopolje, S.S.S.R. 86 52.34 N 67.15 E
Čistovodovka 83 49.24 N 37.20 E
Čita 88 52.03 N 113.30 E
Čita □[4] 88 52.00 N 117.00 E
Citac, Nevado ∧ 248 12.50 S 75.15 W
Citaré ≃ 250 1.11 N 54.41 W
Citeli-Ckaro 84 41.28 N 46.07 E
Cité Universitaire ♉[2] 261 48.49 N 2.20 E
Citlaltépetl, Volcán (Pico de Orizaba) ∧[1] 234 19.01 N 97.16 W
Citra 192 29.25 N 82.06 W
Citronelle 194 31.06 N 88.14 W
Citrus □[6] 220 28.52 N 82.28 W
Citrusdal 158 32.36 S 19.00 E
Citrus Heights 226 38.42 N 121.17 W
Citrus Springs 220 29.00 N 82.27 W
Citrus Tower ♉ 220 28.33 N 81.44 W
Cittadella 64 45.39 N 11.47 E
Città della Pieve 66 42.57 N 12.00 E
Città del Vaticano → Vatican City □[1] 267a 41.54 N 12.27 E
Città di Castello 66 43.27 N 12.14 E
Cittaducale 66 42.23 N 12.57 E
Cittanova 68 38.21 N 16.05 E
Cittareale 66 42.37 N 13.10 E
Città Sant'Angelo 66 42.31 N 14.03 E
Città Universitaria ♉[2] 267a 41.55 N 12.31 E
City Beach 168a 31.56 S 115.45 E
City Bell ◆[8] 258 34.52 S 58.05 W
City College of New York ♉[2] 276 40.49 N 73.57 W
City Island ◆[8] 276 40.51 N 73.47 W
City Mills 283 42.07 N 71.21 W
City of Commerce 280 33.59 N 118.08 W
City of Hope ♉ 280 34.08 N 117.58 W
City Of Industry 280 34.01 N 117.57 W
City of London ◆[8] 260 51.31 N 0.05 W
City of Refuge National Historical Park ♠ 229d 19.25 N 155.54 W
City of Westminster ◆[8] 260 51.30 N 0.09 W
City Point 220 28.24 N 80.45 W
Ciucaș ∧ 38 45.31 N 25.55 E
Ciudad 234 23.44 N 105.42 W
Ciudad Acuña 232 29.18 N 100.55 W
Ciudad Altamirano 234 18.20 N 100.40 W
Ciudad Anáhuac 232 27.14 N 100.09 W
Ciudad Barrios 236 13.46 N 88.16 W
Ciudad Bolívar 246 8.08 N 63.33 W
Ciudad Bolivia 246 8.21 N 70.34 W
Ciudad Camargo, Méx. 232 26.19 N 98.50 W
Ciudad Camargo, Méx. 232 27.40 N 105.10 W
Ciudad Chetumal 232 18.30 N 88.18 W
Ciudad Darío 236 12.43 N 86.08 W
Ciudad de Guayana → Ciudad Guayana 246 8.22 N 62.40 W
Ciudad de la Habana □[4] 240p 23.08 N 82.22 W
Ciudad del Cabo → Cape Town 158 33.55 S 18.22 E
Ciudad del Carmen 232 18.38 N 91.50 W
Ciudad del Maíz 234 22.24 N 99.36 W
Ciudad de los Deportes ♠ 286a 19.23 N 99.11 W
Ciudad del Vaticano → Vatican City □[1] 267a 41.54 N 12.27 E
Ciudad de México 234
286a 19.24 N 99.09 W
Ciudad de Naucalpan de Juárez 286a 19.28 N 99.14 W
Ciudad Deportiva ♠, Cuba 286b 23.07 N 82.22 W
Ciudad Deportiva ♠, Méx. 286a 19.24 N 99.06 W
Ciudad de Valles 234 21.59 N 99.01 W
Ciudad de Villaldama 232 26.30 N 100.26 W
Ciudadela 34 40.02 N 3.50 E
Ciudadela, Parque de la ♠ 266d 41.23 N 2.11 E
Ciudad General Belgrano 288 34.43 S 58.32 W
Ciudad Guayana 246 8.22 N 62.40 W
Ciudad Guerrero 232 28.33 N 107.30 W
Ciudad Guzmán 234 19.41 N 103.29 W
Ciudad Hidalgo, Méx. 234 19.41 N 100.34 W
Ciudad Hidalgo, Méx. 236 14.41 N 92.09 W
Ciudad Ixtepec 234 16.34 N 95.06 W
Ciudad Jiménez 232 27.08 N 104.55 W
Ciudad Juárez 232 31.44 N 106.29 W
Ciudad Lerdo 196 25.32 N 103.32 W
Ciudad Lineal ◆[8] 266a 40.27 N 3.40 W
Ciudad López Mateos 286a 19.33 N 99.15 W
Ciudad Madero 234 22.16 N 97.50 W
Ciudad Mante 234 22.44 N 98.57 W
Ciudad Manuel Doblado 234 20.44 N 101.56 W
Ciudad Melchor Múzquiz 232 27.53 N 101.31 W
Ciudad Mendoza 234 18.48 N 97.11 W
Ciudad Mier 232 26.26 N 99.09 W
Ciudad Miguel Alemán 232 26.23 N 99.01 W
Ciudad Morelos 232 32.38 N 114.52 W
Ciudad Obregón 232 27.29 N 109.56 W
Ciudad Ocampo 234 22.50 N 99.20 W
Ciudad Ojeda (Lagunillas) 246 10.12 N 71.19 W
Ciudad Piar 246 7.27 N 63.19 W
Ciudad Real 34 38.59 N 3.56 W
Ciudad Rodrigo 34 40.36 N 6.32 W
Ciudad Sahagún 234 19.47 N 98.33 W
Ciudad Santos 234 21.36 N 98.58 W
Ciudad Serdán 234 18.59 N 97.27 W
Ciudad Tecún Umán 236 14.40 N 92.09 W
Ciudad Trujillo → Santo Domingo 238 18.28 N 69.54 W
Ciudad Universitaria ◆[8] 266a 40.27 N 3.44 W
Ciudad Universitaria ♉[2], Esp. 266a 40.27 N 3.43 W
Ciudad Universitaria ♉[2], Méx. 286a 19.20 N 99.11 W
Ciudad Universitaria ♉[2], Ven. 286c 10.29 N 66.53 W
Ciudad Victoria, Méx. 204 32.20 N 115.06 W
Ciudad Victoria, Méx. 234 23.44 N 99.08 W
Ciudad Vieja 236 14.31 N 90.46 W
Ciuma 152 13.14 S 15.40 E
Ciurana ≃ 34 41.08 N 0.39 E
Civate 62 45.50 N 9.21 E
Civenna 58 45.56 N 9.16 E
Civetta, Monte ∧ 64 46.23 N 12.03 E
Civezzano 64 46.05 N 11.11 E
Cividale del Friuli 64 46.06 N 13.25 E
Cividate al Piano 62 45.33 N 9.50 E
Cividate Camuno 64 45.57 N 10.17 E
Civil' ≃ 80 56.08 N 47.35 E
Civil'sk 80 55.53 N 47.29 E
Civita 68 39.49 N 16.18 E
Civitacampomarano 66 41.47 N 14.41 E
Civita Castellana 66 42.17 N 12.25 E
Civita di Bagno 66 42.18 N 13.26 E
Civitanova Alta 66 43.19 N 13.40 E
Civitanova del Sannio 66 41.40 N 14.24 E
Civitanova Marche 66 43.18 N 13.44 E
Civitaquana 66 42.19 N 13.54 E
Civitavecchia 66 42.06 N 11.48 E
Civitella del Tronto 66 42.46 N 13.40 E
Civitella di Romagna 66 44.00 N 11.56 E
Civitella in Val di Chiana 66 43.25 N 11.43 E
Civitella Marittima 66 43.00 N 11.17 E
Civitella Roveto 66 41.54 N 13.25 E
Civray 32 46.09 N 0.18 E
Çivril 130 38.18 N 29.45 E
Čivyrkujskij Zaliv ⊂ 88 53.45 N 109.10 E
Cixerri ≃ 71 39.17 N 8.59 E
Cixi 100 30.11 N 121.15 E
Çiyutuo 104 41.31 N 122.53 E
Čiža 24 67.06 N 44.19 E
Čiža Vtoraja 80 50.52 N 49.40 E
Cize 58 46.12 N 5.26 E
Cizhuping 107 29.11 N 103.36 E
Çizre 130 37.20 N 42.12 E
Čkalov → Orenburg 86 51.54 N 55.06 E
Čkalovo, S.S.S.R. 78 46.28 N 34.11 E
Čkalovo, S.S.S.R. 86 53.38 N 70.24 E
Čkalovsk 80 56.46 N 43.16 E
Čkalovskij 265b 55.54 N 38.04 E
Ç K Creek ≃ 202 47.36 N 108.29 W
Čkyně 60 49.07 N 13.49 E
Čl'a, Ozero ◎ 89 53.27 N 140.03 E
Clachan 46 55.45 N 5.34 W
Clackamas 224 45.25 N 122.34 W
Clackamas □[6] 224 45.10 N 122.16 W
Clackamas ≃ 224 45.22 N 122.36 W
Clackamas, Oak Grove Fork ≃ 224 45.05 N 122.03 W
Clackamas Heights 224 45.23 N 122.34 W
Clackline 168a 31.43 S 116.31 E
Clackmannan 46 56.06 N 3.46 W
Clacton-on-Sea 42 51.48 N 1.09 E
Cladich 46 56.21 N 5.05 W
Claerwen ≃ 42 52.44 N 3.37 W
Claerwen Reservoir ◎[1] 42 52.17 N 3.43 W
Claflin 198 38.31 N 98.32 W
Claiborne 194 31.32 N 87.31 W
Clain ≃ 32 46.47 N 0.32 E
Claire, Lake ◎ 176 58.30 N 112.00 W
Claire, Pointe ≻ 275a 45.25 N 73.50 W
Clair Engle Lake ◎[1] 204 40.52 N 122.43 W
Claireville 275b 43.45 N 79.38 W
Claireville Reservoir ◎[1] 275b 43.44 N 79.39 W
Clairfontaine-en-Yvelines 50 48.37 N 1.55 E
Clairis ≃ 50 48.07 N 2.45 E
Clairmarais 50 50.46 N 2.18 E
Clairmont 182 55.16 N 118.47 W
Clairton 214 40.18 N 79.53 W
Clairvaux-les-Lacs 58 46.34 N 5.45 E
Claix 62 45.07 N 5.40 E
Clallam □[6] 224 48.10 N 123.49 W
Clallam Bay 224 48.15 N 124.16 W
Clam ≃, Mich., U.S. 190 44.05 N 85.00 W
Clam ≃, Wis., U.S. 190 45.57 N 92.33 W
Clam, North Fork ≃ 190 45.46 N 92.18 W
Clamart 261 48.48 N 2.16 E
Clamecy 50 47.27 N 3.31 E
Clam Gulch 180 60.15 N 151.22 W
Clam Lake ◎ 184 55.19 N 105.43 W
Clampton 162 29.56 S 119.06 E
Clan Alpine Mountains ⛰ 204 39.40 N 117.55 W
Clandonald 182 53.34 N 110.44 W

Symbol	English	Deutsch	Español	Français	Português
≃	River	Fluss	Río	Rivière	Rio
≋	Canal	Kanal	Canal	Canal	Canal
↳	Waterfall, Rapids	Wasserfall, Stromschnellen	Cascada, Rápidos	Chute d'eau, Rapides	Cascata, Rápidos
⋓	Strait	Meeresstrasse	Estrecho	Détroit	Estreito
⊂	Bay, Gulf	Bucht, Golf	Bahía, Golfo	Baie, Golfe	Baía, Golfo
◎	Lake, Lakes	See, Seen	Lago, Lagos	Lac, Lacs	Lago, Lagos
☷	Swamp	Sumpf	Pantano	Marais	Pântano
⩍	Ice Features, Glacier	Eis- und Gletscherformen	Accidentes Glaciales	Formes glaciaires	Acidentes Glaciares
⊤	Other Hydrographic Features	Andere Hydrographische Objekte	Otros Elementos Hidrográficos	Autres données hydrographiques	Outros Elementos Hidrográficos
✢	Submarine Features	Untermeerische Objekte	Accidentes Submarinos	Formes de relief sous-marin	Acidentes Submarinos
□	Political Unit	Politische Einheit	Unidad Politica	Entité politique	Unidade Política
♉	Cultural Institution	Kulturelle Institution	Institución Cultural	Institution culturelle	Instituição Cultural
⊥	Historical Site	Historische Stätte	Sitio Histórico	Site historique	Sítio Histórico
♠	Recreational Site	Erholungs- und Ferienort	Sitio de Recreo	Centre de loisirs	Sítio de Lazer
⊠	Airport	Flughafen	Aeropuerto	Aéroport	Aeroporto
■	Military Installation	Militäranlage	Instalación Militar	Installation militaire	Instalação Militar
◆	Miscellaneous	Verschiedenes	Misceláneo	Divers	Miscelânea

Name	Page	Lat.°′	Long.°′
Clandon Park ♠	**260**	51.15 N	0.30 W
Clandulla	**170**	32.55 S	149.57 E
Clane	**48**	53.18 N	6.41 W
Clans	**62**	44.00 N	7.09 E
Clanton	**194**	32.50 N	86.38 W
Clanwilliam	**158**	32.11 S	18.54 E
Claonaig	**46**	55.46 N	5.22 W
Clapperton Island I	**190**	46.02 N	82.13 W
Clapp Farm	**214**	41.24 N	79.32 W
Clàr, Loch nan ⊜	**46**	58.17 N	4.08 W
Clara, Arg.	**252**	31.50 S	58.49 W
Clara, Eire	**48**	53.20 N	7.36 W
Clara, Miss., U.S.	**194**	31.35 N	88.42 W
Clara ≃	**166**	18.30 S	141.18 E
Clara City	**198**	44.57 N	95.22 W
Clara Island I	**110**	10.54 N	97.55 E
Claraville	**166**	18.40 S	141.43 E
Claraz	**252**	37.54 S	59.17 W
Clare, Austl.	**166**	33.25 S	143.55 E
Clare, Austl.	**168b**	33.50 S	138.36 E
Clare, Eng., U.K.	**42**	52.25 N	0.35 E
Clare, Mich., U.S.	**190**	43.49 N	84.46 W
Clare □[6]	**48**	52.50 N	9.00 W
Clare ≃, Ont., Can.	**212**	44.28 N	77.17 W
Clare ≃, Eire	**48**	53.20 N	9.03 W
Clarecastle	**48**	52.49 N	8.57 W
Claregalway	**48**	53.21 N	8.57 W
Clare Island I	**48**	53.48 N	10.00 W
Claremont, Ont., Can.	**212**	43.58 N	79.07 W
Claremont, Eng., U.K.	**260**	51.21 N	0.22 W
Claremont, Calif., U.S.	**228**	34.06 N	117.43 W
Claremont, N.H., U.S.	**188**	43.23 N	72.20 W
Claremont, S. Dak., U.S.	**198**	45.40 N	98.01 W
Claremont, Va., U.S.	**208**	37.14 N	76.58 W
Claremont ∧	**204**	39.53 N	120.57 W
Claremont Colleges ʊ[2]	**280**	34.06 N	117.44 W
Claremore	**196**	36.19 N	95.36 W
Claremorris	**48**	53.44 N	9.00 W
Clarence, N.Z.	**172**	42.10 S	173.56 E
Clarence, Ill., U.S.	**216**	40.28 N	87.58 W
Clarence, Iowa, U.S.	**190**	41.53 N	91.04 W
Clarence, Mo., U.S.	**219**	39.44 N	92.16 W
Clarence, N.Y., U.S.	**210**	42.59 N	78.35 W
Clarence, Pa., U.S.	**214**	41.03 N	77.56 W
Clarence ≃, Austl.	**166**	29.25 S	153.22 E
Clarence ≃, N.Z.	**172**	42.10 S	173.57 E
Clarence, Isla I	**254**	54.10 S	71.50 W
Clarence, Port ⊂	**180**	65.15 N	166.40 W
Clarence Cannon Lake ⊜[1]	**219**	39.30 N	91.45 W
Clarence Center	**210**	43.00 N	78.35 W
Clarence Creek	**206**	45.30 N	75.13 W
Clarence E. Hancock Airport ⊠	**212**	43.07 N	76.07 W
Clarence Fahnestook Memorial State Park ♠	**210**	41.26 N	73.50 W
Clarence Island I	**9**	61.09 S	54.06 W
Clarence J. Brown Reservoir ⊜[1]	**218**	39.58 N	83.44 W
Clarence Strait ⩌, Austl.	**164**	12.00 S	131.00 E
Clarence Strait ⩌, Alaska, U.S.	**180**	55.25 N	132.00 W
Clarence Town, Austl.	**170**	32.35 S	151.47 E
Clarence Town, Ba.	**238**	23.06 N	74.59 W
Clarenceville, Qué., Can.	**206**	45.04 N	73.15 W
Clarenceville, Mich., U.S.	**281**	42.27 N	83.19 W
Clarendon, Austl.	**168b**	35.07 S	138.38 E
Clarendon, Ark., U.S.	**194**	34.42 N	91.18 W
Clarendon, N.Y., U.S.	**210**	43.11 N	78.04 W
Clarendon, Pa., U.S.	**214**	41.47 N	79.06 W
Clarendon, Tex., U.S.	**196**	34.56 N	100.53 W
Clarendon Hills	**278**	41.48 N	87.59 W
Clarens	**158**	28.30 S	28.29 E
Clarenville	**186**	48.10 N	53.58 W
Claresholm	**182**	50.02 N	113.35 W
Claret	**62**	43.52 N	3.54 E
Clarholz	**52**	51.54 N	8.11 E
Claridge	**214**	40.22 N	79.37 W
Clarie Coast ●[2]	**9**	66.30 S	133.00 E
Clarin	**116**	9.58 N	124.01 E
Clarinda	**198**	40.44 N	95.02 W
Clarines	**246**	9.56 N	65.10 W
Clarington	**214**	41.20 N	79.07 W
Clarion, Iowa, U.S.	**190**	42.44 N	93.44 W
Clarion, Pa., U.S.	**214**	41.13 N	79.24 W
Clarion □[6]	**214**	41.13 N	79.24 W
Clarion ≃	**214**	41.07 N	79.41 W
Clarión, Isla I	**232**	18.22 N	114.44 W
Clarion, West Branch ≃	**214**	41.29 N	78.41 W
Clarion Fracture Zone ✢	**16**	19.00 N	122.00 W
Clarissa	**198**	46.08 N	94.57 W
Clark, N.J., U.S.	**276**	40.38 N	74.19 W
Clark, Ohio, U.S.	**214**	40.27 N	81.54 W
Clark, S. Dak., U.S.	**198**	44.53 N	97.44 W
Clark, Tex., U.S.	**222**	30.23 N	94.46 W
Clark □[6], Ind., U.S.	**218**	38.17 N	85.44 W
Clark □[6], Ohio, U.S.	**218**	39.56 N	83.49 W
Clark □[6], Wash., U.S.	**224**	45.48 N	122.31 W
Clark, Lake ⊜	**180**	60.15 N	154.15 W
Clark, Mount ∧	**180**	64.25 N	124.12 W
Clark, Point ≻	**190**	44.04 N	81.45 W
Clark Air Base ▪	**116**	15.11 N	120.32 E
Clark Branch ≃	**285**	39.43 N	74.45 W
Clark Creek ≃, Kans., U.S.	**198**	39.05 N	96.42 W
Clark Creek ≃, Pa., U.S.	**208**	40.22 N	76.58 W
Clarkdale	**200**	34.46 N	112.03 W
Clarke ≃	**166**	19.12 S	145.30 E
Clarke City	**186**	50.12 N	66.38 W
Clarke Island I	**166**	40.33 S	148.10 E
Clarke Lake ⊜	**184**	54.25 N	106.51 W
Clarke Range ⩚	**166**	20.50 S	148.33 E
Clarke River	**166**	19.13 S	145.27 E
Clarkfield	**198**	44.48 N	95.48 W
Clark Fork	**202**	48.08 N	116.11 W
Clark Fork ≃	**202**	48.09 N	116.15 W
Clark Hill	**218**	38.18 N	83.12 W
Clark Hill Lake ⊜[1]	**192**	33.50 N	82.20 W
Clarklake	**216**	42.04 N	84.21 W
Clark Lake ⊜	**216**	42.07 N	84.19 W
Clark Mills	**210**	43.06 N	75.22 W
Clark Mountain ∧, Calif., U.S.	**204**	35.32 N	115.35 W
Clark Mountain ∧, Wash., U.S.	**224**	48.03 N	120.57 W
Clarks, La., U.S.	**194**	32.02 N	92.08 W
Clarks, Nebr., U.S.	**198**	41.13 N	97.50 W
Clarks ≃	**194**	37.03 N	88.33 W
Clarks, West Fork ≃	**194**	36.59 N	88.31 W
Clarksboro	**285**	39.48 N	75.14 W
Clarksburg, Ont., Can.	**212**	44.43 N	80.27 W
Clarksburg, Calif., U.S.	**226**	38.25 N	121.32 W
Clarksburg, Ill., U.S.	**219**	39.20 N	88.44 W
Clarksburg, Ind., U.S.	**218**	39.26 N	85.21 W
Clarksburg, Md., U.S.	**208**	39.14 N	77.17 W
Clarksburg, N.J., U.S.	**208**	40.12 N	74.27 W
Clarksburg, Ohio, U.S.	**218**	39.30 N	83.09 W
Clarksburg, W. Va., U.S.	**188**	39.17 N	80.21 W
Clarksburg State Park ♠	**207**	42.43 N	73.06 W
Clarks Creek ≃, Ky., U.S.	**218**	38.40 N	84.44 W
Clarks Creek ≃, Tex., U.S.	**222**	29.11 N	96.53 W
Clarksdale	**194**	34.12 N	90.34 W
Clarks Green	**210**	41.30 N	75.42 W
Clark's Harbour	**186**	43.26 N	65.38 W
Clarks Hill	**216**	40.15 N	86.43 W
Clarks Island I	**283**	42.01 N	70.38 W
Clarks Mills	**214**	41.24 N	80.11 W
Clarkson, Ont., Can.	**275b**	43.31 N	79.37 W
Clarkson, Ky., U.S.	**194**	37.30 N	86.13 W
Clarkson, N.Y., U.S.	**210**	43.14 N	77.56 W
Clarks Point	**180**	58.51 N	158.30 W
Clarks Summit	**210**	41.30 N	75.42 W
Clarkston	**216**	42.44 N	83.25 W
Clark's Town	**241q**	18.25 N	77.34 W
Clarksville, Ark., U.S.	**194**	35.28 N	93.28 W
Clarksville, Del., U.S.	**208**	38.33 N	75.09 W
Clarksville, Ind., U.S.	**218**	38.17 N	85.45 W
Clarksville, Iowa, U.S.	**190**	42.47 N	92.40 W
Clarksville, Md., U.S.	**208**	39.13 N	76.57 W
Clarksville, Mich., U.S.	**216**	42.50 N	85.15 W
Clarksville, Mo., U.S.	**219**	39.22 N	90.54 W
Clarksville, N.Y., U.S.	**210**	42.35 N	73.58 W
Clarksville, Ohio, U.S.	**218**	39.24 N	83.59 W
Clarksville, Tenn., U.S.	**194**	36.32 N	87.21 W
Clarksville, Tex., U.S.	**196**	33.37 N	95.03 W
Clarksville, Va., U.S.	**192**	36.37 N	78.34 W
Clarksville City	**222**	32.32 N	94.34 W
Clarkton, Mo., U.S.	**194**	36.27 N	89.58 W
Clarkton, N.C., U.S.	**192**	34.29 N	78.39 W
Claro ≃, Bra.	**255**	19.06 S	47.52 W
Claro ≃, Bra.	**255**	19.08 S	50.40 W
Claro ≃, Bra.	**255**	15.28 S	51.43 W
Claro, Arroyo ≃	**288**	34.25 S	58.41 W
Claro, Ribeirão ≃	**287b**	23.40 S	46.17 W
Clary	**50**	50.05 N	3.24 E
Claryville	**210**	41.55 N	74.34 W
Clashmore	**48**	52.00 N	7.48 W
Clatskanie	**224**	46.06 N	123.12 W
Clatskanie ≃	**224**	46.08 N	123.14 W
Clatsop □[6]	**224**	46.01 N	123.41 W
Clatteringshaws Lake ⊜	**44**	55.05 N	4.17 W
Claude	**196**	35.07 N	101.22 W
Claudy	**44**	54.54 N	7.09 W
Claughton	**44**	54.06 N	2.40 W
Claussnitz	**54**	50.56 N	12.53 E
Clausthal-Zellerfeld	**52**	51.48 N	10.20 E
Claver	**116**	9.35 N	125.44 E
Claverack	**210**	42.13 N	73.44 W
Claveria, Pil.	**116**	18.37 N	121.05 E
Claveria, Pil.	**116**	8.38 N	124.55 E
Clavet	**184**	52.00 N	106.23 W
Clavey ≃	**226**	37.52 N	120.07 W
Clavos, Laguna de ⊜	**196**	27.37 N	104.52 W
Clawit, Mount ∧	**116**	16.58 N	120.58 E
Clawson	**222**	31.24 N	94.47 W
Claxton	**192**	32.10 N	81.55 W
Clay, Ky., U.S.	**194**	37.29 N	87.49 W
Clay, Tex., U.S.	**222**	30.23 N	96.21 W
Clay, W. Va., U.S.	**188**	38.28 N	81.05 W
Clay □[6]	**219**	38.45 N	88.40 W
Claybank Creek ≃	**194**	31.10 N	85.44 W
Clay Center, Kans., U.S.	**198**	39.23 N	97.08 W
Clay Center, Nebr., U.S.	**198**	40.32 N	98.03 W
Clay Center, Ohio, U.S.	**214**	41.34 N	83.22 W
Clay City, Ill., U.S.	**194**	38.41 N	88.21 W
Clay City, Ind., U.S.	**194**	39.17 N	87.07 W
Clay City, Ky., U.S.	**192**	37.52 N	83.55 W
Clay Creek ≃	**198**	38.06 N	102.31 W
Clay Cross	**44**	53.10 N	1.24 W
Claydon	**42**	52.06 N	1.07 E
Claye-Souilly	**50**	48.57 N	2.42 E
Claygate	**260**	51.22 N	0.20 W
Claygate Cross	**260**	51.16 N	0.19 E
Clayhole Wash ∨	**200**	36.59 N	113.17 W
Clayhurst	**182**	56.15 N	120.01 W
Claymont	**208**	39.48 N	75.28 W
Clayoquot Sound ⩌	**182**	49.11 N	126.08 W
Claypole	**288**	34.48 S	58.20 W
Claypool, Ariz., U.S.	**200**	33.25 N	110.51 W
Claypool, Ind., U.S.	**216**	41.08 N	85.53 W
Claysburg	**214**	40.18 N	78.27 W
Clay Springs	**200**	34.22 N	110.18 W
Claysville	**214**	40.07 N	80.25 W
Clayton, Austl.	**274b**	37.56 S	145.07 E
Clayton, Eng., U.K.	**262**	53.47 N	1.52 W
Clayton, Ala., U.S.	**194**	31.53 N	85.27 W
Clayton, Calif., U.S.	**282**	37.57 N	121.56 W
Clayton, Del., U.S.	**208**	39.17 N	75.38 W
Clayton, Ga., U.S.	**192**	34.53 N	83.23 W
Clayton, Ill., U.S.	**219**	40.02 N	90.57 W
Clayton, Ind., U.S.	**218**	39.41 N	86.31 W
Clayton, Mich., U.S.	**216**	41.52 N	84.14 W
Clayton, Mo., U.S.	**219**	38.39 N	90.20 W
Clayton, N.J., U.S.	**208**	39.39 N	75.06 W
Clayton, N. Mex., U.S.	**196**	36.27 N	103.11 W
Clayton, N.C., U.S.	**192**	35.39 N	78.28 W
Clayton, N.Y., U.S.	**212**	44.14 N	76.05 W
Clayton, Okla., U.S.	**196**	34.35 N	95.21 W
Clayton, Tex., U.S.	**222**	32.06 N	94.28 W
Clayton ≃	**166**	29.06 S	138.05 E
Claytonia	**214**	41.00 N	79.58 W
Clayton-le-Moors	**262**	53.47 N	2.23 W
Clayton-le-Woods	**262**	53.41 N	2.38 W
Clayton Valley ∨	**282**	37.58 N	121.58 W
Claytonville	**216**	40.34 N	87.49 W
Clay Village	**218**	38.11 N	85.07 W
Clayville	**210**	42.59 N	75.15 W
Clear ≃	**182**	56.11 N	119.42 W
Clear, Cape ≻, Eire	**48**	51.24 N	9.30 W
Clear, Cape ≻, Alaska, U.S.	**180**	59.48 N	147.54 W
Clear, Lake ⊜	**212**	45.26 N	77.12 W
Clear, Mount ∧	**171b**	35.52 S	149.04 E
Clear Boggy Creek ≃	**196**	34.03 N	95.47 W
Clearbrook, B.C., Can.	**224**	49.08 N	122.26 W
Clearbrook, Minn., U.S.	**198**	47.42 N	95.26 W
Clear Creek	**218**	39.07 N	86.32 W
Clear Creek ≃, Ala., U.S.	**194**	34.00 N	87.19 W
Clear Creek ≃, Ariz., U.S.	**200**	34.59 N	110.38 W
Clear Creek ≃, Calif., U.S.	**204**	40.31 N	122.22 W
Clear Creek ≃, Calif., U.S.	**280**	34.17 N	118.12 W
Clear Creek ≃, Calif., U.S.	**282**	37.20 N	122.21 W
Clear Creek ≃, Colo., U.S.	**200**	39.50 N	104.57 W
Clear Creek ≃, Ky., U.S.	**218**	38.10 N	85.17 W
Clear Creek ≃, Mo., U.S.	**194**	38.00 N	93.56 W
Clear Creek ≃, Mont., U.S.	**202**	48.46 N	109.25 W
Clear Creek ≃, Nebr., U.S.	**198**	41.08 N	99.06 W
Clear Creek ≃, Ohio, U.S.	**218**	39.33 N	84.20 W
Clear Creek ≃, Oreg., U.S.	**224**	45.23 N	122.29 W
Clear Creek ≃, Oreg., U.S.	**224**	45.09 N	121.31 W
Clear Creek ≃, Tenn., U.S.	**192**	36.05 N	84.42 W
Clear Creek ≃, Tex., U.S.	**196**	33.16 N	97.03 W
Clear Creek ≃, Tex., U.S.	**222**	29.09 N	97.23 W
Clear Creek ≃, Tex., U.S.	**222**	29.33 N	95.05 W
Clear Creek ≃, Wash., U.S.	**224**	46.07 N	122.00 W
Clear Creek ≃, Wyo., U.S.	**202**	44.53 N	106.04 W
Clear Creek State Park ♠	**214**	41.20 N	79.05 W
Clearfield, Iowa, U.S.	**198**	40.48 N	94.29 W
Clearfield, Ky., U.S.	**218**	38.10 N	83.26 W
Clearfield, Pa., U.S.	**214**	41.02 N	78.27 W
Clearfield, Utah, U.S.	**200**	41.07 N	112.01 W
Clearfield □[6]	**214**	41.02 N	78.27 W
Clearfield Creek ≃	**214**	41.02 N	78.24 W
Clear Fork Reservoir ⊜[1]	**214**	40.42 N	82.38 W
Clearing ◆[8]	**278**	41.47 N	87.47 W
Clear Island I	**48**	51.26 N	9.30 W
Clear Lake, Iowa, U.S.	**190**	43.08 N	93.23 W
Clear Lake, S. Dak., U.S.	**198**	44.45 N	96.41 W
Clearlake, Wash., U.S.	**224**	48.28 N	122.14 W
Clear Lake, Wis., U.S.	**190**	45.15 N	92.16 W
Clear Lake ⊜, Man., Can.	**184**	50.42 N	100.00 W
Clear Lake ⊜, Ont., Can.	**212**	44.59 N	79.33 W
Clear Lake ⊜, Ont., Can.	**212**	44.30 N	78.13 W
Clear Lake ⊜, Ont., Can.	**212**	45.14 N	79.57 W
Clear Lake ⊜, Ind., U.S.	**216**	41.44 N	84.50 W
Clear Lake ⊜[1], Calif., U.S.	**204**	39.02 N	122.50 W
Clear Lake ⊜[1], La., U.S.	**194**	31.55 N	93.05 W
Clearlake Highlands	**226**	38.57 N	122.38 W
Clearlake Oaks	**226**	39.07 N	122.40 W
Clearlake Park	**226**	38.58 N	122.39 W
Clear Lake Reservoir ⊜[1]	**204**	41.52 N	121.08 W
Clear Lake Shores	**222**	29.33 N	95.02 W
Clearmont	**202**	44.38 N	106.23 W
Clear Run	**214**	41.08 N	78.45 W
Clear Site	**180**	64.19 N	149.11 W
Clearview, Ohio, U.S.	**214**	41.25 N	82.10 W
Clearview, Wash., U.S.	**224**	47.45 N	122.06 W
Clearview, W. Va., U.S.	**214**	40.09 N	80.41 W
Clearview Estates	**279b**	40.34 N	80.16 W
Clearwater, B.C., Can.	**182**	51.38 N	120.02 W
Clearwater, Man., Can.	**184**	49.08 N	99.01 W
Clearwater, Fla., U.S.	**220**	27.58 N	82.48 W
Clearwater, Kans., U.S.	**198**	37.30 N	97.30 W
Clearwater, Nebr., U.S.	**198**	42.10 N	98.11 W
Clearwater, Wash., U.S.	**224**	47.35 N	124.17 W
Clearwater ≃, Can.	**184**	56.44 N	111.23 W
Clearwater ≃, Alta., Can.	**182**	52.23 N	114.50 W
Clearwater ≃, B.C., Can.	**182**	51.42 N	120.00 W
Clearwater ≃, Idaho, U.S.	**202**	46.25 N	117.02 W
Clearwater ≃, Minn., U.S.	**198**	47.54 N	96.16 W
Clearwater ≃, Mont., U.S.	**202**	46.58 N	113.23 W
Clearwater ≃, Wash., U.S.	**224**	47.33 N	124.21 W
Clearwater, Middle Fork ≃	**202**	46.09 N	115.59 W
Clearwater, North Fork ≃	**202**	46.30 N	116.19 W
Clearwater, South Fork ≃	**202**	46.09 N	115.59 W
Clear Water Bay ⊂	**271d**	22.17 N	114.18 E
Clearwater Beach Island I	**220**	27.59 N	82.49 W
Clearwater Lake ⊜, B.C., Can.	**182**	52.15 N	120.13 W
Clearwater Lake ⊜, Man., Can.	**184**	54.05 N	101.00 W
Clearwater Mountains ⩚	**202**	46.00 N	115.30 W
Clearwater Provincial Park ♠	**184**	54.03 N	101.10 W
Cleator Moor	**44**	54.31 N	3.30 W
Clebit	**196**	34.21 N	94.52 W
Cleburne	**222**	32.21 N	97.23 W
Clee Hills ⩚[2]	**42**	52.25 N	2.35 W
Cle Elum	**224**	47.12 N	120.56 W
Cle Elum ≃	**224**	47.11 N	121.01 W
Cle Elum Lake ⊜[1]	**224**	47.18 N	121.06 W
Cleethorpes	**44**	53.34 N	0.02 W
Cleeve Cloud ∧[2]	**42**	51.34 N	2.00 W
Clefmont	**58**	48.06 N	5.31 E
Cleggan	**48**	53.33 N	10.09 W
Clelles	**62**	44.50 N	5.37 E
Clementon	**285**	39.49 N	74.59 W
Clementsport	**186**	44.40 N	65.37 W
Clemson	**192**	34.41 N	82.50 W
Clemville	**222**	29.00 N	96.08 W
Clendenin	**188**	38.29 N	81.21 W
Clendening Lake ⊜[1]	**214**	40.16 N	81.13 W
Clenze	**54**	52.56 N	10.58 E
Cleobury Mortimer	**42**	52.23 N	2.29 W
Cleona	**208**	40.20 N	76.29 W
Cléon-d'Andran	**62**	44.37 N	4.56 E
Cleopatra Needle ∧	**116**	10.07 N	118.58 E
Clères	**50**	49.36 N	1.07 E
Clerke Rocks II[1]	**244**	55.01 S	34.41 W
Clermont, Austl.	**166**	22.49 S	147.39 E
Clermont, Qué., Can.	**186**	47.41 N	70.14 W
Clermont, Fr.	**50**	49.23 N	2.24 E
Clermont, Fla., U.S.	**220**	28.33 N	81.46 W
Clermont, N.J., U.S.	**285**	39.59 N	74.48 W
Clermont, Pa., U.S.	**214**	41.41 N	78.29 W
Clermont □[6]	**218**	39.05 N	84.11 W
Clermont-en-Argonne	**56**	49.06 N	5.04 E
Clermont-Ferrand	**32**	45.47 N	3.05 E
Clermont State Park ♠	**210**	42.05 N	73.55 W
Clerval	**58**	47.24 N	6.30 E
Clervaux	**56**	50.04 N	6.01 E
Cléry-Saint-André	**50**	47.49 N	1.45 E
Cles	**64**	46.22 N	11.02 E
Cleve	**166**	33.42 S	136.30 E
Clevedon	**42**	51.27 N	2.51 W
Cleveland, Austl.	**171a**	27.32 S	153.17 E
Cleveland, Ala., U.S.	**194**	33.59 N	86.35 W
Cleveland, Fla., U.S.	**220**	26.57 N	82.00 W
Cleveland, Ga., U.S.	**192**	34.36 N	83.46 W
Cleveland, Miss., U.S.	**194**	33.45 N	90.50 W
Cleveland, N.C., U.S.	**192**	35.44 N	80.40 W
Cleveland, N.Y., U.S.	**210**	43.14 N	75.53 W
Cleveland, Ohio, U.S.	**214** / **279a**	41.30 N	81.41 W
Cleveland, Okla., U.S.	**196**	36.19 N	96.28 W
Cleveland, Tenn., U.S.	**194**	35.10 N	84.53 W
Cleveland, Tex., U.S.	**222**	30.21 N	95.05 W
Cleveland, Va., U.S.	**192**	36.57 N	82.09 W
Cleveland □[6]	**44**	54.35 N	1.15 W
Cleveland, Cape ≻	**166**	19.11 S	147.01 E
Cleveland, Mount ∧, Austl.	**166**	41.25 S	145.23 E
Cleveland, Mount ∧, Mont., U.S.	**202**	48.56 N	113.51 W
Cleveland Heights	**214**	41.30 N	81.34 W
Cleveland Hills ⩚[2]	**44**	54.23 N	1.05 W
Cleveland-Hopkins International Airport ⊠	**279a**	41.25 N	81.51 W
Clevelândia	**252**	26.24 S	52.21 W
Clevelândia do Norte	**250**	3.49 N	51.52 W
Cleveland Museum of Art ʊ	**279a**	41.31 N	81.37 W
Cleveland National Forest ♠	**280**	33.47 N	117.38 W
Cleveland Park ◆[8]	**284c**	38.56 N	77.04 W
Cleveland Peninsula ≻[1]	**182**	55.45 N	132.00 W
Cleveland Pond ⊜	**283**	42.07 N	70.58 W
Cleveland State University ʊ[2]	**279a**	41.30 N	81.40 W
Cleveland Zoo ♠	**279a**	41.27 N	81.43 W
Cleveleys	**44**	53.53 N	3.03 W
Cleversburg	**208**	40.02 N	77.28 W
Cleves → Kleve, B.R.D.	**52**	51.48 N	6.09 E
Cleves, Ohio, U.S.	**218**	39.10 N	84.45 W
Clew Bay ⊂	**48**	53.50 N	9.50 W
Clewiston	**220**	26.45 N	80.56 W
Cley next the Sea	**42**	52.58 N	1.03 E
Clichy	**50**	48.54 N	2.18 E
Clichy-sous-Bois	**261**	48.55 N	2.33 E
Clifden	**48**	53.29 N	10.01 W
Clifden Bay ⊂	**48**	53.28 N	10.05 W
Cliffdale Creek ≃	**166**	16.56 S	138.48 E
Cliffdell	**224**	46.44 N	120.42 W
Cliffe	**260**	51.28 N	0.30 E
Cliffe Marshes ≋	**260**	51.28 N	0.30 E
Cliffe Woods	**260**	51.26 N	0.30 E
Clifford, Ont., Can.	**212**	43.58 N	80.58 W
Clifford, S. Afr.	**158**	31.04 S	27.28 E
Clifford, Ind., U.S.	**218**	39.17 N	85.52 W
Clifford, Pa., U.S.	**210**	41.39 N	75.36 W
Clifford Park ♠	**274b**	37.43 S	145.16 E
Cliffside	**210**	42.31 N	74.59 W
Cliffside Park	**276**	40.49 N	73.59 W
Cliffwood	**276**	40.26 N	74.14 W
Cliffwood Beach	**276**	40.27 N	74.14 W
Clifton, Austl.	**171a**	27.56 S	151.54 E
Clifton, Eng., U.K.	**262**	53.46 N	2.49 W
Clifton, Ariz., U.S.	**200**	33.03 N	109.18 W
Clifton, Ill., U.S.	**216**	40.56 N	87.56 W
Clifton, Kans., U.S.	**198**	39.34 N	97.17 W
Clifton, N.J., U.S.	**210**	40.53 N	74.08 W
Clifton, N.Y., U.S.	**210**	43.03 N	77.49 W
Clifton, Oreg., U.S.	**224**	46.12 N	123.27 W
Clifton, Tenn., U.S.	**194**	35.23 N	88.01 W
Clifton, Tex., U.S.	**222**	31.47 N	97.35 W
Clifton, Lake ⊜	**168a**	32.49 S	115.41 E
Clifton Court Forebay ⊜[1]	**226**	37.50 N	121.35 W
Clifton Forge	**192**	37.49 N	79.49 W
Clifton Gorge ∨	**42**	51.28 N	2.37 W
Clifton Heights	**285**	39.56 N	75.18 W
Clifton Hills	**166**	26.52 S	138.50 E
Clifton Knolls	**210**	42.52 N	73.46 W
Clifton Park ♠	**284b**	39.19 N	76.35 W
Clifton Point ≻	**240b**	25.01 N	77.34 W
Clifton Springs	**210**	42.58 N	77.08 W
Clifty, Mount ∧	**224**	47.07 N	121.10 W
Clifty Creek ≃	**218**	39.09 N	85.54 W
Clifty Falls State Park ♠	**218**	38.45 N	85.26 W
Clignon ≃	**50**	49.07 N	3.04 E
Climax, Sask., Can.	**184**	49.13 N	108.23 W
Climax, Colo., U.S.	**200**	39.22 N	106.11 W
Climax, Ga., U.S.	**192**	30.53 N	84.26 W
Climax, Mich., U.S.	**216**	42.14 N	85.20 W
Climax, Pa., U.S.	**214**	40.59 N	79.23 W
Clinch ≃	**192**	35.53 N	84.29 W
Clinchco	**192**	37.10 N	82.22 W
Clingen	**54**	51.14 N	10.55 E
Clingmans Dome ∧	**192**	35.35 N	83.30 W
Clint	**200**	31.35 N	106.14 W
Clinton, B.C., Can.	**182**	51.05 N	121.35 W
Clinton, Ont., Can.	**190**	43.37 N	81.32 W
Clinton, N.Z.	**172**	46.12 S	169.22 E
Clinton, Ala., U.S.	**194**	32.55 N	88.00 W
Clinton, Ark., U.S.	**194**	35.36 N	92.28 W
Clinton, Conn., U.S.	**207**	41.17 N	72.32 W
Clinton, Ill., U.S.	**219**	40.09 N	88.57 W
Clinton, Ind., U.S.	**194**	39.40 N	87.24 W
Clinton, Iowa, U.S.	**190**	41.51 N	90.12 W
Clinton, Ky., U.S.	**194**	36.40 N	89.02 W
Clinton, La., U.S.	**194**	30.52 N	91.01 W
Clinton, Maine, U.S.	**188**	44.38 N	69.30 W
Clinton, Md., U.S.	**208**	38.46 N	76.54 W
Clinton, Mass., U.S.	**207**	42.25 N	71.41 W
Clinton, Mich., U.S.	**216**	42.04 N	83.58 W
Clinton, Minn., U.S.	**198**	45.28 N	96.26 W
Clinton, Miss., U.S.	**194**	32.20 N	90.20 W
Clinton, Mo., U.S.	**194**	38.22 N	93.46 W
Clinton, N.J., U.S.	**210**	40.38 N	74.55 W
Clinton, N.C., U.S.	**192**	35.00 N	78.20 W
Clinton, N.Y., U.S.	**210**	43.03 N	75.23 W
Clinton, Ohio, U.S.	**214**	40.56 N	81.42 W
Clinton, Okla., U.S.	**196**	35.31 N	98.59 W
Clinton, Pa., U.S.	**214**	40.29 N	80.18 W
Clinton, S.C., U.S.	**192**	34.29 N	81.53 W
Clinton, Tenn., U.S.	**192**	36.06 N	84.08 W
Clinton, Tex., U.S.	**222**	33.06 N	96.14 W
Clinton, Wash., U.S.	**224**	47.59 N	122.22 W
Clinton, Wis., U.S.	**216**	42.34 N	88.52 W
Clinton □[6], Ill., U.S.	**219**	38.37 N	89.22 W
Clinton □[6], Ind., U.S.	**216**	40.17 N	86.31 W
Clinton □[6], Mich., U.S.	**216**	42.56 N	84.36 W
Clinton □[6], N.Y., U.S.	**206**	44.57 N	73.42 W
Clinton □[6], Ohio, U.S.	**218**	39.27 N	83.50 W
Clinton □[6], Pa., U.S.	**210**	41.08 N	71.26 W
Clinton ≃	**214**	42.36 N	82.48 W
Clinton, Cape ≻	**166**	22.32 S	150.47 E
Clinton, Middle Branch ≃	**281**	42.36 N	82.54 W
Clinton, North Branch ≃	**214**	42.36 N	82.54 W
Clinton-Colden Lake ⊜	**176**	63.58 N	107.27 W
Clintondale	**210**	41.01 N	77.29 W
Clinton Park	**210**	42.36 N	73.43 W
Clinton Reservoir ⊜[1]	**276**	41.05 N	74.27 W
Clinton Township	**214**	42.33 N	82.53 W
Clintonville, Mich., U.S.	**281**	42.43 N	83.22 W
Clintonville, Pa., U.S.	**214**	41.12 N	79.53 W
Clintonville, Wis., U.S.	**190**	44.37 N	88.46 W
Clintwood	**192**	37.09 N	82.27 W
Clio, Ala., U.S.	**194**	31.43 N	85.36 W
Clio, Mich., U.S.	**190**	43.11 N	83.44 W
Clio, S.C., U.S.	**192**	34.35 N	79.33 W
Clipperton I[1]	**230**	10.17 N	109.13 W
Clipperton Fracture Zone ✢	**16**	10.00 N	112.00 W
Clisham ∧	**46**	57.57 N	6.49 W
Clisson	**32**	47.05 N	1.17 W
Clitheroe	**44**	53.53 N	2.23 W
Clitunno ≃	**66**	42.56 N	12.37 E
Clive, Austl.	**166**	22.46 S	149.18 E
Clive, N.Z.	**172**	39.35 S	176.55 E
Cliza	**248**	17.36 S	65.56 W
Cloates, Point ≻	**162**	22.43 S	113.40 E
Clock Face	**262**	53.25 N	2.43 W
Clocolan	**158**	29.00 S	27.30 E
Clodomira	**252**	27.35 S	64.08 W
Cloe	**214**	40.56 N	78.56 W
Cloete	**196**	27.55 N	101.10 W
Cloghan, Eire	**48**	53.13 N	7.53 W
Cloghan, Eire	**48**	54.51 N	7.56 W
Cloghane	**48**	52.13 N	10.12 W
Clogheen	**48**	52.16 N	8.00 W
Clogher	**48**	54.25 N	7.12 W
Clogher Head ≻	**48**	53.48 N	6.12 W
Cloghjordan	**48**	52.57 N	8.02 W
Cloisters ʊ	**276**	40.52 N	73.56 W
Clonakilty	**48**	51.37 N	8.54 W
Clonakilty Bay ⊂	**48**	51.35 N	8.50 W
Cloncurry	**166**	20.42 S	140.30 E
Cloncurry ≃	**166**	18.37 S	140.40 E
Clondalkin	**48**	53.19 N	6.24 W
Clonee	**48**	53.25 N	6.26 W
Clones	**48**	54.11 N	7.15 W
Clonfert	**48**	53.14 N	8.05 W
Clonmacnois ⊥	**48**	53.20 N	7.59 W
Clonmany	**48**	55.14 N	7.25 W
Clonmel	**48**	52.21 N	7.42 W
Clonroche	**48**	52.27 N	6.43 W
Clontarf	**274a**	33.48 S	151.16 E
Cloone	**48**	53.57 N	7.46 W
Clo-oose	**182**	48.40 N	124.49 W
Cloppenburg	**52**	52.50 N	8.02 E
Cloquallum Creek ≃	**224**	46.58 N	123.24 W
Cloquet	**190**	46.43 N	92.28 W
Cloquet ≃	**190**	46.52 N	92.35 W
Clorinda	**252**	25.17 S	57.43 W
Closter	**276**	40.59 N	73.58 W
Cloudcroft	**200**	32.58 N	105.45 W
Cloud Peak ∧	**202**	44.25 N	107.10 W
Cloudy Bay ⊂	**172**	41.27 S	174.10 E
Cloudy Mountain ∧	**180**	63.11 N	156.05 W
Clough	**48**	54.17 N	5.50 W
Clough Foot	**262**	53.43 N	2.08 W
Clova	**46**	56.50 N	3.06 W
Clova, Glen ∨	**46**	56.49 N	3.04 W
Clove Lakes Park ♠	**276**	40.37 N	74.07 W
Clovelly, Austl.	**274a**	33.55 S	151.16 E
Clovelly, Eng., U.K.	**42**	51.00 N	4.24 W
Clover	**192**	35.07 N	81.14 W
Clover Bank	**210**	42.45 N	78.53 W
Clover Creek ≃	**202**	43.00 N	115.11 W
Cloverdale, B.C., Can.	**224**	49.06 N	122.44 W
Cloverdale, Ala., U.S.	**194**	34.56 N	87.46 W
Cloverdale, Calif., U.S.	**204**	38.48 N	123.01 W
Cloverdale, Ill., U.S.	**278**	41.56 N	88.07 W
Cloverdale, Ind., U.S.	**194**	39.31 N	86.48 W
Cloverdale, Ky., U.S.	**218**	38.10 N	84.53 W
Cloverdale, Mich., U.S.	**216**	42.32 N	85.23 W
Cloverdale, Ohio, U.S.	**216**	41.01 N	84.18 W
Cloverdale, Oreg., U.S.	**224**	45.12 N	123.53 W
Cloverdale Mall ◆[9]	**275b**	43.38 N	79.34 W
Cloverdene	**273d**	26.09 S	28.22 E
Cloverleaf	**222**	29.47 N	95.13 W
Clover Pass	**180**	55.28 N	131.47 W
Cloverport	**194**	37.50 N	86.38 W
Cloverville	**216**	43.11 N	86.10 W
Clovis, Calif., U.S.	**226**	36.49 N	119.42 W
Clovis, N. Mex., U.S.	**196**	34.24 N	103.12 W
Clowbridge Reservoir ⊜[1]	**262**	53.45 N	2.16 W
Clowne	**44**	53.18 N	1.16 W
Cloyes-sur-le-Loir	**50**	48.00 N	1.14 E
Cloyne	**48**	51.51 N	8.08 W
Cluain Meala → Clonmel	**48**	52.21 N	7.42 W
Cluanie, Loch ⊜	**46**	57.07 N	5.05 W
Cluj	**38**	46.47 N	23.36 E
Cluj □[4]	**38**	46.45 N	23.45 E
Clun	**42**	52.26 N	3.00 W
Clun ≃	**42**	52.22 N	2.53 W
Clune	**214**	40.34 N	79.18 W
Clunes	**169**	37.18 S	143.47 E
Clun Forest ◆[3]	**42**	52.28 N	3.07 W
Clunie Water ≃	**46**	57.00 N	3.24 W
Cluny, Austl.	**166**	24.31 S	139.35 E
Cluny, Fr.	**58**	46.26 N	4.39 E
Cluses	**58**	46.04 N	6.36 E
Clusone	**64**	45.53 N	9.57 E
Clute	**222**	29.01 N	95.24 W
Clutha ≃	**172**	46.21 S	169.48 E
Clwyd □[6]	**44**	53.05 N	3.20 W
Clwyd ≃	**44**	53.20 N	3.30 W
Clwyd, Vale of ∨	**44**	53.12 N	3.24 W
Clwydian Range ⩚	**44**	53.10 N	3.20 W
Clydach	**42**	51.43 N	3.50 W
Clyde, Alta., Can.	**182**	54.09 N	113.39 W
Clyde, N.W. Ter., Can.	**176**	70.25 N	68.30 W
Clyde, N.Z.	**172**	45.11 S	169.19 E
Clyde, Calif., U.S.	**226**	38.02 N	122.02 W
Clyde, Kans., U.S.	**198**	39.36 N	97.24 W
Clyde, Mich., U.S.	**281**	42.41 N	83.37 W
Clyde, N.Y., U.S.	**210**	43.05 N	76.52 W
Clyde, Ohio, U.S.	**214**	41.18 N	82.59 W
Clyde, Tex., U.S.	**196**	32.24 N	99.30 W
Clyde ≃, Austl.	**170**	35.23 S	150.15 E
Clyde ≃, N.S., Can.	**186**	43.35 N	65.25 W
Clyde ≃, Ont., Can.	**212**	44.58 N	76.22 W
Clyde ≃, Dom.	**240d**	15.33 N	61.18 W
Clyde ≃, Scot., U.K.	**46**	55.44 N	4.55 W
Clyde ≃, N.Y., U.S.	**210**	43.04 N	77.00 W
Clyde ≃, Vt., U.S.	**188**	44.56 N	72.12 W
Clyde, Firth of ⊂[1]	**46**	55.40 N	5.00 W
Clydebank	**46**	55.54 N	4.24 W
Clydegale Lake ⊜	**212**	45.25 N	78.23 W
Clyde Lake ⊜	**182**	55.18 N	111.28 W
Clyde No.3	**214**	39.59 N	80.03 W
Clyde Park	**202**	45.53 N	110.36 W
Clyde Potts Reservoir ⊜[1]	**276**	40.48 N	74.35 W
Clydesdale	**158**	26.54 S	27.55 E
Clydesdale ∨	**46**	55.42 N	3.50 W
Clymer, N.Y., U.S.	**214**	42.03 N	79.35 W
Clymer, Pa., U.S.	**214**	40.40 N	79.01 W
Clynnog-fawr	**44**	53.01 N	4.23 W
Clywedog ≃, Wales, U.K.	**42**	52.27 N	3.32 W
Clywedog ≃, Wales, U.K.	**42**	53.02 N	2.52 W
Ćmielów	**30**	50.53 N	21.31 E
Cna ≃, S.S.S.R.	**76**	57.33 N	34.36 E
Cna ≃, S.S.S.R.	**76**	52.10 N	27.03 E
Cna ≃, S.S.S.R.	**80**	54.32 N	42.05 E
Cna ≃, S.S.S.R.	**82**	55.25 N	39.10 E
Cnoc Moy ∧[2]	**44**	55.23 N	5.46 W
Côa ≃	**34**	41.05 N	7.06 W
Coacalco □[7]	**286a**	19.37 N	99.06 W
Coacalco de Berriozábal	**286a**	19.37 N	9.05 W
Coachella	**204**	33.41 N	116.10 W
Coachella Canal ⩶	**204**	33.34 N	116.00 W
Coachford	**48**	51.53 N	8.48 W
Coacoyole	**232**	24.31 N	106.34 W
Coacuilco	**234**	21.07 N	98.35 W
Coahoma	**196**	32.18 N	101.18 W
Coahuayana	**234**	18.44 N	103.41 W
Coahuayana, Río de ≃	**234**	18.41 N	103.45 W
Coahuayutla de Guerrero	**234**	18.19 N	101.49 W
Coahuila	**200**	32.12 N	114.59 W
Coahuila □[3]	**232**	27.20 N	102.00 W
Coal ≃	**180**	59.39 N	126.57 W
Coalbrook	**158**	26.51 S	27.53 E
Coalbrookdale	**42**	52.38 N	2.30 W
Coalburg	**214**	41.11 N	80.36 W
Coalburn	**46**	55.36 N	3.54 W
Coal City	**216**	41.17 N	88.17 W
Coalcomán de Matamoros	**234**	18.47 N	103.09 W
Coal Creek	**180**	65.22 N	143.10 W
Coal Creek ≃, Colo., U.S.	**198**	40.30 N	104.26 W
Coal Creek ≃, Ind., U.S.	**194**	39.57 N	87.25 W
Coal Creek ≃, Wash., U.S.	**202**	47.19 N	118.36 W
Coal Creek Flat	**172**	45.29 S	169.18 E
Coaldale, Alta., Can.	**182**	49.43 N	112.37 W
Coaldale, Pa., U.S.	**210**	40.50 N	75.54 W
Coal Fire Creek ≃	**194**	33.15 N	88.18 W
Coal Fork	**188**	38.19 N	81.32 W
Coalgate, N.Z.	**172**	43.29 S	171.58 E
Coalgate, Okla., U.S.	**196**	34.32 N	96.13 W
Coal Grove	**188**	38.30 N	82.39 W
Coal Harbour	**182**	50.36 N	127.35 W
Coal Hill	**194**	35.26 N	93.40 W
Coal Hill Park ♠	**271a**	39.56 N	116.23 E
Coalhurst	**182**	49.45 N	112.56 W
Coalinga	**226**	36.09 N	120.21 W
Coalisland	**48**	54.32 N	6.42 W
Coal Island I	**172**	46.07 S	166.38 E
Coalmont	**182**	49.31 N	120.41 W
Coalpit Heath	**42**	51.32 N	2.28 W
Coalport	**214**	40.45 N	78.32 W
Coal River	**180**	59.45 N	126.55 W
Coal Run ≃	**279b**	40.21 N	80.07 W
Coalspur	**182**	53.11 N	117.01 W
Coalton	**219**	39.17 N	89.19 W
Coaltown	**214**	41.02 N	80.20 W
Coal Valley ∨	**204**	38.56 N	115.25 W
Coalville, S. Afr.	**158**	26.01 S	29.10 E
Coalville, Eng., U.K.	**42**	52.44 S	1.20 W
Coalville, Utah, U.S.	**200**	40.55 N	111.24 W
Coamo	**240m**	18.05 N	66.22 W
Coamo, Lago ⊜[1]	**240m**	18.01 N	66.23 W
Coapilla	**234**	17.08 N	93.10 W
Coaraci	**255**	14.38 S	39.32 W
Coari	**246**	4.05 S	63.08 W
Coari ≃	**246**	4.30 S	63.33 W
Coari, Lago de ⊜	**246**	4.15 S	63.22 W
Coarsegold	**226**	37.16 N	119.42 W
Coast □[4], Kenya	**154**	3.00 N	39.30 E
Coast □[4], Tan.	**154**	7.00 S	39.00 E
Coast Mountains ⩚	**176**	55.00 N	129.00 W
Coast Ranges ⩚	**178**	41.00 N	123.30 W
Coatán ≃	**236**	14.48 N	92.31 W
Coatbridge	**46**	55.52 N	4.01 W
Coatepec	**234**	19.27 N	96.58 W
Coatepec de Harinas	**234**	18.54 N	99.43 W
Coatepeque	**236**	14.42 N	91.52 W
Coatepeque, Lago de ⊜	**236**	13.52 N	89.33 W
Coatepetl, Cerro ∧	**234**	18.25 N	97.35 W
Coates Creek ≃	**212**	44.24 N	79.54 W
Coatesville	**208**	39.59 N	75.49 W
Coaticook	**206**	45.08 N	71.48 W
Coaticook ≃	**206**	45.20 N	71.53 W
Coatsburg	**219**	40.02 N	91.10 W
Coats Island I	**176**	62.30 N	83.00 W
Coats Land ◆[1]	**9**	77.00 S	28.00 W
Coatzacoalcos	**234**	18.09 N	94.25 W
Coatzacoalcos ≃	**234**	18.10 N	94.27 W
Coatzacoalcos, Bahía ⊂	**234**	18.10 N	94.27 W
Coatzintla	**234**	20.29 N	97.27 W
Coayllo	**248**	12.44 S	76.28 W
Coazze	**62**	45.03 N	7.18 E
Cobá ⊥	**232**	20.36 N	87.35 W
Cobadin	**38**	44.04 N	28.13 E
Cobalt, Ont., Can.	**190**	47.24 N	79.41 W
Cobalt, Conn., U.S.	**207**	41.34 N	72.34 W
Cobán	**236**	15.29 N	90.19 W
Çobanlar	**130**	38.41 N	30.47 E
Cobar	**166**	31.30 S	145.49 E
Cobargo	**166**	36.23 S	149.53 E
Cobb	**226**	38.49 N	122.43 W
Cobb Creek ≃	**196**	35.05 N	98.25 W
Cobberas, Mount ∧	**166**	36.52 S	148.10 E
Cobbetts Lake ⊜	**283**	42.48 N	71.17 W
Cobbin's Brook ≃	**260**	51.41 N	0.01 W
Cobb Island	**208**	38.16 N	76.51 W
Cobb Island I, Md., U.S.	**208**	38.16 N	76.51 W
Cobb Island I, Va., U.S.	**208**	37.20 N	75.44 W
Cobbitty	**274a**	34.01 S	150.41 E
Cobbitty ∧[2]	**274a**	33.59 S	150.42 E
Cobble Hill	**224**	48.41 N	123.36 W
Cobble Mountain Reservoir ⊜[1]	**207**	42.08 N	72.55 W
Cobblestone Mountain ∧	**228**	34.37 N	118.52 W
Cobbs Creek ≃	**285**	39.54 N	75.15 W
Cobbs Creek Park ♠	**285**	39.58 N	75.16 W
Cobb Seamount ✢[3]	**16**	46.45 N	130.50 W
Cobden, Austl.	**169**	38.20 S	143.05 E
Cobden, Ont., Can.	**190**	45.38 N	76.53 W
Cobden, Ill., U.S.	**194**	37.32 N	89.15 W
Cobeña	**266a**	40.34 N	3.30 W
Cobequid Bay ⊂	**186**	45.21 N	63.45 W
Cobequid Mountains ⩚	**186**	45.30 N	63.30 W
Cobh	**48**	51.51 N	8.17 W
Cobham, Eng., U.K.	**260**	51.23 N	0.24 E
Cobham, Eng., U.K.	**260**	51.20 N	0.25 W
Cobham ≃	**184**	53.15 N	93.58 W
Cobham Hall ⊥	**260**	51.23 N	0.25 E
Cobija, Bol.	**248**	11.02 S	68.44 W
Cobija, Chile	**252**	22.33 S	70.16 W
Coblenz → Koblenz	**56**	50.21 N	7.35 E
Cobleskill	**210**	42.41 N	74.29 W
Cobleskill Creek ≃	**210**	42.43 N	74.20 W
Coboconk	**212**	44.39 N	78.48 W
Cobo Hall ʊ	**281**	42.19 N	83.03 W
Cobolgo, Gora ∧	**84**	42.50 N	46.23 E
Coboto, Cerro ∧	**200**	31.29 N	112.05 W
Čoboty	**265b**	55.39 N	37.21 E
Cobourg	**212**	43.58 N	78.10 W
Cobourg Peninsula ≻[1]	**164**	11.20 S	132.15 E
Cobquecura	**252**	36.08 S	72.47 W
Cobram	**166**	35.55 S	145.39 E
Cobras, Ilha das I	**287a**	22.54 S	43.10 W
Cobre ≃	**236**	8.01 N	81.18 W
Cóbuè	**154**	12.04 S	34.50 E
Coburg, Austl.	**169**	37.45 S	144.58 E
Coburg, B.R.D.	**56**	50.15 N	10.58 E
Coburg Island I	**176**	76.00 N	79.25 W
Coburn	**210**	40.52 N	77.28 W
Coburn Mountain ∧	**188**	45.28 N	70.06 W
Coca ≃	**246**	0.29 S	76.58 W
Coca, Pizzo di ∧	**64**	46.04 N	10.01 E
Coca, Punta ≻	**236**	12.28 N	83.30 W
Cocachacra	**248**	17.06 S	71.46 W
Cocais ∧	**256**	21.51 S	42.53 W
Cocais, Ribeirão dos ≃	**256**	21.59 S	47.15 W
Cocal	**250**	3.28 S	41.34 W
Cocalico Creek ≃	**208**	40.07 N	76.14 W
Coccaglio	**64**	45.34 N	9.58 E
Cocconato	**62**	45.05 N	8.02 E
Cocentaina	**34**	38.45 N	0.26 W
Cochabamba	**248**	17.24 S	66.09 W
Cochabamba □[5]	**248**	17.30 S	65.40 W
Cochagual	**252**	31.54 S	68.23 W
Čochatauri	**84**	42.01 N	42.15 E
Cochato ≃	**283**	42.10 N	71.01 W
Coche, Isla I	**246**	10.45 N	63.55 W
Cochem	**56**	50.11 N	7.09 E
Cochesett	**283**	42.14 N	70.48 W
Cochetopa Creek ≃	**200**	38.31 N	106.47 W
Cochichewick, Lake ⊜	**283**	42.42 N	71.06 W
Cochin	**122**	9.58 N	76.14 E
Cochinos (Bay of Pigs), Bahía de ⊂	**240p**	22.07 N	81.10 W
Cochinos, Cayos II	**236**	15.57 N	86.33 W
Cochise Head ∧	**200**	32.03 N	109.18 W
Cochituate	**207**	42.19 N	71.22 W
Cochituate, Lake ⊜	**283**	42.17 N	71.22 W
Cochituate State Park ♠	**207**	42.20 N	71.22 W
Cochran	**192**	32.23 N	83.21 W
Cochrane, Alta., Can.	**182**	51.11 N	114.28 W
Cochrane, Ont., Can.	**176**	49.04 N	81.01 W
Cochrane, Wis., U.S.	**190**	44.14 N	91.50 W
Cochrane ≃	**176**	57.52 N	101.38 W
Cochrane, Lago (Lago Pueyrredón) ⊜	**254**	47.20 S	72.00 W
Cochranton	**214**	41.31 N	80.03 W
Cochranville	**208**	39.53 N	75.55 W

Symbols in the index entries represent the broad categories identified in the key at the right. Symbols with superior numbers (⩚[2]) identify subcategories (see complete key on page *I* · *30*).

Kartensymbole in dem Registerverzeichnis stellen die rechts in Schlüssel erklärten Kategorien dar. Symbole mit hochgestellten Ziffern (⩚[2]) bezeichnen Unterabteilungen einer Kategorie (vgl. vollständiger Schlüssel auf Seite *I* · *30*).

Los símbolos incluídos en el texto del índice representan las grandes categorias identificadas con la clave a la derecha. Los símbolos con numeros en su parte superior (⩚[2]) identifican las subcategorías (véase la clave completa en la página *I* · *30*).

Les symboles de l'index représentent les catégories indiquées dans la légende à droite. Les symboles suivis d'un indice (⩚[2]) représentent des sous-catégories (voir légende complète à la page *I* · *30*).

Os símbolos incluídos no texto do índice representam as grandes categorias identificadas com a chave à direita. Os símbolos com números em sua parte superior (⩚[2]) identificam as subcategorias (veja-se a chave completa à página *I* · *30*).

	English	Deutsch	Español	Français	Português
∧	Mountain	Berg	Montaña	Montagne	Montanha
⩚	Mountains	Berge	Montañas	Montagnes	Montanhas
⋈	Pass	Pass	Paso	Col	Passo
∨	Valley, Canyon	Tal, Cañon	Valle, Cañón	Vallée, Canyon	Vale, Canhão
≚	Plain	Ebene	Llano	Plaine	Planície
≻	Cape	Kap	Cabo	Cap	Cabo
I	Island	Insel	Isla	Île	Ilha
II	Islands	Inseln	Islas	Îles	Ilhas
●	Other Topographic Features	Andere Topographische Objekte	Otros Elementos Topográficos	Autres données topographiques	Outros Elementos Topográficos

ESPAÑOL — Nombre / Página / Lat.°′ / Long.°′ W=Oeste
FRANÇAIS — Nom / Page / Lat.°′ / Long.°′ W=Ouest
PORTUGUÊS — Nome / Página / Lat.°′ / Long.°′ W=Oeste

Cochstedt 54 51.53 N 11.24 E
Cockatoo-Inseln → Buccaneer Archipelago ▮▮ 160 16.17 S 123.20 E
Cock Bridge 46 57.09 N 3.14 W
Cockburn 166 32.05 S 141.00 E
Cockburn, Canal ⩦ 254 54.20 S 71.30 W
Cockburn, Cape ❯ 164 11.20 S 132.52 E
Cockburn, Mount ▲ 162 22.46 S 130.36 E
Cockburn Island ▮ 190 45.55 N 83.22 W
Cockburn Sound ⩦ 168a 32.12 S 115.42 E
Cockburnspath 46 55.56 N 2.21 W
Cock Clarks 260 51.42 N 0.37 E
Cockenoe Island ▮ 276 41.05 N 73.21 W
Cockenzie 46 55.58 N 2.58 W
Cockerham 44 53.59 N 2.50 W
Cockermouth 44 54.40 N 3.21 W
Cockeysville 208 39.29 N 76.39 W
Cockfosters ↝[8] 260 51.39 N 0.09 W
Cockpit Country ↝[1] 241q 18.18 N 77.43 W
Cockrell Hill 222 32.45 N 96.54 W
Cockroach Island ▮ 240m 18.24 N 65.04 W
Cockscomb Point ❯ 174u 14.14 S 170.40 W
Coclé □[4] 236 8.30 N 80.15 W
Coclé del Norte ≃ 236 9.05 N 80.35 W
Coclois 50 48.28 N 4.20 E
Coco ≃ 236 15.00 N 83.10 W
Coco, Cayo ▮ 240p 22.30 N 78.28 W
Coco, Isla del ▮ 230 5.32 N 87.04 W
Côco, Rio do ≃ 250 9.27 S 50.02 W
Cocoa 220 28.21 N 80.44 W
Cocoa Beach 220 28.19 N 80.36 W
Cocobeach 152 0.59 N 9.36 E
Coco Channel ⩦ 110 13.45 N 93.00 E
Cococi 250 6.25 S 40.30 W
Cocodrie Lake ⊜[1] 194 30.58 N 92.25 W
Coco Islands ▮▮ 110 14.05 N 93.18 E
Coconino Plateau ▲[1] 200 35.50 N 112.30 W
Cocorocuma, Cayos ↝[2] 236 15.45 N 83.00 W
Côcos 255 14.10 S 44.33 W
Cocos Basin ✦[1] 12 7.00 S 95.00 E
Cocos Bay ⊂ 241r 10.27 N 61.00 W
Cocos Island ▮ 174p 13.14 N 144.39 E
Cocos Islands □[2] 12 12.10 S 96.55 E
Cocos Islands ▮▮ 4 12.10 S 96.55 E
Cocos Ridge ✦[3] 16 5.30 N 87.30 W
Cocotá ↝[8] 287a 22.49 S 43.11 W
Cocotitlán 234 19.14 N 98.52 W
Cocuiza ≃ 246 10.59 N 71.17 W
Cocula, Méx. 234 20.23 N 103.50 W
Cocula, Méx. 234 18.14 N 99.40 W
Cod ≃ 44 54.10 N 1.22 W
Cod, Cape ❯ 207 41.42 N 70.15 W
Codăeşti 38 46.52 N 27.46 E
Codajás 246 3.50 S 62.05 W
Codaruina 71 40.56 N 8.49 E
Coddenham 42 52.09 N 1.07 E
Codera, Cabo ❯ 246 10.35 N 66.05 W
Coderre 184 50.10 N 106.23 W
Coderre, Ruisseau ≃ 275a 45.43 N 73.19 W
Codesa 182 55.45 N 118.04 W
Codfish Island ▮ 172 46.47 S 167.38 E
Codigoro 66 44.49 N 12.08 E
Cod Island ▮ 176 57.45 N 61.50 W
Codlea 38 45.42 N 25.27 E
Codnor 42 53.03 N 1.23 W
Codó 250 4.29 S 43.53 W
Codogno 62 45.09 N 9.42 E
Codorus 208 39.48 N 76.52 W
Codorus Creek ≃ 208 40.03 N 76.38 W
Codorus State Park ♦ 208 39.48 N 76.54 W
Codózinho 250 4.46 S 44.10 W
Codpa 248 18.50 S 69.44 W
Codro 86 50.50 N 88.34 E
Codroipo 64 45.58 N 12.59 E
Codrongianos 71 40.39 N 8.41 E
Codroy 186 47.53 N 59.24 W
Codroy Pond 186 48.04 N 58.52 W
Codsall 42 52.38 N 2.12 W
Cody, Nebr., U.S. 198 42.56 N 101.15 W
Cody, Wyo., U.S. 202 44.32 N 109.03 W
Coeburn 192 36.57 N 82.28 W
Coelemu 252 36.29 S 72.42 W
Coelho da Rocha 256 22.47 S 43.23 W
Coelho Neto 250 4.15 S 43.00 W
Coemba 152 12.08 S 18.05 E
Coen 164 13.56 S 143.12 E
Coen ≃, Austl. 164 13.56 S 142.02 E
Coën ≃, C.R. 236 9.34 N 82.58 W
Coeneo [de la Libertad] 234 19.49 N 101.35 W
Coeroeni ≃ 250 3.21 N 57.31 W
Coesfeld 52 51.56 N 7.10 E
Coetivy Island ▮ 138 7.08 S 56.16 E
Coeur d'Alene 202 47.41 N 116.46 W
Coeur d'Alene ≃ 202 47.28 N 116.48 W
Coeur d'Alene, South Fork ≃ 202 47.33 N 116.15 W
Coeur d'Alene Indian Reservation ↝[4] 202 47.18 N 116.45 W
Coeur d'Alene Lake ⊜[1] 202 47.32 N 116.48 W
Coeur d'Alene Mountains ⋀ 202 47.50 N 116.05 W
Coevorden 52 52.40 N 6.45 E
Coeymans 210 42.28 N 73.48 W
Coffeen 219 39.05 N 89.24 W
Coffeen Lake ⊜[1] 219 39.03 N 89.20 W
Coffeeville 194 33.59 N 89.40 W
Coffeyville 198 37.02 N 95.37 W
Coffin, Île ▮ 186 47.33 N 61.30 W
Coffin Bay ⊂ 162 34.27 S 135.19 E
Coffin Bay Peninsula ❯[1] 162 34.32 S 135.15 E
Coffs Harbour 166 30.18 S 153.08 E
Cofimvaba 158 32.00 S 27.35 E
Cofradía 236 15.24 N 88.09 W
Cofre de Perote, Parque Nacional ♦ 234 19.32 N 97.10 W
Cofrentes 34 39.14 N 1.04 W
Coggeshall 42 51.52 N 0.41 E
Coggiola 62 45.41 N 8.11 E
Coggon 190 42.17 N 91.32 W
Coghinas ≃ 71 40.56 N 8.48 E
Coghinas, Lago del ⊜ 71 40.45 N 9.02 E
Coglians, Monte (Hohe Warte) ▲ 64 46.37 N 12.53 E
Cogliate 266b 45.39 N 9.05 E
Cognac 32 45.42 N 0.20 W
Cogne 62 45.37 N 7.21 E
Cognin 62 45.34 N 5.54 E
Cogoleto 62 44.23 N 8.39 E
Cogolin 62 43.15 N 6.32 E
Cogollo del Cengio 64 45.47 N 11.25 E
Cogolludo 34 40.57 N 3.05 W
Cogolo 64 46.21 N 10.41 E
Cogswell 198 46.07 N 97.47 W
Cogswell Reservoir ⊜[1] 280 34.14 N 117.58 W
Cogtong Bay ⊂ 116 9.51 N 124.33 E
Çogun 130 39.20 N 34.08 E
Cohansey ≃ 208 39.21 N 75.22 W
Cohasset 207 42.14 N 70.48 W
Cohasset Harbor ⊂ 283 42.15 N 70.47 W
Cohenga ≃ 248 10.17 S 73.57 W
Cohoctah 216 42.46 N 83.57 W
Cohocton 210 42.30 N 77.30 W
Cohocton ≃ 210 42.09 N 77.05 W
Cohoe 180 60.23 N 151.18 W
Cohoes 210 42.46 N 73.42 W
Cohoni 248 16.44 S 67.51 W
Cohoon, Lake ⊜[1] 208 36.45 N 76.38 W
Cohuna 166 35.49 S 144.13 E
Coiba, Isla de ▮ 246 7.27 N 81.45 W
Coig ≃ 254 50.58 S 69.11 W
Coigeach, Rubha ❯ 46 58.06 N 5.26 W
Coignières 261 48.45 N 1.55 E
Coihaique 254 45.34 S 72.04 W
Coils Creek ≃ 204 39.32 N 116.16 W
Coimbatore 122 11.00 N 76.58 E
Coimbra, Bra. 248 19.55 S 57.47 W
Coimbra, Bra. 255 20.52 S 42.48 W
Coimbra, Port. 34 40.12 N 8.25 W
Coin, Esp. 34 36.40 N 4.45 W
Coin, Iowa, U.S. 198 40.40 N 95.14 W
Coipasa, Lago ⊜ 248 19.12 S 68.07 W
Coipasa, Salar de ≋ 248 19.26 S 68.09 W
Coire → Chur 58 46.51 N 9.32 E
Coire, Loch ⊜ 46 58.13 N 4.21 W
Coixtlahuaca 234 17.43 N 97.19 W
Čojbalsan, Mong. 88 48.34 N 114.50 E
Čojbalsan (Bajan Tümen), Mong. 88 48.04 N 114.30 E
Čojbalsan Uul ▲ 88 47.49 N 107.00 E
Cojedes 246 9.37 N 68.55 W
Cojedes □[3] 246 9.20 N 68.20 W
Cojimar ↝[8] 286b 23.10 N 82.18 W
Cojimar ≃ 286b 23.10 N 82.17 W
Cojudo Blanco, Cerro ▲ 254 47.05 S 69.20 W
Cojumatlán de Régules 234 20.07 N 102.50 W
Cojutepeque 236 13.43 N 88.56 W
Çokak 130 37.45 N 36.19 E
Cokato 190 45.05 N 94.11 W
Cokeburg 214 40.06 N 80.04 W
Coker 273a 6.29 N 3.20 E
Cokeville 200 42.05 N 110.57 W
Çoki 150 15.30 N 15.59 W
Čoktal 85 42.36 N 76.44 E
Čokurdach 74 70.38 N 147.55 E
Colāba Point ❯ 272c 18.53 N 72.48 E
Colac 169 38.20 S 143.35 E
Colac, Lake ⊜ 169 38.18 S 143.35 E
Çolaklı 130 38.22 N 38.33 E
Colalao del Valle 252 26.22 S 65.57 W
Colán Conhué 254 43.16 S 69.51 W
Colapsin Point ❯ 116 6.38 N 125.25 E
Colares, Bra. 250 0.56 S 48.17 W
Colares, Port. 34 38.48 N 9.27 W
Colares, Ribeira de ≃ 266c 38.49 N 9.28 W
Colatina 255 19.32 S 40.37 W
Cölbe 56 50.51 N 8.48 E
Colbeck, Cape ❯ 9 77.06 S 157.48 W
Colberry Park 281 42.36 N 83.16 W
Colbert 196 33.51 N 96.30 W
Colbinabbin 166 36.35 S 144.49 E
Colbitz 54 52.19 N 11.36 E
Colbitz-Letzlinger Heide ↝[3] 54 52.27 N 11.35 E
Colborne, Ont., Can. 212 42.51 N 80.19 W
Colborne, Ont., Can. 212 44.00 N 77.53 W
Colbún 252 35.42 S 71.25 W
Colburn 216 40.31 N 86.43 W
Colby, Kans., U.S. 198 39.24 N 101.03 W
Colby, Wis., U.S. 190 44.55 N 90.19 W
Colca 248 12.18 S 75.13 W
Colca ≃ 248 15.51 S 72.26 W
Colcamar 248 6.16 S 77.55 W
Colcapirhua 248 17.25 S 66.15 W
Colchester, Ont., Can. 214 41.59 N 82.56 W
Colchester, Eng., U.K. 42 51.54 N 0.54 E
Colchester, Conn., U.S. 207 41.34 N 72.20 W
Colchester, Ill., U.S. 190 40.25 N 90.48 W
Coldbackie 46 58.31 N 4.23 W
Cold Bay 180 55.11 N 162.30 W
Cold Bay ⊂ 180 55.13 N 162.33 W
Coldblow ↝[8] 260 51.26 N 0.10 E
Cold Brook 210 43.15 N 75.03 W
Cold Creek ≃ 212 44.12 N 77.36 W
Colden 210 42.39 N 78.41 W
Cold Fell ▲ 44 54.54 N 2.36 W
Cold Harbor Battlefield (1864) ⊥ 208 37.36 N 77.20 W
Coldingham 46 55.53 N 2.10 W
Colditz 54 51.07 N 12.48 E
Cold Lake 184 54.27 N 110.10 W
Cold Lake ⊜ 184 54.33 N 110.05 W
Cold Lake Indian Reserve ↝[4] 184 54.35 N 110.10 W
Cold Norton 260 51.40 N 0.40 E
Coldrano 64 46.38 N 10.50 E
Cold Spring, Ky., U.S. 218 39.01 N 84.27 W
Cold Spring, Minn., U.S. 190 45.27 N 94.26 W
Cold Spring, N.J., U.S. 208 38.59 N 74.57 W
Cold Spring, N.Y., U.S. 210 41.25 N 73.57 W
Coldspring, Tex., U.S. 222 30.36 N 95.08 W
Cold Spring Harbor 276 40.52 N 73.27 W
Cold Spring Harbor ⊂ 276 40.53 N 73.28 W
Coldsprings, Ont., Can. 212 44.17 N 78.18 W
Cold Springs, N.Y., U.S. 210 43.08 N 76.15 W
Cold Springs Creek ≃ 198 44.32 N 104.06 W
Cold Spring Terrace 276 40.50 N 73.26 W
Coldstream, Austl. 274b 37.44 S 145.23 E
Coldstream, Scot., U.K. 46 55.39 N 2.15 W
Cold Stream ≃ 226 39.35 N 120.22 W
Coldwater, Ont., Can. 212 44.42 N 79.40 W
Coldwater, Kans., U.S. 198 37.16 N 99.19 W
Coldwater, Mich., U.S. 216 41.57 N 85.00 W
Coldwater, Miss., U.S. 194 34.41 N 89.59 W
Coldwater, Ohio, U.S. 216 40.29 N 84.38 W
Coldwater ≃, Ont., Can. 212 44.44 N 79.39 W
Coldwater ≃, Mich., U.S. 216 42.04 N 85.08 W
Coldwater Canyon ∨ 280 34.14 N 117.44 W
Coldwater Indian Reserve ↝[4] 182 50.04 N 120.48 W
Coldwater Lake ⊜ 216 41.49 N 84.58 W
Cole □[6] 219 38.30 N 92.13 W
Cole ≃, Ang. 152 9.07 S 15.50 E
Cole ≃, Eng., U.K. 42 51.42 N 1.42 W
Cole ≃, Eng., U.K. 42 52.28 N 1.41 W
Colebrook, N.H., U.S. 188 44.54 N 71.30 W
Colebrook, Ohio, U.S. 214 41.32 N 80.46 W
Colebrook River Lake ⊜[1] 207 42.03 N 73.04 W
Cole Camp 194 38.28 N 93.12 W
Coledale 170 34.17 S 150.57 E
Coleen ≃ 180 67.05 N 142.31 W
Coleford National Park ♦ 158 29.53 S 29.28 E
Colégio, Morro do ▲ 287b 23.38 S 46.21 W
Coleman, Alta., Can. 182 49.38 N 114.30 W
Coleman, Fla., U.S. 220 28.48 N 82.04 W
Coleman, Md., U.S. 208 39.21 N 76.05 W
Coleman, Mich., U.S. 190 43.46 N 84.35 W
Coleman, Tex., U.S. 196 31.50 N 99.26 W
Coleman, Wis., U.S. 190 45.04 N 88.02 W
Coleman ≃ 164 15.06 S 141.38 E
Colembert 50 50.45 N 1.50 E
Colen Lakes ⊜ 184 54.33 N 95.25 W
Colenso 158 28.50 S 29.44 E
Colerain 214 40.07 N 80.49 W
Coleraine, Austl. 166 37.36 S 141.42 E
Coleraine, N. Ire., U.K. 48 55.08 N 6.40 W
Coleraine, Minn., U.S. 190 47.17 N 93.27 W
Coleridge 198 42.30 N 97.13 W
Coleridge, Lake ⊜ 172 43.17 S 171.30 E
Coleroon ≃ 122 11.23 N 79.46 E
Coles 194 31.17 N 91.03 W
Colesberg 158 30.45 S 25.05 E
Coles Brook ≃ 276 40.55 N 74.02 W
Coleshill, Eng., U.K. 42 52.30 N 1.42 W
Coleshill, Eng., U.K. 260 51.39 N 0.38 W
Coles Point 208 38.09 N 76.38 W
Colesville, Md., U.S. 284c 39.05 N 77.00 W
Colesville, N.J., U.S. 210 41.15 N 74.39 W
Coleto Creek ≃ 196 28.41 N 97.01 W
Coleville, Sask., Can. 184 51.43 N 109.16 W
Coleville ≃ 226 38.33 N 119.30 W
Colfax, Calif., U.S. 226 39.06 N 120.57 W
Colfax, Ill., U.S. 216 40.34 N 88.37 W
Colfax, Ind., U.S. 194 40.12 N 86.40 W
Colfax, Iowa, U.S. 190 41.41 N 93.14 W
Colfax, La., U.S. 194 31.31 N 92.42 W
Colfax, Wash., U.S. 202 46.53 N 117.22 W
Colfax, Wis., U.S. 190 45.00 N 91.44 W
Colfiorito 66 43.02 N 12.55 E
Colgate 216 43.12 N 88.12 W
Colgate Creek ≃ 284b 39.15 N 76.32 W
Colgong 124 25.16 N 87.13 E
Colgrave Sound ⩦ 46 60.37 N 0.58 W
Colhué Huapi, Lago ⊜ 254 45.30 S 68.48 W
Coliban ≃ 169 36.56 S 144.33 E
Colibris, Pointe des ❯, Guad. 241o 16.15 N 61.11 W
Colibris, Pointe des ❯, Guad. 241o 16.17 N 61.06 W
Colico 58 46.08 N 9.22 E
Coligny, Fr. 58 46.23 N 5.21 E
Coligny, S. Afr. 158 26.17 S 26.15 E
Colijnsplaat 52 51.46 N 3.51 E
Colima, Méx. 200 32.25 N 115.05 W
Colima, Méx. 234 19.14 N 103.43 W
Colima □[3] 234 19.10 N 104.00 W
Colima, Nevado de ▲ 234 19.33 N 103.38 W
Colimes ≃ 246 1.32 S 80.00 W
Colin 50 47.08 N 2.32 E
Colina 252 33.12 S 70.41 W
Colinas, Bra. 250 6.02 S 44.14 W
Colinas, Bra. 255 14.12 S 48.03 W
Colinet 186 47.13 N 53.33 W
Colinton, Austl. 171b 35.51 S 149.09 E
Colinton, Alta., Can. 182 54.37 N 113.15 W
Coll ▮ 46 56.38 N 6.34 W
Colla 258 34.04 S 57.21 W
Colla, Arroyo ≃ 258 34.19 S 57.20 W
Collagna 64 44.21 N 10.16 E
Collalbo (Klobenstein) 64 46.32 N 11.28 E
Collalto Sabino 66 42.08 N 13.02 E
Collamer 210 43.06 N 76.04 W
Collarenebri 166 29.33 S 148.35 E
Collarmele 66 42.03 N 13.38 E
Collaroy 274a 33.44 S 151.18 E
Collazzone 66 42.54 N 12.26 E
Collbran 200 39.14 N 107.57 W
Collecchio 64 44.45 N 10.13 E
Collecorvino 66 42.27 N 14.01 E
Colle di Tora 66 42.13 N 12.57 E
Colle di Val d'Elsa 66 43.25 N 11.07 E
Colleen Bawn 154 21.00 S 29.13 E
Colleferro 66 41.44 N 12.59 E
College 180 64.51 N 147.47 W
College City 226 39.00 N 122.00 W
College Corner 218 39.34 N 84.49 W
Collegedale 194 35.04 N 85.03 W
College Meadows 218 39.56 N 86.07 W
College Park, Ga., U.S. 192 33.39 N 84.27 W
College Park, Md., U.S. 208 39.00 N 76.55 W
College Park Airport ✈ 284c 38.58 N 76.55 W
College Place 202 46.03 N 118.23 W
College Point ↝[8] 276 40.47 N 73.51 W
College Station 222 30.37 N 96.21 W
Collegeville, Ind., U.S. 216 40.56 N 87.09 W
Collegeville, Pa., U.S. 208 40.11 N 75.27 W
Collégien 261 48.50 N 2.40 E
Collegno 62 45.05 N 7.34 E
Colle Isarco (Gossensass) 64 46.56 N 11.26 E
Collepardo 66 41.46 N 13.22 E
Collepasso 68 40.04 N 18.10 E
Collepietro 66 42.13 N 13.46 E
Collerina 166 29.41 S 146.38 E
Collesalvetti 66 43.35 N 10.28 E
Colle Sannita 68 41.22 N 14.50 E
Collesano 70 37.55 N 13.56 E
Colletorto 68 41.40 N 14.58 E
Colleymount 182 54.01 N 126.09 W
Colleyville 222 32.53 N 97.09 W
Colliano 68 40.43 N 15.17 E
Collie 162 33.21 S 116.09 E
Colli a Volturno 66 41.36 N 14.06 E
Colli del Tronto 66 42.52 N 13.44 E
Colli di Monte Bove 66 42.06 N 13.09 E
Collie 168a 33.21 S 116.09 E
Collie ≃ 168a 33.18 S 115.44 E
Collier □[6] 220 26.10 N 81.22 W
Collier Bay ⊂ 160 16.10 S 124.15 E
Collier Bridge ↝[5] 220 26.57 N 82.04 W
Collier City 220 26.14 N 80.09 W
Collier Law ▲[2] 44 54.46 N 1.58 W
Collier Range ▲ 162 24.43 S 119.12 E
Collier Row ↝[8] 260 51.36 N 0.10 E
Colliers 214 40.22 N 80.33 W
Collier-Seminole State Park ♦ 220 25.59 N 81.36 W
Colliersville 210 42.29 N 74.59 W
Collierville 194 35.03 N 89.40 W
Collieston 46 57.21 N 1.56 W
Colligan ≃ 48 52.06 N 7.38 W
Collin □[6] 222 33.07 N 96.35 W
Collina, Passo della ✕ 66 44.01 N 10.56 E
Collingbourne Kingston 42 51.18 N 1.13 W
Collingdale 208 39.55 N 75.17 W
Collings Pass ✕ 158 28.13 S 29.38 E
Collingswood 285 39.55 N 75.04 W
Collingwood, Austl. 274b 37.48 S 145.00 E
Collingwood, Ont., Can. 212 44.29 N 80.13 W
Collingwood, N.Z. 172 40.40 S 172.41 E
Collingwood Bay ⊂ 164 9.20 S 149.30 E
Collins, Ga., U.S. 192 32.11 N 82.07 W
Collins, Iowa, U.S. 190 41.54 N 93.18 W
Collins, Miss., U.S. 194 31.39 N 89.33 W
Collins, N.Y., U.S. 210 42.30 N 78.55 W
Collins, Ohio, U.S. 214 41.16 N 82.30 W
Collins ≃ 194 35.48 N 85.37 W
Collins, Mount ▲[2] 190 47.51 N 80.59 W
Collins Bay 212 44.15 N 76.36 W
Collinsburg 214 40.13 N 79.46 W
Collins Center 210 42.30 N 78.51 W
Collins Lake ⊜ 212 44.22 N 76.27 W
Collins Park 208 39.41 N 75.33 W
Collinston 194 32.41 N 91.52 W
Collinsville, Austl. 166 20.34 S 147.51 E
Collinsville, Ala., U.S. 194 34.16 N 85.52 W
Collinsville, Calif., U.S. 282 38.05 N 121.51 W
Collinsville, Conn., U.S. 207 41.49 N 72.55 W
Collinsville, Ill., U.S. 219 38.41 N 89.51 W
Collinsville, Miss., U.S. 194 32.30 N 88.51 W
Collinsville, N.J., U.S. 276 40.49 N 74.28 W
Collinsville, Okla., U.S. 196 36.22 N 95.51 W
Collinwood 194 35.10 N 87.44 W
Collio 64 45.48 N 10.20 E
Collipulli 252 37.57 S 72.26 W
Collique Alto 286d 11.55 S 77.03 W
Collister 202 43.38 N 116.15 W
Collo 148 37.00 N 6.34 E
Collobrières 62 43.14 N 6.18 E
Collombey 58 46.16 N 6.57 E
Collomsville 210 41.09 N 77.09 W
Collon 48 53.47 N 6.29 W
Collonges 58 46.08 N 5.54 E
Collooney 48 54.11 N 8.29 W
Colma 226 37.41 N 122.28 W
Colma Creek ≃ 282 37.38 N 122.23 W
Colman 198 43.59 N 96.49 W
Colmar 58 48.05 N 7.22 E
Colmar Manor 284c 38.56 N 76.57 W
Colmars 62 44.11 N 6.38 E
Colmenar 34 36.54 N 4.20 W
Colmenar de Oreja 34 40.06 N 3.23 W
Colmenar Viejo 34 40.40 N 3.46 W
Colmeneros 234 18.06 N 101.40 W
Colmesneil 194 30.54 N 94.25 W
Colmnitz 54 50.54 N 13.31 E
Colmonell 44 55.08 N 4.55 W
Coln ≃ 42 51.42 N 1.42 W
Colnbrook 260 51.29 N 0.31 W
Colne 44 53.52 N 2.09 W
Colne ≃, Eng., U.K. 42 51.48 N 1.01 E
Colne ≃, Eng., U.K. 260 51.26 N 0.30 W
Colnett, Cabo ❯ 232 30.58 N 116.19 W
Colney Heath 260 51.44 N 0.15 W
Colney Street 260 51.42 N 0.20 W
Colo 190 42.01 N 93.19 W
Colo ≃ 170 33.26 S 150.53 E
Colobraro 68 40.11 N 16.25 E
Cologna Veneta 64 45.18 N 11.23 E
Cologne → Köln, B.R.D. 56 50.56 N 6.59 E
Cologne, Minn., U.S. 190 44.47 N 93.46 W
Cologne, N.J., U.S. 208 39.30 N 74.37 W
Cologno al Serio 62 45.37 N 9.42 E
Cologno Monzese 266b 45.32 N 9.17 E
Cololo, Nevado ▲ 248 14.53 S 69.06 W
Coloma, Calif., U.S. 226 38.48 N 120.53 W
Coloma, Mich., U.S. 216 42.11 N 86.19 W
Coloma, Wis., U.S. 190 44.02 N 89.31 W
Colomas, Ensenada de la ⊂ 240p 22.13 N 83.34 W
Colomb-Béchar → Béchar 148 31.37 N 2.13 W
Colombes 50 48.55 N 2.15 E
Colombey-les-Belles 58 48.32 N 5.54 E
Colombey-les-Deux-Églises 58 48.13 N 4.53 E
Colombia, Col. 246 3.24 N 74.49 W
Colombia, Méx. 196 27.42 N 99.45 W
Colombia □[1] 242
246 4.00 N 72.00 W
Colombie → Colombia □[1] 246 4.00 N 72.00 W
Colombie britannique → British Columbia □[4] 182 54.00 N 125.00 W
Colombier 58 46.58 N 6.52 E
Colombo, Bra. 252 25.17 S 49.14 W
Colombo, S. Lan. 122 6.56 N 79.51 E
Colome 198 43.15 N 99.43 W
Colón, Arg. 252 32.13 S 58.08 W
Colón, Arg. 252 33.53 S 61.07 W
Colón, Cuba 240p 22.43 N 80.54 W
Colón, Pan. 236 9.22 N 79.54 W
Colon, Mich., U.S. 216 41.57 N 85.19 W
Colón, Ur. 252 33.53 S 54.43 W
Colón, Ur. 258 34.48 S 56.14 W
Colón □[4] 236 9.00 N 80.20 W
Colón □[5] 236 15.40 N 85.30 W
Colón, Archipiélago de → Galápagos □[4] 246a 0.30 S 90.30 W
Colón, Archipiélago de (Galapagos Islands) ▮▮ 246a 0.30 S 90.30 W
Colón, Cementerio ↝ 286b 23.08 N 82.23 W
Colón, Isla ▮ 236 9.24 N 82.17 W
Colón, Montañas de ⋀ 236 14.55 N 84.45 W
Colón, Teatro ♦ 288 34.36 S 58.23 W
Colona 162 31.38 S 132.05 E
Colonard-Corubert 50 48.25 N 0.39 E
Colonarie ≃ 241h 13.14 N 61.06 W
Colonelganj 124 27.08 N 81.42 E
Colonet 204 31.05 N 116.10 W
Colongulac, Lake ⊜ 169 38.10 S 143.11 E
Colonia → Köln, B.R.D. 56 50.56 N 6.59 E
Colonia, N.J., U.S. 210 40.35 N 74.18 W
Colonia □[5] 258 34.10 S 57.30 W
Colônia ≃ 255 15.11 S 39.45 W
Colonia, Aeroporto ✈ 258 34.28 S 57.49 W
Colonia, Cuchilla de la ▲[2] 258 34.15 S 57.35 W
Colonia Agrícola Turén 246 9.15 N 69.05 W
Colonia Alvear 252 35.00 S 67.40 W
Colonia Caroya 252 31.02 S 64.05 W
Colonia Cristóbal Obregón 234 16.20 N 93.30 W
Colonia del Sacramento 258 34.28 S 57.51 W
Colonia Dora 252 28.36 S 62.57 W
Colonia Elisa 252 26.56 S 59.32 W
Colonia Guadalupe 204 32.04 N 116.37 W
Colonia Hogar Ricardo Gutiérrez 288 34.51 S 58.51 W
Colonia José Mármol 252 26.59 S 60.44 W
Colonial Acres 208 39.31 N 76.20 W
Colonia Las Heras 254 46.33 S 68.57 W
Colonia Lavalleja 252 31.06 S 57.01 W
Colonial Beach 208 38.15 N 76.58 W
Colonial Crest 208 40.20 N 76.50 W
Colonia Leopoldina 250 8.57 S 35.39 W
Colonial Heights, Ill., U.S. 278 41.05 N 88.01 W
Colonial Heights, Va., U.S. 208 37.15 N 77.25 W
Colonial Manor 285 39.51 N 75.09 W
Colonial National Historical Park ♦ 208 37.12 N 76.45 W
Colonial Park 208 40.18 N 76.49 W
Colonial Village, N.Y., U.S. 210 43.08 N 78.58 W
Colonial Village, Pa., U.S. 285 40.04 N 75.24 W
Colonial Williamsburg ⊥ 208 37.16 N 76.42 W
Colonia Morelos 200 30.50 N 109.10 W
Colonia Nicolich 258 34.50 S 56.02 W
Colonia Progreso, Méx. 204 32.35 N 115.37 W
Colonia Progreso, Méx. 234 23.48 N 103.18 W
Colonia Providencia 240m 17.59 N 66.00 W
Colonias Unidas 252 26.42 S 59.38 W
Colonia Valdense 258 34.20 S 57.14 W
Colonia Villafañe 252 26.12 S 59.05 W
Colonie 210 42.43 N 73.50 W
Colonie Koret 152 0.34 N 23.28 E
Colonna 267a 41.50 N 12.45 E
Colonna, Capo ❯ 68 41.17 N 16.26 E
Colonnata 64 44.05 N 10.10 E
Colonsay 184 51.59 N 105.53 W
Colonsay ▮ 46 56.04 N 6.13 W
Colony 198 38.04 N 95.22 W
Colora 208 39.40 N 76.06 W
Colorada, Punta ❯ 288 34.45 S 58.06 W
Coloradas, Lomas ▲[2] 254 43.24 S 67.24 W
Colorado, C.R. 236 10.46 N 83.35 W
Colorado, Hond. 236 15.47 N 87.19 W
Colorado, Alaska, U.S. 180 63.09 N 149.26 W
Colorado □[6] 222 29.40 N 96.30 W
Colorado □[3] 178 39.30 N 105.30 W
Colorado ≃, Arg. 244 39.50 S 62.08 W
Colorado ≃, Bra. 248 13.03 S 62.20 W
Colorado ≃, N.A. 200 31.54 N 114.57 W
Colorado ≃, Tex., U.S. 196 28.36 N 95.58 W
Colorado ⩦ 286a 19.24 N 98.59 W
Colorado, Arroyo ∨ 200 34.58 N 107.13 W
Colorado, Cerro ▲, Arg. 254 45.02 S 69.38 W
Colorado, Cerro ▲, Chile 286e 33.24 S 70.45 W
Colorado, Cerro ▲, Méx. 232 31.31 N 115.31 W
Colorado, Cerro ▲, Perú 286d 12.07 S 76.55 W
Colorado, North Fork ≃ 200 40.12 N 105.50 W
Colorado, Williams Fork ≃ 200 40.03 N 106.11 W
Colorado City, Ariz., U.S. 200 36.58 N 112.58 W
Colorado City, Tex., U.S. 196 32.24 N 100.52 W
Colorado de Abajo 196 26.28 N 99.54 W
Colorado National Monument ♦ 200 39.04 N 108.25 W
Colorado Plateau ▲[1] 200 36.30 N 108.00 W
Colorado River Aqueduct ⩦[1] 228 33.50 N 117.23 W
Colorado River Indian Reservation ↝[4] 200 34.00 N 114.25 W
Colorado Springs 200 38.50 N 104.49 W
Colorines 234 19.07 N 100.12 W
Colorno 64 44.56 N 10.23 E
Colosimi 68 39.07 N 16.24 E
Colosseo ⊥ 267a 41.54 N 12.29 E
Colotepec ≃ 234 15.47 N 97.03 W
Colotlán 234 22.06 N 103.16 W
Colotlipa 234 17.25 N 99.09 W
Colo Vale 170 34.24 S 150.29 E
Čolpon 85 42.12 N 75.28 E
Čolpon-Ata 85 42.40 N 77.06 E
Colpoy Bay ⊂ 212 44.47 N 81.05 W
Colquechaca 248 18.40 S 66.01 W
Colquencha 248 17.00 S 68.17 W
Colquiri 248 17.25 S 67.08 W
Colquitt 192 31.10 N 84.44 W
Colsterworth 42 52.48 N 0.37 W
Colstrip 202 45.53 N 106.38 W
Colt 194 35.08 N 90.49 W
Colta 248 15.10 S 73.18 W
Coltauco 252 34.18 S 71.06 W
Coltishall 42 52.44 N 1.22 E
Colton, Austl. 162 33.29 S 134.56 E
Colton, Calif., U.S. 228 34.04 N 117.20 W
Colton, Ohio, U.S. 216 41.28 N 83.57 W
Colton, Oreg., U.S. 224 45.10 N 122.26 W
Colton, S. Dak., U.S. 198 43.47 N 96.56 W
Coltons Point 208 38.14 N 76.45 W
Colts Neck 208 40.17 N 74.11 W
Coltsville Center 214 41.05 N 80.34 W
Columbia, Ala., U.S. 192 31.18 N 85.07 W
Columbia, Calif., U.S. 226 38.02 N 120.24 W
Columbia, Conn., U.S. 207 41.42 N 72.18 W
Columbia, Ill., U.S. 219 38.27 N 90.12 W
Columbia, Ind., U.S. 218 39.35 N 85.12 W
Columbia, Ky., U.S. 194 37.06 N 85.18 W
Columbia, La., U.S. 194 32.06 N 92.05 W
Columbia, Md., U.S. 208 39.13 N 76.52 W
Columbia, Miss., U.S. 194 31.15 N 89.56 W
Columbia, Mo., U.S. 219 38.57 N 92.20 W
Columbia, N.J., U.S. 210 40.56 N 75.06 W
Columbia, N.C., U.S. 192 35.55 N 76.15 W
Columbia, Pa., U.S. 208 40.02 N 76.30 W
Columbia, S.C., U.S. 192 34.00 N 81.03 W
Columbia, Tenn., U.S. 194 35.37 N 87.02 W
Columbia □[6], N.Y., U.S. 210 42.15 N 73.47 W
Columbia □[6], Oreg., U.S. 224 45.57 N 123.03 W
Columbia □[6], Pa., U.S. 210 41.00 N 76.28 W
Columbia ≃ 176 46.15 N 124.05 W
Columbia, Cape ❯ 16 83.08 N 70.35 W
Columbia, Mount ▲ 182 52.09 N 117.25 W
Columbia Airport ✈ 279a 41.19 N 81.58 W
Columbia Basin ⩦[1] 202 46.45 N 119.05 W
Columbia Center 279a 41.19 N 81.56 W
Columbia City, Ind., U.S. 216 41.10 N 85.29 W
Columbia City, Oreg., U.S. 224 45.55 N 122.51 W
Columbia Cross Roads 210 41.50 N 76.48 W
Columbia Falls, Maine, U.S. 188 44.39 N 67.44 W
Columbia Falls, Mont., U.S. 202 48.23 N 114.11 W
Columbia Heights 224 46.09 N 122.58 W
Columbia Icefield ⊠ 182 52.10 N 117.30 W
Columbia Lake ⊜ 182 50.15 N 115.57 W
Columbia Lake Indian Reserve ↝[4] 182 50.25 N 115.57 W
Columbia Mountains ⋀ 182 51.30 N 118.30 W
Columbiana, Ala., U.S. 194 33.11 N 86.36 W
Columbiana, Ohio, U.S. 214 40.53 N 80.42 W
Columbiana □[6] 214 40.47 N 80.46 W
Columbia Plateau ▲[1] 202 44.00 N 117.30 W
Columbia Regional Airport ✈ 219 38.50 N 92.13 W
Columbia Road Reservoir ⊜[1] 198 45.45 N 98.15 W
Columbia State Historical Park ♦ 226 38.02 N 120.25 W
Columbia Station 214 41.20 N 81.57 W
Columbia University ⊍[2] 276 40.48 N 73.58 W
Columbiaville, Mich., U.S. 190 43.09 N 83.25 W
Columbiaville, N.Y., U.S. 210 42.19 N 73.45 W
Columbine, Cape ❯ 158 32.47 S 18.52 E
Columbretes, Islas ▮▮ 34 39.52 N 0.40 E
Columbus, Ga., U.S. 192 32.29 N 84.59 W
Columbus, Ind., U.S. 218 39.13 N 85.55 W
Columbus, Kans., U.S. 198 37.10 N 94.50 W
Columbus, Miss., U.S. 194 33.30 N 88.25 W
Columbus, Mont., U.S. 202 45.38 N 109.15 W
Columbus, Nebr., U.S. 198 41.25 N 97.22 W
Columbus, N.J., U.S. 208 40.04 N 74.43 W
Columbus, N. Mex., U.S. 200 31.50 N 107.38 W
Columbus, N.C., U.S. 192 35.15 N 82.12 W
Columbus, N. Dak., U.S. 198 48.54 N 102.47 W
Columbus, Ohio, U.S. 214 39.57 N 83.00 W
Columbus, Pa., U.S. 214 41.56 N 79.35 W
Columbus, Tex., U.S. 222 29.42 N 96.33 W
Columbus, Wis., U.S. 190 43.20 N 89.01 W
Columbus Air Force Base ■ 194 33.38 N 88.26 W
Columbus Grove 216 40.55 N 84.04 W
Columbus Junction 190 41.17 N 91.22 W
Columbus Park ♦ 278 41.53 N 87.47 W
Columbus Point ❯, Ba. 238 24.08 N 75.16 W
Columbus Point ❯, Trin. 241r 11.08 N 60.48 W
Columbus Salt Marsh ≋ 204 38.04 N 117.58 W
Coluna 255 18.14 S 42.50 W
Colusa 226 39.13 N 122.01 W
Colusa □[6] 226 39.13 N 122.01 W
Colusa Trough ⩦ 226 39.02 N 121.59 W
Colver 214 40.33 N 78.47 W
Colville, N.Z. 172 36.38 S 175.28 E
Colville, Wash., U.S. 202 48.33 N 117.54 W
Colville ≃, Alaska, U.S. 180 70.25 N 150.30 W
Colville ≃, Wash., U.S. 202 48.37 N 118.05 W
Colville, Cape ❯ 172 36.28 S 175.21 E
Colville Indian Reservation ↝[4] 202 48.15 N 119.00 W
Colville Lake ⊜ 180 67.10 N 126.00 W
Colwell 44 55.04 N 2.04 W
Colwood 224 48.26 N 123.29 W
Colwyn 285 39.55 N 75.15 W
Colwyn Bay 44 53.18 N 3.43 W
Colyton, Austl. 274a 33.47 S 150.48 E
Colyton, Eng., U.K. 42 50.44 N 3.04 W
Comacchio 66 44.42 N 12.11 E
Comacchio, Valli di ⊂ 66 44.38 N 12.06 E
Comal 115a 6.55 S 109.31 E
Comala 234 19.19 N 103.45 W
Comalapa, Guat. 236 14.44 N 90.53 W
Comalapa, Nic. 236 12.17 N 85.31 W
Comalcalco 234 18.16 N 93.13 W
Comales 232 26.10 N 98.56 W
Comalito, Cerro ▲ 234 20.30 N 104.36 W
Comallo 254 40.40 S 63.30 W
Comallo, Arroyo ≃ 254 40.29 S 70.12 W
Coman, Mount ▲ 9 74.02 S 65.04 W
Comanche, Okla., U.S. 196 34.22 N 97.58 W
Comanche, Tex., U.S. 196 31.54 N 98.36 W
Comanche Creek ≃ 198 39.53 N 104.19 W
Comandante Fontana 252 25.20 S 59.41 W
Comandante Leal 252 30.53 S 65.47 W
Comandante Luis Piedrabuena 254 49.59 S 68.54 W
Comandante Nicanor Otamendi 252 38.07 S 57.51 W
Comăneşti 38 46.25 N 26.26 E
Comanja de Corona 234 21.19 N 101.42 W
Comarapa 248 17.54 S 64.29 W
Comas, Perú 248 11.46 S 75.02 W
Comas, Perú 286d 11.57 S 77.04 W
Comayagua 236 14.25 N 87.37 W
Comayagua □[5] 236 14.30 N 87.40 W
Comayagua, Montañas de ⋀ 236 14.23 N 87.26 W
Combahee ≃ 192 32.30 N 80.31 W
Combarbalá 252 31.11 S 71.02 W
Combeaufontaine 58 47.43 N 5.53 E
Combe Martin 42 51.13 N 4.02 W
Comber, Ont., Can. 214 42.14 N 82.33 W
Comber, N. Ire., U.K. 48 54.33 N 5.45 W
Comberbach 262 53.17 N 2.32 W
Combermere Bay ⊂ 110 19.37 N 93.34 E
Comberton 42 52.11 N 0.02 E
Combe Seamount ✦[3] 14 12.30 S 177.30 W
Comblain-au-Pont 56 50.28 N 5.35 E
Combles 50 50.01 N 2.52 E
Combloux 62 45.54 N 6.39 E
Combourg 32 48.25 N 1.45 W
Comboyne 166 31.36 S 152.29 E
Comboyuro Point ❯ 171a 27.04 S 153.24 E
Combres 50 48.19 N 1.04 E
Combronde 32 45.59 N 3.05 E
Combs 262 53.18 N 1.57 W
Combs-la-Ville 50 48.40 N 2.34 E
Combs Reservoir ⊜[1] 262 53.19 N 1.57 W
Comburg ⊍[1] 56 49.06 N 9.44 E
Comb Wash ∨ 200 37.13 N 109.42 W
Come by Chance 186 47.51 N 53.58 W
Comeglians 64 46.31 N 12.52 E
Comelico Superiore 64 46.35 N 12.30 E
Comendador Gomes 255 19.41 S 49.05 W
Comer 192 34.04 N 83.08 W
Comercinho 255 16.19 S 41.47 W
Comerío 240m 18.13 N 66.14 W
Comet 166 23.37 S 148.33 E
Comet ≃ 166 23.34 S 148.32 E
Cometela 156 21.51 S 34.29 E
Comfort, N.C., U.S. 192 35.00 N 77.30 W
Comfort, Tex., U.S. 196 29.58 N 98.49 W
Comfort, Cape ❯ 176 65.08 N 83.21 W
Comfort, Point ❯ 276 40.27 N 74.08 W
Comfrey 198 44.07 N 94.54 W
Comilla 124 23.27 N 91.12 E
Comines 50 50.46 N 3.01 E
Comino, Capo ❯ 71 40.32 N 9.49 E
Comiskey Park ♦ 278 41.50 N 87.38 W
Comiso 70 36.56 N 14.36 E
Comitán [de Domínguez] 232 16.15 N 92.08 W
Comitini 70 37.24 N 13.39 E
Comloşu Mare 38 45.54 N 20.38 E
Commack 210 40.51 N 73.18 W
Commencement Bay ⊂ 224 47.17 N 122.28 W
Commentry 32 46.17 N 2.44 E
Commerce, Ga., U.S. 192 34.12 N 83.28 W
Commerce, Mich., U.S. 216 42.34 N 83.30 W
Commerce, Okla., U.S. 196 36.56 N 94.53 W
Commerce, Tex., U.S. 196 33.15 N 95.54 W
Commerce City 198 39.49 N 104.55 W
Commerce Lake ⊜ 281 42.35 N 83.30 W
Commerciale Luigi Bocconi, Università ⊍[2] 266b 45.26 N 9.11 E
Commercial Point 218 39.46 N 83.04 W
Commercy 56 48.45 N 5.35 E
Commewijne □[5] 250 5.30 N 55.00 W
Comminges ↝[1] 32 43.15 N 0.45 E
Committee Bay ⊂ 176 68.30 N 86.30 W
Commodore 214 40.43 N 78.57 W
Commondale 158 27.20 S 30.56 E
Common Edge 262 53.47 N 3.02 W
Commonwealth Bay ⊂ 9 66.54 S 142.40 E
Commonwealth Range ▲ 9 84.15 S 172.20 E
Commoron Creek ≃ 166 28.22 S 150.08 E
Community Center 228 34.16 N 118.44 W
Como, Austl. 274a 34.00 S 151.04 E
Como, It. 62 45.47 N 9.05 E
Como, Miss., U.S. 194 34.31 N 90.03 W
Como, N.C., U.S. 208 36.30 N 77.00 W
Como, Tex., U.S. 222 33.03 N 95.28 W
Como, Wis., U.S. 216 42.37 N 88.28 W
Como □[4] 58 45.59 N 9.13 E
Como ≃ 152 0.59 N 9.50 E
Como, Lago di ⊜ 58 46.00 N 9.20 E
Como, Lake ⊜ 216 42.36 N 88.29 W
Como, Mount ▲ 226 39.02 N 119.28 W
Comodoro Py 252 35.19 S 60.31 W
Comodoro Rivadavia 254 45.52 S 67.30 W
Como Lake ⊜ 190 47.55 N 83.30 W
Comologno 58 46.12 N 8.34 E
Comondú 232 26.03 N 111.46 W
Comonfort 234 20.43 N 100.46 W

Symbol	English	Deutsch	Español	Français	Português
≃	River	Fluss	Rio	Rivière	Rio
⩦	Canal	Kanal	Canal	Canal	Canal
⩫	Waterfall, Rapids	Wasserfall, Stromschnellen	Cascada, Rápidos	Chute d'eau, Rapides	Cascata, Rápidos
⩦	Strait	Meeresstrasse	Estrecho	Détroit	Estreito
⊂	Bay, Gulf	Bucht, Golf	Bahía, Golfo	Baie, Golfe	Baía, Golfo
⊜	Lake, Lakes	See, Seen	Lago, Lagos	Lac, Lacs	Lago, Lagos
≋	Swamp	Sumpf	Pantano	Marais	Pântano
⊠	Ice Features, Glacier	Eis- und Gletscherformen	Accidentes Glaciales	Formes glaciaires	Acidentes Glaciares
↝	Other Hydrographic Features	Andere Hydrographische Objekte	Otros Elementos Hidrográficos	Autres données hydrographiques	Outros Elementos Hidrográficos

Symbol	English	Deutsch	Español	Français	Português
✦	Submarine Features	Untermeerische Objekte	Accidentes Submarinos	Formes de relief sous-marin	Acidentes Submarinos
□	Political Unit	Politische Einheit	Unidad Política	Entité politique	Unidade Política
⊍	Cultural Institution	Kulturelle Institution	Institución Cultural	Institution culturelle	Instituição Cultural
⊥	Historical Site	Historische Stätte	Sitio Histórico	Site historique	Sitio Histórico
♦	Recreational Site	Erholungs- und Ferienort	Sitio de Recreo	Centre de loisirs	Sitio de Lazer
✈	Airport	Flughafen	Aeropuerto	Aéroport	Aeroporto
■	Military Installation	Militäranlage	Instalación Militar	Installation militaire	Instalação Militar
↝	Miscellaneous	Verschiedenes	Misceláneo	Divers	Miscelânea

ENGLISH / DEUTSCH

Name	Page	Lat.°′	Long.°′
Comoras → Comoros □[1]	157a	12.10 S	44.10 E
Comores → Comoros □[1]	157a	12.10 S	44.10 E
Comorin, Cape ≻	122	8.04 N	77.34 E
Comoros □[1]	138		
	157a	12.10 S	44.10 E
Comox	182	49.40 N	124.55 W
Companhia Siderúrgica Nacional ⚒[3]	256	22.31 S	44.07 W
Compans	261	49.00 N	2.40 E
Compatsch	58	46.58 N	10.25 E
Compiègne	50	49.25 N	2.50 E
Compo Cove C	276	41.07 N	73.21 W
Compostela, Méx.	234	21.15 N	104.53 W
Compostela, Pil.	116	7.40 N	126.02 E
Comprida, Ilha I, Bra.	252	24.50 S	47.42 W
Comprida, Ilha I, Bra.	287a	23.02 S	43.12 W
Comps-sur-Artuby	62	43.43 N	6.30 E
Compstall	262	53.25 N	2.03 W
Compton, Eng., U.K.	260	51.13 N	0.38 W
Compton, Calif., U.S.	228	33.54 N	118.13 W
Compton, Ill., U.S.	216	41.42 N	89.05 W
Compton □[6]	206	45.20 N	71.25 W
Compton Airport ⊠	280	33.53 N	118.15 W
Compton Creek ≃, Calif., U.S.	280	33.50 N	118.12 W
Compton Creek ≃, N.J., U.S.	276	40.26 N	74.05 W
Comptonville	273d	26.17 S	27.58 E
Comrie	46	56.22 N	4.00 W
Comstock, Mich., U.S.	216	42.16 N	85.31 W
Comstock, Nebr., U.S.	198	41.33 N	99.14 W
Comstock, Tex., U.S.	196	29.41 N	101.11 W
Comstock Park	216	43.02 N	85.40 W
Comunanza	66	42.57 N	13.25 E
Con ≃, S.S.S.R.	76	52.54 N	36.00 E
Con ≃, Viet.	110	19.04 N	105.00 E
Čona ≃, S.S.S.R.	74	62.54 N	111.06 E
Cona ≃, Scot., U.K.	46	56.46 N	5.14 W
Conakry	150	9.31 N	13.43 W
Conambo ≃	246	2.07 S	76.03 W
Conanicut Island I	207	41.32 N	71.21 W
Cona Niyeo	254	41.53 S	67.00 W
Conara Junction	166	41.50 S	147.26 E
Conasauga ≃	192	34.33 N	84.55 W
Conaskonk Point ≻	276	40.27 N	74.11 W
Conca ≃	66	43.58 N	12.43 E
Concarán	252	32.34 S	65.15 W
Concarneau	32	47.52 N	3.55 W
Conceição, Bra.	248	7.24 S	58.05 W
Conceição, Bra.	250	7.33 S	38.31 W
Conceição, Moç.	156	18.45 S	36.10 E
Conceição, Cachoeira ↳	248	9.34 S	64.22 W
Conceição, Ilha da I	287a	22.52 S	43.07 W
Conceição da Aparecida	255	21.06 S	46.12 W
Conceição da Barra	255	18.35 S	39.45 W
Conceição da Ibitipoca	256	21.43 S	43.55 W
Conceição da Pedra	256	22.09 S	45.27 W
Conceição das Alagoas	255	19.55 S	48.23 W
Conceição de Ipanema	255	19.55 S	41.41 W
Conceição de Jacareí	256	23.02 S	44.09 W
Conceição do Almeida	255	12.48 S	39.12 W
Conceição do Araguaia	250	8.15 S	49.17 W
Conceição do Canindé	250	7.54 S	41.34 W
Conceição do Coité	250	11.33 S	39.16 W
Conceição do Formoso	256	21.25 S	43.21 W
Conceição do Mato Dentro	255	19.01 S	43.25 W
Conceição do Maú	246	3.35 N	59.53 W
Conceição do Norte	255	12.13 S	47.18 W
Conceição do Rio Verde	256	21.53 S	45.05 W
Conceição dos Ouros	256	22.25 S	45.47 W
Concepción, Arg.	252	28.23 S	57.53 W
Concepción, Arg.	252	27.20 S	65.35 W
Concepción, Bol.	248	16.15 S	62.04 W
Concepción, Bol.	248	11.29 S	66.31 W
Concepción, Chile	252	36.50 S	73.03 W
Concepción, Col.	246	6.46 N	72.42 W
Concepción, Guat.	236	15.37 N	91.41 W
Concepción, Gui. Ecu.	152	3.23 N	8.46 E
Concepción, Para.	252	23.25 S	57.17 W
Concepción, Perú	248	11.55 S	75.17 W
Concepcion, Pil.	116	15.19 N	120.39 E
Concepcion, Pil.	116	12.24 N	122.06 E
Concepcion, Pil.	116	11.13 N	123.06 E
Concepcion, Pil.	116	10.42 N	123.03 E
Concepción □[5]	252	23.00 S	57.00 W
Concepción, Bahía C	232	26.39 N	111.48 W
Concepción, Estrecho del ⊔	254	50.30 S	74.55 W
Concepción, Laguna ⊜	248	17.29 S	61.25 W
Concepción, Río de la ≃	232	30.32 N	113.02 W
Concepción, Volcán ∧[1]	236	11.34 N	85.37 W
Concepcion Bay C	116	11.15 N	123.07 E
Concepción de Ataco	236	13.52 N	89.51 W
Concepción de Buenos Aires	234	19.58 N	103.16 W
Concepción de la Sierra	252	27.59 S	55.31 W
Concepción de la Vega → La Vega, Rep. Dom.	238	19.13 N	70.31 W
Concepción del Oro	232	24.38 N	101.25 W
Concepción del Uruguay	252	32.29 S	58.14 W
Concepción Quezaltepeque	236	14.06 N	88.58 W
Conception, Point ≻	204	34.27 N	120.27 W
Conception Bay C, Newf., Can.	186	47.45 N	53.00 W
Conception Bay C, Namibia	156	23.53 S	14.28 E
Concession	154	17.22 S	30.57 E
Conchagua	236	13.19 N	87.52 W
Conchagua, Volcán de ∧[1]	236	13.14 N	87.46 W
Conchal	256	22.20 S	47.10 W
Conchal, Ribeirão do ≃	256	22.20 S	47.10 W
Conchalí	286e	33.24 S	70.39 W
Conchas ≃	196	35.23 N	104.18 W
Conchas Dam	196	35.22 N	104.11 W
Conchas Lake ⊜[1]	196	35.25 N	104.14 W
Conche	186	50.53 N	55.54 W
Conches	32	48.51 N	2.43 E
Conches-en-Ouche	50	48.58 N	0.56 E
Conchi	252	22.02 S	68.38 W
Conchillas	258	34.15 S	58.04 W
Conchitas, Arroyo ≃	288	34.45 S	58.09 W
Concho	200	34.28 N	109.36 W
Conchos ≃, Méx.	232	29.35 N	104.25 W
Conchos ≃, Méx.	232	25.07 N	98.32 W
Concise	58	46.51 N	6.43 E
Conco	64	45.48 N	11.36 E
Concón	252	32.55 S	71.31 W
Conconongon Point ≻	116	12.14 N	120.13 E
Concord, Austl.	274a	33.52 S	151.06 E
Concord, Ont., Can.	275b	43.48 N	79.29 W
Concord, Calif., U.S.	226	37.59 N	122.02 W
Concord, Ga., U.S.	192	33.05 N	84.26 W
Concord, Ill., U.S.	219	39.49 N	90.22 W
Concord, Ky., U.S.	218	38.41 N	83.30 W
Concord, Mass., U.S.	207	42.27 N	71.21 W
Concord, Mich., U.S.	216	42.10 N	84.38 W
Concord, Mo., U.S.	219	38.31 N	90.23 W
Concord, N.H., U.S.	188	43.12 N	71.32 W
Concord, N.C., U.S.	192	35.25 N	80.35 W
Concord, Pa., U.S.	214	40.15 N	77.42 W
Concord, Tex., U.S.	222	31.16 N	96.09 W
Concord ≃	283	42.39 N	71.18 W
Concord Battleground ⊥	283	42.28 N	71.21 W
Concordia, Arg.	252	31.24 S	58.02 W
Concórdia, Bra.	246	4.35 S	66.35 W
Concórdia, Bra.	252	27.14 S	52.01 W
Concordia, Méx.	232	25.47 N	103.07 W
Concordia, Méx.	234	23.17 N	106.04 W
Concordia, Perú	246	4.30 S	74.55 W
Concordia, Kans., U.S.	198	39.34 N	97.39 W
Concordia, Mo., U.S.	194	38.59 N	93.34 W
Concordia Gardens	216	41.09 N	85.08 W
Concordia Sagitaria ⊥	64	45.45 N	12.51 E
Concordia sulla Secchia	64	44.55 N	10.59 E
Concord Naval Weapons Station ▪	282	38.03 N	122.02 W
Concordville	285	39.53 N	75.31 W
Concord West	274a	33.51 S	151.05 E
Concorezzo	62	45.35 N	9.20 E
Concrete	224	48.32 N	121.45 W
Con-cuong	110	19.02 N	104.54 E
Conda	152	11.06 S	14.20 E
Condamine	166	26.56 S	150.08 E
Condat-en-Féniers	32	45.21 N	2.46 E
Condé, Ang.	152	10.50 S	14.37 E
Conde, Bra.	255	11.49 S	37.37 W
Condé, Fr.	32	48.51 N	0.33 W
Conde, S. Dak., U.S.	198	45.09 N	98.06 W
Condécourt	261	49.02 N	1.57 E
Condé-en-Brie	50	49.00 N	3.33 E
Condega	236	13.21 N	86.24 W
Condeixa	250	0.54 S	48.36 W
Conderilla Señor	286d	12.02 S	77.05 W
Condé-sur-l'Escaut	50	50.27 N	3.35 E
Condè-sur-Vesgre	261	48.45 N	1.40 E
Condeúba	255	14.53 S	41.59 W
Condino	64	45.53 N	10.36 E
Condobolin	166	33.05 S	147.09 E
Condom	32	43.58 N	0.22 E
Condon	202	45.14 N	120.11 W
Condoto	246	5.06 N	76.37 W
Condove	62	45.07 N	7.18 E
Condrieu	62	45.27 N	4.46 E
Condroz □[9]	56	50.25 N	5.00 E
Cone	196	33.48 N	101.23 W
Conecuh ≃	194	30.58 N	87.14 W
Conegliano	64	45.53 N	12.18 E
Conejos	200	37.05 N	106.01 W
Conejos ≃	200	37.18 N	105.44 W
Conemaugh	214	40.24 N	78.52 W
Conemaugh ≃	214	40.28 N	79.27 W
Conemaugh River Lake ⊜[1]	214	40.28 N	79.17 W
Cone Mountain ∧	180	66.12 N	156.03 W
Conero, Monte ∧	66	43.33 N	13.36 E
Conestoga	208	39.57 N	76.21 W
Conestoga Creek ≃	208	39.56 N	76.23 W
Conestogo	212	43.32 N	80.30 W
Conestogo ≃	212	43.32 N	80.29 W
Conestogo Lake ⊜	212	43.44 N	80.44 W
Conesus	210	42.43 N	77.41 W
Conesus Lake ⊜	210	42.47 N	77.43 W
Conesville	214	40.11 N	81.54 W
Conewago Creek ≃	208	40.07 N	76.42 W
Conewago Lake ⊜	208	40.06 N	76.52 W
Conewango Creek ≃	214	41.50 N	79.09 W
Coney Island ◆[8]	276	40.34 N	74.00 W
Confederation Lake ⊜	184	51.05 N	92.44 W
Configni	66	42.25 N	12.38 E
Conflans-en-Jarnisy	56	49.10 N	5.51 E
Conflans-Sainte-Honorine	50	48.59 N	2.06 E
Conflenti	68	39.04 N	16.17 E
Conflict Group II	164	10.45 S	151.45 E
Confluence	188	39.49 N	79.21 W
Confolens	32	46.01 N	0.41 E
Confraternidad, Parque ♠	286d	12.09 S	77.02 W
Confusion Bay C	186	49.58 N	55.47 W
Confuso ≃	252	25.09 S	57.34 W
Cong	48	53.32 N	9.19 W
Congamond	207	42.01 N	72.46 W
Congaree ≃	192	33.45 N	80.37 W
Congelin	168a	32.50 S	116.54 E
Congers	210	41.09 N	74.11 W
Congers Lake ⊜	276	41.09 N	73.57 W
Cong Hoa Stadium ♠	269c	10.45 N	106.40 E
Conghua	100	23.32 N	113.32 E
Congjiang	102	25.41 N	108.47 E
Congkou	98	36.12 N	120.23 E
Congleton	44	53.10 N	2.13 W
Congo	250	7.48 S	36.40 W
Congo □[1]	10		
	152	1.00 S	15.00 E
Congo, République du → Congo □[1]	152	1.00 S	15.00 E
Congo (Zaire) (Zaïre) ≃	138	6.04 S	12.24 E
Congo, Democratic Republic of the → Zaire □[1]	10	0.00	25.00 E
Congo, Serra do ⋀	152	6.30 S	13.43 E
Congo Basin ⩡[1]	10	0.00	20.00 E
Congonhal	256	22.09 S	46.02 W
Congonhas, Aeroporto de ⊠	256	23.38 S	46.38 W
Congonhinhas	255	23.33 S	50.33 W
Congost ≃	266d	41.33 N	2.15 E
Congregación Cuauhtémoc	234	22.38 N	98.08 W
Congregación Ignacio Zaragoza	234	23.15 N	98.50 W
Congresbury	42	51.23 N	2.48 W
Congress, Sask., Can.	184	49.46 N	106.00 W
Congress, Ohio, U.S.	214	40.55 N	82.03 W
Congyang	100	30.42 N	117.12 E
Conie ≃	50	48.06 N	1.30 E
Conigli, Isola dei I	71a	35.30 N	12.33 E
Coningsby	44	53.07 N	0.10 W
Conisbrough	44	53.29 N	1.13 W
Coniston, Ont., Can.	190	46.29 N	80.51 W
Coniston, Eng., U.K.	44	54.22 N	3.05 W
Coniston Water ⊜	44	54.20 N	3.04 W
Conitaca	232	24.10 N	106.43 W
Conjeeveram → Kānchipuram	122	12.50 N	79.43 E
Conjola	170	35.13 S	150.27 E
Conjola, Lake C	170	35.16 S	150.27 E
Conjuror Bay C	176	65.45 N	118.07 W
Čon-Kemin ≃	85	42.42 N	75.54 E
Conklin, Alta., Can.	182	55.38 N	111.05 W
Conklin, N.Y., U.S.	210	42.02 N	75.48 W
Conklingville Dam ◆[6]	210	43.17 N	74.02 W
Conklin Point ≻	276	40.41 N	73.17 W
Conkouati	152	4.00 S	11.13 E
Conliège	58	46.39 N	5.36 E
Conlin, Lake ⊜	220	28.14 N	81.07 W
Çonlu	130	40.13 N	28.06 E
Conn, Lough ⊜	48	54.04 N	9.20 W
Connah's Quay	44	53.13 N	3.03 W
Connaught □[9]	48	43.45 N	9.00 W
Connaughton	285	40.05 N	75.19 W
Connaughton, Mount ∧[2]	162	22.42 S	122.40 E
Connaught Place ♠	272a	28.38 N	77.12 E
Connaux	62	44.05 N	4.36 E
Conneaut	214	41.57 N	80.34 W
Conneaut Creek ≃	214	41.58 N	80.33 W
Conneaut Lake	214	41.36 N	80.19 W
Conneaut Lake ⊜	214	41.37 N	80.18 W
Conneaut Outlet ≃	214	41.33 N	80.06 W
Conneautville	214	41.36 N	80.18 W
Connecticut □[3]	207		
	178	41.45 N	72.45 W
Connecticut ≃	188	41.17 N	72.21 W
Connell	202	46.40 N	118.52 W
Connell, Mount ∧	182	49.18 N	115.38 W
Connellsville	188	40.01 N	79.35 W
Connelly	210	41.55 N	73.59 W
Connel Park	44	55.23 N	4.12 W
Connemara	166	24.13 S	142.17 E
Connemara ◆[1]	48	53.25 N	9.45 W
Conner	116	17.48 N	121.19 E
Connerré	50	48.03 N	0.30 E
Connersville, Fla., U.S.	220	27.54 N	81.47 W
Connersville, Ind., U.S.	218	39.39 N	85.08 W
Connetquot ≃	276	40.43 N	73.08 W
Connetquot Brook ≃	276	40.45 N	73.09 W
Connetquot River State Park ♠	210	40.46 N	73.09 W
Connewarre, Lake ⊜	169	38.14 S	144.27 E
Conn Island I	284c	39.00 N	77.16 W
Conn Lake ⊜	176	70.34 N	73.30 W
Connoquenessing	214	40.49 N	80.59 W
Connoquenessing Creek ≃	214	40.51 N	80.19 W
Connors Range ⋀	166	21.40 S	149.10 E
Conodoguinet Creek ≃	208	40.17 N	76.55 W
Conon ≃	46	57.34 N	6.26 W
Cononaco ≃	246	1.32 S	75.35 W
Conotton Creek ≃	214	40.34 N	81.23 W
Conover	192	35.42 N	81.12 W
Conowingo	208	39.40 N	76.09 W
Conowingo ◆[6]	208	39.33 N	76.04 W
Conowingo Creek ≃	208	39.41 N	76.12 W
Conowingo Dam ◆[6]	208	39.39 N	76.10 W
Conquest	184	51.32 N	107.17 W
Conquista	255	19.56 S	47.33 W
Conquista, Ribeirão da ≃	256	21.17 S	43.51 W
Conrad, Iowa, U.S.	190	42.14 N	92.52 W
Conrad, Mont., U.S.	202	48.10 N	111.57 W
Conrado	256	22.32 S	43.33 W
Conroe	222	30.19 N	95.27 W
Conroe, Lake ⊜[1]	222	30.25 N	95.37 W
Consandolo	66	44.39 N	11.46 E
Čon-Saryoj	85	42.37 N	76.53 E
Conscience Bay C	276	40.57 N	73.07 W
Consdorf	56	49.46 N	6.20 E
Consecon	212	44.00 N	77.31 W
Conselheiro Lafaiete	255	20.40 S	43.48 W
Conselheiro Paulino	256	22.13 S	42.31 W
Conselheiro Pena	255	19.10 S	41.30 W
Conselice	66	44.31 N	11.49 E
Conselve	64	45.14 N	11.52 E
Conservatória	256	22.18 S	43.57 W
Consett	44	54.51 N	1.49 W
Conshohocken	208	40.05 N	75.18 W
Consolação	256	22.33 S	45.55 W
Consolação ◆[8]	287b	23.33 S	46.39 W
Consolación del Norte	240p	22.45 N	83.33 W
Consolación del Sur	240p	22.30 N	83.31 W
Consolidated Main Reef Mines ◆[7]	273d	26.11 S	27.56 E
Con Son II	110	8.43 N	106.36 E
Consort	184	52.01 N	110.46 W
Constable	206	44.56 N	74.18 W
Constableville	212	43.34 N	75.26 W
Constance → Konstanz	58	47.40 N	9.10 E
Constance, Lake → Bodensee ⊜	58	47.35 N	9.25 E
Constance Lake ⊜	212	45.25 N	75.58 W
Constan Creek ≃	212	45.17 N	76.46 W
Constan Lake ⊜	212	45.24 N	77.00 W
Constanța	38	44.11 N	28.39 E
Constanța □[4]	38	44.20 N	28.20 E
Constantia	210	43.15 N	76.00 W
Constantina	34	37.52 N	5.37 W
Constantine, Alg.	148	36.22 N	6.37 E
Constantine, Mich., U.S.	216	41.50 N	85.40 W
Constantine □[8]	36	36.20 N	6.35 E
Constantine, Cape ≻	180	58.25 N	158.50 W
Constantinople → İstanbul	130	41.01 N	28.58 E
Constânzia	34	39.28 N	8.20 W
Constitución, Chile	252	35.20 S	72.25 W
Constitución, Ur.	252	31.05 S	57.50 W
Constitución ◆[8]	288	34.37 S	58.23 W
Constitucion de 1857, Parque Nacional ♠	204	32.05 N	115.55 W
Constitution, Mount ∧	224	48.40 N	122.50 W
Consuegra	34	39.28 N	3.36 W
Consul	184	49.21 N	109.30 W
Consuma	66	43.47 N	11.35 E
Consuma, Passo della)(	66	43.47 N	11.36 E
Contai	126	21.47 N	87.45 E
Contamana	248	7.15 S	74.54 W
Contarina	64	45.00 N	12.13 E
Contas, Rio de ≃	255	14.17 S	39.01 W
Contee	208	39.05 N	76.52 W
Contendas do Sincorá	255	13.45 S	41.02 W
Contentnea Creek ≃	192	35.21 N	77.23 W
Contes	62	43.49 N	7.19 E
Contigliano	66	42.24 N	12.46 E
Continental	216	41.06 N	84.16 W
Continental Peak ∧	200	42.16 N	108.43 W
Contoocook ≃	188	43.27 N	71.35 W
Contoocook Lake ⊜	207	42.47 N	72.01 W
Contraalmirante Cordero	252	38.44 S	68.10 W
Contra Costa □[6]	226	37.55 N	121.55 W
Contra Costa Canal ⩧	282	38.02 N	121.58 W
Contra Loma Reservoir ⊜[1]	282	37.58 N	121.49 W
Contramaestre	240p	20.18 N	76.15 W
Contramaestre ≃	240p	20.31 N	76.18 W
Contratación	246	6.18 N	73.29 W
Contrecoeur	206	45.51 N	73.14 W
Contre Island ≻[1]	276	40.54 N	73.32 W
Contreras □[7]	286a	19.16 N	99.16 W
Contreras, Embalse de ⊜[1]	34	39.32 N	1.30 W
Contres	50	47.25 N	1.26 E
Contrexéville	58	48.11 N	5.54 E
Contrisson	56	48.48 N	4.57 E
Controller Bay C	180	60.07 N	144.15 W
Contumaza	248	7.22 S	78.49 W
Contursi	68	40.39 N	15.14 E
Contwoyto Lake ⊜	176	65.42 N	110.50 W
Conty	50	49.44 N	2.09 E
Contz-les-Bains	56	49.27 N	6.21 E
Convención	246	8.28 N	73.21 W
Convent	194	30.06 N	90.50 W
Convento	236	9.21 N	83.30 W
Convent Station	276	40.47 N	74.26 W
Conversano	68	40.58 N	17.08 E
Converse	216	40.35 N	85.52 W
Converse Lake ⊜	276	41.08 N	73.39 W
Converse Pond Brook ≃	276	41.03 N	73.40 W
Convoy	216	40.55 N	84.42 W
Conway, P.E.I., Can.	186	46.40 N	63.59 W
Conway, S. Afr.	158	31.43 S	25.16 E
Conway, Wales, U.K.	44	53.17 N	3.50 W
Conway, Ark., U.S.	194	35.05 N	92.26 W
Conway, Fla., U.S.	220	28.31 N	81.20 W
Conway, Mass., U.S.	207	42.31 N	72.42 W
Conway, Mo., U.S.	194	37.30 N	92.49 W
Conway, N.H., U.S.	188	43.59 N	71.07 W
Conway, N.C., U.S.	192	36.26 N	77.20 W
Conway, Pa., U.S.	214	40.40 N	80.14 W
Conway, S.C., U.S.	192	33.50 N	79.03 W
Conway, Wash., U.S.	224	48.21 N	122.21 W
Conway ≃	44	53.17 N	3.50 W
Conway, Cape ≻	166	20.32 S	148.56 E
Conway, Lake ⊜	162	28.17 S	135.35 E
Conway, Lake ⊜[1]	194	35.00 N	92.25 W
Conway, Mount ∧	162	23.45 S	133.25 E
Conway, Vale of ∨	44	53.12 N	3.48 W
Conway Bay C	44	53.18 N	3.55 W
Conway Springs	198	37.24 N	97.39 W
Conyers	192	33.40 N	84.01 W
Conyngham	210	40.59 N	76.03 W
Coo	56	50.24 N	5.52 E
Coober Pedy	162	29.01 S	134.43 E
Cooch Behār	124	26.19 N	89.26 E
Cooch Behār □[5]	124	26.20 N	89.20 E
Coogee Bay C	274a	33.55 S	151.16 E
Coogoon ≃	166	27.19 S	148.50 E
Cook, Ind., U.S.	216	41.22 N	87.26 W
Cook, Minn., U.S.	190	47.51 N	92.41 W
Cook, Nebr., U.S.	198	40.31 N	96.10 W
Cook, Wash., U.S.	224	45.43 N	121.40 W
Cook □[6]	216	41.53 N	87.38 W
Cook, Bahía C	254	55.10 S	70.10 W
Cook, Baie de C	174s	17.29 S	149.49 W
Cook, Cape ≻	182	50.08 N	127.55 W
Cook, Mount ∧	172	43.36 S	170.10 E
Cook, Point ≻	274b	37.55 S	144.48 E
Cookardinia	171b	35.34 S	147.14 E
Cook Bay C, Ont., Can.	212	44.15 N	79.30 W
Cook Bay C, N. Heb.	175f	18.45 S	169.10 E
Cookbundoon ≃	170	34.28 S	150.04 E
Cook Creek ≃	224	47.17 N	124.05 W
Cooke, Mount ∧	168a	32.25 S	116.18 E
Cookernup	168a	33.00 S	115.54 E
Cookes Peak ∧	200	32.32 N	107.44 W
Cookeville	194	36.10 N	85.31 W
Cook Forest State Park ♠	214	41.22 N	79.12 W
Cookham	42	51.34 N	0.43 W
Cookhouse	158	32.44 S	25.48 E
Cook Ice Shelf ⊓	9	68.40 S	152.30 E
Cooking Lake ⊜	182	53.25 N	113.02 W
Cook Inlet C	180	60.30 N	152.00 W
Cook-Inseln → Cook Islands □[2]	14	20.00 S	158.00 W
Cook Island I	174o	1.57 N	157.28 W
Cook Islands □[2]	14	20.00 S	158.00 W
Cook Islands II	14	20.00 S	158.00 W
Cooks ≃	274a	33.56 S	151.10 E
Cooksburg	214	41.20 N	79.12 W
Cooks Falls	210	41.57 N	74.59 W
Cook's Harbour	186	51.36 N	55.52 W
Cookshire	206	45.25 N	71.38 W
Cooksmill Green	260	51.44 N	0.22 E
Cooks Mills	284a	43.00 N	79.11 W
Cookstown, Ont., Can.	212	44.11 N	79.42 W
Cookstown, N. Ire., U.K.	48	54.39 N	6.45 W
Cook Strait ⊔	172	41.15 S	174.30 E
Cooksville, Ill., U.S.	216	40.33 N	88.43 W
Cooksville, Md., U.S.	208	39.19 N	77.01 W
Cooksville, Wis., U.S.	216	42.50 N	89.14 W
Cooksville Creek ≃	275b	43.34 N	79.34 W
Cooktown	164	15.28 S	145.15 E
Cookville	222	33.11 N	94.51 W
Coolaney	48	54.11 N	8.29 W
Coole ≃	50	48.56 N	4.21 E
Cooleemee	192	35.49 N	80.33 W
Cooley Lake ⊜	281	42.37 N	83.27 W
Coolgardie	162	30.57 S	121.10 E
Coolidge, Ariz., U.S.	200	32.59 N	111.31 W
Coolidge, Ga., U.S.	192	31.01 N	83.52 W
Coolidge, Tex., U.S.	222	31.45 N	96.39 W
Coolidge, Mount ∧	198	43.44 N	103.29 W
Coolidge Dam ◆[6]	200	33.00 N	110.20 W
Coolidge Field ⊠	240c	17.09 N	61.47 W
Coolidge Point ≻	283	42.34 N	70.44 W
Coolin	202	48.28 N	116.51 W
Cooling	260	51.27 N	0.32 E
Cooloongup, Lake ⊜	168a	32.18 S	115.47 E
Coolspring	214	41.02 N	79.05 W
Coolumburra, Mount ∧	170	35.01 S	150.10 E
Coombe Cottage ⊥	274b	37.43 S	145.23 E
Coomera ≃	171a	27.53 S	153.24 E
Coon Creek ≃, Calif., U.S.	226	38.51 N	121.34 W
Coon Creek ≃, Ill., U.S.	216	42.15 N	88.48 W
Coon Creek ≃, Tex., U.S.	222	31.59 N	95.52 W
Coon Creek Lake ⊜[1]	222	32.04 N	95.52 W
Coondapoor	122	13.38 N	74.42 E
Coongan ≃	162	20.53 S	119.47 E
Coonoor	122	11.21 N	76.49 E
Coon Rapids, Iowa, U.S.	198	41.52 N	94.41 W
Coon Rapids, Minn., U.S.	190	45.09 N	93.18 W
Coontown	276	40.37 N	74.31 W
Coon Valley	190	43.42 N	91.01 W
Cooper	196	33.23 N	95.35 W
Cooper ≃, N.J., U.S.	285	39.57 N	75.07 W
Cooper ≃, Wash., U.S.	224	47.23 N	121.23 W
Cooper, Mount ∧	162	26.11 S	127.56 E
Cooper, North Branch ≃	285	39.55 N	75.02 W
Cooper Center	216	42.23 N	85.37 W
Cooper Creek ≃	166	28.29 S	137.46 E
Cooper Island I	240m	18.22 N	64.30 W
Cooper Lake ⊜	200	41.37 N	105.50 W
Cooper Landing	180	61.57 N	145.18 W
Cooper Mountain ∧	180	60.23 N	149.51 W
Cooper River Parkway ♠	285	39.55 N	75.03 W
Cooper Road	194	32.35 N	93.48 W
Coopers	194	32.46 N	86.33 W
Coopersale Common	260	51.42 N	0.08 E
Coopersburg	208	40.31 N	75.23 W
Coopers Plains, Austl.	171a	27.34 S	153.02 E
Coopers Plains, N.Y., U.S.	210	42.11 N	77.08 W
Cooperstown, N. Dak., U.S.	198	47.27 N	98.07 W
Cooperstown, N.Y., U.S.	210	42.42 N	74.56 W
Cooperstown, Pa., U.S.	214	40.43 N	79.57 W
Cooperstown, Pa., U.S.	214	41.30 N	79.52 W
Coopersville	216	43.04 N	85.57 W
Coos □[6]	206	45.04 N	71.20 W
Coosa ≃	194	32.30 N	86.16 W
Coosawhatchie ≃	192	32.32 N	80.52 W
Coos Bay	202	43.22 N	124.13 W
Coos Bay C	202	43.23 N	124.16 W
Cootehill	48	54.04 N	7.05 W
Coot-Tha, Mount ∧[2]	171a	27.29 S	152.58 E
Cooyar Creek ≃	171a	27.24 S	152.03 E
Cooyar Mountain ∧	171a	26.57 S	151.47 E
Čop	78	48.26 N	22.10 E
Copacabana, Arg.	252	28.12 S	67.29 W
Copacabana, Bol.	248	16.10 S	69.05 W
Copacabana ◆[8]	287a	22.58 S	43.11 W
Copacabana, Forte de ⊥	287a	22.59 S	43.11 W
Copainalá	234	17.05 N	93.12 W
Copake	210	42.06 N	73.33 W
Copake Falls	210	42.07 N	73.31 W
Copala	234	16.37 N	98.58 W
Copalillo	234	18.02 N	99.07 W
Copalis ≃	224	47.07 N	124.13 W
Copalis Beach	224	47.07 N	124.10 W
Copalita ≃	234	15.46 N	96.03 W
Copalquín	232	25.29 N	107.00 W
Copán, Hond.	236	14.50 N	89.09 W
Copan, Okla., U.S.	196	36.54 N	95.56 W
Copán □[5]	236	14.50 N	89.00 W
Copán ⊥	236	14.50 N	89.09 W
Copanatoyac	234	17.15 N	98.45 W
Copándaro de Galeana	234	19.53 N	101.13 W
Copano Bay C	196	28.05 N	97.05 W
Copatana	246	2.48 S	67.04 W
Cope	198	39.40 N	102.51 W
Copeá, Paraná ≃[1]	246	3.52 S	63.20 W
Copeau ≃	184	52.45 N	103.00 W
Copeland	220	25.57 N	81.22 W
Copeland Island I	44	54.41 N	5.32 W
Copenhagen → København, Dan.	41	55.40 N	12.35 E
Copenhagen, N.Y., U.S.	212	43.54 N	75.41 W
Copenhague → København	41	55.40 N	12.35 E
Copertino	68	40.16 N	18.03 E
Copetonas	252	38.43 S	60.27 W
Copeville	222	33.05 N	96.25 W
Copiague	210	40.41 N	73.24 W
Copiague Neck ≻[1]	276	40.40 N	73.22 W
Copiapó	252	27.22 S	70.20 W
Copinsay I	46	58.54 N	2.40 W
Coplay	208	40.44 N	75.29 W
Copley, Austl.	166	30.32 S	138.25 E
Copley, Ohio, U.S.	214	41.06 N	81.39 W
Copoas, Mount ∧	116	10.48 N	119.17 E
Copolo	152	10.22 S	14.07 E
Çoporito	246	8.56 N	62.00 W
Čopoviči	78	50.49 N	27.58 E
Copparo	64	44.54 N	11.49 E
Coppell	222	32.57 N	97.01 W
Coppename ≃	250	5.48 N	55.55 W
Coppenbrügge	52	52.07 N	9.32 E
Copper ≃	180	60.30 N	144.50 W
Copperas Cove	196	31.08 N	97.54 W
Copperas Mountain ∧	276	41.02 N	74.28 W
Copperbelt □[4]	154	13.00 S	28.00 E
Copper Butte ∧	202	48.42 N	118.28 W
Copper Center	180	61.58 N	145.19 W
Copper Cliff	190	46.28 N	81.04 W
Copper Creek ≃	192	36.40 N	82.45 W
Copper Harbor	190	47.27 N	87.53 W
Coppermine	176	67.50 N	115.05 W
Coppermine ≃	176	67.49 N	115.04 W
Copper Mine Point ≻, Br. Vir. Is.	240m	18.26 N	64.25 W
Coppermine Point ≻, Ont., Can.	190	46.59 N	84.47 W
Copper Mountain	182	49.20 N	120.33 W
Copper Mountain ∧, Alaska, U.S.	180	55.14 N	132.36 W
Copper Mountain ∧, Wyo., U.S.	200	43.27 N	107.57 W
Copperopolis	226	37.59 N	120.38 W
Coppet	58	46.19 N	6.12 E
Copplestone	42	50.49 N	3.45 W
Coppull	262	53.37 N	2.40 W
Copster Green	262	53.48 N	2.30 W
Copton Creek ≃	182	54.16 N	119.15 W
Copton Point ≻	116	10.00 N	123.22 E
Coqueiro Grande, Serra do ∧	256	21.40 S	42.55 W
Coquet ≃	44	55.22 N	1.37 W
Coquet Dale ∨	44	55.16 N	1.50 W
Coquí	240m	17.59 N	66.14 W
Coquilhatville → Mbandaka	152	0.04 N	18.16 E
Coquille	202	43.11 N	124.11 W
Coquille ≃	202	43.07 N	124.26 W
Coquille, East Fork ≃	202	43.06 N	124.04 W
Coquille, Middle Fork ≃	202	43.05 N	124.09 W
Coquille, South Fork ≃	202	43.02 N	124.07 W
Coquimatlán	234	19.12 N	103.48 W
Coquimbo	252	29.58 S	71.21 W
Coquimbo □[4]	252	31.00 S	71.00 W
Corabia	38	43.46 N	24.30 E
Coração de Jesus	255	16.42 S	44.22 W
Coração de Maria	255	12.14 S	38.45 W
Corace ≃	68	38.49 N	16.37 E
Coracora	248	15.02 S	73.47 W
Corail, Mer de → Coral Sea ⊤[2]	14	20.00 S	158.00 E
Çorak Gölü ⊜	130	37.40 N	29.46 E
Coral	214	40.30 N	79.11 W
Coralaque ≃	248	16.26 S	70.45 W
Coral Bay C, Pil.	116	8.25 N	117.20 E
Coral Bay C, Vir. Is., U.S.	240m	18.20 N	64.41 W
Coral Gables	220	25.45 N	80.16 W
Coral Harbour	176	64.08 N	83.10 W
Coral Hills	284c	38.52 N	76.55 W
Coral Sea ⊤[2]	14	20.00 S	158.00 E
Coral Sea Basin ⊹[1]	14	14.00 S	152.00 E
Coral Sea Plateau ⊹[3]	14	17.00 S	149.00 E
Coral Springs	220	26.16 N	80.13 W
Coralville	190	41.40 N	91.35 W
Coralville Lake ⊜[1]	190	41.47 N	91.48 W
Coram, Mont., U.S.	202	48.36 N	114.02 W
Coram, N.Y., U.S.	210	40.52 N	73.00 W
Corangamite, Lake ⊜	169	38.10 S	143.25 E
Corantijn (Corentyne) ≃	250	5.55 N	57.05 W
Coraopolis	214	40.31 N	80.10 W
Coraopolis Heights	279b	40.29 N	80.10 W
Corato	68	41.09 N	16.25 E
Corbara, Lago di ⊜[1]	66	42.43 N	12.15 E
Corbeil-Essonnes	50	48.36 N	2.29 E
Corbenay	58	47.54 N	6.20 E
Corbeny	50	49.28 N	3.49 E
Corbeolona	62	45.10 N	9.22 E
Corbera, Riera de ≃	266d	41.27 N	1.59 E
Corberon	58	47.01 N	4.59 E
Corbett	210	42.03 N	75.02 W
Corbetta	62	45.28 N	8.55 E
Corbettsville	210	42.01 N	75.48 W
Corbie	50	49.55 N	2.30 E
Corbiere Point ≻	43b	49.11 N	2.15 W
Corbières ⋀	32	42.55 N	2.38 E
Corbigny	50	47.15 N	3.40 E
Corbin	192	36.57 N	84.05 W
Corbion	56	49.48 N	5.00 E
Corbola	64	45.00 N	12.05 E
Corbones ≃	34	37.36 N	5.39 W
Corbu	38	44.29 N	24.43 E
Corby	42	52.29 N	0.40 W
Corcaigh → Cork	48	51.54 N	8.28 W
Córcega	240m	18.19 N	67.15 W
Córcega, Isla de → Corse I	36	42.00 N	9.00 E
Corciano	66	43.08 N	12.17 E
Corcieux	58	48.10 N	6.53 E
Corcolle ◆[8]	267a	41.55 N	12.46 E
Corcoran	226	36.06 N	119.33 W
Corcovado ∧	287a	22.57 S	43.13 W
Corcovado, Golfo C	254	43.30 S	73.30 W
Corcovado, Volcán ∧[1]	254	43.12 S	72.48 W
Corcubión	34	42.57 N	9.11 W
Cordâ ≃	250	6.26 S	48.17 W
Cordeaux Reservoir ⊜[1]	170	34.22 S	150.45 E
Cordeiro	255	22.02 S	42.22 W
Cordele, Ga., U.S.	192	31.58 N	83.47 W
Cordele, Tex., U.S.	222	29.08 N	96.38 W
Cordell	196	35.17 N	98.59 W
Cordell Hull Reservoir ⊜[1]	194	36.25 N	85.40 W
Cordenons	64	45.59 N	12.42 E
Corder	194	39.06 N	93.38 W
Cordes	32	44.04 N	1.57 E
Cordignano	64	45.57 N	12.25 E
Cordillera □[5]	252	25.15 S	57.00 W
Cordillo Downs	166	26.43 S	140.38 E
Cordisburgo	255	19.07 S	44.21 W
Córdoba, Arg.	252	31.24 S	64.11 W
Córdoba, Esp.	34	37.53 N	4.46 W
Córdoba, Méx.	234	18.53 N	96.56 W
Córdoba □[4]	252	32.00 S	64.00 W
Córdoba □[5]	246	8 20 N	75.40 W
Córdoba, Península ≻[1]	254	53.20 S	72.50 W
Cordon	116	16.40 N	121.28 E
Cordova → Córdoba, Esp.	34	37.53 N	4.46 W
Córdova, Perú	248	14.04 S	75.03 W
Cordova, Ala., U.S.	194	33.46 N	87.11 W
Cordova, Alaska, U.S.	180	60.33 N	145.46 W
Cordova, Ill., U.S.	190	41.41 N	90.19 W
Cordova, Md., U.S.	208	38.52 N	76.00 W
Cordova Bay C	180	54.55 N	132.35 W
Cordova Lake ⊜	212	44.35 N	77.49 W
Cordova Peak ∧	180	60.51 N	145.16 W
Corea, Estrecho de → Korea Strait ⊔	90	34.00 N	129.00 E
Corea del Norte → Korea, North □[1]	98	40.00 N	127.00 E
Corea del Sur → Korea, South □[1]	98	36.30 N	128.00 E
Coreaú	250	3.33 S	40.39 W
Coreaú ≃	250	2.54 S	40.50 W
Core Creek ≃	285	40.11 N	74.55 W
Corée, Détroit de → Korea Strait ⊔	90	34.00 N	129.00 E
Coree, Mount ∧	171b	35.18 S	148.48 E
Corée du Nord → Korea, North □[1]	98	40.00 N	127.00 E
Corée du Sud → Korea, South □[1]	98	36.30 N	128.00 E
Coreglia Antelminelli	64	44.04 N	10.31 E
Coreinbob	171b	35.13 S	147.38 E
Coremas	250	7.01 S	37.58 W
Corentyne (Corantijn) ≃	250	5.55 N	57.05 W
Corerepe	232	25.40 N	108.40 W
Corese Terra	66	42.10 N	12.42 E
Corey Lake ⊜	216	41.55 N	85.45 W
Corfe Castle	42	50.38 N	2.04 W
Corfield	166	21.43 S	143.22 E
Corfu → Kérkira, Ellás	38	39.36 N	19.56 E
Corfu, N.Y., U.S.	210	42.58 N	78.24 W
Corfu → Kérkira I	38	39.40 N	19.42 E
Cori	66	41.39 N	12.55 E
Coria	34	39.59 N	6.32 W
Coria del Río	34	37.16 N	6.03 W
Coriaí ≃	250	3.18 S	52.04 W
Coribe	255	13.50 S	44.28 W
Coricudgy, Mount ∧	170	32.50 S	150.22 E
Corigliano Calabro	68	39.36 N	16.31 E
Corigliano d'Otranto	68	40.09 N	18.15 E
Corinaldo	66	43.39 N	13.03 E
Corinna	188	44.55 N	69.16 W
Corinne, Pa., U.S.	285	39.54 N	75.40 W
Corinne, Utah, U.S.	200	41.35 N	112.07 W
Corinne, W. Va., U.S.	192	37.34 N	81.22 W
Corinth → Kórinthos, Ellás	38	37.56 N	22.56 E
Corinth, Ky., U.S.	218	38.30 N	84.34 W
Corinth, Miss., U.S.	194	34.56 N	88.31 W
Corinth, N.Y., U.S.	210	43.15 N	73.49 W
Corinth, Gulf of → Korinthiakós Kólpos C	38	38.19 N	22.04 E
Corinth Canal → Korínthou, Dhiórix ⩧	38	37.57 N	22.56 E
Corinto, Bra.	255	18.21 S	44.27 W
Corinto, El Sal.	236	13.49 N	87.58 W
Corinto, Nic.	236	12.29 N	87.10 W
Corio Bay C	169	38.07 S	144.24 E
Coripata	248	16.18 S	67.36 W
Corire	248	16.14 S	72.28 W
Coris	248	9.50 S	77.45 W
Corisco, Isla de I	152	0.53 N	9.20 E
Corixao ≃	248	18.22 S	57.23 W
Cork	48	51.54 N	8.28 W
Cork □[6]	48	52.00 N	8.30 W
Cork Airport ⊠	48	51.51 N	8.29 W
Cork Harbour C	48	51.45 N	8.15 W
Corkscrew	220	26.28 N	81.33 W
Corkscrew Swamp ☷	220	26.25 N	81.34 W
Corlay	32	48.19 N	3.03 W
Corleone	70	37.49 N	13.18 E
Corleto Perticara	68	40.23 N	16.03 E
Çorlu	130	41.09 N	27.48 E
Cormainville	50	48.08 N	1.36 E
Cormano	266b	45.33 N	9.10 E
Cormatin	58	46.33 N	4.41 E
Cormeilles	50	49.15 N	0.23 E
Cormeilles-en-Parisis	50	48.59 N	2.12 E
Cormery	50	47.16 N	0.51 E
Cormons	64	45.58 N	13.28 E
Cormoran Reef ⊹[2]	175b	7.50 N	134.32 E
Cormorant	184	54.14 N	100.35 W
Cormorant Lake ⊜	184	54.13 N	100.47 W
Čormoz	86	58.53 N	56.08 E
Corna	64	45.53 N	10.10 E
Čornaja, S.S.S.R.	24	68.35 N	56.30 E
Čornaja, S.S.S.R.	82	55.45 N	38.04 E
Čornaja Cholunica	86	58.51 N	51.42 E
Čornaja Gr'az', S.S.S.R.	82	54.58 N	36.48 E
Čornaja Gr'az', S.S.S.R.	82	54.31 N	35.52 E
Čornaja Gr'az', S.S.S.R.	265b	55.58 N	37.19 E
Čornaja Rečka	265a	59.56 N	30.58 E
Čornaja Sloboda	24	60.48 N	37.46 E
Cornaredo	266b	45.30 N	9.02 E
Cornas	62	44.58 N	4.51 E
Cornedo Vicentino	64	45.37 N	11.20 E
Cornelia, S. Afr.	158	27.13 S	28.52 E
Cornelia, Ga., U.S.	192	34.31 N	83.32 W
Cornélio Procópio	255	23.08 S	50.39 W
Cornelius, N.C., U.S.	192	35.29 N	80.52 W
Cornelius, Oreg., U.S.	224	45.31 N	123.04 W
Cornelius Grinnell Bay C	176	63.20 N	64.50 W
Cornell, Calif., U.S.	228	34.08 N	118.47 W
Cornell, Ill., U.S.	216	41.00 N	88.44 W
Cornell, Wis., U.S.	190	45.10 N	91.09 W
Cornellá	266d	41.21 N	2.04 E

Symbols in the index entries represent the broad categories identified in the key at the right. Symbols with superior numbers (⋀[2]) identify subcategories (see complete key on page I · 30).

Kartensymbole in dem Registerverzeichnis stellen die rechts in Schlüssel erklärten Kategorien dar. Symbole mit hochgestellten Ziffern (⋀[2]) bezeichnen Unterabteilungen einer Kategorie (vgl. vollständiger Schlüssel auf Seite I · 30).

Los símbolos incluídos en el texto del índice representan las grandes categorías identificadas con la clave a la derecha. Los símbolos con numeros en su parte superior (⋀[2]) identifican las subcategorías (véase la clave completa en la página I · 30).

Les symboles de l'index représentent les catégories indiquées dans la légende à droite. Les symboles suivis d'un indice (⋀[2]) représentent des sous-catégories (voir légende complète à la page I · 30).

Os símbolos incluídos no texto do índice representam as grandes categorias identificadas com a chave à direita. Os símbolos com números em sua parte superior (⋀[2]) identificam as subcategorias (veja-se a chave completa à página I · 30).

Symbol	English	Deutsch	Español	Français	Português
∧	Mountain	Berg	Montaña	Montagne	Montanha
⋀	Mountains	Berge	Montañas	Montagnes	Montanhas
)(	Pass	Pass	Paso	Col	Passo
∨	Valley, Canyon	Tal, Cañon	Valle, Cañón	Vallée, Canyon	Vale, Canhão
⩡	Plain	Ebene	Llano	Plaine	Planície
≻	Cape	Kap	Cabo	Cap	Cabo
I	Island	Insel	Isla	Île	Ilha
II	Islands	Inseln	Islas	Îles	Ilhas
●	Other Topographic Features	Andere Topographische Objekte	Otros Elementos Topográficos	Autres données topographiques	Outros Elementos Topográficos

ESPAÑOL — Nombre | Página | Lat.°′ | Long.°′ W=Oeste
FRANÇAIS — Nom | Page | Lat.°′ | Long.°′ W=Ouest
PORTUGUÊS — Nome | Página | Lat.°′ | Long.°′ W=Oeste

Corner Brook 186 48.57 N 57.57 W
Corner Inlet ⊂ 169 38.43 S 146.20 E
Corner Store 285 40.07 N 75.30 W
Cornes, Lac des ⊜ 206 46.43 N 75.09 W
Cornforth 44 54.42 N 1.31 W
Cornhill 46 57.36 N 2.42 W
Cornholme 262 53.44 N 2.08 W
Cornia ≃ 66 42.57 N 10.33 E
Corniglia 62 44.07 N 9.42 E
Corning, Ark., U.S. 194 36.24 N 90.35 W
Corning, Calif., U.S. 204 39.56 N 122.11 W
Corning, Iowa, U.S. 198 40.59 N 94.44 W
Corning, Kans., U.S. 198 39.39 N 96.02 W
Corning, N.Y., U.S. 210 42.09 N 77.04 W
Corning, Ohio, U.S. 188 39.36 N 82.05 W
Cornish 188 43.48 N 70.48 W
Cornish, Mount ∧ 162 20.13 S 126.28 E
Cornland 219 39.56 N 89.24 W
Çorno ≃ 66 42.49 N 12.55 E
Čornobajevka 78 46.42 N 32.32 E
Çorno Grande ∧ 66 42.28 N 13.34 E
Çornoje, S.S.S.R. 80 57.32 N 46.25 E
Çornoje, S.S.S.R. 86 51.44 N 77.34 E
Čornolesskoje 84 44.42 N 43.42 E
Čornomorskij 78 44.51 N 38.29 E
Čornomorskij Zapovednik ◆[4] 78 46.10 N 32.00 E
Čornomorskoje, S.S.S.R. 78 45.03 N 35.58 E
Čornomorskoje, S.S.S.R. 78 45.30 N 32.42 E
Čornoreck 86 52.45 N 76.40 E
Cornuda 64 45.50 N 12.00 E
Cornwall, Ont., Can. 206 45.02 N 74.44 W
Cornwall, N.Y., U.S. 210 41.26 N 74.01 W
Cornwall, Pa., U.S. 208 40.14 N 76.31 W
Cornwall □[6] 42 50.30 N 4.40 W
Cornwall Bridge 207 41.49 N 73.22 W
Cornwallis Island ▮ 176 75.15 N 94.30 W
Cornwall on the Hudson 210 41.27 N 74.00 W
Cornwell 220 27.23 N 81.05 W
Çornwells Heights 285 40.04 N 74.57 W
Çornyj Jar 80 48.04 N 46.08 E
Çornyj Mys, S.S.S.R. 24 68.20 N 38.37 E
Çornyj Mys, S.S.S.R. 86 55.33 N 80.04 E
Çornyj Ostrov 78 49.32 N 26.46 E
Çornyj Otrog 86 51.55 N 55.59 E
Çornyj Rynok 84 44.24 N 46.33 E
Çornyj Tašlyk ≃ 78 48.11 N 30.51 E
Corny Point 166 34.55 S 137.03 E
Coro 246 11.25 N 69.41 W
Coro, Golfete de ⊂ 241s 11.30 N 69.55 W
Coroaci 255 18.35 S 42.17 W
Coroa Grande 256 22.54 S 43.52 W
Coroatá 250 4.08 S 44.08 W
Çoroca ≃ 152 15.43 S 11.55 E
Čoroch (Çoruh) ≃ 130 41.36 N 41.35 E
Corocoro 248 17.12 S 68.29 W
Corocoro Island ▮ 246 8.30 N 60.10 W
Corofin 48 52.56 N 9.03 W
Coroico 248 16.10 S 67.44 W
Coroico ≃ 248 15.27 S 67.50 W
Coromandel, Bra. 255 18.28 S 47.13 W
Coromandel, N.Z. 172 36.46 S 175.30 E
Coromandel Coast •[2] 122 14.00 N 80.10 E
Coromandel Peninsula ≻[1] 172 36.50 S 175.35 E
Coromandel Range ⛰ 172 37.00 S 175.40 E
Coron 116 12.00 N 120.12 E
Corona, Calif., U.S. 228 33.52 N 117.34 W
Corona, N. Mex., U.S. 200 34.15 N 105.36 W
Corona ◆[8] 276 40.45 N 73.52 W
Coronación, Golfo de la → Coronation Gulf ⊂ 176 68.25 N 110.00 W
Coronación, Isla de la → Coronation Island ▮ 9 60.37 S 45.30 W
Corona del Mar ◆[8] 228 33.36 N 117.52 W
Coronado, Méx. 234 22.55 N 100.56 W
Coronado, Calif., U.S. 228 32.41 N 117.11 W
Coronado, Bahía de ⊂ 236 9.00 N 83.50 W
Coronado National Memorial ♠ 200 31.10 N 110.29 W
Coronado Naval Amphibious Base ■ 228 32.40 N 117.10 W
Coronados, Golfo de los ⊂ 254 41.40 S 74.00 W
Coronation 182 52.05 N 111.27 W
Coronation Gardens ♠ 275b 43.41 N 79.29 W
Coronation Gulf ⊂ 176 68.25 N 110.00 W
Coronation Island ▮, B.A.T. 9 60.37 S 45.30 W
Coronation Island ▮, Alaska, U.S. 180 55.52 N 134.15 W
Coronation Park ♠ 273d 26.06 S 27.47 E
Coron Bay ⊂ 116 11.54 N 120.08 E
Coronda 252 31.58 S 60.55 W
Coronel 252 37.01 S 73.08 W
Coronel Bogado 252 27.11 S 56.18 W
Coronel Brandsen 258 35.10 S 58.14 W
Coronel Dorrego 252 38.42 S 61.17 W
Coronel Du Graty 252 27.40 S 60.56 W
Coronel Eugenio del Busto 252 38.57 S 64.15 W
Coronel Fabriciano 255 19.31 S 42.38 W
Coronel Moldes, Arg. 252 33.38 S 64.36 W
Coronel Moldes, Arg. 252 25.16 S 65.29 W
Coronel Murta 255 16.37 S 42.11 W
Coronel Oviedo 252 25.25 S 56.27 W
Coronel Pacheco 256 21.35 S 43.16 W
Coronel Ponce 255 15.34 S 55.01 W
Coronel Pringles 252 37.58 S 61.22 W
Coronel Suárez 252 37.28 S 61.55 W
Coronel Vidal 252 37.27 S 57.43 W
Coronel Vivida 252 25.58 S 52.34 W
Corongo 248 8.35 S 77.55 W
Corongoros 234 19.17 N 102.48 W
Coronie □[5] 250 5.50 N 56.20 W
Coron Island ▮ 116 11.55 N 120.14 E
Coronita 228 33.52 N 117.36 W
Coropuna, Nevado ∧ 248 15.31 S 72.42 W
Çorovodë 38 40.30 N 20.13 E
Corowa 166 36.02 S 146.23 E
Corozal, Belize 232 18.24 N 88.24 W
Corozal, Col. 246 9.19 N 75.18 W
Corozal, Hond. 236 15.48 N 86.43 W
Corozal, P.R. 240m 18.21 N 66.17 W
Corps 62 44.49 N 5.57 E
Corpus 252 27.07 S 55.31 W
Corpus Christi 196 27.48 N 97.24 W
Corpus Christi, Lake ⊜[1] 196 28.10 N 97.53 W
Corpus Christi Bay ⊂ 196 27.48 N 97.20 W
Corpus Christi Naval Air Station ■ 196 27.42 N 97.16 W
Corque 248 18.21 S 67.42 W
Corquín 236 14.34 N 88.52 W
Corral 254 39.52 S 73.26 W
Corral de Almaguer 34 39.46 N 3.11 W
Corral de Bustos 252 33.17 S 62.12 W
Corralillo 240p 22.59 N 80.35 W
Corralito, Arroyo del ≃ 258 33.39 S 58.03 W
Corralito, Cuchilla del ⛰[2] 258 33.40 S 57.44 W
Corralitos, Méx. 196 26.57 N 104.39 W
Corralitos, Calif., U.S. 226 36.59 N 121.48 W
Corran 46 56.43 N 5.14 W
Corraum Peninsula ≻[1] 48 54.54 N 9.53 W
Correas, Arroyo ≃ 288 34.24 S 58.32 W
Correctionville 198 42.28 N 95.47 W

Corredor 287b 23.27 S 46.19 W
Correggio 64 44.46 N 10.47 E
Corregidor Island ▮ 116 14.23 N 120.35 E
Córrego do Bom Jesus 256 22.38 S 46.02 W
Córrego do Ouro, Bra. 255 16.18 S 50.32 W
Córrego do Ouro, Bra. 256 21.22 S 45.47 W
Córrego Rico 255 15.14 S 47.48 W
Correia de Almeida 256 21.17 S 43.38 W
Corrente 250 10.27 S 45.10 W
Corrente ≃, Bra. 250 4.18 S 42.11 W
Corrente ≃, Bra. 255 19.19 S 50.50 W
Corrente ≃, Bra. 255 13.08 S 43.28 W
Correntes 250 9.08 S 36.19 W
Correntes ≃ 255 17.38 S 55.08 W
Correntes, Cabo das ≻ 156 24.11 S 35.34 E
Correntezas 256 22.30 S 42.31 W
Correnti, Isola delle ▮▮ 70 36.38 N 15.05 E
Correntina 255 13.20 S 44.39 W
Corrèze □[5] 32 45.20 N 1.50 E
Correzzana 266b 45.40 N 9.18 E
Corrib, Lough ⊜ 48 53.05 N 9.10 W
Corridonia 66 43.15 N 13.30 E
Corrientes 252 27.28 S 58.50 W
Corrientes □[4] 252 29.00 S 58.00 W
Corrientes ≃, Arg. 252 30.21 S 59.33 W
Corrientes ≃, S.A. 246 3.43 S 74.35 W
Corrientes, Cabo ≻, Arg. 252 38.01 S 57.32 W
Corrientes, Cabo ≻, Col. 246 5.30 N 77.34 W
Corrientes, Cabo ≻, Cuba 240p 21.45 N 84.31 W
Corrientes, Cabo ≻, Méx. 234 20.25 N 105.42 W
Corrientes, Ensenada de ⊂ 240p 21.51 N 84.36 W
Corrigan 222 31.00 N 94.50 W
Corrigin 162 32.21 S 117.52 E
Corrimal 170 34.22 S 150.54 E
Corringham 260 51.31 N 0.28 E
Corroios 266c 38.38 N 9.09 W
Corropoli 66 42.49 N 13.50 E
Corrotoman ≃ 208 37.40 N 76.29 W
Corry 214 41.56 N 73.39 W
Corryong Creek ≃ 171b 36.06 S 147.59 E
Corryvreckan, Gulf of ⋃ 46 56.09 N 5.44 W
Corsano 68 39.53 N 18.22 E
Corse (Corsica) ▮ 36 42.00 N 9.00 E
Corse, Cap ≻ 62 43.00 N 9.25 E
Corserine ∧ 44 55.09 N 4.22 W
Corsham 42 51.26 N 2.11 W
Corsica, Pa., U.S. 214 41.10 N 79.12 W
Corsica, S. Dak., U.S. 198 43.25 N 98.24 W
Corsica → Corse ▮ 36 42.00 N 9.00 E
Corsicana 222 32.06 N 96.28 W
Corsica River ⊂ 208 39.05 N 76.08 W
Corsico 62 45.26 N 9.07 E
Corsock 44 55.04 N 3.57 W
Corson Inlet ⊂ 208 39.12 N 74.39 W
Cortaccia (Kurtatsch) 64 46.19 N 11.13 E
Cortachy 46 56.43 N 2.58 W
Cort Adelaer, Kap ≻ 176 62.00 N 42.00 W
Cortaderas 252 32.30 S 65.00 W
Cortado, Rio do ≃ 287a 23.00 S 43.25 W
Cortale 68 38.50 N 16.25 E
Cortazar 234 20.29 N 100.56 W
Corte 36 42.18 N 9.08 E
Corte Alto 254 40.57 S 73.10 W
Cortegana 34 37.55 N 6.49 W
Corte Madera 226 37.55 N 122.31 W
Corte Madera Creek ≃ 282 37.23 N 122.14 W
Cortemaggiore 64 44.59 N 9.56 E
Cortemilia 62 44.35 N 8.12 E
Cortes 116 9.17 N 126.11 E
Cortés □[5] 236 15.30 N 88.00 W
Cortés, Ensenada de ⊂ 240p 22.05 N 83.52 W
Cortez, Colo., U.S. 200 37.21 N 108.35 W
Cortez, Fla., U.S. 220 27.28 N 82.41 W
Cortez Mountains ⛰ 204 40.20 N 116.20 W
Cortina Creek ≃ 226 39.06 N 122.02 W
Cortina d'Ampezzo 64 46.32 N 12.08 E
Çortines 258 34.34 S 59.13 W
Čortkov 78 49.01 N 25.48 E
Cortland, Ill., U.S. 216 41.55 N 88.41 W
Cortland, Ind., U.S. 218 38.58 N 85.58 W
Cortland, Nebr., U.S. 198 40.30 N 96.42 W
Cortland, N.Y., U.S. 210 42.36 N 76.11 W
Cortland, Ohio, U.S. 214 41.20 N 80.44 W
Cortland □[6] 210 42.36 N 76.11 W
Corton 42 52.32 N 1.44 E
Cortona 66 43.16 N 11.59 E
Çorubal (Koliba) ≃ 150 11.57 N 15.06 W
Čoruch-Dajron 85 40.24 N 69.40 E
Coruche 34 38.57 N 8.31 W
Çoruh (Čoroch) ≃ 130 41.36 N 41.35 E
Çorum, Tür. 130 39.14 N 28.27 E
Çorum, Tür. 130 40.33 N 34.58 E
Çorum □[4] 130 40.30 N 34.40 E
Corumbá 248 19.01 S 57.39 W
Corumbá ≃ 255 18.19 S 48.55 W
Corumbá de Goiás 255 15.55 S 48.48 W
Corumbaíba 255 18.09 S 48.34 W
Corumbataí ≃ 252 23.55 S 51.57 W
Corumbaú, Ponta de ≻ 255 16.53 S 39.06 W
Corumbiara Antigo ≃ 248 13.13 S 62.06 W
Corumo ≃ 246 6.49 N 60.52 W
Corund 38 46.28 N 25.11 E
Corunna, Ont., Can. 214 42.53 N 82.26 W
Corunna → La Coruña, Esp. 34 43.22 N 8.23 W
Corunna, Ind., U.S. 216 41.26 N 85.09 W
Corunna, Mich., U.S. 216 42.59 N 84.07 W
Corunna Downs 162 21.28 S 119.51 E
Coruripe 250 10.08 S 36.10 W
Corvallis, Mont., U.S. 202 46.19 N 114.07 W
Corvallis, Oreg., U.S. 202 44.34 N 123.16 W
Corvara in Badia 64 46.33 N 11.52 E
Corve ≃ 42 52.22 N 2.43 W
Corve Dale ∨ 42 52.30 N 2.40 W
Corvey, Kloster ⊍[1] 52 51.46 N 9.25 E
Corviale ◆[8] 267a 41.52 N 12.25 E
Corvo ▮ 148a 39.42 N 31.06 W
Corwen 42 52.59 N 3.22 W
Corwin, Cape ≻ 180 59.54 N 165.41 W
Corwith 190 42.59 N 93.57 W
Corydon, Ind., U.S. 218 38.13 N 86.07 W
Corydon, Iowa, U.S. 190 40.45 N 93.19 W
Corydon, Ky., U.S. 194 37.44 N 87.43 W
Coryell 222 31.33 N 97.37 W
Coryell □[6] 222 31.25 N 97.40 W
Coryell Creek ≃ 222 31.23 N 97.35 W
Coryton 260 51.31 N 0.31 E
Coryville 214 41.53 N 78.24 W
Corzu 38 44.28 N 23.10 E
Corzuela 252 26.57 S 60.58 W
Cos → Kos ▮ 38 36.50 N 27.10 E
Cosa (Ansedonia) ⊥ 66 42.25 N 11.18 E
Cosamaloapan [de Carpio] 232 18.22 N 95.48 W
Cosapa 248 18.11 S 68.40 W
Cosby 42 52.33 N 1.11 W
Coscile ≃ 68 39.42 N 16.28 E
Cos Cob 276 41.02 N 73.36 W
Cos Cob Harbor ⊂ 276 41.01 N 73.36 W

Coscomatepec [de Bravo] 234 19.04 N 97.02 W
Cosel → Koźle 30 50.20 N 18.08 E
Coseley 42 52.33 N 2.06 W
Cosenza 68 39.17 N 16.15 E
Cosenza □[4] 68 39.28 N 16.25 E
Cosgrove's Creek ≃ 274a 33.50 S 150.46 E
Coshocton 214 40.16 N 81.51 W
Coshocton □[6] 214 40.16 N 81.51 W
Cosigüina, Punta ≻ 236 12.54 N 87.41 W
Cosigüina, Volcán ∧[1] 236 12.59 N 87.34 W
Coslada 266a 40.25 N 3.34 W
Cosmo ◆[8] 256 22.54 S 43.37 W
Cosmoledo Group ▮▮ 138 9.43 S 47.35 E
Cosmópolis, Bra. 256 22.38 S 47.12 W
Cosmopolis, Wash., U.S. 224 46.57 N 123.46 W
Cosmorama 255 20.28 S 49.47 W
Cosmos ◆[8] 287a 22.55 S 44.37 W
Cosne-sur-Loire 50 47.24 N 2.55 E
Cosoleacaque 234 18.00 N 94.37 W
Cospán 248 7.26 S 78.33 W
Cosquín 252 31.15 S 64.29 W
Cossato 62 45.34 N 8.10 E
Cossatot ≃ 194 33.48 N 94.09 W
Cossayuna 210 43.11 N 73.26 W
Cossayuna Lake ⊜ 210 43.12 N 73.25 W
Cossebaude 54 51.05 N 13.38 E
Çossé-le-Vivien 28 47.57 N 0.55 W
Čošskaja Guba ⊂ 24 67.30 N 46.30 E
Cossoine 71 40.27 N 8.43 E
Cosson ≃ 50 47.30 N 1.15 E
Cossonay 58 46.37 N 6.31 E
Cost 222 29.26 N 97.32 W
Costa, Cayo ▮ 220 26.41 N 82.15 W
Costa, Sierra de la → Coast Ranges ⛰ 178 41.00 N 123.30 W
Costacciaro 66 43.21 N 12.42 E
Costa de Caparica 266c 38.38 N 9.14 W
Costa del Marfil → Ivory Coast □[1] 150 8.00 N 5.00 W
Costa de San José 258 33.51 S 56.53 W
Costa di Rovigo 64 45.03 N 11.42 E
Costa Mesa 228 33.39 N 117.55 W
Costanera, Cadena → Coast Mountains ⛰ 176 55.00 N 129.00 W
Costanero, Canal de ≊ 288 34.28 S 58.28 W
Costa Rica 232 28.55 N 111.36 W
Costa Rica □[1] 230 / 236 10.00 N 84.00 W
Costaros 62 44.54 N 3.50 E
Costas 256 22.39 S 45.56 W
Costello 214 41.36 N 78.03 W
Costelloe 48 53.17 N 9.32 W
Costermansville → Bukavu 154 2.30 S 28.52 E
Costessey 42 52.40 N 1.11 E
Costești 38 44.40 N 24.53 E
Costiera, Catena ⛰ 68 39.20 N 16.05 E
Costigan Lake ⊜ 184 56.56 N 105.55 W
Costigliole d'Asti 62 44.47 N 8.11 E
Costigliole Saluzzo 62 44.34 N 7.29 E
Costilla 200 36.59 N 105.32 W
Costilla Creek ≃ 200 36.59 N 105.43 W
Cosumnes ≃ 226 38.16 N 121.26 W
Cosumnes, Middle Fork ≃ 226 38.33 N 120.51 W
Cosumnes, North Fork ≃ 226 38.33 N 120.51 W
Cosumnes, South Fork ≃ 226 38.33 N 120.49 W
Coswig, D.D.R. 54 51.07 N 13.34 E
Coswig, D.D.R. 54 51.53 N 12.26 E
Cotabambas 248 13.45 S 72.21 W
Cotabato 116 7.13 N 124.15 E
Cotabato □[4] 116 6.40 N 124.45 E
Cotacajes ≃ 248 16.00 S 67.01 W
Cotagaita 248 20.50 S 65.41 W
Cotagaita ≃ 248 21.01 S 65.23 W
Cotahuasi 248 15.12 S 72.56 W
Cotão ∧[2] 266c 38.45 N 9.18 W
Cotati 226 38.20 N 122.42 W
Cotaxtla ≃ 234 19.02 N 96.08 W
Coteau-Landing 206 45.15 N 74.13 W
Coteau-Station 206 45.17 N 74.14 W
Coteaux 238 18.12 N 74.02 W
Côte d'Ivoire → Ivory Coast □[1] 150 8.00 N 5.00 W
Côte-d'Or □[5] 50 47.30 N 4.50 E
Cotegipe 255 12.02 S 44.15 W
Cote Indian Reserve ◆[4] 184 51.38 N 101.53 W
Cotentin ≻[1] 32 49.30 N 1.30 W
Côte-Saint-Luc 275a 45.28 N 73.40 W
Côtes-du-Nord □[5] 32 48.25 N 2.40 W
Côte Visitation ◆[8] 275a 45.33 N 73.36 W
Cothi ≃ 42 51.52 N 4.10 W
Coti ≃ 248 8.36 S 65.33 W
Cotia 256 23.37 S 46.56 W
Cotia □[7] 287b 23.38 S 46.56 W
Cotia ≃ 256 23.31 S 46.51 W
Cotia, Represa de ⊜[1] 287b 23.44 S 46.57 W
Cotignac 62 43.32 N 6.09 E
Cotignola 66 44.23 N 11.56 E
Cotija de la Paz 234 19.49 N 102.43 W
Cotingo ≃ 246 3.55 N 60.30 W
Cotmeana ≃ 38 44.24 N 24.45 E
Cotoca 248 17.49 S 63.03 W
Cotonou 150 6.21 N 2.26 E
Cotopaxi □[4] 246 0.55 S 78.55 W
Cotopaxi ∧[1] 246 0.40 S 78.26 W
Cotorra, Isla ▮ 241r 10.02 N 62.16 W
Cotovêlo, Cachoeira do ⌊ 248 7.08 S 58.43 W
Cotronei 68 39.09 N 16.47 E
Cotswold Hills ⛰[2] 42 51.45 N 2.10 W
Cottage Grove, Ind., U.S. 218 39.36 N 84.52 W
Cottage Grove, Oreg., U.S. 202 43.48 N 123.03 W
Cottage Grove, Wis., U.S. 216 43.05 N 89.12 W
Cottage Hills 219 38.55 N 90.04 W
Cottageville 192 32.56 N 80.29 W
Cottam, Ont., Can. 214 42.08 N 82.45 W
Cottam, Eng., U.K. 262 53.47 N 2.46 W
Cottanello 66 42.24 N 12.41 E
Cottbus 54 51.45 N 14.19 E
Cottbus □[5] 54 51.45 N 14.00 E
Cottekill 210 41.51 N 74.06 W
Cottel Island ▮ 186 48.51 N 53.42 W
Cottenham 42 52.18 N 0.09 E
Cotter 194 36.16 N 92.32 W
Cotter ≃ 171b 35.19 S 148.57 E
Cottiennes, Alpes (Alpi Cozie) ⛰ 62 44.45 N 7.00 E
Cottingham (Haltemprice) 44 53.47 N 0.24 W
Cottleville 219 38.45 N 90.39 W
Cottondale, Ala., U.S. 194 33.11 N 87.27 W
Cottondale, Fla., U.S. 192 30.48 N 85.23 W
Cotton Lake ⊜, Man., Can. 184 55.05 N 96.50 W
Cotton Lake ⊜, Tex., U.S. 222 29.48 N 94.48 W
Cotton Plant 194 35.00 N 91.15 W
Cottonport 194 30.59 N 92.03 W
Cotton Valley 194 32.49 N 93.25 W
Cottonwood, Ariz., U.S. 200 34.45 N 112.01 W
Cottonwood, Calif., U.S. 204 40.23 N 122.17 W

Cottonwood, Idaho, U.S. 202 46.03 N 116.21 W
Cottonwood, Minn., U.S. 198 44.37 N 95.41 W
Cottonwood ≃, Kans., U.S. 198 38.23 N 96.03 W
Cottonwood ≃, Minn., U.S. 198 44.17 N 94.25 W
Cottonwood Creek ≃, Calif., U.S. 226 36.27 N 119.20 W
Cottonwood Creek ≃, Calif., U.S. 226 36.52 N 120.12 W
Cottonwood Creek ≃, Calif., U.S. 228 35.13 N 117.59 W
Cottonwood Creek ≃, Mont., U.S. 202 48.33 N 107.45 W
Cottonwood Creek ≃, Mont., U.S. 202 48.16 N 110.52 W
Cottonwood Creek ≃, N. Dak., U.S. 198 46.16 N 98.15 W
Cottonwood Creek ≃, Okla., U.S. 196 35.54 N 97.27 W
Cottonwood Creek ≃, Oreg., U.S. 202 43.53 N 117.43 W
Cottonwood Creek ≃, S. Dak., U.S. 198 43.59 N 101.46 W
Cottonwood Creek ≃, Tex., U.S. 196 32.48 N 100.21 W
Cottonwood Creek ≃, Tex., U.S. 196 31.23 N 103.46 W
Cottonwood Creek ≃, Utah, U.S. 200 39.09 N 110.55 W
Cottonwood Creek ≃, Wyo., U.S. 202 43.51 N 108.09 W
Cottonwood Creek, Middle Fork ≃ 204 40.23 N 122.20 W
Cottonwood Creek, South Fork ≃ 204 40.23 N 122.20 W
Cottonwood Falls 198 38.22 N 96.32 W
Cottonwood Wash ∨, Ariz., U.S. 200 36.19 N 113.59 W
Cottonwood Wash ∨, Ariz., U.S. 200 35.00 N 110.39 W
Cotubandê 287a 22.51 S 43.01 W
Cotuhé ≃ 246 2.53 S 69.44 W
Cotuí 238 19.03 N 70.09 W
Cotuit 207 41.37 N 70.26 W
Cotulla 196 28.26 N 99.14 W
Cotunduba, Ilha de ▮ 287a 22.58 S 43.09 W
Coubert 261 48.40 N 2.42 E
Coubre, Pointe de la ≻ 32 45.41 N 1.13 W
Coubron 261 48.55 N 2.35 E
Couches-les-Mines 58 46.52 N 4.34 E
Couchiching, Lake ⊜ 212 44.40 N 79.23 W
Coucouron 62 44.48 N 3.58 E
Coucy-le-Château-Auffrique 50 49.31 N 3.19 E
Coudekerque-Branche 50 51.02 N 2.24 E
Coudersport 214 41.46 N 78.01 W
Coudres, Île aux ▮ 186 47.24 N 70.23 W
Couer d'Alene Indian Reservation ◆[4] 202 47.18 N 116.45 W
Couesnon ≃ 32 48.37 N 1.31 W
Couffo ≃ 150 6.35 N 1.59 E
Cougar 224 46.03 N 122.18 W
Cougar Reservoir ⊜[1] 202 44.06 N 122.12 W
Couhé 32 46.18 N 0.11 E
Couillet 50 50.23 N 4.27 E
Couilly-Pont-aux-Dames 261 48.53 N 2.52 E
Coulanges-la-Vineuse 50 47.42 N 3.35 E
Coulanges-sur-Yonne 50 47.31 N 3.32 E
Coulee City 202 47.37 N 119.17 W
Coulee Dam 202 47.58 N 118.59 W
Coulee Dam National Recreation Area ♠ 202 47.48 N 119.45 W
Coulihaut 240d 15.30 N 61.29 W
Coulman Island ▮ 9 73.27 S 169.40 E
Coulmier-le-Sec 58 47.45 N 4.29 E
Coulogne 50 50.55 N 1.53 E
Coulomby 50 50.42 N 2.00 E
Coulommiers 50 48.49 N 3.05 E
Coulon ≃ 62 43.51 N 5.00 E
Coulonge ≃ 190 45.51 N 76.46 W
Coulonge-Est ≃ 190 46.06 N 76.44 W
Coulsdon ◆[8] 260 51.19 N 0.08 W
Coulters 279b 40.18 N 79.48 W
Coulterville, Calif., U.S. 226 37.43 N 120.12 W
Coulterville, Ill., U.S. 194 38.11 N 89.36 W
Council 202 44.44 N 116.26 W
Council Bluffs 198 41.16 N 95.52 W
Council Grove 198 38.40 N 96.29 W
Council Grove Lake ⊜[1] 198 38.42 N 96.31 W
Country Campus 222 30.49 N 95.26 W
Country Club Estates 220 28.03 N 81.57 W
Country Club Hills 278 41.34 N 87.44 W
Country Hills 279b 40.19 N 79.42 W
Country Homes 202 47.45 N 117.24 W
Country Ridge Estates 276 41.02 N 73.41 W
Countryside 278 41.47 N 87.52 W
Countryside Lake ⊜ 278 42.15 N 88.03 W
Countryside Manor 278 42.18 N 87.56 W
County Park ♠ 284a 43.06 N 78.54 W
Coupar Angus 46 56.33 N 3.17 W
Coupeville 224 48.13 N 122.41 W
Coupland 222 30.28 N 97.24 W
Coupon 214 40.32 N 78.31 W
Coupvray 261 48.54 N 2.48 E
Courbevoie 50 48.54 N 2.15 E
Courbons 62 44.06 N 6.12 E
Courçay 50 47.15 N 0.52 E
Courcelle 261 48.42 N 2.06 E
Courcelles, Bel. 50 50.28 N 4.22 E
Courcelles, Fr. 261 49.07 N 2.18 E
Courcelles-Chaussy 56 49.07 N 6.24 E
Courcelles-les-Lens 50 50.25 N 3.01 E
Courcelles-sur-Nied 56 49.04 N 6.18 E
Courchevel 62 45.25 N 6.38 E
Cour-Cheverny 50 47.30 N 1.27 E
Courcibo ≃ 250 4.53 N 53.00 W
Courçon 32 46.15 N 0.49 W
Courcouronnes 261 48.37 N 2.24 E
Courdimanche 261 49.02 N 2.00 E
Cour-et-Buis 62 45.26 N 5.00 E
Courgent 261 48.54 N 1.40 E
Courland → Kurzeme □[9] 76 56.50 N 22.30 E
Courmayeur 62 45.47 N 6.58 E
Couronne, Cap ≻ 62 43.19 N 5.03 E
Couronnement, Île du → Coronation Island ▮ 9 60.37 S 45.30 W
Courpière 62 45.45 N 3.33 E
Courquetaine 261 48.41 N 2.45 E
Course Brook ≃ 283 42.17 N 71.22 W
Courson-les-Carrières 50 47.36 N 3.30 E
Court 58 47.14 N 7.20 E
Courtacon 50 48.42 N 3.17 E
Courtalain 50 48.05 N 1.09 E
Courteilles 50 48.44 N 1.01 E
Courtenay, B.C., Can. 182 49.41 N 125.00 W
Courtenay, Fr. 50 48.02 N 3.03 E
Courthézon 62 44.05 N 4.53 E
Courtice 212 43.55 N 78.46 W
Courtisols 56 48.59 N 4.31 E
Courtland, Ont., Can. 212 42.51 N 80.38 W
Courtland, Ala., U.S. 194 34.40 N 87.18 W
Courtland, Calif., U.S. 226 38.20 N 121.34 W
Courtland, Va., U.S. 208 36.43 N 77.04 W

Courtleigh 284b 39.22 N 76.46 W
Courtmacsherry 48 51.38 N 8.43 W
Courtmacsherry Bay ⊂ 48 51.35 N 8.40 W
Courtney, Pa., U.S. 279b 40.13 N 79.58 W
Courtney, Tex., U.S. 222 30.16 N 96.04 W
Courtney Creek ≃ 196 31.16 N 102.50 W
Courtomer, Fr. 50 48.38 N 0.22 E
Courtomer, Fr. 261 48.39 N 2.54 E
Courtown Harbour 48 52.38 N 6.13 W
Courtrai → Kortrijk 50 50.50 N 3.16 E
Courtright 214 42.49 N 82.28 W
Courtry, Fr. 261 48.33 N 2.46 E
Courtry, Fr. 261 48.55 N 2.36 E
Court-Saint-Étienne 50 50.39 N 4.34 E
Courville-sur-Eure 50 48.27 N 1.15 E
Coushatta 194 32.00 N 93.21 W
Cousin ≃ 50 47.15 N 4.04 E
Cousiño, Parque ♠ 286e 33.28 S 70.40 W
Cousins Lake ⊜ 184 56.49 N 98.32 W
Cousolre 50 50.15 N 4.09 E
Coussegrey 50 47.57 N 4.01 E
Coussey 58 48.25 N 5.41 E
Coustellet 62 43.53 N 5.11 E
Coutances 32 49.03 N 1.26 W
Coutevroult 261 48.52 N 2.51 E
Couto de Magalhães ≃ 255 13.37 S 53.09 W
Couto Magalhães 250 8.17 S 49.16 W
Coutras 32 45.02 N 0.08 W
Coutts 182 49.00 N 111.57 W
Couture, Lac ⊜ 176 60.07 N 75.20 W
Couture-sur-Loir 50 47.45 N 0.41 E
Couves, Ilha das ▮ 256 23.25 S 44.52 W
Couvet 58 46.56 N 6.38 E
Couvin 50 50.03 N 4.29 E
Cova da Piedade 266c 38.40 N 9.10 W
Covane 156 21.22 S 33.56 E
Covasna 38 45.51 N 26.11 E
Covasna □[4] 38 46.00 N 26.00 E
Cove, Scot., U.K. 46 57.51 N 5.42 W
Cove, Oreg., U.S. 202 45.18 N 117.49 W
Covedale 218 39.07 N 84.37 W
Cove Harbor ⊂ 276 41.03 N 73.30 W
Cove Island ▮ 190 45.17 N 81.44 W
Covelo, Ang. 152 12.06 S 13.55 E
Covelo, Calif., U.S. 204 39.48 N 123.15 W
Cove Neck 276 40.53 N 73.31 W
Cove Neck ≻[1] 276 40.53 N 73.30 W
Coventry, Eng., U.K. 42 52.25 N 1.30 W
Coventry, Conn., U.S. 207 41.48 N 72.23 W
Coventry, Del., U.S. 285 39.40 N 75.38 W
Coventry, R.I., U.S. 207 41.41 N 71.34 W
Coventry Cathedral ⊍[1] 42 52.25 N 1.30 W
Coventryville 285 40.10 N 75.41 W
Cove Point 208 38.23 N 76.24 W
Cove Point ≻ 208 38.23 N 76.23 W
Cover ≃ 44 54.17 N 1.46 W
Covered Wells 200 32.10 N 112.08 W
Covert 216 42.17 N 86.16 W
Covigliaio 66 44.08 N 11.18 E
Covilhã 34 40.17 N 7.30 W
Covina 228 34.05 N 117.53 W
Covington, Ind., U.S. 194 40.09 N 87.24 W
Covington, Ky., U.S. 218 39.05 N 84.30 W
Covington, La., U.S. 194 30.29 N 90.06 W
Covington, Ohio, U.S. 218 40.07 N 84.21 W
Covington, Okla., U.S. 196 36.18 N 97.35 W
Covington, Pa., U.S. 210 41.45 N 77.05 W
Covington, Tenn., U.S. 194 35.34 N 89.38 W
Covington, Tex., U.S. 222 32.11 N 97.16 W
Covington, Va., U.S. 192 37.47 N 79.59 W
Covões 266c 38.50 N 9.20 W
Covunco, Arroyo ≃ 252 38.29 S 69.32 W
Cow ≃ 190 47.23 N 83.59 W
Cowal ◆[1] 46 56.05 N 5.08 W
Cowal, Lake ⊜ 166 33.35 S 147.25 E
Cowan, Ky., U.S. 218 38.24 N 83.54 W
Cowan, Tenn., U.S. 194 35.10 N 86.01 W
Cowan, Lake ⊜ 162 31.50 S 121.50 E
Cowanesque 210 41.56 N 77.30 W
Cowanesque ≃ 210 42.00 N 77.07 W
Cowan Heights 280 33.47 N 117.47 W
Cowan Lake ⊜, Sask., Can. 184 54.00 N 107.15 W
Cowan Lake ⊜, Ohio, U.S. 218 39.23 N 83.54 W
Cowan Lake State Park ♠ 218 39.23 N 83.53 W
Cowansburg 279b 40.15 N 79.46 W
Cowanshannock Creek ≃ 214 40.51 N 79.30 W
Cowansville, Qué., Can. 206 45.12 N 72.45 W
Cowansville, Pa., U.S. 214 40.53 N 79.36 W
Cowaramup 162 33.52 S 115.05 E
Coward 192 33.58 N 79.45 W
Coward Springs 166 29.24 S 136.49 E
Cowarie 166 27.43 S 138.20 E
Cow Bayou ≃ 222 31.19 N 97.00 W
Cowbridge 42 51.28 N 3.27 W
Cowburn Tunnel ◆[5] 262 53.21 N 1.52 W
Cow Canyon ∨ 280 34.01 N 120.06 W
Cowcowing Lakes ⊜ 162 31.01 S 117.18 E
Cow Creek ≃, Kans., U.S. 198 38.02 N 97.56 W
Cow Creek ≃, Mont., U.S. 202 47.47 N 108.56 W
Cow Creek ≃, Okla., U.S. 196 34.10 N 98.00 W
Cow Creek ≃, Oreg., U.S. 202 42.57 N 123.20 W
Cow Creek ≃, Wash., U.S. 202 46.45 N 118.09 W
Cowden, Ill., U.S. 219 39.15 N 88.52 W
Cowden, Pa., U.S. 279b 40.19 N 80.13 W
Cowdenbeath 46 56.07 N 3.21 W
Cowell 166 33.41 S 136.55 E
Coweman ≃ 224 46.06 N 122.52 W
Cowen 188 38.25 N 80.34 W
Cowen, Mount ∧ 202 45.23 N 110.29 W
Cowes, Austl. 169 38.27 S 145.14 E
Cowes, Eng., U.K. 42 50.45 N 1.18 W
Cowessess Indian Reserve ◆[4] 184 50.31 N 102.42 W
Coweta 196 35.57 N 95.39 W
Cow Green Reservoir ⊜[1] 44 54.40 N 2.18 W
Cowgulch Creek ≃ 202 46.02 N 107.52 W
Cow Head 186 49.55 N 57.48 W
Cowhouse Creek ≃ 222 31.10 N 97.35 W
Cowichan ≃ 224 48.46 N 123.38 W
Cowichan Bay 182 48.44 N 123.40 W
Cowichan Lake ⊜ 182 48.54 N 124.20 W
Cowiche Creek, North Fork ≃ 224 46.38 N 120.41 W
Cowiche Creek, South Fork ≃ 224 46.38 N 120.41 W
Cowie Water ≃ 46 56.58 N 2.12 W
Cowles Dam ◆[6] 273d 26.13 S 28.28 E
Cowlesville 210 42.51 N 78.28 W
Cowley, Austl. 166 26.54 S 144.49 E
Cowley, Alta., Can. 182 49.34 N 114.05 W
Cowley, Eng., U.K. 42 51.43 N 1.12 W
Cowley, Wyo., U.S. 202 44.53 N 108.28 W
Cowley ◆[8] 260 51.32 N 0.29 W
Cowlitz □[6] 224 46.07 N 122.43 W
Cowlitz ≃ 224 46.05 N 122.53 W
Cowm Reservoir ⊜[1] 262 53.40 N 2.11 W
Cow Palace ⊍ 282 37.42 N 122.25 W
Cowpasture ≃ 188 37.48 N 79.45 W
Cowpens 192 35.01 N 81.48 W
Cowpens National Battlefield ♠ 192 35.06 N 81.46 W
Cowplain 42 50.54 N 1.01 W
Cowra 166 33.50 S 148.41 E

Cox ≃ 164 15.19 S 135.25 E
Cox, Mount ∧[2] 162 24.55 S 125.36 E
Coxá ≃ 255 14.16 S 44.11 W
Cox Creek ≃ 212 43.35 N 80.29 W
Coxheath 260 51.14 N 0.30 E
Coxim 255 18.30 S 54.45 W
Coxim ≃ 255 18.34 S 54.46 W
Coxipi, Lac ⊜ 186 51.33 N 58.25 W
Coxipó da Ponte 248 15.38 S 56.04 W
Coxquihui 234 20.11 N 97.35 W
Coxs ≃ 170 33.57 S 150.25 E
Coxsackie 210 42.21 N 73.48 W
Cox's Bāzār 120 21.26 N 91.59 E
Cox's Cove 186 49.07 N 58.05 W
Coyah 150 9.43 N 13.23 W
Coyame 232 29.28 N 105.06 W
Coyanosa Draw ∨ 196 31.18 N 103.06 W
Coya Sur 252 22.25 S 69.38 W
Coyle, Water of ≃ 44 55.28 N 4.32 W
Coyoacán □[7] 286a 19.19 N 99.11 W
Coyoacán ◆[8] 286a 19.20 N 99.10 W
Coyote 226 37.13 N 121.44 W
Coyote ≃ 232 30.48 N 112.35 W
Coyote Creek ≃, Calif., U.S. 204 33.13 N 116.13 W
Coyote Creek ≃, Calif., U.S. 226 37.28 N 122.03 W
Coyote Creek ≃, Calif., U.S. 280 33.47 N 118.05 W
Coyote Creek, East Fork ≃ 226 37.10 N 121.30 W
Coyote Creek, Middle Fork ≃ 226 37.10 N 121.30 W
Coyote Hills ⛰[2] 282 37.33 N 122.05 W
Coyote Hills Regional Park ♠ 282 37.33 N 122.06 W
Coyote Lake ⊜ 204 35.04 N 116.45 W
Coyote Lake ⊜[1] 226 37.06 N 121.32 W
Coyotepec 234 19.46 N 99.12 W
Coyote Point ≻ 282 37.35 N 122.19 W
Coyote Wash ∨ 200 32.40 N 114.08 W
Coy Pond ⊜ 283 42.36 N 70.49 W
Coyuca de Benítez 234 17.02 N 100.04 W
Coyuca de Catalán 234 18.20 N 100.39 W
Coyutla 234 20.15 N 97.39 W
Cozad 198 40.52 N 99.59 W
Cozes 32 45.35 N 0.50 W
Cozie, Alpi (Alpes Cottiennes) ⛰ 62 44.45 N 7.00 E
Cozoyoapan 234 16.46 N 98.15 W
Cozumel 232 20.31 N 86.55 W
Cozumel, Isla de ▮ 232 20.25 N 86.55 W
Cozy Lake 276 41.01 N 74.30 W
Crab Alley Bay ⊂ 208 38.55 N 76.17 W
Crab Creek ≃ 202 46.49 N 119.55 W
Crab Hill 241g 13.19 N 59.38 W
Crab Meadow ☰ 276 40.55 N 73.20 W
Crab Orchard, Ky., U.S. 192 37.28 N 84.30 W
Crab Orchard, Tenn., U.S. 192 35.55 N 84.53 W
Crab Orchard Lake ⊜[1] 194 37.43 N 89.05 W
Crabtree 214 40.22 N 79.35 W
Crabtree Creek ≃ 279b 40.21 N 79.30 W
Crabtree Mills 206 45.58 N 73.28 W
Craches 261 48.34 N 1.49 E
Crackenback ≃ 171b 36.21 S 148.36 E
Craco 68 40.23 N 16.26 E
Cracovie → Kraków 30 50.03 N 19.58 E
Cračovka 80 52.57 N 52.52 E
Cradle Mountain National Park ♠ 166 42.00 S 146.00 E
Cradock, Austl. 166 32.04 S 138.30 E
Cradock, S. Afr. 158 32.08 S 25.36 E
Crafthole 158 26.24 S 24.03 E
Crafton 214 40.26 N 80.04 W
Crafts Creek ≃ 285 40.07 N 74.46 W
Cragg Vale 262 53.42 N 2.00 W
Cragsmoor 210 41.40 N 74.23 W
Craig, B.C., Can. 224 49.18 N 124.15 W
Craig, Alaska, U.S. 180 55.29 N 133.09 W
Craig, Colo., U.S. 200 40.31 N 107.33 W
Craig, Mo., U.S. 194 40.11 N 95.23 W
Craig, Nebr., U.S. 198 41.47 N 96.22 W
Craig, Point ∧ 162 26.51 S 126.19 E
Craig Air Force Base ■ 194 32.21 N 86.59 W
Craig Beach 214 41.07 N 81.01 W
Craig Creek ≃ 192 37.39 N 79.49 W
Craigellachie 182 50.59 N 118.43 W
Craighall ◆[8] 273d 26.07 S 28.02 E
Craighall Park ◆[8] 273d 26.08 S 28.01 E
Craighouse 46 55.51 N 5.57 W
Craigmont 202 46.15 N 116.28 W
Craigmore 154 20.28 S 32.50 E
Craigmyle 182 51.40 N 112.15 W
Craignish Point ≻ 46 56.07 N 5.37 W
Craignure 46 56.28 N 5.42 W
Craigsville, Pa., U.S. 214 40.51 N 79.39 W
Craigsville, Va., U.S. 192 38.05 N 79.23 W
Craigville 216 40.47 N 85.06 W
Craik 184 51.03 N 105.49 W
Crail 46 56.16 N 2.38 W
Crailsheim 56 49.08 N 10.04 E
Craiova 38 44.19 N 23.48 E
Crake ≃ 44 54.14 N 3.03 W
Craley 208 39.57 N 76.31 W
Cramant 50 48.59 N 3.59 E
Cramlington 44 55.05 N 1.36 W
Cranage 262 53.12 N 2.22 W
Cranberry 214 41.21 N 79.43 W
Cranberry Brook ≃ 283 42.11 N 71.01 W
Cranberry Creek 210 43.09 N 74.14 W
Cranberry Island ▮ 212 44.44 N 81.18 W
Cranberry Lake 210 40.57 N 74.45 W
Cranberry Lake ⊜, Ont., Can. 212 44.26 N 76.19 W
Cranberry Lake ⊜, Ont., Can. 212 44.47 N 75.50 W
Cranberry Lake ⊜, N.Y., U.S. 188 44.10 N 74.50 W
Cranberry Lake ⊜, Wash., U.S. 224 47.17 N 123.05 W
Cranberry Pond ⊜ 276 41.08 N 74.12 W
Cranberry Portage 184 54.35 N 101.23 W
Cranborne Chase ◆[3] 42 50.55 N 2.05 W
Cranbourne 169 38.06 S 145.17 E
Cranbrook, Austl. 162 34.18 S 117.32 E
Cranbrook, B.C., Can. 182 49.31 N 115.46 W
Cranbrook, Eng., U.K. 42 51.06 N 0.33 E
Cranbrook ⊍[3] 281 42.34 N 83.14 W
Cranbury 276 40.19 N 74.31 W
Cranbury Brook ≃ 276 40.19 N 74.37 W
Crandall 222 32.38 N 96.27 W
Crandon 190 45.34 N 88.54 W
Crandon Lakes 210 41.07 N 74.50 W
Crane, Ariz., U.S. 204 32.42 N 114.40 W
Crane, Ind., U.S. 194 38.54 N 86.54 W
Crane, Mo., U.S. 194 36.54 N 93.34 W
Crane, Tex., U.S. 196 31.24 N 102.21 W
Crane Beach •[2] 283 42.41 N 70.46 W
Cranebrook 274a 33.43 S 150.42 E
Crane Creek ≃ 190 43.01 N 91.58 W
Crane Creek Reservoir ⊜[1] 202 44.22 N 116.35 W
Crane Lake ⊜, Ont., Can. 212 45.13 N 79.57 W
Crane Lake ⊜, Sask., Can. 184 50.06 N 109.06 W
Crane Mountain ∧ 202 42.04 N 120.13 W
Crane Neck Point ≻ 276 40.58 N 73.10 W
Crane Prairie Reservoir ⊜ 202 43.44 N 122.02 W
Crane River Indian Reserve ◆[4] 184 51.30 N 99.14 W
Cranesville 214 41.54 N 80.21 W
Cranfield 42 52.05 N 0.35 W

Symbol	English	Deutsch	Español	Français	Português
≃	River	Fluss	Río	Rivière	Rio
≊	Canal	Kanal	Canal	Canal	Canal
⌊	Waterfall, Rapids	Wasserfall, Stromschnellen	Cascada, Rápidos	Chute d'eau, Rapides	Cascata, Rápidos
⋃	Strait	Meeresstrasse	Estrecho	Détroit	Estreito
⊂	Bay, Gulf	Bucht, Golf	Bahía, Golfo	Baie, Golfe	Baía, Golfo
⊜	Lake, Lakes	See, Seen	Lago, Lagos	Lac, Lacs	Lago, Lagos
☰	Swamp	Sumpf	Pantano	Marais	Pântano
⍓	Ice Features, Glacier	Eis- und Gletscherformen	Accidentes Glaciales	Formes glaciaires	Acidentes Glaciares
⊤	Other Hydrographic Features	Andere Hydrographische Objekte	Otros Elementos Hidrográficos	Autres données hydrographiques	Outros Elementos Hidrográficos
⊹	Submarine Features	Untermeerische Objekte	Accidentes Submarinos	Formes de relief sous-marin	Acidentes Submarinos
□	Political Unit	Politische Einheit	Unidad Politica	Entité politique	Unidade Política
⊍	Cultural Institution	Kulturelle Institution	Institución Cultural	Institution culturelle	Instituição Cultural
⊥	Historical Site	Historische Stätte	Sitio Histórico	Site historique	Sitio Histórico
♠	Recreational Site	Erholungs- und Ferienort	Sitio de Recreo	Centre de loisirs	Sítio de Lazer
⊠	Airport	Flughafen	Aeropuerto	Aéroport	Aeroporto
■	Military Installation	Militäranlage	Instalación Militar	Installation militaire	Instalação Militar
◆	Miscellaneous	Verschiedenes	Misceláneo	Divers	Miscelânea

ENGLISH — Name | Page | Lat.°′ | Long.°′
DEUTSCH — Name | Seite | Breite°′ | Länge°′ E = Ost

Cranfills Gap 222 31.46 N 97.50 W
Cranford 210 40.39 N 74.19 W
Crange ✦[8] 263 51.32 N 7.11 E
Cran-Gévrier 58 45.54 N 6.06 E
Crank 262 53.29 N 2.45 W
Cranleigh 42 51.09 N 0.30 W
Crans 58 46.19 N 7.28 E
Cranston 207 41.47 N 71.26 W
Cranston Heights 285 39.38 N 75.38 W
Craolândia 250 7.57 S 47.15 W
Craon 32 47.51 N 0.57 W
Craonne 50 49.26 N 3.47 E
Craponne, Fr. 62 45.44 N 4.43 E
Craponne, Fr. 62 45.20 N 3.51 E
Craponne, Canal de ≅ 62 43.40 N 4.39 E
Crary Mountains ∧∧ 9 76.48 S 117.40 W
Craryville 210 42.11 N 73.35 W
Crasna 38 45.36 N 26.08 E
Crasna (Kraszna) ≃ 38 48.09 N 22.20 E
Crassier 58 46.22 N 6.11 E
Crater Lake @, St. Vin. 241h 13.20 N 61.11 W
Crater Lake @, Oreg., U.S. 202 42.56 N 122.06 W
Crater Lake National Park ✦ 202 42.49 N 122.08 W
Crater Mount ∧ 164 6.30 S 145.10 E
Crater Point ≻ 164 5.22 S 152.09 E
Craters of the Moon National Monument ✦ 202 43.20 N 113.35 W
Crateús 250 5.10 S 40.40 W
Crathie 46 57.02 N 3.12 W
Crati ≃ 68 39.43 N 16.31 E
Crato 250 7.14 S 39.23 W
Crau ✦[1] 62 43.36 N 4.50 E
Crauford, Cape ≻ 176 73.43 N 84.50 W
Craughwell 48 53.13 N 8.43 W
Cravant 50 47.41 N 3.41 E
Cravari ≃ 248 12.06 S 58.03 W
Cravat 219 38.25 N 89.06 W
Craven 184 50.39 N 104.50 W
Craven Arms 42 52.26 N 2.50 W
Cravensville 171b 36.24 S 147.34 E
Cravo Norte 246 6.18 N 70.12 W
Cravo Norte ≃ 246 6.18 N 70.12 W
Cravo Sur ≃ 246 4.42 N 71.36 W
Crawfish ≃ 216 43.00 N 88.49 W
Crawford, Scot., U.K. 44 55.28 N 3.40 W
Crawford, Colo., U.S. 200 38.42 N 107.37 W
Crawford, Miss., U.S. 194 33.18 N 88.37 W
Crawford, Nebr., U.S. 198 42.41 N 103.25 W
Crawford, Tex., U.S. 222 31.32 N 97.27 W
Crawford ☐[6], Ind., U.S. 218 38.20 N 86.28 W
Crawford ☐[6], Ohio, U.S. 214 40.48 N 82.58 W
Crawford ☐[6], Pa., U.S. 214 41.39 N 80.10 W
Crawford Bay 182 49.42 N 116.48 W
Crawford Countryside 278 41.32 N 87.43 W
Crawford Notch State Park ✦ 188 44.13 N 71.25 W
Crawfordsville, Ark., U.S. 194 35.14 N 90.20 W
Crawfordsville, Ind., U.S. 194 40.02 N 86.54 W
Crawfordville, Fla., U.S. 192 30.11 N 84.23 W
Crawfordville, Ga., U.S. 192 33.33 N 82.54 W
Crawinkel 54 50.47 N 10.47 E
Crawley 42 51.07 N 0.12 W
Crawshawbooth 262 53.43 N 2.17 W
Cray 42 51.55 N 3.36 W
Crayford ✦[8] 260 51.27 N 0.11 E
Crays Hill 260 51.36 N 0.28 E
Crazy Mountains ∧∧ 202 46.08 N 110.20 W
Crazy Peak ∧ 202 46.01 N 110.16 W
Crazy Woman Creek ≃ 202 44.29 N 106.08 W
Creagan 46 56.33 N 5.17 W
Creagorry 46 57.26 N 7.19 W
Creal Springs 194 37.37 N 88.50 W
Creamery 285 40.13 N 75.25 W
Crean Lake @ 184 54.05 N 106.10 W
Crêches-sur-Saône 58 46.15 N 4.47 E
Crécy, Forêt de ✦ 261 48.48 N 2.53 E
Crécy-en-Brie 50 48.51 N 2.55 E
Crécy-en-Ponthieu 50 50.15 N 1.53 E
Crécy-sur-Serre 50 49.42 N 3.37 E
Credit ≃ 212 43.33 N 79.35 W
Crediton 42 50.47 N 3.39 W
Cree ≃, Sask., Can. 176 59.00 N 105.47 W
Cree ≃, Scot., U.K. 44 54.52 N 4.20 W
Creede 200 37.51 N 106.56 W
Creedmoor 192 36.07 N 78.41 W
Creedmore 222 30.12 N 97.43 W
Creek Brook ≃ 283 42.47 N 71.08 W
Creek Locks 210 41.52 N 74.03 W
Creekmouth ✦[8] 260 51.31 N 0.06 E
Creekside 214 40.41 N 79.12 W
Creekwood 278 41.39 N 87.59 W
Creel 232 27.45 N 107.38 W
Cree Lake @ 176 57.30 N 106.30 W
Creemore 212 44.19 N 80.06 W
Creetown 44 54.54 N 4.23 W
Cregganbaun 48 53.42 N 9.51 W
Creglingen 56 49.28 N 10.01 E
Crégy-lès-Meaux 261 48.58 N 2.52 E
Créhange 56 49.03 N 6.35 E
Creighton, Sask., Can. 184 54.45 N 101.54 W
Creighton, S. Afr. 158 30.01 S 29.51 E
Creighton, Nebr., U.S. 198 42.28 N 97.54 W
Creighton, Pa., U.S. 214 40.35 N 79.47 W
Creighton Mine 190 46.28 N 81.11 W
Creil, Fr. 50 49.16 N 2.29 E
Creil, Ned. 52 52.45 N 5.40 E
Crema 62 45.22 N 9.41 E
Cremia 58 46.05 N 9.16 E
Crémieu 62 45.43 N 5.15 E
Cremona, Alta., Can. 182 51.33 N 114.29 W
Cremona, It. 64 45.07 N 10.02 E
Cremona ☐[4] 64 45.12 N 10.00 E
Crenshaw, Miss., U.S. 194 34.30 N 90.12 W
Crenshaw, Pa., U.S. 214 41.15 N 78.46 W
Crépieux-la-Pape 62 45.48 N 4.52 E
Crep Nudo ∧ 64 46.13 N 12.24 E
Crepori ≃ 250 5.42 S 57.08 W
Crépy-en-Laonnois 50 49.36 N 3.31 E
Crépy-en-Valois 50 49.14 N 2.54 E
Crequy 50 50.29 N 2.03 E
Creran, Loch C 46 56.31 N 5.20 W
Cres 36 44.58 N 14.25 E
Cres, Otok I 36 44.50 N 14.25 E
Cresaptown 188 39.36 N 78.50 W
Crescent, N.Y., U.S. 210 42.49 N 73.43 W
Crescent, Okla., U.S. 196 35.57 N 97.36 W
Crescent, Oreg., U.S. 202 43.29 N 121.41 W
Crescent, Lake @ 224 48.05 N 123.50 W
Crescent Beach, B.C., Can. 224 49.04 N 122.53 W
Crescent Beach, Fla., U.S. 220 27.15 N 82.32 W
Crescent City, Calif., U.S. 204 41.45 N 124.12 W
Crescent City, Fla., U.S. 192 29.26 N 81.30 W
Crescent City, Ill., U.S. 216 40.46 N 87.51 W
Crescent Ditch ≅ 226 36.29 N 120.07 W
Crescent Group II 108 16.31 N 111.38 E
Crescent Heights 222 32.11 N 95.56 W
Crescentino 62 45.11 N 8.06 E
Crescent Lake @, Fla., U.S. 192 29.28 N 81.30 W
Crescent Lake @, Oreg., U.S. 202 43.29 N 121.59 W
Crescent Lake Estates 281 42.38 N 83.25 W
Crescent Spur 182 53.35 N 120.41 W
Crescentville ✦[8] 285 40.02 N 75.05 W
Crescenzago ✦[8] 266b 45.30 N 9.15 E
Cresco, Iowa, U.S. 190 43.22 N 92.07 W
Cresco, Pa., U.S. 210 41.09 N 75.17 W
Crespano del Grappa 64 45.49 N 11.50 E
Crespian 62 43.53 N 4.06 E
Crespières 261 48.53 N 1.55 E
Crespin 50 50.25 N 3.39 E
Crespino 64 44.59 N 11.53 E
Crespo 252 32.02 S 60.19 W
Cressbrook Creek ≃ 171a 27.05 S 152.27 E
Cressely 261 48.43 N 2.05 E
Cressey 226 37.25 N 120.40 W
Cresskill 276 40.57 N 73.57 W
Cresskill Brook ≃ 276 40.57 N 73.58 W
Cresson, Pa., U.S. 214 40.28 N 78.35 W
Cresson, Tex., U.S. 222 32.32 N 97.37 W
Cressona 208 40.38 N 76.12 W
Cressy 169 38.02 S 143.38 E
Crest 62 44.44 N 5.02 E
Cresta 58 46.28 N 9.31 E
Crested Butte 200 38.52 N 106.59 W
Cresthaven 220 26.19 N 80.05 W
Crest Hill 216 41.32 N 88.07 W
Crestline, Calif., U.S. 228 34.14 N 117.17 W
Crestline, Ohio, U.S. 214 40.47 N 82.44 W
Creston, B.C., Can. 182 49.06 N 116.31 W
Creston, Newf., Can. 186 47.09 N 55.11 W
Creston, Calif., U.S. 226 35.31 N 120.31 W
Creston, Ill., U.S. 216 41.56 N 88.58 W
Creston, Iowa, U.S. 198 41.04 N 94.22 W
Creston, Ohio, U.S. 214 40.59 N 81.54 W
Crestone Peak ∧ 200 37.58 N 105.36 W
Crestview, Fla., U.S. 194 30.46 N 86.34 W
Crestview, Wis., U.S. 216 42.49 N 87.49 W
Crestview Heights 210 42.05 N 76.07 W
Crestwood, Ill., U.S. 278 41.39 N 87.44 W
Crestwood, Ky., U.S. 218 38.19 N 85.28 W
Crestwood, Mo., U.S. 219 38.33 N 90.23 W
Creswell, Eng., U.K. 44 53.16 N 1.12 W
Creswell, Oreg., U.S. 202 43.55 N 123.01 W
Creswell Bay C 176 72.35 N 93.25 W
Creswell Creek ≃ 162 18.10 S 135.11 E
Creswick 169 37.26 S 143.54 E
Creta, Isla de → Kríti I 38 35.29 N 24.42 E
Crete, Ill., U.S. 216 41.27 N 87.38 W
Crete, Nebr., U.S. 198 40.38 N 96.58 W
Crete → Kríti I 38 35.29 N 24.42 E
Crete, Sea of → Kritikón Pélagos ≂[2] 38 35.46 N 23.54 E
Créteil 50 48.48 N 2.28 E
Crétéville 36 36.40 N 10.20 E
Cretin, Cape ≻ 164 6.40 S 147.52 E
Creus, Cabo de ≻ 34 42.19 N 3.19 E
Creuse ☐[5] 32 46.05 N 2.00 E
Creuse ≃ 32 47.00 N 0.34 E
Creussen 60 49.51 N 11.37 E
Creutzwald-la-Croix 56 49.12 N 6.41 E
Creuzburg 56 51.03 N 10.15 E
Crevacuore 62 45.41 N 8.15 E
Crevalcore 64 44.43 N 11.09 E
Creve Coeur, Ill., U.S. 190 40.39 N 89.35 W
Creve Coeur, Mo., U.S. 219 38.40 N 90.27 W
Crèvecœur-en-Auge 50 49.07 N 0.01 E
Crèvecœur-en-Brie 261 48.45 N 2.55 E
Creve Coeur Lake @ 219 38.43 N 90.29 W
Crèvecœur-le-Grand 50 49.36 N 2.05 E
Crevillente 34 38.15 N 0.48 W
Crevoladossola 58 46.09 N 8.18 E
Crewe 192 37.05 N 78.08 W
Crewkerne 42 50.53 N 2.48 W
Crews Lake @ 220 28.23 N 82.31 W
Crewsville 220 27.16 N 81.36 W
Crianlarich 46 56.23 N 4.36 W
Crib Point 169 38.22 S 145.12 E
Cricamola ≃ 236 8.59 N 81.54 W
Criccieth 42 52.55 N 4.14 W
Criciúma 252 28.40 S 49.23 W
Crick 42 52.21 N 1.07 W
Cricket 192 36.11 N 81.12 W
Crickhowell 42 51.53 N 3.07 W
Cricklade 42 51.39 N 1.51 W
Cridersville 216 40.39 N 84.09 W
Crieff 46 56.23 N 3.52 W
Criel-sur-Mer 50 50.01 N 1.19 E
Criffell ∧ 44 54.57 N 3.38 W
Crikvenica 36 45.11 N 14.42 E
Crillon, Mount ∧ 180 58.40 N 137.10 W
Crimea → Krymskij Poluostrov ≻[1] 78 45.00 N 34.00 E
Crimmitschau 54 50.49 N 12.23 E
Crinan 46 56.05 N 5.35 W
Crîngeni 38 44.01 N 24.47 E
Cripple Creek 200 38.45 N 105.11 W
Criques, Grande Île de I 273b 4.20 S 15.25 E
Criquetot-l'Esneval 50 49.39 N 0.16 E
Crirninoso, Monte ∧ 256 21.32 S 43.25 W
Crisenoy 261 48.36 N 2.45 E
Crisfield 208 37.59 N 75.51 W
Crisólia 256 22.15 S 46.25 W
Crisóstomo, Ribeirão ≃ 250 10.19 S 50.26 W
Crispiano 68 40.36 N 17.14 E
Criss Creek 182 51.03 N 120.44 W
Crissiumal 252 27.30 S 54.07 W
Cristal, Monts de ∧∧ 152 0.30 N 10.30 E
Cristal, Sierra del ∧∧ 240p 20.33 N 75.31 W
Cristalândia 250 10.36 S 49.11 W
Cristalina 255 16.45 S 47.36 W
Cristalino ≃ 255 12.38 S 50.40 W
Cristallo ∧ 64 46.34 N 12.12 E
Cristianópolis 255 17.13 S 48.45 W
Cristina 256 22.13 S 45.16 W
Cristinápolis 250 11.29 S 37.46 W
Cristino Castro 250 8.49 S 44.13 W
Cristóbal 236 9.21 N 79.55 W
Cristóbal, Punta de ≻ 240p 22.12 N 81.51 W
Cristóbal Colón, Pico ∧ 246 10.50 N 73.41 W
Cristoforo Colombo, Aeroporto di ⊠ 62 44.25 N 8.49 E
Cristo Redentor ⊥ 252 32.50 S 70.05 W
Cristo Redentor, Estatua do ✦[1] 287a 22.57 S 43.13 W
Cristuru-Secuiesc 38 46.17 N 25.02 E
Crişu Alb ≃ 38 46.42 N 21.17 E
Crişu Negru ≃ 38 46.42 N 21.16 E
Crişu Repede (Sebes Körös) ≃ 38 46.55 N 20.59 E
Crittenden 218 38.47 N 84.36 W
Crivitz, D.D.R. 54 53.35 N 11.38 E
Crivitz, Wis., U.S. 190 45.14 N 88.01 W
Crixalândia 255 15.18 S 47.16 W
Crixás 255 14.27 S 49.58 W
Crixás ≃ 250 11.02 S 48.34 W
Crixás Açu ≃ 255 13.19 S 50.36 W
Crixás Mirim ≃ 255 13.30 S 50.30 W
Črna 61 46.28 N 14.51 E
Crna ≃ 38 41.35 N 21.59 E
Crna Gora ☐[3] 38 42.30 N 19.18 E
Crni vrh ∧ 61 46.29 N 15.14 E
Črnomelj 36 45.34 N 15.11 E
Croachy 46 57.19 N 4.14 W
Croal ≃ 262 53.33 N 2.23 W
Croatia → Hrvatska ☐[3] 36 45.10 N 15.30 E
Croce dello Scrivano, Passo)(68 40.34 N 15.50 E
Croce Domini, Passo di)(64 45.54 N 10.24 E
Crocefieschi 62 44.35 N 9.01 E
Crocetta del Montello 64 45.50 N 12.02 E
Crocheron 208 38.15 N 76.03 W
Crockenhill 260 51.23 N 0.10 E
Crocker 194 37.57 N 92.16 W
Crocker, Banjaran ∧∧ 112 5.40 N 116.14 E
Crockery Creek ≃ 216 43.02 N 86.05 W
Crocketford 44 55.02 N 3.50 W
Crockett, Calif., U.S. 226 38.03 N 122.13 W
Crockett, Tex., U.S. 222 31.19 N 95.28 W
Crockham Hill 260 51.14 N 0.04 E
Crocus Hill → The Valley 238 18.13 N 63.04 W
Croft 262 53.26 N 2.33 W
Crofton, B.C., Can. 224 48.52 N 123.38 W
Crofton, Ky., U.S. 194 37.03 N 87.29 W
Crofton, Md., U.S. 208 39.01 N 76.42 W
Crofton, Nebr., U.S. 198 42.44 N 97.30 W
Croggan 46 56.22 N 5.42 W
Croghan 212 43.54 N 75.24 W
Croglin 44 54.49 N 2.39 W
Croick 46 57.53 N 4.35 W
Croil Islands II 206 44.58 N 74.58 W
Croisette, Cap ≻ 62 43.13 N 5.20 E
Croisilles 50 50.12 N 2.53 E
Croissy-Beaubourg 261 48.50 N 2.40 E
Croissy-sur-Seine 261 48.53 N 2.09 E
Croix 50 50.40 N 3.09 E
Croix, Lac à la @ 186 51.16 N 70.13 W
Croix, Lac la @ 190 48.21 N 92.05 W
Croker, Cape ≻, Austl. 164 10.58 S 132.35 E
Croker, Cape ≻, Ont., Can. 212 44.58 N 80.59 W
Croker Island I 164 11.12 S 132.32 E
Crolles 62 45.17 N 5.53 E
Cromarty 46 57.40 N 4.02 W
Cromarty Firth C[1] 46 57.41 N 4.07 W
Cromby 285 40.09 N 75.32 W
Cromer, Austl. 274a 33.44 S 151.17 E
Cromer, Eng., U.K. 42 52.56 N 1.18 E
Cromínia 255 17.17 S 49.21 W
Cromore 46 58.09 N 6.29 W
Crompton Point ≻ 240d 15.35 N 61.19 W
Cromwell, N.Z. 172 45.03 S 169.12 E
Cromwell, Ala., U.S. 194 32.14 N 88.17 W
Cromwell, Conn., U.S. 207 41.36 N 72.39 W
Cromwell, Ind., U.S. 216 41.24 N 85.37 W
Cromwell Park ✦ 279a 41.28 N 82.08 W
Cronadun 172 42.02 S 171.52 E
Cronenberg ✦[8] 263 51.12 N 7.08 E
Cronin, Mount ∧ 182 54.54 N 126.52 W
Cronton 262 53.23 N 2.46 W
Cronulla Beach ✦[2] 274a 34.02 S 151.11 E
Croob, Slieve ∧[2] 44 54.20 N 5.58 W
Crook, Eng., U.K. 44 54.43 N 1.44 W
Crook, Colo., U.S. 198 40.51 N 102.48 W
Crooked ≃, B.C., Can. 182 54.50 N 122.54 W
Crooked ≃, Mo., U.S. 194 39.13 N 93.49 W
Crooked ≃, Oreg., U.S. 202 44.34 N 121.16 W
Crooked Creek 180 61.52 N 158.08 W
Crooked Creek ≃, U.S. 196 36.57 N 100.06 W
Crooked Creek ≃, Ark., U.S. 194 36.14 N 92.29 W
Crooked Creek ≃, Ill., U.S. 219 38.30 N 89.25 W
Crooked Creek ≃, Ind., U.S. 216 40.45 N 86.30 W
Crooked Creek ≃, Mo., U.S. 219 39.34 N 91.55 W
Crooked Creek ≃, Mont., U.S. 202 47.27 N 107.58 W
Crooked Creek ≃, Pa., U.S. 210 41.55 N 77.08 W
Crooked Creek ≃, Pa., U.S. 214 40.45 N 79.33 W
Crooked Creek Lake @[1] 214 40.42 N 79.30 W
Crooked Creek State Park ✦ 214 40.42 N 79.29 W
Crooked Island I 238 22.45 N 74.13 W
Crooked Island Passage)(238 22.55 N 74.35 W
Crooked Lake, Ind., U.S. 216 41.41 N 85.02 W
Crooked Lake, Mich., U.S. 216 42.29 N 85.25 W
Crooked Lake @, Newf., Can. 186 48.24 N 56.17 W
Crooked Lake @, Sask., Can. 184 50.36 N 102.45 W
Crooked Lake @, N.A. 190 48.13 N 91.50 W
Crooked Lake @, Fla., U.S. 220 27.48 N 81.35 W
Crooked Lake @, Ind., U.S. 216 41.40 N 85.03 W
Crooked River 184 52.51 N 103.44 W
Crookes Point ≻ 276 40.32 N 74.08 W
Crookham 279b 40.12 N 79.59 W
Crook of Alves 46 57.38 N 3.27 W
Crookston 198 47.47 N 96.37 W
Crookstown 48 51.50 N 8.50 W
Crooksville 188 39.46 N 82.06 W
Crookwell 166 34.28 S 149.28 E
Croom 48 52.31 N 8.42 W
Cropalati 68 39.31 N 16.43 E
Cropani 68 38.58 N 16.47 E
Cropper 218 38.19 N 85.07 W
Crosby, Eng., U.K. 262 53.30 N 3.02 W
Crosby, Minn., U.S. 190 46.28 N 93.57 W
Crosby, Miss., U.S. 194 31.17 N 91.04 W
Crosby, N. Dak., U.S. 198 48.55 N 103.18 W
Crosby, Pa., U.S. 214 41.45 N 78.24 W
Crosby, Tex., U.S. 222 29.55 N 95.04 W
Crosby ✦[8] 273d 26.12 S 27.59 E
Crosby, Mount ∧ 202 43.53 N 109.20 W
Crosby Lake @ 212 44.45 N 76.26 W
Crosbyton 196 33.40 N 101.14 W
Crosia 68 39.34 N 16.46 E
Crosne 261 48.43 N 2.28 E
Cross ≃ 146 4.42 N 8.21 E
Cross, Cape ≻ 156 21.49 S 13.57 E
Cross Banks II 283 42.43 N 70.49 W
Cross Bay C 184 53.15 N 99.25 W
Cross Bay Bridge ✦[5] 276 40.35 N 73.49 W
Crossbost 46 58.08 N 6.23 W
Cross City 192 29.39 N 83.07 W
Cross County Center ✦ 276 40.56 N 73.51 W
Cross Creek ≃, Calif., U.S. 226 36.08 N 119.38 W
Cross Creek ≃, Ohio, U.S. 214 40.18 N 80.36 W
Crossen, D.D.R. 54 50.45 N 12.29 E
Crossen → Krosno Odrzańskie, Pol. 30 52.04 N 15.05 E
Crossens 262 53.41 N 2.57 W
Crossett 194 33.08 N 91.58 W
Cross Fell ∧ 44 54.42 N 2.29 W
Crossfield 182 51.26 N 114.02 W
Crossgar 48 54.24 N 5.45 W
Crosshaven 48 51.48 N 8.17 W
Crosshill 44 55.19 N 4.39 W
Crossinsee @ 264a 52.22 N 13.41 E
Cross Island I 272c 18.57 N 72.51 E
Cross Keys 285 39.43 N 75.02 W
Cross Keys Airport ⊠ 285 39.42 N 75.02 W
Cross Lake @, Man., Can. 184 54.45 N 97.30 W
Cross Lake @, Ont., Can. 190 46.53 N 79.57 W
Cross Lake @, N.Y., U.S. 210 43.08 N 76.29 W
Crossley, Mount ∧ 172 42.50 S 172.04 E
Crossmaglen 48 54.05 N 6.37 W
Crossman ≃ 168a 32.47 S 116.32 E
Crossman Peak ∧ 200 34.32 N 114.07 W
Crossmolina 48 54.06 N 9.20 W
Cross Plains, Ind., U.S. 218 38.57 N 85.12 W
Cross Plains, Tex., U.S. 196 32.08 N 99.11 W
Cross Plains, Wis., U.S. 190 43.07 N 89.39 W
Cross Roads 222 32.03 N 95.58 W
Cross Sound)(180 58.10 N 136.30 W
Crossville, Ill., U.S. 194 38.10 N 88.04 W
Crossville, Tenn., U.S. 194 35.58 N 85.02 W
Crosswicks 285 40.09 N 74.39 W
Crosswicks Creek ≃ 208 40.09 N 74.43 W
Crostolo ≃ 64 44.55 N 10.38 E
Croston 262 53.40 N 2.46 W
Croswell 190 43.16 N 82.37 W
Crotch Lake @ 212 44.55 N 76.48 W
Crotenay 58 46.45 N 5.49 E
Crothersville 218 38.48 N 85.50 W
Croton 214 40.14 N 82.41 W
Crotona Park ✦ 276 40.50 N 73.54 W
Crotone 68 39.05 N 17.07 E
Croton Falls 210 41.21 N 73.40 W
Croton-on-Hudson 210 41.12 N 73.54 W
Croton Point ≻ 276 41.10 N 73.54 W
Crottendorf 54 50.30 N 12.56 E
Crouch ≃ 260 51.37 N 0.57 E
Croult ≃ 261 48.57 N 2.25 E
Crouse Run ≃ 279b 40.35 N 79.58 W
Crouy 50 49.24 N 3.22 E
Crow ≃ 190 45.15 N 93.31 W
Crow, North Fork ≃ 190 45.05 N 93.45 W
Crow, South Fork ≃ 190 45.05 N 93.45 W
Crow Agency 202 45.36 N 107.27 W
Crowborough 42 51.03 N 0.09 E
Crow Creek ≃, U.S. 198 40.23 N 104.29 W
Crow Creek ≃, Calif., U.S. 282 37.42 N 122.03 W
Crow Creek ≃, Ill., U.S. 194 40.56 N 89.27 W
Crow Creek ≃, Mont., U.S. 198 45.45 N 105.06 W
Crow Creek ≃, Mont., U.S. 202 46.11 N 111.29 W
Crow Creek ≃, S. Dak., U.S. 198 43.57 N 99.15 W
Crow Creek ≃, Wyo., U.S. 202 43.19 N 109.09 W
Crow Creek Indian Reservation ✦[4] 198 44.11 N 99.30 W
Crowder 196 35.07 N 95.40 W
Crowduck Lake @ 184 50.08 N 95.15 W
Crowdy Head ≻ 166 31.50 S 152.45 E
Crowe ≃ 212 44.22 N 77.46 W
Crowe Lake @ 212 44.29 N 77.46 W
Crowell 196 33.59 N 99.43 W
Crow Hill ∧[2] 262 53.42 N 1.58 W
Crowhurst 260 51.12 N 0.01 W
Crow Indian Reservation ✦[4] 202 45.27 N 108.00 W
Crow Lake 184 49.12 N 93.57 W
Crow Lake @ 212 44.43 N 76.37 W
Crowland 42 52.41 N 0.11 W
Crowl Creek ≃ 166 31.58 S 144.53 E
Crowle 44 53.37 N 0.49 W
Crowley, Calif., U.S. 226 36.21 N 119.17 W
Crowley, La., U.S. 194 30.13 N 92.22 W
Crowley, Tex., U.S. 222 32.35 N 97.22 W
Crowley, Lake @[1] 204 37.37 N 118.44 W
Crowleys Ridge ∧ 194 35.45 N 90.45 W
Crowlin Islands II 46 57.20 N 5.44 W
Crown 214 41.23 N 79.16 W
Crown Hill 212 44.26 N 79.39 W
Crown Island I 164 5.05 S 146.55 E
Crown Mines ✦[7] 273d 26.13 S 28.00 E
Crown Mountain ∧ 240m 18.21 N 64.58 W
Crown Point, Ind., U.S. 216 41.25 N 87.22 W
Crown Point, N.Y., U.S. 188 43.57 N 73.25 W
Crown Point State Park ✦ 224 45.32 N 122.15 W
Crown Prince Frederick Island I 176 70.02 N 86.50 W
Crown Prince Range ∧∧ 175e 6.25 S 155.43 E
Crown Village 276 40.40 N 73.27 W
Crow Peak ∧ 202 46.18 N 111.54 W
Crow Rock Creek ≃ 202 47.06 N 106.15 W
Crows Landing 226 37.24 N 121.04 W
Crowsnest, B.C., Can. 182 49.38 N 114.41 W
Crowsnest Pass)(182 49.39 N 114.45 W
Crows Nest Peak ∧ 198 44.03 N 103.58 W
Crowthorne 42 51.23 N 0.49 W
Crowton 262 53.16 N 2.38 W
Crow Wing ≃ 198 46.19 N 94.20 W
Croxley Green 260 51.39 N 0.27 W
Croxteth Park ✦ 262 53.26 N 2.53 W
Croy 46 57.31 N 4.02 W
Croyde 42 51.07 N 4.13 W
Croydon, Pa., U.S. 208 40.05 N 74.54 W
Croydon ✦[8] 260 51.23 N 0.06 W
Croydon Park 274a 33.54 S 151.07 E
Croydon Peak ∧ 188 43.28 N 72.13 W
Croydon Station 182 53.05 N 119.44 W
Crozet 192 38.04 N 78.42 W
Crozet Basin ✦[1] 6 40.00 S 60.00 E
Crozon 32 48.15 N 4.29 W
Cruachan, Ben ∧ 46 56.25 N 5.08 W
Cruas 62 44.39 N 4.46 E
Crucea 38 44.32 N 28.14 E
Crucero 248 14.21 S 70.00 W
Crucero, Cerro ∧ 234 21.41 N 104.25 W
Cruces, Cuba 240p 22.21 N 80.16 W
Cruces, Méx. 232 29.26 N 107.24 W
Crucible 188 39.57 N 79.58 W
Crucilândia 255 20.23 S 44.21 W
Crucoli 68 39.25 N 17.00 E
Cruden Bay 46 57.25 N 1.50 W
Crudgington 42 52.46 N 2.33 W
Cruger 194 33.14 N 90.14 W
Cruillas 232 24.45 N 98.31 W
Crum Creek ≃ 285 39.51 N 75.19 W
Crumhorn Mountain ∧ 210 42.33 N 74.55 W
Crumlin, Ont., Can. 212 43.01 N 81.09 W
Crumlin, N. Ire., U.K. 48 54.37 N 6.14 W
Crum Lynne 285 39.52 N 75.20 W
Crummock Water @ 44 54.34 N 3.18 W
Crump Lake @ 202 42.17 N 119.50 W
Crumpton 208 39.14 N 75.55 W
Crumstown 216 41.38 N 86.25 W
Crupet 56 50.21 N 4.48 E
Cruseilles 58 46.02 N 6.07 E
Cruser Brook ≃ 276 40.27 N 74.39 W
Crusheen 48 52.58 N 8.53 W
Crusnes 56 49.26 N 5.25 E
Crusnes ≃ 56 49.27 N 5.36 E
Cruz, Arroyo de la ≃, Calif., U.S. 226 35.42 N 121.09 W
Cruz, Arroyo de la ≃, Ur. 258 34.00 S 56.08 W
Cruz, Cabo ≻ 240p 19.51 N 77.44 W
Cruz, Cañada de la ≃ 258 34.09 S 58.58 W
Cruz, Cayo I 240p 22.15 N 77.49 W
Cruz Alta, Arg. 252 33.01 S 61.49 W
Cruz Alta, Bra. 252 28.39 S 53.36 W
Cruz Bay 240m 18.20 N 64.48 W
Cruz das Almas 256 22.44 S 46.51 W
Cruz de Elorza 234 23.49 N 100.29 W
Cruz del Eje 252 30.44 S 64.48 W
Cruz Descoberta 256 22.45 S 46.48 W
Cruzeiro 256 22.34 S 44.58 W
Cruzeiro do Oeste 255 23.46 S 53.04 W
Cruzeiro do Sul 248 7.38 S 72.36 W
Cruzeta 250 6.25 S 36.47 W
Cruz Grande, Chile 252 29.25 S 71.18 W
Cruz Grande, Méx. 234 16.44 N 99.08 W
Cruzília 256 21.50 S 44.48 W
Cruz Machado 252 26.01 S 51.21 W
Cruzy-le-Châtel 50 47.51 N 4.12 E
Crvenka 38 45.39 N 19.28 E
Crymmych 42 51.59 N 4.40 W
Crystal, Minn., U.S. 190 45.00 N 93.25 W
Crystal, N. Dak., U.S. 198 48.36 N 97.40 W
Crystal ≃ 200 39.25 N 107.14 W
Crystal Bay 226 39.15 N 120.00 W
Crystal Bay C 220 28.55 N 82.43 W
Crystal Beach, Ont., Can. 284a 42.52 N 79.04 W
Crystal Beach, Fla., U.S. 220 28.06 N 82.47 W
Crystal Beach, Tex., U.S. 222 29.27 N 94.38 W
Crystal Cave ✦[5] 208 40.32 N 75.51 W
Crystal City, Man., Can. 184 49.09 N 98.56 W
Crystal City, Mo., U.S. 219 38.13 N 90.23 W
Crystal City, Tex., U.S. 196 28.41 N 99.50 W
Crystal Creek ≃ 278 41.58 N 87.51 W
Crystal Falls 190 46.05 N 88.20 W
Crystal Gardens 216 42.14 N 88.23 W
Crystal Lake, Fla., U.S. 220 30.26 N 85.41 W
Crystal Lake, Ill., U.S. 216 42.14 N 88.19 W
Crystal Lake, N.Y., U.S. 210 42.28 N 78.20 W
Crystal Lake, N.Y., U.S. 210 42.31 N 74.12 W
Crystal Lake @, Ont., Can. 212 44.45 N 78.30 W
Crystal Lake @, Mass., U.S. 283 42.29 N 71.05 W
Crystal Lake @, Mass., U.S. 283 42.48 N 71.09 W
Crystal Lake @, Mich., U.S. 190 44.40 N 86.10 W
Crystal Lake @, N.J., U.S. 276 41.02 N 74.15 W
Crystal Lakes 218 39.52 N 84.04 W
Crystal Lawns 216 41.34 N 88.09 W
Crystal Manor 216 42.14 N 88.17 W
Crystal Palace Stadium and Motor Race Track ✦ 260 51.25 N 0.04 W
Crystal River 192 28.54 N 82.36 W
Crystal Spring Lake @ 285 39.43 N 75.01 W
Crystal Springs, Fla., U.S. 220 28.11 N 82.10 W
Crystal Springs, Miss., U.S. 194 31.59 N 90.21 W
Crystal Springs Dam ✦[6] 282 37.32 N 122.22 W
Crystal Vista 216 42.14 N 88.24 W
Csepel ✦[8] 264c 47.24 N 19.14 E
Csepel-sziget I 264c 47.24 N 19.03 E
Cserta ≃ 61 46.35 N 16.36 E
Csesznek ⊥ 30 47.16 N 17.53 E
Csobánka 264c 47.38 N 18.58 E
Csomád 264c 47.40 N 19.15 E
Csömör 264c 47.33 N 19.14 E
Csömöri-patak ≃ 264c 47.36 N 19.07 E
Csongrád 30 46.43 N 20.09 E
Csongrád ☐[6] 30 46.25 N 20.15 E
Csorna 30 47.37 N 17.16 E
Csurgó 30 46.16 N 17.06 E
Ču 85 43.36 N 73.45 E
Ču ≃ 86 45.00 N 67.44 E
Cúa 246 10.10 N 66.54 W
Cuacnopalan 234 18.49 N 97.30 W
Cuácua ≃ 154 17.54 S 36.48 E
Cuadro Nacional 252 34.37 S 68.17 W
Cuajimalpa ☐[7] 286a 19.21 N 99.17 W
Cuajimalpa ✦[8] 286a 19.21 N 99.18 W
Cuajinicuilapa 234 16.28 N 98.25 W
Cuajone 248 17.00 S 70.43 W
Cuale 152 8.06 S 16.03 E
Cua-lo 110 18.49 N 105.43 E
Cuamato 152 17.05 S 15.09 E
Cuambog 116 7.20 N 125.52 E
Cuanavale ≃ 152 15.07 S 19.14 E
Cuando 152 16.32 S 22.07 E
Cuando (Kwando) ≃ 152 18.27 S 23.32 E
Cuando Cubango ☐[5] 152 16.00 S 20.00 E
Cuangar 152 17.36 S 18.39 E
Cuango, Ang. 152 6.17 S 16.41 E
Cuango, Ang. 152 9.10 S 17.58 E
Cuango, Ang. 152 14.30 S 18.59 E
Cuango (Kwango) ≃ 152 3.14 S 17.23 E
Cuanza ≃ 152 9.19 S 13.08 E
Cuanza-Norte ☐[5] 152 8.50 S 14.30 E
Cuanza-Sul ☐[5] 152 10.50 S 14.50 E
Cuao ≃ 246 4.55 N 67.40 W
Cuapiaxtla 234 19.18 N 97.46 W
Cua-rao 110 19.16 N 104.27 E
Cuaró 252 30.37 S 56.54 W
Cuartillo, Arroyo ≃ 258 33.45 S 59.06 W
Cuarto ≃ 252 33.25 S 63.02 W
Cuary ≃ 246 1.30 N 68.11 W
Cuatir ≃ 152 17.01 S 18.09 E
Cuatro Caminos 286b 22.54 N 82.23 W
Cuatro Ciénegas [de Carranza] 196 26.59 N 102.05 W
Cuatro Islands II 116 10.31 N 124.39 E
Cuauhtémoc, Méx. 232 28.25 N 106.52 W
Cuauhtémoc, Méx. 234 19.20 N 103.36 W
Cuautémoc ☐[7] 286a 19.26 N 99.09 W
Cuautepec [de Hinojosa] 234 20.02 N 98.18 W
Cuautepec el Alto ✦[8] 286a 19.34 N 99.08 W
Cuautitlán 234 19.26 N 104.23 W
Cuautitlán ☐[7] 286a 19.39 N 99.13 W
Cuautitlán [de Romero Rubio] 234 19.40 N 99.11 W
Cuautla 234 20.11 N 104.21 W
Cuautla Morelos 234 18.48 N 98.57 W
Cuautzin, Cerro ∧ 286a 19.10 N 99.04 W
Cuba, Port. 34 38.10 N 7.53 W
Cuba, Ala., U.S. 194 32.26 N 88.23 W
Cuba, Ill., U.S. 190 40.30 N 90.12 W
Cuba, Kans., U.S. 198 39.48 N 97.27 W
Cuba, Mo., U.S. 194 38.04 N 91.24 W
Cuba, N. Mex., U.S. 200 36.01 N 107.04 W
Cuba, N.Y., U.S. 210 42.13 N 78.17 W
Cuba ☐[1] 230
240p 21.30 N 80.00 W
Cubabi, Cerro ∧ 200 31.42 N 112.46 W
Cubadak 112 0.19 N 100.00 E
Cubagua, Isla I 246 10.48 N 64.10 W
Cuba Island I 276 40.38 N 73.32 W
Cubal 152 13.02 S 14.19 E
Cubal ≃, Ang. 152 12.42 S 13.56 E
Cubal ≃, Ang. 152 12.13 S 13.39 E
Cubal ≃, Ang. 152 11.19 S 13.48 E
Cuba Lake @ 210 42.15 N 78.18 W
Cubanea 254 41.02 S 70.16 W
Cubango (Okavango) ≃ 138 18.50 S 22.25 E
Cubangui ≃ 152 14.22 S 19.58 E
Čubaricha 86 57.37 N 68.22 E
Čubarovo 82 55.12 N 36.56 E
Cubatão 256 23.53 S 46.25 W
Cubatão, Serra de ✦[4] 256 23.52 S 46.28 W
Cubati 250 6.51 S 36.21 W
Cub Hills ∧∧[2] 184 54.20 N 104.30 W
Cubia ≃ 152 16.01 S 21.50 E
Čublas 24 64.44 N 45.00 E
Cub Run ≃ 208 38.46 N 77.28 W
Çubuk 130 40.15 N 33.02 E
Çubuklu ✦[8] 267b 41.06 N 29.04 E
Cuc ≃ 250 1.22 N 53.33 W
Cucamonga 228 34.06 N 117.35 W
Cucamonga Creek ≃ 280 33.57 N 117.37 W
Cucamonga Peak ∧ 228 34.14 N 117.36 W
Cuccaro Vetere 68 40.09 N 15.18 E
Cucco, Monte ∧ 66 43.22 N 12.45 E
Čučeviči 76 52.35 N 26.52 E
Cuchara, Río de la ≃ 234 16.37 N 97.41 W
Cucharas 234 22.52 N 105.19 W
Cucharas ≃ 198 37.55 N 104.32 W
Cuchi 152 14.36 S 16.58 E
Cuchi ≃ 152 15.28 S 17.21 E
Cuchibi ≃ 152 15.00 S 20.45 E
Cuchilla Alta, Cerro ∧ 236 15.10 N 88.12 W
Cuchilla Águila, Cerro ∧ 234 21.27 N 101.03 W
Cuchillo-Có 252 38.20 S 64.37 W
Cuchillo Negro Creek ≃ 200 33.08 N 107.14 W
Cuchivero ≃ 246 7.40 N 65.57 W
Čuchloma 76 58.45 N 42.41 E
Čuchlomskoje, Ozero @ 76 58.46 N 42.35 E
Cuchumatanes, Sierra de los ∧∧ 236 15.35 N 91.25 W
Cuckels Brook ≃ 276 40.33 N 74.33 W
Cuckfield 42 51.00 N 0.09 W
Cuckney 44 53.15 N 1.08 W
Cuckold Point ≻ 284b 39.14 N 76.24 W
Čučkovo, S.S.S.R. 76 59.36 N 41.14 E
Čučkovo, S.S.S.R. 80 54.17 N 41.26 E
Cucuí 246 1.12 N 66.50 W
Čučuleny 78 47.02 N 28.22 E
Cucumbi 152 10.17 S 19.05 E
Cucuron 62 43.47 N 5.26 E
Cucurpe 232 30.20 N 110.43 W
Cúcuta 246 7.54 N 72.31 W
Cudachar 84 42.21 N 47.11 E
Cudahy, Calif., U.S. 280 33.58 N 118.11 W
Cudahy, Wis., U.S. 216 42.57 N 87.52 W
Cuddalore 122 11.45 N 79.45 E
Cuddapah 122 14.28 N 78.49 E
Cuddeback Lake @ 228 35.18 N 117.28 W
Cuddebackville 210 41.28 N 74.36 W
Cuddia ≃ 70 37.53 N 12.37 E
Cuddington 262 53.14 N 2.36 W
Cuddle Lake @ 184 55.25 N 95.47 W
Cuddy 279b 40.21 N 80.09 W
Cuddy Mountain ∧ 202 44.46 N 116.47 W
Cudgegong ≃ 170 32.37 S 149.43 E
Cudgewa Creek ≃ 171b 36.03 S 147.55 E
Cudham ✦[8] 260 51.19 N 0.05 E
Cudia Park ✦ 275b 43.43 N 79.13 W
Čudin 76 52.44 N 26.59 E
Cudjoe Key I 220 24.40 N 81.30 W
Čudnov 78 50.04 N 28.06 E
Čudovo 76 59.07 N 31.41 E
Čudskoje Ozero (Peipsi Järv) @ 76 58.45 N 27.30 E
Cudworth, Sask., Can. 184 52.30 N 105.45 W
Cudworth, Eng., U.K. 44 53.35 N 1.25 W
Cue 162 27.25 S 117.54 E
Cuebe ≃ 152 15.48 S 17.30 E
Cueio ≃, Ang. 152 15.27 S 21.21 E
Cueio ≃, Ang. 152 16.17 S 17.46 E
Cuelei ≃ 152 15.33 S 17.21 E
Cuéllar 34 41.25 N 4.19 W
Cuenca, Ec. 246 2.53 S 78.59 W
Cuenca, Esp. 34 40.04 N 2.08 W
Cuencamé [de Ceniceros] 232 24.53 N 103.42 W
Cuerámaro 234 20.37 N 101.43 W
Cuernavaca 234 18.55 N 99.15 W
Cuero 222 29.06 N 97.18 W
Cuers 62 43.14 N 6.04 E
Cuervo, Laguna del @ 232 29.17 N 105.57 W
Cuesmes 50 50.26 N 3.55 E
Cuesta Pass)(226 35.21 N 120.38 W
Cueto 240p 20.39 N 75.56 W
Cuetzala del Progreso 234 18.07 N 99.50 W
Cuetzalan del Progreso 234 20.02 N 97.31 W
Cuevas del Almanzora 34 37.18 N 1.53 W
Cuevo 248 20.27 S 63.32 W
Čufarovo 80 54.06 N 47.19 E
Cuffley 260 51.47 N 0.07 W
Cufra → Al-Kufrah ✦[1] 146 24.20 N 23.15 E
Cufré 258 34.12 S 57.06 W
Cufré, Arroyo ≃ 258 34.27 S 57.09 W
Cufré, Cuchilla ∧∧[2] 258 34.20 S 57.10 W
Cuggiono 62 45.31 N 8.49 E
Cugir 38 45.50 N 23.22 E
Cuglieri 71 40.11 N 8.34 E
Čugujev 78 49.50 N 36.41 E
Čugujevka 89 44.08 N 133.53 E
Čugunaš 86 52.52 N 87.46 E
Čuguš, Gora ∧ 84 43.47 N 40.16 E
Cuiabá 248 15.35 S 56.05 W
Cuiabá ≃ 248 17.05 S 56.36 W
Cuiari 246 1.30 N 68.11 W
Cuichapa 234 17.59 N 94.15 W
Cuidado, Punta ≻ 174z 27.08 S 109.19 W
Cuieiras ≃ 246 2.50 S 60.31 W
Cuigezhuang, Zhg. 105 40.02 N 117.54 E
Cuigezhuang, Zhg. 105 40.01 N 116.28 E
Cuihengcun 100 22.28 N 113.32 E
Cuihuangkou 105 39.32 N 117.11 E
Cuijiatun 104 40.57 N 121.09 E
Cuijiazhuang 104 40.57 N 122.44 E
Cuilapa 236 14.17 N 90.18 W
Cuilcagh ∧ 48 54.12 N 7.48 W
Cuilco ≃ 236 15.24 N 91.58 W
Ču-Ilijskije Gory ∧∧ 85 43.52 N 75.00 E
Cuilo (Kwilu) ≃ 152 3.22 S 17.22 E
Cuilo Futa 152 6.25 S 15.44 E
Cuimba 152 6.08 S 14.38 E
Cuio 152 12.58 S 12.58 E
Cuiquiao 98 34.12 N 114.36 E
Cuiseaux 58 46.30 N 5.24 E
Cuisery 58 47.22 N 5.19 E
Cuisy 261 49.01 N 2.46 E
Cuité 250 6.29 S 36.09 W
Cuitláhuac 234 18.49 N 96.43 W
Cuito ≃ 152 18.01 S 20.48 E
Cuito-Cuanavale 152 15.10 S 19.10 E
Cuitzeo, Lago de @ 234 19.55 N 101.05 W
Cuitzeo del Porvenir 234 19.59 N 101.09 W
Cuitzmala 234 19.23 N 104.59 W
Cuiuni ≃ 246 0.45 S 63.07 W
Cuivre ≃ 219 38.56 N 90.42 W
Cuivre, North Fork ≃ 219 39.02 N 90.59 W
Cuivre, West Fork ≃ 219 39.02 N 90.59 W
Cuivre River State Park ✦ 219 39.02 N 90.57 W
Cuixi 100 28.16 N 117.10 E

Symbols in the index entries represent the broad categories identified in the key at the right. Symbols with superior numbers (∧∧[2]) identify subcategories (see complete key on page I · 30).

Kartensymbole in dem Registerverzeichnis stellen die rechts in Schlüssel erklärten Kategorien dar. Symbole mit hochgestellten Ziffern (∧∧[2]) bezeichnen Unterabteilungen einer Kategorie (vgl. vollständiger Schlüssel auf Seite I · 30).

Los símbolos incluidos en el texto del indice representan las grandes categorias identificadas con la clave a la derecha. Los símbolos con numeros en su parte superior (∧∧[2]) identifican las subcategorias (véase la clave completa en la página I · 30).

Les symboles de l'index représentent les catégories indiquées dans la légende à droite. Les symboles suivis d'un indice (∧∧[2]) représentent des sous-catégories (voir légende complète à la page I · 30).

Os símbolos incluídos no texto do índice representam as grandes categorias identificadas com a chave à direita. Os símbolos com números em sua parte superior (∧∧[2]) identificam as subcategorias (veja-se a chave completa à página I · 30).

	English	Deutsch	Español	Français	Português
∧	Mountain	Berg	Montaña	Montagne	Montanha
∧∧	Mountains	Berge	Montañas	Montagnes	Montanhas
)(	Pass	Pass	Paso	Col	Passo
∨	Valley, Canyon	Tal, Cañon	Valle, Cañón	Vallée, Canyon	Vale, Canhão
⌓	Plain	Ebene	Llano	Plaine	Planície
≻	Cape	Kap	Cabo	Cap	Cabo
I	Island	Insel	Isla	Île	Ilha
II	Islands	Inseln	Islas	Îles	Ilhas
✦	Other Topographic Features	Andere Topographische Objekte	Otros Elementos Topográficos	Autres données topographiques	Outros Elementos Topográficos

ESPAÑOL — Nombre / Página / Lat.°′ / Long.°′ W=Oeste
FRANÇAIS — Nom / Page / Lat.°′ / Long.°′ W=Ouest
PORTUGUÊS — Nome / Página / Lat.°′ / Long.°′ W=Oeste

Čuja, S.S.S.R. 86 50.24 N 86.39 E
Čuja, S.S.S.R. 88 59.17 N 112.24 E
Cují 286c 10.28 N 67.02 W
Çukas 112 0.25 S 104.18 E
Čukčagirskoje Ozero 89 52.00 N 136.36 E
Čukotskij, Mys 180 64.14 N 173.10 W
Čukotskij Poluostrov [1] 180 66.00 N 175.00 W
Çukurca 128 37.15 N 43.37 E
Čukurčak 85 41.47 N 71.07 E
Cukurino 83 48.05 N 37.18 E
Culaba 116 11.40 N 124.32 E
Čulak-Kurgan 85 43.46 N 69.12 E
Culaman 116 5.58 N 125.40 E
Culari 250 1.27 N 53.42 W
Culasi, Pil. 116 11.26 N 122.03 E
Culasi, Pil. 116 10.43 N 125.43 E
Culasian 116 8.51 N 117.29 E
Culasi Point 116 11.37 N 122.42 E
Culbertson, Mont., U.S. 198 48.09 N 104.31 W
Culbertson, Nebr., U.S. 198 40.14 N 100.50 W
Culbertson Run 285 40.03 N 75.45 W
Culcheth 262 53.27 N 2.32 W
Culdaff 48 55.18 N 7.11 W
Culdaff Bay 48 55.17 N 7.10 W
Culebra, Isla de 240m 18.19 N 65.17 W
Culebra, Laguna de la 234 22.28 N 98.20 W
Culebra, Sierra de la 34 41.54 N 6.20 W
Culebra Peak 200 37.07 N 105.11 W
Culebrinos 240m 18.24 N 67.11 W
Culebrita, Isla 240m 18.19 N 65.14 W
Culemborg 52 51.56 N 5.13 E
Culgoa 166 29.56 S 146.20 E
Culham Inlet 162 33.55 S 120.04 E
Culiacán 232 24.48 N 107.24 W
Culiacán, Cerro 234 20.20 N 100.58 W
Culiacancito 232 24.50 N 107.32 W
Culion 116 11.53 N 120.01 E
Culion Island 116 11.50 N 119.55 E
Cúllar de Baza 34 37.35 N 2.34 W
Cull Creek 282 37.42 N 122.03 W
Cullen, Scot., U.K. 46 57.41 N 2.49 W
Cullen, La., U.S. 194 32.58 N 93.27 W
Cullen Bullen 170 33.18 S 150.01 E
Cullen Point 164 11.57 S 141.54 E
Culleoka, Tenn., U.S. 194 35.29 N 86.59 W
Culleoka, Tex., U.S. 222 33.08 N 96.29 W
Cullera 34 39.10 N 0.15 W
Cullicudden 46 57.39 N 4.13 W
Cullin, Lough 48 53.57 N 9.12 W
Cullinan 158 25.40 S 28.32 E
Cullin Hills [2] 46 57.15 N 6.15 W
Cullman 194 34.11 N 86.51 W
Culloden Battlesite 46 57.28 N 4.05 W
Cullom 216 40.53 N 88.16 W
Cullompton 42 50.52 N 3.24 W
Cullowhee 192 35.19 N 83.11 W
Cully 58 46.29 N 6.44 E
Çulm 42 50.46 N 3.31 W
Čul'man 74 56.52 N 124.52 E
Cülmen 130 37.19 N 38.48 E
Culmore 284c 38.51 N 77.08 W
Culoz 62 45.51 N 5.47 E
Culpeper 188 38.28 N 77.53 W
Culpina 248 20.50 S 64.58 W
Culrain 46 57.55 N 4.24 W
Cults 46 57.07 N 2.10 W
Cultus Lake 224 49.04 N 121.58 W
Cultus Lake 224 49.03 N 121.58 W
Cultus Lake Provincial Park 224 49.03 N 121.58 W
Culú Culú, Arroyo 258 35.19 S 58.57 W
Culuene 255 12.56 S 52.51 W
Çulukidze 84 42.20 N 42.25 E
Čuluunchoroot 88 49.45 N 114.20 E
Čuluut 102 45.49 N 107.02 E
Čuluut 88 49.11 N 100.41 E
Culvain 46 56.56 N 5.17 W
Culver, Ind., U.S. 216 41.13 N 86.25 W
Culver, Oreg., U.S. 202 44.32 N 121.13 W
Culver, Point 162 32.54 S 124.43 E
Culver City 228 34.01 N 118.24 W
Culverden 172 42.46 S 172.51 E
Culvers Lake 210 41.10 N 74.48 W
Çulverstone Green 260 51.20 N 0.21 E
Čulym 86 55.06 N 80.58 E
Čulym, S.S.S.R. 86 54.38 N 78.16 E
Čulym, S.S.S.R. 86 57.43 N 83.51 E
Čulyšman 86 51.20 N 87.45 E
Čum 24 67.06 N 63.07 E
Cuma 152 12.52 S 15.05 E
Çuma (Cumae) 68 40.50 N 14.06 E
Čumakovo 86 55.41 N 79.02 E
Cumalı 130 36.42 N 27.27 E
Cuman' 78 50.49 N 25.53 E
Cumaná 246 10.28 N 64.10 W
Cumanacoa 246 10.15 N 63.55 W
Cumanayagua 240p 22.09 N 80.12 W
Cumaovası 130 38.15 N 27.09 E
Cumari 255 18.16 S 48.11 W
Cumbal 246 0.54 N 77.47 W
Cumbal, Nevado de 246 0.57 N 77.52 W
Cumbe 250 10.21 S 37.14 W
Cumbee 220 28.04 N 81.55 W
Cumberland, B.C., Can. 182 49.37 N 125.01 W
Cumberland, Iowa, U.S. 198 41.16 N 94.52 W
Cumberland, Ky., U.S. 192 36.59 N 82.59 W
Cumberland, Md., U.S. 188 39.39 N 78.46 W
Cumberland, Va., U.S. 192 37.30 N 78.15 W
Cumberland, Wash., U.S. 224 47.17 N 121.56 W
Cumberland, Wis., U.S. 190 45.32 N 92.01 W
Cumberland □[6], N.J., U.S. 208 39.26 N 75.14 W
Cumberland □[6], Pa., U.S. 208 40.12 N 77.12 W
Cumberland 178 37.09 N 88.25 W
Cumberland, Caney Fork 194 36.09 N 85.52 W
Cumberland, Cape 175f 14.39 S 166.37 E
Cumberland, Lake [1] 194 36.57 N 84.55 W
Cumberland Bay 241h 13.16 N 61.17 W
Cumberland City 194 36.23 N 87.38 W
Cumberland Falls State Park 192 36.50 N 84.20 W
Cumberland Gap 192 36.36 N 83.41 W
Cumberland Gap National Historical Park 192 36.36 N 83.40 W
Cumberland Hill 207 41.59 N 71.28 W
Cumberland House 184 53.58 N 102.16 W
Cumberland Indian Reserve [4] 184 53.04 N 104.50 W
Cumberland Islands 166 20.40 S 149.09 E
Cumberland Lake 184 54.02 N 102.17 W
Cumberland Peninsula [1] 176 66.50 N 64.00 W
Cumberland Plateau [1] 178 36.00 N 85.00 W
Cumberland Sound 176 65.10 N 65.30 W
Cumbernauld 46 55.58 N 3.59 W
Cumbres de Monterrey, Parque Nacional 232 25.31 N 100.18 W
Cumbria □[6] 44 54.30 N 3.00 W
Cumbrian Mountains 44 54.30 N 3.05 W
Čumbur-Kosa 83 46.57 N 38.53 E
Cumby 222 33.08 N 95.50 W
Çumeral Nuevo 200 30.54 N 110.51 W
Čumerna 38 42.47 N 25.58 E
Çumiana 62 44.59 N 7.22 E
Čumikan 89 54.42 N 135.19 E
Cuminá → Paru de Oeste 250 1.30 S 56.00 W
Cuminapanema 250 1.09 S 54.54 W
Cuminestown 46 57.32 N 2.20 W
Cumming 192 34.13 N 84.08 W
Cummings Mountain 228 35.03 N 118.34 W
Cummington 207 42.27 N 72.54 W
Cummins, Mount 182 52.03 N 118.15 W
Cummins Creek 222 29.43 N 96.31 W
Cummins Range 162 19.05 S 127.10 E
Cumnock 44 55.27 N 4.16 W
Cumnor 42 51.44 N 1.20 W
Cumpas 232 30.02 N 109.48 W
Çumra 130 37.34 N 32.48 E
Cumshewa Inlet 182 53.03 N 131.45 W
Cumuripa 232 28.08 N 109.53 W
Çumwhinton 44 54.52 N 2.51 W
Čumyš 86 53.31 N 83.10 E
Č'un' 80 55.44 N 54.16 E
Čun'a, S.S.S.R. 74 61.36 N 96.30 E
Čuna, S.S.S.R. 88 57.47 N 95.26 E
Cunani 250 2.52 N 51.06 W
Cunauaru 246 3.10 S 63.01 W
Cunaviche 246 7.22 N 67.25 W
Cunco 252 38.55 S 72.02 W
Cuncumén 252 31.53 S 70.38 W
Çundinamarca □[5] 246 5.00 N 74.00 W
Čundža 86 43.32 N 79.28 E
Cunene (Kunene) 152 17.20 S 11.50 E
Cuneo 62 44.23 N 7.32 E
Cuneo □[4] 62 44.31 N 7.34 E
Cunewalde 54 51.06 N 14.30 E
Cuney 222 32.02 N 95.25 W
Cung-hau, Cua [1] 110 9.46 N 106.34 E
Çungüş 130 38.13 N 39.17 E
Cunha 256 23.05 S 44.58 W
Cunhambebe 256 23.00 S 44.20 W
Cunha Porã 252 26.54 S 53.09 W
Cunhinga 152 10.38 S 16.48 E
Cunhuã, Igarapé 248 5.46 S 64.36 W
Cunlhat 62 45.38 N 3.35 E
Cunningham, Austl. 171a 28.09 S 151.51 E
Cunningham, Kans., U.S. 198 37.39 N 98.26 W
Cunningham, Lake 240b 25.04 N 77.26 W
Cunninghame □[9] 46 55.40 N 4.30 W
Cunningham Falls State Park 208 39.35 N 77.27 W
Cunningham Park, Mass., U.S. 283 42.15 N 71.03 W
Cunningham Park, N.Y., U.S. 276 40.44 N 73.46 W
Cunninghams Gap National Park 171a 28.01 S 152.22 E
Čunojar 88 57.27 N 97.18 E
Çunqian 100 28.30 N 115.10 E
Čunskij 88 56.05 N 99.41 E
Çuntan 107 29.37 N 106.36 E
Čuny 76 59.39 N 36.04 E
Cuogang 88 49.14 N 118.08 E
Cuokkaraš'ša 24 69.57 N 24.32 E
Çuorgnè 62 45.23 N 7.39 E
Čupa 24 66.16 N 33.00 E
Čupachovka 78 50.23 N 34.36 E
Čupalejka 80 55.11 N 42.33 E
Cupar, Sask., Can. 184 50.57 N 104.12 W
Cupar, Scot., U.K. 46 56.19 N 3.01 W
Cupecê, Ribeirão 287b 23.37 S 46.42 W
Cupello 66 42.04 N 14.40 E
Cuperly 50 49.04 N 4.26 E
Cupertino 226 37.19 N 122.02 W
Cupica, Golfo de 246 6.35 N 77.25 W
Cupins 255 19.51 S 51.03 W
Cupra Marittima 66 43.01 N 13.51 E
Çupramontana 66 43.27 N 13.07 E
Ćuprija 38 43.56 N 21.23 E
Cupsaw Lake 276 41.07 N 74.15 W
Cuqiao 107 30.36 N 103.59 E
Cuquema 152 12.03 S 17.40 E
Cuquenán 246 4.45 N 61.30 W
Çuquío 234 20.55 N 103.02 W
Čur 80 57.07 N 52.58 E
Curaçá 250 8.59 S 39.54 W
Curaçao 241s 12.11 N 69.00 W
Curacautín 252 38.26 S 71.53 W
Çuracaví 252 33.24 S 71.09 W
Čuračiki 80 55.44 N 47.26 E
Curacó 252 38.49 S 64.57 W
Curaglia 58 46.41 N 8.51 E
Curahuara 248 17.40 S 68.02 W
Curanilahue 252 37.28 S 73.21 W
Curanipe 252 35.50 S 72.38 W
Çuranja 248 9.58 S 70.58 W
Čurapča 74 62.00 N 132.24 E
Curapi 250 1.25 N 53.49 W
Çuraray 246 2.20 S 74.05 W
Čurbek 85 39.59 N 69.56 E
Curcani 38 44.12 N 26.35 E
Curcubăta 38 46.27 N 22.42 E
Curdies 169 38.30 S 142.55 E
Cure 50 47.40 N 3.41 E
Curecanti National Recreation Area 200 38.24 N 107.25 W
Curepipe 157c 20.19 S 57.31 E
Curepto 252 35.05 S 72.01 W
Curequetê 248 8.20 S 65.40 W
Curiapo 246 8.33 N 61.00 W
Curib 84 42.14 N 46.49 E
Curicó 252 34.59 S 71.14 W
Curicuriari 246 0.14 S 66.48 W
Curières, Lac 206 46.41 N 74.51 W
Curimatá 250 10.02 S 44.17 W
Curimeo 234 20.01 N 101.42 W
Curinga 68 38.49 N 16.19 E
Curious, Mount 162 27.28 S 114.20 E
Curisevo 255 12.14 S 53.17 W
Curitiba 252 25.25 S 49.15 W
Curitibanos 252 27.18 S 50.36 W
Curiuaú 246 1.51 S 61.14 W
Curiúva 255 24.02 S 50.27 W
Curl Curl 274a 33.46 S 151.18 E
Curoca Norte 152 16.18 S 12.58 E
Curone 62 45.03 N 8.54 E
Curon Venosta (Graun) 64 46.49 N 10.32 E
Čurovići 78 52.10 N 32.01 E
Currais Novos 250 6.15 S 36.31 W
Curralinho 250 1.48 S 49.47 W
Curran 219 39.44 N 89.46 W
Currant Creek, Colo., U.S. 200 38.29 N 105.24 W
Currant Creek, Mont., U.S. 202 46.22 N 108.39 W
Currant Mountain 204 38.55 N 115.25 W
Curreeney 48 52.43 N 8.08 W
Current 190 48.27 N 89.11 W
Current, Jacks Fork 194 37.12 N 91.17 W
Current Islands 192 25.22 N 76.49 W
Currie, Scot., U.K. 46 55.54 N 3.20 W
Currie, Minn., U.S. 198 43.59 N 95.40 W
Currituck 192 36.27 N 76.01 W
Currituck □[6] 208 36.28 N 76.03 W
Currituck Sound 192 36.20 N 75.52 W
Currituok Seamount [3] 14 30.05 S 173.25 W
Curry 180 62.37 N 150.01 W
Curry, Lake [1] 226 38.22 N 122.08 W
Curry Rivel 42 51.02 N 2.52 W
Curryville, Mo., U.S. 219 39.21 N 91.21 W
Curryville, Pa., U.S. 214 40.17 N 78.20 W
Cursi 68 40.09 N 18.18 E
Curslack [8] 52 53.27 N 10.13 E
Curtarolo 64 45.31 N 11.50 E
Curtea-de-Argeș 38 45.08 N 24.41 E
Curtice 214 41.37 N 83.22 W
Curtina 252 32.09 S 56.07 W
Curtis, Esp. 34 43.07 N 8.03 W
Curtis, Ark., U.S. 194 34.00 N 93.06 W
Curtis, Nebr., U.S. 198 40.38 N 100.31 W
Curtis, Port [3] 166 24.00 S 151.30 E
Curtis Bay 284b 39.13 N 76.35 W
Curtis Creek 284b 39.12 N 76.35 W
Curtis Island, Austl. 166 23.38 S 151.09 E
Curtis Island, N.Z. 14 30.30 S 178.34 W
Curtis Lake 176 66.38 N 89.02 W
Curtisville 214 40.37 N 79.50 W
Curu 250 3.22 S 39.04 W
Curuá, Bra. 250 5.23 S 54.22 W
Curuá, Bra. 250 1.55 S 55.07 W
Curuá, Bra. 255 13.51 S 51.38 W
Curuá, Ilha 250 0.48 N 50.10 W
Curuá do Sul 250 2.39 S 54.10 W
Curuaés 250 7.30 S 54.45 W
Curuan 116 7.13 N 122.14 E
Curuá Una 250 2.24 S 54.05 W
Curubandé 236 10.43 N 85.26 W
Curuçá 250 0.43 S 47.50 W
Curuçá [8] 287b 23.30 S 46.25 W
Curuçá 246 4.27 S 71.23 W
Curuçambaba 250 2.08 S 49.18 W
Çurug, Indon. 115a 6.15 S 106.33 E
Čurug, Jugo. 38 45.29 N 20.04 E
Curuguaty 252 24.31 S 55.42 W
Curumo 286c 10.27 N 66.52 W
Curumu 250 1.01 S 51.03 W
Curunga 152 12.51 S 21.12 E
Curup 112 3.28 S 102.32 E
Curupá 250 9.54 S 45.54 W
C'urupinsk 78 46.37 N 32.43 E
Curupira, Sierra de 246 1.25 N 64.30 W
Cururu, Bra. 248 7.12 S 58.03 W
Cururu, Bra. 250 0.39 S 50.11 W
Cururu-Açu 250 8.58 S 57.13 W
Cururupu 250 1.50 S 44.52 W
Curutu 246 5.05 N 63.28 W
Curuzú Cuatiá 252 29.47 S 58.03 W
Curva Grande 250 2.37 S 45.27 W
Curvelo 255 18.45 S 44.25 W
Curwensville 214 40.58 N 78.32 W
Curwensville Lake [1] 214 40.55 N 78.37 W
Curwensville State Park 214 40.55 N 78.34 W
Curwood, Mount [2] 190 46.42 N 88.14 W
Cusago 266b 45.27 N 9.02 E
Cusano Milanino 62 45.33 N 9.11 E
Cusano Mutri 68 41.20 N 14.30 E
Cusapin 236 9.11 N 81.54 W
Cusco → Cuzco 248 13.31 S 71.59 W
Cuscuzeiro, Pico do 256 23.18 S 44.47 W
Cushabatay 248 7.09 S 75.08 W
Cushendall 48 55.06 N 6.04 W
Cushendun 48 55.08 N 6.02 W
Cushina 48 53.11 N 7.05 W
Cushing, Okla., U.S. 196 35.59 N 96.46 W
Cushing, Tex., U.S. 222 31.43 N 94.50 W
Cushman 194 35.53 N 91.45 W
Cushman, Lake [1] 224 47.28 N 123.14 W
Cusiana 246 4.33 N 71.51 W
Cusick 202 48.20 N 117.18 W
Cusihuiriáchic 232 28.14 N 106.50 W
Çusna, Monte 64 44.17 N 10.23 E
Čusovaja 86 58.13 N 56.22 E
Čusovoj 86 58.17 N 57.49 E
Cusseta 192 32.18 N 84.47 W
Cussewago Creek 214 41.38 N 80.11 W
Cussey-sur-l'Ognon 58 47.20 N 5.56 E
Cusso 152 14.16 S 15.36 E
Çust, N.Z. 172 43.19 S 172.22 E
Čust, S.S.S.R. 85 41.00 N 71.15 E
Custar 216 41.17 N 83.51 W
Custer, Mich., U.S. 190 43.58 N 86.14 W
Custer, Mont., U.S. 202 46.08 N 107.33 W
Custer, Okla., U.S. 196 35.40 N 98.53 W
Custer, S. Dak., U.S. 198 43.46 N 103.36 W
Custer, Wash., U.S. 224 48.55 N 122.38 W
Custer Battlefield National Monument 202 45.32 N 107.20 W
Custer City 214 41.54 N 78.39 W
Custer Creek 198 46.42 N 105.29 W
Custer State Park 198 43.43 N 103.23 W
Custines 56 48.48 N 6.09 E
Custódia 250 8.07 S 37.39 W
Custonaci 70 38.04 N 12.41 E
Cut and Shoot 222 30.19 N 95.25 W
Cutato 152 10.33 S 16.48 E
Cut Bank 202 48.38 N 112.20 W
Cutbank 182 54.44 N 118.31 W
Cut Bank Creek, N.A. 198 48.35 N 100.52 W
Cut Bank Creek, Mont., U.S. 202 48.29 N 112.14 W
Çut Beaver Lake 184 53.47 N 102.38 W
Čutejevo 80 55.16 N 47.47 E
Cutervo 248 6.22 S 78.51 W
Cuthand Creek 194 33.23 N 94.57 W
Cuthbert 192 31.46 N 84.48 W
Cut Knife 184 52.44 N 109.01 W
Cutler, Calif., U.S. 226 36.31 N 119.17 W
Cutler, Maine, U.S. 188 44.40 N 67.12 W
Cutler Ridge 220 25.36 N 80.24 W
Çutlerville 216 42.51 N 85.40 W
Čutovo 78 49.43 N 35.10 E
Cutral-Có 252 38.56 S 69.14 W
Cutro 68 39.02 N 16.59 E
Cutrofiano 68 40.07 N 18.12 E
Cuttack 120 20.30 N 85.50 E
Çuttyhunk Island 207 41.25 N 70.56 W
Čutyr' 80 57.24 N 53.17 E
Cutzamalá 234 18.22 N 100.39 W
Cutzamala de Pinzón 234 18.28 N 100.34 W
Çutzio 234 18.39 N 100.54 W
Čuvašskaja Avtonomnaja Sovetskaja Socialističeskaja Respublika □[3] 80 55.30 N 47.00 E
Cuvette □[5] 152 0.30 S 16.00 E
Cuvier, Cape 162 24.05 S 113.22 E
Cuvilly 50 49.33 N 2.42 E
Cuvo 152 10.50 S 13.47 E
Cuxhaven 52 53.52 N 8.42 E
Cuxton 260 51.22 N 0.27 E
Cuyabá → Cuiabá 248 15.35 S 56.05 W
Cuyaguateje 240p 22.05 N 83.58 W
Cuyahoga □[6] 214 41.30 N 81.41 W
Cuyahoga 214 41.30 N 81.42 W
Cuyahoga County Airport 279a 41.34 N 81.29 W
Cuyahoga Falls 214 41.08 N 81.29 W
Cuyahoga Heights 279a 41.26 N 81.39 W
Cuyahoga Ohio Canal 279a 41.26 N 81.40 W
Cuyahoga Valley National Recreation Area 214 41.20 N 81.35 W
Cuyama 204 34.54 N 120.18 W
Cuyamaca Peak 204 32.57 N 116.36 W
Cuyamaca Rancho State Park 204 32.58 N 116.32 W
Cuyamel 236 15.38 N 88.12 W
Cuyapo 116 15.46 N 120.40 E
Cuyk 52 51.44 N 5.52 E
Cuyler 210 42.44 N 75.57 W
Cuylerville 210 42.47 N 77.52 W
Cuyo 116 10.51 N 121.00 E
Cuyo East Pass 116 11.00 N 121.28 E
Cuyo Island 116 10.51 N 121.02 E
Cuyo Islands 116 11.04 N 120.57 E
Cuyo West Pass 116 11.00 N 120.30 E
Cuyubini 246 8.20 N 60.20 W
Cuyuni 246 6.23 N 58.41 W
Cuyutlán, Laguna de 234 19.00 N 104.10 W
Cuzco 248 13.31 S 71.59 W
Çuzco □[5] 248 12.30 S 72.30 W
Čuzik 86 58.03 N 80.37 E
Cuzna 34 38.04 N 4.41 W
Cuzzago 58 46.00 N 8.22 E
Cvetkovo 78 49.11 N 31.33 E
Cvetnogorsk 86 54.14 N 90.27 E
Cvetnoje 78 48.57 N 32.29 E
Cvikov 54 50.48 N 14.40 E
Cwmbran 42 51.39 N 3.00 W
Cyangugu 154 2.29 S 28.54 E
Cybinka 30 52.12 N 14.48 E
Cybulev 78 49.06 N 29.50 E
Cyčevsko-V'azemskije Gr'ady 76 55.35 N 34.00 E
Cyclades → Kikládhes 38 37.30 N 25.00 E
Cyclone 214 41.50 N 78.35 W
Cygnet 216 41.14 N 83.39 W
Cygnet Bay 162 16.35 S 123.05 E
Cygnet Lake 184 56.47 N 94.54 W
Cylburn Park 284b 39.21 N 76.39 W
Cynin 42 51.48 N 4.29 W
Cynthiana, Ky., U.S. 218 38.23 N 84.18 W
Cynthiana, Ohio, U.S. 218 39.10 N 83.21 W
Cynwyl Elfed 42 51.55 N 4.22 W
Cypern → Cyprus □[1] 130 35.00 N 33.00 E
Cypress, Calif., U.S. 280 33.50 N 118.01 W
Cypress, La., U.S. 194 31.36 N 93.02 W
Cypress, Tex., U.S. 222 29.58 N 95.42 W
Cypress Bayou 194 35.03 N 91.42 W
Cypress Creek, Fla., U.S. 220 28.05 N 82.24 W
Cypress Creek, Tex., U.S. 194 30.19 N 93.45 W
Cypress Creek, Tex., U.S. 222 30.02 N 95.19 W
Cypress Gardens 220 28.00 N 81.42 W
Cypress Hills [2] 184 49.40 N 109.30 W
Cypress Hills Provincial Park, Alta., Can. 184 49.39 N 110.10 W
Cypress Hills Provincial Park, Sask., Can. 184 49.39 N 109.30 W
Cypress Island 224 48.35 N 122.42 W
Cypress Lake, Sask., Can. 184 49.28 N 109.29 W
Cypress Lake, Fla., U.S. 220 28.05 N 81.19 W
Cypress Point 226 36.35 N 121.59 W
Cypress Quarters 220 27.16 N 80.48 W
Cypress River 184 49.34 N 99.05 W
Cypress Swamp 208 37.02 N 76.53 W
Cypress Swamp 208 38.30 N 75.17 W
Cyprus □[1] 22; 130 35.00 N 33.00 E
Cyrenaica → Barqah [1] 146 31.00 N 22.30 E
Cyrene 219 39.17 N 91.06 W
Cyrene 146 32.49 N 21.52 E
Cyril 196 34.54 N 98.12 W
Cyrildene [8] 273d 26.11 S 28.06 E
Cyrus Field Bay 176 62.50 N 64.55 W
Cysoing 50 50.34 N 3.13 E
Cythera → Kíthira 38 36.20 N 22.58 E
Czaplinek 30 53.34 N 16.14 E
Czarna Białostocka 30 53.19 N 23.16 E
Czarna Woda 30 53.51 N 18.06 E
Czarne 30 53.42 N 16.57 E
Czarnków 30 52.55 N 16.34 E
Czechoslovakia □[1] 22; 30 49.30 N 17.00 E
Czechowice-Dziedzice 30 49.54 N 19.00 E
Czempiń 30 52.10 N 16.47 E
Czerniejewo 30 52.26 N 17.30 E
Czernowitz → Černovcy 78 48.18 N 25.56 E
Czersk 30 53.48 N 18.00 E
Czerwieńsk 30 52.01 N 15.25 E
Częstochowa 30 50.49 N 19.06 E
Człopa 30 53.06 N 16.08 E
Człuchów 30 53.41 N 17.21 E
Czudec 30 49.57 N 21.50 E

D

Da → Black 110 21.15 N 105.20 E
Daaden 56 50.44 N 7.58 E
Daan, Zhg. 100 27.52 N 117.53 E
Daan, Zhg. 100 23.05 N 115.37 E
Daan, Zhg. 110 23.19 N 110.34 E
Daanbantayan 116 11.14 N 124.00 E
Daanchang 107 29.23 N 106.01 E
Daanping 104 41.10 N 123.25 E
Ḍabāb, Jabal aḍ- 132 31.02 N 35.38 E
Daba Gorayale 144 8.42 N 44.55 E
Dabagou 104 42.27 N 122.00 E
Ḍab'ah, Ra's aḍ- 140 31.05 N 28.26 E
Dabai 150 11.31 N 5.11 E
Dabaiqipu 104 41.52 N 122.36 E
Dabaizhuang 105 39.27 N 117.23 E
Dabajuro 246 11.02 N 70.40 W
Dabakala 150 8.22 N 4.26 W
Dabali 104 41.51 N 120.37 E
Dabaling 100 24.28 N 113.17 E
Dabancheng 86 43.21 N 88.19 E
Dabangdian 100 31.37 N 113.41 E
Dabanyingzi 104 42.11 N 121.55 E
Dabao 98 40.34 N 124.12 E
Dabaojiagangzi 104 42.09 N 123.33 E
Dabaozhuang 105 40.18 N 116.58 E
Dabaozi 105 40.11 N 115.10 E
Dabaro 144 6.11 N 48.22 E
Dabashan 102 31.55 N 109.05 E
Dabasi 107 28.55 N 105.09 E
Dabat 144 12.58 N 37.48 E
Dabayingzi 104 42.11 N 121.35 E
Dabbūrīya 132 32.41 N 35.22 E
Dabegabis 158 28.07 S 18.36 E
Dabeiba 246 7.01 N 76.16 W
Dabeiwa 105 40.48 N 117.31 E
Dabeiyingzi 104 42.05 N 122.08 E
Dabendorf 54 52.14 N 13.26 E
Daber → Dobra 30 53.35 N 15.18 E
Daberas 156 25.38 S 18.29 E
Daberg [8] 263 51.40 N 7.47 E
Dabhoi 120 22.11 N 73.26 E
Dābhol 122 17.36 N 73.10 E
Ḍab'ī, Wādī aḍ- 132 31.42 N 36.42 E
Dąbie 30 52.06 N 18.49 E
Dąbie [8] 54 53.24 N 14.40 E
Dąbie, Jezioro 54 53.27 N 14.40 E
Dabieshan 100 31.00 N 115.40 E
Dabilda 146 12.46 N 14.34 E
Dablān 130 34.52 N 40.34 E
Ďáblice [8] 54 50.08 N 14.29 E
Dabnou 150 14.09 N 5.22 E
Dabo 58 48.39 N 7.14 E
Dabob Bay 224 47.47 N 122.50 W
Dabobeizhuang 105 39.18 N 117.59 E
Dabola 150 10.45 N 11.07 W
Dabola □[4] 150 10.36 N 11.07 W
Dabong 114 5.23 N 102.01 E
Dabou 150 5.19 N 4.23 W
Daboya 150 9.32 N 1.23 W
Dabra 124 25.54 N 78.20 E
Dābri [8] 272a 28.37 N 77.05 E
Dabringhausen 56 51.05 N 7.11 E
Dąbrowa Białostocka 30 53.39 N 23.20 E
Dąbrowa Tarnowska 30 50.11 N 21.00 E
Dabu, Zhg. 100 24.20 N 114.35 E
Dabu, Zhg. 100 23.52 N 116.54 E
Dabus 144 10.48 N 35.10 E
Dabusunhu 102 36.58 N 94.55 E
Dabusutu-Ula, Gora 86 50.44 N 92.40 E
Dacaitun 104 41.38 N 121.18 E
Dacangzigou 104 40.59 N 121.01 E
Dacaocun 105 40.34 N 117.07 E
Dacata 144 7.15 N 42.15 E
Dacca 124 23.43 N 90.25 E
Dacca □[8] 124 24.00 N 90.25 E
Dachaidan 102 37.53 N 95.07 E
Dachakou 100 29.38 N 118.18 E
Dachang, Zhg. 105 39.53 N 116.59 E
Dachang, Zhg. 106 31.18 N 121.25 E
Dachang, Zhg. 106 32.12 N 118.45 E
Dachang Airport 269b 31.18 N 121.25 E
Dachangshandao 98 39.10 N 122.34 E
Dachau 60 48.15 N 11.27 E
Dachauer Moos 60 48.12 N 11.25 E
Dacheng 100 28.34 N 115.31 E
Dachengji 100 33.52 N 119.26 E
Dachenjiabao 106 32.11 N 120.22 E
Dachenshan 106 30.21 N 121.52 E
Dachenxiangtun 104 41.34 N 123.31 E
Dachi 100 25.10 N 116.46 E
Dachongyu 105 40.23 N 117.41 E
Dachsberg [2] 263 51.30 N 6.30 E
Dačice 61 49.05 N 15.26 E
Dac-lac, Cao Nguyen [1] 110 12.50 N 108.05 E
Dačnoje [8] 265a 59.50 N 30.16 E
Dacoma 196 36.40 N 98.34 W
Dacorum □[8] 260 51.45 N 0.30 W
Dacun, Zhg. 102 27.55 N 101.08 E
Dacun, Zhg. 106 31.12 N 119.40 E
Dadal 88 49.01 N 111.07 E
Dadali 175e 8.07 S 159.06 E
Dadanawa 246 2.50 N 59.30 W
Dadaolizhuang 105 39.59 N 116.59 E
Dadaotun 104 41.46 N 122.13 E
Dadar [8] 272c 19.01 N 72.50 E
Daday 130 41.28 N 33.28 E
Dadayungou 104 41.23 N 123.04 E
Daddys Creek 192 36.05 N 84.47 W
Dade □[6] 220 25.33 N 80.32 W
Dade Battlefield State Historic Site 220 28.38 N 82.09 W
Dade City 220 28.22 N 82.12 W
Dadeville 194 32.50 N 85.46 W
Dādhar 120 29.28 N 67.39 E
Dadian 100 33.36 N 117.16 E
Dadiangas → General Santos 116 6.07 N 125.11 E
Dadianzi 104 42.11 N 124.02 E
Dading 102 27.04 N 105.31 E
Dadingjiawopu 104 41.13 N 122.16 E
D'adino 88 55.44 N 105.45 E
Dadle 144 5.23 N 46.57 E
Ḍadnah 128 25.33 N 56.21 E
Dadon 124 27.57 N 78.28 E
Dadonggejiang 105 39.51 N 116.48 E
Dadongzhou 104 41.44 N 124.00 E
Dadou 32 43.44 N 1.49 E
Dādpur, Bhārat 272b 22.42 N 88.33 E
Dādpur, Bhārat 272b 22.54 N 88.31 E
Dādra and Nagar Haveli □[8] 122 20.05 N 73.00 E
Dādri 124 28.34 N 77.33 E
Dādu 120 26.44 N 67.47 E
Dadugang 102 22.23 N 100.55 E
Daduhe 102 29.33 N 103.45 E
Dadukou, Zhg. 100 25.44 N 119.05 E
Dadukou, Zhg. 102 26.40 N 101.39 E
Dadukou, Zhg. 107 28.45 N 105.13 E
Dadukou, Zhg. 107 29.28 N 106.29 E
Daegu → Taegu 98 35.52 N 128.35 E
Daejeon → Taejŏn 98 36.20 N 127.26 E
Daerhanmaoming'anqi (Bailingmiao) 102 41.42 N 110.23 E
Daerhanwangfu 89 44.19 N 122.15 E
Daerhao 98 41.42 N 115.54 E
Daet 116 14.05 N 122.55 E
Daf' 146 28.03 N 19.57 E
Dafan, Zhg. 100 29.41 N 114.40 E
Dafan, Zhg. 104 42.38 N 122.11 E
Dafangshen, Zhg. 104 42.25 N 123.14 E
Dafangshen, Zhg. 104 42.34 N 123.28 E
Dafangshen, Zhg. 104 42.36 N 123.04 E
Dafanpuzi 104 41.37 N 122.50 E
Dafeng (Dazhongji) 100 33.12 N 120.30 E
Dafna 132 33.14 N 35.38 E
Dafoe 184 51.46 N 104.32 W
Dafoe 184 55.55 N 94.48 W
Dafoe Lake 184 55.43 N 96.15 W
Dafosi (Great Buddha Temple) [1] 106 30.16 N 120.09 E
Dafoutuo 105 40.24 N 115.58 E
Dafu 100 29.55 N 118.35 E
Dafushui 100 30.52 N 113.32 E
Dagā 110 16.56 N 94.45 E
Dagana 150 16.31 N 15.30 W
Dagana [1] 146 13.05 N 16.00 E
Dagang, Zhg. 100 33.12 N 120.07 E
Dagang, Zhg. 100 22.49 N 113.23 E
Dagang, Zhg. 106 32.12 N 119.39 E
Dagangtou 100 28.18 N 119.44 E
Daganwangzhai 104 40.49 N 122.33 E
Daganzo de Arriba 266a 40.33 N 3.27 W
Dagaokan 104 40.46 N 122.22 E
Dagaolifangcun 104 41.10 N 122.28 E
Dagaolitun 104 42.26 N 123.53 E
Dagaoyang 106 30.35 N 120.26 E
Daga Post 140 9.12 N 33.58 E
Dagash 140 19.22 N 33.24 E
Dagda 76 56.06 N 27.32 E
Dageløkke 41 55.04 N 10.53 E
Dagenham [8] 260 51.32 N 0.10 E
Dagestanskaja Avtonomnaja Sovetskaja Socialističeskaja Respublika □[3] 84 43.00 N 47.00 E
Dagestanskije Ogni 84 42.07 N 48.12 E
Daggafontein 273d 26.18 S 28.28 E
Daggafontein Mines [7] 273d 26.18 S 28.29 E
Daggett 228 34.52 N 116.53 W
Dagg Sound 172 45.23 S 166.46 E
Daghfalī 140 19.17 N 32.30 E
Dağkızılca 130 38.18 N 27.24 E
Dagmersellen 58 47.13 N 7.59 E
Dagö → Hiiumaa 76 58.52 N 22.40 E
Dagomys 84 43.40 N 39.41 E
Dagongtun 89 42.48 N 121.58 E
Dagoretti 154 1.18 S 36.46 E
Dagsboro 208 38.33 N 75.15 W
Dagshai 123 30.53 N 77.03 E
Dagu 105 38.59 N 117.41 E
Dagua, Col. 246 3.40 N 76.41 W
Dagua, Pap. N. Gui. 164 3.25 S 143.20 E
Daguan, Zhg. 100 31.14 N 117.01 E
Daguan, Zhg. 102 27.44 N 104.16 E
Daguao 240m 18.14 N 65.41 W
Dagufen'gou 105 40.41 N 116.20 E
Daguhe, Zhg. 98 36.42 N 120.26 E
Daguhe, Zhg. 98 37.34 N 121.17 E
D'Aguilar, Mount 171a 27.19 S 152.47 E
D'Aguilar Range 171a 27.10 S 152.45 E
Dagujia 98 42.22 N 124.52 E
Dagujiazi 104 42.20 N 123.20 E
Dagupan 116 16.03 N 120.20 E
Dagus Mines 214 41.21 N 78.37 W
Dagutang 100 29.38 N 116.06 E
Dagwin 110 18.04 N 97.41 E
Dahabān 144 21.55 N 39.04 E
Dahanchang 105 39.29 N 117.05 E
Dahaneh-ye Ghowrī 120 35.54 N 68.30 E
Dahaneh-ye Kāshār 120 35.09 N 66.14 E
Dahan-e Qowmghī 120 34.28 N 66.31 E
Dahantun 104 42.10 N 122.41 E
Dahasah, Wādī 142 28.08 N 31.00 E
Daḥdāḥ, Tall [2] 132 32.36 N 36.03 E
Dahe 106 31.42 N 120.37 E
Daheba 107 30.06 N 106.03 E
Dahebei 105 39.10 N 117.39 E
Daheiyugou 104 41.21 N 121.55 E
Dahekou 106 32.16 N 119.05 E
Dahengdu 100 29.03 N 121.30 E
Daheqiao 100 29.25 N 115.16 E
Dahijuri 126 22.31 N 86.59 E
Dahīrpur [8] 272a 28.43 N 77.12 E
Dahl 56 51.18 N 7.31 E
Dahl [8] 263 51.11 N 6.26 E
Dahlak Archipelago 144 15.45 N 40.30 E
Dahlak Kebir Island 144 15.38 N 40.11 E
Dahle 263 51.18 N 7.45 E
Dahlem 56 50.23 N 6.33 E
Dahlem [8] 264a 52.28 N 13.17 E
Dahlem, Museum 264a 52.27 N 13.18 E
Dahlen 54 51.22 N 12.59 E
Dahlenburg 54 53.11 N 10.44 E
Dahlerau 263 51.13 N 7.19 E
Dahlewitz 54 52.19 N 13.26 E
Dahlgren, Ill., U.S. 194 38.12 N 88.41 W
Dahlgren, Va., U.S. 208 38.20 N 77.03 W
Dahlhausen 54 53.03 N 12.20 E
Dahlia 154 18.35 S 27.08 E
Dahlonega 192 34.32 N 89.59 W
Dahlonega Plateau [1] 192 34.10 N 84.20 W
Dahlwitz-Hoppegarten 54 52.30 N 13.38 E
Dahmarū 142 28.41 N 30.49 E
Dahme, B.R.D. 54 54.13 N 11.04 E
Dahme, D.D.R. 54 51.52 N 13.25 E
Dahme 54 52.25 N 13.35 E
Dahn 56 49.09 N 7.47 E
Dahomey → Benin □[1] 150 9.30 N 2.15 E
Dahong 106 31.53 N 121.17 E
Dahongmen 105 39.47 N 116.20 E
Dahongshan 100 31.30 N 113.00 E
Dahongtaizi 104 41.41 N 121.23 E
Dahoucun 105 38.51 N 115.37 E
Dahra, Lībīya 146 29.34 N 17.50 E
Dahra, Sén. 150 15.21 N 15.29 W
Dahra 148 36.20 N 1.21 E
Dähre 54 52.48 N 10.54 E
Dahsah, Wādī ad- 142 27.19 N 31.26 E
Dahshūr 142 29.45 N 31.14 E
Dahu, Zhg. 100 26.04 N 117.19 E
Dahu, Zhg. 100 26.22 N 119.06 E
Dahu, Zhg. 100 26.10 N 114.57 E
Dahua 102 23.44 N 107.59 E
Dahuan 100 22.33 N 113.29 E
Dahuangdi 104 42.08 N 122.27 E
Dahuangji 98 35.06 N 115.15 E
Dahuangpu 105 39.26 N 117.16 E
Dahuangshanpu 104 41.16 N 121.23 E
Dahuashancun 105 40.17 N 117.04 E
Dahuasi 107 30.05 N 104.08 E
Dahūk 128 36.52 N 43.00 E
Dahuni 164 10.31 S 149.55 E
Dahushan 104 41.37 N 122.09 E
Daḥy, Nafūd ad- [2] 136 22.20 N 45.35 E
Dai, Pulau 164 7.33 S 129.41 E
Daia 38 44.00 N 25.59 E
Daian 94 35.05 N 136.33 E
Daibagnyahāti 126 22.33 N 89.52 E
Daibosatsu-rei 94 35.45 N 138.51 E
Daibu 106 31.18 N 119.30 E
Daiei 96 35.29 N 133.45 E
Daifang 100 27.32 N 115.41 E
Daigo 94 36.46 N 140.21 E
Daigo [8] 270 34.57 N 135.50 E
Daiguantun 105 39.57 N 117.50 E
Daihaiyingzi 104 42.30 N 121.26 E
Daiji 100 33.48 N 115.03 E
Daijiagou 107 30.00 N 106.33 E
Daijiang 100 26.14 N 119.40 E
Daijiasi 107 29.14 N 105.09 E
Daijiayao 100 32.56 N 120.44 E
Daikanbō 96 33.00 N 131.04 E
Daik-U 110 17.47 N 96.40 E
Dā'īl 132 32.45 N 36.08 E
Dailekh 124 28.50 N 81.44 E
Daimanji-san 92 36.15 N 133.19 E
Daimiel 34 39.04 N 3.37 W
Daimon, Nihon 94 36.44 N 137.03 E
Daimon, Nihon 268 35.53 N 139.44 E
Daimuken-zan 94 35.15 N 138.10 E
Dainan 100 32.43 N 120.06 E
Daingean 48 53.18 N 7.17 W
Daingerfield 222 33.02 N 94.44 W
Dainhāt 126 23.37 N 88.04 E
Dainichiga-take 94 36.00 N 136.50 E
Daintree 164 16.15 S 145.19 E
Daiō-zaki 92 34.17 N 136.54 E
Daiqintala 89 45.16 N 121.44 E
Dāira Dīn Panāh 123 30.34 N 70.56 E
Dairago 266b 45.34 N 8.52 E
Daireaux 252 36.36 S 61.45 W
Dairen → Lüda 98 38.53 N 121.35 E
Dairsie 46 56.20 N 2.56 W
Dairy 46 55.43 N 4.43 W
Dairy City → Cypress 280 33.50 N 118.01 W
Dairy Creek, East Fork 224 45.34 N 123.09 W
Dairy Creek, West Fork 224 45.34 N 123.09 W
Dairyland → La Palma, Calif., U.S. 280 33.51 N 118.02 W
Dairyland, N.Y., U.S. 210 41.45 N 74.33 W
Dairyland Reservoir [1] 190 45.30 N 91.00 W
Dairy Valley → Cerritos 280 33.51 N 118.05 W
Dai-sen 96 35.22 N 133.33 E
Dai-sen-oki-kokuritsu-kōen 96 35.20 N 133.35 E
Daisen-zan 96 34.07 N 133.56 E
Daisetta 222 30.07 N 94.39 W
Daishin 94 37.12 N 140.15 E
Daishōji 94 36.18 N 136.15 E
Daisongdao 100 24.03 N 118.03 E
Daitō, Nihon 96 35.19 N 132.58 E
Daitō, Nihon 96 34.42 N 135.38 E
Daiwa, Nihon 96 34.32 N 132.57 E
Daiwa, Nihon 96 34.57 N 132.39 E
Daixi 106 30.40 N 120.01 E
Daixian 102 39.08 N 113.01 E
Daixiqiao 106 31.36 N 120.04 E
Daiya 94 36.45 N 139.46 E
Daiyunshan 100 25.46 N 118.16 E
Dajabón 238 19.33 N 71.42 W
Dājal 120 29.33 N 70.23 E
Da'jānīyah, Jabal ad- 132 30.34 N 35.43 E
Dajan Uul 102 45.20 N 95.30 E

Symbol	English	Deutsch	Español	Français	Português
≃	River	Fluss	Río	Rivière	Rio
≍	Canal	Kanal	Canal	Canal	Canal
ᒪ	Waterfall, Rapids	Wasserfall, Stromschnellen	Cascada, Rápidos	Chute d'eau, Rapides	Cascata, Rápidos
⩊	Strait	Meeresstrasse	Estrecho	Détroit	Estreito
C	Bay, Gulf	Bucht, Golf	Bahía, Golfo	Baie, Golfe	Baía, Golfo
⊜	Lake, Lakes	See, Seen	Lago, Lagos	Lac, Lacs	Lago, Lagos
☷	Swamp	Sumpf	Pantano	Marais	Pântano
⧈	Ice Features, Glacier	Eis- und Gletscherformen	Accidentes Glaciales	Formes glaciaires	Acidentes Glaciares
☛	Other Hydrographic Features	Andere Hydrographische Objekte	Otros Elementos Hidrográficos	Autres données hydrographiques	Outros Elementos Hidrográficos
✧	Submarine Features	Untermeerische Objekte	Accidentes Submarinos	Formes de relief sous-marin	Acidentes Submarinos
□	Political Unit	Politische Einheit	Unidad Politica	Entité politique	Unidade Política
♉	Cultural Institution	Kulturelle Institution	Institución Cultural	Institution culturelle	Instituição Cultural
⊥	Historical Site	Historische Stätte	Sitio Histórico	Site historique	Sitio Histórico
♠	Recreational Site	Erholungs- und Ferienort	Sitio de Recreo	Centre de loisirs	Sítio de Lazer
⊠	Airport	Flughafen	Aeropuerto	Aéroport	Aeroporto
■	Military Installation	Militäranlage	Instalación Militar	Installation militaire	Instalação Militar
◆	Miscellaneous	Verschiedenes	Misceláneo	Divers	Miscelânea

ENGLISH: Name | Page | Lat.°′ | Long.°′
DEUTSCH: Name | Seite | Breite°′ | Länge°′ E=Ost

Name	Page	Lat.°′	Long.°′
Dajarra	166	21.41 S	139.31 E
Dajianshan ∧	102	26.42 N	103.34 E
Dajiao	106	31.51 N	121.13 E
Dajidian	105	38.50 N	115.26 E
Dajin I	100	21.52 N	113.02 E
Dajindian	100	34.24 N	113.01 E
Dajing	100	28.24 N	121.07 E
Dajingjie	100	28.59 N	113.19 E
Dajishan	100	24.38 N	114.26 E
Dajitai	104	42.20 N	121.11 E
Dajiuba	120	36.50 N	89.35 E
Dajiyang ⋓	100	30.54 N	122.18 E
Daju	105	39.12 N	115.31 E
Dak ⊜	128	32.48 N	61.14 E
Dakangpu	104	41.32 N	121.06 E
Dakanzi	104	40.52 N	122.53 E
Dakar	150	14.40 N	17.26 W
Dākātia ≃[1]	126	22.57 N	90.42 E
Dakecihu ⊜	120	31.55 N	87.35 E
Dakendabanshan ⛰	102	38.25 N	95.55 E
Dakengkou	100	24.33 N	113.37 E
Dak-gle	110	15.11 N	107.48 E
Dakhal, Bi'r ad- ⫪[4]	142	28.40 N	32.24 E
Dakhal, Wādī ad- ∨	142	28.49 N	32.45 E
Dakhla	148	23.43 N	15.57 W
Dakingari	150	11.37 N	4.01 E
Dakka → Dacca	124	23.43 N	90.25 E
Dākoānk	110	7.02 N	93.43 E
Dakongcheng	105	39.30 N	117.09 E
Dakongwan	104	40.51 N	122.19 E
Dakoro	150	14.31 N	6.46 E
Dakota City, Iowa, U.S.	190	42.43 N	94.12 W
Dakota City, Nebr., U.S.	198	42.25 N	96.25 W
Dakou	100	34.27 N	112.44 E
Dakouraoua	150	13.58 N	6.15 E
Dakoutun	105	39.35 N	117.14 E
Đakovica	38	42.23 N	20.25 E
Đakovo	38	45.19 N	18.25 E
Dakshingram	126	24.03 N	87.48 E
Dak-to	110	14.42 N	107.51 E
Dakumu	89	48.51 N	124.18 E
Dakunlun	98	36.34 N	117.52 E
Dákura, Laguna ⊂	236	14.24 N	83.15 W
Dakwa	154	4.00 N	26.26 E
Dakwah, Tall ad- ∧[2]	132	33.25 N	36.56 E
Dala, Ang.	152	11.03 S	20.17 E
Dala, Ang.	152	8.05 S	15.50 E
Dala, Sol.is.	175e	8.35 S	160.40 E
Dalaas	58	47.07 N	10.00 E
Dalaba	150	10.42 N	12.15 W
Dalaba □[4]	150	10.45 N	12.18 W
Dalabani	150	10.28 N	9.27 W
Dala Cachibo	152	10.28 S	14.39 E
Dala-Floda	40	60.31 N	14.47 E
Dalaguete	116	9.46 N	123.32 E
Dalahan (Shiqizhan)	89	52.06 N	125.46 E
Dala-Husby	40	60.21 N	16.00 E
Dalai	89	45.28 N	124.18 E
Dala-Järna	26	60.33 N	14.21 E
Dalajchöl	86	47.59 N	90.47 E
Dalaji	89	51.38 N	120.06 E
Dalälven ≃	40	60.38 N	17.27 E
Dalama	130	37.47 N	28.04 E
Dalaman ≃	130	36.40 N	28.45 E
Dalāmī	140	11.52 N	30.28 E
Dalan	100	23.19 N	114.47 E
Dalandzadgad	102	43.35 N	104.30 E
Dalandžargalan	102	45.58 N	108.59 E
Dalane ⬥[1]	26	58.35 N	6.20 E
Dalang	100	22.57 N	113.56 E
Dalantuozi	104	41.28 N	122.47 E
Dalao	150	11.29 N	13.40 W
Dalaodao I	100	25.47 N	119.43 E
Dalarna □[9]	26	61.01 N	14.04 E
Dalarö	40	59.08 N	18.24 E
Dalat, Malay.	112	2.44 N	111.56 E
Da-lat, Viet.	110	11.56 N	108.25 E
Dalatando	152	9.18 S	14.54 E
Dalatehouqi	102	41.09 N	107.58 E
Dalateqi	102	40.28 N	110.02 E
Dalavakasır	130	37.14 N	41.45 E
Dalayaozi	105	40.49 N	117.41 E
Dalbana ≃	250	4.48 N	57.27 W
Dālbandin	128	28.53 N	64.25 E
Dalbeattie	44	54.56 N	3.49 W
D'Albertis Dome ∧	164	5.00 S	142.05 E
Dalbosjön ⊂	26	58.45 N	12.48 E
Dalby, Austl.	166	27.11 S	151.16 E
Dalby, Sve.	41	55.40 N	13.20 E
Dalcahue	254	42.23 S	73.40 W
Dalch ≃	42	50.52 N	3.47 W
Dale, Nor.	26	60.35 N	5.49 E
Dale, Wales, U.K.	42	51.43 N	5.11 W
Dale, Ind., U.S.	194	38.10 N	86.59 W
Dale, Pa., U.S.	214	40.18 N	78.54 W
Dale, Tex., U.S.	222	29.56 N	97.34 W
Dale ≃	168a	32.10 S	116.49 E
Dale Bridge	168a	32.05 S	116.49 E
Dalecarlia → Dalarna □[9]	26	61.01 N	14.04 E
Dale City	208	38.38 N	77.18 W
Dale Hollow Dam ⬥[6]	192	36.25 N	85.30 W
Dale Hollow Lake ⊜[1]	192	36.36 N	85.19 W
Dale Lake ⊜	204	34.08 N	115.42 W
Dalen	26	59.27 N	8.00 E
Dalengtu	98	41.11 N	113.45 E
Daleshankou)(	102	28.12 N	98.08 E
Daleside	158	26.30 S	28.04 E
Dalesville	206	45.42 N	74.24 W
Dalesville ≃	206	45.40 N	74.24 W
Daleszyce	30	50.48 N	20.48 E
Dalet	110	19.59 N	93.51 E
Daleville, Ind., U.S.	218	40.07 N	85.33 W
Daleville, Pa., U.S.	210	41.18 N	75.31 W
Dalfsen	52	52.30 N	6.16 E
Dalgaranga	162	27.46 S	117.02 E
Dalgaranger ∧	162	27.51 S	117.06 E
Dalgety	171b	36.30 S	148.50 E
Dalgety Brook ≃	162	25.07 S	115.47 E
Dalgety Downs	162	25.17 S	116.15 E
Dal Goble	144	9.52 N	49.50 E
Dalgomai	124	26.06 N	90.47 E
Dalhalvaig	46	58.28 N	3.54 W
Dalhart	196	36.04 N	102.31 W
Dalhausen	52	51.37 N	9.17 E
Dalhousie, Bhārat	123	32.32 N	75.59 E
Dalhousie, N.B., Can.	186	48.04 N	66.23 W
Dalhousie, Cape ≻	180	70.14 N	129.42 W
Dalhousie Island I	126	21.35 N	88.45 E
Dalhousie Lake ⊜	212	44.58 N	76.35 W
Dalhousie Square ♠	272b	22.33 N	88.22 E
Dali, Zhg.	102	34.47 N	109.57 E
Dali, Zhg.	102	25.38 N	100.09 E
Daliandao I	100	25.40 N	119.42 E
Daliangdi	98	41.54 N	115.45 E
Daliangshan ⛰	102	28.00 N	103.00 E
Dalianhe	104	40.57 N	123.15 E
Daliankeng	105	40.54 N	117.45 E
Dalianwukou	106	30.17 N	119.00 E
Dalías	34	36.49 N	2.52 W
Dalihe ≃	102	37.05 N	110.20 E
Daliji	100	33.48 N	117.48 E
Dalikou	100	26.52 N	118.00 E
Dalin, Zhg.	89	43.43 N	122.45 E
Dalin, Zhg.	107	30.17 N	104.07 E
Daling	104	41.27 N	121.15 E
Dalingbeigou	104	40.42 N	123.08 E
Dalinghe	104	41.35 N	121.02 E
Dalinghe ≃	98	40.56 N	121.43 E
Dalinghekou ≃[1]	98	40.55 N	121.50 E
Dalipe Point ≻	116	10.46 N	121.55 E
Daliu	105	38.51 N	116.19 E
Daliushugou	104	40.46 N	122.14 E
Daliutai	104	41.25 N	121.55 E
Daliutun	104	42.14 N	122.46 E
Daliuzhen	98	37.44 N	116.50 E
Daliuzhuang, Zhg.	100	33.04 N	114.03 E
Daliuzhuang, Zhg.	105	39.52 N	118.00 E
Dāliyat el Karmel	132	32.42 N	35.03 E
Daliyya	132	32.35 N	35.04 E
Dalizi	98	41.45 N	126.49 E
Dalj	38	45.29 N	18.59 E
Daljā'	142	27.39 N	30.42 E
Dalkarlsberg	40	59.26 N	14.51 E
Dalkeith	46	55.54 N	3.04 W
Dālkola	124	25.52 N	87.51 E
Dall, Mount ∧	180	62.35 N	152.18 W
Dāllah, 'Ayn ⫪[4]	140	27.19 N	27.20 E
Dallardsville	222	30.38 N	94.38 W
Dallas, Scot., U.K.	46	57.33 N	3.28 W
Dallas, Ala., U.S.	194	33.50 N	86.40 W
Dallas, Ga., U.S.	192	33.55 N	84.51 W
Dallas, N.C., U.S.	192	35.19 N	81.11 W
Dallas, Oreg., U.S.	202	44.55 N	123.19 W
Dallas, Pa., U.S.	210	41.20 N	75.58 W
Dallas, Tex., U.S.	222	32.47 N	96.48 W
Dallas, Wis., U.S.	190	45.16 N	91.51 W
Dallas □[6]	222	32.17 N	96.47 W
Dallas Center	190	41.41 N	93.58 W
Dallas City	190	40.38 N	91.10 W
Dallas-Fort Worth Regional Airport ⊠	222	32.54 N	97.01 W
Dallas Naval Air Station ■	222	32.44 N	96.59 W
Dallastown	208	39.54 N	76.39 W
Dallau	56	49.23 N	9.11 E
Dallgow	54	52.32 N	13.05 E
Dalli Rajhāra	122	20.35 N	81.04 E
Dall Island I	180	54.50 N	132.55 W
Dall Lake ⊜	180	60.18 N	163.35 W
Dalmā' I	128	24.30 N	52.20 E
Dalmacija □[9]	36	43.00 N	17.00 E
Dalmacio Vélez Sarsfield	252	32.36 S	63.35 W
Dalmally	46	56.24 N	4.58 W
Dal'mamedli	84	40.42 N	46.34 E
Dalmatia	208	40.39 N	76.54 W
Dalmatia → Dalmacija □[9]	36	43.00 N	17.00 E
Dalmatovo	86	56.16 N	62.56 E
Dalmau	124	26.04 N	81.02 E
Dalmellington	44	55.19 N	4.24 W
Dalmeny	184	52.20 N	106.46 W
Dalmine	62	45.39 N	9.36 E
Dalmose	41	55.18 N	11.26 E
Dal'n'aja	89	45.56 N	142.04 E
Dal'n'aja Muja	88	54.21 N	103.37 E
Dalnaspidal	46	56.50 N	4.14 W
Dal'neje-Konstantinovo	80	55.49 N	44.06 E
Dal'ne-Rusanovo	82	54.15 N	36.45 E
Dal'nik	78	46.28 N	30.34 E
Daloa	150	6.53 N	6.27 W
Daloa □[5]	150	7.00 N	6.45 W
Dalong	120	28.54 N	90.33 E
Dalongchang	105	39.50 N	116.06 E
Dalonghua	105	39.18 N	115.18 E
Dalongtian	100	24.14 N	115.44 E
Dalovice	54	50.11 N	12.55 E
Dalqū	140	20.07 N	30.37 E
Dalroy	182	51.07 N	113.39 W
Dalry, Scot., U.K.	44	55.07 N	4.10 W
Dalry, Scot., U.K.	46	55.43 N	4.44 W
Dalrymple, Mount ∧	166	21.02 S	148.38 E
Dalrymple Creek ≃	171a	27.59 S	151.46 E
Dalrymple Lake ⊜	212	44.38 N	79.07 W
Dalsbruk (Taalintehdas)	26	60.02 N	22.31 E
Dalsingh Sarai	124	25.40 N	85.50 E
Dalsingpara	124	26.47 N	89.22 E
Dalsjöfors	26	57.43 N	13.05 E
Dalsland □[9]	26	58.30 N	12.50 E
Dals-Långed	26	58.55 N	12.18 E
Dal'stroja	180	68.19 N	177.39 W
Dalton, S. Afr.	158	29.20 S	30.40 E
Dalton, Eng., U.K.	262	53.34 N	2.46 W
Dalton, Ga., U.S.	192	34.47 N	84.58 W
Dalton, Mass., U.S.	207	42.29 N	73.09 W
Dalton, Nebr., U.S.	198	41.25 N	102.58 W
Dalton, N.Y., U.S.	210	42.32 N	77.57 W
Dalton, Ohio, U.S.	214	40.48 N	81.42 W
Dalton, Pa., U.S.	210	41.32 N	75.45 W
Dalton City	219	39.43 N	88.48 W
Daltonganj	124	24.02 N	84.04 E
Dalton Gardens	202	47.44 N	116.46 W
Dalton Iceberg Tongue ⍓	9	66.15 S	121.30 E
Dalton-in-Furness	44	54.09 N	3.11 W
Dalu	104	41.27 N	123.19 E
Dalubeikou	105	38.59 N	117.12 E
Daludalu	114	1.05 N	100.15 E
Daluis, Gorges de ∨	62	44.04 N	6.49 E
Dalum, B.R.D.	52	52.35 N	7.14 E
Dalum, Dan.	41	55.22 N	10.22 E
Daluojiazhuang	106	32.09 N	120.08 E
Daluotaozi	104	41.17 N	122.52 E
Daluoxi	100	25.14 N	118.36 E
Daluping	100	26.11 N	114.30 E
Dalupiri Island I, Pil.	116	12.25 N	124.16 E
Dalupiri Island I, Pil.	116	19.05 N	121.14 E
Dalushan I	100	28.06 N	121.25 E
Daluxi	100	24.28 N	117.01 E
Daluzhuang	106	30.06 N	120.15 E
Dalview	273d	26.15 S	28.21 E
Dalvík	24a	65.59 N	18.32 W
Dalwallinu	162	30.17 S	116.40 E
Dalwhinnie	46	56.56 N	4.14 W
Dalworthington Gardens	222	32.42 N	97.10 W
Daly ≃	164	13.20 S	130.19 E
Daly Bay ⊂	176	64.00 N	89.40 W
Daly City	226	37.42 N	122.29 W
Daly Lake ⊜	184	56.33 N	105.40 W
Daly Point ≻	212	44.53 N	80.14 W
Daly River	164	13.45 S	130.50 E
Daly River Aboriginal Reserve ⬥[4]	164	14.20 S	130.00 E
Daly Waters	164	16.15 S	133.22 E
Dāmā, Sūrīy.	132	32.57 N	36.25 E
Dama, Zhg.	100	32.03 N	118.02 E
Dama, Zhg.	100	24.21 N	116.32 E
Damaiyu I	100	25.13 N	119.35 E
Damān	122	20.25 N	72.51 E
Damān □[8]	122	20.10 N	73.00 E
Damang I	100	21.55 N	113.08 E
Damanhūr	142	31.02 N	30.28 E
Damanling	105	40.36 N	115.08 E
Damaopu	104	41.16 N	121.07 E
Damaoshan ⛰	106	31.43 N	119.17 E
Damar	130	41.15 N	41.34 E
Damar, Pulau I, Indon.	164	7.09 S	128.40 E
Damar, Pulau I, Indon.	164	1.00 S	128.24 E
Damara	152	4.58 N	18.42 E
Damaraja	115a	6.55 S	108.05 E
Damaraland □[9]	156	22.34 S	17.06 E
Damariscotta	188	44.02 N	69.32 W
Damāş, Mişr	142	30.48 N	31.20 E
Damas → Dimashq, Sūrīy.	132	33.30 N	36.18 E
Damasco → Dimashq	132	33.30 N	36.18 E
Damascus → Dimashq, Sūrīy.	132	33.30 N	36.18 E
Damascus, Ark., U.S.	194	35.22 N	92.25 W
Damascus, Ga., U.S.	192	31.18 N	84.43 W
Damascus, Md., U.S.	208	39.17 N	77.12 W
Damascus, Ohio, U.S.	214	40.54 N	80.58 W
Damascus, Pa., U.S.	210	41.42 N	75.04 W
Damascus, Va., U.S.	192	36.37 N	81.46 W
Damascus International Airport ⊠	132	33.29 N	36.13 E
Damaskus → Dimashq	132	33.30 N	36.18 E
Damāţ	142	30.57 N	30.57 E
Damāvand	128	35.43 N	52.04 E
Damāvand, Qolleh-ye ∧	128	35.56 N	52.08 E
Damba	152	6.41 S	15.08 E
Dambach-la-Ville	58	48.20 N	7.26 E
Dambarta	150	12.26 N	8.31 E
Dambeck	54	52.48 N	11.09 E
Dambuki	89	54.20 N	121.35 E
Dam-doi	110	8.50 N	105.15 E
Damelevières	58	48.33 N	6.23 E
Damengjialazi	104	41.04 N	120.53 E
Damengzhuang	105	39.32 N	116.59 E
Damergou ⬥[1]	150	15.00 N	8.55 E
Damerham	42	50.57 N	1.52 W
Dämeritzsee ⊜	264a	52.25 N	13.45 E
Damery	50	49.04 N	3.53 E
Dames Quarter	208	38.11 N	75.54 W
Dam Gamad	140	13.17 N	27.28 E
Dāmghān	128	39.09 N	54.22 E
Damianópolis	255	14.33 S	46.10 W
Damianpu	107	30.36 N	104.10 E
Damiao, Zhg.	98	34.20 N	117.23 E
Damiao, Zhg.	98	42.26 N	118.22 E
Damiao, Zhg.	102	37.18 N	104.39 E
Damiao, Zhg.	104	42.33 N	122.18 E
Damiaochang	107	29.39 N	106.05 E
Damiaogou	104	41.06 N	123.52 E
Damiaojiang	106	31.00 N	120.28 E
Damiaoshan	102	25.06 N	109.15 E
Damiaoshang	105	39.56 N	115.12 E
Damiar	84	41.15 N	41.34 E
Dămieneşti	38	46.44 N	26.59 E
Damietta → Dumyāţ	142	31.25 N	31.48 E
Damietta Mouth → Dumyāţ, Maşabb ≃[1]	142	31.32 N	31.51 E
Damin	100	28.56 N	120.29 E
Daming	98	36.19 N	115.06 E
Damintun	104	41.52 N	122.56 E
Dāmiyā	132	32.06 N	35.33 E
Damm	263	51.40 N	6.48 E
Dammai Island I	116	5.47 N	120.25 E
Dammarie	50	48.21 N	1.30 E
Dammarie-lès-Lys	50	48.31 N	2.39 E
Dammartin-en-Goële	50	49.03 N	2.41 E
Dammartin-en-Serve	50	48.54 N	1.37 E
Dammastock ∧	58	46.39 N	8.25 E
Damme, Bel.	50	51.15 N	3.17 E
Damme, B.R.D.	52	52.30 N	8.08 E
Damme, D.D.R.	54	53.17 N	14.01 E
Dāmodar ≃	124	22.17 N	88.05 E
Dāmodar Main Canal ≍	126	23.01 N	87.53 E
Damoh	124	23.50 N	79.27 E
Damon	222	29.17 N	95.45 W
Damongo	150	9.05 N	1.49 W
Damotapāda	272c	19.03 N	73.04 E
Damous	34	36.33 N	1.42 E
Damozhuang	105	39.53 N	115.40 E
Dampar, Tasek ⊜	114	3.02 N	102.43 E
Dampelas → Sabang	112	0.11 N	119.51 E
Dampier	162	20.39 S	116.45 E
Dampier, Cape ≻	164	6.02 S	151.02 E
Dampier, Selat ⋓	164	0.40 S	130.40 E
Dampier Archipelago II	162	20.35 S	116.35 E
Dampier Land ≻[1]	162	17.30 S	122.55 E
Dampierre, Fr.	50	48.42 N	1.59 E
Dampierre, Fr.	58	47.09 N	5.45 E
Dampierre, Château de ⊥	261	48.42 N	1.59 E
Dampierre-en-Burly	50	47.46 N	2.31 E
Dampierre-sur-Linotte	58	47.31 N	6.14 E
Dampierre-sur-Salon	58	47.33 N	5.41 E
Dampier Strait ⋓	164	5.36 S	148.12 E
Dampit	115a	8.13 S	112.45 E
Dampmart	261	48.53 N	2.44 E
Damprichard	58	47.15 N	6.53 E
Dâmrei, Chuŏr Phnum ⛰	110	11.00 N	104.05 E
Damují ≃	240p	22.11 N	80.33 W
Damüls	58	47.17 N	9.53 E
Dāmurhuda	126	23.36 N	88.47 E
Damutougou	98	42.28 N	118.56 E
Damuyang ⊂	100	29.20 N	122.06 E
Damville	50	48.52 N	1.04 E
Damvillers	56	49.20 N	5.24 E
Dan	132	33.14 N	35.39 E
Dan ≃	192	36.42 N	78.45 W
Dana, Cam.	146	10.14 N	15.18 E
Dana, Ind., U.S.	194	39.48 N	87.30 W
Dana, Mount ∧	226	37.54 N	119.13 W
Dana, Pulau I	112	10.50 S	121.16 E
Danai	112	0.29 N	103.26 E
Danajon Bank ⬩[4]	116	10.16 N	124.17 E
Danakil Plain ⌣	144	12.25 N	40.30 E
Danané	150	7.16 N	8.09 W
Danané □[5]	150	7.15 N	8.00 W
Da-nang	110	16.04 N	108.13 E
Danan'gou	105	40.32 N	117.49 E
Da'nanhu	102	42.28 N	93.32 E
Danao, Pil.	116	10.32 N	124.02 E
Danao, Pil.	116	12.29 N	122.39 E
Dana Point	228	33.29 N	117.44 W
Dana Point ≻	228	33.28 N	117.43 W
Dānāpur	124	25.38 N	85.03 E
Danba	102	31.00 N	101.50 E
Danboro	208	40.21 N	75.08 W
Danbury, Eng., U.K.	260	51.44 N	0.33 E
Danbury, Conn., U.S.	207	41.23 N	73.27 W
Danbury, Iowa, U.S.	198	42.14 N	95.43 W
Danbury, Nebr., U.S.	198	40.03 N	100.24 W
Danbury, N.C., U.S.	192	36.24 N	80.12 W
Danbury, Tex., U.S.	222	29.14 N	95.21 W
Danby Lake ⊜	204	34.14 N	115.07 W
Dancheng	100	33.39 N	115.11 E
Danchengji	100	33.47 N	116.17 E
Dand	120	31.37 N	65.41 E
Dandaragan	162	30.40 S	115.42 E
Dande ≃	152	8.28 S	13.21 E
Dandeldhura	124	29.18 N	80.35 E
Dandeli	122	15.15 N	74.37 E
Dandenong	169	37.59 S	145.12 E
Dandenong, Mount ∧	274b	37.50 S	145.21 E
Dandenong Creek ≃	274b	38.01 S	145.05 E
Danderyd	40	59.25 N	18.01 E
Dandīl	142	29.10 N	31.02 E
Dandot	123	32.39 N	72.58 E
Dandridge	192	36.01 N	83.25 W
Dan Dume	150	11.27 N	7.10 E
Dane □[6]	216	43.04 N	89.15 W
Dane ≃	262	53.15 N	2.31 W
Danea	150	11.27 N	13.12 W
Dane County Regional Airport-Truax Field ⊠	216	43.08 N	89.20 W
Dänemark → Denmark □[1]	26	56.00 N	10.00 E
Dänemark-Strasse → Denmark Strait ⋓	10	67.00 N	25.00 W
Danevang	222	29.03 N	96.13 W
Danewitz	264a	52.44 N	13.40 E
Danfeng	102	33.40 N	110.17 E
Danfengzhen	102	24.50 N	103.56 E
Danforth, Ill., U.S.	216	40.49 N	87.59 W
Danforth, Maine, U.S.	188	45.40 N	67.52 W
Danforth Hills ⛰	200	40.15 N	108.00 W
Dānga, Bhārat	272b	22.47 N	88.28 E
Dānga, Bngl.	126	23.54 N	90.36 E
Danga ≃	271c	1.27 N	103.43 E
Dangādiha	126	21.30 N	86.19 E
Danganqundao I	100	22.06 N	113.30 E
Danganqundao II	100	22.00 N	114.14 E
Dan'ganshan I	100	22.03 N	114.16 E
Dangara, S.S.S.R.	85	40.35 N	70.54 E
Dangara, S.S.S.R.	85	38.06 N	69.22 E
Dangba	98	40.46 N	118.32 E
Dangchang	102	34.03 N	104.23 E
Dangcheng	98	38.46 N	114.34 E
Dange, Ang.	152	8.09 S	14.46 E
Dangé, Fr.	32	46.56 N	0.36 E
Dange, Nig.	150	12.52 N	5.21 E
Dange-lá-Menha	152	9.32 S	14.39 E
Danger, Point ≻	171a	28.10 S	153.33 E
Danger Point ≻	158	34.40 S	19.17 E
Dang-Haoussa	152	5.52 N	13.29 E
Danghui	105	40.03 N	117.04 E
Dangkou	106	31.32 N	120.34 E
Dangla	144	11.18 N	36.54 E
Dango	140	10.00 N	24.45 E
Dan Gora	150	11.30 N	8.09 E
Dangshan	98	34.26 N	116.21 E
Dangtu	100	31.34 N	118.30 E
Dan Gulbi	150	11.38 N	6.16 E
Dangxiong	120	30.31 N	91.08 E
Dangyang	102	30.50 N	111.38 E
Dangyu	105	40.00 N	118.01 E
Dani	150	13.43 N	0.10 W
Dania	220	26.03 N	80.09 W
Daniel	200	42.52 N	110.04 W
Daniel, Mount ∧	224	47.34 N	121.11 W
Daniel Boone Home ⊥	219	38.39 N	90.52 W
Daniel Boone Homestead ⊥	208	40.21 N	75.49 W
Daniels	284b	39.26 N	77.03 W
Daniel's Harbour	186	50.14 N	57.35 W
Danielskuil	158	28.11 S	23.33 E
Danielson	207	41.48 N	71.53 W
Daniels Pass)(	200	40.18 N	111.15 W
Daniels Run ≃	284c	38.51 N	77.17 W
Danielsville, Ga., U.S.	192	34.07 N	83.13 W
Danielsville, Pa., U.S.	208	40.48 N	75.32 W
Danilov	80	58.12 N	40.12 E
Danilovka, S.S.S.R.	80	52.33 N	45.23 E
Danilovka, S.S.S.R.	80	50.21 N	44.06 E
Danilovo	82	55.40 N	38.46 E
Danilovskaja Vozvyšennost' ⛰[1]	80	58.12 N	40.16 E
Danilovskoje	82	56.48 N	35.45 E
Daning, Zhg.	102	36.33 N	110.38 E
Daning, Zhg.	102	24.39 N	111.51 E
Daningbashi	85	38.45 N	75.04 E
Dänisch Nienhof	54	54.28 N	10.07 E
Danissa Hills ⛰[2]	154	3.17 N	40.59 E
Daniupucun	104	41.23 N	122.37 E
Danja	150	11.21 N	7.31 E
Danjo-guntō II	92	32.02 N	128.23 E
Danjoutin	58	47.37 N	6.52 E
Ḍank	128	23.33 N	56.17 E
Dankama	150	13.20 N	7.44 E
Dankersen	52	52.17 N	8.58 E
Danki	82	54.55 N	37.34 E
Dankov	76	53.15 N	39.08 E
Dankova, Pik ∧	85	41.05 N	77.38 E
Dankug	144	11.00 N	49.02 E
Danleng, Zhg.	102	29.18 N	103.10 E
Danleng, Zhg.	107	30.01 N	103.30 E
Danlí	236	14.00 N	86.35 W
Danmark → Denmark □[1]	26	56.00 N	10.00 E
Dannebrog	198	41.07 N	98.33 W
Dannemare	41	54.45 N	11.12 E
Dannemarie	58	47.38 N	7.08 E
Dannemora, Sve.	40	60.11 N	17.49 E
Dannemora, N.Y., U.S.	188	44.43 N	73.43 W
Dannenberg	54	53.06 N	11.05 E
Dannenreich	264a	52.19 N	13.45 E
Dannenwalde	54	53.04 N	13.11 E
Dannevirke	172	40.12 S	176.07 E
Dannewerk	41	54.29 N	9.31 E
Dannhauser	158	28.04 S	30.04 E
Danno-ura ♠	96	34.23 N	134.08 E
Dano	150	11.09 N	3.04 W
Danompari	112	0.09 N	115.02 E
Dañoso, Cabo ≻	254	48.50 S	67.13 W
Dan Ryan Woods ♠	278	41.45 N	87.39 W
Dan Sai	110	17.17 N	101.09 E
Danshanzhen	107	30.06 N	104.54 E
Danshui	100	22.49 N	114.27 E
Dansville, Mich., U.S.	216	42.34 N	84.18 W
Dansville, N.Y., U.S.	210	42.34 N	77.42 W
Dāntan	126	21.57 N	87.16 E
Dante, Som.	144	10.25 N	51.16 E
Dante, Va., U.S.	192	36.53 N	82.18 W
Dantewāra	122	18.54 N	81.21 E
Dantuzhen	106	32.12 N	119.31 E
Danube ≃	22	45.20 N	29.40 E
Danube, Mouths of the ≃[1]	38	45.10 N	29.50 E
Danubio → Danube ≃	22	45.20 N	29.40 E
Danubyu	110	17.15 N	95.35 E
Danvers, Ill., U.S.	190	40.32 N	89.11 W
Danvers, Mass., U.S.	207	42.34 N	70.56 W
Danvers ≃	283	42.32 N	70.53 W
Danville, Qué., Can.	206	45.47 N	72.01 W
Danville, Ark., U.S.	194	35.03 N	93.24 W
Danville, Calif., U.S.	226	37.49 N	122.00 W
Danville, Ga., U.S.	192	32.37 N	83.15 W
Danville, Ill., U.S.	194	40.08 N	87.37 W
Danville, Ind., U.S.	218	39.46 N	86.32 W
Danville, Ky., U.S.	194	37.39 N	84.46 W
Danville, Mo., U.S.	219	38.54 N	91.32 W
Danville, Ohio, U.S.	214	40.27 N	82.16 W
Danville, Pa., U.S.	210	40.57 N	76.37 W
Danville, Vt., U.S.	188	44.25 N	66.09 W
Danville, Va., U.S.	192	36.35 N	79.24 W
Danxian, Zhg.	98	34.48 N	116.03 E
Danxian (Nada), Zhg.	110	19.35 N	109.17 E
Danyang, Zhg.	100	26.22 N	119.30 E
Danyang, Zhg.	106	32.00 N	119.35 E
Danyanghu ⊜	106	31.25 N	118.41 E
Danzig → Gdańsk	30	54.23 N	18.40 E
Danzig, Gulf of ⊂	30	54.40 N	19.15 E
Dao	116	10.31 N	121.57 E
Dâo ≃	34	40.20 N	8.11 W
Daocheng	102	29.06 N	100.38 E
Daodemiao	89	43.41 N	120.19 E
Daodi	105	39.32 N	118.11 E
Daofu	102	31.07 N	101.08 E
Daoguanhe	100	30.54 N	114.57 E
Daohu	100	29.42 N	117.29 E
Daolazui	105	40.06 N	115.06 E
Daoliban	104	41.52 N	121.37 E
Daolin	100	27.59 N	112.42 E
Daolinggang	98	34.02 N	114.34 E
Daoliupu	107	30.12 N	105.09 E
Daomaguan	98	39.04 N	114.36 E
Daosa	124	26.53 N	76.20 E
Daoshiwu	106	30.18 N	118.57 E
Daoshui ≃	100	30.44 N	114.39 E
Daoshuqiao	106	31.51 N	119.41 E
Daotiancun	89	48.53 N	130.03 E
Daotou	98	37.14 N	120.20 E
Daoudi	150	14.08 N	13.58 W
Daoukro	150	7.03 N	3.58 W
Daoulas	32	48.22 N	4.15 W
Daoura, Oued ∨	148	29.03 N	4.33 W
Daoxian	102	25.35 N	111.27 E
Daozhen	102	28.42 N	107.56 E
Daozi	89	45.00 N	123.43 E
Dapa	116	9.46 N	126.03 E
Dapango	150	10.52 N	0.12 E
Dapanzhuang	98	37.20 N	115.28 E
Dapaozi	89	45.27 N	122.07 E
Dapdap	116	14.14 N	122.15 E
Dapeng	100	22.34 N	114.29 E
Daphne	194	30.36 N	87.54 W
Dapiak, Mount ∧	116	8.15 N	123.28 E
Daping, Zhg.	100	23.11 N	115.49 E
Daping, Zhg.	100	24.24 N	115.58 E
Dapingshan	102	25.30 N	109.39 E
Dapishi	100	26.30 N	112.54 E
Dapitan	116	8.39 N	123.25 E
Dapitan ≃	116	8.38 N	123.25 E
Dapitan Bay ⊂	116	8.40 N	123.23 E
Dapto	170	34.30 S	150.47 E
Dapu, Zhg.	100	23.16 N	113.32 E
Dapu, Zhg.	100	24.32 N	116.42 E
Dapu, Zhg.	106	31.19 N	119.56 E
Dapujie	100	27.00 N	112.46 E
Daqian	106	30.55 N	120.11 E
Daqiangmen	106	31.29 N	120.27 E
Daqiangzi	104	42.21 N	120.29 E
Daqiao, Zhg.	100	32.21 N	119.41 E
Daqiao, Zhg.	100	29.39 N	121.26 E
Daqiao, Zhg.	100	26.38 N	118.54 E
Daqiao, Zhg.	100	28.11 N	114.16 E
Daqiao, Zhg.	100	24.56 N	113.09 E
Daqiao, Zhg.	106	30.59 N	121.14 E
Daqiaochang	107	28.52 N	105.40 E
Daqiaojie	106	30.46 N	119.14 E
Daqiaokou	100	27.06 N	113.38 E
Daqiaotou	106	30.47 N	120.52 E
Daqiaozhai	102	25.21 N	106.15 E
Daqinggou, Zhg.	98	41.16 N	114.10 E
Daqinggou, Zhg.	98	41.12 N	125.07 E
Daqinghe	98	39.13 N	118.51 E
Daqinghe ≃, Zhg.	98	42.26 N	123.50 E
Daqinghe ≃, Zhg.	105	39.04 N	116.55 E
Daqingshan ∧, Zhg.	89	45.35 N	127.51 E
Daqingshan ∧, Zhg.	104	42.03 N	123.45 E
Daqiu	100	25.24 N	119.39 E
Daqqāq	140	12.56 N	26.58 E
Daquan	102	41.21 N	95.17 E
Daquantou	105	39.31 N	114.46 E
Daquanyan	104	42.37 N	123.32 E
Dāqūf	142	28.24 N	30.38 E
Daqushan I	100	27.48 N	121.08 E
Dar'ā	132	32.37 N	36.06 E
Dar'ā □[8]	132	33.00 N	36.10 E
Dārāb	128	28.45 N	54.34 E
Darāban	120	31.44 N	70.20 E
Darabani	38	48.11 N	26.35 E
Darāfisah	140	13.23 N	31.59 E
Daraga	116	11.54 N	123.52 E
Daragodleh	144	10.10 N	44.57 E
Daraina	157b	13.12 S	49.40 E
Daraj	146	30.09 N	10.26 E
Darājīl	142	30.39 N	30.52 E
Darakeh	267d	35.48 N	51.23 E
Darakht-e Yahyá	120	31.50 N	68.08 E
Daram Island I	116	11.38 N	124.47 E
Dārān	128	32.59 N	50.24 E
Daraoli ⬥[8]	272c	19.11 N	72.48 E
Darap	112	1.13 S	112.03 E
Dār as-Salām	273c	29.59 N	31.13 E
Darasun	88	51.40 N	114.00 E
Daraut-Kurgan	85	39.33 N	72.13 E
Darave	272c	19.02 N	73.01 E
Darāw	140	24.25 N	32.56 E
Darawah	142	30.13 N	31.06 E
Dārayyā	132	33.27 N	36.15 E
Darb al-Ḥājj	142	30.10 N	31.33 E
Darb al-Ḥajj, Jabal ∧	132	30.05 N	35.26 E
Darband, Īrān	267d	35.49 N	51.26 E
Darband, Pāk.	123	34.20 N	72.52 E
Darbāsīyah	130	37.04 N	40.39 E
Darbaza	85	41.35 N	69.02 E
Darbėnai	76	56.01 N	21.15 E
Dar-Beni-Kriche-Bahri	34	35.30 N	5.20 W
Darbhanga	124	26.10 N	85.54 E
Darbhanga □[5]	124	26.00 N	86.00 E
Darboruk	144	9.52 N	44.30 E
Darby, Mont., U.S.	202	46.01 N	114.11 W
Darby, Pa., U.S.	208	39.54 N	75.15 W
Darby, Cape ≻	180	64.20 N	162.22 W
Darby Creek ≃	285	39.52 N	75.18 W
Darbydale	218	39.51 N	83.11 W
Darčeli	84	42.27 N	41.42 E
Darchan	88	49.28 N	105.56 E
D'Archiac, Mount ∧	172	43.28 S	170.35 E
D'Arcy	182	50.33 N	122.29 W
D'Arcy Island I	224	48.34 N	123.17 W
Darda	38	45.37 N	18.41 E
Dardadine	168a	33.14 S	116.50 E
Dardanelle, Ark., U.S.	194	35.13 N	93.09 W
Dardanelle, Calif., U.S.	226	38.20 N	119.50 W
Dardanelle Lake ⊜[1]	194	35.25 N	93.20 W
Dardanelles → Çanakkale Boğazı ⋓	130	40.15 N	26.25 E
Dardanup	168a	33.24 S	115.45 E
Dardara	34	35.08 N	5.15 W
Dardenelles Cone ∧	226	38.25 N	119.53 W
Dardenne Creek ≃	219	38.52 N	90.32 W
Dardenne Lake ⊜	219	38.52 N	90.38 W
Dardesheim	54	51.59 N	10.49 E
Dardistān □[9]	123	35.30 N	74.00 E
Dare	208	37.10 N	76.26 W
Dare ≃	144	7.18 N	42.15 E
Darebin Creek ≃	274b	37.47 S	145.02 E
Dareda	154	4.13 S	35.33 E
Dar-el-Beida → Casablanca	148	33.39 N	7.35 W
Darende	130	38.34 N	37.30 E
Darent ≃	260	51.28 N	0.13 E
Daresbury	262	53.21 N	2.38 W
Dar-es-Salaam	154	6.48 S	39.17 E
Daressalam → Dar-es-Salaam	154	6.48 S	39.17 E
Darfeld	52	52.01 N	7.16 E
Darfo	64	45.53 N	10.11 E
Dārfūr □[4]	140	13.00 N	25.00 E
Dargai	123	34.11 N	71.53 E
Dargan-Ata	74	40.29 N	62.10 E
Dargaville	172	35.56 S	173.53 E
Dargle ≃	48	53.11 N	6.04 W
Dargol	150	13.55 N	1.15 E
Dargun	54	53.54 N	12.51 E
Dari, Sūd.	140	5.48 N	30.21 E
Dari (Jimai), Zhg.	102	33.55 N	99.54 E
Dāriāpur	126	23.36 N	89.27 E
Darıca	130	40.45 N	29.23 E
Darie Hills ⛰[2]	144	8.15 N	47.25 E
Darién, Col.	246	3.56 N	76.31 W
Darien, Conn., U.S.	207	41.05 N	73.28 W
Darien, Ga., U.S.	192	31.22 N	81.26 W
Darien, N.Y., U.S.	210	41.43 N	70.37 W
Darien, Wis., U.S.	216	42.36 N	88.42 W
Darién, Serranía del ⛰	246	8.20 N	77.22 W
Darien Center	210	42.54 N	78.23 W
Darien Lakes State Park ♠	210	42.55 N	78.25 W
Dariense, Cordillera ⛰	236	12.55 N	85.30 W
Dariganga	102	45.21 N	113.38 E
Darigayos Point ≻	116	16.50 N	120.20 E
Darjeeling	124	27.02 N	88.16 E
Darjeeling □[5]	124	26.50 N	88.20 E
Darjevka	83	47.42 N	39.41 E
Darjinskij	86	49.04 N	72.56 E
Darjinskoje	80	51.20 N	51.44 E
Darkan	168a	33.20 S	116.44 E
Darke □[6]	218	40.06 N	84.38 W
Darke Peak	166	33.28 S	136.12 E
Darkhāna	123	30.39 N	72.11 E
Darkhazīneh	128	31.54 N	48.59 E
Dark Head ≻	241h	13.17 N	61.16 W
Darkin ≃	168a	32.00 S	116.14 E
Darkūsh	130	35.59 N	36.23 E
Darlaston	42	52.34 N	2.02 W
Darling, S. Afr.	158	33.23 S	18.23 E
Darling, Miss., U.S.	194	34.22 N	90.23 W
Darling, Pa., U.S.	285	39.54 N	75.28 W
Darling ≃	166	34.07 S	141.55 E
Darling, Lake ⊜[1]	198	48.35 N	101.40 W
Darling Downs ⬥[1]	166	27.30 S	150.30 E
Darlingford	184	49.12 N	98.22 W
Darling Range ⛰	162	32.00 S	116.00 E
Darlington, Austl.	168a	31.55 S	116.05 E
Darlington, Austl.	169	38.00 S	143.03 E
Darlington, Eng., U.K.	44	54.31 N	1.34 W
Darlington, Md., U.S.	208	39.39 N	76.11 W
Darlington, Pa., U.S.	214	40.49 N	80.26 W
Darlington, S.C., U.S.	192	34.18 N	79.52 W
Darlington, Wis., U.S.	190	42.41 N	90.07 W
Darlington Brook ≃	276	41.05 N	74.11 W
Darlington Corners	285	39.55 N	75.34 W
Darlington Range ⛰	171a	27.50 S	153.15 E
Darlot, Lake ⊜	162	27.48 S	121.35 E
Darłowo	30	54.26 N	16.23 E
Darma Pass)(	124	30.29 N	80.34 W
Darmstadt	56	49.53 N	8.40 E
Darmstadt □[5]	56	50.00 N	8.40 E
Darnah	146	32.46 N	22.39 E
Darnah □[4]	146	32.30 N	22.45 E
Darnall	158	29.23 S	31.18 E
Darnétal	50	49.27 N	1.09 E
Darney	58	48.05 N	6.03 E
Darnick	166	32.51 S	143.37 E
Darnley, Cape ≻	9	67.43 S	69.30 E
Darnley Bay ⊂	180	69.35 N	123.30 W
Daroca	34	41.07 N	1.25 W
Darodih	126	23.14 N	86.27 E
Daror ⫪[4]	144	8.13 N	44.40 E
Dar-Ould-Zidouh	148	32.22 N	6.49 W
Darou Mousti	150	15.03 N	16.03 W
Darovoje	82	54.34 N	38.22 E
Darr ≃	166	23.39 S	143.50 E
Darra	171a	27.34 S	152.58 E
Darragh	279b	40.16 N	79.41 W
Darrah, Mount ∧	182	49.28 N	114.35 W
Darrang □[5]	124	25.30 N	89.30 E
Darregueira	252	37.42 S	63.10 W
Darreh Gaz	128	37.27 N	59.07 E
Darrington	224	48.15 N	121.36 W
Darrouzett	196	36.27 N	100.20 W
Darryl Gardens	284b	39.25 N	76.25 W
Dārsana	126	23.32 N	88.52 E
Darscheid	56	50.12 N	6.53 E
Darss ≻[1]	54	54.25 N	12.31 E
Darsser Ort ≻	54	54.29 N	12.31 E
Dart ≃	42	50.20 N	3.33 W
Dart, Cape ≻	9	73.06 S	126.20 W
Dār Ta'izzah	130	36.17 N	36.51 E
Dartford	260	51.27 N	0.14 E
Dartford □[8]	260	51.26 N	0.15 E
Dartford Tunnel ⬥[5]	260	51.28 N	0.16 E
Dartmoor	166	37.55 S	141.17 E
Dartmoor ⬥[3]	42	50.35 N	4.00 W
Dartmoor National Park ♠	42	50.37 N	3.52 W
Dartmouth, N.S., Can.	186	44.40 N	63.34 W
Dartmouth, Eng., U.K.	42	50.21 N	3.35 W
Dartmouth ≃	186	48.53 N	64.34 W
Dartmouth, Lake ⊜	166	26.04 S	145.18 E
Darton	44	53.36 N	1.32 W
Dartuch, Cabo ≻	34	39.56 N	3.48 E
Daru, Pap. N. Gui.	164	9.04 S	143.21 E
Daru, S.L.	150	7.59 N	10.50 W
Daruvar	36	45.36 N	17.13 E
Darvaza	128	40.11 N	58.24 E
Darvāzahgêy	120	31.48 N	67.44 E
Darvazskij Chrebet ⛰	85	38.30 N	71.15 E
Darvel	46	55.37 N	4.18 W
Darvel, Teluk ⊂	112	4.50 N	118.30 E
Darvi	88	47.02 N	93.35 E
Darvinskij Zapovednik ⬥[4]	76	58.50 N	37.40 E
Darwen	262	53.42 N	2.28 W
Darwen ≃	262	53.45 N	2.41 W
Darwendale	154	17.43 S	30.33 E
Dārwha	122	20.19 N	77.46 E
Darwin, Arg.	254	39.12 S	65.46 W
Darwin, Austl.	164	12.28 S	130.50 E
Darwin, Bahía ⊂	254	45.27 S	74.40 W
Darwin, Isla I	246a	1.39 N	92.00 W
Darwin, Volcán ∧[1]	246a	0.10 S	91.18 W
Darwin River	164	12.49 S	130.58 E
Daryābād	124	26.53 N	81.33 E
Darya Khān	123	31.48 N	71.06 E
Daryāpur	120	20.56 N	77.20 E
Darz Āb	120	35.58 N	65.22 E
Darzo	64	45.51 N	10.33 E
Dār Zubi	140	13.07 N	23.40 E
Dās	123	35.05 N	75.05 E
Dās I	128	25.09 N	52.53 E
Dasāda	120	23.19 N	71.50 E
Dasanjiazi, Zhg.	104	42.05 N	122.32 E
Dasanjiazi, Zhg.	104	42.31 N	122.54 E
Dašava	78	49.16 N	24.01 E
Dašbalbar	88	49.36 N	114.24 E
Dasburg	56	50.03 N	6.07 E
Dase → Dese	144	11.05 N	39.41 E
Dašev	78	49.00 N	29.26 E
Dashafa	105	39.19 N	116.19 E
Dashahu ⊜	100	30.11 N	113.46 E
Dashaling	104	41.20 N	123.01 E
Dashalitu	104	42.31 N	122.30 E
Dashankou	105	40.17 N	115.49 E
Dashanpu	107	29.25 N	104.49 E
Dashanzhuang	98	38.02 N	117.39 E
Dashaping	100	29.24 N	113.51 E
Dashazhai	89	46.16 N	121.25 E
Dashengfenchang	106	31.53 N	121.34 E
Dashengpu	104	41.13 N	121.02 E
Dashentang	105	39.13 N	117.56 E
Dashetai	102	40.58 N	109.19 E
Dashields Dam ⬥[6]	214	40.33 N	80.12 W
Dashihe ≃	105	39.35 N	116.05 E
Dashiqiao, Zhg.	100	33.57 N	113.53 E
Dashiqiao, Zhg.	104	41.52 N	123.17 E
Dashiqiao, Zhg.	107	30.28 N	106.29 E
Dashiqiao, Zhg.	107	30.39 N	105.37 E
Dashiqiao, Zhg.	107	30.07 N	106.12 E
Dashitou, Zhg.	89	43.19 N	128.28 E
Dashitou, Zhg.	102	42.49 N	95.19 E
Dashlūţ	142	27.34 N	30.42 E
Dash Point	224	47.19 N	122.26 W
Dasht ≃	128	25.10 N	61.40 E
Dashtīārī ≃	128	25.09 N	61.32 E
Dashu	106	31.13 N	120.56 E
Dashun	100	28.06 N	119.52 E
Dashutang	102	23.00 N	103.55 E
Dashuwan	105	40.37 N	117.19 E
Dasi, Zhg.	100	33.48 N	115.55 E
Dasi (Huangfansi), Zhg.	102	38.15 N	100.22 E
Dašinčilen	88	47.51 N	104.03 E
Dasing	60	48.23 N	11.03 E
Dasizhan	89	45.53 N	130.24 E
Daska	123	32.20 N	74.21 E
Daškesan	84	40.30 N	46.04 E
Daskop	158	33.44 S	22.43 E
Daškovka	76	53.44 N	30.13 E
Dasmina	126	22.17 N	90.35 E
Dasol	116	15.59 N	119.52 E
Dasol Bay ⊂	116	15.53 N	119.51 E
Daspalla	120	20.21 N	84.51 E
Dassalan Island I	116	6.45 N	121.28 E
Dassel, B.R.D.	52	51.48 N	9.41 E
Dassel, Minn., U.S.	190	45.05 N	94.19 W
Dasseneiland I	158	33.26 S	18.04 E
Dasserat, Lac ⊜	190	48.16 N	79.25 W
Dassiefontein	158	31.35 S	24.25 E
Dassow	54	53.50 N	10.59 E
Dasswang	60	49.09 N	11.40 E
Dastakert	84	39.23 N	46.02 E
Dastgardān	128	34.19 N	56.51 E
Daštidžum	85	38.01 N	70.12 E
Daštioburdon	85	39.24 N	69.04 E
Dastjerd	128	34.33 N	50.15 E
Dāsuria	126	24.07 N	89.08 E

Symbols in the index entries represent the broad categories identified in the key at the right. Symbols with superior numbers (⛰[2]) identify subcategories (see complete key on page *I · 30*).

Kartensymbole in dem Registerverzeichnis stellen die rechts in Schlüssel erklärten Kategorien dar. Symbole mit hochgestellten Ziffern (⛰[2]) bezeichnen Unterabteilungen einer Kategorie (vgl. vollständiger Schlüssel auf Seite *I · 30*).

Los símbolos incluidos en el texto del índice representan las grandes categorias identificadas con la clave a la derecha. Los símbolos con numeros en su parte superior (⛰[2]) identifican las subcategorías (véase la clave completa en la página *I · 30*).

Les symboles de l'index représentent les catégories indiquées dans la légende à droite. Les symboles suivis d'un indice (⛰[2]) représentent des sous-catégories (voir légende complète à la page *I · 30*).

Os símbolos incluídos no texto do índice representam as grandes categorias identificadas com a chave à direita. Os símbolos com números em sua parte superior (⛰[2]) identificam as subcategorias (veja-se a chave completa à página *I · 30*).

English	Deutsch	Español	Français	Português
∧ Mountain	Berg	Montaña	Montagne	Montanha
⛰ Mountains	Berge	Montañas	Montagnes	Montanhas
)(Pass	Pass	Paso	Col	Passo
∨ Valley, Canyon	Tal, Cañon	Valle, Cañón	Vallée, Canyon	Vale, Canhão
⌣ Plain	Ebene	Llano	Plaine	Planície
≻ Cape	Kap	Cabo	Cap	Cabo
I Island	Insel	Isla	Île	Ilha
II Islands	Inseln	Islas	Îles	Ilhas
⊥ Other Topographic Features	Andere Topographische Objekte	Otros Elementos Topográficos	Autres données topographiques	Outros Elementos Topográficos

ESPAÑOL

Nombre	Página	Lat.°′	Long.°′ W=Oeste
Dasūya	123	31.49 N	75.38 E
Datachang	107	28.55 N	104.21 E
Datagenoyang	112	2.03 N	115.10 E
Datai	105	39.58 N	115.54 E
Dataizi	104	41.17 N	121.46 E
Datan, Zhg.	98	41.31 N	115.54 E
Datan, Zhg.	98	39.31 N	122.11 E
Datang, Zhg.	100	24.47 N	113.43 E
Datang, Zhg.	102	22.23 N	108.23 E
Datang, Zhg.	102	24.11 N	109.00 E
Datangwei	100	25.17 N	114.56 E
Datça	130	36.45 N	27.40 E
Datchet	260	51.29 N	0.34 W
Date	92a	42.27 N	140.51 E
Date Creek ≃	200	34.13 N	113.29 W
Datia	124	25.40 N	78.28 E
Datia □[5]	124	25.50 N	78.30 E
Datian, Zhg.	100	25.42 N	117.49 E
Datian, Zhg.	100	24.06 N	116.19 E
Datianwei	100	25.54 N	115.10 E
Dativli	272c	19.11 N	73.03 E
D'at'kovo	76	53.36 N	34.20 E
D'atloviči	76	52.20 N	26.50 E
D'atlovo, S.S.S.R.	76	53.28 N	25.24 E
D'atlovo, S.S.S.R.	82	56.14 N	36.16 E
Datong, Zhg.	89	46.03 N	124.50 E
Datong, Zhg.	100	30.48 N	117.45 E
Datong, Zhg.	102	37.03 N	101.45 E
Datong, Zhg.	102	40.08 N	113.13 E
Datonghe ≃	102	36.20 N	102.55 E
Datongshan ⩚	102	38.00 N	99.30 E
Datongzhen	100	32.50 N	118.52 E
Datoushan	98	41.50 N	117.08 E
Dātra	272b	22.58 N	88.16 E
Datta	89	49.18 N	140.22 E
Dattapāra	126	23.01 N	90.53 E
Dattapukur	126	22.45 N	88.33 E
Dattapulia	126	23.14 N	88.43 E
Datteln	52	51.40 N	7.23 E
Datteln-Hamm-Kanal ≊	263	51.39 N	7.21 E
Dattilo	70	37.58 N	12.39 E
Datu, Tanjung ≻	112	2.06 N	109.39 E
Datuan	106	30.58 N	121.44 E
Datumakuta	112	2.32 N	117.51 E
Datun, Zhg.	89	43.49 N	125.12 E
Datun, Zhg.	98	40.37 N	119.57 E
Datun, Zhg.	104	40.59 N	122.55 E
Datuopu	100	28.03 N	112.58 E
Datu Piang	116	7.01 N	124.30 E
Daua (Dawa) ≃	144	4.11 N	42.06 E
Daubiche ≃	89	44.54 N	133.35 E
Daudkāndi	126	23.32 N	90.43 E
Dāūd Khel	123	32.53 N	71.34 E
Daudnagar	124	25.02 N	84.24 E
Daugai	76	54.22 N	24.20 E
Daugård	41	55.44 N	9.43 E
Daugava (Zapadnaja Dvina) ≃	76	57.04 N	24.03 E
Daugavpils	76	55.53 N	26.32 E
Dauin	116	9.12 N	123.16 E
Daulatābād (Shirin Tagāo), Afg.	120	36.26 N	64.55 E
Daulatabad, Bhārat	126	24.08 N	88.22 E
Daulatkhan	126	22.38 N	90.49 E
Daulatpur, Bhārat	272b	22.26 N	88.18 E
Daulatpur, Bngl.	126	24.00 N	88.52 E
Daulatpur (Ramchandrapur), Bngl.	126	23.58 N	89.50 E
Daulatpur, Bngl.	126	22.53 N	89.31 E
Daulatpur, Pāk.	120	26.30 N	67.58 E
Daule, Bhārat	272c	19.10 N	73.03 E
Daule, Ec.	246	1.50 S	79.56 W
Daule, Ec.	246	0.24 N	80.00 W
Daule ≃	246	2.10 S	79.52 W
Daultāla	123	33.12 N	73.09 E
Daulton Creek ≃	226	37.04 N	119.59 W
Daun	56	50.11 N	6.50 E
Daund	122	18.28 N	74.36 E
Daung Kyun I	110	12.14 N	98.05 E
Daunia, Monti della ⩚	68	41.27 N	15.06 E
Dauphin, Man., Can.	184	51.09 N	100.03 W
Dauphin, Pa., U.S.	208	40.22 N	76.56 W
Dauphin □[6]	208	40.15 N	76.52 W
Dauphin ≃	184	51.58 N	98.04 W
Dauphiné □[9]	32	44.50 N	6.00 E
Dauphin Island I	194	30.14 N	88.12 W
Dauphin Lake ⊜	184	51.17 N	99.48 W
Daura	150	13.02 N	8.21 E
Daurija	88	49.56 N	116.52 E
Daurskij Chrebet ⩚	88	50.30 N	112.30 E
Daurskoje	86	55.14 N	92.05 E
Dausenau	56	50.20 N	7.45 E
Dāvangere	122	14.28 N	75.55 E
Davant	194	29.37 N	89.51 W
Davao	116	7.04 N	125.36 E
Davao ≃	116	7.04 N	125.37 E
Davao del Norte □[4]	116	7.10 N	125.50 E
Davao del Sur □[4]	116	6.15 N	125.40 E
Davao Gulf ᑕ	116	6.40 N	125.55 E
Davao Oriental □[4]	116	7.30 N	126.30 E
Dāvar Panāh	128	27.21 N	62.21 E
Dāvarzan	128	36.23 N	56.50 E
Davel	158	26.24 S	29.40 E
Daveluyville	206	46.12 N	72.08 W
Davenda	88	53.33 N	119.18 E
Davenham	262	53.14 N	2.31 W
Davenport, Calif., U.S.	226	37.01 N	122.12 W
Davenport, Fla., U.S.	220	28.10 N	81.36 W
Davenport, Iowa, U.S.	190	41.32 N	90.41 W
Davenport, Nebr., U.S.	198	40.19 N	97.49 W
Davenport, N.Y., U.S.	210	42.28 N	74.51 W
Davenport, Okla., U.S.	196	35.42 N	96.46 W
Davenport, Wash., U.S.	202	47.39 N	118.09 W
Davenport, Mount ∧	162	22.23 S	130.51 E
Davenport Downs	166	24.08 S	141.07 E
Davenport Range ⩚	162	20.47 S	134.48 E
Daventry	42	52.16 N	1.09 W
Davey, Port ᑕ	166	43.19 S	145.55 E
Daveyton Location	273d	26.09 S	28.25 E
David	236	8.26 N	82.26 W
David City	198	41.15 N	97.08 W
David-Gorodok	78	52.03 N	27.14 E
Davido-Nikol'skoje	83	48.30 N	39.50 E
David Point ≻	241k	12.14 N	61.39 W
Davids Island I	276	40.53 N	73.46 W
Davidson, Sask., Can.	184	51.18 N	106.59 W
Davidson, N.C., U.S.	192	35.30 N	80.51 W
Davidson, Okla., U.S.	196	34.14 N	99.05 W
Davidson Creek ≃	222	30.21 N	96.27 W
Davidson Heights	214	40.35 N	80.15 W
Davidson Lake ⊜	184	53.47 N	99.37 W
Davidson Mountains ⩚	180	68.45 N	142.10 W
Davidson Park ♠	274a	33.45 S	151.12 E
Davidsville	214	40.14 N	78.56 W
Davie	220	26.05 N	80.14 W
Davies, Mount ∧	162	26.14 S	129.16 E
Davignab	158	27.32 S	19.48 E
Davila	116	18.29 N	120.35 E
Davilla	222	30.47 N	97.17 W
Davington	44	55.18 N	3.12 W
Davin Lake ⊜	184	56.50 N	103.40 W
Davinópolis	255	15.58 S	50.08 W
Daviot	46	57.25 N	4.08 W
Davis, Calif., U.S.	226	38.33 N	121.44 W
Davis, N.C., U.S.	192	34.48 N	76.28 W
Davis, Okla., U.S.	196	34.30 N	97.03 W
Davis, W. Va., U.S.	188	39.08 N	79.28 W
Davis ≃	162	21.42 S	121.05 E
Davis, Mount ∧	188	39.47 N	79.10 W
Davis Bay ᑕ	9	66.08 S	134.05 E
Davisboro	192	32.59 N	82.36 W
Davisburg	216	42.45 N	83.33 W

FRANÇAIS

Nom	Page	Lat.°′	Long.°′ W=Ouest
Davis City	190	40.38 N	93.49 W
Davis Cove	186	47.40 N	54.18 W
Davis Creek ≃, Mich., U.S.	281	42.27 N	83.43 W
Davis Creek ≃, Mo., U.S.	219	39.12 N	91.53 W
Davis Dam	200	35.11 N	114.35 W
Davis Dam ⬥[6]	200	35.11 N	114.21 W
Davis Island I	279b	40.29 N	80.05 W
Davis Lake ⊜, Ill., U.S.	278	42.16 N	88.05 W
Davis Lake ⊜, Oreg., U.S.	202	43.37 N	121.51 W
Davis-Monthan Air Force Base ■	200	32.11 N	110.53 W
Davis Mountains ⩚	196	30.35 N	104.00 W
Davison	216	43.02 N	83.31 W
Davis Park	210	40.42 N	72.59 W
Davis Point ≻	282	38.03 N	122.15 W
Davis Sea ⍑[2]	9	66.00 S	92.00 E
Davisson Lake ⊜	224	46.30 N	122.20 W
Davis Strait ⋓	176	67.00 N	57.00 W
Davisville	285	40.11 N	75.03 W
Davlekanovo	86	54.13 N	55.03 E
Davoli	68	38.39 N	16.29 E
Davos	58	46.48 N	9.50 E
Davron	261	48.52 N	1.57 E
Davst	86	50.36 N	92.28 E
Davulga	130	38.58 N	31.23 E
Davutlar	130	37.43 N	27.17 E
Davy	192	37.29 N	81.39 W
Davydkovo, S.S.S.R.	82	56.17 N	36.49 E
Davydkovo, S.S.S.R.	265b	55.35 N	37.12 E
Davydov Brod	78	47.14 N	33.12 E
Davydovka	78	51.10 N	39.25 E
Davydovo	82	55.37 N	38.52 E
Davydovskoje	82	55.52 N	36.48 E
Davyhulme	262	53.27 N	2.22 W
Dawa, Zhg.	104	41.00 N	122.03 E
Dawa, Zhg.	104	41.54 N	123.32 E
Dawa (Daua) ≃	144	4.11 N	42.06 E
Dawaki	150	12.06 N	8.20 E
Dawan	102	23.52 N	109.29 E
Dawangcun	106	30.45 N	118.59 E
Dawangdian	105	39.04 N	115.26 E
Dawangdong	105	38.53 N	116.21 E
Dawangji	100	34.00 N	117.46 E
Dawangjiadao I	98	39.27 N	123.07 E
Dawangqiao	98	36.58 N	118.31 E
Dawangsangou	104	41.43 N	121.36 E
Dawangzhuang, Zhg.	105	39.23 N	116.28 E
Dawangzhuang, Zhg.	105	38.59 N	115.56 E
Dawanshan I	100	21.57 N	113.43 E
Dawāsir, Wādī ad- ∨	144	20.24 N	46.29 E
Dawatun	104	41.05 N	121.01 E
Dawei	102	25.09 N	110.21 E
Daweihe	98	36.42 N	118.57 E
Daweizhuang	105	39.34 N	116.53 E
Daweizigou	104	42.38 N	123.09 E
Dawenhe ≃	98	35.38 N	116.24 E
Dawenkou	98	35.59 N	117.07 E
Dawera, Pulau I	164	7.44 S	130.00 E
Dawlan	110	16.44 N	98.01 E
Dawley	42	52.40 N	2.28 W
Dawlish	42	50.35 N	3.28 W
Dawn	208	37.50 N	77.22 W
Dawna Range ⩚	110	16.50 N	98.15 E
Dawrah	140	12.22 N	24.19 E
Daws Heath	260	51.34 N	0.37 E
Dawson, Yukon, Can.	180	64.04 N	139.25 W
Dawson, Ga., U.S.	192	31.47 N	84.26 W
Dawson, Ill., U.S.	219	39.51 N	89.28 W
Dawson, Minn., U.S.	198	44.56 N	96.03 W
Dawson, Nebr., U.S.	198	40.08 N	95.50 W
Dawson, Tex., U.S.	222	31.54 N	96.43 W
Dawson ≃	166	23.38 S	149.46 E
Dawson, Isla I	254	53.55 S	70.45 W
Dawson, Mount ∧	182	51.09 N	117.25 W
Dawson Bay ᑕ	184	52.55 N	100.50 W
Dawson Creek	182	55.46 N	120.14 W
Dawson Inlet ᑕ	176	61.50 N	93.25 W
Dawson-Lambton Glacier ⍓	9	76.15 S	27.30 W
Dawson Range ⩚, Austl.	166	24.20 S	149.45 E
Dawson Range ⩚, Yukon, Can.	180	62.40 N	139.00 W
Dawson Ridge	214	40.42 N	80.22 W
Dawson Springs	194	37.10 N	87.41 W
Dawsonville	192	34.25 N	84.07 W
Dawu	100	31.34 N	114.06 E
Dawudapu	104	41.36 N	123.03 E
Dawuji	105	39.51 N	116.30 E
Dawujiawopeng	104	41.55 N	122.29 E
Dawujiazi	104	42.16 N	121.52 E
Dawulancun	104	41.56 N	121.05 E
Dax	32	43.43 N	1.03 W
Daxi ≃	100	28.18 N	119.44 E
Daxian	102	31.18 N	107.30 E
Daxiaoqindao I	98	38.18 N	120.48 E
Daxin	102	22.50 N	107.26 E
Daxing, Zhg.	98	39.44 N	116.20 E
Daxing (Huangcun), Zhg.	105	39.41 N	116.29 E
Daxing, Zhg.	106	31.50 N	121.40 E
Daxing'anling-shanmai ⩚	89	49.40 N	122.00 E
Daxingchang	107	30.17 N	103.26 E
Daxingcun	106	31.45 N	121.40 E
Daxingji	100	33.55 N	118.29 E
Daxingzhai	102	23.13 N	102.21 E
Daxinji	100	34.03 N	119.28 E
Daxinzhuang, Zhg.	105	39.26 N	118.20 E
Daxinzhuang, Zhg.	105	40.23 N	116.44 E
Daxiyang	106	30.21 N	121.58 E
Daxueshan ⩚	102	30.10 N	101.50 E
Daxujia	98	34.18 N	117.34 E
Daxujie	100	29.32 N	121.52 E
Daya	100	25.24 N	114.22 E
Dayakou	102	22.46 N	100.18 E
Dayanchi	102	27.41 N	101.55 E
Dayang	100	25.56 N	118.48 E
Dayangcha	98	42.04 N	126.43 E
Dayanggou	104	41.14 N	123.51 E
Dayanghe ≃	98	39.54 N	123.40 E
Dayangji	98	36.04 N	116.31 E
Dayangquanzi	104	41.17 N	121.39 E
Dayaniguas, Ensenada de ᑕ	240p	22.20 N	83.15 W
Dayao	102	25.43 N	101.13 E
Dayaopu	100	27.59 N	113.42 E
Dayaoshan	102	24.05 N	110.17 E
Dayboro	171a	27.11 S	152.50 E
Daye	100	30.06 N	114.57 E
Dayghar	272c	19.09 N	73.03 E
Day Heights	218	39.11 N	84.14 W
Dayi	107	30.37 N	103.31 E
Dayiji	100	32.32 N	119.14 E
Daying, Zhg.	98	39.53 N	123.07 E
Daying, Zhg.	98	34.27 N	113.59 E
Daying, Zhg.	98	37.19 N	115.43 E
Daying, Zhg.	98	39.19 N	113.46 E
Daying, Zhg.	100	33.59 N	112.51 E
Dayingzhen	105	39.05 N	116.06 E
Dayingzi, Zhg.	98	41.19 N	118.19 E
Dayingzi, Zhg.	98	41.28 N	120.21 E
Dayingzi, Zhg.	104	41.08 N	122.50 E
Day Island	224	47.15 N	122.33 W
Day Lake ⊜	224	48.23 N	121.58 W
Daylesford	169	37.21 S	144.09 E
Daym Zubayr	140	7.43 N	26.13 E
Dayong, Zhg.	100	22.28 N	113.16 E
Dayong, Zhg.	102	28.59 N	110.15 E
Dayr, Jabal ad- ∧	140	12.27 N	30.42 E
Dayr Abū Sa'īd	132	32.30 N	35.41 E
Dayr al-'Ashā'ir	132	33.32 N	36.01 E
Dayr al-Balaḥ	132	31.25 N	34.21 E
Dayr al-Ghuṣūn	132	32.21 N	35.05 E
Dayr 'Alī	132	33.17 N	36.18 E
Dayr 'Allā	132	32.12 N	35.37 E

PORTUGUÊS

Nome	Página	Lat.°′	Long.°′ W=Oeste
Dayr 'Aṭīyah	130	34.06 N	36.46 E
Dayr az-Zawr	130	35.20 N	40.09 E
Dayr az-Zawr □[8]	130	35.30 N	39.00 E
Dayr Dibwān	132	31.55 N	35.16 E
Dayr Ḥāfir	130	36.09 N	37.42 E
Dayrīk	130	37.10 N	42.08 E
Dayr Jabal aṭ-Ṭayr	142	28.17 N	30.45 E
Dayr Mawās	142	27.38 N	30.51 E
Dayr Qānūn	132	33.36 N	36.08 E
Dayr Sharaf	132	32.15 N	35.11 E
Dayrūṭ, Miṣr	142	27.33 N	30.49 E
Dayrūṭ, Miṣr	142	31.13 N	30.30 E
Dayrūṭ ash-Sharīf	142	27.35 N	30.49 E
Days Island I	284b	39.24 N	76.22 W
Daysland	182	52.52 N	112.15 W
Day Star Indian Reserve ⬥[4]	184	51.43 N	104.14 W
Dayton, Ill., U.S.	216	41.23 N	88.47 W
Dayton, Ind., U.S.	216	40.23 N	86.46 W
Dayton, Iowa, U.S.	190	42.16 N	94.04 W
Dayton, Ky., U.S.	218	39.07 N	84.28 W
Dayton, Mich., U.S.	216	41.48 N	86.26 W
Dayton, Nev., U.S.	226	39.14 N	119.36 W
Dayton, N.J., U.S.	276	40.22 N	74.31 W
Dayton, N.Y., U.S.	210	42.25 N	78.58 W
Dayton, Ohio, U.S.	218	39.45 N	84.15 W
Dayton, Oreg., U.S.	224	45.13 N	123.05 W
Dayton, Pa., U.S.	210	40.35 N	76.39 W
Dayton, Pa., U.S.	214	40.53 N	79.16 W
Dayton, Tenn., U.S.	194	35.30 N	85.00 W
Dayton, Tex., U.S.	222	30.03 N	94.54 W
Dayton, Va., U.S.	188	38.25 N	78.56 W
Dayton, Wash., U.S.	202	46.19 N	117.59 W
Dayton, Wyo., U.S.	202	44.53 N	107.16 W
Daytona Beach	192	29.12 N	81.00 W
Dayu	112	1.59 S	115.04 E
Dayuba	107	29.15 N	103.34 E
Dayudao I	100	22.16 N	113.56 E
Dayuling ⩚	100	25.20 N	114.16 E
Dayushan I	106	30.19 N	121.58 E
Dayville, Conn., U.S.	207	41.51 N	71.53 W
Dayville, Oreg., U.S.	202	44.28 N	119.32 W
Dazaifu	96	33.25 N	130.30 E
Dazaifu ⊥	96	33.31 N	130.31 E
Dazaohuo	102	36.40 N	94.04 E
Dazaoliyingzi	104	42.07 N	121.20 E
Dazaomiao	106	32.06 N	121.29 E
Dazhangzi	98	40.46 N	118.07 E
Dazhaotai	104	41.14 N	123.03 E
Dazhengjiatun	98	39.37 N	122.52 E
Dazhengzhuangzi	105	39.16 N	116.46 E
Dazhi	100	34.29 N	113.17 E
Dazhiba	102	27.09 N	99.52 E
Dazhifang	104	41.21 N	123.12 E
Dazhou	100	28.53 N	118.58 E
Dazhu	102	30.48 N	107.12 E
Dazhuangke	105	40.32 N	115.42 E
Dazhubao	107	28.59 N	103.38 E
Dazhuge	98	35.58 N	118.37 E
Dazhuyuan	100	23.43 N	115.57 E
Dazifangshen	104	42.27 N	124.12 E
Daziling	104	41.21 N	121.26 E
Dazixi ≃	100	25.45 N	118.27 E
Daziying	104	41.42 N	123.36 E
Dazkırı	130	37.55 N	29.52 E
Dazu	107	29.43 N	105.42 E
Dazui	100	30.16 N	114.02 E
Dazuojiao ≻	100	24.54 N	118.58 E
De Aar	158	30.39 S	24.00 E
Dead ≃, Mich., U.S.	190	46.34 N	87.24 W
Dead ≃, N.J., U.S.	276	40.39 N	74.31 W
Deadhorse	180	70.11 N	148.27 W
Dead Horse Point State Park ♠	200	38.28 N	109.44 W
Dead Lake ⊜	184	55.40 N	105.01 W
Deadman ≃	182	50.45 N	120.55 W
Deadman Brook ≃	276	41.08 N	73.22 W
Deadman Creek ≃	226	37.12 N	120.42 W
Deadman Hill ∧	162	23.48 S	119.25 E
Deadmans Cay	238	23.14 N	75.14 W
Deadman's Creek Indian Reserve ⬥[4]	182	50.49 N	121.00 W
Dead Run ≃	284c	38.57 N	77.11 W
Dead Sea (Al-Baḥr al-Mayyit) (Yam HaMelaḥ) ⊜	132	31.30 N	35.30 E
Deadwood	198	44.23 N	103.44 W
Deadwood ≃	202	44.05 N	115.40 W
Deadwood Reservoir ⊜[1]	202	44.19 N	115.40 W
Deagan Island I	116	12.15 N	123.51 E
Deakin	162	30.46 S	128.58 E
Deakin, Mount ∧[2]	162	17.38 S	130.48 E
Deakin Bay ᑕ	9	68.23 S	150.10 E
Deal, Eng., U.K.	42	51.14 N	1.24 E
Deal, N.J., U.S.	208	40.15 N	74.00 W
Deale	208	38.47 N	76.33 W
Dealesville	158	28.40 S	25.37 E
Deal Island	208	38.09 N	75.56 W
Deal Island I	208	38.09 N	75.56 W
Deam Lake ⊜[1]	218	38.28 N	85.51 W
Dean	100	29.20 N	115.46 E
Dean ≃, B.C., Can.	182	52.50 N	126.57 W
Dean ≃, Eng., U.K.	44	53.20 N	2.14 W
Dean, Forest of ⬥[3]	42	51.48 N	2.30 W
Dean Channel ⋓	182	52.33 N	127.13 W
Deane	262	53.34 N	2.28 W
Deán Funes	252	30.26 S	64.21 W
Dean Row	262	53.20 N	2.11 W
Deans	276	40.24 N	74.31 W
Deansboro	210	42.60 N	75.26 W
Deans Dundas Bay ᑕ	176	72.15 N	118.25 W
Deanville	222	30.26 N	96.46 W
Dearborn	216	42.18 N	83.10 W
Dearborn □[6]	218	39.06 N	84.51 W
Dearborn ≃	202	47.07 N	111.55 W
Dearborn Heights, Ill., U.S.	278	41.43 N	87.48 W
Dearborn Heights, Mich., U.S.	216	42.19 N	83.14 W
Dearg, Beinn ∧	46	57.47 N	4.56 W
Dearne ≃	44	53.30 N	1.16 W
Dear Reservoir ⊜[1]	44	55.20 N	3.37 W
Dease ≃	180	59.54 N	128.30 W
Dease Arm ᑕ	180	66.52 N	119.37 W
Dease Lake ⊜	180	58.35 N	130.02 W
Dease Strait ⋓	176	68.40 N	108.00 W
Death Valley	204	36.18 N	116.25 W
Death Valley ∨	204	36.30 N	117.00 W
Death Valley National Monument ♠	204	36.30 N	117.00 W
Deatsville	194	32.37 N	86.24 W
Deauville	50	49.22 N	0.04 E
Debagrām	126	23.41 N	88.18 E
Debal'cevo	83	48.20 N	38.24 E
Debānāndapur	272b	22.56 N	88.22 E
Debao	102	23.21 N	106.31 E
Debar	38	41.31 N	20.30 E
De Bary	220	28.52 N	81.15 W
Debauch Mountain ∧	180	64.31 N	159.52 W
Débé	241r	10.12 N	61.27 W
Deben ≃	42	51.58 N	1.24 E
Debenham	42	52.13 N	1.11 E
De Beque	200	39.20 N	108.13 W
De Berry	194	32.18 N	94.10 W
Debesy	80	57.39 N	53.49 E
Debet ≃	84	41.22 N	44.58 E
Debhāta	124	22.33 N	88.58 E
Dębica	30	50.04 N	21.24 E
De Bilt	52	52.06 N	5.10 E
Debipur	126	24.14 N	88.38 E
Debīr Char	126	22.24 N	90.41 E
Dęblin	30	51.35 N	21.50 E
Dębno	30	52.45 N	14.40 E
Debo, Lac ⊜	150	15.18 N	4.09 W
Deborah, Mount ∧	180	63.38 N	147.15 W
Deborah West, Lake ⊜	162	30.45 S	119.07 E
Deboyne Islands II	164	10.45 S	152.25 E
Debra	126	22.24 N	87.33 E
Debre Birhan	144	9.40 N	39.33 E
Debrecen	30	47.32 N	21.38 E
Debre Markos	144	10.20 N	37.45 E
Debre May	144	11.19 N	37.30 E
Debre Tabor	144	11.50 N	38.05 E
Debre Zebit	144	11.50 N	38.40 E
Debre Zeyt	144	8.47 N	39.00 E
Debrzno	30	53.33 N	17.14 E
Debstedt	52	53.37 N	8.38 E
Decatur, Ala., U.S.	194	34.36 N	86.59 W
Decatur, Ga., U.S.	192	33.46 N	84.18 W
Decatur, Ill., U.S.	219	39.51 N	89.32 W
Decatur, Ind., U.S.	216	40.50 N	84.56 W
Decatur, Mich., U.S.	216	42.17 N	85.58 W
Decatur, Miss., U.S.	194	32.26 N	89.07 W
Decatur, Nebr., U.S.	198	42.00 N	96.15 W
Decatur, Ohio, U.S.	218	38.49 N	83.42 W
Decatur, Tenn., U.S.	192	35.31 N	84.47 W
Decatur, Tex., U.S.	222	33.14 N	97.35 W
Decatur □[6]	218	39.20 N	85.29 W
Decatur, Lake ⊜[1]	219	39.51 N	88.52 W
Decatur Island I	224	48.31 N	122.50 W
Decatur Municipal Airport ⊠	219	39.50 N	88.52 W
Decaturville	194	35.35 N	88.07 W
Decazeville	32	44.34 N	2.15 E
Deccan ⩚[1]	122	14.00 N	77.00 E
Decelles, Réservoir ⊜[1]	190	47.42 N	78.08 W
Deception, Mount ∧	224	47.49 N	123.14 W
Deception Bay ᑕ	171a	27.07 S	153.05 E
Deception Lake ⊜	184	56.33 N	104.15 W
Deception Pass ≊	224	48.24 N	122.38 W
Deception Pass State Park ♠	224	48.24 N	122.39 W
Dechang	102	27.24 N	102.10 E
Dechêne, Lac ⊜	186	51.15 N	67.51 W
Dechenhöhle ⊥[5]	263	51.22 N	7.39 E
Decherd	194	35.13 N	86.05 W
Dechu	120	26.47 N	72.20 E
Déchy	50	50.21 N	3.07 E
Decimomannu	71	39.19 N	8.58 E
Decimoputzu	71	39.20 N	8.55 E
Děčín	54	50.48 N	14.13 E
Děčínské stěny ⩚	54	50.50 N	14.12 E
Decize	32	46.50 N	3.27 E
Decker Lake	182	54.17 N	125.50 W
Decker Lake ⊜[1]	222	30.18 N	97.36 W
Deckers Point	214	40.46 N	78.59 W
Deckerville	190	43.32 N	82.44 W
De Cocksdorp	52	53.08 N	4.52 E
Decollatura	68	39.03 N	16.21 E
Decorah	190	43.18 N	91.48 W
Decs	30	46.17 N	18.46 E
Deda	38	46.57 N	24.53 E
Dedaye	110	16.24 N	95.53 E
Deddington	42	51.59 N	1.19 W
Dededo	174p	13.31 N	144.49 E
Dedegöl Dağı ∧	130	37.39 N	31.17 E
Dedeköy	130	37.58 N	29.36 E
Dedeleben	54	52.03 N	10.25 E
Dedeli	84	39.11 N	43.05 E
Dedelow	54	53.22 N	13.48 E
Dedemsvaart	52	52.36 N	6.28 E
Dedenevo	82	56.15 N	37.31 E
Dedesdorf	52	53.27 N	8.30 E
Dedham	207	42.15 N	71.10 W
Dediāpāda	120	21.38 N	73.35 E
Dedilovskije Vyselki	82	54.20 N	38.03 E
Dedinovo	82	55.03 N	39.07 E
Dedo, Cerro ∧	254	44.49 S	71.52 W
Dedo de Deus ∧	256	22.30 S	43.03 W
De Doorns	158	33.28 S	19.41 E
Dédougou	150	12.28 N	3.28 W
Dedoviči	76	57.32 N	29.56 E
Dedovsk	82	55.52 N	37.07 E
Dedu	89	48.31 N	126.14 E
Deduru ≃	122	7.36 N	79.48 E
Dedza	154	14.22 S	34.20 E
Dee ≃, Eire	48	53.52 N	6.21 W
Dee ≃, U.K.	42	53.11 N	2.53 W
Dee ≃, U.K.	44	53.20 N	3.12 W
Dee ≃, Eng., U.K.	44	54.18 N	2.32 W
Dee ≃, Scot., U.K.	44	54.50 N	4.03 W
Dee ≃, Scot., U.K.	46	57.09 N	2.07 W
Dee, Loch ⊜	44	55.05 N	4.24 W
Deedsville	216	40.55 N	86.06 W
De Efteling ♠	52	51.39 N	5.02 E
Deeg	124	27.28 N	77.20 E
Deelfontein	158	30.59 S	23.48 E
Deelpan	158	26.19 S	25.36 E
Deenwood	192	31.14 N	82.23 W
Deep ≃, Ind., U.S.	216	41.34 N	87.17 W
Deep ≃, N.C., U.S.	192	35.36 N	79.03 W
Deepavaal Brook ≃	276	40.53 N	74.16 W
Deep Bay ᑕ	184	56.25 N	103.00 W
Deep Brook ≃, Mass., U.S.	283	42.38 N	71.22 W
Deep Brook ≃, N.J., U.S.	276	40.58 N	74.09 W
Deep Creek ≃, U.S.	200	41.44 N	113.00 W
Deep Creek ≃, Calif., U.S.	228	34.20 N	117.14 W
Deep Creek ≃, Del., U.S.	208	38.38 N	75.37 W
Deep Creek ≃, Idaho, U.S.	202	42.15 N	116.40 W
Deep Creek ≃, Md., U.S.	284b	39.17 N	76.28 W
Deep Creek ≃, Oreg., U.S.	224	45.23 N	122.26 W
Deep Creek ≃, Tex., U.S.	196	32.31 N	100.55 W
Deep Creek ≃, Tex., U.S.	196	32.45 N	99.10 W
Deep Creek ≃, Utah, U.S.	200	40.10 N	113.50 W
Deep Creek Indian Reserve ⬥[4]	182	52.16 N	122.07 W
Deeping Fen ≣	42	52.44 N	0.13 W
Deep Red Creek ≃	196	34.17 N	98.39 W
Deep River, Ont., Can.	190	46.06 N	77.30 W
Deep River, Conn., U.S.	207	41.23 N	72.26 W
Deep River, Iowa, U.S.	190	41.35 N	92.22 W
Deep River, Wash., U.S.	224	46.21 N	123.41 W
Deep Run ≃, Md., U.S.	284b	39.25 N	76.40 W
Deep Run ≃, Md., U.S.	284b	39.13 N	76.42 W
Deep Run ≃, N.J., U.S.	276	40.26 N	74.22 W
Deep Run ≃, N.J., U.S.	285	39.44 N	74.41 W
Deepwater, Austl.	166	29.27 S	151.51 E
Deepwater, Mo., U.S.	194	38.16 N	93.47 W
Deep Water, N.J., U.S.	208	39.41 N	75.29 W
Deep Well	162	24.25 S	134.05 E
Deer ≃	212	43.56 N	75.34 W
Deer Creek, Ind., U.S.	216	40.37 N	86.23 W
Deer Creek, Minn., U.S.	198	46.24 N	95.19 W
Deer Creek ≃, U.S.	208	39.37 N	76.09 W
Deer Creek ≃, Calif., U.S.	226	35.56 N	119.28 W
Deer Creek ≃, Calif., U.S.	226	39.13 N	121.17 W
Deer Creek ≃, Calif., U.S.	226	38.22 N	121.21 W
Deer Creek ≃, Calif., U.S.	282	37.24 N	122.09 W
Deer Creek ≃, Ill., U.S.	278	41.32 N	87.37 W
Deer Creek ≃, Ind., U.S.	216	40.34 N	86.41 W
Deer Creek ≃, Kans., U.S.	198	39.40 N	99.06 W
Deer Creek ≃, Miss., U.S.	194	32.33 N	90.47 W
Deer Creek ≃, Nebr., U.S.	198	40.28 N	100.00 W
Deer Creek ≃, Ohio, U.S.	218	39.27 N	83.00 W
Deer Creek ≃, Okla., U.S.	196	35.38 N	98.28 W
Deer Creek ≃, Oreg., U.S.	224	45.08 N	123.15 W
Deer Creek ≃, Pa., U.S.	279b	40.32 N	79.51 W
Deer Creek ≃, Wash., U.S.	224	48.16 N	121.55 W
Deer Creek ≃, Wyo., U.S.	200	42.52 N	105.52 W
Deer Creek ≃, Wyo., U.S.	202	43.09 N	107.42 W
Deer Creek Indian Reservation ⬥[4]	190	47.50 N	93.25 W
Deer Creek Lake ⊜[1]	218	39.40 N	83.15 W
Deerfield, Ill., U.S.	216	42.10 N	87.51 W
Deerfield, Ind., U.S.	216	40.17 N	84.59 W
Deerfield, Kans., U.S.	198	37.59 N	101.08 W
Deerfield, Mass., U.S.	207	42.33 N	72.36 W
Deerfield, Mich., U.S.	216	41.53 N	83.47 W
Deerfield, Ohio, U.S.	214	41.02 N	81.03 W
Deerfield, Wis., U.S.	216	43.03 N	89.05 W
Deerfield ≃	207	42.35 N	72.35 W
Deerfield Beach	220	26.19 N	80.06 W
Deerfield Manor	278	42.10 N	87.55 W
Deerfield Street	208	39.31 N	75.14 W
Deer Grove ♠	278	42.09 N	88.04 W
Deer Harbor	224	48.37 N	123.00 W
Deering	180	66.05 N	162.43 W
Deering, Mount ∧[2]	162	24.53 S	129.04 E
Deer Island ≻[1]	283	42.21 N	70.58 W
Deer Island I, N.B., Can.	186	45.00 N	66.57 W
Deer Island I, Alaska, U.S.	180	54.53 N	162.25 W
Deer Island I, Oreg., U.S.	224	45.58 N	122.50 W
Deer Isle	188	44.13 N	68.41 W
Deer Lake, Newf., Can.	186	49.10 N	57.26 W
Deer Lake, Pa., U.S.	208	40.37 N	76.03 W
Deer Lake ⊜, Newf., Can.	186	49.07 N	57.35 W
Deer Lake ⊜, Ont., Can.	184	52.40 N	94.30 W
Deer Lakes Regional Park ♠	279b	40.38 N	79.49 W
Deerlijk	50	50.51 N	3.21 E
Deer Lodge	202	46.24 N	112.44 W
Deer Mountain ∧	188	45.01 N	70.56 W
Deer Park, Austl.	274b	37.47 S	144.47 E
Deer Park, Ala., U.S.	194	31.13 N	88.19 W
Deer Park, Calif., U.S.	226	38.32 N	122.28 W
Deer Park, Fla., U.S.	220	28.05 N	80.54 W
Deer Park, Ill., U.S.	278	42.09 N	88.04 W
Deer Park, N.Y., U.S.	210	40.46 N	73.20 W
Deer Park, Ohio, U.S.	218	39.13 N	84.24 W
Deer Park, Tex., U.S.	222	29.43 N	95.08 W
Deer Park, Wash., U.S.	202	47.57 N	117.28 W
Deer Park Airport ⊠	276	40.46 N	73.19 W
Deerpass Bay ᑕ	176	65.56 N	122.25 W
Deer Pond ⊜, Newf., Can.	186	48.30 N	54.45 W
Deer Pond ⊜, N.J., U.S.	276	40.57 N	74.24 W
Deer River, Minn., U.S.	190	47.20 N	93.48 W
Deer River, N.Y., U.S.	212	43.56 N	75.36 W
Deer Sound ⋓	46	58.58 N	2.48 W
Deersville	214	40.19 N	81.11 W
Deer Trail	198	39.37 N	104.02 W
Deerwood	190	46.28 N	93.54 W
Deesa	120	24.15 N	72.10 E
Dee Why	170	33.45 S	151.17 E
Dee Why Head ≻	274a	33.46 S	151.19 E
Dee Why Lagoon ᑕ	274a	33.45 S	151.18 E
Defengzhuang	98	41.02 N	113.16 E
Defereggen ∨	64	46.55 N	12.25 E
Defereggen Alpen ⩚	64	46.52 N	12.20 E
Deferiet	212	44.02 N	75.41 W
Defiance, Iowa, U.S.	198	41.49 N	95.20 W
Defiance, Ohio, U.S.	216	41.17 N	84.22 W
Defiance, Pa., U.S.	214	40.10 N	78.14 W
Defiance □[6]	216	41.19 N	84.30 W
Defiance, Mount ∧	224	45.38 N	121.43 W
Defiance Plateau ⩚[1]	200	36.00 N	109.15 W
Deflotte, Cap ≻	175f	21.10 S	167.25 E
De Forest	190	43.15 N	89.20 W
De Forest Lake ⊜	276	41.08 N	73.58 W
De Funiak Springs	194	30.43 N	86.07 W
Defurovy Lažany	60	49.27 N	13.40 E
Dega Ahmedo	144	8.00 N	43.00 E
Deganga	126	22.40 N	88.39 E
Deganwy	44	53.18 N	3.47 W
Deganya	132	32.42 N	35.35 E
Dega Werabe	144	8.08 N	45.22 E
Dege	102	31.50 N	98.40 E
Degeberga	26	55.50 N	14.05 E
Degeh-Bur	144	8.14 N	43.35 E
Dégelis (Saint-Rose-du-Dégelis)	186	47.33 N	68.39 W
Degema	150	4.45 N	6.47 E
Degerby	26	60.02 N	20.23 E
Degeres	85	43.14 N	75.49 E
Degerfors	40	59.14 N	14.26 E
Degerhamn	26	56.21 N	16.24 E
Degerndorf	64	47.44 N	12.06 E
Deggendorf	60	48.51 N	12.59 E
Deggingen	56	48.36 N	9.43 E
Degh ≃	123	31.25 N	74.04 E
Değirmendere	130	38.07 N	27.09 E
Degla Reidab	144	2.51 N	42.18 E
Deglunden ⊜	40	60.05 N	13.49 E
Dego	62	44.27 N	8.19 E
Degollado	234	20.28 N	102.09 W
Degoma	144	12.28 N	37.37 E
Degong	114	4.05 N	101.08 E
De Graafschap ⬥[1]	52	52.00 N	6.30 E
De Graff	216	40.19 N	83.55 W
De Gray Lake ⊜[1]	194	34.15 N	93.15 W
De Grey	162	20.10 S	119.12 E
De Grey ≃	162	20.12 S	119.11 E
Degt'ari	78	50.35 N	32.45 E
Degt'arka ≃	265a	59.57 N	30.52 E
Degt'arsk	86	56.42 N	60.06 E
Degtevo	80	49.11 N	40.39 E
Degunino ⬥[8]	265b	55.52 N	37.33 E
De Haan	50	51.16 N	3.02 E
Deharda	126	21.40 N	87.25 E
Deh Bālā	123	34.04 N	70.29 E
Deh Bārez	128	27.26 N	57.12 E
Deh Bīd	128	30.38 N	53.13 E
Dehdez	128	31.43 N	50.17 E
Dehej	120	21.42 N	72.35 E
Dehgolān	128	35.17 N	47.25 E
Dehibat	148	32.01 N	10.42 E
Dehiwala-Mount Lavinia	122	6.51 N	79.52 E
Deh Kord	128	33.49 N	48.53 E
Dehlorān	128	32.41 N	47.16 E
De Hoek	158	32.57 S	18.46 E
De Hoge Veluwe, Nationale Park ♠	52	52.02 N	5.55 E
Dehra Dūn	124	30.19 N	78.02 E
Dehri	124	24.52 N	84.11 E
Dehrn	56	50.25 N	8.05 E
Deh Salm	128	31.12 N	59.19 E
Dehu	122	18.35 N	73.51 W
Dehua	100	25.32 N	118.15 E
Dehuang	98	35.12 N	114.25 E
Dehui	89	44.34 N	125.43 E
Deidesheim	56	49.24 N	8.11 E
Deilbach ≃	263	51.23 N	7.05 E
Deilinghofen	56	51.22 N	7.47 E
Dein	164	5.30 S	146.10 E
Deining	60	49.13 N	11.32 E
Deinze	50	50.59 N	3.32 E
Deir el Asad	132	32.56 N	35.16 E
Deister ⩚	52	52.15 N	9.30 E
Deiva Marina	62	44.13 N	9.30 E
Dej	38	47.09 N	23.52 E
Deje	40	59.36 N	13.28 E
Dejima	94	36.05 N	140.10 E
Dejnau	128	39.15 N	63.11 E
De Jongs, Tanjong ≻	164	6.56 S	138.32 E
Deka ≃	154	18.03 S	26.44 E
De Kalb, Ill., U.S.	216	41.56 N	88.45 W
De Kalb, Miss., U.S.	194	32.46 N	88.39 W
De Kalb, Tex., U.S.	194	33.31 N	94.37 W
De Kalb □[6], Ill., U.S.	216	41.59 N	88.41 W
De Kalb □[6], Ind., U.S.	216	41.22 N	85.04 W
De Kalb Junction	212	44.30 N	75.16 W
Dekan, Hochland von → Deccan ⩚[1]	122	14.00 N	77.00 E
De-Kastri	89	51.28 N	140.47 E
Dekemhare	144	15.05 N	39.02 E
Dekese	152	3.27 S	21.24 E
Dekhgila Military Base ■	142	31.08 N	29.48 E
Dekina	150	7.39 N	7.02 E
Dekoa	152	6.19 N	19.04 E
De Koog	52	53.05 N	4.45 E
De Krim	52	52.38 N	6.38 E
De La Blache, Lac ⊜	186	50.05 N	69.29 W
Delabole	42	50.37 N	4.42 W
Delafield	216	43.04 N	88.24 W
Delai	102	30.54 N	98.56 E
Del Aire	280	33.55 N	118.21 W
Delamere, Austl.	168b	35.35 S	138.11 E
Delamere, Eng., U.K.	262	53.13 N	2.39 W
Delamere Forest ⬥[3]	262	53.14 N	2.38 W
Delami Mayal, Jabal ∧	140	11.38 N	30.23 E
Del Amo Center ⬥[9]	280	33.50 N	118.21 W
De Lancey, N.Y., U.S.	210	42.12 N	74.58 W
De Lancey, Pa., U.S.	214	40.59 N	78.58 W
Delanco	208	40.03 N	74.57 W
De Land	220	29.02 N	81.18 W
Delanggu	115a	7.37 S	110.41 E
Delano, Calif., U.S.	226	35.41 N	119.15 W
Delano, Minn., U.S.	190	45.02 N	93.47 W
Delano, Pa., U.S.	210	40.50 N	76.04 W
Delano Peak ∧	200	38.22 N	112.23 W
Delanson	210	42.45 N	74.11 W
Delaport Point ≻	240b	25.05 N	77.27 W
Delapu	120	31.35 N	91.35 E
Delārām	128	32.11 N	63.25 E
Delareyville	158	26.44 S	25.29 E
Delarof Islands II	181a	51.30 N	178.45 W
Delaronde Lake ⊜	184	54.05 N	107.05 W
Del'atiči	76	53.47 N	25.59 E
Del'atin	78	48.32 N	24.37 E
Delatite ≃	169	37.10 S	146.00 E
Delavan, Ill., U.S.	194	40.22 N	89.33 W
Delavan, Wis., U.S.	216	42.38 N	88.39 W
Delavan Lake	216	42.38 N	88.35 W
Delavan Lake ⊜	216	42.37 N	88.38 W
Delaware, Ont., Can.	214	42.55 N	81.25 W
Delaware, N.J., U.S.	210	40.53 N	75.04 W
Delaware, Ohio, U.S.	214	40.18 N	83.04 W
Delaware, Okla., U.S.	196	36.47 N	95.38 W
Delaware □[3]	208	39.10 N	75.30 W
Delaware □[6], Ind., U.S.	216	40.18 N	85.23 W
Delaware □[6], N.Y., U.S.	210	42.17 N	74.55 W
Delaware □[6], Ohio, U.S.	214	40.18 N	83.04 W
Delaware □[6], Pa., U.S.	208	39.55 N	75.23 W
Delaware □[3]	178	39.10 N	75.30 W
Delaware ≃, U.S.	188	39.20 N	75.25 W
Delaware ≃, Kans., U.S.	198	39.03 N	95.24 W
Delaware, East Branch ≃	210	41.55 N	75.17 W
Delaware, University of ⊌[2]	285	39.41 N	75.45 W
Delaware, West Branch ≃	210	41.56 N	75.17 W
Delaware and Raritan Canal ≊	208	40.29 N	74.26 W
Delaware Aqueduct ≊[1]	210	42.05 N	74.54 W
Delaware Bay ᑕ	208	39.05 N	75.15 W
Delaware City	208	39.34 N	75.36 W
Delaware Lake ⊜[1]	214	40.20 N	83.00 W
Delaware Memorial Bridge ⬥[5]	208	39.41 N	75.31 W
Delaware Mountains ⩚	196	31.35 N	104.40 W
Delaware Park	210	40.43 N	75.11 W
Delaware Park ♠	284a	42.56 N	78.52 W
Delaware Park Race Track ♠	285	39.42 N	75.40 W
Delaware Seashore State Park ♠	208	38.38 N	75.04 W
Delaware State Park ♠	214	40.23 N	83.04 W
Delaware Water Gap	210	40.59 N	75.09 W
Delaware Water Gap National Recreation Area ♠	210	41.08 N	74.55 W
Delbrück	52	51.46 N	8.33 E
Delburne	182	52.12 N	113.14 W
Del Campillo	252	34.22 S	64.29 W
Del Carril	258	35.31 S	59.30 W
Del City	196	35.27 N	97.27 W
Del Dios	228	33.04 N	117.08 W
Delegate	166	37.03 S	148.58 E
Delémont	58	47.22 N	7.21 E
De Leon	196	32.07 N	98.32 W
De Leon Springs	192	29.07 N	81.21 W
de Lesquin, Aéroport ⊠	50	50.35 N	3.07 E
Delet ⋓	26	60.15 N	20.35 E
Delevan	210	42.29 N	78.29 W
Delfim Moreira	256	22.30 S	45.17 W
Delfinópolis	255	20.20 S	46.51 W
Delft	52	52.00 N	4.21 E
Delft Island I	122	9.30 N	79.42 E
Delfzijl	52	53.19 N	6.46 E
Delgada, Punta ≻	254	42.46 S	63.38 W
Delgado, Cabo ≻	154	10.40 S	40.35 E
Del Gallego	116	13.56 N	122.36 E
Delger ≃	88	49.17 N	100.40 E
Delgerchaan Uul ∧	88	49.58 N	106.23 E
Delgerchangaj	102	45.14 N	104.50 E
Delgerchet	102	45.49 N	110.28 E
Delgercogt	102	46.08 N	106.29 E
Delgerech	102	45.49 N	111.12 E
Del Haven	208	39.03 N	74.56 W
Delhi, Bhārat	124		
	272a	28.40 N	77.13 E
Delhi, Ont., Can.	212	42.51 N	80.30 W
Delhi, Calif., U.S.	226	37.26 N	120.46 W
Delhi, Iowa, U.S.	190	42.26 N	91.20 W
Delhi, La., U.S.	194	32.27 N	91.30 W
Delhi, N.Y., U.S.	210	42.17 N	74.55 W
Delhi □[3]	123	28.37 N	77.10 E
Delhi, University of ⊌[2]	272a	28.42 N	77.13 E
Delhi Cantonment	272a	28.36 N	77.08 E
Delhi Hills	218	39.05 N	84.07 W
Delhi Railroad Station ⬥[5]	272a	28.40 N	77.13 E
Delhi Tail Distributary ≊	272a	28.41 N	77.10 E
Deli, Pulau I	115a	7.00 S	105.32 E
Delia, Alta., Can.	182	51.38 N	112.23 W

Symbol	English	Deutsch	Español	Français	Português
≃	River	Fluss	Río	Rivière	Rio
≊	Canal	Kanal	Canal	Canal	Canal
↳	Waterfall, Rapids	Wasserfall, Stromschnellen	Cascada, Rápidos	Chute d'eau, Rapides	Cascata, Rápidos
⋓	Strait	Meeresstrasse	Estrecho	Détroit	Estreito
ᑕ	Bay, Gulf	Bucht, Golf	Bahía, Golfo	Baie, Golfe	Baía, Golfo
⊜	Lake, Lakes	See, Seen	Lago, Lagos	Lac, Lacs	Lago, Lagos
≣	Swamp	Sumpf	Pantano	Marais	Pântano
⍓	Ice Features, Glacier	Eis- und Gletscherformen	Accidentes Glaciales	Formes glaciaires	Acidentes Glaciares
⍑	Other Hydrographic Features	Andere Hydrographische Objekte	Otros Elementos Hidrográficos	Autres données hydrographiques	Outros Elementos Hidrográficos
⤈	Submarine Features	Untermeerische Objekte	Accidentes Submarinos	Formes de relief sous-marin	Acidentes Submarinos
□	Political Unit	Politische Einheit	Unidad Politica	Entité politique	Unidade Política
⊌	Cultural Institution	Kulturelle Institution	Institución Cultural	Institution culturelle	Instituição Cultural
⊥	Historical Site	Historische Stätte	Sitio Histórico	Site historique	Sítio Histórico
♠	Recreational Site	Erholungs- und Ferienort	Sitio de Recreo	Centre de loisirs	Sítio de Lazer
⊠	Airport	Flughafen	Aeropuerto	Aéroport	Aeroporto
■	Military Installation	Militäranlage	Instalación Militar	Installation militaire	Instalação Militar
⬥	Miscellaneous	Verschiedenes	Misceláneo	Divers	Miscelânea

Delia, It. 70 37.21 N 13.55 E
Delia ≃ 70 37.19 N 13.58 E
Delianuova 68 38.14 N 15.55 E
Deliblato 38 44.50 N 21.03 E
Delice 130 39.58 N 34.02 E
Delice ≃ 130 40.28 N 34.10 E
Delices 240d 15.17 N 61.16 W
Deliceto 68 41.13 N 15.23 E
Delicias, Cuba 240p 21.11 N 76.34 W
Delicias, Méx. 232 28.13 N 105.28 W
De Lier 52 51.57 N 4.15 E
Delight 194 34.02 N 93.30 W
Delightful 214 41.18 N 80.57 W
Deliilyas 130 39.20 N 36.48 E
Delījān 128 33.59 N 50.40 E
Delıklıkaya ≻ 130 41.12 N 30.20 E
Deliktaş 130 39.21 N 37.13 E
Délimbé 146 9.53 N 22.37 E
Delingha 102 37.14 N 97.11 E
Dēliņkalns ∧ 76 57.30 N 27.25 E
Déli Pályaudvar ⊸[5] 264c 47.30 N 19.01 E
Delisle 184 51.55 N 107.08 W
Delisle ≃ 206 45.23 N 74.10 W
Delitua 114 3.30 N 98.41 E
Delitzsch 54 51.31 N 12.20 E
Delkern 228 35.21 N 119.01 W
Dell 46 58.30 N 6.20 W
Dellach 64 46.40 N 13.05 E
Dell City 200 31.56 N 105.12 W
Delle 58 47.30 N 7.00 E
Dellenbaugh, Mount ∧ 200 36.07 N 113.32 W
Dellensjöarna ⊜ 26 61.54 N 16.41 E
Delligsen 52 51.57 N 9.48 E
Dello 64 45.25 N 10.04 E
Dell Rapids 198 43.50 N 96.43 W
Dellroy 214 40.33 N 81.12 W
Dellwig 263 51.29 N 7.41 E
Dellwig ⊸[8] 263 51.29 N 6.56 E
Dellwood 219 38.44 N 90.16 W
Dellwood Highlands 278 41.34 N 88.03 W
Dellys 148 36.55 N 3.55 E
Del Mar, Calif., U.S. 228 32.58 N 117.16 W
Delmar, Del., U.S. 208 38.27 N 75.34 W
Delmar, Iowa, U.S. 190 42.00 N 90.37 W
Delmar, Md., U.S. 208 38.27 N 75.34 W
Delmar, N.Y., U.S. 210 42.37 N 73.50 W
Del Mar Heights 226 35.26 N 120.52 W
Del Mar Woods 278 42.12 N 87.51 W
Delmas, Sask., Can. 184 52.55 N 108.36 W
Delmas, S. Afr. 158 26.08 S 28.43 E
Delme 56 48.53 N 6.24 E
Delme ≃ 52 53.05 N 8.40 E
Delmenhorst 52 53.03 N 8.38 E
Delmiro Gouveia 250 9.23 S 37.59 W
Delmont, N.J., U.S. 208 39.13 N 74.57 W
Delmont, Pa., U.S. 214 40.25 N 79.34 W
Delmont, S. Dak., U.S. 198 43.16 N 98.10 W
Del Monte Heights 226 36.36 N 121.50 W
Del Monte Park 226 36.36 N 121.56 W
Delnice 36 45.24 N 14.48 E
Del Norte 200 37.41 N 106.21 W
De-Longa, Ostrova II 74 76.30 N 153.00 E
De Long Mountains ⩘ 180 68.20 N 162.00 W
De-Long-Strasse → Longa, Proliv ⩊ 74 70.20 N 178.00 E
Deloraine, Austl. 166 41.31 S 146.39 E
Deloraine, Man., Can. 184 49.12 N 100.29 W
Delorme, Lac ⊜ 176 54.31 N 69.52 W
Deloro 212 44.31 N 77.37 W
Delos → Dhílos ⊥ 38 37.26 N 25.16 E
Delph 262 53.34 N 2.01 W
Delphi 216 40.36 N 86.41 W
Delphi → Dhelfoí ⊥ 38 38.30 N 22.29 E
Delphi Falls 210 42.53 N 75.55 W
Delphos, Kans., U.S. 198 39.16 N 97.46 W
Delphos, Ohio, U.S. 216 40.50 N 84.20 W
Delph Reservoir ⊜[1] 262 53.38 N 2.27 W
Delportshoop 158 28.22 S 24.20 E
Del Puerto Creek ≃ 226 37.32 N 121.07 W
Delran 285 40.02 N 74.58 W
Delrath 263 51.08 N 6.47 E
Delray ⊸[8] 281 42.18 N 83.08 W
Delray Beach 220 26.28 N 80.04 W
Del Rey 226 36.40 N 119.36 W
Del Rey Oaks 226 36.36 N 121.50 W
Del Rio 196 29.22 N 100.54 W
Del Rosa 228 34.08 N 117.15 W
Delsbo 26 61.48 N 16.35 E
Delson 206 45.22 N 73.33 W
Delstern ⊸[8] 263 51.20 N 7.31 E
Delta, Ont., Can. 212 44.37 N 76.08 W
Delta, Méx. 200 32.22 N 115.12 W
Delta, Colo., U.S. 200 38.44 N 108.04 W
Delta, Mo., U.S. 194 37.12 N 89.44 W
Delta, Ohio, U.S. 216 41.34 N 84.00 W
Delta, Pa., U.S. 208 39.44 N 76.19 W
Delta, Utah, U.S. 200 39.21 N 112.35 W
Delta ≃ 180 64.09 N 146.18 W
Delta Amacuro □[8] 246 8.30 N 61.30 W
Delta Barrage ⊸[6] 142 30.11 N 31.07 E
Delta Beach 184 50.11 N 98.19 W
Delta City 194 33.04 N 90.48 W
Delta Downs 166 17.00 S 141.18 E
Delta Junction 180 64.02 N 145.41 W
Delta Mendota Canal ☰ 226 37.49 N 121.34 W
Delta Peak ∧ 180 56.39 N 129.34 W
Delta Reservoir ⊜[1] 210 43.17 N 75.26 W
Deltaville 208 37.33 N 76.20 W
Delton 216 42.30 N 85.24 W
Deltona 220 28.54 N 81.16 W
Delungra 166 29.39 S 150.50 E
Del'un-Uranskij Chrebet ⩘ 88 56.30 N 114.00 E
Delüün 86 47.42 N 90.59 E
De Luz Creek ≃ 228 33.22 N 117.19 W
Del Valle 222 30.12 N 97.40 W
Delvin 48 53.36 N 7.05 W
Delvinë 38 39.57 N 20.06 E
Del Viso 258 34.27 S 58.48 W
Delyn □[8] 262 53.16 N 3.11 W
Demak 115a 6.53 S 110.38 E
Demaki 80 58.26 N 54.41 E
Demarcation Point ≻ 180 69.40 N 141.15 W
Demarest 276 40.57 N 73.58 W
Demarest Brook ≃ 276 40.57 N 73.58 W
Demavend, Mount → Damāvand, Qolleh-ye ∧ 128 35.56 N 52.08 E
Demba 152 5.30 S 22.16 E
Demba Chio 152 9.41 S 13.41 E
Dembecha 144 10.35 N 37.30 E
Dembi 144 8.05 N 36.27 E
Dembia, Centraf. 154 5.07 N 24.25 E
Dembia, Zaïre 154 3.31 N 25.50 E
Dembidolo 144 8.30 N 34.48 E
Dembo 152 3.56 S 12.35 E
Dême ≃ 50 47.43 N 0.29 E
Demerara ≃ 246 6.48 N 58.10 W
Demerthin 54 52.58 N 12.17 E
Demidov 76 55.16 N 31.31 E
Demidovka 78 50.25 N 25.20 E
Demidovo 76 59.17 N 38.17 E
Deming, N. Mex., U.S. 200 32.16 N 107.45 W
Deming, Wash., U.S. 224 48.49 N 122.13 W
Demini ≃ 246 0.46 S 62.56 W
Demirci 130 39.03 N 28.40 E
Demircidere 130 37.33 N 27.50 E
Demir Kapija ∨ 38 41.24 N 22.15 E
Demirköy 130 41.49 N 27.45 E
Demirtaş 130 40.16 N 29.06 E
Demitz-Thumitz 54 51.09 N 14.14 E
Demjanka ≃ 86 59.34 N 69.20 E
Demjanovka 86 54.04 N 65.22 E
Demjanovo 24 60.22 N 47.03 E
Demjansk 76 57.38 N 32.28 E
Demjanskoje 86 59.36 N 69.18 E
Demjas 80 51.13 N 49.08 E
Demmeltrath ⊸[8] 263 51.11 N 7.03 E
Demmin 54 53.54 N 13.02 E
Demmitt 182 55.26 N 119.54 W
Demnat 148 31.44 N 6.59 W
Democracy, Monument of ⊥ 269a 13.45 N 100.30 E
Democrat Point ≻ 276 40.37 N 73.18 W
Demoiselles, Grotte des •[5] 62 43.55 N 3.45 E
Demone, Val ⊸[1] 70 37.58 N 14.35 E
Demonte 62 44.19 N 7.17 E
De Montigny, Lac ⊜ 190 48.08 N 77.54 W
Demopolis 194 32.31 N 87.50 W
Demorest 192 34.31 N 83.32 W
De Mossville 218 38.48 N 84.25 W
Demotte 216 41.12 N 87.12 W
Dempo, Gunung ∧ 112 4.02 S 103.09 E
Dempster, Point ≻ 162 33.39 S 123.52 E
Demsa 146 9.32 N 13.14 E
Demta 164 2.20 S 140.08 E
Demurino 78 48.10 N 36.29 E
De Naauwte 158 30.08 S 21.42 E
Denain 50 50.20 N 3.23 E
Denair 226 37.32 N 120.47 W
Denali 180 63.11 N 147.28 W
Denan 144 6.30 N 43.30 E
Denare Beach 184 54.40 N 102.05 W
Denau 85 38.16 N 67.54 E
Denbigh, Ont., Can. 212 45.08 N 77.16 W
Denbigh, Wales, U.K. 44 53.11 N 3.25 W
Denbigh, Cape ≻ 180 64.23 N 161.31 W
Den Burg 52 53.03 N 4.48 E
Denby Dale 44 53.35 N 1.38 W
Den Chai 110 17.59 N 100.04 E
Dendang 112 3.05 S 107.54 E
Dendé 152 3.46 S 11.09 E
Dender (Dendre) ≃ 50 51.02 N 4.06 E
Denderleeuw 50 50.53 N 4.04 E
Dendermonde 50 51.02 N 4.07 E
Dendron 208 37.03 N 76.56 W
Dendy Park ♦ 274b 37.56 S 145.00 E
Deneba 144 9.50 N 39.09 E
Denekamp 52 52.23 N 7.00 E
Denenchōfu ⊸[8] 268 35.35 N 139.41 E
Deneysville 158 26.53 S 28.06 E
Deneżnikovo, S.S.S.R. 82 55.26 N 38.07 E
Deneżnikovo, S.S.S.R. 83 49.02 N 38.57 E
Dengcheng 100 33.41 N 114.27 E
Deng Deng 152 5.12 N 13.31 E
Denge 154 3.34 N 28.14 E
Denge Marsh ☷ 42 50.57 N 0.55 E
Dengfeng 100 34.29 N 113.04 E
Denggongchang 107 30.24 N 103.49 E
Dengjingguan 107 29.10 N 104.56 E
Dengke 102 32.31 N 97.59 E
Dengkou 102 40.20 N 106.59 E
Denglongshu 98 41.20 N 115.15 E
Dengmingsi 98 37.53 N 116.42 E
Dengshahe 98 39.13 N 122.04 E
Dengshipuzi 104 42.17 N 123.08 E
Dengta 100 24.01 N 114.49 E
Denguiro 152 5.38 N 23.02 E
Dengxian 102 32.42 N 112.01 E
Dengyoufang 98 41.34 N 114.32 E
Den Haag → 's-Gravenhage 52 52.06 N 4.18 E
Denham, Austl. 162 25.55 S 113.32 E
Denham, Eng., U.K. 260 51.34 N 0.30 W
Denham, Ind., U.S. 216 41.09 N 86.43 W
Denham, Mount ∧ 241q 18.13 N 77.32 W
Denham Aerodrome ⊠ 260 51.36 N 0.31 W
Denham Island I 166 16.43 S 139.09 E
Denham Place ʋ 260 51.34 N 0.30 W
Denham Range ⩘ 166 21.55 S 147.46 E
Denham Sound ⩊ 162 25.40 S 113.15 E
Denham Springs 194 30.29 N 90.57 W
Den Helder 52 52.54 N 4.45 E
Denholme 262 53.48 N 1.54 W
Denia 34 38.51 N 0.07 E
Denial Bay 162 32.06 S 133.32 E
Dénié 150 11.14 N 7.29 W
Deniliquin 166 35.32 S 144.58 E
Deniskoviči, S.S.S.R. 76 52.19 N 31.43 E
Deniskoviči, S.S.S.R. 76 52.44 N 26.41 E
Denison, Iowa, U.S. 198 42.01 N 95.21 W
Denison, Tex., U.S. 196 33.45 N 96.33 W
Denison, Mount ∧ 180 58.25 N 154.27 W
Denison Dam ⊸[6] 196 33.36 N 96.18 W
Denisovka, S.S.S.R. 24 66.14 N 55.20 E
Denisovka, S.S.S.R. 86 52.28 N 61.46 E
Denisovo 82 54.28 N 37.51 E
Denisy 261 48.33 N 1.56 E
Denizli 130 37.46 N 29.06 E
Denizli □[4] 130 37.40 N 29.15 E
Denkanikota 122 12.32 N 77.48 E
Denkendorf, B.R.D. 56 48.41 N 9.19 E
Denkendorf, B.R.D. 60 48.56 N 11.27 E
Denkingen 58 47.53 N 9.19 E
Denklingen, B.R.D. 56 50.55 N 7.39 E
Denklingen, B.R.D. 58 47.55 N 10.51 E
Den'kovo 82 56.01 N 36.21 E
Denman Glacier ⍓ 9 66.45 S 99.25 E
Denmark, Austl. 162 34.57 S 117.21 E
Denmark, S.C., U.S. 192 33.19 N 81.09 W
Denmark, Wis., U.S. 190 44.21 N 87.50 W
Denmark □[1] 22
26 56.00 N 10.00 E
Denmark, Lake ⊜ 276 40.58 N 74.31 W
Denmark Bay C 176 70.33 N 103.20 E
Denmark Strait ⩊ 10 67.00 N 25.00 W
Dennemont 261 49.01 N 1.42 E
Dennery 241f 13.55 N 60.54 W
Dennis 207 41.44 N 70.12 W
Dennis Head ≻ 46 59.23 N 2.23 W
Dennison 214 40.24 N 81.19 W
Dennis Port 207 41.39 N 70.08 W
Denniston 172 41.44 S 171.48 E
Denniston Creek ≃ 282 37.30 N 122.28 W
Dennisville 208 39.12 N 74.49 W
Denny 46 56.02 N 3.55 W
Den Oever 52 52.56 N 5.02 E
Denouval 261 48.58 N 2.03 E
Denpasar 115b 8.39 S 115.13 E
Denshaw 262 53.35 N 2.02 W
Dent Ditch ☰ 279a 41.18 N 82.08 W
Denton, Eng., U.K. 262 53.27 N 2.07 W
Denton, Md., U.S. 208 38.53 N 75.50 W
Denton, Mich., U.S. 281 42.16 N 83.31 W
Denton, Mont., U.S. 202 47.19 N 109.57 W
Denton, Tex., U.S. 222 33.13 N 97.08 W
Denton □[6] 222 33.07 N 97.10 W
Denton Creek ≃ 196 32.58 N 96.57 W
Dentonia Park ♦ 275b 43.42 N 79.17 W
D'Entrecasteaux, Point ≻ 162 34.50 S 116.00 E
D'Entrecasteaux Islands II 164 9.30 S 150.40 E
Dents du Midi ⩘ 58 46.10 N 6.56 E
Denver, Colo., U.S. 200 39.43 N 105.01 W
Denver, Ind., U.S. 216 40.52 N 86.05 W
Denver, Iowa, U.S. 190 42.40 N 92.20 W
Denver, Pa., U.S. 208 40.14 N 76.08 W
Denver City 196 32.58 N 102.50 W
Denville 210 40.53 N 74.29 W
Denzlingen 58 48.04 N 7.52 E
Deoband 124 29.42 N 77.41 E
Deocha 126 24.03 N 87.35 E
Deogarh, Bhārat 120 25.32 N 73.54 E
Deogarh, Bhārat 122 21.32 N 84.44 E
Deogarh, Bhārat 124 24.33 N 78.15 E
Deogarh ∧ 124 23.32 N 82.16 E
Deogarh Hills ⩘[2] 124 23.35 N 82.30 E
Deoghar 124 24.29 N 86.42 E
Deolāli 122 19.57 N 73.50 E
Deoli, Bhārat 120 25.45 N 75.23 E
Deoli, Bhārat 126 22.03 N 86.49 E
Deoli ⊸[8] 272a 28.30 N 77.14 E
Deopāra 126 22.55 N 90.15 E
Deori 124 23.08 N 78.41 E
Deoria 124 26.31 N 83.47 E
Deoria □[5] 124 26.50 N 83.50 E
Deori Khās 124 23.24 N 79.01 E
Deosai Mountains ⩘ 123 35.20 N 75.12 E
Deosil 124 23.42 N 82.15 E
Dep ≃ 89 52.54 N 127.45 E
Depāl 126 21.44 N 87.33 E
De Panne 50 51.06 N 2.35 E
Depāra 272b 22.53 N 88.34 E
Departure Bay 224 49.12 N 123.58 W
DePaul University ʋ[2] 278 41.56 N 87.39 W
Depauville 212 44.08 N 76.04 W
Depauw 218 38.20 N 86.13 W
De Peel ☷ 52 51.25 N 6.00 E
De Pere 190 44.27 N 88.04 W
Depew, N.Y., U.S. 210 42.54 N 78.42 W
Depew, Okla., U.S. 196 35.48 N 96.31 W
Deping 98 37.28 N 116.57 E
De Pinte 50 51.00 N 3.39 E
Depoe Bay 202 44.49 N 124.04 W
Depok 115a 6.24 S 106.50 E
Deport 196 33.32 N 95.19 W
Deposit 210 42.04 N 75.25 W
Depósito 246 3.12 N 60.35 W
Deptford ⊸[8] 260 51.28 N 0.02 W
Deptford Terrace 285 39.48 N 75.09 W
Depuch Island I 162 20.38 S 117.43 E
Depue 190 41.19 N 89.19 W
Deputy 218 38.48 N 85.39 W
Deqin 102 28.38 N 98.52 E
Deqing, Zhg. 102 23.09 N 111.45 E
Deqing, Zhg. 106 30.33 N 120.05 E
De Queen 194 34.02 N 94.21 W
De Quincy 194 30.27 N 93.26 W
Dera, Lak (Lach Dera) ≃ 144 0.15 N 42.17 E
Dera Bugti 120 29.02 N 69.09 E
Derac 238 19.39 N 71.49 W
Dera Ghāzi Khān 123 30.03 N 70.38 E
Dera Gopipur 123 31.54 N 76.13 E
Dera Ismāīl Khān 123 31.50 N 70.54 E
Dera Nānak 123 32.02 N 75.01 E
Dera Nawāb 123 29.06 N 71.06 E
Dera-patak ≃ 264c 47.39 N 19.05 E
Derāwar Fort 123 28.46 N 71.20 E
Deražn'a 78 49.16 N 27.26 E
Derbent 84 42.03 N 48.18 E
Derbesiye 130 37.06 N 40.40 E
Derbeškinskij 80 55.52 N 53.30 E
Derbetovka 80 45.48 N 43.05 E
Der Bodden ⩊ 54 54.16 N 13.12 E
Derby, Austl. 162 17.18 S 123.38 E
Derby, Austl. 166 41.09 S 147.47 E
Derby, S. Afr. 158 25.55 S 27.02 E
Derby, Eng., U.K. 42 52.55 N 1.29 W
Derby, Conn., U.S. 207 41.19 N 73.05 W
Derby, Kans., U.S. 198 37.33 N 97.16 W
Derby, Maine, U.S. 188 45.14 N 68.59 W
Derby, N.Y., U.S. 210 42.41 N 78.58 W
Derby, Ohio, U.S. 218 39.46 N 83.12 W
Derby, Vt., U.S. 206 44.57 N 72.08 W
Derby Acres 226 35.15 N 119.35 W
Derby Line 188 45.00 N 72.06 W
Derbyshire □[6] 262 53.25 N 1.55 W
Derdepoort 156 24.42 S 26.20 E
Derecho ≃ 246 2.38 S 69.54 W
Derečin 76 53.15 N 24.55 E
Derecske 30 47.21 N 21.34 E
Dereishaklı 130 41.03 N 39.08 E
Dereköy, Tür. 130 39.16 N 27.19 E
Dereköy, Tür. 130 40.08 N 37.47 E
Dereköy, Tür. 130 41.56 N 27.21 E
Dereli 130 40.45 N 38.27 E
Derenburg 54 51.52 N 10.54 E
Derendorf ⊸[8] 263 51.15 N 6.48 E
Derenwu 105 39.40 N 116.46 E
Dereseki 267b 41.08 N 29.08 E
Derev'anka 24 61.34 N 34.27 E
Derewa ≃ 164 2.48 S 136.10 E
Derg, Lough ⊜, Eire 48 53.00 N 8.20 W
Derg, Lough ⊜, Eire 48 54.36 N 7.53 W
Dergači, S.S.S.R. 78 50.07 N 36.07 E
Dergači, S.S.S.R. 80 51.14 N 48.46 E
Dergaon 120 26.42 N 93.58 E
Der Grabow C 54 54.23 N 12.50 E
De Ridder 194 30.51 N 93.17 W
De Rijp 52 52.34 N 4.50 E
Derik 130 37.22 N 40.17 E
Derinkuyu 130 38.23 N 34.45 E
Der Kanal → English Channel ⩊ 28 50.20 N 1.00 W
Derkul 80 51.16 N 51.18 E
Derkul ≃ 83 48.35 N 39.41 E
Dermbach 56 50.43 N 10.06 E
Dermott 194 33.32 N 91.26 W
Dermulo 64 46.20 N 11.04 E
Derne 263 51.35 N 7.41 E
Derne ⊸[8] 263 51.34 N 7.31 E
Dernieres, Isles II 194 29.02 N 90.47 W
Dernoviči 78 51.36 N 29.43 E
Deroche 224 49.11 N 122.04 W
Dero Eri 144 9.02 N 46.48 E
Derong 102 28.47 N 99.14 E
Derrame 196 26.19 N 104.23 W
Derravaragh, Lough ⊜ 48 53.40 N 7.24 W
Derre 154 16.56 S 36.11 E
Derrick City 214 41.58 N 78.34 W
Derrinallum 169 37.57 S 143.13 E
Derry → Londonderry, N. Ire., U.K. 48 55.00 N 7.19 W
Derry, N.H., U.S. 188 42.53 N 71.19 W
Derry, Pa., U.S. 214 40.20 N 79.18 W
Derrybrien 48 53.04 N 8.36 W
Derrykeevan 48 55.08 N 6.29 W
Derryveagh Mountains ⩘ 48 55.00 N 8.05 W
Derry West 275b 43.39 N 79.42 W
Der Sārāi ⊸[8] 272a 28.33 N 77.11 E
Dersau 54 54.07 N 10.20 E
Derschlag 56 51.00 N 7.37 E
Dersingham 42 52.51 N 0.30 E
Derudeb 140 17.32 N 36.06 E
De Rust 158 33.30 S 22.32 E
Deruta 66 42.59 N 12.25 E
De Ruyter 210 42.46 N 75.53 W
De Ruyter Reservoir ⊜[1] 210 42.49 N 75.53 W
Der'uzino 82 56.18 N 38.16 E
Derval 32 47.40 N 1.40 W
Derventa 38 44.58 N 17.55 E
Derwent 182 53.39 N 110.58 W
Derwent ≃, Austl. 166 43.03 S 147.22 E
Derwent ≃, Eng., U.K. 42 52.50 N 1.15 W
Derwent ≃, Eng., U.K. 44 53.45 N 0.57 W
Derwent ≃, Eng., U.K. 44 54.57 N 1.41 W
Derwent ≃, Eng., U.K. 44 54.38 N 3.34 W
Derwent Bridge 166 42.08 S 146.13 E
Derwent Reservoir ⊜[1] 44 54.50 N 2.00 W
Derwent Water ⊜ 44 54.34 N 3.08 W
Deržavino 80 53.13 N 52.22 E
Deržavinskij 86 51.03 N 66.19 E
Desaguadero ≃, Arg. 252 34.13 S 66.47 W
Desaguadero ≃, Bol. 248 18.24 S 67.05 W
Deşt 130 39.10 N 39.49 E
Des Allemands 194 29.50 N 90.28 W
Désappointement, Îles du II 14 14.10 S 141.20 W
Des Arc 194 34.58 N 91.30 W
Desborough 42 52.27 N 0.49 W
Descabezado Grande, Volcán ∧[1] 252 35.36 S 70.45 W
Descanso, Bra. 252 26.50 S 53.35 W
Descanso, Calif., U.S. 204 32.51 N 116.37 W
Descanso, Punta ≻ 204 32.16 N 117.03 W
Descanso Gardens ♦ 280 34.12 N 118.13 W
Descartes 32 46.58 N 0.42 E
Deschaillons 206 46.32 N 72.07 W
Deschambault 206 46.39 N 71.56 W
Deschambault Lake 184 54.55 N 103.22 W
Deschambault Lake ⊜ 184 54.40 N 103.35 W
Descharme Lake ⊜ 184 57.05 N 109.13 W
Deschênes 188 45.23 N 75.48 W
Deschenes, Lake ⊜ 212 45.22 N 75.51 W
Deschutes ≃, Oreg., U.S. 202 45.38 N 120.54 W
Deschutes ≃, Wash., U.S. 224 47.02 N 122.54 W
Deschutes-Umatilla Plateau ⩘[1] 202 45.00 N 119.40 W
Descoberto 256 21.27 S 42.58 W
Descoberto, Serra do ∧ 256 21.24 S 42.57 W
Dese 144 11.05 N 39.41 E
Deseado ≃ 254 47.45 S 65.54 W
Deseado, Cabo ≻ 254 52.44 S 74.44 W
Desembarco de los 33 Orientales, Monumento ⊥ 258 33.48 S 58.25 W
Desengaño, Punta ≻ 254 49.15 S 67.37 W
Desenzano del Garda 64 45.28 N 10.32 E
Deseret Peak ∧ 200 40.28 N 112.38 W
Deseronto 212 44.12 N 77.03 W
Désert ≃ 190 46.23 N 75.58 W
Désert, Lac ⊜ 190 46.35 N 76.19 W
Desertas, Ilhas I 148 32.30 N 16.30 W
Desert Creek ≃ 226 38.48 N 119.19 W
Desert Hot Springs 204 33.58 N 116.30 W
Desert Lake ⊜, Ont., Can. 212 44.32 N 76.35 W
Desert Lake ⊜, Nev., U.S. 204 37.58 N 115.15 W
Desert Mountains ⩘ 226 39.16 N 119.00 W
Desert Peak ∧ 200 41.11 N 113.22 W
Desert Valley ∨ 204 41.15 N 118.20 W
Desert View Highlands 228 34.37 N 118.13 W
Desfogue del Lago, Canal de ☰ 286a 19.26 N 99.03 W
Desford 42 52.39 N 1.17 W
Deshaies 241o 16.18 N 61.48 W
Desheng 102 24.45 N 108.28 E
Deshengbo 102 26.58 N 103.59 E
Deshengchang 107 29.06 N 105.25 E
Deshengtai 104 42.14 N 123.45 E
Deshengyingzi 104 41.44 N 123.14 E
Deshler, Nebr., U.S. 198 40.08 N 97.44 W
Deshler, Ohio, U.S. 216 41.12 N 83.54 W
Deshnoke 120 27.48 N 73.21 E
Deshon Manor 214 40.52 N 79.57 W
Deshu 128 30.26 N 63.19 E
Deshun 106 31.58 N 120.29 E
Desiderio Tello 252 31.13 S 66.19 W
Desio 62 45.37 N 9.13 E
Des Lacs ≃ 198 48.17 N 101.25 W
Deslinde, Arroyo ≃ 258 33.44 S 58.52 W
Desmarais 182 55.56 N 113.49 W
De Smet 198 44.23 N 97.33 W
De Smet, Lake ⊜[1] 202 44.29 N 106.45 W
Des Moines, Iowa, U.S. 190 41.35 N 93.37 W
Des Moines, N. Mex., U.S. 196 36.46 N 103.50 W
Des Moines, Wash., U.S. 224 47.24 N 122.19 W
Des Moines ≃ 190 40.22 N 91.26 W
Des Moines, East Fork ≃ 198 42.41 N 94.12 W
Desmoronado, Cerro ∧ 234 20.21 N 104.59 W
Desna 78 50.56 N 30.46 E
Desna ≃, S.S.S.R. 78 50.33 N 30.32 E
Desna ≃, S.S.S.R. 82 55.26 N 37.30 E
Desolación, Isla I 254 53.00 S 74.10 W
Désolation, Cap de la → Disappointment, Cape ≻ 244 54.53 S 36.07 W
Desolation Point ≻ 116 10.28 N 125.39 E
Desor, Mount ∧[2] 190 47.58 N 89.01 W
De Soto, Ill., U.S. 194 37.49 N 89.14 W
De Soto, Ind., U.S. 216 40.15 N 85.17 W
De Soto, Mo., U.S. 194 38.08 N 90.33 W
De Soto, Tex., U.S. 222 32.35 N 96.51 W
De Soto □[6] 220 27.11 N 81.48 W
De Soto City 220 27.27 N 81.24 W
De Soto National Memorial ⊥ 220 27.31 N 82.40 W
De Soto State Park ♦ 194 34.28 N 85.36 W
Despatch 158 33.46 S 25.30 E
Despeñaperros, Desfiladero de)(34 38.24 N 3.30 W
Des Plaines 216 42.02 N 87.54 W
Des Plaines ≃ 216 41.24 N 88.16 W
Despotovac 38 44.05 N 21.33 E
Despujols 116 12.31 N 122.01 E
Desruisseaux 241f 13.47 N 60.56 W
Dessau 54 51.50 N 12.14 E
Dessel 56 51.14 N 5.07 E
Destacado Island I 116 12.16 N 124.06 E
De Steeg 52 52.02 N 6.04 E
Destek 130 40.51 N 36.12 E
Destelbergen 50 51.03 N 3.48 E
Destêrro 250 7.17 S 37.06 W
Destin 194 30.24 N 86.30 W
D'Estrées, Passe du ⩊ 175f 19.38 S 163.23 E
Destruction, Mount ∧[2] 162 24.35 S 127.59 E
Destruction Bay 180 61.15 N 138.48 W
Destruction Island I 224 47.40 N 124.30 W
Desulo 71 40.01 N 9.14 E
Desvres 50 50.40 N 1.50 E
Deta 38 45.24 N 21.13 E
Detčino 82 54.49 N 36.19 E
Dethlingen 52 52.57 N 10.07 E
Detling 260 51.18 N 0.34 E
Detmold 52 51.56 N 8.52 E
Detmold □[6] 52 51.48 N 8.00 E
Detour, Point ≻ 190 45.36 N 86.37 W
Detrital Wash ∨ 200 36.02 N 114.28 W
Detroit, Ill., U.S. 219 39.37 N 90.40 W
Detroit, Mich., U.S. 216
281 42.20 N 83.03 W
Detroit, Tex., U.S. 196 33.40 N 95.16 W
Detroit ≃ 214 42.06 N 83.08 W
Detroit, University of ʋ[2] 281 42.25 N 83.08 W
Detroit Beach 216 41.55 N 83.20 W
Detroit City Airport ⊠ 281 42.25 N 83.01 W
Detroit Institute of Arts ʋ 281 42.22 N 83.04 W
Detroit Lake ⊜[1] 202 44.42 N 122.10 W
Detroit Lakes 198 46.49 N 95.51 W
Detroit Metropolitan-Wayne County Airport ⊠ 281 42.13 N 83.22 W
Detroit Race Course ♦ 281 42.23 N 83.19 W
Detroit-Windsor Tunnel ⊸[5] 281 42.20 N 83.02 W

ENGLISH Name	Page	Lat.°′	Long.°′	DEUTSCH Name	Seite	Breite°′	Länge°′ E=Ost

Detroit Zoological Park ♦ 281 42.29 N 83.09 W
Detskosel'skij 265a 59.44 N 30.28 E
Dett 154 18.38 S 26.50 E
Dettelbach 56 49.48 N 10.09 E
Dettifoss ↳ 24a 65.50 N 16.20 W
Dettingen an der Erms 56 48.32 N 9.20 E
Dettwiller 56 48.45 N 7.28 E
Det Udom 110 14.54 N 105.05 E
Detva 30 48.31 N 19.28 E
Deuben 54 51.06 N 12.04 E
Deuels Corners 284a 42.45 N 78.45 W
Deuil-la-Barre 261 48.59 N 2.20 E
Deūlgaon Rāja 122 20.01 N 76.02 E
Deulpur 272b 22.36 N 88.10 E
Deulti 126 22.26 N 87.56 E
Deurne, Bel. 50 51.13 N 4.28 E
Deurne, Ned. 52 51.28 N 5.47 E
Deusen ⊸[8] 263 51.33 N 7.26 E
Deutsche Bucht C 30 54.30 N 7.30 E
Deutsche Demokratische Republik → German Democratic Republic □[1] 30 52.00 N 12.30 E
Deutsch Eylau → Iława 30 53.37 N 19.33 E
Deutschfeistritz 61 47.11 N 15.20 E
Deutsch Krone → Wałcz 30 53.17 N 16.28 E
Deutschlandsberg 61 46.49 N 15.13 E
Deutsch-Luxemburger-Naturpark ♦ 56 49.55 N 6.15 E
Deutsch-Neudorf 54 50.38 N 13.27 E
Deutsch Wagram 264b 48.18 N 16.34 E
Deutsch Wusterhausen 264a 52.18 N 13.35 E
Deutzen 54 51.06 N 12.26 E
Deux-Montagnes 206 45.32 N 73.53 W
Deux-Montagnes □[6] 206 45.35 N 74.05 W
Deux-Montagnes, Lac des ⊜ 275a 45.28 N 73.59 W
Deux-Sèvres □[5] 32 46.30 N 0.20 W
Deva 38 45.53 N 22.55 E
Devakottai 122 9.57 N 78.49 E
De Valls Bluff 194 34.47 N 91.28 W
Devaprayāg 124 30.09 N 78.37 E
Dev'atern'a 80 56.12 N 53.24 E
Dev'atiny 24 60.56 N 36.46 E
Devault 285 40.05 N 75.32 W
Dévaványa 30 47.02 N 20.58 E
Devecikonağı 130 39.55 N 28.34 E
Devecser 30 47.06 N 17.26 E
Deve Dağı ∧ 130 40.34 N 41.21 E
Develi 130 38.23 N 35.30 E
Deventer 52 52.15 N 6.10 E
Deveron ≃ 46 57.40 N 2.31 W
Devers 222 30.02 N 94.36 W
Devers Canal, West Branch ☰ 222 29.57 N 94.46 W
Deversoir Military Base ■ 142 30.25 N 32.20 E
Devès, Monts du ⩘ 32 45.00 N 3.45 E
Devět Skal ∧ 30 49.40 N 16.02 E
Devgad Bāria 120 22.42 N 73.54 E
De View, Bayou ≃ 194 34.48 N 91.18 W
Devīkot 120 26.42 N 71.12 E
Devil Lake ⊜ 212 44.35 N 76.27 W
Deville 56 49.53 N 4.42 E
Déville-lès-Rouen 50 49.28 N 1.02 E
Devil Peak ∧ 226 37.32 N 119.44 W
Devil River Peak ∧ 172 40.58 S 172.39 E
Devils ≃ 196 29.39 N 100.58 W
Devils Brook ≃ 276 40.20 N 74.37 W
Devils Canyon ∨ 280 34.16 N 117.58 W
Devil's Den State Park ♦ 194 35.46 N 94.16 W
Devils Hole Rapids ↳ 284a 43.08 N 79.03 W
Devil's Hopyard State Park ♦ 207 41.28 N 72.22 W
Devil's Island → Diable, Île du I 250 5.17 N 52.35 W
Devils Lake 198 48.07 N 98.59 W
Devils Lake ⊜, Mich., U.S. 216 41.58 N 84.17 W
Devils Lake ⊜, N. Dak., U.S. 198 48.01 N 98.52 W
Devil's Lake State Park ♦ 190 43.24 N 89.44 W
Devils Paw ∧ 180 58.44 N 133.50 W
Devils Postpile National Monument ♦ 226 37.37 N 119.05 W
Devils's Bridge 42 52.23 N 3.51 W
Devils Tower National Monument ♦ 198 44.31 N 104.57 W
Devil's Water ≃ 44 54.58 N 2.02 W
Devin 38 41.45 N 24.24 E
Devine, B.C., Can. 182 50.32 N 122.30 W
Devine, Tex., U.S. 196 29.08 N 98.54 W
Devizes 42 51.22 N 1.59 W
Devladovo 78 48.07 N 33.45 E
De Voe Lake ⊜ 276 40.23 N 74.23 W
Devoll ≃ 38 40.49 N 19.51 E
Dévoluy ⩘ 62 44.39 N 5.53 E
Devon, Alta., Can. 182 53.22 N 113.44 W
Devon, S. Afr. 158 26.21 S 28.48 E
Devon, Pa., U.S. 285 40.03 N 75.25 W
Devon □[6] 42 50.45 N 3.50 W
Devon ≃, Eng., U.K. 42 53.04 N 0.43 W
Devon ≃, Scot., U.K. 46 56.07 N 3.51 W
Devon Island I 16 75.00 N 87.00 W
Devonport, Austl. 166 41.11 S 146.21 E
Devonport, N.Z. 172 36.49 S 174.48 E
Devonport, Eng., U.K. 42 50.22 N 4.10 W
Devonshire Plaza ⊸[9] 281 42.17 N 83.00 W
Devore 228 34.13 N 117.25 W
Devoto 252 31.24 S 62.19 W
Devrek 130 41.13 N 31.57 E
Devrekâni 130 41.36 N 33.51 E
Devres ≃ 130 41.06 N 34.25 E
Devure ≃ 154 19.50 S 31.45 E
Dewa, Ujung ≻ 114 2.55 N 95.48 E
Dewakang-lompo, Pulau I 112 5.24 S 118.25 E
Dewa-kyūryō ⩘[2] 92 39.05 N 140.10 E
Dewart 210 41.07 N 76.53 W
Dewart Lake ⊜ 216 41.22 N 85.47 W
Dewās 120 22.58 N 76.04 E
Dewas □[5] 124 22.30 N 76.30 E
Dewdney 182 49.10 N 122.12 W
Dewetsdorp 158 29.33 S 26.34 E
Dewey, P.R. 240m 18.18 N 65.18 W
Dewey, Ill., U.S. 216 40.19 N 88.17 W
Dewey, Okla., U.S. 196 36.48 N 95.56 W
Dewey, Wash., U.S. 224 48.25 N 122.37 W
Dewey Beach 208 38.42 N 75.05 W
Deweyville 194 30.18 N 93.45 W
De Witt, Ark., U.S. 194 34.18 N 91.20 W
Dewitt, Ill., U.S. 219 40.11 N 88.47 W
De Witt, Iowa, U.S. 190 41.49 N 90.33 W
De Witt, Mich., U.S. 216 42.51 N 84.34 W
De Witt, Nebr., U.S. 198 40.24 N 96.55 W
De Witt, N.Y., U.S. 210 43.02 N 76.04 W
De Witt □[6], Ill., U.S. 216 40.12 N 88.55 W
De Witt □[6], Tex., U.S. 222 29.07 N 97.20 W
Dewittville 214 42.14 N 79.27 W
Dewsbury 44 53.42 N 1.37 W
Dexing 100 28.54 N 117.36 E
Dexingjie 98 39.54 N 122.50 E
Dexter, Maine, U.S. 188 45.01 N 69.18 W
Dexter, Mich., U.S. 216 42.20 N 83.53 W
Dexter, Mo., U.S. 194 36.48 N 89.57 W
Dexter, N. Mex., U.S. 196 33.12 N 104.22 W
Dexter, N.Y., U.S. 212 44.01 N 76.03 W
Dexterity Fiord C[2] 176 71.11 N 73.03 W
Deyang 102 31.14 N 104.22 E
Dey-Dey, Lake ⊜ 162 29.12 S 131.04 E
Deyhūk 128 33.17 N 57.30 E
Deyyer 128 27.50 N 51.55 E
Dez ≃ 128 31.39 N 48.52 E
Dezadeash Lake ⊜ 180 60.28 N 136.58 W
Dezfūl 128 32.23 N 48.24 E
Dez Gerd 128 30.45 N 51.57 E
Dezhou 98 37.27 N 116.18 E
Dezh Shāhpūr 128 35.31 N 46.10 E
Dežneva, Mys ≻ 180 66.06 N 169.45 W
Dezong 120 32.09 N 90.20 E
Dezzo di Scalve 64 45.59 N 10.05 E
Dhabān Singh 123 31.45 N 73.35 E
Dhāding 124 27.52 N 84.55 E
Dhādkā 126 22.47 N 86.30 E
Dháfna ∧ 267c 38.07 N 23.38 E
Dháfni 38 37.48 N 22.01 E
Dhafníon, Moní ʋ[1] 267c 38.01 N 23.38 E
Dhahab 140 28.29 N 34.32 E
Dhahran → Az-Ẓahrān 128 26.18 N 50.08 E
Dhāka 124 26.41 N 85.10 E
Dhākauli 124 24.45 N 77.51 E
Dhakuria Lake ⊜ 272b 22.31 N 88.22 E
Dhaleswari ≃ 126 23.32 N 90.34 E
Dháli 130 35.01 N 33.25 E
Dhamār 144 14.46 N 44.23 E
Dhampur 124 29.19 N 78.31 E
Dhāmrai 126 23.55 N 90.13 E
Dhamtari 122 20.41 N 81.34 E
Dhāmura 126 22.53 N 90.12 E
Dhanaula 123 30.17 N 75.35 E
Dhanaura 124 28.58 N 78.15 E
Dhānbād 126 23.48 N 86.27 E
Dhānbād □[5] 124 23.47 N 86.26 E
Dhandhuka 120 22.22 N 71.59 E
Dhanera 126 23.25 N 86.39 E
Dhaneswargāti 126 23.25 N 89.20 E
Dhangarhi 124 28.41 N 80.36 E
Dhaniakhāli 126 22.58 N 88.06 E
D'hanis 196 29.20 N 99.17 W
Dhankuta 124 26.59 N 87.20 E
Dhansar 272c 19.07 N 73.05 E
Dhanushkodi 122 9.11 N 79.24 E
Dhānyahānā 272b 22.48 N 88.11 E
Dhār 120 22.36 N 75.18 E
Dharampur 122 20.32 N 73.11 E
Dharān Bāzār 124 26.49 N 87.17 E
Dharangaon 120 21.01 N 75.16 E
Dhārāpuram 122 10.44 N 77.31 E
Dhāri 120 21.20 N 71.01 E
Dhārīwāl 123 31.57 N 75.19 E
Dharmābād 122 18.54 N 77.51 E
Dharmapuri 122 12.08 N 78.10 E
Dharmavaram 122 14.26 N 77.43 E
Dharmjaygarh 124 22.28 N 83.13 E
Dharmkot 123 30.57 N 75.14 E
Dharmsāla 123 32.13 N 76.19 E
Dhārni 120 21.33 N 76.53 E
Dhārwār 122 15.28 N 75.01 E
Dhasān ≃ 124 25.48 N 79.24 E
Dhātrigrām 126 23.15 N 88.20 E
Dhaulāgiri ∧ 124 28.42 N 83.30 E
Dhebar Lake ⊜ 120 24.16 N 74.00 E
Dhelfoí ⊥ 38 38.30 N 22.29 E
Dhenkānāl 120 20.40 N 85.36 E
Dherínia 130 35.03 N 33.57 E
Dhërmiu ʋ[1] 38 40.08 N 19.42 E
Dherue, Loch an ⊜ 46 58.25 N 4.27 W
Dheskáti 38 39.55 N 21.49 E
Dheune ≃ 58 46.54 N 5.00 E
Dhiavolítsion 38 37.18 N 21.58 E
Dhībān 132 31.30 N 35.47 E
Dhidhimótikhon 38 41.21 N 26.30 E
Dhíkti ⩘ 38 35.08 N 25.22 E
Dhílos ⊥ 38 37.26 N 25.16 E
Dhimitsána 38 37.37 N 22.03 E
Dhiónisos 267c 38.06 N 23.53 E
Dhirāsrām 126 23.57 N 90.25 E
Dhirwah, Wādī adh- ∨ 132 31.18 N 36.56 E
Dhodhekánisos (Dodecanese) II 38 36.30 N 27.00 E
Dhodhóni ⊥ 38 39.34 N 20.47 E
Dhokra 272b 22.40 N 88.34 E
Dholka 120 22.43 N 72.28 E
Dholpur 124 26.42 N 77.54 E
Dhomhnull, Sgurr ∧ 46 56.45 N 5.27 W
Dhone 122 15.25 N 77.53 E
Dhopākholai 126 23.08 N 89.10 E
Dhorāji 120 21.44 N 70.27 E
Dhosha 126 22.15 N 88.33 E
Dhowa 126 24.03 N 86.54 E
Dhoxáton 38 41.05 N 24.14 E
Dhrāngadhra 120 22.59 N 71.28 E
Dhrapetsóna 267c 37.57 N 23.37 E
Dhrol 120 22.34 N 70.25 E
Dhron ≃ 56 49.52 N 6.54 E
Dhubāb 144 12.56 N 43.25 E
Dhubri 124 26.02 N 89.58 E
Dhudiāl 123 33.04 N 72.58 E
Dhulāgarh 272b 22.35 N 88.11 E
Dhulāsār 126 21.52 N 90.14 E
Dhule 120 20.54 N 74.47 E
Dhulia → Dhule 120 20.54 N 74.47 E
Dhuliān 124 24.41 N 87.58 E
Dhulikhel 124 27.37 N 85.33 E
Dhūlsīrās ⊸[8] 272a 28.33 N 77.02 E
Dhünn 56 51.06 N 7.16 E
Dhünn-Stausee ⊜[1] 263 51.05 N 7.16 E
Dhupgāri 124 26.36 N 89.01 E
Dhūri 124 30.22 N 75.52 E
Dhutumkhar ≃ 272c 18.54 N 73.00 E
Diabaig 46 57.34 N 5.40 W
Diabakania 150 10.38 N 10.58 W
Diable, Île du (Devil's Island) I 250 5.17 N 52.35 W
Diable, Lac du ⊜ 206 46.31 N 74.20 W
Diable, Morne au ∧ 240d 15.37 N 61.27 W
Diable, Pointe du ≻ 240e 14.47 N 60.54 W
Diable, Rivière du ≃ 206 46.03 N 74.38 W
Diablo, Calif., U.S. 226 37.50 N 121.58 W
Diablo, Wash., U.S. 224 48.43 N 121.09 W
Diablo, Canyon ∨ 200 35.18 N 110.59 W
Diablo, Isla del → Diable, Île du I 250 5.17 N 52.35 W
Diablo, Mount ∧ 226 37.53 N 121.55 W
Diablo, Sierra del ⩘ 196 27.20 N 104.05 W
Diablo Lake ⊜[1] 224 48.43 N 121.08 W
Diablo Plateau ⩘[1] 200 31.30 N 105.30 W
Diablo Range ⩘ 226 37.00 N 121.20 W
Diablotin, Morne ∧ 240d 15.30 N 61.24 W
Diabo 150 7.47 N 5.11 W
Diaca 154 11.30 S 39.59 E
Diadema 256 23.42 S 46.37 W
Diadema □[7] 287b 23.42 S 46.36 W
Diadema Argentina 254 45.46 S 67.40 W
Diafarabé 150 14.09 N 5.01 W
Diagonal 198 40.48 N 94.20 W
Diaka ≃[1] 150 15.13 N 4.14 W
Dialakoto 150 13.19 N 13.18 W
Dialassagou 150 13.45 N 3.37 W
Diamant, Pointe du ≻ 240e 14.27 N 61.03 W
Diamante, Arg. 252 32.04 S 60.39 W
Diamante, It. 68 39.41 N 15.49 E
Diamante ≃ 252 34.31 S 66.56 W
Diamante, Punta del ≻ 234 16.47 N 99.52 W
Diamante de Ubá 256 21.12 S 42.55 W
Diamantina 255 18.15 S 43.36 W
Diamantina ≃ 166 26.45 S 139.10 E
Diamantina Lakes 166 23.46 S 141.09 E
Diamantina Trough ⊹[1] 14 37.00 S 105.00 E
Diamantino 248 14.25 S 56.27 W

Symbols in the index entries represent the broad categories identified in the key at the right. Symbols with superior numbers (⩘²) identify subcategories (see complete key on page I · 30).

Kartensymbole in dem Registerverzeichnis stellen die rechts in Schlüssel erklärten Kategorien dar. Symbole mit hochgestellten Ziffern (⩘²) bezeichnen Unterabteilungen einer Kategorie (vgl. vollständiger Schlüssel auf Seite I · 30).

Los símbolos incluídos en el texto del índice representan las grandes categorias identificadas con la clave a la derecha. Los símbolos con numeros en su parte superior (⩘²) identifican las subcategorias (véase la clave completa en la página I · 30).

Les symboles de l'index représentent les catégories indiquées dans la légende à droite. Les symboles suivis d'un indice (⩘²) représentent des sous-catégories (voir légende complète à la page I · 30).

Os símbolos incluídos no texto do índice representam as grandes categorias identificadas com a chave à direita. Os símbolos com números em sua parte superior (⩘²) identificam as subcategorias (veja-se a chave completa à página I · 30).

	English	Deutsch	Español	Français	Português
∧	Mountain	Berg	Montaña	Montagne	Montanha
⩘	Mountains	Berge	Montañas	Montagnes	Montanhas
)(	Pass	Pass	Paso	Col	Passo
∨	Valley, Canyon	Tal, Cañon	Valle, Cañón	Vallée, Canyon	Vale, Canhão
≚	Plain	Ebene	Llano	Plaine	Planície
≻	Cape	Kap	Cabo	Cap	Cabo
I	Island	Insel	Isla	Île	Ilha
II	Islands	Inseln	Islas	Îles	Ilhas
♦	Other Topographic Features	Andere Topographische Objekte	Otros Elementos Topográficos	Autres données topographiques	Outros Elementos Topográficos

ESPAÑOL — Nombre / Página / Lat.°′ / Long.°′ W=Oeste
FRANÇAIS — Nom / Page / Lat.°′ / Long.°′ W=Ouest
PORTUGUÊS — Nome / Página / Lat.°′ / Long.°′ W=Oeste

Diamond, Ill., U.S. 216 41.17 N 88.15 W
Diamond, Mo., U.S. 194 37.00 N 94.19 W
Diamond, Ohio, U.S. 214 41.06 N 81.01 W
Diamond Bar 228 33.58 N 117.51 W
Diamond Brook ≃ 276 40.56 N 74.08 W
Diamond Creek 274b 37.41 S 145.09 E
Diamond Creek ≃ 169 37.44 S 145.09 E
Diamond Harbour 126 22.12 N 88.12 E
Diamond Head ⁶ 229c 21.16 N 157.49 W
Diamond Hill 207 41.59 N 71.25 W
Diamond Hill Reservoir @¹ 283 42.00 N 71.24 W
Diamond Hill State Park ♦ 283 42.00 N 71.26 W
Diamond Islets II 166 17.25 S 150.58 E
Diamond Lake 216 42.15 N 88.00 W
Diamond Lake @, Ont., Can. 212 45.04 N 78.13 W
Diamond Lake @, Ill., U.S. 278 42.15 N 88.00 W
Diamond Lake @, Mich., U.S. 216 41.54 N 85.59 W
Diamond Lake @, Oreg., U.S. 202 43.10 N 122.09 W
Diamond Peak ∧, Idaho, U.S. 202 44.09 N 113.05 W
Diamond Peak ∧, Oreg., U.S. 202 43.33 N 122.09 W
Diamond Peak ∧, Wash., U.S. 202 46.07 N 117.32 W
Diamond Springs 226 38.42 N 120.49 W
Diamondville 200 41.47 N 110.32 W
Diamonguel 150 15.06 N 12.55 W
Diana 222 32.43 N 94.45 W
Diana, Baie C 176 60.50 N 69.50 W
Dianalund 41 55.32 N 11.30 E
Dianbai (Shuidong) 102 21.33 N 111.16 E
Dianchi @ 102 24.50 N 102.42 E
Diancun 105 39.55 N 116.14 E
Dianfangba 102 32.54 N 103.35 E
Diangounté Kamara 150 14.33 N 9.31 W
Dianhu 100 33.58 N 119.38 E
Dianji 98 36.32 N 120.27 E
Dianjiang 102 30.21 N 107.23 E
Diano, Vallo di ∨ 68 40.21 N 15.36 E
Diano Marina 62 43.54 N 8.05 E
Dianópolis 250 11.38 S 46.50 W
Dianqianhe 100 30.44 N 116.02 E
Dianra 150 8.45 N 6.14 W
Dianshang 106 31.10 N 118.51 E
Dianshanhu @ 106 31.08 N 120.55 E
Diantou 100 27.18 N 120.11 E
Dianxia 100 27.58 N 115.40 E
Dianzi 104 41.37 N 122.05 E
Diaobingshan 104 42.28 N 123.33 E
Diaoebao 105 40.43 N 115.49 E
Diaohetou 105 39.17 N 116.41 E
Diaojiapu 100 32.22 N 119.54 E
Diaoshuilouzi 104 40.59 N 122.22 E
Diaotai 100 29.40 N 119.39 E
Diaouala 150 10.07 N 5.28 W
Diaowo 105 39.30 N 116.04 E
Diapaga 150 12.04 N 1.47 E
Diapangou 150 12.07 N 0.11 E
Dias 256 22.28 S 45.34 W
Diascund Creek Reservoir @¹ 208 37.27 N 76.54 W
Diavolo, Mount ∧ 110 12.42 N 92.55 E
Dibai 124 28.13 N 78.15 E
Dibāng ≃ 120 27.50 N 95.32 E
Dibay
→ Dubayy 128 25.18 N 55.18 E
Dibaya 152 6.30 S 22.57 E
Dibbersen 52 53.22 N 9.52 E
Dibbīn 132 32.26 N 36.34 E
Dibble Iceberg Tongue ⊠ 9 65.40 S 135.10 E
Dibeng 158 27.35 S 22.54 E
D'Iberville 194 30.26 N 88.54 W
Dibete 156 23.45 S 26.26 E
Dibi 144 4.12 N 41.58 E
Dibo 144 6.31 N 41.52 E
Diboll 222 31.11 N 94.47 W
Dibrugarh 120 27.29 N 94.54 E
Dibs 140 12.34 N 24.14 E
Dibs, Bi'r ⁴ 140 22.12 N 29.32 E
Dichāon Kalān ⁸ 272a 28.39 N 76.59 E
Dickelsbach ≃ 263 51.24 N 6.45 E
Dickens 196 33.37 N 100.50 W
Dickerson 208 39.13 N 77.25 W
Dickey, Lake @ 224 48.06 N 124.31 W
Dickey, West Fork ≃ 224 47.55 N 124.42 W
Dickey Lake @ 212 44.47 N 77.44 W
Dickinson, N. Dak., U.S. 198 46.53 N 102.47 W
Dickinson, Pa., U.S. 208 40.07 N 77.20 W
Dickinson, Tex., U.S. 222 29.28 N 95.03 W
Dickinson Bayou ≃ 222 29.28 N 94.58 W
Dickinson Island I 281 42.37 N 82.38 W
Dicks 158 27.43 S 30.10 E
Dickson 194 36.05 N 87.23 W
Dickson City 210 41.27 N 75.37 W
Dicle
→ Tigris ≃ 128 31.00 N 47.25 E
Dicomano 66 43.53 N 11.31 E
Diculom 116 7.54 N 122.14 E
Dicun 100 33.46 N 117.32 E
Didam 52 51.56 N 6.08 E
Didao 89 45.22 N 130.51 E
Didbiran 89 51.58 N 139.20 E
Didcot 42 51.37 N 1.15 W
Didesa ≃ 144 9.56 N 35.45 E
Didiéni 150 13.53 N 8.06 W
Didimbo 152 17.30 S 21.45 E
Didinga Hills ⁂ 154 4.20 N 33.35 E
Didsbury 182 51.40 N 114.08 W
Didsbury ⁸ 262 53.25 N 2.14 W
Didwāna 120 27.24 N 74.34 E
Didy 157b 18.07 S 48.32 E
Didyma ⊥ 130 37.25 N 27.15 E
Die 62 44.45 N 5.22 E
Die Aue ¹ 263 51.40 N 6.35 E
Die Berg ∧ 156 25.12 S 30.09 E
Die Boss 158 31.59 S 19.44 E
Diébougou 150 10.58 N 3.15 W
Dieburg 56 49.54 N 8.50 E
Dieciocho de Julio 252 33.41 S 53.33 W
Dieciocho de Marzo 232 25.38 N 97.50 W
Diecke 150 7.21 N 8.58 W
Diedenhofen
→ Thionville 56 49.22 N 6.10 E
Diedersdorf 264a 52.20 N 13.21 E
Die Erpe ≃ 264a 52.27 N 13.38 E
Diefenbaker, Lake @¹ 184 51.00 N 106.55 W
Diego de Almagro, Isla I 254 51.25 S 75.10 W
Diego de Ocampo, Pico ∧ 238 19.35 N 70.45 W
Diego Garcia I 12 7.20 S 72.25 E
Diego Gaynor 258 34.17 S 59.14 W
Diego Ramirez, Islas II 244 56.30 S 68.44 W
Diégo-Suarez 157b 12.16 S 49.17 E
Diégo-Suarez □⁴ 157b 13.30 S 49.10 E
Die Haard ¹ 263 51.41 N 7.15 E
Diekirch 56 49.53 N 6.10 E
Dieksee @ 54 54.10 N 10.30 E
Dieleemu 86 46.22 N 88.43 E
Dielingen 52 52.26 N 8.20 E
Dielsdorf 58 47.29 N 8.27 E
Diéma 150 14.32 N 9.12 W
Diemansputs 158 29.54 S 21.33 E
Diembéring 150 12.28 N 16.47 W
Diemel ≃ 52 51.39 N 9.27 E
Diemelsee, Naturpark ♦ 56 51.20 N 8.45 E
Diemel-Talsperre ⁶ 56 51.22 N 8.43 E
Diemen 52 52.20 N 4.58 E
Diemuchuoke 120 32.42 N 79.29 E
Dien-bien-phu 110 21.23 N 103.01 E
Diepenau 52 52.25 N 8.44 E
Diepenheim 52 52.12 N 6.33 E
Diepensee 264a 52.22 N 13.31 E
Diepenveen 52 52.18 N 6.08 E
Diepholz 52 52.35 N 8.21 E
Diepoldsau 58 47.23 N 9.38 E
Dieppe, N.B., Can. 186 46.06 N 64.45 W
Dieppe, Fr. 50 49.56 N 1.05 E
Dierbao 98 40.20 N 114.32 E
Dierdorf 56 50.33 N 7.39 E
Dieren 52 52.03 N 6.06 E
Dierhagen 54 54.18 N 12.21 E
Dieringhausen 56 50.59 N 7.31 E
Dierks 194 34.07 N 94.01 W
Diersbach 60 48.25 N 13.34 E
Diersfordt 263 51.42 N 6.33 E
Diesdorf 54 52.45 N 10.52 E
Dieskau 54 51.26 N 12.02 E
Diessem ⁸ 263 51.20 N 6.35 E
Diessen 64 47.56 N 11.06 E
Diessenhofen 58 47.41 N 8.45 E
Diest 56 50.59 N 5.03 E
Dietenheim 58 48.12 N 10.04 E
Dietersburg 60 48.30 N 12.55 E
Dietersdorf 56 50.13 N 10.49 E
Dietfurt 56 48.57 N 10.56 E
Dietfurt an der Altmühl 60 49.02 N 11.35 E
Dietikon 58 47.24 N 8.24 E
Dietkorom 146 13.41 N 12.03 E
Dietmannsried 58 47.49 N 10.17 E
Dietrich 202 42.55 N 114.16 W
Dietzenbach 56 50.01 N 8.47 E
Dieulefit 62 44.31 N 5.04 E
Dieulouard 56 48.51 N 6.04 E
Dieu-sur-Meuse 56 49.04 N 5.25 E
Dieuze 56 48.49 N 6.43 E
Dieveniškės 76 54.12 N 25.37 E
Dievenow
→ Dziwnów 30 54.03 N 14.45 E
Diever 52 52.52 N 6.19 E
Die Ville ⁂² 56 50.40 N 6.55 E
Diez 56 50.22 N 8.01 E
Diez de Octubre 232 24.44 N 104.39 W
Dif 144 1.00 N 41.00 E
Difang 98 35.23 N 117.52 E
Diffa 146 13.19 N 12.37 E
Diffa □⁵ 146 16.00 N 13.30 E
Differdange 56 49.32 N 5.52 E
Difficult Run ≃ 284c 38.58 N 77.14 W
Diffun 116 16.34 N 121.33 E
Difuri I 122 5.24 N 73.38 E
Dīg 118 27.28 N 77.20 E
Digambarpur 126 21.57 N 88.22 E
Digba 154 4.24 N 25.47 E
Digboi 120 27.23 N 95.38 E
Digby Neck ⁻¹ 186 44.30 N 66.10 W
Dige 98 34.22 N 114.28 E
Digerberget ∧² 40 60.35 N 13.25 E
Digges Islands II 176 62.35 N 77.50 W
Diggle 262 53.34 N 1.59 W
Dīghalia 126 23.07 N 89.39 E
Dighipāra 126 21.58 N 88.17 E
Dighode 272c 18.54 N 73.02 E
Dighra 272b 22.47 N 88.32 E
Dighton, Kans., U.S. 198 38.29 N 100.28 W
Dighton, Mass., U.S. 207 41.49 N 71.07 W
Di Giorgio 228 35.15 N 118.51 W
Dīglūr 122 18.33 N 77.36 E
Digmoor 262 53.32 N 2.45 W
Dīgnagar 126 23.27 N 87.41 E
Dignano 64 46.05 N 12.56 E
Digne 62 44.06 N 6.14 E
Digoin 32 46.29 N 3.59 E
Digomi 84 41.47 N 44.44 E
Digong 104 42.11 N 122.03 E
Digor 84 40.23 N 43.24 E
Digora 84 43.10 N 44.09 E
Digos 116 6.45 N 125.20 E
Digpa 272b 22.50 N 88.20 E
Digras 122 20.07 N 77.43 E
Digri 120 25.10 N 69.07 E
Digul ≃ 164 7.07 S 138.42 E
Dih 130 37.46 N 42.11 E
Dihaer 86 42.35 N 89.49 E
Dih Dahot ≃ 144 10.40 N 49.25 E
Dihun 144 7.18 N 42.42 E
Diirmentobe 86 45.44 N 63.37 E
Dijag 24 65.48 N 57.39 E
Dijlah
→ Tigris ≃ 128 31.00 N 47.25 E
Dijlah, Wādī ∨ 142 29.58 N 31.18 E
Dijle (Dyle) ≃ 56 50.53 N 4.42 E
Dijle Kanaal ≅ 56 50.53 N 4.42 E
Dijohan Point ⁻ 116 16.19 N 122.14 E
Dijon 58 47.19 N 5.01 E
Dik 146 9.58 N 17.31 E
Dikaja 76 59.15 N 39.30 E
Dikala 154 4.41 N 31.23 E
Dikan'ka 78 49.49 N 34.32 E
Dikbıyık 130 41.13 N 36.38 E
Dike 190 42.28 N 92.38 W
Dikhil 144 11.06 N 42.22 E
Dikili 130 39.04 N 26.53 E
Dikirnis 142 31.05 N 31.35 E
Dikli 76 57.35 N 25.06 E
Diklosmta, Gora ∧ 84 42.29 N 45.47 E
Dikmen 130 39.53 N 32.50 E
Dikodougou 150 9.04 N 5.46 W
Dikomu Di Kai ∧ 156 24.58 S 24.31 E
Diksmuide (Dixmude) 50 51.02 N 2.52 E
Dikson 74 73.30 N 80.35 E
Dikumbiya 144 14.42 N 37.24 E
Dikwa 146 12.02 N 13.56 E
Dila 144 6.21 N 38.17 E
Dil' al-'Ifrīt ∧² 142 28.23 N 31.09 E
Dilbeek 50 50.51 N 4.16 E
Dile Point ⁻ 116 17.34 N 120.20 E
Dilgarpur 272b 22.51 N 88.10 E
Dili 112 8.33 S 125.35 E
Diligent Strait Ų 110 12.11 N 92.57 E
Di-linh 110 11.35 N 108.04 E
Diližan 84 40.45 N 44.52 E
Diližanskij Zapovednik ♦ 84 40.40 N 45.00 E
Dill ≃ 56 50.33 N 8.29 E
Dill City 196 35.17 N 99.08 W
Dillenburg 56 50.44 N 8.17 E
Diller 198 40.07 N 96.56 W
Dilley, Oreg., U.S. 224 45.29 N 123.07 W
Dilley, Tex., U.S. 196 28.40 N 99.10 W
Dillia ∨ 146 16.53 N 11.00 E
Dillia Téfidinga 146 15.16 N 12.06 E
Dilling 140 12.03 N 29.39 E
Dillingen 56 49.21 N 6.44 E
Dillingen an der Donau 56 48.34 N 10.29 E
Dillingham 180 59.02 N 158.29 W
Dillon, Colo., U.S. 200 39.37 N 106.04 W
Dillon, Mont., U.S. 202 45.13 N 112.38 W
Dillon, S.C., U.S. 192 34.25 N 79.22 W
Dillon ≃ 184 55.56 N 108.57 W
Dillon Bay C 175f 18.48 S 168.58 E
Dillon Cone ∧ 172 42.16 S 173.13 E
Dillon Lake @ 184 55.45 N 109.30 W
Dillon Lake @¹ 188 40.02 N 82.10 W
Dillon Reservoir @¹ 200 39.35 N 106.02 W
Dillon State Park ♦ 188 40.03 N 82.08 W
Dillonvale 214 40.12 N 80.47 W
Dillsboro 218 39.01 N 85.04 W
Dillsburg 208 40.07 N 77.02 W
Dilltown 214 40.29 N 79.00 W
Dillwyn 192 37.32 N 78.27 W
Dilly 150 14.57 N 7.40 W
Dilolo 152 10.42 S 22.20 E
Dilworth 198 46.53 N 96.42 W
Dilworthtown 285 39.54 N 75.34 W
Dima, Ang. 152 15.27 S 20.10 E
Dima, Yai. 144 6.16 N 36.22 E
Dimāpur 120 25.54 N 93.44 E
Dimaro 64 46.20 N 10.52 E
Dimasalang 116 12.12 N 123.51 E
Dimashq (Damascus) 132 33.30 N 36.18 E
Dimashq □⁸ 130 34.00 N 36.45 E
Dimasse, Rass ⁻ 36 35.37 N 11.03 E
Dimataling 116 7.32 N 123.22 E
Dimbelenge 152 5.33 S 23.07 E
Dimbokro 150 6.39 N 4.42 W
Dimbokro □⁵ 150 6.45 N 4.15 W
Dimboola 166 36.27 S 142.02 E
Dimbou 152 1.29 S 11.52 E
Dîmbovița □⁴ 38 45.00 N 25.30 E
Dîmbovița ≃ 38 44.14 N 26.27 E
Dimbulah 166 17.09 S 145.07 E
Dime Box 222 30.21 N 96.50 W
Dimetoka 130 40.16 N 27.17 E
Dimitrov 83 48.15 N 37.18 E
Dimitrovgrad, Blg. 38 42.03 N 25.36 E
Dimitrovgrad, Jugo. 38 43.01 N 22.47 E
Dimitrovgrad, S.S.S.R. 24 54.14 N 49.39 E
Dimitrovo
→ Pernik 38 42.36 N 23.02 W
Dimitrovskoje 85 40.16 N 69.03 E
Dimlang ∧ 146 8.24 N 11.47 E
Dimmitt 196 34.33 N 102.19 W
Dimo 154 5.19 N 29.10 E
Dimock 210 41.45 N 75.32 W
Dimona 132 31.04 N 35.02 E
Dimondale 216 42.39 N 84.39 W
Dinach 144 9.12 N 50.40 E
Dinagat 116 9.59 N 125.35 E
Dinagat Island I 116 10.12 N 125.35 E
Dinagat Sound Ų 116 9.59 N 125.50 E
Dinahican Point ⁻ 116 14.42 N 121.44 E
Dinājpur 124 25.38 N 88.38 E
Dinalupihan 116 14.52 N 120.28 E
Dinamarca
→ Denmark □¹ 26 56.00 N 10.00 E
Dinamarca, Estrecho de → Denmark Strait Ų 10 67.00 N 25.00 W
Dinamarci 68 38.31 N 16.09 E
Dinamita 196 25.43 N 103.38 W
Dinamo 80 50.15 N 41.38 E
Dinamo, Stadion ♦ 265b 55.48 N 37.34 E
Dinan 32 48.27 N 2.02 W
Dīnānagar 123 32.09 N 75.28 E
Dinant 56 50.16 N 4.55 E
Dinar 130 38.04 N 30.10 E
Dinara ⁂ 36 43.50 N 16.35 E
Dinard 32 48.38 N 2.04 W
Dinaric Alps
→ Dinara ⁂ 36 43.50 N 16.35 E
Dinarische Alpen
→ Dinara ⁂ 36 43.50 N 16.35 E
Dinas, Pil. 116 7.38 N 123.20 E
Dinas, Wales, U.K. 42 52.00 N 4.54 W
Dinas Head ⁻ 42 52.02 N 4.55 W
Dinas Powis 42 51.26 N 3.14 W
Dindanko 150 14.08 N 9.30 W
Dindar, Nahr ad- (Dinder) ≃ 140 14.06 N 33.40 E
Dindar National Park ♦ 140 12.40 N 35.20 E
Dindārpur ⁸ 272a 28.36 N 76.59 E
Dinde 152 14.12 S 13.44 E
Dinder (Nahr ad-Dindar) ≃ 140 14.06 N 33.40 E
Dindi ≃ 122 16.21 N 79.13 E
Dindigul 122 10.21 N 77.57 E
Dindima 150 10.18 N 10.12 E
Dindori 120 22.57 N 81.05 E
Dineksaray 130 37.23 N 32.37 E
Dinga, Pāk. 120 25.26 N 67.10 E
Dinga, Pāk. 123 32.38 N 73.43 E
Dinga, Zaïre 152 5.19 S 16.34 E
Dingalan Bay C 116 15.18 N 121.25 E
Dingan 110 19.44 N 110.21 E
Dingba 124 3.24 N 27.55 E
Dingbian 102 37.40 N 107.41 E
Dingbianji 102 36.37 N 108.41 E
Dingden 52 51.46 N 6.37 E
Dinge 152 4.58 S 12.22 E
Dingelsdorf 58 47.44 N 9.09 E
Dingelstädt 54 51.18 N 10.19 E
Dingelstedt 54 51.58 N 10.58 E
Dingeryu 105 39.37 N 114.55 E
Dingfeng 106 31.20 N 121.45 E
Dingfou 106 31.18 N 119.10 E
Dinggou 100 32.34 N 119.39 E
Dinggu 104 40.35 N 122.13 E
Dinggyê 120 28.18 N 88.06 E
Dingjiaao 107 29.24 N 106.09 E
Dingjiagou 104 40.42 N 123.35 E
Dingjiandian 106 32.06 N 120.52 E
Dingjiasuo 100 32.32 N 120.40 E
Dingjiazhuang 106 32.11 N 120.16 E
Dingjie 124 28.29 N 88.06 E
Dingkouzhen 102 39.55 N 106.40 E
Dingla 124 27.21 N 87.08 E
Dingle 58 52.08 N 10.15 W
Dingle ⁸ 262 53.23 N 2.57 W
Dingle Bay C 48 52.05 N 10.15 W
Dingle Peninsula ⁻¹ 48 52.12 N 10.05 W
Dingley 274b 37.58 S 145.07 E
Dinglingen 58 48.20 N 7.50 E
Dingman Creek ≃ 212 42.55 N 81.25 W
Dingmans Ferry 210 41.14 N 74.53 W
Dingnan 100 24.48 N 114.59 E
Dingnanshui ≃ 106 24.28 N 115.26 E
Dingo 166 23.39 S 149.20 E
Dingolfing 60 48.38 N 12.31 E
Dingping 102 31.32 N 95.27 E
Dingras 116 18.06 N 120.42 E
Dingri 120 28.35 N 86.38 E
Dingshan 106 31.17 N 119.50 E
Dingshanqiao 106 31.21 N 119.23 E
Dingtao 98 35.04 N 115.34 E
Dingtuna 40 59.34 N 16.22 E
Dinguira 150 14.24 N 11.16 W
Dinguiraye 150 11.18 N 10.43 W
Dinguiraye □⁴ 150 11.30 N 10.55 W
Dingwall, N.S., Can. 186 46.54 N 60.28 W
Dingwall, Scot., U.K. 46 57.35 N 4.29 W
Dingxi 102 35.38 N 104.29 E
Dingxian 98 38.32 N 114.59 E
Dingxiang 98 38.30 N 112.59 E
Dingxiang 102 25.13 N 105.07 E
Dingxing 105 39.17 N 115.46 E
Dingyan 100 32.23 N 120.45 E
Dingyuan 100 32.32 N 117.40 E
Dingzhouying 105 40.20 N 115.43 E
Dingzichang 107 28.54 N 106.08 E
Dingzigang ≃ 106 36.37 N 120.50 E
Dinh, Mui ⁻ 110 11.22 N 109.01 E
Dīnhāta 124 26.08 N 89.28 E
Dinh-ca 110 21.45 N 106.03 E
Dinh-lap 110 21.33 N 107.06 E
Dinh-lap 48 52.43 N 7.18 W
Dinkel ≃ 52 52.30 N 6.58 E
Dinkelsbühl 56 49.04 N 10.19 E
Dinkelscherben 58 48.21 N 10.35 E
Dinkey Creek ≃ 226 36.54 N 119.07 W
Dinklage 52 52.40 N 8.07 E
Dinnebito Wash ∨ 200 35.29 N 111.14 W
Dinner Point ⁻ 220 28.28 N 82.41 W
Dinnet 46 57.03 N 2.54 W
Dinnington 44 53.22 N 1.12 W
Dinokwe 156 23.24 S 26.40 E
Dinorwic 184 49.41 N 92.30 W
Dinorwic Lake @ 184 49.37 N 92.33 W
Dinosaur 200 40.15 N 109.01 W
Dinosaur National Monument ♦ 200 40.32 N 108.58 W
Dinosaur Provincial Park ♦ 182 50.45 N 111.30 W
Dinskaja 78 45.13 N 39.14 E
Dinslaken 52 51.34 N 6.44 E
Dinslaken □⁸ 263 51.36 N 6.43 E
Dinslakener Bruch 263 51.35 N 6.43 E
Dinslaken-Schwarze Heide, Flughafen ⊠ 263 51.37 N 6.51 E
Dinsmore, Sask., Can. 184 51.20 N 107.26 W
Dinsmore, Fla., U.S. 192 30.26 N 81.46 W
Dinsor 144 2.28 N 43.00 E
Dinteloord 52 51.37 N 4.22 E
Dinuba 226 36.32 N 119.23 W
Dinwiddie 208 37.05 N 77.35 W
Dinwiddie □⁶ 208 37.10 N 77.20 W
Dinxperlo 52 51.52 N 6.29 E
Diō 26 56.38 N 14.13 E
Diobo 152 2.16 N 20.29 E
Diodār 120 24.06 N 71.47 E
Dioīla 150 12.29 N 6.48 W
Diois □⁹ 62 44.40 N 5.20 E
Diomede 180 65.47 N 169.00 W
Dion ≃ 150 10.12 N 8.39 W
Dionisio 255 19.49 S 42.45 W
Dionísio Cerqueira 252 26.15 S 53.38 W
Dionne, Lac @ 186 49.26 N 67.55 W
Dions 62 43.56 N 4.19 E
Diorama 255 16.21 S 51.14 W
Dios 175e 5.33 S 154.58 E
Diósd 264c 47.25 N 18.57 E
Diouloulou 150 13.03 N 16.36 W
Dioumantène 150 12.36 N 16.25 W
Dioundiou 150 12.37 N 3.33 E
Dioungani 150 14.19 N 2.44 W
Dioura 150 14.50 N 5.15 W
Diourbel 150 14.40 N 16.15 W
Diourbel □⁴ 150 15.30 N 15.30 W
Dipaculao 116 15.51 N 121.32 E
Dipai 100 23.50 N 114.06 E
Dīpālpur 123 30.40 N 73.39 E
Dipignano 68 39.15 N 16.15 E
Dipilo, Pizzo ∧ 70 37.57 N 13.59 E
Diplo 120 24.28 N 69.35 E
Dipolog 116 8.35 N 123.20 E
Dippoldiswalde 54 50.54 N 13.40 E
Dipton 172 45.54 S 168.22 E
Dipu 106 30.38 N 119.41 E
Diqiyingzi 104 42.11 N 121.29 E
Dique Florentino Ameghino 254 43.40 S 66.25 W
Dīr 123 35.12 N 71.53 E
Dira, Djebel ∧ 34 36.05 N 3.38 E
Diré 150 16.16 N 3.24 W
Direction, Cape ⁻ 164 12.51 S 143.32 E
Dire Dawa 144 9.37 N 41.52 E
Direkli 130 39.43 N 36.40 E
Diriamba 236 11.51 N 86.14 W
Dirico 152 17.58 S 20.47 E
Diriomo 236 11.52 N 86.03 W
Dirk Hartog Island I 162 25.48 S 113.00 E
Dirkiesdorp 158 27.10 S 30.25 E
Dirkiesrus 158 26.20 S 24.44 E
Dirkou 146 19.01 N 12.53 E
Dirkshorn 52 52.45 N 4.45 E
Dirksland 52 51.44 N 4.06 E
Dirnaich 60 48.27 N 12.30 E
Dirrah 140 13.37 N 26.06 E
Dirranbandi 166 28.35 S 148.14 E
Dirri 144 4.22 N 46.38 E
Ḑirs 144 18.32 N 42.05 E
Dirschau
→ Tczew 30 54.06 N 18.47 E
Dirty Devil ≃ 200 37.53 N 110.24 W
Dīsah 140 12.02 N 34.19 E
Disappointment, Cape ⁻, Falk. Is. 244 54.53 S 36.07 W
Disappointment, Cape ⁻, Wash., U.S. 224 46.18 N 124.03 W
Disappointment, Lake @ 162 23.30 S 122.50 E
Disappointment, Mount ∧ 169 37.25 S 145.18 E
Disappointment Creek ≃ 200 38.01 N 108.51 W
Disaster Bay C 166 37.17 S 150.00 E
Disbrow Drain ≃ 281 42.06 N 83.27 W
Disco 214 42.41 N 83.02 W
Discovery 273d 26.10 S 27.54 E
Discovery, Port C 224 48.05 N 122.52 W
Discovery Bay C 166 38.12 S 141.07 E
Discovery Island I 224 48.25 N 123.15 W
Discovery Passage Ų 182 50.00 N 125.15 W
Discovery Tablemount ⁺³ 8 42.00 S 0.05 E
Disentis 58 46.43 N 8.51 E
Dishāshah 142 28.59 N 30.51 E
Dishergarh 126 23.41 N 86.50 E
Dishman 202 47.39 N 117.17 W
Dishnā 140 26.07 N 32.28 E
Dishna ≃ 180 63.37 N 157.18 W
Disiḍi 130 38.47 N 39.00 E
Disihao 89 50.28 N 124.35 E
Disko I 216 41.00 N 85.57 W
Disko I 176 69.50 N 53.30 W
Disko Bugt C 176 69.15 N 52.00 W
Disley 262 53.21 N 2.02 W
Disley Tunnel ⁵ 262 53.22 N 2.03 W
Dismal ≃ 198 41.50 N 100.05 W
Dismal Lakes @ 176 67.26 N 117.07 W
Dismal Swamp Canal ≅ 208 36.45 N 76.20 W
Disna 76 55.33 N 28.10 E
Disna ≃ 76 55.34 N 28.12 E
Disney 196 36.29 N 95.01 W
Disneyland ♦ 228 33.48 N 117.55 W
Disneyworld ♦ 220 28.27 N 81.28 W
Diso 68 40.00 N 18.23 E
Disputanta 208 37.08 N 77.14 W
Disraëli 206 45.54 N 71.21 W
Diss 42 52.23 N 1.07 E
Dissen 52 52.07 N 8.12 E
Dissimieux, Lac @ 186 49.51 N 69.48 W
Distant 214 40.59 N 79.22 W
Disteghil Sār ∧ 123 36.19 N 75.12 E
Disteln 263 51.36 N 7.09 E
Distington 44 54.36 N 3.32 W
District Heights 284c 38.51 N 76.53 W
District of Columbia □³ 284c
Distrito Especial □⁵ 178 38.54 N 77.01 W
Distrito Federal □⁵, Arg. 246 4.15 N 74.15 W
Distrito Federal □⁵, Bra. 258 34.36 S 58.26 W
Distrito Federal □⁵, Méx. 255 15.45 S 47.45 W
Distrito Federal □⁵, Ven. 234 19.15 N 99.10 W
Distroff 246 10.30 N 66.55 W
Disūq 56 49.20 N 6.16 E
Ditfurt 142 31.08 N 30.39 E
Dithmarschen ¹ 54 51.50 N 11.11 E
Dit Island I 52 54.10 N 9.10 E
Dittaino ≃ 116 11.15 N 120.56 E
Ditton, Eng., U.K. 70 37.25 N 15.00 E
Ditton, Eng., U.K. 260 51.18 N 0.27 E
Ditton ≃ 262 53.22 N 2.45 W
Ditton Priors 206 45.23 N 71.12 W
Ditzingen 42 52.30 N 2.35 W
Ditzum 58 48.50 N 9.04 E
Diu 52 53.18 N 7.16 E
Diuata Mountains ⁂ 120 20.42 N 70.59 E
Diuata Point ⁻ 116 9.10 N 125.47 E
Dīva 116 9.05 N 125.12 E
Divāla 272c 19.11 N 73.02 E
Dīvāndarreh 120 29.05 N 83.11 E
Divčice 128 35.55 N 47.02 E
Dive 61 49.06 N 14.19 E
Divejevo 272c 19.11 N 73.02 E
Divenie 80 55.03 N 43.15 E
Divenskaja 152 2.41 S 12.05 E
Diveria ≃ 76 59.12 N 30.01 E
Divesiom 58 46.09 N 8.19 E
Diviči 32 49.19 N 0.05 W
Dividing Creek 84 41.12 N 48.59 E
Dividing Creek ≃ 208 39.16 N 75.06 W
Dividing Ridge ∧ 208 38.05 N 75.32 W
Divignano 219 39.07 N 90.39 W
Divilican Bay C 266b 45.40 N 8.36 E
Divin 116 17.25 N 122.19 E
Divine Corners 78 51.58 N 24.35 E
Divinhe 210 41.48 N 74.40 W
Divino 156 20.40 S 34.49 E
Divinolândia 255 20.37 S 42.09 W
Divinópolis 256 21.40 S 46.45 W
Divion 255 20.09 S 44.54 W
Divis ∧² 50 50.28 N 2.30 E
Divisa Nova 44 54.37 N 6.01 W
Divisões, Serra das ⁂² 256 21.31 S 46.12 W
Divisor, Serra do (Cordillera Ultraoriental) ⁂¹ 255 17.00 S 51.00 W
Divizija 248 8.20 S 73.30 W
Divnogorsk 78 45.57 N 29.59 E
Divnoje 86 55.58 N 92.22 E
Divo 80 45.55 N 43.22 E
Divo □⁵ 150 5.50 N 5.22 W
Divonne-les-Bains 150 5.40 N 5.30 W
Divriği 58 46.22 N 6.08 E
Dīwāl Qol 130 39.23 N 38.07 E
Dix, Ill., U.S. 120 34.19 N 67.54 E
Dix, Nebr., U.S. 219 38.27 N 88.56 W
Dix ≃ 198 41.14 N 103.29 W
Dix, Lac des @ 192 37.49 N 84.43 W
Dixboro 58 46.03 N 7.24 E
Dixfield 216 42.19 N 83.39 W
Dix Hills 188 44.32 N 70.27 W
Dixie 207 40.49 N 73.22 W
Dixie Square ⁹ 275b 43.36 N 79.36 W
Dixie Valley ∨ 278 41.37 N 87.40 W
Dix-Milles, Lac @ 204 39.50 N 117.55 W
Dixmoor 190 46.46 N 77.45 W
Dixmude 278 41.38 N 87.40 W
→ Diksmuide
Dixon, Calif., U.S. 50 51.02 N 2.52 E
Dixon, Ill., U.S. 226 38.27 N 121.49 W
Dixon, Ky., U.S. 190 41.50 N 89.29 W
Dixon, Mo., U.S. 194 37.31 N 87.41 W
Dixon, N. Mex., U.S. 194 37.60 N 92.06 W
Dixon, Ohio, U.S. 200 36.12 N 105.53 W
Dixon Entrance Ų 216 40.57 N 84.48 W
Dixons Mills 180 54.25 N 132.30 W
Dixons Pond @ 194 32.04 N 87.47 W
Dixonville 276 40.56 N 74.27 W
Dixville 214 40.43 N 79.01 W
Diyadin 206 45.04 N 71.46 W
Diyālā □⁴ 84 39.33 N 43.41 E
Diyālā (Sīrvān) ≃ 128 34.00 N 45.00 E
Diyarbakır 128 33.14 N 44.31 E
Diyarbakır □⁴ 130 37.55 N 40.14 E
Diyarb Najm 130 38.05 N 40.15 E
Diyu al-Wasta 142 30.45 N 31.26 E
Dizangsi 142 30.54 N 31.30 E
Dizhou 104 41.26 N 120.57 E
Dizy 102 23.00 N 106.20 E
Dizzard Point ⁻ 50 49.04 N 3.58 E
Dja ≃ 42 50.45 N 4.38 W
Dja, Réserve de ♦⁴ 152 2.02 N 15.12 E
Djabalpur 152 3.05 N 13.00 E
→ Jabalpur
Djabir 124 23.10 N 79.57 E
Djadié ≃ 152 0.32 N 24.05 E
Djado 152 0.46 N 12.58 E
Djado, Plateau du ⁂¹ 146 21.01 N 12.18 E
Djaipur
→ Jaipur 146 21.45 N 12.50 E
Djakarta
→ Jakarta 120 26.55 N 75.49 E
Djakonovo 269e 6.10 S 106.48 E
Djakovka 82 54.34 N 38.20 E
Djakovo 80 50.43 N 46.48 E
Djakovo ⁸ 83 47.57 N 39.09 E
Djamaa 265b 55.39 N 37.40 E
Djamba, Ang. 148 33.32 N 6.00 E
Djamba, Zaïre 152 16.46 S 13.59 E
Djambala 152 9.45 S 22.07 E
Djamshedpur 152 2.33 S 14.45 E
→ Jamshedpur
Djanet 126 22.48 N 86.11 E
Djangatiti Dafana 148 24.34 N 9.29 E
Djaposten 146 11.46 N 21.19 E
Djaret, Oued ∨ 152 3.25 N 13.32 E
Djaul Island I 148 26.32 N 1.30 E
Djebel Abiod 164 2.56 S 150.55 E
Djebeniana 36 36.58 N 9.05 E
Djebibina 148 35.02 N 10.55 E
Djebobo ∧ 36 36.07 N 10.06 E
Djebren 150 8.20 N 0.35 E
Djedaa 146 11.14 N 19.01 E
Djedda 146 13.31 N 18.34 E
→ Jiddah
Djedi, Oued ∨ 144 21.30 N 39.12 E
Djeffara (Gefara) ≃ 148 34.28 N 6.05 E
Djéké Djéké 146 32.30 N 11.45 E
Djelfa 148 8.25 N 18.12 E
Djelo-Binza 148 34.40 N 3.15 E
Djema 273b 4.23 S 15.16 E
Djember 146 6.03 N 25.19 E
Djemila ⊥ 146 10.25 N 17.50 E
Djemmal 34 36.25 N 5.44 E
Djenein 148 35.38 N 10.46 E
Djenné 148 31.44 N 10.09 E
Djenoun, Garet el ∧ 150 13.54 N 4.33 W
Djeradou 148 25.05 N 5.25 E
Djerba, Île de I 36 36.15 N 10.23 E
Djerem ≃ 148 33.48 N 10.54 E
Djerid, Chott ≅ 152 5.20 N 13.24 E
Dji ≃ 148 33.42 N 8.26 E
Djiba 152 6.47 N 22.14 E
Djibasso 152 1.21 S 13.09 E
Djibo 150 13.07 N 4.10 W
Djibouti 150 14.06 N 1.38 W
Djibouti □¹ 144 11.36 N 43.09 E
Djibouti □¹ 144 11.30 N 43.00 E
Djibrouia 144 11.30 N 43.00
Djidjelli 150 13.13 N 11.14 W
Djibabo Plain ≃ 148 36.48 N 5.46 E
Djohong 144 4.00 N 39.10 E
Djokjakarta 152 6.50 N 14.42 E
→ Yogyakarta
Djokoumatombi 115a 7.48 S 110.22 E
Djokupunda 152 0.47 N 15.22 E
Djolu 152 5.27 S 20.58 E
Djoubé 152 0.37 N 22.21 E
Djoua ≃ 152 1.21 N 20.22 E
Djoué ≃ 152 1.13 N 13.12 E
Djougou 273b 4.19 S 15.14 E
Djouho Battinga 150 9.42 N 1.40 E
Djoum 152 6.38 N 20.34 E
Djourab, Erg du ≃ 152 2.40 N 12.40 E
Dju 146 10.27 N 20.04 E
Djúpivogur 154 1.55 N 30.30 E
Djura 24a 64.40 N 14.10 W
Djurås 40 60.37 N 15.00 E
Djurmo 40 60.33 N 15.08 E
Djurö 40 60.33 N 15.10 E
Djurö I 40 59.19 N 18.42 E
Djursholm 26 58.52 N 13.28 E
Dlouhá Ves, Česko. 40 59.24 N 18.05 E
60 49.12 N 13.31 E
Dmanisi 84 41.22 N 44.12 E
Dmitr'ašovka 76 52.09 N 39.04 E
Dmitrija Lapteva, Proliv Ų 74 73.00 N 142.00 E
Dmitrijevka, S.S.S.R. 83 48.55 N 39.10 E
Dmitrijevka, S.S.S.R. 83 47.56 N 38.56 E
Dmitrijevka, S.S.S.R. 85 43.30 N 77.02 E
Dmitrijevka, S.S.S.R. 86 55.10 N 75.36 E
Dmitrijev-L'govskij 78 52.08 N 35.05 E
Dmitrijevskij 86 49.08 N 57.50 E
Dmitrijevskoje, S.S.S.R. 80 45.48 N 41.54 E
Dmitrijevskoje, S.S.S.R. 82 54.40 N 37.38 E
Dmitrijev Usad, S.S.S.R. 76 54.08 N 43.08 E
Dmitrijev Usad, S.S.S.R. 80 54.14 N 43.18 E
Dmitrijevy Gory 80 55.12 N 41.47 E
Dmitrov 82 56.21 N 37.31 E
Dmitrova Gora 82 56.40 N 36.59 E
Dmitrovcy 82 55.16 N 38.55 E
Dmitroviči 76 53.59 N 29.06 E
Dmitrovka, S.S.S.R. 78 45.29 N 35.04 E
Dmitrovka, S.S.S.R. 78 46.51 N 36.35 E
Dmitrovka, S.S.S.R. 78 48.48 N 32.44 E
Dmitrovskij Pogost 76 55.19 N 39.49 E
Dmitrovsk-Orlovskij 76 52.30 N 35.09 E
Dmuchajlovka 78 49.03 N 34.46 E
Dnepr ≃ 78 46.30 N 32.18 E
Dnepr'any 78 46.44 N 33.16 E
Dneprodzeržinsk 78 48.30 N 34.37 E
Dneprodzeržinskoje Vodochranilišče @¹ 78 48.45 N 34.00 E
Dnepropetrovsk 78 48.27 N 34.59 E
Dneprovka 78 47.26 N 34.38 E
Dneprovskij Liman C¹ 78 46.35 N 31.55 E
Dneprovsko-Bugskij Kanal ≅ 78 52.03 N 25.35 E
Dneprovskoje 76 55.40 N 33.55 E
Dnestr ≃ 78 46.18 N 30.17 E
Dnestrovskij Liman @ 78 46.15 N 30.17 E
Dnieper
→ Dnepr ≃ 78 46.30 N 32.18 E
Dniepropetrovsk
→ Dnepropetrovsk 78 48.27 N 34.59 E
Dniester
→ Dnestr ≃ 78 46.18 N 30.17 E
Dno 76 57.50 N 29.59 E
Do, Lac @ 150 15.54 N 2.45 W
Doa 154 16.44 S 34.32 E
Do Āb-e Mīkh-e Zarrīn 120 35.16 N 68.00 E
Doaktown 186 46.33 N 66.08 W
Doangdoangan-besar, Pulau I 112 5.24 S 117.55 E
Doany 157b 14.22 S 49.31 E
Doba 146 8.39 N 16.51 E
Dobane 140 6.24 N 24.42 E
Dobbertin 54 53.37 N 12.04 E
Dobbiaco (Toblach) 64 46.44 N 12.14 E
Dobbin 222 30.22 N 95.46 W
Dobbins 226 39.22 N 121.12 W
Dobbs Ferry 210 41.01 N 73.52 W
Dobbyn 166 19.48 S 140.00 E
Dobczyce 30 49.54 N 20.06 E
Dobel 56 48.48 N 8.29 E
Dobele 76 56.37 N 23.16 E
Döbeln 54 51.07 N 13.07 E
Doberai, Jazirah (Vogelkop) ⁻¹ 164 1.30 S 132.30 E
Döberitz 264a 52.33 N 13.03 E
Doberlug-Kirchhain 54 51.38 N 13.34 E
Döbern 54 51.37 N 14.36 E
Dobiegniew 30 52.59 N 15.47 E
Döbling ⁸ 264b 48.15 N 16.22 E
Dobo 164 5.46 S 134.13 E
Doboj 38 44.44 N 18.06 E
Dobra, Pol. 30 51.54 N 18.37 E
Dobra, Pol. 30 53.35 N 15.18 E
Dobra ≃ 36 45.33 N 15.31 E
Dobr'anka, S.S.S.R. 78 52.04 N 31.11 E
Dobr'anka, S.S.S.R. 86 58.27 N 56.24 E
Dobr'ankka 78 48.21 N 30.54 E
Dobřany 60 49.40 N 13.18 E
Dobra Stausee @¹ 61 48.35 N 15.20 E
Dobre Miasto 30 53.59 N 20.25 E
Döbriach 64 46.47 N 13.39 E
Dobrič
→ Tolbuhin 38 43.34 N 27.50 E
Dobrinka, S.S.S.R. 80 52.09 N 40.29 E
Dobrinka, S.S.S.R. 80 48.49 N 42.58 E
Dobrinka, S.S.S.R. 80 50.49 N 41.51 E
Dobříš 30 49.47 N 14.11 E
Dobritz 54 52.01 N 12.10 E
Dobrodzień 30 50.44 N 18.27 E
Dobroje, S.S.S.R. 76 57.06 N 32.02 E
Dobroje, S.S.S.R. 76 52.52 N 39.48 E
Dobroměřice 54 50.23 N 13.46 E
Dobromil' 78 49.34 N 22.47 E
Dobropolje 78 48.28 N 37.05 E
Dobroslavka 78 52.24 N 26.15 E
Dobroteasa 38 44.47 N 24.23 E
Dobrotvor 78 50.14 N 24.22 E
Dobroveličkovka 78 48.23 N 31.11 E
Dobrovol' (Schlossberg in Ostpreussen) 76 54.46 N 22.31 E
Dobrovolje 78 48.41 N 36.37 E
Dobrudžansko plato ⁂¹ 38 43.32 N 27.50 E
Dobruš 76 52.25 N 31.19 E
Dobruška 30 50.17 N 16.10 E
Dobryn' 78 51.46 N 29.12 E
Dobrzany 30 53.22 N 15.25 E
Dobrzyń nad Wisłą 30 52.38 N 19.20 E
Dobšiná 30 48.49 N 20.23 E
Dobson 192 36.24 N 80.43 W
Dốc ≃ 88 49.39 N 114.48 E
Doce ≃, Bra. 255 18.26 S 51.05 W
Doce ≃, Bra. 255 19.37 S 39.49 W
Doce de Octubre 196 25.38 N 97.47 W
Doce Leguas, Cayos de las II 240p 20.55 N 79.05 W
Dochart ≃ 46 56.28 N 4.20 W
Docking 42 52.55 N 0.38 E
Dockton 224 47.22 N 122.28 W
Dockweiler 56 50.15 N 6.46 E
Dockweiler State Beach ♦ 280 33.55 N 118.26 W
Doctor Arroyo 234 23.40 N 100.11 W
Doctor Cecilio Báez 252 25.03 S 56.19 W
Doctor Coss 196 25.55 N 99.11 W
Doctor Edmund A. Babler Memorial State Park ♦ 219 38.36 N 90.43 W
Doctor González 232 25.52 N 99.57 W
Doctor Hicks Range ⁂ 162 28.40 S 124.20 E
Doctor Pedro P. Peña 252 22.06 S 62.22 W
Doctors Creek ≃ 208 40.11 N 74.41 W
Doda 123 33.08 N 75.34 E
Doda Betta ∧ 122 11.24 N 76.44 E
Dod Ballāpur 122 13.18 N 77.32 E
Doddinghurst 260 51.40 N 0.18 E
Doddo ≃ 146 7.05 N 19.10 E
Doddridge 194 33.06 N 93.54 W
Doddsville 194 33.39 N 90.31 W
Dodecanese
→ Dhodhekánisos II 38 36.30 N 27.00 E
Dodéo 152 7.29 N 12.04 E
Dodge, Nebr., U.S. 198 41.43 N 96.52 W
Dodge, Tex., U.S. 222 30.45 N 95.24 W
Dodge □⁶ 216 43.14 N 88.40 W
Dodge Brothers State Park Number 4 ♦, Mich., U.S. 281 42.37 N 83.22 W
Dodge Brothers State Park Number 8 ♦, Mich., U.S. 281 42.36 N 83.01 W
Dodge Center 190 44.02 N 92.51 W
Dodge City 198 37.45 N 100.01 W
Dodge Park 284c 38.56 N 76.53 W
Dodger Stadium ♦ 280 34.04 N 118.14 W
Dodgeville 190 42.58 N 90.08 W
Dodman Point ⁻ 42 50.13 N 4.48 W

Symbol	English	Deutsch	Español	Français	Português
≃	River	Fluss	Rio	Rivière	Rio
≅	Canal	Kanal	Canal	Canal	Canal
↳	Waterfall, Rapids	Wasserfall, Stromschnellen	Cascada, Rápidos	Chute d'eau, Rapides	Cascata, Rápidos
Ų	Strait	Meeresstrasse	Estrecho	Détroit	Estreito
C	Bay, Gulf	Bucht, Golf	Bahía, Golfo	Baie, Golfe	Baía, Golfo
@	Lake, Lakes	See, Seen	Lago, Lagos	Lac, Lacs	Lago, Lagos
≡	Swamp	Sumpf	Pantano	Marais	Pântano
⊠	Ice Features, Glacier	Eis- und Gletscherformen	Accidentes Glaciales	Formes glaciaires	Acidentes Glaciares
⁺	Other Hydrographic Features	Andere Hydrographische Objekte	Otros Elementos Hidrográficos	Autres données hydrographiques	Outros Acidentes Hidrográficos
⁺	Submarine Features	Untermeerische Objekte	Accidentes Submarinos	Formes de relief sous-marin	Acidentes Submarinos
□	Political Unit	Politische Einheit	Unidad Política	Entité politique	Unidade Política
⊌	Cultural Institution	Kulturelle Institution	Institución Cultural	Institution culturelle	Instituição Cultural
⊥	Historical Site	Historische Stätte	Sitio Histórico	Site historique	Sítio Histórico
♦	Recreational Site	Erholungs- und Ferienort	Sitio de Recreo	Centre de loisirs	Sitio de Lazer
⊠	Airport	Flughafen	Aeropuerto	Aéroport	Aeroporto
■	Military Installation	Militäranlage	Instalación Militar	Installation militaire	Instalação Militar
◆	Miscellaneous	Verschiedenes	Misceláneo	Divers	Miscelânea

Name	Page	Lat.°′	Long.°′
Dodo	156	18.45 S	25.20 E
Dodo Goei	140	5.57 N	27.26 E
Dodola	144	7.02 N	39.07 E
Dodoma	154	6.11 S	35.45 E
Dodoma □[4]	154	6.00 S	36.00 E
Dodori ≃	154	1.52 S	41.02 E
Dodsland	184	51.48 N	108.49 W
Dodson, La., U.S.	194	32.05 N	92.39 W
Dodson, Mont., U.S.	202	48.24 N	108.15 W
Dodson, Tex., U.S.	196	34.46 N	100.02 W
Dodson Peninsula ≻[1]	9	75.46 S	62.50 W
Dodurga	130	39.48 N	29.55 E
Doe Lake ⊜	212	45.32 N	79.25 W
Doe River	182	56.00 N	120.05 W
Doerun	192	31.19 N	83.55 W
Doesburg	52	52.01 N	6.09 E
Doetinchem	52	51.58 N	6.17 E
Dog ≃	190	48.51 N	89.37 W
Dogāchia	272b	22.58 N	88.31 E
Dogadda	124	29.48 N	78.37 E
Dō ga-mori ∧	96	33.09 N	132.53 E
Doğanbey, Tür.	130	37.48 N	31.54 E
Doğanbey, Tür.	130	37.37 N	27.11 E
Doğanbey, Tür.	130	38.04 N	26.53 E
Doğançay	130	40.37 N	30.20 E
Doganella	66	41.34 N	12.56 E
Doğanhisar	130	38.09 N	31.41 E
Doğanşehir	130	38.06 N	37.53 E
Dog Creek	182	51.35 N	122.15 W
Dog Creek ≃, Mont., U.S.	202	47.44 N	109.36 W
Dog Creek ≃, Ohio, U.S.	216	41.03 N	84.23 W
Dog Ear Creek ≃	198	43.42 N	99.59 W
Dog Islands II	240m	18.29 N	64.28 W
Dog Lake ⊜, Man., Can.	184	51.02 N	98.30 W
Dog Lake ⊜, Ont., Can.	190	48.18 N	84.10 W
Dog Lake ⊜, Ont., Can.	190	48.46 N	89.32 W
Dog Lake ⊜, Ont., Can.	212	44.27 N	76.20 W
Dogliani	62	44.32 N	7.56 E
Dogna	64	46.27 N	13.19 E
Dōgo II	92	36.15 N	133.16 E
Dogondoutchi	150	13.38 N	4.02 E
Dōgo-yama ∧	96	35.04 N	133.14 E
Dogpound Creek ≃	182	51.50 N	114.24 W
Dogs, Isle of I	260	51.29 N	0.01 W
D'ogtevo	78	49.10 N	40.39 E
Doğubayazıt	84	39.32 N	44.08 E
Doguéraoua	150	13.58 N	5.35 E
Dogura	164	10.05 S	150.05 E
Doha → Ad-Dawḥah	128	25.17 N	51.32 E
Dohad	120	22.50 N	74.16 E
Dohār	126	23.35 N	90.09 E
Dohhi	124	24.32 N	84.54 E
Dohna	54	50.57 N	13.51 E
Dohrgaul	263	51.06 N	7.27 E
Dohrīghāt	124	26.16 N	83.31 E
Doi	96	33.57 N	133.30 E
Doi, Kinh ☰	269c	10.43 N	106.37 E
Doigab	144	0.59 N	43.38 E
Doiran, Lake ⊜	38	41.13 N	22.44 E
Dois de Novembro, Cachoeira ᒪ	248	8.52 S	62.16 W
Dois Irmãos	250	9.16 S	49.05 W
Dois Irmãos, Pico ∧	287a	22.59 S	43.14 W
Dois Riachos	250	9.23 S	37.05 W
Dōjō	268	35.51 N	139.32 E
Dōjō ◆[8]	270	34.52 N	135.14 E
Doka, Indon.	164	6.39 S	134.15 E
Doka, Sūd.	140	13.31 N	35.46 E
Doki ≃	96	34.18 N	133.48 E
Dokka	26	60.50 N	10.05 E
Dokkane, Djebel ∧	148	35.23 N	8.00 E
Dokkum	52	53.19 N	6.00 E
Dokmetepe	130	40.19 N	36.18 E
Dokri	120	27.23 N	68.06 E
Dokšicy	76	54.54 N	27.46 E
Dokská pahorkatina ⋀[2]	54	50.30 N	14.45 E
Dokšukino	84	43.33 N	43.50 E
Doksy	54	50.35 N	14.38 E
Dokučajevsk	83	47.44 N	37.40 E
Dol'a, S.S.S.R.	83	47.53 N	37.41 E
Dola, Ohio, U.S.	216	40.47 N	83.42 W
Dolak ≃	164	8.20 S	138.30 E
Doland	198	44.54 N	98.06 W
Dolany	60	49.27 N	13.15 E
Dolavon	254	43.18 S	65.42 W
Dolaybaköy	267b	40.54 N	29.15 E
Dolbeau	176	48.53 N	72.14 W
Dolberg	52	51.42 N	7.55 E
Dolceacqua	62	43.51 N	7.37 E
Dolcedorme, Serra ∧	68	39.53 N	16.13 E
Dol-de-Bretagne	32	48.33 N	1.45 W
Dole	58	47.06 N	5.30 E
Dolega	236	8.34 N	82.25 W
Dolen	222	30.26 N	94.54 W
Dolgaja	86	55.49 N	64.15 E
Dolgaja, Kosa ≻[2]	78	46.43 N	37.41 E
Dolgarrog	44	53.11 N	3.51 W
Dolgelin	54	52.29 N	14.24 E
Dolgellau	42	52.44 N	3.53 W
Dolgen'koje	83	49.01 N	37.19 E
Dolgeville	210	43.06 N	74.46 W
Dolgij, Ostrov I	24	69.15 N	59.04 E
Dolgij Most	88	56.45 N	96.48 E
Dolginovo	76	54.39 N	27.29 E
Dolgoi Island I	180	55.10 N	161.45 W
Dolgoje	78	52.04 N	37.34 E
Dolgoprudnyj	82	55.56 N	37.31 E
Dolgorukovo	76	52.19 N	38.21 E
Dolgoščelje	24	66.03 N	43.24 E
Dolianova	71	39.22 N	9.10 E
Dolina	83	48 59 N	37.27 E
Dolinnyj	80	51.16 N	52.11 E
Dolinovskoje	83	48.36 N	38.33 E
Dolinsk	89	47.21 N	142.48 E
Dolinskaja	78	48.07 N	32.44 E
Dolisie	152	4.12 S	12.41 E
Dolj □[4]	38	44.15 N	23.45 E
Döllach	64	46.58 N	12.54 E
Dollar	46	56.09 N	3.40 W
Dollard-des-Ormeaux	206	45.29 N	73.49 W
Dollar Law ∧	46	55.33 N	3.17 W
Döllbach	56	50.26 N	9.44 E
Dolle	54	52.25 N	11.37 E
Dollern	52	53.32 N	9.32 E
Dollerup	41	54.46 N	9.40 E
Döllnitz	54	51.24 N	12.01 E
Dollnstein	60	48.52 N	11.04 E
Döllstädt	54	51.05 N	10.49 E
Dolmabahçe Sarayı ʋ	267b	41.02 N	29.00 E
Dolmatovka	78	46.13 N	32.26 E
Dolmatovskij	80	57.29 N	42.18 E
Dolni Dâbnik	38	43.24 N	24.26 E
Dolní Jiřetín	54	50.35 N	13.33 E
Dolni Lom	38	43.31 N	22.47 E
Dolni Žandov	60	50.02 N	12.34 E
Dolnomoravský úval ∨	30	49.00 N	17.15 E
Dolný Kubín	30	49.12 N	19.17 E
Dolo, It.	64	45.25 N	12.05 E
Dolo, Som.	144	4.13 N	42.08 E
Dolo Bay	144	4.12 N	42.09 E
Dolokparibuan	114	3.01 N	98.39 E
Dolomites → Dolomiti ⋀	64	46.25 N	11.50 E
Dolomiti (Dolomiten) ⋀	64	46.25 N	11.50 E
Dolon'	86	50.40 N	79.18 E
Dolon ≃	62	45.18 N	4.46 E
Dolon, Pereval)(	85	41.52 N	75.45 E
Dolores, Arg.	252	36.20 S	57.40 W
Dolores, Col.	246	3.33 N	74.54 W
Dolores, Esp.	34	38.08 N	0.46 W
Dolores, Guat.	232	16.31 N	89.25 W
Dolores, Méx.	196	26.20 N	101.29 W
Dolores, Méx.	232	28.53 N	108.27 W
Dolores, Colo., U.S.	200	37.28 N	108.30 W
Dolores, Ur.	252	33.33 S	58.13 W
Dolores, Ven.	246	8.18 N	69.34 W
Dolores ≃, Pil.	116	12.02 N	125.29 E
Dolores ≃, U.S.	200	38.49 N	109.17 W
Dolores, Mission ʋ[1]	282	37.46 N	122.26 W
Dolores Hidalgo	234	21.10 N	100.56 W
Dolphin, Cape ≻	254	51.15 S	58.57 W
Dolphin and Union Strait ɰ	176	69.05 N	114.45 W
Dolphin Head ∧	241q	18.22 N	78.10 W
Dölsach	64	46.49 N	12.51 E
Dolsk	30	52.00 N	17.03 E
Dol'skoje	82	54.47 N	36.26 E
Dolton, Eng., U.K.	42	50.53 N	4.01 W
Dolton, Ill., U.S.	216	41.39 N	87.37 W
Dolwyddelan	42	53.03 N	3.53 W
Dolżak	78	48.41 N	26.32 E
Dolžanskaja, S.S.S.R.	78	46.37 N	37.48 E
Dolžanskaja, S.S.S.R.	83	48.03 N	39.39 E
Dolžicy, S.S.S.R.	76	58.31 N	29.08 E
Dolžicy, S.S.S.R.	76	58.00 N	29.51 E
Dolžik	78	50.13 N	35.55 E
Dom ∧, Indon.	164	2.40 S	136.53 E
Dom ∧, Schw.	58	46.06 N	7.50 E
D'oma ≃	86	54.42 N	55.57 E
Domacha	76	52.28 N	34.58 E
Domačovo	78	51.44 N	23.37 E
Domadare	144	1.48 N	41.13 E
Domaine, Pointe du ≻	275a	45.23 N	73.54 W
Domanevka	78	47.37 N	30.58 E
Domaniç	130	39.48 N	29.37 E
Domaniči	76	53.02 N	33.25 E
Domanico	68	39.13 N	16.12 E
Dom Aquino	255	15.48 S	54.53 W
Domar, Enneri ∨	146	18.11 N	18.04 E
Domariāganj	124	27.13 N	82.40 E
Domart-en-Ponthieu	50	50.04 N	2.07 E
Domasi	154	15.18 S	35.20 E
Domaška	80	53.00 N	50.47 E
Domaso	58	46.09 N	9.19 E
Domat/Ems	58	46.50 N	9.28 E
Domažlice	60	49.27 N	12.56 E
Dombaj	84	43.17 N	41.37 E
Dombarovskij	86	50.46 N	59.32 E
Dombås	26	62.05 N	9.08 E
Dombasle-sur-Meurthe	58	48.38 N	6.21 E
Dombe	156	19.59 S	33.25 E
Dombe Grande	152	12.58 S	13.11 E
Dombes ◆[1]	58	46.00 N	5.03 E
Domboj-Ul'gan, Gora ∧	84	43.14 N	41.41 E
Dombóvár	30	46.23 N	18.08 E
Dombrád	30	48.14 N	21.56 E
Dombresson	58	47.04 N	6.58 E
Domburg	52	51.34 N	3.30 E
Dom Cavati	255	19.23 S	42.06 W
Dome à Collenias	148	27.15 N	9.42 E
Dome Creek	182	53.44 N	121.01 W
Domegge di Cadore	64	46.27 N	12.25 E
Domène	62	45.12 N	5.50 E
Dome Peak ∧, Pil.	116	5.37 N	125.20 E
Dome Peak ∧, Wash., U.S.	224	48.18 N	121.02 W
Domett	172	42.51 S	173.13 E
Domèvre-en-Haye	56	48.49 N	5.55 E
Domeyko	252	28.57 S	70.54 W
Domeyko, Cordillera ⋀	252	24.30 S	69.00 W
Domfront	32	48.36 N	0.39 W
Domiciano Ribeiro	255	16.56 S	47.46 W
Dominal, Parc ♠	62	44.52 N	6.32 E
Domingo M. Irala	252	25.54 S	54.43 W
Domingos Martins	255	20.22 S	40.40 W
Dominguez	280	33.50 N	118.13 W
Dominguez Channel ɰ	280	38.47 N	118.15 W
Dominguez Hills ⋀[2]	280	33.52 N	118.14 W
Dominica □[1]	230		
	240d	15.30 N	61.20 W
Dominica Channel ɰ	238	15.10 N	61.15 W
Dominicain (république) → Dominican Republic □[1]	238	19.00 N	70.40 W
Dominical	236	9.13 N	83.51 W
Dominicana, República → Dominican Republic □[1]	238	19.00 N	70.40 W
Dominican Republic □[1]	230		
	238	19.00 N	70.40 W
Dominikanische Republik → Dominican Republic □[1]	238	19.00 N	70.40 W
Dominion	186	46.13 N	60.01 W
Dominion, Cape ≻	176	66.13 N	74.28 W
Dominion Astrophysical Observatory ʋ[3]	224	48.31 N	123.25 W
Dominique → Dominica □[1]	240d	15.30 N	61.20 W
Domiongo	152	4.37 S	21.15 E
Domitilla, Catacombe di ⊥	267a	41.52 N	12.31 E
Dömitz	54	53.08 N	11.14 E
Dom Joaquim	255	18.57 S	43.16 W
Domleschg ∨	58	46.44 N	9.28 E
Dommartin-lès-Toul	58	48.40 N	5.54 E
Dommartin-Varimont	56	48.58 N	4.46 E
Dommary-Baroncourt	56	49.17 N	5.42 E
Dommel ≃	52	51.40 N	5.20 E
Dommitzsch	54	51.38 N	12.53 E
Domnarvet	40	60.30 N	15.27 E
Domnești	38	44.25 N	25.56 E
Domnino	82	54.10 N	38.11 E
Dom Noi ≃	110	15.17 N	105.28 E
Domo	144	7.54 N	46.52 E
Domodedovo	82	55.26 N	37.46 E
Domodedovo, Aeroport ⊠	82	55.25 N	37.53 E
Domodossola	58	46.07 N	8.17 E
Domohani	124	26.35 N	88.48 E
Domoni	157a	12.15 S	44.32 E
Domont	261	49.02 N	2.20 E
Dompaire	58	48.13 N	6.13 E
Dom Pedrito	252	30.59 S	54.40 W
Dom Pedro	250	4.29 S	44.27 W
Dom Pedro II, Estação ◆[5]	287a	23.54 S	43.12 W
Dompierre-sur-Besbre	32	46.31 N	3.41 E
Dompu	115b	8.32 S	118.28 E
Domremy	184	52.47 N	105.44 W
Domrémy-la-Pucelle	58	48.27 N	5.41 E
Domselaar	258	35.04 S	58.18 W
Dom Silvério	255	20.09 S	42.58 W
Domsjö	26	63.15 N	18.43 E
Domus de Maria	71	38.57 N	8.52 E
Domusnovas	71	39.19 N	8.39 E
Domuyo, Volcán ∧[1]	252	36.38 S	70.26 W
Domvast	50	50.12 N	1.55 E
Dom Viçoso	256	22.13 S	45.09 W
Dom Yai ≃	110	15.18 N	105.10 E
Domžale	36	46.08 N	14.36 E
Don ≃, Bhārat	122	16.17 N	76.27 E
Don ≃, Ont., Can.	212	43.39 N	79.21 W
Don ≃, Lao	110	15.07 N	105.48 E
Don ≃, S.S.S.R.	72	47.04 N	39.18 E
Don ≃, Eng., U.K.	44	53.39 N	0.59 W
Don ≃, Eng., U.K.	262	53.47 N	2.14 W
Don ≃, Scot., U.K.	46	57.08 N	2.05 W
Dona Ana, Moç.	154	17.25 S	35.07 E
Dona Ana, N. Mex., U.S.	200	32.23 N	106.49 W
Donada	64	45.02 N	12.12 E
Donadeu	252	26.43 S	62.44 W
Dona Eusébia	256	21.18 S	42.48 W
Donaghadee	48	54.93 N	5.33 W
Donaghmore	48	54.32 N	6.49 W
Donahoe Creek ≃	222	30.49 N	97.12 W
Donald	166	36.22 S	143.00 E
Donalda	182	52.35 N	112.34 W
Donaldson, Ark., U.S.	194	34.14 N	92.55 W
Donaldson, Ind., U.S.	216	41.22 N	86.27 W
Donaldson, Pa., U.S.	208	40.38 N	76.24 W
Donaldson Crossroads	279b	40.16 N	80.07 W
Donaldsonville	194	30.06 N	90.59 W
Donalsonville	192	31.03 N	84.53 W
Donard, Slieve ∧	48	54.11 N	5.55 W
Donau → Danube ≃	22	45.20 N	29.40 E
Donaueschingen	58	47.57 N	8.29 E
Donaufeld ◆[8]	264b	48.15 N	16.25 E
Donau Kanal ☰	264b	48.10 N	16.30 E
Donaumoos ☷	60	48.30 N	11.15 E
Donaupark ♠	264b	48.14 N	16.25 E
Donauried ◆[1]	56	48.35 N	10.40 E
Donaustadt ◆[8]	264b	48.13 N	16.30 E
Donaustauf	60	49.02 N	12.13 E
Donauturm ʋ	264b	48.14 N	16.25 E
Donauwörth	56	48.43 N	10.46 E
Don Benito	34	38.57 N	5.52 W
Dönberg	263	51.18 N	7.10 E
Don Bosco ◆[8]	258	34.42 S	58.18 W
Doncaster, Austl.	274b	37.47 S	145.08 E
Doncaster, Eng., U.K.	44	53.32 N	1.07 W
Doncaster ≃	206	45.58 N	74.06 W
Doncaster East	274b	37.47 S	145.10 E
Donchêry	56	49.42 N	4.52 E
Doncovka	83	49.35 N	39.16 E
Dondaicha	120	21.20 N	74.34 E
Dondo, Ang.	152	9.38 S	14.25 E
Dondo, Moç.	156	19.36 S	34.44 E
Dondo, Teluk C	112	0.55 N	120.30 E
Dondra Head ≻	122	5.55 N	80.35 E
Don-duong	110	11.51 N	108.35 E
Dond'ušany	78	48.15 N	27.37 E
Doneck, S.S.S.R.	83	48.21 N	40.02 E
Doneck, S.S.S.R.	83	48.00 N	37.48 E
Doneck □[4]	83	48.00 N	37.30 E
Doneck, Aeroport ⊠	83	48.08 N	37.45 E
Doneckij Kr'až ∧	83	48.15 N	38.45 E
Donegal, Eire	48	54.39 N	8.07 W
Donegal, S. Afr.	158	26.10 S	23.58 E
Donegal, Pa., U.S.	214	40.07 N	79.23 W
Donegal □[6]	48	54.50 N	8.00 W
Donegal Bay C	48	54.30 N	8.30 W
Doneraile	48	52.13 N	8.35 W
Donetsk → Doneck	83	48.00 N	37.48 E
Donga ≃	146	8.19 N	9.58 E
Dongan → Mishan, Zhg.	89	45.33 N	131.52 E
Dongan, Zhg.	100	33.24 N	114.24 E
Dongan, Zhg.	102	26.17 N	111.07 E
Dongan, Zhg.	106	30.30 N	118.48 E
Dongan, Zhg.	106	31.35 N	119.44 E
Dongao	100	29.12 N	121.25 E
Dongao I	100	22.01 N	113.43 E
Dongara	162	29.15 S	114.56 E
Dongargarh	120	21.12 N	80.44 E
Dongazhen	98	36.11 N	116.16 E
Dongba, Zhg.	105	39.58 N	116.32 E
Dongba, Zhg.	106	31.18 N	119.03 E
Dongbahe	105	39.58 N	116.27 E
Dongbaimiao	105	40.34 N	116.05 E
Dongbeibao	98	36.06 N	117.08 E
Dongbeicha	98	41.43 N	127.23 E
Dongbulizhadamu	120	34.27 N	93.12 E
Dongchang	106	31.52 N	121.38 E
Dongchangjie	106	32.04 N	119.18 E
Dongchansi	107	30.20 N	105.20 E
Dongcheng	100	28.56 N	121.16 E
Dongchong	100	26.35 N	119.52 E
Dongchuan	102	26.10 N	103.01 E
Dongcun	106	30.57 N	121.46 E
Dongdaban	104	41.43 N	120.49 E
Dongdaoan	98	38.21 N	117.12 E
Dongdu	98	35.50 N	117.42 E
Dongduluo	105	39.04 N	115.15 E
Dongen	52	51.37 N	4.56 E
Dongfang (Basuo)	110	19.05 N	108.39 E
Dongfeng, Zhg.	98	42.40 N	125.28 E
Dongfeng, Zhg.	100	27.20 N	118.53 E
Dongfeng, Zhg.	107	29.59 N	104.48 E
Dongfengtai	105	39.34 N	117.45 E
Donggala	112	0.40 S	119.44 E
Donggang	100	22.58 N	115.57 E
Donggangzi	89	45.53 N	129.49 E
Dongge	124	29.38 N	90.59 E
Donggi	112	1.33 S	122.15 E
Donggongshan ⋀	100	27.36 N	119.26 E
Donggongsuo	106	32.07 N	121.25 E
Donggou, Zhg.	100	33.38 N	119.40 E
Donggou, Zhg.	106	32.17 N	118.59 E
Donggu	100	26.46 N	115.22 E
Dongguan, Zhg.	100	23.03 N	113.46 E
Dongguan, Zhg.	100	27.49 N	116.25 E
Dongguan, Zhg.	106	30.22 N	119.28 E
Dongguanchang	107	30.47 N	106.16 E
Dongguang	98	37.53 N	116.30 E
Dongguanpu	106	31.13 N	120.43 E
Dongguanyingzi	104	41.56 N	120.38 E
Dongguayu I	100	27.38 N	121.07 E
Donggugang	105	39.10 N	116.49 E
Donggui ⊜	106	31.21 N	119.52 E
Dong-hai, Viet.	110	12.34 N	109.14 E
Donghai (Haizhou), Zhg.	98	34.34 N	119.11 E
Donghai → East China Sea ⊤[2]	90	30.00 N	126.00 E
Donghaidao I	102	21.02 N	110.25 E
Donghenghe ☰	106	31.54 N	120.17 E
Dong-hoi	110	17.29 N	106.36 E
Donghu ⊜	120	32.10 N	84.40 E
Donghuanggou	104	40.43 N	123.29 E
Donghuwei	100	26.28 N	113.07 E
Dongi	112	2.02 S	121.28 E
Dongio	58	46.27 N	8.58 E
Dongjia	98	37.18 N	118.24 E
Dongjiadao I	100	25.19 N	119.46 E
Dongjiang	100	25.57 N	113.15 E
Dongjiang ≃	100	23.06 N	114.00 E
Dongjiangkou	102	33.37 N	108.49 E
Dongjidao I	100	28.43 N	121.55 E
Dongjie	100	25.53 N	116.22 E
Dongjielang	100	31.03 N	115.57 E
Dongjingcheng	89	44.07 N	129.09 E
Dongjinghe ≃	100	30.31 N	112.50 E
Dongjingji	98	40.06 N	114.00 E
Dongjiu	120	29.58 N	94.53 E
Dongkaihecheng	104	41.04 N	122.38 E
Dongkalang	112	0.10 N	120.06 E
Dongkeng	100	27.48 N	119.42 E
Dong-khe	110	22.26 N	106.27 E
Dongkou	98	35.29 N	115.20 E
Dongkun	100	25.26 N	119.44 E
Donglan	102	24.40 N	107.18 E
Donglaohuyu	104	42.28 N	124.17 E
Donglaojunpu	104	41.24 N	121.22 E
Dongli	102	20.50 N	110.20 E
Dongliang	104	42.00 N	121.25 E
Dongliangjia	105	40.52 N	118.17 E
Donglidian	98	36.02 N	118.23 E
Donglinchang	107	29.39 N	104.07 E
Dongling	104	41.50 N	123.35 E
Dongling ʋ[1]	104	41.49 N	123.29 E
Dongliu, Zhg.	100	30.14 N	116.53 E
Dongliu, Zhg.	106	32.06 N	118.58 E
Dongliujiazi	104	42.21 N	122.44 E
Donglizhuang	105	39.21 N	116.47 E
Donglong	100	23.36 N	116.50 E
Donglucun	89	49.28 N	128.50 E
Dongmenshi	100	28.29 N	114.02 E
Dongming	98	35.18 N	115 08 E
Dong-nai ≃	110	10.45 N	106.46 E
Dongnangou	104	41.25 N	122.02 E
Dong-nhien, Rach ≃	269c	10.49 N	106.46 E
Dongning	89	44.04 N	131.07 E
Dongo, Ang.	152	14.36 S	15.48 E
Dongo, It.	58	46.07 N	9.17 E
Dongo, Zaïre	152	2.43 N	18.24 E
Dongobe	152	4.37 N	23.12 E
Dongobesh	154	4.04 S	35.23 E
Dongola → Dunqulah	140	19.10 N	30.29 E
Dongon Point ≻	116	12.44 N	120.48 E
Dongou	152	2.02 N	18.04 E
Dongpi	100	27.15 N	116.06 E
Dongping, Zhg.	98	35.55 N	116.18 E
Dongping, Zhg.	100	27.24 N	118.39 E
Dongpinghu ⊜	98	36.00 N	116.12 E
Dongpushi	100	30.03 N	120.34 E
Dongqi ≃	100	25.00 N	118.27 E
Dongqian	106	30.52 N	120.23 E
Dongqiao	100	31.12 N	112.48 E
Dongqing	106	31.49 N	120.03 E
Dongqingduizi	104	41.02 N	122.08 E
Dongsanjiazi	104	41.54 N	122.48 E
Dongsanlintang	106	31.09 N	121.31 E
Dongshaer	120	28.41 N	89.09 E
Dongshahe ≃	104	41.07 N	121.50 E
Dongshajiao	100	30.19 N	122.09 E
Dongshan, Zhg.	100	23.46 N	117.31 E
Dongshan, Zhg.	102	19.50 N	110.14 E
Dongshankou	104	41.31 N	123.28 E
Dongshanqiao	106	31.52 N	118.46 E
Dongshaqundao (Pratas Islands) II	90	20.42 N	116.43 E
Dongshe	106	32.07 N	121.12 E
Dongsheng	102	39.57 N	110.00 E
Dongsheshanzi	104	42.15 N	123.09 E
Dongshi, Zhg.	100	24.43 N	115.59 E
Dongshi, Zhg.	100	24.42 N	118.27 E
Dongshi, Zhg.	105	39.49 N	116.34 E
Dongshuangzhai	98	40.18 N	113.56 E
Dongshuiyan	105	39.15 N	115.23 E
Dongtai	100	32.51 N	120.20 E
Dongtaihu C	106	31.05 N	120.30 E
Dongtaipingzhen	89	45.18 N	122.05 E
Dongtangou	105	39.23 N	118.22 E
Dongtangshu	106	31.33 N	120.51 E
Dongtianmushan ∧	106	30.22 N	119.31 E
Dongtinghu	106	30.53 N	119.30 E
Dongtinghu ⊜	100	29.20 N	112.54 E
Dongtingwei	100	24.59 N	114.54 E
Dongtingxi	102	28.34 N	110.36 E
Dongtingxishan ∧	106	31.07 N	120.16 E
Dongtingzhen	98	38.29 N	115.08 E
Dongtou	100	27.50 N	121.09 E
Dongtoushan I	100	27.50 N	121.08 E
Dong-trieu	110	21.05 N	106.31 E
Dongtuhulu	104	41.55 N	121.33 E
Dongtuoshanzi	104	42.10 N	123.08 E
Dongtuozi	104	41.17 N	121.53 E
Dong-van	110	23.16 N	105.22 E
Dongwangfu	89	44.47 N	120.53 E
Dongwangzhuang	106	32.16 N	120.32 E
Dongwe ≃	152	13.58 S	23.53 E
Dongwenhe ≃	98	35.28 N	118.32 E
Dongwuquan	105	39.20 N	115.43 E
Dongxi, Zhg.	100	28.35 N	120.02 E
Dongxi, Zhg.	102	28.47 N	106.39 E
Dongxi, Zhg.	107	30.24 N	104.33 E
Dongxi, Zhg.	107	28.46 N	104.41 E
Dongxi ≃, Zhg.	100	27.02 N	118.18 E
Dongxi ≃, Zhg.	100	24.36 N	117.37 E
Dongxiacun	106	31.11 N	119.05 E
Dongxiagaogao	104	42.36 N	122 30 E
Dongxiang	100	28.13 N	116.35 E
Dongxiangdao I	100	25.36 N	119.48 E
Dongxiaofangshen	104	40.50 N	122.22 E
Dongxin	106	31.24 N	121.41 E
Dongxing	89	46.23 N	127.52 E
Dongxingchang, Zhg.	107	29.16 N	103.55 E
Dongxingchang, Zhg.	107	29.36 N	105.04 E
Dongxinghe	105	39.46 N	114.49 E
Dongxingsha I	106	31.23 N	121.44 E
Dongxinpu	104	41.00 N	123.18 E
Dongxinzhen	106	31.57 N	121.42 E
Dongyang	100	29.16 N	120.14 E
Dongyangqiao	106	30.52 N	120.34 E
Dongyangzhen	89	48.03 N	124.17 E
Dongyaoji	98	35.56 N	113.58 E
Dongyian	105	39.22 N	115.46 E
Dongyinhe ≃	105	39.09 N	117.43 E
Dongyou	100	27.11 N	118.42 E
Dongyuezhen	107	30.24 N	103.32 E
Dongzhang	100	25.44 N	119.17 E
Dongzhaocun	105	40.02 N	116.46 E
Dongzhaozhuang	105	39.57 N	118.24 E
Dongzhenbeng	106	30.59 N	121.01 E
Dongzhizhuang	105	40.25 N	116.50 E
Dongzhuangpu	105	40.34 N	115.42 E
Dongziya	105	38.50 N	116.44 E
Donie	222	31.29 N	96.13 W
Doninga	150	10.37 N	1.26 W
Donington	42	52.55 N	0.12 W
Doniphan, Mo., U.S.	194	36.37 N	90.50 W
Doniphan, Nebr., U.S.	198	40.46 N	98.22 W
Don Islands II	116	11.05 N	123.38 E
Donja Stubica	36	45.59 N	15.58 E
Donjek ≃	180	62.35 N	140.00 W
Donjezk → Doneck	83	48.00 N	37.48 E
Donji Vakuf	36	44.09 N	17.25 E
Donk	52	51.33 N	5.37 E
Donkerpoort	158	30.32 S	25.30 E
Donkey Creek ≃	198	44.12 N	104.58 W
Donkey Town	260	51.20 N	0.39 W
Don Martín	196	27.32 N	100.37 W
Don Matías	246	6.30 N	75.22 W
Don Mills ◆[8]	275b	43.44 N	79.20 W
Don Mills Centre ◆[9]	275b	43.44 N	79.21 W
Don Muang Airport ⊠	269a	13.56 N	100.37 E
Donna Buang, Mount ∧	169	37.43 S	145.40 E
Donnacona	206	46.40 N	71.47 W
Donnalucata	70	36.45 N	14.38 E
Donnaz	62	45.36 N	7.46 E
Donnellson	219	39.02 N	89.29 W
Donnells Reservoir ⊜[1]	226	38.20 N	119.56 W
Donnelly, Alta., Can.	182	55.44 N	117.06 W
Donnelly, Alaska, U.S.	180	63.41 N	145.53 W
Donnelly, Idaho, U.S.	202	44.44 N	116.05 W
Donnellys Crossing	172	35.43 S	173.37 E
Donnemarie-Dontilly	50	48.29 N	3.08 E
Donner	194	29.42 N	90.58 W
Donner Lake ⊜[1]	226	39.20 N	120.16 W
Donner Memorial State Park ♠	226	39.18 N	120.16 W
Donner Pass)(	226	39.19 N	120.20 W
Donnersberg ∧	56	50.23 N	8.32 E
Donner und Blitzen ≃	202	43.17 N	118.49 W
Donnybrook, Austl.	162	33.35 S	115.49 E
Donnybrook, S. Afr.	158	30.00 S	29.48 E
Donora	214	40.11 N	79.52 W
Donors Hills	166	18.42 S	140.33 E
Donoughmore	48	51.57 N	8.45 W
Donovan	216	40.53 N	87.37 W
Don Peninsula ≻[1]	182	52.30 N	128.10 W
Donque	152	15.28 S	14.06 E
Donskoj, S.S.S.R.	76	53.58 N	38.20 E
Donskoj, S.S.S.R.	83	47.25 N	40.14 E
Donskoje, S.S.S.R.	76	52.37 N	39.00 E
Donskoje, S.S.S.R.	80	45.21 N	41.59 E
Donskoje, S.S.S.R.	83	47.31 N	37.33 E
Donskoje Belogorje ⋀[1]	78	50.30 N	39.45 E
Donsol	116	12.54 N	123.36 E
Don Torcuato	288	34.30 S	58.38 W
Don Torcuato, Aeródromo ⊠	288	34.30 S	58.36 W
Donuzlav Ozero ⊜	78	45.23 N	33.05 E
Donyztau ⋀	86	46.25 N	57.00 E
Donzdorf	56	48.41 N	9.48 E
Donzère	62	44.27 N	4.43 E
Donzy	50	47.22 N	3.08 E
Dooagh	48	53.59 N	10.09 W
Dood Nuur ⊜	88	51.20 N	99.20 E
Doomadgee Aborginal Reserve ◆[4]	166	17.43 S	138.36 E
Doomadgee Mission	166	17.56 S	138.49 E
Doon, Ont., Can.	212	43.23 N	80.26 W
Doon, Iowa, U.S.	198	43.17 N	96.14 W
Doon ≃	44	55.26 N	4.38 W
Doon, Loch ⊜	44	55.15 N	4.22 W
Doonbeg	48	52.44 N	9.32 W
Doonbeg ≃	48	52.44 N	9.34 W
Doondi	166	28.15 S	148.28 E
Doonerak, Mount ∧	180	67.56 N	150.37 W
Doongalla Forest Reserve ♠	274b	37.51 S	145.20 E
Doonside	274a	33.46 S	150.52 E
Dooralong	170	33.12 S	151.22 E
Doorn	52	52.03 N	5.21 E
Doorndam	158	28.03 S	21.03 E
Doornik → Tournai	50	50.36 N	3.23 E
Door Peninsula ≻[1]	190	44.55 N	87.20 W
Dopping Brook ≃	283	42.12 N	71.23 W
Dor	132	32.37 N	34.55 E
Dora	194	33.44 N	87.05 W
Dora, Lake ⊜, Austl.	162	22.05 S	122.55 E
Dora, Lake ⊜, Fla., U.S.	220	29.00 N	81.37 W
Dora Baltea ≃	62	45.11 N	8.05 E
Dora di Rhêmes ≃	62	45.42 N	7.11 E
Dorado	240m	18.28 N	66.15 W
Doraha	123	30.49 N	76.01 E
Dorāh Ān)(	123	36.07 N	71.15 E
Dorain, Beinn ∧	46	56.30 N	4.42 W
Dorândia	256	22.27 S	43.57 W
Dora Riparia ≃	62	45.05 N	7.44 E
Doratama ∧	123	34.54 N	76.00 E
Doraville	192	33.54 N	84.17 W
Dorback Burn ≃	46	57.31 N	3.40 W
Dorchester, N.B., Can.	186	45.54 N	64.31 W
Dorchester, Ont., Can.	212	42.59 N	81.04 W
Dorchester, Eng., U.K.	42	51.39 N	1.10 W
Dorchester, Eng., U.K.	42	50.43 N	2.26 W
Dorchester, Ill., U.S.	219	39.05 N	89.53 W
Dorchester, Nebr., U.S.	198	40.39 N	97.07 W
Dorchester, N.J., U.S.	208	39.17 N	74.58 W
Dorchester, Wis., U.S.	190	45.00 N	90.20 W
Dorchester □[6]	208	38.34 N	76.04 W
Dorchester ◆[8]	283	42.17 N	71.04 W
Dorchester, Cape ≻	176	65.29 N	77.30 W
Dorchester Bay C	283	42.19 N	71.02 W
Dorchester Crossing	186	46.10 N	64.34 W
Dorchester Heights National Historic Site ⊥	283	42.20 N	71.03 W
Dorchheim	56	50.30 N	8.04 E
Dordabis	156	22.52 S	17.38 E
Dordives	50	48.09 N	2.46 E
Dordogne □[5]	32	45.10 N	0.45 E
Dordogne ≃	32	45.02 N	0.35 W
Dordon	42	52.36 N	1.37 W
Dordrecht, Ned.	52	51.49 N	4.40 E
Dordrecht, S. Afr.	158	31.20 S	27.03 E
Doré ≃, Sask., Can.	184	54.56 N	107.45 W
Dore ≃, Fr.	62	45.50 N	3.35 E
Dore ≃, Eng., U.K.	42	51.57 N	2.52 W
Dore, Monts ⋀	32	45.30 N	2.45 E
Doreissou	146	10.33 N	15.08 E
Doré Lake	184	54.31 N	107.06 W
Doré Lake ⊜	184	54.46 N	107.17 W
Dorena	202	43.47 N	122.55 W
Dorena Lake ⊜[1]	202	43.46 N	122.55 W
Dores	46	57.22 N	4.15 W
Dores do Indaiá	255	19.27 S	45.36 W
Dores do Paraibuna	256	21.31 S	43.39 W
Dorf Dienten	64	47.22 N	13.00 E
Dorfen	60	48.17 N	12.08 E
Dorfgastein	64	47.15 N	13.06 E
Dorfmark	52	52.54 N	9.46 E
Dorgali	71	40.17 N	9.35 E
Dori	150	14.02 N	0.02 W
Doring ≃	158	31.54 S	18.39 E
Doringbaai	158	31.48 S	18.15 E
Doringkop ∧	273d	26.15 S	27.50 E
Dorino	82	56.28 N	36.09 E
Dorion-Vaudreuil	206	45.23 N	74.01 W
Dorje Lāpka ∧	124	28.11 N	85.47 E
Dorking	260	51.14 N	0.20 W
Dorloo	210	42.43 N	74.37 W
Dormaa Ahenkro	150	7.17 N	2.53 W
Dormagen	56	51.05 N	6.50 E
Dormans	50	49.04 N	3.38 E
Dormidontovka	89	47.45 N	134.57 E
Dornach	58	47.29 N	7.37 E
Dornap	263	51.15 N	7.04 E
Dornbach ◆[8]	264b	48.14 N	16.18 E
Dornbirn	58	47.25 N	9.44 E
Dorndorf, D.D.R.	54	51.00 N	11.40 E
Dorndorf, D.D.R.	56	50.50 N	10.05 E
Dornecy	50	47.26 N	3.35 E
Dorney	260	51.30 N	0.40 W
Dornhan	58	48.21 N	8.30 E
Dornie	46	57.17 N	5.31 W
Dorno	62	45.09 N	8.57 E
Dornoch	46	57.52 N	4.02 W
Dornoch Firth C[1]	46	57.53 N	4.00 W
Dornod □[4]	88	48.00 N	115.00 E
Dornogov' □[4]	102	44.30 N	110.00 E
Dornsife	208	40.45 N	76.47 W
Dornstadt	58	48.28 N	9.56 E
Dornstetten	58	48.28 N	8.30 E
Dornumersiel	52	53.40 N	7.28 E
Doro, Indon.	115a	7.02 S	109.41 E
Doro, Mali	150	16.09 N	0.51 W
Dorochovo	82	55.33 N	36.23 E
Dorog	30	47.43 N	18.44 E
Dorogobuž	76	54.55 N	33.18 E
Dorohoi	38	47.57 N	26.24 E
Dorokempo	115b	8.33 S	118.15 E
Doromata	115b	8.46 S	118.13 E
Doromo	154	3.49 N	26.17 E
Döröö Nuur ⊜	88	47.40 N	93.30 E
Dorošata	80	57.21 N	51.08 E
Dorošicha	82	56.52 N	35.50 E
Dorotea	26	64.16 N	16.24 E
Dorothy	208	39.24 N	74.49 W
Dorothy, Lake ⊜	224	47.34 N	121.22 W
Dorotockeys Run ≃	276	40.59 N	73.58 W
Dorpat → Tartu	76	58.23 N	26.43 E
Dörpen	52	52.57 N	7.20 E
Dorr	216	42.43 N	85.43 W
Dorrance	198	38.51 N	98.35 W
Dorre Island I	162	25.09 S	113.07 E
Dorridge	42	52.22 N	1.45 W
Dorrigo	166	30.21 S	152.43 E
Dorris	204	41.58 N	121.55 W
Dorset, Ohio, U.S.	214	41.41 N	80.40 W
Dorset, Vt., U.S.	210	43.15 N	73.06 W
Dorset □[6]	42	50.47 N	2.20 W
Dorset Peak ∧	188	43.19 N	73.02 W
Dorsey Run ≃	284b	39.11 N	76.48 W
Dorseyville	279b	40.35 N	79.53 W
Dorsten	52	51.39 N	6.58 E
Dorstfeld ◆[8]	263	51.31 N	7.25 E
Dort → Dordrecht	52	51.49 N	4.40 E
Dortan	58	46.19 N	5.40 E
Dortmund	52		
	263	51.31 N	7.28 E
Dortmund-Ems-Kanal ☰	52	51.32 N	7.27 E
Dortmunder Rieselfelder ◆[1]	263	51.39 N	7.25 E
Dortmund-Wickede, Flughafen ⊠	263	51.32 N	7.35 E
Dorton	192	37.17 N	82.35 W
Dörtyol	130	36.52 N	36.12 E
Dorum	52	53.41 N	8.34 E
Doruma	154	4.44 N	27.42 E
Dorval	206	45.27 N	73.44 W
Dorval, Île I	275a	45.26 N	73.45 W
Dorval Gardens Centre ◆[9]	275a	45.27 N	73.44 W
Dörverden	52	52.51 N	9.13 E
Dörvöldžin	88	48.11 N	93.54 E
Dörzbach	56	49.23 N	9.42 E
Dosara	150	12.32 N	6.09 E
Dosara ∧	123	34.38 N	72.30 E
Dos Arroyos	234	17.02 N	99.40 W
Dosatuj	88	50.23 N	118.38 E
Dos Bahías, Cabo ≻	254	44.55 S	65.32 W
Dos Bocas	240m	18.20 N	66.40 W
Dos Bocas, Lago ⊜[1]	240m	18.19 N	66.40 W
Doščatoje	80	55.23 N	42.07 E
Dosewallips ≃	224	47.42 N	122.53 W
Doshan Tappeh Airfield ⊠	267d	35.42 N	51.28 E
Dos Hermanas	34	37.17 N	5.55 W
Dos Hermanas, Islas II	258	34.05 S	58.17 W
Dōshi	94	35.32 N	139.02 E
Dōshi ≃	94	35.36 N	139.14 E
Doshisha University ʋ[2]	270	35.02 N	135.46 E
Dosi	164	5.56 S	134.34 E
Dösjebro	41	55.49 N	13.01 E
Do-son	110	20.42 N	106.47 E
Dosoris Island ≻[1]	276	40.53 N	73.38 W
Dosoris Pond ⊜	276	40.54 N	73.38 W
Dos Palos	226	36.59 N	120.37 W
Dos Reyes, Punta ≻	252	24.33 S	70.35 W
Dosse ≃	54	53.13 N	12.20 E
Dossin Great Lakes Museum ʋ	281	42.20 N	82.59 W
Dosso	150	13.03 N	3.12 E
Dosso □[5]	150	13.00 N	3.00 E
Dossor	80	47.32 N	53.01 E
Doster	216	42.27 N	85.33 W
Doswell	208	37.52 N	77.27 W
Dothan	194	31.13 N	85.24 W
Doting Cove	186	49.27 N	53.57 W
Dot Lake	180	63.40 N	194.04 W
Dotnuva	76	55.21 N	23.54 E
Dotson	222	32.01 N	94.31 W
Döttingen	58	47.34 N	8.16 E
Doty	224	46.38 N	123.17 W
Douai	50	50.22 N	3.04 E
Douala	152	4.03 N	9.42 E
Douarnenez	32	48.06 N	4.20 W
Doubabougou	150	14.13 N	7.59 W
Double, Lac ⊜	186	50.46 N	70.23 W
Double, Pointe ≻	241o	16.20 N	61.00 W
Double Bayou	222	29.41 N	94.39 W
Double Cone ∧	172	45.04 S	168.48 E
Double Island Point ≻	166	25.56 S	153.11 E
Double Mountain ∧	228	35.02 N	118.29 W
Double Point ≻	166	17.39 S	146.09 E
Double Springs	194	34.09 N	87.24 W
Doubletop Peak ∧	200	43.21 N	110.17 W
Doubs	58	46.56 N	6.21 E
Doubs ≃, Eur.	32	47.10 N	6.25 E
Doubs ≃, Eur.	58	46.54 N	5.02 E
Doubtful Sound ɰ	172	45.17 S	166.51 E
Doubtless Bay C	172	34.55 S	173.25 E
Douchy	50	47.57 N	3.03 E
Douchy-les-Mines	50	50.18 N	3.23 E
Doudeville	50	49.43 N	0.48 E
Doudian	105	39.39 N	116.03 E
Doué ≃[1]	150	16.38 N	15.02 W
Douentza	150	15.00 N	2.57 W
Dougga ⊥	148	36.25 N	9.13 E
Doughboy	170	35.15 S	149.39 E
Doughboy Bay C	172	47.02 S	167.41 E
Douglas, Ont., Can.	212	45.31 N	76.56 W
Douglas, I. of Man	44	54.09 N	4.28 W
Douglas, S. Afr.	158	29.04 S	23.46 E
Douglas, Scot., U.K.	46	55.33 N	3.51 W
Douglas, Alaska, U.S.	180	58.16 N	134.22 W
Douglas, Ariz., U.S.	200	31.21 N	109.33 W
Douglas, Ga., U.S.	192	31.31 N	82.51 W
Douglas, Mich., U.S.	216	42.38 N	86.12 W
Douglas, N. Dak., U.S.	198	47.51 N	101.30 W
Douglas, Wyo., U.S.	200	42.45 N	105.24 W
Douglas □[6]	226	38.55 N	119.39 W
Douglas ≃	262	53.43 N	2.50 W
Douglas, Cape ≻	180	58.52 N	153.18 W
Douglas, Mount ∧	180	58.52 N	153.31 W
Douglas, Mount ∧[2]	162	28.39 S	123.53 E
Douglas Aircraft Company ʋ[3]	280	33.50 N	118.09 W
Douglas Channel ɰ	182	53.30 N	129.12 W
Douglas Creek ≃	200	40.06 N	108.46 W
Douglas Lake	182	50.10 N	120.12 W
Douglas Lake ⊜[1]	192	36.00 N	83.22 W
Douglas Lake Indian Reserve ◆[4]	182	50.10 N	120.49 W
Douglas Park	170	34.11 S	150.43 E
Douglas Park ♠	278	41.52 N	87.42 W
Douglass, Kans., U.S.	198	37.31 N	97.01 W
Douglass, Tex., U.S.	222	31.40 N	94.53 W
Douglass Run ≃	279b	40.15 N	79.48 W
Douglas Station	184	49.53 N	99.46 W
Douglassville	208	40.15 N	75.44 W
Douglasville	192	33.45 N	84.45 W
Douglas Water ≃	46	55.38 N	3.46 W
Dougouro, Ouadi ∨	146	17.53 N	21.31 E
Dougouzi, Zhg.	89	49.57 N	127.01 E
Dougouzi, Zhg.	104	41.16 N	122.34 E
Douhe ≃	105	39.13 N	118.03 E
Doujiapu	104	41.05 N	122.12 E
Doujiazhuang	105	40.22 N	116.59 E
Doulaincourt	58	48.19 N	5.12 E
Doulevant-le-Château	58	48.23 N	4.55 E
Doullens	50	50.09 N	2.21 E
Doumanaba	150	11.40 N	5.56 W
Doumanga	152	2.41 S	12.40 E
Doumba	152	5.05 N	14.18 E
Doumdégué	152	7.29 N	18.58 E
Doumé	152	4.14 N	13.27 E
Doumé ≃	152	4.06 N	14.34 E
Doumen, Zhg.	100	22.14 N	113.11 E
Doumen, Zhg.	105	39.18 N	115.53 E
Douna	150	14.39 N	1.44 W
Doune	46	56.12 N	4.05 W
Doune Castle ⊥	46	56.11 N	4.03 W
Dounguila	152	2.53 S	11.58 E
Doupov	54	50.10 N	13.08 E
Doupovské hory ⋀	54	50.13 N	13.08 E
Dour	50	50.24 N	3.47 E
Doura	150	13.14 N	5.55 W
Dourada, Serra ⋀[1]	255	13.10 S	48.45 W
Douradinho	256	21.45 S	45.46 W
Dourado ≃, Bra.	255	21.22 S	49.41 W
Dourado ≃, Bra.	256	21.43 S	45.44 W
Dourados	255	22.13 S	54.48 W
Dourados ≃	255	21.58 S	54.18 W
Dourbali	146	11.49 N	15.52 E
Dourdan	50	48.32 N	2.01 E

Symbols in the index entries represent the broad categories identified in the key at the right. Symbols with superior numbers (⋀[2]) identify subcategories (see complete key on page *I* · 30).

Kartensymbole in dem Registerverzeichnis stellen die rechts in Schlüssel erklärten Kategorien dar. Symbole mit hochgestellten Ziffern (⋀[2]) bezeichnen Unterabteilungen einer Kategorie (vgl. vollständiger Schlüssel auf Seite *I* · 30).

Los símbolos incluidos en el texto del índice representan las grandes categorias identificadas con la clave a la derecha. Los símbolos con numeros en su parte superior (⋀[2]) identifican las subcategorías (véase la clave completa en la página *I* · 30).

Les symboles de l'index représentent les catégories indiquées dans la légende à droite. Les symboles suivis d'un indice (⋀[2]) représentent des sous-catégories (voir légende complète à la page *I* · 30).

Os símbolos incluídos no texto do índice representam as grandes categorias identificadas com a chave à direita. Os símbolos com números em sua parte superior (⋀[2]) identificam as subcategorias (veja-se a chave completa à página *I* · 30).

∧ Mountain	Berg	Montaña	Montagne	Montanha
⋀ Mountains	Berge	Montañas	Montagnes	Montanhas
)(Pass	Pass	Paso	Col	Passo
∨ Valley, Canyon	Tal, Cañon	Valle, Cañón	Vallée, Canyon	Vale, Canhão
⌣ Plain	Ebene	Llano	Plaine	Planície
≻ Cape	Kap	Cabo	Cap	Cabo
I Island	Insel	Isla	Île	Ilha
II Islands	Inseln	Islas	Îles	Ilhas
⊥ Other Topographic Features	Andere Topographische Objekte	Otros Elementos Topográficos	Autres données topographiques	Outros Elementos Topográficos

ESPAÑOL / FRANÇAIS / PORTUGUÊS

Nombre / Nom / Nome	Página / Page	Lat.°′	Long.°′ W=Oeste / W=Ouest
Dourdou ≃	32	44.00 N	2.41 E
Dourges	50	50.26 N	2.59 E
Dourkoulé	146	14.27 N	22.13 E
Douro (Duero) ≃	34	41.08 N	8.40 W
Doushanhe	100	31.38 N	114.42 E
Dousman	216	43.01 N	88.28 W
Douthat State Park ♠	192	37.55 N	79.50 W
Douvaine	58	46.19 N	6.18 E
Douvres, Fr.	32	49.17 N	0.23 W
Douvres → Dover, Eng., U.K.	42	51.08 N	1.19 E
Douvres, Falaises de ✧[4]	273b	4.06 S	15.25 E
Douvrin	50	50.31 N	2.50 E
Doux ≃	62	45.04 N	4.50 E
Douy-la-Ramée	261	49.04 N	2.53 E
Douyu	98	37.53 N	114.30 E
Douz	148	33.28 N	9.01 E
Douze ≃	32	43.54 N	0.30 W
Douzhangzhuang	105	39.23 N	116.55 E
Douzishan	107	29.04 N	104.57 E
Douzy	56	49.40 N	5.03 E
Dovadola	66	44.07 N	11.53 E
Dovbyš	78	50.22 N	27.59 E
Dove ≃	42	52.50 N	1.35 W
Dove Creek	200	37.46 N	108.54 W
Dove Creek ≃, Tex., U.S.	196	31.20 N	100.36 W
Dove Creek ≃, Utah, U.S.	200	41.37 N	113.15 W
Dove Holes	262	53.18 N	1.53 W
Dove Holes Tunnel ✢[5]	262	53.18 N	1.53 W
Dover, Austl.	166	43.19 S	147.01 E
Dover, S. Afr.	158	27.02 S	27.46 E
Dover, Eng., U.K.	42	51.08 N	1.19 E
Dover, Ark., U.S.	194	35.24 N	93.07 W
Dover, Del., U.S.	208	39.10 N	75.32 W
Dover, Fla., U.S.	220	28.00 N	82.13 W
Dover, Idaho, U.S.	202	48.15 N	116.36 W
Dover, Ky., U.S.	218	38.46 N	83.53 W
Dover, Mass., U.S.	283	42.15 N	71.17 W
Dover, N.H., U.S.	188	43.12 N	70.56 W
Dover, N.J., U.S.	210	40.53 N	74.34 W
Dover, N.C., U.S.	192	35.13 N	77.26 W
Dover, Ohio, U.S.	214	40.32 N	81.29 W
Dover, Okla., U.S.	196	35.59 N	97.55 W
Dover, Pa., U.S.	208	40.00 N	76.51 W
Dover, Tenn., U.S.	194	36.29 N	87.50 W
Dover, Point ≻	162	32.32 S	125.32 E
Dover, Strait of (Pas de Calais) Ʉ	50	51.00 N	1.30 E
Dover Air Force Base ■	208	39.08 N	75.28 W
Dovercourt	42	51.56 N	1.16 E
Dover-Foxcroft	188	45.11 N	69.13 W
Dover Heights	274a	33.53 S	151.17 E
Dover Hills	276	40.52 N	74.33 W
Dover Plains	210	41.44 N	73.35 W
Dovers Hills ∧∧[2]	162	23.10 S	128.45 E
Dove Stone Reservoir ⊜[1]	262	53.32 N	1.58 W
Doveton	274b	38.00 S	145.14 E
Dovey Valley ∨	42	52.35 N	3.50 W
Dovol'noje	86	54.30 N	79.40 E
Dovre	26	61.59 N	9.15 E
Dovrefjell ∧∧	26	62.06 N	9.25 E
Dovsk	76	53.09 N	30.28 E
Dowa	154	13.40 S	33.58 E
Dowagiac	216	41.59 N	86.06 W
Dowagiac ≃	216	41.51 N	86.16 W
Dowagiac Creek ≃	216	41.49 N	86.10 W
Dowally	46	56.36 N	3.37 W
Dow City	198	41.56 N	95.30 W
Dowell	208	38.21 N	76.27 W
Dowerin	162	31.12 S	117.02 E
Dowker, Île I	275a	45.24 N	73.54 W
Dowlatābād, Afg.	120	36.59 N	66.50 E
Dowlatābād, Afg.	120	36.26 N	64.55 E
Dowlatābād, Īrān	128	28.18 N	56.40 E
Dowlatābād, Īrān	267d	35.37 N	51.27 E
Dowlat Yār	120	34.33 N	65.47 E
Dowling Lake ⊜	182	51.44 N	112.00 W
Downe ✢[8]	260	51.20 N	0.03 E
Down East	285	40.03 N	75.32 W
Downers Grove	216	41.48 N	88.01 W
Downey, Calif., U.S.	228	33.56 N	118.08 W
Downey, Idaho, U.S.	202	42.26 N	112.07 W
Downey, Ill., U.S.	278	42.18 N	87.51 W
Downey Creek ≃	224	48.16 N	121.14 W
Downham, Eng., U.K.	42	52.26 N	0.15 E
Downham, Eng., U.K.	260	51.38 N	0.30 E
Downham Market	42	52.36 N	0.23 E
Down House ⊥	260	51.20 N	0.03 E
Downieville	226	39.34 N	120.50 W
Downing	194	40.29 N	92.22 W
Downingtown	208	40.00 N	75.42 W
Downingtown Airport ⊠	285	39.59 N	75.45 W
Downpatrick	48	54.20 N	5.43 W
Downpatrick Head ≻	48	54.20 N	9.20 W
Downs, Ill., U.S.	216	40.24 N	88.52 W
Downs, Kans., U.S.	198	39.30 N	98.33 W
Downs Mountain ∧	200	43.18 N	109.40 W
Downsview Dells Park ♠	275b	43.44 N	79.30 W
Downsville	210	42.05 N	75.00 W
Downsville Dam ✢[6]	210	42.05 N	74.58 W
Downton	42	51.00 N	1.44 W
Downton, Mount ∧	182	52.42 N	124.51 W
Downton Lake ⊜	182	50.51 N	123.00 W
Downwind Acres Airfield ⊠	281	42.09 N	83.34 W
Dow Rūd	128	33.28 N	49.04 E
Dows	190	42.39 N	93.30 W
Dowsārī	128	28.25 N	57.59 E
Dowshī	120	35.37 N	68.41 E
Doyle	204	40.02 N	120.06 W
Doyles	186	47.50 N	59.12 W
Doylesburg	214	40.13 N	77.42 W
Doylestown, Ohio, U.S.	214	40.58 N	81.42 W
Doylestown, Pa., U.S.	208	40.19 N	75.08 W
Doyline	194	32.32 N	93.25 W
Dōzan ≃	96	33.58 N	133.47 E
Dozier	194	31.30 N	86.28 W
Dozois, Réservoir ⊜[1]	190	47.30 N	77.05 W
Dozza	66	44.22 N	11.37 E
Dra, Hamada du ✢[2]	148	29.00 N	6.45 W
Drâa, Cap ≻	148	28.44 N	11.08 W
Drâa, Oued ∨	148	28.43 N	11.09 W
Draa el Mizan	34	36.32 N	3.50 E
Drabble → José Enrique Rodó	258	33.41 S	57.34 W
Drabenderhöhe	56	50.57 N	7.27 E
Drabov	78	49.58 N	32.08 E
Drac ≃	62	45.13 N	5.41 E
Dracena	255	21.32 S	51.29 W
Drachenfels ⊥	56	50.40 N	7.12 E
Drachten	52	53.06 N	6.05 E
Dračie Jaskyně ✧[5]	30	49.05 N	19.35 E
Dracut	207	42.40 N	71.18 W
Dragalina	38	44.26 N	27.20 E
Drăgănești-Olt	38	44.10 N	24.32 E
Drăgănești-Vlașca	38	44.06 N	25.36 E
Drăgășani	38	44.40 N	24.16 E
Drag Lake ⊜	212	45.05 N	78.24 W
Dragone ≃	64	44.23 N	10.37 E
Dragonera, Isla I	34	39.35 N	2.19 E
Dragoni	68	41.16 N	14.18 E
Dragonja ≃	64	45.28 N	13.37 E
Dragons Mouth Ʉ	241r	10.45 N	61.46 W
Dragon Swamp ≃	208	37.33 N	76.34 W
Dragoon	200	32.02 N	110.02 W
Dragør	41	55.36 N	12.41 E
Draguignan	62	43.32 N	6.28 E
Dragvograd	61	46.35 N	15.02 E
Drain	202	43.40 N	123.19 W
Drake, Mo., U.S.	219	38.28 N	91.28 W
Drake, N. Dak., U.S.	198	47.55 N	100.23 W
Drakenburg	52	52.41 N	9.13 E
Drakensberg ∧∧	156	27.00 S	30.00 E
Drake Passage Ʉ	18	58.00 S	70.00 W
Drake Peak ∧	202	42.19 N	120.07 W
Drakesboro	194	37.13 N	87.03 W
Drakes Branch	192	37.00 N	78.36 W
Drakes Brook ≃	276	40.49 N	74.43 W
Drake Well Museum ʊ	214	41.36 N	79.39 W
Drakino	82	54.52 N	37.17 E
Dráma	38	41.09 N	24.08 E
Dramburg → Drawsko Pomorskie	30	53.32 N	15.48 E
Drammen	26	59.44 N	10.15 E
Drancy	50	48.56 N	2.27 E
Dranda	84	42.53 N	41.09 E
Drang ≃	110	13.19 N	107.21 E
Drangajökull ⛋	24a	66.11 N	22.15 W
Drangstedt	52	53.36 N	8.44 E
Dranov, Ostrovul I	38	44.52 N	29.15 E
Dransfeld	52	51.30 N	9.45 E
Dranske	54	54.38 N	13.14 E
Drap	62	43.45 N	7.19 E
Draper, N.C., U.S.	192	36.31 N	79.41 W
Draper, Utah, U.S.	200	40.32 N	111.52 W
Draperstown	48	54.48 N	6.47 W
Drās	123	34.27 N	75.46 E
Drau (Drava) (Dráva) ≃	36	45.33 N	18.55 E
Drava (Drau) (Dráva) ≃	36	45.33 N	18.55 E
Draveil	50	48.41 N	2.25 E
Dravinja ≃	36	46.22 N	15.57 E
Dravosburg	279b	40.21 N	79.51 W
Drawa ≃	30	52.52 N	15.59 E
Drawno	30	53.13 N	15.45 E
Drawsko Pomorskie	30	53.32 N	15.48 E
Drayton, Ont., Can.	212	43.46 N	80.40 W
Drayton, N. Dak., U.S.	198	48.38 N	97.11 W
Drayton, S.C., U.S.	192	34.58 N	81.54 W
Drayton Plains	216	42.41 N	83.23 W
Drayton Valley	182	53.13 N	114.59 W
Draženˇ	60	49.54 N	13.18 E
Draženov	60	49.28 N	12.52 E
Drean	36	36.41 N	7.46 E
Drebach	54	50.40 N	13.01 E
Drebkau	54	51.39 N	14.13 E
Dreifelder Weiher ⊜	56	50.36 N	7.49 E
Dreihausen	56	50.43 N	8.50 E
Dreiherrnspitze (Pico dei Tre Signori) ∧	64	47.04 N	12.15 E
Dreikikir	164	3.35 S	142.45 E
Drejø I	41	54.58 N	10.25 E
Dremsel, Mount ∧	164	2.10 S	146.55 E
Drena	64	45.58 N	10.56 E
Drenovec	38	43.42 N	22.59 E
Drensteinfurt	52	51.48 N	7.44 E
Drenthe □[4]	52	52.45 N	6.30 E
Dresde → Dresden	54	51.03 N	13.44 E
Dresden, Ont., Can.	214	42.35 N	82.11 W
Dresden, D.D.R.	54	51.03 N	13.44 E
Dresden, N.Y., U.S.	210	42.41 N	76.58 W
Dresden, Ohio, U.S.	214	40.07 N	82.01 W
Dresden, Tenn., U.S.	194	36.18 N	88.42 W
Dresden □[5]	54	51.10 N	14.00 E
Dresher	285	40.08 N	75.10 W
Dretun'	76	55.41 N	29.13 E
Dreux	50	48.44 N	1.22 E
Drevenack	263	51.40 N	6.45 E
Drew	194	33.49 N	90.32 W
Drewer	263	51.40 N	7.07 E
Drewitz, D.D.R.	54	52.22 N	13.07 E
Drewitz, D.D.R.	54	52.12 N	12.10 E
Drewitz ✢[8]	264a	52.22 N	13.08 E
Drewryville	208	36.43 N	77.18 W
Drews Reservoir ⊜[1]	202	42.10 N	120.40 W
Drew University ʊ[2]	276	40.46 N	74.25 W
Drexel	218	39.45 N	84.16 W
Drexel Gardens	218	39.44 N	86.15 W
Drexel Hill	285	39.57 N	75.19 W
Drexel University ʊ[2]	285	39.57 N	75.11 W
Drezdenko	30	52.51 N	15.50 E
Drezna	82	55.44 N	38.51 E
Dribin	76	54.08 N	31.06 E
Driebergen	52	52.03 N	5.16 E
Drienov	30	48.53 N	21.17 E
Driesen → Drezdenko	30	52.51 N	15.50 E
Driffield	44	54.00 N	0.27 W
Drifton	210	41.00 N	75.54 W
Driftpile ≃	182	55.23 N	115.40 W
Drift Pile River Indian Reserve ✢[4]	182	55.18 N	115.45 W
Driftwood	214	41.20 N	78.08 W
Driftwood ≃, B.C., Can.	182	55.43 N	126.15 W
Driftwood ≃, Ind., U.S.	218	39.12 N	85.56 W
Driftwood Creek ≃	198	40.11 N	100.39 W
Driggs	202	43.44 N	111.14 W
Drimnin	46	56.36 N	6.00 W
Drimoleague	48	51.38 N	9.14 W
Drin ≃	38	41.17 N	20.02 E
Drina ≃	38	44.53 N	19.21 E
Dringenberg	52	51.40 N	9.02 E
Drinit, Pellg i C	38	41.45 N	19.28 E
Driorejo	115a	7.21 S	112.37 E
Driscoll	196	27.40 N	97.45 W
Driskill Mountain ∧[2]	194	32.25 N	92.54 W
Drissa ≃	76	55.47 N	27.55 E
Drisv'aty, Ozero ⊜	76	55.38 N	26.35 E
Driver	208	36.49 N	76.30 W
Drizzle Lake ⊜	212	45.20 N	78.10 W
Drjanovo	38	42.58 N	25.27 E
Drnholec	61	48.52 N	16.29 E
Drniš	36	43.51 N	16.09 E
Dro	64	45.58 N	10.54 E
Drøbak	26	59.39 N	10.39 E
Drobeta-Turnu-Severin	38	44.38 N	22.39 E
Drobylevo	82	55.44 N	35.53 E
Drobyš'ovo, S.S.S.R.	83	49.02 N	37.44 E
Drobyšovo, S.S.S.R.	86	53.58 N	74.40 E
Drochtersen	52	53.42 N	9.23 E
Drocourt	261	49.03 N	1.46 E
Drogheda	48	53.43 N	6.21 W
Drogičin	76	52.11 N	25.09 E
Drogobyč	78	49.21 N	23.30 E
Drohiczyn	30	52.24 N	22.41 E
Drohobycz → Drogobyč	78	49.21 N	23.30 E
Droichead Átha → Drogheda	48	53.43 N	6.21 W
Droichead Nua	48	53.11 N	6.48 W
Droitwich	42	52.16 N	2.09 W
Drokija	78	48.03 N	27.48 E
Drolshagen	56	51.01 N	7.46 E
Dromahair	48	54.14 N	8.19 W
Dromana	169	38.21 S	144.58 E
Dromara	44	54.23 N	6.01 W
Dromcolliher	48	52.20 N	8.54 W
Drôme □[5]	62	44.35 N	5.10 E
Drôme ≃	62	44.46 N	4.46 E
Drömling ✢[1]	54	52.29 N	11.04 E
Dromod	48	53.51 N	7.55 W
Dromore	48	54.25 N	6.09 W
Dromore West	48	54.15 N	8.53 W
Dronero	62	44.28 N	7.22 E
Dronfield	44	53.19 N	1.27 W
Drongen	50	51.03 N	3.40 E
Dronne ≃	32	45.02 N	0.09 W
Dronninglund	26	57.09 N	10.18 E
Dronrijp	52	53.11 N	5.38 E
Dröschede	263	51.22 N	7.39 E
Drosiá	267c	38.07 N	23.52 E
Drösing	61	48.32 N	16.54 E
Droskovo	76	52.31 N	37.05 E
Drossen → Ośno	30	52.28 N	14.50 E
Drottningholms slott ⊥	40	59.19 N	17.53 E
Droué	50	48.02 N	1.05 E
Droue-sur-Drouette	261	48.36 N	1.42 E
Drouette ≃	261	48.37 N	1.37 E
Drouin	169	38.08 S	145.51 E
Drov'anaja	88	51.35 N	113.02 E
Droylsden	262	53.29 N	2.10 W
Droyssig	54	51.02 N	12.01 E
Drožžanoje	80	54.44 N	47.34 E
Dr. Petru Groza	38	46.32 N	22.28 E
Druid Hill Park ♠	284b	39.19 N	76.39 W
Druja	76	55.47 N	27.27 E
Druk-Yul → Bhutan □[1]	120	27.30 N	90.30 E
Drulingen	56	48.52 N	7.11 E
Drum, Mount ∧	180	62.07 N	144.35 W
Drumbeg	46	58.14 N	5.12 W
Drumbo	212	43.14 N	80.33 W
Drumcliffe	48	54.20 N	8.30 W
Drumheller	182	51.28 N	112.42 W
Drumlish	48	53.48 N	7.46 W
Drummond, N.Z.	172	46.09 S	168.09 E
Drummond, Mont., U.S.	202	46.40 N	113.09 W
Drummond, Wis., U.S.	190	46.20 N	91.15 W
Drummond □[6]	206	45.50 N	72.20 W
Drummond, Lake ⊜	208	36.36 N	76.28 W
Drummond Island I	190	46.00 N	83.40 W
Drummond Range ∧∧	166	23.30 S	147.15 E
Drummondville	206	45.53 N	72.29 W
Drummore	44	54.42 N	4.54 W
Drummoyne	274a	33.51 S	151.09 E
Drumquin	48	54.37 N	7.30 W
Drumright	196	35.59 N	96.36 W
Drumshanbo	48	54.02 N	8.02 W
Drunen	52	51.42 N	5.08 E
Drusenheim	56	48.46 N	7.57 E
Druskininkai	76	54.01 N	23.58 E
Drut' ≃	76	53.03 N	30.42 E
Druten	52	51.54 N	5.36 E
Druyes-les-Belles-Fontaines	50	47.33 N	3.25 E
Družba, S.S.S.R.	86	45.15 N	82.26 E
Družba, S.S.S.R.	265b	55.53 N	37.45 E
Družina	74	68.14 N	145.18 E
Družkovka	83	48.37 N	37.33 E
Družnaja Gorka	76	59.17 N	30.08 E
Drvar	36	44.22 N	16.24 E
Drwęca ≃	30	53.00 N	18.42 E
Dry ≃	164	14.54 S	132.24 E
Dry Arm C	202	47.45 N	106.20 W
Dry Bay C	180	59.08 N	138.25 W
Dryberry Lake ⊜	184	49.33 N	93.53 W
Dryburgh Abbey ʊ[1]	46	55.34 N	2.40 W
Dry Cimarron ≃	196	36.54 N	102.59 W
Dry Creek ≃, Calif., U.S.	204	38.35 N	122.51 W
Dry Creek ≃, Calif., U.S.	226	36.47 N	119.46 W
Dry Creek ≃, Calif., U.S.	226	38.22 N	122.18 W
Dry Creek ≃, Calif., U.S.	226	37.27 N	120.37 W
Dry Creek ≃, Calif., U.S.	226	38.14 N	121.24 W
Dry Creek ≃, Calif., U.S.	226	36.58 N	120.13 W
Dry Creek ≃, Calif., U.S.	226	38.58 N	121.32 W
Dry Creek ≃, Calif., U.S.	226	39.13 N	121.25 W
Dry Creek ≃, Calif., U.S.	226	38.39 N	121.28 W
Dry Creek ≃, Calif., U.S.	282	37.22 N	122.23 W
Dry Creek ≃, Oreg., U.S.	202	43.34 N	117.21 W
Dry Creek ≃, Oreg., U.S.	224	45.30 N	121.03 W
Dry Creek ≃, Tex., U.S.	222	32.46 N	95.28 W
Dry Creek ≃, Wyo., U.S.	200	41.23 N	109.38 W
Dry Creek ≃, Wyo., U.S.	202	44.30 N	108.03 W
Dry Creek ≃, Wyo., U.S.	202	43.13 N	108.54 W
Dry Creek Mountain ∧	204	41.22 N	116.22 W
Dryden, Ont., Can.	184	49.47 N	92.50 W
Dryden, N.Y., U.S.	210	42.29 N	76.18 W
Dryden, Wash., U.S.	224	47.33 N	120.34 W
Dry Devils ≃	196	29.47 N	100.59 W
Dryfe Water ≃	44	55.08 N	3.26 W
Dry Frio ≃	196	29.17 N	99.39 W
Drygalski Island I	9	65.45 S	92.30 E
Dry Lake ⊜	198	48.15 N	98.58 W
Drymen	46	56.04 N	4.27 W
Dry Prong	194	31.35 N	92.32 W
Dry Ridge	218	38.41 N	84.35 W
Dry Run	214	40.10 N	77.45 W
Drysdale	169	38.11 S	144.34 E
Drysdale ≃	164	13.59 S	126.51 E
Dry Tortugas II	220	24.38 N	82.55 W
Drzewica	30	51.27 N	20.28 E
Drzewice	54	52.38 N	14.38 E
Dschang	152	5.27 N	10.04 E
Dschidda → Jiddah	144	21.30 N	39.12 E
Dscuba → Juba ≃	144	0.12 S	42.40 E
Du	150	10.30 N	0.59 W
Dua ≃	152	3.20 N	20.53 E
Duabo	150	5.40 N	8.05 W
Duāigaon	126	24.14 N	90.51 E
Duala → Douala	152	4.03 N	9.42 E
Dualchi	71	40.13 N	8.54 E
Duan	102	24.06 N	108.10 E
Duancun	105	38.52 N	115.56 E
Duane L. Bliss State Park ♠	226	38.59 N	120.06 W
Duanesburg	210	42.46 N	74.08 W
Duanjialing	105	39.59 N	117.09 E
Duaringa	166	23.43 S	149.40 E
Duarte	228	34.08 N	117.58 W
Duarte, Pico ∧	238	19.02 N	70.59 W
Duartina	255	22.24 S	49.25 W
Duas Barras	256	22.02 S	42.32 W
Duayaw Nkwanta	150	7.10 N	2.06 W
Dubá	54	50.34 N	14.33 E
Dubach	194	32.42 N	92.39 W
Dubai → Dubayy	128	25.18 N	55.18 E
Dubawnt ≃	176	64.33 N	100.06 W
Dubawnt Lake ⊜	176	63.08 N	101.30 W
Dubayy	128	25.18 N	55.18 E
Dubbah, Jabal ad- ∧[2]	142	30.26 N	30.38 E
Dubbeldam	52	51.47 N	4.42 E
Dubbo	166	32.15 S	148.36 E
Dubbo Hill ∧	171b	35.25 S	148.36 E
Dubele	154	2.54 N	29.33 E
Dübendorf	58	47.25 N	8.38 E
Dübener Heide ✢[3]	54	51.40 N	12.40 E
Dubenskij	86	51.27 N	56.38 E
Dubh Artach II[1]	46	56.08 N	6.40 W
Dubí	54	50.42 N	13.45 E
Dubi Bheri	272b	22.53 N	88.17 E
Dubica	36	45.11 N	16.48 E
Dubie	154	8.33 S	28.32 E
Dubinino	82	56.09 N	37.01 E
Dubino	58	46.09 N	9.27 E
Dubjazy	80	56.08 N	49.13 E
Dubki, S.S.S.R.	265a	60.00 N	30.00 E
Dubki, S.S.S.R.	265b	55.41 N	37.14 E
Dublin, Austl.	168b	34.27 S	138.21 E
Dublin, Ont., Can.	212	43.31 N	81.17 W
Dublin (Baile Átha Cliath), Eire	28		
	48	53.20 N	6.15 W
Dublin, Calif., U.S.	226	37.42 N	121.56 W
Dublin, Ga., U.S.	192	32.32 N	82.54 W
Dublin, Ind., U.S.	218	39.49 N	85.13 W
Dublin, Md., U.S.	208	39.39 N	76.15 W
Dublin, Ohio, U.S.	214	40.06 N	83.07 W
Dublin, Pa., U.S.	208	40.22 N	75.12 W
Dublin, Tex., U.S.	196	32.05 N	98.21 W
Dublin, Va., U.S.	192	37.06 N	80.41 W
Dublin □[6]	48	53.20 N	6.15 W
Dublin (Collinstown) Airport ⊠	44	53.26 N	6.15 W
Dublin Bay C	48	53.20 N	6.06 W
Dublin Canyon ∨	282	37.42 N	121.59 W
Dublon I	175c	7.23 N	151.53 E
Dubna, S.S.S.R.	82	56.44 N	37.10 E
Dubna, S.S.S.R.	82	54.09 N	36.58 E
Dubna ≃, S.S.S.R.	76	56.22 N	26.10 E
Dubna ≃, S.S.S.R.	82	56.47 N	37.15 E
Dubňany	30	48.55 N	17.06 E
Dubnevo	82	55.06 N	38.08 E
Dubnica nad Váhom	30	48.58 N	18.09 E
Dubno	78	50.26 N	25.44 E
Dubois, Idaho, U.S.	202	44.10 N	112.14 W
Dubois, Ill., U.S.	219	38.13 N	89.13 W
Dubois, Ind., U.S.	194	38.27 N	86.48 W
Du Bois, Nebr., U.S.	198	40.02 N	96.04 W
Du Bois, Pa., U.S.	214	41.07 N	78.46 W
Dubois, Wyo., U.S.	200	43.33 N	109.38 W
Du Bois Reservoir ⊜[1]	214	41.06 N	78.38 W
Duboistown	210	41.13 N	77.04 W
Dub'onki	80	54.27 N	46.18 E
Dubossarskoje Vodochranilišče ⊜[1]	38	48.02 N	28.42 E
Dubossary	78	47.16 N	29.08 E
Dubovaja Rošča	76	53.11 N	36.04 E
Dubov'azovka	78	51.08 N	33.22 E
Dubovići	78	51.38 N	33.35 E
Dubovka, S.S.S.R.	78	51.26 N	41.25 E
Dubovka, S.S.S.R.	80	49.03 N	44.50 E
Dubovoje	76	53.08 N	40.05 E
Dubovskij	80	56.21 N	46.48 E
Dubovskoje	80	47.25 N	42.46 E
Dubovyj Ovrag	80	48.20 N	44.37 E
Dubovyj Umet	80	52.59 N	50.17 E
Duboweitun	89	50.42 N	120.14 E
Dubra	126	23.32 N	86.31 E
Dubrājpur	126	23.48 N	87.23 E
Dubréka	150	9.48 N	13.31 W
Dubreka □[4]	150	10.00 N	13.40 W
Dubrova, S.S.S.R.	76	52.25 N	29.58 E
Dubrova, S.S.S.R.	78	51.47 N	28.13 E
Dubrova, S.S.S.R.	80	57.42 N	55.01 E
Dubrova, S.S.S.R.	80	56.59 N	54.33 E
Dubrovica	78	51.34 N	26.34 E
Dubroviči	80	54.39 N	39.56 E
Dubrovicy	82	56.46 N	39.10 E
Dubrovino	86	55.28 N	83.17 E
Dubrovka, S.S.S.R.	76	59.51 N	30.56 E
Dubrovka, S.S.S.R.	76	53.42 N	33.30 E
Dubrovka, S.S.S.R.	76	59.13 N	36.13 E
Dubrovka, S.S.S.R.	82	54.44 N	36.21 E
Dubrovka, S.S.S.R.	83	47.54 N	39.02 E
Dubrovki	80	53.49 N	43.19 E
Dubrovnik	38	42.38 N	18.07 E
Dubrovno	76	54.35 N	30.41 E
Dubrovnoje, S.S.S.R.	86	57.58 N	69.25 E
Dubrovnoje, S.S.S.R.	86	54.49 N	68.06 E
Dubrovo	76	59.51 N	33.34 E
Dubrovskoje	88	58.45 N	111.10 E
Dubunskaja	86	43.46 N	80.13 E
Dubuque	190	42.30 N	90.41 W
Dubysa ≃	76	55.05 N	23.26 E
Duchana	85	38.02 N	68.13 E
Duchang	100	29.15 N	116.13 E
Duchcov	54	50.37 N	13.45 E
Ducherow	54	53.46 N	13.46 E
Duchesne	200	40.10 N	110.24 W
Duchesne ≃	200	40.05 N	109.41 W
Duchess	166	21.22 S	139.52 E
Duchess Hill	154	18.18 S	30.13 E
Duchovnickoje	80	52.28 N	48.15 E
Duchovščina	76	55.12 N	32.25 E
Duck ≃	194	36.02 N	87.52 W
Duckabush ≃	224	47.38 N	122.56 W
Duck Bay	184	52.10 N	100.09 W
Duck Creek ≃, Ont., Can.	281	42.18 N	82.41 W
Duck Creek ≃, Calif., U.S.	226	37.55 N	121.16 W
Duck Creek ≃, Ind., U.S.	218	40.08 N	85.57 W
Duck Creek ≃, Nev., U.S.	204	40.06 N	114.43 W
Duck Creek ≃, N. Dak., U.S.	198	46.03 N	102.14 W
Duck Creek ≃, Tex., U.S.	196	33.14 N	100.42 W
Duck Creek ≃, Tex., U.S.	222	32.48 N	96.31 W
Duck Creek ≃, Tex., U.S.	222	31.06 N	96.17 W
Duck Creek ≃, Wis., U.S.	190	44.33 N	88.02 W
Duck Hill	194	33.38 N	89.43 W
Duck Island Harbor C	276	40.55 N	73.23 W
Duck Key I	220	24.46 N	80.56 W
Duck Lake, Sask., Can.	184	52.47 N	106.13 W
Duck Lake, Mich., U.S.	216	42.24 N	84.47 W
Duck Lake ⊜, Man., Can.	184	54.52 N	98.11 W
Duck Lake ⊜, Mich., U.S.	216	42.23 N	84.47 W
Duck Lake ⊜, Mich., U.S.	281	42.40 N	83.35 W
Duck Mountain ∧	184	51.35 N	101.00 W
Duck Mountain Provincial Park ♠, Man., Can.	184	51.36 N	100.55 W
Duck Mountain Provincial Park ♠, Sask., Can.	184	51.38 N	101.53 W
Ducktown	192	35.03 N	84.23 W
Duck Valley Indian Reservation ✢[4]	204	42.00 N	116.10 W
Duckwall Mountain ∧	226	37.58 N	120.07 W
Duclair	50	49.29 N	0.53 E
Ducos	240e	14.34 N	60.58 W
Du Couedic, Cape ≻	166	36.04 S	136.42 E
Ducun	106	31.07 N	120.27 E
Duda ≃	246	2.33 N	74.02 W
Dudačkino	76	59.57 N	32.53 E
Dudčany	78	47.12 N	33.46 E
Duddington	42	52.36 N	0.32 W
Duddon ≃	44	54.15 N	3.13 W
Dudelange	56	49.28 N	6.05 E
Dudergofka ≃	265a	59.52 N	30.12 E
Duderstadt	52	51.31 N	10.16 E
Dūdhi	124	24.13 N	83.15 E
Dudh Kosi ≃	124	27.08 N	86.26 E
Dudhnai	124	25.59 N	90.44 E
Dudinka	74	69.25 N	86.15 E
Dudkin	78	47.53 N	40.32 E
Dudley, Eng., U.K.	42	52.30 N	2.05 W
Dudley, Mass., U.S.	207	42.03 N	71.56 W
Dudley, Pa., U.S.	214	40.12 N	78.10 W
Dudley Pond ⊜	283	42.20 N	71.22 W
Dudna ≃	122	19.07 N	76.54 E
Dudo	144	9.20 N	50.14 E
Dudo ≃	144	9.12 N	50.42 E
Dudorovskij	76	53.40 N	35.22 E
Dudullu	267b	41.02 N	29.09 E
Dudweiler	56	49.17 N	7.02 E
Dudzele	50	51.17 N	3.14 E
Due	89	50.50 N	142.06 E
Duékoué	150	6.45 N	7.21 W
Duerbote (Taikang)	89	46.52 N	124.27 E
Dueré	250	11.20 S	49.17 W
Duerji	89	45.39 N	121.49 E
Duerna ≃	34	42.19 N	5.54 W
Duero (Douro) ≃	34	41.08 N	8.40 W
Dueville	64	45.38 N	11.32 E
Due West	192	34.20 N	82.23 W
Dufault, Lac ⊜	190	48.19 N	79.00 W
Duff Dunbar	123	32.15 N	77.12 E
Duffel	50	51.06 N	4.31 E
Dufferin □[6]	212	44.05 N	80.15 W
Duffer Peak ∧	204	41.40 N	118.44 W
Duffield	162	25.50 S	134.40 E
Duffin Creek ≃	212	43.49 N	79.02 W
Dufftown	46	57.26 N	3.08 W
Dufourspitze ∧	58	45.55 N	7.52 E
Dufresne ≃	206	46.16 N	73.59 W
Dufur	224	45.27 N	121.08 W
Duga Resa	36	45.27 N	15.30 E
Dugdemona ≃	194	31.47 N	92.22 W
Dugede	120	30.54 N	90.48 E
Dugger	194	39.04 N	87.16 W
Dugino	83	47.09 N	39.27 E
Dugi Otok I	36	44.00 N	15.04 E
Dugna	82	54.25 N	36.51 E
Dugny	261	48.57 N	2.25 E
Dugny-sur-Meuse	56	49.06 N	5.23 E
Dugort	48	54.01 N	10.01 W
Dug Pond ⊜	283	42.17 N	71.22 W
Du Gué ≃	176	57.21 N	70.45 W
Duğur	130	41.31 N	42.42 E
Duhernal Lake ⊜	276	40.24 N	74.22 W
Duhi	140	7.07 N	28.45 E
Duhnen	52	53.53 N	8.38 E
Duhu	100	22.04 N	112.56 E
Duich, Loch C	46	57.14 N	5.30 W
Duida, Cerro ∧	246	3.25 N	65.40 W
Duifken Point ≻	164	12.33 S	141.38 E
Duilongdeqing	124	29.56 N	90.42 E
Duimianshan ∧	89	47.58 N	129.07 E
Duin Dui	175f	15.24 S	167.46 E
Duingen	52	52.00 N	9.42 E
Duingt	62	45.50 N	6.12 E
Duino	64	45.46 N	13.36 E
Duirinish	46	57.19 N	5.41 W
Duisburg	56		
	263	51.25 N	6.46 E
Duissern ✢[8]	263	51.26 N	6.47 E
Duitama	246	5.50 N	73.02 W
Duiveland I	52	51.38 N	4.00 E
Duiwelskloof	156	23.42 S	30.06 E
Duji	98	34.11 N	115.48 E
Dujiadao I	98	36.44 N	121.27 E
Dujiahang	106	31.03 N	121.29 E
Dujuma	144	1.14 N	42.37 E
Dukana ⍑[4]	154	3.59 N	37.16 E
Dukazi	120	30.54 N	92.52 E
Duke	196	34.40 N	99.34 W
Duke Center	214	41.57 N	78.29 W
Duke Island I	180	54.56 N	131.20 W
Dukelský priesmyk)(	78	49.25 N	21.43 E
Duke of York Bay C	176	65.25 N	84.50 W
Duke of York Island I	164	4.10 S	152.26 E
Dukes □[6]	207	41.23 N	70.31 W
Dukes Brook ≃	276	40.33 N	74.37 W
Duk Fadiat	140	7.45 N	31.25 E
Duk Faiwil	140	7.30 N	31.29 E
Dukhān	128	25.25 N	50.48 E
Dukhmays	142	31.07 N	31.04 E
Duki	120	30.09 N	68.34 E
Dukinfield	262	53.29 N	2.05 W
Dukla	30	49.34 N	21.41 E
Dūkštas	76	55.32 N	26.20 E
Duku, Nig.	146	10.49 N	10.46 E
Duku, Nig.	150	11.10 N	4.55 E
Dula	152	4.41 N	20.22 E
Dūlāb	267d	35.37 N	51.27 E
Dulag	116	10.57 N	125.02 E
Dulāi	124	23.57 N	89.31 E
Dulais ≃	42	51.41 N	3.47 W
Dulan (Chahanwusu)	102	36.16 N	98.28 E
Dulanhu ⊜	102	36.50 N	98.42 E
Dul'apino	80	57.15 N	40.49 E
Dulas ≃, Wales, U.K.	42	52.36 N	3.50 W
Dulas ≃, Wales, U.K.	42	52.16 N	3.22 W
Dulas Bay C	44	53.23 N	4.15 W
Dulata	86	43.26 N	80.50 E
Dulayb, Khawr ∨	140	11.45 N	32.47 E
Dulaym	146	25.58 N	14.03 E
Dulce	200	36.56 N	107.00 W
Dulce ≃	252	30.31 S	62.32 W
Dulce, Arroyo ≃	258	35.28 S	57.41 W
Dulce, Bahía C	234	16.33 N	98.50 W
Dulce, Golfo C	236	8.32 N	83.14 W
Dulce Grande	234	22.59 N	102.14 W
Dulce Nombre de Culmí	236	15.09 N	85.37 W
Dul'durga	88	50.41 N	113.36 E
Dulebino	82	55.47 N	38.32 E
Duleek	48	53.39 N	6.25 W
Dulgalach ≃	74	67.44 N	133.12 E
Dulin	98	38.22 N	116.43 E
Duliu	105	39.13 N	116.16 E
Duliujianhe ≃	105	38.51 N	117.20 E
Duliuzhen	105	39.01 N	116.54 E
Duljo Point ≻	116	9.35 N	123.43 E
Dulkaninna	166	29.01 S	138.27 E
Dülken	56	51.15 N	6.20 E
Dulles International Airport ⊠	208	38.58 N	77.28 W
Dullstroom	156	25.27 S	30.07 E
Dul Madoba	144	9.08 N	45.58 E
Dülmen	52	51.51 N	7.16 E
Dulnain Bridge	46	57.16 N	3.41 W
Dulnan ≃	46	57.18 N	3.40 W
Dulovka	76	57.32 N	28.20 E
Dulovo	38	43.49 N	27.09 E
Dulq Maghār	130	36.22 N	38.39 E
D'ul'tydag, Gora ∧	84	41.58 N	46.56 E
Dulung ≃	126	22.08 N	87.05 E
Duluquin Point ≻	116	7.45 N	122.05 E
Duluth, Ga., U.S.	192	34.00 N	84.09 W
Duluth, Minn., U.S.	190	46.47 N	92.06 W
Dulverton	42	51.03 N	3.33 W
Dulwich ✢[8]	260	51.26 N	0.05 W
Duma, Bots.	156	18.45 S	22.46 E
Dūmā, Lubnān	130	34.12 N	35.50 E
Dūmā, Sūrīy.	132	33.35 N	36.24 E
Duma, Zaïre	154	4.57 N	27.19 E
Dumaguete	116	9.18 N	123.18 E
Dumai	114	1.41 N	101.27 E
Dumalag	116	11.18 N	122.37 E
Dumalinao	116	7.49 N	123.23 E
Dumali Point ≻	116	13.07 N	121.33 E
Dumanjug	116	10.04 N	123.26 E
Dumanquilas Bay C	116	7.34 N	123.04 E
Dumaran Channel Ʉ	116	10.25 N	119.45 E
Dumaran Island I	116	10.33 N	119.51 E
Dumaresq ≃	166	28.40 S	150.28 E
Dumaring	112	1.36 N	118.12 E
Dumas, Ark., U.S.	194	33.53 N	91.29 W
Dumas, Tex., U.S.	196	35.52 N	101.58 W
Ḍumayr	132	33.38 N	36.40 E
Dumayrah	142	31.08 N	31.22 E
Dumbarton	46	55.57 N	4.35 W
Dumbarton Bridge ✢[5]	282	37.31 N	122.07 W
Dumbarton Point ≻	282	37.30 N	122.06 W
Dumbier ∧	30	48.57 N	19.37 E
Dumbleyung	162	33.19 S	117.44 E
Dumbo	152	14.06 S	17.24 E
Dumbrăveni	38	46.14 N	24.35 E
Dum-Dum	126	22.35 N	88.24 E
Dum-Dum International Airport ⊠	126	22.38 N	88.25 E
Dume, Point ≻	228	34.00 N	118.48 W
Dumei	100	24.47 N	117.21 E
Dümeli	130	40.32 N	33.31 E
Dumfries, Scot., U.K.	44	55.04 N	3.37 W
Dumfries, Va., U.S.	208	38.34 N	77.20 W
Dumfries and Galloway □[4]	44	55.00 N	4.00 W
Duminiči	76	53.55 N	35.06 E
Dumjor	272b	22.38 N	88.13 E
Dumka	126	24.16 N	87.15 E
Dumlupınar	130	38.52 N	30.00 E
Dummar	132	33.32 N	36.14 E
Dümmer ⊜	52	52.31 N	8.19 E
Dummer Range ∧∧	162	20.11 S	125.59 E
Dumoga-kecil	112	0.31 N	123.55 E
Dumoine ≃	190	46.13 N	77.51 W
Dumoine, Lac ⊜	190	46.53 N	77.54 W
Dumont, Iowa, U.S.	190	42.45 N	92.58 W
Dumont, N.J., U.S.	210	40.56 N	74.00 W
Dumont, Lac ⊜	190	46.04 N	76.27 W
Dumont d'urville ʊ[3]	9	66.35 S	140.00 E
Dümpelfeld	56	50.27 N	6.56 E
Dümpten ✢[8]	263	51.27 N	6.54 E
Dumpu	164	5.50 S	145.45 E
Dumra	124	26.34 N	85.31 E
Dumraon	124	25.33 N	84.09 E
Dumria	126	22.47 N	89.26 E
Dumuriā	126	22.11 N	86.20 E
Dumyāṭ (Damietta)	142	31.25 N	31.48 E
Dumyāṭ □[4]	142	31.20 N	31.45 E
Dumyāṭ, Far' ≃	142	31.32 N	31.51 E
Dumyāṭ, Maṣabb ≃[1]	142	31.32 N	31.51 E
Dün ∧	54	51.21 N	10.30 E
Duna → Danube ≃	22	45.20 N	29.40 E
Dünaburg → Daugavpils	76	55.53 N	26.32 E
Dunaff Head ≻	48	55.17 N	7.33 W
Dunaföldvár	30	46.48 N	18.55 E
Dunaharaszti	30	47.21 N	19.05 E
Dunaj	265a	59.58 N	30.56 E
Dunaj → Danube ≃	22	45.20 N	29.40 E
Dunaj, Ostrova II	74	73.52 N	124.29 E
Dunajec ≃	30	50.15 N	20.44 E
Dunajevcy	78	48.54 N	26.51 E
Dunajevo	88	52.05 N	117.02 E
Dunajská Streda	30	48.01 N	17.35 E
Dunakeszi	30	47.38 N	19.08 E
Dunany Point ≻	44	53.52 N	6.14 W
Dunărea → Danube ≃	22	45.20 N	29.40 E
Dunărea Veche ≃	38	45.17 N	28.02 E
Duna-Tisza-csatorna ☰	264c	47.21 N	19.05 E
Dunaújváros	30	46.58 N	18.57 E
Dunav → Danube ≃	22	45.20 N	29.40 E
Dunavățu-de-Sus	38	44.59 N	29.13 E
Duna-völgyi-főcsatorna ☰	30	46.12 N	18.56 E
Dunback	172	45.23 S	170.38 E
Dunbar, Scot., U.K.	46	56.00 N	2.31 W
Dunbar, W. Va., U.S.	188	38.22 N	81.45 W
Dunbarton	275b	43.49 N	79.06 W
Dunbeath	46	58.15 N	3.25 W
Dunblane, Sask., Can.	184	51.11 N	106.52 W
Dunblane, Scot., U.K.	46	56.12 N	3.59 W
Duncan, B.C., Can.	182	48.47 N	123.42 W
Duncan, Ariz., U.S.	200	32.43 N	109.06 W
Duncan, Miss., U.S.	194	34.03 N	90.45 W
Duncan, Okla., U.S.	196	34.30 N	97.57 W
Duncan ≃	182	50.11 N	116.57 W
Duncan Dam ✢[6]	182	50.15 N	116.55 W
Duncan Lake ⊜	182	50.20 N	117.00 W
Duncannon	208	40.23 N	77.02 W
Duncan Passage Ʉ	110	11.00 N	92.30 E
Duncans	241q	18.28 N	77.32 W
Duncansby Head ≻	46	58.39 N	3.02 W
Duncan's Creek ≃	274a	33.53 S	150.39 E
Duncanville	222	32.39 N	96.55 W
Dunchurch	42	52.20 N	1.16 W
Duncormick	48	52.14 N	6.39 W
Dundaga	76	57.31 N	22.21 E
Dundāhera	272a	28.38 N	77.26 E
Dundalk, Ont., Can.	212	44.10 N	80.24 W
Dundalk, Eire	48	54.01 N	6.25 W
Dundalk, Md., U.S.	208	39.15 N	76.31 W
Dundalk Bay C	48	53.57 N	6.17 W
Dundas, Austl.	274a	33.48 S	151.02 E
Dundas, Ont., Can.	212	43.16 N	79.58 W
Dundas, Minn., U.S.	190	44.26 N	93.12 W
Dundas □[6]	212	45.00 N	75.20 W
Dundas, Cape ≻	212	44.57 N	81.07 W
Dundas, Lake ⊜	162	32.35 S	121.50 E
Dundas Island I	182	54.33 N	130.55 W
Dundas Peninsula ≻[1]	176	74.50 N	111.30 W
Dundas Strait Ʉ	164	11.20 S	131.35 E
Dún Dealgan → Dundalk	48	54.01 N	6.25 W
Dundee, S. Afr.	158	28.12 S	30.16 E
Dundee, Scot., U.K.	46	56.28 N	3.00 W
Dundee, Fla., U.S.	220	28.07 N	81.37 W
Dundee, Ill., U.S.	216	42.06 N	88.17 W
Dundee, Mich., U.S.	216	41.57 N	83.40 W
Dundee, Miss., U.S.	194	34.32 N	90.27 W
Dundee, N.Y., U.S.	210	42.31 N	76.59 W
Dundee, Ohio, U.S.	214	40.35 N	81.37 W
Dundee, Oreg., U.S.	224	45.17 N	123.01 W
Dundee Creek C	284b	39.21 N	76.22 W
Dundgov' □[4]	102	45.30 N	106.30 E
Dundīṭ	142	30.41 N	31.18 E
Dundoo	166	27.39 S	144.39 E
Dundrum, Eire	48	53.17 N	6.15 W
Dundrum, N. Ire., U.K.	48	54.16 N	5.51 W
Dundrum Bay C	48	54.14 N	5.45 W
Dundurn	184	51.49 N	106.30 W
Dundwa Range ∧∧	124	27.45 N	82.30 E
Duneaton Water ≃	46	55.32 N	3.42 W
Dunedin, N.Z.	172	45.52 S	170.30 E
Dunedin, Fla., U.S.	220	28.00 N	82.47 W
Dunedoo	166	32.01 S	149.24 E
Duneland Beach	216	41.45 N	86.50 W
Dunellen	276	40.35 N	74.28 W
Dunewood	276	40.38 N	73.11 W
Dunfanaghy	48	55.11 N	7.59 W
Dunfermline	46	56.04 N	3.29 W
Du Ngae, Khao ∧	110	15.10 N	98.47 E
Dungannon, N. Ire., U.K.	48	54.31 N	6.46 W
Dungannon, Va., U.S.	192	36.50 N	82.28 W
Dūngarpur	120	23.50 N	73.43 E
Dungarvan	48	52.05 N	7.37 W
Dungarvan Harbour C	48	52.10 N	7.35 W
Dungas	150	13.04 N	9.20 E
Dungau ✢[1]	60	48.50 N	12.40 E
Dungeness ≻	42	50.55 N	0.58 E
Dungeness ≃	224	48.08 N	123.06 W
Dungeness Spit ≻[2]	224	48.10 N	123.09 W
Dungiven	48	54.55 N	6.55 W
Dungloe	48	54.57 N	8.22 W
Dungo, Lagoa do ⊜	152	17.20 S	18.58 E
Dungog	166	32.24 S	151.46 E
Dungu	154	3.37 N	28.34 E
Dungun ≃	114	4.47 N	103.23 E
Dunham	206	45.08 N	72.48 W
Dunham Lake ⊜	281	42.39 N	83.41 W
Dunham-on-the-Hill	262	53.15 N	2.47 W
Dunham Town	262	53.23 N	2.24 W
Dunhe ≃	100	30.27 N	114.11 E
Dunheved, Austl.	274a	33.45 S	150.47 E

	English	Deutsch	Español	Français	Português
≃	River	Fluss	Río	Rivière	Rio
☰	Canal	Kanal	Canal	Canal	Canal
⅃	Waterfall, Rapids	Wasserfall, Stromschnellen	Cascada, Rápidos	Chute d'eau, Rapides	Cascata, Rápidos
Ʉ	Strait	Meeresstrasse	Estrecho	Détroit	Estreito
C	Bay, Gulf	Bucht, Golf	Bahía, Golfo	Baie, Golfe	Baía, Golfo
⊜	Lake, Lakes	See, Seen	Lago, Lagos	Lac, Lacs	Lago, Lagos
☷	Swamp	Sumpf	Pantano	Marais	Pântano
⛋	Ice Features, Glacier	Eis- und Gletscherformen	Accidentes Glaciales	Formes glaciaires	Acidentes Glaciares
⍑	Other Hydrographic Features	Andere Hydrographische Objekte	Otros Elementos Hidrográficos	Autres données hydrographiques	Outros Elementos Hidrográficos

	English	Deutsch	Español	Français	Português
✧	Submarine Features	Untermeerische Objekte	Accidentes Submarinos	Formes de relief sous-marin	Acidentes Submarinos
□	Political Unit	Politische Einheit	Unidad Politica	Entité politique	Unidade Política
ʊ	Cultural Institution	Kulturelle Institution	Institución Cultural	Institution culturelle	Instituição Cultural
⊥	Historical Site	Historische Stätte	Sitio Histórico	Site historique	Sitio Histórico
♠	Recreational Site	Erholungs- und Ferienort	Sitio de Recreo	Centre de loisirs	Sítio de Lazer
⊠	Airport	Flughafen	Aeropuerto	Aéroport	Aeroporto
■	Military Installation	Militäranlage	Instalación Militar	Installation militaire	Instalação Militar
✢	Miscellaneous	Verschiedenes	Misceláneo	Divers	Miscelânea

Name	Page	Lat.°′	Long.°′
Dunheved → Launceston, Eng., U.K.	42	50.38 N	4.21 W
Dunhoucun	100	27.02 N	114.58 E
Dunhua	89	43.21 N	128.13 E
Dunhuang	102	40.12 N	94.41 E
Dunières	62	45.13 N	4.20 E
Dunilovo, S.S.S.R.	76	57.46 N	38.55 E
Dunilovo, S.S.S.R.	80	57.00 N	41.27 E
Dunkeld	46	56.34 N	3.35 W
Dunkeld ⬥[8]	273d	26.09 S	28.03 E
Dunkellin ≃	48	53.12 N	8.54 W
Dunkelsteinerwald ⬥[3]	61	48.15 N	15.29 E
Dunkern @	40	59.09 N	16.52 E
Dunker Pond @	276	41.05 N	74.28 W
Dunkerque	50	51.03 N	2.22 E
Dunkerrin	48	52.55 N	7.55 W
Dunkery Hill ∧[2]	42	51.11 N	3.35 W
Dunkineely	48	54.38 N	8.23 W
Dunkinsville	218	38.51 N	83.30 W
Dunkirk → Dunkerque, Fr.	50	51.03 N	2.22 E
Dunkirk, Ind., U.S.	216	40.23 N	85.13 W
Dunkirk, N.Y., U.S.	214	42.29 N	79.20 W
Dunkirk, Ohio, U.S.	216	40.48 N	83.39 W
Dunk's Green	260	51.15 N	0.19 E
Dunkuj	140	12.50 N	32.49 E
Dunkwa, Ghana	150	5.58 N	1.46 W
Dunkwa, Ghana	150	5.22 N	1.12 W
Dún Laoghaire	48	53.17 N	6.08 W
Dunlap, Iowa, U.S.	198	41.51 N	95.36 W
Dunlap, Tenn., U.S.	194	35.23 N	85.23 W
Dunlap Acres	228	34.03 N	117.06 W
Dunlavin	48	53.02 N	6.41 W
Dunleary → Dún Laoghaire	48	53.17 N	6.08 W
Dunleer	48	53.50 N	6.24 W
Dun-le-Palestel	32	46.17 N	1.48 E
Dunlop	46	55.43 N	4.32 W
Dunloy	48	55.01 N	6.25 W
Dunmanus Bay C	48	51.35 N	9.45 W
Dunmanway	48	51.43 N	9.06 W
Dunmarra	164	16.42 S	133.25 E
Dunmore, Eire	48	53.36 N	8.46 W
Dunmore, Pa., U.S.	210	41.25 N	75.38 W
Dunmore Cave ⊥[5]	48	52.44 N	7.15 W
Dunmore East	48	52.09 N	7.00 W
Dunmore Town	238	25.30 N	76.39 W
Dunmurry	48	54.33 N	6.01 W
Dunn	192	35.19 N	78.37 W
Dunnamanagh	48	54.52 N	7.18 W
Dünnbach ≃	56	50.10 N	7.18 E
Dunnellon	220	29.03 N	82.28 W
Dunnet	46	58.31 N	3.20 W
Dunnet Bay C	46	58.37 N	3.24 W
Dunnet Head ≻	46	58.40 N	3.24 W
Dunnigan	226	38.53 N	121.58 W
Dunning	198	41.50 N	100.06 W
Dunning Creek ≃	214	40.02 N	78.28 W
Dunningtown	279b	40.25 N	79.35 W
Dunn Loring	284c	38.53 N	77.14 W
Dunnockshaw	262	53.45 N	2.17 W
Dunnottar Castle ⊥	46	56.57 N	2.11 W
Dunns Bridge	216	41.13 N	86.59 W
Dunnville	212	42.54 N	79.36 W
Dunolly	169	36.52 S	143.44 E
Dunoon	46	55.57 N	4.56 W
Dunqul ⊤[4]	140	23.26 N	31.37 E
Dunqulah	140	19.10 N	30.29 E
Dunqulah al-Qadīmah	140	18.13 N	30.45 E
Dunqunāb	140	21.06 N	37.05 E
Dunqunāb, Khalīj C	140	21.05 N	37.08 E
Dunrea	184	49.25 N	99.44 W
Dun Rig ∧	46	55.34 N	3.10 W
Duns	46	55.47 N	2.20 W
Dunsandel	172	43.40 S	172.11 E
Dunseith	198	48.50 N	100.02 W
Dunsford	42	50.41 N	3.40 W
Dunsmuir	204	41.13 N	122.16 W
Dunstable, Eng., U.K.	42	51.53 N	0.32 W
Dunstable, Mass., U.S.	207	42.40 N	71.29 W
Dunstaffnage Castle ⊥	46	56.26 N	5.32 W
Dunstan Mountains ∧∧	172	44.57 S	169.32 E
Dunster, B.C., Can.	182	53.08 N	119.50 W
Dunster, Eng., U.K.	42	51.12 N	3.27 W
Dun-sur-Auron	32	46.53 N	2.34 E
Dun-sur-Meuse	56	49.23 N	5.11 E
Duntelchaig, Loch @	46	57.20 N	4.18 W
Dunton Green	260	51.18 N	0.11 E
Dunton Wayletts	260	51.35 N	0.24 E
Duntou	100	29.21 N	119.46 E
Duntroon	172	44.52 S	170.41 E
Duntroon Royal Military College ■	171b	35.18 S	149.12 E
Dunvegan, S. Afr.	273d	26.09 S	28.09 E
Dunvegan, Scot., U.K.	46	57.26 N	6.35 W
Dunvegan, Loch C	46	57.28 N	6.40 W
Dunvegan Castle ⊥	46	57.26 N	6.35 W
Dunvegan Head ≻	46	57.31 N	6.43 W
Dunville	186	47.16 N	53.54 W
Dunwich	171a	27.31 S	153.23 E
Dunyāpur	123	29.48 N	71.44 E
Dünzlau	60	48.47 N	11.20 E
Duobe ≃	150	5.45 N	8.00 W
Duobukulehe ≃	89	49.56 N	125.12 E
Duogu'nao	102	31.32 N	103.14 E
Duojundian	105	39.22 N	117.31 E
Duolun	98	42.15 N	116.18 E
Duolundabohuer	120	33.25 N	93.54 E
Duomaer	120	34.15 N	79.45 E
Duomo ♁[1]	266b	45.27 N	9.11 E
Duomula	120	34.07 N	82.30 E
Duong-dong	110	10.13 N	103.58 E
Duopatela	120	28.28 N	88.14 E
Duoyue	107	30.11 N	103.42 E
Duozhuang	98	35.35 N	118.12 E
Du Page □[6]	216	41.52 N	88.06 W
Du Page ≃	216	41.25 N	88.14 W
Du Page, East Branch ≃	278	41.42 N	88.09 W
Dupangling ∧∧	102	25.32 N	111.11 E
Duparquet, Lac @	190	48.28 N	79.16 W
Dupax	116	16.17 N	121.05 E
Duping	102	27.11 N	108.20 E
Dupl'atka	80	51.07 N	42.20 E
Dupli	82	54.21 N	36.54 E
Dupo	219	38.31 N	90.13 W
Dupont, Ind., U.S.	218	38.53 N	85.31 W
Dupont, Ohio, U.S.	216	41.03 N	84.18 W
Dupont, Pa., U.S.	210	41.20 N	75.45 W
Du Pont, Wash., U.S.	224	47.06 N	122.38 W
Dupree	198	45.03 N	101.36 W
Duque Bacelar	250	4.09 S	42.57 W
Duque de Bragança	152	9.06 S	15.57 E
Duque de Caxias	256	22.47 S	43.18 W
Duque de Caxias □[7]	287a	22.45 S	43.16 W
Duque de York, Isla I	254	50.40 S	75.20 W
Duquesne	214	40.21 N	79.51 W
Duquesne University ♁[2]	279b	40.26 N	79.59 W
DuQuoin	194	38.01 N	89.14 W
Dūrā	132	31.30 N	35.02 E
Durack ≃	164	15.33 S	127.52 E
Durack Range ∧∧	160	17.00 S	128.00 E
Durağan	130	41.25 N	35.04 E
Durak	130	39.42 N	28.17 E
Dural	170	33.41 S	151.02 E
Duran	200	34.28 N	105.24 W
Durance ≃	62	43.55 N	4.44 E
Durand, Ill., U.S.	190	42.26 N	89.20 W
Durand, Mich., U.S.	216	42.55 N	83.59 W
Durand, Wis., U.S.	190	44.38 N	91.58 W
Durand, Récif ✢[2]	175f	22.03 S	168.39 E
Durango, Esp.	34	43.10 N	2.37 W
Durango, Méx.	234	24.02 N	104.40 W
Durango, Colo., U.S.	200	37.16 N	107.53 W
Durango □[3]	234	23.30 N	104.45 W
Duranillin	168a	33.31 S	116.48 E
Durant, Iowa, U.S.	190	41.36 N	90.54 W
Durant, Miss., U.S.	194	33.04 N	89.51 W
Durant, Okla., U.S.	196	34.00 N	96.23 W
Duras	32	44.41 N	0.11 E
Durasovka	80	51.41 N	44.55 E
Duraton ≃	34	41.37 N	4.07 W
Duraur ≃	144	10.40 N	49.25 E
Durazno	252	33.22 S	56.31 W
Durazno, Arroyo ≃	258	34.41 S	58.52 W
Durazzo → Durrës	38	41.19 N	19.26 E
Durbādānga	126	22.57 N	89.15 E
Durban	158	29.55 S	30.56 E
Durban Roodepoort Deep Gold Mines ⬥[7]	273d	26.10 S	27.51 E
Durbanville	158	33.50 S	18.39 E
Durbe	76	56.35 N	21.21 E
D'urbel'džin	85	41.16 N	74.57 E
Durbet-Daba, Pereval)(	86	49.37 N	89.25 E
Durbin	188	38.33 N	79.50 W
Durbo	144	11.30 N	50.18 E
Durbuy	56	50.21 N	5.28 E
Durchholz	263	51.23 N	7.17 E
Durdent ≃	50	49.51 N	0.36 E
Đurđevac	36	46.03 N	17.04 E
Durdur ≃	144	10.38 N	44.02 E
Dureji	120	25.53 N	67.18 E
Düren	56	50.48 N	6.28 E
Durg	120	21.11 N	81.17 E
Durg □[5]	124	22.00 N	81.10 E
Durgāpur	126	23.29 N	87.20 E
Durham, Ont., Can.	212	44.10 N	80.49 W
Durham, Eng., U.K.	44	54.47 N	1.34 W
Durham, Calif., U.S.	204	39.44 N	121.48 W
Durham, Conn., U.S.	207	41.29 N	72.41 W
Durham, Mo., U.S.	219	39.58 N	91.40 W
Durham, N.H., U.S.	188	43.08 N	70.56 W
Durham, N.C., U.S.	192	35.59 N	78.54 W
Durham, Oreg., U.S.	224	45.25 N	122.46 W
Durham □[6], Ont., Can.	212	44.05 N	78.35 W
Durham □[6], Eng., U.K.	44	54.45 N	1.45 W
Durham Cathedral ♁[1]	44	54.46 N	1.36 W
Durham Downs	166	27.05 S	141.54 E
Durham Heights ∧	176	71.08 N	122.56 W
Durham Pond @	276	41.00 N	74.27 W
Durhamville	210	43.07 N	75.40 W
Durian ≃	115a	6.01 S	106.24 E
Durian, Selat ⊔	114	0.42 N	103.42 E
Duriansebatang	112	0.47 S	109.56 E
Durian Tipus	114	3.07 N	102.13 E
D'urinskije Razlivy ☰	80	50.25 N	50.20 E
Durlabhpur	272b	22.47 N	88.29 E
Durlach ⬥[8]	56	49.00 N	8.28 E
Durlešty	78	47.02 N	28.45 E
Durmersheim	56	48.56 N	8.16 E
Durmitor ∧	38	43.08 N	19.01 E
Dürnast	60	49.38 N	11.59 E
Durness	46	58.33 N	4.45 W
Durness, Kyle of C	46	58.34 N	4.49 W
Durnikino	80	51.39 N	42.49 E
Dürnkrut	61	48.28 N	16.51 E
Dürnstein ⊥	61	48.24 N	15.32 E
Durón	34	40.38 N	2.43 W
Duross Heights	285	39.41 N	75.37 W
Dürre Liesing ≃	264b	48.08 N	16.16 E
Durrell	186	49.40 N	54.44 W
Dürrenboden	58	46.57 N	8.50 E
Durrës	38	41.19 N	19.26 E
Durrie	166	25.38 S	140.16 E
Durrington	42	51.13 N	1.45 W
Durris	48	51.36 N	9.31 W
Dürröhrsdorf	54	51.01 N	14.00 E
Durrow	48	52.50 N	7.22 W
Dursey Head ≻	48	51.35 N	10.14 W
Dursley	42	51.42 N	2.21 W
Dursunbey	130	39.35 N	28.38 E
D'urt'uli	86	55.29 N	54.52 E
Duru	154	4.14 N	28.45 E
Duru ∧	144	5.30 N	37.10 E
Dūruḥ	128	32.17 N	60.30 E
Durunkah	142	27.08 N	31.10 E
Durūz, Jabal ad- ∧∧	132	32.40 N	36.44 E
D'Urville Island I	172	40.50 S	173.52 E
Duryea	210	41.21 N	75.45 W
Dury Voe C	46a	60.20 N	1.08 W
Dušak	128	37.13 N	60.02 E
Dušanbe	85	38.35 N	68.48 E
Dušanbe □[4]	85	38.40 N	69.40 E
Dušekan	74	60.39 N	109.03 E
Dušeti	84	42.06 N	44.42 E
Dusetos	76	55.45 N	25.51 E
Dushai ≃	102	32.48 N	110.38 E
Dushan, Zhg.	100	31.36 N	116.14 E
Dushan, Zhg.	102	25.53 N	107.30 E
Dushanbe → Dušanbe	85	38.35 N	68.48 E
Dushanhu @	98	35.06 N	116.52 E
Dushantou	106	30.46 N	119.47 E
Dushanzi	86	44.20 N	84.51 E
Dusheng	98	38.23 N	116.33 E
Dushichang	107	29.10 N	106.31 E
Dushikou	98	41.17 N	115.38 E
Dushore	210	41.31 N	76.24 W
Düshorn	52	52.49 N	9.37 E
Dushu	100	33.21 N	113.09 E
Dushuhu @	106	31.17 N	120.42 E
Dusios Ežeras @	76	54.18 N	23.42 E
Dusky Sound ⊔	172	45.47 S	166.28 E
Dušocha, Gora ∧	85	39.10 N	70.01 E
Duson	194	30.12 N	92.11 W
Dušonovo	82	56.04 N	38.18 E
Düssel	263	51.16 N	7.03 E
Düsselbach ≃	263	51.13 N	6.45 E
Düsseldorf	56		
	263	51.12 N	6.47 E
Düsseldorf □[5]	52	51.15 N	7.00 E
Düsseldorf, Flughafen ⊠	56	51.17 N	6.45 E
Düsseldorf, Universität ♁[2]	263	51.12 N	6.48 E
Düsseldorf-Mettmann □[8]	263	51.16 N	6.58 E
Dusslingen	58	48.27 N	9.03 E
Dussnang	58	47.26 N	8.58 E
Duston	42	52.14 N	0.56 W
Dutaliutexingsishan ∧∧	120	34.15 N	87.00 E
Dutch Creek ≃	194	35.03 N	93.24 W
Dutchess □[6]	210	41.42 N	73.56 W
Dutch Harbor	180	53.53 N	166.32 W
Dutch John	200	40.55 N	109.24 W
Dutchman Creek ≃	226	37.11 N	120.28 W
Dutchman Draw ∨	200	37.00 N	113.29 W
Dutianjie	102	24.38 N	101.31 E
Dutlhe	156	23.55 S	23.47 E
Dutoitspiek ∧	158	33.46 S	19.12 E
Dutou	106	31.19 N	120.54 E
Dutovlje	64	45.46 N	13.50 E
Dutovo	24	63.47 N	56.35 E
Dutsen Wai	150	10.50 N	8.12 E
Dutton, Ont., Can.	214	42.39 N	81.30 W
Dutton, Eng., U.K.	262	53.19 N	2.38 W
Dutton, Mich., U.S.	216	42.50 N	85.35 W
Dutton, Mont., U.S.	202	47.51 N	111.43 W
Dutton ≃	166	20.45 S	143.12 E
Dutton, Mount ∧, Alaska, U.S.	180	55.10 N	162.15 W
Dutton, Mount ∧, Utah, U.S.	200	38.01 N	112.13 W
Dutun	105	39.46 N	117.02 E
Dutzow	219	38.37 N	90.59 W
Duut	86	47.30 N	91.40 E
Duval, Lac @	190	46.19 N	76.55 W
Duvall	224	47.44 N	121.59 W
Duvan	86	55.42 N	57.54 E
Duvanka ≃	83	49.35 N	38.10 E
Duvannyj	84	40.06 N	49.24 E
Duved	26	63.24 N	12.52 E
Duvernay ⬥[8]	275a	45.35 N	73.40 W
Duvno	36	43.43 N	17.14 E
Duwamish	224	47.32 N	122.19 W
Duwaydār, Bi'r ad- ⊤[4]	142	30.55 N	32.31 E
Duxbury	207	42.02 N	70.40 W
Duxbury Bay C	207	42.02 N	70.39 W
Duxun	100	23.55 N	117.37 E
Duyagan Point ≻	116	12.36 N	121.33 E
Duyang	102	23.59 N	107.47 E
Duyun	102	26.12 N	107.31 E
Düzce	130	40.50 N	31.10 E
Duze	100	29.07 N	118.56 E
Dve Mogili	38	43.36 N	25.52 E
Dvina Occidental → Zapadnaja Dvina ≃	76	57.04 N	24.03 E
Dvina Setentrional → Severnaja Dvina ≃	24	64.32 N	40.30 E
Dvinje, Ozero @	76	56.08 N	31.12 E
Dvinsk → Daugavpils	76	55.53 N	26.32 E
Dvinskaja Guba C	24	65.00 N	39.45 E
Dvojnovskij	80	51.03 N	42.27 E
Dvorcy	82	54.37 N	36.00 E
Dvorec	88	58.23 N	101.55 E
Dvoriši	76	58.12 N	35.13 E
Dvornikovo	82	55.30 N	38.38 E
Dvuch Cirkoje, Gora ∧	74	67.35 N	168.07 E
Dvugorbaja, Gora ∧	180	68.30 N	179.20 E
Dvulučnoje	78	50.02 N	38.02 E
Dvůr Králové [nad Labem]	30	50.26 N	15.48 E
Dwangwa ≃	154	12.33 S	34.12 E
Dwarbasini	272b	22.59 N	88.14 E
Dwārka	120	22.14 N	68.58 E
Dwārka ≃	126	23.44 N	88.11 E
Dwārkeswar ≃	126	23.06 N	87.21 E
Dwarli	272c	19.12 N	73.08 E
Dwars Kill ≃	276	40.58 N	73.58 W
Dwellingup	168a	32.43 S	116.02 E
Dwight	216	41.05 N	88.26 W
Dwight D. Eisenhower Lock ⬥[5]	206	45.00 N	74.45 W
Dwina-Bucht → Dvinskaja Guba C	24	65.00 N	39.45 E
Dwingeloo	52	52.50 N	6.21 E
Dwyfor ≃	42	52.55 N	4.17 W
Dwyka	158	33.02 S	21.30 E
Dwyka ≃	158	33.18 S	21.39 E
Dyam ≃	86	46.00 N	85.50 E
Dybbøl	41	54.55 N	9.45 E
Dyberry Creek ≃	210	41.35 N	75.15 W
Dyce	46	57.12 N	2.11 W
Dyche Stadium ♠	278	42.04 N	87.41 W
Dych-Tau, Gora ∧	84	43.03 N	43.08 E
Dyck, Schloss ⊥	263	51.09 N	6.34 E
Dyer, Ind., U.S.	216	41.30 N	87.31 W
Dyer, Tenn., U.S.	194	36.04 N	88.59 W
Dyer, Cape ≻	176	66.37 N	61.18 W
Dyer Bay C	212	45.10 N	81.18 W
Dyer Island I	158	34.41 S	19.25 E
Dyero	150	12.50 N	6.30 W
Dyersburg	194	36.03 N	89.23 W
Dyersville	190	42.29 N	91.08 W
Dyess Air Force Base ■	196	32.25 N	99.51 W
Dyfed □[6]	42	52.00 N	4.30 W
Dyfi ≃	42	52.32 N	4.03 W
Dyje (Thaya) ≃	30	48.37 N	16.56 E
Dyke	46	57.36 N	3.41 W
Dyke Ackland Bay C	164	9.00 S	148.45 E
Dyken Pond @	210	42.43 N	73.26 W
Dykes Pond @	283	42.36 N	70.44 W
Dyle (Dijle) ≃	56	51.04 N	4.25 E
Dyleň ∧	60	49.58 N	12.30 E
Dylym	84	43.04 N	46.38 E
Dymchurch	42	51.02 N	1.00 E
Dyment	184	49.37 N	92.19 W
Dymer	78	50.47 N	30.18 E
Dymock	42	51.59 N	2.26 W
Dynów	30	49.49 N	22.14 E
Dyreborg	41	55.04 N	10.13 E
Dyrnesvågen	26	63.26 N	7.51 E
Dyrotz	264a	52.33 N	12.58 E
Dysart, Sask., Can.	184	50.56 N	104.02 W
Dysart, Scot., U.K.	46	56.08 N	3.08 W
Dysart, Iowa, U.S.	190	42.10 N	92.18 W
Dysart, Pa., U.S.	214	40.36 N	78.31 W
Dýšina	60	49.46 N	13.29 E
Dysnų Ežeras @	76	55.29 N	26.20 E
Dysse-Alin', Chrebet ∧∧	89	52.05 N	135.00 E
Dysselsdorp	158	33.34 S	22.28 E
Dysynni ≃	42	52.36 N	4.05 W
Dzaamar	88	48.10 N	104.50 E
Dzaamaryn Uul ∧∧	88	48.20 N	104.40 E
Džabžur	84	40.54 N	43.58 E
Dzachuj	102	45.00 N	96.32 E
Džagdy, Chrebet ∧∧	89	53.40 N	131.00 E
Džalagaš	86	45.05 N	64.40 E
Džalal-Abad	85	40.56 N	73.00 E
Džalinda	89	53.29 N	123.54 E
Džamantau, Gory ∧∧	85	40.55 N	74.40 E
Džamašuj	85	40.52 N	71.28 E
Džambejty	80	50.16 N	52.35 E
Džambul, S.S.S.R.	80	47.34 N	50.12 E
Džambul, S.S.S.R.	85	42.54 N	71.22 E
Džambul, S.S.S.R.	86	47.12 N	71.42 E
Džambul □[4]	86	44.00 N	72.00 E
Džanga	128	40.00 N	53.03 E
Džangi-Džol	85	41.36 N	72.08 E
Džankoj	78	45.43 N	34.24 E
Džansugurov	86	45.24 N	79.29 E
Džanybek	80	49.25 N	46.51 E
Dzaoudzi	157a	12.47 S	45.17 E
Džardžan	74	68.43 N	124.02 E
Džargalant → Chovd, Mong.	86	48.01 N	91.39 E
Džargalant, Mong.	88	48.47 N	100.43 E
Džargalant, Mong.	88	47.19 N	99.39 E
Džargalant, Mong.	88	48.37 N	99.17 E
Džargalant, Mong.	88	46.57 N	115.15 E
Džargaltchaan	88	47.32 N	109.28 E
Džarylgač, Ostrov I	78	46.02 N	32.55 E
Džarylgačskij Zaliv C	78	46.05 N	32.50 E
Dzaudzhikau → Ordžonikidze	84	43.03 N	44.40 E
Džaur	89	50.02 N	138.30 E
Džava	84	42.24 N	43.54 E
Dzavchan	88	48.48 N	93.07 E
Dzavchan □[4]	88	48.00 N	96.00 E
Dzavchan ≃	88	48.54 N	93.23 E
Dzavchanmandal	88	48.22 N	95.03 E
Džavchlant → Uliastaj	88	47.45 N	96.49 E
Džazator	86	49.45 N	87.23 E
Džbán ∧	54	50.12 N	13.45 E
Džebel	128	39.38 N	54.14 E
Džebrail	84	39.23 N	47.02 E
Dzegamčaj ≃	84	41.00 N	45.59 E
Dželinda	74	70.08 N	114.00 E
Dzemul	232	21.12 N	89.18 W
Dzeng	152	3.45 N	12.00 E
Dženretlen, Mys ≻	180	67.07 N	173.45 W
Dzenzik, Mys ≻	78	46.30 N	36.07 E
Džergetal	85	41.30 N	75.47 E
Džermuk	84	39.51 N	45.41 E
Dzerzhinsk → Dzeržinsk	80	56.15 N	43.24 E
Dzeržinsk, S.S.S.R.	76	53.41 N	27.08 E
Dzeržinsk, S.S.S.R.	78	50.09 N	27.56 E
Dzeržinsk, S.S.S.R.	80	56.15 N	43.24 E
Dzeržinsk, S.S.S.R.	83	48.26 N	37.50 E
Dzeržinskaja, Gora ∧	76	53.51 N	27.03 E
Dzeržinskij, S.S.S.R.	78	48.02 N	39.26 E
Dzeržinskij, S.S.S.R.	82	55.38 N	37.50 E
Dzeržinskij, S.S.S.R.	86	54.01 N	90.12 E
Dzeržinskij ⬥[8]	83	48.02 N	39.26 E
Dzeržinskoje, S.S.S.R.	86	45.50 N	81.07 E
Dzeržinskoje, S.S.S.R.	86	56.49 N	95.18 E
Džetim, Chrebet ∧∧	85	41.35 N	77.05 E
Džetygara	86	52.11 N	61.12 E
Džetyoguz	85	42.27 N	78.14 E
Džezdy	86	48.04 N	67.05 E
Džezkazgan, S.S.S.R.	86	47.53 N	67.27 E
Džezkazgan, S.S.S.R.	86	47.47 N	67.46 E
Dzhambul → Džambul	85	42.54 N	71.22 E
Działdowo	30	53.15 N	20.10 E
Działoszyce	30	50.22 N	20.21 E
Dzibalchén	232	19.31 N	89.45 W
Dzibilchaltun ⊥	232	21.05 N	89.36 W
Džida ≃	88	50.37 N	106.14 E
Džidinskij, Chrebet ∧∧	88	50.10 N	102.00 E
Dzierzgoń	30	53.56 N	19.21 E
Dzierżoniów (Reichenbach)	30	50.44 N	16.39 E
Dzilam González	232	21.17 N	88.56 W
Džilav	85	39.19 N	67.45 E
Džilga	85	41.43 N	69.01 E
Džinst	102	45.22 N	100.35 E
Dzioua	148	33.14 N	5.14 E
Džirgatal'	85	39.13 N	71.12 E
Dzitás	232	20.51 N	88.31 W
Dzitbalché	232	20.19 N	90.03 W
Dziwna ≃[1]	54	54.01 N	14.44 E
Dziwnów	30	54.03 N	14.45 E
Džizak	85	40.06 N	67.50 E
Dzodze	150	6.14 N	1.00 E
Džubga	78	44.20 N	38.43 E
Džugdžur, Chrebet ∧∧	74	58.00 N	136.00 E
Džūkste	76	56.47 N	23.15 E
Džul'fa	84	38.58 N	45.38 E
Džumabazar	85	39.31 N	67.13 E
Džumgoltau, Chrebet ∧∧	85	42.18 N	74.32 E
Dzungarian Basin → Zhuangaerpendi ≚[1]	86	45.00 N	88.00 E
Dzungarian Gate (Džungarskije Vorota))(	86	45.25 N	82.25 E
Džungarskij Alatau, Chrebet ∧∧	86	45.00 N	81.00 E
Džungarskije Vorota → Dzungarian Gate)(	86	45.25 N	82.25 E
Džurak-Sal ≃	80	47.18 N	43.36 E
Dzürch	88	48.55 N	100.10 E
Džurin	78	48.41 N	28.18 E
Džurun	86	49.15 N	57.37 E
Džusaly	86	45.28 N	64.05 E
Dzüünchangaj	88	49.19 N	95.20 E
Dzüüncharaa	88	48.52 N	106.28 E
Dzüüngovy	88	49.55 N	93.52 E
Dzuunmod	88	47.45 N	106.58 E
Dzygovka	78	48.22 N	28.19 E
E			
Eads	198	38.29 N	102.47 W
Eagar	200	34.06 N	109.11 W
Eagle, Alaska, U.S.	180	64.46 N	141.16 W
Eagle, Colo., U.S.	200	39.39 N	106.50 W
Eagle, N.Y., U.S.	210	42.33 N	78.18 W
Eagle, Wis., U.S.	216	42.53 N	88.28 W
Eagle ≃, Newf., Can.	176	53.35 N	57.25 W
Eagle ≃, Yukon, Can.	180	67.20 N	137.10 W
Eagle ≃, Colo., U.S.	200	39.39 N	107.04 W
Eagle, Mount ∧	241n	17.46 N	64.49 W
Eagle Bay	182	50.56 N	119.12 W
Eagle Bend	198	44.10 N	93.53 W
Eagle Bridge	210	42.57 N	73.24 W
Eagle Butte	198	45.00 N	101.14 W
Eagle Chief Creek ≃	196	36.22 N	98.27 W
Eagle Creek	224	45.21 N	122.21 W
Eagle Creek ≃, Sask., Can.	184	52.22 N	107.24 W
Eagle Creek ≃, Ariz., U.S.	200	32.58 N	109.25 W
Eagle Creek ≃, Ind., U.S.	218	39.43 N	86.12 W
Eagle Creek ≃, Ky., U.S.	218	38.36 N	85.04 W
Eagle Creek ≃, Mont., U.S.	202	48.12 N	111.11 W
Eagle Creek ≃, N. Mex., U.S.	196	32.47 N	104.20 W
Eagle Creek ≃, Ohio, U.S.	214	41.18 N	80.53 W
Eagle Creek ≃, Ohio, U.S.	218	38.43 N	83.51 W
Eagle Creek ≃, Oreg., U.S.	202	44.45 N	117.10 W
Eagle Creek ≃, Oreg., U.S.	224	45.21 N	122.23 W
Eagle Creek, East Fork ≃	218	38.47 N	83.43 W
Eagle Creek, West Fork ≃	218	38.47 N	83.43 W
Eagle Creek Reservoir @[1]	218	39.50 N	86.18 W
Eagledale	224	47.37 N	122.32 W
Eagle Farm Airport ⊠	171a	27.27 S	153.11 E
Eagle Grove	190	42.40 N	93.54 W
Eagle Harbor	210	43.15 N	78.15 W
Eaglehawk	169	36.43 S	144.15 E
Eagle Hill ≃	283	42.42 N	70.49 W
Eagle Key I	220	25.09 N	80.36 W
Eagle Lake, Fla., U.S.	220	27.59 N	81.45 W
Eagle Lake, Maine, U.S.	186	47.02 N	68.36 W
Eagle Lake, Mich., U.S.	216	41.48 N	86.02 W
Eagle Lake, Tex., U.S.	222	29.35 N	96.20 W
Eagle Lake @, B.C., Can.	182	51.55 N	124.25 W
Eagle Lake @, Ont., Can.	184	50.39 N	94.54 W
Eagle Lake @, Ont., Can.	184	49.42 N	93.13 W
Eagle Lake @, Ont., Can.	212	44.41 N	76.43 W
Eagle Lake @, Ont., Can.	212	45.08 N	78.29 W
Eagle Lake @, Calif., U.S.	204	40.39 N	120.44 W
Eagle Lake @, Maine, U.S.	186	46.20 N	69.20 W
Eagle Lake @, Mich., U.S.	216	41.48 N	86.02 W
Eagle Lake @, Tex., U.S.	222	29.34 N	96.21 W
Eagle Lake @, Wis., U.S.	216	42.42 N	88.07 W
Eagle Mountain, Calif., U.S.	204	33.49 N	115.27 W
Eagle Mountain, Tex., U.S.	222	32.52 N	97.30 W
Eagle Mountain ∧	202	46.20 N	115.07 W
Eagle Mountain ∧[2]	190	47.54 N	90.33 W
Eagle Mountain Lake @[1]	222	32.55 N	97.30 W
Eagle Nest Butte ∧	198	43.27 N	101.39 W
Eagle Nest Lake @	222	29.13 N	95.37 W
Eagle Pass	196	28.43 N	100.30 W
Eagle Peak ∧, Calif., U.S.	204	41.17 N	120.12 W
Eagle Peak ∧, Calif., U.S.	228	35.15 N	118.28 W
Eagle Peak ∧, Calif., U.S.	282	37.54 N	121.54 W
Eagle River, Alaska, U.S.	180	61.19 N	149.34 W
Eagle River, Mich., U.S.	190	47.24 N	88.18 W
Eagle River, Wis., U.S.	190	45.55 N	89.15 W
Eagle Rock	192	37.38 N	79.48 W
Eagle Rock ⬥[8]	280	34.09 N	118.12 W
Eagle Rock Reservation ♠	276	40.49 N	74.14 W
Eaglesfield	44	55.03 N	3.12 W
Eaglesham, Alta., Can.	182	55.47 N	117.53 W
Eaglesham, Scot., U.K.	46	55.44 N	4.18 W
Eagles Mere	210	41.25 N	76.35 W
Eagle Village	180	64.47 N	141.07 W
Eagleville, Conn., U.S.	207	41.47 N	72.17 W
Eagleville, Pa., U.S.	285	40.10 N	75.24 W
Eagleville, Wis., U.S.	216	42.52 N	88.26 W
Ealing ⬥[8]	260	51.31 N	0.20 W
Eamont ≃	44	54.40 N	2.39 W
Earaheedy	162	25.34 S	121.39 E
Earby	44	53.56 N	2.08 W
Earcroft	262	53.43 N	2.29 W
Eardisley	42	52.08 N	2.59 W
Eardley Lake @	184	52.32 N	96.05 W
Ear Falls	184	50.38 N	93.13 W
Earle	194	35.16 N	90.28 W
Earlestown	262	53.27 N	2.39 W
Earl Grey	184	50.56 N	104.45 W
Earlham	194	41.30 N	94.07 W
Earlimart	226	35.53 N	119.16 W
Earlington	194	37.16 N	87.30 W
Earlish	46	57.34 N	6.23 W
Earl Park	216	40.42 N	87.25 W
Earls Colne	42	51.56 N	0.42 E
Earl Shilton	42	52.35 N	1.20 W
Earl Soham	42	52.14 N	1.16 E
Earlston	46	55.39 N	2.40 W
Earlton	210	42.21 N	73.54 W
Earlville, Ill., U.S.	216	41.35 N	88.55 W
Earlville, N.Y., U.S.	210	42.44 N	75.33 W
Earlville, Pa., U.S.	208	40.19 N	75.44 W
Earlwood	274a	33.56 S	151.08 E
Early	198	42.28 N	95.09 W
Early Winters Creek ≃	224	48.35 N	120.35 W
Earn ≃	46	56.21 N	3.19 W
Earn, Loch @	46	56.23 N	4.14 W
Earnslaw, Mount ∧	172	44.37 S	168.24 E
Earsdon	44	55.03 N	1.29 W
Earth	196	34.14 N	102.24 W
Easington	44	54.47 N	1.19 W
Easingwold	44	54.07 N	1.11 W
Eask, Lough @	48	54.41 N	8.03 W
Easky	48	54.18 N	8.58 W
Easley	192	34.50 N	82.36 W
East ≃, Ont., Can.	212	45.20 N	79.17 W
East ≃, Colo., U.S.	200	38.40 N	106.51 W
East ≃, N.Y., U.S.	276	40.48 N	73.48 W
East, University of the ♁[2]	269f	14.36 N	120.59 E
East Aberthaw	42	51.23 N	3.22 W
East Acton	283	42.29 N	71.25 W
East Allen ≃	44	54.55 N	2.19 W
East Alliance	214	40.55 N	81.04 W
East Alligator ≃	164	12.08 S	132.42 E
East Alton	219	38.53 N	90.06 W
East Amherst	210	43.01 N	78.42 W
East Angus	206	45.29 N	71.40 W
East Arlington	210	43.04 N	73.09 W
East Atlantic Beach	276	40.35 N	73.43 W
East Aurora	210	42.46 N	78.37 W
East Avon	210	42.55 N	77.42 W
East Bangor	210	40.53 N	75.11 W
East Barming	260	51.16 N	0.28 E
East Barnet ⬥[8]	260	51.38 N	0.09 W
East Basin C	279a	41.32 N	81.40 W
East Bay C, Fla., U.S.	192	30.05 N	85.32 W
East Bay C, N.Y., U.S.	210	40.38 N	73.32 W
East Bay C, Tex., U.S.	222	29.30 N	94.35 W
East Bedfont ⬥[8]	260	51.27 N	0.26 W
East Bend	192	36.13 N	80.31 W
East Berbice-Corentyne □[5]	246	5.20 N	57.50 W
East Berkshire	206	44.56 N	72.42 W
East-Berlin → Berlin (Ost), D.D.R.	264a	52.30 N	13.25 E
East Berlin, Conn., U.S.	207	41.37 N	72.43 W
East Berlin, Pa., U.S.	208	39.56 N	76.59 W
East Bernard	222	29.32 N	96.04 W
East Bernstadt	192	37.11 N	84.07 W
East Berwick	210	41.03 N	76.13 W
East Bethany	210	42.56 N	78.06 W
East Bhāgīrath Plain ≚	126	23.30 N	88.30 E
East Billerica	283	42.35 N	71.14 W
East Blackstone	207	42.02 N	71.31 W
East Bloomfield	210	42.54 N	77.26 W
East Boston ⬥[8]	283	42.23 N	71.02 W
Eastbourne, N.Z.	172	41.18 S	174.54 E
Eastbourne, Eng., U.K.	42	50.46 N	0.17 E
East Brady	214	40.59 N	79.37 W
East Braintree	184	49.37 N	95.38 W
East Branch	210	41.59 N	75.08 W
East Branch Clarion River Lake @[1]	214	41.35 N	78.35 W
East Brewster	207	41.46 N	70.04 W
East Brewton	194	31.05 N	87.04 W
East Bridgewater	207	42.02 N	70.58 W
East Brimfield Lake @[1]	207	42.06 N	72.10 W
East Brookfield	207	42.14 N	72.03 W
East Brooklyn	207	41.48 N	71.54 W
East Brother I	271d	22.20 N	113.58 E
East Brunswick	208	40.25 N	74.23 W
East Bucas Island I	116	9.43 N	126.02 E
East Burwood	274b	37.51 S	145.09 E
Eastbury	260	51.37 N	0.25 W
East Butler	214	40.53 N	79.51 W
East Butte ∧	202	48.52 N	111.09 W
East Cache Creek ≃	196	34.08 N	98.16 W
East Caicos I	238	21.41 N	71.30 W
East Calder	46	55.54 N	3.27 W
East Canaan	207	42.01 N	73.17 W
East Canada Creek ≃	210	43.00 N	74.45 W
East Canton	214	40.47 N	81.17 W
East Cape ≻, N.Z.	172	37.41 S	178.33 E
East Cape ≻, Alaska, U.S.	181a	51.21 N	179.29 E
East Cape ≻, Fla., U.S.	220	25.07 N	81.05 W
East Carbon	200	39.33 N	110.25 W
East Carlisle	214	41.19 N	82.05 W
East Caroline Basin ✢[1]	14	3.00 N	147.00 E
East Castor ≃	212	45.16 N	75.17 W
East Catfish Creek ≃	212	42.47 N	81.04 W
East-Central □[3]	150	6.00 N	7.30 E
East Channel ≃[1]	180	69.20 N	134.00 W
East Chatham	210	42.25 N	73.32 W
East Chelmsford	207	42.36 N	71.18 W
Eastchester	210	40.57 N	73.49 W
Eastchester Bay C	276	40.51 N	73.48 W
East Chicago	216	41.38 N	87.27 W
East Chicago Heights	278	40.31 N	87.35 W
East China Sea ⊤[2]	90	30.00 N	126.00 E
Eastchurch	42	51.25 N	0.52 E
East Clandon	260	51.15 N	0.29 W
East Claridon	214	41.32 N	81.07 W
East Cleddau ≃	42	51.46 N	4.52 W
East Cleveland	214	41.32 N	81.35 W
East Coast Bays	172	36.45 S	174.46 E
East Concord	210	42.33 N	78.38 W
East Corinth	188	45.00 N	69.01 W
Eastcote ⬥[8]	260	51.35 N	0.24 W
East Cote Blanche Bay C	194	29.35 N	91.40 W
East Coulée	182	51.20 N	112.19 W
East Creek ≃	276	40.27 N	74.09 W
East Cross Creek ≃	212	44.17 N	78.44 W
East Demerara-West Coast Berbice □[5]	246	6.20 N	58.00 W
East Dennis	207	41.45 N	70.10 W
East Dereham	42	52.41 N	0.56 E
East Detroit	214	42.28 N	82.56 W
East Dismal Swamp ☰	192	35.45 N	76.35 W
East Ditch ☰	276	40.56 N	74.19 W
East Don ≃	275b	43.43 N	79.20 W
East Douglas	207	42.04 N	71.43 W
East Dublin	192	32.32 N	82.52 W
East Dubuque	190	42.30 N	90.39 W
East Dundee	216	42.06 N	88.16 W
East Durham	210	42.22 N	74.06 W
East Ely	204	39.15 N	114.53 W
Eastend, Sask., Can.	184	49.31 N	108.48 W
East End, Vir. Is., U.S.	240m	18.21 N	64.40 W
East End Point ≻	240b	25.03 N	77.16 W
East Enterprise	218	38.52 N	84.59 W
Easter Island → Pascua, Isla de I	174z	27.07 S	109.22 W
Easterly	222	31.06 N	96.23 W
Eastern □[4], Ghana	150	6.30 N	0.30 W
Eastern □[4], Kenya	154	0.05 N	38.00 E
Eastern □[4], S.L.	150	8.15 N	11.00 W
Eastern □[4], Zam.	154	13.00 S	32.15 E
Eastern Bay C	208	38.51 N	76.19 W
Eastern Caprivi Strip □[5]	156	17.45 S	24.00 E
Eastern Channel → Tsushima-kaikyō ⊔	92	34.00 N	129.00 E
Eastern Cove C	168b	35.46 S	137.50 E
Eastern Creek ≃, Austl.	166	20.10 S	141.08 E
Eastern Creek ≃, Austl.	274a	33.39 S	150.51 E
Eastern Division □[5], Fiji	175g	19.00 S	180.00 E
Eastern Division □[5], Sol.is.	175e	10.30 S	162.00 E
Eastern Fields ✢[2]	164	10.20 S	145.45 E
Eastern Ghāts ∧∧	122	14.00 N	78.50 E
Eastern Highlands □[5]	164	6.30 S	145.15 E
Eastern Island I	174g	28.12 N	177.20 W
Eastern Isles II	42a	49.57 N	6.15 W
Eastern Michigan University ♁[2]	281	42.15 N	83.37 W
Eastern Native ⬥[8]	273d	26.13 S	28.05 E
Eastern Neck Island I	208	39.02 N	76.13 W
Eastern Point ≻	283	42.35 N	70.40 W
Eastern Sayans → Vostočnyj Sajan ∧∧	88	53.00 N	97.00 E
Eastern Shore ⬥[1]	208	38.40 N	75.50 W
Eastern Yamuna Canal ☰	272a	28.40 N	77.15 E
East Falkland I	254	51.55 S	59.00 W
East Falls ⬥[8]	285	40.01 N	75.11 W
East Falmouth	207	41.35 N	70.34 W
East Farleigh	260	51.15 N	0.29 E
East Farmingdale	276	40.44 N	73.26 W
East Faxon	210	41.15 N	76.58 W
East Fayetteville	192	35.05 N	78.51 W
East Flat Rock	192	35.17 N	82.32 W
Eastford	207	41.54 N	72.05 W
East Fork Lake @[1]	218	39.02 N	84.07 W
East Foxboro	283	42.04 N	71.12 W
East Freedom	214	40.21 N	78.26 W
East Freetown	207	41.46 N	70.58 W
East Frisian Islands → Ostfriesische Inseln II	52	53.44 N	7.25 E
East Gaffney	192	35.05 N	81.42 W
East Gallatin ≃	202	45.53 N	111.20 W
Eastgate	224	47.34 N	122.08 W
East Germany → German Democratic Republic □[1]	30	52.00 N	12.30 E
East Ghor Canal → Ghawr ash-Sharqīyah, Qanāt al- ☰	132	32.41 N	35.38 E
East Glacier Park	202	48.27 N	113.13 W
East Glenville	210	42.51 N	73.57 W
East Granby	207	41.57 N	72.44 W
East Grand Forks	198	47.56 N	97.01 W
East Grand Rapids	216	42.56 N	85.35 W
East Greenbush	210	42.35 N	73.42 W
East Greenville, Ohio, U.S.	214	40.48 N	81.36 W
East Greenville, Pa., U.S.	208	40.24 N	75.30 W
East Greenwich, N.Y., U.S.	210	43.09 N	73.24 W
East Greenwich, R.I., U.S.	207	41.40 N	71.27 W
East Grinstead	42	51.08 N	0.01 W
East Haddam	207	41.27 N	72.28 W
East Half Hollow Hills	276	40.48 N	73.19 W
Eastham, Eng., U.K.	262	53.19 N	2.58 W
Eastham, Mass., U.S.	207	41.50 N	69.58 W
East Ham ⬥[8]	260	51.32 N	0.03 E
East Hampton, Conn., U.S.	207	41.35 N	72.31 W
Easthampton, Mass., U.S.	207	42.16 N	72.40 W
East Hampton, N.Y., U.S.	207	40.58 N	72.11 W
East Hanningfield	260	51.41 N	0.34 E
East Hanover	276	40.49 N	74.22 W
East Harbor State Park ♠	214	41.32 N	82.49 W
East Harling	42	52.26 N	0.55 E
East Hartford	207	41.46 N	72.39 W
East Hartland	207	42.00 N	72.55 W
East Harwich	207	41.43 N	70.02 W
East Haven	207	41.17 N	72.52 W
East Hazel Crest	278	41.35 N	87.39 W
East Helena	202	46.35 N	111.56 W
East Herkimer	210	43.02 N	74.58 W
East Hertfordshire □[8]	260	51.46 N	0.02 W
East Hickory	214	41.35 N	79.24 W
East Highland Park	208	37.36 N	77.25 W
East Hills, Austl.	274a	33.58 S	150.59 E
East Hills, N.Y., U.S.	276	40.47 N	73.38 W
East Hoathly	42	50.55 N	0.10 E
East Horsley	42	51.15 N	0.26 W

Symbols in the index entries represent the broad categories identified in the key at the right. Symbols with superior numbers (∧∧[2]) identify subcategories (see complete key on page I · 30).

Kartensymbole in dem Registerverzeichnis stellen die rechts in Schlüssel erklärten Kategorien dar. Symbole mit hochgestellten Ziffern (∧∧[2]) bezeichnen Unterabteilungen einer Kategorie (vgl. vollständiger Schlüssel auf Seite I · 30).

Los símbolos incluidos en el texto del índice representan las grandes categorias identificadas con la clave a la derecha. Los símbolos con numeros en su parte superior (∧∧[2]) identifican las subcategorías (véase la clave completa en la página I · 30).

Les symboles de l'index représentent les catégories indiquées dans la légende à droite. Les symboles suivis d'un indice (∧∧[2]) représentent des sous-catégories (voir légende complète à la page I · 30).

Os símbolos incluídos no texto do índice representam as grandes categorias identificadas com a chave à direita. Os símbolos com números em sua parte superior (∧∧[2]) identificam as subcategorias (veja-se a chave completa à página I · 30).

	ENGLISH	DEUTSCH	ESPAÑOL	FRANÇAIS	PORTUGUÊS
∧	Mountain	Berg	Montaña	Montagne	Montanha
∧∧	Mountains	Berge	Montañas	Montagnes	Montanhas
)(	Pass	Pass	Paso	Col	Passo
∨	Valley, Canyon	Tal, Cañon	Valle, Cañón	Vallée, Canyon	Vale, Canhão
≚	Plain	Ebene	Llano	Plaine	Planície
≻	Cape	Kap	Cabo	Cap	Cabo
I	Island	Insel	Isla	Île	Ilha
II	Islands	Inseln	Islas	Îles	Ilhas
⊥	Other Topographic Features	Andere Topographische Objekte	Otros Elementos Topográficos	Autres données topographiques	Outros Elementos Topográficos

ESPAÑOL — Nombre | Página | Lat.°' | Long.°' W=Oeste
FRANÇAIS — Nom | Page | Lat.°' | Long.°' W=Ouest
PORTUGUÊS — Nome | Página | Lat.°' | Long.°' W=Oeste

Nombre / Nom / Nome	Página / Page	Lat.°'	Long.°'
East Humber ≃	212	43.47 N	79.35 W
East Huntington	276	40.52 N	73.24 W
East Ilsley	42	51.32 N	1.17 W
East Irvington	276	41.03 N	73.51 W
East Island ≻[1]	276	40.54 N	73.38 W
East Islip	276	40.44 N	73.11 W
East Jewett	210	42.14 N	74.09 W
East Jordan	190	45.10 N	85.07 W
East Keansburg	276	40.26 N	74.07 W
East Kelowna	182	49.51 N	119.25 W
East Kilbride	46	55.46 N	4.10 W
East Killingly	207	41.51 N	71.49 W
East Kingston	210	41.57 N	73.58 W
Eastlake, Mich., U.S.	190	44.15 N	86.18 W
Eastlake, Ohio, U.S.	214	41.34 N	81.35 W
East Lake @, Ont., Can.	212	43.55 N	77.12 W
East Lake @, N.J., U.S.	276	40.58 N	74.21 W
East Lake Tohopekaliga @	220	28.18 N	81.17 W
East Lamma Channel Џ	271d	22.15 N	114.07 E
Eastland	196	32.24 N	98.49 W
Eastland ◆[9], Mich., U.S.	281	42.27 N	82.56 W
Eastland ◆[9], Pa., U.S.	279b	40.22 N	79.50 W
East Lansdowne	285	39.56 N	75.16 W
East Lansing	216	42.44 N	84.29 W
East Laurinburg	192	34.46 N	79.27 W
Eastleigh	42	50.58 N	1.22 W
East Lewistown	214	40.57 N	80.42 W
East Liberty	216	40.20 N	83.35 W
East Liberty ◆[8]	279b	40.27 N	79.55 W
East Lindfield	274a	33.46 S	151.11 E
East Linton	46	55.59 N	2.39 W
East Liverpool	214	40.38 N	80.35 W
East Loch Roag C	46	58.14 N	6.48 W
East Loch Tarbert C	46	57.52 N	6.45 W
East London (Oos-Londen)	158	33.00 S	27.55 E
East Longmeadow	207	42.04 N	72.31 W
East Loof	42	50.22 N	4.27 W
East Los Angeles	228	34.01 N	118.09 W
East Lyme	207	41.22 N	72.13 W
East Lynn	216	40.28 N	87.48 W
East Lynn Lake @[1]	188	38.05 N	82.20 W
East Machias	188	44.44 N	67.24 W
Eastmain	176	52.15 N	78.30 W
Eastmain ≃	176	52.15 N	78.35 W
East Malling	260	51.17 N	0.26 E
Eastman, Qué., Can.	206	45.18 N	72.19 W
Eastman, Ga., U.S.	192	32.12 N	83.11 W
East Mansfield	283	42.01 N	71.11 W
East Marin Island |	282	37.58 N	122.27 W
East Markham	44	53.15 N	0.54 W
East McKeesport	279b	40.23 N	79.48 W
East Meadow	210	40.43 N	73.34 W
East Meadow ≃	283	42.47 N	71.02 W
East Meadow Brook ≃	276	40.39 N	73.34 W
East Mecca	214	41.24 N	80.45 W
East Mengo □[5]	154	1.00 N	32.30 E
East Meredith	210	42.25 N	74.53 W
East Midlands Airport ⊠	42	52.50 N	1.20 W
East Millbury	207	42.13 N	71.45 W
East Millinocket	188	45.37 N	68.35 W
East Millstone	276	40.30 N	74.35 W
East Missoula	202	46.52 N	113.58 W
East Molesey	260	51.24 N	0.21 W
East Moline	190	41.31 N	90.25 W
East Monongahela	279b	40.12 N	79.55 W
East Mountain	222	32.35 N	94.51 W
East Mustang Creek ≃	222	29.03 N	96.27 W
East Naples	220	26.08 N	81.46 W
East Nassau	210	42.30 N	73.30 W
East Neck	276	40.54 N	73.26 W
East Newark	276	40.45 N	74.10 W
East New Britain □[5]	164	6.00 S	152.00 E
East New Market	208	38.36 N	75.56 W
East New York ◆[8]	276	40.40 N	73.53 W
East Nimār □[5]	124	22.00 N	76.30 E
East Nishnabotna ≃	198	40.39 N	95.37 W
East Nodaway ≃	194	40.38 N	95.01 W
East Norriton	208	40.09 N	75.18 W
East Northfield	207	42.43 N	72.27 W
East Northport	210	40.52 N	73.19 W
East Norwich	210	40.50 N	73.32 W
East Novaya Zemlya Trough ✢[1]	10	74.00 N	62.00 E
East Oakville Creek ≃	275b	43.28 N	79.48 W
East Olympia	224	46.58 N	122.50 W
Easton, Eng., U.K.	42	50.32 N	2.26 W
Easton, Calif., U.S.	226	36.39 N	119.47 W
Easton, Conn., U.S.	207	41.15 N	73.18 W
Easton, Ill., U.S.	219	40.14 N	89.50 W
Easton, Md., U.S.	208	38.46 N	76.04 W
Easton, Mass., U.S.	283	42.02 N	71.06 W
Easton, Pa., U.S.	208	40.42 N	75.12 W
Easton, Tex., U.S.	222	32.23 N	94.35 W
Easton, Wash., U.S.	224	47.14 N	121.11 W
Eastondale	283	42.02 N	71.04 W
Easton Reservoir @[1]	207	41.16 N	73.16 W
East Orange	210	40.46 N	74.13 W
East Orleans	207	41.47 N	69.58 W
East Orne Bank ✢[4]	14	27.45 S	157.25 W
East Otto	210	42.23 N	78.45 W
Eastover	192	33.52 N	80.41 W
East Pacific Basin ✢[1]	14	12.00 N	150.00 W
East Palatka	192	29.40 N	81.35 W
East Palestine	214	40.50 N	80.33 W
East Palo Alto	226	37.27 N	122.07 W
East Park Reservoir @[1]	226	39.21 N	122.30 W
East Parkrose	224	45.33 N	122.32 W
East Peak ∧	116	11.13 N	119.29 E
East Peckham	260	51.15 N	0.23 E
East Pembroke, Mass., U.S.	283	42.05 N	70.46 W
East Pembroke, N.Y., U.S.	210	42.60 N	78.18 W
East Peoria	190	40.40 N	89.34 W
East Pepperell	207	42.40 N	71.34 W
East Petersburg	208	40.06 N	76.21 W
East Pharsalia	210	42.34 N	75.43 W
East Pine	182	55.43 N	121.13 W
East Pines	284c	38.57 N	76.55 W
East Pittsburgh	279b	40.24 N	79.48 W
East Point	192	33.40 N	84.27 W
East Point ≻, P.E.I., Can.	186	46.27 N	61.58 W
East Point ≻, Mass., U.S.	207	42.25 N	70.54 W
East Point ≻, Vir. Is., U.S.	241n	17.45 N	64.34 W
Eastpoint ◆[9]	284b	39.18 N	76.31 W
Eastport, Newf., Can.	186	48.39 N	53.45 W
Eastport, Idaho, U.S.	202	48.59 N	116.11 W
Eastport, Maine, U.S.	188	44.54 N	67.00 W
Eastport, N.Y., U.S.	207	40.49 N	72.44 W
East Porterville	204	36.04 N	118.56 W
East Potomac Park ♠	284c	38.52 N	77.01 W
East Prairie	194	36.47 N	89.23 W
East Prairie ≃	182	55.34 N	116.25 W
East Prospect	208	39.58 N	76.31 W
East Providence	207	41.49 N	71.23 W
East Pryor Mountain ∧	202	45.11 N	108.20 W
East Quogue	207	40.51 N	72.35 W
East Rājasthān Uplands ⩕[1]	124	26.40 N	76.35 E
East Randolph	210	42.10 N	78.57 W
East Retford	44	53.19 N	0.56 W
East Richmond	226	37.57 N	122.19 W
Eastridge Center ◆[9]	282	37.20 N	121.49 W
East Rigaud ≃	206	45.27 N	74.22 W
Eastriggs	44	54.59 N	3.10 W
East River C	208	37.24 N	76.21 W
East Rochester, N.Y., U.S.	210	43.07 N	77.29 W
East Rochester, Ohio, U.S.	214	40.45 N	81.02 W
East Rockaway	276	40.39 N	73.40 W
East Rockingham	192	34.57 N	79.45 W
East Rockwood	216	42.03 N	83.13 W
East Rosebud Creek ≃	202	45.29 N	109.27 W
East Rutherford	276	40.51 N	74.06 W
Eastry	42	51.15 N	1.18 E
East Saint Louis	219	38.38 N	90.09 W
East Salem	208	40.37 N	77.14 W
East Salt Creek ≃	200	39.13 N	108.54 W
East Sandwich	207	41.45 N	70.27 W
East Sandy Creek ≃	214	41.22 N	79.51 W
East Schodack	210	42.34 N	73.38 W
East Scotia Basin ✢[1]	9	57.00 S	35.00 W
East Sepik □[5]	164	4.00 S	143.30 E
East Setauket	210	40.57 N	73.06 W
East Shoal Lake @	184	50.23 N	97.37 W
East Siberian Sea → Vostočno-Sibirskoje More ⊤[2]	12	74.00 N	166.00 E
East Side	210	41.04 N	75.46 W
East Side Canal ☰, Calif., U.S.	226	37.21 N	120.55 W
East Side Canal ☰, Calif., U.S.	226	35.33 N	119.33 W
East Sister Island |	166	39.39 S	148.00 E
East Smethport	214	41.49 N	78.26 W
East Smithfield	210	41.52 N	76.38 W
East Sooke	224	48.22 N	123.43 W
Eastsound	224	48.42 N	122.55 W
East Sound Џ	224	48.39 N	122.53 W
East Sparta	214	40.40 N	81.21 W
East Spencer	192	35.41 N	80.26 W
East Springfield, Ohio, U.S.	214	40.27 N	80.52 W
East Springfield, Pa., U.S.	214	41.57 N	80.28 W
East Stony Creek ≃	210	43.15 N	74.12 W
East Stour ≃	42	51.08 N	0.53 E
East Stroudsburg	210	41.00 N	75.11 W
East Sudbury	283	42.24 N	71.24 W
East Sullivan	188	44.30 N	68.09 W
East Sydenham ≃	214	42.35 N	82.23 W
East Syracuse	210	43.04 N	76.05 W
East Tawas	190	44.17 N	83.29 W
East Templeton	207	42.34 N	78.02 W
East Texas	210	40.33 N	75.33 W
East Thompson	207	42.00 N	71.48 W
East Tilbury	260	51.28 N	0.26 E
East Troy	216	42.47 N	88.24 W
East Tulare	226	36.12 N	119.20 W
East Tustin	280	33.46 N	117.49 W
East Twin ≃	190	44.08 N	87.34 W
Eastvale	214	40.46 N	80.19 W
East Vandergrift	214	40.36 N	79.34 W
Eastview	218	40.19 N	80.38 W
Eastville	208	37.21 N	75.57 W
East Walker ≃	204	38.53 N	119.10 W
East Walpole	207	42.10 N	71.13 W
East Wareham	207	41.46 N	70.40 W
East Washington	214	40.10 N	80.14 W
East Waterford	208	40.22 N	77.36 W
East Wenatchee	202	47.25 N	120.16 W
East Wenonah	285	39.47 N	75.08 W
East White Plains	276	41.03 N	73.47 W
Eastwick ◆[8]	285	39.55 N	75.14 W
East Wickham ◆[8]	260	51.28 N	0.07 E
East Williamson	210	43.14 N	77.09 W
East Williston	276	40.46 N	73.38 W
East Wilmington	192	34.13 N	77.53 W
East Wittering	42	50.41 N	0.53 W
Eastwood, Austl.	274a	33.48 S	151.05 E
Eastwood, Eng., U.K.	44	53.01 N	1.18 W
Eastwood, Eng., U.K.	260	51.34 N	0.40 E
Eastwood, Eng., U.K.	262	53.43 N	2.03 W
Eastwood, Mich., U.S.	216	42.19 N	85.32 W
Eastwood, Pa., U.S.	279b	40.17 N	79.31 W
East Worcester	210	42.37 N	74.40 W
East Yegua Creek ≃	222	30.19 N	96.45 W
East Yellow Creek ≃	194	39.38 N	93.04 W
East York, Ont., Can.	212	43.41 N	79.20 W
East York, Pa., U.S.	208	39.58 N	76.43 W
Eaton, Austl.	168a	33.19 S	115.43 E
Eaton, Colo., U.S.	200	40.32 N	104.42 W
Eaton, Ind., U.S.	216	40.21 N	85.21 W
Eaton, N.Y., U.S.	210	42.51 N	75.37 W
Eaton, Ohio, U.S.	218	39.45 N	84.38 W
Eaton ≃	206	45.28 N	71.39 W
Eaton Estates	214	41.19 N	81.59 W
Eatonia	184	51.13 N	109.23 W
Eaton-Nord ≃	206	45.24 N	71.35 W
Eaton Park	220	28.00 N	81.54 W
Eaton Rapids	216	42.36 N	84.39 W
Eatons Neck	276	40.56 N	73.24 W
Eatons Neck ≻[1]	276	40.57 N	73.23 W
Eatons Neck Point ≻	210	40.57 N	73.24 W
Eaton Socon	42	52.13 N	0.18 W
Eatonton	192	33.20 N	83.23 W
Eatontown	208	40.18 N	74.07 W
Eatonville	224	46.52 N	122.16 W
Eaton Wash ∨	280	34.04 N	118.03 W
Eaton Wash Dam ◆[6]	280	34.10 N	118.06 W
Eau ≃	44	53.31 N	0.44 W
Eaubonne	261	49.00 N	2.17 E
Eau Claire, Mich., U.S.	216	41.59 N	86.18 W
Eau Claire, Pa., U.S.	214	41.08 N	79.48 W
Eau Claire, Wis., U.S.	190	44.49 N	91.31 W
Eau Claire ≃, Wis., U.S.	190	44.49 N	91.31 W
Eau Claire ≃, Wis., U.S.	190	44.55 N	89.37 W
Eau-Claire, Lac à l' @, Qué., Can.	176	56.10 N	74.25 W
Eau-Claire, Lac à l' @, Qué., Can.	206	46.33 N	73.04 W
Eau d'Heure ≃	56	50.18 N	4.24 E
Eau Galle ≃	190	44.37 N	92.00 W
Eau Gallie	220	28.08 N	80.38 W
Eaulne ≃	50	49.54 N	1.07 E
Eauripik |[1]	108	6.42 N	143.03 E
Eauripik Ridge ✢[3]	14	4.00 N	141.30 E
Eauze	32	43.52 N	0.06 E
Ebabaka	152	2.30 S	18.19 E
Eban	150	9.44 N	4.56 E
Ebanga	152	12.44 S	14.44 E
Ebangalakata	152	0.29 S	21.29 E
Ebano	234	22.13 N	98.22 W
Ebba Ksour	148	35.57 N	8.50 E
Ebb and Flow Indian Reserve ◆[4]	184	51.05 N	99.05 W
Ebb and Flow Lake @	184	51.05 N	98.56 W
Ebbegebirge ⩕	56	51.08 N	7.46 E
Ebbegebirge, Naturpark ♠	263	51.06 N	7.45 E
Ebben Creek ≃	283	42.38 N	70.45 W
Ebberup	41	55.15 N	9.59 E
Ebbetts Pass)(	226	38.33 N	119.48 W
Ebbs	64	47.38 N	12.13 E
Ebbw ≃	42	51.33 N	2.59 W
Ebbw Vale	42	51.47 N	3.12 W
Ebebiyin	152	2.09 N	11.20 E
Ebejty, Ozero @	86	54.38 N	71.44 E
Ebel	152	0.07 N	11.05 E
Ebeleben	54	51.17 N	10.43 E
Ebeltoft	41	56.12 N	10.41 E
Ebeltoft Vig C	41	56.10 N	10.36 E
Ebenau	64	47.47 N	13.11 E
Ebendorf	54	52.11 N	11.34 E
Ebene Reichenau	64	46.51 N	13.54 E
Ebenezer	275b	43.46 N	79.40 W
Ebenezer Ridge ∧	218	39.06 N	84.55 W
Eben Junction	190	46.21 N	86.58 W
Ebenrode → Nesterov	76	54.38 N	22.34 E
Ebensburg	214	40.29 N	78.44 W
Ebensee	64	47.48 N	13.46 E
Ebensfeld	56	50.04 N	10.58 E
Eberbach	56	49.28 N	8.59 E
Ebergassing	264b	48.03 N	16.31 E
Eber Gölü @	130	38.38 N	31.12 E
Ebergötzen	52	51.34 N	10.06 E
Ebermannstadt	60	49.43 N	11.13 E
Ebern	56	50.05 N	10.47 E
Eberndorf	61	46.35 N	14.38 E
Ebersbach, B.R.D.	56	48.43 N	9.31 E
Ebersbach, D.D.R.	54	51.00 N	14.35 E
Ebersberg	60	48.05 N	11.58 E
Eberschwang	60	48.09 N	13.34 E
Ebersdorf	52	53.31 N	9.03 E
Ebersdorf bei Coburg	56	50.13 N	11.04 E
Eberstein	61	46.48 N	14.34 E
Eberswalde	54	52.50 N	13.49 E
Ebetsu	92a	43.07 N	141.34 E
Ebian	102	29.10 N	103.20 E
Ebina	94	35.26 N	139.25 E
Ebingen	58	48.13 N	9.01 E
Ebnat	58	47.15 N	9.08 E
Ebo	152	11.02 S	14.41 E
Ebola ≃	152	3.20 N	20.57 E
Eboli	68	40.37 N	15.04 E
Ebolowa	152	2.54 N	11.09 E
Ebon |[1]	14	4.35 N	168.44 E
Ebonda	152	2.12 N	22.21 E
Ebony	156	22.05 S	15.15 E
Eboshi-yama ∧	96	35.04 N	133.04 E
Éboué Stadium ♠	273b	4.16 S	15.16 E
Ebrach	56	49.50 N	10.29 E
Ébrié, Lagune C	150	5.14 N	4.26 W
Ebro ≃	34	40.43 N	0.54 E
Ebro, Delta del ≚[2]	34	40.43 N	0.54 E
Ebro, Embalse del @[1]	34	43.00 N	3.58 W
Ebstorf	52	53.01 N	10.25 E
Ebute-ikorodu	273a	6.37 N	3.30 E
Ebute-Metta ◆[8]	273a	6.29 N	3.23 E
Ecarté, Chenal ≃[1]	214	42.28 N	82.29 W
Ecatepec □[7]	286a	19.36 N	99.04 W
Ecatepec de Morelos	286a	19.35 N	99.04 W
Écaussinnes-d'Enghen	50	50.34 N	4.10 E
Ecclefechan	44	55.03 N	3.17 W
Eccles, Eng., U.K.	260	51.19 N	0.29 E
Eccles, Eng., U.K.	262	53.29 N	2.21 W
Eccles, W. Va., U.S.	192	37.47 N	81.16 W
Ecclesfield	44	53.27 N	1.27 W
Eccleshall	42	52.52 N	2.15 W
Eccleston, Eng., U.K.	262	53.27 N	2.47 W
Eccleston, Eng., U.K.	262	53.39 N	2.44 W
Eccleston, Md., U.S.	284b	39.24 N	76.44 W
Eceabat	130	40.11 N	26.21 E
Echabi	89	53.30 N	142.59 E
Echague	116	16.42 N	121.40 E
Echallens	58	46.38 N	6.38 E
Echaporã	255	22.26 S	50.12 W
Echarcon	261	48.34 N	2.24 E
Échauffour	50	48.44 N	0.23 E
Echeconnee Creek ≃	192	32.39 N	83.36 W
Echeng	100	30.24 N	114.51 E
Échenoz-la-Méline	58	47.36 N	6.08 E
Echi ≃	94	35.13 N	136.07 E
Echigawa	94	35.10 N	136.12 E
Echigo-sammyaku ⩕	92	37.50 N	139.50 E
Echimamish ≃	184	54.20 N	97.27 W
Eching	60	48.18 N	11.37 E
Echizen	94	35.54 N	136.00 E
Echizen-kaga-kaigan-kokutei-kōen ♠	94	36.08 N	136.05 E
Echizen-misaki ≻	94	35.59 N	135.57 E
Echo	198	44.37 N	95.25 W
Echo Bay C	276	40.54 N	73.46 W
Echoing ≃	184	55.51 N	92.05 W
Echoing Lake @	184	54.31 N	92.15 W
Echo Lake @, Ill., U.S.	278	42.13 N	88.05 W
Echo Lake @, N.J., U.S.	276	41.04 N	74.25 W
Echo Summit ∧	226	38.50 N	120.02 W
Echt, Ned.	52	51.06 N	5.52 E
Echt, Scot., U.K.	46	57.08 N	2.26 W
Echterdingen	56	48.41 N	9.10 E
Echternach	56	49.48 N	6.26 E
Echternacherbrück	56	49.49 N	6.25 E
Echuca	166	36.08 S	144.46 E
Echunga	168b	35.07 S	138.48 E
Écija	34	37.32 N	5.05 W
Ecilda Paullier	258	34.22 S	57.04 W
Eck, Loch @	46	56.05 N	5.00 W
Eckartsberga	54	51.07 N	11.34 E
Eckbolsheim	58	48.35 N	7.41 E
Eckenhagen	56	50.59 N	7.41 E
Eckernförde	41	54.28 N	9.50 E
Eckernförder Bucht C	41	54.30 N	10.02 E
Eckerö |	26	60.14 N	19.35 E
Eckington	44	53.19 N	1.21 W
Eckley	210	40.59 N	75.51 W
Eckville	182	52.21 N	114.22 W
Eckwarderhörne	52	53.31 N	8.14 E
Ecleto	222	29.03 N	97.45 W
Ecleto Creek ≃	196	28.52 N	97.45 W
Eclipse Sound Џ	176	72.38 N	79.00 W
Ečmiadzin	84	40.10 N	44.18 E
Ecola State Park ♠	224	45.57 N	123.58 W
École ≃	261	48.32 N	2.33 E
Écommoy	50	47.50 N	0.16 E
Econfina ≃	192	30.02 N	83.55 W
Econlockhatchee ≃	220	28.42 N	81.02 W
Economy, Ind., U.S.	218	39.59 N	85.05 W
Economy, Pa., U.S.	214	40.39 N	80.14 W
Economy Park ♠	279b	40.37 N	80.12 W
Écorce, Lac de l' @[1]	190	47.05 N	76.24 W
Écorces, Lac des @	206	46.00 N	74.32 W
Ecorse	216	42.15 N	83.09 W
Ecorse ≃	281	42.14 N	83.09 W
Ecorse, South Branch ≃	281	42.14 N	83.09 W
Écos	50	49.10 N	1.39 E
Écosse → Scotland □[8]	28	57.00 N	4.00 W
Écouen	50	49.01 N	2.23 E
Écouen, Château d' ⊥	261	49.01 N	2.23 E
Écouis	50	49.19 N	1.26 E
Ecoute, Rû d' ≃	261	48.39 N	2.26 E
Ecquevilly	261	48.57 N	1.55 E
Écrosnes	261	48.33 N	1.44 E
Ecru	194	34.21 N	89.01 W
Ecser	264c	47.27 N	19.20 E
Ecstall ≃	182	54.09 N	129.56 W
Ecuador □[1]	242		
	246	2.00 S	77.30 W
Ecuandureo	234	20.10 N	102.11 W
Écueillé	32	47.05 N	1.21 E
Écuises	58	46.45 N	4.32 E
Ecum Secum	186	44.58 N	62.08 W
Écury-sur-Coole	50	48.54 N	4.20 E
Ed, Sve.	26	58.55 N	11.55 E
Ed, Yai.	144	13.52 N	41.40 E
Eda ◆[8]	268	35.34 N	139.34 E
Edah	162	28.17 S	117.10 E
Edam, Sask., Can.	184	53.12 N	108.46 W
Edam, Ned.	52	52.31 N	5.03 E
Edarene	148	25.27 N	8.22 E
Eday |	46	59.11 N	2.47 W
Edderton	46	57.50 N	4.10 W
Eddington Gardens	285	40.06 N	74.57 W
Eddleston	46	55.43 N	3.13 W
Eddrachillis Bay C	46	58.18 N	5.15 W
Eddy	222	31.18 N	97.15 W
Eddystone	208	39.51 N	75.21 W
Eddystone Point ≻	166	41.00 S	148.21 E
Eddystone Rocks ||[1]	42	50.12 N	4.15 W
Eddyville, Iowa, U.S.	190	41.09 N	92.38 W
Eddyville, Ky., U.S.	194	37.03 N	88.04 W
Eddyville, N.Y., U.S.	210	41.54 N	74.02 W
Ede, Ned.	52	52.03 N	5.40 E
Ede, Nig.	150	7.44 N	4.27 E
Edéa	152	3.48 N	10.08 E
Edebäck	40	60.04 N	13.33 E
Edebo	40	60.01 N	18.34 E
Edegem	52	51.09 N	4.27 E
Edehon Lake @	176	60.25 N	97.15 W
Edéia	255	17.18 S	49.55 W
Edelény	30	48.18 N	20.44 E
Edelsfeld	60	49.34 N	11.42 E
Edelshausen	60	48.37 N	11.17 E
Edelweiss Spitze ∧	64	47.07 N	12.50 E
Edemissen	52	52.23 N	10.16 E
Eden, Austl.	166	37.04 S	149.54 E
Éden, Bra.	287a	22.48 S	43.24 W
Eden, N. Ire., U.K.	48	54.43 N	5.47 W
Eden, Mich., U.S.	216	42.32 N	84.26 W
Eden, Miss., U.S.	194	32.59 N	90.20 W
Eden, N.Y., U.S.	210	42.39 N	78.54 W
Eden, Tex., U.S.	196	31.13 N	99.51 W
Eden, Wyo., U.S.	200	42.03 N	109.26 W
Eden ≃, Eng., U.K.	42	51.10 N	0.11 E
Eden ≃, Eng., U.K.	44	54.57 N	3.01 W
Eden ≃, Scot., U.K.	46	56.22 N	2.50 W
Eden ≃, Wales, U.K.	42	52.48 N	3.53 W
Edenbridge	260	51.12 N	0.04 E
Edenburg	158	29.45 S	25.56 E
Eden Canyon ∨	282	37.42 N	122.01 W
Edendale, N.Z.	172	46.19 S	168.47 E
Edendale, S. Afr.	158	29.39 S	30.18 E
Edenderry	48	53.21 N	7.35 W
Edenfield	262	53.40 N	2.18 W
Eden Hill ∧[2]	207	41.20 N	73.19 W
Edenkoben	56	49.17 N	8.07 E
Eden Lake @	184	56.38 N	100.15 W
Eden Mills	212	43.35 N	80.09 W
Eden Park ◆[8]	260	51.23 N	0.02 W
Edenside ∨	44	54.40 N	2.35 W
Edenton	192	36.04 N	76.39 W
Edenvale	273d	26.08 S	28.09 E
Edenvale Location	273d	26.08 S	28.11 E
Eden Valley, Austl.	168b	34.39 S	139.06 E
Eden Valley, Minn., U.S.	190	45.19 N	94.33 W
Edenville	158	27.37 S	27.34 E
Edeowie	166	31.27 S	138.27 E
Eder ≃	56	51.13 N	9.27 E
Ederkopf ∧	56	50.56 N	8.12 E
Ederny	48	54.32 N	7.39 W
Ederstausee @[1]	56	51.11 N	9.00 E
Eder-Talsperre ◆[6]	56	51.11 N	9.02 E
Edesheim	56	49.16 N	8.08 E
Edessa → Édhessa	38	40.48 N	22.03 E
Edewecht	52	53.07 N	8.02 E
Edfu → Idfū	140	24.58 N	32.52 E
Edgar, Nebr., U.S.	198	40.22 N	97.58 W
Edgar, Wis., U.S.	190	44.55 N	90.00 W
Edgard	194	30.03 N	90.34 W
Edgar Ranges ⩕	162	18.43 S	123.25 E
Edgars Creek ≃	274b	37.44 S	144.58 E
Edgartown	207	41.23 N	70.31 W
Edgartown Harbor C	207	41.24 N	70.30 W
Edgecliff	222	32.39 N	97.22 W
Edgecumbe	172	37.59 S	176.50 E
Edgefield	192	33.47 N	81.56 W
Edge Hill ◆[8]	262	53.24 N	2.57 W
Edge Hill ∧[2]	42	52.08 N	1.27 W
Edgeley, Ont., Can.	275b	43.48 N	79.31 W
Edgeley, N. Dak., U.S.	198	46.22 N	98.43 W
Edgely	285	40.07 N	74.50 W
Edgemere	208	39.14 N	76.27 W
Edgemont, Calif., U.S.	228	33.53 N	117.18 W
Edgemont, Pa., U.S.	285	39.57 N	75.27 W
Edgemont, S. Dak., U.S.	198	43.18 N	103.50 W
Edgemont Park	216	42.44 N	84.36 W
Edge Mountain ∧	180	58.12 N	152.06 W
Edgeroi	166	30.07 S	149.48 E
Edgerton, Alta., Can.	184	52.45 N	110.27 W
Edgerton, Ind., U.S.	216	41.05 N	84.49 W
Edgerton, Minn., U.S.	198	43.53 N	96.08 W
Edgerton, Ohio, U.S.	216	41.27 N	84.45 W
Edgerton, Wis., U.S.	216	42.50 N	89.04 W
Edgerton, Wyo., U.S.	200	43.25 N	106.15 W
Edgewater, Ala., U.S.	194	33.32 N	86.57 W
Edgewater, Fla., U.S.	220	28.60 N	80.54 W
Edgewater, N.J., U.S.	276	40.50 N	73.58 W
Edgewater Heights	281	42.12 N	83.31 W
Edgewater Park	285	40.04 N	74.54 W
Edgewater Park ♠	279a	41.29 N	81.43 W
Edgewater Point ≻	276	40.55 N	73.44 W
Edgewood, B.C., Can.	182	49.47 N	118.08 W
Edgewood, Fla., U.S.	220	28.29 N	81.32 W
Edgewood, Ill., U.S.	194	38.55 N	88.40 W
Edgewood, Ind., U.S.	218	40.06 N	85.44 W
Edgewood, Ind., U.S.	218	39.41 N	86.09 W
Edgewood, Iowa, U.S.	190	42.39 N	91.24 W
Edgewood, Md., U.S.	188	39.25 N	76.18 W
Edgewood, Ohio, U.S.	214	41.52 N	80.46 W
Edgewood, Pa., U.S.	210	40.47 N	76.35 W
Edgewood, Pa., U.S.	279b	40.26 N	79.53 W
Edgewood, Tex., U.S.	222	32.42 N	95.53 W
Edgewood Arsenal ■	208	39.20 N	76.17 W
Edgeworth	214	40.33 N	80.11 W
Edgeworthstown	48	53.42 N	7.36 W
Edgware ◆[8]	260	51.37 N	0.17 W
Edgworth	262	53.39 N	2.24 W
Édhessa	38	40.48 N	22.03 E
Edievale	172	45.48 S	169.22 E
Ediger	56	50.06 N	7.09 E
Edimbourg → Edinburgh	46	55.57 N	3.13 W
Edimburgo → Edinburgh	46	55.57 N	3.13 W
Edina, Liber.	150	6.01 N	10.10 W
Edina, Minn., U.S.	190	44.55 N	93.20 W
Edina, Mo., U.S.	219	40.10 N	92.11 W
Edinboro	214	41.52 N	80.08 W
Edinboro Lake @	214	41.53 N	80.08 W
Edinburg, Ill., U.S.	219	39.39 N	89.23 W
Edinburg, Ind., U.S.	218	39.21 N	85.58 W
Edinburg, Miss., U.S.	194	32.48 N	89.20 W
Edinburg, N. Dak., U.S.	198	48.30 N	97.52 W
Edinburg, N.Y., U.S.	210	43.13 N	74.07 W
Edinburg, Ohio, U.S.	214	41.06 N	81.09 W
Edinburg, Tex., U.S.	196	26.18 N	98.10 W
Edinburg, Va., U.S.	188	38.49 N	78.34 W
Edinburgh	46	55.57 N	3.13 W
Edinburgh (Turnhouse) Airport ⊠	46	55.57 N	3.21 W
Edinburgh Castle ⊥	46	55.56 N	3.14 W
Edinburgh Channel Џ	236	14.45 N	82.40 W
Edinburgh Mountain ∧	224	48.38 N	124.24 W
Edinburgh Reef ✢[2]	236	14.50 N	82.39 W
Edincik	130	40.20 N	27.51 E
Edingen → Enghien	50	50.42 N	4.02 E
Edirne	130	41.40 N	26.34 E
Edirne □[4]	130	41.20 N	26.40 E
Edison, Ga., U.S.	192	31.33 N	84.44 W
Edison, N.J., U.S.	210	40.31 N	74.24 W
Edison, Ohio, U.S.	214	40.33 N	82.52 W
Edison, Pa., U.S.	208	40.17 N	75.07 W
Edison Bridge ◆[5]	214	41.27 N	82.49 W
Edison National Historic Site ⊥	276	40.47 N	74.14 W
Edison Park ◆[8]	278	42.01 N	87.49 W
Edisseja	84	44.03 N	44.33 E
Edisto ≃	192	32.39 N	80.24 W
Edisto, North Fork ≃	192	33.16 N	80.53 W
Edisto, South Fork ≃	192	33.16 N	80.53 W
Edith	170	33.48 S	149.55 E
Edith, Mount ∧	202	46.26 N	111.11 W
Edithburgh	168b	35.06 S	137.44 E
Edith River	164	14.11 S	132.02 E
Edithvale	274b	38.02 S	145.07 E
Edjeleh	148	27.38 N	9.50 E
Edjudina	162	29.48 S	122.23 E
Edmeston	210	42.42 N	75.15 W
Edmond	196	35.39 N	97.29 W
Edmondbyers	44	54.51 N	1.58 W
Edmonds	224	47.48 N	122.22 W
Edmonston	284c	38.57 N	76.56 W
Edmonton, Austl.	166	17.01 S	145.45 E
Edmonton, Alta., Can.	182	53.33 N	113.28 W
Edmonton, Ky., U.S.	194	36.59 N	85.37 W
Edmonton ◆[8]	260	51.37 N	0.04 W
Edmore, Mich., U.S.	190	43.25 N	85.03 W
Edmore, N. Dak., U.S.	198	48.25 N	98.27 W
Edmund	162	23.46 S	116.02 E
Edmund Lake @	184	54.45 N	93.15 W
Edmundson Acres	228	35.14 N	118.49 W
Edmundston	186	47.22 N	68.20 W
Edna, Kans., U.S.	198	37.04 N	95.22 W
Edna, Pa., U.S.	279b	40.19 N	79.39 W
Edna, Tex., U.S.	222	28.59 N	96.39 W
Edna Bay	180	55.57 N	133.40 W
Ednor	208	39.09 N	76.59 W
Edo ≃	94	35.37 N	139.53 E
Edogawa ◆[8]	268	35.42 N	139.52 E
Edolo	64	46.11 N	10.20 E
Edom	222	32.22 N	95.37 W
Edon	216	41.33 N	84.46 W
Edosaki	94	35.57 N	140.19 E
Edremit	130	39.35 N	27.01 E
Edremit Körfezi C	130	39.30 N	26.45 E
Edrengijn Nuruu ⩕	102	44.15 N	97.45 E
Edsbro	40	59.54 N	18.29 E
Edsbruk	26	58.02 N	16.28 E
Edsbyn	26	61.23 N	15.49 E
Edsgatan	40	59.26 N	13.33 E
Edson	182	53.35 N	116.26 W
Edson Butte ∧	202	42.52 N	124.20 W
Eduardo Castex	252	35.54 S	64.18 W
Eduardo VII, Península → Edward VII Peninsula ≻[1]	9	77.40 S	155.00 W
Eduni, Mount ∧	180	64.15 N	128.04 W
Edward, Lake @	154	0.25 S	29.30 E
Edward, Mount ∧	162	23.22 S	131.55 E
Edwardes Park ♠	274b	37.43 S	145.00 E
Edward Island |	190	48.24 N	88.36 W
Edwards, Calif., U.S.	228	34.54 N	117.53 W
Edwards, Miss., U.S.	194	32.20 N	90.36 W
Edwards, N.Y., U.S.	212	44.20 N	75.15 W
Edwards ≃	190	41.09 N	90.59 W
Edwards Air Force Base ■	228	34.54 N	117.52 W
Edwards Airport ⊠	276	40.45 N	73.03 W
Edwardsburg	216	41.48 N	86.05 W
Edwards Butte ∧	224	45.23 N	123.41 W
Edwards Creek	166	28.21 S	135.51 E
Edwards Gardens ♠	275b	43.44 N	79.22 W
Edwards Plateau ⩕[1]	196	31.20 N	101.00 W
Edwards Run ≃	285	39.48 N	75.12 W
Edwardsville, Ill., U.S.	219	38.49 N	89.58 W
Edwardsville, Ind., U.S.	218	38.16 N	85.55 W
Edwardsville, Pa., U.S.	210	41.17 N	75.53 W
Edward VIII Bay C	9	66.50 S	57.00 E
Edward VII Peninsula ≻[1]	9	77.40 S	155.00 W
Edwinstowe	44	53.12 N	1.04 W
Edzell	46	56.48 N	2.39 W
Edziza Peak ∧	180	57.40 N	130.36 W
Eede	52	51.15 N	3.28 E
Eefde	52	52.10 N	6.14 E
Eek	180	60.12 N	162.15 W
Eek ≃	180	60.12 N	162.15 W
Eeklo	50	51.11 N	3.34 E
Eel ≃, Calif., U.S.	204	40.40 N	124.20 W
Eel ≃, Ind., U.S.	194	39.07 N	86.57 W
Eel ≃, Ind., U.S.	216	40.45 N	86.22 W
Eel, Middle Fork ≃	204	39.42 N	123.21 W
Eel, North Fork ≃	204	39.57 N	123.26 W
Eel, South Fork ≃	204	40.22 N	123.55 W
Eel Bay C	212	44.19 N	76.02 W
Eelde	52	53.07 N	6.35 E
Eels Creek ≃	212	44.35 N	78.03 W
Eels Lake @	212	44.54 N	78.08 W
Eemskanaal ☰	52	53.15 N	6.45 E
Eerbeek	52	52.07 N	6.04 E
Eergetu	89	46.12 N	122.43 E
Eergu'nahe (Argun') ≃	74	53.20 N	121.28 E
Eergunaqi	89	50.54 N	121.57 E
Eersel	52	51.22 N	5.19 E
Eexta	52	53.10 N	6.59 E
Efate |	175f	17.40 S	168.25 E
Eferding	61	48.18 N	14.02 E
Éféri	148	24.22 N	9.30 E
Effeltrich	60	49.40 N	11.06 E
Effiakuma	150	5.06 N	1.39 W
Effigy Mounds National Monument ♠	190	43.06 N	91.13 W
Effingham, Eng., U.K.	260	51.16 N	0.24 W
Effingham, Ill., U.S.	194	39.07 N	88.33 W
Effingham, Kans., U.S.	198	39.31 N	95.24 W
Effingham □[6]	219	39.07 N	88.33 W
Effingham Lake @	212	44.59 N	77.22 W
Effon-Alaiye	150	7.40 N	4.56 E
Effort	210	40.56 N	75.26 W
Efiduasi	150	6.51 N	1.24 W
Efkere	130	38.47 N	35.40 E
Eforie	38	44.06 N	28.38 E
Efrikemer ☰[1]	267b	41.03 N	28.58 E
Efringen-Kirchen	58	47.49 N	7.35 E
Ega ≃	34	42.19 N	1.55 W
Egadi, Isole ||	70	37.58 N	12.16 E
Egan	222	32.28 N	97.17 W
Egaña	252	36.59 S	59.06 W
Egan Range ⩕	204	39.00 N	115.00 W
Eganville	190	45.32 N	77.06 W
Egau ≃	58	48.36 N	10.34 E
Egba □[8]	273a	6.41 N	3.23 E
Egbe, Nig.	150	8.16 N	5.31 E
Egbe, Nig.	273a	6.33 N	3.17 E
Egbunda	154	2.44 N	27.12 E
Egede og Rothes Fjord C[2]	176	66.00 N	38.00 W
Egedesminde	176	68.42 N	52.45 W
Égée, Mer → Aegean Sea ⊤[2]	38	38.30 N	25.00 E
Egegik	180	58.13 N	157.22 W
Egeln	54	51.56 N	11.25 E
Egeo, Mar → Aegean Sea ⊤[2]	38	38.30 N	25.00 E
Eger → Cheb, Česko.	54	50.01 N	12.25 E
Eger, Magy.	30	47.54 N	20.23 E
Eger (Ohře) ≃	54	50.32 N	14.08 E
Egeria Mountain ∧	182	53.55 N	130.22 W
Egernsund	41	54.54 N	9.37 E
Egerpohl	263	51.07 N	7.27 E
Egersund	26	58.27 N	6.00 E
Egerta	144	2.10 N	43.14 E
Egerton	262	53.38 N	2.26 W
Egerton, Mount ∧	9	80.50 S	158.50 E
Egeskov ⊥	41	55.10 N	10.30 E
Egestorf	52	53.11 N	10.04 E
Egestorf [am Süntel]	52	52.17 N	9.31 E
Egg	58	47.26 N	9.54 E
Egge ⩕	52	51.40 N	8.55 E
Eggebek	41	54.37 N	9.22 E
Eggelsberg	60	48.05 N	13.00 E
Eggenberg, Schloss ⊥	61	47.05 N	15.25 E
Eggenburg	61	48.39 N	15.50 E
Eggenfelden	60	48.25 N	12.46 E
Eggenstein	56	49.04 N	8.23 E
Eggerscheid	263	51.19 N	6.53 E
Eggersdorf	54	52.32 N	13.49 E
Eggesin	54	53.41 N	14.05 E
Egg Harbor City	208	39.32 N	74.39 W
Egg Island Point ≻	208	39.11 N	75.08 W
Egg Lagoon	166	39.39 S	143.58 E
Egg Lake @, Man., Can.	184	54.21 N	101.26 W
Egg Lake @, Sask., Can.	184	55.05 N	105.30 W
Egglestone Abbey ♁[1]	44	54.32 N	1.54 W
Egglham	60	48.32 N	13.04 E
Egham	260	51.26 N	0.34 W
Éghezée	56	50.36 N	4.54 E
Egijn ≃	88	49.24 N	103.36 E
Eğil	130	38.15 N	40.05 E
Egilsay |	46	59.09 N	2.56 W
Egilsstadir	24a	65.16 N	14.18 W
Egipto → Egypt □[1]	140	27.00 N	30.00 E
Égletons	32	45.24 N	2.03 E
Eglin Air Force Base ■	194	30.29 N	86.30 W
Eglinton	48	55.01 N	7.11 W
Eglisau	58	47.34 N	8.32 E
Egloskerry	42	50.39 N	4.27 W
Égly	261	48.35 N	2.13 E
Egmond aan Zee	52	52.36 N	4.37 E
Egmond-Binnen	52	52.35 N	4.39 E
Egmont, Cape ≻, N.S., Can.	186	46.51 N	60.18 W
Egmont, Cape ≻, N.Z.	172	39.17 S	173.45 E
Egmont, Mount ∧	172	39.18 S	174.04 E
Egmont Bay C	186	46.35 N	64.12 W
Egmont Channel Џ	220	27.36 N	82.45 W
Egmont Key |	220	27.35 N	82.46 W
Egmont National Park ♠	172	39.15 S	174.05 E
Egna (Neumarkt)	64	46.19 N	11.16 E
Egnach	58	47.33 N	9.23 E
Egnazia ⊥	68	40.53 N	17.24 E
Egoryevsk → Jegorjevsk	82	55.23 N	39.02 E
Egota ◆[8]	268	35.43 N	139.40 E
Egra	126	21.54 N	87.32 E
Egremont, Alta., Can.	182	54.02 N	113.08 W
Egremont, Eng., U.K.	44	54.29 N	3.33 W
Eğret	130	38.57 N	30.18 E
Égreville	50	48.10 N	2.52 E
Eğridir	130	37.52 N	30.51 E
Eğridir Gölü @	130	38.02 N	30.53 E
Eğriköy	130	38.44 N	27.21 E
Egton	44	54.26 N	0.45 W
Egtved	41	55.37 N	9.18 E
Éguas, Rio das ≃	255	13.26 S	44.14 W
Éguilles	62	43.34 N	5.22 E
Eguisheim	58	48.03 N	7.18 E
Egum Atoll |[1]	164	9.25 S	151.55 E
Egvekinot	180	66.19 N	179.10 W
Egypt, Mass., U.S.	207	42.13 N	70.46 W
Egypt, Pa., U.S.	208	40.41 N	75.32 W
Egypt, Tex., U.S.	222	29.24 N	96.14 W
Egypt □[1]	136		
	140	27.00 N	30.00 E
Egypt, Lake of @[1]	194	37.35 N	88.55 W
Égypte → Egypt □[1]	140	27.00 N	30.00 E
Egyptian Museum ♁	273c	30.03 N	31.04 E
Eha-Amufu	150	6.40 N	7.46 E
Ehen ≃	44	54.25 N	3.30 W
Ehime □[5]	96	33.40 N	132.50 E
Ehingen	58	48.17 N	9.43 E
Ehingen ◆[8]	263	51.22 N	6.42 E
Ehle ≃	54	52.12 N	11.44 E
Ehmen	54	52.24 N	10.41 E
Ehra-Lessien	54	52.34 N	10.46 E
Ehrang	56	49.49 N	6.41 E
Ehrenberg	200	33.36 N	114.31 W
Ehrenberg Range ⩕	162	23.18 S	130.20 E
Ehrenbreitstein, Feste ⊥	56	50.21 N	7.37 E
Ehrenburg ⊥	56	50.12 N	7.27 E
Ehrenfeld	214	40.22 N	78.47 W
Ehrenfriedersdorf	54	50.38 N	12.58 E
Ehrenhausen	61	46.43 N	15.35 E
Ehreshoven	56	50.58 N	7.20 E
Ehrhardt	192	33.06 N	81.01 W
Ehrhorn	52	53.10 N	9.53 E
Ehringhausen	263	51.11 N	7.33 E
Ehringhausen ◆[8]	263	51.09 N	7.11 E
Ehrwald	58	47.24 N	10.55 E
Ehwa Women's University ♁[2]	271b	37.34 N	126.56 E
Éibar	34	43.11 N	2.28 W
Eibau	54	50.58 N	14.40 E
Eibelshausen	56	50.49 N	8.20 E
Eibelstadt	56	49.43 N	10.00 E
Eibenstock	54	50.29 N	12.35 E
Eibergen	52	52.06 N	6.39 E
Eibsee @	64	47.27 N	10.58 E
Eicha	54	50.21 N	10.34 E
Eich-Berg ∧[2]	264a	52.39 N	13.50 E
Eiche, D.D.R.	264a	52.34 N	13.36 E
Eiche, D.D.R.	264a	52.25 N	12.58 E
Eichenbarleben	54	52.10 N	11.24 E
Eichenbrandt	264a	52.38 N	13.51 E
Eichendorf	60	48.38 N	12.51 E
Eichlinghofen ◆[8]	263	51.29 N	7.24 E
Eichsfeld ◆[1]	56	51.25 N	10.20 E
Eichstädt	264a	52.42 N	13.07 E
Eichstätt	60	48.54 N	11.12 E
Eichstetten	58	48.05 N	7.44 E
Eichtersheim	56	49.14 N	8.46 E
Eichwalde	54	52.22 N	13.37 E
Eickelborn	52	51.39 N	8.13 E
Eicken ◆[8]	263	51.13 N	6.26 E
Eickerend	263	51.13 N	6.34 E
Eickerkopf ∧[2]	263	51.21 N	7.42 E
Eicklingen	52	52.33 N	10.10 E
Eide	26	62.55 N	7.26 E
Eidelstedt ◆[8]	52	53.36 N	9.53 E
Eider ≃	41	54.19 N	8.58 E
Eiderstedt ≻[1]	41	54.22 N	8.50 E
Eidfjord	26	60.28 N	7.05 E
Eidsvåg, Nor.	26	60.27 N	5.21 E
Eidsvåg, Nor.	26	62.47 N	8.03 E
Eidsvold	166	25.22 S	151.07 E
Eidsvoll	26	60.19 N	11.14 E
Eifa	56	50.58 N	8.34 E
Eifel ⩕	56	50.15 N	6.45 E
Eiffel, Tour ⊥	261	48.51 N	2.18 E
Eiffel Flats	154	18.15 S	29.59 E
Eifgenbach ≃	263	51.05 N	7.09 E
Eigen ◆[8]	263	51.33 N	6.57 E
Eigenji	94	35.04 N	136.18 E
Eigenrieden	54	51.11 N	10.22 E
Eiger ∧	58	46.35 N	8.00 E
Eigg |	46	56.54 N	6.10 W
Eigg, Sound of Џ	46	56.51 N	6.13 W
Eighe, Carn ∧	46	57.17 N	5.07 W

Symbol	English	Deutsch	Español	Français	Português
≃	River	Fluss	Río	Rivière	Rio
☰	Canal	Kanal	Canal	Canal	Canal
⌊	Waterfall, Rapids	Wasserfall, Stromschnellen	Cascada, Rápidos	Chute d'eau, Rapides	Cascata, Rápidos
Џ	Strait	Meeresstrasse	Estrecho	Détroit	Estreito
C	Bay, Gulf	Bucht, Golf	Bahía, Golfo	Baie, Golfe	Baía, Golfo
@	Lake, Lakes	See, Seen	Lago, Lagos	Lac, Lacs	Lago, Lagos
☷	Swamp	Sumpf	Pantano	Marais	Pântano
⍓	Ice Features, Glacier	Eis- und Gletscherformen	Accidentes Glaciales	Formes glaciaires	Acidentes Glaciares
⊤	Other Hydrographic Features	Andere Hydrographische Objekte	Otros Elementos Hidrográficos	Autres données hydrographiques	Outros Elementos Hidrográficos
✢	Submarine Features	Untermeerische Objekte	Accidentes Submarinos	Formes de relief sous-marin	Acidentes Submarinos
□	Political Unit	Politische Einheit	Unidad Politica	Entité politique	Unidade Política
♁	Cultural Institution	Kulturelle Institution	Institución Cultural	Institution culturelle	Instituição Cultural
⊥	Historical Site	Historische Stätte	Sitio Histórico	Site historique	Sitio Histórico
♠	Recreational Site	Erholungs- und Ferienort	Sitio de Recreo	Centre de loisirs	Sítio de Lazer
⊠	Airport	Flughafen	Aeropuerto	Aéroport	Aeroporto
■	Military Installation	Militäranlage	Instalación Militar	Installation militaire	Instalação Militar
◆	Miscellaneous	Verschiedenes	Misceláneo	Divers	Miscelânea

Eight Degree Channel ⋃ 122 8.00 N 73.00 E
Eighteenmile Creek ≃, N.Y., U.S. 210 42.43 N 78.58 W
Eighteenmile Creek ≃, N.Y., U.S. 210 43.21 N 78.43 W
Eight Mile Creek ≃, Ont., Can. 284a 43.14 N 79.11 W
Eightmile Creek ≃, Ind., U.S. 216 40.57 N 85.22 W
Eightmile Creek ≃, Oreg., U.S. 224 45.36 N 121.05 W
Eights Coast •[2] 9 73.30 S 93.00 W
Eighty Mile Beach •[2] 162 19.45 S 121.00 E
Eiheiji 94 36.05 N 136.20 E
Eijerlandsche Gat C 52 53.12 N 4.50 E
Eijsden 56 50.47 N 5.43 E
Eik 144 8.58 N 45.09 E
Eikeren ⊜ 26 59.38 N 9.58 E
Eikesdalsvatnet ⊜ 26 62.34 N 8.11 E
Eil 144 8.00 N 49.51 E
Eildon 169 37.14 S 145.56 E
Eildon, Lake ⊜[1] 169 37.11 S 145.55 E
Eilean Gowan Island I 212 45.02 N 79.25 W
Eileen 216 41.17 N 88.15 W
Eilenburg 54 51.27 N 12.37 E
Eil Malk I 175b 7.09 N 134.22 E
Eilpe •[8] 263 51.21 N 7.29 E
Eilsleben 54 52.09 N 11.13 E
Eimbeckhausen 52 52.14 N 9.25 E
Eimke 52 52.58 N 10.19 E
Eina 26 60.38 N 10.36 E
Einasleigh 166 18.31 S 144.05 E
Einasleigh ≃ 166 17.30 S 142.17 E
Einbeck 52 51.49 N 9.52 E
Eindhoven 52 51.26 N 5.28 E
Eine 50 50.52 N 3.37 E
Einme 110 16.54 N 95.11 E
Einöd 56 49.16 N 7.19 E
Einödriegel ∧ 60 48.56 N 13.02 E
Einruhr 56 50.35 N 6.22 E
Einsbach 60 48.16 N 11.16 E
Einsiedel 54 50.46 N 12.58 E
Einsiedeln 58 47.08 N 8.45 E
Einville-au-Jard 58 48.39 N 6.30 E
Eirauli 272c 19.10 N 72.59 E
Eire → Ireland □[1] 28 53.00 N 8.00 W
Eiru ≃ 248 6.42 S 69.52 W
Eirunepé 248 6.40 S 69.52 W
Eisbach ≃ 56 49.38 N 8.22 E
Eisch ≃ 56 49.45 N 6.07 E
Eiseb ≃ 156 20.26 S 20.05 E
Eisenach 54 50.59 N 10.19 E
Eisenberg, B.R.D. 56 49.38 N 8.05 E
Eisenberg, D.D.R. 54 50.58 N 11.53 E
Eisenberg ∧[2] 61 47.12 N 16.24 E
Eisenerzer Alpen ∧∧ 61 47.28 N 14.45 E
Eisenhofen 60 48.21 N 11.17 E
Eisenhower, Mount ∧ 182 51.18 N 115.55 W
Eisenhower Memorial Park ♠ 276 40.44 N 73.34 W
Eisenhüttenstadt 54 52.10 N 14.39 E
Eisenkappel 61 46.29 N 14.35 E
Eisenschmitt 56 50.03 N 6.43 E
Eisentadt 61 47.51 N 16.32 E
Eiserfeld 56 50.50 N 7.59 E
Eisern 56 50.50 N 8.02 E
Eisfeld 54 50.26 N 10.54 E
Eisgarn 61 48.54 N 15.06 E
Eishken 46 58.01 N 6.32 W
Eishort, Loch C 46 57.10 N 5.59 W
Eišiškės 76 54.10 N 25.00 E
Eisk → Jejsk 78 46.42 N 38.16 E
Eisleben 54 51.31 N 11.32 E
Eislingen 56 48.42 N 9.42 E
Eita 174t 1.21 N 173.05 E
Eithon ≃ 42 52.12 N 3.27 W
Eitorf 56 50.46 N 7.26 E
Ejasi → Eyasi, Lake ⊜ 154 3.40 S 35.05 E
Ejby, Dan. 41 55.26 N 9.57 E
Ejby, Dan. 41 55.30 N 12.07 E
Ejea de los Caballeros 34 42.08 N 1.08 W
Ejeda 157b 24.20 S 44.31 E
Ejido 246 8.33 N 71.14 W
Ejigbo, Nig. 150 7.55 N 4.19 E
Ejigbo, Nig. 273a 6.33 N 3.18 E
Ejinaqi 102 41.50 N 100.50 E
Ejstrup 41 55.59 N 9.17 E
Ejura 150 7.23 N 1.22 W
Ejutla de Crespo 234 16.34 N 96.44 W
Ekalaka 198 45.53 N 104.33 W
Ekáli 267c 38.07 N 23.50 E
Ekalla 152 1.27 S 14.00 E
Ekanga 152 2.23 S 23.14 E
Ekas 115b 8.53 S 116.27 E
Ekaterinburg → Sverdlovsk 86 56.51 N 60.36 E
Ekaterinodar → Krasnodar 78 45.02 N 39.00 E
Ekaterinoslav → Dnepropetrovsk 78 48.27 N 34.59 E
Ekeby 41 56.00 N 12.58 E
Ekenäs (Taamisaari) 26 59.58 N 23.26 E
Ekenässjön 26 57.30 N 15.00 E
Ekeren 50 51.17 N 4.25 E
Ekerö I 40 59.18 N 17.43 E
Eket, Nig. 150 4.39 N 7.56 E
Eket, Sve. 41 56.15 N 13.11 E
Eketahuna 172 40.39 S 175.42 E
Ekhínos 38 41.17 N 24.59 E
Ekiatap ≃ 180 68.46 N 179.00 W
Ekiatapskij Chrebet ∧∧ 74 68.30 N 179.00 E
Ekibastuz 86 51.42 N 75.22 E
Ekimčan 89 53.04 N 132.58 E
Ekityki, Ozero ⊜ 180 67.30 N 179.30 E
Ekitykskij Chrebet ∧∧ 180 67.45 N 179.00 E
Ekiya 96 34.30 N 133.26 E
Eko → Lagos 150 6.27 N 3.24 E
Ekoli 152 0.23 S 24.16 E
Ekoln ⊜ 40 59.45 N 17.37 E
Ekolsund 40 59.37 N 17.22 E
Ekolsundsviken C 40 59.35 N 17.24 E
Ekombe 152 1.16 N 21.36 E
Ekonda 74 65.47 N 105.17 E
Ekoungounou 152 0.33 S 15.38 E
Ekovamou 152 0.07 N 16.31 E
Ekpoma 150 6.46 N 6.08 E
Eksāra 272b 22.38 N 88.17 E
Eksel 56 51.09 N 5.23 E
Eksere 130 36.48 N 32.01 E
Eksjö 26 57.40 N 14.57 E
Ekuk 180 58.49 N 158.34 W
Ekuku 152 0.42 S 21.38 E
Ekuta 152 2.59 N 18.42 E
Ekwan ≃ 176 53.14 N 82.13 W
Ekwendeni 154 11.23 S 33.50 E
Ekwok 180 59.22 N 157.30 W
El- → Ad-, Al-, An-, Ar-, As-, Ash-, At-, Az-
Ela 110 19.37 N 96.13 E
El Aaiún 148 27.09 N 13.12 W
El Abiodh Sidi Cheikh 148 32.56 N 0.42 E
El-Adde 144 2.35 N 46.13 E
El Adeb Larache 148 27.22 N 8.52 E
El Adelanto 236 14.10 N 89.50 W
El-Aden Hindi 144 2.18 N 42.00 E
El Affroun 148 36.30 N 2.38 E
El-Afwein 144 9.55 N 47.14 E
El Aguacate 286c 10.28 N 66.59 W
El Aguilar 252 23.12 S 65.42 W
Elaía 38 39.35 N 20.20 E
Elaine 194 34.18 N 90.51 W
El Alamein → Al-'Alamayn 140 30.49 N 28.57 E
El Álamo, Méx. 196 27.32 N 100.52 W
El Álamo, Méx. 196 26.29 N 99.46 W
El Álamo, Méx. 204 31.34 N 116.02 W
El Alia 36 37.10 N 10.03 E
El Alto, Chile 286e 33.30 S 70.43 W
El Alto, Perú 246 4.18 S 81.07 W
Elamanchili 122 17.33 N 82.52 E
El Amparo de Apure 246 7.06 N 70.45 W
Elan ≃, Rom. 38 46.07 N 28.04 E
Elan' ≃, S.S.S.R. 78 51.07 N 41.25 E
Elancourt 261 48.47 N 1.58 E
Elands ≃ 156 25.10 S 29.10 E
Elandsbaai 158 32.19 S 18.21 E
Elandsfontein 273d 26.10 S 28.12 E
Elandskraal 158 28.28 S 30.32 E
Elandsvlei 158 32.19 S 19.33 E
El Angel 246 0.37 N 77.56 W
Elanora Heights 274a 33.42 S 151.17 E
El Aouinet 36 35.52 N 7.54 E
El Arahal 34 37.16 N 5.33 W
El Arba 148 36.37 N 3.13 E
El Arco 232 28.00 N 113.25 W
El Arenal 234 20.47 N 103.42 W
El Aricha 148 34.09 N 1.10 W
El Aroussa 36 36.22 N 9.28 E
El Arrabal Torrelletas 266d 41.21 N 1.57 E
El Arrayán 286e 33.21 S 70.28 W
El Asnam (Orléansville) 148 36.10 N 1.20 E
Elassón 38 39.54 N 22.11 E
Elat 132 29.33 N 34.57 E
Elat, Gulf of → Aqaba, Gulf of C 128 29.00 N 34.40 E
Elat Landing Ground ⊠ 132 29.34 N 34.55 W
El-Avaji 144 3.37 N 47.00 E
El Avila, Cerro ∧ 286c 10.33 N 66.52 W
El Avión 232 24.08 N 106.59 W
Elayu 144 11.13 N 49.00 E
Elâzığ 130 38.41 N 39.14 E
Elâzığ □[4] 130 38.35 N 39.30 E
El Azul, Sierra ∧∧ 234 23.25 N 100.30 W
Elba, Ala., U.S. 194 31.25 N 86.04 W
Elba, Mich., U.S. 216 43.03 N 83.27 W
Elba, N.Y., U.S. 210 43.05 N 78.11 W
Elba → Elbe ≃ 30 53.50 N 9.00 E
Elba, Isola d' I 66 42.46 N 10.17 E
El'ban 89 50.06 N 136.31 E
El Banco 246 9.00 N 73.58 W
El Barco de Avila 34 40.21 N 5.31 W
El Barco de Valdeorras 34 42.25 N 6.59 W
El Barreal 200 31.17 N 107.10 W
El Barril 234 23.02 N 102.08 W
El Barrio 234 16.48 N 95.15 W
Elbasan 38 41.06 N 20.05 E
Elbaşı 130 38.41 N 35.59 E
El Baúl 246 8.57 N 68.17 W
El Bayadh 148 33.40 N 1.01 E
Elbe 224 46.45 N 121.49 W
Elbe (Labe) ≃ 30 53.50 N 9.00 E
Elbe, Île d' → Elba, Isole d' I 66 42.46 N 10.17 E
Elbe-Havel-Kanal ≡ 54 52.24 N 12.23 E
El-Beida → Zāwiyat al-Bayḍā' 146 32.46 N 21.43 E
Elbe-Lübeck-Kanal ≡ 54 53.50 N 10.36 E
El-Berde 144 4.52 N 43.40 E
Elberfeld •[8] 263 51.16 N 7.08 E
Elbert 198 39.13 N 104.32 W
Elbert, Mount ∧ 200 39.07 N 106.27 W
Elberta 190 44.37 N 86.14 W
Elberton 192 34.07 N 82.52 W
Elbeuf 50 49.17 N 1.00 E
Elbeyli 130 36.41 N 37.26 E
Elbing → Elbląg 30 54.10 N 19.25 E
Elbingerode 54 51.45 N 10.46 E
Elbistan 130 38.13 N 37.12 E
Elbląg (Elbing) 30 54.10 N 19.25 E
Elbląski, Kanał ≡ 30 53.43 N 19.53 E
El Bluff 236 11.59 N 83.40 W
El Bolsón 254 41.58 S 71.31 W
El Bonillo 34 38.57 N 2.32 W
El Bordo 246 2.06 N 76.58 W
El-Borj 34 35.43 N 5.40 W
El-Borouj 148 32.30 N 7.10 W
El Bosque 234 17.04 N 92.44 W
El Bosque, Aeropuerto ⊠ 286e 33.34 S 70.42 W
Elbow 184 51.07 N 106.35 W
Elbow ≃ 182 51.03 N 114.02 W
Elbow Cay I 238 23.57 N 80.29 W
Elbow Lake 198 45.59 N 95.58 W
Elbow Lake ⊜ 184 54.50 N 100.53 W
Elbridge 210 43.02 N 76.27 W
El'Brus, Gora (Mount Elbrus) ∧ 84 43.21 N 42.26 E
Elbrus, Mount → El'brus, Gora ∧ 84 43.21 N 42.26 E
El'brusskij 84 43.38 N 42.10 E
Elbsandsteingebirge ∧∧ 54 50.50 N 14.20 E
El-Bur 144 4.40 N 46.40 E
Elburg 52 52.26 N 5.50 E
El Burgo de Osma 34 41.35 N 3.04 W
Elburn 216 41.54 N 88.28 W
Elburz Mountains → Alborz, Reshteh-ye Kūhhā-ye ∧∧ 128 36.00 N 53.00 E
El'buzd ≃ 83 46.53 N 39.43 E
El'buzo 83 46.53 N 39.41 E
El Caburé 252 26.01 S 62.22 W
El Cajon 228 32.48 N 116.58 W
El Callao 246 7.21 N 61.49 W
El Calvario 246 4.22 N 73.40 W
El Calvario •[8] 286b 23.05 N 82.20 W
El Calverio 246 8.59 N 67.00 W
El Campamento 240m 18.22 N 66.28 W
El Campamento •[8] 266a 40.24 N 3.46 W
El Campo 222 29.12 N 96.16 W
El Capitan ∧, Calif., U.S. 226 37.43 N 119.38 W
El Capitan ∧, Mont., U.S. 202 46.01 N 114.23 W
El Capomo 234 21.17 N 105.13 W
El Caribe 286c 10.37 N 66.50 W
El Carmen, Arg. 252 24.23 S 65.16 W
El Carmen, Bol. 248 18.49 S 58.33 W
El Carmen, Chile 286e 33.21 S 70.43 W
El Carmen, Col. 246 8.30 N 73.27 W
El Carmen, Méx. 234 19.19 N 97.40 W
El Carmen, Méx. 234 15.35 N 93.05 W
El Carmen, Perú 248 13.30 S 76.04 W
El Carmen, Ven. 286c 10.24 N 67.01 W
El Carmen, Ven. 286c 10.24 N 66.50 W
El Carmen, Canal ≡ 286e 33.18 S 70.41 W
El Carmen de Bolívar 246 9.43 N 75.08 W
El Carricito 232 28.24 N 103.23 W
El Carril 252 25.05 S 65.28 W
El Carrizal 234 23.00 N 97.50 W
El Carrizo 232 29.58 N 105.16 W
El Casco 196 25.34 N 104.35 W
El Castillo 236 11.01 N 84.24 W
El Cedral 236 16.26 N 90.03 W
El Cedrito 232 29.11 N 101.59 W
El Cenajo, Embalse de ⊜[1] 34 38.25 N 2.00 W
El Centinela 204 32.38 N 115.40 W
El Centinela, Cerro ∧ 234 19.13 N 104.17 W
El Centro 204 32.48 N 115.34 W
El Cerrito, Col. 246 3.42 N 76.19 W
El Cerrito, Calif., U.S. 226 37.55 N 122.18 W
El Cerrito, Calif., U.S. 228 33.49 N 117.31 W
El Cerro, Bol. 248 17.31 S 61.34 W
El Cerro, Ur. 258 34.00 S 58.15 W
El Cerro Del Aripo ∧ 241r 10.43 N 61.15 W
El Chamal 234 23.56 N 97.54 W
El Chante 234 19.41 N 104.10 W
El Charco Largo 232 24.10 N 97.58 W
Elche 34 38.15 N 0.42 W
Elche de la Sierra 34 38.27 N 2.03 W
El Chimborazo, Cerro ∧ 236 13.05 N 85.58 W
El'chkakvun ≃ 180 68.42 N 171.00 E
Elcho 190 45.26 N 89.11 W
El Chocón, Embalse ⊜[1] 254 39.30 S 69.00 W
Elcho Island I 164 11.55 S 135.45 E
El Cholar 252 37.25 S 70.39 W
El Chorrillo 252 33.18 S 66.16 W
El Ciprés 204 31.50 N 116.38 W
El Coacoyul 234 17.37 N 101.26 W
El Cobre 240p 20.03 N 75.57 W
El Cocuy 246 6.25 N 72.27 W
El Cojo 286c 10.37 N 66.53 W
El Cojo, Quebrada ≃ 286c 10.37 N 66.53 W
El Colorado 252 26.18 S 59.22 W
El Colorado, Canal de ≡ 286e 33.34 S 70.32 W
El Cóndor, Cerro ∧ 252 26.38 S 68.22 W
El Congo 236 13.54 N 89.30 W
El Consuelo 232 31.02 N 111.53 W
El Corazón 246 1.12 S 79.06 W
El Corcovado 254 43.32 S 71.36 W
El Corozo 286c 10.35 N 66.58 W
El Corpus 236 13.16 N 87.03 W
El Corte de Madera Creek ≃ 282 37.19 N 122.20 W
El Cortijo 286e 33.22 S 70.42 W
El Coto 240m 18.28 N 66.44 W
El Cotorro •[8] 286b 23.03 N 82.16 W
El Coyote 200 30.50 N 112.40 W
El Cozón 232 31.18 N 112.29 W
El Cristo 240p 20.07 N 75.45 W
El Cubo → Casigua 246 8.46 N 72.30 W
El Cuco 236 13.10 N 88.07 W
El Cuidado 234 22.20 N 103.07 W
El Cuy 254 39.56 S 68.20 W
Elda 34 38.29 N 0.47 W
El Dab 144 8.58 N 46.38 E
Eldagsen 52 52.10 N 9.40 E
El-Dambahaddo 144 3.14 N 46.45 E
El Dátil 232 30.07 N 112.15 W
Elde ≃ 54 53.17 N 12.40 E
Eldekanal ≡ 54 53.24 N 11.36 E
Eldena, D.D.R. 54 53.13 N 11.25 E
Eldena, D.D.R. 54 54.05 N 13.26 E
El Depósito 234 17.44 N 94.23 W
El Der 144 5.08 N 43.08 E
El-Der ≃ 144 9.00 N 47.30 E
Elder Island I 276 40.38 N 73.23 W
Elder Mills 275b 43.49 N 79.38 W
Eldersville 214 40.21 N 80.29 W
Elderton 214 40.42 N 79.21 W
El Descanso 204 32.12 N 116.55 W
El Desemboque, Méx. 232 30.30 N 112.59 W
El Desemboque, Méx. 232 29.30 N 112.27 W
Eldforsen 40 60.26 N 14.13 E
El'dikan 74 60.48 N 135.11 E
Eldingen 52 52.41 N 10.21 E
Eld Inlet C 224 47.04 N 123.01 W
El Diviso 246 1.22 N 78.14 W
El Djem 148 35.18 N 10.43 E
El Djouf •[2] 134 20.30 N 8.00 W
Eldon, Iowa, U.S. 190 40.55 N 92.13 W
Eldon, Mo., U.S. 194 38.21 N 92.35 W
El-Don Far 144 10.35 N 49.02 E
Eldon Hazlett State Park ♠ 219 38.39 N 89.22 W
Eldora, Iowa, U.S. 190 42.19 N 93.26 W
Eldora, Pa., U.S. 279b 40.10 N 79.53 W
Eldorado, Arg. 252 26.24 S 54.38 W
Eldorado, Bra. 252 24.32 S 48.06 W
El Dorado, Méx. 232 24.17 N 107.21 W
El Dorado, Ark., U.S. 194 33.13 N 92.40 W
El Dorado, Calif., U.S. 226 38.41 N 120.51 W
Eldorado, Ill., U.S. 194 37.49 N 88.26 W
El Dorado, Kans., U.S. 198 37.49 N 96.52 W
Eldorado, Ohio, U.S. 218 39.54 N 84.41 W
Eldorado, Okla., U.S. 196 34.28 N 99.39 W
Eldorado, Tex., U.S. 196 30.52 N 100.36 W
El Dorado, Ven. 246 6.44 N 61.38 W
El Dorado □[6] 226 38.43 N 120.48 W
Eldorado Hills 226 38.37 N 120.27 W
El Dorado Park ♠ 280 33.49 N 118.05 W
Eldorado Peak ∧ 224 48.32 N 121.08 W
El Dorado Springs 194 37.52 N 94.01 W
Eldoret 154 0.31 N 35.17 E
Eldred, Ill., U.S. 219 39.17 N 90.33 W
Eldred, N.Y., U.S. 210 41.32 N 74.53 W
Eldred, Pa., U.S. 214 41.57 N 78.23 W
Eldridge 190 41.39 N 90.35 W
Eldridge, Mount ∧ 180 64.46 N 141.48 W
Eldridges Hill 285 39.40 N 75.18 W
Eleanor 188 38.32 N 81.56 W
Eleanor, Lake ⊜[1] 226 37.59 N 119.51 W
Eleazer 158 26.40 S 26.53 E
Electra 196 34.02 N 98.55 W
Electric City 202 47.56 N 119.02 W
Eleele 229b 21.55 N 159.35 W
Elefante, Isla del → Elephant Island I 9 61.10 S 55.14 W
Elefantes, Rio dos (Olifants) ≃ 156 24.10 S 32.40 E
Elegest ≃ 88 51.32 N 94.05 E
El Eglab •[2] 148 26.25 N 5.00 W
Elei, Wādī V 140 22.04 N 34.27 E
Eleja 76 56.26 N 23.42 E
Elektrogorsk 82 55.53 N 38.47 E
Elektrostal' 82 55.47 N 38.28 E
Elektrougli 82 55.43 N 38.13 E
Elektrozavod 80 52.34 N 54.01 E
Elele 150 5.07 N 6.48 E
Elemì 130 41.04 N 35.30 E
Elena 38 42.56 N 25.53 E
El Encantado 286c 10.27 N 66.47 W
El Encanto, Col. 246 1.37 S 73.14 W
El Encanto, Guat. 232 17.17 N 89.34 W
Elend 54 51.44 N 10.41 E
Elepete 273a 6.41 N 3.28 E
Elephanta Caves •[5] 272c 18.58 N 72.56 E
Elephanta Island (Ghārāpuri) I 272c 18.57 N 72.55 E
Elephant Butte Reservoir ⊜[1] 200 33.19 N 107.10 W
Elephant Island I 9 61.10 S 55.14 W
Elephant Lake ⊜ 212 45.08 N 78.07 W
Elephant Mountain ∧ 188 44.46 N 70.46 W
Elesbão Veloso 250 6.13 S 42.08 W
Eleşkirt 130 39.48 N 42.42 E
El Estor 236 15.32 N 89.21 W
El Estribo 234 22.26 N 99.17 W
Elets → Jelec 76 52.37 N 38.30 E
El Eulma 148 36.08 N 5.40 E
Eleusis → Elevsís 38 38.02 N 23.32 E
Eleutério 256 22.19 S 46.43 W
Eleutero ≃ 70 38.06 N 13.29 E
Eleuthera I 238 25.10 N 76.14 W
Eleuthera Point ≻ 238 24.40 N 76.11 W
Eleva 190 44.35 N 91.28 W
Eleven Point ≃ 194 36.09 N 91.05 W
Elevsínos, Kólpos C 267c 38.02 N 23.34 E
Elevsís 38 38.02 N 23.32 E
Elevtheroúpolis 38 40.55 N 24.16 E
El Fahs 36 36.22 N 9.55 E
El Faro, It. 71 40.36 N 8.13 E
El Faro, P.R. 240m 18.00 N 66.47 W
Elfenbeinküste → Ivory Coast □[1] 150 8.00 N 5.00 W
El Ferrol del Caudillo 34 43.29 N 8.14 W
Elfers 220 28.13 N 82.43 W
Elfgen 263 51.05 N 6.32 E
Elfin Cove 180 58.12 N 136.20 W
Elfrida 200 31.44 N 109.42 W
Elfros 184 51.43 N 103.52 W
El Fud 144 7.20 N 42.50 E
El Fuerte 232 26.25 N 108.39 W
El Galpón 252 25.23 S 64.38 W
Elgershausen 56 51.16 N 9.22 E
Elgin, Austl. 168a 33.31 S 115.37 E
Elgin, Ont., Can. 212 44.36 N 76.13 W
Elgin, Scot., U.K. 46 57.39 N 3.20 W
Elgin, Ill., U.S. 216 42.02 N 88.17 W
Elgin, Iowa, U.S. 190 42.57 N 91.38 W
Elgin, Minn., U.S. 190 44.08 N 92.15 W
Elgin, Nebr., U.S. 198 41.59 N 98.05 W
Elgin, N. Dak., U.S. 198 46.24 N 101.51 W
Elgin, Ohio, U.S. 216 40.44 N 84.28 W
Elgin, Oreg., U.S. 202 45.34 N 117.55 W
Elgin, Pa., U.S. 214 41.54 N 79.45 W
Elgin, Tex., U.S. 222 30.21 N 97.22 W
Elgin □[6] 214 42.42 N 81.15 W
Elgin, Lake ⊜ 206 45.45 N 71.20 W
El Gogorrón, Parque Nacional ♠ 234 21.48 N 100.48 W
Elgol 46 57.09 N 6.06 W
El Goléa 148 30.30 N 2.50 E
El Golfete ⊜ 236 15.44 N 88.53 W
El Golfo de Santa Clara 232 31.42 N 114.30 W
El Goloso •[8] 266a 40.33 N 3.42 W
Elgon, Mount ∧ 154 1.08 N 34.33 E
Elgoras, Gora ∧ 24 68.06 N 31.30 E
El Granada 226 37.30 N 122.28 W
El Grove 34 42.30 N 8.52 W
El Grullo 234 19.48 N 104.13 W
El Guaje 232 27.52 N 103.18 W
El Guamo 246 10.02 N 74.59 W
El Guanábano 286c 10.24 N 67.01 W
El Guapo 246 10.09 N 65.58 W
El Guarapo 286c 10.36 N 66.58 W
El Guayabo 246 8.37 N 72.20 W
El Guettâra ⊤[4] 148 22.01 N 2.59 W
El'gygytgyn, Ozero ⊜ 180 67.30 N 172.00 E
El Hadjar 36 36.48 N 7.45 E
El-Hajeb 148 33.43 N 5.13 W
Elham 42 51.10 N 1.07 E
El-Hamurre 144 7.11 N 48.55 E
El Hank •[4] 148 24.30 N 7.00 W
El Haouaria 36 37.03 N 11.02 E
El Hatillo 286c 10.26 N 66.49 W
El Hatillo, Quebrada ≃ 286c 10.27 N 66.47 W
El Havre → Le Havre 50 49.30 N 0.08 E
El Her 144 5.40 N 42.26 E
El Higo 234 21.46 N 98.28 W
Elhovo 38 42.10 N 26.34 E
El Huecú 252 37.37 S 70.36 W
Eliase 164 8.21 S 130.47 E
Elías Piña 238 18.53 N 71.42 W
Elías Romero 258 34.46 S 58.52 W
Eliasville 196 32.57 N 98.46 W
Elida, N. Mex., U.S. 196 33.57 N 103.39 W
Elida, Ohio, U.S. 216 40.47 N 84.12 W
El Idrissia 148 34.30 N 2.37 E
Elila 154 2.43 S 25.53 E
Elila ≃ 154 2.45 S 25.53 E
Elim, Namibia 156 17.48 S 15.31 E
Elim, S. Afr. 158 34.35 S 19.45 E
Elim, Alaska, U.S. 180 64.37 N 162.15 W
Elimsport 210 41.08 N 77.02 W
Elingampangu 152 2.03 S 24.02 E
Elinghu ⊜ 102 34.50 N 97.35 E
Elin Pelin 38 42.40 N 23.36 E
Eliot 188 43.09 N 70.48 W
Elipa 152 0.53 S 24.34 E
Elisabeth-Sophien-Koog 41 54.30 N 8.53 E
Élisabethville, Fr. 261 48.58 N 1.51 E
Élisabethville → Lubumbashi, Zaïre 154 11.40 S 27.28 E
Elisenvaara 24 61.25 N 29.46 E
Eliseu Martins 250 8.13 S 43.42 W
Elista 80 46.16 N 44.14 E
Elizabeth, Austl. 168b 34.43 S 138.40 E
Elizabeth, Colo., U.S. 200 39.22 N 104.36 W
Elizabeth, Ill., U.S. 190 42.19 N 90.13 W
Elizabeth, La., U.S. 194 30.52 N 92.48 W
Elizabeth, N.J., U.S. 210 40.40 N 74.11 W
Elizabeth, Pa., U.S. 214 40.16 N 79.53 W
Elizabeth, W. Va., U.S. 188 39.04 N 81.24 W
Elizabeth ≃, N.J., U.S. 276 40.38 N 74.12 W
Elizabeth ≃, Va., U.S. 208 36.54 N 76.20 W
Elizabeth, Cape ≻ 224 47.22 N 124.22 W
Elizabeth, West Branch ≃ 276 40.42 N 74.14 W
Elizabeth Bay C 156 27.04 S 15.11 E
Elizabeth City 192 36.18 N 76.14 W
Elizabeth Creek ≃ 222 33.02 N 97.14 W
Elizabeth Islands II 207 41.27 N 70.47 W
Elizabeth Lake ⊜ 281 42.38 N 83.23 W
Elizabeth Lake Estates 281 42.38 N 83.22 W
Elizabeth Park ♠ 281 42.07 N 83.11 W
Elizabeth Port C 276 40.41 N 74.09 W
Elizabeth Reef I[1] 160 29.56 S 159.04 E
Elizabethton 192 36.21 N 82.13 W
Elizabethtown, Ill., U.S. 194 37.27 N 88.18 W
Elizabethtown, Ind., U.S. 218 39.08 N 85.49 W
Elizabethtown, Ky., U.S. 194 37.42 N 85.52 W
Elizabethtown, N.C., U.S. 192 34.38 N 78.37 W
Elizabethtown, N.Y., U.S. 188 44.13 N 73.36 W
Elizabethtown, Pa., U.S. 208 40.09 N 76.36 W
Elizabethville 208 40.33 N 76.49 W
Eliza Howell Park ♠ 281 42.24 N 83.16 W
Elizaville, Ind., U.S. 218 40.08 N 86.24 W
Elizaville, N.Y., U.S. 210 42.03 N 73.48 W
El-Jadida (Mazagan) 148 33.16 N 8.30 W
El Jaralito 232 26.07 N 104.10 W
El Jebel 200 39.22 N 107.02 W
El-Jebha 34 35.13 N 4.38 W
El Jícaro 236 13.43 N 86.08 W
El Jícaro ≃ 236 13.31 N 86.00 W
El Jobean 220 26.58 N 82.13 W
Ełk 30 53.50 N 22.22 E
Elk □[6] 214 41.26 N 78.43 W
Elk ≃, Alta., Can. 182 52.55 N 115.40 W
Elk ≃, B.C., Can. 182 49.10 N 115.14 W
Ełk ≃, Pol. 30 53.31 N 22.47 E
Elk ≃, Colo., U.S. 200 40.29 N 106.58 W
Elk ≃, Kans., U.S. 198 37.15 N 95.41 W
Elk ≃, Minn., U.S. 190 45.18 N 93.34 W
Elk ≃, Mo., U.S. 194 36.38 N 94.38 W
Elk ≃, W. Va., U.S. 188 38.21 N 81.38 W
Elk ≃, Wis., U.S. 190 45.42 N 90.37 W
Elkader 190 42.51 N 91.24 W
El Kairouan 148 35.41 N 10.07 E
El Kala 148 36.50 N 8.30 E
El Kantara 148 33.41 N 10.55 E
El-Karafab 140 18.10 N 31.36 E
El Kasserine 148 35.11 N 8.48 E
Elk Bayou ≃ 226 36.06 N 119.24 W
Elk City 196 35.25 N 99.25 W
Elk City Lake ⊜[1] 198 37.25 N 95.55 W
Elk Creek 204 39.36 N 122.32 W
Elk Creek ≃, Okla., U.S. 196 34.48 N 99.09 W
Elk Creek ≃, Oreg., U.S. 202 43.38 N 123.34 W
Elk Creek ≃, Pa., U.S. 214 42.01 N 80.22 W
Elk Creek ≃, S. Dak., U.S. 198 44.15 N 102.22 W
Elk Creek ≃, Wash., U.S. 224 46.38 N 123.17 W
Elkedra ≃ 162 21.08 S 136.22 E
El Kef 148 36.11 N 8.43 E
El Kef □[8] 36 36.00 N 9.00 E
El-Kelâa-des-Srarhna 148 32.02 N 7.23 W
El Kere 144 5.48 N 42.10 E
El Kerma 34 35.36 N 0.35 W
Elk Grove 226 38.25 N 121.22 W
Elk Grove Village 278 42.01 N 87.59 W
Elkhart, Ill., U.S. 219 40.01 N 89.29 W
Elkhart, Ind., U.S. 216 41.41 N 85.58 W
Elkhart, Kans., U.S. 198 37.00 N 101.54 W
Elkhart, Tex., U.S. 222 31.38 N 95.35 W
Elkhart □[6] 216 41.35 N 85.50 W
Elkhart ≃ 216 41.41 N 85.58 W
Elkhart Lake 190 43.50 N 88.01 W
El Khatt •[4] 148 22.40 N 10.05 W
Elkhead Creek ≃ 200 40.31 N 107.26 W
Elkhead Mountains ∧∧ 200 40.50 N 107.05 W
El Khnâchîch •[4] 148 21.50 N 3.45 W
Elkhorn, Man., Can. 184 49.58 N 101.14 W
Elk Horn, Iowa, U.S. 198 41.36 N 95.03 W
Elkhorn, Wis., U.S. 216 42.40 N 88.33 W
Elkhorn ≃ 198 41.07 N 96.19 W
Elkhorn, North Fork ≃ 198 42.00 N 97.21 W
Elkhorn City 192 37.18 N 82.21 W
Elkhorn Creek ≃, Ky., U.S. 218 38.19 N 84.52 W
Elkhorn Creek ≃, Mo., U.S. 219 39.05 N 91.20 W
Elkhorn Peaks ∧∧ 202 43.22 N 111.06 W
Elki 128 37.34 N 43.10 E
Elkin 192 36.16 N 80.51 W
Elkins 188 38.55 N 79.51 W
Elkins Park 208 40.05 N 75.08 W
Elk Island I 184 50.45 N 96.32 W
Elk Island National Park ♠ 182 53.37 N 112.45 W
Elkland 210 41.59 N 77.21 W
Elk Mills 208 39.39 N 75.50 W
Elk Mountain 200 41.41 N 106.25 W
Elk Mountain ∧, Wash., U.S. 224 46.08 N 122.28 W
Elk Mountain ∧, Wyo., U.S. 200 41.38 N 106.32 W
Elk Neck State Park ♠ 208 39.30 N 75.58 W
Elko, B.C., Can. 182 49.18 N 115.07 W
Elko, Nev., U.S. 204 40.50 N 115.46 W
El Kouif 36 35.29 N 8.19 E
Elk Peak ∧ 202 46.27 N 110.46 W
Elk Plain 224 47.04 N 122.24 W
Elk Point, Alta., Can. 182 53.34 N 110.54 W
Elk Point, S. Dak., U.S. 198 42.41 N 96.41 W
Elk Rapids 190 44.54 N 85.25 W
El Krib 36 36.19 N 9.09 E
Elkridge 208 39.13 N 76.42 W
Elk River, Idaho, U.S. 202 46.47 N 116.11 W
Elk River, Minn., U.S. 190 45.18 N 93.35 W
Elk River C 208 39.31 N 75.55 W
El Kseur 148 36.46 N 4.49 E
Elk State Park ♠ 214 41.38 N 78.34 W
Elkton, Ky., U.S. 194 36.49 N 87.09 W
Elkton, Md., U.S. 208 39.36 N 75.50 W
Elkton, Mich., U.S. 190 43.49 N 83.11 W
Elkton, Ohio, U.S. 214 40.46 N 80.42 W
Elkton, S. Dak., U.S. 198 44.14 N 96.29 W
Elkton, Va., U.S. 188 38.25 N 78.38 W
Elkville 194 37.55 N 89.14 W
Ell, Lake ⊜ 162 29.13 S 127.46 E
Elland 262 53.41 N 1.50 W
Ellard Lake ⊜ 184 54.33 N 91.55 W
Ellás → Greece □[1] 38 39.00 N 22.00 E
Ellavalla 162 25.05 S 114.22 E
Ellaville 192 32.15 N 84.18 W
Ellefeld 54 50.29 N 12.23 E
Ellef Ringnes Island I 16 78.30 N 104.00 W
El Leh 144 3.48 N 39.48 E
Elleker 162 35.00 S 117.43 E
Ellemandsbjerg ∧[2] 41 56.07 N 10.32 E
Ellen ≃ 44 54.43 N 3.30 W
Ellen, Mount ∧ 200 38.07 N 110.49 W
Ellendale, Austl. 162 17.56 S 124.48 E
Ellendale, Del., U.S. 208 38.47 N 75.25 W
Ellendale, Minn., U.S. 190 43.52 N 93.18 W
Ellendale, N. Dak., U.S. 198 46.06 N 98.32 W
Ellensburg 202 47.00 N 120.32 W
Ellenton, Fla., U.S. 220 29.47 N 81.26 W
Ellenton, Ga., U.S. 192 31.11 N 83.35 W
Ellenville 210 41.43 N 74.24 W
Eller •[8] 263 51.12 N 6.51 E
Ellerbee 192 35.04 N 79.46 W
Ellero ≃ 62 44.27 N 7.54 E
Ellès 36 35.57 N 9.06 E
Ellesmere 42 52.54 N 2.54 W
Ellesmere, Lake C 172 43.48 S 172.25 E
Ellesmere Island I 16 81.00 N 80.00 W
Ellesmere Park 262 53.29 N 2.20 W
Ellesmere Port 262 53.17 N 2.54 W
Ellesmere Port □[8] 262 53.18 N 2.47 W
Ellettsville 194 39.14 N 86.37 W
Ellewoutsdijk 52 51.24 N 3.49 E
Ellezelles 50 50.44 N 3.41 E
Ellice ≃ 176 68.02 N 103.26 W
Ellice Islands → Tuvalu □[1] 14 8.00 S 178.00 E
Ellichpur → Achalpur 120 21.16 N 77.31 E
Ellicott City 208 39.16 N 76.48 W
Ellicott Creek ≃ 210 43.01 N 78.53 W
Ellicott Creek Park ♠ 284a 43.01 N 78.50 W
Ellicottville 210 42.17 N 78.40 W
Ellijay 192 34.42 N 84.28 W
El Limón, Méx. 234 19.49 N 104.11 W
El Limón, Méx. 234 18.05 N 101.59 W
El Limoncito 286c 10.29 N 66.47 W
El Limón de Talleaché 232 24.16 N 107.04 W
Ellingen 56 49.04 N 10.58 E
Ellinger 222 29.50 N 96.44 W
Ellinghorst •[8] 263 51.34 N 6.57 E
Ellington, Eng., U.K. 44 55.13 N 1.34 W
Ellington, Conn., U.S. 207 41.54 N 72.28 W
Ellington, Mo., U.S. 194 37.14 N 90.58 W
Ellington, N.Y., U.S. 214 42.13 N 79.07 W
Ellinikón 267c 37.53 N 23.44 E
Ellinikón, Aerolimín ⊠ 267c 37.54 N 23.44 E
Ellinwood 198 38.21 N 98.35 W
Elliot 158 31.18 S 27.50 E
Elliot, Mount ∧ 166 19.29 S 146.58 E
Elliotdale 158 31.55 S 28.38 E
Elliotganj 126 23.31 N 90.52 E
Elliot Lake 190 46.23 N 82.39 W
Elliot Lake ⊜ 184 52.55 N 95.20 W
Elliott, Austl. 162 17.33 S 133.32 E
Elliott, Ill., U.S. 216 40.28 N 88.16 W
Elliott, Iowa, U.S. 198 41.09 N 95.10 W
Elliott □[6] 218 38.13 N 83.10 W
Elliott, Mount ∧ 162 20.29 S 126.37 E
Elliott Bay C 224 47.36 N 122.22 W
Elliott Key I 220 25.27 N 80.11 W
Elliottville 218 38.11 N 83.16 W
Ellis 198 38.56 N 99.34 W
Ellis □[6] 222 32.20 N 96.48 W
Ellisburg 212 43.44 N 76.08 W
Ellis Island I 276 40.42 N 74.02 W
Ellis Mountain ∧ 224 48.10 N 124.19 W
Ellison Creek Reservoir ⊜[1] 222 32.56 N 94.43 W
Ellisport 224 47.25 N 122.26 W
Ellisras 156 23.40 S 27.46 E
Elliston, Austl. 162 33.39 S 134.55 E
Elliston, Newf., Can. 186 48.38 N 53.03 W
Elliston, Mont., U.S. 202 46.33 N 112.26 W
Ellisville, Miss., U.S. 194 31.36 N 89.12 W
Ellisville, Mo., U.S. 219 38.35 N 90.35 W
Ellmau 64 47.31 N 12.18 E
Ellmauer Halt ∧ 64 47.34 N 12.18 E
Ellon 46 57.22 N 2.05 W
Ellora 122 20.01 N 75.10 E
Ellore → Elūru 122 16.42 N 81.06 E
Elloree 192 33.32 N 80.34 W
Ellport 214 40.52 N 80.16 W
Ellrich 54 51.35 N 10.40 E
Ellsworth, Ill., U.S. 216 40.27 N 88.43 W
Ellsworth, Kans., U.S. 198 38.44 N 98.14 W
Ellsworth, Maine, U.S. 188 44.33 N 68.26 W
Ellsworth, Mich., U.S. 190 45.10 N 85.15 W
Ellsworth, Minn., U.S. 198 43.31 N 96.01 W
Ellsworth, Ohio, U.S. 214 41.01 N 80.52 W
Ellsworth, Pa., U.S. 214 40.07 N 80.01 W
Ellsworth, Wash., U.S. 224 45.37 N 122.36 W
Ellsworth, Wis., U.S. 190 44.44 N 92.29 W
Ellsworth Air Force Base ■ 198 44.08 N 103.05 W
Ellsworth Land •[1] 9 75.30 S 80.00 W
Ellsworth Mountains ∧∧ 9 79.00 S 85.00 W
El Lucero 196 25.53 N 103.25 W
Ellwangen 56 48.57 N 10.07 E
Ellwanger Berge ∧∧[2] 56 49.00 N 10.15 E
Ellwood City 214 40.50 N 80.17 W
Elm, B.R.D. 52 53.31 N 9.12 E
Elm, Schw. 58 46.55 N 9.11 E
Elm, Eng., U.K. 42 52.38 N 0.10 E
Elm ∧∧[2] 54 52.09 N 10.53 E
Elm ≃, U.S. 198 45.36 N 98.19 W
Elm ≃, Ill., U.S. 194 38.24 N 88.14 W
Elm ≃, N. Dak., U.S. 198 47.15 N 96.50 W
Elma, Iowa, U.S. 190 43.15 N 92.26 W
Elma, N.Y., U.S. 210 42.51 N 78.38 W
Elma, Wash., U.S. 224 47.00 N 123.25 W
El Macero 226 38.33 N 121.41 W
Elmadağ (Küçükyozgat) 130 39.55 N 33.15 E
Elma Dağı ∧ 130 39.49 N 33.00 E
El Maharès 148 34.32 N 10.30 E
El Mahdia 148 35.30 N 11.04 E
El Mahia •[1] 148 22.30 N 2.30 W
El Malah 34 35.24 N 1.05 W
Elmalı 130 36.44 N 29.56 E
El Manchón 236 14.23 N 92.02 W
El Maneadero 232 31.45 N 116.35 W
El Manteco 246 7.27 N 62.32 W
Elmas 71 39.16 N 9.03 E
Elmas Burnu ≻ 267b 41.13 N 29.13 E
Elmaton 222 28.53 N 96.09 W
El Mayoco 254 42.39 S 70.59 W
Elmberg ∧ 64 47.40 N 13.57 E
Elmbridge □[8] 260 51.22 N 0.23 W
Elm Brook ≃ 283 42.29 N 71.16 W
Elm City 192 35.48 N 77.52 W
Elm Creek, Man., Can. 184 49.41 N 98.00 W
Elm Creek, Nebr., U.S. 198 40.43 N 99.22 W
Elm Creek ≃, Minn., U.S. 198 43.45 N 94.11 W
Elm Creek ≃, S. Dak., U.S. 198 44.21 N 102.42 W
Elm Creek ≃, Tex., U.S. 196 33.12 N 98.50 W
Elm Creek ≃, Tex., U.S. 196 32.40 N 99.41 W
Elm Creek ≃, Tex., U.S. 196 28.54 N 100.12 W
Elm Creek ≃, Tex., U.S. 222 29.15 N 97.32 W
El Meco 234 22.35 N 99.20 W
El Médano 232 24.25 N 111.30 W
El Meghaïer 148 33.55 N 5.58 E
El Melón, Sierra ∧∧ 234 23.56 N 99.39 W
Elmen 58 47.20 N 10.32 E
Elmer 208 39.36 N 75.10 W
El Metlaoui 148 34.20 N 8.24 E
Elm Grove 216 43.03 N 88.04 W
Elmhurst, Austl. 169 37.11 S 143.15 E
Elmhurst, Ill., U.S. 216 41.53 N 87.56 W
Elmhurst, Pa., U.S. 210 41.22 N 75.33 W
Elmhurst •[8] 276 40.44 N 73.53 W
El Mijao 286c 10.23 N 66.48 W
El Milagro 252 31.01 S 65.59 W
El Milia 148 36.48 N 6.14 E
El Mimbre 196 25.40 N 102.20 W
Elmina 150 5.05 N 1.21 W
El Minao 240m 18.22 N 66.05 W
Elmira, Ont., Can. 212 43.36 N 80.33 W
Elmira, P.E.I., Can. 186 46.27 N 62.04 W
Elmira, Calif., U.S. 226 38.21 N 121.55 W
Elmira, N.Y., U.S. 210 42.06 N 76.49 W
El Mirage 200 33.36 N 112.19 W
El Mirage Lake ⊜ 228 34.38 N 117.35 W
Elmira Heights 210 42.08 N 76.49 W
Elm Mott 222 31.40 N 97.06 W
Elmo, Mont., U.S. 182 47.50 N 114.21 W
Elmo, Tex., U.S. 222 32.43 N 96.10 W
El Moknine 148 35.38 N 10.54 E
El Molinillo 34 39.28 N 4.13 W
El Molinito 286a 19.27 N 99.15 W
Elmont, N.Y., U.S. 276 40.42 N 73.42 W
Elmont, Va., U.S. 208 37.43 N 77.30 W
El Monte, Chile 252 33.41 S 71.01 W
El Monte, Calif., U.S. 228 34.04 N 118.02 W
El Monte Airport ⊠ 280 34.06 N 118.02 W
Elmora 214 40.36 N 78.45 W
El Moral 196 28.51 N 100.39 W
Elmore, Austl. 166 36.30 S 144.37 E
Elmore, Minn., U.S. 190 43.30 N 94.05 W
Elmore, Ohio, U.S. 214 41.29 N 83.18 W
Elmore City 196 34.37 N 97.24 W
El Morro ⊥ 240m 18.28 N 66.07 W
El Morro National Monument ♠ 200 35.05 N 108.22 W
Elm Point ≻ 276 40.49 N 73.46 W
Elmpt 56 51.13 N 6.10 E
El Mreiti ⊤[4] 148 23.29 N 7.52 W
El Mreyyé •[1] 150 19.30 N 7.00 W
Elmschenhagen •[8] 54 54.18 N 10.12 E
Elmsdale 186 44.58 N 63.30 W
Elmsford 210 41.03 N 73.49 W
Elmshorn 52 53.45 N 9.39 E
Elmstein 56 49.21 N 7.56 E
Elmswell 42 52.15 N 0.53 E
El Mulato 196 29.22 N 104.10 W
Elmvale 212 44.35 N 79.52 W
Elmville 218 38.20 N 84.46 W
Elmwood, Ont., Can. 212 44.14 N 81.03 W
Elmwood, Ill., U.S. 190 40.47 N 89.58 W
Elmwood, Mass., U.S. 283 42.01 N 70.58 W
Elmwood, Nebr., U.S. 198 40.50 N 96.18 W
Elmwood, Wis., U.S. 190 44.47 N 92.09 W
Elmwood •[8] 285 39.56 N 75.14 W
Elmwood Park, Ill., U.S. 216 41.55 N 87.49 W
Elmwood Park, N.J., U.S. 276 40.54 N 74.07 W

Symbols in the index entries represent the broad categories identified in the key at the right. Symbols with superior numbers (∧∧[2]) identify subcategories (see complete key on page I · 30).

Kartensymbole in dem Registerverzeichnis stellen die rechts in Schlüssel erklärten Kategorien dar. Symbole mit hochgestellten Ziffern (∧∧[2]) bezeichnen Unterabteilungen einer Kategorie (vgl. vollständiger Schlüssel auf Seite I · 30).

Los símbolos incluídos en el texto del índice representan las grandes categorías identificadas con la clave a la derecha. Los símbolos con numeros en su parte superior (∧∧[2]) identifican las subcategorías (véase la clave completa en la página I · 30).

Les symboles de l'index représentent les catégories indiquées dans la légende à droite. Les symboles suivis d'un indice (∧∧[2]) représentent des sous-catégories (voir légende complète à la page I · 30).

Os símbolos incluídos no texto do índice representam as grandes categorias identificadas com a chave à direita. Os símbolos com números em sua parte superior (∧∧[2]) identificam as subcategorias (veja-se a chave completa à página I · 30).

Symbol	English	Deutsch	Español	Français	Português
∧	Mountain	Berg	Montaña	Montagne	Montanha
∧∧	Mountains	Berge	Montañas	Montagnes	Montanhas
)(	Pass	Pass	Paso	Col	Passo
V	Valley, Canyon	Tal, Cañon	Valle, Cañón	Vallée, Canyon	Vale, Canhão
≡	Plain	Ebene	Llano	Plaine	Planície
≻	Cape	Kap	Cabo	Cap	Cabo
I	Island	Insel	Isla	Île	Ilha
II	Islands	Inseln	Islas	Îles	Ilhas
•	Other Topographic Features	Andere Topographische Objekte	Otros Elementos Topográficos	Autres données topographiques	Outros Elementos Topográficos

ESPAÑOL

Nombre	Página	Lat.°′	Long.°′ W=Oeste
Elmwood Park, Wis., U.S.	216	42.41 N	87.50 W
El Naranjo, Arg.	252	25.44 S	64.59 W
El Naranjo, Méx.	234	22.30 N	98.38 W
Elne	32	42.36 N	2.58 E
El Negralejo	266a	40.24 N	3.31 W
El Negrito	236	15.16 N	87.41 W
El Nevado, Cerro ∧, Arg.	252	35.35 S	68.30 W
El Nevado, Cerro ∧, Col.	246	3.59 N	74.04 W
El Nido, Pil.	116	11.11 N	119.23 E
El Nido, Calif., U.S.	226	37.08 N	120.29 W
El Niybo	144	4.32 N	39.59 E
Elnora, Alta., Can.	182	51.59 N	113.12 W
Elnora, Ind., U.S.	194	38.53 N	87.05 W
El Oasis	286c	10.35 N	66.59 W
El-Obeid → Al-Ubayyiḍ	140	13.11 N	30.13 E
Elobey, Islas II	152	0.59 N	9.30 E
Eloida, Lake ⊜	212	44.40 N	75.58 W
Elói Mendes	256	21.37 S	45.34 W
Eloise	220	27.60 N	81.44 W
Elokbatindi	152	3.27 N	10.08 E
Elora, Ont., Can.	212	43.41 N	80.26 W
Elora, Tenn., U.S.	194	35.01 N	86.21 W
El Oro □[4]	246	3.30 S	79.50 W
Elortondo	252	33.42 S	61.37 W
Elorza	246	7.03 N	69.31 W
El Oso	246	4.59 N	65.25 W
El Otro Lado	286c	10.24 N	66.49 W
El Oued	148	33.20 N	6.58 E
Eloy	200	32.45 N	111.33 W
Éloyes	58	48.06 N	6.37 E
El Pacayal	232	15.37 N	92.02 W
El Palmar, Bol.	248	21.54 S	63.39 W
El Palmar, Ven.	246	7.58 N	61.53 W
El Palmar, Ven.	286c	10.38 N	66.52 W
El Palomar	288	34.36 S	58.36 W
El Palomar, Base Aérea Militar ■	288	34.37 S	58.37 W
El Palqui	252	30.45 S	70.59 W
El Pantanoso, Arroyo ≃	288	34.47 S	58.40 W
El Pao, Ven.	246	8.01 N	62.38 W
El Pao, Ven.	246	9.38 N	68.08 W
El Paradero	246	10.38 N	69.32 W
El Paraíso, Hond.	236	13.51 N	86.34 W
El Paraíso, Méx.	234	17.25 N	100.15 W
El Paraíso □[5]	236	14.10 N	86.30 W
El Pardo ◆[8]	266a	40.31 N	3.47 W
El Pardo, Monte de ⋀[2]	266a	40.33 N	3.48 W
El Paso, Ill., U.S.	216	40.44 N	89.01 W
El Paso, Tex., U.S.	200	31.45 N	106.29 W
El Paso Creek ≃	228	35.02 N	118.51 W
El Paso de Robles → Paso Robles	226	35.38 N	120.41 W
El Paso Peaks ⋀	204	35.28 N	117.43 W
El Pato	246	2.50 N	74.48 W
El Paují	286c	10.26 N	66.49 W
El Pedregal ◆[8]	286c	10.30 N	66.51 W
El Peñuelo	232	24.34 N	100.46 W
El Peral	286e	33.35 S	70.34 W
El Perú	246	7.19 N	61.49 W
El Pescado, Arroyo ≃	258	34.54 S	57.47 W
Elphin	48	53.51 N	8.12 W
Elphinstone	184	50.33 N	100.19 W
El Picacho, Cerro ∧	234	20.40 N	100.43 W
El Pilar	246	10.32 N	63.09 W
El Pinar, Parque Nacional ♠	286c	10.29 N	66.56 W
El Piñón	246	10.24 N	74.50 W
El Pintado	252	24.38 S	61.27 W
El Piojo, Arroyo ≃	288	34.50 S	58.45 W
El Piquete	252	24.13 S	64.39 W
El Placer	234	23.33 N	106.10 W
El Plantío ◆[8]	266a	40.28 N	3.49 W
El Platanillo	234	18.28 N	101.52 W
El Plomo	200	31.15 N	112.04 W
El Polvorín	240m	18.26 N	66.17 W
El Porcal	266a	40.18 N	3.32 W
El Portal, Calif., U.S.	226	37.41 N	119.47 W
El Portal, Fla., U.S.	220	25.52 N	80.11 W
El Porvenir, Méx.	196	27.33 N	104.57 W
El Porvenir, Méx.	204	32.05 N	116.38 W
El Porvenir, Méx.	232	31.15 N	105.51 W
El Porvenir, Méx.	234	15.44 N	93.22 W
El Potosí	232	24.51 N	100.19 W
El Potosí, Parque Nacional ♠	234	22.00 N	99.58 W
El Potrero	196	26.23 N	100.27 W
El Potro, Cerro ∧	252	28.24 S	69.39 W
El Progreso, Ec.	246a	0.54 S	89.33 W
El Progreso, Guat.	236	14.21 N	89.51 W
El Progreso, Guat.	236	14.51 N	90.04 W
El Progreso, Hond.	236	15.21 N	87.49 W
El Progreso □[5]	236	14.50 N	90.00 W
El Puente del Arzobispo	34	39.48 N	5.10 W
El Puerto de Santa María	34	36.36 N	6.13 W
El Puesto	252	27.57 S	67.38 W
El Quebrachal	252	25.17 S	64.04 W
El Quelite	234	23.32 N	106.28 W
Elquera Bushland ♠	274a	33.42 S	150.04 E
Elqui ≃	252	29.54 S	71.17 W
Elrama	214	40.15 N	79.56 W
El Ranchito	234	18.40 N	103.41 W
El Rastro	246	9.03 N	67.27 W
El Real	246	8.08 N	77.43 W
El Recreo ◆[8]	286c	10.30 N	66.53 W
El Remolino, Méx.	196	28.44 N	101.07 W
El Remolino, Méx.	234	17.39 N	94.13 W
El Reno	196	35.32 N	97.57 W
El Rio	228	34.14 N	119.10 W
El Rito	200	36.21 N	106.11 W
El Rito ≃	200	36.12 N	106.14 W
El Roba	154	3.57 N	40.01 E
El Roble	234	23.32 N	106.14 W
Elrose	184	51.13 N	108.01 W
Elroy	190	43.45 N	90.16 W
El Rucio	234	23.23 N	102.05 W
Elsa, Yukon, Can.	180	63.55 N	135.28 W
Elsa, Tex., U.S.	196	26.18 N	97.59 W
Elsa ≃	66	43.43 N	10.52 E
Elsah	219	38.57 N	90.22 W
El Sahuaro	200	31.05 N	112.55 W
El Salado	252	26.25 S	70.19 W
El Salto, Chile	286e	33.23 S	70.38 W
El Salto, Méx.	234	23.47 N	105.22 W
El Salto, Méx.	234	20.32 N	103.11 W
El Salvador	116	8.34 N	124.32 E
El Salvador □[1]	230		
	236	13.50 N	88.55 W
El Samán de Apure	246	7.55 N	68.44 W
El Santo	240p	22.42 N	79.41 W
Elsass → Alsace □[9]	32	48.30 N	7.30 E
El Sauce	236	12.53 N	86.32 W
El Sauz	232	29.02 N	106.16 W
El Sauzal	232	31.54 N	116.41 W
Elsberry	219	39.10 N	90.47 W
Elsbethen	64	47.45 N	13.05 E
Elsburg	273d	26.15 S	28.12 E
Elsdorf, B.R.D.	52	53.14 N	9.20 E
Elsdorf, B.R.D.	56	50.54 N	6.34 E
El Segundo	228	33.55 N	118.24 W
Elsen	52	51.44 N	8.39 E
Elsey	263	51.22 N	7.34 E
Elsfleth	52	53.14 N	8.28 E
El Siasgo, Arroyo ≃	258	35.33 S	58.33 W
Elsie, Mich., U.S.	216	43.05 N	84.23 W
Elsie, Oreg., U.S.	224	45.52 N	123.35 W
Elsinore → Helsingør, Dan.	41	56.02 N	12.37 E
Elsinore, Utah, U.S.	200	38.41 N	112.09 W
Elsinore, Lake ⊜[1]	228	33.39 N	117.21 W
El Sitio	286c	10.28 N	66.46 W

FRANÇAIS

Nom	Page	Lat.°′	Long.°′ W=Ouest
Elsloo	56	50.56 N	5.46 E
Elsmere, Del., U.S.	208	39.44 N	75.36 W
Elsmere, Ky., U.S.	218	39.00 N	84.36 W
Elsmere, N.Y., U.S.	210	42.38 N	73.49 W
El Sobrante	226	37.58 N	122.19 W
El Socorro	246	8.59 N	65.44 W
El Sombrero	246	9.23 N	67.03 W
Elspe	56	51.09 N	8.04 E
Elspeet	52	52.17 N	5.46 E
Elst	52	51.55 N	5.50 E
Elstal	54	52.32 N	12.59 E
Elstead	42	51.11 N	0.43 W
Elster	54	51.50 N	12.49 E
Elsterberg	54	50.36 N	12.10 E
Elstergebirge ⋀	54	50.15 N	12.20 E
Elsterwerda	54	51.28 N	13.31 E
Elston, Ind., U.S.	216	40.22 N	86.55 W
Elston, Mo., U.S.	219	38.37 N	92.19 W
Elstra	54	51.13 N	14.08 E
Elstree, Eng., U.K.	260	51.39 N	0.16 W
Elstree Aerodrome ⊠	260	51.39 N	0.19 W
El Sueco	232	29.54 N	106.24 W
El Tajín ⊥	234	20.27 N	97.23 W
El Tala	252	26.07 S	65.17 W
El Talar	258	34.27 S	58.39 W
El Tamarindo	236	13.11 N	87.54 W
El Tambo	246	1.26 N	77.23 W
El Tanque	196	26.28 N	99.38 W
El Tapextle	234	23.52 N	105.33 W
El Tarf	36	36.45 N	8.20 E
Elten	52	51.52 N	6.10 E
El Tepozteco, Parque Nacional ♠	234	19.00 N	99.00 W
El Terrero	234	18.58 N	102.28 W
Eltham, Austl.	169	37.44 S	145.09 E
Eltham, N.Z.	172	39.26 S	174.18 E
Eltham ◆[8]	260	51.27 N	0.04 E
Eltham Palace ʋ	260	51.27 N	0.03 E
El Tigre, Col.	246	2.28 N	68.15 W
El Tigre, Ven.	246	8.55 N	64.15 W
El Tigre, Isla I	236	13.16 N	87.38 W
El Tigrito → San José de Guanipa	246	8.54 N	64.09 W
El Timbiriche	234	18.38 N	101.31 W
El Tisey, Cerro ∧	236	12.59 N	86.22 W
Eltmann	56	49.58 N	10.40 E
El Tocuyo	246	9.47 N	69.48 W
El Tofo	252	29.27 S	71.15 W
El'ton, S.S.S.R.	80	49.08 N	46.50 E
Elton, Eng., U.K.	262	53.16 N	2.49 W
Elton, La., U.S.	194	30.29 N	92.42 W
Elton, Pa., U.S.	214	40.17 N	78.48 W
El'ton, Ozero ⊜	80	49.16 N	46.35 E
El Toreo ♠	286a	19.27 N	99.13 W
El Toro	228	33.38 N	117.42 W
El Toro ∧	240m	18.16 N	65.49 W
El Toro I	234	21.26 N	97.31 W
El Toro Marine Corps Air Station ■	228	33.41 N	117.44 W
El Tranco, Embalse de ⊜[1]	34	38.10 N	2.45 W
El Tránsito, Chile	252	28.52 S	70.17 W
El Tránsito, El Sal.	236	13.22 N	88.21 W
El Trapiche	246	3.03 N	77.33 W
El Trébol	252	32.12 S	61.42 W
El Triunfo, Hond.	236	13.06 N	87.00 W
El Triunfo, Hond.	236	15.46 N	87.26 W
El Triunfo, Méx.	232	23.47 N	110.08 W
El Tuito	234	20.19 N	105.22 W
El Tunal	252	24.48 S	65.45 W
El Turbio	254	51.41 S	72.05 W
Eltville	56	50.02 N	8.07 E
Eltz, Burg ⊥	56	50.12 N	7.20 E
Elunchanzizhiqi (Alihe)	89	50.34 N	123.40 E
Elunchunzizhiqi (Xiaoergou)	89	49.30 N	123.47 E
Elura → Ellora	122	20.01 N	75.10 E
Elūru	122	16.42 N	81.06 E
Elva	76	58.13 N	26.25 E
El Valle	236	8.36 N	80.08 W
El Valle ◆[8]	286c	10.27 N	66.55 W
Elvas	34	38.53 N	7.10 W
Elvas ≃	256	21.12 S	44.08 W
Elven	32	47.44 N	2.35 W
El Venado, Isla I	236	11.57 N	83.44 W
El Verano	226	38.18 N	122.29 W
El Verde	234	23.21 N	106.09 W
Elverdissen	52	52.05 N	8.38 E
Elverlingsen	263	51.17 N	7.42 E
Elverta	226	38.43 N	121.28 W
Elverum	26	60.53 N	11.34 E
El Viejo	236	12.40 N	87.10 W
El Vigía	246	8.38 N	71.39 W
El Vigía, Cerro ∧	234	21.19 N	104.03 W
Elvira	258	35.14 S	59.29 W
Elvo ≃	62	45.23 N	8.21 E
El Volcán, Arg.	252	33.15 S	66.12 W
El Volcán, Chile	252	33.49 S	70.11 W
El Wak, Kenya	154	2.49 N	40.56 E
El-Wak, Som.	144	2.50 N	41.03 E
El-Wanot	144	4.07 N	47.07 E
El-Warre	144	3.39 N	45.18 E
Elwha ≃	224	48.10 N	123.35 W
Elwood, Austl.	274b	37.53 S	144.59 E
Elwood, Ill., U.S.	216	41.24 N	88.07 W
Elwood, Ind., U.S.	216	40.17 N	85.50 W
Elwood, Kans., U.S.	198	39.45 N	94.52 W
Elwood, Nebr., U.S.	198	40.36 N	99.52 W
Elwood, N.J., U.S.	208	39.35 N	74.43 W
Elwood, N.Y., U.S.	207	40.51 N	73.20 W
Elwood Park, Fla., U.S.	220	27.28 N	82.30 W
Elwood Park, Pa., U.S.	279b	40.10 N	80.17 W
Elwy ≃	44	53.16 N	3.26 W
Elwyn	285	39.54 N	75.24 W
Elxleben	54	51.02 N	10.56 E
Ely, Eng., U.K.	42	52.24 N	0.16 E
Ely, Minn., U.S.	190	47.54 N	91.51 W
Ely, Mo., U.S.	219	39.41 N	91.39 W
Ely, Nev., U.S.	204	39.15 N	114.53 W
Ely, Isle of ◆[1]	42	52.24 N	0.10 E
El Yagual	246	7.29 N	68.25 W
Ely Cathedral ʋ[1]	42	52.24 N	0.16 E
El Yopal	246	5.21 N	72.23 W
Elyria	214	41.22 N	82.06 W
Elyria Airport ⊠	279a	41.20 N	82.06 W
Elysburg	210	40.52 N	76.33 W
Elysian Park ♠	280	34.05 N	118.14 W
El Yunque ∧	240m	18.19 N	65.48 W
Elywood Park ♠	279a	41.23 N	82.06 W
Elz	56	50.25 N	8.02 E
Elz ≃	58	48.21 N	7.45 E
Elzach	58	48.10 N	8.04 E
El Zamural	286c	10.27 N	67.00 W
El Zapotal	234	15.27 N	93.10 W
El Zapotán	234	18.41 N	103.39 W
El Zapote de Calabacillas	232	25.42 N	106.32 W
Elzbach ≃	56	50.12 N	7.22 E
Elze, B.R.D.	52	52.35 N	9.44 E
Elze, B.R.D.	52	52.07 N	9.44 E
El Zig-Zag	286c	10.33 N	66.58 W
Emadle	144	5.13 N	46.56 E
Emae I	175f	17.04 S	168.24 E
Emajõgi ≃	76	58.26 N	27.15 E
Emali	154	2.05 S	37.38 E
Emalı Bendi ◆[6]	267b	41.04 N	29.06 E
Emån ≃	26	57.08 N	16.30 E
Émancé	261	48.35 N	1.44 E
Emau I	175f	17.28 S	168.30 E
Emba	86	48.50 N	58.08 E
Emba ≃	80	46.38 N	53.14 E
Embarcación	252	23.13 S	64.06 W
Embarras ≃, Alta., Can.	182	53.27 N	116.37 W
Embarras ≃, Ill., U.S.	194	38.39 N	87.37 W

PORTUGUÊS

Nome	Página	Lat.°′	Long.°′ W=Oeste
Embarras, North Fork ≃	194	38.55 N	87.59 W
Embarrass	190	44.40 N	88.42 W
Embarrass ≃, Minn., U.S.	190	47.24 N	92.25 W
Embarrass ≃, Wis., U.S.	190	44.23 N	88.45 W
Embarrass, Middle Branch ≃	190	44.43 N	88.55 W
Embetsu	92a	44.44 N	141.47 E
Embid	34	40.58 N	1.43 W
Embira ≃	248	7.19 S	70.15 W
Embleton	44	55.30 N	1.37 W
Embo	46	57.54 N	3.59 W
Emboabas	256	21.18 S	44.08 W
Embondo	152	0.15 N	19.38 E
Embrach	58	47.30 N	8.36 E
Embreeville, Pa., U.S.	285	39.56 N	75.44 W
Embreeville, Tenn., U.S.	192	36.11 N	82.28 W
Embro	212	43.09 N	80.54 W
Embrun, Ont., Can.	212	45.16 N	75.17 W
Embrun, Fr.	62	44.34 N	6.30 E
Embry	50	50.29 N	1.58 E
Embu, Bra.	256	23.39 S	46.51 W
Embu, Kenya	154	0.32 S	37.27 E
Embu □[7]	287b	23.40 S	46.50 W
Embu-Guaçu	256	23.49 S	46.48 W
Embu-Guacu □[7]	287b	23.48 S	46.48 W
Embu-Mirim ≃	287b	23.39 S	46.51 W
Emden, B.R.D.	52	53.22 N	7.12 E
Emden, Ill., U.S.	194	40.18 N	89.29 W
Emden, Mo., U.S.	219	39.48 N	91.52 W
Emei	107	29.36 N	103.31 E
Emeigh	214	40.42 N	78.47 W
Emel' ≃	86	46.20 N	81.46 E
Emelle	194	32.44 N	88.19 W
Emerado	198	47.55 N	97.22 W
Émerainville	261	48.49 N	2.37 E
Emerald, Austl.	166	23.32 S	148.10 E
Emerald, Austl.	169	37.56 S	145.26 E
Emerald Basin ✚[1]	6	57.00 S	161.00 E
Emerald Bay State Park ♠	226	38.57 N	120.05 W
Emerald Lake	226	37.28 N	122.16 W
Emero ≃	248	13.19 S	67.17 W
Emerson, Man., Can.	184	49.00 N	97.12 W
Emerson, Ark., U.S.	194	33.06 N	93.11 W
Emerson, Ga., U.S.	192	34.08 N	84.45 W
Emerson, Iowa, U.S.	198	41.01 N	95.24 W
Emerson, Mo., U.S.	219	39.53 N	91.42 W
Emerson, Nebr., U.S.	198	42.17 N	96.44 W
Emerson, N.J., U.S.	276	40.58 N	74.02 W
Emery, S. Dak., U.S.	198	43.36 N	97.37 W
Emery, Utah, U.S.	200	38.55 N	111.15 W
Emeryville, Ont., Can.	214	42.18 N	82.45 W
Emeryville, Calif., U.S.	226	37.50 N	122.17 W
Emet	130	39.20 N	29.15 E
Emgayet	146	29.04 N	12.58 E
Emhouse	222	32.09 N	96.35 W
Emi	88	50.36 N	97.49 E
Emigrant Gap	226	39.19 N	120.38 W
Emigrant Gap)(	226	39.18 N	120.40 W
Emigsville	208	40.01 N	76.44 W
Emiliano Zapata, Méx.	232	17.45 N	91.46 W
Emiliano Zapata, Méx.	234	16.10 N	94.01 W
Emilia-Romagna □[4]	66	44.35 N	11.00 E
Emílio de Carvalho	152	5.55 S	12.57 E
Emin	86	46.27 N	83.23 E
Eminābād	123	32.02 N	74.16 E
Emine, nos ≻	38	42.42 N	27.51 E
Eminence, Ky., U.S.	218	38.22 N	85.11 W
Eminence, Mo., U.S.	194	37.09 N	91.22 W
Emira Island I	164	1.40 S	150.00 E
Emiralem	130	38.36 N	27.09 E
Emiratos Arabes Unidos → United Arab Emirates □[1]	128	24.00 N	54.00 E
Emirdağ	130	39.01 N	31.10 E
Emır Dağları ⋀	130	38.50 N	31.15 E
Emirhan	130	39.42 N	37.46 E
Emisou, Tarso ∧	146	21.13 N	18.32 E
Emita	166	40.00 S	147.54 E
Emlembe ∧	158	25.57 S	31.11 E
Emlenton	214	41.11 N	79.43 W
Emlichheim	52	52.36 N	6.50 E
Emmaån ≃	40	58.44 N	15.35 E
Emmaboda	26	56.38 N	15.32 E
Emmarentia ◆[8]	273d	26.10 S	28.01 E
Emmaste	76	58.42 N	22.36 E
Emmaus, S.S.S.R.	82	56.47 N	36.07 E
Emmaus, Pa., U.S.	208	40.32 N	75.30 W
Emmaville	166	29.26 S	151.36 E
Emme ≃	58	47.13 N	7.34 E
Emmeline Lake ⊜	184	55.00 N	106.22 W
Emmeloord	52	52.43 N	5.45 E
Emmen	52	52.47 N	7.00 E
Emmenbrücke	58	47.04 N	8.17 E
Emmendingen	58	48.07 N	7.50 E
Emmental ∨	58	46.56 N	7.45 E
Emmer ≃	52	52.03 N	9.23 E
Emmer-Compascuum	52	52.48 N	7.02 E
Emmer-Erfscheidenveen	52	52.48 N	7.01 E
Emmerich	52	51.50 N	6.15 E
Emmerstedt	54	52.15 N	10.58 E
Emmet, Austl.	166	24.40 S	144.28 E
Emmet, Ark., U.S.	194	33.44 N	93.28 W
Emmetsburg	198	43.07 N	94.41 W
Emmett, Idaho, U.S.	202	43.52 N	116.30 W
Emmett, Mich., U.S.	214	42.59 N	82.46 W
Emmiganūru	122	15.44 N	77.29 E
Emmitsburg	208	39.42 N	77.20 W
Emmonak	180	62.46 N	164.30 W
Emneth	42	52.38 N	0.11 E
Emo	190	48.38 N	93.50 W
Emőd	30	47.56 N	20.49 E
Emory	222	32.52 N	95.46 W
Emory ≃	192	35.56 N	84.29 W
Emory Peak ∧	196	29.13 N	103.17 W
Empalme	232	27.58 N	110.51 W
Empalme Escobedo	234	20.41 N	100.44 W
Empalme Purísima	234	23.55 N	105.05 W
Empalme San Vicente	258	34.58 S	58.22 W
Empangeni	158	28.50 S	31.48 E
Empedrado, Arg.	252	27.57 S	58.48 W
Empedrado, Chile	252	35.36 S	72.17 W
Emperor Jimmu, Tomb Of ⊥	270	34.29 N	135.47 E
Emperor Nintoku, Tomb of ⊥	270	34.34 N	135.29 E
Emperor Range ⋀	175e	5.45 S	154.55 E
Emperor Seamount Chain ✚[3]	6	45.00 N	170.00 E
Emperor Tenchi, Tomb of ⊥	270	34.59 N	135.48 E
Empfingen	58	48.24 N	8.42 E
Empire, Calif., U.S.	226	37.38 N	120.54 W
Empire, Nev., U.S.	204	40.37 N	119.21 W
Empire, Ohio, U.S.	214	40.31 N	80.37 W
Empire, Oreg., U.S.	202	43.23 N	124.17 W
Empoli	66	43.43 N	10.57 E
Emporia, Kans., U.S.	198	38.24 N	96.11 W
Emporia, Va., U.S.	208	36.41 N	77.32 W
Emporium	214	41.31 N	78.14 W
Empress	184	50.57 N	110.00 W
Empress Augusta Bay C	175e	6.25 S	155.05 E
Emptinne	56	50.19 N	5.07 E
Emrekom	84	39.58 N	41.57 E
Ems ≃	52	53.30 N	7.00 E
Emscher ≃	263	51.34 N	6.42 E
Emscher Bruch ◆[1]	263	51.34 N	7.09 E
Emsdetten	52	52.10 N	7.31 E
Ems-Jade-Kanal Ξ	52	53.19 N	7.10 E
Emskirchen	56	49.33 N	10.43 E

Nome	Página	Lat.°′	Long.°′ W=Oeste
Emsland ◆[1]	52	52.50 N	7.20 E
Emst ◆[8]	263	51.21 N	7.30 E
Emstek	52	52.50 N	8.09 E
Emsworth, Eng., U.K.	42	50.51 N	0.56 W
Emsworth, Pa., U.S.	214	40.30 N	80.04 W
Emu Creek ≃	171a	26.56 S	152.19 E
Emu Downs	168b	33.54 S	138.59 E
Emuerhe ≃	89	53.24 N	124.00 E
Emukae	92	33.18 N	129.38 E
Emu Park	166	23.15 S	150.50 E
Emu Plains	274a	33.45 S	150.41 E
Emuren	273a	6.40 N	3.31 E
Emusuo	89	43.45 N	128.10 E
Emyvale	48	54.20 N	6.59 W
En (Inn) ≃	32	48.35 N	13.28 E
Ena	94	35.29 N	137.40 E
Enana	156	17.29 S	16.19 E
Enånger	26	61.32 N	17.00 E
Enaratoli	164	3.55 S	136.21 E
Enard Bay C	46	58.05 N	5.20 W
Ena-san ∧	94	35.26 N	137.36 E
Enbacka	40	60.25 N	15.36 E
Enborne ≃	42	51.24 N	1.06 W
Encampment	200	41.12 N	106.47 W
Encampment ≃	200	41.18 N	106.43 W
Encantado	252	29.15 S	51.53 W
Encantado ◆[8]	287a	22.54 S	43.18 W
Encanto, Cape ≻	116	15.44 N	121.37 E
Encarnação ◆[8]	266c	38.47 N	9.06 W
Encarnación	252	27.20 S	55.54 W
Encarnación de Díaz	234	21.31 N	102.14 W
Encha	98	37.25 N	115.42 E
Enchenberg	56	49.01 N	7.20 E
Enchi	150	5.49 N	2.49 W
Enchilayas	200	30.50 N	112.50 W
Enchovas, Enseada das C	256	23.57 S	45.18 W
Enciastraia, Monte ∧	62	44.22 N	6.53 E
Encinal	196	28.02 N	99.21 W
Encinas	196	25.40 N	101.08 W
Encinitas	228	33.03 N	117.17 W
Encino, N. Mex., U.S.	200	34.39 N	105.28 W
Encino, Tex., U.S.	196	26.57 N	98.08 W
Encino ◆[8]	280	34.09 N	118.30 W
Encino Reservoir ⊜[1]	280	34.05 N	118.31 W
Encontrados	246	9.03 N	72.14 W
Encounter Bay C	168b	35.35 S	138.44 E
Encrucijada, Cuba	240p	22.37 N	79.52 W
Encrucijada, Méx.	234	18.18 N	93.29 W
Encruzilhada	255	15.31 S	40.54 W
Encruzilhada do Sul	252	30.32 S	52.31 W
Encs	30	48.20 N	21.08 E
Endako	182	54.05 N	125.02 W
Endako ≃	182	54.05 N	124.55 W
Endau ≃	114	2.39 N	103.38 E
Ende	115b	8.50 S	121.39 E
Ende, Teluk C	115b	8.52 S	121.30 E
Endeavor, Pa., U.S.	214	41.35 N	79.23 W
Endeavor, Wis., U.S.	190	43.43 N	89.29 W
Endeavour	184	52.08 N	102.40 W
Endeavour Strait Ц	164	10.50 S	142.15 E
Endelave I	41	55.46 N	10.17 E
Enderbury I[1]	14	3.08 S	171.05 W
Enderby, B.C., Can.	182	50.33 N	119.08 W
Enderby, Eng., U.K.	42	52.36 N	1.12 W
Enderby Land ◆[1]	9	67.30 S	53.00 E
Enderlin	198	46.37 N	97.36 W
Endicott, N.Y., U.S.	210	42.06 N	76.03 W
Endicott, Wash., U.S.	202	46.56 N	117.41 W
Endicott Mountains ⋀	180	67.50 N	152.00 W
Endimari ≃	248	8.46 S	66.07 W
Endine	64	45.46 N	9.59 E
Endine Gaiano	64	45.48 N	9.59 E
Endingen	58	48.09 N	7.42 E
Endja, Oued ≃	34	36.31 N	6.15 E
Endō	268	35.23 N	139.27 E
Endola	156	17.37 S	15.50 E
'En Dor	132	32.39 N	35.25 E
Endorf in Oberbayern	64	47.54 N	12.18 E
Endre ≃	62	43.28 N	6.36 E
Endrick ∧	170	35.12 S	150.12 E
Endwell	210	42.07 N	76.02 W
Ene ≃	248	11.09 S	74.19 W
Enemonzo	64	46.25 N	12.53 E
Enez	130	40.44 N	26.04 E
Enfer, Pointe d' ≻	240e	14.24 N	60.52 W
Enfida	36	36.07 N	10.23 E
Enfield, Austl.	168b	34.53 S	138.35 E
Enfield, Austl.	274a	33.53 S	151.06 E
Enfield, N.Z.	172	45.03 S	170.52 E
Enfield, Conn., U.S.	207	41.58 N	72.36 W
Enfield, N.H., U.S.	188	43.34 N	71.57 W
Enfield, N.C., U.S.	192	36.11 N	77.47 W
Enfield, Va., U.S.	208	37.43 N	77.12 W
Enfield ◆[8]	260	51.40 N	0.05 W
Engadine	170	34.04 S	151.01 E
Engaño, Cabo ≻	238	18.37 N	68.20 W
Engaru	92a	44.03 N	143.31 E
Engažimo	88	57.51 N	114.56 E
Engcobo	158	31.37 S	28.00 E
'En Gedi	132	31.27 N	35.23 E
Engelberg	58	46.49 N	8.25 E
Engelhard	192	35.31 N	76.02 W
Engelhartszell	60	48.31 N	13.44 E
Engel's	80	51.30 N	46.07 E
Engelsberg	60	49.19 N	11.38 E
Engelschmanplaat I	52	53.28 N	6.02 E
Engelsdorf	54	51.20 N	12.29 E
Engelskirchen	56	50.59 N	7.24 E
Engel's'ovo	83	48.22 N	39.23 E
Engen	58	47.51 N	8.46 E
Engenheiro Passos	256	22.30 S	44.41 W
Engenheiro Paulo de Frontin	256	22.33 S	43.41 W
Engenho	248	15.10 S	56.25 W
Engenho, Ilha do I	287a	22.50 S	43.07 W
Engenho de Dentro ◆[8]	287a	22.54 S	43.18 W
Engenho do Mato	287a	22.52 S	43.01 W
Engenho Nôvo	256	21.49 S	43.00 W
Engenho Nôvo ◆[8]	287a	22.55 S	43.17 W
Enger	52	52.08 N	8.34 E
Engestofte	41	54.46 N	11.34 E
Engesvang	41	56.10 N	9.21 E
'En Gev	132	32.47 N	35.38 E
Enggano, Pulau I	112	5.24 S	102.16 E
Enghershatu ∧	144	16.40 N	38.20 E
Enghien (Edingen), Bel.	50	50.42 N	4.02 E
Enghien (Les-Bains), Fr.	50	48.58 N	2.19 E
Enghien-Moisselles, Aéroport d' ⊠	261	49.02 N	2.21 E
Engiadina Bassa ∨	58	46.50 N	10.20 E
Engis	56	50.35 N	5.25 E
Engizek Dağı ∧	130	37.50 N	37.10 E
Engjan	26	63.09 N	8.32 E
England	194	34.33 N	91.58 W
England □[8]	28	52.30 N	1.30 W
England Air Force Base ■	194	31.20 N	92.33 W
Englebright Lake ⊜[1]	226	39.15 N	121.15 W
Englee	186	50.44 N	56.06 W
Englefield, Cape ≻	176	69.51 N	85.39 W
Englefield Green	260	51.26 N	0.35 W
Englefontaine	50	50.11 N	3.39 E
Englehart	190	47.49 N	79.52 W
Englehart ≃	190	47.51 N	79.50 W
Englewood, B.C., Can.	182	50.33 N	126.53 W
Englewood, Colo., U.S.	200	39.39 N	104.59 W
Englewood, Fla., U.S.	220	26.58 N	82.21 W
Englewood, Ind., U.S.	218	38.50 N	86.31 W
Englewood, Kans., U.S.	198	37.02 N	100.01 W
Englewood, N.J., U.S.	210	40.54 N	73.59 W

Nome	Página	Lat.°′	Long.°′ W=Oeste
Englewood, Ohio, U.S.	218	39.53 N	84.18 W
Englewood, Tenn., U.S.	192	35.26 N	84.29 W
Englewood ◆[8]	278	41.47 N	87.39 W
Englewood Cliffs	276	40.53 N	73.57 W
Englewood Reservoir ⊜[1]	218	39.58 N	84.18 W
English, Ind., U.S.	218	38.20 N	86.28 W
English, Ky., U.S.	218	38.37 N	85.08 W
English ≃, Ont., Can.	176	50.12 N	95.00 W
English ≃, N.A.	206	45.13 N	73.50 W
English ≃, Iowa, U.S.	190	41.29 N	91.30 W
English Bay	180	59.22 N	151.55 W
English Bāzār	124	25.00 N	88.09 E
English Center	210	41.26 N	77.17 W
English Channel (La Manche) Ц	28	50.20 N	1.00 W
English Coast ◆[2]	9	73.45 S	73.00 W
English Harbour West	186	47.28 N	55.29 W
Englishman ≃	224	49.22 N	124.18 W
Englishtown	208	40.18 N	74.22 W
Engong	152	0.36 N	10.06 E
Engter	52	52.23 N	8.04 E
Enguera	34	38.59 N	0.41 W
Engum	41	55.44 N	9.40 E
Engure	76	57.10 N	23.13 E
Engures Ezers ⊜	76	57.16 N	23.06 E
Engwilen	58	47.37 N	9.05 E
'En Ḥarod	132	32.33 N	35.23 E
'En HaShofet	132	32.35 N	35.06 E
Enid	196	36.19 N	97.48 W
Enid Lake ⊜[1]	194	34.10 N	89.50 W
Enilda	182	55.25 N	116.18 W
Eningen unter Achalm	58	48.29 N	9.16 E
Eninogorsk	86	54.36 N	52.30 E
Eniwa	92a	42.45 N	141.33 E
Eniwetok I[1]	14	11.30 N	162.15 E
Enka	192	35.32 N	82.38 W
Enkeldoorn	154	19.01 S	30.53 E
Enkenbach	56	49.29 N	7.54 E
Enkhuizen	52	52.42 N	5.17 E
Enkirch	56	49.59 N	7.07 E
Enköping	40	59.38 N	17.04 E
Enle	102	24.02 N	101.09 E
Enmedio	196	29.04 N	103.29 W
Enmelen	180	65.01 N	175.54 W
Enmore	246	6.46 N	57.59 W
Enna	70	37.34 N	14.16 E
Enna □[4]	70	37.35 N	14.26 E
Ennadai Lake ⊜	176	60.53 N	101.15 W
Enné, Ouadi ∨	146	14.24 N	18.45 E
Ennedi ⋀[1]	146	17.15 N	22.00 E
Ennell, Lough ⊜	48	53.28 N	7.24 W
Ennenda	58	47.01 N	9.05 E
Ennepe ≃	263	51.22 N	7.27 E
Ennepe-Ruhr-Kreis □[8]	263	51.21 N	7.15 E
Ennepestausee ⊜[1]	263	51.14 N	7.25 E
Ennepetal	56	51.18 N	7.22 E
Ennerdale Water ⊜	44	54.31 N	3.23 W
Ennery	261	49.05 N	2.06 E
'En Netafim	132	29.35 N	34.53 E
Enngonia	166	29.19 S	145.51 E
Enniger	52	51.50 N	7.56 E
Ennigerloh	52	51.50 N	8.02 E
Ennigloh	52	52.12 N	8.34 E
Ennis, Eire	48	52.50 N	8.59 W
Ennis, Mont., U.S.	202	45.21 N	111.44 W
Ennis, Tex., U.S.	222	32.20 N	96.38 W
Enniscorthy	48	52.30 N	6.34 W
Enniskillen	48	54.21 N	7.38 W
Ennis Lake ⊜[1]	202	45.26 N	111.41 W
Ennistymon	48	52.57 N	9.15 W
Enns	61	48.13 N	14.29 E
Enns ≃	61	48.14 N	14.32 E
Ennstaler Alpen ⋀	61	47.37 N	14.35 E
Eno	26	62.48 N	30.09 E
Enø I	41	55.10 N	11.40 E
Eno ≃	96	34.53 N	132.41 E
Enochs	196	33.52 N	102.46 W
Enoggera Army Base ■	171a	27.25 S	152.58 E
Enola	208	40.17 N	76.56 W
Enon	218	39.53 N	83.56 W
Enontekiö	24	68.23 N	23.38 E
Enon Valley	214	40.51 N	80.28 W
Enoree ≃	192	34.26 N	81.25 W
Enosburg Falls	188	44.55 N	72.48 W
Eno-shima I	94	35.18 N	139.29 E
Enping	102	22.11 N	112.17 E
Enragé, Point ≻	186	44.16 N	64.15 W
Enrekang	112	3.34 S	119.47 E
Enrile	116	17.34 N	121.42 E
Enrique Fynn	258	34.50 S	59.08 W
Enrique Urien	252	27.34 S	60.32 W
Enriquillo	238	17.54 N	71.14 W
Enriquillo, Lago ⊜	238	18.27 N	71.39 W
Ens	52	52.38 N	5.50 E
Ensay	166	37.23 S	147.50 E
Ensay I	46	57.46 N	7.05 W
Enschede	52	52.12 N	6.53 E
Ensdorf	60	49.21 N	11.56 E
Enseada	256	23.29 S	45.05 W
Ensenada, Arg.	258	34.51 S	57.55 W
Ensenada, Méx.	232	31.52 N	116.37 W
Ensenada, P.R.	240m	17.58 N	66.56 W
Ensenada □[5]	288	34.50 S	58.00 W
Enshi	102	30.17 N	109.19 E
Enshū-nada ⍑[2]	92	34.27 N	137.38 E
Ensisheim	58	47.52 N	7.21 E
Enstaberga	40	58.45 N	16.51 E
Entebbe	154	0.04 N	32.28 E
Entenbühl ∧	60	49.46 N	12.24 E
Enter	52	52.18 N	6.34 E
Enterprise, Guy.	246	6.56 N	58.24 W
Enterprise, Ala., U.S.	194	31.19 N	85.51 W
Enterprise, Calif., U.S.	204	39.32 N	121.22 W
Enterprise, Kans., U.S.	198	38.54 N	97.07 W
Enterprise, Miss., U.S.	194	32.10 N	88.49 W
Enterprise, Oreg., U.S.	202	45.25 N	117.17 W
Enterprise, Utah, U.S.	200	37.34 N	113.43 W
Entiat ≃	202	47.40 N	120.14 W
Entiat, Lake ⊜	202	47.40 N	120.12 W
Entiat Mountains ⋀	224	48.00 N	120.42 W
Entinas, Punta ≻	34	36.41 N	2.46 W
Entlebuch	58	47.00 N	8.04 E
Entlebuch ∨	58	46.58 N	8.00 E
Entracque	62	44.14 N	7.24 E
Entraigues-sur-Sorgue	62	44.00 N	4.55 E
Entrains-sur-Nohain	50	47.27 N	3.15 E
Entrance, Cape ≻	164	2.21 S	150.12 E
Entraunes	62	44.11 N	6.45 E
Entraygues	32	44.39 N	2.34 E
Entrechaux	62	44.13 N	5.08 E
Entrée, Île d' I	186	47.17 N	61.42 W
Entremont-le-Vieux	62	45.26 N	5.53 E
Entrepeñas, Embalse de ⊜[1]	34	40.34 N	2.42 W
Entre Ríos, Bol.	248	21.32 S	64.12 W
Entre Rios, Bra.	255	11.56 S	38.05 W
Entre-Rios, Moç.	154	14.57 S	37.20 E
Entre Ríos □[4]	252	32.00 S	59.00 W
Entre Rios de Minas	255	20.41 S	44.04 W
Entrevaux	62	43.57 N	6.49 E
Entrèves	62	45.49 N	6.57 E
Entriken	214	40.20 N	78.12 W
Entringen	56	48.33 N	8.58 E
Entroncamento	34	39.28 N	8.28 W
Entupido	256	22.30 S	44.51 W
Entwistle	182	53.36 N	115.00 W
Entzheim, Aéroport d' ⊠	58	48.32 N	7.38 E
Enu, Pulau I	164	7.05 S	134.30 E
Enugu	150	6.27 N	7.27 E

Nome	Página	Lat.°′	Long.°′ W=Oeste
Enumclaw	224	47.12 N	121.59 W
Enurmino	180	66.57 N	171.49 W
Envalira, Port d')(	34	42.35 N	1.45 E
Envermeu	50	49.54 N	1.16 E
Envies, Rivière des ≃	206	46.37 N	72.24 W
Envigado	246	6.10 N	75.35 W
Envira	248	7.18 S	70.13 W
'En Yahav	132	30.38 N	35.11 E
Enyamba	154	3.40 S	24.58 E
Enyanghe	102	31.48 N	106.31 E
Enyellé	152	2.49 N	18.06 E
Enys, Mount ∧	172	43.14 S	171.38 E
Enz ≃	56	49.01 N	9.07 E
Enza ≃	64	44.54 N	10.31 E
Enzan	94	35.42 N	138.44 E
Enzaran, Bir ⍑[4]	148	23.56 N	14.33 W
Enzbach ≃	56	49.54 N	6.25 E
Enzenkirchen	60	48.23 N	13.39 E
Enzesfeld	61	47.55 N	16.10 E
Enzklösterle	56	48.40 N	8.28 E
Enzweihingen	56	48.55 N	8.58 E
Eo ≃	34	43.28 N	7.03 W
Eola	224	44.55 N	123.07 W
Eolia	219	39.14 N	91.01 W
Eolie o Lipari, Isole II	70	38.30 N	14.50 E
Epanomí	38	40.26 N	22.56 E
Épars, Bois de l' ♠	261	48.45 N	1.45 E
Epazote, Cerro ∧	232	24.35 N	105.07 W
Epe, B.R.D.	52	52.11 N	7.02 E
Epe, Ned.	52	52.21 N	6.00 E
Epe, Nig.	150	6.37 N	3.59 E
Epecuén, Lago ⊜	252	37.10 S	62.54 W
Epéna	152	1.22 N	17.29 E
Épernay	50	49.03 N	3.57 E
Épernon	50	48.37 N	1.41 E
Épernon, Les Taillis d' ♠	261	48.40 N	1.45 E
Epes	194	32.42 N	88.07 W
Ephesus ⊥	130	37.55 N	27.17 E
Ephraim	200	39.22 N	111.35 W
Ephrata, Pa., U.S.	208	40.11 N	76.10 W
Ephrata, Wash., U.S.	202	47.19 N	119.33 W
Ephrata Cloister ⊥	208	40.12 N	76.09 W
Ephratah	210	43.00 N	74.32 W
Epi I	175f	16.43 S	168.15 E
Épiais-lès-Louvres	261	49.02 N	2.33 E
Épila	34	41.36 N	1.17 W
Épinac-les-Mines	58	46.59 N	4.31 E
Épinal	58	48.11 N	6.27 E
Épinay-sous-Sénart	261	48.42 N	2.31 E
Épinay-sur-Orge	261	48.40 N	2.20 E
Épinay-sur-Seine	261	48.57 N	2.19 E
Episcopia	68	40.04 N	16.06 E
Episkopí	130	34.40 N	32.54 E
Epo	164	8.40 S	146.30 E
Époisses	50	47.30 N	4.10 E
Epomeo, Monte ∧	68	40.44 N	13.54 E
Épône	261	48.57 N	1.49 E
Eport, Loch C	46	57.33 N	7.11 W
Eppalock, Lake ⊜[1]	169	36.52 S	144.31 E
Eppendorf	54	50.48 N	13.14 E
Eppendorf ◆[8]	263	51.27 N	7.11 E
Eppenhausen ◆[8]	263	51.21 N	7.31 E
Eppeville	50	49.44 N	3.03 E
Epping, Austl.	169	37.39 S	145.02 E
Epping, Austl.	274a	33.46 S	151.05 E
Epping, Eng., U.K.	260	51.43 N	0.07 E
Epping, N.H., U.S.	188	43.02 N	71.04 W
Eppingen	56	49.08 N	8.54 E
Epping Forest □[8]	260	51.43 N	0.10 E
Epping Forest ♠	260	51.40 N	0.03 E
Epping Green, Eng., U.K.	260	51.45 N	0.07 W
Epping Green, Eng., U.K.	260	51.44 N	0.05 E
Epping Upland	260	51.43 N	0.06 E
Epsom	260	51.20 N	0.16 W
Epsom and Ewell □[8]	260	51.20 N	0.16 W
Epsom Downs Race Course ♠	260	51.19 N	0.15 W
Epte ≃, Fr.	50	49.04 N	1.37 E
Epte ≃, Zhg.	86	44.55 N	83.37 E
Épuisay	50	47.54 N	0.56 E
Epukiro	156	21.41 S	19.08 E
Epukiro ≃	156	20.45 S	21.05 E
Epupa Falls L	152	16.55 S	13.10 E
Epuyén	254	42.14 S	71.21 W
Epworth	44	53.32 N	0.49 W
Eqlīd	128	30.55 N	52.39 E
Equality	194	37.44 N	88.20 W
Equata	152	0.13 S	9.18 E
Équateur □[4]	152	1.00 N	20.30 E
Equateur → Ecuador □[1]	246	2.00 S	77.30 W
Equatorial Guinea □[1]	10		
	152	2.00 N	9.00 E
Équihen-Plage	50	50.41 N	1.34 E
Equimina ≃	152	13.11 S	12.47 E
Equinunk	210	41.51 N	75.14 W
Equi Terme	64	44.09 N	10.10 E
Era ≃, It.	66	43.40 N	10.38 E
Era ≃, Pap. N. Gui.	164	7.35 S	144.41 E
Erac Creek ≃	166	26.56 S	145.48 E
Eraclea	64	45.35 N	12.40 E
Eraclea ⊥	68	40.13 N	16.40 E
Eraclea Minoa ⊥	70	37.23 N	13.17 E
Eradu	162	28.41 S	115.02 E
Éragny	261	49.01 N	2.06 E
Eramosa ≃	212	43.32 N	80.14 W
Eran Bay C	116	9.06 N	117.43 E
Eranga	152	1.52 S	18.56 E
Erangal ◆[8]	272c	19.10 N	72.47 E
Erap	164	6.35 S	146.40 E
Erath	194	29.58 N	92.02 W
Erave	164	6.40 S	143.50 E
Erave ≃	164	6.40 S	143.55 E
Erba	62	45.48 N	9.15 E
Erba, Jabal ∧, Sūd.	140	19.04 N	36.46 E
Erba, Jabal ∧, Sūd.	140	20.45 N	36.50 E
Erbaa	130	40.42 N	36.36 E
Erbach, B.R.D.	56	49.40 N	8.59 E
Erbach, B.R.D.	58	48.20 N	9.53 E
Erbendorf	60	49.50 N	12.03 E
Erbenheim	56	50.03 N	8.18 E
Erbeskopf ∧	56	49.44 N	7.05 E
Erchie	68	40.26 N	17.44 E
Erčimijn Nuruu ⋀	88	49.24 N	100.00 E
Erciş	84	39.02 N	43.22 E
Erciyeş Dağı ∧	130	38.32 N	35.28 E
Ercolano	68	40.48 N	14.21 E
Ercolano (Herculaneum) ⊥	68	40.46 N	14.20 E
Érd	30	47.23 N	18.56 E
Erdaobaihe ≃	98	42.34 N	128.08 E
Erdaofang, Zhg.	104	41.37 N	122.34 E
Erdaofang, Zhg.	104	41.54 N	123.57 E
Erdaofangshen	104	42.09 N	123.17 E
Erdaogangzi, Zhg.	104	41.57 N	122.09 E
Erdaogangzi, Zhg.	104	42.04 N	123.06 E
Erdaohe	89	43.37 N	127.35 E
Erdaohezi, Zhg.	89	45.07 N	127.16 E
Erdaohezi, Zhg.	89	45.08 N	129.39 E
Erdaohuayuantun	98	42.17 N	127.07 E
Erdaojingzi	104	41.49 N	122.20 E
Erdaoliangzi, Zhg.	98	40.50 N	119.04 E
Erdaoliangzi, Zhg.	105	40.31 N	118.03 E
Erdaowan	89	47.58 N	124.33 E
Erdek	130	40.24 N	27.48 E
Erdemli	130	36.37 N	34.18 E
Erdene, Mong.	88	47.48 N	107.55 E
Erdene, Mong.	102	44.40 N	111.05 E
Erdene, Mong.	102	45.08 N	97.40 E
Erdenebulgan	88	50.07 N	101.35 E
Erdenebüren	86	48.26 N	91.27 E
Erdenedalaj	102	46.02 N	104.58 E
Erdenemandal	88	48.32 N	101.19 E
Erdenheim	285	40.05 N	75.13 W
Erdevik	38	45.07 N	19.25 E

English	Deutsch	Español	Français	Português
River	Fluss	Río	Rivière	Rio
Canal	Kanal	Canal	Canal	Canal
Waterfall, Rapids	Wasserfall, Stromschnellen	Cascada, Rápidos	Chute d'eau, Rapides	Cascata, Rápidos
Strait	Meeresstrasse	Estrecho	Détroit	Estreito
Bay, Gulf	Bucht, Golf	Bahía, Golfo	Baie, Golfe	Baía, Golfo
Lake, Lakes	See, Seen	Lago, Lagos	Lac, Lacs	Lago, Lagos
Swamp	Sumpf	Pantano	Marais	Pântano
Ice Features, Glacier	Eis- und Gletscherformen	Accidentes Glaciales	Formes glaciaires	Acidentes Glaciares
Other Hydrographic Features	Andere Hydrographische Objekte	Otros Elementos Hidrográficos	Autres données hydrographiques	Outros Elementos Hidrográficos

English	Deutsch	Español	Français	Português
Submarine Features	Untermeerische Objekte	Accidentes Submarinos	Formes de relief sous-marin	Acidentes Submarinos
Political Unit	Politische Einheit	Unidad Politica	Entité politique	Unidade Política
Cultural Institution	Kulturelle Institution	Institución Cultural	Institution culturelle	Instituição Cultural
Historical Site	Historische Stätte	Sitio Histórico	Site historique	Sitio Histórico
Recreational Site	Erholungs- und Ferienort	Sitio de Recreo	Centre de loisirs	Sítio de Lazer
Airport	Flughafen	Aeropuerto	Aéroport	Aeroporto
Military Installation	Militäranlage	Instalación Militar	Installation militaire	Instalação Militar
Miscellaneous	Verschiedenes	Misceláneo	Divers	Miscelânea

Name	Page	Lat.	Long.
Erdhausen	56	50.45 N	8.34 E
Erdiao	106	32.12 N	121.12 E
Erding	60	48.18 N	11.54 E
Erdinger Moos ☷	60	48.22 N	11.52 E
Erdnijevskij	80	46.52 N	46.17 E
Erebato ≃	246	5.54 N	64.16 W
Erebus, Mount ∧	9	77.32 S	167.09 E
Erechim	252	27.38 S	52.17 W
Ereğli, Tür.	130	37.31 N	34.04 E
Ereğli, Tür.	130	41.17 N	31.25 E
Eregun	273a	6.36 N	3.22 E
Erei, Monti ⩓	70	37.27 N	14.19 E
Eremita	256	21.35 S	45.04 W
Erenas	116	12.25 N	124.19 E
Erenköy	130	40.58 N	38.08 E
Erenköy ⬩[8]	267b	40.58 N	29.04 E
Erepecu, Lago do ⊜	250	1.20 S	56.35 W
Eresma ≃	34	41.26 N	4.45 W
Eressós	38	39.18 N	25.51 E
Erétria	38	38.24 N	23.48 E
Erez	132	31.34 N	34.34 E
Érezée	56	50.18 N	5.33 E
Erfa ≃	56	49.40 N	9.23 E
Erfde	41	54.19 N	9.19 E
Erfenisdam ⬩[6]	158	28.33 S	26.50 E
Erfoud	148	31.28 N	4.10 W
Erft ≃	56	51.11 N	6.44 E
Erftstadt	56	50.48 N	6.46 E
Erfurt	54	50.58 N	11.01 E
Erfurt □[5]	54	51.10 N	10.45 E
Ergani	130	38.17 N	39.46 E
Erg el Agreb	148	30.48 N	5.30 E
Ergene ≃	130	41.01 N	26.22 E
Ergenzingen	58	48.29 N	8.48 E
Erges (Erjas) ≃	34	39.40 N	7.01 E
Ergig ≃	146	11.22 N	15.24 E
Ērgļi	76	56.54 N	25.38 E
Ergolding	60	48.35 N	12.10 E
Ergoldsbach	60	48.41 N	12.12 E
Ergste	56	51.25 N	7.34 E
Erguvejem ≃	180	65.20 N	176.00 W
Erhai ⊜	102	25.48 N	100.11 E
Érherhi, Ahzar ∨	150	14.56 N	3.24 E
Erhlin	100	23.54 N	120.22 E
Erhshui	100	23.49 N	120.36 E
Erhulai	98	41.23 N	125.08 E
Eria ≃	34	42.03 N	5.44 W
Erial	208	39.46 N	75.01 W
Eriba	140	16.37 N	36.04 E
Eriboll	46	58.28 N	4.41 W
Eriboll, Loch C	46	58.31 N	4.41 W
Erica, Austl.	169	37.59 S	146.22 E
Erica, Ned.	52	52.43 N	6.55 E
Erice	70	38.02 N	12.35 E
Ericeira	34	38.59 N	9.25 W
Erichsen Lake ⊜	176	70.38 N	80.21 W
Erichshagen	52	52.40 N	9.14 E
Ericht, Loch ⊜	46	56.48 N	4.24 W
Erick	196	35.13 N	99.52 W
Erickson, B.C., Can.	182	49.05 N	116.28 W
Erickson, Man., Can.	184	50.30 N	99.55 W
Ericson	198	41.47 N	98.41 W
Erie, Colo., U.S.	200	40.03 N	105.03 W
Erie, Ill., U.S.	190	41.39 N	90.05 W
Erie, Kans., U.S.	198	37.34 N	95.15 W
Erie, Mich., U.S.	216	41.48 N	83.30 W
Erie, Pa., U.S.	214	42.08 N	80.04 W
Erie □[6], N.Y., U.S.	210	42.54 N	78.53 W
Erie □[6], Ohio, U.S.	214	41.27 N	82.42 W
Erie □[6], Pa., U.S.	214	42.08 N	80.04 W
Erie, Lake ⊜	190	42.15 N	81.00 W
Erieau	214	42.16 N	81.56 W
Erie Basin C	276	40.40 N	74.01 W
Erie Beach, Ont., Can.	214	42.16 N	82.00 W
Erie Beach, Ont., Can.	284a	42.53 N	78.57 W
Erie Canal → New York State Barge Canal ≍	210	43.05 N	78.43 W
Erie International Airport ⊠	214	42.05 N	80.11 W
Erigavo	144	10.37 N	47.24 E
Eriksberg ⊥	40	58.56 N	16.22 E
Eriksdale	184	50.52 N	98.06 W
Erímanthos ∧	38	37.59 N	21.51 E
Erimo-misaki ≻	92a	41.55 N	143.15 E
Erin, Ont., Can.	212	43.45 N	80.07 W
Erin, N.Y., U.S.	210	42.11 N	76.40 W
Erindale	275b	43.32 N	79.39 W
Ering	60	48.18 N	13.09 E
Eriskay I	46	57.04 N	7.18 W
Erisort, Loch C	46	58.07 N	6.24 W
Eriswil	58	47.05 N	7.51 E
Erith ⬩[8]	260	51.29 N	0.10 E
Erithraí	38	38.13 N	23.19 E
Eritrea □[4]	144	15.20 N	39.00 E
Erivan → Jerevan	84	40.11 N	44.30 E
Erjas (Erges) ≃	34	39.40 N	7.01 W
Erjia	106	32.02 N	121.13 E
Erkelenz	56	51.05 N	6.19 E
Erken ⊜	40	59.51 N	18.34 E
Erken-Jurt	84	44.27 N	41.54 E
Erkheim	58	48.02 N	10.20 E
Erkilet	130	38.49 N	35.27 E
Erkina ≃	48	52.51 N	7.23 W
Erkner	54	52.25 N	13.45 E
Erkner, Forst ⬩[3]	264a	52.22 N	13.47 E
Erkowit	140	18.46 N	37.07 E
Erkrath	56	51.13 N	6.55 E
Erl	64	47.41 N	12.11 E
Erlach, Öst.	61	47.43 N	16.13 E
Erlach, Schw.	58	47.03 N	7.06 E
Erlands Point	224	47.36 N	122.42 W
Erlangchang	107	30.18 N	106.00 E
Erlangen	60	49.36 N	11.01 E
Erlanger	218	39.01 N	84.37 W
Erlanghe	100	30.19 N	116.04 E
Erlangmiao	100	33.46 N	112.23 E
Erlau ≃	60	48.34 N	13.36 E
Erlauf ≃	61	48.12 N	15.11 E
Erlbach	54	50.18 N	12.22 E
Erldunda	162	25.14 S	133.12 E
Erle ⬩[8]	263	51.33 N	7.05 E
Erli	62	44.08 N	8.06 E
Erlian	102	43.46 N	112.05 E
Erling	106	31.53 N	119.36 E
Erling, Lake ⊜[1]	194	33.05 N	93.35 W
Erlistoun	162	28.20 S	122.08 E
Erlongshan, Zhg.	89	48.28 N	126.31 E
Erlongshan, Zhg.	89	50.04 N	126.47 E
Erlongshan, Zhg.	89	47.20 N	132.28 E
Erlsbach	64	46.55 N	12.15 E
Erma	208	38.59 N	74.54 W
Ermana, Chrebet ⩓	88	50.00 N	113.30 E
Ermatingen	58	47.41 N	9.06 E
Erme ≃	42	50.18 N	3.56 W
Ermelik	130	39.42 N	39.02 E
Ermelindo Matarazo ⬩[8]	287b	23.29 S	46.29 W
Ermelo, Ned.	52	52.17 N	5.37 E
Ermelo, S. Afr.	158	26.34 S	29.58 E
Ermenak	130	36.38 N	32.54 E
Ermendegou	104	42.02 N	121.56 E
Ermenonville	50	49.08 N	2.42 E
Ermidas	34	38.00 N	8.23 W
Ermil Post	140	13.37 N	27.36 E
Ermineskin Indian Reserve ⬩[4]	182	52.52 N	113.30 W
Ermington	274a	33.48 S	151.04 E
Ermita de los Correa	234	22.54 N	103.01 W
Ermitaž ♉	265a	59.56 N	30.20 E
Ermont	50	48.59 N	2.16 E
Ermoúpolis	38	37.26 N	24.56 E
Ermsleben	54	51.44 N	11.21 E
Ernaballa Mission	162	26.17 S	132.07 E
Ernākulam	122	9.59 N	76.17 E
Erndtebrück	56	50.59 N	8.15 E
Erne, Lower Lough ⊜	48	54.26 N	7.46 W
Erne, Upper Lough ⊜	48	54.14 N	7.32 W
Ernée	32	48.18 N	0.56 W
Ernest	214	40.41 N	79.10 W
Ernestina	258	35.16 S	59.34 W
Ernest Legouve Reef ✢[2]	14	35.10 S	150.40 W
Ernest Sound Џ	182	55.52 N	132.10 W
Erni, Uad ∨	148	26.45 N	10.47 W
Ernici, Monti ⩓	66	41.48 N	13.22 E
Ernst-Thälman, Pioneerpark ♣	264a	52.28 N	13.33 E
Ernst-Thälmann-Stadion ♣	264a	52.23 N	13.05 E
Erode	122	11.21 N	77.44 E
Eromanga	166	26.40 S	143.16 E
Eromanga I	175f	18.45 S	169.05 E
Erongo	156	21.44 S	15.53 E
Erongoberge ⩓	156	21.45 S	15.37 E
Eroto	144	16.13 N	37.57 E
Erp	56	50.46 N	6.43 E
Erpfendorf	64	47.35 N	12.28 E
Erpuzi	105	40.29 N	115.33 E
Erquelinnes	50	50.18 N	4.07 E
Err, Piz d' ∧	58	46.33 N	9.41 E
Errabiddy	162	25.28 S	117.07 E
Erramala Range ⩓	122	15.30 N	78.10 E
Errego	154	16.02 S	37.14 E
Errer ≃	144	7.32 N	42.05 E
Er-Riad → Ar-Riyāḍ	128	24.38 N	46.43 E
Errigal ∧	48	55.02 N	8.07 W
Errington	224	49.17 N	124.22 W
Erris Head ≻	48	54.19 N	10.00 W
Errochty, Loch ⊜	46	56.45 N	4.12 W
Errogie	46	57.16 N	4.22 W
Errol Heights	224	45.29 N	122.33 W
Ersekë	38	40.20 N	20.41 E
Ershijiazi	104	41.17 N	120.32 E
Ershilipu	105	40.07 N	117.24 E
Ershiqizhan	89	53.23 N	123.16 E
Ershiwuzhan	89	53.22 N	123.55 E
Erskine	198	47.40 N	96.00 W
Erskine, Lake ⊜	276	41.06 N	74.15 W
Erskine Inlet C	176	76.15 N	102.20 W
Erskine Park	274a	33.49 S	150.47 E
Erstein	58	48.26 N	7.40 E
Erstfeld	58	46.49 N	8.39 E
Ertai, Zhg.	86	44.14 N	80.52 E
Ertai, Zhg.	86	46.07 N	90.06 E
Ertaizi, Zhg.	104	42.05 N	123.35 E
Ertaizi, Zhg.	104	42.35 N	124.00 E
Ertaizi, Zhg.	104	41.52 N	121.56 E
Ertaizi, Zhg.	104	40.47 N	120.54 E
Ertil'	78	51.51 N	40.49 E
Ertingen	58	48.06 N	9.28 E
Erto	64	46.16 N	12.22 E
Ertuğrul	130	39.34 N	27.43 E
Ertvelde	50	51.11 N	3.45 E
Erua	172	39.14 S	175.24 E
Eruar	126	23.28 N	87.52 E
Erudina	166	31.28 S	139.23 E
Erundu	156	20.36 S	16.25 E
Erunkan	273a	6.37 N	3.24 E
Erva, Ponta da ≻	266c	38.50 N	8.58 W
Erval	252	32.02 S	53.24 W
Ervalla	40	59.22 N	15.15 E
Erving	207	42.36 N	72.24 W
Ervy-le-Châtel	50	48.02 N	3.55 E
Erwin, N.C., U.S.	192	35.20 N	78.41 W
Erwin, Tenn., U.S.	192	36.09 N	82.25 W
Erwitte	52	51.37 N	8.20 E
Erwood	184	52.50 N	102.10 W
Erxleben	54	52.13 N	11.14 E
Érythrée → Eritrea □[4]	144	15.20 N	39.00 E
Eryuan	102	26.06 N	99.55 E
Erzaohang	106	31.05 N	121.49 E
Erzbach ≃	61	47.36 N	14.44 E
Erzberg ⬩[7]	61	47.32 N	14.54 E
Erzgebirge (Krušné hory) ⩓	54	50.30 N	13.10 E
Erzhan	89	43.58 N	128.44 E
Erzhou I	100	22.00 N	114.11 E
Erzhuang	105	39.24 N	117.22 E
Erzin	88	50.15 N	95.10 E
Erzincan	130	39.44 N	39.29 E
Erzincan □[4]	130	39.40 N	39.30 E
Erzingen	58	47.39 N	8.25 E
Erzurum	130	39.55 N	41.17 E
Erzurum □[4]	130	40.00 N	41.30 E
Esa-Ala	164	9.44 S	150.49 E
Esambo	152	3.40 S	23.24 E
Esan-saki ≻	92a	41.49 N	141.11 E
Esashi, Nihon	92	39.12 N	141.09 E
Esashi, Nihon	92	41.52 N	140.07 E
Esashi, Nihon	92a	44.56 N	142.35 E
Esbiye	130	40.57 N	38.44 E
Esbjerg	26	55.28 N	8.27 E
Esbly	261	48.54 N	2.49 E
Esbo → Espoo	26	60.13 N	24.40 E
Esborn	263	51.23 N	7.20 E
Esca ≃	34	42.37 N	1.03 W
Escada	250	8.22 S	35.14 W
Escalada	258	34.10 S	59.07 W
Escalante, Pil.	116	10.50 N	123.33 E
Escalante, Utah, U.S.	200	37.47 N	111.36 W
Escalante ≃, Utah, U.S.	200	37.17 N	110.53 W
Escalante ≃, Ven.	246	9.15 N	71.50 W
Escalante Desert ⬩[2]	200	37.50 N	113.30 W
Escalaplano	71	39.37 N	9.21 E
Escalón, Méx.	232	26.45 N	104.20 W
Escalon, Calif., U.S.	226	37.48 N	121.00 W
Escalona	34	40.10 N	4.24 W
Escambia ≃	194	30.32 N	87.11 W
Escanaba	190	45.45 N	87.04 W
Escanaba ≃	190	45.47 N	87.04 W
Escanaba, East Branch ≃	190	46.16 N	87.27 W
Escanaba, Middle Branch ≃	190	46.16 N	87.27 W
Escandón, Puerto de)(	34	40.17 N	1.00 W
Escárcega de Matamoros	232	18.37 N	90.43 W
Escarpada Point ≻	116	18.31 N	122.13 E
Escarpado Peak ∧	116	8.36 N	117.22 E
Escatawpa ≃	194	30.25 N	88.35 W
Escaudain	50	50.20 N	3.21 E
Escaut (Schelde) ≃	50	51.22 N	4.15 E
Esch ≃	56	48.54 N	6.04 E
Eschach	58	47.44 N	9.36 E
Eschau	58	48.29 N	7.43 E
Eschebrügge	52	52.37 N	6.46 E
Eschede	52	52.44 N	10.14 E
Eschen	58	47.13 N	9.31 E
Eschenau	60	49.34 N	11.12 E
Eschenbach	60	49.45 N	11.49 E
Eschenlohe	64	47.36 N	11.11 E
Eschershausen	52	51.56 N	9.38 E
Eschlkam	60	49.18 N	12.55 E
Escholzmatt	58	46.55 N	7.56 E
Eschscholtz Bay C	180	66.18 N	161.25 W
Esch-sur-Alzette	56	49.30 N	5.59 E
Esch-sur-Sûre	56	49.55 N	5.55 E
Eschwege	56	51.11 N	10.04 E
Eschweiler	56	50.49 N	6.16 E
Esclave, Grand Lac de l' → Great Slave Lake ⊜	176	61.30 N	114.00 W
Esclavo, Gran Lago del → Great Slave Lake ⊜	176	61.30 N	114.00 W
Escobal	236	9.09 N	79.58 W
Escobar □[5]	288	34.23 S	58.46 W
Escobar, Arroyo ≃	288	34.21 S	58.44 W
Escobedo	196	27.13 N	101.21 W
Escocesa, Bahía C	238	19.25 N	69.45 W
Escoheag	207	41.35 N	71.32 W
Escondido	228	33.07 N	117.05 W
Escondido ≃, Méx.	196	28.39 N	100.34 W
Escondido ≃, Nic.	236	12.04 N	83.45 W
Escondido Canal ≍	228	33.11 N	116.58 W
Escondido Creek ≃	228	33.01 N	117.15 W
Escorial → San Lorenzo de El Escorial	34	40.35 N	4.09 W
Escoutay ≃	62	44.29 N	4.42 E
Escravos ≃[1]	150	5.35 N	5.10 E
Escrick	44	53.53 N	1.02 W
Escuadrón 201 ⬩[8]	286a	19.22 N	99.06 W
Escudero, Arroyo ≃	258	34.20 S	57.05 W
Escudo de Veraguas, Isla I	236	9.06 N	81.33 W
Escuinapa [de Hidalgo]	234	22.51 N	105.48 W
Escuintla, Guat.	236	14.18 N	90.47 W
Escuintla, Méx.	232	15.20 N	92.38 W
Escuintla □[5]	236	14.10 N	91.00 W
Escuminac, Point ≻	186	47.04 N	64.46 W
Escurial, Serra do ∧	250	10.04 S	41.05 W
Esebi	154	2.57 N	30.39 E
Eséka	152	3.39 N	10.46 E
Esenler	267b	41.02 N	28.51 E
Esenli	130	40.41 N	37.24 E
Esens	52	53.39 N	7.37 E
Ésera ≃	34	42.06 N	0.15 E
Esesi	130	39.49 N	39.19 E
Eşfahān (Isfahan)	128	32.40 N	51.38 E
Eşfahān □[4]	128	32.30 N	53.00 E
Esgueva ≃	34	41.40 N	4.43 W
Eshan	102	24.11 N	102.22 E
Esher	260	51.23 N	0.22 W
Eshkāshem	123	36.42 N	71.34 E
Eshowe	158	28.58 S	31.29 E
Esh-Sham → Dimashq	132	33.30 N	36.18 E
Eshta'ol	132	31.47 N	35.00 E
Esiama	150	4.56 N	2.21 W
Esine	64	45.55 N	10.15 E
Esino ≃	66	43.39 N	13.22 E
Esira	157b	24.20 S	46.42 E
Esirgâh	130	39.48 N	38.52 E
Esk	171a	27.15 S	152.25 E
Esk ≃, N.Z.	172	43.06 S	171.57 E
Esk ≃, U.K.	44	54.58 N	3.04 W
Esk ≃, Eng., U.K.	44	54.29 N	0.37 W
Esk ≃, Eng., U.K.	44	54.21 N	3.23 W
Esk ≃, Scot., U.K.	46	55.57 N	3.03 W
Eskdale, N.Z.	172	39.24 S	176.50 E
Eskdale, W. Va., U.S.	188	38.05 N	81.27 W
Eskdale ∨	44	55.10 N	3.00 W
Eski Dzhumaya → Târgovište	38	43.15 N	26.34 E
Eskifjördur	24a	65.04 N	13.59 W
Eskiikan	85	43.12 N	68.31 E
Eskiköy	130	36.36 N	30.34 E
Eskilstrup	41	54.51 N	11.54 E
Eskilstuna	40	59.22 N	16.30 E
Eski Malatya	130	38.26 N	38.23 E
Eskimo Lakes ⊜	180	69.15 N	132.17 W
Eskimo Point	176	61.07 N	94.03 W
Eskipazar	130	40.58 N	32.33 E
Eskişehir	130	39.46 N	30.32 E
Eskişehir □[4]	130	39.35 N	31.10 E
Eskridge	198	38.52 N	96.06 W
Esla ≃	34	41.29 N	6.03 W
Eslām Qal'eh	128	34.40 N	61.04 E
Eslarn	60	49.35 N	12.32 E
Eslohe	56	51.15 N	8.09 E
Eslöv	41	55.50 N	13.20 E
Esmā'īlābād	128	28.48 N	56.39 E
Eşme	130	38.24 N	28.59 E
Esmeralda, Austl.	166	18.50 S	142.34 E
Esmeralda, Cuba	240p	21.51 N	78.07 W
Esmeralda, Méx.	196	25.40 N	103.30 W
Esmeralda, Ven.	246	3.10 N	65.33 W
Esmeralda, Isla I	254	48.57 S	75.25 W
Esmeraldas	246	0.59 N	79.42 W
Esmeraldas □[4]	246	0.40 N	79.30 W
Esmeraldas ≃	246	0.58 N	79.38 W
Esmirna → İzmir	130	38.25 N	27.09 E
Esmond, N. Dak., U.S.	198	48.02 N	99.46 W
Esmond, R.I., U.S.	207	41.53 N	71.30 W
Esnagi Lake ⊜	190	48.38 N	84.32 W
Esneux	56	50.32 N	5.34 E
Esong	152	2.09 N	10.58 E
Esopus Creek ≃	210	42.04 N	73.56 W
Espada, Punta ≻	246	12.05 N	71.07 W
Espagne → Spain □[1]	34	40.00 N	4.00 W
Espalion	32	44.31 N	2.46 E
Espaly-Saint-Marcel	62	45.03 N	3.52 E
España → Spain □[1]	34	40.00 N	4.00 W
Espanola, Ont., Can.	190	46.15 N	81.46 W
Espanola, N. Mex., U.S.	200	36.06 N	106.02 W
Española, Isla I	246a	1.25 S	89.42 W
Esparta	236	9.59 N	84.40 W
Esparto	226	38.42 N	122.01 W
Espasingen	58	47.49 N	9.00 E
Espe, Dan.	41	55.12 N	10.25 E
Espe, S.S.S.R.	85	43.52 N	74.10 E
Espejo	34	37.41 N	4.33 W
Espejo, Canal de ≍	286e	33.32 S	70.43 W
Espelkamp	52	52.25 N	8.36 E
Espenberg, Cape ≻	180	66.33 N	163.36 W
Espenhain	54	51.11 N	12.29 E
Espera, Arroyo ≃[1]	288	34.24 S	58.36 W
Espera Feliz	255	20.39 S	41.55 W
Esperança, Bra.	246	4.24 S	69.52 W
Esperança, Bra.	250	7.01 S	35.51 W
Esperance, Austl.	162	33.51 S	121.53 E
Esperance, N.Y., U.S.	210	42.46 N	74.15 W
Esperance Bay C	162	33.51 S	121.53 E
Esperantina	250	3.54 S	42.14 W
Esperantinópolis	250	4.53 S	44.53 W
Esperanza, Arg.	252	31.27 S	60.56 W
Esperanza, Méx.	232	27.35 N	109.56 W
Esperanza, Méx.	234	18.52 N	97.24 W
Esperanza, Pil.	116	8.43 N	125.36 E
Esperanza, Pil.	116	11.44 N	124.03 E
Esperanza, P.R.	240m	18.06 N	65.28 W
Esperanza, S. Afr.	158	30.21 S	30.40 E
Esperanza Inlet C	182	49.48 N	127.10 W
Espergærde	41	56.00 N	12.34 E
Esperia	66	41.23 N	13.41 E
Esperito, Arroyo ≃[1]	288	34.23 S	58.36 W
Espevær	26	59.36 N	5.10 E
Espichel, Cabo ≻	34	38.25 N	9.13 W
Espinal, Col.	246	4.09 N	74.53 W
Espinal, Méx.	234	16.29 N	95.03 W
Espinar	248	14.47 S	71.29 W
Espinazo	196	26.16 N	101.06 W
Espinazo, Sierra del → Espinhaço, Serra do ⩓	255	17.30 S	43.30 W
Espinazo del Diablo, Sierra ⩓	234	23.55 N	106.00 W
Espingarda ≃	250	10.03 S	47.13 W
Espinhaço, Serra do ⩓	255	17.30 S	43.30 W
Espinho	34	41.00 N	8.39 W
Espinillo	252	24.58 S	58.34 W
Espinillo, Arroyo ≃	258	34.59 S	57.36 W
Espinillo, Punta ≻	258	34.50 S	56.26 W
Espino	246	8.34 N	66.01 W
Espinosa	255	14.56 S	42.50 W
Espinos de Judio	234	19.52 N	104.35 W
Espírito Santo → Vila Velha	250	3.13 N	51.13 W
Espírito Santo □[3]	255	19.30 S	40.30 W
Espírito Santo do Dourado	256	22.03 S	45.58 W
Espíritu Santo I	175f	15.50 S	166.50 E
Espíritu Santo, Bahía del C	232	19.20 N	87.35 W
Espíritu Santo, Isla del I	232	24.30 N	110.22 W
Espita	232	21.01 N	88.19 W
Esplanada	255	11.47 S	37.57 W
Esplugas	266d	41.23 N	2.06 E
Espoir, Bay d' C	186	47.50 N	55.51 W
Espoo (Esbo)	26	60.13 N	24.40 E
Esposende	34	41.32 N	8.47 W
Esposizione Universale di Roma ♣	267a	41.50 N	12.28 E
Espumoso	252	28.44 S	52.51 W
Espungabera	156	20.29 S	32.48 E
Espy	210	41.01 N	76.25 W
Espyville Station	214	41.36 N	80.29 W
Esquatzel Coulee ∨	202	46.17 N	119.07 W
Esquel	254	42.54 S	71.19 W
Esquimalt	182	48.26 N	123.24 W
Esquina	252	30.01 S	59.32 W
Esquina Negra	258	35.02 S	58.03 W
Esquipulas, Guat.	236	14.34 N	89.21 W
Esquipulas, Nic.	236	12.40 N	85.47 W
Esquiú	252	29.23 S	65.17 W
Esrum Sø ⊜	41	56.00 N	12.24 E
Essa ≃	76	54.53 N	28.40 E
Essaoui Mellene, Oued ∨	148	27.26 N	6.40 E
Essaouira (Mogador)	148	31.30 N	9.47 W
Essarts	261	48.30 N	1.46 E
Essé	152	4.05 N	11.53 E
Esse ≃	66	43.16 N	11.54 E
Esseg → Osijek	38	45.33 N	18.41 E
Essel ⬩[8]	263	51.37 N	7.15 E
Essen, Bel.	50	51.28 N	4.28 E
Essen, B.R.D.	52	52.43 N	7.57 E
Essen, B.R.D.	56		
	263	51.28 N	7.01 E
Essenbach	60	48.37 N	12.13 E
Essenberg	263	51.26 N	6.42 E
Essendon, Austl.	169	37.46 S	144.55 E
Essendon, Eng., U.K.	260	51.46 N	0.09 W
Essendon, Mount ∧	162	24.59 S	120.28 E
Essendon Airport ⊠	169	37.43 S	144.53 E
Essen-Mülheim, Flughafen ⊠	263	51.24 N	6.58 E
Essentuki → Jessentuki	84	44.03 N	42.51 E
Essequibo ≃	246	6.59 N	58.23 W
Es Sers	36	36.04 N	9.02 E
Essex, Ont., Can.	214	42.10 N	82.49 W
Essex, Conn., U.S.	207	41.21 N	72.24 W
Essex, Ill., U.S.	216	41.11 N	88.11 W
Essex, Iowa, U.S.	198	40.50 N	95.18 W
Essex, Md., U.S.	208	39.18 N	76.29 W
Essex, Mass., U.S.	207	42.38 N	70.47 W
Essex, Mo., U.S.	194	36.49 N	95.52 W
Essex, Mont., U.S.	182	48.17 N	113.37 W
Essex □[6], Ont., Can.	214	42.10 N	82.50 W
Essex □[6], Eng., U.K.	42	51.48 N	0.40 E
Essex □[6], Mass., U.S.	207	42.31 N	70.55 W
Essex □[6], N.J., U.S.	210	40.48 N	74.12 W
Essex □[6], Vt., U.S.	206	44.57 N	71.43 W
Essex □[6], Va., U.S.	208	37.55 N	76.55 W
Essex ≃	283	42.39 N	70.46 W
Essex Bay C	283	42.39 N	70.44 W
Essex Fells	276	40.50 N	74.17 W
Essex Junction	188	44.29 N	73.07 W
Essex Skypark ⊠	284b	39.18 N	76.28 W
Essexvale	154	20.18 S	28.56 E
Essexville	190	43.37 N	83.50 W
Essig	56	50.40 N	6.54 E
Essing	60	48.56 N	11.47 E
Essington	285	39.52 N	75.18 W
Essling ⬩[8]	264b	48.13 N	16.32 E
Esslingen	56	48.45 N	9.16 E
Es Smala es Souassi	36	35.21 N	10.33 E
Esson Lake ⊜	212	45.02 N	78.16 W
Essonne □[5]	50	48.36 N	2.20 E
Essonne ≃	50	48.37 N	2.29 E
Essoyes	58	48.04 N	4.32 E
Es-Suki	140	13.20 N	33.54 E
Essvik	26	62.19 N	17.24 E
Est □[5]	150	12.00 N	1.00 E
Est ⬩[5]	261	48.53 N	2.22 E
Est, Canal de l' ≍	58	48.45 N	5.35 E
Est, Cap ≻	157b	15.16 S	50.29 E
Est, Île de l' I	186	47.37 N	61.26 W
Est, Pointe de l' ≻	186	49.08 N	61.41 W
Estacada	224	45.17 N	122.20 W
Estaca de Bares, Punta de la ≻	34	43.46 N	7.42 W
Estacado, Llano ≚	196	33.30 N	102.40 W
Estados, Isla de los (Staten Island) I	254	54.47 S	64.15 W
Estados Unidos → United States □[1]	178	38.00 N	97.00 W
Eşţahbānāt	128	29.08 N	54.04 E
Estaires	50	50.38 N	2.43 E
Estambul → İstanbul	130	41.01 N	28.58 E
Estância, Bra.	250	11.16 S	37.26 W
Estancia, Pil.	116	11.28 N	123.09 E
Estancia, S. Afr.	158	26.17 S	29.52 E
Estancia, N. Mex., U.S.	200	34.45 N	106.04 W
Estancia de los López	234	20.53 N	104.31 W
Estandarte	250	1.26 S	45.32 W
Estanislao del Campo	252	25.03 S	60.06 W
Estanzuelas	236	13.38 N	88.30 W
Estarreja	34	40.45 N	8.34 W
Estats, Pique d' ∧	34	42.40 N	1.24 E
Estavayer-le-Lac	58	46.51 N	6.50 E
Estcourt	158	29.01 S	29.52 E
Este	64	45.14 N	11.39 E
Este ≃	52	53.32 N	9.47 E
Este, Parque Nacional del ♣	286c	10.30 N	66.50 W
Este, Punta ≻	240m	18.08 N	65.16 W
Esteban Echeverría	258	34.50 S	58.28 W
Esteban Echeverría □[5]	288	34.51 S	58.32 W
Estefanía, Lago → Stefanie, Lake ⊜	144	4.40 N	36.50 E
Esteio	252	29.51 S	51.10 W
Estelí	236	13.05 N	86.23 W
Estelí □[5]	236	13.10 N	86.20 W
Estella	34	42.40 N	2.02 W
Estelline, S. Dak., U.S.	198	44.35 N	96.54 W
Estelline, Tex., U.S.	196	34.33 N	100.26 W
Estell Manor	208	39.23 N	74.48 W
Estèng	62	44.14 N	6.45 E
Estepa	34	37.18 N	4.54 W
Estepona	34	36.26 N	5.08 W
Ester	180	64.51 N	148.01 W
Esterel ⩓	62	43.30 N	6.50 E
Esterháza ⊥	30	47.37 N	16.53 E
Esterhazy	184	50.40 N	102.08 W
Esterias, Cap ≻	152	0.37 N	9.20 E
Esternay	50	48.44 N	3.34 E
Estero	220	26.26 N	81.49 W
Estero Bay C, Calif., U.S.	226	35.24 N	120.53 W
Estero Bay C, Fla., U.S.	220	26.25 N	81.52 W
Estero Island I	220	26.26 N	81.56 W
Estéron ≃	62	43.49 N	7.11 E
Esteros	252	26.37 S	63.39 W
Esterwegen	52	52.59 N	7.38 E
Estes Park	200	40.23 N	105.31 W
Este Sudeste, Cayos del II	236	12.26 N	81.27 W
Estevan	184	49.07 N	103.05 W
Estevan Group II	182	53.05 N	129.40 W

ENGLISH

Name	Page	Lat.°′	Long.°′
Estevan Point	182	49.23 N	126.33 W
Esther Island I	180	60.50 N	148.05 W
Estherville	198	43.24 N	94.50 W
Estí ≃	236	8.28 N	82.16 W
Estill	192	32.45 N	81.14 W
Estissac	50	48.16 N	3.49 E
Estiva	256	22.28 S	46.02 W
Estiva, Ribeirão da ≃	287b	23.44 S	46.23 W
Estling, Lake ⊜	276	40.53 N	74.30 W
Estocolmo → Stockholm	40	59.20 N	18.03 E
Eston, Sask., Can.	184	51.10 N	108.46 W
Eston, Eng., U.K.	44	54.34 N	1.07 W
Estonian Soviet Socialist Republic → Estonskaja Sovetskaja Socialističeskaja Respublika □[3]	76	59.00 N	26.00 E
Estonskaja Sovetskaja Socialističeskaja Respublika □[3]	76	59.00 N	26.00 E
Estoril	266c	38.42 N	9.23 W
Estrasburgo → Strasbourg	58	48.35 N	7.45 E
Estrées-Saint-Denis	50	49.26 N	2.39 E
Estrêla	252	29.29 S	51.58 W
Estrela ∧	34	40.19 N	7.37 W
Estrêla ≃	287a	22.43 S	43.13 W
Estrela, Serra da ⩓	34	40.20 N	7.38 W
Estrêla do Indaiá	255	19.31 S	45.47 W
Estrêla do Leste	255	16.17 S	53.34 W
Estrêla do Norte	255	13.49 S	49.04 W
Estrêla do Sul	255	18.46 S	47.42 W
Estrella ≃	226	35.45 N	120.41 W
Estrella, Cerro de la ∧	286a	19.20 N	99.05 W
Estrella, Punta ≻	232	30.55 N	114.43 W
Estremadura □[9]	34	39.15 N	9.10 W
Estremoz	34	38.51 N	7.35 W
Estrondo, Serra do ⩓[1]	250	9.00 S	48.45 W
Estuaire □[4]	152	0.10 S	10.00 E
Estuary	184	50.56 N	109.46 W
Esumba, Île I	152	2.00 N	21.12 E
Eszék → Osijek	38	45.33 N	18.41 E
Esztergom	30	47.48 N	18.45 E
Étables	32	48.38 N	2.50 W
Etadunna	166	28.43 S	138.38 E
Etah, Bhārat	124	27.38 N	78.40 E
Etah, Grn.	16	78.19 N	72.38 W
Etah □[5]	124	27.40 N	78.50 E
Étain	56	49.13 N	5.38 E
Etajima	96	34.15 N	132.30 E
Eta-jima I	96	34.15 N	132.28 E
Étalle	56	49.41 N	5.36 E
Étampes	50	48.26 N	2.09 E
Etamunbanie, Lake ⊜	166	26.15 S	139.44 E
Étaples	50	50.31 N	1.39 E
États-Unis → United States □[1]	178	38.00 N	97.00 W
Etāwah, Bhārat	124	25.32 N	76.22 E
Etāwah, Bhārat	124	26.46 N	79.02 E
Etāwah □[5]	124	26.40 N	79.20 E
Etchemin ≃	186	46.46 N	71.14 W
Etchojoa	232	26.55 N	109.38 W
Etchoropo	232	26.41 N	109.40 W
Etéké	152	1.29 S	11.35 E
Etembue	152	1.17 N	9.25 E
Eten	248	6.54 S	79.52 W
Etendard, Pic de l' ∧	62	45.09 N	6.09 E
Eternity Range ⩓	9	69.46 S	64.34 W
Ethan	198	43.33 N	103.59 W
Ethel	194	33.07 N	89.34 W
Ethel ≃	162	24.09 S	118.26 E
Ethelbert	184	51.31 N	100.22 W
Ethel Creek	162	22.54 S	120.09 E
Ethel Lake ⊜	180	63.21 N	136.00 W
Etherow ≃	262	53.24 N	2.03 W
Ethiopia □[1]	136		
	144	9.00 N	39.00 E
Ethiopie → Ethiopia □[1]	144	9.00 N	39.00 E
Ethnikón Mousíon ♉	267c	37.59 N	23.44 E
Ethridge, Mont., U.S.	182	48.34 N	112.07 W
Ethridge, Tenn., U.S.	194	35.19 N	87.18 W
Eticoga	150	11.09 N	16.08 W
Eticuera Creek ≃	226	38.41 N	122.16 W
Etili	130	39.59 N	26.54 E
Etimesğut	130	39.57 N	32.40 E
Étiolles	261	48.38 N	2.29 E
Etiopía → Ethiopia □[1]	144	9.00 N	39.00 E
Etive, Loch ⊜	46	56.29 N	5.09 W
Etiwanda	228	34.08 N	117.31 W
Etjo ∧	156	21.09 S	16.30 E
Etna, Calif., U.S.	204	41.27 N	122.54 W
Etna, N.Y., U.S.	210	42.29 N	76.23 W
Etna, Pa., U.S.	214	40.30 N	79.57 W
Etna, Wyo., U.S.	200	43.02 N	111.00 W
Etna, Monte (Mongibello) ∧	70	37.50 N	14.55 E
Etna Green	216	41.17 N	86.03 W
Etne	26	59.40 N	5.56 E
Etobicoke	212	43.39 N	79.34 W
Etobicoke Creek ≃	212	43.35 N	79.32 W
Etoile	154	11.38 S	27.34 E
Étoile, Chaîne de l' ⩓	62	43.22 N	5.30 E
Etoka	152	0.10 N	23.23 E
Etolin Island I	180	56.08 N	132.26 W
Etolin Strait Џ	180	60.20 N	165.15 W
Etomami ≃	184	52.48 N	102.33 W
Eton, Austl.	166	21.16 S	148.58 E
Eton, Eng., U.K.	260	51.31 N	0.37 W
Eton College ♉[2]	260	51.30 N	0.36 W
Etondo	152	7.46 S	23.36 E
Etonia Creek ≃	192	29.42 N	81.39 W
Etorofu-tō → Iturup, Ostrov I	92a	44.54 N	147.30 E
Etosha National Park ⬩[4]	156	18.45 S	15.00 E
Etoshapan ≚	156	18.45 S	16.15 E
Etoumbi	152	0.01 S	14.57 E
Etowah	192	35.20 N	84.32 W
Etowah ≃	192	34.15 N	85.11 W
Étréchy	50	48.30 N	2.12 E
Étrépagny	50	49.18 N	1.37 E
Étretat	50	49.42 N	0.12 E
Etrotroka	157b	22.53 S	47.36 E
Etroubles	62	45.49 N	7.14 E
Etsch → Adige ≃	64	45.10 N	12.20 E
Eţ Ţaiyiba	132	32.16 N	35.01 E
Ettal	64	47.34 N	11.05 E
Ettalong	170	33.31 S	151.21 E
Ettelbruck	56	49.52 N	6.05 E
Ettenheim	58	48.15 N	7.49 E
Etten-Leur	52	51.34 N	4.38 E
Etterbeek	50	50.50 N	4.23 E
Etters	208	40.09 N	76.45 W
Ettington	42	52.09 N	1.36 W
Eţ Ţīra	132	32.14 N	34.57 E
Ettlingen	56	48.56 N	8.24 E
Ettrema Creek ≃	170	34.50 S	150.22 E
Ettrick	208	37.14 N	77.25 W
Ettrick Forest ⬩[3]	46	55.30 N	3.00 W
Ettrick Pen ∧	44	55.22 N	3.16 W
Ettrick Water ≃	46	55.31 N	2.55 W
Ettringen, B.R.D.	56	50.21 N	7.13 E
Ettringen, B.R.D.	58	48.06 N	10.39 E
Etuku	154	3.43 S	25.44 E
Etuokeqi	102	39.08 N	108.00 E

DEUTSCH

Name	Seite	Breite°′	Länge°′ E=Ost
Etyka	88	51.00 N	116.50 E
Etzatlán	234	20.46 N	104.05 W
Etzikom Coulee ≃	184	49.25 N	111.10 W
Etzná-Tixmucuy ⊥	232	19.35 N	90.15 W
Eu	50	50.03 N	1.25 E
Eua I	14	21.22 S	174.56 W
Eua Iki I	174w	21.07 S	174.59 W
Eubank Acres	222	30.23 N	97.42 W
Eubanque	256	21.33 S	43.30 W
Euboea → Évvoia I	38	38.34 N	23.50 E
Eucalyptus Hills	228	32.56 N	116.56 W
Euchiniko ≃	182	53.20 N	123.50 W
Eucla	162	31.43 S	128.52 E
Euclid, Ohio, U.S.	214	41.34 N	81.32 W
Euclid, Pa., U.S.	214	41.00 N	79.56 W
Euclid Center	216	42.08 N	86.24 W
Euclid Creek ≃	279a	41.35 N	81.35 W
Euclid Creek Reservation ♣	279a	41.33 N	81.32 W
Euclides da Cunha	250	10.31 S	39.01 W
Eucumbene	171b	36.07 S	148.38 E
Eucumbene ≃	171b	36.21 S	148.38 E
Eucumbene, Lake ⊜[1]	171b	36.05 S	148.45 E
Eucumbene Dam ⬩[5]	171b	36.07 S	148.40 E
Eudistes, Lac des ⊜	186	50.30 N	65.15 W
Eudora, Ark., U.S.	194	33.07 N	91.16 W
Eudora, Kans., U.S.	198	38.57 N	95.06 W
Eudunda	168b	34.11 S	139.04 E
Eufaula, Ala., U.S.	194	31.54 N	85.09 W
Eufaula, Okla., U.S.	196	35.17 N	95.35 W
Eufaula Lake ⊜[1]	196	35.17 N	95.31 W
Eufrates → Euphrates ≃	128	31.00 N	47.25 E
Euganei, Colli ⩓[2]	64	45.19 N	11.40 E
Eugendorf	64	47.52 N	13.07 E
Eugene	202	44.02 N	123.05 W
Eugenia, Punta ≻	232	27.50 N	115.05 W
Eugenia Lake ⊜	212	44.20 N	80.30 W
Eugenio Bustos	252	33.46 S	69.04 W
Eugênio de Melo	256	23.09 S	45.47 W
Eugenópolis	255	21.06 S	42.11 W
Eugmo I	26	63.49 N	22.45 E
Eugowra	166	33.26 S	148.23 E
Euijeongbu → Ŭijŏngbu	98	37.44 N	127.03 E
Euless	222	32.50 N	97.05 W
Eulo	166	28.10 S	145.03 E
Eulogio Sánchez Errázuriz, Aeropuerto ⊠	286e	33.27 S	70.33 W
Eume ≃	34	43.25 N	8.08 W
Eumemmerring Creek ≃	274b	38.03 S	145.10 E
Eumungerie	166	31.57 S	148.37 E
Eungela National Park ♣	166	21.00 S	148.30 E
Eunice, La., U.S.	194	30.30 N	92.25 W
Eunice, N. Mex., U.S.	196	32.26 N	103.09 W
Eupen	56	50.38 N	6.02 E
Euphrat → Euphrates ≃	128	31.00 N	47.25 E
Euphrates (Fırat) (Al-Furāt) ≃	128	31.00 N	47.25 E
Eupora	194	33.32 N	89.16 W
Eure	208	36.26 N	76.51 W
Eure □[5]	50	49.10 N	1.00 E
Eure ≃	50	49.18 N	1.12 E
Eure-et-Loir □[5]	50	48.30 N	1.30 E
Eureka, Alaska, U.S.	180	65.11 N	150.13 W
Eureka, Calif., U.S.	204	40.47 N	124.09 W
Eureka, Ill., U.S.	190	40.43 N	89.16 W
Eureka, Kans., U.S.	198	37.49 N	96.17 W
Eureka, Mo., U.S.	219	38.30 N	90.38 W
Eureka, Mont., U.S.	202	48.53 N	115.03 W
Eureka, Nev., U.S.	204	39.31 N	115.58 W
Eureka, Pa., U.S.	214	40.15 N	78.46 W
Eureka, Pa., U.S.	285	40.15 N	75.11 W
Eureka, S. Dak., U.S.	198	45.46 N	99.38 W
Eureka, Tex., U.S.	222	32.01 N	96.18 W
Eureka, Utah, U.S.	200	39.57 N	112.07 W
Eureka, Mount ∧	162	26.34 S	121.32 E
Eureka Springs	194	36.24 N	93.44 W
Eurialo, Castello ⊥	70	37.06 N	15.14 E
Eurinilla Creek ≃	166	30.50 S	140.01 E
Euroa	169	36.45 S	145.35 E
Europa, Île I	138	22.20 S	40.22 E
Europa, Picos de ⩓	34	43.12 N	4.48 W
Europabrücke ⬩[5]	64	47.11 N	11.23 E
Europa Point ≻	34	36.10 N	5.22 W
Europe ⚲[1]	4	50.00 N	28.00 E
Europe ⚲[1]	10	50.00 N	20.00 E
Europoort ⬩[5]	52	51.58 N	4.00 E
Eursinge	52	52.46 N	6.28 E
Eurville	58	48.35 N	5.02 E
Euseigne	58	46.10 N	7.25 E
Euskirchen	56	50.39 N	6.47 E
Eustace	222	32.18 N	96.01 W
Eustis, Fla., U.S.	220	28.51 N	81.41 W
Eustis, Nebr., U.S.	198	40.40 N	100.02 W
Eustis, Lake ⊜	220	28.50 N	81.44 W
Euston	166	34.35 S	142.44 E
Euston Station ⬩[5]	260	51.32 N	0.08 W
Eutaw	194	32.50 N	87.53 W
Eutin	54	54.08 N	10.37 E
Eutingen	56	48.28 N	8.44 E
Eutsuk Lake ⊜	182	53.20 N	126.44 W
Eutzsch	54	51.49 N	12.38 E
Euxton	262	53.40 N	2.41 W
Euzet-les-Bains	62	44.04 N	4.14 E
Eva	194	34.20 N	86.46 W
Evadale	194	30.21 N	94.04 W
Eva Downs	162	18.01 S	134.52 E
Evale	152	16.33 S	15.44 E
Evällen ⊜	40	60.03 N	18.20 E
Evançon ≃	62	45.40 N	7.41 E
Evandale	166	41.34 S	147.14 E
Evans, Lac ⊜	176	50.55 N	77.00 W
Evans, Mount ∧	200	39.35 N	105.38 W
Evansburg, Alta., Can.	182	53.36 N	115.01 W
Evansburg, Pa., U.S.	285	40.11 N	75.26 W
Evans Center	210	42.39 N	79.02 W
Evans City	214	40.45 N	80.03 W
Evans Creek ≃	202	42.25 N	123.11 W
Evansdale	190	42.30 N	92.17 W
Evans Head ≻	166	29.07 S	153.26 E
Evans Mills	212	44.05 N	75.48 W
Evansport	216	41.25 N	84.24 W
Evans Strait Џ	176	63.15 N	82.00 W
Evanston, Ill., U.S.	216	42.03 N	87.42 W
Evanston, Pa., U.S.	279b	40.16 N	79.41 W
Evanston, Wyo., U.S.	200	41.16 N	110.58 W
Evansville, Ill., U.S.	194	38.05 N	89.56 W
Evansville, Ind., U.S.	194	37.58 N	87.35 W
Evansville, Wis., U.S.	216	42.47 N	89.18 W
Evansville, Wyo., U.S.	200	42.52 N	106.16 W
Evant	196	31.29 N	98.09 W
Evanton	46	57.40 N	4.20 W
Eva Perón → La Plata	258	34.55 S	57.57 W
Evart	190	43.54 N	85.08 W
Evarts	192	36.52 N	83.12 W
Evaton	158	26.31 S	27.54 E
Evaz	128	27.46 N	53.59 E
Ève	261	49.05 N	2.42 E
Evecquemont	261	49.02 N	1.57 E
Eveking	263	51.14 N	7.44 E
Eveleth	190	47.28 N	92.32 W
Evelyn, Mount ∧[2]	164	13.36 S	132.53 E
Evening Shade	194	36.04 N	91.37 W
Evenkamp	263	51.40 N	7.39 E
Evenkijskij Nacionalnyj Okrug □[8]	88	59.15 N	104.00 E
Evenlode ≃	42	51.47 N	1.21 W
Evensk	74	61.57 N	159.14 E
Even Yehuda	132	32.16 N	34.53 E
Everard, Lake ⊜	162	31.25 S	135.05 E

Symbols in the index entries represent the broad categories identified in the key at the right. Symbols with superior numbers (⩓[2]) identify subcategories (see complete key on page *I* · *30*).

Kartensymbole in dem Registerverzeichnis stellen die rechts in Schlüssel erklärten Kategorien dar. Symbole mit hochgestellten Ziffern (⩓[2]) bezeichnen Unterabteilungen einer Kategorie (vgl. vollständiger Schlüssel auf Seite *I* · *30*).

Los símbolos incluídos en el texto del índice representan las grandes categorias identificadas con la clave a la derecha. Los símbolos con numeros en su parte superior (⩓[2]) identifican las subcategorías (véase la clave completa en la página *I* · *30*).

Les symboles de l'index représentent les catégories indiquées dans la légende à droite. Les symboles suivis d'un indice (⩓[2]) représentent des sous-catégories (voir légende complète à la page *I* · *30*).

Os símbolos incluídos no texto do índice representam as grandes categorias identificadas com a chave à direita. Os símbolos com números em sua parte superior (⩓[2]) identificam as subcategorias (veja-se a chave completa à página *I* · *30*).

Symbol	English	Deutsch	Español	Français	Português
∧	Mountain	Berg	Montaña	Montagne	Montanha
⩓	Mountains	Berge	Montañas	Montagnes	Montanhas
)(	Pass	Pass	Paso	Col	Passo
∨	Valley, Canyon	Tal, Cañon	Valle, Cañón	Vallée, Canyon	Vale, Canhão
≚	Plain	Ebene	Llano	Plaine	Planície
≻	Cape	Kap	Cabo	Cap	Cabo
I	Island	Insel	Isla	Île	Ilha
II	Islands	Inseln	Islas	Îles	Ilhas
⚲	Other Topographic Features	Andere Topographische Objekte	Otros Elementos Topográficos	Autres données topographiques	Outros Elementos Topográficos

ESPAÑOL — Nombre, Página, Lat.°′, Long.°′ W=Oeste · FRANÇAIS — Nom, Page, Lat.°′, Long.°′ W=Ouest · PORTUGUÊS — Nome, Página, Lat.°′, Long.°′ W=Oeste

Everard, Mount ⋀, Austl. 162 26.16 S 132.04 E
Everard, Mount ⋀, B.C., Can. 182 51.05 N 125.45 W
Everard Ranges ⋀ 162 27.05 S 132.28 E
Evercreech 42 51.09 N 2.30 W
Evere 56 50.52 N 4.24 E
Everek 128 38.23 N 35.30 E
Everest 198 39.41 N 95.26 W
Everest, Mount (Zhumulangmafeng) ⋀ 124 27.59 N 86.56 E
Everett, Ont., Can. 212 44.11 N 79.57 W
Everett, Mass., U.S. 207 42.24 N 71.03 W
Everett, N.J., U.S. 276 40.21 N 74.09 W
Everett, Pa., U.S. 188 40.01 N 78.23 W
Everett, Wash., U.S. 224 47.59 N 122.13 W
Everett, Mount ⋀ 207 42.06 N 73.25 W
Everett Mountains ⋀ 176 62.45 N 67.12 W
Evergem 50 51.07 N 3.42 E
Everglades City 220 25.52 N 81.23 W
Everglades National Park ♠ 220 25.27 N 80.53 W
Evergreen, Ala., U.S. 194 31.26 N 86.57 W
Evergreen, Calif., U.S. 204 35.54 N 120.26 W
Evergreen, Mont., U.S. 202 48.13 N 114.18 W
Evergreen, Tex., U.S. 222 30.33 N 95.14 W
Evergreen Lake ⊜[1] 216 40.40 N 89.02 W
Evergreen Park 216 41.43 N 87.42 W
Evergreen Plaza ✈[9] 278 41.43 N 87.41 W
Everly 198 43.10 N 95.20 W
Everman 222 32.38 N 97.17 W
Everöd 26 55.54 N 14.06 E
Eversael 263 51.33 N 6.39 E
Eversberg 56 51.21 N 8.20 E
Everse 52 52.45 N 10.02 E
Everson, Pa., U.S. 214 40.06 N 79.35 W
Everson, Wash., U.S. 224 48.55 N 122.21 W
Everswinkel 52 51.55 N 7.50 E
Everton 218 39.34 N 85.05 W
Everton ✈[8] 262 53.25 N 2.58 W
Everton Football Ground ♠ 262 53.26 N 2.58 W
Evesen 52 52.17 N 8.59 E
Evesham, Sask., Can. 184 52.24 N 109.50 W
Evesham, Eng., U.K. 42 52.06 N 1.56 W
Evesham, Vale of ⋁ 42 52.06 N 1.50 W
Évian-les-Bains 58 46.23 N 6.35 E
Evijärvi 26 63.22 N 23.29 E
Evinayong 152 1.27 N 10.34 E
Eving ✈[8] 263 51.33 N 7.29 E
Evingsen 263 51.18 N 7.44 E
Evionnaz 58 46.11 N 7.01 E
Evisa 36 42.15 N 8.47 E
Evje 26 58.36 N 7.51 E
Evolène 58 46.07 N 7.30 E
Évora 34 38.34 N 7.54 W
Evoron, Ozero ⊜ 89 51.28 N 136.30 E
Evpatorija → Jevpatorija 78 45.12 N 33.22 E
Évrange 56 49.30 N 6.12 E
Évreux 50 49.01 N 1.09 E
Évrieu 62 45.35 N 5.34 E
'Evron 132 32.59 N 35.06 E
Évros (Marica) (Meriç) ≃ 38 40.52 N 26.12 E
Evrótas ≃ 38 36.48 N 22.40 E
Évry 50 48.38 N 2.27 E
Évry-les-Châteaux 261 48.39 N 2.38 E
Evungu 154 4.27 S 25.12 E
Évvoia I 38 38.34 N 23.50 E
Évzonos ⋀ 267c 37.57 N 23.49 E
Ewa 229c 21.21 N 158.02 W
Ewa Beach 229c 21.20 N 158.04 W
Ewan 285 39.42 N 75.11 W
Ewaninga 162 23.58 S 133.58 E
Ewan Lake ⊜ 285 39.42 N 75.11 W
Ewansville 285 39.59 N 74.44 W
Ewarton 241q 18.11 N 77.05 W
Ewbank 158 26.14 S 23.35 E
Ewe, Loch C 46 57.48 N 5.40 W
Ewell, Eng., U.K. 260 51.21 N 0.15 W
Ewell, Md., U.S. 208 37.59 N 76.02 W
Ewen 190 46.32 N 89.17 W
Ewersbach 56 50.50 N 8.19 E
Ewes Water ≃ 44 55.08 N 3.00 W
Ewing, Ky., U.S. 218 38.26 N 83.52 W
Ewing, Mo., U.S. 219 40.00 N 91.43 W
Ewing, Nebr., U.S. 198 42.16 N 98.21 W
Ewing, Va., U.S. 192 36.38 N 83.26 W
Ewingsville 279b 40.24 N 80.06 W
Ewing Township 208 40.16 N 74.44 W
Ewo 152 0.53 S 14.49 E
Ewu 273a 6.33 N 3.19 E
Exaltación 248 13.16 S 65.15 W
Excelda 158 32.16 S 22.08 E
Excello 218 39.29 N 84.25 W
Excelsior 158 28.56 S 27.06 E
Excelsior Mountain ⋀ 226 38.02 N 119.18 W
Excelsior Park ♠ 274a 33.45 S 151.01 E
Excelsior Springs 194 39.20 N 94.13 W
Excenevex 58 46.21 N 6.21 E
Exchange 210 41.07 N 76.41 W
Exchange Station ✈[5] 262 53.29 N 2.15 W
Excursion Inlet 180 58.25 N 135.27 W
Exe ≃ 42 50.37 N 3.25 W
Executive Committee Range ⋀ 9 76.50 S 126.00 W
Exeter, Austl. 170 34.38 S 150.19 E
Exeter, Ont., Can. 190 43.21 N 81.29 W
Exeter, Eng., U.K. 42 50.43 N 3.31 W
Exeter, Calif., U.S. 226 36.18 N 119.09 W
Exeter, Nebr., U.S. 198 40.39 N 97.27 W
Exeter, N.H., U.S. 188 42.59 N 70.57 W
Exeter, Pa., U.S. 210 41.20 N 75.49 W
Exeter, R.I., U.S. 207 41.35 N 71.32 W
Exeter ≃ 188 43.02 N 70.55 W
Exeter Sound 𝕌 176 66.14 N 62.00 W
Exford 42 51.08 N 3.38 W
Exhibition Park ♠ 275b 43.38 N 79.25 W
Exhibition Stadium ♠ 275b 43.38 N 79.25 W
Exincourt 58 47.30 N 6.50 E
Exing 60 48.38 N 12.37 E
Exira 198 41.35 N 94.52 W
Exline Slough ≃ 216 41.05 N 87.47 W
Exloërmond 52 52.54 N 6.57 E
Exmes 50 48.46 N 0.11 E
Exminster 42 50.41 N 3.29 W
Exmoor ✈[3] 42 51.10 N 3.45 W
Exmoor National Park ♠ 42 51.12 N 3.46 W
Exmore 208 37.32 N 75.50 W
Exmouth 42 50.37 N 3.25 W
Exmouth Gulf C 162 22.23 S 114.07 E
Exmouth Gulf C 162 22.00 S 114.20 E
Expedition Range ⋀ 166 24.30 S 149.05 E
Experiment 192 33.16 N 84.17 W
Exploits ≃ 186 49.05 N 55.20 W
Exploits, Bay of C 186 49.24 N 55.00 W
Exploits Dam ✈[6] 186 48.45 N 56.30 W
Export 214 40.25 N 79.37 W
Exshaw 182 51.03 N 115.09 W
Extension 224 49.06 N 123.57 W
Exter 52 52.08 N 8.46 E
Externsteine ⊥ 52 51.52 N 8.55 E
Extertal 52 52.04 N 9.07 E
Exton 208 40.02 N 75.37 W
Extorás ≃ 234 21.06 N 99.23 W
Extrema 256 22.51 S 46.19 W
Extremadura □[9] 34 39.00 N 6.00 W
Exu 250 7.31 S 39.43 W
Exuma Sound 𝕌 238 24.15 N 76.00 W
Eyak 180 60.32 N 145.36 W
Eyam 44 53.17 N 1.41 W
Eyasi, Lake ⊜ 154 3.40 S 35.05 E
Eydehavn 26 58.31 N 8.53 E
Eye, Eng., U.K. 42 52.19 N 1.09 E
Eye, Eng., U.K. 42 52.35 N 0.10 W
Eyebrow 184 50.47 N 106.09 W
Eyemouth 46 55.52 N 2.06 W
Eye Peninsula ⋟[1] 46 58.13 N 6.13 W
Eyers Grove 210 41.05 N 76.31 W
Eye Water ≃ 46 55.53 N 2.06 W
Eygalières 62 43.45 N 4.57 E
Eyguières 62 43.42 N 5.02 E
Eyhorne Street 260 51.16 N 0.38 E
Eyjafjörður C[2] 24a 65.54 N 18.15 W
Eylar Mountain ⋀ 204 37.28 N 121.33 W
Eymet 32 44.40 N 0.24 E
Eymir 130 40.02 N 35.14 E
Eymoutiers 32 45.44 N 1.44 E
Eynhallow Sound 𝕌 46 59.08 N 3.06 W
Eynort, Loch C 46 57.13 N 7.18 W
Eynsford 260 51.22 N 0.13 E
Eynsham 42 51.48 N 1.22 W
Eyota 190 43.59 N 92.14 W
Eyrarbakki 24a 63.53 N 21.05 W
Eyre 162 32.15 S 126.18 E
Eyrecourt 48 53.11 N 8.07 W
Eyre Creek ≃ 166 26.40 S 139.00 E
Eyre Mountains ⋀ 172 45.20 S 168.30 E
Eyre North, Lake ⊜ 166 28.40 S 137.10 E
Eyre Peninsula ⋟[1] 162 34.00 S 135.45 E
Eyre South, Lake ⊜ 166 29.30 S 137.20 E
Eyrieux ≃ 62 44.48 N 4.48 E
Eystrup 52 52.46 N 9.13 E
Eythorne 42 51.11 N 1.17 E
Eythra 54 51.14 N 12.17 E
Eyüp ✈[8] 267b 41.03 N 28.55 E
Eyvānakī 128 35.20 N 52.04 E
Ezanville 261 49.02 N 2.22 E
Ezbekīyah ✈[8] 273c 30.03 N 31.15 E
Eze 62 43.43 N 7.22 E
Ezeiza 258 34.51 S 58.32 W
Ezeiza, Aeropuerto Internacional de ⊠ 288 34.49 S 58.32 W
Ezere 76 56.26 N 22.22 E
Ežerėlis 76 54.53 N 23.37 E
Ezeriș 38 45.24 N 21.53 E
Ezine 130 39.47 N 26.20 E
Ezinepazarı 130 40.34 N 36.09 E
Ezop, Chrebet ⋀ 89 52.56 N 133.37 E
Ezpeleta 258 34.46 S 58.15 W
Ezva 24 61.47 N 50.40 E
Ézy-sur-Eure 50 48.52 N 1.25 E
Ezzell 222 29.17 N 96.58 W

F

Faaa Airport ⊠ 174s 17.33 S 149.36 W
Faaone 174s 17.40 S 149.18 W
Fabala 150 9.44 N 9.05 W
Fabbrico 64 44.52 N 10.50 E
Fabens 200 31.30 N 106.10 W
Fåberg 26 61.10 N 10.24 E
Faber Lake ⊜ 176 63.56 N 117.15 W
Fabert Shoal ✈[2] 14 24.30 S 158.05 W
Fabius 210 42.50 N 75.59 W
Fåborg 41 55.06 N 10.15 E
Fábrega, Cerro ⋀ 236 9.07 N 82.52 W
Fabrègues 62 43.33 N 3.46 E
Fabreville ✈[8] 275a 45.34 N 73.50 W
Fabriano 66 43.20 N 12.54 E
Fabrica 116 10.54 N 123.23 E
Fabrica di Roma 66 42.20 N 12.18 E
Fabričnyj 85 43.11 N 76.24 E
Fabrizia 68 38.29 N 16.18 E
Facatativá 246 4.49 N 74.22 W
Facha 146 29.27 N 17.18 E
Faches-Thumesnil 50 50.35 N 3.04 E
Fachi 146 18.06 N 11.34 E
Facpi Point ⋟ 174p 13.20 N 144.38 E
Factoryville 210 41.34 N 75.47 W
Facundo 254 45.18 S 69.58 W
Fada 146 17.14 N 21.33 E
Fada, Lochan ⊜ 46 57.41 N 5.18 W
Fadalto 64 46.05 N 12.20 E
Fada Ngourma 150 12.04 N 0.21 E
Fadd 40 46.28 N 18.50 E
Faddeja, Zaliv C 74 76.40 N 107.20 E
Faddejevskij, Ostrov I 74 75.30 N 144.00 E
Faddoi 140 8.07 N 32.07 E
Fadian Point ⋟ 174p 13.26 N 144.49 E
Fadiffolu Atoll I[1] 122 5.25 N 73.30 E
Fadit 140 9.58 N 32.13 E
Faedis 64 46.10 N 13.20 E
Faenø I 41 55.29 N 9.42 E
Faenza 66 44.17 N 11.53 E
Faeroe Islands □[2] 22 62.00 N 7.00 W
Faerøerne → Faeroe Islands □[2] 22 62.00 N 7.00 W
Faete, Monte ⋀ 267a 41.45 N 12.44 E
Fafa 150 15.20 N 0.43 E
Fafadur 144 2.11 N 41.32 E
Fafakourou 150 13.04 N 14.34 W
Fafalog 174p 13.37 N 144.51 E
Fafe 34 41.27 N 8.10 W
Fafen ≃ 144 6.07 N 44.20 E
Faga ≃ 150 13.15 N 0.55 E
Fagaitua 174u 14.16 S 170.37 W
Fagaloa Bay C 175a 13.54 S 171.28 W
Fagamalo 175a 13.25 S 172.21 W
Făgăraș 38 45.51 N 24.58 E
Făgăraș, Munții ⋀ 38 45.35 N 25.00 E
Fagasa 174u 14.17 S 170.43 W
Fagel 42 54.27 N 9.31 E
Fagernes 26 60.59 N 9.15 E
Fagersta 40 60.00 N 15.47 E
Fagertärn ✈[4] 40 58.46 N 14.42 E
Fagerviken 40 60.33 N 17.45 E
Fāget 38 45.51 N 22.10 E
Faggen Bach ≃ 64 47.05 N 10.40 E
Faggo 150 11.23 N 9.57 E
Fagnano, Lago ⊜ 254 54.35 S 68.00 W
Fagnano Castello 68 39.34 N 16.03 E
Fagnano Olona 62 45.40 N 8.52 E
Fagnières 50 48.58 N 4.19 E
Faguibine, Lac ⊜ 150 16.45 N 3.54 W
Fagundes ≃ 256 22.12 S 43.11 W
Fagurhólsmýri 24a 63.54 N 16.38 W
Fagwir 140 9.33 N 30.25 E
Fahan 48 55.05 N 7.28 W
Fahl, Oued el ⋁ 148 31.15 N 4.41 E
Fahraj 128 28.58 N 58.52 E
Fährdorf 54 53.58 N 11.28 E
Fahrland 54 52.28 N 13.01 E
Fahrländer See ⊜ 264a 52.27 N 13.01 E
Fahrn → Varna 64 46.44 N 11.38 E
Fahrnau 58 47.39 N 7.50 E
Fahuaqiao 106 30.52 N 121.25 E
Faial I 148a 38.34 N 28.42 W
Fā'id 142 30.19 N 32.19 E
Fā'id Military Base ■ 142 30.20 N 32.16 E
Faido 58 46.29 N 8.48 E
Faillon, Lac ⊜ 190 48.21 N 76.38 W
Failsworth 262 53.31 N 2.09 W
Fains-les-Sources 56 48.47 N 5.08 E
Fairbairn Park ♠ 274b 37.47 S 144.55 E
Fairbank 190 42.38 N 92.03 W
Fairbanks, Alaska, U.S. 180 64.51 N 147.43 W
Fairbanks, La., U.S. 194 30.00 N 92.02 W
Fair Bluff 192 34.19 N 79.02 W
Fairborn 218 39.49 N 84.02 W
Fairbourne 42 52.41 N 4.03 W
Fairburn 192 33.34 N 84.35 W
Fairbury, Ill., U.S. 216 40.45 N 88.31 W
Fairbury, Nebr., U.S. 198 40.08 N 97.11 W
Fairchance 188 39.49 N 79.45 W
Fairchild 190 44.36 N 90.58 W
Fairchild Air Force Base ■ 202 47.38 N 117.38 W
Fairchild Creek ≃ 212 43.07 N 80.07 W
Fairdale 216 42.06 N 88.56 W
Faire 116 17.53 N 121.34 E
Fairfax, Ala., U.S. 194 32.48 N 85.11 W
Fairfax, Calif., U.S. 226 37.59 N 122.35 W
Fairfax, Del., U.S. 285 39.47 N 75.32 W
Fairfax, Minn., U.S. 198 44.32 N 94.31 W
Fairfax, Okla., U.S. 196 36.34 N 96.42 W
Fairfax, S.C., U.S. 192 33.01 N 81.18 W
Fairfax, S. Dak., U.S. 198 43.02 N 98.54 W
Fairfax, Vt., U.S. 188 44.40 N 73.01 W
Fairfax, Va., U.S. 208 38.51 N 77.18 W
Fairfax □[6] 208 38.45 N 77.15 W
Fairfax State Recreation Area ♠ 218 39.02 N 86.29 W
Fairfax Station 284c 38.48 N 77.20 W
Fairfield, Austl. 170 33.52 S 150.57 E
Fairfield, Ala., U.S. 194 33.29 N 86.55 W
Fairfield, Calif., U.S. 226 38.15 N 122.03 W
Fairfield, Conn., U.S. 210 41.09 N 73.15 W
Fairfield, Idaho, U.S. 202 43.21 N 114.48 W
Fairfield, Ill., U.S. 194 38.23 N 88.22 W
Fairfield, Iowa, U.S. 190 40.56 N 91.57 W
Fairfield, Maine, U.S. 188 44.35 N 69.36 W
Fairfield, Mont., U.S. 202 47.37 N 111.59 W
Fairfield, Nebr., U.S. 198 40.26 N 98.06 W
Fairfield, N.J., U.S. 276 40.53 N 74.17 W
Fairfield, N.Y., U.S. 210 43.08 N 74.55 W
Fairfield, Ohio, U.S. 218 39.20 N 84.33 W
Fairfield, Pa., U.S. 214 39.47 N 77.22 W
Fairfield, Tex., U.S. 222 31.44 N 96.10 W
Fairfield □[6] 207 41.11 N 73.11 W
Fairfield University ✈[2] 276 41.09 N 73.15 W
Fairford 42 51.44 N 1.47 W
Fairgrove 190 43.31 N 83.33 W
Fair Harbor 210 40.38 N 73.11 W
Fairhaven, Mass., U.S. 207 41.39 N 70.54 W
Fair Haven, Mich., U.S. 214 42.41 N 82.39 W
Fair Haven, N.J., U.S. 208 40.23 N 74.03 W
Fair Haven, N.Y., U.S. 210 43.19 N 76.42 W
Fairhaven, Ohio, U.S. 218 39.38 N 84.47 W
Fair Haven, Vt., U.S. 188 43.36 N 73.16 W
Fairhaven, Va., U.S. 284c 38.47 N 77.05 W
Fairhaven Bay ⊜ 283 42.26 N 71.21 W
Fair Head ⋟ 48 55.13 N 6.09 W
Fairhope, Ala., U.S. 194 30.31 N 87.54 W
Fairhope, Ohio, U.S. 214 40.51 N 81.19 W
Fairhope, Pa., U.S. 214 40.07 N 79.50 W
Fair Isle I 46 59.32 N 1.39 W
Fairland, Ind., U.S. 218 39.35 N 85.52 W
Fairland, Md., U.S. 284c 39.05 N 76.58 W
Fairland, Okla., U.S. 196 36.45 N 94.51 W
Fairlane Town ✈[9] 281 42.19 N 83.13 W
Fair Lawn, N.J., U.S. 210 40.56 N 74.07 W
Fairlawn, Ohio, U.S. 214 41.08 N 81.36 W
Fairlee 284c 38.52 N 77.16 W
Fairleigh Dickinson University ✈[2], N.J., U.S. 276 40.50 N 74.07 W
Fairleigh Dickinson University (Teaneck) ✈[2], N.J., U.S. 276 40.53 N 74.02 W
Fairleigh Dickinson University (Madison) ✈[2], N.J., U.S. 276 40.46 N 74.26 W
Fairless Hills 208 40.11 N 74.50 W
Fairlie, N.Z. 172 44.06 S 170.50 E
Fairlie, Scot., U.K. 46 55.46 N 4.51 W
Fairlight 42 50.53 N 0.40 E
Fairmont, Ill., U.S. 216 41.34 N 88.04 W
Fairmont, Minn., U.S. 198 43.39 N 94.28 W
Fairmont, Nebr., U.S. 198 40.38 N 97.35 W
Fairmont, N.C., U.S. 192 34.30 N 79.07 W
Fairmont, Pa., U.S. 279b 40.29 N 79.54 W
Fairmont, Wash., U.S. 224 48.54 N 122.16 W
Fairmont, W. Va., U.S. 188 39.29 N 80.09 W
Fairmont City 219 38.40 N 90.06 W
Fairmont Hot Springs 182 50.19 N 115.53 W
Fairmont Reservoir ⊜[1] 228 34.43 N 118.26 W
Fairmont Terrace 282 37.43 N 122.07 W
Fairmount, Ga., U.S. 192 34.26 N 84.42 W
Fairmount, Ill., U.S. 194 40.03 N 87.56 W
Fairmount, Ind., U.S. 216 40.25 N 85.39 W
Fairmount, N. Dak., U.S. 198 46.03 N 96.36 W
Fairmount, N.Y., U.S. 210 43.04 N 76.15 W
Fairmount City 214 41.01 N 79.19 W
Fairmount Heights 208 38.54 N 76.55 W
Fairmount Park ♠ 285 40.00 N 75.12 W
Fair Ness ⋟ 176 63.24 N 72.05 W
Fair Oaks, Calif., U.S. 226 38.39 N 121.16 W
Fair Oaks, Ga., U.S. 192 33.55 N 84.32 W
Fair Oaks, Ind., U.S. 216 41.05 N 87.15 W
Fair Oaks, Pa., U.S. 279b 40.35 N 80.13 W
Fairoaks Airport ⊠ 260 51.21 N 0.32 W
Fair Plain 216 42.05 N 86.28 W
Fairplay 200 39.19 N 105.60 W
Fairpoint 214 40.07 N 80.56 W
Fairport, Ont., Can. 275b 43.49 N 79.05 W
Fairport, N.Y., U.S. 210 43.06 N 77.27 W
Fairport Beach 275b 43.48 N 79.06 W
Fairport Harbor 214 41.45 N 81.17 W
Fairseat 260 51.20 N 0.20 E
Fairton 208 39.23 N 75.13 W
Fairview, Austl. 164 15.33 S 144.19 E
Fairview, Alta., Can. 182 56.04 N 118.23 W
Fairview, Ga., U.S. 192 34.58 N 85.16 W
Fairview, Ill., U.S. 190 40.38 N 90.10 W
Fairview, Ind., U.S. 216 40.18 N 85.11 W
Fairview, Kans., U.S. 198 39.50 N 95.44 W
Fairview, Md., U.S. 208 39.09 N 76.29 W
Fairview, Mich., U.S. 190 44.44 N 84.03 W
Fairview, Mont., U.S. 198 47.51 N 104.03 W
Fairview, N.J., U.S. 276 40.49 N 74.00 W
Fairview, N.J., U.S. 285 39.53 N 74.49 W
Fairview, N.Y., U.S. 210 41.44 N 73.56 W
Fairview, N.Y., U.S. 276 41.03 N 73.48 W
Fairview, Ohio, U.S. 214 40.03 N 81.14 W
Fairview, Okla., U.S. 196 36.16 N 98.29 W
Fairview, Pa., U.S. 214 41.01 N 79.44 W
Fairview, Pa., U.S. 214 42.03 N 80.15 W
Fairview, Tenn., U.S. 194 35.59 N 87.07 W
Fairview, Utah, U.S. 200 39.38 N 111.26 W
Fairview, W. Va., U.S. 188 39.36 N 80.15 W
Fairview Heights 219 38.36 N 90.00 W
Fairview Lanes 214 41.23 N 82.40 W
Fairview Mall ✈[9] 275b 43.47 N 79.21 W
Fairview Park, Ind., U.S. 194 39.41 N 87.25 W
Fairview Park, Ohio, U.S. 214 41.27 N 81.51 W
Fairview Park, Pa., U.S. 214 41.10 N 75.53 W
Fairview Peak ⋀, Nev., U.S. 204 39.14 N 118.08 W
Fairview Peak ⋀, Oreg., U.S. 202 43.35 N 122.39 W
Fairview Pointe Claire Centre ✈[9] 275a 45.28 N 73.50 W
Fairview Shores 220 28.36 N 81.23 W
Fairview Village 285 40.10 N 75.23 W
Fairvilla 220 28.35 N 81.24 W
Fairville 285 39.51 N 75.38 W
Fairweather, Mount ⋀ 180 58.54 N 137.32 W
Fairy Lake ⊜ 212 45.20 N 79.11 W
Fairy Meadow 170 34.23 S 150.54 E
Fairy Stone State Park ♠ 192 36.48 N 80.06 W
Fairy Water ≃ 48 54.37 N 7.20 W
Fais I 108 9.46 N 140.31 E
Faison 192 35.07 N 78.08 W
Faistós ⊥ 38 35.01 N 24.48 E
Faith 198 45.02 N 102.02 W
Faiyum → Al-Fayyūm 142 29.19 N 30.50 E
Faizābād 124 26.47 N 82.08 E
Faizābād □[5] 124 26.30 N 82.30 E
Fajansovyj 76 54.04 N 34.24 E
Fajardo 240m 18.20 N 65.39 W
Fajou, Îlet à I 241o 16.21 N 61.35 W
Fajr, Wādī ⋁ 128 30.06 N 38.18 E
Fajzabad 85 38.34 N 69.19 E
Fak 130 37.51 N 39.05 E
Fakahatchee Strand ≡ 220 25.59 N 81.25 W
Fakaofo I[1] 14 9.22 S 171.14 W
Fakarava I[1] 14 16.20 S 145.37 W
Fakejev 80 48.57 N 49.56 E
Fakel 80 57.38 N 53.02 E
Fakenham 42 52.50 N 0.51 E
Fakfak 116 2.55 S 132.18 E
Fakılı 130 39.13 N 35.00 E
Fakirganj 124 25.58 N 90.02 E
Fakī Ṣādiq 140 12.08 N 23.55 E
Fakrinkotti 140 18.01 N 31.20 E
Fakse 41 55.15 N 12.08 E
Fakse Bugt C 41 55.10 N 12.15 E
Fakse Ladeplads 41 55.13 N 12.11 E
Faku 104 42.30 N 123.24 E
Fal ≃ 42 50.08 N 5.02 W
Falaba 150 9.51 N 11.19 W
Faladyé 150 13.08 N 8.20 W
Falaise 32 48.54 N 0.12 W
Falākāta 124 26.32 N 89.12 E
Falalu I 14 7.38 N 151.41 E
Falam 110 22.55 N 93.40 E
Falāvarjān 128 32.33 N 51.30 E
Falcade 64 46.21 N 11.51 E
Falcão 256 22.17 S 44.16 W
Falciu 38 46.18 N 28.08 E
Falck 56 49.14 N 6.38 E
Falcognana di Sotto ✈[8] 267a 41.45 N 12.33 E
Falcón □[3] 246 11.00 N 69.50 W
Falcon, Cap ⋟ 148 35.46 N 0.48 W
Falcon, Cape ⋟ 224 45.46 N 123.59 W
Falconara Albanese 68 39.16 N 16.05 E
Falconara Alta 66 43.37 N 13.24 E
Falconara Marittima 66 43.37 N 13.24 E
Falconbridge 190 46.35 N 80.48 W
Falcone 70 38.07 N 15.05 E
Falcone, Capo di ⋟ 71 40.58 N 8.12 E
Falconer 214 42.07 N 79.12 W
Falcon Heights 202 42.08 N 121.45 W
Falcon Reservoir (Presa Falcón) ⊜[1] 196 26.37 N 99.11 W
Falconwood 210 43.00 N 78.57 W
Faldsled 41 55.09 N 10.09 E
Faléa 150 12.16 N 11.17 W
Faleasao 174y 14.13 S 169.32 W
Falelima 175a 13.32 S 172.41 W
Falémé ≃ 150 14.46 N 12.14 W
Falenki 80 58.22 N 51.35 E
Falerii Novi ⊥ 66 42.16 N 12.20 E
Falerna 68 39.00 N 16.10 E
Falerone 66 43.06 N 13.28 E
Faleşty 78 47.34 N 27.43 E
Falevai 175a 13.55 S 171.59 W
Falfurrias 196 27.14 N 98.09 W
Falher 182 55.44 N 117.12 W
Falicon 62 43.45 N 7.17 E
Fálirou, Órmos C 267c 37.56 N 23.40 E
Falkenau 54 50.51 N 13.07 E
Falkenberg, B.R.D. 60 48.28 N 12.43 E
Falkenberg, B.R.D. 60 49.52 N 12.14 E
Falkenberg, D.D.R. 54 52.48 N 13.58 E
Falkenberg, D.D.R. 54 51.35 N 13.14 E
Falkenberg → Niemodlin, Pol. 30 50.39 N 17.37 E
Falkenberg, Sve. 26 56.54 N 12.28 E
Falkenberg ✈[8] 264a 52.34 N 13.33 E
Falkenburg → Złocieniec 30 53.33 N 16.01 E
Falkenhagen, D.D.R. 54 53.12 N 12.12 E
Falkenhagen, D.D.R. 54 52.26 N 14.19 E
Falkenhagener See ⊜ 264a 52.34 N 13.08 E
Falkenrehde 264a 52.30 N 12.56 E
Falkensee 54 52.33 N 13.04 E
Falkenstein, B.R.D. 60 49.06 N 12.30 E
Falkenstein, D.D.R. 54 50.29 N 12.22 E
Falkenthal 54 52.54 N 13.17 E
Falkirk 46 56.00 N 3.48 W
Falkland, B.C., Can. 182 50.30 N 119.33 W
Falkland, Scot., U.K. 46 56.15 N 3.12 W
Falkland-Inseln → Falkland Islands (Islas Malvinas) □[2] 254 51.45 S 59.00 W
Falkland Islands □[2] 254 51.45 S 59.00 W
Falkland Plateau ✈[3] 4 52.00 S 50.00 W
Falkland Sound 𝕌 254 51.45 S 59.25 W
Falköping 26 58.10 N 13.31 E
Fall ≃, Ont., Can. 212 44.59 N 76.22 W
Fall ≃, Kans., U.S. 198 37.24 N 95.40 W
Fall ≃, Wash., U.S. 224 46.47 N 123.30 W
Falla 40 58.41 N 15.45 E
Fallais 56 50.37 N 5.10 E
Fallbrook 228 33.23 N 117.15 W
Fallbrook Square ✈[9] 280 34.12 N 118.38 W
Fall City 224 47.34 N 121.53 W
Fall Creek 190 44.46 N 91.17 W
Fall Creek ≃, Ind., U.S. 218 39.47 N 86.11 W
Fall Creek ≃, N.Y., U.S. 210 42.28 N 76.31 W
Fallen Jerusalem I 240m 18.25 N 64.27 W
Fallen Leaf 226 38.53 N 120.04 W
Fallen Leaf Reservoir ⊜[1] 226 38.54 N 120.03 W
Fallentimber 214 40.41 N 78.30 W
Fallentimber Creek ≃ 182 51.45 N 114.59 W
Fallen Timbers State Memorial ⊥ 216 41.33 N 83.42 W
Fallersleben 54 52.25 N 10.43 E
Falling ≃ 192 37.01 N 78.55 W
Fallingbostel 52 52.52 N 9.41 E
Falling Creek ≃ 208 37.26 N 77.26 W
Falling Water ≃ 194 36.02 N 85.47 W
Fallon, Mont., U.S. 198 46.50 N 105.07 W
Fallon, Nev., U.S. 204 39.28 N 118.47 W
Fall River, Kans., U.S. 198 37.36 N 96.02 W
Fall River, Mass., U.S. 207 41.43 N 71.08 W
Fall River, Wis., U.S. 190 43.23 N 89.03 W
Fall River Lake ⊜[1] 198 37.42 N 96.08 W
Fall River Mills 204 41.00 N 121.26 W
Falls 210 41.28 N 75.52 W
Falls □[6] 222 31.17 N 96.55 W
Fallsburg 210 41.44 N 74.36 W
Falls Church 208 38.53 N 77.11 W
Falls City, Nebr., U.S. 198 40.03 N 95.36 W
Falls City, Oreg., U.S. 202 44.52 N 123.26 W
Falls Creek, Austl. 170 34.59 S 150.35 E
Falls Creek, Pa., U.S. 214 41.09 N 78.48 W
Falls Creek ≃ 226 37.57 N 119.46 W
Fallsington 285 40.12 N 74.49 W
Falls Pond ⊜ 283 41.58 N 71.20 W
Falls Run ≃ 284b 39.22 N 76.52 W
Fallston 208 39.31 N 76.25 W
Falls Village 207 41.57 N 73.22 W
Falmouth, Antig. 240f 17.01 N 61.47 W
Falmouth, Jam. 241q 18.30 N 77.39 W
Falmouth, Eng., U.K. 42 50.08 N 5.04 W
Falmouth, Ky., U.S. 218 38.40 N 84.20 W
Falmouth, Maine, U.S. 188 43.39 N 70.16 W
Falmouth, Mass., U.S. 207 41.34 N 70.38 W
Falmouth, Va., U.S. 208 38.19 N 77.28 W
Falmouth Bay C 42 50.07 N 3.36 W
Falmouth Heights 207 41.33 N 70.36 W
Falsa Chipana, Punta ⋟ 248 21.20 S 70.06 W
False Cape ⋟, Fla., U.S. 220 28.35 N 80.34 W
False Cape ⋟, Va., U.S. 208 36.39 N 76.51 W
False Divi Point ⋟ 122 15.43 N 80.49 E
False Ducks Islands II 212 43.57 N 76.49 W
False Pass 180 54.52 N 163.24 W
Falset 34 41.08 N 0.49 E
Falsino ≃ 250 0.56 N 51.35 W
Fal'šivyj Gelendžik 78 44.31 N 38.09 E
Falso, Cabo ⋟, Hond. 236 15.12 N 83.20 W
Falso, Cabo ⋟, Rep. Dom. 238 17.47 N 71.41 W
Falso Cabo de Hornos ⋟ 254 55.43 S 68.05 W
Falster I 41 54.48 N 11.58 E
Falsterbo 41 55.24 N 12.50 E
Falsterbokanalen ≅ 41 55.24 N 12.56 E
Falstone 44 55.11 N 2.25 W
Falta 126 22.17 N 88.07 E
Falterona, Monte ⋀ 66 43.52 N 11.42 E
Fălticeni 38 47.28 N 26.18 E
Falun, Sve. 40 60.36 N 15.38 E
Falun, Zhg. 107 29.58 N 104.29 E
Falzarego, Passo di ⋊ 64 46.31 N 12.00 E
Fam, Kepulauan II 164 0.40 S 130.15 E
Fama, Ouadi ⋁ 146 15.22 N 20.34 E
Famadas 266d 41.21 N 2.05 E
Famagusta → Ammókhostos 130 35.07 N 33.57 E
Famaillá 252 27.03 S 65.24 W
Famatina 252 28.55 S 67.31 W
Famatina, Sierra de ⋀ 252 29.00 S 67.51 W
Fambach 54 50.44 N 10.22 E
Fameck 56 49.18 N 6.07 E
Famenne □[9] 56 50.10 N 5.15 E
Familleureux 50 50.31 N 4.12 E
Family Lake ⊜ 184 51.54 N 95.30 W
Fana 150 12.47 N 6.57 W
Fanaco, Lago ⊜ 70 37.39 N 13.33 E
Fanad Head ⋟ 48 55.16 N 7.38 W
Fanado ≃ 255 17.10 S 42.40 W
Fanambana 157b 13.34 S 50.00 E
Fanan I 175c 7.11 N 151.59 E
Fanano 64 44.12 N 10.47 E
Fanārah 142 30.17 N 32.21 E
Fanchang 100 31.07 N 118.12 E
Fanch'eng → Xiangfan 102 32.03 N 112.01 E
Fancher, Ill., U.S. 219 39.16 N 88.47 W
Fancher, N.Y., U.S. 210 43.15 N 66.06 W
Fancy 241h 13.22 N 61.11 W
Fancy Creek ≃ 198 39.28 N 96.45 W
Fancy Prairie 219 39.59 N 89.36 W
Fandango Creek ≃ 196 26.58 N 99.09 W
Fandriana 157b 20.14 S 47.23 E
Fane ≃ 48 53.56 N 6.23 W
Fanepura 123 31.29 N 72.54 E
Faneroménis, Moní ✈[1] 267c 37.59 N 23.26 E
Fang 110 19.55 N 99.13 E
Fangaga ⋀ 144 17.30 N 38.01 E
Fangak 140 9.04 N 30.53 E
Fangbian 106 31.42 N 119.06 E
Fangcheng, Zhg. 100 33.16 N 112.59 E
Fangcheng, Zhg. 102 21.49 N 108.22 E
Fangcheng, Zhg. 105 39.16 N 115.08 E
Fangcun, Zhg. 100 29.04 N 118.36 E
Fangcun, Zhg. 100 27.01 N 118.06 E
Fangcunkou 100 26.50 N 118.15 E
Fängersee ⊜ 264a 52.35 N 13.50 E
Fangguan 105 39.20 N 115.58 E
Fanghe ≃ 98 35.05 N 118.24 E
Fangji 100 31.54 N 115.35 E
Fangjiachang 107 30.05 N 104.16 E
Fangjiazhuang 106 30.45 N 119.53 E
Fangliao 100 22.22 N 120.35 E
Fangmujie 98 42.34 N 124.34 E
Fangniu 102 27.40 N 100.25 E
Fangshan, T'aiwan 100 22.16 N 120.39 E
Fangshan, Zhg. 98 39.42 N 115.58 E
Fangshan ≃ 106 31.40 N 119.16 E
Fangshan ⋀[2] 106 31.29 N 119.09 E
Fangshanzhen 104 41.54 N 122.05 E
Fangshen 104 42.02 N 124.04 E
Fangshengpu 107 30.20 N 104.54 E
Fangtai 105 39.20 N 116.13 E
Fangtang 100 28.23 N 114.38 E
Fangxian 102 32.02 N 110.45 E
Fangxianqiao 106 32.00 N 119.44 E
Fangzheng 89 45.50 N 128.50 E
Fangzi 98 36.36 N 119.07 E
Fanhe ≃ 104 42.16 N 123.40 E
Fanhões 266c 38.53 N 9.09 W
Fanipol' 76 53.45 N 27.20 E
Fanjakana 157b 21.10 S 46.53 E
Fanjiadai 106 32.04 N 120.15 E
Fanjiadian 104 41.41 N 121.50 E
Fanjiatun 89 43.43 N 125.06 E
Fanjiazhen 106 36.14 N 117.01 E
Fanjiazhuang 105 39.50 N 116.27 E
Fannaråken ⋀ 26 61.31 N 7.55 E
Fannettsburg 214 40.04 N 77.50 W
Fannich, Loch ⊜ 46 57.38 N 5.00 W
Fanning Island I[1] 14 3.52 N 159.20 W
Fanrem 63 63.16 N 9.50 E
Fanny, Mount ⋀ 202 45.18 N 117.36 W
Fanny Bay 182 49.30 N 124.50 W
Fano 66 43.50 N 13.01 E
Fanø I 26 55.25 N 8.25 E
Fanqiao 100 28.48 N 121.10 E
Fans, Col des ⋊ 62 44.56 N 4.47 E
Fanshan 100 32.40 N 119.42 E
Fanshanbao 105 40.13 N 115.25 E
Fanshang 100 31.40 N 120.01 E
Fanshawe Lake ⊜ 212 43.05 N 81.10 W
Fansher Creek ≃ 214 42.37 N 82.01 W
Fanshui 100 33.07 N 119.25 E
Fan-si-pan ⋀ 110 22.15 N 103.46 E
Fanthyttan 40 59.40 N 15.06 E
Fanwood 276 40.37 N 74.25 W
Fanxian 98 35.57 N 115.38 E
Faoileann, Bàgh nam C 46 56.23 N 7.17 W
Faqīrah, Wādī ⋁ 142 28.52 N 30.57 E
Faqqū'ah 132 32.30 N 35.24 E
Faqūs 142 30.44 N 31.48 E
Fara I 175e 8.06 S 159.35 E
Farab 85 39.14 N 67.28 E
Faraday, Mount ⋀ 172 42.02 S 171.34 E
Faraday Seamount Group ✈[3] 10 49.00 N 28.00 W
Faradje 154 3.44 N 29.43 E
Farafangana 157b 22.49 S 47.50 E
Farāh 128 32.22 N 62.07 E
Farāh □[4] 128 33.00 N 62.30 E
Farāh ≃ 128 31.29 N 61.24 E
Farahābād 267d 35.47 N 51.27 E
Farahalana 157b 14.26 S 50.10 E
Farā'id, Jabal al- ⋀ 140 23.31 N 35.20 E
Fara in Sabina 66 42.12 N 12.43 E
Farallon de Medinilla I 108 16.01 N 146.04 E
Farallon de Pajaros I 108 20.32 N 144.54 E
Farallon Island II 204 37.43 N 123.03 W
Faramana 150 12.03 N 4.40 W
Faranah 150 10.02 N 10.44 W
Faranah □[4] 150 10.00 N 10.50 W
Fara Novarese 62 45.33 N 8.27 E
Faras, Qārat al- ⋀[2] 142 29.35 N 30.58 E
Farasān, Jazā'ir II 144 16.48 N 41.54 E
Farasān al-Kabīr I 144 16.42 N 42.00 E
Faratsiho 157b 19.24 S 46.57 E
Faraulep I[1] 108 8.36 N 144.33 E
Farazād 267d 35.47 N 51.21 E
Farber 219 39.17 N 91.34 W
Farbovano 78 50.09 N 31.51 E
Farcăul ⋀ 38 47.56 N 24.27 E
Farchant 64 47.32 N 11.06 E
Farcy 261 48.31 N 2.37 E
Fardes ≃ 34 37.35 N 3.00 W
Fare ≃ 50 47.39 N 0.14 E
Fareara, Pointe ⋟ 174s 17.52 S 149.39 W
Fareham 42 50.51 N 1.10 W
Fårevejle 41 55.48 N 11.27 E
Farewell 180 62.31 N 153.53 W
Farewell, Cape ⋟ 172 40.30 S 172.41 E
Farewell Spit ⋟[2] 172 40.31 S 172.52 E
Färgelanda 26 58.34 N 11.59 E
Fargniers 50 49.39 N 3.19 E
Fargo 198 46.52 N 96.48 W
Far Hills 276 40.41 N 74.38 W
Faria ≃ 287a 22.53 S 43.15 W
Fāri'ah, Wādī al- ⋁ 132 32.06 N 35.31 E
Faribault 190 44.18 N 93.16 W
Faribault, Lac ⊜ 176 59.00 N 72.00 W
Farīdābād 124 28.26 N 77.19 E
Farīdganj 126 23.08 N 90.45 E
Farīdkot 123 30.40 N 74.45 E
Farīdnagar 124 28.46 N 77.37 E
Farīdpur, Bhārat 124 28.13 N 79.33 E
Farīdpur, Bngl. 124 24.10 N 89.26 E
Farīdpur, Bngl. 126 23.36 N 89.50 E
Farīdpur Station 126 24.10 N 89.10 E
Farié Haoussa 150 13.48 N 1.38 E
Fārigh, Wādī al- ⋁ 146 29.00 N 21.11 E
Färila 26 61.48 N 15.51 E
Farilhão Point ⋟ 156 22.15 S 14.15 E
Farilhões II 34 39.28 N 9.34 W
Farim 150 12.27 N 15.17 W
Farīmān 128 35.43 N 59.53 E
Farina 219 38.50 N 88.46 W
Faringdon 42 51.40 N 1.35 W
Farington 262 53.43 N 2.42 W
Farinha ≃ 250 6.51 S 47.30 W
Farini d'Olmo 62 44.43 N 9.34 E
Fariš 85 40.35 N 66.52 E
Fariske 130 36.37 N 32.38 E
Fāriskūr 142 31.20 N 31.43 E
Färjestaden 26 56.39 N 16.27 E
Farkwa 154 5.24 S 35.36 E
Farleigh 260 51.19 N 0.02 W
Farley 190 42.27 N 91.00 W
Farley Green 260 51.12 N 0.29 W
Farmahīn 128 34.30 N 49.41 E
Farmer City 216 40.15 N 88.39 W
Farmers Branch 222 32.56 N 96.53 W
Farmersburg 194 39.15 N 87.23 W
Farmers Fork 208 38.02 N 76.45 W
Farmers Retreat 218 38.58 N 85.06 W
Farmersville, Calif., U.S. 226 36.18 N 119.12 W
Farmersville, Ill., U.S. 219 39.26 N 89.39 W
Farmersville, Pa., U.S. 208 40.08 N 76.10 W
Farmersville, Tex., U.S. 222 33.10 N 96.22 W
Farmersville Station 210 42.26 N 78.22 W
Farmerville 194 32.47 N 92.24 W
Farmingdale 208 40.12 N 74.10 W
Farmington, Calif., U.S. 226 37.56 N 120.59 W
Farmington, Conn., U.S. 207 41.43 N 72.50 W
Farmington, Del., U.S. 208 38.52 N 75.35 W
Farmington, Ill., U.S. 190 40.42 N 90.00 W
Farmington, Iowa, U.S. 190 40.38 N 91.44 W
Farmington, Maine, U.S. 188 44.40 N 70.09 W
Farmington, Mich., U.S. 216 42.28 N 83.22 W
Farmington, Minn., U.S. 190 44.38 N 93.08 W
Farmington, Mo., U.S. 194 37.47 N 90.25 W
Farmington, N.H., U.S. 188 43.24 N 71.04 W
Farmington, N. Mex., U.S. 200 36.44 N 108.12 W
Farmington, Utah, U.S. 200 40.59 N 111.53 W
Farmington ≃ 207 41.51 N 72.38 W
Farmington, West Branch ≃ 207 41.52 N 72.57 W
Farmington Hills 281 42.28 N 83.23 W
Farmington Reservoir ⊜[1] 226 37.55 N 120.55 W
Farmingville 210 40.39 N 73.02 W
Farmland 218 40.11 N 85.08 W
Far Mountain ⋀ 182 52.46 N 125.17 W
Farm Pond ⊜, Mass., U.S. 283 42.14 N 71.21 W
Farm Pond ⊜, Mass., U.S. 283 42.17 N 71.26 W
Farmville, N.C., U.S. 192 35.36 N 77.35 W
Farmville, Va., U.S. 192 37.18 N 78.24 W
Färna 40 59.47 N 15.51 E
Farnam 198 40.42 N 100.13 W
Farnawā 142 30.58 N 30.34 E
Farnborough 42 51.17 N 0.46 W
Farnborough ✈[8] 260 51.21 N 0.04 E
Farncombe 260 51.12 N 0.36 W
Färnebofjärden ⊜ 40 60.14 N 16.47 E
Farne Islands II 44 55.38 N 1.38 W
Farnham, Qué., Can. 206 45.17 N 72.59 W
Farnham, Eng., U.K. 42 51.13 N 0.49 W
Farnham, N.Y., U.S. 214 42.36 N 79.05 W
Farnham, Va., U.S. 208 37.53 N 76.38 W
Farnham, Mount ⋀ 182 50.29 N 116.30 W
Farnham Common 260 51.33 N 0.37 W
Farnham Royal 260 51.32 N 0.37 W
Farnhamville 198 42.17 N 94.24 W
Farningham 260 51.23 N 0.13 E
Farnroda 54 50.56 N 10.23 E
Farnworth 262 53.33 N 2.24 W
Faro, Bra. 250 2.11 S 56.44 W
Faro, Port. 34 37.01 N 7.56 W
Faro ≃ 146 9.21 N 12.55 E
Faro, Punta ⋟ 246 11.07 N 74.51 W
Faro, Punta del ⋟ 70 38.16 N 15.39 E
Färöer → Faeroe Islands □[2] 22 62.00 N 7.00 W
Fårön I 26 57.56 N 19.08 E
Fårösund 26 57.52 N 19.03 E
Farquhar, Cape ⋟ 162 23.37 S 113.37 E
Farquhar Group II 138 10.10 S 51.10 E
Farr 46 57.21 N 4.12 W
Farra d'Isonzo 64 45.56 N 12.31 E
Farragut 198 40.43 N 95.29 W
Farragut State Recreation Area ♠ 202 47.55 N 116.35 W
Farrandsville 210 41.10 N 77.31 W
Farrar ≃ 46 57.24 N 4.50 W
Farrar Pond ⊜ 283 42.25 N 71.21 W
Farrars Creek ≃ 166 25.35 S 140.43 E
Farrāshband 128 28.53 N 52.06 E
Farrell 214 41.13 N 80.30 W
Farrell Flat 168b 33.50 S 138.47 E
Farrer Park ♠ 271c 1.19 N 103.51 E
Farrington Lake ⊜ 276 40.26 N 74.28 W
Farrington Lake Heights 276 40.26 N 74.27 W
Far Rockaway ✈[8] 276 40.36 N 73.45 W
Farrukhābād 124 27.24 N 79.34 E
Farrukhābād □[5] 124 27.15 N 79.35 E
Farrukhnagar, Bhārat 124 28.27 N 76.49 E
Farrukhnagar, Bhārat 272a 28.43 N 77.23 E
Fārs □[4] 128 29.00 N 53.00 E
Fársala 38 39.18 N 22.23 E
Farschviller 56 49.06 N 6.54 E
Farsī 128 33.47 N 63.15 E
Farsīs 142 30.40 N 31.14 E

≃ River — Fluss — Río — Rivière — Rio
≅ Canal — Kanal — Canal — Canal — Canal
⌊ Waterfall, Rapids — Wasserfall, Stromschnellen — Cascada, Rápidos — Chute d'eau, Rapides — Cascata, Rápidos
𝕌 Strait — Meeresstrasse — Estrecho — Détroit — Estreito
C Bay, Gulf — Bucht, Golf — Bahía, Golfo — Baie, Golfe — Baía, Golfo
⊜ Lake, Lakes — See, Seen — Lago, Lagos — Lac, Lacs — Lago, Lagos
≡ Swamp — Sumpf — Pantano — Marais — Pântano
⊓ Ice Features, Glacier — Eis- und Gletscherformen — Accidentes Glaciales — Formes glaciaires — Acidentes Glaciares
✈ Other Hydrographic Features — Andere Hydrographische Objekte — Otros Elementos Hidrográficos — Autres données hydrographiques — Outros Elementos Hidrográficos

✈ Submarine Features — Untermeerische Objekte — Accidentes Submarinos — Formes de relief sous-marin — Acidentes Submarinos
□ Political Unit — Politische Einheit — Unidad Política — Entité politique — Unidade Política
✈ Cultural Institution — Kulturelle Institution — Institución Cultural — Institution culturelle — Instituição Cultural
⊥ Historical Site — Historische Stätte — Sitio Histórico — Site historique — Sítio Histórico
♠ Recreational Site — Erholungs- und Ferienort — Sitio de Recreo — Centre de loisirs — Sítio de Lazer
⊠ Airport — Flughafen — Aeropuerto — Aéroport — Aeroporto
■ Military Installation — Militäranlage — Instalación Militar — Installation militaire — Instalação Militar
✈ Miscellaneous — Verschiedenes — Misceláneo — Divers — Miscelânea

ENGLISH (Name, Page, Lat.°′, Long.°′) — DEUTSCH (Name, Seite, Breite°′, Länge°′ E=Ost)

Name	Page	Lat.°′	Long.°′
Farsø	26	56.47 N	9.21 E
Farsta	40	59.14 N	18.04 E
Farsund	26	58.05 N	6.48 E
Fartak, Ra's >	118	15.38 N	52.15 E
Fartura, Rio da ≃	256	21.37 S	46.55 W
Farukolu I	122	6.12 N	73.16 E
Farum	41	55.48 N	12.22 E
Fårvang	41	56.16 N	9.44 E
Farvel, Kap >	16	59.45 N	44.00 W
Farwell, Mich., U.S.	190	43.50 N	84.52 W
Farwell, Tex., U.S.	196	34.23 N	103.02 W
Fāryāb □[4]	128	36.00 N	65.00 E
Fasā	128	28.56 N	53.42 E
Fasano	68	40.50 N	17.22 E
Faščovka	83	48.16 N	38.37 E
Fashkhah, 'Ayn ⫪[4]	132	31.43 N	35.27 E
Fåsjön ⊜	40	59.36 N	14.58 E
Fasmund >[1]	41	54.32 N	13.35 E
Fassa	150	13.26 N	8.15 W
Fassberg	52	52.54 N	10.10 E
Fasterholt	41	56.01 N	9.07 E
Fastnet Rock I[2]	48	51.24 N	9.35 W
Fastov	78	50.06 N	29.55 E
Fastoveckaja	78	45.56 N	40.09 E
Fatagar, Tanjung >	164	2.46 S	131.57 E
Fataki	154	4.46 S	28.11 E
Fatala ≃	150	10.13 N	14.00 W
Fat Deer Key I	220	24.44 N	81.00 W
Fate	222	32.56 N	96.23 W
Fatehābād, Bhārat	123	29.31 N	75.27 E
Fatehābād, Bhārat	124	27.01 N	78.19 E
Fatehgarh, Bhārat	124	27.22 N	79.38 E
Fatehgarh, Bhārat	124	24.48 N	76.58 E
Fatehgarh Chūriān	123	31.52 N	74.58 E
Fatehjang	123	33.34 N	72.39 E
Fatehpur, Bhārat	120	27.59 N	74.57 E
Fatehpur, Bhārat	124	27.10 N	81.13 E
Fatehpur, Bhārat	124	25.56 N	80.48 E
Fatehpur, Bhārat	126	22.17 N	88.14 E
Fatehpur, Pāk.	123	31.09 N	71.13 E
Fatehpur □[5]	124	25.50 N	81.00 E
Fatehpur Sīkri	124	27.06 N	77.40 E
Fathai	140	8.05 N	31.48 E
Fathepur	126	24.05 N	87.44 E
Fatikli	130	36.08 N	36.12 E
Fatima, Arg.	258	34.26 S	59.00 W
Fátima, Bra.	248	16.11 S	54.58 W
Fátima, Port.	34	39.37 N	8.39 W
Fāṭimah, Wādī V	144	21.27 N	39.09 E
Fatoto	150	13.26 N	13.52 W
Fat'ož	78	52.07 N	35.52 E
Fatsa	130	41.02 N	37.31 E
Fatshan → Foshan	100	23.03 N	113.09 E
Fatulla	126	23.38 N	90.29 E
Fatuma	174w	21.13 S	175.07 W
Fatunda	152	4.08 S	17.13 E
Fatwā	124	25.31 N	85.19 E
Fauabu	175e	8.34 S	160.43 E
Faucigny	58	46.07 N	6.22 E
Faucille, Col de la)(	58	46.22 N	6.02 E
Faucilles, Monts ΛΛ	58	48.07 N	6.16 E
Faucogney	58	47.51 N	6.34 E
Faucon-de-Barcelonnette	62	44.24 N	6.41 E
Fauglia	66	43.34 N	10.31 E
Fauldhouse	46	55.50 N	3.37 W
Faulkton	198	45.02 N	99.08 W
Faulquemont	56	49.03 N	6.36 E
Fauquembergues	50	50.36 N	2.05 E
Fauquier	182	49.53 N	118.05 W
Fauquier □[6]	208	38.35 N	77.35 W
Făurei	38	45.06 N	27.14 E
Faure Island I	162	25.51 S	113.52 E
Fauresmith	158	29.42 S	25.21 E
Fauro I	175e	6.55 S	156.04 E
Fauske	24	67.15 N	15.24 E
Faust	182	55.19 N	115.38 W
Faustovo	82	55.26 N	38.29 E
Fauville-en-Caux	50	49.39 N	0.35 E
Fauvillers	56	49.51 N	5.40 E
Faux-Cap	157b	25.33 S	45.32 E
Fauza ≃	82	56.25 N	36.04 E
Fåvang	26	61.27 N	10.11 E
Favara	70	37.19 N	13.39 E
Faverges	62	45.45 N	6.18 E
Faverney	58	47.46 N	6.06 E
Faversham	42	51.20 N	0.53 E
Favières	261	48.46 N	2.47 E
Favignana	70	37.56 N	12.20 E
Favignana, Isola I	70	37.56 N	12.19 E
Favoriten ◆[8]	264b	48.11 N	16.23 E
Favourable Lake ⊜	184	52.53 N	93.56 W
Favrieux	261	48.57 N	1.39 E
Fawcett	182	54.32 N	114.05 W
Fawcett Lake ⊜	182	55.19 N	113.57 W
Fawkham Green	260	51.22 N	0.17 E
Fawkner	274b	37.43 S	144.58 E
Fawkner Park ♠	274b	37.50 S	144.59 E
Fawley	42	50.49 N	1.20 W
Fawn ≃, Ont., Can.	176	55.22 N	88.20 W
Fawn ≃, U.S.	216	41.51 N	85.40 W
Fawn Grove	208	39.44 N	76.27 W
Fawnie Nose Λ	182	53.16 N	125.08 W
Fawnie Range ΛΛ	182	53.10 N	125.00 W
Fawsett Farms	284c	38.59 N	77.14 W
Faxaflói C	24a	64.25 N	23.00 W
Faxälven ≃	26	63.13 N	17.13 E
Faxinal	255	23.59 S	51.22 W
Faxinal do Soturno	252	29.37 S	53.26 W
Faxon	210	41.15 N	76.58 W
Fayd	128	27.07 N	42.27 E
Fayence	62	43.37 N	6.41 E
Fayerweather Island I	276	41.08 N	73.13 W
Fayette, Ala., U.S.	194	33.42 N	87.50 W
Fayette, Iowa, U.S.	190	42.51 N	91.48 W
Fayette, Miss., U.S.	194	31.42 N	91.04 W
Fayette, Mo., U.S.	194	39.09 N	92.41 W
Fayette, N.Y., U.S.	210	42.49 N	76.49 W
Fayette, Ohio, U.S.	216	41.40 N	84.20 W
Fayette □[6], Ill., U.S.	219	38.58 N	89.06 W
Fayette □[6], Ind., U.S.	218	39.39 N	85.08 W
Fayette □[6], Ky., U.S.	218	38.07 N	84.30 W
Fayette □[6], Ohio, U.S.	218	39.32 N	83.26 W
Fayette □[6], Pa., U.S.	214	40.05 N	79.39 W
Fayette □[6], Tex., U.S.	222	29.50 N	96.57 W
Fayette City	214	40.06 N	79.50 W
Fayetteville, Ark., U.S.	194	36.04 N	94.10 W
Fayetteville, Ga., U.S.	192	33.27 N	84.27 W
Fayetteville, Ill., U.S.	219	38.22 N	89.48 W
Fayetteville, N.C., U.S.	192	35.03 N	78.54 W
Fayetteville, N.Y., U.S.	210	43.02 N	76.00 W
Fayetteville, Ohio, U.S.	218	39.11 N	83.56 W
Fayetteville, Pa., U.S.	208	39.55 N	77.33 W
Fayetteville, Tenn., U.S.	194	35.09 N	86.35 W
Fayetteville, Tex., U.S.	222	29.54 N	96.41 W
Fayetteville, W. Va., U.S.	188	38.03 N	81.06 W
Faylakah I	128	29.25 N	48.22 E
Fayl-Billot	58	47.47 N	5.36 E
Fayrā	144	13.17 N	43.25 E
Fay-sur-Lignon	62	44.59 N	4.14 E
Fayville	207	42.18 N	71.31 W
Fayyum → Al-Fayyūm	142	29.19 N	30.50 E
Fažana	64	44.55 N	13.49 E
Fazao	150	8.42 N	0.46 E
Fazao, Forêt Classée du ◆[4]	150	8.40 N	0.42 E
Fazeka	144	14.08 N	43.05 E
Fazenda de Cima	248	15.56 S	56.37 W
Fazenda Libongo	152	8.24 S	13.24 E
Fazenda Nova	255	16.11 S	50.48 W
Fāzilka	123	30.24 N	74.02 E
Fāzilpur	120	29.18 N	70.27 E
Fazzān (Fezzan) ◆[1]	146	26.00 N	14.00 E
Fdérik	148	22.41 N	12.43 W
Feale ≃	48	52.28 N	9.40 W
Fear, Cape >	192	33.50 N	77.58 W
Fearnhead	262	53.25 N	2.33 W
Feasterville	208	40.09 N	75.00 W
Feather ≃	204	38.47 N	121.36 W
Feather, Middle Fork ≃	204	39.34 N	125.26 W
Feather, North Fork ≃	204	39.34 N	121.28 W
Feather, North Fork, East Branch ≃	204	40.01 N	121.13 W
Feather, South Fork ≃	204	39.33 N	121.28 W
Featherbed Top Λ	262	53.26 N	1.52 W
Featherston	172	41.07 S	175.20 E
Featherstone, Eng., U.K.	44	53.41 N	1.21 W
Featherstone, Zimb.	154	18.42 S	30.49 E
Feathertop, Mount Λ	166	36.54 S	147.08 E
Fécamp	50	49.45 N	0.22 E
Fedala → Mohammedia	148	33.44 N	7.24 W
Feddet >[1]	41	55.09 N	12.07 E
Federación	252	31.00 S	57.54 W
Federal, Arg.	252	30.57 S	58.48 W
Federal, Pa., U.S.	279b	40.23 N	80.09 W
Federalsburg	208	38.42 N	75.47 W
Federal Way	224	47.20 N	122.20 W
Federation Forest State Park ♠	224	47.09 N	121.40 W
Federsee ⊜	58	48.05 N	9.38 E
Fedeshk	128	32.45 N	58.50 E
Fedjadj, Chott el ☵	148	33.55 N	9.10 E
Fedje	26	60.47 N	4.42 E
Fedons Camp Λ	241k	12.07 N	61.42 W
Fedorino	82	55.08 N	36.06 E
Fedosejevka	80	46.53 N	44.00 E
Fedosejevskaja	24	62.07 N	40.42 E
Fedosicha	86	54.47 N	81.54 E
Fedosjino	82	55.08 N	38.30 E
Fedotovo	82	55.41 N	39.12 E
Feeagh, Lough ⊜	48	53.55 N	9.36 W
Feeding Hills	207	42.04 N	72.41 W
Feehanville	278	42.05 N	87.54 W
Feesburg	218	38.52 N	83.58 W
Fefan I	175c	7.21 N	151.51 E
Fehérgyarmat	30	47.58 N	22.32 E
Fehmarn I	54	54.28 N	11.08 E
Fehmarn Belt (Femer Bælt) ⋓	41	54.35 N	11.15 E
Fehmarnsund ⋓	54	54.24 N	11.07 E
Fehrbellin	54	52.49 N	12.46 E
Feia, Lagoa C	255	22.00 S	41.20 W
Feicheng	98	36.15 N	116.46 E
Feichten	58	47.02 N	10.44 E
Feidong (Dianfu)	100	31.52 N	117.29 E
Feignies	50	50.18 N	3.55 E
Feigumfossen ↳	26	61.23 N	7.26 E
Feihekou	100	33.36 N	115.36 E
Feihuanghekou ≃[1]	100	34.16 N	120.18 E
Feijó	248	8.09 S	70.21 W
Feiketu	89	45.46 N	127.09 E
Feilding	172	40.13 S	175.34 E
Feiler Λ	58	47.07 N	10.52 E
Feiliqiao	106	31.05 N	119.05 E
Feilitzsch	54	50.22 N	11.56 E
Feilnbach	64	47.46 N	12.00 E
Feilong, Zhg.	107	30.36 N	105.54 E
Feilong, Zhg.	107	30.25 N	106.20 E
Feilongguan	107	28.57 N	105.05 E
Feiluan	100	26.35 N	119.35 E
Feio ≃	255	21.03 S	51.47 W
Feira	154	15.37 S	30.25 E
Feira de Santana	255	12.15 S	38.57 W
Feistritz ≃	61	47.01 N	16.08 E
Feistritz an der Gail	64	46.34 N	13.36 E
Feixi	100	31.42 N	117.10 E
Feixian	98	35.18 N	117.57 E
Feixiang	98	36.34 N	114.49 E
Feiyunjiang ≃	100	27.48 N	120.36 E
Fejér □[6]	30	47.10 N	18.35 E
Fejø I	41	54.57 N	11.26 E
Feklistova, Ostrov I	89	55.02 N	136.55 E
Felâhiye	130	39.06 N	35.35 E
Felanitx	34	39.28 N	3.08 E
Felbertauren-Tunnel ◆[5]	64	47.08 N	12.31 E
Felda	220	26.33 N	81.26 W
Felda ≃	56	50.42 N	9.03 E
Feldafing	64	47.57 N	11.17 E
Feldaist ≃	61	48.19 N	14.34 E
Feld am See	64	46.47 N	13.45 E
Feldbach	61	46.57 N	15.54 E
Feldberg, B.R.D.	58	47.51 N	8.02 E
Feldberg, D.D.R.	54	53.20 N	13.26 E
Feldberg Λ	58	47.52 N	7.59 E
Felderbach ≃	263	51.22 N	7.08 E
Feldhausen	263	51.37 N	6.59 E
Feldis	58	46.48 N	9.26 E
Feldkirch	58	47.14 N	9.36 E
Feldkirchen	64	47.54 N	11.50 E
Feldkirchen in Kärnten	61	46.43 N	14.05 E
Feldmark	263	51.41 N	6.38 E
Feldstetten	58	48.28 N	9.37 E
Felhit	144	16.43 N	38.02 E
Feliciano	240m	18.28 N	67.08 W
Feliciano, Arroyo ≃	252	31.06 S	59.54 W
Felicity	218	38.51 N	84.06 W
Felino	64	44.42 N	10.15 E
Felipe Carrillo Puerto	232	19.35 N	88.03 W
Felix, Cape >	176	69.54 N	97.50 W
Felix, Rio ≃	196	33.08 N	104.19 W
Felixburg	154	19.29 S	30.51 E
Félix Gómez	232	29.50 N	111.30 W
Felixlândia	255	18.47 S	44.55 W
Felixstowe	42	51.58 N	1.20 E
Felixton	158	28.50 S	31.53 E
Félix U. Gómez	232	30.35 N	105.50 W
Felizzano	62	44.54 N	8.26 E
Fella ≃	64	46.21 N	13.07 E
Fellbach	56	48.48 N	9.15 E
Felletin	32	45.53 N	2.10 E
Felling	44	54.57 N	1.33 W
Fellingsbro	40	59.26 N	15.35 E
Fellows	226	35.11 N	119.32 W
Fellows Creek ≃	281	42.17 N	83.26 W
Fellowship	285	39.56 N	74.58 W
Fellsburg	214	40.11 N	79.49 W
Fellsmere	220	27.46 N	80.36 W
Fellwick	285	40.08 N	75.11 W
Felpham	42	50.47 N	0.39 W
Felsberg	56	51.08 N	9.25 E
Felsenmeer, Naturschutzgebiet ♠	263	51.25 N	7.45 E
Felszabadulási Emlékmű ⊥	264c	47.29 N	19.03 E
Feltham ◆[8]	260	51.27 N	0.24 W
Felt Lake ⊜	282	37.23 N	122.11 W
Felton, Calif., U.S.	226	37.03 N	122.04 W
Felton, Del., U.S.	208	39.01 N	75.35 W
Felton, Pa., U.S.	208	39.51 N	76.34 W
Feltre	64	46.01 N	11.54 E
Felts Mills	212	44.01 N	75.46 W
Fêmeas, Rio das ≃	255	12.27 S	45.12 W
Femer Bælt (Fehmarn Belt) ⋓	41	54.35 N	11.15 E
Femme Osage Creek ≃	219	38.39 N	90.44 W
Femmøller	41	56.14 N	10.35 E
Femø I	41	54.58 N	11.33 E
Femunden ⊜	26	62.12 N	11.52 E
Femundsenden	26	61.55 N	11.55 E
Femundsmarka Nasjonalpark ♠	26	62.20 N	12.07 E
Fena Valley Reservoir ⊜[1]	174p	13.21 N	144.42 E
Fendaozi	104	41.35 N	120.51 E
Fen Ditton	42	52.13 N	0.10 E
Fenelon Falls	212	44.32 N	78.45 W
Fenelton	214	40.52 N	79.44 W
Fener ◆[8]	267b	41.02 N	28.56 E
Fenerbahçe Stadyumu ♠	267b	40.59 N	29.02 E
Fener Burnu >	130	41.07 N	39.25 E
Fénérive	157b	17.22 S	49.25 E
Fener Tepesi Λ[2]	267b	41.09 N	28.47 E
Fenerwa	144	13.05 N	38.58 E
Fenestrelle	62	45.02 N	7.03 E
Fénétrange	56	48.51 N	7.01 E
Fengcheng, Zhg.	98	40.28 N	124.00 E
Fengcheng, Zhg.	100	28.10 N	115.46 E
Fengcheng, Zhg.	106	30.55 N	121.38 E
Fengchengpu	102	38.32 N	101.50 E
Fengdengwu	105	39.42 N	117.55 E
Fengdian	107	30.41 N	104.51 E
Fengdu	102	29.58 N	107.41 E
Fengfeng	98	36.28 N	114.14 E
Fenggang, Zhg.	100	28.34 N	116.34 E
Fenggang, Zhg.	102	27.58 N	107.47 E
Fenggaopu	107	29.24 N	105.41 E
Fenghe ≃	105	39.25 N	116.57 E
Fenghua	100	29.40 N	121.24 E
Fenghuang, Zhg.	100	23.58 N	116.44 E
Fenghuang, Zhg.	102	27.58 N	109.19 E
Fenghuang, Zhg.	102	24.25 N	107.17 E
Fenghuangchang	107	29.44 N	106.19 E
Fenghuangshan Λ	107	28.54 N	106.35 E
Fenghuanjing	100	31.11 N	117.49 E
Fenghuizhen	100	29.56 N	120.58 E
Fengjia, Zhg.	98	37.03 N	121.42 E
Fengjia, Zhg.	104	42.35 N	122.30 E
Fengjiabao	102	36.12 N	104.49 E
Fengjiakou	98	38.11 N	116.44 E
Fengjianjiao	106	30.41 N	120.51 E
Fengjiatun	104	41.14 N	122.00 E
Fengjiawopeng	104	42.19 N	123.40 E
Fengjiaxiang	106	30.56 N	121.06 E
Fengjing	106	30.53 N	121.01 E
Fengkou	100	30.05 N	113.18 E
Fengle, Zhg.	89	45.47 N	125.26 E
Fengle, Zhg.	100	27.13 N	118.11 E
Fenglehe	102	31.28 N	112.20 E
Fenglezhen	98	36.14 N	114.18 E
Fengliang	100	23.59 N	116.14 E
Fenglin, T'aiwan	100	23.44 N	121.27 E
Fenglin, Zhg.	100	28.19 N	120.46 E
Fengling)(	100	28.14 N	118.29 E
Fenglingtou	100	28.26 N	117.50 E
Fengman	89	43.46 N	126.41 E
Fengmingdao I	98	39.24 N	121.22 E
Fengnan (Xugezhuang)	105	39.34 N	118.06 E
Fengning	98	41.12 N	116.32 E
Fengpin	100	23.36 N	121.31 E
Fengpingzi	102	32.46 N	105.12 E
Fengqiao, Zhg.	100	29.46 N	120.26 E
Fengqiao, Zhg.	106	31.19 N	120.33 E
Fengqing	102	24.46 N	99.52 E
Fengqiu	98	35.05 N	114.25 E
Fengrun (Xugezhuang)	105	39.50 N	118.07 E
Fengshan, Zhg.	89	46.22 N	128.30 E
Fengshan, Zhg.	98	41.14 N	117.05 E
Fengshan, Zhg.	102	22.01 N	109.59 E
Fengshi	100	24.42 N	116.34 E
Fengshun	100	23.48 N	116.11 E
Fengtai, Zhg.	100	32.44 N	116.43 E
Fengtai, Zhg.	105	39.51 N	116.16 E
Fengtian	100	27.24 N	114.43 E
Fengtien → Shenyang	104	41.48 N	123.27 E
Fengting	100	25.16 N	118.54 E
Fengwan	100	24.48 N	113.50 E
Fengxi	102	31.48 N	109.50 E
Fengxian, Zhg.	98	34.42 N	116.34 E
Fengxian, Zhg.	102	33.57 N	106.44 E
Fengxian, Zhg.	106	30.55 N	121.27 E
Fengxiang	102	34.29 N	107.29 E
Fengxin	100	28.43 N	115.23 E
Fengyang, Zhg.	100	24.49 N	117.53 E
Fengyang, Zhg.	100	32.52 N	117.34 E
Fengyi	102	31.44 N	103.53 E
Fengyu	100	26.31 N	119.18 E
Fengzhen	102	40.24 N	113.09 E
Fengzhou	100	25.41 N	113.52 E
Fengzhuangtou	106	31.00 N	118.39 E
Fenholloway ≃	192	29.59 N	83.47 W
Fenhu ⊜	106	31.00 N	120.47 E
Feni	124	23.00 N	91.24 E
Feni Islands II	14	4.05 S	153.42 E
Fenimore Pass ⋓	180	52.00 N	175.35 W
Fenino	265b	55.44 N	37.57 E
Fenis	62	45.44 N	7.29 E
Feniscowles	262	53.43 N	2.32 W
Fenjie	106	32.17 N	120.20 E
Fennimore	190	42.59 N	90.39 W
Fennville	216	42.36 N	86.06 W
Fenny Compton	42	52.09 N	1.20 W
Fenny Stratford	42	52.00 N	0.43 W
Feno, Capo di >	36	41.57 N	8.36 E
Fenoarivo, Madag.	157b	20.52 S	46.53 E
Fenoarivo, Madag.	157b	21.43 S	46.24 E
Fenoarivo, Madag.	157b	18.26 S	46.34 E
Fensfjorden C[2]	26	60.51 N	4.50 E
Fenshui	100	29.56 N	119.25 E
Fenshui'ao	100	25.20 N	114.43 E
Fenshuidunshen	106	31.30 N	120.01 E
Fenshuiling, Zhg.	107	28.51 N	105.35 E
Fenshuiling, Zhg.	107	30.20 N	105.15 E
Fenshuiling ΛΛ	104	40.52 N	123.25 E
Fenshuipu	107	30.05 N	104.05 E
Fenshuizhen	107	29.44 N	103.55 E
Fenshuizui	100	30.35 N	113.38 E
Fensmark	41	55.17 N	11.49 E
Fenton, Mich., U.S.	216	42.48 N	83.42 W
Fenton, Mo., U.S.	219	38.32 N	90.22 W
Fenton, Lake ⊜	216	42.50 N	83.43 W
Fentou	105	38.53 N	116.32 E
Fentress	222	29.45 N	97.47 W
Fenway Park ♠	283	42.21 N	71.06 W
Fenwick	188	38.14 N	80.35 W
Fenwick Island >[1]	208	38.25 N	75.03 W
Fenyang	102	37.18 N	111.41 E
Fenyi	100	27.47 N	114.42 E
Feodosija	78	45.02 N	35.23 E
Feodosijskij Zaliv C	78	45.05 N	35.35 E
Fépin	56	50.01 N	4.44 E
Fer, Cap de >	148	37.05 N	7.10 E
Ferbane	48	53.15 N	7.49 W
Ferbitz	264a	52.30 N	13.01 E
Ferch	264a	52.19 N	12.56 E
Fercher Berge Λ[2]	264a	52.19 N	12.57 E
Ferchland	54	52.26 N	12.00 E
Ferdinand	194	38.14 N	86.52 W
Ferdinandshof	54	53.39 N	13.53 E
Ferdows	128	34.00 N	58.09 E
Fère-Champenoise	50	48.45 N	3.59 E
Fère-en-Tardenois	50	49.12 N	3.31 E
Ferencváros ◆[8]	264c	47.28 N	19.06 E
Ferentillo	66	42.37 N	12.47 E
Ferentino	66	41.42 N	13.15 E
Ferfer	144	5.06 N	45.09 E
Fergana	85	40.23 N	71.46 E
Fergana □[4]	85	40.30 N	71.20 E
Ferganskaja Dolina V	85	40.50 N	71.30 E
Ferganskij Chrebet ΛΛ	85	41.00 N	74.00 E
Fergus	212	43.42 N	80.22 W
Fergus Falls	198	46.17 N	96.04 W
Ferguson, Austl.	168a	33.26 S	115.51 E
Ferguson, B.C., Can.	182	50.41 N	117.28 W
Ferguson, Ky., U.S.	192	37.03 N	84.36 W
Ferguson, Mo., U.S.	219	38.46 N	90.19 W
Fergusonville	285	40.07 N	74.54 W
Fergusson Island I	164	9.30 S	150.40 E
Fériana	148	34.57 N	8.34 E
Ferihegyi Repülőtér ⊠	264c	47.26 N	19.15 E
Ferkéssédougou	150	9.36 N	5.12 W
Ferkéssédougou □[5]	150	9.30 N	4.50 W
Ferla	70	37.07 N	14.56 E
Ferlach	61	46.31 N	14.18 E
Ferleiten	64	47.10 N	12.49 E
Ferlo ◆[1]	150	0.15 N	0.14 W
Ferlo, Vallée du V	150	15.42 N	15.30 W
Fermiers, Île aux I	275a	45.40 N	73.27 W
Fermignano	66	43.40 N	12.39 E
Fermin, Point >	228	33.42 N	118.18 W
Fermo	66	43.09 N	13.43 E
Fermoselle	34	41.19 N	6.23 W
Fermoy	48	52.08 N	8.16 W
Fernandes Belo	250	1.07 S	46.19 W
Fernández	252	27.55 S	63.54 W
Fernández Leal	200	30.51 N	108.17 W
Fernandina, Isla I	246a	0.25 S	91.30 W
Fernandina Beach	192	30.40 N	81.27 W
Fernando de la Mora	252	25.19 S	57.36 W
Fernando de Noronha □[3]	250	3.51 S	32.25 W
Fernando de Noronha, Ilha I	250	3.51 S	32.25 W
Fernandópolis	255	20.16 S	50.14 W
Fernando Póo → Bioko I	152	3.30 N	8.40 E
Fernán-Núñez	34	37.40 N	4.43 W
Fernão Veloso, Baía de C	154	14.20 S	40.45 E
Ferndale, S. Afr.	273d	26.05 S	27.59 E
Ferndale, Calif., U.S.	204	40.35 N	124.16 W
Ferndale, Fla., U.S.	220	28.37 N	81.42 W
Ferndale, Md., U.S.	208	39.11 N	76.38 W
Ferndale, Mich., U.S.	216	42.28 N	83.08 W
Ferndale, N.Y., U.S.	210	41.46 N	74.44 W
Ferndale, Pa., U.S.	208	40.32 N	75.11 W
Ferndale, Pa., U.S.	210	40.47 N	76.35 W
Ferndale, Pa., U.S.	214	40.18 N	78.55 W
Ferndale, Wash., U.S.	202	48.51 N	122.36 W
Ferndale Lake ⊜	222	32.57 N	95.05 W
Ferndown	42	50.48 N	1.55 W
Ferney-Voltaire	58	46.15 N	6.07 E
Fern Glen	210	40.57 N	76.10 W
Fernhatten ΛΛ[2]	41	56.15 N	10.48 E
Fernie	182	49.30 N	115.03 W
Fernilee	262	53.18 N	1.58 W
Fernilee Reservoir ⊜[1]	262	53.17 N	1.59 W
Fernley	204	39.36 N	119.15 W
Ferno	62	45.37 N	8.45 E
Fernow, Mount Λ	224	47.45 N	121.14 W
Fern Park	220	28.41 N	81.20 W
Fernpass)(	58	47.22 N	10.50 E
Fern Ridge Lake ⊜[1]	202	44.05 N	123.18 W
Ferns	48	52.35 N	6.31 W
Ferntree Gully National Park ♠	169	37.53 S	145.19 E
Fernvale	171a	27.27 S	152.39 E
Fernway, Ill., U.S.	278	41.36 N	87.50 W
Fernway, Pa., U.S.	214	40.41 N	80.07 W
Fernwood, Idaho, U.S.	202	47.07 N	116.23 W
Fernwood, N.Y., U.S.	210	43.16 N	73.40 W
Ferny Creek	274b	37.53 S	145.21 E
Feroé, Islas → Faeroe Islands □[2]	22	62.00 N	7.00 W
Feroës → Faeroe Islands □[2]	22	62.00 N	7.00 W
Ferokh	122	11.11 N	75.51 E
Feroleto Antico	68	38.58 N	16.23 E
Feroleto della Chiesa	68	38.28 N	16.04 E
Ferozepore → Fīrozpur	123	30.55 N	74.36 E
Férrai	130	40.54 N	26.10 E
Ferrandina	68	40.29 N	16.28 E
Ferrara	64	44.50 N	11.35 E
Ferrara □[4]	64	44.48 N	11.50 E
Ferrat, Cap >	148	35.54 N	0.23 W
Ferrato, Capo >	71	39.18 N	9.38 E
Ferraz de Vasconcelos	256	23.32 S	46.22 W
Ferraz de Vasconcelos □[7]	287b	23.33 S	46.21 W
Ferrazzano	66	41.32 N	14.40 E
Ferré, Cap >	240e	14.28 N	60.49 W
Ferreira, Ang.	152	12.53 S	22.48 E
Ferreira, S. Afr.	158	29.13 S	26.10 E
Ferreira, Riacho ≃	250	10.06 S	42.13 W
Ferreira do Alentejo	34	38.03 N	8.07 W
Ferreira Gomes	250	0.48 N	51.08 W
Ferreiros	256	22.25 S	43.34 W
Ferrell	285	39.41 N	75.12 W
Ferrell's Bridge Dam ◆[6]	222	32.45 N	94.30 W
Ferreñafe	248	6.38 S	79.45 W
Ferrera Erbognone	62	45.07 N	8.52 E
Ferret	58	45.55 N	7.06 E
Ferret, Cap >	32	44.37 N	1.15 W
Ferreyra	252	31.28 S	64.08 W
Ferriday	194	31.38 N	91.33 W
Ferriere	62	44.38 N	9.30 E
Ferrière-la-Grande	50	50.15 N	4.00 E
Ferrières	50	48.05 N	2.47 E
Ferrières-en-Brie	50	48.49 N	2.43 E
Ferris	222	32.32 N	96.40 W
Ferritslev	41	55.18 N	10.36 E
Ferro ≃	255	12.27 S	54.31 W
Ferrol → El Ferrol del Caudillo	34	43.29 N	8.14 W
Ferrol, Península de >[1]	248	9.10 S	78.37 W
Ferron	200	39.05 N	111.08 W
Ferron Creek ≃	200	39.09 N	110.55 W
Ferros	255	19.14 S	43.02 W
Ferru, Monte Λ	71	39.44 N	9.38 E
Ferruzzano	68	38.02 N	16.05 E
Ferry, Pointe >	241o	16.17 N	61.49 W
Ferryhill	44	54.41 N	1.33 W
Ferryland	186	47.02 N	52.53 W
Ferry Point Park ♠	276	40.49 N	73.50 W
Ferrysburg	216	43.05 N	86.11 W
Ferry Village	284a	43.58 N	78.57 W
Ferryville → Menzel Bourguiba	148	37.10 N	9.48 E
Feršampenuaz	86	53.32 N	59.51 E
Fertile	198	47.32 N	96.17 W
Fertilia, Aeroporto di ⊠	71	40.37 N	8.15 E
Fertő (Neusiedler See) ⊜	61	47.50 N	16.45 E
Ferulargiu, Monte Λ	71	40.31 N	9.34 E
Ferzikovo	82	54.32 N	36.45 E
Fès	148	34.05 N	4.57 W
Feshi	152	6.07 S	18.10 E
Feshie ≃	46	57.08 N	3.55 W
Fessenden	198	47.39 N	99.38 W
Festenberg → Twardogóra	30	51.22 N	17.28 E
Festus	219	38.13 N	90.24 W
Fetcham	260	51.17 N	0.22 W
Fet Dom, Tanjung >	164	1.53 S	129.43 E
Fété Bowé	150	14.56 N	13.30 W
Fetești	38	44.23 N	27.50 E
Fethaland, Point of >	46a	60.38 N	1.18 W
Fethard	48	52.27 N	7.41 W
Fethiye	130	36.37 N	29.07 E
Fethiye Körfezi C	130	36.40 N	29.00 E
Fetisovo	72	42.46 N	52.38 E
Fetlar I	46a	60.37 N	0.52 W
Fetsund	26	59.56 N	11.10 E
Fetterangus	46	57.33 N	2.01 W
Fettercairn	46	56.51 N	2.34 W
Fetzara, Lac ⊜	148	36.52 N	7.22 E
Feucherolles	261	48.52 N	1.58 E
Feucht	60	49.22 N	11.13 E
Feuchtwangen	56	49.10 N	10.20 E
Feudingen	56	50.56 N	8.19 E
Feuerland → Tierra del Fuego, Isla Grande de I	254	54.00 S	69.00 W
Feuet	146	24.57 N	10.04 E
Feuilles, Baie aux C	176	58.55 N	69.20 W
Feuilles, Rivière aux ≃	176	58.47 N	70.04 W
Feuquières-en-Vimeu	50	50.04 N	1.36 E
Feura Bush	210	42.35 N	73.53 W
Feurs	62	45.45 N	4.14 E
Fevik	26	58.23 N	8.42 E
Fevzipaşa	130	37.07 N	36.37 E
Féy	56	49.02 N	6.06 E
Feyen	56	49.44 N	6.38 E
Feyẕābād, Afg.	120	37.06 N	70.34 E
Feyẕābād, Īrān	128	35.01 N	58.46 E
Feyzin	62	45.40 N	4.51 E
Fez → Fès	148	34.05 N	4.57 W
Fezzan → Fazzān ◆[1]	146	26.00 N	14.00 E
Ffestiniog	42	52.58 N	3.55 W
Fforest Fawr ◆[1]	42	51.52 N	3.36 W
F. Gilbert Hills State Forest ♠	283	42.03 N	71.17 W
Fiambalá	252	27.41 S	67.38 W
Fiamignano	66	42.16 N	13.07 E
Fian	150	10.23 N	2.29 W
Fianarantsoa	157b	21.26 S	47.05 E
Fianarantsoa □[4]	157b	22.00 S	47.00 E
Fianga	146	9.55 N	15.09 E
Fiano	62	45.13 N	7.31 E
Fiantsonana	157b	19.09 S	46.12 E
Fiastra, Abbazia di ɷ[1]	66	43.13 N	13.25 E
Fiavè	64	46.00 N	10.50 E
Ficarazzi	70	38.05 N	13.28 E
Ficarolo	64	44.57 N	11.26 E
Ficarra	70	38.06 N	14.50 E
Fiche	144	9.52 N	38.46 E
Fichtelberg Λ	54	50.26 N	12.57 E
Fichtenau	264a	52.27 N	13.42 E
Ficksburg	158	28.57 S	27.50 E
Ficulle	66	42.50 N	12.04 E
Ficuzza ≃	70	37.00 N	14.20 E
Fidalgo ≃	250	7.28 S	42.32 W
Fiddlers Hamlet	260	51.41 N	0.08 E
Fiddletown	226	38.30 N	120.46 W
Fiddyment Creek ≃	278	41.36 N	88.03 W
Fidelity	219	39.09 N	90.10 W
Fidenza	64	44.52 N	10.03 E
Fidīmīn	142	29.23 N	30.46 E
Fiditi	150	7.45 N	3.53 E
Fidji → Fiji □[1]	175g	18.00 S	175.00 E
Fidler Lake ⊜	184	57.11 N	96.57 W
Fidschi → Fiji □[1]	175g	18.00 S	175.00 E
Fiè (Völs)	64	46.31 N	11.30 E
Fieberbrunn	64	47.29 N	12.33 E
Field	182	51.24 N	116.29 W
Fieldale	192	36.42 N	79.57 W
Field Museum ɷ	278	41.53 N	87.37 W
Fieldon	219	39.07 N	90.30 W
Fieldsboro	285	40.08 N	74.44 W
Fieldstone	276	40.44 N	74.33 W
Fiemme, Val di V	64	46.24 N	11.25 E
Fiener Bruch ☵	54	52.19 N	12.10 E
Fienvillers	50	50.07 N	2.14 E
Fier	38	40.43 N	19.34 E
Fier ≃	58	45.56 N	5.50 E
Fiéra Campionaria ♠	266b	45.28 N	9.09 E
Fiera di Primiero	64	46.10 N	11.49 E
Fierenana	157b	18.29 S	48.24 E
Fiery Creek ≃, Austl.	166	18.23 S	139.52 E
Fiery Creek ≃, Austl.	169	37.44 S	142.56 E
Fiesch	58	46.20 N	8.10 E
Fiesole	66	43.48 N	11.17 E
Fiesso d'Artico	64	45.24 N	12.02 E
Fiesso Umbertiano	64	44.56 N	11.36 E
Fife	224	47.14 N	122.22 W
Fife □[4]	46	56.13 N	3.02 W
Fife Lake, Sask., Can.	184	49.12 N	105.43 W
Fife Lake, Mich., U.S.	190	44.35 N	85.21 W
Fife Lake ⊜	184	49.14 N	105.53 W
Fife Ness >	46	56.17 N	2.36 W
Fifield	190	45.53 N	90.25 W
Fifteenmile Creek ≃, Oreg., U.S.	224	45.37 N	121.07 W
Fifteenmile Creek ≃, Wyo., U.S.	202	44.01 N	108.01 W
Fifth Cataract → Ash-Shallāl al-Khāmis ↳	140	18.23 N	33.47 E
Fifth Depot Lake ⊜	212	44.36 N	76.52 W
Figeac	32	44.37 N	2.02 E
Figeholm	26	57.22 N	16.33 E
Fig Garden	226	36.48 N	119.47 W
Fighting Island I	281	42.13 N	83.07 W
Figline Valdarno	66	43.37 N	11.28 E
Figtree	154	20.24 S	28.21 E
Figueira → Governador Valadares, Bra.	255	18.51 S	41.56 W
Figueira, Bra.	287a	22.42 S	43.27 W
Figueira, Cachoeira ↳	250	9.49 S	58.13 W
Figueira da Foz	34	40.09 N	8.52 W
Figueras	34	42.16 N	2.58 E
Figuig	148	32.10 N	1.15 W
Fihaonana	157b	18.36 S	47.12 E
Fiherenana ≃	157b	23.19 S	43.37 E
Fiji □[1]	14; 175g	18.00 S	175.00 E
Fiji Islands II	14	18.00 S	178.00 E
Fijnaart	52	51.37 N	4.31 E
Fik	144	8.10 N	42.18 E
Fiktūriyā, Bi'r ⫪[4]	142	30.24 N	30.36 E
Filabusi	154	20.34 S	29.20 E
Filadélfia, Bra.	250	7.21 S	47.30 W
Filadelfia, C.R.	236	10.26 N	85.34 W
Filadelfia, It.	68	38.48 N	16.18 E
Filadelfia → Philadelphia, Pa., U.S.	208	39.57 N	75.07 W
Fil'akovo	30	48.17 N	19.51 E
Filandari	68	38.37 N	16.02 E
Filatova Gora	76	57.40 N	28.10 E
Filchner Ice Shelf ⊓	9	79.00 S	40.00 W
File Lake ⊜	184	54.53 N	100.20 W
Filettino	66	41.53 N	13.19 E
Filey	44	54.12 N	0.17 W
Filey Bay C	44	54.12 N	0.16 W
Fili ◆[8]	265b	55.45 N	37.31 E
Filí ⊥	38	38.10 N	23.40 E
Filiano	68	40.49 N	15.42 E
Filiași	38	44.33 N	23.31 E
Filiatrá	38	37.10 N	21.35 E
Filicudi, Isola I	70	38.34 N	14.34 E
Filimonki	82	55.33 N	37.21 E
Filimonovo	86	56.12 N	95.28 E
Filingué	150	14.21 N	3.19 E
Filipinas → Philippines □[1]	116	13.00 N	122.00 E
Filipinas, Mar de → Philippine Sea ⫪[2]	14	20.00 N	135.00 E
Fílippoi ⊥	38	41.00 N	24.16 E
Filippo Reef ✢[2]	14	5.30 S	151.50 W
Filippovka	80	53.59 N	49.46 E
Filippovo	80	58.18 N	50.30 E
Filippovskoje, S.S.S.R.	82	56.48 N	39.07 E
Filippovskoje, S.S.S.R.	82	56.06 N	38.37 E
Filipstad	40	59.43 N	14.10 E
Filisola	234	17.50 N	94.19 W
Fillmore, Sask., Can.	184	49.50 N	103.25 W
Fillmore, Calif., U.S.	228	34.24 N	118.55 W
Fillmore, Ill., U.S.	219	39.07 N	89.17 W
Fillmore, N.Y., U.S.	210	42.28 N	78.07 W
Fillmore, Utah, U.S.	200	38.58 N	112.20 W
Fillmore Glen State Park ♠	210	42.42 N	76.20 W
Filogaso	68	38.41 N	16.14 E
Filomeno Mata	234	20.12 N	97.42 W
Filonovskaja	80	50.34 N	42.46 E
Filottrano	66	43.26 N	13.21 E
Filskov	41	55.48 N	9.02 E
Filton	42	51.31 N	2.35 W
Filzbach	58	47.07 N	9.08 E
Fimi ≃	152	3.01 S	16.58 E
Fina, Réserve de ◆[4]	150	12.50 N	8.30 W
Finaalspan	273d	26.17 S	28.15 E
Finale Emilia	64	44.50 N	11.17 E
Finale Ligure	62	44.10 N	8.20 E
Finca El Rey, Parque Nacional ♠	252	25.00 S	64.40 W
Fincastle	192	37.30 N	79.53 W
Finch	206	45.11 N	75.07 W
Finch Lake ⊜	184	56.34 N	100.57 W
Finchley ◆[8]	260	51.36 N	0.10 W
Findel, Aéroport de ⊠	56	49.37 N	6.10 E
Finderne	276	40.34 N	74.35 W
Findhorn	46	57.39 N	3.36 W
Findhorn ≃	46	57.38 N	3.38 W
Findlay, Ill., U.S.	219	39.31 N	88.45 W
Findlay, Ohio, U.S.	216	41.02 N	83.39 W
Findlay, Mount Λ	182	50.04 N	116.28 W
Findlay Creek ≃	182	50.20 N	115.52 W
Findley Lake	214	42.07 N	79.44 W
Findley Lake ⊜	214	42.06 N	79.43 W
Finedon	42	52.20 N	0.39 W
Finejevo	82	56.02 N	38.53 E
Finesville	210	40.36 N	75.10 W
Fingal, Austl.	166	41.39 S	147.58 E
Fingal, Ont., Can.	214	42.43 N	81.19 W
Fingal, N. Dak., U.S.	198	46.46 N	97.47 W
Finger Lake ⊜	184	53.09 N	93.30 W
Fingoè	154	15.12 S	31.50 E
Finike	130	36.18 N	30.09 E
Finike Körfezi C	130	36.17 N	30.16 E
Finisk ≃	48	52.07 N	7.50 W
Finistère □[5]	32	48.20 N	4.00 W
Finisterre	196	25.59 N	103.15 W
Finisterre → Land's End >	42	50.03 N	5.44 W
Finisterre, Cabo de >	34	42.53 N	9.16 W
Finisterre Range ΛΛ	164	5.50 S	146.05 E
Finja	41	56.10 N	13.41 E
Finjasjön ⊜	41	56.08 N	13.42 E
Finke	162	25.34 S	134.35 E
Finke ≃	162	26.20 S	136.00 E
Finke, Mount Λ[2]	162	30.55 S	134.02 E
Finkenkrug	264a	52.34 N	13.03 E
Finkenwerder ◆[8]	52	53.31 N	9.52 E
Finksburg	208	39.30 N	76.54 W
Finland □[1]	22; 24	64.00 N	26.00 E
Finland, Gulf of (Suomenlahti) (Finskij Zaliv) C	26	60.00 N	27.00 E
Finlande → Finland □[1]	24	64.00 N	26.00 E
Finlandia → Finland □[1]	24	64.00 N	26.00 E
Finlandia, Golfo de → Finland, Gulf of C	26	60.00 N	27.00 E
Finl'andskij Vokzal ◆[5]	265a	59.57 N	30.22 E
Finlas, Loch ⊜	44	55.15 N	4.25 W
Finlay ≃	176	57.00 N	125.05 W
Finley, Austl.	166	35.39 S	145.35 E
Finley, N. Dak., U.S.	198	47.31 N	97.50 W
Finley Creek ≃	194	36.58 N	93.22 W
Finleyville, Pa., U.S.	214	40.09 N	78.11 W
Finleyville, Pa., U.S.	214	40.15 N	80.00 W
Finleyville Airport ⊠	279b	40.15 N	80.01 W
Finmoore	182	53.59 N	123.37 W
Finn ≃	28	54.50 N	7.29 W
Finne ◆[1]	54	51.13 N	11.19 E
Finnegan	182	51.07 N	112.05 W
Finnentrop	56	51.09 N	7.58 E
Finnerödja	40	58.56 N	14.26 E
Finney Creek ≃	224	48.31 N	121.51 W
Finnhamn	40	59.28 N	18.50 E
Finnie Bay C	176	65.13 N	77.30 W
Finnis, Cape >	162	33.38 S	134.51 E
Finnischer Meerbusen → Finland, Gulf of C	26	60.00 N	27.00 E
Finniss	168b	35.24 S	138.49 E
Finniss ≃	168b	35.30 S	138.53 E
Finnland → Finland □[1]	24	64.00 N	26.00 E
Finnmark □[6]	24	70.00 N	25.00 E
Finn Mountain Λ	180	60.37 N	157.11 W
Finno Λ[2]	154	3.27 N	41.32 E
Finnskogen ◆[3]	26	60.40 N	12.40 E
Finnsnes	24	69.14 N	17.59 E
Finocchio ◆[8]	267a	41.53 N	12.41 E
Finow	54	52.50 N	13.43 E
Finowfurt	54	52.51 N	13.41 E
Finowkanal ☲	54	52.51 N	13.24 E
Fins, Fr.	50	50.02 N	3.03 E
Fins, 'Umān	128	22.56 N	59.13 E
Finsbury	273d	26.13 S	27.39 E
Finschhafen	164	6.35 S	147.50 E
Finse	26	60.36 N	7.30 E
Finskij Zaliv → Finland, Gulf of C	26	60.00 N	27.00 E
Finspång	40	58.43 N	15.47 E
Finsta	40	59.44 N	18.30 E
Finsteraarhorn Λ	58	46.32 N	8.08 E
Finsterwalde	54	51.38 N	13.42 E
Finsterwolde	52	53.12 N	7.04 E
Fintel	52	53.10 N	9.40 E
Fintona	48	54.30 N	7.19 W
Fintown	48	54.52 N	8.08 W
Finvoy	48	55.00 N	6.30 W
Fionn Loch ⊜	46	57.46 N	5.29 W
Fiora ≃	66	42.20 N	11.34 E
Fiorano Modenese	64	44.32 N	10.49 E
Fiordland National Park ♠	172	45.30 S	167.20 E
Fiorenzuola d'Arda	62	44.56 N	9.55 E
Fiorenzuola di Focara	66	43.57 N	12.48 E
Fiorito ◆[8]	288	34.42 S	58.27 W
Fīq	132	32.47 N	35.42 E
Fırat → Euphrates ≃	128	31.00 N	47.25 E
Firavitoba	246	5.40 N	73.00 W
Fircrest	224	47.14 N	122.31 W
Fire ≃	190	48.52 N	83.21 W
Firebaugh	226	36.52 N	120.27 W
Firebrick	218	38.41 N	83.03 W
Fire Island Inlet C	276	40.38 N	73.16 W
Fire Island National Seashore ♠	210	40.38 N	73.08 W
Fire Island Pines	276	40.40 N	73.04 W
Fire Islands II	276	40.40 N	73.11 W
Firenze (Florence)	64; 66	43.46 N	11.15 E
Firenze □[4]	66	43.50 N	11.20 E

Symbols in the index entries represent the broad categories identified in the key at the right. Symbols with superior numbers (ΛΛ[2]) identify subcategories (see complete key on page I · 30).

Kartensymbole in dem Registerverzeichnis stellen die rechts in Schlüssel erklärten Kategorien dar. Symbole mit hochgestellten Ziffern (ΛΛ[2]) bezeichnen Unterabteilungen einer Kategorie (vgl. vollständiger Schlüssel auf Seite I · 30).

Los símbolos incluídos en el texto del índice representan las grandes categorías identificadas con la clave a la derecha. Los símbolos con numeros en su parte superior (ΛΛ[2]) identifican las subcategorías (véase la clave completa en la página I · 30).

Les symboles de l'index représentent les catégories indiquées dans la légende à droite. Les symboles suivis d'un indice (ΛΛ[2]) représentent des sous-catégories (voir légende complète à la page I · 30).

Os símbolos incluídos no texto do índice representam as grandes categorias identificadas com a chave à direita. Os símbolos com números em sua parte superior (ΛΛ[2]) identificam as subcategorias (veja-se a chave completa à página I · 30).

Symbol	English	Deutsch	Español	Français	Português
Λ	Mountain	Berg	Montaña	Montagne	Montanha
ΛΛ	Mountains	Berge	Montañas	Montagnes	Montanhas
)(	Pass	Pass	Paso	Col	Passo
V	Valley, Canyon	Tal, Cañon	Valle, Cañón	Vallée, Canyon	Vale, Canhão
≚	Plain	Ebene	Llano	Plaine	Planície
>	Cape	Kap	Cabo	Cap	Cabo
I	Island	Insel	Isla	Île	Ilha
II	Islands	Inseln	Islas	Îles	Ilhas
⊥	Other Topographic Features	Andere Topographische Objekte	Otros Elementos Topográficos	Autres données topographiques	Outros Elementos Topográficos

ESPAÑOL / FRANÇAIS / PORTUGUÊS

Nombre / Nom / Nome	Página / Page	Lat.°′	Long.°′ W=Oeste / W=Ouest
Firenzuola	66	44.07 N	11.23 E
Firesteel Creek ≃	198	43.43 N	97.58 W
Firgrove	262	53.37 N	2.08 W
Firmat	252	33.27 S	61.29 W
Firminópolis	255	16.40 S	50.19 W
Firminy	62	45.23 N	4.18 E
Firmo	68	39.43 N	16.10 E
Firovo	76	57.29 N	33.40 E
Fīrozābād	124	27.09 N	78.25 E
Fīrozpur	123	30.55 N	74.36 E
Fīrozpur Jhirka	124	27.48 N	76.57 E
Firsanovka	265b	55.57 N	37.15 E
Firsovo	88	52.20 N	118.06 E
First Broad ≃	192	35.11 N	81.37 W
First Cataract ⌊	140	24.01 N	32.52 E
First Cliff ▪[4]	283	42.12 N	70.43 W
First Connecticut Lake ⊜	206	45.05 N	71.15 W
First Herring Brook ≃	283	42.11 N	70.45 W
First King	162	31.49 S	124.21 E
First Watchung Mountain ∧	276	40.55 N	74.10 W
Firth	198	40.33 N	96.37 W
Firth ≃	180	69.32 N	139.22 W
Fir'uza	128	37.56 N	58.04 E
Fīrūzābād	128	28.50 N	52.36 E
Fīrūz Bahram	267d	35.38 N	51.15 E
Fīrūz Kūh	128	35.45 N	52.47 E
Fischa ≃	264b	48.04 N	16.35 E
Fischbach, B.R.D.	56	49.44 N	7.23 E
Fischbach, B.R.D.	60	49.25 N	11.12 E
Fischbachau	64	47.43 N	11.57 E
Fischbacher Alpen Ʌ	61	47.28 N	15.30 E
Fischbeck, B.R.D.	52	52.09 N	9.17 E
Fischbeck, D.D.R.	54	52.32 N	12.01 E
Fischeln ⬥[8]	263	51.18 N	6.35 E
Fischen	58	47.28 N	10.16 E
Fischhausen → Primorsk	76	54.44 N	20.01 E
Fischland ▪[2]	54	54.22 N	12.25 E
Fish ≃, Austl.	170	33.29 S	149.37 E
Fish ≃, Namibia	156	28.07 S	17.45 E
Fish ≃, Ala., U.S.	194	30.25 N	87.50 W
Fishbourne	42	50.44 N	1.12 W
Fish Brook ≃, Mass., U.S.	283	42.38 N	70.58 W
Fish Brook ≃, Mass., U.S.	283	42.42 N	71.13 W
Fish Camp	226	37.29 N	119.38 W
Fish Canyon V	280	34.11 N	117.55 W
Fish Creek ≃, Ont., Can.	212	43.13 N	81.13 W
Fish Creek ≃, U.S.	216	41.28 N	84.45 W
Fish Creek ≃, Mont., U.S.	202	46.17 N	109.13 W
Fish Creek ≃, N.Y., U.S.	212	43.12 N	75.43 W
Fish Creek ≃, Oreg., U.S.	224	45.09 N	122.09 W
Fish Creek, East Branch ≃	212	43.16 N	75.38 W
Fish Creek, West Branch ≃	212	43.16 N	75.38 W
Fish Creek Mountain ∧	224	45.05 N	122.08 W
Fisheating Creek ≃	220	26.57 N	81.07 W
Fisher, Austl.	162	30.33 S	130.58 E
Fisher, Ark., U.S.	194	35.30 N	90.58 W
Fisher, Ill., U.S.	216	40.19 N	88.21 W
Fisher, La., U.S.	194	31.30 N	93.28 W
Fisher, Pa., U.S.	214	41.16 N	79.15 W
Fisher ≃, Man., Can.	184	51.26 N	97.18 W
Fisher ≃, Mont., U.S.	202	48.22 N	115.19 W
Fisher Bay C, Man., Can.	184	51.30 N	97.16 W
Fisher Bay C, Mich., U.S.	281	42.36 N	82.39 W
Fisher Branch	184	51.05 N	97.37 W
Fisher Channel Џ	182	52.10 N	127.42 W
Fisher Glacier ◹	9	73.15 S	66.00 E
Fisher Heights	279b	40.10 N	79.54 W
Fishermans Island I	208	37.06 N	75.58 W
Fisherman's Wharf ⬥	282	37.48 N	122.25 W
Fishermens Bend Airfield ⊠	274b	37.50 S	144.55 E
Fisher Peak ∧	192	36.33 N	80.50 W
Fisher River Indian Reserve ⬥[4]	184	51.26 N	97.20 W
Fishers, Ind., U.S.	218	39.57 N	86.01 W
Fishers, N.Y., U.S.	210	43.00 N	77.28 W
Fishers Island I	207	41.16 N	72.02 W
Fishers Peak ∧	196	37.06 N	104.28 W
Fisher Strait Џ	176	63.15 N	83.30 W
Fishertown	214	40.08 N	78.35 W
Fisherville, Ont., Can.	275b	43.47 N	79.28 W
Fisherville, Pa., U.S.	285	40.01 N	75.45 W
Fishguard	42	51.59 N	4.59 W
Fishhook	219	39.48 N	90.53 W
Fish House	210	43.08 N	74.08 W
Fishing Bay C	208	38.18 N	76.01 W
Fishing Creek	208	38.20 N	76.14 W
Fishing Creek ≃, Ky., U.S.	192	37.06 N	84.41 W
Fishing Creek ≃, N.C., U.S.	192	35.57 N	77.31 W
Fishing Creek ≃, Pa., U.S.	210	41.07 N	77.29 W
Fishing Creek ≃, S.C., U.S.	192	34.36 N	80.54 W
Fishing Islands II	212	44.45 N	81.20 W
Fishing Lake ⊜, Man., Can.	184	52.07 N	95.25 W
Fishing Lake ⊜, Sask., Can.	184	51.50 N	103.32 W
Fishkill	210	41.32 N	73.53 W
Fishkill Creek ≃	210	41.29 N	73.59 W
Fish Lake	216	41.34 N	86.33 W
Fish Lake ⊜, Ont., Can.	212	44.06 N	77.11 W
Fish Lake ⊜, Mich., U.S.	216	42.03 N	85.52 W
Fish Lake ⊜, Wash., U.S.	224	47.50 N	120.42 W
Fishmoor Reservoir ⊜[1]	262	53.44 N	2.28 W
Fish Point >	214	41.43 N	82.40 W
Fishpool	262	53.35 N	2.17 W
Fish River	166	17.55 S	137.45 E
Fishs Eddy	210	41.58 N	75.10 W
Fisk	194	36.47 N	90.12 W
Fiskárdhon	38	38.27 N	20.35 E
Fiskdale	207	42.07 N	72.07 W
Fiskebäckskil	26	58.15 N	11.27 E
Fismes	50	49.18 N	3.41 E
Fišt, Gora ∧	84	43.58 N	39.54 E
Fitchburg	207	42.35 N	71.48 W
Fitchville, Conn., U.S.	207	41.34 N	72.09 W
Fitchville, Ohio, U.S.	214	41.06 N	82.29 W
Fitful Head >	46a	59.54 N	1.23 W
Fitiuta	174y	14.13 S	169.27 W
Fito, Mount ∧	175a	13.55 S	171.44 W
Fitri, Lac ⊜	146	12.50 N	17.28 E
Fittja	40	59.15 N	17.52 E
Fittleworth	42	50.58 N	0.35 W
Fitu	144	5.05 N	40.42 E
Fitzgerald	192	31.43 N	83.15 W
Fitz Henry	279b	40.10 N	79.45 W
Fitz Hugh Sound Џ	182	51.40 N	127.57 W
Fitzmaurice ≃	164	14.50 S	129.44 E
Fitz Roy, Arg.	254	47.02 S	67.15 W
Fitzroy, Austl.	274b	37.48 S	144.59 E
Fitzroy ≃, Austl.	162	17.31 S	123.35 E
Fitzroy ≃, Austl.	166	23.32 S	150.52 E
Fitzroy, Monte (Cerro Chaltel) ∧	254	49.17 S	73.05 W
Fitzroy Crossing	162	18.11 S	125.35 E
Fitzwilliam	207	42.47 N	72.08 W
Fitzwilliam Island I	190	45.30 N	81.45 W
Fiuggi	66	41.48 N	13.13 E
Fiumalbo	64	44.11 N	10.39 E
Fiume → Rijeka	36	45.20 N	14.27 E
Fiumedinisi	70	38.02 N	15.23 E
Fiumefreddo Bruzio	68	39.14 N	16.04 E
Fiumefreddo di Sicilia	70	37.47 N	15.12 E
Fiumesino	66	43.38 N	13.22 E
Fiume Veneto	64	45.56 N	12.44 E
Fiumicino	36	41.46 N	12.14 E
Fiumicino ⬥[8]	66	41.46 N	12.14 E
Five Corners	283	42.01 N	71.07 W
Five Dock	274a	33.52 S	151.08 E
Five Islands	186	45.25 N	64.02 W
Five Islands Harbour C	240c	17.06 N	61.54 W
Fivemile ≃	276	41.03 N	73.27 W
Fivemile Creek ≃, N.Y., U.S.	210	42.22 N	77.22 W
Fivemile Creek ≃, Oreg., U.S.	224	45.36 N	121.05 W
Fivemile Creek ≃, Wyo., U.S.	202	43.14 N	108.12 W
Fivemile Point	210	42.06 N	75.48 W
Fivemiletown	48	54.23 N	7.18 W
Five Penny Borve	46	58.25 N	6.25 W
Five Points, Calif., U.S.	226	36.26 N	120.06 W
Five Points, Ind., U.S.	218	39.35 N	86.20 W
Five Points, N. Mex., U.S.	200	35.04 N	106.41 W
Five Points, Ohio, U.S.	218	39.41 N	83.12 W
Five Points, Pa., U.S.	214	40.34 N	80.15 W
Five Points, Pa., U.S.	285	39.50 N	75.42 W
Fivizzano	64	44.14 N	10.08 E
Fiwila Mission	154	13.58 S	29.36 E
Fixin	58	47.15 N	4.58 E
Fix-Saint-Geneys	62	45.08 N	3.40 E
Fizi	154	4.18 S	28.57 E
Fizuli	84	39.37 N	47.08 E
Fjællebroen	41	55.03 N	10.24 E
Fjærlandsfjorden C[2]	26	61.17 N	6.40 E
Fjällåsen	24	67.29 N	20.10 E
Fjällbacka	26	58.36 N	11.17 E
Fjällsjöälven ≃	26	63.29 N	16.50 E
Fjärdhundra	40	59.47 N	16.56 E
Fjärdhundra □[9]	40	59.47 N	16.55 E
Fjenneslev	41	55.26 N	11.40 E
Fjerritslev	26	57.05 N	9.16 E
Fjugesta	40	59.10 N	14.52 E
Fkih-ben-Salah	148	32.32 N	6.40 W
Flachsmeer	52	53.07 N	7.28 E
Flacksta	40	59.23 N	16.27 E
Fladnitz	61	46.59 N	15.47 E
Fladså ≃	41	55.19 N	8.54 E
Fladungen	56	50.31 N	10.08 E
Flag Creek ≃	278	41.43 N	87.55 W
Flagler	198	39.18 N	103.04 W
Flagler Beach	192	29.29 N	81.07 W
Flagstaff, S. Afr.	158	31.05 S	29.29 E
Flagstaff, Ariz., U.S.	200	35.12 N	111.39 W
Flagstaff Lake ⊜	188	45.10 N	70.15 W
Flagtown	276	40.31 N	74.41 W
Flaken-See ⊜	264a	52.25 N	13.46 E
Flåm	26	60.50 N	7.07 E
Flambeau ≃	190	45.18 N	91.15 W
Flambeau, South Fork ≃	190	45.39 N	90.48 W
Flamborough Head >	44	54.07 N	0.04 W
Fläming ⬥[1]	54	52.00 N	12.30 E
Flaming Gorge National Recreation Area ♠	200	41.30 N	109.30 W
Flaming Gorge Reservoir ⊜[1]	200	41.15 N	109.30 W
Flamingo	220	25.09 N	80.56 W
Flamingo, Teluk C	164	5.33 S	138.00 E
Flammersfeld	56	50.38 N	7.32 E
Flanagan	216	40.53 N	88.52 W
Flanagan ≃	184	52.50 N	93.28 W
Flanagan Passage Џ	240m	18.18 N	64.39 W
Flanders, Ont., Can.	190	48.44 N	92.05 W
Flanders, N.J., U.S.	276	40.51 N	74.42 W
Flanders, N.Y., U.S.	207	40.49 N	72.36 W
Flanders (Flandre) (Vlaanderen) □[9]	50	51.00 N	3.00 E
Flanders Airport ⊠	276	40.50 N	74.41 W
Flandes	246	4.18 N	74.49 W
Flandorf	264b	48.21 N	16.23 E
Flandre → Flanders □[9]	50	51.00 N	3.00 E
Flandreau	198	44.03 N	96.36 W
Flannan Islands II	46	58.18 N	7.36 W
Flåren ⊜	26	57.02 N	14.06 E
Flasher	198	46.27 N	101.14 W
Flåsjön ⊜	26	64.06 N	15.51 E
Flat, Alaska, U.S.	180	62.27 N	158.01 W
Flat, Tex., U.S.	222	31.19 N	97.38 W
Flat ≃, N.W. Ter., Can.	180	61.33 N	125.18 W
Flat ≃, Mich., U.S.	190	42.56 N	85.20 W
Flat ≃, N.C., U.S.	192	36.05 N	78.49 W
Flat Bay	186	48.24 N	58.36 W
Flatbush ⬥[8]	276	40.39 N	73.56 W
Flat Creek ≃, Ky., U.S.	218	38.17 N	83.48 W
Flat Creek ≃, Mo., U.S.	194	36.45 N	93.31 W
Flat Creek ≃, Mont., U.S.	202	47.43 N	109.50 W
Flat Creek ≃, N.J., U.S.	276	40.27 N	74.10 W
Flat Creek ≃, Va., U.S.	192	37.24 N	77.53 W
Flat Creek Reservoir ⊜[1]	222	32.14 N	95.45 W
Flatey	24a	65.19 N	23.07 W
Flateyri	24a	65.59 N	23.42 W
Flathead ≃	202	47.22 N	114.47 W
Flathead, North Fork ≃	202	48.28 N	114.04 W
Flathead, South Fork ≃	202	48.23 N	114.04 W
Flathead Indian Reservation ⬥[4]	202	47.30 N	114.25 W
Flathead Lake ⊜	202	47.52 N	114.08 W
Flat Holm I	42	51.23 N	3.08 W
Flat Island I	157c	19.52 S	57.40 E
Flat Lake ⊜	182	54.39 N	112.55 W
Flat Lick	192	36.50 N	83.46 W
Flatonia	222	29.47 N	97.06 W
Flatow, D.D.R.	264a	52.44 N	12.57 E
Flatow → Złotów, Pol.	30	53.22 N	17.02 E
Flat River, P.E.I., Can.	186	46.01 N	62.52 W
Flat River, Mo., U.S.	194	37.51 N	90.31 W
Flat River Reservoir ⊜[1]	207	41.42 N	71.37 W
Flat Rock, Ala., U.S.	194	34.46 N	85.42 W
Flat Rock, Ill., U.S.	194	38.54 N	87.40 W
Flat Rock, Ind., U.S.	218	39.22 N	85.50 W
Flat Rock, Mich., U.S.	216	42.06 N	83.18 W
Flat Rock, Ohio, U.S.	214	41.14 N	82.52 W
Flatrock ≃	218	39.12 N	85.56 W
Flatrock Creek ≃	216	41.10 N	84.27 W
Flatrock Lake ⊜	184	55.37 N	100.47 W
Flatruet Ʌ[2]	26	62.45 N	12.50 E
Flats	222	32.50 N	95.53 W
Flattery, Cape >, Austl.	164	14.58 S	145.21 E
Flattery, Cape >, Wash., U.S.	224	48.23 N	124.43 W
Flatts	240a	32.19 N	64.44 W
Flatwillow Creek ≃	202	46.56 N	107.55 W
Flatwood	194	32.09 N	87.31 W
Flatwoods	188	38.31 N	82.43 W
Flaugherty Run ≃	279b	40.33 N	80.13 W
Flaunden	260	51.42 N	0.32 W
Flavigny-sur-Moselle	58	48.34 N	6.11 E
Flavigny-sur-Ozerain	58	47.30 N	4.32 E
Flavy-le-Martel	50	49.43 N	3.12 E
Flawil	58	47.24 N	9.12 E
Flaxcombe	184	51.29 N	109.36 W
Flaxman Island I	180	70.13 N	146.00 W
Flax Pond ⊜, Mass., U.S.	283	42.29 N	70.57 W
Flax Pond ⊜, N.Y., U.S.	276	40.58 N	73.08 W
Flaxton	198	48.54 N	102.24 W
Flaxville	198	48.49 N	105.10 W
Flechas Point >	116	10.22 N	119.34 E
Flechtingen	54	52.20 N	11.14 E
Fleckeby	41	54.29 N	9.41 E
Flecken Zechlin	54	53.09 N	12.46 E
Fleesensee ⊜	54	53.30 N	12.29 E
Fleet	42	51.16 N	0.50 W
Fleet ≃	46	57.57 N	4.05 W
Fleet Point >	276	40.40 N	73.20 W
Fleets Bay C	208	37.40 N	76.19 W
Fleetville	210	41.36 N	75.43 W
Fleetwing Estates	285	40.07 N	74.51 W
Fleetwood, Eng., U.K.	44	53.56 N	3.01 W
Fleetwood, Pa., U.S.	208	40.27 N	75.49 W
Flehe ⬥[8]	263	51.12 N	6.47 E
Flehingen	56	49.05 N	8.46 E
Fleischhacker Zoo ♠	282	37.44 N	122.30 W
Fleischmanns	210	42.09 N	74.32 W
Flekkefjord	26	58.17 N	6.41 E
Fleming, Colo., U.S.	198	40.41 N	102.50 W
Fleming, Pa., U.S.	214	40.55 N	77.52 W
Fleming □[6]	218	38.21 N	83.42 W
Fleming Creek ≃, Ont., Can.	214	42.26 N	81.43 W
Fleming Creek ≃, Ky., U.S.	218	38.22 N	83.57 W
Fleming Creek ≃, Mich., U.S.	281	42.16 N	83.40 W
Flemingsburg	218	36.25 N	83.44 W
Flemington, N.J., U.S.	210	40.31 N	74.52 W
Flemington, Pa., U.S.	210	41.07 N	77.28 W
Flemington Racecourse ♠	274b	37.47 S	144.55 E
Flemish Cap ⊹[3]	16	48.00 N	45.00 W
Flemsdorf	54	53.02 N	14.10 E
Flen	40	59.04 N	16.35 E
Flensburg	41	54.47 N	9.26 E
Flensburger Förde C	41	54.49 N	9.45 E
Fleres (Boden)	64	46.58 N	11.21 E
Flers	32	48.45 N	0.34 W
Flers-sur-Noye	50	49.44 N	2.15 E
Flesherton	212	44.16 N	80.33 W
Flesko, Tanjung >	112	0.29 N	124.30 E
Fletcher, Ont., Can.	214	42.18 N	82.18 W
Fletcher, N.C., U.S.	192	35.26 N	82.30 W
Fletcher, Ohio, U.S.	218	40.09 N	84.07 W
Fletcher, Okla., U.S.	196	34.52 N	98.17 W
Fletcher Islands II	9	72.40 S	94.10 W
Fletcher Moss Museum ʊ	262	53.25 N	2.14 W
Fletcher Pond ⊜[1]	190	44.58 N	83.52 W
Fletchers Creek ≃	275b	43.38 N	79.42 W
Fleurance	32	43.50 N	0.40 E
Fleur-de-Lys	186	50.07 N	56.08 W
Fleurier	58	46.54 N	6.35 E
Fleurus	56	50.29 N	4.33 E
Fleurville	58	46.27 N	4.53 E
Fleury-les-Aubrais	50	47.56 N	1.55 E
Fleury-Mérogis	261	48.38 N	2.22 E
Fleury-sur-Andelle	50	49.22 N	1.22 E
Fleuth ≃	263	51.32 N	6.26 E
Fleuve □[4]	150	16.00 N	14.30 W
Flexanville	261	48.51 N	1.44 E
Flexenpass)(	58	47.09 N	10.10 E
Fley ⬥[8]	263	51.23 N	7.30 E
Flieden	56	50.25 N	9.33 E
Flierich	263	51.35 N	7.48 E
Flight Locks ʊ[3]	284a	43.08 N	79.12 W
Flimby	44	54.41 N	3.31 W
Flims	58	46.50 N	9.17 E
Flinders ≃	166	17.36 S	140.36 E
Flinders Bay C	162	34.23 S	115.19 E
Flinders Chase ♠	166	35.54 S	136.40 E
Flinders Island I	166	40.00 S	148.00 E
Flinders Peak ∧	171a	27.49 S	152.49 E
Flinders Peak ∧[2]	169	37.51 S	144.24 E
Flinders Range Ʌ	14	31.25 S	138.45 E
Flinders Reefs ⊹[2]	166	17.37 S	148.31 E
Flinders Street Station ⬥[5]	274b	37.49 S	144.58 E
Flinesjön ⊜	40	60.23 N	16.06 E
Flines-lèz-Râches	50	50.25 N	3.11 E
Flin Flon	184	54.46 N	101.53 W
Flingern ⬥[8]	263	51.14 N	6.49 E
Flins-sur-Seine	261	48.58 N	1.52 E
Flint, Wales, U.K.	44	53.15 N	3.07 W
Flint, Mich., U.S.	216	43.01 N	83.41 W
Flint, Tex., U.S.	222	32.12 N	95.21 W
Flint I	14	11.26 S	151.48 W
Flint ≃, Ga., U.S.	192	30.52 N	84.38 W
Flint ≃, Mich., U.S.	190	43.21 N	84.03 W
Flint, South Branch ≃	216	43.10 N	83.23 W
Flint Castle ⊥	262	53.16 N	3.07 W
Flint Creek ≃, Ala., U.S.	194	34.30 N	86.57 W
Flint Creek ≃, Mont., U.S.	202	46.39 N	113.08 W
Flint Creek ≃, N.Y., U.S.	210	42.57 N	77.03 W
Flint Creek Range Ʌ	202	46.20 N	113.05 W
Flint Hill	219	38.52 N	90.52 W
Flint Hills Ʌ[2]	198	38.50 N	100.00 W
Flint Lake ⊜, N.W. Ter., Can.	176	69.10 N	74.20 W
Flint Lake ⊜, Ind., U.S.	216	41.31 N	87.03 W
Flinton, Austl.	166	27.54 S	149.34 E
Flinton, Pa., U.S.	214	40.43 N	78.31 W
Flint Peak ∧	280	34.10 N	118.12 W
Flint Pond ⊜	283	42.40 N	71.26 W
Flinträngan Џ	41	55.34 N	12.50 E
Flintridge	228	34.11 N	118.11 W
Flintville	194	34.59 N	86.25 W
Flipper Point >	174a	19.18 N	166.35 E
Flirey	56	48.53 N	5.50 E
Flirsch	58	47.09 N	10.24 E
Flisa	26	60.34 N	12.06 E
Flitwick	42	52.00 N	0.29 W
Flixecourt	50	50.01 N	2.05 E
Flize	56	49.42 N	4.46 E
Flobecq (Vloesberg)	50	50.44 N	3.44 E
Floby	26	58.08 N	13.20 E
Floda, Sve.	26	57.48 N	12.22 E
Floda, Sve.	40	59.04 N	16.21 E
Flodden	44	55.38 N	2.10 W
Flodden Field Battlesite (1513) ⊥	44	55.38 N	2.13 W
Flogny	50	47.57 N	3.52 E
Flöha	54	50.51 N	13.04 E
Flöha ≃	54	50.51 N	13.04 E
Floing	56	49.43 N	4.56 E
Flomaton	194	31.00 N	87.16 W
Flomborn	56	49.41 N	8.08 E
Flomot	196	34.14 N	100.59 W
Floodwood	190	46.55 N	92.56 W
Flora, Ill., U.S.	194	38.40 N	88.29 W
Flora, Ind., U.S.	216	40.33 N	86.31 W
Flora, Miss., U.S.	194	32.33 N	90.19 W
Florac	32	44.19 N	3.36 E
Florala	194	31.00 N	86.20 W
Floral City	220	28.45 N	82.18 W
Floral Park, Mont., U.S.	202	45.57 N	112.26 W
Floral Park, N.Y., U.S.	210	40.43 N	73.42 W
Florange	56	49.20 N	6.07 E
Florânia	250	6.08 S	36.49 W
Flora Vista	200	36.48 N	108.02 W
Flore, Piton ∧	241f	13.58 N	60.57 W
Floreffe	56	50.26 N	4.45 E
Florence → Firenze, It.	66	43.46 N	11.15 E
Florence, Ala., U.S.	194	34.49 N	87.40 W
Florence, Ariz., U.S.	200	33.02 N	111.23 W
Florence, Calif., U.S.	228	33.58 N	118.15 W
Florence, Colo., U.S.	200	38.23 N	105.08 W
Florence, Kans., U.S.	198	38.15 N	96.56 W
Florence, Ky., U.S.	218	39.00 N	84.38 W
Florence, N.J., U.S.	285	40.07 N	74.49 W
Florence, N.J., U.S.	285	39.44 N	74.55 W
Florence, Oreg., U.S.	202	43.58 N	124.07 W
Florence, Pa., U.S.	214	40.26 N	80.26 W
Florence, S.C., U.S.	192	34.12 N	79.46 W
Florence, Tex., U.S.	222	30.51 N	97.48 W
Florence, Wis., U.S.	190	45.56 N	88.07 W
Florencia, Col.	246	1.36 N	75.36 W
Florencia → Firenze, It.	66	43.46 N	11.15 E
Florencio Sánchez	258	33.53 S	57.24 W
Florencio Varela	258	34.49 S	58.17 W
Florencio Varela □[5]	288	34.52 S	58.15 W
Florennes	56	50.15 N	4.37 E
Florentia	273d	26.16 S	28.08 E
Florentino Ameghino, Embalse ⊜[1]	254	43.55 S	66.20 W
Florenville	56	49.42 N	5.18 E
Florenz → Firenze	66	43.46 N	11.15 E
Flores, Bra.	250	7.51 S	37.59 W
Flores, Perú	286d	12.01 S	77.01 W
Flores □[5]	258	33.48 S	56.50 W
Flores ⬥[8]	288	34.38 S	58.28 W
Flores I, Indon.	115b	8.30 S	121.00 E
Flores I, Port.	148a	39.26 N	31.13 W
Flores, Cachoeira das ⌊	255	14.19 S	53.32 W
Flores, Laut (Flores Sea) ⫧[2]	112	8.00 S	120.00 E
Flores, Rio das ≃	256	22.05 S	43.34 W
Flores, Selat Џ	115b	8.25 S	122.55 E
Flores da Cunha	252	29.02 S	51.11 W
Flôres de Goiás	255	14.34 S	47.04 W
Flores Island I	182	49.20 N	126.10 W
Flores Sea → Flores, Laut ⫧[2]	112	8.00 S	120.00 E
Floresta, Bra.	250	8.36 S	38.34 W
Floresta, It.	70	37.59 N	14.55 E
Floresta ⬥[8]	288	34.38 S	58.29 W
Floresta Azul	255	14.51 S	39.41 W
Florestina	255	18.29 S	48.01 W
Floreşty	78	47.53 N	28.17 E
Floresville	196	29.08 N	98.10 W
Florham Park	210	40.47 N	74.23 W
Floriano, Bra.	250	6.47 S	43.01 W
Floriano, Bra.	256	22.27 S	44.18 W
Floriano Peixoto, Bra.	248	9.03 S	67.24 W
Floriano Peixoto, Bra.	250	9.32 S	35.36 W
Florianópolis	252	27.35 S	48.34 W
Florida, Col.	246	3.21 N	76.15 W
Florida, Cuba	240p	21.32 N	78.14 W
Florida, Hond.	236	15.01 N	88.50 W
Florida, Perú	248	5.50 S	77.55 W
Florida, P.R.	240m	18.22 N	66.34 W
Florida, P.R.	240m	18.14 N	65.47 W
Florida, S. Afr.	273d	26.11 S	27.55 E
Florida, Ind., U.S.	218	40.10 N	85.42 W
Florida, N.Y., U.S.	210	41.20 N	74.22 W
Florida, Ohio, U.S.	216	41.20 N	84.12 W
Florida, Ur.	258	34.06 S	56.13 W
Florida ⬥[8]	288	34.31 S	58.30 W
Florida □[3]	178		
	192	28.00 N	82.00 W
Florida ≃	200	37.03 N	107.52 W
Florida, Cape >	220	25.40 N	80.09 W
Florida, Cerro la ∧	234	23.13 N	99.15 W
Florida, Straits of Џ	238	25.00 N	79.45 W
Florida Bay C	220	25.00 N	80.45 W
Floridablanca	246	7.04 N	73.06 W
Florida City	220	25.27 N	80.29 W
Florida Island I	175e	9.05 S	160.15 E
Florida Keys II	220	24.45 N	81.00 W
Florida Ridge	220	27.35 N	80.23 W
Florida State Indian Reservation ⬥[4]	220	26.10 N	80.50 W
Floridia	70	37.05 N	15.09 E
Florido ≃	232	27.43 N	105.10 W
Floridsdorf ⬥[8]	264b	48.16 N	16.24 E
Floridsdorfer Brücke ⬥[5]	264b	48.14 N	16.23 E
Florien	194	31.27 N	93.27 W
Florin	226	38.30 N	121.24 W
Flórina	38	40.47 N	21.24 E
Florisbad	158	28.46 S	26.06 E
Florissant	219	38.48 N	90.20 W
Floriston	226	39.24 N	120.01 W
Florø	26	61.36 N	5.00 E
Flörsheim	56	50.01 N	8.26 E
Florvåg	26	60.25 N	5.14 E
Flosaille	62	45.39 N	5.18 E
Floss	60	49.44 N	12.17 E
Flossach ≃, B.R.D.	58	48.24 N	10.25 E
Flossach ≃, B.R.D.	64	48.13 N	10.30 E
Flossenbürg	60	49.44 N	12.21 E
Flossmoor	216	41.33 N	87.40 W
Flotantes, Jardines ♠	286a	19.16 N	99.06 W
Flöthbach ≃	263	51.17 N	6.26 E
Flotta I	46	58.50 N	3.07 W
Flotten Lake ⊜	184	54.38 N	108.30 W
Flourtown	285	40.07 N	75.13 W
Flowerfield	278	41.52 N	88.02 W
Flower Hill	276	40.49 N	73.41 W
Flower Mound	222	33.02 N	97.04 W
Flower's Cove	186	51.18 N	56.44 W
Flowery Branch	192	34.11 N	83.55 W
Floyd, N. Mex., U.S.	196	34.13 N	103.35 W
Floyd, Tex., U.S.	222	33.09 N	96.15 W
Floyd, Va., U.S.	192	36.55 N	80.19 W
Floyd □[6]	218	38.18 N	85.49 W
Floyd ≃	198	42.29 N	96.23 W
Floydada	196	33.59 N	101.20 W
Floyds Fork ≃	194	38.00 N	85.41 W
Fluchthorn ∧	58	46.53 N	10.13 E
Flüela Pass)(	58	46.45 N	9.57 E
Flüelen	58	46.54 N	8.38 E
Fluessen ⊜	52	52.57 N	5.30 E
Flühli	58	46.53 N	8.01 E
Flumen ≃	34	41.43 N	0.09 W
Flumendosa ≃	71	39.26 N	9.37 E
Flumendosa, Lago Alto del ⊜	71	39.56 N	9.26 E
Flumeri	68	41.05 N	15.09 E
Flumet	62	45.49 N	6.30 E
Fluminimaggiore	71	39.26 N	8.30 E
Flums	58	47.05 N	9.20 E
Flüren	263	51.41 N	6.33 E
Flushing → Vlissingen, Ned.	52	51.26 N	3.35 E
Flushing, Mich., U.S.	216	43.04 N	83.51 W
Flushing, Ohio, U.S.	214	40.09 N	81.04 W
Flushing ⬥[8]	276	40.45 N	73.49 W
Flushing Airport ⊠	276	40.47 N	73.50 W
Flushing Bay C	276	40.47 N	73.51 W
Flushing Meadow-Corona Park ♠	276	40.45 N	73.51 W
Fluvanna, N.Y., U.S.	214	42.07 N	79.18 W
Fluvanna, Tex., U.S.	196	32.53 N	101.09 W
Fluvia ≃	34	42.12 N	3.07 E
Fly ≃	164	8.30 S	143.41 E
Fly Creek	210	42.43 N	74.59 W
Fly Creek ≃	202	45.59 N	107.59 W
Flyinge	41	55.45 N	13.21 E
Flying Fish Cove	112	10.25 S	105.43 E
Flying "w" Ranch Airport ⊠	285	39.56 N	74.48 W
Flynn	222	31.09 N	96.08 W
Foam Lake	184	51.39 N	103.33 W
Fobaochang	107	28.47 N	106.05 E
Fobbing	260	51.32 N	0.29 E
Fobello	62	45.53 N	8.10 E
Foča, Jugo.	38	43.31 N	18.46 E
Foça, Tür.	130	38.39 N	26.46 E
Focene ⬥[8]	267a	41.48 N	12.14 E
Fochabers	46	57.37 N	3.05 W
Fochville	158	26.30 S	27.30 E
Fockbek	41	54.18 N	9.36 E
Focşani	38	45.41 N	27.11 E
Fodda, Oued ≃	34	35.14 N	1.28 E
Fodé	152	5.29 N	23.18 E
Fodécontea	150	10.50 N	14.22 W
Fodingshan ∧	102	27.08 N	108.02 E
F'odorovka, S.S.S.R.	78	49.23 N	35.07 E
F'odorovka, S.S.S.R.	78	47.33 N	36.33 E
F'odorovka, S.S.S.R.	80	53.28 N	49.38 E
F'odorovka, S.S.S.R.	80	52.21 N	52.55 E
F'odorovka, S.S.S.R.	80	51.09 N	51.59 E
F'odorovka, S.S.S.R.	82	56.15 N	37.14 E
F'odorovka, S.S.S.R.	83	47.20 N	38.23 E
F'odorovka, S.S.S.R.	86	53.38 N	62.42 E
F'odorovka, S.S.S.R.	86	53.22 N	76.18 E
F'odorovka, S.S.S.R.	86	53.11 N	55.11 E
F'odorovka, S.S.S.R.	86	56.05 N	78.49 E
F'odorovskoje, S.S.S.R.	82	56.19 N	37.40 E
F'odorovskoje, S.S.S.R.	82	56.44 N	36.58 E
F'odorovskoje, S.S.S.R.	82	56.07 N	38.52 E
F'odorovskoje, S.S.S.R.	82	56.08 N	38.04 E
Foëcy	50	47.10 N	2.10 E
Foeni	38	45.30 N	20.53 E
Fogang (Shijiao)	100	23.52 N	113.32 E
Fogdön >[1]	40	59.25 N	16.52 E
Fogelevo	85	42.03 N	69.32 E
Fogelsville	208	40.35 N	75.38 W
Foggaret el Arab	148	27.03 N	2.59 E
Foggaret ez Zoua	148	27.20 N	3.00 E
Foggia	68	41.27 N	15.34 E
Foggia □[4]	68	41.30 N	15.30 E
Foggy Island Bay C	180	70.15 N	147.30 W
Foglia ≃	66	43.55 N	12.54 E
Foglianise	68	41.10 N	14.40 E
Fogliano, Lago di C	66	41.24 N	12.54 E
Foglizzo	62	45.16 N	7.49 E
Fogo	186	49.43 N	54.17 W
Fogo I	150a	14.55 N	24.25 W
Fogo, Cape >	186	49.39 N	54.00 W
Fogo Island I	186	49.40 N	54.13 W
Fogolawa	150	12.19 N	8.41 E
Fogueteiro	266c	38.37 N	9.07 W
Fohnsdorf	61	47.13 N	14.41 E
Föhr I	30	54.43 N	8.30 E
Foia ∧	34	37.19 N	8.36 W
Foiano della Chiana	66	43.15 N	11.49 E
Foiano di Val Fortore	68	41.21 N	14.59 E
Foins, Lac aux ⊜	190	47.05 N	78.11 W
Foivre ≃	56	49.30 N	4.32 E
Foix	32	42.58 N	1.36 E
Foix ⬥[1]	32	43.00 N	1.40 E
Fojnica	36	43.58 N	17.54 E
Foki	80	56.42 N	54.21 E
Fokino	76	53.27 N	34.24 E
Fokku	150	11.40 N	4.31 E
Folakara	157b	18.20 S	45.02 E
Folamasi	104	41.56 N	121.27 E
Folarskardhuten ∧	26	60.37 N	7.45 E
Folcroft	285	39.54 N	75.17 W
Folda C[2]	24	67.36 N	14.50 E
Foldingbro	41	55.26 N	9.01 E
Folembray	50	49.33 N	3.17 E
Foley, Ala., U.S.	194	30.25 N	87.41 W
Foley, Minn., U.S.	190	45.40 N	93.55 W
Foley, Mo., U.S.	219	39.03 N	90.44 W
Foleyet	190	48.16 N	82.30 W
Foley Island I	176	68.35 N	75.10 W
Folgares	152	14.54 S	15.08 E
Folgaria	64	45.55 N	11.10 E
Folgefonni ◹	26	60.00 N	6.20 E
Folger Hill ∧[2]	207	41.17 N	70.01 W
Foligno	66	42.57 N	12.42 E
Folk	219	38.26 N	92.06 W
Folkärna	40	60.09 N	16.19 E
Folkestone	42	51.05 N	1.11 E
Folkingham	42	52.54 N	0.24 W
Folkston	192	30.50 N	82.01 W
Folkwangmuseum ʊ	263	51.27 N	7.00 E
Follafoss	26	63.59 N	11.06 E
Follainville-Dennemont	261	49.01 N	1.43 E
Follansbee	214	40.20 N	80.36 W
Folldal	26	62.08 N	10.03 E
Folle Anse, Pointe de >	241o	15.57 N	61.20 W
Follebu	26	61.14 N	10.17 E
Follets Island I	222	29.02 N	95.10 W
Follett	196	36.26 N	100.08 W
Follina	64	45.57 N	12.07 E
Föllinge	26	63.40 N	14.37 E
Follonica	66	42.55 N	10.45 E
Follonica, Golfo di C	66	42.54 N	10.43 E
Folly Branch ≃	284b	38.56 N	76.49 W
Folmhusen	52	53.10 N	7.28 E
Folschviller	56	49.04 N	6.41 E
Folsom, Calif., U.S.	226	38.41 N	121.15 W
Folsom, N.J., U.S.	208	39.38 N	74.51 W
Folsom, Pa., U.S.	285	39.54 N	75.19 W
Folsom Lake ⊜[1]	226	38.43 N	121.08 W
Folsom Lake State Recreation Area ♠	226	38.46 N	121.06 W
Fomboni	157a	12.16 S	43.45 E
Fomento, Cuba	240p	22.06 N	79.43 W
Fomento, Ur.	258	34.26 S	57.14 W
Fomin	80	46.58 N	43.38 E
Fominiči	76	54.07 N	34.41 E
Fominki	80	55.57 N	42.22 E
Fominskaja	24	61.17 N	48.40 E
Fominskoje, S.S.S.R.	76	58.59 N	39.06 E
Fominskoje, S.S.S.R.	76	59.43 N	42.05 E
Fomkino	80	54.25 N	50.30 E
Foncine-le-Bas	58	46.38 N	6.03 E
Fonda, Iowa, U.S.	198	42.35 N	94.51 W
Fonda, N.Y., U.S.	210	42.57 N	74.22 W
Fondachelli	70	37.58 N	15.11 E
Fond d'Or Bay C	241f	13.56 N	60.54 W
Fond du Lac, Sask., Can.	176	59.19 N	107.10 W
Fond du Lac, Wis., U.S.	190	43.47 N	88.27 W
Fond du Lac ≃	176	59.17 N	106.00 W
Fond du Lac Indian Reservation ⬥[4]	190	46.45 N	92.37 W
Fondi	66	41.21 N	13.25 E
Fondi, Lago di C	66	41.19 N	13.20 E
Fondo	64	46.26 N	11.08 E
Fondouk el Aouareb	36	35.34 N	9.46 E
Fongfong	140	12.56 N	23.14 E
Fonni	71	40.07 N	9.15 E
Fonsagrada	34	43.08 N	7.04 W
Fonseca	246	10.54 N	72.51 W
Fonseca, Golfo de C	236	13.10 N	87.40 W
Fons-outre-Gardon	62	43.54 N	4.11 E
Font ≃	44	55.10 N	1.44 W
Fontaine, Fr.	58	47.40 N	7.00 E
Fontaine, Fr.	62	45.11 N	5.40 E
Fontainebleau, Fr.	50	48.24 N	2.42 E
Fontainebleau, S. Afr.	273d	26.07 S	27.59 E
Fontaine-Française	58	47.31 N	5.22 E
Fontaine-le-Dun	50	49.49 N	0.51 E
Fontaine-lès-Dijon	58	47.21 N	5.01 E
Fontaine-lès-Grès	50	48.25 N	3.54 E
Fontaine-lès-Luxeuil	58	47.51 N	6.20 E
Fontaines	58	46.51 N	4.46 E
Fontaines-sur-Saône	62	45.50 N	4.51 E
Fontan	62	44.00 N	7.33 E
Fontana, Arg.	252	27.25 S	59.02 W
Fontana, Calif., U.S.	228	34.06 N	117.26 W
Fontana, Wis., U.S.	216	42.33 N	88.35 W
Fontana, Lago ⊜	254	44.56 S	71.30 W
Fontanafredda	64	45.58 N	12.34 E
Fontana Lake ⊜[1]	192	35.26 N	83.38 W
Fontanarosa	68	41.01 N	15.01 E
Fontanarossa, Aeroporto di ⊠	70	37.29 N	15.03 E
Fontanelas	266c	38.51 N	9.26 W
Fontanelice	66	44.15 N	11.33 E
Fontanella	64	45.27 N	9.48 E
Fontanellato	64	44.53 N	10.10 E
Fontanelle	198	41.17 N	94.34 W
Fontanetto Po	62	45.12 N	8.11 E
Fontanigorda	62	44.33 N	9.19 E
Fontarabie, Lac ⊜	186	51.10 N	66.25 W
Fontas ≃	176	58.20 N	121.50 W
Fonte, Bra.	287b	23.25 S	46.21 W
Fonte, It.	64	45.47 N	11.53 E
Fonte, It.	66	41.46 N	13.13 E
Fonte Avellana, Monastero di ʊ[1]	66	43.29 N	12.45 E
Fonte Blanda	66	42.34 N	11.10 E
Fonte Boa	246	2.32 S	66.01 W
Fonte Colombo, Convento di ʊ[1]	66	42.23 N	12.50 E
Fontenay, Abbaye de ʊ[1]	50	47.39 N	4.24 E
Fontenay-aux-Roses	261	48.47 N	2.17 E
Fontenay-en-Parisis	261	49.03 N	2.27 E
Fontenay-le-Comte	32	46.28 N	0.48 W
Fontenay-le-Fleury	261	48.49 N	2.03 E
Fontenay-lès-Briis	261	48.37 N	2.09 E
Fontenay-le-Vicomte	261	48.33 N	2.24 E
Fontenay-Saint-Père	261	49.02 N	1.45 E
Fontenay-sous-Bois	261	48.51 N	2.29 E
Fontenay-Trésigny	50	48.42 N	2.52 E
Fontenelle	186	48.52 N	64.52 W
Fontenelle Creek ≃	200	42.05 N	110.08 W
Fontenelle Reservoir ⊜[1]	200	42.05 N	110.06 W
Fontespina	66	43.17 N	13.45 E
Fontevivo	64	44.51 N	10.10 E
Font Hill Manor	284b	39.17 N	76.52 W
Fontibón	246	4.40 N	74.09 W
Fonti del Clitunno ⫧[4]	66	42.49 N	12.46 E
Fontoy	56	49.21 N	6.00 E
Fontur >	24a	66.23 N	14.30 W
Fontvieille	62	43.43 N	4.43 E
Fonzaso	64	46.01 N	11.48 E
Foochow → Fuzhou	100	26.06 N	119.17 E
Foot Creek ≃	198	45.26 N	98.29 W
Foothill Farms	226	38.40 N	121.21 W
Foothills	182	53.04 N	116.48 W
Footprint Lake ⊜	184	55.47 N	98.53 W
Footscray	169	37.48 S	144.54 E
Footville	216	42.40 N	89.12 W
Foping	102	33.22 N	108.19 E
Foppolo	64	46.03 N	9.45 E
Fora, Ponta de >	287a	22.57 S	43.07 W
Foraker, Mount ∧	180	62.56 N	151.26 W
Forbach, B.R.D.	56	48.41 N	8.21 E
Forbach, Fr.	56	49.11 N	6.54 E
Forbes	166	33.23 S	148.01 E
Forbes, Lac ⊜	206	46.31 N	74.12 W
Forbes, Mount ∧	182	51.52 N	116.56 W
Forbes Field ♠	279b	40.27 N	79.57 W
Forbesganj	124	26.18 N	87.15 E
Forbes Reef	158	26.10 S	31.05 E
Forbes Road	214	40.21 N	79.32 W
Forbestown	226	39.31 N	121.16 W
Forbidden City ♠	271a	39.55 N	116.23 E
Forcados	150	5.22 N	5.24 E
Forcados ≃[1]	150	5.25 N	5.19 E
Forcalquier	62	43.58 N	5.47 E
Force	214	41.15 N	78.30 W
Forchheim, B.R.D.	60	49.43 N	11.04 E
Forchheim, D.D.R.	54	50.43 N	13.16 E
Forclaz, Col de la)(	58	46.04 N	7.00 E
Ford, Scot., U.K.	46	56.10 N	5.26 W
Ford, Kans., U.S.	198	37.38 N	99.45 W
Ford □[6]	216	40.27 N	88.06 W
Ford ≃	190	45.40 N	87.09 W
Ford, Cape >	164	13.26 S	129.52 E
Ford City, Calif., U.S.	226	35.09 N	119.27 W
Ford City, Pa., U.S.	214	40.46 N	79.32 W
Ford City ⬥[9]	278	41.46 N	87.44 W
Ford Cliff	214	40.45 N	79.32 W
Ford Dam ⬥[6]	281	42.13 N	83.33 W
Ford Dry Lake ⊜	204	33.38 N	115.00 W
Førde, Nor.	26	61.27 N	5.52 E
Førde, Nor.	26	59.36 N	5.29 E
Førdefjorden C[2]	26	61.28 N	5.39 E
Forden	42	52.36 N	3.08 W
Förderstedt	54	51.54 N	11.38 E
Fordham University ʊ[2]	276	40.51 N	73.53 W
Fordingbridge	42	50.56 N	1.47 W
Ford Lake ⊜	281	42.13 N	83.36 W
Ford Mansion ⊥	276	40.48 N	74.28 W
Ford Motor Company (River Rouge Plant) ʊ[3]	281	42.18 N	83.10 W
Ford Museum ʊ	281	42.18 N	83.14 W
Fordongianus	71	39.59 N	8.48 E
Ford Ranges Ʌ	9	77.00 S	145.00 W
Fords	276	40.32 N	74.19 W
Fords Bridge	166	29.45 S	145.26 E
Fordsburg ⬥[8]	273d	26.13 S	28.02 E
Fords Prairie	224	46.47 N	123.05 W
Fordsville	194	37.38 N	86.43 W
Fordville	198	48.13 N	97.47 W
Fordyce	194	33.49 N	92.25 W
Fordyce Lake ⊜[1]	226	39.23 N	120.28 W
Foré	150	13.08 N	10.42 W
Forécariah	150	9.26 N	13.06 W
Forécariah □[4]	150	9.30 N	13.15 W
Forel, Mont ∧	176	67.00 N	37.00 W
Foreland Point >	42	51.16 N	3.47 W
Foreman	194	33.43 N	94.24 W
Foremost	184	49.29 N	111.25 W
Forenza	68	40.51 N	15.51 E
Forepaugh Airport ⊠[2]	279a	41.21 N	81.30 W
Foresman	216	40.52 N	87.18 W
Forest, Bel.	50	50.48 N	4.19 E
Forest, Ont., Can.	190	43.06 N	82.00 W
Forest, Ind., U.S.	216	40.22 N	86.20 W
Forest, Miss., U.S.	194	32.22 N	89.28 W
Forest, Ohio, U.S.	216	40.48 N	83.31 W
Forest □[6]	214	41.29 N	79.27 W
Forest ≃	198	48.21 N	97.09 W
Forest, Middle Branch ≃	198	48.13 N	97.48 W
Forest Acres	192	34.01 N	80.58 W
Forestburg	182	52.35 N	112.04 W
Forest City, Iowa, U.S.	190	43.16 N	93.39 W
Forest City, N.C., U.S.	192	35.20 N	81.52 W
Forest City, Pa., U.S.	210	41.39 N	75.28 W
Forest Creek ≃	226	38.23 N	120.28 W
Forest Gate ⬥[8]	260	51.33 N	0.02 E
Forest Glade	222	31.39 N	96.31 W
Forest Grove, B.C., Can.	182	51.46 N	121.06 W
Forest Grove, Oreg., U.S.	224	45.31 N	123.07 W
Forest Grove, Pa., U.S.	279b	40.18 N	75.04 W
Forest Heights	284c	38.49 N	77.00 W
Forest Hill, Austl.	171a	27.35 S	152.22 E

Symbol	English	Deutsch	Español	Français	Português
≃	River	Fluss	Río	Rivière	Rio
≊	Canal	Kanal	Canal	Canal	Canal
⌊	Waterfall, Rapids	Wasserfall, Stromschnellen	Cascada, Rápidos	Chute d'eau, Rapides	Cascata, Rápidos
Џ	Strait	Meeresstrasse	Estrecho	Détroit	Estreito
C	Bay, Gulf	Bucht, Golf	Bahía, Golfo	Baie, Golfe	Baía, Golfo
⊜	Lake, Lakes	See, Seen	Lago, Lagos	Lac, Lacs	Lago, Lagos
≋	Swamp	Sumpf	Pantano	Marais	Pântano
◹	Ice Features, Glacier	Eis- und Gletscherformen	Accidentes Glaciales	Formes glaciaires	Acidentes Glaciares
⫧	Other Hydrographic Features	Andere Hydrographische Objekte	Otros Elementos Hidrográficos	Autres données hydrographiques	Outros Elementos Hidrográficos
⊹	Submarine Features	Untermeerische Objekte	Accidentes Submarinos	Formes de relief sous-marin	Acidentes Submarinos
□	Political Unit	Politische Einheit	Unidad Política	Entité politique	Unidade Política
ʊ	Cultural Institution	Kulturelle Institution	Institución Cultural	Institution culturelle	Instituição Cultural
⊥	Historical Site	Historische Stätte	Sitio Histórico	Site historique	Sitio Histórico
♠	Recreational Site	Erholungs- und Ferienort	Sitio de Recreo	Centre de loisirs	Sítio de Lazer
⊠	Airport	Flughafen	Aeropuerto	Aéroport	Aeroporto
▪	Military Installation	Militäranlage	Instalación Militar	Installation militaire	Instalação Militar
⬥	Miscellaneous	Verschiedenes	Misceláneo	Divers	Miscelânea

ENGLISH / DEUTSCH

Name	Page	Lat.°′	Long.°′
Forest Hill, Austl.	171b	35.09 S	147.27 E
Forest Hill, Austl.	274b	37.50 S	145.11 E
Foresthill, Calif., U.S.	226	39.01 N	120.49 W
Forest Hill, Md., U.S.	208	39.35 N	76.23 W
Forest Hill, Tex., U.S.	222	32.40 N	97.16 W
Forest Hill ◆[8]	275b	43.42 N	79.24 W
Forest Hill Park ♠	279a	41.31 N	81.35 W
Forest Hill Parkway ♠	279a	41.33 N	81.36 W
Forest Hills	279b	40.26 N	79.52 W
Forest Hills ◆[8]	276	40.42 N	73.51 W
Forest Home	194	31.52 N	86.50 W
Forestier Peninsula ≻[1]	166	42.57 S	147.55 E
Forest Lake, Ill., U.S.	216	42.13 N	88.03 W
Forest Lake, Minn., U.S.	190	45.17 N	92.59 W
Forest Lake ⊜, Ill., U.S.	278	42.13 N	88.03 W
Forest Lake ⊜, Mass., U.S.	283	42.43 N	71.15 W
Forest Lawn Memorial Park ◆	280	34.09 N	118.19 W
Forest Park, Ga., U.S.	192	33.37 N	84.22 W
Forest Park, Ill., U.S.	278	41.53 N	87.50 W
Forest Park, Ohio, U.S.	218	39.16 N	84.34 W
Forest Park ◆[8]	284b	39.19 N	76.41 W
Forest Park ♠	276	40.42 N	73.51 W
Forest River	278	42.05 N	87.54 W
Forest Row	42	51.06 N	0.02 E
Forest View	278	41.49 N	87.47 W
Forestville, Austl.	274a	33.46 S	151.13 E
Forestville, Qué., Can.	186	48.45 N	69.06 W
Forestville, Md., U.S.	284c	38.50 N	76.52 W
Forestville, N.Y., U.S.	214	42.26 N	79.10 W
Forestville, Pa., U.S.	214	41.06 N	80.00 W
Forestville, Wis., U.S.	190	44.41 N	87.29 W
Forêt l'Orient, Lac de la ⊜[1]	50	48.17 N	4.20 E
Forêt-Noire → Schwarzwald ⛰	58	48.00 N	8.15 E
Forez, Monts du ⛰	32	45.35 N	3.48 E
Forfar	46	56.38 N	2.54 W
Forfry	261	49.03 N	2.51 E
Forgan	196	36.54 N	100.32 W
Forgaria	64	46.13 N	12.58 E
Forge Acres	284b	39.25 N	76.27 W
Forges-les-Bains	261	48.38 N	2.06 E
Forges-les-Eaux	50	49.37 N	1.33 E
Forget, Pointe ≻	275a	45.27 N	73.58 W
Forge Village	207	42.35 N	71.29 W
Forggensee ⊜	58	47.36 N	10.44 E
Forillon, Parc National (Forillon National Park) ♠	186	48.55 N	64.25 W
Forino	68	40.52 N	14.44 E
Foristell	219	38.49 N	90.57 W
Fork	208	39.28 N	76.27 W
Forked Creek ≃	216	41.19 N	88.09 W
Forked Deer ≃	194	35.56 N	89.35 W
Forked Deer, Middle Fork ≃	194	36.01 N	89.13 W
Forked Deer, North Fork ≃	194	36.00 N	89.26 W
Forked Deer, South Fork ≃	194	36.00 N	89.26 W
Forked River	208	39.51 N	74.12 W
Forks	224	47.57 N	124.23 W
Forkston	210	41.31 N	76.07 W
Forksville	210	41.29 N	76.36 W
Forleti, Arroyo ≃	288	34.35 S	58.41 W
Forlì	66	44.13 N	12.03 E
Forlì □[4]	64	44.05 N	12.02 E
Forlimpopoli	66	44.11 N	12.07 E
Forman	198	46.07 N	97.38 W
Formazza	58	46.22 N	8.26 E
Formby	262	53.34 N	3.05 W
Formby Hills ⛰[2]	262	53.34 N	3.06 W
Formby Point ≻	262	53.33 N	3.06 W
Formentera I	34	38.42 N	1.28 E
Formentor, Cabo de ≻	34	39.58 N	3.12 E
Formerie	50	49.39 N	1.44 E
Former Imperial Palace ♉	270	35.01 N	135.46 E
Formia	66	41.15 N	13.37 E
Formiga	255	20.27 S	45.25 W
Formiga ≃	256	22.18 S	42.52 W
Formigine	64	44.34 N	10.51 E
Formignana	64	44.50 N	11.51 E
Formosa, Arg.	252	26.11 S	58.11 W
Formosa, Bra.	255	15.32 S	47.20 W
Formosa □[4]	252	25.00 S	60.00 W
Formosa → Taiwan □[1]	100	23.30 N	121.00 E
Formosa → T'aiwan I	100	23.30 N	121.00 E
Formosa, Serra ⛰[1]	250	12.00 S	55.00 W
Formosa Bay C	154	2.45 S	40.20 E
Formosa Strait ⩌	100	24.00 N	119.00 E
Formoso ≃, Bra.	250	10.34 S	49.56 W
Formoso ≃, Bra.	255	13.26 S	44.14 W
Formoso ≃, Bra.	255	18.25 S	52.28 W
Formoso ≃, Bra.	255	17.25 S	44.57 W
Formoso ≃, Bra.	256	21.20 S	43.10 W
Fornelli	71	41.00 N	8.14 E
Forney	222	32.45 N	96.28 W
Forni Avoltri	64	46.35 N	12.46 E
Forni di sopra	64	46.25 N	12.35 E
Forni di sotto	64	46.23 N	12.40 E
Forni di Val d'Astico	64	45.51 N	11.22 E
Forno	64	46.21 N	11.37 E
Forno Alpi Graie	62	45.22 N	7.13 E
Forno di Zoldo	64	46.21 N	12.11 E
Fornosovo	76	59.35 N	30.35 E
Fornovo di Taro	64	44.42 N	10.06 E
Foro Romano ⊥	267a	41.54 N	12.29 E
Føroyar → Faeroe Islands □[2]	22	62.00 N	7.00 W
Forpost	86	56.47 N	72.10 E
Forres, Arg.	252	27.53 S	63.58 W
Forres, Scot., U.K.	46	57.37 N	3.38 W
Forrest, Austl.	162	30.51 S	128.06 E
Forrest, Ill., U.S.	216	40.45 N	88.25 W
Forrest ≃	164	15.18 S	128.04 E
Forrest, Mount ∧	162	24.48 S	127.45 E
Forrestal Research Center ♉[3]	276	40.21 N	74.37 W
Forrest City	194	35.01 N	90.47 W
Forrester Island I	180	54.48 N	133.32 W
Forrest Lakes ⊜	162	29.12 S	128.46 E
Forreston, Ill., U.S.	190	42.08 N	89.35 W
Forreston, Tex., U.S.	222	32.16 N	96.52 W
Fors	40	60.13 N	16.18 E
Forsan	196	32.07 N	101.22 W
Forsayth	166	18.35 S	143.36 E
Forsbacka	40	60.37 N	16.53 E
Forsby	26	60.30 N	25.56 E
Forserum	26	57.42 N	14.28 E
Forshaga	40	59.32 N	13.28 E
Forsmark	40	60.22 N	18.09 E
Forssa	26	60.49 N	23.38 E
Forst	54	51.44 N	14.39 E
Förste	52	51.44 N	10.10 E
Forster	166	32.11 S	152.31 E
Forstwald ◆[8]	263	51.18 N	6.30 E
Forsyth, Ga., U.S.	192	33.02 N	83.56 W
Forsyth, Ill., U.S.	219	39.56 N	88.57 W
Forsyth, Mo., U.S.	194	36.41 N	93.06 W
Forsyth, Mont., U.S.	202	46.16 N	106.41 W
Forsyth Island I	164	16.50 S	139.06 E
Fort ◆[8]	272c	18.56 N	72.50 E
Fort Abbās	123	29.12 N	72.52 E
Fort Adams	194	31.05 N	91.33 W
Fort Albany	176	52.15 N	81.37 W
Fort Alexander Indian Reserve ◆[4]	184	50.27 N	96.15 W
Fortaleza	250	3.43 S	38.30 W
Fortaleza ≃	248	10.40 S	77.52 W
Fortaleza de Santa Teresa ♠	252	33.59 S	53.32 W
Fortaleza do Ituxi	248	7.29 S	66.20 W
Fortaleza dos Nogueiras	250	6.54 S	46.09 W
Fort Allen ■	240m	18.01 N	66.30 W
Fort Amherst National Historic Park ♠	186	46.15 N	63.06 W
Fort Ancient State Memorial ⊥	218	39.24 N	84.06 W
Fort Anne National Historic Park ♠	186	44.44 N	65.26 W
Fort Apache Indian Reservation ◆[4]	200	34.01 N	110.28 W
Fort-Archambault → Sarh	146	9.09 N	18.23 E
Fort Assiniboine	182	54.20 N	114.46 W
Fort Atkinson	216	42.56 N	88.50 W
Fort Augusta ⊥	210	40.53 N	76.46 W
Fort Augustus	46	57.09 N	4.41 W
Fort Baker ■	282	37.50 N	122.29 W
Fort Battleford National Historic Park ♠	184	52.42 N	108.15 W
Fort Bayard → Zhanjiang	102	21.16 N	110.28 E
Fort Beaufort	158	32.46 S	26.40 E
Fort Beauséjour National Historic Park ♠	186	45.53 N	64.10 W
Fort Belknap Agency	202	48.30 N	108.46 W
Fort Belknap Indian Reservation ◆[4]	202	48.16 N	108.38 W
Fort Belvoir ■	208	38.44 N	77.10 W
Fort Bend □[6]	222	29.32 N	95.47 W
Fort Benjamin Harrison ■	218	39.52 N	86.01 W
Fort Benning ■	192	32.22 N	84.50 W
Fort Benton	202	47.49 N	110.40 W
Fort Berthold Indian Reservation ◆[4]	198	47.40 N	102.25 W
Fort Bidwell	204	41.52 N	120.09 W
Fort Bragg	204	39.26 N	123.48 W
Fort Bragg ■	192	35.09 N	78.59 W
Fort Branch	194	38.15 N	87.35 W
Fort Bridger	200	41.19 N	110.23 W
Fort Campbell ■	194	36.39 N	87.29 W
Fort Canby State Park ♠	224	46.17 N	124.04 W
Fort Canning ■	271c	1.18 N	103.51 E
Fort-Carnot	157b	21.53 S	47.28 E
Fort Caroline National Memorial ⊥	192	30.20 N	81.30 W
Fort Carson ■	200	38.44 N	104.48 W
Fort Casey Historical State Park ♠	224	48.10 N	122.40 W
Fort Chambly National Historic Park ♠	206	45.27 N	73.17 W
Fort-Chimo	176	58.06 N	68.25 W
Fort Chipewyan	176	58.42 N	111.08 W
Fort Churchill Historic State Monument ⊥	226	39.18 N	119.17 W
Fort Clatsop National Memorial ⊥	224	46.08 N	123.54 W
Fort Cobb	196	35.06 N	98.26 W
Fort Cobb Reservoir ⊜[1]	196	35.12 N	98.29 W
Fort Collins	200	40.35 N	105.05 W
Fort Columbia Historical State Park ♠	224	46.15 N	123.56 W
Fort Constantine	166	20.28 S	140.37 E
Fort-Coulonge	188	45.51 N	76.44 W
Fort Covington	188	44.59 N	74.30 W
Fort-Crampel	152	6.59 N	19.11 E
Fort Custer State Recreation Area ♠	216	42.18 N	85.20 W
Fort-Dauphin	157b	25.02 S	47.00 E
Fort Davis, Ala., U.S.	194	32.15 N	85.43 W
Fort Davis, Tex., U.S.	196	30.35 N	103.54 W
Fort Davis National Historic Site ⊥	196	30.33 N	103.53 W
Fort de Douaumont ⊥	56	49.13 N	5.25 E
Fort Defiance	200	35.45 N	109.05 W
Fort-de-France	240e	14.36 N	61.05 W
Fort-de-France, Baie de C	240e	14.34 N	61.04 W
Fort-de-France-Lamentin, Aérodrome de ⊠	240e	14.35 N	61.00 W
Fort Deposit	194	31.59 N	86.35 W
Fort de Possel	152	5.01 N	19.15 E
Fort Detrick ■	208	39.27 N	77.26 W
Fort de Vaux ⊥	56	49.12 N	5.28 E
Fort Devens ■	207	42.32 N	71.37 W
Fort Dix ■	208	40.00 N	74.33 W
Fort Dodge	190	42.30 N	94.10 W
Fort Donelson National Military Park ♠	194	36.26 N	87.49 W
Fort Duchesne	200	40.17 N	109.52 W
Fort Dupont Park ♠	284c	38.53 N	76.57 W
Forte, Monte ∧	71	40.43 N	8.15 E
Forteau	186	51.28 N	56.58 W
Forte dei Marmi	64	43.57 N	10.10 E
Forte de Magoito	266c	38.52 N	9.27 W
Fort Edward	210	43.16 N	73.35 W
Forte República	152	7.45 S	16.23 E
Fort Erie	212	42.54 N	78.56 W
Fort Erie Race Track ♠	284a	42.55 N	78.56 W
Fortescue ≃	162	21.00 S	116.06 E
Fort Eustis ■	208	37.09 N	76.35 W
Fortevoit	46	56.20 N	3.32 W
Fortezza (Franzensfeste)	64	46.47 N	11.37 E
Fort Fairfield	186	46.46 N	67.50 W
Fort Fitzgerald	176	59.53 N	111.37 W
Fort Flatters → Zaouia el Kahla	148	28.09 N	6.43 E
Fort Foote Village	284c	38.46 N	77.01 W
Fort-Foureau	146	12.05 N	15.02 E
Fort Frances	190	48.36 N	93.24 W
Fort Franklin	180	65.11 N	123.46 W
Fort Fraser	182	54.04 N	124.33 W
Fort Frederica National Monument ♠	192	31.12 N	81.26 W
Fort Gaines	192	31.37 N	85.03 W
Fort Gardel	148	24.52 N	8.21 E
Fort Garland	200	37.26 N	105.26 W
Fort Gay	188	38.07 N	82.36 W
Fort-George	176	53.50 N	79.00 W
Fort George ⊥	284a	43.15 N	79.04 W
Fort George G. Meade ■	208	39.05 N	76.50 W
Fort Gibson	196	35.48 N	95.15 W
Fort Gibson Lake ⊜[1]	196	36.00 N	95.18 W
Fort Good Hope	180	66.15 N	128.38 W
Fort Gordon ■	192	33.25 N	82.11 W
Fort-Gourand → Fdérik	148	22.41 N	12.43 W
Fort Green	220	27.36 N	81.57 W
Forth, B.R.D.	60	49.36 N	11.14 E
Forth, Scot., U.K.	46	55.47 N	3.41 W
Forth ≃	46	56.03 N	3.44 W
Forth, Carse of ∨	46	56.08 N	4.05 W
Forth, Firth of C	46	56.10 N	2.45 W
Förtha	56	50.56 N	10.14 E
Fort Hall, Kenya	154	0.43 S	37.09 E
Fort Hall, Idaho, U.S.	202	43.02 N	112.26 W
Fort Hall Indian Reservation ◆[4]	202	43.10 N	112.10 W
Fort Hamilton ■	276	40.37 N	74.02 W
Forth Bridge ◆[5]	46	56.00 N	3.25 W
Fort Hertz → Putao	102	27.21 N	97.24 E
Fort Hill → Chitipa	154	9.43 S	33.16 E
Fort Hill State Memorial ⊥	218	39.07 N	83.25 W
Fort Hood ■	222	31.08 N	97.46 W
Fort Howard	208	39.12 N	76.27 W
Fort Huachuca ■	200	31.33 N	110.20 W
Fort Hunter	210	42.57 N	74.17 W
Fortierville	206	46.29 N	72.02 W
Fortin, Lac ⊜	186	50.50 N	67.46 W
Fortín Ayacucho	248	19.58 S	59.47 W
Fortín Coroneles Sanchez	248	19.20 S	59.58 W
Fortín de las Flores	234	18.54 N	97.00 W
Fortín Florida	248	20.45 S	59.17 W
Fortín Garrapatal	248	21.27 S	61.30 W
Fortín Teniente Montanía	252	22.04 S	59.57 W
Fortín Uno	252	38.51 S	65.17 W
Fort Jackson ■	192	34.01 N	80.57 W
Fort Jameson → Chipata	154	13.39 S	32.40 E
Fort Jefferson National Monument ♠	220	24.37 N	82.54 W
Fort Jennings	216	40.54 N	84.18 W
Fort Jeudy, Point of ≻	241k	12.00 N	61.42 W
Fort Johnson	210	42.57 N	74.14 W
Fort Johnston → Mangoche	154	14.28 S	35.16 E
Fort Jones	204	41.36 N	122.51 W
Fort Kent	186	47.15 N	68.36 W
Fort Klamath	202	42.42 N	122.00 W
Fort Knox ■	194	37.54 N	85.57 W
Fort Lallemand	148	31.13 N	6.17 E
Fort-Lamy → Ndjamena	146	12.07 N	15.03 E
Fort Langley	224	49.10 N	122.35 W
Fort Langley National Historic Park ♠	224	49.10 N	122.35 W
Fort Laramie	200	42.13 N	104.31 W
Fort Laramie National Historic Site ♠	198	42.09 N	104.41 W
Fort Lauderdale	220	26.07 N	80.08 W
Fort Lauderdale-Hollywood International Airport ⊠	220	26.04 N	80.09 W
Fort Laurens State Memorial ⊥	214	40.38 N	81.27 W
Fort Leavenworth ■	198	39.21 N	94.55 W
Fort Le Boeuf ⊥	214	41.56 N	79.59 W
Fort Lee	210	40.51 N	73.58 W
Fort Lee ■	208	37.14 N	77.20 W
Fort Lennox National Historic Park ♠	206	45.06 N	73.16 W
Fort Leonard Wood ■	194	37.45 N	92.07 W
Fort Lewis ■	224	47.05 N	122.37 W
Fort Liard	176	60.15 N	123.28 W
Fort Ligonier ⊥	214	40.15 N	79.14 W
Fort Lincoln State Park ♠	198	46.45 N	100.52 W
Fort Littleton	214	40.04 N	77.58 W
Fort Loramie	216	40.21 N	84.22 W
Fort Loudoun Lake ⊜[1]	192	35.45 N	84.10 W
Fort Lupton	200	40.05 N	104.49 W
Fort Macleod	182	49.43 N	113.25 W
Fort Mac Mahon	148	29.51 N	1.45 E
Fort Madison	190	40.38 N	91.27 W
Fort Maguire	154	13.08 S	34.52 E
Fort-Mahon-Plage	50	50.21 N	1.34 E
Fort Malden National Historic Park ♠	281	42.06 N	83.07 W
Fort Matanzas National Monument ♠	192	29.40 N	81.18 W
Fort McClellan ■	194	34.43 N	85.47 W
Fort McDermitt Indian Reservation ◆[4]	202	42.00 N	117.32 W
Fort McDowell Indian Reservation ◆[4]	200	33.38 N	111.41 W
Fort McHenry National Monument ♠	208	39.16 N	76.35 W
Fort Mckinley	218	39.48 N	84.17 W
Fort McMurray	184	56.44 N	111.23 W
Fort McNair ■	284c	38.52 N	77.04 W
Fort McPherson	180	67.27 N	134.53 W
Fort Meade	220	27.45 N	81.48 W
Fort Mill	192	35.01 N	80.57 W
Fort Miller	210	43.10 N	73.35 W
Fort Miribel	148	29.31 N	2.55 E
Fort Mitchell	218	39.03 N	84.33 W
Fort Mojave Indian Reservation ◆[4]	200	34.55 N	114.35 W
Fort Monmouth ■	208	40.19 N	74.02 W
Fort Monroe ■	208	37.00 N	76.18 W
Fort Montgomery	210	41.20 N	73.59 W
Fort Morgan	198	40.15 N	103.48 W
Fort Myer ■	284c	38.53 N	77.05 W
Fort Myers	220	26.37 N	81.54 W
Fort Myers Beach	220	26.27 N	81.57 W
Fort Myers Shores	220	26.43 N	81.45 W
Fort Myers Villas	220	26.34 N	81.52 W
Fort Necessity National Battlefield ⊥	188	39.47 N	79.39 W
Fort Neck ≻[1]	276	40.39 N	73.28 W
Fort Nelson	176	58.49 N	122.39 W
Fort Nelson ≃	176	59.30 N	124.00 W
Fort Niagara Beach	284a	43.16 N	79.03 W
Fort Niagara State Park ♠	284a	43.16 N	79.03 W
Fort Nonsense ⊥	276	40.48 N	74.29 W
Fort Norman	180	64.54 N	125.34 W
Fort Nottingham	158	29.25 S	29.55 E
Fort Ogden	220	27.05 N	81.57 W
Fort Ord ■	226	36.40 N	121.48 W
Fortore ≃	68	41.55 N	15.17 E
Fort Parker State Park ♠	222	31.36 N	96.33 W
Fort Payne	194	34.27 N	85.43 W
Fort Peck	202	48.01 N	106.27 W
Fort Peck Dam ◆[6]	202	47.52 N	106.38 W
Fort Peck Indian Reservation ◆[4]	202	48.22 N	105.40 W
Fort Peck Lake ⊜[1]	202	47.45 N	106.50 W
Fort Pierce	220	27.27 N	80.20 W
Fort Pierce Inlet C	220	27.28 N	80.18 W
Fort Pierre	198	44.21 N	100.22 W
Fort Pitt Tunnel ◆[5]	279b	40.25 N	80.00 W
Fort Plain	210	42.56 N	74.38 W
Fort Point National Historical Site ⊥	282	37.48 N	122.28 W
Fort Polk ■	194	31.04 N	93.11 W
Fort Portal	154	0.40 N	30.17 E
Fort Providence	176	61.21 N	117.39 W
Fort Pulaski National Monument ♠	192	32.01 N	80.59 W
Fort Qu'Appelle	184	50.56 N	103.09 W
Fort Raleigh National Historic Site ⊥	192	35.55 N	75.40 W
Fort Randall Dam ◆[6]	198	42.48 N	98.35 W
Fort Recovery	216	40.25 N	84.47 W
Fort Reliance	176	62.42 N	109.08 W
Fort Resolution	176	61.10 N	113.40 W
Fortress Mountain ∧	202	44.20 N	109.47 W
Fortress of Louisburg National Historic Park ♠	186	45.56 N	59.57 W
Fort Riley ■	198	39.04 N	96.47 W
Fort Ritchie ■	208	39.43 N	77.30 W
Fort Rixon	154	20.01 S	29.18 E
Fort Rodd Hill National Historic Park ♠	224	48.26 N	123.28 W
Fortrose, N.Z.	172	46.34 S	168.48 E
Fortrose, Scot., U.K.	46	57.34 N	4.09 W
Fort Rosebery → Mansa	154	11.12 S	28.53 E
Fort Rucker ■	194	31.20 N	85.42 W
Fort Saint	148	30.19 N	9.30 E
Fort Saint James	182	54.26 N	124.15 W
Fort Saint John	182	56.15 N	120.51 W
Fort Salonga	276	40.55 N	73.18 W
Fort Sandeman	120	31.20 N	69.27 E
Fort Saskatchewan	182	53.43 N	113.13 W
Fort Scott	198	37.50 N	94.42 W
Fort Şeneca	214	41.13 N	83.10 W
Fort-Ševčenko	84	44.31 N	50.16 E
Fort Severn	176	56.00 N	87.38 W
Fort Shawnee	216	40.42 N	84.07 W
Fort Sheridan ■	216	42.13 N	87.48 W
Fort-Sibut	152	5.44 N	19.05 E
Fort Sill ■	196	34.40 N	98.25 W
Fort Simcoe Historical State Park ♠	224	46.21 N	120.50 W
Fort Simpson	176	61.52 N	121.23 W
Fort Smith, N.W. Ter., Can.	176	60.00 N	111.53 W
Fort Smith, Ark., U.S.	194	35.23 N	94.25 W
Fort Steele	182	49.37 N	115.38 W
Fort Stevens State Park ♠	224	46.10 N	124.00 W
Fort Stewart ■	192	31.52 N	81.37 W
Fort Stockton	196	30.53 N	102.53 W
Fort Sumner	196	34.28 N	104.15 W
Fort Sumter National Monument ♠	192	32.44 N	79.46 W
Fort Supply	196	36.35 N	99.35 W
Fort Tejon State Historical Park ♠	228	34.52 N	118.53 W
Fort Thomas, Ariz., U.S.	200	33.02 N	109.58 W
Fort Thomas, Ky., U.S.	218	39.04 N	84.26 W
Fort Thompson	198	44.03 N	99.26 W
Fort Tilden ■	276	40.33 N	73.53 W
Fort Totten Indian Reservation ◆[4]	198	47.53 N	98.50 W
Fort Totten Park ♠	284c	38.57 N	77.00 W
Fort Towson	196	34.01 N	95.16 W
Fort-Trinquet → Bir Mogreïn	148	25.14 N	11.35 W
Fortuna, Arg.	252	35.07 S	65.23 W
Fortuna, Calif., U.S.	204	40.36 N	124.09 W
Fortuna, Río de la ≃	248	16.36 S	58.46 W
Fortuna Ledge (Marshall)	180	61.53 N	162.05 W
Fortune	186	47.04 N	55.50 W
Fortune Bay C	186	47.25 N	55.25 W
Fortune Ditch ≊	279a	41.20 N	82.03 W
Fortune Harbour	186	49.31 N	55.15 W
Fort Union National Monument ♠	200	35.55 N	105.01 W
Fort Valley	192	32.33 N	83.53 W
Fort Vancouver National Historic Site ⊥	224	45.38 N	122.37 W
Fort Vermilion	176	58.24 N	116.00 W
Fort Victoria	154	20.05 S	30.50 E
Fortville	218	39.56 N	85.51 W
Fort Wadsworth ■	276	40.36 N	74.04 W
Fort Walton Beach	194	30.25 N	86.36 W
Fort Washakie	200	43.00 N	108.53 W
Fort Washington	208	40.09 N	75.13 W
Fort Washington Forest	208	38.43 N	76.59 W
Fort Washington State Historical Park ♠	285	40.07 N	75.14 W
Fort Wayne	216	41.04 N	85.09 W
Fort Wayne Military Museum ♉	281	42.18 N	83.06 W
Fort Wayne Municipal Airport (Baer Field) ⊠	216	40.59 N	85.11 W
Fort Wellington	246	6.24 N	57.36 W
Fort Wellington National Historic Park ♠	212	44.44 N	75.31 W
Fort White	192	29.55 N	82.43 W
Fort William → Thunder Bay, Ont., Can.	190	48.23 N	89.15 W
Fort William, Scot., U.K.	46	56.49 N	5.07 W
Fort William ⊥	272b	22.33 N	88.20 E
Fort Worth	222	32.45 N	97.20 W
Fort Yates	198	46.05 N	100.38 W
Forty Foot Drain ≊	42	52.28 N	0.05 W
Forty Fort	210	41.17 N	75.53 W
Fort Yukon	180	66.34 N	145.17 W
Fort Yuma Indian Reservation ◆[4]	204	32.48 N	114.34 W
Forum ♠, Qué., Can.	275a	45.29 N	73.35 W
Forum ♠, Calif., U.S.	280	33.57 N	118.20 W
Forūr, Jazīreh-ye I	128	26.17 N	54.32 E
Forza d'Agrò	70	37.55 N	15.20 E
Foscagno, Passo di)(	64	46.30 N	10.08 E
Fosdinovo	64	44.08 N	10.01 E
Fosforitnyj	82	55.19 N	38.54 E
Foshan	100	23.03 N	113.09 E
Fosna ≻[1]	24	64.00 N	10.30 E
Fosnavåg	26	62.21 N	5.39 E
Foso	150	5.42 N	1.17 W
Foss	46	56.41 N	3.58 W
Foss ≃, Eng., U.K.	44	53.57 N	1.06 W
Foss ≃, Wash., U.S.	224	47.43 N	121.18 W
Fossacesia	66	42.15 N	14.29 E
Fossacesia Marina	66	42.15 N	14.30 E
Fossa Eugeniana ≊	263	51.33 N	6.36 E
Fossano	62	44.33 N	7.43 E
Fossanova, Abbazia di ♉[1]	66	41.29 N	13.13 E
Fossato, Colle di)(	66	43.19 N	12.47 E
Fossato di Vico	66	43.18 N	12.46 E
Fossé	56	49.27 N	5.00 E
Fosse-Martin	261	49.05 N	2.54 E
Fosses	261	49.06 N	2.29 E
Fosses-la-Ville	56	50.24 N	4.42 E
Fossil	202	45.00 N	120.13 W
Fossil Butte National Monument ♠	202	41.50 N	110.40 W
Fossil Downs	162	18.08 S	125.38 E
Fossil Lake ⊜	202	43.18 N	120.15 W
Fossombrone	66	43.41 N	12.48 E
Fosston	198	47.35 N	95.45 W
Fos-sur-Mer	62	43.26 N	4.57 E
Foster, Austl.	169	38.39 S	146.12 E
Foster, Ky., U.S.	218	38.48 N	84.13 W
Foster, R.I., U.S.	207	41.47 N	71.44 W
Foster ≃	184	55.47 N	105.49 W
Foster, Mount ∧	180	59.48 N	135.29 W
Foster Brook	214	41.59 N	78.37 W
Foster City	226	37.34 N	122.16 W
Foster Creek ≃	198	44.34 N	98.12 W
Fosterdale	210	41.42 N	74.58 W
Foster Joseph Sayers Reservoir ⊜[1]	214	41.02 N	77.40 W
Foster Park	228	34.21 N	119.18 W
Fosters	194	33.06 N	87.41 W
Fosters Pond ⊜	283	42.37 N	71.08 W
Foster Street	260	51.46 N	0.09 E
Foster Village	229c	21.22 N	157.56 W
Fostoria	214	41.09 N	83.25 W
Fót	264c	47.37 N	19.12 E
Fotadrevo	157b	24.03 S	45.01 E
Fotan	100	24.12 N	117.53 E
Fothergill	44	54.42 N	3.30 W
Fóti-Somlyó ∧[2]	264c	47.38 N	19.13 E
Foucarmont	50	49.51 N	1.34 E
Fou-Chouen → Fushun	104	41.52 N	123.53 E
Fouesnant	32	47.54 N	4.01 W
Foug	56	48.41 N	5.47 E
Fougamou	152	1.13 S	10.36 E
Fougères	32	48.21 N	1.12 W
Fougères-sur-Bièvre	50	47.27 N	1.21 E
Fougerolles	58	47.53 N	6.24 E
Fouhsin → Fuxinshi	104	42.03 N	121.46 E
Fouju	261	48.35 N	2.47 E
Fouke	194	33.16 N	93.53 W
Foula I	46a	60.08 N	2.05 W
Foulain	58	48.02 N	5.13 E
Foulalaba	150	10.41 N	7.22 W
Foula Mori	150	12.10 N	13.51 W
Foul Bay C	140	23.30 N	35.39 E
Foulertons Brook ≃	276	40.50 N	74.20 W
Fouling → Fuling	102	29.42 N	107.21 E
Foulness ≃	44	53.47 N	0.43 W
Foulness Island I	42	51.36 N	0.55 E
Foulness Point ≻	42	51.38 N	0.57 E
Foulpointe	157b	17.41 S	49.31 E
Foulsham	42	52.48 N	1.01 E
Foulwind, Cape ≻	172	41.45 S	171.28 E
Foumban	152	5.43 N	10.55 E
Foumbot	152	5.30 N	10.38 E
Foumbouni	157a	11.50 S	43.30 E
Foum el Alba, Passe de)(	148	20.27 N	3.36 W
Foum-el-Hassane	148	28.59 N	8.55 W
Foum-Zguid	148	30.04 N	6.54 W
Foundiougne	150	14.08 N	16.28 W
Fountain	198	38.41 N	104.42 W
Fountain □[6]	216	40.17 N	87.13 W
Fountain City, Ind., U.S.	218	39.57 N	84.55 W
Fountain City, Wis., U.S.	190	44.08 N	91.43 W
Fountain Creek ≃	219	38.20 N	90.22 W
Fountain Green	200	39.38 N	111.38 W
Fountain Hill	208	40.36 N	75.24 W
Fountain Inn	192	34.42 N	82.12 W
Fountain Park	216	41.50 N	84.32 W
Fountain Peak ∧	204	34.57 N	115.32 W
Fountain Place	194	30.31 N	91.09 W
Fountains Abbey ♉[1]	44	54.07 N	1.34 W
Fountaintown	218	39.42 N	85.47 W
Fountain Valley	228	33.43 N	117.57 W
Fouquières-lès-Béthune	50	50.31 N	2.37 E
Fourche LaFave ≃	194	34.58 N	92.35 W
Fourche Maline ≃	194	34.55 N	94.55 W
Fourchu	186	45.43 N	60.15 W
Four Elms	260	51.13 N	0.06 E
Four Hole Swamp ≃	192	33.03 N	80.24 W
Fouriesburg	158	28.38 S	28.14 E
Fourmies	50	50.00 N	4.03 E
Four Mile Creek ≃, Ont., Can.	284a	43.15 N	79.08 W
Fourmile Creek ≃, N.Y., U.S.	284a	43.17 N	79.00 W
Four Mile Creek ≃, Ohio, U.S.	218	39.26 N	84.32 W
Four Mile Creek State Campsite ♠	284a	43.16 N	79.00 W
Fourmile Draw ∨	196	32.40 N	104.18 W
Four Mile Lake ⊜	212	44.40 N	78.44 W
Four Mile Run ≃	284c	38.50 N	77.02 W
Four Mountains, Islands of the II	180	52.50 N	170.00 W
Fournaise, Piton de la ∧	157c	21.14 S	55.43 E
Fourneau, Pointe à ≻	275a	45.22 N	73.51 W
Fourneaux, Fr.	50	47.53 N	1.48 E
Fourneaux, Fr.	62	45.11 N	6.39 E
Fournier, Lac ⊜	186	51.33 N	65.25 W
Fournière, Lac ⊜	190	48.04 N	78.03 W
Foúrnoi I	130	37.34 N	26.30 E
Four Oaks	192	35.27 N	78.26 W
Fourqueux	261	48.53 N	2.04 E
Fours	32	46.49 N	3.43 E
Fourteenmile Creek ≃	218	38.26 N	85.37 W
Fourteen Streams	158	28.04 S	24.53 E
Fourth Cataract → Ash-Shallāl ar-Rābi'	140	18.47 N	32.03 E
Fourth Cliff ◆[4]	283	42.09 N	70.42 W
Four Towns	281	42.37 N	83.25 W
Fous, Pointe des ≻	240d	15.12 N	61.20 W
Foussard ◆[1]	50	48.16 N	1.17 E
Fouta Djallon ◆[1]	150	11.30 N	12.30 W
Fou-Tcheou → Fuzhou	100	26.06 N	119.17 E
Fouyang → Fuyang	100	30.03 N	119.57 E
Fouzon ≃	50	47.16 N	1.27 E
Foveaux Strait ⩌	172	46.35 S	168.00 E
Foveran	46	57.18 N	2.02 W
Fowey	42	50.20 N	4.38 W
Fowler, Calif., U.S.	226	36.38 N	119.41 W
Fowler, Colo., U.S.	198	38.08 N	104.01 W
Fowler, Ind., U.S.	216	40.37 N	87.19 W
Fowler, Kans., U.S.	198	37.23 N	100.12 W
Fowler, Mich., U.S.	216	43.00 N	84.44 W
Fowler, Ohio, U.S.	214	41.19 N	80.40 W
Fowler, Point ≻	162	32.02 S	132.29 E
Fowler Creek ≃	281	42.17 N	83.30 W
Fowlers Bay	162	31.59 S	132.27 E
Fowlerton	196	28.28 N	98.48 W
Fowlerville	216	42.40 N	84.04 W
Fowliang → Jingdezhen	100	29.16 N	117.11 E
Fowman	128	37.13 N	49.19 E
Fox ≃, Man., Can.	184	56.03 N	93.18 W
Fox ≃, U.S.	194	40.18 N	91.30 W
Fox ≃, U.S.	216	41.21 N	88.50 W
Fox ≃, Ill., U.S.	194	38.32 N	88.08 W
Fox ≃, Wis., U.S.	190	44.32 N	88.01 W
Fox, Cape ≻	182	54.47 N	130.51 W
Foxboro, Ont., Can.	212	44.15 N	77.26 W
Foxboro, Mass., U.S.	207	42.04 N	71.16 W
Fox Brook ≃	276	41.03 N	74.13 W
Foxburg	214	41.09 N	79.41 W
Fox Chapel	279b	40.30 N	79.55 W
Fox Chase ◆[8]	285	40.04 N	75.05 W
Fox Chase Manor	285	40.05 N	75.06 W
Fox Creek ≃, Ky., U.S.	218	38.16 N	83.41 W
Fox Creek ≃, N.Y., U.S.	210	42.41 N	74.18 W
Foxe Basin C	176	68.25 N	77.00 W
Foxe-Becken → Foxe Basin C	176	68.25 N	77.00 W
Foxe Channel ⩌	176	64.30 N	80.00 W
Foxen ⊜	26	59.23 N	11.52 E
Foxe Peninsula ≻[1]	176	65.00 N	76.00 W
Foxford	48	53.58 N	9.08 W
Fox Glacier	172	43.28 S	170.00 E
Fox Harbour	186	52.22 N	55.41 W
Foxholes	44	54.08 N	0.28 W
Fox Hollow Lake ⊜	276	41.02 N	74.40 W
Fox Island I, Ont., Can.	212	44.28 N	78.24 W
Fox Island I, Wash., U.S.	224	47.16 N	122.37 W
Fox Islands II	180	54.00 N	168.00 W
Fox Lake, Ill., U.S.	216	42.24 N	88.11 W
Fox Lake, Wis., U.S.	190	43.34 N	88.55 W
Fox Lake ⊜	216	42.25 N	88.09 W
Fox Mountain ∧	180	61.55 N	133.22 W
Foxpark	200	41.05 N	106.09 W
Fox Point	216	43.09 N	87.54 W
Fox Point ≻	276	40.54 N	73.35 W
Fox River Estates	216	41.58 N	88.20 W
Fox River Grove	216	42.12 N	88.13 W
Foxton	172	40.28 S	175.18 E
Foxton Beach	172	40.28 S	175.13 E
Foxvale	283	42.03 N	71.14 W
Fox Valley, Austl.	274a	33.45 S	151.06 E
Fox Valley, Sask., Can.	184	50.29 N	109.28 W
Foxwells	208	37.38 N	76.18 W
Foxwist Green	262	53.12 N	2.34 W
Foxworth	194	31.14 N	89.52 W
Foyedong	98	40.41 N	119.12 E
Foyers	46	57.14 N	4.29 W
Foyle ≃	44	55.04 N	7.15 W
Foyle, Lough C	48	55.06 N	7.08 W
Foynes	48	52.37 N	9.06 W
Foza	64	45.54 N	11.38 E
Foz do Cunene	152	17.16 S	11.50 E
Foz do Iguaçu	252	25.33 S	54.35 W
Foz do Jordão	248	9.23 S	71.56 W
Foz Giraldo	34	40.00 N	7.43 W
Foziling	100	31.20 N	116.17 E
Frabosa Soprana	62	44.17 N	7.48 E
Fracción del Refugio	234	21.57 N	100.02 W
Frackville	208	40.47 N	76.14 W
Fraction Run ≃	278	41.34 N	88.04 W
Fraga, Arg.	252	33.30 S	65.48 W
Fraga, Esp.	34	41.31 N	0.21 E
Fragagnano	68	40.26 N	17.28 E
Fragneto Monforte	68	41.15 N	14.46 E
Fragoso, Cayo I	240p	22.44 N	79.30 W
Fragua, Sierra de la ⛰	196	26.41 N	102.13 W
Fraile Muerto	252	32.31 S	54.32 W
Fraïn, Chott el ⊜	34	35.57 N	5.38 E
Fraire	50	50.16 N	4.30 E
Fraisans	58	47.09 N	5.46 E
Fraisse	62	45.23 N	4.15 E
Fraize	58	48.11 N	7.00 E
Frameries	50	50.24 N	3.54 E
Framingham	207	42.17 N	71.25 W
Framlingham	42	52.13 N	1.21 E
Frammersbach	56	50.04 N	9.28 E
Framnes Mountains ⛰	9	67.50 S	62.35 E
Frampol	30	50.41 N	22.40 E
Frampton on Severn	42	51.46 N	2.22 W
França, Bra.	250	11.34 S	40.36 W
Franca, Bra.	255	20.32 S	47.24 W
Français, Récif de ◆[2]	175f	19.40 S	163.20 E
Francavilla al Mare	66	42.25 N	14.17 E
Francavilla Angitola	68	38.46 N	16.16 E
Francavilla d'Ete	66	43.11 N	13.32 E
Francavilla di Sicilia	70	37.54 N	15.08 E
Francavilla Fontana	68	40.31 N	17.35 E
Francavilla in Sinni	68	40.05 N	16.12 E
Francavilla Marittima	68	39.49 N	16.23 E
France □[1]	22		
	32	46.00 N	2.00 E
Frances ≃	180	60.12 N	129.02 W
Francés, Cabo ≻	240p	21.54 N	84.02 W
Francés, Punta ≻	240p	21.38 N	83.12 W
Francês dos Carvalhos	256	22.05 S	44.29 W
Frances Lake ⊜	180	61.25 N	129.30 W
Francés Viejo, Cabo ≻	238	19.39 N	69.55 W
Francesville	216	40.59 N	86.53 W
Franceville	152	1.38 S	13.35 E
Francfort-sur-Main → Frankfurt am Main	56	50.07 N	8.40 E
Franche-Comté □[9]	58	47.00 N	6.00 E
Francia	252	32.33 S	56.37 W
Francia → France □[1]	22	46.00 N	2.00 E
Francia, Estación de ◆[5]	266d	41.23 N	2.11 E
Francia, Peña de ∧	34	42.35 N	8.02 W
Francis	184	50.05 N	103.55 W
Francis, Lake ⊜	206	45.02 N	71.20 W
Francisca, Punta ≻	232	21.34 N	87.21 W
Francis Case, Lake ⊜[1]	198	43.15 N	99.00 W
Francisco A. Berra	258	35.23 S	58.51 W
Francisco Alvarez	258	34.38 S	58.52 W
Francisco Beltrão	252	26.05 S	53.04 W
Francisco de Orellana	246	0.28 S	76.58 W
Francisco González Villarreal	232	25.22 N	97.53 W
Francisco I. Madero, Méx.	232	24.32 N	104.22 W
Francisco I. Madero, Méx.	232	25.45 N	103.21 W
Francisco I. Madero, Méx.	234	16.50 N	93.50 W
Francisco I. Madero, Méx.	234	21.36 N	104.49 W
Francisco José, Tierra → Zemľa Franca-Iosifa II	12	81.00 N	55.00 E
Francisco Morato	256	23.16 S	46.45 W
Francisco Morazán □[5]	236	14.15 N	87.15 W
Francisco Perito Moreno, Parque Nacional ♠	254	47.50 S	72.08 W
Francisco Primo Verdad	234	21.48 N	101.55 W
Francisco Sá	255	16.28 S	43.30 W
Francisco Zarco	234	32.06 N	116.30 W
Francistown	156	21.11 S	27.32 E
Francitas	222	28.52 N	96.20 W
Franco da Rocha	256	23.20 S	46.43 W
Francofonte	70	37.14 N	14.53 E
François	186	47.35 N	56.45 W
François, Lacs à ⊜	186	51.40 N	65.49 W
François-Joseph, Chutes	152	7.34 S	17.17 E
François-Joseph, îles du → Zeml'a Franca-Iosifa II	12	81.00 N	55.00 E
François Lake	182	54.04 N	125.44 W
François Lake ⊜	182	54.00 N	125.40 W
Francolise	68	41.11 N	14.03 E
Franconia Notch State Park ♠	188	44.06 N	71.43 W
Franconville	261	48.59 N	2.14 E
Francs Peak ∧	202	43.58 N	109.20 W
Francueil	50	47.19 N	1.05 E
Franeker	52	53.11 N	5.32 E
Frangy	58	46.01 N	5.56 E
Frank	279b	40.16 N	79.48 W
Frank and Poet Drain ≊	281	42.06 N	83.12 W
Frankby	262	53.22 N	3.08 W
Frankel City	196	32.23 N	102.47 W
Frankenau	56	51.05 N	8.56 E
Frankenbach	56	50.40 N	8.34 E
Frankenberg	54	50.54 N	13.01 E
Frankenberg-Eder	56	51.03 N	8.48 E
Frankenburg	60	48.05 N	13.30 E
Frankenheim	56	50.32 N	10.04 E
Frankenhöhe ⛰	56	49.15 N	10.15 E
Frankenmarkt	64	47.59 N	13.25 E
Frankenmuth	190	43.20 N	83.44 W
Frankenstein, B.R.D.	56	49.26 N	7.58 E
Frankenstein → Ząbkowice Śląskie, Pol.	30	50.36 N	16.53 E
Frankenthal	56	49.32 N	8.21 E
Frankenwald ⛰	54	50.18 N	11.36 E
Frankfield	241q	18.09 N	77.22 W
Frankford, Ont., Can.	212	44.12 N	77.36 W
Frankford, Del., U.S.	208	38.31 N	75.14 W
Frankford, Mo., U.S.	219	39.29 N	91.19 W
Frankford ◆[8]	285	40.01 N	75.05 W

Symbols in the index entries represent the broad categories identified in the key at the right. Symbols with superior numbers (⛰[2]) identify subcategories (see complete key on page I · 30).

Kartensymbole in dem Registerverzeichnis stellen die rechts in Schlüssel erklärten Kategorien dar. Symbole mit hochgestellten Ziffern (⛰[2]) bezeichnen Unterabteilungen einer Kategorie (vgl. vollständiger Schlüssel auf Seite I · 30).

Los símbolos incluídos en el texto del índice representan las grandes categorias identificadas con la clave a la derecha. Los símbolos con numeros en su parte superior (⛰[2]) identifican las subcategorias (véase la clave completa en la página I · 30).

Les symboles de l'index représentent les catégories indiquées dans la légende à droite. Les symboles suivis d'un indice (⛰[2]) représentent des sous-catégories (voir légende complète à la page I · 30).

Os símbolos incluídos no texto do índice representam as grandes categorias identificadas com a chave à direita. Os símbolos com números em sua parte superior (⛰[2]) identificam as subcategorias (veja-se a chave completa à página I · 30).

	English	Deutsch	Español	Français	Português
∧	Mountain	Berg	Montaña	Montagne	Montanha
⛰	Mountains	Berge	Montañas	Montagnes	Montanhas
)(	Pass	Pass	Paso	Col	Passo
∨	Valley, Canyon	Tal, Cañon	Valle, Cañón	Vallée, Canyon	Vale, Canhão
≃	Plain	Ebene	Llano	Plaine	Planicie
≻	Cape	Kap	Cabo	Cap	Cabo
I	Island	Insel	Isla	Île	Ilha
II	Islands	Inseln	Islas	Îles	Ilhas
◆	Other Topographic Features	Andere Topographische Objekte	Otros Elementos Topográficos	Autres données topographiques	Outros Elementos Topográficos

ESPAÑOL Nombre	Página	Lat.°′	Long.°′ W=Oeste
FRANÇAIS Nom	Page	Lat.°′	Long.°′ W=Ouest
PORTUGUÊS Nome	Página	Lat.°′	Long.°′ W=Oeste

Frankfort, S. Afr. 158 32.44 S 27.26 E
Frankfort, S. Afr. 158 27.17 S 28.30 E
Frankfort, Ill., U.S. 216 41.30 N 87.51 W
Frankfort, Ind., U.S. 216 40.17 N 86.31 W
Frankfort, Kans., U.S. 198 39.42 N 96.25 W
Frankfort, Ky., U.S. 218 38.12 N 84.52 W
Frankfort, Maine, U.S. 188 44.36 N 68.53 W
Frankfort, Mich., U.S. 190 44.38 N 86.14 W
Frankfort, N.Y., U.S. 210 43.02 N 75.04 W
Frankfort, Ohio, U.S. 218 39.24 N 83.11 W
Frankfort, S. Dak., U.S. 198 44.53 N 98.18 W
Frankfort Springs 214 40.30 N 80.25 W
Frankfurt □⁵ 54 52.30 N 14.00 E
Frankfurt am Main 56 50.07 N 8.40 E
Frankfurt am Main, Flughafen ⊠ 56 50.02 N 8.33 E
Frankfurt an der Oder 54 52.20 N 14.33 E
Fränkische Alb ⩘ 30 49.00 N 11.30 E
Fränkische Rezat ≃ 56 49.11 N 11.01 E
Fränkische Saale ≃ 56 50.03 N 9.42 E
Fränkische Schweiz ✦¹ 60 49.45 N 11.25 E
Frank Key I 220 25.07 N 80.54 W
Frankland ≃ 162 34.58 S 116.49 E
Frankleben 54 51.18 N 11.56 E
Franklin, S. Afr. 158 30.18 S 29.30 E
Franklin, Ariz., U.S. 200 32.42 N 109.05 W
Franklin, Ga., U.S. 192 33.17 N 85.08 W
Franklin, Idaho, U.S. 202 40.31 N 111.48 W
Franklin, Ill., U.S. 219 39.37 N 90.03 W
Franklin, Ind., U.S. 218 39.29 N 86.03 W
Franklin, Ky., U.S. 194 36.43 N 86.35 W
Franklin, La., U.S. 194 29.48 N 91.30 W
Franklin, Maine, U.S. 188 44.32 N 68.09 W
Franklin, Mass., U.S. 207 42.05 N 71.24 W
Franklin, Minn., U.S. 198 44.32 N 94.53 W
Franklin, Nebr., U.S. 198 40.06 N 98.57 W
Franklin, N.H., U.S. 188 43.27 N 71.39 W
Franklin, N.J., U.S. 210 41.07 N 74.35 W
Franklin, N.C., U.S. 192 35.11 N 83.23 W
Franklin, N.Y., U.S. 210 42.20 N 75.10 W
Franklin, Ohio, U.S. 218 39.34 N 84.18 W
Franklin, Pa., U.S. 214 41.24 N 79.50 W
Franklin, Tenn., U.S. 194 35.55 N 86.52 W
Franklin, Tex., U.S. 222 31.02 N 96.29 W
Franklin, Vt., U.S. 206 44.59 N 72.55 W
Franklin, Va., U.S. 208 36.41 N 76.55 W
Franklin, W. Va., U.S. 188 38.39 N 79.20 W
Franklin, Wis., U.S. 216 42.54 N 88.03 W
Franklin □⁵ 176 72.00 N 100.00 W
Franklin □⁶, Ind., U.S. 218 39.25 N 85.01 W
Franklin □⁶, Ky., U.S. 218 38.14 N 84.52 W
Franklin □⁶, Mass., U.S. 207 42.36 N 72.36 W
Franklin □⁶, Mo., U.S. 219 38.25 N 91.03 W
Franklin □⁶, N.Y., U.S. 206 44.57 N 74.18 W
Franklin □⁶, Ohio, U.S. 218 39.57 N 83.00 W
Franklin □⁶, Pa., U.S. 208 39.56 N 77.40 W
Franklin □⁶, Tex., U.S. 222 33.07 N 95.13 W
Franklin □⁶, Vt., U.S. 206 44.57 N 72.52 W
Franklin, Mount ⋀ 171b 35.29 S 148.47 E
Franklin, Point ≻ 180 70.54 N 158.48 W
Franklin Canyon Reservoir ⊜¹ 280 34.06 N 118.25 W
Franklin Delano Roosevelt, Parque Nacional ♠ 258 34.52 S 56.03 W
Franklin Delano Roosevelt Lake ⊜¹ 202 48.20 N 118.10 W
Franklin Delano Roosevelt Park ♠ 285 39.54 N 75.11 W
Franklin Farms 279b 40.10 N 80.16 W
Franklin Grove 190 41.50 N 89.18 W
Franklin Harbor C 166 33.42 S 136.56 E
Franklin Island I 212 45.24 N 80.20 W
Franklin Lake ⊜, N.W. Ter., Can. 176 66.56 N 96.03 W
Franklin Lake ⊜, Nev., U.S. 204 40.24 N 115.12 W
Franklin Lake ⊜, N.J., U.S. 276 40.59 N 74.13 W
Franklin Lakes 276 41.01 N 74.12 W
Franklin Mountains ⩘, N.W. Ter., Can. 176 63.15 N 123.30 W
Franklin Mountains ⩘, N.Z. 172 44.55 S 167.45 E
Franklin Park, Ill., U.S. 216 41.56 N 87.49 W
Franklin Park, N.J., U.S. 276 40.26 N 74.32 W
Franklin Park, N.Y., U.S. 210 43.05 N 76.05 W
Franklin Park, Pa., U.S. 279b 40.35 N 80.06 W
Franklin Park, Va., U.S. 284c 38.55 N 77.09 W
Franklin Park ♠ 283 42.18 N 71.06 W
Franklin Pond ⊜ 275 41.06 N 74.35 W
Franklin Ridge ⋀ 282 38.00 N 122.10 W
Franklin River 224 49.06 N 124.49 W
Franklin Roosevelt Park ✦⁸ 273d 26.09 S 27.59 E
Franklin Springs 210 43.02 N 75.24 W
Franklin Square 210 40.43 N 73.40 W
Franklin State Forest ♠ 283 42.04 N 71.26 W
Franklin Strait ⊔ 176 72.00 N 96.00 W
Franklinton, La., U.S. 194 30.51 N 90.09 W
Franklinton, N.C., U.S. 192 36.06 N 78.27 W
Franklintown 208 40.05 N 77.02 W
Franklinville, N.J., U.S. 208 39.37 N 75.05 W
Franklinville, N.Y., U.S. 210 42.20 N 78.28 W
Frankreich → France □¹ 22 46.00 N 2.00 E
Frankston, Austl. 169 38.08 S 145.07 E
Frankston, Tex., U.S. 222 32.03 N 95.30 W
Franksville 216 42.46 N 87.55 W
Frankton 216 40.13 N 85.46 W
Frankville 194 31.39 N 88.09 W
Fränö 26 62.54 N 17.50 E
Fr'anovo 82 56.08 N 38.27 E
Franschhoek 158 33.55 S 19.09 E
Fransfontein 156 20.12 S 15.01 E
Fränsta 26 62.30 N 16.09 E
Františkovy Lázně 54 50.04 N 12.21 E
Franvillers 50 49.58 N 2.30 E
Franzburg 54 54.11 N 12.52 E
Franzensburg ⊥ 264b 48.04 N 16.22 E
Franzensfeste → Fortezza 64 46.47 N 11.37 E
Franz Josef Glacier 172 43.24 S 170.11 E
Franz Josef Land → Zeml'a Franca-Iosifa II 12 81.00 N 55.00 E
Franz-Josefs-Bahnhof ✦⁵ 264b 48.13 N 16.21 E
Franz-Josefs-Höhe ♠ 64 47.04 N 12.45 E
Fanzösische Süd- und Antarktis-Gebiete → French Southern and Antarctic Territories □² 6 49.30 S 69.30 E
Französisch-Polynesien → French Polynesia □² 14 15.00 S 140.00 W
Frasca, Capo della ≻ 71 39.46 N 8.27 E
Frascati 66 41.48 N 12.41 E

Frascineto 68 39.50 N 16.16 E
Frasdorf 64 47.48 N 12.16 E
Fraser 200 39.57 N 105.49 W
Fraser ≃, B.C., Can. 182 49.09 N 123.12 W
Fraser ≃, Newf., Can. 176 56.35 N 61.55 W
Fraser ≃, Colo., U.S. 200 40.06 N 105.58 W
Fraser, Mount ⋀ 162 25.39 S 118.23 E
Fraserburg 158 31.55 S 21.30 E
Fraserburgh 46 57.42 N 2.00 W
Fraser Island I 166 25.15 S 153.10 E
Fraser Lake 182 54.04 N 124.51 W
Fraser Lake ⊜ 182 54.05 N 124.35 W
Fraser Mills 224 49.14 N 122.52 W
Fraser National Park ♠ 169 37.10 S 145.50 E
Fraser Plateau ⩘¹ 182 51.30 N 122.00 W
Fraser Range 162 32.03 S 122.48 E
Frasertown 172 38.58 S 177.24 E
Frasne 58 46.51 N 6.10 E
Frasnes-lez-Buissenal 50 50.40 N 3.36 E
Frassine ≃ 64 45.18 N 11.37 E
Frassinoro 64 44.18 N 10.34 E
Frati, Monte dei ⋀ 66 43.40 N 12.10 E
Frattamaggiore 68 40.57 N 14.16 E
Frattócchie 267a 41.46 N 12.37 E
Frauenburg → Frombork 30 54.22 N 19.41 E
Frauenfeld 58 47.34 N 8.54 E
Frauenstein 54 50.48 N 13.32 E
Frauenwald 54 50.35 N 10.51 E
Fraulautern 56 49.19 N 6.46 E
Fraureuth 54 50.42 N 12.20 E
Fray Bentos 252 33.08 S 58.18 W
Fray Luis Beltrán 252 39.19 S 65.46 W
Fray Marcos 252 34.11 S 55.44 W
Frazee 198 46.44 N 95.42 W
Frazer, Mont., U.S. 202 48.03 N 106.02 W
Frazer, Pa., U.S. 208 40.02 N 75.33 W
Frazeysburg 214 40.07 N 82.07 W
Frazier Mountain ⋀ 228 34.47 N 118.58 W
Frazier Park 228 34.49 N 118.56 W
Fr'azino 82 55.58 N 38.04 E
Frazzanò 70 38.04 N 14.44 E
Frecheiras 250 2.51 S 42.05 W
Frecheirinha 250 3.46 S 40.48 W
Frechen 56 50.54 N 6.49 E
Frechilla 34 42.08 N 4.50 W
Freckenhorst 52 51.55 N 7.58 E
Freckleton 262 53.45 N 2.52 W
Freddo ≃ 70 38.01 N 12.54 E
Fredeburg 56 51.11 N 8.18 E
Freden 52 51.56 N 9.54 E
Fredensborg 41 55.58 N 12.24 E
Fredensborg Slot ⊥ 41 55.58 N 12.23 E
Frederic 190 45.40 N 92.28 W
Frederica 208 39.01 N 75.28 W
Fredericia 41 55.35 N 9.46 E
Frederick, Ill., U.S. 219 40.04 N 90.26 W
Frederick, Md., U.S. 208 39.25 N 77.25 W
Frederick, Okla., U.S. 196 34.23 N 99.01 W
Frederick, S. Dak., U.S. 198 45.50 N 98.30 W
Frederick □⁶ 208 39.25 N 77.25 W
Frederick Hills ⩘² 164 12.41 S 136.00 E
Frederick House ≃ 190 49.19 N 81.16 W
Frederick House Lake ⊜ 190 48.40 N 80.55 W
Frederick Island I 162 34.04 S 122.00 E
Frederick Reef ✢² 166 20.58 S 154.23 E
Fredericksburg, Ind., U.S. 218 38.26 N 86.11 W
Fredericksburg, Iowa, U.S. 190 42.58 N 92.12 W
Fredericksburg, Ohio, U.S. 214 40.41 N 81.52 W
Fredericksburg, Pa., U.S. 214 40.27 N 76.26 W
Fredericksburg, Tex., U.S. 196 30.17 N 98.52 W
Fredericksburg, Va., U.S. 208 38.18 N 77.29 W
Fredericksburg Battlefield (1862) ⊥ 208 38.17 N 77.28 W
Frederick Sound ⊔ 180 57.00 N 133.00 W
Fredericktown, Mo., U.S. 194 37.33 N 90.18 W
Fredericktown, Ohio, U.S. 214 40.29 N 82.33 W
Frederico Westphalen 252 27.22 S 53.24 W
Fredericton 186 45.58 N 66.39 W
Fredericton Junction 186 45.40 N 66.37 W
Frederik Hendrik-Eiland → Yos Sudarsa, Pulau I 164 7.50 S 138.30 E
Frederiksberg, Dan. 41 55.25 N 11.34 E
Frederiksberg, Dan. 41 55.41 N 12.32 E
Frederiksborg □⁶ 41 55.56 N 12.18 E
Frederiksborg Slot ⊥ 41 55.56 N 12.19 E
Frederikshåb 176 62.00 N 49.43 W
Frederikshavn 26 57.26 N 10.32 E
Frederikssund 41 55.50 N 12.04 E
Frederiksted 241n 17.43 N 64.53 W
Frederiksværk 41 55.58 N 12.02 E
Frederik Willem IV Vallen ⊾ 250 3.28 N 57.37 W
Fredersdorf bei Berlin 54 52.31 N 13.44 E
Fredonia, Col. 246 5.55 N 75.41 W
Fredonia, Ariz., U.S. 200 36.57 N 112.32 W
Fredonia, Kans., U.S. 198 37.32 N 95.49 W
Fredonia, N. Dak., U.S. 198 46.20 N 99.06 W
Fredonia, N.Y., U.S. 214 42.27 N 79.20 W
Fredonia, Pa., U.S. 214 41.20 N 80.14 W
Fredrika 26 64.05 N 18.24 E
Fredriksborg 40 60.08 N 14.23 E
Fredrikstad 26 59.13 N 10.57 E
Freeburg, Ill., U.S. 219 38.26 N 89.55 W
Freeburg, Mo., U.S. 219 38.19 N 91.55 W
Freeburg, Pa., U.S. 208 40.46 N 76.57 W
Freedom, Calif., U.S. 226 36.55 N 121.48 W
Freedom, Pa., U.S. 214 40.41 N 80.15 W
Freehold, N.J., U.S. 208 40.16 N 74.17 W
Freehold, N.Y., U.S. 210 42.22 N 74.03 W
Freeland, Mich., U.S. 190 43.32 N 84.07 W
Freeland, Pa., U.S. 210 41.01 N 75.47 W
Freeland, Wash., U.S. 224 48.01 N 122.32 W
Freeland Park 216 40.37 N 87.30 W
Freeling, Mount ⋀ 162 22.35 S 133.06 E
Freel Peak ⋀ 226 38.52 N 119.54 W
Freels, Cape ≻, Newf., Can. 186 49.15 N 53.28 W
Freels, Cape ≻, Newf., Can. 186 46.37 N 53.33 W
Freeman 198 43.21 N 97.26 W
Freeman ≃ 182 54.20 N 114.47 W
Freeman, Lake ⊜ 216 40.42 N 86.43 W
Freemansburg 210 40.39 N 75.22 W
Freemount 48 52.16 N 8.53 W
Freeport, Ba. 238 26.30 N 78.45 W
Freeport, N.S., Can. 186 44.17 N 66.19 W
Freeport, Ont., Can. 212 43.25 N 80.25 W
Freeport, Fla., U.S. 194 30.30 N 86.08 W
Freeport, Ill., U.S. 190 42.17 N 89.36 W
Freeport, Maine, U.S. 188 43.51 N 70.06 W
Freeport, Mich., U.S. 216 42.45 N 85.19 W
Freeport, N.Y., U.S. 210 40.39 N 73.35 W
Freeport, Ohio, U.S. 214 40.13 N 81.16 W
Freeport, Pa., U.S. 188 40.40 N 79.41 W
Freeport, Tex., U.S. 222 28.58 N 95.22 W
Freer 196 27.53 N 98.37 W
Freest 54 54.08 N 13.43 E
Freeston 222 31.32 N 96.15 W
Freestone 171a 28.08 S 152.08 E
Freestone □⁶ 222 31.44 N 96.10 W
Freetown, Antig. 240c 17.03 N 61.42 W

Freetown, S.L. 150 8.30 N 13.15 W
Freetown, Ind., U.S. 218 38.58 N 86.08 W
Freetown, N.Y., U.S. 207 40.58 N 72.11 W
Freeville 210 42.31 N 76.21 W
Freewood Acres 208 40.10 N 74.15 W
Freezeout Lake ⊜ 202 47.40 N 112.03 W
Fregenal de la Sierra 34 38.10 N 6.39 W
Fregene ✦⁸ 66 41.51 N 12.12 E
Freiberg 54 50.54 N 13.20 E
Freiberger Mulde ≃ 54 51.10 N 12.48 E
Freiburg → Świebodzice, Pol. 30 50.52 N 16.19 E
Freiburg → Fribourg, Schw. 58 46.48 N 7.09 E
Freiburg □⁵ 58 48.00 N 8.25 E
Freiburg an der Elbe 52 53.49 N 9.17 E
Freiburger Mulde ≃ 54 51.10 N 12.48 E
Freiburg im Breisgau 58 47.59 N 7.51 E
Freiendiez 56 50.23 N 8.02 E
Freienfels 60 49.53 N 12.07 E
Freienhufen 54 51.35 N 13.58 E
Freienwalde in Pommern → Chociwel 30 53.28 N 15.19 E
Freie Universität ✦² 264a 52.26 N 13.16 E
Freihung 60 49.37 N 11.55 E
Freiland 61 47.58 N 15.34 E
Freilassing 64 47.50 N 12.59 E
Freilingen 56 50.33 N 7.50 E
Freinberg 60 48.34 N 13.31 E
Freinsheim 56 49.30 N 8.13 E
Freirina 252 28.30 S 71.06 W
Freisen 56 49.33 N 7.14 E
Freisenbruch ✦⁸ 263 51.27 N 7.06 E
Freising 60 48.23 N 11.44 E
Freisinger Moos ≡ 60 48.23 N 11.42 E
Freistadt, Öst. 61 48.31 N 14.31 E
Freistadt → Kożuchów, Pol. 30 51.45 N 15.35 E
Freistett 56 48.41 N 7.56 E
Freital 54 51.00 N 13.39 E
Freiwaldau → Gozdnica 30 51.26 N 15.06 E
Freiwalde 54 51.58 N 13.44 E
Freixial 266c 38.54 N 9.09 W
Fréjorgues, Aéroport de ⊠ 62 43.33 N 4.00 E
Fréjus 62 43.26 N 6.44 E
Fréjus, Tunnel du ✦⁵ 62 45.13 N 6.42 E
Fremainville 261 49.04 N 1.52 E
Fremantle 168a 32.03 S 115.45 E
Fremdingen 56 48.58 N 10.27 E
Fremington 42 51.04 N 4.07 W
Fremont, Calif., U.S. 226 37.34 N 122.01 W
Fremont, Ind., U.S. 216 41.44 N 84.56 W
Fremont, Iowa, U.S. 190 41.13 N 92.26 W
Fremont, Mich., U.S. 190 43.28 N 85.57 W
Fremont, Nebr., U.S. 198 41.26 N 96.30 W
Fremont, N.C., U.S. 192 35.33 N 77.58 W
Fremont, Ohio, U.S. 214 41.21 N 83.07 W
Fremont, Wis., U.S. 190 44.16 N 88.52 W
Fremont ≃ 200 38.24 N 110.42 W
Fremont Airport ⊠ 282 37.28 N 121.56 W
Fremont Canyon ∨ 280 33.48 N 117.42 W
Fremont Island I 200 41.09 N 112.20 W
Fremont Lake ⊜ 202 42.57 N 109.49 W
Fremont Peak ⋀, Calif., U.S. 226 36.46 N 121.30 W
Fremont Peak ⋀, Calif., U.S. 228 35.12 N 117.27 W
Fremont Valley ∨ 228 35.10 N 118.00 W
French ≃ 190 45.56 N 80.54 W
French Broad ≃ 192 35.57 N 83.51 W
Frenchburg 192 37.57 N 83.37 W
French Camp 226 37.53 N 121.16 W
Frenchcap Cay I 240m 18.14 N 64.51 W
French Creek ≃, Man., Can. 184 57.02 N 92.12 W
French Creek ≃, U.S. 214 41.25 N 79.50 W
French Creek ≃, Ohio, U.S. 279a 41.27 N 82.07 W
French Creek ≃, Pa., U.S. 208 40.08 N 75.31 W
French Creek ≃, S. Dak., U.S. 198 43.38 N 102.55 W
French Creek, South Branch ≃, Pa., U.S. 214 41.54 N 79.54 W
French Creek, South Branch ≃, Pa., U.S. 285 40.10 N 75.42 W
French Creek, West Branch ≃ 214 41.58 N 79.52 W
French Creek State Park ♠ 208 40.13 N 75.47 W
French Frigate Shoals ✢² 14 23.45 N 166.10 W
French Guiana □² 242
 250 4.00 N 53.00 W
French Island I 169 38.21 S 145.21 E
French Lick 194 38.33 N 86.37 W
Frenchman Bay C, Ont., Can. 212 43.49 N 79.05 W
Frenchman Bay C, Maine, U.S. 188 44.25 N 68.10 W
Frenchman Butte 184 53.35 N 109.38 W
Frenchman Creek ≃, Ont., Can. 284a 42.56 N 78.59 W
Frenchman Creek ≃, N.A. 202 48.24 N 107.05 W
Frenchman Creek ≃, U.S. 198 40.13 N 100.50 W
Frenchman Flat ≡ 204 36.50 N 115.55 W
Frenchman Lake ⊜ 204 36.48 N 116.56 W
Frenchman Point ≻ 212 44.35 N 80.55 W
Frenchmans Cap ⋀ 166 42.16 S 145.50 E
Frenchmans Creek ≃ 282 37.19 N 122.27 W
Frenchpark 48 53.52 N 8.26 W
French Pass 172 40.56 S 173.50 E
French Polynesia □² 14 15.00 S 140.00 W
Frenchs Forest 274a 33.45 S 151.14 E
French Southern and Antarctic Territories □² 6 49.30 S 69.30 E
French Stream ≃ 283 42.07 N 70.53 W
Frenchtown 210 40.32 N 75.04 W
Frenda 148 35.02 N 1.01 E
Freneuse 261 49.03 N 1.36 E
Frensdorferhaar 52 52.25 N 7.03 E
Frenštát pod Radhoštěm 30 49.33 N 18.14 E
Frentani, Monti dei ⋀ 66 41.54 N 14.37 E
Frépillon 261 49.03 N 2.12 E
Frere 158 28.52 S 29.47 E
Freren 52 52.29 N 7.32 E
Fresco 150 5.05 N 5.34 W
Fresco ≃ 250 6.39 S 51.59 W
Freshfield 262 53.34 N 3.04 W
Freshfield, Mount ⋀ 182 51.44 N 116.57 W
Freshford 48 52.43 N 7.24 W
Fresh Meadows ✦⁸ 276 40.44 N 73.48 W
Fresh Pond ⊜, Mass., U.S. 283 42.23 N 71.09 W
Fresh Pond ⊜, N.Y., U.S. 276 40.55 N 73.18 W
Freshwater 42 50.40 N 1.30 W
Freshwater Creek ≃ 226 39.12 N 122.04 W
Fresia 254 41.09 S 73.27 W
Fresnes 261 48.45 N 2.19 E
Fresne-Saint-Mamès 58 47.33 N 5.52 E
Fresnes-en-Woëvre 56 49.08 N 5.39 E
Fresnes-sur-Escaut 50 50.26 N 3.35 E
Fresnes-sur-Marne 261 48.56 N 2.45 E
Fresnillo 234 23.10 N 102.53 W
Fresno, Col. 246 5.09 N 75.01 W
Fresno, Calif., U.S. 226 36.45 N 119.45 W
Fresno, Ohio, U.S. 214 40.20 N 81.44 W

Fresno, Tex., U.S. 222 29.32 N 95.27 W
Fresno □⁶ 226 36.38 N 119.45 W
Fresno ≃ 226 37.05 N 120.33 W
Fresno, Lewis Fork ≃ 226 37.20 N 119.39 W
Fresno, Portillo del ⨯ 34 42.38 N 3.46 W
Fresno Air Terminal ⊠ 226 36.46 N 119.43 W
Fresno Reservoir ⊜¹ 202 48.41 N 109.57 W
Fresno Slough ≃ 226 36.47 N 120.22 W
Fresnoy-Folny 50 49.53 N 1.26 E
Fresnoy-le-Grand 50 49.57 N 3.25 E
Fressenneville 50 50.04 N 1.34 E
Fressin 50 50.27 N 2.03 E
Freswick 46 58.35 N 3.05 W
Fréteval 50 47.53 N 1.13 E
Frétigney-et-Velloreille 58 47.29 N 5.56 E
Fretin 50 50.33 N 3.08 E
Frettes 58 47.41 N 5.34 E
Freu, Cabo del ≻ 34 39.45 N 3.27 E
Freudenberg, B.R.D. 56 50.54 N 7.52 E
Freudenberg, B.R.D. 56 49.44 N 9.19 E
Freudenberg, D.D.R. 264a 52.42 N 13.49 E
Freudenstadt 58 48.28 N 8.25 E
Frévent 50 50.16 N 2.17 E
Frew ≃ 162 20.00 S 135.38 E
Frewash ≃ 42 52.53 N 1.14 W
Frewena 162 19.25 S 135.25 E
Frewsburg 214 42.03 N 79.10 W
Freyburg 54 51.13 N 11.46 E
Freycinet, Cape ≻ 162 34.06 S 114.59 E
Freycinet Estuary C¹ 162 26.25 S 113.45 E
Freycinet Peninsula ≻¹ 166 42.13 S 148.18 E
Freyenstein 54 53.17 N 12.20 E
Freyre 252 31.10 S 62.06 W
Freystadt 60 49.12 N 11.20 E
Freyung 60 48.48 N 13.33 E
Fria 150 10.05 N 13.32 W
Fria □⁴ 150 10.30 N 13.40 W
Fria, Cape ≻ 152 18.30 S 12.01 E
Friant 226 36.59 N 119.43 W
Friant Dam ✦⁶ 226 37.00 N 119.43 W
Friant-Kern Canal ≚ 226 35.22 N 119.06 W
Friars Point 194 34.22 N 90.38 W
Frías, Arg. 252 28.39 S 65.09 W
Frías, Perú 248 4.52 S 79.57 W
Fribourg (Freiburg) 58 46.48 N 7.09 E
Fribourg (Freiburg) □³ 58 46.45 N 7.05 E
Frick 58 47.31 N 8.01 E
Frickhofen 56 50.30 N 8.07 E
Frick Park ♠ 279b 40.26 N 79.54 W
Friday 222 31.07 N 95.15 W
Friday Harbor 224 48.32 N 123.01 W
Fridaythorpe 44 54.01 N 0.40 W
Fridingen an der Donau 58 48.01 N 8.56 E
Fridley 190 45.06 N 93.15 W
Fridolfing 60 48.00 N 12.49 E
Fridtjof Nansen, Mount ⋀ 9 85.21 S 167.33 W
Friedberg, B.R.D. 56 50.20 N 8.45 E
Friedberg, B.R.D. 58 48.21 N 10.58 E
Friedberg, Öst. 61 47.27 N 16.03 E
Friedburg 60 48.01 N 13.15 E
Friedeberg in der Neumark → Strzelce Krajeńskie 30 52.53 N 15.32 E
Friedeburg [/ Saale] 54 51.37 N 11.44 E
Friedenau ✦⁸ 264a 52.28 N 13.20 E
Friedensfels 60 49.53 N 11.17 E
Friedens 214 40.03 N 79.00 W
Friedensburg 208 40.36 N 76.14 W
Friedersdorf, D.D.R. 54 51.39 N 12.21 E
Friedersdorf, D.D.R. 54 51.01 N 14.34 E
Friedersdorf, D.D.R. 54 52.17 N 13.47 E
Friedesheim 158 27.55 S 26.43 E
Friedland, B.R.D. 56 51.25 N 9.55 E
Friedland, D.D.R. 54 53.40 N 13.33 E
Friedland, D.D.R. 54 52.06 N 14.16 E
Friedland → Mieroszów, Pol. 30 50.41 N 16.10 E
Friedrich-Ebert-Brücke ✦⁵ 263 51.28 N 6.43 E
Friedrich Krupp-Aktiengesellschaft ✦³ 263 51.28 N 7.00 E
Friedrichroda 54 50.52 N 10.34 E
Friedrichsbrunn 54 51.41 N 11.02 E
Friedrichsdorf 56 50.15 N 8.38 E
Friedrichsfeld 263 51.38 N 6.39 E
Friedrichsfelde ✦⁸ 264a 52.31 N 13.31 E
Friedrichshafen 58 47.39 N 9.28 E
Friedrichshagen ✦⁸ 264a 52.27 N 13.38 E
Friedrichshain ✦⁸ 264a 52.31 N 13.27 E
Friedrichshof 264a 52.19 N 13.46 E
Friedrichsort ✦⁸ 52 54.24 N 10.11 E
Friedrichsruh, Schloss ⊥ 52 53.32 N 10.20 E
Friedrichsruhe 54 53.31 N 11.45 E
Friedrichstadt 41 54.22 N 9.05 E
Friedrichsthal 56 49.19 N 7.05 E
Friedrichstrasse, Bahnhof ✦⁵ 264a 52.31 N 13.24 E
Friedrichswalde 54 53.02 N 13.42 E
Frielas 266c 38.49 N 9.09 W
Frielendorf 56 50.58 N 9.19 E
Friemersheim 263 51.23 N 6.42 E
Friend, Nebr., U.S. 198 40.38 N 97.17 W
Friend, Oreg., U.S. 224 45.21 N 121.16 W
Friends Colony ✦⁸ 272a 28.34 N 77.16 E
Friendship, N.Y., U.S. 210 42.12 N 78.08 W
Friendship, Tenn., U.S. 194 35.55 N 89.14 W
Friendship, Wis., U.S. 190 43.58 N 89.49 W
Friendship Creek ≃ 285 39.55 N 74.43 W
Friendship Shoal ✢² 112 5.58 N 112.38 E
Friends Meeting House State Memorial ⊥ 214 40.09 N 80.47 W
Friendswood 222 29.32 N 95.12 W
Friern Barnet ✦⁸ 260 51.37 N 0.10 W
Fries 192 36.43 N 80.59 W
Friesach 61 46.57 N 14.24 E
Friesack 54 52.44 N 12.34 E
Friesenheim 58 48.22 N 7.53 E
Friesenhofen 58 47.45 N 10.04 E
Friesenried 58 47.52 N 10.31 E
Friesland □⁴ 52 53.03 N 5.45 E
Fries Mills 285 39.39 N 75.03 W
Friesoythe 52 53.01 N 7.51 E
Frigento 68 41.01 N 15.06 E
Frignano 68 40.59 N 14.11 E
Frignano ✦¹ 64 44.20 N 10.51 E
Friguia 150 12.03 N 10.56 W
Friitala 26 61.26 N 21.52 E
Frillendorf ✦⁸ 263 51.28 N 7.03 E
Frindsbury 260 51.24 N 0.30 E
Frinsted 260 51.17 N 0.43 E
Frinton-on-Sea 42 51.50 N 1.14 E
Frintrop ✦⁸ 263 51.29 N 6.55 E
Frio ≃, N.A. 236 11.08 N 84.46 W
Frio ≃, Tex., U.S. 196 28.30 N 98.10 W
Frio, Cabo ≻ 255 22.53 S 42.00 W
Friockheim 46 56.38 N 2.38 W
Frio Draw ∨ 196 34.50 N 102.19 W
Friona 196 34.38 N 102.43 W
Frisa, Loch ⊜ 46 56.34 N 6.05 W
Frisange 56 49.32 N 6.12 E
Frisches Haff → Vislinskij Zaliv C 30 54.27 N 19.40 E
Frisco, Pa., U.S. 214 40.51 N 80.16 W
Frisco, Tex., U.S. 222 33.09 N 96.49 W
Frisco City 194 31.26 N 87.24 W
Frisco Creek ≃ 196 36.34 N 101.23 W
Frisian Islands II 22 53.35 N 6.40 E

Fristad 26 57.50 N 13.01 E
Fritch 196 35.38 N 101.36 W
Fritsla 26 57.33 N 12.47 E
Fritzlar 56 51.08 N 9.16 E
Friuli □⁹ 64 46.00 N 13.00 E
Friuli-Venezia Giulia □⁴ 64 46.00 N 13.00 E
Friza, Proliv ⊔ 74 45.30 N 149.10 E
Frizington 44 54.32 N 3.30 W
Frobisher 184 49.12 N 102.26 W
Frobisher Bay 176 63.44 N 68.28 W
Frobisher Bay C 176 62.30 N 66.00 W
Frobisher Lake ⊜ 184 56.25 N 108.20 W
Frodsham 262 53.18 N 2.44 W
Frog Lake ⊜ 184 53.55 N 110.18 W
Frohavet ⊔ 26 63.52 N 9.26 E
Frohburg 54 51.03 N 12.33 E
Frohlinde ✦⁸ 263 51.32 N 7.21 E
Frohnau ✦⁸ 264a 52.38 N 13.18 E
Frohnhausen 263 51.29 N 7.48 E
Frohnhausen ✦⁸ 263 51.27 N 6.58 E
Frohnleiten 61 47.16 N 15.19 E
Frohse 54 52.02 N 11.43 E
Froid 198 48.20 N 104.30 W
Froid, Ruisseau ≃ 206 46.23 N 74.46 W
Froidmont-Cohartille 50 49.41 N 3.42 E
Froidos 56 49.03 N 5.07 E
Froissy 50 49.34 N 2.13 E
Froitzheim 56 50.42 N 6.34 E
Frolišči, S.S.S.R. 80 56.25 N 42.39 E
Frolišči, S.S.S.R. 82 56.18 N 39.13 E
Frolovo 80 49.47 N 43.39 E
Froman Run ≃ 279b 40.12 N 80.00 W
Fromberg 202 45.23 N 108.54 W
Frombork 30 54.22 N 19.41 E
Frome, Eng., U.K. 42 51.14 N 2.20 W
Frome ≃, Austl. 166 29.06 S 137.52 E
Frome ≃, Eng., U.K. 42 52.03 N 2.38 W
Frome ≃, Eng., U.K. 42 50.41 N 2.04 W
Frome, Lake ⊜ 166 30.48 S 139.48 E
Frome Downs 166 31.13 S 139.46 E
Fromelennes 56 50.08 N 4.52 E
Fromentières 50 48.54 N 3.52 E
Frömern 263 51.30 N 7.44 E
Frommern 58 48.15 N 8.52 E
Fröndenberg 56 51.28 N 7.46 E
Frönsberg 263 51.21 N 7.46 E
Fronteiras 250 7.05 S 40.37 W
Frontenac 220 28.27 N 80.46 W
Frontenac □⁶, Ont., Can. 212 44.40 N 76.45 W
Frontenac □⁶, Qué., Can. 206 45.42 N 71.15 W
Frontenard 58 46.55 N 5.10 E
Frontenex-Villard-Rosset 62 45.38 N 6.19 E
Frontenhausen 60 48.33 N 12.32 E
Frontera 234 18.32 N 92.38 W
Frontera, Punta ≻ 234 18.36 N 92.42 W
Fronteras 200 30.56 N 109.31 W
Frontier, Sask., Can. 184 49.12 N 108.34 W
Frontier, Mich., U.S. 216 41.47 N 84.36 W
Frontier, Wyo., U.S. 200 41.49 N 110.32 W
Frontignan 62 43.27 N 3.45 E
Frontino 246 6.46 N 76.08 W
Frontino, Páramo ⋀ 246 6.28 N 76.04 W
Frontón, Isla I 286d 12.07 S 77.11 W
Front Range ⩘ 200 39.45 N 105.45 W
Front Royal 188 38.55 N 78.11 W
Frose 54 51.48 N 11.23 E
Frosinone 66 41.38 N 13.19 E
Frosinone □⁴ 66 41.37 N 13.27 E
Frosna ≻¹ 26 63.45 N 10.25 E
Frosolone 68 41.36 N 14.27 E
Frösön 26 63.11 N 14.32 E
Frost 222 32.05 N 96.48 W
Frostavallen 41 55.58 N 13.30 E
Frostburg 188 39.39 N 78.56 W
Frost Creek ≃ 276 40.54 N 73.37 W
Frostproof 220 27.44 N 81.32 W
Frotheim 52 52.21 N 8.40 E
Frouard 56 48.46 N 6.08 E
Fröví 40 59.28 N 15.22 E
Frøya I 24 63.43 N 8.42 E
Fruges 50 50.31 N 2.08 E
Fruita 200 39.09 N 108.44 W
Fruitdale, Ala., U.S. 194 31.20 N 88.25 W
Fruitdale, Oreg., U.S. 202 42.24 N 123.20 W
Fruithurst 194 33.44 N 85.25 W
Fruitland, Idaho, U.S. 202 44.00 N 116.55 W
Fruitland, Md., U.S. 208 38.19 N 75.37 W
Fruitland Park 220 28.51 N 81.54 W
Fruitport 216 43.07 N 86.09 W
Fruitvale, B.C., Can. 182 49.07 N 117.33 W
Fruitvale, Tex., U.S. 222 32.41 N 95.48 W
Fruitvale, Wash., U.S. 202 46.37 N 120.33 W
Fruitville 192 27.20 N 82.30 W
Frumușița 38 45.40 N 28.04 E
Frunze, S.S.S.R. 78 46.16 N 34.52 E
Frunze, S.S.S.R. 83 48.40 N 38.45 E
Frunze, S.S.S.R. 85 42.54 N 74.36 E
Frunze, S.S.S.R. 85 40.07 N 71.44 E
Frunze □⁴ 85 42.50 N 74.00 E
Frunzovka 78 47.20 N 29.44 E
Frutal 255 20.02 S 48.55 W
Frutigen 58 46.35 N 7.39 E
Frutillar 254 41.07 S 73.03 W
Fryburg 214 41.21 N 79.26 W
Frýdek-Místek 30 49.41 N 18.22 E
Frýdlant 30 50.56 N 15.05 E
Frye 279b 40.11 N 79.56 W
Fryeburg 188 44.01 N 70.59 W
Fryerning 260 51.41 N 0.22 E
Fryingpan ≃ 200 39.22 N 107.02 W
Fuaamotu 174w 21.16 S 175.08 W
Fuaamotu Airfield ⊠ 174w 21.17 S 175.08 W
Fuan, Zhg. 100 32.41 N 120.41 E
Fuan, Zhg. 100 27.08 N 119.40 E
Fuanjie 100 25.29 N 117.53 E
Fubine 62 44.58 N 8.26 E
Fucecchio 66 43.44 N 10.48 E
Fucheng 100 30.06 N 113.08 E
Fucheng 98 37.52 N 116.08 E
Fuchikou 100 29.51 N 115.27 E
Fuchinobe (United States), Camp ■ 268 35.34 N 139.10 E
Fuchow → Fuzhou 100 28.01 N 116.20 E
Fuchs-Berg ⋀² 264a 52.27 N 13.51 E
Fuchskaute ⋀ 56 50.37 N 7.52 E
Füchtorf 52 52.03 N 8.02 E
Fuchū, Nihon 94 36.39 N 137.10 E
Fuchū, Nihon 94 35.40 N 139.29 E
Fuchū, Nihon 96 34.34 N 133.14 E
Fuchū, Nihon 96 34.24 N 132.30 E
Fuchu Air Station (United States) ■ 268 35.41 N 139.29 E
Fuchunjiang ≃ 106 30.10 N 120.09 E
Fucine 64 46.18 N 10.44 E
Fucino, Conca del ⩘ 66 42.01 N 13.31 E
Fuday I 46 57.03 N 7.23 W
Fuding 107 27.21 N 120.12 E
Fuduhe ≃ 107 29.59 N 116.33 E
Fuefuki ≃ 94 35.33 N 138.28 E
Fuelbeckestausee ⊜¹ 263 51.15 N 7.40 E
Fuencaliente 34 38.24 N 4.18 W
Fuencarral ✦⁸ 266a 40.30 N 3.41 W
Fuenlabrada 266a 40.17 N 3.48 W
Fuensalida 34 40.03 N 4.12 W
Fuensanta, Embalse de ⊜¹ 34 38.23 N 2.13 W
Fuente 196 28.40 N 100.32 W
Fuente de Cantos 34 38.15 N 6.18 W
Fuente de Oro 246 3.28 N 73.37 W
Fuente-obejuna 34 38.16 N 5.25 W
Fuentesaúco 34 41.14 N 5.30 W
Fuentes de Ebro 34 41.31 N 0.38 W

Fuerli 105 39.40 N 116.41 E
Fuerte ≃ 232 25.54 N 109.22 W
Fuerte Olimpo 248 21.02 S 57.54 W
Fuerteventura I 148 28.20 N 14.00 W
Fuerza, Castillo de la ⊥ 286b 23.09 N 82.21 W
Fufeng 102 34.20 N 107.51 E
Fuga Island I 116 18.52 N 121.22 E
Fugama, Wādī ∨ 140 14.43 N 24.36 E
Fügen 64 47.21 N 11.51 E
Fuglebjerg 41 55.18 N 11.34 E
Fugløysund ⊔ 24 70.12 N 20.20 E
Fugong 102 27.09 N 98.52 E
Fuguo 98 34.04 N 114.24 E
Fuguozhen 98 37.42 N 118.08 E
Fuhe 100 23.22 N 113.37 E
Fuhlenbrock ✦⁸ 263 51.32 N 6.54 E
Fuhlsbüttel, Flughafen ⊠ 52 53.38 N 10.00 E
Fuhrberg 52 52.34 N 9.50 E
Fuhrn 60 49.21 N 12.17 E
Fuhse ≃ 52 52.37 N 10.03 E
Fuhsien → Fuxian 98 39.37 N 122.01 E
Fuhu 100 29.11 N 118.04 E
Fuji, Nihon 94 35.09 N 138.39 E
Fuji, Zhg. 98 34.24 N 114.48 E
Fuji ≃ 94 35.07 N 138.39 E
Fuji, Mount → Fuji-san ⋀¹ 94 35.22 N 138.44 E
Fujiachang 107 29.57 N 104.18 E
Fujiafeng 105 39.11 N 117.32 E
Fujian □⁴ 100 26.00 N 118.00 E
Fujiang ≃ 102 29.59 N 106.16 E
Fujiatun 104 41.42 N 123.44 E
Fujiawopu 104 40.58 N 122.14 E
Fujiazhuangcun 104 41.15 N 122.20 E
Fujichang 107 29.09 N 105.23 E
Fujie 106 31.09 N 119.27 E
Fujieda 94 34.52 N 138.16 E
Fuji-hakone-izu-kokuritsu-kōen ♠ 94 35.21 N 138.44 E
Fujiidera 96 34.34 N 135.36 E
Fujikawa 94 35.08 N 138.37 E
Fujikubo 268 35.50 N 139.32 E
Fujimi, Nihon 94 35.51 N 139.33 E
Fujimi, Nihon 94 36.27 N 139.05 E
Fujimi, Nihon 94 35.55 N 138.15 E
Fujin 89 47.14 N 132.00 E
Fujino 94 35.37 N 139.10 E
Fujinomiya 94 35.12 N 138.38 E
Fujioka, Nihon 94 35.12 N 137.12 E
Fujioka, Nihon 94 36.15 N 139.05 E
Fuji-san ⋀¹ 94 35.22 N 138.44 E
Fujisawa 94 35.21 N 139.29 E
Fujishiro 94 35.55 N 140.07 E
Fujiwara, Nihon 94 36.49 N 136.30 E
Fujiwara, Nihon 94 36.51 N 139.44 E
Fujiwara-dam ✦⁶ 94 36.49 N 139.02 E
Fujiyama → Fuji-san ⋀¹ 94 35.22 N 138.44 E
Fuji-yoshida 94 35.38 N 138.42 E
Fukagawa 92a 43.43 N 142.03 E
Fukagawa ✦⁸ 268 35.40 N 139.48 E
Fukami 268 35.28 N 139.28 E
Fukang 86 44.10 N 87.59 E
Fukasaka-tunnel ✦⁵ 94 35.35 N 136.10 E
Fukashan ⋀ 89 47.55 N 120.53 E
Fukaya 94 36.12 N 139.17 E
Fukiage 94 36.06 N 139.27 E
Fukiai ≃ 270 34.42 N 135.12 E
Fukien → Fujian □⁴ 100 26.00 N 118.00 E
Fukou, Zhg. 100 26.28 N 117.40 E
Fukou, Zhg. 100 25.45 N 118.28 E
Fukube 95 35.33 N 134.18 E
Fukuchiyama 96 35.18 N 135.07 E
Fukude 94 34.40 N 137.53 E
Fukue 92 32.41 N 128.50 E
Fukuei Chiao ≻ 100 25.19 N 121.34 E
Fukue-shima I 92 32.40 N 128.45 E
Fukui, Nihon 94 36.04 N 136.13 E
Fukui, Nihon 270 34.51 N 135.34 E
Fukui □⁵ 92 36.00 N 136.15 E
Fukuma 96 33.46 N 130.28 E
Fukumitsu 94 36.33 N 136.52 E
Fukuno 94 36.35 N 136.55 E
Fukuoka, Nihon 92 40.16 N 141.18 E
Fukuoka, Nihon 94 35.52 N 139.32 E
Fukuoka, Nihon 94 35.34 N 137.27 E
Fukuoka, Nihon 94 36.42 N 136.56 E
Fukuoka, Nihon 96 33.35 N 130.24 E
Fukuoka □⁵ 96 33.45 N 130.30 E
Fukuroda-no-taki ⊾ 94 36.46 N 140.25 E
Fukuroi 94 34.45 N 137.55 E
Fukushima, Nihon 92 37.45 N 140.28 E
Fukushima, Nihon 92a 41.29 N 140.15 E
Fukushima □⁵ 94 37.08 N 140.00 E
Fukushima ✦⁸ 270 34.42 N 135.29 E
Fukusumi 270 34.37 N 135.32 E
Fukuta 268 35.21 N 140.04 E
Fukutani ✦⁸ 270 34.43 N 135.02 E
Fukuyama 96 34.29 N 133.22 E
Fukuzaki 96 34.57 N 134.45 E
Fulacunda 150 11.44 N 15.03 W
Fūlādī, Kūh-e ⋀ 120 34.38 N 67.32 E
Fūlād Maḥalleh 128 36.02 N 53.44 E
Fulaerji 89 47.13 N 123.39 E
Fulanga I 175g 19.08 S 178.34 W
Fulanga Passage ⊔ 175g 19.00 S 178.40 W
Fulda, B.R.D. 56 50.33 N 9.41 E
Fulda, Minn., U.S. 198 43.52 N 95.36 W
Fulda ≃ 30 51.25 N 9.39 E
Fulda ≃ 58 46.37 N 10.22 E
Fulechang 102 25.27 N 104.19 E
Fulerum ✦⁸ 263 51.26 N 6.57 E
Fulford Harbour 224 48.46 N 123.27 W
Fulgatore 70 37.57 N 12.42 E
Fulham ✦⁸ 260 51.29 N 0.12 W
Fuli 100 23.12 N 121.16 E
Fuliji 100 33.46 N 116.58 E
Fuling 102 29.42 N 107.21 E
Fulitun 89 46.42 N 131.10 E
Fullarton ≃ 166 20.15 S 141.10 E
Fullen ⊜ 52 52.52 N 7.09 E
Fuller Springs 222 31.18 N 94.41 W
Fullerton, Calif., U.S. 228 33.52 N 117.55 W
Fullerton, Ky., U.S. 218 38.43 N 82.58 W
Fullerton, Nebr., U.S. 198 41.22 N 97.58 W
Fullerton, Pa., U.S. 208 40.38 N 75.28 W
Fullerton Municipal Airport ⊠ 280 33.52 N 117.59 W
Fullerton Point ≻ 240c 17.06 N 61.54 W
Fulmer 260 51.33 N 0.34 W
Fulong 102 22.57 N 107.41 E
Fulongchang 107 30.03 N 103.38 E
Fulpmes 64 47.10 N 11.21 E
Fulshear 222 29.41 N 95.54 W
Fulton, Ala., U.S. 194 31.47 N 87.43 W
Fulton, Ark., U.S. 194 33.37 N 93.49 W
Fulton, Ill., U.S. 190 41.52 N 90.11 W
Fulton, Ind., U.S. 216 40.57 N 86.16 W
Fulton, Kans., U.S. 198 38.01 N 94.43 W
Fulton, Ky., U.S. 194 36.30 N 88.53 W
Fulton, Md., U.S. 208 39.09 N 76.56 W
Fulton, Mich., U.S. 216 42.06 N 85.22 W
Fulton, Miss., U.S. 194 34.16 N 88.24 W
Fulton, Mo., U.S. 219 38.52 N 91.57 W
Fulton, N.Y., U.S. 210 43.19 N 76.25 W
Fulton, Ohio, U.S. 214 40.28 N 82.50 W
Fulton, Tex., U.S. 196 28.04 N 97.02 W
Fulton □⁶, Ga., U.S. 192 33.47 N 84.24 W
Fulton □⁶, Ill., U.S. 219 40.28 N 90.13 W
Fulton □⁶, Ind., U.S. 216 41.04 N 86.13 W
Fulton □⁶, N.Y., U.S. 210 43.00 N 74.27 W
Fulton □⁶, Ohio, U.S. 216 41.36 N 84.10 W
Fulton □⁶, Pa., U.S. 214 40.06 N 78.04 W
Fulton ≃ 182 54.48 N 126.07 W
Fultondale 194 33.36 N 86.48 W
Fultonham 210 42.31 N 75.03 W
Fultonville 210 42.57 N 74.22 W
Fuluchang, Zhg. 107 29.18 N 103.40 E

≃ River	Fluss	Río	Rivière	Rio	✢ Submarine Features	Untermeerische Objekte	Accidentes Submarinos	Formes de relief sous-marin	Acidentes Submarinos
≚ Canal	Kanal	Canal	Canal	Canal	□ Political Unit	Politische Einheit	Unidad Política	Entité politique	Unidade Política
⊾ Waterfall, Rapids	Wasserfall, Stromschnellen	Cascada, Rápidos	Chute d'eau, Rapides	Cascata, Rápidos	✦ Cultural Institution	Kulturelle Institution	Institución Cultural	Institution culturelle	Instituição Cultural
⊔ Strait	Meeresstrasse	Estrecho	Détroit	Estreito	⊥ Historical Site	Historische Stätte	Sitio Histórico	Site historique	Sítio Histórico
C Bay, Gulf	Bucht, Golf	Bahía, Golfo	Baie, Golfe	Baía, Golfo	♠ Recreational Site	Erholungs- und Ferienort	Sitio de Recreo	Centre de loisirs	Sítio de Lazer
⊜ Lake, Lakes	See, Seen	Lago, Lagos	Lac, Lacs	Lago, Lagos	⊠ Airport	Flughafen	Aeropuerto	Aéroport	Aeroporto
≡ Swamp	Sumpf	Pantano	Marais	Pântano	■ Military Installation	Militäranlage	Instalación Militar	Installation militaire	Instalação Militar
⩘ Ice Features, Glacier	Eis- und Gletscherformen	Accidentes Glaciales	Formes glaciaires	Acidentes Glaciares	✦ Miscellaneous	Verschiedenes	Misceláneo	Divers	Miscelânea
⊤ Other Hydrographic Features	Andere Hydrographische Objekte	Otros Elementos Hidrográficos	Autres données hydrographiques	Outros Elementos Hidrográficos					

Fuluchang, Zhg. 107 29.38 N 106.08 E
Fulufjället ∧ 26 61.33 N 12.43 E
Fulwood 262 53.47 N 2.41 W
Fumaça 256 22.17 S 44.19 W
Fumane 156 24.29 S 33.58 E
Fumay 56 49.59 N 4.42 E
Fumel 32 44.29 N 0.57 E
Fumin, Zhg. 102 25.16 N 102.26 E
Fumin, Zhg. 106 31.54 N 121.10 E
Fumintun 98 42.29 N 126.22 E
Fuminzhen 106 31.37 N 121.39 E
Funa ≃ 273b 4.23 S 15.19 E
Funabashi, Nihon 94 35.42 N 139.59 E
Funabashi, Nihon 94 36.42 N 137.19 E
Funafuti I 14 8.31 S 179.13 E
Funagawa
→ Oga 92 39.53 N 139.51 E
Funan, Zhg. 100 32.39 N 115.32 E
Funan, Zhg. 102 22.32 N 107.56 E
Funaoka 96 35.23 N 134.14 E
Funasaka 270 34.49 N 135.17 E
Funäsdalen 26 62.32 N 12.33 E
Funchal 148 32.38 N 16.54 W
Fundación 246 10.31 N 74.11 W
Fundão, Bra. 255 19.55 S 40.24 W
Fundão, Port. 34 40.08 N 7.30 W
Fundão, Ilha do I 287a 22.51 S 43.14 W
Funde 272c 18.54 N 72.58 E
Fundición de Avalos 232 28.35 N 106.00 W
Fundo ≃ 250 10.12 S 44.39 W
Fundo, Arroio ≃ 287a 22.58 S 43.22 W
Fundo, Córrego ≃ 287b 23.46 S 46.47 W
Funduq Bin Ghashīr 146 32.41 N 13.11 E
Fundy, Bay of C 186 45.00 N 66.00 W
Fundy National Park ♠ 186 45.38 N 65.00 W
Fünfkirchen
→ Pécs 30 46.05 N 18.13 E
Funhalouro 156 23.03 S 34.25 E
Funil, Ribeirão do ≃ 256 22.02 S 43.46 W
Funil, Rio do ≃ 256 22.58 S 44.34 W
Funing, Zhg. 98 39.54 N 119.14 E
Funing, Zhg. 100 33.47 N 119.48 E
Funing, Zhg. 102 23.33 N 105.35 E
Funiuchang 107 29.03 N 106.33 E
Funiushan ⋏ 100 33.40 N 112.30 E
Funk Island I 186 49.46 N 53.10 W
Funks Creek ≃ 226 39.19 N 122.11 W
Funkturm ʋ 264a 52.31 N 13.16 E
Funne ≃ 263 51.42 N 7.36 E
Funnel Creek ≃ 166 22.18 S 148.57 E
Funnel Hill ∧[2] 272c 18.54 N 73.07 E
Funo 96 34.53 N 132.47 E
Funshinagh, Lough ◎ 48 53.31 N 8.07 W
Funsi 150 10.17 N 1.58 W
Funtana Coberta ⊥ 71 39.34 N 9.21 E
Funtua 150 11.31 N 7.17 E
Funyan Goba 144 4.22 N 37.58 E
Fuorn, Pass dal (Ofenpass))(58 46.37 N 10.15 E
Fuping 102 34.47 N 109.07 E
Fuqiao 106 31.36 N 121.12 E
Fuqikou 100 29.44 N 117.48 E
Fuqing 100 25.44 N 119.22 E
Fuqiu 98 34.54 N 117.56 E
Fuquay-Varina 192 35.35 N 78.48 W
Füramoos 58 48.00 N 9.53 E
Furancungo 154 14.55 S 33.35 E
Furano 92a 43.21 N 142.24 E
Furci Siculo 70 37.57 N 15.23 E
Furculești 38 43.52 N 25.09 E
Fures 62 45.19 N 5.30 E
Fūrg 128 28.18 N 55.13 E
Furkapass)(58 46.34 N 8.25 E
Furlong 208 40.18 N 75.05 W
Furmanov 80 57.15 N 41.07 E
Furmanovka 86 44.17 N 72.57 E
Furmanovo 80 49.42 N 49.28 E
Furn, Wādī al- ∨ 142 30.13 N 31.40 E
Furnace 46 56.09 N 5.10 W
Furnace Brook ≃ 283 42.06 N 70.43 W
Furnace Creek ≃ 284b 39.11 N 76.35 W
Furnace Pond ◎ 283 42.03 N 70.49 W
Furnari 70 38.07 N 15.08 E
Furnas, Represa de ◎[1] 255 20.45 S 46.00 W
Furn ash-Shubbāk 132 33.52 N 35.31 E
Furneaux Group II 166 40.10 S 148.05 E
Furnes
→ Veurne 50 51.04 N 2.40 E
Furness Abbey ʋ[1] 44 54.07 N 3.12 W
Furness Fells ⋏[2] 44 54.18 N 3.07 W
Furongshan ∧ 100 27.30 N 115.52 E
Furqlus 130 34.36 N 37.05 E
Fürstenau, B.R.D. 52 51.50 N 9.19 E
Fürstenau, B.R.D. 52 52.31 N 7.40 E
Fürstenberg, B.R.D. 52 51.44 N 9.24 E
Fürstenberg, D.D.R. 54 52.09 N 14.40 E
Fürstenberg / Havel 54 53.11 N 13.08 E
Fürstenfeld 61 47.03 N 16.05 E
Fürstenfeldbruck 60 48.10 N 11.15 E
Fürstenfelde
→ Boleszkowice 30 52.44 N 14.36 E
Fürstenhagen 56 51.12 N 9.41 E
Fürstenstein 60 48.43 N 13.20 E
Fürstenwalde 54 52.21 N 14.04 E
Fürstenwerder 54 53.24 N 13.34 E
Fürstenzell 60 48.32 N 13.19 E
Furtei 71 39.34 N 8.57 E
Fürth, B.R.D. 56 49.28 N 10.59 E
Fürth, B.R.D. 56 49.39 N 8.47 E
Furth im Wald 60 49.18 N 12.51 E
Furtwangen 58 48.03 N 8.12 E
Furuba ≃ 256 23.21 S 44.57 W
Furubō-san ∧[2] 270 34.53 N 135.19 E
Furudal 26 61.10 N 15.08 E
Furudono 94 37.05 N 140.34 E
Furukawa, Nihon 92 38.34 N 140.58 E
Furukawa, Nihon 94 36.14 N 137.11 E
Furulund 41 55.46 N 13.04 E
Furusund 40 59.40 N 18.55 E
Furu-tone ≃ 94 35.58 N 139.51 E
Furuvik 40 60.39 N 17.20 E
Furuyakami 268 35.55 N 139.32 E
Fürwiggestausee ◎[1] 263 51.09 N 7.41 E
Fury and Hecla Strait ⊔ 176 69.56 N 84.00 W
Fusagasugá 246 4.21 N 74.22 W
Fusain ≃ 50 48.09 N 2.45 E
Fusan
→ Pusan 98 35.06 N 129.03 E
Fuscaldo 68 39.25 N 16.02 E
Fusch 64 47.13 N 12.49 E
Fuschl am See 64 47.48 N 13.18 E
Fuschun
→ Fushun 104 41.52 N 123.53 E
Fuse
→ Higashiōsaka, Nihon 96 34.39 N 135.35 E
Fuse, Nihon 268 35.53 N 139.01 E
Fushan, Zhg. 98 37.29 N 121.16 E
Fushan, Zhg. 102 36.02 N 111.48 E
Fushan, Zhg. 106 31.49 N 120.46 E
Fushimi ⬥[8] 270 34.55 N 135.46 E
Fushino ≃ 96 34.03 N 131.24 E
Fushui 100 31.21 N 113.40 E
Fushui ≃ 100 29.52 N 115.28 E
Fushun, Zhg. 104 41.52 N 123.53 E
Fushun, Zhg. 107 29.11 N 105.00 E
Fushuncheng 104 41.53 N 123.51 E
Fusignano 66 44.28 N 11.57 E
Fusilier 184 51.51 N 109.46 W
Fusin
→ Fuxinshi 104 42.03 N 121.46 E
Fusine in Valromana 64 46.30 N 13.39 E
Fusio 58 46.27 N 8.40 E
Fusō 94 35.21 N 136.55 E
Fusong 98 42.18 N 127.20 E
Fussa 94 35.45 N 139.20 E
Füssen 64 47.34 N 10.42 E
Fuste, Picacho del ∧ 196 27.35 N 102.47 W
Futa, Passo della)(66 44.05 N 11.17 E
Futaba 94 35.41 N 138.30 E
Futago-san ∧ 96 33.35 N 131.36 E
Futamata
→ Tenryū 94 34.52 N 137.49 E
Futamatagawa 268 35.28 N 139.33 E
Futami, Nihon 94 34.30 N 136.47 E
Futami, Nihon 96 33.41 N 132.38 E
Futang, Zhg. 102 24.26 N 112.09 E
Futang, Zhg. 106 30.40 N 119.35 E
Futan University ʋ[2] 269b 31.17 N 121.29 E
Futaoi-jima I 96 34.06 N 130.47 E
Futatabi-yama ∧ 270 34.43 N 135.11 E
Futatsubashi 268 35.28 N 139.30 E
Futatsu-ne I[2] 174f 24.46 N 141.18 E
Fu Tau Pun Chau I 271d 22.21 N 114.22 E
Futian, Zhg. 100 27.22 N 112.47 E
Futian, Zhg. 100 27.26 N 114.56 E
Futianhe 100 31.30 N 115.05 E
Futianqiao 100 29.16 N 114.58 E
Futiga 174u 14.21 S 170.45 W
Futjāni ≃ 126 24.06 N 90.09 E
Futschou
→ Fuzhou 100 26.06 N 119.17 E
Futtsu 94 35.19 N 139.49 E
Futtsu-misaki ≻ 268 35.17 N 139.48 E
Futuna I, N. Heb. 175f 19.32 S 170.14 E
Futuna I, Wal./F. 14 14.15 S 178.09 W
Futunxi ≃ 100 26.51 N 117.46 E
Futuyu 105 39.19 N 114.54 E
Fuveau 62 43.27 N 5.34 E
Fuwah 142 31.12 N 30.33 E
Fuwen 86 47.13 N 89.39 E
Fuxi, Zhg. 100 25.14 N 113.52 E
Fuxi, Zhg. 100 27.14 N 119.50 E
Fuxian, Zhg. 98 39.37 N 122.01 E
Fuxian, Zhg. 102 36.02 N 109.13 E
Fuxianhu ◎ 102 24.30 N 102.55 E
Fuxin 104 42.08 N 121.45 E
Fuxing, Zhg. 107 30.27 N 106.04 E
Fuxing, Zhg. 107 30.24 N 104.53 E
Fuxingchang, Zhg. 107 29.40 N 105.13 E
Fuxingchang, Zhg. 107 29.54 N 105.43 E
Fuxingdao I 269b 31.17 N 121.33 E
Fuxingdao Park ♠ 269b 31.17 N 121.33 E
Fuxinghao 104 42.35 N 120.32 E
Fuxinshi 104 42.03 N 121.46 E
Fuyang, Zhg. 100 32.52 N 115.42 E
Fuyang, Zhg. 100 23.36 N 116.37 E
Fuyang, Zhg. 100 30.03 N 119.57 E
Fuyanghe ≃ 98 38.14 N 116.05 E
Fuyaoshan I 100 26.57 N 120.21 E
Fuyishui ≃ 102 25.08 N 110.13 E
Fuyouertuoshan ∧ 89 45.52 N 119.48 E
Fuyu, Zhg. 89 47.49 N 124.27 E
Fuyu, Zhg. 89 45.10 N 124.50 E
Fuyuan, Zhg. 89 47.40 N 132.30 E
Fuyuan, Zhg. 102 25.39 N 104.12 E
Fuyuanzhen 89 48.21 N 134.18 E
Fuzhai 100 29.32 N 120.02 E
Fuzhong 102 24.28 N 111.22 E
Fuzhou (Foochow), Zhg. 100 26.06 N 119.17 E
Fuzhou, Zhg. 100 28.01 N 116.20 E
Fuzhouwan C 98 39.18 N 121.35 E
Fuzhuang 98 38.02 N 116.08 E
Fyfield 260 51.45 N 0.16 E
Fylde □[8] 262 53.46 N 2.53 W
Fylde ≻[1] 262 53.47 N 2.56 W
Fylland ≻[1] 41 56.00 N 9.15 E
Fyn □[6] 41 55.20 N 10.25 E
Fyn I 41 55.20 N 10.30 E
Fyne, Loch C 46 55.56 N 5.24 W
Fyns Hoved ≻ 41 55.37 N 10.36 E
Fyresvatn ◎ 26 59.06 N 8.12 E
Fyrisån ≃ 40 59.47 N 17.39 E
Fysingen ◎ 40 59.34 N 17.55 E
Fyvie 46 57.25 N 2.23 W

G

Ga 150 9.47 N 2.30 W
Gaaden 264b 48.03 N 16.12 E
Gaanderen 52 51.56 N 6.21 E
Gabah 144 8.10 N 50.06 E
Gabal 144 8.30 N 47.55 E
Gabaldon 116 15.28 N 121.19 E
Gabare 38 43.19 N 23.55 E
Gabarus 186 45.50 N 60.09 W
Gabarus Bay C 186 45.51 N 60.07 W
Gabas ≃ 32 43.46 N 0.42 W
Gabbs 204 38.52 N 117.55 W
Gabby Heights 214 40.09 N 80.15 W
Gabela 152 10.48 S 14.20 E
Gaberones
→ Gaborone 156 24.45 S 25.55 E
Gabès 148 33.53 N 10.07 E
Gabès □[5] 148 33.15 N 9.00 E
Gabès, Golfe de C 148 34.00 N 10.25 E
Gabia 152 4.34 S 17.07 E
Gabiarra 255 16.15 S 39.41 W
Gabicce Mare 66 43.58 N 12.46 E
Gabii ⊥ 267a 41.54 N 12.43 E
Gabil 146 11.09 N 18.12 E
Gabilan Range ⋏ 226 36.30 N 121.15 W
Gąbin 30 52.25 N 19.44 E
Gabir 140 8.35 N 24.40 E
Gable Mountain ∧ 182 54.30 N 121.40 W
Gablenz 54 51.41 N 14.31 E
Gablingen 58 48.27 N 10.49 E
Gablitz 264b 48.14 N 16.09 E
Gablonz
→ Jablonec nad Nisou 30 50.44 N 15.10 E
Gabon □[1] 138
152 1.00 S 11.45 E
Gabon, Estuaire du C[1] 152 0.25 N 9.20 E
Gaborone 156 24.45 S 25.55 E
Gabras 140 10.16 N 26.14 E
Gabria 64 45.52 N 13.34 E
Gabriel 250 11.14 S 41.53 W
Gabriel Strait ⊔ 176 61.45 N 65.30 W
Gabriel y Galan, Embalse de ◎[1] 34 40.15 N 6.15 W
Gabriel Zamora 234 19.05 N 102.05 W
Gābrīk 128 25.44 N 58.28 E
Gabriola 224 49.12 N 123.50 W
Gabriola Island I 224 49.10 N 123.47 W
Gabrovo 38 42.52 N 25.19 E
Gabun
→ Gabon □[1] 152 1.00 S 11.45 E
Gaby 62 45.43 N 7.53 E
Gacé 50 48.48 N 0.18 E
Gachetá 246 4.49 N 73.36 W
Gachsārān 128 30.12 N 50.47 E
Gackle 198 46.38 N 99.09 W
Gacko 38 43.10 N 18.32 E
Gad'ač 78 50.22 N 34.00 E
Gadag 122 15.25 N 75.37 E
Gadamai 140 17.09 N 36.06 E
Gādarwāra 124 22.55 N 78.47 E
Gadbjerg 41 55.46 N 9.20 E
Gäddede 26 64.30 N 14.09 E
Gadderbaum 52 52.00 N 8.31 E
Gade ≃ 260 51.38 N 0.28 W
Gadebusch 54 53.42 N 11.07 E
Gadein 140 8.11 N 28.44 E
Gadera ≃ 64 46.47 N 11.54 E
Gadernheim 56 49.43 N 8.44 E
Gadevang 41 55.58 N 12.18 E
Gadiloviči 76 53.05 N 30.16 E
Gadis ≃ 114 1.03 N 98.55 E
Gadmen 58 46.44 N 8.21 E
Gádor 34 36.57 N 2.29 W
Gádor, Sierra de ⋏ 34 36.54 N 2.47 W
Gadra 120 25.40 N 70.37 E
Gadrut 84 39.32 N 47.02 E
Gadsden, Ala., U.S. 194 34.02 N 86.02 W
Gadsden, Ariz., U.S. 200 32.33 N 108.47 W
Gadwāl 122 16.14 N 77.48 E
Gadzi 152 4.47 N 16.42 E
Gaer (Geeryasha) 120 31.44 N 80.21 E
Gaerwen 44 53.13 N 4.16 W
Găești 38 44.43 N 25.19 E
Gaeta 66 41.12 N 13.35 E
Gaeta, Golfo di C 66 41.06 N 13.30 E
Gaferut I 108 9.14 N 145.23 E
Gaffney 192 35.05 N 81.39 W
Gafour 36 36.18 N 9.19 E
Gafsa 148 34.25 N 8.48 E
Gag, Pulau I 164 0.27 S 129.52 E
Gagal 146 9.01 N 15.08 E
Gagan 175e 5.14 S 154.37 E
Gagarawa 150 12.25 N 9.32 E
Gagarin 76 55.33 N 35.00 E
Gage 196 36.19 N 99.45 W
Gages Lake 278 42.21 N 87.59 W
Gages Lake ◎ 278 42.21 N 88.00 W
Gagetown 186 45.47 N 66.09 W
Gaggenau 56 48.48 N 8.19 E
Gaggi 70 37.51 N 15.13 E
Gaggiano 62 45.24 N 9.02 E
Gaghamni 140 11.41 N 28.19 E
Gagi I 175e 7.25 S 158.13 E
Gagil 174q 9.33 N 138.10 E
Gagil-Tomil I 174q 9.32 N 138.10 E
Gagino 80 55.14 N 45.02 E
Gagliano Castelferrato 70 37.43 N 14.32 E
Gagliano del Capo 68 39.50 N 18.22 E
Gagnef 40 60.35 N 15.04 E
Gagnia 152 1.28 S 16.02 E
Gagnoa 150 6.08 N 5.56 W
Gagnoa □[5] 150 6.15 N 5.40 W
Gagnon 176 51.53 N 68.10 W
Gagnon, Lac ◎ 206 46.07 N 75.07 W
Gagny 261 48.53 N 2.32 E
Gago Coutinho 152 14.08 S 21.25 E
Gagra 84 43.20 N 40.15 E
Gagret 123 31.40 N 76.04 E
Gagrinskij Chrebet ⋏ 84 43.27 N 40.24 E
Gahanna 218 40.01 N 82.53 W
Gahini 154 1.50 S 30.30 E
Gahlen 52 51.40 N 6.52 E
Gahmen ⬥[8] 263 51.36 N 7.32 E
Gaiab ≃ 156 28.31 S 19.35 E
Gaiarine 64 45.52 N 12.29 E
Gaibānda 124 25.19 N 89.33 E
Gaichtpass)(58 47.27 N 10.37 E
Gaigalava 76 56.40 N 27.18 E
Gaighāta 126 22.56 N 88.44 E
Gaijiatun 104 40.50 N 122.37 E
Gail 196 32.46 N 101.27 W
Gail ≃ 64 46.36 N 13.53 E
Gailberg Sattel)(64 46.43 N 12.58 E
Gail Creek ≃ 222 31.07 N 95.23 W
Gaildorf 56 49.00 N 9.46 E
Gaillac 32 43.54 N 1.55 E
Gaillard, Château ⊥ 50 48.09 N 1.54 E
Gaillard, Lac ◎ 186 50.06 N 68.47 W
Gaillard, Lake ◎ 207 41.21 N 72.46 W
Gaillefontaine 50 49.39 N 1.37 E
Gaillon, Fr. 50 49.10 N 1.20 E
Gaillon, Fr. 261 49.02 N 1.54 E
Gaima 164 8.20 S 142.55 E
Gaimán 254 43.17 S 65.29 W
Gaimersheim 60 48.49 N 11.22 E
Gaines, Mich., U.S. 216 42.52 N 83.55 W
Gaines, Pa., U.S. 210 41.45 N 77.34 W
Gainesboro 194 36.21 N 85.39 W
Gainesville, Fla., U.S. 192 29.40 N 82.20 W
Gainesville, Ga., U.S. 192 34.18 N 83.50 W
Gainesville, Mo., U.S. 194 36.36 N 92.26 W
Gainesville, N.Y., U.S. 210 42.39 N 78.08 W
Gainesville, Tex., U.S. 196 33.37 N 97.08 W
Gainford 44 54.32 N 1.44 W
Gainsborough, Sask., Can. 184 49.10 N 101.26 W
Gainsborough, Eng., U.K. 44 53.24 N 0.46 W
Gainsborough Creek ≃ 184 49.10 N 101.02 W
Gaiole in Chianti 66 43.28 N 11.26 E
Gaiping 98 40.24 N 122.22 E
Gairdner ≃ 162 34.17 S 119.28 E
Gairdner, Lake ◎ 162 31.35 S 136.00 E
Gairloch 46 57.42 N 5.40 W
Gairloch, Loch C 46 57.44 N 5.44 W
Gairn ≃ 46 57.03 N 3.05 W
Gais, It. 64 46.50 N 11.57 E
Gais, Schw. 58 47.22 N 9.27 E
Gaisberg ∧ 64 47.48 N 13.07 E
Gaisbeuren 58 47.54 N 9.43 E
Gaisstein ∧ 64 47.20 N 12.30 E
Gaital, Cerro ∧ 236 8.37 N 80.07 W
Gaither 208 39.21 N 77.01 W
Gaithersburg 208 39.09 N 77.12 W
Gaiziņkalns ∧[2] 76 56.52 N 25.57 E
Gaj, Jugo. 36 45.29 N 17.02 E
Gaj, S.S.S.R. 86 51.27 N 58.27 E
Gajā 272b 22.52 N 88.10 E
Gajčur ≃ 78 47.57 N 36.11 E
Gajendragarh 122 15.44 N 75.59 E
Gajiram 146 12.30 N 13.12 E
Gajny 24 60.15 N 54.15 E
Gājol 124 25.13 N 88.12 E
Gajsin 78 48.48 N 29.24 E
Gaj Singhpur 123 29.40 N 73.27 E
Gajuapara ≃ 250 4.17 S 47.25 W
Gajutino 76 58.42 N 38.32 E
Gajvoron 78 48.22 N 29.52 E
Gakona 180 62.18 N 145.18 W
Gākuch 123 36.10 N 73.45 E
Gakugsa 24 61.34 N 36.26 E
Gal, Punta de ≻ 34 39.10 N 1.05 E
Gāla 126 24.18 N 89.54 E
Galaassija 128 39.52 N 64.27 E
Galāchipa 126 22.10 N 90.25 E
Galahad 182 52.31 N 111.56 W
Galamares 266c 38.48 N 9.25 W
Galán, Cerro ∧ 252 25.55 S 66.52 W
Galana ≃ 154 3.09 S 40.08 E
Galangue 152 13.48 S 16.09 E
Galanta 30 48.12 N 17.43 E
Galápagos □[4] 246a 0.30 S 90.30 W
Galapagos Islands
→ Colón, Archipiélago de II 246a 0.30 S 90.30 W
Galapagos Rise ⬥[3] 18 3.00 N 95.00 W
Galaroza 34 37.55 N 6.42 W
Galas ≃ 114 5.31 N 102.12 E
Galashiels 46 55.37 N 2.49 W
Galata ⬥[8] 267b 41.01 N 28.58 E
Galata Köprüsü ⬥[5] 267b 41.00 N 28.57 E
Galata Kulesi ʋ 267b 41.01 N 28.58 E
Galatea 172 38.25 S 176.45 E
Galați 38 45.26 N 28.03 E
Galați □[4] 38 45.45 N 27.45 E
Galatia 194 37.51 N 88.37 W
Galatina 68 40.10 N 18.10 E
Galatone 68 40.09 N 18.04 E
Galatro 68 38.28 N 16.06 E
Galátsion 267c 38.01 N 23.45 E
Galatz
→ Galați 38 45.26 N 28.03 E
Galaure ≃ 62 45.11 N 4.49 E
Gala Water ≃ 46 55.37 N 2.47 W
Galax 192 36.40 N 80.56 W
Galaxídhion 38 38.22 N 22.23 E
Galbyn Gov' ⬥[2] 102 42.30 N 107.00 E
Galdhøpiggen ∧ 26 61.37 N 8.17 E
Gale, Lac ◎ 190 46.46 N 76.51 W
Galeairy Lake ◎ 212 45.29 N 78.17 W
Galeana, Méx. 232 24.50 N 100.04 W
Galeana, Méx. 232 30.07 N 107.38 W
Galeão, Aeroporto do ⊠ 256 22.50 S 43.15 W
Galeata 66 44.00 N 11.55 E
Galegu 140 12.36 N 35.02 E
Galeh Dār 128 27.38 N 52.42 E
Galela 108 1.50 N 127.50 E
Galena, Austl. 162 27.50 S 114.41 E
Galena, Alaska, U.S. 180 64.44 N 156.57 W
Galena, Ill., U.S. 190 42.25 N 90.26 W
Galena, Ind., U.S. 218 38.21 N 85.56 W
Galena, Kans., U.S. 198 37.04 N 94.38 W
Galena, Md., U.S. 208 39.20 N 75.55 W
Galena, Mo., U.S. 194 36.48 N 93.28 W
Galena, Ohio, U.S. 214 40.13 N 82.53 W
Galena Park 222 29.44 N 95.14 W
Galenbecker See ◎ 54 53.38 N 13.43 E
Galeota Point ≻ 241r 10.08 N 60.59 W
Galera ≃ 248 14.25 S 60.07 W
Galera, Punta ≻, Chile 254 39.59 S 73.43 W
Galera, Punta ≻, Ec. 246 0.49 N 80.03 W
Galera Point ≻ 241r 10.49 N 60.55 W
Galeria ⊥ 267a 42.02 N 12.18 E
Galeria, Fosso la ≃ 267a 41.48 N 12.21 E
Galesburg, Ill., U.S. 190 40.57 N 90.22 W
Galesburg, Mich., U.S. 216 42.14 N 85.25 W
Gales Creek 224 45.39 N 123.13 W
Gales Creek ≃ 224 45.29 N 123.06 W
Gales Ferry 207 41.26 N 72.05 W
Gales Point ≻ 283 42.33 N 70.47 W
Galesville, Md., U.S. 208 38.50 N 76.31 W
Galesville, Wis., U.S. 190 44.05 N 91.21 W
Galeton 214 41.44 N 77.39 W
Galeville 210 43.05 N 76.11 W
Galgash 144 0.14 N 41.37 E
Galgate 44 54.00 N 2.47 W
Galheirão ≃ 255 12.23 S 45.05 W
Galheiros 255 13.18 S 46.25 W
Gali 84 42.38 N 41.44 E
Gali, Torrente de ≃ 266d 41.28 N 2.00 E
Galiano 224 48.52 N 123.21 W
Galiano Island I 224 48.56 N 123.29 W
Galibier, Col du)(62 45.04 N 6.24 E
Galič, S.S.S.R. 78 49.08 N 24.43 E
Galič, S.S.S.R. 80 58.23 N 42.21 E
Galicia □[9] 34 43.00 N 8.00 W
Galičsko-Čuchlomskaja Vozvyšennost' ⋏[2] 24 58.25 N 42.20 E
Galičskoje, Ozero ◎ 80 58.24 N 42.18 E
Galiema, Baie de C 273b 4.19 S 15.16 E
Galien 216 41.48 N 86.30 W
Galien ≃ 216 41.48 N 86.45 W
Galilee 207 41.23 N 71.30 W
Galilee
→ HaGalil ⬥[1] 132 32.54 N 35.20 E
Galilee, Lake ◎ 166 22.21 S 145.48 E
Galilee, Sea of
→ Kinneret, Yam ◎ 132 32.48 N 35.35 E
Galiléia 255 19.00 S 41.33 W
Galim 152 7.06 N 12.29 E
Galina Point ≻ 241q 18.24 N 76.53 W
Galindo Creek ≃ 282 37.58 N 122.02 W
Galion 214 40.44 N 82.47 W
Galion, Baie du C 240e 14.44 N 60.57 W
Galion, Rivière du ≃ 240e 14.44 N 60.57 W
Galis 115a 7.08 S 113.33 E
Galisteo Creek ≃ 200 35.31 N 106.22 W
Galite, Canal de la ⊔ 36 37.20 N 9.00 E
Galiuro Mountains ⋏ 200 32.40 N 110.20 W
Galižana 64 44.56 N 13.52 E
Galka'yo 144 6.49 N 47.23 E
Galkhausen 263 51.05 N 6.58 E
Galkin, Ostrov I 80 45.45 N 48.18 E
Galkino, S.S.S.R. 82 54.46 N 35.49 E
Galkino, S.S.S.R. 86 52.14 N 78.20 E
Galkino, S.S.S.R. 86 55.36 N 62.55 E
Gall'aaral 85 40.02 N 67.35 E
Gallan Head ≻ 46 58.14 N 7.03 W
Gallarate 62 45.40 N 8.47 E
Gallardon 50 48.32 N 1.42 E
Gallatin, Mo., U.S. 194 39.55 N 93.58 W
Gallatin, Pa., U.S. 279b 40.12 N 79.53 W
Gallatin, Tenn., U.S. 194 36.24 N 86.27 W
Gallatin, Tex., U.S. 222 31.54 N 95.09 W
Gallatin □[6] 218 38.45 N 84.51 W
Gallatin ≃ 202 45.56 N 111.29 W
Gallatin Range ⋏ 202 45.15 N 111.05 W
Galle 122 6.02 N 80.13 E
Gállego ≃ 34 41.39 N 0.51 W
Gallegos ≃ 254 51.36 S 68.59 W
Gallegos Canyon ∨ 200 36.41 N 108.07 W
Galles
→ Wales □[8] 28 52.30 N 3.30 W
Galleyend 260 51.42 N 0.29 E
Galley Head ≻ 48 51.30 N 8.57 W
Galleywood 260 51.42 N 0.28 E
Galliate 62 45.29 N 8.42 E
Gallicano 64 44.04 N 10.26 E
Gallicano nel Lazio 267a 41.52 N 12.49 E
Gallicchio 68 40.17 N 16.08 E
Gallico 68 38.10 N 15.41 E
Galliera Veneta 64 45.39 N 11.49 E
Gallimh
→ Galway 48 53.16 N 9.03 W
Gallinara I 62 44.02 N 8.14 E
Gallinas ≃ 196 35.10 N 104.55 W
Gallinas, Punta ≻ 246 12.28 N 71.40 W
Gallinas Creek ≃ 282 38.01 N 122.30 W
Gallio 64 45.53 N 11.33 E
Gallipoli, Austl. 166 19.10 S 137.55 E
Gallipoli, It. 68 40.03 N 17.58 E
Gallipoli
→ Gelibolu, Tür. 130 40.24 N 26.40 E
Gallipoli Peninsula
→ Gelibolu Yarımadası ≻[1] 130 40.20 N 26.30 E
Gallipolis 188 38.49 N 82.12 W
Gallitzin 214 40.29 N 78.33 W
Gallivaggio 58 46.21 N 9.21 E
Gällivare 24 67.07 N 20.45 E
Gällö 26 62.55 N 15.14 E
Gallo, Capo ≻ 70 38.13 N 13.19 E
Gallo, Lago del ◎[1] 64 46.07 N 10.10 E
Gallo, Lago di ◎[1] 58 46.37 N 10.10 E
Gallo Arroyo ∨ 200 33.55 N 105.00 W
Galloo Island I 212 43.54 N 76.25 W
Galloupes Point ≻ 283 42.28 N 70.53 W
Galloway □[9] 44 55.00 N 4.25 W
Galloway, Mull of ≻ 44 54.38 N 4.50 W
Galloway Creek ≃, Md., U.S. 284b 39.18 N 76.23 W
Galloway Creek ≃, Mich., U.S. 281 42.39 N 83.12 W
Galluis 261 48.48 N 1.48 E
Gallup 200 35.32 N 108.44 W
Gallupville 210 42.40 N 74.14 W
Gallur 34 41.52 N 1.19 W
Gallura ⬥[1] 71 41.00 N 9.13 E
Galluzzo ⬥[8] 66 43.44 N 11.13 E
Gally, Rû de ≃ 261 48.53 N 1.53 E
Gälnan ⊔ 40 59.31 N 18.45 E
Gålö I 40 59.05 N 18.17 E
Galop Island I 212 44.46 N 75.24 W
Galoppo, Ippodromo del ♠ 266b 45.28 N 9.07 E
Galougo 150 13.50 N 11.04 W
Galsi 126 23.20 N 87.42 E
Galston 46 55.36 N 4.24 W
Galt, Mong. 88 48.46 N 99.53 E
Galt, Calif., U.S. 226 38.15 N 121.18 W
Gal Tardo 144 3.37 N 45.58 E
Galtelli 71 40.23 N 9.37 E
Galten 41 56.09 N 9.55 E
Galten C 40 59.27 N 16.09 E

ENGLISH

Name | Page | Lat.°′ | Long.°′

Galtür 58 46.58 N 10.11 E
Galtymore ∧ 48 52.22 N 8.10 W
Galty Mountains ⋏ 48 52.25 N 8.10 W
Galūgāh-e Āsīyeh 128 34.01 N 59.55 E
Galugur 114 2.34 N 99.39 E
Galula 154 8.36 S 33.02 E
Galuut 88 48.30 N 113.20 E
Galva, Ill., U.S. 190 41.10 N 90.03 W
Galva, Iowa, U.S. 198 42.30 N 95.25 W
Galvarino 252 38.24 S 72.47 W
Galveston, Ind., U.S. 216 40.35 N 86.11 W
Galveston, Tex., U.S. 222 29.18 N 94.48 W
Galveston □[6] 222 29.20 N 94.53 W
Galveston Bay C 222 29.36 N 94.57 W
Galveston Island I 222 29.13 N 94.55 W
Gálvez 252 32.02 S 61.13 W
Galvin, Austl. 274b 37.51 S 144.49 E
Galvin, Wash., U.S. 224 46.45 N 123.02 W
Galway, Eire 48 53.16 N 9.03 W
Galway, N.Y., U.S. 210 43.01 N 74.02 W
Galway □[6] 48 53.20 N 9.00 W
Galway Bay C 48 53.10 N 9.15 W
Gam ≃ 110 21.55 N 105.12 E
Gam, Pulau I 164 0.27 S 130.36 E
Gama, Isla I 254 40.29 S 62.12 W
Gamaches 50 49.59 N 1.33 E
Gamagōri 94 34.50 N 137.14 E
Gamalejevka 80 52.16 N 53.26 E
Gamaliel 194 36.38 N 85.48 W
Gaman 130 41.10 N 36.20 E
Gamare, Lake ◎ 144 11.30 N 41.40 E
Gamarra 246 8.20 N 73.45 W
Gamay 116 12.23 N 125.18 E
Gamay Bay C 116 12.21 N 125.21 E
Gambaga 150 10.32 N 0.26 W
Gambais 261 48.46 N 1.40 E
Gambaiseuil 261 48.45 N 1.44 E
Gambang 114 3.43 N 103.06 E
Gambara, It. 64 45.15 N 10.18 E
Gámbara, Méx. 234 18.55 N 102.05 W
Gambarie 68 38.10 N 15.50 E
Gambassi 66 43.32 N 10.57 E
Gambatesa 66 41.30 N 14.54 E
Gambela 144 8.18 N 34.37 E
Gambell 180 63.46 N 171.46 W
Gambellara 64 45.28 N 11.20 E
Gamber 208 39.28 N 76.56 W
Gambia □[1] 134
150 13.30 N 15.30 W
Gambia (Gambie) ≃ 150 13.28 N 16.34 W
Gambi Aṭrash 140 10.03 N 33.47 E
Gambie
→ Gambia □[1] 150 13.30 N 15.30 W
Gambie (Gambia) ≃ 150 13.28 N 16.34 W
Gambier 214 40.23 N 82.24 W
Gambier, Îles II 14 21.20 S 136.30 W
Gamble Mansion State Historic Site ⊥ 220 27.32 N 82.32 W
Gambo, Newf., Can. 186 48.46 N 54.14 W
Gambo, Centraf. 152 4.39 N 22.16 E
Gamboa 236 9.07 N 79.42 W
Gamboli 120 29.50 N 68.26 E
Gambolò 62 45.15 N 8.51 E
Gamboma 152 1.53 S 15.51 E
Gamboula 152 4.08 N 15.09 E
Gambrill State Park ♠ 208 39.30 N 77.30 W
Game Creek ≃ 285 39.41 N 75.28 W
Gamen-see ◎ 264a 52.40 N 13.51 E
Gaming 61 47.56 N 15.06 E
Gamka ≃, Namibia 156 28.15 S 17.26 E
Gamka ≃, S. Afr. 158 33.18 S 21.39 E
Gamlakarleby
→ Kokkola 26 63.50 N 23.07 E
Gamla Uppsala 40 59.54 N 17.38 E
Gamleby 26 57.54 N 16.24 E
Gammel Estrup ⊥ 26 56.26 N 10.21 E
Gammelstad ʋ[1] 26 65.38 N 22.01 E
Gammertingen 58 48.15 N 9.13 E
Gammon ≃ 184 51.07 N 95.09 W
Gammon, Point ≻ 207 41.36 N 70.16 W
Gamō, Nihon 94 35.03 N 136.11 E
Gamō, Nihon 268 35.52 N 139.48 E
Gamoep 158 29.55 S 18.25 E
Gamon 150 13.20 N 12.55 W
Gamova, Mys ≻ 89 42.35 N 131.12 E
Gamph, Slieve ⋏ 48 54.05 N 9.00 W
Gampoko 273b 4.16 S 15.10 E
Gampola 122 7.10 N 80.34 E
Gampongbatak 114 4.48 N 97.39 E
Gampoul 273b 4.08 S 15.22 E
Gams 58 47.12 N 9.28 E
Gamsfeld ∧ 64 47.37 N 13.29 E
Gamtoos ≃ 158 33.58 S 25.01 E
Gamud ∧ 144 4.05 N 38.03 E
G'amyš, Gora ∧ 84 40.18 N 46.23 E
Ganacker 60 48.43 N 12.41 E
Ganado, Ariz., U.S. 200 35.43 N 109.33 W
Ganado, Tex., U.S. 222 29.02 N 96.31 W
Ganano ≃ 116 16.45 N 121.44 E
Gananoque 212 44.20 N 76.10 W
Gananoque ≃ 212 44.19 N 76.09 W
Gananoque Lake ◎ 212 44.27 N 76.09 W
Ganaraska ≃ 212 43.57 N 78.18 W
Ganargua Creek ≃ 210 43.04 N 77.00 W
Ganassi 116 7.49 N 124.06 E
Gancevići 76 52.45 N 26.26 E
Ganchangba 107 28.52 N 103.41 E
Ganči 85 39.58 N 69.08 E
Gand
→ Gent 50 51.03 N 3.43 E
Ganda 152 4.05 N 23.32 E
Gandadiwata, Bulu ∧ 112 2.42 S 119.27 E
Gandajika 152 6.45 S 23.57 E
Gandak ≃ 124 25.40 N 85.13 E
Gandara 258 35.26 S 58.06 W
Gāndarbal 123 34.14 N 74.47 E
Ganda Singhwāla 123 31.02 N 74.31 E
Gandāva 120 28.37 N 67.29 E
Gandavaroyi Falls ʟ 154 17.17 S 29.07 E
Gānde 126 24.10 N 86.26 E
Gander 186 48.57 N 54.37 W
Gander ≃ 186 49.15 N 54.30 W
Gander Bay 186 49.18 N 54.29 W
Gander Bay C 186 49.25 N 54.28 W
Ganderkesee 52 53.02 N 8.32 E
Gander Lake ◎ 186 48.55 N 54.40 W
Gandesa 34 41.03 N 0.26 E
Gandevi 120 20.49 N 72.59 E
Gāndhi Sāgar ◎[1] 120 24.18 N 75.21 E
Gandi 150 12.55 N 5.49 E
Gandi, Wādī ∨ 140 11.23 N 24.31 E
Gandía 34 38.58 N 0.11 W
Gandino 62 45.49 N 9.54 E
Gando 152 12.30 S 17.25 E
Gandou 152 2.24 N 17.27 E
Gandrange 56 49.16 N 6.08 E
Gandria 58 46.01 N 9.00 E
Gandu 255 13.45 S 39.30 W
Gandy Bridge ⬥[5] 220 27.53 N 82.34 W
G'andžačaj ≃ 84 40.54 N 46.28 E
Gandzha
→ Kirovabad 84 40.40 N 46.22 E
Ganfang 100 28.40 N 114.51 E
Ganfosi 107 29.36 N 104.03 E
Ganga
→ Ganges ≃ 124 23.22 N 90.32 E
Gangādharpur 272b 22.36 N 88.11 E
Gangafani 150 14.23 N 2.24 W
Gangājalghāti 126 23.25 N 87.07 E
Gangala-Na-Bodio 154 3.41 N 29.08 E
Gangalingolo 273b 4.20 S 15.09 E
Gan Gan 254 42.30 S 68.16 W
Ganganagar
→ Sri Gangānagar 123 29.55 N 73.53 E
Gangāpur, Bhārat 120 25.13 N 74.16 E
Gangāpur, Bhārat 122 19.41 N 75.01 E
Gangāpur, Bhārat 124 26.29 N 76.43 E

DEUTSCH

Name | Seite | Breite°′ | Länge°′ E=Ost

Gangara, Niger 150 13.33 N 7.14 E
Gangara, Niger 150 14.36 N 8.30 E
Gāngārāmpur 124 25.24 N 88.31 E
Ganga Sāgar 126 21.38 N 88.05 E
Gangaw 110 22.11 N 94.07 E
Gangāwati 122 15.26 N 76.32 E
Gangaw Range ⋏ 110 24.50 N 96.40 E
Ganga-Yamuna Doāb ⋏[1] 124 26.40 N 79.30 E
Gangbukou 98 35.48 N 118.37 E
Gangcha 102 37.15 N 100.28 E
Gangchengtun 98 35.52 N 116.52 E
Gangdaba, Tchabal ⋏ 152 7.44 N 12.45 E
Gangdhār 120 23.57 N 75.37 E
Gangdisishan ∧ 120 31.29 N 80.45 E
Gangdisishanmai ⋏ 120 29.30 N 87.00 E
Gangelt 56 50.59 N 5.59 E
Ganges, B.C., Can. 182 48.51 N 123.30 W
Ganges, Fr. 62 43.56 N 3.42 E
Ganges (Ganga) (Padma) ≃ 124 23.22 N 90.32 E
Ganges, Mouths of the ≃[1] 120 22.00 N 89.00 E
Ganges Delta ⏝[2] 124 23.00 N 89.00 E
Ganghu 120 32.05 N 87.00 E
Gangi 70 37.41 N 14.10 E
Gangkofen 60 48.26 N 12.34 E
Gangkou, Zhg. 100 29.45 N 115.44 E
Gangkou, Zhg. 100 29.21 N 117.58 E
Gangkou, Zhg. 100 22.38 N 113.22 E
Gangkou, Zhg. 106 30.44 N 118.54 E
Gangkouzhen 100 22.36 N 114.54 E
Gangkov 100 29.32 N 118.56 E
Ganglasishan ⋏ 120 31.00 N 82.50 E
Ganglingshan ⋏ 120 32.00 N 83.00 E
Gang Mills 210 42.09 N 77.07 W
Gāngnāpur 126 23.09 N 88.38 E
Gangneung
→ Kangnŭng 98 37.45 N 128.54 E
Gango ≃ 152 9.48 S 15.40 E
Gangoh 124 29.46 N 77.15 E
Gangotri 120 30.56 N 79.02 E
Gan'goumen 98 41.40 N 116.35 E
Gan'gouyi 102 36.01 N 105.03 E
Gan'gouzhen 98 40.30 N 119.27 E
Gangqiao 107 30.13 N 105.22 E
Gang Ranch 182 51.33 N 122.20 W
Gangshang 100 28.06 N 116.30 E
Gangtok 124 27.20 N 88.37 E
Gangtou 98 38.04 N 113.56 E
Gangtouli 106 31.42 N 119.02 E
Gangu 102 34.38 N 105.27 E
Gangwa, Zaïre 152 3.30 S 20.55 E
Gangwa, Zhg. 105 39.48 N 116.10 E
Gangwei 100 24.20 N 118.01 E
Ganhe ≃ 89 49.12 N 125.03 E
Ganhezi 86 44.08 N 88.32 E
Ganhu 102 44.33 N 94.09 E
Gani 164 0.47 S 128.13 E
Ganina Gar' 88 57.06 N 91.31 E
Ganišob 85 39.03 N 70.47 E
Ganj Dundwara 124 27.44 N 78.57 E
Ganjiang 107 29.42 N 103.38 E
Ganjiang ≃ 100 29.12 N 116.00 E
Ganjingzi 89 49.40 N 119.40 E
Gankui (Dayangshu) 89 49.45 N 124.35 E
Ganlanshan ∧ 124 29.54 N 90.02 E
Ganlu 106 31.32 N 120.35 E
Ganluo 102 29.03 N 102.59 E
Ganluzhen 107 29.54 N 104.47 E
Gannahoek 158 26.44 S 24.08 E
Gannan 89 47.54 N 123.30 E
Gannano, Lago di ◎ 68 40.19 N 16.26 E
Gannapan 158 30.23 S 22.12 E
Gannat 32 46.06 N 3.12 E
Gannett Peak ∧ 200 43.11 N 109.39 W
Gannovka 83 48.33 N 38.35 E
Gannvalley 198 44.02 N 98.59 W
Ganongga I 175e 8.05 S 156.34 E
Ganos Dağı ∧ 130 40.47 N 27.16 E
Ganpingsi 102 35.13 N 102.30 E
Ganpu 106 30.24 N 120.53 E
Ganquan 102 36.25 N 109.16 E
Gansbaai 158 34.35 S 19.22 E
Gänsbrunnen 58 47.16 N 7.28 E
Gansen 120 37.25 N 92.15 E
Gänserndorf 61 48.20 N 16.43 E
Gansevoort 210 43.12 N 73.39 W
Ganshoren 50 50.52 N 4.18 E
Ganso Azul 248 8.51 S 74.44 W
Gansu □[4] 102 37.00 N 103.00 E
Ganta 150 7.15 N 8.59 W
Gantan 100 29.37 N 119.34 E
Gantang, Zhg. 100 26.56 N 119.40 E
Gantang, Zhg. 102 22.58 N 109.00 E
Gante
→ Gent 50 51.03 N 3.43 E
Gantheaume, Cape ≻ 166 36.05 S 137.27 E
Gantheaume Bay C 162 27.44 S 114.07 E
Gantheaume Point ≻ 162 17.59 S 122.10 E
Gantiadi 84 43.24 N 40.06 E
Gantian 100 27.30 N 113.10 E
Gantt 194 31.25 N 86.29 W
Gantung 112 2.58 S 108.09 E
Gantung, Mount ∧ 116 8.57 N 117.48 E
Ganu Mór ∧ 46 58.25 N 4.53 W
Gan'uškino 80 46.36 N 49.16 E
Ganwé 150 8.11 N 7.51 W
Ganwo 150 11.13 N 4.42 E
Ganxi, Zhg. 100 28.08 N 118.06 E
Ganxi, Zhg. 102 29.02 N 109.32 E
Ganyabao 102 36.45 N 105.25 E
Ganyesa 158 26.35 S 24.10 E
Ganyu 98 34.52 N 119.10 E
Ganzhe 100 26.12 N 119.06 E
Ganzhenyi 100 30.33 N 113.21 E
Ganzhou, Zhg. 100 25.54 N 114.55 E
Ganzhou
→ Zhangye, Zhg. 102 38.57 N 100.37 E
Ganzhoujie 100 28.49 N 115.25 E
Ganzhu 100 26.58 N 116.16 E
Ganzhuermiao 88 48.24 N 118.08 E
Ganzi 102 31.40 N 100.01 E
Ganzlin 54 53.23 N 12.15 E
Gao 150 16.16 N 0.03 W
Gao □[4] 150 18.15 N 1.00 W
Gaoan 100 28.25 N 115.22 E
Gaobaita 271a 39.53 N 116.30 E
Gaobeidian, Zhg. 105 39.20 N 115.51 E
Gaobeidian, Zhg. 271a 39.54 N 116.33 E
Gaochang 107 28.49 N 104.24 E
Gaocheng, Zhg. 98 38.04 N 114.49 E
Gaocheng, Zhg. 100 31.57 N 113.25 E
Gaocheng, Zhg. 106 31.28 N 119.48 E
Gaochengzhai 104 41.24 N 123.43 E
Gaochun 106 31.20 N 118.52 E
Gaodianzi 102 30.40 N 110.01 E
Gaofeng ∧ 106 30.34 N 118.40 E
Gaofu 100 27.48 N 117.01 E
Gaogongmiao 100 33.25 N 115.53 E
Gaogou 100 34.03 N 119.15 E
Gaogucheng 102 38.20 N 101.50 E
Gaohe 100 22.47 N 112.57 E
Gaohebu 100 30.44 N 116.50 E
Gaojiabao 102 38.30 N 110.11 E
Gaojiachang 107 30.16 N 104.09 E
Gaojiadian 98 42.40 N 124.28 E
Gaojian 100 29.04 N 121.14 E
Gaojiapuzi 104 41.22 N 123.36 E
Gaojiaqiao 106 30.43 N 120.38 E
Gaojiatun 104 41.06 N 121.19 E
Gaojiawopeng 104 41.28 N 122.10 E
Gaojiawopu 104 41.50 N 122.47 E
Gaojiazao 105 39.58 N 114.47 E
Gaojiazhen 102 30.05 N 107.51 E
Gaokan 104 40.55 N 122.14 E
Gaokeng 100 27.40 N 113.58 E

Symbols in the index entries represent the broad categories identified in the key at the right. Symbols with superior numbers (⋏[2]) identify subcategories (see complete key on page *I · 30*).

Kartensymbole in dem Registerverzeichnis stellen die rechts in Schlüssel erklärten Kategorien dar. Symbole mit hochgestellten Ziffern (⋏[2]) bezeichnen Unterabteilungen einer Kategorie (vgl. vollständiger Schlüssel auf Seite *I · 30*).

Los símbolos incluídos en el texto del índice representan las grandes categorias identificadas con la clave a la derecha. Los símbolos con numeros en su parte superior (⋏[2]) identifican las subcategorias (véase la clave completa en la página *I · 30*).

Les symboles de l'index représentent les catégories indiquées dans la légende à droite. Les symboles suivis d'un indice (⋏[2]) représentent des sous-catégories (voir légende complète à la page *I · 30*).

Os símbolos incluídos no texto do índice representam as grandes categorias identificadas com a chave à direita. Os símbolos com números em sua parte superior (⋏[2]) identificam as subcategorias (veja-se a chave completa à página *I · 30*).

∧	Mountain	Berg	Montaña	Montagne	Montanha
⋏	Mountains	Berge	Montañas	Montagnes	Montanhas
)(	Pass	Pass	Paso	Col	Passo
∨	Valley, Canyon	Tal, Cañon	Valle, Cañón	Vallée, Canyon	Vale, Canhão
⏝	Plain	Ebene	Llano	Plaine	Planície
≻	Cape	Kap	Cabo	Cap	Cabo
I	Island	Insel	Isla	Île	Ilha
II	Islands	Inseln	Islas	Îles	Ilhas
⊥	Other Topographic Features	Andere Topographische Objekte	Otros Elementos Topográficos	Autres données topographiques	Outros Elementos Topográficos

ESPAÑOL

Nombre	Página	Lat.	Long. W=Oeste
Gaolan	102	36.25 N	103.56 E
Gaolandao ▮	100	21.55 N	113.15 E
Gaolao	104	41.54 N	120.59 E
Gaoli	105	39.17 N	115.38 E
Gaoliangzhen	107	29.45 N	105.15 E
Gaoliban	104	41.39 N	121.58 E
Gaolifangshen	104	42.27 N	123.21 E
Gaolimen	98	40.22 N	124.02 E
Gaolingtun	105	40.37 N	117.06 E
Gaolinying	105	39.06 N	115.38 E
Gaoliying	105	40.10 N	116.29 E
Gaoliyingzi	104	41.56 N	124.17 E
Gaolong	100	26.56 N	113.45 E
Gaolou	105	39.59 N	116.50 E
Gaolouchang, Zhg.	107	30.03 N	105.58 E
Gaolouchang, Zhg.	107	29.51 N	104.41 E
Gaoluo	98	37.27 N	113.55 E
Gaomi	98	36.23 N	119.44 E
Gaona	252	25.12 S	64.05 W
Gaopi, Zhg.	100	24.14 N	116.39 E
Gaopi, Zhg.	100	26.37 N	114.38 E
Gaoping, Zhg.	102	35.48 N	112.52 E
Gaoping, Zhg.	107	30.28 N	105.42 E
Gaopingba	107	30.47 N	106.06 E
Gaoqiao, Zhg.	100	26.36 N	117.46 E
Gaoqiao, Zhg.	100	30.08 N	119.56 E
Gaoqiao, Zhg.	102	28.06 N	106.36 E
Gaoqiao, Zhg.	104	40.55 N	121.00 E
Gaoqiao, Zhg.	106	31.21 N	121.34 E
Gaoqiao, Zhg.	106	32.14 N	119.38 E
Gaoqiao, Zhg.	107	30.24 N	103.37 E
Gaoqiaomen	106	32.01 N	118.51 E
Gaoqipu	104	41.32 N	121.40 E
Gaosha	100	26.27 N	117.56 E
Gaoshaling	105	38.51 N	117.36 E
Gaoshan, Zhg.	100	25.29 N	119.34 E
Gaoshan, Zhg.	107	29.26 N	104.28 E
Gaoshanbao, Zhg.	98	41.43 N	115.41 E
Gaoshanbao, Zhg.	105	40.40 N	117.29 E
Gaoshangbao	98	39.11 N	118.30 E
Gaoshanpu	102	27.10 N	105.14 E
Gaoshantai	104	42.22 N	122.28 E
Gaoshanzi	104	41.34 N	122.02 E
Gaoshengchang	107	29.59 N	105.31 E
Gaoshengzhen	104	41.20 N	122.12 E
Gaoshichang	107	29.36 N	104.45 E
Gaoshikan	107	29.12 N	105.04 E
Gaosichang	107	30.17 N	104.52 E
Gaotai	102	39.20 N	99.58 E
Gaotaishan	104	42.05 N	122.50 E
Gaotan, Zhg.	100	30.23 N	117.23 E
Gaotan, Zhg.	100	23.12 N	115.22 E
Gaotang, Zhg.	98	36.54 N	116.14 E
Gaotang, Zhg.	100	32.24 N	116.01 E
Gaotanzi	102	32.22 N	108.36 E
Gaotingsi	100	26.05 N	112.53 E
Gaotingzhen	100	30.14 N	122.12 E
Gaotuozi	104	41.08 N	122.40 E
Gaoua	150	10.20 N	3.11 W
Gaoual	150	11.45 N	13.12 W
Gaoual □[4]	150	11.45 N	13.12 W
Gaoxian	102	28.20 N	104.38 E
Gaoxing	100	26.28 N	115.14 E
Gaoya	98	36.22 N	118.49 E
Gaoyang	98	34.30 N	114.40 E
Gaoyapu	107	29.14 N	106.19 E
Gaoyazi	102	36.54 N	106.12 E
Gaoyi	98	37.36 N	114.36 E
Gaoyou	100	32.47 N	119.27 E
Gaoyouhu ◉	100	32.50 N	119.20 E
Gaoyoushi	100	28.25 N	115.31 E
Gaozhangjia	102	36.06 N	107.18 E
Gaozhou	102	21.55 N	110.50 E
Gaozhuangzi	105	39.19 N	117.10 E
Gaozi	106	32.11 N	119.18 E
Gaoziba	107	29.01 N	106.00 E
Gaozuo	100	33.57 N	118.03 E
Gap, Fr.	62	44.34 N	6.05 E
Gap, Pa., U.S.	208	39.59 N	76.01 W
Gapālnagar	272b	22.49 N	88.08 E
Gapan	116	15.19 N	120.57 E
Gapeau ≃	62	43.07 N	6.11 E
Gapern ◉	40	59.31 N	13.40 E
Gara, Lough ◉	48	53.55 N	8.25 W
Garachiné	246	8.04 N	78.22 W
Garachiné, Punta ≻	246	8.06 N	78.25 W
Garad	144	6.54 N	49.20 E
Gārādāha	126	24.14 N	89.34 E
Garagoa	246	5.05 N	73.21 W
Garaguso	68	40.33 N	16.14 E
Garah	166	29.04 S	149.38 E
Garai ≃[1]	126	23.32 N	89.31 E
Garaina	164	7.50 S	147.10 E
Garamba ≃	154	3.53 N	29.12 E
Garamba, Parc National de la ♠	154	4.10 N	29.30 E
Gara Muleta ∧	144	9.17 N	41.47 E
Garānberia	272b	22.24 N	88.34 E
Garancières	261	48.49 N	1.46 E
Garango	150	11.48 N	0.34 W
Garanhuns	250	8.54 S	36.29 W
Garapan	174n	15.12 N	145.43 E
Garautha	124	25.34 N	79.18 E
Garba	146	9.12 N	20.30 E
Garbagna	266b	45.23 N	8.39 E
Garbagnate Milanese	266b	45.35 N	9.05 E
Garba Harre	144	3.20 N	42.17 E
Garbatella ◂[8]	267a	41.52 N	12.29 E
Garba Tula	154	0.32 N	38.31 E
Garber	196	36.26 N	97.35 W
Garberville	204	40.06 N	123.48 W
Garbokaraj	88	54.09 N	99.52 E
Garboldisham	42	52.24 N	0.56 E
Garbsen	52	52.25 N	9.34 E
Garça	255	22.14 S	49.37 W
Garças, Rio das ≃	255	15.54 S	52.16 W
Garcevo	76	52.45 N	32.59 E
Garches	261	48.51 N	2.11 E
Garching	60	48.15 N	11.39 E
Garching an der Alz	60	48.08 N	12.34 E
Garchitorena	116	13.52 N	123.40 E
García	232	29.59 N	108.20 W
García, Laguna ◉	288	34.58 S	58.09 W
García de la Cadena	234	21.09 N	103.28 W
García de Sola, Embalse de ◉[1]	34	39.15 N	5.05 W
Garcia Hernandez	116	9.37 N	124.18 E
Garcias	255	20.34 S	52.13 W
Gard □[5]	62	44.00 N	4.00 E
Gard ≃	62	43.51 N	4.37 E
Gard, Pont du ◂[5]	62	43.56 N	4.36 E
Garda	64	45.34 N	10.42 E
Garda, Lago di ◉	64	45.40 N	10.41 E
Gardabani	84	41.28 N	45.06 E
Gardanne	62	43.27 N	5.28 E
Garde, Lac la ◉	190	46.46 N	78.14 W
Gardelegen	54	52.31 N	11.23 E
Garden ≃	190	46.32 N	84.09 W
Gardena	228	33.53 N	118.18 W
Gardena, Val ∨	64	46.35 N	11.35 E
Garden Acres	226	37.58 N	121.13 W
Garden City, Ga., U.S.	192	32.06 N	81.09 W
Garden City, Kans., U.S.	198	37.58 N	100.53 W
Garden City, Mich., U.S.	216	42.20 N	83.20 W
Garden City, Mo., U.S.	194	38.34 N	94.12 W
Garden City, N.Y., U.S.	210	40.43 N	73.37 W
Garden City, Tex., U.S.	196	31.52 N	101.29 W
Garden City Park	276	40.44 N	73.40 W
Gardendale	194	33.39 N	86.49 W
Garden Farms	226	35.24 N	120.07 W
Garden Gate Village	282	37.20 N	122.02 W
Garden Grove, Calif., U.S.	228	33.46 N	117.57 W
Garden Grove, Iowa, U.S.	190	40.50 N	93.36 W
Garden Home	224	45.26 N	122.47 W

FRANÇAIS

Nom	Page	Lat.	Long. W=Ouest
Garden Island ▮, Austl.	168a	32.13 S	115.41 E
Garden Island ▮, Mich., U.S.	190	45.49 N	85.30 W
Garden Peninsula ≻[1]	190	45.45 N	86.35 W
Garden Prairie	216	42.15 N	88.44 W
Garden Reach	126	22.33 N	88.17 E
Gardenside	218	38.03 N	84.33 W
Garden State Arts Center ʊ	276	40.24 N	74.11 W
Garden State Park ♠	285	39.55 N	75.02 W
Garden State Plaza ◂[9]	276	40.55 N	74.05 W
Gardenton	184	49.05 N	96.40 W
Garden Valley	226	38.51 N	120.51 W
Garden View	210	41.16 N	77.03 W
Gardenville	208	40.22 N	75.07 W
Gardermoen	26	60.13 N	11.06 E
Gardey	252	37.17 S	59.21 W
Gardēz	120	33.37 N	69.07 E
Gardinas → Grodno	76	53.41 N	23.50 E
Gardiner, Maine, U.S.	188	44.14 N	69.46 W
Gardiner, Mont., U.S.	202	45.02 N	110.42 W
Gardiner, N.Y., U.S.	210	41.41 N	74.09 W
Gardiner, Oreg., U.S.	202	43.44 N	124.07 W
Gardiner, Wash., U.S.	224	48.03 N	122.55 W
Gardiner Dam ◂[6]	184	51.17 N	106.51 W
Gardiner Range ⩘	162	23.50 S	131.46 E
Gardiners Bay C	207	41.08 N	72.10 W
Gardiners Creek ≃	274b	37.50 S	145.02 E
Gardiners Island ▮	207	41.05 N	72.07 W
Garding	41	54.20 N	8.46 E
Gardner, Ill., U.S.	216	41.11 N	88.18 W
Gardner, Kans., U.S.	198	38.49 N	94.56 W
Gardner, Mass., U.S.	207	42.34 N	72.00 W
Gardner ▮[1]	14	4.40 S	174.32 W
Gardner Canal C	182	53.28 N	128.15 W
Gardner Lake ◉	207	41.31 N	72.13 W
Gardner Pinnacles ▮▮[1]	14	25.00 N	167.55 W
Gardnersville	218	38.46 N	84.30 W
Gardnertown	210	41.32 N	74.04 W
Gardnerville	226	38.56 N	119.45 W
Gardno	54	53.15 N	14.38 E
Gardo	144	9.30 N	49.03 E
Gardolo	64	46.07 N	11.05 E
Gardon d'Alès ≃	62	44.02 N	4.08 E
Gardon d'Anduze ≃	62	44.02 N	4.08 E
Gardone Riviera	64	45.37 N	10.34 E
Gardone Val Trompia	64	45.41 N	10.11 E
Gårdsjö	40	58.52 N	14.19 E
Gårdskär	40	60.37 N	17.35 E
Gardunha, Serra da ⩘	34	40.05 N	7.31 W
Gare Loch C	46	56.01 N	4.48 W
Garelochhead	46	56.05 N	4.50 W
Gareloi Island ▮	181a	51.47 N	178.48 W
Garenfeld	263	51.24 N	7.31 E
Garešnica	36	45.35 N	16.56 E
Garessio	62	44.12 N	8.02 E
Garfield, Kans., U.S.	198	38.05 N	99.14 W
Garfield, N.J., U.S.	210	40.53 N	74.07 W
Garfield, N. Mex., U.S.	200	32.46 N	107.16 W
Garfield, Wash., U.S.	202	47.01 N	117.09 W
Garfield Heights	214	41.26 N	81.37 W
Garfield Mountain ∧	202	44.31 N	112.37 W
Garfield Park ♠, Ill., U.S.	278	41.53 N	87.43 W
Garfield Park ♠, Ohio, U.S.	279a	41.26 N	81.36 W
Garfield Peak ∧	200	42.47 N	107.18 W
Garforth	44	53.48 N	1.22 W
Garga	88	54.26 N	110.33 E
Gargaliánoi	38	37.04 N	21.39 E
Gargano, Promontorio del ≻	68	41.50 N	16.00 E
Gargano, Testa del ≻	68	41.49 N	16.12 E
Gargantua, Cape ≻	190	47.36 N	85.02 W
Gargazzone (Gargazon)	64	46.35 N	11.12 E
Gargellen	58	46.58 N	9.56 E
Gargenville	261	49.00 N	1.49 E
Garges-lès-Gonesse	261	48.58 N	2.25 E
Gargnano	64	45.41 N	10.40 E
Gargouna	150	15.56 N	0.13 E
Gargrave	44	53.59 N	2.06 W
Gargždai	76	55.43 N	21.24 E
Garhākota	124	23.46 N	79.09 E
Garhbeta	126	22.51 N	87.19 E
Garhdīwāla	123	31.44 N	75.45 E
Garhi Jasaya	272a	28.46 N	77.16 E
Garhi Katiya	272a	28.45 N	77.16 E
Garhi Khairo	120	28.04 N	67.59 E
Garhi Malehra	124	25.02 N	79.40 E
Garhmuktesar	124	28.48 N	78.06 E
Garhshankar	123	31.13 N	76.08 E
Garhwal □[5]	124	30.00 N	78.50 E
Gari	86	59.26 N	62.21 E
Garibaldi, Bra.	252	29.15 S	51.32 W
Garibaldi, B.C., Can.	182	49.58 N	123.09 W
Garibaldi, Oreg., U.S.	224	45.34 N	123.55 W
Garibaldi, Casa di ⊥	71	41.13 N	9.27 E
Garibaldi, Mount ∧	182	49.51 N	123.01 W
Garibaldi Provincial Park ♠	182	50.00 N	122.50 W
Garies	158	30.30 S	18.00 E
Garigliano	68	41.13 N	13.45 E
Gariglione, Monte ∧	68	39.09 N	16.41 E
Garín	258	34.26 S	58.44 W
Garín, Arroyo ≃	288	34.23 S	58.43 W
Garinin	46	58.21 N	6.50 W
Garin Regional Park ♠	282	37.38 N	122.03 W
Garipçe Burnu ≻	267b	41.13 N	29.07 E
Garissa	154	0.28 S	39.38 E
Garita Palmera	236	13.44 N	90.05 W
Gariya	272b	22.28 N	88.23 E
Gārji	272b	22.51 N	88.19 E
Garkida	146	10.25 N	12.36 E
Garko	150	11.38 N	8.48 E
Garland, Ala., U.S.	194	31.33 N	86.49 W
Garland, Md., U.S.	284b	39.11 N	76.39 W
Garland, Pa., U.S.	214	41.49 N	79.27 W
Garland, Tex., U.S.	222	32.54 N	96.39 W
Garland, Utah, U.S.	200	41.45 N	112.10 W
Garland Park ♠	275b	43.44 N	79.35 W
Garland Peak ∧	224	48.01 N	120.43 W
Garlasco	62	45.12 N	8.55 E
Garlate	62	45.49 N	9.23 E
Garlate, Lago di ◉	58	45.49 N	9.24 E
Garliava	76	54.49 N	23.52 E
Garlieston	44	54.48 N	4.22 W
Garlin	32	43.34 N	0.15 W
Garm	85	39.02 N	70.22 E
Garm Āb	120	32.14 N	65.01 E
Garmal	144	8.35 N	50.24 E
Gärmersdorf	60	49.26 N	11.54 E
Garmisch-Partenkirchen	64	47.29 N	11.05 E
Garmouth	46	57.40 N	3.07 W
Garmsar	128	35.20 N	52.13 E
Garnavillo	190	42.52 N	91.14 W
Garne	261	48.41 N	1.58 E
Garner, Iowa, U.S.	190	43.06 N	93.36 W
Garner, N.C., U.S.	192	35.43 N	78.37 W
Garnet Bay C	176	65.17 N	75.15 W
Garnet Range ⩘	202	46.45 N	113.15 W
Garnett	198	38.17 N	95.14 W
Garni Habibullāh Khan	123	34.24 N	73.22 E

PORTUGUÊS

Nome	Página	Lat.	Long. W=Oeste
Garnijskij Zapovednik ♠	84	40.00 N	44.55 E
Garnish	186	47.14 N	55.22 W
Garnock ≃	46	55.38 N	4.42 W
Garoe	144	8.25 N	48.33 E
Garona → Garonne ≃	32	45.02 N	0.36 W
Garonne ≃	32	45.02 N	0.36 W
Garou, Lac ◉	150	16.04 N	2.45 W
Garoua, Cam.	146	9.18 N	13.24 E
Garoua, Niger	146	13.53 N	13.11 E
Garoua Boulaï	152	5.53 N	14.33 E
Garoumélé	146	14.07 N	12.58 E
Garove Island ▮	164	4.40 S	149.30 E
Garpenberg	40	60.19 N	16.12 E
Garphyttan	40	59.19 N	14.56 E
Garphyttans Nationalpark ♠	40	59.17 N	14.51 E
Garraf, Costa de ⊹[2]	266d	41.16 N	2.02 E
Garrapata Creek ≃	226	36.25 N	121.55 W
Garrattsville	210	42.39 N	75.10 W
Garrel	52	52.57 N	8.01 E
Garret Mountain Reservation ♠	276	40.54 N	74.11 W
Garretson	198	43.43 N	96.30 W
Garrett, Ind., U.S.	216	41.21 N	85.08 W
Garrett, Ky., U.S.	192	37.29 N	82.50 W
Garrett Creek ≃	222	32.57 N	95.44 W
Garrett Lake ◉	184	53.39 N	90.59 W
Garrett Park	208	39.02 N	77.06 W
Garrettsville	214	41.17 N	81.06 W
Garrison, N. Ire., U.K.	48	54.25 N	8.05 W
Garrison, Ky., U.S.	218	38.36 N	83.10 W
Garrison, Md., U.S.	208	39.24 N	76.45 W
Garrison, Mont., U.S.	202	46.31 N	112.57 W
Garrison, N. Dak., U.S.	198	47.40 N	101.25 W
Garrison, N.Y., U.S.	210	41.23 N	73.57 W
Garrison, Tex., U.S.	222	31.49 N	94.30 W
Garrison Dam ◂[6]	198	47.22 N	101.25 W
Garron Point ≻	48	55.03 N	5.55 W
Garros	46	57.37 N	6.11 W
Garrovillas	34	39.43 N	6.33 W
Garry ≃	46	56.43 N	3.47 W
Garry, Loch ◉	206	45.15 N	74.43 W
Garry Bay C	176	68.55 N	85.05 W
Garry Lake ◉	176	66.00 N	100.00 W
Garsdale Head	44	54.19 N	2.20 W
Garsen	154	2.16 S	40.07 E
Garskolk	158	30.41 S	22.02 E
Gårslev	41	55.38 N	9.43 E
Garson	190	46.34 N	80.52 W
Garson Lake ◉	184	56.19 N	110.02 W
Garstang	44	53.55 N	2.47 W
Garstedt	52	53.41 N	9.58 E
Garston	260	51.41 N	0.23 W
Garston ◂[8]	262	53.21 N	2.53 W
Garswood	262	53.29 N	2.40 W
Gartempe ≃	32	46.48 N	0.50 E
Gartenstadt ◂[8]	263	51.30 N	7.26 E
Garthby Station (Beaulac)	206	45.50 N	71.23 W
Gartow	54	53.02 N	11.29 E
Gartrop-Bühl	263	51.40 N	6.49 E
Gartz	54	53.12 N	14.23 E
Garu	150	10.51 N	0.11 W
Garub	156	26.33 S	16.00 E
Garubhāsa	124	26.33 N	90.22 E
Gārulia	126	22.49 N	88.22 E
Garut	115a	7.13 S	107.54 E
Garve	46	57.37 N	4.42 W
Garvellachs ▮▮	46	56.14 N	5.47 W
Garvie Mountains ⩘	172	45.30 S	168.50 E
Garwa	124	24.11 N	83.49 E
Garwin	190	42.06 N	92.40 W
Garwolin	30	51.54 N	21.37 E
Garwood, N.J., U.S.	276	40.39 N	74.19 W
Garwood, Tex., U.S.	222	29.27 N	96.24 W
Gary, Ind., U.S.	216		
	278	41.36 N	87.20 W
Gary, S. Dak., U.S.	198	44.48 N	96.27 W
Gary, Tex., U.S.	194	32.07 N	94.22 W
Gary Harbor C	278	41.38 N	87.20 W
Gary Municipal Airport ⊠	278	41.37 N	87.25 W
Garysburg	208	36.27 N	77.33 W
Garz	54	54.19 N	13.20 E
Garza	252	28.09 S	63.32 W
Garza Ayala	196	26.29 N	100.02 W
Garza-Little Elm Reservoir ◉[1]	196	33.08 N	97.00 W
Garzas Creek ≃	226	37.13 N	120.57 W
Garzeno	58	46.08 N	9.15 E
Garzón, Col.	246	2.12 N	75.38 W
Garzón, Ur.	252	34.36 S	54.33 W
Gas	261	48.34 N	1.40 E
Gasan	116	13.19 N	121.51 E
Gasan-Kuli	128	37.27 N	53.59 E
Gas City	216	40.29 N	85.37 W
Gascogne, Golfe de → Biscay, Bay of C	32	44.00 N	4.00 W
Gasconade	219	38.40 N	91.34 W
Gasconade □[6]	219	38.27 N	91.30 W
Gasconade ≃	194	38.40 N	91.33 W
Gasconade, Osage Fork ≃	194	37.45 N	92.26 W
Gascoyne ≃	162	24.52 S	113.37 E
Gascoyne, Mount ∧	162	24.58 S	116.38 E
Gascoyne Junction	162	25.03 S	115.12 E
Gash (Nahr al-Qāsh) ≃	140	16.48 N	35.51 E
Gashaka	146	7.21 N	11.27 E
Gasherbrum ∧	123	35.40 N	76.40 E
Gashua	146	12.54 N	11.00 E
Gashunhu (Juyanhai) ◉	102	42.22 N	100.34 E
Gasi	154	4.25 S	39.30 E
Gasline	284a	42.53 N	79.11 W
Gasny	50	49.05 N	1.36 E
Gaspar	252	26.56 S	48.58 W
Gasparilla Island ▮	220	26.46 N	82.16 W
Gasparilla Sound ⊔	220	26.48 N	82.15 W
Gaspé	186	48.50 N	64.29 W
Gaspé, Baie de ≃	186	48.46 N	64.17 W
Gaspé, Cap de ≻	186	48.45 N	64.10 W
Gaspé, Péninsule de ≻[1]	186	48.30 N	65.00 W
Gaspereau Lake ◉	186	44.57 N	64.34 W
Gasperina	68	38.44 N	16.30 E
Gaspésie, Parc de la ♠	186	48.55 N	66.00 W
Gaspoltshofen	60	48.08 N	13.46 E
Gasport	210	43.12 N	78.35 W
Gaspra	78	44.27 N	34.07 E
Gassan	150	12.49 N	3.12 W
Gas-san ∧	92	38.32 N	140.01 E
Gassaway	188	38.40 N	80.47 W
Gasselte	52	52.57 N	6.46 E
Gassen → Jasień	30	51.46 N	15.01 E
Gassin	62	43.13 N	6.35 E
Gassino Torinese	62	45.08 N	7.49 E
Gastein → Badgastein	64	47.07 N	13.08 E
Gasteiner Tal ∨	64	47.11 N	13.06 E
Gastello	89	49.07 N	142.58 E
Gaston, Ind., U.S.	216	40.19 N	85.30 W
Gaston, N.C., U.S.	192	36.30 N	77.38 W
Gaston, Oreg., U.S.	224	45.26 N	123.08 W
Gaston, Lake ◉[1]	192	36.35 N	78.00 W
Gastonia, N.C., U.S.	192	35.16 N	81.11 W
Gastonia, Tex., U.S.	222	32.37 N	96.24 W
Gastonville	279b	40.15 N	79.59 W
Gastoúni	38	37.51 N	21.16 E
Gastre	254	42.17 S	69.14 W
Gästrikland □[9]	40	60.30 N	16.27 E
Gat	132	31.37 N	34.47 E
Gata, Cabo de ≻	34	36.43 N	2.12 W
Gata, Sierra de ⩘	34	40.14 N	6.45 W
Gătaia	38	45.26 N	21.26 E
Gátas, Akrotírion ≻	130	34.34 N	33.02 E
Gatčina	76	59.34 N	30.08 E
Gate	196	36.51 N	100.04 W
Gateacre ◂[8]	262	53.23 N	2.51 W
Gate City	192	36.38 N	82.35 W
Gatehouse of Fleet	44	54.53 N	4.11 W
Gatere	175e	7.55 S	159.06 E
Gatere, Mount ∧	175e	7.49 S	158.54 E
Gatersleben	54	51.49 N	11.17 E
Gates, N.C., U.S.	208	36.30 N	76.46 W
Gates, N.Y., U.S.	210	43.09 N	77.41 W
Gates □[6]	208	36.28 N	76.43 W
Gateshead	44	54.58 N	1.37 W
Gateshead Island ▮	176	70.22 N	100.27 W
Gates Mills	279a	41.31 N	81.24 W
Gatesville, N.C., U.S.	192	36.19 N	76.45 W
Gatesville, Tex., U.S.	222	31.26 N	97.45 W
Gateway	200	38.41 N	108.59 W
Gateway Arch ʊ	219	38.37 N	90.12 W
Gateway National Recreation Area ♠	276	40.34 N	74.16 W
Gateway of India ⊥	272c	18.55 N	72.50 E
Gaths Mine	154	20.00 S	30.31 E
Gathurst	262	53.34 N	2.42 W
Gatié Loumo	150	15.28 N	4.37 W
Gâtine, Hauteurs de ⩘[2]	32	46.40 N	0.50 W
Gatineau ≃	176	45.27 N	75.40 W
Gatineau, Parc ♠	188	45.30 N	76.05 W
Gatley	262	53.23 N	2.14 W
Gatlinburg	192	35.43 N	83.31 W
Gato, Arroyo del ≃, Arg.	288	34.51 S	57.56 W
Gato, Arroyo del ≃, Arg.	288	34.55 S	58.37 W
Ga'ton	132	33.00 N	35.13 E
Gato Negro	286c	10.33 N	66.57 W
Gatooma	154	18.21 S	29.55 E
Gatow ◂[8]	264a	52.29 N	13.11 E
Gatow, Flugplatz ⊠	264a	52.28 N	13.08 E
Gattendorf	61	48.01 N	16.59 E
Gattières	62	43.46 N	7.11 E
Gattinara	62	45.37 N	8.22 E
Gatton	171a	27.33 S	152.17 E
Gattorna	62	44.26 N	9.11 E
Gatukai ▮	175e	8.46 S	158.11 E
Gatún, Lago ◉[1]	236	9.12 N	79.55 W
Gatun Locks ◂[5]	236	9.16 N	79.55 W
Gatvand	128	32.15 N	48.50 E
Gau-Algesheim	56	49.57 N	8.01 E
Gauchy	50	49.49 N	3.16 E
Gaucín	34	36.31 N	5.19 W
Gauer Lake ◉	184	57.00 N	97.50 W
Gauguin's House, Site of ⊥	174s	17.37 S	149.36 W
Gauhāti	120	26.11 N	91.44 E
Gauja ≃	76	57.09 N	24.16 E
Gaujiėna	76	57.30 N	26.40 E
Gaukler Point ≻	281	42.27 N	82.52 W
Gaula ≃	26	63.21 N	10.14 E
Gauley ≃	188	38.10 N	81.12 W
Gauley Bridge	188	38.10 N	81.11 W
Gaunless ≃	44	54.40 N	1.41 W
Gau-Odernheim	56	49.47 N	8.11 E
Gaura Barhaj	124	26.17 N	83.44 E
Gaurain-Ramecroix	50	50.35 N	3.29 E
Gaurama	252	27.34 S	52.03 W
Gaurambha	126	22.39 N	89.34 E
Gaurela	124	22.45 N	81.54 E
Gaurhāti	126	22.46 N	87.48 E
Gauribaradia	126	23.45 N	89.52 E
Gauribidanūr	122	13.37 N	77.31 E
Gauri Phanta	124	28.41 N	80.33 E
Gauripur	124	26.05 N	89.58 E
Gauri Sankar ∧	124	27.57 N	86.21 E
Gaurnadi	126	22.58 N	90.14 E
Gause	222	30.47 N	96.43 W
Gausta ∧	26	59.50 N	8.35 E
Gauthiot, Chutes ↳	146	9.43 N	14.34 E
Gauting	60	48.04 N	11.23 E
Gavá	34	41.18 N	2.01 E
Gāvanpāda	272c	18.57 N	73.01 E
Gavardo	64	45.35 N	10.26 E
Gávdhos ▮	136	34.50 N	24.06 E
Gávea ◂[8]	287a	22.58 S	43.14 W
Gávea, Hipódromo da ♠	287a	22.58 S	43.13 W
Gave d'Aspe ≃	32	43.12 N	0.36 W
Gavel-långsjön ◉	40	59.50 N	18.18 E
Gavello	64	45.01 N	11.55 E
Gavet	62	45.04 N	5.52 E
Gavi	62	44.41 N	8.49 E
Gavia, Arroyo de la ≃	266a	40.21 N	3.40 W
Gavião ≃	255	14.06 S	41.01 W
Gavião, Pico do ∧	256	21.37 S	44.50 W
Gavilán	286c	10.24 N	66.51 W
Gavinana	66	44.05 N	10.45 E
Gavins Point Dam ◂[6]	198	42.48 N	97.40 W
Gaviões	256	22.34 S	42.33 W
Gavirate	62	45.50 N	8.43 E
Gavja ≃	76	53.49 N	25.35 E
Gāvkhūnī, Bāṭlāq-e ☷	128	32.06 N	52.52 E
Gāv Koshī	128	28.38 N	57.12 E
Gävle	40	60.40 N	17.10 E
Gävleborgs Län □[6]	26	61.30 N	16.15 E
Gävlebukten C	40	60.42 N	17.20 E
Gavnø	41	55.11 N	11.44 E
Gavoi	71	40.10 N	9.12 E
Gavorrano	66	42.55 N	10.54 E
Gavriila, Guba C	180	62.25 N	179.15 E
Gavrilov-Jam	80	57.18 N	39.51 E
Gavrilovka	83	48.37 N	37.31 E
Gavrilovka Vtoraja	80	52.53 N	42.46 E
Gavrilov Posad	80	56.33 N	40.07 E
Gávrion	38	37.52 N	24.46 E
Gavry	76	56.55 N	27.53 E
Gawachab	156	27.03 S	17.50 E
Gawān	124	24.37 N	85.55 E
Gaweinstal	61	48.28 N	16.35 E
Gāwīlgarh Hills ⩘[2]	122	21.20 N	77.00 E
Gawler	168b	34.37 S	138.44 E
Gawler ≃	168b	34.41 S	138.27 E
Gawler Ranges ⩘	162	32.30 S	136.00 E
Gawso	150	6.48 N	2.31 W
Gawsworth	262	53.13 N	2.10 W
Gawthorpe Hall ⊥	262	53.48 N	2.18 W
Gawu	150	9.14 N	6.52 E
Gaya, Bhārat	124	24.47 N	85.00 E
Gaya, Nig.	150	11.53 N	9.02 E
Gaya, Niger	150	11.53 N	3.27 E
Gaya □[5]	124	24.50 N	84.50 E
Gay City State Park ♠	207	41.42 N	72.28 W
Gayéri	150	12.39 N	0.29 E
Gay Head	207	41.21 N	70.49 W
Gay Hill	222	30.16 N	96.30 W
Gaylord, Mich., U.S.	190	45.02 N	84.40 W
Gaylord, Minn., U.S.	190	44.33 N	94.13 W
Gaylordsville	207	41.39 N	73.29 W
Gayly	279b	40.27 N	80.09 W
Gayndah	166	25.37 S	151.36 E
Gays Mills	190	43.19 N	90.51 W
Gayton, Eng., U.K.	42	52.45 N	0.34 E
Gayton, Eng., U.K.	262	53.19 N	3.06 W
Gayt on Sands ⊹[4]	262	53.17 N	3.07 W
Gaywood	42	52.46 N	0.26 E
Gaza □[5]	156	23.30 S	32.45 E
Gazalkent	85	41.33 N	69.47 E
Gazaoua	150	13.32 N	7.55 E
Gaza Strip □[9]	132	31.25 N	34.20 E
Gaza Strip □[2]	132	31.25 N	34.20 E
Gazelle, Récif de la ⊹[2]	175f	20.11 S	165.27 E
Gazelle Channel ⊔	164	2.50 S	150.55 E
Gazelle Peninsula ≻[1]	164	4.40 S	152.00 E
Gazeran	261	48.38 N	1.46 E
Gazeran, Bois de ♠	261	48.40 N	1.45 E
Gazi	154	1.04 N	24.31 E
Gaziantep	130	37.05 N	37.22 E
Gaziantep □[4]	130	37.00 N	37.20 E
Gazimur ≃	88	52.57 N	120.22 E
Gazimurskij Chrebet ⩘	88	52.00 N	119.00 E
Gazimurskij Zavod	88	51.33 N	118.22 E
Gazipaşa	130	36.17 N	32.20 E
Gāzīpura	126	22.46 N	90.43 E
Gazira Sportin Club ♠	273c	30.04 N	31.13 E
Gaznau	85	40.10 N	71.02 E
Gazoldo degli Ippoliti	64	45.12 N	10.35 E
Gazos Creek ≃	226	37.10 N	122.22 W
Gazzada	62	45.47 N	8.51 E
Gazzaniga	62	45.48 N	9.50 E
Gazzuolo	64	45.04 N	10.35 E
Gbangbama	150	7.42 N	12.19 W
Gbanka	150	7.00 N	9.29 W
Gbogbo	273a	6.36 N	3.31 E
Gboko	150	7.20 N	8.57 E
Gbon	150	9.50 N	6.27 W
Gbongan	150	7.29 N	4.21 E
Gbwado	152	3.54 N	20.46 E
Gcoverega	156	19.08 S	24.15 E
Gdańsk (Danzig)	30	54.23 N	18.40 E
Gden'	78	51.20 N	30.25 E
Gdov	76	58.44 N	27.48 E
Gdyel	148	35.48 N	0.26 W
Gdynia	30	54.32 N	18.33 E
Gearhart	224	46.01 N	123.55 W
Gearhart Mountain ∧	202	42.30 N	120.53 W
Gearhartville	214	40.53 N	78.15 W
Geary, N.B., Can.	186	45.46 N	66.29 W
Geary, Okla., U.S.	196	35.38 N	98.19 W
Geauga □[6]	214	41.35 N	81.12 W
Geauga Lake Park ♠	279a	41.21 N	81.23 W
Gêba ≃	150	11.46 N	15.36 W
Gebaberg ∧	56	50.36 N	10.16 E
Gebe, Pulau ▮	164	0.05 S	129.20 E
Gebeler	130	39.26 N	29.00 E
Gebeme	130	40.38 N	37.48 E
Gebenbach	60	49.32 N	11.53 E
Gebesee	54	51.07 N	10.56 E
Gebi	84	42.46 N	43.30 E
Geblelu	144	10.40 N	41.31 E
Gebra	54	51.24 N	10.35 E
Gebweiler → Guebwiller	58	47.55 N	7.12 E
Gebze	130	40.48 N	29.25 E
Gecha	144	7.31 N	35.22 E
Gechang	106	31.05 N	119.27 E
Gecun	106	32.10 N	119.37 E
Geddes, Mich., U.S.	281	42.16 N	83.40 W
Geddes, S. Dak., U.S.	198	43.15 N	98.42 W
Gede, Gunung ∧	115a	6.47 S	106.59 E
Gede National Monument ♠	154	3.19 S	40.03 E
Gedera	132	31.49 N	34.46 E
Gedern	56	50.25 N	9.12 E
Gedian	100	30.32 N	114.38 E
Gedinne	56	49.59 N	4.56 E
Gediz	130	39.02 N	29.25 E
Gediz ≃	130	38.35 N	26.48 E
Gedo	144	8.58 N	37.27 E
Gedongdalem	112	5.04 S	105.25 E
Gedongtataan	115a	5.23 S	105.05 E
Gedser	41	54.35 N	11.57 E
Gedser Odde ≻	41	54.34 N	11.59 E
Geduld	273d	26.15 S	28.25 E
Geduld Dam ◂[6]	273d	26.13 S	28.25 E
Gedun	100	27.39 N	118.26 E
Geebung	171a	27.22 S	153.03 E
Gee Cross	262	53.26 N	2.04 W
Geehi	171b	36.24 S	148.11 E
Geehi ≃	171b	36.11 S	148.02 E
Geel	56	51.10 N	5.00 E
Geelong	169	38.08 S	144.21 E
Geelong West	169	38.08 S	144.20 E
Geelvink Channel ⊔	162	28.30 S	114.10 E
Geer ≃	56	50.51 N	5.42 E
Ge'ermu	102	36.23 N	94.50 E
Geertruidenberg	52	51.43 N	4.52 E
Geeste ≃	52	53.32 N	8.35 E
Geesthacht	52	53.26 N	10.22 E
Geeveston	166	43.10 S	146.55 E
Gefara (Djeffara) ≚	146	32.30 N	11.45 E
Gefell	54	50.26 N	11.52 E
Gefle → Gävle	40	60.40 N	17.10 E
Gefrees	54	50.06 N	11.44 E
Gegang	100	30.04 N	117.38 E
Gegečkori	84	42.25 N	42.22 E
Gegenmiao	89	45.58 N	122.15 E
Gegongzhen	100	30.02 N	117.05 E
Gegou	98	35.24 N	118.32 E
Gegu	105	38.59 N	117.30 E
Gehackte Berge ⩘[2]	264a	52.41 N	13.30 E
Gehlenburg → Biała Piska	30	53.37 N	22.04 E
Gehrden	52	52.18 N	9.36 E
Gehren	54	50.39 N	10.59 E
Gehu	100	27.46 N	119.16 E
Gehu ◉	106	31.36 N	119.51 E
Gehua	164	10.20 S	150.25 E
Geidam	146	12.57 N	11.57 E
Geiger	194	32.52 N	88.18 W
Geigertown	208	40.13 N	75.50 W
Geihoku	96	34.44 N	132.17 E
Geikie ≃	176	57.45 N	103.52 W
Geilenkirchen	56	50.57 N	6.07 E
Geilo	26	60.31 N	8.12 E
Geilo Hills ⩘[2]	154	3.36 N	41.17 E
Geinō	94	34.48 N	136.25 E
Geiranger	26	62.06 N	7.12 E
Geisa	56	50.43 N	9.57 E
Geisberg ∧	60	49.53 N	11.03 E
Geisecke	263	51.27 N	7.37 E
Geisei	96	33.31 N	133.49 E
Geiselhöring	60	48.50 N	12.23 E
Geisenfeld	60	48.41 N	11.37 E
Geisenhausen	60	48.28 N	12.15 E
Geisenheim	56	49.59 N	7.58 E
Geising	54	50.45 N	13.47 E
Geisingen	58	47.55 N	8.38 E
Geislingen an der Steige	56	48.36 N	9.50 E
Geismar	52	51.31 N	9.57 E
Geispolsheim	58	48.31 N	7.39 E
Geistenbeck ◂[8]	263	51.09 N	6.27 E
Geistown	214	40.17 N	78.52 W
Geist Reservoir ◉[1], Ind., U.S.	218	39.56 N	85.56 W
Geist Reservoir ◉[1], Pa., U.S.	285	39.57 N	75.24 W
Geisweid	56	50.55 N	8.01 E
Geita	154	2.52 S	32.10 E
Geithain	54	51.03 N	12.41 E
Geiyō-shotō ▮▮	96	34.10 N	132.45 E
Gejah	272a	28.31 N	77.23 E
Gejiaji	98	37.08 N	121.50 E
Gejiatun	98	40.27 N	119.55 E
Gejinhe ≃	98	38.12 N	117.46 E
Gejiu (Kokiu)	102	23.22 N	103.06 E
Geka, Mys ≻	180	64.26 N	178.10 E
Gela	70	37.04 N	14.15 E
Gela ≃	70	37.03 N	14.15 E
Gela, Golfo di C	70	37.03 N	14.10 E
Geladi	144	6.58 N	44.30 E
Gelai ∧[1]	154	2.33 S	36.05 E
Gelanchang	102	30.03 N	107.04 E
Gelang, Tanjong ≻	114	3.58 N	103.26 E
Gelaochang	107	29.36 N	103.39 E
Gelasa, Selat ⊔	112	2.40 S	107.15 E
Gelber Fluss → Huanghe ≃	100	32.19 N	115.02 E
Gelbes Meer → Yellow Sea ⍑[2]	90	36.00 N	123.00 E
Gelderland □[4]	52	52.10 N	5.50 E
Geldermalsen	52	51.53 N	5.17 E
Geldern	52	51.31 N	6.20 E
Geldern □[8]	263	51.25 N	6.27 E
Geldrop	52	51.25 N	5.33 E
Geleen	56	50.58 N	5.52 E
Gelegra	130	40.01 N	31.50 E
Gelemso	144	8.48 N	40.35 E
Gelenau	54	50.42 N	12.58 E
Gelenbe	130	39.10 N	27.50 E
Gelendost	130	38.07 N	31.01 E
Gelendžik	78	44.33 N	38.06 E
Gélengdeng	146	10.56 N	15.32 E
Gelfingen	58	47.13 N	8.16 E
Gelgaudiškis	76	55.05 N	23.00 E
Gelib → Jilib	144	0.28 N	42.50 E
Gelibolu	130	40.24 N	26.40 E
Gelibolu Yarımadası (Gallipoli Peninsula) ≻[1]	130	40.20 N	26.30 E
Gelidonya Burnu ≻	130	36.13 N	30.25 E
Gelinden	56	50.46 N	5.15 E
Gélise ≃	32	44.11 N	0.17 E
Geliting	115b	8.39 S	122.18 E
Geliting, Teluk C	115b	8.36 S	122.17 E
Gellenstrom ⊔	54	54.28 N	13.03 E
Gellep-Stratum ◂[8]	263	51.20 N	6.41 E
Gellibrand	169	38.32 S	143.32 E
Gellibrand ≃	169	38.41 S	143.09 E
Gellibrand, Point ≻	274b	37.52 S	144.54 E
Gellingen → Ghislenghien	50	50.39 N	3.52 E
Gellinsor	144	6.24 N	46.46 E
Gel'm'azov	78	49.49 N	31.49 E
Gelnhausen	56	50.11 N	9.11 E
Gelså ≃	41	55.19 N	8.54 E
Gelsdorf	56	50.35 N	7.02 E
Gelsenkirchen	52	51.31 N	7.07 E
Gelsenkirchen-Horst, Galopprennbahn ♠	263	51.32 N	7.02 E
Gelsted	41	55.24 N	9.59 E
Gelt ≃	44	54.56 N	2.47 W
Geltendorf	60	48.07 N	11.01 E
Gelterkinden	58	47.28 N	7.51 E
Gelting	41	54.45 N	9.53 E
Geltow	54	52.22 N	12.58 E
Gel Turfo	144	3.05 N	45.58 E
Geluk	158	27.01 S	24.18 E
Geluksburg	158	28.30 S	29.33 E
Geluwe	50	50.48 N	3.04 E
Gelveri	130	38.17 N	34.23 E
Gemas	114	2.35 N	102.37 E
Gem Beach	214	41.35 N	82.50 W
Gembloux	56	50.34 N	4.41 E
Gembrook	169	37.57 S	145.33 E
Gemen	52	51.51 N	6.52 E
Gemena	152	3.15 N	19.46 E
Gemengchi ◉	120	31.15 N	89.15 E
Gémenos	62	43.18 N	5.38 E
Gemerek	130	39.11 N	36.05 E
Gemert	52	51.34 N	5.40 E
Gemla	26	56.52 N	14.38 E
Gemlik	130	40.26 N	29.09 E
Gemlik Körfezi C	130	40.25 N	28.55 E
Gemolong	115a	7.24 S	110.50 E
Gemona del Friuli	64	46.16 N	13.09 E
Gemonio	62	45.53 N	8.40 E
Gemu Gofa □[4]	144	4.45 N	37.00 E
Gemünd	56	50.34 N	6.30 E
Gemünden, B.R.D.	56	50.03 N	9.41 E
Gemünden, B.R.D.	56	49.54 N	7.28 E
Gemünden, B.R.D.	56	50.58 N	8.58 E
Gemuzhakechi ◉	120	33.47 N	85.30 E
Genadendal	158	34.02 S	19.33 E
Genale ≃	144	5.43 N	40.53 E
Genappe	50	50.36 N	4.27 E
Genarp	41	55.36 N	13.23 E
Genazzano	66	41.50 N	12.58 E
Genç	130	38.46 N	40.35 E
Gençay	32	46.23 N	0.24 E
Gencek	130	37.27 N	31.33 E
Gending	115a	7.48 S	113.18 E
Gendrey	58	47.12 N	5.41 E
Gendringen	52	51.52 N	6.22 E
Gendt	52	51.53 N	5.59 E
Genegantslet Creek ≃	210	42.18 N	75.48 W
Genemuiden	52	52.37 N	6.07 E
General Acha	252	37.23 S	64.36 W
General Alvear, Arg.	252	34.58 S	67.42 W
General Alvear, Arg.	252	36.03 S	60.01 W
General Aquino	252	24.26 S	56.42 W
General Arenales	252	34.18 S	61.18 W
General Belgrano	252	35.46 S	58.30 W
General Bravo	232	25.48 N	99.10 W
General Butler State Park ♠	218	38.40 N	85.10 W
General Cabrera	252	32.48 S	63.52 W
General Câmara	252	29.54 S	51.46 W
General Campos	252	31.32 S	58.24 W
General Carneiro	255	15.42 S	52.45 W
General Carrera, Lago (Lago Buenos Aires) ◉	254	46.35 S	72.00 W
General Cepeda	232	25.23 N	101.27 W
General Conesa, Arg.	252	36.30 S	57.20 W
General Conesa, Arg.	254	40.06 S	64.26 W
General Daniel Cerri	252	38.42 S	62.24 W
General del Sur, Cementerio ◂	286c	10.28 N	66.55 W
General Elizardo Aquino	252	26.53 S	56.17 W
General Enrique Martínez	252	33.12 S	53.48 W
General Enrique Mosconi	252	22.36 S	63.49 W
General Escobedo, Méx.	196	25.49 N	100.20 W
General Escobedo, Méx.	232	25.30 N	105.15 W
General Eugenio A. Garay, Para.	248	20.31 S	62.08 W
General Eugenio A. Garay, Para.	252	25.55 S	56.11 W
General Galarza	252	32.43 S	59.24 W
General Guido	252	36.40 S	57.46 W
General Gutiérrez	252	32.57 S	68.48 W
General Hornos	258	34.53 S	58.56 W
General Island ▮	116	9.25 N	126.00 E
General José de San Martín	252	26.33 S	59.21 W
General Juan Madariaga	252	37.00 S	57.09 W
General La Madrid	252	37.16 S	61.17 W
General Las Heras	258	34.56 S	58.57 W
General Las Heras □[5]	288	34.56 S	58.51 W
General Lavalle	252	36.24 S	56.58 W
General Levalle	252	34.01 S	63.56 W
General Lorenzo Vintter	254	40.44 S	64.29 W
General Luna	116	9.47 N	126.09 E
General MacArthur (Pambuhan Sur)	116	11.15 N	125.32 E
General Machado	152	12.03 S	17.30 E
General Mansilla (Bartolomé Bavio)	258	35.05 S	57.45 W
General Manuel Belgrano, Cerro ∧	252	29.01 S	67.49 W
General Martín Miguel de Güemes	252	24.40 S	65.03 W
General Mitchell Field ⊠	216	42.57 N	87.54 W

Symbol	English	Deutsch	Español	Français	Português
≃	River	Fluss	Río	Rivière	Rio
≊	Canal	Kanal	Canal	Canal	Canal
↳	Waterfall, Rapids	Wasserfall, Stromschnellen	Cascada, Rápidos	Chute d'eau, Rapides	Cascata, Rápidos
⊔	Strait	Meeresstrasse	Estrecho	Détroit	Estreito
C	Bay, Gulf	Bucht, Golf	Bahía, Golfo	Baie, Golfe	Baía, Golfo
◉	Lake, Lakes	See, Seen	Lago, Lagos	Lac, Lacs	Lago, Lagos
☷	Swamp	Sumpf	Pantano	Marais	Pântano
⊼	Ice Features, Glacier	Eis- und Gletscherformen	Accidentes Glaciales	Formes glaciaires	Acidentes Glaciares
⍑	Other Hydrographic Features	Andere Hydrographische Objekte	Otros Elementos Hidrográficos	Autres données hydrographiques	Outros Elementos Hidrográficos

Symbol	English	Deutsch	Español	Français	Português
⊹	Submarine Features	Untermeerische Objekte	Accidentes Submarinos	Formes de relief sous-marin	Acidentes Submarinos
□	Political Unit	Politische Einheit	Unidad Politica	Entité politique	Unidade Política
ʊ	Cultural Institution	Kulturelle Institution	Institución Cultural	Institution culturelle	Instituição Cultural
⊥	Historical Site	Historische Stätte	Sitio Histórico	Site historique	Sitio Histórico
♠	Recreational Site	Erholungs- und Ferienort	Sitio de Recreo	Centre de loisirs	Sítio de Lazer
⊠	Airport	Flughafen	Aeropuerto	Aéroport	Aeroporto
▪	Military Installation	Militäranlage	Instalación Militar	Installation militaire	Instalação Militar
◂	Miscellaneous	Verschiedenes	Misceláneo	Divers	Miscelânea

General Motors Corporation (Pontiac Division) ♉[3] 281 42.49 N 83.17 W
General Motors Proving Grounds ♉[3] 281 42.35 N 83.41 W
General Motors Technical Center ♉[3] 281 42.31 N 83.02 W
General'nyj ≃ 265a 60.00 N 30.32 E
General O'Brien 252 34.54 S 60.45 W
General Pacheco 288 34.28 S 58.38 W
General Panfilo Natera 234 22.40 N 102.06 W
General Paz, Arg. 252 27.45 S 57.37 W
General Paz, Arg. 258 35.31 S 58.19 W
General Pico 252 35.40 S 63.44 W
General Pinedo 252 27.19 S 61.17 W
General Pinto 252 34.46 S 61.53 W
General Pizarro 252 24.13 S 64.01 W
General Plaza (Limón) 246 2.58 S 78.25 W
General Roca 252 39.02 S 67.35 W
General Rodríguez 258 34.36 S 58.57 W
General Rojo 252 33.28 S 60.17 W
General Saavedra 248 17.15 S 63.10 W
General Sampaio 250 4.02 S 39.29 W
General San Martín, Arg. 252 37.59 S 63.34 W
General San Martín, Arg. 258 34.34 S 58.32 W
General San Martín □[5] 288 34.34 S 58.34 W
General Santos (Dadiangas) 116 6.07 N 125.11 E
General Sarmiento 258 34.33 S 58.43 W
General Sarmiento □[5] 288 34.32 S 58.43 W
General'skoje 83 47.28 N 39.35 E
General Terán 232 25.16 N 99.41 W
General Tinio 116 15.21 N 121.03 E
General Toševo 38 43.42 N 28.02 E
General Treviño 196 26.14 N 99.29 W
General Urquiza ◆[8] 288 34.34 S 58.29 W
General Vargas 252 29.42 S 54.40 W
General Viamonte (Los Toldos) 252 35.01 S 61.01 W
General Villegas 252 35.02 S 63.01 W
General Vintter, Lago (Lago Palena) ⊜ 254 43.55 S 71.40 W
General Warren Village 285 40.02 N 75.32 W
General Zuazua 196 25.54 N 100.07 W
Gênes → Genova 62 44.25 N 8.57 E
Genesee, Idaho, U.S. 202 46.33 N 116.56 W
Genesee, Pa., U.S. 214 41.59 N 77.52 W
Genesee, Wis., U.S. 216 42.58 N 88.21 W
Genesee □[6], Mich., U.S. 216 42.56 N 83.41 W
Genesee □[6], N.Y., U.S. 210 43.00 N 78.11 W
Genesee ≃ 210 43.16 N 77.36 W
Geneseo, Ill., U.S. 190 41.27 N 90.09 W
Geneseo, Kans., U.S. 198 38.31 N 98.09 W
Geneseo, N.Y., U.S. 210 42.48 N 77.49 W
Geneva → Genève, Schw. 58 46.12 N 6.09 E
Geneva, S. Afr. 158 27.50 S 27.08 E
Geneva, Ala., U.S. 194 31.02 N 85.52 W
Geneva, Fla., U.S. 220 28.44 N 81.07 W
Geneva, Ill., U.S. 216 41.53 N 88.18 W
Geneva, Ind., U.S. 216 40.36 N 84.58 W
Geneva, Nebr., U.S. 198 40.32 N 97.36 W
Geneva, N.Y., U.S. 210 42.52 N 77.00 W
Geneva, Ohio, U.S. 214 41.48 N 80.57 W
Geneva, Pa., U.S. 214 41.35 N 80.14 W
Geneva, Wash., U.S. 224 48.45 N 122.24 W
Geneva, Lake (Lac Léman) (Lac de Gèneve) ⊜, Eur. 58 46.25 N 6.30 E
Geneva, Lake ⊜, Wis., U.S. 216 42.34 N 88.30 W
Geneva-on-the-lake 214 41.52 N 80.57 W
Genève (Geneva) 58 46.12 N 6.09 E
Genève □[3] 58 46.15 N 6.10 E
Genève, Lac de → Geneva, Lake ⊜ 58 46.25 N 6.30 E
Genève-Cointrin, Aéroport ⊠ 58 46.14 N 6.06 E
Genevia 194 34.43 N 92.13 W
Genevois ◆[1] 58 46.03 N 6.14 E
Genévriers, Île des I 186 51.15 N 58.26 W
Genf → Genève 58 46.12 N 6.09 E
Genga 66 43.26 N 12.56 E
Gengenbach 58 48.24 N 8.01 E
Genghis Khan, Wall of ⊥ 88 49.00 N 116.00 E
Gengji 100 33.47 N 112.47 E
Gengkou 100 29.12 N 113.19 E
Gengma 102 23.34 N 99.06 E
Gengputou 106 31.12 N 119.55 E
Gengzhuangzi 104 40.59 N 122.42 E
Genhe ≃ 89 50.16 N 119.22 E
Geničesk 78 46.11 N 34.48 E
Génicourt 261 49.05 N 2.04 E
Génicourt-sur-Meuse 56 49.02 N 5.26 E
Genil ≃ 34 37.42 N 5.19 W
Génissiat 58 46.03 N 5.47 E
Genk 56 50.58 N 5.30 E
Genkai 96 33.51 N 130.30 E
Genkai-kokutei-kōen ♣ 96 33.54 N 130.31 E
Genkai-nada ⊤[2] 92 34.00 N 130.00 E
Genkanyj, Chrebet ⛰ 180 66.15 N 172.20 W
Genlis 58 47.14 N 5.13 E
Gennach ≃ 58 48.10 N 10.43 E
Gennargentu, Monti del ⛰ 71 40.01 N 9.19 E
Gennebreck 263 51.19 N 7.12 E
Gennep 52 51.42 N 5.58 E
Genner 41 55.07 N 9.26 E
Gennes 32 47.20 N 0.14 W
Gennevilliers 261 48.56 N 2.18 E
Genoa, Austl. 166 37.29 S 149.35 E
Genoa → Genova, It. 62 44.25 N 8.57 E
Genoa, Ill., U.S. 216 42.06 N 88.42 W
Genoa, Nebr., U.S. 198 41.27 N 97.44 W
Genoa, Nev., U.S. 226 39.00 N 119.51 W
Genoa, N.Y., U.S. 210 42.40 N 76.32 W
Genoa, Ohio, U.S. 214 41.31 N 83.22 W
Genoa, Wis., U.S. 190 43.35 N 91.13 W
Genoa, Arroyo ≃ 254 44.58 S 70.06 W
Genoa City 216 42.30 N 88.20 W
Genoa Peak ∧ 226 39.03 N 119.53 W
Genola 62 44.35 N 7.39 E
Génolhac 62 44.21 N 3.57 E
Genova (Genoa) 62 44.25 N 8.57 E
Genova □[4] 62 44.30 N 9.04 E
Genova, Golfo di C 62 44.10 N 8.55 E
Genova, Val V 64 46.11 N 10.40 E
Genovesa, Isla I 246a 0.20 N 89.58 W
Genrijetty, Ostrov I 74 77.06 N 156.30 E
Gensan → Wŏnsan 98 39.09 N 127.25 E
Gens de Terre ≃ 190 46.53 N 76.00 W
Genshagen 264a 52.19 N 13.19 E
Genshagener Heide ◆[3] 264a 52.20 N 13.18 E
Genshiryoku-kenkyūsho ♉[3] 94 36.27 N 140.36 E
Gensingen 56 49.53 N 7.55 E
Gensungen 56 51.08 N 9.26 E
Gent (Gand) 50 51.03 N 3.43 E
Gentbrugge 50 51.03 N 3.45 E
Gent-Brugge, Kanaal ≋ 50 51.03 N 3.43 E
Genteng 115a 8.22 S 114.09 E
Genteng, Gili I 115a 7.12 S 113.54 E
Genteng, Tanjung ≻ 115a 7.23 S 106.24 E
Genthin 54 52.24 N 12.09 E
Gentilly 261 48.49 N 2.21 E
Gentilly ≃ 206 46.24 N 72.21 W
Genting 114 3.42 N 98.10 E
Gentio do Ouro 250 11.25 S 42.30 W
Gentioux 32 45.47 N 1.59 E
Gent naar Terneuzen, Kanaal van ≋ 50 51.04 N 3.44 E
Gentofte 41 55.45 N 12.33 E
Gentry, Lake ⊜ 220 28.08 N 81.15 W
Genua → Genova 62 44.25 N 8.57 E
Genuang 114 2.29 N 102.53 E
Genval 50 50.43 N 4.29 E
Genyem 164 2.46 S 140.12 E
Genzano di Lucania 68 40.51 N 16.02 E
Genzano di Roma 66 41.42 N 12.41 E
Geographe Bay C 162 33.35 S 115.15 E
Geographe Channel ⊔ 162 24.40 S 113.20 E
Geokčaj 84 40.39 N 47.44 E
Geokčaj ≃ 84 40.39 N 47.45 E
Geok-Tepe 128 38.09 N 57.58 E
Geonkhāli 126 22.12 N 88.03 E
George, S. Afr. 158 33.58 S 22.24 E
George, Iowa, U.S. 198 43.21 N 96.00 W
George, Tex., U.S. 222 30.59 N 96.07 W
George ≃, Austl. 162 20.50 S 117.28 E
George ≃, Qué., Can. 176 58.49 N 66.10 W
George, Cape ≻ 186 45.53 N 61.53 W
George, Lake ⊜, Austl. 162 22.37 S 123.38 E
George, Lake ⊜, Austl. 166 35.05 S 149.25 E
George, Lake ⊜, N.A. 190 46.28 N 84.10 W
George, Lake ⊜, Ug. 154 0.02 N 30.12 E
George, Lake ⊜, U.S. 216 41.45 N 85.00 W
George, Lake ⊜, Fla., U.S. 192 29.17 N 81.36 W
George, Lake ⊜, Ind., U.S. 216 41.40 N 87.30 W
George, Lake ⊜, N.Y., U.S. 188 43.35 N 73.35 W
George, Lake ⊜[1] 222 29.29 N 95.38 W
George Air Force Base ■ 228 34.35 N 117.22 W
George B. Stevenson Dam ◆[6] 214 41.25 N 78.01 W
George Gill Range ⛰ 162 24.15 S 131.36 E
George H. Crosby-Manitou State Park ♣ 190 47.29 N 91.10 W
George Island I 254 52.19 S 59.45 W
George Mason University ♉[2] 284c 38.50 N 77.17 W
Georgensgmünd 56 49.11 N 11.00 E
Georgenthal 54 50.49 N 10.40 E
Georges ≃ 170 33.57 S 150.58 E
Georges Bank ✢[4] 16 41.00 N 67.00 W
Georges Hall 274a 33.55 S 150.59 E
Georges Island I 283 42.19 N 70.56 W
George Sound ⊔ 172 44.50 S 167.23 E
Georges River Bridge ◆[5] 274a 34.00 S 151.07 E
Georges Run 214 40.21 N 80.37 W
Georges Run ≃ 279b 40.23 N 80.06 W
Georgetown, Austl. 166 18.18 S 143.33 E
George Town, Austl. 166 41.06 S 146.50 E
Georgetown, Ont., Can. 212 43.39 N 79.55 W
Georgetown, P.E.I., Can. 186 46.11 N 62.32 W
Georgetown, Cay. Is. 238 19.18 N 81.23 W
Georgetown, Gam. 150 13.30 N 14.47 W
Georgetown, Guy. 246 6.48 N 58.10 W
George Town (Pinang), Malay. 114 5.25 N 100.20 E
Georgetown, St. Vin. 241h 13.16 N 61.08 W
Georgetown, Calif., U.S. 226 38.54 N 120.50 W
Georgetown, Conn., U.S. 207 41.16 N 73.26 W
Georgetown, Del., U.S. 208 38.42 N 75.23 W
Georgetown, Fla., U.S. 192 29.23 N 81.38 W
Georgetown, Ga., U.S. 192 31.53 N 85.06 W
Georgetown, Idaho, U.S. 202 42.29 N 111.22 W
Georgetown, Ill., U.S. 194 39.59 N 87.38 W
Georgetown, Ind., U.S. 218 38.18 N 85.58 W
Georgetown, Ky., U.S. 218 38.13 N 84.33 W
Georgetown, Mass., U.S. 207 42.43 N 71.00 W
Georgetown, Miss., U.S. 194 31.52 N 90.10 W
Georgetown, N.J., U.S. 285 40.05 N 74.39 W
Georgetown, N.Y., U.S. 210 42.46 N 75.44 W
Georgetown, Ohio, U.S. 218 38.52 N 83.54 W
Georgetown, Pa., U.S. 214 40.39 N 80.30 W
Georgetown, S.C., U.S. 192 33.23 N 79.17 W
Georgetown, Tex., U.S. 222 30.38 N 97.41 W
Georgetown ◆[8] 284c 38.54 N 77.03 W
Georgetown Lake ⊜ 202 46.11 N 113.17 W
Georgetown Rowley State Forest ♣ 283 42.42 N 70.58 W
Georgetown University ♉[2] 284c 38.54 N 77.04 W
George V Coast •[2] 9 68.30 S 147.30 E
George VI Sound ⊔ 9 71.00 S 68.00 W
George Washington Birthplace National Monument ♣ 208 38.11 N 76.56 W
George Washington Bridge ◆[5] 276 40.51 N 73.57 W
George Washington Carver National Monument ♣ 194 37.00 N 94.19 W
George Washington University ♉[2] 284c 38.54 N 77.03 W
George West 196 28.20 N 98.07 W
Georgia □[3] 178
192 32.50 N 83.15 W
Georgia, Strait of ⊔ 182 49.20 N 124.00 W
Georgia del Sur, Isla de → South Georgia I 244 54.15 S 36.45 W
Georgia Heights 278 41.32 N 87.20 W
Georgiana 194 31.33 N 86.44 W
Georgian Bay C 190 45.15 N 80.50 W
Georgian Bay Islands National Park ♣ 190 44.54 N 79.52 W
Georgian Soviet Socialist Republic → Gruzinskaja Sovetskaja Socialističeskaja Respublika □[3] 84 42.00 N 44.00 E
Géorgie du Sud → South Georgia I 244 54.15 S 36.45 W
Georgijevka, S.S.S.R. 80 53.18 N 51.01 E
Georgijevka, S.S.S.R. 83 48.26 N 39.17 E
Georgijevka, S.S.S.R. 85 43.03 N 74.43 E
Georgijevka, S.S.S.R. 85 42.11 N 70.00 E
Georgijevka, S.S.S.R. 86 49.19 N 81.35 E
Georgijevsk 84 44.09 N 43.28 E
Georgina ≃ 166 23.30 S 139.47 E
Georgina Island I 212 44.23 N 79.17 W
Georgina Islands Indian Reserve ◆[4] 212 44.22 N 79.19 W
Georgiu-Dež (Liski) 78 50.59 N 39.30 E
Georgsmarienhütte 52 52.12 N 8.02 E
Gera 54 50.52 N 12.04 E
Gera □[5] 54 50.45 N 11.45 E
Gera ≃ 54 51.08 N 10.56 E
Geraardsbergen 50 50.46 N 3.52 E
Geraberg 54 50.43 N 10.50 E
Gerabronn 56 49.15 N 9.55 E
Gerace 68 38.16 N 16.13 E
Geraci Siculo 70 37.51 N 14.09 E
Gerais, Chapada dos ⛰[1] 255 17.40 S 45.20 W
Gerais, Serra dos ∧ 256 21.54 S 44.06 W
Geral, Serra •[4], Bra. 250 11.15 S 46.30 W
Geral, Serra •[4], Bra. 252 26.30 S 50.30 W
Gerald 219 38.24 N 91.20 W
Geral de Goiás, Serra •[4] 255 13.00 S 46.15 W
Geraldine, N.Z. 172 44.05 S 171.14 E
Geraldine, Mont., U.S. 202 47.36 N 110.16 W
Geraldton, Austl. 162 28.46 S 114.36 E
Geraldton, Ont., Can. 176 49.44 N 86.57 W
Gerale 144 6.20 N 42.32 E
Gerard, Lake ⊜ 276 41.06 N 74.33 W
Gerard, Mount ∧ 162 27.13 S 122.41 E
Gérardmer 58 48.04 N 6.53 E
Gerasa ⊥ 132 32.17 N 35.53 E
Gerasdorf 264b 48.18 N 16.28 E
Gerasimovka 86 58.37 N 71.53 E
Gerber 204 40.03 N 122.09 W
Gerber Reservoir ⊜[1] 202 42.12 N 121.06 W
Gerbéviller 58 48.30 N 6.31 E
Gerblingerode 52 51.29 N 10.15 E
Gerbstedt 54 51.38 N 11.37 E
Gerca 78 48.09 N 26.16 E
Gerchsheim 56 49.42 N 9.47 E
Gercüş 130 37.34 N 41.23 E
Gerdau 158 26.28 S 26.06 E
Gerdine, Mount ∧ 180 61.35 N 152.26 W
Gerdview 273d 26.10 S 28.11 E
Gère ≃ 62 45.32 N 4.54 E
Gerede 130 40.48 N 32.12 E
Gerenzano 266b 45.38 N 9.00 E
Gereshk 120 31.48 N 64.34 E
Geretsried 64 47.51 N 11.28 E
Gérgal 34 37.07 N 2.33 W
Gergebil' 84 42.31 N 47.05 E
Gerger 130 38.02 N 39.02 E
Geria Nij 126 23.56 N 86.55 E
Gerik 114 5.25 N 101.08 E
Gering 198 41.50 N 103.40 W
Geringswalde 54 51.04 N 12.54 E
Geriş 130 36.58 N 31.44 E
Gerlachovský štít ∧ 30 49.12 N 20.08 E
Gerlafingen 58 47.10 N 7.34 E
Gerli ◆[8] 288 34.41 S 58.23 W
Gerlingen 56 48.48 N 9.03 E
Gerlogubi 144 6.51 N 45.05 E
Gerlos 64 47.14 N 12.02 E
Gerlos Pass)(64 47.14 N 12.08 E
Gerlova Huť 60 49.10 N 13.17 E
Germa (Jarmah) ⊥ 146 26.33 N 13.04 E
Germagnano 62 45.15 N 7.28 E
Germaine Bank ✢[4] 16 5.05 N 107.35 W
Germán 232 25.10 N 97.54 W
German Democratic Republic □[1] 22
30 52.00 N 12.30 E
Germania 214 41.39 N 77.40 W
Germano 214 40.25 N 80.57 W
Germanoviči 76 55.25 N 27.44 E
Germansen, Mount ∧ 182 55.37 N 124.50 W
Germansen Lake ⊜ 182 55.41 N 124.53 W
Germansen Landing 182 55.47 N 124.43 W
Germansville 208 40.42 N 75.42 W
Germantown, Ill., U.S. 219 38.33 N 89.32 W
Germantown, Ky., U.S. 218 38.39 N 83.58 W
Germantown, N.Y., U.S. 210 42.08 N 73.54 W
Germantown, Ohio, U.S. 218 39.38 N 84.22 W
Germantown, Tenn., U.S. 194 35.05 N 89.49 W
Germantown, Wis., U.S. 216 43.14 N 88.06 W
Germantown ◆[8] 285 40.03 N 75.11 W
Germantown Reservoir ⊜[1] 218 39.40 N 84.30 W
Germany, Federal Republic of □[1] 22
30 51.00 N 9.00 E
Germany Flats ≚ 276 41.05 N 74.39 W
Germay 58 48.25 N 5.21 E
Germencik 130 37.51 N 27.37 E
Germendorf 54 52.45 N 13.10 E
Germersheim 56 49.13 N 8.22 E
Germfask 190 46.15 N 85.55 W
Germī 128 39.01 N 48.03 E
Germili 130 39.06 N 38.49 E
Germiston 158
273d 26.15 S 28.05 E
Germiter 130 38.28 N 37.36 E
Gernrode 54 51.43 N 11.08 E
Gernsbach 56 48.46 N 8.19 E
Gernsheim 56 49.44 N 8.29 E
Gero 94 35.48 N 137.14 E
Geroda 56 50.17 N 9.53 E
Gerola Alta 58 46.03 N 9.32 E
Geroldsgrün 54 50.20 N 11.35 E
Geroldstein 56 50.06 N 7.56 E
Gerolfing 60 48.45 N 11.21 E
Gerolsbach 60 48.30 N 11.22 E
Gerolstein 56 50.13 N 6.40 E
Gerolzhofen 56 49.54 N 10.21 E
Gerona, Esp. 34 41.59 N 2.49 E
Gerona, Pil. 116 15.36 N 120.36 E
Gerpinnes 50 50.20 N 4.31 E
Gerrards Cross 260 51.35 N 0.34 W
Gerrei ◆[1] 71 39.28 N 9.17 E
Gerresheim ◆[8] 263 51.14 N 6.52 E
Gerringong 170 34.45 S 150.50 E
Gerry 214 42.12 N 79.15 W
Gers □[5] 32 43.40 N 0.30 E
Gers ≃ 32 44.09 N 0.39 E
Gersau 58 47.00 N 8.32 E
Gersdorf 54 50.45 N 12.42 E
Gersfeld 56 50.27 N 9.55 E
Gershøj 41 55.43 N 11.59 E
Gersprenz ≃ 56 49.59 N 9.04 E
Gerstetten 56 48.37 N 10.01 E
Gersthofen 58 48.25 N 10.53 E
Gerstungen 56 50.58 N 10.04 E
Gertak Sanggul, Tanjong ≻ 114 5.15 N 100.11 E
Gerthe ◆[8] 263 51.31 N 7.17 E
Gerufa 156 19.17 S 26.02 E
Gervais 224 45.07 N 122.54 W
Gerwisch 54 52.10 N 11.44 E
Gerza 142 29.26 N 31.11 E
Gerze 130 41.48 N 35.12 E
Gerzen 60 48.31 N 12.25 E
Gerzensee 58 46.51 N 7.33 E
Gescher 52 51.57 N 6.59 E
Geschriebenstein (Írottkő) ∧ 61 47.21 N 16.26 E
Geschwenda 54 50.44 N 10.49 E
Gesees 60 49.54 N 11.32 E
Geseke 52 51.38 N 8.31 E
Geser 164 3.53 S 130.54 E
Gesher HaZiw 132 33.02 N 35.06 E
Gesi 115a 7.20 S 111.01 E
Gesoa 164 8.25 S 143.35 E
Gespunsart 56 49.49 N 4.50 E
Gessertshausen 58 48.20 N 10.44 E
Gesso ≃ 62 44.24 N 7.33 E
Gessopalena 66 42.03 N 14.16 E
Gesten 41 55.31 N 9.12 E
Gesualdo 68 41.00 N 15.04 E
Geta 26 60.23 N 19.50 E
Getafe 34 40.18 N 3.43 W
Getafe, Aeropuerto ⊠ 266a 40.18 N 3.43 W
Gethaoli 272c 19.08 N 73.01 E
Gethsémani 186 50.13 N 60.40 W
Geti 154 1.13 N 30.12 E
Getinge 26 56.49 N 12.44 E
Gettorf 41 54.24 N 9.58 E
Gettysburg, Ohio, U.S. 218 40.07 N 84.30 W
Gettysburg, Pa., U.S. 208 39.50 N 77.14 W
Gettysburg, S. Dak., U.S. 198 45.01 N 99.57 W
Gettysburg National Military Park ♣ 208 39.49 N 77.15 W
Getulândia 256 22.40 S 44.06 W
Getulina 255 21.49 S 49.55 W
Getulio 116 10.45 N 122.40 E
Getúlio Vargas 252 27.50 S 52.16 W
Getz Ice Shelf ⊓ 9 75.00 S 129.00 W
Getzville 210 43.01 N 78.46 W
Geudubang 114 4.54 N 97.23 E
Geumpang 114 4.48 N 96.09 E
Geureudong, Gunung ∧ 114 4.48 N 96.48 E
Gevān 128 26.03 N 57.17 E
Gevaş 128 38.16 N 43.07 E
Gevelsberg 56 51.19 N 7.20 E
Gevgelija 38 41.08 N 22.30 E
Gévora ≃ 34 38.53 N 6.57 W
Gevrey-Chambertin 58 47.14 N 4.57 E
Gewani 144 10.16 N 40.44 E
Geweke ◆[8] 263 51.22 N 7.25 E
Gex 58 46.20 N 6.04 E
Geyer 54 50.37 N 12.55 E
Geyer Ditch ≋ 216 41.36 N 86.25 W
Geyikli 130 39.48 N 26.12 E
Geysdorp 158 26.32 S 25.18 E
Geyser 202 47.16 N 110.30 W
Geyser, Banc du ✢[2] 138 12.25 S 46.25 E
Geyserville 204 38.42 N 122.54 W
Geyuan 100 28.31 N 117.44 E
Geyve 130 40.30 N 30.18 E
Gézenti 146 21.41 N 18.18 E
Gezer 132 31.52 N 34.55 E
Gez Gölü ⊜ 130 38.35 N 33.06 E
Gezihu ⊜ 120 38.10 N 90.42 E
Ghabāghib 132 33.10 N 36.13 E
Ghābat al-'Arab 140 9.02 N 29.29 E
Ghadaf, Wādī al- V 132 31.46 N 36.50 E
Ghafe 272c 19.05 N 73.07 E
Ghaggar ≃ 123 29.30 N 74.53 E
Ghaghar Reservoir ⊜[1] 124 24.38 N 83.11 E
Ghāghra ≃ 124 25.47 N 84.37 E
Ghāgra 124 23.17 N 84.33 E
Ghairatganj 124 23.24 N 78.13 E
Ghakhar 123 32.18 N 74.09 E
Ghallah, Wādī al- V 140 10.25 N 27.32 E
Ghammāzah al-Kubrā 142 29.43 N 31.18 E
Ghamrīn 142 30.30 N 30.55 E
Ghana □[1] 134
150 8.00 N 2.00 W
Ghansoli 272c 19.08 N 72.59 E
Ghanzi 156 21.38 S 21.45 E
Ghanzi □[5] 156 22.00 S 23.00 E
Ghārāpuri 272c 18.54 N 72.56 E
Gharaunda 124 29.33 N 76.58 E
Gharbah, Wādī V 142 29.40 N 31.58 E
Gharbi, Île I 148 34.39 N 11.03 E
Ghardaïa 148 32.31 N 3.37 E
Ghardimaou 36 36.26 N 8.27 E
Gharghoda 124 22.10 N 83.21 E
Gharībwāl 123 32.41 N 73.10 E
Gharīfah 132 33.38 N 35.33 E
Gharig 140 10.47 N 27.33 E
Ghārīyat al-Gharbīyah 132 32.41 N 36.13 E
Ghārīyat ash-Sharqīyah 132 32.40 N 36.16 E
Gharo 120 24.44 N 67.35 E
Gharrāf, Shaṭṭ al- ≃ 128 32.30 N 45.48 E
Gharrah, Jabal ∧[2] 142 30.12 N 32.15 E
Gharroli ◆[8] 272a 28.37 N 77.20 E
Gharw, Jazīrat I 142 31.21 N 30.06 E
Gharyān 146 32.10 N 13.01 E
Gharyān □[4] 146 30.50 N 12.00 E
Ghaṣm 132 32.33 N 36.22 E
Ghāt 146 24.58 N 10.11 E
Ghātākhān 126 23.02 N 90.26 E
Ghātāl 126 22.40 N 87.43 E
Ghatampur 272b 22.54 N 88.10 E
Ghātkopar ◆[8] 272c 19.05 N 72.54 E
Ghātprabha ≃ 122 16.20 N 75.48 E
Ghātsīla 126 22.36 N 86.29 E
Ghats Occidentales → Western Ghāts ⛰ 122 14.00 N 75.00 E
Ghats Orientales → Eastern Ghāts ⛰ 122 14.00 N 78.50 E
GHawdex I 36 36.03 N 14.15 E
Ghawr ash-Sharqīyah, Qanāt al- ≋ 132 32.41 N 35.38 E
Ghaylah ∧[1] 132 33.11 N 37.05 E
Ghayl Bā Wazīr 144 14.48 N 49.21 E
Ghayth, Wādī V 132 30.59 N 36.00 E
Ghazāl, Baḥr al- □[4] 140 8.00 N 28.00 E
Ghazāl, Baḥr al- ≃ 140 9.31 N 30.25 E
Ghazal, Bahr el V 146 13.01 N 15.28 E
Ghazālat al-Khīs 142 30.34 N 31.34 E
Ghazaouet 148 35.06 N 1.51 W
Ghāziābād 123 28.40 N 77.26 E
Ghāzīpur, Bhārat 124 25.35 N 83.34 E
Ghazipur, Bhārat 272b 22.36 N 88.34 E
Ghāzīpur □[5] 124 25.40 N 83.20 E
Ghāzipur ◆[8] 272a 28.38 N 77.19 E
Ghazīr 130 34.01 N 35.40 E
Ghazlūna 120 31.33 N 68.48 E
Ghaznī 120 33.33 N 68.26 E
Ghaznī □[4] 120 33.00 N 68.00 E
Ghaznī ≃ 120 32.35 N 67.58 E
Ghazni Khel 123 32.33 N 70.44 E
Ghazzah (Gaza), Gaza 132 31.30 N 34.28 E
Ghazzah, Lubnān 132 33.40 N 35.49 E
Gheā ≃ 272b 22.52 N 88.19 E
Ghedi 64 45.24 N 10.16 E
Ghemme 62 45.37 N 8.25 E
Ghennes Heights 279b 40.09 N 79.56 W
Ghent → Gent, Bel. 50 51.03 N 3.43 E
Ghent, Ky., U.S. 218 38.44 N 85.04 W
Ghent, N.Y., U.S. 210 42.20 N 73.37 W
Ghent, Ohio, U.S. 214 41.09 N 81.38 W
Gheora ◆[8] 272a 28.42 N 77.01 E
Gheorghe Gheorghiu-Dej 38 46.14 N 26.44 E
Gheorgheni 38 46.43 N 25.36 E
Gherla 38 47.02 N 23.55 E
Ghesar 272c 19.09 N 73.05 E
Ghigo 62 44.53 N 7.03 E
Ghilarza 71 40.07 N 8.50 E
Ghīn, Tall ∧ 132 32.39 N 36.43 E
Ghior 126 23.54 N 89.53 E
Ghislenghien 50 50.39 N 3.52 E
Ghisonàccia 36 42.00 N 9.25 E
Ghizar ≃ 123 36.15 N 73.25 E
Ghlin 50 50.28 N 3.53 E
Ghlò, Beinn a ∧ 46 56.50 N 3.43 W
Gholson 222 31.43 N 97.12 W
Ghonda ◆[8] 272a 28.41 N 77.16 E
Ghondi ◆[8] 272a 28.42 N 77.16 E
Ghorāsahan 124 26.50 N 85.08 E
Ghorāsāl 126 23.56 N 90.38 E
Ghoshpur, Bhārat 272b 22.23 N 88.29 E
Ghoshpur, Bngl. 126 23.27 N 89.39 E
Ghotki 120 28.01 N 69.19 E
Ghowr □[4] 128 34.00 N 65.00 E
Ghubaysh 140 12.09 N 27.21 E
Ghubbet Raguda C 144 10.55 N 46.35 E
Ghudāf, Wādī al- V 128 32.56 N 43.30 E
Ghudāmis 146 30.08 N 9.30 E
Ghunthur 130 34.23 N 37.09 E
Ghurāb, Jabal ∧[2] 142 28.58 N 31.16 E
Ghurayrah 144 18.37 N 42.41 E
Ghūrīān 128 34.21 N 61.30 E
Ghurrān, Farsh al- ⛰[1] 142 29.38 N 31.38 E
Ghushuri 272b 22.37 N 88.22 E
Ghuwaybah, Wādī V 142 29.36 N 32.20 E
Ghuwayr, 'Ayn al- ⊤[4] 132 31.37 N 35.25 E
Ghuzzayil, Sabkhat ⊜ 146 29.50 N 19.35 E
Gia-dinh 110 10.48 N 106.42 E
Giaginskaja 78 44.53 N 40.05 E
Giang ≃ 110 17.40 N 106.30 E
Giannutri, Isola di I 66 42.15 N 11.06 E
Giano, Monte ∧ 66 42.25 N 13.06 E
Giano dell'Umbria 66 42.50 N 12.35 E
Giant City State Park ♣ 194 37.39 N 89.12 W
Giant Mountain ∧ 188 44.10 N 73.44 W
Giant's Castle ∧ 158 29.21 S 29.27 E
Giants Castle Game Reserve ◆[4] 158 29.16 S 29.30 E
Giant's Causeway ♣ 44 55.14 N 6.30 W
Giants Neck 207 41.18 N 72.11 W
Giants Tomb Island I 212 44.55 N 80.00 W
Gianyar 115b 8.32 S 115.20 E
Gia-rai 110 9.14 N 105.28 E
Giardinello 70 38.05 N 13.09 E
Giardinetto 68 41.19 N 15.24 E
Giardini 70 37.50 N 15.17 E
Giarratana 70 37.03 N 14.48 E
Giarre 70 37.43 N 15.11 E
Giaveno 62 45.02 N 7.21 E
Giazza 64 45.39 N 11.07 E
Giba 71 39.04 N 8.38 E
Gibara 240p 21.07 N 76.08 W
Gibbon, Minn., U.S. 190 44.32 N 94.31 W
Gibbon, Nebr., U.S. 198 40.45 N 98.51 W
Gibbons 182 53.50 N 113.20 W
Gibbonsville 202 45.33 N 113.55 W
Gibb River 164 15.39 S 126.38 E
Gibbs, Mount ∧ 162 32.55 S 120.00 E
Gibbsboro 285 39.50 N 74.58 W
Gibbstown 208 39.50 N 75.17 W
Gibellina 70 37.47 N 12.58 E
Gibeon 156 25.09 S 17.43 E
Gibeon □[5] 156 25.00 S 19.00 E
Gibilmanna, Santuario di ♉[1] 70 37.59 N 14.02 E
Gibraleón 34 37.23 N 6.58 W
Gibraltar, Gib. 34 36.09 N 5.21 W
Gibraltar, Mich., U.S. 216 42.06 N 83.12 W
Gibraltar, Pa., U.S. 208 40.17 N 75.52 W
Gibraltar □[2] 22
34 36.11 N 5.22 W
Gibraltar, Strait of (Estrecho de Gibraltar) ⊔ 34 35.57 N 5.36 W
Gibraltar Point ≻, Ont., Can. 275b 43.36 N 79.23 W
Gibraltar Point ≻, Eng., U.K. 44 53.05 N 0.19 E
Gibsland 194 32.33 N 93.03 W
Gibson, Austl. 162 33.39 S 121.48 E
Gibson, Ga., U.S. 192 33.14 N 82.36 W
Gibson, N.Y., U.S. 210 42.08 N 76.59 W
Gibson, Pa., U.S. 210 41.44 N 75.38 W
Gibson ≃ 212 44.58 N 79.51 W
Gibsonburg 214 41.23 N 83.19 W
Gibson City 216 40.28 N 88.22 W
Gibson Desert ◆[2] 162 24.30 S 126.00 E
Gibson Hill ∧[2] 214 41.51 N 80.10 W
Gibsonia 214 40.38 N 79.59 W
Gibson Indian Reserve ◆[4] 212 45.01 N 79.44 W
Gibson Island I 208 39.05 N 76.26 W
Gibsons 182 49.24 N 123.30 W
Gibsonton 220 27.51 N 82.23 W
Gidajevo 24 59.57 N 52.22 E
Gidami 144 9.58 N 34.37 E
Gidari 146 9.17 N 16.40 E
Giddalūr 122 15.21 N 78.55 E
Giddarbāha 123 30.12 N 74.40 E
Giddings 222 30.11 N 96.56 W
Gide 144 9.40 N 35.16 E
Gideälven ≃ 26 63.20 N 19.08 E
Gidea Park ◆[8] 260 51.35 N 0.12 E
Gideåvallen 26 63.29 N 18.58 E
Gideon 194 36.27 N 89.55 W
Gidgee 162 27.16 S 119.22 E
Gidgi, Lake ⊜ 162 29.16 S 126.03 E
Gidhni 126 22.29 N 86.51 E
Gidole 144 5.38 N 37.30 E
Gidrotorf 80 56.28 N 43.33 E
Gidžaki, Gora ∧ 84 40.25 N 49.01 E
Giebelstadt 56 49.39 N 9.56 E
Gieboldehausen 52 51.36 N 10.13 E
Giedraičiai 76 55.05 N 25.15 E
Gielow 54 53.42 N 12.44 E
Gielsdorf 264a 52.36 N 13.52 E
Gien 50 47.42 N 2.38 E
Giengen 56 48.37 N 10.14 E
Giens 62 43.02 N 6.08 E
Gier ≃ 62 45.35 N 4.46 E
Gierath 263 51.07 N 6.33 E
Gierle 56 51.16 N 4.51 E
Giesebitz → Izbica 30 54.42 N 17.26 E
Gieselwerder 52 51.36 N 9.33 E
Giesenkirchen ◆[8] 263 51.09 N 6.30 E
Giesing ◆[8] 64 48.06 N 11.35 E
Giessen 56 50.35 N 8.40 E
Gieten 52 53.00 N 6.46 E
Giethoorn 52 52.43 N 6.05 E
Gièvres 50 47.16 N 1.40 E
Giez 62 45.45 N 6.15 E
Giffone 68 38.27 N 16.10 E
Giffoni Valle Piana 68 40.44 N 14.56 E
Gifford, Scot., U.K. 46 55.54 N 2.45 W
Gifford, Fla., U.S. 220 27.41 N 80.25 W
Gifford, Ill., U.S. 216 40.18 N 88.01 W
Gifford, Ind., U.S. 216 41.06 N 87.01 W
Gifford, Pa., U.S. 214 41.51 N 78.36 W
Gifford ≃ 176 70.21 N 83.05 W
Gifford Creek 162 24.05 S 116.11 E
Gifford Fjord C[2] 176 69.57 N 81.55 W
Gifford Pinchot State Park ♣ 208 40.04 N 76.53 W
Giffre ≃ 58 46.05 N 6.30 E
Gifhorn 52 52.29 N 10.33 E
Giflitz 56 51.09 N 9.07 E
Gif-sur-Yvette 261 48.42 N 2.08 E
Gifu 94 35.25 N 136.45 E
Gifu □[5] 94 35.45 N 137.00 E
Gigant 80 46.30 N 41.20 E
Giganta, Cerro ∧ 232 26.07 N 111.36 W
Giganta, Sierra de la ⛰ 232 25.30 N 111.15 W
Gigante 246 2.23 N 75.33 W
Gigante Islands II 116 11.36 N 123.20 E
Gigatangan Island I 116 11.34 N 124.16 E
Gigen 38 43.42 N 24.29 E
Gigena → Alcira 252 32.45 S 64.20 W
Giggleswick 44 54.04 N 2.17 W
Gigha, Sound of ⊔ 46 55.41 N 5.42 W
Gigha Isles II 46 55.41 N 5.46 W
Gig Harbor 224 47.20 N 122.35 W
Giglio, Isola del I 66 42.21 N 10.54 E
Giglio Castello 66 42.22 N 10.54 E
Gigliola 66 44.51 N 12.14 E
Giglio Porto 66 42.22 N 10.55 E
Gigmoto 116 13.47 N 124.23 E
Gignod 62 45.46 N 7.17 E
Gihu → Gifu 94 35.25 N 136.45 E
Gijón 34 43.32 N 5.40 W
Gijunabena Islands II 175e 7.31 S 158.42 E
Gikongoro 154 2.29 S 29.34 E
Gila ≃ 200 32.43 N 114.33 W
Gila, Middle Fork ≃ 200 33.14 N 108.14 W
Gila Bend 200 32.57 N 112.43 W
Gila Bend Mountains ⛰ 200 33.10 N 113.10 W
Gila Cliff Dwellings National Monument ♣ 200 33.02 N 108.16 W
Gila Mountains ⛰ 200 33.05 N 109.50 W
Gīlān □[4] 128 37.00 N 49.00 E
Gīlān-e Gharb 128 34.08 N 45.55 E
Gila River Indian Reservation ◆[4] 200 33.12 N 112.00 W
Gilātala 126 22.36 N 89.41 E
Gilbert, La., U.S. 194 32.03 N 91.39 W
Gilbert, Minn., U.S. 190 47.29 N 92.28 W
Gilbert ≃, Austl. 166 16.35 S 141.15 E
Gilbert ≃, Austl. 168b 34.22 S 138.40 E
Gilbert, Mount ∧ 182 50.51 N 124.20 W
Gilbert Airport ⊠ 279a 41.22 N 81.58 W
Gilbert Island I 219 39.35 N 91.11 W
Gilbert Islands II 14 0.30 S 174.00 E
Gilbert Islands → Kiribati □[1] 14 0.00 175.00 E
Gilbert Lake ⊜ 281 42.34 N 83.17 W
Gilbert Lake State Park ♣ 210 42.36 N 75.08 W
Gilberton 210 40.48 N 76.13 W
Gilbertown 194 31.53 N 88.19 W
Gilbert Peak ∧ 224 46.30 N 121.25 W
Gilbert Plains 184 51.09 N 100.29 W
Gilbert River 166 18.09 S 142.52 E
Gilberts 216 42.06 N 88.23 W
Gilbert Seamount ✢[3] 16 52.50 N 150.05 W
Gilbertsville, N.Y., U.S. 210 42.28 N 75.20 W
Gilbertsville, Pa., U.S. 208 40.19 N 75.37 W
Gilbertville 207 42.19 N 72.12 W
Gilbjerg Hoved ≻ 41 56.08 N 12.17 E
Gilboa 216 41.01 N 83.55 W
Gilboa', Hare ⛰[2] 132 32.30 N 35.23 E
Gilbués 250 9.50 S 45.21 W
Gilching 60 48.07 N 11.17 E
Gildehaus 52 52.18 N 7.06 E
Gildford 202 48.34 N 110.18 W
Gilead 216 41.48 N 85.09 W
Giles, Arroyo de ≃ 258 34.20 S 59.23 W
Giles Creek ≃ 162 17.25 S 130.50 E
Giles Point ≻ 168b 35.03 S 137.45 E
Gilette 62 43.51 N 7.10 E
Gilford 48 54.23 N 6.22 W
Gilford Island I 182 50.45 N 126.25 W
Gilford Park 208 39.58 N 74.08 W
Gilgai 162 31.15 S 119.56 E
Gilgandra 166 31.42 S 148.39 E
Gilgil 154 0.30 S 36.19 E
Gil Gil Creek ≃ 166 29.10 S 148.51 E
Gilgit 123 35.55 N 74.18 E
Gilgit ≃ 123 35.44 N 74.38 E
Gilgit Wazārat □[8] 123 35.10 N 74.55 E
Gilgo Island I 276 40.38 N 73.25 W
Gilgo State Park ♣ 276 40.38 N 73.22 W
Gilima 154 3.55 N 28.22 E
Gilimanuk 115a 8.10 S 114.26 E
Gil Island I 182 53.13 N 129.15 W
Gill, Lough ⊜ 48 54.16 N 8.24 W
Gillam 184 56.21 N 94.43 W
Gilleland Creek ≃ 222 30.13 N 97.32 W
Gilleleje 41 56.07 N 12.19 E
Gillen, Lake ⊜ 162 26.11 S 124.38 E
Gilles, Lake ⊜ 166 32.50 S 136.45 E
Gillespie 219 39.07 N 89.49 W
Gillespie Point ≻ 172 43.24 S 169.50 E
Gillett, Ark., U.S. 194 34.07 N 91.22 W
Gillett, Pa., U.S. 210 41.57 N 76.48 W
Gillett, Wis., U.S. 190 44.54 N 88.18 W
Gillette, N.J., U.S. 276 40.41 N 74.28 W
Gillette, Wyo., U.S. 198 44.18 N 105.30 W
Gillette Castle State Park ♣ 207 41.26 N 72.25 W
Gillian, Lake ⊜ 176 69.32 N 75.23 W
Gillingham, Eng., U.K. 42 51.02 N 2.17 W
Gillingham, Eng., U.K. 260 51.24 N 0.33 E
Gillingham □[8] 260 51.22 N 0.35 E
Gilman, Conn., U.S. 207 41.34 N 72.16 W
Gilman, Ill., U.S. 216 40.46 N 87.59 W
Gilman, Iowa, U.S. 190 41.53 N 92.47 W
Gilman, Wis., U.S. 190 45.10 N 90.48 W
Gilman Hot Springs 228 33.50 N 116.59 W
Gilmer, Ill., U.S. 278 42.14 N 88.02 W
Gilmer, Tex., U.S. 222 32.44 N 94.57 W
Gilmer Park 216 41.36 N 86.15 W
Gilmore 171b 35.20 S 148.11 E
Gilmore City 198 42.44 N 94.27 W
Gilmore Creek ≃ 171b 35.18 S 148.13 E
Gilo ≃ 144 8.10 N 33.15 E
Gilroy 226 37.00 N 121.34 W
Gilserberg 56 50.57 N 9.04 E
Gilsizer Slough ≃ 226 38.58 N 121.44 W
Gilston Park ♣ 260 51.48 N 0.04 E
Giltner 198 40.47 N 98.09 W
Gil'uj ≃ 89 53.58 N 127.30 E
Giluwe, Mount ∧ 164 6.05 S 143.50 E
Gilwern 42 51.51 N 3.06 W
Gilze 52 51.33 N 4.57 E
Gimån ≃ 26 62.28 N 16.20 E
Gimbi 144 9.10 N 35.42 E
Gimborn 56 51.03 N 7.28 E
Gimcheon → Kimch'ŏn 98 36.07 N 128.05 E
Gimie, Mount ∧ 241f 13.52 N 61.01 W
Gimigliano 68 38.58 N 16.32 E
Gimlet 218 38.13 N 83.09 W
Gimli 184 50.38 N 96.59 W
Gimo 40 60.11 N 18.11 E
Gimoly 24 63.03 N 32.19 E
Gimone ≃ 32 44.00 N 1.06 E
Gimont 32 43.38 N 0.53 E
Gimpu 112 1.36 S 120.02 E
Ginaldag, Gora ∧ 84 40.20 N 45.57 E
Ginderich 263 51.39 N 6.32 E
Ginebra → Genève 58 46.12 N 6.09 E
Gineste, Col de la)(62 43.15 N 5.27 E
Gingell 216 42.43 N 83.17 W
Gingera, Mount ∧ 171b 35.35 S 148.47 E
Ginger Hill 279b 40.12 N 80.00 W
Ginger Island I 240m 18.24 N 64.28 W
Gingin, Austl. 162 31.21 S 115.42 E
Gin Gin, Austl. 166 25.00 S 151.58 E
Gingindlovu 158 29.02 S 31.30 E
Gingoog 116 8.50 N 125.07 E
Gingoog Bay C 116 8.59 N 125.05 E
Gingst 54 54.27 N 13.16 E
Ginir 144 7.07 N 40.46 E
Ginkakuji Temple ♉[1] 270 35.03 N 135.47 E

Symbols in the index entries represent the broad categories identified in the key at the right. Symbols with superior numbers (⛰[2]) identify subcategories (see complete key on page *I* · *30*).

Kartensymbole in dem Registerverzeichnis stellen die rechts in Schlüssel erklärten Kategorien dar. Symbole mit hochgestellten Ziffern (⛰[2]) bezeichnen Unterabteilungen einer Kategorie (vgl. vollständiger Schlüssel auf Seite *I* · *30*).

Los símbolos incluídos en el texto del índice representan las grandes categorias identificadas con la clave a la derecha. Los símbolos con numeros en su parte superior (⛰[2]) identifican las subcategorías (véase la clave completa en la página *I* · *30*).

Les symboles de l'index représentent les catégories indiquées dans la légende à droite. Les symboles suivis d'un indice (⛰[2]) représentent des sous-catégories (voir légende complète à la page *I* · *30*).

Os símbolos incluídos no texto do índice representam as grandes categorias identificadas com a chave à direita. Os símbolos com números em sua parte superior (⛰[2]) identificam as subcategorias (veja-se a chave completa à página *I* · *30*).

Symbol	English	Deutsch	Español	Français	Português
∧	Mountain	Berg	Montaña	Montagne	Montanha
⛰	Mountains	Berge	Montañas	Montagnes	Montanhas
)(	Pass	Pass	Paso	Col	Passo
V	Valley, Canyon	Tal, Cañon	Valle, Cañón	Vallée, Canyon	Vale, Canhão
≚	Plain	Ebene	Llano	Plaine	Planície
≻	Cape	Kap	Cabo	Cap	Cabo
I	Island	Insel	Isla	Île	Ilha
II	Islands	Inseln	Islas	Îles	Ilhas
•	Other Topographic Features	Andere Topographische Objekte	Otros Elementos Topográficos	Autres données topographiques	Outros Elementos Topográficos

ESPAÑOL: Nombre — Página — Lat. °′ — Long. °′ W=Oeste
FRANÇAIS: Nom — Page — Lat. °′ — Long. °′ W=Ouest
PORTUGUÊS: Nome — Página — Lat. °′ — Long. °′ W=Oeste

Nombre	Página	Lat.	Long.
Ginkgo State Park	202	46.59 N	120.01 W
Ginnosar	132	32.51 N	35.31 E
Ginosa	68	40.35 N	16.46 E
Ginostra	70	38.47 N	15.11 E
Ginowan	174m	26.17 N	127.46 E
Ginter	214	40.46 N	78.23 W
Ginza	268	35.40 N	139.47 E
Ginzo de Limia	34	42.03 N	7.43 W
Gioi	68	40.17 N	15.13 E
Gioia dei Marsi	66	41.57 N	13.42 E
Gioia del Colle	68	40.48 N	16.56 E
Gioia Tauro	68	38.26 N	15.54 E
Gioia Vecchio	66	41.54 N	13.44 E
Gioiosa Ionica	68	38.20 N	16.18 E
Gioiosa Marea	70	38.10 N	14.54 E
Gion	96	34.26 N	132.28 E
Giornico	58	46.24 N	8.52 E
Giovi, Passo dei	62	44.33 N	8.57 E
Giovinazzo	68	41.11 N	16.40 E
Giporlos	116	11.07 N	125.27 E
Gipping	42	52.04 N	1.10 E
Gipsy	214	40.48 N	78.53 W
Giraglia, Île de la	62	43.02 N	9.24 E
Giralia	162	22.41 S	114.21 E
Giraltovce	30	49.07 N	21.31 E
Girard, Ill., U.S.	219	39.27 N	89.47 W
Girard, Kans., U.S.	198	37.31 N	94.51 W
Girard, Mich., U.S.	216	42.02 N	85.00 W
Girard, Ohio, U.S.	214	41.10 N	80.42 W
Girard, Pa., U.S.	214	42.00 N	80.19 W
Girard, Tex., U.S.	196	33.22 N	100.40 W
Girardot	246	4.18 N	74.48 W
Girardville	208	40.47 N	76.17 W
Giraud, Pointe	240d	15.19 N	61.15 W
Giraul	152	15.04 S	12.08 E
Giraumont	56	49.10 N	5.55 E
Girbovu	38	44.44 N	23.21 E
Gird Gwalior	124	26.00 N	78.00 E
Girdletree	208	38.06 N	75.24 W
Girdwood	180	60.57 N	149.10 W
Giresun	130	40.55 N	38.24 E
Giresun	130	40.30 N	38.30 E
Girgarre	166	36.24 S	144.59 E
Girgaum	272c	18.57 N	72.48 E
Girgenti → Agrigento	70	37.27 N	13.30 E
Girgir, Cape	164	3.50 S	144.34 E
Gīr Hills	120	21.18 N	71.00 E
Giri	152	0.28 N	17.59 E
Giridih	126	24.11 N	86.18 E
Girifalco	68	38.49 N	16.25 E
Girilambone	166	31.15 S	146.54 E
Girimira	130	37.07 N	41.26 E
Girna	122	21.08 N	75.19 E
Giro, Nig.	150	11.06 N	4.46 E
Giro, Zaïre	154	3.08 N	29.15 E
Giromagny	58	47.45 N	6.50 E
Girón, Ec.	246	3.10 S	79.08 W
Giron, Fr.	58	46.14 N	5.46 E
Gironde	32	44.45 N	0.35 W
Gironde	32	45.20 N	0.45 W
Gironville-sous-les-Côtes	56	48.48 N	5.40 E
Girou	32	43.46 N	1.23 E
Girouxville	182	55.45 N	117.20 W
Girtys Run	279b	40.28 N	79.58 W
Giru	166	19.31 S	147.06 E
Giruá	252	28.02 S	54.21 W
Girvan	44	55.15 N	4.51 W
Girvan, Water of	44	55.15 N	4.51 W
Girvas	24	62.30 N	33.40 E
Girvas, Vodopad	24	62.27 N	33.40 E
Girwa	124	28.15 N	81.05 E
Gisborne, Austl.	169	37.29 S	144.35 E
Gisborne, N.Z.	172	38.40 S	178.01 E
Gisborne Lake	186	47.48 N	54.50 W
Giscome	182	54.04 N	122.22 W
Gisenyi	154	1.42 S	29.15 E
Gislaved	26	57.18 N	13.32 E
Gislev	41	55.13 N	10.37 E
Gislinge	41	55.44 N	11.33 E
Gislövs läge	41	55.21 N	13.14 E
Gisors	50	49.17 N	1.47 E
Gissar	85	38.33 N	68.35 E
Gissarskij Chrebet	85	39.00 N	68.40 E
Gisselfeld	41	55.18 N	11.59 E
Gissi	66	42.01 N	14.33 E
Gisslarbo	40	59.38 N	15.49 E
Gistel	50	51.10 N	2.57 E
Giswil	58	46.50 N	8.11 E
Gitambo	154	4.21 N	24.45 E
Gitarama	154	2.07 S	29.45 E
Gitega	154	3.26 S	29.56 E
Gittelde	52	51.48 N	10.10 E
Giuba, Isole	144	0.50 S	42.15 E
Giudicarie, Valli	64	45.58 N	10.45 E
Giugliano in Campania	68	40.56 N	14.12 E
Giuliana	70	37.40 N	13.14 E
Giulianova	66	42.45 N	13.57 E
Giulie, Alpi → Julian Alps	36	46.00 N	14.00 E
Giulietti, Lake	144	13.15 N	40.55 E
Giumbo → Jumbo	144	0.12 S	42.38 E
Giurgiu	38	43.53 N	25.57 E
Giussano	62	45.42 N	9.14 E
Giv'atayim	132	32.04 N	34.48 E
Giv'at Brenner	132	31.52 N	34.48 E
Give	41	55.51 N	9.15 E
Giverny	50	49.04 N	1.32 E
Givet	56	50.08 N	4.50 E
Givors	62	45.35 N	4.46 E
Givrine, Col de la	58	46.27 N	6.05 E
Givry	58	46.47 N	4.45 E
Givry-en-Argonne	56	48.57 N	4.53 E
Givry Island	175c	7.07 N	151.53 E
Giyon	144	8.30 N	38.00 E
Giza → Al-Jīzah	142	30.01 N	31.13 E
Gīzāb	120	33.23 N	66.16 E
Gižduvan	128	40.06 N	64.41 E
Gizen	140	10.49 N	34.48 E
Gizeux	50	47.24 N	0.12 E
Gižiga	74	62.03 N	160.30 E
Gižiginskaja Guba	74	61.30 N	158.00 E
Gizo	175e	8.06 S	156.51 E
Gizo Island	175e	8.04 S	156.48 E
Giżycko	30	54.03 N	21.47 E
Gizzeria	68	38.59 N	16.12 E
Gjedved	41	55.56 N	9.51 E
Gjern	41	56.14 N	9.45 E
Gjirokastër	38	40.05 N	20.10 E
Gjoa Haven	176	68.38 N	95.57 W
Gjøvik	26	60.48 N	10.42 E
Gjuesevo	38	42.14 N	22.28 E
Gjuhëzës, Kep i	38	40.25 N	19.18 E
Glace Bay	186	46.12 N	59.57 W
Glacier, B.C., Can.	182	51.16 N	117.31 W
Glacier, Wash., U.S.	224	48.53 N	121.57 W
Glacier Bay	180	58.40 N	136.00 W
Glacier Bay National Monument	180	58.45 N	136.30 W
Glacier Hills	276	40.51 N	74.28 W
Glacier National Park, B.C., Can.	182	51.15 N	117.35 W
Glacier National Park, Mont., U.S.	202	48.35 N	113.40 W
Glacier Peak	224	48.07 N	121.07 W
Glad'	76	59.07 N	32.06 E
Gl'ad'anskoje	86	54.54 N	65.06 E
Gladbach → Mönchengladbach	56	51.12 N	6.28 E
Gladbeck	52	51.34 N	6.59 E
Gladbrook	190	42.11 N	92.43 W
Gladden	279b	40.21 N	80.11 W
Gladden Heights	279b	40.22 N	80.15 W
Glade Creek	202	45.54 N	119.42 W
Gladenbach	56	50.46 N	8.34 E
Glades	220	26.59 N	81.12 W
Glade Spring	192	36.47 N	81.47 W
Gladesville	274a	33.50 S	151.08 E
Gladewater	222	32.33 N	94.56 W
Gladewater, Lake	222	32.35 N	94.57 W
Gladkovka	78	46.23 N	32.36 E
Gladsakse	41	55.44 N	12.29 E
Gladstone, Austl.	166	33.17 S	138.22 E
Gladstone, Austl.	166	23.51 S	151.16 E
Gladstone, Man., Can.	184	50.13 N	98.57 W
Gladstone, Mich., U.S.	190	45.50 N	87.03 W
Gladstone, Mo., U.S.	194	39.13 N	94.34 W
Gladstone, N.J., U.S.	210	40.43 N	74.40 W
Gladstone, Oreg., U.S.	224	45.23 N	122.36 W
Gladstone Brook	276	40.43 N	74.40 W
Gladwin	190	43.59 N	84.29 W
Gladwyne	285	40.02 N	75.17 W
Gladys Lake	180	59.55 N	132.55 W
Glænø	41	55.12 N	11.28 E
Glafsfjorden	26	59.34 N	12.37 E
Gláma	24a	65.47 N	23.00 W
Glåma	26	59.12 N	10.57 E
Glamis	46	56.36 N	3.00 W
Glamis Castle	46	56.37 N	3.00 W
Glamoč	36	44.03 N	16.51 E
Glamor Lake	212	44.58 N	78.23 W
Glamsbjerg	41	55.16 N	10.07 E
Glan	116	5.49 N	125.10 E
Glan	40	58.37 N	15.58 E
Glan, B.R.D.	56	49.47 N	7.43 E
Glan, Öst.	61	46.36 N	14.25 E
Glan, Pil.	116	5.50 N	125.12 E
Glanamman	42	51.48 N	3.54 W
Gland	58	46.26 N	6.16 E
Gland	50	49.55 N	4.05 E
Glandon, Col du	62	45.14 N	6.11 E
Glandorf, B.R.D.	52	52.05 N	7.59 E
Glandorf, Ohio, U.S.	216	41.07 N	84.05 W
Glâne	58	46.47 N	7.08 E
Glanegg	61	46.44 N	14.11 E
Glanerbrug	52	52.13 N	6.58 E
Glanshammar	40	59.19 N	15.24 E
Glanum	62	43.49 N	4.47 E
Glan-y-don	262	53.19 N	3.15 W
Glaris → Glarus	58	47.02 N	9.04 E
Glarner Alpen	58	46.55 N	9.00 E
Glärnisch	58	47.00 N	9.00 E
Glarus	58	47.02 N	9.04 E
Glarus	58	47.00 N	9.03 E
Glascarnoch, Loch	46	57.40 N	4.50 W
Glasco, Kans., U.S.	198	39.22 N	97.50 W
Glasco, N.Y., U.S.	210	42.03 N	73.57 W
Glasgow, Scot., U.K.	46	55.53 N	4.15 W
Glasgow, Ill., U.S.	219	39.33 N	90.29 W
Glasgow, Ky., U.S.	194	37.00 N	85.55 W
Glasgow, Mo., U.S.	194	39.14 N	92.50 W
Glasgow, Mont., U.S.	202	48.12 N	106.38 W
Glasgow, Pa., U.S.	214	40.42 N	78.27 W
Glasgow, Va., U.S.	192	37.38 N	79.27 W
Glasgow (Abbotsinch) Airport	46	55.52 N	4.26 W
Glashütte, B.R.D.	52	53.41 N	10.02 E
Glashütte, D.D.R.	54	50.51 N	13.47 E
Glashütte	263	51.13 N	6.52 E
Glaslyn	184	53.21 N	108.22 W
Glaslyn	42	52.56 N	4.06 W
Glas Maol	46	56.52 N	3.22 W
Glasow	54	52.20 N	13.28 E
Glass, Loch	46	57.43 N	4.30 W
Glassboro	208	39.42 N	75.07 W
Glassboro State College	285	39.42 N	75.07 W
Glass House Mountains	171a	26.53 S	152.58 E
Glassmanor	284c	38.49 N	76.59 W
Glass Mountains	196	30.25 N	103.15 W
Glasson	48	53.28 N	7.52 W
Glassport	214	40.19 N	79.54 W
Glastonbury, Eng., U.K.	42	51.06 N	2.43 W
Glastonbury, Conn., U.S.	207	41.43 N	72.37 W
Glatt	58	47.34 N	8.28 E
Glatten	58	48.26 N	8.31 E
Glattfelden	58	47.33 N	8.30 E
Glatz → Kłodzko	30	50.27 N	16.39 E
Glaubitz	54	51.19 N	13.22 E
Glauchau	54	50.49 N	12.32 E
Glaven	42	52.58 N	1.03 E
Glaze Brook	262	53.25 N	2.27 W
Glazebury	262	53.28 N	2.30 W
Glaževo	76	59.41 N	32.05 E
Glazok	80	53.06 N	40.42 E
Glazov	80	58.09 N	52.40 E
Glazovo, S.S.S.R.	82	54.57 N	37.22 E
Glazovo, S.S.S.R.	82	55.38 N	35.46 E
Glazovo, S.S.S.R.	82	54.47 N	37.34 E
Glazunovka	76	52.30 N	36.19 E
Glazunovskaja	80	49.50 N	42.51 E
Gleason	194	36.13 N	88.37 W
Glebovka	78	46.38 N	39.59 E
Glebovo, S.S.S.R.	82	56.39 N	38.42 E
Glebovo, S.S.S.R.	82	56.54 N	37.43 E
Gleed	224	46.40 N	120.37 W
Glehn	263	51.10 N	6.35 E
Gleichen	182	50.52 N	113.03 W
Gleidingen	52	52.16 N	9.50 E
Gleinalpe	61	47.15 N	15.30 E
Gleisdorf	61	47.06 N	15.44 E
Gleiwitz → Gliwice	30	50.17 N	18.40 E
Glejbjerg	41	55.33 N	8.50 E
Glemsford	42	52.06 N	0.41 E
Glen, Eire	48	54.38 N	8.40 W
Glen, Eng., U.K.	42	52.51 N	0.06 W
Glen Afton	172	37.37 S	175.02 E
Glen Alice	170	33.02 S	150.13 E
Glen Allen	208	37.40 N	77.30 W
Glen Alpine	192	35.44 N	81.47 W
Glenamaddy	48	53.37 N	8.35 W
Glenamoy	48	54.14 N	9.42 W
Glenarchy	275b	43.29 N	79.46 W
Glenarden	208	38.56 N	76.52 W
Glenarm, N. Ire., U.K.	48	54.58 N	5.57 W
Glen Arm, Md., U.S.	284b	39.27 N	76.30 W
Glen Aubrey	210	42.15 N	76.01 W
Glenavon, Sask., Can.	184	50.10 N	103.10 W
Glen Avon, S. Afr.	158	31.43 S	26.12 E
Glen Avon Heights	228	34.01 N	117.29 W
Glenavy, N.Z.	172	44.55 S	171.06 E
Glenavy, N. Ire., U.K.	48	54.35 N	6.13 W
Glenbeigh	48	52.02 N	9.58 W
Glenboro	184	49.32 N	99.15 W
Glenbrook	170	33.46 S	150.37 E
Glenbrook Heights	226	39.15 N	121.02 W
Glenburn, N. Dak., U.S.	198	48.31 N	101.13 W
Glenburn, Pa., U.S.	210	41.31 N	75.44 W
Glen Burnie	208	39.10 N	76.37 W
Glen Burnie Park	208	39.09 N	76.38 W
Glen Campbell	214	40.49 N	78.50 W
Glen Canyon	200	37.05 N	111.41 W
Glen Canyon	200	37.10 N	110.50 W
Glen Canyon Dam	200	36.48 N	111.13 W
Glen Canyon National Recreation Area	200	37.00 N	111.20 W
Glen Carbon	219	38.45 N	89.59 W
Glenclova	154	19.59 S	31.26 E
Glencoe, Austl.	166	37.42 S	140.37 E
Glencoe, Ont., Can.	214	42.45 N	81.43 W
Glencoe, S. Afr.	158	28.12 S	30.07 E
Glencoe, Ala., U.S.	194	33.57 N	85.56 W
Glencoe, Ill., U.S.	216	42.08 N	87.45 W
Glencoe, Ky., U.S.	218	38.43 N	84.49 W
Glencoe, Md., U.S.	208	39.33 N	76.38 W
Glencoe, Minn., U.S.	190	44.46 N	94.09 W
Glencolumbkille	48	54.43 N	8.45 E
Glencoul, Loch	46	58.14 N	4.58 W
Glen Cove	210	40.52 N	73.37 W
Glendale, Ariz., U.S.	200	33.32 N	112.11 W
Glendale, Calif., U.S.	228	34.10 N	118.17 W
Glendale, Mass., U.S.	207	42.17 N	73.21 W
Glendale, Mo., U.S.	219	38.33 N	90.22 W
Glendale, Oreg., U.S.	202	42.44 N	123.26 W
Glendale, R.I., U.S.	207	41.58 N	71.38 W
Glendale, Tex., U.S.	222	31.01 N	95.18 W
Glendale, Utah, U.S.	200	37.19 N	112.36 W
Glendale, Wis., U.S.	216	43.07 N	87.57 W
Glendale, Zimb.	154	17.21 S	31.04 E
Glendale Heights	278	41.55 N	88.03 W
Glendale Lake	214	40.41 N	78.32 W
Glendalough	48	53.01 N	6.26 W
Glen Davis	170	33.08 S	150.17 E
Glendive	198	47.06 N	104.43 W
Glendive Creek	198	47.08 N	104.41 W
Glendo	200	42.30 N	105.02 W
Glendoe Forest	46	57.06 N	4.37 W
Glendon, Alta., Can.	182	54.15 N	111.10 W
Glendon, Pa., U.S.	208	40.40 N	75.14 W
Glendora, Calif., U.S.	228	34.08 N	117.52 W
Glendora, N.J., U.S.	285	39.50 N	75.04 W
Glendo Reservoir	198	42.31 N	104.58 W
Glendo State Park	198	42.33 N	104.58 W
Glendowan	48	54.58 N	7.57 W
Glen Eagle, Austl.	168a	32.17 S	116.11 E
Gleneagle, Austl.	171a	27.57 S	152.59 E
Glen Echo	284c	38.58 N	77.08 W
Glen Echo Amusement Park	284c	38.58 N	77.08 W
Gleneden Beach	202	44.53 N	124.02 W
Glen Elder	198	39.30 N	98.18 W
Glenelg, Austl.	168b	34.59 S	138.31 E
Glenelg, Scot., U.K.	46	57.13 N	5.38 W
Glenelg	166	38.03 S	141.00 E
Glen Ellen	226	38.22 N	122.31 W
Glenelly	48	54.44 N	7.18 W
Glen Ellyn	278	41.52 N	88.03 W
Glen Ellyn Countryside	278	41.55 N	88.04 W
Glenfarg	46	56.16 N	3.24 W
Glenfarne	48	54.17 N	7.59 W
Glenfield, Austl.	274a	33.58 S	150.54 E
Glenfield, Eng., U.K.	42	52.39 N	1.12 W
Glenfield, N.Y., U.S.	212	43.43 N	75.24 W
Glenfield, Pa., U.S.	279b	40.31 N	80.08 W
Glenfinnan	46	56.52 N	5.27 W
Glen Flora	222	29.21 N	96.12 W
Glen Florrie	162	22.55 S	115.59 E
Glenford	210	42.00 N	74.07 W
Glen Forest	168a	31.54 S	116.06 E
Glengallan Creek	171a	28.09 S	151.53 E
Glen Gardner	210	40.42 N	74.56 W
Glengarriff	48	51.45 N	9.33 W
Glengarry	206	45.15 N	74.40 W
Glengarry Range	162	26.13 S	118.59 E
Glengyle	166	24.48 S	139.37 E
Glenham	210	41.31 N	73.56 W
Glenhaven	274a	33.42 S	151.00 E
Glen Head	276	40.50 N	73.37 W
Glen Hills	208	39.04 N	77.12 W
Glenhope	172	41.39 S	172.39 E
Glenhuntly	274b	37.54 S	145.03 E
Glen Innes	166	29.44 S	151.44 E
Glen Island	276	40.53 N	73.47 W
Glen Lake	224	48.26 N	123.31 W
Glenluce	44	54.53 N	4.49 W
Glenluce Abbey	44	54.53 N	4.50 W
Glen Lyon	210	41.10 N	76.05 W
Glen Miller	212	44.08 N	77.35 W
Glen Mills	285	39.55 N	75.30 W
Glenmont, N.Y., U.S.	210	42.36 N	73.46 W
Glenmont, Ohio, U.S.	214	40.31 N	82.06 W
Glenmoor	214	40.40 N	80.37 W
Glenmoore, Pa., U.S.	208	40.05 N	75.46 W
Glen Moore, Pa., U.S.	208	40.03 N	76.18 W
Glenmora	194	30.59 N	92.35 W
Glenmore	284b	39.11 N	76.36 W
Glenmorgan	166	27.15 S	149.41 E
Glenn, Calif., U.S.	226	39.31 N	122.01 W
Glenn, Mich., U.S.	216	42.31 N	86.14 W
Glenn	226	39.29 N	122.18 W
Glennallen	180	62.07 N	145.33 W
Glenn-Colusa Canal	226	39.07 N	122.08 W
Glenn Dale	284c	38.59 N	76.49 W
Glenns Creek	218	38.09 N	84.52 W
Glenns Ferry	202	42.57 N	115.18 W
Glennville	192	31.56 N	81.56 W
Glen Oak	278	41.53 N	88.02 W
Glenolden	285	39.54 N	75.17 W
Glenoma	224	46.31 N	122.09 W
Glenorchy	172	44.51 S	168.23 E
Glenore Grove	171a	27.32 S	152.24 E
Glenorie	170	33.33 S	151.00 E
Glenormiston	166	22.55 S	138.48 E
Glen Park	212	44.00 N	75.57 W
Glenreagh	166	30.03 S	152.59 E
Glen Richey	214	40.57 N	78.29 W
Glen Riddle	285	39.54 N	75.26 W
Glenridge, Mass., U.S.	283	42.15 N	71.20 W
Glen Ridge, N.J., U.S.	276	40.49 N	74.13 W
Glen Robertson	206	45.21 N	74.30 W
Glen Rock, N.J., U.S.	276	40.58 N	74.08 W
Glen Rock, Pa., U.S.	208	39.48 N	76.44 W
Glenrock, Wyo., U.S.	200	42.52 N	105.52 W
Glen Rose	222	32.14 N	97.45 W
Glen Ross	212	44.16 N	77.36 W
Glenrothes	46	56.12 N	3.10 W
Glenroy, Austl.	162	17.22 S	126.06 E
Glenroy, Austl.	162	21.46 S	114.49 E
Glenroy, Austl.	274b	37.42 S	144.55 E
Glenroy	172	42.00 S	172.20 E
Glens Falls	210	43.19 N	73.39 W
Glenshaw	214	40.31 N	79.57 W
Glenshee	46	56.48 N	3.30 W
Glenside, S. Afr.	158	29.25 S	30.47 E
Glenside, N.J., U.S.	208	39.40 N	75.29 W
Glenside, Pa., U.S.	208	40.06 N	75.09 W
Glen Spey	210	41.29 N	74.49 W
Glen Stewart Park	275b	43.41 N	79.18 W
Glenties	48	54.47 N	8.17 W
Glen Ullin	198	46.49 N	101.50 W
Glenview	216	42.04 N	87.48 W
Glenview Countryside	278	42.04 N	87.50 W
Glenview Naval Air Station	216	42.05 N	87.50 W
Glenville, Eire	48	52.03 N	8.26 W
Glenville, Minn., U.S.	190	43.34 N	93.17 W
Glenville, N.Y., U.S.	276	41.04 N	73.50 W
Glenville, W. Va., U.S.	188	38.56 N	80.50 W
Glen Waverley	274b	37.53 S	145.10 E
Glen White	192	37.44 N	81.17 W
Glen Wild	210	41.29 N	74.49 W
Glen Wild Lake	276	41.02 N	74.20 W
Glenwillard	214	40.34 N	80.13 W
Glen Williams	212	43.40 N	79.55 W
Glenwillow	214	41.22 N	81.28 W
Glenwood, N.B., Can.	186	48.59 N	54.52 W
Glenwood, Ala., U.S.	194	31.40 N	86.10 W
Glenwood, Ark., U.S.	194	34.20 N	93.33 W
Glenwood, Ga., U.S.	192	32.11 N	82.40 W
Glenwood, Ill., U.S.	278	41.33 N	87.37 W
Glenwood, Ind., U.S.	218	39.37 N	85.18 W
Glenwood, Iowa, U.S.	198	41.03 N	95.45 W
Glenwood, Minn., U.S.	198	45.39 N	95.23 W
Glenwood, N.J., U.S.	210	41.15 N	74.29 W
Glenwood, N. Mex., U.S.	200	33.19 N	108.53 W
Glenwood, N.Y., U.S.	210	42.37 N	78.39 W
Glenwood, Oreg., U.S.	224	45.39 N	123.16 W
Glenwood, Tex., U.S.	222	32.39 N	94.51 W
Glenwood, Utah, U.S.	200	38.46 N	111.59 W
Glenwood, Va., U.S.	192	36.35 N	79.22 W
Glenwood, Wash., U.S.	224	46.01 N	121.17 W
Glenwood City	190	45.04 N	92.10 W
Glenwood Landing	276	40.50 N	73.39 W
Glenwood Park	284c	38.58 N	76.50 W
Glenwood Springs	200	39.33 N	107.19 W
Glenwoodville	182	49.22 N	113.21 W
Gleschendorf	54	54.02 N	10.40 E
Glesien	54	51.27 N	12.13 E
Gletsch	58	46.34 N	8.22 E
Gleussen	56	50.08 N	10.53 E
Glew	258	34.53 S	58.23 W
Glidden, Iowa, U.S.	198	42.04 N	94.44 W
Glidden, Tex., U.S.	222	29.42 N	96.35 W
Glidden, Wis., U.S.	190	46.09 N	90.34 W
Glide	202	43.18 N	123.06 W
Gliener Berg	264a	52.42 N	13.00 E
Glienicke, D.D.R.	54	52.13 N	14.05 E
Glienicke, D.D.R.	54	52.37 N	13.19 E
Glífa	38	38.57 N	22.58 E
Glifádha	267c	37.52 N	23.45 E
Glimåkra	26	56.18 N	14.08 E
Glimmingehus	26	55.30 N	14.13 E
Glin	48	52.34 N	9.17 W
Glina	36	45.20 N	16.06 E
Glina	36	45.26 N	16.07 E
Glin'any	78	49.49 N	24.30 E
Glinde	52	53.32 N	10.13 E
Glindow	54	52.21 N	12.54 E
Glindowsee	264a	52.21 N	12.56 E
Glinka	76	54.39 N	32.52 E
Glinkovo	85	42.55 N	69.40 E
Glittertinden	26	61.39 N	8.33 E
Gliwice (Gleiwitz)	30	50.17 N	18.40 E
Gliwicki, Kanał	30	50.22 N	18.05 E
Globe, Ariz., U.S.	200	33.24 N	110.47 W
Globe, Ky., U.S.	218	38.17 N	83.14 W
Globino	78	49.23 N	33.17 E
Glod'any	78	47.47 N	27.31 E
Glodeanu-Siliştea	38	44.50 N	26.48 E
Glodok	269e	6.08 S	106.48 E
Glogau → Głogów	30	51.40 N	16.05 E
Gloggnitz	61	47.40 N	15.57 E
Glogn	58	46.46 N	9.12 E
Głogów, Pol.	30	50.10 N	21.58 E
Głogów, Pol.	30	51.40 N	16.05 E
Głogówek	30	50.22 N	17.51 E
Glommersträsk	26	65.16 N	19.38 E
Glonn	64	47.59 N	11.52 E
Glonn	60	48.26 N	11.36 E
Glorenza (Glurns)	64	46.40 N	10.33 E
Glória	250	9.11 S	38.18 W
Gloria, Bahía de la	240p	21.50 N	77.40 W
Gloria, Sierra de la	196	26.45 N	101.10 W
Glória de Dourados	255	22.21 S	54.13 W
Gloria Glens Park	214	41.03 N	81.54 W
Glorieta	200	35.35 N	105.46 W
Glorieuses, Îles	138	11.30 S	47.20 E
Glörstausee	263	51.14 N	7.29 E
Glos-la-Ferrière	50	48.51 N	0.36 E
Glossop	262	53.27 N	1.57 W
Glossopteris, Mount	9	84.44 S	113.51 W
Gloster	194	31.12 N	91.01 W
Glostrup	41	55.40 N	12.24 E
Glotovka	80	53.57 N	46.42 E
Glotovo	24	63.30 N	49.23 E
Gloucester, Austl.	166	31.59 S	151.58 E
Gloucester, Eng., U.K.	42	51.53 N	2.14 W
Gloucester, Mass., U.S.	207	42.41 N	70.39 W
Gloucester, Va., U.S.	208	37.25 N	76.32 W
Gloucester, N.J., U.S.	208	39.50 N	75.10 W
Gloucester, Va., U.S.	208	37.25 N	76.30 W
Gloucester, Cape	164	5.27 S	148.25 E
Gloucester, Vale of	42	51.55 N	2.10 W
Gloucester City	285	39.54 N	75.07 W
Gloucester Fisherman	283	42.36 N	70.40 W
Gloucester Harbor	207	42.36 N	70.40 W
Gloucester Island	166	20.01 S	148.27 E
Gloucester Point	208	37.16 N	76.30 W
Gloucester Pool	212	44.51 N	79.43 W
Gloucestershire	42	51.47 N	2.15 W
Glouster	188	39.30 N	82.05 W
Glover-Archbold Park	284c	38.55 N	77.05 W
Glover Creek	194	34.02 N	94.56 W
Glover Island	186	48.44 N	57.45 W
Glovers Reef	232	16.49 N	87.48 W
Gloversville	210	43.03 N	74.20 W
Glovertown	186	48.41 N	54.02 W
Glowe	54	54.35 N	13.28 E
Glöwen	54	52.55 N	12.05 E
Głowno	30	51.58 N	19.44 E
Głubczyce	30	50.13 N	17.49 E
Glubokij, S.S.S.R.	78	48.31 N	40.19 E
Glubokij, S.S.S.R.	80	47.01 N	42.47 E
Glubokij, S.S.S.R.	89	52.53 N	129.44 E
Glubokoje, S.S.S.R.	76	55.08 N	27.41 E
Glubokoje, S.S.S.R.	82	54.32 N	38.32 E
Glubokoje, S.S.S.R.	86	50.06 N	82.19 E
Głuchołazy	30	50.20 N	17.22 E
Gluchov	78	51.41 N	33.53 E
Gluchovo	265b	55.46 N	37.16 E
Glückauf-Kampfbahn	263	51.32 N	7.05 E
Glücksburg	41	54.50 N	9.33 E
Glückstadt, B.R.D.	52	53.47 N	9.25 E
Gluckstadt, S. Afr.	158	27.57 S	31.02 E
Glud	41	55.49 N	10.00 E
Glumslöv	41	55.56 N	12.48 E
Glumsø	41	55.21 N	11.42 E
Gluša	76	53.05 N	28.52 E
Glusk	76	52.54 N	28.41 E
Gluškeviči	78	51.34 N	27.47 E
Gluškovo	78	51.22 N	34.38 E
Glybokaja	78	48.07 N	25.56 E
Glyde	48	53.52 N	6.21 W
Glyder Fawr	42	53.06 N	4.01 W
Glyme	42	51.49 N	1.22 W
Glyndebourne	50	50.52 N	0.04 E
Glyndon, Md., U.S.	208	39.29 N	76.49 W
Glyndon, Minn., U.S.	198	46.52 N	96.35 W
Glyngøre	26	56.46 N	8.52 E
Glynneath	42	51.46 N	3.38 W
Gmelinka	80	50.24 N	46.54 E
Gmünd, Öst.	61	48.47 N	15.00 E
Gmünd, Öst.	64	46.54 N	13.32 E
Gmund am Tegernsee	64	47.45 N	11.44 E
Gmunden	64	47.55 N	13.48 E
Gnadenhutten	214	40.22 N	81.26 W
Gnadenhutten Monument	214	40.21 N	81.25 W
Gnalta	166	31.03 S	142.20 E
Gnaraloo	162	23.51 S	113.31 E
Gnarp	26	62.03 N	17.16 E
Gnarpurt, Lake	169	38.03 S	143.24 E
Gnarrenburg	52	53.22 N	9.00 E
Gnaw Bone	218	39.12 N	86.09 W
Gnesen → Gniezno	30	52.31 N	17.37 E
Gnesta	40	59.03 N	17.18 E
Gnezdovo	76	54.47 N	31.47 E
Gniben	41	56.01 N	11.18 E
Gniew	30	53.51 N	18.49 E
Gniewkowo	30	52.54 N	18.25 E
Gniezno	30	52.31 N	17.37 E
Gnilaja Lipa	78	49.07 N	24.44 E
Gnilec	76	52.22 N	36.01 E
Gniloj Jelanec	78	47.20 N	31.44 E
Gniloj Tikič	78	48.47 N	30.53 E
Gnivan'	78	49.06 N	28.20 E
Gnjilane	38	42.28 N	21.29 E
Gnoien	54	53.58 N	12.42 E
Gnosjö	26	57.22 N	13.44 E
Gnowangerup	162	33.56 S	117.59 E
Gō	96	35.02 N	132.13 E
Goa	116	13.42 N	123.29 E
Goa	122	14.20 N	74.00 E
Goageb	156	26.44 S	17.15 E
Goalen Head	166	36.40 S	150.05 E
Goāliar	126	24.07 N	90.18 E
Goālpāra	124	26.10 N	90.37 E
Goāltor	126	22.43 N	87.10 E
Goalundo Ghāt	126	23.43 N	89.46 E
Goan	150	13.14 N	5.09 W
Goangoa	140	5.48 N	25.09 E
Goascorán	236	13.36 N	87.45 W
Goascorán	236	13.25 N	87.48 W
Goat Fell	46	55.39 N	5.11 W
Goathland	44	54.23 N	0.44 W
Goat Island	284a	43.05 N	79.04 W
Goat Mountain	202	47.21 N	113.21 W
Goat Peak	224	46.56 N	121.16 W
Goba	144	7.02 N	40.00 E
Gobabis	156	22.30 S	18.58 E
Gobabis	156	22.00 S	19.00 E
Gobai	126	23.37 N	86.28 E
Gobardānga	126	22.53 N	88.45 E
Göbel	130	40.00 N	28.09 E
Guinea-Bissau	60	48.06 N	13.32 E
Guinea-Bissau	258	34.10 S	59.19 W
Gobernador Costa	254	44.04 S	70.35 W
Gobernador Gregores	254	48.46 S	70.15 W
Gobernador Ingeniero Valentín Virasoro	252	28.03 S	56.02 W
Gobernador Juan E. Martínez	252	28.55 S	58.56 W
Gobernador Monteverde	288	34.48 S	58.16 W
Gobernador Racedo	252	31.34 S	60.04 W
Gobernador Udaondo	258	35.18 S	58.36 W
Gobi Desert	102	43.00 N	106.00 E
Gobindapur, Bhārat	126	23.16 N	87.58 E
Gobindapur, Bhārat	272b	22.23 N	88.25 E
Gobindapur, Bhārat	272b	22.55 N	88.12 E
Gobindgarh	123	30.41 N	76.18 E
Gobindpur	126	23.50 N	86.31 E
Gobles	216	42.21 N	85.53 W
Gobō	96	33.53 N	135.10 E
Gobra	126	23.45 N	89.12 E
Gobur	154	4.20 N	31.04 E
Gobza	76	55.16 N	31.31 E
Göçbeyli	130	39.13 N	27.25 E
Goceano, Catena del	71	40.28 N	9.02 E
Goce Delčev	38	41.34 N	23.44 E
Goch	52	51.41 N	6.10 E
Gochas	156	24.55 S	18.55 E
Gochsheim	56	50.01 N	10.16 E
Go-cong	269c	10.50 N	106.50 E
Göcsej	61	46.43 N	16.42 E
Goðafoss	24a	65.40 N	17.30 W
Godāgāri	124	24.28 N	88.20 E
Godalming	42	51.11 N	0.37 W
Godalo	144	4.36 N	43.27 E
Godar	128	28.12 N	63.14 E
Godāvari	122	17.00 N	81.45 E
Godāvari, Mouths of the	122	16.25 N	82.00 E
Godbout	186	49.19 N	67.37 W
Godda	124	24.50 N	87.13 E
Goddard	218	38.22 N	83.37 W
Goddard Space Flight Center	284c	39.00 N	76.52 W
Goddelau	56	49.50 N	8.30 E
Goddua	146	26.26 N	14.18 E
Godeffroy	210	41.27 N	74.37 W
Godega di Sant'Urbano	64	45.56 N	12.24 E
Godegård	40	58.44 N	15.09 E
Godelheim	52	51.44 N	9.22 E
Gödene	130	36.34 N	30.21 E
Godere	144	5.05 N	43.50 E
Goderich	190	43.45 N	81.43 W
Goderville	50	49.39 N	0.22 E
Godfrey	219	38.57 N	90.11 W
Godhavn	176	69.15 N	53.33 W
Godhra	120	22.45 N	73.38 E
Godinlave	144	5.54 N	46.40 E
Godinne	56	50.21 N	4.52 E
Godley	222	32.27 N	97.32 W
Godmanchester	42	52.19 N	0.11 W
Godo, Indon.	115b	8.33 S	118.40 E
Gōdo, Nihon	94	35.25 N	136.36 E
Gōdo, Nihon	268	35.51 N	139.44 E
Gödöllő	264c	47.36 N	19.22 E
Gödöllői Dombvidék	264c	47.37 N	19.16 E
Godong	115a	7.02 S	110.46 E
Godoy Cruz	252	32.55 S	68.50 W
Godramstein	56	49.12 N	8.05 E
Godrano	70	37.54 N	13.26 E
Gods	184	56.22 N	92.51 W
Godshill	42	50.38 N	1.14 W
Godshorn	52	52.26 N	9.43 E
Gods Lake	184	54.40 N	94.09 W
Gods Lake	184	54.40 N	94.20 W
Gods Mercy, Bay of	176	63.30 N	86.10 W
Godstone	260	51.15 N	0.04 W
Godthåb	176	64.11 N	51.44 W
Godunovo	82	56.29 N	39.02 E
Godwin Austen (K2)	123	35.53 N	76.30 E
Goedemoed	158	30.33 S	26.26 E
Goedgegun	158	27.06 S	31.12 E
Goéland, Lac au	176	49.47 N	76.48 W
Goélands, Lac aux	176	55.27 N	64.17 W
Goeree	52	51.50 N	3.55 E
Goes	52	51.30 N	3.54 E
Goetzenbruck	56	48.59 N	7.23 E
Goff, Som.	144	2.42 N	41.03 E
Goff, Kans., U.S.	198	39.40 N	95.56 W
Goff Creek	196	36.43 N	101.29 W
Goffle Brook	276	40.56 N	74.08 W
Goff's Oak	260	51.43 N	0.05 W
Goffstown	188	43.01 N	71.36 W
Gofoundurei	144	4.31 N	46.46 E
Gogama	190	47.40 N	81.43 W
Gogeb	144	7.10 N	37.27 E
Gogebic, Lake	190	46.30 N	89.35 W
Gogebic Range	190	46.45 N	89.25 W
Gogeh	144	8.12 N	38.27 E
Göggingen	58	48.20 N	10.52 E
Gogha	120	21.41 N	72.17 E
Gogland, Ostrov	76	60.04 N	27.00 E
Goglio	58	46.18 N	8.16 E
Gogoi	156	20.17 S	33.08 E
Gogolevka	76	54.17 N	31.58 E
Gogolevo	78	49.56 N	33.48 E
Gogolin	30	50.30 N	18.02 E
Gogonou	150	10.50 N	2.50 E
Gogo-shima	96	33.54 N	132.41 E
Gogrial	140	8.32 N	28.07 E
Gohad	124	26.26 N	78.27 E
Gohāla	126	23.15 N	89.59 E
Gohāla	126	24.08 N	89.35 E
Gohāna	124	29.08 N	76.42 E
Gohfeld	52	52.12 N	8.45 E
Gohitafla	150	7.30 N	5.53 W
Göhl	54	54.17 N	10.56 E
Gohoku	96	33.39 N	133.21 E
Go Home Lake	212	45.00 N	79.51 W
Gohpur	120	26.53 N	93.38 E
Gohr	263	51.06 N	6.43 E
Göhrde	54	53.08 N	10.52 E
Göhren	54	54.20 N	13.44 E
Goiana, Bra.	250	7.33 S	34.59 W
Goianá, Bra.	256	21.32 S	43.12 W
Goianápolis	255	16.30 S	49.01 W
Goiandira	255	18.08 S	48.06 W
Goianésia	255	15.18 S	49.07 W
Goiânia	255	16.40 S	49.16 W
Goianinha	250	6.16 S	35.12 W
Goianira	255	16.30 S	49.26 W
Goianorte	250	8.35 S	48.56 W
Goiás	255	15.56 S	50.08 W
Goiás	255	15.00 S	49.00 W
Goiatuba	255	18.01 S	49.22 W
Goichran	120	31.04 N	78.07 E
Goikul	175b	7.22 N	134.36 E
Goil, Loch	46	56.08 N	4.52 W
Goio-Erê	252	24.12 S	53.01 W
Goio-Erê	252	24.14 S	53.21 W
Goirle	52	51.32 N	5.04 E
Góis, Bra.	256	22.33 S	46.18 W
Góis, Port.	34	40.09 N	8.07 W
Goito	64	45.15 N	10.40 E
Gojam	144	11.00 N	37.00 E
Gojō	96	34.21 N	135.42 E
Gojōme	92	39.56 N	140.07 E
Gojra	123	31.09 N	72.41 E
Gojtchskij, Pereval	84	44.18 N	39.18 E
Gokāk	122	16.10 N	74.50 E
Gokarna	126	24.03 N	88.07 E
Gokase	92	32.35 N	131.42 E
Gökçe	130	40.11 N	25.55 E
Gökçeada	130	40.10 N	25.50 E
Gökçen	130	38.07 N	27.53 E
Gökdere, Tür.	130	38.44 N	40.13 E
Gökdere, Tür.	130	40.29 N	36.47 E
Gōkōmutsumi	268	35.48 N	139.59 E
Göksholm	40	59.16 N	15.33 E
Göksu, Tür.	84	39.19 N	42.17 E
Göksu, Tür.	130	36.20 N	34.05 E
Göksu, Tür.	130	37.37 N	35.35 E
Göksu Deresí	267b	41.06 N	29.03 E
Göksun	130	38.03 N	36.30 E
Göktepe	130	37.15 N	28.36 E
Gök Tepe	130	36.53 N	29.17 E
Gokwe	154	18.07 S	28.58 E
Gol	26	60.42 N	8.57 E
Gol, Khawr	140	6.55 N	30.16 E
Gola	48	55.05 N	8.22 W
Golabāri	272b	22.36 N	88.20 E
Golāghāt	120	26.31 N	93.58 E
Gola Gokaran Nath	124	28.05 N	80.28 E
Golaja Pristan'	78	46.31 N	32.31 E
Gołańcz	30	52.57 N	17.18 E
Golan Heights	132	32.55 N	35.42 E
Golāshkerd	128	27.59 N	57.16 E
Gölbaşı, Tür.	130	39.48 N	32.49 E
Gölbası, Tür.	130	37.50 N	37.40 E
Golborne	262	53.29 N	2.36 W
Golcar	262	53.39 N	1.51 W
Gol'čicha	74	71.43 N	83.36 E
Golconda, Ill., U.S.	194	37.22 N	88.29 W
Golconda, Nev., U.S.	204	40.57 N	117.30 W
Gölcük, Tür.	130	40.44 N	29.48 E
Gölcuk, Tür.	130	39.18 N	27.59 E
Golczewo	54	53.49 N	14.59 E
Gołdap	30	54.19 N	22.19 E
Goldau	58	47.03 N	8.33 E
Gold Bar	224	47.51 N	121.42 W
Gold Beach	202	42.25 N	124.25 W
Goldbeck	54	52.43 N	11.52 E
Goldberg, D.D.R.	54	53.35 N	12.05 E
Goldberg → Złotoryja, Pol.	30	51.08 N	15.55 E
Goldberger See	54	53.36 N	12.07 E
Goldbergtunnel	263	51.01 N	7.28 E
Goldbey	58	48.12 N	6.26 E
Goldboro	186	45.11 N	61.39 W
Gold Bridge	182	50.51 N	122.50 W
Gold Coast → Southport	171a	27.58 S	153.25 E
Gold Coast, Afr.	150	5.10 N	1.00 W
Gold Coast, Ghana	150	5.20 N	0.45 W
Gold Creek	180	62.46 N	149.41 W
Gold Creek	182	49.04 N	115.12 W
Golden, B.C., Can.	182	51.18 N	116.58 W
Golden, Eire	48	52.29 N	7.58 W
Golden, Colo., U.S.	200	39.46 N	105.13 W
Golden, Ill., U.S.	219	40.07 N	91.01 W
Golden Bay	172	40.40 S	172.50 E
Golden Beach	220	25.58 N	80.09 W
Golden Brook	283	42.44 N	71.19 W
Golden City	194	37.24 N	94.05 W
Goldendale	224	45.49 N	120.50 W
Golden Ears Provincial Park	182	49.30 N	122.25 W
Goldene Aue	54	51.25 N	11.00 E
Golden Gate	220	26.09 N	81.43 W
Golden Gate	226	37.49 N	122.29 W
Golden Gate Bridge	282	37.49 N	122.28 W
Golden Gate Fields Race Track	282	37.53 N	122.19 W
Golden Gate Highlands National Park	158	28.30 S	28.40 E
Golden Gate National Recreation Area	282	37.49 N	122.31 W
Golden Gate Park	282	37.46 N	122.28 W
Golden Green	260	51.12 N	0.21 E
Golden Hill Creek	210	43.22 N	78.28 W
Golden Hinde	182	49.40 N	125.45 W
Golden Horn → Haliç	267b	41.02 N	28.58 E
Golden Lake	190	45.35 N	77.20 W
Golden Meadow	194	29.23 N	90.16 W
Golden Prairie	184	50.14 N	109.38 W
Golden Rock	122	10.48 N	78.44 E
Goldenrod	220	28.37 N	81.18 W
Golden Spike National Historic Site	202	41.38 N	112.35 W
Goldenstedt	52	52.48 N	8.25 E
Golden Valley	42	52.02 N	2.56 W
Golders Green	260	51.35 N	0.12 W
Goldfield, Iowa, U.S.	190	42.44 N	93.55 W
Goldfield, Nev., U.S.	204	37.42 N	117.14 W
Gold Lake	212	44.43 N	78.17 W
Goldlauter	54	50.38 N	10.44 E
Gold Mountain	204	37.15 N	117.18 W
Goldney	258	34.37 S	59.18 W
Goldonna	194	32.01 N	92.54 W
Goldpan Peak	180	61.12 N	153.22 W
Gold River	182	49.41 N	126.08 W
Gold Rock	184	49.27 N	92.43 W
Gold Run	226	39.10 N	120.52 W
Goldsand Lake	184	57.02 N	101.08 W
Goldsboro, Md., U.S.	208	39.02 N	75.47 W
Goldsboro, N.C., U.S.	192	35.23 N	77.59 W
Goldsmith, Ind., U.S.	216	40.17 N	86.09 W
Goldsmith, Tex., U.S.	196	31.59 N	102.40 W
Goldsmith, Lake	169	37.32 S	143.21 E
Goldston	192	35.36 N	79.20 W
Goldstone Lake	228	35.22 N	116.54 W
Goldstream Provincial Park	224	48.29 N	123.33 W

Symbol	English	Deutsch	Español	Français	Português
≃	River	Fluss	Río	Rivière	Rio
	Canal	Kanal	Canal	Canal	Canal
	Waterfall, Rapids	Wasserfall, Stromschnellen	Cascada, Rápidos	Chute d'eau, Rapides	Cascata, Rápidos
	Strait	Meeresstrasse	Estrecho	Détroit	Estreito
	Bay, Gulf	Bucht, Golf	Bahía, Golfo	Baie, Golfe	Baía, Golfo
	Lake, Lakes	See, Seen	Lago, Lagos	Lac, Lacs	Lago, Lagos
	Swamp	Sumpf	Pantano	Marais	Pântano
	Ice Features, Glacier	Eis- und Gletscherformen	Accidentes Glaciales	Formes glaciaires	Acidentes Glaciares
	Other Hydrographic Features	Andere Hydrographische Objekte	Otros Elementos Hidrográficos	Autres données hydrographiques	Outros Elementos Hidrográficos
	Submarine Features	Untermeerische Objekte	Accidentes Submarinos	Formes de relief sous-marin	Acidentes Submarinos
□	Political Unit	Politische Einheit	Unidad Politica	Entité politique	Unidade Política
	Cultural Institution	Kulturelle Institution	Institución Cultural	Institution culturelle	Instituição Cultural
	Historical Site	Historische Stätte	Sitio Histórico	Site historique	Sitio Histórico
	Recreational Site	Erholungs- und Ferienort	Sitio de Recreo	Centre de loisirs	Sítio de Lazer
⊠	Airport	Flughafen	Aeropuerto	Aéroport	Aeroporto
■	Military Installation	Militäranlage	Instalación Militar	Installation militaire	Instalação Militar
	Miscellaneous	Verschiedenes	Misceláneo	Divers	Miscelânea

ENGLISH / DEUTSCH

Name	Page / Seite	Lat.°′ / Breite°′	Long.°′ / Länge°′ E=Ost
Goldsworthy, Mount ∧[2]	162	20.21 S	119.32 E
Goldthwaite	196	31.27 N	98.34 W
Golec, Gora ∧	88	58.39 N	94.10 E
Golec-Davydov, Gora ∧	88	52.34 N	107.25 E
Golec-In'aptuk, Gora ∧	88	56.22 N	110.11 E
Golec-Korolenko, Gora ∧	88	58.15 N	115.01 E
Golec-Longdor, Gora ∧	88	58.24 N	116.47 E
Golec-Načinskij, Gora ∧	89	52.24 N	118.53 E
Golec-Skalistyj, Gora ∧	88	56.24 N	119.12 E
Golec-Talakanskij, Gora ∧	88	51.52 N	119.24 E
Golec-Urgučenskij, Gora ∧	88	53.30 N	118.08 E
Golec-Ušmunskij, Gora ∧	89	51.40 N	118.35 E
Goleen	48	51.28 N	9.43 W
Golela	158	27.20 S	31.55 E
Goleniów	30	53.36 N	14.50 E
Goleta	204	34.27 N	119.50 W
Goleta, Cerro ∧	234	18.38 N	100.04 W
Golf, Fla., U.S.	220	26.31 N	80.06 W
Golf, Ill., U.S.	278	42.03 N	87.48 W
Golfcrest	216	41.57 N	83.22 W
Golfe-Juan	62	43.34 N	7.05 E
Golfito	236	8.38 N	83.11 W
Golf Manor	285	39.42 N	75.28 W
Golf Mill ⬥[9]	278	42.03 N	87.50 W
Golfo Aranci	71	40.59 N	9.38 E
Golf Park Terrace	278	42.03 N	87.51 W
Golfside	281	42.15 N	83.41 W
Golf View	208	39.43 N	75.28 W
Golfview Heights	220	26.43 N	80.07 W
Golfview Hills	278	41.47 N	87.56 W
Goliad	196	28.40 N	97.23 W
Goliad □[6]	222	28.52 N	97.22 W
Golicyno, S.S.S.R.	80	53.38 N	44.07 E
Golicyno, S.S.S.R.	82	55.37 N	36.59 E
Golina	30	52.16 N	18.05 E
Golinda	222	31.25 N	97.05 W
Goljama Kamčija ≃	38	43.03 N	27.29 E
Goljam Perelik ∧	38	41.36 N	24.34 E
Goljanovo ⬥[8]	265b	55.49 N	37.48 E
Goljevo	265b	55.48 N	37.19 E
Gölköy	130	40.42 N	37.38 E
Gollach ≃	56	49.31 N	10.00 E
Gollel	158	27.20 S	31.55 E
Göllersbach ≃	61	48.22 N	16.11 E
Göllet	130	40.45 N	42.18 E
Golling an der Salzach	64	47.36 N	13.10 E
Gollnow → Goleniów	30	53.36 N	14.50 E
Golm	264a	52.24 N	12.57 E
Gölmarmara	130	38.42 N	27.56 E
Golmberg ∧[2]	54	52.01 N	13.21 E
Gol'movskij	83	48.25 N	38.05 E
Golo ≃	32	42.31 N	9.32 E
Goloby	78	51.06 N	24.59 E
Golodnaja Guba, Ozero ⊜	24	67.52 N	52.48 E
Gologory ⩕	78	49.45 N	24.35 E
Golo Island I	116	13.40 N	120.22 E
Golok (Kolok) ≃	114	6.15 N	102.05 E
Golongoso	146	9.00 N	19.09 E
Golovacovka	85	42.52 N	71.13 E
Golovanevsk	78	48.23 N	30.28 E
Golovanovo, S.S.S.R.	80	56.09 N	54.07 E
Golovanovo, S.S.S.R.	80	54.55 N	40.27 E
Golovčin	76	54.04 N	29.55 E
Golovčino	78	50.32 N	35.47 E
Golovin	180	64.33 N	163.02 W
Golovinka	84	43.48 N	39.28 E
Golovino, S.S.S.R.	80	55.58 N	40.26 E
Golovino, S.S.S.R.	82	56.01 N	39.11 E
Golovinščino	80	53.18 N	43.59 E
Golovinskaja	88	53.26 N	102.43 E
Golovnino	82	54.23 N	36.10 E
Golovno	78	51.21 N	24.04 E
Golovskoje	88	55.30 N	105.32 E
Golpara □[5]	124	26.25 N	89.25 E
Golpāyegān	128	33.27 N	50.18 E
Gölpazarı	130	40.15 N	30.19 E
Golra	123	33.42 N	72.58 E
Golrān	128	35.06 N	61.41 E
Gol'šany	76	54.15 N	26.01 E
Gölsdorf	54	51.59 N	12.39 E
Golspie, Austl.	170	34.17 S	149.40 E
Golspie, Scot., U.K.	46	57.58 N	3.58 W
Golssen	54	51.58 N	13.36 E
Gol't'ajevo	82	55.13 N	36.02 E
Gol't'avino	88	58.26 N	98.27 E
Golub-Dobrzyń	30	53.08 N	19.02 E
Golubi	76	59.28 N	41.39 E
Golubinskij	80	48.52 N	43.34 E
Golubovka, S.S.S.R.	78	48.53 N	35.19 E
Golubovka, S.S.S.R.	86	53.09 N	74.12 E
Golubovka ⬥[8]	83	48.38 N	38.39 E
Goluin	144	1.43 N	44.38 E
Golumet'	88	53.03 N	102.21 E
Golungo Alto	152	9.08 S	14.46 E
Golva	198	46.44 N	103.51 W
Gölveren	130	37.48 N	33.52 E
Golynki	76	54.52 N	31.23 E
Golyšmanovo, S.S.S.R.	86	56.28 N	68.38 E
Golyšmanovo, S.S.S.R.	86	56.23 N	68.23 E
Golzheim ⬥[8]	263	51.15 N	6.46 E
Golzow, D.D.R.	54	52.16 N	12.36 E
Golzow, D.D.R.	54	52.34 N	14.29 E
Goma, Yai.	144	8.25 N	36.53 E
Goma, Zaïre	154	1.41 S	29.14 E
Gomagoi	64	46.35 N	10.32 E
Gomanodan-zan ∧	96	34.03 N	135.34 E
Gomaringen	58	48.27 N	9.05 E
Gomas, Sierra de ⩕	196	26.23 N	100.32 W
Gomati ≃	124	25.32 N	83.10 E
Gomati Plain ⌣	124	26.30 N	81.10 E
Goma Tsétsé	273b	4.14 S	15.08 E
Gombari	154	2.43 N	29.04 E
Gombe, Nig.	146	10.19 N	11.02 E
Gombe, Zaïre	152	0.42 S	17.35 E
Gombe ≃	154	4.38 S	31.40 E
Gombi	146	10.10 N	12.45 E
Gomboro	150	13.29 N	2.46 W
Gomel'	76	52.25 N	31.00 E
Gomel' □[4]	78	52.00 N	29.00 E
Gömele	130	40.02 N	30.34 E
Gomer	216	40.51 N	84.11 W
Gomera I	148	28.06 N	17.08 W
Gometra I	46	56.29 N	6.17 W
Gometz-la-Ville	261	48.40 N	2.08 E
Gometz-le-Châtel	261	48.41 N	2.08 E
Gomez	220	27.06 N	80.09 W
Gómez Farías, Méx.	232	29.18 N	107.40 W
Gómez Farías, Méx.	234	19.47 N	103.29 W
Gómez Palacio	232	25.34 N	103.30 W
Gómez Plata	246	6.41 N	75.12 W
Gomīshān	128	37.04 N	54.06 E
Gommécourt	261	49.05 N	1.36 E
Gommern	54	52.04 N	11.50 E
Gomogomo	164	6.40 S	134.43 E
Gomoh	126	23.52 N	86.10 E
Gompa	123	35.02 N	77.20 E
Goms ∨	58	46.27 N	8.15 E
Gomshall	260	51.13 N	0.27 W
Gomumu, Pulau I	164	1.49 S	127.38 E
Gona	164	8.37 S	148.17 E
Gonābād	128	34.20 N	58.42 E
Gonaïves	238	19.27 N	72.41 W
Gonaka	152	2.56 S	13.14 E
Gonam	74	57.21 N	131.12 E
Gonam ≃	74	57.21 N	131.14 E
Gonars	64	45.53 N	13.13 E
Gonäs	40	60.09 N	15.06 E
Gonâve, Golfe de la C	238	19.00 N	73.30 W
Gonâve, Île de la I	238	18.51 N	73.03 W
Gonbad-e Qābūs	128	37.17 N	55.17 E
Gonçalves	256	22.40 S	45.51 W
Gonçalves Dias	250	4.57 S	44.14 W
Gončarovka	78	50.32 N	39.28 E
Goncelin	62	45.20 N	5.59 E
Gonda	124	27.08 N	81.56 E
Gonda □[5]	124	27.10 N	82.10 E
Gondal	120	21.58 N	70.48 E
Gondang	115a	7.24 S	111.06 E
Gondar → Gonder	144	12.40 N	37.30 E
Gonder	144	12.40 N	37.30 E
Gondey	146	9.09 N	19.19 E
Gondia	120	21.27 N	80.12 E
Gondola	156	19.10 S	33.40 E
Gondomar	34	41.09 N	8.32 W
Gondrecourt-le-Château	58	48.31 N	5.30 E
Gondreville	58	48.42 N	5.58 E
Gondrexange, Étang de ⊜	58	48.42 N	6.54 E
Gönen, Tür.	130	40.06 N	27.39 E
Gonen, Yis.	132	33.08 N	35.39 E
Gonesse	50	48.59 N	2.27 E
Gonfaron	62	43.19 N	6.17 E
Gongan	102	30.02 N	112.04 E
Gonganbao	86	44.59 N	86.18 E
Gonganpucun	104	41.19 N	123.27 E
Gongbuchang	105	40.17 N	116.15 E
Gongchangling	104	41.06 N	123.30 E
Gongcheng	102	24.49 N	110.46 E
Gongchenqiao	106	30.20 N	120.08 E
Gongchuan, Zhg.	100	26.06 N	117.24 E
Gongchuan, Zhg.	102	23.40 N	107.50 E
Gongcun	105	39.28 N	116.10 E
Gongdaoqiao	100	32.36 N	119.22 E
Gongdian	100	28.06 N	116.56 E
Gongen-yama ∧	94	35.40 N	139.01 E
Gongfang	100	27.36 N	115.34 E
Gonggashan (Minya Konka) ∧	102	29.35 N	101.51 E
Gongge	120	29.17 N	90.46 E
Gonggeershan ∧	120	38.37 N	75.20 E
Gonghe	102	36.20 N	100.48 E
Gonghui	98	41.12 N	114.37 E
Gongjialu	106	31.17 N	121.40 E
Gongjiasha	106	31.52 N	121.04 E
Gongjiatun	104	40.55 N	120.37 E
Gongjiazhai	104	41.57 N	124.01 E
Gongjing	107	29.21 N	104.43 E
Gongjingying	105	39.12 N	116.11 E
Gongjue	102	30.43 N	98.19 E
Gongkou	98	35.38 N	119.47 E
Gongli	98	35.55 N	117.24 E
Gongling	100	26.18 N	119.40 E
Gongliu	86	43.30 N	82.15 E
Gonglushan ∧	106	30.39 N	119.18 E
Gongogi	255	14.19 S	39.29 W
Gongola ≃	146	9.30 N	12.04 E
Gongoué	152	0.32 S	9.12 E
Gongo-Yembe	152	1.58 S	18.40 E
Gongpengzi	89	45.09 N	125.39 E
Gongpi	100	27.38 N	115.52 E
Gongping	100	23.05 N	115.24 E
Gongpingwei	100	26.12 N	112.51 E
Gongshan	102	25.50 N	103.13 E
Gongshiya	120	31.25 N	84.37 E
Gongshui ≃	100	26.00 N	115.22 E
Gongsiqiao	106	32.15 N	121.20 E
Gongsizhen	106	31.41 N	121.48 E
Gongtangtou	106	31.48 N	118.42 E
Gongxian	102	34.48 N	113.03 E
Gongyefu	98	42.16 N	118.32 E
Gongyemiao	89	43.40 N	121.06 E
Gongyingzi	98	40.54 N	119.41 E
Gongzhutun	104	42.10 N	123.00 E
Gongzui	107	29.19 N	103.28 E
Goni, It.	71	39.34 N	9.17 E
Goñi, Ur.	252	33.31 S	56.24 W
Goniądz	30	53.30 N	22.45 E
Goniānamandi	123	30.19 N	74.54 E
Göniksuyu ≃	84	38.55 N	40.34 E
Gonini ≃	250	4.10 N	54.24 W
Goniri	146	11.30 N	12.20 E
Gonnesa	71	39.16 N	8.28 E
Gonnosfanadiga	71	39.29 N	8.39 E
Gonnostramatza	71	39.41 N	8.50 E
Gonochovo	86	52.57 N	81.20 E
Gonoles, Vodochranilišče ⊜[1]	76	53.58 N	27.22 E
Gōnoura	92	33.45 N	129.41 E
Gonubie	158	32.57 S	28.01 E
Gonža	89	53.36 N	125.19 E
Gonzaga, It.	64	44.57 N	10.49 E
Gonzaga, Pil.	116	18.16 N	122.00 E
Gonzales, Calif., U.S.	226	36.31 N	121.32 W
Gonzales, La., U.S.	194	30.14 N	90.55 W
Gonzales, Tex., U.S.	222	29.30 N	97.27 W
Gonzales □[6]	222	29.28 N	97.30 W
González	258	34.14 S	56.52 W
González, Riacho ≃	252	22.48 S	57.54 W
González Catán	258	34.46 S	58.39 W
González Chaves	252	38.02 S	60.06 W
González Moreno	252	35.33 S	63.22 W
González Ortega	204	32.40 N	115.23 W
González Risos	258	34.52 S	59.13 W
Gonzanamá	246	4.15 S	79.27 W
Goobarragandra ≃	171b	35.20 S	148.15 E
Goochland	192	37.41 N	77.53 W
Goode, Mount ∧	180	61.20 N	148.02 W
Good Easter	260	51.47 N	0.21 E
Goodells	214	42.59 N	82.40 W
Goode Mountain ∧	224	48.29 N	120.55 W
Goodenough, Mount ∧	180	67.56 N	135.31 W
Goodenough Bay C	164	9.55 S	150.00 E
Goodenough Island I	164	9.20 S	150.15 E
Gooderham	212	44.54 N	78.23 W
Goodeve	184	51.04 N	103.10 W
Goodfellow Air Force Base ▪	196	31.26 N	100.25 W
Good Hope, S. Afr.	158	31.51 S	21.55 E
Good Hope, Ohio, U.S.	218	39.27 N	83.22 W
Good Hope, Cape of ≻	158	34.24 S	18.30 E
Goodhope Bay C	180	66.10 N	163.45 W
Good Hope Mountain ∧	182	51.09 N	124.10 W
Goodhouse	158	28.57 S	18.13 E
Goodhue	190	44.24 N	92.37 W
Gooding	202	42.56 N	114.43 W
Goodison	214	42.44 N	83.10 W
Goodland, Fla., U.S.	220	25.55 N	81.39 W
Goodland, Ind., U.S.	216	40.46 N	87.18 W
Goodland, Kans., U.S.	198	39.21 N	101.43 W
Goodlands	184	49.05 N	100.35 W
Goodlow Park	222	32.07 N	96.14 W
Goodman, Miss., U.S.	194	32.58 N	89.55 W
Goodman, Wis., U.S.	190	45.38 N	88.21 W
Goodman Bay C	240b	25.05 N	77.24 W
Goodna	171a	27.37 S	152.54 E
Goodnews Bay	180	59.07 N	161.35 W
Goodooga	166	29.07 S	147.27 E
Goodradigbee ≃	171b	35.08 S	148.41 E
Goodrich, Mich., U.S.	216	42.55 N	83.30 W
Goodrich, N. Dak., U.S.	198	47.28 N	100.08 W
Goodrich, Tex., U.S.	222	30.36 N	94.57 W
Good Spirit Lake ⊜	184	51.34 N	102.40 W
Good Spirit Lake Provincial Park ♠	184	51.36 N	102.45 W
Good Thunder	190	44.00 N	94.04 W
Goodview	190	44.04 N	91.41 W
Goodville	208	40.08 N	76.00 W
Goodwater	194	33.04 N	86.03 W
Goodwell	196	36.36 N	101.38 W
Goodwick	42	52.00 N	5.00 W
Goodwin, Lake ⊜	224	48.08 N	122.18 W
Goodwives ≃	276	41.04 N	73.28 W
Goodwood	212	44.02 N	79.12 W
Goodyear	200	33.26 N	112.21 W
Gooie Hoop,, Kaap die → Good Hope, Cape of ≻	158	34.24 S	18.30 E
Goole	44	53.42 N	0.52 W
Goolgowi	166	33.59 S	145.42 E
Goolwa	168b	35.31 S	138.47 E
Goomalling	162	31.19 S	116.49 E
Goombalie	166	29.59 S	145.23 E
Goombungee	171a	27.18 S	151.51 E
Goomburra	171a	28.03 S	152.07 E
Goonda	156	19.51 S	34.00 E
Goondiwindi	166	28.32 S	150.19 E
Goongarrie	162	30.03 S	121.09 E
Goor	52	52.14 N	6.35 E
Goose ≃, Alta., Can.	182	54.58 N	117.11 W
Goose ≃, N. Dak., U.S.	198	47.28 N	96.52 W
Goose Bay	176	53.20 N	60.25 W
Goose Bay C	281	42.35 N	82.41 W
Gooseberry Creek ≃	202	43.55 N	108.04 W
Goose Creek ≃, U.S.	202	42.33 N	113.46 W
Goose Creek ≃, Ky., U.S.	192	37.16 N	83.38 W
Goose Creek ≃, Nebr., U.S.	198	42.02 N	100.03 W
Goose Creek ≃, N.Y., U.S.	214	42.06 N	79.22 W
Goose Creek ≃, Va., U.S.	208	39.06 N	77.29 W
Goose Island I	182	51.55 N	128.25 W
Goose Lake ⊜, Man., Can.	184	54.26 N	101.30 W
Goose Lake ⊜, Ont., Can.	184	51.46 N	93.00 W
Goose Lake ⊜, Ont., Can.	212	44.25 N	78.52 W
Goose Lake ⊜, Ont., Can.	214	42.31 N	82.31 W
Goose Lake ⊜, Sask., Can.	184	51.45 N	107.23 W
Goose Lake ⊜, U.S.	204	41.57 N	120.25 W
Goose Lake Canal ≍	226	35.50 N	119.37 W
Goose Lake Prairie State Park ♠	216	41.21 N	88.18 W
Gooseprairie	224	46.54 N	121.15 W
Goostrey	262	53.13 N	2.20 W
Gooty	122	15.07 N	77.38 E
Gopālganj, Bhārat	124	26.28 N	84.26 E
Gopālganj, Bngl.	124	23.01 N	89.50 E
Gopālnagar, Bhārat	126	23.03 N	88.45 E
Gopālnagar, Bhārat	272b	22.50 N	88.14 E
Gopālpur, Bhārat	272b	22.38 N	88.27 E
Gopālpur, Bngl.	126	24.12 N	89.01 E
Gopeng	114	4.28 N	101.10 E
Göpfritz	61	48.43 N	15.24 E
Gopīballabhpur	126	22.13 N	86.54 E
Gopichettipālaiyam	122	11.28 N	77.27 E
Gopinagar	272b	22.50 N	88.07 E
Goppenstein	58	46.22 N	7.45 E
Göppingen	56	48.42 N	9.40 E
Gor	123	35.32 N	74.31 E
Góra, Pol.	30	51.40 N	16.33 E
Gora, S.S.S.R.	76	60.02 N	41.43 E
Gor'ačegorsk	86	55.24 N	88.55 E
Gor'ačij Kl'uč	84	44.37 N	39.07 E
Gor'ačinsk	88	52.59 N	108.18 E
Goradit	144	11.25 N	38.25 E
Goradiz	84	39.27 N	47.20 E
Gora Imandan-Makit ∧	89	54.06 N	117.50 E
Góra Kalwaria	30	51.59 N	21.12 E
Gorakhpur	124	26.45 N	83.22 E
Gor'any	76	55.25 N	29.02 E
Goras	124	25.32 N	76.56 E
Goražde	38	43.40 N	18.56 E
Gorbačevo Michajlovka	83	47.50 N	38.00 E
Gorbatov	80	56.08 N	43.04 E
Gorbatovka	80	56.15 N	43.45 E
Gorbica	88	53.06 N	119.13 E
Gorboviči	76	53.49 N	30.41 E
Gorčucha	80	57.43 N	43.43 E
Gorda, Punta ≻, Chile	248	19.18 S	70.18 W
Gorda, Punta ≻, Méx.	234	19.14 N	96.11 W
Gorda, Punta ≻, Nic.	236	14.21 N	83.12 W
Gorda, Punta ≻, Nic.	236	11.26 N	83.48 W
Gordejevka	76	52.59 N	31.58 E
Gordes, Fr.	62	43.54 N	5.12 E
Gördes, Tür.	130	38.54 N	28.18 E
Gordil	146	9.44 N	21.35 E
Gørding	41	55.29 N	8.48 E
Gordium ⊥	130	39.41 N	32.01 E
Gordo	194	33.19 N	87.54 W
Gordo, Cerro ∧	234	20.46 N	102.35 W
Gordola	58	46.11 N	8.52 E
Gordon, Scot., U.K.	46	55.41 N	2.34 W
Gordon, Ga., U.S.	192	32.53 N	83.20 W
Gordon, Nebr., U.S.	198	42.48 N	102.12 W
Gordon, Ohio, U.S.	218	39.56 N	84.31 W
Gordon, Pa., U.S.	208	40.45 N	76.21 W
Gordon, Wis., U.S.	190	46.15 N	91.48 W
Gordon ≃	224	48.35 N	124.24 W
Gordon, Isla I	254	54.58 S	69.35 W
Gordon Creek ≃	198	42.49 N	100.40 W
Gordon Downs	162	18.44 S	128.35 E
Gordon Heights	207	40.51 N	72.58 W
Gordon Horne Peak ∧	182	51.46 N	118.50 W
Gordon Indian Reserve ⬥[4]	184	51.16 N	104.16 W
Gordon Lake ⊜, Alta., Can.	184	56.30 N	110.25 W
Gordon Lake ⊜, Sask., Can.	184	55.50 N	106.26 W
Gordon Lakes	276	41.03 N	74.22 W
Gordon Pass C	220	26.06 N	81.48 W
Gordon River	224	48.47 N	124.21 W
Gordon's Bay	158	34.10 S	18.52 E
Gordonsville	188	38.08 N	78.11 W
Gordonton	172	37.40 S	175.18 E
Gordonvale	166	17.05 S	145.47 E
Gordonville	220	27.57 N	81.49 W
Gore, Austl.	166	28.17 S	151.29 E
Gore, N.S., Can.	186	45.07 N	63.43 W
Gore, N.Z.	172	46.06 S	168.58 E
Goré, Tchad	146	7.53 N	16.40 E
Gore, Yai.	144	8.08 N	35.33 E
Gore Bay	190	45.55 N	82.28 W
Gorebridge	46	55.51 N	3.02 W
Goreda	164	3.39 S	134.58 E
Goree	196	33.28 N	99.31 W
Goreeis	156	20.00 S	15.45 E
Gore Hill	274a	33.49 S	151.11 E
Görele	130	41.02 N	39.00 E
Gorelki	82	54.15 N	37.37 E
Goreloje, S.S.S.R.	80	52.57 N	41.28 E
Goreloje, S.S.S.R.	84	41.14 N	43.42 E
Gorelovo	265a	59.47 N	30.08 E
Gorelyj ≃	265a	59.58 N	30.28 E
Göreme ⊥	130	38.26 N	34.54 E
Gore Mountain ∧	188	44.55 N	71.48 W
Goreng Pass)(	124	30.17 N	90.14 E
Gorenki	265b	55.48 N	37.55 E
Gore Point ≻, Austl.	166	17.38 S	139.56 E
Gore Point ≻, Alaska, U.S.	180	59.12 N	151.00 W
Goretovka ≃	265b	55.56 N	37.20 E
Goreville	194	37.33 N	88.58 W
Gorey, Eire	48	52.40 N	6.18 W
Gorey, Jersey	43b	49.12 N	2.02 W
Gorgān	128	36.50 N	54.29 E
Gorgān ≃	128	36.59 N	54.05 E
Gorgany ⩕	78	48.30 N	24.00 E
Gorge Lake ⊜[1]	224	48.42 N	121.13 W
Görgeshausen	56	50.24 N	7.56 E
Gorgoglione	68	40.23 N	16.09 E
Gorgol Blanc ≃	150	16.14 N	12.58 W
Gorgol Noir ≃	150	16.13 N	12.58 W
Gorgona, Isla I	246	2.59 N	78.12 W
Gorgonzola	62	45.32 N	9.24 E
Gorgor	248	10.35 S	77.02 W
Gorgora	144	12.13 N	37.16 E
Gorgota	38	44.47 N	26.05 E
Gorgova	38	45.11 N	29.10 E
Gorham, Maine, U.S.	188	43.41 N	70.26 W
Gorham, N.H., U.S.	188	44.23 N	71.10 W
Gorham, N.Y., U.S.	210	42.48 N	77.08 W
Gorhambury House ⊥	260	51.47 N	0.24 W
Gori	84	41.58 N	44.07 E
Goria	272b	22.24 N	88.29 E
Gorica → Gorizia	64	45.57 N	13.38 E
Goricy	76	57.09 N	36.44 E
Gorin ≃	89	50.45 N	137.50 E
Gorinchem	52	51.50 N	5.00 E
Goring	42	51.32 N	1.09 W
Goring-by-Sea	42	50.49 N	0.25 W
Goring Gap ∨	42	51.32 N	1.08 W
Goris	84	39.31 N	46.23 E
Göritz	54	53.24 N	13.54 E
Göritzhain	54	50.58 N	12.47 E
Gorizia	64	45.57 N	13.38 E
Gorizia □[4]	64	45.55 N	13.30 E
Gorj □[4]	38	45.00 N	23.20 E
Gorjani	38	45.24 N	18.21 E
Gor'kaja Balka	84	44.17 N	43.59 E
Gor'kaja Balka ∨	84	44.38 N	45.00 E
Görke	54	53.51 N	13.38 E
Gorki, S.S.S.R.	76	54.17 N	30.59 E
Gorki, S.S.S.R.	80	57.38 N	45.05 E
Gorki → Gor'kij, S.S.S.R.	80	56.20 N	44.00 E
Gorki, S.S.S.R.	82	55.30 N	37.45 E
Gorki, S.S.S.R.	82	54.18 N	36.08 E
Gor'kij (Gorky)	80	56.20 N	44.00 E
Gorki Vtoryje	265b	55.44 N	37.11 E
Gor'kiy → Gor'kij	80	56.20 N	44.00 E
Gor'koje, Ozero ⊜	86	52.30 N	81.20 E
Gor'ko-Solenoje, Ozero ⊜	80	49.20 N	46.05 E
Gor'kovskoje	86	55.22 N	74.24 E
Gor'kovskoje Vodochranilišče ⊜[1]	80	57.00 N	43.10 E
Gorky → Gor'kij	80	56.20 N	44.00 E
Gorlago	62	45.40 N	9.49 E
Gorla Maggiore	266b	45.40 N	8.53 E
Gorla Minore	266b	45.39 N	8.54 E
Gorleston on Sea	42	52.36 N	1.43 E
Gørlev	41	55.32 N	11.14 E
Gorlice	30	49.40 N	21.10 E
Görlitz	54	51.09 N	14.59 E
Gorlosen	54	53.11 N	11.27 E
Gorlovka	83	48.18 N	38.03 E
Gorlovo	76	53.50 N	39.02 E
Gorm, Loch ⊜	46	55.48 N	6.25 W
Gorman, Calif., U.S.	228	34.48 N	118.51 W
Gorman, Tex., U.S.	196	32.12 N	98.41 W
Gorman Creek ≃	228	34.38 N	118.45 W
Görmin	54	53.59 N	13.16 E
Gorn'ackij, S.S.S.R.	24	67.32 N	64.03 E
Gorn'ackij, S.S.S.R.	78	48.17 N	40.55 E
Gorn'ackij, S.S.S.R.	78	47.42 N	34.09 E
Gorna Dzhumaya → Blagoevgrad	38	42.01 N	23.06 E
Gornaja Prolejka	80	49.24 N	44.59 E
Gorn'ak, S.S.S.R.	76	53.36 N	39.29 E
Gorn'ak, S.S.S.R.	78	50.20 N	24.10 E
Gorn'ak, S.S.S.R.	83	48.04 N	37.24 E
Gorn'ak, S.S.S.R.	86	51.00 N	81.29 E
Gornalunga ≃	70	37.24 N	15.03 E
Gorna Orjahovica	38	43.07 N	25.41 E
Gornau	54	50.46 N	13.02 E
Gornergrat ♠	58	45.49 N	7.47 E
Gornja Radgona	61	46.41 N	16.00 E
Gornji Grad	36	46.18 N	14.49 E
Gornji Milanovac	38	44.01 N	20.27 E
Gornji Vakuf	36	43.56 N	17.35 E
Gorno-Altajsk	86	51.58 N	85.58 E
Gorno-Altajskaja Avtonomnaja Oblast' □[8]	86	51.00 N	86.00 E
Gorno-Badachšanskaja Avtonomnaja Oblast' □[4]	85	38.30 N	73.00 E
Gorno-Čujskij	88	59.12 N	112.25 E
Gornoje	86	48.29 N	85.00 E
Gorno-Lesnoj Zapovednik ♠	85	41.10 N	69.55 E
Gornopravdinsk	86	60.07 N	69.54 E
Gornostajevka	78	47.01 N	33.44 E
Gorno-Vod'anoje	80	49.16 N	44.56 E
Gornozavodsk, S.S.S.R.	86	58.20 N	58.32 E
Gornozavodsk, S.S.S.R.	89	46.34 N	141.49 E
Gornyj, S.S.S.R.	80	51.46 N	48.34 E
Gornyj, S.S.S.R.	89	50.48 N	136.29 E
Gornyj, S.S.S.R.	89	44.57 N	133.59 E
Gornyj Balyklej	80	49.34 N	45.04 E
Gornyj Tikič ≃	78	48.47 N	30.53 E
Goro, It.	64	44.51 N	12.18 E
Goro, N. Cal.	175f	22.16 S	167.02 E
Goro, Tchad	146	8.37 N	18.08 E
Goro, Yai.	144	6.56 N	40.32 E
Gorochan ∧	144	9.22 N	37.04 E
Gorochov	78	50.30 N	24.45 E
Gorochovatka	83	49.21 N	37.31 E
Gorochovec	80	56.12 N	42.40 E
Gorochovje	76	56.31 N	30.29 E
Gorodec, S.S.S.R.	76	52.58 N	30.21 E
Gorodec, S.S.S.R.	76	53.33 N	30.02 E
Gorodec, S.S.S.R.	76	52.12 N	24.40 E
Gorodec, S.S.S.R.	76	58.32 N	29.47 E
Gorodec, S.S.S.R.	78	51.17 N	26.19 E
Gorodec, S.S.S.R.	80	56.38 N	43.30 E
Gorodeja	76	53.19 N	26.32 E
Gorodenka	38	48.41 N	25.29 E
Gorodišče, S.S.S.R.	76	53.44 N	29.48 E
Gorodišče, S.S.S.R.	76	53.19 N	26.00 E
Gorodišče, S.S.S.R.	76	59.38 N	32.08 E
Gorodišče, S.S.S.R.	78	49.17 N	31.27 E
Gorodišče, S.S.S.R.	78	51.09 N	38.04 E
Gorodišče, S.S.S.R.	80	48.48 N	44.29 E
Gorodišče, S.S.S.R.	80	53.17 N	45.42 E
Gorodišče, S.S.S.R.	82	54.53 N	38.13 E
Gorodišče, S.S.S.R.	82	56.47 N	38.52 E
Gorodišče, S.S.S.R.	83	48.19 N	38.39 E
Gorodišče, S.S.S.R.	83	49.03 N	39.38 E
Gorodišči	82	55.52 N	39.05 E
Gorodkovka	78	48.23 N	28.42 E
Gorodn'a, S.S.S.R.	78	51.53 N	31.36 E
Gorodn'a, S.S.S.R.	82	56.43 N	36.19 E
Gorodn'a, S.S.S.R.	82	54.57 N	38.49 E
Gorodnica	78	50.48 N	27.20 E
Gorodno	76	57.32 N	29.35 E
Gorodok, S.S.S.R.	76	55.28 N	29.59 E
Gorodok, S.S.S.R.	78	49.10 N	26.34 E
Gorodok, S.S.S.R.	78	49.47 N	23.39 E
Gorod'onka	78	48.41 N	25.29 E
Goroka	164	6.05 S	145.25 E
Gorokan	170	33.16 S	151.30 E
Gorom-Gorom	150	14.26 N	0.14 W
Gorong, Pulau I	164	3.59 S	131.25 E
Gorongosa ≃	156	20.30 S	34.40 E
Gorongosa, Parque Nacional da ♠	156	18.45 S	34.15 E
Gorongosa, Serra da ∧	154	18.30 S	34.03 E
Gorontalo	112	0.33 N	123.03 E
Goronyo	150	13.29 N	5.39 E
Górowo Iławeckie	30	54.17 N	20.30 E
Gorple Reservoirs ⊜[1]	262	53.47 N	2.06 W
Gorran ⊜	40	59.43 N	17.32 E
Gorredijk	52	53.00 N	6.05 E
Gorror	174q	9.27 N	138.04 E
Görsdorf	54	51.54 N	13.29 E
Goršečnoje	78	51.32 N	38.02 E
Gorsedd	262	53.17 N	3.16 W
Gorseinon	42	51.40 N	4.02 W
Gorskaja	265a	60.03 N	29.59 E
Gorskoje	83	48.46 N	38.30 E
Gorškovo	82	54.26 N	37.59 E
Gorst	224	47.32 N	122.42 W
Gort	48	53.04 N	8.50 W
Gortahork	48	55.08 N	8.09 W
Gorton ⬥[8]	262	53.27 N	2.10 W
Görtschitz ≃	61	46.45 N	14.32 E
Görukle	130	40.14 N	28.50 E
Gorul, Muntele ∧	38	45.48 N	26.25 E
Gorumna Island I	48	53.14 N	9.40 W
Gorutuba ≃	255	14.57 S	43.33 W
Görwihl	58	47.39 N	8.04 E
Gory, S.S.S.R.	76	54.16 N	31.13 E
Gory, S.S.S.R.	80	48.38 N	51.46 E
Goryn' ≃	78	52.08 N	27.17 E
Görz → Gorizia	64	45.57 N	13.38 E
Gorzano, Monte ∧	66	42.37 N	13.24 E
Gorze	56	49.03 N	6.00 E
Görzig	54	51.40 N	12.00 E
Görzke	54	52.10 N	12.22 E
Górzno	30	53.13 N	19.38 E
Gorzów Śląski	30	51.02 N	18.24 E
Gorzów Wielkopolski (Landsberg an der Warthe)	30	52.44 N	15.15 E
Górzyca	54	52.29 N	14.40 E
Gosāba	126	22.10 N	88.48 E
Gosainthan ∧	120	28.22 N	85.50 E
Gosairhāt	126	23.05 N	90.26 E
Gosaldo	64	46.13 N	11.58 E
Gosau	64	47.34 N	13.31 E
Gosauseen ⊜	64	47.32 N	13.31 E
Gosberg	60	49.42 N	11.07 E
Gošča	78	50.36 N	26.41 E
Göschenen	58	46.40 N	8.35 E
Goschen Strait ⊍	164	10.09 S	150.56 E
Gose	96	34.27 N	135.44 E
Gosen, D.D.R.	264a	52.24 N	13.43 E
Gosen, Nihon	92	37.44 N	139.11 E
Gosford	170	33.26 S	151.21 E
Gosforth, Eng., U.K.	44	55.01 N	1.37 W
Gosforth, Eng., U.K.	44	54.26 N	3.27 W
Gosforth Park ♠	273d	26.14 S	28.10 E
Gosforth Park Race Course ♠	273d	26.14 S	28.08 E
Goshabi	140	17.58 N	31.06 E
Goshen, N.S., Can.	186	45.23 N	61.59 W
Goshen, Calif., U.S.	226	36.21 N	119.25 W
Goshen, Conn., U.S.	207	41.50 N	73.14 W
Goshen, Ind., U.S.	216	41.35 N	85.50 W
Goshen, Mass., U.S.	207	42.27 N	72.48 W
Goshen, N.J., U.S.	208	39.08 N	74.51 W
Goshen, N.Y., U.S.	210	41.24 N	74.20 W
Goshen, Ohio, U.S.	218	39.14 N	84.10 W
Goshiki	96	34.24 N	134.47 E
Goshogawara	92	40.48 N	140.27 E
Goshute Indian Reservation ⬥[4]	200	39.53 N	114.08 W
Goshute Lake ⊜	204	40.08 N	114.38 W
Goshute Valley ∨	204	40.40 N	114.30 W
Goslar	52	51.54 N	10.25 E
Gosnells	168a	32.04 S	116.00 E
Gospić	36	44.33 N	15.23 E
Gosport, Eng., U.K.	42	50.48 N	1.08 W
Gosport, Ind., U.S.	194	39.21 N	86.40 W
Gossa	54	51.40 N	12.26 E
Gossas	150	14.30 N	16.04 W
Gossau	58	47.25 N	9.15 E
Gosse ⬥[8]	263	51.08 N	7.01 E
Gosselies	56	50.28 N	4.25 E
Gössenheim	56	50.01 N	9.46 E
Gossensass → Colle Isarco	64	46.56 N	11.26 E
Gosser Hill	279b	40.37 N	79.37 W
Gossi	150	15.49 N	1.17 W
Gossinga	140	8.39 N	25.59 E
Gössl	64	47.38 N	13.54 E
Gössnitz	54	50.53 N	12.26 E
Gossolengo	62	44.59 N	9.37 E
Gössweinstein	60	49.46 N	11.20 E
Gostagajevskaja	78	45.01 N	37.30 E
Gostilovo	82	55.18 N	38.36 E
Gostiščevo	78	50.47 N	36.39 E
Gostivar	38	41.47 N	20.54 E
Göstling	61	47.48 N	14.55 E
Gostyń	30	51.53 N	17.00 E
Gostynin	30	52.26 N	19.29 E
Gosudarev Bajrak	83	48.21 N	38.08 E
Göta älv ≃	26	57.42 N	11.52 E
Göta kanal ≍	40	58.50 N	13.58 E
Gotanno ⬥[8]	268	35.46 N	139.49 E
Gotchen Creek ≃	224	46.00 N	121.30 W
Got Creek ≃	284a	43.03 N	78.42 W
Gotebo	196	35.04 N	98.53 W
Göteborg (Gothenburg)	26	57.43 N	11.58 E
Göteborgs Och Bohus län □[6]	26	58.30 N	11.30 E
Gotel Mountains ⩕	152	6.55 N	11.15 E
Gotemba	94	35.18 N	138.56 E
Götene	26	58.32 N	13.29 E
Gotešty	78	46.09 N	28.10 E
Gotha, D.D.R.	54	50.57 N	10.41 E
Gotha, Fla., U.S.	220	28.32 N	81.31 W
Gothem	26	57.35 N	18.43 E
Gothenburg → Göteborg, Sve.	26	57.43 N	11.58 E
Gothenburg, Nebr., U.S.	198	40.56 N	100.09 W
Gothèye	150	13.52 N	1.34 E
Gotland I	26	57.30 N	18.33 E
Gotlands Län □[6]	26	57.30 N	18.30 E
Gotoputovo	86	56.46 N	70.10 E
Gotō-rettō II	92	32.50 N	129.00 E
Gotska Sandön I	26	58.23 N	19.16 E
Gōtsu	96	35.00 N	132.14 E
Gottenheim	58	48.03 N	7.44 E
Götterswickerhamm	263	51.35 N	6.40 E
Gottesbrücke	264a	52.25 N	13.49 E
Gotthard Tunnel ⬥[5]	58	46.35 N	8.35 E
Göttin	264a	52.27 N	12.54 E
Götting	64	47.52 N	11.56 E
Göttingen, B.R.D.	52	51.32 N	9.55 E
Göttingen, B.R.D.	56	50.52 N	8.46 E
Göttin See ⊜	264a	52.28 N	12.54 E
Gottmadingen	58	47.44 N	8.47 E
Gottolengo	64	45.17 N	10.16 E
Gottorf, Schloss ⊥	41	54.30 N	9.32 E
Gottsbüren	52	51.35 N	9.30 E
Gottsdorf	60	48.32 N	13.44 E
Gottvaterkapelle ♁[1]	60	49.42 N	11.41 E
Gottwaldov	30	49.13 N	17.41 E
Götzendorf	264b	48.01 N	16.35 E
Götzis	58	47.20 N	9.38 E
Gouala ≃	150	10.14 N	8.38 W
Gouarec	32	48.13 N	3.11 W
Goubangzi	104	41.22 N	121.46 E
Goubone	146	20.43 N	17.08 E
Gouchang	102	27.00 N	105.44 E
Gouda, Ned.	52	52.01 N	4.43 E
Gouda, S. Afr.	158	33.19 S	19.04 E
Goudet	62	44.53 N	3.55 E
Goudge	252	34.40 S	68.08 W
Goudhurst	42	51.07 N	0.28 E
Goudiry	150	14.11 N	12.43 W
Goudoumaria	146	13.42 N	11.10 E
Goudswaard	52	51.47 N	4.16 E
Gouéké	150	8.02 N	8.43 W
Goûfi, Djebel el ∧	34	36.57 N	6.27 E
Gougezhuang	105	38.53 N	116.11 E
Gough Island I	10	40.20 S	10.00 W
Gough Lake ⊜	182	52.02 N	112.28 W
Gouin, Réservoir ⊜[1]	176	48.38 N	74.54 W
Goujiachang	107	30.36 N	106.33 E
Goujiawopeng	104	40.48 N	122.29 E
Goukou	89	48.39 N	122.06 E
Goulais ≃	190	46.43 N	84.27 W
Goulbin ⬥[1]	150	14.00 N	7.00 E
Goulburn	170	34.45 S	149.43 E
Goulburn ≃	169	36.41 S	145.12 E
Goulburn Islands II	164	11.33 S	133.26 E
Goulburn Weir ⊜[1]	169	36.45 S	145.08 E
Gould	194	33.59 N	91.34 W
Gould City	190	46.06 N	85.42 W
Gould Park	214	40.04 N	82.53 W
Goulds	220	25.33 N	80.23 W
Gouldsboro	210	41.44 N	75.28 W
Gouldsboro State Park ♠	210	41.13 N	75.28 W
Goulet Lake ⊜	184	55.23 N	96.18 W
Goulia	150	10.01 N	7.11 W
Goulicun	106	31.40 N	120.00 E
Goulimime	148	28.56 N	10.04 W
Goulmima	148	31.02 N	5.00 W
Goumbati ∧[2]	150	13.08 N	12.06 W
Goumbou, Gabon	152	3.11 S	10.45 E
Goumbou, Mali	150	14.59 N	7.27 W
Gouménissa	38	40.57 N	22.27 E
Goumois	58	47.16 N	6.57 E
Gouna	146	8.32 N	13.34 E
Gounda ≃	146	9.25 N	20.57 E
Goundam	150	16.25 N	3.40 W
Goundi	146	9.22 N	17.22 E
Gounou Gaya	146	9.38 N	15.31 E
Goupillières	261	48.53 N	1.46 E
Gouraya	34	36.34 N	1.55 E
Gourbassi	150	13.24 N	11.38 W
Gourbeyre	241o	16.00 N	61.42 W
Gourdhead Run ≃	279b	40.33 N	79.57 W
Gourdon, Fr.	32	44.44 N	1.23 E
Gourdon, Fr.	62	43.43 N	6.59 E
Gouré	150	13.58 N	10.18 E
Gourey	150	13.13 N	2.21 W
Gouri, Ruins of ⊥	124	24.53 N	88.07 E
Gourin	32	48.08 N	3.36 W
Gouripur	124	24.46 N	90.34 E
Gourits ≃	158	34.21 S	21.52 E
Gourlay Lake ⊜	190	48.52 N	84.54 W
Gourma Rharous	150	16.53 N	1.55 W
Gournay-en-Bray	50	49.29 N	1.44 E
Gournay-sur-Marne	261	48.52 N	2.34 E
Gouro	146	19.33 N	19.33 E
Gourock	46	55.58 N	4.49 W
Goussainville	50	49.01 N	2.28 E
Goussonville	261	48.55 N	1.46 E
Goutou	105	39.49 N	117.11 E
Gouvêa	255	18.27 S	43.44 W
Gouveia	266c	38.50 N	9.26 W
Gouverneur	212	44.20 N	75.28 W
Gouyadong	100	25.10 N	112.55 E
Gov'altaj □[4]	102	45.30 N	96.00 E
Govan	184	51.18 N	105.00 W
Go-vap	269c	10.49 N	106.41 E
Govardhan	124	27.30 N	77.28 E
Gove	198	38.58 N	100.29 W
Govea ≃	286b	22.56 N	82.30 W
Govenlock	184	49.15 N	109.48 W
Goverla, Gora ∧	78	48.10 N	24.32 E
Governador, Ilha do I	287a	22.48 S	43.12 W
Governador Portela	256	22.29 S	43.30 W
Governador Valadares	255	18.51 S	41.56 W
Government Camp	224	45.18 N	21.45 W
Governor Dodge State Park ♠	190	43.00 N	90.07 W
Governor Generoso	116	6.39 N	126.05 E
Governor Head ≻	170	35.07 S	150.46 E
Governors Harbour	238	25.10 N	76.14 W
Governors Island I	276	40.41 N	74.01 W
Govind Balabh Pant Sāgar ⊜[1]	124	24.05 N	82.50 E
Govindgarh	124	24.23 N	81.18 E
Govind Sāgar ⊜[1]	123	31.20 N	76.45 E
Gowan ≃	184	55.49 N	94.08 W
Gowanda	210	42.28 N	78.56 W
Gowan Range ⩕	166	25.00 S	145.00 E
Gowen City	208	40.45 N	76.32 W
Gower ≻[1]	42	51.36 N	4.10 W
Gowerton	42	51.39 N	4.01 W
Gowk	128	29.51 N	57.44 E
Gowmal (Gumal) ≃	120	31.56 N	70.22 E
Gowmal Kalay	120	32.29 N	68.55 E
Gowna, Lough ⊜	48	53.51 N	7.34 W
Gowrie	198	42.17 N	94.17 W
Gowy ≃	262	53.17 N	2.51 W
Goya	252	29.08 S	59.16 W
Goyania → Goiânia	255	16.40 S	49.16 W
Goyatz	54	52.01 N	14.09 E
Goyave	241o	16.08 N	61.34 W
Goyaves, Îlets à II	241o	16.10 N	61.48 W
Goyder ≃	164	12.38 S	135.11 E
Goyder Creek ≃	162	25.39 S	134.47 E
Goyelle, Lac ⊜	186	50.47 N	60.45 W
Goyeneche	258	35.20 S	58.43 W
Goyerkāta	124	26.42 N	89.02 E
Göykazi	130	36.14 N	29.59 E
Göynücek	130	40.24 N	35.32 E
Göynük	130	40.24 N	30.47 E
Goyt ≃	262	53.24 N	2.09 W
Goz Beïda	146	12.13 N	21.25 E
Gozdnica	30	51.26 N	15.06 E
Gozdowice	54	52.45 N	14.18 E
Gozenyama	94	36.32 N	140.20 E
Gözne	130	36.59 N	34.34 E
Gozo → GĦawdex I	36	36.03 N	14.15 E
Göz Tepe ∧[2]	267b	41.06 N	29.06 E
Gozzano	62	45.45 N	8.26 E
Graaff-Reinet	158	32.14 S	24.32 E
Graafwater	158	32.00 S	18.37 E
Graauw	52	51.20 N	4.05 E
Grabc'ovo	82	54.34 N	36.22 E
Graben	56	49.09 N	8.29 E
Grabenstätt	64	47.51 N	12.32 E
Grabill	216	41.13 N	84.58 W
Grabo	150	4.55 N	7.30 W
Grabouw	158	34.09 S	19.02 E
Grabovaja Balka, Les ♠	83	48.09 N	38.37 E
Grabovo	86	53.07 N	74.52 E
Grabow	54	53.16 N	11.34 E
Grabowiec	30	50.50 N	23.33 E
Grabów nad Prosną	30	51.31 N	18.06 E
Gračac	36	44.18 N	15.51 E
Gračanica	38	44.42 N	18.19 E
Gračanica, Manastir ♁[1]	38	42.36 N	21.09 E
Graçay	50	47.08 N	1.51 E
Grace	202	42.35 N	111.44 W
Gracefield	188	46.06 N	76.03 W
Graceham	208	39.37 N	77.24 W
Graceton	214	40.30 N	79.10 W
Graceville, Fla., U.S.	192	30.58 N	85.31 W
Graceville, Minn., U.S.	198	45.34 N	96.26 W
Gračevka	82	55.06 N	36.49 E
Gračev Kust	80	51.59 N	49.50 E
Grächen	58	46.12 N	7.50 E
Grachovo	80	56.04 N	51.58 E
Grači	80	49.49 N	43.33 E
Gracia ⬥[8]	266d	41.23 N	2.09 E
Gracias	236	14.35 N	88.35 W
Gracias a Dios □[5]	236	15.10 N	84.20 W

Symbols in the index entries represent the broad categories identified in the key at the right. Symbols with superior numbers (⩕[2]) identify subcategories (see complete key on page *I · 30*).

Kartensymbole in dem Registerverzeichnis stellen die rechts in Schlüssel erklärten Kategorien dar. Symbole mit hochgestellten Ziffern (⩕[2]) bezeichnen Unterabteilungen einer Kategorie (vgl. vollständiger Schlüssel auf Seite *I · 30*).

Los símbolos incluídos en el texto del índice representan las grandes categorias identificadas con la clave a la derecha. Los símbolos con numeros en su parte superior (⩕[2]) identifican las subcategorías (véase la clave completa en la página *I · 30*).

Les symboles de l'index représentent les catégories indiquées dans la légende à droite. Les symboles suivis d'un indice (⩕[2]) représentent des sous-catégories (voir légende complète à la page *I · 30*).

Os símbolos incluídos no texto do índice representam as grandes categorias identificadas com a chave à direita. Os símbolos com números em sua parte superior (⩕[2]) identificam as subcategorias (veja-se a chave completa à página *I · 30*).

	English	Deutsch	Español	Français	Português
∧	Mountain	Berg	Montaña	Montagne	Montanha
⩕	Mountains	Berge	Montañas	Montagnes	Montanhas
)(	Pass	Pass	Paso	Col	Passo
∨	Valley, Canyon	Tal, Cañon	Valle, Cañón	Vallée, Canyon	Vale, Canhão
⌣	Plain	Ebene	Llano	Plaine	Planície
≻	Cape	Kap	Cabo	Cap	Cabo
I	Island	Insel	Isla	Île	Ilha
II	Islands	Inseln	Islas	Îles	Ilhas
⊥	Other Topographic Features	Andere Topographische Objekte	Otros Elementos Topográficos	Autres données topographiques	Cutros Elementos Topográficos

ESPAÑOL

Nombre	Página	Lat.°′	Long.°′ W=Oeste
Gracias a Dios, Cabo ≻	236	15.00 N	83.10 W
Gračiki ≃	83	48.30 N	39.52 E
Graciosa I	148a	39.04 N	28.00 W
Graciosa, Isla I	148	29.15 N	13.30 W
Gračov	80	49.26 N	41.32 E
Gračovka	80	52.07 N	40.01 E
Gradačac	38	44.53 N	18.26 E
Gradara	66	43.57 N	12.46 E
Gradaús	250	7.43 S	51.11 W
Gradaús, Serra dos ⛰[1]	250	8.00 S	50.45 W
Gr'adcy	76	56.24 N	31.55 E
Gräddö	40	59.46 N	19.02 E
Gradisca d'Isonzo	64	45.53 N	13.30 E
Gradižsk	78	49.13 N	33.07 E
Grado, Esp.	34	43.23 N	6.04 W
Grado, It.	64	45.40 N	13.23 E
Grado, Laguna di C	64	45.43 N	13.20 E
Gradoli	66	42.39 N	11.51 E
Grady, Ark., U.S.	194	34.05 N	91.42 W
Grady, N. Mex., U.S.	196	34.49 N	103.19 W
Gradyville	285	39.57 N	75.28 W
Graemsay I	46	58.56 N	3.17 W
Græsted	41	56.04 N	12.17 E
Graettinger	198	43.14 N	94.45 W
Gräfelfing	60	48.07 N	11.25 E
Grafenau	60	48.52 N	13.25 E
Gräfenberg	60	49.39 N	11.15 E
Grafenberg ◆[8]	263	51.14 N	6.50 E
Gräfenhainichen	54	51.44 N	12.27 E
Gräfenroda	54	50.45 N	10.48 E
Gräfenthal	54	50.31 N	11.18 E
Gräfentonna	54	51.05 N	10.44 E
Grafenwöhr	60	49.43 N	11.54 E
Graffignano	66	42.34 N	12.12 E
Grafham Water ⊜	42	52.17 N	0.20 W
Gräfinau-Angstedt	54	50.42 N	11.01 E
Grafing bei München	60	48.02 N	11.59 E
Gråfjell ∧	26	60.16 N	9.29 E
Graford	196	32.56 N	98.14 W
Gräfrath ◆[8]	263	51.13 N	7.04 E
Grafschaft Bentheim □[9]	52	52.30 N	7.00 E
Grafton, Austl.	166	29.41 S	152.56 E
Grafton, Ont., Can.	212	44.00 N	78.01 W
Grafton, Ill., U.S.	219	38.58 N	90.26 W
Grafton, Mass., U.S.	207	42.12 N	71.41 W
Grafton, N. Dak., U.S.	198	48.25 N	97.25 W
Grafton, N.Y., U.S.	210	42.46 N	73.27 W
Grafton, Ohio, U.S.	214	41.16 N	82.04 W
Grafton, W. Va., U.S.	188	39.20 N	80.01 W
Grafton, Wis., U.S.	190	43.19 N	87.56 W
Grafton, Cape ≻	166	16.52 S	145.55 E
Grafton Lakes State Park ♠	210	42.48 N	73.28 W
Grafty Green	260	51.12 N	0.41 E
Graglia	62	45.33 N	7.59 E
Gragnano	68	40.41 N	14.31 E
Gragnano Trebbiense	62	45.01 N	9.34 E
Graham, Calif., U.S.	280	33.58 N	118.15 W
Graham, N.C., U.S.	192	36.05 N	79.25 W
Graham, Tex., U.S.	196	33.06 N	98.35 W
Graham, Wash., U.S.	224	47.03 N	122.15 W
Graham, Mount ∧	200	32.42 N	109.52 W
Graham Cave State Park ♠	219	38.55 N	91.32 W
Graham Creek ≃	218	38.49 N	85.39 W
Graham Island I	182	53.40 N	132.30 W
Graham Lake ⊜, Ont., Can.	212	44.34 N	75.53 W
Graham Lake ⊜, Maine, U.S.	186	44.40 N	68.25 W
Graham Land ◆[1]	9	66.00 S	63.30 W
Graham Memorial Park ♠	284b	39.25 N	76.30 W
Graham Moore, Cape ≻	176	72.52 N	76.04 W
Graham Moore Bay C	176	75.26 N	101.25 W
Grahamstad → Grahamstown	158	33.19 S	26.31 E
Grahamstown	158	33.19 S	26.31 E
Grahamsville	210	41.51 N	74.33 W
Grahn	218	38.17 N	83.05 W
Graïba	148	34.30 N	10.13 E
Graie, Alpi (Alpes Grées) ⛰	62	45.30 N	7.10 E
Grain	260	51.28 N	0.43 E
Grain, Isle of I	42	51.27 N	0.41 E
Grain Coast ⌖[2]	150	5.00 N	9.00 W
Grainfield	198	39.07 N	100.28 W
Grajagan	115a	8.35 S	114.13 E
Grajagan, Teluk C	115a	8.40 S	114.18 E
Grajaú	250	5.49 S	46.08 W
Grajaú ≃	250	3.41 S	44.48 W
Grajewo	30	53.39 N	22.27 E
Grajvoron	78	50.28 N	35.39 E
Gram	41	55.17 N	9.04 E
Gramacho	287a	22.44 S	43.18 W
Gramada	38	43.50 N	22.39 E
Gramado	252	29.24 S	50.54 W
Gramalote	246	7.53 N	72.48 W
Gramat	32	44.47 N	1.43 E
Gramatneusiedl	264b	48.02 N	16.29 E
Grambling	194	32.32 N	92.43 W
Gramilla	252	27.18 S	64.37 W
Gramínea	256	22.10 S	46.38 W
Grammer	218	39.09 N	85.43 W
Grammichele	70	37.13 N	14.38 E
Grammont → Geraardsbergen	50	50.46 N	3.52 E
Gramoteino	86	54.31 N	86.22 E
Grampian	214	40.58 N	78.37 W
Grampian □[4]	46	57.15 N	2.45 W
Grampian Mountains ⛰	46	56.55 N	4.00 W
Gramschatz	56	49.56 N	9.58 E
Gramsh	38	40.52 N	20.11 E
Gramzow	54	53.12 N	14.00 E
Gran → Esztergom	30	47.48 N	18.45 E
Grana ≃	62	44.25 N	7.27 E
Granaatboskolk	158	30.02 S	19.51 E
Granada, Col.	246	3.34 N	73.45 W
Granada, Esp.	34	37.13 N	3.41 W
Granada, Nic.	236	11.56 N	85.57 W
Granada, Pil.	116	10.40 N	123.02 E
Granada, Colo., U.S.	198	38.04 N	102.19 W
Granada, Minn., U.S.	190	43.42 N	94.21 W
Granada □[5]	236	11.50 N	86.00 W
Granada → Grenada □[1]	241k	12.07 N	61.40 W
Granada Hills ◆[8]	280	34.16 N	118.31 W
Granadella	34	41.21 N	0.40 E
Granado	286d	12.04 S	76.57 W
Granaglione	66	44.07 N	10.58 E
Gran Altiplanicie Central ⛰[1]	254	48.55 S	69.25 W
Granard	48	53.47 N	7.30 W
Granarolo dell'Emilia	64	44.33 N	11.27 E
Granatello	70	37.53 N	12.32 E
Gran Bahía Australiana → Great Australian Bight C[3]	162	35.00 S	135.00 E
Gran Bajo de San Julián ∨	254	49.30 S	68.30 W
Gran Barrera de Arrecifes → Great Barrier Reef ⟡[2]	160	18.00 S	145.50 E
Granbergsdal	40	59.24 N	14.35 E
Granbury	222	32.27 N	97.47 W
Granbury, Lake ⊜[1]	222	32.25 N	97.45 W
Granby, Qué., Can.	206	45.24 N	72.44 W
Granby, Colo., U.S.	200	40.05 N	105.56 W
Granby, Conn., U.S.	207	41.57 N	72.47 W
Granby, Mass., U.S.	207	42.15 N	72.31 W
Granby, Mo., U.S.	194	36.55 N	94.15 W
Granby ≃	182	49.03 N	118.25 W
Granby, Lake ⊜[1]	200	40.09 N	105.50 W

FRANÇAIS

Nom	Page	Lat.°′	Long.°′ W=Ouest
Gran Canal del Desagüe ☰	286a	19.29 N	99.05 W
Gran Canaria I	148	28.00 N	15.36 W
Grancey-le-Château	58	47.40 N	5.02 E
Gran Chaco ⊻	18	23.00 S	60.00 W
Grand	58	48.23 N	5.29 E
Grand ≃, Ont., Can.	212	42.51 N	79.34 W
Grand ≃, U.S.	194	39.23 N	93.06 W
Grand ≃, Mich., U.S.	216	43.04 N	86.15 W
Grand ≃, Ohio, U.S.	214	41.46 N	81.17 W
Grand ≃, S. Dak., U.S.	198	45.40 N	100.32 W
Grand ≃, Wis., U.S.	190	43.45 N	89.16 W
Grand, East Fork ≃	194	40.12 N	94.21 W
Grand, Lac ⊜	190	47.10 N	76.57 W
Grand, North Fork ≃	198	45.47 N	102.16 W
Grand, South Fork ≃	198	45.43 N	102.17 W
Grand Aféri	150	6.19 N	3.57 W
Grandas	34	43.13 N	6.52 W
Grandas de Salime, Embalse de ⊜[1]	34	43.10 N	6.45 W
Grand Bahama I	238	26.38 N	78.25 W
Grand Ballon ∧	58	47.55 N	7.08 E
Grand Bank	186	47.06 N	55.46 W
Grand Bank ⟡[4]	16	47.00 N	52.00 W
Grand Bassa □[6]	150	6.00 N	9.30 W
Grand-Bassam	150	5.12 N	3.44 W
Grand Bay, N.B., Can.	186	45.18 N	66.12 W
Grand Bay, Ala., U.S.	194	30.29 N	88.21 W
Grand Bay C	240d	15.14 N	61.19 W
Grand Beach	184	50.35 N	96.40 W
Grand Bend	190	43.15 N	81.45 W
Grand Blanc	216	42.56 N	83.38 W
Grand-Bourg	241o	15.53 N	61.19 W
Grand Bruit	186	47.41 N	58.13 W
Grand Caille Point ≻	241f	13.52 N	61.05 W
Grand Calumet ≃	278	41.38 N	87.34 W
Grand-Calumet, Île du I	188	45.44 N	76.41 W
Grand Canal ☰, Eire	48	53.21 N	6.14 W
Grand Canal → Yunhe ☰, Zhg.	90	32.12 N	119.31 E
Grand Cane	194	32.05 N	93.49 W
Grand Cañon du Verdon ♠	62	43.47 N	6.27 E
Grand Canyon	200	36.03 N	112.09 W
Grand Canyon ∨	200	36.10 N	112.45 W
Grand Canyon National Park ♠	200	36.15 N	112.58 W
Grand Canyon of Pennsylvania ♠	210	41.43 N	77.28 W
Grand Cape Mount □[6]	150	7.00 N	11.00 W
Grand Cayman I	238	19.20 N	81.15 W
Grand Central Terminal ◆[5]	276	40.45 N	73.59 W
Grand Centre	184	54.25 N	110.13 W
Grand Cess	150	4.36 N	8.10 W
Grandchamp, Fr.	58	47.43 N	5.27 E
Grandchamp, Fr.	261	48.43 N	1.37 E
Grand-Charmont	58	47.32 N	6.50 E
Grand Chenier	194	29.46 N	92.58 W
Grand Combin ∧	58	45.56 N	7.18 E
Grand Coulee	202	47.56 N	119.00 W
Grand Coulee ∨	202	47.45 N	119.15 W
Grand Coulee Dam ◆[6]	202	47.57 N	118.59 W
Grand-Couronne	50	49.21 N	1.00 E
Grand Cul-de-Sac Marin C	241o	16.20 N	61.35 W
Grande ≃, Arg.	252	36.52 S	69.45 W
Grande ≃, Arg.	252	24.12 S	64.42 W
Grande ≃, Bol.	248	15.51 S	64.39 W
Grande ≃, Bra.	242	11.05 S	43.09 W
Grande ≃, Bra.	255	19.52 S	50.20 W
Grande ≃, Bra.	287a	22.55 S	43.25 W
Grande ≃, Bra.	287b	23.45 S	46.22 W
Grande ≃, Qué., Can.	186	48.24 N	64.30 W
Grande ≃, Chile	252	30.35 S	71.11 W
Grande ≃, Esp.	34	39.07 N	0.44 W
Grande ≃, It.	70	37.55 N	13.13 E
Grande ≃, Méx.	234	17.43 N	96.56 W
Grande ≃, Méx.	234	16.47 N	95.52 W
Grande ≃, Méx.	234	17.13 N	100.55 W
Grande ≃, Pan.	236	8.18 N	80.24 W
Grande ≃, Perú	248	14.59 S	75.29 W
Grande ≃, S.A.	254	53.48 S	67.40 W
Grande, Arroyo ≃, Arg.	258	34.37 S	59.25 W
Grande, Arroyo ≃, Arg.	288	34.45 S	58.08 W
Grande, Arroyo ≃, Méx.	234	23.55 N	98.44 W
Grande, Arroyo ≃, Ur.	258	33.37 S	57.09 W
Grande, Bahía C[3]	254	50.45 S	68.45 W
Grande, Boca C	220	26.43 N	82.16 W
Grande, Boca ≃[1]	246	8.38 N	60.30 W
Grande, Cañada ≃, Arg.	258	35.19 S	57.48 W
Grande, Cañada ≃, Arg.	258	35.15 S	59.23 W
Grande, Cayo I	240p	20.59 N	79.09 W
Grande, Cerro ∧, Méx.	234	20.41 N	101.12 W
Grande, Cerro ∧, Méx.	234	21.45 N	103.05 W
Grande, Cerro ∧, Méx.	234	20.30 N	103.02 W
Grande, Cerro ∧, Méx.	234	23.39 N	100.51 W
Grande, Corixa (Curiche Grande) ≋	248	17.10 S	58.20 W
Grande, Cuchilla ∧	252	33.15 S	55.07 W
Grande, Igarapé ≃	250	3.37 S	48.53 W
Grande, Ilha I, Bra.	252	23.45 S	54.03 W
Grande, Ilha I, Bra.	256	23.09 S	44.14 W
Grande, Isola I	70	37.53 N	12.26 E
Grande, Lago ⊜, Arg.	254	47.44 S	68.04 W
Grande, Lago ⊜, Bra.	250	2.16 S	54.17 W
Grande, Laguna ⊜	286b	23.05 N	82.30 W
Grande, Laguna ⊜	258	34.14 S	58.53 W
Grande, Mare (Taranto) C	68	40.27 N	17.12 E
Grande, Naviglio ☰	266b	45.35 N	8.42 E
Grande, Ponta ≻	255	16.22 S	39.01 W
Grande, Praia ⌖[2]	256	24.05 S	46.30 W
Grande, Punta ≻	252	25.06 S	70.30 W
Grande, Ribeirão ≃	256	22.11 S	43.19 W
Grande, Rio (Bravo del Norte) ≃	178	25.55 N	97.09 W
Grande, Salina ≋	68	40.26 N	17.18 E
Grande, Serra ⛰	250	6.00 S	40.52 W
Grande, Serra → Geral, Serra ⌖[4]	250	11.15 S	46.30 W
Grande, Sierra ⛰	196	29.40 N	104.55 W
Grande, Volcán ∧[1]	234	20.06 N	101.38 W
Grande-Anse, N.B., Can.	186	47.48 N	65.11 W
Grande Anse, Guad.	241o	16.18 N	61.04 W
Grande Anse C	275a	45.23 N	73.53 W
Grande Anse Bay C	241k	12.02 N	61.45 W
Grande Casse, Pointe de la ∧	62	45.24 N	6.50 E
Grande Cayemite I	238	18.37 N	73.45 W
Grande-Chartreuse, Couvent de la ψ[1]	62	45.22 N	5.50 E
Grande Comore I	157a	11.35 S	43.20 E
Grande da Botija, Ilha I	246	3.58 S	62.53 W
Grande de Añasco ≃	240m	18.16 N	67.11 W
Grande de Arecibo ≃	240m	18.29 N	66.42 W

PORTUGUÊS

Nome	Página	Lat.°′	Long.°′ W=Oeste
Grande de Jutaí, Ilha I	250	3.15 S	49.37 W
Grande de Lipez ≃	248	20.47 S	67.14 W
Grande de Loíza ≃	240m	18.27 N	65.53 W
Grande de Manacapuru, Lago ⊜	246	3.04 S	61.25 W
Grande de Manatí ≃	240m	18.29 N	66.32 W
Grande de Matagalpa ≃	236	12.54 N	83.32 W
Grande de Santa Marta, Ciénaga C	246	10.50 N	74.25 W
Grande de Santiago ≃	234	21.36 N	105.26 W
Grande de Tarija ≃	248	22.53 S	64.21 W
Grande de Térraba ≃	236	9.03 N	83.40 W
Grande do Curuaí, Lago ⊜	250	2.15 S	55.20 W
Grande do Gurupá, Ilha I	250	1.00 S	51.30 W
Grande do Tapará, Ilha I	250	2.14 S	54.39 W
Grande Fausse Passe ⋃	175f	19.45 S	163.59 E
Grande Île I	275a	45.29 N	73.17 W
Grande Île de la Ndjili I	273b	4.19 S	15.24 E
Grande Inferior, Cuchilla ⛰[2]	258	33.50 S	56.27 W
Grand-Entrée	186	47.33 N	61.34 W
Grande Pointe ≻	241o	15.58 N	61.38 W
Grande-Prairie	182	55.10 N	118.48 W
Grand Erg de Bilma ◆[2]	146	18.30 N	14.00 E
Grand Erg Occidental ◆[2]	148	30.30 N	0.30 E
Grand Erg Oriental ◆[2]	148	30.30 N	7.00 E
Grande-Rivière	186	48.24 N	64.30 W
Grande Rivière à Goyaves ≃	241o	16.18 N	61.37 W
Grande Rivière de la Baleine ≃	176	55.16 N	77.47 W
Grande Ronde ≃	202	46.05 N	116.59 W
Grandes, Salinas ⊻	252	30.05 S	65.05 W
Grandes Antillas, Islas → Greater Antilles II	238	20.00 N	74.00 W
Grandes Antilles, Îles → Greater Antilles II	238	20.00 N	74.00 W
Grande Sassière, Aiguille de la ∧	62	45.30 N	7.00 E
Grande Sauldre ≃	50	47.22 N	1.55 E
Gran Desierto de Arena → Great Sandy Desert ◆[2]	162	21.30 S	125.00 E
Gran Desierto Victoria → Great Victoria Desert ◆[2]	162	28.30 S	127.45 E
Grandes-Piles	206	46.41 N	72.44 W
Grand-Étang	186	46.33 N	61.02 W
Grande-Terre I	241o	16.20 N	61.25 W
Grande Vigie, Pointe de la ≻	241o	16.31 N	61.28 W
Grand Eyvia ≃	62	45.42 N	7.14 E
Grand Falls, N.B., Can.	186	47.03 N	67.44 W
Grand Falls, Newf., Can.	186	48.56 N	55.40 W
Grandfalls, Tex., U.S.	196	31.20 N	102.51 W
Grandfather Mountain ∧	192	36.07 N	81.48 W
Grandfield	196	34.13 N	98.41 W
Grand Forks, B.C., Can.	182	49.02 N	118.27 W
Grand Forks, N. Dak., U.S.	198	47.55 N	97.03 W
Grand Forks Air Force Base ■	198	47.57 N	97.25 W
Grand-Fort-Philippe	50	50.00 N	2.06 E
Grand-Fougeray	32	47.44 N	1.44 W
Grand-Gallargues	62	43.43 N	4.10 E
Grand Gedeh □[6]	150	6.00 N	8.00 W
Grand Gorge	210	42.22 N	74.30 W
Grand-Halleux	56	50.19 N	5.54 E
Grand Haven	216	43.04 N	86.13 W
Grand Haven State Park ♠	216	43.02 N	86.13 W
Grand Hers ≃	32	43.47 N	1.20 E
Grandiči	76	53.43 N	23.49 E
Grandin, Lac ⊜	176	63.59 N	119.00 W
Grandioznyj, Pik ∧	88	53.50 N	96.11 E
Grand Island, Fla., U.S.	220	28.53 N	81.44 W
Grand Island, Nebr., U.S.	198	40.55 N	98.21 W
Grand Island, N.Y., U.S.	212	43.01 N	78.58 W
Grand Island I, Ont., Can.	212	44.34 N	78.50 W
Grand Island I, Mich., U.S.	190	46.30 N	86.40 W
Grand Island I, N.Y., U.S.	210	43.02 N	78.58 W
Grand Isle	194	29.14 N	90.00 W
Grand Isle □[6]	206	44.57 N	73.17 W
Grand Junction, Colo., U.S.	200	39.05 N	108.33 W
Grand Junction, Iowa, U.S.	198	42.02 N	94.14 W
Grand Junction, Mich., U.S.	216	42.24 N	86.04 W
Grand Junction, Tenn., U.S.	194	35.03 N	89.10 W
Grand lac des Îles ⊜	206	46.43 N	73.30 W
Grand Lac du Nord ⊜	186	50.54 N	67.06 W
Grand lac Germain ⊜	186	51.12 N	66.41 W
Grand Lac Salé → Great Salt Lake ⊜	200	41.10 N	112.30 W
Grand lac Victoria ⊜	190	47.31 N	77.30 W
Grand-Lahou	150	5.08 N	5.01 W
Grand Lake	200	40.15 N	105.49 W
Grand Lake ⊜, N.B., Can.	186	45.42 N	66.05 W
Grand Lake ⊜, Newf., Can.	186	49.00 N	57.25 W
Grand Lake ⊜, N.A.	186	45.43 N	67.50 W
Grand Lake ⊜, La., U.S.	194	29.55 N	92.47 W
Grand Lake ⊜, Maine, U.S.	188	45.15 N	67.50 W
Grand Lake ⊜, Mich., U.S.	190	45.18 N	83.30 W
Grand Lake ⊜, Ohio, U.S.	216	40.30 N	84.32 W
Grand Lake-Saint Marys State Park ♠	216	40.33 N	84.27 W
Grand Ledge	216	42.45 N	84.45 W
Grand Lieu, Lac de ⊜	32	47.06 N	1.40 W
Grand Manan Channel ⋃	186	44.45 N	66.52 W
Grand Manan Island I	186	44.40 N	66.50 W
Grand Marais, Mich., U.S.	190	46.40 N	85.59 W
Grand Marais, Minn., U.S.	190	47.45 N	90.20 W
Grand Meadow	190	43.42 N	92.34 W
Grand'Mère	206	46.37 N	72.41 W
Grand Mesa ∧	200	39.00 N	108.00 W
Grandmesnil, Lac ⊜	186	51.19 N	67.33 W
Grand Morié	150	5.59 N	4.08 W
Grand Morin ≃	50	48.54 N	2.50 E
Grandola, It.	58	46.02 N	9.13 E
Grândola, Port.	34	38.10 N	8.34 W
Grand-Pabos, Riviére du ≃	186	48.21 N	64.43 W
Grand Palace ψ	269a	13.45 N	100.30 E
Grand Passage ⋃	175f	18.45 S	163.10 E
Grand-Popo	150	6.17 N	1.50 E
Grand Portage	190	47.58 N	89.41 W
Grand Portage Indian Reservation ◆[4]	190	47.55 N	89.45 W
Grand Portage National Monument ♠	190	48.02 N	89.57 W
Grand Prairie	222	32.45 N	96.59 W
Grandpré	56	49.20 N	4.52 E
Grand Pré National Historic Park ♠	186	45.08 N	64.18 W
Grand Prix Airport ⊠	281	42.33 N	83.11 W
Grand Rapids, Man., Can.	184	53.08 N	99.20 W
Grand Rapids, Mich., U.S.	216	42.58 N	85.40 W
Grand Rapids, Minn., U.S.	190	47.14 N	93.31 W
Grand Rapids, Ohio, U.S.	216	41.25 N	83.52 W
Grand Récif de Cook ⟡[2]	175f	19.25 S	163.50 E
Grand Récif Mathieu ⟡[2]	175f	20.51 S	164.20 E
Grand Rhône ≃	62	43.20 N	4.50 E
Grand Ridge	216	41.14 N	88.50 W
Grandrieu, Bel.	50	50.12 N	4.10 E
Grandrieu, Fr.	62	44.47 N	3.38 E
Grand River	214	41.44 N	81.17 W
Grand' Rivière	240e	14.52 N	61.11 W
Grand Ronde	224	45.04 N	123.37 W
Grand Roy	241k	12.08 N	61.45 W
Grand Ruisseau ≃	275a	45.39 N	73.12 W
Grand-Saint-Bernard, Col du)(	58	45.50 N	7.10 E
Grand-Saint-Bernard, Tunnel du ◆[5]	58	45.51 N	7.11 E
Grand Saline	222	32.41 N	95.43 W
Grand Saline Creek ≃	222	32.41 N	95.36 W
Grandson	58	46.49 N	6.38 E
Grand Terrace	228	34.03 N	117.20 W
Grand Teton ∧	202	43.44 N	110.48 W
Grand Teton National Park ♠	202	43.30 N	43.57 W
Grand Tower	194	37.38 N	89.30 W
Grand Traverse Bay C	190	45.02 N	85.30 W
Grand Traverse Bay, East Arm C	190	44.52 N	85.28 W
Grand Traverse Bay, West Arm C	190	44.52 N	85.35 W
Grandtully	46	56.39 N	3.46 W
Grand Turk	238	21.28 N	71.08 W
Grand Union Canal ☰	260	51.30 N	0.02 W
Grand Valley, Ont., Can.	212	43.54 N	80.19 W
Grand Valley, Colo., U.S.	200	39.27 N	108.03 W
Grand Valley, Pa., U.S.	214	41.43 N	79.32 W
Grandview, Man., Can.	184	51.10 N	100.45 W
Grandview, Ill., U.S.	219	39.49 N	89.37 W
Grandview, Mo., U.S.	194	38.53 N	94.32 W
Grandview, Pa., U.S.	279b	40.10 N	79.52 W
Grandview, Tex., U.S.	222	32.16 N	97.11 W
Grandview, Wash., U.S.	202	46.15 N	119.54 W
Grand View, Wis., U.S.	190	46.22 N	91.06 W
Grandview Beach	216	41.50 N	83.24 W
Grandview Heights, Ohio, U.S.	218	40.01 N	83.03 W
Grandview Heights, Pa., U.S.	208	40.03 N	76.17 W
Grandview Homes	216	40.44 N	84.04 W
Grand View-on-Hudson	276	41.44 N	73.55 W
Grandvillars	58	47.33 N	6.58 E
Grandville	216	42.54 N	85.46 W
Grandvilliers	50	49.40 N	1.56 E
Grand Wash Cliffs ⌖[4]	200	35.40 N	113.50 W
Grand Winterberg ∧	56	48.59 N	7.37 E
Grandyle Village	210	43.01 N	78.57 W
Grâne	62	44.44 N	4.55 E
Grañén	34	41.56 N	0.22 W
Graneros	252	34.04 S	70.44 W
Graney, Lough ⊜	48	52.59 N	8.40 W
Grangärde	40	60.16 N	14.59 E
Grange, Austl.	168b	34.54 S	138.30 E
Grange, Eng., U.K.	262	53.23 N	3.09 W
Grange, Bois de la ♠	261	48.45 N	2.30 E
Grange-Bléneau, Château de la ⊥	50	48.41 N	2.55 E
Grange Hill	260	51.37 N	0.05 E
Grangemouth	46	56.02 N	3.45 W
Grängen ⊜	40	59.45 N	14.47 E
Grangent, Lac de ⊜[1]	62	45.25 N	4.15 E
Grange-over-Sands	44	54.12 N	2.55 W
Granger, Tex., U.S.	222	30.43 N	97.27 W
Granger, Utah, U.S.	200	40.42 N	111.57 W
Granger, Wash., U.S.	202	46.21 N	120.11 W
Granger, Wyo., U.S.	200	41.35 N	109.58 W
Granges → Grenchen	58	47.11 N	7.24 E
Grångesberg	40	60.05 N	14.59 E
Granges-sur-Vologne	58	48.09 N	6.47 E
Grangeville, Idaho, U.S.	202	45.56 N	116.07 W
Grangeville, Pa., U.S.	208	39.47 N	76.58 W
Grangousier Hill ∧[2]	190	47.35 N	84.56 W
Gran Guardia	252	25.52 S	58.53 W
Granite, Md., U.S.	284b	39.21 N	76.51 W
Granite, Okla., U.S.	196	34.58 N	99.23 W
Granite City	219	38.42 N	90.09 W
Granite Creek ≃	224	48.43 N	120.55 W
Granite Dam ◆[6]	186	48.06 N	57.20 W
Granite Dome ∧	226	38.13 N	119.44 W
Granite Downs	162	26.57 S	133.30 E
Granite Falls, Minn., U.S.	198	44.49 N	95.33 W
Granite Falls, N.C., U.S.	192	35.48 N	81.26 W
Granite Falls, Wash., U.S.	224	48.05 N	121.58 W
Granite Lake ⊜[1]	186	48.08 N	57.05 W
Granite Mountain ∧, Austl.	171b	35.44 S	148.13 E
Granite Mountain ∧, Alaska, U.S.	180	65.26 N	161.14 W
Granite Mountain ∧, Alaska, U.S.	182	55.30 N	132.35 W
Granite Mountains ⛰	202	42.35 N	107.30 W
Granite Pass)(	202	44.38 N	107.30 W
Granite Peak	162	25.38 S	121.21 E
Granite Peak ∧, Mont., U.S.	202	45.34 N	112.02 W
Granite Peak ∧, Mont., U.S.	202	45.10 N	109.48 W
Granite Peak ∧, Nev., U.S.	204	41.40 N	117.35 W
Granite Peak ∧, Nev., U.S.	204	40.48 N	119.25 W
Granite Range ⛰	204	41.00 N	119.35 W
Graniteville, Mass., U.S.	207	42.36 N	71.28 W
Graniteville, S.C., U.S.	192	33.34 N	81.48 W
Graniteville, Vt., U.S.	188	44.08 N	72.29 W
Graniti	70	37.53 N	15.14 E
Granitnoje	83	47.27 N	37.52 E
Granito	250	7.43 S	39.36 W
Granitogorsk	85	42.44 N	73.27 E
Granitola, Capo ≻	70	37.34 N	12.41 E
Granitola Torretta	70	37.34 N	12.40 E
Granity	172	41.38 S	171.51 E
Granitzenbach ≃	61	47.11 N	14.46 E
Granja, Bra.	250	3.06 S	40.50 W
Granja, Port.	266c	38.51 N	9.06 W
Gran Khingan → Daxing'anlingshan mai ⛰	89	49.40 N	122.00 E
Granki	76	54.51 N	31.27 E
Grankulla (Kauniainen)	26	60.13 N	24.45 E
Gran Lago Salado → Great Salt Lake ⊜	200	41.10 N	112.30 W
Gran Laguna Salada ⊜	254	44.24 S	67.23 W
Granma □[4]	240p	21.20 N	76.50 W
Gränna	26	58.01 N	14.28 E
Grannoch, Loch ≃	44	55.00 N	4.17 W
Granollers	34	41.37 N	2.18 E
Granön	26	64.15 N	19.19 E
Granov	78	48.52 N	29.34 E
Gran Pajonal ⛰	248	10.45 S	74.30 W
Gran Paradiso ∧	62	45.32 N	7.16 E
Gran Paradiso, Parco Nazionale del ♠	62	45.34 N	7.18 E
Gran Piedra ∧	240p	20.01 N	75.38 W
Gran Pilastro (Hochfeiler) ∧	64	46.58 N	11.44 E
Gran Quivira National Monument ♠	200	34.05 N	106.14 W
Gran Rio ≃	250	4.01 N	55.31 W
Gran Sasso d'Italia ⛰	66	42.27 N	13.42 E
Gransee	54	53.00 N	13.09 E
Grant, Fla., U.S.	220	27.56 N	80.32 W
Grant, Mich., U.S.	190	43.20 N	85.49 W
Grant, Nebr., U.S.	198	40.50 N	101.56 W
Grant □[6], Ind., U.S.	216	40.33 N	85.40 W
Grant □[6], Ky., U.S.	218	38.39 N	84.39 W
Grant ≃	190	42.40 N	90.45 W
Grant, Lake ⊜	218	39.00 N	83.53 W
Grant, Mount ∧	204	38.34 N	118.48 W
Grant, Point ≻	169	38.31 S	145.07 E
Granta ≃	42	52.10 N	0.06 E
Grant Birthplace State Memorial ⊥	218	38.54 N	84.14 W
Grant City	194	40.29 N	94.25 W
Grantham, Austl.	171a	27.34 S	152.12 E
Grantham, Eng., U.K.	42	52.55 N	0.39 W
Grantham, Pa., U.S.	208	40.09 N	77.00 W
Grant-Kohrs Ranch National Historic Site ⊥	202	46.25 N	112.40 W
Grant Lake ⊜[1]	226	37.50 N	119.07 W
Grant Mills	283	41.57 N	71.26 W
Granton	46	55.59 N	3.14 W
Grantorto	64	45.36 N	11.43 E
Grantown on Spey	46	57.20 N	3.58 W
Grant Park	216	41.14 N	87.39 W
Grant Park ♠	278	41.52 N	87.37 W
Grant Point ≻[1]	176	68.19 N	98.53 W
Grant Range ⛰	204	38.25 N	115.30 W
Grants	200	35.09 N	107.52 W
Grantsburg, Ind., U.S.	218	38.17 N	86.28 W
Grantsburg, Wis., U.S.	190	45.47 N	92.41 W
Grantshouse	46	55.53 N	2.19 W
Grants Pass	202	42.26 N	123.19 W
Grants Patch	162	30.27 S	121.07 E
Grant-Suttie Bay C	176	69.47 N	77.15 W
Grantsville, Utah, U.S.	200	40.36 N	112.28 W
Grantsville, W. Va., U.S.	188	38.55 N	81.06 W
Grantville, Ga., U.S.	192	33.14 N	84.50 W
Grantville, Pa., U.S.	208	40.23 N	76.39 W
Granum	182	49.52 N	113.30 W
Granville, Austl.	274a	33.50 S	151.01 E
Granville, Fr.	32	48.50 N	1.36 W
Granville, Ill., U.S.	190	41.16 N	89.14 W
Granville, Mass., U.S.	207	42.04 N	72.52 W
Granville, Mo., U.S.	219	39.34 N	92.06 W
Granville, N. Dak., U.S.	198	48.16 N	100.47 W
Granville, N.Y., U.S.	188	43.24 N	73.16 W
Granville, Ohio, U.S.	214	40.04 N	82.31 W
Granville, Pa., U.S.	208	40.33 N	77.38 W
Granville, W. Va., U.S.	188	39.39 N	79.59 W
Granville Lake ⊜	184	56.18 N	100.30 W
Granvin	26	60.33 N	6.43 E
Granzin, D.D.R.	54	53.25 N	12.53 E
Granzin, D.D.R.	54	53.30 N	11.56 E
Grão Mogol	255	16.34 S	42.54 W
Grape Creek ≃	200	38.26 N	105.16 W
Grape Island I	283	42.16 N	70.55 W
Grapeland	222	31.29 N	95.29 W
Grapeview	224	47.20 N	122.50 W
Grapeville	214	40.19 N	79.36 W
Grapevine	222	32.56 N	97.06 W
Grapevine Lake ⊜[1]	222	32.59 N	97.06 W
Grapevine Peak ∧	204	36.57 N	117.09 W
Grappa, Monte ∧	64	45.52 N	11.48 E
Grappenhall	262	53.22 N	2.32 W
Gras, Lac de ⊜	176	64.30 N	110.30 W
Grasbult	150	30.52 S	21.47 E
Grasdorf	52	52.06 N	10.09 E
Graskop	156	24.58 S	30.49 E
Grasleben	54	52.18 N	11.01 E
Grasmere, S. Afr.	158	26.26 S	27.52 E
Grasmere, Eng., U.K.	44	54.28 N	3.02 W
Grasmere Lake ⊜	276	40.36 N	74.05 W
Gräsö	40	60.21 N	18.28 E
Gräsö I	40	60.24 N	18.25 E
Grasonville	208	38.57 N	76.13 W
Grass ≃, Man., Can.	184	56.03 N	96.33 W
Grass ≃, N.Y., U.S.	188	44.59 N	74.46 W
Grass, South Branch ≃	188	44.25 N	75.06 W
Grassano	68	40.38 N	16.18 E
Grassau	64	47.47 N	12.27 E
Grass Creek ≃	202	43.56 N	108.39 W
Grasscroft	262	53.32 N	2.02 W
Grasse	62	43.40 N	6.55 E
Grassendale ◆[8]	262	53.21 N	2.54 W
Grassflat	214	41.00 N	78.07 W
Grass Hassock Channel ⋃	276	40.36 N	73.48 W
Grasshopper Creek ≃	202	45.06 N	112.47 W
Grassi Lagoon C	175e	8.12 S	157.40 E
Grassington	44	54.04 N	1.59 W
Grass Island I	276	40.39 N	73.18 W
Grässjön ⊜	40	59.52 N	13.43 E
Grass Lake	216	42.15 N	84.13 W
Grass Lake ⊜	216	42.27 N	88.10 W
Grass Patch	162	33.14 S	121.43 E
Grassrange	202	47.01 N	108.48 W
Grassridge Dam ◆[6]	158	31.45 S	25.29 E
Grass River Provincial Park ♠	184	54.40 N	100.50 W
Grass Valley, Austl.	168a	31.38 S	116.48 E
Grass Valley, Calif., U.S.	226	39.13 N	121.04 W
Grass Valley, Oreg., U.S.	224	45.22 N	120.47 W
Grassy	166	40.03 S	144.04 E
Grassy	190	48.42 N	81.27 W
Grassy Bay C	276	40.38 N	73.48 W
Grassy Brook ≃	284a	43.03 N	79.07 W
Grassy Creek ≃	216	40.55 N	86.30 W
Grassy Hill ∧	271d	22.25 N	114.09 E
Grassy Island I	276	41.04 N	73.23 W
Grassy Island Lake ⊜	184	51.50 N	110.20 W
Grassy Key I	220	24.46 N	80.57 W
Grassy Lake	182	49.49 N	111.43 W
Grassy Lake ⊜	220	27.13 N	81.20 W
Grassy Plains	182	53.57 N	125.54 W
Grassy Sprain Reservoir ⊜[1]	276	40.58 N	73.51 W
Gråsten	41	54.55 N	9.36 E
Grästorp	26	58.20 N	12.40 E
Graterford	285	40.13 N	75.27 W
Graterford State Correctional Institution ψ	285	40.14 N	75.26 W
Grates Point ≻	186	48.09 N	52.57 W
Gratis	218	39.39 N	84.32 W
Gratitunon	115a	7.43 S	113.00 E
Gratkorn	61	47.08 N	15.21 E
Gratz, Ky., U.S.	218	38.28 N	84.57 W
Gratz, Pa., U.S.	208	40.37 N	76.43 W
Gratztown	279b	40.14 N	79.47 W
Graubünden (Grischun) □[3]	58	46.45 N	9.30 E
Graudenz → Grudziądz	30	53.29 N	18.45 E
Graue Hörner ∧	58	46.57 N	9.23 E
Graukogel ∧	64	47.06 N	13.10 E
Graulinster	56	49.45 N	6.18 E
Graun → Curon Venosta	64	46.49 N	10.32 E
Graupa	54	51.00 N	13.54 E
Gravatá	250	8.12 S	35.34 W
Gravatá ≃	255	16.53 S	42.10 W
Grave	52	51.45 N	5.44 E
Gravedona	58	46.09 N	9.18 E
Gravelbourg	184	49.53 N	106.34 W
Gravel Creek ≃	202	42.39 N	123.35 W
Gravelines	50	50.59 N	2.07 E
Gravellona-Toce	58	45.55 N	8.26 E
Gravell Point ≻	176	67.10 N	76.43 W
Gravelly Bay C	284a	42.52 N	79.15 W
Gravelly Brook ≃	276	40.25 N	74.13 W
Gravelly Pond ⊜	283	42.36 N	70.48 W
Gravelotte, Fr.	56	49.07 N	6.01 E
Gravelotte, S. Afr.	156	23.56 S	30.34 E
Gravenhurst	212	44.55 N	79.22 W
Grävenwiesbach	56	50.23 N	8.27 E
Grave Peak ∧	202	46.24 N	114.44 W
Gravesend, Austl.	166	29.35 S	150.19 E
Gravesend, Eng., U.K.	260	51.27 N	0.24 E
Gravesend Bay C	276	40.36 N	74.01 W
Gravesham □[8]	260	51.25 N	0.24 E
Gravette	194	36.26 N	94.27 W
Gravigny	50	49.03 N	1.10 E
Gravina di Matera ≃	68	40.37 N	16.49 E
Gravina in Puglia	68	40.49 N	16.25 E
Gravina Island I	182	55.17 N	131.45 W
Gray, Fr.	58	47.27 N	5.35 E
Gray, Ga., U.S.	192	33.01 N	83.32 W
Gray, Ky., U.S.	192	36.57 N	84.00 W
Gray, Maine, U.S.	188	43.53 N	70.20 W
Gray, Pa., U.S.	214	40.08 N	79.05 W
Grayback Mountain ∧, Alaska, U.S.	180	57.08 N	153.54 W
Grayback Mountain ∧, Oreg., U.S.	202	42.07 N	123.18 W
Grayland	224	46.48 N	124.06 W
Grayling, Alaska, U.S.	180	62.57 N	160.03 W
Grayling, Mich., U.S.	190	44.40 N	84.43 W
Grays	260	51.29 N	0.20 E
Grays ≃	224	46.18 N	123.41 W
Grays Harbor □[6]	224	47.09 N	123.45 W
Grays Harbor C	224	46.56 N	124.05 W
Grayshott	42	51.11 N	0.45 W
Grayslake	216	42.21 N	88.03 W
Grays Lake ⊜	278	42.21 N	88.03 W
Grays Lake ≋	202	43.04 N	111.26 W
Grays Lake Outlet ≃	202	43.22 N	111.46 W
Grayson, Sask., Can.	184	50.44 N	102.40 W
Grayson, Ala., U.S.	194	34.15 N	87.24 W
Grayson, Calif., U.S.	226	37.33 N	121.10 W
Grayson, Ky., U.S.	218	38.20 N	82.57 W
Grayson Lake ⊜[1]	218	38.13 N	83.00 W
Grayson Lake State Park ♠	218	38.13 N	83.02 W
Grays Peak ∧	200	39.37 N	105.45 W
Grays Point	274a	34.04 S	151.05 E
Grays River	224	46.21 N	123.37 W
Grays Thurrock	42	51.29 N	0.20 E
Gray Summit	219	38.29 N	90.49 W
Graysville	194	35.27 N	85.05 W
Graytown	214	41.33 N	83.16 W
Grayville	194	38.16 N	87.59 W
Gray Wolf ≃	224	47.55 N	123.07 W
Graz	61	47.05 N	15.27 E
Grazalema	34	36.46 N	5.22 W
Graždanka ◆[8]	265a	60.00 N	30.24 E
Gr'azeva ≃	265b	55.34 N	37.21 E
Gr'azi	80	52.29 N	39.57 E
Grazierville	214	40.40 N	78.16 W
Gr'aznoje	82	54.02 N	39.07 E
Gr'aznovo, S.S.S.R.	82	54.18 N	36.49 E
Gr'aznovo, S.S.S.R.	265b	55.57 N	37.34 E
Gr'aznyj Irtek	80	51.56 N	53.11 E
Gr'azovec	76	58.53 N	40.14 E
Grdelica	38	42.54 N	22.04 E
Greaca, Lacul ⊜	38	44.05 N	26.23 E
Greåker	26	59.16 N	11.02 E
Greasby	262	53.23 N	3.07 W
Great ≃	241k	12.08 N	61.36 W
Great Abaco I	238	26.28 N	77.05 W
Great Adventure ♠	208	40.09 N	74.27 W
Great Altcar	262	53.33 N	3.01 W
Great America ♠	216	42.21 N	87.55 W
Great Amwell	260	51.48 N	0.01 W
Great Artesian Basin ⊻[1]	160	25.00 S	143.00 E
Great Astrolabe Reef ⟡[2]	175g	18.52 S	178.31 E
Great Australian Bight C[3]	162	35.00 S	135.00 E
Great Bacolet Point ≻	241k	12.04 N	61.37 W
Great Baddow	260	51.43 N	0.29 E
Great Bahama Bank ⟡[4]	238	23.15 N	78.00 W
Great Barrier Island I	172	36.10 S	175.25 E
Great Barrier Reef ⟡[2]	160	18.00 S	145.50 E
Great Barrington	207	42.12 N	73.22 W
Great Barrow	262	53.12 N	2.48 W
Great Basin ⊻[1]	178	40.00 N	117.00 W
Great Bay C	208	39.30 N	74.23 W
Great Bear ≃	180	64.54 N	125.35 W
Great Bear Lake ⊜	176	66.00 N	120.00 W
Great Beaver Lake ⊜	182	54.25 N	123.45 W
Great Bend, Kans., U.S.	198	38.22 N	98.46 W
Great Bend, N.Y., U.S.	210	44.02 N	75.43 W
Great Bend, Pa., U.S.	210	41.58 N	75.45 W
Great Bernera I	46	58.13 N	6.49 W
Great Bitter Lake → al-Murrah al-Kubrā, Al-Buḥayrah ⊜	142	30.20 N	32.23 E
Great Blasket Island I	48	52.05 N	10.32 W
Great Blue Hill ∧[2]	207	42.13 N	71.07 W
Great Bookham	260	51.16 N	0.22 W
Great Braxted	260	51.48 N	0.42 E

Symbol	English	Deutsch	Español	Français	Português
≃	River	Fluss	Río	Rivière	Rio
☰	Canal	Kanal	Canal	Canal	Canal
↳	Waterfall, Rapids	Wasserfall, Stromschnellen	Cascada, Rápidos	Chute d'eau, Rapides	Cascata, Rápidos
⋃	Strait	Meeresstrasse	Estrecho	Détroit	Estreito
C	Bay, Gulf	Bucht, Golf	Bahía, Golfo	Baie, Golfe	Baía, Golfo
⊜	Lake, Lakes	See, Seen	Lago, Lagos	Lac, Lacs	Lago, Lagos
≋	Swamp	Sumpf	Pantano	Marais	Pântano
⊼	Ice Features, Glacier	Eis- und Gletscherformen	Accidentes Glaciales	Formes glaciaires	Acidentes Glaciares
⊡	Other Hydrographic Features	Andere Hydrographische Objekte	Otros Elementos Hidrográficos	Autres données hydrographiques	Outros Elementos Hidrográficos
⟡	Submarine Features	Untermeerische Objekte	Accidentes Submarinos	Formes de relief sous-marin	Acidentes Submarinos
□	Political Unit	Politische Einheit	Unidad Política	Entité politique	Unidade Política
ψ	Cultural Institution	Kulturelle Institution	Institución Cultural	Institution culturelle	Instituição Cultural
⊥	Historical Site	Historische Stätte	Sitio Histórico	Site historique	Sitio Histórico
♠	Recreational Site	Erholungs- und Ferienort	Sitio de Recreo	Centre de loisirs	Sitio de Lazer
⊠	Airport	Flughafen	Aeropuerto	Aéroport	Aeroporto
■	Military Installation	Militäranlage	Instalación Militar	Installation militaire	Instalação Militar
◆	Miscellaneous	Verschiedenes	Misceláneo	Divers	Miscelânea

Great Brewster Island I 283 42.20 N 70.53 W
Great Brook ≃ 276 40.42 N 74.31 W
Great Budworth 262 53.18 N 2.30 W
Great Burnt Lake ⊜ 186 48.20 N 56.13 W
Great Burso Bank ✣[4] 262 53.29 N 3.06 W
Great Burstead 260 51.36 N 0.25 E
Great Camanoe I 240m 18.29 N 64.32 W
Great Captain Island I 276 40.59 N 73.38 W
Great Central Lake ⊜ 182 49.27 N 125.12 W
Great Channel ⩌ 110 6.25 N 94.20 E
Great Chazy ≃ 206 44.56 N 73.23 W
Great Chazy, North Branch ≃ 206 44.57 N 73.38 W
Great Clifton 44 54.31 N 3.29 W
Great Coco Island I 110 14.05 N 93.24 E
Great Coharie Creek ≃ 192 34.50 N 78.22 W
Great Cove C 276 40.43 N 73.14 W
Great Crosby 262 53.29 N 3.01 W
Great Crossing 218 38.08 N 84.38 W
Great Cumbrae I 46 55.46 N 4.57 W
Great Cumbrae Island I 46 55.46 N 4.55 W
Great Dismal Swamp ☷ 192 36.30 N 76.30 W
Great Ditch ⌶ 276 40.24 N 74.31 W
Great Divide Basin ≚[1] 202 42.00 N 108.10 W
Great Dividing Range ⩕ 160 25.00 S 147.00 E
Great Duck Island I 190 45.40 N 82.58 W
Great Dunmow 42 51.53 N 0.22 E
Great Eau ≃ 44 53.25 N 0.13 E
Great Egg Harbor ≃ 208 39.18 N 74.40 W
Great Egg Harbor Bay C 208 39.18 N 74.37 W
Great Egg Harbor Inlet C 208 39.20 N 74.34 W
Greater Antilles II 238 20.00 N 74.00 W
Greater Bombay □[5] 272c 19.08 N 72.51 E
Greater Buffalo International Airport ⊠ 210 42.56 N 78.44 W
Greater Cincinnati Airport ⊠ 218 39.03 N 84.40 W
Greater Khingan Mountains → Daxing'anling-shanmai ⩕ 89 49.40 N 122.00 E
Greater London □[6] 260 51.30 N 0.10 W
Greater Manchester □[6] 262 53.30 N 2.18 W
Greater Pittsburgh International Airport ⊠ 214 40.29 N 80.14 W
Greater Sunda Islands II 108 2.00 S 110.00 E
Greater Wilmington Airport ⊠ 208 39.41 N 75.36 W
Greater Wollongong → Wollongong 170 34.25 S 150.54 E
Great Exuma I 238 23.32 N 75.50 W
Great Falls, Man., Can. 184 50.27 N 96.02 W
Great Falls, Mont., U.S. 202 47.30 N 111.17 W
Great Falls, S.C., U.S. 192 34.34 N 80.54 W
Great Falls, Va., U.S. 284c 39.00 N 77.17 W
Great Falls L 284c 39.00 N 77.16 W
Great Falls Park ♠ 284c 39.00 N 77.15 W
Great Fish Point ≻ 158 33.30 S 27.10 E
Great Gable ∧ 44 54.28 N 3.12 W
Great Gaddesden 260 51.47 N 0.30 W
Great Grimsby → Grimsby 44 53.35 N 0.05 W
Great Guana Cay I 238 24.00 N 76.20 W
Great Hameldon ∧[2] 262 53.45 N 2.19 W
Great Harwood 262 53.48 N 2.24 W
Greathead Bay C 241h 13.08 N 61.14 W
Great Himalaya Range ⩕ 120 29.00 N 83.00 E
Greathouse Peak ∧ 202 46.46 N 109.21 W
Great Inagua I 238 21.05 N 73.18 W
Great Indian Desert (Thar Desert) ◆[2] 120 28.00 N 72.00 E
Great Island I, N.Y., U.S. 276 41.05 N 73.44 W
Great Island I, N.Y., U.S. 276 40.38 N 73.30 W
Great Karroo (Groot Karroo) ⩕[1] 158 32.25 S 22.40 E
Great Kills ◆[8] 276 40.33 N 74.10 W
Great Kills Harbor C 276 40.32 N 74.08 W
Great Kills Park ♠ 276 40.33 N 74.08 W
Great La Cloche Island I 190 46.01 N 81.52 W
Great Lake ⊜ 166 41.52 S 146.45 E
Great Lakes Naval Training Center ■ 216 42.18 N 87.50 W
Great Lakes Steel Works ʋ[3] 281 42.15 N 83.08 W
Great Machipongo Inlet C 208 37.22 N 75.43 W
Great Malvern (Malvern) 42 52.07 N 2.19 W
Great Marsh ☷ 208 36.32 N 75.57 W
Great Marton 262 53.48 N 3.02 W
Great Massingham 42 52.46 N 0.40 E
Great Meadows 210 40.52 N 74.55 W
Great Meadows National Wildlife Refuge ◆[4] 283 42.29 N 71.20 W
Great Mercury Island I 172 36.37 S 175.48 E
Great Meteor Tablemount ✣[3] 10 30.00 N 28.30 W
Great Miami ≃ 188 39.06 N 84.49 W
Great Mills 208 38.14 N 76.30 W
Great Misery Island I 283 42.33 N 70.48 W
Great Missenden 42 51.43 N 0.43 W
Great Mis Tor ∧ 42 50.34 N 4.01 W
Great Mosque ʋ[1] 146 32.46 N 22.40 E
Great Namaland □[9] 156 25.00 S 17.00 E
Great Neck 276 40.47 N 73.44 W
Great Neck ≻[1], Mass., U.S. 283 42.42 N 70.48 W
Great Neck ≻[1], N.Y., U.S. 276 40.50 N 73.45 W
Great Neck Estates 276 40.47 N 73.44 W
Great Nicobar I 110 7.00 N 93.50 E
Great North East Channel ⩌ 164 9.30 S 143.25 E
Great Notch Reservoir ⊜[1] 276 40.53 N 74.12 W
Great Ormes Head ≻ 44 53.21 N 3.52 W
Great Ouse ≃ 42 52.47 N 0.22 E
Great Oxney Green 260 51.44 N 0.25 E
Great Palm Island I 166 18.43 S 146.37 E
Great Parndon 260 51.45 N 0.05 E
Great Patchogue Lake ⊜ 276 40.46 N 73.01 W
Great Peconic Bay C 207 40.56 N 72.30 W
Great Piece Meadows ☷ 276 40.54 N 74.19 W
Great Plain of the Koukdjuak ≚ 176 66.00 N 73.00 W
Great Plains ≚ 16 42.00 N 100.00 W
Great Point ≻ 207 41.23 N 70.03 W
Great Pubnico Lake ⊜ 186 43.42 N 65.43 W
Great Quittacas Pond ⊜ 207 41.48 N 70.54 W
Great River 276 40.45 N 73.10 W
Great Ruaha ≃ 154 7.56 S 37.52 E
Great Sacandaga Lake ⊜ 210 43.08 N 74.10 W
Great Saint Bernard Pass → Grand-Saint-Bernard, Col du)(58 45.50 N 7.10 E
Great Sale Cay I 192 27.00 N 78.12 W
Great Salt Lake ⊜ 200 41.10 N 112.30 W
Great Salt Lake Desert ◆[2] 200 40.40 N 113.30 W
Great Salt Plains Lake ⊜[1] 196 36.44 N 98.12 W
Great Sand Dunes National Monument ♠ 200 37.43 N 105.36 W
Great Sand Hills ⩕[2] 184 50.35 N 109.05 W
Great Sandy Desert ◆[2], Austl. 162 21.30 S 125.00 E
Great Sandy Desert ◆[2], Oreg., U.S. 202 43.35 N 120.15 W
Great Sankey 262 53.23 N 2.39 W
Great Santa Cruz Island I 116 6.52 N 122.03 E
Great Scarcies (Kolenté) ≃ 150 8.55 N 13.08 W
Great Sea Reef ✣[2] 175g 16.15 S 179.00 E
Great Seneca Creek ≃ 208 39.08 N 77.20 W
Great Shelford 42 52.09 N 0.09 E
Great Sitkin Island I 180 52.03 N 176.07 W
Great Slave Lake ⊜ 176 61.30 N 114.00 W
Great Smoky Mountains ⩕ 192 35.35 N 83.30 W
Great Smoky Mountains National Park ♠ 192 35.39 N 83.30 W
Great Sound ⩌, Ber. 240a 32.17 N 64.51 W
Great Sound ⩌, N.J., U.S. 208 39.06 N 74.47 W
Great South Bay C 210 40.40 N 73.17 W
Great Stour ≃ 42 51.19 N 1.15 E
Great Sutton 262 53.17 N 2.56 W
Great Swamp National Wildlife Refuge ◆[4] 276 40.43 N 74.28 W
Great Tenasserim ≃ 110 12.24 N 98.37 E
Great Thatch Island I 240m 18.23 N 64.43 W
Great Tobago I 240m 18.27 N 64.48 W
Great Torrington 42 50.57 N 4.08 W
Great Totham 260 51.47 N 0.43 E
Great Tsau ∧ 156 21.14 S 22.45 E
Great Usutu (Maputo) ≃ 158 26.11 S 32.42 E
Great Valley 210 42.13 N 78.38 W
Great Victoria Desert ◆[2] 162 28.30 S 127.45 E
Great Wall → Changcheng ⊥ 98 40.30 N 117.00 E
Great Waltham 260 51.48 N 0.28 E
Great Warley 260 51.35 N 0.17 E
Great Whernside ∧ 44 54.09 N 1.59 W
Great Wicomico ≃ 208 37.48 N 76.18 W
Great World ʋ 269b 31.14 N 121.23 E
Great Yarmouth 42 52.37 N 1.44 E
Great Zab (Büyükzap) (Az-Zāb al-Kabīr) ≃ 128 36.00 N 43.21 E
Grebbestad 26 58.42 N 11.15 E
Grebenhain 56 50.29 N 9.19 E
Grebenka 78 50.07 N 32.25 E
Grebenstein 56 51.26 N 9.24 E
Grebnevo 265b 55.58 N 38.05 E
Greb'onki 78 49.57 N 30.12 E
Gréboun, Mont ∧ 150 20.00 N 8.35 E
Grecale, Capo ≻ 71a 35.31 N 12.38 E
Grèce → Greece □[1] 38 39.00 N 22.00 E
Grecia 236 10.05 N 84.18 W
Grecia → Greece □[1] 38 39.00 N 22.00 E
Grečiškino 83 48.52 N 38.54 E
Grecken ⊜ 40 59.35 N 14.44 E
Greco 252 32.48 S 57.03 W
Greco ◆[8] 266b 45.30 N 9.13 E
Greco, Monte ∧ 66 41.48 N 14.00 E
Greco Island I 282 37.31 N 122.11 W
Greding 60 49.03 N 11.21 E
Gredos, Sierra de ⩕ 34 40.18 N 5.05 W
Gredstedbro 41 55.24 N 8.45 E
Greece 210 43.14 N 77.38 W
Greece □[1] 22
38 39.00 N 22.00 E
Greeley, Colo., U.S. 200 40.25 N 104.42 W
Greeley, Kans., U.S. 198 38.22 N 95.08 W
Greeley, Nebr., U.S. 198 41.33 N 98.32 W
Greeley, Pa., U.S. 210 41.25 N 75.00 W
Greeleyville 192 33.35 N 79.58 W
Green □[6] 216 42.48 N 89.25 W
Green ≃, N.B., Can. 186 47.18 N 68.09 W
Green ≃, S. Afr. 158 30.40 S 23.17 E
Green ≃, U.S. 200 38.11 N 109.53 W
Green ≃, U.S. 207 42.35 N 72.36 W
Green ≃, Ill., U.S. 190 41.28 N 90.23 W
Green ≃, Ill., U.S. 216 41.46 N 89.10 W
Green ≃, Ky., U.S. 194 37.55 N 87.30 W
Green ≃, N. Dak., U.S. 198 46.52 N 102.35 W
Green ≃, Vt., U.S. 210 43.06 N 73.13 W
Green ≃, Wash., U.S. 224 46.20 N 122.34 W
Green ≃, Wash., U.S. 224 47.33 N 122.20 W
Greenacres 202 47.39 N 117.06 W
Green Acres ◆[9] 276 40.40 N 73.43 W
Greenacres City 220 26.37 N 80.07 W
Greenbackville 208 38.01 N 75.23 W
Greenbank 224 48.06 N 122.34 W
Green Bay 190 44.30 N 88.01 W
Green Bay C, Newf., Can. 186 49.43 N 55.58 W
Green Bay C, Ont., Can. 212 44.38 N 76.36 W
Green Bay C, U.S. 190 45.00 N 87.30 W
Greenbelt 284c 39.01 N 76.53 W
Greenbelt Park ♠ 284c 38.59 N 76.54 W
Greenbo Lake ⊜ 218 38.29 N 82.54 W
Greenbo Lake State Park ♠ 218 38.29 N 82.54 W
Greenbooth Reservoir ⊜[1] 262 53.38 N 2.13 W
Greenbrae 226 37.57 N 122.31 W
Greenbrier, Ark., U.S. 194 35.14 N 92.23 W
Green Brier, Tenn., U.S. 194 36.27 N 86.49 W
Greenbrier ≃ 188 37.49 N 80.30 W
Greenbrier State Park ♠ 208 39.33 N 77.38 W
Green Brook 276 40.36 N 74.29 W
Green Brook ≃ 276 40.33 N 74.32 W
Greenburg 194 30.51 N 90.40 W
Greenbush, Mass., U.S. 207 42.11 N 70.45 W
Greenbush, Minn., U.S. 198 48.42 N 96.11 W
Greenbush, Va., U.S. 208 37.45 N 75.41 W
Greenbushes 162 33.51 S 116.03 E
Green Camp 214 40.32 N 83.13 W
Green Cape ≻ 166 37.15 S 150.03 E
Greencastle, Eire 48 55.12 N 6.59 W
Greencastle, Ind., U.S. 194 39.38 N 86.52 W
Greencastle, Pa., U.S. 188 39.47 N 77.44 W
Green City 194 40.16 N 92.57 W
Green Cove Springs 192 30.00 N 81.41 W
Green Creek 208 39.03 N 74.54 W
Green Creek ≃, Ohio, U.S. 214 41.26 N 83.01 W
Green Creek ≃, Pa., U.S. 285 39.53 N 75.28 W
Greencrest Park 214 41.23 N 80.24 W
Greendale, Austl. 274a 33.55 S 150.39 E
Greendale, Ind., U.S. 218 39.07 N 84.52 W
Greendale, Wis., U.S. 216 42.57 N 88.00 W
Greene, B.R.D. 52 51.52 N 9.56 E
Greene, Iowa, U.S. 190 42.54 N 92.48 W
Greene, Maine, U.S. 188 44.11 N 70.08 W
Greene, N.Y., U.S. 210 42.20 N 75.46 W
Greene, R.I., U.S. 207 41.41 N 71.44 W
Greene □[6], Ill., U.S. 219 39.18 N 90.24 W
Greene □[6], N.Y., U.S. 210 42.13 N 73.52 W
Greene □[6], Ohio, U.S. 218 39.41 N 83.56 W
Greeneville 192 36.10 N 82.50 W
Green Farms 276 41.07 N 73.19 W
Greenfield, Eng., U.K. 262 53.32 N 2.01 W
Greenfield, Wales, U.K. 44 53.18 N 3.13 W
Greenfield, Calif., U.S. 226 36.19 N 121.15 W
Greenfield, Ill., U.S. 219 39.21 N 90.12 W
Greenfield, Ind., U.S. 218 39.47 N 85.46 W
Greenfield, Iowa, U.S. 198 41.18 N 94.28 W
Greenfield, Mass., U.S. 207 42.36 N 72.36 W
Greenfield, Mo., U.S. 194 37.25 N 93.51 W
Greenfield, Ohio, U.S. 218 39.21 N 83.23 W
Greenfield, Tenn., U.S. 194 36.09 N 88.48 W
Greenfield, Wis., U.S. 216 42.58 N 88.02 W
Greenfield Park, Qué., Can. 275a 45.29 N 73.29 W
Greenfield Park, N.Y., U.S. 210 41.44 N 74.29 W
Greenfields Village 285 75.10 N 39.49 W
Greenfield Village ⊥ 281 42.18 N 83.14 W
Greenford ◆[8] 260 51.32 N 0.21 W
Green Forest 194 36.20 N 93.26 W
Green Harbor 207 42.05 N 70.39 W
Green Harbor ≃ 283 42.05 N 70.39 W
Green Head ≻ 162 30.05 S 114.58 E
Green Hill 285 39.59 N 75.36 W
Greenhill ◆[8] 260 51.35 N 0.20 W
Greenhills 218 39.16 N 84.31 W
Greenhithe 260 51.27 N 0.17 E
Greenhorn Creek ≃ 198 38.08 N 104.38 W
Greenhurst 214 42.07 N 79.19 W
Green Hut Park 276 40.50 N 74.39 W
Green Island, N.Z. 172 45.54 S 170.26 E
Greenisland, N. Ire., U.K. 48 54.42 N 5.52 W
Green Island, N.Y., U.S. 210 42.45 N 73.41 W
Green Island I 241k 12.14 N 61.35 W
Green Island Bay C 116 10.12 N 119.22 E
Green Islands II 14 4.30 S 154.10 E
Green Knoll 276 40.36 N 74.36 W
Green Lake, Sask., Can. 184 54.17 N 107.47 W
Green Lake, Wis., U.S. 190 43.51 N 88.57 W
Green Lake ⊜, B.C., Can. 182 51.24 N 121.15 W
Green Lake ⊜, Sask., Can. 184 54.10 N 107.43 W
Green Lake ⊜, Mich., U.S. 281 42.36 N 83.25 W
Green Lake ⊜, N.Y., U.S. 284a 42.45 N 78.45 W
Green Lake ⊜, Wis., U.S. 190 43.41 N 88.57 W
Green Lakes State Park ♠ 212 43.03 N 75.58 W
Greenlal (Saint-Grégoire-de-Greenlay) 206 45.34 N 72.01 W
Greenland 190 46.46 N 89.06 W
Greenland □[2] 16 70.00 N 40.00 W
Greenland Basin ✣[1] 16 77.00 N 0.00
Greenland-Iceland Rise ✣[3] 10 67.00 N 27.00 W
Greenlands 158 27.07 S 27.40 E
Greenland Sea ⍑[2] 16 77.00 N 1.00 W
Green Lane 208 40.20 N 75.28 W
Green Lane Reservoir ⊜[1] 208 40.22 N 75.29 W
Greenlaw 46 55.43 N 2.28 W
Greenlawn 276 40.52 N 73.22 W
Greenleaf 198 39.44 N 96.59 W
Green Lookout Mountain ∧ 224 45.52 N 122.08 W
Green Manorville 207 42.00 N 72.32 W
Green Meadows 284c 38.58 N 76.57 W
Greenmount, Austl. 168a 31.54 S 116.03 E
Greenmount, Austl. 171a 27.47 S 151.54 E
Greenmount, Eng., U.K. 262 53.37 N 2.20 W
Greenmount, Md., U.S. 208 39.38 N 76.52 W
Green Mountain Reservoir ⊜[1] 200 39.52 N 106.17 W
Green Mountains ⩕ 188 43.45 N 72.45 W
Green Oak Lake ⊜ 281 42.27 N 83.43 W
Green Oaks 278 42.18 N 87.55 W
Greenock, Austl. 168b 34.27 S 138.55 E
Greenock, Scot., U.K. 46 55.57 N 4.45 W
Greenock, Pa., U.S. 279b 40.19 N 79.48 W
Greenodd 44 54.14 N 3.04 W
Greenore Point ≻ 48 52.15 N 6.18 W
Greenough 162 28.57 S 114.44 E
Greenough ≃ 162 28.51 S 114.38 E
Greenough, Mount ∧ 180 69.10 N 141.35 W
Green Park 208 40.23 N 77.19 W
Green Peter Lake ⊜[1] 202 44.28 N 122.30 W
Green Point ≻ 276 40.43 N 73.06 W
Green Pond 276 41.01 N 74.29 W
Green Pond ⊜ 276 41.00 N 74.30 W
Green Pond Brook ≃ 276 40.53 N 74.34 W
Green Pond Mountain ∧ 276 40.58 N 74.33 W
Greenport 207 41.06 N 72.22 W
Green Ridge 285 39.51 N 75.25 W
Green River, Pap. N. Gui. 164 3.55 S 141.10 E
Green River, Utah, U.S. 200 38.59 N 110.10 W
Green River, Wyo., U.S. 200 41.32 N 109.28 W
Green River Gorge V 224 47.19 N 121.54 W
Green River Lake ⊜[1] 194 37.15 N 85.15 W
Greensboro, Ala., U.S. 194 32.42 N 87.36 W
Greensboro, Fla., U.S. 192 30.34 N 84.45 W
Greensboro, Ga., U.S. 192 33.35 N 83.11 W
Greensboro, Md., U.S. 188 38.59 N 75.48 W
Greensboro, N.C., U.S. 192 36.04 N 79.47 W
Greensburg, Ind., U.S. 218 39.20 N 85.29 W
Greensburg, Kans., U.S. 198 37.36 N 99.18 W
Greensburg, Ky., U.S. 194 37.16 N 85.30 W
Greensburg, Ohio, U.S. 214 40.56 N 81.28 W
Greensburg, Pa., U.S. 214 40.18 N 79.33 W
Greens Fork 218 39.54 N 85.02 W
Greenside ◆[8] 273d 26.09 S 28.01 E
Greens Lake C 222 29.16 N 94.59 W
Greens Peak ∧ 200 34.07 N 109.35 W
Greenspond 186 49.04 N 53.34 W
Green Springs 214 41.15 N 83.03 W
Greenstead 260 51.42 N 0.14 E
Greenstone 208 39.45 N 77.27 W
Greenstone Point ≻ 46 57.55 N 5.38 W
Green Street 260 51.40 N 0.16 W
Green Street Green ◆[8] 260 51.21 N 0.04 E
Greensville □[6] 208 36.40 N 77.30 W
Green Swamp ☷, Fla., U.S. 220 28.20 N 81.48 W
Green Swamp ☷, N.C., U.S. 192 34.10 N 78.20 W
Greentown, Ind., U.S. 216 40.29 N 85.58 W
Greentown, Ohio, U.S. 214 40.56 N 81.28 W
Greentown, Pa., U.S. 210 41.19 N 75.18 W
Green Tree, Pa., U.S. 279b 40.25 N 80.05 W
Green Tree, Pa., U.S. 285 40.02 N 75.30 W
Greenup, Ill., U.S. 194 39.15 N 88.10 W
Greenup, Ky., U.S. 218 38.34 N 82.50 W
Greenup □[6] 218 38.33 N 83.00 W
Greenvale 276 40.49 N 73.38 W
Green Valley, Ont., Can. 206 45.16 N 74.36 W
Green Valley, Ill., U.S. 190 40.24 N 89.38 W
Green Valley Creek ≃ 226 38.13 N 122.08 W
Greenview 219 40.05 N 89.44 W
Green Village, N.J., U.S. 276 40.44 N 74.27 W
Greenvillage, Pa., U.S. 208 40.00 N 77.36 W
Greenville, Liber. 150 5.01 N 9.03 W
Greenville, Ala., U.S. 194 31.50 N 86.38 W
Greenville, Calif., U.S. 204 40.08 N 120.57 W
Greenville, Fla., U.S. 192 30.28 N 83.38 W
Greenville, Ill., U.S. 219 38.53 N 89.25 W
Greenville, Ind., U.S. 218 38.23 N 85.59 W
Greenville, Ky., U.S. 194 37.12 N 87.11 W
Greenville, Maine, U.S. 188 45.28 N 69.35 W
Greenville, Mich., U.S. 190 43.11 N 85.15 W
Greenville, Miss., U.S. 194 33.25 N 91.05 W
Greenville, Mo., U.S. 194 37.08 N 90.27 W
Greenville, N.H., U.S. 188 42.46 N 71.49 W
Greenville, N.C., U.S. 192 35.37 N 77.23 W
Greenville, N.Y., U.S. 210 42.25 N 74.01 W
Greenville, N.Y., U.S. 276 41.00 N 73.49 W
Greenville, Ohio, U.S. 218 40.06 N 84.38 W
Greenville, Pa., U.S. 214 41.24 N 80.23 W
Greenville, R.I., U.S. 207 41.52 N 71.33 W
Greenville, S.C., U.S. 192 34.51 N 82.23 W
Greenville, Tex., U.S. 222 33.08 N 96.07 W
Greenville Creek ≃ 218 40.07 N 84.22 W
Green Water ≃, S. Afr. 158 29.00 S 22.10 E
Greenwater ≃, Wash., U.S. 224 47.09 N 121.39 W
Greenwater Lake Provincial Park ♠ 184 52.33 N 103.33 W
Greenwell Point 170 34.55 S 150.44 E
Greenwich, Austl. 274a 33.50 S 151.11 E
Greenwich, Conn., U.S. 207 41.01 N 73.38 W
Greenwich, N.J., U.S. 208 39.24 N 75.21 W
Greenwich, N.Y., U.S. 210 43.05 N 73.30 W
Greenwich, Ohio, U.S. 214 41.02 N 82.31 W
Greenwich ◆[8] 260 51.28 N 0.02 E
Greenwich Cove C 276 41.01 N 73.35 W
Greenwich Creek ≃ 276 41.02 N 73.37 W
Greenwich Observatory ʋ[3] 260 51.28 N 0.00
Greenwich Point ≻ 276 41.00 N 73.34 W
Greenwich Village ◆[8] 276 40.44 N 74.00 W
Greenwood, B.C., Can. 182 49.05 N 118.41 W
Greenwood, Ark., U.S. 194 35.13 N 94.15 W
Greenwood, Calif., U.S. 226 38.54 N 120.55 W
Greenwood, Del., U.S. 208 38.49 N 75.35 W
Greenwood, Ind., U.S. 218 39.37 N 86.07 W
Greenwood, Mass., U.S. 283 42.29 N 71.04 W
Greenwood, Miss., U.S. 194 33.31 N 90.11 W
Greenwood, Nebr., U.S. 198 40.58 N 96.27 W
Greenwood, N.Y., U.S. 210 42.08 N 77.39 W
Greenwood, Pa., U.S. 214 40.32 N 78.21 W
Greenwood, S.C., U.S. 192 34.12 N 82.10 W
Greenwood, Wis., U.S. 190 44.46 N 90.36 W
Greenwood, Lake ⊜[1] 192 34.15 N 82.02 W
Greenwood Cemetery ◆ 276 40.39 N 73.59 W
Greenwood Lake 210 41.14 N 74.18 W
Greenwood Lake ⊜, U.S. 210 41.11 N 74.19 W
Greenwood Lake ⊜, Mass., U.S. 283 42.00 N 71.17 W
Greenwood Race Track ♠ 275b 43.40 N 79.19 W
Greer, Ohio, U.S. 214 40.31 N 82.13 W
Greer, S.C., U.S. 192 34.56 N 82.14 W
Greers Ferry Lake ⊜[1] 194 35.30 N 92.10 W
Greerton 172 37.43 S 176.08 E
Grées, Alpes (Alpi Graie) ⩕ 62 45.30 N 7.10 E
Greeson, Lake ⊜[1] 194 34.10 N 93.45 W
Greetland 262 53.41 N 1.52 W
Greetsiel 52 53.30 N 7.05 E
Greffiers 261 48.37 N 1.51 E
Gréfodé 152 5.43 N 21.33 E
Grefrath, B.R.D. 56 51.20 N 6.20 E
Grefrath, B.R.D. 263 51.10 N 6.38 E
Gregadoo 171b 35.14 S 147.27 E
Gregbe 150 6.48 N 6.43 W
Gregg 279b 40.24 N 80.10 W
Gregg □[6] 222 32.30 N 94.50 W
Greggio 62 45.27 N 8.23 E
Greg Greg 171b 36.03 S 148.02 E
Gregoire Lake Indian Reserve ◆[4] 184 56.28 N 111.10 W
Gregório ≃ 248 6.50 S 70.46 W
Gregory, Mich., U.S. 216 42.28 N 84.05 W
Gregory, S. Dak., U.S. 198 43.14 N 99.26 W
Gregory, Tex., U.S. 196 27.55 N 97.17 W
Gregory ≃ 166 17.53 S 139.17 E
Gregory, Lake ⊜, Austl. 162 25.38 S 119.58 E
Gregory, Lake ⊜, Austl. 166 28.55 S 139.00 E
Gregory, Port ⍑[3] 162 28.10 S 114.14 E
Gregory Lake ⊜ 162 20.10 S 127.20 E
Gregory Range ⩕ 166 19.00 S 143.05 E
Grégy-sur-Yerre 261 48.40 N 2.37 E
Greifenberg → Gryfice 30 53.56 N 15.12 E
Greifenburg 64 46.45 N 13.11 E
Greifendorf 54 51.01 N 13.06 E
Greifenhagen → Gryfino 30 53.12 N 14.30 E
Greifensee 58 47.22 N 8.41 E
Greifensee ⊜ 58 47.21 N 8.41 E
Greifenstein 264b 48.21 N 16.25 E
Greiffenberg 54 53.05 N 13.58 E
Greiffenburg ⊥ 263 51.20 N 6.38 E

ENGLISH — Name | Page | Lat.°′ | Long.°′

Greifswald 54 54.05 N 13.23 E
Greifswalder Bodden C 54 54.15 N 13.35 E
Greifswalder Oie I 54 54.14 N 13.55 E
Greimberg ∧ 61 47.15 N 14.09 E
Grein 61 48.14 N 14.51 E
Greinsheim 56 49.18 N 8.16 E
Greiz 54 50.39 N 12.12 E
Grejdernoje 80 46.53 N 45.01 E
Grejsdal 41 55.45 N 9.32 E
Grekov 80 47.24 N 43.41 E
Grekovo 83 48.54 N 40.14 E
Grem'ačij 88 57.01 N 108.12 E
Grem'ačinsk, S.S.S.R. 86 58.34 N 57.51 E
Grem'ačinsk, S.S.S.R. 88 52.48 N 107.57 E
Grem'ačje 78 51.29 N 39.00 E
Grem'aščevo 82 54.14 N 36.15 E
Gremersdorf 54 54.20 N 10.55 E
Gremicha 24 68.03 N 39.27 E
Grenå 26 56.25 N 10.53 E
Grenada 194 33.47 N 89.55 W
Grenada □[1] 230
241k 12.07 N 61.40 W
Grenada Lake ⊜[1] 194 33.50 N 89.40 W
Grenade → Grenada □[1] 241k 12.07 N 61.40 W
Grenadier Island I 212 44.03 N 76.22 W
Grenadier Pond ⊜ 275b 43.38 N 79.28 W
Grenadine Islands II 238 12.40 N 61.15 W
Grenagh 48 52.00 N 8.37 W
Grenay 50 50.27 N 2.44 E
Grenchen 58 47.11 N 7.24 E
Grenell 212 44.16 N 76.04 W
Grenfell, Austl. 166 33.54 S 148.10 E
Grenfell, Sask., Can. 184 50.25 N 102.56 W
Grenoble 62 45.10 N 5.43 E
Grenola 198 37.21 N 96.27 W
Grenora 198 48.37 N 103.56 W
Grenoside 44 53.27 N 1.30 W
Grenville, Qué., Can. 206 45.37 N 74.36 W
Grenville, Gren. 241k 12.07 N 61.37 W
Grenville □[6] 212 44.50 N 75.40 W
Grenville, Cape ≻ 164 11.58 S 143.14 E
Grenville Bay 206 45.38 N 74.36 W
Grenville Bay C 241k 12.07 N 61.36 W
Grenville Channel ⩌ 182 53.40 N 129.40 W
Grenzaa ≃ 52 52.39 N 6.45 E
Grenz-Berg ∧[2] 264a 52.27 N 13.44 E
Grenzlandring ♠ 56 51.11 N 6.17 E
Gréolières 62 43.48 N 6.57 E
Gréoux-les-Bains 62 43.45 N 5.53 E
Greppin 54 51.39 N 12.18 E
Gresenhorst 54 54.09 N 12.26 E
Gresham 224 45.30 N 122.26 W
Gresham Park 192 33.42 N 84.19 W
Gresik, Indon. 112 2.18 S 103.57 E
Gresik, Indon. 115a 7.09 S 112.38 E
Gressåmoen Nasjonalpark ♠ 26 64.15 N 13.08 E
Gresse-en-Vercors 62 44.54 N 5.34 E
Gressey 261 48.50 N 1.37 E
Gressitt 208 37.29 N 76.43 W
Gressk 76 53.10 N 27.29 E
Gressoney, Val di V 62 45.47 N 7.49 E
Gressoney-la-Trinité 62 45.50 N 7.49 E
Gressoney-Saint-Jean 62 45.47 N 7.49 E
Gressy 261 48.58 N 2.41 E
Gresten 61 48.00 N 15.02 E
Grésy-sur-Aix 62 45.43 N 5.57 E
Grésy-sur-Isère 62 45.36 N 6.15 E
Greta 170 32.41 S 151.24 E
Greta ≃, Eng., U.K. 44 54.09 N 2.36 W
Greta ≃, Eng., U.K. 44 54.36 N 3.10 W
Greta ≃, Eng., U.K. 44 54.32 N 1.53 W
Gretna, Man., Can. 184 49.02 N 97.35 W
Gretna, La., U.S. 194 29.55 N 90.03 W
Gretna, Va., U.S. 192 36.57 N 79.22 W
Gretna Green 44 54.59 N 3.04 W
Gretz-Armainvilliers 50 48.44 N 2.44 E
Greussen 54 51.14 N 10.57 E
Greve, Dan. 41 55.36 N 12.15 E
Greve, It. 66 43.35 N 11.19 E
Greve ≃ 66 43.46 N 11.13 E
Grevel ◆[8] 263 51.34 N 7.33 E
Grevelingen ⩌ 52 51.45 N 4.00 E
Grevelingendam ◆[5] 52 51.40 N 4.10 E
Greven 52 52.05 N 7.36 E
Grevená 38 40.05 N 21.25 E
Grevenbroich 56 51.05 N 6.35 E
Grevenbroich □[8] 263 51.08 N 6.38 E
Greven-Granzin 54 53.29 N 10.48 E
Grevenmacher 56 49.42 N 6.20 E
Grevesmühlen 54 53.51 N 11.10 E
Greve Strand 41 55.35 N 12.14 E
Greville Bay C 186 45.22 N 64.38 W
Grevinge 41 55.48 N 11.34 E
Grey □[6] 212 44.20 N 80.45 W
Grey ≃, Newf., Can. 186 47.38 N 57.05 W
Grey ≃, N.Z. 172 42.27 S 171.12 E
Grey, Cape ≻ 164 13.00 S 136.40 E
Grey, Point ≻, Austl. 169 38.34 S 143.59 E
Grey, Point ≻, B.C., Can. 224 49.16 N 123.16 W
Greyabbey 48 54.32 N 5.30 W
Greybull 202 44.30 N 108.03 W
Greybull ≃ 202 44.28 N 108.03 W
Grey Eagle 190 45.50 N 94.45 W
Grey Islands II 186 50.50 N 55.37 W
Greylingstad 158 26.44 S 28.45 E
Greylock, Mount ∧ 207 42.38 N 73.10 W
Greymont ◆[8] 273d 26.10 S 27.58 E
Greymouth 172 42.28 S 171.12 E
Grey Range ⩕ 166 27.00 S 143.35 E
Greys ≃ 202 43.10 N 111.00 W
Greystanes 274a 33.49 S 150.55 E
Greystoke 44 54.40 N 2.52 W
Greystones 48 53.09 N 6.04 W
Greyton 158 34.04 S 19.38 E
Greytown, N.Z. 172 41.05 S 175.27 E
Greytown → San Juan del Norte, Nic. 236 10.55 N 83.42 W
Greytown, S. Afr. 158 29.07 S 30.30 E
Grez-Doiceau 56 50.44 N 4.42 E
Grez-sur-Loing 50 48.19 N 2.42 E
Grezzana 64 45.31 N 11.01 E
Gribanovskij 80 51.27 N 41.58 E
Gribb Bank ✣[4] 9 61.30 S 88.00 E
Gribbel Island I 182 53.25 N 129.00 W
Gribbin Head ≻ 42 50.19 N 4.40 W
Gribingui ≃ 146 8.33 N 19.05 E
Gribovka 82 54.19 N 38.27 E
Gricev 78 49.58 N 27.14 E
Gridley, Calif., U.S. 226 39.22 N 121.42 W
Gridley, Ill., U.S. 216 40.45 N 88.53 W
Griebnitz See ⊜ 264a 52.24 N 13.06 E
Griechenland → Greece □[1] 38 39.00 N 22.00 E
Griekwastad 158 28.49 S 23.15 E
Grier City 210 40.50 N 76.04 W
Gries am Brenner 64 47.03 N 11.29 E
Griesbach 60 48.36 N 12.35 E
Griesbach im Rottal 60 48.28 N 13.11 E
Griesen 64 47.29 N 10.56 E
Griesheim 56 49.50 N 8.34 E
Gries im Sellrain 64 47.12 N 11.09 E
Grieskirchen 60 48.14 N 13.50 E
Griessem 52 52.00 N 9.12 E
Griesspitzen ∧ 64 47.22 N 10.58 E
Griffen 61 46.42 N 14.44 E
Griffin, Sask., Can. 184 49.40 N 103.26 W
Griffin, Ga., U.S. 192 33.15 N 84.16 W
Griffin, Lake ⊜ 220 28.52 N 81.51 W
Griffin Bay C 224 48.30 N 122.58 W
Griffiss Air Force Base ■ 210 43.14 N 75.26 W

DEUTSCH — Name | Seite | Breite°′ | Länge°′ E=Ost

Griffith, Austl. 166 34.17 S 146.03 E
Griffith, Ind., U.S. 216 41.32 N 87.25 W
Griffith Airport ⊠ 278 41.31 N 87.23 W
Griffith Island I, N.W. Ter., Can. 176 74.35 N 95.30 W
Griffith Island I, Ont., Can. 212 44.51 N 80.54 W
Griffith Park ♠ 280 34.09 N 118.17 W
Grifton 192 35.23 N 77.26 W
Griggs Drain ⌶ 281 42.11 N 83.26 W
Griggs Reservoir ⊜[1] 214 40.03 N 83.06 W
Griggstown 276 40.26 N 74.37 W
Griggsville 219 39.42 N 90.43 W
Grignan 62 44.25 N 4.54 E
Grignano 64 45.42 N 13.43 E
Grignasco 62 45.41 N 8.20 E
Grigno 64 46.01 N 11.38 E
Grignols 32 44.23 N 0.03 W
Grignon 261 48.51 N 1.51 E
Grigny 62 45.37 N 4.47 E
Grigoriopol' 78 47.10 N 29.18 E
Grigorjevka, S.S.S.R. 78 46.17 N 33.44 E
Grigorjevka, S.S.S.R. 83 47.27 N 38.23 E
Grigorjevka, S.S.S.R. 85 42.43 N 77.30 E
Grigorjevskoje, S.S.S.R. 82 54.49 N 37.59 E
Grigorjevskoje, S.S.S.R. 82 54.48 N 39.15 E
Grigorovka, S.S.S.R. 78 51.03 N 32.51 E
Grigorovka, S.S.S.R. 78 50.05 N 30.39 E
Grigorovka, S.S.S.R. 82 54.38 N 36.20 E
Grigorovo 82 56.42 N 37.35 E
Grigorovskoje 82 54.17 N 36.21 E
Grijalva ≃ 232 18.36 N 92.39 W
Grijpskerk 52 53.15 N 6.18 E
Grillbach ≃ 263 51.11 N 6.44 E
Grillby 40 59.37 N 17.15 E
Grillenburg 54 50.57 N 13.31 E
Grim, Cape ≻ 166 40.41 S 144.41 E
Grima 152 3.59 N 17.06 E
Grimajlov 78 49.20 N 26.01 E
Grimaldi 68 39.08 N 16.14 E
Grimari 152 5.44 N 20.03 E
Grimaud 62 43.16 N 6.31 E
Grimbergen 50 50.56 N 4.23 E
Grimeford Village 262 53.36 N 2.34 W
Grimes 226 39.04 N 121.54 W
Grimes □[6] 222 30.35 N 96.00 W
Grimlinghausen ◆[8] 263 51.10 N 6.44 E
Grimma 54 51.14 N 12.43 E
Grimmen 54 54.07 N 13.02 E
Grimmenstein 61 47.38 N 16.06 E
Grimmialp 58 46.34 N 7.29 E
Grimnitzsee ⊜ 54 52.58 N 13.47 E
Grimsargh 262 53.48 N 2.38 W
Grimsby, Ont., Can. 212 43.12 N 79.34 W
Grimsby, Eng., U.K. 44 53.35 N 0.05 W
Grimselpass)(58 46.34 N 8.21 E
Grimselsee ⊜ 58 46.34 N 8.18 E
Grímsey I 24a 66.34 N 18.00 W
Grimshaw 182 56.11 N 117.36 W
Grímsstaðir 24a 65.40 N 16.01 W
Grimstad 26 58.20 N 8.36 E
Grimstead 208 37.30 N 76.18 W
Grin'ava 78 47.59 N 24.49 E
Grindavík 24a 63.52 N 22.27 W
Grindelwald 58 46.37 N 8.02 E
Grindsted 41 55.45 N 8.56 E
Grindstone Island (Cap-aux-Meules) 186 47.23 N 61.52 W
Grindstone Island I 212 44.16 N 76.07 W
Grinnell 190 41.45 N 92.43 W
Grinnell, Lake ⊜ 276 41.06 N 74.38 W
Grinnell Peninsula ≻[1] 176 76.40 N 95.00 W
Grin'ovo 76 52.35 N 33.04 E
Grintavec ∧ 61 46.21 N 14.32 E
Grinzing ◆[8] 264b 48.15 N 16.21 E
Grip 26 63.14 N 7.37 E
Gripsholms slott ⊥ 40 59.15 N 17.13 E
Gripsholmsviken C 40 59.17 N 17.20 E
Griqualand East ◆[1] 158 30.30 S 29.00 E
Griqualand West ◆[1] 158 28.20 S 23.30 E
Grisdale 224 47.22 N 123.37 W
Grisee → Gresik 115a 7.09 S 112.38 E
Grišino 82 56.13 N 37.40 E
Griškovcy 78 49.56 N 28.36 E
Gris-Nez, Cap ≻ 50 50.52 N 1.35 E
Grisolia 68 39.43 N 15.51 E
Grisons → Graubünden □[3] 58 46.45 N 9.30 E
Grisslehamn 40 60.06 N 18.50 E
Grissom Air Force Base ■ 216 40.40 N 86.08 W
Gristow 54 54.10 N 13.20 E
Griswold, Man., Can. 184 49.45 N 100.25 W
Griswold, Iowa, U.S. 198 41.14 N 95.08 W
Griswold Creek ≃ 279a 41.27 N 81.23 W
Griswoldville 207 42.39 N 72.49 W
Grisy-Suisnes 261 48.41 N 2.40 E
Grivai Pamia 152 7.03 N 19.26 E
Grivenskaja 78 45.38 N 38.09 E
Grizzana 64 44.15 N 11.09 E
Grizzly Bay C 226 38.07 N 122.01 W
Grizzly Bear Mountain ∧ 176 65.22 N 121.00 W
Grizzly Creek ≃ 282 37.52 N 122.06 W
Grizzly Flats 226 38.38 N 120.31 W
Grizzly Island I 282 38.08 N 121.58 W
Grizzly Mountain ∧, Idaho, U.S. 202 47.43 N 116.06 W
Grizzly Mountain ∧, Oreg., U.S. 202 44.26 N 120.57 W
Grizzly Mountain ∧, Wash., U.S. 202 48.25 N 118.30 W
Grizzly Slough ≃ 282 38.06 N 121.53 W
Grmeč ⩕ 36 44.40 N 16.30 E
Groaíras 250 3.53 S 40.23 W
Groais Island I 186 50.57 N 55.35 W
Grobbendonk 56 51.12 N 4.43 E
Gröben 264a 52.17 N 13.10 E
Gröbener-See ⊜ 264a 52.17 N 13.11 E
Gröbenzell 60 48.11 N 11.22 E
Grobina 76 56.33 N 21.10 E
Groblersdal 156 25.15 S 29.25 E
Groblershoop 158 28.55 S 20.59 E
Gröbming 64 47.26 N 13.54 E
Grobogan 115a 7.01 S 110.55 E
Gröbzig 54 51.41 N 11.52 E
Grodekovo 85 42.49 N 71.29 E
Grödig 64 47.44 N 13.02 E
Gröditsch 54 52.03 N 13.59 E
Gröditz 54 51.24 N 13.27 E
Grodków 30 50.43 N 17.22 E
Grodno 76 53.41 N 23.50 E
Grodno □[4] 24 54.45 N 26.00 E
Grodovka 83 48.15 N 37.23 E
Grodz'anka 76 53.33 N 28.45 E
Grodzisk Mazowiecki 30 52.07 N 20.37 E
Grodzisk [wielkopolski] 30 52.14 N 16.22 E
Groede 52 51.23 N 3.30 E
Groen ≃ 156 30.40 S 23.17 E
Groënland → Greenland □[2] 16 70.00 N 40.00 W
Groenlandia → Greenland □[2] 16 70.00 N 40.00 W
Groenlo 52 52.03 N 6.38 E
Groenvlei 158 27.27 S 30.13 E
Groesbeck, Ohio, U.S. 218 39.13 N 84.35 W
Groesbeck, Tex., U.S. 222 31.31 N 96.32 W
Groesbeek 52 51.47 N 5.55 E
Grofa, Gora ∧ 78 48.37 N 23.56 E
Grogol, Kali ≃ 269e 6.10 S 106.47 E
Grogol-hilir ◆[8] 269e 6.13 S 106.47 E
Grohnde 52 52.01 N 9.25 E
Groitzsch 54 51.09 N 12.16 E

Symbols in the index entries represent the broad categories identified in the key at the right. Symbols with superior numbers (⩕[2]) identify subcategories (see complete key on page I · 30).

Kartensymbole in dem Registerverzeichnis stellen die rechts in Schlüssel erklärten Kategorien dar. Symbole mit hochgestellten Ziffern (⩕[2]) bezeichnen Unterabteilungen einer Kategorie (vgl. vollständiger Schlüssel auf Seite I · 30).

Los símbolos incluidos en el texto del índice representan las grandes categorias identificadas con la clave a la derecha. Los símbolos con numeros en su parte superior (⩕[2]) identifican las subcategorías (véase la clave completa en la página I · 30).

Les symboles de l'index représentent les catégories indiquées dans la légende à droite. Les symboles suivis d'un indice (⩕[2]) représentent des sous-catégories (voir légende complète à la page I · 30).

Os símbolos incluídos no texto do índice representam as grandes categorias identificadas com a chave à direita. Os símbolos com números em sua parte superior (⩕[2]) identificam as subcategorias (veja-se a chave completa à página I · 30).

Symbol	English	Deutsch	Español	Français	Português
∧	Mountain	Berg	Montaña	Montagne	Montanha
⩕	Mountains	Berge	Montañas	Montagnes	Montanhas
)(	Pass	Pass	Paso	Col	Passo
V	Valley, Canyon	Tal, Cañon	Valle, Cañón	Vallée, Canyon	Vale, Canhão
≚	Plain	Ebene	Llano	Plaine	Planície
≻	Cape	Kap	Cabo	Cap	Cabo
I	Island	Insel	Isla	Île	Ilha
II	Islands	Inseln	Islas	Îles	Ilhas
⊥	Other Topographic Features	Andere Topographische Objekte	Otros Elementos Topográficos	Autres données topographiques	Outros Elementos Topográficos

ESPAÑOL
Nombre Página Lat.°′ Long.°′ W=Oeste

Groix 32 47.38 N 3.28 W
Groix, Île de I 32 47.38 N 3.27 W
Grójec 30 51.52 N 20.52 E
Grokgak 115a 8.11 S 114.47 E
Grolley 58 46.50 N 7.05 E
Grombalia 148 36.36 N 10.30 E
Grömitz 54 54.09 N 10.58 E
Gromo 64 45.58 N 9.56 E
Gromokleja ≃ 78 47.21 N 32.14 E
Gromoslavka 80 48.12 N 43.37 E
Gromovka 78 46.19 N 34.06 E
Gronau, B.R.D. 52 52.13 N 7.00 E
Gronau, B.R.D. 52 52.05 N 9.46 E
Grondines (Saint-Charles-des-Grondines) 206 46.36 N 72.03 W
Grondneus 158 28.06 S 20.48 E
Grone 52 51.32 N 9.53 E
Grönenbach 58 47.52 N 10.13 E
Grong 24 64.28 N 12.18 E
Grongemouth 44 56.01 N 3.44 W
Gröningen, D.D.R. 54 51.56 N 11.13 E
Groningen, Ned. 52 53.13 N 6.33 E
Groningen, Sur. 250 5.48 N 55.28 W
Groningen □4 52 53.15 N 6.45 E
Grønland → Greenland □2 16 70.00 N 40.00 W
Gronlid 184 53.06 N 104.28 W
Grønsund ⩍ 41 54.53 N 12.08 E
Grönwohld 52 53.39 N 10.25 E
Groom 196 35.12 N 101.06 W
Groom Lake ⊜ 204 37.15 N 115.48 W
Groot ≃, S. Afr. 158 33.54 S 21.39 E
Groot ≃, S. Afr. 158 33.45 S 24.36 E
Groot-Berg ≃ 158 32.47 S 18.08 E
Groot-Brakrivier 158 34.01 S 21.46 E
Grootbruintjies-hoogte ⛰ 158 32.32 S 25.20 E
Grootebroek 52 52.43 N 5.13 E
Groote Eylandt I 164 14.00 S 136.40 E
Groot Elandsvlei 273d 26.08 S 27.40 E
Grootfontein 156 19.32 S 18.05 E
Grootfontein □5 156 19.00 S 20.00 E
Groot-Karasberge ⛰ 158 27.20 S 18.40 E
Groot Karroo → Great Karroo ⛰1 158 32.25 S 22.40 E
Groot-Kei ≃ 158 32.41 S 28.22 E
Groot Laagte ≃ 156 20.37 S 21.37 E
Groot Letaba ≃ 156 23.58 S 31.50 E
Groot-marico 156 25.37 S 26.26 E
Grootpan 158 25.58 S 26.33 E
Grootrivierhoogte ⛰ 158 33.15 S 24.22 E
Groot Shingwidzi (Singuédeze) ≃ 156 23.53 S 32.17 E
Groot-Swartberge ⛰ 158 33.22 S 22.20 E
Groot-Vis ≃ 158 33.30 S 27.08 E
Grootvlei 158 26.44 S 28.32 E
Grootvloer ⊜ 158 30.00 S 20.40 E
Groot Winterhoekbergé ⛰ 158 33.36 S 24.58 E
Gröpelingen ◂8 52 53.07 N 8.46 E
Gropello Cairoli 62 45.11 N 9.00 E
Gros Bois, Parc de ♠ 261 48.44 N 2.32 E
Groscavallo 62 45.22 N 7.15 E
Grose ≃ 170 33.36 S 150.41 E
Grosio 64 46.18 N 10.16 E
Gros Islet 241f 14.05 N 60.58 W
Gros Islet Bay C 241f 14.05 N 60.58 W
Groslay 261 48.59 N 2.21 E
Gros Mécatina, Cap du ≻ 186 50.45 N 59.00 W
Gros-Morne 240e 14.43 N 61.01 W
Gros Morne Λ 186 49.36 N 57.48 W
Gros Morne National Park ♠ 186 49.40 N 57.45 W
Grosne ≃ 58 46.42 N 4.56 E
Grosnez Point ≻ 43b 49.16 N 2.15 W
Grosotto 64 46.17 N 10.15 E
Gros Piton Λ 241f 13.49 N 61.04 W
Grosrouvre 261 48.47 N 1.46 E
Grossa, Ponta ≻, Bra. 256 23.35 S 45.13 W
Grossa, Ponta ≻, Bra. 287a 22.47 S 43.11 W
Grossaitingen 58 48.14 N 10.47 E
Grossalmerode 56 51.15 N 9.46 E
Grossalsleben 54 51.59 N 11.13 E
Gross Ammensleben 54 52.14 N 11.31 E
Grossarl 64 47.14 N 13.12 E
Grossauheim 56 50.06 N 8.56 E
Gross-Beeren 54 52.21 N 13.18 E
Gross Berkel 52 52.04 N 9.19 E
Gross-Bieberau 56 49.48 N 8.49 E
Grossbodungen 54 51.28 N 10.28 E
Gross Börnecke 54 51.50 N 11.29 E
Grossbothen 54 51.11 N 12.44 E
Grossbottwar 56 49.00 N 9.17 E
Grossbreitenbach 54 50.35 N 11.02 E
Grossburgwedel 52 52.29 N 9.51 E
Grossdeuben 54 51.14 N 12.23 E
Grossdubrau 54 51.15 N 14.28 E
Gross Düngen 52 52.06 N 10.01 E
Grosse Antillen → Greater Antilles II 238 20.00 N 74.00 W
Grosse Australische Bucht → Great Australian Bight C3 162 35.00 S 135.00 E
Grossebersdorf 54 50.47 N 11.57 E
Grosse Ebene → Great Plains ⊻ 16 42.00 N 100.00 W
Grosse Herrenwiese ☷ 264a 52.17 N 13.20 E
Grosse Ile 216 42.08 N 83.09 W
Grosse Île I, Qué., Can. 186 47.37 N 61.31 W
Grosse Ile I, Mich., U.S. 216 42.08 N 83.09 W
Grosse Laaber ≃ 60 48.56 N 12.30 E
Grossenbaum ◂8 263 51.22 N 6.47 E
Grossenbrode 54 54.22 N 11.05 E
Grossen-Buseck 56 50.36 N 8.47 E
Grossengottern 54 51.09 N 10.34 E
Grossengstingen 58 48.23 N 9.17 E
Grossenhain 54 51.17 N 13.31 E
Grossenheidorn 52 52.27 N 9.23 E
Grossenkneten 52 52.56 N 8.16 E
Grossen-Linden 56 50.31 N 8.39 E
Grossenlüder 56 50.35 N 9.32 E
Grossenritte 56 51.15 N 9.23 E
Grossenwiehe 41 54.43 N 9.15 E
Gross-Enzersdorf 264b 48.12 N 16.33 E
Grosse Pointe 214 42.24 N 82.55 W
Grosse Pointe ≻ 241o 16.01 N 61.16 W
Grosse Pointe Farms 214 42.25 N 82.53 W
Grosse Pointe Park 214 42.23 N 82.56 W
Grosse Pointe Shores 214 42.26 N 82.53 W
Grosse Pointe Woods 214 42.27 N 82.55 W
Grosser Arber Λ 60 49.07 N 13.07 E
Grosser Bären-See → Great Bear Lake ⊜ 176 66.00 N 120.00 W
Grosser Beerberg Λ 54 50.37 N 10.44 E
Grosser Bösenstein Λ 61 47.26 N 14.24 E
Grosser Buchstein Λ 61 47.36 N 14.35 E
Grosser Chingan → Daxing'anling-shanmai ⛰ 89 49.40 N 122.00 E
Grosser Feldberg Λ 56 50.14 N 8.26 E
Grosser Galtenberg Λ 64 47.20 N 11.58 E

FRANÇAIS
Nom Page Lat.°′ Long.°′ W=Ouest

Grosser Gleichberg Λ 54 50.23 N 10.35 E
Grosser Graben ≍ 264a 52.28 N 13.03 E
Grosser Heuberg ⛰1 58 48.06 N 8.55 E
Grosser Inselsberg Λ 54 50.52 N 10.28 E
Grosser Jasmunder Bodden C 54 54.31 N 13.29 E
Grosser Knallstein Λ 61 47.19 N 13.58 E
Grosser Königstuhl Λ 64 46.57 N 13.47 E
Grosser Müggelsee ⊜ 54 52.26 N 13.39 E
Grosse Röder ≃ 54 51.30 N 13.25 E
Grosser oder Kaiser-Kanal → Yunhe ≍ 90 32.12 N 119.31 E
Grosse Rodl ≃ 61 48.20 N 14.09 E
Grosser Peilstein Λ 61 48.18 N 15.06 E
Grosser Plessower See ⊜ 264a 52.23 N 12.54 E
Grosser Plöner See ⊜ 54 54.06 N 10.25 E
Grosser Priel Λ 61 47.43 N 14.04 E
Grosser Rachel Λ 60 48.59 N 13.24 E
Grosser Ravens-Berg Λ2 264a 52.21 N 13.04 E
Grosser Riedelstein Λ 60 49.10 N 12.59 E
Grosser Salz-See → Great Salt Lake ⊜ 200 41.10 N 112.30 W
Grosser Seddiner See ⊜ 264a 52.17 N 13.02 E
Grosser Selchower See ⊜ 54 52.14 N 13.53 E
Grosser Sklaven-See → Great Slave Lake ⊜ 176 61.30 N 114.00 W
Grosser Walfisch-Fluss → Grande Rivière de la Baleine ≃ 176 55.16 N 77.47 W
Grosser Wannsee ⊜ 264a 52.26 N 13.11 E
Grosser Winterberg Λ2 54 50.54 N 14.16 E
Grosser Zern-See ⊜ 264a 52.24 N 12.56 E
Grosse Sandspitze Λ 64 46.46 N 12.49 E
Grosse Sandwüste → Great Sandy Desert ◂2 162 21.30 S 125.00 E
Grosse Saualpe Λ 61 46.51 N 14.39 E
Grosses Barrier-Riff → Great Barrier Reef ✢2 160 18.00 S 145.50 E
Grosses Meer ⊜ 52 53.25 N 7.17 E
Grosses Moor ◂3, B.R.D. 52 52.35 N 8.45 E
Grosses Moor ◂3, B.R.D. 52 52.40 N 8.20 E
Grosses Schulerloch ♠ 60 48.55 N 11.48 E
Grosse Sundainseln → Greater Sunda Islands II 108 2.00 S 110.00 E
Grosses Walsertal V 58 47.14 N 9.56 E
Grosse Syrte → Surt, Khalīj C 146 31.30 N 18.00 E
Grosseto 66 42.46 N 11.08 E
Grosseto □4 66 42.50 N 11.15 E
Grosse Tulln ≃ 61 48.20 N 16.02 E
Grossevići 89 47.59 N 139.30 E
Gross-Gerau 56 49.55 N 8.29 E
Gross-Gerungs 61 48.34 N 14.57 E
Gross Gleidingen 54 52.14 N 10.25 E
Gross Glienicke 264a 52.28 N 13.07 E
Gross-Glienicker See ⊜ 264a 52.28 N 13.06 E
Grossglockner Λ 64 47.04 N 12.42 E
Grossgmain 64 47.43 N 12.55 E
Grossgörschen 54 51.13 N 12.11 E
Gross Grönau 54 53.46 N 10.44 E
Grosshansdorf 52 53.40 N 10.17 E
Grosshartmannsdorf 54 50.48 N 13.19 E
Gross-Hehlen 52 52.39 N 10.03 E
Grossheide 52 53.35 N 7.20 E
Grosshennersdorf 54 50.59 N 14.47 E
Grosshöchstetten 58 46.55 N 7.38 E
Grossholzleute 58 47.41 N 10.05 E
Grossjedlersdorf ◂8 264b 48.17 N 16.25 E
Grosskayna 54 51.17 N 11.56 E
Gross Kienitz 264a 52.19 N 13.28 E
Gross-Kollmar 52 53.44 N 9.30 E
Grosskorbetha 54 51.16 N 12.01 E
Gross Kreutz 54 52.24 N 12.46 E
Grosskrut 61 48.38 N 16.43 E
Grosslehna 54 51.18 N 12.10 E
Gross Leine 54 52.00 N 14.03 E
Grosslittgen 56 50.02 N 6.47 E
Grossmachnow 54 52.16 N 13.28 E
Grossmehring 60 48.46 N 11.32 E
Gross Möllen → Mielno 30 54.16 N 16.01 E
Grossmont 228 32.47 N 116.59 W
Gross Muckrow 54 52.04 N 14.26 E
Grössnöbach 60 48.21 N 11.35 E
Gross Oesingen 52 52.38 N 10.29 E
Grossörner 54 51.37 N 11.29 E
Grossos 250 4.59 S 37.09 W
Grossostheim 56 49.55 N 9.04 E
Grosspostwitz 54 51.07 N 14.26 E
Grossquenstedt 54 51.56 N 11.07 E
Grossraming 61 47.53 N 14.33 E
Grossräschen 54 51.35 N 14.00 E
Gross Rhüden 52 51.56 N 10.07 E
Grossrinderfeld 56 49.39 N 9.44 E
Gross Rodensleben 54 52.08 N 11.25 E
Grossröhrsdorf 54 51.08 N 14.01 E
Gross Rosenburg 54 51.55 N 11.53 E
Grossrückerswalde 54 50.38 N 13.07 E
Grossrudestedt 54 51.05 N 11.06 E
Grosssachsenheim 56 48.58 N 9.04 E
Gross-Sarau 54 53.45 N 10.44 E
Grossschirma 54 50.58 N 13.17 E
Grossschönau 54 50.54 N 14.40 E
Gross Schönebeck 54 52.54 N 13.32 E
Gross-Schulzendorf 264a 52.16 N 13.21 E
Grosssölk 64 47.25 N 13.58 E
Gross Strehlitz → Strzelce Opolskie 30 50.31 N 18.19 E
Grosstimmern 56 49.52 N 8.50 E
Gross-Umstadt 56 49.52 N 8.55 E
Grossvenediger Λ 64 47.06 N 12.21 E
Grosswardein → Oradea 38 47.03 N 21.57 E
Gross Wartenberg → Syców 30 51.19 N 17.43 E
Grosswell 64 47.41 N 11.18 E
Gross Windgällen Λ 58 46.49 N 8.44 E
Gross Wittensee 41 54.24 N 9.46 E
Gross Ziethen, D.D.R. 264a 52.24 N 13.27 E
Gross Ziethen, D.D.R. 264a 52.44 N 13.01 E
Grosszimmern 56 49.52 N 8.50 E
Grostenquin 56 48.59 N 6.44 E
Grosvenor, Lake ⊜ 180 58.40 N 155.15 W
Grosvenor Dale 207 41.58 N 71.54 W
Gros Ventre ≃ 202 43.33 N 110.46 W
Groswater Bay C 176 54.20 N 57.30 W
Grote Nete ≃ 56 51.07 N 4.34 E
Groton, Conn., U.S. 207 41.19 N 72.12 W
Groton, Mass., U.S. 207 42.37 N 71.34 W
Groton, N.Y., U.S. 210 42.35 N 76.22 W
Groton, S. Dak., U.S. 198 45.27 N 98.06 W
Grottaferrata 66 41.47 N 12.40 E

PORTUGUÊS
Nome Página Lat.°′ Long.°′ W=Oeste

Grottaglie 68 40.32 N 17.26 E
Grottaminarda 68 41.04 N 15.02 E
Grottammare 66 42.59 N 13.52 E
Grotte 70 37.24 N 13.42 E
Grotte di Castro 66 42.40 N 11.52 E
Grotteria 68 38.22 N 16.17 E
Grottkau → Grodków 30 50.43 N 17.22 E
Grottoes 188 38.16 N 78.56 W
Grottole 68 40.36 N 16.23 E
Grouard Mission 182 55.31 N 116.09 W
Groundbirch 182 55.47 N 120.55 W
Groundhog ≃ 176 49.43 N 81.58 W
Grouse Creek 200 41.42 N 113.53 W
Grouse Creek ≃, Kans., U.S. 198 37.00 N 96.55 W
Grouse Creek ≃, Utah, U.S. 200 41.22 N 113.55 W
Grouse Creek Mountain Λ 202 44.22 N 113.54 W
Grouw 52 53.05 N 5.45 E
Grove, Okla., U.S. 196 36.36 N 94.46 W
Grove, Pa., U.S. 285 40.01 N 75.38 W
Grove City, Fla., U.S. 220 26.56 N 82.20 W
Grove City, Minn., U.S. 198 45.09 N 94.41 W
Grove City, Ohio, U.S. 218 39.53 N 83.06 W
Grove City, Pa., U.S. 214 41.10 N 80.05 W
Grove Hill 194 31.42 N 87.47 W
Groveland, Calif., U.S. 226 37.50 N 120.14 W
Groveland, Fla., U.S. 220 28.34 N 81.51 W
Groveland, Mass., U.S. 207 42.46 N 71.02 W
Groveland, N.Y., U.S. 210 42.40 N 77.46 W
Grovely Ridge Λ 42 51.08 N 2.04 W
Grove Mountains ⛰ 9 72.53 S 74.53 E
Grove Park ◂8 260 51.26 N 0.01 E
Groveport 218 39.51 N 82.53 W
Grover 210 41.37 N 76.52 W
Grover City 204 35.07 N 120.37 W
Grover Cleveland Birthplace ⊥ 276 40.50 N 74.16 W
Grover Cleveland Park ♠ 284a 42.57 N 78.49 W
Grover Hill 216 41.01 N 84.29 W
Grovers Mills 276 40.19 N 74.37 W
Groves 194 29.57 N 93.55 W
Groveton, N.H., U.S. 188 44.36 N 71.31 W
Groveton, Pa., U.S. 279b 40.30 N 80.06 W
Groveton, Tex., U.S. 222 31.03 N 95.08 W
Groveton, Va., U.S. 284c 38.46 N 77.05 W
Grovetown 192 33.27 N 82.12 W
Groveville 208 40.11 N 74.40 W
Growler Peak Λ 200 32.24 N 113.07 W
Growler Wash V 200 32.35 N 113.30 W
Groznoje 85 42.36 N 71.12 E
Groznyj 84 43.20 N 45.42 E
Groznyy → Groznyj 84 43.20 N 45.42 E
Grube, B.R.D. 54 54.14 N 11.01 E
Grube, D.D.R. 264a 52.26 N 12.57 E
Grubišno Polje 36 45.42 N 17.10 E
Grubweg 60 48.35 N 13.29 E
Grudovo 38 42.21 N 27.10 E
Grudziądz 30 53.29 N 18.45 E
Gruesa, Punta ≻ 248 20.22 S 70.11 W
Gruetli 194 35.22 N 85.40 W
Grugapark ♠ 263 51.26 N 7.00 E
Grugliasco 62 45.04 N 7.35 E
Gruia 38 44.16 N 22.42 E
Gruinard Bay C 46 57.53 N 5.31 W
Gruinart, Loch C 46 55.52 N 6.20 W
Gruiten 56 51.14 N 7.01 E
Gruitrode 56 51.05 N 5.35 E
Grulla 196 26.16 N 98.39 W
Grumello del Monte 62 45.38 N 9.52 E
Grumento Nova 68 40.17 N 15.53 E
Grumentum ⊥ 68 40.17 N 15.55 E
Grumman-Bethpage Airport ⊠ 276 40.45 N 73.29 W
Grumman Corporation ♥3 276 40.45 N 73.30 W
Grumme ◂8 263 51.30 N 7.14 E
Grumo Appula 68 41.01 N 16.42 E
Grums 26 59.21 N 13.06 E
Grun' 78 50.16 N 34.36 E
Grüna 54 50.49 N 12.47 E
Grünau 156 27.47 S 18.23 E
Grünau ◂8 264a 52.25 N 13.34 E
Grünau im Almtal 64 47.51 N 13.57 E
Grunavat, Loch ⊜ 46 58.10 N 6.55 W
Grünbach 54 50.26 N 12.22 E
Grünberg, B.R.D. 56 50.35 N 8.58 E
Grünberg → Zielona Góra, Pol. 30 51.56 N 15.31 E
Grundlsee ⊜ 64 47.38 N 13.52 E
Grundy 192 37.17 N 82.06 W
Grundy □6 216 41.22 N 88.26 W
Grundy Center 190 42.22 N 92.47 W
Grundy Lake Provincial Park ♠ 190 45.48 N 80.34 W
Grünefeld 264a 52.41 N 12.58 E
Grünenplan 52 51.57 N 9.44 E
Grünewald, B.R.D. 263 51.13 N 7.37 E
Grünewald, D.D.R. 54 51.24 N 14.00 E
Grunewald ◂8 264a 52.30 N 13.17 E
Grunewald, Jagdschloss ⊥ 264a 52.28 N 13.16 E
Grünhain 54 50.35 N 12.48 E
Grünhainichen 54 50.46 N 13.08 E
Grünheide 54 52.25 N 13.49 E
Grünsfeld 56 49.36 N 9.44 E
Grünstadt 56 49.34 N 8.10 E
Grüntal 264a 52.45 N 13.44 E
Grunthal 184 49.25 N 96.52 W
Grünwald 60 48.02 N 11.31 E
Gruševka 78 47.55 N 40.40 E
Gruševka ≃ 83 47.26 N 40.00 E
Gruševskaja 83 47.26 N 39.57 E
Grušino 76 59.27 N 44.09 E
Gruting 46 60.14 N 1.30 W
Gruver 196 36.16 N 101.24 W
Gruyère, Lac de la ⊜ 58 46.38 N 7.06 E
Gruyères 58 46.35 N 7.05 E
Gruzdžiai 76 56.06 N 23.16 E
Gruzinskaja Sovetskaja Socialističeskaja Respublika Λ 84 42.00 N 44.00 E
Gruznovka 88 55.09 N 105.12 E
Gruzskaja Balka 78 46.25 N 40.19 E
Gruzskij Jelančik ≃ 83 47.07 N 38.04 E
Gruzskoje 83 48.33 N 37.18 E
Gruzsko-Zor'anskoje 83 47.56 N 38.06 E
Grybów 30 49.38 N 20.56 E
Grycken ⊜ 40 60.27 N 16.13 E
Gryfice 30 53.56 N 15.12 E
Gryfino 30 53.12 N 14.30 E
Grytdalen Nasjonalpark ♠ 26 63.25 N 9.45 E
Grytgöl 40 58.48 N 15.33 E
Grythyttan 40 59.42 N 14.32 E
Gschnitz 64 47.03 N 11.22 E
Gschütt, Pass)(64 47.35 N 13.30 E
Gschwend 56 48.56 N 9.44 E
Gstaad 58 46.28 N 7.17 E
Gsteig 58 46.23 N 7.16 E
Gua 124 22.12 N 85.23 E
Guabaria ≃1 126 22.10 N 90.30 E
Guabito 236 9.30 N 82.37 W
Guabu 106 32.16 N 118.53 E
Guacanayabo, Golfo de C 240p 20.28 N 77.30 W
Guacara 246 10.14 N 67.53 W
Guacarí 246 3.46 N 76.20 W
Gu Achi 200 32.20 N 112.02 W
Guachinango 234 20.32 N 104.24 W
Guachiría ≃ 246 5.27 N 70.36 W
Guachochic 232 26.51 N 107.05 W
Guaçuí 255 20.46 S 41.41 W
Guadajira ≃ 34 38.52 N 6.41 W
Guadajoz ≃ 34 37.50 N 4.51 W
Guadalajara, Esp. 34 40.38 N 3.10 W
Guadalajara, Méx. 234 20.40 N 103.20 W
Guadalamar ≃ 34 38.05 N 3.06 W
Guadalaviar ≃ 34 40.21 N 1.08 W
Guadalcanal 34 38.06 N 5.49 W
Guadalcanal I 175e 9.32 S 160.12 E
Guadalcázar 234 22.37 N 100.24 W
Guadalén ≃ 34 38.05 N 3.32 W
Guadalén, Embalse de ⊜1 34 38.25 N 3.15 W
Guadalentin ≃ 34 37.59 N 1.04 W
Guadalete ≃ 34 36.35 N 6.13 W
Guadalhorce ≃ 34 36.41 N 4.27 W
Guadalmena ≃ 34 38.19 N 2.56 W
Guadalmez ≃ 34 38.46 N 5.04 W
Guadalope ≃ 34 41.15 N 0.03 W
Guadalquivir ≃ 34 36.47 N 6.22 W
Guadalupe, Bol. 248 18.33 S 64.05 W
Guadalupe, Col. 246 2.01 N 75.45 W
Guadalupe, C.R. 236 9.57 N 84.03 W
Guadalupe, Méx. 196 28.09 N 100.36 W
Guadalupe, Méx. 232 16.16 N 91.27 W
Guadalupe, Méx. 232 25.41 N 100.15 W
Guadalupe, Méx. 234 22.45 N 102.31 W
Guadalupe, Perú 248 7.15 S 79.29 W
Guadalupe, Calif., U.S. 204 34.58 N 120.34 W
Guadalupe □6 222 29.37 N 97.45 W
Guadalupe ◂8 287a 22.50 S 43.23 W
Guadalupe → Guadeloupe □2 241o 16.15 N 61.35 W
Guadalupe ≃, Méx. 204 32.05 N 116.53 W
Guadalupe ≃, Calif., U.S. 282 37.25 N 121.58 W
Guadalupe ≃, Tex., U.S. 196 28.30 N 96.53 W
Guadalupe, Basílica de ♥1 286a 19.29 N 99.07 W
Guadalupe, Isla de I 178 29.00 N 118.16 W
Guadalupe, Presa de ⊜1 286a 19.37 N 99.16 W
Guadalupe, Sierra de ⛰, Esp. 34 39.26 N 5.25 W
Guadalupe, Sierra de ⛰, Méx. 286a 19.35 N 99.08 W
Guadalupe [Bravos] 232 31.23 N 106.07 W
Guadalupe del Norte ≍ 286a 19.34 N 99.01 W
Guadalupe de Ramírez 234 17.45 N 98.10 W
Guadalupe Garzarón 232 24.35 N 101.15 W
Guadalupe Mountains ⛰ 196 32.20 N 105.00 W
Guadalupe Mountains National Park ♠ 196 31.55 N 104.55 W
Guadalupe Peak Λ 196 31.50 N 104.52 W
Guadalupe Seamount ✢3 14 27.55 N 168.50 W
Guadalupe Slough ≃ 282 37.27 N 122.02 W
Guadalupe Victoria, Méx. 196 27.47 N 101.04 W
Guadalupe Victoria, Méx. 232 24.27 N 104.07 W
Guadalupe Victoria, Méx. 234 19.17 N 97.21 W
Guadalupe Victoria, Presa ⊜1 234 23.50 N 104.46 W
Guadalupita 200 36.08 N 105.14 W
Guadarrama ≃ 34 39.53 N 4.10 W
Guadarrama, Puerto de)(34 40.43 N 4.10 W
Guadarrama, Sierra de ⛰ 34 40.55 N 4.00 W
Guadazaón ≃ 34 39.42 N 1.36 W
Guadeloupe □2 230
241o 16.15 N 61.35 W
Guadeloupe Passage ⩍ 238 16.45 N 61.30 W
Guadiana ≃ 34 37.14 N 7.22 W
Guadiana, Ensenada de C 240p 22.05 N 84.24 W
Guadiana Menor ≃ 34 37.56 N 3.15 W
Guadiaro ≃ 34 36.17 N 5.17 W
Guadiela ≃ 34 40.22 N 2.49 W
Guadix 34 37.18 N 3.08 W
Guafo, Isla I 254 43.36 S 74.43 W
Guagnano 68 40.24 N 17.57 E
Guagua 116 14.58 N 120.38 E
Guahe 105 39.12 N 115.00 E
Guaianases ◂8 287b 23.33 S 46.25 W
Guaíba 252 30.06 S 51.19 W
Guaíba C1 252 30.15 S 51.12 W
Guaicaipuro □5 286c 10.25 N 66.57 W
Guaihezhen 100 33.28 N 112.59 E
Guaimaca 236 14.32 N 86.51 W
Guáimaro 240p 21.03 N 77.21 W
Guaimoreto, Laguna de C 236 15.58 N 85.55 W
Guaimozi 98 41.31 N 125.26 E
Guainía □5 246 2.30 N 69.00 W
Guainía ≃ 246 2.01 N 67.07 W
Guaió ≃ 287b 23.31 S 46.19 W
Guaipava 256 21.40 S 45.43 W
Guaiquica 256 22.25 S 47.14 W
Guaiquinima, Cerro Λ 246 5.49 N 63.40 W
Guaíra, Bra. 252 24.04 S 54.15 W
Guaíra, Bra. 255 20.19 S 48.18 W
Guairá □5 252 25.45 S 56.30 W
Guaire ≃ 286c 10.25 N 66.46 W
Guáitara ≃ 246 1.34 N 77.27 W
Guaitecas, Islas II 254 43.57 S 73.50 W
Guaiúba 250 4.02 S 38.38 W
Guajaba, Cayo I 240p 21.50 N 77.30 W
Guajará ≃ 250 1.48 S 53.02 W
Guajará-Açu 250 1.38 S 48.07 W
Guajará-Miri 250 1.29 S 48.17 W
Guajará-Mirim 248 10.48 S 65.22 W
Guajataca, Lago de ⊜1 240m 18.23 N 66.55 W
Guajiasi 104 41.15 N 120.54 E
Gualaca 236 8.32 N 82.18 W
Gualaceo 246 2.54 S 78.47 W
Gualala 204 38.46 N 123.32 W
Gualán 236 15.08 N 89.22 W
Gualaquiza 246 3.24 S 78.33 W
Gualdo Tadino 66 43.14 N 12.47 E
Gualeguay 252 33.09 S 59.20 W
Gualeguay ≃ 252 33.19 S 59.39 W
Gualeguaychú 252 33.01 S 58.31 W
Gualicho, Salina ⊻ 254 40.24 S 65.15 W
Gualjaina 254 42.42 S 70.30 W
Gualtieri 64 44.54 N 10.38 E
Guam □2 14
174p 13.28 N 144.47 E
Guamá ≃, Bra. 250 1.29 S 48.30 W
Guamá ≃, Cuba 240p 22.11 N 83.41 W
Guamal, Col. 246 9.09 N 74.14 W
Guamal, Col. 246 3.52 N 73.44 W
Guamal, Quebrada ≃ 286c 10.31 N 66.59 W
Guamblin, Isla I 254 44.51 S 75.05 W
Guaminí 252 37.02 S 62.25 W
Guamo 246 4.02 N 74.58 W
Guamo Embarcadero 240p 20.37 N 76.58 W
Guamote 246 1.56 S 78.43 W
Guamúchil 234 23.55 N 106.05 W
Guamués ≃ 246 0.32 N 76.33 W
Gua Musang 114 4.53 N 101.58 E
Gu'an 105 39.26 N 116.18 E
Guanábana 240m 18.01 N 67.07 W
Guanabara, Baía de C 287a 22.50 S 43.10 W
Guanabara, Palácio de ♥ 287a 22.56 S 43.11 W
Guanacaste □4 236 10.30 N 85.15 W
Guanacaste, Cordillera de ⛰ 236 10.45 N 85.05 W
Guanacaure, Cerro Λ 236 13.14 N 87.07 W
Guanaceví 232 25.56 N 105.57 W
Guanache ≃ 248 5.53 S 74.21 W
Guanahacabibes, Golfo de C 240p 22.08 N 84.35 W
Guanahacabibes, Península de ≻1 240p 21.57 N 84.35 W
Guana Island I 240m 18.29 N 64.34 W
Guanaja 236 16.27 N 85.54 W
Guanaja, Isla de I 236 16.30 N 85.55 W
Guanajay 240p 22.55 N 82.42 W
Guanajibo ≃ 240m 18.10 N 67.11 W
Guanajibo, Punta ≻ 240m 18.10 N 67.11 W
Guanajuato 234 21.01 N 101.15 W
Guanajuato □3 234 21.00 N 101.00 W
Guanambi 255 14.13 S 42.47 W
Guañape, Isla I 248 8.33 S 78.57 W
Guanare 246 9.03 N 69.45 W
Guanare ≃ 246 8.13 N 67.46 W
Guanare Viejo ≃ 246 8.19 N 68.10 W
Guanarito 246 8.42 N 69.12 W
Guanay 248 15.28 S 67.52 W
Guanbuqiao 100 29.56 N 114.21 E
Guanchao 100 26.41 N 114.58 E
Guancheng 107 30.01 N 103.54 E
Guancun 106 31.30 N 119.43 E
Guandacol 252 29.31 S 68.32 W
Guandanghu 100 30.06 N 113.37 E
Guandi, Zhg. 98 42.37 N 118.27 E
Guandi, Zhg. 98 41.48 N 116.52 E
Guandian 100 32.40 N 118.04 E
Guandu 100 24.17 N 113.53 E
Guanduchang 107 30.04 N 106.25 E
Guane 240p 22.12 N 84.05 W
Guang'an 107 30.28 N 106.39 E
Guangchang 100 26.50 N 116.14 E
Guangde 106 30.54 N 119.26 E
Guangdeguan 102 27.23 N 104.29 E
Guangdong □4 90 23.00 N 113.00 E
Guangfeng 100 28.25 N 118.11 E
Guangfu, Zhg. 106 31.18 N 120.23 E
Guangfu, Zhg. 107 30.13 N 104.41 E
Guangfuyingzi 104 42.14 N 120.58 E
Guanghan 102 31.00 N 104.18 E
Guanghua 102 32.25 N 111.36 E
Guangji 100 29.52 N 115.34 E
Guangling, Zhg. 98 39.47 N 114.17 E
Guangling, Zhg. 106 32.06 N 120.13 E
Guangludao I 98 39.09 N 122.21 E
Guangmaoshan Λ 102 27.02 N 100.58 E
Guangnan 102 24.10 N 105.06 E
Guangningsi 98 39.08 N 121.45 E
Guangping 98 36.30 N 114.57 E
Guangrao 98 37.02 N 118.25 E
Guangshan 100 32.02 N 114.52 E
Guangshui 100 31.40 N 114.00 E
Guangxing 107 29.04 N 106.33 E
Guangxi Zhuang Zizhiqu □4 102 24.00 N 109.00 E
Guangyuan 102 32.23 N 105.58 E
Guangze 100 27.32 N 117.20 E
Guangzhen 106 30.45 N 121.07 E
Guangzhou (Canton) 100 23.06 N 113.16 E
Guangzong 98 37.06 N 115.08 E
Guanhaiwei 100 30.11 N 121.25 E
Guanhe ≃, Zhg. 100 34.29 N 119.49 E
Guanhe ≃, Zhg. 100 32.16 N 115.42 E
Guanhekou ≃1 100 34.29 N 119.50 E
Guanhu 98 34.26 N 117.59 E
Guánica 240m 17.58 N 66.55 W
Guánica, Laguna de ⊜ 240m 18.00 N 66.56 W
Guanipa ≃ 246 9.56 N 62.26 W
Guanjianhe ≃ 107 30.00 N 106.01 E
Guankou, Zhg. 100 30.35 N 115.20 E
Guankou, Zhg. 107 30.40 N 103.28 E
Guanlin 106 31.32 N 119.42 E
Guanling 102 25.57 N 105.29 E
Guanlipu 104 41.37 N 123.18 E
Guanmenshan 89 47.23 N 122.20 E
Guannan 98 34.07 N 119.23 E
Guano 246 1.35 S 78.38 W
Guano Creek ≃ 202 42.12 N 119.31 W
Guanpata 236 15.01 N 85.02 W
Guanputou 105 38.58 N 117.04 E
Guanqian, Zhg. 100 25.57 N 116.33 E
Guanqian, Zhg. 100 27.48 N 118.31 E
Guanqian, Zhg. 100 26.12 N 117.57 E
Guanqian, Zhg. 100 30.42 N 117.39 E
Guanqiao, Zhg. 98 34.58 N 117.14 E
Guanqiao, Zhg. 100 25.03 N 118.06 E
Guanqiaopu 100 31.08 N 112.54 E
Guanshan I 100 27.21 N 120.36 E
Guanshanchang 107 28.46 N 103.42 E
Guanshi 100 26.43 N 112.53 E
Guanshui 98 40.55 N 124.33 E
Guanta 246 10.14 N 64.36 W
Guantánamo 240p 20.08 N 75.12 W
Guantánamo □4 240p 20.20 N 75.00 W
Guantánamo ≃ 240p 19.55 N 75.12 W
Guantánamo, Bahía de C 240p 20.00 N 75.08 W
Guantanamo Bay Naval Station ■ 240p 19.55 N 75.10 W
Guantang 106 31.37 N 119.06 E
Guantangqiao 106 32.09 N 119.27 E
Guantao 98 36.35 N 115.19 E
Guanting, Zhg. 100 34.19 N 113.47 E
Guanting, Zhg. 105 40.13 N 115.37 E
Guantingshuiku ⊜1 105 40.20 N 115.38 E
Guantou, Zhg. 100 27.58 N 120.46 E
Guantou, Zhg. 100 26.08 N 119.33 E
Guantunbao 98 40.28 N 113.24 E
Guanxian, Zhg. 98 36.30 N 115.27 E
Guanxian, Zhg. 102 31.00 N 103.40 E
Guanxun 100 24.19 N 117.45 E
Guanyin 107 29.50 N 105.57 E
Guanyinao 100 26.18 N 115.32 E
Guanyinchang, Zhg. 107 29.15 N 104.02 E
Guanyinchang, Zhg. 107 29.06 N 104.24 E
Guanyinchang, Zhg. 107 30.28 N 105.16 E
Guanyingzicun 104 41.52 N 121.53 E
Guanyinpu, Zhg. 107 30.16 N 103.51 E
Guanyinpu, Zhg. 107 28.58 N 104.53 E
Guanyinqiao, Zhg. 100 26.42 N 112.44 E
Guanyinqiao, Zhg. 107 29.46 N 104.12 E
Guanyinqiao, Zhg. 107 29.05 N 104.46 E
Guanyinshan 106 32.01 N 120.58 E
Guanyinsi, Zhg. 106 31.48 N 118.57 E
Guanyinsi, Zhg. 107 30.33 N 104.11 E
Guanyintan 107 29.35 N 105.14 E
Guanyintang, Zhg. 98 34.26 N 115.27 E
Guanyintang, Zhg. 100 31.01 N 112.35 E
Guanyintang, Zhg. 105 39.52 N 116.31 E
Guanyintang, Zhg. 106 32.09 N 121.09 E
Guanyinzhou 100 29.30 N 113.09 E
Guanyun (Dayishan) 98 34.20 N 119.17 E
Guanzhuang, Zhg. 98 37.12 N 114.30 E
Guanzhuang, Zhg. 100 28.58 N 117.24 E
Guanzhuang, Zhg. 100 32.49 N 114.16 E
Guaotou 100 27.37 N 120.33 E
Guapi 246 2.36 N 77.54 W
Guapiaçu ≃ 256 22.40 S 42.55 W
Guapiara 255 24.10 S 48.32 W
Guápiles 236 10.13 N 83.46 W
Guapimirim 256 22.32 S 42.59 W
Guapimirim ≃ 256 22.40 S 42.58 W
Guapó 255 16.49 S 49.32 W
Guapo Bay C 241r 10.12 N 61.40 W
Guaporé 252 28.51 S 51.54 W
Guaporé ≃, Bra. 252 29.10 S 51.54 W
Guaporé (Iténez) ≃, S.A. 248 11.54 S 65.01 W
Guaqui 248 16.35 S 68.51 W
Guará ≃ 255 12.59 S 44.49 W
Guara, Sierra de ⛰ 34 42.17 N 0.10 W
Guarabira 250 6.51 S 35.29 W
Guaraçaí 255 21.02 S 51.11 W
Guaracarumbo 286c 10.34 N 66.59 W
Guaraci, Bra. 255 20.29 S 48.57 W
Guaraci, Bra. 255 22.57 S 51.40 W
Guaraciaba do Norte 250 4.10 S 40.46 W
Guaraciama 255 17.03 S 43.41 W
Guaraguara, Punta ≻ 241r 10.31 N 62.19 W
Guaraí ≃ 287a 22.42 S 43.02 W
Guaramirim 252 26.27 S 49.00 W
Guaranda 246 1.36 S 79.00 W
Guaranésia 256 21.18 S 46.48 W
Guarani 256 21.22 S 43.03 W
Guaraniaçu 252 25.06 S 52.52 W
Guarani das Missões 252 28.08 S 54.34 W
Guarani de Goiás 255 13.59 S 46.31 W
Guarapari 255 20.40 S 40.30 W
Guarapiranga, Barragem do ◂6 287b 23.41 S 46.43 W
Guarapiranga, Reservatório de ⊜1 256 23.44 S 46.44 W
Guarapuava 252 25.23 S 51.27 W
Guaraqueçaba 252 25.17 S 48.21 W
Guarará 256 21.43 S 43.02 W
Guarará ≃ 287b 23.39 S 46.30 W
Guararé 246 7.49 N 80.17 W
Guararema 256 23.25 S 46.02 W
Guaratiba, Morro de Λ 287a 23.04 S 43.33 W
Guaratinguetá 256 22.49 S 45.13 W
Guaratinguetá, Ribeirão de ≃ 256 22.49 S 45.13 W
Guaratuba 252 25.54 S 48.34 W
Guar Chempedak 114 5.52 N 100.28 E
Guarcino 66 41.48 N 13.19 E
Guarda 34 40.32 N 7.16 W
Guardado de Abajo 196 26.22 N 98.57 W
Guardafui, Cape → Asir,ras ≻ 144 11.48 N 51.22 E
Guardavalle 68 38.30 N 16.30 E
Guardea 66 42.37 N 12.18 E
Guardia Escolta 252 28.59 S 62.08 W
Guardiagrele 66 42.11 N 14.13 E
Guardia Lombardi 68 40.57 N 15.12 E
Guardia Mitre 254 40.26 S 63.41 W
Guardia Sanframondi 68 41.15 N 14.36 E
Guardiato ≃ 34 38.20 N 5.22 W
Guardia Vieja, Arroyo de la ≃ 258 33.37 S 57.07 W
Guardo 34 42.47 N 4.50 W
Guareí ≃ 255 22.40 S 53.34 W
Guareim (Quaraí) ≃ 252 30.12 S 57.36 W
Guareña 34 38.51 N 6.06 W
Guareña ≃ 34 41.29 N 5.23 W
Guarenas 246 10.28 N 66.37 W
Guariba ≃ 248 7.41 S 60.18 W
Guarico 246 9.32 N 69.48 W
Guárico □3 246 8.40 N 66.35 W
Guárico ≃ 246 7.55 N 67.23 W
Guárico, Embalse del ⊜1 246 9.05 N 67.25 W
Guarico, Punta ≻ 240p 20.37 N 74.44 W
Guarizama 236 14.55 N 86.20 W
Guarujá 256 24.00 S 46.16 W
Guarulhos 256 23.28 S 46.32 W
Guarulhos □7 287b 23.26 S 46.29 W
Guasare ≃ 246 11.03 N 72.02 W
Guasave 232 25.34 N 108.27 W
Guasdualito 246 7.15 N 70.44 W
Guasila 71 39.34 N 9.03 E
Guasipati 246 7.28 N 61.54 W
Guastalla 64 44.55 N 10.39 E
Guāsuba ≃1 126 21.38 N 88.53 E
Guatajiagua 236 13.40 N 88.13 W
Guatemala 236 14.38 N 90.31 W
Guatemala □5 236 14.40 N 90.30 W
Guatemala □1 230
236 15.30 N 90.15 W
Guatemala Basin ✢1 18 8.00 N 95.00 W
Guateque 246 5.00 N 73.28 W
Guatimozín 252 33.27 S 62.27 W
Guatire 246 10.28 N 66.32 W
Guatopo, Parque Nacional ♠ 246 10.05 N 66.25 W
Guatraché 252 37.40 S 63.32 W
Guaugurina 164 10.37 S 150.28 E
Guaviare ≃ 246 4.03 N 67.44 W
Guaxindiba ≃ 287a 22.44 S 43.02 W
Guaxupé 256 21.18 S 46.42 W
Guayabal, Cuba 240p 20.42 N 77.36 W
Guayabal, Ven. 246 8.00 N 67.24 W
Guayabal, Lago ⊜1 240m 18.06 N 66.30 W
Guayabero ≃ 246 2.36 N 72.47 W
Guayabo 232 26.00 N 107.26 W
Guayabo Colorado 234 19.02 N 101.35 W
Guayacán 252 29.58 S 71.22 W
Guayaguayare 241r 10.08 N 61.02 W
Guayama 240m 17.59 N 66.07 W
Guayambre ≃ 236 14.26 N 86.02 W
Guayameo 234 18.12 N 101.19 W
Guayana → Ciudad Guayana 246 8.22 N 62.40 W
Guayana → Guyana □1 246 5.00 N 59.00 W
Guayaneco, Archipiélago II 254 47.45 S 75.10 W
Guayanés, Punta ≻ 240m 18.04 N 65.48 W
Guayanilla 240m 18.01 N 66.47 W
Guayanilla, Bahía de C 240m 18.00 N 66.46 W
Guayape 236 14.45 N 86.52 W
Guayape ≃ 236 14.26 N 85.58 W
Guayapo ≃ 246 4.30 N 67.35 W
Guayaquil 246 2.10 S 79.50 W
Guayaramerín 248 10.48 S 65.23 W
Guayas □4 246 2.00 S 80.00 W
Guayas ≃, Col. 246 1.23 N 74.50 W
Guayas ≃, Ec. 246 2.36 S 79.52 W
Guaycora 232 28.50 N 109.21 W
Guaycurú, Arroyo ≃ 258 34.00 S 56.50 W
Guaymallén 252 32.54 S 68.47 W
Guaymas 232 27.56 N 110.54 W
Guaynabo 240m 18.22 N 66.07 W
Guayquiraró ≃ 252 30.10 S 58.34 W
Guayuriba ≃ 246 3.55 N 73.05 W
Guazacapán 236 14.04 N 90.25 W
Guazapares 232 27.22 N 108.15 W
Guazárachic 232 26.57 N 106.43 W
Guazhou 106 32.15 N 119.23 E
Guazunamby, Arroyo ≃ 288 34.24 S 58.38 W
Guba, Yai. 144 10.16 N 35.17 E
Guba, Zaïre 154 10.40 S 26.26 E
Gubacha 86 58.52 N 57.36 E
Gubam 164 8.40 S 141.55 E
Gubany 76 56.37 N 30.40 E
Gubari 80 51.32 N 42.33 E
Gubat 116 12.55 N 124.07 E
Gubbi 122 13.19 N 76.56 E
Gubbio 66 43.21 N 12.35 E
Gubeikou 105 40.42 N 117.09 E
Gubentaoligai 104 42.16 N 122.13 E
Gubin 30 51.56 N 14.45 E
Gubinicha 78 48.48 N 35.15 E
Gubino, S.S.S.R. 80 53.19 N 48.44 E
Gubino, S.S.S.R. 82 55.42 N 39.07 E
Gubio 146 12.29 N 12.48 E
Gubkin 78 51.18 N 37.32 E
Gubug 115a 7.03 S 110.40 E
Gucheng, Zhg. 98 37.22 N 115.56 E
Gucheng, Zhg. 100 25.53 N 116.11 E
Gucheng, Zhg. 100 32.46 N 118.32 E
Gucheng, Zhg. 100 33.59 N 117.29 E
Gucheng, Zhg. 102 32.18 N 111.35 E
Gucheng, Zhg. 105 39.08 N 115.42 E
Gucheng, Zhg. 105 40.32 N 116.02 E
Gucheng, Zhg. 106 30.29 N 119.46 E
Guchengcang 100 32.34 N 115.20 E

Symbol	English	Deutsch	Español	Français	Português
≃	River	Fluss	Río	Rivière	Rio
≍	Canal	Kanal	Canal	Canal	Canal
↳	Waterfall, Rapids	Wasserfall, Stromschnellen	Cascada, Rápidos	Chute d'eau, Rapides	Cascata, Rápidos
⩍	Strait	Meeresstrasse	Estrecho	Détroit	Estreito
C	Bay, Gulf	Bucht, Golf	Bahía, Golfo	Baie, Golfe	Baía, Golfo
⊜	Lake, Lakes	See, Seen	Lago, Lagos	Lac, Lacs	Lago, Lagos
☷	Swamp	Sumpf	Pantano	Marais	Pântano
⌓	Ice Features, Glacier	Eis- und Gletscherformen	Accidentes Glaciales	Formes glaciaires	Acidentes Glaciares
⊤	Other Hydrographic Features	Andere Hydrographische Objekte	Otros Elementos Hidrográficos	Autres données hydrographiques	Outros Elementos Hidrográficos
✢	Submarine Features	Untermeerische Objekte	Accidentes Submarinos	Formes de relief sous-marin	Acidentes Submarinos
□	Political Unit	Politische Einheit	Unidad Politica	Entité politique	Unidade Política
♥	Cultural Institution	Kulturelle Institution	Institución Cultural	Institution culturelle	Instituição Cultural
⊥	Historical Site	Historische Stätte	Sitio Histórico	Site historique	Sitio Histórico
♠	Recreational Site	Erholungs- und Ferienort	Sitio de Recreo	Centre de loisirs	Sítio de Lazer
⊠	Airport	Flughafen	Aeropuerto	Aéroport	Aeroporto
■	Military Installation	Militäranlage	Instalación Militar	Installation militaire	Instalação Militar
◂	Miscellaneous	Verschiedenes	Misceláneo	Divers	Miscelânea

ENGLISH: Name | Page | Lat.°′ | Long.°′ — DEUTSCH: Name | Seite | Breite°′ | Länge°′ E=Ost

Name	Page	Lat.°′	Long.°′
Guchenghu ⊜	106	31.17 N	118.54 E
Guchengzi, Zhg.	104	42.33 N	123.45 E
Guchengzi, Zhg.	104	40.58 N	122.36 E
Guchengzi, Zhg.	104	41.44 N	123.35 E
Guchengzi, Zhg.	104	40.40 N	120.31 E
Gučin-Us	102	45.30 N	102.28 E
Gücük	130	38.12 N	37.29 E
Gūdalūr, Bhārat	122	9.41 N	77.16 E
Gūdalūr, Bhārat	122	11.30 N	76.30 E
Gúdar, Sierra de ⋀	34	40.27 N	0.42 W
Gudauta	84	43.06 N	40.37 E
Gudbrandsdalen ∨	26	61.30 N	10.00 E
Gudensberg	56	51.10 N	9.22 E
Gudermes	84	43.20 N	46.08 E
Guderup	41	54.59 N	9.53 E
Gudhjem	26	55.13 N	14.59 E
Gudianzi	100	31.49 N	116.05 E
Gudivāda	122	16.27 N	80.59 E
Gudiyāttam	122	12.57 N	78.52 E
Gudme	41	55.09 N	10.43 E
Gudow	54	53.33 N	10.46 E
Güdül	130	40.13 N	32.15 E
Gūdūr	122	14.08 N	79.51 E
Gudvangen	26	60.52 N	6.50 E
Guebwiller (Gebweiler)	58	47.55 N	7.12 E
Guéckédou	150	8.33 N	10.09 W
Guéckédou □[4]	150	8.40 N	10.15 W
Gué-de-Longroi	261	48.30 N	1.43 E
Gué-d'Hossus	50	49.57 N	4.32 E
Guédi, Mont ∧	146	12.14 N	18.58 E
Guéguen, Lac ⊜	190	48.06 N	77.13 W
Guéhenno, Calvaire de ✝[1]	32	47.56 N	2.42 W
Guéherville	261	48.32 N	1.53 E
Güejar ≃	246	2.55 N	73.14 W
Guelma	148	36.28 N	7.26 E
Guelph	212	43.33 N	80.15 W
Guelta Zemmur	148	25.15 N	12.20 W
Guéméné-sur-Scorff	32	48.04 N	3.12 W
Güemes	234	23.56 N	99.00 W
Guemes Island I	224	48.33 N	122.37 W
Guené	150	11.44 N	3.13 E
Guenguel ≃	254	45.41 S	70.20 W
Guer	28	47.54 N	2.07 W
Güera	148	20.48 N	17.08 W
Guera □[5]	146	11.30 N	18.30 E
Guéra, Massif de ⋀	146	11.55 N	18.12 E
Guérande	32	47.20 N	2.26 W
Guerara	148	32.46 N	4.34 E
Guerban'angeer	102	37.45 N	97.30 E
Guercif	148	34.15 N	3.21 W
Guerdjoumane, Djebel ∧	34	36.25 N	2.51 E
Guéré	146	9.12 N	18.10 E
Güere ≃	246	9.50 N	65.08 W
Guéréda	146	14.31 N	22.05 E
Guéret	32	46.10 N	1.52 E
Guérin Kouka	150	9.41 N	0.37 E
Guerla Mandatashan ∧	120	30.26 N	81.20 E
Guermantes	261	48.51 N	2.42 E
Guerne	214	40.46 N	81.54 W
Guernes	261	49.01 N	1.38 E
Guerneville	204	38.30 N	123.00 W
Guernica	258	34.56 S	58.25 W
Guernica y Luno	34	43.19 N	2.41 W
Guernsey	200	42.16 N	104.45 W
Guernsey □[6]	214	40.08 N	81.30 W
Guernsey □[2]	22		
	43b	49.28 N	2.35 W
Guernsey I	32	49.27 N	2.35 W
Guernsey Reservoir ⊜[1]	198	42.19 N	104.48 W
Guernsey State Park ♦	198	42.20 N	104.50 W
Guerrero	196	28.20 N	100.23 W
Guerrero □[3]	234	17.40 N	100.00 W
Guerville	261	48.57 N	1.44 E
Guerzim	148	29.45 N	1.47 W
Guesle ≃	261	48.36 N	1.40 E
Guessou-Sud	150	10.03 N	2.38 E
Guest Peninsula ≻[1]	9	76.18 S	148.00 W
Gueydan	194	30.02 N	92.30 W
Guéyo	150	5.49 N	6.36 W
Gufang	100	29.04 N	119.32 E
Guffin Bay ⊂	212	44.01 N	76.09 W
Guga	89	52.43 N	137.35 E
Gugang	100	28.17 N	113.46 E
Guge ∧	144	6.10 N	37.26 E
Gugera	123	30.58 N	73.19 E
Gugging	264b	48.19 N	16.15 E
Güglia, Pass dal)(	58	46.28 N	9.44 E
Güglingen	56	49.04 N	9.00 E
Guglionesi	66	41.55 N	14.55 E
Guguan	102	40.27 N	99.13 E
Guguan I	108	17.19 N	145.51 E
Guhe	100	31.54 N	117.58 E
Guhrau → Góra	30	51.40 N	16.33 E
Guia	248	15.22 S	56.14 W
Guia de Pacobaíba	256	22.43 S	43.10 W
Guialana, Cerro ∧	234	16.52 N	96.30 W
Guia Lopes da Laguna	248	21.26 S	56.07 W
Guiana Basin ✢[1]	18	10.00 N	50.00 W
Guiana Island I	240c	17.07 N	61.44 W
Guibéroua	150	6.14 N	6.10 W
Guibes	156	26.41 S	16.42 E
Güicán	246	6.28 N	72.25 W
Guichen	32	47.58 N	1.48 W
Guichi	100	30.40 N	117.28 E
Guichicovi	234	16.58 N	95.06 W
Guichón	252	32.21 S	57.12 W
Guicun	100	33.37 N	114.11 E
Guide (Heyin)	102	36.03 N	101.28 E
Guider	146	9.56 N	13.57 E
Guide Rock	198	40.04 N	98.20 W
Guidexiang	107	29.51 N	104.47 E
Guidigri	150	13.40 N	9.51 E
Guidimouni	150	13.42 N	9.30 E
Guiding	102	26.28 N	107.07 E
Guidizzolo	64	45.19 N	10.35 E
Guidong	100	26.05 N	113.57 E
Guidonia	66	42.01 N	12.45 E
Guidouma	152	1.37 S	10.41 E
Guiers ≃	62	45.37 N	5.37 E
Guiers, Lac de ⊜	150	16.12 N	15.50 W
Guifujie	100	27.20 N	120.01 E
Guiglia	64	44.26 N	10.58 E
Guiglo	150	6.33 N	7.29 W
Guiglo □[5]	150	6.20 N	7.45 W
Guignes-Rabutin	50	48.38 N	2.48 E
Guihuayuan	107	30.37 N	105.25 E
Guihulngan	116	10.07 N	123.16 E
Güija, Lago de ⊜	236	14.17 N	89.31 W
Guijalo	116	13.44 N	123.52 E
Guijingqiao	106	31.21 N	119.40 E
Guijuelo	34	40.33 N	5.40 W
Guil ≃	62	44.40 N	6.36 E
Guilarte, Monte ∧	240m	18.09 N	66.46 W
Guilderland	210	42.42 N	73.54 W
Guildford, Austl.	274a	33.51 S	150.59 E
Guildford, Eng., U.K.	260	51.14 N	0.35 W
Guildford □[8]	260	51.16 N	0.32 W
Guildford Cathedral ✝[1]	260	51.14 N	0.35 W
Guildhall	188	44.34 N	71.34 W
Guildtown	46	56.28 N	3.24 W
Guilford, Conn., U.S.	207	41.17 N	72.41 W
Guilford, Ind., U.S.	218	39.10 N	84.55 W
Guilford, Maine, U.S.	188	45.14 N	69.29 W
Guilford, N.Y., U.S.	210	42.24 N	75.29 W
Guilford Courthouse National Military Park ♦	192	36.01 N	79.45 W
Guilherand	62	44.56 N	4.52 E
Guilherme Capelo	152	5.13 S	12.08 E
Guilin (Kweilin)	102	25.11 N	110.09 E
Guilinchang	107	30.13 N	105.50 E
Guilinzhen	107	30.15 N	104.53 E
Guiliuhe	89	46.11 N	121.45 E
Guillaume-Delisle, Lac ⊜	176	56.15 N	76.17 W
Guillaumes	62	44.05 N	6.51 E
Guillermo E. Hudson	288	34.47 S	58.10 W
Guillestre	62	44.40 N	6.39 E
Guillon	50	47.31 N	4.06 E
Guilsfield	42	52.42 N	3.09 W
Guilvinec	32	47.47 N	4.17 W
Guimarães, Bra.	250	2.08 S	44.36 W
Guimarães, Port.	34	41.27 N	8.18 W
Guimaras Island I	116	10.35 N	122.37 E
Guimaras Strait ⊔	116	10.30 N	122.44 E
Guimba	116	15.40 N	120.46 E
Guimbal	116	10.40 N	122.19 E
Guimeishan	100	24.44 N	114.52 E
Guimuzhang ∧	100	24.40 N	116.48 E
Guin	194	33.58 N	87.55 W
Guina-Bissau → Guinea-Bissau □[1]	150	12.00 N	15.00 W
Guinan	102	35.24 N	100.57 E
Guinayang	269f	14.42 N	121.08 E
Guinayangan	116	13.54 N	122.27 E
Guinda	226	38.50 N	122.12 W
Guindulman	116	9.46 N	124.29 E
Guindulman Bay ⊂	116	9.44 N	124.29 E
Guiné → Guinea-Bissau □[1]	150	12.00 N	15.00 W
Guinea	208	38.08 N	77.26 W
Guinea □[1]	134		
	150	11.00 N	10.00 W
Guinea, Gulf of ⊂	10	2.00 N	2.30 E
Guinea Basin ✢[1]	10	0.30 N	5.00 W
Guinea-Bissau □[1], Afr.	134		
	150	12.00 N	15.00 W
Guineacor Creek ≃	170	34.21 S	150.05 E
Guinea Ecuatorial → Equatorial Guinea □[1]	152	2.00 N	9.00 E
Guinea Rise ✢[3]	10	3.00 S	0.30 W
Guinecourt, Lac ⊜	186	50.55 N	69.16 W
Guinée → Guinea □[1]	150	11.00 N	10.00 W
Guinée-Bissau → Guinea-Bissau □[1]	150	12.00 N	15.00 W
Guinée équitoriale → Equatorial Guinea □[1]	152	2.00 N	9.00 E
Güines, Cuba	240p	22.50 N	82.02 W
Guînes, Fr.	50	50.52 N	1.52 E
Guingamp	32	48.33 N	3.11 W
Guinguinéo	150	14.16 N	15.57 W
Guinobatan	116	13.11 N	123.36 E
Güinope	236	13.51 N	86.55 W
Guintacan Island I	116	11.19 N	123.54 E
Guintinguintin, Mount ∧	116	12.25 N	122.24 E
Guintinua Island I	116	14.26 N	122.51 E
Guiones, Punta ≻	236	9.54 N	85.41 W
Guiong	116	6.25 N	122.01 E
Guiperreux	261	48.40 N	1.42 E
Guiperreux, Étang de ⊜	261	48.40 N	1.43 E
Guiping	102	23.20 N	110.09 E
Guipúzcoa □[4]	34	43.10 N	2.10 W
Guir, Hamada du ⬥[2]	148	30.45 N	3.15 W
Guir, Oued ∨	148	30.29 N	2.17 W
Güira de Melena	240p	22.48 N	82.30 W
Guiratinga	255	16.21 S	53.45 W
Guirenji	100	33.42 N	118.12 E
Güiria	246	10.34 N	62.18 W
Guiricema	255	21.00 S	42.43 W
Guisachan Forest ⬥[3]	46	57.17 N	4.55 W
Guisanbourg	250	4.25 N	51.56 W
Guisborough	44	54.32 N	1.04 W
Guiscard	50	49.39 N	3.03 E
Guise	50	49.54 N	3.38 E
Guiseley	44	53.53 N	1.42 W
Guishui ≃	100	28.27 N	112.47 E
Guisijan	116	11.05 N	122.03 E
Güisisil, Cerro ∧	236	12.37 N	86.13 W
Guist Creek ≃	218	38.09 N	85.13 W
Guita Koulouba	152	5.56 N	23.19 E
Guitiriz	34	43.11 N	7.54 W
Guitou	100	24.58 N	113.25 E
Guitrancourt	261	49.01 N	1.47 E
Guîtres	32	45.03 N	0.11 W
Guitri	150	5.31 N	5.14 W
Guiuan	116	11.02 N	125.43 E
Guixian	102	23.06 N	109.39 E
Guiyang, Zhg.	100	25.46 N	112.43 E
Guiyang (Kweiyang), Zhg.	102	26.35 N	106.43 E
Güiza ≃	246	1.22 N	78.36 W
Guizhou □[4]	102	27.00 N	107.00 E
Gujarat □[3]	120	22.00 N	72.00 E
Gūjar Khān	123	33.16 N	73.19 E
Gujiabeng	106	30.45 N	120.59 E
Gujiang	100	27.11 N	114.49 E
Gujiaqiao	100	32.51 N	116.33 E
Gujiatun	104	40.39 N	124.08 E
Gujiatuo	107	29.14 N	106.12 E
Gujiazi, Zhg.	104	42.02 N	123.01 E
Gujiazi, Zhg.	104	41.44 N	124.11 E
Gujrānwāla	123	32.26 N	74.33 E
Gujrāt	123	32.34 N	74.05 E
Gukas'an	84	41.03 N	43.52 E
Gukou	100	26.27 N	118.38 E
Gukovo	83	48.03 N	39.56 E
Gul, Tanjong ≻	271c	1.17 N	103.39 E
Gul'a	88	54.41 N	121.01 E
Gul'aj-Borisovka	78	46.38 N	40.13 E
Gul'ajevskije Koški, Ostrova II	24	68.55 N	55.10 E
Gul'ajpole	78	47.38 N	36.16 E
Gulang	102	37.36 N	102.58 E
Gulangyu I	100	24.28 N	118.04 E
Gulaothi	124	28.36 N	77.47 E
Gulargambone	166	31.20 S	148.28 E
Gulbarga	122	17.20 N	76.50 E
Gulbene	76	57.11 N	26.45 E
Gul'ča	85	40.19 N	73.26 E
Gul'ča ≃	85	40.20 N	73.26 E
Gulch	144	14.43 N	36.45 E
Guldborg	41	54.52 N	11.45 E
Guldborg Sund ⊔	41	54.48 N	11.48 E
Guldsmedshyttan	40	59.42 N	15.06 E
Gülebağdı	130	39.52 N	39.50 E
Guledagudda	122	16.03 N	75.48 E
Guleicheng	100	23.47 N	117.36 E
Guleta	144	6.21 N	37.10 E
Gulf □[5]	164	7.00 S	145.00 E
Gulf Gate Estates	220	27.15 N	82.31 W
Gulf Hammock	192	29.15 N	82.43 W
Gulf Harbors	220	28.14 N	82.45 W
Gulf of Alaska Seamount Province ✢	16	55.00 N	144.00 W
Gulfport, Fla., U.S.	220	27.44 N	82.43 W
Gulfport, Miss., U.S.	194	30.22 N	89.06 W
Gulf Shores	194	30.17 N	87.41 W
Gulf Stream ≃	212	43.51 N	75.56 W
Gulgong	166	32.22 S	149.32 E
Gulicun, Zhg.	106	31.52 N	118.41 E
Gulicun, Zhg.	106	31.38 N	120.50 E
Gul Imām	123	32.16 N	70.32 E
Guling	100	23.45 N	114.26 E
Gulistān, Pāk.	120	30.36 N	66.35 E
Gulistan, S.S.S.R.	85	40.30 N	68.46 E
Gulistan Palace ✝	267d	35.41 N	51.25 E
Guljanci	38	43.38 N	24.42 E
Gulkana	180	62.16 N	145.23 W
Gull ≃	212	44.37 N	78.49 W
Gulland Rock II[1]	42	50.34 N	4.59 W
Gullane	46	56.02 N	2.50 W
Gullfoss ∟	24a	64.24 N	20.08 W
Gullholmen	26	58.11 N	11.24 E
Gullion, Slieve ∧	48	54.08 N	6.26 W
Gull Island I	281	42.32 N	82.41 W
Gullivan Bay ⊂	220	25.52 N	81.38 W
Gull Lake	184	50.08 N	108.27 W
Gull Lake ⊜, Alta., Can.	182	52.35 N	114.00 W
Gull Lake ⊜, Ont., Can.	184	51.18 N	91.58 W
Gull Lake ⊜, Ont., Can.	212	44.51 N	78.47 W
Gull Lake ⊜, Mich., U.S.	216	42.24 N	85.25 W
Gull Lake ⊜, Minn., U.S.	190	46.25 N	94.20 W
Gullrock Lake ⊜	184	50.58 N	93.40 W
Gullspång	40	58.59 N	14.06 E
Güllü Dağı ∧	130	41.21 N	42.10 E
Güllük	130	37.14 N	27.36 E
Gulmarg	123	34.03 N	74.23 E
Gulnam	140	6.55 N	29.30 E
Gülnar	130	36.20 N	33.25 E
Gulong	89	45.51 N	124.14 E
Gulpen	56	50.48 N	5.54 E
Gülper See ⊜	54	52.44 N	12.14 E
Gulph Mills	285	40.04 N	75.21 W
Gülpınar	130	39.32 N	26.07 E
Gul'ripši	84	42.57 N	41.06 E
Gul'šad	86	46.39 N	74.24 E
Gülşehir	130	38.45 N	34.38 E
Gulsvik	26	60.23 N	9.35 E
Gulu, Ug.	154	2.47 N	32.18 E
Gulu, Zhg.	120	28.06 N	89.17 E
Gulukguluk	115a	7.04 S	113.40 E
Guluogongba	120	34.20 N	84.50 E
Gulwe	154	6.30 S	36.29 E
Gumaca	116	13.55 N	122.06 E
Gumahang	116	12.35 N	123.16 E
Gumal (Gowmal) ≃	120	31.56 N	70.22 E
Gumare	156	19.21 S	22.12 E
Gumba, Ang.	152	11.40 S	16.34 E
Gumba, Zaïre	152	2.57 N	21.26 E
Gumbinnen → Gusev	76	54.36 N	22.12 E
Gumbiro	154	10.16 S	35.39 E
Gumel	150	12.39 N	9.22 E
Gumeracha	168b	34.49 S	138.53 E
Gümgüm	84	39.10 N	41.28 E
Gumiao	100	32.26 N	113.16 E
Gumieńce ⬥[8]	54	53.51 N	14.30 E
Gumla	124	23.03 N	84.33 E
Gumma □[5]	94	36.30 N	139.00 E
Gummersbach	56	51.02 N	7.34 E
Gummi	150	12.09 N	5.09 E
Gumpas Pond ⊜	283	42.44 N	71.22 W
Gumpas Pond Brook ≃	283	42.42 N	71.21 W
Gumpoldskirchen	264b	48.03 N	16.17 E
Gumrak	80	48.47 N	44.22 E
Gum Swamp Creek ≃	192	32.08 N	82.55 W
Gumti ≃	126	23.32 N	90.43 E
Gümüşhacıköy	130	40.53 N	35.14 E
Gümüşhane	130	40.27 N	39.29 E
Gümüshane □[4]	130	40.15 N	39.45 E
Gümüşköy	267b	41.14 N	28.58 E
Gun ≃	216	42.28 N	85.40 W
Guna, Bhārat	124	24.39 N	77.19 E
Guna, Yai.	144	8.19 N	39.51 E
Guna □[5]	124	24.30 N	77.30 E
Guna ∧	144	11.42 N	38.12 E
Gunbar	166	34.01 S	145.25 E
Gun Barrel City	222	32.20 N	96.10 W
Gun Creek ≃	284a	43.03 N	78.55 W
Gunda	88	52.47 N	111.44 E
Gundagai	166	35.04 S	148.07 E
Gundelfingen, B.R.D.	56	48.33 N	10.22 E
Gundelfingen, B.R.D.	58	48.03 N	7.52 E
Gundelsdorf	60	48.33 N	11.03 E
Gundelsheim	56	49.17 N	9.09 E
Gundertshausen	60	48.05 N	12.59 E
Gundik	115a	7.12 S	110.54 E
Gundji	152	2.05 N	21.27 E
Gundlakamma ≃	122	15.32 N	80.14 E
Gündlkoferau	60	48.31 N	12.02 E
Gundlupet	122	11.48 N	76.41 E
Gündüzlü	130	40.53 N	37.43 E
Guneh Ghar ∧	123	35.19 N	71.47 E
Güney	130	38.09 N	29.05 E
Gungartan ∧	171b	36.18 S	148.24 E
Gungi	152	6.21 S	19.15 E
Gungo	152	11.48 S	14.08 E
Güngören	267b	41.01 N	28.53 E
Gungu	152	5.44 S	19.19 E
Gunib	84	42.25 N	46.57 E
Gunisao ≃	184	53.54 N	97.58 W
Gunisao Lake ⊜	184	53.33 N	96.15 W
Gunjrauliya	124	26.35 N	84.34 E
Gun Lake ⊜	216	42.37 N	85.32 W
Gunma	94	36.24 N	139.00 E
Gunnar	176	59.23 N	108.53 W
Günnarijn	102	45.38 N	102.01 E
Gunnarn	26	65.00 N	17.40 E
Gunnbjørns Fjeld ∧	16	68.55 N	29.53 W
Gunnebo	26	57.43 N	16.32 E
Gunnedah	166	30.59 S	150.15 E
Gunning Island I	276	40.22 N	73.59 W
Gunnislake	42	50.31 N	4.12 W
Gunnison, Colo., U.S.	200	38.33 N	106.56 W
Gunnison, Utah, U.S.	200	39.09 N	111.49 W
Gunnison ≃	200	39.03 N	108.35 W
Gunnison, Lake Fork ≃	200	38.28 N	107.19 W
Gunnison, North Fork ≃	200	38.47 N	107.50 W
Gunn Peak ∧	224	47.49 N	121.27 W
Gunpowder Creek ≃, Austl.	166	19.14 S	139.58 E
Gunpowder Creek ≃, Ky., U.S.	218	38.53 N	84.47 W
Gunpowder Falls ≃	208	39.24 N	76.22 W
Gunpowder River ⊂	208	39.22 N	76.22 W
Gunpowder State Park ♦	208	39.37 N	76.40 W
Gunsan → Kunsan	98	35.58 N	126.41 E
Gunskirchen	60	48.08 N	13.57 E
Gunston Cove ⊂	208	38.40 N	77.09 W
Guntakal	122	15.10 N	77.23 E
Güntersberge	54	51.38 N	10.59 E
Guntersblum	56	49.47 N	8.21 E
Guntersdorf	61	48.39 N	16.03 E
Guntersville	194	34.21 N	86.18 W
Guntersville Dam ⬥[6]	194	34.13 N	86.23 W
Guntersville Lake ⊜[1]	194	34.45 N	86.03 W
Guntingsaga	114	2.33 N	99.39 E
Guntramsdorf	264b	48.03 N	16.19 E
Guntung	114	1.38 N	101.34 E
Guntūr	122	16.18 N	80.27 E
Gunungkencana	115a	6.34 S	106.04 E
Gunungmegang	112	3.27 S	103.52 E
Gunungsahilan	112	0.06 N	101.18 E
Gunungsitoli	114	1.17 N	97.37 E
Gunungtua	114	1.30 N	99.37 E
Gunupur	122	19.05 N	83.49 E
Gunyidi	162	30.08 S	116.04 E
Günz ≃	58	48.27 N	10.16 E
Gunza ≃	152	11.10 S	13.50 E
Günzburg	58	48.27 N	10.16 E
Gunzenhausen	56	49.07 N	10.45 E
Gunzigou	104	41.31 N	123.58 E
Guodian	106	30.27 N	120.33 E
Guoerbenaobao	102	43.14 N	112.28 E
Guoguantun	98	35.29 N	115.54 E
Gu Oidak Wash ∨	200	31.57 N	112.21 W
Guoji	100	32.59 N	113.06 E
Guojiadian	104	41.51 N	121.30 E
Guojiajiang	106	32.17 N	120.50 E
Guojiatun, Zhg.	98	41.31 N	117.02 E
Guojiatun, Zhg.	104	42.00 N	122.51 E
Guojiatun, Zhg.	104	40.52 N	122.04 E
Guojiawopeng	104	42.03 N	122.46 E
Guojiayao	105	40.37 N	115.39 E
Guojiayuan	106	32.10 N	120.35 E
Guojiga	86	43.47 N	80.48 E
Guokuishan ∧	89	45.17 N	129.30 E
Guoleizhuang	98	40.44 N	114.36 E
Guoluoshan ⋀	102	33.14 N	99.50 E
Guolutan	100	32.04 N	115.40 E
Guosu	98	38.24 N	114.00 E
Guoxian	102	38.54 N	112.50 E
Guoyang	100	33.32 N	116.12 E
Guozhangzi	98	40.43 N	118.47 E
Guozhuang	98	35.25 N	117.10 E
Guozhuangmiao	106	31.49 N	119.01 E
Gupeizhou	98	34.09 N	117.54 E
Gupis	123	36.14 N	73.26 E
Gura	80	57.18 N	51.25 E
Gura, Wādī ∨	140	17.28 N	35.10 E
Gurabo	240m	18.16 N	65.58 W
Guraferdo	144	6.50 N	35.06 E
Gurag ∧	144	8.15 N	38.21 E
Gura-Galbena	78	46.43 N	28.42 E
Gurahonț	38	46.16 N	22.21 E
Gura Humorului	38	47.33 N	25.54 E
Gurais	123	34.38 N	74.50 E
Guran	88	54.46 N	100.38 E
Gurara ≃	150	8.12 N	6.41 E
Gurdāspur	123	32.02 N	75.31 E
Gurdon	194	33.55 N	93.09 W
Gurdžaani	84	41.43 N	45.48 E
Güre	130	38.39 N	29.10 E
Gurejev	80	47.21 N	43.16 E
G'urg'an	84	40.23 N	50.19 E
Gurgaon	124	28.28 N	77.02 E
Gurgaon □[5]	124	28.20 N	77.00 E
Gurgei, Jabal ∧	140	13.50 N	24.19 E
Gurghiului, Munții ⋀	38	46.41 N	25.12 E
Gurguan Point ≻	174n	15.00 N	145.35 E
Gurguéia ≃	250	6.50 S	43.24 W
Gurgura	144	7.50 N	41.30 E
Gūrha	120	14.14 N	74.50 E
Guri, Embalse ⊜[1]	246	7.30 N	62.50 W
Gurjev	80	47.07 N	51.56 E
Gurjev □[4]	86	45.00 N	53.00 E
Gurjevo	82	54.42 N	36.28 E
Gurjevsk, S.S.S.R.	76	54.47 N	20.38 E
Gurjevsk, S.S.S.R.	86	54.17 N	85.56 E
Gurk	61	46.52 N	14.18 E
Gurk ≃	61	46.36 N	14.31 E
Gurk ✝[1]	61	46.52 N	14.15 E
Gurkha	124	28.00 N	84.37 E
Gurktaler Alpen ⋀	64	46.55 N	14.00 E
Gurla Mandhata → Guerla Mandatashan ∧	120	30.26 N	81.20 E
Gurlevo	76	59.28 N	28.54 E
Gurnee	216	42.22 N	87.55 W
Gurnet Point ≻	283	42.01 N	70.34 W
Gurnley Football Ground ♦	262	53.47 N	2.14 W
Gursarai	124	25.37 N	79.11 E
Gurskøy I	26	62.15 N	5.41 E
Gürsu	130	40.13 N	29.12 E
Guru	120	29.34 N	66.43 E
Guru Har Sahāi	123	30.43 N	74.25 E
Gurun, Malay.	114	5.49 N	100.29 E
Gürün, Tür.	130	38.43 N	37.17 E
Gurupá	250	1.25 S	51.39 W
Gurupi	250	11.43 S	49.04 W
Gurupi ≃	250	1.13 S	46.06 W
Guru Sikhar ∧	120	24.39 N	72.46 E
Gurvanbulag	88	47.38 N	103.31 E
Gurvansajchan	102	45.22 N	107.00 E
Gurvan Sajchan Uul ⋀	102	43.50 N	103.30 E
Gurvan-Tes	102	43.28 N	101.21 E
Gurzuf	78	44.33 N	34.17 E
Gus' ≃	80	55.00 N	41.11 E
Gusar	85	39.28 N	67.50 E
Gušari	85	38.55 N	68.51 E
Gusarka	78	47.23 N	36.31 E
Gusasale	144	6.30 N	43.00 E
Gus'atin	78	49.05 N	26.11 E
Gusau	150	12.12 N	6.40 E
Gus'-Chrustal'nyj	80	55.37 N	40.40 E
Guselka	80	50.27 N	45.09 E
Güsen	54	52.21 N	11.59 E
Gusen ≃	61	48.15 N	14.30 E
Gusev, S.S.S.R.	76	54.36 N	22.12 E
Gusev, S.S.S.R.	78	48.27 N	40.32 E
Gusevo	76	56.06 N	33.21 E
Gusevskij	80	55.40 N	40.34 E
Gushan, Zhg.	98	39.53 N	123.36 E
Gushan, Zhg.	98	36.30 N	116.53 E
Gushan, Zhg.	106	31.44 N	120.33 E
Gushan ∧, Zhg.	100	26.05 N	119.22 E
Gushan ∧, Zhg.	104	41.18 N	120.35 E
Gushanbeizifu	104	42.10 N	120.30 E
Gushankou	105	39.38 N	115.49 E
Gushantun	89	48.18 N	123.47 E
Gushanzi, Zhg.	98	40.22 N	120.03 E
Gushanzi, Zhg.	104	41.03 N	123.03 E
Gushi, Zhg.	100	28.34 N	119.24 E
Gushi, Zhg.	100	32.12 N	115.41 E
Gushiago	150	9.55 N	0.12 W
Gushichan	174m	26.07 N	127.45 E
Gushikawa	174m	26.21 N	127.52 E
Gushu, Zhg.	98	34.15 N	115.48 E
Gushu, Zhg.	104	42.36 N	123.26 E
Gusi	112	6.07 N	117.08 E
Gusino	76	54.44 N	31.22 E
Gusinoje, Ozero ⊜	88	51.12 N	106.24 E
Gusinoje Ozero	88	51.09 N	106.10 E
Gusinoozersk	88	51.17 N	106.30 E
Guskef	85	39.02 N	69.20 E
Guskhara	126	23.30 N	87.45 E
Gus'-Khrustal'nyy → Gus'-Chrustal'nyj	80	55.37 N	40.40 E
Gusong	102	28.18 N	105.14 E
Guspini	71	39.32 N	8.37 E
Gussago	64	45.35 N	10.09 E
Gusselby	40	59.39 N	15.14 E
Güssing	61	47.04 N	16.20 E
Gussola	64	45.00 N	10.20 E
Gustav Holm, Kap ≻	176	67.00 N	34.00 W
Gustavo A. Madero □[7]	286a	19.29 N	99.08 W
Gustavsberg	40	59.19 N	18.23 E
Gustavus	180	58.25 N	135.44 W
Güsten	54	51.49 N	11.35 E
Gustia	272b	22.59 N	88.26 E
Gustine, Calif., U.S.	226	37.16 N	121.00 E
Gustine, Tex., U.S.	196	31.51 N	98.24 W
Gustorf	56	51.04 N	6.34 E
Güstrow	54	53.48 N	12.10 E
Gusum	26	58.16 N	16.29 E
Gus'-Železnyj	80	55.03 N	41.10 E
Gutach	58	48.15 N	8.13 E
Gutaj	88	49.59 N	108.12 E
Gutara ≃	88	54.50 N	97.23 E
Gutarskij Chrebet ⋀	88	54.30 N	97.40 E
Gutcher	46	60.40 N	1.00 W
Gutenfels, Burg ⊥	56	50.07 N	7.46 E
Guten Hoffnung, Kap der → Good Hope, Cape of ≻	158	34.24 S	18.30 E
Güterfelde	264a	52.22 N	13.12 E
Gütersloh	52	51.54 N	8.23 E
Guthrie, Ind., U.S.	218	38.59 N	86.31 W
Guthrie, Ky., U.S.	194	36.39 N	87.10 W
Guthrie, Okla., U.S.	196	35.53 N	97.25 W
Guthrie, Tex., U.S.	196	33.37 N	100.19 W
Guthrie Center	198	41.41 N	94.30 W
Guthrie Lake ⊜	184	55.17 N	100.38 W
Gutian, Zhg.	100	26.36 N	118.46 E
Gutian, Zhg.	100	25.43 N	116.57 E
Gutian, Zhg.	100	25.15 N	116.46 E
Gutianxi ≃	100	26.22 N	118.42 E
Gutiérrez	248	19.25 S	63.34 W
Gutiérrez Zamora	234	20.27 N	97.05 W
Gutland □[9]	56	49.40 N	6.10 E
Gutland ⬥[1]	56	49.40 N	6.10 E
Guton, Gora ∧	84	41.51 N	46.45 E
Guttannen	58	46.39 N	8.18 E
Guttau	54	51.15 N	14.34 E
Guttenberg, Iowa, U.S.	190	42.47 N	91.06 W
Guttenberg, N.J., U.S.	276	40.48 N	74.01 W
Guttentag → Dobrodzień	30	50.44 N	18.27 E
Guttstadt → Dobre Miasto	30	53.59 N	20.25 E
Gutu	154	19.38 S	31.10 E
Gutujevskij, Ostrov I	265a	59.54 N	30.14 E
Gutulia Nasjonalpark ♦	26	62.02 N	12.12 E
Guty	78	50.08 N	35.21 E
Gützkow	54	53.56 N	13.24 E
Güvem	130	40.36 N	32.40 E
Guwen	107	29.11 N	104.26 E
Guxhagen	56	51.12 N	9.28 E
Guxian, Zhg.	100	32.26 N	113.37 E
Guxian, Zhg.	100	27.09 N	115.31 E
Guxiandu	100	29.06 N	116.50 E
Guxianji	100	31.57 N	116.15 E
Guxihe	107	30.18 N	105.52 E
Guxiong	106	31.55 N	118.38 E
Guy	222	29.21 N	95.47 W
Guyana □[1]	242		
	246	5.00 N	59.00 W
Guyancourt	261	48.46 N	2.04 E
Guyancourt, Aéroport de ⊠	261	48.45 N	2.05 E
Guyane → Guyana □[1]	246	5.00 N	59.00 W
Guyane française → French Guiana □[2]	250	4.00 N	53.00 W
Guyang, Zhg.	98	34.58 N	114.58 E
Guyang, Zhg.	102	41.10 N	110.02 E
Guye	105	39.44 N	118.25 E
Guyenne □[9]	32	44.30 N	1.00 E
Guyi	100	25.38 N	118.47 E
Guyin	102	23.58 N	105.47 E
Guyizhen	107	30.22 N	103.33 E
Guymon	196	36.41 N	101.29 W
Guyonne, Ruisseau la ≃	261	48.49 N	1.52 E
Guyot, Mount ∧	192	35.42 N	83.15 W
Guyra	166	30.14 S	151.40 E
Guysborough	186	45.23 N	61.30 W
Guys Mills	214	41.38 N	79.59 W
Guyton	192	32.20 N	81.24 W
Guyuan, Zhg.	98	41.30 N	115.35 E
Guyuan, Zhg.	102	35.58 N	106.45 E
Guzar	72	38.36 N	66.15 E
Güzel ≃	84	39.44 N	43.01 E
Güzelbahçe	130	38.21 N	26.54 E
Güzelsu	130	36.54 N	31.53 E
Guzhang	102	28.31 N	109.57 E
Guzhen	100	33.19 N	117.21 E
Guzishan	98	41.42 N	118.06 E
Guzmán, Méx.	232	31.13 N	107.27 W
Guzmán → Ciudad Guzmán, Méx.	234	19.41 N	103.29 W
Guzmán, Laguna de ⊜	232	31.20 N	107.30 W
Gvardejsk	76	54.39 N	21.05 E
Gvardejskoje, S.S.S.R.	78	45.07 N	34.01 E
Gvardejskoje, S.S.S.R.	78	49.20 N	26.42 E
Gvardejskoje, S.S.S.R.	78	48.44 N	35.19 E
Gvardejsk [Tapiau]	76	54.39 N	21.05 E
Gvazda	78	50.44 N	40.30 E
Gvozdec	78	48.34 N	25.17 E
Gwa	110	17.36 N	94.35 E
Gwabegar	166	30.36 S	148.58 E
Gwadabawa	150	13.20 N	5.15 E
Gwādar	128	25.07 N	62.19 E
Gwagwada	150	10.14 N	7.14 E
Gwai	154	19.15 S	27.42 E
Gwai ≃	154	17.59 S	26.52 E
Gwalangu	152	2.19 N	18.11 E
Gwalchmai	44	53.15 N	4.25 W
Gwāl Haidarzai	120	30.45 N	68.53 E
Gwalia	162	28.55 S	121.20 E
Gwalior	124	26.13 N	78.10 E
Gwambygine	168a	31.59 S	116.48 E
Gwanara	150	8.55 N	3.09 E
Gwanda	154	20.57 S	29.01 E
Gwandu	150	12.30 N	4.41 E
Gwane	154	4.43 N	25.50 E
Gwangju → Kwangju	98	35.09 N	126.54 E
Gwarzo	150	11.56 N	7.56 E
Gwasero	150	9.29 N	3.30 E
Gwash ≃	42	52.39 N	0.27 W
Gwātar Bay ⊂	128	25.04 N	61.36 E
Gwatt	58	46.43 N	7.38 E
Gwaun ≃	42	52.00 N	4.58 W
Gwda ≃	30	53.04 N	16.44 E
Gweebarra ≃	48	54.50 N	8.20 W
Gweebarra Bay ⊂	48	54.52 N	8.20 W
Gweedore	48	55.03 N	8.14 W
Gweesalla	48	54.07 N	9.54 W
Gwelo	154	19.27 S	29.49 E
Gwelo ≃	154	18.45 S	28.36 E
Gwembe	154	16.30 S	27.35 E
Gwendraeth Fâch ≃	42	51.44 N	4.18 W
Gwendraeth Fawr ≃	42	51.43 N	4.18 W
Gwent □[6]	42	51.43 N	2.57 W
Gwinn	190	46.17 N	87.26 W
Gwobu	154	2.37 N	26.13 E
Gwydir ≃	166	29.27 S	149.48 E
Gwynedd	285	40.12 N	75.15 W
Gwynedd □[6]	44	53.20 N	4.00 W
Gwynedd Square	285	40.13 N	75.18 W
Gwynedd Valley	285	40.11 N	75.15 W
Gwynn	208	37.30 N	76.17 W
Gwynneville	218	39.40 N	85.39 W
Gwynn Island I	208	37.30 N	76.17 W
Gwynn Oak Amusement Park ♦	284b	39.20 N	76.43 W
Gwynns Falls ≃	284b	39.16 N	76.37 W
Gwynns Falls Park ♦	284b	39.18 N	76.41 W
Gyál	264c	47.23 N	19.14 E
Gya La)(	124	28.44 N	84.40 E
Gyáli-patak ≃	264c	47.24 N	19.07 E
Gyangtse → Jiangzi	120	28.57 N	89.35 E
Gybdan	80	56.33 N	51.39 E
Gyda	74	70.52 N	78.30 E
Gydanskaja Guba ⊂	74	71.20 N	76.30 E
Gydanskij Poluostrov ≻[1]	74	70.50 N	79.00 E
Gyebu	164	3.03 S	133.51 E
Gyemo Chen ∧	124	27.20 N	88.52 E
Gyeongju → Kyŏngju	98	35.51 N	129.14 E
Gyldenløves Fjord ⊂[2]	176	64.30 N	41.30 W
Gyldenløveshøj ∧[2]	41	55.33 N	11.52 E
Gy [les-Nonains]	58	47.24 N	5.49 E
Gylling	41	55.53 N	10.11 E
Gymea Bay	274a	34.02 S	151.05 E
Gympie	166	26.11 S	152.40 E
Gyobingauk	110	18.13 N	95.39 E
Gyōda	94	36.08 N	139.28 E
Gyoma	30	46.56 N	20.50 E
Gyöngyös	30	47.47 N	19.56 E
Gyöngyös ≃	61	47.14 N	16.55 E
Győr	30	47.42 N	17.38 E
Győr-Sopron □[6]	30	47.35 N	17.15 E
Gypsey Race ≃	44	54.05 N	0.12 W
Gypsum, Colo., U.S.	200	39.39 N	106.57 W
Gypsum, Kans., U.S.	198	38.42 N	97.26 W
Gypsum, Ohio, U.S.	214	41.30 N	82.52 W
Gypsum Creek ≃, U.S.	200	37.09 N	109.52 W
Gypsum Creek ≃, Kans., U.S.	198	38.51 N	97.25 W
Gypsum Hills ⋀[2]	196	36.25 N	99.20 W
Gypsum Point ≻	176	61.53 N	114.35 W
Gypsumville	184	51.45 N	98.35 W
Gyrbovec	78	46.50 N	29.21 E
Gysinge	40	60.17 N	16.53 E
Gyttorp	40	59.31 N	14.58 E
Gyula	30	46.39 N	21.17 E
Gyulafehérvár → Alba-Iulia	38	46.04 N	23.35 E
Gžat' ≃	76	55.56 N	34.33 E
Gžatsk	86	55.42 N	78.11 E
Gžel'	82	55.36 N	38.24 E
Gzhatsk → Gagarin	76	55.33 N	35.00 E
H			
Haag → 's-Gravenhage, Ned.	52	52.06 N	4.18 E
Haag, Öst.	61	48.07 N	14.34 E
Haag am Hausruck	60	48.11 N	13.38 E
Haagen	58	47.38 N	7.40 E
Haag in Oberbayern	60	48.10 N	12.11 E
Haaksbergen	52	52.09 N	6.44 E
Haalenberg	156	26.52 S	15.30 E
Haaltert	50	50.54 N	4.00 E
Haamstede	52	51.43 N	3.45 E
Haan	56	51.11 N	7.00 E
Haapajärvi	26	63.45 N	25.20 E
Haapajärvi ⊜	26	63.33 N	27.00 E
Haapamäki	26	62.15 N	24.28 E
Haapavesi	26	64.08 N	25.22 E
Haapsalu	76	58.56 N	23.33 E
Haar	60	48.06 N	11.44 E
Haar ⬥[8]	263	51.26 N	7.13 E
Ha'Arava (Wādī al-Jayb) ∨	132	31.04 N	35.27 E
Haardt ⋀	56	49.15 N	8.00 E
Haaren, B.R.D.	52	51.34 N	8.44 E
Haaren, Ned.	52	51.36 N	5.12 E
Haarlem, Ned.	52	52.23 N	4.38 E
Haarlem, S. Afr.	158	33.44 S	23.20 E
Haarlemmermeer ⬥[1]	52	52.15 N	4.38 E
Haarzopf ⬥[8]	263	51.25 N	6.58 E
Haast	172	43.53 S	169.03 E
Haast ≃	172	43.50 S	169.02 E
Haast Bluff	162	23.30 S	131.50 E
Haast Pass)(	172	44.06 S	169.21 E
Haatinao, Pointe ≻	174x	9.47 S	138.51 W
Haava, Canal ⊔	174x	9.53 S	139.04 W
Habahe	86	47.53 N	86.12 E
Habaqi, Zhg.	104	42.38 N	122.02 E
Habaqi, Zhg.	104	42.36 N	122.52 E
Habaqila	102	42.01 N	106.02 E
Habartov	54	50.08 N	12.33 E
Habaswein	154	1.01 N	39.29 E
Ḥabawna, Wādī ∨	144	17.51 N	44.59 E
Habay-la-Neuve	56	49.44 N	5.39 E
Ḥabbān	144	14.21 N	47.05 E
Ḥabbānīyah, Hawr al- ⊜	128	33.17 N	43.29 E
Ḥabbūsh	132	33.24 N	35.29 E
Habelschwerdt → Bystrzyca Kłodzka	30	50.18 N	16.38 E
Habère-Poche	58	46.15 N	6.29 E
Haberfield	274a	33.53 S	151.08 E
Habermehl Peak ∧	9	71.49 S	6.38 E
Haberskirchen	60	48.31 N	12.39 E
Ḥabīb, Wādī ∨	142	27.20 N	31.30 E
Habichtswald, Naturpark ♦	56	51.20 N	9.15 E
Habiganj	120	24.23 N	91.25 E
Habikino	96	34.33 N	135.37 E
Habīlah	140	12.41 N	22.33 E
Habinghorst ⬥[8]	263	51.35 N	7.18 E
Hab Nadi Chowki	120	25.01 N	66.53 E
Habo	26	57.55 N	14.04 E
Habob, Wādī ∨	140	18.07 N	35.01 E
Habomai-shotō → Malaja Kuril'skaja Gr'ada II	92a	43.30 N	146.10 E
Haboro	92a	44.22 N	141.42 E
Hābra	126	22.50 N	88.38 E
Habsburg ⊥	58	47.28 N	8.13 E
Habsheim	58	47.44 N	7.25 E
Habshīyah, Jabal ⋀	144	16.40 N	49.40 E
Habu	270	34.27 N	135.24 E
Habutaki	270	34.25 N	135.26 E
Hache, Lac la ⊜	182	51.50 N	121.30 W
Hachen	56	51.22 N	7.59 E
Hachenburg	56	50.39 N	7.50 E
Hachi	120	27.46 N	94.01 E
Hachijō	270	34.37 N	135.48 E
Hachijō-jima I	90	33.05 N	139.48 E
Hachiman, Nihon	94	35.45 N	136.57 E
Hachiman → Ōmi-hachiman, Nihon	94	35.08 N	136.06 E
Hachiman-misaki ≻	94	35.08 N	140.19 E
Hachinohe	92	40.30 N	141.29 E
Hachiōji	94	35.39 N	139.20 E
Hachmühlen	52	52.10 N	9.28 E
Hacıbektaş	130	38.57 N	34.35 E
Hacienda Heights	228	33.58 N	117.58 W
Hacienda Miravalles	236	10.41 N	85.14 W
Hacihamza	130	41.05 N	34.28 E
Hacıishaklı	130	36.11 N	33.40 E
Hacıköy	130	40.04 N	35.31 E
Hacılar	130	38.39 N	35.27 E
Hackås	26	62.55 N	14.31 E
Hackberry, Ariz., U.S.	200	35.22 N	113.44 W
Hackberry, La., U.S.	194	29.59 N	93.21 W
Hackberry Creek ≃, Kans., U.S.	198	38.48 N	100.03 W
Hackberry Creek ≃, Tex., U.S.	222	31.53 N	97.12 W
Hackensack	210	40.53 N	74.03 W
Hackensack ≃	276	40.43 N	74.06 W
Hacketstown	48	52.52 N	6.33 W
Hackett, Ark., U.S.	194	35.11 N	94.25 W
Hackett, Pa., U.S.	279b	40.15 N	80.01 W
Hacketts	260	51.45 N	0.05 W
Hackettstown	210	40.51 N	74.50 W
Hacking ≃	274a	34.04 S	151.06 E
Hacking, Port ⊂	274a	34.05 S	151.09 E
Hackleburg	194	34.17 N	87.50 W
Hackney ⬥[8]	260	51.33 N	0.03 W
Hack Point	208	39.28 N	75.53 W
Håckren ⊜	26	63.11 N	13.35 E
Haçlı Gölü ⊜	130	39.00 N	42.18 E
Haco	152	10.12 S	15.44 E
Hacreş Dağları ⋀	130	38.38 N	41.37 E
Hadāli	123	32.18 N	72.12 E
Hadalīya	140	16.10 N	36.06 E
Hadamar	56	50.27 N	8.02 E
Hadano	94	35.22 N	139.14 E
Ḥadāribah, Ra's al- ≻	140	22.04 N	36.54 E
HaDarom □[5]	132	30.40 N	34.50 E
Hadayingzi	104	42.22 N	121.40 E
Ḥadd, Ra's al- ≻	118	22.32 N	59.48 E
Haddad, Ouadi ∨	146	14.40 N	18.46 E

Symbols in the index entries represent the broad categories identified in the key at the right. Symbols with superior numbers (⋀[2]) identify subcategories (see complete key on page *I* · *30*).

Kartensymbole in dem Registerverzeichnis stellen die rechts in Schlüssel erklärten Kategorien dar. Symbole mit hochgestellten Ziffern (⋀[2]) bezeichnen Unterabteilungen einer Kategorie (vgl. vollständiger Schlüssel auf Seite *I* · *30*).

Los símbolos incluídos en el texto del índice representan las grandes categorias identificadas con la clave a la derecha. Los símbolos con numeros en su parte superior (⋀[2]) identifican las subcategorias (véase la clave completa en la página *I* · *30*).

Les symboles de l'index représentent les catégories indiquées dans la légende à droite. Les symboles suivis d'un indice (⋀[2]) représentent des sous-catégories (voir légende complète à la page *I* · *30*).

Os símbolos incluídos no texto do índice representam as grandes categorias identificadas com a chave à direita. Os símbolos com números em sua parte superior (⋀[2]) identificam as subcategorias (veja-se a chave completa à página *I* · *30*).

∧ Mountain	Berg	Montaña	Montagne	Montanha
⋀ Mountains	Berge	Montañas	Montagnes	Montanhas
)(Pass	Pass	Paso	Col	Passo
∨ Valley, Canyon	Tal, Cañon	Valle, Cañón	Vallée, Canyon	Vale, Canhão
═ Plain	Ebene	Llano	Plaine	Planície
≻ Cape	Kap	Cabo	Cap	Cabo
I Island	Insel	Isla	Île	Ilha
II Islands	Inseln	Islas	Îles	Ilhas
⊥ Other Topographic Features	Andere Topographische Objekte	Otros Elementos Topográficos	Autres données topographiques	Outros Elementos Topográficos

ESPAÑOL | FRANÇAIS | PORTUGUÊS

Nombre / Nom / Nome	Página / Page	Lat.°′	Long.°′ W=Oeste / W=Ouest
Ḥaddādīn, Qārat al- ∧[2]	142	30.04 N	30.58 E
Haddam, Conn., U.S.	207	41.29 N	72.31 W
Haddam, Kans., U.S.	198	39.51 N	97.18 W
Haddenham, Eng., U.K.	42	52.22 N	0.09 E
Haddenham, Eng., U.K.	42	51.46 N	0.56 W
Haddington	46	55.58 N	2.47 W
Haddock	192	33.02 N	83.26 W
Haddon Downs	166	26.21 S	140.50 E
Haddonfield	208	39.54 N	75.02 W
Haddon Heights	208	39.52 N	75.02 W
Hadejia	150	12.30 N	9.59 E
Hadejia ≃	146	12.50 N	10.51 E
Hadeln, Land ◆[1]	52	53.45 N	8.45 E
Haden	171a	27.14 S	151.53 E
Ḥadera	132	32.26 N	34.55 E
Ḥadera ≃	132	32.27 N	34.53 E
Hadersdorf ◆[8]	264b	48.13 N	16.14 E
Hadersfeld	264b	48.20 N	16.15 E
Haderslev	41	55.15 N	9.30 E
Haderslev Fjord C	41	55.17 N	9.40 E
Hadfield, Austl.	274b	37.42 S	144.56 E
Hadfield, Eng., U.K.	262	53.28 N	1.58 W
Hadībū	118	12.38 N	54.02 E
Ḥadīd, Jabal ∧[2]	142	30.20 N	30.06 E
Ḥadīd, Jabal al- ∧[2]	142	28.47 N	31.04 E
Hadım	130	36.59 N	32.28 E
Hadīyah	128	25.34 N	38.41 E
Hadjeb el Aïoun	36	35.24 N	9.33 E
Hadjout	34	36.31 N	2.25 E
Hadleigh	260	51.33 N	0.37 E
Hadleigh Castle ⊥	260	51.33 N	0.36 E
Hadley, Mass., U.S.	207	42.21 N	72.35 W
Hadley, Mich., U.S.	216	42.57 N	83.24 W
Hadley, N.Y., U.S.	210	43.19 N	73.51 W
Hadley, Pa., U.S.	214	41.25 N	80.14 W
Hadley Bay C	176	72.30 N	107.45 W
Hadley Creek ≃	219	39.37 N	91.12 W
Hadlock	202	48.02 N	122.46 W
Hadlow	260	51.14 N	0.20 E
Hadlyme	207	41.25 N	72.25 W
Hadmersleben	54	51.59 N	11.18 E
Hadong, Taehan	98	35.05 N	127.44 E
Ha-dong, Viet.	110	20.58 N	105.46 E
Ḥaḍramawt ◆[1]	144	15.00 N	50.00 E
Ḥaḍramawt, Wādī ∨	144	15.55 N	50.00 E
Hadrian's Wall ⊥	44	54.59 N	2.26 W
Hadsten	41	56.20 N	10.03 E
Hadsund	26	56.43 N	10.07 E
Haḍūr Shu'ayb ∧	144	15.18 N	43.59 E
Hadyai → Hat Yai	110	7.01 N	100.28 E
Haeju	98	38.02 N	125.42 E
Haemgon-ni ◆[8]	271b	37.35 N	126.49 E
Haena	229b	22.14 N	159.34 W
Haenam	98	34.34 N	126.35 E
Haena Point ❯	229b	22.14 N	159.34 W
Haenertsburg	156	24.00 S	29.50 E
Haengyŏng-ni	98	42.33 N	129.56 E
Haerbin (Harbin)	89	45.45 N	126.41 E
Haerhonghe ≃	102	42.40 N	110.42 E
Haerlikeshan ∧	102	43.08 N	94.20 E
Haernao	104	41.46 N	120.28 E
Haertao	104	42.21 N	122.04 E
Hafeïra, Oued el- ∨	148	25.18 N	10.48 W
Hafelekar Spitze ∧	64	47.19 N	11.23 E
Haffen-Mehr	52	51.44 N	6.28 E
Haffkrug-Scharbeutz	54	54.03 N	10.44 E
Hafford	184	52.48 N	107.20 W
Haffouz	36	35.38 N	9.41 E
Hafik	130	39.52 N	37.24 E
Ḥafīra, Qā' al- ≚	132	31.06 N	36.14 E
Ḥafīrat al-'Aydā	128	26.26 N	39.10 E
Ḥafīt, Jabal ∧	128	24.03 N	55.46 E
Ḥāfiẓ, Bi'r ⊤[4]	142	30.51 N	31.40 E
Hāfizābād	123	32.04 N	73.41 E
Hafızbey	130	37.12 N	30.31 E
Hāflong	120	25.11 N	93.02 E
Hafnarfjörđur	24a	64.03 N	21.56 W
Haft Gel	128	31.27 N	49.27 E
Hafun, Ras ❯	136	10.27 N	51.26 E
Hafun Bay North C	144	10.45 N	51.15 E
Hafun Bay South C	144	10.10 N	51.05 E
Haga, Nihon	94	36.32 N	140.04 E
Haga, Nihon	96	35.09 N	134.33 E
HaGadol, HaMakhtesh •[7]	132	30.56 N	34.59 E
Haga-Haga	158	32.46 S	28.14 E
Hagal	98	40.23 N	127.15 E
HaGalil (Galilee) ◆[1]	132	32.54 N	35.20 E
Hagaman	210	42.59 N	74.09 W
Hagan	192	32.09 N	81.56 W
Hagari ≃	122	15.45 N	76.56 E
Hagar Shores	216	42.13 N	86.22 W
Hagarstown	219	38.57 N	89.10 W
Hagau	60	48.43 N	11.22 E
Hage	52	53.36 N	7.17 E
Hagelberg ∧[2]	54	52.08 N	12.32 E
Hagemeister Island I	180	58.40 N	161.00 W
Hagen, B.R.D.	52	52.12 N	7.59 E
Hagen, B.R.D.	52	52.34 N	9.26 E
Hagen, B.R.D.	56	51.22 N	7.28 E
Hagenbrunn	264b	48.20 N	16.25 E
Hagen-Gebirge ⩕	64	47.32 N	13.07 E
Hagenow	54	53.26 N	11.11 E
Hagensborg	182	52.23 N	126.33 W
Hagenwerder	54	51.04 N	14.58 E
Hagerman, Idaho, U.S.	202	42.49 N	114.54 W
Hagerman, N. Mex., U.S.	196	33.07 N	104.20 W
Hagerman Corners	275b	43.50 N	79.18 W
Hagerstown, Ind., U.S.	218	39.55 N	85.10 W
Hagerstown, Md., U.S.	188	39.39 N	77.43 W
Hagersville	212	42.58 N	80.03 W
Hagetmau	32	43.40 N	0.35 W
Hagfors	40	60.02 N	13.42 E
Haggen ◎	40	60.06 N	15.13 E
Haggetts Pond ◎	283	42.39 N	71.12 W
Haggin, Mount ∧	202	46.05 N	113.05 W
Hagi	96	34.24 N	131.25 E
Ha-giang	110	22.50 N	104.59 E
Hagitani	270	34.54 N	135.35 E
Hagiwara	94	35.52 N	137.12 E
Hagley	42	52.26 N	2.08 W
Hagondange	56	49.15 N	6.10 E
HaGosherim	132	33.13 N	35.37 E
Hags Head ❯	48	52.57 N	9.30 W
Hague, Sask., Can.	184	52.30 N	106.25 W
Hague, N. Dak., U.S.	198	46.02 N	99.59 W
Hague, Cap de la ❯	32	49.43 N	1.57 W
Haguenau	56	48.49 N	7.47 E
Hagues Peak ∧	200	40.29 N	105.38 W
Hahaia	157a	11.33 S	43.17 E
Hahajima-rettō II	14	26.37 N	142.10 E
Hāhipur	272b	22.47 N	88.10 E
Hahira	192	30.57 N	83.22 W
Hahlen	52	52.18 N	8.50 E
Hahn	56	50.31 N	7.53 E
Hahnbach	60	49.32 N	11.48 E
Hahnenberg	263	51.12 N	7.24 E
Hahnenkamm ∧	64	47.25 N	12.22 E
Hahnenklee-Bockswiese	52	51.51 N	10.20 E
Hahnerberg ◆[8]	263	51.13 N	7.09 E
Hahnstätten	56	50.18 N	8.04 E
Hahntown	279b	40.19 N	79.44 W
Haho ≃	150	6.17 N	1.23 E
Hahyŏn-ni	98	38.33 N	127.57 E
Haian	100	32.34 N	120.28 E
Haianshan ⩕	100	22.40 N	114.20 E
Haian Shanmo ⩕	100	23.25 N	121.25 E
Haiba	106	32.04 N	120.38 E
Haibara, Nihon	94	34.32 N	135.57 E
Haibara, Nihon	94	34.44 N	138.13 E
Haibatpur	272a	28.37 N	77.26 E
Haibei	89	47.39 N	126.51 E
Haicheng, Zhg.	100	24.25 N	117.51 E
Haicheng, Zhg.	104	40.52 N	122.45 E
Haichenghe ≃	104	40.56 N	122.21 E
Haidargarh	124	26.37 N	81.22 E
Haidārpur ◆[8]	272a	28.43 N	77.09 E
Haidennaab ≃	60	49.36 N	12.08 E
Haiderabad → Hyderābād, Bhārat	122	17.23 N	78.29 E
Haiderabad → Hyderābād, Pāk.	120	25.22 N	68.22 E
Haidhof	60	49.50 N	11.39 E
Haidian	105	39.59 N	116.18 E
Haiding	60	48.13 N	13.58 E
Haidmühle	60	48.50 N	13.46 E
Haïdra	36	35.34 N	8.27 E
Haidstein ∧	60	49.13 N	12.48 E
Haidun	100	29.36 N	121.49 E
Hai-duong	110	20.56 N	106.19 E
Haifa → Ḥefa	132	32.50 N	35.00 E
Haifa, Bay of → Ḥefa, Mifraẓ C	132	32.52 N	35.03 E
Haifeng	100	22.59 N	115.21 E
Haifengzheng	106	31.53 N	121.46 E
Haifuzhen	106	31.59 N	121.42 E
Haig	162	31.01 S	126.05 E
Haig, Mount ∧	182	49.17 N	114.29 W
Haiger	56	50.44 N	8.13 E
Haigerloch	58	48.22 N	8.48 E
Haigh	262	53.35 N	2.36 W
Haigler	198	40.01 N	101.56 W
Haihezhen	100	33.44 N	120.02 E
Haijima	268	35.42 N	139.21 E
Haik, Lake ◎	144	11.19 N	39.41 E
Haikang (Leizhou)	102	20.56 N	110.04 E
Haikou, Zhg.	100	25.43 N	119.28 E
Haikou, Zhg.	100	29.04 N	117.46 E
Haikou, Zhg.	100	28.20 N	120.06 E
Haikou, Zhg.	102	20.06 N	110.21 E
Haiku	229a	20.55 N	156.20 W
Ḥā'il	128	27.33 N	41.42 E
Hailaer	89	49.12 N	119.42 E
Hailaerhe ≃	90	49.35 N	117.55 E
Hailākāndi	120	24.41 N	92.34 E
Hailar → Hailaer	89	49.12 N	119.42 E
Hailasen	89	46.13 N	121.00 E
Hailesboro	212	44.18 N	75.27 W
Hailey, Eng., U.K.	260	51.46 N	0.01 W
Hailey, Idaho, U.S.	202	43.31 N	114.19 W
Haileybury	190	47.27 N	79.38 W
Hailin	89	44.35 N	129.22 E
Hailing	60	48.45 N	12.33 E
Haillicourt	50	50.28 N	2.35 E
Hailsham	42	50.52 N	0.16 E
Hailun	89	47.28 N	126.58 E
Hailuoto	26	65.00 N	24.43 E
Hailuoto I	26	65.02 N	24.42 E
Haiman Tepesi ∧[2]	267b	41.12 N	29.15 E
Haimen, Zhg.	100	28.41 N	121.27 E
Haimen, Zhg.	100	23.14 N	116.38 E
Haimen, Zhg.	106	31.55 N	121.10 E
Haimenwan C	100	23.09 N	116.34 E
Haimhausen	60	48.19 N	11.34 E
Haimi	175d	24.15 N	123.52 E
Haimiao	98	37.13 N	119.51 E
Haiming	58	47.15 N	10.53 E
Haina	56	51.02 N	8.58 E
Hainan → Hainandao I	110	19.00 N	109.30 E
Hainandao I	110	19.00 N	109.30 E
Hainault ◆[8]	260	51.36 N	0.06 E
Hainaut □[4]	50	50.30 N	3.50 E
Hainburg an der Donau	61	48.09 N	16.57 E
Hainchen	56	50.51 N	8.12 E
Haines, Alaska, U.S.	180	59.15 N	135.25 W
Haines, Oreg., U.S.	202	44.55 N	117.56 W
Haines City	220	28.07 N	81.37 W
Haines Falls	210	42.12 N	74.06 W
Haines Junction	180	60.45 N	137.30 W
Hainesport	208	39.59 N	74.50 W
Hainesville	278	42.21 N	88.04 W
Hainewalde	54	50.54 N	14.41 E
Hainfeld	61	48.02 N	15.46 E
Hainich ⩕	54	51.05 N	10.27 E
Hainichen	54	50.58 N	13.07 E
Haining	106	30.25 N	120.32 E
Hainleite ⩕	54	51.20 N	10.48 E
Hainsbach	60	48.44 N	12.25 E
Hainsberg	54	50.59 N	13.38 E
Hainzenberg	64	47.13 N	11.54 E
Hai-phong	110	20.52 N	106.41 E
Haiqiao	106	31.47 N	121.19 E
Haiqing	89	47.53 N	134.40 E
Haitandao I	100	25.33 N	119.48 E
Haitangxi	107	29.33 N	106.35 E
Haitanxia ⋓	100	25.27 N	119.38 E
Haiti □[1]	230		
	238	19.00 N	72.25 W
Haitou, Zhg.	98	35.00 N	119.12 E
Haitou, Zhg.	110	19.34 N	108.58 E
Haitouji	98	35.23 N	115.19 E
Haitun	102	38.50 N	96.41 E
Haiwee Reservoir ◎[1]	204	36.10 N	117.57 W
Haiyan, Zhg.	102	36.54 N	101.12 E
Haiyan, Zhg.	106	30.31 N	120.57 E
Haiyang (Dongcun)	98	36.46 N	121.10 E
Haiyangdao I	98	39.02 N	123.14 E
Haiyingzi	98	41.22 N	115.05 E
Haiyuan	102	36.32 N	105.52 E
Haizhou	100	22.40 N	113.10 E
Haizhoumiao	104	42.00 N	121.39 E
Haizhouyingzi	104	42.07 N	121.46 E
Ḥajar, Tall al- ∧[2]	132	33.21 N	37.03 E
Ḥajar Banga	140	11.30 N	23.00 E
Hajdú-Bihar □[6]	30	47.25 N	21.30 E
Hajdúböszörmény	30	47.41 N	21.30 E
Hajdúnánás	30	47.51 N	21.26 E
Hajdúszoboszló	30	47.27 N	21.24 E
Hajiadian	98	41.32 N	117.10 E
Hājīganj	126	23.15 N	90.50 E
Hajiki-saki ❯	92	38.19 N	138.31 E
Hājīpur, Bhārat	124	25.41 N	85.13 E
Hājīpur, Bhārat	126	22.49 N	87.38 E
Hajipur, Bhārat	272b	22.57 N	88.19 E
Ḥājj, Wādī al- ∨	142	30.03 N	32.45 E
Hajnówka	30	52.45 N	23.36 E
Ḥajūl, Wādī ∨	142	29.42 N	32.22 E
Haka	110	22.39 N	93.37 E
Hakachi-zaki ❯	94	34.41 N	138.45 E
HaKarmel, Har (Mount Carmel) ∧	132	32.44 N	35.02 E
Hakata	96	34.07 N	132.57 E
Hakata-jima I	96	34.13 N	133.05 E
Hakataramea ≃	172	44.44 S	170.29 E
Hakendover	56	50.48 N	4.59 E
Haki	96	33.20 N	130.50 E
Hakkâri	128	37.34 N	43.45 E
Hakken-san ∧	92	34.10 N	135.54 E
Hakkōda-san ∧	92	40.40 N	140.53 E
Hak Kok Tau ❯	271d	22.16 N	114.15 E
Hako-dake ∧	92a	44.40 N	142.25 E
Hakodate	92a	41.45 N	140.43 E
Hakone	94	35.12 N	139.06 E
Hakoneno-seki ⊥	94	35.10 N	139.02 E
Hakone-tōge)(	94	35.11 N	139.01 E
Hakone-yama ∧	94	35.14 N	139.02 E
Håksberg	40	60.11 N	15.12 E
Hakskeenpan ◎	158	26.48 S	20.12 E
Hakuba	94	36.42 N	137.52 E
Hakui	94	36.53 N	136.47 E
Hakupu	174v	19.06 S	169.50 W
Hakusan	94	34.38 N	136.21 E
Haku-san ∧	94	36.09 N	136.46 E
Haku-san-kokuritsu-kōen ♠	94	36.12 N	136.47 E
Hakushū	94	35.48 N	138.20 E
Hakuta	96	35.21 N	133.17 E
Hakuta ≃	96	35.26 N	133.15 E
Hāla	120	25.49 N	68.25 E
Halaaobao	102	42.11 N	107.20 E
Ḥalab (Aleppo)	130	36.12 N	37.10 E
Ḥalab □[8]	130	36.00 N	37.00 E
Ḥalabjah	128	35.10 N	45.59 E
Halachó	232	20.29 N	90.05 W
Halaerjige	104	42.24 N	122.11 E
Halagetu	104	42.34 N	122.40 E
Halagigie Point ❯	174v	19.03 S	169.57 W
Halahai	89	44.39 N	125.07 E
Halahu (Heihai) ◎	102	38.15 N	97.40 E
Halahushao	104	42.11 N	121.44 E
Ḥalā'ib	140	22.13 N	36.38 E
Halalii Lake ◎	229b	21.52 N	160.11 W
Halamutai	86	46.10 N	84.52 E
Halasa	140	14.26 N	30.39 E
Halas-patak ≃	264c	47.24 N	19.20 E
Halasu	89	48.09 N	122.25 E
Halataojie	104	42.30 N	122.06 E
Halatiekeshan ⩕	85	40.30 N	77.05 E
Halaula	229d	20.14 N	155.46 W
Hålaveden ⩕[2]	26	58.05 N	14.45 E
Halawa, Cape ❯	229a	21.10 N	156.43 W
Halawa Bay C	229a	21.10 N	156.44 W
Halawa Heights	229c	21.23 N	157.55 W
Halawotelake	120	37.17 N	90.20 E
Ḥalbā	130	34.33 N	36.05 E
Halbach ◆[8]	263	51.12 N	7.12 E
Halbau → Iłowa	30	51.30 N	15.12 E
Halbe	54	52.06 N	13.42 E
Halberstadt	54	51.54 N	11.02 E
Halbert, Lake ◎[1]	222	32.04 N	96.25 W
Halberton	42	50.55 N	3.25 W
Halbrite	184	49.20 N	103.32 W
Ḥalbūn	132	33.40 N	36.15 E
Halbury	168b	34.05 S	138.31 E
Halcombe	172	40.09 S	175.30 E
Halcon, Mount ∧	116	13.16 N	121.00 E
Halcottsville	210	42.12 N	74.36 W
Haldeman	218	38.15 N	83.19 W
Halden	26	59.09 N	11.23 E
Halden ◆[8]	263	51.23 N	7.31 E
Haldensleben	54	52.18 N	11.26 E
Haldern	52	51.46 N	6.27 E
Haldi ≃	126	22.01 N	88.03 E
Haldībāri	124	26.20 N	88.46 E
Haldībunia	126	22.26 N	89.38 E
Haldimand □[6]	212	42.57 N	79.50 W
Haldwāni	124	29.13 N	79.31 E
Hale, Eng., U.K.	262	53.20 N	2.48 W
Hale, Eng., U.K.	262	53.23 N	2.21 W
Hale, Mo., U.S.	194	39.36 N	93.20 W
Hale ≃	162	24.56 S	135.53 E
Haleakala Crater •[6]	229a	20.43 N	156.13 W
Haleakala National Park ♠	229a	20.44 N	156.13 W
Haleb → Ḥalab	130	36.12 N	37.10 E
Halebarns	262	53.22 N	2.19 W
Haleb Island I	144	12.55 N	42.59 E
Hale Center	196	34.04 N	101.51 W
Hale Creek ≃	282	37.23 N	122.06 W
Haledon	276	40.56 N	74.11 W
Haledon Reservoir ◎[1]	276	40.59 N	74.12 W
Hale Eddy	210	42.00 N	75.23 W
Hale Head ∧	262	53.19 N	2.48 W
Haleiwa	229c	21.35 N	158.07 W
Halekii-Pihana Heiaus State Monument ⊥	229a	20.54 N	156.29 W
Halenkov	30	49.19 N	18.08 E
Hales Corners	216	42.55 N	88.03 W
Halesite	207	40.52 N	73.25 W
Halesowen	42	52.26 N	2.05 W
Hale Street	260	51.13 N	0.24 E
Halesworth	42	52.21 N	1.30 E
Halethorpe	284b	39.15 N	76.41 W
Halewood	262	53.22 N	2.49 W
Haleyville	194	34.14 N	87.37 W
Half Assini	150	5.03 N	2.53 W
Ḥalfāyah, Naqb al- (Halfaya Pass))(	140	31.30 N	25.11 E
Halfaya Pass → Ḥalfāyah, Naqb al-)(	140	31.30 N	25.11 E
Half Day	278	42.12 N	87.56 W
Halfeti	130	37.15 N	37.52 E
Half Hollow Hills	276	40.48 N	73.21 W
Halfing	64	47.57 N	12.16 E
Halfmoon Bay, B.C., Can.	182	49.31 N	123.54 W
Half-Moon Bay, N.Z.	172	46.54 S	168.08 E
Half Moon Bay, Calif., U.S.	226	37.28 N	122.26 W
Halfmoon Bay C, Austl.	274b	37.58 S	145.00 E
Half Moon Bay C, Calif., U.S.	282	37.29 N	122.28 W
Half Moon Bay Airport ⊠	282	37.31 N	122.30 W
Half Moon Bay Beaches ♠	282	37.29 N	122.27 W
Halfway, Md., U.S.	188	39.37 N	77.46 W
Halfway, Oreg., U.S.	202	44.53 N	117.07 W
Halfway Lake ◎	184	55.03 N	98.24 W
Halgån ≃	40	60.16 N	13.27 E
Ḥalḥūl	132	31.35 N	35.07 E
Ḥalī ⊤[4]	144	18.42 N	41.20 E
Haliburton	212	45.03 N	78.03 W
Haliburton □[6]	212	44.10 N	78.30 W
Haliburton Lake ◎	212	45.12 N	78.24 W
Halibut Point ❯	283	42.42 N	70.38 W
Haliç C	267b	41.02 N	28.58 E
Halicarnassus ⊥	130	37.03 N	27.23 E
Halicz ∧	78	49.05 N	22.48 E
Halifax, Austl.	166	18.35 S	146.18 E
Halifax, N.S., Can.	186	44.39 N	63.36 W
Halifax, Eng., U.K.	44		
	262	53.44 N	1.52 W
Halifax, Mass., U.S.	207	41.59 N	70.52 W
Halifax, N.C., U.S.	192	36.20 N	77.35 W
Halifax, Pa., U.S.	208	40.28 N	76.56 W
Halifax, Va., U.S.	192	36.46 N	78.56 W
Halifax Bay C	166	18.50 S	146.30 E
Halifax Citadel National Historic Park ♠	186	44.40 N	63.36 W
Halifax Harbour C	186	44.35 N	63.31 W
Haliimaile	229a	20.52 N	156.20 W
Ḥalīl ≃	128	27.28 N	58.44 E
Halimatazi	104	42.37 N	122.35 E
Halimiye	130	36.40 N	32.45 E
Halim Perdanakusuma Airfield ■	269e	6.16 S	106.54 E
Halimun, Gunung ∧	115a	6.42 S	106.26 E
Halin	144	9.08 N	48.47 E
Halingen	263	51.27 N	7.44 E
Hālisahar	126	22.56 N	88.25 E
Haliyāl	122	15.20 N	74.46 E
Haljala	76	59.26 N	26.16 E
Halkalı	267b	41.02 N	28.47 E
Halkett, Cape ❯	180	70.49 N	152.12 W
Halkirk	46	58.30 N	3.30 W
Halkyn	262	53.14 N	3.11 W
Halkyn Mountain ∧	262	53.14 N	3.13 W
Hall, Austl.	171b	35.10 S	149.04 E
Hall, Ind., U.S.	218	39.33 N	86.32 W
Hall, N.Y., U.S.	210	42.48 N	77.04 W
Hällabrottet	40	59.07 N	15.12 E
Halladale ≃	46	58.33 N	3.55 W
Hallam	274b	38.01 S	145.06 E
Hallam Peak ∧	182	52.11 N	118.46 W
Halland □[9]	26	57.00 N	12.40 E
Hallandale	220	25.60 N	80.09 W
Hallandsås ⩕[2]	26	56.23 N	13.00 E
Hallands Län □[6]	26	56.45 N	13.00 E
Hallands Väderö I	26	56.26 N	12.33 E
Halla-san ∧	90	33.22 N	126.32 E
Hallau	58	47.42 N	8.27 E
Hällberga	40	59.19 N	16.36 E
Hällbybrunn	40	59.24 N	16.25 E
Halle, Bel.	50	50.44 N	4.13 E
Halle, B.R.D.	52	52.04 N	8.22 E
Halle, B.R.D.	52	51.59 N	9.33 E
Halle, D.D.R.	54	51.29 N	11.58 E
Halle □[5]	54	51.30 N	11.45 E
Halleberg ∧[2]	26	58.23 N	12.27 E
Hällefors	40	59.47 N	14.30 E
Hälleforsnäs	40	59.10 N	16.30 E
Hallein	64	47.41 N	13.06 E
Hällekis	26	58.38 N	13.25 E
Hallen	26	63.11 N	14.05 E
Hallenberg	56	51.06 N	8.37 E
Hallencourt	50	49.59 N	1.53 E
Hallertau ◆[1]	60	48.35 N	11.45 E
Hällestad	40	58.44 N	15.34 E
Hallett, Cape ❯	9	72.19 S	170.18 E
Hallettsville	222	29.27 N	96.56 W
Halliday	198	47.21 N	102.20 W
Halligen II	30	54.35 N	8.35 E
Halling	260	51.21 N	0.27 E
Hallingdalselvi ≃	26	60.24 N	9.35 E
Hällingsåfallet L	26	64.20 N	14.20 E
Hall Island I	180	60.40 N	173.05 W
Hall Islands II	14	8.37 N	152.00 E
Halliste ≃	76	58.31 N	25.03 E
Hall-i'-th'-Wood	262	53.36 N	2.26 W
Hall Lake ◎	176	68.41 N	82.17 W
Hall Meadow Brook Reservoir ◎[1]	207	41.52 N	73.10 W
Hall Mountain ∧	202	48.49 N	117.15 W
Hällnäs	26	64.19 N	19.38 E
Hallock	198	48.47 N	96.57 W
Hallowell	188	44.17 N	69.48 W
Hall Peninsula ❯[1]	176	63.30 N	66.00 W
Halls	194	35.53 N	89.24 W
Halls Bayou ≃	222	29.12 N	95.07 W
Hallsberg	40	59.04 N	15.07 E
Halls Brook ≃	283	42.00 N	70.43 W
Halls Creek	162	18.16 S	127.46 E
Halls Creek ≃	200	37.18 N	110.45 W
Hållsfjärden C[2]	40	59.08 N	17.40 E
Halls Lake ◎	212	45.07 N	78.45 W
Halls Stream ≃	206	45.01 N	71.30 W
Hållsta	40	59.18 N	16.27 E
Hallstadt	56	49.55 N	10.52 E
Hallstahammar	40	59.37 N	16.13 E
Hallstatt	64	47.33 N	13.39 E
Hallstätter See ◎	64	47.35 N	13.39 E
Hallstavik	40	60.03 N	18.36 E
Hallstead	210	41.58 N	75.45 W
Hallsville, Mo., U.S.	219	39.07 N	92.13 W
Hallsville, Tex., U.S.	222	32.30 N	94.34 W
Halluin	50	50.47 N	3.08 E
Hallwiler See ◎	58	47.18 N	8.13 E
Hallwood	208	37.53 N	75.35 W
Halma	56	50.05 N	5.08 E
Halmahera I	108	1.00 N	128.00 E
Halmahera, Laut (Halmahera Sea) ⊤[2]	108	1.00 S	129.00 E
Halmstad	26	56.39 N	12.50 E
Hals	26	57.00 N	10.19 E
Halsafjorden C[2]	26	63.03 N	8.11 E
Halsall	262	53.35 N	2.57 W
Halsbrücke	54	50.57 N	13.21 E
Halsey, Nebr., U.S.	198	41.54 N	100.16 W
Halsey, Oreg., U.S.	202	44.23 N	123.07 W
Halsey Harbor C	116	11.45 N	119.56 E
Halsey Valley	210	42.08 N	76.27 W
Hälsingborg → Helsingborg	41	56.03 N	12.42 E
Hälsingland □[9]	26	61.30 N	17.00 E
Halstad	198	47.21 N	96.50 W
Halstead, Eng., U.K.	42	51.57 N	0.38 E
Halstead, Eng., U.K.	260	51.20 N	0.08 E
Halstead, Kans., U.S.	198	38.00 N	97.30 W
Halstenbek	52	53.38 N	9.50 E
Halsteren	52	51.32 N	4.16 E
Halstow Marshes ≡	260	51.29 N	0.33 E
Haltern	52	51.46 N	7.10 E
Haltiatunturi ∧	24	69.18 N	21.16 E
Haltom City	222	32.48 N	97.16 W
Halton	262	53.20 N	2.42 W
Halton □[6]	212	43.30 N	79.53 W
Halton □[8]	262	53.20 N	2.44 W
Haltwhistle	44	54.58 N	2.27 W
Halura, Pulau I	115b	10.19 S	120.07 E
Halūzonī, Wādī al- ∨	273c	30.05 N	31.24 E
Halvarsgårdarna	40	60.24 N	15.23 E
Halvarsnoren ◎	40	59.35 N	14.36 E
Halver	56	51.11 N	7.30 E
Halvorson, Mount ∧	182	53.15 N	120.33 W
Halwell	42	50.22 N	3.43 W
Ham, Fr.	50	49.45 N	3.04 E
Ham, Tchad	146	10.00 N	15.41 E
Ham ◆[8]	260	51.26 N	0.19 W
Ham, Oued el ≃	34	35.42 N	4.52 E
Ḥamad	140	15.19 N	33.43 E
Hamada	96	34.53 N	132.05 E
Hamada ◆[1]	148	27.30 N	9.00 W
Hamadān	128	34.48 N	48.30 E
Hamadān □[8]	128	35.00 N	48.40 E
Ḥamāh	130	35.08 N	36.45 E
Ḥamāh □[8]	130	35.10 N	37.00 E
Hamahika-jima I	174m	26.19 N	127.57 E
Hamakeza	89	47.05 N	120.52 E
Hamakita	94	34.48 N	137.47 E
Hamale	150	10.59 N	2.44 W
Hamam	130	39.30 N	35.24 E
Hamamatsu	94	34.42 N	137.44 E
Hamamözü	130	40.48 N	35.02 E
Haman	98	35.15 N	128.24 E
Hamanaka	92a	43.05 N	145.10 E
Hamana-ko ◎	94	34.45 N	137.34 E
Hamano	268	35.33 N	140.08 E
Hamaoka	94	34.39 N	138.08 E
Hamar	26	60.48 N	11.06 E
Hamasaka	96	35.37 N	134.27 E
Ḥamāṭah, Jabal ∧	140	24.12 N	35.00 E
Hamatang	98	40.12 N	124.20 E
Hama-tombetsu	92a	45.07 N	142.23 E
Hambach	56	49.04 N	7.02 E
Hambaek-san ∧	98	37.09 N	128.55 E
Hambantota	122	6.07 N	81.07 E
Hamberg	273d	26.11 S	27.53 E
Hambergen	52	53.18 N	8.49 E
Hamber Provincial Park ♠	182	52.25 N	117.40 W
Hamble	42	50.52 N	1.19 W
Hambledon	42	50.56 N	1.04 W
Hambleton Hills ⩕[2]	44	54.16 N	1.12 W
Hambly Lake ◎	212	44.28 N	76.41 W
Hamborn ◆[8]	263	51.29 N	6.46 E
Hambourg → Hamburg	52	53.33 N	9.59 E
Hambridge National Park ♠	166	33.25 S	136.00 E
Hamburg, B.R.D.	52	53.33 N	9.59 E
Hamburg, S. Afr.	158	33.17 S	27.28 E
Hamburg, Ark., U.S.	194	33.14 N	91.48 W
Hamburg, Conn., U.S.	207	41.23 N	72.21 W
Hamburg, Ill., U.S.	219	39.14 N	90.43 W
Hamburg, Iowa, U.S.	198	40.36 N	95.39 W
Hamburg, Mich., U.S.	216	42.27 N	83.48 W
Hamburg, N.J., U.S.	210	41.09 N	74.35 W
Hamburg, N.Y., U.S.	210	42.43 N	78.50 W
Hamburg, Pa., U.S.	208	40.34 N	75.59 W
Hamburg □[3]	52	53.35 N	10.00 E
Hamburg Airport ⊠	284a	42.42 N	78.55 W
Hamburg Ditch ≆	208	36.31 N	76.33 W
Hamburger Hallig ❯[1]	41	54.36 N	8.49 E
Hamburg Mountains ⩕	276	41.08 N	74.32 W
Hamburgo → Hamburg	52	53.33 N	9.59 E
Hamburgsund	26	58.33 N	11.16 E
Ḥamḍ, Wādī al- ∨	128	25.54 N	36.38 E
Ḥamḍah	144	19.02 N	43.36 E
Hamdallay Timbou	150	12.03 N	10.37 W
Hamdam Āb, Dasht-e ≚	128	34.45 N	61.30 E
Ḥamdānah ⊤[4]	144	19.58 N	40.35 E
Hamden, Conn., U.S.	207	41.21 N	72.56 W
Hamden, N.Y., U.S.	210	42.12 N	75.00 W
Hamden, Ohio, U.S.	188	39.10 N	82.32 W
Hamdilaye	150	13.34 N	2.24 E
Häme ◆[1]	26	61.30 N	24.30 E
Hämeenkangas ◆[3]	26	61.45 N	22.40 E
Hämeenkylä	26	60.16 N	24.47 E
Hämeen lääni □[4]	26	61.30 N	24.30 E
Hämeenlinna	26	61.00 N	24.27 E
Hameiershan ⩕	102	37.34 N	96.15 E
Hamel	168a	32.52 S	115.55 E
HaMelah, Yam → Dead Sea ◎	132	31.30 N	35.30 E
Hämelerwald	52	52.22 N	10.05 E
Hamelin Pool	162	26.26 S	114.11 E
Hamelin Pool C	162	26.15 S	114.05 E
Hameln	52	52.06 N	9.21 E
HaMerkaz □[5]	132	32.05 N	34.55 E
Hamer Koke	144	5.12 N	36.45 E
Hamero Hadad	144	7.34 N	42.18 E
Hamersleben	54	52.04 N	11.05 E
Hamersley Range ⩕	162	21.53 S	116.46 E
Hamersville	218	38.55 N	83.59 W
Hames Creek ≃	226	35.53 N	120.50 W
Hamgyŏng Namdo □[4]	98	40.00 N	127.30 E
Hamgyŏng-pukdo □[4]	98	41.45 N	129.50 E
Hamgyŏng-sanmaek ⩕	98	41.50 N	128.30 E
Ham House ⊥	260	51.27 N	0.19 W
Hamhŭng	98	39.54 N	127.32 E
Hami	102	42.47 N	93.32 E
Hamidiye	130	41.09 N	26.40 E
Hamiguitan, Mount ∧	116	6.44 N	126.11 E
Hamilton, Austl.	166	37.45 S	142.02 E
Hamilton, Ber.	240a	32.17 N	64.46 W
Hamilton, Ont., Can.	212	43.15 N	79.51 W
Hamilton, N.Z.	172	37.47 S	175.17 E
Hamilton, Scot., U.K.	46	55.47 N	4.03 W
Hamilton, Ala., U.S.	194	34.09 N	88.06 W
Hamilton, Alaska, U.S.	180	62.54 N	163.53 W
Hamilton, Ga., U.S.	192	32.45 N	84.53 W
Hamilton, Ill., U.S.	190	40.24 N	91.21 W
Hamilton, Ind., U.S.	216	41.32 N	84.55 W
Hamilton, Kans., U.S.	198	37.59 N	96.10 W
Hamilton, Mass., U.S.	207	42.37 N	70.52 W
Hamilton, Mich., U.S.	216	42.41 N	86.00 W
Hamilton, Mo., U.S.	194	39.45 N	94.01 W
Hamilton, Mont., U.S.	202	46.15 N	114.09 W
Hamilton, N.C., U.S.	192	35.57 N	77.12 W
Hamilton, N.Y., U.S.	210	42.50 N	75.33 W
Hamilton, Ohio, U.S.	218	39.26 N	84.30 W
Hamilton, R.I., U.S.	207	41.33 N	71.26 W
Hamilton, Tex., U.S.	196	31.42 N	98.07 W
Hamilton, Wash., U.S.	224	48.31 N	121.59 W
Hamilton □[6], Ind., U.S.	218	40.03 N	86.01 W
Hamilton □[6], N.Y., U.S.	210	43.24 N	74.25 W
Hamilton □[6], Ohio, U.S.	218	39.06 N	84.31 W
Hamilton ◆[8]	284b	39.21 N	76.33 W
Hamilton ≃	166	23.30 S	139.47 E
Hamilton, Lake ◎	220	28.03 N	81.39 W
Hamilton, Lake ◎[1]	194	34.30 N	93.05 W
Hamilton, Mount ∧, Alaska, U.S.	180	61.10 N	159.46 W
Hamilton, Mount ∧, Calif., U.S.	226	37.21 N	121.38 W
Hamilton, Mount ∧, Nev., U.S.	204	39.14 N	115.32 W
Hamilton Acres	180	64.51 N	147.40 W
Hamilton Air Force Base ■	282	38.03 N	122.31 W
Hamilton City	204	39.45 N	122.01 W
Hamilton Creek ≃	162	26.40 S	135.19 E
Hamilton Creek Indian Reserve ◆[4]	182	50.11 N	120.30 W
Hamilton Dome	200	43.46 N	108.34 W
Hamilton Harbour C	212	43.17 N	79.50 W
Hamilton Hill	168a	32.05 S	115.46 E
Hamilton Hotel	166	22.50 S	140.35 E
Hamilton Inlet C	176	54.00 N	57.30 W
Hamilton Lake ◎	216	41.33 N	84.55 W
Hamilton Mountain ∧	188	43.25 N	74.22 W
Hamilton Park, Ind., U.S.	216	40.17 N	85.19 W
Hamilton Park, Pa., U.S.	208	40.02 N	76.20 W
Hamilton Sound ⋓	186	49.30 N	54.30 W
Hamilton Square	285	40.14 N	74.40 W
Ḥamīm, Wādī al- ∨	146	30.10 N	21.32 E
Hamina	26	60.34 N	27.12 E
Hamiota	184	50.11 N	100.36 W
Ḥamir, Wādī ∨	128	31.37 N	42.12 E
Hamīrpur, Bhārat	123	31.41 N	76.31 E
Hamīrpur, Bhārat	124	25.57 N	80.09 E
Hamīrpur □[5]	124	25.30 N	26.40 E
Hamjong-ni	98	38.59 N	125.17 E
Hamler	216	41.14 N	84.02 W
Hamlet, Ind., U.S.	216	41.23 N	86.35 W
Hamlet, N.C., U.S.	192	34.53 N	79.42 W
Hamlet, Ohio, U.S.	218	39.01 N	84.12 W
Hamlet, Mount ∧	180	68.47 N	165.57 W
Hamley Bridge	168b	34.21 S	138.41 E
Hamlin, N.Y., U.S.	210	43.18 N	77.55 W
Hamlin, Pa., U.S.	210	41.24 N	75.24 W
Hamlin, Tex., U.S.	196	32.53 N	100.08 W
Hamlin, W. Va., U.S.	188	38.17 N	82.06 W
Hamlin Beach State Park ♠	210	43.22 N	77.58 W
Hamlin Lake ◎	190	44.03 N	86.27 W
Hamlin Valley Wash ∨	200	38.53 N	114.01 W
Hamm, B.R.D.	52	51.43 N	7.10 E
Hamm, B.R.D.	52		
	263	51.41 N	7.49 E
Hamm ◆[8], B.R.D.	263	51.15 N	6.25 E
Hamm ◆[8], B.R.D.	263	51.23 N	7.03 E
Hamm ◆[8], B.R.D.	263	51.12 N	6.44 E
Ḥammād, Wādī ∨	142	29.45 N	32.24 E
Hamma Hamma ≃	224	47.33 N	123.03 W
Ḥammām at-Turkumān	130	36.32 N	39.03 E
Hammamet, Alg.	36	35.27 N	7.58 E
Hammamet, Tun.	148	36.24 N	10.37 E
Hammamet, Golfe de C	148	36.05 N	10.40 E
Hammami ◆[1]	148	23.03 N	11.30 W
Hammam Lif	148	36.44 N	10.20 E
Ḥammānā	132	33.49 N	35.44 E
Hammar	40	58.49 N	14.57 E
Ḥammār, Hawr al- ◎	128	30.50 N	47.10 E
Hammarby	40	60.33 N	16.34 E
Hammarn	40	59.45 N	14.30 E
Hammarö	40	59.20 N	13.31 E
Hammarön I	40	59.19 N	13.31 E
Hammarstrand	26	63.06 N	16.21 E
Hamme	50	51.06 N	4.08 E
Hamme ≃	52	53.10 N	8.44 E
Hammel	41	56.15 N	9.52 E
Hammelburg	56	50.07 N	9.53 E
Hamme-Mille	56	50.47 N	4.43 E
Hammerbrücke	54	50.26 N	12.25 E
Hammerdal	26	63.36 N	15.21 E
Hammerfest	24	70.40 N	23.42 E
Hammermühle → Kępice	30	54.15 N	16.52 E
Hämmern	263	51.08 N	7.21 E
Hammershus ⊥	26	55.16 N	14.45 E
Hammersley Inlet C	224	47.12 N	123.00 W
Hammersmith ◆[8]	260	51.30 N	0.14 W
Hammerstein → Czarne	30	53.42 N	16.57 E
Hammerum	41	56.08 N	9.04 E
Hamminkeln	52	51.44 N	6.35 E
Hammon	196	35.38 N	99.23 W
Hammonasset ≃	207	41.16 N	72.33 W
Hammond, Ind., U.S.	216	41.36 N	87.30 W
Hammond, La., U.S.	194	30.30 N	90.28 W
Hammond, N.Y., U.S.	212	44.27 N	75.42 W
Hammond, Oreg., U.S.	224	46.12 N	123.57 W
Hammond, Wis., U.S.	190	44.59 N	92.26 W
Hammond Island I, Austl.	164	10.35 S	142.13 E
Hammond Island I, Calif., U.S.	282	38.06 N	121.57 W
Hammond Pond Park ♠	283	42.19 N	71.11 W
Hammondsport	210	42.25 N	77.13 W
Hammondsville	214	40.33 N	80.43 W
Hammondville	274a	33.57 S	150.57 E
Hammonia	158	28.43 S	27.49 E
Hammonton	208	39.38 N	74.48 W
Hamningberg	24	70.31 N	30.37 E
Ham-Nord	206	45.54 N	71.39 W
Hamo	130	39.36 N	38.11 E
Hamoir	56	50.26 N	5.32 E
Hamont	56	51.15 N	5.33 E
HaMore, Giv'at ∧	132	32.37 N	35.21 E
Hamorton	285	39.52 N	75.39 W
Hamoyet, Jabal ∧	144	17.33 N	38.02 E
Hampden, Austl.	168b	34.09 S	139.03 E
Hampden, Newf., Can.	186	49.33 N	56.51 W
Hampden, N.Z.	172	45.19 S	170.49 E
Hampden, Maine, U.S.	188	44.45 N	68.50 W
Hampden, Mass., U.S.	207	42.04 N	72.25 W
Hampden, N. Dak., U.S.	198	48.32 N	98.40 W
Hampden □[6]	207	42.07 N	72.36 W
Hampetorp	40	59.09 N	15.40 E
Hampshire	216	42.06 N	88.32 W
Hampshire □[6], Eng., U.K.	42	51.05 N	1.15 W
Hampshire □[6], Mass., U.S.	207	42.19 N	72.38 W
Hampshire Downs ⩕[1]	42	51.15 N	1.17 W
Hampshire Heights	279b	40.20 N	79.33 W
Hampstead, Qué., Can.	275a	45.29 N	73.38 W
Hampstead, N.C., U.S.	192	34.22 N	77.49 W
Hampstead ◆[8]	260	51.33 N	0.11 W
Hampstead Heath ♠	260	51.34 N	0.10 W
Hampton, Austl.	274b	37.56 S	145.00 E
Hampton, N.B., Can.	186	45.32 N	65.51 W
Hampton, Ont., Can.	212	43.58 N	78.45 W
Hampton, Ark., U.S.	194	33.32 N	92.28 W
Hampton, Conn., U.S.	207	41.47 N	72.03 W
Hampton, Fla., U.S.	192	29.52 N	82.07 W
Hampton, Ga., U.S.	192	33.23 N	84.17 W
Hampton, Iowa, U.S.	190	42.45 N	93.12 W
Hampton, Nebr., U.S.	198	40.53 N	97.53 W
Hampton, N.H., U.S.	188	42.56 N	70.50 W
Hampton, N.J., U.S.	210	40.42 N	74.58 W
Hampton, Pa., U.S.	208	39.56 N	77.04 W
Hampton, S.C., U.S.	192	32.52 N	81.07 W
Hampton, Va., U.S.	208	37.01 N	76.22 W
Hampton ◆[8]	260	51.25 N	0.22 W
Hampton Bays	207	40.53 N	72.31 W
Hampton Butte ∧	202	43.46 N	120.17 W
Hampton Court Palace ⊌	260	51.24 N	0.20 W
Hampton Harbour C	162	20.40 S	116.30 E
Hampton National Historic Site ⊥	284b	39.25 N	76.35 W
Hampton Park	274b	38.02 S	145.15 E
Hampton Roads ⊤[3]	208	36.58 N	76.20 W
Hampton Roads Bridge-Tunnel ◆[5]	208	37.00 N	76.18 W
Hampton Tableland ⩕[1]	162	32.10 S	126.10 E
Hamp'yŏng	98	35.05 N	126.30 E
Hamr	54	50.35 N	13.35 E
Hamra	26	61.39 N	15.00 E
Hamra, Ouadi ∨	146	12.52 N	21.15 E
Hamra, Saguia el ∨	148	27.15 N	13.21 W
Ḥamrah, Jabal al- ∧	132	29.39 N	34.47 E
Ḥamran, Har ∧	132	30.41 N	34.34 E
Hamra Nationalpark ♠	26	61.45 N	14.55 E
Ḥamrat ash-Shaykh	140	14.35 N	27.58 E
Hamrivier	158	28.08 S	19.18 E
Hams Bluff •[4]	241n	17.46 N	64.52 W
Hams Fork ≃	200	41.35 N	109.59 W
Ham-Sud	206	45.46 N	71.36 W
Ham-tan	110	10.40 N	107.46 E
Hamtramck	216	42.24 N	83.03 W
Hamur	84	39.36 N	42.59 E
Hamura	94	35.45 N	139.19 E
Hamyang	98	35.32 N	127.42 E
Ḥamzah, Jabal al- ∧[2]	142	30.14 N	31.38 E
Han	150	10.41 N	2.27 W
Han, Grottes de •[5]	56	50.08 N	5.15 E
Han, Nong ◎	110	17.12 N	104.11 E
Hana	229a	20.45 N	155.59 W
Hanábana ≃	240p	22.23 N	80.58 W
Hanahan	192	32.55 N	80.00 W
Hanailike	85	39.16 N	76.26 E
Ḥanak	128	25.33 N	36.56 E
Hanakaoo Point ❯	229a	20.55 N	156.42 W
Hanalei	229b	22.07 N	159.30 W
Hanalei Bay C	229b	22.13 N	159.31 W
Hanamaki	92	39.23 N	141.07 E
Hanamaulu	229b	21.59 N	159.22 W
Hanamenu, Baie C	174x	9.46 S	139.08 W
Hanam-ni	98	38.23 N	126.43 E
Hanang ∧	154	4.26 S	35.24 E
Hanapepe	229b	21.55 N	159.35 W
Hanapepe ≃	229b	21.54 N	159.36 W
Hanapepe Bay C	229b	21.54 N	159.35 W
Hānār Char	126	23.08 N	90.38 E
Hanataka-sen ∧	96	35.24 N	132.45 E
Hana Teio	174x	9.59 S	139.06 W
Hanatetena	174x	9.58 S	139.04 W
Hana Tuuna	174x	10.00 S	139.07 W
Hanau	56	50.08 N	8.55 E
Hanaui	174x	9.45 S	139.05 W
Hanawa, Nihon	92	40.11 N	140.47 E
Hanawa, Nihon	94	36.57 N	140.25 E
Hanawa, Nihon	268	35.13 N	139.53 E
Hanbury ≃	176	63.37 N	104.33 W
Hanceville, B.C., Can.	182	51.55 N	123.03 W
Hanceville, Ala., U.S.	194	34.04 N	86.46 W
Hanchang	107	30.26 N	103.43 E
Hancheng, Zhg.	102	35.29 N	110.25 E
Hancheng, Zhg.	105	39.39 N	118.02 E
Hanches	261	48.36 N	1.39 E
Hanchō	270	34.47 N	135.27 E
Han-ch'ŏn C	271b	37.33 N	127.02 E
Hanchuan	100	30.39 N	113.48 E
Hanchung → Hanzhong	102	32.59 N	107.11 E
Hancock, Md., U.S.	188	39.42 N	78.11 W

English	Deutsch	Español	Français	Português
≃ River	Fluss	Río	Rivière	Rio
≆ Canal	Kanal	Canal	Canal	Canal
L Waterfall, Rapids	Wasserfall, Stromschnellen	Cascada, Rápidos	Chute d'eau, Rapides	Cascata, Rápidos
⋓ Strait	Meeresstrasse	Estrecho	Détroit	Estreito
C Bay, Gulf	Bucht, Golf	Bahía, Golfo	Baie, Golfe	Baía, Golfo
◎ Lake, Lakes	See, Seen	Lago, Lagos	Lac, Lacs	Lago, Lagos
≡ Swamp	Sumpf	Pantano	Marais	Pântano
◪ Ice Features, Glacier	Eis- und Gletscherformen	Accidentes Glaciales	Formes glaciaires	Acidentes Glaciares
⊤ Other Hydrographic Features	Andere Hydrographische Objekte	Otros Elementos Hidrográficos	Autres données hydrographiques	Outros Elementos Hidrográficos

English	Deutsch	Español	Français	Português
✢ Submarine Features	Untermeerische Objekte	Accidentes Submarinos	Formes de relief sous-marin	Acidentes Submarinos
□ Political Unit	Politische Einheit	Unidad Política	Entité politique	Unidade Política
⊌ Cultural Institution	Kulturelle Institution	Institución Cultural	Institution culturelle	Instituição Cultural
⊥ Historical Site	Historische Stätte	Sitio Histórico	Site historique	Sítio Histórico
♠ Recreational Site	Erholungs- und Ferienort	Sitio de Recreo	Centre de loisirs	Sítio de Lazer
⊠ Airport	Flughafen	Aeropuerto	Aéroport	Aeroporto
■ Military Installation	Militäranlage	Instalación Militar	Installation militaire	Instalação Militar
◆ Miscellaneous	Verschiedenes	Misceláneo	Divers	Miscelânea

Hancock, Mich., U.S. 190 47.07 N 88.35 W
Hancock, Minn., U.S. 198 45.30 N 95.48 W
Hancock, N.Y., U.S. 210 41.57 N 75.17 W
Hancock, Wis., U.S. 190 44.08 N 89.31 W
Hancock □[6], Ind., U.S. 218 39.47 N 85.46 W
Hancock □[6], Ohio, U.S. 216 41.02 N 83.39 W
Hancock □[6], W. Va., U.S. 214 40.30 N 80.33 W
Hancock, Lake ◎ 220 27.58 N 81.50 W
Hancock International Airport ⊠ 210 43.07 N 76.07 W
Hancocks Bridge 208 39.31 N 75.28 W
Hancun 105 39.24 N 116.36 E
Handa, Nihon 94 34.53 N 136.56 E
Handa, Nihon 96 34.02 N 134.02 E
Handa I 46 58.22 N 5.12 W
Handan 98 36.37 N 114.29 E
Handaokou 98 34.16 N 116.24 E
Handawor 123 34.24 N 74.17 E
Handen 40 59.10 N 18.08 E
Handeni 154 5.26 S 38.01 E
Handforth 262 53.21 N 2.13 W
Handig Point ≻ 116 10.49 N 125.42 E
Handlová 30 48.44 N 18.46 E
Hando 144 10.39 N 51.08 E
Handöl 26 63.16 N 12.26 E
Handorf 52 51.59 N 7.41 E
Handsworth 184 49.48 N 103.00 W
Handub 140 19.14 N 37.16 E
Handzame 50 51.02 N 3.00 E
Handzell 60 48.34 N 11.04 E
Haneda Airport ⊠ 268 35.33 N 139.46 E
HaNegev ➛[1] 132 30.30 N 34.55 E
Haney 182 49.13 N 122.36 W
Hane-yama ∧ 96 33.14 N 131.08 E
Hane-zaki ≻ 96 33.22 N 134.02 E
Hanford 226 36.20 N 119.39 W
Han'gang 98 34.39 N 114.38 E
Han-gang ≃ 98 37.45 N 126.11 E
Hangang, First Bridge ➛[5] 271b 37.32 N 126.56 E
Hangang, Second Bridge ➛[5] 271b 37.34 N 126.54 E
Hangang, Third Bridge ➛[5] 271b 37.32 N 127.00 E
Hanga Roa 174z 27.09 S 109.26 W
Hangatiki 172 38.15 S 175.10 E
Hangbu 100 28.53 N 118.49 E
Hangchow → Hangzhou 106 30.15 N 120.10 E
Hangchow Bay → Hangzhouwan C 100 30.20 N 121.00 E
Hang Hau Town 271d 22.19 N 114.16 E
Hanging Gardens ♠ 272c 18.58 N 72.48 E
Hanging Rock State Park ♠ 192 36.25 N 80.15 W
Hangingstone Hill ∧[2] 42 50.39 N 3.57 W
Hanging Woman Creek ≃ 202 45.19 N 106.31 W
Hangjinhouqi 102 40.41 N 106.59 E
Hangjinqi 102 39.59 N 108.57 E
Hangklip, Kaap ≻ 158 34.26 S 18.48 E
Hangkou 100 29.03 N 114.27 E
Hangö (Hanko) 26 59.50 N 22.57 E
Hang-Tcheou → Hangzhou 106 30.15 N 120.10 E
Hangtou 106 31.01 N 121.35 E
Hangtschou → Hangzhou 106 30.15 N 120.10 E
Hangu, Pāk. 123 33.32 N 71.04 E
Hangu, Zhg. 105 39.15 N 117.47 E
Hanguang 100 24.16 N 113.08 E
Hanguchang 107 29.32 N 106.21 E
Hangugang 105 39.15 N 116.56 E
Hangxian (Linping) 106 30.25 N 120.18 E
Hangyu 106 30.35 N 119.23 E
Hangzhou (Hangchow) 106 30.15 N 120.10 E
Hangzhouwan C 100 30.20 N 121.00 E
Hani 130 38.24 N 40.24 E
Hänigsen 52 52.29 N 10.05 E
Hanimadu I 122 6.45 N 73.09 E
Hanīn 144 15.50 N 48.19 E
Ḥanīsh, Jazā'ir II 144 13.45 N 42.45 E
Ḥanita 132 33.05 N 35.10 E
Hanjalipan 112 2.15 S 112.47 E
Hanjiagou 104 40.42 N 120.47 E
Hanjiang, Zhg. 100 25.30 N 119.06 E
Hanjiang, Zhg. 100 24.48 N 118.38 E
Hanjiang ≃ 100 23.41 N 116.38 E
Hanjiapuzi 104 40.48 N 123.14 E
Hanjiashu 105 39.11 N 117.04 E
Hanjiawa 106 31.16 N 119.18 E
Hankamer 222 29.51 N 94.38 W
Hankasalmi 26 62.23 N 26.26 E
Hanke 26 59.12 N 10.47 E
Hankensbüttel 54 52.44 N 10.36 E
Hankey 158 33.50 S 24.52 E
Hankins 210 41.49 N 75.05 W
Hankinson 198 46.04 N 96.54 W
Hanko → Hangö 26 59.50 N 22.57 E
Hankow → Wuhan 100 30.36 N 114.17 E
Hanköyü 130 38.35 N 39.04 E
Hanks Pond ◎ 276 41.05 N 74.26 W
Hanku → Hangu 105 39.15 N 117.47 E
Hānle 120 32.48 N 79.00 E
Hanley 184 51.37 N 106.27 W
Hanmer 190 46.30 N 80.56 W
Hanmer Springs 172 42.31 S 172.49 E
Hanmiao 89 44.33 N 119.59 E
Hann ≃ 164 17.10 S 126.10 E
Hanna, Alta., Can. 182 51.38 N 111.54 W
Hanna, Ind., U.S. 216 41.25 N 86.47 W
Hanna, Okla., U.S. 196 35.12 N 95.53 W
Hanna, Wyo., U.S. 200 41.52 N 106.34 W
Hanna City 190 40.42 N 89.48 W
Hannaford 198 47.19 N 98.11 W
Hannah 198 48.58 N 98.42 W
Hannah Bay C 176 51.05 N 79.45 W
Hannastown 214 40.21 N 79.30 W
Hannibal, Mo., U.S. 219 39.42 N 91.22 W
Hannibal, N.Y., U.S. 210 43.19 N 76.35 W
Hanningfield Reservoir ◎[1] 260 51.39 N 0.31 E
Hannington, Lake ◎ 154 0.15 N 36.06 E
Hannō 94 35.51 N 139.19 E
Hannover 52 52.24 N 9.44 E
Hannover □[6] 52 52.30 N 9.00 E
Hannut 56 50.40 N 5.05 E
Hanö I 26 56.00 N 14.50 E
Hanobası 130 38.35 N 33.50 E
Hanöbukten C 26 55.45 N 14.30 E
Ha-noi 110 21.02 N 105.51 E
Hanönü 130 41.38 N 34.28 E
Hanoura 96 33.57 N 134.38 E
Hanover → Hannover, B.R.D. 52 52.24 N 9.44 E
Hanover, Ont., Can. 212 44.09 N 81.02 W
Hanover, S. Afr. 158 31.04 S 24.29 E
Hanover, Conn., U.S. 207 41.38 N 72.04 W
Hanover, Ill., U.S. 190 42.15 N 90.17 W
Hanover, Ind., U.S. 218 38.43 N 85.28 W
Hanover, Kans., U.S. 198 39.54 N 96.53 W
Hanover, Mass., U.S. 207 42.07 N 70.49 W
Hanover, Mich., U.S. 216 42.06 N 84.33 W
Hanover, N.H., U.S. 188 43.42 N 72.18 W
Hanover, Ohio, U.S. 214 40.04 N 82.15 W
Hanover, Pa., U.S. 208 39.48 N 76.59 W
Hanover, Va., U.S. 208 37.46 N 77.22 W
Hanover, Wis., U.S. 216 42.38 N 89.10 W
Hanover □[6] 208 37.42 N 77.20 W
Hanover, Isla I 254 51.00 S 74.40 W
Hanover Airport ⊠ 276 40.50 N 74.21 W
Hanover Center 283 42.07 N 70.51 W
Hanover Park 216 42.00 N 88.09 W
Hanover Road 158 30.58 S 24.33 E
Hanoverton 214 40.45 N 80.56 W
Hanovre → Hannover 52 52.24 N 9.44 E
Hansanjiazi 104 41.44 N 122.57 E
Hansantai 86 45.23 N 84.06 E
Hansard 182 54.05 N 121.52 W
Hansa-Viertel ʊ 264a 52.31 N 13.21 E
Hanscom Air Force Base ■ 283 42.28 N 71.17 W
Hans Creek ≃ 210 43.06 N 74.08 W
Hānsdiha 124 24.36 N 87.05 E
Hansen Dam ➛[6] 280 34.16 N 118.23 W
Hansen Flood Control Basin ≚[1] 228 34.16 N 118.23 W
Hansenide Colony ʊ 174b 0.32 S 166.57 E
Hanshan 100 31.44 N 118.08 E
Hansharo ⊥ 94 35.02 N 138.56 E
Hanshui ≃ 100 30.35 N 114.17 E
Hansi, Bhārat 120 32.27 N 77.50 E
Hānsi, Bhārat 123 29.06 N 75.58 E
Hansia 272b 22.48 N 88.24 E
Hanska 198 44.09 N 94.30 W
Hānskhāli 126 23.21 N 88.37 E
Hans Lollik Island I 240m 18.24 N 64.55 W
Hans Meyer Range ⋀⋀ 164 4.20 S 152.55 E
Hanson 207 42.05 N 70.53 W
Hanson ≃ 162 20.15 S 133.25 E
Hanson Lake ◎ 184 54.42 N 102.49 W
Hanstholm 26 57.07 N 8.38 E
Han-sur-Lesse 56 50.08 N 5.11 E
Han-sur-Nied 56 48.59 N 6.26 E
Hansville 224 47.55 N 122.33 W
Hansweert 52 51.26 N 4.00 E
Hantaj 88 49.35 N 103.13 E
Hāntālbunia 126 22.44 N 89.31 E
Hantamsberg ⋀⋀ 158 31.22 S 19.45 E
Hantan → Handan 98 36.37 N 114.29 E
Hantes ≃ 50 50.19 N 4.11 E
Hant's Harbour 186 48.01 N 53.16 W
Hantsport 186 45.04 N 64.11 W
Hantu, Pulau I 271c 1.14 N 103.45 E
Hantu, Tanjong ≻ 114 4.18 N 100.34 E
Hantzsch ≃ 176 67.32 N 72.25 W
Hanumānnagar 124 26.30 N 86.51 E
Hanušovce nad Topl'ou 30 49.02 N 21.30 E
Hanušovice 30 50.05 N 16.55 E
Hanveden ⋀⋀[2] 40 59.07 N 18.00 E
Hanwood 166 34.20 S 146.03 E
Hanworth ➛[8] 260 51.26 N 0.23 W
Hanxinzhuang 105 40.16 N 116.44 E
Hanyang 102 30.35 N 114.00 E
Hanyangba 107 29.44 N 103.44 E
Hanyangping 102 32.41 N 108.34 E
Hanyin 102 32.42 N 108.50 E
Hanyū 94 36.10 N 139.32 E
Hanyuan 102 29.22 N 102.38 E
Hanyuangai 102 29.30 N 102.31 E
Hanzan 96 33.16 N 133.51 E
Hanzhong 102 32.59 N 107.11 E
Hanzhuang 98 34.38 N 117.24 E
Hao I[1] 14 18.15 S 140.54 W
Haohekou 100 28.38 N 112.49 E
Haojiadian 100 31.47 N 113.44 E
Haoli → Hegang 89 47.24 N 130.17 E
Haoluqi 106 30.38 N 119.34 E
HaOn 132 32.43 N 35.38 E
Haouach, Ouadi ∨ 146 16.45 N 19.35 E
Haoxi ≃ 100 28.27 N 119.56 E
Haozhikou 107 29.36 N 105.02 E
Haparanda 26 65.50 N 24.10 E
Hapatoni, Baie C 174x 9.58 S 139.07 W
Hapert 52 51.23 N 5.15 E
Hapeville 192 33.40 N 84.24 W
Hap Hawkins Lake ◎[1] 202 44.58 N 112.51 W
Happ'o-ri 98 40.40 N 127.49 E
Happy 196 34.45 N 101.52 W
Happy Camp 204 41.48 N 123.22 W
Happy Jack 200 34.45 N 111.11 W
Happy Valley Race Course ♠ 271d 22.16 N 114.10 E
Hapsford 262 53.16 N 2.48 W
Hapsu 98 41.13 N 128.51 E
Hapton 262 53.47 N 2.19 W
Hāpur 124 28.43 N 77.47 E
HaQatan, HaMakhtesh ⊥[7] 132 30.58 N 35.12 E
Ḥaql 128 29.18 N 34.57 E
Haquira 248 14.13 S 72.11 W
Har 164 5.20 S 133.10 E
Har, Laga ≃ 154 1.40 N 39.36 E
Hara, Nihon 94 35.07 N 138.48 E
Hara, Nihon 94 35.58 N 138.33 E
Hara, Nihon 268 35.50 N 139.46 E
Ḥaraḍ, Ar. Sa. 128 24.08 N 49.05 E
Härad, Sve. 40 59.23 N 16.55 E
Ḥaraḍ, Yaman 144 16.28 N 43.04 E
Harai ≃ 96 33.45 N 131.01 E
Haraiki I[1] 14 17.28 S 143.27 W
Harajuku 268 35.54 N 139.21 E
Haraldsted 41 55.30 N 11.47 E
Haramachida 268 35.33 N 139.27 E
Haramosh ∧ 123 35.50 N 74.53 E
Haranomachi 92 37.38 N 140.58 E
Harappa 123 30.38 N 72.52 E
Harappa Road 123 30.36 N 72.55 E
Harar → Harer 144 9.18 N 42.08 E
Harardera 144 4.32 N 47.53 E
Ḥarash, Bi'r al- ⊤[4] 146 25.30 N 22.12 E
Ḥarastā al-Baṣal 132 33.34 N 36.22 E
Hārāt 272b 22.53 N 88.11 E
Ḥārat Ḥurayk 132 33.51 N 35.30 E
Haraz 146 13.57 N 19.26 E
Haraze 146 9.55 N 20.48 E
Harbāti 272b 22.55 N 88.33 E
Harbert 216 41.52 N 86.38 W
Harbeson 208 38.43 N 75.17 W
Harbin → Haerbin 89 45.45 N 126.41 E
Harbiye 130 36.11 N 36.05 E
Harbke 54 52.12 N 11.03 E
Harbo 40 60.06 N 17.12 E
Harbonnières 50 49.51 N 2.40 E
Harboør 26 56.37 N 8.12 E
Harbor 202 42.03 N 124.15 W
Harbor Beach 190 43.51 N 82.39 W
Harbor City ➛[8] 280 33.48 N 118.17 W
Harborcreek 214 42.10 N 79.57 W
Harbord 170 33.45 S 151.26 E
Harbor Isle 276 40.36 N 73.40 W
Harbor Side 228 32.37 N 117.05 W
Harbor Springs 190 45.26 N 85.00 W
Harborton 208 37.40 N 75.50 W
Harbor Tunnel ➛[5] 284b 39.15 N 76.34 W
Harbor View 214 41.42 N 83.27 W
Harbour Breton 186 47.29 N 55.48 W
Harbour Buffett 186 47.31 N 54.05 W
Harbour Deep 186 50.22 N 56.31 W
Harbour Grace 186 47.42 N 53.13 W
Harbours, Bay of C 254 52.15 S 59.15 W
Harbourville 186 45.09 N 64.49 W
Harburg 56 48.47 N 10.41 E
Harburg ➛[8] 52 53.28 N 9.59 E
Harburger Berge, Naturpark ♠ 52 53.25 N 9.50 E
Hårby 41 55.13 N 10.07 E
Harchies 50 50.29 N 3.41 E
Harcourt, Austl. 169 37.00 S 144.15 E
Harcourt, Fr. 50 49.10 N 0.48 E
Harcuvar Mountains ⋀⋀ 200 34.00 N 113.30 W
Hard 58 47.29 N 9.41 E
Harda 124 22.20 N 77.06 E
Hardangerfjorden C[2] 26 60.10 N 6.00 E
Hardangerjøkulen ⊓ 26 60.33 N 7.26 E
Hardangervidda ⋀⋀[1] 26 60.20 N 7.30 E
Hardangervidda Nasjonalpark ♠ 26 60.15 N 7.05 E
Hardap Dam ➛[6] 156 24.28 S 17.48 E
Hardee □[6] 220 27.29 N 81.48 W
Hardeeville 192 32.17 N 81.05 W
Hardegarijp 52 53.13 N 5.56 E
Hardegsen 52 51.39 N 9.49 E
Hardelot-Plage 50 50.38 N 1.35 E
Hardenberg 52 52.34 N 6.37 E
Harderwijk 52 52.21 N 5.36 E
Hardesty 196 36.37 N 101.12 W
Hardey ≃ 162 22.45 S 116.07 E
Hardgrave, Mount ∧[2] 171a 27.30 S 153.29 E
Hardheim 56 49.36 N 9.28 E
Hardin, Ill., U.S. 219 39.09 N 90.37 W
Hardin, Mont., U.S. 202 45.44 N 107.37 W
Hardin, Tex., U.S. 222 30.09 N 94.44 W
Hardin □[6], Ohio, U.S. 216 40.39 N 83.36 W
Hardin □[6], Tex., U.S. 222 30.20 N 94.35 W
Harding, S. Afr. 158 30.34 S 29.58 E
Harding, Ill., U.S. 216 41.31 N 88.51 W
Harding, Mass., U.S. 283 42.12 N 71.27 W
Harding, Lake ◎[1] 192 32.40 N 85.06 W
Harding Lake ◎ 184 56.13 N 98.23 W
Harding Lakes 208 39.27 N 74.45 W
Hardinsburg, Ind., U.S. 218 38.28 N 86.17 W
Hardinsburg, Ky., U.S. 194 37.47 N 86.28 W
Hardiro 144 9.03 N 49.54 E
Hardisty 182 52.40 N 111.18 W
Hardisty Lake ◎ 176 64.30 N 117.45 W
Hardoi 124 27.25 N 80.07 E
Hardricourt 261 49.01 N 1.54 E
Hardscrabble Wash ∨ 200 34.39 N 109.28 W
Hardt 263 51.07 N 6.58 E
Hardteck → Krasnolesje 76 54.24 N 22.23 E
Hardtner 198 37.01 N 98.39 W
Hardwār 124 29.58 N 78.10 E
Hardwick, Ga., U.S. 192 33.09 N 83.13 W
Hardwick, Mass., U.S. 207 42.21 N 72.12 W
Hardwick, Vt., U.S. 188 44.30 N 72.22 W
Hardwicke Island I 182 50.30 N 125.30 W
Hardwood Ridge ∧ 210 41.15 N 75.23 W
Hardy, Ark., U.S. 194 36.19 N 91.29 W
Hardy, Nebr., U.S. 198 40.01 N 97.56 W
Hardy, Península ≻[1] 254 55.25 S 68.30 W
Hardy Bay C 176 75.02 N 115.16 W
Hardy Creek ≃ 214 42.52 N 81.52 W
Hardy Lake ◎[1] 218 38.47 N 85.42 W
Hardy Lake State Recreation Area ♠ 218 38.44 N 86.26 W
Hardys Pond ◎ 283 42.25 N 71.15 W
Hare Bay 186 48.51 N 54.01 W
Hare Bay C 186 51.18 N 55.50 W
Harefield ➛[8] 260 51.36 N 0.29 W
Hareid 26 62.22 N 6.02 E
Hare Indian ≃ 176 66.18 N 128.38 W
Harelbeke 50 50.51 N 3.18 E
Haren, B.R.D. 52 52.47 N 7.14 E
Haren, Ned. 52 53.10 N 6.35 E
Hareøen I 176 70.25 N 54.50 W
Harer 144 9.18 N 42.08 E
Harerge □[4] 144 8.00 N 43.00 E
Hareskov 41 55.46 N 12.25 E
Hareto 144 9.20 N 37.06 E
Harewood 172 43.29 S 172.35 E
Harfaz 130 38.01 N 41.19 E
Harfleur 50 49.30 N 0.12 E
Harford 210 42.26 N 76.14 W
Harford □[6] 208 39.32 N 76.21 W
Harford Heights 279b 40.22 N 79.46 W
Harford Mills 210 42.25 N 76.12 W
Harg, Sve. 40 59.49 N 18.57 E
Harg, Sve. 40 60.11 N 18.24 E
Hargeisa □[4] 144 9.40 N 44.20 E
Hargele 144 5.20 N 42.05 E
Hargeville 261 48.53 N 1.45 E
Hargeysa 144 9.30 N 44.03 E
Harghita □[4] 38 46.35 N 25.30 E
Hargrave ≃ 184 54.24 N 98.48 W
Hargrave Lake ◎ 184 54.29 N 99.40 W
Hargshamn 40 60.10 N 18.28 E
Harhur 130 37.49 N 42.20 E
Hāriabhānga ≃[1] 126 21.43 N 89.05 E
Hariāna 123 31.38 N 75.51 E
Hariarapitu 114 2.33 N 98.35 E
Ḥarīb 144 14.57 N 45.30 E
Haribes 156 24.20 S 17.40 E
Haricha, Hamâda el ➛[2] 148 22.36 N 3.31 W
Harigabessho 270 34.37 N 135.58 E
Harihar 122 14.31 N 75.48 E
Harihari 172 43.09 S 170.33 E
Hariharpāra 126 24.02 N 88.27 E
Hariharpur Garhi 124 27.19 N 85.29 E
Harike 123 31.10 N 74.57 E
Ḥārim 130 36.12 N 36.31 E
Ḥarim, Jabal al- ∧ 128 23.58 N 56.14 E
Harima 96 34.42 N 134.53 E
Harima-nada ⊤[2] 96 34.29 N 134.35 E
Harinagab 124 27.09 N 84.19 E
Harinākunda 126 23.39 N 89.03 E
Haringey ➛[8] 260 51.35 N 0.07 W
Hāringhāta ≃[1] 124 21.54 N 89.57 E
Haringvliet ⊔ 52 51.47 N 4.10 E
Haringvlietbrug ➛[5] 52 51.43 N 4.20 E
Haripād 122 9.18 N 76.28 E
Haripāl 272b 22.49 N 88.07 E
Haripur, Bhārat 126 24.18 N 87.05 E
Haripur, Bhārat 272b 22.56 N 88.14 E
Harīpur, Pāk. 123 33.59 N 72.56 E
Ḥarīr, Wādī al- ∨ 132 32.44 N 35.54 E
Harirāmpur 126 23.42 N 89.57 E
Harīrūd (Tedżen) ≃ 128 37.24 N 60.38 E
Haris 156 22.48 S 16.52 E
Harischandra Range ⋀⋀ 122 19.15 N 74.05 E
Ḥārithān 130 36.16 N 37.05 E
Harjavalta 26 61.19 N 22.08 E
Härjedalen □[9] 26 62.20 N 13.00 E
Harkaway 274b 38.00 S 145.21 E
Härkeberga 40 59.42 N 17.11 E
Harkema-Opeinde 52 53.11 N 6.08 E
Harker Heights 222 31.05 N 97.40 W
Harkers Island 192 34.42 N 76.34 W
Harker Village 285 39.51 N 75.09 W
Harkness Memorial State Park ♠ 207 41.18 N 72.07 W
Harkortsee ◎ 263 51.24 N 7.25 E
Harlaching ➛[8] 60 48.06 N 11.33 E
Harlan, Ind., U.S. 216 41.12 N 84.55 W
Harlan, Iowa, U.S. 198 41.39 N 95.19 W
Harlan, Ky., U.S. 192 36.51 N 83.19 W
Harlan County Lake ◎[1] 198 40.04 N 99.16 W
Harlech 42 52.52 N 4.07 W
Harlem, Fla., U.S. 220 26.44 N 80.58 W
Harlem, Ga., U.S. 192 33.25 N 82.19 W
Harlem, Mont., U.S. 202 48.32 N 108.47 W
Harlem ➛[8] 276 40.49 N 73.56 W
Harlem River ⊔ 276 40.48 N 73.54 W
Harlem Springs 214 40.31 N 81.02 W
Harlesden ➛[8] 260 51.32 N 0.15 W
Harlesiel 52 53.43 N 7.49 E
Harleston 42 52.24 N 1.18 E
Harleton 222 32.41 N 94.35 W
Hårlev 41 55.21 N 12.15 E
Harleysville 208 40.17 N 75.23 W
Harlin 171a 26.59 S 152.22 E
Harlingen, Ned. 52 53.10 N 5.24 E
Harlingen, Tex., U.S. 196 26.11 N 97.42 W
Harlinger Land ➛[1] 52 53.40 N 7.30 E
Harlingerode 54 51.54 N 10.31 E
Harlington ➛[8] 260 51.29 N 0.26 W
Harlösa 41 55.43 N 13.32 E
Harlow 260 51.47 N 0.08 E
Harlow □[8] 260 51.44 N 0.07 E
Harlowton 202 46.26 N 109.50 W
Harlpur 272b 22.42 N 88.10 E
Harman 188 38.55 N 79.32 W
Harmånger 26 61.56 N 17.13 E
Harmanli, Blg. 38 41.56 N 25.54 E
Harmanlı, Tür. 130 37.51 N 37.45 E
Harmar Heights 279b 40.33 N 79.49 W
Harmarville 279b 40.32 N 79.51 W
Hármashatár-hegy ∧ 264c 47.33 N 19.00 E
Harmelen 52 52.05 N 4.58 E
Harmonsburg 214 41.40 N 80.19 W
Harmonville 285 40.06 N 75.17 W
Harmony, Calif., U.S. 226 35.35 N 121.01 W
Harmony, Ind., U.S. 194 39.32 N 87.04 W
Harmony, Maine, U.S. 188 44.58 N 69.33 W
Harmony, Minn., U.S. 190 43.33 N 92.01 W
Harmony, N.J., U.S. 210 40.45 N 75.09 W
Harmony, Pa., U.S. 214 40.48 N 80.06 W
Harmony, R.I., U.S. 207 41.53 N 71.36 W
Harmony Brook ≃ 276 40.48 N 74.34 W
Harmony Heights 220 27.29 N 80.21 W
Harmony Hills 285 39.42 N 75.41 W
Harnai, Bhārat 122 17.48 N 73.06 E
Harnai, Pāk. 120 30.06 N 67.56 E
Harnäs 40 60.39 N 17.22 E
Harnātānr 124 27.19 N 84.01 E
Harndrup 41 55.28 N 10.02 E
Harnes 50 50.27 N 2.54 E
Härnevi 40 59.44 N 17.05 E
Harney ≃ 220 25.25 N 81.10 W
Harney, Lake ◎ 220 28.45 N 81.03 W
Harney Basin ≚[1] 202 43.15 N 120.40 W
Harney Lake ◎ 202 43.14 N 119.07 W
Harney Peak ∧ 198 44.00 N 103.30 W
Harney Pond Canal ≍ 220 27.00 N 81.04 W
Härnösand 26 62.38 N 17.56 E
Haro 34 42.35 N 2.51 W
Harod ≃ 132 32.31 N 35.33 E
Harola 272a 28.36 N 77.19 E
Harold Hill ➛[8] 260 51.36 N 0.13 E
Harold Parker State Forest ♠ 283 42.37 N 71.05 W
Haroldswick 46a 60.41 N 0.50 W
Harold Wood ➛[8] 260 51.36 N 0.14 E
Haro Strait ⊔ 224 48.30 N 123.15 W
Haroué 58 48.28 N 6.11 E
Harpālpur 124 25.17 N 79.20 E
Harpanahalli 122 14.48 N 75.59 E
Harpen ➛[8] 263 51.29 N 7.16 E
Harpenden 42 51.49 N 0.22 W
Harper, Liber. 150 4.25 N 7.43 W
Harper, Kans., U.S. 198 37.17 N 98.01 W
Harper, Tex., U.S. 196 30.18 N 99.15 W
Harper, Wash., U.S. 224 47.31 N 122.46 W
Harper, Mount ∧ 180 64.14 N 143.50 W
Harper Lake ◎ 228 35.02 N 117.17 W
Harpers Ferry National Historical Park ♠ 188 39.13 N 77.45 W
Harpersfield 210 42.26 N 74.41 W
Harper Town 44 54.55 N 2.31 W
Harper Woods 214 42.24 N 82.55 W
Harpille ∧ 62 43.50 N 6.48 E
Harpstedt 52 52.54 N 8.35 E
Harpster 214 40.44 N 83.15 W
Harpsund ʊ 40 59.06 N 16.29 E
Harpurhey ➛[8] 262 53.31 N 2.13 W
Harpur Hill 262 53.14 N 1.54 W
Harpursville 210 42.11 N 75.38 W
Harquahala Mountain ∧ 200 33.49 N 113.21 W
Ḥarrah 144 14.57 N 50.19 E
Ḥārrah, Jabal al- ∧ 132 33.04 N 35.59 E
Harrai 124 22.37 N 79.13 E
Harran 130 36.51 N 39.00 E
Ḥarrān al-'Awāmīd 132 33.27 N 36.34 E
Harray, Loch of ◎ 46 59.01 N 3.13 W
Harrell 194 33.31 N 92.24 W
Harricana ≃ 176 51.15 N 79.45 W
Harrietfield 46 56.25 N 3.39 W
Harrietsham 260 51.15 N 0.41 E
Harriman, N.Y., U.S. 210 41.18 N 74.09 W
Harriman, Tenn., U.S. 192 35.56 N 84.33 W
Harriman Reservoir ◎[1] 207 42.50 N 72.53 W
Harriman State Park ♠ 210 41.14 N 74.09 W
Harrington, Eng., U.K. 44 54.37 N 3.34 W
Harrington, Del., U.S. 208 38.56 N 75.35 W
Harrington, Maine, U.S. 188 44.37 N 67.49 W
Harrington, Wash., U.S. 202 47.29 N 118.15 W
Harrington Creek ≃ 282 37.19 N 122.18 W
Harrington Drain ≍ 281 42.36 N 82.54 W
Harrington Park 276 40.59 N 73.59 W
Harris, Sask., Can. 184 51.44 N 107.35 W
Harris, Scot., U.K. 46 56.59 N 6.20 W
Harris, Minn., U.S. 190 45.35 N 92.59 W
Harris, N.Y., U.S. 210 41.43 N 74.44 W
Harris, R.I., U.S. 207 41.44 N 71.32 W
Harris □[6] 222 29.50 N 95.22 W
Harris ≃ 168a 33.18 S 116.09 E
Harris ➛[1] 46 57.55 N 6.50 W
Harris, Lake ◎, Austl. 162 31.08 S 135.14 E
Harris, Lake ◎, Fla., U.S. 220 28.46 N 81.49 W
Harris, Sound of ⊔ 46 57.45 N 7.10 W
Harris Bay C 212 45.23 N 77.50 W
Harris Brook ≃ 283 42.44 N 71.13 W
Harrisburg, Ark., U.S. 194 35.34 N 90.43 W
Harrisburg, Ill., U.S. 194 37.44 N 88.33 W
Harrisburg, Ind., U.S. 218 39.41 N 85.11 W
Harrisburg, Nebr., U.S. 198 41.33 N 103.44 W
Harrisburg, Ohio, U.S. 214 40.53 N 81.14 W
Harrisburg, Oreg., U.S. 202 44.16 N 123.10 W
Harrisburg, Pa., U.S. 208 40.16 N 76.52 W
Harrisburg International Airport ⊠ 208 40.12 N 76.45 W
Harris Creek C 208 38.45 N 76.18 W
Harris Creek ≃ 222 32.33 N 95.08 W
Harrisfield 274b 37.57 S 145.11 E
Harris Hill 210 42.58 N 78.40 W
Harrislee 41 54.48 N 9.22 E
Harrismith, Austl. 162 32.56 S 117.52 E
Harrismith, S. Afr. 158 28.18 S 29.03 E
Harrison, Ark., U.S. 194 36.14 N 93.07 W
Harrison, Idaho, U.S. 202 47.27 N 116.47 W
Harrison, Ill., U.S. 216 42.25 N 89.11 W
Harrison, Mich., U.S. 190 44.01 N 84.48 W
Harrison, Nebr., U.S. 198 42.41 N 103.53 W
Harrison, N.J., U.S. 276 40.45 N 74.10 W
Harrison, N.Y., U.S. 210 40.58 N 73.43 W
Harrison, Ohio, U.S. 218 39.16 N 84.49 W
Harrison □[6], Ind., U.S. 218 38.17 N 86.07 W
Harrison □[6], Ky., U.S. 218 38.25 N 84.19 W
Harrison □[6], Ohio, U.S. 214 40.16 N 81.05 W
Harrison □[6], Tex., U.S. 222 32.35 N 94.35 W
Harrison ≃ 224 49.14 N 121.57 W

ENGLISH

Name Page Lat.°′ Long.°′
Harrison, Cape ≻ 176 54.55 N 57.55 W
Harrison Bay C 180 70.30 N 151.30 W
Harrisonburg, La., U.S. 194 31.46 N 91.49 W
Harrisonburg, Va., U.S. 188 36.34 N 78.58 W
Harrison City 279b 40.21 N 79.39 W
Harrison Hot Springs 224 49.18 N 121.47 W
Harrison Islands II 176 69.13 N 90.30 W
Harrison Lake ◎ 182 49.30 N 121.50 W
Harrison Mills 224 49.14 N 121.57 W
Harrisons Brook ≃ 276 40.38 N 74.34 W
Harrison Tomb State Memorial ⊥ 218 39.09 N 84.46 W
Harrison Valley 214 41.57 N 77.39 W
Harrisonville, Md., U.S. 284b 39.23 N 77.50 W
Harrisonville, Mo., U.S. 194 38.39 N 94.21 W
Harrisonville, N.J., U.S. 285 39.41 N 75.16 W
Harris Park 274a 33.49 S 151.01 E
Harris Pond ◎ 283 42.45 N 71.16 W
Harris Reservoir ◎[1] 222 29.14 N 95.33 W
Harriston, Ont., Can. 212 43.54 N 80.53 W
Harriston, Miss., U.S. 194 31.44 N 91.02 W
Harristown 219 39.51 N 89.05 W
Harrisville, Austl. 171a 27.49 S 152.40 E
Harrisville, Mich., U.S. 190 44.39 N 83.17 W
Harrisville, N.Y., U.S. 212 44.09 N 75.19 W
Harrisville, Ohio, U.S. 214 40.11 N 80.53 W
Harrisville, Pa., U.S. 214 41.08 N 80.01 W
Harrisville, R.I., U.S. 207 41.58 N 71.41 W
Harrisville, W. Va., U.S. 188 39.13 N 81.03 W
Harrod 216 40.43 N 83.55 W
Harrodsburg 194 37.46 N 84.51 W
Harrods Creek ≃ 218 38.20 N 85.38 W
Harrogate 44 54.00 N 1.33 W
Harrold 196 34.05 N 99.02 W
Harrop Lake ◎ 184 52.38 N 95.58 W
Harrow 214 42.02 N 82.55 W
Harrow ➛[8] 260 51.35 N 0.21 W
Harrow on the Hill ➛[8] 260 51.34 N 0.20 W
Harrow School ʊ[2] 260 51.34 N 0.20 W
Harrowsmith 212 44.24 N 76.40 W
Harry Truman Field ⊠ 240m 18.21 N 64.59 W
Harry W. Nice Memorial Bridge □[3] 208 38.22 N 77.00 W
Harsefeld 52 53.27 N 9.30 E
Harsens Island 214 42.34 N 82.34 W
Harsens Island I 281 42.35 N 82.38 W
Harsewinkel 52 51.58 N 8.13 E
Harsīn 128 34.16 N 47.35 E
Harşit ≃ 130 41.01 N 38.52 E
Harskamp 52 52.07 N 5.45 E
Harsleben 54 51.52 N 11.05 E
Harstad 24 68.46 N 16.30 E
Harstena 26 58.16 N 17.01 E
Harsūd 124 22.06 N 76.44 E
Harsum 52 52.12 N 9.57 E
Hart, Tür. 130 40.24 N 40.09 E
Hart, Mich., U.S. 190 43.42 N 86.22 W
Hart, Tex., U.S. 196 34.23 N 102.07 W
Hart ≃ 180 65.51 N 136.22 W
Hart, Lake ◎, Austl. 166 31.08 S 136.24 E
Hart, Lake ◎, Fla., U.S. 220 28.22 N 81.13 W
Ḥartā 132 32.42 N 35.51 E
Hartbees ≃ 158 28.45 S 20.32 E
Hartbeesfontein 158 26.42 S 26.26 E
Hartbeespoort 158 25.44 S 27.52 E
Hartberg 61 47.17 N 15.59 E
Hartenholm 52 53.54 N 10.03 E
Hartenstein 54 50.39 N 12.40 E
Hart Fell ∧ 44 55.25 N 3.25 W
Hartfield 208 37.33 N 76.27 W
Hartford, Eng., U.K. 262 53.15 N 2.33 W
Hartford, Ala., U.S. 194 31.06 N 85.42 W
Hartford, Ark., U.S. 194 35.01 N 94.23 W
Hartford, Conn., U.S. 207 41.46 N 72.41 W
Hartford, Ill., U.S. 219 38.50 N 90.06 W
Hartford, Ind., U.S. 218 38.59 N 84.58 W
Hartford, Kans., U.S. 198 38.18 N 95.58 W
Hartford, Ky., U.S. 194 37.27 N 86.55 W
Hartford, Mich., U.S. 216 42.12 N 86.10 W
Hartford, N.J., U.S. 285 39.58 N 74.54 W
Hartford, N.Y., U.S. 210 43.21 N 73.22 W
Hartford, Ohio, U.S. 214 41.19 N 80.34 W
Hartford, Pa., U.S. 210 41.47 N 75.42 W
Hartford, S. Dak., U.S. 198 43.37 N 96.57 W
Hartford, Wis., U.S. 190 43.19 N 88.22 W
Hartford □[6] 207 41.46 N 72.41 W
Hartford City 216 40.27 N 85.22 W
Hartha 54 51.05 N 12.58 E
Hartington 198 42.37 N 97.16 W
Hart Island I, Md., U.S. 208 39.15 N 76.23 W
Hart Island I, N.Y., U.S. 276 40.51 N 73.46 W
Hart Lake ◎ 202 42.24 N 119.51 W
Hartland, N.B., Can. 186 46.18 N 67.32 W
Hartland, Eng., U.K. 42 50.59 N 4.29 W
Hartland, Ill., U.S. 216 42.22 N 88.31 W
Hartland, Maine, U.S. 188 44.53 N 69.27 W
Hartland, Mich., U.S. 216 42.39 N 83.45 W
Hartland, N.Y., U.S. 210 43.14 N 78.35 W
Hartland, Wis., U.S. 216 43.06 N 88.21 W
Hartland Point ≻ 42 51.02 N 4.31 W
Hartlepool 44 54.42 N 1.11 W
Hartleton 210 40.54 N 77.10 W
Hartley, Austl. 170 33.33 S 150.11 E
Hartley, Eng., U.K. 260 51.23 N 0.19 E
Hartley, Iowa, U.S. 198 43.11 N 95.29 W
Hartley, Tex., U.S. 196 35.53 N 102.24 W
Hartley, Zimb. 154 18.10 S 30.14 E
Hartley Bay 182 53.25 N 129.15 W
Hartlip 260 51.21 N 0.39 E
Hart Lot 210 43.01 N 76.28 W
Hartly 208 39.10 N 75.43 W
Hartmanice 60 49.10 N 13.27 E
Hartmannsdorf 54 50.53 N 12.48 E
Hartmannshain 56 50.28 N 9.16 E
Hart Mountain ∧ 184 52.29 N 101.25 W
Hartney 184 49.28 N 100.30 W
Hartola 26 61.35 N 26.01 E
Harts ≃ 158 28.24 S 24.17 E
Hartsburg 219 38.42 N 92.18 W
Hartsdale 210 41.01 N 73.48 W
Hartselle 194 34.27 N 86.56 W
Härtsfeld ➛[1] 56 48.50 N 10.15 E
Hartshill 42 52.37 N 1.32 W
Hartshorne 196 34.51 N 95.34 W
Harts Range 162 23.00 S 134.55 E
Hartstene Island I 224 47.14 N 122.53 W
Hartstown 214 41.33 N 80.23 W
Hartsville, Ind., U.S. 218 39.16 N 85.42 W
Hartsville, Pa., U.S. 285 40.14 N 75.05 W
Hartsville, S.C., U.S. 192 34.23 N 80.04 W
Hartsville, Tenn., U.S. 194 36.24 N 86.10 W
Hartswater 158 27.34 S 24.43 E
Hartville, Mo., U.S. 194 37.15 N 92.31 W
Hartville, Ohio, U.S. 214 40.58 N 81.20 W
Hartwell 192 34.21 N 82.56 W
Hartwell Lake ◎[1] 192 34.30 N 82.55 W
Hartwick 210 42.40 N 75.03 W
Hartwick Pines State Park ♠ 190 44.47 N 84.41 W
Hartz Mountain's National Park ♠ 166 43.15 S 146.50 E
Harue 94 36.08 N 136.14 E
Haruku, Pulau I 164 3.34 S 128.29 E
Hārūn 140 11.20 N 25.43 E
Haruna 94 36.23 N 138.53 E
Hārūnābād 123 29.37 N 73.08 E
Haruna-san ∧ 94 36.28 N 138.52 E
Haruniye 130 37.17 N 36.27 E

DEUTSCH

Name Seite Breite°′ Länge°′ E=Ost
Haruno, Nihon 94 34.57 N 137.53 E
Haruno, Nihon 96 33.30 N 133.30 E
Harūr 122 12.04 N 78.30 E
Hārūt ≃ 128 31.35 N 61.18 E
Harvard, Ill., U.S. 216 42.25 N 88.37 W
Harvard, Mass., U.S. 207 42.30 N 71.35 W
Harvard, Nebr., U.S. 198 40.37 N 98.06 W
Harvard University ʊ[2] 283 42.22 N 71.07 W
Harvel, Eng., U.K. 260 51.21 N 0.22 E
Harvel, Ill., U.S. 219 39.21 N 89.32 W
Harvest, Mount ∧[2] 162 25.54 S 126.28 E
Harvey, Austl. 168a 33.05 S 115.54 E
Harvey, N.B., Can. 186 45.43 N 64.43 W
Harvey, Ill., U.S. 216 41.37 N 87.39 W
Harvey, N. Dak., U.S. 198 47.47 N 99.56 W
Harvey ≃ 168a 32.46 S 115.43 E
Harvey Estuary C[1] 168a 32.43 S 115.42 E
Harvey Mountain ∧ 207 42.18 N 73.25 W
Harvey Reservoir ◎[1] 168a 33.05 S 115.58 E
Harveysburg 218 39.30 N 84.01 W
Harveys Lake 210 41.23 N 76.02 W
Harwell 42 51.37 N 1.18 W
Harwich, Eng., U.K. 42 51.57 N 1.17 E
Harwich, Mass., U.S. 207 41.41 N 70.01 W
Harwich Port 207 41.40 N 70.05 W
Harwick 279b 40.34 N 79.48 W
Harwinton 207 41.46 N 73.04 W
Harwood, Eng., U.K. 262 53.35 N 2.23 W
Harwood, Tex., U.S. 222 29.40 N 97.30 W
Harwood Heights 278 41.59 N 87.48 W
Harwood Mines 210 40.57 N 76.01 W
Harwood Park 284b 39.12 N 76.44 W
Haryana □[3] 120 29.20 N 76.20 E
Harz ⋀⋀ 54 51.45 N 10.30 E
Harz, Naturpark ♠ 54 51.44 N 10.30 E
Harzgerode 54 51.38 N 11.08 E
Ḥaṣā, Bi'r al- ⊤[4] 140 22.58 N 35.40 E
Ḥasā, Wādī al- ∨ 132 31.05 N 35.27 E
Hasafen 86 45.14 N 90.20 E
Ḥaṣāh, Wādī al- ∨ 132 30.38 N 37.09 E
Hasaki 94 35.44 N 140.50 E
Ḥasanābād 267d 35.44 N 51.19 E
Ḥasanābād-e Khāleşeh 267d 35.37 N 51.12 E
Hasan Abdāl 123 33.49 N 72.41 E
Hasançelebi 130 38.58 N 37.54 E
Hasan Dağı ∧ 130 38.08 N 34.12 E
Hasankale → Pasinler 130 39.59 N 41.41 E
Hasankeyf 130 37.43 N 41.25 E
Ḥasan Kīādeh 128 37.24 N 49.58 E
Hasanparti 122 18.04 N 79.32 E
Hasanpur 124 28.43 N 78.17 E
Hasayaz 130 40.15 N 33.20 E
Ḥāṣbānī, Nahr al- ≃ 132 33.11 N 35.37 E
Ḥāṣbayyā 132 33.24 N 35.41 E
Hasbek 130 39.33 N 35.33 E
Hasbergen, B.R.D. 52 53.05 N 8.40 E
Hasbergen, B.R.D. 52 52.14 N 7.57 E
Hasbrouck Heights 276 40.52 N 74.04 W
Hascosay I 46 60.37 N 0.59 W
Hasdo ≃ 120 21.44 N 82.44 E
Hasdo-Rāmpur Basin ≚[1] 124 22.50 N 82.35 E
Hase, Nihon 94 35.47 N 138.06 E
Hase, Nihon 270 34.32 N 135.54 E
Hase ≃, B.R.D. 52 52.41 N 7.18 E
Hase ≃, Nihon 270 34.34 N 135.38 E
Hasel ≃ 54 50.32 N 10.27 E
Haselberg → Krasnoznamensk 76 54.57 N 22.30 E
Häselgehr 58 47.19 N 10.30 E
Haselhorst ➛[8] 264a 52.33 N 13.15 E
Haselünne 52 52.40 N 7.29 E
Hasenheide, Volkspark ♠ 264a 52.29 N 13.25 E
Hasenkamp 252 31.31 S 59.51 W
Hashā, Jabal al- ∧ 144 13.43 N 44.31 E
Ĥasharād 128 37.30 N 47.16 E
HaShefela ➛[1] 132 31.40 N 34.55 E
Hashima 94 35.19 N 136.42 E
Hashimoto, Nihon 96 34.19 N 135.37 E
Hashimoto, Nihon 270 34.26 N 135.23 E
Hashır 128 37.54 N 42.36 E
Hashira-jima I 96 34.01 N 132.25 E
Hashiri-jima I 96 34.21 N 133.27 E
Hashīshah, Thamad Bū ⊤[4] 146 26.23 N 18.47 E
Hashitai 89 49.24 N 125.18 E
Hashtpar 128 37.48 N 48.55 E
Hasht Sāl ➛[8] 272a 28.38 N 77.03 E
Hasil, Pulau I 164 1.06 S 128.24 E
Hāsilpur 123 29.43 N 72.33 E
Hāsīn-e Bozorg 84 39.23 N 44.42 E
Haskayne 262 53.34 N 2.58 W
Haskeir Islands II 46 57.42 N 7.41 W
Haskell, Okla., U.S. 196 35.50 N 95.40 W
Haskell, Tex., U.S. 196 33.10 N 99.44 W
Haskell Pond ◎ 283 42.37 N 70.44 W
Hasketh Bank 262 53.43 N 2.51 W
Haskins 216 41.28 N 83.42 W
Haskovo 38 41.56 N 25.33 E
Hasköy, Tür. 130 41.38 N 26.41 E
Hasköy, Tür. 130 40.59 N 42.52 E
Hasköy ➛[8] 267b 41.02 N 28.58 E
Haslach im Kinzigtal 58 48.16 N 8.06 E
Hasle, Dan. 41 55.11 N 14.43 E
Hasle, Schw. 58 47.01 N 7.39 E
Haslemere 42 51.06 N 0.43 W
Haslett 216 42.45 N 84.19 W
Haslev 41 55.20 N 11.58 E
Haslingden 262 53.43 N 2.18 W
Haslingden Grane 262 53.42 N 2.21 W
Haslital ∨ 58 46.42 N 8.10 E
Hasmark 41 55.33 N 10.28 E
Ḥasmat 'Umar, Bi'r ⊤[4] 140 21.46 N 34.00 E
Hāsnābād 126 22.35 N 88.55 E
Hasnācha 272b 22.26 N 88.09 E
Haspe ➛[8] 263 51.21 N 7.26 E
Hasper-Stausee ◎[1] 263 51.18 N 7.25 E
Haspres 50 50.15 N 3.25 E
Hasras 130 37.57 N 42.16 E
Ḥaṣṣ, Jabal al- ∧[2] 130 35.52 N 37.22 E
Hassa 130 36.50 N 36.29 E
Hassan 122 13.00 N 76.05 E
Ḥassān, Tallat ∧ 142 27.33 N 31.47 E
Hassard 219 39.39 N 91.40 W
Hassayampa ≃ 200 33.20 N 112.43 W
Hassberge ⋀⋀[2] 56 50.12 N 10.29 E
Hassbergen 52 52.44 N 9.13 E
Hasseïra ⋀⋀[1] 150 17.28 N 11.41 W
Hassel 52 52.48 N 9.11 E
Hassel ➛[8] 263 51.36 N 7.03 E
Hasselbeck-Schwarzbach 263 51.16 N 6.53 E
Hasselfelde 54 51.41 N 10.51 E
Hasselfors 40 59.05 N 14.39 E
Hassels ➛[8] 263 51.10 N 6.53 E
Hasselt, Bel. 56 50.56 N 5.20 E
Hasselt, Ned. 52 52.35 N 6.05 E
Hassfurt 56 50.02 N 10.31 E
Hassi Amdakane ⊤[4] 148 28.23 N 2.19 W
Hassi Bel Guebbour 148 28.46 N 6.27 E
Hassi el Ghella 34 35.28 N 1.03 W
Hassi Mameche 34 35.52 N 0.04 E
Hassi Messaoud 148 31.43 N 5.59 E
Hassi R'Mel 148 32.35 N 3.24 E
Hassi Zehana 34 35.01 N 0.53 W
Hassleben 54 53.13 N 13.41 E
Hässleholm 41 56.09 N 13.46 E
Hasslinghausen 56 51.20 N 7.17 E
Hassloch 56 49.22 N 8.16 E
Hasson Heights 214 41.26 N 79.41 W
Hästbo 40 60.27 N 16.27 E
Hästen ➛[8], B.R.D. 263 51.09 N 7.06 E
Hasten ➛[8], B.R.D. 263 51.12 N 7.09 E
Hastière-Lavaux 56 50.13 N 4.50 E
Hastings, Austl. 169 38.18 S 145.11 E

Symbols in the index entries represent the broad categories identified in the key at the right. Symbols with superior numbers (⋀⋀[2]) identify subcategories (see complete key on page I · 30).

Kartensymbole in dem Registerverzeichnis stellen die rechts in Schlüssel erklärten Kategorien dar. Symbole mit hochgestellten Ziffern (⋀⋀[2]) bezeichnen Unterabteilungen einer Kategorie (vgl. vollständiger Schlüssel auf Seite I · 30).

Los símbolos incluídos en el texto del índice representan las grandes categorias identificadas con la clave a la derecha. Los símbolos con numeros en su parte superior (⋀⋀[2]) identifican las subcategorías (véase la clave completa en la página I · 30).

Les symboles de l'index représentent les catégories indiquées dans la légende à droite. Les symboles suivis d'un indice (⋀⋀[2]) représentent des sous-catégories (voir légende complète à la page I · 30).

Os símbolos incluídos no texto do índice representam as grandes categorias identificadas com a chave à direita. Os símbolos com números em sua parte superior (⋀⋀[2]) identificam as subcategorias (veja-se a chave completa à página I · 30).

	English	Deutsch	Español	Français	Português
∧	Mountain	Berg	Montaña	Montagne	Montanha
⋀⋀	Mountains	Berge	Montañas	Montagnes	Montanhas
)(	Pass	Pass	Paso	Col	Passo
∨	Valley, Canyon	Tal, Cañon	Valle, Cañón	Vallée, Canyon	Vale, Canhão
≚	Plain	Ebene	Llano	Plaine	Planície
≻	Cape	Kap	Cabo	Cap	Cabo
I	Island	Insel	Isla	Île	Ilha
II	Islands	Inseln	Islas	Îles	Ilhas
⊥	Other Topographic Features	Andere Topographische Objekte	Otros Elementos Topográficos	Autres données topographiques	Outros Elementos Topográficos

ESPAÑOL

Nombre | Página | Lat.°′ | Long.°′ W=Oeste

Hastings, Barb. 241g 13.04 N 59.35 W
Hastings, Ont., Can. 212 44.18 N 77.57 W
Hastings, N.Z. 172 39.38 S 176.51 E
Hastings, Eng., U.K. 42 50.51 N 0.36 E
Hastings, Fla., U.S. 192 29.40 N 81.30 W
Hastings, Ill., U.S. 278 41.41 N 87.58 W
Hastings, Mich., U.S. 216 42.39 N 85.17 W
Hastings, Minn., U.S. 190 44.44 N 92.51 W
Hastings, Nebr., U.S. 198 40.35 N 98.23 W
Hastings, N.Y., U.S. 210 43.22 N 76.09 W
Hastings, Pa., U.S. 214 40.40 N 78.42 W
Hastings □[6] 212 44.45 N 77.40 W
Hastings Battlesite (1066) ⊥ 42 50.53 N 0.31 E
Hastings-on-Hudson 276 40.60 N 73.53 W
Hastingwood 260 51.45 N 0.09 E
Hastrup 41 55.26 N 12.11 E
Hasty 198 38.07 N 102.58 W
Hasuda 94 35.59 N 139.40 E
Hasumi 96 34.52 N 132.37 E
Haswell 198 38.27 N 103.09 W
Hata 94 36.11 N 137.51 E
Ha-tan 110 18.30 N 105.20 E
Hatanagi-dam ◆[6] 94 35.18 N 138.12 E
Hatashō 94 35.10 N 136.15 E
Hatay □[4] 130 36.30 N 36.15 E
Hatboro 208 40.11 N 75.06 W
Hatch, N. Mex., U.S. 200 32.40 N 107.09 W
Hatch, Utah, U.S. 200 37.39 N 112.26 W
Hatches Creek 162 20.56 S 135.12 E
Hatchet Creek ≃ 194 32.52 N 86.20 W
Hatchet Lake 186 44.35 N 63.40 W
Hatchie ≃ 194 35.35 N 89.53 W
Hatchineha, Lake ◎ 220 28.02 N 81.25 W
Hatchlands ⊥ 260 51.15 N 0.28 W
Hatchmere 262 53.15 N 2.40 W
Hatchville 207 41.38 N 70.34 W
Hatch Wash ∨ 200 38.32 N 109.36 W
Hat Creek ≃, U.S. 198 43.16 N 103.36 W
Hat Creek ≃, Calif., U.S. 204 40.59 N 121.33 W
Haţeg 38 45.37 N 22.57 E
Hateruma-shima I 175d 24.03 N 123.47 E
Hatfield, Austl. 166 33.52 S 143.45 E
Hatfield, Eng., U.K. 260 51.46 N 0.13 W
Hatfield, Ark., U.S. 194 34.29 N 94.23 W
Hatfield, Mass., U.S. 207 42.22 N 72.36 W
Hatfield Aerodrome ⊠ 260 51.46 N 0.16 W
Hatfield House ⊥ 260 51.46 N 0.13 W
Hatfield Peverel 260 51.47 N 0.35 E
Hatfield Swamp ☷ 276 40.50 N 74.20 W
Hathāla 123 32.03 N 70.34 E
Hathaway Mead 224 45.27 N 123.47 W
Hathaway Pines 226 38.07 N 120.28 W
Hatherleigh 42 50.49 N 4.04 W
Hathersage 44 53.19 N 1.38 W
Hathob, Oued el ∨ 36 35.23 N 9.32 E
Hāthras 124 27.36 N 78.03 E
Hātia Ʉ 124 22.30 N 91.15 E
Hātia Island I 124 22.40 N 91.00 E
Hātiāra 272b 22.37 N 88.27 E
Ḥāṭibah, Ra's > 144 21.55 N 38.58 E
Ha-tien 110 10.23 N 104.29 E
Hatillo 240m 18.29 N 66.49 W
Ha-tinh 110 18.20 N 105.54 E
Hatinoe → Hachinohe 92 40.30 N 141.29 E
Hatiozi → Hachiōji 94 35.39 N 139.20 E
Hatip 130 37.46 N 32.25 E
Hātisāla 272b 22.33 N 88.32 E
Hato 241s 12.12 N 68.57 W
Hato, Bocht van C 241s 12.13 N 68.58 W
Hato del Volcán 236 8.46 N 82.38 W
Hatogaya 94 35.50 N 139.44 E
Hato Mayor [del Rey] 238 18.46 N 69.15 W
Hato Rey 240m 18.25 N 66.03 W
Hatoyama 94 35.59 N 139.20 E
Hāt Pīplia 124 22.46 N 76.18 E
Hatsukaichi 96 34.21 N 132.20 E
Hatsu-shima I 94 35.02 N 139.10 E
Hatsutomi 268 35.46 N 140.01 E
Hatta 124 24.07 N 79.36 E
Hattah Lakes National Park ♠ 166 34.40 S 142.30 E
Hattem 52 52.28 N 6.04 E
Hatten, B.R.D. 52 53.02 N 8.22 E
Hatten, Fr. 56 48.54 N 7.59 E
Hattenhofen 60 48.13 N 11.07 E
Hatteras 192 35.13 N 75.42 W
Hatteras, Cape > 192 35.13 N 75.32 W
Hatteras Island I 192 35.25 N 75.30 W
Hattiesburg 194 31.19 N 89.16 W
Hatting 41 55.51 N 9.46 E
Hattingen 56 51.23 N 7.10 E
Hattingspruit 158 28.09 S 30.11 E
Hatton, Eng., U.K. 262 53.20 N 2.36 W
Hatton, Scot., U.K. 46 57.25 N 1.54 W
Hatton, Ala., U.S. 194 32.06 N 86.35 W
Hatton, N. Dak., U.S. 198 47.38 N 97.27 W
Hatton ◆[8] 260 51.28 N 0.25 W
Hatton Fields 226 36.33 N 121.54 W
Hattorf [am Harz] 52 51.39 N 10.14 E
Hattori, Nihon 270 34.46 N 135.27 E
Hattori, Nihon 270 34.52 N 135.36 E
Hattstatt 58 48.01 N 7.17 E
Hattstedt 41 54.31 N 9.01 E
Hatunsaray 130 37.35 N 32.21 E
Hatvan 30 47.40 N 19.41 E
Hat Yai 110 7.01 N 100.28 E
Hatzfeld ◆[8] 263 51.17 N 7.11 E
Hatzic 224 49.09 N 122.15 W
Hatzic Lake ◎ 224 49.10 N 122.14 W
Hauachil Island I 144 15.08 N 40.15 E
Hau-bon (Cheo-reo) 110 13.24 N 108.27 E
Haubourdin 50 50.36 N 2.59 E
Haubstadt 194 38.12 N 87.34 W
Hau-duc 110 15.20 N 108.13 E
Hāudullāpur 272b 22.25 N 88.33 E
Hauge 26 58.18 N 6.15 E
Haugesund 26 59.25 N 5.18 E
Haugh of Urr 44 54.58 N 3.52 W
Haughton Green 262 53.27 N 2.06 W
Haugsdorf 61 48.42 N 16.05 E
Hauhungaroa Range ⋀ 172 38.50 S 175.34 E
Haukeligrend 26 59.45 N 7.31 E
Haukipudas 26 65.11 N 25.21 E
Haukivesi ◎ 26 62.06 N 28.28 E
Haukivuori 26 62.01 N 27.13 E
Hauldres, Rû des ≃ 261 48.37 N 2.28 E
Haulerwijk 52 53.04 N 6.20 E
Haultain ≃ 184 55.51 N 106.46 W
Haune ≃ 56 50.52 N 9.43 E
Haunersdorf 60 48.36 N 12.43 E
Haunstetten 58 48.18 N 10.54 E
Haunts Creek Ʉ 276 40.37 N 73.31 W
Hauppauge 210 40.49 N 73.12 W
Hauptsrus 158 26.33 S 26.18 E
Hauraki Gulf C 172 36.20 S 175.05 E
Hauroko, Lake ◎ 172 46.00 S 167.20 E
Hauru, Pointe > 174s 17.29 S 149.55 W
Haus 64 47.25 N 13.49 E
Hausa, Nig. 273a 6.37 N 3.21 E
Hausa, Sah. Occ. 148 27.06 N 10.55 W
Hausham 64 47.45 N 11.50 E
Hausruck ⋀ 60 48.07 N 13.35 E
Haussee ◎ 264a 52.38 N 13.41 E
Haussömmern 54 51.11 N 10.49 E
Haut, Isle au I 188 44.03 N 68.38 W
Haut Atlas ⋀ 148 31.30 N 6.00 W
Haut-Barr, Château du ⊥ 58 48.43 N 7.21 E
Haut-Bassins □[5] 150 12.30 N 2.30 W
Haut-Bout 261 48.32 N 1.55 E
Haute Colme, Canal de la Ξ 50 50.50 N 2.12 E
Hautecombe, Abbaye de ʊ[1] 62 45.45 N 5.50 E
Haute-Corse □[5] 36 42.30 N 9.00 E

FRANÇAIS

Nom | Page | Lat.°′ | Long.°′ W=Ouest

Haute-Garonne □[5] 32 43.25 N 1.30 E
Haute-Kotto □[5] 152 7.00 N 23.00 E
Haute-Loire □[5] 32 45.05 N 3.50 E
Hauteluce 62 45.45 N 6.35 E
Haute-Marne □[5] 58 48.05 N 5.10 E
Hauterive 186 49.12 N 68.16 W
Hauterives 62 45.15 N 5.02 E
Hautes-Alpes □[5] 62 44.40 N 6.30 E
Haute-Sangha □[5] 152 4.30 N 16.00 E
Haute-Saône □[5] 58 47.40 N 6.10 E
Haute-Savoie □[5] 32 46.00 N 6.20 E
Haute Seine, Canal de la Ξ 50 48.34 N 3.43 E
Hautes Fagnes ⋀ 56 50.30 N 6.05 E
Hautes-Pyrénées □[5] 32 43.00 N 0.10 E
Haute-Vienne □[5] 32 45.50 N 1.15 E
Hauteville-Lompnes 58 45.58 N 5.36 E
Haute-Volta → Upper Volta □[1] 150 13.00 N 2.00 W
Haut-Kœnigsburg, Château du ⊥ 58 48.14 N 7.22 E
Haut-Mbomou □[5] 140 6.00 N 26.00 E
Hautmont 50 50.15 N 3.56 E
Haut-Ogooué □[4] 152 2.00 S 14.00 E
Haut-Rhin □[5] 58 47.53 N 7.13 E
Hauts-de-Seine □[5] 261 48.50 N 2.11 E
Hautvillers 50 49.05 N 3.57 E
Haut-Zaïre □[4] 154 2.20 N 27.00 E
Hauula 229c 21.37 N 157.55 W
Hauzenberg 60 48.39 N 13.38 E
Hauz Khas ⊥ 272a 28.36 N 77.09 E
Hauz Rāni ◆[8] 272a 28.32 N 77.13 E
Havana → La Habana, Cuba 240p 23.08 N 82.22 W
Havana, Ark., U.S. 194 35.07 N 93.32 W
Havana, Fla., U.S. 192 30.38 N 84.25 W
Havana, Ill., U.S. 194 40.18 N 90.04 W
Havana, N. Dak., U.S. 198 45.57 N 97.37 W
Havane, La → La Habana 240p 23.08 N 82.22 W
Havannah, Canal de la Ʉ 175f 22.22 S 167.01 E
Havannah Harbour C 175f 17.33 S 168.16 E
Havant 42 50.51 N 0.59 W
Havasu, Lake ◎[1] 200 34.30 N 114.20 W
Havasu Creek ≃ 200 36.19 N 112.46 W
Havasupai Indian Reservation ◆[4] 200 36.13 N 112.40 W
Havdrup 41 55.32 N 12.08 E
Havel ≃ 54 52.53 N 11.58 E
Havelange 56 50.23 N 5.14 E
Havelberg 54 52.50 N 12.04 E
Havelberg ∧[2] 264a 52.28 N 13.12 E
Haveli 123 30.27 N 73.42 E
Haveliān 123 34.03 N 73.10 E
Havelland ◆[1] 54 52.25 N 12.45 E
Havelländisches Luch ☷ 54 52.40 N 12.40 E
Havelock, Ont., Can. 212 44.26 N 77.53 W
Havelock, N.Z. 172 41.17 S 173.46 E
Havelock, Swaz. 158 25.56 S 31.06 E
Havelock, N.C., U.S. 192 34.53 N 76.54 W
Havelock Island I 110 11.58 N 93.00 E
Havelock North 172 39.40 S 176.53 E
Haven 198 37.54 N 97.47 W
Haverford 285 40.01 N 75.18 W
Haverford College ʊ[2] 285 40.00 N 75.18 W
Haverfordwest 42 51.49 N 4.58 W
Haverhill, Eng., U.K. 42 52.05 N 0.26 E
Haverhill, Mass., U.S. 207 42.47 N 71.05 W
Haverhill Airport ⊠ 283 42.48 N 71.04 W
Haverhill-Riverside Airport ⊠ 283 42.46 N 71.02 W
Hāveri 122 14.48 N 75.24 E
Haverigg 44 54.11 N 3.17 W
Havering ◆[8] 260 51.34 N 0.14 E
Havering-atte-Bower ◆[8] 260 51.37 N 0.11 E
Havering's Grove 260 51.38 N 0.23 E
Havern ◎ 26 62.17 N 15.07 E
Haverö 26 62.24 N 15.05 E
Haverstraw 210 41.12 N 73.58 W
Havertown 208 39.59 N 75.18 W
Haviland, Kans., U.S. 198 37.37 N 99.06 W
Haviland, Ohio, U.S. 216 41.01 N 84.35 W
Haviland Brook ≃ 276 41.07 N 73.33 W
Havilhanları 130 38.09 N 41.47 E
Ḥavīq 128 38.10 N 48.54 E
Havířov 30 49.47 N 18.27 E
Havixbeck 52 51.58 N 7.25 E
Hävla 40 58.55 N 15.52 E
Havlíčkův Brod 30 49.36 N 15.35 E
Havnbjerg 41 55.02 N 9.48 E
Havnsø 41 55.45 N 11.20 E
Havran 130 39.33 N 27.06 E
Havré, Bel. 50 50.28 N 4.02 E
Havre → Le Havre, Fr. 50 49.30 N 0.08 E
Havre, Mont., U.S. 202 48.33 N 109.41 W
Havre-Aubert 186 47.14 N 61.51 W
Havre de Grace 188 39.33 N 76.06 W
Havre de Grace Heights 208 39.35 N 76.07 W
Havre-Saint-Pierre 186 50.14 N 63.36 W
Havsa 130 41.33 N 26.49 E
Havza 130 40.58 N 35.41 E
Haw ≃ 192 35.36 N 79.03 W
Hawaii □[3] 229d 20.00 N 157.45 W
Hawaii I 229d 19.30 N 155.30 W
Hawaiian Gardens 280 33.50 N 118.04 W
Hawaiian Islands II 14 24.00 N 167.00 W
Hawaiian Ridge ✢[3] 14 24.00 N 165.00 W
Hawaii Volcanoes National Park ♠ 229d 19.23 N 155.17 W
Hawal ≃ 146 10.00 N 12.05 E
Hawarden, Sask., Can. 184 51.23 N 106.36 W
Hawarden, N.Z. 172 42.56 S 172.38 E
Hawarden, Wales, U.K. 44 53.11 N 3.02 W
Hawarden, Iowa, U.S. 198 43.00 N 96.29 W
Ḥawashīyah, Wādī ∨ 142 28.31 N 32.58 E
Haw Creek ≃ 218 39.11 N 85.55 W
Hawea, Lake ◎ 172 44.30 S 169.17 E
Hawera 172 39.35 S 174.17 E
Hawes 44 54.18 N 2.12 W
Hawesville 194 37.54 N 86.45 W
Haweswater Reservoir ◎ 44 54.32 N 2.48 W
Ḥawf, Jabal ⋀[2] 273c 29.55 N 31.21 E
Ḥawf, Wādī ∨ 142 29.53 N 31.18 E
Hawi 229d 20.14 N 155.50 W
Hawick 44 55.25 N 2.47 W
Hawk Creek ≃ 198 44.44 N 95.25 W
Hawkdun Range ⋀ 172 44.46 S 170.00 E
Hawke, Cape > 166 32.13 S 152.34 E
Hawke Bay C 172 39.20 S 177.30 E
Hawker 166 31.53 S 138.25 E
Hawkes, Mount ∧ 9 83.56 S 55.45 W
Hawkes Brook ≃ 283 42.45 N 71.08 W
Hawkesbury 206 45.36 N 74.37 W
Hawkesbury ≃ 170 33.30 S 151.10 E
Hawkesbury Island I 182 53.38 N 129.00 W
Hawkes Pond ◎ 283 42.30 N 71.02 W
Hawkeye 190 42.56 N 91.57 W
Hawkhurst 42 51.02 N 0.30 E
Hawkins, Tex., U.S. 222 32.35 N 95.12 W
Hawkins, Wis., U.S. 190 45.31 N 90.43 W
Hawkins Island I 180 60.30 N 146.00 W
Hawkinsville 192 32.17 N 83.28 W
Hawk Junction 190 48.05 N 84.34 W
Hawk Lake 184 49.48 N 93.59 W
Haw Knob ∧ 192 35.19 N 84.02 W
Hawk Point 219 38.58 N 91.08 W
Hawk Run 214 40.55 N 78.13 W
Hawksbill ∧ 188 38.33 N 78.23 W

PORTUGUÊS

Nome | Página | Lat.°′ | Long.°′ W=Oeste

Hawksbill Creek C 192 26.32 N 78.43 W
Hawks Nest Point > 238 24.09 N 75.32 W
Hawkwell 260 51.36 N 0.40 E
Hawkwood 166 25.47 S 150.50 E
Hawley, Eng., U.K. 260 51.25 N 0.14 E
Hawley, Minn., U.S. 198 46.53 N 96.19 W
Hawley, Pa., U.S. 210 41.28 N 75.11 W
Hawleyton 210 42.01 N 75.55 W
Hawleyville 207 41.26 N 73.21 W
Haworth 276 40.58 N 73.59 W
Haw Par Villa ʊ 271c 1.16 N 103.47 E
Hawr 142 27.52 N 30.44 E
Hawrān, Wādī ∨ 128 33.58 N 42.34 E
Ḥawsh 'Īsā 142 30.55 N 30.17 E
Ḥawsh Mūsá 132 33.43 N 35.56 E
Hawthorn, Austl. 274b 37.49 S 145.02 E
Hawthorn, Pa., U.S. 214 41.01 N 79.17 W
Hawthorne, Calif., U.S. 228 33.55 N 118.21 W
Hawthorne, Fla., U.S. 192 29.36 N 82.05 W
Hawthorne, Nev., U.S. 204 38.32 N 118.38 W
Hawthorne, N.J., U.S. 210 40.57 N 74.09 W
Hawthorne, N.Y., U.S. 210 41.07 N 73.48 W
Hawthorne Lake ◎ 276 41.03 N 74.35 W
Hawthorne Municipal Airport ⊠ 280 33.55 N 118.20 W
Hawthorne Race Track ♠ 278 41.50 N 87.45 W
Hawthorn Woods 278 42.13 N 88.03 W
Ḥawwārah 132 32.32 N 35.54 E
Ḥawwārat 'Adlān 142 29.12 N 30.58 E
Ḥawwārat al-Maqṭa' 142 29.15 N 30.54 E
Hawzen 144 13.56 N 39.28 E
Haxtun 198 40.39 N 102.38 W
Hay 166 34.30 S 144.51 E
Hay ≃, Austl. 166 25.14 S 138.00 E
Hay ≃, Can. 176 60.52 N 115.44 W
Hay ≃, Wis., U.S. 190 44.59 N 91.51 W
Hay, Cape > 176 74.25 N 113.00 W
Hay, Mount ∧, Austl. 162 23.28 S 133.05 E
Hay, Mount ∧, Austl. 170 33.37 S 150.26 E
Hay, Mount ∧, N.A. 180 59.15 N 137.37 W
Hay, South Fork ≃ 190 45.03 N 91.57 W
Haya 164 3.27 S 129.33 E
Haya ≃ 94 35.14 N 139.09 E
Hayachine-san ∧ 92 39.34 N 141.29 E
Haya'er 120 37.00 N 93.18 E
Hayakawa 94 35.25 N 138.22 E
Hayama, Nihon 94 35.16 N 139.35 E
Hayama, Nihon 96 33.26 N 133.13 E
Hayang 98 35.55 N 128.47 E
Hayange 56 49.20 N 6.03 E
HaYarden → Jordan ≃ 132 31.46 N 35.33 E
Hayashima 96 34.36 N 133.50 E
Haybān 140 11.13 N 30.31 E
Haybān, Jabal ∧ 140 11.15 N 30.31 E
Hay Bay C 212 44.10 N 76.55 W
Haybes 56 50.00 N 4.43 E
Haydān, Wādī al- ∨ 132 31.27 N 35.36 E
Haydaran 130 39.14 N 39.43 E
Haydarlı 130 38.16 N 30.23 E
Haydarpaşa ◆[8] 267b 40.58 N 29.02 E
Haydarpaşa Garı ◆[5] 267b 41.00 N 29.01 E
Hayden, Ariz., U.S. 200 33.00 N 110.47 W
Hayden, Colo., U.S. 200 40.30 N 107.16 W
Hayden, Ind., U.S. 218 38.59 N 85.44 W
Hayden Peak ∧ 202 42.59 N 116.39 W
Haydenville, Mass., U.S. 207 42.22 N 72.42 W
Haydenville, Ohio, U.S. 188 39.29 N 82.20 W
Haydock 262 53.28 N 2.39 W
Haydock Park Race Course ♠ 262 53.29 N 2.37 W
Haydon Bridge 44 54.58 N 2.14 W
Haye, La → 's-Gravenhage 52 52.06 N 4.18 E
Hayes ◆[8], Eng., U.K. 260 51.31 N 0.25 W
Hayes ◆[8], Eng., U.K. 260 51.23 N 0.01 E
Hayes ≃, Man., Can. 184 57.03 N 92.09 W
Hayes ≃, N.W. Ter., Can. 176 67.18 N 95.02 W
Hayes, Mount ∧ 180 63.37 N 146.43 W
Hayes Center 198 40.31 N 101.01 W
Hayes State Memorial ⊥ 214 41.21 N 83.08 W
Hayesville, N.C., U.S. 192 35.03 N 83.49 W
Hayesville, Ohio, U.S. 214 40.46 N 82.16 W
Hayesville, Oreg., U.S. 224 44.59 N 122.58 W
Hayfield, Eng., U.K. 262 53.23 N 1.57 W
Hayfield, Minn., U.S. 190 43.53 N 92.51 W
Hayford Peak ∧ 204 36.40 N 115.11 W
Hayfork 204 40.33 N 123.11 W
Hayfork Bally ∧ 204 40.39 N 123.13 W
Hayfork Creek ≃ 204 40.37 N 123.26 W
Hay Island I 212 44.53 N 80.58 W
Hay Lake ◎ 212 45.23 N 78.11 W
Hay Lakes 182 53.13 N 113.03 W
Haymakers Run ≃ 279b 40.25 N 79.43 W
Haymana 130 39.27 N 32.30 E
Haynau → Chojnów 30 51.17 N 15.56 E
Haynes 194 34.53 N 90.47 W
Haynes Creek ≃ 285 39.53 N 74.50 W
Haynesville, La., U.S. 194 32.58 N 93.08 W
Haynesville, Va., U.S. 208 37.57 N 76.40 W
Hayneville 194 32.06 N 86.35 W
Hay-on-Wye 42 52.04 N 3.07 W
Hayrabolu 130 41.12 N 27.06 E
Hayrat 84 40.40 N 40.24 E
Hay River 176 60.51 N 115.40 W
Hays, Alta., Can. 182 50.06 N 111.48 W
Hays, Kans., U.S. 198 38.53 N 99.20 W
Hays, Mont., U.S. 202 48.03 N 108.43 W
Hays □[6] 222 30.02 N 97.45 W
Hays ◆[8] 279b 40.23 N 79.56 W
Hays Mill Creek ≃ 285 39.44 N 74.50 W
Hay Springs 198 42.41 N 102.41 W
Haystack Mountain ∧ 204 41.39 N 115.38 W
Haysville, Kans., U.S. 198 37.34 N 97.21 W
Haysville, Pa., U.S. 279b 40.32 N 80.09 W
Hayti, Mo., U.S. 194 36.14 N 89.44 W
Hayti, Pa., U.S. 208 39.59 N 75.51 W
Hayti, S. Dak., U.S. 198 44.40 N 97.12 W
Hayward, Calif., U.S. 226 37.40 N 122.05 W
Hayward, Wis., U.S. 190 46.01 N 91.29 W
Hayward Brook ≃ 283 42.22 N 71.20 W
Hayward Municipal Airport ⊠ 282 37.40 N 122.08 W
Haywards Heath 42 51.00 N 0.06 W
Ḥayy, Jabal al- ∧ 142 29.43 N 31.35 E
HaẒafon □[5] 132 32.50 N 35.20 E
Hazak 130 37.21 N 41.54 E
Hazapin Gölü ◎ 84 41.15 N 43.12 E
Hazara □[8] 123 35.00 N 73.20 E
Hazard 192 37.15 N 83.12 W
Hazardville 207 41.59 N 72.33 W
Hazāreh Toghāy 120 37.11 N 67.13 E
Hazar Gölü ◎ 130 38.30 N 39.25 E
Hazāribāgh 124 23.59 N 85.21 E
Hazāribāgh □[5] 126 24.00 N 85.30 E
Hazāribāgh Plateau ⋀[1] 124 24.00 N 85.10 E
Haze, Cape > 220 26.46 N 82.10 W
Hazebrouck 50 50.43 N 2.32 E
Hazel ≃ 188 38.33 N 77.51 W
Hazelbrook 170 33.44 S 150.27 E
Hazel Crest 278 41.35 N 87.40 W
Hazel Dell 224 45.39 N 122.41 W
Hazel Green, Ill., U.S. 278 41.41 N 87.45 W
Hazel Green, Wis., U.S. 190 42.32 N 90.26 W
Hazelgrove, Austl. 170 33.40 S 149.52 E
Hazel Grove, Eng., U.K. 262 53.23 N 2.08 W
Hazel Hurst 214 41.42 N 78.35 W
Hazel Kirk 279b 40.11 N 79.57 W

Hazel Park 216 42.29 N 83.06 W
Hazel Park Race Track ♠ 281 42.29 N 83.05 W
Hazelton, B.C., Can. 182 55.15 N 127.40 W
Hazelton, Idaho, U.S. 202 42.41 N 114.08 W
Hazelton, N. Dak., U.S. 198 46.29 N 100.17 W
Hazelton Mountains ⋀ 182 55.00 N 128.00 W
Hazelton Peak ∧ 202 44.06 N 107.03 W
Hazelwood, Mo., U.S. 219 38.46 N 90.22 W
Hazelwood, N.C., U.S. 192 35.28 N 83.00 W
Hazelwood ◆[8] 279b 40.25 N 79.56 W
Hazen, Ark., U.S. 194 34.47 N 91.35 W
Hazen, Nev., U.S. 226 39.34 N 119.03 W
Hazen, N. Dak., U.S. 198 47.18 N 101.38 W
Hazen, Pa., U.S. 214 41.12 N 78.58 W
Hazen Bay C 180 61.00 N 165.10 W
Ḥazerim 132 31.14 N 34.43 E
Hazlehurst, Ga., U.S. 192 31.52 N 82.36 W
Hazlehurst, Miss., U.S. 194 31.52 N 90.24 W
Hazlet, Sask., Can. 184 50.25 N 108.36 W
Hazlet, N.J., U.S. 208 40.26 N 74.13 W
Hazleton, Iowa, U.S. 190 42.37 N 91.54 W
Hazleton, Pa., U.S. 210 40.58 N 75.59 W
Hazlett, Lake ◎ 162 21.30 S 128.48 E
Ḥazor 132 32.59 N 35.33 E
Hazro, Pāk. 123 33.54 N 72.29 E
Hazro, Tür. 130 38.15 N 40.47 E
Hazu 94 34.47 N 137.08 E
Hazzo 130 38.11 N 41.29 E
Heacham 42 52.55 N 0.30 E
Head ≃ 212 44.44 N 79.15 W
Head Bay d'Espoir 186 47.56 N 55.45 W
Headcorn 42 51.11 N 0.37 E
Headford 48 53.28 N 9.05 W
Headington 42 51.45 N 1.13 W
Head Lake ◎ 212 44.45 N 78.55 W
Headland 194 31.21 N 85.20 W
Headlands 154 18.14 S 32.03 E
Headley, Eng., U.K. 42 51.07 N 0.50 W
Headley, Eng., U.K. 260 51.17 N 0.16 W
Headley, Mount ∧ 202 47.44 N 115.15 W
Head of the Harbor 276 40.54 N 73.10 W
Heald Green 262 53.22 N 2.14 W
Heald Moor ◆[3] 262 53.44 N 2.10 W
Healdsburg 204 38.37 N 122.52 W
Healdton 196 34.14 N 97.29 W
Healesville 169 37.40 S 145.31 E
Healy, Alaska, U.S. 180 63.52 N 148.58 W
Healy, Kans., U.S. 198 38.36 N 100.37 W
Healy, Mount ∧ 180 63.46 N 149.01 W
Healy Lake ◎ 212 45.10 N 79.55 W
Heani, Mont ∧ 174x 9.47 S 139.04 W
Heanna 174m 26.19 N 127.54 E
Heanor 44 53.01 N 1.22 W
Heany Junction 154 20.06 S 28.54 E
Heanza-banare I 174m 26.21 N 127.57 E
Heard Pond ◎ 283 42.21 N 71.22 W
Hearne 222 30.53 N 96.36 W
Hearst 176 49.41 N 83.40 W
Hearst Island I 9 69.25 S 62.10 W
Hearst San Simeon State Historical Park ♠ 226 35.42 N 121.10 W
Heart ≃, Alta., Can. 182 56.14 N 117.17 W
Heart ≃, N. Dak., U.S. 198 46.47 N 100.51 W
Heart Lake ◎, Alta., Can. 182 55.02 N 111.30 W
Heart Lake ◎, Ont., Can. 275b 43.44 N 79.48 W
Heart Lake Indian Reserve ◆[4] 182 55.02 N 111.30 W
Heart Pond ◎ 283 42.34 N 71.23 W
Heart's Content 186 47.53 N 53.22 W
Heath, Mass., U.S. 207 42.40 N 72.49 W
Heath, Ohio, U.S. 214 39.58 N 82.29 W
Heath, Tex., U.S. 222 32.50 N 96.29 W
Heath, Pointe > 186 49.05 N 61.42 W
Heathcote, Austl. 169 36.55 S 144.42 E
Heathcote, Austl. 274a 34.05 S 151.01 E
Heathcote Brook ≃ 276 40.23 N 74.37 W
Heath End 42 51.22 N 1.09 W
Heatherton 274b 37.58 S 145.06 E
Heathfield 42 50.59 N 0.17 E
Heathmont 274b 37.49 S 145.15 E
Heath Springs 192 34.36 N 80.40 W
Heathsville 208 37.55 N 76.28 W
Heatley 262 53.24 N 2.27 W
Heaton Hall ⊥ 262 53.32 N 2.15 W
Heaton Moor 262 53.25 N 2.11 W
Heaven, Temple of ʊ[1] 271a 39.53 N 116.25 E
Heavener 194 34.53 N 94.36 W
Heaven Park ♠ 271a 39.52 N 116.24 E
Heaverham 260 51.18 N 0.15 E
Heaviley 262 53.24 N 2.09 W
Hebaochang 107 29.33 N 105.32 E
Hebaodao I 100 21.52 N 113.09 E
Hebbronville 196 27.18 N 98.41 W
Hebburn 44 54.59 N 1.30 W
Hebbville 284b 39.20 N 77.46 W
Hebden Bridge 262 53.45 N 2.00 W
Hebden Water ≃ 262 53.44 N 2.00 W
Hebei, Zhg. 104 40.43 N 122.12 E
Hebei, Zhg. 104 41.01 N 123.51 E
Hebei □[4] 98 38.00 N 116.00 E
Hebeitun 105 39.35 N 117.07 E
Hebel 166 28.59 S 147.48 E
Heber, Ariz., U.S. 200 34.26 N 110.36 W
Heber, Calif., U.S. 204 32.44 N 115.32 W
Heber City 200 40.30 N 111.25 W
Heber Springs 194 35.30 N 92.02 W
Hebgen Lake ◎[1] 202 44.47 N 111.14 W
Hebi 98 35.59 N 114.11 E
Hebianchang 107 30.29 N 105.08 E
Hebo, Oreg., U.S. 224 45.14 N 123.52 W
Hebo, Zhg. 102 31.29 N 98.58 E
Hebo, Mount ∧ 224 45.12 N 123.45 W
Hébridas, Islas → Hebrides II 46 57.00 N 6.30 W
Hebrides II 46 57.00 N 6.30 W
Hebrides, Sea of the ⊤[2] 46 57.07 N 6.55 W
Hebron, Conn., U.S. 207 41.39 N 72.22 W
Hebron, Ill., U.S. 216 42.28 N 88.26 W
Hebron, Ind., U.S. 216 41.19 N 87.12 W
Hebron, Ky., U.S. 218 39.04 N 84.42 W
Hebron, Md., U.S. 188 38.25 N 75.41 W
Hebron, Nebr., U.S. 198 40.10 N 97.35 W
Hebron, N. Dak., U.S. 198 46.54 N 102.03 W
Hebron, Pa., U.S. 208 40.21 N 76.24 W
Hebron, Tex., U.S. 222 33.01 N 96.52 W
Hebron, Wis., U.S. 216 42.56 N 88.42 W
Hebron → Al-Khalīl, Urd. 132 31.32 N 35.06 E
Hebu 100 27.50 N 115.22 E
Hebukesaier 86 46.47 N 85.43 E
Hebutu 104 42.19 N 122.20 E
Heby 40 59.56 N 16.53 E
Hecao 105 40.21 N 116.47 E
Hecate Strait Ʉ 182 53.00 N 131.00 W
Hecelchakán 232 20.10 N 90.08 W
Heceta Island I 180 55.45 N 133.35 W
Hechi 102 24.51 N 107.59 E
Hechiceros 196 28.33 N 103.38 W
Hechingen 58 48.21 N 8.58 E
Hechtel 56 51.08 N 5.21 E
Hechthausen 52 53.38 N 9.14 E
Hechuan 107 30.00 N 106.16 E
Heckelberg 54 52.44 N 13.50 E
Hecker 219 38.18 N 90.00 W
Heckington 42 52.59 N 0.18 W
Hecklingen 54 51.51 N 11.32 E
Heckscher State Park ♠ 210 40.43 N 73.10 W
Hecla 198 45.53 N 98.09 W
Hecla Island I 184 51.08 N 96.45 W

Hectanooga 186 44.06 N 66.02 W
Hector, N.Z. 172 41.36 S 171.53 E
Hector, Minn., U.S. 198 44.45 N 94.43 W
Hector, Mount ∧ 172 40.57 S 175.17 E
Heda 94 34.58 N 138.46 E
Hedal 26 60.37 N 9.42 E
Hedaru 154 4.30 S 37.54 E
Heddal ʊ[1] 26 59.35 N 9.11 E
Hedding 285 40.06 N 74.44 W
Hédé, Fr. 32 48.18 N 1.48 W
Hede, Sve. 26 62.25 N 13.30 E
Hedehusene 41 55.39 N 12.12 E
Hedel 52 51.45 N 5.15 E
Hedemora 40 60.17 N 15.59 E
Hedemünden 56 51.23 N 9.46 E
Hedensted 41 55.46 N 9.42 E
Hedersleben 54 51.51 N 11.15 E
Hedesunda 40 60.24 N 16.59 E
Hedesundafjärdarna ◎ 40 60.20 N 17.00 E
He Devil ∧ 202 45.21 N 116.33 W
Hedgerley 260 51.35 N 0.36 W
Hedian 100 32.45 N 114.18 E
Hedley, B.C., Can. 182 49.21 N 120.04 W
Hedley, Tex., U.S. 196 34.52 N 100.39 W
Hedmark □[6] 26 61.30 N 11.45 E
Hednesford 42 52.43 N 2.00 W
Hedo 174m 26.51 N 128.16 E
Hedo-misaki > 174m 26.52 N 128.16 E
Hedon 44 53.44 N 0.12 W
Hedrick 190 41.11 N 92.19 W
Hedströmmen ≃ 40 59.28 N 16.04 E
Hedutne 272c 19.10 N 73.06 E
Hedwig Village 222 29.47 N 95.27 W
Heek 52 52.07 N 7.06 E
Heel 52 51.11 N 5.53 E
Heel Point > 174a 19.19 N 166.37 E
Heemskerk 52 52.31 N 4.40 E
Heemstede 52 52.21 N 4.37 E
Heepen 52 52.01 N 8.35 E
Heer, Bel. 56 50.10 N 4.50 E
Heer, Ned. 56 50.50 N 5.44 E
Heerde 52 52.23 N 6.03 E
Heerdt ◆[8] 263 51.13 N 6.43 E
Heerenveen 52 52.57 N 5.55 E
Heeren-Werve 52 51.35 N 7.43 E
Heeres-Museum ʊ 264b 48.11 N 16.23 E
Heerkan 107 29.32 N 103.56 E
Heerlen 56 50.54 N 5.59 E
Heesch 52 51.44 N 5.32 E
Heeslingen 52 53.19 N 9.20 E
Heessen 52 51.42 N 7.50 E
Heeze 52 51.24 N 5.35 E
Ḥefa (Haifa) 132 32.50 N 35.00 E
Ḥefa □[5] 132 32.35 N 35.00 E
Ḥefa, Mifraẕ C 132 32.53 N 35.03 E
Ḥefa, Sede-Te'ufa ⊠ 132 32.49 N 35.02 E
Hefei 100 31.51 N 117.17 E
Hefengchang 107 30.26 N 104.43 E
Heffron Park ♠ 274a 33.57 S 151.15 E
Heflin 194 33.39 N 85.35 W
Hegang 89 47.24 N 130.17 E
Hegau ◆[1] 58 47.50 N 8.45 E
Hégenheim 58 47.34 N 7.32 E
Hegewisch ◆[8] 278 41.40 N 87.33 W
Hegins 208 40.39 N 76.30 W
Hegra 26 63.28 N 11.07 E
Heguaizi 102 39.39 N 106.41 E
Heguri 270 34.38 N 135.42 E
Hehe, Zhg. 98 36.54 N 116.26 E
Hehe, Zhg. 106 31.55 N 121.32 E
Hehlen 52 51.59 N 9.28 E
Heho 110 20.43 N 96.49 E
Hehou 100 28.40 N 114.28 E
Heicheng (Karakhoto) ⊥ 102 41.47 N 101.03 E
Heichengzhen 102 36.18 N 106.32 E
Heichengzi 104 42.10 N 121.01 E
Heicunzhen 98 35.05 N 118.44 E
Heidayingzi 98 40.52 N 116.12 E
Heidberg ∧[2] 263 51.15 N 7.21 E
Heide 30 54.12 N 9.06 E
Heide ◆[8], B.R.D. 263 51.31 N 6.52 E
Heide ◆[8], B.R.D. 263 51.26 N 7.01 E
Heideck 60 49.08 N 11.07 E
Heidelberg, Austl. 169 37.45 S 145.04 E
Heidelberg, B.R.D. 56 49.25 N 8.43 E
Heidelberg, Ont., Can. 212 43.31 N 80.37 W
Heidelberg, S. Afr. 158 34.06 S 20.59 E
Heidelberg, S. Afr. 158 26.32 S 28.18 E
Heidelberg, Miss., U.S. 194 31.53 N 88.59 W
Heidelberg, Pa., U.S. 279b 40.23 N 80.05 W
Heidelberg, Schloss ⊥ 56 49.24 N 8.42 E
Heidelberg Raceway ♠ 279b 40.23 N 80.06 W
Heidelsheim 56 49.06 N 8.38 E
Heiden, B.R.D. 52 51.59 N 8.50 E
Heiden, Schw. 58 47.27 N 9.33 E
Heiden, Port C 180 56.55 N 158.45 W
Heidenau, B.R.D. 52 53.19 N 9.39 E
Heidenau, D.D.R. 54 50.59 N 13.52 E
Heidenheim 56 49.01 N 10.44 E
Heidenheim an der Brenz 56 48.40 N 10.08 E
Heidenheimer 222 31.01 N 97.18 W
Heidenoldendorf 52 51.57 N 8.50 E
Heidenreichenstein 61 48.52 N 15.07 E
Heider Ditch Ξ 279a 41.31 N 82.01 W
Heiderscheid 56 49.53 N 5.54 E
Heidhausen ◆[8] 263 51.23 N 7.01 E
Heidhof ◆[8] 263 51.11 N 7.11 E
Heidlersburg 208 39.57 N 77.09 W
Heidouwo 105 39.42 N 117.15 E
Heigenbrücken 56 50.02 N 9.23 E
Heigoutaicun 104 41.30 N 123.01 E
Heigun-tō I 96 33.47 N 132.14 E
Heihai → Halahu ◎ 102 38.15 N 97.40 E
Heihe → Aihun, Zhg. 89 50.13 N 127.33 E
Heihe (Naquka), Zhg. 120 31.34 N 92.00 E
Heihe ≃ 105 40.44 N 116.27 E
Heijō → P'yŏngyang 98 39.01 N 125.45 E
Heike ga-dake ∧ 96 34.19 N 131.54 E
Heikendorf 54 54.22 N 10.12 E
Heil 263 51.38 N 7.35 E
Heilangkou 105 39.37 N 117.24 E
Heilbron 158 27.21 S 27.58 E
Heilbronn 56 49.08 N 9.13 E
Heilenbecker-Stausee ◎[1] 263 51.15 N 7.22 E
Heiligenbeil → Mamonovo 76 54.28 N 19.57 E
Heiligenberg 58 47.49 N 9.19 E
Heiligenblut 64 47.02 N 12.50 E
Heiligendamm 54 54.08 N 11.50 E
Heiligenhafen 54 54.22 N 10.58 E
Heiligenhaus 56 51.19 N 6.59 E
Heiligensee ◆[8] 264a 52.36 N 13.13 E
Heiligenstadt, B.R.D. 60 49.51 N 11.10 E
Heiligenstadt, D.D.R. 56 51.23 N 10.09 E
Heilongguan 102 36.19 N 111.11 E
Heilongjiang □[4] 89 48.00 N 128.00 E
Heilongjiang (Amur) ≃ 89 52.56 N 141.10 E
Heilongtan, Zhg. 105 40.44 N 116.31 E
Heilongtan, Zhg. 105 40.02 N 116.11 E
Heiloo 52 52.36 N 4.43 E
Heilsberg → Lidzbark Warmiński 30 54.09 N 20.35 E
Heilsbronn 56 49.20 N 10.47 E
Heiltz-le-Maurupt 56 48.48 N 4.49 E

Heilungkiang → Heilongjiang □[4] 89 48.00 N 128.00 E
Heilwood 214 40.37 N 78.55 W
Heimaey I 24a 63.26 N 20.17 W
Heimbach 56 50.38 N 6.28 E
Heimbuchenthal 56 49.53 N 9.17 E
Heimburg 54 51.49 N 10.54 E
Heimdal 26 63.21 N 10.22 E
Heimenkirch 58 47.37 N 9.53 E
Heimsheim 56 48.48 N 8.51 E
Heinävesi 26 62.26 N 28.36 E
Heinersdorf, D.D.R. 54 52.27 N 14.13 E
Heinersdorf, D.D.R. 264a 52.23 N 13.20 E
Heinersdorf ◆[8] 264a 52.34 N 13.27 E
Heining 60 48.35 N 13.24 E
Heiniuyingzi 98 41.07 N 120.19 E
Heino 52 52.26 N 6.14 E
Heinola 26 61.13 N 26.02 E
Heinrichshorst 54 52.20 N 11.42 E
Heinrichswalde → Slavsk 76 55.03 N 21.41 E
Heinsberg 56 51.03 N 6.05 E
Heiquanyi 102 39.32 N 99.42 E
Heirnkut 110 25.14 N 94.45 E
Heis 144 10.50 N 46.54 E
Heisfelde 52 53.15 N 7.26 E
Heishan 104 41.41 N 122.07 E
Heishanbao 102 38.37 N 103.25 E
Heishanguan 98 38.33 N 113.41 E
Heishantou, Zhg. 89 50.13 N 119.28 E
Heishantou, Zhg. 98 42.28 N 125.33 E
Heishui 98 42.09 N 119.28 E
Heishuisi 102 36.08 N 108.42 E
Heisingen ◆[8] 263 51.25 N 7.04 E
Heisker Islands II 46 57.31 N 7.40 W
Heisler 182 52.41 N 112.13 W
Heislerville 208 39.15 N 75.07 W
Heissen ◆[8] 263 51.26 N 6.56 E
Heist-aan-Zee 50 51.21 N 3.15 E
Heist-op-den-Berg 56 51.05 N 4.43 E
Heitang 102 26.29 N 105.09 E
Heitersheim 58 47.53 N 7.40 E
Heiwa 94 35.12 N 136.44 E
Heiyanghebao 105 39.07 N 118.15 E
Heiyantang 102 27.28 N 101.11 E
Heiyanzi 105 39.13 N 118.08 E
Heiyuguan 98 40.39 N 117.32 E
Hejaz → Al-Ḥijāz ◆[1] 118 24.30 N 38.30 E
Hejiachang 107 29.24 N 104.56 E
Hejian, Zhg. 98 38.26 N 116.05 E
Hejian, Zhg. 105 39.25 N 116.25 E
Hejiang 107 28.49 N 105.50 E
Hejiangzhen 107 29.16 N 104.16 E
Hejiaqiao 100 27.24 N 113.21 E
Hejiashi 106 31.39 N 121.01 E
Hejiawopeng 104 41.32 N 122.07 E
Hejiaying 105 39.55 N 118.19 E
Hejin 102 35.39 N 110.40 E
Hejlsminde 41 55.22 N 9.37 E
Hejnsvig 41 55.41 N 8.59 E
Hekelgem 50 50.54 N 4.06 E
Hekili Point > 229a 20.48 N 156.37 W
Hekimhan 130 38.49 N 37.56 E
Hekinan 94 34.51 N 136.58 E
Hekla ∧[1] 24a 64.00 N 19.39 W
Hekou, Zhg. 100 32.09 N 116.04 E
Hekou, Zhg. 100 31.22 N 114.26 E
Hekou, Zhg. 102 28.22 N 108.14 E
Hekou, Zhg. 102 29.57 N 111.04 E
Hekou, Zhg. 102 36.09 N 103.22 E
Hekou, Zhg. 102 22.38 N 103.56 E
Hekouchang 107 29.21 N 104.21 E
Hekoujie 102 26.31 N 100.39 E
Hekura-jima I 92 37.51 N 136.55 E
Hel 30 54.37 N 18.48 E
Helagsfjället ∧ 26 62.55 N 12.27 E
Helaluo 102 33.56 N 102.10 E
Helangou 104 41.00 N 123.25 E
Helanshan ⋀ 102 38.40 N 105.57 E
Helbe ≃ 54 51.13 N 11.06 E
Helbra 54 51.33 N 11.29 E
Helchteren 56 51.03 N 5.22 E
Heldburg 54 50.17 N 10.44 E
Helden 56 51.07 N 7.56 E
Heldenbergen 56 50.14 N 8.52 E
Heldra 56 51.07 N 10.11 E
Heldrungen 54 51.18 N 11.13 E
Helechos, Cañada de los ≃ 286a 19.22 N 99.12 W
Helemano Stream ≃ 229c 21.35 N 158.06 W
Helen, Mount ∧ 166 21.34 S 141.13 E
Helena, Ark., U.S. 194 34.32 N 90.35 W
Helena, Mont., U.S. 202 46.36 N 112.01 W
Helena, N.Y., U.S. 206 44.55 N 74.44 W
Helena, Ohio, U.S. 214 41.21 N 83.18 W
Helena, Okla., U.S. 196 36.33 N 98.16 W
Helena ≃ 168a 31.54 S 116.00 E
Helena Reservoir ◎[1] 168a 31.59 S 116.13 E
Helendale 228 34.45 N 117.18 W
Helenenberg 56 49.51 N 6.32 E
Helenental ◆[1] 264b 48.01 N 16.11 E
Helen Island I 108 2.58 N 131.49 E
Helensburgh, Austl. 170 34.11 S 150.59 E
Helensburgh, Scot., U.K. 46 56.01 N 4.44 W
Helen Springs 162 18.26 S 133.52 E
Helensville 172 36.40 S 174.28 E
Helenville 216 43.01 N 88.41 W
Helenwood 192 36.26 N 84.32 W
Heleẕ 132 31.35 N 34.40 E
Helfenberg 61 48.32 N 14.08 E
Helfenstein 208 40.45 N 76.27 W
Helfta 54 51.30 N 11.34 E
Helgaå ≃ 26 55.53 N 14.08 E
Helgenæs I 41 56.08 N 10.32 E
Helgoland I 30 54.12 N 7.53 E
Helgoländer Bucht C 30 54.10 N 8.04 E
Helicoide ◆[9] 286c 10.29 N 66.55 W
Helidon 171a 27.33 S 152.08 E
Helingeer 102 40.26 N 111.55 E
Heliodora 256 22.04 S 45.32 W
Heliópolis 287a 22.45 S 43.25 W
Heliopolis → Mişr al-Jadīdah ◆[8] 273c 30.06 N 31.20 E
Heliopolis (On) ⊥ 142 30.08 N 31.17 E
Heliopolis Aerodrome ⊠ 273c 30.04 N 31.19 E
Heliopolis Racing Club ♠ 273c 30.06 N 31.19 E
Helishan ⋀ 102 39.30 N 100.30 E
Heliu 100 33.02 N 116.57 E
Helixi 106 30.40 N 118.59 E
Helizhen 89 47.05 N 130.16 E
Hell 26 63.26 N 10.54 E
Hellam 208 40.00 N 76.36 W
Hellberge ⋀[2] 54 52.34 N 11.17 E
Hellbrunn, Schloss ⊥ 64 47.46 N 13.04 E
Hellebæk 41 56.04 N 12.34 E
Ḥelleh ≃ 128 29.10 N 50.40 E
Hellemmes-Lille 50 50.37 N 3.07 E
Hellen Blazes, Lake ◎ 220 28.01 N 80.47 W
Hellendoorn 52 52.24 N 6.26 E
Hellenthal 56 50.29 N 6.26 E
Hellerau ◆[8] 54 51.07 N 13.44 E
Hellern 52 52.15 N 7.58 E
Hellersen 263 51.12 N 7.39 E
Hellertown 208 40.35 N 75.21 W
Hellesylt 26 62.05 N 6.54 E
Hellevad 41 55.05 N 9.13 E
Hellevoetsluis 52 51.49 N 4.08 E
Hell Gate Ʉ 276 40.47 N 73.56 W
Hell Hole Reservoir ◎[1] 226 39.04 N 120.22 W
Hellifield 44 54.01 N 2.12 W
Hellín 34 38.31 N 1.41 W

Symbol	English	Deutsch	Español	Français	Português
≃	River	Fluss	Río	Rivière	Rio
Ξ	Canal	Kanal	Canal	Canal	Canal
⌊	Waterfall, Rapids	Wasserfall, Stromschnellen	Cascada, Rápidos	Chute d'eau, Rapides	Cascata, Rápidos
Ʉ	Strait	Meeresstrasse	Estrecho	Détroit	Estreito
C	Bay, Gulf	Bucht, Golf	Bahía, Golfo	Baie, Golfe	Baía, Golfo
◎	Lake, Lakes	See, Seen	Lago, Lagos	Lac, Lacs	Lago, Lagos
☷	Swamp	Sumpf	Pantano	Marais	Pântano
⊓	Ice Features, Glacier	Eis- und Gletscherformen	Accidentes Glaciales	Formes glaciaires	Acidentes Glaciares
⊤	Other Hydrographic Features	Andere Hydrographische Objekte	Otros Elementos Hidrográficos	Autres données hydrographiques	Outros Elementos Hidrográficos

Symbol	English	Deutsch	Español	Français	Português
✢	Submarine Features	Untermeerische Objekte	Accidentes Submarinos	Formes de relief sous-marin	Acidentes Submarinos
□	Political Unit	Politische Einheit	Unidad Politica	Entité politique	Unidade Política
ʊ	Cultural Institution	Kulturelle Institution	Institución Cultural	Institution culturelle	Instituição Cultural
⊥	Historical Site	Historische Stätte	Sitio Histórico	Site historique	Sitio Histórico
♠	Recreational Site	Erholungs- und Ferienort	Sitio de Recreo	Centre de loisirs	Sítio de Lazer
⊠	Airport	Flughafen	Aeropuerto	Aéroport	Aeroporto
■	Military Installation	Militäranlage	Instalación Militar	Installation militaire	Instalação Militar
◆	Miscellaneous	Verschiedenes	Misceláneo	Divers	Miscelânea

ENGLISH | DEUTSCH

Name / Name	Page / Seite	Lat.°′ / Breite°′	Long.°′ / Länge°′ E=Ost
Helli Ness ≻	46	60.02 N	1.10 W
Hellmonsödt	61	48.26 N	14.18 E
Hells Canyon ∨	202	45.20 N	116.45 W
Hellsee ⊜	264a	52.45 N	13.35 E
Hells Gate ♠	182	49.47 N	121.27 W
Hell-Ville	157b	13.25 S	48.16 E
Hellweg ➜[1]	52	51.32 N	7.47 E
Helm	226	36.32 N	120.06 W
Helmand □[4]	128	31.00 N	64.00 E
Helmand ≃	128	31.12 N	61.34 E
Helmbrechts	54	50.14 N	11.43 E
Helmcken Falls L	182	51.57 N	120.11 W
Helmeringhausen	156	25.54 S	16.57 E
Helmetta	276	40.22 N	74.26 W
Helmetta Pond ⊜	276	40.23 N	74.26 W
Helmond	52	51.29 N	5.40 E
Helmsburg	218	39.16 N	86.18 W
Helmsdale	46	58.07 N	3.40 W
Helmsdale ≃	46	58.07 N	3.40 W
Helmshore	262	53.41 N	2.20 W
Helmsley	44	54.14 N	1.04 W
Helmstedt	54	52.13 N	11.00 E
Helnæs I	41	55.08 N	10.02 E
Helong	98	42.32 N	128.59 E
Helper	200	39.41 N	110.51 W
Helpmekaar	158	28.29 S	30.29 E
Helpter Berg ∧[2]	54	53.30 N	13.36 E
Helsby	262	53.16 N	2.46 W
Helsby Hill ∧[2]	262	53.16 N	2.46 W
Helsingborg	41	56.03 N	12.42 E
Helsinge	41	56.01 N	12.12 E
Helsingfors → Helsinki	26	60.10 N	24.58 E
Helsingør (Elsinore)	41	56.02 N	12.37 E
Helsinki (Helsingfors)	26	60.10 N	24.58 E
Helska, Mierzeja ≻[2]	30	54.45 N	18.39 E
Helston	42	50.05 N	5.16 W
Heltonville	218	38.56 N	86.23 W
Helvecia	252	31.06 S	60.05 W
Helvellyn ∧	44	54.31 N	3.01 W
Helvick Head ≻	48	52.03 N	7.33 W
Helvoirt	52	51.38 N	5.13 E
Hem ≃	50	50.51 N	2.06 E
Hemar, Naḥal ∨	132	31.08 N	35.22 E
Hemau	60	49.03 N	11.47 E
Hemāvati ≃	122	12.31 N	76.27 E
Hembe	152	1.54 N	22.42 E
Hemel Hempstead	260	51.46 N	0.28 W
Hemelingen ➜[8]	52	53.03 N	8.53 E
Hemeln	52	51.30 N	9.36 E
Hemer	56	51.23 N	7.46 E
Hemet	228	33.45 N	116.58 W
Hemfjärden C	40	59.17 N	15.20 E
Hemford	186	44.30 N	64.47 W
Hemfurth-Edersee	56	51.10 N	9.02 E
Hemiksem	50	51.09 N	4.21 E
Héming	58	48.42 N	6.57 E
Hemingford	198	42.19 N	103.04 W
Hemingway	192	33.45 N	79.27 W
Hemlock, Ind., U.S.	216	40.25 N	86.03 W
Hemlock, N.Y., U.S.	210	42.48 N	77.36 W
Hemlock Lake ⊜	210	42.43 N	77.37 W
Hemmerde	52	51.33 N	7.48 E
Hemmerden	263	51.07 N	6.36 E
Hemmingen-Westerfeld	52	52.19 N	9.45 E
Hemmoor	52	53.41 N	9.08 E
Hemphill	194	31.20 N	93.51 W
Hempnall	42	52.30 N	1.19 E
Hempstead, N.Y., U.S.	210	40.42 N	73.37 W
Hempstead, Tex., U.S.	222	30.06 N	96.05 W
Hempstead Harbor C	276	40.50 N	73.39 W
Hempstead Lake ⊜	276	40.41 N	73.38 W
Hempstead Lake State Park ♠	276	40.41 N	73.38 W
Hemse	26	57.14 N	18.22 E
Hemsedal	26	60.52 N	8.34 E
Hemsön I	26	62.43 N	18.05 E
Hemstreet Park	210	42.54 N	73.41 W
Hemsworth	44	53.38 N	1.21 W
Hemujing	98	37.54 N	115.22 E
Henan	102	34.46 N	101.49 E
Henan □[4]	90	34.00 N	114.00 E
Hen and Chickens II	172	35.55 S	174.45 E
Henares ≃	34	40.24 N	3.30 W
Henbury, Austl.	162	24.35 S	133.15 E
Henbury, Eng., U.K.	262	53.15 N	2.11 W
Hendek	130	40.48 N	30.45 E
Henderson, Arg.	252	36.18 S	61.43 W
Henderson, Ind., U.S.	218	39.40 N	85.31 W
Henderson, Ky., U.S.	194	37.50 N	87.35 W
Henderson, Minn., U.S.	190	44.31 N	93.55 W
Henderson, Nebr., U.S.	198	40.47 N	97.49 W
Henderson, Nev., U.S.	204	36.02 N	114.59 W
Henderson, N.C., U.S.	192	36.20 N	78.25 W
Henderson, N.Y., U.S.	212	43.51 N	76.11 W
Henderson, Tenn., U.S.	194	35.27 N	88.38 W
Henderson, Tex., U.S.	222	32.09 N	94.48 W
Henderson □[6]	222	32.13 N	95.50 W
Henderson Bay C	212	43.54 N	76.10 W
Henderson Creek ≃	194	40.52 N	91.02 W
Henderson Island I	6	24.22 S	128.19 W
Hendersonville, N.C., U.S.	192	35.19 N	82.28 W
Hendersonville, Pa., U.S.	214	40.18 N	80.09 W
Hendersonville, Tenn., U.S.	194	36.18 N	86.37 W
Hendījān	128	30.14 N	49.43 E
Hendon ➜[8]	260	51.35 N	0.14 W
Hendorābī, Jazīreh-ye I	128	26.40 N	53.37 E
Hendricks, Minn., U.S.	198	44.30 N	96.25 W
Hendricks, W. Va., U.S.	188	39.05 N	79.38 W
Hendricks □[6]	218	39.46 N	86.26 W
Hendrina	158	26.11 S	29.45 E
Hendry □[6]	220	26.36 N	81.13 W
Hendrysburg	214	40.04 N	81.10 W
Hendy	42	51.43 N	4.04 W
Henefer	200	41.01 N	111.30 W
Henfield	42	50.56 N	0.17 W
Hengām, Jazīreh-ye I	128	26.39 N	55.53 E
Henganofi	164	6.15 S	145.35 E
Hengchow → Hengyang	102	26.51 N	112.30 E
Hengcun	100	27.10 N	116.48 E
Hengdaochuan	98	41.15 N	125.31 E
Hengdaohe	89	43.18 N	127.18 E
Hengdaohezi, Zhg.	89	43.13 N	126.44 E
Hengdaohezi, Zhg.	104	42.07 N	123.49 E
Hengelo	52	52.15 N	6.45 E
Hengersberg	60	48.47 N	13.03 E
Hengfan	106	30.20 N	119.45 E
Hengfeng	100	28.24 N	117.34 E
Henggang	100	29.32 N	115.27 E
Henggong	106	31.52 N	120.03 E
Henggouzi	89	43.12 N	124.47 E
Henghutou	104	42.05 N	124.00 E
Hengjie	106	31.13 N	119.30 E
Hengjing	106	31.11 N	120.32 E
Hengjinghong	106	30.34 N	120.59 E
Hengli	100	23.12 N	114.37 E
Henglin	106	31.42 N	120.06 E
Henglu	98	41.26 N	126.04 E
Henglutou	106	30.19 N	119.19 E
Hengmian	106	31.09 N	121.38 E
Hengoed	42	51.39 N	3.10 W
Hengsen	263	51.29 N	7.38 E
Hengsha I	106	31.20 N	121.50 E
Hengshan, Zhg.	100	27.15 N	112.51 E
Hengshan, Zhg.	102	37.56 N	108.53 E
Hengshan, Zhg.	106	31.01 N	120.32 E
Hengshan ∧	100	27.16 N	112.35 E
Hengshan ⩘	102	39.30 N	113.45 E
Hengshanchang	107	30.33 N	105.24 E
Hengshanqiao	106	31.46 N	120.07 E
Hengshanxia	106	30.18 N	118.44 E
Hengshi, Zhg.	100	26.05 N	114.38 E
Hengshi, Zhg.	100	23.52 N	113.15 E
Hengshitan	100	29.32 N	114.41 E
Hengshui	98	37.43 N	115.40 E
Hengshui ≃	107	28.57 N	105.22 E
Hengsteysee ⊜[1]	263	51.25 N	7.28 E
Hengtangshi	106	31.41 N	121.02 E
Hengtianchi	107	29.07 N	105.01 E
Hengtianxi	107	29.05 N	105.03 E
Hengxi, Zhg.	100	29.42 N	121.35 E
Hengxi, Zhg.	100	28.46 N	120.29 E
Hengxi, Zhg.	106	31.43 N	118.46 E
Hengxian	102	22.42 N	109.13 E
Hengxiang	106	32.12 N	120.15 E
Hengxikou	100	29.26 N	121.26 E
Hengyan	100	29.25 N	118.34 E
Hengyang	102	26.51 N	112.30 E
Hénin-Beaumont	50	50.25 N	2.56 E
Henley Beach	168b	34.55 S	138.30 E
Henley-in-Arden	42	52.17 N	1.46 W
Henley-on-Thames	42	51.32 N	0.56 W
Henlopen, Cape ≻	208	38.48 N	75.05 W
Henlow	42	52.02 N	0.18 W
Hennan ⊜	26	62.06 N	15.46 E
Hennaya	34	34.58 N	1.22 W
Henneberg	54	50.29 N	10.21 E
Hennebont	32	47.48 N	3.17 W
Hennef	56	50.46 N	7.16 E
Hennen	56	51.27 N	7.39 E
Hennenman	158	27.59 S	27.01 E
Hennepin	190	41.15 N	89.21 W
Hennepin, Point ≻	281	42.12 N	83.09 W
Hennersdorf	264b	48.07 N	16.22 E
Hennessey	196	36.06 N	97.54 W
Hennessey, Lake ⊜[1]	226	38.29 N	122.22 W
Hennickendorf	54	52.30 N	13.51 E
Henniez	58	46.44 N	6.54 E
Hennigsdorf	54	52.38 N	13.12 E
Henniker	188	43.11 N	71.49 W
Henning, Ill., U.S.	216	40.18 N	87.42 W
Henning, Minn., U.S.	198	46.19 N	95.27 W
Henning, Tenn., U.S.	194	35.41 N	89.34 W
Henri ≃	206	46.30 N	71.47 W
Henri, Cap ≻	186	49.48 N	64.23 W
Henri-Chapelle	56	50.40 N	5.56 E
Henrichemont	50	47.18 N	2.32 E
Henrichenburg	263	51.35 N	7.19 E
Henrico □[6]	208	37.30 N	77.20 W
Henrietta, N.Y., U.S.	210	43.03 N	77.37 W
Henrietta, Tex., U.S.	196	33.49 N	98.12 W
Henrietta Maria, Cape ≻	176	55.09 N	82.20 W
Henry, Ill., U.S.	190	41.47 N	89.41 W
Henry, S. Dak., U.S.	198	44.53 N	97.28 W
Henry □[6], Ind., U.S.	218	39.55 N	85.22 W
Henry □[6], Ky., U.S.	218	38.26 N	85.09 W
Henry □[6], Ohio, U.S.	216	41.20 N	84.04 W
Henry ≃	162	22.40 S	115.40 E
Henry, Cape ≻	208	36.55 N	76.01 W
Henry, Mount ∧	202	48.53 N	115.31 W
Henry, Mount ∧[2]	274a	33.50 S	150.38 E
Henry, Point ≻	162	34.29 S	119.23 E
Henry Cowell Redwoods State Park ♠	226	37.02 N	122.03 W
Henryetta	196	35.27 N	95.59 W
Henry Island I	224	48.35 N	123.11 W
Henry Kater, Cape ≻	176	69.05 N	66.44 W
Henry Mountains ⩘	200	38.00 N	110.50 W
Henry Pittier, Parque Nacional ♠	246	10.25 N	67.43 W
Henrys Bend	214	41.28 N	79.37 W
Henrys Fork ≃, U.S.	200	41.00 N	109.39 W
Henrys Fork ≃, Idaho, U.S.	202	43.45 N	111.56 W
Henryville, Qué., Can.	206	45.08 N	73.11 W
Henryville, Ind., U.S.	218	38.32 N	85.46 W
Henry W. Coe State Park ♠	226	37.12 N	121.30 W
Hensall	190	43.26 N	81.30 W
Henshaw, Lake ⊜[1]	204	33.15 N	116.45 W
Hensley	194	34.30 N	92.12 W
Henslow, Cape ≻	175e	9.56 S	160.38 E
Henson Creek ≃	284b	38.46 N	77.00 W
Hensonville	210	42.17 N	74.13 W
Henstedt-Ulzburg	52	53.47 N	9.58 E
Henstridge	42	50.59 N	2.24 W
Hentiesbaai	156	22.08 S	14.18 E
Hentona	174m	26.45 N	128.10 E
Henty	166	35.31 S	147.02 E
Henzada	110	17.38 N	95.28 E
Hepburn	184	52.31 N	106.43 W
Hepburn Springs	169	37.19 S	144.09 E
Hephzibah	192	33.19 N	82.06 W
Heping, Zhg.	100	27.10 N	117.18 E
Heping, Zhg.	100	22.01 N	112.59 E
Heping (Yangmingzhen), Zhg.	100	24.28 N	114.58 E
Heping, Zhg.	100	23.17 N	116.29 E
Heping, Zhg.	100	23.54 N	114.38 E
Hepo	100	23.28 N	115.56 E
Heppenheim an der Bergstrasse	56	49.39 N	8.38 E
Heppner	202	45.21 N	119.33 W
Heptonstall	262	53.45 N	2.01 W
Heptonstall Moor ≃	262	53.46 N	2.05 W
Hepu (Lianzhou)	102	21.39 N	109.11 E
Hepworth	212	44.37 N	81.09 W
Heqi	106	31.03 N	119.49 E
Heqiao	106	31.30 N	119.53 E
Heqing	102	26.30 N	100.20 E
Hequ	102	39.29 N	111.19 E
Héraðsflói C	24a	65.45 N	14.10 W
Hera Lacinia, Tempio di ⊥	68	39.01 N	17.13 E
Herāt	128	34.20 N	62.12 E
Herāt □[4]	128	34.30 N	62.00 E
Hérault □[5]	32	43.40 N	3.30 E
Hérault ≃	32	43.17 N	3.26 E
Herbasse ≃	62	45.02 N	4.57 E
Herbault	50	47.36 N	1.08 E
Herbede	56	51.25 N	7.16 E
Herbern	52	51.44 N	7.39 E
Herbert, Sask., Can.	184	50.26 N	107.12 W
Herbert, N.Z.	172	45.14 S	170.47 E
Herbert ≃	166	18.32 S	146.17 E
Herbertabad	110	11.43 N	92.37 E
Herbert Hoover National Historic Site ⊥	190	41.38 N	91.23 W
Herbertingen	58	48.04 N	9.26 E
Herbert Island I	180	52.45 N	170.10 W
Herberton	166	17.23 S	145.23 E
Herbert Peak ∧	172	43.41 S	172.44 E
Herbertsdale	158	34.01 S	21.46 E
Herbeumont	56	49.47 N	5.14 E
Herbignac	32	47.27 N	2.19 W
Herb Lake	184	54.47 N	99.47 W
Herblay	50	49.00 N	2.10 E
Herblet Lake ⊜	184	54.56 N	99.54 W
Herbolzheim	58	48.13 N	7.47 E
Herborn	56	50.40 N	8.17 E
Herbrechtingen	56	48.37 N	10.10 E
Herbsleben	54	51.07 N	10.50 E
Herbstein	56	50.34 N	9.20 E
Herceg-Novi	38	42.27 N	18.32 E
Herculaneum	219	38.16 N	90.23 W
Hercules	282	38.01 N	122.17 W
Herdecke	56	51.24 N	7.26 E
Herdorf	56	50.46 N	7.56 E
Herdringen	56	51.25 N	7.58 E
Herđubreid ∧	24a	65.13 N	16.18 W
Heredia	236	10.00 N	84.07 W
Heredia □[4]	236	10.30 N	84.00 W
Hereford, Eng., U.K.	42	52.04 N	2.43 W
Hereford, Ariz., U.S.	200	31.26 N	110.06 W
Hereford, Md., U.S.	208	39.35 N	76.40 W
Hereford, Tex., U.S.	196	34.49 N	102.24 W
Hereford and Worcester □[6]	42	52.10 N	2.30 W
Hereford Cathedral ♉[1]	42	52.04 N	2.43 W
Hereford Mountain ∧	206	45.05 N	71.36 W
Hereke	130	40.48 N	29.39 E
Herekino	172	35.15 S	173.13 E
Herencia	34	39.21 N	3.22 W
Herentals	56	51.11 N	4.50 E
Herfølge	41	55.25 N	12.10 E
Herford	52	52.06 N	8.40 E
Hergatz	58	47.39 N	9.50 E
Hergisdorf	54	51.32 N	11.28 E
Hergla	36	36.02 N	10.31 E
Herhahn	56	50.33 N	6.26 E
Herheri	130	37.41 N	39.00 E
Héricourt	58	47.35 N	6.45 E
Hérimoncourt	58	47.26 N	6.53 E
Heringen	54	51.27 N	10.52 E
Heringsdorf	54	54.18 N	11.00 E
Herington	198	38.40 N	96.57 W
Heriot	172	45.50 S	169.16 E
Herisau	58	47.23 N	9.17 E
Heritage Range ⩘	9	79.30 S	84.00 W
Herk ≃	56	50.58 N	5.07 E
Herk-de-Stad	56	50.56 N	5.10 E
Herkimer	210	43.02 N	74.59 W
Herkimer □[6]	210	43.02 N	74.59 W
Herleshausen	56	51.00 N	10.09 E
Herlev	41	55.43 N	12.27 E
Herlong	204	40.09 N	120.08 W
Herlufmagle	41	55.19 N	11.46 E
Herlufsholm	41	55.15 N	11.46 E
Hermagor	64	46.37 N	13.22 E
Herman, Minn., U.S.	198	45.49 N	96.08 W
Herman, Nebr., U.S.	198	41.40 N	96.13 W
Herman, Pa., U.S.	214	40.50 N	79.49 W
Herman, Lake ⊜	282	38.05 N	122.09 W
Hermana Mayor Island I	116	15.48 N	119.48 E
Hermanas	196	27.13 N	101.14 W
Herma Ness ≻	46a	60.50 N	0.55 W
Hermann	219	38.42 N	91.27 W
Hermann Eckstein Park ♠	273d	26.10 S	28.02 E
Hermannsburg, Austl.	162	23.57 S	132.45 E
Hermannsburg, B.R.D.	52	52.50 N	10.05 E
Hermannsdenkmal ⊥	52	51.55 N	8.50 E
Hermannskogel ∧	264b	48.16 N	16.18 E
Hermannstadt → Sibiu	38	45.48 N	24.09 E
Hermannstein	56	50.35 N	8.29 E
Hermano Peak ∧	200	37.13 N	108.48 W
Heřmanova Hut	60	49.44 N	13.04 E
Hermansverk	26	61.11 N	6.51 E
Hermansville	190	45.42 N	87.37 W
Hermanus	158	34.25 S	19.16 E
Hermanville	194	31.58 N	90.50 W
Hermeray	261	48.38 N	1.41 E
Hermes	50	49.22 N	2.15 E
Hermeskeil	56	49.39 N	6.56 E
Hermidale	166	31.33 S	146.43 E
Hermies	50	50.07 N	3.02 E
Herminie	214	40.16 N	79.43 W
Hermiston	202	45.51 N	119.17 W
Hermitage, Newf., Can.	186	47.33 N	55.56 W
Hermitage, N.Z.	172	43.44 S	170.06 E
Hermitage, Ark., U.S.	194	33.27 N	92.10 W
Hermitage, Mo., U.S.	194	37.56 N	93.19 W
Hermitage Bay C	186	47.35 N	56.05 W
Hermitage Park	284c	39.05 N	77.04 W
Hermit Islands II	164	1.30 S	145.05 E
Hermleigh	196	32.38 N	100.46 W
Hermon, S. Afr.	158	33.27 S	18.59 E
Hermon, N.Y., U.S.	212	44.28 N	75.14 W
Hermon,, Mount → Shaykh, Jabal ash- ∧	132	33.26 N	35.51 E
Hermosa Beach	280	33.52 N	118.24 W
Hermosillo, Méx.	200	32.30 N	114.59 W
Hermosillo, Méx.	232	29.04 N	110.58 W
Hermoso, Cerro ∧	246	1.10 S	78.12 W
Hermsdorf	54	50.54 N	11.52 E
Hermsdorf ➜[8]	264a	52.37 N	13.18 E
Hermyingyi	110	14.15 N	98.21 E
Hernád (Hornád) ≃	30	47.56 N	21.08 E
Hernals ➜[8]	264b	48.13 N	16.20 E
Hernandarias	252	25.22 S	54.45 W
Hernández	234	23.01 N	102.01 W
Hernandez Reservoir ⊜[1]	226	36.22 N	120.49 W
Hernando, Arg.	252	32.25 S	63.44 W
Hernando, Fla., U.S.	220	28.54 N	82.22 W
Hernando, Miss., U.S.	194	34.49 N	89.59 W
Hernando □[6]	220	28.34 N	82.22 W
Hernani	116	11.20 N	125.37 E
Herndon, Calif., U.S.	226	36.49 N	119.54 W
Herndon, Kans., U.S.	198	39.55 N	100.47 W
Herndon, Va., U.S.	208	38.58 N	77.23 W
Herndon Canal ≆	226	36.46 N	119.46 W
Herne	52	51.32 N	7.13 E
Herne Bay	42	51.23 N	1.08 E
Herne Hill	168a	31.50 S	116.01 E
Herning	41	56.08 N	8.59 E
Hernwood Heights	284b	39.22 N	77.50 W
Heroica Caborca	232	30.37 N	112.06 W
Heroica Nogales	232	31.20 N	110.56 W
Herongate	260	51.36 N	0.21 E
Herongen	56	51.24 N	6.15 E
Heron Lake	198	43.47 N	95.19 W
Hérons, Île aux I	275a	45.25 N	73.35 W
Heronsgate	260	51.38 N	0.31 W
Hérouville	261	49.06 N	2.08 E
Herowābād	128	37.37 N	48.32 E
Herpf	54	50.34 N	10.20 E
Herradura	252	26.29 S	58.18 W
Herräng	40	60.08 N	18.39 E
Herreid	198	45.50 N	100.04 W
Herrenalb	56	48.48 N	8.26 E
Herrenberg	56	48.35 N	8.52 E
Herrenchiemsee, Schloss ⊥	64	47.52 N	12.23 E
Herrera	252	28.29 S	63.04 W
Herrera □[4]	236	7.54 N	80.38 W
Herrera del Duque	34	39.10 N	5.03 W
Herrera de Pisuerga	34	42.36 N	4.20 W
Herrick, Austl.	166	41.06 S	147.52 E
Herrick, Ill., U.S.	219	39.13 N	88.59 W
Herrick Creek ≃	182	54.20 N	121.30 W
Herrick Grove	212	44.04 N	76.12 W
Herricks	276	40.45 N	73.40 W
Herrieden	56	49.14 N	10.30 E
Herrin	194	37.48 N	89.02 W
Herring ≃	283	42.10 N	70.44 W
Herring Bay C	208	38.44 N	76.33 W
Herring Cove, N.S., Can.	186	44.34 N	63.34 W
Herring Cove, Alaska, U.S.	180	55.21 N	131.41 W
Herring Creek ≃	208	37.49 N	77.07 W
Herringen	52	51.40 N	7.44 E
Herring Run ≃	284b	39.18 N	76.31 W
Herring Run Park ♠	284b	39.19 N	76.33 W
Herritslev	41	54.42 N	11.41 E
Herrlingen	58	48.25 N	9.53 E
Herrljunga	26	58.05 N	13.02 E
Herrnburg	54	53.47 N	10.45 E
Herrnhut	54	51.01 N	14.44 E
Herrnstadt → Wąsosz	30	51.34 N	16.42 E
Herrsching am Ammersee	60	48.00 N	11.10 E
Herrs Island I	279b	40.28 N	79.58 W
Herrskogen	40	59.32 N	16.15 E
Herry	50	47.13 N	2.57 E
Hersbruck	60	49.30 N	11.26 E
Herschbach	56	50.34 N	7.44 E
Herscheid	56	51.10 N	7.44 E
Herschel	184	51.38 N	108.21 W
Herschel Island I	180	69.35 N	139.05 W
Herscher	216	41.03 N	88.06 W
Herselt	56	51.03 N	4.53 E
Herserange	56	49.31 N	5.47 E
Hersham	260	51.22 N	0.23 W
Hershey, Nebr., U.S.	198	41.10 N	101.00 W
Hershey, Pa., U.S.	208	40.17 N	76.39 W
Hersman	219	39.57 N	90.44 W
Herstadberg	40	58.38 N	16.10 E
Herstal	56	50.40 N	5.38 E
Herstmonceux	42	50.53 N	0.20 E
Herten	52	51.35 N	7.07 E
Hertford, Eng., U.K.	260	51.48 N	0.05 W
Hertford, N.C., U.S.	192	36.11 N	76.28 W
Hertford □[6]	208	36.28 N	77.01 W
Hertfordshire □[6]	42	51.50 N	0.10 W
Hertingfordbury	260	51.48 N	0.06 W
Hertsmere □[8]	260	51.41 N	0.17 W
Hertzogville	158	28.08 S	25.33 E
Heruncun	104	40.58 N	123.27 E
Hervás	34	40.16 N	5.51 W
Herve	56	50.38 N	5.48 E
Hervel d'Oeste	252	27.13 S	51.34 W
Hervest	263	51.40 N	7.01 E
Hervey Bay C	166	25.00 S	153.00 E
Herxheim	56	49.09 N	8.13 E
Héry	50	47.54 N	3.38 E
Héry-sur-Ugines	62	45.46 N	6.28 E
Herzberg, D.D.R.	54	51.41 N	13.14 E
Herzberg, D.D.R.	54	52.54 N	12.58 E
Herzberg am Harz	52	51.39 N	10.20 E
Herzebrock	52	51.53 N	8.14 E
Herzfeld	52	51.40 N	8.08 E
Herzfelde	54	52.29 N	13.50 E
Herzhausen	56	51.11 N	8.53 E
Herzliyya	132	32.10 N	34.51 E
Herznach	58	47.28 N	8.03 E
Herzogenaurach	56	49.34 N	10.53 E
Herzogenbuchsee	58	47.12 N	7.41 E
Herzogenburg	61	48.17 N	15.42 E
Herzsprung	54	53.04 N	12.28 E
Ḥeṣār, Kūh-e ⩘	120	34.50 N	66.35 E
Hesarak	267d	35.47 N	51.19 E
Hesdin	50	50.22 N	2.02 E
Heseerhe ≃	85	39.29 N	76.29 E
Hesel	52	53.18 N	7.35 E
Hesepe	52	52.26 N	7.58 E
Heshachang	107	30.37 N	105.40 E
Heshangqiao	100	34.15 N	113.47 E
Heshaoqiao	100	32.55 N	118.22 E
Heshe	110	19.41 N	109.42 E
Heshengqiao	100	30.00 N	114.22 E
Heshi	100	25.04 N	118.37 E
Heshituoluogai	86	46.35 N	86.01 E
Heshui, Zhg.	100	24.24 N	114.56 E
Heshui, Zhg.	102	22.18 N	111.52 E
Heshui, Zhg.	102	22.48 N	112.29 E
Heshuijian	100	30.33 N	116.05 E
Heshun, Zhg.	100	27.30 N	117.24 E
Heshun, Zhg.	102	37.21 N	113.35 E
Heshuo	86	42.15 N	86.53 E
Hesketh Bank	262	53.42 N	2.51 W
Hesketh Out Marsh ≣	262	53.43 N	2.55 W
Heskin Green	262	53.38 N	2.42 W
Hesler	218	38.28 N	84.47 W
Hesperange	56	49.34 N	6.09 E
Hesperia, Calif., U.S.	228	34.25 N	117.18 W
Hesperia, Mich., U.S.	190	43.34 N	86.04 W
Hesperus Mountain ∧	200	37.27 N	108.05 W
Hess ≃	180	63.34 N	133.57 W
Hesselager	41	55.10 N	10.45 E
Hesselø I	41	56.12 N	11.43 E
Hesselte	52	52.25 N	7.22 E
Hessen	54	52.02 N	10.15 E
Hessen □[3]	30	50.30 N	9.15 E
Hessen Cassal	216	41.00 N	85.05 W
Hessenthal	56	49.55 N	9.17 E
Hessische Rhön, Naturpark ♠	56	50.35 N	9.50 E
Hessisch Lichtenau	56	51.12 N	9.43 E
Hessisch Oldendorf	52	52.10 N	9.15 E
Hessle	44	53.44 N	0.26 W
Hesso	166	32.08 S	137.27 E
Hess Tablemount ✣[3]	14	18.30 N	174.30 W
Hesston, Kans., U.S.	198	38.08 N	97.26 W
Hesston, Pa., U.S.	214	40.26 N	78.07 W
Heston ➜[8]	260	51.29 N	0.22 W
Heswall	262	53.20 N	3.06 W
Het ≃	110	20.49 N	104.01 E
Hetai	102	23.22 N	112.19 E
Hetanbu	100	28.21 N	117.11 E
Hetang, Zhg.	100	26.40 N	119.09 E
Hetang, Zhg.	106	31.43 N	120.27 E
Hetang, Zhg.	107	28.58 N	106.03 E
Hetch Hetchy Aqueduct ≆[1]	226	37.29 N	122.19 W
Hetch Hetchy Reservoir ⊜[1]	226	37.57 N	119.43 W
Hetian, Zhg.	100	25.41 N	116.26 E
Hetian, Zhg.	100	23.19 N	115.38 E
Hetian, Zhg.	120	37.08 N	79.54 E
Hetianhe ≃	90	40.30 N	80.45 E
Het Loo, Paleis ♉	52	52.14 N	5.56 E
Hetou	100	24.18 N	113.29 E
Hetoudian	98	37.02 N	120.35 E
Hetoupu	100	30.50 N	116.03 E
Hetouxi ≃	100	23.58 N	117.24 E
Hettange-Grande	56	49.24 N	6.09 E
Hettenleidelheim	56	49.32 N	8.04 E
Hettick	219	39.21 N	90.02 W
Hettingen	58	48.13 N	9.14 E
Hettinger	198	46.00 N	102.39 W
Hetton-le-Hole	44	54.50 N	1.27 W
Hettstedt	54	51.38 N	11.30 E
Hetzendorf ➜[8]	264b	48.10 N	16.18 E
Hetzerath	56	49.52 N	6.49 E
Het Zoute	50	51.21 N	3.18 E
Heuchin	50	50.28 N	2.16 E
Heudeber	54	51.54 N	10.50 E
Heule	50	50.50 N	3.14 E
Heuningspruit	158	27.26 S	27.28 E
Heusden	50	51.02 N	5.16 E
Heustreu	56	50.21 N	10.15 E
Heusweiler	56	49.20 N	6.55 E
Heuvelton	212	44.37 N	75.25 W
Hève, Cap de la ≻	50	49.31 N	0.04 E
Heven ➜[8]	263	51.26 N	7.17 E
Heverlee	56	50.52 N	4.42 E
Heves	30	47.36 N	20.17 E
Heves □[6]	30	47.50 N	20.15 E
Hewitt, N.J., U.S.	210	41.08 N	74.18 W
Hewitt, Tex., U.S.	222	31.28 N	97.12 W
Hewlett, N.Y., U.S.	276	40.38 N	73.42 W
Hewlett, Va., U.S.	208	37.55 N	77.35 W
Hewlett Bay Park	276	40.38 N	73.42 W
Hewlett Harbor	276	40.38 N	73.41 W
Hewlett Neck	276	40.37 N	73.42 W
Hewlett Point ≻	276	40.50 N	73.45 W
Hewopu	104	41.14 N	122.24 E
Hewu	100	26.41 N	113.40 E
Hexen Kopf ∧	58	47.01 N	10.28 E
Hexham	44	54.58 N	2.06 W
Hexi, Zhg.	100	31.21 N	114.02 E
Hexi, Zhg.	100	24.52 N	117.15 E
Hexi, Zhg.	105	40.35 N	117.52 E
Hexian, Zhg.	100	31.43 N	118.22 E
Hexian, Zhg.	102	24.15 N	111.43 E
Hexibao	102	38.34 N	102.11 E
Hexingchang	107	30.05 N	104.35 E
Hexingjie	106	31.55 N	120.36 E
Hexiwu	105	39.38 N	116.58 E
Hex-Rivierberge ⩘	158	33.25 S	19.37 E
Hextable	260	51.25 N	0.11 E
Hexton	172	38.37 S	177.58 E
Hexue	102	30.00 N	112.20 E
Heyan	104	42.30 N	120.29 E
Heyang, Zhg.	98	35.27 N	118.33 E
Heyang, Zhg.	102	35.15 N	110.06 E
Heybeli ➜[8]	267b	40.53 N	29.05 E
Heybeliada I	267b	40.53 N	29.05 E
Heybridge	260	51.44 N	0.41 E
Heyburn	202	42.34 N	113.46 W
Heyburn State Recreation Area ♠	202	47.20 N	116.49 W
Heyderbreck → Kędzierzyn	30	50.20 N	18.12 E
Heyerode	54	51.10 N	10.25 E
Heyrieux	62	45.38 N	5.03 E
Heysham	44	54.02 N	2.54 W
Heyuan	100	23.44 N	114.41 E
Heywood, Austl.	166	38.08 S	141.38 E
Heywood, Eng., U.K.	262	53.36 N	2.13 W
Heyworth	216	40.19 N	88.59 W
Hezan	130	38.21 N	40.38 E
Heze	98	35.17 N	115.27 E
Hezhang	102	27.00 N	104.37 E
Hezhao	98	37.08 N	115.17 E
Hezhen	100	29.56 N	120.10 E
Hezheng	102	35.25 N	103.10 E
Hezijian	105	40.13 N	116.03 E
Heziwei	100	24.54 N	115.14 E
Hiale	110	15.55 N	107.34 E
Hialeah	220	25.49 N	80.17 W
Hialeah Park Race Track ♠	220	25.51 N	80.17 W
Hiawassee	192	34.58 N	83.46 W
Hiawatha, Kans., U.S.	198	39.51 N	95.32 W
Hiawatha, Utah, U.S.	200	39.29 N	111.01 W
Hiba-dōgo-taishaku-kokutei-kōen ♠	96	35.07 N	133.08 E
Hibaiyo	116	10.16 N	123.20 E
Hibaldstow	44	53.31 N	0.32 W
Hibbing	190	47.25 N	92.56 W
Hibbs, Point ≻	166	42.38 S	145.15 E
Hibernia	276	40.57 N	74.30 W
Hibernia Reef ✣[2]	160	12.00 S	123.23 E
Hibiki-nada ⫪[2]	96	34.00 N	130.30 E
Hiburi-shima I	96	33.10 N	132.17 E
Hibuson Island I	116	10.27 N	125.29 E
Hickam Air Force Base ■	229c	21.20 N	157.57 W
Hickman, Calif., U.S.	226	37.37 N	120.45 W
Hickman, Ky., U.S.	194	36.34 N	89.11 W
Hickman, Nebr., U.S.	198	40.37 N	96.38 W
Hickman, Pa., U.S.	279b	40.23 N	80.09 W
Hickman's Harbour	186	48.06 N	53.44 W
Hickory, Miss., U.S.	194	32.19 N	89.01 W
Hickory, N.C., U.S.	192	35.44 N	81.21 W
Hickory, Pa., U.S.	214	40.18 N	80.18 W
Hickory Corners	216	42.27 N	85.22 W
Hickory Creek ≃, Mich., U.S.	216	42.05 N	86.29 W
Hickory Creek ≃, Tex., U.S.	222	31.29 N	95.07 W
Hickory Hills	216	41.43 N	87.49 W
Hickory Run State Park ♠	210	41.02 N	75.41 W
Hickory Township	214	41.15 N	80.27 W
Hicks, Point ≻	166	37.48 S	149.17 E
Hicks Bay	172	37.36 S	178.18 E
Hickson Lake ⊜	184	56.17 N	104.25 W
Hicksville, N.Y., U.S.	210	40.46 N	73.32 W
Hicksville, Ohio, U.S.	216	41.18 N	84.46 W
Hico	196	31.59 N	98.02 W
Hicpochee, Lake ⊜	220	26.50 N	81.10 W
Hida → Hita	96	33.19 N	130.56 E
Hidaka, Nihon	94	35.54 N	139.21 E
Hidaka, Nihon	96	33.55 N	135.09 E
Hidaka, Nihon	96	35.28 N	134.47 E
Hidaka ≃	96	33.52 N	135.09 E
Hidaka-sammyaku ⩘	92a	42.35 N	142.45 E
Hida-kiso-gawa-kokutei-kōen ♠	94	35.37 N	137.15 E
Hida-kōchi ⩘[1]	94	36.16 N	137.05 E
Hidalgo, Méx.	232	25.59 N	100.27 W
Hidalgo, Méx.	232	27.47 N	99.52 W
Hidalgo, Méx.	232	24.15 N	99.26 W
Hidalgo, Méx.	234	23.10 N	103.13 W
Hidalgo □[3]	234	20.30 N	99.00 W
Hidalgo del Parral	232	26.56 N	105.40 W
Hidalgo Yalalag	234	17.11 N	96.11 W
Hida-sammyaku ⩘	94	36.25 N	137.40 E
Hiddenhausen	52	52.08 N	8.38 E
Hidden Hills	228	34.09 N	118.43 W
Hiddensee I	54	54.33 N	13.07 E
Hidden Valley, Calif., U.S.	226	38.46 N	121.09 W
Hidden Valley, Tex., U.S.	222	29.54 N	95.25 W
Hiddesen	52	51.55 N	8.50 E
Hiddinghausen	263	51.22 N	7.17 E
Hidilola	144	5.52 N	43.42 E
Hidrolândia	255	16.58 S	49.14 W
Hidrolina	255	14.37 S	49.25 W
Hieflau	61	47.36 N	14.44 E
Hienghène	175f	20.41 S	164.56 E
Hienheim	60	48.52 N	11.46 E
Hierapolis ⊥	130	37.58 N	29.19 E
Hierges	56	50.06 N	4.44 E
Hierro (Ferro) I	148	27.45 N	18.00 W
Hiesfeld	263	51.33 N	6.46 E
Hietzing ➜[8]	264b	48.11 N	16.18 E
Higashi ➜[8]	270	34.41 N	135.31 E
Higashibetsuin	270	34.58 N	135.34 E
Higashifuji-enshūjō ■	94	35.17 N	138.51 E
Higashiichiki	92	31.40 N	130.20 E
Higashiiyayama	96	33.52 N	133.54 E
Higashiizu	94	34.48 N	139.04 E
Higashi-jima I	174f	24.47 N	141.23 E
Higashimatsuyama	94	36.02 N	139.24 E
Higashimonzen	268	35.56 N	139.40 E
Higashimurayama	94	35.46 N	139.29 E
Higashinada ➜[8]	270	34.43 N	135.16 E
Higashinakano	268	35.38 N	139.25 E
Higashinari ➜[8]	270	34.40 N	135.33 E
Higashine	92	38.26 N	140.24 E
Higashinose	270	34.55 N	135.30 E
Higashiōizumi ➜[8]	268	35.45 N	139.36 E
Higashiōsaka	96	34.39 N	135.35 E
Higashishirakawa	94	35.39 N	137.19 E
Higashisumiyoshi ➜[8]	270	34.37 N	135.32 E
Higashitokonoo-san ∧	96	35.25 N	134.55 E
Higashitsuno	96	33.23 N	133.02 E
Higashiura	94	34.59 N	136.58 E
Higashiyama ➜[8]	270	34.52 N	135.48 E
Higashiyodogawa ➜[8]	270	34.44 N	135.29 E
Higashiyoshino	94	34.24 N	135.58 E
Higbee	194	39.19 N	92.31 W
Higganum	207	41.30 N	72.34 W
Higgins	196	36.07 N	100.02 W
Higgins, Mount ∧	224	48.19 N	121.45 W
Higgins Lake ⊜	190	44.30 N	84.45 W
Higginsport	218	38.47 N	83.58 W
Higginsville, Austl.	162	31.45 S	121.43 E
Higginsville, Mo., U.S.	194	39.04 N	93.43 W
Higgs' Hope	158	29.19 S	23.16 E
Higham Ferrers	42	52.18 N	0.36 W
Higham Upshire	260	51.26 N	0.28 E
Highbank	222	31.10 N	96.50 W
High Bank Creek ≃	216	42.37 N	85.11 W
High Bar Indian Reserve ➜[4]	182	51.06 N	122.00 W
High Beach	260	51.39 N	0.02 E
High Bentham	44	54.08 N	2.30 W
Highbridge, Eng., U.K.	42	51.13 N	2.49 W
High Bridge, N.J., U.S.	210	40.40 N	74.54 W
Highbury	164	16.25 S	143.09 E
Highcliff	279b	40.32 N	80.03 W
Higher Ballam	262	53.46 N	2.59 W
Higher Broughton ➜[8]	262	53.30 N	2.15 W
Higher Hogshead ∧[2]	262	53.42 N	2.09 W
Higher Penwortham	262	53.45 N	2.44 W
Higher Walton, Eng., U.K.	262	53.45 N	2.38 W
Higher Walton, Eng., U.K.	262	53.22 N	2.37 W
Higher Whitley	262	53.19 N	2.35 W
Highett	274b	37.57 S	145.03 E
High Falls	210	41.50 N	74.08 W
High Falls L	212	43.56 N	75.23 W
Highfield	154	17.50 S	31.00 E
High Force L	44	54.38 N	2.13 W
Highgate	214	42.30 N	81.49 W
Highgate Center	206	44.58 N	73.03 W
Highgate Springs	206	44.58 N	72.59 W
Highgrove	228	34.01 N	117.20 W
High Halstow	260	51.27 N	0.34 E
High Hesket	44	54.48 N	2.48 W
High Hill	219	38.53 N	91.23 W
High Hill ∧[2]	276	40.49 N	73.25 W
High Hill ≃, Can.	184	56.45 N	110.30 W
High Hill ≃, Man., Can.	184	55.52 N	94.42 W
High Hill Lake ⊜	184	55.34 N	95.40 W
High Island I	190	45.42 N	85.40 W
High Island Creek ≃	190	44.35 N	93.54 W
High Knob ∧	188	39.08 N	78.26 W
Highland, Calif., U.S.	228	34.08 N	117.12 W
Highland, Ill., U.S.	219	38.44 N	89.41 W
Highland, Ind., U.S.	216	41.33 N	87.27 W
Highland, Kans., U.S.	198	39.52 N	95.16 W
Highland, Md., U.S.	208	39.11 N	76.57 W
Highland, Mich., U.S.	281	42.38 N	83.37 W
Highland, N.Y., U.S.	210	41.43 N	73.58 W
Highland, Ohio, U.S.	218	39.21 N	83.36 W
Highland, Pa., U.S.	279b	40.33 N	80.04 W
Highland □[4]	46	57.40 N	5.00 W
Highland □[6]	218	39.12 N	83.37 W
Highland Beach	220	26.25 N	80.04 W
Highland City	220	27.58 N	81.53 W
Highland Creek ≃	226	38.24 N	121.14 W
Highland Creek Park ♠	275b	43.47 N	79.12 W
Highland Falls	210	41.22 N	73.58 W
Highland Heights, Ky., U.S.	218	39.04 N	84.27 W
Highland Heights, Ohio, U.S.	214	41.32 N	81.29 W
Highland Hills	278	41.52 N	88.01 W
Highland Home	194	31.57 N	86.19 W
Highland Lake, Ill., U.S.	278	42.21 N	88.04 W
Highland Lake, Mass., U.S.	283	42.41 N	72.37 W
Highland Lake, N.Y., U.S.	210	41.32 N	74.51 W
Highland Lake ⊜, Conn., U.S.	207	41.54 N	73.06 W
Highland Lake ⊜, Ill., U.S.	278	42.22 N	88.04 W
Highland Lake ⊜, N.J., U.S.	276	41.10 N	74.28 W
Highland Lakes	210	41.10 N	74.28 W
Highland Park, Ill., U.S.	216	42.11 N	87.48 W
Highland Park, Md., U.S.	284c	38.54 N	76.54 W
Highland Park, Mich., U.S.	216	42.24 N	83.06 W
Highland Park, N.J., U.S.	210	40.30 N	74.26 W
Highland Park, Pa., U.S.	210	40.38 N	77.35 W
Highland Park, Tex., U.S.	222	32.50 N	96.48 W
Highland Park ➜[8]	280	34.07 N	118.13 W
Highland Park ♠, Mass., U.S.	283	42.30 N	70.55 W
Highland Park ♠, Pa., U.S.	279b	40.29 N	79.55 W
Highland Peak ∧	226	38.33 N	119.45 W
Highland Point ≻	220	25.30 N	81.12 W
Highlands, N.J., U.S.	208	40.24 N	73.59 W
Highlands, N.C., U.S.	192	35.03 N	83.12 W
Highlands, Tex., U.S.	222	29.49 N	95.04 W
Highlands □[6]	220	27.20 N	81.16 W
Highlands Hammock State Park ♠	220	27.28 N	81.33 W
Highland Silver Lake ⊜[1]	219	38.47 N	89.39 W
Highlands North ➜[8]	273d	26.09 S	28.05 E
Highland Springs	208	37.33 N	77.20 W
Highlands Reservoir ⊜[1]	222	29.50 N	95.02 W
Highland State Recreation Area ♠	216	42.39 N	83.33 W
Highlandtown ➜[8]	284b	39.17 N	76.33 W
Highland Village	222	29.45 N	95.27 W
High Laver	260	51.45 N	0.13 E
High Legh	262	53.21 N	2.27 W
Highmore	198	44.31 N	99.27 W
High Ongar	260	51.43 N	0.16 E
High Park ♠	275b	43.39 N	79.28 W
High Peak □[8]	262	53.23 N	1.55 W
High Peak ∧, Pil.	116	15.29 N	120.07 E
High Peak ∧, N.Y., U.S.	210	42.09 N	74.05 W
High Peak ➜[1]	262	53.24 N	1.50 W
High Plains ≚	178	38.30 N	103.00 W
High Point, Fla., U.S.	220	27.55 N	82.42 W
High Point, N.C., U.S.	192	35.58 N	80.01 W
Highpoint, Ohio, U.S.	218	39.14 N	84.24 W
High Point ∧, N.J., U.S.	210	41.19 N	74.40 W
High Point ∧, Wyo., U.S.	202	41.37 N	107.47 W
High Point State Park ♠	210	41.18 N	74.41 W
High Prairie	182	55.26 N	116.29 W
High Ridge	219	38.27 N	90.32 W
High River	182	50.35 N	113.52 W
High Rock	192	26.36 N	76.18 W
High Rock ∧	188	39.33 N	79.06 W
Highrock Indian Reserve ➜[4]	184	55.54 N	100.30 W
Highrock Lake ⊜, Man., Can.	184	55.45 N	100.30 W
Highrock Lake ⊜, Sask., Can.	184	57.04 N	105.30 W
High Rock Lake ⊜[1]	192	35.40 N	80.17 W
High Seat ∧	44	54.24 N	2.18 W
High Spire	208	40.13 N	76.48 W
High Springs	192	29.50 N	82.36 W
High Street ∧	44	54.29 N	2.52 W
Hightown	262	53.32 N	3.04 W
Hightstown	208	40.16 N	74.31 W
High View	210	41.33 N	74.27 W
Highwater	206	45.01 N	72.26 W
Highway City	226	36.49 N	119.54 W
High Willhays ∧	42	50.41 N	3.59 W
Highwood, Ill., U.S.	216	42.13 N	87.48 W
Highwood, Mont., U.S.	202	47.35 N	110.47 W
Highwood ≃	182	50.49 N	113.47 W
Highwood Baldy ∧	202	47.27 N	110.37 W
Highwood Creek ≃	202	47.40 N	111.00 W

Symbols in the index entries represent the broad categories identified in the key at the right. Symbols with superior numbers (⩘[2]) identify subcategories (see complete key on page I · 30).

Kartensymbole in dem Registerverzeichnis stellen die rechts in Schlüssel erklärten Kategorien dar. Symbole mit hochgestellten Ziffern (⩘[2]) bezeichnen Unterabteilungen einer Kategorie (vgl. vollständiger Schlüssel auf Seite I · 30).

Los símbolos incluídos en el texto del índice representan las grandes categorias identificadas con la clave a la derecha. Los símbolos con numeros en su parte superior (⩘[2]) identifican las subcategorías (véase la clave completa en la página I · 30).

Les symboles de l'index représentent les catégories indiquées dans la légende à droite. Les symboles suivis d'un indice (⩘[2]) représentent des sous-catégories (voir légende complète à la page I · 30).

Os símbolos incluídos no texto do índice representam as grandes categorias identificadas com a chave à direita. Os símbolos com números em sua parte superior (⩘[2]) identificam as subcategorias (veja-se a chave completa à página I · 30).

Symbol	English	Deutsch	Español	Français	Português
∧	Mountain	Berg	Montaña	Montagne	Montanha
⩘	Mountains	Berge	Montañas	Montagnes	Montanhas
)(	Pass	Pass	Paso	Col	Passo
∨	Valley, Canyon	Tal, Cañon	Valle, Cañón	Vallée, Canyon	Vale, Canhão
≚	Plain	Ebene	Llano	Plaine	Planície
≻	Cape	Kap	Cabo	Cap	Cabo
I	Island	Insel	Isla	Île	Ilha
II	Islands	Inseln	Islas	Îles	Ilhas
⏏	Other Topographic Features	Andere Topographische Objekte	Otros Elementos Topográficos	Autres données topographiques	Outros Elementos Topográficos

ESPAÑOL — Nombre | Página | Lat.°′ | Long.°′ W=Oeste

Highwood Mountains ⋀ 202 47.25 N 110.30 W
Highworth 42 51.38 N 1.43 W
High Wycombe 42 51.38 N 0.46 W
Higlet 154 1.04 S 40.19 E
Higuera Blanca 234 19.42 N 105.10 W
Higuera de Zaragoza 232 25.59 N 109.16 W
Higuera Gorda 234 22.04 N 104.29 W
Higueras 196 25.58 N 100.01 W
Higüero, Punta ≻ 240m 18.22 N 67.16 W
Higuerote 246 10.29 N 66.06 W
Higuito ≃ 236 14.43 N 88.40 W
Hihyā 142 30.40 N 31.36 E
Hii ≃ 96 35.26 N 132.54 E
Hiiumaa ▮ 76 58.52 N 22.40 E
Hījānah, Buḥayrat al- ◎ 132 33.18 N 36.36 E
Híjar 34 41.10 N 0.27 W
Ḥijāz, Jabal al- ⋀ 144 19.45 N 41.55 E
Hiji 96 33.22 N 131.32 E
Hiji ≃ 96 33.36 N 132.29 E
Hijikawa 96 33.27 N 132.41 E
Hikami 96 35.10 N 135.02 E
Hikari, Nihon 94 35.39 N 140.30 E
Hikari, Nihon 96 33.58 N 131.56 E
Hikarigaoka 268 35.50 N 139.58 E
Hikawa 96 35.25 N 132.50 E
Hikawa Shrine ʊ[1] 268 35.54 N 139.38 E
Hiketa 96 34.13 N 134.24 E
Hiki ≃ 96 33.33 N 135.27 E
Hikigawa 96 33.34 N 135.27 E
Hikimi 96 34.34 N 132.01 E
Hikimi ≃ 96 34.37 N 131.48 E
Hikiura 270 34.33 N 134.58 E
Hikone 94 35.15 N 136.15 E
Hikone-jō ⊥ 94 35.15 N 136.14 E
Hiko-san ∧ 96 33.27 N 130.54 E
Hikueru ▮[1] 14 17.36 S 142.37 W
Hikurangi 172 35.36 S 174.18 E
Hikurangi ∧ 172 38.21 S 176.51 E
Hikutaia 172 37.17 S 175.39 E
Hikutivake 174v 18.56 S 169.53 W
Hila 112 7.35 S 127.24 E
Hilaban Island ▮ 116 12.03 N 125.34 E
Hilāl, Jabal ⋀ 132 34.40 N 31.00 E
Hilāl, Ra's al- ≻ 146 32.57 N 22.10 E
Hilbersdorf 54 50.55 N 13.23 E
Hilbert 190 44.09 N 88.10 W
Hilbre Islands ▮▮ 262 53.23 N 3.13 W
Hilbre Point ≻ 262 53.23 N 3.12 W
Hilchenbach 56 51.00 N 8.06 E
Hilda 184 50.28 N 110.03 W
Hildburghausen 54 50.25 N 10.44 E
Hilden 56 51.10 N 6.56 E
Hildenborough 260 51.13 N 0.15 E
Hilders 56 50.34 N 10.00 E
Hildesheim 52 52.09 N 9.57 E
Hildesheim □[6] 52 51.40 N 10.00 E
Hildreth 198 40.20 N 99.03 W
Hilgen 263 51.06 N 7.09 E
Hiligeo 114 1.22 N 97.10 E
Hiliotaluwa 114 0.44 N 97.53 E
Hill □[6] 222 32.02 N 97.10 W
Hillaby, Mount ∧ 241g 13.12 N 59.35 W
Hill Air Force Base ■ 202 41.05 N 111.58 W
Hillandale, S. Afr. 158 33.06 S 20.36 E
Hillandale, Md., U.S. 284c 39.01 N 76.58 W
Hill Bank 232 17.35 N 88.42 W
Hillbrow ◆[8] 273d 26.11 S 28.03 E
Hillburn 210 41.08 N 74.10 W
Hill City, Kans., U.S. 198 39.22 N 99.51 W
Hill City, Minn., U.S. 190 46.59 N 93.36 W
Hill City, S. Dak., U.S. 198 43.56 N 103.35 W
Hill Creek ≃ 200 39.55 N 109.40 W
Hillcrest, Ill., U.S. 216 41.57 N 89.04 W
Hillcrest, N.Y., U.S. 210 42.09 N 75.53 W
Hillcrest, N.Y., U.S. 210 41.09 N 74.02 W
Hillcrest Center 228 35.23 N 118.57 W
Hillcrest Heights 284c 38.52 N 76.57 W
Hillcrest Mines 182 49.34 N 114.23 W
Hillcrest Orchard 216 41.51 N 83.29 W
Hillcrest Park 226 38.07 N 122.16 W
Hill Cumorah ⊥ 210 43.01 N 77.15 W
Hille, B.R.D. 52 52.20 N 8.44 E
Hille, Sve. 40 60.44 N 17.11 E
Hillegom 52 52.18 N 4.35 E
Hillegossen 52 51.59 N 8.37 E
Hillen ◆[8] 263 51.37 N 7.13 E
Hillerød 41 55.56 N 12.19 E
Hillers Creek ≃ 219 38.38 N 91.54 W
Hillesheim 56 50.18 N 6.38 E
Hilli 124 25.17 N 89.01 E
Hilliard, Fla., U.S. 192 30.41 N 81.55 W
Hilliard, Ohio, U.S. 214 40.02 N 83.10 W
Hilliards 214 41.05 N 79.50 W
Hillingdon ◆[8] 260 51.32 N 0.27 W
Hillisburg 216 40.17 N 86.20 W
Hill Island Lake ◎ 176 60.29 N 109.50 W
Hillister 194 30.40 N 94.23 W
Hillman 190 45.04 N 83.54 W
Hillmersdorf 54 51.42 N 13.29 E
Hill of Fearn 46 57.45 N 3.56 W
Hills 198 43.32 N 96.21 W
Hills and Dales 214 39.42 N 84.13 W
Hillsboro, Ill., U.S. 219 39.09 N 89.29 W
Hillsboro, Kans., U.S. 198 38.21 N 97.12 W
Hillsboro, Ky., U.S. 218 38.18 N 83.40 W
Hillsboro, Md., U.S. 208 38.55 N 75.50 W
Hillsboro, Mo., U.S. 219 38.14 N 90.34 W
Hillsboro, N.H., U.S. 188 43.07 N 71.54 W
Hillsboro, N. Mex., U.S. 200 32.55 N 107.34 W
Hillsboro, N. Dak., U.S. 198 47.26 N 97.03 W
Hillsboro, Ohio, U.S. 218 39.12 N 83.37 W
Hillsboro, Oreg., U.S. 224 45.31 N 122.59 W
Hillsboro, Tex., U.S. 222 32.01 N 97.08 W
Hillsboro, Wis., U.S. 190 43.39 N 90.21 W
Hillsboro Beach 220 26.18 N 80.05 W
Hillsboro Canal Ξ 220 26.19 N 80.05 W
Hillsborough, N.B., Can. 186 45.56 N 64.39 W
Hillsborough, N. Ire., U.K. 48 54.28 N 6.05 W
Hillsborough, Calif., U.S. 226 37.34 N 122.20 W
Hillsborough, N.C., U.S. 192 36.05 N 79.07 W
Hillsborough □[6], Fla., U.S. 220 27.55 N 82.15 W
Hillsborough □[6], N.H., U.S. 207 42.49 N 71.41 W
Hillsborough ≃ 220 27.56 N 82.27 W
Hillsborough, Cape ≻ 166 20.54 S 149.03 E
Hillsborough Bay C, P.E.I., Can. 186 46.10 N 63.05 W
Hillsborough Bay C, Fla., U.S. 220 27.52 N 82.27 W
Hillsborough River State Park ♠ 220 28.09 N 82.14 W
Hillsburgh 212 43.47 N 80.09 W
Hills Creek Lake ◎[1] 202 43.40 N 122.26 W
Hillsdale, Mich., U.S. 216 41.55 N 84.38 W
Hillsdale, N.J., U.S. 276 41.00 N 74.02 W
Hillsdale, N.Y., U.S. 210 42.11 N 73.31 W
Hillsdale, Pa., U.S. 214 40.45 N 78.53 W
Hillsdale □[6] 216 41.53 N 84.36 W
Hillsdale ◆[9] 282 37.32 N 122.18 W
Hillsdale Park ♠ 284b 39.19 N 76.42 W
Hills Flat 226 39.14 N 121.03 W
Hillsgrove 210 41.27 N 76.42 W
Hillside, Austl. 162 21.44 S 119.23 E
Hillside, Ill., U.S. 278 41.52 N 87.54 W
Hillside, Md., U.S. 284c 38.52 N 76.55 W
Hillside, N.J., U.S. 276 40.42 N 74.13 W
Hillside ◆[8] 276 40.42 N 73.47 W
Hillside Gardens 216 42.16 N 84.27 W
Hillside Heights 285 39.41 N 75.41 W
Hillston 166 33.29 S 145.32 E

FRANÇAIS — Nom | Page | Lat.°′ | Long.°′ W=Ouest

Hillsville, Pa., U.S. 214 41.01 N 80.30 W
Hillsville, Va., U.S. 192 36.46 N 80.44 W
Hillswick 46a 60.28 N 1.30 W
Hilltop 208 39.49 N 75.04 W
Hilltop Center ◆[9] 282 37.59 N 122.19 W
Hilltown, N. Ire., U.K. 48 54.12 N 6.08 W
Hilltown, Pa., U.S. 208 40.20 N 75.14 W
Hillview 219 39.27 N 90.33 W
Hillview Reservoir ◎[1] 276 40.55 N 73.52 W
Hillwood 284c 38.52 N 77.10 W
Hilmar 226 37.25 N 120.51 W
Hilo 229d 19.43 N 155.05 W
Hilo Bay C 229d 19.44 N 155.05 W
Hilonghilong, Mount ∧ 116 9.06 N 125.44 E
Hilongos 116 10.23 N 124.45 E
Hilo Point ≻ 174n 15.02 N 145.36 E
Hilpotstein 60 49.12 N 11.12 E
Hilpsford Point ≻ 44 54.03 N 3.12 W
Hils ∧ 52 51.55 N 9.40 E
Hilshire Village 222 29.49 N 95.26 W
Hiltaba, Mount ∧ 162 32.09 S 135.03 E
Hilter 52 52.08 N 8.08 E
Hilton, N.Y., U.S. 210 43.17 N 77.48 W
Hilton, Pa., U.S. 208 40.00 N 76.49 W
Hilton Head Island ▮ 192 32.12 N 80.45 W
Hiltpolstein 60 49.40 N 11.19 E
Hiltrop ◆[8] 263 51.30 N 7.15 E
Hiltrup 52 51.54 N 7.38 E
Hilvarenbeek 52 51.29 N 5.09 E
Hilversum 52 52.14 N 5.10 E
Hima 192 37.07 N 83.47 W
Himachal Pradesh □[8] 120 32.00 N 77.00 E
Himalayas ⋀ 120 28.00 N 84.00 E
Himalchuli ∧ 124 28.25 N 84.39 E
Himamaylan 116 10.06 N 122.52 E
Himanka 26 64.04 N 23.39 E
Himarë 38 40.07 N 19.44 E
Himatnagar 120 23.36 N 72.57 E
Himberg 264b 48.05 N 16.26 E
Hime ≃ 94 37.02 N 137.49 E
Himeji 96 34.49 N 134.42 E
Hime-shima ▮ 96 33.43 N 131.40 E
Himeville 158 29.44 S 29.31 E
Himi 94 36.51 N 136.59 E
Himmelbjerget ⋀[2] 41 56.06 N 9.42 E
Himmelgeist ◆[8] 263 51.10 N 6.49 E
Himmelpforten 52 53.36 N 9.18 E
Himmelsthür 52 52.09 N 9.55 E
Himmerfjärden C[2] 40 59.00 N 17.43 E
Himmerland ◆[1] 26 56.50 N 9.45 E
Himmetdede 130 38.55 N 35.07 E
Himrod 210 42.35 N 76.57 W
Ḥimṣ (Homs) 130 34.44 N 36.43 E
Ḥimṣ □[8] 130 34.15 N 38.00 E
Ḥimṣ, Baḥrat ◎[1] 130 34.39 N 36.34 E
Hinabangan 116 11.42 N 125.04 E
Hīnah 132 33.21 N 35.56 E
Hinako, Kepulauan ▮▮ 114 0.52 N 97.21 E
Hinase 96 34.44 N 134.16 E
Hinatuan 116 8.23 N 126.20 E
Hinatuan Island ▮ 116 9.47 N 125.43 E
Hinatuan Passage ⋓ 116 9.45 N 125.47 E
Hinche 238 19.09 N 72.01 W
Hinchinbrook Entrance ⋓ 180 60.25 N 146.50 W
Hinchinbrook Island ▮, Austl. 166 18.23 S 146.17 E
Hinchinbrook Island ▮, Alaska, U.S. 180 60.22 N 146.30 W
Hinckley, Eng., U.K. 42 52.33 N 1.21 W
Hinckley, Ill., U.S. 216 41.46 N 88.38 W
Hinckley, Minn., U.S. 190 46.01 N 92.56 W
Hinckley, Ohio, U.S. 214 41.14 N 81.45 W
Hinckley, Utah, U.S. 200 39.20 N 112.40 W
Hinckley Reservoir ◎[1] 210 43.20 N 75.05 W
Hincks, Murlong, and Nicholls National Park ♠ 166 33.50 S 136.00 E
Hindan ≃ 272a 28.30 N 77.27 E
Hindang 116 10.26 N 124.44 E
Hindaun 124 26.43 N 77.01 E
Hindelang 58 47.30 N 10.22 E
Hindelbank 58 47.03 N 7.32 E
Hindeloopen 52 52.56 N 5.24 E
Hindenburg → Zabrze 30 50.18 N 18.46 E
Hindhead 42 51.07 N 0.44 W
Hindley 262 53.32 N 2.35 W
Hindley Green 262 53.31 N 2.32 W
Hindman 192 37.20 N 82.59 W
Hindmarsh, Lake ◎ 166 36.03 S 141.55 E
Hindmarsh Island ▮ 168b 35.32 S 138.52 E
Hindmarsh Valley 168b 35.30 S 138.38 E
Hindon 42 51.06 N 2.08 W
Hinds 172 44.00 S 171.34 E
Hindsholm ▮ 41 55.33 N 10.40 E
Hinds Lake ◎ 186 48.57 N 57.00 W
Hindubāgh 120 30.49 N 67.45 E
Hindu Kush ⋀ 120 36.00 N 71.30 E
Hindu Malkot 123 30.09 N 73.55 E
Hindupur 122 13.49 N 77.29 E
Hines 202 43.34 N 119.05 W
Hines Creek 182 56.15 N 118.36 W
Hines Creek ≃ 182 55.54 N 118.37 W
Hines Peak ∧ 228 34.31 N 119.05 W
Hinesville 192 31.51 N 81.36 W
Hinganghāt 122 20.34 N 78.50 E
Hingatungan 116 10.35 N 125.11 E
Hingham 207 42.14 N 70.53 W
Hingham Bay C 207 42.17 N 70.55 W
Hingham Harbor C 283 42.15 N 70.53 W
Hingol ≃ 128 25.23 N 65.28 E
Hingoli 122 19.43 N 77.09 E
Hinigaran 116 10.17 N 122.51 E
Hınıs 130 39.22 N 41.44 E
Hınıs ≃ 84 39.18 N 42.12 E
Hinish Bay C 46 56.28 N 6.50 W
Hinkley 228 34.56 N 117.12 W
Hinkson Creek ≃ 219 38.56 N 92.23 W
Hinkston Creek ≃ 218 38.18 N 84.14 W
Hinnerjoki 26 61.00 N 22.00 E
Hinnerup 41 56.16 N 10.04 E
Hinnøya ▮ 24 68.30 N 16.00 E
Hino, Nihon 94 35.41 N 139.24 E
Hino, Nihon 94 35.00 N 136.15 E
Hino, Nihon 96 35.14 N 133.27 E
Hino ≃, Nihon 94 35.09 N 136.02 E
Hino ≃, Nihon 94 36.04 N 136.11 E
Hino ≃, Nihon 96 35.27 N 133.23 E
Hinoba-an 116 9.35 N 122.28 E
Hinode 94 35.45 N 139.14 E
Hinoemata 94 37.01 N 139.23 E
Hinohara 94 35.43 N 139.09 E
Hinojosa del Duque 34 38.30 N 5.09 W
Hinokage 92 32.39 N 131.24 E
Hino-misaki ≻, Nihon 96 33.53 N 135.04 E
Hinomi-saki ≻, Nihon 96 35.26 N 132.38 E
Hinsbeck 56 51.21 N 6.17 E
Hinsdale, Ill., U.S. 216 41.48 N 87.56 W
Hinsdale, Mass., U.S. 207 42.26 N 73.08 W
Hinsdale, Mont., U.S. 202 48.24 N 107.05 W
Hinsdale, N.H., U.S. 188 42.47 N 72.29 W
Hinsdale, N.Y., U.S. 210 42.10 N 78.23 W
Hinsel ◆[8] 263 51.26 N 7.05 E
Hinsen ◎ 40 60.39 N 16.05 E
Hinte 52 53.25 N 7.11 E
Hinterbichl 64 47.01 N 12.20 E
Hinterbrühl 264b 48.05 N 16.15 E
Hinterhermsdorf 54 50.55 N 14.22 E
Hinterrhein 58 46.32 N 9.12 E
Hinterrhein ≃ 58 46.49 N 9.25 E
Hinterriss 64 47.28 N 11.28 E
Hintersdorf 264b 48.18 N 16.13 E

PORTUGUÊS — Nome | Página | Lat.°′ | Long.°′ W=Oeste

Hintersee, B.R.D. 64 47.36 N 12.50 E
Hintersee, D.D.R. 54 53.37 N 14.16 E
Hintersee, Öst. 64 47.42 N 13.17 E
Hinterstoder 61 47.41 N 14.09 E
Hintertux 64 47.07 N 11.41 E
Hinterweidenthal 56 49.12 N 7.45 E
Hinterzarten 58 47.54 N 8.06 E
Hinton, Alta., Can. 182 53.25 N 117.34 W
Hinton, Mo., U.S. 219 39.03 N 92.21 W
Hinton, Okla., U.S. 196 35.28 N 98.21 W
Hinton, W. Va., U.S. 192 37.41 N 80.53 W
Hi-numa ◎ 94 36.16 N 140.30 E
Hinuma ≃ 94 36.16 N 140.28 E
Hinundayan 116 10.21 N 125.15 E
Hinwil 58 47.18 N 8.51 E
Hinzik 84 40.08 N 40.58 E
Hípico, Club ♠ 286e 33.28 S 70.41 W
Hipólito 232 25.41 N 101.26 W
Hipólito Yrigoyen 252 32.55 S 66.20 W
Hippolytushoef 52 52.54 N 4.57 E
Hirado 92 33.22 N 129.33 E
Hirado-shima ▮ 92 33.20 N 129.30 E
Hiraiwa-hana ≻ 174f 24.48 N 141.18 E
Hiraizumi 92 38.59 N 141.07 E
Hirakata, Nihon 96 34.48 N 135.38 E
Hirakata, Nihon 268 35.56 N 139.33 E
Hirakawa, Nihon 268 35.23 N 140.03 E
Hirakawa, Nihon 270 34.52 N 135.47 E
Hirakubo 175d 24.35 N 124.19 E
Hīrākud 122 21.31 N 83.57 E
Hīrākud ◎[1] 120 21.31 N 83.52 E
Hiram, Maine, U.S. 188 43.53 N 70.49 W
Hiram, Ohio, U.S. 214 41.19 N 81.09 W
Hiraman ≃ 154 1.07 S 39.55 E
Hiran □[4] 144 4.10 N 45.20 E
Hirane-zaki ≻ 96 33.43 N 132.08 E
Hirao 96 33.56 N 132.04 E
Hirao-dai ♠ 96 33.48 N 130.51 E
Hiraoka → Higashiōsaka 96 34.39 N 135.35 E
Hīrāpur 124 24.22 N 79.13 E
Hirara 175d 24.48 N 125.17 E
Hirata, Nihon 94 35.15 N 136.38 E
Hirata, Nihon 96 35.26 N 132.49 E
Hiratsuka 94 35.19 N 139.21 E
Hiraya 94 35.19 N 137.37 E
Hirfanlı Barajı ◆[6] 130 39.18 N 33.29 E
Hirhafok 148 23.49 N 5.45 E
Hiriyūr 122 13.58 N 76.36 E
Ḥirjillah 132 33.22 N 36.18 E
Hîrlău 38 47.25 N 26.54 E
Hīrmand, Hāmūn-e ◎ 128 30.45 N 61.10 E
Hirokawa, Nihon 96 33.15 N 130.32 E
Hirokawa, Nihon 96 34.01 N 135.11 E
Hirok Sāmi 128 26.02 N 63.25 E
Hiromi 96 32.50 N 132.43 E
Hiroo 92a 42.17 N 143.19 E
Hirooka 268 35.15 N 140.04 E
Hirosaki 92 40.35 N 140.28 E
Hiroschima → Hiroshima 96 34.24 N 132.27 E
Hirose 96 35.22 N 133.10 E
Hiroshima 96 34.24 N 132.27 E
Hiroshima □[5] 96 34.30 N 133.00 E
Hiro-shima ▮ 96 34.22 N 133.43 E
Hiroshima-wan C 96 34.06 N 132.20 E
Hirosima → Hiroshima 96 34.24 N 132.27 E
Hirota 270 34.45 N 135.21 E
Hirsau 56 48.44 N 8.44 E
Hirschaid 56 49.49 N 10.59 E
Hirschau 60 49.33 N 11.57 E
Hirschbach 54 50.33 N 10.44 E
Hirschberg, D.D.R. 54 50.24 N 11.49 E
Hirschberg → Jelenia Góra, Pol. 30 50.55 N 15.46 E
Hirschfeld 54 51.23 N 13.37 E
Hirschfelde, D.D.R. 54 50.57 N 14.53 E
Hirschfelde, D.D.R. 264a 52.38 N 13.48 E
Hirschhorn 56 49.27 N 8.53 E
Hirschstetten ◆[8] 264b 48.14 N 16.29 E
Hirshfeld Brook ≃ 276 40.57 N 74.02 W
Hirsingue 58 47.35 N 7.15 E
Hirson 50 49.55 N 4.05 E
Hîrşova 38 44.41 N 27.57 E
Hirtshals 26 57.35 N 9.58 E
Hirtzfelden 58 47.55 N 7.27 E
Hirukawa 94 35.31 N 137.23 E
Hiru-zen ∧ 96 35.19 N 133.40 E
Hirwaun 42 51.45 N 3.30 W
Hisābpur 272b 22.51 N 88.32 E
Hisai, Nihon 94 34.40 N 136.28 E
Hisai, Nihon 270 34.25 N 135.28 E
Hisār 123 29.10 N 75.43 E
Hisarköy 130 39.48 N 29.37 E
Hisarönü 130 41.33 N 32.02 E
Ḥisbān 132 31.48 N 35.48 E
Hisiu 164 9.05 S 146.45 E
Ḥismā ≚ 128 29.00 N 35.40 E
Ḥiṣn al-'Abr 144 16.05 N 47.22 E
Ḥiṣn al-Qarn 144 15.11 N 49.05 E
Hispaniola ▮ 238 19.00 N 71.00 W
Histon 42 52.15 N 0.06 E
Hisua 124 24.50 N 85.25 E
Ḥisyah 130 34.24 N 36.45 E
Hīt 128 33.38 N 42.49 E
Hita 96 33.19 N 130.56 E
Hitachi 94 36.36 N 140.39 E
Hitachi-ōta 94 36.32 N 140.31 E
Hitati → Hitachi 94 36.36 N 140.39 E
Hitchcock 222 29.21 N 95.01 W
Hitchin 42 51.57 N 0.17 W
Hitchins 218 38.17 N 82.55 W
Hither Green ◆[8] 260 51.27 N 0.01 W
Hither Hills State Park ♠ 207 41.01 N 72.01 W
Hitiaa 174s 17.36 S 149.18 W
Hitokura 270 34.55 N 135.25 E
Hitotsubashi University ʊ[2] 268 35.42 N 139.27 E
Hitoyoshi 92 32.13 N 130.45 E
Hitra ▮ 26 63.33 N 8.45 E
Hittarp 41 56.06 N 12.38 E
Hittisau 58 47.27 N 9.57 E
Hitzacker 54 53.09 N 11.02 E
Hitze-Berge ⋀[2] 264a 52.35 N 13.07 E
Hiuchiga-take ∧ 94 36.57 N 139.17 E
Hiuchi-nada ⍑[2] 96 34.05 N 133.20 E
Hiūnchuli Pātan ∧ 124 28.50 N 82.37 E
Hiva Oa ▮ 174x 9.45 S 139.00 W
Hi Vista 228 34.44 N 117.47 W
Hivris 130 38.18 N 42.10 E
Hiw ▮ 175f 13.10 S 166.35 E
Hiwa 96 34.59 N 132.59 E
Hiwannee 194 31.43 N 88.48 W
Hiwasa 96 33.44 N 134.32 E
Hiwassee ≃ 192 35.19 N 84.47 W
Hiwassee Lake ◎[1] 192 35.10 N 84.05 W
Hixon 182 53.27 N 122.36 W
Hixson 192 35.09 N 85.14 W
Hiyoshi, Nihon 94 35.53 N 137.45 E
Hiyoshi, Nihon 96 35.09 N 135.31 E
Hiyoshi, Nihon 96 33.20 N 132.48 E
Hiyoshi ◆[8] 268 35.33 N 139.39 E
Ḥiyyon, Naḥal V 132 30.12 N 35.07 E
Hizaonna 174m 26.24 N 127.50 E
Hjälmare kanal Ξ 40 59.24 N 15.56 E
Hjälmaren ◎ 40 59.15 N 15.45 E
Hjälmaresund ⋓ 40 59.15 N 16.06 E
Hjarnø ▮ 41 55.50 N 10.05 E
Hjelm ▮ 41 56.08 N 10.48 E
Hjelmelandsvågen 26 59.14 N 6.11 E
Hjeltefjorden C[2] 26 60.40 N 4.55 E
Hjembæk 41 55.42 N 11.25 E
Hjo 26 58.18 N 14.17 E
Hjøllund 41 56.05 N 9.25 E
Hjordkær 41 55.01 N 9.19 E
Hjørring 26 57.28 N 9.59 E
Hjort Basin ✧[1] 9 59.00 S 158.00 E
Hjortkvarn 40 58.53 N 15.25 E
Hjørundfjorden C[2] 26 62.21 N 6.23 E
Hlabisa 158 28.08 S 31.52 E
Hlaingbwe 110 17.08 N 97.50 E
Hlatikulu 158 27.00 S 31.25 E
Hlegu 110 17.06 N 96.14 E
Hlinsko 30 49.45 N 15.55 E
Hlobane 158 27.42 S 31.00 E
Hlohovec 30 48.25 N 17.47 E
Hlohovice 60 49.53 N 13.38 E
Hluboká ⊥ 61 49.05 N 14.25 E
Hluboká nad Vltavou 61 49.03 N 14.27 E
Hlučín 30 49.54 N 18.12 E
Hluhluwe 158 28.01 S 32.15 E
Hluhluwe Game Reserve ◆[4] 158 28.05 S 32.04 E
Hluti 158 27.13 S 31.35 E
Hmawbi 110 17.06 N 96.02 E
Hnilec ≃ 30 48.53 N 21.01 E
Ho 150 6.35 N 0.30 E
Hoa-binh 110 20.50 N 105.20 E
Hoa-da 110 11.11 N 108.33 E
Hoagland 216 40.57 N 85.00 W
Hoagland Ditch Ξ 216 40.48 N 86.48 W
Hoai-nhon 110 14.26 N 109.01 E
Hoanib ≃ 156 19.27 S 12.46 E
Hoare Bay C 176 65.20 N 62.30 W
Hoarusib ≃ 156 19.03 S 12.36 E
Hoa-thoi 269c 10.44 N 106.35 E
Hoback ≃ 202 43.19 N 110.44 W
Hobart, Austl. 166 42.53 S 147.19 E
Hobart, Ind., U.S. 216 41.32 N 87.15 W
Hobart, N.Y., U.S. 210 42.22 N 74.40 W
Hobart, Okla., U.S. 196 35.01 N 99.06 W
Hobart, Wash., U.S. 224 47.25 N 121.58 W
Hobbs, Ind., U.S. 216 40.17 N 85.57 W
Hobbs, N. Mex., U.S. 196 32.42 N 103.08 W
Hobbs Coast •[2] 9 74.45 S 131.00 W
Hobe Sound 220 27.04 N 80.08 W
Hobgood 192 36.02 N 77.24 W
Hobo 246 2.35 N 75.27 W
Hoboken, Bel. 50 51.10 N 4.21 E
Hoboken, N.J., U.S. 210 40.45 N 74.03 W
Hobro 26 56.38 N 9.48 E
Hobson 202 47.00 N 109.52 W
Hobson Lake ◎ 182 52.30 N 120.20 W
Hobsons Bay C 274b 37.51 S 144.56 E
Hoburgen ≻ 26 56.55 N 18.07 E
Hocaköy, Tür. 130 41.03 N 30.17 E
Hocaköy, Tür. 130 37.08 N 32.16 E
Hocalar 130 38.34 N 30.00 E
Hocalı 130 38.41 N 27.41 E
Hochalmspitze ∧ 64 47.01 N 13.19 E
Hochandochtla Mountain ∧ 180 65.32 N 154.50 W
Höchberg 56 49.49 N 9.51 E
Hochburg 60 48.07 N 12.52 E
Hochdahl 56 51.13 N 6.56 E
Hochdorf 58 47.10 N 8.17 E
Höchenschwand 58 47.44 N 8.10 E
Hochfeiler (Gran Pilastro) ∧ 64 46.58 N 11.44 E
Hochfeld 156 21.28 S 17.58 E
Hochfeld ◆[8] 263 51.25 N 6.46 E
Hochfelden 56 48.45 N 7.34 E
Hochfilzen 64 47.28 N 12.37 E
Hochfinstermünz 58 46.56 N 10.29 E
Hochgern ∧ 64 47.45 N 12.30 E
Hochgolling ∧ 64 47.16 N 13.45 E
Hochheide 263 51.27 N 6.41 E
Hochheim, B.R.D. 56 50.01 N 8.20 E
Hochheim, Tex., U.S. 222 29.19 N 97.17 W
Hochkirch 54 51.09 N 14.34 E
Hochkönig ∧ 64 47.25 N 13.04 E
Hochkreuz ∧ 64 46.49 N 13.04 E
Hochlantsch ∧ 61 47.21 N 15.25 E
Hochlar ◆[8] 263 51.36 N 7.10 E
Hochlarmark ◆[8] 263 51.34 N 7.11 E
Hochneukirch 56 51.06 N 6.26 E
Hochobir ∧ 61 46.30 N 14.29 E
Hochreichart ∧ 61 47.22 N 14.41 E
Hochries ∧ 64 47.45 N 12.14 E
Hochschwab ∧ 61 47.37 N 15.09 E
Hochschwab ⋀ 61 47.36 N 15.05 E
Hochsimmer ∧ 56 50.21 N 7.12 E
Hochspeyer 56 49.26 N 7.54 E
Höchst, B.R.D. 56 49.48 N 8.59 E
Höchst, Öst. 58 47.28 N 9.38 E
Höchst ◆[8] 56 50.07 N 8.33 E
Höchstadt an der Aisch 56 49.42 N 10.44 E
Höchstädt an der Donau 56 48.36 N 10.34 E
Höchsten 263 51.27 N 7.29 E
Höchstenbach 56 50.38 N 7.44 E
Hochstuhl (Veliki Stol) ∧ 61 46.26 N 14.10 E
Hochtaunus, Naturpark ♠ 56 50.20 N 8.20 E
Hochtor)(64 47.05 N 12.51 E
Hoch'uan → Hechuan 107 30.00 N 106.16 E
Ho Chung 271d 22.22 N 114.14 E
Hochvogel ∧ 58 47.23 N 10.26 E
Hockanum ≃ 207 41.45 N 72.39 W
Hockenheim 56 49.19 N 8.33 E
Hockeroda 54 50.35 N 11.26 E
Hockessin 285 39.47 N 75.42 W
Hocking ≃ 188 39.12 N 81.45 W
Hockley, Eng., U.K. 260 51.37 N 0.40 E
Hockley, Tex., U.S. 222 30.02 N 95.51 W
Hockomock Swamp ☷ 283 41.59 N 71.05 W
Hodal 124 27.54 N 77.22 E
Hōdatsu-san ∧ 94 36.47 N 136.49 E
Hodder ≃ 44 53.50 N 2.25 W
Hoddesdon 260 51.46 N 0.01 W
Hoddlesden 262 53.42 N 2.26 W
Hodeida → Al-Ḥudaydah 144 14.48 N 42.57 E
Hodenhagen 52 52.46 N 9.35 E
Hodge 194 32.17 N 92.43 W
Hodgenville 194 37.34 N 85.44 W
Hodges, Lake ◎[1] 228 33.03 N 117.05 W
Hodges Brook ≃ 283 41.58 N 71.14 W
Hodges Creek ≃ 219 39.15 N 90.13 W
Hodges Hill ∧[2] 186 49.04 N 55.53 W
Hodgeville 184 50.08 N 106.58 W
Hodgkins 278 41.46 N 87.51 W
Hodgkins Seamount ✧[3] 16 53.20 N 135.45 W
Hodgson 184 51.13 N 97.34 W
Hodgson ≃ 164 14.48 S 134.35 E
Hodgson, Mount ∧[2] 162 22.26 S 121.10 E
Hodh ◆[1] 150 16.10 N 8.40 W
Hod HaSharon 132 32.09 N 34.53 E
Hódmezővásárhely 30 46.25 N 20.20 E
Hodmo ≃ 144 10.45 N 46.23 E
Hodna, Chott el ◎ 148 35.25 N 4.45 E
Hodna, Monts du ⋀ 148 35.50 N 4.50 E
Hodna, Plaine du ≚ 34 35.38 N 4.30 E
Hodnet 42 52.51 N 2.35 W
Hodogaya ◆[8] 268 35.27 N 139.36 E
Hodogaya Baseball Ground ♠ 268 35.27 N 139.35 E
Hodonín 30 48.51 N 17.08 E
Hodoš 61 46.50 N 16.20 E
Hodzana ≃ 180 66.15 N 147.48 W
Hoed 41 56.19 N 10.49 E
Hoedekenskerke 52 51.25 N 3.55 E
Hoehne 198 37.17 N 104.23 W
Hoek van Holland 52 51.59 N 4.09 E
Hoeningen 263 51.05 N 6.41 E
Hoensbroek 56 50.55 N 5.55 E
Hœrdt 58 48.42 N 7.47 E
Hoerstgen 263 51.30 N 6.27 E
Hoeryŏng 98 42.27 N 129.44 E
Hoeyang 98 38.43 N 127.36 E
Hof, B.R.D. 54 50.18 N 11.55 E
Hof, Ísland 24a 64.34 N 14.39 W
Hofburg ʊ 264b 48.12 N 16.22 E
Höfđakaupstađur 24a 65.50 N 20.19 W
Hofei → Hefei 100 31.51 N 117.17 E
Hofeld 56 49.30 N 7.09 E
Höfen, B.R.D. 56 50.32 N 6.15 E
Höfen, B.R.D. 60 49.08 N 11.21 E
Hoffman, Ill., U.S. 219 38.32 N 89.16 W
Hoffman, Minn., U.S. 198 45.50 N 95.48 W
Hoffman Estates 216 42.03 N 88.05 W
Hoffman Island ▮ 276 40.35 N 74.03 W
Hoffmans 210 42.54 N 74.05 W
Hoffman Station 284a 43.04 N 78.50 W
Hoffnung 263 51.07 N 7.13 E
Hofgeismar 52 51.30 N 9.22 E
Hofheim 56 50.07 N 8.26 E
Hofheim in Unterfranken 56 50.08 N 10.31 E
Hofkirchen an der Trattnac 60 48.13 N 13.44 E
Höflein an der Donau 264b 48.21 N 16.17 E
Hofmeyr 158 31.39 S 25.50 E
Höfn 24a 64.17 N 15.10 W
Hofors 40 60.33 N 16.17 E
Hofsjökull ⍓ 24a 64.48 N 18.50 W
Hofstade 50 50.58 N 4.02 E
Hofstede ◆[8] 263 51.30 N 7.12 E
Hofstra University ʊ[2] 276 40.43 N 73.36 W
Hōfu 96 34.03 N 131.34 E
Hofuf → Al-Hufūf 128 25.22 N 49.34 E
Hofweier 58 48.25 N 7.55 E
Hogalbāria 126 23.53 N 88.51 E
Höganäs 41 56.12 N 12.33 E
Hogan Lake ◎ 190 45.52 N 78.30 W
Hogansburg 206 44.59 N 74.40 W
Hogansville 192 33.11 N 84.55 W
Hogarth, Mount ∧[2] 166 21.48 S 136.58 E
Hogatza ≃ 180 66.00 N 155.29 W
Hogback Mountain ∧, U.S. 207 42.43 N 72.25 W
Hogback Mountain ∧, Mont., U.S. 202 44.54 N 112.07 W
Hogback Mountain ∧, S.C., U.S. 192 35.10 N 82.17 W
Högbo 40 60.40 N 16.48 E
Hog Canyon V 226 35.42 N 120.35 W
Hog Creek ≃ 222 31.32 N 97.18 W
Högfors 40 59.59 N 15.01 E
Hoggar → Ahaggar ⋀ 148 23.00 N 6.30 E
Hoghton 262 53.44 N 2.35 W
Hoghton Tower ⊥ 262 53.44 N 2.34 W
Hog Island ▮, Mass., U.S. 283 42.40 N 70.46 W
Hog Island ▮, Mich., U.S. 190 45.48 N 85.22 W
Hog Island ▮, Vt., U.S. 206 44.57 N 73.13 W
Hog Island ▮, Va., U.S. 208 37.25 N 75.41 W
Hog Island Bay C 208 37.27 N 75.46 W
Hogoro 154 5.57 S 36.27 E
Hog Point ≻ 116 5.18 N 119.15 E
Hogs Back •[4] 42 51.13 N 0.40 W
Högsby 26 57.10 N 16.02 E
Högsjö 40 59.02 N 15.41 E
Hoh ≃ 224 47.45 N 124.29 W
Hoh, South Fork ≃ 224 47.46 N 124.01 W
Hohe Acht ∧ 56 50.23 N 7.00 E
Hohebach 56 49.22 N 9.44 E
Hohegeiss 54 51.40 N 10.40 E
Hohelimburg, Schloss ⊥ 263 51.21 N 7.34 E
Hohe Mark, Naturpark ♠ 263 51.38 N 6.49 E
Hohenaschau 64 47.45 N 12.19 E
Hohenau 252 27.05 S 55.45 W
Hohenau an der March 61 48.36 N 16.55 E
Hohenberg 60 49.16 N 11.30 E
Hohenbrunn 60 48.03 N 11.42 E
Hohenbucko 54 51.46 N 13.28 E
Hohenbudberg ◆[8] 263 51.23 N 6.40 E
Hohendorf 54 54.01 N 13.44 E
Hohenebra 54 51.18 N 10.49 E
Hoheneggelsen 52 52.13 N 10.10 E
Hohenems 58 47.22 N 9.41 E
Hohenfels 60 49.12 N 11.51 E
Hohenfurch 58 47.51 N 10.54 E
Hohengüstow 54 53.14 N 13.59 E
Hohenhameln 52 52.15 N 10.03 E
Hohenheide 263 51.29 N 7.47 E
Hohenirlach 60 49.22 N 12.13 E
Hohenkammer 60 48.25 N 11.32 E
Hohenkirchen, B.R.D. 52 53.39 N 7.55 E
Hohenkirchen, B.R.D. 56 51.23 N 9.29 E
Hohenkirchen, D.D.R. 54 53.51 N 11.17 E
Hohenkirchen, D.D.R. 54 50.51 N 10.41 E
Hohenleipisch 54 51.30 N 13.34 E
Hohenleuben 54 50.43 N 12.03 E
Hohenlimburg 56 51.21 N 7.35 E
Hohenlimburg, Schloss ⊥ 263 51.21 N 7.34 E
Hohenlinden 60 48.09 N 12.00 E
Hohenmölsen 54 51.09 N 12.06 E
Hohen Neuendorf 54 52.40 N 13.16 E
Hohenpolding 60 48.23 N 12.08 E
Hohensalza → Inowrocław 30 52.48 N 18.15 E
Hohenschönhausen ◆[8] 264a 52.33 N 13.30 E
Hohenseeden 54 52.19 N 12.01 E
Hohenseefeld 54 51.53 N 13.18 E
Hohenstaufen 56 48.44 N 9.43 E
Hohenstein → Olsztynek 30 53.36 N 20.17 E
Hohenstein-Ernstthal 54 50.48 N 12.42 E
Hohensyburg ⊥ 56 51.25 N 7.29 E
Hohentauern 61 47.26 N 14.29 E
Hohenthurm 54 51.31 N 12.05 E
Hohenthurn 64 46.33 N 13.40 E
Hohentwiel ∧ 58 47.46 N 8.49 E
Hohenwald 194 35.33 N 87.33 W
Hohenwart 60 48.36 N 11.23 E
Hohenwarte-Stausee ◎[1] 54 50.32 N 11.30 E
Hohenwarthe 54 52.13 N 11.42 E
Hohenwutzen 54 52.51 N 14.07 E
Hohenzethen 54 53.03 N 10.49 E
Hohenzollern, Burg ⊥ 58 48.19 N 8.58 E
Hohenzollernkanal Ξ 264a 52.32 N 13.20 E
Hoher Bogen ∧ 60 49.15 N 12.55 E
Hoher Dachstein ∧ 64 47.28 N 13.35 E
Hoher Freschen ∧ 58 47.18 N 9.46 E
Hohe Rhön ⋀ 56 50.30 N 10.00 E
Hoher Ifen ∧ 58 47.21 N 10.05 E
Hoherlehme 264a 52.19 N 13.37 E
Hoher Mechtin ∧[2] 54 53.03 N 10.55 E
Hoher Meissner ∧ 52 51.12 N 9.50 E
Hoher Peissenberg ∧ 60 47.48 N 11.02 E
Hoher Riffler ∧ 58 47.07 N 10.22 E
Hoher Sonnblick ∧ 64 47.03 N 12.57 E
Hoher Zinken ∧ 64 47.40 N 13.20 E
Hohe Tauern ⋀ 64 47.10 N 12.30 E
Hohe Warte (Monte Coglians) ∧ 64 46.37 N 12.53 E
Hoh Head ≻ 224 47.46 N 124.29 W
Höhn 56 50.37 N 8.00 E
Hohndorf 54 50.45 N 12.40 E
Hohne 52 52.35 N 10.22 E
Hohneck, Le ∧ 58 48.02 N 7.01 E
Hohnstein 54 50.59 N 14.10 E
Hohoe 150 7.09 N 0.28 E
Hōhoku 96 34.17 N 130.57 E
Ho-Ho-Kus 276 41.00 N 74.07 W
Hohokus Brook ≃ 276 40.57 N 74.06 W
Hoholitna ≃ 180 61.31 N 157.00 W
Höhscheid ◆[8] 263 51.09 N 7.04 E
Hohultslätt 26 56.58 N 15.39 E
Hohwacht 54 54.19 N 10.41 E
Hohwachter Bucht C 41 54.20 N 10.45 E
Hoi-an 110 15.52 N 108.19 E
Hoihow → Haikou 102 20.06 N 110.21 E
Hoima 154 1.26 N 31.21 E
Hoisdorf 52 53.39 N 10.20 E
Hoisington 198 38.31 N 98.47 W
Hoisten 263 51.08 N 6.42 E
Hoi-xuan 110 20.22 N 105.07 E
Hojāi 120 26.00 N 92.51 E
Højby, Dan. 41 55.55 N 11.37 E
Højby, Dan. 41 55.20 N 10.27 E
Höje 40 59.54 N 13.33 E
Højer 26 54.58 N 8.43 E
Højerup 41 55.17 N 12.27 E
Hōjō, Nihon 96 33.58 N 132.46 E
Hōjō → Kasai, Nihon 96 34.56 N 134.50 E
Hoka 130 40.21 N 40.55 E
Hokah 190 43.45 N 91.21 W
Hokang → Hegang 89 47.24 N 130.17 E
Hökåsen 40 59.40 N 16.35 E
Hokendauqua 208 40.39 N 75.29 W
Hökensås ⋀[2] 26 58.11 N 14.08 E
Hokes Bluff 194 34.00 N 85.52 W
Hoketçe 130 38.16 N 36.13 E
Hōki ≃ 94 36.47 N 140.08 E
Hokianga Harbour C 172 35.32 S 173.22 E
Hokitika 172 42.43 S 170.58 E
Hokkaidō □[5] 92a 44.00 N 143.00 E
Hokkaidō ▮ 92a 44.00 N 143.00 E
Hokksund 26 59.47 N 9.59 E
Hoko ≃ 224 48.17 N 124.22 W
Hōkōji 270 34.52 N 135.07 E
Hököpinge 41 55.30 N 13.00 E
Hokota 94 36.09 N 140.31 E
Hok So Wan 271d 22.13 N 114.14 E
Hokubo 96 34.57 N 133.38 E
Hokudan 96 34.32 N 134.56 E
Hokura ≃ 94 37.10 N 138.16 E
Hokuriku-tunnel ◆[5] 94 35.42 N 136.10 E
Hokusei 94 35.09 N 136.31 E
Hola 154 1.29 S 40.02 E
Holalkere 122 14.02 N 76.11 E
Holanda → Netherlands □[1] 30 52.15 N 5.30 E
Holbæk 41 55.43 N 11.43 E
Holbeach 42 52.49 N 0.01 E
Holbeach Marsh ☷ 42 52.52 N 0.05 E
Holberg 182 50.31 N 128.01 W
Holborn ◆[8] 260 51.31 N 0.07 W
Holbrook, Austl. 171b 35.44 S 147.19 E
Holbrook, Ariz., U.S. 200 34.54 N 110.10 W
Holbrook, Ill., U.S. 278 41.32 N 87.38 W
Holbrook, Md., U.S. 284b 39.24 N 76.51 W
Holbrook, Mass., U.S. 207 42.09 N 71.01 W
Holbrook, Nebr., U.S. 198 40.18 N 100.01 W
Holbrook, N.Y., U.S. 210 40.48 N 73.05 W
Holbrook Mountain ∧[2] 212 44.25 N 77.51 W
Holckenhavn 41 55.17 N 10.47 E
Holcomb, Ill., U.S. 216 42.04 N 89.06 W
Holcomb, N.Y., U.S. 210 42.54 N 77.25 W
Holcomb Creek ≃ 228 34.17 N 117.08 W
Holden, Alta., Can. 182 53.14 N 112.14 W
Holden, Mass., U.S. 207 42.21 N 71.52 W
Holden, Mo., U.S. 194 38.43 N 94.01 W
Holden, Utah, U.S. 200 39.06 N 112.16 W
Holden, W. Va., U.S. 188 37.50 N 82.04 W
Holden, Mount ∧[2] 216 41.40 N 87.03 W
Holdenstedt 52 52.55 N 10.31 E
Holden Village 224 48.12 N 120.47 W
Holdenville 196 35.05 N 96.24 W
Holder 220 28.58 N 82.25 W
Holderness ≻[1] 44 53.47 N 0.10 W
Holdfast 184 50.58 N 105.25 W
Holdich 254 45.57 S 68.13 W
Holdingford 190 45.44 N 94.26 W
Holdorf 52 52.35 N 8.07 E
Holdrege 198 40.26 N 99.22 W
Holeby 41 54.43 N 11.28 E
Hole in the Mountain Peak ∧ 204 40.55 N 115.05 W
Hole Narsipur 122 12.47 N 76.15 E
Holešov 30 49.20 N 17.35 E
Holetown 241g 13.11 N 59.39 W
Holgate, S. Afr. 158 33.59 S 22.21 E
Holgate, Ohio, U.S. 216 41.15 N 84.08 W
Holguín 240p 20.53 N 76.15 W
Holguín □[4] 240p 20.55 N 75.50 W
Hol-Hol, Dji. 144 11.19 N 42.57 E
Holhol, Tür. 130 39.14 N 40.03 E
Holič 30 48.49 N 17.10 E
Holice 30 50.04 N 15.59 E
Holiday Beach Provincial Park ♠ 214 42.02 N 83.05 W
Holiday Hills 216 42.18 N 88.13 W
Holiday Lake Amusement Park ♠ 285 40.02 N 74.56 W
Holiday Shores 219 38.55 N 89.56 W
Holitna ≃ 180 61.40 N 157.12 W
Höljes 26 60.54 N 12.36 E
Hollabrunn 61 48.34 N 16.05 E
Holladay 200 40.40 N 111.49 W
Hollage 52 52.20 N 7.58 E
Hollam's Bird Island ▮ 156 24.45 S 14.34 E
Holland, Man., Can. 184 49.32 N 98.55 W
Holland, Mich., U.S. 216 42.47 N 86.07 W
Holland, N.Y., U.S. 210 42.38 N 78.33 W
Holland, Ohio, U.S. 216 41.37 N 83.43 W
Holland, Pa., U.S. 285 40.10 N 74.59 W
Holland, Tex., U.S. 222 30.53 N 97.24 W
Holland, Va., U.S. 208 36.41 N 76.47 W
Holland □[9] 52 52.20 N 4.45 E
Holland → Netherlands □[1] 30 52.15 N 5.30 E
Holland ≃ 212 44.12 N 79.31 W
Holland, Mount ∧ 162 32.12 S 119.44 E
Hollandale 194 33.10 N 90.58 W
Hollande, Étang de ◎ 261 48.44 N 1.48 E
Holland Fen ☷ 42 53.00 N 0.10 W
Hollandia → Jayapura 164 2.32 S 140.42 E
Holland Landing 212 44.06 N 79.29 W
Holland-on-Sea 42 51.48 N 1.13 E
Holland Park 171a 27.31 S 153.03 E
Holland Patent 210 43.14 N 75.15 W
Holland Point ≻ 208 38.43 N 76.32 W
Holland Pond State Park ♠ 207 42.04 N 72.09 W
Hollands Diep ⋓ 52 51.42 N 4.30 E
Hollandstoun 46 59.21 N 2.16 W
Holland Straits ⋓ 208 38.08 N 76.02 W
Holland Tunnel ◆[5] 276 40.44 N 74.02 W
Hollansburg 218 39.59 N 84.48 W
Holleben 54 51.26 N 11.53 E
Hollenfels, Château ⊥ 56 49.43 N 6.03 E
Höllengebirge ⋀ 64 47.48 N 13.39 E
Hollenstedt 52 53.22 N 9.43 E
Hollenstein an der Ybbs 61 47.48 N 14.46 E
Höllenstein Berg ∧ 264b 48.06 N 16.11 E
Höllental V 61 47.45 N 15.47 E
Hollern 52 53.36 N 9.32 E
Holleton 162 31.57 S 119.02 E
Holley 210 43.14 N 78.02 W
Hollfeld 60 49.56 N 11.18 E
Hollick-Kenyon Plateau ⋀[1] 9 79.00 S 97.00 W
Holliday, Mo., U.S. 219 39.29 N 92.08 W
Holliday, Tex., U.S. 196 33.49 N 98.42 W

Symbol	English	Deutsch	Español	Français	Português
≃	River	Fluss	Río	Rivière	Rio
Ξ	Canal	Kanal	Canal	Canal	Canal
ʟ	Waterfall, Rapids	Wasserfall, Stromschnellen	Cascada, Rápidos	Chute d'eau, Rapides	Cascata, Rápidos
⋓	Strait	Meeresstrasse	Estrecho	Détroit	Estreito
C	Bay, Gulf	Bucht, Golf	Bahía, Golfo	Baie, Golfe	Baía, Golfo
◎	Lake, Lakes	See, Seen	Lago, Lagos	Lac, Lacs	Lago, Lagos
☷	Swamp	Sumpf	Pantano	Marais	Pântano
⍓	Ice Features, Glacier	Eis- und Gletscherformen	Accidentes Glaciales	Formes glaciaires	Acidentes Glaciares
⍑	Other Hydrographic Features	Andere Hydrographische Objekte	Otros Elementos Hidrográficos	Autres données hydrographiques	Outros Elementos Hidrográficos

Symbol	English	Deutsch	Español	Français	Português
✧	Submarine Features	Untermeerische Objekte	Accidentes Submarinos	Formes de relief sous-marin	Acidentes Submarinos
□	Political Unit	Politische Einheit	Unidad Politica	Entité politique	Unidade Política
ʊ	Cultural Institution	Kulturelle Institution	Institución Cultural	Institution culturelle	Instituição Cultural
⊥	Historical Site	Historische Stätte	Sitio Histórico	Site historique	Sitio Histórico
♠	Recreational Site	Erholungs- und Ferienort	Sitio de Recreo	Centre de loisirs	Sítio de Lazer
⊠	Airport	Flughafen	Aeropuerto	Aéroport	Aeroporto
■	Military Installation	Militäranlage	Instalación Militar	Installation militaire	Instalação Militar
◆	Miscellaneous	Verschiedenes	Misceláneo	Divers	Miscelânea

Holliday Creek ≃ 196 33.55 N 98.28 W
Holliday Park ♦ 281 42.21 N 83.24 W
Hollidaysburg 214 40.26 N 78.23 W
Hollingbourne 260 51.16 N 0.38 E
Hollingstedt 41 54.27 N 9.19 E
Hollingworth 262 53.28 N 1.59 W
Hollingworth Lake ⊜ 262 53.38 N 2.06 W
Hollins 262 53.34 N 2.17 W
Hollins Green 262 53.25 N 2.27 W
Hollinswood 284c 38.55 N 77.13 W
Hollis, N.H., U.S. 207 42.44 N 71.35 W
Hollis, Okla., U.S. 196 34.41 N 99.55 W
Hollis ⊥8 276 40.43 N 73.46 W
Hollister 226 36.51 N 121.24 W
Holliston 207 42.12 N 71.26 W
Hollman, Cape ≻ 164 4.59 S 150.06 E
Holloman Air Force Base ■ 200 32.51 N 106.05 W
Holloway 214 40.10 N 81.08 W
Holloway Terrace 285 39.42 N 75.33 W
Hollow Rock 194 36.02 N 88.16 W
Hollowville 210 42.12 N 73.42 W
Hollsopple 214 40.13 N 78.56 W
Hollum 52 53.26 N 5.37 E
Höllviken C 41 55.26 N 12.54 E
Höllviksnäs 41 55.25 N 12.57 E
Holly, Colo., U.S. 198 38.03 N 102.07 W
Holly, Mich., U.S. 216 42.48 N 83.38 W
Holly, Wash., U.S. 224 47.34 N 122.58 W
Holly, Mount ∧2 285 40.00 N 74.47 W
Holly Grove 194 34.36 N 91.12 W
Holly Hill, Fla., U.S. 192 29.14 N 81.02 W
Holly Hill, S.C., U.S. 192 33.19 N 80.25 W
Holly Park 208 39.53 N 74.10 W
Holly Pond ⊜ 276 41.03 N 73.30 W
Holly River State Park ♦ 188 38.40 N 80.21 W
Holly Run ≃ 285 39.47 N 75.03 W
Holly Springs 194 34.41 N 89.26 W
Holly State Recreation Area ♦ 216 42.49 N 83.32 W
Hollywood, Eire 48 53.06 N 6.35 W
Hollywood, Fla., U.S. 220 26.00 N 80.09 W
Hollywood, Md., U.S. 208 38.21 N 76.34 W
Hollywood, Pa., U.S. 285 40.05 N 75.06 W
Hollywood ⊥8 228 34.06 N 118.21 W
Hollywood, Mount ∧ 280 34.08 N 118.18 W
Hollywood Bowl ♦ 280 34.07 N 118.20 W
Hollywood-Burbank Airport ⊠ 228 34.12 N 118.21 W
Hollywood Heights 219 38.39 N 89.59 W
Hollywood Indian Reservation ⊥4 220 26.02 N 80.13 W
Hollywood Park Race Track ♦ 280 33.57 N 118.20 W
Hollywood Reservoir ⊜1 280 34.07 N 118.20 W
Holman Island 176 70.43 N 117.43 W
Hólmavík 24a 65.43 N 21.43 W
Holmdel 208 40.21 N 74.11 W
Holme, Dan. 41 56.07 N 10.11 E
Holme, Eng., U.K. 262 53.33 N 1.50 W
Holme ≃ 44 53.41 N 1.43 W
Holme Chapel 262 53.45 N 2.11 W
Holmen, Nor. 26 60.40 N 10.22 E
Holmen, Wis., U.S. 190 43.58 N 91.15 W
Holmenkollen 26 59.58 N 10.40 E
Holmes, N.Y., U.S. 210 41.31 N 73.39 W
Holmes, Pa., U.S. 285 39.54 N 75.19 W
Holmes □6 214 40.33 N 81.55 W
Holmes, Mount ∧ 202 44.49 N 110.51 W
Holmes Beach 220 27.31 N 82.43 W
Holmesburg ⊥8 285 40.02 N 75.03 W
Holmes Creek ≃ 194 30.30 N 85.47 W
Holmesglen 274b 37.53 S 145.06 E
Holmes Harbor C 224 48.04 N 122.32 W
Holmes Lake ⊜ 184 57.05 N 96.45 W
Holmes Reefs ⊥2 164 16.27 S 148.00 E
Holmes Run ≃ 284c 38.48 N 77.07 W
Holmes Run Acres 284c 38.51 N 77.13 W
Holmestrand 26 59.29 N 10.18 E
Holmesville, N.Y., U.S. 210 42.31 N 75.24 W
Holmesville, Ohio, U.S. 214 40.38 N 81.55 W
Holmeswood 262 53.39 N 2.52 W
Holmfirth 44 53.35 N 1.46 W
Holmia 246 4.58 N 59.35 W
Holmön I 26 63.47 N 20.53 E
Holmsbu 26 59.33 N 10.27 E
Holmsjön ⊜, Sve. 26 62.25 N 15.20 E
Holmsjön ⊜, Sve. 26 62.41 N 16.33 E
Holmsund 26 63.42 N 20.21 E
Holnstein 60 49.33 N 11.39 E
Hölö 40 59.01 N 17.35 E
Holod 38 46.47 N 22.08 E
Holoit, Punta ≻ 232 21.37 N 88.08 W
Holon 132 32.01 N 34.46 E
Holoog 156 27.22 S 17.55 E
Holopaw 220 28.08 N 81.04 W
Holroyd 274a 33.50 S 150.58 E
Holroyd ≃ 164 14.10 S 141.36 E
Holsloot 52 52.44 N 6.48 E
Holstebro 26 56.21 N 8.38 E
Holsted 41 55.30 N 8.55 E
Holstein 198 42.29 N 95.33 W
Holsteinborg ⊥ 41 55.13 N 11.28 E
Holsteinische Schweiz ⊥1 54 54.11 N 10.36 E
Holsteinsborg 176 66.55 N 53.40 W
Holsterhausen 263 51.41 N 6.57 E
Holston ≃ 192 35.57 N 83.51 W
Holston High Knob ∧ 192 36.27 N 82.05 W
Holsworthy 42 50.49 N 4.21 W
Holt, Wales, U.K. 42 53.05 N 2.53 W
Holt, Ala., U.S. 194 33.15 N 87.29 W
Holt, Calif., U.S. 226 37.56 N 121.26 W
Holt, Fla., U.S. 194 30.43 N 86.45 W
Holt, Mich., U.S. 216 42.39 N 84.31 W
Holt Creek ≃ 198 42.28 N 98.50 W
Holte 41 55.49 N 12.28 E
Holtemme ≃ 54 51.57 N 11.10 E
Holten 52 52.17 N 6.25 E
Holten ⊥8 263 51.31 N 6.48 E
Holtenau ⊥8 54 54.22 N 10.08 E
Holter Lake ⊜1 202 46.55 N 111.57 W
Holthausen, B.R.D. 52 52.33 N 7.17 E
Holthausen, B.R.D. 263 51.23 N 7.13 E
Holthausen ⊥8 263 51.34 N 7.26 E
Holthusen 52 53.08 N 7.18 E
Holton, Ind., U.S. 218 39.04 N 85.23 W
Holton, Kans., U.S. 198 39.28 N 95.44 W
Holtorf 52 52.40 N 9.13 E
Holts Summit 219 38.39 N 92.07 W
Holtsville 210 40.49 N 73.02 W
Holtug 41 55.21 N 12.25 E
Holtville 204 32.49 N 115.23 W
Holtwick 52 52.00 N 7.05 E
Holtwood 208 39.50 N 76.19 W
Holwerd 52 53.22 N 5.54 E
Holycross, Eire 48 52.38 N 7.52 W
Holy Cross, Alaska, U.S. 180 62.12 N 159.47 W
Holy Cross Mountain ∧ 182 53.47 N 120.47 W
Holyhead 44 53.19 N 4.38 W
Holyhead Bay C 44 53.23 N 4.37 W
Holy Island I, Eng., U.K. 44 55.41 N 1.48 W
Holy Island I, Scot., U.K. 46 55.32 N 5.05 W
Holy Island I, Wales, U.K. 44 53.18 N 4.37 W
Holy Island I, Mass., U.S. 283 42.43 N 70.50 W
Holyoke, Colo., U.S. 198 40.35 N 102.18 W
Holyoke, Mass., U.S. 207 42.12 N 72.37 W
Holyrood 198 38.35 N 98.25 W
Holyrood Palace ⊌ 46 55.56 N 3.12 W
Holy Sepulchre, The Church of the ⊌1 132 31.46 N 35.14 E
Holýšov 60 49.36 N 13.05 E
Holywell 44 53.17 N 3.13 W
Holywell Green 262 53.41 N 1.52 W
Holywood 48 54.38 N 5.49 W
Holzbüttgen 263 51.12 N 6.37 E
Holzen 56 51.26 N 7.31 E
Holzgau 58 47.16 N 10.21 E
Holzgerlingen 56 48.38 N 9.00 E
Holzhausen, B.R.D. 52 52.17 N 8.32 E
Holzhausen, B.R.D. 56 52.01 N 8.44 E
Holzhausen, B.R.D. 52 52.13 N 8.01 E
Holzhausen, D.D.R. 54 51.18 N 12.28 E
Holzhausen an der Haide 56 50.13 N 7.55 E
Holzheim 56 51.09 N 6.39 E
Holzkirchen 64 47.52 N 11.42 E
Holzminden 52 51.50 N 9.27 E
Holzweissig 54 51.36 N 12.18 E
Holzwickede 52 51.30 N 7.36 E
Homa 130 38.14 N 30.01 E
Homa Bay 154 0.31 S 34.27 E
Homalin 110 24.52 N 94.55 E
Homathko ≃ 182 50.55 N 124.50 W
Homathko Snowfield ⊠ 182 51.05 N 124.30 W
Homāyūnshahr 128 32.41 N 51.31 E
Homberg, B.R.D. 56 51.28 N 6.38 E
Homberg, B.R.D. 56 50.43 N 8.59 E
Homberg, B.R.D. 56 51.02 N 9.24 E
Homberg, B.R.D. 263 51.18 N 6.56 E
Hombori 150 15.17 N 1.42 W
Hombori Tondo ∧ 150 15.16 N 1.40 W
Hombourg-haut 56 49.08 N 6.46 E
Hombre Muerto, Salar del ≃ 252 25.23 S 67.06 W
Hombruch ⊥8 263 51.29 N 7.26 E
Homburg, B.R.D. 56 49.19 N 7.20 E
Homburg → Bad Homburg vor der Höhe, B.R.D. 56 50.13 N 8.37 E
Home, Pa., U.S. 214 40.44 N 79.06 W
Home, Wash., U.S. 224 47.17 N 122.46 W
Homeacre 214 40.51 N 79.55 W
Home Bay C, N.W. Ter., Can. 176 68.45 N 67.10 W
Home Bay C, Kiribati 174d 0.53 S 169.35 E
Homebush Bay C 274a 33.50 S 151.05 E
Home Corner 216 40.32 N 85.40 W
Homécourt 56 49.14 N 5.59 E
Home Creek ≃ 196 31.29 N 99.14 W
Homedale, Idaho, U.S. 202 43.37 N 116.56 W
Homedale, Ohio, U.S. 214 40.04 N 83.02 W
Home Gardens 228 33.53 N 117.30 W
Home Hill 166 19.40 S 147.25 E
Homeland, Calif., U.S. 228 33.44 N 117.07 W
Homeland, Fla., U.S. 220 27.49 N 81.49 W
Homeland Canal ≅ 226 35.57 N 119.27 W
Home of Franklin Delano Roosevelt National Historic Site ⊥1 210 41.46 N 73.56 W
Home Place 218 39.55 N 86.07 W
Homer, Alaska, U.S. 180 59.39 N 151.33 W
Homer, Ga., U.S. 192 34.20 N 83.30 W
Homer, La., U.S. 194 32.48 N 93.04 W
Homer, Mich., U.S. 216 42.09 N 84.49 W
Homer, Nebr., U.S. 198 42.19 N 96.29 W
Homer, N.Y., U.S. 210 42.38 N 76.11 W
Homer, Ohio, U.S. 214 40.15 N 82.31 W
Homer, Tex., U.S. 222 31.18 N 94.36 W
Homer City 214 40.32 N 79.10 W
Homert ∧2 263 51.11 N 7.39 E
Homert, Naturpark ♦ 56 51.15 N 8.10 E
Homer Tunnel ⊥5 172 44.45 S 168.00 E
Homerville, Ga., U.S. 192 31.02 N 82.45 W
Homerville, Ohio, U.S. 214 41.02 N 82.08 W
Homer Wash ∨ 204 34.20 N 115.02 W
Homer Youngs Peak ∧ 202 45.19 N 113.41 W
Home Seamount ⊥3 14 12.30 S 176.40 W
Homestead, Austl. 166 20.22 S 145.39 E
Homestead, Fla., U.S. 220 25.29 N 80.29 W
Homestead Air Force Base ■ 220 25.29 N 80.23 W
Homestead National Monument of America ♦ 198 40.14 N 96.54 W
Homestead Valley 282 37.54 N 122.32 W
Hometown, Ill., U.S. 278 41.44 N 87.44 W
Hometown, Pa., U.S. 210 40.49 N 75.59 W
Homewood, Ala., U.S. 194 33.29 N 86.48 W
Homewood, Calif., U.S. 226 39.05 N 120.10 W
Homewood, Ill., U.S. 216 41.34 N 87.40 W
Homewood, Ohio, U.S. 218 39.23 N 84.33 W
Homewood ⊥8 279b 40.27 N 79.54 W
Homewood Acres 278 41.34 N 87.43 W
Homeworth 214 40.50 N 81.04 W
Hominy 196 36.25 N 96.24 W
Hominy Creek ≃ 196 36.20 N 96.00 W
Hommersåk 26 58.58 N 5.42 E
Hommura 92 34.22 N 139.15 E
Homnābād 122 17.46 N 77.08 E
Homo Bay C 175f 15.57 S 168.11 E
Homochitto ≃ 194 31.09 N 91.31 W
Homoine 156 23.52 S 35.09 E
Homonhon Island I 116 10.44 N 125.43 E
Homosassa 220 28.47 N 82.37 W
Homosassa Bay C 220 28.45 N 82.43 W
Homosassa Springs 220 28.48 N 82.35 W
Homs → Al-Khums, Lībiya 146 32.39 N 14.16 E
Homs → Ḥimṣ, Sūrīy. 130 34.44 N 36.43 E
Honai 96 33.30 N 132.25 E
Honaker 192 37.01 N 81.59 W
Honami 96 33.36 N 130.42 E
Honan → Luoyang 102 34.41 N 112.28 E
Honan → Henan □4 90 34.00 N 114.00 E
Honāvar 122 14.17 N 74.27 E
Honaz 130 37.45 N 29.17 E
Honbetsu 92a 43.07 N 143.37 E
Hon-chong 110 10.10 N 104.37 E
Honda 246 5.12 N 74.45 W
Honda, Bahía C, Col. 246 12.21 N 71.47 W
Honda, Bahía C, Cuba 240p 22.57 N 83.10 W
Honda, Cañada ≃ 258 33.57 S 59.21 W
Honda Bay C 116 9.53 N 118.49 E
Honddu ≃, Wales, U.K. 42 51.57 N 3.23 W
Honddu ≃, Wales, U.K. 42 51.54 N 2.58 W
Hondeklipbaai 156 30.20 S 17.18 E
Honderfontein 158 32.12 S 21.22 E
Hon-dien, Nui ∧ 110 11.33 N 108.38 E
Hondo, Alta., Can. 182 55.04 N 114.02 W
Hondo, Nihon 96 32.27 N 130.12 E
Hondo, N. Mex., U.S. 200 33.23 N 105.16 W
Hondo, Tex., U.S. 196 29.21 N 99.09 W
Hondo ≃, Cuba 286b 22.55 N 82.16 W
Hondo ≃, Méx. 286a 19.26 N 99.15 W
Hondo ≃, N.A. 232 18.29 N 88.19 W
Hondo, Arroyo ≃ 226 37.28 N 121.47 W
Hondo, Rio ≃, Calif., U.S. 280 33.55 N 118.10 W
Hondo, Rio ≃, N. Mex., U.S. 196 33.22 N 104.24 W
Hondo Creek ≃ 196 28.45 N 99.11 W
Hondoji Temple ⊌1 268 35.51 N 139.56 E
Hondschoote 50 50.59 N 2.35 E
Hondsrug ⊥2 52 52.55 N 6.50 E
Honduras □1 230
Honduras 236 15.00 N 86.30 W
Honduras, Cabo de ≻ 236 16.01 N 86.02 W
Honduras, Gulf of C 236 16.10 N 87.50 W
Honduras, Port C 236 16.13 N 88.41 W
Honea Path 192 34.27 N 82.24 W
Hönebach 56 50.56 N 9.56 E
Hønefoss 26 60.10 N 10.18 E
Honeoye 210 42.47 N 77.31 W
Honeoye Creek ≃ 210 42.58 N 77.43 W
Honeoye Falls 210 42.57 N 77.36 W
Honeoye Lake ⊜ 210 42.45 N 77.31 W
Honesdale 210 41.34 N 75.16 W
Honey Brook 208 40.06 N 75.55 W
Honey Creek 216 42.45 N 88.19 W
Honey Creek ≃, Iowa, U.S. 190 42.09 N 93.03 W
Honey Creek ≃, Mo., U.S. 194 39.53 N 93.34 W
Honey Creek ≃, Ohio, U.S. 214 41.05 N 83.12 W
Honey Creek ≃, Pa., U.S. 208 40.36 N 77.35 W
Honey Creek ≃, Wis., U.S. 216 42.41 N 88.17 W
Honeydew 273d 26.05 S 27.55 E
Honeygo Run ≃ 284b 39.22 N 76.25 W
Honey Grove 196 33.35 N 95.55 W
Honey Lake ⊜ 204 40.16 N 120.19 W
Honeymoon Bay 182 48.49 N 124.10 W
Honeyville 200 41.38 N 112.04 W
Honfleur 50 49.25 N 0.14 E
Høng 41 55.31 N 11.18 E
Honga 152 15.09 S 15.12 E
Hon-gai 110 20.57 N 107.05 E
Hongan 100 31.18 N 114.37 E
Honga River C 208 38.19 N 76.10 W
Hongawa 96 33.43 N 133.19 E
Hongchang 100 34.05 N 113.20 E
Hongch'ŏn 98 37.42 N 127.52 E
Hongchoudai 100 29.03 N 121.11 E
Hongcun 106 31.01 N 119.15 E
Hongdong 102 36.19 N 111.39 E
Honge ≃ 100 32.25 N 115.35 E
Hongen 56 51.02 N 6.57 E
Honggun 98 40.46 N 128.27 E
Hong-ha → Red ≃ 110 20.17 N 106.34 E
Honghaiwan C 100 22.40 N 115.10 E
Honghe 102 23.23 N 102.35 E
Hongheercun 89 48.09 N 119.19 E
Honghu 100 29.48 N 113.27 E
Honghu ⊜ 100 29.52 N 113.23 E
Honghuaerji 89 48.15 N 120.01 E
Honghuaji 100 33.52 N 114.26 E
Honghualiangzi 89 48.06 N 123.12 E
Honghuamu 89 48.33 N 125.39 E
Hongjiang, Zhg. 100 26.49 N 120.03 E
Hongjiang, Zhg. 102 27.00 N 109.51 E
Hong Kong → Victoria 271d 22.17 N 114.09 E
Hong Kong □2 90
Hong Kong 271d 22.15 N 114.10 E
Hong Kong I 271d 22.15 N 114.11 E
Hong Kong, University of ⊌2 271d 22.17 N 114.08 E
Hongkou Park ♦ 269b 31.16 N 121.28 E
Hongkou Stadium ♦ 269b 31.16 N 121.28 E
Honglai 100 25.08 N 118.32 E
Honglanbu 106 31.37 N 118.57 E
Honglinqiao 106 30.59 N 118.59 E
Hongliutai 85 39.48 N 77.26 E
Hongliuyuan 102 41.04 N 95.26 E
Honglongdian 106 30.30 N 119.00 E
Honglu 100 25.44 N 119.20 E
Hongluan 100 28.31 N 117.01 E
Hongluoshan ∧ 104 40.56 N 120.42 E
Hongluoxian 104 41.01 N 120.53 E
Hongmeichang 105 39.50 N 115.51 E
Hongmendu 102 26.10 N 102.37 E
Hongmenkou 102 27.22 N 100.30 E
Hongmenpu 107 30.37 N 104.08 E
Hongmiaozi 107 28.47 N 104.02 E
Hong-ngu 110 10.48 N 105.21 E
Hongō, Nihon 96 36.15 N 137.59 E
Hongō, Nihon 96 34.24 N 132.59 E
Hongō, Nihon 96 34.17 N 132.02 E
Hongpailou 107 30.38 N 104.01 E
Hongqiao, Zhg. 100 28.14 N 121.01 E
Hongqiao, Zhg. 100 32.16 N 119.26 E
Hongqiao, Zhg. 105 39.50 N 117.34 E
Hongqiao, Zhg. 106 31.29 N 121.49 E
Hongqiao, Zhg. 269b 31.12 N 121.22 E
Hongqiao Airport ⊠ 269b 31.12 N 121.23 E
Hongrie → Hungary □1 30 47.00 N 20.00 E
Hongrui 98 35.08 N 118.38 E
Hongshan, Zhg. 89 48.02 N 128.00 E
Hongshan, Zhg. 98 36.37 N 118.00 E
Hongshi 98 41.21 N 119.32 E
Hongshidou 104 41.52 N 122.11 E
Hongshilazi 89 43.00 N 127.04 E
Hongshili 98 40.41 N 125.03 E
Hongshuibao 102 37.24 N 104.00 E
Hongshuichuan 105 40.06 N 117.55 E
Hongshuihe ≃ 102 23.45 N 109.30 E
Hongshuyangzi 105 40.36 N 116.36 E
Hongsibao 102 37.18 N 106.02 E
Hongsŏng 98 36.36 N 126.39 E
Hongtang 100 26.06 N 119.14 E
Hongtian 100 25.52 N 117.15 E
Hongtugou 128 38.08 N 91.10 E
Hongtuwan 98 41.03 N 113.39 E
Hongtuzhang ∧ 100 23.46 N 115.56 E
Honguedo, Détroit d' ⊔ 186 49.15 N 64.00 W
Hongwŏn 98 40.02 N 127.57 E
Hongxingqiao 106 30.55 N 119.52 E
Hongxinpu 100 32.43 N 117.42 E
Hongya 102 29.58 N 103.31 E
Hongyang, Zhg. 100 23.28 N 116.13 E
Hongyang, Zhg. 100 26.32 N 119.27 E
Hongyanzi 104 40.38 N 120.31 E
Hongyōtoku 268 35.41 N 139.55 E
Hongze 100 33.19 N 118.53 E
Hongzehu ⊜ 100 33.16 N 118.34 E
Honiara 175e 9.26 S 159.57 E
Honiton 42 50.48 N 3.13 W
Honjō, Nihon 92 39.23 N 140.03 E
Honjō, Nihon 94 36.24 N 138.01 E
Honjō, Nihon 94 36.14 N 139.11 E
Honkamäki ∧2 26 62.58 N 27.05 E
Hon-kawane 94 35.07 N 138.09 E
Honker Bay C 282 38.04 N 121.56 W
Hönne ≃ 263 51.28 N 7.46 E
Honnecourt-sur-Escaut 50 50.02 N 3.12 E
Honningsvåg 24 70.59 N 25.59 E
Honnō 94 35.29 N 140.18 E
Hōnō 26 57.42 N 11.39 E
Honokaa 229d 20.05 N 155.28 W
Honokahua 229d 21.00 N 156.39 W
Honokawai 229a 20.57 N 156.41 W
Honolulu 229c 21.19 N 157.52 W
Honolulu □6 229c 21.19 N 157.52 W
Honolulu International Airport ⊠ 229c 21.20 N 157.55 W
Honomu 229d 19.52 N 155.07 W
Honouliuli 229c 21.22 N 158.02 W
Hönow 54 52.32 N 13.38 E
Hon-shima I 96 34.23 N 133.47 E
Honshū I 92 36.00 N 138.00 E
Hontoon Island State Park ♦ 220 28.59 N 81.22 W
Höntrop ⊥8 263 51.27 N 7.08 E
Honuapo Bay C 229d 19.05 N 155.33 W
Honyakushiji Temple ⊌1 270 34.26 N 135.47 E
Hoo 260 51.25 N 0.34 E
Hood 226 38.22 N 121.31 W
Hood □6 222 32.25 N 97.45 W
Hood ≃, N.W. Ter., Can. 176 67.26 N 108.53 W
Hood ≃, Oreg., U.S. 224 45.42 N 121.30 W
Hood, East Fork ≃ 224 45.36 N 121.38 W
Hood, Mount ∧ 224 45.23 N 121.41 W
Hood Canal C 224 47.35 N 123.00 W
Hood Canal Floating Bridge ⊥5 224 47.52 N 122.38 W
Hoodoo Peak ∧ 202 48.15 N 120.19 W
Hood Point ≻, Austl. 162 34.23 S 119.34 E
Hood Point ≻, Pap. N. Gui. 164 10.05 S 147.45 E
Hood Pond ⊜ 283 42.40 N 70.57 W
Hood River 224 45.43 N 121.31 W
Hood River □6 224 45.30 N 121.40 W
Hoodsport 224 47.24 N 123.09 W
Hoods Range ⊥ 166 28.35 S 144.30 E
Hoof 56 51.17 N 9.20 E
Hoogerheide 52 51.25 N 4.20 E
Hoogeveen 52 52.43 N 6.29 E
Hoogeveense Vaart ≅ 52 52.42 N 6.11 E
Hoogezand 52 53.09 N 6.47 E
Hooghly □5 126 22.50 N 88.15 E
Hooghly ≃1 126 21.55 N 88.05 E
Hooghly-Chinsura 126 22.54 N 88.24 E
Hoogkerk 52 53.13 N 6.30 E
Hooglede 50 50.59 N 3.05 E
Hoogstede 52 52.34 N 6.56 E
Hoogstraten 56 51.24 N 4.46 E
Hoogte 158 27.28 S 28.03 E
Hoogvliet 52 51.52 N 4.21 E
Hook 42 51.17 N 0.58 W
Hook ⊥8 260 51.22 N 0.18 W
Hooker 196 36.52 N 101.13 W
Hooker, Bi'r ⊤4 142 30.23 N 30.20 E
Hooker Creek 162 18.20 S 130.40 E
Hook Head ≻ 48 52.07 N 6.55 W
Hookina 166 31.45 S 138.20 E
Hook Island I 166 20.08 S 148.55 E
Hook Mountain State Park ♦ 276 41.09 N 73.55 W
Hook Point ≻ 166 25.48 S 153.05 E
Hooks 194 33.28 N 94.15 W
Hooksiel 52 53.38 N 8.01 E
Hoolehua 229a 21.10 N 157.06 W
Hoonah 180 58.07 N 135.26 W
Hoopa 204 41.03 N 123.40 W
Hoopa Valley Indian Reservation ⊥4 204 41.08 N 123.40 W
Hooper 198 41.37 N 96.33 W
Hooper Bay 180 61.31 N 166.06 W
Hooper Islands II 208 38.20 N 76.13 W
Hooper Strait ⊔ 208 38.12 N 76.03 W
Hoopersville 208 38.16 N 76.11 W
Hoopes Reservoir ⊜1 285 39.47 N 75.37 W
Hoopeston 216 40.28 N 87.40 W
Hooping Harbour 186 50.37 N 56.17 W
Hoople 198 48.32 N 97.38 W
Hoopstad 158 27.54 S 25.58 E
Hoopstick Brook ≃ 276 40.39 N 74.41 W
Höör 41 55.56 N 13.32 E
Hoorn 52 52.38 N 5.04 E
Hoorn, Kap → Hornos, Cabo de ≻ 254 55.59 S 67.16 W
Hoosac Range ⊥ 207 42.45 N 73.02 W
Hoosac Tunnel ⊥5 207 42.41 N 73.03 W
Hoosic ≃ 210 42.54 N 73.39 W
Hoosick 210 42.52 N 73.20 W
Hoosick Falls 210 42.54 N 73.21 W
Hooton 262 53.18 N 2.57 W
Hoover Dam ⊥6 200 36.00 N 114.27 W
Hoover Reservoir ⊜1 214 40.08 N 82.53 W
Hooversville 214 40.09 N 78.55 W
Hopa 130 41.25 N 41.24 E
Hopatcong 210 40.56 N 74.39 W
Hopatcong, Lake ⊜ 210 40.57 N 74.38 W
Hopatcong State Park ♦ 276 40.55 N 74.40 W
Hop Bottom 210 41.42 N 75.46 W
Hop Brook ≃ 276 40.19 N 74.08 W
Hope, B.C., Can. 182 49.23 N 121.26 W
Hope, Alaska, U.S. 180 60.55 N 149.38 W
Hope, Ark., U.S. 194 33.40 N 93.36 W
Hope, Ind., U.S. 218 39.18 N 85.46 W
Hope, N.J., U.S. 210 40.55 N 74.58 W
Hope, N. Dak., U.S. 198 47.19 N 97.43 W
Hope, R.I., U.S. 207 41.44 N 71.34 W
Hope, Ben ∧ 46 58.24 N 4.37 W
Hope, Loch ⊜ 46 58.27 N 4.39 W
Hope, Point ≻ 180 68.21 N 166.50 W
Hope Bay C 212 44.55 N 81.08 W
Hopedale, Newf., Can. 176 55.28 N 60.13 W
Hopedale, Ill., U.S. 194 40.25 N 89.25 W
Hopedale, La., U.S. 194 29.51 N 89.41 W
Hopedale, Mass., U.S. 207 42.08 N 71.33 W
Hopedale, Ohio, U.S. 214 40.20 N 80.54 W
Hope Farm 210 41.44 N 73.40 W
Hopefield 158 33.04 S 18.22 E
Hopeh → Hebei □4 98 38.00 N 116.00 E
Hope Island I, B.C., Can. 182 50.55 N 127.53 W
Hope Island I, Ont., Can. 212 44.55 N 80.12 W
Hopeland 208 40.14 N 76.16 W
Hopelawn 276 40.32 N 74.18 W
Hopelchén 232 19.46 N 89.51 W
Hopeman 46 57.42 N 3.25 W
Hope Mills 192 34.59 N 78.57 W
Hopen I 10 76.35 N 25.10 E
Hopes Advance, Baie C 176 59.25 N 69.40 W
Hopes Advance, Cap ≻ 176 61.04 N 69.34 W
Hopetoun, Austl. 162 33.57 S 120.07 E
Hopetoun, Austl. 166 35.44 S 142.22 E
Hopetown 158 29.34 S 24.03 E
Hope Valley, Austl. 168b 34.50 S 138.44 E
Hope Valley, R.I., U.S. 207 41.30 N 71.43 W
Hopewell, N.J., U.S. 208 40.23 N 74.46 W
Hopewell, Pa., U.S. 214 40.08 N 78.16 W
Hopewell, Va., U.S. 208 37.18 N 77.17 W
Hopewell Islands II 176 58.25 N 78.00 W
Hopewell Junction 210 41.35 N 73.48 W
Hopewell Village National Historic Site ⊥ 208 40.12 N 75.46 W
Hopfgarten 64 47.27 N 12.10 E
Hopfgarten in Defereggen 64 46.55 N 12.31 E
Hopi → Hebi 98 35.59 N 114.11 E
Hopi Buttes ∧ 200 35.20 N 110.15 W
Hopi Indian Reservation ⊥4 200 35.45 N 110.35 W
Hopingzhen 106 30.50 N 119.54 E
Hopkins, Mich., U.S. 216 42.37 N 85.45 W
Hopkins, Mo., U.S. 190 40.33 N 94.49 W
Hopkins □6 222 33.07 N 95.35 W
Hopkins, Lake ⊜ 162 24.15 S 128.50 E
Hopkins Creek ≃ 284a 43.17 N 78.46 W
Hopkinsville 194 36.52 N 87.29 W
Hopkinton, Iowa, U.S. 190 42.21 N 91.15 W
Hopkinton, Mass., U.S. 207 42.13 N 71.31 W
Hopkinton, R.I., U.S. 207 41.28 N 71.47 W
Hopland 204 38.58 N 123.07 W
Hopohoponga, Mui ≻ 174w 21.09 S 175.02 W
Ho Poi 271d 22.25 N 114.03 E
Hoppegarten 264a 52.31 N 13.40 E
Hoppenrade 264a 52.32 N 12.56 E
Hopper Canyon ∨ 228 34.22 N 118.51 W
Hoppo → Hepu 102 21.39 N 109.11 E
Hopsten 52 52.23 N 7.36 E
Hoptrup 41 55.11 N 9.28 E
Hopwood, Mount ∧ 166 21.49 S 144.26 E
Hoque 152 14.39 S 13.54 E
Hoquiam 224 46.59 N 123.53 W
Hoquiam ≃ 224 46.58 N 123.54 W
Horace Mountain ∧ 180 67.40 N 149.06 W
Horado 94 35.36 N 136.50 E
Hōrai 94 34.56 N 137.34 E
Horakelifo 144 8.50 N 43.10 E
Horanchia 144 6.35 N 38.46 E
Horasan 130 40.03 N 42.11 E
Horatio 194 33.56 N 94.21 W
Horatio Gardens 278 42.10 N 87.57 W
Horažďovice 60 49.20 N 13.43 E
Horb am Neckar 58 48.26 N 8.41 E
Horbelev 41 54.49 N 12.04 E
Hörbering 60 48.23 N 12.33 E
Horbourg 58 48.05 N 7.23 E
Hörby 41 55.51 N 13.39 E
Horconcitos 236 8.19 N 82.10 W
Hordaland □6 26 60.15 N 6.30 E
Hörde ⊥8 263 51.29 N 7.30 E
Horden 44 54.46 N 1.18 W
Horden ≃ 164 3.50 S 141.25 E
Hordio 144 10.32 N 51.08 E
Horezu 38 45.08 N 23.59 E
Horgen 58 47.15 N 8.36 E
Hořice 30 50.22 N 15.38 E
Horicon 190 43.27 N 88.38 W
Horigane 268 35.50 N 139.27 E
Horine 219 38.16 N 90.26 W
Horinouchi 94 37.14 N 138.56 E
Horinouchi ⊥8 268 35.41 N 139.40 E
Horio 144 5.00 N 47.26 E
Horizon Tablemount ⊥3 14 19.30 N 169.00 W
Horizontina 252 27.37 S 54.19 W
Horka 54 51.16 N 14.56 E
Hörken 40 60.02 N 14.56 E
Horley 42 51.11 N 0.11 W
Horlick Mountains ⊥ 9 85.23 S 121.00 W
Hormigueros 240m 18.09 N 67.08 W
Hormoz, Jazīreh-ye I 128 27.04 N 56.28 E
Hormuz, Strait of ⊔ 128 26.34 N 56.15 E
Horn, B.R.D. 52 51.52 N 8.56 E
Horn, Öst. 61 48.40 N 15.40 E
Horn ⊥8 52 53.38 N 10.05 E
Horn ≻ 24a 66.28 N 22.28 W
Horn ≃, N.W. Ter., Can. 176 61.30 N 118.01 W
Horn ≃, Eur. 56 49.15 N 7.20 E
Horn, Ben ∧2 46 58.01 N 4.02 W
Horn, Cape → Hornos, Cabo de ≻ 254 55.59 S 67.16 W
Hornád (Hernád) ≃ 30 47.56 N 21.08 E
Hornaday ≃ 180 69.22 N 123.50 W
Hornafjördur C 24a 64.17 N 15.16 W
Hornavan ⊜ 24 66.10 N 17.30 E
Hornbach 56 49.11 N 7.22 E
Hornbæk 41 56.05 N 12.28 E
Hornbeak 194 36.20 N 89.18 W
Hornbeck 194 31.20 N 93.24 W
Hornberg 58 48.13 N 8.13 E
Hornbrook 204 41.55 N 122.33 W
Hornburg 54 52.01 N 10.36 E
Hornby, Ont., Can. 275b 43.33 N 79.50 W
Hornby, N.Z. 172 43.33 S 172.32 E
Hornby Bay C 176 66.35 N 117.50 W
Horncastle 44 53.13 N 0.07 W
Hornchurch ⊥8 260 51.34 N 0.12 E
Horndal 40 60.18 N 16.25 E
Horndean 42 50.55 N 1.00 W
Horndon on the Hill 260 51.31 N 0.25 E
Horne 41 55.06 N 10.11 E
Horne, Îles de II 14 14.16 S 178.05 W
Hornebach ≃ 263 51.39 N 7.38 E
Horneburg, B.R.D. 52 53.30 N 9.34 E
Horneburg, B.R.D. 263 51.38 N 7.18 E
Hörnefors 26 63.38 N 19.54 E
Hornell 210 42.19 N 77.40 W
Hornepayne 176 49.13 N 84.47 W
Hornerstown 208 40.06 N 74.31 W
Hornhausen 54 52.02 N 11.10 E
Horn Head ≻ 48 55.14 N 7.59 W
Horn Hill 260 51.37 N 0.32 W
Horní Jiretín 54 50.35 N 13.32 E
Hornindal 26 61.58 N 6.31 E
Hornindalsvatnet ⊜ 26 61.56 N 6.22 E
Hørning 41 56.05 N 10.03 E
Hörningsholm 40 59.03 N 17.40 E
Horní Počernice 54 50.06 N 14.38 E
Hornisgrinde ∧ 58 48.36 N 8.12 E
Horn Island I, Austl. 164 10.37 S 142.17 E
Horn Island I, Miss., U.S. 194 30.13 N 88.38 W
Horní Slavkov 54 50.07 N 12.46 E
Hornito, Cerro ∧ 236 8.42 N 82.06 W
Hornitos 226 37.30 N 120.14 W
Horní Vltavice 60 48.57 N 13.46 E
Horn Lake 194 34.58 N 90.02 W
Horn Lake ⊜ 212 45.24 N 79.36 W
Hornomoravský úval ∨ 30 49.25 N 17.20 E
Hornos, Cabo de (Cape Horn) ≻ 254 55.59 S 67.16 W
Hornos, Isla I 254 55.57 S 67.17 W
Hornos, Islas de II 288 34.25 S 57.55 W
Hornow 54 51.38 N 14.31 E
Hornoy 50 49.51 N 1.54 E
Horn Plateau ⊥1 176 62.15 N 119.15 W
Horn Pond ⊜ 283 42.28 N 71.09 W
Hornsby, Austl. 170 33.42 S 150.06 E
Hornsby, Ill., U.S. 219 39.10 N 89.45 W
Hornsbyville 208 37.12 N 76.28 W
Hornsea 44 53.55 N 0.10 W
Hornsey ⊥8 260 51.35 N 0.07 W
Hornslet 41 56.19 N 10.20 E
Hornstorf 54 53.54 N 11.32 E
Hornsyld 41 55.45 N 9.51 E
Horntown 208 37.58 N 75.28 W
Hornu 50 50.26 N 3.49 E
Horoizumi 92a 42.01 N 143.09 E
Horoshiri-dake ∧ 92a 42.43 N 142.41 E
Horotiu 172 37.43 S 175.12 E
Hořovice 60 49.50 N 13.54 E
Horqueta 252 23.24 S 56.53 W
Horrabridge 42 50.31 N 4.05 W
Horrelville 172 43.20 S 172.20 E
Horrem 263 51.06 N 6.48 E
Horseback Knob ∧2 218 39.14 N 82.56 W
Horse Cave 194 37.11 N 85.54 W
Horse Creek 200 41.25 N 105.11 W
Horse Creek ≃, Colo., U.S. 198 38.05 N 103.19 W
Horse Creek ≃, Fla., U.S. 220 27.06 N 81.58 W
Horse Creek ≃, Ill., U.S. 219 39.45 N 89.34 W
Horse Creek ≃, Mo., U.S. 194 37.46 N 93.53 W
Horse Creek ≃, Wyo., U.S. 198 41.57 N 103.58 W
Horse Creek ≃, Wyo., U.S. 200 42.52 N 110.03 W
Horsefly 182 52.20 N 121.24 W
Horsefly Lake ⊜ 182 52.25 N 121.00 W
Horsehead Branch ≃ 284b 39.23 N 76.46 W
Horsehead Creek ≃ 198 43.17 N 103.22 W
Horsehead Lake ⊜ 198 47.02 N 99.47 W
Horseheads 210 42.10 N 76.50 W
Horse Heaven Hills ⊥2 202 46.10 N 119.45 W
Horse Islands II 186 50.13 N 55.45 W
Horsell 260 51.19 N 0.34 W
Horseneck Brook ≃ 276 41.01 N 73.38 W
Horsens 41 55.52 N 9.52 E
Horsens Fjord C 41 55.50 N 10.05 E
Horse Prairie Creek ≃ 202 44.59 N 112.52 W
Horse Shoe Bend 202 43.55 N 116.12 W
Horseshoe Bend National Military Park ♦ 194 33.00 N 85.46 W
Horseshoe Cove C 276 40.27 N 74.00 W
Horseshoe Creek ≃ 198 42.27 N 104.58 W
Horseshoe Falls ⌊ 284a 43.05 N 79.04 W
Horseshoe Lake ⊜, Man., Can. 184 52.12 N 95.50 W
Horseshoe Lake ⊜, N.J., U.S. 276 40.52 N 74.38 W
Horse Shoe Reef ⊥2 240m 18.40 N 64.12 W
Horsfjärden C 40 59.04 N 18.09 E
Horsforth 44 53.51 N 1.39 W
Horsham, Austl. 166 36.43 S 142.13 E
Horsham, Eng., U.K. 42 51.04 N 0.21 W
Horsham, Pa., U.S. 208 40.11 N 75.06 W
Horsham Saint Faith 42 52.41 N 1.16 E
Hørsholm 41 55.53 N 12.30 E
Hörsingen 54 52.16 N 11.09 E
Horsley, Austl. 274a 33.51 S 150.51 E
Horsley, Eng., U.K. 260 51.16 N 0.26 W
Horslunde 41 54.54 N 11.14 E
Horšovský Týn 60 49.32 N 12.56 E
Horst, B.R.D. 52 53.48 N 9.37 E
Horst, D.D.R. 54 53.22 N 10.37 E
Horst, Ned. 52 51.27 N 6.04 E
Horst ⊥8 263 51.32 N 7.02 E
Horsted Keynes 42 51.02 N 0.01 W
Hörstel 52 52.18 N 7.35 E
Horsthausen ⊥8 263 51.33 N 7.13 E
Horstmar 52 52.05 N 7.17 E
Horstmar ⊥8 263 51.36 N 7.33 E
Horsunlu 130 37.55 N 28.36 E
Horta 148a 38.32 N 28.38 W
Horta ⊥8 266d 41.26 N 2.00 E
Horta, Ouadi ∨ 146 17.51 N 21.52 E
Hortaleza ⊥8 266a 40.28 N 3.39 W
Horten 26 59.25 N 10.30 E
Hortobágy □9 30 47.35 N 21.00 E
Horton, Eng., U.K. 260 51.28 N 0.32 W
Horton, Ind., U.S. 218 40.05 N 86.09 W
Horton, Kans., U.S. 198 39.40 N 95.32 W
Horton, Mich., U.S. 216 42.09 N 84.31 W
Horton ≃ 180 70.00 N 126.53 W
Horton in Ribblesdale 44 54.09 N 2.17 W
Horton Kirby 260 51.23 N 0.15 E
Horton Lake ⊜ 176 67.30 N 122.28 W
Hortonville, N.Y., U.S. 210 41.46 N 75.02 W
Hortonville, Wis., U.S. 190 44.20 N 88.38 W
Horumersiel 52 53.41 N 8.00 E
Hørup 41 54.56 N 9.55 E
Hørve 41 55.45 N 11.28 E
Horw 58 47.01 N 8.18 E
Horwich 262 53.37 N 2.33 W
Horwood Lake ⊜ 190 48.03 N 82.20 W
Hory Matky Boží 60 49.16 N 13.27 E
Horzum 130 37.10 N 29.30 E
Hosaina 144 7.38 N 37.52 E
Hoşalay 130 42.00 N 33.27 E
Hösbach 56 50.00 N 9.12 E
Hosei University ⊌2 268 35.42 N 139.44 E
Hösel 56 51.19 N 6.54 E
Hosena 54 51.27 N 14.01 E
Hoséré Vokré ∧ 146 8.20 N 13.15 E
Hoseynābād 128 35.33 N 47.08 E
Hoseynīyeh-ye Khodā-Dād 128 32.42 N 48.14 E
Hosford 192 30.23 N 84.48 W
Hoshāb 128 26.01 N 63.56 E
Hoshangābād 124 22.45 N 77.43 E
Hoshangābād □5 124 22.30 N 77.30 E
Hoshangābād Plain ≃ 124 22.35 N 77.25 E
Hoshiārpur, Bhārat 123 31.32 N 75.54 E
Hoshiārpur, Bhārat 272a 28.35 N 77.22 E
Hoshigajō ∧ 96 34.31 N 134.19 E
Hosingen 56 50.01 N 6.05 E
Hosjö 40 60.35 N 15.46 E
Hoskins 164 5.27 S 150.30 E
Hosmer, B.C., Can. 182 49.35 N 114.57 W
Hosmer, S. Dak., U.S. 198 45.34 N 99.28 W
Hosoe 94 34.49 N 137.39 E
Hospental 58 46.37 N 8.34 E
Hospers 198 43.04 N 95.54 W
Hospet 122 15.16 N 76.24 E
Hospital 48 52.29 N 8.25 W
Hospital de Orbigo 34 42.28 N 5.53 W
Hospitalet 34 41.22 N 2.08 E
Hossegor 32 43.40 N 1.27 W
Hosston 194 32.53 N 93.53 W
Hosta Butte ∧ 200 35.35 N 108.12 W
Hoste, Isla I 254 55.15 S 69.00 W
Hostěradice 61 48.57 N 16.15 E
Hostetter 214 40.16 N 79.24 W
Hostigrām 272b 22.26 N 88.31 E
Hostivař ⊥8 54 50.01 N 14.32 E
Hostivice 54 50.04 N 14.15 E
Host'ka 54 50.30 N 14.20 E
Hostomice 54 50.35 N 13.46 E
Hostotipaquillo 234 21.04 N 104.04 W
Hostouň 60 49.34 N 12.46 E
Hosūr 122 12.43 N 77.49 E
Hot 110 18.06 N 98.36 E
Hota 268 35.08 N 139.51 E
Hotagen 26 63.59 N 14.15 E
Hotagen ⊜ 26 63.53 N 14.29 E
Hotagsfjällen ∧ 26 64.20 N 14.30 E
Hotaka 94 36.20 N 137.53 E
Hotaka-dake ∧ 94 36.17 N 137.39 E
Hotamış 130 37.36 N 33.13 E
Hotarele 38 44.10 N 26.22 E
Hotazel 158 27.15 S 23.00 E
Hotchkiss 200 38.48 N 107.43 W
Hotchkissville 207 41.46 N 73.13 W
Hot Creek Range ⊥ 204 38.30 N 116.25 W
Hötensleben 54 52.08 N 11.01 E
Hotevilla 200 35.56 N 110.41 W
Hotham ≃ 168a 32.58 S 116.22 E
Hotham Inlet C 180 66.45 N 162.00 W
Hotham Peak ∧ 180 66.48 N 160.42 W
Hoting 26 64.07 N 16.10 E
Hot Springs, Mont., U.S. 202 47.37 N 114.40 W
Hot Springs → Truth or Consequences, N. Mex., U.S. 200 33.08 N 107.15 W
Hot Springs, N.C., U.S. 192 35.54 N 82.50 W
Hot Springs, S. Dak., U.S. 198 43.26 N 103.29 W
Hot Springs, Va., U.S. 192 38.00 N 79.50 W
Hot Springs National Park 194 34.30 N 93.03 W
Hot Springs Peak ∧, Calif., U.S. 204 40.22 N 120.07 W
Hot Springs Peak ∧, Nev., U.S. 204 41.22 N 117.26 W
Hot Sulphur Springs 200 40.04 N 106.06 W
Hottah Lake ⊜ 176 65.04 N 118.29 W
Hotte, Massif de la ⊥ 238 18.25 N 73.55 W
Hottentot Bay C 156 26.05 S 14.58 E
Hottentotskloof 158 33.15 S 19.40 E
Hotton 56 50.16 N 5.27 E
Hötzum 54 52.13 N 10.37 E
Houailou 175i 21.17 S 165.38 E
Houa Khong □4 102 21.00 N 101.00 E
Houamuang 110 20.09 N 103.38 E

Symbols in the index entries represent the broad categories identified in the key at the right. Symbols with superior numbers (⊥2) identify subcategories (see complete key on page I · 30).

Kartensymbole in dem Registerverzeichnis stellen die rechts in Schlüssel erklärten Kategorien dar. Symbole mit hochgestellten Ziffern (⊥2) bezeichnen Unterabteilungen einer Kategorie (vgl. vollständiger Schlüssel auf Seite I · 30).

Los símbolos incluidos en el texto del índice representan las grandes categorías identificadas con la clave a la derecha. Los símbolos con numeros en su parte superior (⊥2) identifican las subcategorías (véase la clave completa en la página I · 30).

Les symboles de l'index représentent les catégories indiquées dans la légende à droite. Les symboles suivis d'un indice (⊥2) représentent des sous-catégories (voir légende complète à la page I · 30).

Os símbolos incluídos no texto do índice representam as grandes categorias identificadas com a chave à direita. Os símbolos com números em sua parte superior (⊥2) identificam as subcategorias (veja-se a chave completa à página I · 30).

English	Deutsch	Español	Français	Português
∧ Mountain	Berg	Montaña	Montagne	Montanha
∧∧ Mountains	Berge	Montañas	Montagnes	Montanhas
)(Pass	Pass	Paso	Col	Passo
∨ Valley, Canyon	Tal, Cañon	Valle, Cañón	Vallée, Canyon	Vale, Canhão
≃ Plain	Ebene	Llano	Plaine	Planície
≻ Cape	Kap	Cabo	Cap	Cabo
I Island	Insel	Isla	Île	Ilha
II Islands	Inseln	Islas	Îles	Ilhas
⊥ Other Topographic Features	Andere Topographische Objekte	Otros Elementos Topográficos	Autres données topographiques	Outros Elementos Topográficos

Symbol substitutions used below: ≃ river, ☲ canal, ↳ waterfall/rapids, ⋓ strait, C bay/gulf, ⊜ lake, ☷ swamp, ⍓ glacier, ⍑ other hydrographic feature, ∧ mountain, ⛰ mountains, ≻ cape, ▮ island, ▮▮ islands, V valley,)(pass, □ political unit, ⚜ cultural institution, ⊥ historical site, ♠ recreational site, ⊠ airport, ▪ military installation, ◂ miscellaneous, • other feature; [n] = printed superscript.

ESPAÑOL: Nombre — Página — Lat.°′ — Long.°′ W=Oeste
FRANÇAIS: Nom — Page — Lat.°′ — Long.°′ W=Ouest
PORTUGUÊS: Nome — Página — Lat.°′ — Long.°′ W=Oeste

Nombre / Nom / Nome	Página / Page	Lat.°′	Long.°′ W=Oeste
Houa Phan □[4]	102	20.30 N	104.00 E
Houbaishu	106	31.49 N	119.10 E
Houbao	98	41.54 N	125.14 E
Houcheng	106	31.55 N	120.26 E
Houdahepao	104	41.49 N	123.01 E
Houdain	50	50.27 N	2.32 E
Houdan	50	48.47 N	1.36 E
Houdelaincourt	58	48.33 N	5.28 E
Houdeng-Aimeries	50	50.29 N	4.08 E
Houeillès	32	44.12 N	0.02 E
Houffalize	56	50.08 N	5.47 E
Hough Green	262	53.23 N	2.47 W
Houghton, Mich., U.S.	190	47.06 N	88.34 W
Houghton, N.Y., U.S.	210	42.25 N	78.10 W
Houghton, Wash., U.S.	224	47.40 N	122.12 W
Houghton ◂[8]	273d	26.10 S	28.04 E
Houghton Green	262	53.25 N	2.34 W
Houghton Lake	190	44.18 N	84.45 W
Houghton Lake ⊜	190	44.20 N	84.45 W
Houghton-le-Spring	44	54.51 N	1.28 W
Houghton Regis	42	51.55 N	0.31 W
Houguangzhengtai	104	41.13 N	122.07 E
Hougujiazi	104	42.21 N	123.22 E
Houhai ⊜	271a	39.57 N	116.22 E
Hou Hoi Wan C	100	22.28 N	113.56 E
Houhuangtukan	104	41.02 N	122.29 E
Houillères de la Sarre, Canal des ☲	56	48.42 N	6.55 E
Houilles	261	48.56 N	2.11 E
Houjia	98	37.02 N	122.06 E
Houjiangfushan	105	40.03 N	117.09 E
Houjie	100	22.58 N	113.39 E
Houjiumen	104	42.38 N	123.18 E
Houkou	98	37.34 N	115.09 E
Houliujia	104	40.47 N	122.19 E
Houlka	194	34.02 N	89.01 W
Houlton	188	46.08 N	67.51 W
Houluan	105	39.13 N	116.32 E
Houlung	100	24.39 N	120.47 E
Houma, Tonga	174w	21.09 S	175.19 W
Houma, La., U.S.	194	29.36 N	90.43 W
Houma, Zhg.	102	35.40 N	111.29 E
Houmanzhoutun	104	42.29 N	123.14 E
Houmen	100	22.51 N	115.09 E
Houmont Park	222	29.50 N	95.13 W
Hound Creek ≃	202	47.13 N	111.23 W
Houndé	150	11.30 N	3.31 W
Hounslow ◂[8]	260	51.29 N	0.22 W
Houplines	50	50.42 N	2.55 E
Houqianjiayu	104	40.50 N	120.41 E
Houqiao	105	40.04 N	116.39 E
Hourn, Loch C	46	57.08 N	5.36 W
Housatonic	207	42.16 N	73.22 W
Housatonic ≃	207	41.10 N	73.07 W
House	196	34.39 N	103.54 W
House ≃	184	56.13 N	112.31 W
Houserville	214	40.50 N	77.50 W
House Springs	219	38.24 N	90.34 W
Houshan	106	31.03 N	120.21 E
Houshenfou	106	30.49 N	120.00 E
Houston, B.C., Can.	182	54.24 N	126.38 W
Houston, Del., U.S.	208	38.55 N	75.30 W
Houston, Minn., U.S.	190	43.45 N	91.34 W
Houston, Miss., U.S.	194	33.54 N	89.00 W
Houston, Mo., U.S.	194	37.22 N	91.58 W
Houston, Ohio, U.S.	216	40.15 N	84.20 W
Houston, Pa., U.S.	214	40.15 N	80.13 W
Houston, Tex., U.S.	222	29.46 N	95.22 W
Houston □[6]	222	31.20 N	95.20 W
Houston ≃	194	30.16 N	93.13 W
Houston, Lake ⊜[1]	222	29.58 N	95.07 W
Houston Creek ≃	218	38.13 N	84.15 W
Houston Intercontinental Airport ⊠	222	29.59 N	95.27 W
Houston Ship Channel ☲	222	29.21 N	94.47 W
Hout ≃	156	23.04 S	29.36 E
Houthalen	56	51.02 N	5.22 E
Houthulst	50	50.59 N	2.57 E
Houtkop	158	26.36 S	27.52 E
Houtkraal	158	30.23 S	24.05 E
Houtskär ▮	26	60.12 N	21.22 E
Houtzdale	214	40.49 N	78.21 W
Houwaterdam ◂[6]	158	30.20 S	23.39 E
Houwuliangdian	104	41.31 N	121.55 E
Houwutaigou	104	41.46 N	121.42 E
Houx	261	48.34 N	1.37 E
Houxi	100	28.46 N	118.49 E
Houxinlitun	104	41.05 N	122.33 E
Houxinqiu	104	42.34 N	122.43 E
Houyatai	104	41.26 N	121.49 E
Houying, Zhg.	98	40.24 N	123.50 E
Houying, Zhg.	105	39.51 N	117.15 E
Houying, Zhg.	105	39.42 N	118.18 E
Houyouzha	106	32.02 N	121.05 E
Houzhangcun	105	40.08 N	116.11 E
Houzhou	106	31.35 N	119.22 E
Houzitun	104	41.04 N	121.18 E
Hov	41	55.55 N	10.16 E
Hova	40	58.52 N	14.13 E
Hovborg	41	55.36 N	8.57 E
Høve, Dan.	41	55.50 N	11.30 E
Hove, Eng., U.K.	42	50.49 N	0.10 W
Hovedgård	41	55.57 N	9.58 E
Hövelhof	52	51.49 N	8.40 E
Hoven, Dan.	41	55.51 N	8.46 E
Hoven, S. Dak., U.S.	198	45.15 N	99.47 W
Hovenweep National Monument ♠	200	37.24 N	108.59 W
Hoveyzeh	128	31.27 N	48.04 E
Hovmantorp	26	56.47 N	15.08 E
Hovran ⊜	40	60.16 N	16.03 E
Hovsta	40	59.21 N	15.13 E
Howa, Ouadi (Wādī Howar) ↳	140	17.30 N	27.08 E
Howar, Wādī (Ouadi Howa) ↳	140	17.30 N	27.08 E
Howard, Austl.	166	25.19 S	152.34 E
Howard, Kans., U.S.	198	37.28 N	96.16 W
Howard, Ohio, U.S.	214	40.25 N	82.20 W
Howard, Pa., U.S.	214	41.01 N	77.40 W
Howard, S. Dak., U.S.	198	44.01 N	97.32 W
Howard, Wis., U.S.	190	44.33 N	88.04 W
Howard □[6], Ind., U.S.	216	40.29 N	86.08 W
Howard □[6], Md., U.S.	208	39.16 N	76.48 W
Howard Beach ◂[8]	276	40.40 N	73.51 W
Howard City	190	43.24 N	85.28 W
Howard Draw V	196	30.08 N	101.35 W
Howard Hanson Reservoir ⊜[1]	224	47.15 N	121.45 W
Howard Heights	284b	39.17 N	76.50 W
Howardian Hills ⛰[2]	44	54.07 N	1.00 W
Howard Island ▮	164	12.10 S	135.24 E
Howard Lake	190	45.04 N	94.04 W
Howard Pass)(	180	68.13 N	156.55 W
Howard Prairie Lake ⊜[1]	202	42.15 N	122.20 W
Howard University ⚜[2]	284c	38.55 N	77.01 W
Howden	44	53.45 N	0.52 W
Howe	216	41.43 N	85.25 W
Howe, Cape ≻	166	37.31 S	149.59 E
Howe Caverns •[5]	210	42.42 N	74.25 W
Howe Green	260	51.42 N	0.32 E
Howe Island ▮	212	44.17 N	76.15 W
Howeke	150	4.50 N	7.45 W
Howell	216	42.36 N	83.55 W
Howell Airport ⊠	278	41.39 N	87.45 W
Howell Island ▮	219	38.40 N	90.42 W
Howells	198	41.43 N	97.00 W
Howells Pond ⊜	276	41.03 N	74.42 W
Howes Cave	210	42.41 N	74.23 W
Howe Sound ⋓	182	49.22 N	123.18 W
Howe's Range ⛰	170	33.08 S	150.47 E
Howes Valley	170	32.50 S	150.51 E
Howey In The Hills	220	28.43 N	81.47 W
Howick, Qué., Can.	206	45.11 N	73.51 W
Howick, S. Afr.	158	29.28 S	30.14 E
Howitt, Mount ∧	166	37.10 S	146.40 E
Howland	188	45.14 N	68.40 W
Howland Island ▮	14	0.48 N	176.38 W
Howley	186	49.10 N	57.07 W
Howley, Mount ∧	186	48.17 N	58.26 W
Howmore	46	57.18 N	7.23 W
Howqua ≃	169	37.14 S	146.08 E
Howrah	126	22.35 N	88.20 E
Howrah □[5]	126	22.36 N	88.10 E
Howrah Bridge ◂[5]	272b	22.35 N	88.21 E
Howrah Railroad Station ◂[5]	272b	22.35 N	88.21 E
Howse Peak ∧	182	51.49 N	116.41 W
Howser	182	50.18 N	116.57 W
Howson Peak ∧	182	54.25 N	127.44 W
Howth, Eire	48	53.23 N	6.04 W
Howth, Tex., U.S.	222	30.10 N	96.04 W
Howth Head ≻	44	53.22 N	6.03 W
Hoxie, Ark., U.S.	194	36.03 N	90.58 W
Hoxie, Kans., U.S.	198	39.21 N	100.26 W
Höxter	52	51.46 N	9.23 E
Hoxton Park	274a	33.55 S	150.51 E
Hoxton Park Aerodrome ⊠	274a	33.54 S	150.50 E
Hoy ▮	46	58.51 N	3.18 W
Hoya, B.R.D.	52	52.48 N	9.08 E
Hōya, Nihon	94	35.43 N	139.34 E
Høyanger	26	61.13 N	6.05 E
Hoyerswerda	54	51.26 N	14.14 E
Hoylake	262	53.23 N	3.11 W
Hoyleton, Austl.	168b	34.01 S	138.33 E
Hoyleton, Ill., U.S.	219	38.27 N	89.16 W
Hoym	54	51.47 N	11.19 E
Hōyo-kaikyō ⋓	96	33.18 N	131.59 E
Hoyos	34	40.10 N	6.43 W
Hōyo-shotō ▮▮	96	33.52 N	132.18 E
Hoyran	130	38.19 N	30.59 E
Hoyran Gölü ⊜	130	38.12 N	30.50 E
Höytiäinen ⊜	26	62.48 N	29.39 E
Hoyt Lakes	190	47.31 N	92.08 W
Hoytville, Mich., U.S.	216	42.45 N	84.53 W
Hoytville, Ohio, U.S.	216	41.11 N	83.47 W
Hozain ≃	50	48.16 N	4.06 E
Hozat	130	39.07 N	39.14 E
Hozumi	94	35.24 N	136.41 E
Hpru-so	110	19.25 N	97.08 E
Hracholusky, údolní nádrž ⊜[1]	60	49.47 N	13.07 E
Hradec Králové	30	50.12 N	15.50 E
Hrádek nad Nisou	54	50.48 N	14.51 E
Hradiště ∧	54	50.13 N	13.08 E
Hranice, Česko.	30	49.33 N	17.44 E
Hranice, Česko.	54	50.15 N	12.10 E
Hrdlovka	54	50.36 N	13.40 E
Hřensko	54	50.50 N	14.14 E
Hriňová	30	48.36 N	19.31 E
Hrob	54	50.39 N	13.44 E
Hron ≃	30	47.49 N	18.45 E
Hronov	30	50.29 N	16.12 E
Hrotovice	61	49.06 N	16.07 E
Hrubieszów	30	50.49 N	23.55 E
Hrubý Jeseník ⛰	30	50.00 N	17.20 E
Hrušovany	61	48.50 N	16.23 E
Hrvatska (Croatia) □[3]	36	45.10 N	15.30 E
Hsenwi	110	23.18 N	97.58 E
Hsiakuan → Xiaguan	102	25.34 N	100.14 E
Hsiamen → Xiamen	100	24.28 N	118.07 E
Hsian → Xi'an	102	34.15 N	108.52 E
Hsiangt'an → Xiangtan	100	27.51 N	112.54 E
Hsiangyang → Xiangfan	102	32.03 N	112.01 E
Hsiaohungt'ou Hsü ▮	100	21.57 N	121.35 E
Hsichih	269d	25.04 N	121.39 E
Hsichi Hsü ▮	100	23.15 N	119.37 E
Hsich'üan Tao ▮	100	25.59 N	119.57 E
Hsientung	269d	25.09 N	121.44 E
Hsienyang → Xianyang	102	34.22 N	108.42 E
Hsi-hseng	110	20.09 N	97.15 E
Hsilo	100	23.49 N	120.27 E
Hsilo Ch'i ≃	100	23.47 N	120.15 E
Hsinch'eng	100	24.08 N	121.39 E
Hsinchu	100	24.48 N	120.58 E
Hsinchuang	100	25.02 N	121.26 E
Hsinghua → Xinghua	100	32.57 N	119.50 E
Hsingt'ai → Xingtai	98	37.04 N	114.29 E
Hsinhailien → Xinhailian	98	34.39 N	119.16 E
Hsinhsiang → Xinxiang	98	35.20 N	113.51 E
Hsinhua	100	23.01 N	120.20 E
Hsining → Xining	102	36.38 N	101.55 E
Hsinkao Shan ∧	100	23.28 N	120.57 E
Hsinking → Changchun	89	43.53 N	125.19 E
Hsinpeit'ou	269d	25.08 N	121.30 E
Hsinp'u → Xinhailian	98	34.39 N	119.16 E
Hsinshih	100	23.05 N	120.17 E
Hsintien	100	24.58 N	121.33 E
Hsintien Hsi ≃	269d	25.00 N	121.32 E
Hsinyang → Xinyang	100	32.19 N	114.01 E
Hsipaw	110	22.37 N	97.18 E
Hsip'ing Hsü ▮	100	23.14 N	119.36 E
Hsiukuluan Ch'i ≃	100	23.28 N	121.29 E
Hsiyü	100	23.36 N	119.30 E
Hsüanhua → Xuanhua	105	40.37 N	115.03 E
Hsüch'ang → Xuchang	100	34.03 N	113.49 E
Hsüchou → Xuzhou	98	34.16 N	117.11 E
Hsüehchia	100	23.14 N	120.11 E
Hsüehweng Shan ∧	100	24.24 N	121.12 E
Hsuphāng	110	20.18 N	98.42 E
Huaan	100	25.02 N	117.34 E
Huab ≃	156	20.52 S	13.25 E
Huabu	100	29.00 N	118.20 E
Huaca Juliana ⊥	286d	12.07 S	77.02 W
Huacaña	248	14.02 S	74.02 W
Huacaraje	248	13.33 S	63.45 W
Huachacalla	248	18.45 S	68.17 W
Huacheng	100	24.04 N	115.38 E
Huachi, Laguna ⊜	248	14.11 S	63.30 W
Huachipa	286d	12.00 S	76.56 W
Huacho	248	11.07 S	77.37 W
Huachón	248	10.40 S	75.57 W
Huachos	248	13.12 S	75.31 W
Huachuan (Hunanying)	89	46.13 N	130.32 E
Huachuca City	200	31.34 N	110.21 W
Huaco	252	30.09 S	68.31 W
Huacrachuco	248	8.39 S	77.05 W
Huade	98	41.46 N	114.16 E
Huadian	89	42.58 N	126.43 E
Huadingshan ∧	100	29.15 N	121.05 E
Huafeng	106	32.14 N	121.16 E
Huaguchang	107	28.58 N	104.30 E
Huagutang	106	30.55 N	119.18 E
Hua Hin	110	12.34 N	99.58 E
Hua Hsü ▮	100	23.24 N	119.20 E
Huaiá-Miçu ≃	250	10.52 S	53.15 W
Huaian, Zhg.	98	40.39 N	114.27 E
Huaian, Zhg.	100	33.32 N	119.10 E
Huaibin (Wulongji)	100	32.28 N	115.24 E
Huaide, Zhg.	89	43.32 N	124.50 E
Huaide, Zhg.	107	28.59 N	105.15 E
Huaidezhen	89	43.54 N	124.47 E
Huaihe ≃, Zhg.	98	37.28 N	114.55 E
Huaihe ≃, Zhg.	100	32.58 N	118.17 E
Huaihuazhenshi	106	31.05 N	119.41 E
Huaiji	102	24.01 N	112.18 E
Huailai	105	40.23 N	115.33 E
Huailinzhen	100	31.26 N	117.36 E
Huaillati	248	14.05 S	72.31 W
Huainan	100	32.40 N	117.00 E
Huaining	100	30.25 N	116.38 E
Huairou	105	40.19 N	116.37 E
Huaite → Huaide	89	43.32 N	124.50 E
Huaiyang	100	33.44 N	114.53 E
Huaiyin	100	33.35 N	119.02 E
Huai Yot	110	7.45 N	99.37 E
Huaiyuan	100	32.57 N	117.12 E
Huaiyushan ⛰	100	28.50 N	117.50 E
Huaji	100	32.46 N	115.20 E
Huajiang	102	25.50 N	110.21 E
Huajianzi	104	40.48 N	122.12 E
Huajiaodao ▮	98	39.26 N	121.17 E
Huajiapuzi	104	40.52 N	123.14 E
Huajiayingzi	104	42.20 N	121.00 E
Huajimic	234	21.42 N	104.20 W
Huajintepec	234	16.36 N	98.14 W
Huajuapan de León	234	17.48 N	97.46 W
Huakou	100	25.13 N	117.35 E
Hualahuises	232	24.53 N	99.41 W
Hualalai ∧[1]	229d	19.42 N	155.52 W
Hualañé	252	34.59 S	71.49 W
Hualapai Indian Reservation ◂[4]	200	35.38 N	113.30 W
Hualapai Mountains ⛰	200	34.50 N	113.55 W
Hualapai Peak ∧	200	35.04 N	113.54 W
Hualfín	252	27.14 S	66.50 W
Hualgayoc	248	6.46 S	78.37 W
Hualien	100	23.58 N	121.36 E
Hualin	89	44.35 N	129.35 E
Hualingpuzi	104	41.31 N	123.54 E
Hualla	248	13.44 S	73.55 W
Huallaga ≃	248	5.10 S	75.32 W
Huallanca, Perú	248	9.51 S	76.56 W
Huallanca, Perú	248	8.49 S	77.52 W
Hualong	102	36.05 N	102.36 E
Huamachuco	248	7.48 S	78.04 W
Huamanquiquia	248	13.44 S	74.15 W
Huamantla	234	19.19 N	97.56 W
Huambo (Nova Lisboa), Ang.	152	12.44 S	15.47 E
Huambo, Perú	248	15.44 S	72.07 W
Huambo □[5]	152	12.30 S	15.40 E
Huambo ≃	248	7.04 S	77.10 W
Huambos	248	6.28 S	78.58 W
Huameiao	100	26.32 N	115.47 E
Huameishan ∧	100	25.28 N	113.58 E
Huamugou	98	42.34 N	117.14 E
Huamuxtitlán	234	17.49 N	98.34 W
Huancabamba, Perú	248	5.14 S	79.28 W
Huancabamba, Perú	248	10.21 S	75.32 W
Huancané	248	15.12 S	69.46 W
Huancapi	248	13.41 S	74.04 W
Huancarama	248	13.39 S	73.05 W
Huancarqui	248	16.06 S	72.29 W
Huancavelica	248	12.46 S	75.02 W
Huancavelica □[5]	248	13.00 S	75.00 W
Huancaybamba	248	9.05 S	76.50 W
Huancayo	248	12.04 S	75.14 W
Huanchaca	248	20.20 S	66.39 W
Huanchaca, Serranía de ⛰	248	14.30 S	60.39 W
Huandacareo	234	19.59 N	101.17 W
Huando	248	12.29 S	74.58 W
Huang'aicun	106	31.43 N	118.40 E
Huang'anshi	100	29.06 N	113.34 E
Huangbai	98	41.17 N	126.21 E
Huangbaozi	102	39.54 N	99.26 E
Huangbeipu	104	42.21 N	123.25 E
Huangbi	100	28.48 N	120.06 E
Huangcaoping	100	25.42 N	113.27 E
Huang Chi ≃	269d	25.14 N	121.43 E
Huangchong	100	22.18 N	113.03 E
Huangchuan	100	32.09 N	115.03 E
Huangcun	105	39.56 N	116.11 E
Huangdai	106	31.26 N	120.33 E
Huangdan	107	29.10 N	103.44 E
Huangdao ▮	100	27.58 N	121.06 E
Huangdayang ⋓	100	30.03 N	122.26 E
Huangdi, Zhg.	98	40.14 N	120.15 E
Huangdi, Zhg.	105	40.57 N	118.24 E
Huangdu, Zhg.	106	31.16 N	121.13 E
Huangdu, Zhg.	106	30.47 N	118.51 E
Huangduqiao	100	29.18 N	120.55 E
Huanggaihu ⊜	100	29.44 N	113.23 E
Huanggang, Zhg.	90	30.27 N	114.52 E
Huanggang, Zhg.	98	34.39 N	116.03 E
Huanggang, Zhg.	100	28.32 N	114.33 E
Huanggang, Zhg.	100	30.27 N	114.52 E
Huanggangshi	100	33.09 N	115.55 E
Huanggu'an	98	35.28 N	115.42 E
Huangguayingzi	104	41.46 N	120.46 E
Huangguoshu	102	26.02 N	105.32 E
Huanghai → Yellow Sea ⍑[2]	90	36.00 N	123.00 E
Huanghe ≃, Zhg.	90	37.32 N	118.19 E
Huanghe ≃, Zhg.	100	32.19 N	115.02 E
Huangheya	98	37.19 N	116.19 E
Huangho → Huanghe ≃	100	32.19 N	115.02 E
Huang Hsi ≃	100	23.57 N	121.36 E
Huanghu	106	30.27 N	119.48 E
Huanghua, Zhg.	98	38.22 N	117.21 E
Huanghua, Zhg.	100	28.14 N	113.14 E
Huanghuadianzi, Zhg.	98	42.15 N	126.26 E
Huanghuadianzi, Zhg.	104	41.44 N	122.48 E
Huangji	98	34.26 N	116.59 E
Huangjiadao ▮	98	36.43 N	121.37 E
Huangjialing	104	42.12 N	122.55 E
Huangjialu	106	31.00 N	121.45 E
Huangjiangshui ≃	100	22.54 N	115.18 E
Huangjiatun	104	41.11 N	122.54 E
Huangjiazhai	106	32.01 N	121.36 E
Huangjinbu	100	28.27 N	116.47 E
Huangjing	106	31.39 N	121.06 E
Huangjinjing	107	29.44 N	104.38 E
Huangjinzi	89	50.02 N	127.20 E
Huangjueshu	107	29.50 N	106.27 E
Huangkan	105	40.22 N	116.28 E
Huangkeng	100	27.35 N	117.39 E
Huangkou	102	42.46 N	93.58 E
Huanglaomen	100	29.30 N	115.49 E
Huangli	106	31.39 N	119.42 E
Huanglian	107	29.17 N	106.18 E
Huangling	102	35.41 N	109.09 E
Huanglingji	100	30.25 N	114.03 E
Huanglong, Zhg.	100	23.34 N	116.58 E
Huanglong, Zhg.	102	35.45 N	109.42 E
Huanglongdang	100	31.58 N	112.28 E
Huanglongxi	107	30.19 N	103.58 E
Huangmao	100	28.07 N	114.04 E
Huangmapi	100	23.30 N	114.33 E
Huangmei	100	30.04 N	115.56 E
Huangnihe, Zhg.	89	43.32 N	127.59 E
Huangnihe, Zhg.	100	31.06 N	117.22 E
Huangnixi ≃	100	24.48 N	116.31 E
Huangpi, Zhg.	100	26.39 N	115.51 E
Huangpi, Zhg.	100	30.53 N	114.22 E
Huangpujiang ≃	106	31.24 N	121.31 E
Huangqi	100	26.21 N	119.54 E
Huangqiao	106	32.15 N	120.13 E
Huangshabao	100	25.08 N	112.44 E
Huangshahe	102	26.03 N	110.58 E
Huangshajie	100	29.03 N	113.08 E
Huangshan	98	36.57 N	122.18 E
Huangshan ∧	100	30.07 N	118.10 E
Huangshanguan	98	37.32 N	120.16 E
Huangshapu	100	26.50 N	113.26 E
Huangshaqiao	100	28.56 N	114.40 E
Huangshatuo	104	41.12 N	122.31 E
Huangshi, Zhg.	100	26.15 N	115.54 E
Huangshi, Zhg.	100	25.23 N	119.04 E
Huangshi, Zhg.	100	30.13 N	115.05 E
Huangshi, Zhg.	102	29.00 N	111.02 E
Huangshidu	100	27.44 N	116.44 E
Huangshuihe	107	30.32 N	103.55 E
Huangsonggang	100	22.49 N	113.51 E
Huangtan, Zhg.	100	27.44 N	119.58 E
Huangtan, Zhg.	100	26.41 N	117.17 E
Huangtang, Zhg.	100	23.44 N	114.58 E
Huangtang, Zhg.	106	31.46 N	120.21 E
Huangtang, Zhg.	106	31.47 N	119.40 E
Huangtanghu ⊜	100	30.00 N	114.12 E
Huangtankou	100	28.50 N	118.53 E
Huangtantuan	100	30.53 N	113.33 E
Huangtian	100	23.52 N	114.58 E
Huangtianfan	100	29.10 N	120.08 E
Huangtu	100	27.36 N	118.00 E
Huangtuchang	107	30.41 N	104.18 E
Huangtugang	100	31.25 N	115.05 E
Huangtukan	104	41.21 N	122.45 E
Huangtuliangzi	98	41.14 N	118.39 E
Huangtuling	100	27.18 N	113.30 E
Huangtupo	105	39.47 N	116.16 E
Huanguelén	252	37.02 S	61.57 W
Huangxian	98	37.38 N	120.29 E
Huangxu	106	32.06 N	119.37 E
Huangyaguan	105	40.14 N	117.26 E
Huangyan	100	28.39 N	121.15 E
Huangyanzhuang	105	40.01 N	118.21 E
Huangyuan	102	36.42 N	101.25 E
Huangyuzeng	104	42.05 N	124.11 E
Huangze	100	29.35 N	120.55 E
Huangzeshan ▮	100	30.31 N	122.16 E
Huangzeyang ⋓	100	30.36 N	122.28 E
Huangzhai	100	29.27 N	120.00 E
Huangzhawan	102	40.36 N	96.55 E
Huangzhong	102	36.31 N	101.40 E
Huangzhu	110	19.29 N	110.24 E
Huangzhuang, Zhg.	100	34.05 N	112.15 E
Huangzhuang, Zhg.	105	39.29 N	117.31 E
Huangzhuangwa ⊜	105	39.33 N	117.33 E
Huangzhuangzhen	105	39.53 N	117.05 E
Huaning	102	24.14 N	102.56 E
Huaniqueo [de Morales]	234	19.54 N	101.26 W
Huaniugouzi	104	41.34 N	122.35 E
Huaniupuzi	104	41.23 N	123.31 E
Huanjiang	102	24.54 N	108.21 E
Huanren	98	41.14 N	125.21 E
Huanshan	100	28.10 N	121.12 E
Huanshui ≃	100	30.40 N	114.05 E
Huanta	248	12.56 S	74.15 W
Huantai	98	36.59 N	118.06 E
Huantan	100	31.49 N	113.04 E
Huántar	248	9.26 S	77.15 W
Huánuco	248	9.55 S	76.14 W
Huánuco □[5]	248	9.30 S	75.50 W
Huanuni	248	18.16 S	66.51 W
Huanxi	100	26.34 N	113.36 E
Huanxian	102	36.39 N	107.18 E
Huanxianghe ≃	105	39.34 N	117.45 E
Huanxiling	104	41.17 N	123.54 E
Huanzo, Cordillera de ⛰	248	14.30 S	73.20 W
Huapí, Serranía ⛰	236	12.30 N	85.00 W
Huap'ing Hsü ▮	100	25.24 N	121.58 E
Huaqiao, Zhg.	100	27.54 N	118.48 E
Huaqiao, Zhg.	100	28.56 N	121.27 E
Huaqiao, Zhg.	100	29.32 N	117.11 E
Huaqiao, Zhg.	102	27.28 N	110.02 E
Huaqiao, Zhg.	107	30.47 N	106.41 E
Huaqiaozi	107	30.30 N	103.53 E
Huara	248	19.59 S	69.47 W
Huaral	248	11.30 S	77.12 W
Huarás	248	9.32 S	77.32 W
Huari, Bol.	248	19.00 S	66.48 W
Huari, Perú	248	9.20 S	77.14 W
Huariaca	248	10.27 S	76.07 W
Huaribamba	248	12.16 S	74.57 W
Huarina	248	16.12 S	68.38 W
Huarmey	248	10.04 S	78.10 W
Huarochirí	248	12.09 S	76.14 W
Huarocondo	248	13.25 S	72.13 W
Huarong	100	29.30 N	112.34 E
Huásabas	232	29.47 N	109.18 W
Huasaga ≃	246	3.42 S	76.26 W
Hua Sai	110	8.02 N	100.18 E
Huasamota	234	22.30 N	104.30 W
Huascarán, Nevado ∧	248	9.07 S	77.37 W
Huasco	252	28.28 S	71.14 W
Huasco ≃	252	28.27 S	71.13 W
Huashan	98	34.39 N	116.44 E
Huashaoying	98	40.12 N	114.36 E
Huashishan ⛰	100	24.24 N	113.38 E
Huashu	106	31.50 N	120.28 E
Huatabampo	232	26.50 N	109.38 W
Huatangpu	100	25.48 N	112.52 E
Huating	102	35.09 N	107.10 E
Huatong	102	23.01 N	106.36 E
Huatunas, Lagunas ⊜	248	13.06 S	66.15 W
Huatusco de Chicuellar	234	19.09 N	96.57 W
Huauchinango	234	20.11 N	98.03 W
Huaura	248	11.04 S	77.36 W
Huaura ≃	248	11.06 S	77.39 W
Huautla	234	21.02 N	98.17 W
Huautla de Jiménez	234	18.08 N	96.51 W
Huaxian, Zhg.	98	35.37 N	114.32 E
Huaxian, Zhg.	100	23.22 N	113.12 E
Huaxian, Zhg.	102	34.30 N	109.40 E
Huayan	107	30.01 N	105.02 E
Huayang, Zhg.	102	33.25 N	107.44 E
Huayang, Zhg.	107	30.32 N	104.04 E
Huayingtai	104	40.43 N	122.19 E
Huayllay	248	11.01 S	76.21 W
Huayna Potosí, Nevado ∧	248	16.16 S	68.11 W
Huaytará	248	13.36 S	75.22 W
Huayuan, Zhg.	100	31.16 N	113.58 E
Huayuan, Zhg.	100	33.00 N	118.16 E
Huayuan, Zhg.	102	28.34 N	109.13 E
Huayuri, Pampa de ☷	248	14.30 S	75.30 W
Huazhou	102	21.40 N	110.33 E
Huazi	104	41.25 N	123.29 E
Huazigou	104	41.50 N	121.01 E
Huazikou	106	32.13 N	118.57 E
Huazolotitlán	234	16.17 N	97.56 W
Ḥubārah, Wādī V	142	27.21 N	31.39 E
Ḥubayṭah, Bi'r ⍑[4]	142	30.27 N	32.27 E
Hubbard, Iowa, U.S.	190	42.18 N	93.18 W
Hubbard, Ohio, U.S.	214	41.10 N	80.34 W
Hubbard, Oreg., U.S.	224	45.11 N	122.48 W
Hubbard, Tex., U.S.	222	31.51 N	96.48 W
Hubbard Creek ≃	196	32.54 N	98.53 W
Hubbard Creek Reservoir ⊜[1]	196	32.45 N	99.00 W
Hubbard Lake ⊜	190	44.49 N	83.34 W
Hubbards	186	44.38 N	64.04 W
Hubbardston	207	42.29 N	72.01 W
Hubbard Woods	278	42.06 N	87.44 W
Hubbell	190	47.11 N	88.26 W
Hubbelrath	263	51.16 N	6.55 E
Hubei □[4]	90	31.00 N	112.00 E
Huben, Öst.	64	46.56 N	12.34 E
Huben, Öst.	64	47.03 N	10.58 E
Huberdeau	206	45.58 N	74.38 W
Huber Heights	218	39.50 N	84.07 W
Hublersburg	210	40.58 N	77.37 W
Hubli	122	15.21 N	75.10 E
Hubuleng	102	41.19 N	111.08 E
Hucaogang	106	32.00 N	120.29 E
Hucclecote	42	51.51 N	2.11 W
Hucha	106	31.16 N	119.47 E
Huch'ang	98	41.25 N	127.03 E
Huchi	100	31.08 N	117.40 E
Huchow → Huzhou	106	30.52 N	120.06 E
Huckarde ◂[8]	263	51.32 N	7.24 E
Hückelhoven-Ratheim	56	51.04 N	6.10 E
Hückeswagen	56	51.08 N	7.20 E
Hucking	260	51.18 N	0.39 E
Huckingen ◂[8]	263	51.22 N	6.43 E
Huckitta Creek ≃	162	22.38 S	135.30 E
Huckleberry Island ▮	276	40.53 N	73.45 W
Huckleberry Mountain ∧	202	43.51 N	122.19 W
Huckleberry Mountain ∧[2]	212	44.28 N	75.28 W
Hucknall	42	53.02 N	1.11 W
Hucqueliers	50	50.34 N	1.54 E
Hucun	105	39.02 N	115.56 E
Hudangtou	106	30.48 N	121.22 E
Huddart Park ♠	282	37.26 N	122.19 W
Hudderfield Narrow Canal ☲	262	53.29 N	2.06 W
Huddersfield	262	53.39 N	1.47 W
Huddinge	40	59.14 N	17.59 E
Huddle Park Golf Course ♠	273d	26.09 S	28.07 E
Huddunge	40	60.03 N	16.59 E
Hude	52	53.07 N	8.27 E
Hudgin Creek ≃	194	33.40 N	91.59 W
Hūdī	140	17.42 N	34.17 E
Hudiksvall	26	61.44 N	17.07 E
Hudingshan	100	33.45 N	113.17 E
Hudong	100	22.51 N	115.56 E
Hudoutun	98	42.06 N	124.50 E
Hudson, Qué., Can.	206	45.27 N	74.09 W
Hudson, Fla., U.S.	220	28.22 N	82.42 W
Hudson, Ill., U.S.	216	40.36 N	88.59 W
Hudson, Ind., U.S.	216	41.32 N	85.05 W
Hudson, Iowa, U.S.	190	42.24 N	92.28 W
Hudson, Md., U.S.	208	38.35 N	76.15 W
Hudson, Mass., U.S.	207	42.24 N	71.35 W
Hudson, Mich., U.S.	216	41.51 N	84.21 W
Hudson, N.H., U.S.	188	42.46 N	71.26 W
Hudson, N.C., U.S.	192	35.51 N	81.30 W
Hudson, N.Y., U.S.	210	42.15 N	73.47 W
Hudson, Ohio, U.S.	214	41.15 N	81.26 W
Hudson, S. Dak., U.S.	198	43.08 N	96.27 W
Hudson, Tex., U.S.	222	31.19 N	94.50 W
Hudson, Wis., U.S.	190	44.53 N	92.45 W
Hudson, Wyo., U.S.	200	42.54 N	108.35 W
Hudson □[6]	276	40.44 N	74.02 W
Hudson ≃, U.S.	188	40.42 N	74.02 W
Hudson ≃, Ga., U.S.	192	34.14 N	83.10 W
Hudson, Lake ⊜[1]	194	36.20 N	95.05 W
Hudson Bay	184	52.52 N	102.25 W
Hudson Bay C	176	60.00 N	86.00 W
Hudson Falls	210	43.18 N	73.35 W
Hudson Highlands State Park ♠	210	41.26 N	73.58 W
Hudson Hope	182	56.02 N	121.55 W
Hudson Lake	216	41.43 N	86.32 W
Hudson Mountains ⛰	9	74.32 S	99.20 W
Hudsons Peak ∧	171b	36.26 S	149.10 E
Hudson Strait ⋓	176	62.30 N	72.00 W
Hudsonville	216	42.52 N	85.52 W
Hudun	144	9.08 N	47.32 E
Hudwin Lake ⊜	184	53.12 N	95.42 W
Hudžirt	86	47.05 N	91.10 E
Hue	110	16.28 N	107.36 E
Huebra ≃	34	41.02 N	6.48 W
Huechucuicui, Punta ≻	254	41.47 S	74.02 W
Huechulafquén, Lago ⊜	254	39.46 S	71.28 W
Huedin	38	46.52 N	23.02 E
Huehuetán	236	15.01 N	92.22 W
Huehuetenango	236	15.20 N	91.28 W
Huehuetenango □[5]	236	15.40 N	91.35 W
Huehuetlán el Chico	234	18.21 N	98.42 W
Huejúcar	234	22.21 N	103.13 W
Huejuquilla el Alto	234	22.36 N	103.52 W
Huejutla de Reyes	234	21.08 N	98.25 W
Huelgoat	32	48.22 N	3.45 W
Huelma	34	37.39 N	3.27 W
Huelva	34	37.16 N	6.57 W
Huelva, Río de ≃	34	37.27 N	6.00 W
Huenque ≃	248	16.12 S	69.44 W
Huentelauquén	252	31.35 S	71.32 W
Huércal-Overa	34	37.23 N	1.57 W
Huerfano ≃	198	38.14 N	104.15 W
Huerhuero Creek ≃	226	35.40 N	120.42 W
Huerhuero Creek, East Branch ≃	226	35.31 N	120.32 W
Huerhuero Creek, Middle Branch ≃	226	35.31 N	120.32 W
Huerlumada	120	32.45 N	90.00 E
Huerva ≃	34	41.39 N	0.52 W
Huesca	34	42.08 N	0.25 W
Huesca □[4]	34	42.05 N	0.00
Huéscar	34	37.49 N	2.32 W
Hueston Woods State Park ♠	218	39.34 N	84.44 W
Huetamo de Núñez	234	18.35 N	100.53 W
Huete	34	40.08 N	2.41 W
Huey	219	38.36 N	89.17 W
Hueyapan	234	18.52 N	98.40 W
Hueyapan de Ocampo	234	18.07 N	95.09 W
Hueytown	194	33.27 N	86.59 W
Hufengchang	107	29.43 N	106.07 E
Hüffenhardt	56	49.18 N	9.04 E
Huffman	222	30.01 N	95.05 W
Huffman Dam ◂[6]	218	39.48 N	84.05 W
Hüfingen	58	47.55 N	8.29 E
Ḥufrat an-Naḥās	140	9.45 N	24.19 E
Hügel, Villa ⚜	263	51.25 N	7.01 E
Huggins, Mount ∧	9	78.17 S	162.28 E
Hugh ≃	162	25.01 S	134.01 E
Hugh Butler Lake ⊜[1]	198	40.22 N	100.42 W
Hughenden	166	20.51 S	144.12 E
Hughes, Austl.	162	30.42 S	129.31 E
Hughes, Alaska, U.S.	180	66.03 N	154.16 W
Hughes, Ark., U.S.	194	34.57 N	90.28 W
Hughes ≃	184	56.46 N	100.01 W
Hughes, South Fork ≃	188	39.08 N	81.20 W
Hughes Airport ⊠	280	33.58 N	118.25 W
Hughes Creek ≃	169	36.53 S	145.08 E
Hughes Springs	222	33.05 N	94.38 W
Hughesville	210	41.14 N	76.44 W
Hughson	226	37.36 N	120.52 W
Hughsonville	210	41.35 N	73.56 W
Hugh Town	42a	49.55 N	6.17 W
Hugo, Colo., U.S.	198	39.08 N	103.28 W
Hugo, Okla., U.S.	196	34.01 N	95.31 W
Hugoton	198	37.11 N	101.21 W
Hugouji	100	33.23 N	117.08 E
Huguenot	210	41.25 N	74.38 W
Huguenot Lake ⊜	276	40.56 N	73.47 W
Huguf	144	9.59 N	45.50 E
Huhehaote (Huhehot)	102	40.51 N	111.40 E
Huhehot → Huhehaote	102	40.51 N	111.40 E
Huhsi	100	23.32 N	119.38 E
Huian, Zhg.	100	25.04 N	118.47 E
Huian, Zhg.	106	31.47 N	121.45 E
Huiarau Range ⛰	172	38.45 S	177.00 E
Huib-Hochplato ⛰[1]	156	27.00 S	16.45 E
Huibieyang ⋓	100	30.08 N	121.44 E
Huibu	100	28.18 N	115.15 E
Huichang, Zhg.	100	25.34 N	115.49 E
Huichang, Zhg.	105	39.04 N	115.04 E
Huichapan	234	20.23 N	99.39 W
Hŭich'ŏn	98	40.10 N	126.17 E
Huichou → Huiyang	100	23.05 N	114.24 E
Huichuan (Guanbao)	102	35.11 N	104.02 E
Huicungo	248	7.17 S	76.48 W
Huidong	102	26.41 N	102.36 E
Huidui	105	39.04 N	117.16 E
Huihe	106	31.45 N	121.43 E
Huijihe ≃	100	33.53 N	115.36 E
Huíla	152	15.04 S	13.32 E
Huíla □[5], Ang.	152	15.20 S	15.00 E
Huila □[5], Col.	246	2.30 N	75.45 W
Huila, Nevado del ∧	246	3.00 N	76.00 W
Huilai	100	23.04 N	116.18 E
Huili	102	26.43 N	102.10 E
Huiliuji	100	32.50 N	115.58 E
Huillapima	252	28.44 S	65.59 W
Huilong, Zhg.	100	23.46 N	114.34 E
Huilong, Zhg.	100	27.30 N	118.24 E
Huilong, Zhg.	100	25.22 N	116.24 E
Huilong, Zhg.	100	24.09 N	113.58 E
Huilong, Zhg.	107	30.28 N	105.26 E
Huilong, Zhg.	107	30.35 N	105.49 E
Huilongchang, Zhg.	107	30.18 N	103.39 E
Huilongchang, Zhg.	107	29.41 N	104.17 E
Huilongchang, Zhg.	107	29.17 N	105.01 E
Huilongchang, Zhg.	107	30.41 N	106.34 E
Huilotas, Sierra de las ⛰	196	28.08 N	102.03 W
Huimanguillo	234	17.51 N	93.23 W
Huimin	98	37.29 N	117.29 E
Huinan	98	42.40 N	126.00 E
Huinca Renancó	252	34.50 S	64.23 W
Hüinghausen	263	51.11 N	7.48 E
Huining	102	35.41 N	105.08 E
Huisachal	196	26.47 N	101.07 W
Huisduinen	52	52.56 N	4.44 E
Huishan	106	31.35 N	120.16 E
Huishui	102	26.07 N	106.24 E
Huismes	50	47.14 N	0.15 E
Huisne ≃	50	47.59 N	0.11 E
Huissen	52	51.57 N	5.56 E
Huistepec	234	16.39 N	98.20 W
Huiting	98	34.05 N	116.04 E
Huitiupan	234	17.13 N	92.39 W
Huitong	102	26.54 N	109.31 E
Huitongqiao	102	24.43 N	98.56 E
Huittinen (Lauttakylä)	26	61.11 N	22.42 E
Huitzilán	234	19.58 N	97.41 W
Huitzuco de los Figueroa	234	18.18 N	99.21 W
Huixian	102	33.47 N	106.16 E
Huixquilucan □[7]	286a	19.24 N	99.18 W
Huixtla	232	15.09 N	92.28 W
Huiyang (Huizhou)	100	23.05 N	114.24 E
Huiyao	100	27.16 N	118.05 E
Huizache	234	22.55 N	100.25 W
Huize	102	26.27 N	103.09 E
Huizen	52	52.17 N	5.14 E
Huizhou → Huiyang	100	23.05 N	114.24 E
Hujia, Zhg.	104	41.20 N	121.52 E
Hujia, Zhg.	106	31.25 N	121.37 E
Hujiadian	107	29.41 N	104.07 E
Hujiajie	104	41.06 N	122.10 E
Hujiasi	107	29.16 N	105.13 E
Hujiawopu	104	42.34 N	122.11 E
Hujiayu	105	39.28 N	115.27 E
Hujiazhuang	105	39.51 N	117.07 E
Hujie	102	24.56 N	100.32 E
Ḥukayyim, Bi'r al- ⍑[4]	146	31.36 N	23.29 E
Hukeng	100	27.29 N	114.18 E
Hukou	100	29.45 N	116.13 E
Hŭksan-chedo ▮▮	98	34.30 N	125.20 E
Hukui → Fukui	94	36.04 N	136.13 E
Ḥukūmah	140	13.52 N	36.07 E
Hukuntsi	156	24.02 S	21.48 E
Hukuoka → Fukuoka	96	33.35 N	130.24 E
Hukusima → Fukushima	92	37.45 N	140.28 E
Hukuyama → Fukuyama	96	34.29 N	133.22 E
Hula	144	6.29 N	38.34 E
Ḥula, 'Emeq ☷[1]	132	33.08 N	35.37 E
Hulahula ≃	180	70.00 N	144.01 W
Hulan	89	46.00 N	126.38 E
Hulanhe ≃	89	45.55 N	126.41 E
Hulbert, Mich., U.S.	190	46.21 N	85.09 W
Hulbert, Okla., U.S.	194	35.56 N	95.09 W
Hulberton	210	43.15 N	78.04 W
Ḥulda	132	31.50 N	34.53 E
Huldrefossen ↳	26	61.28 N	5.58 E
Huldsessen	60	48.24 N	12.42 E
Hulei	100	24.50 N	116.48 E
Huleia Stream ≃	229b	21.57 N	159.22 W
Hulett	198	44.41 N	104.36 W
Hulim	114	1.12 N	99.31 E
Hulín	30	49.19 N	17.28 E
Huliuhe ≃	98	40.10 N	114.33 E
Hull, Qué., Can.	212	45.26 N	75.43 W
Hull → Kingston upon Hull, Eng., U.K.	44	53.45 N	0.20 W
Hull, Ill., U.S.	219	39.43 N	91.13 W
Hull, Iowa, U.S.	198	43.11 N	96.08 W
Hull, Mass., U.S.	207	42.17 N	70.53 W
Hull, Tex., U.S.	222	30.09 N	94.39 W
Hull □[6]	212	45.40 N	75.35 W
Hull ▮[1]	14	4.29 S	172.10 W
Hull ≃	44	53.44 N	0.19 W
Hullavington	42	51.33 N	2.09 W
Hull Bay C	283	42.18 N	70.53 W
Hullbridge	260	51.37 N	0.38 E
Hull Glacier ⍓	9	75.05 S	137.15 W
Hullo	76	59.00 N	23.14 E
Hulmeville	285	40.08 N	74.55 W
Hulot, Lac ⊜	186	50.14 N	69.18 W
Hüls, B.R.D.	56	51.22 N	6.30 E
Hüls, B.R.D.	263	51.40 N	7.08 E
Hülscheid	56	51.16 N	7.34 E
Hülser Berg ◂[8]	263	51.24 N	6.31 E
Hülser Berg ∧[2]	263	51.23 N	6.33 E
Hulst	52	51.17 N	4.03 E
Hult	40	58.40 N	16.07 E
Hultsfred	26	57.29 N	15.50 E
Huludao	104	40.43 N	121.00 E
Hulufa	105	39.42 N	116.12 E
Hulun → Hailaer	89	49.12 N	119.42 E
Hulunchi ⊜	88	49.01 N	117.32 E
Huluyu	105	40.14 N	116.53 E
Ḥulwān	142	29.51 N	31.20 E
Ḥulwān Military Installation ▪	142	29.50 N	31.19 E
Ḥulwān Observatory ⚜[3]	142	29.52 N	31.21 E
Huma	89	51.43 N	126.38 E
Humacao	240m	18.09 N	65.50 W
Humaerhe ≃	89	51.40 N	126.44 E
Humahuaca	252	23.12 S	65.21 W
Humaitá, Bra.	248	7.31 S	63.02 W
Humaitá, Para.	252	27.03 S	58.33 W
Humaitá ≃	248	8.16 S	72.44 W
Humansdorp	158	34.02 S	24.46 E
Humansville	194	37.48 N	93.35 W
Humara, Jabal al- ∧	140	16.16 N	30.59 E
Humarock	283	42.08 N	70.41 W
Ḥumaydah	140	14.22 N	22.31 E
Humayingzi	98	41.06 N	116.48 E
Humayun's Tomb ⊥	272a	28.36 N	77.15 E
Humbe	152	16.40 S	14.55 E
Humbe, Serra do ⛰	152	12.13 S	15.25 E
Humbeek	50	50.58 N	4.23 E
Humber ≃, Ont., Can.	212	43.38 N	79.28 W
Humber ≃, Eng., U.K.	44	53.40 N	0.10 W
Humber, Mouth of the ≃[1]	44	53.32 N	0.08 E
Humber Bay C	275b	43.38 N	79.29 W
Humberside □[6]	44	53.55 N	0.40 W
Humberto de Campos	250	2.37 S	43.27 W
Humberto Primo	252	30.52 S	61.22 W

Symbol	English	Deutsch	Español	Français	Português
≃	River	Fluss	Río	Rivière	Rio
☲	Canal	Kanal	Canal	Canal	Canal
↳	Waterfall, Rapids	Wasserfall, Stromschnellen	Cascada, Rápidos	Chute d'eau, Rapides	Cascata, Rápidos
⋓	Strait	Meeresstrasse	Estrecho	Détroit	Estreito
C	Bay, Gulf	Bucht, Golf	Bahía, Golfo	Baie, Golfe	Baía, Golfo
⊜	Lake, Lakes	See, Seen	Lago, Lagos	Lac, Lacs	Lago, Lagos
☷	Swamp	Sumpf	Pantano	Marais	Pântano
⍓	Ice Features, Glacier	Eis- und Gletscherformen	Accidentes Glaciales	Formes glaciaires	Acidentes Glaciares
⍑	Other Hydrographic Features	Andere Hydrographische Objekte	Otros Elementos Hidrográficos	Autres données hydrographiques	Outros Elementos Hidrográficos
⇸	Submarine Features	Untermeerische Objekte	Accidentes Submarinos	Formes de relief sous-marin	Acidentes Submarinos
□	Political Unit	Politische Einheit	Unidad Politica	Entité politique	Unidade Política
⚜	Cultural Institution	Kulturelle Institution	Institución Cultural	Institution culturelle	Instituição Cultural
⊥	Historical Site	Historische Stätte	Sitio Histórico	Site historique	Sitio Histórico
♠	Recreational Site	Erholungs- und Ferienort	Sitio de Recreo	Centre de loisirs	Sítio de Lazer
⊠	Airport	Flughafen	Aeropuerto	Aéroport	Aeroporto
▪	Military Installation	Militäranlage	Instalación Militar	Installation militaire	Instalação Militar
◂	Miscellaneous	Verschiedenes	Misceláneo	Divers	Miscelânea

Humber Valley Park ♠ 275b 43.39 N 79.30 W
Humbird 190 44.32 N 90.53 W
Humble, Dan. 41 54.50 N 10.42 E
Humble, Tex., U.S. 222 30.00 N 95.16 W
Humboldt, Sask., Can. 184 52.12 N 105.07 W
Humboldt, Ariz., U.S. 200 34.30 N 112.14 W
Humboldt, Ill., U.S. 194 39.36 N 88.19 W
Humboldt, Iowa, U.S. 190 42.44 N 94.13 W
Humboldt, Kans., U.S. 198 37.49 N 95.26 W
Humboldt, Nebr., U.S. 198 40.10 N 95.57 W
Humboldt, S. Dak., U.S. 198 43.39 N 97.04 W
Humboldt, Tenn., U.S. 194 35.49 N 88.55 W
Humboldt ≃ 204 40.02 N 118.31 W
Humboldt, Mont ∧ 175f 21.53 S 166.25 E
Humboldt, North Fork ≃ 204 40.56 N 115.32 W
Humboldt, Parque ♠ 286c 10.28 N 66.54 W
Humboldt, Planetario ʋ 286c 10.30 N 66.50 W
Humboldt, South Fork ≃ 204 40.47 N 115.53 W
Humboldt Bay C 204 40.47 N 124.11 W
Humboldt Lake ⊜ 204 39.58 N 118.38 W
Humboldt Mountains ⩕ 9 71.45 S 11.30 E
Humboldt Park ♠ 278 41.54 N 87.42 W
Humboldt Redwoods State Park ♠ 204 40.19 N 124.00 W
Humboldt Salt Marsh ☷ 204 39.50 N 117.55 W
Humboldt-Universität ʋ[2] 264a 52.31 N 13.24 E
Hume, Calif., U.S. 204 36.47 N 118.55 W
Hume, N.Y., U.S. 210 42.29 N 78.08 W
Hume, Lake ⊜[1] 166 36.06 S 147.05 E
Hume and Hovell Lookout ♠ 169 37.15 S 144.59 E
Hume and Hovell Memorial ⊥ 170 34.10 S 150.47 E
Humeburn 166 27.24 S 145.14 E
Hūmedān 128 25.24 N 59.39 E
Humen 100 22.49 N 113.41 E
Humen C[1] 100 22.44 N 113.40 E
Humenné 30 48.56 N 21.55 E
Húmera 266a 40.26 N 3.47 W
Humeston 190 40.52 N 93.30 W
Humla Karnāli ≃ 124 29.38 N 81.52 E
Humlebæk 41 55.58 N 12.33 E
Hummelfjell ∧ 26 62.27 N 11.17 E
Hummelo 52 52.00 N 6.14 E
Hummelstown 208 40.16 N 76.43 W
Hummels Wharf 210 40.50 N 76.50 W
Hümmling ⩕ 52 52.52 N 7.31 E
Humos, Isla I 254 45.38 S 73.59 W
Humpata 152 15.02 S 13.24 E
Hümpfershausen 56 50.40 N 10.13 E
Humphrey, Ark., U.S. 194 34.25 N 91.42 W
Humphrey, Nebr., U.S. 198 41.41 N 97.29 W
Humphrey Creek ≃ 284b 39.14 N 76.30 W
Humphreys, Mount ∧ 204 37.17 N 118.40 W
Humphreys Peak ∧ 200 35.20 N 111.40 W
Humpolec 30 49.32 N 15.22 E
Humppila 26 60.56 N 23.22 E
Humptulips 224 47.14 N 123.57 W
Humptulips ≃ 224 47.03 N 124.03 W
Humptulips, East Fork ≃ 224 47.15 N 123.54 W
Humptulips, West Fork ≃ 224 47.15 N 123.54 W
Humptulips Ridge ∧ 224 47.20 N 123.45 W
Ḥumrat Shaybūn, Jabal ⩕[2] 142 29.06 N 31.16 E
Humula 171b 35.29 S 147.45 E
Humuqiao 106 31.09 N 121.14 E
Humuya ≃ 236 15.13 N 87.57 W
Hūn 146 29.07 N 15.56 E
Hunabasi → Funabashi 94 35.42 N 139.59 E
Húnaflói C 24a 65.50 N 20.50 W
Hunan □[4] 102 28.00 N 111.00 E
Ḥunayshāt, Ghurd al- •[8] 142 30.07 N 29.47 E
Hunchun 98 42.54 N 130.22 E
Huncoat 262 53.46 N 2.20 W
Hundeluft 54 51.58 N 12.20 E
Hundested 41 55.58 N 11.52 E
Hundewāli 123 31.55 N 72.38 E
Hundezler 130 40.45 N 40.15 E
Hundorp 26 61.33 N 9.54 E
Hundred 188 39.41 N 80.28 W
Hundred End 262 53.42 N 2.53 W
Hundred Island National Park ♠ 116 16.13 N 120.01 E
Hundred Islands II 116 16.13 N 120.03 E
Hundslund 41 55.55 N 10.04 E
Hundstein ∧ 64 47.20 N 12.54 E
Hundwil 58 47.22 N 9.19 E
Hunedoara 38 45.45 N 22.54 E
Hunedoara □[4] 38 45.45 N 23.00 E
Hünfeld 56 50.40 N 9.46 E
Hungary □[1] 22
30 47.00 N 20.00 E
Hungchiang → Hongjiang 102 27.00 N 109.51 E
Hungen 56 50.28 N 8.54 E
Hungerford, Austl. 166 29.00 S 144.25 E
Hungerford, Eng., U.K. 42 51.26 N 1.30 W
Hungerford, Tex., U.S. 222 29.24 N 96.05 W
Hungf'ou Hsü I 100 22.03 N 121.33 E
Hŭngho-ri 98 37.14 N 127.44 E
Hŭngin-ni 98 39.03 N 126.26 E
Hung-long 269c 10.40 N 106.39 E
Hungmao 100 24.55 N 120.58 E
Hŭngnam 98 39.50 N 127.38 E
Hungria → Hungary □[1] 30 47.00 N 20.00 E
Hungry Horse 202 48.23 N 114.04 W
Hungry Horse Dam ◆[6] 202 48.14 N 114.04 W
Hungry Horse Reservoir ⊜[1] 202 48.15 N 113.50 W
Hungry Lake ⊜ 212 44.48 N 76.53 W
Hungry Law 44 55.21 N 2.24 W
Hung-yen 110 20.39 N 106.04 E
Hunhe 104 41.43 N 123.26 E
Hunhe ≃ 98 41.01 N 122.27 E
Huningue 58 47.36 N 7.35 E
Hunish, Rubha ≻ 46 57.41 N 6.21 W
Huni Valley 150 5.28 N 1.55 W
Hunjiang 98 41.56 N 126.29 E
Hunker 279b 40.12 N 79.38 W
Ḥunkurāb, Ra's ≻ 140 24.34 N 35.10 E
Hunn ⊜ 40 58.51 N 15.57 E
Hunneberg ∧[2] 26 58.20 N 12.27 E
Hunnebostrand 26 58.27 N 11.18 E
Hunnewell 219 39.40 N 91.52 W
Hunnewell Lake ⊜ 219 39.42 N 91.52 W
Hunsberge ⩕ 156 27.45 S 17.12 E
Hunseby 41 54.48 N 11.32 E
Hunshuitang 102 25.12 N 102.58 E
Hunspach 56 48.57 N 7.57 E
Hunsrück ⩕ 56 49.50 N 6.40 E
Hunstanton 42 52.57 N 0.30 E
Hunstein Range ⩕ 164 4.30 S 142.40 E
Hunsūr 122 12.18 N 76.17 E
Hunswinkel 263 51.05 N 7.48 E
Hunt □[6] 222 33.03 N 96.05 W
Hunte ≃ 52 52.30 N 8.19 E
Hunter, N. Dak., U.S. 198 47.12 N 97.13 W
Hunter, N.Y., U.S. 210 42.13 N 74.13 W
Hunter ≃, Austl. 170 32.50 S 151.42 E
Hunter ≃, N.Z. 172 44.22 S 169.25 E
Hunter, Mount ∧ 180 62.57 N 151.05 W
Hunter, Port C 170 32.55 S 151.48 E
Hunterdon □[6] 208 40.31 N 74.52 W
Hunter Island I, Austl. 166 40.32 S 144.45 E
Hunter Island I, B.C., Can. 182 51.55 N 128.05 W
Hunter Island I, N. Cal. 14 22.24 S 172.03 E
Hunter Island I, N.Y., U.S. 276 40.53 N 73.47 W
Hunter Island Ridge ⊹[3] 14 21.30 S 175.00 E
Hunter Liggett Military Reservation ■ 226 35.55 N 121.15 W
Hunter Mountain ∧ 210 42.10 N 74.14 W
Hunter Mountains ⩕ 172 45.42 S 167.25 E
Hunter River 186 46.21 N 63.21 W
Hunters Bay C 110 19.57 N 93.19 E
Hunters Creek Village 222 29.46 N 95.24 W
Huntersfield Mountain ∧ 210 42.21 N 74.21 W
Hunters Hill 274a 33.50 S 151.09 E
Hunters Point ≻ 282 37.43 N 122.22 W
Hunter's Quay 46 55.58 N 4.55 W
Hunters Road 154 19.09 S 29.48 E
Hunters Run 208 40.05 N 77.11 W
Huntersville 192 35.25 N 80.50 W
Huntertown 216 41.14 N 85.10 W
Hunterville 172 39.56 S 175.34 E
Hunter Wash ∨ 200 36.17 N 108.34 W
Huntingburg 194 38.18 N 86.57 W
Hunting Creek ≃ 208 39.33 N 77.20 W
Huntingdon, B.C., Can. 224 49.00 N 122.16 W
Huntingdon, Qué., Can. 206 45.05 N 74.10 W
Huntingdon, Eng., U.K. 42 52.20 N 0.12 W
Huntingdon, Pa., U.S. 214 40.29 N 78.01 W
Huntingdon, Tenn., U.S. 194 36.00 N 88.26 W
Huntingdon □[6], Qué., Can. 206 45.05 N 74.00 W
Huntingdon □[6], Pa., U.S. 214 40.29 N 78.01 W
Huntingdon Valley Creek ≃ 285 40.07 N 75.04 W
Hunting Island State Park ♠ 192 32.20 N 80.30 W
Huntington, Eng., U.K. 44 54.01 N 1.04 W
Huntington, Ind., U.S. 216 40.53 N 85.30 W
Huntington, Mass., U.S. 207 42.14 N 72.53 W
Huntington, N.Y., U.S. 210 40.51 N 73.25 W
Huntington, Oreg., U.S. 202 44.21 N 117.16 W
Huntington, Tex., U.S. 222 31.17 N 94.34 W
Huntington, Utah, U.S. 200 39.20 N 110.58 W
Huntington, Va., U.S. 284c 38.48 N 77.15 W
Huntington, W. Va., U.S. 188 38.25 N 82.26 W
Huntington □[6] 216 40.53 N 85.30 W
Huntington Bay 276 40.54 N 73.25 W
Huntington Bay C 276 40.55 N 73.25 W
Huntington Beach, Calif., U.S. 228 33.39 N 118.01 W
Huntington Beach, N.Y., U.S. 276 40.54 N 73.23 W
Huntington Creek ≃, Nev., U.S. 204 40.37 N 115.43 W
Huntington Creek ≃, Pa., U.S. 210 41.06 N 76.22 W
Huntington Creek ≃, Utah, U.S. 200 39.09 N 110.55 W
Huntington Harbor C 276 40.54 N 73.26 W
Huntington Lake 226 37.15 N 119.14 W
Huntington Lake ⊜[1], Calif., U.S. 226 37.14 N 119.12 W
Huntington Lake ⊜[1], Ind., U.S. 216 40.50 N 85.25 W
Huntington Library ʋ[3] 280 34.08 N 118.07 W
Huntington Mills 210 41.11 N 76.14 W
Huntington Park 228 33.59 N 118.13 W
Huntington Park ♠ 279a 41.29 N 81.56 W
Huntington Station 210 40.51 N 73.25 W
Huntington Woods 281 42.29 N 83.10 W
Huntingtown 208 38.37 N 76.37 W
Hunting Valley 279a 41.31 N 81.23 W
Huntingville 206 45.20 N 71.51 W
Huntley, Ill., U.S. 216 42.10 N 88.26 W
Huntley, Mont., U.S. 202 45.54 N 108.19 W
Huntly, N.Z. 172 37.33 S 175.10 E
Huntly, Scot., U.K. 28
46 57.27 N 2.47 W
Hunt Mountain ∧ 202 44.44 N 107.45 W
Hunton 260 51.13 N 0.28 E
Huntsburg 214 41.32 N 81.03 W
Hunt's Cross ◆[8] 262 53.21 N 2.51 W
Hunts Point 224 47.39 N 122.14 W
Huntsville, Ont., Can. 212 45.20 N 79.13 W
Huntsville, Ala., U.S. 194 34.44 N 86.35 W
Huntsville, Ark., U.S. 194 36.05 N 93.44 W
Huntsville, Ill., U.S. 219 40.11 N 90.52 W
Huntsville, Ind., U.S. 218 40.01 N 85.44 W
Huntsville, Mo., U.S. 194 39.26 N 92.33 W
Huntsville, Ohio, U.S. 216 40.26 N 83.49 W
Huntsville, Tenn., U.S. 192 36.25 N 84.29 W
Huntsville, Tex., U.S. 222 30.43 N 95.33 W
Huntsville, Utah, U.S. 200 41.16 N 111.46 W
Huntsville State Park ♠ 222 30.37 N 95.32 W
Hunū, Kathīb al- •[8] 142 30.37 N 32.49 E
Hunucmá 232 21.01 N 89.52 W
Hunut 130 40.39 N 41.09 E
Hünxe 52 51.38 N 6.46 E
Hünxer Wald ♠ 263 51.40 N 6.50 E
Hunyani (Panhame) ≃ 154 15.37 S 30.39 E
Hunyuan 98 39.48 N 113.41 E
Hun-yung 98 42.53 N 130.12 E
Hunza ≃ 123 35.55 N 74.22 E
Huobuxunhu ⊜ 102 36.39 N 96.20 E
Huocheng 86 44.12 N 80.26 E
Huoergeluo 89 45.35 N 120.56 E
Huoerpahu ⊜ 120 34.32 N 81.03 E
Huokou 100 26.28 N 119.16 E
Huolehe ≃ 89 44.55 N 122.35 E
Huolong 106 32.04 N 121.17 E
Huolongmen 89 49.48 N 125.47 E
Huolu 98 38.05 N 114.18 E
Huong-hoa 110 16.37 N 106.45 E
Huong-khe 110 18.13 N 105.41 E
Huong-thuy 110 16.25 N 107.40 E
Huon Gulf C 164 7.10 S 147.25 E
Huon Peninsula ≻[1] 164 6.25 S 147.25 E
Huonville 166 43.01 S 147.02 E
Huoqiu 100 32.20 N 116.16 E
Huorili 89 49.00 N 124.41 E
Huoshan 100 31.25 N 116.20 E
Huoshan ⩕ 102 36.40 N 111.50 E
Huoshaoliao 100 25.00 N 121.45 E
Huoshao Tao I 100 22.40 N 121.30 E
Huotong 100 26.53 N 119.25 E
Huotongxi ≃ 100 26.50 N 119.32 E
Huotuolaihuduke 102 40.19 N 104.18 E
Huoxi ≃ 100 25.20 N 117.21 E
Huoxian, Zhg. 102 36.37 N 111.40 E
Huoxian, Zhg. 105 39.46 N 116.46 E
Huoyan 100 33.42 N 113.40 E
Hupeh → Hubei □[4] 90 31.00 N 112.00 E
Hupu 106 31.45 N 120.54 E
Huqiao 106 31.26 N 119.26 E
Hura 126 23.18 N 86.39 E
Hūrand 84 38.51 N 47.22 E
Hurao (Hulin) 89 45.46 N 132.59 E
Hurāsāgar ≃ 126 24.04 N 89.40 E
Ḥuraydīn, Wādī ∨ 132 30.59 N 33.53 E
Ḥuraymilā 128 25.08 N 46.08 E
Hūrayn 142 30.39 N 31.08 E
Hurd, Cape ≻ 190 45.13 N 81.44 W
Hurdalssjøen ⊜ 26 60.20 N 11.05 E
Hurdland 219 40.08 N 92.18 W
Hurdsfield 262 53.16 N 2.06 W
Hurepoix ◆[1] 261 48.40 N 2.10 E
Hurffville 285 39.46 N 75.07 W
Huriel 32 46.23 N 2.29 E
Hurley, Miss., U.S. 194 30.40 N 88.30 W
Hurley, N. Mex., U.S. 200 32.42 N 108.08 W
Hurley, N.Y., U.S. 210 41.55 N 74.04 W
Hurley, S. Dak., U.S. 198 43.17 N 97.05 W
Hurley, Wis., U.S. 190 46.28 N 90.08 W
Hurleyville 210 41.44 N 74.40 W
Hurlford 46 55.36 N 4.28 W
Hurliness 46 58.47 N 3.15 W
Hurlingham 258 34.36 S 58.38 W
Hurlock 188 38.38 N 75.52 W
Hurmāgai 128 28.18 N 64.26 E
Huron, Calif., U.S. 226 36.12 N 120.06 W
Huron, Ohio, U.S. 214 41.24 N 82.33 W
Huron, S. Dak., U.S. 198 44.22 N 98.13 W
Huron □[6], Ont., Can. 212 43.45 N 81.10 W
Huron □[6], Ohio, U.S. 214 41.15 N 82.37 W
Huron ≃ 216 42.03 N 83.14 W
Huron, East Branch ≃ 214 41.17 N 82.38 W
Huron, Lake ⊜ 190 44.30 N 82.15 W
Huron, Point ≻ 214 42.34 N 82.47 W
Huron, West Branch ≃ 214 41.17 N 82.38 W
Huron Gardens 216 42.38 N 83.20 W
Huron Mountains ⩕[2] 190 46.45 N 87.45 W
Hurons, Rivière des ≃ 206 45.28 N 73.16 W
Hurricane, Alaska, U.S. 180 62.59 N 149.38 W
Hurricane, Utah, U.S. 200 37.11 N 113.17 W
Hurricane, W. Va., U.S. 188 38.26 N 82.01 W
Hurricane Bayou ≃ 222 31.21 N 95.35 W
Hurricane Creek ≃, Ark., U.S. 194 34.05 N 92.23 W
Hurricane Creek ≃, Ga., U.S. 192 31.23 N 82.19 W
Hurricane Creek ≃, Ill., U.S. 219 38.53 N 89.13 W
Hurricane Wash ∨ 200 37.00 N 113.23 W
Hurshi 126 24.17 N 88.28 E
Hursley 42 51.02 N 1.24 W
Hurso 144 9.38 N 41.38 E
Hurst 222 32.49 N 97.09 W
Hurstbourne Tarrant 42 51.17 N 1.23 W
Hurstbridge 169 37.38 S 145.12 E
Hurstpierpoint 42 50.56 N 0.11 W
Hurstville 170 33.58 S 151.06 E
Hurstwood Reservoir ⊜[1] 262 53.47 N 2.10 W
Hurtado ≃ 252 30.35 S 71.11 W
Hürth 56 50.52 N 6.51 E
Hurtsboro 194 32.14 N 85.25 W
Hurunui ≃ 172 42.55 S 173.17 E
Hurup 26 56.45 N 8.25 E
Husainābād 124 24.32 N 84.01 E
Husainīwāla 123 30.59 N 74.34 E
Husainpur 124 24.25 N 90.40 E
Húsavík 24a 66.04 N 17.18 W
Husby-Långhundra 40 59.45 N 18.01 E
Huse → Higashiōsaka 96 34.39 N 135.35 E
Husen ◆[8] 263 51.33 N 7.36 E
Hüseyinli 130 40.21 N 33.59 E
Hushan, Zhg. 89 45.35 N 130.35 E
Hushan, Zhg. 100 22.09 N 113.10 E
Hushan, Zhg. 100 28.36 N 118.59 E
Husheib 140 14.54 N 35.07 E
Hushi 107 28.57 N 105.22 E
Hushiha 105 40.52 N 116.59 E
Hushitai 104 41.57 N 123.30 E
Hushu, Zhg. 106 31.52 N 118.59 E
Hushu, Zhg. 106 30.18 N 120.08 E
Hushuguan 106 31.23 N 120.30 E
Huşi 38 46.40 N 28.04 E
Husinec 60 49.03 N 13.58 E
Huskisson 170 35.02 S 150.40 E
Huskvarna 26 57.48 N 14.16 E
Huslia 180 65.42 N 156.25 W
Hussar 182 51.03 N 112.41 W
Hussigny-Godbrange 56 49.29 N 5.52 E
Hustisford 190 43.21 N 88.36 W
Huston ≃ 220 25.42 N 81.17 W
Hustontown 214 40.03 N 78.02 W
Hustopeče 61 48.57 N 16.44 E
Husum, B.R.D. 41 54.28 N 9.03 E
Husum, Sve. 26 63.20 N 19.10 E
Husum, Wash., U.S. 224 45.49 N 121.29 W
Hutangqiao 106 31.46 N 119.57 E
Hutan Melintang 114 3.53 N 100.56 E
Hutanopan 114 0.41 N 99.42 E
Hutaym, Ḥarrat •[9] 128 26.15 N 40.20 E
Hutberg ∧[2] 54 52.09 N 14.33 E
Hutchins 222 32.39 N 96.43 W
Hutchinson, S. Afr. 158 31.30 S 23.09 E
Hutchinson, Kans., U.S. 198 38.05 N 97.56 W
Hutchinson, Minn., U.S. 190 44.54 N 94.22 W
Hutchinson, Pa., U.S. 214 40.13 N 79.44 W
Hutchinson ≃ 276 40.52 N 73.50 W
Hutchinson Island I 220 27.25 N 80.17 W
Hutch Mountain ∧ 200 34.47 N 111.22 W
Huthwaite 44 53.09 N 1.17 W
Hutou, Zhg. 100 26.04 N 118.46 E
Hutou, Zhg. 100 25.15 N 118.03 E
Hutou, Zhg. 106 31.37 N 119.37 E
Hutou, Zhg. 106 32.14 N 120.17 E
Hutouxi ≃ 100 25.57 N 118.02 E
Hutouya 98 37.13 N 119.46 E
Hutsonville 194 39.07 N 87.39 W
Hüttau 64 47.25 N 13.18 E
Hütteldorf ◆[8] 264b 48.12 N 16.16 E
Hüttener Berge ⩕[2] 41 54.26 N 9.40 E
Hüttenheim ◆[8] 263 51.22 N 6.43 E
Hüttental 56 50.54 N 8.02 E
Hutte Sauvage, Lac de la ⊜ 176 56.15 N 64.45 W
Huttig 194 33.02 N 92.11 W
Hütting 60 48.48 N 11.07 E
Hutto 222 30.33 N 97.33 W
Hutton, Eng., U.K. 260 51.38 N 0.22 E
Hutton, Eng., U.K. 262 53.44 N 2.46 W
Hutton, Mount ∧ 166 25.51 S 148.20 E
Huttonsville 212 43.38 N 79.48 W
Huttrop ◆[8] 263 51.27 N 7.03 E
Hüttschlag 64 47.10 N 13.14 E
Huttwil 58 47.07 N 7.51 E
Hutubi 86 44.07 N 86.57 E
Hutuohe ≃ 98 38.14 N 116.05 E
Huu 115b 8.48 S 118.25 E
Huvalu Forest ◆[3] 174v 19.03 S 169.51 W
Huveaune ≃ 62 43.15 N 5.23 E
Hüvek 130 37.22 N 38.31 E
Huvudskär I 40 58.57 N 18.34 E
Huwan, Zhg. 100 31.41 N 114.53 E
Huwan, Zhg. 100 27.55 N 116.31 E
Huwei 100 23.42 N 120.24 E
Huwun 144 4.23 N 40.08 E
Ḥuwwārah 132 32.09 N 35.15 E
Huxford 194 31.13 N 87.28 W
Huxi 100 26.12 N 114.44 E
Huxian 102 34.09 N 108.32 E
Huxley 182 51.56 N 113.14 W
Huy 56 50.31 N 5.14 E
Huy ∧ 54 51.57 N 10.57 E
Huyang 100 25.26 N 118.27 E
Huyangzhen 100 32.25 N 112.45 E
Huyton-with-Roby 262 53.25 N 2.52 W
Huyuesi 106 30.23 N 118.45 E
Hüyük 130 37.57 N 31.37 E
Huyutou 100 26.44 N 119.49 E
Huzhen 100 28.50 N 120.15 E
Huzhou 106 30.52 N 120.06 E
Huzhu 102 37.00 N 102.00 E
Huzhuangtun 104 40.43 N 122.33 E
Huzi 100 30.56 N 113.42 E
Huzisawa → Fujisawa 94 35.21 N 139.29 E
Hvalsø 41 55.36 N 11.50 E
Hvannadalshnúkur ∧ 24a 64.01 N 16.41 W
Hvar 36 43.10 N 16.27 E
Hvar, Otok I 36 43.09 N 16.45 E
Hvarski Kanal ⊔ 36 43.15 N 16.37 E
Hveragerdi 24a 64.03 N 21.10 W
Hvide Sande 26 55.59 N 8.08 E
Hvidovre 41 55.39 N 12.29 E
Hvittingfoss 26 59.29 N 10.01 E
Hvolsvöllur 24a 63.45 N 20.10 W
Hwach'ŏn 98 38.06 N 127.41 E
Hwach'ŏn-chŏsuji ⊜ 98 38.07 N 127.52 E
Hwach'ŏn-ni 98 39.01 N 126.02 E
Hwainan → Huainan 100 32.40 N 117.00 E
Hwaining → Anqing 100 30.31 N 117.02 E
Hwanggong-ni 98 40.03 N 129.27 E
Hwanghae Namdo □[4] 98 38.15 N 125.30 E
Hwanghae Pukdo □[4] 98 38.30 N 126.25 E
Hwang Ho → Huanghe ≃ 90 37.32 N 118.19 E
Hwangju 98 38.42 N 125.46 E
Hwangshih → Huangshi 100 30.13 N 115.05 E
Hyak 224 47.24 N 121.24 W
Hyakuna 174m 26.08 N 127.48 E
Hyakuri-ga-take ∧ 94 35.23 N 135.49 E
Hyannis, Mass., U.S. 207 41.39 N 70.17 W
Hyannis, Nebr., U.S. 198 41.59 N 101.44 W
Hyannis Port 207 41.38 N 70.18 W
Hyattsville 284c 38.56 N 76.56 W
Hyattville 202 44.15 N 107.36 W
Hybla Valley 208 38.45 N 77.05 W
Hyco Lake ⊜[1] 192 36.30 N 79.05 W
Hydaburg 180 55.12 N 132.49 W
Hyde, N.Z. 172 45.18 S 170.15 E
Hyde, Eng., U.K. 262 53.27 N 2.04 W
Hyde, Pa., U.S. 214 41.00 N 78.28 W
Hyden, Austl. 162 32.27 S 118.53 E
Hyden, Ky., U.S. 192 37.10 N 83.22 W
Hyde Park, Guy. 246 6.30 N 58.16 W
Hyde Park, N.Y., U.S. 210 41.47 N 73.56 W
Hyde Park, Vt., U.S. 188 44.36 N 72.37 W
Hyde Park ◆[8], Ill., U.S. 278 41.48 N 87.36 W
Hyde Park ◆[8], Mass., U.S. 283 42.15 N 71.08 W
Hyde Park ♠, Austl. 274a 33.53 S 151.13 E
Hyde Park ♠, Eng., U.K. 260 51.20 N 0.10 W
Hyde Park ♠, N.Y., U.S. 284a 43.06 N 79.01 W
Hyder 180 55.55 N 130.01 W
Hyderābād, Bhārat 122 17.23 N 78.29 E
Hyderābād, Pāk. 120 25.22 N 68.22 E
Hydetown 214 41.40 N 79.44 W
Hydra → Ídhra I 38 37.20 N 23.32 E
Hydraulic 182 52.36 N 121.42 W
Hyen ⊜ 40 60.36 N 16.12 E
Hyères 62 43.07 N 6.07 E
Hyères, Îles d' II 62 43.00 N 6.20 E
Hyères-Plage 62 43.06 N 6.10 E
Hyesan 98 41.23 N 128.12 E
Hyland ≃ 180 59.50 N 128.10 W
Hylestad 26 59.05 N 7.32 E
Hyllekrog I 41 54.36 N 11.30 E
Hyllinge, Dan. 41 55.16 N 11.37 E
Hyllinge, Sve. 41 56.06 N 12.51 E
Hyllstofta 41 56.08 N 13.16 E
Hyltebruk 26 57.00 N 13.14 E
Hymera 194 39.11 N 87.18 W
Hyndburn □[8] 262 53.45 N 2.23 W
Hyndman 188 39.49 N 78.44 W
Hyndman Peak ∧ 202 43.50 N 114.10 W
Hyne Field ⊠ 281 42.34 N 83.47 W
Hyōgo □[5] 96 35.00 N 135.00 E
Hyōgo ◆[8] 270 34.47 N 135.10 E
Hyŏn-ni 98 37.57 N 128.20 E
Hyōno-sen ∧ 96 35.21 N 134.31 E
Hyŏpch'ŏn 98 35.35 N 128.08 E
Hyrra Banda 152 5.57 N 22.04 E
Hyrum 200 41.38 N 111.51 W
Hyrynsalmi 26 64.40 N 28.32 E
Hysham 202 46.18 N 107.14 W
Hythe, Austl. 166 43.25 S 146.59 E
Hythe, Alta., Can. 182 55.20 N 119.33 W
Hythe, Eng., U.K. 42 51.05 N 1.05 E
Hythe End 260 51.27 N 0.32 W
Hyūga 92 32.25 N 131.38 E
Hyūga-nada ⊤[2] 92 32.00 N 131.35 E
Hyvinge → Hyvinkää 26 60.38 N 24.52 E
Hyvinkää 26 60.38 N 24.52 E

I

I □[4] 150 17.00 N 7.15 W
Iacanga 255 21.54 S 49.01 W
Iaciara 255 14.09 S 46.40 W
Iaco (Yaco) ≃ 248 9.03 S 68.34 W
Iaçu 255 12.45 S 40.13 W
Iaeger 192 37.28 N 81.49 W
Iago 222 29.17 N 95.58 W
Iakora 157b 23.06 S 46.40 E
Ialomiţa □[4] 38 44.30 N 27.20 E
Ialomiţa ≃ 38 44.42 N 27.51 E
Ialomiţei, Balta ☷ 38 44.30 N 28.00 E
Iamonia, Lake ⊜ 192 30.38 N 84.14 W
Iango 152 9.11 S 17.39 E
Iano, Monte ∧ 267a 41.46 N 12.44 E
Iapó ≃ 252 24.30 S 50.24 W
Iapu 255 19.26 S 42.13 W
Iaşi 38 47.10 N 27.35 E
Iaşi □[4] 38 47.15 N 27.15 E
Iato 70 37.58 N 13.07 E
Iatt, Lake ⊜[1] 194 31.35 N 92.40 W
Iauaretê 246 0.36 N 69.12 W
Iaú-Iabu ≃ 250 3.06 S 51.46 W
Iazu 38 44.44 N 27.25 E
Ib ≃ 120 21.34 N 83.48 E
Iba, Pil. 116 15.20 N 119.58 E
Iba, Zaïre 152 3.05 S 17.38 E
'Ibādah, Wādī ∨ 142 27.49 N 30.54 E
Ibadan 150 7.17 N 3.30 E
Ibagué 246 4.27 N 75.14 W
Ibaiti 255 23.50 S 50.10 W
Ibajay 116 11.49 N 122.10 E
Ibajay ≃ 116 11.49 N 122.10 E
Ibaka 152 4.16 S 23.12 E
Ibambi 154 2.22 N 27.37 E
Ibanda 154 0.08 S 30.29 E
Ibăneşti 38 48.04 N 26.22 E
Ibans, Laguna de C 236 15.53 N 84.52 W
Ibanshe 152 4.58 S 21.30 E
Ibapah Peak ∧ 200 39.50 N 113.55 W
Ibar ≃ 38 43.44 N 20.45 E

ENGLISH
Name Page Lat.°' Long.°'

Ibara 96 34.36 N 133.28 E
Ibaraki, Nihon 94 36.17 N 140.26 E
Ibaraki, Nihon 96 34.49 N 135.34 E
Ibaraki □[5] 94 36.30 N 140.30 E
Ibarra 246 0.21 N 78.07 W
Ibarreta 252 25.13 S 59.51 W
Ibaruma 175d 24.30 N 124.17 E
Ibb 144 14.01 N 44.10 E
Ibba 154 4.48 N 29.06 E
Ibba ≃ 140 7.09 N 28.41 E
Ibbenbüren 52 52.16 N 7.43 E
Ibeke Gembo 152 1.24 S 18.51 E
Ibembo 152 2.38 N 23.37 E
Ibenga ≃ 152 2.20 N 18.08 E
Iberia, Mo., U.S. 194 38.05 N 92.18 W
Iberia, Ohio, U.S. 214 40.40 N 82.51 W
Ibérica, Península ≻[1] 4 40.00 N 5.00 W
Ibérico, Sistema ⩕ 34 41.00 N 2.30 W
Iberoamericana, Universidad ʋ[2] 286a 19.21 N 99.08 W
Ibertioga 256 21.25 S 43.58 W
Iberville 206 45.18 N 73.14 W
Iberville □[6] 206 45.15 N 73.10 W
Iberville, Lac d' ⊜ 176 55.55 N 73.15 W
Iberville, Mont d' ∧ 176 58.53 N 63.43 W
Ibese 273a 6.33 N 3.29 E
Ibeto 150 10.29 N 5.09 E
Ibi 150 8.12 N 9.45 E
Ibi ≃ 94 35.03 N 136.42 E
Ibiá 255 19.29 S 46.32 W
Ibiapaba, Serra da ⩕ 250 4.00 S 41.00 W
Ibiapina 250 3.55 S 40.54 W
Ibiara 250 7.30 S 38.25 W
Ibicaraí 255 14.51 S 39.36 W
Ibicuí 255 14.51 S 39.59 W
Ibicuí ≃ 252 29.25 S 56.47 W
Ibicuicito, Arroyo ≃ 258 33.49 S 58.49 W
Ibicuy 258 33.44 S 59.10 W
Ibigawa 94 35.29 N 136.34 E
Ibipetuba 250 11.00 S 44.32 W
Ibipira 250 6.31 S 44.38 W
Ibiquera 255 12.38 S 40.57 W
Ibiraci 255 20.28 S 47.08 W
Ibiraçu 255 19.50 S 40.22 W
Ibirama 252 27.04 S 49.31 W
Ibirapuã 255 17.39 S 40.07 W
Ibirapuera ◆[8] 287b 23.37 S 46.40 W
Ibirapuera, Parque ♠ 287b 23.35 S 46.39 W
Ibirapuitã ≃ 252 29.22 S 55.57 W
Ibirataia 255 14.04 S 39.38 W
Ibiri 154 4.56 S 32.33 E
Ibirubá 252 28.38 S 53.06 W
Ibitiara 255 12.39 S 42.13 W
Ibitiguaia 256 21.57 S 43.25 W
Ibitinga 255 21.45 S 48.49 W
Ibitiúra De Minas 256 22.04 S 46.26 W
Ibituporanga 256 22.45 S 43.47 W
Ibiúna 256 23.39 S 47.13 W
Ibiza 34 38.54 N 1.26 E
Ibiza I 34 39.00 N 1.25 E
Iblei, Monti ⩕ 70 37.10 N 14.55 E
Ibnahs 142 30.34 N 31.07 E
Ibn Hānī', Ra's ≻ 130 35.35 N 35.43 E
Ibn Şirār, Bi'r ⊤[4] 144 19.30 N 42.41 E
Ibo 154 12.20 S 40.35 E
Ibo ≃ 96 34.46 N 134.35 E
Ibo, Ilha do I 154 12.20 S 40.36 E
Ibondo 154 2.38 S 32.40 E
Ibonma 164 3.28 S 133.28 E
Ibor ≃ 34 39.49 N 5.33 W
Ibotirama 255 12.11 S 43.13 W
Iboundji, Mont ∧ 152 1.08 S 11.48 E
İbradı 130 37.06 N 31.36 E
Ibrah, Wādī ∨ 140 10.36 N 24.58 E
İbrala 130 37.09 N 33.31 E
Ibresi 80 55.18 N 47.03 E
'Ibrī 128 23.14 N 56.30 E
İbriktepe 130 41.00 N 26.30 E
Ibshān 142 31.10 N 31.10 E
Ibshawāy 142 29.22 N 30.41 E
Ibstock 42 52.42 N 1.23 W
Ibta' 132 32.47 N 36.09 E
Ibu 174m 26.45 N 128.19 E
Ibuki 94 35.24 N 136.23 E
Ibuki-jima I 96 34.08 N 133.32 E
Ibuki-sanchi ⩕ 94 35.35 N 136.18 E
Ibuki-yama ∧ 94 35.25 N 136.24 E
Iburg 52 52.09 N 8.02 E
Ibusuki 93b 31.16 N 130.39 E
Ibwe Munyama 154 16.09 S 28.34 E
Ibychen, Gora ∧ 88 51.36 N 109.45 E
Ica 248 14.04 S 75.42 W
Ica □[5] 248 14.20 S 75.30 W
Ica ≃, Perú 248 14.54 S 75.34 W
Içá (Putumayo) ≃, S.A. 246 3.07 S 67.58 W
Ića ≃, S.S.S.R. 76 56.52 N 26.59 E
Icabarú ≃ 246 4.45 N 62.15 W
Icadambanauan Island I 116 10.49 N 119.38 E
Icamaquã ≃ 252 28.34 S 56.00 W
Icamole 196 25.55 N 100.43 W
Içana 246 0.21 N 67.19 W
Içana (Isana) ≃ 246 0.26 N 67.19 W
Icaño, Arg. 252 28.41 S 62.54 W
Icaño, Arg. 252 28.54 S 65.19 W
Icatu 250 2.46 S 44.04 W
Icatuaçu 256 23.44 S 46.24 W
Iceberg Pass)(200 40.25 N 105.45 W
Ice House Reservoir ⊜[1] 226 38.49 N 120.23 W
İçel □[4] 130 36.45 N 34.00 E
Iceland □[1] 22
24a 65.00 N 18.00 W
Icém 255 20.21 S 49.12 W
Ice Mountain ∧ 182 54.25 N 121.08 W
Ičera 88 58.32 N 109.47 E
İçerenköy ◆[8] 267b 40.58 N 29.06 E
Ichalkaranji 122 16.42 N 74.28 E
Ichāmāti ≃, Bhārat 126 22.35 N 88.57 E
Ichāmati ≃, Pāk. 126 24.00 N 89.15 E
Ichang → Yichang 102 30.42 N 111.11 E
Ichāpur 126 22.50 N 88.24 E
Ichawaynochaway Creek ≃ 192 31.10 N 84.28 W
Ich Bajan Ajrag ∧ 88 47.55 N 95.02 E
Ich Bogd Uul ⩕ 90 44.55 N 100.20 E
Ichbulag 102 45.26 N 113.10 E
Ich Buural Uul ∧ 88 48.00 N 94.30 E
Ichchāpuram 122 19.07 N 84.42 E
Ichdžargalan 102 45.31 N 108.50 E
Ichenhausen 58 48.22 N 10.18 E
Ichenheim 58 48.26 N 7.49 E
Ichhāwar 124 23.01 N 77.01 E
Ichi ≃ 96 34.46 N 134.41 E
Ichiba 96 34.05 N 134.17 E
Ichigaya, Camp ■ 268 35.44 N 139.41 E
Ichihara 94 35.31 N 140.05 E
Ichikai 94 36.32 N 140.06 E
Ichikawa, Nihon 94 35.44 N 139.55 E
Ichikawa, Nihon 96 34.59 N 134.46 E
Ichikawa-daimon 94 35.34 N 138.30 E
Ichilo ≃ 248 15.57 S 64.42 W
Ichinohe 92 40.13 N 141.17 E
Ichinomiya, Nihon 94 35.39 N 138.41 E
Ichinomiya, Nihon 94 35.18 N 136.48 E
Ichinomiya, Nihon 94 35.22 N 140.22 E
Ichinomiya, Nihon 96 35.06 N 134.35 E
Ichinomiya, Nihon 96 32.57 N 131.07 E
Ichinomiya, Nihon 96 34.28 N 134.51 E
Ichinomoto 270 34.37 N 135.50 E
Ichinose 270 35.53 N 135.10 E
Ichinoseki 92 38.55 N 141.08 E
Ichino-tani ⊥ 96 34.39 N 135.07 E
Ichino-tani Battlefield ⊥ 270 34.39 N 135.07 E
Ichiu 96 33.57 N 134.04 E

DEUTSCH
Name Seite Breite°' Länge°' E=Ost

Ichkeul, Garaet ⊜ 36 37.10 N 9.40 E
Ichoca 248 17.12 S 67.17 W
Ich'on, C.M.I.K. 98 38.30 N 126.50 E
Ich'ŏn, Taehan 98 37.17 N 127.27 E
Ichtamir 88 47.30 N 100.52 E
Ichtegem 50 51.06 N 3.00 E
Ichtershausen 54 50.52 N 10.58 E
Ich'un → Yichun 90 47.42 N 128.55 E
Ich-Uul, Mong. 88 49.27 N 101.27 E
Ich-Uul, Mong. 88 48.33 N 98.40 E
Icicle Creek ≃ 224 47.34 N 120.40 W
Ička, Gora ∧[2] 80 51.13 N 50.15 E
Ickenham ◆[8] 260 51.34 N 0.27 W
Ickern ◆[8] 263 51.36 N 7.21 E
Ickesburg 208 40.27 N 77.21 W
Icking 64 47.57 N 11.25 E
İçme 130 38.37 N 39.34 E
Ičn'a 78 50.52 N 32.24 E
Icó 250 6.24 S 38.51 W
Icoca 152 6.11 S 16.19 E
Iconha 255 20.48 S 40.48 W
Icoraci 250 1.18 S 48.28 W
Icy Bay C 180 60.00 N 141.15 W
Icy Cape ≻ 180 70.20 N 161.52 W
Icy Strait ⊔ 180 58.18 N 135.30 W
Ida, Som. 144 0.14 N 42.15 E
Ida, Mich., U.S. 216 41.55 N 83.34 W
Ida ≃ 88 53.10 N 103.20 E
Ida, Mount ∧, Austl. 162 29.14 S 120.25 E
Ida, Mount ∧, Jam. 241q 17.58 N 77.43 W
Idabel 194 33.54 N 94.50 W
Idaga Hamus 144 14.12 N 39.48 E
Ida Grove 198 42.21 N 95.28 W
Idah 150 7.07 N 6.43 E
Idaho □[3] 178
202 45.00 N 115.00 W
Idaho City 202 43.50 N 115.50 W
Idaho Falls 202 43.30 N 112.02 W
Idaho Springs 200 39.45 N 105.31 W
Idalou 196 33.40 N 101.41 W
Idanha-a-Nova 34 39.55 N 7.14 W
Idāppādi 122 11.35 N 77.51 E
Idar 120 23.50 N 73.00 E
Idarkopf ∧ 56 49.51 N 7.16 E
Idar-Oberstein 56 49.42 N 7.19 E
Idarwald ◆[3] 56 49.20 N 7.15 E
Idaville, Ind., U.S. 216 40.46 N 86.39 W
Idaville, Oreg., U.S. 224 45.31 N 123.53 W
Iddan 144 6.03 N 49.01 E
Iddo ◆[8] 273a 6.28 N 3.23 E
Ide 96 34.47 N 135.49 E
Idehan •[8] 146 28.00 N 11.30 E
Idehan ◆[2] 146 28.00 N 11.00 E
Idel' 24 64.08 N 34.14 E
Idelès 148 23.58 N 5.53 E
Idemba 152 2.38 S 11.38 E
Iden 54 52.46 N 11.55 E
Ider 88 48.13 N 97.23 E
Iderijn ≃ 88 49.16 N 100.41 E
Idermeg 88 47.36 N 111.15 E
Idfīnā 142 31.18 N 30.31 E
Idfū 140 24.58 N 32.52 E
Ídhi Óros ∧ 38 35.18 N 24.43 E
Ídhra 38 37.20 N 23.29 E
Ídhra I 38 37.20 N 23.32 E
Idi 114 4.57 N 97.46 E
Idice ≃ 64 44.35 N 11.49 E
Idi-cut 114 4.59 N 97.42 E
Idifina Barrage ◆[6] 142 31.17 N 30.31 E
Idimu 273a 6.35 N 3.17 E
Idio 116 11.37 N 122.06 E
Idiofa 152 5.02 S 19.36 E
Iditarod ≃ 180 63.02 N 158.58 W
Idkerberget 40 60.23 N 15.14 E
Idkū 142 31.18 N 30.18 E
Idkū, Buḥayrat ⊜ 142 31.16 N 30.17 E
Idle Hill 260 51.15 N 0.08 E
Idlib 130 35.55 N 36.38 E
Idlib □[8] 130 35.50 N 36.40 E
Idmū 142 28.09 N 30.41 E
Idnah 132 31.34 N 34.59 E
Idodi 154 7.47 S 35.11 E
Ídolo, Isla del I 234 21.25 N 97.27 W
Idomogu 273a 6.43 N 3.30 E
Idre 26 61.52 N 12.43 E
Idria 226 36.25 N 120.40 W
Idrica 76 56.21 N 28.53 E
Idrigill Point ≻ 46 57.20 N 6.35 W
Idrija 36 46.00 N 14.01 E
Idrijca ≃ 64 46.09 N 13.45 E
Idrinskoje 86 54.21 N 92.07 E
Idro 64 45.44 N 10.29 E
Idro, Lago d' ⊜ 64 45.47 N 10.30 E
Idroscalo ⊜ 266b 45.28 N 9.18 E
Idstedt 41 54.35 N 9.31 E
Idstein 56 50.13 N 8.16 E
Idutywa 158 32.02 S 28.16 E
Idyllwild 204 33.45 N 116.43 W
Idylside 216 41.31 N 88.07 W
Idylwood 284c 38.54 N 77.12 W
Idževan 84 40.53 N 45.07 E
Iecava 76 56.36 N 24.12 E
Iecava ≃ 76 56.41 N 23.42 E
Ielsi 66 41.30 N 14.48 E
Ienne 66 41.53 N 13.10 E
Iepê 255 22.40 S 51.05 W
Ieper (Ypres) 50 50.51 N 2.53 E
Ierápetra 38 35.00 N 25.45 E
Ierisós 38 40.24 N 23.52 E
Ierón Asklipioú ⊥ 38 37.37 N 23.02 E
Ierzu 71 39.47 N 9.31 E
Ieshima 96 34.40 N 134.32 E
Ieshima-shotō II 96 34.40 N 134.32 E
Iesi 66 43.31 N 13.14 E
Iesolo 64 45.32 N 12.38 E
If, Château d' ⊥ 62 43.17 N 5.19 E
Ifakara 154 8.08 S 36.41 E
Ifako 273a 6.39 N 3.20 E
Ifalik I[1] 108 7.15 N 144.27 E
Ifanadiana 157b 21.19 S 47.39 E
Ifata 148 25.29 N 7.58 E
Ife 150 7.30 N 4.30 E
Iferouâne 150 19.04 N 8.24 E
Iferten → Yverdon 58 46.47 N 6.39 E
Iffezheim 56 48.49 N 8.08 E
Ifni □[9] 148 29.20 N 10.00 W
Ifon 150 6.58 N 5.45 E
Iforas, Adrar des ⩕ 150 20.00 N 2.00 E
Ifould Lake ⊜ 162 30.53 S 132.09 E
Ifta 56 51.04 N 10.11 E
Ifugao □[4] 116 16.45 N 121.15 E
Iga 94 34.49 N 136.13 E
Iga ≃ 94 34.45 N 136.01 E
Igaci 250 9.33 S 36.38 W
Igal 30 46.31 N 17.55 E
Igalula, Tan. 154 5.38 S 32.38 E
Igalula, Tan. 154 5.14 S 33.00 E
Igan 112 2.49 N 111.43 E
Igan ≃ 112 2.51 N 111.39 E
Igana 150 7.59 N 3.14 E
Iganga 154 0.37 N 33.29 E
Iganmu ◆[8] 273a 6.29 N 3.22 E
Igaporã 255 13.46 S 42.43 W
Igara 250 10.24 S 40.07 W
Igaraí 256 21.25 S 46.49 W
Igara Paraná ≃ 246 2.09 S 71.47 W
Igarapé-Açu 250 1.07 S 47.37 W
Igarapé Grande 250 4.41 S 44.58 W
Igarapé-Miri 250 1.59 S 48.58 W
Igaratá 256 23.12 S 46.07 W
Igarka 74 67.28 N 86.35 E
Igarra 150 7.18 N 6.07 E
Igarukiro 154 3.08 S 33.31 E
Igatpuri 122 19.42 N 73.33 E
Igaun 273a 6.42 N 3.23 E
Igawa 154 8.35 S 34.28 E
Igbaja 150 8.23 N 4.52 E
Igbobi 273a 6.32 N 3.22 E
Igboho 150 8.51 N 3.45 E

Symbols in the index entries represent the broad categories identified in the key at the right. Symbols with superior numbers (⩕[2]) identify subcategories (see complete key on page I · 30).

Kartensymbole in dem Registerverzeichnis stellen die rechts in Schlüssel erklärten Kategorien dar. Symbole mit hochgestellten Ziffern (⩕[2]) bezeichnen Unterabteilungen einer Kategorie (vgl. vollständiger Schlüssel auf Seite I · 30).

Los símbolos incluídos en el texto del índice representan las grandes categorias identificadas con la clave a la derecha. Los símbolos con numeros en su parte superior (⩕[2]) identifican las subcategorías (véase la clave completa en la página I · 30).

Les symboles de l'index représentent les catégories indiquées dans la légende à droite. Les symboles suivis d'un indice (⩕[2]) représentent des sous-catégories (voir légende complète à la page I · 30).

Os símbolos incluídos no texto do índice representam as grandes categorias identificadas com a chave à direita. Os símbolos com números em sua parte superior (⩕[2]) identificam as subcategorias (veja-se a chave completa à página I · 30).

	English	Deutsch	Español	Français	Português
∧	Mountain	Berg	Montaña	Montagne	Montanha
⩕	Mountains	Berge	Montañas	Montagnes	Montanhas
)(	Pass	Pass	Paso	Col	Passo
∨	Valley, Canyon	Tal, Cañon	Valle, Cañón	Vallée, Canyon	Vale, Canhão
⩡	Plain	Ebene	Llano	Plaine	Planície
≻	Cape	Kap	Cabo	Cap	Cabo
I	Island	Insel	Isla	Île	Ilha
II	Islands	Inseln	Islas	Îles	Ilhas
•	Other Topographic Features	Andere Topographische Objekte	Otros Elementos Topográficos	Autres données topographiques	Outros Elementos Topográficos

ESPAÑOL

Nombre	Página	Lat. °′	Long. °′ W=Oeste
Igbologun	273a	6.25 N	3.20 E
Igbo-Ora	150	7.26 N	3.17 E
Igbor	150	7.27 N	8.34 E
Igdir, Īrān	84	39.20 N	47.30 E
Iğdır, Tür.	84	39.55 N	44.02 E
Iğdır, Tür.	130	40.16 N	35.38 E
Igdy	128	39.54 N	56.54 E
Igea Marina	66	44.08 N	12.29 E
Igel	56	49.42 N	6.32 E
Igelfors	40	58.51 N	15.41 E
Igelsberg	58	48.32 N	8.26 E
Igel'vejem ≃	180	65.40 N	172.50 W
Igersheim	56	49.29 N	9.49 E
Iggensbach	60	48.44 N	13.08 E
Iggesund	26	61.38 N	17.04 E
Ighil Izane	148	35.44 N	0.30 E
Ightham	260	51.17 N	0.17 E
Ightham Mote ⊥	260	51.15 N	0.16 E
Igirma	88	56.59 N	103.37 E
Igiugig	180	59.20 N	155.55 W
Iglau → Jihlava	30	49.24 N	15.36 E
Iglesia	252	30.24 S	69.13 W
Iglesias	71	39.19 N	8.32 E
Iglesiente ✣[1]	71	39.18 N	8.40 E
Igli	148	30.25 N	2.12 W
Iglino	86	54.50 N	56.26 E
Igloolik	176	69.24 N	81.49 W
Iglovo	82	55.47 N	36.40 E
Igls	64	47.14 N	11.25 E
Ignacej	78	47.41 N	28.40 E
Ignacio, Calif., U.S.	226	38.05 N	122.32 W
Ignacio, Colo., U.S.	200	37.07 N	107.38 W
Ignacio de la Llave	234	18.43 N	95.59 W
Ignacio Zaragoza, Méx.	232	29.35 N	107.30 W
Ignacio Zaragoza, Méx.	234	23.55 N	103.42 W
Ignalina	76	55.21 N	26.10 E
Ignašino	89	53.28 N	122.23 E
Ignatjevcy	80	57.32 N	51.39 E
Ignatovka	80	53.57 N	47.38 E
Ignatovo	82	56.10 N	37.32 E
İğneada	130	41.52 N	27.58 E
İğneada Burnu ≻	130	41.54 N	28.03 E
Igney	58	48.17 N	6.24 E
Ignon ≃	58	47.31 N	5.10 E
Igny	261	48.45 N	2.14 E
Igodovo	80	58.01 N	42.21 E
Igoumenítsa	38	39.30 N	20.16 E
Igra	80	57.33 N	53.04 E
Igreja Nova	250	10.07 S	36.39 W
Iguaçu ≃, Bra.	287a	22.45 S	43.14 W
Iguaçu ≃, S.A.	252	25.36 S	54.36 W
Iguaçu, Saltos do ⌊	252	25.41 S	54.26 W
Iguaí	255	14.45 S	40.04 W
Iguala	234	18.21 N	99.32 W
Igualada	34	41.35 N	1.38 E
Iguana ≃	246	7.54 N	65.46 W
Iguana, Sierra de la ⩘	196	26.45 N	100.20 W
Iguape	252	24.43 S	47.33 W
Iguará ≃	250	3.28 S	43.55 W
Iguaraçu	255	23.11 S	51.50 W
Iguassu Falls → Iguaçu, Saltos do ⌊	252	25.41 S	54.26 W
Iguatemi	255	23.40 S	54.34 W
Iguatemi ≃	255	23.55 S	54.10 W
Iguatu	250	6.22 S	39.18 W
Iguazú (Iguaçu), Parque Nacional ♠	252	25.35 S	54.20 W
Iguéla	152	1.55 S	9.19 E
Iguetti, Sebkhet ≚	148	25.05 N	9.50 W
Iguidi, Erg ⍛[8]	148	26.35 N	5.40 W
Iguig	116	17.45 N	121.44 E
Igumale	150	6.49 N	7.59 E
Igumnovo	82	55.37 N	38.18 E
Igvak, Cape ≻	180	57.26 N	156.00 W
Igžej	88	53.59 N	103.10 E
Ihavandiffulu Atoll ❙[1]	122	7.00 N	72.55 E
Iheya-shima ❙	93b	27.00 N	127.56 E
Ihiala	150	5.51 N	6.51 E
Ihirène, Oued ∨	148	20.25 N	4.35 E
Ihle ≃	54	52.17 N	11.52 E
Ihlienworth	52	53.44 N	8.55 E
Ihmert	56	51.20 N	7.44 E
Ihnāsiyat al-Madīnah	142	29.05 N	30.56 E
Ihorombe	157b	23.00 S	47.33 E
Ihosy	157b	22.24 S	46.08 E
Ihosy ≃	157b	21.58 S	43.38 E
Ihotry, Lac ⊚	157b	21.56 S	43.41 E
Ihringen	58	48.02 N	7.39 E
Ihringshausen	56	51.21 N	9.31 E
Ihrlerstein	60	48.56 N	11.52 E
İhsangazi	130	41.11 N	33.33 E
Ihtiman	38	42.26 N	23.49 E
Ihu	164	7.55 S	145.25 E
Ihugh	150	7.02 N	9.00 E
Ihwah	142	29.03 N	31.00 E
Ii	26	65.19 N	25.22 E
II ☐[4]	150	16.30 N	10.00 W
Iida	94	35.31 N	137.50 E
III ☐[4]	150	16.15 N	11.45 W
III Internacional	80	49.49 N	47.06 E
Iijima	94	35.40 N	137.56 E
Iijoki ≃	24	65.20 N	25.17 E
Iiktu, Gora Λ	86	49.51 N	87.40 E
Iinan	94	34.27 N	136.24 E
Iinashi ≃	96	35.27 N	133.13 E
Iioka	94	35.42 N	140.43 E
Iisaku	76	59.06 N	27.19 E
Iisalmi	26	63.34 N	27.11 E
Ii-shima ❙	174m	26.43 N	127.47 E
Ii-suido ⩌	174m	26.42 N	127.51 E
Iisvesi	26	62.40 N	27.02 E
Iitaka	94	34.26 N	136.21 E
Iittala	26	61.04 N	24.10 E
Iivaara Λ[2]	26	65.47 N	29.40 E
Iiyama	94	36.51 N	138.22 E
Iizuka	96	33.38 N	130.41 E
Ij ≃	88	52.34 N	96.10 E
Ija ≃	88	55.05 N	101.05 E
Ijaiye	273a	6.40 N	3.18 E
Ijaji	144	8.59 N	37.13 E
Ijara	154	1.36 S	40.31 E
Ijebu-Igbo	150	6.56 N	4.01 E
Ijebu-Ode	150	6.50 N	3.56 E
Ijesa-Tedo	273a	6.30 N	3.19 E
Ijill, Kediet Λ	148	22.38 N	12.33 W
Ijill, Sebkhet ⊚	148	22.47 N	12.53 W
Ijin	98	42.05 N	130.08 E
Ijira	94	35.31 N	136.44 E
IJmuiden	52	52.27 N	4.36 E
IJssel ≃	52	52.30 N	6.00 E
IJsselmeer (Zuiderzee) ⍑[2]	52	52.45 N	5.25 E
IJsselmuiden	52	52.34 N	5.56 E
IJsselstein	52	52.02 N	5.03 E
Ijuh	174b	0.30 S	166.57 E
Ijuí	252	28.23 S	53.55 W
Ijuí ≃	252	27.58 S	55.20 W
Iju Junction	273a	6.40 N	3.19 E
Iju Water Works ʊ[3]	273a	6.40 N	3.20 E
IJzendijke	52	51.19 N	3.38 E
IJzer (Yser) ≃	50	51.09 N	2.43 E
Ik ≃	80	55.55 N	52.36 E
Ik, Ozero ⊚	86	56.03 N	71.33 E
Ika	88	59.18 N	106.12 E
Ikaalinen	26	61.46 N	23.03 E
Ikahavo, Plateau de l' ⩘[1]	157b	17.25 S	45.50 E
Ikaho	94	36.30 N	138.55 E
Ikalamavony	157b	21.09 S	46.35 E
Ikali	152	2.02 S	21.02 E
Ikalou	152	4.03 S	11.48 E
Ikamatua	172	42.16 S	171.41 E
Ikang	150	4.50 N	8.32 E
Ikara	150	11.12 N	8.15 E

FRANÇAIS

Nom	Page	Lat. °′	Long. °′ W=Ouest
Ikare	150	7.32 N	5.45 E
Ikaría ❙	38	37.41 N	26.20 E
Ikari-dam ✣[6]	94	36.52 N	139.42 E
Ikari-ko ⊚	94	36.56 N	139.41 E
Ikaruga	96	34.36 N	135.44 E
Ikast	41	56.08 N	9.10 E
Ikatan	180	54.45 N	163.19 W
Ikatskij Chrebet ⩘	88	54.00 N	111.00 E
Ikawa	94	35.13 N	138.15 E
Ikawa-dam ✣[6]	94	35.12 N	138.13 E
Ikawhenua Range ⩘	172	38.20 S	176.56 E
Ikazaki	96	33.32 N	132.39 E
Ikeda, Nihon	92a	42.55 N	143.27 E
Ikeda, Nihon	94	36.25 N	137.53 E
Ikeda, Nihon	94	35.26 N	136.34 E
Ikeda, Nihon	94	35.53 N	136.21 E
Ikeda, Nihon	96	34.01 N	133.48 E
Ikeda, Nihon	96	34.49 N	135.25 E
Ikegawa	96	33.36 N	133.11 E
Ikej	88	54.12 N	100.04 E
Ikeja	150	6.36 N	3.21 E
Ikeja ☐[8]	273a	6.30 N	3.25 E
Ikela	152	1.11 S	23.16 E
Ikélemba	152	1.14 N	16.31 E
Ikelemba ≃	152	0.07 N	18.17 E
Ikema-shima ❙	175d	24.56 N	125.16 E
Ikepa ≃	157b	17.01 S	46.45 E
Ikerre	150	7.31 N	5.14 E
Ike-shima ❙	174m	26.23 N	128.00 E
Ikeura	270	34.30 N	135.25 E
Iki ❙	92	33.47 N	129.43 E
Iki-Burul	80	45.49 N	44.39 E
Ikimba, Lake ⊚	154	1.28 S	31.30 E
Īkinjī Maryūt	142	31.00 N	29.45 E
Ikire	150	7.23 N	4.12 E
Ikirun	150	7.55 N	4.41 E
İkitelli	267b	41.04 N	28.47 E
İkizce	130	39.36 N	32.40 E
İkizdere	130	40.47 N	40.33 E
Iko	152	0.35 S	16.01 E
Ikole	150	7.49 N	5.30 E
Ikolik, Cape ≻	180	57.17 N	154.48 W
Ikom	150	5.58 N	8.42 E
Ikoma, Nihon	96	34.41 N	135.42 E
Ikoma, Tan.	154	2.04 S	34.37 E
Ikoma-sanchi ⩘	270	34.40 N	135.40 E
Ikoma-tunnel ✣[5]	270	34.41 N	135.41 E
Ikoma-yama Λ	270	34.40 N	135.41 E
Ikon-Chal'	84	44.18 N	41.55 E
Ikorec ≃	78	50.58 N	39.45 E
Ikorodu	150	6.37 N	3.31 E
Ikot Ekpene	150	5.12 N	7.40 E
Ikoy ≃	152	0.53 S	10.36 E
Ikoyi ✣[8]	273a	6.27 N	3.26 E
Ikoyi Prison ʊ	273a	6.25 N	3.25 E
Ikozi	154	2.32 S	27.37 E
Ikpikpuk ≃	180	70.50 N	154.25 W
Ikra	126	23.42 N	87.07 E
Ikr'anoje	80	46.06 N	47.45 E
Ikrāsh	142	30.45 N	31.30 E
Ikša	82	56.10 N	37.31 E
Iksa ≃	86	57.48 N	82.36 E
Iksāl	132	32.41 N	35.19 E
Ikti, Cape ≻	180	56.00 N	158.30 W
Ikuata	273a	6.25 N	3.22 E
Ikuchi-shima ❙	96	34.17 N	133.07 E
Ikuji-hana ≻	94	36.54 N	137.25 E
Ikuktlitlig Mountain Λ	180	59.16 N	161.27 W
Ikungu	154	1.34 S	33.40 E
Ikuno	96	35.10 N	134.48 E
Ikuno ✣[8]	270	34.39 N	135.33 E
Ikurangi, Mount Λ	174k	21.13 S	159.45 W
Ikusaka	94	36.25 N	137.56 E
Ikusu ≃	273b	4.24 S	15.14 E
Ikuta	268	35.37 N	139.33 E
Ikuta ✣[8]	270	34.42 N	135.11 E
Ikva ≃, Magy.	61	47.42 N	16.58 E
Ikva ≃, S.S.S.R.	78	50.33 N	25.24 E
Ikwah	142	30.41 N	31.28 E
Ila, Nig.	150	8.01 N	4.55 E
Ila, Zaïre	152	2.53 S	21.05 E
Ilabaya	248	17.25 S	70.31 W
Ilacaon Point ≻	116	11.00 N	123.12 E
Ilad	144	10.09 N	47.52 E
Ilagala	154	5.12 S	29.50 E
Ilagan	116	17.10 N	121.54 E
Ilagan ≃	116	17.09 N	121.54 E
Ilaiyānkudi	122	9.38 N	78.38 E
Ilaka, Madag.	157b	19.33 S	48.52 E
Ilaka, Madag.	157b	20.20 S	47.09 E
Īlām, Īrān	128	33.38 N	46.26 E
Ilām, Nepāl	124	26.55 N	87.56 E
Ilam → Sri Lanka ☐[1]	122	7.00 N	81.00 E
Ilām Bāzār	126	23.38 N	87.32 E
Ilan	100	24.45 N	121.44 E
Ilan Ch'uan ≃	100	24.42 N	121.48 E
Ilanskij	88	56.14 N	96.03 E
Ilanz	58	46.46 N	9.12 E
Ilara	273a	6.42 N	3.27 E
Ilaro	150	6.53 N	3.03 E
Ilasco	219	39.40 N	91.19 W
Iława	30	53.37 N	19.33 E
Ilawe	150	7.37 N	5.06 E
Ilay	58	46.37 N	5.53 E
Ilbenge	74	62.49 N	124.24 E
Ilberstedt	54	51.48 N	11.40 E
Ilbunga	162	26.25 S	135.03 E
Il Catalano	71	39.53 N	8.17 E
Ilchester, Eng., U.K.	42	51.01 N	2.41 W
Ilchester, Md., U.S.	284b	39.15 N	76.46 W
Ildefonso, Islas ❙❙	254	55.44 S	69.26 W
Île-à-la-Crosse	184	55.27 N	107.53 W
Île-à-la-Crosse, Lac ⊚	184	55.40 N	107.45 W
Île-aux-Tourtes, Pont ✣[5]	275a	45.25 N	73.59 W
Ilebo (Port-Francqui)	152	4.19 S	20.35 E
Île-Cadieux	275a	45.25 N	74.01 W
Île-de-France ☐[9]	50	49.00 N	2.20 E
Île de la Camargue ☐[9]	62	43.34 N	4.34 E
Ilek	80	51.30 N	53.22 E
Ilek ≃	72	51.30 N	53.20 E
Ilen ≃	48	51.33 N	9.19 W
Île-Perrot	206	45.23 N	73.57 W
Ileret	154	4.19 N	36.13 E
Îles, Lac des ⊚, Qué., Can.	206	46.06 N	74.02 W
Îles, Lac des ⊚, Sask., Can.	184	54.26 N	109.25 W
Ilesha, Nig.	150	8.56 N	3.25 E
Ilesha, Nig.	150	7.38 N	4.45 E
Ilet' ≃	80	55.56 N	48.14 E
Ilevskij Pogost	24	60.41 N	43.46 E
Ileza	24	60.43 N	43.54 E
Ilfeld	54	51.34 N	10.47 E
Ilford, Austl.	170	32.58 S	149.51 E
Ilford, Man., Can.	184	56.04 N	95.35 W
Ilford ✣[8]	260	51.33 N	0.05 E
Ilfov ☐[4]	38	44.30 N	26.00 E
Ilfracombe, Austl.	166	23.30 S	144.30 E
Ilfracombe, Eng., U.K.	42	51.13 N	4.08 W
Il Fuorn	58	46.40 N	10.12 E
Ilga ≃	88	55.00 N	105.04 E
Ilgaz	130	40.56 N	33.38 E
Ilgaz Dağları ⩘	130	41.00 N	33.35 E
Ilgın	130	38.17 N	31.55 E
Ilha ✣[8]	256	23.00 S	43.33 W
Ilhabela	256	23.47 S	45.21 W
Ilha das Flôres	250	10.27 S	36.33 W
Ilha Grande	246	0.27 S	65.02 W
Ilha Grande, Baía da C	256	23.09 S	44.30 W
Ilhas, Cachoeira das ⌊	250	1.03 S	57.33 W
Ilhavo	34	40.36 N	8.40 W
Ilhéos → Ilhéus	255	14.49 S	39.02 W

PORTUGUÊS

Nome	Página	Lat. °′	Long. °′ W=Oeste
Ilhéus	255	14.49 S	39.02 W
Ili ≃	86	45.24 N	74.02 E
Ilia	38	45.56 N	22.39 E
Iliamna	180	59.45 N	154.54 W
Iliamna Lake ⊚	180	59.30 N	155.00 W
Ilian, Mount Λ	116	10.26 N	119.33 E
Iliatenco	234	16.58 N	98.40 W
İliç	130	39.28 N	38.34 E
Ilıca, Tür.	130	39.57 N	41.07 E
Ilıca, Tür.	130	39.52 N	27.46 E
Ilicínea	255	20.56 S	45.50 W
Iliff	198	40.45 N	103.04 W
Iliff, Lake ⊚	276	41.02 N	74.43 W
Iligan	116	8.14 N	124.14 E
Iligan Bay C	116	8.25 N	124.05 E
Ilijan	116	13.38 N	121.04 E
Ilim ≃	88	57.38 N	102.34 E
Ilimsk	88	56.46 N	103.52 E
Ilin	116	12.15 N	121.02 E
Ilin Island ❙	116	12.14 N	121.05 E
Ilinka	82	54.04 N	38.12 E
Ilinta ≃	157b	25.02 S	44.05 E
Ilion	210	43.01 N	75.02 W
Ilio Point ≻	229a	21.13 N	157.15 W
Ilioúpolis	267c	37.56 N	23.45 E
Ilir	88	55.13 N	100.40 E
Ilirska Bistrica	36	45.34 N	14.15 E
İlisira	130	37.12 N	33.02 E
Ilisós ≃	267c	37.57 N	23.41 E
Ilja	76	54.25 N	27.18 E
Iljak	86	60.11 N	77.59 E
Iljičevsk	84	39.33 N	44.58 E
Iljičovsk	78	46.18 N	30.39 E
Iljincy	78	49.07 N	29.12 E
Iljinka, S.S.S.R.	80	48.32 N	41.05 E
Iljinka, S.S.S.R.	88	52.08 N	101.17 E
Iljino	76	55.57 N	31.40 E
Iljinskij, S.S.S.R.	24	61.02 N	32.41 E
Iljinskij, S.S.S.R.	86	58.35 N	55.41 E
Iljinskij, S.S.S.R.	88	52.05 N	114.10 E
Iljinskij, S.S.S.R.	89	47.58 N	142.12 E
Iljinskij, S.S.S.R.	265b	55.37 N	38.06 E
Iljinskij Pogost	82	55.28 N	38.54 E
Iljinskoje, S.S.S.R.	76	58.47 N	44.36 E
Iljinskoje, S.S.S.R.	76	56.58 N	37.11 E
Iljinskoje, S.S.S.R.	76	57.19 N	38.32 E
Iljinskoje, S.S.S.R.	76	53.14 N	35.26 E
Iljinskoje, S.S.S.R.	80	56.29 N	52.49 E
Iljinskoje, S.S.S.R.	82	56.34 N	35.57 E
Iljinskoje, S.S.S.R.	82	54.59 N	36.11 E
Iljinskoje, S.S.S.R.	265b	55.46 N	37.15 E
Iljinskoje-Chovanskoje	80	56.58 N	39.46 E
Iljinsko-Podomskoje	24	61.08 N	47.56 E
Iljinsko-Zaborskoje	80	57.16 N	44.23 E
Iljiny Gory ⩘[2]	76	56.34 N	34.12 E
Il'ka	88	51.43 N	108.32 E
Ilkal	122	15.58 N	76.08 E
Ilkeston	42	52.59 N	1.18 W
Il'kino	80	55.13 N	41.36 E
Ilkley	44	53.55 N	1.50 W
Ill ≃, Fr.	58	48.40 N	7.53 E
Ill ≃, Öst.	58	47.17 N	9.33 E
Illabot Creek ≃	224	48.29 N	121.30 W
Illampu, Nevado Λ	248	15.50 S	68.34 W
Illana Bay C	116	7.25 N	123.45 E
Illapel	252	31.38 S	71.10 W
Illarionovo	78	48.25 N	35.16 E
Illasi	64	45.28 N	11.10 E
Illawarra, Lake C	170	34.32 S	150.50 E
Illbillee, Mount Λ	162	27.02 S	132.30 E
Ille-et-Vilaine ☐[5]	32	48.10 N	1.30 W
Illéla	150	14.28 N	5.15 E
Iller ≃	58	48.23 N	9.58 E
Illertissen	58	48.13 N	10.06 E
Illescas, Esp.	34	40.07 N	3.50 W
Illescas, Méx.	234	23.13 N	102.07 W
Illfurth	58	47.40 N	7.16 E
Illhaeusern	58	48.11 N	7.26 E
Illi, Ba ≃	146	10.44 N	15.21 E
Illiers	50	48.18 N	1.15 E
Illimani, Nevado Λ	248	16.39 S	67.48 W
Illimo	248	6.28 S	79.51 W
Illingen	56	48.57 N	8.55 E
Illingworth	262	53.45 N	1.54 W
Illinois ☐[3]	178	40.00 N	89.00 W
Illinois ≃, Ill., U.S.	194	38.58 N	90.27 W
Illinois ≃, Oreg., U.S.	202	42.33 N	124.03 W
Illinois, University of (Circle Campus) ʊ[2]	278	41.52 N	87.39 W
Illinois and Michigan Canal ☰	278	41.32 N	88.05 W
Illinois Beach State Park ♠	216	42.26 N	87.48 W
Illinois Institute of Technology ʊ[2]	278	41.50 N	87.38 W
Illinois Peak Λ	202	47.02 N	115.04 W
Illiopolis	219	39.51 N	89.15 W
Illizi	148	26.29 N	8.28 E
Illkirch-Graffenstaden	58	48.32 N	7.43 E
Illminster	42	50.56 N	2.55 W
Illovo	158	30.05 S	30.50 E
Illzach	58	47.47 N	7.20 E
Ilm ≃, B.R.D.	60	48.49 N	11.45 E
Ilm ≃, D.D.R.	54	51.07 N	11.40 E
Ilmajoki	26	62.44 N	22.34 E
Il'men', Ozero ⊚	76	58.17 N	31.20 E
Ilmenau	54	50.41 N	10.55 E
Ilmenau ≃	54	53.23 N	10.10 E
Il'menskij, Zapovednik ♠	86	55.16 N	60.17 E
Il'mino	80	53.47 N	45.40 E
Ilo	248	17.38 S	71.20 W
Ilobasco	236	13.51 N	88.51 W
Ilobu	150	7.51 N	4.30 E
Iloc Island ❙	116	11.18 N	119.41 E
Ilocos Norte ☐[4]	116	18.10 N	120.45 E
Ilocos Sur ☐[4]	116	17.05 N	120.35 E
Iloilo	116	10.42 N	122.34 E
Iloilo ☐[4]	116	11.00 N	122.35 E
Iloilo Strait ⩌	116	10.43 N	122.36 E
Ilomantsi	26	62.40 N	30.55 E
Ilondola Mission	154	10.42 S	31.47 E
Ilongero	154	4.40 S	34.52 E
Ilop	164	2.54 S	141.13 E
Ilopango, Lago de ⊚	236	13.40 N	89.03 W
Ilora	150	7.45 N	3.50 E
Ilorin	150	8.30 N	4.32 E
Iloron, Cerro Λ	234	20.57 N	104.22 W
Ilovajsk	83	47.56 N	38.13 E
Ilovatka	80	50.31 N	45.55 E
Ilovka	78	50.43 N	38.38 E
Ilovl'a	80	49.18 N	43.59 E
Ilovl'a ≃	80	49.14 N	43.54 E
Iłowa	30	51.30 N	15.12 E
Il Palone Λ	64	46.02 N	11.04 E
Il'pyrskij	74	59.56 N	164.10 E
Ilsan-ni	271b	37.41 N	126.46 E
Ilse ≃	54	52.06 N	10.35 E
Ilsenburg	54	51.52 N	10.40 E
Ilshofen	56	49.10 N	9.55 E
Il'skij	78	44.51 N	38.35 E
Ilskov	41	56.14 N	9.06 E
Il Telegrafo Λ	66	42.22 N	11.10 E
Ilten	52	52.21 N	9.55 E
Ilu	152	4.12 N	23.02 E
Ilubabor ☐[4]	144	6.50 N	35.20 E
Iluhār	126	22.48 N	90.06 E
Ilūkste	76	55.58 N	26.18 E
Ilverich	263	51.17 N	6.42 E
Ilwaco	224	46.19 N	124.03 W
Ilwaki	112	7.56 S	126.26 E
İlyasbey	130	40.13 N	29.52 E
Ilz ≃	60	48.35 N	13.29 E
Iłża	30	51.11 N	21.14 E
Ima	88	55.13 N	115.55 E
Imabari	96	34.03 N	133.00 E
Imadomi	268	35.28 N	140.06 E
Imaichi	94	36.43 N	139.41 E
Imajō	94	35.46 N	136.12 E
Imajuku	268	35.58 N	139.21 E
Imajuku ✣[8]	268	35.29 N	139.32 E
Imaki	270	34.24 N	135.46 E
Imaloto ≃	157b	23.27 S	45.13 E
Imambara ʊ[1]	272b	22.54 N	88.25 E
İmamlar	130	40.47 N	30.59 E
Iman	89	45.55 N	133.43 E
Iman ≃	89	45.57 N	133.42 E
Imanbaj ⊥	86	43.13 N	60.25 E
Imandan-Makit, Gora Λ	88	54.15 N	117.38 E
Imandra, Ozero ⊚	24	67.30 N	33.00 E
Imanombo	157b	24.26 S	45.49 E
Imantau	86	52.58 N	68.22 E
Imari	92	33.16 N	129.53 E
Imaruí	252	28.21 S	48.49 W
Imaruí, Lagoa C	252	28.21 S	48.52 W
Imasa	140	18.01 N	36.12 E
Imatra	26	61.10 N	28.46 E
Imavere	76	58.44 N	25.48 E
Imaza ≃	248	5.05 S	78.19 W
Imazu	94	35.24 N	136.02 E
Imbābah	142	30.04 N	31.13 E
Imbabura ☐[4]	246	0.22 N	78.25 W
Imbariê	256	22.39 S	43.13 W
Imbituba	252	28.14 S	48.40 W
Imbituva	252	25.12 S	50.35 W
Imboassu, Canal ☰	287a	22.48 S	43.04 W
Imboden	194	36.12 N	91.10 W
Imbonga	152	0.43 S	19.46 E
Imbundi	152	5.44 S	16.16 E
Ime, Beinn Λ	46	56.14 N	4.49 W
Imeni Abaja	86	50.44 N	69.30 E
Imeni Babuškina	76	59.45 N	43.07 E
Imeni Čapajeva	85	43.28 N	76.50 E
Imeni C'urupy	82	55.30 N	38.39 E
Imeni Džambula, S.S.S.R.	86	45.26 N	74.24 E
Imeni Džambula, S.S.S.R.	86	47.43 N	74.09 E
Imeni Frunze	86	46.23 N	77.20 E
Imeni Il-go Okt'abr'a	88	55.54 N	119.36 E
Imeni Kalinina, S.S.S.R.	80	51.51 N	52.43 E
Imeni Kalinina, S.S.S.R.	85	41.28 N	76.22 E
Imeni Kalinina, S.S.S.R.	85	43.16 N	74.03 E
Imeni Kalinina, S.S.S.R.	86	43.40 N	59.07 E
Imeni Karla Libknechta	78	51.37 N	35.27 E
Imeni Kirova, S.S.S.R.	86	51.27 N	77.32 E
Imeni Kirova, S.S.S.R.	86	46.27 N	77.13 E
Imeni Leninskogo Komsomola	86	50.45 N	66.44 E
Imeni Marta	86	46.57 N	58.58 E
Imeni Michajla Ivanoviča Kalinina	80	57.59 N	45.07 E
Imeni Morozova	265a	59.59 N	31.02 E
Imeni Moskvy, Kanal ☰	82	56.43 N	37.08 E
Imeni M.V. Lomonosova, Universitet ʊ[2]	265b	55.43 N	37.32 E
Imeni Panfilova	85	43.23 N	77.07 E
Imeni Poliny Osipenko	89	52.25 N	136.28 E
Imeni Sardarova Karachana	85	38.26 N	68.46 E
Imeni Şeredy	83	46.52 N	40.03 E
Imeni Ševčenko	86	45.58 N	61.04 E
Imeni S.M. Kirova, Stadion ♠	265a	59.58 N	30.14 E
Imeni Stepana Razina	80	54.54 N	44.18 E
Imeni Tel'mana	89	48.36 N	134.59 E
Imeni Timir'azeva	86	53.39 N	65.31 E
Imeni Vladimira Iljiča Lenina	80	53.36 N	46.58 E
Imeni Vorovskogo, S.S.S.R.	80	55.43 N	41.06 E
Imeni Vorovskogo, S.S.S.R.	82	55.43 N	38.20 E
Imeni XXI Partsjezda	86	50.43 N	67.50 E
Imeni Žel'abova	76	58.57 N	36.36 E
Imera ⊥	70	37.59 N	13.49 E
İmerhav	84	41.25 N	42.14 E
Imerimandroso	157b	17.23 S	48.38 E
Imese	152	2.07 N	18.06 E
Imgenbroich	56	50.34 N	6.16 E
Imi	144	6.28 N	42.18 E
Imías	240p	20.04 N	74.38 W
Imilac	252	24.14 S	68.53 W
Imilili ⍑[4]	148	23.18 N	15.54 W
Imi-n'tanout	148	31.10 N	8.50 W
Imišli	84	39.52 N	48.04 E
Imittós	267c	37.57 N	23.45 E
Imittós Óros Λ	267c	37.55 N	23.47 E
Imjin-gang ≃	98	37.47 N	126.40 E
Imlay	204	40.39 N	118.09 W
Imlay City	190	43.02 N	83.05 W
Imlaystown	208	40.10 N	74.31 W
Imler	214	40.12 N	78.31 W
Immarna	162	30.30 S	132.09 E
Immendingen	58	47.56 N	8.44 E
Immenhausen	56	51.25 N	9.28 E
Immensen	52	52.23 N	10.04 E
Immenstaad	58	47.40 N	9.22 E
Immenstadt	58	47.33 N	10.13 E
Immigrath	263	51.06 N	6.57 E
Immingham Dock	44	53.37 N	0.12 W
Immokalee	220	26.25 N	81.25 W
Imnaha ≃	202	45.49 N	116.46 W
Imo ≃	150	4.36 N	7.35 E
Imogiri	115a	7.55 S	110.23 E
Imokt'an	98	38.50 N	126.41 E
Imola	66	44.21 N	11.42 E
Imore	273a	6.26 N	3.17 E
Imoro	273a	6.43 N	3.30 E
Im Ostholz ✣[8]	263	51.26 N	7.12 E
Imotski	36	43.27 N	17.13 E
Imp'a	98	35.59 N	126.49 E
Impasugong	116	8.19 N	125.00 E
Impe	152	2.44 S	15.17 E
Impendle	158	29.37 S	29.55 E
Impenekuim, Gora Λ	180	65.42 N	176.30 E
Imperatore, Campo ≚	66	42.25 N	13.40 E
Imperatriz	250	5.32 S	47.29 W
Imperia	62	43.53 N	8.03 E
Imperia ☐[4]	62	43.58 N	7.47 E
Imperial, Sask., Can.	184	51.22 N	105.27 W
Imperial, Perú	248	13.04 S	76.21 W
Imperial, Calif., U.S.	204	32.51 N	115.34 W
Imperial, Mo., U.S.	219	38.22 N	90.23 W
Imperial, Nebr., U.S.	198	40.31 N	101.39 W
Imperial, Pa., U.S.	214	40.27 N	80.15 W
Imperial, Tex., U.S.	196	31.16 N	102.41 W
Imperial ≃	254	38.48 S	73.24 W
Imperial Beach	228	32.35 N	117.08 W
Imperial Dam ✣[6]	204	32.55 N	114.30 W
Imperial de Aragón, Canal ☰	34	42.02 N	1.33 W
Imperiale	68	40.07 N	16.35 E
Imperial Mills	182	55.00 N	111.44 W
Imperial Palace ʊ	268	35.41 N	139.45 E
Imperial Valley ∨	204	32.50 N	115.30 W
Impflingen	56	49.10 N	8.07 E
Impfondo	152	1.37 N	18.04 E
Imphāl	120	24.49 N	93.57 E
Impilachti	24	61.40 N	31.04 E
Imprensa, Gruta da ⍛[6]	287a	23.00 S	43.15 W
Impruneta	66	43.41 N	11.15 E
Impulo	152	13.53 S	13.39 E
İmralı ❙	130	40.32 N	28.32 E
İmranlı	130	39.54 N	38.07 E
İmron	130	38.12 N	38.53 E
Imsil	98	35.37 N	127.15 E
Imst	58	47.14 N	10.44 E
Imtān	132	32.24 N	36.49 E
Imuris	232	30.47 N	110.52 W
Imuruan Bay C	116	10.40 N	119.16 E
Imuruk Basin ⊚	180	65.06 N	165.36 W
Imuruk Lake ⊚	180	65.36 N	163.10 W
Imute	273a	6.42 N	3.29 E
Imwŏn-ni	98	37.15 N	129.20 E
Ina, Nihon	94	35.50 N	137.57 E
Ina, Nihon	94	35.59 N	140.03 E
Ina, Nihon	94	37.10 N	139.32 E
Ina, Nihon	268	35.59 N	139.38 E
In'a, S.S.S.R.	74	59.24 N	144.48 E
In'a, S.S.S.R.	86	50.48 N	86.37 E
In'a, S.S.S.R.	86	53.31 N	82.40 E
Ina, Ill., U.S.	194	38.09 N	88.54 W
Ina ≃, Nihon	96	34.43 N	135.28 E
Ina ≃, Pol.	54	53.32 N	14.38 E
In'a ≃, S.S.S.R.	86	54.59 N	82.59 E
Inaba	270	34.26 N	135.27 E
Inabe	94	35.07 N	136.33 E
Ina-bonchi ≚[1]	94	35.45 N	137.57 E
Inabu	94	35.13 N	137.30 E
Inaccessible Island ❙	10	37.17 S	12.45 W
Inada	270	34.54 N	135.08 E
Inagawa	96	34.53 N	135.22 E
Inagawan	116	9.33 N	118.39 E
Inage	268	35.38 N	140.05 E
Inagi	94	35.38 N	139.30 E
Inajá	250	8.54 S	37.49 W
Inajá ≃	250	8.53 S	49.44 W
In'akino	80	54.26 N	41.07 E
Inakona	175e	9.49 S	160.02 E
Inala	171a	27.35 S	152.58 E
Inamangando ≃	152	14.03 S	12.23 E
Inambari ≃	248	12.41 S	69.44 W
In Aménas	148	28.05 N	9.30 E
In Amguel	148	23.40 N	5.10 E
Inami, Nihon	94	36.33 N	136.58 E
Inami, Nihon	96	33.48 N	135.13 E
Inami, Nihon	96	34.45 N	134.54 E
Inamuragasaki Point ⊥	268	35.18 N	139.32 E
Inanda	273d	26.07 S	28.03 E
Inangahua Junction	172	41.51 S	171.57 E
Inanwatan	164	2.08 S	132.10 E
Inaouene, Oued ≃	148	34.12 N	4.54 W
Iñapari	248	10.57 S	69.35 W
Inaporok	164	8.15 S	141.55 E
Inarajan	174p	13.16 N	144.45 E
Inari	24	68.54 N	27.01 E
Inari ⊚	24	69.00 N	28.00 E
Inarigda	74	63.14 N	107.27 E
Inas, Gunong Λ	114	5.15 N	100.56 E
Inasa	94	34.50 N	137.40 E
Inatsuke ✣[8]	268	35.46 N	139.43 E
Inatsuki	96	33.36 N	130.43 E
Inauaia	164	8.40 S	146.35 E
Inauini ≃	248	8.30 S	67.24 W
Inawasiro-ko ⊚	92	37.29 N	140.06 E
Inazawa	94	35.15 N	136.47 E
Inba	94	35.46 N	140.14 E
Inba-numa ⊚	94	35.46 N	140.12 E
In Belbel	148	27.54 N	1.10 E
Inca	34	39.43 N	2.54 E
Inca de Oro	252	26.45 S	69.54 W
Incaguasi	252	29.13 S	71.03 W
Ince	262	53.17 N	2.49 W
Ince Blundell	262	53.31 N	3.02 W
İnce Burun ≻	130	42.07 N	34.56 E
Ince-in-Makerfield	262	53.32 N	2.37 W
İncekum Burnu ≻	130	36.13 N	33.58 E
İncesu	130	38.38 N	35.11 E
Inch	48	52.08 N	9.59 W
Inchard, Loch C	46	58.27 N	5.04 W
Inchas Military Base ■	142	30.20 N	31.27 E
Inchbare	46	56.47 N	2.38 W
Inchcape ❙[2]	46	56.55 N	2.50 W
Inchini	144	8.48 N	37.43 E
Inchmarnock ❙	46	55.47 N	5.09 W
Inchnadamph	46	58.09 N	4.59 W
Inch'ŏn	98		
	271b	37.28 N	126.38 E
Inchture	46	56.26 N	3.10 W
Inchwagh Lake ⊚	281	42.27 N	83.41 W
İncirliova	130	37.50 N	27.43 E
Incisa in Val d'Arno	66	43.40 N	11.27 E
Incline Village	226	39.16 N	119.56 W
Incomati (Komati) ≃	156	25.46 S	32.43 E
Inconfidência	256	22.16 S	43.13 W
Inconfidentes	256	22.20 S	46.20 W
Inčoun	180	66.18 N	170.17 W
Incudine	64	46.14 N	10.22 E
Incudine, l' Λ	36	41.51 N	9.12 E
Incy	24	65.48 N	40.26 E
Indaal, Loch C	46	55.45 N	6.21 W
Indaiá ≃	255	18.27 S	45.22 W
Indaiatuba	256	23.05 S	47.14 W
Indalsälven ≃	26	62.31 N	17.27 E
Indanan	116	5.58 N	120.59 E
Indaparapeo	234	19.47 N	100.58 W
Inda Silase	144	14.05 N	38.20 E
Indaw	110	23.40 N	94.46 E
Indawgyi Lake ⊚	110	25.10 N	96.19 E
Indé	232	25.54 N	105.13 W
Inde → India ☐[1]	118	20.00 N	77.00 E
Inde ≃	56	50.54 N	6.21 E
Indemini	58	46.06 N	8.50 E
Independence, Calif., U.S.	204	36.48 N	118.12 W
Independence, Ind., U.S.	216	40.20 N	87.10 W
Independence, Iowa, U.S.	190	42.28 N	91.54 W
Independence, Kans., U.S.	198	37.13 N	95.42 W
Independence, Ky., U.S.	218	38.57 N	84.32 W
Independence, La., U.S.	194	30.38 N	90.30 W
Independence, Mo., U.S.	194	39.05 N	94.24 W
Independence, Ohio, U.S.	279a	41.23 N	81.39 W
Independence, Oreg., U.S.	202	44.51 N	123.11 W
Independence, Pa., U.S.	214	40.15 N	80.31 W
Independence, Tex., U.S.	222	30.19 N	96.21 W
Independence, Va., U.S.	192	36.37 N	81.09 W
Independence, Wis., U.S.	190	44.21 N	91.25 W
Independence ≃	188	43.45 N	75.20 W
Independence Creek ≃	196	30.27 N	101.44 W
Independence Hall ⊥	285	39.57 N	75.09 W
Independence Lake ⊚[1]	226	39.26 N	120.18 W
Independence Mountains ⩘	204	41.15 N	116.05 W
Independencia, Bol.	248	17.07 S	66.53 W
Independência, Bra.	250	5.23 S	40.19 W
Independencia, Isla ❙	248	14.15 S	76.12 W
Independenţa	38	43.58 N	28.05 E
Inder, Ozero ⊚	80	48.27 N	51.54 E
Inderborskij	80	48.33 N	51.44 E
In der Bredde	263	51.20 N	7.23 E
İnderesi	130	37.50 N	35.40 E
Index	224	47.50 N	121.33 W
Index, Mount Λ	224	47.46 N	121.35 W
Indi	122	17.10 N	75.58 E
India ☐[1]	118	20.00 N	77.00 E
India Brook ≃	276	40.47 N	74.37 W
India Gate ⊥	272a	28.37 N	77.18 E
Indialantic	220	28.05 N	80.34 W
Indian ≃, Ont., Can.	212	44.13 N	78.08 W
Indian ≃, Ont., Can.	212	45.16 N	76.14 W
Indian ≃, Del., U.S.	208	38.36 N	75.10 W
Indian ≃, Mass., U.S.	283	42.47 N	70.58 W
Indian ≃, Mich., U.S.	190	45.59 N	86.15 W
Indian ≃, N.Y., U.S.	212	43.58 N	75.17 W
Indiana	214	40.37 N	79.09 W
Indiana ☐[6]	214	40.37 N	79.09 W
Indiana ☐[3]	178		
	194	40.00 N	86.15 W
Indiana Dunes National Lakeshore ♠	216	41.40 N	87.00 W
Indiana Dunes State Park ♠	216	41.40 N	87.02 W
Indian Agricultural Research Institute ʊ[3]	272a	28.38 N	77.10 E
Indiana Harbor C	278	41.40 N	87.27 W
Indiana Harbor Canal ☰	278	41.40 N	87.27 W
Indianapolis	218	39.46 N	86.09 W
Indianapolis (Weir Cook) Municipal Airport ⊠	218	39.43 N	86.16 W
Indianapolis Motor Speedway ♠	218	39.48 N	86.14 W
Indian Bayou ≃	194	34.14 N	91.52 W
Indian Brook	186	46.23 N	60.32 W
Indian Caverns ⍛[5]	214	40.38 N	78.05 W
Indian Church	232	17.45 N	88.40 W
Indian Creek	278	42.14 N	87.59 W
Indian Creek ≃, U.S.	218	39.19 N	84.38 W
Indian Creek ≃, Calif., U.S.	228	35.18 N	118.26 W
Indian Creek ≃, Ill., U.S.	216	41.26 N	88.46 W
Indian Creek ≃, Ill., U.S.	219	39.56 N	90.32 W
Indian Creek ≃, Ill., U.S.	278	42.11 N	87.55 W
Indian Creek ≃, Ind., U.S.	216	40.55 N	86.42 W
Indian Creek ≃, Ind., U.S.	218	39.23 N	86.29 W
Indian Creek ≃, Ind., U.S.	218	38.10 N	86.14 W
Indian Creek ≃, Ind., U.S.	218	38.43 N	85.06 W
Indian Creek ≃, Md., U.S.	284c	38.59 N	76.55 W
Indian Creek ≃, Mo., U.S.	194	36.33 N	94.29 W
Indian Creek ≃, N. Mex., U.S.	200	36.11 N	108.23 W
Indian Creek ≃, N.Y., U.S.	276	40.43 N	73.06 W
Indian Creek ≃, Ohio, U.S.	279a	41.17 N	81.31 W
Indian Creek ≃, S. Dak., U.S.	198	44.39 N	103.19 W
Indian Creek ≃, Tenn., U.S.	194	35.13 N	88.08 W
Indian Creek Lake ⊚[1]	222	31.44 N	95.58 W
Indianford	216	42.49 N	88.35 W
Indian Grave Mountain Λ[2]	192	32.59 N	84.21 W
Indian Grove Brook ≃	276	40.44 N	74.33 W
Indian Harbour Beach	220	28.10 N	80.35 W
Indian Head	184	50.32 N	103.40 W
Indian Head Brook ≃	283	42.04 N	70.52 W
Indian Head Park	278	41.47 N	87.54 W
Indian Head Pond ⊚	283	42.03 N	70.51 W
Indian Heights	216	40.25 N	86.08 W
Indian Island ❙	224	48.04 N	122.43 W
Indian Kentuck Creek ≃	218	38.43 N	85.16 W
Indian Lake, Mich., U.S.	216	41.59 N	86.12 W
Indian Lake, N.Y., U.S.	188	43.47 N	74.16 W
Indian Lake ⊚, Ont., Can.	190	47.08 N	82.08 W
Indian Lake ⊚, Mich., U.S.	190	45.59 N	86.20 W
Indian Lake ⊚, Mich., U.S.	216	42.09 N	85.29 W
Indian Lake ⊚, Mich., U.S.	216	42.00 N	86.13 W
Indian Lake ⊚, N.J., U.S.	276	40.53 N	74.29 W
Indian Lake ⊚, Ohio, U.S.	216	40.29 N	83.53 W
Indian Lake Estates	220	27.48 N	81.19 W
Indian Lakes ⊚	216	41.33 N	85.25 W
Indian Lake State Park ♠	216	40.29 N	83.52 W
Indian Mills Brook ≃	285	39.47 N	74.44 W
Indian Mills Lake ⊚	285	39.48 N	74.44 W
Indian Neck	207	41.15 N	72.46 W
Indian Ocean ⍑[1]	4		
	6	10.00 S	70.00 E
Indianola, Iowa, U.S.	190	41.22 N	93.34 W
Indianola, Miss., U.S.	194	33.27 N	90.39 W
Indianola, Nebr., U.S.	198	40.14 N	100.25 W
Indianola, Pa., U.S.	279b	40.34 N	79.51 W
Indianola, Wash., U.S.	224	47.45 N	122.31 W
Indianópolis	255	19.02 S	47.55 W
Indianópolis ✣[8]	287b	23.36 S	46.38 W
Indian Peak Λ, Utah, U.S.	200	38.16 N	113.53 W
Indian Peak Λ, Wyo., U.S.	202	44.47 N	109.51 W
Indian Point ≻	212	44.37 N	78.49 W
Indian Prairie Canal ☰	220	27.02 N	80.57 W
Indian River	190	45.25 N	84.37 W
Indian River ☐[6]	220	27.43 N	80.36 W
Indian River C	220	28.00 N	80.30 W
Indian River Bay C	208	38.36 N	75.05 W
Indian River Inlet C	208	38.37 N	75.03 W
Indian Rock Λ	224	45.59 N	120.49 W
Indian Rock Paintings ⊥	224	46.38 N	120.31 W
Indian Rocks Beach	220	27.53 N	82.51 W
Indian Springs, Nev., U.S.	204	36.34 N	115.40 W
Indian Springs, Va., U.S.	284c	38.49 N	77.10 W
Indian Stream ≃	206	45.03 N	71.26 W
Indiantown	220	27.01 N	80.28 W
Indian Town Point ≻	240c	17.06 N	61.40 W
Indian Village, Ind., U.S.	218	40.10 N	85.22 W
Indian Village, N.Y., U.S.	210	42.57 N	76.10 W
Indiaporã	255	19.57 S	50.17 W
Indiaroba	250	11.32 S	37.31 W
Indico, Océano → Indian Ocean ⍑[1]	6	10.00 S	70.00 E
Indien → India ☐[1]	118	20.00 N	77.00 E
Indien, Océan → Indian Ocean ⍑[1]	6	10.00 S	70.00 E
Indien, territoires britanniques de l'Ocean → British Indian Ocean Territory ☐[2]	12	7.00 S	72.00 E

Symbol	English	Deutsch	Español	Français	Português
≃	River	Fluss	Río	Rivière	Rio
☰	Canal	Kanal	Canal	Canal	Canal
⌊	Waterfall, Rapids	Wasserfall, Stromschnellen	Cascada, Rápidos	Chute d'eau, Rapides	Cascata, Rápidos
⩌	Strait	Meeresstrasse	Estrecho	Détroit	Estreito
C	Bay, Gulf	Bucht, Golf	Bahía, Golfo	Baie, Golfe	Baía, Golfo
⊚	Lake, Lakes	See, Seen	Lago, Lagos	Lac, Lacs	Lago, Lagos
≚	Swamp	Sumpf	Pantano	Marais	Pântano
⍓	Ice Features, Glacier	Eis- und Gletscherformen	Accidentes Glaciales	Formes glaciaires	Acidentes Glaciares
⍑	Other Hydrographic Features	Andere Hydrographische Objekte	Otros Elementos Hidrográficos	Autres données hydrographiques	Outros Elementos Hidrográficos
✢	Submarine Features	Untermeerische Objekte	Accidentes Submarinos	Formes de relief sous-marin	Acidentes Submarinos
☐	Political Unit	Politische Einheit	Unidad Política	Entité politique	Unidade Política
ʊ	Cultural Institution	Kulturelle Institution	Institución Cultural	Institution culturelle	Instituição Cultural
⊥	Historical Site	Historische Stätte	Sitio Histórico	Site historique	Sitio Histórico
♠	Recreational Site	Erholungs- und Ferienort	Sitio de Recreo	Centre de loisirs	Sítio de Lazer
⊠	Airport	Flughafen	Aeropuerto	Aéroport	Aeroporto
■	Military Installation	Militäranlage	Instalación Militar	Installation militaire	Instalação Militar
✣	Miscellaneous	Verschiedenes	Misceláneo	Divers	Miscelânea

Name	Page	Lat.°′	Long.°′
Indiera Alta	240m	18.09 N	66.53 W
Indiga	24	67.41 N	49.00 E
Indigirka ≃	74	70.48 N	148.54 E
Inđija	38	45.03 N	20.05 E
Indin	120	20.16 N	92.57 E
Indio	204	33.43 N	116.13 W
Indio ≃, Nic.	236	10.57 N	83.44 W
Indio ≃, Pan.	236	9.12 N	80.11 W
Indio, Punta ≻	258	35.16 S	57.13 W
Indischer Ozean → Indian Ocean ⍑[1]	6	10.00 S	70.00 E
Indispensable Reefs ⊸[2]	160	12.40 S	160.25 E
Indispensable Strait ⊔	175e	9.00 S	160.30 E
Indo → Indus ≃	120	24.20 N	67.47 E
Indochina ⊸[1]	12	16.00 N	107.00 E
Indom	24	64.36 N	55.22 E
Indonesia □[1]	108	5.00 S	120.00 E
Indonesia, University of ʊ[2]	269e	6.12 S	106.51 E
Indonesian Culture, Museum of ʊ[3]	269e	6.09 N	106.49 E
Indonésie → Indonesia □[1]	108	5.00 S	120.00 E
Indonesien → Indonesia □[1]	108	5.00 S	120.00 E
Indooroopilly	171a	27.30 S	152.58 E
Indore	120	22.43 N	75.50 E
Indpur	126	23.10 N	86.56 E
Indragiri ≃	112	0.22 S	103.26 E
Indramayu	115a	6.20 S	108.19 E
Indramayu, Tanjung ≻	115a	6.14 S	108.17 E
Indrapuri	114	5.26 N	95.27 E
Indrāvati ≃	122	18.44 N	80.16 E
Indre □[5]	32	46.45 N	1.30 E
Indre ≃	32	47.16 N	0.19 E
Indre-et-Loire □[5]	32	47.15 N	0.45 E
Indrois ≃	50	47.13 N	0.56 E
Indungo	152	14.48 S	16.17 E
Induno Olona	62	45.52 N	8.51 E
Indur → Indore	120	22.43 N	75.50 E
Indura	76	53.27 N	23.53 E
Indus ≃	120	24.20 N	67.47 E
Industria ⊸[8]	273d	26.12 S	27.59 E
Industry, Ill., U.S.	194	40.20 N	90.36 W
Industry, Pa., U.S.	214	40.39 N	80.25 W
Industry, Tex., U.S.	222	29.58 N	96.30 W
Indwe	158	31.27 S	27.23 E
Ine	96	35.39 N	135.17 E
İnebolu	130	41.58 N	33.46 E
İnece	130	41.41 N	27.04 E
İnecik	130	40.56 N	27.16 E
In Ecker	148	24.09 N	5.03 E
In Edjejou, Oued ∨	148	22.46 N	4.05 E
İnegöl	130	40.05 N	29.31 E
İnekollar	130	39.33 N	28.56 E
Inerie, Gunung ∧	115b	8.52 S	120.56 E
Inés, Monte ∧	254	48.29 S	69.40 W
Ineu	38	46.26 N	21.49 E
İnevi	130	38.40 N	32.56 E
Inez, Ky., U.S.	192	37.52 N	82.32 W
Inez, Tex., U.S.	222	28.54 N	96.47 W
Inez, Lake ◎	276	41.01 N	74.17 W
In Ezzane	148	23.28 N	11.12 E
Infanta, Pil.	116	15.50 N	119.55 E
Infanta, Pil.	116	14.45 N	121.39 E
Infantas	286d	11.57 S	77.04 W
Infante, Kaap ≻	158	34.29 S	20.51 E
Inferior, Laguna C	234	16.20 N	94.40 W
Inferno, Cachoeira do ⌊	250	1.00 S	56.04 W
Infiernillo, Canal del ⊔	232	29.09 N	112.15 W
Infiernillo, Presa del ◎[1]	234	18.35 N	101.45 W
Infiesto	34	43.21 N	5.22 W
Infreschi, Punta d' ≻	68	39.59 N	15.25 E
Ing ≃	110	20.13 N	100.27 E
Ingá	250	7.17 S	35.36 W
Ingabu	110	17.49 N	95.16 E
Ingaí	256	21.24 S	44.55 W
Ingaí ≃	256	21.23 S	44.52 W
I-n-Gall	150	16.47 N	6.56 E
Ingalls	218	39.58 N	85.48 W
Ingalls Creek ≃	224	47.28 N	120.39 W
Ingalls Park	216	41.32 N	88.03 W
Inganda	152	0.05 S	20.57 E
Inganno ≃	70	38.04 N	14.37 E
Ingarö I	40	59.16 N	18.28 E
Ingatestone	42	51.41 N	0.22 E
Ingatestone Hall ⊥	260	51.39 N	0.23 E
Ingelfingen	56	49.18 N	9.39 E
Ingelheim	56	49.59 N	8.05 E
Ingelmunster	50	50.55 N	3.15 E
Ingelstad	26	56.45 N	14.55 E
Ingende	152	0.15 S	18.57 E
Ingeniero Budge ⊸[8]	288	34.43 S	58.28 W
Ingeniero Jacobacci	254	41.18 S	69.35 W
Ingeniero Juan Allan	258	34.53 S	58.11 W
Ingeniero Luiggi	252	35.25 S	64.29 W
Ingeniero Maschwitz	258	34.23 S	58.44 W
Ingeniero Romulo Otamendi	258	34.13 S	58.54 W
Ingeniero White	252	38.47 S	62.16 W
Ingeniero Williams	258	34.54 S	59.22 W
Ingenio La Esperanza	252	24.13 S	64.51 W
Ingenio Santa Ana	252	27.28 S	65.41 W
Ingeringbach ≃	61	47.12 N	14.49 E
Ingersheim	58	48.06 N	7.18 E
Ingersoll	212	43.02 N	80.53 W
Ingham	166	18.39 S	146.10 E
Ingham □[6]	216	42.37 N	84.22 W
Ingička	85	39.52 N	67.20 E
Ingleborough ∧	44	54.11 N	2.23 W
Ingleburn	170	34.00 S	150.52 E
Inglesa, Costa → English Coast ⍛[2]	9	73.45 S	73.00 W
Inglesby Lake ◎	212	44.27 N	77.03 W
Ingleside, Austl.	274a	33.41 S	151.13 E
Ingleside, Ont., Can.	206	45.00 N	75.00 W
Ingleside, Ill., U.S.	216	42.23 N	88.09 W
Ingleside, Tex., U.S.	196	27.53 N	97.13 W
Ingleside ⊸[8]	282	37.43 N	122.28 W
Ingleton	44	54.10 N	2.27 W
Inglewood, Austl.	166	28.25 S	151.05 E
Inglewood, Austl.	166	36.34 S	143.52 E
Inglewood, Ont., Can.	212	43.47 N	79.56 W
Inglewood, N.Z.	172	39.09 S	174.12 E
Inglewood, Calif., U.S.	228	33.58 N	118.21 W
Inglewood, Wash., U.S.	224	47.44 N	122.15 W
Inglewood Forest ⊸[3]	44	54.45 N	2.50 W
Inglis, Man., Can.	184	50.57 N	101.15 W
Inglis, Fla., U.S.	220	29.02 N	82.40 W
Inglis Lock ⊸[5]	220	29.02 N	82.37 W
Ingoda ≃	88	51.42 N	115.48 E
Ingogo	158	27.32 S	29.56 E
Ingolstadt	60	48.46 N	11.27 E
Ingonish	186	46.42 N	60.22 W
Ingornachoix Bay C	186	50.38 N	57.20 W
Ingraham, Lake ◎	220	25.09 N	81.08 W
Ingram, Pa., U.S.	279b	40.26 N	80.04 W
Ingram, Tex., U.S.	196	30.04 N	99.14 W
Ingram Bay C	208	37.48 N	76.17 W
Ingrave	260	51.36 N	0.21 E
Ingrid Christensen Coast ⍛[2]	9	69.30 S	76.00 E
In Guezzam	150	19.32 N	5.42 E
Ingul ≃	78	47.00 N	31.59 E
Ingulec	78	47.43 N	33.14 E
Ingulec ≃	78	46.41 N	32.48 E
Ingulo-Kamenka	78	48.17 N	32.30 E
Inguri ≃	84	42.24 N	41.33 E
Inguzet	86	58.50 N	83.52 E
Ingvallsbenning	40	60.15 N	15.53 E
Ingwavuma	158	27.09 S	32.00 E
Ingwavuma ≃	158	26.58 S	32.17 E
Ingwe	154	13.02 S	26.25 E
Ingwiller	56	48.52 N	7.29 E
Inhaca	156	26.01 S	32.58 E
Inhaca, Ilha da I	158	26.03 S	32.57 E
Inhafenga	156	20.35 S	33.53 E
Inhambane	156	23.51 S	35.29 E
Inhambane □[5]	156	23.00 S	34.30 E
Inhambane, Baía de C	156	23.58 S	35.51 E
Inhambupe	255	11.47 S	38.21 W
Inhaminga	156	18.24 S	35.00 E
Inhapim	255	19.33 S	42.07 W
Inharrime	156	24.29 S	35.01 E
Inharrime ≃	156	24.29 S	35.01 E
Inhassoro	156	21.33 S	35.11 E
Inhaúma	255	19.29 S	44.22 W
Inhaúma ⊸[8]	287a	22.52 S	43.17 W
İnhisar	130	40.03 N	30.23 E
Inhoaíba ⊸[8]	256	22.54 S	43.36 W
Inhobi ≃	255	23.45 S	54.40 W
Inhomirim	256	22.35 S	43.10 W
Inhuma	250	6.40 S	41.42 W
Inhumas	255	16.22 S	49.30 W
Ini ≃	146	9.30 N	12.20 E
Iniesta	34	39.26 N	1.45 W
Inimutaba	255	18.45 S	44.22 W
Ining → Yining	86	43.55 N	81.14 E
Inini ≃	250	3.39 N	54.00 W
Inírida ≃	246	3.55 N	67.52 W
Inisa	150	7.52 N	4.20 E
Inishbofin I, Eire	48	55.09 N	8.11 W
Inishbofin I, Eire	48	53.37 N	10.15 W
Inisheer I	48	53.02 N	9.26 W
Inishmaan I	48	53.05 N	9.32 W
Inishmore I	48	53.07 N	9.45 W
Inishowen Head ≻	44	55.14 N	6.56 W
Inishowen Peninsula ≻[1]	48	55.12 N	7.20 W
Inishowen Point ≻	48	55.14 N	6.56 W
Inishshark I	48	53.37 N	10.18 W
Inishtrahull I[2]	48	55.26 N	7.14 W
Inishturk I	48	53.43 N	10.08 W
Inistioge	48	52.29 N	7.04 W
Initao	116	8.30 N	124.18 E
Injasuti ∧	156	29.09 S	29.23 E
Inje	98	38.05 N	128.09 E
Injibara	144	11.00 N	36.59 E
Injune	166	25.51 S	148.34 E
Inkeroinen	26	60.42 N	26.51 E
Inketete	152	2.37 S	21.53 E
Inkisi (Zadi) ≃	152	4.46 S	14.52 E
Inkom	202	42.48 N	112.15 W
Inkster, Mich., U.S.	216	42.17 N	83.17 W
Inkster, N. Dak., U.S.	198	48.09 N	97.39 W
Inland Kaikoura Range ⋀	172	42.00 S	173.40 E
Inland Lake ◎, Man., Can.	184	52.17 N	99.42 W
Inland Lake ◎, Alaska, U.S.	180	66.27 N	159.47 W
Inland Sea → Seto-naikai ⍑[2]	92	34.20 N	133.30 E
Inle Lake ◎	110	20.32 N	96.55 E
Inmaculadita	232	29.55 N	111.48 W
Inman, Kans., U.S.	198	38.14 N	97.47 W
Inman, S.C., U.S.	192	35.03 N	82.05 W
Inman Mills	192	35.02 N	82.06 W
Inman Valley	168b	35.30 S	138.28 E
Inn (En) ≃	32	48.35 N	13.28 E
Innamincka	166	27.45 S	140.44 E
Innellan	46	55.54 N	4.57 W
Inner Bay C	214	42.37 N	80.24 W
Innerbraz	58	47.09 N	9.55 E
Innerferrera	58	46.31 N	9.28 E
Innerfragant	64	46.58 N	13.04 E
Inner Harbor C	276	40.52 N	73.28 W
Inner Hebrides II	46	56.30 N	6.00 W
Innerkip	212	43.13 N	80.42 W
Innerleithen	46	55.38 N	3.05 W
Inner Mongolia → Neimenggu Zizhiqu □[4]	90	43.00 N	115.00 E
Inner Sound ⊔	46	57.25 N	5.56 W
Innerste ≃	52	52.15 N	9.50 E
Innerste-Talsperre ⊸[6]	52	51.55 N	10.17 E
Innerthal	58	47.06 N	8.56 E
Innertkirchen	58	46.42 N	8.14 E
Innervillgraten	64	46.48 N	12.23 E
Innichen → San Candido	64	46.44 N	12.17 E
Inning	60	48.05 N	11.09 E
Inniscrone	48	54.12 N	9.06 W
Innisfail, Austl.	166	17.32 S	146.02 E
Innisfail, Alta., Can.	182	52.02 N	113.57 W
Innisfil Creek ≃	212	44.07 N	79.59 W
Innisfree	182	53.22 N	111.32 W
Innisplain	171a	28.10 S	152.55 E
Innokentjevka	89	49.42 N	136.57 E
Innokentjevskij	89	48.37 N	140.10 E
Innoko ≃	180	62.14 N	159.45 W
Innolovo	265a	59.47 N	29.59 E
Innoshima	96	34.20 N	133.10 E
Inno-shima I	96	34.19 N	133.10 E
Innsbruck	64	47.16 N	11.24 E
Innviertel ⊸[1]	60	48.10 N	13.15 E
Inny ≃, Eire	48	53.33 N	7.48 W
Inny ≃, Eng., U.K.	42	50.35 N	4.17 W
Ino, Nihon	96	33.33 N	133.26 E
Ino, Va., U.S.	208	37.46 N	76.48 W
Inoã	256	22.55 S	42.57 W
Inobonto	112	0.52 N	123.57 E
Inocência	255	19.47 S	51.48 W
Inokashira Park ♠	268	35.42 N	139.34 E
Inokovka	80	52.33 N	42.34 E
Inola	196	36.09 N	95.31 W
Ino-misaki ≻	96	33.01 N	133.06 E
Inongo	152	1.57 S	18.16 E
Inoni	152	3.04 S	15.39 E
İnönü	130	39.48 N	30.09 E
Inoue	270	34.48 N	135.08 E
In Ouzzal, Oued ∨	148	21.35 N	2.00 E
Inowrocław	30	52.48 N	18.15 E
Inozemcevo	84	44.06 N	43.06 E
Inp'ung-dong	98	41.25 N	126.34 E
Inrath ⊸[8]	263	51.21 N	6.32 E
In Rhar	148	27.10 N	1.59 E
Ins	58	47.00 N	7.06 E
In Salah	148	27.12 N	2.28 E
Insan-ni	98	41.01 N	127.21 E
Insar	80	53.52 N	44.21 E
Insar ≃	80	54.43 N	45.18 E
Insch	46	57.21 N	2.37 W
Inscription, Cape ≻	162	25.29 S	112.59 E
Inscription Point ≻	274a	34.00 S	151.13 E
Insein	110	16.53 N	96.07 E
Insel Man → Isle of Man □[2]	44	54.15 N	4.30 W
Inshar	150	8.49 N	9.40 E
Inshāṣ ar-Raml	142	30.23 N	31.27 E
Insjön	26	60.41 N	15.05 E
Ińsko	30	53.27 N	15.33 E
In Sokki, Oued ∨	148	29.37 N	4.13 E
Inspiration	200	33.25 N	110.53 W
Insterburg → Čern'achovsk	76	54.38 N	21.49 E
Instow	184	49.44 N	108.16 W
Insurgente José María Morelos, Parque Nacional ♠	234	19.51 N	101.18 W
Inta	24	66.02 N	60.08 E
I-n-Tebezas ⍑[4]	150	17.49 N	1.53 E
Intendente Alvear	252	35.14 S	63.35 W
İntepe	130	40.00 N	26.20 E
Intercession City	220	28.16 N	81.30 W
Intercourse	208	40.02 N	76.06 W
Interlagos ⊸[8]	287b	23.42 S	46.42 W
Interlaken, Schw.	58	46.41 N	7.51 E
Interlaken, Mass., U.S.	210	42.19 N	73.20 W
Interlaken, N.J., U.S.	208	40.14 N	74.01 W
Interlaken, N.Y., U.S.	210	42.37 N	76.44 W
Interlândia	255	16.12 S	49.02 W
International Amphitheatre ʊ	278	41.49 N	87.39 W
International Falls	190	48.36 N	93.25 W
International Peace Garden ♠	198	49.00 N	100.04 W
Interstate Park ♠	190	45.23 N	92.40 W
Inthanon, Doi ∧	110	18.35 N	98.29 E
Intibucá	236	14.16 N	88.10 W
Intibucá □[5]	236	14.20 N	88.15 W
Intipucá	236	13.12 N	88.04 W
Intiyaco	252	28.39 S	60.05 W
Intracoastal Waterway ≅, U.S.	192	33.40 N	79.00 W
Intracoastal Waterway ≅, U.S.	196	28.45 N	95.40 W
Intragna	58	46.10 N	8.42 E
Intrånget	40	60.20 N	16.09 E
Introbio	58	45.57 N	9.27 E
Introdacqua	66	42.00 N	13.54 E
Intschŏn → Inch'ŏn	98	37.28 N	126.38 E
Intu	112	0.15 S	115.21 E
Intuto	246	3.39 S	74.44 W
Inubō-saki ≻	94	35.42 N	140.53 E
Inukai	96	33.04 N	131.38 E
Inútil, Bahía C	254	53.30 S	69.50 W
Inuvik	180	68.25 N	133.30 W
Inuya ≃	248	10.41 S	73.30 W
Inuyama	94	35.23 N	136.56 E
In'va ≃	86	58.59 N	55.40 E
Inver	46	57.49 N	3.55 W
Inveralochy	170	34.57 S	149.39 E
Inveraray	46	56.13 N	5.05 W
Inverarity	46	56.35 N	2.53 W
Inverbervie	46	56.51 N	2.17 W
Invercargill	172	46.24 S	168.21 E
Inverdruie	46	57.10 N	3.48 W
Inverell	166	29.47 S	151.07 E
Invergarry	46	57.02 N	4.47 W
Invergordon	46	57.42 N	4.10 W
Inverkeilor	46	56.38 N	2.32 W
Inverkeithing	46	56.02 N	3.25 W
Inverkeithny	46	57.30 N	2.37 W
Inverleigh	169	38.06 S	144.03 E
Inverloch	169	38.38 S	145.43 E
Invermay	184	51.48 N	103.09 W
Invermere	182	50.30 N	116.02 W
Invermoriston	46	57.13 N	4.38 W
Inverness, N.S., Can.	186	46.14 N	61.18 W
Inverness, Qué., Can.	206	46.15 N	71.31 W
Inverness, Scot., U.K.	46	57.27 N	4.15 W
Inverness, Calif., U.S.	204	38.06 N	122.51 W
Inverness, Fla., U.S.	220	28.51 N	82.20 W
Inverness, Ill., U.S.	216	42.07 N	88.05 W
Inverness, Miss., U.S.	194	33.21 N	90.35 W
Inveruglas	46	56.15 N	4.43 W
Inveruno	62	45.31 N	8.51 E
Inverurie	46	57.17 N	2.23 W
Inverway	162	17.50 S	129.38 E
Investigator Group II	162	33.45 S	134.30 E
Investigator Strait ⊔	166	35.25 S	137.10 E
Inwood, Man., Can.	184	50.34 N	97.32 W
Inwood, Ont., Can.	214	42.49 N	81.59 W
Inwood, Fla., U.S.	220	28.02 N	81.46 W
Inwood, Ind., U.S.	216	41.19 N	86.12 W
Inwood, Iowa, U.S.	198	43.18 N	96.26 W
Inwood, N.Y., U.S.	276	40.37 N	73.45 W
Inwood Hill Park ♠	276	40.52 N	73.56 W
Inyanga	154	18.13 S	32.46 E
Inyanga Mountains ⋀	154	18.00 S	33.00 E
Inyangani ∧	154	18.20 S	32.50 E
Inyan Kara Mountain ∧	198	44.13 N	104.21 W
Inyantue	154	18.32 S	26.41 E
Inyati	154	19.39 S	28.54 E
Inyazura	154	18.43 S	32.10 E
Inyo, Mount ∧	204	36.44 N	117.59 W
Inyokern	204	35.39 N	117.49 W
Inyo Mountains ⋀	204	36.40 N	118.10 W
Inyonga	154	6.43 S	32.04 E
Inywa	110	23.56 N	96.17 E
Inza	80	53.51 N	46.21 E
Inza ≃	80	53.54 N	45.44 E
Inzago	62	45.32 N	9.29 E
Inzai	94	35.50 N	140.09 E
Inzana Lake ◎	182	54.58 N	124.40 W
Inžavino	80	52.19 N	42.30 E
Inzell	64	47.46 N	12.44 E
Inzer	86	54.14 N	57.34 E
Inzer ≃	86	54.30 N	56.28 E
Inzersdorf ⊸[8]	264b	48.09 N	16.21 E
Inzia ≃	152	3.45 S	17.57 E
Ioanna, Gora ∧	180	64.50 N	178.08 E
Ioánnina	38	39.40 N	20.50 E
Ioco	224	49.18 N	122.52 W
Iō-jima I, Nihon	93b	30.48 N	130.18 E
Iō-jima I, Nihon	174f	24.47 N	141.20 E
Iokanga	24	68.00 N	39.37 E
Iokanga ≃	24	68.00 N	39.43 E
Iola, Kans., U.S.	198	37.55 N	95.24 W
Iola, Pa., U.S.	210	45.08 N	76.32 W
Iola, Tex., U.S.	222	30.46 N	96.05 W
Iola, Wis., U.S.	190	44.36 N	89.08 W
Iolgo, Chrebet ⋀	86	51.30 N	86.25 E
Iolotan'	72	37.18 N	62.21 E
Ioma	164	8.20 S	147.50 E
Iôna, Ang.	152	16.50 S	12.20 E
Iona, N.S., Can.	186	45.58 N	60.48 W
Iona, Idaho, U.S.	202	43.32 N	111.56 W
Iona I	46	56.19 N	6.25 W
Iôna, Parque Nacional do ♠	152	16.30 S	12.00 E
Iona, Sound of ⊔	46	56.19 N	6.24 W
Iona College ʊ[2]	276	40.56 N	73.47 W
Ionaivo ≃	157b	22.56 S	46.54 E
Ione, Calif., U.S.	226	38.21 N	120.56 W
Ione, Oreg., U.S.	202	45.30 N	119.50 W
Ione, Wash., U.S.	202	48.45 N	117.25 W
Ionia, Mich., U.S.	216	42.59 N	85.04 W
Ionia, N.Y., U.S.	210	42.56 N	77.30 W
Ionia □[6]	216	42.56 N	85.04 W
Ionian Islands → Iónioi Nísoi II	38	38.30 N	20.30 E
Ionian Sea ⍑[2]	22	39.00 N	19.00 E
Ionia State Park ♠	216	42.58 N	85.36 W
Ionico, Mare → Ionian Sea ⍑[2]	22	39.00 N	19.00 E
Ionienne, Mer → Ionian Sea ⍑[2]	22	39.00 N	19.00 E
Iónioi Nísoi II	38	38.30 N	20.30 E
Ionisches Meer → Ionian Sea ⍑[2]	22	39.00 N	19.00 E
Ionivejem ≃	180	66.12 N	174.00 W
Iony, Ostrov I	74	56.26 N	143.25 E
Ioppolo	68	38.35 N	15.53 E
Ioppolo Giancaxio	70	37.23 N	13.33 E
Iordan	85	39.58 N	71.46 E
Iori ≃	84	41.03 N	46.17 E
Iory	85	39.30 N	67.53 E
Íos	38	36.44 N	25.17 E
Íos I	38	36.42 N	25.24 E
Ioscoe, Lake ◎	276	41.02 N	74.19 W
Iosegun ≃	182	54.44 N	117.11 W
Iosegun Lake	182	54.29 N	116.50 W
Iovlevo	82	56.10 N	38.20 E
Iowa	194	30.14 N	93.01 W
Iowa □[3]	178	42.15 N	93.15 W
Iowa ≃	190	41.10 N	91.02 W
Iowa, South Fork ≃	190	42.18 N	93.04 W
Iowa City	190	41.40 N	91.32 W
Iowa Falls	190	42.31 N	93.16 W
Iowa Park	196	33.57 N	98.40 W
Iō-zan ∧	94	36.31 N	136.48 E
I Pak	271d	22.19 N	114.00 E
Ipala	154	4.30 S	32.53 E
Ipameri	255	17.43 S	48.09 W
Ipanema ⊸[8]	256	22.59 S	43.12 W
Ipanema ≃	250	9.53 S	37.15 W
Ipanguaçu	250	5.30 S	36.52 W
Ipat, P.I.T.T.	174r	6.58 N	158.12 E
Ipat, S.S.S.R.	24	66.13 N	56.33 E
Ipatinga	255	19.30 S	42.32 W
Ipatovo	80	45.43 N	42.53 E
Ipaumirim	250	6.47 S	38.43 W
Ipava	194	40.21 N	90.19 W
Ípeiros ⊸[1]	38	39.40 N	20.50 E
Ipel'(Ipoly) ≃	30	47.49 N	18.52 E
Iperu	150	6.52 N	3.38 E
Iphigenia Bay C	180	55.40 N	133.55 W
Iphofen	56	49.42 N	10.15 E
Ipiabas	256	22.23 S	43.53 W
Ipiales	246	0.50 N	77.37 W
Ipiaú	255	14.08 S	39.44 W
Ipiíba	256	22.52 S	42.57 W
Ipil	116	7.47 N	122.35 E
Ipin → Yibin	107	28.47 N	104.38 E
Ipirá	255	12.10 S	39.44 W
Ipiranga, Bra.	246	3.12 S	66.01 W
Ipiranga, Bra.	252	25.01 S	50.35 W
Ipiranga, Bra.	287a	22.43 S	43.12 W
Ipiranga ⊸[8]	287b	23.36 S	46.35 W
Ipiranga ≃, Bra.	256	23.21 S	45.10 W
Ipiranga ≃, Bra.	287a	22.48 S	43.37 W
Ipiranga, Canal ≅	287a	22.46 S	43.37 W
Ipiranga, Museu do ʊ	287b	23.35 S	46.36 W
Ipitá	248	19.20 S	63.32 W
Ipitinga ≃	250	0.02 N	53.01 W
Ipixuna	250	4.22 S	44.34 W
Ipixuna ≃, Bra.	248	5.45 S	63.02 W
Ipixuna ≃, Bra.	248	6.16 S	61.52 W
Ipixuna ≃, Bra.	248	7.11 S	71.51 W
Ipixuna, Igarapé ≃	250	4.32 S	52.40 W
İpkaiye	130	40.12 N	27.06 E
Ipoh	114	4.35 N	101.05 E
Ipojuca	250	8.24 S	35.04 W
Ipojuca ≃	250	8.25 S	34.58 W
Ipokera	154	8.03 S	35.41 E
Ipole	154	5.47 S	32.44 E
Ipoly (Ipel') ≃	30	47.49 N	18.52 E
Iporã, Bra.	255	23.59 S	53.37 W
Iporá, Bra.	255	16.28 S	51.07 W
Ippa ≃	76	52.13 N	29.08 E
Ippari ≃	70	36.52 N	14.26 E
Ippinghausen	56	51.17 N	9.08 E
Ippy	152	6.15 N	21.12 E
İpsala	130	40.55 N	26.23 E
İpsile	130	40.14 N	37.33 E
Ipswich, Austl.	171a	27.36 S	152.46 E
Ipswich, Eng., U.K.	42	52.04 N	1.10 E
Ipswich, Mass., U.S.	207	42.41 N	70.50 W
Ipswich, S. Dak., U.S.	198	45.27 N	99.02 W
Ipswich ≃	207	42.42 N	70.48 W
Ipswich Bay C	207	42.41 N	70.42 W
Ipu	250	4.20 S	40.42 W
Ipubi	250	7.39 S	40.07 W
Ipueiras	250	4.33 S	40.43 W
Ipuh	112	3.00 S	101.30 E
Ipuiúna	256	22.06 S	46.11 W
Ipun, Isla I	254	44.37 S	74.46 W
Ipupiara	255	11.49 S	42.37 W
Iput' ≃	76	52.26 N	31.02 E
Iqfahṣ	142	28.47 N	30.49 E
Iquique	248	20.13 S	70.10 W
Iquitos	246	3.46 S	73.15 W
Ira	196	32.35 N	101.00 W
Iraan, Pil.	116	9.04 N	117.42 E
Iraan, Tex., U.S.	196	30.54 N	101.54 W
Irabu-jima I	175d	24.50 N	125.10 E
Iracema	250	5.48 S	38.18 W
Iracoubo	250	5.29 N	53.13 W
Irago-misaki ≻	94	34.35 N	137.01 E
Irago-suidō ⊔	94	34.35 N	137.00 E
Iraí	252	27.11 S	53.15 W
Irajá ⊸[8]	287a	22.51 S	43.19 W
Irajá ≃	287a	22.49 S	43.17 W
Irajol'	24	64.27 N	55.08 E
Irak → Iraq □[1]	128	33.00 N	44.00 E
Iráklion, Ellás	38	35.20 N	25.09 E
Iráklion, Ellás	267c	38.04 N	23.46 E
Irámuco	234	19.57 N	100.55 W
Iran (Īrān) □[1]	118		
	128	32.00 N	53.00 E
Iran, Pegunungan ⋀	112	2.05 N	114.55 E
Īrānshahr	128	27.13 N	60.41 E
Irapa	246	10.34 N	62.35 W
Irapuato	234	20.41 N	101.21 W
Iraq □[1]	118	33.00 N	44.00 E
Irará	255	12.02 S	38.46 W
Iratapuru ≃	250	0.36 S	52.35 W
Irati	252	25.27 S	50.39 W
Irati ≃	34	42.35 N	1.16 W
Irauçuba	250	3.45 S	39.47 W
Irāwan, Wādī ∨	146	26.35 N	12.45 E
Irazú, Volcán ∧[1]	236	9.58 N	83.53 W
Irba	88	58.07 N	99.00 E
Irbejskoje	88	55.39 N	95.28 E
Irbeni Väin (Irves Šaurums) ⊔	76	57.48 N	22.05 E
Irbid	132	32.33 N	35.51 E
Irbid □[8]	132	32.33 N	35.51 E
Irbīl	128	36.11 N	44.01 E
Irbīl □[4]	128	36.10 N	44.00 E
Irbit	86	57.41 N	63.03 E
Irby	262	53.21 N	3.07 W
Irdning	61	47.33 N	14.01 E
Irdyn'	78	49.23 N	31.44 E
Irebu	152	0.37 S	17.45 E
Irecê	250	11.18 S	41.52 W
Iredame	144	10.29 N	49.21 E
Iregua ≃	34	42.27 N	2.24 W
Ireland □[1]	22		
	48	53.00 N	8.00 W
Ireland Brook ≃	276	40.25 N	74.29 W
Ireland Island I	240a	32.19 N	64.50 W
Iren' ≃	86	57.27 N	56.56 E
Irene, S. Afr.	158	25.51 S	28.13 E
Irene, S. Dak., U.S.	198	43.05 N	97.10 W
Irene, Tex., U.S.	222	31.59 N	96.52 W
Ireng (Maú) ≃	246	3.33 N	59.51 W
İresi	130	39.09 N	39.53 E
Iresick Brook ≃	276	40.24 N	74.22 W
Ireton	198	42.58 N	96.19 W
Irfon ≃	42	52.09 N	3.24 W
Irgakly	84	44.22 N	44.45 E
Irgiz	86	48.37 N	61.16 E
Irgiz ≃	86	48.13 N	62.08 E
Irharrhar, Oued ∨, Alg.	148	20.25 N	6.10 E
Irharrhar, Oued ∨, Alg.	148	28.03 N	6.15 E
Iri	98	35.56 N	126.57 E
Irian Jaya □[4]	164	5.00 S	138.00 E
Iriba	146	15.07 N	22.15 E
Irié	150	8.17 N	9.11 W
Iriga	116	13.25 N	123.25 E
Irigny	62	45.40 N	4.49 E
Irîgui ⊸[1]	150	16.43 N	5.30 W
Iriklinskij	86	51.39 N	58.38 E
Iringa	154	7.46 S	35.42 E
Iringa □[4]	154	9.00 S	35.00 E
Irinjālakuda	122	10.20 N	76.14 E
Iriomote-jima I	175d	24.20 N	123.50 E
Iriona	236	15.57 N	85.11 W
Iriri ≃, Bra.	250	3.52 S	52.37 W
Iriri ≃, Bra.	287a	22.41 S	43.05 W
Iriri Novo ≃	250	8.46 S	53.22 W
Irische See → Irish Sea ⍑[2]	28	53.30 N	5.20 W
Irish, Mount ∧	204	37.38 N	115.24 W
Irish Sea ⍑[2]	28	53.30 N	5.20 W
Irishtown	166	40.55 S	145.08 E
Irituia	250	1.46 S	47.26 W
Iriyamazu	268	35.16 N	139.39 E
Irkās, Wādī ∨	142	28.57 N	32.00 E
Irkeštam	85	39.41 N	73.55 E
Irkinejeva ≃	88	58.30 N	96.48 E
Irkinejevo	88	58.30 N	96.49 E
Irklijev	78	49.32 N	32.18 E
Irklijevskaja	78	45.51 N	39.39 E
Irkoutsk → Irkutsk	88	52.16 N	104.20 E
Irkut ≃	88	52.18 N	104.15 E
Irkutsk	88	52.16 N	104.20 E
Irkutsk □[4]	88	56.00 N	106.00 E
Irlam	44	53.28 N	2.25 W
Irland → Ireland □[1]	28	53.00 N	8.00 W
Irlanda, Mar de → Irish Sea ⍑[2]	28	53.30 N	5.20 W
Irlande → Ireland □[1]	28	53.00 N	8.00 W
Irlande,, Mer d' → Irish Sea ⍑[2]	28	53.30 N	5.20 W
Irma	182	52.55 N	111.14 W
Irmauw	164	7.25 S	131.42 E
Irminio ≃	70	36.46 N	14.36 E
Irmino	83	48.36 N	38.36 E
Irnijärvi ◎	26	65.36 N	29.05 E
Irnsum	52	53.05 N	5.47 E
Iro, Lac ◎	146	10.06 N	19.25 E
Iroise C	32	48.15 N	4.55 W
Iron Baron	166	32.59 S	137.09 E
Iron Belt	190	46.25 N	90.19 W
Iron Bottom Sound ⊔	175e	9.15 S	160.00 E
Iron Bridge, Ont., Can.	190	46.17 N	83.14 W
Iron Bridge, Eng., U.K.	42	52.38 N	2.29 W
Iron Bridge Dam ⊸[6]	222	32.50 N	95.54 W
Iron City	194	35.01 N	87.35 W
Iron Cove C	274a	33.52 S	151.10 E
Iron Creek ≃	182	52.43 N	111.14 W
Irondale, Ala., U.S.	194	33.32 N	86.42 W
Irondale, Mo., U.S.	194	37.50 N	90.41 W
Irondale, Ohio, U.S.	214	40.34 N	80.44 W
Irondale ≃	212	44.49 N	78.37 W
Irondequoit	210	43.12 N	77.36 W
Irondequoit Bay C	210	43.12 N	77.32 W
Iron Gate ∨	38	44.41 N	22.31 E
Iron Gate Reservoir ◎[1]	38	44.30 N	22.00 E
Ironia	276	40.50 N	74.38 W
Iron Knob	166	32.44 S	137.08 E
Iron Mountain	190	45.49 N	88.04 W
Iron Mountain ∧, Ariz., U.S.	200	33.27 N	111.10 W
Iron Mountain ∧, Calif., U.S.	280	34.17 N	117.43 W
Iron Mountains ⋀	192	36.30 N	81.50 W
Iron Range	164	12.42 S	143.18 E
Iron River, Mich., U.S.	190	46.05 N	88.39 W
Iron River, Wis., U.S.	190	46.34 N	91.24 W
Iron Springs	208	39.46 N	77.25 W
Ironstone Kopje ∧	156	25.08 S	24.05 E
Ironton, Minn., U.S.	190	46.28 N	93.59 W
Ironton, Mo., U.S.	194	37.36 N	90.38 W
Ironton, Ohio, U.S.	188	38.31 N	82.40 W
Ironwood	190	46.27 N	90.10 W
Ironworks Creek ≃	285	40.10 N	74.59 W
Iroquois, Ont., Can.	212	44.51 N	75.19 W
Iroquois, Ill., U.S.	216	40.50 N	87.35 W
Iroquois, S. Dak., U.S.	198	44.22 N	97.51 W
Iroquois □[6]	216	40.47 N	87.44 W
Iroquois ≃	216	41.05 N	87.49 W
Iroquois Falls	190	48.46 N	80.41 W
Iroquois Lock and Dam ⊸[5]	212	44.45 N	75.23 W
Írottkő (Geschriebenstein) ∧	61	47.21 N	16.26 E
Irō-zaki ≻	94	34.36 N	138.51 E
Irpen'	78	50.31 N	30.15 E
Irpen' ≃	78	50.34 N	30.16 E
Irrawaddy □[8]	110	17.00 N	95.00 E
Irrawaddy ≃	110	15.50 N	95.06 E
Irregully Creek ≃	162	23.06 S	116.21 E
Irrel	56	49.51 N	6.28 E
Irricana	182	51.19 N	113.37 W
Irrigon	202	45.54 N	119.30 W
Irrua	150	6.46 N	6.14 E
Irša ≃	78	50.45 N	29.30 E
Iršava	78	48.20 N	23.03 E
Irschenberg	64	47.50 N	11.55 E
Irsee	58	47.54 N	10.34 E
Irsina	68	40.45 N	16.15 E
Irt ≃	44	54.22 N	3.26 W
Irt'aš, Ozero ◎	86	55.50 N	60.45 E
Irtek ≃	80	51.28 N	52.39 E
Irthing ≃	44	54.55 N	2.50 W
Irthlingborough	42	52.20 N	0.37 W
Irtyš	86	54.29 N	74.22 E
Irtyš ≃	74	61.04 N	68.52 E
Irtysch → Irtyš ≃	72	61.04 N	68.52 E
Irtysh → Irtyš ≃	72	61.04 N	68.52 E
Irtyšsk	86	53.21 N	75.27 E
Irubaj	80	50.11 N	51.21 E
Iruma	94	35.50 N	139.28 E
Iruma ≃	94	35.57 N	139.30 E
Iruma Air Base ■	268	35.50 N	139.24 E
Irumu	154	1.27 N	29.52 E
Irún	34	43.21 N	1.47 W
Irupana	248	16.28 S	67.28 W
Irurzun	34	42.55 N	1.50 W
Irves Šaurums (Irbeni Väin) ⊔	76	57.48 N	22.05 E
Irvine, Alta., Can.	184	49.57 N	110.16 W
Irvine, Scot., U.K.	46	55.37 N	4.40 W
Irvine, Calif., U.S.	228	33.41 N	117.46 W
Irvine, Ky., U.S.	192	37.42 N	83.58 W
Irvine, Pa., U.S.	214	41.50 N	79.17 W
Irvine ≃	46	55.37 N	4.41 W
Irvine, Mount ∧	210	42.03 N	78.40 W
Irvine Creek ≃	212	43.41 N	80.25 W
Irvine Park ♠	280	33.48 N	117.45 W
Irvines Landing	182	49.38 N	124.03 W
Irvinestown	48	54.28 N	7.38 W
Irving, Ill., U.S.	219	39.12 N	89.24 W
Irving, N.Y., U.S.	214	42.34 N	79.07 W
Irving, Tex., U.S.	222	32.49 N	96.56 W
Irving Park ⊸[8]	278	41.57 N	87.43 W
Irvington, Ill., U.S.	219	38.26 N	89.10 W
Irvington, Ky., U.S.	194	37.53 N	86.17 W
Irvington, N.J., U.S.	210	40.44 N	74.14 W
Irvington, N.Y., U.S.	210	41.02 N	73.52 W
Irvington, Ohio, U.S.	218	39.51 N	84.15 W
Irvington, Va., U.S.	208	37.40 N	76.25 W
Irvington ⊸[8]	284b	39.17 N	76.41 W
Irvona	214	40.46 N	78.33 W
Irwell ≃	44	53.27 N	2.17 W
Irwin, Austl.	162	29.12 S	115.04 E
Irwin, Ohio, U.S.	218	40.07 N	83.29 W
Irwin, Pa., U.S.	279b	40.20 N	79.42 W
Irwin ≃	162	29.15 S	114.56 E
Irwin, Point ≻	162	35.04 S	116.56 E
Irwindale	280	34.06 N	117.56 W
Irwinton	192	32.49 N	83.10 W
Irwŏl-san ∧	98	36.50 N	129.06 E
Is	86	58.48 N	59.43 E
Is, Jabal ∧	140	21.49 N	35.39 E
Isa	150	13.14 N	6.24 E
'Īsā, Ra's ≻	144	15.11 N	42.39 E
Isaac ≃	166	22.52 S	149.20 E
Isaac Lake ◎, B.C., Can.	182	53.10 N	120.50 W

Name	Seite	Breite°′	Länge°′ E=Ost
Isaac Lake ◎, Ont., Can.	212	44.47 N	81.14 W
Isaba	34	42.52 N	0.55 W
Isabel, Pil.	116	10.56 N	124.26 E
Isabel, S. Dak., U.S.	198	45.24 N	101.26 W
Isabel, Bahía C	246a	0.38 S	91.27 W
Isabela, Pil.	116	10.12 N	122.59 E
Isabela (Basilan), Pil.	116	6.42 N	121.58 E
Isabela, P.R.	240m	18.30 N	67.01 W
Isabela □[4]	116	17.00 N	122.00 E
Isabela, Cabo ≻	238	19.56 N	71.01 W
Isabela, Canal ⊔	246a	0.20 S	90.55 W
Isabela, Isla I, Ec.	246a	0.30 S	91.06 W
Isabela, Isla I, Méx.	234	21.51 N	105.55 W
Isabelia, Cordillera ⋀	236	13.45 N	85.15 W
Isabella Lake ◎	212	45.24 N	79.49 W
Isabella Lake ◎[1]	204	35.40 N	118.26 W
Isabelle ≃	190	47.50 N	91.41 W
Isábena ≃	34	42.11 N	0.21 E
Isaccea	38	45.16 N	28.28 E
Ísafjarðardjúp C[2]	24a	66.10 N	23.00 W
Ísafjörður	24a	66.08 N	23.13 W
Isāgarh	124	24.50 N	77.53 E
Isagatedo	273a	6.32 N	3.20 E
Isahaya	92	32.50 N	130.03 E
Isak	114	4.28 N	96.55 E
Isaka, Tan.	154	3.54 S	32.56 E
Isaka, Zaïre	152	2.35 S	18.48 E
Isaka-Buku	152	3.55 S	22.03 E
Īsa Khel	123	32.42 N	71.16 E
Isakly	80	54.08 N	51.32 E
Isakovka	86	55.45 N	74.24 E
Isakovo, S.S.S.R.	76	55.11 N	34.40 E
Isakovo, S.S.S.R.	76	60.30 N	41.13 E
Isakovo, S.S.S.R.	82	54.36 N	37.02 E
Isakovo, S.S.S.R.	265b	55.59 N	37.23 E
Işalniţa	38	44.24 N	23.44 E
Isalo, Parc National de l' ♠	157b	22.45 S	45.15 E
Isana (Içana) ≃	246	0.26 N	67.19 W
Īsānagar	124	27.54 N	81.13 E
Isandhlwana ⊥	158	28.21 S	30.39 E
Isandja Etat	152	2.59 S	22.00 E
Isando	273d	26.09 S	28.12 E
Isanga	152	1.26 S	22.18 E
Isangano Game Reserve ⊸[4]	154	11.10 S	30.40 E
Isangi	152	0.46 N	24.15 E
Is'angulovo	86	52.12 N	56.36 E
Isanlu Makutu	150	8.17 N	5.46 E
Isan-ni	98	40.46 N	128.55 E
Isanti	190	45.29 N	93.15 W
Isar ≃	30	48.49 N	12.58 E
Isara	150	6.59 N	3.41 E
Isarco (Eisack) ≃	64	46.27 N	11.18 E
Isarco, Valle ∨	64	46.45 N	11.37 E
Isarog, Mount ∧	116	13.39 N	123.23 E
Isasi	273a	6.40 N	3.23 E
Isawa	94	35.39 N	138.38 E
Isbergues	50	50.37 N	2.27 E
Isbister	46	60.36 N	1.19 W
İşcehisar	130	38.51 N	30.45 E
Isčerskaja	84	43.43 N	45.08 E
Ischgl	58	47.01 N	10.17 E
Ischia	68	40.44 N	13.57 E
Ischia, Isola d' I	68	40.43 N	13.54 E
Ischia di Castro	66	42.33 N	11.45 E
Ischim → Išim ≃	86	57.45 N	71.12 E
Ischitella	68	41.54 N	15.54 E
Ischma → Ižma ≃	24	65.19 N	52.54 E
Ischodnaja, Gora ∧	180	64.50 N	173.26 W
Ischua	210	42.15 N	78.24 W
Ischua Creek ≃	210	42.10 N	78.23 W
Iscuandé ≃	246	2.38 N	78.04 W
Isdes	50	47.40 N	2.15 E
Ise (Uji-yamada)	94	34.29 N	136.42 E
Ise ≃	54	52.30 N	10.33 E
Isebania	154	1.15 S	34.33 E
Isefjord C	41	55.52 N	11.49 E
Isehara	94	35.24 N	139.18 E
Išejevka	80	54.25 N	48.16 E
Iseke	154	6.25 S	35.01 E
Isel ≃	64	46.50 N	12.47 E
Iselin, N.J., U.S.	210	40.34 N	74.19 W
Iselin, Pa., U.S.	214	40.34 N	79.24 W
Iselle	58	46.12 N	8.12 E
Iseltwald	58	46.43 N	7.58 E
Isen	60	48.13 N	12.04 E
Isen ≃	60	48.15 N	12.40 E
Isenbajevo	80	56.03 N	53.25 E
Isenbüttel	52	52.26 N	10.34 E
Isenyela	154	8.36 S	33.30 E
Iseo	64	45.39 N	10.03 E
Iseo, Lago d' ◎	64	45.43 N	10.04 E
Iseramagazi	154	4.40 S	32.09 E
Iseran, Col de l')(	62	45.25 N	7.02 E
Isère □[5]	62	45.10 N	5.50 E
Isère ≃	62	44.59 N	4.51 E
Iseri	273a	6.39 N	3.23 E
Iseri-Oke	273a	6.38 N	3.23 E
Iseri-Osun	273a	6.31 N	3.17 E
Iserlohn	56	51.22 N	7.41 E
Iserlohn □[8]	263	51.24 N	7.36 E
Iserlohnerheide ⊸[8]	263	51.24 N	7.42 E
Isernia	66	41.36 N	14.14 E
Isernia □[4]	66	41.40 N	14.15 E
Isesaki	94	36.19 N	139.12 E
Ise-shima-kokuritsu-kōen ♠	92	34.23 N	136.48 E
Iset' ≃	86	56.36 N	66.24 E
Isetskoje	86	56.29 N	65.21 E
Ise-wan C	94	34.43 N	136.43 E
Iseyin	150	7.58 N	3.36 E
Isezaki → Isesaki	92	36.19 N	139.12 E
Isfahan → Eşfahān	128	32.40 N	51.38 E
Isfana	85	39.50 N	69.31 E
Isfana ≃	85	40.13 N	69.26 E
Isfara	85	40.07 N	70.38 E
'Isfiyā	132	32.43 N	35.04 E
Ishenga Oswe	152	3.46 S	22.34 E
Isheri-Olofin	273a	6.35 N	3.17 E
Isherton	246	2.19 N	59.22 W
Ishi ≃	270	34.35 N	135.38 E
Ishibashi	94	36.26 N	139.52 E
Ishibe	94	35.00 N	136.04 E
Ishigaki	175d	24.20 N	124.09 E
Ishigaki-shima I	175d	24.24 N	124.12 E
Ishige	94	36.07 N	139.58 E
Ishii	96	34.04 N	134.26 E
Ishikari ≃	90	43.15 N	141.23 E
Ishikari-dake ∧	92a	44.33 N	143.02 E
Ishikari-heiya ≚	92a	43.15 N	141.23 E
Ishikari-wan C	92a	43.25 N	141.01 E
Ishikawa, Nihon	94	37.09 N	140.27 E
Ishikawa, Nihon	174m	26.25 N	127.50 E
Ishikawa □[5]	94	36.45 N	136.45 E
Ishiki	94	34.48 N	137.01 E
Ishikiri	270	34.41 N	135.39 E
I-shima I	96	33.51 N	134.49 E
Ishinomaki	92	38.25 N	141.18 E
Ishioka	94	36.11 N	140.16 E
Ishiyama	270	34.58 N	135.55 E
Ishizuchi-kokutei-kōen ♠	96	33.45 N	133.08 E
Ishizuchi-san ∧	96	33.46 N	133.07 E
Ishkumān	123	36.32 N	73.49 E
Ishmant	142	29.12 N	31.11 E
Ishpeming	190	46.30 N	87.40 W
Ishua	150	7.24 N	5.57 E
Ishuizu ≃	270	34.33 N	135.27 E
Ishurdi	124	24.08 N	89.05 E
Isidro Casanova	288	34.42 S	58.35 W
Isigny	32	49.19 N	1.06 W
Işıklı	130	38.19 N	29.51 E
Isili	71	39.44 N	9.06 E
Isil'kul'	86	54.55 N	71.16 E

Symbols in the index entries represent the broad categories identified in the key at the right. Symbols with superior numbers (⋀[2]) identify subcategories (see complete key on page *I · 30*).

Kartensymbole in dem Register-verzeichnis stellen die rechts in Schlüssel erklärten Kategorien dar. Symbole mit hochgestellten Ziffern (⋀[2]) bezeichnen Unterabteilungen einer Kategorie (vgl. vollständiger Schlüssel auf Seite *I · 30*).

Los símbolos incluídos en el texto del índice representan las grandes categorias identificadas con la clave a la derecha. Los símbolos con numeros en su parte superior (⋀[2]) identifican las subcategorías (véase la clave completa en la página *I · 30*).

Les symboles de l'index représentent les catégories indiquées dans la légende à droite. Les symboles suivis d'un indice (⋀[2]) représentent des sous-catégories (voir légende complète à la page *I · 30*).

Os símbolos incluídos no texto do índice representam as grandes categorias identificadas com a chave à direita. Os símbolos com números em sua parte superior (⋀[2]) identificam as subcategorias (veja-se a chave completa à página *I · 30*).

	English	Deutsch	Español	Français	Português
∧	Mountain	Berg	Montaña	Montagne	Montanha
⋀	Mountains	Berge	Montañas	Montagnes	Montanhas
)(	Pass	Pass	Paso	Col	Passo
∨	Valley, Canyon	Tal, Cañon	Valle, Cañón	Vallée, Canyon	Vale, Canhão
≚	Plain	Ebene	Llano	Plaine	Planície
≻	Cape	Kap	Cabo	Cap	Cabo
I	Island	Insel	Isla	Île	Ilha
II	Islands	Inseln	Islas	Îles	Ilhas
⍛	Other Topographic Features	Andere Topographische Objekte	Otros Elementos Topográficos	Autres données topographiques	Outros Elementos Topográficos

ESPAÑOL

Nombre	Página	Lat.°′	Long.°′ W=Oeste
Išim	86	56.09 N	69.27 E
Išim ≃	86	57.45 N	71.12 E
Išimbaj	86	53.28 N	56.02 E
Išimka	86	51.24 N	67.08 E
Išimskaja Step' ≚	86	55.00 N	70.00 E
Isimu	112	0.40 N	122.51 E
Isinga	88	52.55 N	112.00 E
Isinga, Ozero ⊜	88	52.55 N	111.57 E
Isiolo	154	0.21 N	37.35 E
Isipingo Beach	158	29.59 S	30.57 E
Isiro (Paulis)	154	2.47 N	27.37 E
Isis	166	25.12 S	152.13 E
Isisford	166	24.16 S	144.26 E
Iskander	85	41.36 N	69.43 E
Iskâr, Jazovir ⊜[1]	38	43.23 N	27.29 E
Iskaten', Chrebet ⛰	180	66.30 N	179.00 W
Iškejevo	80	55.51 N	50.56 E
İskenderun	130	36.37 N	36.07 E
İskenderun Körfezi C	130	36.30 N	35.40 E
Iske R'az'ap	80	54.36 N	49.42 E
İskilip	130	40.45 N	34.29 E
Iski-Naukat	85	40.16 N	72.36 E
Iskininskij	80	47.13 N	52.41 E
Iskitim	86	54.38 N	83.18 E
Iskona ≃	82	55.34 N	36.05 E
Iskushuban	144	10.13 N	50.14 E
Iskut ≃	180	56.42 N	131.45 W
Isla	234	18.01 N	95.30 W
Isla ≃	46	57.30 N	2.47 W
Isla, Salar de la ≚	252	25.49 S	68.53 W
Isla Cristina	34	37.12 N	7.19 W
Isla de Maipo	252	33.45 S	70.54 W
İslâhiye	130	37.03 N	36.36 E
Islāmābād → Anantnāg, Bhārat	123	33.44 N	75.09 E
Islāmābād, Pāk.	123	33.42 N	73.10 E
Isla Mala	258	34.12 S	56.21 W
Islāmkot	120	24.42 N	70.11 E
Islamorada	220	24.56 N	80.37 W
Islāmpur, Bhārat	124	25.09 N	85.12 E
Islāmpur, Bhārat	124	26.16 N	88.12 E
Islāmpur, Bhārat	126	24.09 N	88.28 E
Islāmpur, Bhārat	126	21.43 N	87.39 E
Isla Mujeres	232	21.12 N	86.43 W
Island	194	37.27 N	87.09 W
Island □[6]	224	48.07 N	122.36 W
Island → Iceland □[1]	24a	65.00 N	18.00 W
Island ≃	262	53.44 N	2.51 W
Island Bay C	116	9.06 N	118.10 E
Island Beach State Park ♠	208	39.50 N	74.06 W
Island Bend	171b	36.19 S	148.29 E
Island Channel ⋓	276	40.36 N	73.53 W
Island Creek	283	42.01 N	70.43 W
Island Falls, Sask., Can.	184	55.32 N	102.21 W
Island Falls, Maine, U.S.	188	46.00 N	68.16 W
Island Heights	208	39.57 N	74.09 W
Islandia → Iceland □[1]	24a	65.00 N	18.00 W
Island Lagoon ⊜	166	31.30 S	136.40 E
Island Lake, Man., Can.	184	53.58 N	94.47 W
Island Lake, Ill., U.S.	216	42.17 N	88.12 W
Island Lake, Mich., U.S.	216	42.31 N	83.44 W
Island Lake ⊜	184	53.47 N	94.25 W
Island Lake State Recreation Area ♠	216	42.30 N	83.43 W
Island Park, Idaho, U.S.	202	44.24 N	111.19 W
Island Park, N.Y., U.S.	276	40.36 N	73.40 W
Island Park, R.I., U.S.	207	41.37 N	71.14 W
Island Park Reservoir ⊜[1]	202	44.25 N	111.29 W
Island Point ≻	162	30.20 S	115.02 E
Island Pond	188	44.49 N	71.53 W
Island Pond ⊜	186	48.25 N	56.23 W
Islands, Bay of C, Newf., Can.	186	49.10 N	58.15 W
Islands, Bay Of C, N.Z.	172	35.12 S	174.10 E
Island View	216	40.31 N	83.53 W
Isla Patrulla	252	32.59 S	54.35 W
Islas de la Bahía □[5]	236	16.20 N	86.30 W
Islas Malvinas → Falkland Islands □[2]	254	51.45 S	59.00 W
Isla Verde	252	33.14 S	62.24 W
Isla Vista	204	34.25 N	119.53 W
Islay I	46	55.48 N	6.12 W
Islay, Punta ≻	248	17.01 S	72.07 W
Islay, Sound of ⋓	46	55.50 N	6.01 W
Islay Creek ≃	226	35.17 N	120.53 W
Isle	190	46.08 N	93.29 W
Isle ≃, Fr.	32	44.55 N	0.15 W
Isle ≃, Eng., U.K.	42	50.59 N	2.53 W
Isle-Adam, Forêt de l' ♠	261	49.05 N	2.15 E
Isleat, Sound of ⋓	46	57.05 N	5.52 W
Isle-aux-Morts	186	47.35 N	58.59 W
Isle of Hope	192	31.58 N	81.05 W
Isle of Man □[2]	22		
	44	54.15 N	4.30 W
Isle of Palms	192	32.47 N	79.48 W
Isle of Wight	208	36.54 N	76.43 W
Isle of Wight □[6], Eng., U.K.	42	50.40 N	1.20 W
Isle of Wight □[6], Va., U.S.	208	36.50 N	76.42 W
Isle of Wight Bay C	208	38.22 N	75.06 W
Isle Royale National Park ♠	190	48.00 N	89.00 W
Isles, Lake of the ⊜	212	44.19 N	75.59 W
Isle Saint George	214	41.43 N	82.49 W
Islesboro Island I	188	44.20 N	68.53 W
Isleta	200	34.55 N	106.42 W
Isleta Indian Reservation ◆[4]	200	34.55 N	106.45 W
Isleton	226	38.10 N	121.37 W
Islets Caribou	186	49.30 N	67.14 W
Isleworth ◆[8]	260	51.28 N	0.20 W
Islington	207	42.13 N	71.11 W
Islington ◆[8], Ont., Can.	275b	43.39 N	79.32 W
Islington ◆[8], Eng., U.K.	42	51.34 N	0.06 W
Islip, Eng., U.K.	42	51.50 N	1.14 W
Islip, N.Y., U.S.	276	40.44 N	73.13 W
Islip-MacArthur Airport ⊠	210	40.48 N	73.06 W
Islip Terrace	276	40.46 N	73.13 W
Islivig	46	58.05 N	7.11 W
Isloč' ≃	76	53.55 N	26.13 E
Islón	252	29.54 S	71.12 W
Ismael Cortinas (Arroyo Grande)	258	33.58 S	57.06 W
Ismailia → Al-Ismā'īlīyah	142	30.35 N	32.16 E
Ismā'īlīyah ◆[8]	273c	30.03 N	31.14 E
Ismā'īlīyah, Tur'at al- ≡	142	30.04 N	31.16 E
İsmailli	130	38.56 N	27.13 E
Ismailly	84	40.47 N	48.09 E
Ismailovo	80	55.34 N	54.39 E
Ismanning	60	48.14 N	11.41 E
Isnā	140	25.18 N	32.33 E
Isny	58	47.41 N	10.02 E
Isoanala	157b	23.50 S	45.44 E
Isobe	94	34.22 N	136.49 E
Isogo ◆[8]	268	35.23 N	139.37 E
Isojoki	26	62.07 N	21.58 E
Isoka	154	10.10 S	32.35 E
Isokyrö	26	63.00 N	22.19 E
Isola, Fr.	62	44.11 N	7.03 E
Isola, Miss., U.S.	194	33.16 N	90.36 W

FRANÇAIS

Nom	Page	Lat.°′	Long.°′ W=Ouest
Isola, Monte ∧	64	45.42 N	10.05 E
Isola d'Asti	62	44.50 N	8.11 E
Isola del Cantone	62	44.39 N	8.57 E
Isola del Gran Sasso d'Italia	66	42.30 N	13.40 E
Isola della Scala	64	45.16 N	11.00 E
Isola del Liri	66	41.41 N	13.34 E
Isola di Capo Rizzuto	68	38.58 N	17.06 E
Isola Dovarese	64	45.10 N	10.18 E
Isola Farnese ◆[8]	66	42.01 N	12.23 E
Isola Vicentina	64	45.38 N	11.25 E
Isoletta	66	41.30 N	13.34 E
Isolillock Peak ∧	224	49.18 N	121.27 W
Isolo	273a	6.32 N	3.19 E
Isone	58	46.08 N	8.59 E
Isonzo (Soča) ≃	64	45.47 N	13.32 E
Isorella	64	45.18 N	10.19 E
Isosyöte ∧[2]	26	65.37 N	27.35 E
Iso-zaki ≻	94	36.23 N	140.38 E
İspanak	130	36.52 N	37.07 E
Ispani	68	40.08 N	15.34 E
Isparta	130	37.46 N	30.33 E
Isparta □[4]	130	38.00 N	31.00 E
Isperih	38	43.43 N	26.50 E
Ispica	70	36.47 N	14.55 E
Ispica, Cava d' ●[5]	70	36.51 N	14.51 E
Ispikān	128	26.14 N	62.12 E
İspir	130	40.29 N	41.00 E
Ispra	62	45.49 N	8.37 E
Ispringen	56	48.55 N	8.40 E
Israel □[1]	118		
	132	31.30 N	35.00 E
Israel ≃	188	44.29 N	71.35 W
Issa	80	53.52 N	44.51 E
Issa ≃	76	56.58 N	28.47 E
Issano	246	5.49 N	59.25 W
Issaquah	224	47.32 N	122.02 W
Issaran, Ra's ≻	142	28.48 N	32.47 E
Issel (Oude IJssel) ≃	52	52.00 N	6.10 E
Isselburg	52	51.51 N	6.28 E
Isselhorst	52	51.57 N	8.24 E
Issen, Oued ≃	34	36.52 N	3.48 E
Isser, Oued ≃	34	35.08 N	1.28 W
Issia	150	6.29 N	6.35 W
Issigeac	32	44.44 N	0.36 E
Issime	62	45.41 N	7.51 E
Issogne	62	45.39 N	7.41 E
Issoire	32	45.33 N	3.15 E
Issole ≃	62	43.27 N	6.12 E
Issou	261	48.59 N	1.48 E
Issoudun	32	46.57 N	2.00 E
Issum	52	51.32 N	6.25 E
Issuna	154	5.23 S	34.46 E
Is-sur-Tille	58	47.31 N	5.06 E
Issy	50	48.50 N	2.18 E
Issyk	85	43.22 N	77.28 E
Issyk-Kul', Ozero ⊜	85	42.25 N	77.15 E
Issy-les-Moulineaux	261	48.49 N	2.17 E
Īstādeh-ye Moqor, Āb-e ⊜	120	32.32 N	67.57 E
İstanbul	130		
	267b	41.01 N	28.58 E
İstanbul □[4]	38	41.25 N	29.00 E
İstanbul (Yeşilköy) hava alani ⊠	267b	40.58 N	28.49 E
İstanbul Boğazı (Bosporus) ⋓	130	41.06 N	29.04 E
İstanbul Üniversitesi ♉[2]	267b	41.00 N	28.58 E
Isṭanhā	142	30.28 N	31.07 E
Istead Rise	260	51.24 N	0.22 E
Isteren ⊜	26	61.58 N	11.48 E
Isthmus Bay C	212	45.00 N	81.15 W
Istiaía	38	38.57 N	23.09 E
İstilil	130	37.14 N	41.04 E
İstinye ◆[8]	267b	41.06 N	29.03 E
Istisu	84	39.57 N	45.59 E
Istmina	246	5.10 N	76.39 W
Isto, Mount ∧	180	69.12 N	143.48 W
Istobensk	80	58.25 N	48.48 E
Istobnoje, S.S.S.R.	78	51.08 N	37.21 E
Istobnoje, S.S.S.R.	78	51.16 N	38.39 E
Istok	38	42.47 N	20.29 E
Istokpoga, Lake ⊜	220	27.22 N	81.17 W
Istra	82	55.55 N	36.52 E
Istra ≻[1]	36	45.15 N	14.00 E
Istra ≃	82	55.44 N	37.08 E
Istrana	64	45.41 N	12.07 E
Istranca Dağları ⛰	130	41.50 N	27.30 E
Istres	62	43.31 N	4.59 E
Istria → Istra ≻[1]	36	45.15 N	14.00 E
Istrinskoje Vodochranilišče ⊜[1]	82	56.04 N	36.49 E
Isumi	94	35.17 N	140.19 E
Isumi ≃	94	35.18 N	140.29 E
Isumrud Strait ⋓	164	4.45 S	145.50 E
Isunba	273a	6.27 N	3.17 E
Iswarīpur	126	22.19 N	89.07 E
Iswepe	158	26.50 S	30.31 E
Itá	252	25.29 S	57.21 W
Itabaiana, Bra.	250	10.41 S	37.26 W
Itabaiana, Bra.	250	7.20 S	35.20 W
Itabaiana, Bra.	250	11.16 S	37.47 W
Itabapoana	255	21.18 S	40.58 W
Itabashi ◆[8]	268	35.45 N	139.43 E
Itaberá	255	23.51 S	49.09 W
Itaberaba	255	12.32 S	40.18 W
Itaberaí	255	16.02 S	49.48 W
Itabi	250	10.08 S	37.06 W
Itabira	255	19.37 S	43.13 W
Itaboca	256	22.03 S	44.05 W
Itaboraí	256	22.45 S	42.52 W
Itaboraí □[7]	287a	22.43 S	43.00 W
Itabuna	255	14.48 S	39.16 W
Itacaiunas ≃	250	5.21 S	49.08 W
Itacajá	250	8.19 S	47.46 W
Itacambiruçu ≃	255	16.44 S	42.45 W
Itacaré	255	14.18 S	39.00 W
Itacoatiara	250	3.08 S	58.25 W
Itacoatiara, Ponta de ≻	287a	22.59 S	43.02 W
Itacuaí ≃	246	4.20 S	70.12 W
Itacurubí del Rosario	252	24.29 S	56.41 W
Itacuruça, Ilha de I	256	22.56 S	43.53 W
Itacurussá	256	22.55 S	43.55 W
Itaetê	255	12.59 S	40.58 W
Itagacaba ≃	256	22.34 S	44.56 W
Itagi	255	14.10 S	40.01 W
Itaguaçu	255	19.48 S	40.51 W
Itaguaí	256	22.52 S	43.47 W
Itaguajé	255	22.37 S	51.59 W
Itaguara	255	20.23 S	44.29 W
Itaguaré, Pico do ∧	256	22.30 S	45.10 W
Ítaguari ≃	255	14.11 S	44.40 W
Itaguaru	255	15.44 S	49.37 W
Itaguatins	250	5.47 S	47.29 W
Itagüí	246	6.10 N	75.36 W
Itaí	255	23.24 S	49.06 W
Itá-Ibaté	252	27.26 S	57.20 W
Itaiçaba	250	4.40 S	37.51 W
Itaim	256	22.24 S	45.53 W
Itaim ≃, Bra.	250	7.02 S	42.02 W
Itaim ≃, Bra.	256	22.19 S	45.51 W
Itaim ≃, Bra.	256	23.07 S	45.08 W
Itainópolis	250	7.24 S	41.31 W
Itaiópolis	252	26.20 S	49.56 W
Itaipava	256	22.23 S	43.08 W
Itaipu, Bra.	256	22.58 S	43.02 W
Itaipu, Bra.	287a	22.44 S	43.26 W
Itaipu, Lagoa de C	287a	22.58 S	43.02 W
Itaipu, Ponta de ≻	287a	22.59 S	43.03 W
Itaituba	250	4.17 S	55.59 W
Itajá	255	19.07 S	51.37 W
Itajaí	252	26.53 S	48.39 W
Itajaí do Sul ≃	252	27.12 S	49.39 W
Itajubá	256	22.26 S	45.27 W
Itaju do Colônia	255	15.09 S	39.44 W
Itajuípe	255	14.41 S	39.22 W

PORTUGUÊS

Nome	Página	Lat.°′	Long.°′ W=Oeste
Itaka, S.S.S.R.	88	53.53 N	118.42 E
Itaka, Tan.	154	8.52 S	32.47 E
Itaki	273a	6.43 N	3.17 E
Itako	94	35.56 N	140.33 E
Itakura, Nihon	94	37.03 N	138.18 E
Itakura, Nihon	94	36.13 N	139.26 E
Italia → Italy □[1]	36	42.50 N	12.50 E
Itálica ⊥	34	37.30 N	6.05 W
Italie → Italy □[1]	36	42.50 N	12.50 E
Italien → Italy □[1]	36	42.50 N	12.50 E
Italy	222	32.11 N	96.53 W
Italy □[1]	22		
	36	42.50 N	12.50 E
Itamaraju	255	17.05 S	39.31 W
Itamarandiba	255	17.51 S	42.51 W
Itamarandiba ≃	255	17.18 S	42.48 W
Itamarati	256	21.25 S	42.49 W
Itamari	255	13.47 S	39.37 W
Itamataré	250	2.16 S	46.24 W
Itambacuri	255	18.01 S	41.42 W
Itambé	255	15.15 S	40.37 W
Itambi	256	22.44 S	42.58 W
Itami	96	34.46 N	135.25 E
Itami, Camp ■	270	34.47 N	135.24 E
Itamonte	256	22.17 S	44.53 W
Itampolo	157b	24.41 S	43.57 E
Itandéua, Lago ⊜	250	2.01 S	55.10 W
Itandrano	157b	21.47 S	45.17 E
Itanhaém	255	24.11 S	46.47 W
Itanhandu	256	22.18 S	44.57 W
Itanhauã ≃	248	4.45 S	63.48 W
Itanhém	255	17.09 S	40.20 W
Itanhém ≃	255	17.32 S	39.12 W
Itanhomi	255	19.10 S	41.52 W
Itano	96	34.07 N	134.28 E
Itany (Litani) ≃	250	3.40 N	54.00 W
Itaobim	255	16.34 S	41.30 W
Itaocaia	287a	22.58 S	43.01 W
Itapaci	255	14.57 S	49.34 W
Itapagé	250	3.41 S	39.34 W
Itapagipe	255	19.54 S	49.22 W
Itapanhaú ≃	256	23.51 S	46.10 W
Itaparaná ≃	248	5.47 S	63.03 W
Itapaya	248	17.34 S	66.21 W
Itapé	255	14.54 S	39.26 W
Itapebi	255	15.56 S	39.32 W
Itapecerica	255	20.28 S	45.07 W
Itapecerica da Serra	256	23.43 S	46.50 W
Itapecerica da Serra □[7]	287b	23.44 S	46.52 W
Itapechinga	256	22.58 S	46.35 W
Itapecuru ≃	250	2.52 S	44.12 W
Itapecuru-Mirim	250	3.24 S	44.20 W
Itapemirim	255	21.01 S	40.50 W
Itapera	250	2.32 S	43.47 W
Itaperina, Pointe ≻	157b	24.59 S	47.06 E
Itaperuna	255	21.12 S	41.54 W
Itapeteiú	256	22.54 S	42.47 W
Itapetim	250	7.22 S	37.11 W
Itapetinga	255	15.15 S	40.15 W
Itapetininga	255	23.36 S	48.03 W
Itapetininga ≃	255	23.35 S	48.27 W
Itapeva, Bra.	255	23.58 S	48.52 W
Itapeva, Bra.	256	22.46 S	46.13 W
Itapevi	256	23.33 S	46.56 W
Itapevi □[7]	287b	23.31 S	46.55 W
Itapicuru	250	11.19 S	38.15 W
Itapicuru ≃	250	11.47 S	37.32 W
Itapipoca	250	3.30 S	39.35 W
Itapira	256	22.26 S	46.50 W
Itapiranga, Bra.	250	2.45 S	58.01 W
Itapiranga, Bra.	252	27.08 S	53.43 W
Itapirapuã	255	15.52 S	50.36 W
Itapitanga	255	14.26 S	39.34 W
Itapiúna	250	4.33 S	38.57 W
Itápolis	255	21.35 S	48.46 W
Itaporã	255	22.01 S	54.54 W
Itaporã de Goiás	250	8.02 S	48.39 W
Itaporanga, Bra.	250	7.18 S	38.10 W
Itaporanga, Bra.	255	23.42 S	49.29 W
Itaporanga d'Ajuda	250	10.59 S	37.18 W
Itapúa □[5]	252	26.50 S	55.50 W
Itapuranga	255	15.35 S	49.59 W
Itaquaciara	287b	23.47 S	46.51 W
Itaquaquecetuba	256	23.29 S	46.21 W
Itaquaquecetuba □[7]	287b	23.28 S	46.20 W
Itaquara	255	13.27 S	39.57 W
Itaquari	255	20.20 S	40.22 W
Itaquera ◆[8]	256	23.32 S	46.27 W
Itaquera, Ribeirão ≃	287b	23.28 S	46.26 W
Itaqui	252	29.08 S	56.33 W
Itaqui, Serra do ∧	287b	23.28 S	46.55 W
Itaquyry	252	24.56 S	55.13 W
Itarantim	255	15.39 S	40.03 W
Itararé	255	24.07 S	49.20 W
Itararé ≃	252	23.10 S	49.42 W
Itārsi	124	22.37 N	77.45 E
Itarumã	255	18.42 S	51.25 W
Itasca, Ill., U.S.	278	41.58 N	87.59 W
Itasca, Tex., U.S.	222	32.10 N	97.09 W
Itasca State Park ♠	198	47.18 N	95.18 W
Itatá ≃, Bra.	250	3.28 S	51.57 W
Itata ≃, Chile	252	36.23 S	72.52 W
Itatí	252	27.16 S	58.15 W
Itatiaia	256	22.30 S	44.34 W
Itatiaia, Parque Nacional do ♠	256	22.28 S	44.37 W
Itatiba	256	23.00 S	46.51 W
Itatinga	255	23.07 S	48.36 W
Itatira	250	4.30 S	39.37 W
Itatka	86	56.49 N	85.37 E
Itatori	94	35.42 N	136.38 E
Itatskij	86	56.04 N	89.05 E
Itatupã	250	0.37 S	51.12 W
Itaú	250	5.50 S	37.59 W
Itauaiuri, Serra ∧[2]	250	1.47 S	54.06 W
Itauçu	255	16.13 S	49.37 W
Itaueira	250	7.36 S	43.02 W
Itaueiras ≃	250	6.41 S	42.55 W
Itaúna	255	20.04 S	44.34 W
Itaúna, Morro do ∧[2]	287a	22.46 S	43.02 W
Itazuke-kūkō ⊠	96	33.52 N	130.28 E
Itbayat Island I	108	20.46 N	121.50 E
Itchen Lake ⊜	176	65.33 N	112.50 W
Ité ≃	246	7.00 N	74.15 W
Itéa	38	38.26 N	22.24 E
Iténez (Guaporé) ≃	248	11.54 S	65.01 W
Ith ∧	52	52.05 N	9.35 E
Ithaca, Mich., U.S.	190	43.18 N	84.36 W
Ithaca, N.Y., U.S.	210	42.27 N	76.30 W
Itháki	38	38.23 N	20.42 E
Itháki I	38	38.24 N	20.42 E
Ithan Creek ≃	285	40.00 N	75.21 W
Ithnayn	142	30.41 N	32.21 E
Itigi	154	5.42 S	34.29 E
Itikawa → Ichikawa	94	35.44 N	139.55 E
Itimādpur	124	27.15 N	78.12 E
Itimbiri ≃	152	2.02 N	22.44 E
Itinga	255	16.36 S	41.47 W
Itinga ≃	255	16.35 S	41.45 W
Itinomiya → Ichinomiya	94	35.18 N	136.48 E
Itipo	152	0.50 S	18.35 E
Itiquira	255	17.12 S	54.07 W
Itiquira ≃	248	17.18 S	56.44 W
Itirapina	255	22.15 S	47.49 W
Itire	273a	6.31 N	3.21 E
Itiruçu	255	13.31 S	40.09 W
Itiúba	250	10.43 S	39.51 W
Itkillik ≃	180	70.08 N	150.57 W
Itlar'	82	56.51 N	39.17 E
Itlīdim	142	27.52 N	30.48 E
Itmīdah	142	30.46 N	31.20 E
Itmurynkol', Ozero ⊜	80	49.30 N	52.22 E
Itō	94	34.58 N	139.05 E
Itobi	256	21.44 S	46.58 W
Itobo	154	4.10 S	33.01 E
Itóca, Ilha de I	287a	22.46 S	43.04 W
Itóculo	154	14.42 S	40.18 E
Itoigawa	94	37.02 N	137.51 E
Itoko	152	1.00 S	21.45 E
Itomamo, Lac ⊜	186	49.11 N	70.28 W
Itoman	174m	26.08 N	127.40 E
Iton ≃	50	49.09 N	1.12 E
Itonamas ≃	248	12.28 S	64.24 W
Itororó	255	15.07 S	40.06 W
Itri	66	41.17 N	13.32 E
Iṭsā	142	29.15 N	30.48 E
Itsukaichi, Nihon	94	35.44 N	139.13 E
Itsukaichi, Nihon	96	34.24 N	132.22 E
Itsuki	92	32.24 N	130.50 E
Itsuku-shima I	96	34.16 N	132.19 E
Itsuwa	92	32.30 N	130.10 E
Itta Bena	194	33.30 N	90.20 W
Ittel, Oued ∨	148	34.19 N	6.01 E
Itter ≃	263	51.09 N	6.52 E
Ittersum	52	52.28 N	6.07 E
Itteville	261	48.31 N	2.21 E
Ittiḥād al-Imārāt al-'Arabīyah → United Arab Emirates □[1]	128	24.00 N	54.00 E
Ittiri	71	40.36 N	8.34 E
Ittygran, Ostrov I	180	64.36 N	172.40 W
Itu	255	23.16 S	47.19 W
Itu ≃	252	29.25 S	55.51 W
Ituaçu	255	13.49 S	41.18 W
Ituango	246	7.04 N	75.45 W
Ituberá	255	13.44 S	39.09 W
Itucumã ≃	248	6.59 S	69.48 W
Itueta	255	19.23 S	41.11 W
Ituí	256	21.32 S	42.55 W
Ituí ≃	246	4.38 S	70.19 W
Ituim ≃	252	28.35 S	51.20 W
Ituiutaba	255	18.58 S	49.28 W
Itula	154	3.29 S	27.52 E
Itumbiara	255	18.25 S	49.13 W
Itumirim	256	21.19 S	44.53 W
Itum-Kale	84	42.43 N	45.35 E
Ituna	184	51.10 N	103.30 W
Itungi Port	154	9.35 S	33.56 E
Itupeva	256	23.09 S	47.04 W
Itupeva ≃	256	22.03 S	47.15 W
Itupiranga	250	5.09 S	49.20 W
Ituporanga	252	27.25 S	49.36 W
Iturama	255	19.44 S	50.11 W
Iturbe	252	26.01 S	56.30 W
Iturbide	232	19.40 N	89.37 W
Ituri ≃	154	1.40 N	27.01 E
Iturup, Ostrov (Etorofu-tō) I	92a	44.54 N	147.30 E
Itutinga	256	21.18 S	44.40 W
Ituverava	255	20.20 S	47.47 W
Ituxi ≃	248	7.18 S	64.51 W
Ituzaingó, Arg.	252	27.36 S	56.41 W
Ituzaingó, Arg.	258	34.40 S	58.40 W
Ituzaingó, Ur.	258	34.25 S	56.26 W
Itwa	124	27.20 N	82.42 E
Ityāy al-Bārūd	142	30.53 N	30.40 E
Itz ≃	56	49.58 N	10.52 E
Itzehoe	52	53.55 N	9.31 E
I'udkovo	24	54.36 N	34.43 E
Iuka, Ill., U.S.	219	38.37 N	88.47 W
Iuka, Miss., U.S.	194	34.49 N	88.11 W
Iul'tin	180	67.50 N	178.48 W
Iul'tin, Gora ∧	180	67.50 N	178.25 W
Iúna	255	20.21 S	41.32 W
Iupeba	256	23.41 S	46.22 W
IV □[4]	150	15.45 N	13.00 W
Iva	192	34.19 N	82.40 W
Ivacevići	76	52.43 N	25.21 E
Ivačovo	76	60.32 N	36.22 E
Ivahona	157b	23.27 S	46.10 E
Ivaí ≃	255	23.18 S	53.42 W
Ivaiporã	252	24.15 S	51.45 W
Ivajlovgrad	38	41.32 N	26.08 E
Ivakoany, Massif de l' ⛰	157b	23.50 S	46.25 E
Ivalo	24	68.42 N	27.30 E
Ivalojoki ≃	24	68.43 N	27.36 E
Ivancevo	82	55.58 N	36.07 E
Ivančice	61	49.06 N	16.23 E
Ivancovo	82	56.39 N	35.50 E
Ivanec	36	46.13 N	16.08 E
Ivane-Puste	78	48.39 N	26.11 E
Ivangorod	76	59.24 N	28.10 E
Ivangrad	38	42.50 N	19.52 E
Ivanhoe, Austl.	166	32.54 S	144.18 E
Ivanhoe, Austl.	274b	37.46 S	145.03 E
Ivanhoe, Calif., U.S.	226	36.23 N	119.13 W
Ivanhoe, Ill., U.S.	278	42.17 N	88.02 W
Ivanhoe, Minn., U.S.	198	44.28 N	96.15 W
Ivanhoe, Va., U.S.	192	36.50 N	80.58 W
Ivanhoe ≃	190	48.40 N	82.11 W
Ivanhoe Lake ⊜	190	48.05 N	82.38 W
Ivanica	78	50.47 N	32.36 E
Ivanić Grad	36	45.42 N	16.24 E
Ivaniči	78	50.39 N	24.20 E
Ivanišči, S.S.S.R.	76	56.36 N	35.13 E
Ivanišči, S.S.S.R.	80	55.46 N	40.26 E
Ivanjica	38	43.35 N	20.14 E
Ivankov	78	50.56 N	29.54 E
Ivankovcy	89	49.06 N	134.28 E
Ivan'kovo	82	54.44 N	37.57 E
Ivan'kovskij	80	56.39 N	40.05 E
Ivan'kovskoje Vodochranilišče ⊜[1]	82	56.37 N	36.32 E
Ivanof Bay	180	55.54 N	159.29 W
Ivano-Frankovo	78	49.55 N	23.43 E
Ivano-Frankovsk	78	48.55 N	24.43 E
Ivanopol'	78	49.52 N	28.12 E
Ivanopolje	83	48.28 N	37.46 E
Ivano-šamševo	83	46.52 N	39.54 E
Ivanovka, S.S.S.R.	78	46.43 N	34.33 E
Ivanovka, S.S.S.R.	78	46.58 N	30.28 E
Ivanovka, S.S.S.R.	80	52.51 N	53.48 E
Ivanovka, S.S.S.R.	80	52.15 N	41.35 E
Ivanovka, S.S.S.R.	80	51.54 N	43.46 E
Ivanovka, S.S.S.R.	83	48.14 N	38.58 E
Ivanovka, S.S.S.R.	83	47.35 N	37.19 E
Ivanovka, S.S.S.R.	85	42.54 N	75.05 E
Ivanovka, S.S.S.R.	89	43.58 N	132.30 E
Ivanovka, S.S.S.R.	89	50.22 N	128.02 E
Ivanovo, S.S.S.R.	78	52.09 N	25.32 E
Ivanovo, S.S.S.R.	80	57.00 N	40.59 E
Ivanovo-Voznesensk → Ivanovo	80	57.00 N	40.59 E
Ivanovskaja, S.S.S.R.	24	60.48 N	55.52 E
Ivanovskaja, S.S.S.R.	78	45.17 N	38.29 E
Ivanovskoje, S.S.S.R.	76	59.17 N	28.49 E
Ivanovskoje, S.S.S.R.	78	51.37 N	34.57 E
Ivanovskoje, S.S.S.R.	82	55.05 N	37.50 E
Ivanovskoje, S.S.S.R.	82	56.23 N	37.07 E
Ivanovskoje, S.S.S.R.	82	54.55 N	36.50 E
Ivanovskoje, S.S.S.R.	82	55.52 N	36.55 E
Ivanovskoje, S.S.S.R.	265a	59.46 N	30.47 E
Ivan-Ozero	82	54.04 N	38.20 E
Ivan-Ozero, Ozero ⊜	82	54.07 N	38.17 E
Ivanpah Lake ⊜	204	35.35 N	115.25 W
Ivantejevka, S.S.S.R.	80	52.16 N	49.07 E
Ivantejevka, S.S.S.R.	82	55.58 N	37.55 E
Ivantejevo	76	57.48 N	33.09 E
Ivato	157b	20.37 S	47.12 E
Ivatuva	255	23.37 S	52.13 W
Ivdel'	72	60.42 N	60.24 E
Ivenec	76	53.53 N	26.45 E
Iver	260	51.31 N	0.30 W
Iver Heath	260	51.32 N	0.31 W
Iverny	261	49.00 N	2.47 E
Ivigtut	176	61.12 N	48.10 W
Ivindo ≃	152	0.09 S	12.09 E
Ivinheima ≃	255	23.14 S	53.42 W
Ivje	76	53.56 N	25.46 E
Ivn'a	78	51.04 N	36.08 E
Ivnica	78	50.09 N	29.03 E
Ivo	248	20.27 S	63.26 W
Ivohibe	157b	22.29 S	46.52 E
Ivolginsk	88	51.45 N	107.14 E
Ivon ≃	248	11.06 S	66.08 W
Ivondro	157b	24.47 S	46.52 E
Ivor	208	36.54 N	76.54 W
Ivorogbo	150	5.30 N	6.21 E
Ivory Coast □[1]	134		
	150	8.00 N	5.00 W
Ivory Coast ●[2]	150	5.10 N	5.00 W
Ivoryton	207	41.21 N	72.27 W
Ivösjön ⊜	26	56.06 N	14.27 E
Ivot, S.S.S.R.	76	53.42 N	34.12 E
Ivot, S.S.S.R.	78	51.58 N	33.28 E
Ivotka ≃	78	51.57 N	33.22 E
Ivrea	62	45.28 N	7.52 E
İvrindi	130	39.34 N	27.29 E
Ivry-la-Bataille	50	48.53 N	1.28 E
Ivry[-sur-Seine]	50	48.49 N	2.23 E
Ivujivik	176	62.24 N	77.55 W
Ivybridge	42	50.23 N	3.56 W
Ivy Hatch	260	51.16 N	0.16 E
Ivyland	285	40.12 N	75.04 W
Ivywild	198	39.49 N	104.51 W
Iwade	96	34.15 N	135.19 E
Iwafune, Nihon	94	36.19 N	139.40 E
Iwafune, Nihon	270	34.44 N	135.54 E
Iwagi	96	34.15 N	133.09 E
Iwai	94	36.03 N	139.54 E
Iwai-shima I	96	33.47 N	131.58 E
Iwaizumi	92	39.50 N	141.48 E
Iwaki (Taira)	94	37.03 N	140.55 E
Iwaki-san ∧	92	40.39 N	140.18 E
Iwakuni	96	34.09 N	132.11 E
Iwakuni Marine Corps Air Station (United States) ■	96	34.08 N	132.14 E
Iwakura	94	35.17 N	136.52 E
Iwama	94	36.18 N	140.16 E
Iwami, Nihon	96	34.53 N	132.26 E
Iwami, Nihon	96	35.35 N	134.20 E
Iwami-kōgen ⛰[1]	96	35.00 N	132.30 E
Iwami-kokubun-ji ♉[1]	96	34.59 N	132.13 E
Iwamizawa	92a	43.12 N	141.46 E
Iwamura	94	35.22 N	137.26 E
Iwanai	92a	42.58 N	140.30 E
Iwanowo → Ivanovo	80	57.00 N	40.59 E
Iwanuma	92	38.06 N	140.52 E
Iwaoka ◆[8]	270	34.44 N	134.58 E
iwase, Nihon	94	36.21 N	140.06 E
Iwase, Nihon	268	35.17 N	139.52 E
Iwata	94	34.42 N	137.48 E
Iwataki	96	35.34 N	135.09 E
Iwate □[5]	92	39.37 N	141.22 E
Iwate-san ∧	92	39.51 N	141.00 E
Iwatsuki	94	35.57 N	139.42 E
Iwaya → Awaji, Nihon	96	34.35 N	135.01 E
Iwaya, Nihon	270	34.35 N	135.02 E
Iwayama	270	34.52 N	135.52 E
Iwazono	270	34.45 N	135.19 E
Iwo	150	7.38 N	4.11 E
Iwo Jima → Iō-jima I	174f	24.47 N	141.20 E
Iwo Jima Air Base ■	174f	24.47 N	141.19 E
Iwŏn	98	40.19 N	128.39 E
Iwuy	50	50.14 N	3.19 E
Ixcán ≃	236	16.07 N	91.05 W
Ixchiguán	236	15.12 N	91.53 W
Ixcuintepec ≃	234	17.21 N	95.24 W
Ixelles	50	50.50 N	4.22 E
Ixhuatlán del Café	234	19.04 N	96.59 W
Ixiamas	248	13.45 S	68.09 W
Iximché ⊥	236	14.44 N	90.59 W
Ixmiquilpan	234	20.29 N	99.14 W
Ixonia	216	43.09 N	88.36 W
Ixopo	158	30.08 S	30.00 E
Ixtacalco □[7]	286a	19.24 N	99.06 W
Ixtacalco ◆[8]	286a	19.23 N	99.07 W
Ixtacihuatl y Popocatépetl, Parques Nacionales ♠	234	19.10 N	98.38 W
Ixtaltepec	234	16.30 N	95.03 W
Ixtapa, Punta ≻	234	17.39 N	101.40 W
Ixtapalapa □[7]	286a	19.21 N	99.04 W
Ixtapalapa ◆[8]	286a	19.21 N	99.06 W
Ixtapan de la Sal	234	18.50 N	99.41 W
Ixtlahuacán del Río	234	20.52 N	103.15 W
Ixtlán	234	20.11 N	102.24 W
Ixtlán de Juárez	234	17.20 N	96.29 W
Ixtlán del Río	234	21.02 N	104.22 W
Ixworth	42	52.18 N	0.50 E
Iya ≃	96	33.58 N	133.47 E
'Iyādh	144	14.59 N	46.51 E
'Iyāl Bakhīt	140	13.25 N	28.41 E
Iyang, Taehan	98	34.53 N	127.01 E
Iyang → Yiyang, Zhg.	102	28.36 N	112.20 E
Iyang, Gili I	115a	6.59 S	114.10 E
Iyo	96	33.46 N	132.42 E
Iyo-mishima	96	33.58 N	133.33 E
Iyo-nada ⫪[2]	96	33.40 N	132.20 E
Iž ≃	80	55.58 N	52.38 E
Iza ≃	38	47.54 N	23.57 E
Izabal	236	15.24 N	89.08 W
Izabal □[5]	236	15.30 N	89.00 W
Izabal, Lago de ⊜	236	15.30 N	89.10 W
'Izab al-Baṣāriṭah	142	31.23 N	31.47 E
Īzad Khvāst	128	31.31 N	52.07 E
Izalco	236	13.45 N	89.40 W
'Izam, Jabal al- ∧	132	30.51 N	35.46 E
Izapa ⊥	232	14.55 N	92.10 W
Izasa-misaki ≻	96	35.40 N	134.32 E
Iz'aslav	78	50.07 N	26.51 E
'Izbat Abū Ṣuql	132	31.09 N	33.49 E
Izberbaš	84	42.33 N	47.52 E
Izbica, Pol.	30	50.54 N	23.09 E
Izbica, Pol.	30	54.42 N	17.26 E
Izd'oškovo	76	55.08 N	33.37 E
Izegem	50	50.55 N	3.12 E
Īzeh	128	31.50 N	49.50 E
Izena-shima I	174m	26.56 N	127.56 E
Izendy	86	45.48 N	59.28 E
Izernore	58	46.13 N	5.33 E
Iževsk	80	56.51 N	53.14 E
Iževskoje	80	54.34 N	40.53 E
Izhevsk → Iževsk	80	56.51 N	53.14 E
Izkī	128	22.56 N	57.46 E
Ižma	24	65.02 N	53.55 E
Ižma ≃	24	65.19 N	52.54 E
Izmail	78	45.21 N	28.50 E
Izmajlovo	80	53.43 N	47.14 E
Izmajlovo ◆[8]	265b	55.48 N	37.46 E
Izmajlovskij Park ♠	265b	55.46 N	37.47 E
Izmalkovo	76	52.41 N	37.58 E
İzmir	130	38.25 N	27.09 E
İzmir □[4]	130	38.30 N	27.15 E
İzmir Körfezi C	130	38.30 N	26.50 E
İzmit (Kocaeli)	130	40.46 N	29.55 E
İzmit Körfezi C	130	40.45 N	29.35 E
Ižmorskij	86	56.11 N	86.38 E
Iznajar, Embalse de ⊜[1]	34	37.15 N	4.30 W
Iznalloz	34	37.23 N	3.31 W
İznik	130	40.26 N	29.43 E
İznik Gölü ⊜	130	40.26 N	29.30 E
Iznoski	76	54.59 N	35.19 E
Izola	64	45.32 N	13.40 E
Izoplit	82	56.38 N	36.12 E
Izopo, Punta ≻	236	15.48 N	87.23 W
Ižora ≃	265a	59.48 N	30.36 E
Izozog, Bañados de ☷	248	18.48 S	62.10 W
Izra'	132	32.51 N	36.15 E
Izsák	30	46.48 N	19.22 E
Iztaccíhuatl ∧[1]	234	19.11 N	98.39 W
Iztapa	236	13.56 N	90.43 W
Izúcar de Matamoros	234	18.36 N	98.28 W
Izu-hantō ≻[1]	94	34.45 N	139.00 E
Izuhara	92	34.12 N	129.17 E
Iz'um	83	49.12 N	37.19 E
Izumi, Nihon	92	32.05 N	130.22 E
Izumi, Nihon	94	35.54 N	136.40 E
Izumi, Nihon	96	34.29 N	135.26 E
Izumi ◆[8]	268	35.25 N	139.30 E
Izumi-ōtsu	96	34.30 N	135.24 E
Izumi-sano	96	34.25 N	135.19 E
Izumizaki	94	37.09 N	140.17 E
Izumo	96	35.22 N	132.46 E
Izumo ≃	94	34.38 N	136.33 E
Izumrud	86	57.05 N	61.23 E
Izu-nagaoka	94	35.02 N	138.56 E
Izushi	96	35.28 N	134.52 E
Izu-shotō II	90	32.00 N	140.00 E
Izuwara	270	34.53 N	135.32 E
Izvarino	83	48.17 N	39.52 E
Izvestij CIK, Ostrova II	74	75.55 N	82.30 E
Izvestkovyj	89	48.59 N	131.33 E

J

Nome	Página	Lat.°′	Long.°′ W=Oeste
Ja'ār, Birkat al- ⊜	142	30.28 N	30.10 E
Jääsjärvi ⊜	26	61.36 N	26.07 E
Jabā, Sūrīy.	132	33.10 N	35.56 E
Jaba, Yai.	144	6.17 N	35.12 E
Jabābīn, Tallāt al- ⛰[2]	142	30.31 N	30.07 E
Jabal	146	28.36 N	19.58 E
Jabal,, Baḥr al- → Mountain Nile ≃	136	9.30 N	30.30 E
Jabal Abyad Plateau ⛰[1]	140	19.00 N	29.00 E
Jabal al-Awliyā'	140	15.14 N	32.30 E
Jabal an-Nūr	142	28.57 N	31.02 E
Jabal aṭ-Ṭayr	142	28.14 N	30.45 E
Jabal Dūd	140	13.25 N	33.09 E
Jabal Lubnān □[4]	132	33.50 N	35.40 E
Jabalón ≃	34	38.53 N	4.05 W
Jabal Os Sarāj	120	35.07 N	69.14 E
Jabalpur	124	23.10 N	79.57 E
Jabal Qerri	140	16.15 N	32.48 E
Jabal Ṣabāyā I	144	18.35 N	41.03 E
Jabal 'Uwaybid	142	30.09 N	32.12 E
Jabālyah	132	31.32 N	34.29 E
Jabavu	273d	26.15 S	27.53 E
Jabbān, Arḍ al- ◆[1]	132	32.08 N	36.35 E
Jabbeke	50	51.11 N	3.05 E
Jabbi	123	33.08 N	72.38 E
Jabbūl, Sabkhat al- ⊜	130	36.03 N	37.39 E
Jabel	54	53.32 N	12.32 E
Jabi	114	2.32 N	102.48 E
Jabjabah, Wādī ∨	140	22.37 N	33.17 E
Jablah	130	35.21 N	35.55 E
Jablanac	36	44.42 N	14.54 E
Jablanica	36	43.39 N	17.45 E
Jablanica ≃	38	43.07 N	21.57 E
Jablaničko Jezero ⊜[1]	36	43.40 N	17.50 E
Jablines	261	48.55 N	2.46 E
Jabločnoje	78	50.18 N	35.14 E
Jabločnyj	89	47.10 N	142.04 E
Jablonec nad Nisou	30	50.44 N	15.10 E
Jablonica	30	48.37 N	17.25 E
Jabłonka	30	49.29 N	19.41 E
Jablonné v Podještědí	54	50.48 N	14.47 E
Jablonoj → Jablonovyj Chrebet ⛰	88	53.30 N	115.00 E
Jablonov	78	48.24 N	24.57 E
Jablonovo	88	51.51 N	112.49 E
Jablonovyj Chrebet ⛰	88	53.30 N	115.00 E
Jabłonowo	30	53.24 N	19.09 E
Jablònowy-Gebirge → Jablonovyj Chrebet ⛰	88	53.30 N	115.00 W
Jablunkov	30	49.35 N	18.47 E
Jablunkovský průsmyk)(	30	49.32 N	18.45 E
Jaboatão	250	8.07 S	35.01 W
Jaboncillos	232	28.57 N	102.39 W
Jaboncillos Creek ≃	196	27.23 N	97.45 W
Jabonga	116	9.20 N	125.32 E
Jaborandi	255	20.40 S	48.25 W
Jabori	123	34.36 N	73.16 E
Jaboticabal	255	21.16 S	48.19 W
Jabrat Sa'īd ⫪[4]	140	16.06 N	31.50 E
Jabrīn ⫪[4]	118	23.17 N	48.58 E
Jabron ≃	62	44.33 N	4.45 E
Jabron, Torrent le ≃	62	44.09 N	5.57 E
Jabung	115a	5.29 S	105.40 E
Jabung, Tanjung ≻	112	1.01 S	104.22 E
Jaca	34	42.34 N	0.33 W
Jacala de Ledesma	234	21.01 N	99.11 W
Jacaleapa	236	14.00 N	86.40 W
Jacaltenango	236	15.40 N	91.44 W
Jacana	274b	37.42 S	144.55 E
Jacaraci	255	14.51 S	42.26 W
Jacaré	256	21.20 S	42.51 W
Jacaré ≃, Bra.	248	5.49 S	63.35 W
Jacaré ≃, Bra.	250	10.03 S	42.13 W
Jacaré ≃, Bra.	255	13.50 S	40.42 W
Jacaré ≃, Bra.	287a	22.56 S	43.04 W
Jacareí	256	23.19 S	45.58 W
Jacareí ≃	256	22.54 S	46.28 W
Jacarepaguá ◆[8]	256	22.56 S	43.20 W
Jacarepaguá, Lagoa de C	256	22.59 S	43.24 W
Jacarèzinho	255	23.09 S	49.59 W
Jaceruba	256	22.35 S	43.34 W
Jáchal ≃	252	30.44 S	68.08 W
Jachenau	64	47.36 N	11.25 E
Jachniki	78	50.26 N	33.10 E
Jachroma	82	56.17 N	37.30 E
Jachroma ≃	82	56.31 N	37.07 E
Jáchymov	54	50.20 N	12.55 E
Jaciara	255	15.59 S	54.57 W
Jacinto	255	16.10 S	40.17 W
Jacinto Aráuz	252	38.04 S	63.26 W
Jacinto City	222	29.46 N	95.16 W
Jacinto Machado	252	29.00 S	49.46 W
Jaci Paraná	248	9.15 S	64.23 W
Jaciparaná ≃	248	9.22 S	64.22 W
Jackass Creek ≃	226	37.22 N	119.23 W
Jack Creek ≃	202	42.59 N	121.32 W
Jackfish Lake ⊜	184	53.05 N	108.25 W
Jackhead Harbour	184	51.52 N	97.16 W
Jack Lake ⊜	212	44.42 N	78.03 W
Jack London State Historical Park ♠	226	38.21 N	122.32 W
Jackman	188	45.38 N	70.16 W
Jackman Creek ≃	224	48.30 N	121.43 W
Jackman Station	188	45.37 N	70.15 W
Jack Mountain ∧, Mont., U.S.	202	46.21 N	112.18 W
Jack Mountain ∧, Wash., U.S.	224	48.47 N	120.57 W
Jackpot	204	41.59 N	114.40 W
Jacksboro, Tenn., U.S.	192	36.20 N	84.11 W
Jacksboro, Tex., U.S.	196	33.13 N	98.10 W
Jacks Creek ≃	208	40.35 N	77.33 W
Jacks Island I	279b	40.37 N	79.43 W
Jacks Mountain ∧	210	40.45 N	77.30 W
Jackson, Ala., U.S.	194	31.31 N	87.53 W
Jackson, Calif., U.S.	226	38.21 N	120.46 W
Jackson, Ga., U.S.	192	33.18 N	83.58 W
Jackson, Ky., U.S.	192	37.33 N	83.23 W
Jackson, La., U.S.	194	30.50 N	91.13 W
Jackson, Mich., U.S.	216	42.15 N	84.24 W

	English	Deutsch	Español	Français	Português
≃	River	Fluss	Río	Rivière	Rio
≡	Canal	Kanal	Canal	Canal	Canal
ᒪ	Waterfall, Rapids	Wasserfall, Stromschnellen	Cascada, Rápidos	Chute d'eau, Rapides	Cascata, Rápidos
⋓	Strait	Meeresstrasse	Estrecho	Détroit	Estreito
C	Bay, Gulf	Bucht, Golf	Bahía, Golfo	Baie, Golfe	Baía, Golfo
⊜	Lake, Lakes	See, Seen	Lago, Lagos	Lac, Lacs	Lago, Lagos
☷	Swamp	Sumpf	Pantano	Marais	Pântano
⩍	Ice Features, Glacier	Eis- und Gletscherformen	Accidentes Glaciales	Formes glaciaires	Acidentes Glaciares
⫪	Other Hydrographic Features	Andere Hydrographische Objekte	Otros Elementos Hidrográficos	Autres données hydrographiques	Outros Elementos Hidrográficos

	English	Deutsch	Español	Français	Português
✣	Submarine Features	Untermeerische Objekte	Accidentes Submarinos	Formes de relief sous-marin	Acidentes Submarinos
□	Political Unit	Politische Einheit	Unidad Politica	Entité politique	Unidade Política
♉	Cultural Institution	Kulturelle Institution	Institución Cultural	Institution culturelle	Instituição Cultural
⊥	Historical Site	Historische Stätte	Sitio Histórico	Site historique	Sitio Histórico
♠	Recreational Site	Erholungs- und Ferienort	Sitio de Recreo	Centre de loisirs	Sítio de Lazer
⊠	Airport	Flughafen	Aeropuerto	Aéroport	Aeroporto
■	Military Installation	Militäranlage	Instalación Militar	Installation militaire	Instalação Militar
◆	Miscellaneous	Verschiedenes	Misceláneo	Divers	Miscelânea

Jackson, Minn., U.S. 198 43.37 N 95.01 W
Jackson, Miss., U.S. 194 32.18 N 90.12 W
Jackson, Mo., U.S. 194 37.23 N 89.40 W
Jackson, N.J., U.S. 208 40.06 N 74.23 W
Jackson, N.C., U.S. 192 36.23 N 77.25 W
Jackson, Ohio, U.S. 188 39.03 N 82.39 W
Jackson, Pa., U.S. 210 41.50 N 75.36 W
Jackson, S.C., U.S. 192 33.20 N 81.47 W
Jackson, Tenn., U.S. 194 35.37 N 88.49 W
Jackson, Wyo., U.S. 200 43.29 N 110.38 W
Jackson □[6], Ind., U.S. 218 38.53 N 86.03 W
Jackson □[6], Mich., U.S. 216 42.15 N 84.24 W
Jackson □[6], Tex., U.S. 222 29.00 N 96.35 W
Jackson ≐ 188 37.47 N 79.46 W
Jackson, Cape ≻ 172 41.00 S 174.18 E
Jackson, Lake @, Fla., U.S. 220 27.29 N 81.28 W
Jackson, Lake @, Fla., U.S. 220 27.55 N 81.10 W
Jackson, Mount ∧, Ant. 9 71.23 S 63.22 W
Jackson, Mount ∧, Austl. 162 30.15 S 119.16 E
Jackson, Port C 274a 33.50 S 151.16 E
Jackson Bay C 172 43.58 S 168.42 E
Jackson Brook ≐ 276 40.53 N 74.34 W
Jackson Butte ∧ 226 38.20 N 120.43 W
Jackson Center, Ohio, U.S. 216 40.27 N 84.02 W
Jackson Center, Pa., U.S. 214 41.16 N 80.09 W
Jackson Creek ≐, Can. 184 49.18 N 100.50 W
Jackson Creek ≐, Calif., U.S. 226 38.18 N 121.01 W
Jackson Creek ≐, Ill., U.S. 216 41.26 N 88.10 W
Jackson Heights ➔[8] 276 40.45 N 73.53 W
Jackson Lake @[1], Ga., U.S. 192 33.22 N 83.52 W
Jackson Lake @[1], Wyo., U.S. 202 43.55 N 110.40 W
Jackson Mountain ∧ 188 44.46 N 70.32 W
Jackson Park ♠, Ont., Can. 281 42.17 N 83.01 W
Jackson Park ♠, Ill., U.S. 278 41.47 N 87.35 W
Jackson's Arm 186 49.52 N 56.47 W
Jacksons Creek ≐ 169 37.40 S 144.48 E
Jacksons Head ≻ 172 43.58 S 168.37 E
Jacksonville, Ala., U.S. 194 33.49 N 85.46 W
Jacksonville, Ark., U.S. 194 34.52 N 92.07 W
Jacksonville, Fla., U.S. 192 30.20 N 81.40 W
Jacksonville, Ill., U.S. 219 39.44 N 90.14 W
Jacksonville, N.C., U.S. 192 34.45 N 77.26 W
Jacksonville, N.Y., U.S. 210 42.31 N 76.37 W
Jacksonville, Oreg., U.S. 202 42.19 N 122.57 W
Jacksonville, Tex., U.S. 222 31.58 N 95.17 W
Jacksonville, Vt., U.S. 207 42.47 N 72.49 W
Jacksonville, Lake @[1] 222 31.55 N 95.17 W
Jacksonville Beach 192 30.18 N 81.24 W
Jacks Reef 210 43.06 N 76.25 W
Jacks Run ≐ 279b 40.19 N 79.45 W
Jacktown Acres 279b 40.13 N 79.35 W
Jacmel 238 18.14 N 72.32 W
Jacob, Morne ∧ 240e 14.46 N 61.06 W
Jacobābād 120 28.17 N 68.26 E
Jacobina 250 11.11 S 40.31 W
Jacob Island I 212 44.28 N 78.28 W
Jacob Riis Park ♠ 276 40.34 N 73.52 W
Jacobs Creek ≐ 214 40.07 N 79.44 W
Jacobsdal 158 29.13 S 24.41 E
Jacobus 208 39.53 N 76.43 W
Jacona de Plancarte 234 19.57 N 102.16 W
Jacques, Lac à @ 180 66.10 N 127.25 W
Jacques-Cartier ≐ 206 46.40 N 71.45 W
Jacques-Cartier, Détroit de 𝔲 186 50.00 N 63.30 W
Jacques-Cartier, Mont ∧ 186 48.59 N 65.57 W
Jacques-Cartier, Pont ➔[5] 275a 45.31 N 73.32 W
Jacquet River 186 47.55 N 66.00 W
Jacqueville 150 5.12 N 4.25 W
Jacquinot Bay C 164 5.35 S 151.30 E
Jacu ≐, Bra. 250 6.13 S 35.09 W
Jacú ≐, Bra. 256 23.05 S 45.08 W
Jacu, Rio do ≐ 287b 23.29 S 46.27 W
Jacuba ≐ 255 18.25 S 52.28 W
Jacuecanga 256 23.01 S 44.13 W
Jacuí ≐ 252 30.02 S 51.15 W
Jacuipe 255 12.29 S 38.38 W
Jacuípe ≐ 255 12.30 S 39.05 W
Jacumba 204 32.37 N 116.11 W
Jacundá 250 4.33 S 49.28 W
Jacundá ≐ 250 1.57 S 50.26 W
Jacupiranga 252 24.42 S 48.00 W
Jacurici ≐ 250 10.57 S 39.35 W
Jacutinga 256 22.17 S 46.37 W
Jada 146 8.46 N 12.09 E
Jada'ah, Jabal ⩕[2] 142 29.58 N 30.40 E
Jadal ➔[1] 150 19.00 N 4.15 E
Jaddi, Rās ≻ 128 25.14 N 63.31 E
Jade 52 53.20 N 8.14 E
Jade Buddha, Temple of the (Yufosi) ➔[1] 269b 31.14 N 121.26 E
Jadebusen C 52 53.30 N 8.10 E
Jäder 40 59.25 N 16.41 E
Jäderfors 40 60.41 N 16.40 E
Jade Run ≐ 285 39.56 N 74.45 W
Jadīdah 128 34.01 N 42.28 E
Jadito Wash V 200 35.22 N 110.50 W
J.A.D. Jensens Nunatakker ∧ 176 62.45 N 48.00 W
Jadotville → Likasi 154 10.59 S 26.44 E
Jadraque 34 40.55 N 2.55 W
Jadrin 80 55.56 N 46.12 E
Jadromino 82 55.57 N 36.36 E
Jādū 146 31.57 N 12.01 E
Jaduty 78 51.22 N 32.19 E
Jægerspris 41 55.51 N 11.59 E
Jaeger Summit ∧ 154 2.52 S 35.47 E
Ja'el ≐ 144 10.56 N 51.09 E
Jaén, Esp. 34 37.46 N 3.47 W
Jaén, Perú 248 5.42 S 78.47 W
Jæren ➔[1] 26 58.45 N 5.45 E
Jāfarābād, Bhārat 120 20.52 N 71.22 E
Ja'farābād, Īrān 128 35.43 N 50.43 E
Jāfarpur 126 22.29 N 89.06 E
Jāfarpur ➔[8] 272a 28.40 N 77.01 E
Jaffa, Cape ≻ 166 36.58 S 139.40 E
Jaffa, Tel Aviv- → Tel Aviv-Yafo 132 32.04 N 34.46 E
Jaffārah, Qūr al- ⩕[2] 142 30.25 N 29.35 E
Jaffna 122 9.40 N 80.00 E
Jaffna Lagoon C 122 9.35 N 80.15 E
Jaffrey 207 42.48 N 72.01 W
Jafjaf aṣ-Ṣaghīr ⩕[2] 146 20.50 N 21.35 E
Jafr, Qā' al- ≍[2] 132 30.17 N 36.20 E
Jagādhri 124 30.10 N 77.18 E
Jagala ≐ 76 59.29 N 25.09 E
Jagalūr 122 14.32 N 76.21 E
Jāgan 120 28.05 N 68.30 E
Jagannāthganj Ghāt 124 24.45 N 89.49 E
Jagannāthpūr 126 22.48 N 88.24 E
Jagati 120 23.54 N 89.06 E
Jagatnagar 272b 22.47 N 88.13 E
Jagatpur ➔[8] 272a 28.44 N 77.14 E
Jagatsingpur 120 20.16 N 86.10 E
Jagdalpur 122 19.04 N 82.02 E
Jagdīspur 124 25.29 N 84.25 E
Jagel 41 54.25 N 9.32 E
Jägerndorf → Krnov 30 50.05 N 17.41 E
Jagersfontein 158 29.44 S 25.29 E
Jaggayyapeta 122 16.54 N 80.06 E
Jagged Mountain ∧ 180 58.38 N 162.02 W
Jaghbūb ≂[4] 146 29.40 N 24.43 E
Jagnob ≐ 85 39.15 N 68.35 E
Jagny-sous-Bois 261 49.05 N 2.27 E
Jagodnoje, S.S.S.R. 74 62.33 N 149.40 E
Jagodnoje, S.S.S.R. 80 53.36 N 49.04 E
Jagodnyj 86 59.44 N 65.04 E
Jagorlyckij Liman C 78 46.24 N 31.50 E
Jagotin 78 50.17 N 31.46 E
Jagraon 123 30.47 N 75.29 E
Jagst ≐ 56 49.14 N 9.11 E
Jagsthausen 56 49.19 N 9.28 E
Jagstzell 56 49.02 N 10.05 E
Jagtiāl 122 18.48 N 78.56 E
Jaguaquara 255 13.32 S 39.58 W
Jaguarão 252 32.34 S 53.23 W
Jaguarão (Yaguarón) ≐ 252 32.39 S 53.12 W
Jaguarari 250 10.16 S 40.12 W
Jaguaretama 250 5.37 S 38.46 W
Jaguari 252 29.30 S 54.41 W
Jaguari ≐ 256 23.10 S 45.55 W
Jaguariaíva 252 24.15 S 49.42 W
Jaguaribara 250 5.40 S 38.37 W
Jaguaribe 250 5.53 S 38.37 W
Jaguaribe ≐ 250 4.25 S 37.45 W
Jaguari-Mirim ≐ 256 21.59 S 47.17 W
Jaguaripe 255 13.06 S 38.53 W
Jaguariúna 256 22.41 S 46.59 W
Jaguaruana 250 4.50 S 37.47 W
Jaguaruna 252 28.36 S 49.02 W
Jagüé 252 28.38 S 68.24 W
Jagüey Grande 240p 22.32 N 81.08 W
Jāguli 126 22.56 N 88.32 E
Jāgulia 272b 22.44 N 88.32 E
Jagungal, Mount ∧ 171b 36.09 S 148.23 E
Jagunovskij 86 55.17 N 85.59 E
Jahānābād, Bhārat 124 25.13 N 84.59 E
Jahānābād, Pāk. 123 32.11 N 72.29 E
Jahāngīra 123 33.55 N 72.13 E
Jahāngīrābād 124 28.25 N 78.06 E
Jahangirpur ➔[8] 272a 28.44 N 77.13 E
Jahānia 123 30.02 N 71.49 E
Jahannam, Qārat ⩕[2] 142 29.19 N 30.09 E
Jahnsdorf 54 50.44 N 12.51 E
Jahrom 128 28.31 N 53.33 E
Jahú → Jaú 255 22.18 S 48.33 W
Jai ≐ 250 3.58 N 54.49 W
Jaicós 250 7.21 S 41.08 W
Jaidak 120 31.58 N 66.43 E
Jaihti ≐ 126 24.08 N 86.47 E
Jaijōn 123 31.21 N 76.09 E
Jailolo 108 1.05 N 127.30 E
Jaimanitas ≐ 286b 23.05 N 82.29 W
Jainti 124 26.42 N 89.36 E
Jaintiāpur 120 25.08 N 92.07 E
Jaipur 120 26.55 N 75.49 E
Jaipur □[5] 124 27.00 N 76.10 E
Jāis 124 26.15 N 81.32 E
Jaisalmer 120 26.55 N 70.54 E
Jaisan 86 50.51 N 56.14 E
Jaito 123 30.28 N 74.53 E
Jaja 86 56.12 N 86.26 E
Jaja ≐ 86 56.58 N 86.23 E
Jājarkot 124 28.42 N 82.12 E
Jājarm 128 36.58 N 56.27 E
Jajce 36 44.21 N 17.16 E
Jajichi 174m 26.47 N 128.13 E
Jajjha 123 28.45 N 70.34 E
Jajl'u 86 51.48 N 87.36 E
Jajpan 85 40.23 N 70.48 E
Jājpur 120 20.51 N 86.20 E
Jajva 86 59.20 N 57.15 E
Jajva ≐ 86 59.13 N 56.40 E
Jakarta 115a / 269e 6.10 S 106.48 E
Jakarta, Teluk C 115a 6.05 S 106.48 E
Jakarta Kota Station ➔[5] 269e 6.08 S 106.49 E
Jakarta Raya □[4] 115a 6.10 S 106.45 E
Jakdūl @ 140 17.39 N 32.59 E
Jake Creek Mountain ∧ 204 41.13 N 116.54 W
Jakenan 115a 6.45 S 111.11 E
Jākhal 123 29.48 N 75.50 E
Jakhau 120 23.13 N 68.43 E
Jakkonen 24 66.33 N 29.52 E
Jakobsberg 40 59.26 N 17.50 E
Jakobsdalsberget ∧[2] 40 58.41 N 16.07 E
Jakobshagen → Dobrzany 30 53.22 N 15.25 E
Jakobshavn 176 69.13 N 51.06 W
Jakobstad (Pietarsaari) 26 63.40 N 22.42 E
Jakovleviči 76 54.20 N 30.31 E
Jakovlevka 89 44.26 N 133.28 E
Jakovlevo 82 54.48 N 37.26 E
Jaksa 24 61.48 N 56.49 E
Jakšanga 80 58.23 N 45.56 E
Jakšur-Bodja 80 57.11 N 53.09 E
Jakupica ⩕ 38 41.43 N 21.26 E
Jakutsk 74 62.13 N 129.49 E
Jakutskaja □[8] 88 58.00 N 121.00 E
Jal 196 32.07 N 103.12 W
Jala 234 21.05 N 104.26 W
Jalacingo 234 19.48 N 97.18 W
Jalajala 116 14.21 N 121.19 E
Jalājil 128 25.41 N 45.28 E
Jalālābād, Afg. 120 34.26 N 70.28 E
Jalālābād, Bhārat 123 30.37 N 74.15 E
Jalālābād, Bhārat 124 27.43 N 79.40 E
Jalālat al-Baḥrīyah, Jabal ∧[1] 142 29.20 N 32.00 E
Jalālat al-Qiblīyah, Jabal ∧[1] 142 28.42 N 32.22 E
Jalaliyeh Race Track ♠ 267d 35.43 N 51.24 E
Jalālpur, Bhārat 124 26.19 N 82.44 E
Jalālpur, Pāk. 123 32.38 N 74.12 E
Jalālpur Pīrwāla 123 29.30 N 71.13 E
Jalama 84 41.44 N 48.34 E
Jalan' 86 58.21 N 91.53 E
Jalán ≐ 236 14.39 N 86.12 W
Jalan Besar Stadium ♠ 271c 1.18 N 103.52 E
Jalangi 126 24.08 N 88.42 E
Jalangi ≐ 126 23.25 N 88.22 E
Jalan Kayu 271c 1.24 N 103.52 E
Jalapa, Guat. 236 14.38 N 89.59 W
Jalapa, Méx. 234 17.43 N 92.49 W
Jalapa, Nic. 236 13.55 N 86.08 W
Jalapa □[5] 236 14.35 N 89.55 W
Jalapa de Díaz 234 18.04 N 96.32 W
Jalapa Enríquez 234 19.32 N 96.55 W
Jalasjärvi 26 62.30 N 22.45 E
Jalaud ≐ 116 10.45 N 122.40 E
Jālaun 124 26.09 N 79.21 E
Jal'čiki 80 55.09 N 48.01 E
Jalcocotán 234 21.28 N 105.07 W
Jalcomulco ≐ 234 19.20 N 96.33 W
Jalda 126 21.56 N 87.30 E
Jalea de Catalán 234 17.26 N 99.51 W
Jalesar 124 27.29 N 78.19 E
Jaleshwar 124 26.38 N 85.48 E
Jaleswar 126 21.49 N 87.13 E
Jālgaon, Bhārat 122 21.01 N 75.34 E
Jālgaon, Bhārat 122 21.03 N 76.32 E
Jal'gelevo 265a 59.34 N 29.57 E
Jalhay 56 50.34 N 5.58 E
Jalīrpār 126 23.13 N 89.58 E
Jalisco 234 21.27 N 104.54 W
Jalisco □[3] 234 20.20 N 103.40 W
Jallas ≐ 34 42.54 N 9.08 W
Jallieu 62 45.35 N 5.16 E
Jālna 122 19.50 N 75.53 E
Jalón ≐ 34 41.47 N 1.04 W
Jālor 120 25.21 N 72.37 E
Jalostotitlán 234 21.12 N 102.28 W
Jalpa 234 21.38 N 102.58 W
Jalpa de Méndez 234 18.08 N 93.05 W
Jalpaiguri 124 26.31 N 88.44 E
Jalpaiguri □[5] 124 26.40 N 89.00 E
Jalpan 234 21.14 N 99.29 W
Jalpug ≐ 78 45.41 N 28.35 E
Jalpug, Ozero @ 38 45.25 N 28.37 E
Jalta (Yalta), S.S.S.R. 78 44.30 N 34.10 E
Jalta, S.S.S.R. 83 46.58 N 37.16 E
Jaltenango de la Paz 234 15.55 N 92.43 W
Jaltepec ≐ 234 17.26 N 94.59 W
Jáltipan 234 17.58 N 94.42 W
Jaltocán 234 21.09 N 98.32 W
Jaltuškov 78 48.58 N 27.30 E
Jālū 146 29.02 N 21.32 E
Jālū, Wāḥat ≂[4] 146 29.02 N 21.32 E
Jaluit I[1] 14 6.00 N 169.35 E
Jalutorovsk 86 56.40 N 66.18 E
Jam, S.S.S.R. 82 55.29 N 37.45 E
Jam, S.S.S.R. 85 40.07 N 68.11 E
Jama 83 48.52 N 38.06 E
Jamaare ≐ 150 12.06 N 10.14 E
Jāmāibāti 272b 22.51 N 88.08 E
Jamaica 240p 20.12 N 75.09 W
Jamaica ➔[8] 276 40.42 N 73.47 W
Jamaica □[1] 230 / 241q 18.15 N 77.30 W
Jamaica Bay C 210 40.36 N 73.51 W
Jamaica Channel 𝔲 238 18.00 N 75.30 W
Jamaica Plain ➔[8] 283 42.19 N 71.06 W
Jamaika → Jamaica □[1] 241q 18.15 N 77.30 W
Jamaïque → Jamaica □[1] 241q 18.15 N 77.30 W
Jamal, Poluostrov ≻[1] 74 70.00 N 70.00 E
Jam-Alin', Chrebet ∧ 89 53.00 N 134.36 E
Jamālīyah ➔[8] 273c 30.03 N 31.16 E
Jamalo-Neneckij Nacionalnyj Okrug □[8] 24 66.30 N 64.00 E
Jamālpur, Bhārat 124 25.18 N 86.30 E
Jamālpur, Bngl. 124 24.55 N 89.56 E
Jamālpurganj 126 23.04 N 87.59 E
Jamame 144 0.04 N 42.46 E
Jamanari ≐ 246 2.58 S 68.53 W
Jamanchalinka 80 47.40 N 51.35 E
Jamantau, Gora ∧ 72 54.15 N 58.06 E
Jamanxim ≐ 250 4.43 S 56.18 W
Jamapará 256 21.55 S 42.43 W
Jamari ≐ 248 8.27 S 63.30 W
Jamari, Lago @ 246 1.26 S 56.35 W
Jamarovka 88 50.38 N 110.16 E
Jamašurma 80 55.58 N 49.36 E
Jamay 234 20.18 N 102.43 W
Jamba 152 13.50 S 15.30 E
Jāmbād 126 22.42 N 86.35 E
Jambeiro 256 23.16 S 45.41 W
Jambeiro, Serra do ⩕[2] 256 23.13 S 45.38 W
Jambelí, Canal de 𝔲 246 3.00 S 80.00 W
Jamberoo 170 34.39 S 150.47 E
Jambes 56 50.28 N 4.52 E
Jambi □[4] 112 1.30 S 103.00 E
Jambin 166 24.12 S 150.22 E
Jamboeye ≐ 114 5.16 N 97.29 E
Jambol 38 42.29 N 26.30 E
Jambol □[4] 130 42.10 N 26.30 E
Jambongan, Pulau I 112 6.40 N 117.27 E
Jambuair, Tanjung ≻ 114 5.16 N 97.30 E
Jambusar 120 22.03 N 72.48 E
James ≐, Austl. 166 20.36 S 137.41 E
James ≐, Alta., Can. 182 51.55 N 114.34 W
James ≐, U.S. 198 42.52 N 97.18 W
James ≐, Mo., U.S. 194 36.45 N 93.30 W
James ≐, Va., U.S. 192 36.57 N 76.26 W
James, Isla I 254 44.57 S 74.07 W
James, Lake @ 216 41.42 N 85.02 W
James, Lake @[1] 192 35.45 N 81.55 W
Jamesābād 120 25.17 N 69.15 E
James Bay C 176 53.00 N 80.30 W
Jamesburg 208 40.21 N 74.26 W
James City, N.C., U.S. 192 35.05 N 77.02 W
James City, Pa., U.S. 214 41.37 N 78.50 W
James City □[6] 208 37.17 N 76.48 W
James Craik 252 32.09 S 63.28 W
James Creek 214 40.23 N 78.10 W
James Gardens ♠ 275b 43.40 N 79.31 W
James Island 284 48.37 N 123.22 W
James Island I 208 38.31 N 76.20 W
James M. Cox Dayton Municipal Airport ⊠ 218 39.54 N 84.13 W
Jameson Raid Memorial ⊥ 273d 26.11 S 27.49 E
James Point ≻ 192 25.21 N 76.24 W
Jamesport 194 39.58 N 93.48 W
James Price Point ≻ 162 17.30 S 122.08 E
James Ranges ⩕ 162 24.06 S 132.30 E
James River Bridge ➔[5] 208 37.00 N 76.30 W
James Ross, Cape ≻ 176 74.40 N 114.25 W
James Ross Island I 9 64.15 S 57.45 W
James Ross Strait 𝔲 176 69.40 N 95.30 W
James Smith Indian Reserve ➔[4] 184 53.08 N 104.52 W
Jamestown, Austl. 166 33.12 S 138.36 E
Jamestown, Eire 48 53.55 N 8.02 W
Jamestown, S. Afr. 158 31.06 S 26.45 E
Jamestown, Calif., U.S. 226 37.57 N 120.25 W
Jamestown, Kans., U.S. 198 39.36 N 97.52 W
Jamestown, Ky., U.S. 194 36.59 N 85.04 W
Jamestown, Mich., U.S. 216 42.50 N 85.51 W
Jamestown, N.C., U.S. 192 35.59 N 79.56 W
Jamestown, N. Dak., U.S. 198 46.54 N 98.42 W
Jamestown, N.Y., U.S. 214 42.06 N 79.14 W
Jamestown, Ohio, U.S. 218 39.39 N 83.44 W
Jamestown, Pa., U.S. 214 41.29 N 80.27 W
Jamestown, R.I., U.S. 207 41.30 N 71.22 W
Jamestown, Tenn., U.S. 194 36.26 N 84.57 W
Jamestown ⊥ 208 37.12 N 76.46 W
Jamestown Festival Park ♠ 208 37.14 N 76.48 W
Jamestown Reservoir @[1] 198 47.15 N 98.40 W
Jamesville, N.Y., U.S. 210 42.59 N 76.04 W
Jamesville, Va., U.S. 208 37.31 N 75.56 W
Jamet, Lac @ 206 46.34 N 74.30 W
Jametz 56 49.26 N 5.23 E
Jamgarh ∧ 123 34.35 N 73.37 E
Jamieson ≐ 169 37.18 S 146.08 E
Jamiltepec 234 16.17 N 97.49 W
Jaminauá ≐ 248 9.20 S 70.59 W
Jaminsk 76 52.46 N 28.16 E
Jaminskij 80 50.21 N 42.14 E
Jāmira ≐ 126 21.45 N 87.02 E
Jamira ≐[1] 126 21.35 N 88.28 E
Jamison 208 40.16 N 75.05 W
Jamison City 210 41.18 N 76.22 W
Jamison Town 274a 33.46 S 150.41 E
Jam-Ižora 265a 59.42 N 30.36 E
Jamjodhpur 120 21.54 N 70.01 E
Jamkhandi 122 16.31 N 75.18 E
Jamki 86 59.33 N 66.47 E
Jamkino 82 55.55 N 38.24 E
Jamm 76 58.26 N 28.03 E
Jammalamadugu 122 14.50 N 78.24 E
Jammerbugten C 26 57.20 N 9.30 E
Jammerland Bugt C 41 55.35 N 11.05 E
Jammu 123 32.42 N 74.52 E
Jammu Airport ⊠ 123 32.42 N 74.51 E
Jammu and Kashmir □[2] 120 34.00 N 76.00 E
Jāmnagar 120 22.28 N 70.04 E
Jamnotri 120 31.01 N 78.27 E
Jamoigne 56 49.42 N 5.25 E
Jamor ≐ 266c 38.42 N 9.15 W
Jampang-kulon 115a 7.16 S 106.37 E
Jampol', S.S.S.R. 78 48.16 N 28.17 E
Jampol', S.S.S.R. 78 49.58 N 26.14 E
Jampol', S.S.S.R. 78 51.57 N 33.46 E
Jampol', S.S.S.R. 83 48.56 N 37.58 E
Jāmpur, Bhārat 272b 22.56 N 88.12 E
Jāmpur, Pāk. 123 29.39 N 70.36 E
Jämsä 26 61.52 N 25.12 E
Jamsah 140 27.38 N 33.35 E
Jämsänkoski 26 61.55 N 25.11 E
Jamshedpur 126 22.48 N 86.11 E
Jamsk 74 59.35 N 154.10 E
Jamskaja Sloboda 82 55.29 N 36.01 E
Jāmtāra 126 23.57 N 86.48 E
Jämtland □[9] 26 63.30 N 14.00 E
Jämtlands Län □[6] 24 63.00 N 14.40 E
Jamuāni 126 21.57 N 86.14 E
Jamuga 82 56.24 N 36.40 E
Jamūi 124 24.55 N 86.13 E
Jamuna ≐ 124 23.51 N 89.45 E
Jamundí 246 3.15 N 76.32 W
Jāmuria 126 23.44 N 87.02 E
Jāmurki 126 24.09 N 90.02 E
Jana ≐ 74 71.31 N 136.32 E
Janai 272b 22.43 N 88.16 E
Janāj 142 31.00 N 30.46 E
Janajkino 80 50.43 N 51.06 E
Janas 266c 38.49 N 9.26 W
Janauacá, Lago @ 246 3.28 S 60.17 W
Janaúba 255 15.48 S 43.19 W
Janaucu, Ilha I 250 0.30 N 50.10 W
Janaul 86 56.16 N 54.56 E
Jand 123 33.26 N 72.01 E
Janda, Laguna de la @ 34 36.15 N 5.51 W
Jandaia 255 17.06 S 50.07 W
Jandaia do Sul 255 23.36 S 51.39 W
Jandaíra 250 11.34 S 37.47 W
Jandalī, Wādī al- V 142 30.05 N 31.52 E
Jandaq 128 34.02 N 54.26 E
Jandelsbrunn 60 48.44 N 13.42 E
Jandiāla 123 31.36 N 75.03 E
Jandiatuba ≐ 246 3.28 S 68.42 W
Jandira 256 23.31 S 46.54 W
Jandira □[7] 287b 23.32 S 46.54 W
Jandowae 166 26.47 S 151.06 E
Jandrakinot 180 64.54 N 172.32 W
Jándula ≐ 34 38.03 N 4.06 W
Jándula, Embalse de @[1] 34 38.30 N 4.00 W
Janeiro, Rio de ≐ 250 11.51 S 45.09 W
Jane Peak ∧ 172 45.20 S 168.19 E
Janes Island I 208 38.00 N 75.52 W
Janes Island State Park ♠ 208 38.00 N 75.52 W
Janesville, Calif., U.S. 204 40.18 N 120.32 W
Janesville, Minn., U.S. 190 44.07 N 93.42 W
Janesville, Wis., U.S. 216 42.41 N 89.01 W
Janetstown 46 58.16 N 3.22 W
Jangal Bādhāl 126 23.07 N 89.21 E
Jangamo 156 24.06 S 35.21 E
Jangany 157b 23.14 S 45.27 E
Jangaon 122 17.43 N 79.11 E
Jangarej 24 68.46 N 61.25 E
Jangel'skij 86 53.08 N 58.59 E
Jangel'urta, Gora ∧[2] 24 67.33 N 38.02 E
Jangeru 112 2.20 S 116.29 E
Jangiabad 85 41.08 N 70.05 E
Jangi-Bazar 85 41.40 N 70.53 E
Jangijer 85 40.17 N 68.50 E
Jangijul' 85 41.07 N 69.03 E
Jangikišlak 85 40.25 N 67.10 E
Jangikurgan, S.S.S.R. 85 40.34 N 71.09 E
Jangikurgan, S.S.S.R. 85 41.12 N 71.44 E
Jangipāra 126 22.45 N 88.04 E
Jangipur 124 24.28 N 88.04 E
Jangjong 114 4.23 N 96.48 E
Jangulovo 80 56.26 N 50.25 E
Janikowo 30 52.45 N 18.07 E
Janīn 132 32.28 N 35.18 E
Janīn, Sabkhat al- @ 146 30.30 N 21.00 E
Janina → Ioánnina 38 39.40 N 20.50 E
Janino 265a 59.56 N 30.36 E
Janisjarvi, Ozero @ 24 61.59 N 30.57 E
Janiuay 116 10.58 N 122.30 E
Janja 38 44.40 N 19.15 E
Janjina, Jugo. 36 42.56 N 17.26 E
Janjina, Madag. 157b 20.30 S 45.50 E
Janka 126 21.52 N 87.56 E
Janka ≐ 76 55.22 N 27.31 E
Jankan, Chrebet ⩕ 88 55.45 N 118.00 E
Jankāpur 126 21.54 N 87.23 E
Jan Kempdorp (Andalusia) 158 27.55 S 24.51 E
Jan Lake @ 184 54.55 N 102.55 W
Janlohong 112 2.15 N 117.03 E
Jan Mayen I 10 71.00 N 8.20 W
Jannale 144 1.50 N 44.42 E
Jannali 274a 34.01 S 151.04 E
Jannali Park ♠ 274a 34.01 S 151.03 E
Janos 232 30.54 N 108.10 W
Janos, Río de ≐ 232 30.56 N 108.08 W
Jánoshalma 30 46.18 N 19.20 E
Jánosháza 30 47.08 N 17.10 E
János-hegy ∧ 264c 47.31 N 18.58 E
Janov 78 49.28 N 28.21 E
Janovice nad Úhlavou 60 49.21 N 13.14 E
Janoviči 76 55.17 N 30.42 E
Janowiec Wielkopolski 30 52.46 N 17.31 E
Janów Lubelski 30 50.43 N 22.24 E
Jānsath 124 29.20 N 77.51 E
Jansen 184 51.47 N 104.43 W
Jansenville 158 32.57 S 24.40 E
Janskij 74 68.28 N 134.48 E
Janskij Zaliv C 74 71.50 N 136.00 E
Jantarnyj 76 54.52 N 19.57 E
Jantetelco 234 18.42 N 98.46 W
Jantikovo 80 55.32 N 47.48 E
Jantra ≐ 38 43.38 N 25.34 E
Januária 255 15.29 S 44.22 W
Januário Cicco 250 6.09 S 35.35 W
Jan Van Riebeeck Park ♠ 273d 26.10 S 27.59 E
Janvarcevo 80 51.26 N 52.15 E
Janville 50 48.12 N 1.53 E
Janville-sur-Juine 261 48.31 N 2.16 E
Janvry 261 48.39 N 2.09 E
Jany-Kurgan 85 43.55 N 67.15 E
Janzé 50 47.58 N 1.30 W
Janzūr 142 30.41 N 31.02 E
Jaora 120 23.38 N 75.08 E
Japan □[1] 90 / 92 36.00 N 138.00 E
Japan, Sea of ≂[2] 90 40.00 N 135.00 E
Japan Basin ⊹[1] 12 40.00 N 135.00 E
Japanisches Meer → Japan, Sea of ≂[2] 90 40.00 N 135.00 E
Japaratinga 250 9.05 S 35.15 W
Japaratuba 250 10.35 S 36.57 W
Japeri 256 22.39 S 43.40 W
Japi 250 6.27 S 35.56 W
Japiim 248 7.37 S 72.54 W
Japla 124 24.33 N 84.01 E
Japoatã 250 10.20 S 36.48 W
Japon → Japan □[1] 92 36.00 N 138.00 E
Japón, Mar del → Japan, Sea of ≂[2] 90 40.00 N 135.00 E
Japtiksal'a 74 69.21 N 72.32 E
Japuíba 256 22.35 S 42.42 W
Japurá 246 1.48 S 66.30 W
Japurá (Caquetá) ≐ 246 3.08 S 64.46 W
Jaqué 246 7.31 N 78.10 W
Jaqui 248 15.30 S 74.26 W
Jar 80 58.15 N 52.06 E
Jarābulus 130 36.49 N 38.01 E
Jarad 144 18.59 N 41.24 E
Jaradū 142 29.18 N 30.42 E
Jaraguá 255 15.45 S 49.20 W
Jaraguá ➔[8] 287b 23.27 S 46.44 W
Jaraguá, Pico do ∧ 287b 23.26 S 46.46 W
Jaraguá do Sul 252 26.29 S 49.04 W
Jaraicejo 34 39.40 N 5.49 W
Jaraiz de la Vera 34 40.04 N 5.45 W
Jaral del Progreso 234 20.22 N 101.04 W
Jarales 200 34.37 N 106.46 W
Jarama ≐ 34 40.02 N 3.39 W
Jarama, Canal del ≐ 266a 40.18 N 3.32 W
Jaramānah 132 33.29 N 36.21 E
Jaramillo 254 47.11 S 67.09 W
Jaramor 80 56.07 N 48.44 E
Jaran' ≐ 80 57.35 N 48.14 E
Jarandilla 34 40.08 N 5.39 W
Jaransk 80 57.19 N 47.54 E
Jarānwāla 123 31.20 N 73.26 E
Jarash 132 32.17 N 35.54 E
Jarawī, Wādī V 142 29.47 N 31.19 E
Jarbah, Jabal al- ∧ 142 30.16 N 32.03 E
Jarbah, Wāḥat ≂[4] 140 29.21 N 25.20 E
Jarbidge ≐ 202 42.19 N 115.39 W
Järbo 40 60.43 N 16.36 E
Jarcevo 76 55.04 N 32.41 E
Jardas al-'Abīd 146 32.19 N 20.56 E
Jardim, Bra. 248 21.28 S 56.09 W
Jardim, Bra. 250 7.35 S 39.16 W
Jardim América ➔[8] 287b 23.34 S 46.41 W
Jardim de Angicos 250 5.39 S 35.59 W
Jardim de Piranhas 250 6.22 S 37.20 W
Jardim do Seridó 250 6.35 S 36.46 W
Jardim Paulista ➔[8] 287b 23.35 S 46.40 W
Jardín América 252 27.03 S 55.14 W
Jardines de la Reina, Archipiélago de los II 240p 20.50 N 78.55 W
Jardinópolis 255 21.02 S 47.46 W
Jardymly 84 38.55 N 48.15 E
Jaredi 150 12.46 N 5.05 E
Jarega 24 63.27 N 53.26 E
Jaremča 78 48.27 N 24.33 E
Jarenga 24 62.43 N 49.30 E
Jarensk 24 62.11 N 49.02 E
Järfälla 40 59.24 N 17.50 E
Jargara 78 46.27 N 28.27 E
Jargeau 50 47.52 N 2.07 E
Jari ≐, Bra. 248 5.07 S 62.21 W
Jari ≐, Bra. 250 1.09 S 51.54 W
Jari, Lago @ 246 5.00 S 62.19 W
Jāria Jhānjail 124 25.02 N 90.39 E
Jaridih 124 23.38 N 86.04 E
Jarinu 256 23.06 S 46.44 W
Jarkino 88 59.08 N 99.23 E
Jarkovo 86 57.24 N 67.05 E
Jarkul'-Mat'uškino 86 55.51 N 76.06 E
Järlåsa 40 59.53 N 17.12 E
Jarmah 146 26.33 N 13.04 E
Jarmen 54 53.55 N 13.20 E
Jarmolincy 78 49.12 N 26.50 E
Järna 40 59.06 N 17.34 E
Jarnac 32 45.41 N 0.10 W
Jarny 56 49.09 N 5.53 E
Jaro 116 11.11 N 124.47 E
Jarochta 88 58.58 N 98.58 E
Jarocin 30 51.59 N 17.31 E
Jaroměř 30 50.21 N 15.55 E
Jaroměřice 61 49.05 N 15.53 E
Jaropolec 82 56.08 N 35.49 E
Jaroslavec 78 51.33 N 33.40 E
Jaroslavl' 80 57.37 N 39.52 E
Jaroslavl' □[4] 82 56.45 N 38.45 E
Jaroslavskaja 84 44.36 N 40.27 E
Jaroslavskij 89 44.10 N 132.13 E
Jaroslavskij Vokzal ➔[5] 265b 55.47 N 37.39 E
Jarosław 30 50.02 N 22.42 E
Jarovaja 83 49.03 N 37.37 E
Järpen 26 63.21 N 13.29 E
Jarrahdale 168a 32.20 S 116.04 E
Jarratt 208 36.48 N 77.28 W
Jarrell 222 30.49 N 97.36 W
Jarrettsville 208 39.36 N 76.29 W
Jarrīs 142 27.55 N 30.46 E
Jarrow 44 54.59 N 1.29 W
Jarry, Parc ♠ 275a 45.32 N 73.38 W
Jar-Sale 74 66.50 N 70.50 E
Jarsomovy 86 60.15 N 73.38 E
Jaru 248 10.26 S 62.27 W
Jaruu 88 48.08 N 96.45 E
Järva-Jaani 76 59.02 N 25.53 E
Järvakandi 76 58.47 N 24.49 E
Järvelä 26 60.52 N 25.17 E
Järvenpää 26 60.28 N 25.06 E
Jarvie 182 54.27 N 113.59 W
Jarville-la-Malgrange 58 48.40 N 6.13 E
Jarvis 212 42.53 N 80.06 W
Jarvisburg 192 36.09 N 75.52 W
Jarvis Island I 14 0.23 S 160.02 W
Järvsö 26 61.43 N 16.10 E
Jarw, Tallat al- ⩕[2] 142 30.36 N 30.13 E
Jarwa 124 27.39 N 82.31 E
Jasaan 116 8.39 N 124.45 E
Jasai 272c 18.56 N 73.01 E
Jašalta 80 46.20 N 42.17 E
Jašašnaja Tašla 80 53.55 N 48.16 E
Jaša Tomić 38 45.27 N 20.51 E
Jasdan 120 22.02 N 71.12 E
Jasel'da ≐ 76 52.07 N 26.28 E
Jasenevo ➔[8] 265b 55.36 N 37.33 E
Jasenki 78 51.32 N 38.12 E
Jasenovoje 82 54.10 N 36.47 E
Jasenovskij 83 48.10 N 39.10 E
Jasenskaja 78 46.22 N 38.16 E
Jashpurnagar 124 22.54 N 84.09 E
Jāshpur Pāts ➔[1] 124 22.55 N 84.00 E
Jasidih 124 24.31 N 86.39 E
Jasień 30 51.46 N 15.01 E
Jasienica 54 53.37 N 14.32 E
Jasikan 150 7.24 N 0.28 E
Jašil'kul', Ozero @ 120 37.45 N 72.55 E
Jasin 114 2.19 N 102.26 E
Jasin'a 78 48.16 N 24.20 E
Jasinga 115a 6.29 S 106.27 E
Jasinovataja 83 48.08 N 37.51 E
Jasinovka 83 48.08 N 37.57 E
Jāsk 128 25.38 N 57.46 E
Jaskhar 272c 18.54 N 72.59 E
Jaškino 86 55.54 N 85.26 E
Jaškul' 80 46.11 N 45.21 E
Jasło 30 49.45 N 21.29 E
Jasmine Estates 220 28.17 N 82.42 W
Jasmund ≻[1] 54 54.32 N 13.35 E
Jasnogorka 83 48.47 N 37.33 E
Jasnogorsk 82 54.29 N 37.42 E
Jasnomorskij 89 46.45 N 141.54 E
Jasnyj, S.S.S.R. 86 51.04 N 59.58 E
Jasnyj, S.S.S.R. 89 53.17 N 127.59 E
Jason Islands II 254 51.05 S 61.00 W
Jason Peninsula ≻[1] 9 66.10 S 61.00 W
Jasonville 194 39.10 N 87.12 W
Jasper, Alta., Can. 182 52.53 N 118.05 W
Jasper, Ala., U.S. 194 33.50 N 87.17 W
Jasper, Ark., U.S. 194 36.00 N 93.11 W
Jasper, Fla., U.S. 192 30.31 N 82.57 W
Jasper, Ga., U.S. 192 34.28 N 84.26 W
Jasper, Ind., U.S. 194 38.24 N 86.56 W
Jasper, Mich., U.S. 216 41.48 N 84.02 W
Jasper, Minn., U.S. 198 43.51 N 96.24 W
Jasper, Mo., U.S. 194 37.20 N 94.18 W
Jasper, N.Y., U.S. 210 42.07 N 77.30 W
Jasper, Tenn., U.S. 194 35.04 N 85.38 W
Jasper, Tex., U.S. 194 30.55 N 94.01 W
Jasper □[6] 216 40.57 N 87.09 W
Jasper Lake @ 182 53.07 N 118.00 W
Jasper National Park ♠ 182 52.53 N 118.03 W
Jaspur 124 29.17 N 78.49 E
Jasra 124 25.17 N 81.48 E
Jassans-Riottier 58 45.59 N 4.45 E
Jassar 123 32.06 N 74.57 E
Jassy → Iași 38 47.10 N 27.35 E
Jastarnia 30 54.43 N 18.40 E
Jastrebarsko 36 45.40 N 15.39 E
Jastrebovka, S.S.S.R. 78 51.27 N 37.32 E
Jastrebovka, S.S.S.R. 82 54.36 N 36.24 E
Jastrow → Jastrowie 30 53.26 N 16.49 E
Jastrowie 30 53.26 N 16.49 E
Jaswantnagar 124 26.53 N 78.55 E
Jászapáti 30 47.31 N 20.09 E
Jászberény 30 47.30 N 19.55 E
Jat, Uad el V 148 26.45 N 13.03 W
Jataí 255 17.53 S 51.43 W
Jatapu ≐ 246 2.13 S 58.17 W
Jataté ≐ 236 16.15 N 91.17 W
Jati, Bra. 250 7.41 S 39.01 W
Jāti, Pāk. 120 24.21 N 68.16 E
Jatibarang 115a 6.28 S 108.17 E
Jatibonico 240p 21.56 N 79.10 W
Jatibonico del Sur ≐ 240p 21.33 N 79.09 W
Jatilawang 115a 7.32 S 109.06 E
Jatinegara ➔[8] 269e 6.13 S 106.52 E
Jatiroto 115a 8.07 S 113.21 E
Jatisrono 115a 7.49 S 111.07 E
Játiva 34 38.59 N 0.31 W
Jatiwangi 115a 6.44 S 108.15 E
Jatni 120 20.10 N 85.42 E
Jatobá ≐ 255 12.23 S 54.07 W
Jatoi Janūbi 123 29.31 N 70.51 E
Jātrāpur 126 22.44 N 89.45 E
Jatt (Tel Gat) 132 32.24 N 35.02 E
Jatung 124 27.29 N 88.55 E
Jatznick 54 53.35 N 13.56 E
Jāu, Ang. 152 15.12 S 13.31 E
Jaú, Bra. 255 22.18 S 48.33 W
Jaú ≐ 246 1.54 S 61.26 W
Jauaperi ≐ 246 1.26 S 61.35 W
Jauer → Jawor 30 51.03 N 16.11 E
Jauerling ∧ 61 48.20 N 15.20 E
Jaugrām 126 23.06 N 88.05 E
Jauja 248 11.48 S 75.30 W
Jauli 272a 28.44 N 77.21 E
Jaumave 234 23.25 N 99.23 W
Jaúna ≐ 248 6.24 S 59.57 W
Jaunde → Yaoundé 152 3.52 N 11.31 E
Jaune, Mer → Yellow Sea ≂[2] 90 36.00 N 123.00 E
Jaungulbene 76 57.04 N 26.36 E
Jaunjelgava 76 56.37 N 25.05 E
Jaunpass X 58 46.36 N 7.20 E
Jaunpiebalga 76 57.11 N 26.03 E
Jaunpils 76 56.44 N 23.01 E
Jaunpur 124 25.44 N 82.41 E
Jaunpur □[5] 124 25.40 N 82.40 E
Jaupaci 255 16.18 S 50.54 W
Jauquara ≐ 248 15.06 S 57.06 W
Jáuregui 258 34.36 S 59.10 W
Jauru ≐, Bra. 248 16.22 S 57.46 W
Jauru ≐, Bra. 255 18.40 S 54.36 W
Jausiers 62 44.25 N 6.44 E
Jauza ≐ 265b 55.45 N 37.38 E
Java 198 45.30 N 99.53 W
Java Center 210 42.39 N 78.23 W
Javādi Hills ⩕[2] 122 12.35 N 78.50 E
Javalambre ∧ 34 40.06 N 1.03 W
Javan 85 38.19 N 69.02 E
Javari (Yavarí) ≐ 242 4.21 S 70.02 W
Javas 80 54.26 N 42.51 E
Java Sea → Jawa I 115a 7.30 S 110.00 E
Java Sea → Jawa, Laut ≂[2] 112 5.00 S 110.00 E
Java Trench ⊹[1] 12 10.00 S 110.00 E
Java Village 210 42.40 N 78.26 W
Jávea 34 38.47 N 0.10 E
Jävenitz 54 52.31 N 11.30 E
Javier, Isla I 254 47.06 S 74.24 W
Javkino 78 47.16 N 32.37 E
Javlenka 86 54.21 N 68.27 E
Javor ⩕ 38 44.05 N 18.55 E
Javořice ∧ 61 49.14 N 15.20 E
Javorie ∧ 30 48.27 N 19.18 E
Javorná 60 49.13 N 13.18 E
Javorník 30 50.23 N 17.00 E
Javorníky ⩕ 30 49.20 N 18.20 E
Javorov 78 49.56 N 23.23 E
Javorová skála ∧ 30 49.31 N 14.30 E
Javr ≐ 24 68.09 N 30.06 E
Jävre 26 65.09 N 21.59 E
Jawa (Java) I 115a 7.30 S 110.00 E
Jawa, Laut (Java Sea) ≂[2] 112 5.00 S 110.00 E
Jawa Barat □[4] 115a 7.00 S 107.00 E
Jawāla Mukhi 123 31.53 N 76.19 E
Jaw'alīyāt, Jabal al- ∧ 132 31.26 N 36.26 E
Jawa Tengah □[4] 115a 7.30 S 110.00 E
Jawa Timur □[4] 115a 8.00 S 113.00 E
Jawbar 132 33.31 N 36.19 E
Jawf, Wādī al- V 144 15.50 N 45.35 E
Jawi 112 0.48 S 109.16 E
Jawor 30 51.03 N 16.11 E
Jaworzno 30 50.13 N 19.15 E
Jay, Fla., U.S. 194 30.57 N 87.09 W
Jay, Okla., U.S. 196 36.25 N 94.48 W
Jay □[6] 216 40.26 N 84.59 W
Jaya, Puncak ∧ 164 4.05 S 137.11 E
Jayamkondacholapuram 122 11.13 N 79.22 E
Jayanca 248 6.24 S 79.50 W
Jayapura (Sukarnapura) 164 2.32 S 140.42 E
Jay Cooke State Park ♠ 190 46.41 N 92.23 W
Jaydebpur 124 24.00 N 90.26 E
Jaynagar 126 22.36 N 90.42 E
Jaynagar Majilpur 126 22.11 N 88.25 E
Jaynes 200 32.16 N 111.01 W
Jay Peak ∧ 188 44.55 N 72.32 W
Jaypur 126 23.03 N 87.27 E
Jayrūd 130 33.49 N 36.44 E
Jayton 196 33.15 N 100.34 W
Jayuya 240m 18.13 N 66.36 W
Jaywick 42 51.47 N 1.08 E
Jaz 80 54.54 N 45.13 E
Jaželbicy 76 58.02 N 32.58 E
Jazevec 24 65.43 N 46.30 E
Jazgulem ≐ 85 38.12 N 71.21 E
Jazīrat Muḥammad 273c 30.07 N 31.12 E
Jazjavan 85 40.39 N 71.24 E

Symbols in the index entries represent the broad categories identified in the key at the right. Symbols with superior numbers (⩕[2]) identify subcategories (see complete key on page *I* · *30*).

Kartensymbole in dem Registerverzeichnis stellen die rechts in Schlüssel erklärten Kategorien dar. Symbole mit hochgestellten Ziffern (⩕[2]) bezeichnen Unterabteilungen einer Kategorie (vgl. vollständiger Schlüssel auf Seite *I* · *30*).

Los símbolos incluidos en el texto del índice representan las grandes categorías identificadas con la clave a la derecha. Los símbolos con numeros en su parte superior (⩕[2]) identifican las subcategorías (véase la clave completa en la página *I* · *30*).

Les symboles de l'index représentent les catégories indiquées dans la légende à droite. Les symboles suivis d'un indice (⩕[2]) représentent des sous-catégories (voir légende complète à la page *I* · *30*).

Os símbolos incluídos no texto do índice representam as grandes categorias identificadas com a chave à direita. Os símbolos com números em sua parte superior (⩕[2]) identificam as subcategorias (veja-se a chave completa à página *I* · *30*).

	English	Deutsch	Español	Français	Português
∧	Mountain	Berg	Montaña	Montagne	Montanha
⩕	Mountains	Berge	Montañas	Montagnes	Montanhas
X	Pass	Pass	Paso	Col	Passo
V	Valley, Canyon	Tal, Cañon	Valle, Cañón	Vallée, Canyon	Vale, Canhão
≍	Plain	Ebene	Llano	Plaine	Planície
≻	Cape	Kap	Cabo	Cap	Cabo
I	Island	Insel	Isla	Île	Ilha
II	Islands	Inseln	Islas	Îles	Ilhas
≐	Other Topographic Features	Andere Topographische Objekte	Otros Elementos Topográficos	Autres données topographiques	Outros Elementos Topográficos

ESPAÑOL

Nombre	Página	Lat.°′	Long.°′ W=Oeste
Jažma	24	66.56 N	44.29 E
Jaz Mūrīān, Hāmūn-e ⊜	128	27.20 N	58.55 E
Jazovaja	86	49.27 N	85.20 E
Jazykovo	80	54.18 N	47.24 E
Jazzīn	132	33.32 N	35.34 E
Jbā'	132	33.29 N	35.31 E
J B Thomas, Lake ⊜[1]	196	32.35 N	101.10 W
J. C. Murphey Lake ⊜	216	40.58 N	87.30 W
Jdiouia	34	35.57 N	0.50 E
Jeanerette	194	29.55 N	91.40 W
Jeanesville	210	40.56 N	75.58 W
Jeannette	214	40.20 N	79.35 W
Jebāl Bārez, Kūh-e ⩘	128	28.30 N	58.20 E
Jebba	150	9.08 N	4.50 E
Jebel	38	45.33 N	21.14 E
Jeber-Bergfrieden	54	51.59 N	12.20 E
Jeberos	248	5.17 S	76.13 W
Jebri	120	27.18 N	65.44 E
Jebus	112	1.44 S	105.29 E
Jechegnadzor	84	39.46 N	45.21 E
Jedarma	88	58.44 N	102.36 E
Jedburgh	44	55.29 N	2.34 W
Jedburgh Abbey ʊ[1]	44	55.27 N	2.34 W
Jeddore Lake ⊜[1]	186	48.03 N	55.55 W
Jedelevo	80	53.24 N	47.45 E
Jedepo	150	5.16 N	8.20 W
Jedincy	78	48.10 N	27.19 E
Jedisa	84	42.31 N	44.16 E
Jedlesee ◆[8]	264b	48.16 N	16.23 E
Jednevo	82	56.06 N	36.14 E
Jedogon	88	54.15 N	100.15 E
Jedrovo	76	57.55 N	33.38 E
Jędrzejów	30	50.39 N	20.18 E
Jedwabne	30	53.17 N	22.19 E
Jed Water ≃	46	55.32 N	2.33 W
Jeetzel (Jeetze) ≃	54	53.09 N	11.04 E
Jefawa	140	10.57 N	23.48 E
Jeffers	198	44.03 N	95.12 W
Jefferson, Ga., U.S.	192	34.07 N	83.35 W
Jefferson, Ind., U.S.	216	40.17 N	86.36 W
Jefferson, Iowa, U.S.	198	42.01 N	94.23 W
Jefferson, Md., U.S.	208	39.22 N	77.32 W
Jefferson, Mass., U.S.	207	42.22 N	71.53 W
Jefferson, N.J., U.S.	285	39.45 N	75.13 W
Jefferson, N.C., U.S.	192	36.26 N	81.28 W
Jefferson, N.Y., U.S.	210	42.29 N	74.37 W
Jefferson, N.Y., U.S.	210	42.14 N	73.54 W
Jefferson, Ohio, U.S.	214	41.44 N	80.46 W
Jefferson, Oreg., U.S.	202	44.43 N	123.01 W
Jefferson, Pa., U.S.	279b	39.56 N	80.04 W
Jefferson, S.C., U.S.	192	34.39 N	80.23 W
Jefferson, S. Dak., U.S.	198	42.36 N	96.34 W
Jefferson, Tex., U.S.	194	32.46 N	94.21 W
Jefferson, Wis., U.S.	216	43.00 N	88.48 W
Jefferson □[6], Ill., U.S.	219	38.19 N	88.55 W
Jefferson □[6], Ind., U.S.	218	38.44 N	85.23 W
Jefferson □[6], Ky., U.S.	218	38.14 N	85.10 W
Jefferson □[6], Mo., U.S.	219	38.20 N	90.34 W
Jefferson □[6], N.Y., U.S.	212	43.59 N	75.55 W
Jefferson □[6], Ohio, U.S.	214	40.22 N	80.37 W
Jefferson □[6], Pa., U.S.	214	41.09 N	79.05 W
Jefferson □[6], Wash., U.S.	224	47.50 N	122.36 W
Jefferson □[6], Wis., U.S.	216	43.02 N	88.46 W
Jefferson ≃	202	45.56 N	111.30 W
Jefferson, Mount ∧, U.S.	202	44.34 N	111.30 W
Jefferson, Mount ∧, Idaho, U.S.	202	44.34 N	111.30 W
Jefferson, Mount ∧, Nev., U.S.	204	38.46 N	116.55 W
Jefferson, Mount ∧, Oreg., U.S.	202	44.40 N	121.47 W
Jefferson City, Mo., U.S.	219	38.34 N	92.10 W
Jefferson City, Tenn., U.S.	192	36.07 N	83.30 W
Jefferson Park ◆[8]	278	41.59 N	87.46 W
Jefferson Proving Ground ■	218	38.50 N	85.25 W
Jeffersonton	188	38.38 N	77.55 W
Jeffersontown	218	38.12 N	85.35 W
Jefferson Village	284c	38.52 N	77.10 W
Jeffersonville, Ga., U.S.	192	32.41 N	83.20 W
Jeffersonville, Ind., U.S.	218	38.17 N	85.44 W
Jeffersonville, N.Y., U.S.	210	41.20 N	73.47 W
Jeffersonville, Ohio, U.S.	218	39.39 N	83.34 W
Jeffrey City	200	42.29 N	107.49 W
Jefimovka	80	52.13 N	52.03 E
Jefimovskij	76	59.30 N	35.02 E
Jefremov	76	53.09 N	38.07 E
Jefremova	82	56.13 N	38.59 E
Jefremovka	83	47.19 N	38.29 E
Jefremovo-Stepanovka	78	48.43 N	40.50 E
Jefremovskaja	82	55.25 N	38.59 E
Jega	150	12.15 N	4.23 E
Jegenstorf	58	47.03 N	7.30 E
Jegindybulak, S.S.S.R.	86	49.45 N	76.23 E
Jegindybulak, S.S.S.R.	86	48.42 N	81.48 E
Jegorjevka	89	50.42 N	127.42 E
Jegorjevsk	82	55.23 N	39.02 E
Jegorlyk ≃	80	46.33 N	41.52 E
Jehol → Chengde	105	40.58 N	117.53 E
Jeja ≃	78	46.41 N	38.36 E
Jejsk	78	46.42 N	38.16 E
Jejskij Liman C	78	46.42 N	38.25 E
Jeju → Cheju	90	33.31 N	126.32 E
Jejur	272b	22.53 N	88.08 E
Jēkabpils	76	56.29 N	25.51 E
Jekaterinburg → Sverdlovsk	86	56.51 N	60.36 E
Jekaterinino	76	55.49 N	33.58 E
Jekaterininskoje	86	56.53 N	74.34 E
Jekaterinoslav → Dnepropetrovsk	78	48.27 N	34.59 E
Jekaterinoslavka	89	50.23 N	129.08 E
Jekaterinovka, S.S.S.R.	78	46.42 N	38.46 E
Jekaterinovka, S.S.S.R.	80	52.03 N	44.21 E
Jekaterinovka, S.S.S.R.	80	46.32 N	41.42 E
Jekaterinovka, S.S.S.R.	80	53.04 N	49.28 E
Jekaterinovka, S.S.S.R.	83	47.33 N	38.23 E
Jekaterinovka, S.S.S.R.	86	54.36 N	70.58 E
Jekaterinovka ◆[8]	265b	55.46 N	37.23 E
Jekaterinovskaja	78	46.20 N	39.58 E
Jekateriny, Proliv ⊔	74	53.53 N	140.25 E
Jekimoviči	76	54.07 N	33.18 E
Jekpindykurylys	80	47.49 N	47.17 E
Jekyll Island ▮	192	31.04 N	81.25 W
Jekyll Island State Park ♠	192	31.02 N	81.25 W
Jelabuga	80	55.47 N	52.04 E
Jelai ≃, Indon.	112	2.59 S	110.45 E
Jelai ≃, Malay.	114	4.04 N	102.20 E

FRANÇAIS

Nom	Page	Lat.°′	Long.°′ W=Ouest
Jelan', S.S.S.R.	80	52.13 N	44.11 E
Jelan', S.S.S.R.	80	50.57 N	43.44 E
Jelan', S.S.S.R.	83	48.41 N	39.47 E
Jelan', S.S.S.R.	86	57.39 N	63.42 E
Jelan' ≃, S.S.S.R.	80	51.07 N	41.26 E
Jelan' ≃, S.S.S.R.	80	50.56 N	43.45 E
Jelancy	88	52.49 N	106.25 E
Jelanec	78	47.42 N	31.51 E
Jelanka	86	55.37 N	75.18 E
Jelan'-Koleno	78	51.09 N	41.14 E
Jelan'-Kolenovskij	78	51.10 N	41.10 E
Jelatak	174r	6.56 N	158.17 E
Jelat'ma	80	54.58 N	41.45 E
Jelaur, S.S.S.R.	80	54.34 N	50.21 E
Jelaur, S.S.S.R.	80	53.50 N	48.48 E
Jelchovka	80	53.51 N	50.18 E
Jel'covka	86	53.15 N	86.15 E
Jel'cy, S.S.S.R.	76	56.40 N	33.51 E
Jel'cy, S.S.S.R.	82	56.11 N	38.46 E
Jelec	76	52.37 N	38.30 E
Jeleckij	24	67.03 N	64.10 E
Jelenia Góra (Hirschberg)	30	50.55 N	15.46 E
Jelenskij	76	53.29 N	35.23 E
Jelgava	76	56.39 N	23.42 E
Jelgavkrasti	76	57.28 N	24.26 E
Jelisejevka	78	47.02 N	36.24 E
Jelizarovo, S.S.S.R.	78	48.12 N	34.33 E
Jelizarovo, S.S.S.R.	80	58.33 N	44.50 E
Jelizavetgradka	78	48.48 N	32.24 E
Jelizavetinka, S.S.S.R.	86	51.46 N	59.45 E
Jelizavetinka, S.S.S.R.	86	51.28 N	71.12 E
Jelizavetopol'skoje	86	52.51 N	60.36 E
Jelizavetovka	78	46.39 N	38.53 E
Jelizavety, Mys ≻	89	54.27 N	142.42 E
Jelizovo	76	53.24 N	29.01 E
Jelli	154	5.22 N	31.48 E
Jellico	192	36.35 N	84.08 W
Jelling	41	55.45 N	9.26 E
Jelloway	214	40.33 N	82.18 W
Jelm Mountain ∧	200	41.06 N	105.58 W
Jel'n'a	76	54.35 N	33.11 E
Jelnat'	80	57.20 N	42.49 E
Jel'niki	80	54.37 N	43.53 E
Jeloguj ≃	74	63.13 N	87.45 E
Jel'onovka, S.S.S.R.	83	48.39 N	38.01 E
Jel'onovka, S.S.S.R.	83	47.50 N	37.40 E
Jelošnoje	86	55.27 N	66.44 E
Jelovo	80	57.03 N	54.54 E
Jels	41	55.21 N	9.12 E
Jelšanka, S.S.S.R.	80	52.35 N	47.59 E
Jelšanka, S.S.S.R.	80	51.49 N	46.23 E
Jelšanka Pervaja	80	52.53 N	52.02 E
Jelšava	30	48.39 N	20.14 E
Jel'sk	78	51.48 N	29.09 E
Jemaa	150	9.27 N	8.23 E
Jemaja, Pulau ▮	112	2.55 N	105.45 E
Jemaluang	114	2.17 N	103.52 E
Jemantajevo	80	53.34 N	53.50 E
Jemanželinsk	86	54.45 N	61.20 E
Jemappes	50	50.27 N	3.53 E
Jember	115a	8.10 S	113.42 E
Jemca	24	63.04 N	40.20 E
Jemca ≃	24	63.15 N	41.20 E
Jemeljanovka	78	45.32 N	34.53 E
Jemeljanovo	86	56.11 N	92.40 E
Jemel'stan	24	61.13 N	52.29 E
Jemen → Yemen □[1]	144	15.00 N	44.00 E
Jemen, Volksrepublik → Yemen, People's Democratic Republic of □[1]	144	15.00 N	48.00 E
Jemeppe	56	50.37 N	5.30 E
Jemez ≃	200	35.22 N	106.31 W
Jemez Springs	200	35.46 N	106.42 W
Jemgum	52	53.16 N	7.23 E
Jemil'čino	78	50.52 N	27.48 E
Jemnice	61	49.01 N	15.35 E
Jemniště ⊥	30	49.45 N	14.48 E
Jempang, Danau ⊜	112	0.26 S	116.12 E
Jena, D.D.R.	54	50.56 N	11.35 E
Jena, La., U.S.	194	31.41 N	92.08 W
Jenakijevo	83	48.14 N	38.13 E
Jenašimskij Polkan, Gora ∧	74	59.50 N	92.52 E
Jenaz	58	46.55 N	9.45 E
Jenbach	64	47.24 N	11.47 E
Jenbek	86	48.53 N	77.12 E
Jendarata	114	3.55 N	100.57 E
Jendongin	88	53.27 N	113.01 E
Jendouba (Souk el Arba)	148	36.30 N	8.47 E
Jendouba □[8]	36	36.30 N	8.45 E
Jeneponto	112	5.41 S	119.42 E
Jenera	216	40.54 N	83.44 W
Jeniang	114	5.49 N	100.38 E
Jenisej ≃	72	71.50 N	82.40 E
Jenisejsk	86	58.27 N	92.10 E
Jenisejskij Kr'až ⩘	74	59.00 N	93.00 E
Jenisejskij Zaliv C	74	72.30 N	80.00 E
Jenison	216	42.54 N	85.47 W
Jenkins	222	32.59 N	94.44 W
Jenkins, Mount ∧	162	25.36 S	129.41 E
Jenkinson Lake ⊜[1]	226	38.44 N	120.33 W
Jenkinsville	192	34.16 N	81.17 W
Jenkintown	208	40.06 N	75.08 W
Jenks	196	36.01 N	95.58 W
Jenli	100	23.15 N	120.08 E
Jenners	214	40.09 N	79.03 W
Jennersdorf	61	46.57 N	16.08 E
Jennerstown	214	40.10 N	79.04 W
Jennifer Branch ≃	284b	39.25 N	76.30 W
Jennings, Fla., U.S.	192	30.36 N	83.06 W
Jennings, La., U.S.	194	30.13 N	92.39 W
Jennings, Mo., U.S.	219	38.44 N	90.17 W
Jennings □[6]	218	38.59 N	85.36 W
Jennings Creek ≃	216	40.53 N	84.17 W
Jennings Lodge	224	45.24 N	122.38 W
Jenotajevka	80	47.15 N	47.03 E
Jensen	200	40.22 N	109.17 W
Jensen Beach	220	27.15 N	80.14 W
Jens Munk Island ▮	176	69.42 N	79.30 W
Jenu	112	0.36 S	109.52 E
Jen'uka	88	57.58 N	121.42 E
Jenya	144	4.12 N	37.32 E
Jeonju → Chŏnju	98	35.49 N	127.08 E
Jepač	24	66.58 N	61.22 E
Jepara	115a	6.35 S	110.39 E
Jeparit	166	36.09 S	141.59 E
Jepelacio	248	6.07 S	76.57 W
Jepichin	80	48.16 N	45.14 E
Jepifan'	76	53.49 N	38.33 E
Jeppener	258	35.17 S	58.12 W
Jeptha Knob ∧[2]	218	38.11 N	85.07 W
Jepua (Jeppo)	26	63.24 N	22.37 E
Jequeri	255	20.27 S	42.40 W
Jequetepeque ≃	248	7.21 S	79.36 W
Jequié	255	13.51 S	40.05 W
Jequitaí	255	17.15 S	44.28 W
Jequitinhonha	255	16.26 S	41.00 W
Jequitinhonha ≃	255	15.51 S	38.53 W
Jerachtur	80	54.43 N	41.09 E
Jerada	148	34.17 N	2.13 W
Jerangle	171b	35.52 S	149.22 E
Jeransang	114	3.52 N	102.22 E
Jerantut	114	3.56 N	102.22 E
Jerbar	140	5.39 N	31.05 E
Jerbent	128	39.19 N	58.36 E
Jerbogačon	74	61.16 N	108.00 E
Jercevo	24	60.48 N	40.05 E
Jerdenevo	82	54.55 N	36.27 E
Jerécuaro	234	20.09 N	100.31 W
Jeremejevka	83	46.58 N	39.33 E
Jeremejevo	82	55.57 N	37.01 E
Jérémie	238	18.39 N	74.07 W
Jeremino	82	56.27 N	37.58 E
Jeremoabo	250	10.04 S	38.21 W

PORTUGUÊS

Nome	Página	Lat.°′	Long.°′ W=Oeste
Jeremy Hill ∧[2]	207	42.45 N	71.21 W
Jeremy Point ≻	207	41.53 N	70.04 W
Jerevan	84	40.11 N	44.30 E
Jerez ≃	234	22.15 N	103.11 W
Jerez, Punta ≻	234	22.54 N	97.46 W
Jerez de García Salinas	234	22.39 N	103.00 W
Jerez de la Frontera	34	36.41 N	6.08 W
Jerez de los Caballeros	34	38.19 N	6.46 W
Jergač	86	57.28 N	56.39 E
Jergak-Targak-Tajga, Chrebet ⩘	88	53.25 N	95.30 E
Jergalan ≃	86	44.55 N	83.08 E
Jergeni ⩘[2]	80	47.00 N	44.00 E
Jergeninskij	80	47.07 N	44.28 E
Jericho, Austl.	166	23.36 S	146.08 E
Jericho, N.J., U.S.	285	39.48 N	75.09 W
Jericho, N.Y., U.S.	210	40.48 N	73.32 W
Jericho → Arīḥā, Urd.	132	31.52 N	35.27 E
Jerichow	54	52.30 N	12.01 E
Jericó, Bra.	250	6.33 S	37.48 W
Jericó, Col.	246	5.47 N	75.47 W
Jerid, Chott ☷	148	33.42 N	8.26 E
Jerik ≃	83	48.59 N	38.30 E
Jerilderie	166	35.22 S	145.44 E
Jerimoth Hill ∧[2]	207	41.52 N	71.47 W
Jerki	78	48.59 N	31.00 E
Jermak	86	52.02 N	76.55 E
Jermakovo	80	53.11 N	49.38 E
Jermakovskaja	80	48.03 N	41.17 E
Jermakovskoje	86	53.16 N	92.24 E
Jermekejevo	80	54.05 N	53.40 E
Jermentau	86	51.38 N	73.10 E
Jermentau ⩘	86	51.10 N	73.10 E
Jermica	24	66.56 N	52.15 E
Jermilovka	86	57.40 N	72.55 E
Jermiš'	80	54.46 N	42.16 E
Jermolajevo, S.S.S.R.	86	55.13 N	92.10 E
Jermolajevo, S.S.S.R.	86	52.43 N	55.48 E
Jermolino, S.S.S.R.	82	55.57 N	36.54 E
Jermolino, S.S.S.R.	82	56.48 N	37.49 E
Jermolino, S.S.S.R.	82	55.12 N	36.36 E
Jermolino, S.S.S.R.	86	57.20 N	64.43 E
Jermyn	210	41.31 N	75.32 W
Jernhatten ∧[2]	41	56.15 N	10.48 E
Jernih	114	4.25 N	97.43 E
Jeroaquara	255	15.23 S	50.25 W
Jerofej Pavlovič	89	53.58 N	122.01 E
Jerome, Ariz., U.S.	200	34.45 N	112.07 W
Jerome, Idaho, U.S.	202	42.43 N	114.31 W
Jerome, Ill., U.S.	219	39.46 N	89.41 W
Jerome, Mich., U.S.	216	42.01 N	84.28 W
Jerome, Pa., U.S.	214	40.13 N	78.59 W
Jeromesville	214	40.48 N	82.12 W
Jer'omino	86	58.35 N	79.25 E
Jerônimo Monteiro	255	20.47 S	41.24 W
Jerónimos de Belém, Mosteiro dos ʊ[1]	266c	38.42 N	9.12 W
Jeropol	74	65.15 N	168.40 E
Jerpoint Abbey ⊥	48	53.29 N	7.08 W
Jerry City	216	41.15 N	83.36 W
Jerry Slough ≃	226	35.33 N	119.31 W
Jersale	144	2.41 N	45.26 E
Jersey	214	40.03 N	82.46 W
Jersey □[6]	219	39.07 N	90.20 W
Jersey □[2]	22 / 43b	49.15 N	2.10 W
Jersey City	210	40.44 N	74.02 W
Jersey City State College ʊ[2]	276	40.43 N	74.05 W
Jersey Mountain ∧	202	45.29 N	115.34 W
Jersey Shore	210	41.12 N	77.16 W
Jersey Village	222	29.52 N	95.35 W
Jerseyville	219	39.07 N	90.20 W
Jerši	76	54.24 N	34.12 E
Jeršiči	76	53.40 N	32.44 E
Jeršov	80	51.20 N	48.17 E
Jeršovka	86	54.07 N	64.59 E
Jeršovo	82	55.46 N	36.52 E
Jeršovskij	86	52.29 N	59.08 E
Jertarskij	86	56.47 N	64.18 E
Jerte ≃	34	39.58 N	6.17 W
Jerteh	114	5.45 N	102.30 E
Jertom	24	63.32 N	47.48 E
Jerumenha	250	7.05 S	43.30 W
Jerusalem → Yerushalayim	132	31.46 N	35.14 E
Jerusalim (Talusan)	116	7.26 N	122.49 E
Jeruslan ≃	80	50.15 N	45.42 E
Jervaulx Abbey ʊ[1]	44	54.16 N	1.43 W
Jervis, Cape ≻	168b	35.38 S	138.06 E
Jervis Bay	170	35.08 S	150.42 E
Jervis Bay C	170	35.05 S	150.44 E
Jervis Inlet C	182	49.46 N	124.10 W
Jervois Range ⩘	162	22.38 S	136.05 E
Jerxheim	54	52.05 N	10.54 E
Jerykly	80	55.11 N	51.26 E
Jerzens	58	47.10 N	10.45 E
Jesaulovka	83	48.03 N	39.02 E
Jesenakaty ≃	80	50.32 N	51.47 E
Jesenice, Česko.	54	50.04 N	13.29 E
Jesenice, Jugo.	61	46.27 N	14.04 E
Jesenice, údolní nádrž ⊜[1]	60	50.04 N	12.27 E
Jesenická Přehradová Nádrž ⊜[1]	54	50.02 N	12.30 E
Jeseník	30	50.14 N	17.13 E
Jesenoviči	76	57.17 N	34.14 E
Jesensaj	80	49.54 N	51.28 E
Ješera	84	43.04 N	40.55 E
Jeserig bei Wiesenburg	54	52.05 N	12.27 E
Jesi → Iesi	66	43.31 N	13.14 E
Jesil'	86	51.58 N	66.24 E
Jes'ki	76	57.56 N	36.23 E
Jesönbulag → Altaj	90	46.25 N	96.20 E
Jessej	74	68.29 N	102.10 E
Jesselton → Kota Kinabalu	112	5.59 N	116.04 E
Jessen	54	51.47 N	12.58 E
Jessentuki	84	44.03 N	42.51 E
Jesser Point ≻	158	27.32 S	32.40 E
Jessheim	26	60.09 N	11.11 E
Jessnitz	54	51.41 N	12.17 E
Jessore	124	23.10 N	89.13 E
Jessup	210	41.28 N	75.34 W
Jessup, Lake ⊜	220	28.43 N	81.14 W
Jessup Park ♠	280	34.15 N	118.24 W
Jestetten	58	47.39 N	8.34 E
Jestřebí	54	50.38 N	14.36 E
Jesuânia	256	22.00 S	45.18 W
Jésuite, Lac du ⊜	206	46.53 N	72.36 W
Jesup, Ga., U.S.	192	31.36 N	81.53 W
Jesup, Iowa, U.S.	190	42.29 N	92.04 W
Jesús	252	27.03 S	55.47 W
Jésus, Île ▮	206	45.35 N	73.45 W
Jesús Carranza	234	17.26 N	95.02 W
Jesús del Monte ◆[8]	286b	23.06 N	82.22 W
Jesús de Otoro	236	14.26 N	87.59 W
Jesús María, Arg.	252	30.59 S	64.06 W
Jesús María, Méx.	232	25.06 N	107.28 W
Jesús María, Méx.	234	21.58 N	102.21 W
Jesús María, Perú	286d	12.04 S	77.04 W
Jesús María ≃	234	21.51 N	104.42 W
Jesús María, Punta ≻	258	34.39 S	56.55 W
Jet	196	36.40 N	98.11 W
Jeta, Ilha de ▮	150	11.53 N	16.15 W
Jetafe	116	10.09 N	124.09 E
Jetmore	198	38.03 N	99.54 W
Jet Propulsion Laboratory ʊ[3]	280	34.12 N	118.11 W
Jetpur	120	21.44 N	70.37 E
Jetřichovice	54	50.49 N	14.25 E
Jett	218	38.11 N	84.49 W
Jette	50	50.52 N	4.20 E

Name	Page	Lat.	Long.
Jettingen	58	48.23 N	10.26 E
Jeumont	50	50.18 N	4.06 E
Jeune Landing	182	50.27 N	127.30 W
Jeunieb	114	5.10 N	96.29 E
Jever	52	53.34 N	7.54 E
Jeverland ◆[1]	52	53.35 N	8.00 E
Jevgaščino	86	56.26 N	74.41 E
Jevgenjevka	85	43.31 N	77.40 E
Jevíčko	30	49.38 N	16.43 E
Jevišovka ≃	61	48.49 N	16.28 E
Jevlach	84	40.36 N	47.09 E
Jevlaš'ovo	80	53.07 N	46.51 E
Jevnaker	26	60.15 N	10.28 E
Jevpatorija	78	45.12 N	33.22 E
Jevra	86	59.56 N	64.27 E
Jevrejskaja Avtonomnaja Oblast' □[8]	89	48.30 N	132.00 E
Jevsug	83	49.13 N	39.18 E
Jevsug ≃	83	48.47 N	39.19 E
Jewel Cave National Monument ♠	198	43.42 N	103.50 W
Jewell, Iowa, U.S.	190	42.20 N	93.39 W
Jewell, Kans., U.S.	198	39.40 N	98.10 W
Jewell, N.Y., U.S.	210	43.13 N	75.48 W
Jewell, Ohio, U.S.	216	41.20 N	84.17 W
Jewell, Oreg., U.S.	224	45.56 N	123.30 W
Jewell Ridge	192	37.11 N	81.48 W
Jewell Village	218	39.10 N	85.51 W
Jewett, Ill., U.S.	194	39.13 N	88.15 W
Jewett, Ohio, U.S.	214	40.22 N	81.00 W
Jewett, Tex., U.S.	222	31.22 N	96.09 W
Jewett City	207	41.36 N	71.59 W
Jewett Creek ≃	212	44.22 N	75.45 W
Jewett Lake ⊜	184	56.09 N	104.40 W
Jewettville	284a	42.43 N	78.52 W
Jeypore	122	18.51 N	82.35 E
Jezerce ∧	38	42.26 N	19.49 E
Jezerišče	76	55.50 N	29.59 E
Jezerní hora ∧	60	49.10 N	13.11 E
Ježicha	80	58.06 N	47.40 E
Jeziorany	30	53.58 N	20.46 E
Ježovo	80	58.02 N	52.14 E
Jezreel, Valley of → Yizre'el, 'Emeq ⊻	132	32.36 N	35.14 E
Jhābua	120	22.46 N	74.36 E
Jhāhtipahāri	126	23.22 N	86.54 E
Jhajha	124	24.46 N	86.22 E
Jhajjar	124	28.37 N	76.39 E
Jhal	120	28.17 N	67.27 E
Jhālakāti	124	22.39 N	90.12 E
Jhālawār	124	24.36 N	76.09 E
Jhālawār □[5]	124	24.30 N	76.20 E
Jhalida	124	23.22 N	85.58 E
Jhal Jhao	120	26.18 N	65.35 E
Jhālod	120	23.06 N	74.09 E
Jhālrapātan	124	24.33 N	76.10 E
Jhang Maghiāna	123	31.16 N	72.19 E
Jhānsi	124	25.26 N	78.35 E
Jhānsi Post	123	33.54 N	71.24 E
Jhāpa	124	26.29 N	87.51 E
Jhārgrām	126	22.27 N	86.59 E
Jharia	126	23.45 N	86.24 E
Jhārpokhariā	126	22.10 N	86.38 E
Jhārsuguda	120	21.51 N	84.02 E
Jhawāni	124	27.35 N	84.31 E
Jhawāriān	123	32.22 N	72.38 E
Jhelum	123	32.56 N	73.44 E
Jhelum ≃	123	31.12 N	72.08 E
Jhenida	124	23.33 N	89.10 E
Jhenkāri	272b	22.46 N	88.18 E
Jhikra	126	22.37 N	87.55 E
Jhilimili	126	22.49 N	86.37 E
Jhil Kuranga ◆[8]	272a	28.40 N	77.17 E
Jhilla ≃[1]	126	21.58 N	88.56 E
Jhingergācha	126	23.07 N	89.07 E
Jhinkpāni	124	22.25 N	85.47 E
Jhok Rind	120	31.27 N	70.26 E
Jhūnjhunu	120	28.08 N	75.24 E
Jiaban, Zhg.	102	25.38 N	107.07 E
Jiaban, Zhg.	102	25.10 N	107.03 E
Jiabong	116	11.46 N	124.57 E
Jiacha	120	29.11 N	92.44 E
Jiading	106	31.23 N	121.15 E
Jiaganj	126	24.14 N	88.16 E
Jiagedan	89	51.35 N	120.55 E
Jiahashitai	89	46.25 N	122.17 E
Jiahe	102	25.43 N	112.05 E
Jiajiachang, Zhg.	107	30.26 N	104.21 E
Jiajiachang, Zhg.	107	29.44 N	105.06 E
Jiajiagou, Zhg.	104	41.44 N	120.58 E
Jiajiagou, Zhg.	104	42.20 N	121.46 E
Jiajiang	107	29.45 N	103.34 E
Jiajiayuan	106	32.18 N	120.55 E
Jiakou	100	30.10 N	119.03 E
Jialalassi	144	3.25 N	45.40 E
Jiali	120	30.47 N	93.24 E
Jialingjiang ≃	102	30.02 N	106.18 E
Jialou	100	32.54 N	113.26 E
Jialu	106	30.26 N	118.51 E
Jiamingzhen	107	29.16 N	105.20 E
Jiamusi (Kiamusze)	89	46.50 N	130.21 E
Jiamuyingzi	104	41.56 N	121.43 E
Ji'an, Zhg.	98	41.06 N	126.08 E
Ji'an, Zhg.	100	27.07 N	114.58 E
Jianba	106	31.59 N	120.35 E
Jianbi	106	32.11 N	119.35 E
Jianbing (Hongzidian)	98	38.21 N	113.49 E
Jianchang, Zhg.	98	39.58 N	122.35 E
Jianchang, Zhg.	98	40.51 N	119.46 E
Jianchang, Zhg.	98	41.16 N	124.29 E
Ji'anchang, Zhg.	107	30.32 N	105.58 E
Jianchangying	98	40.06 N	118.49 E
Jianchapu	105	39.06 N	116.31 E
Jianchaxi, Zhg.	102	28.08 N	108.04 E
Jianchaxi, Zhg.	107	30.22 N	104.03 E
Jianchuan	102	26.34 N	99.53 E
Jiande	100	29.32 N	119.30 E
Jiang'an	107	28.44 N	105.05 E
Jiangba	100	33.08 N	118.45 E
Jiangbei, Zhg.	100	26.20 N	115.26 E
Jiangbei, Zhg.	107	29.47 N	106.31 E
Jiangbian	102	24.03 N	103.37 E
Jiangbianzhai	102	23.49 N	100.11 E
Jiangcha	102	34.02 N	103.05 E
Jiangcheng, Zhg.	102	22.40 N	101.48 E
Jiangcheng, Zhg.	105	38.52 N	115.22 E
Jiangcun	100	28.17 N	117.49 E
Jiangda	102	31.27 N	98.15 E
Jiangdi	102	25.08 N	104.45 E
Jiangdihe	102	25.55 N	101.31 E
Jiangdu	100	32.26 N	119.34 E
Jiangduo	100	32.22 N	120.15 E
Jiange	102	32.06 N	105.29 E
Jianggeer	120	36.41 N	76.07 E
Jianghua (Shuikou)	102	24.58 N	111.38 E
Jianghuaqiao	106	32.05 N	120.00 E
Jiangjia, Zhg.	106	31.58 N	121.28 E
Jiangjia, Zhg.	106	31.40 N	121.09 E
Jiangjiadian	104	41.41 N	121.03 E
Jiangjiagou	104	41.44 N	121.44 E
Jiangjiaji, Zhg.	100	31.59 N	115.16 E
Jiangjiaji, Zhg.	100	32.19 N	115.44 E
Jiangjiatun, Zhg.	104	41.42 N	122.02 E
Jiangjiatun, Zhg.	104	41.42 N	122.25 E
Jiangjin	107	29.17 N	106.16 E
Jiangjing	100	25.34 N	119.25 E
Jiangjunguan)(	105	40.15 N	117.16 E
Jiangjunling	100	28.17 N	116.28 E
Jiangjunmiao	86	44.43 N	90.05 E
Jiangjunqiao	102	31.18 N	100.55 E
Jiangkou, Zhg.	100	27.27 N	118.03 E
Jiangkou, Zhg.	100	25.29 N	119.12 E
Jiangkou, Zhg.	100	29.43 N	121.25 E
Jiangkou, Zhg.	100	25.54 N	114.20 E
Jiangkou, Zhg.	100	27.21 N	115.31 E
Jiangkou, Zhg.	102	33.39 N	107.12 E
Jiangkou, Zhg.	102	30.26 N	111.42 E

Name	Page	Lat.	Long.
Jiangkou (Shuangjiangzhen), Zhg.	102	23.31 N	110.17 E
Jiangkou, Zhg.	102	27.37 N	108.48 E
Jiangkou, Zhg.	107	30.14 N	103.55 E
Jiangkouji	100	32.50 N	116.16 E
Jiangkoutang	100	27.30 N	112.44 E
Jiangle	100	26.42 N	117.25 E
Jiangling	102	30.20 N	112.06 E
Jianglingxi	102	31.28 N	107.13 E
Jiangmen	100	22.35 N	113.05 E
Jiangmifeng	89	43.58 N	126.45 E
Jiangning	106	31.58 N	118.50 E
Jiangpu	100	32.04 N	118.37 E
Jiangqiao	89	46.45 N	123.41 E
Jiangqiaotou	106	30.37 N	120.38 E
Jiangshan	100	28.45 N	118.37 E
Jiangshan'gang ≃	100	28.57 N	118.50 E
Jiangshe	106	31.34 N	120.08 E
Jiangshui	98	37.13 N	113.59 E
Jiangsu □[4]	90	33.00 N	120.00 E
Jiangtian	100	25.52 N	119.34 E
Jiangtun, Zhg.	102	23.41 N	112.37 E
Jiangtun, Zhg.	104	41.37 N	122.22 E
Jiangwakou	105	39.31 N	117.42 E
Jiangwan, Zhg.	100	29.25 N	118.02 E
Jiangwan, Zhg.	106	31.18 N	121.29 E
Jiangxi □[4]	100	28.00 N	116.00 E
Jiangxiacun	106	31.44 N	121.50 E
Jiangxiang	100	32.16 N	117.37 E
Jiangxikou	100	27.36 N	118.23 E
Jiangxizhai	102	22.51 N	101.50 E
Jiangya	102	29.17 N	110.39 E
Jiangyan	100	32.31 N	120.09 E
Jiangyi	100	29.12 N	115.46 E
Jiangyin	106	31.55 N	120.16 E
Jiangying	100	33.27 N	119.40 E
Jiangyou	102	31.53 N	104.51 E
Jiangyu, Zhg.	98	36.16 N	118.40 E
Jiangyu, Zhg.	100	27.50 N	112.46 E
Jiangyuanzhen	107	30.35 N	103.48 E
Jiangzaogang	106	32.01 N	121.03 E
Jiangzhasiji	120	30.28 N	88.55 E
Jiangzhong	120	29.10 N	93.32 E
Jiangzi	120	28.57 N	89.35 E
Jianhe	102	26.27 N	108.33 E
Jianhe ≃	104	40.59 N	121.51 E
Jianhezhuang	105	39.14 N	118.03 E
Jianhu	100	33.28 N	119.50 E
Jiankou	102	29.38 N	110.20 E
Jianli	100	29.49 N	112.53 E
Jianlingdian	100	32.45 N	113.12 E
Jianning	100	26.50 N	116.49 E
Jianou	100	27.03 N	118.19 E
Jianping	98	41.24 N	119.37 E
Jianqiao, Zhg.	98	37.57 N	116.16 E
Jianqiao, Zhg.	106	30.20 N	120.12 E
Jianqigou	104	40.54 N	123.17 E
Jianshan, Zhg.	100	29.14 N	120.44 E
Jianshan, Zhg.	100	29.58 N	120.16 E
Jianshi	102	30.36 N	109.38 E
Jianshui	102	23.38 N	102.49 E
Jiantiao	100	29.04 N	121.36 E
Jiantou, Zhg.	98	34.35 N	117.34 E
Jiantou, Zhg.	105	39.26 N	115.41 E
Jianwei	107	29.12 N	103.57 E
Jianxi ≃	100	26.38 N	118.12 E
Jianyang, Zhg.	100	27.22 N	118.04 E
Jianyang, Zhg.	107	30.24 N	104.32 E
Jianzha	102	35.59 N	102.02 E
Jiaocheng	102	37.33 N	112.02 E
Jiaodao	105	39.39 N	116.06 E
Jiaodianzi	104	41.32 N	121.49 E
Jiaodonggou	104	40.50 N	123.58 E
Jiaohe	89	43.42 N	127.19 E
Jiaojiapuzi	104	40.47 N	123.48 E
Jiaolianhe ≃	89	43.43 N	123.05 E
Jiaoling	100	24.41 N	116.10 E
Jiaonan	98	35.51 N	119.59 E
Jiaoshan ▮	106	31.21 N	120.06 E
Jiaoshanhe	100	29.38 N	112.33 E
Jiaotinghu Xuhongqu ⊜[1]	100	32.45 N	114.39 E
Jiaowei	100	24.32 N	117.54 E
Jiaoxi	106	31.49 N	120.10 E
Jiaoxian	98	36.18 N	119.58 E
Jiaoyang	100	27.56 N	119.16 E
Jiaozhuang	100	33.14 N	114.02 E
Jiaozuo	102	35.15 N	113.18 E
Jiapu	106	31.06 N	119.56 E
Jiashan, Zhg.	100	32.47 N	118.00 E
Jiashan, Zhg.	106	30.51 N	120.54 E
Jiashi	85	39.28 N	76.45 E
Jiashunhu ⊜	120	34.35 N	86.05 E
Jiasiqiao	107	29.07 N	106.26 E
Jiatan	107	30.12 N	106.29 E
Jiatanchang	107	29.09 N	106.16 E
Jiawang	98	34.27 N	117.27 E
Jiaxian, Zhg.	100	34.00 N	113.12 E
Jiaxian, Zhg.	102	38.01 N	110.31 E
Jiaxing	106	30.46 N	120.45 E
Jiayin	89	48.53 N	130.24 E
Jiayu	100	29.58 N	113.55 E
Jiayunhu ⊜	120	35.02 N	85.40 E
Jiaze	106	31.42 N	119.47 E
Jiazhai	98	34.33 N	115.48 E
Jiazhuang	105	39.19 N	117.22 E
Jiazi	100	22.55 N	116.04 E
Jiazier, Zhg.	85	38.40 N	76.33 E
Jiazier, Zhg.	120	38.55 N	76.09 E
Jiaziwan C	100	22.52 N	116.05 E
Jibacoa ≃	240p	20.15 N	77.12 W
Jibaganleh	144	8.05 N	48.37 E
Jibalei	144	10.10 N	50.54 E
Jibannagar	126	23.25 N	88.50 E
Jíbaro, Arroyo ≃	286b	23.03 N	82.23 W
Jibat ∧	144	8.45 N	37.29 E
Jibiya	150	13.05 N	7.12 E
Jiboa ≃	236	13.22 N	89.04 W
Jibóia, Ilha da ▮	256	23.03 S	44.22 W
Jibuti → Djibouti	144	11.36 N	43.09 E
Jicarilla Indian Reservation ◆[4]	200	36.40 N	107.00 W
Jicarón, Isla ▮	246	7.16 N	81.47 W
Jicatuyo ≃	236	14.43 N	88.39 W
Jicheng	105	39.23 N	116.17 E
Jičín	30	50.26 N	15.21 E
Jicotea ≃	286b	23.01 N	82.14 W
Jidād	140	11.05 N	24.44 E
Jiddah	144	21.30 N	39.12 E
Jidingxilin	120	32.52 N	92.21 E
Jidy, Wādī al- ∨	142	30.13 N	32.46 E
Jiebu	100	28.15 N	115.02 E
Jiedihe ≃	98	38.36 N	117.33 E
Jiedong	100	26.02 N	113.00 E
Jiegou	100	33.21 N	117.55 E
Jiehe	98	35.16 N	117.04 E
Jiejiang	106	31.58 N	120.43 E
Jiejinkou	89	47.57 N	132.50 E
Jielingkou	98	40.09 N	119.15 E
Jielongchang	107	29.13 N	106.32 E
Jielongqiao	107	30.25 N	104.45 E
Jiemian	100	25.56 N	118.02 E
Jiepai, Zhg.	100	32.15 N	117.50 E
Jiepai, Zhg.	100	29.34 N	115.06 E
Jiepai, Zhg.	100	26.41 N	112.46 E
Jiepai, Zhg.	106	30.55 N	119.32 E
Jiepai, Zhg.	107	29.28 N	104.43 E
Jierjialang	89	43.06 N	122.54 E
Jiesheng	100	22.45 N	115.25 E
Jieshi	100	22.51 N	115.49 E
Jieshichang	107	29.27 N	105.17 E
Jieshiwan C	100	22.46 N	115.40 E
Jieshou, Zhg.	100	33.00 N	119.27 E
Jieshou, Zhg.	100	27.22 N	117.40 E
Jieshou, Zhg.	100	33.18 N	115.20 E
Jieshui	100	27.46 N	114.49 E
Jietou	100	33.33 N	118.24 E
Jiexiu	102	37.05 N	111.51 E
Jieyang	100	23.35 N	116.21 E

Name	Page	Lat.	Long.
Jiezhongdian	100	32.41 N	112.29 E
Jieznas	76	54.36 N	24.10 E
Jifjāfah, Bi'r ⊤[4]	140	30.27 N	33.11 E
Jiftūn, Jazā'ir ▮▮	140	27.13 N	33.56 E
Jiggalong Creek ≃	162	22.53 S	120.14 E
Jiggalong Mission	162	23.25 S	120.47 E
Jighuiling	105	40.22 N	117.27 E
Jigley	144	4.26 N	45.23 E
Jigongying	102	26.18 N	104.48 E
Jigongzhen	98	34.02 N	115.32 E
Jiguaní	240p	20.22 N	76.26 W
Jiguanshan, Zhg.	98	40.32 N	123.55 E
Jiguanshan, Zhg.	104	41.18 N	123.36 E
Jiguanshan, Zhg.	104	42.08 N	124.15 E
Jigüey, Bahía de C	240p	22.08 N	78.05 W
Jihe	100	32.15 N	112.48 E
Jiheier	85	38.11 N	75.46 E
Jihlava	30	49.24 N	15.36 E
Jihlava ≃	61	48.55 N	16.37 E
Jihočeský Kraj □[4]	30	49.05 N	14.30 E
Jihomoravský Kraj □[4]	30	49.10 N	16.40 E
Jihyüeht'an	100	23.52 N	120.53 E
Jijia ≃	38	46.54 N	28.05 E
Jijiadian	98	35.32 N	119.05 E
Jijiamiao	107	29.18 N	104.06 E
Jijiapuzi	104	41.16 N	124.12 E
Jijiashi	106	32.08 N	120.18 E
Jijiaying	105	40.20 N	115.24 E
Jijiga	144	9.22 N	42.47 E
Jijona	34	38.32 N	0.30 W
Jike	102	31.00 N	99.41 E
Jikkoku-tōge)(	94	36.06 N	138.39 E
Jilalin	89	51.19 N	119.55 E
Jilantai	102	39.47 N	105.45 E
Jilantaiyanchi ⊜	102	39.43 N	105.41 E
Jilemutu	89	52.14 N	120.47 E
Jilib	144	0.28 N	42.50 E
Jilibulake	120	33.05 N	93.10 E
Jilin (Kirin)	89	43.51 N	126.33 E
Jilin □[4]	90	44.00 N	126.00 E
Jilintuo	102	30.58 N	109.05 E
Jilliby Creek ≃	170	33.16 S	151.24 E
Jiloca ≃	34	41.21 N	1.39 W
Jilong	120	28.29 N	85.20 E
Jilotepec de Abasolo	234	19.58 N	99.32 W
Jilotlán de los Dolores	234	19.14 N	102.59 W
Jílové	54	50.46 N	14.07 E
Jima	144	7.36 N	36.50 E
Jimbaran	115b	8.46 S	115.11 E
Jimbolia	38	45.47 N	20.43 E
Jimboomba	171a	27.50 S	153.02 E
Jimei	100	24.37 N	118.07 E
Jimena de la Frontera	34	36.26 N	5.27 W
Jiménez, Méx.	232	29.02 N	100.41 W
Jimenez, Pil.	116	8.20 N	123.50 E
Jiménez, Arroyo ≃	288	34.44 S	58.13 W
Jiménez, Laguna de ⊜	258	35.26 S	59.01 W
Jiménez del Teúl	234	23.10 N	104.05 W
Jimi ≃	164	5.20 S	144.20 E
Jimingcun	105	39.19 N	116.09 E
Jiminghe	100	30.36 N	115.32 E
Jim Ned Creek ≃	196	31.50 N	99.07 W
Jimo	98	36.23 N	120.27 E
Jim Thorpe	210	40.52 N	75.45 W
Jimuganayaji	85	38.36 N	75.39 E
Jimunai	86	47.32 N	85.38 E
Jimusaer	86	44.00 N	89.04 E
Jināḥ	140	25.20 N	30.31 E
Jinan (Tsinan), Zhg.	98	36.40 N	116.57 E
Jin'an, Zhg.	100	28.38 N	119.18 E
Jinbang	100	25.01 N	118.01 E
Jinbaoshan ∧	102	34.09 N	111.29 E
Jinbohe ≃	107	28.54 N	103.40 E
Jincang	89	43.20 N	130.30 E
Jince	60	49.47 N	13.59 E
Jinchanggouliang	98	41.56 N	120.19 E
Jincheng, Zhg.	102	35.30 N	112.50 E
Jincheng, Zhg.	102	26.43 N	111.00 E
Jinchengshan ∧	107	30.47 N	106.32 E
Jinchuan	102	31.25 N	102.08 E
Jinchuanqiao	102	27.18 N	101.48 E
Jīnd	123	29.19 N	76.19 E
Jindabyne	171b	36.25 S	148.38 E
Jindabyne, Lake ⊜[1]	171b	36.22 S	148.37 E
Jindaichang	107	29.43 N	104.49 E
Jindālī, Bi'r ⊤[4]	142	29.55 N	31.40 E
Jindřichovice	54	50.15 N	12.37 E
Jindřichův Hradec	30	49.09 N	15.00 E
Jinfeng	100	26.01 N	119.36 E
Jinfosi	102	39.29 N	99.00 E
Jing'an	100	28.52 N	115.20 E
Jin'gangpo	107	29.38 N	106.25 E
Jingangtou	100	27.54 N	113.40 E
Jin'gangtuo	107	29.10 N	106.07 E
Jing'anji	98	34.30 N	116.55 E
Jingbian	102	37.25 N	108.21 E
Jingbohu ≃	89	43.54 N	128.54 E
Jingcheng	100	24.36 N	117.30 E
Jingde	100	30.19 N	118.31 E
Jingdezhen (Kingtechen)	100	29.16 N	117.11 E
Jingdong	102	24.28 N	100.52 E
Jingellic	171b	35.56 S	147.42 E
Jingeryu	105	39.43 N	115.36 E
Jinggang	100	28.28 N	112.46 E
Jinggangshan	100	26.36 N	114.05 E
Jinggangshan-guanliju	100	26.45 N	114.06 E
Jinggongqiao	100	29.45 N	117.11 E
Jinggu	102	23.32 N	100.41 E
Jingguan	107	29.55 N	106.33 E
Jinghai, Zhg.	100	23.03 N	116.31 E
Jinghai, Zhg.	105	38.56 N	116.55 E
Jinghaigang C	100	23.01 N	116.34 E
Jinghaiwei	98	36.52 N	122.13 E
Jinghe	86	44.39 N	82.50 E
Jinghe ≃, Zhg.	102	34.28 N	109.00 E
Jinghe ≃, Zhg.	107	29.09 N	104.57 E
Jinghong	102	22.01 N	100.49 E
Jingjiang	106	32.01 N	120.15 E
Jingjiangjie	102	26.19 N	100.33 E
Jingjiayu	104	41.40 N	123.51 E
Jingjing	100	28.31 N	113.25 E
Jingkou	106	31.47 N	120.33 E
Jinglou	100	32.39 N	112.56 E
Jingmen	102	31.00 N	112.09 E
Jingning, Zhg.	100	27.59 N	119.38 E
Jingning, Zhg.	102	35.25 N	105.56 E
Jin'gou	104	41.38 N	120.35 E
Jin'goutun	98	41.03 N	117.27 E
Jingshan	100	31.02 N	113.05 E
Jingshan ⩘	102	31.45 N	111.22 E
Jingshanshi	106	30.43 N	120.03 E
Jingtai	102	37.17 N	104.09 E
Jingu	100	25.13 N	118.07 E
Jingxi	102	23.08 N	106.29 E
Jingxian, Zhg.	98	37.42 N	116.16 E
Jingxian, Zhg.	100	30.42 N	118.24 E
Jingxian, Zhg.	102	26.40 N	109.25 E
Jingxin	100	24.14 N	115.56 E
Jingxing, Zhg.	89	47.04 N	123.01 E
Jingxing, Zhg.	98	38.02 N	114.01 E
Jingyan	107	29.40 N	104.04 E
Jingyu	98	42.22 N	126.50 E
Jingyuan, Zhg.	102	36.38 N	104.37 E
Jingyuan, Zhg.	102	35.30 N	106.48 E
Jingzhi	98	36.19 N	119.23 E
Jingzichang	107	29.00 N	104.41 E
Jinhae → Chinhae	98	35.09 N	128.40 E
Jinhe	89	51.33 N	121.55 E
Jinhua	100	29.07 N	119.39 E
Jinhuajiang ≃	100	29.06 N	119.39 E
Jinhui	106	30.59 N	121.29 E
Jinín	60	49.13 N	13.58 E
Jining, Zhg.	98	35.25 N	116.36 E
Jining, Zhg.	102	41.06 N	112.58 E
Jinja	154	0.26 N	33.12 E

≃ River	Fluss	Río	Rivière	Rio
⊼ Canal	Kanal	Canal	Canal	Canal
⌊ Waterfall, Rapids	Wasserfall, Stromschnellen	Cascada, Rápidos	Chute d'eau, Rapides	Cascata, Rápidos
⊔ Strait	Meeresstrasse	Estrecho	Détroit	Estreito
C Bay, Gulf	Bucht, Golf	Bahía, Golfo	Baie, Golfe	Baía, Golfo
⊜ Lake, Lakes	See, Seen	Lago, Lagos	Lac, Lacs	Lago, Lagos
☷ Swamp	Sumpf	Pantano	Marais	Pântano
⊠ Ice Features, Glacier	Eis- und Gletscherformen	Accidentes Glaciales	Formes glaciaires	Acidentes Glaciares
⊤ Other Hydrographic Features	Andere Hydrographische Objekte	Otros Elementos Hidrográficos	Autres données hydrographiques	Outros Elementos Hidrográficos

✣ Submarine Features	Untermeerische Objekte	Accidentes Submarinos	Formes de relief sous-marin	Acidentes Submarinos
□ Political Unit	Politische Einheit	Unidad Política	Entité politique	Unidade Política
ʊ Cultural Institution	Kulturelle Institution	Institución Cultural	Institution culturelle	Instituição Cultural
⊥ Historical Site	Historische Stätte	Sitio Histórico	Site historique	Sitio Histórico
♠ Recreational Site	Erholungs- und Ferienort	Sitio de Recreo	Centre de loisirs	Sítio de Lazer
⊠ Airport	Flughafen	Aeropuerto	Aéroport	Aeroporto
■ Military Installation	Militäranlage	Instalación Militar	Installation militaire	Instalação Militar
◆ Miscellaneous	Verschiedenes	Misceláneo	Divers	Miscelânea

Jinjero 144 4.40 N 36.29 E
Jinjiadian 98 41.39 N 118.18 E
Jinjiang (Qingyang) 100 24.50 N 118.35 E
Jinjiang ≃, Zhg. 100 24.54 N 118.35 E
Jinjiang ≃, Zhg. 100 24.48 N 113.35 E
Jinjiang ≃, Zhg. 100 28.24 N 115.49 E
Jinjiangjie 110 26.19 N 100.33 E
Jinjiangzhen (Dengjiabu) 100 28.11 N 116.47 E
Jinjiawopeng 104 41.38 N 122.16 E
Jinjiawopu 104 42.32 N 122.10 E
Jinjiazhen 89 42.49 N 123.40 E
Jinjing 100 24.37 N 118.36 E
Jinjini 150 7.26 N 2.39 W
Jinju → Chinju 98 35.11 N 128.05 E
Jinkeng 100 27.15 N 117.14 E
Jinkichi-mori ∧ 96 33.41 N 134.07 E
Jinkou, Zhg. 98 36.35 N 120.46 E
Jinkou, Zhg. 100 29.18 N 115.15 E
Jinkou, Zhg. 100 30.22 N 114.10 E
Jinkuang 102 28.20 N 101.54 E
Jinlijing 107 29.48 N 104.45 E
Jinlingsi 104 41.42 N 120.49 E
Jinlingyu 105 40.06 N 117.32 E
Jinlonggou 89 51.45 N 125.51 E
Jinning (Jiukunyang) 102 24.41 N 102.35 E
Jinniu, Zhg. 100 31.24 N 117.12 E
Jinniu, Zhg. 100 29.59 N 114.38 E
Jinotega 236 13.06 N 86.00 W
Jinotega □[5] 236 14.00 N 85.25 W
Jinotepe 236 11.51 N 86.12 W
Jinping, Zhg. 102 22.50 N 103.10 E
Jinping, Zhg. 102 26.38 N 109.03 E
Jinpingchang 107 28.54 N 104.43 E
Jinpo 105 39.18 N 115.15 E
Jinqiao 100 31.46 N 116.50 E
Jinrui 100 27.57 N 114.12 E
Jinseki 96 34.48 N 133.11 E
Jinsen → Inch'ŏn 98 37.28 N 126.38 E
Jinsha, Zhg. 100 26.12 N 118.39 E
Jinsha, Zhg. 102 27.18 N 106.10 E
Jinsha, Zhg. 106 32.06 N 121.05 E
Jinshajiang ≃ 102 28.50 N 104.36 E
Jinshan, Zhg. 89 51.51 N 126.30 E
Jinshan, Zhg. 106 30.54 N 121.09 E
Jinshanwei 106 30.44 N 121.19 E
Jinshanxiang 107 30.35 N 104.52 E
Jinshanzui 106 30.44 N 121.22 E
Jinshi 102 29.33 N 111.50 E
Jinshijing 107 29.23 N 104.08 E
Jinshui ≃ 100 32.05 N 112.25 E
Jinshuzhen 106 31.23 N 120.24 E
Jinsiniangqiao 106 30.43 N 121.15 E
Jinsuozhen 100 33.39 N 118.17 E
Jinta 102 40.03 N 98.53 E
Jintan 106 31.45 N 119.34 E
Jintang, Zhg. 102 30.54 N 104.19 E
Jintang, Zhg. 102 30.19 N 102.19 E
Jintian 100 27.10 N 114.27 E
Jintotolo Channel U 116 11.48 N 123.05 E
Jintotolo Island I 116 11.51 N 123.08 E
Jinxi, Zhg. 100 27.54 N 116.43 E
Jinxi, Zhg. 104 40.45 N 120.50 E
Jinxi ≃ 100 26.51 N 117.46 E
Jinxian, Zhg. 98 38.02 N 115.02 E
Jinxian, Zhg. 98 39.04 N 121.40 E
Jinxian, Zhg. 100 29.40 N 119.01 E
Jinxian, Zhg. 100 28.22 N 116.14 E
Jinxian, Zhg. 104 41.11 N 121.22 E
Jinxiang 98 35.05 N 116.18 E
Jinxianyan ∧ 100 26.55 N 118.38 E
Jinya ⊥ 94 36.06 N 137.15 E
Jinyun 100 28.40 N 120.03 E
Jinz, Qā' al- ≚ 132 30.45 N 36.04 E
Jinze 106 31.02 N 120.56 E
Jinzhai 100 31.44 N 115.54 E
Jinzhaizhen 100 31.32 N 115.46 E
Jinzhenwei 100 27.26 N 120.35 E
Jinzhonghe ≃ 105 39.08 N 117.42 E
Jinzhou (Chinchou) 104 41.07 N 121.08 E
Jinzisi 107 29.09 N 106.22 E
Jinzū ≃ 92 36.46 N 137.13 E
Jiō 270 34.58 N 133.28 E
Jiparaná ≃ 248 8.03 S 62.52 W
Jipengqundao II 100 21.52 N 114.00 E
Jipijapa 246 1.20 S 80.35 W
Jipioca, Ilha I 250 1.53 N 50.12 W
Jiquilisco 236 13.19 N 88.35 W
Jiquilisco, Bahía de C 236 13.10 N 88.28 W
Jiquilpan de Juárez 234 19.59 N 102.43 W
Jiquipilas 234 16.40 N 93.39 W
Jiquipilco 234 19.32 N 99.36 W
Jiquiriçá 255 13.14 S 39.36 W
Jiquiriçá ≃ 255 13.12 S 38.57 W
Jirāfī, Wādī al- (Naḥal Paran) V 132 30.24 N 35.10 E
Jirbān 140 11.03 N 30.36 E
Jire 144 5.22 N 48.05 E
Jiřetín 54 50.50 N 14.35 E
Jiřikov 54 50.59 N 13.35 E
Jirjā 140 26.20 N 31.53 E
Jirkov 54 50.30 N 13.27 E
Jīsh (Gush Ḥalav) 132 33.02 N 35.27 E
Jishou 102 28.17 N 109.29 E
Jishui 100 27.14 N 115.06 E
Jishuiji 100 33.46 N 115.24 E
Jisr ash-Shughūr 130 35.48 N 36.19 E
Jitai 86 44.01 N 89.28 E
Jitan 100 24.59 N 115.44 E
Jitarning 162 32.48 S 117.59 E
Jitaúna 255 14.01 S 39.57 W
Jitianpu 107 30.19 N 104.01 E
Jitotol 234 17.02 N 92.52 W
Jitra 114 6.16 N 100.25 E
Jituo 120 34.15 N 82.05 E
Jiu ≃ 38 43.47 N 23.48 E
Jiuanji 106 30.43 N 119.41 E
Jiuantu 98 42.32 N 128.18 E
Jiubao 100 25.57 N 115.48 E
Jiubingtai 104 41.39 N 124.07 E
Jiuchangshan 98 36.54 N 117.50 E
Jiucheng, Zhg. 98 37.13 N 116.02 E
Jiucheng, Zhg. 105 39.23 N 116.44 E
Jiuchengzhen 98 38.12 N 117.18 E
Jiuchuchang 107 29.55 N 104.38 E
Jiudaoliang 102 31.35 N 110.12 E
Jiudhara 126 22.24 N 89.44 E
Jiudian 106 32.10 N 120.57 E
Jiudongle 102 38.49 N 101.05 E
Jiudu 106 30.31 N 119.53 E
Jiufeng, Zhg. 100 24.20 N 117.02 E
Jiufeng, Zhg. 100 25.33 N 119.08 E
Jiugang, Zhg. 105 39.03 N 116.12 E
Jiugang, Zhg. 105 39.49 N 116.27 E
Jiuganyu 98 34.54 N 119.07 E
Jiugongan 102 29.52 N 112.00 E
Jiugongkou 105 39.51 N 114.47 E
Jiugongshan ∧ 100 29.26 N 114.42 E
Jiuguan, Zhg. 98 37.26 N 121.53 E
Jiuguan, Zhg. 106 30.51 N 120.16 E
Jiuguantao 98 36.40 N 115.25 E
Jiuhe 100 23.32 N 115.04 E
Jiuhongshui 102 37.14 N 103.57 E
Jiuhuaian 98 40.24 N 114.31 E
Jiuhuanghekou ≃[1] 98 38.15 N 118.05 E
Jiuhuashan 100 30.25 N 117.51 E
Jiuhuaxian 100 23.30 N 113.16 E
Jiuhuinan 98 42.37 N 126.14 E
Jiujiang, Zhg. 100 22.51 N 113.02 E
Jiujiang, Zhg. 100 29.44 N 115.59 E
Jiujiawopeng 104 40.59 N 121.22 E
Jiujiji 98 35.09 N 114.48 E
Jiujing 107 29.05 N 103.54 E
Jiukou 100 30.52 N 112.38 E
Jiulianshan ∧∧ 100 24.40 N 114.46 E
Jiuliguan 100 31.50 N 114.14 E
Jiulingshan ∧∧ 100 28.46 N 114.45 E
Jiulong → Kowloon, H.K. 271d 22.18 N 114.10 E
Jiulong, Zhg. 100 24.08 N 112.55 E
Jiulong, Zhg. 102 29.00 N 101.50 E
Jiulong, Zhg. 106 31.54 N 121.34 E
Jiulongchang 107 29.32 N 106.05 E
Jiulonggang 100 32.38 N 117.03 E
Jiulongpo 107 29.29 N 106.32 E
Jiulongxi ≃ 100 25.59 N 117.18 E
Jiumangya 120 37.40 N 91.50 E
Jiumen 98 40.42 N 120.27 E
Jiumianyang 100 30.16 N 113.13 E
Jiumu 100 28.11 N 118.27 E
Jiuninghe 105 39.28 N 117.46 E
Jiuningyang 100 25.38 N 117.21 E
Jiupeixian 98 34.28 N 117.59 E
Jiupengxi ≃ 100 25.00 N 117.32 E
Jiupingnan 100 27.01 N 119.03 E
Jiupu 105 40.21 N 115.18 E
Jiuqidong 98 37.03 N 117.36 E
Jiuqingcheng 98 37.12 N 117.40 E
Jiuquan (Suzhou) 102 39.45 N 98.34 E
Jiurongcheng 98 37.21 N 122.32 E
Jiushangshui 100 33.32 N 114.32 E
Jiushenqiu 100 33.11 N 115.08 E
Jiusiyang 100 33.41 N 118.39 E
Jiusongyu 105 40.27 N 116.58 E
Jiutai 89 44.08 N 125.50 E
Jiutaozhou 102 34.45 N 103.14 E
Jiuwuqing 105 39.31 N 116.52 E
Jiuxian, Zhg. 100 33.32 N 113.17 E
Jiuxian, Zhg. 100 33.15 N 115.35 E
Jiuxian, Zhg. 100 25.54 N 113.22 E
Jiuxian, Zhg. 100 25.14 N 116.31 E
Jiuxian, Zhg. 100 31.11 N 118.04 E
Jiuxian, Zhg. 105 40.14 N 116.10 E
Jiuxian, Zhg. 107 30.27 N 103.51 E
Jiuxianchang 107 29.51 N 106.13 E
Jiuxiangcheng 100 33.13 N 114.49 E
Jiuxianxiang 107 30.19 N 106.46 E
Jiuxianzhen 98 37.53 N 117.06 E
Jiuyaoshan 98 37.23 N 114.41 E
Jiuyingkou 105 39.42 N 114.44 E
Jiuyingzi 104 42.03 N 121.38 E
Jiuyuanqu 102 35.09 N 111.51 E
Jiuyunjie 86 44.12 N 88.05 E
Jiuyutai 98 34.59 N 116.29 E
Jiuzhan 89 43.57 N 126.29 E
Jiuzhen, Zhg. 98 37.06 N 117.57 E
Jiuzhen, Zhg. 100 24.05 N 117.42 E
Jiuzhi (Zhiqingsongduo) 102 33.57 N 100.52 E
Jiuzhou 105 39.30 N 116.33 E
Jiuzhuangwo 105 40.11 N 115.36 E
Jiwangtun 104 41.02 N 122.58 E
Jīwani 128 25.03 N 61.45 E
Jiwuer 89 50.32 N 123.15 E
Jixi, Zhg. 89 45.17 N 130.59 E
Jixi, Zhg. 100 30.06 N 118.35 E
Jixian, Zhg. 98 35.26 N 114.05 E
Jixian, Zhg. 98 37.36 N 115.31 E
Jixian, Zhg. 105 40.03 N 117.24 E
Jixiangsi 107 30.39 N 105.32 E
Jixiashi 100 28.22 N 118.44 E
Jixingji 100 32.55 N 116.46 E
Jiyang, Zhg. 98 36.59 N 117.11 E
Jiyang, Zhg. 100 27.10 N 118.07 E
Jiyang, Zhg. 105 39.38 N 115.59 E
Jiyizhen 102 35.55 N 110.15 E
Jiyuan 102 35.08 N 112.35 E
Jiyuyang @ 106 30.56 N 120.25 E
Jiz', Wādī V 144 16.19 N 52.00 E
Jīzah, Tur'at al- ≡ 273c 29.50 N 31.16 E
Jizayy 142 30.28 N 30.51 E
Jizera ≃ 54 50.10 N 14.43 E
Jizhuang 100 34.25 N 116.34 E
Jizl, Wādī al- V 128 25.38 N 38.21 E
Jizō-dake ∧ 94 36.36 N 139.28 E
Jizō-zaki ≻ 96 35.34 N 133.20 E
Joaçaba 252 27.10 S 51.30 W
Joachimsthal → Jáchymov, Česko. 54 50.20 N 12.55 E
Joachimsthal, D.D.R. 54 52.58 N 13.44 E
Joaíma 255 16.39 S 41.02 W
Joal 150 14.10 N 16.51 W
Joana Coeli 250 1.58 S 49.23 W
Joana Peres 250 3.18 S 49.42 W
Joanes 250 0.51 S 48.31 W
Joanésia 255 19.12 S 42.40 W
Joanicó 258 34.36 S 56.15 W
Joanna 192 34.25 N 81.49 W
Joanópolis 256 22.56 S 46.17 W
João Alfredo 250 7.52 S 35.35 W
João Belo 156 25.02 S 33.34 E
João Câmara 250 5.32 S 35.48 W
João de Tiba ≃ 255 16.16 S 39.01 W
João Mendes ≃ 287a 22.57 S 43.03 W
João Neiva 255 19.45 S 40.24 W
João Pessoa 250 7.07 S 34.52 W
João Pinheiro 255 17.45 S 46.10 W
Joaquim Távora 255 23.30 S 49.58 W
Joaquin 194 31.58 N 94.03 W
Joaquín Gorina ◆[8] 258 34.54 S 58.02 W
Joaquin Miller Park ♠ 282 37.49 N 122.11 W
Joaquín Suárez 258 34.44 S 56.02 W
Joaquín V. González 252 25.05 S 64.11 W
Job 62 45.37 N 3.45 E
Jobabo 240p 20.54 N 77.17 W
Jobat 120 22.25 N 74.34 E
Jobo Point ≻ 116 8.42 N 126.15 E
Jobos 240m 17.58 N 66.10 W
Jobos, Bahía de C 240m 17.56 N 66.13 W
Job Peak ∧ 204 39.35 N 118.14 W
Jobstown 285 40.02 N 74.42 W
Jochberg 64 47.23 N 12.24 E
Jock ≃ 212 45.16 N 75.43 W
Jocketa 54 50.33 N 12.10 E
Jocko ≃ 202 47.20 N 114.17 W
Jocolí 252 32.35 S 68.41 W
Jo Co Marsh ≡ 276 40.37 N 73.47 W
Jocón 236 15.17 N 86.58 W
Jocoro 236 13.37 N 88.01 W
Jocotán 236 14.49 N 89.23 W
Jocotepec 234 20.18 N 103.26 W
Jocotitlán 234 19.42 N 99.48 W
Jocuixtita 232 24.15 N 106.16 W
Jódar 34 37.50 N 3.21 W
Jodhpur 120 26.17 N 73.02 E
Jodiya 120 22.42 N 70.18 E
Jodoigne 56 50.43 N 4.52 E
Jodrell Bank Radio Telescope ɤ[3] 262 53.14 N 2.18 W
Joe ≃ 220 25.17 N 81.05 W
Joe Batt's Arm 186 49.44 N 54.10 W
Joel 158 28.42 S 28.21 E
Joensuu 26 62.36 N 29.46 E
Joes Hill ∧[2] 174o 1.48 N 157.19 W
Jœuf 56 49.14 N 6.01 E
Jofane 156 21.17 S 34.16 E
Joffre, Mount ∧ 182 50.32 N 115.13 W
Jōganji ≃ 94 36.46 N 137.18 E
Jōga-shima I 94 35.08 N 139.37 E
Jōgawara 268 35.42 N 139.22 E
Jōge 96 34.42 N 133.07 E
Jogeshvari ◆[8] 272c 19.08 N 72.51 E
Jogeshvari Cave •[5] 272c 19.08 N 72.51 E
Jõgeva 76 58.45 N 26.24 E
Jog Falls L 122 14.13 N 74.45 E
Joggins 186 45.42 N 64.27 W
Joghatāy 128 36.36 N 57.01 E
Jogindarnagar 123 31.59 N 76.46 E
Jōhana 94 36.31 N 136.57 E
Johannesburg, S. Afr. 158 273d 26.15 S 28.00 E
Johannesburg, Calif., U.S. 228 35.22 N 117.38 W
Johannesburg (Jan Smuts) Airport ⊠ 273d 26.08 S 28.14 E
Johanngeorgenstadt 54 50.26 N 12.43 E
Johannisburg → Pisz 30 53.38 N 21.49 E
Johanniskreuz 56 49.20 N 7.49 E
Johannisthal ◆[8] 264a 52.26 N 13.30 E
Johar 144 2.48 N 45.33 E
Jōhen 92 32.57 N 132.35 E
Johi 120 26.41 N 67.37 E
Johilla ≃ 124 23.37 N 81.14 E
John ≃ 180 66.55 N 151.35 W
John Boyd Thacher State Park ♠ 210 42.38 N 74.01 W
John Carroll University ɤ[2] 279a 41.29 N 81.32 W
John Day 202 44.25 N 118.57 W
John Day ≃ 202 45.44 N 120.39 W
John Day, Middle Fork ≃ 202 44.55 N 119.18 W
John Day, North Fork ≃ 202 44.45 N 119.38 W
John Day, South Fork ≃ 202 44.28 N 119.31 W
John Day Dam ◆[6] 224 45.43 N 120.41 W
John Day Fossil Beds National Monument ♠ 202 44.34 N 119.39 W
Johney Creek ≃ 196 28.27 N 98.54 W
John Fitzgerald Kennedy International Airport ⊠ 210 40.38 N 73.47 W
John Fitzgerald Kennedy Space Center ɤ[3] 220 28.40 N 80.40 W
John Fitzgerald Kennedy Stadium ♠ 285 39.54 N 75.10 W
John Forrest National Park ♠ 168a 31.53 S 116.06 E
John Hancock Center ɤ 278 41.55 N 87.37 W
John J. Duffy Preserve ♠ 278 41.39 N 87.55 W
John Martin Reservoir @[1] 198 38.05 N 103.02 W
John McLaren Park ♠ 282 37.43 N 122.25 W
John Muir National Historical Site ⊥ 282 37.59 N 122.08 W
Johnny Run ≃ 216 41.17 N 88.21 W
John O'groats 46 58.38 N 3.05 W
John Pennekamp Coral Reef State Park ♠ 220 25.11 N 80.15 W
John Redmond Reservoir @[1] 198 38.18 N 95.55 W
Johns ≃ 224 46.54 N 124.01 W
Johns Creek ≃ 192 37.30 N 80.06 W
Johnshaven 46 56.47 N 2.20 W
Johns Hopkins University ɤ[2] 284b 39.20 N 76.37 W
Johnson, Kans., U.S. 198 37.34 N 101.45 W
Johnson, Nebr., U.S. 198 40.24 N 96.01 W
Johnson, N.Y., U.S. 210 41.22 N 74.30 W
Johnson, Vt., U.S. 188 44.38 N 72.41 W
Johnson □[6], Ind., U.S. 218 39.29 N 86.03 W
Johnson □[6], Tex., U.S. 222 32.20 N 97.20 W
Johnson, Mount ∧ 226 36.37 N 121.19 W
Johnson Bay C 208 38.03 N 75.20 W
Johnsonburg, N.J., U.S. 210 40.58 N 74.53 W
Johnsonburg, N.Y., U.S. 210 42.44 N 78.18 W
Johnsonburg, Pa., U.S. 214 41.29 N 78.41 W
Johnson City, N.Y., U.S. 210 42.07 N 75.57 W
Johnson City, Tenn., U.S. 192 36.19 N 82.21 W
Johnson City, Tex., U.S. 196 30.17 N 98.25 W
Johnson Creek, N.Y., U.S. 210 43.15 N 78.31 W
Johnson Creek, Wis., U.S. 216 43.05 N 88.47 W
Johnson Creek ≃, Idaho, U.S. 202 44.58 N 115.30 W
Johnson Creek ≃, Ky., U.S. 218 38.27 N 84.04 W
Johnson Creek ≃, N.Y., U.S. 210 43.22 N 78.16 W
Johnson Creek ≃, Tex., U.S. 222 32.02 N 94.59 W
Johnson Creek ≃, Wash., U.S. 224 46.35 N 121.42 W
Johnsondale 204 35.58 N 118.32 W
Johnson Drain ≡ 281 42.26 N 83.28 W
Johnson Draw V, Tex., U.S. 196 30.08 N 101.07 W
Johnson Draw V, Tex., U.S. 196 31.58 N 101.41 W
Johnson Hall ⊥ 210 43.01 N 74.23 W
Johnson Park ♠ 276 40.30 N 74.27 W
Johnson Point ≻ 241h 13.07 N 61.12 W
Johnsons Crossing 180 60.29 N 133.16 W
Johnsons Point ≻ 240c 17.02 N 61.53 W
Johnsons Pond @ 283 42.44 N 71.03 W
Johnsons Station 222 32.42 N 97.08 W
Johnsonville, N.Z. 172 41.14 S 174.47 E
Johnsonville, N.Y., U.S. 210 42.55 N 73.31 W
Johnsonville, S.C., U.S. 192 33.49 N 79.27 W
Johnston, Wales, U.K. 42 51.46 N 5.00 W
Johnston, Iowa, U.S. 190 41.40 N 93.42 W
Johnston, R.I., U.S. 207 41.50 N 71.30 W
Johnston, S.C., U.S. 192 33.50 N 81.48 W
Johnston, Lake @ 162 32.25 S 120.30 E
Johnston City 194 37.49 N 88.56 W
Johnstone 46 55.50 N 4.31 W
Johnstone Peak ∧ 280 34.10 N 117.48 W
Johnstone Strait U 182 50.25 N 126.00 W
Johnston Falls L 154 10.35 S 28.40 E
Johnston Island I 14 17.00 N 168.30 W
Johnstown, Colo., U.S. 200 40.20 N 104.54 W
Johnstown, N.Y., U.S. 210 43.00 N 74.22 W
Johnstown, Ohio, U.S. 214 40.09 N 82.41 W
Johnstown, Pa., U.S. 214 40.20 N 78.55 W
Johnstown Center 216 42.42 N 88.50 W
Johnstown Flood National Memorial ⊥ 214 40.21 N 78.47 W
John Tyler Arboretum ♠ 285 39.56 N 75.26 W
Jōhoku 94 36.28 N 140.22 E
Johol 114 2.36 N 102.16 E
Johor □[3] 114 2.00 N 103.30 E
Johor ≃ 114 1.27 N 104.02 E
Johor, Selat U 271c 1.28 N 103.48 E
Johor Baharu 114 271c 1.28 N 103.45 E
Jöhstadt 54 50.30 N 13.05 E
Joice Island I 282 38.08 N 122.02 W
Joigny 50 47.59 N 3.24 E
Joiner 194 35.31 N 90.09 W
Joinerville 222 32.11 N 94.55 W
Joinvile 252 26.18 S 48.50 W
Joinville 58 48.27 N 5.08 E
Joinville, Lac @ 206 46.18 N 75.12 W
Joinville Island I 9 63.15 S 55.45 W
Joinville-le-Pont 261 48.49 N 2.28 E
Jojogan 115a 6.58 S 111.46 E
Jojutla 234 18.37 N 99.11 W
Joka 272b 22.27 N 88.18 E
Jokaj I 174r 6.59 N 158.11 E
Jokaj Passage U 174r 7.01 N 158.11 E
Jokau 140 8.24 N 33.49 E
Jokau ≃ 144 8.22 N 33.47 E
Jokela 26 60.44 N 25.02 E
Jokioinen 26 60.49 N 23.28 E
Jokkmokk 24 66.37 N 19.50 E
Jökulsá á Brú ≃ 24a 65.41 N 14.13 W
Jolārpettai 122 12.34 N 78.35 E
Jolfā 84 38.57 N 45.38 E
Joliet, Ill., U.S. 216 41.32 N 88.05 W
Joliet, Mont., U.S. 202 45.29 N 108.58 W
Joliett 208 40.37 N 76.27 W
Joliette 206 46.01 N 73.27 W
Joliette □[6] 206 46.25 N 74.00 W
Jolietville 218 40.03 N 86.15 W
Jöllenbeck 52 52.11 N 8.45 E
Jolly's Lookout National Park ♠ 171a 27.25 S 152.45 E
Jollyville 222 30.27 N 97.47 W
Jolo 116 6.03 N 121.00 E
Jolo Group II 116 6.00 N 121.09 E
Jolo Island I 116 5.58 N 121.06 E
Jølstravatnet @ 26 61.32 N 6.13 E
Jomalig Island I 116 14.42 N 122.22 E
Jombang 115a 7.33 S 112.14 E
Jombo ≃ 152 10.36 S 17.32 E
Jonacatepec 234 18.41 N 98.48 W
Jonah 222 30.38 N 97.32 W
Jönåker 40 58.44 N 16.40 E
Jonathan Dickinson State Park ♠ 220 27.01 N 80.08 W
Jonava 76 55.05 N 24.17 E
Jones, Pil. 116 16.33 N 121.42 E
Jones, Mich., U.S. 216 41.54 N 85.48 W
Jones, Okla., U.S. 196 35.34 N 97.17 W
Jones ≃ 283 42.00 N 70.42 W
Jones and Laughlin Steel Corporation ɤ[3], Pa., U.S. 279b 40.37 N 80.14 W
Jones and Laughlin Steel Corporation ɤ[3], Pa., U.S. 279b 40.26 N 79.58 W
Jones Beach State Park ♠ 210 40.35 N 73.31 W
Jonesboro, Ark., U.S. 194 35.50 N 90.42 W
Jonesboro, Ga., U.S. 192 33.32 N 84.21 W
Jonesboro, Ill., U.S. 194 37.27 N 89.16 W
Jonesboro, Ind., U.S. 216 40.29 N 85.38 W
Jonesboro, La., U.S. 194 32.15 N 92.43 W
Jonesboro, Maine, U.S. 188 44.40 N 67.35 W
Jonesboro, Tenn., U.S. 192 36.18 N 82.28 W
Jonesburg 219 38.51 N 91.18 W
Jones Creek 222 28.58 N 95.27 W
Jones Creek ≃, Ont., Can. 212 44.30 N 75.49 W
Jones Creek ≃, Tex., U.S. 222 29.08 N 96.03 W
Jones Falls ≃ 284b 39.18 N 76.37 W
Jones Falls, Moores Branch ≃ 284b 39.23 N 76.40 W
Jones Falls, North Branch ≃ 284b 39.25 N 76.42 W
Jones Falls, Slaughterhouse Branch ≃ 284b 39.24 N 76.40 W
Jones Inlet C 210 40.35 N 73.34 W
Jones Mill 194 34.27 N 92.50 W
Jones Mountains ∧∧ 9 73.32 S 94.00 W
Jonesport 188 44.32 N 67.36 W
Jones Sound U 176 76.00 N 85.00 W
Jonestown 194 34.14 N 90.28 W
Jonesville, Ind., U.S. 218 39.04 N 85.53 W
Jonesville, La., U.S. 194 31.38 N 91.49 W
Jonesville, Mich., U.S. 216 41.59 N 84.40 W
Jonesville, N.C., U.S. 192 36.15 N 80.51 W
Jonesville, N.Y., U.S. 210 42.55 N 73.49 W
Jonesville, S.C., U.S. 192 34.50 N 81.41 W
Jonesville, Va., U.S. 192 36.41 N 83.07 W
Jong ≃ 150 7.32 N 12.23 W
Jonggol 115a 6.28 S 107.03 E
Jongkha 120 28.57 N 85.15 E
Jongunjärvi @ 26 65.17 N 27.15 E
Jónico, Mar → Ionian Sea ⊤[2] 22 39.00 N 19.00 E
Joniškėlis 76 56.02 N 24.10 E
Joniškis 76 56.14 N 23.37 E
Jonkersberg 158 33.55 S 22.15 E
Jönköping 26 57.47 N 14.11 E
Jönköpings Län □[6] 26 57.30 N 14.30 E
Jonquière 186 48.24 N 71.15 W
Jonquières 62 44.07 N 4.54 E
Jonsdorf 54 50.51 N 14.43 E
Jonstorp 41 56.14 N 12.40 E
Jontoy 144 0.05 S 42.35 E
Jonuta 232 18.05 N 92.08 W
Jonvilliers 261 48.34 N 1.42 E
Jonzac 32 45.27 N 0.26 W
Joplin, Mo., U.S. 194 37.06 N 94.31 W
Joplin, Mont., U.S. 202 48.34 N 110.46 W
Joppa, Ill., U.S. 194 37.12 N 88.51 W
Joppa, Md., U.S. 208 39.26 N 76.22 W
Jóquei Clube ♠ 287b 23.35 S 46.41 W
Joquicingo 234 19.03 N 99.33 W
Jora 124 26.20 N 77.49 E
Jordan, Pil. 116 10.40 N 122.35 E
Jordan, Minn., U.S. 190 44.40 N 93.37 W
Jordan, Mont., U.S. 202 47.19 N 106.55 W
Jordan, N.Y., U.S. 210 43.04 N 76.28 W
Jordan □[1] 118 128 31.00 N 36.00 E
Jordan (Nahr al-Urdunn) (HaYarden) ≃, As. 132 31.46 N 35.33 E
Jordan ≃, B.C., Can. 224 48.26 N 124.08 W
Jordan ≃, Utah, U.S. 200 40.49 N 112.08 W
Jordan Bay C 186 43.45 N 65.12 W
Jordan Creek ≃ 202 42.52 N 117.38 W
Jordânia 255 15.54 S 40.11 W
Jordania → Jordan □[1] 128 31.00 N 36.00 E
Jordanie → Jordan □[1] 128 31.00 N 36.00 E
Jordanien → Jordan □[1] 128 31.00 N 36.00 E
Jordan Lake @ 216 42.46 N 85.09 W
Jordanów 30 49.40 N 19.50 E
Jordans 260 51.37 N 0.36 W
Jordan Valley 202 42.58 N 117.03 W
Jordanville 210 42.55 N 74.57 W
Jordão ≃ 252 25.46 S 52.07 W
Jordbro 40 59.09 N 18.07 E
Jördenstorf 54 53.52 N 12.37 E
Jordet 26 61.25 N 12.09 E
Jorge Grego, Ilha I 256 23.13 S 44.09 W
Jorge Montt, Isla I 254 51.20 S 74.45 W
Jorge Montt, Ventisquero ⊓ 254 48.17 S 73.30 W
Jorge V, Costade → George V Coast •[2] 9 68.30 S 147.30 E
Jorge VI, Estrecho de → George VI Sound U 9 71.00 S 68.00 W
Jorhāt 120 26.45 N 94.13 E
Jörlfeld 41 54.38 N 9.15 E
Jorm 120 36.52 N 70.51 E
Jörn 26 65.04 N 20.02 E
Jornado del Muerto ◆[2] 200 33.20 N 106.50 W
Joroinen 26 62.11 N 27.50 E
Jorong 112 3.58 S 114.56 E
Jöröö 88 49.43 N 106.42 E
Jöröö ≃ 88 49.54 N 106.08 E
Jørpeland 26 59.01 N 6.03 E
J'orzovka 80 48.56 N 44.38 E
Jos 150 9.55 N 8.53 E
Jose Abad Santos 116 5.38 N 125.27 E
José Batlle y Ordóñez 252 33.28 S 55.07 W
José Bonifácio 255 21.03 S 49.41 W
José Cardel 234 19.22 N 96.22 W
José C. Paz 258 34.30 S 58.45 W

ENGLISH

Name **Page** **Lat.°'** **Long.°'**

José de Freitas 250 4.45 S 42.35 W
José de San Martín 254 44.02 S 70.29 W
José Enrique Rodó (Drabble) 258 33.41 S 57.34 W
José Francisco Vergara 252 22.28 S 69.38 W
Joselândia 248 16.32 S 56.12 W
José María Blanco (Tres Lomas) 252 36.27 S 62.51 W
José Martí, Aeropuerto Internacional ⊠ 286b 23.00 N 82.24 W
Jose Panganiban 116 14.17 N 122.41 E
José Pedro Varela 252 33.27 S 54.32 W
Joseph 202 45.21 N 117.14 W
Joseph, Lac @ 176 52.45 N 65.15 W
Joseph, Lake @ 212 45.14 N 79.45 W
Joseph Bonaparte Gulf C 164 14.15 S 128.30 E
Joseph City 200 34.57 N 110.20 W
Joseph Creek ≃ 202 46.03 N 117.01 W
Josephine, Pa., U.S. 214 40.29 N 79.11 W
Josephine, Tex., U.S. 222 33.04 N 96.19 W
Josephine, Lake @ 220 27.24 N 81.26 W
Josephine Peak ∧ 280 34.17 N 118.09 W
Josephstaal 164 4.44 S 145.01 E
José Santos Arévalo 258 35.10 S 59.14 W
Jōshima 96 33.15 N 130.26 E
Joshīmath 120 30.34 N 79.34 E
Jōshin'etsu-kōgen-kokuritsu-kōen ♠ 94 36.46 N 138.40 E
Joshua 222 32.28 N 97.23 W
Joshua Creek ≃ 275b 43.29 N 79.37 W
Joshua Tree 204 34.08 N 116.19 W
Joshua Tree National Monument ♠ 204 33.55 N 116.00 W
Joshua Trees State Park ♠ 228 34.41 N 117.47 W
Joškar-Ola 80 56.38 N 47.52 E
Jos Plateau ∧∧[1] 150 9.30 N 9.00 E
Jossa 56 50.14 N 9.35 E
Josselin 32 47.57 N 2.33 W
Jossigny 50 48.50 N 2.45 E
Jostedalsbreen ⊓ 26 61.40 N 7.00 E
Jost Van Dyke I 240m 18.28 N 64.45 W
Jōtō, Nihon 96 34.42 N 134.04 E
Jōtō, Nihon 96 35.03 N 135.17 E
Jōtō ◆[8] 270 34.42 N 135.34 E
Jotunheimen ∧∧ 26 61.38 N 8.18 E
Jotunheimen Nasjonalpark ♠ 26 61.35 N 8.30 E
Jouan, Récif ✧[2] 175f 20.39 S 167.01 E
Jouarre 50 48.56 N 3.08 E
Jouars-Pontchartrain 261 48.47 N 1.54 E
Joubertina 158 33.50 S 23.51 E
Joué-lès-Tours 50 47.21 N 0.40 E
Jougne 58 46.46 N 6.24 E
Jouques 62 43.38 N 5.38 E
Jourdanton 196 28.55 N 98.33 W
Joure 52 52.57 N 5.47 E
Joutsa 26 61.44 N 26.07 E
Joutseno 26 61.06 N 28.30 E
Joutsijärvi 24 66.40 N 28.00 E
Joux, Lac de @ 58 46.38 N 6.18 E
Joux, Vallée de V 58 46.35 N 6.15 E
Jouy 50 48.31 N 1.33 E
Jouy-en-Josas 261 48.46 N 2.10 E
Jouy-le-Moutier 261 49.01 N 2.03 E
Jouy-le-Potier 50 47.45 N 1.49 E
Jovellanos 240p 22.48 N 81.12 W
Jovellar 116 13.04 N 123.36 E
Jovet, Mont ∧ 62 45.30 N 6.39 E
Joviânia 255 17.49 S 49.30 W
Jowai 120 25.27 N 92.12 E
Jowlaenga, Mount ∧ 162 17.21 S 122.56 E
Jowzjān □[4] 120 36.30 N 66.00 E
Joy 190 41.12 N 90.55 W
Joy, Mount ∧ 180 63.46 N 132.55 W
Joya, Laguna de la C 234 15.55 N 93.40 W
Joyeuse 62 44.29 N 4.14 E
Jōyō 96 34.51 N 135.47 E
Joyous Pavilion Park ♠ 271a 39.52 N 116.22 E
Joyuda 240m 18.07 N 67.11 W
Józefów 30 52.09 N 21.12 E
Jozini Dam ◆[6] 158 27.25 S 32.05 E
Juaba 250 2.23 S 49.33 W
Juagdan 116 10.00 N 124.35 E
Juami ≃ 246 1.45 S 67.30 W
Ju'an 100 31.45 N 113.11 E
Juanacatlán 234 20.31 N 103.10 W
Juana Díaz 240m 18.03 N 66.31 W
Juan Aldama 232 24.19 N 103.21 W
Juan Anchorena ◆[8] 288 34.29 S 58.30 W
Juana Ramírez, Isla I 234 21.50 N 97.40 W
Juan Atucha 258 35.32 S 59.21 W
Juan B. Arruabarrena 252 30.20 S 58.19 W
Juan Blanco, Arroyo ≃ 258 35.05 S 57.26 W
Juancheng 98 35.35 N 115.29 E
Juan de Fuca, Strait of U 224 48.18 N 124.00 W
Juan de Garay 254 38.52 S 64.34 W
Juan de Mena 252 24.55 S 56.44 W
Juan de Nova, Île I 138 17.03 S 42.45 E
Juan Díaz Covarrubias 234 18.07 N 95.09 W
Juan E. Barra 252 37.48 S 60.29 W
Juan Eugenio 232 25.10 N 103.20 W
Juan Fernández, Archipiélago II 244 33.00 S 80.00 W
Juan González Grande, Arroyo ≃ 258 34.00 S 58.14 W
Juan González Romero ◆[8] 286a 19.30 N 99.04 W
Juangriego 246 11.05 N 63.57 W
Juan Gualberto Gómez 240p 22.52 N 81.33 W
Juan Guerra 248 6.35 S 76.21 W
Juanita, Méx. 234 17.47 N 95.09 W
Juanita, Wash., U.S. 224 47.42 N 122.13 W
Juan Jorba 252 33.37 S 65.16 W
Juan José Castelli 252 25.57 S 60.37 W
Juanjuí 248 7.11 S 76.45 W
Juankoski 26 63.04 N 28.21 E
Juan-les-Pins 62 43.34 N 7.06 E
Juan L. Lacaze 258 34.26 S 57.27 W
Juan N. Fernández 252 38.00 S 59.16 W
Juan Perez Sound U 182 52.30 N 131.18 W
Juan Rodríguez Clara 234 18.00 N 95.25 W
Juan Tronconi 258 35.30 S 59.15 W
Juan Viñas 236 9.54 N 83.45 W
Juanziba 107 30.32 N 104.59 E
Juárez, Arg. 252 37.40 S 59.48 W
Juárez → Ciudad Juárez, Méx. 232 31.44 N 106.29 W
Juárez, Méx. 232 27.37 N 100.44 W
Juárez, Méx. 234 17.39 N 93.10 W
Juárez, Cerro ∧ 234 20.37 N 99.17 W
Juárez, Sierra de ∧∧ 232 32.00 N 115.50 W
Juarzon 150 5.20 N 8.52 W
Juatinga, Ponta de ≻ 256 23.17 S 44.30 W
Juàzeirinho 250 7.04 S 36.35 W
Juàzeiro 250 9.25 S 40.30 W
Juàzeiro do Norte 250 7.12 S 39.20 W
Jūbā 154 4.51 N 31.37 E
Juba ≃, Afr. 144 0.12 S 42.40 E
Juba ≃, Bra. 248 14.59 S 57.44 W
Jubachstausee @[1] 263 51.10 N 7.37 E
Jūbāl, Maḍīq (Strait of Jubal) U 140 27.40 N 33.55 E
Jubal, Strait of → Jūbāl, Maḍīq U 140 27.40 N 33.55 E
Jubayl (Byblos) 130 34.07 N 35.39 E

DEUTSCH

Name **Seite** **Breite°'** **Länge°' E=Ost**

Jubayl, Jabal ∧[2] 142 27.25 N 30.32 E
Jubayt 140 18.57 N 36.50 E
Jubbah 128 28.02 N 40.56 E
Jubb al-Jarrāḥ 130 34.49 N 37.19 E
Jubbātā al-Khashab 132 33.13 N 35.49 E
Jubb Jannīn 132 33.37 N 35.47 E
Jubbulpore → Jabalpur 124 23.10 N 79.57 E
Jubbulpore □[5] 124 23.30 N 80.10 E
Jubilee Downs 162 18.22 S 125.17 E
Jubilee Lake @, Austl. 162 29.12 S 126.38 E
Jubilee Lake @, Newf., Can. 186 48.04 N 55.11 W
Jubones ≃ 246 3.13 S 79.57 W
Jubundha ≃ 126 24.06 N 90.20 E
Jūbu-san ∧ 270 34.50 N 135.55 E
Juby, Cap ≻ 148 27.58 N 12.55 W
Jucá ≃ 250 6.22 S 40.08 W
Júcar ≃ 34 39.09 N 0.14 W
Juçara 255 15.53 S 50.51 W
Júcaro 240p 21.37 N 78.51 W
Jucás 250 6.32 S 39.32 W
Jüchen 56 51.06 N 6.30 E
Juchhöh 54 50.24 N 11.52 E
Juchipila 234 21.25 N 103.07 W
Juchipila ≃ 234 21.03 N 103.25 W
Juchitán [de Zaragoza] 234 16.26 N 95.01 W
Juchitepec 234 19.06 N 98.53 W
Juchitlán 234 20.05 N 104.07 W
Juchnov 76 54.45 N 35.14 E
Juchoviči 76 56.02 N 28.39 E
Jucuapa 236 13.31 N 88.24 W
Jucurucu ≃ 255 17.21 S 39.13 W
Jucurutu 250 6.02 S 37.01 W
Judaea ◆[1] 132 31.35 N 35.00 E
Judas, Punta ≻ 236 9.31 N 84.32 W
Judaydat al-Khās 132 33.24 N 36.33 E
Judaydat 'Arṭūz 132 33.26 N 36.10 E
Juddah → Jiddah 144 21.30 N 39.12 E
Jude Island I 186 47.15 N 54.59 W
Judenau 61 48.17 N 16.00 E
Judenburg 61 47.10 N 14.40 E
Judian 102 27.20 N 99.36 E
Judinki, S.S.S.R. 82 55.27 N 35.48 E
Judinki, S.S.S.R. 82 54.37 N 37.17 E
Judino, S.S.S.R. 76 58.43 N 39.17 E
Judino, S.S.S.R. 80 55.51 N 48.55 E
Judino, S.S.S.R. 82 54.09 N 38.19 E
Judino, S.S.S.R. 265b 55.40 N 37.12 E
Judío, Rambla del ≃ 34 38.15 N 1.27 W
Judique 186 45.52 N 61.30 W
Judith ≃ 202 47.44 N 109.38 W
Judith, Point ≻ 207 41.22 N 71.29 W
Judith Gap 202 46.41 N 109.45 W
Judith Mountains ∧∧ 202 47.12 N 109.15 W
Judith Peak ∧ 202 47.13 N 109.13 W
Judoma ≃ 74 59.08 N 135.06 E
Judson, S.C., U.S. 192 34.50 N 82.27 W
Judson, Tex., U.S. 222 32.35 N 94.45 W
Judsonia 194 35.16 N 91.38 W
Juehedian 105 39.26 N 117.06 E
Juelsminde 41 55.43 N 10.01 E
Jueshui ≃ 100 31.42 N 113.20 E
Juexi, Zhg. 100 29.27 N 121.57 E
Juexi, Zhg. 107 28.55 N 104.16 E
Jufari ≃ 246 1.13 S 62.00 W
Jufayr, Bi'r al- ⊤[4] 142 30.49 N 32.40 E
Jufiang ≃ 107 28.58 N 106.16 E
Jufrah, Jabal al- ∧ 142 30.09 N 31.55 E
Jufrah, Wādī al- V 142 30.24 N 31.35 E
Jug 86 57.43 N 56.10 E
Jug ≃ 24 60.45 N 46.20 E
Jughna 140 12.24 N 25.06 E
Jugo-Kamskij 86 57.42 N 55.35 E
Jugon 32 48.25 N 2.20 W
Jugo-Osetinskaja Avtonomnaja Oblast' □[8] 84 42.20 N 44.00 E
Jugorskij Šar, Proliv U 72 69.45 N 60.35 E
Jugoslavija → Yugoslavia □[1] 22 44.00 N 19.00 E
Jugoslawien → Yugoslavia □[1] 22 44.00 N 19.00 E
Jugo-Zapad ◆[8] 265b 55.40 N 37.32 E
Juḥā 144 16.41 N 42.54 E
Juhe ≃ 105 39.45 N 117.35 E
Jühnsdorf 264a 52.18 N 13.23 E
Jühnsdorfer Heide ◆[3] 264a 52.19 N 13.24 E
Juhu ◆[8] 272c 19.07 N 72.49 E
Juhuadao I 98 40.29 N 120.47 E
Juhu Airport ⊠ 272c 19.06 N 72.50 E
Jui 272c 19.01 N 73.05 E
Juigalpa 236 12.05 N 85.24 W
Juile 234 17.45 N 94.59 W
Juillac 32 45.19 N 1.19 E
Juilly 261 49.01 N 2.42 E
Juiná ≃ 248 12.36 S 58.57 W
Juine ≃ 50 48.32 N 2.23 E
Juist 52 53.40 N 6.59 E
Juist I 52 53.40 N 7.00 E
Juisui 100 23.29 N 121.23 E
Juiz de Fora 256 21.45 S 43.20 W
Jujurieux 58 46.02 N 5.25 E
Jujū-san ∧ 96 33.05 N 131.15 E
Jujuy → San Salvador de Jujuy 252 24.11 S 65.18 W
Jujuy □[4] 252 23.00 S 66.00 W
Jukagirskoje Ploskogorje ∧∧[1] 74 66.00 N 155.00 E
Jukamenskoje 80 57.53 N 52.15 E
Jukonda ≃ 86 59.38 N 67.26 E
Juksa 86 56.55 N 85.10 E
Juksejevo 24 59.52 N 54.19 E
Jukskei ≃ 273d 26.06 S 28.06 E
Jukte 74 63.23 N 105.41 E
Jula ≃ 24 63.49 N 44.44 E
Julāna 124 29.08 N 76.25 E
Julayfah, Bi'r al- ⊤[4] 142 30.43 N 29.35 E
Julbach 60 48.40 N 13.52 E
Juldybajevo 86 52.20 N 57.52 E
Julebao 98 40.09 N 113.36 E
Julesburg 198 40.59 N 102.16 W
Juli 248 16.13 S 69.27 W
Juliaca 248 15.30 S 70.08 W
Julia Creek 166 20.39 S 141.45 E
Julia Creek ≃ 166 20.00 S 141.11 E
Julian 214 40.52 N 77.56 W
Juliana, Lake @ 220 28.07 N 81.48 W
Julianakanaal ≡ 56 51.05 N 5.50 E
Julian Alps ∧∧ 36 46.00 N 14.00 E
Juliana Top ∧ 250 3.41 N 56.32 W
Julianehåb 176 60.43 N 46.01 W
Julia Pfeiffer Burns State Park ♠ 226 36.10 N 120.40 W
Jülich 56 50.55 N 6.21 E
Juliénas 58 46.14 N 4.43 E
Julijske Alpe → Julian Alps ∧∧ 36 46.00 N 14.00 E
Julimes 232 28.25 N 105.27 W
Júlio de Castilhos 252 29.14 S 53.41 W
Julio Prestes, Estação ◆[5] 287b 23.32 S 46.38 W
Julita ɤ 40 59.09 N 16.02 E
Juliuhe 104 42.03 N 122.55 E
Juliustown 285 40.01 N 74.40 W
Jullundur 123 31.19 N 75.34 E
Julu 98 37.13 N 115.01 E
Juma 24 65.07 N 33.16 E
Juma ≃ 248 4.57 S 64.31 W
Jumaguzino 86 52.54 N 56.23 E
Jumahe ≃ 98 39.14 N 115.45 E
Jumapolo 115a 7.42 S 111.00 E
Jumaševo 80 54.59 N 54.25 E
Jumay, Volcán ∧[1] 236 14.41 N 89.59 W

Symbols in the index entries represent the broad categories identified in the key at the right. Symbols with superior numbers (∧∧[2]) identify subcategories (see complete key on page *I · 30*).

Kartensymbole in dem Registerverzeichnis stellen die rechts in Schlüssel erklärten Kategorien dar. Symbole mit hochgestellten Ziffern (∧∧[2]) bezeichnen Unterabteilungen einer Kategorie (vgl. vollständiger Schlüssel auf Seite *I · 30*).

Los símbolos incluídos en el texto del índice representan las grandes categorias identificadas con la clave a la derecha. Los símbolos con numeros en su parte superior (∧∧[2]) identifican las subcategorías (véase la clave completa en la página *I · 30*).

Les symboles de l'index représentent les catégories indiquées dans la légende à droite. Les symboles suivis d'un indice (∧∧[2]) représentent des sous-catégories (voir légende complète à la page *I · 30*).

Os símbolos incluídos no texto do índice representam as grandes categorias identificadas com a chave à direita. Os símbolos com números em sua parte superior (∧∧[2]) identificam as subcategorias (veja-se a chave completa à página *I · 30*).

	English	Deutsch	Español	Français	Português
∧	Mountain	Berg	Montaña	Montagne	Montanha
∧∧	Mountains	Berge	Montañas	Montagnes	Montanhas
)(	Pass	Pass	Paso	Col	Passo
V	Valley, Canyon	Tal, Cañon	Valle, Cañón	Vallée, Canyon	Vale, Canhão
≚	Plain	Ebene	Llano	Plaine	Planície
≻	Cape	Kap	Cabo	Cap	Cabo
I	Island	Insel	Isla	Île	Ilha
II	Islands	Inseln	Islas	Îles	Ilhas
•	Other Topographic Features	Andere Topographische Objekte	Otros Elementos Topográficos	Autres données topographiques	Outros Elementos Topográficos

ESPAÑOL

Nombre	Página	Lat.°′	Long.°′ W=Oeste
Jumbilla	248	5.54 S	77.45 W
Jumbo, Som.	144	0.12 S	42.38 E
Jumbo, Zimb.	154	17.28 S	30.55 E
Jumbo Peak ∧	204	36.12 N	114.11 W
Jumeauville	261	48.55 N	1.47 E
Jumentos Cays ❙❙	238	22.42 N	75.55 W
Jumet	50	50.26 N	4.25 E
Jumièges	50	49.26 N	0.49 E
Jumilla	34	38.29 N	1.17 W
Jumla	124	29.17 N	82.10 E
Jummayzat Banī ʻAmr	142	30.48 N	31.32 E
Jump ≃	190	45.17 N	91.05 W
Jump, North Fork ≃	190	45.25 N	90.40 W
Jump, South Fork ≃	190	45.25 N	90.40 W
Jūn	132	33.35 N	35.27 E
Junāgadh	120	21.31 N	70.28 E
Ju'nan	98	35.11 N	118.51 E
Junaynah, Ra's al- ∧, Miṣr	132	29.28 N	34.02 E
Junaynah, Ra's al- ∧, Miṣr	140	29.01 N	33.58 E
Junaynat al-ʻAṭash ∧[2]	142	28.51 N	31.47 E
Juncal, Isla ❙	258	33.58 S	58.24 W
Juncal, Serra do ∧	256	22.45 S	45.55 W
Juncal do Norte ☷	266c	38.52 N	8.59 W
Juncal do Sul ☷	266c	38.51 N	8.58 W
Juncheng	98	38.57 N	114.41 E
Juncos	240m	18.14 N	65.55 W
Junction, Tex., U.S.	196	30.29 N	99.46 W
Junction, Utah, U.S.	200	38.14 N	112.13 W
Junction City, Ark., U.S.	194	33.01 N	92.43 W
Junction City, Ill., U.S.	219	40.45 N	89.36 W
Junction City, Kans., U.S.	198	39.02 N	96.50 W
Junction City, Ky., U.S.	194	37.35 N	84.48 W
Junction City, Oreg., U.S.	202	44.13 N	123.12 W
Junction City, Wash., U.S.	224	46.58 N	123.46 W
Jundī, Qārat al- ∧[2]	142	29.39 N	30.58 E
Jundiaí	256	23.11 S	46.52 W
Jundiaí ≃, Bra.	256	23.32 S	46.15 W
Jundiaí ≃, Bra.	256	23.11 S	47.16 W
Jundiaí do Sul	255	23.27 S	50.17 W
Jundiaí-Mirim ≃	256	23.10 S	46.56 W
Jundiapeba	256	23.33 S	46.15 W
Jundushan ⛰	105	40.30 N	116.05 E
Juneau, Alaska, U.S.	180	58.20 N	134.27 W
Juneau, Wis., U.S.	190	43.24 N	88.42 W
Junee	166	34.52 S	147.35 E
June in Winter, Lake ◎	220	27.18 N	81.24 W
June Lake	226	37.47 N	119.04 W
June Park	220	28.04 N	80.41 W
Jungapeo	234	19.27 N	100.29 W
Jungbluth Ditch ⩧	279a	41.27 N	82.07 W
Jungfernheide ♠	264a	52.34 N	13.17 E
Jungfern-Inseln → Virgin Islands □[2]	240m	18.20 N	64.50 W
Jungfern-See ◎	264a	52.25 N	13.05 E
Jungfrau ∧	58	46.32 N	7.58 E
Jungfraujoch ◆[5]	58	46.33 N	7.58 E
Jungle Habitat ♠	276	41.08 N	74.21 W
Junglinster	56	49.43 N	6.15 E
Jungshāhi	120	24.51 N	67.46 E
Juniata	198	40.36 N	98.30 W
Juniata □[6]	208	40.34 N	77.24 W
Juniata ◆[8]	285	40.01 N	75.07 W
Juniata ≃	188	40.24 N	77.01 W
Juniata, Frankstown Branch ≃	214	40.34 N	78.03 W
Juniata, Raystown Branch ≃	214	40.25 N	77.58 W
Juniata Gap	214	40.33 N	78.26 W
Juniata Terrace	208	40.35 N	77.34 W
Junín, Arg.	252	34.35 S	60.57 W
Junín, Ec.	246	0.56 S	80.13 W
Junín, Perú	248	11.10 S	76.00 W
Junín □[5]	248	11.30 S	75.00 W
Junín, Lago ◎	248	11.02 S	76.06 W
Junín de los Andes	254	39.56 S	71.05 W
Junior	188	38.59 N	79.57 W
Juniper	186	46.33 N	67.13 W
Junipero Serra Peak ∧	226	36.08 N	121.25 W
Juniville	50	49.24 N	4.23 E
Jūniyah	130	33.59 N	35.38 E
Jun Kharchanai	123	36.52 N	75.01 E
Junkou	100	26.42 N	116.49 E
Junliangcheng	105	39.04 N	117.27 E
Junnar	122	19.12 N	73.53 E
Juno Beach	220	26.52 N	80.04 W
Junokommunarskoje ◆[8]	83	48.13 N	38.18 E
Junqueiro	250	9.56 S	36.29 W
Junqueirópolis	255	21.32 S	51.26 W
Junsele	26	63.41 N	16.54 E
Junxian, Zhg.	98	35.43 N	114.31 E
Junxian, Zhg.	102	32.42 N	111.13 E
Junzhuang	105	40.00 N	116.06 E
Jūō	94	36.40 N	140.41 E
Juodkrantė	76	55.33 N	21.08 E
Juodupė	76	56.05 N	25.37 E
Juojärvi ◎	26	62.43 N	28.33 E
Juparanã, Lagoa ◎	255	19.35 S	40.18 W
Jupilingo ≃	236	14.48 N	89.14 W
Jupille	56	50.39 N	5.38 E
Jupiter	220	26.56 N	80.06 W
Jupiter ≃	186	49.29 N	63.37 W
Jupiter Inlet C	220	26.57 N	80.04 W
Jupiter Island ❙	220	27.04 N	80.07 W
Juqueri ≃	256	23.24 S	46.52 W
Juqueri-Mirim	256	23.21 S	46.37 W
Juqueriquerê, Serra do ⛰	256	23.43 S	45.37 W
Juquiá	252	24.19 S	47.38 W
Juquiá-Guaçu ≃	256	24.00 S	47.16 W
Juquila	234	16.14 N	97.18 W
Juquitiba	256	23.57 S	47.03 W
Jur, Česko.	30	48.15 N	17.13 E
Jur, S.S.S.R.	74	59.52 N	137.39 E
Jura □[3]	58	47.20 N	7.15 E
Jura □[5]	58	46.50 N	5.50 E
Jura ⛰	58	46.45 N	6.30 E
Jura ❙	46	56.00 N	5.54 W
Jūra ≃	76	55.03 N	29.09 E
Jura, Sound of ⋓	46	55.57 N	5.48 W
Juramento	255	16.50 S	43.35 W
Juratiški	76	54.02 N	25.54 E
Jurays wa 'Izbatuhā	142	30.19 N	30.55 E
Jurbarkas	76	55.05 N	22.48 E
Jurcevo	76	60.02 N	32.36 E
Juréia	256	21.17 S	46.22 W
Jurenino	76	59.24 N	42.47 E
Jurevići	78	51.57 N	29.32 E
Jurga	86	55.42 N	84.51 E
Jurgamyš	86	55.21 N	64.28 E
Jurgenson Woods ♠	278	41.34 N	87.36 W
Juriesfontein	158	31.40 S	22.08 E
Juring	164	6.26 S	134.20 E
Jurino	80	56.18 N	46.18 E
Jurja	24	59.03 N	49.14 E
Jurjev → Tartu	76	58.23 N	26.43 E
Jurjevec	80	57.18 N	43.06 E
Jurjevka, S.S.S.R.	78	48.44 N	36.02 E
Jurjevka, S.S.S.R.	83	48.30 N	39.00 E
Jurjev-Pol'skij	80	56.30 N	39.41 E
Jurjevskoje	82	55.05 N	36.13 E
Jurla	86	59.17 N	54.19 E
Jurlovo, S.S.S.R.	82	55.54 N	37.16 E
Jurlovo, S.S.S.R.	82	55.19 N	35.52 E
Jūrmala	76	56.58 N	23.42 E
Jurong, Sing.	271c	1.21 N	103.42 E

FRANÇAIS

Nom	Page	Lat.°′	Long.°′ W=Ouest
Jurong, Zhg.	106	31.57 N	119.10 E
Jurong ≃	271c	1.18 N	103.44 E
Jurovo, S.S.S.R.	78	51.22 N	27.50 E
Jurovo, S.S.S.R.	80	57.30 N	43.50 E
Jurovo, S.S.S.R.	82	55.30 N	38.22 E
Jurovskoje	86	59.29 N	69.02 E
Jursla	40	58.40 N	16.11 E
Jurty	88	56.03 N	97.37 E
Juruá	246	3.27 S	66.03 W
Juruá ≃	242	2.37 S	65.44 W
Juruaia	256	21.15 S	46.35 W
Juruá Mirim ≃	248	8.08 S	72.48 W
Juruena ≃	248	7.20 S	58.03 W
Jurujuba, Enseada de C	287a	22.56 S	43.07 W
Jurupari ≃	248	7.45 S	70.10 W
Jurupari, Arquipélago do ❙❙	250	0.07 N	50.30 W
Jurupari, Ilha ❙	250	0.20 N	50.07 W
Juruti	250	2.09 S	56.04 W
Jur'uzan'	86	54.52 N	58.26 E
Jur'uzan' ≃	86	55.42 N	57.00 E
Jurva	26	62.41 N	21.59 E
Jušala	86	57.04 N	64.17 E
Juscelândia	255	15.20 S	51.19 W
Jusepín	246	9.45 N	63.31 W
Jushiguan	102	24.47 N	97.38 E
Jūshiyama	94	35.06 N	136.46 E
Jushui ≃	100	30.38 N	114.51 E
Juskatla	182	53.37 N	132.18 W
Jus'ki	80	56.39 N	53.05 E
Juškovo	76	59.46 N	45.11 E
Juškozero	24	64.44 N	32.06 E
Jussey	58	47.49 N	5.54 E
Justa	80	47.07 N	46.18 E
Justice	278	41.45 N	87.50 W
Justin	222	33.05 N	97.18 W
Justineberg ∧[2]	40	58.43 N	15.04 E
Justiniano Posse	252	32.53 S	62.40 W
Justo Daract	252	33.52 S	65.11 W
Justus	214	40.42 N	81.35 W
Jusut ≃	80	56.12 N	48.23 E
Jus'va	24	58.56 N	54.57 E
Jutaí	248	5.11 S	68.54 W
Jutaí ≃	242	2.43 S	66.57 W
Jutaza	80	54.35 N	53.16 E
Jütchendorf	264a	52.16 N	13.10 E
Jüterbog	54	51.59 N	13.04 E
Juththah, Jabal al- ∧	132	30.12 N	35.36 E
Juti	255	22.52 S	54.37 W
Jutiapa	236	14.17 N	89.54 W
Jutiapa □[5]	236	14.10 N	89.50 W
Juticalpa	236	14.42 N	86.15 W
Jutiquile	236	14.45 N	86.08 W
Jutland → Jylland ≻[1]	26	56.00 N	9.15 E
Jutogh	123	31.06 N	77.07 E
Jutphaas	52	52.03 N	5.05 E
Jutrosin	30	51.40 N	17.10 E
Juupajoki	26	61.47 N	24.27 E
Juuru	76	59.04 N	24.59 E
Juva	26	61.54 N	27.51 E
Juventud, Isla de la (Isla de Pinos) ❙	240p	21.40 N	82.50 W
Juvisy-sur-Orge	50	48.41 N	2.23 E
Juvuln ◎	26	63.43 N	13.09 E
Juwana	115a	6.42 S	111.09 E
Juwangi	115a	7.10 S	110.45 E
Juwayzah	132	33.02 N	35.51 E
Juxi	100	27.30 N	119.08 E
Juxian	98	35.37 N	118.54 E
Juxing	106	31.56 N	121.33 E
Juxtlahuaca	234	17.20 N	98.01 W
Juyanhai → Gashunhu ◎	102	42.22 N	100.34 E
Juye	98	35.23 N	116.06 E
Jūyom	128	28.10 N	53.52 E
Juyongguan	105	40.18 N	116.04 E
Juža	80	56.35 N	42.01 E
Juzennecourt	58	48.11 N	4.59 E
Juziers	261	49.00 N	1.51 E
Juzihe ≃	98	40.18 N	123.35 E
Južno-Aleksandrovka	88	55.51 N	96.10 E
Južno-Aličurskij Chrebet ⛰	120	37.30 N	73.20 E
Južno-Jenisejskij	86	58.48 N	94.39 E
Južno-Mujskij Chrebet ⛰	88	55.40 N	114.00 E
Južno-Sachalinsk	89	46.58 N	142.42 E
Južno-Suchokumsk	84	44.37 N	45.34 E
Južno-Ural'sk	86	54.26 N	61.15 E
Južnyj, S.S.S.R.	80	56.08 N	44.09 E
Južnyj, S.S.S.R.	80	47.20 N	41.51 E
Južnyj, S.S.S.R.	86	49.21 N	73.01 E
Južnyj, S.S.S.R.	86	53.14 N	83.42 E
Južnyj, S.S.S.R.	86	53.33 N	60.02 E
Južnyj, Mys ≻	74	57.45 N	156.45 E
Južnyj-Alamyšik	85	40.46 N	72.38 E
Južnyj Bug ≃	78	46.59 N	31.58 E
Južnyj Golodnostepskij Kanal ⩧	85	40.15 N	69.08 E
Južnyj Prijut	84	43.12 N	41.55 E
Južnyj Ural ⛰	86	54.00 N	58.30 E
Juzovka → Doneck	83	48.00 N	37.48 E
Jwālahari ◆[8]	272a	28.40 N	77.06 E
Jwayyā	132	33.14 N	35.19 E
Jyderup	41	55.40 N	11.26 E
Jylland ≻[1]	26	56.00 N	9.15 E
Jyllinge	41	55.45 N	12.07 E
Jyväskylä	26	62.14 N	25.44 E

K

Nom	Page	Lat.°′	Long.°′ W=Ouest
K2 → Godwin Austen ∧	123	35.53 N	76.30 E
Ka ≃	150	11.40 N	4.10 E
Kaaawa	229c	21.33 N	157.51 W
Kaabong	154	3.31 N	34.08 E
Kaachka	128	37.21 N	59.36 E
Kaala ∧	229c	21.31 N	158.09 W
Kaala Djerda	36	35.40 N	8.36 E
Kaalaea	229c	21.28 N	157.51 W
Kaala-Gomen	175f	20.40 S	164.25 E
Kaalspruit	158	29.15 S	26.10 E
Kaalualu Bay C	229d	18.58 N	155.37 W
Kaapahu Bay C	229a	20.39 N	156.05 W
Kaapmuiden	156	25.33 S	31.20 E
Kaap Plato ⛰[1]	158	28.20 S	23.57 E
Kaappunt ≻	158	34.21 S	18.30 E
Kaapstad → Cape Town	158	33.55 S	18.22 E
Kaariye Camii ▽[1]	267b	41.01 N	28.55 E
Kaarli	76	59.24 N	26.27 E
Kaarssen	54	53.12 N	11.02 E
Kaarst	56	51.14 N	6.37 E
Kaaterskill Creek ≃	210	42.13 N	73.53 W
Kaatoan, Mount ∧	116	8.07 N	124.55 E
Kaatsheuvel	52	51.40 N	5.02 E
Kaavi	26	62.59 N	28.30 E
Kaba	150	10.09 N	11.40 W
Kaba, Goulbin ∨	150	13.42 N	6.19 E
Kabacan	116	7.08 N	124.49 E
Kabacan ≃	116	7.08 N	124.50 E
Kabadak	126	22.13 N	89.19 E
Kabadak ≃[1]	126	22.13 N	89.18 E
Kabadüz	130	40.53 N	37.56 E
Kabaena, Pulau ❙	112	5.15 S	121.55 E
Kabaena, Selat ⋓	112	5.00 S	122.00 E
Kabah ⊥	232	20.07 N	89.29 W
Kabala	150	9.35 N	11.33 W
Kabale	154	1.15 S	29.59 E
Kabali, Indon.	112	1.42 S	121.54 E
Kabalı, Tür.	130	41.52 N	35.05 E
Kabalo	154	6.03 S	26.55 E
Kabambare	154	4.42 S	27.43 E
Kaban'	86	54.39 N	66.28 E

PORTUGUÊS

Nome	Página	Lat.°′	Long.°′ W=Oeste
Kabanjahe	114	3.06 N	98.30 E
Kabanje	83	49.13 N	38.12 E
Kabanjifa	144	3.34 N	43.30 E
Kabankalan	116	9.59 N	122.49 E
Kabanovka	80	53.39 N	51.18 E
Kabanovo	86	55.20 N	70.52 E
Kabansk	88	52.03 N	106.39 E
Kabardinka	78	44.39 N	37.57 E
Kabardino-Balkarskaja Avtonomnaja Sovetskaja Socialističeskaja Respublika □[3]	84	43.30 N	43.30 E
Kabasalan	116	7.48 N	122.45 E
Kabayan	116	16.37 N	120.51 E
Kabba	150	7.50 N	6.03 E
Kabbani ≃	122	12.13 N	76.54 E
Kabberi	132	33.01 N	35.09 E
Kåbdalis	24	66.10 N	20.00 E
Kabd aṣ-Ṣārim ◆[1]	130	34.34 N	39.33 E
Kabd Warqah ◆[1]	130	34.20 N	39.37 E
Kabel ◆[8]	263	51.24 N	7.29 E
Kabenung Lake ◎	190	48.16 N	85.00 W
Kabetogama Lake ◎	190	48.28 N	92.59 W
Kabeya	154	5.40 S	27.58 E
Kab-hegy ∧	30	46.58 N	17.30 E
Kabia ≃	146	9.54 N	15.10 E
Kabilcevaz	130	38.20 N	41.25 E
Kabinakagami Lake ◎	190	48.54 N	84.25 W
Kabin Buri	110	13.59 N	101.43 E
Kabinda	152	6.08 S	24.29 E
Kabinu	112	4.00 N	116.05 E
Kabir	112	8.17 S	124.13 E
Kabīr Kili	123	33.11 N	71.19 E
Kabīr Kūh ⛰	128	33.25 N	46.45 E
Kabīrwāla	123	30.24 N	71.52 E
Kabkābīyah	140	13.39 N	24.05 E
Kablow	264a	52.18 N	13.44 E
Kablower Ziegelei	264a	52.19 N	13.43 E
Kablukovo, S.S.S.R.	82	56.02 N	38.10 E
Kablukovo, S.S.S.R.	82	56.50 N	36.12 E
Kablungu, Cape ≻	164	6.20 S	150.00 E
Kabna	140	19.10 N	32.41 E
Kabo	152	7.39 N	18.37 E
Kabobo	154	5.07 S	29.03 E
Kabompo ≃	152	14.10 S	23.11 E
Kabondo-Dianda	154	8.53 S	25.40 E
Kabongo, Zaïre	154	7.19 S	25.35 E
Kabongo, Zaïre	154	8.43 S	28.11 E
Kaboro	152	6.59 N	17.33 E
Kabot	150	10.48 N	14.57 W
Kabotshome	154	3.46 S	26.54 E
Kabou	150	9.27 N	0.49 E
Kaboudia, Ras ≻	148	35.14 N	11.10 E
Kaboul → Kābul	120	34.31 N	69.12 E
Kabr	140	10.54 N	26.50 E
Kabūd Gonbad	128	37.00 N	59.45 E
Kabūd Rāhang	128	35.12 N	48.44 E
Kābul	120	34.31 N	69.12 E
Kābul □[4]	120	34.30 N	69.00 E
Kābul ≃	120	33.55 N	72.14 E
Kabunda	154	12.25 S	29.22 E
Kabunga	154	1.42 S	28.08 E
Kabura ≃	94	36.17 N	139.04 E
Kaburuang, Pulau ❙	108	3.48 N	126.48 E
Kabūshīyah	140	16.53 N	33.42 E
Kabwanga	152	7.01 S	22.37 E
Kabwe (Broken Hill)	154	14.27 S	28.27 E
Kabwe-Katanda	152	7.59 S	24.29 E
Kabylie ◆[1]	34	36.30 N	4.30 E
Kača	78	44.47 N	33.32 E
Kačalinskaja	80	49.07 N	44.03 E
Kačanik	38	42.13 N	21.14 E
Kačanovo	76	57.28 N	27.46 E
Kacbachskij	86	52.58 N	59.40 E
Kačerginė	76	54.56 N	23.44 E
Kacha ≃[1]	126	22.23 N	89.54 E
Kachagalau ∧	154	2.19 N	35.03 E
Kach'ang-ni	98	38.24 N	126.11 E
Kachati	84	42.30 N	41.46 E
Kachemak Bay C	180	59.35 N	151.30 W
Kachess Lake ◎[1]	224	47.20 N	121.14 W
Kachhwa	124	25.13 N	82.43 E
Kachi	84	41.26 N	46.56 E
Kachia	150	9.53 N	7.58 E
Kachib	84	42.25 N	46.36 E
Kachin □[3]	102	26.00 N	97.30 E
Kach'i-ri	98	34.27 N	126.08 E
Kachisi	144	9.39 N	37.50 E
Kachovka	78	46.47 N	33.30 E
Kachovskoje Vodochranilišče ◎[1]	78	47.25 N	34.10 E
Kachowka-Stausee → Kachovskoje Vodochranilišče ◎[1]	78	47.25 N	34.10 E
Kach Pass)(	123	36.56 N	72.37 E
K'achta	88	50.26 N	106.25 E
Kachua, Bngl.	126	22.39 N	89.53 E
Kachua, Bngl.	126	23.21 N	90.54 E
Kačiry	86	53.05 N	76.07 E
Kačkanar	86	58.42 N	59.38 E
Kačkanar, Gora ∧	86	58.47 N	59.23 E
Kaçkar Dağı ∧	130	40.50 N	41.10 E
Kačkarovka	78	47.06 N	33.44 E
Kačug	88	53.58 N	105.52 E
Kada ≃	88	54.22 N	103.10 E
Kadada ≃	80	53.09 N	46.01 E
Kadaingti	110	17.37 N	97.32 E
Kadaiyanallūr	122	9.05 N	77.21 E
Kadaň	54	50.20 N	13.15 E
Kadanai (Kadaney) ≃	120	31.02 N	66.09 E
Kadaney (Kadanai) ≃	120	31.02 N	66.09 E
Kadan Kyun ❙	110	12.30 N	98.22 E
Kadapongan, Pulau ❙	112	4.43 S	115.44 E
Kadarbana	124	26.46 N	85.20 E
Kadassa ≃	115b	9.24 S	120.02 E
Kaddam ◎[1]	122	19.07 N	78.46 E
Kade	150	6.05 N	0.50 W
Kadeï ≃	152	3.31 N	16.05 E
Kadena Airfield ⊠	174m	26.22 N	127.45 E
Kadeshiki	80	58.08 N	49.11 E
Kadetrenden (Kadet Rinne) ⋓	41	54.30 N	12.15 E
Kadgo, Lake ◎	162	26.42 S	127.18 E
Kadhimain → Al-Kāẓimīyah	128	33.22 N	44.20 E
Kadi	120	23.18 N	72.20 E
Kadiana	150	10.45 N	6.30 W
Kadijevka	83	48.34 N	38.40 E
Kadıköy	130	40.46 N	26.46 E
Kadıköy ◆[8]	267b	40.59 N	29.01 E
Kadina	168b	33.58 S	137.43 E
Kading ≃	110	18.19 N	104.00 E
Kadınhanı	130	38.15 N	32.14 E
Kadiolo	150	10.33 N	5.46 W
Kadipaten	115a	6.46 S	108.10 E
Kādīpur	124	26.10 N	82.23 E
Kadiri	122	14.07 N	78.10 E
Kadirli	130	37.23 N	36.05 E
Kadışehri	130	40.00 N	35.49 E
Kadiyevka → Kadijevka	83	48.34 N	38.40 E
Kadja, Ouadi (Wādī Kaja) ∨	146	12.02 N	22.28 E
Kadkan	128	35.35 N	58.50 E
Kadnikov	76	59.30 N	40.20 E
Kadnikovskij	76	60.19 N	40.15 E
Kado	150	7.39 N	9.44 E
Kadodo	140	11.04 N	29.31 E
Kadoka	198	43.50 N	101.31 W
Kadom	80	54.34 N	42.30 E
Kadoma	96	34.44 N	135.35 E
Kadoškino	80	54.01 N	44.25 E
Kadov	60	49.24 N	13.47 E
Kaduj	76	59.12 N	37.09 E
Kadumbul ≃	115b	9.42 S	120.32 E
Kaduna	150	10.33 N	7.27 E
Kaduna ≃	150	8.45 N	5.45 E
Kāduqlī	140	11.01 N	29.43 E
Kadūr	122	13.34 N	76.01 E
Kadyj	80	57.47 N	43.11 E
Kadykčan	74	63.02 N	146.50 E
Kadyšovo	80	54.20 N	46.45 E
Kadžaran	84	39.11 N	46.08 E
Kadžerom	24	64.41 N	55.54 E
Kadži-Saj	85	42.08 N	77.10 E
Kaech'ŏn	98	39.42 N	125.53 E
Kaédi	150	16.09 N	13.30 W
Kaedo-ri	98	34.35 N	127.39 E
Kaegudeck Lake ◎	186	48.07 N	55.11 W
Kaélé	146	10.07 N	14.27 E
Kaena Point ≻	229c	21.35 N	158.17 W
Kaeo	172	35.06 S	173.47 E
Kaesŏng	98	37.59 N	126.33 E
Kaesŏng □[4]	98	38.00 N	126.30 E
Kāf	128	31.24 N	37.24 E
Kafakumba	152	9.41 S	23.44 E
Kafan	84	39.13 N	46.24 E
Kafanchan	150	9.36 N	8.17 E
Kaffraria □[9]	158	31.30 S	28.30 E
Kaffrine	150	14.06 N	15.33 W
Kafia Kingi	140	9.16 N	24.25 E
Kafin	150	9.30 N	7.04 E
Kafinda	154	12.39 S	30.20 E
Kafin Madaki	150	10.41 N	9.46 E
Kafirévs, Ákra ≻	38	38.09 N	24.36 E
Kafirnigan ≃	120	36.58 N	68.02 E
Kafr ad-Dawwār	142	31.08 N	30.07 E
Kafr ash-Shaykh	142	31.07 N	30.56 E
Kafr ash-Shaykh □[4]	142	31.15 N	30.50 E
Kafr az-Zayyāt	142	30.49 N	30.49 E
Kafrein Dam ◆[6]	132	31.51 N	35.44 E
Kafr el-Zaiyat → Kafr az-Zayyāt	142	30.49 N	30.49 E
Kafr Ḥūnah	132	33.29 N	35.35 E
Kafr Kannā	132	32.45 N	35.20 E
Kafr Nabrakh	132	33.42 N	35.38 E
Kafr Naffākh	132	33.04 N	35.44 E
Kafr Nāsij	132	33.09 N	36.03 E
Kafr Shīmā	132	33.49 N	35.32 E
Kafr Sūsah	132	33.29 N	36.16 E
Kafr Takhārīm	130	36.07 N	36.31 E
Kafr Yāsīf	132	32.57 N	35.10 E
Kafta	144	13.56 N	37.13 E
Kafu ≃	154	1.08 N	31.05 E
Kafue	154	15.47 S	28.11 E
Kafue ≃	154	15.56 S	28.55 E
Kafue Flats ≚	154	15.40 S	27.25 E
Kafue Gorge ∨	154	15.54 S	28.34 E
Kafue National Park ♠	154	14.30 S	26.10 E
Kafulwe Mission	154	9.00 S	29.02 E
Kafumba	152	5.23 S	18.55 E
Kafwira	154	12.10 S	27.33 E
Kaga	94	36.18 N	136.18 E
Kagalaska Island ❙	181a	51.47 N	176.23 W
Kagal'nickaja	83	46.53 N	40.09 E
Kagal'nik	83	47.05 N	39.19 E
Kagal'nik ≃	83	47.04 N	39.18 E
Kagami	96	33.37 N	133.26 E
Kagamigahara	94	35.24 N	136.54 E
Kagamil Island ❙	180	53.00 N	169.43 W
Kāgān, Pāk.	123	34.47 N	73.32 E
Kagan, S.S.S.R.	128	39.43 N	64.33 E
Kagarko	150	9.29 N	7.41 E
Kagarlyk	78	49.51 N	30.50 E
Kagawa □[5]	96	31.25 N	134.00 E
Kagawong Lake ◎	190	45.49 N	82.18 W
Kagaznagar	122	19.18 N	79.50 E
Kåge	26	64.50 N	20.59 E
Kagelike	120	37.20 N	87.02 E
Kagera ≃	154	0.57 S	31.47 E
Kagera, Parc National de la ♠	154	1.30 S	30.35 E
Kågeröd	41	56.01 N	13.06 E
Kâğıthane	267b	41.04 N	28.58 E
Kâğıthane ≃	267b	41.03 N	28.56 E
Kagitumba	154	1.04 S	30.27 E
Kağızman	84	40.09 N	43.08 E
Käglan ⛰[2]	40	59.23 N	15.31 E
Kagmar	140	14.24 N	30.25 E
Kagopal	146	8.17 N	16.27 E
Kagoshima	92	31.36 N	130.33 E
Kagoshima-wan C	92	31.25 N	130.38 E
Kagran ◆[8]	264b	48.15 N	16.27 E
Kagul	78	45.54 N	28.11 E
Kagulu	154	1.15 N	33.18 E
Kagyo-ri	98	34.25 N	126.48 E
Kahak	128	34.23 N	50.32 E
Kahalīya, Jabal ∧	142	29.55 N	32.09 E
Kahaluu	229c	21.28 N	157.50 W
Kahama	154	3.50 S	32.36 E
Kahana Bay C	229c	21.34 N	157.52 W
Kahayan ≃	112	3.20 S	114.04 E
Kahe	154	3.30 S	37.26 E
Kahemba	152	7.17 S	19.00 E
Kahia	154	6.21 S	28.24 E
Kahiu Point C	229a	21.13 N	156.58 W
Kahk	142	29.25 N	30.38 E
Kahl ≃	56	50.04 N	9.00 E
Kahla	54	50.48 N	11.35 E
Kahl am Main	56	50.04 N	9.00 E
Kahlenberg ∧	264b	48.16 N	16.21 E
Kahler Asten ∧	56	51.11 N	8.29 E
Kāhna	123	31.22 N	74.22 E
Kahnūj	128	27.58 N	57.45 E
Kahoka	194	40.25 N	91.43 W
Kahoku-gata ◎	94	36.40 N	136.41 E
Kahoolawe ❙	229a	20.33 N	156.37 W
Kahouanne, Îlet à ❙	241o	16.22 N	61.47 W
Kahoué, Mont ∧	150	7.06 N	7.15 W
Kahror Pakka	123	29.37 N	71.55 E
Kahshe Lake ◎	212	44.52 N	79.16 W
Kahuku	229c	21.41 N	157.57 W
Kahuku Point ≻	229c	21.43 N	157.59 W
Kahului	229a	20.54 N	156.28 W
Kahului Airport ⊠	229a	20.54 N	156.26 W
Kahului Bay C	229a	20.54 N	156.28 W
Kahurangi Point ≻	172	40.47 S	172.13 E
Kahūta	123	33.35 N	73.23 E
Kahyŏn-bong ∧	271b	37.38 N	126.39 E
Kahyŏn-ni	271b	37.32 N	126.44 E
Kai	164	2.15 S	136.32 E
Kai, Kepulauan ❙❙	164	5.35 S	132.45 E
Kai, Tanjung ≻	112	2.52 S	118.45 E
Kaia, Wādī ∨	140	11.31 N	24.15 E
Kaiai, Jabal ∧	140	19.54 N	36.48 E
Kaiama	150	9.37 N	3.58 E
Kaiapit	164	6.15 S	146.15 E
Kaiapoi	172	43.23 S	172.40 E
Kaibab Gulch ∨	200	37.01 N	111.52 W
Kaibab Indian Reservation ◆[4]	200	36.55 N	112.40 W
Kaibab Plateau ⛰[1]	200	36.30 N	112.15 W
Kaibara	96	35.08 N	135.05 E
Kai Besar ❙	164	5.35 S	133.00 E
Kaibing	61	47.12 N	15.50 E
Kaibito Plateau ⛰[1]	200	36.40 N	111.20 W
Kaichengqiao	100	31.18 N	117.44 E
Kaida	94	35.56 N	137.36 E
Kaidori	268	35.37 N	139.27 E
Kaiedin	140	9.45 N	32.11 E
Kaieteur Fall ʟ	246	5.10 N	59.28 W
Kaifeng	98	34.51 N	114.21 E
Kaifu ≃	96	33.35 N	134.22 E
Kaihe	98	35.42 N	116.20 E
Kaihu	172	35.46 S	173.42 E
Kaihua	100	29.09 N	118.23 E
Kai-iwi	172	39.51 S	174.56 E
Kaijian	102	23.42 N	111.48 E
Kaijiang	102	31.05 N	107.55 E
Kaijo → Kaesŏng	98	37.59 N	126.33 E
Kaijō-jieitai-kasuga-kōkūkichi ■	96	33.31 N	130.28 E
Kaijō-jieitai-shimofusa-kōkūkichi (Shimofusa Naval Air Base) ■	94	35.48 N	140.02 E
Kai Kecil ❙	164	5.45 S	132.40 E
Kaikche	172	35.25 S	173.48 E
Kaikoura	172	42.25 S	173.41 E
Kaikoura Peninsula ≻[1]	172	42.26 S	173.42 E
Kailahun	150	8.17 N	10.34 W
Kailāshahar	120	24.20 N	92.01 E
Kaili	102	26.22 N	108.01 E
Kailu	89	43.36 N	121.14 E
Kailua	229c	21.24 N	157.44 W
Kailua Bay C	229c	21.25 N	157.44 W
Kailua Kona	229d	19.39 N	155.59 W
Kaim ≃	164	6.40 S	141.45 E
Kaïmakchalán ∧	38	40.58 N	21.48 E
Kaimana	164	3.39 S	133.45 E
Kaimanawa Mountains ⛰	172	39.15 S	175.54 E
Kaiman-Inseln → Cayman Islands □[2]	238	19.30 N	80.40 W
Kaimenshan	104	41.03 N	123.08 E
Kaimganj	124	27.34 N	79.21 E
Kaimon-dake ∧	92	31.11 N	130.32 E
Kain	50	50.38 N	3.22 E
Käina	76	58.50 N	22.45 E
Kainach ≃	61	46.54 N	15.31 E
Kainan, Nihon	96	34.09 N	135.12 E
Kainan, Nihon	96	33.36 N	134.22 E
Kainantu	164	6.15 S	145.55 E
Kainda	85	42.50 N	73.41 E
Kai-Ndunda	152	5.42 S	12.42 E
Kaingan ≃	115a	7.44 S	107.54 E
Kainji Dam ◆[6]	150	9.55 N	4.35 E
Kainji Lake ◎[1]	150	10.30 N	4.35 E
Kaintragarh	120	20.43 N	84.32 E
Kaioba	112	5.20 S	122.37 E
Kaipara Harbour C	172	36.25 S	174.13 E
Kaiparowits Plateau ⛰[1]	200	37.20 N	111.15 W
Kaiping	105	39.41 N	118.16 E
Kairābani	126	24.08 N	87.02 E
Kairaku-en ♠	94	36.22 N	140.27 E
Kairāna	124	29.24 N	77.12 E
Kairiru Island ❙	164	3.20 S	143.35 E
Kairo → Al-Qāhirah	142	30.03 N	31.15 E
Kairouan → El Kairouan	148	35.41 N	10.07 E
Kairouan □[8]	36	35.30 N	9.55 E
Kairuku	164	8.50 S	146.35 E
Kairy	78	46.57 N	33.43 E
Kaisarganj	124	27.15 N	81.33 E
Kaisarianí	267c	37.58 N	23.47 E
Kaisarianí, Moní ▽[1]	267c	37.58 N	23.47 E
Kaisergebirge ⛰	64	47.36 N	12.20 E
Kaiserhaus	64	47.32 N	11.55 E
Kaisermühlen ◆[8]	264b	48.14 N	16.26 E
Kaiser Pass)(	226	37.17 N	119.06 W
Kaisersesch	56	50.14 N	7.08 E
Kaiserslautern	56	49.26 N	7.46 E
Kaiserstuhl ∧	58	48.06 N	7.40 E
Kaiserswerth ◆[8]	263	51.18 N	6.44 E
Kaiser-Wilhelm-Museum ▽	263	51.20 N	6.34 E
Kaisheim	56	48.46 N	10.48 E
Kaišiadorys	76	54.52 N	24.27 E
Kait, Tanjung ≻	112	3.14 S	106.05 E
Kaitaia	172	35.07 S	173.16 E
Kai Tak Airport ⊠	271d	22.20 N	114.12 E
Kaitangata	172	46.18 S	169.51 E
Kaitersberg ⛰	60	49.11 N	12.57 E
Kaithal	124	29.48 N	76.23 E
Kaituma ≃	246	8.11 N	59.41 W
Kaiwaka	172	36.10 S	174.27 E
Kaiwatu	164	8.07 S	127.49 E
Kaiwi Channel ⋓	229b	21.15 N	157.30 W
Kaixian	102	31.13 N	108.25 E
Kaiyang	102	26.58 N	106.40 E
Kaiyuan, Zhg.	102	23.44 N	103.11 E
Kaiyuan, Zhg.	104	42.37 N	124.04 E
Kaiyuancheng	98	42.37 N	124.04 E
Kaiyuh Mountains ⛰	180	64.00 N	158.00 W
Kaizhou	104	41.22 N	121.19 E
Kaizuka	96	34.27 N	135.21 E
Kaja, Wādī (Ouadi Kadja) ∨	146	12.02 N	22.28 E
Kajaani	26	64.14 N	27.41 E
Kajabbi	166	20.02 S	140.02 E
Kajakī, Band-e ◎[1]	128	32.22 N	65.16 E
Kājālia	126	23.01 N	89.57 E
Kajang, Indon.	112	5.20 S	120.21 E
Kajang, Malay.	114	2.59 N	101.47 E
Kajasan	86	55.12 N	62.16 E
Kajasula	84	44.19 N	44.59 E
Kajen	115a	7.02 S	109.34 E
Kajgy	86	50.55 N	64.43 E
Kajiado	154	1.51 S	36.47 E
Kājlāgarh	126	22.02 N	87.47 E
Kajmanačicha	86	53.32 N	75.11 E
Kajmonovo	88	56.50 N	104.54 E
Kajmysovy	86	59.48 N	76.31 E
Kajnar	86	49.12 N	77.25 E
Kajnupil'gyn, Laguna C	180	63.30 N	178.50 E
Kajo Kaji	154	3.53 N	31.40 E
Kajrakkum	85	40.16 N	69.49 E
Kajrakkumskoje Vodochranilišce ◎[1]	85	40.20 N	70.10 E
Kajrakty	86	48.31 N	73.14 E
Kajsackoje	80	49.44 N	46.51 E
Kajuru	150	10.21 N	7.40 E
Kaka, Centraf.	140	6.01 N	26.30 E
Kākā, Sūd.	140	10.36 N	32.11 E
Kakabia, Pulau ❙	112	6.54 S	122.13 E
Kakagi Lake ◎	184	49.13 N	93.52 W
Kakamas	158	28.45 S	20.33 E
Kakamega	154	0.17 N	34.45 E
Kakana	110	9.07 N	92.49 E
Kakanui Mountains ⛰	172	45.09 S	170.26 E
Kaka Point	172	46.23 S	169.47 E
Kaka Point ≻	229a	20.31 N	156.33 W
Kakaramea	172	39.43 S	174.27 E
Kakasa	164	9.20 S	148.45 E
Kakata	150	6.35 N	10.19 W
Kakatahi	172	39.41 S	175.20 E
Kākdwīp	126	21.53 N	88.11 E
Kake, Alaska, U.S.	180	56.58 N	133.46 W
Kakehashi ≃	94	36.25 N	136.25 E
Kakelwe ∧	154	4.49 S	29.00 E
Kakenge	152	4.51 S	21.55 E
Kakhonak	180	59.26 N	154.51 W
Kakhra	126	21.38 N	87.27 E
Kākī	128	28.19 N	51.34 E
Kākināda	122	16.56 N	82.13 E
Kakino	80	55.12 N	44.53 E
Kakisa Lake ◎	176	60.55 N	117.40 W
Kako ≃, Guy.	246	5.46 N	60.35 W
Kako ≃, Nihon	96	34.44 N	134.49 E
Kakoaka	156	18.40 S	24.22 E
Kakogawa	96	34.46 N	134.51 E
Kakrāla	272a	28.33 N	77.25 E
Kāksa	126	23.28 N	87.28 E
Kaktovik	180	70.08 N	143.37 W
Kakui-shima ❙	96	34.43 N	134.19 E
Kakuma	154	3.43 N	34.52 E
Kakus ≃	112	2.46 N	113.01 E
Kakwa ≃	182	54.36 N	118.28 W
Kala, Nig.	146	12.05 N	14.27 E
Kala, Zhg.	120	36.47 N	83.48 E
Kala, Zhg.	124	28.16 N	89.23 E
Kala ≃	122	8.18 N	79.50 E
Kalaa Kebira	148	35.52 N	10.32 E
Kalaa Srira	36	35.49 N	10.33 E
Kālābagh	123	32.58 N	71.34 E
Kalabahi	112	8.13 S	124.31 E
Kalabáka	38	39.42 N	21.43 E
Kalabakan	112	4.25 N	117.29 E
Kalabo	152	14.57 S	22.40 E
Kalabula	86	43.24 N	83.06 E
Kalač	78	50.25 N	41.01 E
Kalacık	130	37.17 N	39.02 E
Kalačinsk	86	55.03 N	74.34 E
Kalač-Kurtlak	80	49.00 N	42.26 E
Kalač-na-Donu	80	48.43 N	43.31 E
Kalačskaja Vozvyšennost' ⛰[1]	80	50.30 N	41.30 E
Kaladan ≃	110	20.09 N	92.57 E
Kaladar	212	44.39 N	77.07 W
Kalae	229a	21.10 N	157.00 W
Ka Lae ≻	229d	18.55 N	155.41 W
Kalaeerqisihe ≃	86	47.52 N	84.50 E
Kalaena ≃	112	2.40 S	120.53 E
Kalagan	89	50.30 N	119.55 E
Kalagwe	110	22.31 N	96.31 E
Kalahai ◎	102	35.16 N	99.26 E
Kalahari Desert ◆[2]	156	24.00 S	21.30 E
Kalahari Gemsbok National Park ♠	156	25.30 S	20.30 E
Kālahasti	122	13.45 N	79.43 E
Kalaheo	229b	21.56 N	159.32 W
Kālaia	126	22.23 N	90.36 E
Kalai-Chumb	85	38.28 N	70.46 E
Kalai-Mor	128	35.39 N	62.33 E
Kalais	80	52.38 N	42.38 E
Kalaiya	124	27.02 N	85.00 E
Kalajka	88	58.28 N	111.46 E
Kalajoki	26	64.15 N	23.57 E
Kalajoki ≃	26	64.17 N	23.55 E
Kalakamate	156	20.39 S	27.21 E
Kalakan	88	55.08 N	116.45 E
Kalakan ≃	88	55.07 N	116.46 E
Kalakashihe ≃	120	37.00 N	79.45 E
Kalakepen	114	2.45 N	97.50 E
Kalām	123	35.28 N	72.35 E
Kalama, Wash., U.S.	224	46.01 N	122.51 W
Kalama, Zaïre	154	2.55 S	28.33 E
Kalama ≃	224	46.02 N	122.52 W
Kalama, Pulau ❙	112	3.15 N	125.28 E
Kalámai	38	37.04 N	22.07 E
Kalamaki	130	36.15 N	29.24 E
Kalamákion	267c	37.55 N	23.43 E
Kalamalka Lake ◎	182	50.09 N	119.22 W
Kalamariá	38	40.35 N	22.58 E
Kalamazoo	216	42.17 N	85.32 W
Kalamazoo □[6]	216	42.14 N	85.32 W
Kalamazoo ≃	216	42.40 N	86.10 W
Kalamazoo, North Branch ≃	216	42.14 N	84.44 W
Kalamazoo, South Branch ≃	216	42.14 N	84.44 W
Kalamazoo Lake C	216	42.39 N	86.13 W
Kalamba	152	0.26 S	18.17 E
Kalambau, Pulau ❙	112	4.55 S	115.39 E
Kalambo Falls ʟ	154	8.36 S	31.14 E
Kalamboli	272c	19.01 N	73.06 E
Kalamitskij Zaliv C	78	45.05 N	33.23 E
Kalamo	216	42.32 N	85.01 W
Kalampáka	38	39.42 N	21.39 E
Kalampising	112	3.44 N	116.42 E
Kalamunda	168a	31.57 S	116.03 E
Kalan	84	39.07 N	39.32 E
Kalan □[4]	84	39.20 N	39.30 E
Kalana	150	10.47 N	8.12 W
Kalančak	78	46.16 N	33.17 E
Kalang ≃	271c	1.19 N	103.52 E
Kalange-Bushimaie ≃	152	7.55 S	23.11 E
Kalankalan	150	10.07 N	8.54 W
Kalannie	162	30.21 S	117.04 E
Kālānwāli	123	29.51 N	74.57 E
Kalao, Pulau ❙	112	7.18 S	120.58 E
Kalaong	116	6.04 N	124.28 E
Kalaotoa, Pulau ❙	112	7.22 S	121.47 E
Kalapana	229d	19.22 N	154.58 W
Kalapāra	126	21.59 N	90.14 E
Kalaqinqi	98	41.56 N	118.36 E
Kalar ≃	88	55.23 N	116.18 E
Kalaraš	78	47.16 N	28.19 E
Kälarne	26	62.59 N	16.05 E
Kalāroa	126	22.52 N	89.02 E
Kalasarv	84	39.11 N	48.03 E
Kalashankou	120	35.06 N	91.51 E
Kalashayinshan ∧	102	35.28 N	97.55 E
Kalasi	86	48.43 N	86.59 E
Kalasin, Indon.	112	0.12 N	114.16 E
Kalasin, Thai	110	16.29 N	103.30 E
Kalašnikovo	76	57.17 N	35.13 E
Kalāt	120	29.02 N	66.35 E
Kalatungan Mountain ∧	116	7.58 N	124.47 E
Kalaupapa	229a	21.11 N	156.59 W
Kalaupapa Peninsula ≻[1]	229a	21.13 N	156.58 W
Kalauri	84	41.49 N	45.42 E
Kalaus ≃	80	45.43 N	44.07 E
Kalaus-Kr'akovka	83	48.46 N	38.52 E
Kalavárdha	38	36.20 N	27.57 E
Kalávrita	38	38.01 N	22.06 E
Kalaw	110	20.38 N	96.34 E
Kal'azin	76	57.15 N	37.52 E
Kalb, Nahr al- ≃	132	33.57 N	35.35 E
Kalb, Ra's al- ≻	144	14.02 N	48.40 E
Kalbā'	128	25.03 N	56.21 E
Kalbar	171a	27.56 S	152.37 E
Kalbe	54	52.40 N	11.25 E
Kalbinskij Chrebet ⛰	86	49.10 N	83.00 E
Kalchās	120	29.21 N	69.42 E
Kal'čik ≃	83	47.07 N	37.36 E
Kaldırım ≃	267b	41.10 N	29.12 E
Kaldygajty ≃	80	49.20 N	52.38 E
Kale, Tür.	130	40.23 N	39.39 E
Kale, Tür.	130	37.26 N	28.51 E
Kalecik	130	40.06 N	33.25 E
Kaleden	182	49.23 N	119.35 W
Kaledupa, Pulau ❙	112	5.32 S	123.47 E
Kalegauk Island ❙	110	15.32 N	97.40 E
Kalehe	154	2.06 S	28.55 E
Kaleindaung ≃	110	18.50 N	94.00 E
Kalema, Tan.	154	1.12 S	31.50 E
Kalema, Zaïre	152	4.08 S	24.15 E
Kalemie (Albertville)	154	5.56 S	29.12 E
Kalemyo	120	23.12 N	94.10 E
Kalene Hill	152	11.11 S	24.10 E
Kaleščatovka	83	49.35 N	39.55 E
Kaletwa	110	21.45 N	92.48 E
Kalety	30	50.34 N	18.54 E
Kalevala	24	65.13 N	31.08 E
Kalewa	110	23.12 N	94.17 E
Kale Water ≃	46	55.32 N	2.28 W
Kaleybar	84	38.47 N	47.02 E
Kálfafell	24a	63.58 N	17.40 W
Kalga	88	50.57 N	118.48 E
Kalgačicha	24	63.20 N	36.44 E
Kalgan, Austl.	162	34.53 S	118.01 E
Kalgan → Zhangjiakou, Zhg.	105	40.50 N	114.53 E
Kalgin Island ❙	180	60.28 N	151.55 W
Kalgoorlie	162	30.45 S	121.28 E
Kalhe	272c	18.52 N	73.06 E
Kali	150	12.10 N	11.29 W
Kāli (Sārda) ≃	124	27.21 N	81.23 E
Kālia	126	23.03 N	89.38 E
Kāliāghaj ≃	126	22.10 N	87.50 E
Kāliākair	126	24.05 N	90.14 E
Kaliakra, nos ≻	38	43.21 N	28.27 E
Kalianda	115a	5.45 S	105.38 E
Kalianget	115a	7.03 S	113.56 E
Kalibek, Ozero ◎	86	53.52 N	70.40 E

Symbol	English	Deutsch	Español	Français	Português
≃	River	Fluss	Río	Rivière	Rio
⩧	Canal	Kanal	Canal	Canal	Canal
ʟ	Waterfall, Rapids	Wasserfall, Stromschnellen	Cascada, Rápidos	Chute d'eau, Rapides	Cascata, Rápidos
⋓	Strait	Meeresstrasse	Estrecho	Détroit	Estreito
C	Bay, Gulf	Bucht, Golf	Bahía, Golfo	Baie, Golfe	Baía, Golfo
◎	Lake, Lakes	See, Seen	Lago, Lagos	Lac, Lacs	Lago, Lagos
☷	Swamp	Sumpf	Pantano	Marais	Pântano
⊓	Ice Features, Glacier	Eis- und Gletscherformen	Accidentes Glaciales	Formes glaciaires	Acidentes Glaciares
⊤	Other Hydrographic Features	Andere Hydrographische Objekte	Otros Elementos Hidrográficos	Autres données hydrographiques	Outros Elementos Hidrográficos

Symbol	English	Deutsch	Español	Français	Português
⊹	Submarine Features	Untermeerische Objekte	Accidentes Submarinos	Formes de relief sous-marin	Acidentes Submarinos
□	Political Unit	Politische Einheit	Unidad Politica	Entité politique	Unidade Política
▽	Cultural Institution	Kulturelle Institution	Institución Cultural	Institution culturelle	Instituição Cultural
⊥	Historical Site	Historische Stätte	Sitio Histórico	Site historique	Sitio Histórico
♠	Recreational Site	Erholungs- und Ferienort	Sitio de Recreo	Centre de loisirs	Sítio de Lazer
⊠	Airport	Flughafen	Aeropuerto	Aéroport	Aeroporto
■	Military Installation	Militäranlage	Instalación Militar	Installation militaire	Instalação Militar
◆	Miscellaneous	Verschiedenes	Misceláneo	Divers	Miscelânea

Kālībhīt Hills ⛰[2] 124 22.10 N 77.30 E
Kalibo 116 11.43 N 122.22 E
Kalida 216 40.59 N 84.12 W
Kalifornien,, Golf von → California, Golfo de C 232 28.00 N 112.00 W
Kāli Gandaki ≃ 124 27.42 N 84.25 E
Kāliganga ≃ 126 23.43 N 90.15 E
Kāli Ganga ≃[1] 126 23.40 N 89.12 E
Kāliganj, Bhārat 126 23.44 N 88.14 E
Kālīganj, Bngl. 126 23.25 N 89.08 E
Kālīganj, Bngl. 126 22.28 N 89.02 E
Kalihiwai ≃ 229b 22.13 N 159.26 W
Kalijati 115a 6.32 S 107.40 E
Kālikāpur, Bhārat 126 22.37 N 86.17 E
Kālikāpur, Bhārat 272b 22.29 N 88.32 E
Kālikāpur, Bngl. 126 22.43 N 89.26 E
Kālikāpur, Bngl. 126 23.46 N 89.55 E
Kalikino, S.S.S.R. 76 52.57 N 39.50 E
Kalikino, S.S.S.R. 80 52.55 N 54.05 E
Kalima 154 2.34 S 26.37 E
Kalimantan → Borneo I 112 0.30 N 114.00 E
Kalimantan Barat □[4] 112 0.30 N 110.00 E
Kalimantan Selatan □[4] 112 2.30 S 115.30 E
Kalimantan Tengah □[4] 112 2.00 S 113.30 E
Kalimantan Timur □[4] 112 1.30 N 116.30 E
Kálimnos 38 36.57 N 26.59 E
Kálimnos I 38 37.00 N 27.00 E
Kālimpong 124 27.04 N 88.29 E
Kalina ✦[8] 273b 4.18 S 15.16 E
Kalina, Pointe de ≻ 273b 4.18 S 15.16 E
Kālīnadi ≃ 122 14.50 N 74.08 E
Kālinagar 126 22.26 N 88.51 E
Kalinga-Apayao □[4] 116 17.50 N 121.10 E
Kalinga Bil @ 272b 22.33 N 88.33 E
Kalinin, S.S.S.R. 80 47.11 N 42.10 E
Kalinin, S.S.S.R. 82 56.52 N 35.55 E
Kalinin □[4] 82 56.45 N 36.30 E
Kalininabad 85 39.45 N 69.08 E
Kaliningrad (Königsberg), S.S.S.R. 76 54.43 N 20.30 E
Kaliningrad, S.S.S.R. 82 55.55 N 37.49 E
Kalinku 154 11.12 S 33.12 E
Kalinovik 38 43.31 N 18.26 E
Kalipara 126 22.09 N 89.16 E
Kālipur 272b 22.41 N 88.17 E
Kaliro 154 0.54 N 33.30 E
Kalis 144 8.20 N 49.47 E
Kalisch → Kalisz 30 51.46 N 18.06 E
Kāli Sindh ≃ 124 25.32 N 76.17 E
Kalispell 202 48.12 N 114.19 W
Kalistraticha 86 52.59 N 83.35 E
Kalisz 30 51.46 N 18.06 E
Kalisz Pomorski 30 53.19 N 15.54 E
Kalitva ≃ 78 48.10 N 40.46 E
Kaliua 154 5.04 S 31.48 E
Kaliveli Tank @[1] 122 12.05 N 79.50 E
Kalix 26 65.51 N 23.08 E
Kalixälven ≃ 24 65.50 N 23.11 E
Kāliyāganj 124 25.38 N 88.19 E
Kālka 123 30.50 N 76.56 E
Kālkāji ✦[8] 272a 28.33 N 77.16 E
Kalkaman 86 51.58 N 76.02 E
Kalkar 52 50.36 N 6.46 E
Kalkaska 190 44.44 N 85.11 W
Kalkfeld 156 20.53 S 16.11 E
Kalkfontein 156 22.08 S 20.53 E
Kalkfonteindam ✦[6] 158 29.30 S 25.15 E
Kalkhorst 54 53.58 N 11.02 E
Kālkini 126 23.06 N 90.16 E
Kalkmond 158 28.40 S 20.26 E
Kalkrand 156 24.03 S 17.33 E
Kalksburg ✦[8] 264b 48.08 N 16.15 E
Kalk-See @ 264a 52.26 N 13.46 E
Kalkstasie 158 30.00 S 18.55 E
Kalkum 263 51.18 N 6.46 E
Kalkutta → Calcutta 126 22.32 N 88.22 E
Kall 56 50.32 N 6.32 E
Kallakkurichchi 122 11.44 N 78.58 E
Kallakoopah Creek ≃ 166 27.29 S 138.15 E
Kållandsö I 26 58.40 N 13.09 E
Kallar Kahār 123 32.47 N 72.42 E
Kallaste 76 58.39 N 27.09 E
Kallavesi @ 26 62.50 N 27.45 E
Kalletal 52 52.06 N 8.56 E
Källfallet 40 59.50 N 15.31 E
Kallhäll 40 59.27 N 17.48 E
Kalliecahoolie Lake @ 184 54.14 N 95.29 W
Kallies → Kalisz Pomorski 30 53.19 N 15.54 E
Kallinge 26 56.14 N 15.17 E
Kallista 274b 37.53 S 145.22 E
Kallithéa 267c 37.57 N 23.42 E
Kallmünz 60 49.09 N 11.58 E
Kallnach 58 47.01 N 7.14 E
Kallsjön @ 26 63.37 N 13.00 E
Kalmakkora 86 44.03 N 78.44 E
Kalmakkyrgan ≃ 86 46.58 N 64.30 E
Kalmar 26 56.40 N 16.22 E
Kalmar Län □[6] 26 57.20 N 16.00 E
Kalmarsund ⋓ 26 56.40 N 16.25 E
Kalmit ∧ 56 49.19 N 8.05 E
Kal'mius ≃ 83 47.05 N 37.34 E
Kalmthout 50 51.23 N 4.28 E
Kalmyckaja Avtonomnaja Sovetskaja Socialističeskaja Respublika □[3] 80 46.30 N 45.30 E
Kalmyckije Mysy 86 51.53 N 82.16 E
Kalmykov 80 49.01 N 42.49 E
Kalmykovka, S.S.S.R. 83 49.17 N 38.39 E
Kalmykovka, S.S.S.R. 83 49.17 N 39.52 E
Kalmykovo 80 49.03 N 51.47 E
Kālna 126 23.13 N 88.22 E
Kalnciems 76 56.50 N 23.37 E
Kal'niboloto 78 48.44 N 31.00 E
Kalnibolotskaja 78 46.01 N 40.28 E
Kalničko Gorje ⛰ 36 46.10 N 16.30 E
Kalo 164 10.00 S 147.45 E
Kalocsa 30 46.32 N 18.59 E
Kalofer 38 42.37 N 24.59 E
Kalohi Channel ⋓ 229a 21.00 N 156.56 W
Kaloko 154 6.47 S 25.48 E
Kālol, Bhārat 120 23.15 N 72.29 E
Kālol, Bhārat 120 22.36 N 73.27 E
Kalole 154 3.42 S 27.22 E
Kalolio 112 0.11 S 121.38 E
Kaloli Point ≻ 229d 19.38 N 154.57 W
Kalomo 154 17.02 S 26.30 E
Kalomo ≃ 154 17.57 S 26.24 E
Kalona 190 41.29 N 91.43 W
Kalonda 152 4.48 S 17.33 E
Kalone Peak ∧ 182 52.38 N 126.37 W
Kalonga 154 9.10 S 27.25 E
Kalorama 274b 37.49 S 145.22 E
Kaloran 115a 7.15 S 110.15 E
Kalø Vig C 41 56.15 N 10.25 E
Kalpáki 38 39.55 N 20.20 E
Kalpeni Island I 122 10.05 N 73.38 E
Kālpi 124 26.07 N 79.44 E
Kāl Qal'eh 128 32.38 N 62.32 E
Kalri 123 31.39 N 72.33 E
Kalskag 180 61.30 N 160.23 W
Kalsūbai ∧ 122 19.36 N 73.43 E
Kaltag 180 64.20 N 158.44 W
Kaltan 86 53.30 N 87.17 E
Kaltbrunn 58 47.12 N 9.02 E
Kalte Herberge ∧ 56 50.03 N 7.59 E
Kaltenbrunn 60 49.39 N 11.57 E
Kalteneber 56 51.19 N 10.08 E
Kaltenhouse 56 48.48 N 7.50 E
Kaltenkirchen 52 53.50 N 9.58 E
Kaltenleutgeben 264b 48.07 N 16.12 E
Kaltennordheim 56 50.38 N 10.10 E
Kaltensundheim 56 50.36 N 10.10 E
Kalter Gang ≃ 264b 48.02 N 16.25 E
Kalthof 263 51.26 N 7.40 E
Kal'tino 265a 59.58 N 30.40 E
Kaluga 82 54.31 N 36.16 E
Kaluga □[4] 82 54.45 N 36.30 E
Kalugino, S.S.S.R. 80 48.22 N 51.33 E
Kalugino, S.S.S.R. 82 54.59 N 37.11 E
Kalukalukuang, Pulau I 112 5.14 S 117.38 E
Kalulushi 154 12.50 S 28.03 E
Kalumba, Mount ∧ 166 31.49 S 146.22 E
Kalumburu 164 14.18 S 126.39 E
Kalundborg 41 55.41 N 11.06 E
Kalundborg Fjord C 41 55.41 N 11.00 E
Kālundri 272c 18.59 N 73.08 E
Kalundu, Zaïre 154 3.26 S 29.08 E
Kalundu, Zam. 154 10.16 S 29.24 E
Kālupāra 126 22.58 N 90.10 E
Kalūr Kot 123 32.09 N 71.16 E
Kaluš 78 49.03 N 24.23 E
Kałuszyn 30 52.13 N 21.49 E
Kalutara 122 6.35 N 79.58 E
Kalvåg 26 61.46 N 4.53 E
Kalvarija 76 54.21 N 23.14 E
K'alvaz 84 38.39 N 48.18 E
Kalvehave 41 55.00 N 12.10 E
Kälviä 26 63.52 N 23.26 E
Kalwa 272c 19.12 N 72.59 E
Kalwang 61 47.26 N 14.46 E
Kalwaria Zebrzydowska 30 49.52 N 19.41 E
Kalyān 122 19.15 N 73.09 E
Kalyāndrug 122 14.33 N 77.06 E
Kam ≃ 146 8.15 N 11.00 E
Kama, Mya. 110 19.02 N 95.06 E
Kama, S.S.S.R. 80 56.19 N 54.06 E
Kama, S.S.S.R. 86 60.08 N 62.10 E
Kama, Zaïre 154 3.32 S 27.07 E
Kama ≃ 72 55.45 N 52.00 E
Kamachumu 154 1.35 S 31.37 E
Kamado-zaki ≻ 96 33.04 N 132.17 E
Kamae 92 32.48 N 131.56 E
Kamagaya 94 35.45 N 140.01 E
Kamaiki Point ≻ 229a 20.46 N 156.50 W
Kamaishi 92 39.16 N 141.53 E
Kama-iwa I 174f 24.47 N 141.17 E
Kamajai 76 55.49 N 25.30 E
Kamakou ∧ 229a 21.07 N 156.52 W
Kamakura 94 35.19 N 139.33 E
Kamakwie 150 9.30 N 12.14 W
Kamal 115a 7.10 S 112.42 E
Kamālia 123 30.44 N 72.39 E
Kamamaung 110 17.21 N 97.40 E
Kāman, Bhārat 124 27.39 N 77.16 E
Kaman, Tür. 130 39.22 N 33.44 E
Kaman ≃ 110 14.48 N 106.51 E
Kamana 154 5.59 S 24.56 E
Kamanashi ≃ 94 35.33 N 138.28 E
Kamango 154 0.39 N 29.53 E
Kamaniskeg Lake @ 212 45.25 N 77.42 W
Kamanjab 156 19.35 S 14.51 E
Kamapanda 152 12.00 S 24.10 E
Kamaraerdő ✦[3] 264c 47.26 N 19.00 E
Kamarān I 144 15.21 N 42.34 E
Kamaran, Hadjer ∧ 146 12.41 N 21.46 E
Kamarang ≃ 246 5.53 N 60.35 W
Kāmāreddi 122 18.19 N 78.21 E
Kāmārhāti 272b 22.40 N 88.22 E
Kamarik 130 39.37 N 39.18 E
Kāmārkhāli Ghāt 126 23.32 N 89.33 E
Kāmārkunda 272b 22.49 N 88.13 E
Kamas 200 40.38 N 111.17 W
Kamata ✦[8] 268 35.33 N 139.43 E
Kamatsi Lake @ 184 56.10 N 102.15 W
Kamay 196 33.51 N 98.48 W
Kamba, Nig. 150 11.53 N 3.36 E
Kamba, Zhg. 120 28.17 N 88.32 E
Kambakota 152 7.10 N 17.54 E
Kamballie 162 30.48 S 121.30 E
Kambam 122 9.44 N 77.18 E
Kambang 112 1.42 S 100.42 E
Kambanga 152 13.23 S 23.03 E
Kambar 120 27.36 N 68.00 E
Kambara I 175g 18.57 S 178.57 W
Kambara-tunnel ✦[5] 94 35.02 N 138.31 E
Kambarka 80 56.17 N 54.12 E
Kambia 150 9.07 N 12.55 W
Kambja 76 58.14 N 26.42 E
Kambolé 150 8.45 N 1.36 E
Kambole Mission 154 8.46 S 30.46 E
Kambove 154 10.52 S 26.38 E
Kambu 115b 8.23 S 118.20 E
Kambuye 152 7.18 S 22.50 E
Kamčatka ≃ 74 56.15 N 162.30 E
Kamčatka, Poluostrov ≻[1] 74 56.00 N 160.00 E
Kamčatskij Zaliv C 74 55.35 N 162.21 E
Kâmchay Méa 110 11.35 N 105.40 E
Kamčija ≃ 38 43.02 N 27.53 E
Kāmdebpur, Bhārat 272b 22.54 N 88.20 E
Kāmdebpur, Bhārat 272b 22.47 N 88.30 E
Kamdēsh 123 35.24 N 71.20 E
Kameari ✦[8] 268 35.46 N 139.51 E
Kameel 158 26.38 S 24.58 E
Kame-gamori-yama ∧ 96 33.47 N 133.12 E
Kameido ✦[8] 268 35.42 N 139.50 E
Kamelik ≃ 80 52.06 N 49.30 E
Kamen, B.R.D. 52 51.35 N 7.40 E
Kamen', S.S.S.R. 76 55.01 N 28.53 E
Kamen', Gora ∧ 74 69.06 N 94.48 E
Kamenda 154 6.28 S 24.33 E
Kamenec 76 52.24 N 23.49 E
Kamenec-Podol'skij 78 48.41 N 26.36 E
Kamenický Šenov 54 50.45 N 14.29 E
Kamen' Ignatija, Ostrov I 84 39.38 N 49.43 E
Kamenjak, Rt ≻ 36 44.46 N 13.55 E
Kamenka ✦[8] 265a 60.03 N 30.11 E
Kamenka ≃, S.S.S.R. 78 47.39 N 34.02 E
Kamenka ≃, S.S.S.R. 78 49.47 N 30.01 E
Kamenka ≃, S.S.S.R. 83 47.30 N 38.54 E
Kamenka ≃, S.S.S.R. 83 49.35 N 39.05 E
Kamenka ≃, S.S.S.R. 88 58.33 N 95.51 E
Kamenka ≃, S.S.S.R. 265a 60.01 N 30.12 E
Kamenka-Bugskaja 78 50.07 N 24.20 E
Kamenka-Dneprovskaja 78 47.29 N 34.25 E
Kamen'-Kaširskij 78 51.38 N 24.58 E
Kamen'-na-Obi 86 53.47 N 81.20 E
Kamennogorsk 24 60.58 N 29.07 E
Kamennoje, S.S.S.R. 78 47.53 N 35.25 E
Kamennoje, S.S.S.R. 78 51.31 N 27.38 E
Kamennomostskij 84 44.18 N 40.12 E
Kamennougol'naja Gr'ada ⛰ 24 65.30 N 51.00 E
Kamennyj Brod, S.S.S.R. 78 50.25 N 27.49 E
Kamennyj Brod, S.S.S.R. 83 47.26 N 39.51 E
Kamenskoje, S.S.S.R. 74 62.30 N 166.12 E
Kamenskoje, S.S.S.R. 78 45.49 N 29.16 E
Kamenskoje, S.S.S.R. 82 55.16 N 36.50 E
Kamensk-Šachtinskij 83 48.21 N 40.19 E
Kamensk-Ural'skij 86 56.28 N 61.54 E
Kamenz 54 51.16 N 14.06 E
Kamerik 52 52.06 N 4.54 E
Kamerun → Cameroon □[1] 134 6.00 N 12.00 E
Kamerunberg → Cameroun, Mont ∧ 150 4.12 N 9.11 E
Kames 46 55.54 N 5.15 W
Kameškovo 80 56.21 N 41.00 E
Kāmet ∧ 120 30.54 N 79.37 E
Kameur, Bahr ≃ 146 9.26 N 20.50 E
Kamiah 202 46.14 N 116.02 W
Kamiakatsuka ✦[8] 268 35.46 N 139.39 E
Kamiak Butte ∧ 202 46.52 N 117.10 W
Kamień Krajeńskie 30 53.33 N 17.32 E
Kamienna ≃ 30 51.06 N 21.47 E
Kamienna Góra 30 50.47 N 16.01 E
Kamień Pomorski 30 53.58 N 14.46 E
Kamieńsk 30 51.12 N 19.30 E
Kamieskroon 156 30.09 S 17.56 E
Kamifukuoka 268 35.52 N 139.31 E
Kamigyō ✦[8] 270 35.02 N 135.45 E
Kamiigusa Stadium ♦ 268 35.43 N 139.37 E
Kamikamagari-jima I 96 34.11 N 132.44 E
Kamikitazawa ✦[8] 268 35.40 N 139.38 E
Kâmil 130 41.07 N 34.47 E
Kamilukuak Lake @ 176 62.22 N 101.40 W
Kamina 154 8.44 S 25.00 E
Kaminak Lake @ 176 62.10 N 95.00 W
Kaminaljuyú ⊥ 236 14.38 N 90.33 W
Kaminskij 80 57.10 N 41.28 E
Kaminuriak Lake @ 176 63.00 N 95.40 W
Kamioka 94 36.16 N 137.18 E
Kamioyamada 268 35.35 N 139.24 E
Kámiros ⊥ 38 36.19 N 27.57 E
Kamiryūzu-zaki ≻ 96 33.30 N 133.34 E
Kamisato 94 36.15 N 139.09 E
Kamishak Bay C 180 59.15 N 153.45 W
Kamishii 94 36.04 N 136.24 E
Kami-shima I 94 34.33 N 136.59 E
Kamishinden 270 34.49 N 135.30 E
Kamiš-Samarskich Ozer, Razlivy ☰ 80 48.50 N 50.50 E
Kamituga 154 3.04 S 28.11 E
Kamiyama-shima I 174m 26.15 N 127.35 E
Kamīzgān 84 38.58 N 47.44 E
Kamkhat Muḩaywir ∧[2] 132 31.08 N 36.30 E
Kamku 120 27.30 N 96.30 E
Kamla ≃ 124 26.22 N 85.53 E
Kamlach ≃ 58 48.30 N 10.22 E
Kamloops 182 50.40 N 120.20 W
Kamloops Indian Reserve ✦[4] 182 50.42 N 120.20 W
Kamloops Lake @ 182 50.43 N 120.33 W
Kammanassieberg ⛰ 158 33.39 S 22.43 E
Kammon-kyō ✦[5] 96 33.56 N 130.55 E
Kammuri-yama ∧ 92 34.28 N 132.05 E
Kamnik 36 46.13 N 14.37 E
Kamniokan 88 56.17 N 111.57 E
Kamo, N.Z. 172 35.41 S 174.19 E
Kamo ≃, Nihon 94 35.06 N 140.06 E
Kamo ≃, Nihon 96 33.56 N 133.09 E
Kamoa Mountains ⛰ 246 1.37 N 59.00 W
Kamoda-misaki ≻ 96 33.50 N 134.45 E
Kamohio Bay C 229a 20.31 N 156.36 W
Kamoshida ✦[8] 268 35.34 N 139.30 E
Kamp 56 50.14 N 7.37 E
Kamp ≃ 61 48.23 N 15.48 E
Kāmpa 272b 22.56 N 88.28 E
Kampala 154 0.19 N 32.25 E
Kampar 114 4.18 N 101.09 E
Kampar ≃ 112 0.32 N 103.08 E
Kamparkalns ∧[2] 76 57.18 N 22.47 E
Kampar-kanan ≃ 112 0.16 N 101.41 E
Kampen 52 52.33 N 5.54 E
Kampene 154 3.36 S 26.40 E
Kampfe, Lake @ 276 41.02 N 74.21 W
Kamphaeng, Khao ∧ 110 14.37 N 99.18 E
Kamphaeng Phet 110 16.28 N 99.30 E
Kampil 124 27.37 N 79.17 E
Kampinoska, Puszcza ✦[3] 30 52.20 N 20.30 E
Kampinoski Park Narodowy ♦ 30 52.20 N 20.35 E
Kampire Dior ∧ 123 36.43 N 74.17 E
Kampli 122 15.24 N 76.37 E
Kamp-Lintfort 52 51.30 N 6.31 E
Kamp'o 98 35.48 N 129.29 E
Kampolombo, Lake @ 154 11.37 S 29.42 E
Kampong Ayer Puteh 114 4.16 N 103.12 E
Kampong Baharu 114 3.43 N 103.17 E
Kampong Benta 114 3.32 N 103.22 E
Kampong Buloh 114 5.32 N 102.45 E
Kâmpóng Cham 110 12.00 N 105.27 E
Kampong Chenor 114 3.29 N 102.36 E
Kâmpóng Chhnăng 110 12.15 N 104.40 E
Kampong Dong 114 3.54 N 101.54 E
Kampong Guchil 114 5.33 N 102.14 E
Kampong Jabor 114 3.57 N 103.20 E
Kampong Jerangau 114 4.51 N 103.12 E
Kampong Kandang 114 2.11 N 102.18 E
Kâmpóng Kântuŏt 110 11.26 N 104.49 E
Kampong Kenyam 114 4.31 N 102.28 E
Kampong Kranji 271c 1.26 N 103.46 E
Kampong Kuala Kemaman 114 4.14 N 103.27 E
Kampong Lamir 114 3.36 N 103.21 E
Kampong Lawa 114 5.40 N 101.42 E
Kampong Loyang 271c 1.22 N 103.58 E
Kampong Mengkarak 114 3.19 N 102.27 E
Kampong Merang 114 5.32 N 102.57 E
Kampong Nuri 114 5.02 N 102.23 E
Kampong Penarek 114 5.37 N 102.48 E
Kampong Raja 114 5.48 N 102.35 E
Kampong Renggong 114 4.33 N 102.35 E
Kâmpóng Saôm 110 10.38 N 103.30 E
Kâmpóng Saôm, Chhâk C 110 10.50 N 103.32 E
Kampong Sebuyau 112 1.31 N 110.56 E
Kampong Sekendi 114 3.43 N 100.56 E
Kampong Surau 114 5.49 N 100.54 E
Kampong Tanjong Batu 114 3.12 N 103.27 E
Kampong Tanjong Keling 271c 1.18 N 103.42 E
Kampong Tebing Runtoh 271c 1.26 N 103.40 E
Kâmpóng Thum 110 12.42 N 104.54 E
Kâmpóng Trâlach 110 11.54 N 104.47 E
Kampong Ulu 110 10.03 N 98.33 E
Kampong Ulu Chalok 114 5.26 N 102.50 E
Kâmpôt 110 10.37 N 104.11 E
Kampsville 194 39.18 N 90.37 W
Kampti 150 10.08 N 3.27 W
Kâmpŭchéa □[1] 108 / 110 13.00 N 105.00 E
Kampung ≃ 164 5.44 S 138.24 E
Kampungbaru 112 1.12 S 102.57 E
Kampung Sailolof 164 1.15 S 130.46 E
Kampville 219 38.51 N 90.33 W
Kāmrānga 126 23.14 N 90.47 E
Kamrau, Teluk C 164 3.32 S 133.37 E
Kamrup □[5] 124 26.30 N 90.00 E
Kamsack 184 51.34 N 101.54 W
Kamsdorf 54 50.38 N 11.28 E
Kamskij 24 60.04 N 53.13 E
Kamskoje Ustje 80 55.13 N 49.16 E
Kamskoje Vodochranilišče @[1] 86 58.52 N 56.15 E
Kam Summa 144 0.18 N 42.48 E
Kamsu-ri 98 38.03 N 125.54 E
Kāmthi 120 21.14 N 79.12 E
Kam Tin 271d 22.27 N 114.03 E
Kamuchawie Lake @ 184 56.18 N 101.59 W
Kamudilo 154 7.42 S 27.18 E
Kamuela (Waimea) 229d 20.01 N 155.41 W
Kamui-misaki ≻ 92a 43.20 N 140.21 E
Kámuk, Cerro ∧ 236 9.17 N 83.04 W
Kamuli 154 0.57 N 33.07 E
Kamundan ≃ 164 2.17 S 132.39 E
Kamutambaie ≃ 152 7.17 S 23.41 E
Kamwandu 152 6.04 S 22.42 E
Kamyšet 88 55.12 N 98.42 E
Kamyšev, S.S.S.R. 80 46.39 N 42.38 E
Kamyšev, S.S.S.R. 80 46.53 N 42.31 E
Kamyševacha, S.S.S.R. 78 47.43 N 35.32 E
Kamyševacha, S.S.S.R. 83 48.42 N 38.23 E
Kamyševaja ≃ 80 46.15 N 45.05 E
Kamyševatskaja 78 46.25 N 37.57 E
Kamyševskaja 80 47.37 N 41.49 E
Kamyšin 80 50.06 N 45.24 E
Kamyškurgon 85 40.34 N 70.24 E
Kamyšla 80 54.07 N 52.10 E
Kamyšlov 86 56.52 N 62.43 E
Kamyšlovskij Log ∨ 86 55.00 N 71.00 E
Kamyslybas 86 46.11 N 61.57 E
Kamyslybas, Ozero @ 86 46.12 N 61.48 E
Kamyšnaja ≃ 83 48.55 N 39.55 E
Kamyšnoje 86 51.58 N 61.47 E
Kamyšovyj 80 46.26 N 45.12 E
Kamyš-Zar'a 78 47.19 N 36.42 E
Kamyz'ak 80 46.07 N 48.05 E
Kamyz'ak ≃ 80 46.00 N 48.06 E
Kan, Īrān 128 35.45 N 51.16 E
Kan, Sūd. 140 9.01 N 31.47 E
Kana ≃ 154 18.30 S 27.22 E
Kanaaupscow ≃ 176 53.39 N 77.09 W
Kanab 200 37.03 N 112.32 W
Kanab Creek ≃ 200 36.24 N 112.38 W
Kanada 96 33.41 N 130.47 E
Kanada → Canada □[1] 176 60.00 N 95.00 W
Kanadej 80 53.10 N 47.30 E
Kanae 94 35.30 N 137.49 E
Kanafis 140 9.48 N 25.40 E
Kanaga Island I 180 51.45 N 177.10 W
Kanaga Volcano ∧[1] 180 51.50 N 177.09 W
Kanagawa 268 35.28 N 139.38 E
Kanagawa □[5] 94 35.30 N 139.30 E
Kanagi 96 34.53 N 132.11 E
Kanai 268 35.35 N 139.28 E
Kānāipur 126 23.33 N 89.47 E
Kanairiktok ≃ 176 55.05 N 60.20 W
Kanā'is, Ra's al- ≻ 140 31.15 N 27.51 E
Kanajevka, S.S.S.R. 80 52.12 N 49.40 E
Kanajevka, S.S.S.R. 80 53.07 N 45.35 E
Kanaka Creek ≃ 226 39.25 N 120.57 W
Kanakapura 122 12.33 N 77.25 E
Kanakeswar 126 23.09 N 90.25 E
Kanákia I 267c 37.55 N 23.24 E
Kanākir 132 33.15 N 36.05 E
Kanal 64 46.05 N 13.38 E
Kanal-Inseln → Channel Islands II 28 49.20 N 2.20 W
Kanam 164 3.25 S 152.10 E
Kanamachi ✦[8] 268 35.56 N 139.53 E
Kanamori 268 35.32 N 139.28 E
Kanan 270 34.29 N 135.38 E
Kananaskis ≃ 182 51.05 N 115.03 W
Kananga (Luluabourg) 152 5.54 S 22.25 E
Kananggar 115b 10.03 S 120.22 E
Kanangra Walls •[4] 170 34.00 S 150.07 E
Kananikol'skoje 86 52.47 N 57.29 E
Kanaoka 270 34.33 N 135.32 E
Kanapou Bay C 229a 20.33 N 156.33 W
Kanarase-yama ∧ 96 33.26 N 131.15 E
Kanarraville 200 37.32 N 113.11 W
Kanaš 80 55.31 N 47.30 E
Kanasagō 94 36.33 N 140.28 E
Kanathea I 175g 17.16 S 179.09 W
Kanaudi 124 23.36 N 81.23 E
Kanava, S.S.S.R. 24 61.07 N 54.58 E
Kanava, S.S.S.R. 80 47.13 N 45.24 E
Kanavka 80 50.19 N 48.33 E
Kanawha 190 42.56 N 93.48 W
Kanawha ≃ 188 38.50 N 82.08 W
Kanazawa ✦[8] 268 35.20 N 139.38 E
Kanbalu 110 23.12 N 95.31 E
Kanbauk 110 14.36 N 98.02 E
Kanbe 110 16.42 N 96.01 E
Kančalan ≃ 180 65.08 N 176.25 E
Kanchanaburi 110 14.01 N 99.32 E
Kanchanadit 110 9.10 N 99.28 E
Kānchenjunga ∧ 124 27.42 N 88.08 E
Kānchipuram 122 12.50 N 79.43 E
Kanchow → Ganzhou 100 25.54 N 114.55 E
Kānchrāpāra 126 22.57 N 88.28 E
Kańczuga 30 49.59 N 22.24 E
Kandabulak 80 53.58 N 50.44 E
Kandagač 86 49.28 N 57.25 E
Kandāghat 123 30.59 N 77.07 E
Kandahar 184 51.46 N 104.21 W
Kandāhu 120 27.33 N 69.24 E
Kanda-Kanda 152 6.56 S 23.36 E
Kandala 152 6.02 S 19.24 E
Kandalakša 24 67.09 N 32.21 E
Kandalakšskaja Guba C 24 66.55 N 32.45 E
Kandang 114 3.03 N 97.20 E
Kandangan 112 2.47 S 115.16 E
Kandanghaur 115a 6.21 S 108.06 E
Kandat 86 57.08 N 89.02 E
Kandava 76 57.05 N 22.49 E
Kandavu I 175g 19.03 S 178.13 E
Kandavu Passage ⋓ 175g 18.45 S 178.00 E
Kandé 150 9.57 N 1.03 E
Kandel 56 49.05 N 8.11 E
Kandel ∧ 58 48.04 N 8.01 E
Kander ≃ 58 46.43 N 7.38 E
Kandern 58 47.43 N 7.40 E
Kandersteg 58 46.30 N 7.40 E
Kandhkot 120 28.14 N 69.11 E
Kāndhla 124 29.19 N 77.16 E
Kandi, Benin 150 11.08 N 2.56 E
Kāndi, Bhārat 126 23.57 N 88.02 E
Kandi, Tanjung ≻ 112 1.19 N 121.28 E
Kandia ≃ 123 35.30 N 73.17 E
Kandiāro 120 27.04 N 68.13 E
Kandik ≃ 180 65.24 N 142.34 W
Kandilli ✦[8] 267b 41.04 N 29.03 E
Kandıra 130 41.04 N 30.09 E
Kandivli ✦[8] 272c 19.12 N 72.51 E
Kando ≃ 96 35.22 N 132.40 E
Kandor, Ouadi ∨ 146 17.13 N 20.52 E
Kandos 170 32.52 S 149.58 E
Kāndra 126 23.44 N 87.58 E
Kandrāch 120 25.29 N 65.29 E
Kāndrāng Garhi 124 27.43 N 84.47 E
Kandreho 157b 17.29 S 46.06 E
Kandrian 164 6.15 S 149.35 E
Kandry 80 54.34 N 54.07 E
Kandufuri I 122 7.05 N 72.48 E
Kandukūr 122 15.13 N 79.55 E
Kandute I 122 6.20 N 72.57 E
Kandy 122 7.18 N 80.38 E
Kane, Ill., U.S. 219 39.11 N 90.21 W
Kane, Pa., U.S. 214 41.40 N 78.49 W
Kane □[6] 216 41.53 N 88.18 W
Kaneilio Point ≻ 229c 21.27 N 158.12 W
Kanektok ≃ 180 59.45 N 161.55 W
Kanem □[5] 146 15.00 N 16.00 E
Kanemi 116 6.55 N 123.58 E
Kanenmyvejem ≃ 180 66.04 N 178.40 W
Kaneohe 229c 21.25 N 157.48 W
Kaneohe Bay C 229c 21.28 N 157.49 W
Kaneohe Bay Marine Corps Air Station ■ 229c 21.27 N 157.46 W
Kaneville 216 41.50 N 88.31 W
Kanevskaja 78 46.05 N 38.57 E
Kanfanar 64 45.07 N 13.51 E
Kang 156 23.41 S 22.50 E
Kangaba 150 11.56 N 8.25 W
Kangal 130 39.15 N 37.24 E
Kangalassy 74 62.23 N 129.59 E
Kangān 128 27.50 N 52.03 E

ENGLISH Name	Page	Lat.°′	Long.°′

Kānganheri ✦[8] 272a 28.33 N 76.59 E
Kanganpur 123 30.46 N 74.08 E
Kangar 114 6.26 N 100.12 E
Kangaré 150 11.35 N 8.10 W
Kangarilla 168b 35.09 S 138.40 E
Kangaroo ≃ 170 34.46 S 150.18 E
Kangaroo Flat 168b 34.33 S 138.40 E
Kangaroo Ground 274b 37.41 S 145.13 E
Kangaroo Island I 166 35.50 S 137.06 E
Kangaroo Range National Park ♦ 166 29.35 S 152.10 E
Kangaroo Valley 170 34.44 S 150.32 E
Kangasala 26 61.28 N 24.05 E
Kangasniemi 26 61.59 N 26.38 E
Kangāvar 128 34.30 N 47.58 E
Kangaz 78 46.07 N 28.33 E
Kangbao 98 41.53 N 114.40 E
Kangdarenshan 104 41.32 N 123.41 E
Kangding 102 30.03 N 102.02 E
Kangdong 98 39.09 N 126.05 E
Kangdu 100 27.00 N 116.36 E
Kangean, Kepulauan II 112 6.55 S 115.30 E
Kangean, Pulau I 112 6.54 S 115.20 E
Kangen ≃ 140 6.47 N 33.09 E
Kanggezhuang 105 40.26 N 116.44 E
Kanggup'o 98 41.07 N 127.31 E
Kanggye 98 40.58 N 126.34 E
Kanggyŏng 98 36.10 N 127.00 E
Kanghwa 98 37.45 N 126.30 E
Kanghwa-do I 98 37.40 N 126.27 E
Kanghwa-man C 98 37.20 N 126.35 E
Kangil 88 52.15 N 116.20 E
Kangjin 98 34.39 N 126.45 E
Kangjinjing 89 46.12 N 126.48 E
Kangkar Lenggor 114 2.16 N 103.44 E
Kangkar Teberau 114 1.32 N 103.45 E
Kangley 216 41.09 N 88.53 W
Kangly 85 40.07 N 67.54 E
Kangma 120 28.34 N 89.51 E
Kangmaer 124 30.45 N 85.34 E
Kangnichumike 120 33.10 N 80.59 E
Kangnŭng 98 37.45 N 128.54 E
Kango 152 0.09 N 10.08 E
Kango Caves •[5] 158 33.23 S 22.14 E
Kangoku-iwa I 174f 24.48 N 141.17 E
Kangombe 152 14.03 S 23.40 E
Kangongo 152 17.57 S 21.02 E
Kangowa 152 9.55 S 22.48 E
Kangping 98 42.44 N 123.21 E
Kāngpokpi 120 25.08 N 93.58 E
Kangpu 102 27.43 N 99.00 E
Kāngra 123 32.06 N 76.16 E
Kāngra □[5] 123 32.00 N 76.15 E
Kangshan 100 22.51 N 120.17 E
Kangsŏ 98 38.58 N 125.26 E
Kangsŏ-ri 98 38.06 N 126.58 E
Kangsu 85 39.45 N 75.02 E
Kangto ∧ 120 27.52 N 92.30 E
Kangtuyingzi 104 41.47 N 121.31 E
Känguruh-Insel → Kangaroo Island I 166 35.50 S 137.06 E
Kangwŏn Do □[4], C.M.I.K. 98 38.45 N 127.35 E
Kangwŏn Do □[4], Taehan 98 37.45 N 128.15 E
Kangxianzhuang 105 39.06 N 116.27 E
Kangyidaung 110 16.56 N 94.54 E
Kangzhuang 105 40.23 N 115.53 E
Kanhangad 122 12.19 N 75.04 E
Kanhar ≃ 124 24.28 N 83.08 E
Kanheri Caves •[5] 272c 19.13 N 72.52 E
Kanholmsfjärden ⋓ 40 59.20 N 18.47 E
Kanhsien → Ganzhou 100 25.54 N 114.55 E
Kani, C. Iv. 150 8.29 N 6.36 W
Kani, Mya. 110 22.26 N 94.50 E
Kaniama 152 7.31 S 24.11 E
Kaniamba 154 7.27 S 26.57 E
Kanibadam 85 40.17 N 70.25 E
Kaniepa 154 9.00 S 27.21 E
Kaniere 172 42.45 S 171.00 E
Kaniere, Lake @ 172 42.50 S 171.09 E
Kaniet Islands II 164 0.53 S 145.30 E
Kanif 174q 9.31 N 138.05 E
Kanigiri 122 15.24 N 79.31 E
Kanihāula ✦[8] 272a 28.44 N 77.01 E
Kanin 54 52.17 N 12.50 E
Kanin, Poluostrov ≻[1] 24 68.00 N 45.00 E
Kanina 124 28.20 N 76.19 E
Kaningo 154 0.49 S 38.32 E
Kanin Kamen' ∧ 24 68.18 N 45.00 E
Kanin Nos 24 68.39 N 43.14 E
Kanin Nos, Mys ≻ 24 68.39 N 43.16 E
Kânireş 130 39.18 N 41.01 E
Kaniva 166 36.23 S 141.15 E
Kanjiža 38 46.04 N 20.04 E
Kānjur ✦[8] 272c 19.08 N 72.56 E
Kanjut Sār ∧ 123 36.14 N 75.22 E
Kankaanpää 26 61.48 N 22.25 E
Kankakee 216 41.07 N 87.52 W
Kankakee □[6] 216 41.07 N 87.52 W
Kankakee ≃ 216 41.23 N 88.16 W
Kankakee River State Park ♦ 216 41.12 N 87.59 W
Kankan 150 10.23 N 9.18 W
Kankan □[4] 150 10.10 N 9.15 W
Kankar ✦[8] 272a 28.46 N 77.06 E
Kankéla 150 10.50 N 6.40 W
Kānker 122 20.17 N 81.29 E
Kankō → Hamhŭng 98 39.54 N 127.32 E
Kankossa 150 15.56 N 11.31 W
Kankunskij 74 57.37 N 126.08 E
Kanlıavşar 130 37.13 N 38.16 E
Kanlıca ✦[8] 267b 41.06 N 29.04 E
Kanmaw Kyun I 110 11.40 N 98.28 E
Kanmen 100 28.06 N 121.16 E
Kanmon-kaikyō ⋓ 96 33.56 N 130.56 E
Kanmuri-shima I 96 35.41 N 135.25 E
Kanmuri-yama ∧ 96 34.28 N 132.05 E
Kanna ≃ 94 36.17 N 139.09 E
Kannabe-yama ∧[2] 270 34.48 N 135.44 E
Kannack 110 14.07 N 108.37 E
Kannad 122 20.16 N 75.08 E
Kanna-kō C 174m 26.28 N 127.58 E
Kannapolis 192 35.30 N 80.37 W
Kannauj 124 27.04 N 79.55 E
Kanniyākumāri 122 8.05 N 77.34 E
Kannod 124 22.40 N 76.44 E
Kannonkoski 26 62.58 N 25.15 E
Kannon-zaki ≻ 268 35.15 N 139.45 E
Kannose ≃ 96 34.54 N 132.49 E
Kannus 26 63.54 N 23.54 E
Kano, Nig. 150 12.00 N 8.30 E
Kano, Nihon 96 34.14 N 131.49 E
Kano □[3] 150 11.45 N 9.00 E
Kano ≃ 94 35.05 N 138.52 E
Kanona, N.Y., U.S. 210 42.22 N 77.22 W
Kanona, Zam. 154 13.04 S 30.38 E
Kanoneiland 158 28.39 S 21.05 E
Kanonerskij, Ostrov I 265a 59.54 N 30.13 E
Kanopolis 198 38.43 N 98.09 W
Kanopolis Lake @[1] 198 38.38 N 98.00 W
Kanorado 198 39.20 N 102.02 W
Kanosh 200 38.48 N 112.26 W
Kanouse Brook ≃ 276 41.02 N 74.26 W
Kanouse Mountain ∧ 276 41.04 N 74.25 W
Kan'ov 78 49.44 N 31.28 E
Kan'ovka 24 67.08 N 39.40 E
Kanowit 112 2.06 N 112.09 E
Kanowna 162 30.36 S 121.36 E
Kanoya 92 31.23 N 130.51 E
Kanō-zan ∧ 268 35.15 N 139.57 E
Kanpetlet 110 21.12 N 94.02 E
Kanpoli 272c 19.04 N 73.09 E
Kānpur 124 26.28 N 80.21 E

DEUTSCH Name	Seite	Breite°′	Länge°′ E=Ost

Kānpur □[5] 124 26.30 N 80.00 E
Kansa ≃ 94 34.55 N 137.34 E
Kansai University ✓[2] 270 34.46 N 135.31 E
Kansaj 85 40.30 N 69.41 E
Kansanshi 154 12.05 S 26.26 E
Kānsāripāra 272b 22.56 N 88.14 E
Kansas, Ill., U.S. 194 39.33 N 87.56 W
Kansas, Ohio, U.S. 214 41.15 N 83.17 W
Kansas □[3] 178 / 198 38.45 N 98.15 W
Kansas ≃ 198 39.07 N 94.36 W
Kansas City, Kans., U.S. 198 39.07 N 94.39 W
Kansas City, Mo., U.S 194 39.05 N 94.35 W
Kansau 110 23.50 N 93.35 E
Kansenia 154 10.19 S 26.02 E
Kanshan 106 30.12 N 120.25 E
Kanshi 100 24.56 N 116.54 E
Kansk 86 56.13 N 95.41 E
Kansŏng 98 38.22 N 128.29 E
Kansu → Gansu □[4] 102 37.00 N 103.00 E
Kansyat 164 2.15 S 138.51 E
Kant 85 42.55 N 74.55 E
Kantābānji 122 20.29 N 82.55 E
Kantabrisches Gebirge → Cantábrica, Cordillera ⛰ 34 43.00 N 5.00 W
Kantalvi 272c 18.54 N 73.03 E
Kantang 110 7.25 N 99.31 E
Kāntāphor 124 22.35 N 76.34 E
Kantchari 150 12.29 N 1.31 E
Kantché 150 13.33 N 8.28 E
Kantemirovka, S.S.S.R. 83 49.41 N 39.51 E
Kantemirovka, S.S.S.R. 85 42.51 N 70.20 E
Kānth, Bhārat 124 29.04 N 78.38 E
Kanth → Kąty Wrocławskie, Pol. 30 51.02 N 16.46 E
Kantharalak 110 14.39 N 104.39 E
Kānthi Coastal Plain ⊻ 126 21.45 N 87.45 E
Kantishna ≃ 180 64.45 N 149.58 W
Kantner 214 40.06 N 78.56 W
Kantō-heiya ⊻ 94 36.00 N 139.30 E
Kanton → Guangzhou 100 23.06 N 113.16 E
Kantong 100 32.59 N 116.19 E
Kantorp 40 59.01 N 16.28 E
Kantō-sammyaku ⛰ 92 35.50 N 138.50 E
Kantō-sanchi ⛰ 94 35.59 N 138.43 E
Kantu-long 110 19.57 N 97.36 E
Kantunilkín 232 21.06 N 87.29 W
Kanturk 48 52.10 N 8.55 W
Kanuku Mountains ⛰ 246 3.12 N 59.30 W
Kanuma 94 36.33 N 139.44 E
Kanus 156 27.54 S 18.40 E
Kanuti ≃ 180 66.26 N 153.02 W
Kan'utino 76 55.33 N 33.14 E
Kanye 156 24.59 S 25.19 E
Kanygtokynmankyn, Laguna C 180 69.20 N 178.45 E
Kanyu 156 20.05 S 24.39 E
Kanyutkwin 110 18.21 N 96.30 E
Kanzaki ≃ 270 34.42 N 135.25 E
Kanzanavolok 24 62.23 N 36.58 E
Kanzenze 154 10.31 S 25.12 E
Kanzi 98 39.34 N 122.39 E
Kaohiung → Kaohsiung 100 22.38 N 120.17 E
Kaohsiung 100 22.38 N 120.17 E
Kaohsiung Ch'uan C 100 22.37 N 120.12 E
Kaohsiunghsien 100 22.38 N 120.21 E
Kaoje 150 11.14 N 4.07 E
Kaoko Otavi 156 18.14 S 13.40 E
Kaokoveld □[5] 156 18.00 S 13.30 E
Kaokoveld ⛰[1] 156 21.00 S 14.20 E
Kaolack 150 14.09 N 16.04 W
Kaolun → Kowloon 271d 22.18 N 114.10 E
Kaonga 273b 4.09 S 15.12 E
Kaongweshi ≃ 152 7.53 S 22.20 E
Kaoping → Changzhi 102 36.11 N 113.08 E
Kaoshandian 100 30.54 N 114.32 E
Kaoshanji 105 40.11 N 117.17 E
Kaouar ✦[1] 146 19.00 N 12.40 E
Kapaa 229b 22.05 N 159.19 W
Kapadvanj 120 23.01 N 73.04 E
Kapal 86 45.08 N 79.03 E
Kapalong 116 7.35 N 125.42 E
Kapan 112 9.44 S 124.17 E
Kapanga, Zaïre 152 8.21 S 22.35 E
Kapanga, Zaïre 152 5.04 S 16.58 E
Kapangan 116 16.35 N 120.35 E
Kapaonik ⛰ 38 43.20 N 20.50 E
Kāpāsia 126 24.07 N 90.32 E
Kapatagan 116 7.52 N 123.44 E
Kapatu 154 9.43 S 30.42 E
Kapčagaj 85 43.53 N 77.12 E
Kapčagajskoje Vodochranilišče @[1] 86 43.50 N 78.00 E
Kapcagajtuj 88 49.57 N 118.37 E
Kapchorwa 154 1.24 N 34.27 E
Kapelle 52 51.28 N 3.58 E
Kapellen, Bel. 50 51.19 N 4.26 E
Kapellen, B.R.D. 52 51.34 N 6.22 E
Kapellen, B.R.D. 56 51.25 N 6.35 E
Kapellen, B.R.D. 263 51.08 N 6.38 E
Kapellen, Öst. 61 47.38 N 15.37 E
Kapelle-op-den-Bos 50 51.01 N 4.22 E
Kapellerfeld 264b 48.19 N 16.30 E
Kapelln 61 48.15 N 15.45 E
Kapellskär 40 59.43 N 19.04 E
Kapema 154 10.42 S 28.24 E
Kapenguria 154 1.04 N 35.07 E
Kapfenberg 61 47.26 N 15.18 E
Kapia 152 4.17 S 19.46 E
Kapıdağı Yarımadası ≻[1] 130 40.28 N 27.50 E
Kapikik Lake @ 184 51.32 N 91.57 W
Kapikog Lake @ 212 45.09 N 79.53 W
Kapilavastu 124 27.28 N 83.16 E
Kapilmuni 126 22.42 N 89.20 E
Kapingamarangi I[1] 14 1.04 N 154.46 E
Kapiri Mposhi 154 13.58 S 28.41 E
Kāpīsā □[4] 120 34.45 N 69.30 E
Kapiskau ≃ 176 52.47 N 81.55 W
Kapit 112 2.01 N 112.56 E
Kapitanovka 78 48.54 N 31.42 E
Kapiti Island I 172 40.52 S 174.54 E
Kapiura ≃ 164 5.45 S 150.35 E
Kapka, Massif du ⛰ 146 15.07 N 21.45 E
Kapkataš 85 40.23 N 74.20 E
Kapkatas, Chrebet ⛰ 85 41.50 N 76.10 E
Kapkinka 80 48.08 N 43.51 E
Kaplan 194 30.00 N 92.17 W
Kaplice 61 48.45 N 14.30 E
Kapoe 110 9.35 N 98.40 E
Kapoeta 154 4.47 N 33.35 E
Kapogere 164 9.50 S 147.45 E
Kapona 154 7.11 S 29.09 E
Kaponga 172 39.26 S 174.09 E
Kaporskoje 265a 59.45 N 29.58 E
Kapos ≃ 30 46.44 N 18.30 E
Kaposvár 30 46.22 N 17.47 E
Kaposvar Creek ≃ 184 50.31 N 101.55 W
Kapotn'a ✦[8] 265b 55.38 N 37.48 E
Kapowsin 224 46.59 N 122.13 W
Kapowsin, Lake @ 224 46.58 N 122.13 W
Kapp 26 60.42 N 10.52 E
Kappar 128 25.19 N 62.42 E
Kappel 56 50.00 N 7.21 E
Kappeln 41 54.40 N 9.56 E

Symbols in the index entries represent the broad categories identified in the key at the right. Symbols with superior numbers (⛰[2]) identify subcategories (see complete key on page *I · 30*).

Kartensymbole in dem Registerverzeichnis stellen die rechts in Schlüssel erklärten Kategorien dar. Symbole mit hochgestellten Ziffern (⛰[2]) bezeichnen Unterabteilungen einer Kategorie (vgl. vollständiger Schlüssel auf Seite *I · 30*).

Los símbolos incluídos en el texto del índice representan las grandes categorias identificadas con la clave a la derecha. Los símbolos con numeros en su parte superior (⛰[2]) identifican las subcategorías (véase la clave completa en la página *I · 30*).

Les symboles de l'index représentent les catégories indiquées dans la légende à droite. Les symboles suivis d'un indice (⛰[2]) représentent des sous-catégories (voir légende complète à la page *I · 30*).

Os símbolos incluídos no texto do índice representam as grandes categorias identificadas com a chave à direita. Os símbolos com números em sua parte superior (⛰[2]) identificam as subcategorias (veja-se a chave completa à página *I · 30*).

	English	Deutsch	Español	Français	Português
∧	Mountain	Berg	Montaña	Montagne	Montanha
⛰	Mountains	Berge	Montañas	Montagnes	Montanhas
)(	Pass	Pass	Paso	Col	Passo
∨	Valley, Canyon	Tal, Cañon	Valle, Cañón	Vallée, Canyon	Vale, Canhão
⊻	Plain	Ebene	Llano	Plaine	Planície
≻	Cape	Kap	Cabo	Cap	Cabo
I	Island	Insel	Isla	Île	Ilha
II	Islands	Inseln	Islas	Îles	Ilhas
•	Other Topographic Features	Andere Topographische Objekte	Otros Elementos Topográficos	Autres données topographiques	Outros Elementos Topográficos

ESPAÑOL
Nombre | Página | Lat.°′ | Long.°′ W=Oeste

Kappelshamn 26 57.51 N 18.47 E
Kapps 156 22.22 S 17.52 E
Kaprijke 50 51.13 N 3.36 E
Kaprun 64 47.16 N 12.46 E
Kapsabet 154 0.12 N 35.06 E
Kapsan 98 41.04 N 128.19 E
Kap Shui Mun Ʉ 271d 22.19 N 114.04 E
Kapstadt
→ Cape Town 158 33.55 S 18.22 E
Kapsukas 76 54.33 N 23.21 E
Kaptai 120 22.21 N 92.17 E
Kaptipada 126 21.31 N 86.32 E
Kaptol 38 45.26 N 17.44 E
Kapuas ≃, Indon. 112 0.25 S 109.40 E
Kapuas ≃, Indon. 112 3.01 S 114.20 E
Kapuas Hulu, Pegunungan ⩕ 112 1.25 N 113.30 E
Kapulo 154 8.18 S 29.15 E
Kapunda 168b 34.21 S 138.54 E
Kapūrthala 123 31.23 N 75.23 E
Kapur Utara, Pegunungan ⩕ 115a 6.52 S 111.30 E
Kapuskasing 176 49.25 N 82.26 W
Kapuskasing ≃ 176 49.49 N 82.00 W
Kapuskasing Lake @ 190 48.30 N 82.55 W
Kapustin Jar 80 48.36 N 45.45 E
Kapustino 78 48.57 N 31.14 E
Kapuvár 30 47.36 N 17.02 E
Kap Verde
→ Cape Verde □[1] 150a 16.00 N 24.00 W
Kapyrevščina 76 55.15 N 32.53 E
Kapytdžuch, Gora ∧ 84 39.13 N 46.00 E
Kara, Mali 150 12.56 N 6.15 W
Kara, S.S.S.R. 74 69.14 N 65.00 E
Kara, Yai. 144 5.50 N 37.08 E
Kara ≃ 150 10.01 N 0.25 E
Karaali 130 39.40 N 32.57 E
Karaaul 86 48.57 N 79.15 E
Karabachskij Chrebet ⩕ 84 39.42 N 46.36 E
Karabagl'ar 84 39.26 N 45.12 E
Kara-Balty 85 42.50 N 73.52 E
Karabanovo 82 56.19 N 38.42 E
Karabaš, S.S.S.R. 80 54.42 N 52.36 E
Karabaš, S.S.S.R. 86 55.29 N 60.14 E
Karabau 80 48.26 N 52.54 E
Karabekaul 128 38.30 N 64.08 E
Karabiğa 130 40.24 N 27.18 E
Karabil', Vozvyšennost' ⩕[1] 128 36.25 N 64.00 E
Kara-Bogaz-Gol, Zaliv C 72 41.00 N 53.15 E
Karabudachkent 84 42.41 N 47.34 E
Karabük 130 41.12 N 32.37 E
Karabula 88 58.08 N 97.23 E
Karabula ≃ 88 58.22 N 97.02 E
Karabulak, S.S.S.R. 85 39.51 N 69.38 E
Karabulak, S.S.S.R. 85 42.32 N 69.46 E
Karabulak, S.S.S.R. 86 44.54 N 78.30 E
Karabulak, S.S.S.R. 86 47.34 N 84.41 E
Karabulduk 130 40.50 N 38.34 E
Karabutak 86 49.59 N 60.10 E
Karacadağ 130 41.57 N 27.40 E
Karaca Dağ ∧ 130 37.40 N 39.50 E
Karačaj ≃ 84 41.28 N 49.00 E
Karačajevo-Čerkesskaja Avtonomnaja Oblast' □[4] 84 44.00 N 42.00 E
Karačajevsk 84 43.45 N 41.54 E
Karacaköy 130 41.24 N 28.22 E
Karačala 84 39.48 N 48.57 E
Karačev 76 53.07 N 35.00 E
Karāchi 120 24.52 N 67.03 E
Karachtaj 85 40.55 N 69.46 E
Karači 80 57.59 N 50.28 E
Karād 122 17.17 N 74.12 E
Karadarja ≃ 85 40.54 N 71.45 E
Karadeniz
→ Black Sea ⊤[2] 22 43.00 N 35.00 E
Karaftit 88 54.12 N 111.54 E
Karagaj, S.S.S.R. 80 48.39 N 47.38 E
Karagaj, S.S.S.R. 80 58.16 N 54.56 E
Karagajly 86 49.20 N 75.48 E
Karaganda 86 49.50 N 73.10 E
Karagel 128 39.23 N 53.11 E
Karagičevskij 80 50.11 N 42.55 E
Karaginskij, Ostrov I 74 58.50 N 164.00 E
Karaginskij Zaliv C 74 58.50 N 164.00 E
Karagola Road 124 25.29 N 87.23 E
Karagölü @ 130 36.42 N 29.50 E
Karagoš, Gora ∧ 86 51.44 N 89.24 E
Karagužicha 86 50.47 N 83.00 E
Karahallı 130 38.20 N 29.32 E
Karaia 124 25.54 N 78.01 E
Karaičev 80 48.37 N 42.13 E
Karaidel' 86 55.50 N 56.53 E
Karaidel'skij 86 55.49 N 57.05 E
Kāraikkudi 122 10.04 N 78.47 E
Karaisalı 130 37.16 N 35.03 E
Karaitivu I 122 8.23 N 79.47 E
Karaj 128 35.48 N 50.59 E
Karaj, Rūdkhāneh-ye ≃ 267d 35.35 N 51.11 E
Karajantak 85 40.03 N 67.54 E
Karak 114 3.24 N 102.02 E
Karakabak 86 50.33 N 75.09 E
Karakain 85 41.26 N 74.19 E
Kara-Kala 128 38.26 N 56.18 E
Karakalpakskaja Avtonomnaja Sovetskaja Socialističeskaja Respublika □[3] 86 43.00 N 59.00 E
Karakastek 85 43.08 N 76.06 E
Karakavak 85 39.41 N 72.43 E
Karakecili 130 39.36 N 33.23 E
Karakelong, Pulau I 108 4.15 N 126.48 E
Karakendža 85 39.14 N 71.31 E
Karakišlak 85 39.44 N 67.40 E
Karakitang, Pulau I 112 3.11 N 125.32 E
Karakoin, Ozero @ 86 46.10 N 68.45 E
Karakojsu ≃ 84 42.33 N 46.58 E
Karakojun ≃ 85 41.10 N 75.45 E
Karakol', Ozero @ 86 45.35 N 64.22 E
Karakolka 85 41.32 N 77.23 E
Karakoram Range ⩕ 120 35.30 N 77.00 E
Karakoro ≃ 150 14.43 N 12.03 W
Karaköse 84 39.44 N 43.03 E
Karaksar 88 51.16 N 115.58 E
Karakudžur ≃ 85 41.59 N 75.42 E
Karakul', S.S.S.R. 85 39.02 N 73.33 E
Karakul', S.S.S.R. 86 57.26 N 70.51 E
Karakul', S.S.S.R. 128 39.32 N 63.50 E
Karakul', Ozero @ 85 39.05 N 73.25 E
Karakulak 130 39.59 N 40.01 E
Kara-Kul'dža 85 40.37 N 73.35 E
Karakulino 80 56.01 N 53.43 E
Karakul'skoje 86 54.04 N 62.26 E
Karakum 86 46.49 N 79.33 E
Karakumskij Kanal ☲ 128 37.35 N 61.50 E
Karakumy ◆[2] 72 39.00 N 60.00 E
Karakuni 270 34.28 N 135.28 E
Karakurt 130 40.10 N 42.36 E
Karakuwisa 156 18.56 S 19.40 E
Karala 272a 28.44 N 77.02 E
Karalat 80 45.55 N 48.18 E
Karalon 88 57.02 N 115.52 E
Karam 88 55.09 N 107.37 E
Karama ≃ 112 2.18 S 119.06 E
Karamağara 130 39.42 N 35.31 E
Karamai
→ Kelamayi 86 45.37 N 84.53 E
Karaman, Tür. 130 37.05 N 29.20 E

FRANÇAIS
Nom | Page | Lat.°′ | Long.°′ W=Ouest

Karaman, Tür. 130 37.11 N 33.14 E
Karamanlı 130 37.22 N 29.49 E
Karambu 112 3.51 S 116.04 E
Karamea 172 41.15 S 172.07 E
Karamea ≃ 172 41.16 S 172.06 E
Karamea Bight C[3] 172 41.30 S 171.40 E
Karamıkbataklığı ☰ 130 38.25 N 30.50 E
Karamoja □[5] 154 2.50 N 34.15 E
Karamürsel 130 40.42 N 29.36 E
Karamurt 85 42.19 N 69.58 E
Karamyš ≃ 80 51.20 N 45.00 E
Karamyševo, S.S.S.R. 76 57.45 N 28.45 E
Karamyševo, S.S.S.R. 82 54.46 N 36.07 E
Karamyševo, S.S.S.R. 88 57.34 N 100.55 E
Karamzino 76 56.00 N 34.33 E
Karang, Gunung ∧ 115a 6.16 S 106.03 E
Karang, Tanjung › 112 0.38 S 119.44 E
Karangana 150 12.13 N 5.02 W
Karangbolong, Tanjung › 115a 7.46 S 109.03 E
Karangnunggal 115a 7.38 S 108.06 E
Karangpandan 115a 7.37 S 111.04 E
Karangsembung 115a 6.51 S 108.39 E
Kāranja 122 20.29 N 77.29 E
Karanjia 120 21.47 N 85.58 E
Karanti 130 40.15 N 27.07 E
Karaoba, S.S.S.R. 86 53.17 N 65.06 E
Karaoba, S.S.S.R. 86 47.03 N 56.20 E
Karaoglan 130 39.14 N 39.13 E
Karaozek, S.S.S.R. 85 43.43 N 77.23 E
Karaozek, S.S.S.R. 86 43.16 N 58.40 E
Karaozek, S.S.S.R. 86 45.03 N 65.18 E
Karapınar, Tür. 130 41.30 N 32.12 E
Karapınar, Tür. 130 37.43 N 33.33 E
Karapyši 78 49.38 N 30.47 E
Karaš 80 56.54 N 39.24 E
Karas, Pulau I 164 3.27 S 132.40 E
Kara-Sal ≃ 80 47.22 N 43.38 E
Karaşar 130 40.20 N 32.00 E
Karasburg 156 28.00 S 18.43 E
Kara Sea
→ Karskoje More ⊤[2] 72 76.00 N 80.00 E
Karašjåkka ≃ 24 69.26 N 25.49 E
Karasjok 24 69.27 N 25.30 E
Karasor, Ozero @, S.S.S.R. 86 49.54 N 75.32 E
Karasor, Ozero @, S.S.S.R. 86 51.57 N 75.45 E
Karasu, S.S.S.R. 86 51.20 N 62.21 E
Karasu, Tür. 130 41.06 N 30.41 E
Karasu ≃, Nihon 94 36.15 N 139.17 E
Karasu ≃, S.S.S.R. 84 40.13 N 47.42 E
Karasu ≃, Tür. 130 39.42 N 39.25 E
Karasuk ≃ 86 53.35 N 77.30 E
Karata 84 42.35 N 46.21 E
Karatá, Laguna C 236 13.56 N 83.30 W
Karatal, S.S.S.R. 86 45.07 N 77.54 E
Karatal, S.S.S.R. 86 47.36 N 85.12 E
Karatal ≃ 86 46.26 N 77.10 E
Karataş 130 36.36 N 35.21 E
Karatau 85 43.10 N 70.28 E
Karatau, Chrebet ⩕, S.S.S.R. 85 38.10 N 69.00 E
Karatau, Chrebet ⩕, S.S.S.R. 85 43.50 N 68.30 E
Karateginskij Chrebet ⩕ 85 38.50 N 69.40 E
Karatepe ⊥ 130 37.17 N 36.13 E
Karatia 126 24.14 N 89.58 E
Karatoya ≃ 124 24.13 N 89.36 E
Karatschi
→ Karāchi 120 24.52 N 67.03 E
Karatsu 92 33.26 N 129.58 E
Karau 164 3.45 S 144.20 E
Karauli 124 26.30 N 77.01 E
Karault'ob'o 85 40.33 N 75.57 E
Karaun'ur ≃ 85 40.54 N 72.20 E
Karaurğan 130 40.15 N 42.17 E
Karavás 38 36.21 N 22.57 E
Karave 272c 19.01 N 73.01 E
Karawa 152 3.20 N 20.18 E
Karawanken ⩕ 36 46.30 N 14.25 E
Karayaka 130 40.45 N 36.37 E
Karaye 150 11.48 N 8.02 E
Karayün 130 39.41 N 37.19 E
Karbalā' 128 32.36 N 44.02 E
Karbalā' □[4] 128 32.15 N 43.07 E
Karbenning 40 60.02 N 16.04 E
Kårberg 40 58.58 N 14.57 E
Karbeyaz 130 36.02 N 36.12 E
Kårböle 26 61.59 N 15.19 E
Karby 40 59.34 N 18.13 E
Karcag 30 47.19 N 20.56 E
Karçal Silsilesi ⩕ 84 41.25 N 42.02 E
Karczew 30 52.06 N 21.15 E
Kardail ≃ 80 50.43 N 42.54 E
Karden 56 50.11 N 7.17 E
Kardhámaina 38 36.47 N 27.09 E
Kardhámila 38 38.32 N 26.05 E
Kardhítsa 38 39.21 N 21.55 E
Kärdla 76 59.00 N 22.45 E
Kardymovo 76 54.54 N 32.26 E
Kârdžali 38 41.39 N 25.22 E
Kardžin 84 43.16 N 44.16 E
Karé 146 10.07 N 19.48 E
Karea 272b 22.42 N 88.33 E
Kareeberge ⩕ 158 30.53 S 21.57 E
Kareedouw 158 33.57 S 24.18 E
Kareke 85 38.23 N 76.58 E
Kareli, Bhārat 124 22.55 N 79.04 E
Kareli, S.S.S.R. 84 42.01 N 43.54 E
Karel'skij Gorodok, S.S.S.R. 76 58.04 N 36.30 E
Karel'skij Gorodok, S.S.S.R. 76 57.11 N 33.44 E
Karema, Pap. N. Gui. 164 9.12 S 147.14 E
Karema, Tan. 154 6.49 S 30.26 E
Karen 110 12.51 N 92.53 E
Karen □[3] 110 17.30 N 97.45 E
Karenga ≃ 88 54.28 N 116.32 E
Karepino 24 61.02 N 57.02 E
Karera 272a 28.41 N 77.23 E
Karesuando 24 68.25 N 22.30 E
Karêt ◆[1] 148 24.00 N 7.30 W
Kärevere 76 58.26 N 26.29 E
Kargali 80 55.12 N 50.54 E
Kargalinskaja 84 43.44 N 46.30 E
Karganaj 180 65.21 N 175.25 E
Kargapazarı Dağları ⩕ 84 40.07 N 41.35 E
Kargapolje 86 55.57 N 64.27 E
Kargasok 86 59.07 N 80.53 E
Kargat 86 55.10 N 80.17 E
Kargat ≃ 86 54.37 N 78.12 E
Kargı 130 41.08 N 34.30 E
Kargil 123 34.34 N 76.06 E
Karginskaja 80 49.21 N 41.38 E
Karginskij ≃ 265a 59.50 N 30.01 E
Kargopol' 24 61.30 N 38.58 E
Karguéri 146 13.27 N 10.25 E
Karhal 124 27.01 N 78.57 E
Karhijärvi @ 26 61.35 N 22.30 E
Karhula 26 60.31 N 26.57 E
Karia-ba-Mohammed 148 34.19 N 5.10 W
Kariaí 38 40.16 N 24.15 E
Karianga 157b 22.22 S 47.26 E
Kariba 154 16.30 S 28.45 E
Kariba, Lake @[1] 154 17.00 S 28.00 E
Kariba Dam ◆[6] 154 16.30 S 28.50 E
Karibib 156 21.58 S 15.51 E
Karibib □[5] 156 22.20 S 16.00 E
Karibisches Meer
→ Caribbean Sea ⊤[2] 238 15.00 S 73.00 W
Karibumba 154 0.22 N 29.22 E
Kariega ≃ 158 33.03 S 23.28 E
Karigasniemi 24 69.24 N 25.50 E
Kārikāl 122 10.55 N 79.50 E
Karikari, Cape › 172 34.47 S 173.24 E
Karimata 175d 24.54 N 125.17 E

PORTUGUÊS
Nome | Página | Lat.°′ | Long.°′ W=Oeste

Karimata, Kepulauan II 112 1.25 S 109.05 E
Karimata, Pulau I 112 1.36 S 108.55 E
Karimata, Selat (Karimata Strait) Ʉ 112 2.05 S 108.40 E
Karīmnagar 122 18.26 N 79.09 E
Karīmpur 126 23.58 N 88.37 E
Karimun, Pulau I 114 1.03 N 103.22 E
Karimunjawa, Kepulauan II 115a 5.50 S 110.25 E
Karimunjawa, Pulau I 115a 5.51 S 110.27 E
Karin 144 10.51 N 45.45 E
Karino 82 54.42 N 38.56 E
Karin Seamount ✣[3] 14 18.00 N 169.00 W
Karinskoje 82 55.42 N 36.41 E
Karintorf 80 58.33 N 50.11 E
Karis (Karjaa) 26 60.05 N 23.40 E
Karise 41 55.18 N 12.13 E
Karisimbi, Volcan ∧[1] 154 1.30 S 29.27 E
Káristos 38 38.00 N 24.24 E
Kariya 94 34.59 N 136.59 E
Kariyangwe 154 17.57 S 27.30 E
Kārīz 128 34.49 N 60.47 E
Kārīz-e Elyās 128 35.25 N 61.20 E
Karjaa
→ Karis 26 60.05 N 23.40 E
Karjala ◆[1] 26 64.00 N 32.00 E
Karjepolje 24 65.34 N 43.40 E
Karkabet 144 16.13 N 37.30 E
Kārkal 122 13.12 N 74.59 E
Karkalaj 80 57.00 N 52.24 E
Karkaralinsk 86 49.23 N 75.21 E
Karkar Dūmān ◆[8] 272a 28.39 N 77.18 E
Karkar Island I 164 4.40 S 146.00 E
Karkar Mountains ⩕ 144 9.50 N 49.30 E
Karkas, Kūh-e ∧ 128 33.27 N 51.48 E
Karkheh ≃ 128 31.46 N 47.55 E
Kārkīn Dar 128 25.47 N 59.15 E
Karkinitskij Zaliv C 78 45.55 N 33.00 E
Karkkila 26 60.32 N 24.11 E
Karkku 26 61.25 N 23.01 E
Karkom, Har ∧ 132 30.17 N 34.44 E
Karkonoski Park Narodowy ♠ 30 50.45 N 15.35 E
Karkur 132 32.28 N 35.00 E
Kärla 76 58.20 N 22.15 E
Karlholmsbruk 40 60.31 N 17.35 E
Karlino 30 54.03 N 15.51 E
Karl-Marx-Stadt (Chemnitz) 54 50.50 N 12.55 E
Karl-Marx-Stadt □[5] 54 50.45 N 12.45 E
Karlobag 36 44.32 N 15.05 E
Karlo-Libknechtovsk 83 48.42 N 38.04 E
Karlo-marksovo 83 48.16 N 38.09 E
Karloske ≃ 184 55.41 N 93.56 W
Karlovac 36 45.29 N 15.34 E
Karlovka 78 49.27 N 35.08 E
Karlovo 38 42.38 N 24.48 E
Karlovy Vary (Carlsbad) 54 50.11 N 12.52 E
Karlsbad
→ Karlovy Vary 54 50.11 N 12.52 E
Karlsborg, Sve. 26 58.32 N 14.31 E
Karlsborg, Sve. 26 65.48 N 23.17 E
Karlsburg
→ Alba-Iulia 38 46.04 N 23.35 E
Karlsby 40 58.38 N 15.08 E
Karlsdalssjön @ 40 59.27 N 14.42 E
Karlsfeld 60 48.13 N 11.28 E
Karlshafen 52 51.38 N 9.27 E
Karlshamn 26 56.10 N 14.51 E
Karlshorst ◆[8] 264a 52.29 N 13.32 E
Karlshorst, Trabrennbahn ♠ 264a 52.29 N 13.31 E
Karlshuld 60 48.41 N 11.18 E
Karlskoga 40 59.20 N 14.31 E
Karlskrona 26 56.10 N 15.35 E
Karlslunde 41 55.34 N 12.14 E
Karlsöarna II 26 57.17 N 17.58 E
Karlsruhe 56 49.03 N 8.24 E
Karlsruhe □[5], B.R.D. 56 49.20 N 8.45 E
Karlsruhe □[5], B.R.D. 58 48.30 N 8.30 E
Karlstad, Sve. 40 59.22 N 13.30 E
Karlstad, Minn., U.S. 198 48.35 N 96.31 W
Karlstadt 56 49.57 N 9.45 E
Karlstift 61 48.35 N 14.45 E
Karl'uk, S.S.S.R. 85 38.12 N 67.42 E
Karluk, S.S.S.R. 88 53.27 N 105.58 E
Karluk, Alaska, U.S. 180 57.34 N 154.28 W
Karma 150 13.40 N 1.49 E
Karma, Ouadi V 146 15.38 N 20.01 E
Karmah 140 19.38 N 30.25 E
Karmāla 122 18.25 N 75.12 E
Karmanovka 80 49.24 N 50.22 E
Karmanovo 76 55.52 N 34.52 E
Karmansbo 40 59.42 N 15.44 E
Karmatānr 126 24.05 N 86.42 E
Karmi'el 132 32.55 N 35.18 E
Karmiyya 132 31.36 N 34.33 E
Karmøy I 26 59.15 N 5.15 E
Karnack 194 32.40 N 94.10 W
Karnak
→ Al-Karnak, Mişr 140 25.43 N 32.39 E
Karnak, Ill., U.S. 194 37.18 N 88.58 W
Karnāl 124 29.41 N 76.59 E
Karnāl □[5] 124 29.40 N 76.50 E
Karnāla Fort ⊥ 272c 18.53 N 73.07 E
Karnāli ≃ 124 28.45 N 81.16 E
Karnap 263 51.09 N 6.56 E
Karnaphuli Reservoir @[1] 120 22.42 N 92.12 E
Karnauchovka 78 48.28 N 34.44 E
Karnes □[6] 222 29.00 N 97.47 W
Karnes City 196 28.53 N 97.54 W
Karni 150 10.40 N 2.37 W
Karniki 82 54.12 N 38.05 E
Karnische Alpen (Alpi Carniche) ⩕ 64 46.40 N 13.00 E
Karnobat 38 42.39 N 26.59 E
Karns City 214 41.00 N 79.44 W
Kärnten □[3] 30 46.50 N 13.50 E
Karnzow 54 52.59 N 12.26 E
Karoi 154 16.50 S 29.40 E
Karokh 128 34.28 N 62.35 E
Karolinenhof ◆[8] 264a 52.23 N 13.38 E
Karomatan 116 7.46 N 123.44 E
Karompa-lompo, Pulau I 112 7.15 S 121.45 E
Karon 126 24.07 N 86.44 E
Karonga 154 9.56 S 33.56 E
Karonie 162 30.58 S 122.32 E
Karoonda 166 35.06 S 139.54 E
Karor 123 31.13 N 70.57 E
Karora 140 17.42 N 38.22 E
Karos 158 28.24 S 21.35 E
Karosa 112 1.48 S 119.20 E
Karotho Post 154 5.11 N 35.50 E
Karou 150 15.07 N 0.39 E
Karow, D.D.R. 54 53.32 N 12.15 E
Karow, D.D.R. 54 52.20 N 12.15 E
Karow ◆[8] 264a 52.37 N 13.29 E
Karpathen
→ Carpathian Mountains ⩕ 22 48.00 N 24.00 E
Kárpathos 38 35.30 N 27.14 E
Kárpathos I 38 35.40 N 27.10 E
Karpedo 154 1.10 N 36.06 E
Karpenísion 38 38.55 N 21.40 E
Karpinsk 86 59.45 N 60.01 E
Karpogory 24 64.00 N 44.24 E
Karpovka, S.S.S.R. 83 47.57 N 39.36 E
Karpovka, S.S.S.R. 83 49.10 N 37.43 E
Karpovo, S.S.S.R. 76 60.02 N 36.43 E
Karpovo, S.S.S.R. 82 55.35 N 38.34 E
Karpuninskij 86 58.43 N 61.50 E
Karrats Isfjord C[2] 176 71.20 N 54.00 W
Karre, Monts ⩕ 152 6.33 N 15.40 E

Karrebæksminde 41 55.11 N 11.40 E
Karres 58 47.13 N 10.47 E
Kärrgruvan 40 60.05 N 15.56 E
Karridale 162 34.13 S 115.05 E
Kars 84 40.36 N 43.05 E
Kars □[4] 130 40.30 N 42.45 E
Karša 80 49.48 N 51.27 E
Karsakpaj 86 47.49 N 66.41 E
Karsakuwigamak Lake @ 184 56.22 N 99.30 W
Kärsämäki 26 63.58 N 25.46 E
Karsantı 130 37.33 N 35.24 E
Kārsava 76 56.47 N 27.40 E
Kars Çayı ≃ 84 40.37 N 43.41 E
Karsdorf 54 51.17 N 11.39 E
Karši 128 38.53 N 65.48 E
Karsin 30 53.54 N 17.56 E
Karšinskaja Step' ⌣ 128 39.10 N 65.00 E
Karşıyaka 130 38.27 N 27.07 E
Karskije Vorota, Proliv Ʉ 72 70.30 N 58.00 E
Karskoje More (Kara Sea) ⊤[2] 72 76.00 N 80.00 E
Karsovaj 80 58.14 N 53.11 E
Karst
→ Kras ⩕[1] 64 45.48 N 14.00 E
Kårsta, Sve. 40 59.39 N 18.14 E
Kärsta, Sve. 40 59.40 N 16.49 E
Karstädt 54 53.09 N 11.44 E
Karstula 26 62.52 N 24.47 E
Karsun 80 54.11 N 46.59 E
Kartajol' 24 64.32 N 53.14 E
Kartal 130 40.53 N 29.10 E
Kartala ∧ 157a 11.45 S 43.22 E
Kartalinskij Chrebet ⩕ 84 42.10 N 44.55 E
Kartaly 86 53.03 N 60.40 E
Kartārpur 123 31.27 N 75.30 E
Karthaus 214 41.07 N 78.07 W
Kartosuro 115a 7.33 S 110.44 E
Karttula 26 62.53 N 26.58 E
Kartun 89 45.53 N 134.58 E
Kartuzy 30 54.20 N 18.12 E
Kartzow 54 52.29 N 12.58 E
Käru 76 58.50 N 25.11 E
Karufa 164 3.50 S 133.27 E
Karuizawa 94 36.21 N 138.38 E
Karumai 92 40.19 N 141.28 E
Karumba 166 17.29 S 140.50 E
Kārūn ≃ 128 30.26 N 48.10 E
Karungi 26 66.03 N 23.57 E
Karungu, Kenya 154 0.51 S 34.09 E
Karungu, Tan. 154 1.08 S 33.59 E
Karuni 115b 9.26 S 119.19 E
Karunjie 164 16.18 S 127.12 E
Karunki 26 66.02 N 24.01 E
Karup 41 56.18 N 9.10 E
Karup Å ≃ 41 56.18 N 9.10 E
Karūr 122 10.57 N 78.05 E
Karuscia, Punta › 70 36.49 N 11.59 E
Karvala 265a 59.41 N 30.09 E
Karviná 30 49.50 N 18.30 E
Kārwār 122 14.48 N 74.08 E
Karwendelgebirge ⩕ 64 47.27 N 11.20 E
Karwi 124 25.12 N 80.54 E
Karym 86 60.07 N 66.41 E
Karymskoje, S.S.S.R. 88 54.07 N 101.49 E
Karymskoje, S.S.S.R. 88 51.37 N 114.21 E
Karza 86 58.35 N 80.50 E
Karzachi 84 41.15 N 43.16 E
Kas, Sūd. 140 12.30 N 24.17 E
Kaş, Tür. 130 36.12 N 29.38 E
Kas ≃ 86 57.40 N 90.00 E
Kasaan 180 55.32 N 132.24 W
Kasabi 152 14.48 S 23.42 E
Kasach ≃ 84 40.03 N 43.52 E
Kasadi ≃ 272c 18.59 N 72.59 E
Kasado-shima I 96 33.57 N 131.51 E
Kasagi 94 34.45 N 135.56 E
Kasagi-sanchi ⩕ 270 34.45 N 135.56 E
Kasagi-yama ∧ 94 35.31 N 137.21 E
Kasahara 94 35.17 N 137.09 E
Kasahata 268 35.54 N 139.25 E
Kasai 96 34.56 N 134.50 E
Kasai ◆[8] 268 35.39 N 139.53 E
Kasai (Cassai) ≃, Afr. 152 3.06 S 16.57 E
Kāsai ≃, Bhārat 124 22.09 N 87.50 E
Kasai-Occidental □[4] 152 5.30 S 21.40 E
Kasai-Oriental □[4] 152 4.30 S 24.00 E
Kasaji 152 10.22 S 23.27 E
Kasakake 94 36.23 N 139.17 E
Kasama, Nihon 94 36.23 N 140.16 E
Kasama, Zam. 154 10.13 S 31.12 E
Kasamatsu 94 35.22 N 136.46 E
Kasan
→ Kazan', S.S.S.R. 80 55.45 N 49.08 E
Kasan, S.S.S.R. 128 39.02 N 65.35 E
Kasan-dong 98 41.18 N 126.55 E
Kasane 156 17.50 S 25.05 E
Kasanga 154 8.28 S 31.09 E
Kasangale 152 6.20 S 22.42 E
Kasangeshi ≃ 152 8.24 S 21.56 E
Kasangulu 152 4.36 S 15.10 E
Kasanka Game Reserve ◆[4] 154 12.35 S 30.12 E
Kasano-misaki › 94 36.21 N 136.18 E
Kasansaj 85 41.15 N 71.32 E
Kasansaj ≃ 85 40.57 N 71.30 E
Kasaoka 96 34.30 N 133.30 E
Kāsaragod 122 12.30 N 75.00 E
Kasari ≃ 76 58.45 N 23.49 E
Kašary 78 49.03 N 41.00 E
Kasatori-yama ∧, Nihon 94 34.44 N 136.18 E
Kasatori-yama ∧, Nihon 96 33.33 N 132.55 E
Kasauli 123 30.55 N 76.57 E
Kasba 124 25.51 N 87.33 E
Kasbagoas 126 24.11 N 88.30 E
Kasba Kamarda 126 21.46 N 87.21 E
Kasba Lake @ 176 60.18 N 102.07 W
Kasba Mirgoda 126 21.42 N 87.28 E
Kasba Nārāyangarh 126 22.10 N 87.23 E
Kasba Patāspur 126 22.02 N 87.32 E
Kasba-Tadla 148 32.34 N 6.18 W
Kaschau
→ Košice 30 48.43 N 21.15 E
Kaşçiftliği 130 36.36 N 29.45 E
Kåseberga 26 55.23 N 14.04 E
Kasempa 154 13.27 S 25.50 E
Kasenga 154 10.22 S 28.38 E
Kasenyi 154 1.24 N 30.26 E
Kasese, Ug. 154 0.10 N 30.05 E
Kasese, Zaïre 154 1.38 S 27.07 E
Kaset Sombun 110 16.17 N 101.57 E
Kasfareet Military Base ■ 142 30.15 N 32.24 E
Kāsganj 124 27.49 N 78.39 E
Kash ≃ 86 43.40 N 81.45 E
Kashabowie Lake @ 190 48.42 N 90.25 W
Kashaf ≃ 128 35.58 N 61.07 E
Kashagawigamog Lake @ 212 44.59 N 78.37 W
Kāshān 128 33.59 N 51.29 E
Kashasha 154 1.44 S 31.37 E
Kashegelok 180 60.50 N 157.50 W
Kashgar
→ Kashi 85 39.29 N 75.59 E
Kashi (Shufu) (Kashgar) 85 39.29 N 75.59 E
Kashierhe ≃ 85 39.38 N 74.38 E
Kashigaerhe ≃ 85 39.40 N 78.00 E
Kashihara 96 34.27 N 135.46 E
Kashiji Plain ⌣ 152 13.20 S 22.30 E
Kashileshi ≃ 152 9.46 S 23.05 E
Kashima-jingū ʋ[1] 94 35.59 N 140.40 E
Kashima-nada ⊤[2] 94 36.15 N 140.45 E
Kashima-yariga-take ∧ 94 36.37 N 137.45 E

Kashing
→ Jiaxing 106 30.46 N 120.45 E
Kashio ◆[8] 268 35.25 N 139.33 E
Kashīpur, Bhārat 124 29.13 N 78.57 E
Kāshipur, Bhārat 126 23.26 N 86.40 E
Kashitu 154 13.42 S 28.40 E
Kashiwa 94 35.52 N 139.59 E
Kashiwara 96 34.35 N 135.37 E
Kashiwazaki, Nihon 92 37.22 N 138.33 E
Kashiwazaki, Nihon 268 35.56 N 139.42 E
Kāshmar 128 35.12 N 58.27 E
Kashmir
→ Jammu and Kashmir □[2] 120 34.00 N 76.00 E
Kashmir, Vale of V 123 34.00 N 75.00 E
Kashmor 120 28.26 N 69.35 E
Kashunuk ≃ 180 61.18 N 165.36 W
Kashwakamak Lake @ 212 44.50 N 77.04 W
Kasia 124 26.45 N 83.55 E
Kāsiāni 126 23.14 N 89.45 E
Kasiāri 126 22.08 N 87.14 E
Kasidiji ≃ 152 7.57 S 23.12 E
Kasigau ∧ 154 3.50 S 38.40 E
Kasigluk 180 60.52 N 162.32 W
Kasilof 180 60.23 N 151.18 W
Kasilovo 78 50.38 N 35.37 E
Kasimbar 112 0.09 S 120.00 E
Kasimov 80 54.56 N 41.24 E
Kāsimpur, Bhārat 272b 22.46 N 88.31 E
Kāsimpur, Bngl. 126 23.59 N 90.19 E
Kašin 76 57.21 N 37.37 E
Kāsināthpur, Bhārat 272b 22.35 N 88.31 E
Kāsināthpur, Bngl. 126 23.58 N 89.37 E
Kasinge 154 6.20 S 26.59 E
Kasinka 156 18.13 S 24.22 E
Kāsipur 272b 22.25 N 88.10 E
Kasır 130 37.10 N 40.52 E
Kašira 82 54.51 N 38.10 E
Kaširka ≃ 82 54.52 N 38.13 E
Kasiruta, Pulau I 108 0.25 S 127.12 E
Kasiui, Pulau I 164 4.30 S 131.40 E
Kasiwa
→ Kashiwa 94 35.52 N 139.59 E
Kaskabulak 86 49.34 N 79.52 E
Kaškadarjinskaja Oblast' □[4] 85 39.00 N 66.00 E
Kaskaden-Kette
→ Cascade Range ⩕ 202 45.00 N 121.30 W
Kaskana 85 40.45 N 69.36 E
Kaskaskia ≃ 194 37.59 N 89.56 W
Kaskaskia, East Fork ≃ 219 38.43 N 89.09 W
Kaskaskia, North Fork ≃ 219 38.46 N 89.09 W
Kaskattama ≃ 176 57.03 N 90.07 W
Kaskelen 85 43.12 N 76.37 E
Kaskelen ≃ 85 43.53 N 77.08 E
Kaskinen
→ Kaskö 26 62.23 N 21.13 E
Kaskö (Kaskinen) 26 62.23 N 21.13 E
Kašlagač ≃ 83 47.45 N 37.16 E
Kaslātu ∧ 124 23.58 N 84.54 E
Kasli 86 55.53 N 60.46 E
Kaslo 182 49.55 N 116.55 W
Käsmark
→ Kežmarok 30 49.08 N 20.25 E
Kasn'a 76 55.24 N 34.20 E
Kasn'a ≃ 76 55.51 N 34.25 E
Kaso ≃ 115a 7.25 S 106.40 E
Kasongo 154 4.27 S 26.40 E
Kasongo-Lunda 152 6.28 S 16.49 E
Kásos I 38 35.22 N 26.56 E
Kasota 190 44.18 N 93.57 W
Kašperovka 78 49.26 N 29.41 E
Kašperske Hory 60 49.09 N 13.33 E
Kaspi 84 41.57 N 44.25 E
Kaspijsk 84 42.52 N 47.38 E
Kaspijskij 22 45.22 N 47.24 E
Kaspijskoje More
→ Caspian Sea ⊤[2] 72 42.00 N 50.30 E
Kašpirovka 80 53.03 N 48.27 E
Kaspische Senke
→ Prikaspijskaja Nizmennost' ⌣ 80 48.00 N 52.00 E
Kaspisches Meer
→ Caspian Sea ⊤[2] 72 42.00 N 50.30 E
Kaspl'a 76 55.00 N 31.38 E
Kaspl'a ≃ 76 55.24 N 30.43 E
Kasr, Ra's › 140 18.02 N 38.35 E
Kasrat Muraybiţ 130 36.02 N 38.08 E
Kasrik 130 38.13 N 41.54 E
Kassa
→ Košice 30 48.43 N 21.15 E
Kassab 130 35.56 N 35.59 E
Kassai
→ Cassai (Kasai) ≃ 152 3.02 S 16.57 E
Kassalā 140 15.28 N 36.24 E
Kassalā □[4] 140 18.00 N 36.00 E
Kassándra ›[1] 38 40.06 N 23.22 E
Kassándras, Kólpos C 38 40.06 N 23.30 E
Kassel 56 51.19 N 9.29 E
Kassel □[5] 56 51.10 N 9.20 E
Kasserine
→ El Kasserine 148 35.11 N 8.48 E
Kasserine □[8] 36 35.30 N 8.45 E
Kasshabog Lake @ 212 44.38 N 77.58 W
Kassikaityu ≃ 246 1.49 N 58.32 W
Kassinger 140 18.45 N 31.54 E
Kassîr, Sabkhat al- @ 130 35.03 N 41.07 E
Kasslerfeld ◆[8] 263 51.26 N 6.45 E
Kasson 190 44.03 N 92.45 W
Kassoum 150 13.05 N 3.18 W
Kastamonu 130 41.22 N 33.47 E
Kastamonu □[4] 130 41.40 N 33.45 E
Kastanéai 38 41.38 N 26.28 E
Kastelholm 26 60.14 N 20.04 E
Kastellaun 56 50.04 N 7.26 E
Kastellórizon I 130 36.08 N 29.34 E
Kasterlee 56 51.15 N 4.57 E
Kastl 60 49.22 N 11.42 E
Kastorf 52 53.44 N 10.34 E
Kastoría 38 40.31 N 21.15 E
Kastorías, Límni @ 38 40.30 N 21.17 E
Kastornoje 78 51.50 N 38.06 E
Kastrávion, Tekhnití Límni @[1] 38 38.50 N 21.20 E
Kastrup Lufthavn ⊠ 41 55.38 N 12.39 E
Kasuga, Nihon 94 35.28 N 136.29 E
Kasuga, Nihon 96 33.32 N 130.27 E
Kasuga, Nihon 96 35.10 N 135.06 E
Kasugai, Nihon 94 35.39 N 138.39 E
Kasugai, Nihon 94 35.14 N 136.58 E
Kasuga Shrine ʋ[1] 270 34.41 N 135.51 E
Kasuka 158 33.40 S 26.41 E
Kasukabe 94 35.58 N 139.45 E
Kasukawa 94 36.24 N 139.13 E
Kasulu 154 4.34 S 30.06 E
Kasumba 154 12.12 S 27.48 E
Kasumiga-ura @ 94 36.00 N 140.25 E
Kasum-Ismailov 84 40.36 N 46.47 E
Kasumkent 84 41.41 N 48.07 E
Kasungan 112 1.58 S 113.24 E
Kasungu 154 13.01 S 33.30 E
Kasungu National Park ♠ 154 12.55 S 33.15 E
Kasupe 154 15.10 S 35.15 E
Kasūr 123 31.07 N 74.27 E
Kasym
→ Kazym ≃ 74 63.54 N 65.50 E
Kaszuby ◆[1] 30 54.10 N 18.15 E
Kata 88 58.46 N 106.40 E
Kataba 154 16.05 S 25.10 E
Kataeregi 150 9.22 N 6.17 E
Katahdin, Mount ∧ 188 45.55 N 68.55 W
Katai 272c 19.10 N 73.05 E
Katajevo 88 50.57 N 108.41 E

Katajsk 86 56.18 N 62.35 E
Katako-Kombe 152 3.24 S 24.25 E
Katakwi 154 1.55 N 33.57 E
Katale 154 4.59 S 31.03 E
Katalla 180 60.12 N 144.31 W
Katanda 154 0.50 S 29.22 E
Katanga □[9] 154 10.00 S 26.00 E
Katanga ≃ 88 58.18 N 104.10 E
Katanga Plateau ⩕[1] 138 10.30 S 25.30 E
Katangi 124 23.27 N 79.47 E
Katanglad Mountains ⩕ 116 8.06 N 124.54 E
Katangli 89 51.42 N 143.14 E
Katanimara 126 22.17 N 87.11 E
Katanning 162 33.42 S 117.33 E
Katano 270 34.48 N 135.42 E
Katano-hana › 174f 24.49 N 141.20 E
Katanti 154 2.18 S 27.08 E
Katapakishi 152 8.15 S 22.49 E
Katar
→ Qatar □[1] 128 25.00 N 51.10 E
Katara, Depresión de
→ Qaţţārah, Munkhafaḑ al- •[7] 140 30.00 N 27.30 E
Katarniān Ghāt 124 28.20 N 81.09 E
Katase 268 35.19 N 139.29 E
Katashina 94 36.46 N 139.14 E
Katašin 76 52.36 N 32.10 E
Katav-Ivanovsk 86 54.45 N 58.12 E
Katayama ◆[8] 268 35.46 N 139.34 E
Katchall Island I 110 7.57 N 93.22 E
Katchewanooka Lake @ 212 44.27 N 78.16 W
Katchin-wan C 174m 26.18 N 127.53 E
Katchirga 150 14.03 N 0.06 E
Katech 84 41.39 N 46.34 E
Kateel ≃ 180 65.28 N 157.35 W
Katélé 150 10.38 N 5.37 W
Katepwa Beach 184 50.42 N 103.38 W
Katerbow 54 52.59 N 12.39 E
Kateríni 38 40.16 N 22.30 E
Katerinopol' 78 48.56 N 30.59 E
Katerloch •[5] 61 47.16 N 15.32 E
Katernberg ◆[8], B.R.D. 263 51.29 N 7.04 E
Katernberg ◆[8], B.R.D. 263 51.16 N 7.06 E
Katesbridge 48 54.17 N 6.08 W
Kates Needle ∧ 180 57.03 N 132.03 W
Katešovo 82 54.08 N 37.00 E
Katete, Malawi 154 12.17 S 33.39 E
Katete, Zam. 154 14.05 S 32.07 E
Katghora 124 22.30 N 82.33 E
Katha 110 24.11 N 96.21 E
Kathal 61 47.06 N 14.42 E
Kathangor, Jabal ∧ 140 5.45 N 33.59 E
Katherine 164 14.28 S 132.16 E
Katherine ≃ 164 14.39 S 131.42 E
Katherine Creek ≃ 166 23.48 S 143.42 E
Kāthgodām 124 29.16 N 79.32 E
Kathiār 120 25.32 N 87.35 E
Kāthiāwār ›[1] 120 22.00 N 71.00 E
Kathla 123 31.59 N 76.47 E
Kathleen 220 28.07 N 82.02 W
Kathleen Valley 162 27.23 S 120.38 E
Kathlow 54 51.43 N 14.29 E
Kathmandu, Nepāl 124 27.43 N 85.19 E
Kathor 120 21.18 N 72.56 E
Kathrabbā 132 31.08 N 35.37 E
Kathua 123 32.22 N 75.31 E
Kāthuli 126 23.52 N 88.40 E
Kati 150 12.44 N 8.04 W
Kātiādi 126 24.15 N 90.48 E
Katibas ≃ 112 2.01 N 112.33 E
Katihār 124 25.32 N 87.35 E
Katikati 172 37.33 S 175.55 E
Katima Mulilo 152 17.27 S 24.14 E
Katimik Lake @ 184 52.54 N 99.22 W
Katiola 150 8.08 N 5.06 W
Katiola □[5] 150 8.30 N 4.45 W
Katipunan 116 8.31 N 123.17 E
Kātlang 123 34.22 N 72.05 E
Katlenburg-Duhm 52 51.41 N 10.06 E
Katmai, Mount ∧ 180 58.17 N 154.56 W
Katmai National Monument ♠ 180 58.30 N 155.00 W
Kātmāndu
→ Kathmandu, Nepāl 124 27.43 N 85.19 E
Katni
→ Murwāra, Bhārat 124 23.51 N 80.24 E
Katni, S.S.S.R. 80 57.59 N 47.46 E
Káto Akhaïa 38 38.09 N 21.32 E
Kātol 120 21.16 N 78.35 E
Katompi 154 6.11 S 26.20 E
Katonah 210 41.16 N 73.41 W
Katonga ≃ 154 0.34 N 31.50 E
Katon-Karagaj 86 49.11 N 85.37 E
Katoomba 170 33.42 S 150.18 E
Katopa 154 2.45 S 25.06 E
Katori-jingū ʋ[1] 94 35.52 N 104.35 E
Katoúna 38 38.47 N 21.07 E
Katovice 60 49.16 N 13.49 E
Katowice 30 50.16 N 19.00 E
Katra 123 32.59 N 74.57 E
Kātrās 126 23.48 N 86.17 E
Katričev 80 49.23 N 45.33 E
Katrīnah, Jabal ∧ 140 28.31 N 33.57 E
Katrine, Loch @ 46 56.15 N 4.31 W
Katrineholm 40 59.00 N 16.12 E
Katsch, Golf von
→ Kutch, Gulf of C 120 22.36 N 69.30 E
Katschbach ≃ 61 47.08 N 14.17 E
Katschberg)(64 47.03 N 13.37 E
Katscher
→ Kietrz 30 50.05 N 18.01 E
Katsepe 157b 15.45 S 46.15 E
Katshungu 154 2.27 S 27.23 E
Katsina 150 13.00 N 7.32 E
Katsina Ala ≃ 152 7.48 N 8.52 E
Katsur ≃ 270 34.53 N 135.42 E
Katsura ◆[8] 270 34.59 N 135.42 E
Katsura ≃, Nihon 94 35.36 N 139.15 E
Katsura ≃, Nihon 96 34.02 N 134.35 E
Katsuragi-san ∧ 96 34.20 N 135.27 E
Katsushika ◆[8] 268 35.43 N 139.51 E
Katsuta, Nihon 94 36.24 N 140.30 E
Katsuta, Nihon 96 35.04 N 134.11 E
Kattakurgan 72 39.55 N 66.15 E
Kattara-Senke
→ Qaţţārah, Munkhafaḑ al- •[7] 140 30.00 N 27.30 E
Kattarp 41 56.09 N 12.46 E
Katta-Taldyk 85 40.19 N 73.12 E
Kattaviá 38 35.57 N 27.46 E
Kattegat Ʉ 26 57.00 N 11.00 E
Katternberg ◆[8] 263 51.09 N 7.02 E
Katthammarsvik 26 57.26 N 18.50 E
Kattonghu @ 120 35.30 N 92.00 E
Kattowitz
→ Katowice 30 50.16 N 19.00 E
Kattrup 41 55.57 N 9.56 E
Kāttuputtūr 122 10.59 N 78.14 E
Katul, Jabal ∧ 140 14.16 N 29.23 E
Katuma 154 6.10 S 30.34 E
Katumba 154 7.45 S 25.18 E
Katunino 80 58.01 N 45.39 E
Katunki 80 56.50 N 43.14 E
Kātūria 124 24.44 N 86.43 E
Katushan ∧ 86 45.40 N 82.55 E
Katusice 54 50.26 N 14.50 E
Kātwa 126 23.39 N 88.08 E
Katwijk aan de Rijn 52 52.11 N 4.26 E
Katwijk aan Zee 52 52.13 N 4.24 E
Katy 222 29.47 N 95.49 W
Kąty Wrocławskie 30 51.02 N 16.46 E
Katzenbuckel ∧ 56 49.28 N 9.02 E
Katzenelnbogen 56 50.17 N 7.59 E
Katzenfurt 56 50.37 N 8.21 E
Katzhütte 54 50.33 N 11.03 E

Symbol	English	Deutsch	Español	Français	Português
≃	River	Fluss	Río	Rivière	Rio
☲	Canal	Kanal	Canal	Canal	Canal
⌞	Waterfall, Rapids	Wasserfall, Stromschnellen	Cascada, Rápidos	Chute d'eau, Rapides	Cascata, Rápidos
Ʉ	Strait	Meeresstrasse	Estrecho	Détroit	Estreito
C	Bay, Gulf	Bucht, Golf	Bahía, Golfo	Baie, Golfe	Baía, Golfo
@	Lake, Lakes	See, Seen	Lago, Lagos	Lac, Lacs	Lago, Lagos
☰	Swamp	Sumpf	Pantano	Marais	Pântano
⊓	Ice Features, Glacier	Eis- und Gletscherformen	Accidentes Glaciales	Formes glaciaires	Acidentes Glaciares
⊤	Other Hydrographic Features	Andere Hydrographische Objekte	Otros Elementos Hidrográficos	Autres données hydrographiques	Outros Elementos Hidrográficos

Symbol	English	Deutsch	Español	Français	Português
✣	Submarine Features	Untermeerische Objekte	Accidentes Submarinos	Formes de relief sous-marin	Acidentes Submarinos
□	Political Unit	Politische Einheit	Unidad Política	Entité politique	Unidade Política
ʋ	Cultural Institution	Kulturelle Institution	Institución Cultural	Institution culturelle	Instituição Cultural
⊥	Historical Site	Historische Stätte	Sitio Histórico	Site historique	Sitio Histórico
♠	Recreational Site	Erholungs- und Ferienort	Sitio de Recreo	Centre de loisirs	Sítio de Lazer
⊠	Airport	Flughafen	Aeropuerto	Aéroport	Aeroporto
■	Military Installation	Militäranlage	Instalación Militar	Installation militaire	Instalação Militar
◆	Miscellaneous	Verschiedenes	Misceláneo	Divers	Miscelânea

Kauai □[6] 229b 21.59 N 159.22 W
Kauai I 229b 22.00 N 159.30 W
Kauai Channel ʯ 229b 21.45 N 158.50 W
Kaub 56 50.05 N 7.46 E
Kau Desert ⬥[2] 229d 19.21 N 155.19 W
Kaufbeuren 58 47.53 N 10.37 E
Kaufering 58 48.05 N 10.52 E
Kauffung → Wojcieszów 30 50.58 N 15.56 E
Kaufman 222 32.35 N 96.19 W
Kaufman □[6] 222 32.38 N 96.18 W
Kaugama 150 12.28 N 9.44 E
Kauhajoki 26 62.26 N 22.11 E
Kauhava 26 63.06 N 23.05 E
Kauiki Head > 229a 20.45 N 155.59 W
Kaukapakapa 172 36.37 S 174.30 E
Kaukasus → Bol'šoj Kavkaz ∧∧ 84 42.30 N 45.00 E
Kaukauai 175e 6.52 S 155.36 E
Kau Kau Bay C 175e 9.42 S 160.40 E
Kaukauna 190 44.17 N 88.17 W
Kaukauveld ∧∧[1] 156 20.00 S 20.30 E
Kaukhāli 126 22.38 N 90.04 E
Kaukura I[1] 14 15.45 S 146.42 W
Kaula Island I 229d 21.45 N 160.30 W
Kaulakahi Channel ʯ 229b 22.00 N 159.53 W
Kaulille 56 51.11 N 5.31 E
Kauliranta 24 66.27 N 23.41 E
Kaŭl-li 98 37.58 N 124.37 E
Kaulsdorf 54 50.37 N 11.26 E
Kaulsdorf ⬥[8] 264a 52.31 N 13.33 E
Kaulsdorf-Süd ⬥[8] 264a 52.29 N 13.34 E
Kau Lung Peak ∧ 271d 22.21 N 114.13 E
Kaumakani 229b 21.06 N 157.02 W
Kaumalapau 229a 20.47 N 156.59 W
Kaunakakai 229a 21.06 N 157.01 W
Kaunas 76 54.54 N 23.54 E
Kauneonga Lake 210 41.41 N 74.50 W
Kauner Tal ∨ 58 47.01 N 10.44 E
Kaunghein 110 25.40 N 95.26 E
Kauniainen → Grankulla 26 60.13 N 24.45 E
Kaunuunui Point > 229b 21.56 N 160.10 W
Kaup 164 3.50 S 144.00 E
Kaupanger 26 61.11 N 7.14 E
Kaura Namoda 150 12.35 N 6.35 E
Kauriāla Ghāt 124 28.23 N 81.02 E
Kauru 150 10.33 N 8.12 E
Kausa 272c 19.10 N 73.02 E
Kau Sai Chau I 271d 22.22 N 114.18 E
Kausala 26 60.54 N 26.22 E
Kaušany 78 46.38 N 29.25 E
Kaustinen 26 63.32 N 23.42 E
Kauswagan 116 8.11 N 124.05 E
Kautokeino 24 69.00 N 23.02 E
Kauttua 26 61.06 N 22.10 E
Kau-ye Kyun I 110 11.01 N 98.32 E
Kavača 74 60.16 N 169.51 E
Kavacık 130 39.40 N 28.30 E
Kavadarci 38 41.26 N 22.00 E
Kavajë 38 41.11 N 19.33 E
Kavak, Tür. 130 38.24 N 39.26 E
Kavak, Tür. 130 39.18 N 37.30 E
Kavak, Tür. 130 41.05 N 36.03 E
Kavakköy 130 40.13 N 27.46 E
Kavaklıdere 130 37.26 N 28.22 E
Kavalerovo 89 44.15 N 135.04 E
Kāvali 122 14.55 N 79.59 E
Kavála 38 40.56 N 24.25 E
Kavaratti Island I 122 10.33 N 72.38 E
Kavarna 38 43.25 N 28.20 E
Kaverino, S.S.S.R. 80 54.10 N 41.47 E
Kaverino, S.S.S.R. 82 56.11 N 36.15 E
Kavieng 164 2.35 S 150.50 E
Kavimba 156 18.02 S 24.38 E
Kavīr, Dasht-e ⬥[2] 128 34.40 N 54.30 E
Kavkazskij Zapovednik ♠ 84 43.55 N 40.30 E
Kävlinge 41 55.48 N 13.06 E
Kävlingeån ≃ 41 55.47 N 13.06 E
Kavuu ≃ 154 7.40 S 31.46 E
Kavykuči-Gazimurskije 88 51.22 N 118.10 E
Kaw, Guy. fr. 250 4.29 N 52.02 W
Kaw, Okla., U.S. 196 36.46 N 96.50 W
Kawa 110 17.05 N 96.28 E
Kawachi-nagano 96 34.25 N 135.32 E
Kawagama Lake ⊜ 212 45.18 N 78.45 W
Kawagoe 94 35.55 N 139.29 E
Kawaguchi 94 35.48 N 139.43 E
Kawaguchi-ko ⊜ 94 35.31 N 138.45 E
Kawaihae Bay C 229d 20.02 N 155.50 W
Kawaihoa Point > 229b 21.47 N 160.12 W
Kawaikini ∧ 229b 22.05 N 159.29 W
Kawailoa 229c 21.36 N 158.05 W
Kawailoa Beach 229c 21.37 N 158.05 W
Kawakawa 172 35.23 S 174.04 E
Kawama Mission 154 10.04 S 28.37 E
Kawambwa 154 9.47 S 29.05 E
Kawanishi, Nihon 94 36.22 N 138.10 E
Kawanishi, Nihon 94 36.09 N 136.09 E
Kawanishi, Nihon 96 34.49 N 135.24 E
Kawanishi, Nihon 270 34.45 N 135.47 E
Kawanoe 96 34.01 N 133.34 E
Kawara Débé 150 12.20 N 3.26 E
Kawardha 124 22.01 N 81.15 E
Kawartha Park 212 44.32 N 78.12 W
Kawasaki, Nihon 94 35.32 N 139.43 E
Kawasaki, Nihon 96 33.35 N 130.49 E
Kawasaki Stadium ♠ 268 35.32 N 139.43 E
Kawashima ⬥[8] 268 35.28 N 139.35 E
Kawashiri-misaki > 96 34.26 N 130.58 E
Kawau Island I 172 36.25 S 174.51 E
Kawawa ⬥[8] 268 35.31 N 139.33 E
Kawayan 116 11.41 N 124.21 E
Kawbein 110 16.33 N 97.52 E
Kawdut 110 15.31 N 97.47 E
Kawe, Pulau I 164 0.03 S 130.07 E
Kaweka ∧ 172 39.17 S 176.23 E
Kaweka Range ∧∧ 172 39.15 S 176.20 E
Kawerau 172 38.03 S 176.43 E
Kawhia 172 38.04 S 174.49 E
Kawhia Harbour C 172 38.05 S 174.50 E
Kawich Peak ∧ 204 37.58 N 116.27 W
Kawich Range ∧∧ 204 37.40 N 116.30 W
Kawin 164 2.45 S 150.45 E
Kawinaw Lake ⊜ 184 52.52 N 99.30 W
Kawio, Kepulauan II 112 4.30 N 125.30 E
Kawit 269f 14.27 N 120.54 E
Kawkabān 144 15.40 N 43.52 E
Kawkareik 110 16.33 N 98.14 E
Kawludo 110 18.29 N 97.19 E
Kawm 140 13.31 N 22.50 E
Kawm al-Farā'in (Buto) ⊥ 142 31.11 N 30.45 E
Kawm ar-Rāhib 142 28.20 N 30.37 E
Kawm Birah 273c 30.05 N 31.08 E
Kawm Dafanah (Daphnæ) ⊥ 142 30.52 N 32.11 E
Kawm Ḥamādah 142 30.46 N 30.42 E
Kawm Ishfīn 273c 30.11 N 31.15 E
Kawm Ishū 142 31.07 N 30.00 E
Kawm Ju'ayf (Naucratis) ⊥ 142 30.54 N 30.36 E
Kawm Umbū 140 24.28 N 32.57 E
Kawnipi Lake ⊜ 190 48.24 N 91.14 W
Kayaapu 112 5.26 S 102.24 E
Kayadibi, Tür. 130 39.55 N 34.15 E
Kayadibi, Tür. 130 39.29 N 36.43 E
Kayah □[3] 110 19.15 N 97.30 E
Kayak Island I 180 59.52 N 144.30 W
Kāyalpattinam 122 8.34 N 78.07 E
Kāyamba 272b 22.41 N 88.32 E
Kayambi 154 9.27 S 31.58 E
Kayan 110 16.54 N 96.34 E
Kayan ≃ 112 2.55 N 117.35 E
Kayangel Islands II 108 8.04 N 134.43 E
Kayankulam 122 9.11 N 76.30 E
Kayapa 116 16.22 N 120.53 E
Kayaş 130 39.56 N 32.58 E
Kaya-san ∧ 98 35.49 N 128.07 E
Kaycee 200 43.43 N 106.38 W
Kayeli 164 3.23 S 127.06 E
Kayembe-Mukulu 152 9.03 S 23.57 E
Kayen 115a 6.54 S 110.59 E
Kayes, Congo 152 4.25 S 11.41 E
Kayes, Mali 150 14.27 N 11.26 W
Kayes □[4] 150 14.00 N 11.00 W
Kayima 150 8.53 N 11.10 W
Kayış Dağı ∧ 267b 40.59 N 29.09 E
Kaymakçı 130 38.10 N 28.08 E
Kaymaz 130 39.31 N 31.11 E
Kayna 54 50.59 N 12.14 E
Kaynak 130 37.43 N 39.37 E
Kayō, Nihon 96 34.51 N 133.42 E
Kayō, Nihon 174m 26.33 N 128.07 E
Kayoa, Pulau I 164 0.05 S 127.25 E
Kayombo 154 9.36 S 25.37 E
Kay Point > 180 69.18 N 138.22 W
Kayser Gebergte ∧∧ 250 3.03 N 56.35 W
Kayseri 130 38.43 N 35.30 E
Kayseri □[4] 130 38.30 N 35.55 E
Kaysersberg 58 48.08 N 7.15 E
Kaysville 200 41.02 N 111.56 W
Kayuadi, Pulau I 112 6.49 S 120.47 E
Kayuagung 112 3.24 S 104.50 E
Kayumas 115a 7.50 S 114.08 E
Kayuta Lake ⊜ 210 43.25 N 75.12 W
Kayuyu 154 3.39 S 26.21 E
Kazach 84 41.06 N 45.22 E
Kazachskaja Sovetskaja Socialističeskaja Respublika □[3] 72 48.00 N 68.00 E
Kazachskij Melkosopočnik ∧∧[2] 86 49.00 N 72.00 E
Kazachstan 80 51.09 N 53.00 E
Kazačij 83 46.58 N 40.03 E
Kazačinskoje, S.S.S.R. 86 57.49 N 93.17 E
Kazačinskoje, S.S.S.R. 88 56.16 N 107.36 E
Kazačja Lopan' 78 50.21 N 36.11 E
Kazačje 74 70.44 N 136.13 E
Kazačji Lageri 78 46.42 N 32.59 E
Kazačka 80 51.28 N 43.56 E
Kazackij 86 49.20 N 58.31 E
Kazackoje 78 51.18 N 33.29 E
Kazakdarja 86 43.27 N 59.46 E
Kazakevičevo 89 48.17 N 134.46 E
Kazakh Soviet Socialist Republic → Kazachskaja Sovetskaja Socialističeskaja Respublika □[3] 72 48.00 N 68.00 E
Kazaki 76 52.38 N 38.16 E
Kazaklija 78 46.00 N 28.37 E
Kazal'cevo 86 59.18 N 80.30 E
Kazalinsk 86 45.46 N 62.07 E
Kazan' 80 55.45 N 49.08 E
Kazan ≃ 176 64.02 N 95.30 W
Kazanbulak 84 40.38 N 46.41 E
Kazancı 130 36.30 N 32.53 E
Kazandžik 128 39.16 N 55.32 E
Kazanga 152 5.10 N 23.06 E
Kazanka, S.S.S.R. 78 47.50 N 32.49 E
Kazanka, S.S.S.R. 86 53.20 N 67.27 E
Kazanka ≃ 80 55.48 N 49.01 E
Kazanlăk 38 42.38 N 25.21 E
Kazan Lake ⊜ 184 55.33 N 108.21 W
Kazanlı 130 36.50 N 34.45 E
Kazanovka 76 53.46 N 38.34 E
Kazan-rettō II 14 25.00 N 141.00 E
Kazanskaja 78 49.48 N 41.09 E
Kazanskij Vokzal ⬥[5] 265b 55.46 N 37.40 E
Kazantip, Mys > 78 45.28 N 35.51 E
Kazarman 85 41.24 N 74.03 E
Kazatin 78 49.43 N 28.50 E
Kazatkul' 86 55.02 N 76.03 E
Kazbegi 84 42.39 N 44.39 E
Kazbek, Gora ∧ 84 42.42 N 44.31 E
Kaz Dağı ∧ 130 39.42 N 26.50 E
Kazembe 154 12.11 S 32.37 E
Kāzerūn 128 29.37 N 51.38 E
Kazgorodok, S.S.S.R. 86 49.56 N 71.36 E
Kazgorodok, S.S.S.R. 86 52.53 N 70.42 E
Kažim 24 60.20 N 51.30 E
Kazima 154 5.16 N 26.11 E
Kazi-Magomed 84 40.03 N 48.56 E
Kazimierza Wielka 30 50.16 N 20.30 E
Kazimierz Dolny 30 51.20 N 21.58 E
Kazincbarcika 30 48.16 N 20.37 E
Kazinga Channel ≃ 154 0.13 S 29.53 E
Kazinka, S.S.S.R. 76 52.32 N 39.42 E
Kazinka, S.S.S.R. 78 50.14 N 37.50 E
Kāzipāra 272b 22.43 N 88.31 E
Kāzīr Char 126 22.46 N 90.33 E
Kaziza 152 10.42 S 23.52 E
Kazlų Rūda 76 54.46 N 23.30 E
Kaz'minskoje 84 44.35 N 41.41 E
Kaznačejevo 82 54.31 N 37.16 E
Kaz'onnyj Torec ≃ 83 48.54 N 37.46 E
Kaztalovka 80 49.46 N 48.42 E
Kazumba 152 6.25 S 22.02 E
Kazungula 154 17.45 S 25.20 E
Kazvin → Qazvīn 128 36.16 N 50.00 E
Kazy 128 39.13 N 57.30 E
Kazym ≃ 74 63.54 N 65.50 E
Kazymskaja Kul'tbaza 74 63.40 N 67.14 E
Kazzī, Qārat ∧[2] 146 21.26 N 24.30 E
Kbal Dâmrei 110 14.07 N 105.21 E
Kbelnice 60 49.18 N 13.59 E
Kbely ⬥[8] 54 50.07 N 14.32 E
Kchucin 89 46.04 N 137.51 E
Kcynia 30 53.00 N 17.30 E
Kdyně 60 49.23 N 13.02 E
Kéa 38 37.38 N 24.21 E
Kéa I 38 37.34 N 24.22 E
Keaau 229d 19.37 N 155.02 W
Keady 48 54.15 N 6.42 W
Keahole Point > 229d 19.44 N 156.03 W
Keal, Loch na C 46 56.28 N 6.04 W
Kealaikahiki Channel ʯ 229a 20.37 N 156.50 W
Kealaikahiki Point > 229a 20.32 N 156.42 W
Kealakekua Bay C 229d 19.28 N 155.56 W
Kealia 229b 22.06 N 159.19 W
Keams Canyon 200 35.49 N 110.12 W
Keanae 229a 20.52 N 156.09 W
Keanapapa Point > 229a 20.54 N 157.04 W
Kean College of New Jersey ⱴ[2] 276 40.41 N 74.14 W
Keansburg 208 40.27 N 74.08 W
Kearney, Mo., U.S. 194 39.22 N 94.22 W
Kearney, Nebr., U.S. 198 40.42 N 99.05 W
Kearney, Pa., U.S. 214 40.08 N 78.12 W
Kearns 200 40.39 N 111.59 W
Kearny, Ariz., U.S. 200 33.03 N 110.55 W
Kearny, N.J., U.S. 210 40.46 N 74.09 W
Kearsley 262 53.32 N 2.23 W
Kearsley Creek ≃ 216 43.04 N 83.40 W
Keasbey 276 40.31 N 74.19 W
Keb' ≃ 76 57.44 N 28.28 E
Kebajoran ⬥[8] 269e 6.13 S 106.46 E
Keban 130 38.48 N 38.45 E
Keban Gölü ⊜[1] 130 38.50 N 39.15 E
Kebanyartimur 115a 7.09 S 112.52 E
Kébara 152 2.27 S 14.25 E
Kebbe 150 12.08 N 4.44 E
Kebeiti 120 36.47 N 79.29 E
Kébémer 150 15.22 N 16.27 W
Kébi, Mayo ≃ 146 9.18 N 13.33 E
Kebili 148 33.42 N 8.58 E
Kebîr, Oued el ≃ 34 36.50 N 6.07 E
Kebnekaise ∧ 24 67.53 N 18.33 E
Kebock Head > 46 58.01 N 6.20 W
Kebri Dehar 144 6.47 N 44.17 E
Kebumen 115a 7.40 S 109.39 E
Keb'uty 80 45.50 N 44.14 E
Keče 85 43.14 N 71.22 E
Kecel 30 46.32 N 19.16 E
Kech ≃ 128 26.00 N 62.44 E
Kechika ≃ 176 59.36 N 127.05 W
Keçiborlu 130 37.57 N 30.18 E
Kecksburg 214 40.11 N 79.28 W
Kecskemét 30 46.54 N 19.42 E
Kedabek 84 40.34 N 45.49 E
Kedada 144 5.20 N 36.00 E
Kedah □[3] 114 6.00 N 100.40 E
Kėdainiai 76 55.17 N 24.00 E
Kédange-sur-Canner 56 49.19 N 6.20 E
Kedarnath 124 30.44 N 79.04 E
Kedārpur 126 23.18 N 90.27 E
Kedawung 115a 6.42 S 108.31 E
Kedges Straits ʯ 208 38.03 N 76.02 W
Kedgwick 186 47.39 N 67.21 W
Kédhron 38 39.13 N 22.03 E
Kedianpo 100 31.23 N 112.51 E
Kediri 115a 7.49 S 112.01 E
Kedjebi 150 8.12 N 0.25 E
Kedon 74 64.08 N 159.14 E
Kedong 89 48.02 N 126.15 E
Kédougou 150 12.33 N 12.11 W
Kedrasju 24 64.36 N 60.24 E
Kedrovka 86 55.32 N 86.03 E
Kedu 102 26.33 N 104.21 E
Kedungdung 115a 7.06 S 113.15 E
Kedungjati 115a 7.10 S 110.37 E
Kedungwuni 115a 6.58 S 109.39 E
Kedvavom 24 64.15 N 53.27 E
Kędzierzyn 30 50.20 N 18.12 E
Keecheus Lake ⊜ 224 47.22 N 121.22 W
Keefer 218 38.32 N 84.38 W
Keefers 182 50.02 N 121.33 W
Keego Harbor 216 42.37 N 83.21 W
Keele 42 53.00 N 2.17 W
Keele ≃ 180 64.24 N 124.50 W
Keele Peak ∧ 180 63.26 N 130.19 W
Keeley Lake ⊜ 184 54.54 N 108.08 W
Keels 186 48.36 N 53.24 W
Keelung → Chilung 100 25.08 N 121.44 E
Keen, Mount ∧ 46 56.58 N 2.54 W
Keene, Ont., Can. 212 44.15 N 78.10 W
Keene, Calif., U.S. 228 35.13 N 118.33 W
Keene, Ky., U.S. 192 37.57 N 84.38 W
Keene, N.H., U.S. 188 42.56 N 72.17 W
Keene, Ohio, U.S. 214 40.21 N 81.52 W
Keene, Tex., U.S. 222 32.24 N 97.20 W
Keenesburg 200 40.07 N 104.31 W
Keeney Knob ∧ 192 37.47 N 80.42 W
Keeneyville 278 41.59 N 88.07 W
Keeper Hill ∧ 48 52.45 N 8.16 W
Keerbergen 56 51.00 N 4.37 E
Keerqinyouzhongqi (Gaoliban) 89 44.53 N 121.58 E
Keerqinzuohouqi 89 42.58 N 122.20 E
Keerqinzuozhongqi (Baokang) 89 44.07 N 123.18 E
Keer-weer, Cape > 164 13.58 S 141.30 E
Keerzong 120 32.11 N 79.59 E
Keeseg ∧ 64 46.58 N 12.14 E
Keeseville 188 44.30 N 73.29 W
Keetmanshoop 156 26.36 S 18.08 E
Keetmanshoop □[5] 156 26.30 S 19.00 E
Keewatin, Ont., Can. 184 49.46 N 94.34 W
Keewatin, Minn., U.S. 190 47.24 N 93.05 W
Keewatin □[5] 176 65.00 N 95.00 W
Kefa □[4] 144 6.50 N 36.00 E
Kefallinía I 38 38.15 N 20.35 E
Kéfalos 38 36.45 N 27.00 E
Kefamenanu 112 9.27 S 124.29 E
Kefar 'Azza 132 31.29 N 34.32 E
Kefar Blum 132 33.10 N 35.36 E
Kefar 'Eqron 132 31.51 N 34.49 E
Kefar Sava 132 32.10 N 34.54 E
Kefar Shammay 132 32.57 N 35.27 E
Kefar Syrkin 132 32.04 N 34.56 E
Kefar Szold 132 33.11 N 35.39 E
Kefar Vitkin 132 34.23 N 34.53 E
Kefar Warburg 132 31.43 N 34.44 E
Keferdiz 130 38.19 N 39.03 E
Kefermarkt 61 48.26 N 14.32 E
Keffi 150 8.51 N 7.52 E
Keffin Hausa 150 12.15 N 9.58 E
Keflavík 24a 64.02 N 22.36 W
Kega 24 65.10 N 36.54 E
Ke-ga, Mui >, Viet. 110 12.53 N 109.28 E
Ke-ga, Mui >, Viet. 110 10.42 N 107.58 E
Kegalla 122 7.15 N 80.21 E
Kégashka, Lac ⊜ 186 50.20 N 61.25 W
Kegaska 186 50.12 N 61.17 W
Kegičovka 78 49.17 N 35.46 E
Keglo, Baie C 176 59.10 N 65.50 W
Kegnæs I 41 54.52 N 9.59 E
Kegon-no-taki ᒪ 94 36.44 N 139.31 E
Kegonsa, Lake ⊜ 216 42.58 N 89.15 W
Kegonzhake 120 33.00 N 87.53 E
Keg River 176 57.48 N 117.52 W
Kegums 76 56.46 N 24.45 E
Kegworth 42 52.50 N 1.16 W
Kehdingen, Land ⬥[1] 52 53.45 N 9.15 E
Kehe 89 50.38 N 122.08 E
Kehiwin Indian Reserve ⬥[4] 182 54.07 N 110.48 W
Kehl 56 48.35 N 7.50 E
Kehlen 58 47.41 N 9.33 E
Kehoe 218 38.28 N 83.03 W
Kehra 76 59.20 N 25.20 E
Kehrigk 54 52.09 N 13.55 E
Ke-hsi Mānsām 110 21.56 N 97.50 E
Keig 46 57.15 N 2.39 W
Keighley 44 53.52 N 1.54 W
Keihoku 96 35.09 N 135.38 E
Keijō → Sŏul 98 37.33 N 126.58 E
Keila 76 59.18 N 24.25 E
Keilor 169 37.43 S 144.50 E
Keimoes 158 28.41 S 21.00 E
Kei Mouth 158 32.41 S 28.22 E
Keio University ⱴ[2] 268 35.38 N 139.45 E
Kei Road 158 32.42 S 27.32 E
Keiser 194 35.41 N 90.06 W
Keiskammahoek 158 32.41 S 27.09 E
Keiskammapunt > 158 32.40 S 27.10 E
Keïta 150 14.46 N 5.46 E
Kéita, Bahr ≃ 146 9.14 N 18.21 E
Keitele 26 63.11 N 26.22 E
Keitele ⊜ 26 62.55 N 26.00 E
Keith, Austl. 166 36.06 S 140.21 E
Keith, Scot., U.K. 46 57.32 N 2.57 W
Keith Arm C 176 65.20 N 122.15 W
Keithley Creek 182 52.45 N 121.24 W
Keithsburg 190 41.06 N 90.56 W
Keiyasi 175g 17.54 S 177.45 E
Keizer 224 44.57 N 123.01 W
Kejaman 112 2.39 N 113.45 E
Kejimkujik National Park ♠ 186 44.21 N 65.18 W
Kejni, Gora ∧ 180 64.30 N 174.54 W
Kejvy ∧∧ 24 67.35 N 38.00 E
Kekaha 229b 21.58 N 159.43 W
Kekek ≃ 190 48.24 N 75.48 W
Kekerengu 172 42.00 S 174.01 E
Kekertaluk Island I 176 68.10 N 66.30 W
Kékes ∧ 30 47.55 N 20.02 E
Kekexili 120 35.11 N 93.35 E
Kekexilishanmai ∧∧ 120 35.20 N 90.00 E
Kekeyaer 85 38.02 N 75.05 E
Keklau 175b 7.35 N 134.39 E
Kek Lok Si ⱴ[1] 114 5.23 N 100.14 E
Kekpāra 126 22.27 N 86.35 E
Kekri 120 25.58 N 75.09 E
Kekurnoi, Cape > 180 57.44 N 155.15 W
Kelafo 144 5.40 N 44.20 E
Kelai ≃ 112 2.10 N 117.29 E
Kelalihu ⊜ 120 34.36 N 87.16 E
Kelam 144 4.48 N 36.06 E
Kelamayi 86 45.37 N 84.53 E
Kela Met 144 16.04 N 38.43 E
Kelan 102 39.48 N 111.39 E
Kelanang 114 2.48 N 101.26 E
Kelang 114 3.02 N 101.27 E
Kelang, Pulau I, Indon. 164 3.12 S 127.44 E
Kelang, Pulau I, Malay. 114 3.00 N 101.18 E
Kelani ≃ 122 6.58 N 79.52 E
Kelantan 114 0.51 N 101.40 E
Kelantan □[3] 114 5.20 N 102.00 E
Kelantan ≃ 114 6.11 N 102.15 E
Kelapa 112 1.52 S 105.42 E
Kelaqinzuoqi 98 41.08 N 119.38 E
Kelasuri 84 43.08 N 41.13 E
Kelat 218 38.32 N 84.19 W
Kelayres 210 40.54 N 76.00 W
Kelb, Ouadi ∨ 146 15.19 N 18.51 E
Kel'badžar 84 40.07 N 46.02 E
Kelberg 56 50.17 N 6.55 E
Kelbia, Sebkra ⊜ 36 35.51 N 10.16 E
Kelbra 54 51.26 N 11.02 E
Keld Ula ∧ 86 43.20 N 85.25 E
Kel'd'ušovo 80 55.01 N 44.59 E
Kélékélé 273b 4.20 S 15.08 E
Kelenföld ⬥[8] 264c 47.28 N 19.03 E
Kelenken', Gora ∧ 180 66.07 N 170.52 W
Keles, S.S.S.R. 85 41.24 N 69.12 E
Keles, Tür. 130 39.55 N 29.14 E
Keles ≃ 85 41.02 N 68.37 E
Kéléso 150 10.57 N 3.59 W
Keleti-főcsatorna ≋ 30 48.01 N 21.20 E
Keleti Pályaudvar ⬥[5] 264c 47.30 N 19.06 E
Kelheim 60 48.55 N 11.52 E
Kelibia 148 36.51 N 11.06 E
Kelif 128 37.21 N 66.15 E
Keliyahe ≃ 120 39.00 N 81.40 E
Kelkheim 56 50.08 N 8.26 E
Kelkit ≃ 130 40.46 N 36.32 E
Kell 219 38.30 N 88.54 W
Kellé 152 0.06 S 14.33 E
Kellen 52 51.48 N 6.10 E
Kellenhusen 54 54.11 N 11.03 E
Keller, Tex., U.S. 222 32.56 N 97.15 W
Keller, Va., U.S. 208 37.37 N 75.46 W
Kellerberg 64 46.40 N 13.42 E
Kellerberrin 162 31.38 S 117.43 E
Keller Joch ∧ 64 47.19 N 11.46 E
Keller Lake ⊜, N.W. Ter., Can. 176 64.00 N 121.30 W
Keller Lake ⊜, Sask., Can. 184 56.04 N 106.46 W
Keller Peak ∧ 228 34.12 N 117.03 W
Kellett, Cape > 176 71.59 N 125.34 W
Kellettville 214 41.33 N 79.16 W
Kelleys Island 214 41.36 N 82.42 W
Kelleys Island I 214 41.36 N 82.42 W
Kelliher 184 51.15 N 103.44 W
Kellinghusen 52 53.57 N 9.43 E
Kellmünz 58 48.07 N 10.08 E
Kellogg, Idaho, U.S. 202 47.32 N 116.07 W
Kellogg, Iowa, U.S. 190 41.43 N 92.54 W
Kellogg, Minn., U.S. 190 44.18 N 91.59 W
Kellogg Marsh 224 48.05 N 122.07 W
Kelloggsville 214 41.52 N 80.36 W
Kellojärvi ⊜ 26 64.16 N 29.03 E
Kelloselkä 24 66.56 N 28.50 E
Kells → Ceanannus Mór 48 53.44 N 6.53 W
Kelly Lake ⊜ 180 65.30 N 126.10 W
Kelly Run ≃, Pa., U.S. 279b 40.13 N 79.45 W
Kelly Run ≃, Pa., U.S. 279b 40.15 N 79.55 W
Kellyville, Austl. 274a 33.43 S 150.57 E
Kellyville, Okla., U.S. 196 35.57 N 96.13 W
Kelmė 76 55.38 N 22.56 E
Kel'mency 78 48.27 N 26.50 E
Kelmscott 168a 32.07 S 116.01 E
Kélo 146 9.19 N 15.48 E
Kelolokan 112 1.08 N 117.54 E
Kelottijärvi 24 68.31 N 22.04 E
Kelowna 182 49.53 N 119.29 W
Kelsall 44 53.13 N 2.43 W
Kelsey Bay 182 50.24 N 125.57 W
Kelsey Head > 42 50.24 N 5.08 W
Kelsey Lake ⊜ 184 53.37 N 101.02 W
Kelseyville 204 38.59 N 122.50 W
Kelso, Scot., U.K. 46 55.36 N 2.25 W
Kelso, Wash., U.S. 224 46.09 N 122.54 W
Kelsterbach 56 50.04 N 8.32 E
Kel'temašat 85 42.30 N 70.17 E
Keltie Inlet C 176 64.28 N 73.28 W
Keluang 114 2.02 N 103.19 E
Keluang, Tanjung > 112 3.02 S 110.39 E
Kelud, Gunung ∧ 115a 7.56 S 112.18 E
Kelulunhe → Kerulen ≃ 90 48.48 N 117.00 E
Keluocun 89 49.16 N 125.44 E
Keluohe ≃ 89 49.22 N 125.15 E
Kelvedon 42 51.51 N 0.42 E
Kelvedon Hatch 260 51.40 N 0.16 E
Kelvington 184 52.10 N 103.30 W
Kelvin Seamount ⬥[3] 16 39.00 N 64.00 W
Kelyehed 144 8.44 N 49.10 E
Kelzenberg 263 51.07 N 6.30 E
Kem' 24 64.57 N 34.36 E
Kem' ≃, S.S.S.R. 24 64.57 N 34.41 E
Kem' ≃, S.S.S.R. 86 58.31 N 92.04 E
Kéma, Congo 273b 4.11 S 15.13 E
Kema, Indon. 112 1.23 N 125.04 E
Kema ≃, S.S.S.R. 76 59.21 N 44.29 E
Kema ≃, S.S.S.R. 76 60.16 N 37.20 E
Ké Macina 150 13.58 N 5.22 W
Kemah, Tür. 130 39.36 N 39.02 E
Kemah, Tex., U.S. 222 29.32 N 95.01 W
Kemaliye 130 39.16 N 38.29 E
Kemalpaşa, Tür. 130 41.30 N 41.30 E
Kemalpaşa, Tür. 130 38.25 N 27.26 E
Kemano 182 53.34 N 127.56 W
Kemasik 114 4.25 N 103.27 E
Kemayan 114 3.08 N 102.22 E
Kemayoran Airport ⊠ 269e 6.09 S 106.51 E
Kembani 112 1.34 S 122.54 E
Kembé 152 4.36 N 21.54 E
Kemberg 54 51.46 N 12.38 E
Kemblesville 208 39.45 N 75.50 W
Kembolcha 144 11.02 N 39.43 E
Kembs 58 47.41 N 7.30 E
Kembul 164 5.55 S 150.40 E
Kemčug ≃ 86 57.14 N 90.31 E
Kemena ≃ 112 3.10 N 113.03 E
Kemeneshát ∧∧[2] 61 46.58 N 16.40 E
Kemer 130 36.38 N 29.21 E
Kemer ≃ 267b 41.04 N 29.07 E
Kemer Barajı ⬥[6] 130 37.34 N 28.31 E
Kemerburgaz 267b 41.09 N 28.54 E
Kemerhisar 130 37.49 N 34.36 E
Kemerovo 86 55.20 N 86.05 E
Kemi 24 65.49 N 24.32 E
Kemie 26 62.14 N 30.20 E
Kemijärvi 24 66.40 N 27.25 E
Kemijärvi ⊜ 24 66.36 N 27.24 E
Kemijoki ≃ 26 65.47 N 24.30 E
Kemiö → Kimito 26 60.10 N 22.45 E
Keml'a 80 54.42 N 45.15 E
Kemmel 50 50.47 N 2.49 E
Kemmelberg ∧[2] 50 50.47 N 2.50 E
Kemmerer 200 41.48 N 110.32 W
Kemminghausen ⬥[8] 263 51.34 N 7.29 E
Kemmuna I 36 36.00 N 14.20 E
Kemnath 60 49.52 N 11.54 E
Kemnitz 54 54.04 N 13.31 E
Kemo-Gribingui □[5] 152 7.00 N 19.00 E
Kemp 222 32.26 N 96.14 W

ENGLISH

Name Page Lat.°′ Long.°′

Kemp, Lake ⊜[1] 196 33.45 N 99.13 W
Kemparana 150 12.50 N 4.56 W
Kemp Coast ⊥[2] 9 67.10 S 58.00 E
Kempele 26 64.55 N 25.30 E
Kempen 56 51.22 N 6.25 E
Kempen □[9] 56 51.10 N 5.20 E
Kempener Land ⬥[1] 263 51.19 N 6.29 E
Kempenfelt Bay C 212 44.23 N 79.36 W
Kempenich 56 50.25 N 7.07 E
Kempen-Krefeld □[8] 263 51.17 N 6.31 E
Kemper → Quimper 32 48.00 N 4.06 W
Kempisch Kanaal ≋ 56 51.10 N 4.49 E
Kempner 196 31.05 N 98.00 W
Kemp Peninsula >[1] 9 73.08 S 60.15 W
Kemps Bay 238 24.02 N 77.33 W
Kemps Creek ≃ 274a 33.51 S 150.46 E
Kempsey 166 31.05 S 152.50 E
Kempston 42 52.07 N 0.30 W
Kempt, Lac ⊜ 176 47.25 N 74.22 W
Kempten (Allgäu) 58 47.43 N 10.19 E
Kempton, Ill., U.S. 216 40.56 N 88.14 W
Kempton, Ind., U.S. 216 40.17 N 86.14 W
Kempton Park 158 26.06 S 28.14 E
Kempton Park Race Course ♠ 260 51.25 N 0.23 W
Kemptville 212 45.01 N 75.38 W
Kemptville Creek ≃ 212 45.03 N 75.39 W
Kemsing 260 51.18 N 0.14 E
Kemubu 114 5.18 N 102.01 E
Kemujan, Pulau I 115a 5.48 S 110.28 E
Kemul, Kong ∧ 112 1.52 N 116.11 E
Ken ≃ 124 25.46 N 80.31 E
Ken, Loch ⊜ 44 55.02 N 4.02 W
Ken, Water of ≃ 44 55.04 N 4.08 W
Kena ≃ 24 62.05 N 39.06 E
Kenadsa 148 31.48 N 2.26 W
Kenaf 144 1.37 N 41.36 E
Kenai 180 60.33 N 151.15 W
Kenai Mountains ∧∧ 180 60.00 N 150.00 W
Kenai Peninsula >[1] 180 60.10 N 150.00 W
Kenamuke Swamp ≋ 140 5.55 N 33.48 E
Kenansville, Fla., U.S. 220 27.53 N 80.59 W
Kenansville, N.C., U.S. 192 34.58 N 77.58 W
Kenaral 85 42.32 N 72.08 E
Kenašči 80 50.32 N 53.20 E
Kenashiga-sen ∧ 96 35.14 N 133.31 E
Kenaston 184 51.30 N 106.18 W
Kenberma 283 42.17 N 70.52 W
Kenbridge 192 36.58 N 78.08 W
Kenda 126 23.12 N 86.32 E
Kendai 124 22.45 N 82.37 E
Kendal, Sask., Can. 184 50.15 N 103.37 W
Kendal, Indon. 115a 6.55 S 110.12 E
Kendal, S. Afr. 158 26.04 S 28.58 E
Kendal, Eng., U.K. 44 54.20 N 2.45 W
Kendall, Austl. 166 31.38 S 152.43 E
Kendall, Fla., U.S. 220 25.41 N 80.19 W
Kendall, Mich., U.S. 216 42.22 N 85.49 W
Kendall, N.Y., U.S. 210 43.20 N 78.02 W
Kendall, Wis., U.S. 190 43.48 N 90.21 W
Kendall □[6] 216 41.38 N 88.27 W
Kendall, Cape > 176 63.36 N 87.09 W
Kendall, Mount ∧ 172 41.22 S 172.24 E
Kendall Park 208 40.25 N 74.34 W
Kendallville 216 41.27 N 85.16 W
Kendari 112 3.57 S 122.35 E
Kendari, Teluk C 112 3.57 S 122.38 E
Kendawangan 112 2.32 S 110.12 E
Kende 150 11.30 N 4.12 E
Kendenup 162 34.29 S 117.39 E
Kendghāta 126 24.05 N 87.10 E
Kendikolu I 122 5.57 N 73.24 E
Kendiktas ∧∧ 85 43.35 N 74.45 E
Kendleton 222 29.27 N 96.00 W
Kendrāpāra 120 20.30 N 86.25 E
Kendrew 158 32.32 S 24.30 E
Kendrick, Fla., U.S. 192 29.22 N 82.12 W
Kendrick, Idaho, U.S. 202 46.37 N 116.39 W
Kendrick Creek ≃ 226 38.00 N 119.50 W
Kendua 272b 22.34 N 88.10 E
Kendu Bay 154 0.22 S 34.39 E
Kendyrlisor, Solončak ≋ 86 42.50 N 54.30 E
Kenedy 196 28.49 N 97.51 W
Kenefick 222 30.07 N 94.51 W
Kenema 150 7.52 N 11.12 W
Kenes, S.S.S.R. 85 43.41 N 67.49 E
Kenes, S.S.S.R. 85 43.59 N 73.35 E
Kenge 152 4.52 S 16.59 E
Kengeja 154 5.25 S 39.44 E
Kēng Hkam, Mya. 110 21.01 N 98.29 E
Keng Hkam, Mya. 110 21.27 N 97.03 E
Kengkou, Zhg. 100 29.48 N 117.22 E
Kengkou, Zhg. 100 28.27 N 120.26 E
Kengtian 100 25.54 N 119.26 E
Kēng Tung 110 21.17 N 99.36 E
Kenhardt 158 29.19 S 21.12 E
Kenhorst 208 40.18 N 75.57 W
Kenia 152 2.43 S 17.04 E
Kenia → Kenya □[1] 154 1.00 N 38.00 E
Kenia → Kenya, Mount ∧ 154 0.10 S 37.20 E
Kéniéba 150 12.50 N 11.14 W
Kenilworth, Eng., U.K. 42 52.21 N 1.34 W
Kenilworth, Ill., U.S. 278 42.05 N 87.43 W
Kenilworth, N.J., U.S. 276 40.41 N 74.18 W
Kenilworth, Pa., U.S. 208 40.14 N 75.38 W
Kenilworth Castle ⊥ 42 52.21 N 1.34 W
Keningau 112 5.20 N 116.10 E
Kenitra 148 34.16 N 6.40 W
Kenley ⬥[8] 260 51.19 N 0.06 W
Kenly 192 35.36 N 78.07 W
Kenmare, Eire 48 51.53 N 9.35 W
Kenmare, N. Dak., U.S. 198 48.40 N 102.05 W
Kenmare River ≃ 48 51.45 N 10.00 W
Kenmawr 279b 40.29 N 80.07 W
Kenmore, Scot., U.K. 46 56.34 N 3.59 W
Kenmore, N.Y., U.S. 210 42.58 N 78.53 W
Kenmore, Wash., U.S. 224 47.46 N 122.14 W
Kennard, Ind., U.S. 218 39.54 N 85.31 W
Kennard, Pa., U.S. 214 41.28 N 80.20 W
Kennard, Tex., U.S. 222 31.22 N 95.11 W
Kennebec 198 43.54 N 99.52 W
Kennebec ≃ 188 44.00 N 69.50 W
Kennebecasis Bay C 186 45.25 N 66.00 W
Kennebec Lake ⊜ 212 44.43 N 77.00 W
Kennebunk 188 43.23 N 70.33 W
Kennedale 222 32.39 N 97.13 W
Kennedy, Ala., U.S. 194 33.35 N 87.59 W
Kennedy, N.Y., U.S. 214 42.10 N 79.06 W
Kennedy, Zimb. 154 18.52 S 27.10 E
Kennedy, Cape → Canaveral, Cape > 220 28.27 N 80.32 W
Kennedy, Mount ∧ 180 60.30 N 139.00 W
Kennedy Entrance ʯ 180 59.00 N 152.00 W
Kennedy Lake ⊜ 182 49.05 N 125.40 W
Kennedy Peak ∧ 110 23.19 N 93.45 E
Kennedy Range ∧∧ 162 24.30 S 115.00 E
Kennedyville 208 39.18 N 76.00 W
Kenner 194 29.59 N 90.15 W
Kennerdell 214 41.16 N 79.51 W
Kennet ≃, Eng., U.K. 42 51.28 N 0.57 W
Kennet ≃, Eng., U.K. 42 52.26 N 0.28 E
Kennetcook 186 45.11 N 63.44 W
Kenneth City 220 27.49 N 82.44 W
Kennett 194 36.14 N 90.03 W
Kennett Square 208 39.51 N 75.43 W
Kennewick 202 46.12 N 119.07 W
Kenney 219 40.06 N 89.05 W
Kenney Dam ⬥[6] 182 53.37 N 124.58 W
Kennington 42 51.10 N 0.54 E

DEUTSCH

Name Seite Breite°′ Länge°′ E=Ost

Kennisis Lake ⊜ 212 45.13 N 78.39 W
Kenn Reef ⬥[2] 160 21.12 S 155.46 E
Kenny 222 30.03 N 96.20 W
Kennydale 224 47.31 N 122.12 W
Kennywood Amusement Park ♠ 279b 40.23 N 79.52 W
Kénogami 186 48.26 N 71.14 W
Kenogami ≃ 176 51.06 N 84.28 W
Kenogamissi Lake ⊜ 190 48.15 N 81.31 W
Keno Hill 180 63.55 N 135.18 W
Kenora 184 49.47 N 94.29 W
Kenosha 216 42.35 N 87.49 W
Kenosha □[6] 216 42.06 N 88.04 W
Kenova 188 38.24 N 82.35 W
Kenoza Lake 210 41.44 N 74.57 W
Kenoza Lake ⊜ 283 42.47 N 71.03 W
Kenozero, Ozero ⊜ 24 62.03 N 38.14 E
Ken Rock 216 42.15 N 89.03 W
Kensal 198 47.18 N 98.44 W
Kense 86 46.49 N 68.20 E
Kensico Reservoir ⊜[1] 210 41.05 N 73.46 W
Kensington, Austl. 274a 33.55 S 151.14 E
Kensington, P.E.I., Can. 186 46.26 N 63.38 W
Kensington, Calif., U.S. 226 37.54 N 122.16 W
Kensington, Conn., U.S. 207 41.38 N 72.46 W
Kensington, Kans., U.S. 198 39.46 N 99.02 W
Kensington, Md., U.S. 284c 39.02 N 77.03 W
Kensington, Ohio, U.S. 214 40.44 N 80.57 W
Kensington ⬥[8], S. Afr. 273d 26.12 S 28.06 E
Kensington ⬥[8], N.Y., U.S. 276 40.39 N 73.58 W
Kensington ⬥[8], Pa., U.S. 285 39.58 N 75.08 W
Kensington and Chelsea ⬥[8] 260 51.29 N 0.11 W
Kensington Metropolitan Park ♠ 281 42.32 N 83.39 W
Kensington Park 220 27.22 N 82.31 W
Kent, S.L. 150 8.10 N 13.10 W
Kent, Conn., U.S. 207 41.43 N 73.29 W
Kent, N.Y., U.S. 210 43.20 N 78.08 W
Kent, Ohio, U.S. 214 41.09 N 81.22 W
Kent, Oreg., U.S. 224 45.12 N 120.42 W
Kent, Wash., U.S. 224 47.23 N 122.14 W
Kent □[6], Ont., Can. 214 42.25 N 82.10 W
Kent □[6], Eng., U.K. 42 51.15 N 0.40 E
Kent □[6], Del., U.S. 208 39.10 N 75.32 W
Kent □[6], Md., U.S. 208 39.13 N 76.04 W
Kent □[6], Mich., U.S. 216 42.56 N 85.33 W
Kent □[6], R.I., U.S. 207 41.40 N 71.38 W
Kent ≃ 44 54.15 N 2.48 W
Kent, Vale of ∨ 42 51.10 N 0.30 E
Kent Acres 208 39.08 N 75.31 W
Kentallen 46 56.39 N 5.15 W
Kentani 158 32.31 S 28.19 E
Kentau 85 43.36 N 68.36 E
Kent Bay C 176 69.59 N 96.02 W
Kent Bridge 214 42.31 N 82.04 W
Kent County Airport ⊠ 216 42.54 N 85.39 W
Kentfield 282 37.57 N 122.33 W
Kent Group II 166 39.27 S 147.20 E
Kenthurst 274a 33.40 S 151.00 E
Kent Island I 208 38.55 N 76.20 W
Kent Lake ⊜ 216 42.32 N 83.40 W
Kentland, Ind., U.S. 216 40.46 N 87.27 W
Kentland, Md., U.S. 284c 38.55 N 76.53 W
Kenton, Eng., U.K. 42 50.38 N 3.28 W
Kenton, Del., U.S. 208 39.14 N 75.40 W
Kenton, Mich., U.S. 190 46.28 N 88.54 W
Kenton, Ohio, U.S. 216 40.39 N 83.36 W
Kenton, Tenn., U.S. 194 36.12 N 89.01 W
Kenton □[6] 218 38.56 N 84.33 W
Kent Park 283 42.06 N 70.41 W
Kent Park Golf Course ♠ 273d 26.08 S 28.04 E
Kent Peninsula >[1] 176 68.30 N 107.00 W
Kent Point > 208 38.50 N 76.22 W
Kentucky □[3] 178 37.30 N 85.15 W
Kentucky ≃ 218 38.41 N 85.11 W
Kentucky, Middle Fork ≃ 192 37.35 N 83.40 W
Kentucky, North Fork ≃ 192 37.34 N 83.42 W
Kentucky, South Fork ≃ 192 37.34 N 83.42 W
Kentucky Lake ⊜[1] 194 36.25 N 88.05 W
Kentucky State Horse Park ♠ 218 38.08 N 84.31 W
Kentville 186 45.05 N 64.30 W
Kentwood, La., U.S. 194 30.56 N 90.31 W
Kentwood, Mich., U.S. 216 42.53 N 85.35 W
Kent Woodlands 282 37.57 N 122.34 W
Kenvil 276 40.53 N 74.38 W
Kenwick 168a 32.02 S 115.58 E
Kenwood, Calif., U.S. 226 38.25 N 122.33 W
Kenwood, Ohio, U.S. 218 39.12 N 84.23 W
Kenwood ⬥[8] 278 41.49 N 87.36 W
Kenwood ⊥ 260 51.34 N 0.10 W
Kenya □[1] 10
154 1.00 N 38.00 E
Kenya, Mount ∧, Kenya 154 0.10 S 37.20 E
Kenya, Mount → Kirinyaga ∧, Kenya 154 2.43 N 36.51 E
Kenyon, Eng., U.K. 262 53.27 N 2.34 W
Kenyon, Minn., U.S. 190 44.16 N 92.59 W
Kenyon, R.I., U.S. 207 41.27 N 71.38 W
Kenzingen 58 48.11 N 7.46 E
Kenzou 152 4.10 N 15.02 E
Keokea 229a 20.24 N 156.21 W
Keokuk 190 40.24 N 91.24 W
Keonchi 124 22.38 N 81.47 E
Keo Neua, Col de)(110 18.23 N 105.09 E
Keonjhar □[5] 124 22.00 N 85.30 E
Keonjhargarh 120 21.38 N 85.35 E
Keon Park 274b 37.42 S 145.01 E
Keosauqua 190 40.44 N 91.58 W
Keota, Iowa, U.S. 190 41.21 N 91.57 W
Keota, Okla., U.S. 196 35.15 N 94.55 W
Kepahiang 112 3.39 S 102.34 E
Kepala Batas 114 5.31 N 100.26 E
Kepanjen 115a 8.07 S 112.34 E
Kepi 164 6.32 S 139.19 E
Kępice 30 54.15 N 16.52 E
Kepina 24 65.24 N 41.50 E
Kepingshan ∧∧ 85 40.00 N 77.10 E
Kępno 30 51.17 N 17.59 E
Kepo 112 2.56 S 106.33 E
Keppel Bay C 166 23.21 S 150.55 E
Keppel Harbour C 271c 1.16 N 103.50 E
Kepsut 130 39.41 N 28.09 E
Keptown 219 39.05 N 88.40 W
Kequan 98 36.04 N 114.00 E
Kerala □[3] 122 10.00 N 76.30 E
Keramian, Pulau I 112 5.04 S 114.36 E
Kerandin 112 0.12 S 104.46 E
Kerang 166 35.44 S 143.55 E
Keranyo 144 5.04 N 38.18 E
Keratéa 38 37.48 N 23.59 E
Keratsínion 267c 37.58 N 23.37 E
Keraudren, Cape > 162 19.57 S 119.45 E
Kerava 26 60.24 N 25.07 E
Keravat 164 4.19 S 152.01 E
Kerbat ≃ 114 5.01 N 102.51 E
Kerbela → Karbalā' 128 32.36 N 44.02 E
Kerbi ≃ 89 52.28 N 136.25 E
Kerburan 130 37.33 N 41.44 E

Symbols in the index entries represent the broad categories identified in the key at the right. Symbols with superior numbers (∧∧[2]) identify subcategories (see complete key on page *I · 30*).

Kartensymbole in dem Registerverzeichnis stellen die rechts in Schlüssel erklärten Kategorien dar. Symbole mit hochgestellten Ziffern (∧∧[2]) bezeichnen Unterabteilungen einer Kategorie (vgl. vollständiger Schlüssel auf Seite *I · 30*).

Los símbolos incluídos en el texto del índice representan las grandes categorias identificadas con la clave a la derecha. Los símbolos con numeros en su parte superior (∧∧[2]) identifican las subcategorías (véase la clave completa en la página *I · 30*).

Les symboles de l'index représentent les catégories indiquées dans la légende à droite. Les symboles suivis d'un indice (∧∧[2]) représentent des sous-catégories (voir légende complète à la page *I · 30*).

Os símbolos incluídos no texto do índice representam as grandes categorias identificadas com a chave à direita. Os símbolos com números em sua parte superior (∧∧[2]) identificam as subcategorias (veja-se a chave completa à página *I · 30*).

	English	Deutsch	Español	Français	Português
∧	Mountain	Berg	Montaña	Montagne	Montanha
∧∧	Mountains	Berge	Montañas	Montagnes	Montanhas
)(	Pass	Pass	Paso	Col	Passo
∨	Valley, Canyon	Tal, Cañon	Valle, Cañón	Vallée, Canyon	Vale, Canhão
≚	Plain	Ebene	Llano	Plaine	Planície
>	Cape	Kap	Cabo	Cap	Cabo
I	Island	Insel	Isla	Île	Ilha
II	Islands	Inseln	Islas	Îles	Ilhas
⊥	Other Topographic Features	Andere Topographische Objekte	Otros Elementos Topográficos	Autres données topographiques	Outros Elementos Topográficos

ESPAÑOL / FRANÇAIS / PORTUGUÊS

Nombre / Nom / Nome	Página / Page	Lat.°′	Long.°′ W=Oeste / W=Ouest
Kerby	202	42.12 N	123.39 W
Kerč'	78	45.22 N	36.27 E
Kerčemja	24	61.28 N	53.50 E
Kerčenskij Poluostrov	78	45.15 N	36.00 E
Kerčenskij Proliv	78	45.22 N	36.38 E
Kerčevskij	24	59.55 N	56.17 E
Kerch → Kerč'	78	45.22 N	36.27 E
Kerckhoff Lake	226	37.09 N	119.31 W
Kerec, Mys	24	65.20 N	39.40 E
Kerema	164	8.00 S	145.45 E
Keremeos	182	49.12 N	119.50 W
Kerem Maharal	132	32.39 N	34.59 E
Kerempe Burnu	130	42.01 N	33.21 E
Keren	144	15.46 N	38.28 E
Kerend	128	34.16 N	46.15 E
Kerens	222	32.08 N	96.14 W
Kerepes	264c	47.34 N	19.18 E
Keret'	24	66.16 N	33.34 E
Keret', Ozero	24	65.55 N	32.56 E
Kerewan	150	13.29 N	16.10 W
Kerga	24	62.39 N	46.00 E
Kergez	84	40.18 N	49.38 E
Kerguélen, Îles	6	49.15 S	69.10 E
Kerguelen-Gaussberg Ridge	6	55.00 S	75.00 E
Kerhonkson	210	41.46 N	74.11 W
Kerian	114	5.10 N	100.26 E
Kericho	154	0.22 S	35.17 E
Keri Kera	140	12.21 N	32.46 E
Kerikeri	172	35.13 S	173.58 E
Kerimäki	26	61.55 N	29.17 E
Kerinci, Gunung	112	1.42 S	101.16 E
Kerio	154	2.59 N	36.07 E
Kerion	38	37.40 N	20.48 E
Keritang	112	0.51 S	102.39 E
Kerka	61	46.28 N	16.36 E
Kerkdriel	52	51.46 N	5.20 E
Kerken	56	51.27 N	6.22 E
Kerkenna, Îles	148	34.44 N	11.12 E
Kerkhove	50	50.48 N	3.30 E
Kerkhoven	198	45.12 N	95.19 W
Kerki, S.S.S.R.	24	63.43 N	54.05 E
Kerki, S.S.S.R.	128	37.50 N	65.12 E
Kérkira (Corfu)	38	39.36 N	19.56 E
Kérkira	38	39.40 N	19.42 E
Kerkrade [-Holz]	56	50.52 N	6.04 E
Kerling	114	3.35 N	101.36 E
Kermadec Islands	14	29.16 S	177.55 W
Kermadec Ridge	14	31.00 S	177.30 W
Kermadec Trench	14	30.30 S	176.00 W
Kermajärvi	26	62.28 N	28.40 E
Kermān, Īrān	128	30.17 N	57.05 E
Kerman, Calif., U.S.	226	36.43 N	120.04 W
Kermān	128	29.00 N	57.30 E
Kermānshāh	128	34.19 N	47.04 E
Kermānshāhān	128	34.30 N	47.00 E
Kerme Körfezi	130	36.50 N	28.00 E
Kermit	196	31.51 N	103.06 W
Kermit Roosevelt Seamount	16	39.45 N	145.50 W
Kermode, Mount	182	52.57 N	131.51 W
Kern	228	35.20 N	118.55 W
Kern	204	35.13 N	119.17 W
Kern, South Fork	204	35.40 N	118.27 W
Kern City	228	35.18 N	119.05 W
Kernersville	192	36.07 N	80.04 W
Kernforschungszentrum	56	49.07 N	8.26 E
Kernhof	61	47.49 N	15.32 E
Kern Island Canal	228	35.22 N	119.01 W
Kern River Channel	226	35.49 N	119.40 W
Kernville	204	35.43 N	118.26 W
Keroh	114	5.43 N	101.00 E
Keros	24	60.44 N	52.50 E
Kérou	150	10.50 N	2.06 E
Kérouané	150	9.16 N	9.01 W
Kérouané	150	9.10 N	8.50 W
Kerowagi	164	5.50 S	144.50 E
Kerpe Burnu	130	41.10 N	30.11 E
Kerpen	56	50.52 N	6.41 E
Kerpinen'	78	46.47 N	28.22 E
Kerr	214	41.03 N	78.25 W
Kerre	140	5.19 N	25.40 E
Kerrera	46	56.23 N	5.34 W
Kerridge	262	53.17 N	2.06 W
Kerridge Hill	262	53.17 N	2.06 W
Kerrobert	184	51.55 N	109.08 W
Kerr Reservoir	192	36.35 N	70.28 W
Kerrtown	214	41.38 N	80.10 W
Kerruish Park	279a	41.26 N	81.34 W
Kerrville	196	30.03 N	99.08 W
Kerry	42	52.30 N	3.16 W
Kerry	48	52.10 N	9.30 W
Kerry Head	48	52.25 N	9.57 W
Kersa	144	9.28 N	41.53 E
Kersbrook	168b	34.47 S	138.51 E
Kersey	214	41.22 N	78.36 W
Kershaw	192	34.33 N	80.35 W
Kersinyane	150	15.24 N	10.10 W
Kersley	182	52.49 N	122.25 W
Kerspestausee	263	51.08 N	7.30 E
Kerstenhausen	56	51.04 N	9.13 E
Kert, Oued	34	35.15 N	3.15 W
Kerteh	114	4.31 N	103.27 E
Kerteminde	41	55.27 N	10.40 E
Kerulen (Cherlen) (Kelulunhe)	90	48.48 N	117.00 E
Kerva	80	55.37 N	39.35 E
Kerzaz	148	29.30 N	1.37 W
Kerzendorf	264a	52.16 N	13.17 E
Keržeпec	80	56.28 N	44.26 E
Keržeпec	80	56.05 N	45.03 E
Kerzers	58	46.58 N	7.12 E
Kesabpur	126	22.55 N	89.13 E
Ke-sach	110	9.46 N	105.59 E
Kesagami Lake	176	50.23 N	80.15 W
Kesälahti	26	61.54 N	29.50 E
Keşan	130	40.51 N	26.37 E
Keşap	130	40.55 N	38.31 E
Kesbern	263	51.20 N	7.42 E
Kesch, Piz	58	46.38 N	9.52 E
Kesennuma	92	38.54 N	141.35 E
Kesh	48	54.32 N	7.43 W
Keshan	89	48.02 N	125.51 E
Keshena	190	44.52 N	88.38 W
Keshequa Creek	210	42.43 N	77.50 W
Keshitage	120	37.23 N	78.05 E
Keshod	120	21.18 N	70.15 E
Keşirlik	130	41.58 N	27.12 E
Keşiş Dağları	130	39.50 N	39.45 E
Keskastel	56	48.58 N	7.02 E
Keskin	130	39.41 N	33.37 E
Keski-Suomen lääni	26	62.30 N	25.30 E
Keskozero	24	61.24 N	33.12 E
Keskuvejem, Gora	180	66.12 N	177.40 W
Kes'ma	76	58.27 N	37.04 E
Kesova Gora	76	57.35 N	37.17 E
Kespur	126	22.35 N	87.29 E
Kesra	36	35.49 N	9.22 E
Kessebüren	263	51.31 N	7.43 E
Kessel	56	51.08 N	4.37 E
Kesselsdorf	54	51.02 N	13.35 E
Kessingland	42	52.25 N	1.42 E
Kesswil	58	47.36 N	9.20 E
Kestel Gölü	130	37.26 N	30.28 E
Kestell	158	28.19 S	28.38 E
Kesten'ga	24	65.55 N	31.47 E
Kestep	130	36.27 N	29.16 E
Kestilä	26	64.21 N	26.17 E
Keston	260	51.22 N	0.02 E
Keswick, Ont., Can.	212	44.15 N	79.28 W
Keswick, Eng., U.K.	44	54.37 N	3.08 W
Keszthely	30	46.46 N	17.15 E
Ket'	86	58.55 N	81.32 E
Keta	150	5.55 N	1.00 E
Keta	94	34.56 N	137.50 E
Keta, Ozero	74	68.44 N	90.00 E
Ketaka	96	35.30 N	134.03 E
Keta Lagoon	150	5.54 N	0.56 E
Ketam, Pulau	271c	1.24 N	103.57 E
Ketama	34	34.50 N	4.37 W
Ketang	100	22.58 N	115.28 E
Ketaun	112	3.23 S	101.49 E
Ketchikan	180	55.21 N	131.35 W
Ketchum	202	43.41 N	114.22 W
Kete Krachi	150	7.46 N	0.03 W
Ketelmeer	52	52.35 N	5.45 E
Keti Bandar	120	24.08 N	67.27 E
Ketingwan	154	0.40 N	35.50 E
Ketoj, Ostrov	74	47.20 N	152.28 E
Kétou	150	7.22 N	2.36 E
Ketovo	86	55.21 N	65.18 E
Kętrzyn (Rastenburg)	30	54.06 N	21.23 E
Ketsch	56	49.22 N	8.31 E
Ketta	152	1.28 N	15.56 E
Kettering, Eng., U.K.	42	52.24 N	0.44 W
Kettering, Ohio, U.S.	218	39.41 N	84.10 W
Kettinge	41	54.42 N	11.45 E
Kettle, N.A.	182	48.42 N	118.07 W
Kettle, Minn., U.S.	190	45.52 N	46.45 W
Kettle Creek, Ont., Can.	212	42.40 N	81.13 W
Kettle Creek, Pa., U.S.	210	41.18 N	77.51 W
Kettle Creek Lake	214	41.20 N	78.08 W
Kettle Creek State Park	214	41.23 N	77.56 W
Kettle Falls	202	48.36 N	118.03 W
Kettleman City	226	36.06 N	119.58 W
Kettleman Hills	226	36.00 N	120.00 W
Kettle River Range	202	48.30 N	118.40 W
Kettlersville	216	40.22 N	84.16 W
Kettleshulme	262	53.19 N	2.01 W
Kettlewell	44	54.09 N	2.02 W
Kettwig	56	51.22 N	6.56 E
Kęty	30	49.53 N	19.13 E
Ketzin	54	52.28 N	12.50 E
Keudemane	114	5.15 N	96.55 E
Keudepasi	114	4.18 N	95.56 E
Keudeteunom	114	4.27 N	95.48 E
Keudeunga	114	5.01 N	95.22 E
Keuka Lake	210	42.27 N	77.10 W
Keuka Lake, West Branch	210	42.33 N	77.09 W
Keuka Park	210	42.37 N	77.06 W
Keukenhof	52	52.16 N	4.33 E
Keul'	88	58.25 N	102.49 E
Keula	54	51.20 N	10.31 E
Keum	86	59.32 N	70.35 E
Keurboomsrivier	158	34.00 S	23.24 E
Keurusselkä	26	62.10 N	24.40 E
Keuruu	26	62.16 N	24.42 E
Kevdo-Mel'sitovo	80	53.09 N	43.54 E
Kevelaer	52	51.35 N	6.15 E
Kevin	202	48.45 N	111.58 W
Kevsala	80	45.48 N	42.41 E
Kew, Austl.	169	37.49 S	145.02 E
Kew, S. Afr.	273d	26.08 S	28.06 E
Kew, T./C. Is.	238	21.54 N	72.02 W
Kewanee	190	41.14 N	89.56 W
Kewanna	216	41.01 N	86.25 W
Kewāre	124	27.57 N	83.47 E
Kewaunee	190	44.27 N	87.30 W
Keweenaw Bay	190	46.56 N	88.23 W
Keweenaw Peninsula	190	47.12 N	88.25 W
Keweenaw Point	190	47.30 N	87.50 W
Kew Gardens, Ont., Can.	275b	43.40 N	79.18 W
Kew Gardens, Eng., U.K.	260	51.28 N	0.18 W
Keyala	154	4.27 N	32.52 E
Keyangkeershan	120	31.20 N	87.13 E
Keya Paha	198	42.54 N	99.00 W
Key Biscayne	220	25.42 N	80.10 W
Keyes, Calif., U.S.	226	37.33 N	120.54 W
Keyes, Okla., U.S.	196	36.49 N	102.15 W
Keyesport	219	38.44 N	89.17 W
Keyhole Reservoir	198	44.21 N	104.51 W
Keyhole State Park	198	44.19 N	104.48 W
Key Indian Reserve	184	51.45 N	102.08 W
Key Largo	220	25.04 N	80.28 W
Key Largo	220	25.16 N	80.19 W
Keymer	42	50.55 N	0.08 W
Keyneton	168b	34.34 S	139.08 E
Keynsham	42	51.26 N	2.30 W
Keynshamburg	154	19.15 S	29.39 E
Keyport, N.J., U.S.	276	40.26 N	74.12 W
Keyport, Wash., U.S.	224	47.42 N	122.38 W
Keyport Harbor	276	40.26 N	74.12 W
Keysborough	274b	38.00 S	145.10 E
Keysbrook	168a	32.26 S	115.59 E
Keyser	188	39.26 N	78.59 W
Keystone, Ind., U.S.	216	40.36 N	85.16 W
Keystone, Iowa, U.S.	190	42.00 N	92.12 W
Keystone, S. Dak., U.S.	198	43.54 N	103.25 W
Keystone, W. Va., U.S.	192	37.25 N	81.27 W
Keystone Lake, Okla., U.S.	196	36.15 N	96.25 W
Keystone Lake, Pa., U.S.	214	40.45 N	79.15 W
Keystone Peak	200	31.53 N	111.13 W
Keystone State Park	214	40.23 N	79.24 W
Keysun	130	37.34 N	37.50 E
Keysville, Fla., U.S.	220	27.52 N	82.06 W
Keysville, Va., U.S.	192	37.04 N	78.29 W
Keytesville	194	39.26 N	92.56 W
Key West	220	24.33 N	81.48 W
Key West Island	220	24.33 N	81.47 W
Key West Naval Air Station	220	24.34 N	81.41 W
Kez	80	57.53 N	53.43 E
Kezar Stadium	282	37.46 N	122.27 W
Kezhen	98	41.57 N	118.03 E
Kezi	154	20.58 S	28.32 E
Kežma	88	58.59 N	101.09 E
Kežmarok	30	49.08 N	20.25 E
Kgalagadi	156	25.00 S	22.00 E
Kgatleng	156	24.28 S	26.05 E
Kgun Lake	180	61.32 N	163.45 W
Khabab	132	33.00 N	36.16 E
Khabtrat Umm Judhām	142	30.24 N	31.58 E
Khābūr, Nahr al-	130	35.08 N	40.26 E
Khādar	272a	28.33 N	77.22 E
Khadari, Wādī al-	140	10.29 N	26.15 E
Khadaungnge Taung	110	18.57 N	94.37 E
Khadki (Kirkee)	122	18.34 N	73.52 E
Khadra	34	36.15 N	0.35 E
Khafūrī, Wādī	142	29.37 N	32.04 E
Khagaria	124	25.30 N	86.29 E
Khagdon	126	22.09 N	90.05 E
Khāgrāmuri	272b	22.26 N	88.14 E
Khaïdhárion	267c	37.33 N	22.53 E
Khaidik Gol	86	42.55 N	84.01 E
Khair	124	27.57 N	77.50 E
Khairābād	124	27.32 N	80.45 E
Khairāgarh	120	21.25 N	80.58 E
Khairbani	126	24.14 N	87.05 E
Khairna	272c	19.06 N	73.01 E
Khairpur, Pāk.	120	27.32 N	68.46 E
Khairpur, Pāk.	123	29.35 N	72.14 E
Khajrāho	120	24.50 N	79.58 E
Khājuri	126	21.52 N	87.58 E
Khajuri	272a	28.43 N	77.16 E
Kha Khaeng	110	14.55 N	99.07 E
Khakhea	156	24.51 S	23.20 E
Khalándrion	267c	38.01 N	23.48 E
Khalatse	123	34.20 N	76.49 E
Khālidī, Khirbat al-	132	29.39 N	35.14 E
Khālid Ibn al-Walīd	132	32.43 N	35.41 E
Khalkhalah	132	33.04 N	36.32 E
Khálki	130	36.17 N	27.35 E
Khalkidhikí	38	40.25 N	23.27 E
Khalkís	38	38.28 N	23.36 E
Khālsar	120	34.31 N	77.41 E
Khambhāliya	120	22.12 N	69.39 E
Khambhāt, Gulf of	122	21.00 N	72.30 E
Khāmgaon	122	20.41 N	76.34 E
Khamir	144	16.05 N	43.55 E
Khamīs Mushayṭ	144	18.18 N	42.44 E
Khamkeut	110	18.15 N	104.43 E
Khamma	70	36.47 N	12.02 E
Khammam	122	17.15 N	80.09 E
Khan	156	22.37 S	14.56 E
Khāna	126	23.20 N	87.44 E
Khānābād	120	36.41 N	69.07 E
Khān Abū Shāmāt	132	33.40 N	36.54 E
Khānākul	126	22.43 N	87.51 E
Khān al-Baghdādī	128	33.51 N	42.33 E
Khānaqīn	128	34.21 N	45.22 E
Khān Arnabah	132	33.11 N	35.53 E
Khancoban	171b	36.12 S	148.05 E
Khandaghosh	126	23.13 N	87.41 E
Khandela	120	27.36 N	75.30 E
Khandla	158	28.37 S	31.05 E
Khandwa	124	21.50 N	76.20 E
Khāneh Khvodī	128	36.05 N	56.04 E
Khānewāl	123	30.18 N	71.56 E
Khāngāh Dogrān	123	31.50 N	73.37 E
Khāngarh, Pāk.	120	28.22 N	71.43 E
Khāngarh, Pāk.	123	29.55 N	71.10 E
Khangkhai	110	19.28 N	103.15 E
Khanh-hoa	110	12.15 N	109.06 E
Khanh-hung	110	9.36 N	105.58 E
Khaniá	38	35.31 N	24.02 E
Khaníon, Kólpos	38	35.34 N	23.48 E
Khānkurda	126	22.00 N	87.25 E
Khanna	123	30.42 N	76.13 E
Khannā, Qā'	132	32.04 N	36.26 E
Khānozai	120	30.37 N	67.19 E
Khānpur, Bhārat	272b	22.40 N	88.16 E
Khānpur, Pāk.	123	28.39 N	70.39 E
Khānpur, Bhārat	272a	28.34 N	77.01 E
Khānpur, Bhārat	272a	28.31 N	77.14 E
Khān Shaykhūn	130	35.26 N	36.38 E
Khanty-Mansiysk → Chanty-Mansijsk	74	61.00 N	69.06 E
Khān Yūnus	132	31.21 N	34.19 E
Khanzira, Ras	144	10.55 N	45.47 E
Khao Saming	110	12.21 N	102.27 E
Khao Yoi	110	13.14 N	99.50 E
Khapalu	123	35.10 N	76.20 E
Kharabā	132	32.34 N	36.27 E
Kharagdiha	124	24.25 N	86.10 E
Kharagpur, Bhārat	124	25.07 N	86.33 E
Kharagpur, Bhārat	126	22.20 N	87.20 E
Kharak	123	33.07 N	71.06 E
Khārān	120	28.35 N	65.25 E
Kharānaq	128	32.20 N	54.39 E
Kharar, Bhārat	123	30.45 N	76.39 E
Kharar, Bhārat	126	22.42 N	87.41 E
Khāravli	272c	18.54 N	72.55 E
Kharāyij, Sabkhat al-	130	35.40 N	37.20 E
Kharaz, Jabal	144	12.44 N	44.09 E
Kharbatā	132	31.57 N	35.04 E
Kharbine → Haerbin	89	45.45 N	126.41 E
Khardah	126	22.44 N	88.22 E
Khārghar	272c	19.03 N	73.04 E
Khargon	120	21.49 N	75.36 E
Khāriān	123	32.49 N	73.52 E
Khariār Road	122	20.54 N	82.31 E
Kharīm, Jabal	132	30.17 N	33.58 E
Kharīṭ, Wādī al-	140	24.26 N	33.03 E
Khārk, Jazīreh-ye	128	29.15 N	50.20 E
Kharkov → Char'kov	78	50.00 N	36.15 E
Kharkurī, Jabal al-	144	13.57 N	47.09 E
Kharmān, Kūh-e	128	29.13 N	53.35 E
Kharri	272b	22.55 N	88.14 E
Kharsāwān	124	22.48 N	85.50 E
Kharsia	124	21.58 N	83.07 E
Khartoum → Al-Khurṭūm	140	15.36 N	32.32 E
Khartoum North → Al-Khurṭūm Baḥrī	140	15.38 N	32.33 E
Khartum → Al-Khurṭūm	140	15.36 N	32.32 E
Kharumwa	154	3.12 S	32.39 E
Khasebake	156	20.41 S	24.29 E
Khāsh, Afg.	128	31.31 N	62.52 E
Khāsh, Īrān	128	28.14 N	61.14 E
Khāsh	128	31.11 N	62.05 E
Khāsh, Dasht-e	128	31.50 N	62.30 E
Khashab, Jabal al-	142	29.56 N	31.01 E
Khashm al-Qirbah	140	14.58 N	35.55 E
Khashm al-Qirbah, Khazzān	140	14.40 N	35.55 E
Khashshab, Tur'at al-	273c	29.53 N	31.17 E
Khashum	140	12.27 N	28.02 E
Khaskovo → Haskovo	38	41.56 N	25.33 E
Khaur	123	33.16 N	72.28 E
Khawrah	144	14.26 N	46.09 E
Khawsa	110	15.03 N	97.50 E
Khaybar	128	25.42 N	39.31 E
Khaybar, Ḥarrat	128	25.30 N	39.45 E
Khayl, Kathīb al-	142	30.33 N	32.28 E
Khayra Bil	272b	22.52 N	88.29 E
Khayung	110	15.07 N	104.42 E
Khazar, Baḥr-e → Caspian Sea	72	42.00 N	50.30 E
Khe-bo	110	19.08 N	104.41 E
Khemis el Khechna	34	36.39 N	3.20 E
Khemis Miliana	148	36.16 N	2.13 E
Khemisset	148	33.50 N	6.03 W
Khemmarat	110	16.03 N	105.13 E
Khenchela	148	35.28 N	7.11 E
Khenifra	148	33.00 N	5.40 W
Khenjān	120	35.36 N	70.59 E
Khera	272a	28.46 N	77.08 E
Kheri	124	28.10 N	80.40 E
Kherrata	148	36.31 N	5.26 E
Khersan	128	31.33 N	50.22 E
Kherson → Cherson	78	46.38 N	32.35 E
Khevāj	120	38.13 N	71.02 E
Khewāri	120	26.36 N	68.52 E
Khewra	123	32.39 N	73.01 E
Kheyr Khāneh	128	34.57 N	63.37 E
Khichīwāra Plateau	124	24.25 N	77.30 E
Khichripur	272a	28.37 N	77.19 E
Khimki → Chimki	82	55.54 N	37.26 E
Khíos	38	38.22 N	26.08 E
Khíos	38	38.22 N	26.00 E
Khipro	120	25.50 N	69.22 E
Khirbat Abū Qashṭah	132	31.16 N	34.16 E
Khirbat al-Ghazālah	132	32.44 N	36.12 E
Khirbat 'Awwād	132	32.19 N	36.43 E
Khirbat Qanāfār	132	33.38 N	35.43 E
Khirbat Umm as-Surab	132	32.26 N	36.19 E
Khirbitā	142	30.45 N	30.40 E
Khiri Mat	110	16.50 N	99.48 E
Khirpai	126	22.42 N	87.37 E
Khisfīn	132	32.51 N	35.49 E
Khiuri Khala	124	29.58 N	81.18 E
Khiva → Chiva	72	41.24 N	60.22 E
Khivach	85	38.13 N	71.02 E
Khīyāv	128	38.24 N	47.40 E
Khlong Khlung	110	16.12 N	99.43 E
Khlong Thom	110	7.56 N	99.09 E
Khlong Yai	110	11.46 N	102.54 E
Khlung	110	12.27 N	102.14 E
Khmel'nitskiy → Chmel'nickij	78	49.25 N	27.00 E
Khoai, Hon	110	8.26 N	104.50 E
Khogali	140	6.08 N	27.47 E
Khojāng	124	28.41 N	85.09 E
Khok Kloi	110	8.17 N	98.19 E
Khok Pho	110	6.43 N	101.06 E
Khoksa	126	23.48 N	89.17 E
Khok Samrong	110	15.04 N	100.44 E
Kholargós	267c	38.00 N	23.48 E
Kholm	120	36.42 N	67.41 E
Khomām	128	37.22 N	49.40 E
Khomas Highland	156	22.30 S	16.30 E
Khombole	150	14.46 N	16.42 W
Khomeyn	128	33.38 N	50.04 E
Khomodimo	156	22.46 S	23.52 E
Khondmāl Hills	122	20.20 N	84.00 E
Khon Kaen	110	16.26 N	102.50 E
Khóra	38	37.04 N	21.43 E
Khorāsān	128	35.00 N	58.00 E
Khóra Sfakíon	38	35.12 N	24.09 E
Khorramābād	128	33.30 N	48.20 E
Khorram Daraq	128	36.26 N	48.36 E
Khorramshahr	128	30.25 N	48.11 E
Khouribga	148	32.54 N	6.57 W
Khoutsiri	156	21.22 S	20.08 E
Khowst	120	33.22 N	69.57 E
Khrisokhoús, Kólpos	130	35.06 N	32.25 E
Khrisoúpolis	38	40.58 N	24.42 E
Khudiān	123	30.59 N	74.17 E
Khuff, Ar. Sa.	128	24.57 N	44.42 E
Khuff, Lībīya	146	28.20 N	18.48 E
Khugaung	110	26.07 N	98.18 E
Khūgīānī Sānī	120	31.31 N	66.12 E
Khuis	156	26.37 S	21.45 E
Khu Khan	110	14.42 N	104.12 E
Khulna	124	22.48 N	89.33 E
Khulna	124	22.30 N	89.45 E
Khŭm Bathéay	110	11.59 N	104.57 E
Khumbur Khūlē Ghar	120	32.49 N	68.47 E
Khungdugang	124	27.31 N	89.02 E
Khunjerab Pass	123	36.52 N	75.27 E
Khun Tan, Doi	110	18.30 N	99.20 E
Khunti	124	23.05 N	85.17 E
Khun Yuam	110	18.49 N	97.57 E
Khūr	128	32.57 N	58.26 E
Khuralji Khās	272a	28.39 N	77.17 E
Khurayyif, Minqār	142	28.55 N	30.26 E
Khuria Tank	124	22.25 N	81.36 E
Khurja	124	28.15 N	77.51 E
Khurli	120	28.59 N	65.52 E
Khurramshahr → Khorramshahr	128	30.25 N	48.11 E
Khūryān Mūryān	118	17.30 N	56.00 E
Khūsf	128	32.46 N	58.53 E
Khushāb	123	32.18 N	72.21 E
Khushk Khurd	272a	28.46 N	77.10 E
Khutshwe	156	23.19 S	24.29 E
Khutubi	86	44.45 N	86.25 E
Khuwayy	140	13.05 N	29.14 E
Khuzdār	120	27.48 N	66.37 E
Khūzestān	128	31.00 N	49.00 E
Khvāf	128	34.33 N	60.08 E
Khvājeh Moḥammad, Kūh-e	120	36.22 N	70.17 E
Khvājeh Ra'ūf	120	33.19 N	64.43 E
Khvor	128	33.47 N	55.03 E
Khvormūj	128	28.39 N	51.23 E
Khvoy	128	38.33 N	44.58 E
Khwae Noi	110	14.01 N	99.32 E
Khyber	123	34.00 N	71.00 E
Khyber Pass	123	34.05 N	71.10 E
Kia	175e	7.33 S	158.26 E
Kialwe	154	9.22 S	27.08 E
Kiama, Austl.	170	34.41 S	150.51 E
Kiama, Zaïre	152	7.15 S	17.44 E
Kiamba	116	5.59 N	124.37 E
Kiambi	154	7.20 S	28.01 E
Kiamboni, Kap → Chiamboni, Ras	144	1.38 S	41.36 E
Kiambu	154	1.10 S	36.50 E
Kiamesha Lake	210	41.41 N	74.40 W
Kiamichi	194	33.57 N	95.14 W
Kiamika	206	46.38 N	75.15 W
Kiamika, Barrage	206	46.37 N	75.08 W
Kiamika, Réservoir	206	46.40 N	75.05 W
Kiamusze → Jiamusi	89	46.50 N	130.21 E
Kian → Ji'an	100	27.07 N	114.58 E
Kiana	180	66.59 N	160.25 W
Kiandra	171b	35.53 S	148.30 E
Kiangara	157b	17.58 S	47.02 E
Kiangarow, Mount	166	26.49 S	151.33 E
Kiangsi → Jiangxi	100	28.00 N	116.00 E
Kiangsu → Jiangsu	90	33.00 N	120.00 E
Kiantajärvi	26	65.03 N	29.07 E
Kiaohsien → Jiaoxian	98	36.18 N	119.58 E
Kibæk	41	56.02 N	8.51 E
Kibali	154	3.37 N	28.34 E
Kibamba	154	4.53 S	26.33 E
Kibanga Port	154	0.11 N	32.52 E
Kibangou	152	3.27 S	12.21 E
Kibanseke I	273b	4.26 S	15.23 E
Kibar	120	32.20 N	78.01 E
Kibara	154	2.09 S	33.27 E
Kibāsī	128	30.34 N	47.50 E
Kibau Iyayi	154	8.52 S	34.32 E
Kibawe	116	7.34 N	125.00 E
Kibaya	154	5.18 S	36.34 E
Kibbie	216	42.25 N	86.12 W
Kibenga	152	7.55 S	17.35 E
Kiberashi	154	5.23 S	37.26 E
Kiberege	154	7.57 S	36.52 E
Kiberi	164	7.25 S	143.48 E
Kibi, Ghana	150	6.10 N	0.33 W
Kibi, Nihon	96	34.39 N	133.51 E
Kibi-kōgen	96	34.45 N	133.15 E
Kibila	154	8.14 S	26.23 E
Kibiti	154	7.44 S	38.57 E
Kiboga	154	1.02 N	30.58 E
Kiboko	154	2.15 S	37.42 E
Kibombo	154	3.54 S	25.55 E
Kibondo	154	3.35 S	30.42 E
Kibouendé, Congo	273b	4.19 S	15.11 E
Kibouendé, Congo	273b	4.17 S	15.09 E
Kibouendé I	273b	4.11 S	15.09 E
Kibouendé II	273b	4.12 S	15.09 E
Kibre Mengist	144	5.52 N	39.00 E
Kıbrıs → Cyprus	130	35.00 N	33.00 E
Kibumbu	154	3.32 S	29.45 E
Kibungo	154	2.10 S	30.32 E
Kibuye, Bdi.	154	3.40 S	29.59 E
Kibuye, Rw.	154	2.03 S	29.21 E
Kibwesa	154	6.28 S	29.57 E
Kibwezi	154	2.25 S	37.58 E
Kibworth Beauchamp	42	52.32 N	1.00 W
Kičevo	38	41.31 N	20.57 E
Kichčik	74	53.24 N	156.03 E
Kichijōji	268	35.42 N	139.35 E
Kickany	78	46.47 N	29.36 E
Kickapoo	190	43.05 N	90.53 W
Kickapoo Creek, Ill., U.S.	194	40.08 N	89.27 W
Kickapoo Creek, Tex., U.S.	196	31.31 N	99.58 W
Kickapoo Creek, Tex., U.S.	222	30.47 N	95.08 W
Kickapoo Creek, Tex., U.S.	222	32.16 N	95.28 W
Kicking Horse Pass	182	51.27 N	116.18 W
Kičkino	80	47.05 N	44.02 E
Kičma	80	57.12 N	48.55 E
Kicman'	78	48.27 N	25.44 E
Kičmengskij Gorodok	24	59.59 N	45.48 E
Kičuj	80	55.13 N	51.16 E
Kidal	150	18.26 N	1.24 E
Kidapawan	116	7.01 N	125.03 E
Kidatu	154	7.42 S	36.57 E
Kidbrooke	260	51.28 N	0.02 E
Kidderminster	42	52.23 N	2.14 W
Kidderpore	272b	22.31 N	88.19 E
Kidderpore Docks	272b	22.33 N	88.19 E
Kidepo National Park	154	3.50 N	33.40 E
Kidete	154	6.25 S	37.16 E
Kidira	150	14.28 N	12.13 W
Kidlington	42	51.50 N	1.17 W
Kidnappers, Cape	172	39.39 S	177.07 E
Kido	164	9.15 S	146.55 E
Kidron	214	40.44 N	81.45 W
Kidugallo	154	6.47 S	38.12 E
Kidul, Pegunungan	115a	8.13 S	112.00 E
Kidwelly	42	51.45 N	4.18 W
Kiefersfelden	64	47.37 N	12.11 E
Kiekebusch	264a	52.21 N	13.33 E
Kiel, B.R.D.	41, 54	54.20 N	10.08 E
Kiel, Wis., U.S.	190	43.55 N	88.02 W
Kiel Canal → Nord-Ostsee-Kanal	30	53.53 N	9.08 E
Kielce	30	50.52 N	20.37 E
Kielder	44	55.14 N	2.35 W
Kieler Bucht (Kiel Bay)	41	54.35 N	10.35 E
Kieler Förde	41	54.24 N	10.12 E
Kiembara	150	13.15 N	2.44 W
Kienberg	264a	52.40 N	12.54 E
Kien-binh	110	9.55 N	105.19 E
Kienge	154	10.34 S	27.33 E
Kien-hung	110	9.43 N	105.17 E
Kienitz	54	52.40 N	14.26 E
Kiens → Chienes	64	46.48 N	11.50 E
Kiental	58	46.35 N	7.43 E
Kierling	264b	48.19 N	16.17 E
Kierspe	56	51.08 N	7.35 E
Kierspe-Bahnhof	263	51.08 N	7.37 E
Kiester	190	43.32 N	93.42 W
Kieta	175e	6.13 S	155.38 E
Kietrz	30	50.05 N	18.01 E
Kietz	54	52.34 N	14.36 E
Kiev → Kijev	78	50.26 N	30.31 E
Kiew → Kijev	78	50.26 N	30.31 E
Kifār 'Aşyūn	132	31.39 N	35.08 E
Kifaya	150	12.10 N	13.04 W
Kiffa	150	16.37 N	11.24 W
Kifisiá	38	38.04 N	23.48 E
Kifisós	267c	38.06 N	23.45 E
Kifrī	128	34.42 N	44.58 E
Kifrī, Jabal	142	27.48 N	32.50 E
Kigač	80	46.28 N	49.12 E
Kigali	154	1.57 S	30.04 E
Kigezi	154	1.00 S	29.45 E
Kiği	130	39.19 N	40.21 E
Kigille	140	8.40 N	34.02 E
Kigoma	154	4.52 S	29.38 E
Kigoma	154	4.30 S	30.30 E
Kigun, Cape	180	52.00 N	175.21 W
Kigwa	154	5.10 S	33.08 E
Kığzı	128	38.18 N	43.25 E
Kihei	229a	20.47 N	156.28 W
Kihikihi	172	38.02 S	175.21 E
Kihniö	26	62.12 N	23.11 E
Kihnu	76	58.08 N	24.00 E
Kiholo Bay	229d	19.52 N	155.56 W
Kihundo	154	9.25 S	38.59 E
Kihurio	154	4.28 S	38.04 E
Kii-hantō	96	34.00 N	135.45 E
Kiik	86	47.31 N	72.55 E
Kiiminkinjoki	26	65.12 N	25.18 E
Kiirun → Chilung	100	25.08 N	121.44 E
Kii-sanchi	92	34.00 N	135.50 E
Kii-suidō	96	33.55 N	134.55 E
Kija	86	56.52 N	86.39 E
Kijabe	154	0.56 S	36.34 E
Kijal	114	4.21 N	103.29 E
Kijasovo	80	56.21 N	53.07 E
Kijev (Kiev)	78	50.26 N	30.31 E
Kijevka, S.S.S.R.	80	50.46 N	48.28 E
Kijevka, S.S.S.R.	80	46.05 N	42.57 E
Kijevka, S.S.S.R.	86	50.16 N	71.34 E
Kijevskij Vokzal	265b	55.45 N	37.34 E
Kijevskoje	78	45.03 N	37.52 E
Kijevskoje Polesje	78	51.00 N	30.00 E
Kijevskoje Vodochranilišče	78	51.00 N	30.25 E
Kijima-chosuichi	96	35.04 N	132.44 E
Kijimadaira	94	36.51 N	138.24 E
Kijima-dam	96	35.02 N	132.34 E
Kijkašor	24	60.46 N	49.24 E
Kijma	86	51.35 N	67.34 E
Kijoka	174m	26.42 N	128.09 E
Kikagati	154	1.02 S	30.40 E
Kikai-shima	93b	28.19 N	129.59 E
Kikale	154	7.50 S	39.12 E
Kikati	152	14.48 S	12.28 E
Kikenka	265a	59.52 N	30.04 E
Kikerino	76	59.28 N	29.35 E
Kikerk Lake	176	67.20 N	113.20 W
Kikimi	273b	4.26 S	15.25 E
Kikimorka	80	58.10 N	49.27 E
Kikinda	38	45.50 N	20.28 E
Kikládhes	38	37.30 N	25.00 E
Kiklah	146	32.05 N	12.41 E
Kiknur	80	57.19 N	47.14 E
Kikombo, Zaïre	152	5.59 S	18.09 E
Kikombo, Zaïre	152	5.40 S	18.48 E
Kikongo	152	4.16 S	17.11 E
Kikori	164	7.25 S	144.15 E
Kikori	164	7.10 S	144.05 E
Kikorze	54	53.39 N	15.01 E
Kiku	94	34.39 N	138.04 E
Kikuchi	96	32.59 N	130.45 E
Kikuchi	96	32.56 N	130.35 E
Kikugawa, Nihon	94	34.45 N	138.05 E
Kikugawa, Nihon	96	34.07 N	131.02 E
Kikuka	96	33.02 N	130.46 E
Kikuma	96	34.03 N	132.53 E
Kikuna	268	35.10 N	139.40 E
Kikusui	96	32.58 N	130.36 E
Kikvidze, S.S.S.R.	80	50.53 N	42.46 E
Kikvidze, S.S.S.R.	80	50.44 N	43.03 E
Kikvorsberg	158	31.17 S	25.20 E
Kikwit	152	5.02 S	18.49 E
Kil	26	59.30 N	13.19 E
Kilaån	40	58.44 N	17.01 E
Kılaban	128	37.27 N	42.51 E
Kilafors	26	61.14 N	16.34 E
Kīlakarai	122	9.14 N	78.47 E
Kila Kila	164	9.30 S	147.10 E
Kilambé, Cerro	236	13.34 N	85.42 W
Kılandıras	130	38.34 N	30.11 E
Kilauea	229b	22.13 N	159.25 W
Kilauea Crater	229d	19.25 N	155.17 W
Kilauea Point	229b	22.14 N	159.24 W
Kilb	61	48.06 N	15.24 E
Kilbaha	48	52.33 N	9.52 W
Kilbarchan	46	55.50 N	4.33 W
Kılbasan	130	37.20 N	33.12 E
Kilbeggan	48	53.22 N	7.29 W
Kilbirnie	46	55.46 N	4.41 W
Kilbourne, Ill., U.S.	219	40.09 N	90.01 W
Kilbourne, Ohio, U.S.	214	40.20 N	82.58 W
Kilbrannan Sound	46	55.40 N	5.25 W
Kilbride	46	57.05 N	7.27 W
Kilbuck Mountains	180	60.30 N	159.45 W
Kilbuck Run	279b	40.31 N	80.08 W
Kilcar	48	54.38 N	8.35 W
Kilchberg	58	47.19 N	8.33 E
Kilchis	224	45.30 N	123.52 W
Kilchoan	46	56.42 N	6.06 W
Kilchreest	48	53.10 N	8.38 W
Kilchrenan	46	56.21 N	5.11 W
Kilchu	98	40.58 N	129.20 E
Kilcolgan	48	53.13 N	8.52 W
Kilconnell	48	53.20 N	8.25 W
Kilcormac	48	53.10 N	7.43 W
Kilcoy	171a	26.57 S	152.33 E
Kilcullen	48	53.08 N	6.45 W
Kildare (Saint-Ambroise-de-Kildare), Qué., Can.	206	46.05 N	73.32 W
Kildare, Eire	48	53.10 N	6.55 W
Kildare	48	53.15 N	6.45 W
Kildare, Cape	186	46.52 N	63.58 W
Kildeer	278	42.10 N	88.03 W
Kil'dinstroj	24	68.48 N	33.06 E
Kildonan, B.C., Can.	182	49.00 N	125.00 W
Kildonan, Scot., U.K.	46	58.10 N	3.51 W
Kildonan, Zimb.	154	17.21 S	30.37 E
Kildonan, Strath of	46	58.09 N	3.51 W
Kildorrery	48	52.14 N	8.26 W
Kildrummy	46	57.14 N	2.52 W
Kildrummy Castle	46	57.14 N	2.52 W
Kildurk	164	16.26 S	129.37 E
Kildysart	48	52.41 N	9.06 W
Kilemary	80	56.47 N	46.52 E
Kilembe, Ug.	154	0.12 N	30.00 E
Kilembe, Zaïre	152	5.42 S	19.55 E
Kilfenora	48	52.59 N	9.13 W
Kilfinane	48	52.21 N	8.28 W
Kilgard	224	49.03 N	122.12 W
Kilgarvan	48	51.45 N	9.26 W
Kilgore, Ohio, U.S.	214	40.28 N	81.00 W
Kilgore, Tex., U.S.	222	32.23 N	94.53 W
Kilham	44	54.04 N	0.23 W
Kili	14	5.39 N	169.04 E
Kilian Island	176	73.35 N	107.53 W
Kilibo	150	8.34 N	2.36 E
Kilifi	154	3.38 S	39.51 E
Kilija	78	45.27 N	29.16 E
Kilijskoje Girlo	78	45.18 N	29.40 E
Kilikoiiūr	122	8.54 N	76.39 E
Kilima	154	0.59 S	29.12 E
Kilimanjaro	154	3.45 S	37.45 E
Kilimanjaro	154	3.04 S	37.22 E
Kilimatinde	154	5.51 S	34.57 E
Kilimavony	157b	23.48 S	43.41 E
Kilimli	130	41.28 N	31.50 E
Kılınç	130	40.38 N	29.23 E
Kılınç Tepesi	130	40.32 N	38.10 E
Kilindoni	154	7.55 S	39.39 E
Kilingi-Nõmme	76	58.09 N	24.58 E
Kilis	130	36.44 N	37.05 E
Kilkare Woods	282	37.38 N	121.55 W
Kilkee	48	52.41 N	9.38 W
Kilkeel	48	54.04 N	6.00 W
Kilkelly	48	53.53 N	8.51 W
Kilkenny	48	52.39 N	7.15 W
Kilkenny	48	52.40 N	7.20 W
Kilkerrin	48	53.33 N	8.34 W
Kilkhampton	42	50.53 N	4.29 W
Kilkieran	48	53.19 N	9.43 W
Kilkieran Bay	48	53.15 N	9.45 W
Kilkís	38	41.00 N	22.53 E
Killadoon	48	53.42 N	9.56 W
Killala	48	54.13 N	9.13 W
Killala Bay	48	54.15 N	9.10 W
Killaloe	48	52.48 N	8.27 W
Killaloe Station	190	45.33 N	77.25 W
Killam	182	52.47 N	111.51 W
Killara	274a	33.46 S	151.09 E
Killarney, Austl.	166	28.20 S	152.18 E
Killarney, Man., Can.	184	49.12 N	99.42 W
Killarney, Ont., Can.	190	45.58 N	81.31 W
Killarney, Eire	48	51.53 N	9.30 W
Killarney, Lake	240b	25.03 N	77.27 W
Killarney, Lakes of	48	52.01 N	9.30 W
Killarney Heights	274a	33.46 S	151.13 E
Killarney Provincial Park	190	46.05 N	81.30 W
Killashandra	48	54.00 N	7.32 W
Killavally	48	53.45 N	9.23 W
Killawog	210	42.24 N	76.01 W
Killbear Point Provincial Park	212	45.21 N	80.12 W
Kill Buck, N.Y., U.S.	210	42.10 N	78.41 W
Killbuck, Ohio, U.S.	214	40.30 N	81.59 W
Killbuck Creek, Ill., U.S.	216	42.10 N	89.06 W
Killbuck Creek, Ind., U.S.	218	40.07 N	85.41 W
Killbuck Creek, Ohio, U.S.	214	40.20 N	81.57 W
Killdeer	198	47.22 N	102.45 W
Killearn	46	56.03 N	4.22 W
Killeen	222	31.08 N	97.44 W
Killen	194	34.52 N	87.32 W
Killenaule	48	52.34 N	7.40 W
Killeter	48	54.40 N	7.41 W
Kıllı Dağ	84	40.21 N	42.10 E
Killik	180	69.00 N	153.58 W
Killilan	46	57.19 N	5.25 W
Killimor	48	53.10 N	8.17 W
Killin	46	56.28 N	4.19 W
Killington Mountain	188	43.36 N	72.49 W
Killingworth	207	41.21 N	72.30 W
Killíni	38	37.55 N	21.09 E
Killíni	38	37.57 N	22.23 E
Killinkoski	26	62.24 N	23.52 E
Killorglin	48	52.06 N	9.47 W
Killough	48	54.16 N	5.39 W
Killucan	48	53.31 N	7.07 W
Kill Van Kull	276	40.39 N	74.05 W
Killybegs	48	54.38 N	8.27 W
Killyleagh	48	54.24 N	5.39 W
Kilmacolm	46	55.54 N	4.38 W
Kilmacthomas	48	52.12 N	7.25 W
Kilmaine	48	53.34 N	9.09 W
Kilmallie	46	56.47 N	5.07 W
Kilmallock	48	52.23 N	8.34 W
Kilmaluag	46	57.41 N	6.17 W
Kilmarnock, Scot., U.K.	46	55.36 N	4.30 W
Kilmarnock, Va., U.S.	208	37.43 N	76.23 W
Kilmartin	46	56.07 N	5.29 W
Kilmar Tor	42	50.33 N	4.28 W
Kilmaurs	46	55.39 N	4.32 W
Kilmelford	46	56.16 N	5.29 W
Kil'mez'	80	57.01 N	51.22 E
Kil'mez'	80	56.58 N	50.28 E
Kilmichael	194	33.27 N	89.34 W
Kilmichael Point	48	52.44 N	6.10 W
Kilmore	169	37.18 S	144.57 E

English	Deutsch	Español	Français	Português
River	Fluss	Río	Rivière	Rio
Canal	Kanal	Canal	Canal	Canal
Waterfall, Rapids	Wasserfall, Stromschnellen	Cascada, Rápidos	Chute d'eau, Rapides	Cascata, Rápidos
Strait	Meeresstrasse	Estrecho	Détroit	Estreito
Bay, Gulf	Bucht, Golf	Bahía, Golfo	Baie, Golfe	Baía, Golfo
Lake, Lakes	See, Seen	Lago, Lagos	Lac, Lacs	Lago, Lagos
Swamp	Sumpf	Pantano	Marais	Pântano
Ice Features, Glacier	Eis- und Gletscherformen	Accidentes Glaciales	Formes glaciaires	Acidentes Glaciares
Other Hydrographic Features	Andere Hydrographische Objekte	Otros Elementos Hidrográficos	Autres données hydrographiques	Outros Elementos Hidrográficos
Submarine Features	Untermeerische Objekte	Accidentes Submarinos	Formes de relief sous-marin	Acidentes Submarinos
Political Unit	Politische Einheit	Unidad Politica	Entité politique	Unidade Política
Cultural Institution	Kulturelle Institution	Institución Cultural	Institution culturelle	Instituição Cultural
Historical Site	Historische Stätte	Sitio Histórico	Site historique	Sitio Histórico
Recreational Site	Erholungs- und Ferienort	Sitio de Recreo	Centre de loisirs	Sítio de Lazer
Airport	Flughafen	Aeropuerto	Aéroport	Aeroporto
Military Installation	Militäranlage	Instalación Militar	Installation militaire	Instalação Militar
Miscellaneous	Verschiedenes	Misceláneo	Divers	Miscelânea

Kilmore Creek ≃ 216 40.20 N 86.38 W
Kilnaleck 48 53.52 N 7.19 W
Kilninver 46 56.20 N 5.31 W
Kilo 115b 8.21 S 118.24 E
Kilokri ➝[8] 272a 28.35 N 77.16 E
Kiloli 154 6.50 S 33.23 E
Kilombero ≃ 154 8.31 S 37.22 E
Kilomines 154 1.48 N 30.14 E
Kilondo 154 9.46 S 34.21 E
Kilosa 154 6.50 S 36.59 E
Kilpisjärvi 24 69.03 N 20.48 E
Kilrenny 46 56.14 N 2.41 W
Kilrush 48 52.39 N 9.30 W
Kilsbergen ⛰[2] 40 59.20 N 14.47 E
Kilsmo 40 59.04 N 15.31 E
Kilsyth, Austl. 274b 37.48 S 145.19 E
Kilsyth, Scot., U.K. 46 55.59 N 4.04 W
Kiltān I 122 11.29 N 73.00 E
Kiltealy 48 52.34 N 6.45 W
Kiltimagh 48 53.51 N 9.01 W
Kiltoom 48 53.28 N 8.01 W
Kiltu-ri 98 34.35 N 127.20 E
Kilwa 154 9.18 S 28.25 E
Kilwa Island I 154 9.20 S 28.33 E
Kilwinning 44 55.40 N 4.42 W
Kim 198 37.15 N 103.21 W
Kim ≃ 152 5.28 N 11.07 E
Kima 154 1.26 S 26.43 E
Kimaam 164 7.58 S 138.53 E
Kimamba 154 6.47 S 37.08 E
Kimande 154 7.22 S 35.30 E
Kīmān Fāris (Crocodilopolis) (Arsinoe) ⊥ 142 29.19 N 30.50 E
Kimba 166 33.09 S 136.25 E
Kimball, Minn., U.S. 190 45.19 N 94.18 W
Kimball, Nebr., U.S. 198 41.14 N 103.40 W
Kimball, S. Dak., U.S. 198 43.45 N 98.57 W
Kimball, Mount ▲ 180 63.14 N 144.39 W
Kimbanda 152 4.07 S 17.59 E
Kimbe Bay C 164 5.30 S 150.30 E
Kimberley, B.C., Can. 182 49.41 N 115.59 W
Kimberley, S. Afr. 158 28.43 S 24.46 E
Kimberley Plateau ⛰[1] 160 17.00 S 127.00 E
Kimberly, Idaho, U.S. 202 42.32 N 114.22 W
Kimberly, Wis., U.S. 190 44.17 N 88.20 W
Kimberton 208 40.08 N 75.34 W
Kimbolton, N.Z. 172 40.03 S 175.47 E
Kimbolton, Eng., U.K. 42 52.18 N 0.24 W
Kimbolton, Ohio, U.S. 214 40.09 N 81.34 W
Kimbongo 152 6.08 S 18.01 E
Kimbwala 273b 4.22 S 15.12 E
Kimch'aek (Sŏngjin) 98 40.41 N 129.12 E
Kimch'ŏn 98 36.07 N 128.05 E
Kimerka ≃ 82 56.52 N 37.22 E
Kimhae 98 35.14 N 128.52 E
Kimhwa 98 38.26 N 127.36 E
Kimi, Cam. 152 6.05 N 11.30 E
Kími, Ellás 38 38.37 N 24.06 E
Kimil'tej 88 54.08 N 101.59 E
Kimito (Kemiö) 26 60.10 N 22.45 E
Kimi-tōge ▲[2] 270 34.43 N 135.06 E
Kimi-tōge)(96 34.23 N 135.37 E
Kimitsu 94 35.20 N 139.54 E
Kimiwan Lake ⊜ 182 55.45 N 116.54 W
Kim Kim ≃ 271c 1.26 N 103.58 E
Kimmell 216 41.24 N 85.33 W
Kim-me-ni-oli Wash V 200 36.07 N 108.11 W
Kímolos I 38 36.48 N 24.34 E
Kimongo 152 4.29 S 12.58 E
Kimovsk 76 53.58 N 38.32 E
Kimpangu 152 5.51 S 15.01 E
Kim Plan 279b 40.20 N 79.44 W
Kimp'o 271b 37.37 N 126.43 E
Kimp'o Airport ⊠ 271b 37.33 N 126.48 E
Kimpombo 273b 4.17 S 15.10 E
Kimpō-zan ▲ 94 35.53 N 138.38 E
Kimry 82 56.52 N 37.21 E
Kimsquit 182 52.49 N 126.58 W
Kimstad 40 58.32 N 15.58 E
Kimu ≃ 94 34.39 N 138.04 E
Kimuenza 273b 4.27 S 15.17 E
Kimvula 152 5.44 S 15.58 E
Kimwanga 154 7.08 S 28.42 E
Kinabalian, Mount ▲ 116 8.14 N 125.25 E
Kinabalu, Gunong ▲ 112 6.05 N 116.33 E
Kinabatangan ≃ 112 5.42 N 118.23 E
Kınalı ➝[8] 267b 40.55 N 29.03 E
Kınalıada I 267b 40.55 N 29.03 E
Kinangaly ▲ 157b 19.12 S 45.40 E
Kinango 154 4.08 S 39.19 E
Kinapusan Island I 116 5.13 N 120.40 E
Kinara 164 2.16 S 132.44 E
Kínaros I 130 36.59 N 26.17 E
Kinasa 94 36.42 N 138.01 E
Kinaūni 272a 28.39 N 77.23 E
Kinbasket Lake ⊜ 182 51.58 N 118.03 W
Kinbrace 46 58.15 N 3.56 W
Kinbuck 46 56.13 N 3.57 W
Kincaid, Sask., Can. 184 49.39 N 107.00 W
Kincaid, Ill., U.S. 219 39.35 N 89.25 W
Kincaid, Lake ⊜[1] 219 39.35 N 89.30 W
Kincardine, Ont., Can. 190 44.11 N 81.38 W
Kincardine, Scot., U.K. 46 56.04 N 3.44 W
Kinchafoonee Creek ≃ 192 31.38 N 84.10 W
Kinchang 110 26.32 N 98.02 E
Kinchara 272b 22.53 N 88.32 E
Kincheloe Air Force Base ■ 190 46.15 N 84.28 W
Kincolith 182 55.00 N 129.57 W
Kincraig 46 57.08 N 3.55 W
Kinda, Zaïre 152 4.47 S 21.48 E
Kinda, Zaïre 154 9.18 S 25.04 E
Kindadal 112 1.35 S 123.11 E
Kindanba 152 3.44 S 14.31 E
Kindarun Mountain ▲ 170 32.49 S 150.41 E
Kindberg 61 47.31 N 15.27 E
Kinde 190 43.56 N 83.00 W
Kindel'a 80 51.36 N 52.58 E
Kindel'a ≃ 80 52.31 N 52.41 E
Kindelbrück 54 51.16 N 11.05 E
Kindele 152 8.39 S 24.11 E
Kinder 194 30.29 N 92.51 W
Kinderhook, Ill., U.S. 219 39.42 N 91.09 W
Kinderhook, Mich., U.S. 216 41.48 N 85.00 W
Kinderhook, N.Y., U.S. 210 42.24 N 73.42 W
Kinderhook Creek ≃ 210 42.19 N 73.45 W
Kinder Reservoir ⊜[1] 262 53.23 N 1.55 W
Kinder Scout ▲ 44 53.23 N 1.52 W
Kindersley 184 51.27 N 109.10 W
Kindia 150 10.04 N 12.51 W
Kindia □[4] 150 10.00 N 12.45 W
Kindikan 88 56.02 N 115.15 E
Kinding 60 49.00 N 11.23 E
Kindley Field ⊠ 240a 32.22 N 64.40 W
Kindred 198 46.39 N 97.01 W
Kindu 154 2.57 S 25.56 E
Kinel' 80 53.14 N 50.39 E
Kinel'-Čerkassy 80 53.29 N 51.29 E
Kinel'skije Gory ⛰[1] 80 53.42 N 52.00 E
Kineo, Mount ▲ 188 45.42 N 69.44 W
Kinesi 154 1.28 S 33.52 E
Kinešma 80 57.26 N 42.09 E
Kineton 42 52.10 N 1.30 W
Kinfauns 46 56.22 N 3.21 W
King 192 36.17 N 80.22 W
King □[6] 224 47.26 N 121.48 W
King ≃, Austl. 164 14.41 S 131.59 E
King ≃, Austl. 169 36.41 S 146.25 E
King, Lake ⊜ 162 25.38 S 120.06 E
King, Mount ▲ 166 25.10 S 147.31 E
Kingabwa ➝[8] 273b 4.19 S 15.20 E
King and Queen □[6] 208 37.42 N 76.50 W
King and Queen Court House 208 37.40 N 76.53 W
Kingaroy 166 26.33 S 151.50 E
Kingarth 46 55.46 N 5.03 W
King City, Ont., Can. 212 43.56 N 79.32 W
King City, Calif., U.S. 226 36.13 N 121.08 W
King City, Mo., U.S. 194 40.03 N 94.31 W
Kingcome Inlet C 182 50.50 N 126.10 W
King Cove 180 55.04 N 162.19 W
King Ditch ≍ 279a 41.17 N 82.07 W
Kingdom City 219 38.58 N 91.56 W
King Edward ≃ 164 14.14 S 126.35 E
Kingersheim 58 47.48 N 7.20 E
King Ferry 210 42.40 N 76.37 W
Kingfield 188 44.57 N 70.09 W
Kingfisher 196 35.52 N 97.56 W
King George 208 38.16 N 77.11 W
King George □[6] 208 38.15 N 77.10 W
King George, Mount ▲ 182 50.35 N 115.24 W
King George Bay C 254 51.33 S 60.37 W
King George Island I 9 62.00 S 58.15 W
King George Islands II 176 57.20 N 78.25 W
King George's Dock ➝[5] 272b 22.32 N 88.18 E
King George Sound ⋓ 162 35.03 S 117.57 E
King George's Reservoir ⊜[1] 260 51.39 N 0.01 W
King Hill 202 43.00 N 115.12 W
Kingie ≃ 46 57.04 N 5.08 W
Kingisepp 76 59.22 N 28.36 E
King Island I, Austl. 166 39.50 S 144.00 E
King Island I, B.C., Can. 182 52.12 N 127.42 W
King Island I, Alaska, U.S. 180 64.58 N 168.05 W
Kinglake National Park ♠ 169 37.35 S 145.25 E
King Lear Peak ▲ 204 41.12 N 118.34 W
King Leopold Ranges ⛰ 160 17.30 S 125.45 E
Kingman, Ariz., U.S. 200 35.12 N 114.04 W
Kingman, Kans., U.S. 198 37.39 N 98.07 W
Kingman, Maine, U.S. 188 45.33 N 68.12 W
Kingman Reef ✣[2] 14 6.24 N 162.22 W
King Mountain ▲, B.C., Can. 180 58.17 N 128.54 W
King Mountain ▲, Qué., Can. 212 45.29 N 75.52 W
King Mountain ▲, Oreg., U.S. 202 42.42 N 123.14 W
King Mountain ▲, Oreg., U.S. 202 43.49 N 118.52 W
King of Prussia 208 40.05 N 75.23 W
King of Prussia Plaza ➝[9] 285 40.05 N 75.25 W
Kingoonya 162 30.54 S 135.18 E
Kingoué 152 3.43 S 14.09 E
King Peak ▲ 204 40.10 N 124.08 W
Kingri 120 30.27 N 69.49 E
Kings 216 42.00 N 89.06 W
Kings □[6], Calif., U.S. 226 36.20 N 119.39 W
Kings □[6], N.Y., U.S. 210 40.42 N 74.00 W
Kings ≃, Ark., U.S. 194 36.29 N 93.35 W
Kings ≃, Calif., U.S. 226 36.03 N 119.49 W
Kings ≃, Nev., U.S. 204 41.31 N 118.08 W
Kings, Middle Fork ≃ 204 36.50 N 118.52 W
Kings, North Fork ≃ 226 36.18 N 119.52 W
Kings, South Fork ≃ 226 36.18 N 119.52 W
King Salmon 180 58.14 N 157.24 W
King Salmon ≃ 180 58.15 N 157.30 W
Kingsbarns 46 56.18 N 2.39 W
Kings Beach 226 39.14 N 120.01 W
Kingsbridge 42 50.17 N 3.46 W
Kingsburg 226 36.31 N 119.33 W
Kingsbury, Eng., U.K. 42 52.35 N 1.40 W
Kingsbury, Ind., U.S. 216 41.31 N 86.42 W
Kingsbury ➝[8] 260 51.35 N 0.17 W
Kings Canyon National Park ♠ 204 36.48 N 118.30 W
Kingsclere 42 51.20 N 1.14 W
Kingscourt 48 53.53 N 6.48 W
Kings Creek 218 40.10 N 83.44 W
King's Creek ≃, Austl. 171a 27.57 S 151.42 E
Kings Creek ≃, Tex., U.S. 222 32.25 N 96.15 W
King's Cross Station ➝[5] 260 51.32 N 0.07 W
Kings Dominion ♠ 208 37.51 N 77.27 W
Kingsdown 42 51.11 N 1.25 E
Kings Falls ↳ 212 43.55 N 75.38 W
Kingsford, Austl. 274a 33.56 S 151.14 E
Kingsford, Mich., U.S. 190 45.48 N 88.04 W
Kingsford Heights 216 41.29 N 86.42 W
Kingsford Smith Airport ⊠ 170 33.57 S 151.11 E
Kingsgate 182 49.00 N 116.11 W
Kingshill 241n 17.44 N 64.48 W
Kingshouse 46 56.21 N 4.19 W
Kings Island ♠ 218 39.21 N 84.16 W
Kingskerswell 42 50.30 N 3.33 W
Kingsland, Eng., U.K. 42 52.15 N 2.47 W
Kingsland, Ark., U.S. 194 33.52 N 92.18 W
Kingsland, Ga., U.S. 192 30.48 N 81.41 W
Kingsland, Va., U.S. 208 37.24 N 77.26 W
Kings Langley 42 51.43 N 0.28 W
Kingsley, S. Afr. 158 27.55 S 30.33 E
Kingsley, Eng., U.K. 42 53.01 N 1.59 W
Kingsley, Eng., U.K. 262 53.16 N 2.40 W
Kingsley, Iowa, U.S. 198 42.35 N 95.58 W
Kingsley, Mich., U.S. 190 44.35 N 85.32 W
Kingsley, Pa., U.S. 210 41.46 N 75.45 W
Kingsley Dam ➝[6] 198 41.11 N 101.39 W
King's Lynn 42 52.45 N 0.24 E
Kings Mills 218 39.21 N 84.15 W
Kings Mountain 192 35.15 N 81.20 W
Kings Mountain National Military Park ♠ 192 35.07 N 81.33 W
King Solomon's Mines ⊥ 132 29.45 N 34.56 E
King Sound ⋓ 162 17.00 S 123.30 E
Kings Park, N.Y., U.S. 210 40.53 N 73.16 W
Kings Park, Va., U.S. 284c 38.48 N 77.15 W
Kings Park ♠, Austl. 168a 31.57 S 116.49 E
King's Park ♠, H.K. 271d 22.19 N 114.10 E
Kings Peak ▲ 200 40.46 N 110.22 W
Kings Plaza ➝[9] 276 40.37 N 73.55 W
King's Point, Newf., Can. 186 49.35 N 56.11 W
Kings Point, N.Y., U.S. 210 40.49 N 73.45 W
Kingsport 192 36.32 N 82.33 W
King's Sutton 42 52.01 N 1.16 W
Kingsteignton 42 50.33 N 3.35 W
King Sterndale 262 53.15 N 1.52 W
Kingston, N.S., Can. 186 44.59 N 64.57 W
Kingston, Ont., Can. 212 44.14 N 76.30 W
Kingston, Jam. 241q 18.00 N 76.48 W
Kingston, N.Z. 172 45.20 S 168.42 E
Kingston, Norf. I. 174c 29.03 S 167.58 E
Kingston, Eng., U.K. 28 51.25 N 0.19 W
Kingston, Ga., U.S. 192 34.15 N 84.57 W
Kingston, Ill., U.S. 216 42.06 N 88.46 W
Kingston, Mass., U.S. 207 41.59 N 70.43 W
Kingston, Mo., U.S. 194 39.39 N 94.02 W
Kingston, N.J., U.S. 276 40.23 N 74.37 W
Kingston, N.Y., U.S. 210 41.56 N 74.00 W
Kingston, Ohio, U.S. 218 39.28 N 82.55 W
Kingston, Okla., U.S. 196 34.00 N 96.43 W
Kingston, Pa., U.S. 210 41.16 N 75.54 W
Kingston, R.I., U.S. 207 41.29 N 71.31 W
Kingston, Tenn., U.S. 192 35.52 N 84.31 W
Kingston, Wash., U.S. 224 47.48 N 122.30 W
Kingston ➝[8] 42 51.25 N 0.19 W
Kingston Bay C 283 42.00 N 70.42 W
Kingston Mills 212 44.17 N 76.27 W
Kingston Southeast 166 36.50 S 139.51 E
Kingston upon Hull (Hull) 44 53.45 N 0.20 W
Kingston upon Thames ➝[8] 260 51.25 N 0.19 W
Kingstown → Dún Laoghaire, Eire 48 53.17 N 6.08 W
Kingstown, St. Vin. 241h 13.09 N 61.14 W
Kingstown Bay C 241h 13.09 N 61.15 W
Kingstree 192 33.40 N 79.50 W
Kingsville, Ont., Can. 214 42.02 N 82.45 W
Kingsville, Md., U.S. 284b 39.27 N 76.25 W
Kingsville, Ohio, U.S. 214 41.53 N 80.41 W
Kingsville, Tex., U.S. 196 27.31 N 97.52 W
Kingswear 42 50.21 N 3.34 W
Kingswinford 42 52.29 N 2.10 W
Kingswood, Eng., U.K. 42 51.27 N 2.22 W
Kingswood, Eng., U.K. 260 51.17 N 0.13 W
Kingswood Park 285 40.07 N 74.51 W
King's Worthy 42 51.06 N 1.18 W
Kingtechen → Jingdezhen 100 29.16 N 117.11 E
Kington 42 52.12 N 3.01 W
Kingunda 152 6.34 S 16.58 E
Kingungi 152 5.24 S 17.56 E
Kingussie 46 57.05 N 4.03 W
King William 208 37.41 N 77.01 W
King William □[6] 208 37.42 N 77.05 W
King William Island I 176 69.00 N 97.30 W
King William's Town 158 32.51 S 27.22 E
Kingwood 188 39.28 N 79.41 W
Kinh-duc 110 11.49 N 107.58 E
Kinhwa → Jinhua 100 29.07 N 119.39 E
Kınık 130 39.05 N 27.23 E
Kinira ≃ 158 31.12 S 29.17 E
Kinistino 184 52.57 N 105.00 W
Kinjar Khās 123 29.55 N 70.58 E
Kinkala 152 4.22 S 14.46 E
Kinker Creek ≃ 282 38.02 N 121.52 W
Kinkony, Lac ⊜ 157b 16.08 S 45.50 E
Kinkora 285 40.07 N 74.45 W
Kinldchleven 46 56.42 N 4.58 W
Kinleith 172 38.16 S 175.54 E
Kinlochbervie 46 58.28 N 5.03 W
Kinlocheil 46 56.51 N 5.20 W
Kinlochewe 46 57.36 N 5.20 W
Kinloch Hourn 46 57.06 N 5.22 W
Kinloch Rannoch 46 56.42 N 4.11 W
Kinmount 212 44.47 N 78.39 W
Kinmundy 219 38.46 N 88.51 W
Kinn 26 61.36 N 4.45 E
Kinna 26 57.30 N 12.41 E
Kinnaird 182 49.17 N 117.39 W
Kinnairds Head ▸ 46 57.42 N 2.00 W
Kinnegad 48 53.26 N 7.05 W
Kinnekulle ▲[2] 26 58.35 N 13.23 E
Kinnelon 210 40.59 N 74.23 W
Kinnel Water ≃ 44 55.08 N 3.25 W
Kinneret 132 32.43 N 35.33 E
Kinneret, Yam (Sea of Galilee) ⊜ 132 32.48 N 35.35 E
Kinnerley 42 52.47 N 2.59 W
Kinniconick Creek ≃ 218 38.37 N 83.09 W
Kinnula 26 63.22 N 24.58 E
Kino ≃ 96 34.13 N 135.09 E
Kino, Bahía C 232 28.47 N 111.58 W
Kinoe 96 34.14 N 132.55 E
Kinogitan 116 9.00 N 124.48 E
Kinojévis ≃ 190 48.23 N 78.21 W
Kinomoto 94 35.30 N 136.13 E
Kinonge ≃ 206 45.39 N 74.55 W
Kinoni 154 0.39 S 30.27 E
Kinosaki 96 35.37 N 134.49 E
Kinpoku-san ▲ 92 38.05 N 138.22 E
Kinross, S. Afr. 158 26.22 S 29.03 E
Kinross, Scot., U.K. 46 56.13 N 3.27 W
Kinsale, Eire 48 51.42 N 8.32 W
Kinsale, Va., U.S. 208 38.02 N 76.35 W
Kinsale, Old Head of ▸ 48 51.36 N 8.32 W
Kinsale Harbour C 48 51.41 N 8.30 W
Kinsarvik 26 60.23 N 6.43 E
Kinschasa → Kinshasa 152 4.18 S 15.18 E
Kinshasa 152
273b 4.18 S 15.18 E
Kinshasa □[4] 152 4.18 S 15.18 E
Kinshasa (Ndjili) Airport ⊠, Zaïre 273b 4.23 S 15.27 E
Kinshasa (Ndolo) Airport ⊠, Zaïre 273b 4.20 S 15.19 E
Kinshasa-Est ➝[8] 273b 4.18 S 15.18 E
Kinshasa-Quest ➝[8] 273b 4.20 S 15.15 E
Kinsley 198 37.55 N 99.25 W
Kinsman, Ill., U.S. 216 41.11 N 88.34 W
Kinsman, Ohio, U.S. 214 41.27 N 80.36 W
Kinsoundi 273b 4.10 S 15.15 E
Kinston 192 35.16 N 77.35 W
Kintamani 115b 8.14 S 115.19 E
Kintamo, Rapides de ↳ 273b 4.19 S 15.15 E
Kintampo 150 8.03 N 1.43 W
Kintap 112 3.51 S 115.13 E
Kintari, Mont ▲[2] 273b 4.08 S 15.23 E
Kintélé 273b 4.09 S 15.21 E
Kintinian 150 11.36 N 9.23 W
Kintinku 154 5.53 S 35.14 E
Kintobongo-Bunge 154 8.54 S 26.23 E
Kintore 46 57.13 N 2.21 W
Kintore, Mount ▲ 162 26.34 S 130.30 E
Kintore Range ⛰ 162 23.25 S 129.20 E
Kintsana 273b 4.19 S 15.10 E
Kintus 86 60.09 N 71.25 E
Kintyre ▸[1] 46 55.35 N 5.35 W
Kintyre, Mull of ▸ 44 55.17 N 5.55 W
Kinu ≃ 94 35.56 N 139.57 E
Kinuseo Falls ↳ 182 54.47 N 121.12 W
Kinuso 182 55.20 N 115.25 W
Kinvara 48 53.08 N 8.55 W
Kinver 42 52.27 N 2.14 W
Kinwood 222 29.56 N 95.23 W
Kinyangiri 154 4.27 S 34.37 E
Kinyeti ▲ 154 3.57 N 32.54 E
Kinzia 152 3.36 S 18.26 E
Kinzig ≃, B.R.D. 56 50.08 N 8.54 E
Kinzig ≃, B.R.D. 58 48.37 N 7.49 E
Kinzua 202 44.59 N 120.03 W
Kinzua Creek ≃ 214 41.47 N 78.50 W
Kinzua Dam ➝[6] 214 41.50 N 79.01 W
Kioa I 175g 16.39 S 179.55 E
Kioga-See → Kyoga, Lake ⊜ 154 1.30 N 33.00 E
Kioshkokwi Lake ⊜ 190 46.05 N 78.52 W
Kioto → Kyōto 94 35.00 N 135.45 E
Kiowa, Colo., U.S. 198 39.21 N 104.28 W
Kiowa, Kans., U.S. 198 37.01 N 98.29 W
Kiowa, Okla., U.S. 196 34.43 N 95.54 W
Kiowa Creek ≃, U.S. 196 36.46 N 99.55 W
Kiowa Creek ≃, Colo., U.S. 198 40.20 N 104.05 W
Kipahigan Lake ⊜ 184 55.20 N 101.55 W
Kipandi 152 5.19 S 16.46 E
Kipanga 154 6.14 S 35.21 E
Kiparissía 38 37.14 N 21.40 E
Kiparissiakós Kólpos C 38 37.37 N 21.24 E
Kipatimu 154 8.29 S 38.56 E
Kipawa ≃ 190 47.03 N 79.23 W
Kipawa, Lac ⊜ 190 46.55 N 79.00 W
Kipawa, Parc de ♠ 190 47.15 N 78.15 W
Kipembawe 154 7.39 S 33.24 E
Kipengere Range ⛰ 154 9.10 S 34.15 E
Kiperčeny 78 47.32 N 28.50 E
Kipijevo 24 65.40 N 54.23 E
Kipili 154 7.26 S 30.36 E
Kipini 154 2.32 S 40.31 E
Kipling 184 50.10 N 102.38 W
Kipnuk 180 59.56 N 164.03 W
Kippen 46 56.08 N 4.11 W
Kippenheim 58 48.17 N 7.49 E
Kippure ▲ 48 53.10 N 6.18 W
Kípros → Cyprus □[1] 130 35.00 N 33.00 E
Kipsdorf 54 50.47 N 13.32 E
Kipton 214 41.16 N 82.18 W
Kipushi 154 11.46 N 27.14 E
Kipushia, Zaïre 154 6.10 S 25.12 E
Kipushia, Zaïre 154 12.58 S 29.30 E
Kira, Nihon 94 34.49 N 137.05 E
Kir'a, S.S.S.R. 80 55.04 N 46.53 E
Kira Kira 175e 10.27 S 161.55 E
Kirane 150 15.25 N 10.14 W
Kiranlık 130 39.07 N 41.41 E
Kiranomena 157b 18.17 S 46.03 E
Kīratpur 124 29.31 N 78.12 E
Kiraz 130 38.13 N 28.13 E
Kirazlı 130 40.02 N 26.41 E
Kırbaçbayırı ▲ 267b 40.56 N 29.10 E
Kirbla 76 58.44 N 23.57 E
Kirbymoorside 44 54.16 N 0.55 W
Kirby Muxloe 42 52.38 N 1.13 W
Kirbyville 194 30.40 N 93.54 W
Kırçal 130 41.39 N 35.16 E
Kırcasalih 130 41.23 N 26.48 E
Kirchardt 56 49.12 N 8.59 E
Kirchbach in Steiermark 61 46.54 N 15.44 E
Kirchberg, B.R.D. 56 49.56 N 7.24 E
Kirchberg, B.R.D. 56 49.12 N 9.58 E
Kirchberg, B.R.D. 60 48.54 N 13.11 E
Kirchberg, D.D.R. 54 50.37 N 12.32 E
Kirchberg, Schw. 58 47.05 N 7.35 E
Kirchberg, Schw. 58 47.25 N 9.03 E
Kirch-Berg ▲[2] 264a 52.27 N 13.02 E
Kirchberg am Wagram 61 48.26 N 15.53 E
Kirchberg in Tirol 64 47.27 N 12.19 E
Kirchbichl 64 47.31 N 12.05 E
Kirchderne ➝[8] 263 51.33 N 7.30 E
Kirchdorf, B.R.D. 52 52.36 N 8.49 E
Kirchdorf, D.D.R. 54 54.00 N 11.26 E
Kirchdorf an der Krems 61 47.56 N 14.07 E
Kirchdorf im Wald 60 48.55 N 13.16 E
Kircheib 56 50.42 N 7.28 E
Kirchende 263 51.25 N 7.26 E
Kirchenlaibach 60 49.53 N 11.46 E
Kirchenlamitz 54 50.09 N 11.56 E
Kirchenthumbach 60 49.45 N 11.43 E
Kirchen-Wehbach 56 50.48 N 7.53 E
Kirchhain 56 50.49 N 8.55 E
Kirchham 60 48.21 N 13.16 E
Kirchheiligen 54 51.11 N 10.42 E
Kirchheim 60 48.12 N 13.23 E
Kirchheimbolanden 56 49.40 N 8.00 E
Kirchheim in Schwaben 58 48.10 N 10.30 E
Kirchheim unter Teck 56 48.39 N 9.27 E
Kirchhellen 52 51.36 N 6.55 E
Kirchhellen Heide ➝[3] 263 51.36 N 6.53 E
Kirchhofen 264a 52.22 N 13.53 E
Kirchhörde ➝[8] 263 51.27 N 7.27 E
Kirchhundem 56 51.05 N 8.05 E
Kirchlinde ➝[8] 263 51.32 N 7.22 E
Kirchlinteln 52 52.56 N 9.19 E
Kirchmöser 54 52.22 N 12.25 E
Kirchohsen 52 52.03 N 9.23 E
Kirchroth 60 48.57 N 12.33 E
Kirchschlag in der Buckligen Welt 61 47.31 N 16.18 E
Kirchseeon 60 48.04 N 11.54 E
Kirchveischede 56 51.05 N 7.59 E
Kirchwalsede 52 53.01 N 9.23 E
Kirchwerder ➝[8] 52 53.25 N 10.11 E
Kirchweyhe 52 52.59 N 8.52 E
Kirchzarten 58 47.58 N 7.56 E
Kircubbin 48 54.24 N 5.28 W
Kirda 85 41.06 N 69.00 E
Kirdāsah 142 30.02 N 31.07 E
Kireç, Tür. 130 39.33 N 28.22 E
Kirec, Tür. 130 40.59 N 39.10 E
Kirej ≃ 88 54.12 N 100.40 E
Kirenga ≃ 88 57.47 N 108.07 E
Kirgali 130 37.55 N 40.00 E
Kirghiz Soviet Socialist Republic → Kirgizskaja Sovetskaja Socialističeskaja Respublika □[3] 85 41.30 N 75.00 E
Kirgiz-Mijaki 86 53.38 N 54.47 E
Kirgizskaja Sovetskaja Socialističeskaja Respublika □[3] 85 41.30 N 75.00 E
Kirgizskij Chrebet ⛰ 85 42.30 N 74.00 E
Kirguises,, Estepas de → Kirgizskij Chrebet ⛰ 85 42.30 N 74.00 E
Kiri 152 1.27 S 19.00 E
Kiribati □[1] 14 0.00 174.00 E
Kirigalpotta Mountain ▲ 122 6.48 N 80.46 E
Kiriga-mine ▲ 94 36.06 N 138.12 E
Kiriis West 158 26.34 S 19.00 E
Kırıkhan, Tür. 130 36.32 N 36.19 E
Kırıkhan, Tür. 130 39.32 N 41.20 E
Kirikiri Prisons ɤ 273a 6.27 N 3.19 E
Kırıkkale 130 39.50 N 33.31 E
Kirin → Jilin 89 43.51 N 126.33 E
Kirin → Jilin □[4] 90 44.00 N 126.00 E
Kirínia (Kyrenia) 130 35.20 N 33.19 E
Kirishima-yaku-kokuritsu-kōen ♠ 92 31.55 N 130.51 E
Kirishima-yama ▲ 92 31.56 N 130.52 E
Kirizume-tōge ▲[2] 270 34.56 N 135.16 E
Kirjanovskaja Kontora 88 58.18 N 104.13 E
Kirka 130 39.17 N 30.33 E
Kirkabister 46 60.07 N 1.08 W
Kırkağaç 130 39.06 N 27.40 E
Kirkbride 44 54.54 N 3.12 W
Kirkburton 44 53.37 N 1.42 W
Kirkby 44 53.29 N 2.54 W
Kirkby Lonsdale 44 54.13 N 2.36 W
Kirkby Malzeard 44 54.11 N 1.38 W
Kirkby Stephen 44 54.28 N 2.20 W
Kirkcaldy 46 56.07 N 3.10 W
Kirkcolm 44 54.58 N 5.05 W
Kirkconnel 44 55.23 N 4.00 W
Kirkcudbright 44 54.50 N 4.03 W
Kirkcudbright Bay C 44 54.48 N 4.04 W
Kirkdale ➝[8] 262 53.26 N 2.59 W
Kirkeby 41 56.09 N 9.27 E
Kirkee → Khadki 122 18.34 N 73.52 E
Kirkenær 26 60.28 N 12.03 E
Kirkenes 24 69.40 N 30.03 E
Kirke Stillinge 41 55.26 N 11.15 E
Kirkham 44 53.47 N 2.53 W
Kirkhill 46 57.28 N 4.26 W
Kirkintilloch 46 55.57 N 4.10 W
Kirkjubæjarklaustur 24a 63.47 N 18.04 W

ENGLISH

Name | Page | Lat.°′ | Long.°′

Kirkkonummi → Kyrkslätt 26 60.07 N 24.26 E
Kirkland, Qué., Can. 275a 45.27 N 73.52 W
Kirkland, Ill., U.S. 216 42.06 N 88.51 W
Kirkland, Tex., U.S. 196 34.23 N 100.04 W
Kirkland, Wash., U.S. 224 47.41 N 122.12 W
Kirkland Creek ≃ 200 34.32 N 113.00 W
Kirkland Lake 190 48.09 N 80.02 W
Kırklar Dağı ▲ 84 40.34 N 40.35 E
Kırklareli 130 41.44 N 27.12 E
Kırklareli □[4] 130 41.40 N 27.30 E
Kirklees □[8] 262 53.36 N 1.52 W
Kirkleyditch 262 53.18 N 2.12 W
Kirklin 194 40.12 N 86.22 W
Kirkliston 46 55.58 N 3.25 W
Kirkmichael 46 56.43 N 3.29 W
Kirkness Lake ⊜ 184 51.32 N 93.56 W
Kirkpatrick, Mount ▲ 9 84.20 S 166.19 E
Kirkpatrick Lake ⊜ 182 51.52 N 111.18 W
Kirkstile 44 55.12 N 3.00 W
Kirksville, Ill., U.S. 219 39.34 N 88.40 W
Kirksville, Mo., U.S. 194 40.12 N 92.35 W
Kirkton of Culsalmond 46 57.23 N 2.34 W
Kirkton of Glenisla 46 56.44 N 3.17 W
Kirktown of Auchterless 46 57.27 N 2.28 W
Kirkūk 128 35.28 N 44.28 E
Kirkūk □[4] 128 35.00 N 44.35 E
Kirkville 210 43.05 N 75.57 W
Kirkwall 46 58.59 N 2.58 W
Kirkwood, S. Afr. 158 33.22 S 25.15 E
Kirkwood, Del., U.S. 208 39.34 N 75.42 W
Kirkwood, Ill., U.S. 190 40.52 N 90.45 W
Kirkwood, Mo., U.S. 219 38.35 N 90.24 W
Kirkwood, N.J., U.S. 285 39.50 N 75.01 W
Kirkwood, N.Y., U.S. 210 42.02 N 75.48 W
Kırmıt 130 37.11 N 35.41 E
Kirn 56 49.47 N 7.28 E
Kirnāhar 126 23.45 N 87.52 E
Kirotshe 154 1.37 S 29.02 E
Kirov, S.S.S.R. 76 54.05 N 34.20 E
Kirov, S.S.S.R. 80 58.38 N 49.42 E
Kirova, Zaliv C 84 39.09 N 49.03 E
Kirovabad 84 40.40 N 46.22 E
Kirovakan 84 40.48 N 44.30 E
Kirovgrad 86 57.26 N 60.04 E
Kirovo-Čepeck 80 58.33 N 50.01 E
Kirovograd 78 48.30 N 32.18 E
Kirovograd □[4] 38 48.10 N 30.20 E
Kirovsk, S.S.S.R. 24 67.37 N 33.35 E
Kirovsk, S.S.S.R. 76 53.16 N 29.29 E
Kirovsk, S.S.S.R. 83 48.38 N 38.39 E
Kirovsk, S.S.S.R. 83 49.01 N 37.56 E
Kirovsk, S.S.S.R. 84 38.48 N 48.43 E
Kirovsk, S.S.S.R. 128 37.42 N 60.23 E
Kirovsk, S.S.S.R. 265a 59.52 N 31.00 E
Kirovskije Ostrova II 265a 59.58 N 30.15 E
Kirpičnyj Zavod 265a 60.01 N 30.48 E
Kirpil'skaja 78 45.23 N 39.43 E
Kirriemuir 46 56.41 N 3.01 W
Kirs 86 59.21 N 52.14 E
Kirsanov 80 52.38 N 42.43 E
Kirsanovka 80 52.30 N 52.53 E
Kirschau 54 51.04 N 14.27 E
Kırşehir 130 39.09 N 34.10 E
Kırşehir □[4] 130 39.20 N 34.10 E
Kirtachi Seybou 150 12.48 N 2.29 E
Kīrthar Range ⛰ 120 27.00 N 67.10 E
Kirtland, N. Mex., U.S. 200 36.44 N 108.21 W
Kirtland, Ohio, U.S. 214 41.34 N 81.18 W
Kirtland Air Force Base ■ 200 35.02 N 106.37 W
Kirtland Hills 214 41.37 N 81.24 W
Kirtle Water ≃ 44 54.58 N 3.05 W
Kirton 42 52.56 N 0.04 W
Kirton of Largo 46 56.13 N 2.55 W
Kirtorf 56 50.46 N 9.06 E
Kiruna 24 67.51 N 20.16 E
Kirundu 154 0.44 S 25.32 E
Kirurumo 154 5.53 S 34.11 E
Kirvin 222 31.46 N 96.20 W
Kirwan Heights 279b 40.22 N 80.06 W
Kirwee 172 43.30 S 172.13 E
Kirwin 198 39.40 N 99.07 W
Kirwin Reservoir ⊜[1] 198 39.39 N 99.50 W
Kiryandongo 154 1.53 N 32.03 E
Kiryū 94 36.24 N 139.20 E
Kiržač 82 56.09 N 38.52 E
Kisa, Nihon 96 34.43 N 132.59 E
Kisa, Sve. 26 57.59 N 15.37 E
Kisabe 270 34.47 N 135.41 E
Kisai 94 36.06 N 139.35 E
Kisaichi 270 34.46 N 135.42 E
Kisakata 92 39.13 N 139.54 E
Kisaki 154 7.28 S 37.36 E
Kišaly 76 54.23 N 43.12 E
Kisambo 152 6.25 S 18.14 E
Kisanga 154 2.29 N 26.35 E
Kisangani (Stanleyville) 154 0.30 S 25.12 E
Kisantu 152 5.07 S 15.05 E
Kisar, Pulau I 112 8.05 S 127.10 E
Kisaralik ≃ 180 60.51 N 161.16 W
Kisaran 114 2.59 N 99.37 E
Kisarawe 154 6.54 S 39.04 E
Kisarazu 94 35.23 N 139.55 E
Kisarazu Air Base ■ 268 35.24 N 139.55 E
Kisawa 96 33.49 N 134.18 E
K.I. Sawyer Air Force Base ■ 190 46.21 N 87.25 W
Kisbér 30 47.30 N 18.02 E
Kisbey 184 49.38 N 102.41 W
Kise ≃ 94 35.06 N 138.53 E
Kiselevsk → Kisel'ovsk 86 54.00 N 86.39 E
Kisel'ovka 80 47.18 N 44.07 E
Kisel'ovsk 86 54.00 N 86.39 E
Kisengwa 154 6.00 S 25.50 E
Kisen-yama ▲[2] 270 34.54 N 135.51 E
Kiser Lake ⊜ 218 40.11 N 83.58 W
Kisha 130 40.28 N 41.28 E
Kishanda 154 1.42 S 31.34 E
Kishanganga ≃ 123 34.18 N 73.28 E
Kishangarh ➝[8] 272a 28.31 N 77.08 E
Kishar Bāla 267d 35.49 N 51.13 E
Kishb, Ḥarrat al- ⊕[9] 144 23.00 N 41.25 E
Kishi, Nig. 150 9.05 N 3.52 E
Kishi, Zaïre 154 10.04 S 26.26 E
Kishida ≃ 96 35.08 N 134.27 E
Kishigawa 96 34.13 N 135.20 E
Kishikas ≃ 184 52.45 N 91.43 W
Kishimoto 96 35.23 N 133.25 E
Kishinev → Kišin'ov 78 47.00 N 28.50 E
Kishiwada 96 34.28 N 135.22 E
Kishorganj 124 24.26 N 90.46 E
Kishorn, Loch C 46 57.21 N 5.41 W
Kishtwār 123 33.19 N 75.46 E
Kishwaukee ≃ 216 42.11 N 89.08 W
Kishwaukee, South Branch ≃ 216 42.12 N 88.59 W
Kisia 152 4.35 S 18.22 E
Kisigo ≃ 154 7.03 S 35.50 E
Kisii 154 0.41 S 34.46 E
Kisiju 154 7.24 S 39.20 E
Kiši-Karoj, Ozero ⊜ 86 54.03 N 71.20 E
Kısıklı ➝[8] 267b 41.01 N 29.03 E
Kišin 78 51.08 N 27.41 E
Kišin'ov 78 47.00 N 28.50 E
Kısır Dağı ▲ 84 40.58 N 43.06 E
Kısırkaya 267b 41.14 N 28.58 E
Kısırmandıra 267b 41.14 N 28.49 E
Kisiwada → Kishiwada 96 34.28 N 135.22 E
Kisiwani 154 4.08 S 37.57 E
Kisizi 154 1.00 S 29.56 E
Kiska Island I 181a 52.00 N 178.30 E

DEUTSCH

Name | Seite | Breite°′ | Länge° E=Ost

Kıskanlı 84 39.32 N 41.58 E
Kiskatinaw ≃ 182 56.06 N 120.08 W
Kiska Volcano ▲[1] 181a 52.07 N 177.36 E
Kis-Kevély ▲[2] 264c 47.38 N 18.59 E
Kiski Lake ⊜ 184 54.46 N 98.55 W
Kiskimere 279b 40.37 N 79.35 W
Kiskiminetas ≃ 214 40.41 N 79.40 W
Kiskittogisu Lake ⊜ 184 54.13 N 98.20 W
Kiskitto Lake ⊜ 184 54.16 N 98.34 W
Kiskőrös 30 46.38 N 19.17 E
Kiskunfélegyháza 30 46.43 N 19.52 E
Kiskunhalas 30 46.26 N 19.30 E
Kiskunmajsa 30 46.30 N 19.45 E
Kışla 130 40.51 N 30.57 E
Kisl'akovka 78 46.44 N 31.59 E
Kisl'akovskaja 78 46.27 N 39.40 E
Kislovka 83 49.38 N 37.53 E
Kislovo 80 49.54 N 45.25 E
Kislovodsk 84 43.55 N 42.44 E
Kismayu 144 0.23 S 42.30 E
Kismet 276 40.38 N 73.12 W
Kisnema 76 60.20 N 37.39 E
Kiso, Nihon 94 35.56 N 137.47 E
Kiso, Nihon 268 35.34 N 139.26 E
Kiso ≃ 94 35.02 N 136.45 E
Kisofukushima 94 35.51 N 137.42 E
Kisogawa 94 35.20 N 136.47 E
Kisoro 154 1.17 S 29.41 E
Kiso-sammyaku ⛰ 94 35.43 N 137.50 E
Kisozaki 94 35.04 N 136.44 E
Kispest ➝[8] 264c 47.27 N 19.08 E
Kispiox 182 55.21 N 127.41 W
Kispiox ≃ 182 55.16 N 127.41 W
Kispiox Mountain ▲ 182 55.25 N 127.57 W
Kissamos 38 35.30 N 23.38 E
Kissena Park ♠ 276 40.45 N 73.49 W
Kisseynew Lake ⊜ 184 54.58 N 101.35 W
Kissidougou 150 9.11 N 10.06 W
Kissidougou □[4] 150 9.15 N 9.55 W
Kissimmee 220 28.18 N 81.24 W
Kissimmee ≃ 220 27.10 N 80.53 W
Kissimmee, Lake ⊜ 220 27.55 N 81.16 W
Kissing 60 48.18 N 10.59 E
Kississing 184 55.07 N 101.07 W
Kississing Lake ⊜ 184 55.10 N 101.20 W
Kisslegg 58 47.47 N 9.53 E
Kissū, Jabal ▲ 140 21.35 N 25.09 E
Kista 80 46.05 N 43.06 E
Kistanje 36 43.59 N 15.58 E
Kistarcsa 264c 47.33 N 19.16 E
Kistendej 80 52.08 N 43.39 E
Kistigan Lake ⊜ 184 54.38 N 92.37 W
Kistler 214 40.22 N 77.51 W
Kistruss 80 54.28 N 40.34 E
Kisújszállás 30 47.13 N 20.46 E
Kisuki 96 35.17 N 132.54 E
Kisumu 154 0.06 S 34.45 E
Kisvárda 30 48.13 N 22.05 E
Kiswere 154 9.26 S 39.33 E
Kita 150 13.03 N 9.29 W
Kita ➝[8], Nihon 268 35.45 N 139.44 E
Kita ➝[8], Nihon 270 35.03 N 135.45 E
Kita ➝[8], Nihon 270 34.42 N 135.30 E
Kita-daitō-jima I 90 25.57 N 131.18 E
Kitafuji-enshūjō ■ 94 35.25 N 138.48 E
Kitagi-shima I 96 34.23 N 133.32 E
Kitain Temple ɤ[1] 268 35.54 N 139.30 E
Kita-iō-jima I 14 25.26 N 141.17 E
Kitakami ≃ 92 38.25 N 141.19 E
Kitakami-sanchi ⛰ 92 39.30 N 141.30 E
Kitakyuschu → Kitakyūshū 96 33.53 N 130.50 E
Kitakyūshū 96 33.53 N 130.50 E
Kitale 154 1.01 N 35.00 E
Kitamachi ➝[8] 268 35.46 N 139.39 E
Kitamba ➝[8] 273b 4.19 S 15.14 E
Kitami 92a 43.48 N 143.54 E
Kitami-sanchi ⛰ 92a 44.22 N 142.43 E
Kitanagato-kaigan-kokutei-kōen ♠ 96 34.24 N 131.16 E
Kitanda, Zaïre 154 9.59 S 27.28 E
Kitanda, Zaïre 154 6.36 S 26.27 E
Kitangari 154 10.39 S 39.20 E
Kitangiri, Lake ⊜ 154 4.05 S 34.19 E
Kitangua 152 6.17 S 20.22 E
Kitan-kaikō ⋓ 96 34.17 N 135.00 E
Kita-ura ⊜ 94 36.00 N 140.34 E
Kitava Island I 164 8.40 S 151.20 E
Kitaya 154 10.39 S 40.10 E
Kit Carson, Calif., U.S. 226 38.41 N 120.07 W
Kit Carson, Colo., U.S. 198 38.46 N 102.48 W
Kitchener, Austl. 162 31.02 S 124.11 E
Kitchener, Ont., Can. 212 43.27 N 80.29 W
Kitee 26 62.06 N 30.09 E
Kitega → Gitega 154 3.26 S 29.56 E
Kiteiyab 144 17.12 N 33.43 E
Kitenda 152 6.53 S 17.21 E
Kitenevo 82 56.21 N 36.13 E
Kitengo 152 7.26 S 24.08 E
Kitgum 154 3.18 N 32.53 E
Kíthira 38 36.09 N 23.00 E
Kíthira I 38 36.20 N 22.58 E
Kíthnos 38 37.26 N 24.26 E
Kíthnos I 38 37.25 N 24.28 E
Kithraía 130 35.15 N 33.29 E
Kitimat 182 54.03 N 128.33 W
Kitimat ≃ 182 54.06 N 128.38 W
Kitimat Ranges ⛰ 182 53.30 N 128.50 W
Kitinen ≃ 24 67.08 N 27.29 E
Kitíou, Akrotírion ▸ 130 34.48 N 33.36 E
Kiti Point ▸ 174r 6.51 N 158.09 E
Kitlope ≃ 182 53.10 N 127.45 W
Kitlope Lake ⊜ 182 53.07 N 127.47 W
Kitoj 88 52.36 N 103.50 E
Kitoj ≃ 88 52.39 N 103.56 E
Kitojskije Gol'cy ⛰ 88 52.10 N 101.20 E
Kitridge Point ▸ 241g 13.09 N 59.25 W
Kitsap □[6] 224 47.41 N 122.44 W
Kitscoty 184 53.20 N 110.20 W
Kitshua-Nseke 152 4.26 S 19.36 E
Kittanning 214 40.49 N 79.32 W
Kittatinny Mountain ▲ 123 34.18 N 73.28 E
Kittatinny Tunnel ➝[5] 214 40.09 N 77.41 W
Kittendorf 54 53.37 N 12.54 E
Kittery 188 43.05 N 70.45 W
Kittery Point 188 43.05 N 70.41 W
Kitt Green 262 53.33 N 2.41 W
Kittilä 24 67.40 N 24.54 E
Kittitas 202 46.59 N 120.25 W
Kittitas □[6] 224 47.13 N 121.01 W
Kitu 154 7.38 S 27.42 E
Kitui 154 1.22 S 38.01 E
Kitumbeine ▲[1] 154 2.44 S 36.16 E
Kitunda 154 6.48 S 33.13 E
Kitutu 154 3.17 S 28.05 E
Kitwanga 182 55.06 N 128.03 W
Kitwangar Indian Reserve ➝[4] 182 55.06 N 128.04 W
Kitwe 154 12.49 S 28.13 E
Kityang → Jieyang 100 23.35 N 116.21 E
Kitzbühel 64 47.27 N 12.23 E
Kitzbüheler Alpen ⛰ 64 47.20 N 12.20 E
Kitzingen 56 49.44 N 10.09 E
Kitzscher 54 51.09 N 12.33 E
Kiukiang → Jiujiang 100 29.44 N 115.59 E
Kiukiu, Pointe ▸ 174x 9.47 S 139.09 W
Kiul 124 25.09 N 86.06 E
Kiunga, Kenya 154 1.45 S 41.29 E
Kiunga, Pap. N. Gui. 164 6.10 S 141.15 E
Kiuruvesi 26 63.39 N 26.37 E
Kiuschu → Kyūshū I 92 33.00 N 131.00 E
Kiu Tsui Chau I 271d 22.22 N 114.17 E

Symbols in the index entries represent the broad categories identified in the key at the right. Symbols with superior numbers (⛰[2]) identify subcategories (see complete key on page I · 30).

Kartensymbole in dem Registerverzeichnis stellen die rechts in Schlüssel erklärten Kategorien dar. Symbole mit hochgestellten Ziffern (⛰[2]) bezeichnen Unterabteilungen einer Kategorie (vgl. vollständiger Schlüssel auf Seite I · 30).

Los símbolos incluídos en el texto del índice representan las grandes categorias identificadas con la clave a la derecha. Los símbolos con numeros en su parte superior (⛰[2]) identifican las subcategorías (véase la clave completa en la página I · 30).

Les symboles de l'index représentent les catégories indiquées dans la légende à droite. Les symboles suivis d'un indice (⛰[2]) représentent des sous-catégories (voir légende complète à la page I · 30).

Os símbolos incluídos no texto do índice representam as grandes categorias identificadas com a chave à direita. Os símbolos com números em sua parte superior (⛰[2]) identificam as subcategorias (veja-se a chave completa à página I · 30).

	English	Deutsch	Español	Français	Português
▲	Mountain	Berg	Montaña	Montagne	Montanha
⛰	Mountains	Berge	Montañas	Montagnes	Montanhas
)(	Pass	Pass	Paso	Col	Passo
V	Valley, Canyon	Tal, Cañon	Valle, Cañón	Vallée, Canyon	Vale, Canhão
≚	Plain	Ebene	Llano	Plaine	Planície
▸	Cape	Kap	Cabo	Cap	Cabo
I	Island	Insel	Isla	Île	Ilha
II	Islands	Inseln	Islas	Îles	Ilhas
⊕	Other Topographic Features	Andere Topographische Objekte	Otros Elementos Topográficos	Autres données topographiques	Outros Elementos Topográficos

ESPAÑOL · **FRANÇAIS** · **PORTUGUÊS**

Nombre / Nom / Nome	Página / Page / Página	Lat. °′	Long. °′ W=Oeste / W=Ouest / W=Oeste
Kivač, Vodopad ᒪ	24	62.16 N	33.59 E
Kivak	180	64.16 N	172.57 W
Kivalina	180	67.59 N	164.33 W
Kivercy	78	50.50 N	25.27 E
Kiveriči	76	57.22 N	36.36 E
Kivijärvi	26	63.04 N	25.03 E
Kivijärvi ⊜	26	63.10 N	25.09 E
Kivik	26	55.41 N	14.15 E
Kiviõli	76	59.21 N	26.57 E
Kivu □[4]	154	2.30 S	27.00 E
Kivu, Lac ⊜	154	2.00 S	29.10 E
Kiwai Island I	164	8.30 S	143.25 E
Kiwalik	180	66.02 N	161.50 W
Kiwanis Lake	214	41.28 N	81.09 W
Kiyama	96	33.25 N	130.32 E
Kīyāmakī Dāgh ▲	84	38.47 N	45.53 E
Kiyan-saki ≻	174m	26.05 N	127.39 E
Kıyıköy	130	41.38 N	28.05 E
Kiyiu Lake ⊜	184	51.38 N	108.55 W
Kiyosawa	94	35.03 N	138.15 E
Kiyose	94	35.47 N	139.32 E
Kiyosu	94	35.13 N	136.50 E
Kiyosumi-yama ▲	94	35.09 N	140.09 E
Kiyotani	270	34.52 N	134.59 E
Kiyotsu ≃	94	37.03 N	138.41 E
Kizel	86	59.03 N	57.40 E
Kizhake Chālakudi	122	10.18 N	76.20 E
Kiziguro	154	1.46 S	30.23 E
Kızıl ≃	130	41.44 N	35.58 E
Kızıl Adalar II	130	40.52 N	29.05 E
Kızılcabölük	130	37.37 N	29.01 E
Kızılcahamam	130	40.28 N	32.39 E
Kızılçakçak	84	40.46 N	43.37 E
Kızıldağ ▲	130	36.25 N	32.42 E
Kızıldikme	130	39.05 N	37.01 E
Kızılhisar	130	37.33 N	29.18 E
Kiziljurt	84	43.12 N	46.53 E
Kızıloğlan	130	41.20 N	34.52 E
Kizil'skoje	86	52.44 N	58.54 E
Kızıltoprak ⊸[8]	267b	40.58 N	29.03 E
Kizimkazi	154	6.27 S	39.28 E
Kižinga	88	51.51 N	109.55 E
Kızkalesi ⊥	130	36.28 N	34.04 E
Kızkulesi ⊸[5]	267b	41.01 N	29.00 E
Kizl'ar	84	43.50 N	46.40 E
Kizl'arskij Zaliv C	84	44.33 N	46.55 E
Kizner	80	56.17 N	51.31 E
Kiz'oma	24	61.08 N	44.50 E
Kizu ≃	94	34.53 N	135.42 E
Kizyl-Ajak	128	37.40 N	65.23 E
Kizyl-Arvat	128	38.58 N	56.15 E
Kizyl-Atrek	128	37.36 N	54.46 E
Kizyl-Su	128	39.48 N	53.01 E
Kjellerup	41	56.17 N	9.26 E
Kjøbenhavn → København	41	55.40 N	12.35 E
Kjustendil	38	42.17 N	22.41 E
Klaarstroom	158	33.20 S	22.32 E
Klaaswaal	52	51.46 N	4.26 E
Klabat, Gunung ▲	112	1.28 N	125.02 E
Kladanj	38	44.13 N	18.41 E
Kladbišči	80	55.32 N	45.33 E
Kläden	54	52.38 N	11.39 E
Kladkovo	82	55.24 N	38.51 E
Kladno	54	50.08 N	14.05 E
Kladovo	38	44.37 N	22.37 E
Kladow ⊸[8]	264a	52.27 N	13.09 E
Kladruby	60	49.43 N	12.59 E
Klaeng	110	12.47 N	101.39 E
Klaffenbach	54	50.45 N	12.54 E
Klagan	112	5.58 N	117.27 E
Klagenfurt	61	46.37 N	14.18 E
Klågerup	41	55.36 N	13.15 E
Klagshamn	41	55.32 N	12.55 E
Klagstorp	41	55.24 N	13.22 E
Klahoose Indian Reserve ⊸[4]	182	50.31 N	124.19 W
Klaipėda (Memel)	76	55.43 N	21.07 E
Klais	64	47.29 N	11.14 E
Klakah	115a	7.59 S	113.15 E
Klamath	204	41.32 N	124.02 W
Klamath ≃	204	41.33 N	124.04 W
Klamath Falls	202	42.13 N	121.46 W
Klamath Marsh ☰	202	42.54 N	121.44 W
Klamath Mountains ⛰	204	41.40 N	123.20 W
Klämmingen ⊜	40	59.07 N	17.15 E
Klamm Pass)(	64	47.17 N	13.05 E
Klamono	164	1.08 S	131.30 E
Klang → Kelang	114	3.02 N	101.27 E
Klangpi	110	22.59 N	93.20 E
Klarälven (Trysilelva) ≃	26	59.23 N	13.32 E
Klardorf	60	49.16 N	12.07 E
Kl'as'ma	265b	55.59 N	37.50 E
Klášterec	54	50.24 N	13.10 E
Kl'asticy	76	55.53 N	28.36 E
Klaten	115a	7.42 S	110.35 E
Klatovy	60	49.24 N	13.18 E
Klatt Road	180	61.05 N	149.48 W
Klausdorf, B.R.D.	54	54.18 N	10.15 E
Klausdorf, D.D.R.	54	54.20 N	13.01 E
Klausenburg → Cluj	38	46.47 N	23.36 E
Klausenpass)(	58	46.52 N	8.51 E
Kl'avlino	80	54.17 N	52.01 E
Klawer	158	31.44 S	18.36 E
Klawock	180	55.33 N	133.06 W
Klazienaveen	52	52.44 N	7.00 E
Kl'az'ma	82	55.58 N	37.27 E
Kl'az'ma ≃	80	56.10 N	42.58 E
Kl'az'minskoje Vodochranilišče ⊜[1]	265b	55.59 N	37.35 E
Kleberg	222	32.40 N	96.37 W
Kleck	76	53.04 N	26.38 E
Kłecko	30	52.38 N	17.26 E
Kleczew	30	52.23 N	18.10 E
Kledering ⊸[8]	264b	48.08 N	16.26 E
Kleef	263	51.11 N	6.56 E
Kleena Kleene	182	51.58 N	124.59 W
Kleinasien → Asia Minor ⊸[1]	22	39.00 N	32.00 E
Kleinbeeren	264a	52.22 N	13.20 E
Kleinbegin	158	28.50 S	21.36 E
Klein Blesbokspruit ≃	273d	26.16 S	28.29 E
Kleinbodungen	54	51.28 N	10.32 E
Klein Bonaire I	241s	12.10 N	68.18 W
Klein Bünzow	54	53.53 N	13.48 E
Kleinburg	275b	43.50 N	79.38 W
Klein Curaçao I	241s	12.00 N	68.40 W
Kleine Elster ≃	54	51.32 N	13.23 E
Kleine Emme ≃	58	47.04 N	8.17 E
Kleine Emscher ≃	263	51.31 N	6.43 E
Kleine Erlauf ≃	61	48.07 N	15.08 E
Kleineichen	263	51.08 N	7.21 E
Kleine Laaber ≃	60	48.55 N	12.31 E
Klein Elandsvlei	273d	26.09 S	27.39 E
Kleinenberg	52	51.35 N	8.58 E
Kleinenbroich	263	51.12 N	6.35 E
Kleiner Jasmunder Bodden C	54	54.28 N	13.32 E
Kleiner Ravens-Berg ▲[2]	264a	52.22 N	13.04 E
Kleiner Wannsee ⊜	264a	52.25 N	13.10 E
Kleiner Zern-See ⊜	264a	52.26 N	12.55 E
Kleine Spree ≃	54	51.31 N	14.24 E
Kleines Walsertal ∨	64	47.23 N	10.12 E
Kleinfeltersville	208	40.18 N	76.15 W
Klein Glödnitz	61	46.51 N	14.08 E
Kleinhammer	263	51.14 N	7.46 E
Kleinhöbing	60	49.04 N	11.18 E
Klein-Jukskei ≃	273d	26.08 S	27.56 E
Klein-Karas	156	27.32 S	18.06 E
Klein Karroo → Little Karroo ⛰[1]	158	33.45 S	21.30 E
Klein Kienitz	264a	52.18 N	13.29 E
Klein Lafferde	52	52.14 N	10.14 E
Klein-Linden	56	50.34 N	8.38 E
Kleinlützel	58	47.26 N	7.25 E
Kleinmachnow	54	52.24 N	13.15 E
Klein Marzehns	54	52.01 N	12.37 E
Kleinmond	158	34.21 S	19.03 E
Kleinschönebeck	264a	52.29 N	13.43 E
Klein-Soutpan	158	30.26 S	22.26 E
Klein Stöckheim	54	52.12 N	10.31 E
Klein Wanzleben	54	52.04 N	11.21 E
Klein-Winterhoekberge ⛰	158	33.13 S	25.05 E
Klein Ziethen	264a	52.23 N	13.27 E
Klein Ziethener-Berge ▲[2]	264a	52.22 N	13.26 E
Klekovača ▲	36	44.26 N	16.31 E
Klementjevka	86	50.16 N	80.56 E
Klementjevo	82	55.38 N	36.01 E
Klemme	190	43.01 N	93.36 W
Klemtu	182	52.36 N	128.31 W
Klenau	60	48.29 N	11.19 E
Klenovka	80	57.45 N	54.19 E
Klenovo	82	55.19 N	37.21 E
Klerksdorp	158	26.58 S	26.39 E
Klerkskraal	158	26.15 S	27.10 E
Klesov	78	51.19 N	26.54 E
Klet' ▲	61	48.52 N	14.17 E
Kletn'a	76	53.23 N	33.12 E
Kletskaja	80	49.19 N	43.04 E
Kletsko-Počtovskij	80	49.36 N	43.03 E
Klettwitz	54	51.32 N	13.53 E
Klevan'	78	50.44 N	26.02 E
Kleve	52	51.48 N	6.09 E
Klevenka	80	52.07 N	49.33 E
Kley ⊸[8]	263	51.30 N	7.22 E
Klibreck, Ben ▲	46	58.14 N	4.22 W
Kličev	76	53.29 N	29.21 E
Klička	88	50.26 N	118.00 E
Klickitat	224	45.49 N	121.09 W
Klickitat □[6]	224	45.50 N	121.07 W
Klickitat ≃	224	45.42 N	121.17 W
Kliedbruch ⊸[1]	263	51.22 N	6.33 E
Klietz	54	52.40 N	12.04 E
Klimino	88	58.39 N	98.42 E
Klimoviči	76	53.37 N	31.58 E
Klimovo, S.S.S.R.	76	52.23 N	32.11 E
Klimovo, S.S.S.R.	82	55.22 N	38.52 E
Klimovsk	82	55.22 N	37.32 E
Klimovskoje	82	54.42 N	37.48 E
Klimov Zavod	76	54.50 N	34.55 E
Klimpfjäll	24	65.04 N	14.52 E
Klin, S.S.S.R.	82	56.20 N	36.44 E
Klin, S.S.S.R.	82	55.19 N	36.20 E
Klinaklini ≃	182	51.05 N	125.36 W
Klin-Bel'din	82	54.45 N	39.13 E
Klincovka	80	51.41 N	49.11 E
Klincy	76	52.47 N	32.14 E
Kline Ditch ≅	279a	41.28 N	82.04 W
Kling	116	5.58 N	124.42 E
Klingbach ≃	56	50.17 N	9.22 E
Klingen	60	48.26 N	11.09 E
Klingenberg	54	50.55 N	13.31 E
Klingenberg am Main	56	49.47 N	9.11 E
Klingenbrunn	60	48.56 N	13.19 E
Klingenmünster	56	49.08 N	8.01 E
Klingenthal	54	50.21 N	12.28 E
Klinger Lake ⊜	216	41.47 N	85.33 W
Klingerstown	208	40.40 N	76.41 W
Klinghardtsberge ▲	156	27.18 S	15.48 E
Klingnau	58	47.35 N	8.15 E
Klink	54	53.29 N	12.37 E
Klinkino	83	47.17 N	38.15 E
Klínovec ▲	54	50.24 N	12.58 E
Klinsko-Dmitrovskaja Gr'ada ▲	82	56.10 N	37.15 E
Klintehamn	26	57.24 N	18.12 E
Klintsy → Klincy	76	52.47 N	32.14 E
Klipbakken	158	28.50 S	21.21 E
Klipdale	158	34.19 S	19.57 E
Klipdam	158	27.35 S	19.56 E
Klipdrifdam ⊸[6]	158	26.36 S	27.20 E
Kliplev	41	54.56 N	9.25 E
Klippan	41	56.08 N	13.06 E
Klipriviersberg ⛰	273d	26.17 S	28.02 E
Kliškovcy	78	48.26 N	26.15 E
Klisura	38	42.42 N	24.27 E
Klitmøller	26	57.02 N	8.31 E
Klitten	54	51.20 N	14.36 E
Klixbüll	41	54.48 N	8.53 E
Ključ	36	44.32 N	16.47 E
Klobbicke	264a	52.46 N	13.48 E
Kłobuck	30	50.55 N	18.57 E
Klobuticy	76	58.35 N	29.35 E
Kłodawa	30	52.16 N	18.55 E
Kłodzko	30	50.27 N	16.39 E
Kløfta	26	60.04 N	11.09 E
Kłomnice	30	50.56 N	19.21 E
Klondike	216	40.29 N	86.57 W
Klondike ≃	180	64.05 N	139.26 W
Klondike □[9]	180	63.30 N	139.00 W
Klöntaler See ⊜	58	47.02 N	8.58 E
Klooga	76	59.19 N	24.16 E
Kloosterveen	52	52.59 N	6.33 E
Kloosterzande	52	51.22 N	4.02 E
Klopein	61	46.36 N	14.35 E
Kloster	54	54.35 N	13.06 E
Klosterfelde	54	52.48 N	13.28 E
Klosterhardt ⊸[8]	263	51.31 N	6.53 E
Klösterle	58	47.08 N	10.05 E
Klostermansfeld	54	51.35 N	11.29 E
Klosterneuburg	264b	48.18 N	16.20 E
Kloster Oesede	52	52.12 N	8.07 E
Klosters	58	46.54 N	9.53 E
Klostertal ∨	58	47.08 N	9.59 E
Klosterwappen ▲	30	47.46 N	15.48 E
Kloster Zinna	54	52.01 N	13.07 E
Kloten, Schw.	58	47.27 N	8.35 E
Kloten, Sve.	40	59.54 N	15.17 E
Klotz, Lac ⊜	176	60.32 N	73.40 W
Klötze	54	52.38 N	11.10 E
Klouto	150	6.57 N	0.34 E
Kluane Lake ⊜	180	61.15 N	138.40 W
Kluang	112	2.41 S	103.54 E
Kl'učevaja	24	65.16 N	41.32 E
Kl'učevskaja Sopka, Vulkan ▲[1]	74	56.04 N	160.38 E
Kluchorskij, Pereval)(	84	43.15 N	41.54 E
Kluczbork	30	50.59 N	18.13 E
Kluess	54	53.46 N	12.14 E
Klukwan	180	59.24 N	135.54 W
Klundert	52	51.40 N	4.32 E
Klungkung	115b	8.32 S	115.24 E
Klüppelberg	56	51.06 N	7.28 E
Kluterhöhle ⍛[5]	52	51.18 N	7.21 E
Klutina Lake ⊜	180	61.37 N	146.55 W
Klütz	54	53.58 N	11.10 E
Knaben gruver	26	58.39 N	7.04 E
Knaddah	130	35.45 N	36.12 E
Kn'aginino	80	55.49 N	45.03 E
Knaik ≃	46	56.14 N	3.52 W
Knapdaar	158	30.43 S	26.09 E
Knapdale ⊸[1]	46	55.55 N	5.30 W
Knaphill	260	51.19 N	0.37 W
Knapp	190	44.57 N	92.05 W
Knapp Creek	210	42.00 N	78.30 W
Knappenberg	61	46.56 N	14.35 E
Knäred	26	56.32 N	13.19 E
Knaresborough	44	54.00 N	1.27 W
Knargram	126	24.01 N	87.59 E
Knauertown	285	40.10 N	75.44 W
Knauthain ⊸[8]	54	51.16 N	12.18 E
Kn'ažaja-Bajgora	76	52.23 N	40.02 E
Kn'ažji Gory	76	56.05 N	35.14 E
Kn'ažovo	76	59.40 N	43.54 E
Knebel	41	56.13 N	10.30 E
Knebworth	42	51.52 N	0.12 W
Kneehills Creek ≃	182	51.30 N	112.50 W
Knee Lake ⊜, Man., Can.	184	55.03 N	94.40 W
Knee Lake ⊜ Sask., Can.	184	55.51 N	107.00 W
Knesebeck	54	52.41 N	10.42 E
Knesselare	50	51.08 N	3.25 E
Knetzgau	56	50.00 N	10.33 E
Knevicy	76	57.56 N	32.14 E
Kneža	38	43.30 N	24.05 E
Knić	38	43.55 N	20.43 E
Knickerbocker	196	31.16 N	100.38 W
Kniebis	58	48.28 N	8.17 E
Knife ≃	198	47.20 N	101.23 W
Knife Lake ⊜	184	53.47 N	91.20 W
Knight Inlet C	182	50.41 N	125.40 W
Knight Island I	180	60.20 N	147.45 W
Knighton	42	52.21 N	3.03 W
Knightsen	226	37.58 N	121.40 W
Knights Landing	226	38.48 N	121.43 W
Knightstown	218	39.48 N	85.32 W
Knightville Reservoir ⊜[1]	207	42.19 N	72.52 W
Knik Arm C	180	61.25 N	149.45 W
Knin	36	44.02 N	16.12 E
Knippa	196	29.18 N	99.38 W
Knislinge	26	56.11 N	14.05 E
Knittelfeld	61	47.14 N	14.50 E
Knittlingen	56	49.01 N	8.45 E
Knivsbjerg ▲[2]	41	55.08 N	9.27 E
Knivsta	40	59.43 N	17.48 E
Knjaževac	38	43.34 N	22.16 E
Knob, Cape ≻	162	34.32 S	119.16 E
Knobby Head ≻	162	29.40 S	114.58 E
Knob Noster	194	38.46 N	93.33 W
Knob Peak ▲	116	12.28 N	121.21 E
Knoc	48	52.38 N	9.20 W
Knock	46	57.33 N	2.45 W
Knockholt	260	51.18 N	0.06 E
Knockholt Pound	260	51.19 N	0.08 E
Knocklayd ▲	44	55.09 N	6.15 W
Knocklong	48	52.26 N	8.24 W
Knockmealdown Mountains ⛰	48	52.10 N	8.00 W
Knokke	50	51.21 N	3.17 E
Knole ⊥	260	51.16 N	0.12 E
Knolls Green	262	53.19 N	2.18 W
Knollwood, Conn., U.S.	207	41.17 N	72.13 W
Knollwood, Ill., U.S.	278	42.17 N	87.53 W
Knollwood, Ohio, U.S.	218	39.43 N	84.04 W
Knollwood Park	216	42.14 N	84.22 W
Knolvlei	156	19.10 S	19.23 E
Knon ⊜	40	60.12 N	13.40 E
Knoppiesfontein	273d	26.05 S	28.25 E
Knossos ⊥	38	35.20 N	25.10 E
Knottingley	44	53.43 N	1.14 W
Knott's Berry Farm ♠	280	33.50 N	118.00 W
Knotts Island	208	36.01 N	75.55 W
Knotty Ash ⊸[8]	262	53.25 N	2.54 W
Knotty Green	260	51.37 N	0.39 W
Knowland State Arboretum and Park ♠	282	37.45 N	122.09 W
Knowle	42	52.23 N	1.43 W
Knowlesville	210	43.14 N	78.19 W
Knowltonwood	285	39.53 N	75.24 W
Knowsley	262	53.27 N	2.51 W
Knowsley □[8]	262	53.27 N	2.50 W
Knowsley Hall ⚲	262	53.26 N	2.50 W
Knowsley Park ♠	262	53.27 N	2.49 W
Knox, Austl.	169	37.53 S	145.18 E
Knox, Ind., U.S.	216	41.18 N	86.37 W
Knox, N.Y., U.S.	210	42.40 N	74.07 W
Knox, Pa., U.S.	214	41.14 N	79.32 W
Knox □[6], Ohio, U.S.	214	40.23 N	82.29 W
Knox □[6], Mo., U.S.	219	40.08 N	92.09 W
Knox, Cape ≻	182	54.11 N	133.04 W
Knoxboro	210	42.60 N	75.36 W
Knox City, Mo., U.S.	219	40.09 N	92.01 W
Knox City, Tex., U.S.	196	33.25 N	99.49 W
Knox Coast ⍛[2]	9	66.30 S	105.00 E
Knox Dale	214	41.05 N	79.02 W
Knoxville, Ga., U.S.	192	32.44 N	84.01 W
Knoxville, Ill., U.S.	190	40.55 N	90.17 W
Knoxville, Iowa, U.S.	190	41.19 N	93.06 W
Knoxville, Pa., U.S.	210	41.57 N	77.26 W
Knoxville, Tenn., U.S.	192	35.58 N	83.56 W
Knuckles ▲	122	7.24 N	80.48 E
Knudshoved Odde ≻[1]	41	55.03 N	11.45 E
Knüll ▲	56	50.53 N	9.24 E
Knutby	40	59.55 N	18.15 E
Knuthenborg	41	54.50 N	11.30 E
Knutsford	44	53.19 N	2.22 W
Knysna	158	34.02 S	23.02 E
Knyszyn	30	53.19 N	22.55 E
Koala Sanctuary ⊸[4]	274a	33.40 S	151.10 E
Koani	154	6.08 S	39.17 E
Kob'	88	55.25 N	101.24 E
Koba	112	2.29 S	106.24 E
Kob'aj	74	63.34 N	126.30 E
Kőbánya ⊸[8]	264c	47.29 N	19.10 E
Kobarid	36	46.15 N	13.35 E
Kobar Sink ⍛[7]	144	14.00 N	40.30 E
Kobayashi	92	31.59 N	130.59 E
Kōbe	96		
	270	34.41 N	135.10 E
Kōbe-kō C	270	34.40 N	135.12 E
Kobel'aki	78	49.09 N	34.12 E
København (Copenhagen)	41	55.40 N	12.35 E
København □[6]	41	55.45 N	12.25 E
Kobernausser Wald ⊸[3]	60	48.04 N	13.14 E
Kobe University ⚲[2]	270	34.43 N	135.14 E
Kobi	84	42.33 N	44.32 E
Koblenz, B.R.D.	56	50.21 N	7.35 E
Koblenz, Schw.	58	47.37 N	8.14 E
Koblenz □[5]	56	50.10 N	7.30 E
Kobo, Yai.	144	12.11 N	39.33 E
Kobo, Zaïre	152	4.54 S	17.09 E
Ko-boke ♠	96	33.50 N	133.46 E
Koboko	154	3.25 N	30.58 E
Koboldo	89	52.58 N	132.42 E
Kobona	76	60.01 N	31.36 E
Kobou ≃	152	6.13 N	23.19 E
Kobowen Swamp ☰	144	5.38 N	33.54 E
Koboža	76	58.49 N	35.01 E
Koboža ≃	76	58.52 N	36.17 E
Kobra	24	60.03 N	50.44 E
Kobrin	76	52.13 N	24.21 E
Kobrinskoje	76	59.25 N	30.07 E
Kobroor, Pulau I	164	6.12 S	134.32 E
Kobuchizawa	94	35.52 N	138.19 E
Kobuga-hara ♠	94	36.40 N	139.35 E
Kobuk	180	66.54 N	156.52 W
Kobuk ≃, Alaska, U.S.	180	66.45 N	161.00 W
Kobuk ≃, Zhg.	86	45.50 N	86.20 E
Kobuleti	84	41.50 N	41.47 E
Kobushiga-take ▲	94	35.54 N	138.44 E
Kobylanka	54	53.19 N	14.50 E
Kobylin	30	51.43 N	17.13 E
Kobyl'nik	76	54.56 N	26.41 E
Kobyžča	78	50.49 N	31.30 E
Köca ≃	130	36.16 N	29.15 E
Kocaali	130	41.03 N	30.52 E
Kocaaliler	130	37.19 N	30.44 E
Kocaeli → İzmit	130	40.46 N	29.55 E
Kocaeli □[4]	130	40.55 N	29.55 E
Koçali	130	37.55 N	38.15 E
Kočani	38	41.55 N	22.25 E
Koçarlı	130	37.45 N	27.42 E
Kocasinan	267b	41.01 N	28.50 E
Kočečum ≃	74	64.17 N	100.10 E
Kočelajevo	80	54.01 N	44.02 E
Kočemary	80	54.50 N	40.58 E
Kočen'ajevka	80	53.52 N	46.59 E
Kočen'ga, S.S.S.R.	76	60.09 N	43.33 E
Kočenga, S.S.S.R.	88	55.55 N	104.06 E
Kočenga ≃	88	55.55 N	104.06 E
Kočerga	88	55.15 N	103.46 E
Kočerov	78	50.21 N	29.21 E
Kočetovka, S.S.S.R.	80	52.58 N	40.29 E
Kočetovka, S.S.S.R.	80	55.16 N	46.07 E
Kočevar	76	60.26 N	42.11 E
Kočevje	36	45.38 N	14.52 E
Kočevo	86	59.36 N	54.18 E
Koch'am-ni	98	41.06 N	129.23 E
Kŏch'ang, Taehan	98	35.41 N	127.55 E
Kŏch'ang, Taehan	98	35.26 N	126.42 E
Kochanoviči	76	55.52 N	28.08 E
Kochanovo	76	54.28 N	30.01 E
Kochel	64	47.39 N	11.22 E
Kochelsee ⊜	64	47.38 N	11.20 E
Kochena	158	27.00 S	18.50 E
Kocher ≃	56	49.14 N	9.12 E
Kōchi	96	33.33 N	133.33 E
Kōchi □[5]	96	33.40 N	133.30 E
Kōchi-dani ♠	94	34.34 N	136.10 E
Kochinda	174m	26.08 N	127.43 E
Koch Island I	176	69.38 N	78.15 W
Kochiu → Gejtu	102	23.22 N	103.06 E
Kochma	80	56.56 N	41.06 E
Koch Peak ▲	202	45.02 N	111.28 W
Kochugaon	124	26.34 N	90.04 E
Kock	30	51.39 N	22.27 E
Kočkor-Ata	85	41.04 N	72.29 E
Kočkorka	85	42.14 N	75.45 E
Kocksoord	273d	26.13 S	27.39 E
Kočkurovo	80	54.02 N	45.26 E
Kočmes	24	66.12 N	60.44 E
Kočon'ovo	86	55.02 N	82.12 E
Kočov	60	49.49 N	12.44 E
Kočubejevskoje	84	44.41 N	41.41 E
Kōda, Nihon	94	34.52 N	137.10 E
Kōda, Nihon	96	34.42 N	132.45 E
Kodačdikost	24	63.11 N	55.49 E
Kodaikānal	122	10.14 N	77.29 E
Kodaira	94	35.44 N	139.29 E
Kodama	94	36.11 N	139.08 E
Kodar, Chrebet ⛰	88	57.15 N	118.10 E
Kodari	124	27.56 N	85.56 E
Kodarma	124	24.28 N	85.36 E
Koddo ≃	152	7.05 N	19.10 E
Kodera ⊸[8]	270	34.41 N	135.04 E
Kodersdorf	54	51.15 N	14.53 E
Kodi	152	3.34 S	22.12 E
Kodiak	180	57.48 N	152.23 W
Kodiak Island I	180	57.30 N	153.30 W
Kodiang	114	6.24 N	100.18 E
Kodinār	120	20.47 N	70.42 E
Kodino	24	63.43 N	39.41 E
Kodo, Jabal ▲	140	12.26 N	23.38 E
Kodok	140	9.53 N	32.07 E
Kodori ≃	84	42.47 N	41.10 E
Kodorskij Chrebet ⛰	84	43.00 N	42.00 E
Kodra	78	50.36 N	29.34 E
Kodry ▲[2]	78	47.10 N	28.25 E
Kodyma	78	48.07 N	29.07 E
Kodyma ≃	78	48.01 N	30.48 E
Kodžori	84	41.40 N	44.41 E
Koega ≃	158	33.37 S	22.14 E
Koegas	158	29.16 S	22.20 E
Koehn Lake ⊜	228	35.20 N	117.53 W
Koekelare	50	51.05 N	2.58 E
Koekenaap	158	31.30 S	18.18 E
Koeltztown	219	38.19 N	92.03 W
Koenigsmacker	56	49.24 N	6.17 E
Koersel	56	51.04 N	5.16 E
Koes	156	25.59 S	19.08 E
Kofa Mountains ⛰	200	33.20 N	114.00 W
Kofeld	58	47.44 N	9.41 E
Köfering	60	48.56 N	12.12 E
Koffiefontein	158	29.30 S	25.00 E
Kofiau, Pulau I	164	1.11 S	129.50 E
Köflach	61	47.04 N	15.05 E
Koforidua	150	6.03 N	0.17 W
Kōfu, Nihon	94	35.39 N	138.35 E
Kōfu, Nihon	96	35.17 N	133.30 E
Koga, Nihon	94	36.11 N	139.43 E
Koga, Nihon	96	33.40 N	130.30 E
Koga, Tan.	154	6.14 S	32.25 E
Kogaluc ≃	176	59.40 N	77.35 W
Kogaluc, Baie C	176	59.20 N	77.50 W
Kogaluk ≃	176	56.12 N	61.44 W
Kogan	166	27.03 S	150.46 E
Kogane	268	35.50 N	139.56 E
Koganei	94	35.42 N	139.32 E
Kogarah	274a	33.58 S	151.08 E
Kogarah Bay C	274a	33.59 S	151.07 E
Køge, Dan.	41	55.27 N	12.11 E
Kōge, Nihon	96	35.24 N	134.15 E
Køge Bugt C, Dan.	41	55.30 N	12.20 E
Køge Bugt C, Grn.	176	65.00 N	40.30 W
Kogil'nik ≃	78	45.51 N	29.38 E
Kogin Baba	146	7.55 N	11.30 E
Kogo	152	1.05 N	9.42 E
Kogon ≃	150	11.09 N	14.42 W
Kogoni	150	14.44 N	6.02 W
Kohak	128	25.44 N	62.33 E
Kohala Mountains ⛰	229d	20.05 N	155.45 W
Kohāt	123	33.35 N	71.26 E
Kohāt ≃	123	33.24 N	71.48 E
Kohatk Wash ∨	200	32.38 N	111.55 W
Kohila	76	59.10 N	24.45 E
Kohīma	120	25.40 N	94.07 E
Kohistān □[9]	123	35.00 N	72.30 E
Kohlberg ▲[2]	263	51.18 N	7.46 E
Kohler	190	43.44 N	87.46 W
Kohlfurt → Węgliniec	30	51.17 N	15.13 E
Kohlstädt	52	51.50 N	8.52 E
Kōhoku ⊸[8]	268	35.31 N	139.38 E
Kohren-Sahlis	54	51.01 N	12.36 E
Kohsān	128	34.39 N	61.12 E
Kohtla-Järve	76	59.24 N	27.15 E
Kohu → Kōfu	94	35.39 N	138.35 E
Kohukohu	172	35.21 S	173.32 E
Kohŭng	98	34.37 N	127.16 E
Kohuratahi	172	39.06 S	174.46 E
Koidern	180	61.58 N	140.25 W
Koigi	76	58.50 N	25.45 E
Koihoa	110	8.12 N	93.29 E
Koil-Aligargh → Alīgarh	124	27.53 N	78.05 E
Koilkuntla	122	15.14 N	78.19 E
Koindu	150	8.26 N	10.19 W
Koin-ni	98	40.28 N	126.22 E
Koitere ⊜	26	62.58 N	30.45 E
Koito ≃	94	35.21 N	139.52 E
Kojā ≃	128	25.34 N	61.13 E
Kojandy	86	49.51 N	75.40 E
Kojda	24	66.23 N	42.31 E
Kŏje-do I	98	34.52 N	128.37 E
Kojetin	30	49.21 N	17.18 E
Kojgorodok	24	60.26 N	50.58 E
Ko-jima I	92a	41.22 N	139.48 E
Kojima-ko ⊜[1]	96	34.37 N	134.00 E
Kojnatchyn, Ozero ⊜	180	65.20 N	180.00 E
Kojŏ	98	38.57 N	127.51 E
Kojonup	162	33.50 S	117.09 E
Kojsary	85	42.33 N	78.10 E
Kojsug	83	47.07 N	39.41 E
Kokai ≃	94	35.52 N	140.08 E
K'okajgyr	85	40.43 N	75.37 E
Kokalaat	86	49.47 N	64.15 E
Kokand	85	40.33 N	70.57 E
Kokanee Glacier Provincial Park ♠	182	49.47 N	117.10 W
Kokankišlak	85	40.56 N	72.30 E
Kökar I	26	59.56 N	20.55 E
Kokas	164	2.42 S	132.26 E
Kokašice	60	49.53 N	12.57 E
Kokava nad Rimavicou	30	48.34 N	19.50 E
K'okbel'	85	40.17 N	72.55 E
Kokčetav	86	53.17 N	69.25 E
Kokčetavskaja Vozvyšennost' ⛰[1]	86	52.50 N	69.00 E
Kokee State Park ♠	229b	22.08 N	159.40 W
Kokemäenjoki ≃	26	61.33 N	21.42 E
Kokemäki	26	61.15 N	22.21 E
Ko Kha	110	18.11 N	99.24 E
Kokhav	132	31.38 N	34.40 E
Kokiu → Gejiu	102	23.22 N	103.06 E
Kok-Jangak	85	41.02 N	73.12 E
Kokka	140	20.00 N	30.35 E
Kokkilai Lagoon C	122	9.00 N	80.56 E
Kokkola (Gamlakarleby)	26	63.50 N	23.07 E
Kokku	98	40.22 N	128.44 E
Koknese	76	56.39 N	25.29 E
Koko	150	11.26 N	4.32 E
Kokoda	164	8.52 S	147.45 E
Koko Head ≻	229c	21.16 N	157.42 W
Kokola	154	0.47 N	29.36 E
Kokole Point ≻	229b	21.59 N	159.46 W
Kokolik ≃	180	69.46 N	165.00 W
Kokolopozo	150	5.08 N	6.05 W
K'ok'omeren ≃	85	41.43 N	73.54 E
Kokomo, Ind., U.S.	216	40.29 N	86.08 W
Kokomo, Miss., U.S.	194	31.12 N	90.00 W
Kokonau	164	4.43 S	136.26 E
Kokong	156	24.27 S	23.03 E
Kokonoe	96	33.10 N	131.10 E
Koko Nor → Qinghai ⊜	102	36.50 N	100.20 E
Kokopo	164	4.20 S	152.15 E
Kokorevka	76	52.35 N	34.16 E
Kokosing ≃	214	40.22 N	82.12 W
Kokos-Inseln → Cocos (Keeling) Islands □[2]	12	12.10 S	96.55 E
Kokoškinskij	265b	55.38 N	37.11 E
Kokpāra Narsinghgarh	126	22.31 N	86.33 E
Kokpaš	86	51.12 N	87.45 E
Kokpekty	86	48.45 N	82.24 E
Kokrajhar	124	26.24 N	90.16 E
Kokrines	180	64.56 N	154.42 W
Kokrines Hills ⛰[2]	180	65.15 N	154.00 W
Koksa ≃	86	50.16 N	85.36 E
Kokšaalatau, Chrebet ⛰	72	41.00 N	78.00 E
Kokšamary	80	56.10 N	47.45 E
Koksan	98	38.46 N	126.40 E
Koksaraj	85	42.40 N	68.08 E
Kokšekol, Ozero ⊜	86	46.05 N	62.00 E
Koksijde	50	51.07 N	2.38 E
Koksilah	224	48.40 N	123.38 W
Koksoak ≃	176	58.32 N	68.10 W
Koksŏng	98	35.17 N	127.17 E
Koksovyj	78	48.12 N	40.39 E
Kokstad	158	30.32 S	29.29 E
Koksu, S.S.S.R.	85	41.27 N	68.01 E
Koksu, S.S.S.R.	86	44.59 N	77.56 E
Koktal	86	44.09 N	79.48 E
Kokterek	80	49.25 N	49.15 E
Koktubek	86	48.07 N	56.51 E
Kokubu	92	31.44 N	130.46 E
Kokubunji, Nihon	94	35.42 N	139.29 E
Kokubunji, Nihon	96	34.18 N	133.58 E
Kokubunji Temple ⚲[1]	268	35.44 N	139.55 E
Kokufu	96	35.28 N	134.16 E
Kokuj	88	52.13 N	117.33 E
Kokujbel' ≃	85	38.21 N	72.46 E
Kōkū-jieitai-chikujō-kichi ■	92	33.41 N	131.03 E
Kōkū-jieitai-hamamatsukita-kichi ■	94	34.45 N	137.42 E
Kōkū-jieitai-hyakuri-kichi ■	94	36.11 N	140.25 E
Kōkū-jieitai-iruma-kichi (Iruma Air Base) ■	94	35.50 N	139.24 E
Kōkū-jieitai-kisarazu-kichi (Kisarazu Air Base) ■	94	35.24 N	139.55 E
Kōkū-jieitai-shindenbaru-kichi ■	92	32.04 N	130.30 E
Kōkū-jietai-chikujō-kichi ■	96	33.41 N	131.03 E
Kokžar	86	49.01 N	60.10 E
Kol ≃	128	27.59 N	55.47 E
Kola, Indon.	164	5.26 S	134.29 E
Kola, S.S.S.R.	24	68.53 N	33.01 E
Kola ≃	24	68.53 N	33.02 E
Kolāba □[5]	272c	18.56 N	73.07 E
Kolachel	122	8.10 N	77.15 E
Kolāchi ≃	120	27.08 N	67.02 E
Kol'adovka	83	49.05 N	39.12 E
Kolageran	84	40.58 N	44.37 E
Kolahun	150	8.24 N	10.02 W
Kolaka	112	4.03 S	121.36 E
Kolambo	152	7.34 S	21.58 E
Kolambugan	116	8.07 N	123.55 E
Kolanguj	88	51.01 N	116.31 E
Kola Peninsula → Kol'skij Poluostrov ≻[1]	24	67.30 N	37.00 E
Kolār	122	13.08 N	78.08 E
Kolāras	124	25.14 N	77.36 E
Kolār Gold Fields	122	12.55 N	78.17 E
Kolari	24	67.20 N	23.48 E
Kolarovgrad → Šumen	38	43.16 N	26.55 E
Kolárovo	30	47.52 N	18.02 E
Kolašin	38	42.49 N	19.31 E
Kolāyat	120	27.50 N	72.57 E
Kolbači	89	54.22 N	123.02 E
Kolbäck	40	59.34 N	16.15 E
Kolbäcksån ≃	40	59.32 N	16.16 E
Kolbano	112	10.02 S	124.31 E
Kolbasnaja	78	47.47 N	29.13 E
Kolbča	76	53.39 N	29.14 E
Kolberg → Kołobrzeg	30	54.12 N	15.33 E
Kolbermoor	64	47.51 N	12.04 E
Kolbio	144	1.10 S	41.15 E
Kolbnitz	64	46.52 N	13.19 E
Kolbotn	26	59.49 N	10.48 E
Kolbuszowa	30	50.15 N	21.47 E
Kolby Kås	41	55.48 N	10.33 E
Kolchida ☰	84	42.15 N	42.00 E
Kolchozabad	120	37.27 N	68.31 E
Kol'covo	82	54.27 N	36.40 E
Kol'čuga	82	55.43 N	37.12 E
Kol'čugino	80	56.18 N	39.23 E
Kołczewo	54	53.58 N	14.38 E
Kolda	150	12.53 N	14.57 W
Kolding	41	55.31 N	9.29 E
Kolding Fjord C	41	55.30 N	9.35 E
Kole, Zaïre	152	3.27 S	22.29 E
Kole, Zaïre	154	2.07 N	25.26 E
Kolea	34	36.38 N	2.46 E
Kolebira	124	22.43 N	84.42 E
Kole Kalyan	272c	19.06 N	72.59 E
Kolenfeld	52	52.24 N	9.27 E
Koleno	80	51.52 N	44.07 E
Kolenté	150	10.06 N	12.37 W
Kolenté (Great Scarcies) ≃	150	8.55 N	13.08 W
Kolga	76	59.32 N	25.42 E
Kolgujev, Ostrov I	24	69.05 N	49.15 E
Kolhāpur, Bhārat	122	16.06 N	78.16 E
Kolhāpur, Bhārat	122	16.42 N	74.13 E
Kolho	26	62.08 N	24.31 E
Koli	76	59.30 N	34.30 E
Koli ▲[2]	26	63.06 N	29.48 E
Koli, Jabal ▲	140	14.05 N	25.31 E
Kolia	150	9.46 N	6.28 W
Koliba (Corubal) ≃	150	11.57 N	15.06 W
Koliganek	180	59.48 N	157.25 W
Kolima ⊜	26	63.16 N	25.50 E
Kolimbine ≃	150	15.00 N	11.00 W
Kolín	30	50.01 N	15.13 E
Kolka	76	57.45 N	22.35 E
Kølkær	41	56.04 N	9.06 E
Kolkas Rags ≻	76	57.47 N	22.36 E
Kolki, S.S.S.R.	78	51.37 N	26.37 E
Kolki, S.S.S.R.	78	51.07 N	25.41 E
Kolkwitz	54	51.45 N	14.15 E
Koll ≃	60	48.36 N	12.58 E
Kölleda	54	51.11 N	11.15 E
Kollegāl	122	12.09 N	77.07 E
Kolleru Lake ⊜	122	16.39 N	81.13 E
Kollum	52	53.16 N	6.09 E
Kollund	41	54.51 N	9.27 E
Kolmanskop	156	26.40 S	15.12 E
Kolmården	40	58.40 N	16.23 E
Kolmården ⛰[2]	40	58.41 N	16.35 E
Kolmårdens Djurpark ♠	40	58.40 N	16.29 E
Kolme	144	5.17 N	37.22 E
Kolmogorovo	86	59.15 N	91.20 E
Köln (Cologne)	56	50.56 N	6.59 E
Köln □[5]	56	50.55 N	6.40 E
Köln-Bonn, Flughafen ⊠	56	50.50 N	7.10 E
Kolno	30	53.25 N	21.56 E
Kolo, Niger	150	13.14 N	2.20 E
Koło, Pol.	30	52.12 N	18.38 E
Kolo, Tan.	154	4.44 S	35.50 E
Koloa	229b	21.55 N	159.28 W
Kolobovo	80	56.42 N	41.21 E
Kołobrzeg	30	54.12 N	15.33 E
Koloč' ≃	82	55.34 N	35.52 E
Kolochau	54	51.44 N	13.16 E
Kolodn'a	76	54.48 N	32.09 E
Kologriv	76	58.51 N	44.17 E
Kologrivovka	80	51.44 N	45.20 E
Kolojar	80	52.34 N	46.58 E
Kolok (Golok) ≃	114	6.15 N	102.05 E
Kolokani	150	13.35 N	8.02 W
Koloko	150	11.05 N	5.19 W
Kolokol'covka, S.S.S.R.	80	52.36 N	49.48 E
Kolokol'covka, S.S.S.R.	80	51.12 N	44.36 E
Kolo Lagoon C	175e	8.37 S	158.07 E
Kolom'agi ⊸[8]	265a	60.00 N	30.17 E
Kolom'agi, Areoport ⊠	265a	60.01 N	30.17 E
Kolomak	78	49.50 N	35.18 E
Kolombangara I	175e	8.00 S	157.05 E
Kolomea → Kolomyja	78	48.32 N	25.04 E
Kolomenka ≃	82	55.06 N	38.46 E
Kolomenskaja Sloboda	82	54.22 N	38.15 E
Kolomenskoje ⊸[8]	265b	55.40 N	37.41 E
Kolomna	82	55.05 N	38.49 E
Kolomyja	78	48.32 N	25.04 E
Kolondiéba	150	11.05 N	6.54 W
Kolonga	174w	21.08 S	175.04 W
Kolonie Stolp	264a	52.28 N	13.46 E
Kolono	112	4.18 S	122.41 E
Kolonodale	112	2.00 S	121.19 E
Kolora	272b	22.55 N	88.22 E
Kolosib	120	24.14 N	92.42 E
Kol'osnoje	78	46.02 N	29.56 E
Kolosovka	86	56.28 N	73.36 E
Kolovai	174w	21.06 S	175.20 W
Kolovertnoje	80	50.36 N	51.06 E
Kolovrat, Mount ▲	175e	9.10 S	161.05 E
Kolowana Watobo, Teluk C	112	5.00 S	123.06 E
Kolozsvár → Cluj	38	46.47 N	23.36 E
Kolp' ≃	76	59.20 N	36.49 E
Kolpaševo	86	58.20 N	82.50 E
Kolpino	76	59.45 N	30.36 E
Kölpinsee ⊜	54	53.30 N	12.34 E
Kolpny	76	52.15 N	37.02 E
Kölsa	54	51.28 N	12.13 E
Kol'skij Poluostrov (Kola Peninsula) ≻[1]	24	67.30 N	37.00 E
Kolsnaren ⊜	40	59.02 N	16.01 E
Kolsva	40	59.36 N	15.50 E
Kolubara ≃	38	44.40 N	20.15 E
Kol'učinskaja Guba C	180	66.40 N	174.30 W
Koluel Kayke	254	46.43 S	68.14 W
Kölük	130	37.46 N	38.36 E
Kolumbien → Colombia □[1]	246	4.00 N	72.00 W
Koluszki	30	51.44 N	19.49 E
Koluton ≃	86	51.42 N	69.10 E
Kolva ≃	24	65.55 N	57.15 E
Kolvereid	24	64.51 N	11.32 E
Kølvrå	41	56.18 N	9.08 E
Kolwezi	154	10.43 S	25.28 E
Kolyma ≃	74	69.30 N	161.00 E
Kolymskaja Nizmennost' ☰	74	68.30 N	154.00 E
Kom → Qom	128	34.39 N	50.54 E
Kom ▲	38	43.10 N	23.03 E
Kom ≃	152	2.18 N	11.40 E
Koma, Mya.	110	15.39 N	98.12 E
Koma, S.S.S.R.	86	55.02 N	91.19 E
Koma ≃	94	35.59 N	139.26 E
Komadougou Yobé (Komadugu Yobe) ≃	146	13.43 N	13.20 E
Komadugu Gana ≃	146	13.05 N	12.24 E
Komadugu Yobe (Komadougou Yobé) ≃	146	13.43 N	13.20 E
Komae	94	35.38 N	139.35 E
Komagane	94	35.43 N	137.55 E
Komaga-take ▲, Nihon	92a	42.04 N	140.41 E
Komaga-take ▲, Nihon	94	35.45 N	138.14 E
Komaga-take ▲, Nihon	94	35.47 N	137.48 E
Komagome ⊸[8]	268	35.44 N	139.45 E
Komaki	94	35.17 N	136.55 E
Komandorskije Ostrova II	74	55.00 N	167.00 E
Komandorski Village	226	37.43 N	121.54 W
Komariči	76	52.27 N	34.47 E
Komárno, Česko.	30	47.45 N	18.09 E
Komárom	30	47.44 N	18.08 E
Komárom □[6]	30	47.40 N	18.15 E
Komati (Incomati) ≃	156	25.46 S	32.43 E
Komatipoort	156	25.25 S	31.55 E
Komatsu, Nihon	94	36.24 N	136.27 E
Komatsu, Nihon	96	33.53 N	133.07 E
Komatsu-kūkō ⊠	94	36.24 N	136.26 E
Komatsushima	96	34.00 N	134.35 E
Kombani	157a	11.37 S	43.23 E
Kombissiri	150	12.04 N	1.20 W
Kombo	152	0.20 S	12.22 E
Kombone	152	4.37 N	9.19 E
Komdhārā	272b	22.53 N	88.14 E
Komebail Lagoon C	175b	7.24 N	134.27 E
Kome Island I	154	0.06 S	32.45 E
Komen	64	45.49 N	13.44 E
Komenda	150	5.03 N	1.29 W
Komenoi	268	35.55 N	140.01 E
Komering ≃	112	2.59 S	104.50 E
Komeshia	154	8.01 S	27.07 E
Komfane	164	5.39 S	134.44 E
Komga	158	32.35 S	27.55 E
Komi	175d	24.19 N	123.54 E
Kominato → Amatsu-kominato	94	35.07 N	140.10 E

Symbol	English	Deutsch	Español	Français	Português
≃	River	Fluss	Río	Rivière	Rio
≅	Canal	Kanal	Canal	Canal	Canal
ᒪ	Waterfall, Rapids	Wasserfall, Stromschnellen	Cascada, Rápidos	Chute d'eau, Rapides	Cascata, Rápidos
)(	Strait	Meeresstrasse	Estrecho	Détroit	Estreito
C	Bay, Gulf	Bucht, Golf	Bahía, Golfo	Baie, Golfe	Baía, Golfo
⊜	Lake, Lakes	See, Seen	Lago, Lagos	Lac, Lacs	Lago, Lagos
☰	Swamp	Sumpf	Pantano	Marais	Pântano
⍓	Ice Features, Glacier	Eis- und Gletscherformen	Accidentes Glaciales	Formes glaciaires	Acidentes Glaciares
⍑	Other Hydrographic Features	Andere Hydrographische Objekte	Otros Elementos Hidrográficos	Autres données hydrographiques	Outros Elementos Hidrográficos
✢	Submarine Features	Untermeerische Objekte	Accidentes Submarinos	Formes de relief sous-marin	Acidentes Submarinos
□	Political Unit	Politische Einheit	Unidad Política	Entité politique	Unidade Política
⚲	Cultural Institution	Kulturelle Institution	Institución Cultural	Institution culturelle	Instituição Cultural
⊥	Historical Site	Historische Stätte	Sitio Histórico	Site historique	Sitio Histórico
♠	Recreational Site	Erholungs- und Ferienort	Sitio de Recreo	Centre de loisirs	Sítio de Lazer
⊠	Airport	Flughafen	Aeropuerto	Aéroport	Aeroporto
■	Military Installation	Militäranlage	Instalación Militar	Installation militaire	Instalação Militar
⊸	Miscellaneous	Verschiedenes	Misceláneo	Divers	Miscelânea

Name	Page	Lat.°′	Long.°′
Komin Yanga	150	11.42 N	0.08 E
Komi-Perm'ackij Nacional'nyj Okrug □[8]	24	60.00 N	54.30 E
Komissarovo	89	44.59 N	131.46 E
Komkans	158	31.16 S	18.09 E
Komló	30	46.12 N	18.16 E
Kommadagga	158	33.09 S	25.55 E
Kommandodrif	158	27.30 S	26.14 E
Kommandokraal	158	33.06 S	22.51 E
Kommetjie	158	34.08 S	18.21 E
Kommunal'naja	88	52.03 N	115.06 E
Kommunarka	265b	55.34 N	37.29 E
Kommunarsk	83	48.30 N	38.47 E
Kommunizma, Pik ∧	85	38.57 N	72.01 E
Komodo	115b	8.35 S	119.30 E
Komodo, Pulau I	115b	8.36 S	119.30 E
Komoé ≃	150	5.12 N	3.44 W
Komoka	214	42.57 N	81.26 W
Komono, Congo	152	3.15 S	13.14 E
Komono, Nihon	94	35.00 N	136.31 E
Komoran, Pulau I	164	8.18 S	138.45 E
Komoren → Comoros □[1]	157a	12.10 S	44.10 E
Komorin, Kap → Comorin, Cape ≻	122	8.04 N	77.34 E
Komorn → Komárno	30	47.45 N	18.09 E
Komoro	94	36.19 N	138.26 E
Komotau → Chomutov	54	50.28 N	13.26 E
Komotiní	38	41.08 N	25.25 E
Komovi ⛰	38	42.40 N	19.40 E
Kompasberg ∧	158	31.45 S	24.32 E
Kompiam	164	5.20 S	143.55 E
Kompot	112	0.24 N	124.10 E
Komsberg ⛰	158	32.40 S	20.50 E
Komsomolabad	85	38.52 N	69.57 E
Komsomolec	86	53.45 N	62.02 E
Komsomolec, Ostrov I	74	80.30 N	95.00 E
Komsomolec, Zaliv C	72	45.30 N	52.45 E
Komsomol'sk-na-Amure	89	50.35 N	137.02 E
Komsomol'sk-na-Ust'urte	86	44.03 N	58.20 E
Komsomol'skoje, S.S.S.R.	80	50.46 N	47.03 E
Komsomol'skoje, S.S.S.R.	83	47.40 N	38.05 E
Komsomol'skoje, S.S.S.R.	88	52.29 N	111.06 E
Komsomol'skoj Pravdy, Ostrova II	74	77.20 N	107.40 E
Kömürcüpınar	267b	41.15 N	28.51 E
Komusan	98	42.08 N	129.41 E
Kona, Bhārat	272b	22.37 N	88.18 E
Kona, Mali	150	14.57 N	3.53 W
Kona Coast •[2]	229d	19.25 N	155.55 W
Konagkend	84	41.04 N	48.37 E
Konakpınar	130	39.26 N	27.53 E
Konan, C. Iv.	150	8.21 N	8.00 W
Konan → Hŭngnam, C.M.I.K.	98	39.50 N	127.38 E
Kōnan, Nihon	94	35.20 N	136.53 E
Kōnan, Nihon	94	34.28 N	135.40 E
Konar (Kunar) ≃	123	34.26 N	70.32 E
Konārak	120	19.54 N	86.07 E
Konār Dam ◆[6]	124	23.58 N	85.45 E
Konar-e Khāṣ	120	34.39 N	70.54 E
Konarha □[4]	120	35.15 N	71.00 E
Konawa	196	34.58 N	96.45 W
Končanskoje-Suvorovskoje	76	58.39 N	34.04 E
Konceba	78	48.07 N	29.56 E
Konch	124	25.59 N	79.09 E
Konda	74	61.20 N	63.58 E
Konda ≃, S.S.S.R.	86	60.40 N	69.46 E
Konda ≃, S.S.S.R.	88	53.30 N	113.32 E
Kondagaon	122	19.36 N	81.40 E
Kondakovskij	88	57.59 N	94.12 E
Konde	154	4.57 S	39.45 E
Kondega	76	60.14 N	33.30 E
Kondiaronk, Lac ⊜	190	46.56 N	76.45 W
Kondinin	162	32.30 S	118.16 E
Kondinskoje	86	59.40 N	67.22 E
Kondli ◆[8]	272a	28.37 N	77.19 E
Kondoa	154	4.54 S	35.47 E
Kondolole	154	1.20 N	25.58 E
Konduga	146	11.39 N	13.24 E
Kondurča ≃	80	53.31 N	50.24 E
Koné	175f	21.04 S	164.52 E
Koné, Passe de ⋓	175f	21.08 S	164.41 E
Konecbor	24	64.52 N	57.44 E
Konergino	180	65.54 N	178.50 W
Konevskij, Ostrov I	80	45.43 N	48.30 E
Konfara	150	11.55 N	8.50 W
Kong, C. Iv.	150	9.09 N	4.37 W
Køng, Dan.	41	55.07 N	11.50 E
Kŏng, Kaôh I	110	11.20 N	103.00 E
Kongakut ≃	180	69.48 N	141.50 W
Kongbo	152	4.44 N	21.23 E
Kongcheng	100	31.02 N	117.05 E
Kongeå ≃	41	55.23 N	8.40 E
Kongens Lyngby	41	55.46 N	12.31 E
Kongfang	100	27.58 N	116.53 E
Kongiganak	180	59.58 N	162.45 W
Konginkangas	26	62.46 N	25.48 E
Kongjiamatou	105	39.07 N	116.10 E
Kongjiatun	104	40.42 N	124.04 E
Kongjiawopeng	89	43.58 N	122.41 E
Kongjiazhuang	105	40.47 N	114.48 E
Kongjisihe ≃	86	43.55 N	80.55 E
Kongju	98	36.27 N	127.07 E
Konglong	100	29.56 N	115.54 E
Konglongshan	105	40.33 N	117.17 E
Kongmoon → Jiangmen	100	22.35 N	113.05 E
Kongo → Congo ≃	138	6.04 S	12.24 E
Kongō-ikoma-kokutei-kōen ♠	96	34.28 N	135.40 E
Kongolo, Zaïre	154	5.26 S	24.49 E
Kongolo, Zaïre	154	5.23 S	27.00 E
Kongor	140	7.10 N	31.21 E
Kongō-sanchi ⛰	270	34.27 N	135.41 E
Kongoussi	150	13.19 N	1.32 W
Kongō-zan ∧	96	34.25 N	135.41 E
Kongquehe ≃	90	40.40 N	90.10 E
Kongsberg	26	59.39 N	9.39 E
Kongsvinger	26	60.12 N	12.00 E
Kongsvoll	26	62.18 N	9.37 E
Kongsvoll-Hjerkinn Nasjonalpark ♠	26	62.15 N	9.35 E
Kongtongdao I	98	37.33 N	121.27 E
Kongwa	154	6.12 S	36.25 E
Kongyangcun	106	31.23 N	118.54 E
Kongzhen	106	31.29 N	119.00 E
Koni	154	10.42 S	27.15 E
Koniakari	150	14.34 N	10.54 W
Konice	30	49.35 N	16.53 E
Koniecpol	30	50.48 N	19.41 E
Königgrätz → Hradec Králové	30	50.12 N	15.50 E
Königheim	56	49.37 N	9.35 E
Königin Alexandra-Kette → Queen Alexandra Range ⛰	9	84.00 S	168.00 E
Königin Fabiola-Gebirge → Queen Fabiola Mountains ⛰	9	71.30 S	35.40 E
Königin Mary-Küste → Queen Mary Coast •[2]	9	67.00 S	96.00 E
Königin Maud-Land → Queen Maud Land ◆[1]	9	72.30 S	12.00 E
König-Otto-Höhle •[5]	60	49.15 N	11.42 E
Königsbach	56	48.58 N	8.36 E
Königsberg, B.R.D.	56	50.05 N	10.34 E
Königsberg → Chojna, Pol.	30	52.58 N	14.28 E
Königsberg → Kaliningrad, S.S.S.R.	76	54.43 N	20.30 E
Königsborn	263	51.33 N	7.41 E
Königsbrück	54	51.16 N	13.54 E
Königsbrunn, B.R.D.	58	48.16 N	10.53 E
Königsbrunn, Öst.	264b	48.21 N	16.25 E
Königsdorf	64	47.49 N	11.28 E
Königsee	54	50.39 N	11.05 E
Königsfelden ʊ[1]	58	47.29 N	8.14 E
Königsfeld im Schwarzwald	58	48.08 N	8.25 E
Königshain	54	51.11 N	14.52 E
Königshardt ◆[8]	263	51.33 N	6.51 E
Königshofen	56	49.32 N	9.44 E
Königshofen im Grabfeld	56	50.18 N	10.29 E
Königslutter	54	52.15 N	10.49 E
Königsmoor ◆[3]	52	53.15 N	9.40 E
Königssee	64	47.33 N	12.58 E
Königsstuhl •[4]	54	54.34 N	13.40 E
Königstein, B.R.D.	56	50.11 N	8.29 E
Königstein, B.R.D.	60	49.37 N	11.38 E
Königstein, D.D.R.	54	50.55 N	14.04 E
Königstetten	264b	48.18 N	16.09 E
Königswalde	54	50.33 N	13.02 E
Königswartha	54	51.18 N	14.20 E
Königswinter	56	50.40 N	7.11 E
Königs Wusterhausen	54	52.18 N	13.37 E
Konin	30	52.13 N	18.16 E
Konispol	38	39.39 N	20.10 E
Kónitsa	38	40.02 N	20.45 E
Köniz	58	46.56 N	7.25 E
Konjic	38	43.39 N	17.57 E
Konka ≃	78	47.40 N	35.22 E
Könkämäälv ≃	24	68.29 N	22.17 E
Konkapot ≃	210	42.03 N	73.20 W
Konkiep ≃	156	28.03 S	17.21 E
Konkō	96	34.32 N	133.37 E
Kon'-Kolodez'	76	52.08 N	39.11 E
Konkouré ≃	150	9.58 N	13.42 W
Kon'kovo	83	47.20 N	38.10 E
Konkudera	88	57.33 N	112.30 E
Kon-Kuk University ʊ[2]	271b	37.32 N	127.05 E
Konnagar	126	22.42 N	88.22 E
Könnern	54	51.40 N	11.46 E
Konnevesi ⊜	26	62.40 N	26.35 E
Konnur	122	16.12 N	74.45 E
Kōno	94	35.49 N	136.04 E
Konobejevo	82	55.24 N	38.40 E
Konohana ◆[8]	270	34.41 N	135.16 E
Kōnoike	270	34.42 N	135.37 E
Konolfingen	58	46.53 N	7.38 E
Konongo	150	6.37 N	1.11 W
Konoša	24	60.58 N	40.15 E
Kōno-shima I	96	34.28 N	133.31 E
Kōnosu	94	36.03 N	139.31 E
Konotop	78	51.14 N	33.12 E
Konovalovka	80	53.06 N	51.34 E
Konpienga ≃	150	10.52 N	0.51 E
Konradshöhe ◆[8]	264a	52.35 N	13.14 E
Konradsreuth	54	50.16 N	11.50 E
Konsankoro	150	9.02 N	9.00 W
Konsen-daichi ⛰	92a	63.25 N	144.52 E
Końskie	30	51.12 N	20.26 E
Konstadt → Wołczyn	30	51.01 N	18.03 E
Konstantinopel → İstanbul	130	41.01 N	28.58 E
Konstantinovka, S.S.S.R.	78	47.51 N	31.09 E
Konstantinovka, S.S.S.R.	78	49.57 N	35.07 E
Konstantinovka, S.S.S.R.	80	56.41 N	50.53 E
Konstantinovka, S.S.S.R.	83	47.52 N	37.24 E
Konstantinovka, S.S.S.R.	83	48.32 N	37.43 E
Konstantinovka, S.S.S.R.	265a	59.47 N	30.08 E
Konstantinovo	82	56.33 N	38.02 E
Konstantinovskij, S.S.S.R.	76	57.50 N	39.36 E
Konstantinovskij, S.S.S.R.	80	47.35 N	41.06 E
Konstantinovskije Porogi	76	60.34 N	37.04 E
Konstantynów Łódzki	30	51.45 N	19.20 E
Konstanz	58	47.40 N	9.10 E
Konstein	60	48.50 N	11.04 E
Kontagora	150	10.24 N	5.28 E
Kontcha	152	7.58 N	12.14 E
Kontejevo	80	58.26 N	41.21 E
Kontha	110	19.30 N	96.03 E
Kontich	50	51.08 N	4.27 E
Kontiolahti	26	62.46 N	29.51 E
Kontiomäki	26	64.21 N	28.09 E
Konto	115a	7.46 S	112.19 E
Kontum	110	14.21 N	108.00 E
Kontum, Plateau du ⛰[1]	110	13.55 N	108.05 E
Kōnu	96	34.42 N	133.05 E
Kon'uchovo	86	55.08 N	70.38 E
Konus, Gora ∧	180	67.34 N	178.10 E
Konya	130	37.52 N	32.31 E
Konya □[4]	130	38.00 N	33.00 E
Konyr	80	50.25 N	53.25 E
Konyrat	80	49.36 N	47.01 E
Konyrolen	86	44.16 N	79.19 E
Konyševka	78	51.51 N	35.18 E
Konystanu	80	48.51 N	53.20 E
Konz	56	49.42 N	6.34 E
Konza	154	1.45 S	37.07 E
Konžakovskij Kamen', Gora ∧	86	59.38 N	59.08 E
Konzell	60	49.04 N	12.43 E
Koocanusa, Lake ⊜[1]	202	49.00 N	115.10 W
Koog [aan de Zaan]	52	52.27 N	4.49 E
Kookynie	162	29.20 S	121.29 E
Koolamarra	166	20.12 S	140.14 E
Koolatah	164	15.53 S	142.27 E
Koolau Range ⛰	229c	21.35 N	158.00 W
Kooloonong	166	34.53 S	143.09 E
Koolskamp	50	51.00 N	3.12 E
Koombana Bay C	168a	33.18 S	115.36 E
Koonga	76	58.35 N	24.12 E
Koontz Lake	216	41.25 N	86.29 W
Koontz Lake ⊜	216	41.25 N	86.28 W
Koopan-Noord	158	26.53 S	20.41 E
Koopan-Suid	158	27.15 S	20.22 E
Koopmansfontein	158	28.14 S	24.01 E
Koosa	76	58.33 N	27.07 E
Koosfontein	158	27.22 S	25.27 E
Koosharem	200	38.31 N	111.53 W
Kooskia	202	46.09 N	115.59 W
Koossa	150	9.32 N	8.32 W
Kootenai (Kootenay) ≃	182	49.15 N	117.39 W
Kootenay (Kootenai) ≃	182	49.15 N	117.39 W
Kootenay Indian Reserve ◆[4]	182	49.37 N	115.45 W
Kootenay Lake ⊜	182	49.35 N	116.50 W
Kootenay National Park ♠	182	51.00 N	116.00 W
Kootjieskolk	158	31.15 S	20.21 E
Kootwijk	52	52.12 N	5.45 E
Kopa	85	43.32 N	75.50 E
Kopa ≃	85	43.40 N	76.15 E
Kopāganj	124	26.01 N	83.34 E
Kopāi ≃	126	23.48 N	87.47 E
Kopajgorod	78	48.51 N	27.48 E
Kopanbulak	86	48.56 N	80.52 E
Kopang	115b	8.39 S	116.21 E
Kopanovka	80	47.27 N	46.48 E
Kopanskaja	78	46.17 N	38.29 E
Kopapan	80	50.20 N	50.26 E
Kopargaon	122	19.53 N	74.29 E
Koparkhairna	272c	19.06 N	72.59 E
Koparpāda	272c	19.02 N	73.04 E
Kópasker	24a	66.20 N	16.24 W
Kopatkeviči	76	52.19 N	28.49 E
Kópavogur	24a	64.06 N	21.50 W
Kopceviči	78	52.14 N	28.19 E
Kop Dağı ∧	84	40.01 N	40.28 E
Kopdağı Geçidi)(	130	40.03 N	40.33 E
Kopejsk	86	55.07 N	61.37 E
Kopenhagen → København	41	55.40 N	12.35 E
Köpenick ◆[8]	54	52.27 N	13.34 E
Köpenick, Schloss ʊ	264a	52.27 N	13.34 E
Koper	36	45.33 N	13.44 E
Köpernitz	54	53.04 N	12.56 E
Kopervik	26	59.17 N	5.18 E
Kopeysk → Kopejsk	86	55.07 N	61.37 E
Kopice	54	53.44 N	14.32 E
Köping	40	59.31 N	16.00 E
Kopisty	54	50.34 N	13.35 E
Kopjevo	86	55.03 N	89.50 E
Koplik	38	42.13 N	19.26 E
Köpmanholmen	26	63.10 N	18.34 E
Kopnino	82	56.53 N	38.29 E
Kopondei, Tanjung ≻	115b	8.04 S	122.52 E
Koporje	76	59.44 N	29.01 E
Koporskij Zaliv C	76	59.52 N	28.55 E
Koppal	122	15.21 N	76.09 E
Koppang	26	61.34 N	11.04 E
Koppány ≃	30	46.35 N	18.26 E
Kopparberg	40	59.52 N	14.59 E
Kopparbergs Län □[6]	26	61.00 N	14.30 E
Koppeh Dāgh ⛰	128	37.50 N	58.00 E
Koppel	214	40.50 N	80.20 W
Kopperå	26	63.24 N	11.51 E
Kopperby	41	54.38 N	9.56 E
Kopperl	222	32.04 N	97.30 W
Koppi	89	48.32 N	140.07 E
Koppi ≃	89	48.33 N	140.08 E
Koppies	158	27.20 S	27.30 E
Koppom	26	59.43 N	12.09 E
Kopri	272c	19.11 N	72.58 E
Koprivnica	36	46.10 N	16.50 E
Köprü ≃	130	36.49 N	31.10 E
Köprüören	130	39.30 N	29.47 E
Kopt'ovo	80	56.43 N	40.31 E
Kor ≃	128	29.36 N	53.18 E
Kōra	94	35.12 N	136.15 E
Korab ⛰	38	41.47 N	20.34 E
Kor Aban	144	3.53 N	42.40 E
Korablino	80	53.55 N	40.01 E
Korahe	144	6.35 N	44.23 E
Kor'akovka	86	52.24 N	77.08 E
Kor'akskoje Nagorje ⛰	74	62.30 N	172.00 E
Kōraku-en ♠	96	34.38 N	133.53 E
Korakuen Stadium ♠	268	35.43 N	139.45 E
Korallenmeer → Coral Sea ⊤[2]	14	20.00 S	158.00 E
Koralpe ∧	61	46.47 N	14.58 E
Koralpe ⛰	61	46.50 N	14.58 E
Korannaberg ⛰	158	27.25 S	22.32 E
Korapun	164	5.25 S	152.00 E
Koraput	122	18.49 N	82.43 E
Koraraika, Baie de C	157b	17.45 S	43.57 E
Korarou, Lac ⊜	150	15.15 N	3.16 W
Korashir	144	3.20 N	46.22 E
Korat → Nakhon Ratchasima	110	14.58 N	102.07 E
Koratla	122	18.49 N	78.43 E
Kor'ažma	24	61.18 N	47.06 E
Korba, Bhārat	124	22.21 N	82.41 E
Korba, Tun.	36	36.35 N	10.52 E
Korbach	56	51.16 N	8.52 E
Korbeta	144	13.03 N	39.43 E
Korbol	146	10.01 N	17.43 E
Korbous	36	36.49 N	10.35 E
Korbu, Gunong ∧	114	4.43 N	101.17 E
Korçë	38	40.37 N	20.46 E
Korcevo	76	58.52 N	42.13 E
Korčula	36	42.58 N	17.08 E
Korčula, Otok I	36	42.57 N	16.50 E
Korčulanski Kanal ⋓	36	43.03 N	16.40 E
Kordestān □[4]	128	35.30 N	47.00 E
Kord Kūy	128	36.48 N	54.07 E
Kordovo	86	54.06 N	93.17 E
Korea □[1]	4	38.00 N	127.00 E
Korea, North □[1]	90		
	98	40.00 N	127.00 E
Korea, South □[1]	90		
	98	36.30 N	128.00 E
Korea Bay C	98	39.00 N	124.00 E
Korea Strait ⋓	90	34.00 N	129.00 E
Korea University ʊ[2]	271b	37.36 N	127.02 E
Korec	78	50.37 N	27.09 E
Korekozevo	82	54.20 N	36.11 E
Korelakša	24	65.33 N	32.22 E
Koreliči	76	53.34 N	26.08 E
Korem	144	12.30 N	39.30 E
Koré Mayroua	150	13.18 N	3.55 E
Koren (Die Wurzen))(	64	46.31 N	13.45 E
Korenkovo	78	45.07 N	36.24 E
Koren'ovo	78	51.25 N	34.55 E
Korenovsk	78	45.29 N	39.28 E
Korf	74	60.19 N	165.50 E
Korfovskij	89	48.14 N	135.02 E
Korga	158	30.12 S	20.28 E
Korgan	130	40.44 N	37.13 E
Korgašino	82	54.45 N	37.41 E
Kõrgessaare	76	58.59 N	22.28 E
Korgus	140	19.13 N	33.29 E
Korhogo	150	9.27 N	5.38 W
Korhogo □[5]	150	9.30 N	5.45 W
Kōri	270	34.47 N	135.39 E
Koridhallós	267c	37.59 N	23.39 E
Korido	164	0.50 S	135.35 E
Koriella	169	37.10 S	145.39 E
Korienzé	150	15.24 N	3.47 W
Korim	164	0.54 S	136.02 E
Korima, Oued el ∨	148	33.51 N	0.23 W
Koringberg	158	33.01 S	18.40 E
Koringplaas	158	32.48 S	20.58 E
Korinth	41	55.08 N	10.21 E
Korinthiakós Kólpos C	38	38.19 N	22.04 E
Kórinthos (Corinth)	38	37.56 N	22.56 E
Korínthou, Dhiórix ≍	38	37.57 N	22.56 E
Kóris-hegy ∧	30	47.18 N	17.45 E
Koritsa → Korçë	38	40.37 N	20.46 E
Köritz	54	52.51 N	12.27 E
Kōriyama, Nihon	92	37.24 N	140.23 E
Kōriyama → Yamato-Kōriyama, Nihon	96	34.38 N	135.47 E
Korizo, Passe de)(	146	22.28 N	15.27 E
Korkino, S.S.S.R.	86	54.54 N	61.23 E
Korkino, S.S.S.R.	88	54.23 N	105.14 E
Korkinskoje, Ozero ⊜	265a	59.55 N	30.44 E
Korkuteli	130	37.04 N	30.13 E
Korla → Kuerle	90	41.44 N	86.09 E
Korl'aki	80	57.06 N	46.57 E
Korliki	74	61.31 N	82.22 E
Körlin → Karlino	30	54.03 N	15.51 E
Korma, S.S.S.R.	76	53.08 N	30.48 E
Korma, S.S.S.R.	76	52.21 N	31.31 E
Kormakíti, Akrotírion ≻	130	35.24 N	32.56 E
Körmend	61	47.01 N	16.37 E
Kormilovka	86	55.00 N	74.06 E
Kormovoje	80	46.17 N	43.30 E
Kornat, Otok I	36	43.50 N	15.16 E
Körnebach ≃	263	51.35 N	7.38 E
Kornelimünster	56	50.43 N	6.11 E
Körner	54	51.13 N	10.35 E
Kornešty	78	47.22 N	27.59 E
Korneuburg	264b	48.21 N	16.20 E
Kórnik	30	52.17 N	17.04 E
Kornilovo	86	53.32 N	81.05 E
Kornin	78	50.06 N	29.32 E
Kornouchovo	80	55.33 N	49.53 E
Korn'ovo	265a	60.03 N	30.45 E
Kornsjø	26	58.57 N	11.39 E
Kornwestheim	56	48.52 N	9.11 E
Koro, C. Iv.	150	8.34 N	7.28 W
Koro, Mali	150	14.04 N	3.05 W
Koro I	175g	17.19 S	179.23 E
Koroba	164	5.40 S	142.45 E
Koroča	78	50.48 N	37.11 E
Korodougou	150	12.26 N	6.17 W
Köroglu Tepesi ∧	130	40.31 N	31.53 E
Korogwe	154	5.09 S	38.29 E
Koroit	166	38.17 S	142.22 E
Korolevskij Belok, Gora ∧	86	51.00 N	83.43 E
Korolevu	175g	18.13 S	177.44 E
Korol'ovo	78	48.09 N	23.08 E
Korol'ovščina	76	55.49 N	31.45 E
Korom, Bahr ≃	146	10.35 N	19.45 E
Koromba ∧	175g	17.53 S	177.34 E
Koromiri I	174k	21.15 S	159.43 W
Koromo → Toyota	94	35.05 N	137.09 E
Koronadal	116	6.30 N	124.51 E
Kor'onevo	265b	55.40 N	38.00 E
Koróni	38	36.48 N	21.56 E
Korónia, Límni ⊜	38	40.41 N	23.05 E
Koronowo	30	53.19 N	17.57 E
Korop	78	51.34 N	32.56 E
Koropele	152	4.44 N	17.11 E
Koropíon	38	37.54 N	23.53 E
Koror	175b	7.20 N	134.29 E
Koror I	175b	7.20 N	134.30 E
Kororoit Creek ≃	274b	37.52 S	144.52 E
Körös ≃	30	46.43 N	20.12 E
Koro Sea ⊤[2]	175g	18.00 S	179.50 E
Korosten'	78	50.57 N	28.39 E
Korostyšev	78	50.19 N	29.03 E
Korotkova	88	56.43 N	107.55 E
Korotojak	78	50.59 N	39.10 E
Koro Toro	146	16.05 N	18.30 E
Korotovo	76	58.57 N	37.28 E
Korotyš	76	52.22 N	37.27 E
Korovincy	78	50.48 N	33.45 E
Korovin Island I	180	55.25 N	160.15 W
Korovin Volcano ∧[1]	180	52.22 N	174.10 W
Korovou	175g	17.57 S	178.21 E
Koroyanitu, Mount ∧	175g	17.40 S	177.35 E
Korožečna ≃	76	57.32 N	38.18 E
Korpela	24	66.15 N	30.01 E
Korpilahti	26	62.01 N	25.33 E
Korpo (Korppoo)	26	60.10 N	21.34 E
Korså	40	60.38 N	16.08 E
Korsakov	89	46.38 N	142.46 E
Korsakovo	76	53.16 N	37.21 E
Korschen → Korsze	30	54.10 N	21.09 E
Korschenbroich	56	51.11 N	6.31 E
Korselbränna	26	64.27 N	15.35 E
Korševo	78	51.11 N	40.07 E
Korsika → Corse I	36	42.00 N	9.00 E
Korsnäs, Suomi	26	62.47 N	21.12 E
Korsnäs, Sve.	40	60.35 N	15.43 E
Korso	26	60.21 N	25.06 E
Korsør	41	55.20 N	11.09 E
Körsüleymanlı	130	38.17 N	38.01 E
Korsun'	83	48.12 N	38.05 E
Koršunovo	88	58.37 N	110.10 E
Korsun'-Ševčenkovskij	78	49.26 N	31.16 E
Korsze	30	54.10 N	21.09 E
Kortelisy	78	51.51 N	24.25 E
Kortemark	50	51.02 N	3.02 E
Kortgene	52	51.34 N	3.48 E
Kortkeros	24	61.49 N	51.28 E
Kortrijk (Courtrai)	50	50.50 N	3.16 E
Korucu	130	39.28 N	27.22 E
Kor'ukovka	78	51.46 N	32.14 E
Korumburra	169	38.26 S	145.49 E
Korwai	124	24.08 N	78.03 E
Kōryō	96	34.33 N	135.45 E
Koryŏng	98	35.44 N	128.15 E
Koryst'	78	50.35 N	27.01 E
Koryta	60	49.24 N	13.13 E
Korženevskoj, Pik ∧	85	39.04 N	72.00 E
Koržeuc'	78	48.13 N	27.02 E
Korževka	80	54.12 N	46.22 E
Kos	38	36.53 N	27.18 E
Kos I	38	36.50 N	27.10 E
Kosa, S.S.S.R.	88	54.47 N	108.52 E
Kosa, Yai.	144	7.51 N	36.51 E
Kosa ≃, S.S.S.R.	24	60.11 N	55.10 E
Kosa ≃, S.S.S.R.	80	58.26 N	51.15 E
Kosa ⊥	150	15.50 N	7.00 W
Koš-Agač	86	50.00 N	88.40 E
Kosai	94	34.43 N	137.33 E
Kosaja, Šivera ⌞	88	58.24 N	97.48 E
Kosaja Gora	82	54.07 N	37.33 E
Kosaka	92	40.19 N	140.44 E
Kosa-Meečkyn, Ostrov I	180	65.26 N	178.00 W
Kosan	98	38.52 N	127.24 E
Košankol'	80	49.56 N	48.11 E
Kosčagyl	86	46.51 N	53.48 E
Kösching	60	48.49 N	11.30 E
Kościan	30	52.06 N	16.38 E
Kościerzyna	30	54.08 N	18.00 E
Kosciusko	194	32.58 N	89.35 W
Kosciusko □[6]	216	41.14 N	85.51 W
Kosciusko, Mount ∧	171b	36.27 S	148.16 E
Kosciusko National Park ♠	171b	36.10 S	148.15 E
Kösdağı ∧	130	40.59 N	34.25 E
Kosdaulet, Peski ◆[2]	80	47.45 N	49.30 E
Kose, Nihon	270	34.25 N	135.46 E
Kose, S.S.S.R.	76	59.11 N	25.10 E
Köse, Tür.	130	40.13 N	39.39 E
Kösefakılı	130	39.36 N	34.09 E
Koševka	82	55.09 N	38.05 E
Košelicha	80	55.02 N	43.33 E
Košerovo	82	55.38 N	38.22 E
Koserow	54	54.03 N	13.59 E
Kosha	140	20.49 N	30.32 E
Koshien Stadium ♠	270	34.42 N	135.22 E
Koshigaya	94	35.54 N	139.48 E
Koshigoe	268	35.18 N	139.30 E
Koshikijima-rettō II	92	31.45 N	129.49 E
Koshino	94	36.02 N	136.01 E
Koshk-e Kohneh	128	34.52 N	62.31 E
Koshkonong	194	36.36 N	91.39 W
Koshkonong, Lake ⊜	216	42.52 N	88.58 W
Koshkonong Creek ≃	216	42.53 N	88.59 W
Koshlong Lake ⊜	212	44.58 N	78.29 W
Kōshoku	94	36.38 N	138.06 E
Koshu → Kwangju	98	35.09 N	126.54 E
Kosi	124	27.48 N	77.26 E
Kosi, Lake ⊜	158	26.55 S	32.52 E
Košice	30	48.43 N	21.15 E
Kosigi	122	15.51 N	77.16 E
Kosikovo	76	59.52 N	43.23 E
Kosino, S.S.S.R.	80	58.23 N	51.17 E
Kosino, S.S.S.R.	82	55.43 N	37.52 E
Kosju	24	65.38 N	59.03 E
Kosju ≃	24	66.18 N	59.53 E
Kosjuvom	24	66.17 N	59.50 E
Köşk	130	37.51 N	28.03 E
Koskaecodde Lake ⊜	186	48.00 N	55.20 W
Koškar	86	47.27 N	53.29 E
Koški, S.S.S.R.	80	54.12 N	50.28 E
Koski, Suomi	26	60.39 N	23.09 E
Koškino	80	56.20 N	50.49 E
Koskol'	86	49.31 N	67.05 E
Koskuduk	86	44.06 N	77.22 E
Koskullskulle	24	67.12 N	20.50 E
Koslan	24	63.28 N	48.52 E
Köslin → Koszalin	30	54.12 N	16.09 E
Kosmonosy	54	50.26 N	15.00 E
Kosmosa, Monument ⊥	265b	55.49 N	37.38 E
Kosmynino	80	57.35 N	40.46 E
Kosogor	80	57.07 N	47.34 E
Kosolapovo	80	56.57 N	49.37 E
Kosŏng	98	34.58 N	128.18 E
Kosor	130	40.39 N	42.39 E
Kosov	78	48.19 N	25.05 E
Kosovska Mitrovica	38	42.53 N	20.52 E
Kosový potok ≃	60	49.46 N	12.48 E
Kösreli	130	37.11 N	35.59 E
Kossanto	150	13.08 N	11.58 W
Kossdorf	54	51.29 N	13.14 E
Kosse	222	31.18 N	96.38 W
Kössen	64	47.40 N	12.24 E
Kösslarn	60	48.22 N	13.07 E
Kossol Passage ⋓	175b	7.52 N	134.36 E
Kossol Reef ✢[2]	175b	7.57 N	134.41 E
Kossovo	76	52.45 N	25.09 E
Kossuth	214	41.17 N	79.35 W
Kosta	26	56.51 N	15.23 E
Košt'ahy	54	50.39 N	13.45 E
Kostajnica	36	45.14 N	16.33 E
Koš-Tegirmen	85	42.47 N	73.53 E
Kostelec nad Labem	54	50.11 N	14.35 E
Kostenec	38	42.16 N	23.49 E
Koster	158	25.57 S	26.42 E
Kosterevo	80	55.56 N	39.37 E
Kosteröarna I	26	58.54 N	11.02 E
Kostešty	78	46.52 N	28.44 E
Koštice	54	50.24 N	13.55 E
Kostino, S.S.S.R.	80	52.24 N	51.39 E
Kostino, S.S.S.R.	80	52.11 N	51.20 E
Kostino, S.S.S.R.	82	56.18 N	37.43 E
Kostino, S.S.S.R.	265b	55.55 N	37.51 E
Kostino-Otdelec	78	51.33 N	41.26 E
Kost'kovo	76	60.02 N	33.14 E
Košt'ob'o	85	41.06 N	74.15 E
Kostonjärvi ⊜	26	65.47 N	28.27 E
Kostopol'	78	50.53 N	26.26 E
Kostriževka	78	48.38 N	25.41 E
Kostroma	76	57.46 N	40.55 E
Kostroma ≃	24	57.47 N	40.55 E
Kostrovo	82	55.53 N	36.42 E
Kostrzyn	30	52.37 N	14.39 E
Kost'ukoviči	76	53.20 N	32.03 E
Kost'ukovka	76	52.32 N	30.56 E
Kosugaya ◆[8]	268	35.22 N	139.33 E
Kosuge	94	35.45 N	138.57 E
Kosugi	94	36.43 N	137.06 E
Kosum Phisai	110	16.13 N	103.01 E
Koszalin (Köslin)	30	54.12 N	16.09 E
Kőszeg	61	47.23 N	16.33 E
Koszyce	30	50.11 N	20.35 E
Kota, Bhārat	120	25.11 N	75.50 E
Kota, Bhārat	124	22.18 N	82.02 E
Kota, Malay.	114	5.35 N	100.23 E
Kota, Malay.	114	2.31 N	102.10 E
Kota □[5]	124	25.00 N	76.30 E
Kotabaharu, Indon.	112	0.48 S	111.33 E
Kota Baharu, Malay.	114	6.08 N	102.15 E
Kotabaru → Jayapura, Indon.	164	2.32 S	140.42 E
Kot Addu	123	30.28 N	70.58 E
Kotagiri	122	11.26 N	76.53 E
Kot'ajevka	80	46.33 N	48.46 E
Kotake	96	33.30 N	130.40 E
Kota Kinabalu (Jesselton)	112	5.59 N	116.04 E
Kota Kota → Nkhota Kota	154	12.57 S	34.17 E
Kotālpur	126	23.02 N	87.36 E
Kotamobagu	112	0.46 N	124.19 E
Kotapinang	114	1.53 N	100.05 E
Kotari ⛰	36	44.05 N	15.30 E
Kota Sarang Semut	114	5.59 N	100.24 E
Kotatengah	114	1.05 N	100.33 E
Kota Tinggi	114	1.44 N	103.54 E
Kotawaringin	112	2.29 S	111.25 E
Kotchāndpur	124	23.24 N	89.01 E
Kotcho Lake ⊜	176	59.05 N	121.10 W
Kot Chutta	123	29.53 N	70.39 E
Kotdwāra	124	29.45 N	78.32 E
Kotel	38	42.53 N	26.27 E
Kotel'nyj, Ostrov I	74	75.45 N	138.44 E
Kot Fateh	123	30.07 N	75.05 E
Köthen	54	51.45 N	11.58 E
Koti → Kōchi	96	33.33 N	133.33 E
Kotido	154	3.00 N	34.06 E
Kotka	26	60.28 N	26.55 E
Kot Kapūra	123	30.35 N	74.54 E
Kotla, Bhārat	123	32.15 N	76.02 E
Kotla, Lībīya	146	28.33 N	18.58 E
Kotlas	24	61.16 N	46.35 E
Kotlenski prohod)(	38	42.53 N	26.27 E
Kotli	123	33.31 N	73.55 E
Kotlik	180	63.02 N	163.33 W
Kotlin, Ostrov I	265a	60.00 N	29.46 E
Kot Mūmin	123	32.11 N	73.02 E
Kōtō ◆[8]	268	35.41 N	139.48 E
Koto ≃, Nihon	96	34.21 N	134.02 E
Koto ≃, Nihon	96	33.58 N	131.13 E
Kotobiki-san ∧	96	35.03 N	132.47 E
Kotohira ʊ[1]	96	34.11 N	133.49 E
Kotohira-yama ∧	96	34.11 N	133.48 E
Koton-Karifi	150	8.08 N	6.48 E
Kotonkoro	150	11.02 N	5.58 E
Kotor	38	42.25 N	18.46 E
Kotoriba	36	46.21 N	16.49 E
Kotorovo	80	54.54 N	41.35 E
Kotor Varoš	36	44.37 N	17.23 E
Kotovka	78	49.08 N	34.57 E
Kotovo	80	50.18 N	44.50 E
Kotovsk, S.S.S.R.	78	46.49 N	28.34 E
Kotovsk, S.S.S.R.	78	47.45 N	29.33 E
Kotovsk, S.S.S.R.	80	52.36 N	41.32 E
Kot Pūtli	124	27.43 N	76.12 E
Kotra, Bhārat	120	24.22 N	73.10 E
Kotra, Bhārat	272b	22.46 N	88.34 E
Kot Rādha Kishan	123	31.10 N	74.06 E
Kotri	120	25.22 N	68.18 E
Kotri Allahrakhio	120	24.24 N	67.50 E
Kotrung → Uttarpara-Kotrung	272b	22.40 N	88.21 E
Kötschach	64	46.40 N	13.00 E
Kot Sultān	123	30.46 N	70.56 E
Kōtsu-zan ∧	96	34.01 N	134.12 E
Kottagūdem	122	17.33 N	80.38 E
Kottai Malai ∧	122	9.30 N	77.24 E
Kottas Mountains ⛰	9	74.20 S	12.00 W
Kottayam	122	9.35 N	76.31 E
Kotte	122	6.54 N	79.54 E
Kottenforst, Naturpark ♠	56	50.20 N	6.55 E

Name	Seite	Breite°′	Länge°′ E=Ost
Kotto ≃	152	4.14 N	22.02 E
Kotton	144	9.37 N	50.32 E
Kottūr	122	10.32 N	76.59 E
Kottūru	122	14.49 N	76.13 E
Kotuj ≃	74	71.55 N	102.05 E
Kotum	130	38.25 N	42.18 E
Kot'užen'	78	47.51 N	28.36 E
Kotwālīpāra	126	22.59 N	89.59 E
Kotzebue	180	66.53 N	162.39 W
Kotzebue Sound ⋓	180	66.20 N	163.00 W
Kotzenau → Chocianów	30	51.25 N	15.55 E
Kötzting	60	49.11 N	12.52 E
Koualé	150	11.24 N	7.01 W
Kouan	106	32.19 N	119.52 E
Kouandé	150	10.20 N	1.42 E
Kouango	152	4.58 N	19.59 E
Koubansaki	273b	4.22 S	15.09 E
Koubia	150	11.35 N	11.54 W
Kouchibouguac Bay C	186	46.50 N	64.50 W
Kouchibouguac National Park ♠	186	46.50 N	65.00 W
Koudougou	150	12.15 N	2.22 W
Kouéré	150	10.27 N	3.59 W
Koueveldberge ⛰	158	32.10 S	24.08 E
Kouga	146	9.56 N	21.03 E
Kougaberge ⛰	158	33.40 S	23.50 E
Kougarok Mountain ∧	180	65.41 N	165.13 W
K'ouhu	100	23.35 N	120.10 E
Kouilou □[5]	152	4.00 S	12.00 E
Kouilou ≃	152	4.28 S	11.41 E
Koukdjuak ≃	176	66.45 N	73.09 W
Kouki	152	7.10 N	17.18 E
Koúklia	130	34.42 N	32.34 E
Koukourou ≃	152	7.32 N	19.42 E
Koula-Moutou	152	1.08 S	12.29 E
Koulia Ba	150	14.11 N	14.28 W
Koulikoro	150	12.53 N	7.33 W
Koulouguidi	150	13.27 N	11.03 W
Koulountou ≃	150	13.15 N	13.37 W
Koumac	175f	20.33 S	164.17 E
Koumala	166	21.37 S	149.15 E
Koumameyong	152	0.11 N	11.51 E
Koumankou Markala	150	12.06 N	6.08 W
Koumbakara	150	12.42 N	14.29 W
Koumbal	146	9.26 N	22.39 E
Koumbala ≃	146	9.14 N	20.42 E
Koumban	152	7.43 N	15.12 E
Koumbia, Guinée	150	11.48 N	13.30 W
Koumbia, H. Vol.	150	11.14 N	3.42 W
Koumbisaleh ⊥	150	15.55 N	8.05 W
Koumbouma	150	10.24 N	12.56 W
Koumi	94	36.05 N	138.29 E
Koumou ∧	140	9.34 N	23.38 E
Koumpenntoum	150	13.59 N	14.34 W
Koumra	146	8.55 N	17.33 E
Koun	150	7.29 N	3.15 W
Kounda Ko ≃	150	12.13 N	11.03 W
Koundara	150	12.29 N	13.18 W
Koundara □[4]	150	12.25 N	13.10 W
Koundé	152	6.07 N	14.38 E
Koundougou	150	11.44 N	4.31 W
Koungheul	150	13.59 N	14.48 W
Koungoulou	152	3.32 S	13.20 E
Kouniohou	150	7.40 N	0.48 E
Kounradskij	86	46.59 N	75.00 E
Kountze	194	30.23 N	94.19 W
Koupé, Mont ∧	152	4.47 N	9.43 E
Koupéla	150	12.11 N	0.21 W
Kouqian	89	43.40 N	126.30 E
Kour, Oued n' ≃	34	35.14 N	3.45 W
Kouragué	150	12.18 N	10.02 W
Kourak	86	54.50 N	84.40 E
Kouriles,, Détroit des → Pervyj Kuril'skij Proliv ⋓	74	50.50 N	156.36 E
Kouri-shima I	174m	26.42 N	128.01 E
Kourou	250	5.09 N	52.39 W
Kouroukoto	150	12.35 N	10.05 W
Kourouma	150	11.37 N	4.48 W
Kourouninkoto	150	13.52 N	9.35 W
Kouroussa	150	10.39 N	9.53 W
Kouroussa □[4]	150	10.40 N	9.55 W
Kourtiagou, Réserve de ◆[4]	150	11.35 N	1.30 E
Koury	150	12.11 N	4.48 W
Koussanar	150	13.52 N	14.05 W
Koussané, Mali	150	14.53 N	11.14 W
Koussane, Sén.	150	14.08 N	12.26 W
Kousser, Massif ∧	148	32.02 N	5.59 W
Koussi, Emi ∧	146	19.50 N	18.30 E
Koussili	150	13.30 N	11.38 W
Koutiala	150	12.23 N	5.28 W
Kouto	150	9.53 N	6.25 W
Koutomo I	175f	22.40 S	167.33 E
Koutou	98	38.35 N	114.24 E
Koutouba	150	8.41 N	3.12 W
Kouts	216	41.19 N	87.02 W
Kouvola	26	60.52 N	26.42 E
Kouya ≃	150	10.09 N	9.45 W
Kouyou ≃	152	0.45 S	16.38 E
Kova	88	58.18 N	100.21 E
Kova ≃	88	58.18 N	100.18 E
Kovaksa	80	55.31 N	43.30 E
Koval'ovka	78	47.16 N	31.43 E
Kovarskas	76	55.26 N	24.55 E
Kovarzino	76	60.09 N	38.33 E
Kovdor	24	67.34 N	30.22 E
Kovdozero, Ozero ⊜	24	66.47 N	32.00 E
Kovel'	78	51.14 N	24.41 E
Kovernino	80	57.07 N	43.49 E
Kovilpatti	122	9.10 N	77.52 E
Kovin	38	44.45 N	20.59 E
Kovno → Kaunas	76	54.54 N	23.54 E
Kovpyta	78	51.23 N	30.50 E
Kovrina Vtoraja	80	47.01 N	41.44 E
Kovrov	80	56.22 N	41.18 E
Kovševata	78	49.29 N	30.38 E
Kovsug ≃	83	48.48 N	39.17 E
Kovūr	122	14.29 N	79.59 E
Kovvur	122	17.01 N	81.44 E
Kovylkin	80	48.16 N	41.28 E
Kovylkino	80	54.02 N	43.56 E
Kovža	24	61.09 N	38.58 E
Kovžinskij Zavod	76	60.24 N	37.04 E
Kowa	164	7.53 S	140.32 E
Kowal	30	52.32 N	19.09 E
Kowalewo Pomorskie	30	53.10 N	18.53 E
Kowangge	115b	8.16 S	118.32 E
Kowār	126	24.13 N	86.11 E
Koweït → Kuwait □[1]	128	29.30 N	47.45 E
Kowel → Kovel'	78	51.14 N	24.41 E
Kowhitirangi	172	42.52 S	171.01 E
Kowie → Port Alfred	158	33.36 S	26.55 E
Kowkcheh ≃	120	37.10 N	69.23 E
Kowloon (Jiulong)	271d	22.18 N	114.10 E
Kowloon City	271d	22.19 N	114.11 E
Kowmung ≃	170	33.52 S	150.16 E
Kowŏn	98	39.26 N	127.14 E
Kowt-e 'Ashrow	120	34.27 N	68.48 E
Kōya	96	34.12 N	135.35 E
Koyadaira	96	33.56 N	134.13 E
Kōyaguchi	96	34.18 N	135.33 E
Koyama ◆[8]	268	35.37 N	139.43 E
Koyama-ike ⊜	96	35.30 N	134.09 E
Kōyama-misaki ≻	96	34.40 N	131.36 E
Koyambattur → Coimbatore	122	11.00 N	76.58 E
Koyang-ni	98	37.42 N	126.56 E
Köyceğiz	130	36.57 N	28.41 E
Köyceğiz Gölü ⊜	130	36.55 N	28.40 E
Koyna Reservoir ⊜[1]	122	17.25 N	73.45 E
Koyra ≃[1]	126	22.27 N	89.16 E
Koyuk	180	64.56 N	161.08 W

Symbols in the index entries represent the broad categories identified in the key at the right. Symbols with superior numbers (⛰[2]) identify subcategories (see complete key on page *I* · *30*).

Kartensymbole in dem Registerverzeichnis stellen die rechts in Schlüssel erklärten Kategorien dar. Symbole mit hochgestellten Ziffern (⛰[2]) bezeichnen Unterabteilungen einer Kategorie (vgl. vollständiger Schlüssel auf Seite *I* · *30*).

Los símbolos incluídos en el texto del índice representan las grandes categorias identificadas con la clave a la derecha. Los símbolos con numeros en su parte superior (⛰[2]) identifican las subcategorías (véase la clave completa en la página *I* · *30*).

Les symboles de l'index représentent les catégories indiquées dans la légende à droite. Les symboles suivis d'un indice (⛰[2]) représentent des sous-catégories (voir légende complète à la page *I* · *30*).

Os símbolos incluídos no texto do índice representam as grandes categorias identificadas com a chave à direita. Os símbolos com números em sua parte superior (⛰[2]) identificam as subcategorias (veja-se a chave completa à página *I* · *30*).

	English	Deutsch	Español	Français	Português
∧	Mountain	Berg	Montaña	Montagne	Montanha
⛰	Mountains	Berge	Montañas	Montagnes	Montanhas
)(	Pass	Pass	Paso	Col	Passo
∨	Valley, Canyon	Tal, Cañon	Valle, Cañón	Vallée, Canyon	Vale, Canhão
⌣	Plain	Ebene	Llano	Plaine	Planície
≻	Cape	Kap	Cabo	Cap	Cabo
I	Island	Insel	Isla	Île	Ilha
II	Islands	Inseln	Islas	Îles	Ilhas
•	Other Topographic Features	Andere Topographische Objekte	Otros Elementos Topográficos	Autres données topographiques	Outros Elementos Topográficos

ESPAÑOL

Nombre	Página	Lat.°′	Long.°′ W=Oeste
Koyuk ≃	180	64.55 N	161.12 W
Koyukuk	180	64.53 N	157.43 W
Koyukuk ≃	180	64.56 N	157.30 W
Koyukuk, Middle Fork ≃	180	67.03 N	151.04 W
Koyukuk, North Fork ≃	180	67.03 N	151.04 W
Koyukuk, South Fork ≃	180	66.35 N	151.57 W
Koyulhisar	130	40.18 N	37.51 E
Koyuneli	130	39.50 N	27.15 E
Köyyeri	130	38.30 N	36.30 E
Koza, Nihon	174m	26.20 N	127.50 E
Koža, S.S.S.R.	80	57.47 N	48.57 E
Kozağacı	130	39.24 N	31.50 E
Kozakai	94	34.48 N	137.22 E
Kōzaki	94	35.54 N	140.24 E
Kō-zaki ›	92	34.05 N	129.13 E
Kozaklı	130	39.14 N	34.49 E
Kōzan, Nihon	96	34.35 N	133.03 E
Kozan, Tür.	130	37.27 N	35.49 E
Kozáni	38	40.18 N	21.47 E
Kožanka	78	49.58 N	29.46 E
Kožany, S.S.S.R.	76	52.48 N	31.44 E
Koz'any, S.S.S.R.	76	55.18 N	26.52 E
Kozara ⛰	36	45.00 N	16.50 E
Kozarac	36	44.58 N	16.51 E
Kozdinga	24	63.43 N	47.32 E
Kozelec	78	50.55 N	31.08 E
Kozel'ščina	78	49.13 N	33.51 E
Kozel'sk	82	54.02 N	35.48 E
Koževnikovo	86	56.16 N	84.00 E
Kozhikode → Calicut	122	11.15 N	75.46 E
Koziegłowy	30	50.36 N	19.09 E
Kozienice	30	51.35 N	21.33 E
Kožim	24	65.48 N	59.28 E
Kožimiz, Gora ∧	24	63.12 N	58.48 E
Kozin	78	50.14 N	30.39 E
Kozino	265b	55.54 N	37.11 E
Kozjak (Possruck) ⛰	61	46.37 N	15.28 E
Koźle	30	50.20 N	18.08 E
Kozlov	78	49.33 N	25.20 E
Kozlov Bereg	76	58.57 N	27.44 E
Kozlovka, S.S.S.R.	78	51.39 N	41.16 E
Kozlovka, S.S.S.R.	78	50.52 N	40.27 E
Kozlovka, S.S.S.R.	80	52.33 N	45.41 E
Kozlovka, S.S.S.R.	80	55.52 N	48.14 E
Kozlovo, S.S.S.R.	76	57.34 N	35.29 E
Kozlovo, S.S.S.R.	82	56.31 N	36.16 E
Kozlovščina	76	53.19 N	25.18 E
Kozlu, Tür.	130	41.26 N	31.46 E
Kozlu, Tür.	130	40.37 N	36.30 E
Koźmin	30	51.50 N	17.28 E
Koz'mino	24	61.56 N	48.19 E
Koz'modemjansk	80	56.20 N	46.36 E
Koz'mogorodskoje	24	65.32 N	44.55 E
Kozova	78	49.26 N	25.09 E
Kožpos'olok	24	63.10 N	38.06 E
Kožuchovo	265b	55.43 N	37.54 E
Kożuchów	30	51.45 N	15.35 E
Kozuka	268	35.09 N	139.57 E
Kōzuki	96	34.59 N	134.20 E
Kozukue ✦[8]	268	35.30 N	139.36 E
Kozul'ka	86	56.10 N	91.24 E
Kožurla	86	55.21 N	79.02 E
Kōzu-shima I	92	34.13 N	139.10 E
Kozuya	270	34.52 N	135.45 E
Kožva	24	65.07 N	56.57 E
Kpandae	150	8.28 N	0.01 W
Kpandu	150	7.00 N	0.18 E
Kpong	150	6.09 N	0.04 E
Kra, Isthmus of ✦[3]	110	10.20 N	99.00 E
Kraai ≃	158	30.40 S	26.45 E
Kraaifontein	158	33.50 S	18.43 E
Kraal	158	26.34 S	28.26 E
Kraankuil	158	29.52 S	24.10 E
Krabbendijke	52	51.26 N	4.07 E
Krabi	110	8.04 N	98.55 E
Krâchéh	110	12.29 N	106.01 E
Krackow	54	53.20 N	14.16 E
Kraftsdorf	54	50.52 N	11.55 E
Kragan	115a	6.42 S	111.37 E
Kragenæs	41	54.55 N	11.22 E
Kragerø	26	58.52 N	9.25 E
Kraghave	41	54.48 N	11.53 E
Kragujevac	38	44.01 N	20.55 E
Krahenhöhe ✦[8]	263	51.10 N	7.06 E
Kraiburg	60	48.10 N	12.26 E
Kraichgau □[9]	56	49.10 N	8.50 E
Krainburg → Kranj	36	46.15 N	14.21 E
Krainka	82	54.07 N	36.21 E
Krai-Russkije	80	57.23 N	46.50 E
Krajenka	30	53.19 N	17.00 E
Krajeva	89	44.54 N	131.08 E
Krajneje	80	47.29 N	46.01 E
Krajnik Dolny	54	53.05 N	14.25 E
Krajnovka	84	43.57 N	47.24 E
Krakatau ∧[1]	115a	6.07 S	105.24 E
Krakatoa → Krakatau ∧[1]	115a	6.07 S	105.24 E
Krakau → Kraków	30	50.03 N	19.58 E
Krâkôr	110	12.32 N	104.12 E
Krakovec	78	49.57 N	23.07 E
Krakovo	80	53.36 N	50.51 E
Krakow, D.D.R.	54	53.39 N	12.16 E
Kraków, Pol.	30	50.03 N	19.58 E
Krakower See @	54	53.37 N	12.17 E
Kraksaan	115a	7.46 S	113.25 E
Kraksdorf	54	54.18 N	11.04 E
Kralendijk	241s	12.10 N	68.17 W
Kraljevica	36	45.16 N	14.34 E
Kraljevo	38	43.43 N	20.41 E
Kralovice	60	49.59 N	13.29 E
Královské Vinohrady ✦[8]	54	50.01 N	14.29 E
Kralupy nad Vltavou	54	50.11 N	14.18 E
Kralupy u Chomutova	54	50.25 N	13.20 E
Kramatorsk	83	48.43 N	37.32 E
Kramer	216	40.20 N	87.17 W
Kramfors	26	62.56 N	17.47 E
Krammer Ʉ	52	51.38 N	4.15 E
Krampen	61	47.40 N	15.32 E
Krampnitz	264a	52.28 N	13.04 E
Krampnitzsee @	264a	52.27 N	13.03 E
Kramsach	64	47.27 N	11.52 E
Kranebitten, Flughafen ⊠	64	47.16 N	11.20 E
Kranenburg	52	51.47 N	6.03 E
Krångede	26	63.09 N	16.05 E
Kranichfeld	54	50.51 N	11.12 E
Kranídhion	38	37.22 N	23.10 E
Kranj	36	46.15 N	14.21 E
Kranji	271c	1.26 N	103.45 E
Kranji ≃	271c	1.26 N	103.45 E
Kranji War Memorial ⊥	271c	1.26 N	103.45 E
Kranjska Gora	64	46.29 N	13.47 E
Kranskop	158	29.00 S	30.47 E
Kranskop ∧	158	27.43 S	29.41 E
Kranzberg	156	21.55 S	15.43 E
Krapina	36	46.10 N	15.52 E
Krapivinskij	86	55.00 N	86.49 E
Krapivna	76	53.38 N	35.31 E
Krapkowice	30	50.29 N	17.56 E
Krapperup	41	56.16 N	12.31 E
Krappitz → Krapkowice	30	50.29 N	17.56 E
Krapuh	114	3.39 N	98.10 E
Kras ⛰[1]	64	45.48 N	14.00 E
Krasavino	24	60.58 N	46.26 E
Krasavka	80	51.11 N	43.24 E
Krasieo ≃	110	14.49 N	100.05 E
Krasilov	78	49.39 N	26.59 E
Krasino	72	70.45 N	54.27 E
Krasivaja Meča ≃	76	52.55 N	39.03 E
Krasivka	80	52.16 N	42.31 E
Krasivoje	86	51.54 N	66.46 E

FRANÇAIS

Nom	Page	Lat.°′	Long.°′ W=Ouest
Kraskino	89	42.44 N	130.48 E
Kraskovo	265b	55.39 N	37.59 E
Krāslava	76	55.54 N	27.10 E
Kraslice	54	50.18 N	12.31 E
Krasnaja ≃	83	49.01 N	38.15 E
Krasnaja Gora, S.S.S.R.	76	60.16 N	35.42 E
Krasnaja Gora, S.S.S.R.	76	53.01 N	31.37 E
Krasnaja Gorbatka	80	55.52 N	41.46 E
Krasnaja Gorka	80	56.12 N	43.04 E
Krasnaja Jaranga	180	65.40 N	172.50 W
Krasnaja Jaruga	78	50.48 N	35.39 E
Krasnaja Pachra	82	55.27 N	37.17 E
Krasnaja Pol'ana, S.S.S.R.	78	47.33 N	37.05 E
Krasnaja Pol'ana, S.S.S.R.	80	46.06 N	41.30 E
Krasnaja Pol'ana, S.S.S.R.	80	56.15 N	51.09 E
Krasnaja Pol'ana, S.S.S.R.	80	52.13 N	53.38 E
Krasnaja Poljana	84	43.41 N	40.13 E
Krasnaja Popovka	83	49.08 N	38.09 E
Krasnaja Sloboda, S.S.S.R.	76	52.51 N	27.10 E
Krasnaja Sloboda, S.S.S.R.	84	41.24 N	48.31 E
Krasnaja Talovka	83	48.51 N	39.51 E
Krasnaja Vol'a	76	52.23 N	27.04 E
Krasnaja Zar'a	76	52.47 N	37.41 E
Krásná Lípa	54	50.54 N	14.31 E
Krasn'anka	80	51.04 N	47.56 E
Krasneno	180	64.38 N	174.48 E
Kraśnik	30	50.56 N	22.13 E
Kraśnik Fabryczny	30	50.58 N	22.12 E
Krasnoarmejsk, S.S.S.R.	80	51.02 N	45.42 E
Krasnoarmejsk, S.S.S.R.	80	48.31 N	44.30 E
Krasnoarmejsk, S.S.S.R.	82	56.08 N	38.08 E
Krasnoarmejsk, S.S.S.R.	83	48.17 N	37.11 E
Krasnoarmejskaja	78	45.23 N	38.12 E
Krasnobród	30	50.33 N	23.13 E
Krasnobrodskij	86	54.10 N	86.28 E
Krasnodar	78	45.02 N	39.00 E
Krasnodar □[8]	80	44.10 N	40.30 E
Krasnodarskij	83	48.15 N	39.51 E
Krasnodon	83	48.17 N	39.48 E
Krasnofarfornyj	76	59.08 N	31.51 E
Krasnoflotskoje	80	50.04 N	41.14 E
Krasnogorka	85	43.15 N	75.10 E
Krasnogorodskoje	76	56.50 N	28.17 E
Krasnogorovka	83	48.00 N	37.31 E
Krasnogorsk, S.S.S.R.	82	55.50 N	37.20 E
Krasnogorsk, S.S.S.R.	89	48.24 N	142.06 E
Krasnogorskij, S.S.S.R.	80	56.09 N	48.20 E
Krasnogorskij, S.S.S.R.	85	41.09 N	69.39 E
Krasnogorskij, S.S.S.R.	86	54.36 N	61.15 E
Krasnogorskoje, S.S.S.R.	80	57.42 N	52.30 E
Krasnogorskoje, S.S.S.R.	86	52.18 N	86.12 E
Krasnogovardejskij	86	57.22 N	62.20 E
Krasnograd	78	49.22 N	35.27 E
Krasnogvardejsk	85	39.46 N	67.16 E
Krasnoil'sk	78	48.01 N	25.34 E
Krasnojar	80	48.54 N	51.46 E
Krasnojarka, S.S.S.R.	86	59.26 N	60.30 E
Krasnojarka, S.S.S.R.	86	55.20 N	73.04 E
Krasnoj Armii, Proliv Ʉ	74	80.00 N	94.35 E
Krasnojarovo	89	51.27 N	128.28 E
Krasnojarsk	86	56.01 N	92.50 E
Krasnojarsk □[7]	88	56.00 N	94.00 E
Krasnojarskij	86	51.58 N	59.55 E
Krasnojarskoje Vodochranilišče @[1]	86	55.00 N	92.00 E
Krasnoje, S.S.S.R.	24	59.12 N	47.49 E
Krasnoje, S.S.S.R.	76	52.51 N	38.47 E
Krasnoje, S.S.S.R.	76	53.06 N	33.55 E
Krasnoje, S.S.S.R.	76	54.14 N	27.05 E
Krasnoje, S.S.S.R.	78	46.44 N	39.34 E
Krasnoje, S.S.S.R.	78	46.38 N	29.50 E
Krasnoje, S.S.S.R.	78	50.56 N	38.41 E
Krasnoje, S.S.S.R.	78	50.21 N	38.50 E
Krasnoje, S.S.S.R.	82	54.26 N	38.38 E
Krasnoje, S.S.S.R.	83	48.23 N	39.31 E
Krasnoje, S.S.S.R.	83	48.25 N	37.19 E
Krasnoje, S.S.S.R.	86	54.37 N	85.23 E
Krasnoje, Ozero @	74	64.30 N	174.24 E
Krasnoje Echo	80	55.48 N	40.42 E
Krasnoje Gorodišče	82	54.04 N	38.44 E
Krasnoje-na-Volge	80	57.31 N	41.14 E
Krasnoje Selo, S.S.S.R.	80	48.46 N	42.20 E
Krasnoje Selo, S.S.S.R.	80	48.02 N	45.13 E
Krasnoje Selo, S.S.S.R.	265a	59.44 N	30.05 E
Krasnoje Znam'a, S.S.S.R.	76	57.26 N	35.13 E
Krasnoje Znam'a, S.S.S.R.	128	36.58 N	62.30 E
Krasnokamsk	86	58.04 N	55.48 E
Krasnokutsk	78	50.06 N	35.09 E
Krasnokutskoje	86	53.01 N	75.59 E
Krasnolesje	76	54.24 N	22.23 E
Krasnolesnyj	78	51.53 N	39.35 E
Krasnoluki	76	54.37 N	28.50 E
Krasnomajskij	76	57.37 N	34.22 E
Krasnookt'abr'skij, S.S.S.R.	80	56.40 N	47.45 E
Krasnookt'abr'skij, S.S.S.R.	80	48.53 N	44.45 E
Krasnookt'abr'skij, S.S.S.R.	85	42.50 N	74.18 E
Krasnooskol'skoje Vodochranilišče @[1]	83	49.17 N	37.37 E
Krasnoostrovskij	76	60.18 N	28.40 E
Krasnopavlovka	78	49.08 N	36.19 E
Krasnoperekopsk	78	45.57 N	33.47 E
Krasnopolje, S.S.S.R.	76	53.20 N	31.24 E
Krasnopolje, S.S.S.R.	78	50.46 N	35.16 E
Krasnorečenskij	89	44.41 N	135.14 E
Krasnoščelje	24	67.21 N	37.02 E
Krasnoščokovo	86	51.40 N	82.45 E
Krasnosel'kup	74	65.41 N	82.28 E
Krasnosel'sk	84	40.36 N	45.21 E
Krasnosel'skij	76	53.15 N	24.25 E
Krasnosel'skoje	78	45.25 N	32.42 E
Krasnosielc	30	53.03 N	21.10 E
Krasnoslobodsk, S.S.S.R.	80	48.42 N	44.34 E
Krasnoslobodsk, S.S.S.R.	80	54.26 N	43.48 E
Krasnotorka	83	48.41 N	37.31 E
Krasnoturansk	86	54.16 N	91.29 E
Krasnoturjinsk	86	59.46 N	60.12 E
Krasnoural'sk	86	58.21 N	60.03 E
Krasnousol'skij	86	53.54 N	56.27 E
Krasnovidovo	80	55.21 N	49.04 E
Krasnovišersk	24	60.23 N	56.59 E
Krasnovka, S.S.S.R.	83	47.24 N	37.26 E
Krasnovka, S.S.S.R.	83	48.47 N	40.07 E
Krasnovodsk	128	40.00 N	53.00 E
Krasnovodskij Poluostrov ›[1]	128	40.30 N	53.15 E
Krasnovodskij Zaliv C	128	39.55 N	53.15 E
Krasnoyarsk → Krasnojarsk	86	56.01 N	92.50 E

PORTUGUÊS

Nome	Página	Lat.°′	Long.°′ W=Oeste
Krasnozatonskij	24	61.41 N	50.58 E
Krasnozavodsk	82	56.27 N	38.25 E
Krasnoznamensk	76	54.57 N	22.30 E
Krasnoznamenskij	86	51.03 N	69.30 E
Krasnoz'orskoje	86	53.59 N	79.14 E
Krásný Dvůr	54	50.10 N	13.24 E
Krasnyj	76	54.34 N	31.26 E
Krasnyj Aul	86	51.03 N	81.02 E
Krasnyj Bazar	84	39.41 N	46.58 E
Krasnyj Bogatyr'	80	56.02 N	41.08 E
Krasnyj Bor, S.S.S.R.	80	55.17 N	43.59 E
Krasnyj Bor, S.S.S.R.	80	55.53 N	53.06 E
Krasnyj Bor, S.S.S.R.	265a	59.41 N	30.41 E
Krasnyj Cholm, S.S.S.R.	76	58.03 N	37.07 E
Krasnyj Cholm, S.S.S.R.	80	54.11 N	40.42 E
Krasnyj Cholm, S.S.S.R.	86	51.35 N	54.09 E
Krasnyj Čhuduk	80	46.18 N	46.56 E
Krasnyj Čikoj	88	50.22 N	108.15 E
Krasnyje Baki	80	57.08 N	45.10 E
Krasnyje Barrikady	80	46.14 N	47.53 E
Krasnyje Četai	80	55.42 N	46.09 E
Krasnyje Gory	76	58.57 N	29.29 E
Krasnyje Okny	78	47.32 N	29.27 E
Krasnyje Partizany	78	50.57 N	31.47 E
Krasnyje Tkač	76	55.28 N	39.05 E
Krasnyje Tkači	80	57.30 N	39.45 E
Krasnyj Gul'aj	80	54.01 N	48.22 E
Krasnyj Jar, S.S.S.R.	80	50.42 N	44.46 E
Krasnyj Jar, S.S.S.R.	80	46.33 N	48.21 E
Krasnyj Jar, S.S.S.R.	80	53.30 N	50.22 E
Krasnyj Jar, S.S.S.R.	80	51.38 N	46.25 E
Krasnyj Jar, S.S.S.R.	80	50.37 N	45.47 E
Krasnyj Jar, S.S.S.R.	86	57.07 N	84.33 E
Krasnyj Jar, S.S.S.R.	86	55.14 N	72.56 E
Krasnyj Jar, S.S.S.R.	86	55.54 N	86.57 E
Krasnyj Jar, S.S.S.R.	86	53.20 N	69.14 E
Krasnyj Kl'uč	86	55.26 N	56.12 E
Krasnyj Kut, S.S.S.R.	80	50.57 N	46.58 E
Krasnyj Kut, S.S.S.R.	83	48.12 N	38.48 E
Krasnyj Liman, S.S.S.R.	78	51.32 N	39.50 E
Krasnyj Liman, S.S.S.R.	83	48.59 N	37.49 E
Krasnyj Log	78	51.23 N	39.46 E
Krasnyj Luč, S.S.S.R.	76	57.04 N	30.05 E
Krasnyj Luč, S.S.S.R.	83	48.08 N	38.56 E
Krasnyj Majak	80	56.03 N	41.23 E
Krasnyj Manyč, S.S.S.R.	80	46.59 N	41.07 E
Krasnyj Manyč, S.S.S.R.	80	45.31 N	44.42 E
Krasnyj Manyč, S.S.S.R.	80	46.33 N	42.10 E
Krasnyj Meliorator	80	50.02 N	46.06 E
Krasnyj Okt'abr', S.S.S.R.	80	56.06 N	41.23 E
Krasnyj Okt'abr', S.S.S.R.	80	51.33 N	45.42 E
Krasnyj Okt'abr', S.S.S.R.	82	56.07 N	38.53 E
Krasnyj Okt'abr', S.S.S.R.	82	55.37 N	36.30 E
Krasnyj Okt'abr', S.S.S.R.	83	48.56 N	39.23 E
Krasnyj Okt'abr', S.S.S.R.	83	48.15 N	38.12 E
Krasnyj Okt'abr', S.S.S.R.	86	55.37 N	64.48 E
Krasnyj Okt'abr', S.S.S.R.	86	46.50 N	75.59 E
Krasnyj Oskol	83	49.11 N	37.26 E
Krasnyj Partizan	80	46.20 N	43.10 E
Krasnyj Perekop	78	46.41 N	33.46 E
Krasnyj Profintern	80	57.45 N	40.27 E
Krasnyj Rog	76	52.57 N	33.45 E
Krasnyj Steklovar	80	56.13 N	48.47 E
Krasnyj Stroitel' ✦[8]	265b	55.35 N	37.37 E
Krasnyj Sulin	83	47.54 N	40.03 E
Krasnyj Tekstil'ščik	80	51.23 N	45.50 E
Krasnyj Tkač	82	55.28 N	39.05 E
Krasnystaw	30	50.59 N	23.10 E
Krasnyy Luch → Krasnyj Luč	83	48.08 N	38.56 E
Krasucha	76	57.23 N	33.12 E
Kras'ukovskaja	83	47.31 N	40.06 E
Kraszna (Crasna) ≃	38	48.09 N	22.20 E
Kratke Range ⛰	164	6.25 S	145.35 E
Kratovo	38	42.05 N	22.11 E
Krauchenwies	58	48.01 N	9.14 E
Kraul Mountains ⛰	9	73.10 S	14.10 W
Krauschwitz	54	51.31 N	14.41 E
Kräuterin ⛰	61	47.41 N	15.05 E
Krautheim	56	49.23 N	9.38 E
Kravaře	54	50.38 N	14.23 E
Krawang	115a	6.19 S	107.17 E
Kray ✦[8]	263	51.28 N	7.05 E
Kražiai	76	55.36 N	22.40 E
Krbava ✦[1]	36	44.40 N	15.35 E
Kreamer Island I	220	26.46 N	80.44 W
Kreba	54	51.20 N	14.40 E
Krebs	196	34.56 N	95.43 W
Krečetovo	24	60.56 N	38.30 E
Krečevicy	76	58.37 N	31.21 E
Krefeld	56		
	263	51.20 N	6.34 E
Kregme	41	55.57 N	12.04 E
Kreiensen	52	51.51 N	9.58 E
Kreischa	54	50.56 N	13.45 E
Kreitzer Glacier ⍓	9	70.25 S	72.30 E
Kremastón, Tekhnití Límni @[1]	38	38.55 N	21.30 E
Kremenčug	78	49.04 N	33.25 E
Kremenčugskoje Vodochranilišče @[1]	78	49.20 N	32.30 E
Kremenec	78	50.07 N	25.45 E
Kremeneckaja Vozvyšennost' ⛰[1]	78	50.15 N	26.00 E
Kremennaja	83	49.03 N	38.14 E
Kremen'ovka	83	47.20 N	37.29 E
Kremenskoj	80	47.49 N	41.08 E
Kremenskoje	82	55.06 N	35.57 E
Kremges	78	49.04 N	33.15 E
Kreml' ⊎	265b	55.45 N	37.37 E
Kremmen	54	52.45 N	13.01 E
Kremmling	200	40.03 N	106.24 W
Kremnica	30	48.43 N	18.54 E
Krempe	52	53.50 N	9.29 E
Krems ≃, Öst.	61	48.25 N	15.36 E
Krems ≃, Öst.	61	48.14 N	14.19 E
Krems an der Donau	61	48.25 N	15.36 E
Kremsbrücke	64	46.57 N	13.37 E
Kremsmünster	61	48.03 N	14.08 E
Krenitzin Islands II	180	54.08 N	166.00 W
Krensitz	54	51.29 N	12.27 E
Krepenskij	83	48.06 N	39.03 E
Krepkaja ≃	83	47.35 N	39.23 E
Krepoljin	38	44.16 N	21.37 E
Kresgeville	210	40.54 N	75.30 W
Kress	196	34.22 N	101.45 W
Kressbronn	58	47.35 N	9.36 E
Kressey Lake @	285	39.44 N	75.07 W
Kresta, Zaliv C	180	66.00 N	180.00 E
Krestcy, S.S.S.R.	76	58.15 N	32.31 E
Krestcy, S.S.S.R.	76	58.23 N	39.00 E
Krestjanskoje, S.S.S.R.	80	45.34 N	42.56 E
Krestjanskoje, S.S.S.R.	85	40.32 N	69.02 E
Krest-Major	74	67.37 N	144.45 E
Krestovaja Guba	72	74.07 N	55.33 E
Krestovo-Gorodišče	80	54.10 N	48.36 E
Krestovyj, Pereval)(	84	42.32 N	44.28 E
Kresty	82	55.16 N	37.06 E
Kreta → Kríti I	38	35.29 N	24.42 E
Kretek	115a	7.59 S	110.19 E

Nome	Página	Lat.°′	Long.°′ W=Oeste
Kretinga	76	55.53 N	21.13 E
Kreuth	64	47.38 N	11.44 E
Kreuz an der Ostbahn → Krzyż	30	52.54 N	16.01 E
Kreuzberg	263	51.09 N	7.27 E
Kreuzberg ✦[8]	264a	52.30 N	13.23 E
Kreuzberg ∧	56	50.22 N	9.58 E
Kreuzburg → Kluczbork	30	50.59 N	18.13 E
Kreuzeck-Gruppe ⛰	64	46.51 N	13.06 E
Kreuzen	64	46.40 N	13.35 E
Kreuzlingen	58	47.39 N	9.11 E
Kreuznach → Bad Kreuznach	56	49.52 N	7.51 E
Kreuztal	56	50.58 N	7.59 E
Krevo	76	54.19 N	26.17 E
Kreyenhagen	54	52.55 N	10.52 E
Krian	115a	7.24 S	112.35 E
Kría Vrísi	38	40.41 N	22.18 E
Kribi	152	2.57 N	9.55 E
Kričov	76	53.42 N	31.43 E
Kriebstein, Burg ⊥	54	51.02 N	13.00 E
Kriel	158	26.16 S	29.14 E
Kriens	58	47.02 N	8.17 E
Krigujgun, Mys ›	180	65.30 N	171.05 W
Kriljon, Mys ›	89	45.53 N	142.05 E
Krim → Krymskij Poluostrov ›[1]	78	45.00 N	34.00 E
Křimice	60	49.46 N	13.15 E
Krim Krim	146	8.58 N	15.48 E
Krimml	64	47.13 N	12.11 E
Krimnicksee @	264a	52.18 N	13.39 E
Krimpen aan de IJssel	52	51.54 N	4.35 E
Kriničcno-Lugskoje	83	47.45 N	39.12 E
Kriničķi	78	48.22 N	34.27 E
Kriničnaja	83	48.08 N	38.02 E
Kriničnoje	78	45.32 N	28.40 E
Krishna ≃	122	15.57 N	80.59 E
Krishna, Mouths of the ≃[1]	122	15.43 N	80.55 E
Krishnachaadrapur	126	21.50 N	86.49 E
Krishnagiri	122	12.32 N	78.14 E
Krishnamāti	272b	22.40 N	88.32 E
Krishnanagar, Bhārat	126	23.24 N	88.30 E
Krishnanagar, Bhārat	126	23.13 N	87.33 E
Krishnapur, Bhārat	272b	22.36 N	88.26 E
Krishnapur, Bngl.	126	23.30 N	89.56 E
Krishnarāja Sāgara @[1]	122	12.30 N	76.26 E
Krishnarāmpur	126	22.43 N	88.14 E
Kristdala	26	57.24 N	16.11 E
Kristiania → Oslo	26	59.55 N	10.45 E
Kristianopel	26	56.15 N	16.02 E
Kristiansand	26	58.10 N	8.00 E
Kristianstad	26	56.02 N	14.08 E
Kristianstads Län □[6]	26	56.15 N	14.00 E
Kristiansund	26	63.07 N	7.45 E
Kristiinankaupunki → Kristinestad	26	62.17 N	21.23 E
Kristineberg	26	65.04 N	18.35 E
Kristinehamn	40	59.20 N	14.07 E
Kristinestad (Kristiinankaupunki)	26	62.17 N	21.23 E
Kríti I	38	35.29 N	24.42 E
Kritikón Pélagos ⊤[2]	38	35.46 N	23.54 E
Kritzendorf	264b	48.20 N	16.18 E
Kriul'any	78	47.13 N	29.09 E
Kriuša	82	54.28 N	36.24 E
Kriv'ačka	80	58.40 N	45.27 E
Krivaja ≃	38	44.27 N	18.09 E
Krivaja, Kosa ›[2]	83	47.02 N	38.06 E
Krivaja Ruda	78	49.31 N	32.59 E
Kriv'anskaja	83	47.24 N	40.10 E
Kriva Palanka	38	42.12 N	22.20 E
Krivcy	82	55.28 N	38.12 E
Kriviči	76	54.43 N	27.17 E
Krivinka	86	51.08 N	78.10 E
Krivodol	38	43.23 N	23.29 E
Krivoj Buzan	80	46.31 N	48.33 E
Krivoje Ozero	78	47.56 N	30.21 E
Krivoj Rog	78	47.55 N	33.21 E
Krivoj Torec ≃	83	48.39 N	37.32 E
Křivoklát	60	50.02 N	13.54 E
Krivonosovo	78	49.55 N	39.16 E
Krivorožje, S.S.S.R.	78	48.31 N	38.40 E
Krivorožje, S.S.S.R.	78	48.51 N	40.45 E
Krivošeino	86	57.20 N	83.57 E
Krivošin	76	52.52 N	26.08 E
Krivoy Rog → Krivoj Rog	78	47.55 N	33.21 E
Kriwoi-Rog → Krivoj Rog	78	47.55 N	33.21 E
Križevci	36	46.02 N	16.33 E
Krizskoje	83	49.28 N	39.38 E
Krk, Otok I	36	45.05 N	14.35 E
Krn ∧	64	46.16 N	13.40 E
Krnov	30	50.05 N	17.41 E
Krobia	30	51.47 N	16.58 E
Krøderen @	26	60.15 N	9.38 E
Krogager	41	55.42 N	8.51 E
Krögis	54	51.07 N	13.22 E
Kröhstorf	60	48.37 N	12.57 E
Krojanke → Krajenka	30	53.19 N	17.00 E
Krokek	40	58.40 N	16.24 E
Kroken	24	65.22 N	14.20 E
Krokodil ≃, S. Afr.	156	24.12 S	26.52 E
Krokodil ≃, S. Afr.	156	25.26 S	31.58 E
Krokom	26	63.19 N	14.30 E
Krokowa	30	54.48 N	18.11 E
Krolevec	78	51.33 N	33.23 E
Kröller-Müller, Rijksmuseum ⊎	52	52.05 N	5.50 E
Krölpa	54	50.41 N	11.32 E
Krombi Pits	156	19.30 S	25.02 E
Kroměříž	30	49.18 N	17.24 E
Krommenie	52	52.29 N	4.45 E
Krompachy	30	48.56 N	20.52 E
Kromy	76	52.43 N	35.46 E
Kron ≃	86	47.37 N	87.25 E
Kronach	54	50.14 N	11.20 E
Kronberg	56	50.10 N	8.30 E
Kronborg Slot ⊥	41	56.02 N	12.38 E
Krone ✦[8]	263	51.27 N	7.20 E
Krŏng Kaôh Kŏng	110	11.37 N	102.59 E
Krŏng Kêb	110	10.29 N	104.19 E
Kronobergs Län □[6]	26	56.40 N	14.40 E
Kronoby (Kruunupyy)	26	63.43 N	23.02 E
Kronockij Zaliv C	74	54.12 N	160.36 E
Kronoki	74	54.36 N	161.10 E
Kronshagen	41	54.20 N	10.05 E
Kronstadt → Brașov, Rom.	38	45.39 N	25.37 E
Kronštadt, S.S.S.R.	76	59.59 N	29.45 E
Kronwa	110	15.25 N	98.26 E
Kroondal	158	25.45 S	27.19 E
Kroonstad	158	27.46 S	27.12 E
Kröpelin	54	54.04 N	11.48 E
Kropotkin, S.S.S.R.	72	45.26 N	40.34 E
Kropotkin, S.S.S.R.	88	58.30 N	115.17 E
Kropotkina, Gora ∧	88	53.43 N	117.32 E
Kropp	41	54.24 N	9.31 E
Kroppefjäll ∧[2]	26	58.40 N	12.13 E
Kroppenstedt	54	51.56 N	11.18 E
Kropstädt	54	51.58 N	12.44 E
Kropufino	76	60.23 N	39.10 E
Krościenko	30	49.27 N	20.26 E
Kröslin	54	54.07 N	13.45 E
Krošn'a	78	50.18 N	28.39 E
Krośniewice	30	52.16 N	19.10 E
Krośno	30	49.42 N	21.46 E
Krosno Odrzańskie	30	52.04 N	15.05 E
Krossen	54	50.58 N	11.59 E
Krostitz	54	51.28 N	12.27 E
Krotoszyn	30	51.42 N	17.26 E
Krotovka	80	53.18 N	51.12 E
Krotovo	86	56.57 N	69.20 E

Nome	Página	Lat.°′	Long.°′ W=Oeste
Krotz Springs	194	30.32 N	91.45 W
Kröv	56	49.59 N	7.05 E
Kroya	115a	7.38 S	109.14 E
Krško	36	45.58 N	15.29 E
Krsy	60	49.54 N	13.03 E
Kr'učkov	80	48.01 N	45.40 E
Kr'učkovo	76	57.03 N	35.34 E
Kruckow	54	53.54 N	13.14 E
Krudenburg	263	51.39 N	6.45 E
Kruenggeukueh	114	5.15 N	97.02 E
Kruengluak	114	2.50 N	97.45 E
Kruft	56	50.23 N	7.20 E
Kruger National Park ♣	156	24.00 S	31.40 E
Krugersdorp	158	26.05 S	27.35 E
Krugersdorp Race Course ♣	273d	26.08 S	27.45 E
Krugersdorp West	273d	26.06 S	27.45 E
Krugloje, S.S.S.R.	76	54.15 N	29.48 E
Krugloje, S.S.S.R.	83	47.01 N	39.15 E
Krugloozernyj	80	51.06 N	51.17 E
Kruglyži	80	58.31 N	47.42 E
Krugzell	58	47.47 N	10.16 E
Krui	112	5.11 S	103.56 E
Kruidfontein	158	32.51 S	21.57 E
Kruiningen	52	51.27 N	4.02 E
Kruisfontein	158	34.00 S	24.43 E
Kruishoutem	50	50.54 N	3.31 E
Kruisland	52	51.34 N	4.24 E
Kruisrivier	158	33.26 S	21.55 E
Kruisvallei	158	33.53 S	23.10 E
Krujë	38	41.30 N	19.48 E
Kr'ukov	80	47.24 N	42.28 E
Kr'ukovo, S.S.S.R.	74	66.30 N	159.31 E
Kr'ukovo, S.S.S.R.	82	55.28 N	36.32 E
Kr'ukovo, S.S.S.R.	82	55.59 N	37.10 E
Kr'ukovo, S.S.S.R.	83	47.40 N	39.13 E
Krukut, Kali ≃	269e	6.12 S	106.48 E
Krulevščina	76	55.02 N	27.45 E
Krumasye	164	1.40 S	133.09 E
Krumbach, B.R.D.	58	47.58 N	9.02 E
Krumbach, B.R.D.	58	48.14 N	10.22 E
Krumme Lanke @	264a	52.27 N	13.14 E
Krummendammer Heide ✦[3]	264a	52.28 N	13.39 E
Krummenerl	263	51.05 N	7.45 E
Krummensee	264a	52.36 N	13.42 E
Krumme Steyrling ≃	61	47.54 N	14.14 E
Krummhörn ✦[1]	52	53.25 N	7.10 E
Krumovgrad	38	41.28 N	25.39 E
Krumroy	214	39.58 N	81.24 W
Krün	64	47.30 N	11.16 E
Krung Thep	110		
	269a	13.45 N	100.31 E
Krung Thep Mahanakhon □[4]	269a	13.47 N	100.43 E
Krung Thon Bridge ✦[5]	269a	13.47 N	100.30 E
Krupá	54	50.08 N	13.41 E
Krupec	78	51.38 N	34.21 E
Krüpel-See @	264a	52.18 N	13.42 E
Krupka	54	50.43 N	13.46 E
Krupki	76	54.19 N	29.08 E
Kruså	41	54.50 N	9.25 E
Krusenstern, Cape ›	180	67.07 N	163.43 W
Kruševac	38	43.35 N	21.20 E
Kruševo	38	41.22 N	21.14 E
Krušinovka	76	53.14 N	29.50 E
Krušné hory (Erzgebirge) ⛰	54	50.30 N	13.15 E
Kruszwica	30	52.41 N	18.19 E
Krutaja, S.S.S.R.	24	63.02 N	54.38 E
Krutaja, S.S.S.R.	86	57.24 N	76.27 E
Krutaja Gorka	86	55.25 N	73.15 E
Krutcy	76	57.10 N	29.23 E
Krutec, S.S.S.R.	76	60.17 N	39.25 E
Krutec, S.S.S.R.	82	56.10 N	38.33 E
Krutinka	86	56.01 N	71.31 E
Krutoje	76	52.26 N	37.28 E
Krutoj Log	86	57.53 N	58.14 E
Krutoj Majdan	80	55.35 N	44.04 E
Krutyje Verchi	82	54.19 N	36.26 E
Kruunupyy → Kronoby	26	63.43 N	23.02 E
Kruzenšterna, Proliv Ʉ	74	48.30 N	153.50 E
Kruzof Island I	180	57.10 N	135.40 W
Krydor	184	52.47 N	107.03 W
Krylbo	40	60.08 N	16.13 E
Krylovskaja	78	46.07 N	39.19 E
Krym	83	47.19 N	39.31 E
Krymsk	78	44.56 N	37.59 E
Krymskaja Oblast' □[4]	78	45.00 N	34.00 E
Krymskij	78	47.40 N	40.46 E
Krymskije Gory ⛰	78	44.45 N	34.25 E
Krymskij Poluostrov ›[1]	78	45.00 N	34.00 E
Krymskij Zapovednik ✦[4]	78	44.42 N	34.12 E
Krymskoje	83	48.45 N	38.48 E
Krynica	30	49.25 N	20.56 E
Krynka ≃	83	47.36 N	38.47 E
Kryžina, Chrebet ⛰	88	54.00 N	95.00 E
Kryžopol'	78	48.23 N	28.52 E
Krzepice	30	50.58 N	18.44 E
Krzeszowice	30	50.09 N	19.39 E
Krzeszyce	54	52.36 N	15.01 E
Krzna ≃	30	52.08 N	23.31 E
Krzywiń	30	51.58 N	16.49 E
Krzyż	30	52.54 N	16.01 E
Ksar Chellala	148	35.13 N	2.18 E
Ksar el Barka	150	18.24 N	12.13 W
Ksar el Boukhari	148	35.51 N	2.52 E
Ksar-el-Kebir	148	35.01 N	5.54 W
Ksar-es-Seghir	34	35.50 N	5.32 W
Ksar-es-Souk	148	31.58 N	4.25 W
Ksar Hellal	36	35.39 N	10.54 E
Ksar Rhilane	148	33.00 N	9.38 E
Ksaverovka	78	50.03 N	30.12 E
Ksel, Djebel ∧	148	33.44 N	1.10 E
Kšen' ≃	76	52.23 N	37.44 E
Ksenjevka	88	53.34 N	118.44 E
Ksenofontova	24	60.58 N	56.12 E
Kšenskij	78	51.52 N	37.43 E
Książ Wielkopolski	30	52.05 N	17.14 E
Ksob, Oued ≃, Alg.	34	35.46 N	4.34 E
Ksob, Oued ≃, Alg.	36	35.49 N	7.53 E
Ksour, Monts des ⛰	148	32.45 N	0.30 W
Ksour Essaf	148	35.25 N	11.00 E
Kstovo	80	56.11 N	44.11 E
Kū', Wādī al- ∨	140	13.37 N	25.15 E
Kuah	114	6.19 N	99.51 E
Kuaidamaozi	98	41.40 N	125.44 E
Kuaijishan ⛰	100	29.32 N	120.30 E
Kuala, Indon.	112	2.55 N	105.48 E
Kuala, Indon.	114	3.32 N	98.24 E
Kuala ≃	114	2.45 N	100.00 E
Kualabee	114	4.24 N	96.03 E
Kuala Berang	114	5.04 N	103.01 E
Kualacenako	112	0.28 S	102.40 E
Kuala Dungun	114	4.47 N	103.26 E
Kuala Kangsar	114	4.46 N	100.56 E
Kualakapuas	112	3.01 S	114.21 E
Kuala Kedah	114	6.06 N	100.18 E
Kuala Kelawang	114	2.56 N	102.05 E
Kuala Kerai	114	5.32 N	102.12 E
Kuala Kerau	114	3.43 N	102.22 E
Kualakeriau	112	0.50 N	113.20 E
Kuala Ketil	114	5.36 N	100.39 E
Kuala Kubu Baharu	114	3.34 N	101.39 E
Kuala Kurau	114	5.01 N	100.26 E
Kualakurun	112	1.07 S	113.53 E
Kualalangsa	114	4.32 N	98.01 E
Kuala Lipis	114	4.11 N	102.03 E
Kuala Lumpur	114	3.10 N	101.42 E
Kualamanjual	112	1.25 S	112.00 E
Kuala Nerang	114	6.15 N	100.36 E
Kualapesaguan	112	2.01 S	110.08 E

Nome	Página	Lat.°′	Long.°′ W=Oeste
Kuala Pilah	114	2.44 N	102.15 E
Kualapuu	229a	21.09 N	157.01 W
Kuala Selangor	114	3.21 N	101.15 E
Kualasimpang	114	4.17 N	98.03 E
Kuala Terengganu	114	5.20 N	103.08 E
Kualu ≃	114	2.45 N	100.00 E
Kuamut	112	5.13 N	117.30 E
Kuamut ≃	112	5.13 N	117.32 E
Kuanbang	98	40.29 N	120.04 E
Kuancheng	105	40.38 N	118.27 E
Kuandang	112	0.52 N	122.55 E
Kuandian	98	40.43 N	124.44 E
Kuando → Cuando ≃	152	18.27 S	23.32 E
Kuanhsi	100	24.48 N	121.10 E
Kuanmiao	100	22.58 N	120.19 E
Kuanshan	100	23.03 N	121.09 E
Kuan Shan ∧	100	23.14 N	120.54 E
Kuantan	114	3.48 N	103.20 E
Kuantan ≃	114	3.50 N	103.17 E
Kuanyin	100	25.02 N	121.04 E
Kuanyün → Guanyun	98	34.20 N	119.17 E
Kuanza → Cuanza ≃	152	9.19 S	13.08 E
Kuba	84	41.22 N	48.31 E
Kuba → Cuba □[1]	240p	21.30 N	80.00 W
Kuban' ≃	72	45.20 N	37.30 E
Kubatly	84	39.22 N	46.34 E
Kubbī	140	11.08 N	25.14 E
Kubbum	140	11.47 N	23.47 E
Kubena ≃	76	59.36 N	39.39 E
Kubenskoje	76	59.26 N	39.40 E
Kubenskoje, Ozero @	76	59.40 N	39.25 E
Kubiki	94	37.11 N	138.20 E
Kubinka	82	55.35 N	36.43 E
Kubitzer Bodden C	54	54.24 N	13.12 E
Küblis	58	46.55 N	9.47 E
Kubn'a ≃	80	55.31 N	48.27 E
Kubokawa	96	33.12 N	133.08 E
Kubor, Mount ∧	164	6.05 S	144.45 E
Kubr' ≃	82	56.52 N	38.17 E
Kubrat	38	43.48 N	26.30 E
Kubu	115b	8.16 S	115.35 E
Kubuchaj	88	50.30 N	114.48 E
Kubu Gajah	114	5.10 N	100.41 E
Kubumesaai	112	1.31 N	115.06 E
Kubura	175d	24.27 N	122.57 E
Kubutambahan	115b	8.05 S	115.10 E
Kučema	24	65.37 N	42.28 E
Kučen'ajevo	80	54.44 N	46.24 E
Kučevo	38	44.27 N	21.44 E
Kuchaiburi	126	22.16 N	86.10 E
Kuchāman	120	27.09 N	74.52 E
Kuch'ang-ni	98	40.09 N	124.46 E
Kuche	90	41.43 N	82.54 E
Kuchelebai	154	1.29 N	35.01 E
Kuchen Spitze ∧	58	47.03 N	10.14 E
Kuchinarai	110	16.32 N	104.04 E
Kuching	112	1.33 N	110.20 E
Kuchinoerabu-jima I	93b	30.28 N	130.12 E
Kuchino-shima I	93b	29.57 N	129.57 E
Kuchiwa	96	34.53 N	132.55 E
Kuchl	64	47.37 N	13.09 E
Kūchnay Darvīshān	128	30.59 N	64.11 E
Kuchterin Lug	89	52.25 N	128.05 E
Kuchtinka	82	54.29 N	38.10 E
Kučino	265b	55.45 N	37.58 E
Kučkak	85	40.15 N	70.20 E
Kučki	80	53.01 N	44.29 E
Kuçovë → Stalin	38	40.48 N	19.54 E
Küçük Ağrı Dağı ∧	84	39.38 N	44.25 E
Küçükbahce	130	38.33 N	26.24 E
Küçükbakkal	267b	40.58 N	29.06 E
Küçükçekmece	267b	40.59 N	28.46 E
Küçükköy	267b	41.04 N	28.54 E
Küçükkuyu	130	39.32 N	26.36 E
Kučukskoje, Ozero @	86	52.42 N	79.46 E
Kucur, Tanjung ›	115a	8.39 S	114.34 E
Kučurgan ≃	78	46.43 N	29.53 E
Kūd	123	33.05 N	75.17 E
Kuda ≃	88	52.25 N	104.08 E
Kudaka-shima I	174m	26.09 N	127.54 E
Kudamatsu	96	34.00 N	131.52 E
Kudanggou	104	41.06 N	124.00 E
Kudap	114	1.17 N	102.26 E
Kudara, S.S.S.R.	85	38.25 N	72.41 E
Kudara, S.S.S.R.	88	52.13 N	106.39 E
Kudara ≃	85	38.19 N	72.28 E
Kudara-Somon	88	50.10 N	107.25 E
Kudat	112	6.53 N	116.50 E
Kudbrooke ✦[8]	260	51.28 N	0.03 E
Kudejevskij	86	54.52 N	56.46 E
Kudene	164	6.14 S	134.39 E
Kudever'	76	56.47 N	29.23 E
Kūdī, Qārat ⛰[2]	146	23.30 N	23.52 E
Kudinovo	82	55.45 N	38.12 E
Kudirkos Naumiestis	76	54.46 N	22.53 E
Kudongho	98	35.31 N	126.29 E
Kudoyama	96	34.17 N	135.34 E
Kudremukh ∧	122	13.08 N	75.16 E
Kudrovo	265a	59.54 N	30.31 E
Kudus	115a	6.48 S	110.50 E
Kudyat al-Islām	142	27.32 N	30.45 E
Kudymkar	86	59.01 N	54.37 E
Kuee Ruins ⊥	229d	19.21 N	155.23 W
Kueishan Tao I	100	24.50 N	121.56 E
Kueisui → Huhehaote	102	40.51 N	111.40 E
Kueiyang → Guiyang	102	26.35 N	106.43 E
Kuekvun' ≃	180	69.14 N	179.25 E
Kuënlun → Kunlunshanmai ⛰	120	36.30 N	88.00 E
Kuerbin	89	49.25 N	128.59 E
Kuerchahanbo @	102	43.37 N	114.40 E
K'uerhlo → Kuerle	90	41.44 N	86.09 E
Kuerle	90	41.44 N	86.09 E
Kuerleikehu @	102	37.20 N	96.54 E
Kufayr Yabūs	132	33.42 N	36.01 E
Küfre	130	38.02 N	42.00 E
Kufrinjah	132	32.18 N	35.42 E
Kufstein	64	47.35 N	12.10 E
Kufūr Bilshāy	142	30.51 N	30.48 E
Kufūr Najm	142	30.44 N	31.35 E
Kuga	96	34.05 N	132.05 E
Kugaluk ≃	180	69.10 N	131.00 W
Kugaly	86	44.29 N	78.40 E
Kugarčino	80	55.33 N	50.29 E
Kugart ≃	85	40.52 N	72.53 E
Kugas	85	38.21 N	70.48 E
Kugej	83	46.53 N	39.19 E
Kugesi	80	56.02 N	47.18 E
Kugmallit Bay C	180	69.33 N	133.25 W
Kugo-Jeja ≃	78	46.34 N	39.38 E
Kuguno	94	36.03 N	137.16 E
Kuḥaylī	140	19.25 N	32.50 E
Kühbach	60	48.29 N	11.11 E
Kūhdasht	128	33.32 N	47.36 E
Kūh-e-Geyshtasar ∧	84	38.51 N	47.14 E
Kuḥlīyah, Wādī ∨	142	30.05 N	31.58 E
Kühlungsborn	54	54.09 N	11.43 E
Kuhmo	26	64.08 N	29.31 E
Kuhmoinen	26	61.34 N	25.11 E
Kühnhausen	54	51.02 N	10.58 E
Kühnsdorf	61	46.37 N	14.37 E
Kūhpāyeh	128	32.43 N	52.26 E
Kūhrān, Kūh-e ∧	128	26.46 N	58.12 E
Kühren	54	51.20 N	12.50 E
Kuhstedt	52	53.23 N	8.58 E
Kui	164	7.30 S	147.15 E
Kuibyschew → Kujbyšev	80	53.12 N	50.09 E

Symbol	English	Deutsch	Español	Français	Português
≃	River	Fluss	Río	Rivière	Rio
≍	Canal	Kanal	Canal	Canal	Canal
ʟ	Waterfall, Rapids	Wasserfall, Stromschnellen	Cascada, Rápidos	Chute d'eau, Rapides	Cascata, Rápidos
Ʉ	Strait	Meeresstrasse	Estrecho	Détroit	Estreito
C	Bay, Gulf	Bucht, Golf	Bahía, Golfo	Baie, Golfe	Baía, Golfo
@	Lake, Lakes	See, Seen	Lago, Lagos	Lac, Lacs	Lago, Lagos
☷	Swamp	Sumpf	Pantano	Marais	Pântano
⍓	Ice Features, Glacier	Eis- und Gletscherformen	Accidentes Glaciales	Formes glaciaires	Acidentes Glaciares
⊤	Other Hydrographic Features	Andere Hydrographische Objekte	Otros Elementos Hidrográficos	Autres données hydrographiques	Outros Elementos Hidrográficos
✢	Submarine Features	Untermeerische Objekte	Accidentes Submarinos	Formes de relief sous-marin	Acidentes Submarinos
□	Political Unit	Politische Einheit	Unidad Politica	Entité politique	Unidade Política
⊎	Cultural Institution	Kulturelle Institution	Institución Cultural	Institution culturelle	Instituição Cultural
⊥	Historical Site	Historische Stätte	Sitio Histórico	Site historique	Sítio Histórico
♣	Recreational Site	Erholungs- und Ferienort	Sitio de Recreo	Centre de loisirs	Sítio de Lazer
⊠	Airport	Flughafen	Aeropuerto	Aéroport	Aeroporto
▪	Military Installation	Militäranlage	Instalación Militar	Installation militaire	Instalação Militar
✦	Miscellaneous	Verschiedenes	Misceláneo	Divers	Miscelânea

Kuidesu 98 41.46 N 119.29 E
Kuidou 100 25.10 N 118.11 E
Kuikui, Cape ≻ 229a 20.36 N 156.35 W
Kuikukang 89 53.07 N 124.46 E
Kuilāpāl 126 22.50 N 86.38 E
Kuinre 52 52.47 N 5.50 E
Kuiseb ≃ 156 22.59 S 14.31 E
Kuishi-yama ∧, Nihon 96 33.40 N 133.31 E
Kuishi-yama ∧, Nihon 96 33.51 N 133.35 E
Kuitan 100 23.05 N 115.58 E
Kuito 152 12.22 S 16.56 E
Kuitun 86 44.24 N 84.58 E
Kuiu Island I 180 57.45 N 134.10 W
Kuivaniemi 26 65.35 N 25.11 E
Kuivastu 76 58.35 N 23.22 E
Kuja, S.S.S.R. 24 67.46 N 53.10 E
Kuja, S.S.S.R. 24 65.05 N 40.06 E
Kujal'nickij Liman ⊜ 78 46.40 N 30.42 E
Kujang 98 39.52 N 126.01 E
Kujani Game Reserve ✦[4] 150 7.10 N 0.50 W
Kujasovo 24 56.21 N 53.07 E
Kujawy ✦[1] 30 52.45 N 18.30 E
Kujbyšev, S.S.S.R. 80 53.12 N 50.09 E
Kujbyšev, S.S.S.R. 80 54.57 N 49.05 E
Kujbyšev, S.S.S.R. 86 55.27 N 78.19 E
Kujbyševka 78 47.37 N 31.42 E
Kujbyševo, S.S.S.R. 78 44.38 N 33.52 E
Kujbyševo, S.S.S.R. 78 47.22 N 36.39 E
Kujbyševo, S.S.S.R. 83 47.49 N 38.55 E
Kujbyševo, S.S.S.R. 85 40.22 N 71.17 E
Kujbyševskij 72 37.52 N 68.44 E
Kujbyševskij Zaton 80 55.09 N 49.12 E
Kujbyševskoje Vodochranilišče ⊜[1] 80 53.40 N 49.00 E
Kujbyshevskij 120 37.52 N 68.44 E
Kujeda 86 56.26 N 55.35 E
Kujgan 86 45.25 N 74.10 E
Kujgenkol' 80 49.17 N 47.59 E
Kuji 92 40.11 N 141.46 E
Kuji ≃ 94 36.29 N 140.37 E
Kujirai 268 35.56 N 139.27 E
Kujl'uk 85 41.15 N 69.20 E
Kujman' 76 52.52 N 39.16 E
Kujŏng-ni 98 37.53 N 125.54 E
Kujtun 88 54.21 N 101.29 E
Kujū 96 33.01 N 131.18 E
Kujūkuri 94 35.35 N 140.30 E
Kujūkuri-hama ⊥[2] 94 35.45 N 140.30 E
Kujū-san ∧ 96 33.05 N 131.15 E
Kujvikej, Gora ∧ 180 67.05 N 173.12 E
Kuk ∧ 64 46.16 N 13.45 E
Kuk ≃ 180 70.36 N 160.00 W
Kukaklek Lake ⊜ 180 59.09 N 155.20 W
Kukalaya ≃ 236 13.39 N 83.37 W
Kukan 89 49.12 N 133.28 E
Kukarino 82 55.31 N 35.59 E
Kukawa 146 12.56 N 13.35 E
Kukerin 162 33.11 S 118.05 E
Kukës 38 42.05 N 20.24 E
Kukeshan ∧∧ 85 40.00 N 75.00 E
Kuki 94 36.04 N 139.40 E
Kukipi 164 8.10 S 146.05 E
Kukkola 26 65.59 N 24.04 E
Kukmor 80 56.13 N 50.54 E
Kukoboj 76 58.42 N 39.54 E
Kukol' 76 59.52 N 32.35 E
Kükong → Shaoguan 100 24.50 N 113.37 E
Kukpowruk ≃ 180 69.35 N 163.00 W
Kukpuk ≃ 180 68.23 N 166.20 W
Kukshi 120 22.12 N 74.45 E
Kukuj 76 59.21 N 32.33 E
Kuku-Nor → Qinghai ⊜ 102 36.50 N 100.20 E
Kukunuoerling ∧∧ 102 37.06 N 99.05 E
Kukup 114 1.19 N 103.27 E
Kuku Point ≻ 174a 19.18 N 166.34 E
Kukuri Mukuri Char I 126 21.56 N 90.39 E
Kukuštan 86 57.38 N 56.30 E
Kula, Blg. 38 43.53 N 22.31 E
Kula, Jugo. 38 45.36 N 19.32 E
Kula, Tür. 130 38.32 N 28.40 E
Kula, Haw., U.S. 229a 20.46 N 156.20 W
Kul'ab 120 37.55 N 69.46 E
Kulāchi 123 31.56 N 70.27 E
Kulagi 76 52.56 N 32.24 E
Kula Gulf U 175e 8.05 S 157.18 E
Kulai 114 1.40 N 103.36 E
Kulaj 86 57.42 N 75.15 E
Kula Kangri ∧ 124 28.03 N 90.27 E
Kulākh 144 21.18 N 40.41 E
Kulakovo, S.S.S.R. 82 55.06 N 37.28 E
Kulakovo, S.S.S.R. 86 58.06 N 93.57 E
Kulakši 86 47.12 N 55.24 E
Kulal, Mount ∧ 154 2.43 N 36.56 E
Kulanak 85 41.22 N 75.31 E
Kulandy 86 46.08 N 59.31 E
Kulanutpes ≃ 86 50.21 N 69.15 E
Kulasekharapatnam 122 8.24 N 78.03 E
Kulassein Island I 116 6.25 N 120.41 E
Kulautuva 76 54.58 N 23.38 E
Kulaykilī 140 11.21 N 25.36 E
Kul'či 89 53.33 N 139.36 E
Kuldīga 76 56.58 N 21.59 E
Kuldja → Yining 86 43.55 N 81.14 E
Kul'dur 89 49.13 N 131.38 E
Kule 156 23.05 S 20.05 E
Kulebaki 80 55.24 N 42.32 E
Kulejevo 86 59.40 N 80.59 E
Kulen Vakuf 36 44.34 N 16.06 E
Kulešovka 83 47.05 N 39.33 E
Kulevčinskij 86 53.12 N 61.26 E
Kulgam 123 33.39 N 75.01 E
Kulgera 162 25.50 S 133.18 E
Kulgunino 86 53.35 N 56.56 E
Kuligi 80 58.11 N 53.46 E
Kulik Lake ⊜ 180 68.55 N 155.00 W
Kulikov 78 49.58 N 24.04 E
Kulikovka, S.S.S.R. 78 51.23 N 31.37 E
Kulikovka, S.S.S.R. 80 52.14 N 47.36 E
Kulikovo 76 52.14 N 39.35 E
Kulikovskij 80 50.51 N 42.34 E
Kulim 114 5.22 N 100.34 E
Kulin 162 32.40 S 118.10 E
Kuliushucun 105 40.07 N 116.34 E
Kulju 26 61.23 N 23.46 E
Kulkyne Creek ≃ 166 30.16 S 144.12 E
Kullaberg ∧∧[2] 41 56.18 N 12.30 E
Kullamaa 76 58.53 N 24.05 E
Küllenhahn ✦[8] 263 51.14 N 7.08 E
Küllstedt 56 51.16 N 10.17 E
Kulm 198 46.24 N 98.57 W
Kulmbach 54 50.06 N 11.27 E
Kulnura 170 33.14 S 151.13 E
Kuloj, S.S.S.R. 24 64.58 N 43.28 E
Kuloj, S.S.S.R. 24 61.02 N 42.29 E
Kuloj ≃ 76 60.25 N 42.30 E
Kuloli 85 39.22 N 68.03 E
Kulongshan 98 41.43 N 116.54 E
Kulongshanpuzi 104 41.16 N 123.59 E
Kulotino 76 58.27 N 33.21 E
Kulpahār 124 25.19 N 79.39 E
Kulpara 168b 34.04 S 138.02 E
Kulpawn ≃ 150 10.21 N 1.05 W
Kulpi 126 22.06 N 88.15 E
Kul'pino 82 56.18 N 37.09 E
Kulpmont 208 40.48 N 76.28 W
Kulpsville 285 40.15 N 75.20 W
Kul'sary 86 46.59 N 54.01 E
Kulsbjerge ∧∧[2] 41 55.01 N 12.01 E
Külsheim 56 49.40 N 9.31 E
Kültepe ⊥ 130 38.44 N 35.34 E
Kulti 126 23.44 N 86.51 E
Kultikri 126 22.10 N 87.09 E
Kultuk 88 51.44 N 103.42 E
Kulu, Bhārat 123 31.58 N 77.06 E
Kulu, Tür. 130 39.06 N 33.05 E
Kuluha, Jabal ∧ 140 15.31 N 23.25 E
Kulumadau 164 9.03 S 152.43 E
Kulunda 86 52.35 N 78.57 E
Kulunda ≃ 86 52.59 N 79.48 E
Kulundinskaja Step' ✦[1] 86 53.00 N 79.00 E
Kulundinskoje, Ozero ⊜ 86 53.00 N 79.36 E
Kulunqi 98 42.44 N 121.40 E
Kuluqi 89 50.23 N 124.13 E
Kulwin 166 35.02 S 142.33 E
Kuma 96 33.39 N 132.54 E
Kuma ≃, Nihon 92 32.30 N 130.34 E
Kumagaya 94 36.08 N 139.23 E
Kumai, Indon. 112 3.23 S 112.33 E
Kumai, Indon. 112 2.44 S 111.43 E
Kumai, Teluk ⊂ 112 3.00 S 111.43 E
Kumaishi 92a 42.08 N 139.59 E
Kumak 86 51.10 N 60.08 E
Kumakanda 88 52.44 N 116.55 E
Kumalarang 116 7.44 N 123.08 E
Kumamba, Kepulauan II 164 1.36 S 138.45 E
Kumamoto 92 32.48 N 130.43 E
Kumamoto □[5] 96 32.58 N 130.55 E
Kumani, Ostrov I 84 39.33 N 49.35 E
Kumano, Nihon 92 33.54 N 136.05 E
Kumano, Nihon 96 34.15 N 132.36 E
Kumano ≃ 92 33.44 N 136.01 E
Kumano-nada ⊤[2] 92 33.47 N 136.20 E
Kumanovo 38 42.08 N 21.43 E
Kumār ≃[1], Bngl. 126 23.11 N 90.10 E
Kumār ≃[1], Bngl. 126 23.31 N 89.28 E
Kumara, N.Z. 172 42.38 S 171.11 E
Kumara, S.S.S.R. 89 51.37 N 126.47 E
Kumārapālaiyam 122 11.28 N 77.43 E
Kumarganj 126 22.59 N 87.44 E
Kumārgrām 124 26.37 N 89.50 E
Kumāri ≃ 126 22.57 N 86.48 E
Kumārkhāli 124 23.51 N 89.15 E
Kumarl 162 32.47 S 121.33 E
Kumasi 150 6.41 N 1.35 W
Kumatori 270 34.24 N 135.22 E
Kumawa, Pegunungan ∧∧ 164 3.50 S 132.50 E
Kumba 152 4.38 N 9.25 E
Kumbakonam 122 10.58 N 79.23 E
Kumbar 140 12.03 N 30.16 E
Kumbarilla 166 27.19 S 150.53 E
Kumbe 164 8.21 S 140.13 E
Kumbel' 85 42.30 N 73.11 E
Kumbher 124 28.16 N 81.24 E
Kumbo 152 6.12 N 10.40 E
Kŭmch'ŏn 98 38.10 N 126.29 E
Kum-Dag 128 39.16 N 54.35 E
Kumdah ⊤[4] 144 20.23 N 45.05 E
Kumdan ∧ 123 35.09 N 77.35 E
Kume 96 35.03 N 133.54 E
Kumenan 96 34.56 N 133.58 E
Kumeny 80 58.07 N 49.56 E
Kumertau 86 52.46 N 55.47 E
Kume-shima I 93b 26.20 N 126.47 E
Kŭmgang-san ∧ 98 38.35 N 128.10 E
Kumha Pits 156 18.45 S 24.45 E
Kŭmhwa 98 38.17 N 127.28 E
Kumi 154 1.29 N 33.56 E
Kumihama 96 35.36 N 134.55 E
Kuminovskoje 86 57.48 N 64.07 E
Kuminskij 86 58.40 N 66.04 E
Kumiyama 270 34.53 N 135.45 E
Kumizawa ✦[8] 268 35.23 N 139.31 E
Kŭmje 98 35.48 N 126.52 E
Kumköy 267b 41.15 N 29.02 E
Kumla 40 59.08 N 15.08 E
Kumli 84 43.58 N 46.04 E
Kumlinge I 26 60.16 N 20.47 E
Kumluca, Tür. 130 41.27 N 32.28 E
Kumluca, Tür. 130 36.22 N 30.18 E
Kummelnäs 40 59.21 N 18.17 E
Kummerow 54 54.17 N 12.53 E
Kummerower See ⊜ 54 53.49 N 12.52 E
Kümmersbruck 60 49.25 N 11.53 E
Kumo 146 10.03 N 11.13 E
Kumon Range ∧∧ 102 26.30 N 97.15 E
Kumora 88 55.53 N 111.13 E
Kumosō-yama ∧ 96 33.54 N 134.18 E
Kumotori-yama ∧ 94 35.51 N 138.57 E
Kumphawapi 110 17.07 N 103.01 E
Kumrābād 126 24.10 N 87.16 E
Kŭmsan 98 36.07 N 127.30 E
Kŭmsan-ni 98 37.55 N 125.41 E
Kumsenga 154 3.47 S 30.25 E
Kumta 122 14.25 N 74.24 E
Kumu 154 3.04 N 25.09 E
Kumu ≃ 114 1.24 N 100.43 E
Kumuch 84 42.11 N 47.07 E
Kumukahi, Cape ≻ 229d 19.31 N 154.49 W
Kumukuli 120 37.33 N 88.50 E
Kumushi 86 42.14 N 88.11 E
Kumusi ≃ 164 8.35 S 148.00 E
Kumylženskaja 80 49.53 N 42.36 E
Kumzār 128 26.20 N 56.25 E
Kuna 202 43.30 N 116.25 W
Kunar (Konar) ≃ 123 34.26 N 70.32 E
Kunašak 86 55.43 N 61.36 E
Kunašir, Ostrov (Kunashiri-tō) I 92a 44.10 N 146.00 E
Kunayr, Wādī ∨ 146 27.36 N 15.04 E
Kun'batar 84 44.17 N 45.34 E
Kunchenghu ⊜ 106 31.35 N 120.45 E
Kunchha 124 28.08 N 84.20 E
Kunc'ovo ✦[8] 265b 55.44 N 37.26 E
Kunda, S.S.S.R. 76 59.29 N 26.32 E
Kunda, Zaïre 154 3.57 S 26.35 E
Kunda Hills ∧∧[2] 122 11.10 N 76.30 E
Kundahit 126 23.58 N 87.10 E
Kundam 124 23.13 N 80.21 E
Kundar ≃, As. 120 31.56 N 69.19 E
Kundar ≃, Pāk. 123 34.18 N 73.28 E
Kundara 122 8.57 N 76.41 E
Kundat 86 55.14 N 87.51 E
Kunderu ≃ 122 14.38 N 78.42 E
Kundi 154 1.08 S 40.41 E
Kundiān 123 32.27 N 71.28 E
Kundiawa 164 6.00 S 145.00 E
Kundima 164 4.14 S 143.52 E
Kundip 162 33.42 S 120.10 E
Kundl 64 47.28 N 11.59 E
Kundla 120 21.20 N 71.18 E
Kundr'učje ≃ 83 47.52 N 40.15 E
Kundur, Pulau I 112 0.45 N 103.26 E
Kune ✦[7] 94 35.05 N 137.51 E
Kunene (Cunene) ≃ 152 17.20 S 11.50 E
Kunersdorf, Forst ✦[3] 264a 52.17 N 12.59 E
Kunes 24 70.21 N 26.31 E
Kunga ≃[1] 124 21.45 N 89.30 E
Kungälv 26 57.52 N 11.58 E
Kungana 146 7.50 N 10.42 E
Kungchuling → Huaide 89 43.32 N 124.50 E
Kungej-Alatau, Chrebet ∧∧ 85 42.50 N 77.00 E
Kunghit Island I 182 52.06 N 131.04 W
Kunghsi 100 24.39 N 121.18 E
Kung-pei-tien 269d 25.05 N 121.39 E
Kungrad 86 43.06 N 58.54 E
Kungribingri)(124 30.37 N 80.16 E
Kungsängen 40 59.29 N 17.45 E
Kungsbacka 26 57.29 N 12.04 E
Kungsgården 40 60.36 N 16.37 E
Kungshamn 26 58.22 N 11.15 E
Kungsör 40 59.25 N 16.05 E
Kungu 152 2.47 N 19.12 E
Kungur 72 57.25 N 56.57 E
Kungurri 166 21.05 S 148.44 E
Kungus ≃ 88 55.39 N 95.44 E
Kungwe Mount ∧ 138 6.07 S 29.48 E
Kunhegyes 30 47.22 N 20.38 E
Kunhing 110 21.18 N 98.26 E
Kuni 94 36.35 N 138.38 E
Kunia 229c 21.29 N 158.07 W
Kunimi 96 33.41 N 131.36 E
Kuningan 115a 6.59 S 108.29 E
Kunisaki 96 33.33 N 131.45 E
Kunisaki-hantō ≻[1] 96 33.30 N 131.40 E
Kuni Vyselki 82 54.18 N 38.41 E
Kunja 76 56.18 N 30.59 E
Kunja ≃, S.S.S.R. 76 57.09 N 31.10 E
Kunja ≃, S.S.S.R. 82 56.31 N 38.12 E
Kunjāh 123 32.32 N 73.59 E
Kunje 83 49.23 N 37.15 E
Kunkle 216 41.38 N 84.30 W
Kunkletown 210 40.51 N 75.27 W
Kunkuri 124 22.45 N 83.57 E
Kunlong 110 23.25 N 98.39 E
Kunlunshanmai ∧∧ 120 36.30 N 88.00 E
Kunming 102 25.05 N 102.40 E
Kunminghu ⊜ 271a 39.59 N 116.15 E
Kunnamkulam 122 10.39 N 76.05 E
Kunost' 76 60.01 N 37.38 E
Kunovice 30 49.03 N 17.29 E
Kunow 54 53.00 N 12.07 E
Kunowice 54 52.20 N 14.50 E
Kunrau 54 52.35 N 11.01 E
Kunsan 98 35.58 N 126.41 E
Kunsangen Flygplats ⊠ 40 58.36 N 16.15 E
Kunshan 106 31.23 N 120.57 E
Kunstmuseum ⊌ 263 51.14 N 6.46 E
Kunszentmárton 30 46.51 N 20.18 E
Kuntair 150 13.32 N 16.13 W
Kuntaur 150 13.40 N 14.48 W
Kuntiki 86 58.29 N 76.24 E
Kunting 100 29.48 N 121.56 E
Kuntshankoie 152 3.20 S 23.34 E
Kuntuolun 102 45.13 N 115.21 E
Kununurra 164 15.47 S 128.44 E
Kunwi 98 36.15 N 128.34 E
Kunya 150 12.14 N 8.34 E
Kunžak 61 49.07 N 15.11 E
Künzelsau 56 49.16 N 9.41 E
Künzing 60 48.40 N 13.05 E
Kunzulu 152 3.29 S 16.09 E
Kuocangshan ∧∧ 100 28.30 N 118.46 E
Kuohsing 100 24.02 N 120.51 E
Kuokegan 120 37.30 N 89.55 E
Kuolajarvi 24 66.58 N 29.12 E
Kuop Atoll I[1] 175c 7.03 N 151.56 E
Kuopio 26 62.54 N 27.41 E
Kuopion lääni □[4] 26 63.00 N 27.30 E
Kuortane 26 62.48 N 23.30 E
Kupa ≃ 36 45.28 N 16.24 E
Kup'abal 271b 37.39 N 126.54 E
Kup'ačeje 83 48.10 N 39.37 E
Kupang 112 10.10 S 123.35 E
Kupang, Teluk ⊂ 112 10.04 S 123.40 E
Kup'ansk 83 49.42 N 37.38 E
Kupanskoje 82 56.51 N 38.43 E
Kup'ansk-Uzlovoj 83 49.39 N 37.39 E
Kuparuk ≃ 180 70.25 N 148.55 W
Kupava 80 51.07 N 42.57 E
Kupavna 265b 55.45 N 38.08 E
Kuper Island I 224 48.58 N 123.39 W
Kupferberg 263 51.09 N 7.27 E
Kupferdreh ✦[8] 263 51.23 N 7.05 E
Kupfermühle 41 54.50 N 9.24 E
Kupferzell 56 49.14 N 9.41 E
Kupičev 78 51.00 N 24.44 E
Kupino 86 54.22 N 77.18 E
Kupiškis 76 55.50 N 24.58 E
Küplü, Tür. 130 41.07 N 26.21 E
Küplu, Tür. 130 40.06 N 30.00 E
Kupol, Gora ∧ 180 68.38 N 174.45 E
Kuppenheim 56 48.49 N 8.15 E
Kupper Airport ⊠ 276 40.31 N 74.36 W
Kupreanof Island I 180 56.50 N 133.30 W
Kupreanof Point ≻ 180 55.34 N 159.35 W
Kupres 36 44.00 N 17.17 E
Küps 54 50.11 N 11.16 E
Kupuri 89 54.44 N 130.30 E
Kur ≃ 89 48.44 N 134.14 E
Kur, Pulau I 164 5.20 S 132.00 E
Kura (Kuruçay) ≃, As. 84 39.24 N 49.24 E
Kura ≃, S.S.S.R. 84 44.06 N 44.57 E
Kurabuchi 94 36.25 N 138.48 E
Kur'ačevka, S.S.S.R. 83 49.22 N 39.36 E
Kur'ačevka, S.S.S.R. 83 49.39 N 38.42 E
Kurach 84 41.36 N 47.46 E
Kurach ≃ 84 41.40 N 48.11 E
Kurachovka 83 48.02 N 37.23 E
Kurachovo 83 47.59 N 37.16 E
Kuragaty 85 43.06 N 72.59 E
Kuragaty ≃ 85 43.57 N 73.34 E
Kuragino 86 53.53 N 92.40 E
Kurahashi 96 34.06 N 132.30 E
Kurahashi-jima I 96 34.08 N 132.31 E
Kuraj 86 56.42 N 95.29 E
Kurajlysaj 80 50.07 N 51.51 E
Kurakake-tōge)(94 35.12 N 136.25 E
Kurakaki 270 34.59 N 135.28 E
Kurakino, S.S.S.R. 80 52.33 N 44.03 E
Kurakino, S.S.S.R. 82 54.30 N 35.48 E
Kurakovo 82 54.05 N 37.14 E
Kūrāli 123 30.50 N 76.35 E
Kuram 85 43.33 N 78.08 E
Kuramā', Ḥarrat ⊥[9] 128 24.30 N 40.15 E
Kurama-yama ∧ 96 35.07 N 135.46 E
Kuraminskij Chrebet ∧∧ 85 40.45 N 70.10 E
Kuramo Waters ⊂ 273a 6.26 N 3.26 E
Kuranami 268 35.27 N 140.00 E
Kurāon 124 24.59 N 82.05 E
Kurar ✦[8] 272c 19.11 N 72.52 E
Kurašasaj 86 50.18 N 56.55 E
Kurashiki 96 34.35 N 133.46 E
Kurasiki → Kurashiki 96 34.35 N 133.46 E
Kurate 96 33.47 N 130.41 E
Kurauli 124 27.24 N 78.59 E
Kuraymah 140 18.33 N 31.51 E
Kurayoshi 96 35.26 N 133.49 E
Kurayyimah 132 32.16 N 35.36 E
Kurba 80 57.34 N 39.32 E
Kurba ≃ 88 52.02 N 108.30 E
Kurbağa Gölü ⊜ 130 38.21 N 35.17 E
Kurbalı Dere ≃ 267b 40.59 N 29.02 E
Kurbatovo 86 55.34 N 91.10 E
Kurbulik 88 53.45 N 108.57 E
Kurčaloj 84 43.12 N 46.05 E
Kur-Čilik ≃ 85 43.50 N 78.06 E
Kurčum 86 48.37 N 83.40 E
Kurdaj 85 43.21 N 74.59 E
K'urdamir 84 40.21 N 48.08 E
Kurdgelauri 84 41.58 N 45.32 E
Kurdistan □[9] 118 37.00 N 45.00 E
Kurdufān □[4] 140 13.00 N 30.00 E
Kurd'umovka 83 48.28 N 37.59 E
Kurduvādi 122 18.05 N 75.26 E
Kure, Nihon 96 34.14 N 132.34 E
Küre, Tür. 130 41.48 N 33.43 E
Kure Island I[1] 6 28.25 N 178.25 W
Kurejka ≃ 74 66.30 N 87.12 E
Kurejskaja 88 58.56 N 111.20 E
Kuren' 78 51.09 N 32.44 E
Kurenalus 26 65.21 N 26.59 E
Kurenec 76 54.33 N 26.57 E
Kurgal'džino 86 50.36 N 70.01 E
Kurgan 86 55.26 N 65.18 E
Kurgan Mečetnyj, Gora ∧[2] 83 48.06 N 39.21 E
Kurgan-T'ube 120 37.50 N 68.48 E
Kurgasyn 86 49.15 N 66.43 E
Kurgatej 88 54.23 N 99.27 E
Kurgolovo 76 59.46 N 28.06 E
Kuria I 14 0.14 N 173.25 E
Kuria Muria Islands → Khūryān Mūryān II 118 17.30 N 56.00 E
Kuriasol 126 22.06 N 86.39 E
Kuridala 166 21.17 S 140.30 E
Kurīgrām 124 25.49 N 89.39 E
Kurihama 268 35.13 N 139.43 E
Kurihashi 94 36.08 N 139.42 E
Kurikka 26 62.37 N 22.25 E
Kurilen → Kuril'skije Ostrova II 74 46.10 N 152.00 E
Kurilen-Strasse → Pervyj Kuril'skij Proliv U 74 50.50 N 156.36 E
Kuriles, Islas → Kuril'skije Ostrova II 74 46.10 N 152.00 E
Kuril Islands → Kuril'skije Ostrova II 74 46.10 N 152.00 E
Kurilovka 80 50.44 N 48.02 E
Kuril'sk 74 45.14 N 147.53 E
Kuril'skije Ostrova (Kuril Islands) II 74 46.10 N 152.00 E
Kuril Strait → Pervyj Kuril'skij Proliv U 74 50.50 N 156.36 E
Kuril Trench ✧[1] 6 47.00 N 155.00 E
Kuřim 30 49.18 N 16.32 E
Kurimoto 94 35.49 N 140.30 E
Ku-ring-gai 170 33.45 S 151.08 E
Ku-ring-gai Chase National Park ♠ 170 33.38 S 151.15 E
Kuring Kuru 152 17.38 S 18.35 E
Kurinjippadi 122 11.34 N 79.36 E
Kurinskaja Kosa ≻[2] 84 39.03 N 49.13 E
Kurinwás ≃ 236 12.49 N 83.41 W
Kuripapango 172 39.23 S 176.21 E
Kuriyama, Nihon 92a 43.03 N 141.47 E
Kuriyama, Nihon 94 36.52 N 139.37 E
Kurja, S.S.S.R. 24 61.42 N 57.09 E
Kurja, S.S.S.R. 86 51.36 N 82.19 E
Kurjanovskaja 76 60.19 N 41.33 E
Kurkino, S.S.S.R. 76 53.26 N 38.40 E
Kurkino, S.S.S.R. 265b 55.53 N 37.23 E
Kurkliai 76 55.25 N 25.03 E
Kurl ✦[8] 263 51.35 N 7.35 E
Kurla ✦[8] 272c 19.05 N 72.53 E
Kurlackoje 83 47.21 N 39.03 E
Kurleja 88 52.11 N 119.11 E
Kurlin 80 51.48 N 51.00 E
Kurlovskij 80 55.27 N 40.36 E
Kurmanajevka 80 52.31 N 52.06 E
Kurmani 126 22.47 N 89.53 E
Kurmankol' 80 49.09 N 48.27 E
Kurmenty 85 42.48 N 78.15 E
Kurmitala Airport ⊠ 126 23.46 N 90.23 E
Kurmuk 140 10.33 N 34.17 E
Kurnell 274a 34.01 S 151.13 E
Kurnool 122 15.50 N 78.03 E
Kurobane 94 36.51 N 140.07 E
Kurobe 94 36.51 N 137.26 E
Kurobe ≃ 94 36.55 N 137.25 E
Kurobe-dam ✦[6] 94 36.36 N 137.38 E
Kurodashō 96 35.01 N 135.00 E
Kurogi 96 33.12 N 130.40 E
Kurohone 94 36.30 N 139.17 E
Kuroishi 92 40.38 N 140.36 E
Kuroiso 94 36.58 N 140.03 E
Kuroo-tōge)(96 35.11 N 134.12 E
Kuropatkino, S.S.S.R. 80 46.32 N 45.20 E
Kuropatkino, S.S.S.R. 85 39.57 N 67.27 E
Kurort Darasun 88 51.12 N 113.44 E
Kurose 96 34.19 N 132.40 E
Kurose ≃ 96 34.13 N 132.36 E
Kuro-shima I, Nihon 93b 30.50 N 129.57 E
Kuro-shima I, Nihon 175d 24.19 N 124.05 E
Kurosu 268 35.51 N 139.23 E
Kurovo 82 55.49 N 36.00 E
Kurovskoje 82 55.34 N 38.55 E
Kurow 172 44.44 S 170.28 E
Kuroya 268 35.55 N 139.44 E
Kurrajong 170 33.33 S 150.40 E
Kurram 120 30.06 N 66.31 E
Kurram □[5] 123 33.45 N 70.25 E
Kurram ≃ 123 32.36 N 71.20 E
Kurri Kurri 170 32.49 S 151.29 E
Kursavka 84 44.28 N 42.31 E
Kursela 124 25.27 N 87.15 E
Kuršėnai 76 56.00 N 22.56 E
Kurseong 120 26.53 N 88.17 E
Kursk 78 51.42 N 36.12 E
Kursk □[4] 76 52.14 N 35.30 E
Kurskaja 84 44.03 N 44.27 E
Kurskaja Kosa ≻[2] 76 55.18 N 21.00 E
Kurskij Vokzal ✦[5] 265b 55.46 N 37.40 E
Kurskij Zaliv ⊂ 76 55.00 N 21.00 E
Kursole 144 2.16 N 45.28 E
Kuršumlija 38 43.08 N 21.17 E
Kurşunlu, Tür. 130 40.51 N 33.16 E
Kurşunlu, Tür. 130 38.40 N 37.51 E
Kurtalan 130 37.57 N 41.42 E
Kurtamyš 86 54.55 N 64.27 E
Kurtatsch → Cortaccia 64 46.19 N 11.13 E
Kurten 222 30.47 N 96.16 W
Kürteşe 130 41.14 N 33.44 E
Kurthasanlı 130 38.20 N 32.11 E
Kurth Lake ⊜ 222 31.26 N 94.42 W
Kūrtī 140 18.07 N 31.33 E
Kurtino 82 54.59 N 38.17 E
Kurtistown 229d 19.36 N 155.04 W
Kurtumo 144 7.28 N 49.00 E
Kurty ≃ 85 44.16 N 76.42 E
Kurtz 218 38.58 N 86.12 W
Kuru, Sūd. 140 7.43 N 26.31 E
Kuru, Suomi 26 61.52 N 23.44 E
Kuru ≃ 140 9.08 N 26.57 E
Kuruca Geçidi)(130 38.58 N 40.16 E
Kurucaşile 130 41.50 N 32.43 E
Kuruçay 130 39.39 N 38.29 E
Kuruçay (Kura) ≃ 84 39.24 N 49.24 E
Kuruçeşme ✦[8] 267b 41.03 N 29.02 E
Kurudu, Pulau I 164 1.51 S 137.01 E
Kurukshetra 124 29.59 N 76.51 E
Kurum 164 4.45 S 145.55 E
Kuruman 158 27.28 S 23.28 E
Kuruman ≃ 158 26.56 S 20.39 E
Kuruman Heuwels ∧∧[2] 158 27.40 S 23.25 E
Kurumazaka-tōge)(94 36.24 N 138.28 E
Kurumdy, Gora ∧ 85 39.28 N 73.32 E
Kurume, Nihon 96 33.19 N 130.31 E
Kurume, Nihon 268 35.45 N 139.32 E
Kurumkan 88 54.18 N 110.18 E
Kurun ≃ 144 5.30 N 34.17 E
Kurunegala 122 7.29 N 80.22 E
Kurungbaja, Tanjung ≻ 115b 8.15 S 120.35 E
Kurung Tank ⊜[1] 124 22.19 N 82.14 E
Kurunzulaj 88 51.00 N 117.10 E
Kuruqi 89 48.58 N 123.50 E
Kurur, Jabal ∧ 140 20.31 N 31.32 E
Kurusaj 85 40.35 N 69.24 E
Kurushima-kaikyo U 96 34.07 N 133.00 E
Kuruson-zan ∧ 96 34.21 N 130.51 E
Kurylys 86 48.38 N 60.47 E
Kuryŏng-gang ≃ 98 39.43 N 125.47 E
Kuryongp'o 98 35.59 N 129.32 E
Kurzeme □[9] 76 56.50 N 22.30 E
Kusa 86 55.20 N 59.29 E
Kusabe 270 34.31 N 135.29 E
Kuşadası 130 37.51 N 27.15 E
Kuşadası Körfezi ⊂ 130 37.50 N 27.08 E
Kusaie I 14 5.19 N 162.59 E
Kušalino 76 57.07 N 36.05 E
Kusan 98 36.18 N 128.55 E
Kusan-ni 98 37.43 N 128.49 E

ENGLISH

Name | Page | Lat.°′ | Long.°′

Kusary 84 41.27 N 48.25 E
Kusathu ⊜ 120 35.43 N 92.45 E
Kusatsu, Nihon 94 35.00 N 135.57 E
Kusatsu, Nihon 94 36.37 N 138.36 E
Kusawa Lake ⊜ 180 60.20 N 136.15 W
Kusaybah, Bi'r ⊤[4] 140 22.41 N 29.55 E
Kuščovskaja 78 46.33 N 39.37 E
Kuse 96 35.04 N 133.45 E
Kusel 56 49.32 N 7.24 E
Kušen'ki 78 48.53 N 34.07 E
Kusey 54 52.36 N 11.05 E
Kuş Gölü ⊜ 130 40.10 N 27.57 E
Kushaka 150 10.32 N 6.48 E
Kushālgarh 120 23.10 N 74.27 E
Kusheriki 150 10.33 N 6.28 E
Kushi 174m 26.31 N 128.01 E
Kushida ≃ 94 34.36 N 136.34 E
Kushigata 94 35.36 N 138.28 E
Kushihiki 268 35.55 N 139.36 E
Kushikino 92 31.44 N 130.16 E
Kushima 92 31.29 N 131.14 E
Kushimoto 92 33.28 N 135.47 E
Kushira 270 34.28 N 135.43 E
Kushiro 92a 42.58 N 144.23 E
Kushog Lake ⊜ 212 45.05 N 78.48 W
Kushtia 124 23.55 N 89.07 E
Kushu 105 39.55 N 117.35 E
Kushui 102 42.11 N 94.25 E
Kusiro → Kushiro 92a 42.58 N 144.23 E
Kusiyāra ≃ 120 24.36 N 91.44 E
Kuška 128 35.16 N 62.20 E
Kuška ≃ 128 36.00 N 62.40 E
Kuskokwim ≃ 180 60.17 N 162.27 W
Kuskokwim, North Fork ≃ 180 63.06 N 154.37 W
Kuskokwim, South Fork ≃ 180 63.06 N 154.37 W
Kuskokwim Bay ⊂ 180 59.45 N 162.25 W
Kuskokwim Mountains ∧∧ 180 62.30 N 156.00 W
Kuskovo ✦[8] 265b 55.44 N 37.49 E
Kuškušara 24 64.58 N 40.21 E
Kusma 124 28.14 N 83.41 E
Kušmurun 86 52.27 N 64.36 E
Kušmurun, Ozero ⊜ 86 52.40 N 64.48 E
Küsnacht 58 47.19 N 8.35 E
Kušnarenkovo 86 55.06 N 55.22 E
Kušnica 78 48.27 N 23.14 E
Kusŏng 98 39.59 N 125.15 E
Kusria 272b 22.58 N 88.14 E
Kussharo-ko ⊜ 92a 43.38 N 144.21 E
Küssnacht 58 47.05 N 8.27 E
Kustanaj 86 53.10 N 63.35 E
Kustar'ovka 80 54.16 N 42.16 E
Küsten-Gebirge → Coast Mountains ∧∧ 176 55.00 N 129.00 W
Küstenkanal ≅ 52 52.57 N 7.18 E
Küsten-Ketten → Coast Ranges ∧∧ 178 41.00 N 123.30 W
Kusthalia 126 23.29 N 87.03 E
Kūstī 140 13.10 N 32.40 E
Küstrin → Kostrzyn 30 52.37 N 14.39 E
Kusu, Nihon 94 34.55 N 136.38 E
Kusu, Nihon 96 33.16 N 131.09 E
Kušugum 78 47.42 N 35.14 E
Kušum ≃ 80 48.54 N 50.32 E
Kusumba 272b 22.27 N 88.24 E
Kusumbāni ∧ 126 21.57 N 86.26 E
Kušumskij 80 51.38 N 48.21 E
Kusunoki 96 34.03 N 131.15 E
K'us'ur 74 70.39 N 127.15 E
Kušva 86 58.18 N 59.45 E
Kut, Ko I 110 11.40 N 102.35 E
Kuta 150 9.52 N 6.43 E
Kuta ≃ 88 56.46 N 105.40 E
Kutabaru 112 0.44 S 102.56 E
Kutabuloh 114 3.28 N 97.04 E
Kutacane 114 3.30 N 97.48 E
Kütahya 130 39.25 N 29.59 E
Kütahya □[4] 130 39.20 N 29.30 E
Kutais 78 44.32 N 39.18 E
Kutaisi 84 42.15 N 42.40 E
Kutāmat al-Ghābah 142 30.55 N 30.54 E
Kutanibong 114 3.53 N 96.22 E
Kutaradja → Banda Aceh 114 5.34 N 95.20 E
Kutarere 172 38.03 S 177.09 E
Kutasawang 114 5.08 N 96.54 E
Kutch, Gulf of ⊂ 120 22.36 N 69.30 E
Kutchan 92a 42.54 N 140.45 E
Kutcharo-ko ⊜ 92a 45.09 N 142.19 E
Kutejnikovo, S.S.S.R. 83 47.34 N 39.46 E
Kutejnikovo, S.S.S.R. 83 47.49 N 38.18 E
Kutenholz 52 53.29 N 9.19 E
Kutima 88 57.10 N 108.16 E
Kutima ≃ 88 57.08 N 108.14 E
Kutina 36 45.29 N 16.46 E
Kutiyāna 120 21.38 N 69.59 E
Kutjino 82 55.26 N 37.27 E
Kutkai 110 23.27 N 97.56 E
Kutkašen 84 40.59 N 47.50 E
Kutluškino 80 55.14 N 50.24 E
Kutná Hora 30 49.57 N 15.16 E
Kutno 30 52.15 N 19.23 E
Kutoarjo 115a 7.43 S 109.54 E
Kutomara 88 51.06 N 118.49 E
Kutsuki 94 35.21 N 135.55 E
Küttigen 58 47.25 N 8.03 E
Kuttura 24 68.24 N 26.28 E
Kuttusoja 24 67.46 N 28.50 E
Kuttuzi 265a 59.45 N 30.04 E
Kutu 152 2.44 S 18.09 E
Kutubdia Island I 120 21.50 N 91.52 E
Kutubu, Lake ⊜ 164 6.23 S 143.18 E
Kutukovo 80 54.26 N 40.31 E
Kutulik 88 53.21 N 102.48 E
Kutulo, Lagh ≃ 154 2.08 N 40.56 E
Kutuluk ≃ 80 53.19 N 51.09 E
Kutum 140 14.12 N 24.40 E
Kutu-Moke 152 3.12 S 17.21 E
Kúty, Česko. 30 48.40 N 17.03 E
Kuty, S.S.S.R. 78 48.16 N 25.10 E
Kutztown 210 40.31 N 75.47 W
Kuuli-Majak 128 40.14 N 52.42 E
Kuurne 50 50.51 N 3.17 E
Kuusamo 26 65.58 N 29.11 E
Kuusankoski 26 60.54 N 26.38 E
Kuva 85 40.32 N 72.05 E
Kuvak-Nikol'skoje 80 53.37 N 43.30 E
Kuvandyk 86 51.28 N 57.21 E
Kuvasaj 85 40.18 N 71.58 E
Kuvet ≃ 180 69.14 N 175.00 E
Kuvšinovo 76 57.02 N 34.10 E
Kuwabara 270 34.53 N 135.15 E
Kuwait □[1] 118; 128 29.30 N 47.45 E
Kuwait Bay → Kuwayt, Khalīj al- ⊂ 128 29.30 N 48.00 E
Kuwana 94 35.04 N 136.42 E
Kuwayt, Khalīj al- ⊂ 128 29.30 N 48.00 E
Kuyāli 126 22.31 N 86.11 E
Kuybyshev → Kujbyšev 80 53.12 N 50.09 E
Kūysanjaq 128 36.05 N 44.38 E
Kuyucak, Tür. 130 37.55 N 28.28 E
Kuyucak, Tür. 130 37.51 N 38.21 E
Kuyuwini ≃ 246 2.16 N 58.16 W
Kuyuyukak, Cape ≻ 180 56.54 N 156.50 W
Kuzaranda 24 62.22 N 35.37 E
Kuze 94 35.33 N 136.30 E
Kuze ✦[8] 270 34.57 N 135.49 E
Kuzedejevo 86 53.20 N 87.10 E
Kuzemino 78 50.09 N 34.39 E
Kuzemovka 83 49.31 N 37.59 E
Kužener 80 56.48 N 48.56 E

DEUTSCH

Name | Seite | Breite°′ | Länge°′ E=Ost

Kuženkino 76 57.44 N 33.59 E
Kuzitrin ≃ 180 65.10 N 165.28 W
Kuzkejevo 80 55.46 N 52.48 E
Kuz'miniči 76 54.16 N 33.42 E
Kuz'minka ≃ 265a 59.48 N 30.31 E
Kuz'minki ✦[8] 265b 55.42 N 37.48 E
Kuzmino, S.S.S.R. 82 55.09 N 37.53 E
Kuz'mino, S.S.S.R. 82 56.36 N 37.55 E
Kuzmiščevo 82 54.46 N 37.12 E
Kuz'movka 74 62.19 N 92.02 E
Kuznečicha 80 54.43 N 49.38 E
Kuznečikovo 82 56.13 N 36.35 E
Kuzneck, S.S.S.R. 80 53.07 N 46.36 E
Kuzneck → Novokuzneck, S.S.S.R. 86 53.45 N 87.06 E
Kuzneckij Alatau ∧∧ 86 54.45 N 88.00 E
Kuznecova 89 46.16 N 138.03 E
Kuznecovka 76 56.18 N 28.33 E
Kuznecovo, S.S.S.R. 82 55.27 N 36.57 E
Kuznecovo, S.S.S.R. 82 55.30 N 38.21 E
Kuznecovo, S.S.S.R. 86 59.15 N 63.28 E
Kuznecovo-Michajlovka 83 47.27 N 38.13 E
Kuznecovskij 80 47.25 N 40.57 E
Kuznecy 82 55.51 N 38.40 E
Kuznetsk → Kuzneck 80 53.07 N 46.36 E
Kuzomen', S.S.S.R. 24 66.17 N 36.54 E
Kuzomen', S.S.S.R. 24 64.17 N 42.53 E
Kuzovatovo 80 53.33 N 47.41 E
Kuztekke 130 41.48 N 33.16 E
Kuzucubelen 130 36.51 N 34.27 E
Kuzuha 270 34.52 N 135.41 E
Kuzuryū ≃ 94 36.13 N 136.08 E
Kuzuu 94 36.24 N 139.37 E
Kvænangen ⊂[2] 24 70.05 N 21.13 E
Kværndrup 41 55.10 N 10.32 E
Kvaisi 84 42.31 N 43.40 E
Kvaløya I, Nor. 24 69.40 N 18.30 E
Kvaløya I, Nor. 24 70.37 N 23.52 E
Kvam 26 61.40 N 9.42 E
Kvanløse 41 55.39 N 11.41 E
Kvanndal 26 60.29 N 6.36 E
Kvareli 84 41.56 N 45.54 E
Kvarner ⊂ 36 44.45 N 14.15 E
Kvarnerić U 36 44.45 N 14.35 E
Kvarnsveden 40 60.31 N 15.24 E
Kvarntorp 40 59.08 N 15.15 E
Kvarsa 80 56.58 N 53.57 E
Kvarsebo 40 58.39 N 16.39 E
Kvašenki 82 56.48 N 37.33 E
Kvenna ≃ 26 60.01 N 7.56 E
Kverkfjöll ∧ 24a 64.43 N 16.38 W
Kvichak Bay ⊂ 180 58.48 N 157.30 W
Kvicksund 40 59.27 N 16.19 E
Kvidinge 41 56.08 N 13.04 E
Kvien ⊜ 40 60.24 N 13.48 E
Kvikkjokk 24 66.55 N 17.50 E
Kvilda 60 49.01 N 13.35 E
Kvina ≃ 26 58.17 N 6.56 E
Kvismare kanal ≅ 40 59.12 N 15.11 E
Kvissleby 26 62.17 N 17.21 E
Kvistbro 40 59.09 N 14.49 E
Kvistgård 41 55.59 N 12.30 E
Kvitok 88 56.03 N 98.30 E
Kwa ≃ 152 3.10 S 16.11 E
Kwachaga 154 5.38 S 38.08 E
Kwada 164 6.09 S 141.53 E
Kwahae-ri ✦[8] 271b 37.33 N 126.50 E
Kwahu Plateau ∧∧[1] 150 6.30 N 0.30 W
Kwajalein I[1] 14 9.05 N 167.20 E
Kwajok 140 8.19 N 28.00 E
Kwakhanai 156 21.41 S 21.19 E
Kwakoegron 250 5.15 N 55.20 W
Kwale, Kenya 154 4.11 S 39.27 E
Kwale, Nig. 150 5.46 N 6.26 E
Kwali 150 8.56 N 7.00 E
Kwambilo ≃ 273b 4.26 S 15.20 E
Kwa-Mbonambi 158 28.36 S 32.05 E
Kwamisa ∧ 150 7.08 N 1.53 W
Kwamouth 152 3.10 S 16.12 E
Kwa Mtoro 154 5.14 S 35.26 E
Kwanak-san ∧ 271b 37.27 N 126.58 E
Kwando (Cuando) ≃ 152 18.27 S 23.32 E
Kwangchow → Guangzhou 100 23.06 N 113.16 E
Kwangju 98 35.09 N 126.54 E
Kwangnaru Bridge ✦[5] 271b 37.33 N 127.05 E
Kwango (Cuango) ≃ 152 3.14 S 17.23 E
Kwangsi Chuang Autonomous Region → Guangxi Zhuang Zizhiqu □[4] 102 24.00 N 109.00 E
Kwangtung → Guangdong □[4] 90 23.00 N 113.00 E
Kwangwazi 154 7.47 S 38.15 E
Kwangyang 98 34.59 N 127.34 E
Kwanmo-bong ∧ 98 41.42 N 129.13 E
Kwansan-ni 271b 37.43 N 126.51 E
Kwansei Gakuin University ⊌[2] 270 34.46 N 135.21 E
Kwanto Plain → Kantō-heiya ⌣ 94 36.00 N 139.30 E
Kwara □[3] 150 9.00 N 4.30 E
Kware 150 13.12 N 5.14 E
Kwa-Thema 273d 26.18 S 28.23 E
Kwatisore 164 3.15 S 134.57 E
Kweichow → Guizhou □[4] 102 27.00 N 107.00 E
Kweihwa → Huhehaote 102 40.51 N 111.40 E
Kweijang → Guiyang 102 26.35 N 106.43 E
Kweilin → Guilin 102 25.11 N 110.09 E
Kweisui → Huhehaote 102 40.51 N 111.40 E
Kweiyang → Guiyang 102 26.35 N 106.43 E
Kweneng □[5] 156 24.00 S 24.00 E
Kwenge (Caengo) ≃ 152 4.50 S 18.42 E
Kwesimintim 150 4.54 N 1.47 W
Kwethluk 180 60.49 N 161.27 W
Kwethluk ≃ 180 60.46 N 161.26 W
Kwidzyn 30 53.45 N 18.56 E
Kwiello 150 11.16 N 7.00 E
Kwigillingok 180 59.51 N 163.08 W
Kwiguk 180 62.45 N 164.28 W
Kwiha 144 13.31 N 39.32 E
Kwilu (Cuilo) ≃ 152 3.22 S 17.22 E
Kwinana 168a 32.15 S 115.48 E
Kwisa ≃ 30 51.35 N 15.25 E
Kwitaro ≃ 246 3.19 N 58.47 W
Kwobrup 162 33.37 S 117.46 E
Kwoka, Gunung ∧ 164 0.31 S 132.27 E
Kwolla 150 9.00 N 9.15 E
Kyabé 146 9.27 N 18.57 E
Kyabra 166 26.18 S 143.10 E
Kyabra Creek ≃ 166 25.36 S 142.55 E
Kyabram 166 36.19 S 145.03 E
Kyaikkami 110 16.04 N 97.34 E
Kyaiklat 110 16.26 N 95.44 E
Kyaikto 110 17.18 N 97.01 E
Kya-in 110 16.02 N 98.08 E
Kyaka 154 1.16 S 31.25 E
Kyancutta 166 33.08 S 135.34 E
Ky-anh 110 18.05 N 106.18 E
Kyat-aw 110 12.29 N 98.19 E
Kyaukhnyat 110 18.15 N 97.31 E
Kyaukkyi 110 18.19 N 96.46 E
Kyaukme 110 22.32 N 97.02 E
Kyaukpa 110 13.05 N 98.59 E
Kyaukpyu, Mya. 110 19.05 N 93.52 E
Kyaukpyu, Mya. 110 19.26 N 93.33 E
Kyaukse 110 21.36 N 96.08 E

Symbols in the index entries represent the broad categories identified in the key at the right. Symbols with superior numbers (∧∧[2]) identify subcategories (see complete key on page *I* · *30*).

Kartensymbole in dem Registerverzeichnis stellen die rechts in Schlüssel erklärten Kategorien dar. Symbole mit hochgestellten Ziffern (∧∧[2]) bezeichnen Unterabteilungen einer Kategorie (vgl. vollständiger Schlüssel auf Seite *I* · *30*).

Los símbolos incluídos en el texto del índice representan las grandes categorias identificadas con la clave a la derecha. Los símbolos con numeros en su parte superior (∧∧[2]) identifican las subcategorías (véase la clave completa en la página *I* · *30*).

Les symboles de l'index représentent les catégories indiquées dans la légende à droite. Les symboles suivis d'un indice (∧∧[2]) représentent des sous-catégories (voir légende complète à la page *I* · *30*).

Os símbolos incluídos no texto do índice representam as grandes categorias identificadas com a chave à direita. Os símbolos com números em sua parte superior (∧∧[2]) identificam as subcategorias (veja-se a chave completa à página *I* · *30*).

	English	Deutsch	Español	Français	Português
∧	Mountain	Berg	Montaña	Montagne	Montanha
∧∧	Mountains	Berge	Montañas	Montagnes	Montanhas
)(	Pass	Pass	Paso	Col	Passo
∨	Valley, Canyon	Tal, Cañon	Valle, Cañón	Vallée, Canyon	Vale, Canhão
⌣	Plain	Ebene	Llano	Plaine	Planície
≻	Cape	Kap	Cabo	Cap	Cabo
I	Island	Insel	Isla	Île	Ilha
II	Islands	Inseln	Islas	Îles	Ilhas
⊥	Other Topographic Features	Andere Topographische Objekte	Otros Elementos Topográficos	Autres données topographiques	Outros Elementos Topográficos

Nombre / Nom / Nome	Página / Page / Página	Lat.°′	Long.°′ W=Oeste / W=Ouest / W=Oeste
Kyauktaw	110	20.51 N	92.59 E
Kyaunggon	110	17.06 N	95.11 E
Kybartai	76	54.39 N	22.45 E
Kybean	171b	36.22 S	149.25 E
Kybeyan Range ▲	171b	36.20 S	149.32 E
Kyburz	226	38.47 N	120.18 W
Kydra	171b	36.27 S	149.23 E
Kyeamba	171b	35.26 S	147.37 E
Kyeamba Creek ≃	171b	35.06 S	147.29 E
Kyebaiwa	154	0.33 N	34.48 E
Kyebang-san ▲	98	37.43 N	128.29 E
Kyegegwa	154	0.29 N	31.03 E
Kyeikdon	110	16.00 N	98.24 E
Kyeintali	110	18.00 N	94.29 E
Kyenjojo	154	0.37 N	30.38 E
Kyes Peak ▲	224	47.57 N	121.19 W
Kyffhäuser-Denkmal ⊥	54	51.23 N	11.06 E
Kyffhäuser Gebirge ✶	54	51.23 N	11.05 E
Kyidaunggan	110	19.53 N	96.12 E
Kyindwe	110	20.58 N	93.51 E
Kyje ◆8	54	50.04 N	14.32 E
Kyjov	30	49.01 N	17.08 E
Kykladen → Kikládhes II	38	37.30 N	25.00 E
Kykva	80	57.22 N	53.50 E
Kylâs ▲	124	25.18 N	90.45 E
Kyle, Sask., Can.	184	50.50 N	108.02 W
Kyle, S. Dak., U.S.	198	43.26 N	102.10 W
Kyle, Tex., U.S.	196	29.59 N	97.53 W
Kyle □8	46	55.32 N	4.25 W
Kyle, Lake @1	154	20.14 S	31.00 E
Kyleakin	46	57.16 N	5.44 W
Kyle National Park ♦	154	20.14 S	31.00 E
Kyle of Lochalsh	46	57.17 N	5.43 W
Kylerhea	46	57.14 N	5.41 W
Kylertown	214	41.00 N	78.10 W
Kylestrome	46	58.16 N	5.02 W
Kyll ≃	56	49.48 N	6.42 E
Kyllburg	56	50.02 N	6.35 E
Kym ≃	42	52.14 N	0.17 W
Kymen lääni □4	26	61.00 N	28.00 E
Kymijoki ≃	26	60.30 N	26.52 E
Kymynejvejem ≃	180	67.26 N	175.28 W
Kyn	86	57.52 N	58.38 E
Kyndby	41	55.48 N	11.56 E
Kyneton	169	37.15 S	144.27 E
Kynnefjäll ▲2	26	58.42 N	11.41 E
Kynšperk nad Ohří	54	50.04 N	12.32 E
Kynuna	166	21.35 S	141.55 E
Kyoga, Lake @	154	1.30 N	33.00 E
Kyōga-saki ➤	96	35.46 N	135.13 E
Kyogle	166	28.37 S	153.00 E
Kyoha-ri	271b	37.46 N	126.46 E
Kyohyŏn-ni	271b	37.43 N	126.58 E
Kyom ≃	140	8.58 N	28.13 E
Kyŏmip'o → Songnim	98	38.44 N	125.38 E
Kyonan	94	35.07 N	139.50 E
Kyondo	110	16.35 N	98.03 E
Kyongbok Palace ✶	271b	37.36 N	126.57 E
Kyŏnggi Do □4	98	37.30 N	127.15 E
Kyŏnggi-man C	98	37.25 N	126.00 E
Kyŏngju	98	35.51 N	129.14 E
Kyŏngsan	98	35.48 N	128.43 E
Kyŏngsang Namdo □4	98	35.15 N	128.30 E
Kyŏngsang Pukdo □4	98	36.15 N	128.45 E
Kyŏngsŏng, C.M.I.K.	98	41.35 N	129.36 E
Kyŏngsŏng → Sŏul, Taehan	98	37.33 N	126.58 E
Kyŏngwŏn	98	42.48 N	130.09 E
Kyŏnkadun	110	16.04 N	95.38 E
Kyonmange	110	16.30 N	95.50 E
Kyonpyaw	110	17.18 N	95.12 E
Kyotera	154	0.33 S	31.19 E
Kyōto	94 / 270	35.00 N	135.45 E
Kyōto □5	94	35.05 N	135.45 E
Kyōto-bonchi ✶	270	35.03 N	135.45 E
Kyoto Race Club ♣	270	34.54 N	135.44 E
Kyoto University ◆2	270	35.02 N	135.46 E
Kyōwa	94	36.19 N	140.03 E
Kyŏyomi-dake ▲	96	33.31 N	131.02 E
Kyra	88	49.36 N	111.58 E
Kyra ≃	88	49.27 N	112.13 E
Kyrčany	80	57.37 N	50.10 E
Kyren	88	51.41 N	102.08 E
Kyrenia → Kirinia	130	35.20 N	33.19 E
Kyritz	54	52.56 N	12.23 E
Kyrkheden	40	60.10 N	13.29 E
Kyrkkazyk	85	42.30 N	72.20 E
Kyrksæterøra	26	63.17 N	9.06 E
Kyrkslätt (Kirkkonummi)	26	60.07 N	24.26 E
Kyrö	26	60.42 N	22.45 E
Kyrönjoki ≃	26	63.14 N	21.45 E
Kyrösjärvi @	26	61.45 N	23.10 E
Kyröskoski	26	61.40 N	23.11 E
Kyrta	24	64.04 N	57.42 E
Kyrykkuduk	80	49.51 N	51.54 E
Kyštovka	86	56.33 N	76.38 E
Kyštym	86	55.42 N	60.34 E
Kysykkamys	80	49.14 N	50.19 E
Kyte ≃	194	42.00 N	89.19 W
Kytym	86	59.30 N	59.12 E
Kytmanovo	86	53.28 N	85.28 E
Kyūhōji	270	34.38 N	135.35 E
Kyūhōji ◆8	270	34.38 N	135.35 E
Kyunchaung	110	15.33 N	98.15 E
Kyundon	110	20.31 N	95.44 E
Kyungyi I	110	15.04 N	97.44 E
Kyunhla	110	23.21 N	95.18 E
Kyuquot	182	50.02 N	127.23 W
Kyuquot Sound ∐	182	50.05 N	127.15 W
Kyūroku-jima I	92	40.32 N	139.29 E
Kyū-shizudani-gakkō ⊥	96	34.45 N	134.13 E
Kyūshū I	92	33.00 N	131.00 E
Kyushu-Palau Ridge ◆3	14	13.00 N	135.00 E
Kyūshū-sanchi ✶	92	32.35 N	131.17 E
Kywebwe	110	18.42 N	96.25 E
Kywong	166	34.59 S	146.44 E
Kyyjärvi	26	63.02 N	24.34 E
Kyzyl	88	51.42 N	94.27 E
Kyzylagačskij Zapovednik ◆4	84	39.10 N	49.00 E
Kyzylagaš	85	45.54 N	81.37 E
Kyzylaryk	85	43.57 N	70.42 E
Kyzylbejit	85	41.30 N	72.24 E
Kyzyl-Chaja	86	50.03 N	89.54 E
Kyzyl-Chem ≃	88	51.15 N	96.54 E
Kyzyl-Džar	85	41.17 N	72.02 E
Kyzylemgek	85	41.57 N	74.56 E
Kyzylkak, Ozero @	86	53.25 N	73.48 E
Kyzyl-Kija	85	40.16 N	72.08 E
Kyzylkum ◆2	72	42.00 N	64.00 E
Kyzylkup	128	40.38 N	53.58 E
Kyzyl-Mažalyk	86	51.10 N	90.32 E
Kyzyloba	80	49.37 N	50.38 E
Kyzylraj, Gora ▲	86	48.27 N	75.32 E
Kyzylsu ≃	85	39.17 N	71.23 E
Kyzyltas, Gory ✶	86	48.30 N	74.50 E
Kyzylt'ob'o	85	42.13 N	75.16 E
Kyzylžar	86	48.17 N	69.39 E
Kzyl-Kuga	80	48.28 N	53.01 E
Kzyl-Orda	86	44.48 N	65.28 E
Kzyl-Orda □4	85	45.00 N	65.00 E
Kzyltu	86	53.38 N	72.20 E
L			
La'a	102	29.44 N	101.26 E
Laa an der Thaya	61	48.43 N	16.23 E
Laaben	61	48.06 N	15.52 E
Laaber	60	49.04 N	11.53 E
Laaberberg	60	48.46 N	12.01 E
Laab im Walde	264b	48.09 N	16.11 E
Laacher See @	56	50.25 N	7.16 E
Laaerberg ▲2	264b	48.09 N	16.24 E
Laage	54	53.56 N	12.20 E
La Aguada, Zanjón de ≃	286e	33.30 S	70.47 W
La Aguja, Cabo de ➤	246	11.18 N	74.12 W
Laakajärvi @	26	63.50 N	27.55 E
Laaken ◆8	263	51.15 N	7.15 E
Laakirchen	64	47.58 N	13.49 E
La Albuera	34	38.43 N	6.49 W
La Albufera @	34	39.20 N	0.22 W
La Alcarria ◆1	34	40.30 N	2.45 W
La Aldea	234	20.54 N	101.29 W
La Aldehuela	266a	40.18 N	3.36 W
La Algaba	34	37.28 N	6.01 W
La Almarcha	34	39.41 N	2.22 W
La Almunia de Doña Godina	34	41.29 N	1.22 W
Laanecoorie Reservoir @1	169	36.52 S	143.53 E
La Antorcha, Cerro ▲	234	21.43 N	102.45 W
Laar ◆8	263	51.28 N	6.43 E
La Arena	236	7.58 N	80.28 W
Laas → Lasa	64	46.37 N	10.42 E
Laase	54	53.04 N	11.18 E
Laasphe	56	50.56 N	8.24 E
La Asunción	246	11.02 N	63.53 W
Laatzen	52	52.19 N	9.47 E
Laau Point ➤	229a	21.06 N	157.19 W
La Aurora	286e	33.36 S	70.38 W
La Azufrosa	196	28.14 N	100.50 W
Laba ≃	78	45.11 N	39.42 E
La Babia	232	28.34 N	102.04 W
L'Abacou, Pointe ➤	238	18.03 N	73.47 W
Labadie	219	38.32 N	90.51 W
Labadieville	194	29.50 N	90.57 W
La Baie	186	48.19 N	70.53 W
La Balme-de-Sillingy	58	45.58 N	6.02 E
La Balme-les-Grottes	62	45.51 N	5.20 E
Laban	208	37.24 N	76.17 W
La Banda	252	27.44 S	64.15 W
La Bandera	286e	33.34 S	70.39 W
La Bañeza	34	42.18 N	5.54 W
La Barca	234	20.17 N	102.34 W
La Barge	200	42.16 N	110.12 W
LaBarge Creek ≃	200	42.14 N	110.10 W
La Barre-en-Ouche	50	48.57 N	0.40 E
La Barr Meadows	226	39.11 N	121.02 W
Labason	116	8.04 N	122.31 E
La Bassée	50	50.32 N	2.48 E
Labastide-Murat	32	44.39 N	1.34 E
La Bastide-Puylaurent	62	44.36 N	3.54 E
La Bâte	261	48.35 N	2.01 E
La Baule	32	47.17 N	2.24 W
La Bazoche-Gouet	50	48.08 N	0.59 E
L'Abbé	261	48.34 N	1.50 E
Labbezanga	150	14.57 N	0.42 E
Labé	150	11.19 N	12.17 W
Labé □4	150	11.23 N	12.07 W
Labe (Elbe) ≃	30	53.50 N	9.00 E
Labégude	62	44.39 N	4.22 E
La Bégude-Blanche	62	43.55 N	6.08 E
La Bégude-de-Mazenc	62	44.32 N	4.56 E
Labelle, Qué., Can.	206	46.16 N	74.44 W
La Belle, Fla., U.S.	220	26.46 N	81.26 W
La Belle, Mo., U.S.	219	40.07 N	91.55 W
Labelle □6	206	46.20 N	75.00 W
Labelle, Lac @, Qué., Can.	206	46.13 N	74.52 W
La Belle, Lac @, Wis., U.S.	216	43.08 N	88.31 W
Labengke, Pulau I	112	3.27 S	122.25 E
La Bérarde	62	44.56 N	6.18 E
Laberge, Lake @	180	61.11 N	135.12 W
Laberinto de las Doce Leguas I	240p	20.35 N	78.30 W
La Berra ▲	58	46.41 N	7.11 E
Laberweinting	60	48.48 N	12.19 E
Labes → Łobez	30	53.39 N	15.36 E
La Besace	56	49.34 N	4.58 E
Labette Creek ≃	194	37.03 N	95.05 W
Labi	112	4.25 N	114.22 E
La Biche ≃	182	55.01 N	112.44 W
Labico	66	41.47 N	12.53 E
Labin	36	45.05 N	14.07 E
Labinsk	84	44.38 N	40.44 E
Labis	114	2.23 N	103.02 E
La Bisbal	34	41.57 N	3.03 E
Łabiszyn	30	52.57 N	17.55 E
Lablābah, Wādī al- V	273c	30.02 N	31.19 E
La Blanca	286e	33.31 S	70.41 W
Labnâ ⊥	232	20.11 N	89.34 W
Labo	116	14.09 N	122.51 E
Labo ≃	116	14.11 N	122.56 E
Labo, Mount ▲	116	14.01 N	122.48 E
La Boca	234	23.56 N	99.17 W
Laboe	54	54.24 N	10.15 E
La Boissière	261	48.46 N	1.59 E
La Boissière-Ecole	261	48.41 N	1.39 E
La Bollène-Vésubie	62	43.59 N	7.20 E
La Bonneville-sur-Iton	50	49.00 N	1.02 E
Laboratory	214	40.09 N	80.13 W
Laborde, Arg.	252	33.09 S	62.51 W
La Borde, Fr.	261	48.32 N	2.50 E
Laborec ≃	30	48.31 N	21.54 E
Laborie	241f	13.45 N	61.00 W
Laborie Bay C	241f	13.45 N	61.01 W
Labouchere, Mount ▲	162	25.12 S	118.18 E
Labouheyre	32	44.13 N	0.55 W
Laboulaye	252	34.07 S	63.24 W
La Bouverie	50	50.24 N	3.52 E
La Boyera	286c	10.25 N	66.50 W
Lābpur	126	23.50 N	87.49 E
Labrador ◆1	176	54.00 N	62.00 W
Labrador Basin ◆1	16	54.00 N	47.00 W
Labrador City	176	52.57 N	66.55 W
Labrador Sea ◆2	176	57.00 N	53.00 W
Lábrea, Bra.	248	7.16 S	64.47 W
La Brea, Trin.	241r	10.15 N	61.37 W
Labrède	32	44.41 N	0.31 W
La Bresse	58	48.00 N	6.53 E
La Brévine	58	46.59 N	6.36 E
Labrieville, Parc de ♦	186	49.20 N	69.40 W
La Brigue-de-Nice	62	44.04 N	7.37 E
La Brillanne	62	43.55 N	5.53 E
Labrit	32	44.07 N	0.33 W
La Broquerie	184	49.28 N	96.27 W
Labroye	50	50.17 N	1.59 E
Labry	56	49.10 N	5.52 E
Labuan, Pulau I	112	5.21 N	115.13 E
Labuchongshan ✶	120	30.30 N	85.00 E
Labuha	164	0.37 S	127.29 E
Labuhan	115a	6.22 S	105.50 E
Labuhanbadjo	115b	8.29 S	119.54 E
Labuhanbatu	114	2.12 N	100.12 E
Labuhanbilik	114	2.31 N	100.10 E
Labuhanhaji, Indon.	114	3.33 N	97.00 E
Labuhanhaji, Indon.	115b	8.42 S	116.34 E
Labuhanmarege	112	7.06 S	120.40 E
Labuhanmaringgai	115a	5.21 S	105.48 E
Labuhanpandan	115b	8.23 S	116.43 E
Labuhanruku	114	3.13 N	99.35 E
Labuhanwaiharu	112	5.44 S	104.26 E
Labuk ≃	112	5.54 N	117.30 E
Labuk, Teluk C	112	6.07 N	117.46 E
Labu Kananga	115b	8.08 S	117.47 E
Labutta	110	16.09 N	94.46 E
Labytnangi	72	66.39 N	66.21 E
Laç, Shq.	38	41.38 N	19.43 E
Lac, S.S.S.R.	24	63.18 N	54.28 E
Lac □5	146	13.30 N	14.15 E
Laća, Ozero @	24	61.20 N	38.48 E
La Cadena	196	25.53 N	104.12 W
L'Acadie	275a	45.19 N	73.21 W
L'Acadie ≃	206	45.29 N	73.16 W
La Cadière-d'Azur	62	43.12 N	5.46 E
Lacadivas, Islas → Laccadive Islands II	122	10.00 N	73.00 E
La Cal ≃	248	17.27 S	58.15 W
Lac-à-la-Tortue	206	46.37 N	72.38 W
La Calera, Chile	252	32.47 S	71.12 W
La Calera, Perú	286d	12.12 S	76.54 W
Lac Allard	186	50.38 N	63.28 W
Lacamas Creek ≃	224	46.20 N	122.55 W
Lacamas Lake @	224	45.37 N	122.26 W
La Campana, Esp.	34	37.34 N	5.26 W
La Campana, Méx.	234	22.45 N	105.35 W
La Cañada, Méx.	234	20.37 N	100.19 W
La Canada, Calif., U.S.	228	34.12 N	118.12 W
La Canada Verde Creek ≃	280	33.52 N	118.02 W
Lacanau	32	44.59 N	1.05 W
Lacanau, Étang de C	32	44.58 N	1.07 E
La Candelaria, Arg.	252	26.06 S	65.06 W
La Candelaria, Méx.	200	31.07 N	106.29 W
La Cañiza	34	42.13 N	8.16 W
La Canourgue	32	44.26 N	3.13 E
Lacantum ≃	232	16.36 N	90.39 W
La Capelle-en-Thiérache	50	49.58 N	3.55 E
La Capelle-lès-Boulogne	50	50.44 N	1.42 E
Lacapelle-Marival	32	44.44 N	1.54 E
La Capilla, Méx.	234	18.30 N	96.40 W
La Capilla, Méx.	234	23.59 N	98.25 W
La Carlota, Arg.	252	33.26 S	63.18 W
La Carlota, Pil.	116	10.25 N	122.55 E
La Carlota, Aeropuerto ⊠	286c	10.29 N	66.50 W
Lacarne	214	41.31 N	83.03 W
La Carolina	34	38.15 N	3.37 W
La Casita	234	23.43 N	104.46 W
La Castellana	116	10.20 N	123.03 E
La Castrina, Aeropuerto ⊠	286e	33.31 S	70.38 W
Lacaune	32	43.43 N	2.42 E
La Cavalerie	32	44.00 N	3.10 E
Lac-Bellemare	206	46.34 N	72.55 W
Lac-Brome	206	45.13 N	72.31 W
Laccadive, Minicoy, and Amīndīvi → Lakshadweep □3	122	10.00 N	73.00 E
Laccadive Islands II	122	10.00 N	73.00 E
Laccadive Sea ◆2	12	7.00 N	76.00 E
Lacchiarella	62	45.19 N	9.08 E
Lacco Ameno	68	40.45 N	13.54 E
Lac Courte Oreilles Indian Reservation ◆4	190	45.55 N	91.19 W
Lac du Flambeau	190	45.58 N	89.53 W
Lac du Flambeau Indian Reservation ◆4	190	45.59 N	89.53 W
Lacedonia	68	41.03 N	15.25 E
La Ceiba, Hond.	236	15.47 N	86.50 W
La Ceiba, Ven.	246	9.28 N	71.04 W
La Celle-les-Bordes	261	48.38 N	1.57 E
La Celle-Saint-Cyr	50	47.58 N	3.18 E
La Center, Ky., U.S.	194	37.04 N	88.58 W
La Center, Wash., U.S.	224	45.52 N	122.40 W
Lacepede Bay C	166	36.47 S	139.45 E
Lacerdónia	156	18.01 S	35.30 E
Laces (Latsch)	64	46.37 N	10.52 E
Lac-Etchemin	186	46.24 N	70.30 W
Lacey	224	47.07 N	122.49 W
Lacey Creek ≃	278	41.50 N	88.03 W
Laceyville	210	41.39 N	76.10 W
Lac-Frontière	186	46.42 N	70.00 W
Lac-giao	110	12.40 N	108.03 E
La Chaise-Dieu	62	45.19 N	3.42 E
La Chambre	62	45.22 N	6.18 E
La Chapelle-d'Angillon	50	47.22 N	2.26 E
La Chapelle-en-Vercors	62	44.58 N	5.25 E
La Chapelle-Gauthier	261	48.33 N	2.54 E
La Chapelle-la-Reine	50	48.19 N	2.35 E
La Chapelle-Saint-Mesmin	50	47.53 N	1.50 E
La Chapelle-Vendômoise	50	47.40 N	1.15 E
La Charité-sur-Loire	50	47.11 N	3.01 E
La Chartre-sur-le-Loir	50	47.44 N	0.35 E
La Châtaigneraie	32	46.39 N	0.44 W
La Châtre	32	46.35 N	1.59 E
Lachaussée, Étang de C	56	49.02 N	5.48 E
La Chaux-de-Fonds	58	47.06 N	6.50 E
Lachay, Punta ➤	248	11.18 S	77.39 W
Lach Dennis	262	53.15 N	2.26 W
Lachdenpochja	24	61.31 N	30.08 E
Lachen	58	47.12 N	8.51 E
Lachendorf	52	52.37 N	10.14 E
Lachhmangarh Sīkar	120	27.49 N	75.02 E
L'achi	80	55.20 N	41.56 E
Lachine	206	45.26 N	73.40 W
Lachine, Canal de ≡	275a	45.26 N	73.40 W
Lachine, Rapides de ↳	275a	45.25 N	73.36 W
La Chira, Punta ➤	286d	12.13 S	77.03 W
La Chivera	286c	10.37 N	66.54 W
Lachkaltsap Indian Reserve ◆4	182	55.03 N	129.34 W
Lachlan ≃	166	34.21 S	143.57 E
Lachlan, Loch C	46	56.05 N	5.18 W
La Chorrera, Col.	246	0.44 S	73.01 W
La Chorrera, Pan.	236	8.53 N	79.47 W
L'achoviči, S.S.S.R.	76	53.02 N	26.16 E
L'achoviči, S.S.S.R.	76	52.23 N	27.55 E
L'achovskije Ostrova II	74	73.30 N	141.00 E
La Choza	258	34.47 S	59.07 W
La Choza, Arroyo ≃	258	34.40 S	58.58 W
Lachta ◆8	265a	60.00 N	30.09 E
Lachtinskij Razliv, Ozero @	265a	60.00 N	30.11 E
Lachute	206	45.38 N	74.20 W
Lachva	78	52.13 N	27.04 E
La Ciénaga	252	27.30 S	66.57 W
La Ciénega	234	16.54 N	96.46 W
La Cinta Creek ≃	196	35.24 N	104.06 W
La Ciotat	62	43.10 N	5.36 E
La Cisterna	286e	33.33 S	70.41 W
La Citadelle ⊥	238	19.35 N	72.14 W
La Ciudad, Parque Nacional ♦	234	23.55 N	105.35 W
Lack	48	54.33 N	7.35 W
Lackawanna	210	42.49 N	78.50 W
Lackawanna □6	210	41.24 N	75.40 W
Lackawanna ≃	210	41.21 N	75.47 W
Lackawanna, Lake @	276	40.57 N	74.42 W
Lackawanna State Park ♦	210	41.33 N	75.44 W
Lackawaxen	210	41.29 N	74.59 W
Lackawaxen ≃	210	41.29 N	74.59 W
Lackey	208	37.14 N	76.33 W
Lackland Air Force Base ■	196	29.27 N	98.37 W
Läckö	26	58.41 N	13.13 E
Lackoje	76	58.05 N	38.08 E
Lac La Belle	216	43.09 N	88.32 W
Lac la Biche	182	54.46 N	111.58 W
Lac la Hache	182	51.49 N	121.28 W
Lac la Ronge Provincial Park ♦	184	55.14 N	104.45 W
La Clayette	32	46.18 N	4.19 E
Laclede, Idaho, U.S.	182	49.58 N	116.45 W
La Clede, Ill., U.S.	219	38.53 N	88.43 W
Laclede, Mo., U.S.	194	39.47 N	93.10 W
La Clotilde	252	27.08 S	60.40 W
La Clusaz	62	45.54 N	6.25 E
La Cluse	58	46.10 N	5.34 E
La Cluse-et-Mijoux	58	46.53 N	6.23 E
Lacmalac	171b	35.19 S	148.19 E
Lac-Masson	206	46.02 N	74.04 W
Lac-Mégantic	188	45.36 N	70.53 W
Lacob ti-duyong, Mount ▲	116	17.35 N	121.09 E
La Cocha	252	27.47 S	65.34 W
Lacolle	206	45.05 N	73.22 W
Lacolle ≃	206	45.04 N	73.20 W
La Colle-sur-Loup	62	43.41 N	7.06 E
La Colmena	286a	19.36 N	99.18 W
La Colorada	232	28.41 N	110.25 W
La Columna → Bolivar, Pico ▲	246	8.30 N	71.02 W
Lacombe	182	52.28 N	113.44 W
Lacon	190	41.02 N	89.24 W
Lacona, Iowa, U.S.	190	41.12 N	93.23 W
Lacona, N.Y., U.S.	212	43.39 N	76.04 W
La Concepción, Méx.	234	18.15 N	102.27 W
La Concepción, Pan.	236	8.31 N	82.37 W
La Concepción, Ven.	246	10.38 N	71.50 W
La Condamine-Châtelard	62	44.27 N	6.45 E
Laconi	71	39.51 N	9.03 E
Laconia	188	43.31 N	71.29 W
La Conner	224	48.23 N	122.30 W
La Consulta	252	33.44 S	69.07 W
Lacoochee	220	28.28 N	82.10 W
La Coruña	34	43.22 N	8.23 W
Lacoste, Fr.	62	43.50 N	5.18 E
La Coste, Tex., U.S.	196	29.19 N	98.49 W
La Côte-Saint-André	62	45.23 N	5.15 E
La Courneuve	261	48.56 N	2.23 E
La Couronne	62	43.20 N	5.03 E
La Courtine	32	45.42 N	2.16 E
Lac qui Parle ≃	198	45.01 N	95.53 W
Lac qui Parle, West Branch ≃	198	44.55 N	96.02 W
La Crau	62	43.09 N	6.04 E
Lacre Punt ➤	241s	12.02 N	68.15 W
La Crescent	190	43.50 N	91.19 W
La Crescenta	228	34.12 N	118.12 W
La Croft	214	40.39 N	80.35 W
Lacroix-Saint-Ouen	50	49.21 N	2.47 E
La Crosse, Ind., U.S.	216	41.19 N	86.53 W
La Crosse, Kans., U.S.	198	38.32 N	99.18 W
La Crosse, Va., U.S.	192	36.42 N	78.06 W
Lacrosse, Wash., U.S.	202	46.49 N	117.53 W
La Crosse, Wis., U.S.	190	43.49 N	91.15 W
La Crosse ≃	190	43.49 N	91.16 W
La Cruz, Arg.	252	29.10 S	56.38 W
La Cruz, Col.	246	1.35 N	76.58 W
La Cruz, C.R.	236	11.04 N	85.39 W
La Cruz, Méx.	196	28.33 N	100.48 W
La Cruz, Ur.	258	33.56 S	56.15 W
La Cruz de Río Grande	236	13.06 N	84.10 W
Lac-Saguay	206	46.30 N	75.09 W
Lac Seul	184	50.20 N	92.16 W
Lac Seul Indian Reserve ◆4	184	50.15 N	92.10 W
La Cuchilla	234	18.54 N	103.19 W
La Cuesta, C.R.	236	8.30 N	82.50 W
La Cuesta, Méx.	234	20.10 N	104.51 W
La Cuesta, P.R.	240m	18.25 N	66.49 W
La Cumbre, Arg.	252	30.58 S	64.30 W
La Cumbre, Ven.	286c	10.32 N	66.57 W
La Cure	58	46.28 N	6.05 E
Lacy Fork ≃	222	32.24 N	96.08 W
La Cygne	198	38.21 N	94.46 W
Lacy-Lakeview	222	31.37 N	97.06 W
Lada, Teluk C	115a	6.29 S	105.44 E
Ladainha	255	17.39 S	41.44 W
Ladākh Range ✶	120	34.00 N	78.00 E
Ladan	78	50.31 N	32.35 E
La Dang, Ko I	114	6.33 N	99.18 E
Ladang Jagor	114	4.42 N	101.35 E
Ladário	248	19.01 S	57.35 W
Ladbergen	52	52.08 N	7.44 E
Ladby	41	55.26 N	10.38 E
Ladd	190	41.23 N	89.13 W
Ladder Creek ≃	198	38.48 N	100.52 W
Laddingford	260	51.12 N	0.25 E
Laddonia	219	39.15 N	91.39 W
Ladeburg	264a	52.42 N	13.35 E
La Défense ◆	261	48.53 N	2.15 E
La Dehesa	286e	33.22 S	70.33 W
La Dent d'Oche ▲	58	46.21 N	6.44 E
Ladera Heights	280	33.59 N	118.22 W
Ladesi	100	33.33 N	115.53 E
La Désirade I	241o	16.19 N	61.03 W
Lādhi	38	41.27 N	26.17 E
Ladhu I	175f	15.07 S	167.08 E
Ladhurka	126	23.22 N	86.32 E
La Digue I	138	4.21 S	55.50 E
Lādik	130	40.55 N	35.55 E
L'adiny	24	61.33 N	38.20 E
Ladismith	158	33.30 S	21.16 E
Ladispoli	66	41.56 N	12.05 E
Lādīz	128	28.56 N	61.19 E
Ladner	182	49.05 N	123.05 W
Lādnun	120	27.39 N	74.23 E
Ladoga	194	39.55 N	86.48 W
Ladoga, Lake → Ladožskoje Ozero @	24	61.00 N	31.30 E
La Dolorita	286c	10.29 N	66.47 W
Ladon	50	48.00 N	2.32 E
Ladonia	196	33.25 N	95.57 W
La Dorada	246	5.27 N	74.40 W
La Dormida	252	33.21 S	67.55 W
Lado Sarāi ◆8	272a	28.31 N	77.12 E
L'adova ≃	78	48.28 N	27.37 E
Ladovskaja Balka	80	45.38 N	41.25 E
Ladožskaja	78	45.19 N	39.54 E
Ladožskoje Ozero	76	60.08 N	30.01 E
Ladožskoje Ozero (Lake Ladoga) @	24	61.00 N	31.30 E
Lādpur ◆8	272a	28.44 N	76.59 E
Ladrillero, Golfo C	254	49.20 S	75.37 W
Ladue ≃	180	63.09 N	140.25 W
Ladue	219	38.38 N	90.23 W
Laduškin	76	54.36 N	20.11 E
Ladva	24	61.21 N	34.34 E
Ladva-Vetka	24	61.21 N	34.27 E
Ladvozero	24	65.00 N	29.50 E
Ladwa	124	29.59 N	77.03 E
Lady, Fr.	261	48.35 N	2.54 E
L'ady, S.S.S.R.	76	58.35 N	28.55 E
L'ady, S.S.S.R.	76	58.38 N	28.47 E
Lady Ann Strait ∐	176	75.40 N	79.50 W
Ladybank	46	56.16 N	3.08 W
Lady Barron	166	40.12 S	148.14 E
Ladybower Reservoir @1	44	53.20 N	1.45 W
Ladybrand	158	29.19 S	27.25 E
Lady Elliot Island I	166	24.07 S	152.42 E
Lady Evelyn Lake @	190	47.20 N	80.10 W
Lady Frere	158	31.44 S	27.16 E
Lady Grey	158	30.45 S	27.13 E
Lady Lake	220	28.55 N	81.55 W
Ladysmith, Austl.	171b	35.12 S	147.31 E
Ladysmith, B.C., Can.	182	48.58 N	123.49 W
Ladysmith, S. Afr.	158	28.34 S	29.45 E
Ladysmith, Wis., U.S.	190	45.28 N	91.12 W
Ladyženka	86	51.00 N	68.42 E
Ladyžin	78	48.41 N	29.15 E
Ladžanurges	78	42.47 N	42.50 E
Lae	164	6.45 S	147.00 E
Lae I1	14	8.56 N	166.14 E
Laem, Khao ▲	110	14.27 N	101.30 E
Laem Ngop	110	12.10 N	102.26 E
La Encantada, Cerro de ▲	232	31.00 N	115.24 W
La Encarnacion	234	23.23 N	98.01 W
Laer	52	52.03 N	7.21 E
Laer ◆8	263	51.28 N	7.16 E
Lærdalsøyri	26	61.06 N	7.29 E
La Escondida, Méx.	196	26.17 N	99.46 W
La Escondida, Méx.	232	25.40 N	98.18 W
La Esmeralda, Méx.	232	27.17 N	103.39 W
La Esmeralda, Para.	252	22.13 S	62.38 W
Læsø I	26	57.16 N	11.01 E
La Esperanza, Cuba	240p	22.46 N	83.44 W
La Esperanza, Cuba	240p	22.27 N	80.06 W
La Esperanza, Hond.	236	14.20 N	88.10 W
La Esperanza, Méx.	196	26.46 N	104.00 W
La Esperanza, Méx.	200	32.06 N	114.47 W
La Esperanza, P.R.	240m	18.22 N	66.07 W
La Esperanza ◆8	286b	23.03 N	82.22 W
La Estación	266d	41.34 N	2.14 E
La Estación ◆8	266a	40.27 N	3.48 W
La Estancia	234	18.05 N	101.25 W
La Estrada	34	42.41 N	8.29 W
La Estrella, Bol.	248	16.30 S	63.45 W
La Estrella, Ven.	286c	10.25 N	66.48 W
Lafa	89	43.50 N	127.19 E
La Falda	252	31.05 S	64.30 W
La Farge	190	43.35 N	90.38 W
LaFargeville	212	44.12 N	75.58 W
Lafayette, Fr.	62	45.35 N	5.04 E
Lafayette, Ala., U.S.	194	32.54 N	85.24 W
Lafayette, Calif., U.S.	226	37.54 N	122.07 W
Lafayette, Colo., U.S.	198	40.00 N	105.05 W
Lafayette, Ga., U.S.	192	34.42 N	85.17 W
Lafayette, Ind., U.S.	216	40.25 N	86.53 W
Lafayette, La., U.S.	194	30.14 N	92.01 W
Lafayette, Minn., U.S.	190	44.27 N	94.24 W
La Fayette, N.J., U.S.	210	41.06 N	74.41 W
La Fayette, N.Y., U.S.	210	42.54 N	76.06 W
La Fayette, Ohio, U.S.	216	40.46 N	83.57 W
Lafayette, Oreg., U.S.	224	45.15 N	123.07 W
La Fayette, R.I., U.S.	207	41.34 N	71.29 W
La Fayette, Tenn., U.S.	194	36.32 N	86.01 W
La Fayette, Tex., U.S.	222	32.54 N	94.51 W
Lafayette, Mount ▲	188	44.10 N	71.38 W
Lafayette Hill	285	40.05 N	75.15 W
Lafayette Reservoir @1	282	37.53 N	122.08 W
Lafayette Water Tunnel ◆5	282	37.54 N	122.12 W
La Fère	50	49.40 N	3.22 E
La Feria	196	26.09 N	97.50 W
Laferrere	288	34.45 S	58.35 W
La Ferrière-sur-Risle	50	48.59 N	0.48 E
La Ferté-Alais	50	48.29 N	2.21 E
La Ferté-Bernard	50	48.11 N	0.40 E
La Ferté-Frênel	50	48.50 N	0.30 E
La Ferté-Gaucher	50	48.47 N	3.18 E
La Ferté-Macé	32	48.36 N	0.22 W
La Ferté-Milon	50	49.10 N	3.07 E
La Ferté-Saint-Aubin	50	47.43 N	1.56 E
La Ferté-sous-Jouarre	50	48.57 N	3.08 E
La Ferté-sur-Amance	58	47.50 N	5.42 E
La Ferté-Vidame	50	48.37 N	0.55 E
La Ferté-Villeneuil	50	47.59 N	1.21 E
Lafferty	214	40.07 N	81.01 W
Laffrey	62	45.02 N	5.46 E
Lafia	150	8.30 N	8.30 E
Lafiagi	150	8.52 N	5.25 E
Laflamme ≃	190	48.56 N	77.18 W
Laflèche, Qué., Can.	275a	45.30 N	73.28 W
Laflèche, Sask., Can.	184	49.43 N	106.35 W
La Flèche, Fr.	32	47.42 N	0.05 W
La Floresta	266d	41.27 N	2.04 E
La Florida, Chile	286e	33.33 S	70.34 W
La Florida, Esp.	266d	41.31 N	2.12 E
La Florida, Guat.	232	16.33 N	90.27 W
Lafnitz ≃, Eur.	30 / 61	46.57 N	16.16 E
La Foa	175f	21.43 S	165.50 E
La Foce	62	44.08 N	9.47 E
La Follette	192	36.23 N	84.07 W
Lafon	154	5.02 N	32.27 E
Lafontaine, Qué., Can.	206	45.48 N	74.01 W
La Fontaine, Ind., U.S.	216	40.40 N	85.43 W
Lafontaine, Parc ♦	275a	45.32 N	73.34 W
La Fortuna	236	10.30 N	84.35 W
Lafourche, Bayou ≃	194	29.05 N	90.14 W
La Foux, Fr.	62	43.16 N	6.35 E
La Foux, Fr.	62	44.17 N	6.34 E
La Fragua	252	26.05 S	64.20 W
La Francia	252	31.24 S	62.38 W
La Fregeneda	34	40.59 N	6.52 W
La Frette-sur-Seine	261	48.58 N	2.11 E
La Fría	246	8.13 N	72.15 W
Lafrimbolle	58	48.36 N	7.01 E
La Fuente de San Esteban	34	40.48 N	6.15 W
Laga, Monti della ✶	66	42.37 N	13.24 E
Lagaip ≃	164	5.05 S	142.40 E
La Galite I	148	37.32 N	8.56 E
La Gallareta	252	29.34 S	60.23 W
La Gallega	34	41.54 N	3.16 W
Lagan	26	56.55 N	13.59 E
Lagan ≃, Sve.	26	56.33 N	12.56 E
Lagan ≃, N. Ire., U.K.	44	54.37 N	5.53 W
Lagangzong	120	28.05 N	91.04 E
Lagantu	102	42.20 N	108.22 E
La Garde	62	43.07 N	6.01 E
La Garde-Freinet	62	43.19 N	6.28 E
La Garenne-Colombes	261	48.55 N	2.15 E
Lagarina, Val V	64	45.50 N	11.10 E
La Garita	234	19.43 N	103.10 W
Lagarto, Bra.	250	10.54 S	37.41 W
Lagarto, C.R.	236	10.07 N	84.56 W
Lagarto Creek ≃	196	28.08 N	97.56 W
Lagay	116	14.06 N	122.12 E
Lagayan	116	17.43 N	120.42 E
Lage, B.R.D.	52	51.59 N	8.48 E
Lage, Esp.	34	43.13 N	9.00 W
Lage, Zhg.	120	29.26 N	85.51 E
Lagechi @	124	30.42 N	81.16 E
Lagedu	102	26.24 N	101.11 E
Lågen ≃, Nor.	26	59.03 N	10.05 E
Lågen ≃, Nor.	26	61.08 N	10.25 E
Lägerdorf	52	53.53 N	9.34 E
Lageuen	114	4.44 N	95.31 E
Lage Zwaluwe	52	51.43 N	4.41 E
Laggan	46	57.02 N	4.16 W
Laggan, Loch @1	46	56.57 N	4.28 W
Laggan Bay C	46	55.41 N	6.19 W
Lagginhorn ▲	58	46.11 N	8.01 E
Laghmān □4	120	35.00 N	70.15 E
Laghouat	148	33.50 N	2.59 E
Laghy	48	54.37 N	8.05 W
Lagič	84	40.51 N	48.24 E
La Giettaz	62	45.52 N	6.30 E
La Giustiniana ◆8	267a	41.59 N	12.24 E
La Gleize	56	50.25 N	5.51 E
La Gloria	246	8.37 N	73.48 W
Lagnieu	58	45.54 N	5.21 E
Lagny, Fr.	32	49.37 N	2.55 E
Lagny, Fr.	50	48.52 N	2.43 E
Lagny-le-Sec	261	49.05 N	2.45 E
Lago	68	39.10 N	16.09 E
Lago, Mount ▲	224	48.51 N	120.32 W
Lagoa	256	23.18 S	45.36 W
Lagoa Branca	256	21.54 S	47.02 W
Lagoa da Prata	255	20.01 S	45.33 W
Lagoa Dourada	255	20.55 S	44.05 W
Lagoa Formosa	255	18.47 S	46.24 W
Lago Argentino → Calafate	254	50.20 S	72.18 W
Lagoa Santa	255	19.38 S	43.53 W
Lagoa Vermelha	252	28.13 S	51.32 W
Lago Blanco	254	45.55 S	71.15 W
Lago da Pedra	250	4.20 S	45.10 W
Lago de Camécuaro, Parque Nacional ♦	234	19.51 N	102.18 W
Lagodechi	84	41.49 N	46.18 E
Lagodechskij Zapovednik ♦	84	41.53 N	46.22 E
Lago Futalaufquen	254	42.53 S	71.37 W
Lagoinha	256	23.06 S	45.11 W
Lagolândia	255	15.37 S	49.02 W
Lagolovo	265a	59.42 N	30.00 E
La Gomera	236	14.05 N	91.03 W
Lagonegro	68	40.07 N	15.46 E
Lagonglong	116	8.48 N	124.47 E
Lagonoy	116	13.44 N	123.31 E
Lagonoy Gulf C	116	13.35 N	123.45 E
Lagopesole, Castel di ⊥	68	40.48 N	15.45 E
Lago Posadas	254	47.32 S	71.45 W
Lagorai, Catena del ✶	64	46.18 N	11.35 E
La Gorgue	50	50.38 N	2.42 E
Lagos, Ang.	152	16.04 S	17.03 E
Lagos, Nig.	150 / 273a	6.27 N	3.24 E
Lagos, Port.	34	37.06 N	8.40 W
Lagos □8	150	6.30 N	3.30 E
Lagos (Ikeja) Airport ⊠	273a	6.35 N	3.20 E
Lagos, University of ◆2	273a	6.32 N	3.24 E
Lagosanto	66	44.46 N	12.08 E
Lagos de Moreno	234	21.21 N	101.55 W
Lagos Harbour C	273a	6.26 N	3.24 E
Lagos Island I	273a	6.27 N	3.26 E
Lagos Lagoon C	273a	6.30 N	3.26 E
Lagos Terminus ◆5	273a	6.28 N	3.23 E
La Goulette	148	36.49 N	10.18 E
Lago Viedma	254	49.48 S	72.07 W
La Grand Baie C	275a	45.29 N	74.00 W
La Grand'Combe	62	44.13 N	4.02 E
La Grande	202	45.20 N	118.05 W
La Grande ≃	176	53.50 N	79.00 W
La Grande Anse C	241o	16.19 N	61.48 W
La Grande Moucherolle ▲	62	45.00 N	5.34 E
La Grange, Austl.	162	18.41 S	121.45 E
LaGrange, Calif., U.S.	226	37.40 N	120.28 W
La Grange, Ga., U.S.	192	33.02 N	85.02 W
La Grange, Ill., U.S.	216	41.49 N	87.55 W
Lagrange, Ind., U.S.	216	41.39 N	85.25 W
La Grange, Ky., U.S.	218	38.24 N	85.23 W
La Grange, Maine, U.S.	188	45.10 N	68.51 W
La Grange, Mo., U.S.	219	40.03 N	91.35 W
La Grange, N.C., U.S.	192	35.19 N	77.47 W
Lagrange, Ohio, U.S.	214	41.14 N	82.07 W
La Grange, Tex., U.S.	222	29.54 N	96.52 W
Lagrange, Wyo., U.S.	198	41.38 N	104.10 W
Lagrange □6	216	41.39 N	85.25 W
Lagrange Bay C	162	18.38 S	121.42 E
La Grange Highlands	278	41.48 N	87.53 W
La Grange Lock and Dam ◆5	219	39.57 N	90.32 W
La Grange Park	278	41.50 N	87.52 W
Lagrangeville	210	41.39 N	73.46 W
La Granja	286e	33.32 S	70.39 W
La Gran Sabana ✶	246	5.30 N	61.30 W
La Grave	62	45.03 N	6.18 E
La Grita	246	8.08 N	71.59 W
Lagro	216	40.50 N	85.44 W
La Groise	50	50.05 N	3.41 E
La Grue Bayou ≃	194	34.05 N	91.10 W
Lagu	102	26.26 N	101.30 E
La Guadeloupe (Saint Evariste)	188	45.57 N	70.56 W
La Guaira	246 / 286c	10.36 N	66.56 W
La Guajira □5	246	11.30 N	72.30 W
La Guajira, Peninsula de ➤1	246	12.00 N	71.40 W
La Guardia, Arg.	252	29.33 S	65.27 W
La Guardia, Bol.	248	17.54 S	63.20 W
Laguardia, Esp.	34	42.33 N	2.35 W
La Guardia, Esp.	34	41.54 N	8.53 W
La Guardia Airport ⊠	210	40.46 N	73.53 W
Lagubu	124	29.08 N	87.14 E
La Gudiña	34	42.04 N	7.08 W
La Guépière	261	48.35 N	1.50 E
La Guerche-de-Bretagne	32	47.56 N	1.14 W
La Guerche-sur-l'Aubois	32	46.57 N	2.57 E
Laguiole	32	44.41 N	2.51 E
Laguna, Bra.	252	28.29 S	48.47 W
Laguna, N. Mex., U.S.	200	35.02 N	107.23 W
Laguna □4	116	14.10 N	121.20 E
Laguna ≃, Bra.	250	1.17 S	50.50 W
Laguna ≃, Calif., U.S.	226	38.16 N	121.23 W
Laguna, Ilha da I	250	1.40 S	51.00 W
Laguna Beach	228	33.33 N	117.51 W
Laguna Blanca	240p	20.27 N	76.07 W
Laguna Carapã	255	22.27 S	55.01 W
Laguna Creek ≃	200	36.54 N	109.45 W
Laguna Dam ◆5	200	32.50 N	114.31 W
Laguna de Jaco	232	27.50 N	104.00 W
Laguna Hills	228	33.37 N	117.43 W
Laguna Indian Reservation ◆4	200	35.00 N	107.20 W
Laguna Lake @	226	35.16 N	120.42 W
Laguna Larga	252	31.46 S	63.48 W
Laguna Limpia	252	26.29 S	59.41 W
Laguna Park	222	31.52 N	97.23 W
Lagunas	248	5.14 S	75.38 W
Lagundo	64	46.41 N	11.08 E
Lagunillas, Bol.	248	19.38 S	63.43 W
Lagunillas, Méx.	234	21.34 N	99.35 W
Lagunillas, Ven.	246	8.31 N	71.24 W
Lagunillas → Ciudad Ojeda, Ven.	246	10.12 N	71.19 W
Lagunillas, Laguna @	248	15.44 S	70.43 W
Laguntara C	236	15.12 N	83.30 W
L'agušje	86	54.24 N	77.59 E
Laguyu	104	41.43 N	123.49 E
Laha	89	48.10 N	124.39 E
La Habana	240p / 286b	23.08 N	82.22 W
La Habana □4	240p	22.45 N	82.10 W
La Habana, Bahía de C	286b	23.08 N	82.20 W
La Habana, Universidad de ◆2	286b	23.08 N	82.22 W
La Habra	228	33.56 N	117.57 W
La Habra Heights	280	33.57 N	117.57 W
Lahad Datu	112	5.02 N	118.19 E
Lahaina	229a	20.52 N	156.41 W
Laham	112	0.22 N	115.24 E
Lahār	124	26.12 N	78.57 E
La Harpe, Ill., U.S.	190	40.35 N	90.58 W
La Harpe, Kans., U.S.	198	37.55 N	95.18 W
Lāharpur	124	27.43 N	80.54 E
Lahaska	208	40.21 N	75.02 W
Lahat, Indon.	112	3.48 S	103.32 E
Lahat, Malay.	114	4.33 N	101.02 E
Lahaul and Spiti □5	123	32.40 N	77.15 E
La Hauteville	261	48.42 N	1.37 E
La Havane → La Habana	240p	23.08 N	82.22 W
La Have ≃	186	44.14 N	64.20 W
La Have Islands II	186	44.12 N	64.23 W
La Haye → 's-Gravenhage	52	52.06 N	4.18 E
La Haye-du-Puits	32	49.18 N	1.33 W
La Haÿ-les-Roses	261	48.47 N	2.21 E

Symbol	English	Deutsch	Español	Français	Português
≃	River	Fluss	Rio	Rivière	Rio
≡	Canal	Kanal	Canal	Canal	Canal
↳	Waterfall, Rapids	Wasserfall, Stromschnellen	Cascada, Rápidos	Chute d'eau, Rapides	Cascata, Rápidos
∐	Strait	Meeresstrasse	Estrecho	Détroit	Estreito
C	Bay, Gulf	Bucht, Golf	Bahía, Golfo	Baie, Golfe	Baía, Golfo
@	Lake, Lakes	See, Seen	Lago, Lagos	Lac, Lacs	Lago, Lagos
≋	Swamp	Sumpf	Pantano	Marais	Pântano
⊼	Ice Features, Glacier	Eis- und Gletscherformen	Accidentes Glaciales	Formes glaciaires	Acidentes Glaciares
≑	Other Hydrographic Features	Andere Hydrographische Objekte	Otros Elementos Hidrográficos	Autres données hydrographiques	Outros Elementos Hidrográficos
◆	Submarine Features	Untermeerische Objekte	Accidentes Submarinos	Formes de relief sous-marin	Acidentes Submarinos
□	Political Unit	Politische Einheit	Unidad Politica	Entité politique	Unidade Política
✈	Cultural Institution	Kulturelle Institution	Institución Cultural	Institution culturelle	Instituição Cultural
⊥	Historical Site	Historische Stätte	Sitio Histórico	Site historique	Sítio Histórico
♦	Recreational Site	Erholungs- und Ferienort	Sitio de Recreo	Centre de loisirs	Sítio de Lazer
⊠	Airport	Flughafen	Aeropuerto	Aéroport	Aeroporto
■	Military Installation	Militäranlage	Instalación Militar	Installation militaire	Instalação Militar
◆	Miscellaneous	Verschiedenes	Misceláneo	Divers	Miscelânea

Lähden 52 52.45 N 7.34 E
Lãhe 110 26.20 N 95.26 E
Laheria Sarai 124 26.07 N 85.54 E
Lahewa 114 1.24 N 97.11 E
Lahfān, Bi'r ⊤[4] 132 31.01 N 33.52 E
Lahi, Ava ⊔ 174w 21.02 S 175.11 W
La Higuera 252 29.30 S 71.17 W
Laḥij 144 13.02 N 44.54 E
Lāhījān 128 37.12 N 50.01 E
Lāhitah 132 32.59 N 36.35 E
Lähn → Wleń 30 51.01 N 15.40 E
Lahn ≃ 56 50.18 N 7.37 E
Laholm 26 56.31 N 13.02 E
Laholmsbukten C 26 56.35 N 12.50 E
La Honda 226 37.19 N 122.16 W
La Honda Creek ≃ 282 37.18 N 122.16 W
Lahontan Reservoir ⊜[1] 226 39.23 N 119.09 W
Lahontan State Recreation Area ♠ 226 39.28 N 119.03 W
Lāhor, Pāk. 123 34.03 N 72.22 E
Lahor → Lahore, Pāk. 123 31.35 N 74.18 E
Lahore 123 31.35 N 74.18 E
La Horqueta 246 3.06 N 72.50 W
La Horqueta, Arroyo ≃ 288 34.41 S 58.51 W
La Houssaye-en-Brie 261 48.45 N 2.53 E
Lahr 58 48.20 N 7.52 E
Lahri 120 29.11 N 68.13 E
Laḥṭah, Wādī ∨ 142 29.44 N 32.45 E
Lahti 26 60.58 N 25.40 E
La Huaca 248 4.54 S 80.57 W
La Huacana 234 18.58 N 101.49 W
La Huerta 234 19.28 N 104.39 W
La Hunière 261 48.36 N 1.52 E
Lahuy Island I 116 13.56 N 123.50 E
Laï 146 9.24 N 16.18 E
Laiagam 164 5.30 S 143.20 E
Laian 100 32.27 N 118.25 E
Laibach → Ljubljana 36 46.03 N 14.31 E
Laibin 102 23.42 N 109.22 E
Lai-chau 110 22.02 N 103.10 E
Laichingen 58 48.29 N 9.41 E
Laichow Bay → Laizhouwan C 98 37.36 N 119.30 E
Laide 46 57.52 N 5.32 W
Laidley 171a 27.38 S 152.24 E
Laidley Creek ≃ 171a 27.31 S 152.24 E
Laidon, Loch ⊜ 46 56.39 N 4.40 W
Laie 229c 21.39 N 157.56 W
Laifang 100 25.56 N 116.54 E
Laifeng 102 29.31 N 109.15 E
Laifengchang 107 30.14 N 105.17 E
Laifengyi 107 29.26 N 106.13 E
L'Aigle 50 48.45 N 0.38 E
L'Aigle Creek ≃ 194 33.12 N 92.08 W
Laignes 50 47.50 N 4.22 E
Laigou 100 33.56 N 117.06 E
Laigueglia 62 43.58 N 8.09 E
Laihia 26 62.58 N 22.01 E
Lai-hka 110 21.16 N 97.40 E
Laijiaqiao 107 29.38 N 106.23 E
Lailly-en-Val 50 47.46 N 1.41 E
Lainate 62 45.34 N 9.02 E
Lainbach 61 47.38 N 14.46 E
La Independencia, Bahía de C 248 14.15 S 76.10 W
Laindon 42 51.34 N 0.26 E
Laingsburg, S. Afr. 158 33.11 S 20.51 E
Laingsburg, Mich., U.S. 216 42.54 N 84.21 W
Laingsnek ◆[1] 158 27.28 S 29.55 E
Lainioälven ≃ 24 67.22 N 23.39 E
Laino Borgo 68 39.57 N 15.59 E
Lainville 261 49.04 N 1.49 E
Lainz ◆[8] 264b 48.11 N 16.17 E
Lainzer Tiergarten ♠ 264b 48.10 N 16.14 E
Lair, Scot., U.K. 46 57.29 N 5.20 W
Lair, Ky., U.S. 218 38.20 N 84.20 W
Laird Hill 222 32.21 N 94.54 W
Lairdsville 210 41.14 N 76.37 W
Lairg 46 58.01 N 4.25 W
Laïri 146 10.49 N 17.06 E
Laïri, Batha de ≃ 146 12.28 N 16.45 E
Lais, Indon. 112 3.32 S 102.03 E
Lais, Indon. 112 0.47 N 120.27 E
Lais, Pil. 116 6.20 N 125.39 E
La Isabela 240p 22.57 N 80.01 W
Laisamis 154 1.36 N 37.48 E
Laiševo 80 55.24 N 49.32 E
Laishan 98 37.24 N 121.23 E
Laishui 105 39.23 N 115.42 E
Laissac 32 44.23 N 2.49 E
Laissey 58 47.18 N 6.14 E
Laisuchang 107 29.16 N 105.47 E
Laisvall 24 66.05 N 17.10 E
Laitan 107 29.06 N 106.10 E
Laitila 26 60.53 N 21.41 E
Laives (Leifers) 64 46.26 N 11.20 E
Laiwu 98 36.12 N 117.42 E
Laiwui 164 1.22 S 127.40 E
Laixi 98 36.51 N 120.29 E
Laiya 116 13.40 N 121.24 E
Laiyang 98 36.58 N 120.44 E
Laiyuan, Zhg. 98 39.18 N 114.44 E
Laiyuan, Zhg. 100 25.36 N 117.01 E
Laizhouwan C 98 37.36 N 119.30 E
Laja ≃ 24 66.20 N 56.16 E
Laja, Laguna de la ⊜ 252 37.21 S 71.19 W
Laja, Río de la ≃ 234 20.30 N 100.46 W
Laja, Salto del ⌊ 252 37.22 S 72.25 W
La Jalca 248 6.29 S 77.43 W
La Jara 200 37.16 N 105.58 W
La Jara ◆[1] 34 39.42 N 4.54 W
La Jara Canyon ∨ 200 36.50 N 107.30 W
La Jara Creek ≃ 200 37.22 N 105.46 W
La Jarita 232 28.03 N 103.20 W
La Jarrie 32 46.08 N 1.00 W
Lajas, Méx. 234 23.07 N 105.07 W
Lajas, P.R. 240m 18.03 N 67.04 W
La Javie 62 44.10 N 6.21 E
Laje 255 13.10 S 39.25 W
Laje, Ilha da I 287a 22.57 S 43.09 W
Laje, Ponta da ≻ 266c 38.40 N 9.19 W
Laje, Ribeira de ≃ 266c 38.41 N 9.19 W
Lajeado 252 29.27 S 51.58 W
Lajeado Velho ◆[8] 287b 23.32 S 46.23 W
Lajedo 250 8.40 S 36.19 W
Lajes, Bra. 250 5.41 S 36.14 W
Lajes, Bra. 252 27.48 S 50.19 W
Lajes, Ribeirão das ≃ 256 22.38 S 43.42 W
Lajinha 255 20.09 S 41.37 W
Lajishan ⛰ 102 36.13 N 102.15 E
Lajkovo 265b 55.42 N 37.13 E
La Jolla 228 32.51 N 117.16 W
La Jolla, Point ≻ 228 32.51 N 117.17 W
Lajord 184 50.14 N 104.09 W
La Jose 214 40.50 N 78.41 W
Lajosmizse 30 47.02 N 19.34 E
La Joya, Méx. 196 26.26 N 101.08 W
La Joya, Méx. 232 32.08 N 114.01 W
La Joya, Perú 248 16.44 S 71.51 W
Lajtamak 86 58.25 N 67.25 E
Lajturi 84 41.55 N 41.55 E
La Junta, Méx. 232 28.28 N 107.20 W
La Junta, Colo., U.S. 198 37.59 N 103.33 W
Lakaband 120 31.00 N 69.30 E
Lakahia, Teluk C 164 4.00 S 134.38 E
Lakamané 150 14.31 N 9.55 W
Lakazangbuhe ≃ 124 29.24 N 87.58 E
Lake 194 32.21 N 89.20 W
Lake □[6], Calif., U.S. 226 39.01 N 122.33 W
Lake □[6], Fla., U.S. 220 28.42 N 81.39 W
Lake □[6], Ill., U.S. 216 42.22 N 87.50 W
Lake □[6], Ind., U.S. 216 41.25 N 87.22 W
Lake □[6], Ohio, U.S. 214 41.43 N 81.15 W
Lake Accotink Park ♠ 284c 38.48 N 77.14 W
Lake Albert 171b 35.10 S 147.23 E
Lake Alfred 220 28.05 N 81.44 W
Lake Alpine 226 38.28 N 120.00 W
Lake Andes 198 43.09 N 98.32 W
Lake Angelus 281 42.42 N 83.19 W
Lake Ariel 210 41.27 N 75.23 W
Lake Arrowhead 228 34.15 N 117.12 W
Lake Arthur, La., U.S. 194 30.05 N 92.41 W
Lake Arthur, N. Mex., U.S. 196 33.00 N 104.22 W
Lake Barcroft 284c 38.51 N 77.09 W
Lake Bathurst 170 35.01 S 149.36 E
Lake Benton 198 44.16 N 96.17 W
Lake Beseck 207 41.30 N 72.14 W
Lake Biddy 162 33.00 S 118.57 E
Lake Bluff 216 42.16 N 87.50 W
Lake Buena Vista 220 28.23 N 81.31 W
Lake Burragorang ⊜[1] 170 33.57 S 150.26 E
Lake Butler 192 30.01 N 82.20 W
Lake Cable 214 40.52 N 81.27 W
Lake Camm 162 32.59 S 119.35 E
Lake Cargelligo 166 33.18 S 146.23 E
Lake Carmel 210 41.27 N 73.40 W
Lake Charles 194 30.13 N 93.12 W
Lake Chelan National Recreation Area ♠ 224 48.20 N 120.40 W
Lake City, Ark., U.S. 194 35.49 N 90.26 W
Lake City, Colo., U.S. 200 38.02 N 107.19 W
Lake City, Fla., U.S. 192 30.12 N 82.38 W
Lake City, Ill., U.S. 219 39.45 N 88.43 W
Lake City, Iowa, U.S. 198 42.16 N 94.44 W
Lake City, Mich., U.S. 190 44.20 N 85.13 W
Lake City, Minn., U.S. 190 44.27 N 92.16 W
Lake City, Pa., U.S. 214 42.01 N 80.21 W
Lake City, S.C., U.S. 192 33.52 N 79.45 W
Lake City, Tenn., U.S. 192 36.13 N 84.09 W
Lake Clarke Shores 220 26.39 N 80.04 W
Lake Coleridge 172 43.22 S 171.32 E
Lake Como, N.Y., U.S. 210 42.41 N 76.18 W
Lake Como, Pa., U.S. 210 41.51 N 75.20 W
Lake Cowichan 182 48.50 N 124.03 W
Lake Creek ≃, Oreg., U.S. 202 44.04 N 123.47 W
Lake Creek ≃, Tex., U.S. 222 30.16 N 95.29 W
Lake Crescent 224 48.06 N 123.50 W
Lake Crystal 190 44.06 N 94.13 W
Lake Dalecarlia 216 41.20 N 87.24 W
Lake Dallas 222 33.07 N 97.02 W
Lake Delta 210 43.17 N 75.28 W
Lake Delton 190 43.35 N 89.47 W
Lakedemonovka 83 47.12 N 38.33 E
Lake Denison State Park ♠ 207 42.38 N 72.05 W
Lake District ◆[1] 44 54.30 N 3.10 W
Lake District National Park ♠ 44 54.30 N 3.05 W
Lake Eliza 216 41.26 N 87.10 W
Lake Elsinore 228 33.40 N 117.20 W
Lake Elsinore State Recreation Area ♠ 228 33.41 N 117.22 W
Lake Entrance ⊔ 170 33.05 S 151.39 E
Lake Errock 224 49.13 N 122.02 W
Lake Fenton 216 42.52 N 83.43 W
Lakefield, Ont., Can. 212 44.26 N 78.16 W
Lakefield, S. Afr. 273d 26.11 S 28.18 E
Lakefield, Minn., U.S. 198 43.41 N 95.10 W
Lake Forest, Fla., U.S. 192 30.24 N 81.41 W
Lake Forest, Ill., U.S. 216 42.15 N 87.50 W
Lake Forest, N.J., U.S. 276 40.58 N 74.36 W
Lake Forest Park 224 47.45 N 122.17 W
Lake Fork 219 39.58 N 89.21 W
Lake Fork ≃ 200 40.13 N 110.07 W
Lake Fork Creek ≃ 222 32.36 N 95.21 W
Lake Front Park ♠ 278 42.03 N 87.40 W
Lake Garfield 220 27.54 N 81.47 W
Lake Geneva 216 42.36 N 88.26 W
Lake George 188 43.26 N 73.43 W
Lake Grace 162 33.06 S 118.28 E
Lake Grinnell 276 41.06 N 74.38 W
Lake Grove 276 40.51 N 73.07 W
Lake Hamilton 220 28.07 N 81.42 W
Lake Harbor 220 26.42 N 80.48 W
Lake Harbour 176 62.51 N 69.53 W
Lake Harmony 210 41.04 N 75.36 W
Lake Hattie Reservoir ⊜[1] 200 41.15 N 105.55 W
Lake Havasu City 200 34.27 N 114.22 W
Lake Helen 220 28.59 N 81.14 W
Lake Hiawatha 210 40.53 N 74.23 W
Lake Hill 210 42.04 N 74.11 W
Lake Hills, Ind., U.S. 216 41.28 N 87.27 W
Lake Hills, Wash., U.S. 224 47.36 N 122.08 W
Lake Hopatcong 210 40.55 N 74.39 W
Lake Hughes 228 34.40 N 118.26 W
Lake Huntington 210 41.41 N 75.00 W
Lakehurst 208 40.01 N 74.19 W
Lakehurst Naval Air Station ■ 208 40.01 N 74.18 W
Lake Illawarra 170 34.33 S 150.52 E
Lake Intervale 276 40.53 N 74.25 W
Lake in the Hills 216 42.11 N 88.20 W
Lake Isabella 204 35.39 N 118.28 W
Lake Jackson 222 29.02 N 95.27 W
Lake Jem 220 28.45 N 81.40 W
Lakekamu ≃ 164 8.10 S 146.15 E
Lake Katrine 210 41.59 N 73.59 W
Lake King 162 33.05 S 119.40 E
Lake Lackawanna 210 40.57 N 74.42 W
Lakeland, Fla., U.S. 220 28.03 N 81.57 W
Lakeland, Ga., U.S. 192 31.02 N 83.04 W
Lakeland, Mich., U.S. 216 42.28 N 83.51 W
Lakeland, N.Y., U.S. 210 43.06 N 76.15 W
Lakeland Park 216 42.21 N 88.17 W
Lakeland Village 228 33.39 N 117.22 W
Lake Lenape 210 41.01 N 74.44 W
Lake Linden 190 47.11 N 88.26 W
Lake Lookover 276 41.09 N 74.24 W
Lake Loramie State Park ♠ 216 40.23 N 84.20 W
Lake Louise, Alta., Can. 182 51.26 N 116.11 W
Lake Louise, Wash., U.S. 224 47.05 N 122.36 W
Lake Lucerne 214 41.24 N 81.21 W
Lake Luzerne 210 43.19 N 73.50 W
Lake Magdalene 220 28.05 N 82.28 W
Lake Manyara National Park ♠ 154 3.30 S 36.25 E
Lake Mary 220 28.46 N 81.19 W
Lakemba 274a 33.55 S 151.05 E
Lakemba I 175g 18.13 S 178.47 W
Lakemba Passage ⊔ 175g 17.53 S 178.32 W
Lake Mead National Recreation Area ♠ 200 36.00 N 114.30 W
Lake Mills, Iowa, U.S. 190 43.25 N 93.32 W
Lake Mills, Wis., U.S. 216 43.05 N 88.55 W
Lake Milton 214 41.06 N 80.58 W
Lake Minchumina 180 63.53 N 152.19 W
Lake Monroe 220 28.50 N 81.19 W
Lakemont, N.Y., U.S. 210 42.31 N 76.56 W
Lakemont, Pa., U.S. 214 40.31 N 78.23 W
Lakemoor 216 42.20 N 88.12 W
Lakemore 214 41.01 N 81.25 W
Lake Murray State Park ♠ 196 34.01 N 97.00 W
Lake Nakuru National Park ♠ 154 0.20 S 36.05 E
Lake Nash 166 21.00 S 137.55 E
Lake Nepessing 216 43.02 N 83.22 W
Lakenheath 42 52.25 N 0.31 E
Lake Norden 198 44.35 N 97.13 W
Lake Normandy Estates 284c 39.03 N 77.11 W
Lake Odessa 216 42.47 N 85.08 W
Lake of the Ozarks State Park ♠ 194 38.08 N 92.40 W
Lake of the Woods 216 41.26 N 86.14 W
Lake Orion 216 42.47 N 83.14 W
Lake Orion Heights 216 42.46 N 83.18 W
Lake Oroville State Recreational Area ♠ 226 39.32 N 121.27 W
Lake Oswego 224 45.26 N 122.39 W
Lake Ozark 194 38.12 N 92.38 W
Lakepa 174v 18.59 S 169.48 W
Lake Panasoffkee 220 28.46 N 82.07 W
Lake Paringa 172 43.43 S 169.29 E
Lake Park, Fla., U.S. 220 26.49 N 80.04 W
Lake Park, Iowa, U.S. 198 43.27 N 95.19 W
Lake Park, Minn., U.S. 198 46.53 N 96.06 W
Lake Pine 208 39.52 N 74.51 W
Lake Placid, Fla., U.S. 220 27.18 N 81.22 W
Lake Placid, N.Y., U.S. 188 44.17 N 73.59 W
Lake Pleasant 188 43.28 N 74.25 W
Lakeport, Calif., U.S. 204 39.03 N 122.55 W
Lakeport, Mich., U.S. 190 43.07 N 82.30 W
Lakeport, N.Y., U.S. 210 43.09 N 75.52 W
Lake Preston 198 44.22 N 97.23 W
Lake Providence 194 32.48 N 91.11 W
Lake Pukaki 172 44.11 S 170.09 E
Lakeridge, Nev., U.S. 226 39.02 N 119.57 W
Lake Ridge, N.J., U.S. 276 40.24 N 74.15 W
Lake Riviera 208 40.03 N 74.10 W
Lake Saint Louis 219 38.48 N 90.45 W
Lake Sammamish State Park ♠ 224 47.33 N 122.03 W
Lake San Marcos 228 33.09 N 117.12 W
Lake Sawyer 224 47.20 N 122.03 W
Lakes Bay C 208 39.22 N 74.30 W
Lakes Entrance 166 37.53 S 147.59 E
Lake Shawnee 276 40.59 N 74.36 W
Lakeshore, Calif., U.S. 226 37.15 N 119.12 W
Lake Shore, Fla., U.S. 192 30.17 N 81.43 W
Lake Shore, Mich., U.S. 216 42.38 N 86.14 W
Lake Shore, Wash., U.S. 224 45.42 N 122.42 W
Lakeside, N.S., Can. 186 44.38 N 63.41 W
Lakeside, S. Afr. 273d 26.06 S 28.09 E
Lakeside, Ariz., U.S. 200 34.09 N 109.58 W
Lakeside, Calif., U.S. 228 32.52 N 116.55 W
Lakeside, Conn., U.S. 207 41.26 N 73.16 W
Lakeside, Conn., U.S. 207 41.41 N 73.15 W
Lakeside, Mich., U.S. 216 41.51 N 86.40 W
Lakeside, Mont., U.S. 202 48.01 N 114.13 W
Lakeside, Ohio, U.S. 214 41.32 N 82.45 W
Lakeside, Oreg., U.S. 202 43.34 N 124.11 W
Lakeside, Va., U.S. 208 37.37 N 77.28 W
Lakeside Center ◆[9] 281 42.37 N 83.00 W
Lakeside Village 222 32.02 N 97.30 W
Lakes National Park ♠ 166 38.05 S 147.40 E
Lake Station 216 41.34 N 87.15 W
Lake Stevens 224 48.01 N 122.04 W
Lake Stockholm 276 41.04 N 74.31 W
Lake Success 276 40.46 N 73.43 W
Lake Superior Provincial Park ♠ 190 47.32 N 84.50 W
Lake Swannanoa 276 41.01 N 74.31 W
Lake Taghkanic State Park ♠ 210 42.06 N 73.43 W
Lake Tahoe Airport ⊠ 226 38.54 N 120.00 W
Lake Tahoe-Nevada State Park ♠ 226 39.13 N 119.55 W
Lake Tamarack 210 41.06 N 74.32 W
Lake Tekapo 172 44.01 S 170.30 E
Lake Telemark 276 40.57 N 74.30 W
Lake Temescal Regional Park ♠ 282 37.51 N 122.14 W
Laketon 216 40.58 N 85.50 W
Laketown 200 41.49 N 111.19 W
Lake Varley 162 32.46 S 119.27 E
Lakeview, Calif., U.S. 228 33.50 N 117.07 W
Lakeview, Ga., U.S. 192 34.59 N 85.16 W
Lake View, Iowa, U.S. 198 42.18 N 95.03 W
Lakeview, Mich., U.S. 216 42.18 N 85.11 W
Lake View, N.Y., U.S. 210 42.43 N 78.56 W
Lakeview, Ohio, U.S. 216 40.29 N 83.56 W
Lakeview, Oreg., U.S. 202 42.11 N 120.21 W
Lake View, S.C., U.S. 192 34.21 N 79.10 W
Lakeview, Tex., U.S. 194 29.55 N 93.54 W
Lakeview, Tex., U.S. 196 34.40 N 100.42 W
Lakeview, Wash., U.S. 224 47.10 N 122.30 W
Lakeview ◆[8] 278 41.57 N 87.39 W
Lakeview Mountain ∧, B.C., Can. 182 49.03 N 120.09 W
Lakeview Mountain ∧, Wash., U.S. 224 46.22 N 121.24 W
Lake Village, Ark., U.S. 194 33.20 N 91.17 W
Lake Village, Ind., U.S. 216 41.08 N 87.27 W
Lakeville, Conn., U.S. 207 41.58 N 73.27 W
Lakeville, Ind., U.S. 216 41.31 N 86.16 W
Lakeville, Mich., U.S. 214 42.49 N 83.09 W
Lakeville, Minn., U.S. 190 44.39 N 93.14 W
Lakeville, N.Y., U.S. 210 42.50 N 77.42 W
Lakeville, Ohio, U.S. 214 40.40 N 82.07 W
Lakeville Lake ⊜ 214 42.50 N 83.09 W
Lake Wales 220 27.54 N 81.35 W
Lake Whitney State Park ♠ 222 31.55 N 97.22 W
Lake Wilson 198 43.59 N 95.57 W
Lake Winola 210 41.30 N 75.50 W
Lakewood, Calif., U.S. 228 33.50 N 118.08 W
Lakewood, Colo., U.S. 200 39.44 N 105.06 W
Lakewood, Ill., U.S. 216 39.19 N 88.54 W
Lakewood, Mich., U.S. 216 42.18 N 85.31 W
Lakewood, N.J., U.S. 208 40.06 N 74.13 W
Lakewood, N.Y., U.S. 214 42.06 N 79.20 W
Lakewood, Ohio, U.S. 214 41.29 N 81.48 W
Lakewood, Pa., U.S. 210 41.51 N 75.22 W
Lakewood, Wash., U.S. 224 48.09 N 122.12 W
Lakewood, Wis., U.S. 190 45.18 N 88.31 W
Lakewood Center 224 47.10 N 122.31 W
Lakewood Center ◆[9] 280 33.51 N 118.09 W
Lakewood Park 198 48.04 N 98.56 W
Lakewood Park ♠ 279a 41.29 N 81.47 W
Lakewood Shores 216 41.17 N 88.10 W
Lake Worth, Fla., U.S. 220 26.37 N 80.03 W
Lake Worth, Tex., U.S. 222 32.49 N 97.27 W
Lake Zurich 216 42.12 N 88.06 W
Lakhdaria 34 36.34 N 3.35 E
Lākheri 124 25.40 N 76.10 E
Lakhīmpur 124 27.57 N 80.46 E
Lakhipur, Bhārat 120 24.48 N 93.01 E
Lakhipur, Bhārat 124 26.02 N 90.18 E
Lakhish 132 31.34 N 34.51 E
Lakhish ∨ 132 31.48 N 34.38 E
Lakhnādon 124 22.36 N 79.36 E
Lakhpat 120 23.49 N 68.47 E
Lakhya ≃ 126 23.35 N 90.31 E
L'aki 84 40.34 N 47.26 E
Laki ≃ 115a 7.30 S 107.25 E
Lakin 198 37.56 N 101.15 W
Lakinskij 80 56.01 N 39.57 E
Lakkadiven → Laccadive Islands II 122 10.00 N 73.00 E
Lakki 123 32.36 N 70.55 E
Laknau → Lucknow 124 26.51 N 80.55 E
Lakonikós Kólpos C 38 36.25 N 22.37 E
Lakor, Pulau I 164 8.14 S 128.10 E
Lakota, C. Iv. 150 5.51 N 5.41 W
Lakota, Iowa, U.S. 190 43.23 N 94.06 W
Lakota, N. Dak., U.S. 198 48.02 N 98.21 W
Laksefjorden C[2] 24 70.58 N 27.00 E
Lakselv 24 70.04 N 24.56 E
Lakshadweep □[3] 122 10.00 N 73.00 E
Lakshamannāth 126 21.51 N 87.13 E
Lakshmanpur 272b 22.38 N 88.16 E
Lakshmeshwar 122 15.08 N 75.28 E
Lakshmi, Char I 126 21.57 N 90.33 E
Lakshmikantapur 126 22.07 N 88.20 E
Lakshmīpur 126 22.57 N 90.50 E
Lakshmisāgar 126 22.55 N 87.01 E
Lakulu 152 14.22 S 23.17 E
Lala 116 7.59 N 123.46 E
Lalafuta ≃ 154 13.57 S 24.41 E
La Laguna → San Cristóbal de la Laguna 148 28.29 N 16.19 W
La Lajilla 232 26.47 N 99.37 W
Lāla Mūsa 123 32.42 N 73.58 E
Lalapanzi 154 19.16 S 30.15 E
Lâlapaşa 130 41.50 N 26.44 E
Lalatuncun 104 41.44 N 122.00 E
Lalbenque 32 44.20 N 1.33 E
Laleham 260 51.25 N 0.30 W
Lāleh Zār, Kūh-e ∧ 128 29.24 N 56.46 E
Lâleli 130 41.03 N 37.37 E
La Leona 196 25.52 N 101.05 W
La Leonesa 252 27.03 S 58.43 W
Lalevade-d'Ardèche 62 44.39 N 4.19 E
Lālganj 124 25.52 N 85.11 E
Lālgarh 126 22.35 N 87.03 E
Lāliān 123 31.49 N 72.48 E
Lalibela 144 12.02 N 39.02 E
La Libertad, El Sal. 236 13.29 N 89.19 W
La Libertad, Guat. 232 16.47 N 90.07 W
La Libertad, Hond. 236 14.43 N 87.36 W
La Libertad, Nic. 236 12.13 N 85.10 W
La Libertad □[5] 248 8.00 S 78.30 W
La Ligua 252 32.27 S 71.14 W
La Lima, Hond. 236 15.24 N 87.56 W
La Lima, It. 66 44.04 N 10.46 E
La Limpia, Laguna ⊜ 258 35.37 S 57.49 W
Lalín 34 42.39 N 8.07 W
Lalinde 32 44.51 N 0.44 E
Lalindi 115b 10.12 S 120.10 E
Lalindu ≃ 112 3.28 S 122.05 E
La Línea 34 36.10 N 5.19 W
Lalinhe ≃ 89 45.29 N 125.26 E
L'alino 82 54.29 N 39.06 E
La Lisa ◆[8] 286b 23.04 N 82.26 W
Lalitpur, Bhārat 124 24.41 N 78.25 E
Lalitpur, Nepāl 124 27.41 N 85.20 E
La Llagosta 266d 41.31 N 2.12 E
Lalla Khedidja, Tamgout de ∧ 34 36.27 N 4.15 E
Lālmai 124 23.19 N 91.07 E
Lālmanir Hāt 124 25.54 N 89.27 E
Laloa 112 4.50 S 121.54 E
La Loche 184 56.29 N 109.27 W
La Loche, Lac ⊜ 184 56.25 N 109.30 W
Laloki 164 9.25 S 147.15 E
La Loma 234 22.53 N 105.51 W
La Londe 62 43.08 N 6.14 E
Lalo Point ≻ 174n 14.55 N 145.38 E
La Lora ⛰[1] 34 42.45 N 4.00 W
Lalor Park 274a 33.45 S 150.56 E
La Loupe 50 48.28 N 1.01 E
Lalouvesc 62 45.07 N 4.32 E
La Louvière 50 50.28 N 4.11 E
L'Alpe-d'Huez 62 45.06 N 6.04 E
Lālpur, Bhārat 120 22.12 N 69.58 E
Lālpur, Bngl. 126 24.11 N 88.58 E
Lal'sk 24 60.44 N 47.34 E
Lālsot 124 26.34 N 76.20 E
La Luz 196 25.52 N 97.37 W
Lam 60 49.12 N 13.03 E
Lama ≃ 82 56.29 N 36.10 E
Lama, Ozero ⊜ 74 69.30 N 90.30 E
L'Amable Lake ⊜ 212 45.01 N 77.49 W
La Macarena, Serranía de ⛰ 246 2.45 N 73.55 W
La Maddalena 71 41.13 N 9.24 E
Lama dei Peligni 66 42.02 N 14.11 E
La Madeleine 50 50.39 N 3.04 E
Lamadong 98 40.39 N 119.39 E
La Madrague 62 43.14 N 5.22 E
La Madrid, Arg. 252 27.38 S 65.15 W
Lamadrid, Méx. 196 27.05 N 101.50 W
Lamag 112 5.29 N 117.49 E
La Magdalena, Río de ≃ 286a 19.21 N 99.11 W
Lamagoumen 105 40.52 N 116.39 E
Lamahuang 104 42.27 N 121.33 E
La Mailleraye-sur-Seine 50 49.29 N 0.46 E
La Majada 286c 10.27 N 67.01 W
Lama-Kara 150 9.33 N 1.12 E
La Malbaie 186 47.39 N 70.10 W
La Malinche, Parque Nacional ♠ 234 19.15 N 98.05 W
Lamaline 186 46.52 N 55.49 W
La Malmaison ⊥ 261 48.52 N 2.10 E
Lamaload Reservoir ⊜[1] 262 53.16 N 2.02 W
Lama Mocogno 64 44.18 N 10.45 E
La Mancha 232 24.52 N 102.47 W
La Mancha ◆[1] 34 39.05 N 3.00 W
La Mancha, Canal de → English Channel ⊔ 28 50.20 N 1.00 W
La Manche (English Channel) ⊔ 28 50.20 N 1.00 W
Lamandau ≃ 112 2.42 S 111.34 E
La Mansión 236 10.06 N 85.22 W
Lamap 175f 16.26 S 167.43 E
Lamar, Colo., U.S. 198 38.05 N 102.37 W
Lamar, Mo., U.S. 194 37.29 N 94.17 W
Lamar, Pa., U.S. 210 41.01 N 77.32 W
Lamar, S.C., U.S. 192 34.10 N 80.04 W
Lamar ≃ 202 44.56 N 110.24 W
La Mar, Parque ♠ 286d 12.04 S 77.02 W
La Marañosa 266a 40.17 N 3.35 W
Lamarche 58 48.04 N 5.47 E
Lamarche-sur-Saône 58 47.16 N 5.23 E
La Mare, Pointe ≻ 240e 14.47 N 61.13 W
La Mariposa, Embalse ⊜[1] 286c 10.24 N 66.56 W
La Mariscala 252 34.03 S 54.47 W
La Marolle-en-Sologne 50 47.35 N 1.47 E
La Maroma 196 28.34 N 100.45 W
Lamarque, Arg. 252 39.24 S 65.42 W
La Marque, Tex., U.S. 222 29.22 N 94.58 W
La Marsa 36 36.53 N 10.20 E
La Martre 62 43.46 N 6.36 E
Lamas 248 6.25 S 76.35 W
La Masica 236 15.37 N 87.07 W
Lamastre 62 44.59 N 4.35 E
La Matanza → San Justo 258 34.40 S 58.33 W
Lama Temple ♆[1] 271a 39.56 N 116.25 E
La Mauricie, Parc National de (La Mauricie National Park) ♠ 206 46.50 N 73.00 W
L'Amaury 50 48.47 N 1.49 E
La Maya, Cuba 240p 20.10 N 75.39 W
Lamaya, Zhg. 102 29.50 N 99.53 E
Lamayingzi 104 42.09 N 121.50 E
Lambach 60 48.05 N 13.53 E
Lamballe 32 48.28 N 2.31 W
Lambaréné 152 0.42 S 10.13 E

ENGLISH

Name Page Lat.°′ Long.°′
Lambari 256 21.58 S 45.21 W
Lambari ≃, Bra. 255 19.30 S 45.00 W
Lambari ≃, Bra. 256 21.47 S 45.13 W
Lambasa 175g 16.26 S 179.24 E
Lambayeque 248 6.42 S 79.55 W
Lambayeque □[5] 248 6.20 S 80.00 W
Lambayeque ≃ 248 6.43 S 79.54 W
Lambay Island I 48 53.29 N 6.01 W
Lambe 273a 6.42 N 3.21 E
Lambersart 50 50.39 N 3.02 E
Lambert, Miss., U.S. 194 34.12 N 90.24 W
Lambert, Mont., U.S. 198 47.41 N 104.37 W
Lambert, Cape ≻, Austl. 162 20.35 S 117.10 E
Lambert, Cape ≻, Pap. N. Gui. 164 4.12 S 151.32 E
Lambert Glacier ⊓ 9 71.00 S 70.00 E
Lamberton 198 44.14 N 95.16 W
Lambert-Saint Louis International Airport ⊠ 219 38.45 N 90.22 W
Lambertsbaai → Lambert's Bay 158 32.05 S 18.17 E
Lambert's Bay 158 32.05 S 18.17 E
Lambertville, Mich., U.S. 216 41.46 N 83.35 W
Lambertville, N.J., U.S. 208 40.22 N 74.57 W
Lambesc 62 43.39 N 5.16 E
Lambeth 214 42.54 N 81.18 W
Lambeth ◆[8] 42 51.30 N 0.07 W
L'ambir' 80 54.17 N 45.07 E
Lambo Katenga 154 5.02 S 28.48 E
Lambomakondro 157b 22.41 S 44.44 E
Lambourn 42 51.31 N 1.31 W
Lambourne ≃ 42 51.24 N 1.18 W
Lambourne End 260 51.38 N 0.08 E
Lambrama 248 13.52 S 72.46 W
Lambrate ◆[8] 266b 45.29 N 9.15 E
Lambrecht 56 50.08 N 8.56 E
Lambrechten 60 48.19 N 13.31 E
Lambrechts Drift 158 28.31 S 21.43 E
Lambro ≃ 62 45.08 N 9.32 E
Lambro, Parco ♠ 266b 45.30 N 9.15 E
Lambs Creek 210 41.51 N 77.06 W
Lambs Terrace 285 39.46 N 75.02 W
Lambton 273d 26.15 S 28.10 E
Lambton □[6] 214 42.45 N 82.15 W
Lambton, Cape ≻ 176 71.05 N 123.10 W
Lambu 164 3.09 S 151.41 E
Lambunao 116 11.03 N 122.29 E
Lambwe Valley Game Reserve ◆[4] 154 0.37 S 34.15 E
L'amca 24 64.27 N 37.04 E
Lamdessar-Timur 164 7.12 S 131.58 E
Lame, Nig. 150 10.23 N 9.13 E
Lamé, Tchad 146 9.15 N 14.32 E
La Meca → Makkah 144 21.27 N 39.49 E
La Mecque → Makkah 144 21.27 N 39.49 E
Lame Deer 202 45.37 N 106.40 W
La Méditerranée → Mediterranean Sea ⊤[2] 10 35.00 N 20.00 E
Lamego 34 41.06 N 7.49 W
La Meije ∧ 62 45.00 N 6.18 E
La Membrolle-sur-Choisille 50 47.26 N 0.38 E
La Mendieta 252 24.19 S 64.58 W
L'amen'ga 76 59.51 N 44.31 E
Lamentin 241o 16.16 N 61.38 W
Lamenu 175f 16.34 S 168.11 E
Lamèque 186 47.47 N 64.38 W
La Merced, Arg. 252 24.58 S 65.29 W
La Merced, Arg. 252 28.10 S 65.41 W
La Merced, Perú 248 11.03 S 75.19 W
Lameroo 166 35.20 S 140.31 E
La Mesa, Pan. 236 8.09 N 81.11 W
La Mesa, Calif., U.S. 228 32.46 N 117.01 W
La Mesa, N. Mex., U.S. 200 32.07 N 106.42 W
Lamesa, Tex., U.S. 196 32.44 N 101.57 W
La Mesa, Cerro ∧ 232 26.59 N 113.44 W
La Mesa Dam ◆[6] 269f 14.43 N 121.04 E
La Meta ∧ 66 41.41 N 13.56 E
Lamía 38 38.54 N 22.26 E
L'amin ≃ 74 61.18 N 71.48 E
Lamine ≃ 194 38.59 N 92.51 W
La Minerve 206 46.15 N 74.56 W
Lamingbach ≃ 61 47.25 N 15.16 E
Lamington ≃ 210 40.38 N 74.41 W
Lamington National Park ♠ 166 28.15 S 153.12 E
Laminusa 116 5.33 N 120.55 E
La Mira 234 18.02 N 102.19 W
La Mirada 228 33.54 N 118.01 W
La Mirada Creek ≃ 280 33.53 N 118.01 W
La Misión 204 32.05 N 116.50 W
Lamitan 116 6.39 N 122.08 E
Lamlam, Mount ∧ 174p 13.20 N 144.40 E
Lamlash 46 55.32 N 5.08 W
Lammefjord C 41 55.48 N 11.43 E
Lammerlaw Top ∧ 172 45.40 S 169.38 E
Lammermuir ◆[1] 46 55.50 N 2.25 W
Lammermuir Hills ⛰[2] 46 55.50 N 2.44 W
Lammeulo 114 5.15 N 95.56 E
Lammhult 26 57.10 N 14.35 E
Lammi 26 61.05 N 25.01 E
Lamming Mills 182 53.22 N 120.18 W
Lamogai 164 5.50 S 149.20 E
La Moille, Ill., U.S. 190 41.32 N 89.17 W
Lamoille, Nev., U.S. 204 40.44 N 115.29 W
Lamoille ≃ 188 44.35 N 73.10 W
La Moine ≃ 194 39.59 N 90.31 W
La Moine, East Fork ≃ 194 40.24 N 90.56 W
La Molina 286d 12.05 S 76.57 W
Lamon Bay C 116 14.25 N 122.00 E
La Moncada 234 20.16 N 100.48 W
Lamone ≃ 66 44.31 N 12.15 E
Lamongan 115a 7.07 S 112.25 E
Lamongan, Gunung ∧ 115a 7.58 S 113.20 E
Lamoni 190 40.37 N 93.56 W
Lamont, Alta., Can. 182 53.46 N 112.48 W
Lamont, Calif., U.S. 228 35.15 N 118.55 W
Lamont, Iowa, U.S. 190 42.36 N 91.39 W
Lamont, Mich., U.S. 216 43.01 N 86.09 W
Lamont, Okla., U.S. 196 36.41 N 97.33 W
La Monte 194 38.46 N 93.25 W
La Mothe, Réservoir ⊜[1] 186 48.46 N 71.09 W
La Mothe-Achard 32 46.37 N 1.40 W
La Mothe-Saint-Héraye 32 46.22 N 0.07 W
Lamotrek I[1] 14 7.30 N 146.20 E
La Mott 285 40.04 N 75.08 W
La Motte, Lac ⊜ 190 48.24 N 78.03 W
Lamotte-Beuvron 50 47.36 N 2.01 E
La Motte-Chalançon 62 44.29 N 5.23 E
La Motte-du-Caire 62 44.21 N 6.02 E
Lamoura 58 46.24 N 5.58 E
La Moure 198 46.21 N 98.18 W
La Moustique ≃ 241o 16.11 N 61.35 W
Lampa 248 15.21 S 70.22 W
Lampang 110 18.18 N 99.31 E
Lampasas ≃ 196 30.59 N 97.24 W
Lampedusa 71a 35.30 N 12.56 E
Lampedusa, Isola di I 71a 35.31 N 12.35 E
Lampertheim 56 49.35 N 8.28 E
Lampeter, Wales, U.K. 42 52.07 N 4.05 W
Lampeter, Pa., U.S. 208 39.58 N 76.14 W
Lamphun 110 18.35 N 99.01 E
Lampinsaari 26 64.25 N 25.09 E
Lampione, Isolotto di I 71a 35.34 N 12.19 E
Lampman 184 49.23 N 102.45 W

DEUTSCH

Name Seite Breite°′ Länge°′ E=Ost
Lamprechtshausen 64 47.59 N 12.57 E
Lampung, Teluk C 115a 5.40 S 105.20 E
Lamskoje 76 52.57 N 38.02 E
Lamspringe 52 51.58 N 10.00 E
Lamstedt 52 53.38 N 9.05 E
Lāmta 124 22.08 N 80.07 E
Lamu, Kenya 154 2.16 S 40.54 E
Lāmu, Mya. 110 19.14 N 94.10 E
Lamud 2[illegible]3 6.09 S 77.55 W
La Muerte, Cerro ∧ 236 9.33 N 83.44 W
Lamu Island I 154 2.17 S 40.52 E
Lam Uk Wei 271d 22.26 N 114.22 E
La Mure 62 44.54 N 5.47 E
Lamure-sur-Azergues 58 46.04 N 4.30 E
La Mutua 234 22.23 N 99.18 W
Lan' ≃ 76 52.09 N 27.18 E
Lan, Loi ∧ 110 19.40 N 97.55 E
Lana 64 46.37 N 11.09 E
Lana, Río de la ≃ 234 17.49 N 95.09 W
Lanai I 229a 20.50 N 156.55 W
Lanai City 229a 20.50 N 156.55 W
Lanaihale ∧ 229a 20.49 N 156.52 W
Lanaken 56 50.53 N 5.39 E
Lanalhue, Lago ⊜ 252 37.55 S 73.18 W
La Nana, Bayou ≃ 222 31.27 N 94.43 W
Lanao, Lake ⊜ 116 7.53 N 124.15 E
Lanao del Norte □[4] 116 8.00 N 124.00 E
Lanao del Sur □[4] 116 7.50 N 124.25 E
La Napoule 62 43.31 N 6.56 E
Lanarce 62 44.44 N 4.00 E
Lanark, Ont., Can. 212 45.01 N 76.22 W
Lanark, Scot., U.K. 46 55.41 N 3.46 W
Lanark, Ill., U.S. 190 42.06 N 89.50 W
Lanark, Pa., U.S. 208 40.33 N 75.26 W
Lanark □[6] 212 45.05 N 76.20 W
La Nartelle 62 43.19 N 6.39 E
Lanas 112 5.20 N 116.30 E
La Nava de Ricomalillo 34 39.39 N 4.59 W
Lanbi Kyun I 110 10.50 N 98.15 E
Lanboyan Point ≻ 116 8.18 N 122.56 E
Lancang 102 23.00 N 100.02 E
Lancangjiang → Mekong ≃ 12 10.33 N 105.24 E
Lancashire □[6] 44 53.45 N 2.40 W
Lancashire Plain ⊻ 44 53.40 N 2.45 W
Lancaster, Ont., Can. 206 45.08 N 74.30 W
Lancaster, Eng., U.K. 44 54.03 N 2.48 W
Lancaster, Calif., U.S. 228 34.42 N 118.08 W
Lancaster, Ky., U.S. 192 37.37 N 84.35 W
Lancaster, Mass., U.S. 207 42.28 N 71.41 W
Lancaster, Minn., U.S. 198 48.52 N 96.48 W
Lancaster, Mo., U.S. 194 40.31 N 92.32 W
Lancaster, N.H., U.S. 188 44.29 N 71.34 W
Lancaster, N.Y., U.S. 210 42.54 N 78.40 W
Lancaster, Ohio, U.S. 188 39.43 N 82.36 W
Lancaster, Pa., U.S. 208 40.02 N 76.19 W
Lancaster, S.C., U.S. 192 34.43 N 80.46 W
Lancaster, Tex., U.S. 222 32.36 N 96.46 W
Lancaster, Va., U.S. 208 37.46 N 76.28 W
Lancaster, Wis., U.S. 190 42.51 N 90.43 W
Lancaster □[6], Pa., U.S. 208 40.02 N 76.19 W
Lancaster □[6], Va., U.S. 208 37.45 N 76.30 W
Lancaster Canal ≡ 262 53.46 N 2.43 W
Lancaster Sound ⊔ 176 74.13 N 84.00 W
Lančchuti 84 42.06 N 42.01 E
Lance Creek 200 43.02 N 104.39 W
Lance Creek ≃ 198 43.22 N 104.16 W
Lancefield 169 37.17 S 144.44 E
Lancelot, Mount ∧ 162 26.13 S 123.12 E
Lancey 62 45.14 N 5.53 E
Lanchang 114 3.30 N 102.11 E
Lanchow → Lanzhou 102 36.03 N 103.41 E
Lanciano 66 42.14 N 14.23 E
Lancin, Fr. 62 45.43 N 5.24 E
Lančin, S.S.S.R. 78 48.34 N 24.45 E
Lancing 42 50.50 N 0.19 W
Lanco 254 39.24 S 72.46 W
Lancones 246 4.35 S 80.30 W
Łańcut 30 50.05 N 22.13 E
Lancy 58 46.11 N 6.07 E
Landang Gua 116 6.58 N 122.15 E
Landau 56 49.12 N 8.07 E
Landau an der Isar 60 48.40 N 12.43 E
Landay 128 30.31 N 63.47 E
Land Between the Lakes ♠ 194 36.55 N 88.05 W
Landeck 58 47.08 N 10.34 E
Landeck in Westpreussen → Lędyczek 30 53.33 N 16.58 E
Landen 56 50.45 N 5.05 E
Landenberg 208 39.47 N 75.46 W
Landenhausen 56 50.36 N 9.28 E
Lander 200 42.50 N 108.44 W
Lander ≃ 162 20.25 S 132.00 E
Landerneau 32 48.27 N 4.15 W
Landes □[5] 32 44.20 N 1.00 W
Landesbergen 52 52.33 N 9.07 E
Landeskrone ∧[2] 54 51.08 N 14.56 E
Landess 216 40.37 N 85.34 W
Landete 34 39.54 N 1.22 W
Landham Brook ≃ 283 42.22 N 71.25 W
Landhausen 263 51.24 N 7.45 E
Landi 98 36.35 N 119.59 E
Landi Kotal 123 34.06 N 71.09 E
Landina 86 59.12 N 67.02 E
Landing 210 40.54 N 74.40 W
Landing Lake ⊜ 184 55.17 N 97.26 W
Landingville 208 40.38 N 76.07 W
Landis, Sask., Can. 184 52.12 N 108.28 W
Landis, N.C., U.S. 192 35.33 N 80.37 W
Landisburg 208 40.20 N 77.18 W
Landisville 208 40.06 N 76.25 W
Landivisiau 32 48.31 N 4.04 W
Landkirchen 54 54.27 N 11.08 E
Landl 64 47.35 N 12.02 E
Lando 192 34.43 N 81.01 W
Land O'Lakes, Fla., U.S. 220 28.11 N 82.34 W
Land O'lakes, Wis., U.S. 190 46.10 N 89.13 W
Landor 162 25.09 S 116.54 E
Landos 62 44.51 N 3.50 E
Landösjön ⊜ 26 63.35 N 14.04 E
Landquart 58 46.58 N 9.33 E
Landquart ≃ 58 46.58 N 9.32 E
Landrecies 50 50.08 N 3.42 E
Landres 56 49.19 N 5.48 E
Landreth Draw ∨ 196 31.14 N 102.29 W
Landriano 62 45.19 N 9.15 E
Landri Sales 250 7.16 S 43.55 W
Landro (Höhlenstein) 64 46.39 N 12.14 E
Landrum 192 35.11 N 82.11 W
Landry 62 45.34 N 6.45 E
Landsberg 54 51.31 N 12.10 E
Landsberg am Lech 58 48.05 N 10.55 E
Landsberg an der Warthe → Gorzów Wielkopolski 30 52.44 N 15.15 E
Landsberg in Oberschlesien → Gorzów Śląski 30 51.02 N 18.24 E
Landsberg in Ostpreussen → Górowo Iławeckie 30 54.17 N 20.30 E
Landsborough 166 26.49 S 152.58 E
Landsborough Creek ≃ 166 22.30 S 144.33 E
Landsbro 26 57.22 N 14.54 E
Land's End ≻, Eng., U.K. 42 50.03 N 5.44 W
Lands End ≻, R.I., U.S. 207 41.27 N 71.19 W
Landshut 60 48.33 N 12.09 E
Landskrona 41 55.52 N 12.50 E

Symbols in the index entries represent the broad categories identified in the key at the right. Symbols with superior numbers (⛰[2]) identify subcategories (see complete key on page I · 30).

Kartensymbole in dem Registerverzeichnis stellen die rechts in Schlüssel erklärten Kategorien dar. Symbole mit hochgestellten Ziffern (⛰[2]) bezeichnen Unterabteilungen einer Kategorie (vgl. vollständiger Schlüssel auf Seite I · 30).

Los símbolos incluídos en el texto del índice representan las grandes categorías identificadas con la clave a la derecha. Los símbolos con numeros en su parte superior (⛰[2]) identifican las subcategorías (véase la clave completa en la página I · 30).

Les symboles de l'index représentent les catégories indiquées dans la légende à droite. Les symboles suivis d'un indice (⛰[2]) représentent des sous-catégories (voir légende complète à la page I · 30).

Os símbolos incluídos no texto do índice representam as grandes categorias identificadas com a chave à direita. Os símbolos com números em sua parte superior (⛰[2]) identificam as subcategorias (veja-se a chave completa à página I · 30).

Symbol	English	Deutsch	Español	Français	Português
∧	Mountain	Berg	Montaña	Montagne	Montanha
⛰	Mountains	Berge	Montañas	Montagnes	Montanhas
)(	Pass	Pass	Paso	Col	Passo
∨	Valley, Canyon	Tal, Cañon	Valle, Cañón	Vallée, Canyon	Vale, Canhão
⊻	Plain	Ebene	Llano	Plaine	Planície
≻	Cape	Kap	Cabo	Cap	Cabo
I	Island	Insel	Isla	Île	Ilha
II	Islands	Inseln	Islas	Îles	Ilhas
⊥	Other Topographic Features	Andere Topographische Objekte	Otros Elementos Topográficos	Autres données topographiques	Outros Elementos Topográficos

ESPAÑOL Nombre / FRANÇAIS Nom / PORTUGUÊS Nome	Página / Page / Página	Lat.°′	Long.°′ W=Oeste / W=Ouest / W=Oeste
Landsman Creek ≃	198	39.35 N	102.19 W
Landsmeer	52	52.26 N	4.52 E
Landstuhl	56	49.25 N	7.34 E
Landweg	263	51.29 N	7.37 E
Landwehrbach ≃	263	51.26 N	6.26 E
Land Wursten ⬥[1]	52	53.40 N	8.35 E
Lane	219	40.07 N	88.51 W
Lane City	222	29.13 N	96.02 W
Lane Cove	274a	33.49 S	151.10 E
Lane Cove C	274a	33.48 S	151.09 E
Lane Cove National Park ♠	274a	33.47 S	151.09 E
La Negra	252	23.45 S	70.19 W
Lane Mountain ∧	228	35.05 N	116.56 W
Lanersbach	64	47.09 N	11.44 E
Lanesboro, Mass., U.S.	207	42.31 N	73.14 W
Lanesboro, Minn., U.S.	190	43.43 N	91.59 W
Lanesboro, Pa., U.S.	210	41.58 N	75.35 W
Lanesville, Ind., U.S.	218	38.14 N	85.59 W
Lanesville, N.Y., U.S.	210	42.08 N	74.16 W
Lanesville, Va., U.S.	208	37.37 N	76.59 W
Lanett	194	32.57 N	85.12 W
La Neuveville	58	47.04 N	7.06 E
Laneville	222	31.58 N	94.49 W
Lanexa	208	37.24 N	76.55 W
Lanezi Lake ⊜	182	53.03 N	120.56 W
Lang	184	49.56 N	104.23 W
La-nga ≃	110	11.12 N	107.16 E
Langadhás	38	40.45 N	23.04 E
Langádhia	38	37.41 N	22.02 E
Langa-Langa	152	3.54 S	15.56 E
Langan Creek ≃	216	40.57 N	87.49 W
Langano, Lake ⊜	144	7.35 N	38.48 E
Lan'gao	102	32.13 N	109.02 E
Langar, Afg.	120	37.02 N	73.47 E
L'angar, S.S.S.R.	85	40.25 N	73.07 E
L'angar, S.S.S.R.	123	37.02 N	72.42 E
Langara	112	4.02 S	123.00 E
Langara Island I	182	54.14 N	133.00 W
Langarūd	128	37.11 N	50.10 E
L'angasovo	80	58.32 N	49.30 E
Langau	61	48.49 N	15.42 E
Langavat, Loch ⊜	46	58.04 N	6.48 W
Långban	40	59.51 N	14.15 E
Langbank	184	50.05 N	102.20 W
Lang Bay	182	49.47 N	124.21 W
Langburkersdorf	54	51.02 N	14.14 E
Langchuhe (Sutlej) ≃	120	29.23 N	71.02 E
Langda	102	31.12 N	96.59 E
Langdai	102	26.06 N	105.20 E
Langdale	194	32.44 N	85.11 W
Langdon	198	48.46 N	98.22 W
Langdondale	214	40.08 N	78.15 W
Langdonggangzi	104	41.40 N	122.20 E
Langdon Hills	260	51.34 N	0.25 E
Langeac	32	45.06 N	3.30 E
Langeais	50	47.20 N	0.24 E
Langebaan	158	33.06 S	18.02 E
Langeberg ⩕, S. Afr.	158	28.20 S	22.35 E
Langeberg ⩕, S. Afr.	158	34.00 S	20.40 E
Lange Berge ⩕[2]	56	50.20 N	10.55 E
Langebrück	54	51.07 N	13.50 E
Langeland I	41	55.00 N	10.50 E
Langelands Bælt ʊ	41	54.50 N	10.55 E
Längelmävesi ⊜	26	61.32 N	24.22 E
Langeloth	214	40.23 N	80.24 W
Langelsheim	52	51.56 N	10.19 E
Langemark	50	50.55 N	2.55 E
Langen, B.R.D.	52	53.36 N	8.35 E
Langen, B.R.D.	56	49.59 N	8.41 E
Langenargen	58	47.35 N	9.32 E
Langenau, B.R.D.	58	48.30 N	10.07 E
Langenau, D.D.R.	54	50.50 N	13.18 E
Langenberg, B.R.D.	52	51.46 N	8.19 E
Langenberg, B.R.D.	56	51.21 N	7.09 E
Langenbernsdorf	54	50.45 N	12.19 E
Langenbielau → Bielawa	30	50.41 N	16.38 E
Langenbochum	263	51.37 N	7.07 E
Langenbruck	58	47.21 N	7.46 E
Langenbrücken	56	49.12 N	8.38 E
Langenburg, B.R.D.	56	49.15 N	9.50 E
Langenburg, Sask., Can.	184	50.50 N	101.43 W
Langendorf	54	51.11 N	11.58 E
Langendreer ⬥[8]	263	51.28 N	7.19 E
Langeneichstädt	54	51.20 N	11.41 E
Langenfeld, B.R.D.	56	51.07 N	6.56 E
Längenfeld, Öst.	64	47.04 N	10.58 E
Langenhagen	52	52.27 N	9.44 E
Langenhagen, Flughafen ⊠	52	52.27 N	9.42 E
Langenhessen	54	50.45 N	12.22 E
Langenhorn	41	54.41 N	8.53 E
Langenhorst	263	51.22 N	7.02 E
Langenlois	61	48.28 N	15.40 E
Langennaundorf	54	51.36 N	13.20 E
Langenneufnach	58	48.16 N	10.36 E
Langenselbold	56	50.10 N	9.02 E
Langensteinach	56	49.30 N	10.10 E
Langenthal	58	47.13 N	7.47 E
Langenweddingen	54	52.02 N	11.31 E
Langenwetzendorf	54	50.41 N	12.05 E
Langenzenn	56	49.30 N	10.48 E
Langenzersdorf	264b	48.18 N	16.22 E
Langeoog	52	53.45 N	7.29 E
Langeoog I	52	53.46 N	7.32 E
Langerfeld ⬥[8]	263	51.16 N	7.15 E
Langer See ⊜	264a	52.25 N	13.38 E
Langerwehe	56	50.49 N	6.22 E
Langeskov	41	55.22 N	10.36 E
Langesund	26	59.00 N	9.45 E
Langevåg	26	62.27 N	6.12 E
Langewiesen	54	50.40 N	10.58 E
Langfeng	89	48.02 N	121.12 E
Langfjorden C[2]	26	62.43 N	7.30 E
Langford, B.C., Can.	224	48.27 N	123.30 W
Langford, Eng., U.K.	260	51.45 N	0.40 E
Langford, N.Y., U.S.	210	42.35 N	78.51 W
Langford, S. Dak., U.S.	198	45.36 N	97.50 W
Langford Creek C	208	39.06 N	76.09 W
Langförden	52	52.47 N	8.14 E
Langgam	112	0.15 N	101.43 E
Langgapayung	114	1.43 N	99.59 E
Lang-Göns	56	50.30 N	8.40 E
Långhalsen ⊜	40	58.56 N	16.41 E
Langham	184	52.22 N	106.57 W
Langhe □[9]	62	44.30 N	8.00 E
Langhirano	64	44.37 N	10.16 E
Langho	262	53.48 N	2.27 W
Langholm	44	55.09 N	3.00 W
Langhorne	208	40.10 N	74.55 W
Langhorne Acres	284c	38.51 N	77.16 W
Langhorne Creek	168b	35.18 S	139.02 E
Langhorne Gardens	285	40.11 N	74.53 W
Langhorne Manor	285	40.10 N	74.55 W
Langhorne Terrace	285	40.10 N	74.57 W
Langia Mountains ⩕	154	3.35 N	33.40 E
Langjishan I	100	28.32 N	121.36 E
Langjökull ⊓	24a	64.42 N	20.12 W
Langju	100	27.52 N	116.36 E
Lang Ka, Doi ∧	110	19.00 N	99.24 E
Langkawi, Pulau I	114	6.22 N	99.50 E
Langkazi	124	28.59 N	90.25 E
Langkesi, Kepulauan II	112	5.18 S	124.20 E
Langklip	158	28.12 S	20.20 E
Langkuli Pamier ⩕	85	38.40 N	74.30 E
Langlade I	186	46.50 N	56.20 W
Langley, B.C., Can.	182	49.06 N	122.39 W
Langley, Eng., U.K.	260	51.30 N	0.33 W
Langley, Eng., U.K.	262	53.15 N	2.05 W
Langley, S.C., U.S.	192	33.31 N	81.50 W
Langley, Va., U.S.	284c	38.57 N	77.10 W
Langley, Wash., U.S.	224	48.02 N	122.25 W
Langley Air Force Base ■	208	37.05 N	76.21 W
Langley Hill ∧[2]	282	37.20 N	122.14 W
Langley Park	284c	38.59 N	76.59 W
Langleyville	219	39.34 N	89.21 W
Langlo ≃	166	26.26 S	146.05 E
Langlois	202	42.56 N	124.27 W
Langmazong	120	30.52 N	89.58 E
Lang-mo	110	17.14 N	106.27 E
Langmusi	102	34.02 N	102.30 E
Långnäs	26	60.03 N	22.28 E
Langnau	58	46.57 N	7.47 E
Lango □[5]	154	2.10 N	33.00 E
Langogne	62	44.43 N	3.51 E
Langon	32	44.33 N	0.15 W
Langøya I	24	68.44 N	14.50 E
Lang-phuoc-hai	110	10.26 N	107.18 E
Langping	102	30.38 N	110.21 E
Langport	42	51.02 N	2.50 W
Langqi	100	26.06 N	119.34 E
Langqiaohe	100	30.30 N	118.24 E
Langquaid	60	48.49 N	12.03 E
Langreo → Sama [de Langreo]	34	43.18 N	5.41 W
Langres	58	47.52 N	5.20 E
Langres, Plateau de ⩕[1]	58	47.41 N	5.03 E
Langruth	184	50.24 N	98.38 W
Langruzong	120	31.50 N	91.25 E
Langsa	114	4.28 N	97.58 E
Langsa, Teluk C	114	4.35 N	98.00 E
Langschede	263	51.29 N	7.43 E
Långsele	26	63.11 N	17.04 E
Langshan	102	41.12 N	107.22 E
Langshan ⩕	102	41.10 N	106.30 E
Langshantun	105	40.22 N	115.41 E
Långshyttan	40	60.27 N	16.01 E
Långsjön ⊜	40	59.00 N	17.27 E
Langsnek ⊥	158	27.29 S	29.52 E
Lang-son	110	21.50 N	106.44 E
Langst-Kierst	263	51.18 N	6.43 E
Lang Suan	110	9.57 N	99.04 E
Långsvan ⊜	40	59.43 N	15.49 E
Langtian	100	25.11 N	113.28 E
Langting	120	25.30 N	93.07 E
Langton	212	42.45 N	80.35 W
Langtoutun	89	46.51 N	121.54 E
Langtuozi	104	41.01 N	121.43 E
Langu	100	27.56 N	118.11 E
Langue	236	13.37 N	87.39 W
Languedoc □[9]	32	44.00 N	4.00 E
L'Anguille ≃	194	34.44 N	90.40 W
Langui y Layo, Laguna de ⊜	248	14.29 S	71.13 W
Langula	54	51.09 N	10.25 E
Langundu, Tanjung ≻	115b	8.49 S	118.58 E
Langwarden	52	53.36 N	8.19 E
Langweer	52	52.57 N	5.43 E
Langweid	58	48.29 N	10.51 E
Langweiler	56	49.40 N	7.31 E
Langwies	58	46.49 N	9.43 E
Langwo	104	41.13 N	121.44 E
Langwozhuang	105	39.05 N	115.37 E
Langxi	106	31.08 N	119.10 E
Langzhaogou	98	40.49 N	124.36 E
Langzhong	102	31.35 N	105.59 E
Langzishan	104	41.02 N	123.23 E
Lanham	284c	38.58 N	76.52 W
Lanhil Island I	116	6.46 N	122.22 E
Lanibga, Mount ∧	116	10.27 N	123.56 E
Lanigan	184	51.52 N	105.02 W
Lanín, Parque Nacional ♠	254	39.36 S	71.24 W
Lanín, Volcán ∧[1]	254	39.38 S	71.30 W
Lanjiangzhen	107	30.24 N	105.11 E
Lanjiaweizi	104	41.16 N	123.31 E
Lankao	98	34.50 N	114.49 E
Lanker See ⊜	54	54.12 N	10.17 E
Lankeys Creek	171b	35.49 S	147.39 E
Länkipohja	26	61.44 N	24.48 E
Lanklaar	56	51.01 N	5.44 E
Lankou	100	23.59 N	115.05 E
Lankwitz ⬥[8]	264a	52.26 N	13.21 E
Lanling	89	45.15 N	126.12 E
Lannabruk	40	59.14 N	14.56 E
Lännaholm	40	59.53 N	17.57 E
Lan Nai Wan	271d	22.24 N	114.20 E
Lannaja	78	49.21 N	35.16 E
Lannemezan	32	43.08 N	0.23 E
Lannilis	32	48.34 N	4.31 W
Lannion	32	48.44 N	3.28 W
Lannon	216	43.09 N	88.10 W
L'Annonciation	206	46.25 N	74.52 W
Lanoka Harbor	208	39.52 N	74.10 W
Lanoraie	206	45.58 N	73.13 W
La Noria	258	35.10 S	58.48 W
Lanovcy	78	49.52 N	26.05 E
Lanping	102	26.29 N	99.23 E
Lanqibao	104	40.56 N	122.25 E
Lanqikoucun	104	40.52 N	122.26 E
Lanqipuzi	104	42.12 N	123.25 E
Lanquín	236	15.34 N	89.58 W
Lans, Montagnes de ⩕	62	44.52 N	5.29 E
Lansdale	208	40.15 N	75.17 W
Lansdowne, Austl.	162	17.53 S	126.39 E
Lansdowne, Austl.	274a	33.54 S	150.59 E
Lansdowne, Bhārat	124	29.50 N	78.41 E
Lansdowne, Ont., Can.	212	44.24 N	76.01 W
Lansdowne, Md., U.S.	284b	39.15 N	76.40 W
L'Anse, Mich., U.S.	190	46.45 N	88.27 W
Lanse, Pa., U.S.	214	40.59 N	78.08 W
L'anse Creuse Bay C	214	42.34 N	82.49 W
L'Anse Indian Reservation ⬥[4]	190	46.48 N	88.22 W
Lans-en-Vercors	62	45.07 N	5.35 E
Lansford, N. Dak., U.S.	198	48.38 N	101.23 W
Lansford, Pa., U.S.	210	40.50 N	75.53 W
Lanshan	102	25.18 N	111.52 E
Lanshantou	98	35.07 N	119.21 E
Lansing, Ill., U.S.	216	41.35 N	87.32 W
Lansing, Iowa, U.S.	190	43.22 N	91.13 W
Lansing, Mich., U.S.	216	42.43 N	84.34 W
Lansing, N.Y., U.S.	210	42.32 N	76.30 W
Lansing, Ohio, U.S.	214	40.04 N	80.47 W
Lansing ⬥[8]	275b	43.45 N	79.25 W
Lansing, Lake ⊜	216	42.46 N	84.25 W
Lanškroun	30	49.55 N	16.37 E
Lanslebourg	62	45.17 N	6.52 E
Lanslevillard	62	45.17 N	6.55 E
Lanstrop ⬥[8]	263	51.34 N	7.34 E
Lantana	220	26.35 N	80.03 W
Lantang	100	23.25 N	114.56 E
Lan Tao I	271d	22.17 N	113.59 E
Lanta Yai, Ko I	110	7.35 N	99.05 E
Lantian	102	34.03 N	109.12 E
Lantianba	107	28.52 N	105.28 E
Lantianchang	271a	39.58 N	116.17 E
Lantianchang ⊠	271a	39.58 N	116.15 E
Lantsch → Laces, It.	64	46.37 N	10.52 E
Lantsch, Schw.	58	46.41 N	9.34 E
Lantschou → Lanzhou	102	36.03 N	103.41 E
Lantzville	224	49.15 N	124.05 W
La Nurra ⬥[1]	71	40.45 N	8.15 E
Lanús	258	34.43 S	58.24 W
Lanús □[5]	288	34.42 S	58.28 W
Lanusei	71	39.53 N	9.32 E
Lanuvio	66	41.40 N	12.42 E
Lanuza	116	9.14 N	126.04 E
Lanuza Bay C	116	9.17 N	126.04 E
Lanxi, Zhg.	89	46.15 N	126.14 E
Lanxi, Zhg.	100	29.12 N	119.28 E
Lanxian	102	38.22 N	111.46 E
Lány	54	50.06 N	13.58 E
Lanzada	64	46.15 N	9.51 E
Lanzarote I	148	29.00 N	13.40 W
Lanzendorf	264b	48.06 N	16.26 E
Lanzhou (Lanchow)	102	36.03 N	103.41 E
Lanzo Torinese	62	45.16 N	7.28 E
Lao → Laos □[1]	110	18.00 N	105.00 E
Lao ≃, It.	68	39.47 N	15.48 E
Lao ≃, Thai	110	19.55 N	99.54 E
Laoag	116	18.12 N	120.36 E
Laoag ≃	116	18.12 N	120.31 E
Laoang	116	12.34 N	125.00 E
Laoang Island I	116	12.35 N	125.01 E
Lao-bao	110	16.37 N	106.36 E
Laobian	104	41.58 N	123.10 E
Laobieshan ⩕	102	23.49 N	99.11 E
La Obra	286e	33.36 S	70.30 W
Lao-cai	110	22.30 N	103.57 E
Laochang, Zhg.	102	24.34 N	104.11 E
Laochang, Zhg.	107	29.30 N	106.36 E
Laodafang	104	41.40 N	122.40 E
Laodaodian	89	51.16 N	126.40 E
Laodaohe ≃	100	28.16 N	112.58 E
Laodicea ⊥	130	37.56 N	29.02 E
Laofengkou	86	46.11 N	83.38 E
Laofu	98	42.13 N	118.17 E
Laogang	106	31.01 N	121.49 E
Laoge	100	32.49 N	119.52 E
Laoguan	100	27.38 N	113.36 E
Laoguanpu	104	40.53 N	120.51 E
Laohaotuo	104	41.25 N	122.46 E
Laoheba	107	28.51 N	103.49 E
Laoheishan	89	43.45 N	130.52 E
Laoheshangtai	104	40.43 N	120.49 E
Laohokow → Guanghua	102	32.25 N	111.36 E
Laohuk'ou	100	24.53 N	121.03 E
Laohumiao	271a	39.58 N	116.20 E
Laohutuozi	104	42.25 N	122.34 E
Laoighis □[6]	48	53.00 N	7.30 W
Laojie	102	25.31 N	99.31 E
Laojunguan	105	40.22 N	114.47 E
Laojunmiao → Yumen	102	39.56 N	97.51 E
Laoka	89	52.47 N	125.52 E
Laoling ∧	89	43.27 N	130.11 E
Laolonghe ≃	106	32.11 N	120.00 E
Laolongtan	107	30.01 N	104.48 E
Laomocun	106	30.51 N	119.11 E
Laon	50	49.34 N	3.40 E
Laona, N.Y., U.S.	214	42.25 N	79.19 W
Laona, Wis., U.S.	190	45.34 N	88.40 W
La Orotava	148	28.23 N	16.31 W
La Oroya	248	11.32 S	75.54 W
Laos □[1]	108		
	110	18.00 N	105.00 E
Laoshanwan C	98	36.24 N	122.45 E
Laosolu	114	3.11 N	98.02 E
Laotto	216	41.17 N	85.12 W
Laou, Oued ≃	34	35.29 N	5.04 W
Laowangpo Xuhongqu ⊜[1]	100	33.28 N	114.00 E
Laowushi	106	31.43 N	121.00 E
Laoxinkou	100	30.12 N	112.50 E
Laoyemiao	98	41.03 N	119.53 E
Laoyezhuang	106	32.16 N	120.04 E
Laoyingpan	100	26.34 N	115.10 E
Laozha	106	31.35 N	121.07 E
Laozhen	100	31.34 N	118.19 E
Laozhong	98	33.56 N	114.51 E
Laozhouwan C	98	36.00 N	120.30 E
Laozhuangzizhen	105	39.44 N	118.05 E
Laozishan	100	33.11 N	118.36 E
Lapa	252	25.45 S	49.42 W
Lapa ⬥[8], Bra.	287a	22.55 S	43.11 W
Lapa ⬥[8], Bra.	287b	23.32 S	46.42 W
Lapac Island I	116	5.32 N	120.47 E
Lapai	150	9.06 N	6.45 E
Lapaich, Sgurr na ∧	46	57.21 N	5.04 W
Lapalisse	32	46.15 N	3.38 E
La Palma, Col.	246	5.22 N	74.24 W
La Palma, El Sal.	236	14.19 N	89.11 W
La Palma, Esp.	266d	41.25 N	1.58 E
La Palma, Méx.	234	20.09 N	102.46 W
La Palma, Méx.	234	17.05 N	99.29 W
La Palma, Méx.	234	22.49 N	103.57 W
La Palma, Pan.	246	7.42 N	80.12 W
La Palma, Pan.	246	8.25 N	78.09 W
La Palma, Calif., U.S.	280	33.51 N	118.02 W
La Palma I	148	28.40 N	17.52 W
La Palma ≃	240p	23.03 N	80.54 W
La Palma del Condado	34	37.23 N	6.33 W
La Palmita	196	25.57 N	99.18 W
La Paloma	252	34.40 S	54.10 W
La Palud	62	43.47 N	6.20 E
La Pampa □[4]	252	37.00 S	66.00 W
La Panza Range ⩕	226	35.18 N	120.18 W
Lapão	250	11.24 S	41.50 W
La Paragua	246	6.50 N	63.20 W
Laparan Island I	116	5.54 N	119.59 E
La Parota, Méx.	234	18.20 N	101.08 W
La Parota, Méx.	234	18.19 N	103.02 W
La Parotita	234	19.07 N	101.15 W
La Paternal ⬥[8]	288	34.36 S	58.28 W
La Patrie	206	45.24 N	71.15 W
La Paz, Arg.	252	30.45 S	59.39 W
La Paz, Arg.	252	33.28 S	67.33 W
La Paz, Bol.	248	16.30 S	68.09 W
La Paz, Col.	246	10.23 N	73.10 W
La Paz, Hond.	236	14.16 N	87.40 W
La Paz, Méx.	232	24.10 N	110.18 W
La Paz, Méx.	234	23.41 N	100.43 W
La Paz, Pil.	116	8.19 N	125.43 E
Lapaz, Ind., U.S.	216	41.28 N	86.18 W
La Paz, Ur.	258	34.21 S	57.18 W
La Paz, Ur.	258	34.46 S	56.15 W
La Paz □[5], Bol.	248	15.30 S	68.00 W
La Paz □[5], Hond.	236	14.15 N	87.50 W
La Paz, Bahía de C	232	24.09 N	110.25 W
La Paz, Río de ≃	248	16.27 S	67.19 W
La Paz Centro	236	12.20 N	86.41 W
Lape	115b	8.39 S	117.37 E
La Pedrera	246	1.18 S	69.43 W
Lapeer	216	43.03 N	83.19 W
Lapeer □[6]	216	42.59 N	85.20 W
Lapel	218	40.04 N	85.51 W
Lapela	250	3.44 S	44.45 W
La Penne-sur-Huveaune	62	43.17 N	5.31 E
La Perla, Méx.	232	28.18 N	104.38 W
La Perla, Perú	286d	12.05 S	77.08 W
La Perouse	170	33.59 S	151.14 E
La Perouse, Bahía C	174z	27.04 S	109.18 W
La Perouse Bay C	229a	20.35 N	156.25 W
La Perouse Strait ʊ	89	45.45 N	142.00 E
La Pesca	234	23.46 N	97.47 W
La Pesse	58	46.18 N	5.51 E
La Petite-Pierre	56	48.52 N	7.19 E
Lapford	42	50.55 N	3.47 W
Lapham Hill ∧[2]	216	43.02 N	88.24 W
L'apičev	80	48.30 N	43.32 E
La Piedad [Cavadas]	234	20.21 N	102.00 W
La Piedra	236	9.29 N	83.40 W
La Pimienta	234	21.28 N	99.01 W
La Pine	202	43.40 N	121.30 W
Lapinin Island I	116	10.06 N	124.34 E
Lapinjärvi (Lappträsk)	26	60.38 N	26.13 E
Lapin lääni □[4]	26	66.00 N	27.00 E
Lapinlahti	26	63.22 N	27.24 E
Lapino	82	54.57 N	37.49 E
La Pintada	236	8.36 N	80.27 W
Lápithos	130	35.20 N	33.10 E
La Place	219	39.48 N	88.43 W
Lap Lae	110	17.39 N	100.02 E
La Plaine	240d	15.20 N	61.15 W
Lapland ⬥[1]	24	68.00 N	25.00 E
Laplandija	24	68.16 N	33.19 E
Laplandskij Zapovednik ⬥[4]	24	67.50 N	32.10 E
La Plata, Arg.	258		
	288	34.55 S	57.57 W
La Plata, Col.	246	2.23 N	75.53 W
La Plata, Md., U.S.	188	38.32 N	76.59 W
La Plata, Mo., U.S.	194	40.02 N	92.29 W
La Plata □[5]	288	34.55 S	58.04 W
La Plata ≃	200	36.54 N	108.15 W
La Plata, Isla de I	246	1.16 S	81.06 W
La Plata, Lago ⊜	254	44.53 S	71.50 W
La Plata, Universidad Nacional de ʋ[2]	288	35.55 S	57.57 W
La Playa ⬥[8]	286b	23.06 N	82.27 W
La Plonge Indian Reserve ⬥[4]	184	55.15 N	107.36 W
La Plume	210	41.34 N	75.45 W
La Pocatière	186	47.22 N	68.41 W
La Poile Bay C	186	47.38 N	58.20 W
Lapominka	24	64.48 N	40.28 E
La Pomme	62	43.25 N	5.35 E
Laponie → Lapland ⬥[1]	24	68.00 N	25.00 E
Laporte, Colo., U.S.	200	40.38 N	105.08 W
La Porte, Ind., U.S.	216	41.36 N	86.43 W
Laporte, Pa., U.S.	210	41.25 N	76.30 W
La Porte, Tex., U.S.	222	29.40 N	95.01 W
La Porte □[6]	216	41.36 N	86.43 W
La Porte City	190	42.19 N	92.12 W
Laposa, Bukit ∧	112	4.29 S	119.47 E
La Potherie, Lac ⊜	176	58.50 N	74.24 W
Lapoutroie	58	48.09 N	7.10 E
La Poveda	266a	40.19 N	3.29 W
Lappago (Lappach)	64	46.55 N	11.48 E
Lappajärvi	26	63.12 N	23.38 E
Lappajärvi ⊜	26	63.08 N	23.40 E
Lappeenranta	26	61.04 N	28.11 E
Lappfjärd (Lapväärtti)	26	62.15 N	21.32 E
Lappi	26	61.06 N	21.50 E
Lappland → Lapland ⬥[1]	24	68.00 N	25.00 E
Lappträsk → Lapinjärvi	26	60.38 N	26.13 E
La Prairie	206	45.25 N	73.30 W
Laprairie □[6]	206	45.20 N	73.35 W
La Prele Creek ≃	198	42.50 N	105.30 W
La Presa	228	32.48 N	117.01 W
Laprida, Arg.	252	37.33 S	60.49 W
Laprida, Arg.	252	28.23 S	64.33 W
La Pryor	196	28.57 N	99.51 W
Lapšanga	80	57.27 N	45.03 E
Lâpseki	130	40.20 N	26.41 E
Laptev Sea → Laptevych, More ⊤[2]	74	76.00 N	126.00 E
Laptevych, More (Laptev Sea) ⊤[2]	74	76.00 N	126.00 E
Lapua	26	62.57 N	23.00 E
Lapuanjoki ≃	26	63.34 N	22.30 E
La Puebla	34	39.46 N	3.01 E
La Puebla de Cazalla	34	37.14 N	5.19 W
La Puebla de Montalbán	34	39.52 N	4.21 W
La Puente	228	34.01 N	117.57 W
La Puerta	252	28.10 S	65.48 W
Lapu-Lapu (Opon)	116	10.19 N	123.57 E
La Punt	58	46.35 N	9.55 E
La Punta	286d	12.05 S	77.11 W
La Purísima, Chile	286e	33.34 S	70.39 W
La Purísima, Méx.	232	26.10 N	112.04 W
Lăpuş	38	47.30 N	24.01 E
La Push	224	47.55 N	124.38 W
Lapuyan	116	7.36 N	123.12 E
Lapväärtti → Lappfjärd	26	62.15 N	21.32 E
Lapwai	202	46.24 N	116.48 W
Łapy	30	53.00 N	22.53 E
La Quemada ⊥	234	22.27 N	102.45 W
La Queue-en-Brie	261	48.47 N	2.35 E
La Queue-lès-yvelines	261	48.48 N	1.46 E
La Quiaca	252	22.06 S	65.37 W
L'Aquila	66	42.22 N	13.22 E
L'Aquila □[4]	66	42.05 N	13.40 E
Lār	128	27.41 N	54.17 E
Lara, Austl.	169	38.01 S	144.24 E
Lara, Gabon	152	0.22 N	11.28 E
Lara □[3]	246	10.10 N	69.50 W
Larabanga	150	9.13 N	1.51 W
Laracha	34	43.15 N	8.35 W
Larache	148	35.12 N	6.10 W
Laragne-Montéglin	62	44.19 N	5.49 E
Lārak, Jazīreh-ye I	128	26.52 N	56.22 E
Laramate	248	14.15 S	74.52 W
La Rambla	34	37.36 N	4.44 W
Laramie	200	41.19 N	105.35 W
Laramie ≃	200	42.12 N	104.32 W
Laramie Mountains ⩕	200	42.00 N	105.40 W
Laramie Peak ∧	200	42.17 N	105.27 W
Laranjal	255	21.22 S	42.28 W
Laranjal ≃	255	23.12 S	53.45 W
Laranjeiras	250	10.48 S	37.10 W
Laranjeiras ⬥[8]	287a	22.56 S	43.11 W
Laranjeiras do Sul	252	25.25 S	52.25 W
Larantuka	115b	8.21 S	122.59 E
Laraos	248	12.17 S	75.50 W
Larap	116	14.18 N	122.39 E
Larat	164	7.09 S	131.45 E
Larat, Pulau I	164	7.10 S	131.50 E
Laravale	171a	28.05 S	152.56 E
La Raya, Abra)(	248	14.35 S	70.59 W
L'Arbaa Naït Irathen	34	36.38 N	4.12 E
Larb Creek ≃	202	48.25 N	107.16 W
L'Arbresle	62	45.50 N	4.37 E
Lärbro	26	57.47 N	18.47 E
Larbut, Jazīrat I	140	18.47 N	37.33 E
Larche, Col de (Colle della Maddalena))(	62	44.25 N	6.53 E
Larchmont	210	40.55 N	73.44 W
Larchmont Harbor C	276	40.55 N	73.45 W
Larchwood	198	43.27 N	96.26 W
Lardaro	64	45.58 N	10.39 E
Larde	154	16.28 S	39.43 E
Lardeau	182	50.09 N	116.57 W
Larderello	66	43.14 N	10.53 E
Larder Lake ⊜	190	48.05 N	79.36 W
Lardier, Cap ≻	62	43.09 N	6.37 E
L'Ardoise	186	45.37 N	60.45 W
Lardy	261	48.31 N	2.16 E
Lare	154	0.20 N	37.56 E
La Reculée	148	28.00 N	9.30 E
Laredo, Esp.	34	43.24 N	3.25 W
Laredo, Tex., U.S.	196	27.31 N	99.30 W
Laredo Sound ʊ	182	52.32 N	128.53 W
La Reforma	232	25.06 N	108.05 W
La Reina	286e	33.27 S	70.33 W
Laren	52	52.15 N	5.14 E
Larena	116	9.15 N	123.35 E
La Réole	32	44.35 N	0.02 W
Lares, Perú	248	13.04 S	72.05 W
Lares, P.R.	240m	18.18 N	66.53 W
Larga	78	48.23 N	26.50 E
Larga, Laguna ⊜	286b	23.08 N	82.12 W
Large, Île du I	275a	45.19 N	73.52 W
Largeau	146	17.55 N	19.07 E
Largentière	62	44.32 N	4.18 E
L'Argentière-la-Bessée	62	44.47 N	6.33 E
Lar Gerd	120	35.29 N	66.40 E
Largo, S. Afr.	273d	26.16 S	28.31 E
Largo, Fla., U.S.	220	27.55 N	82.47 W
Largo, Cañon V	200	36.40 N	107.43 W
Largo, Cayo I	240p	21.38 N	81.28 W
Largo Creek ≃	200	34.29 N	108.51 W
Largoward	46	56.15 N	2.51 W
Largs	46	55.48 N	4.52 W
Largue ≃	62	43.51 N	5.52 E
Lārī, Īrān	128	38.30 N	47.49 E
Lari, It.	66	43.34 N	10.35 E
Lari, Perú	248	15.37 S	71.46 W
Lariang	112	1.26 S	119.17 E
Lariang ≃	112	1.25 S	119.17 E
La Ricamarie	62	45.24 N	4.22 E
Larimer	214	40.21 N	79.44 W
Larimore	198	47.54 N	97.38 W
La Rinconada	286d	12.05 S	76.57 W
Larino, It.	66	41.48 N	14.54 E
Larino, S.S.S.R.	83	47.53 N	37.56 E
La Rioja, Arg.	252	29.26 S	66.51 W
La Rioja, Cuba	240p	20.46 N	76.36 W
La Rioja □[4]	252	30.00 S	67.30 W
La Rioja ⬥[1]	34	42.20 N	0.22 W
Lárisa	38	39.38 N	22.25 E
Lárisa, Stathmós ⬥[5]	267c	37.58 N	23.42 E
Larjak	74	61.16 N	80.15 E
Larjan	76	59.30 N	33.47 E
Larjegan ≃	86	60.30 N	77.44 E
Lārkāna	120	27.33 N	68.13 E
Larkhall	46	55.45 N	3.59 W
Lark Harbour	186	49.06 N	58.23 W
Larkhill	42	51.12 N	1.50 W
Larkspur	226	37.56 N	122.32 W
Larksville	210	41.16 N	75.57 W
Larnaca → Lárnax	130	34.55 N	33.38 E
Lárnakos, Kólpos C	130	34.55 N	33.45 E
Lárnax (Larnaca)	130	34.55 N	33.38 E
Larne	48	54.51 N	5.49 W
Larned	198	38.11 N	99.06 W
Larne Lake ⊜	44	54.47 N	5.45 W
Laro	146	8.17 N	12.18 E
La Robla	34	42.48 N	5.37 W
La Roca de la Sierra	34	39.07 N	6.41 W
La Roche	58	46.42 N	7.08 E
La Roche-Bernard	32	47.31 N	2.18 W
La Roche-de-Rame	62	44.45 N	6.35 E
La Roche-des-Arnauds	62	44.34 N	5.57 E
La Roche-en-Ardenne	56	50.11 N	5.35 E
La Roche-en-Brenil	50	47.22 N	4.10 E
La Rochefoucauld	32	45.45 N	0.23 E
La Roche-Guyon	50	49.05 N	1.38 E
La Rochelle	32	46.10 N	1.10 W
Laroche-Saint-Cydroine	50	47.58 N	3.31 E
La Roche-sur-Foron	58	46.04 N	6.19 E
La Roche-sur-Yon	32	46.40 N	1.26 W
La Rochette, Fr.	62	45.28 N	6.07 E
La Rochette, Fr.	261	48.30 N	2.40 E
Larochette, Lux.	56	49.47 N	6.15 E
La Roda	34	39.13 N	2.09 W
La Romana	238	18.25 N	68.58 W
Larona	112	2.45 S	121.20 E
La Ronge	184	55.06 N	105.17 W
Laroquebrou	32	44.58 N	2.11 E
La Roquebrussanne	62	43.20 N	5.59 E
Larose	194	29.35 N	90.23 W
La Route	261	48.48 N	2.47 E
Larrabee State Park ♠	224	48.41 N	122.29 W
Larreynaga	236	12.40 N	86.34 W
Larrey Point ≻	162	19.58 S	119.07 E
Larrimah	164	15.35 S	133.12 E
Larringes	58	46.22 N	6.35 E
Larrison Creek ≃	222	31.27 N	95.03 W
Larrys Creek ≃	210	41.13 N	77.13 W
Larrys River	186	45.13 N	61.23 W
Larsen Air Park ⊠	281	42.11 N	83.33 W
Larsen Bay	180	57.33 N	154.04 W
Larsen Ice Shelf ⊓	9	68.30 S	62.30 W
Larteh Aheneasi	150	5.56 N	0.04 E
La Rubia	252	30.06 S	61.48 W
La Rue, Ohio, U.S.	214	40.35 N	83.23 W
Larue, Tex., U.S.	222	32.07 N	95.41 W
La Rumorosa	204	32.34 N	116.06 W
Laruns	32	42.59 N	0.25 W
Larus Lake ⊜	184	51.17 N	94.40 W
Larvik	26	59.04 N	10.00 E
Larwill	216	41.11 N	85.38 W
Larzac, Causse du ⩕[1]	32	44.00 N	3.15 E
Lasa (Laas), It.	64	46.37 N	10.42 E
Lasa (Lhasa), Zhg.	120	29.40 N	91.09 E
La Sabana	252	27.52 S	59.57 W
Las Adjuntas	286c	10.26 N	67.01 W
La Sagne	58	47.03 N	6.48 E
La Sagra ∧	34	37.57 N	2.34 W
La Sal	200	38.19 N	109.15 W
La Salada	234	18.01 N	101.58 W
La Salette-Fallavaux	62	44.51 N	5.59 E
La Salle, Ont., Can.	214	42.14 N	83.06 W
La Salle, Qué., Can.	206	45.26 N	73.38 W
Lasalle, Fr.	62	44.03 N	3.51 E
La Salle, It.	62	45.45 N	7.04 E
La Salle, Colo., U.S.	200	40.21 N	104.42 W
La Salle, Ill., U.S.	216	41.20 N	89.06 W
La Salle □[6]	216	41.21 N	88.51 W
Lasalle, Parc ♠	275a	45.26 N	73.40 W
La Salle College ʋ[2]	285	40.02 N	75.09 W
La Salle Gardens	216	42.39 N	83.21 W
La Sal Mountains ⩕	200	38.30 N	109.10 W
Lasan	112	1.14 N	115.13 E
Lasanga Island I	164	7.25 S	147.16 E
Las Animas	198	38.04 N	103.13 W
Las Ánimas, Punta ≻	232	28.50 N	113.15 W
Las Anod	144	8.26 N	47.24 E
La Santa, Cerro ∧	240m	18.07 N	66.03 W
Las Arenas	240m	18.02 N	67.09 W
La Sarraz	58	46.40 N	6.31 E
La Sarre	190	48.48 N	79.12 W
La Sarre ≃	190	48.43 N	79.16 W
Las Arrias	252	30.21 S	63.35 W
La Sauceda	196	28.26 N	100.38 W
La Saulce	62	44.25 N	6.01 E
Las Auras	196	26.25 N	99.20 W
Las Blancas	196	25.42 N	97.35 W
Las Bonitas	246	7.52 N	65.40 W
Las Breñas	252	27.05 S	61.05 W
Låsby	41	56.09 N	9.49 E
Las Cabezas de San Juan	34	36.59 N	5.56 W
Las Cabras	252	34.18 S	71.19 W
Las Canadas, Parque Nacionale ♠	148	28.15 N	16.30 W
Lascano	252	33.40 S	54.12 W
Lascar, Volcán ∧[1]	252	23.23 S	67.45 W
Lascari	70	38.00 N	13.56 E
Las Casas → San Cristóbal de las Casas	234	16.45 N	92.38 W
Las Casitas, Cerro ∧	232	23.32 N	109.59 W
Las Casuarinas	252	31.48 S	68.19 W
Las Catitas	252	33.18 S	68.02 W
Las Catonas, Arroyo ≃	288	34.37 S	58.43 W
Lascaux, Grotte de •[5]	32	45.01 N	1.08 E
Las Cejas	252	26.53 S	64.44 W
L'Ascension	206	46.33 N	74.50 W
L'aščevka	78	49.33 N	32.41 E
Las Chacras	258	35.05 S	59.10 W
Las Choapas	234	17.55 N	94.05 W
Las Chorreras	232	28.50 N	105.18 W
Las Cidras	234	19.15 N	101.08 W
La Scie	186	49.57 N	55.36 W
Las Colimas	232	25.21 N	98.40 W
Las Coloradas	254	39.33 S	70.35 W
Las Condes	286e	33.22 S	70.31 W
Lascone, Monte ∧[2]	267a	41.59 N	12.23 E
Las Cruces, Méx.	234	18.45 N	102.16 W
Las Cruces, N. Mex., U.S.	200	32.23 N	106.29 W
Las Cruces, Estero de ≃	286e	33.21 S	70.47 W
Las Cuevas	232	29.38 N	101.19 W
Las Dawa'o	144	10.22 N	49.03 E
Las Delicias	232	15.58 N	91.50 W
Las Dureh	144	10.10 N	46.01 E
La Selva Beach	226	36.55 N	121.51 W
Lasem	115a	6.42 S	111.26 E
La Sentinelle	50	50.21 N	3.29 E
La Serena	252	29.54 S	71.16 W
La Serena ⬥[1]	34	38.45 N	5.30 W
Las Escobas	232	30.33 N	115.56 W
La Seyne	32	43.06 N	5.53 E
La Seyne-sur-Mer	62	43.06 N	5.53 E
Las Flores, Arg.	252	30.19 S	69.12 W
Las Flores, Arg.	252	36.03 S	59.07 W
Las Flores, Méx.	234	18.22 N	93.10 W
Las Flores, P.R.	240m	18.03 N	66.22 W
Las Flores, Ven.	286c	10.34 N	66.56 W
Las Flores Canyon V	280	34.03 N	118.38 W
Las Garcitas	252	26.35 S	59.48 W
Las Guayabas	232	24.00 N	97.45 W
Lasham	42	51.11 N	1.03 W
Las Harquetas, Arroyo ≃	288	34.29 S	58.38 W
Lashburn	184	53.08 N	109.36 W
Lāsh-e Joveyn	128	31.43 N	61.37 E
Las Heras	252	32.51 S	68.49 W
Las Higueras	234	23.41 N	106.06 W
Lashio	110	22.56 N	97.45 E
Lashkar → Gwalior	124	26.13 N	78.10 E
Lashkarak	267d	35.49 N	51.36 E
Lashkar Gāh	128	31.30 N	64.21 E
Lasht	123	36.48 N	73.01 E
Lasia, Pulau I	114	2.10 N	96.39 E
La Sierra, Montaña ⩕	236	14.04 N	87.54 W
Las Iglesias	196	27.35 N	101.21 W
La Sila ⩕	68	39.15 N	16.30 E
La Siligata	66	43.56 N	12.45 E
La Silla de Caracas ∧	286c	10.33 N	66.51 W
Łasin	30	53.32 N	19.05 E
Lašino	80	58.16 N	49.59 E
Lāsjerd	128	35.24 N	53.04 E
Las Julianas, Presa ⊜[1]	286a	19.28 N	99.18 W
Las Juntas	236	10.16 N	85.00 W
Łask	30	51.36 N	19.07 E
Łaskarzew	30	51.48 N	21.35 E
L'askel'a	24	61.45 N	30.59 E
Las Khoreh	144	11.10 N	48.16 E
Laško	36	46.09 N	15.14 E
L'askoviči	78	52.07 N	28.09 E
Las Lajas, Arg.	252	38.31 S	70.22 W
Las Lajas, Pan.	236	8.15 N	81.52 W
Las Lajitas	252	24.41 S	64.15 W
Las Lomas	246	4.40 S	80.15 W
Las Lomitas	252	24.42 S	60.36 W
Lašma	80	54.56 N	41.09 E
Las Malvinas	252	34.50 S	68.15 W
Lašmanka	80	54.44 N	51.28 E
Las Mareas	240m	17.56 N	66.09 W
Las Margaritas	232	16.19 N	91.59 W
Las Margaritas, Laguna ⊜	258	35.28 S	57.56 W
Las Marianas	258	35.04 S	59.31 W
Las Marías	240m	18.15 N	67.00 W
Las Marismas ≣	34	37.00 N	6.15 W
Las Mayas	286c	10.26 N	66.56 W
Las Mercedes	246	9.07 N	66.24 W
Las Mesas	234	17.00 N	99.30 W
Las Minas	286c	10.27 N	66.52 W
Las Minas, Cerro ∧	236	14.33 N	88.39 W
Las Moras Creek ≃	196	29.00 N	100.39 W
Las Mulas, Laguna ⊜	258	35.32 S	57.54 W
Las Navas	116	12.21 N	125.02 E
Las Nieves	232	26.24 N	105.22 W
La Solana	34	38.56 N	3.14 W
Lasolo	112	3.29 S	122.04 E
Lasolo ≃	112	3.28 S	122.06 E
Las Ortegas, Arroyo ≃	288	34.45 S	58.32 W
Las Ovejas	252	37.01 S	70.45 W
Las Palmas, Arg.	252	27.04 S	58.42 W
Las Palmas, Arg.	258	34.05 S	59.10 W
Las Palmas, Pan.	236	8.08 N	81.27 W
Las Palmas, P.R.	240m	17.59 N	66.02 W
Las Palmas de Gran Canaria	148	28.06 N	15.24 W
Las Peñas	234	18.03 N	102.30 W
Las Perdices, Canal de ≍	286e	33.31 S	70.33 W
La Spezia	62	44.07 N	9.50 E
La Spezia □[4]	62	44.13 N	9.40 E
Las Piedras, Bol.	248	11.06 S	66.10 W
Las Piedras, P.R.	240m	18.11 N	65.52 W
Las Piedras, Ur.	258	34.44 S	56.13 W
Las Piedras, Río de ≃	248	12.30 S	69.14 W
Las Piñas, Pil.	269f	14.29 N	120.59 E
Las Piñas, P.R.	240m	18.15 N	65.55 W
Las Plumas	254	43.43 S	67.15 W
Lasqueti Island I	182	49.29 N	124.17 W
Las Raices Creek ≃	196	28.09 N	99.02 W
Las Ramas	246	1.50 S	79.48 W
Las Rejas	286e	33.28 S	70.44 W
Las Rosas, Arg.	252	32.28 S	61.34 W
Las Rosas, Chile	286e	33.35 S	70.37 W
Las Rosas, Méx.	232	16.24 N	92.23 W
Las Rozas de Madrid	266a	40.30 N	3.52 W
Las Salinas de Zipaquirá ʋ[1]	246	5.04 N	73.56 W
Lassan	54	53.57 N	13.50 E
Lassance	255	17.54 S	44.34 W
Lassater	222	32.60 N	94.30 W
Lassay	32	48.26 N	0.30 W
Lassee	61	48.13 N	16.49 E
Lassellsville	210	43.03 N	74.36 W
Lassen Peak ∧[1]	204	40.29 N	121.31 W
Lassen Volcanic National Park ♠	204	40.30 N	121.19 W
Lassigny	50	49.35 N	2.51 E
Lassnitz ≃	61	46.46 N	15.32 E
Lasso ∧[2]	174n	15.02 N	145.38 E
L'Assomption	206	45.50 N	73.25 W
L'Assomption □[6]	206	45.48 N	73.35 W
L'Assomption ≃	206	45.43 N	73.29 W
Lasswade	46	55.53 N	3.08 W
Lassy	261	49.06 N	2.27 E
Las Tablas	246	7.46 N	80.17 W
Las Taperas	248	17.54 S	60.23 W
Las Termas	252	27.29 S	64.52 W
Las Tinajas	252	27.27 S	62.55 W
Last Mountain ∧	184	51.07 N	104.54 W
Last Mountain Lake ⊜	184	51.05 N	105.10 W
Las Torres	236	13.28 N	85.48 W
Las Tórtolas, Cerro ∧	252	29.56 S	69.54 W
Las Toscas	252	28.21 S	59.17 W
Lastoursville	152	0.49 S	12.42 E
Lastovo, Otok I	36	42.45 N	16.53 E
Lastovski Kanal ʊ	36	42.50 N	16.59 E
Lastra a Signa	66	43.46 N	11.06 E
Las Trampas Creek ≃	282	37.53 N	122.03 W
Las Trampas Peak ∧	282	37.50 N	122.03 W
Las Trampas Regional Park ♠	282	37.50 N	122.03 W
Las Trampas Ridge ∧	282	37.49 N	122.02 W
Las Tres Vírgenes, Volcán ∧[1]	232	27.27 N	112.34 W
Lästringe	40	58.54 N	17.18 E
Las Truchas	234	17.55 N	102.12 W
Lastrup	52	52.48 N	7.52 E
Las Tunas □[4]	240p	21.00 N	77.00 W
Las Tunas, Arroyo ≃	288	34.27 S	58.41 W
Las Tunas, Punta ≻	240m	18.30 N	66.38 W

Symbol	English	Deutsch	Español	Français	Português
≃	River	Fluss	Río	Rivière	Rio
≍	Canal	Kanal	Canal	Canal	Canal
L	Waterfall, Rapids	Wasserfall, Stromschnellen	Cascada, Rápidos	Chute d'eau, Rapides	Cascata, Rápidos
ʊ	Strait	Meeresstrasse	Estrecho	Détroit	Estreito
C	Bay, Gulf	Bucht, Golf	Bahía, Golfo	Baie, Golfe	Baía, Golfo
⊜	Lake, Lakes	See, Seen	Lago, Lagos	Lac, Lacs	Lago, Lagos
≣	Swamp	Sumpf	Pantano	Marais	Pântano
⊓	Ice Features, Glacier	Eis- und Gletscherformen	Accidentes Glaciales	Formes glaciaires	Acidentes Glaciares
⊤	Other Hydrographic Features	Andere Hydrographische Objekte	Otros Elementos Hidrográficos	Autres données hydrographiques	Outros Elementos Hidrográficos
✦	Submarine Features	Untermeerische Objekte	Accidentes Submarinos	Formes de relief sous-marin	Acidentes Submarinos
□	Political Unit	Politische Einheit	Unidad Politica	Entité politique	Unidade Política
ʋ	Cultural Institution	Kulturelle Institution	Institución Cultural	Institution culturelle	Instituição Cultural
⊥	Historical Site	Historische Stätte	Sitio Histórico	Site historique	Sitio Histórico
♠	Recreational Site	Erholungs- und Ferienort	Sitio de Recreo	Centre de loisirs	Sítio de Lazer
⊠	Airport	Flughafen	Aeropuerto	Aéroport	Aeroporto
■	Military Installation	Militäranlage	Instalación Militar	Installation militaire	Instalação Militar
⬥	Miscellaneous	Verschiedenes	Misceláneo	Divers	Miscelânea

ENGLISH — DEUTSCH

Name	Page	Lat.°′	Long.°′
Las Tunas Grandes, Laguna @	252	35.58 S	62.25 W
Las Tunas State Beach ♠	280	34.02 N	118.36 W
La Suze	32	47.54 N	0.02 E
Las Varas, Méx.	232	29.29 N	108.01 W
Las Varas, Méx.	234	21.10 N	105.10 W
Las Varillas	252	31.52 S	62.43 W
Las Vegas, Hond.	236	14.49 N	88.06 W
Las Vegas, P.R.	240m	18.11 N	67.02 W
Las Vegas, Nev., U.S.	204	36.11 N	115.08 W
Las Vegas, N. Mex., U.S.	200	35.36 N	105.13 W
Las Vegas, Ven.	246	9.35 N	68.37 W
Las Vigas	234	19.38 N	97.05 W
Las Vizcachas	286e	33.36 S	70.32 W
Lata ∧	174y	14.14 S	169.29 W
La Tabatière	186	50.50 N	58.58 W
Latacunga	246	0.56 S	78.37 W
Latady Island I	9	70.45 S	74.35 W
La Tagua	246	0.03 S	74.40 W
Latakia → Al-Lādhiqīyah	130	35.31 N	35.47 E
Latambar	123	33.07 N	70.52 E
La Tapona	234	22.48 N	100.38 W
La Tasajera	236	13.16 N	88.52 W
Låtefossen ∟	26	59.57 N	6.37 E
Lātehār	124	23.45 N	84.30 E
Lately Common	262	53.29 N	2.30 W
Latera	66	42.38 N	11.50 E
Laterina	66	43.31 N	11.43 E
Laterns	58	47.16 N	9.43 E
Laterrière	186	48.18 N	71.06 W
Laterza	68	40.37 N	16.48 E
La Teste-de-Buch	32	44.38 N	1.09 W
Latexo	222	31.24 N	95.29 W
Latgale □9	76	56.20 N	27.10 E
Latham, Austl.	162	29.45 S	116.26 E
Latham, Ill., U.S.	219	39.58 N	89.10 W
Latham, N.Y., U.S.	210	42.45 N	73.46 W
Latham, Ohio, U.S.	218	39.06 N	83.15 W
Lathan ≃	50	47.27 N	0.08 E
Lathen	52	52.52 N	7.19 E
Lāthi	120	21.43 N	71.23 E
Lathrop, Calif., U.S.	226	37.49 N	121.16 W
Lathrop, Mo., U.S.	194	39.33 N	94.20 W
Lathrup Village	281	42.29 N	83.14 W
La Thuile	62	45.43 N	6.57 E
La Tiama	286c	10.26 N	66.46 W
Latian, Mount ∧	116	6.13 N	125.30 E
Latiano	68	40.33 N	17.43 E
Latimer, Eng., U.K.	260	51.41 N	0.33 W
Latimer, Iowa, U.S.	190	42.46 N	93.22 W
Latina	66	41.28 N	12.52 E
Latina □4	66	41.27 N	13.06 E
Latino Americana, Universidad Militar ʋ2	286a	19.20 N	99.15 W
Latiri	140	9.10 N	25.43 E
Latisana	64	45.47 N	13.00 E
Latjuga	24	64.16 N	48.46 E
Latnaja	78	51.43 N	38.55 E
Latok ∧	123	35.56 N	75.45 E
La Toma	252	33.03 S	65.37 W
Laton	226	36.26 N	119.41 W
Latonovo	83	47.29 N	38.38 E
Latorica ≃	30	48.28 N	21.50 E
Latornell ≃	182	54.58 N	118.00 W
La Torrecilla ∧	240m	18.12 N	66.20 W
La Tortuga, Isla I	246	10.56 N	65.20 W
Latouche Island I	180	60.00 N	147.55 W
Latouche Treville, Cape ≻	162	18.27 S	121.49 E
La Tour	62	43.57 N	7.11 E
La Tour-d'Aigues	62	43.44 N	5.33 E
La Tour-d'Auvergne	32	45.32 N	2.41 E
La Tour-de-Peilz	58	46.27 N	6.49 E
La Tour-du-Pin	62	45.34 N	5.27 E
La Tourette Park ♠	276	40.35 N	74.08 W
Latowicz	30	52.02 N	21.48 E
Lat Phrao, Khlong ≋	269a	13.48 N	100.35 E
La Tremblade	32	45.46 N	1.08 W
La Trimouille	32	46.28 N	1.02 E
La Trinidad, Arg.	252	27.24 S	65.31 W
La Trinidad, Nic.	236	12.58 N	86.14 W
La Trinidad, Pil.	116	16.28 N	120.35 E
La Trinidad, Ven.	286c	10.27 N	66.52 W
La Trinidad de Orichuna	246	7.07 N	69.45 W
La Trinité	240e	14.44 N	60.58 W
Latrobe, Austl.	166	41.14 S	146.24 E
Latrobe, Pa., U.S.	214	40.19 N	79.23 W
La Trobe ≃	169	38.10 S	146.32 E
La Tronche	62	45.12 N	5.44 E
Latronico	68	40.05 N	16.01 E
Latta	192	34.21 N	79.26 W
Lattarico	68	39.28 N	16.08 E
Lattasburg	214	40.53 N	82.06 W
Latterbach	58	46.40 N	7.35 E
Lattingtown	276	40.54 N	73.36 W
Latty	216	41.05 N	84.35 W
La Tuilerie	261	48.34 N	2.08 E
La Tuilière	62	44.11 N	5.32 E
Latuna	112	8.23 S	124.06 E
La Tuque	176	47.26 N	72.47 W
Lātūr	122	18.24 N	76.35 E
La Turbie	62	43.45 N	7.24 E
Latvian Soviet Socialist Republic → Latvijskaja Sovetskaja Socialističeskaja Respublika □3	76	57.00 N	25.00 E
Latvijskaja Sovetskaja Socialističeskaja Respublika □3	76	57.00 N	25.00 E
Lau	164	5.50 S	151.20 E
Laubach	56	50.33 N	8.59 E
Lauban → Lubań	30	51.08 N	15.18 E
Laubenthal	60	48.59 N	11.03 E
Laubusch	54	51.28 N	14.10 E
Laubuseschbach	56	50.24 N	8.20 E
Lauca ≃	248	19.10 S	68.10 W
Laucha	54	51.13 N	11.41 E
Lauchhammer	54	51.30 N	13.47 E
Lauchheim	56	48.52 N	10.14 E
Lauda	56	49.34 N	9.41 E
Lauder	46	55.43 N	2.45 W
Lauderdale	194	32.31 N	88.31 W
Lauderdale V	46	55.43 N	2.42 W
Lauderdale-by-the-Sea	220	26.12 N	80.07 W
Lauderdale Lakes	220	26.11 N	80.12 W
Lauderhill	220	26.10 N	80.14 W
Laudun	62	44.06 N	4.40 E
Lauenbrück	52	53.12 N	9.33 E
Lauenburg, B.R.D.	52	53.22 N	10.33 E
Lauenburg → Lębork, Pol.	30	54.33 N	17.44 E
Lauenburgische Seen, Naturpark ♠	54	53.38 N	10.45 E
Lauenförde	52	51.39 N	9.23 E
Lauenstein, B.R.D.	52	52.04 N	9.33 E
Lauenstein, B.R.D.	54	50.31 N	11.20 E
Lauenstein, D.D.R.	54	50.47 N	13.49 E
Lauer ≃	56	50.18 N	10.10 E
Lauerzer See @	58	47.02 N	8.36 E
Lauf an der Pegnitz	60	49.30 N	11.17 E
Läufelfingen	58	47.24 N	7.51 E
Laufen, B.R.D.	64	47.57 N	12.56 E
Laufen, Schw.	58	47.25 N	7.30 E
Laufenburg (Baden), B.R.D.	58	47.35 N	8.04 E
Laufenburg (Baden), Schw.	58	47.33 N	8.04 E
Laufersfort, Schloss ⊥	263	51.25 N	6.37 E
Lauffen	64	47.40 N	13.37 E
Lauffen am Neckar	56	49.05 N	9.10 E
Laugharne	42	51.47 N	4.28 W
Laughery Creek ≃	218	39.02 N	84.53 W
Laughlen, Mount ∧	162	23.23 S	134.23 E
Laughlin Air Force Base ■	196	29.22 N	100.47 W
Laughlin Peak ∧	196	36.38 N	104.12 W
Laughlintown	214	40.13 N	79.12 W
Lau Group II	175g	18.20 S	178.30 W
Lauingen	56	48.34 N	10.25 E
Lauis → Lugano	58	46.01 N	8.58 E
Laukaa	26	62.25 N	25.57 E
Laukuva	76	55.37 N	22.14 E
Laulii	174u	14.17 S	170.39 W
Laul'u	89	45.46 N	135.16 E
Laun	110	10.07 N	98.46 E
Launceston, Austl.	166	41.26 S	147.08 E
Launceston, Eng., U.K.	42	50.38 N	4.21 W
Laundi, Tanjung ≻	115b	9.28 S	120.12 E
Laune ≃	48	52.07 N	9.48 W
Launglon	110	13.58 N	98.07 E
Laungowāl	123	30.13 N	75.41 E
La Unión, Chile	254	40.17 S	73.05 W
La Unión, Col.	246	1.36 N	77.09 W
La Unión, El Sal.	236	13.20 N	87.51 W
La Unión, Esp.	34	37.37 N	0.52 W
La Unión, Méx.	234	17.58 N	101.49 W
La Unión, Perú	248	5.24 S	80.45 W
La Unión, Perú	248	9.46 S	76.48 W
La Union, Pil.	116	6.42 N	126.05 E
La Union, N. Mex., U.S.	200	31.57 N	106.39 W
La Unión, Ven.	246	8.13 N	67.46 W
La Unión, Ven.	286c	10.25 N	66.48 W
La Union □4	116	16.35 N	120.25 E
La Unión de Coto	236	8.36 N	83.03 W
Launois-sur-Vence	56	49.39 N	4.32 E
Launsdorf	61	46.46 N	14.27 E
Laupen	58	46.54 N	7.14 E
Laupendahl	263	51.21 N	6.56 E
Laupheim	58	48.14 N	9.52 E
Laur	116	15.35 N	121.11 E
Laura, Austl.	164	15.34 S	144.28 E
Laura, Ohio, U.S.	218	40.00 N	84.25 W
La Urbana	246	7.08 N	66.56 W
Laureana di Borrello	68	38.30 N	16.05 E
Laurel, Del., U.S.	208	38.33 N	75.34 W
Laurel, Fla., U.S.	220	27.08 N	82.27 W
Laurel, Ind., U.S.	218	39.30 N	85.11 W
Laurel, Md., U.S.	188	39.06 N	76.51 W
Laurel, Miss., U.S.	194	31.42 N	89.08 W
Laurel, Mont., U.S.	202	45.40 N	108.46 W
Laurel, Nebr., U.S.	198	42.26 N	97.06 W
Laurel, Va., U.S.	208	37.38 N	77.31 W
Laurel, Wash., U.S.	224	45.57 N	121.23 W
Laurel ≃	192	36.57 N	84.18 W
Laurel, Mount ∧2	285	39.56 N	74.53 W
Laurel Bay	192	32.27 N	80.48 W
Laureldale, N.J., U.S.	208	39.30 N	74.41 W
Laureldale, Pa., U.S.	208	40.23 N	75.55 W
Laureles	252	31.22 S	55.51 W
Laurel Gardens	279b	40.31 N	80.01 W
Laurel Hill	171b	35.37 S	148.05 E
Laurel Hill ∧	214	40.02 N	79.17 W
Laurel Hollow	276	40.52 N	73.28 W
Laurel Reservoir @1	276	41.10 N	73.33 W
Laurel Ridge State Park ♠	188	39.58 N	79.23 W
Laurel Run	210	41.13 N	75.57 W
Laurel Run ≃	208	40.20 N	77.20 W
Laurel Springs	285	39.49 N	75.00 W
Laurelton	210	40.53 N	77.12 W
Laurelville, Ohio, U.S.	188	39.28 N	82.44 W
Laurelville, Pa., U.S.	214	40.09 N	79.29 W
Laurenburg	56	50.20 N	7.54 E
Laurence Harbor	276	40.27 N	74.15 W
Laurencekirk	46	56.50 N	2.29 W
Laurens, Iowa, U.S.	198	42.51 N	94.51 W
Laurens, N.Y., U.S.	210	42.32 N	75.06 W
Laurens, S.C., U.S.	192	34.30 N	82.01 W
Laurentides	206	45.51 N	73.46 W
Laurentides ⛰1	16	50.00 N	70.00 W
Laurentides, Parc des ♠	186	47.40 N	71.30 W
Laurentum ⊥	66	41.43 N	12.20 E
Laurenzana	68	40.28 N	15.58 E
Lauria	68	40.02 N	15.50 E
Laurie Island I	9	60.45 S	44.35 W
Laurie Lake @	184	56.34 N	101.54 W
Laurier, Man., Can.	184	50.54 N	99.33 W
Laurier, Qué., Can.	206	46.32 N	71.38 W
Laurière	32	46.05 N	1.28 E
Laurierville	206	46.18 N	71.39 W
Laurinburg	192	34.47 N	79.27 W
Laurino	68	40.20 N	15.20 E
Laurito	68	40.10 N	15.24 E
Lauritsala	26	61.04 N	28.16 E
Lauritzen Bay C	9	69.05 S	156.50 E
Laurium	190	47.14 N	88.26 W
Lauriya Nandangarh	124	26.59 N	84.24 E
Lauro, Monte ∧	70	37.07 N	14.49 E
Lauro Müller	252	28.24 S	49.23 W
Laurys Station	208	40.43 N	75.32 W
Lausanne	58	46.31 N	6.38 E
Lauscha	54	50.28 N	11.10 E
Laut	86	59.18 N	66.02 E
Laut, Pulau I, Indon.	112	4.43 N	107.59 E
Laut, Pulau I, Indon.	112	3.40 S	116.10 E
Laut, Selat Ʊ	112	3.25 S	116.03 E
Lauta	54	51.27 N	14.04 E
Lautaro	252	38.31 S	72.27 W
Lautenbach	58	47.57 N	7.09 E
Lautenthal	52	51.52 N	10.17 E
Lauter ≃, B.R.D.	56	49.39 N	7.35 E
Lauter ≃, Eur.	56	48.58 N	8.11 E
Lauterach	58	47.29 N	9.44 E
Lauterbach, B.R.D.	56	50.38 N	9.24 E
Lauterbach, B.R.D.	58	48.14 N	8.20 E
Lauterbach, B.R.D.	60	48.23 N	11.33 E
Lauterbourg	56	48.59 N	8.11 E
Lauterbrunnen	58	46.36 N	7.55 E
Lauterecken	56	49.39 N	7.35 E
Lauterhofen	60	49.22 N	11.37 E
Lauter [Sachsen]	54	50.33 N	12.44 E
Lauthala I	175g	16.45 S	179.41 W
Laut Kecil, Kepulauan II	112	4.50 S	115.45 E
Lautoka	175g	17.37 S	177.27 E
Lau Trough ⊹1	14	20.00 S	177.00 W
Lauttakylä → Huittinen	26	61.11 N	22.42 E
Lauwe	50	50.48 N	3.11 E
Lauwerszee C	52	53.20 N	6.12 E
Lauzerte	32	44.15 N	1.08 E
Lauzon	206	46.50 N	71.10 W
Lauzun	32	44.38 N	0.28 E
Lava (Łyna) ≃	76	54.37 N	21.14 E
Lava, Nosy I	157b	14.33 S	47.36 E
Lava Beds National Monument ♠	204	41.42 N	121.30 W
Lavaca □6	222	29.22 N	96.55 W
Lavaca ≃	196	28.50 N	96.36 W
Lavaca Bay C	196	28.35 N	96.35 W
La Vacherie	62	44.53 N	5.11 E
Lavagh More ∧	48	54.45 N	8.05 W
Lavagna	62	44.18 N	9.20 E
Lavagna ≃	62	44.21 N	9.20 E
Lava Hot Springs	202	42.37 N	112.01 W
Lavaisse	252	33.49 S	65.25 W
Laval, Qué., Can.	206	45.35 N	73.45 W
Laval, Fr.	32	48.04 N	0.46 W
Laval-des-Rapides ⊹8	275a	45.33 N	73.42 W
La Valette → Valletta	36	35.54 N	14.31 E
La Valette-du-Var	62	43.08 N	5.59 E
Lavalle, Arg.	252	29.01 S	59.11 W
Lavalle, Arg.	252	28.12 S	65.08 W
Lavalleja → Minas	252	34.23 S	55.14 W
Lavallette	208	39.58 N	74.04 W
La Valley	200	37.06 N	105.22 W
Laval-Ouest ⊹8	275a	45.33 N	73.52 W
Lavaltrie	206	45.53 N	73.17 W
Lāvān, Jazīreh-ye I	128	26.48 N	53.15 E
Lavanono	157b	25.24 S	44.55 E
Lavant ≃	61	46.38 N	14.57 E
Lavantbach ≃	61	46.50 N	14.21 E
Lavapié, Punta ≻	252	37.09 S	73.35 W
Lávara	38	41.16 N	26.22 E
Lavaraty	157b	23.16 S	46.59 E
Lavardac	32	44.11 N	0.18 E
Lāvar Meydān ≚	128	30.20 N	54.30 E
Lavarone	64	45.56 N	11.15 E
Lavassaare	76	58.31 N	24.22 E
Lava Tudo ≃	252	28.26 S	50.25 W
Laveaga Peak ∧	226	36.53 N	121.11 W
La Vecilla de Curueño	34	42.51 N	5.24 W
La Vega	238	19.13 N	70.31 W
La Vega ⊹8	286c	10.28 N	66.57 W
Lavela, S.S.S.R.	24	63.38 N	45.31 E
La Vela, Ven.	246	11.27 N	69.34 W
La Vela, Cabo de ≻	246	12.15 N	72.11 W
Lavelanet	32	42.56 N	1.51 E
Lavelle	208	40.46 N	76.22 W
Lavello	68	41.03 N	15.48 E
Laven	41	56.07 N	9.43 E
La Venada	196	25.50 N	97.30 W
Lavendon	42	52.11 N	0.40 W
Lavenham	42	52.06 N	0.47 E
Laveno	58	45.55 N	8.37 E
Lavenone	64	45.44 N	10.26 E
La Venta ⊥	234	18.08 N	94.03 W
Laventie	50	50.38 N	2.46 E
La Ventura	232	24.38 N	100.54 W
Laver ≃	44	54.08 N	1.30 W
Lavéra	62	43.23 N	5.02 E
La Vera ⊹1	34	40.20 N	5.30 W
La Verde, Arg.	252	27.08 S	59.23 W
La Verde, Arg.	258	34.44 S	59.16 W
Laverdière, Lac @	206	46.50 N	74.28 W
L'Averdy, Cape ≻	175e	5.33 S	155.04 E
La Vérendrye, Parc de ♠	190	47.30 N	77.30 W
La Verna ʋ1	66	43.42 N	11.54 E
La Verne, Calif., U.S.	280	34.06 N	117.46 W
Laverne, Okla., U.S.	196	36.43 N	99.54 W
La Verne College ʋ2	280	34.07 N	117.47 W
La Vernia	196	29.21 N	98.07 W
Laverock	285	40.05 N	75.11 W
La Verpillière	62	45.38 N	5.09 E
La Verrière	261	48.45 N	1.57 E
Lavers Hill	169	38.40 S	143.24 E
Laverton, Austl.	162	28.38 S	122.25 E
Laverton, Austl.	169	37.52 S	144.45 E
Laverton Royal Australian Air Force Base ■	169	37.52 S	144.43 E
La Veta	200	37.31 N	105.00 W
Lavezares	116	12.32 N	124.20 E
Lavezzola	66	44.34 N	11.52 E
Lavia	26	61.36 N	22.36 E
Laviano	68	40.47 N	15.18 E
Lavic Lake @	204	34.40 N	116.21 W
La Victoria, Perú	286d	12.04 S	77.02 W
La Victoria, Ven.	246	10.14 N	67.20 W
Lavieille, Lake @	190	45.51 N	78.14 W
Lavik	26	61.06 N	5.30 E
La Villa	64	46.36 N	11.54 E
La Villa ≃	236	7.59 N	80.23 W
La Ville-du-Bois	261	48.40 N	2.16 E
La Villeneuve-Saint-Martin	261	49.04 N	1.58 E
Lavillette	186	47.16 N	65.18 W
Lavin	58	46.46 N	10.06 E
La Viña, Arg.	252	25.27 S	65.35 W
Lavina, Mont., U.S.	202	46.18 N	108.56 W
Lavinio Lido di Enea	66	41.30 N	12.05 E
Laviolette, Lac @	206	46.51 N	73.58 W
La Virginia	246	4.54 N	75.53 W
Lavis	64	46.08 N	11.07 E
La Volla	204	32.51 N	117.16 W
Lavon	222	33.02 N	96.26 W
Lavonia	192	34.26 N	83.06 W
Lavon Lake @1	222	33.05 N	96.28 W
La Voulte-sur-Rhône	62	44.48 N	4.47 E
Lavoûte-sur-Loire	62	45.07 N	3.54 E
Lavoutte, Anse C	241f	14.06 N	60.56 W
Lavras	256	21.14 S	45.00 W
Lavras ≃	287a	23.00 S	43.33 W
Lavras da Mangabeira	250	6.45 S	38.57 W
Lavras do Sul	252	30.49 S	53.55 W
Lavrentija	180	65.35 N	171.00 W
Lavrentija, Zaliv C	180	65.40 N	171.15 W
Lavrinhas	256	22.35 S	44.54 W
Lávrion	38	37.44 N	24.04 E
Lavushi Manda Game Reserve ⊹4	154	12.20 S	30.50 E
Lawa	116	6.12 N	125.41 E
Lawai	229b	21.55 N	159.31 W
Lawang	115a	7.49 S	112.42 E
La Wantzenau	58	48.40 N	7.50 E
La Ward	222	28.51 N	96.28 W
Lawatu	112	2.53 S	120.18 E
Lawdar	144	13.53 N	45.52 E
Lawele	112	5.13 S	122.57 E
Lawers, Ben ∧	46	56.34 N	4.13 W
Laweueng	114	5.31 N	95.52 E
Lawford Lake @	184	54.30 N	96.43 W
Lawgi	166	24.34 S	150.39 E
Lawin	114	5.18 N	101.04 E
Lawin, Pulau I	164	1.31 S	128.44 E
Lawksawk	110	21.15 N	96.52 E
Lawler	190	43.04 N	92.09 W
Lawlor, Mount ∧	280	34.16 N	118.06 W
Lawn, Newf., Can.	186	46.57 N	55.32 W
Lawn, Pa., U.S.	208	40.13 N	76.32 W
Lawn, Tex., U.S.	196	32.08 N	99.49 W
Lawn Bay C	186	46.53 N	55.35 W
Lawndale, Calif., U.S.	228	33.54 N	118.21 W
Lawndale, Ill., U.S.	219	40.13 N	89.17 W
Lawndale, N.C., U.S.	192	35.25 N	81.34 W
Lawndale ⊹8, Ill., U.S.	278	41.51 N	87.43 W
Lawndale ⊹8, Pa., U.S.	285	40.03 N	75.05 W
Lawnes Creek ≃	208	37.08 N	76.40 W
Lawn Hill	166	18.35 S	138.35 E
Lawn Hill Creek ≃	166	18.03 S	139.09 E
Lawnside	285	39.52 N	75.03 W
Lawowa	112	4.26 S	122.56 E
Lawqah	128	29.49 N	42.45 E
Lawra	150	10.39 N	2.52 W
Lawrence, N.Z.	172	45.55 S	169.41 E
Lawrence, Ind., U.S.	218	39.50 N	86.02 W
Lawrence, Kans., U.S.	198	38.58 N	95.14 W
Lawrence, Mass., U.S.	207		
	283	42.42 N	71.09 W
Lawrence, Mich., U.S.	216	42.13 N	86.03 W
Lawrence, Nebr., U.S.	198	40.17 N	98.16 W
Lawrence, N.Y., U.S.	276	40.38 N	73.42 W
Lawrence, Pa., U.S.	279b	40.18 N	80.09 W
Lawrence, Tex., U.S.	222	32.45 N	96.21 W
Lawrence □6, Ind., U.S.	218	38.52 N	86.29 W
Lawrence □6, Pa., U.S.	214	41.00 N	80.20 W
Lawrence, Lake @	224	46.51 N	122.34 W
Lawrence Brook ≃	276	40.29 N	74.24 W
Lawrenceburg, Ind., U.S.	218	39.06 N	84.51 W
Lawrenceburg, Ky., U.S.	218	38.02 N	84.54 W
Lawrenceburg, Tenn., U.S.	194	35.15 N	87.20 W
Lawrence Institute of Technology ʋ2	281	42.28 N	83.15 W
Lawrence Marsh ≋	276	40.36 N	73.42 W
Lawrence Municipal Airport ⊠	283	42.43 N	71.07 W
Lawrence Park	214	42.09 N	80.01 W
Lawrencepur	123	33.50 N	72.30 E
Lawrenceville, Ill., U.S.	194	38.44 N	87.41 W
Lawrenceville, N.J., U.S.	208	40.18 N	74.44 W
Lawrenceville, Pa., U.S.	210	42.00 N	77.08 W
Lawrenceville, Va., U.S.	192	36.45 N	77.51 W
Lawrenceville ⊹8	279b	40.28 N	79.57 W
Lawson, Austl.	170	33.43 S	150.26 E
Lawson, Mo., U.S.	194	39.26 N	94.12 W
Lawson Heights	214	40.18 N	79.23 W
Lawsons Creek ≃	170	32.35 S	149.43 E
Lawtey	192	30.03 N	82.04 W
Lawton, Ky., U.S.	218	38.16 N	83.13 W
Lawton, Mich., U.S.	216	42.10 N	85.50 W
Lawton, N. Dak., U.S.	198	48.18 N	98.22 W
Lawton, Okla., U.S.	196	34.37 N	98.25 W
Lawton ⊹8	286b	23.06 N	82.21 W
Lawu, Gunung ∧	115a	7.38 S	111.11 E
Lawyer Creek ≃	202	46.14 N	116.01 W
Lawyersville	210	42.42 N	74.30 W
Lawz, Jabal al- ∧	128	28.40 N	35.18 E
Laxå	40	58.59 N	14.37 E
Laxay	46	58.09 N	6.35 W
Laxenburg	264b	48.04 N	16.21 E
Laxenburger Park ♠	264b	48.04 N	16.22 E
Laxey	44	54.14 N	4.23 W
Laxford, Loch C	46	58.23 N	5.06 W
Laxou	58	48.41 N	6.09 E
Layang Layang	114	1.49 N	103.29 E
Laye ≃	62	43.54 N	5.48 E
La Yesca	234	21.19 N	104.02 W
Layhill	208	39.05 N	77.03 W
Laylā	144	22.17 N	46.45 E
Layou	241h	13.12 N	61.17 W
Layou ≃	240d	15.23 N	61.26 W
Lay-Saint-Christophe	56	48.45 N	6.12 E
Laysan Island I	14	25.50 N	171.50 W
Layton, N.J., U.S.	210	41.13 N	74.50 W
Layton, Utah, U.S.	200	41.04 N	111.58 W
Laytons Lake @	285	39.42 N	75.26 W
Laytonville	204	39.41 N	123.29 W
Laž	80	57.11 N	49.14 E
La Zarca	232	25.50 N	104.44 W
Lazarev	89	52.13 N	141.32 E
Lazarevo	80	56.49 N	50.15 E
Lazarevskoje	84	43.55 N	39.20 E
Lazarivo	157b	23.54 S	44.59 E
Lazaro Cárdenas	196	25.23 N	103.10 W
Lázaro Cárdenas, Presa @1	232	25.35 N	105.02 W
Lazdijai	76	54.14 N	23.31 E
Lazha	102	26.26 N	101.50 E
Lazhulong	120	35.08 N	81.33 E
Lazi, Pil.	116	9.08 N	123.38 E
Lazi, Zhg.	120	29.10 N	87.42 E
Lazio □4	66	42.00 N	12.30 E
Lazise	64	45.30 N	10.44 E
Lázně Kynžvart	60	50.01 N	12.38 E
Lazo	89	43.25 N	133.55 E
Lazorki	78	50.06 N	32.39 E
La Zorra, Quebrada ≃	286c	10.36 N	67.03 W
Lazzaro	68	37.58 N	15.40 E
Lazzate	266b	45.40 N	9.05 E
Lea ≃	42	51.30 N	0.01 E
Léach	110	12.21 N	103.46 E
Leach ≃	42	51.41 N	1.39 W
Leach Pond @	283	42.04 N	71.09 W
Leachville	194	35.56 N	90.15 W
Leacock	208	40.05 N	76.12 W
Lead	198	44.21 N	103.46 W
Leadbetter Point ≻	224	46.38 N	124.03 W
Leadburn	46	55.47 N	3.14 W
Leadenham	42	53.05 N	0.34 W
Leaden Roding	260	51.48 N	0.19 E
Leader	184	50.53 N	109.31 W
Leader Water ≃	46	55.36 N	2.41 W
Leadgate	44	54.52 N	1.48 W
Lead Hill ∧2	194	37.06 N	92.38 W
Leadhills	44	55.25 N	3.47 W
Leadon ≃	42	51.53 N	2.16 W
Leadore	202	44.41 N	113.21 W
Leadville	200	39.15 N	106.20 W
Leaf ≃, Minn., U.S.	198	46.29 N	94.53 W
Leaf ≃, Miss., U.S.	194	31.00 N	88.45 W
Leaf Lake @	184	53.02 N	102.07 W
League ∧	48	54.39 N	8.44 W
League City	222	29.31 N	95.05 W
Leakesville	194	31.09 N	88.33 W
Leakey	196	29.44 N	99.46 W
Leakin Park ♠	284b	39.18 N	76.42 W
Leak Run ≃	279b	40.27 N	79.47 W
Leaksville	192	36.29 N	79.53 W
Lealman	220	27.50 N	82.41 W
Lealui	152	15.10 S	23.02 E
Leam ≃	42	52.17 N	1.14 W
Agnews Hill ∧2	214	42.03 N	82.36 W
Leamington Spa → Royal Leamington Spa	42	52.18 N	1.31 W
Lean	100	27.24 N	115.48 E
Leán ≃	236	15.47 N	87.20 W
Leander Point ≻	162	29.16 S	114.56 E
Leandro	250	5.59 S	44.55 W
Leandro, Serra do ⛰	256	22.55 S	43.55 W
Leandro N. Alem	252	27.36 S	55.19 W
Leane, Lough @	48	52.05 N	9.35 W
Leannan ≃	48	55.02 N	7.38 W
Leano, Monte ∧	66	41.20 N	13.13 E
Leary	192	31.29 N	84.31 W
Leaside □8	275b	43.42 N	79.22 W
Leask	184	53.00 N	106.45 W
Leatherhead	42	51.18 N	0.20 W
Leatherman Peak ∧	202	44.05 N	113.44 W
Leatherwood Creek ≃	218	38.49 N	86.30 W
Lea Town	262	53.46 N	2.48 W
Leavenworth, Kans., U.S.	198	39.19 N	94.55 W
Leavenworth, Wash., U.S.	224	47.36 N	120.40 W
Leavesden Aerodrome ⊠	260	51.42 N	0.27 W
Leavittsburg	214	41.14 N	80.53 W
Leawood	194	37.03 N	94.31 W
Łeba	30	54.47 N	17.33 E
Łeba ≃	30	54.47 N	17.33 E
Lebach	56	49.24 N	6.54 E
Lebak	116	6.32 N	124.03 E
Lebam	224	46.34 N	123.33 W
Lébamba	152	2.12 S	11.30 E
Lebango	152	0.22 N	14.49 E
Lebanon, Conn., U.S.	207	41.38 N	72.13 W
Lebanon, Ill., U.S.	219	38.36 N	89.49 W
Lebanon, Ind., U.S.	218	40.03 N	86.28 W
Lebanon, Kans., U.S.	198	39.49 N	98.33 W
Lebanon, Ky., U.S.	194	37.34 N	85.15 W
Lebanon, Mo., U.S.	194	37.41 N	92.40 W
Lebanon, N.H., U.S.	188	43.38 N	72.15 W
Lebanon, N.J., U.S.	210	40.39 N	74.50 W
Lebanon, N.Y., U.S.	210	42.47 N	75.39 W
Lebanon, Ohio, U.S.	218	39.26 N	84.13 W
Lebanon, Oreg., U.S.	202	44.32 N	122.54 W
Lebanon, Pa., U.S.	208	40.20 N	76.25 W
Lebanon, S. Dak., U.S.	198	45.04 N	99.46 W
Lebanon, Tenn., U.S.	194	36.12 N	86.18 W
Lebanon, Va., U.S.	192	36.54 N	82.05 W
Lebanon □6	208	40.20 N	76.25 W
Lebanon □1	118		
	128	33.50 N	35.50 E
Lebanon Junction	194	37.50 N	85.44 W
Lebanon Mountains → Lubnān, Jabal ⛰	132	34.00 N	36.00 E
Lebanon Springs	210	42.29 N	73.23 W
Le Ban-Saint-Martin	56	49.07 N	6.09 E
Le Bar-sur-le-Loup	62	43.42 N	6.59 E
Leb'ažje, S.S.S.R.	80	57.25 N	49.32 E
Leb'ažje, S.S.S.R.	86	51.28 N	77.46 E
Leb'ažje, S.S.S.R.	86	55.16 N	66.29 E
Lebbeke	50	51.00 N	4.08 E
Le Béage	62	44.51 N	4.07 E
Le Beausset	62	43.12 N	5.48 E
Lebec	228	34.50 N	118.52 W
Lebed'an'	76	53.01 N	39.09 E
Lebedevka, S.S.S.R.	80	51.06 N	47.09 E
Lebedevka, S.S.S.R.	86	56.48 N	66.57 E
Lebedevka, S.S.S.R.	86	50.09 N	54.07 E
Lebedi	78	51.17 N	37.38 E
Lebedin, S.S.S.R.	78	48.59 N	31.31 E
Lebedin, S.S.S.R.	78	50.36 N	34.30 E
Lebedino	80	55.14 N	49.50 E
Leben, Oued el V	148	34.37 N	10.01 E
Lebesby	24	70.34 N	26.59 E
Le Bessat	62	45.22 N	4.31 E
Le Bihan Falls ∟	158	29.51 S	28.03 E
Le Biot	58	46.16 N	6.38 E
Lebir ≃	114	5.33 N	102.12 E
Le Blanc	32	46.38 N	1.04 E
Le Blanc-Mesnil	261	48.56 N	2.28 E
Le Bleymard	62	44.29 N	3.44 E
Leblon ⊹8	287a	22.59 S	43.13 W
Lebo, Kans., U.S.	198	38.25 N	95.51 W
Lebo, Zaïre	152	4.29 N	23.57 E
Le Bois-de-Cise	50	50.05 N	1.26 E
Le Bois-Dieu	261	48.39 N	1.43 E
Le Bois-d'Oingt	58	45.55 N	4.35 E
Lebombo Mountains ⛰2	156	25.15 S	32.00 E
Lebongtandai	112	3.01 S	101.54 E
Lebon Régis	252	26.56 S	50.42 W
Le Boréon	62	44.07 N	7.17 E
Lębork	30	54.33 N	17.44 E
Le Boulay	261	48.47 N	1.40 E
Le Bourg-d'Oisans	62	45.03 N	6.02 E
Le Bourget	261	48.56 N	2.26 E
Le Bourget-du-Lac	62	45.39 N	5.52 E
Le Brassus	58	46.35 N	6.13 E
Lebrija	34	36.55 N	6.04 W
Lebrija ≃	246	8.08 N	73.47 W
Le Broc	62	43.49 N	7.10 E
Le Brugeron	62	45.43 N	3.43 E
Le Brusc	62	43.04 N	5.48 E
Łebsko, Jezioro C	30	54.44 N	17.24 E
Lebu	252	37.37 S	73.39 W
Le Bugue	32	44.55 N	0.56 E
Le Buisson de Massoury ♠	261	48.30 N	2.43 E
Lebus	54	52.25 N	14.32 E
Leça	112	8.45 S	126.34 E
Le Caire → Al-Qāhirah	142	30.03 N	31.15 E
Le Camp-du-Castellet	62	43.15 N	5.45 E
Le Cannet	62	43.34 N	7.01 E
Lecanto	220	28.51 N	82.29 W
Le Cap → Cap-Haïtien, Haï.	238	19.45 N	72.12 W
Le Cap → Cape Town, S. Afr.	158	33.55 S	18.22 E
Le Carbet	240e	14.43 N	61.11 W
Le Cateau	50	50.06 N	3.33 E
Le Catelet	50	50.00 N	3.15 E
Lecce	68	40.23 N	18.11 E
Lecce □4	68	40.13 N	18.10 E
Lecce, Tavoliere di ≚	68	40.30 N	17.35 E
Lecce nei Marsi	66	41.56 N	13.41 E
Lečchumskij Chrebet ⛰	84	42.45 N	43.05 E
Lecco	62	45.51 N	9.23 E
Lecco, Lago di @	58	45.55 N	9.19 E
Le Center	190	44.24 N	93.44 W
Lech	58	47.12 N	10.09 E
Lech ≃	30	48.44 N	10.56 E
Le Châble, Fr.	58	46.06 N	6.06 E
Le Châble, Schw.	58	46.05 N	7.12 E
L'Échalp	62	44.45 N	7.00 E
Le Chambon-Feugerolles	62	45.24 N	4.19 E
Le Chambon-sur-Lignon	62	45.03 N	4.18 E
Le Champ-Renault	261	49.06 N	2.31 E
Lechang	100	25.09 N	113.21 E
Le Chasseral ∧	58	47.08 N	7.03 E
Le-Château-d'Oléron	32	45.53 N	1.11 W
Le Châtelard, Fr.	62	45.41 N	6.08 E
Le Châtelard, Schw.	58	46.04 N	6.58 E
Le Châtelet	32	46.39 N	2.17 E
Le Châtelet-en-Brie	50	48.30 N	2.48 E
Lechbruck	58	47.42 N	10.47 E
Leche, Laguna de la C	240p	22.13 N	78.38 W
Le Chêne-Rogneux	261	48.46 N	1.46 E
Lecheng	110	19.14 N	110.34 E
Le Chesnay	261	48.50 N	2.07 E
Le Chesne	56	49.31 N	4.46 E
Le Cheylard	62	44.54 N	4.25 E
Lechfeld ≚	58	48.10 N	10.50 E
Lechiguanas, Islas de las II	252	33.26 S	59.42 W
Lechiguiri, Cerro ∧	234	16.43 N	95.30 W
Lechlade	42	51.43 N	1.41 W
Lechleiten	58	47.16 N	10.12 E
Lechta	24	60.49 N	48.28 E
Lechtaler Alpen ⛰	64	47.15 N	10.30 E
Lechuga, Arroyo ≃	286b	23.01 N	82.16 W
Lechuguila, Cerro ∧	234	22.19 N	104.15 W
Lecinone, Monte ∧	267a	41.59 N	12.48 E
Leck	41	54.46 N	8.58 E
Le Claire	190	41.36 N	90.21 W
l'Ecole	50	48.48 N	2.04 E
Lecompte	194	31.05 N	92.24 W
Léconi	152	1.35 S	14.14 E
Léconi ≃	152	1.11 S	13.16 E
Le Conquet	32	48.22 N	4.46 W
Lecontes Mills	214	41.05 N	78.17 W
Le Cornate ∧	66	43.10 N	10.57 E
Le Coudray-Montceaux	261	48.34 N	2.31 E
Le Coudray-Saint-Germer	50	49.25 N	1.50 E
Le Creusot	58	46.48 N	4.26 E
Le Croci di Acerno)(	68	40.47 N	15.02 E
Le Croisic	32	47.18 N	2.31 W
Le Crotoy	50	50.13 N	1.37 E
Łęczna	30	51.19 N	22.52 E
Łęczyca	30	52.04 N	19.13 E
Leda ≃	52	53.12 N	7.26 E
Led'anaja, Gora ∧	74	61.53 N	171.09 W
Ledang, Gunong ∧	114	2.22 N	102.37 E
Ledava ≃	61	46.29 N	16.35 E
Ledbetter	222	30.09 N	96.48 W
Ledbury	42	52.02 N	2.25 W
Ledce	60	49.49 N	13.20 E
Lede	50	50.58 N	3.58 E
Lederach	285	40.16 N	75.24 W
Le Deschaux	58	46.57 N	5.30 E
Ledesma	34	41.05 N	6.00 W
Ledgewood	276	40.53 N	74.39 W
Ledi, Ben ∧	46	56.15 N	4.19 W
Le Diamant	240e	14.29 N	61.02 W
Lediba	152	3.03 S	16.32 E
Lédignan	62	43.59 N	4.06 E
Ledkovo	24	67.14 N	50.30 E
Ledo, Bhārat	120	27.18 N	95.44 E
Ledo, Indon.	112	1.02 N	109.36 E
Lêdo, Cabo ≻	152	9.41 S	13.12 E
Ledong	110	18.45 N	109.12 E
Le Donjon	32	46.21 N	3.48 E
Le Dorat	32	46.13 N	1.05 E
Le Doré, Lac @	186	51.17 N	61.23 W
Ledra ≃	64	46.13 N	13.02 E
Ledsham	262	53.16 N	2.58 W
Ledu	102	36.32 N	102.25 E
Leduc	182	53.16 N	113.33 W
Lędyczek	30	53.33 N	16.58 E
Lee, Ill., U.S.	216	41.48 N	88.56 W
Lee, Mass., U.S.	207	42.19 N	73.15 W
Lee □6, Fla., U.S.	220	26.34 N	81.55 W
Lee □6, Ill., U.S.	216	41.50 N	89.29 W
Lee □6, Tex., U.S.	222	30.20 N	96.55 W
Lee ≃	48	51.54 N	8.22 W
Lee Center	210	43.18 N	75.31 W
Leechburg	214	40.38 N	79.36 W
Leechburg Airport ⊠	279b	40.37 N	79.34 W
Leech Lake @, Sask., Can.	184	51.04 N	102.30 W
Leech Lake @, Minn., U.S.	190	47.09 N	94.23 W
Leech Lake Indian Reservation ⊹4	190	47.30 N	94.27 W
Leechtown	224	48.30 N	123.42 W
Leedey	196	35.52 N	99.21 W
Leeds, Eng., U.K.	44	53.50 N	1.35 W
Leeds, Ala., U.S.	194	33.33 N	86.33 W
Leeds, N. Dak., U.S.	198	48.17 N	99.27 W
Leeds, N.Y., U.S.	210	42.15 N	73.54 W
Leeds □6	212	44.35 N	76.00 W
Leeds and Bradford (Yeadon) Airport ⊠	44	53.52 N	1.38 W
Leeds and Liverpool Canal ≋	262	53.25 N	2.59 W
Leeds Point	208	39.30 N	74.26 W
Leeds Pond @	276	40.49 N	73.42 W
Leedstown	42	50.10 N	5.22 W
Leegebruch	54	52.43 N	13.11 E
Leek	52	53.09 N	6.24 E
Leelanau, Lake @	190	44.55 N	85.43 W
Leen ≃	42	52.57 N	1.11 W
Leenaun	48	53.36 N	9.45 W
Leende	52	51.21 N	5.33 E
Lee-on-the-Solent	42	50.47 N	1.12 W
Lee Park	210	41.14 N	75.55 W
Leeper	214	41.22 N	79.18 W
Leer	52	53.14 N	7.26 E
Leerdam	52	51.54 N	5.05 E
Leerhafe	52	53.32 N	7.47 E
Leersum	52	52.01 N	5.26 E
Lees	262	53.32 N	2.04 W
Leesburg, Fla., U.S.	220	28.49 N	81.53 W
Leesburg, Ga., U.S.	192	31.44 N	84.10 W
Leesburg, Ind., U.S.	216	41.20 N	85.51 W
Leesburg, N.J., U.S.	208	39.15 N	74.59 W
Leesburg, Ohio, U.S.	218	39.21 N	83.33 W
Leesburg, Tex., U.S.	222	32.59 N	95.05 W
Leesburg, Va., U.S.	208	39.07 N	77.34 W
Lees Creek ≃	218	39.21 N	83.29 W
Leese	52	52.30 N	9.06 E
Leesport	208	40.27 N	75.58 W
Lees Summit	194	38.55 N	94.23 W
Leeste	52	52.59 N	8.49 E
Leeston	172	43.46 S	172.18 E
Leesville, Ill., U.S.	216	41.01 N	87.33 W
Leesville, Ind., U.S.	218	38.51 N	86.18 W
Leesville, La., U.S.	194	31.08 N	93.16 W
Leesville, Ohio, U.S.	214	40.27 N	81.13 W
Leesville, Tex., U.S.	222	29.24 N	97.45 W
Leesville Lake @1, Ohio, U.S.	214	40.30 N	81.10 W
Leesville Lake @1, Va., U.S.	192	37.05 N	79.25 W
Leeton	166	34.33 S	146.24 E
Leetonia	214	40.53 N	80.45 W
Leetsdale	214	40.34 N	80.13 W
Leeudoringstad	158	27.15 S	26.10 E
Leeu-Gamka	158	32.47 S	21.59 E
Leeupan @	158	26.34 S	28.59 E
Leeuwarden	52	53.12 N	5.46 E
Leeuwin, Cape ≻	162	34.22 S	115.08 E
Leeuwpan ≚	273d	26.14 S	28.19 E
Lee Vining	226	37.58 N	119.07 W
Leeward Islands II	238	17.00 N	63.00 W
Le Faouët	28	48.02 N	3.29 W
Le Fayet	58	45.55 N	6.42 E
Lefèvre, Cap ≻	175f	20.54 S	167.01 E
Leffe	62	45.48 N	9.53 E
Lefferts, Lake @	276	40.25 N	74.14 W
Léfini ≃	152	2.57 S	16.10 E
Léfini, Réserve de Chasse de la ⊹4	152	2.58 S	15.25 E
Le Focette	64	43.55 N	10.13 E
Leforest	50	50.26 N	3.04 E
Lefors	196	35.26 N	100.48 W
Le François	240e	14.37 N	60.54 W
Le Freney-d'Oisans	62	45.02 N	6.07 E
Lefroy	212	44.16 N	79.34 W
Lefroy, Lake @	162	31.15 S	121.40 E
Leftrook Lake @	184	56.05 N	98.36 W
Lefu ≃	89	44.32 N	132.30 E
Legal	182	53.57 N	113.35 W
Leganés	266a	40.20 N	3.46 W
Legaspi → Legazpi	116	13.08 N	123.44 E
Legau	58	47.51 N	10.07 E
Legazpi	116	13.08 N	123.44 E
Legden	52	52.02 N	7.07 E
Légé	32	46.53 N	1.36 W
Lege Hida	144	7.55 N	41.00 E
Legendre ≃	206	45.44 N	71.08 W
Legendre Island I	162	20.23 S	116.54 E
Léger	50	48.43 N	1.46 E
Legges Tor ∧	166	41.32 S	147.40 E
Leggett, Calif., U.S.	204	39.52 N	123.43 W
Leggett, Tex., U.S.	222	30.49 N	94.52 W
Leghorn → Livorno	66	43.33 N	10.19 E
Legion Mine	154	21.23 S	28.33 E
Legion of Honor, Palace of the ʋ	282	37.47 N	122.30 W
Legionowo	30	52.25 N	20.56 E
L'Église	50	47.22 N	3.56 E
Legnago	64	45.11 N	11.18 E
Legnano	62	45.36 N	8.54 E
Legnica (Liegnitz)	30	51.13 N	16.09 E
Le Gosier	241o	16.12 N	61.30 W
Le Grand	226	37.14 N	120.15 W
LeGrand, Cape ≻	162	34.01 S	122.06 E
Le Grand-Lucé	50	47.52 N	0.28 E
Le Grand-Quevilly	50	49.25 N	1.02 E
Le Grand-Serre	62	45.16 N	5.06 E
Le Grand Wintersberg ∧2	56	48.59 N	7.37 E
Le Grau-du-Roi	62	43.32 N	4.08 E
Le Gua	62	45.01 N	5.37 E
Le Guelta	34	36.22 N	0.50 E
Leguga	154	3.23 N	25.02 E
Legume	166	28.25 S	152.19 E
Legundi, Pulau I	115a	5.50 S	105.16 E
Leh	123	34.10 N	77.35 E
Le Havre	50	49.30 N	0.08 E
Lehčevo	38	43.32 N	23.32 E
Le Hérie-la-Viéville	50	49.49 N	3.38 E
Lehesten	54	50.29 N	11.28 E
Lehi	200	40.24 N	111.51 W
Lehigh, Iowa, U.S.	190	42.22 N	94.03 W
Lehigh, Okla., U.S.	196	34.28 N	96.13 W
Lehigh □6	208	40.36 N	75.29 W
Lehigh ≃	210	40.41 N	75.12 W
Lehigh Acres	220	26.36 N	81.39 W
Lehighton	210	40.49 N	75.45 W

DEUTSCH: Name — Seite — Breite°′ — Länge°′ E=Ost

Symbols in the index entries represent the broad categories identified in the key at the right. Symbols with superior numbers (⛰2) identify subcategories (see complete key on page I · 30).

Kartensymbole in dem Registerverzeichnis stellen die rechts in Schlüssel erklärten Kategorien dar. Symbole mit hochgestellten Ziffern (⛰2) bezeichnen Unterabteilungen einer Kategorie (vgl. vollständiger Schlüssel auf Seite I · 30).

Los símbolos incluídos en el texto del índice representan las grandes categorías identificadas con la clave a la derecha. Los símbolos con numeros en su parte superior (⛰2) identifican las subcategorías (véase la clave completa en la página I · 30).

Les symboles de l'index représentent les catégories indiquées dans la légende à droite. Les symboles suivis d'un indice (⛰2) représentent des sous-catégories (voir légende complète à la page I · 30).

Os símbolos incluídos no texto do índice representam as grandes categorias identificadas com a chave à direita. Os símbolos com números em sua parte superior (⛰2) identificam as subcategorias (veja-se a chave completa à página I · 30).

	English	Deutsch	Español	Français	Português
∧	Mountain	Berg	Montaña	Montagne	Montanha
⛰	Mountains	Berge	Montañas	Montagnes	Montanhas
)(	Pass	Pass	Paso	Col	Passo
V	Valley, Canyon	Tal, Cañon	Valle, Cañón	Vallée, Canyon	Vale, Canhão
≚	Plain	Ebene	Llano	Plaine	Planície
≻	Cape	Kap	Cabo	Cap	Cabo
I	Island	Insel	Isla	Île	Ilha
II	Islands	Inseln	Islas	Îles	Ilhas
⊥	Other Topographic Features	Andere Topographische Objekte	Otros Elementos Topográficos	Autres données topographiques	Outros Elementos Topográficos

ESPAÑOL Nombre / FRANÇAIS Nom / PORTUGUÊS Nome	Página / Page	Lat.°′	Long.°′ W=Oeste / W=Ouest
Lehman Caves National Monument ♠	204	39.01 N	114.14 W
Lehman College ʊ[2]	276	40.52 N	73.54 W
Lehnin	54	52.19 N	12.44 E
Lehnitz	54	52.44 N	13.15 E
Lehnitz See ⊜	264a	52.45 N	13.16 E
Leho	140	7.07 N	33.52 E
Le Hohwald	58	48.24 N	7.20 E
Le Houlme	50	49.31 N	1.02 E
Lehr	198	46.17 N	99.21 W
Lehra Gāga	123	29.55 N	75.49 E
Lehrbach	56	50.47 N	9.04 E
Lehrberg	56	49.21 N	10.30 E
Lehre	54	52.19 N	10.40 E
Lehrte	52	52.22 N	9.59 E
Lehtar	123	33.42 N	73.26 E
Lehtimäki	26	62.47 N	23.55 E
Lehtse	76	59.15 N	25.50 E
Lehua Island ❙	229b	22.01 N	160.06 W
Lehututu	156	23.58 S	21.51 E
Leiah	123	30.58 N	70.56 E
Leião	266c	38.44 N	9.18 W
Leibnitz	61	46.47 N	15.32 E
Leibo	102	28.19 N	103.21 E
Leicester, Eng., U.K.	42	52.38 N	1.05 W
Leicester, Mass., U.S.	207	42.15 N	71.55 W
Leicester, N.Y., U.S.	210	42.46 N	77.54 W
Leicestershire □[6]	42	52.40 N	1.10 W
Leichhardt	274a	33.53 S	151.07 E
Leichhardt ≃	166	17.35 S	139.48 E
Leichhardt Falls ⌊	166	18.14 S	139.53 E
Leichhardt Range ⛰	166	20.40 S	147.25 E
Leichlingen	56	51.06 N	7.01 E
Leiden	52	52.09 N	4.30 E
Leiderdorp	52	52.09 N	4.32 E
Leidschendam	52	52.05 N	4.24 E
Leie (Lys) ≃	50	51.03 N	3.43 E
Leiferde	52	52.26 N	10.26 E
Leigh, N.Z.	172	36.17 S	174.49 E
Leigh, Eng., U.K.	44	53.30 N	2.33 W
Leigh, Eng., U.K.	260	51.12 N	0.13 E
Leigh Canal ☰	262	53.28 N	2.21 W
Leigh Creek	166	30.28 S	138.25 E
Leighlinbridge	48	52.44 N	6.59 W
Leigh-on-Sea	42	51.33 N	0.38 E
Leighton	194	34.42 N	87.32 W
Leighton Buzzard	42	51.55 N	0.40 W
Leikanger	26	61.10 N	6.52 E
Leiktho	110	19.13 N	96.35 E
Leimbach	54	51.36 N	11.28 E
Leimstruth	56	50.59 N	8.19 E
Lein ≃	56	48.54 N	10.01 E
Leinan	184	50.30 N	107.46 W
Leinburg	60	49.27 N	11.19 E
Leinefelde	54	51.23 N	10.20 E
Leinfelden	56	48.41 N	9.08 E
Leinster □[9]	48	55.05 N	7.00 W
Leinster, Mount ∧	48	52.37 N	6.44 W
Leintwardine	42	52.23 N	2.51 W
Leipalingis	76	54.05 N	23.51 E
Leipheim	58	48.27 N	10.13 E
Leipoldtville	158	32.14 S	18.30 E
Leipsic, Del., U.S.	208	39.14 N	75.31 W
Leipsic, Ind., U.S.	218	38.40 N	86.22 W
Leipsic, Ohio, U.S.	216	41.06 N	83.59 W
Leipsic ≃	208	39.15 N	75.24 W
Leipzig	54	51.19 N	12.20 E
Leipzig □[5]	54	51.15 N	12.45 E
Leiria	34	39.45 N	8.48 W
Leirvik	26	59.45 N	5.30 E
Leisach	64	46.48 N	12.45 E
Leishendian	107	28.58 N	106.40 E
Leishui ≃	100	26.54 N	112.39 E
Leisi	76	58.34 N	22.39 E
Leisler, Mount ∧	162	23.28 S	129.17 E
Leisnig	54	51.09 N	12.56 E
Leisure City	220	25.30 N	80.26 W
Leitariegos, Puerto de)(	34	43.00 N	6.25 W
Leitchfield	194	37.29 N	86.18 W
Leiters Ford	216	41.07 N	86.23 W
Leith	46	55.59 N	3.10 W
Leith, Water of ≃	46	55.59 N	3.11 W
Leitha (Lajta) ≃, Eur.	30	47.54 N	17.17 E
Leitha ≃, Öst.	264b	48.00 N	16.35 E
Leithagebirge ⛰	61	47.52 N	16.35 E
Leithe ↞[8]	263	51.29 N	7.06 E
Leith Hill ∧[2]	42	51.11 N	0.23 W
Leitre	164	2.50 S	141.40 E
Leitrim	48	54.00 N	8.04 W
Leitrim □[6]	48	54.20 N	8.20 W
Leitzkau	54	52.03 N	11.57 E
Lei U Mun ⋓	271d	22.16 N	114.14 E
Leiva	246	5.38 N	73.34 W
Leixi	100	27.10 N	112.52 E
Leiyang	100	26.24 N	112.51 E
Leizhoubandao ≻[1]	102	21.15 N	110.09 E
Leizhuang	98	39.47 N	118.34 E
Lejasciems	76	57.17 N	26.35 E
Lek ≃	52	52.00 N	6.00 E
Lékana	152	2.19 S	14.36 E
Le Kef → El Kef	148	36.11 N	8.43 E
Lékéti ≃	152	1.36 S	14.57 E
Lékéti, Monts de la ⛰	152	2.34 S	14.17 E
Lekhainá	38	37.56 N	21.17 E
Lekir	114	4.07 N	100.44 E
Lekitobi	112	1.58 S	124.33 E
Lekkeroog	158	30.43 S	20.00 E
Lekkerwater	156	23.38 S	17.14 E
Lekkous, Oued ≃	34	34.58 N	5.52 W
Lekma ≃	80	58.18 N	52.04 E
Łęknice	54	51.35 N	14.45 E
Lekotero	152	0.46 S	23.51 E
Lékoumou □[5]	152	3.00 S	13.00 E
Le Kreïder	148	34.06 N	0.02 E
Le Kremlin-Bicêtre	261	48.49 N	2.21 E
Leksand	26	60.44 N	14.59 E
Leksberg	40	59.41 N	13.49 E
Leksozero, Ozero ⊜	24	63.46 N	30.58 E
Leksvik	26	63.40 N	10.37 E
Lela	152	5.03 S	12.29 E
Le Lac-d'Issarlès	62	44.49 N	4.04 E
Le Lamentin	240e	14.37 N	61.01 W
Leland, Ill., U.S.	216	41.37 N	88.48 W
Leland, Mich., U.S.	190	45.01 N	85.45 W
Leland, Miss., U.S.	194	33.24 N	90.54 W
Leland Grove	219	39.47 N	89.41 W
Leland Lake ⊜	224	47.53 N	122.53 W
Lelång ⊜	26	59.08 N	12.10 E
Lelant	42	50.11 N	5.26 W
Le Laus	62	44.31 N	6.09 E
Le Lauzet-Ubaye	62	44.26 N	6.26 E
Le Lavandou	62	43.08 N	6.22 E
Lel'čicy	78	51.47 N	28.19 E
Leleiwi Point ≻	229d	19.44 N	155.00 W
Lelepa ❙	175f	17.36 S	168.13 E
Leleque	254	42.23 S	71.03 W
Leles	115a	7.07 S	107.53 E
Lelewau	112	3.02 S	121.05 E
Lélex	58	46.18 N	5.57 E
Le Liège	50	47.13 N	1.06 E
Leling	98	37.45 N	117.12 E
Lelingluang	164	7.09 S	131.43 E
Lelintah	164	2.03 S	130.16 E
Le Lion-d'Angers	32	47.38 N	0.43 W
Lelishan ∧	120	33.26 N	81.42 E
Le Locle	58	47.03 N	6.45 E
Lelogama	112	9.44 S	123.57 E
Le Lorrain	240e	14.50 N	61.04 W
Le Luc	62	43.23 N	6.19 E
Le Lude	50	47.39 N	0.09 E
Lelystad	52	52.31 N	5.27 E
Lema	150	12.57 N	4.14 E
Le Madonie ⛰	70	37.52 N	13.58 E
Lemahabang	115a	6.17 S	107.27 E
Le Maire, Estrecho de ⋓	254	54.50 S	65.00 W
Léman, Lac → Geneva, Lake ⊜	58	46.25 N	6.30 E
Lemanmanu Mission	175e	5.02 S	154.35 E
Le Mans	50	48.00 N	0.12 E
Le Marin	240e	14.28 N	60.53 W
Le Markstein	58	47.56 N	7.02 E
Le Mars	198	42.47 N	96.10 W
Lema Shilindi	144	4.55 N	42.02 E
Lemay	219	38.32 N	90.17 W
Lemay, Lac ⊜	186	50.35 N	68.25 W
Le Mayet-de-Montagne	32	46.05 N	3.40 E
Lembach	56	49.00 N	7.48 E
Lembach im Mühlkreis	60	48.29 N	13.53 E
Lembak	112	0.52 N	117.32 E
Lembang	115a	6.49 S	107.36 E
Lembeck	52	51.45 N	7.00 E
Lembeek	50	50.43 N	4.13 E
Lembeh, Pulau ❙	112	1.26 N	125.13 E
Lembeni	154	3.47 S	37.37 E
Lemberg, Sask., Can.	184	50.44 N	103.13 W
Lemberg, Fr.	56	49.00 N	7.23 E
Lemberg → L'vov, S.S.S.R.	78	49.50 N	24.00 E
Lemberg ∧	58	48.09 N	8.45 E
Lembruch	52	52.31 N	8.22 E
Lembu, Gunung ∧	114	4.12 N	97.24 E
Leme	255	22.12 S	47.24 W
Leme, Morro do ∧[2]	287a	22.58 S	43.10 W
Le Mée-sur-Seine	261	48.32 N	2.38 E
Lemei Rock ∧	224	46.01 N	121.46 W
Lemele	52	52.27 N	6.25 E
Le Mêle-sur-Sarthe	50	48.31 N	0.21 E
Lemene ≃	64	45.37 N	12.53 E
Lemeris, Cape ≻	164	3.15 S	152.03 E
Le Merlerault	50	48.42 N	0.18 E
Lemery	116	13.53 N	120.55 E
Lemeškino	80	51.01 N	44.27 E
Le Mesle	261	48.43 N	1.41 E
Le Mesnil-Amelot	261	49.01 N	2.36 E
Le Mesnil-Aubry	261	49.03 N	2.24 E
Le Mesnil-le-Roi	261	48.56 N	2.08 E
Le Mesnil-Saint-Denis	261	48.45 N	1.58 E
Le Mesnil-sur-Oger	50	48.57 N	4.01 E
Lemesós (Limassol)	130	34.40 N	33.02 E
Lemešovka	78	52.04 N	31.38 E
Lemeta	180	64.52 N	147.44 W
Lemförde	52	52.28 N	8.22 E
Lemfu	152	5.18 S	15.13 E
Lemgo	52	52.02 N	8.54 E
Lemhi ≃	202	45.12 N	113.53 W
Lemhi Pass)(	202	44.58 N	113.27 W
Lemhi Range ⛰	202	44.30 N	113.25 W
Lemie	62	45.14 N	7.17 E
Lemierzyce	54	52.35 N	14.56 E
Lemieux Islands ❙❙	176	64.30 N	64.40 W
Lemin	102	21.11 N	109.42 E
Leming	196	29.04 N	98.29 W
Lemitar	200	34.09 N	106.55 W
Lemke	52	52.39 N	9.09 E
Lemmatsi	76	58.20 N	26.37 E
Lemmenjoen Kansallispuisto ♠	24	68.40 N	26.00 E
Lemmer	52	52.50 N	5.42 E
Lemmon	198	45.56 N	102.10 W
Lemmon, Mount ∧	200	32.26 N	110.47 W
Lemnos → Límnos ❙	38	39.54 N	25.21 E
Lemoenshoek	158	33.51 S	20.51 E
Lemoine, Lac ⊜	190	48.00 N	78.00 W
Lemon, Lake ⊜	218	39.16 N	86.25 W
Le Monastier	62	44.56 N	4.00 E
Lemoncove	204	36.23 N	119.01 W
Lemon Creek ≃	276	40.31 N	74.12 W
Le Monêtier-les-Bains	62	44.59 N	6.31 E
Lemon Grove	228	32.44 N	117.02 W
Lemon Heights	280	33.46 N	117.48 W
Lemont, Ill., U.S.	216	41.40 N	88.00 W
Lemont, Pa., U.S.	214	40.49 N	77.49 W
Le Montet	32	46.25 N	3.03 E
Le Mont Saint-Michel ʊ[1]	32	48.38 N	1.32 W
Lemoore	226	36.18 N	119.47 W
Lemoore Naval Air Station ▪	226	36.15 N	119.57 W
Lemoro	112	1.25 S	121.05 E
Lemotol Bay C	175c	7.21 N	151.35 E
Le Moule	241o	16.20 N	61.21 W
Le Moutier	261	48.50 N	1.42 E
LeMoyne, Qué., Can.	275a	45.31 N	73.29 W
Lemoyne, Ohio, U.S.	214	41.30 N	83.28 W
Lemoyne, Pa., U.S.	208	40.15 N	76.54 W
Lempa ≃	236	13.14 N	88.49 W
Lempäälä	26	61.19 N	23.45 E
Lempe	112	1.40 S	120.14 E
Lempira □[5]	236	14.20 N	88.40 W
Lemro ≃	110	20.25 N	93.20 E
Lemsid ⍑[4]	148	26.32 N	13.49 W
Lemukutan, Pulau ❙	112	0.45 N	108.43 E
Le Murge ⛰[1]	68	40.52 N	16.42 E
Lemutan	112	3.03 N	115.49 E
Le Muy	62	43.28 N	6.33 E
Lemva ≃	24	66.30 N	61.48 E
Lemvig	26	56.32 N	8.18 E
Lemyethna	110	17.36 N	95.09 E
Len ≃	260	51.16 N	0.31 E
Lena, Ill., U.S.	190	42.23 N	89.50 W
Lena, Wis., U.S.	190	44.57 N	88.03 W
Lena ≃	74	72.25 N	126.40 E
Lenakel	175f	19.32 S	169.16 E
Lenangguar	115b	8.44 S	117.24 E
Lenape	285	39.55 N	75.38 W
Lenart	61	46.35 N	15.50 E
Lenawee □[6]	216	41.53 N	84.04 W
Lencloître	32	46.49 N	0.20 E
Lençóis	255	12.34 S	41.23 W
Lend	64	47.18 N	13.04 E
Lenda ≃	154	1.20 N	28.01 E
Lendelede	50	50.53 N	3.14 E
Lendery	24	63.26 N	31.03 E
Lendinara	64	45.05 N	11.36 E
Lendorf	64	46.50 N	13.26 E
Lendringsen	56	51.24 N	7.49 E
Le Neubourg	50	49.09 N	0.55 E
Lenga	114	2.17 N	102.49 E
Lengduqiao	106	30.27 N	119.15 E
Lengede	52	52.12 N	10.18 E
Lengefeld	54	50.43 N	13.11 E
Lengelscheid	263	51.08 N	7.40 E
Lengenfeld, D.D.R.	54	50.34 N	12.22 E
Lengenfeld, D.D.R.	56	51.13 N	10.13 E
Lenger	85	42.12 N	69.54 E
Lengerich, B.R.D.	52	52.11 N	7.50 E
Lengerich, B.R.D.	52	52.33 N	7.32 E
Lenggor ≃	114	2.25 N	103.37 E
Lenggries	64	47.41 N	11.34 E
Lenghu	90	38.30 N	93.15 E
Lengjiagou	104	41.40 N	121.37 E
Lengkong	115a	7.32 S	112.04 E
Lenglingen ⊜	26	64.14 N	13.45 E
Lengnau	58	47.11 N	7.22 E
Lengoué	152	1.13 N	15.43 E
Lengshuichang	107	29.27 N	106.26 E
Lengshuikeng	100	27.55 N	117.08 E
Lengshuitan	102	26.14 N	111.29 E
Lengua de Vaca, Punta ≻	252	30.14 S	71.38 W
Lengulu	154	3.15 N	26.30 E
Lengzipu	104	41.42 N	122.47 E
Lenham	260	51.14 N	0.43 E
Lenhartsville	208	40.34 N	75.53 W
Lenhovda	26	57.00 N	15.17 E
Lenina, Gora ∧[2]	265b	55.42 N	37.31 E
Lenina, Ozero ⊜	78	48.33 N	35.12 E
Lenina, Pik ∧	85	39.20 N	72.55 E
Leninabad	85	40.17 N	69.37 E
Leninakan	84	40.48 N	43.50 E
Lenindżol	85	41.03 N	72.38 E
Leningori	84	42.07 N	44.29 E
Leningrad	76		
	265a	59.55 N	30.15 E
Leningrad □[4]	265a	59.55 N	30.15 E
Leningrad, Aeroport ⊠	265a	59.48 N	30.16 E
Leningrad, Gorod □[7]	265a	59.55 N	30.15 E
Leningrado → Leningrad	76	59.55 N	30.15 E
Leningradskaja	78	46.19 N	39.24 E
Leningradskij Vokzal ↞[5]	265b	55.47 N	37.39 E
Leningradskoje	86	53.33 N	71.35 E
Lenino	78	45.18 N	35.47 E
Lenino ↞[8]	265b	55.37 N	37.41 E
Leninogorsk, S.S.S.R.	80	54.36 N	52.30 E
Leninogorsk, S.S.S.R.	86	50.27 N	83.32 E
Leninpol'	85	42.29 N	71.55 E
Leninsk, S.S.S.R.	78	45.16 N	35.54 E
Leninsk, S.S.S.R.	80	46.08 N	43.46 E
Leninsk, S.S.S.R.	80	48.42 N	45.11 E
Leninsk, S.S.S.R.	85	40.38 N	72.15 E
Leninsk, S.S.S.R.	86	54.55 N	59.54 E
Leninskaja Sloboda	80	56.05 N	44.28 E
Leninskij, S.S.S.R.	78	47.53 N	28.23 E
Leninskij, S.S.S.R.	80	56.34 N	45.58 E
Leninskij, S.S.S.R.	80	46.31 N	44.28 E
Leninskij, S.S.S.R.	82	54.18 N	37.28 E
Leninskij, S.S.S.R.	83	48.05 N	39.31 E
Leninskij, S.S.S.R.	86	52.13 N	76.47 E
Leninsk-Kuzneckij	86	54.38 N	86.10 E
Leninskoje, S.S.S.R.	78	51.27 N	33.18 E
Leninskoje, S.S.S.R.	80	58.19 N	47.06 E
Leninskoje, S.S.S.R.	80	49.03 N	49.56 E
Leninskoje, S.S.S.R.	85	41.45 N	69.23 E
Leninskoje, S.S.S.R.	85	40.42 N	73.11 E
Leninskoje, S.S.S.R.	86	50.44 N	57.53 E
Leninskoje, S.S.S.R.	89	47.56 N	132.38 E
Lenin-Stausee → Kujbyševskoje Vodochranilišče ⊜[1]	80	53.40 N	49.00 E
Leninžol	80	49.20 N	47.05 E
Lenk	58	46.28 N	7.27 E
Lenkerville	208	40.32 N	76.58 W
Len'ki	86	52.57 N	80.26 E
Lenkoran'	84	38.45 N	48.50 E
Lenkoranskaja Nizmennost' ≚	84	38.50 N	48.50 E
Lenmalu	164	1.44 S	130.13 E
Lenne ≃	56	51.25 N	7.30 E
Lennegebirge ⛰	52	51.15 N	8.00 E
Lennep	56	51.11 N	7.15 E
Lennep ↞[8]	52	51.12 N	7.15 E
Lenni	285	39.54 N	75.27 W
Lennon	216	42.59 N	83.56 W
Lennonville	162	27.58 S	117.50 E
Lennox, Calif., U.S.	228	33.56 N	118.21 W
Lennox, S. Dak., U.S.	198	43.21 N	96.53 W
Lennox □[9]	46	56.02 N	4.15 W
Lennox, Isla ❙	254	55.18 S	66.50 W
Lennox and Addington □[6]	212	44.30 N	77.00 W
Lennoxtown	46	55.59 N	4.12 W
Lennoxville	206	45.22 N	71.51 W
Leno	64	45.22 N	10.13 E
Lenoir	192	35.55 N	81.32 W
Lenoir City	192	35.48 N	84.16 W
Le Noirmont	58	47.13 N	6.58 E
Lenola	66	41.24 N	13.28 E
Lenora	60	48.55 N	13.54 E
Lenore Lake ⊜	184	52.30 N	105.00 W
Le Nouvion-en-Thiérache	50	50.01 N	3.47 E
Lenox, Ga., U.S.	192	31.16 N	83.28 W
Lenox, Iowa, U.S.	198	40.53 N	94.34 W
Lenox, Mass., U.S.	207	42.22 N	73.17 W
Lenox, Tenn., U.S.	194	36.05 N	89.30 W
Lenox Dale	207	42.20 N	73.15 W
Lens	50	50.26 N	2.50 E
Lensahn	54	54.13 N	10.52 E
Lensk	74	61.00 N	114.50 E
Lenskoje	86	58.09 N	63.11 E
Lenswood	168b	34.55 S	138.49 E
Lentate sul Seveso	266b	45.41 N	9.07 E
Lentechi	84	42.48 N	42.44 E
Lenti	61	46.37 N	16.33 E
Lenting	60	48.48 N	11.28 E
Lentini	70	37.17 N	15.00 E
Lentner	219	39.43 N	92.09 W
Lentua ⊜	26	64.14 N	29.36 E
Lentvaris	76	54.39 N	25.03 E
Lenwood	228	34.53 N	117.07 W
Lenya	110	11.28 N	99.00 E
Lenya ≃	110	11.40 N	98.43 E
Lenz	273d	26.19 S	27.49 E
Lenzburg	58	47.23 N	8.11 E
Lenzen	54	53.05 N	11.28 E
Lenzerheide (Lai)	58	46.44 N	9.33 E
Lenzinghausen	52	52.07 N	8.28 E
Lenzkirch	58	47.52 N	8.12 E
Léo, H. Vol.	150	11.06 N	2.06 W
Leo, Ind., U.S.	216	41.13 N	85.01 W
Leoben	61	47.23 N	15.06 E
Leobschütz → Głubczyce	30	50.13 N	17.49 E
Leo Carrillo State Beach ♠	228	34.03 N	118.56 W
Léogâne	238	18.31 N	72.38 W
Leogang	64	47.26 N	12.45 E
Leola, Ark., U.S.	194	34.10 N	92.35 W
Leola, Pa., U.S.	208	40.05 N	76.11 W
Leola, S. Dak., U.S.	198	45.43 N	98.56 W
Leominster, Eng., U.K.	42	52.14 N	2.45 W
Leominster, Mass., U.S.	207	42.32 N	71.45 W
León, Esp.	34	42.36 N	5.34 W
Léon, Fr.	32	43.53 N	1.18 W
León, Nic.	236	12.26 N	86.53 W
Leon, Pil.	116	10.47 N	122.23 E
Leon, Iowa, U.S.	190	40.44 N	93.45 W
Leon, Kans., U.S.	198	37.42 N	96.46 W
Leon, N.Y., U.S.	210	42.18 N	79.01 W
León □[5]	236	12.35 N	86.35 W
Leon □[6]	222	31.18 N	95.55 W
León □[9]	34	42.00 N	6.00 W
Leon ≃	196	30.59 N	97.24 W
Leon, Arroyo ≃	282	37.28 N	122.25 W
León, Montes de ⛰	34	42.30 N	6.18 W
Leona	222	31.09 N	95.58 W
Leona ≃	196	28.45 N	99.11 W
Leona, Punta ≻	236	9.41 N	84.41 W
Leonard, Mich., U.S.	214	42.52 N	83.09 W
Leonard, Mo., U.S.	219	39.54 N	92.11 W
Leonard, N. Dak., U.S.	198	46.39 N	97.15 W
Leonard, Tex., U.S.	196	33.23 N	96.15 W
Leonardo	276	40.25 N	74.03 W
Leonardo da Vinci, Aeroporto Intercontinentale ⊠	66	41.48 N	12.13 E
Leonardsburg	214	40.21 N	82.59 W
Leonardsville	210	42.49 N	75.15 W
Leonardtown	188	38.17 N	76.38 W
Leonardville, Namibia	156	23.29 S	18.49 E
Leonardville, Kans., U.S.	198	39.22 N	96.51 W
Leonárison	130	35.28 N	34.08 E
Leona Vicario	200	32.10 N	115.10 W
Leonberg	56	48.48 N	9.01 E
Leonbronn	56	49.03 N	8.53 E
Leon Creek ≃	196	31.11 N	102.45 W
Leondárion	267c	37.59 N	23.51 E
León [de los Aldamas]	234	21.07 N	101.40 W
Leonding	61	48.16 N	14.15 E
Leone	174u	14.20 S	170.47 W
Leone, Golfo del → Lion, Golfe du C	32	43.00 N	4.00 E
Leone, Monte ∧	58	46.15 N	8.06 E
Leones	252	32.39 S	62.18 W
Leonessa	66	42.34 N	12.58 E
Leonforte	70	37.38 N	14.23 E
Leongatha	169	38.29 S	145.57 E
León Guzmán	196	25.31 N	103.34 W
Leonia	276	40.52 N	73.59 W
Leonicha	76	59.37 N	38.51 E
Leonidas	216	42.01 N	85.21 W
Leonídhion	38	37.10 N	22.52 E
Leonidovo	89	49.17 N	142.50 E
Leon Junction	222	31.20 N	97.36 W
Leonora	162	28.53 S	121.20 E
Leonovo	82	55.26 N	38.42 E
León Rougés	252	27.13 S	65.32 W
Leontjev Bajrak, Uročišče ♠	83	48.03 N	38.48 E
Leontjevka	85	43.03 N	69.50 E
Leontjevo	76	58.58 N	36.37 E
Leonville	194	30.29 N	91.59 W
Leopard	285	40.01 N	75.27 W
Leopold	169	38.11 S	144.28 E
Leopold, Camp ▪	273b	4.18 S	15.17 E
Léopold, Mont ∧[2]	273b	4.19 S	15.15 E
Leopold and Astrid Coast •[2]	9	67.10 S	84.10 E
Leopoldau ↞[8]	264b	48.16 N	16.27 E
Leopold Downs	162	17.52 S	125.25 E
Léopold II, Lac → Mai-Ndombe, Lac ⊜	152	2.00 S	18.20 E
Leopoldina	256	21.32 S	42.38 W
Leopoldkanaal ☰	50	51.14 N	3.46 E
Leopoldo de Bulhões	255	16.37 S	48.46 W
Leopoldo y Astrid, Costa → Leopold and Astrid Coast •[2]	9	67.10 S	84.10 E
Leopoldsburg	56	51.07 N	5.15 E
Leopoldsdorf	264b	48.06 N	16.24 E
Leopoldshagen	54	53.46 N	13.53 E
Leopoldstadt ↞[8]	264b	48.13 N	16.23 E
Léopoldville → Kinshasa	152	4.18 S	15.18 E
Leoti	198	38.29 N	101.21 W
Leoville	184	53.37 N	107.35 W
Leovo	78	46.29 N	28.15 E
Le Pailly	58	47.48 N	5.25 E
Le Palais	32	47.21 N	3.09 W
Lepanto, C.R.	236	9.57 N	85.02 W
Lepanto → Návpaktos, Ellás	38	38.23 N	21.50 E
Lepanto, Ark., U.S.	194	35.36 N	90.20 W
Lepar, Pulau ❙	112	2.57 S	106.50 E
Le Parcq	50	50.23 N	2.06 E
Le Pâté	261	48.32 N	2.18 E
Lepe	34	37.15 N	7.12 W
Le Péage-de-Roussillon	62	45.22 N	4.48 E
Le Pecq	261	48.54 N	2.07 E
Lepel'	76	54.53 N	28.42 E
Le Pellerin	32	47.12 N	1.45 W
Lepembusu, Keli ∧	115b	8.40 S	121.49 E
Le Perray-en-Yvelines	261	48.42 N	1.51 E
Le Perreux-sur-Marne	261	48.51 N	2.30 E
Leper Settlement ʊ	229a	21.12 N	156.58 W
Lepeški	82	56.05 N	38.07 E
Le Petit-Clamart ʊ	261	48.47 N	2.14 E
Le Petit-Couronne	50	49.23 N	1.01 E
Le Petit-Quevilly	50	49.26 N	1.02 E
Lephepe	156	23.20 S	25.50 E
Lépi	152	12.52 S	15.26 E
Le Piastre	66	44.00 N	10.50 E
Lepihué	254	41.37 S	73.36 W
Le Pin	261	48.55 N	2.38 E
Le Pin-au-Haras	50	48.44 N	0.09 E
L'Épine, Fr.	56	48.58 N	4.28 E
L'Épine, Fr.	261	48.32 N	2.21 E
Leping	100	28.57 N	117.05 E
Lepini, Monti ⛰	66	41.35 N	13.00 E
Lépin-le-Lac	62	45.32 N	5.47 E
L'Épiphanie	206	45.51 N	73.30 W
Lepl'avo	78	49.48 N	31.32 E
Le Plessis-aux-Bois	261	49.00 N	2.46 E
Le Plessis-Belleville	50	49.06 N	2.46 E
Le Plessis-Bouchard	261	49.00 N	2.14 E
Le Plessis-Pâté	261	48.37 N	2.20 E
Le Plessis-Trévise	261	48.49 N	2.34 E
Lépo, Lagoa de ⊜	152	17.08 S	19.00 E
Le Poët	62	44.17 N	5.53 E
Le Pont	58	46.40 N	6.20 E
Le Pont-de-Beauvoisin	62	45.32 N	5.40 E
Le Pont-de-Montvert	62	44.22 N	3.45 E
Le Pontel	261	48.49 N	1.53 E
Lepontine, Alpi ⛰	58	46.25 N	8.40 E
Leporano	68	40.23 N	17.20 E
Le Port	157c	20.55 S	55.18 E
Le Portel	50	50.42 N	1.34 E
Le Port-Marly	261	48.53 N	2.06 E
Le Pouzin	62	44.45 N	4.45 E
Leppävirta	26	62.29 N	27.47 E
Lepperton	172	39.04 S	174.13 E
Leppin	54	52.53 N	11.34 E
Leppington	274a	33.58 S	150.49 E
Le Pradet	62	43.06 N	6.01 E
Lepreau, Point ≻	186	45.04 N	66.27 W
Le Prêcheur	240e	14.48 N	61.14 W
Le Pré-Saint-Gervais	261	48.53 N	2.25 E
Le Prese	58	46.18 N	10.04 E
Lepsinsk	86	45.32 N	80.37 E
Lepsy, S.S.S.R.	86	46.15 N	78.55 E
Lepsy, S.S.S.R.	86	46.18 N	78.20 E
Leptis Magna ⊥	146	32.38 N	14.18 E
Le Puy	62	45.02 N	3.53 E
Leqing	100	28.08 N	120.58 E
Lequeitio	34	43.22 N	2.30 W
Le Quesnoy	50	50.15 N	3.38 E
Léraba ≃	150	9.42 N	4.35 W
Le Raincy	261	48.54 N	2.31 E
Le Rayol-Canadel-sur-Mer	62	43.10 N	6.28 E
Le Raysville	210	41.51 N	76.11 W
Lerberget	41	56.11 N	12.33 E
Lercara Friddi	70	37.45 N	13.36 E
Lerche	263	51.37 N	7.43 E
Lerderderg ≃	169	37.42 S	144.30 E
Lerdo → Ciudad Lerdo	196	25.32 N	103.32 W
Lerdo de Tejada	234	18.37 N	95.31 W
Léré, Fr.	50	47.28 N	2.52 E
Léré, Mali	150	15.43 N	4.55 W
Lere, Nig.	150	9.43 N	9.21 E
Léré, Tchad	146	9.39 N	14.13 E
Lereh	164	3.08 S	139.54 E
Lerek ∧	114	3.47 N	102.47 E
Le Renne, Rivière ≃	206	45.41 N	72.39 W
Le Reposoir	58	46.00 N	6.33 E
Leri ≃	42	52.32 N	4.02 W
Leribe	158	28.58 S	28.00 E
Lerici	64	44.04 N	9.55 E
Lérida, Col.	246	0.10 N	70.42 W
Lérida, Esp.	34	41.37 N	0.37 E
Lerik	84	38.46 N	48.25 E
Lérins, Îles de ❙❙	62	43.31 N	7.03 E
Lerma	34	42.02 N	3.45 W
Lerma ≃	234	20.13 N	102.46 W
Lermontovka	89	47.10 N	134.20 E
Lermoos	58	47.24 N	10.53 E
Lerno, Monte ∧	71	40.37 N	9.10 E
Le Robert	240e	14.41 N	60.57 W
Léros ❙, Ellás	38	37.08 N	26.52 E
Léros ❙, Ellás	267c	37.59 N	23.34 E
Lérouville	56	48.47 N	5.33 E
Leroux Wash ∨	200	34.54 N	110.12 W
Leroy, Ind., U.S.	216	41.22 N	87.16 W
Le Roy, Kans., U.S.	198	38.05 N	95.38 W
Le Roy, Minn., U.S.	190	43.31 N	92.30 W
Le Roy, N.Y., U.S.	210	42.59 N	77.59 W
Le Roy, Pa., U.S.	210	41.41 N	76.43 W
Leroy, Tex., U.S.	222	31.44 N	97.01 W
Lerum	26	57.46 N	12.16 E
Le Russey	58	47.10 N	6.44 E
Lerwick	46a	60.09 N	1.09 W
Léry	206	45.21 N	73.48 W
Lesa	62	45.50 N	8.34 E
Les Abrets	62	45.32 N	5.35 E
Les Abymes	241o	16.16 N	61.31 W
Lesage, Lac ⊜	206	46.19 N	75.03 W
Le Saint-Esprit	240e	14.34 N	60.57 W
Les Aix-d'Angillon	50	47.12 N	2.34 E
Les Allues	62	45.26 N	6.33 E
Les Alluets-le-Roi	261	48.55 N	1.55 E
Les Andelys	50	49.15 N	1.25 E
Les Anses-d'Arlets	240e	14.29 N	61.05 W
Le Sappey-en-Chartreuse	62	45.16 N	5.47 E
Les Arcs	62	43.27 N	6.29 E
Lesatima, Ol Doinyo ∧	154	0.19 S	36.37 E
Le Sauze	62	44.22 N	6.41 E
Les Baux-en-Provence	62	43.45 N	4.48 E
Les Bézards	50	47.48 N	2.44 E
Les Bordes	261	48.39 N	1.58 E
Lesbos → Lésvos ❙	38	39.10 N	26.20 E
Les Bouchoux	58	46.18 N	5.49 E
Les Bréviaires	261	48.42 N	1.49 E
Lesbury	44	55.24 N	1.36 W
L'Escarène	62	43.50 N	7.21 E
L'Escaut	50	50.27 N	3.35 E
Les Cayes	238	18.12 N	73.45 W
Les Chaises	261	48.39 N	1.42 E
Les Chapieux	62	45.42 N	6.44 E
Leschenault, Cape ≻	162	31.18 S	115.27 E
Leschenault Inlet C	168a	33.15 S	115.42 E
Lesches	261	48.54 N	2.47 E
Leščinovka	78	49.16 N	34.14 E
Les Clayes-sous-Bois	261	48.49 N	1.59 E
Les Contamines-Montjoie	62	45.50 N	6.44 E
Les Diablerets	58	46.21 N	7.10 E
Les Diablerets ∧	58	46.19 N	7.12 E
Les Écharmeaux	58	46.10 N	4.27 E
Les Échelles	62	45.26 N	5.45 E
Les Écureuils	206	46.39 N	71.43 W
Le Semnoz ∧	62	45.48 N	6.07 E
Leseru	154	0.35 N	35.10 E
Les Essarts	32	46.46 N	1.14 W
Les Essarts-le-Roi	261	48.43 N	1.54 E
Les Estables	62	44.54 N	4.10 E
Les Étangs	56	49.09 N	6.23 E
Lesever, Mount ∧	162	30.10 S	115.11 E
Les Fonts	266d	41.32 N	2.02 E
Les Fourgs	58	46.50 N	6.25 E
Les Galleries d'Anjou ↞[9]	275a	45.35 N	73.34 W
Les Gâtines	261	48.48 N	1.58 E
Les Gets	58	46.09 N	6.40 E
Les Granges-le-Roi	261	48.30 N	2.01 E
Les Halles	62	45.43 N	4.26 E
Leshan	107	29.34 N	103.45 E
Les Haudères	58	46.05 N	7.31 E
Les Hautes-Rivières	56	49.53 N	4.50 E
Les Herbiers	32	46.52 N	1.01 W
Les Houches	62	45.53 N	6.48 E
Leshui ≃	100	26.54 N	113.12 E
Lesignano de'Bagni	64	44.39 N	10.18 E
Lésigny	261	48.45 N	2.37 E
Lesima, Monte ∧	62	44.41 N	9.15 E
Lesina	68	41.52 N	15.21 E
Lesina, Lago di C	68	41.53 N	15.26 E
Les Islettes	56	49.06 N	5.00 E
Lesjaskog	26	62.15 N	8.22 E
Lesjöfors	40	59.59 N	14.11 E
Lesken	84	43.16 N	43.48 E
Les'ki	78	49.19 N	32.13 E
Lesko	30	49.29 N	22.21 E
Leskovac	38	42.59 N	21.57 E
Leskov Island ❙	9	56.40 S	28.10 W
Les Laumes	58	47.32 N	4.27 E
Les Lecques	62	43.11 N	5.40 E
Leslie, S. Afr.	158	26.27 S	28.55 E
Leslie, Scot., U.K.	46	56.12 N	3.13 W
Leslie, Ark., U.S.	194	35.50 N	92.34 W
Leslie, Ga., U.S.	192	31.57 N	84.05 W
Leslie, Mich., U.S.	216	42.27 N	84.26 W
Leslie, W. Va., U.S.	188	38.03 N	80.43 W
Les Lilas	261	48.53 N	2.25 E
Les Loges	261	48.34 N	2.03 E
Les Loges-en-Josas	261	48.46 N	2.09 E
Lesmahagow	46	55.39 N	3.55 W
Les Marécottes	58	46.07 N	7.00 E
Les Mées	62	44.02 N	5.59 E
Les Mesnuls	50	48.45 N	1.50 E
Lesmo	266b	45.39 N	9.18 E
Les Molières	261	48.40 N	2.04 E
Les Monges ∧	62	44.16 N	6.12 E
Lesmont	50	48.26 N	4.25 E
Les Moroubas	152	6.11 N	20.13 E
Les Mosses	58	46.24 N	7.07 E
Les Mureaux	261	49.00 N	1.55 E
Leśna	30	51.02 N	15.16 E
Lesna ≃	76	52.10 N	23.33 E
Lesnaja	76	52.59 N	25.46 E
Les Neyrolles	58	46.08 N	5.38 E
Lešnica	38	44.39 N	19.19 E
Lesnoj, S.S.S.R.	80	54.11 N	40.27 E
Lesnoj, S.S.S.R.	86	56.57 N	67.15 E
Lesnoj ↞[8]	265a	60.00 N	30.19 E
Lesnoje	76	58.17 N	35.32 E
Lesnoje Konobejevo	80	54.02 N	41.55 E
Lesnoje Mat'unino	80	53.27 N	47.26 E
Lesnoj Gorodok	265b	55.39 N	37.13 E
Lesnoj Park ♠	265a	59.59 N	30.21 E
Lesný ∧	60	50.02 N	12.37 E
Lesnyje Pol'any, S.S.S.R.	24	58.58 N	52.26 E
Lesnyje Pol'any, S.S.S.R.	265b	55.57 N	37.53 E
Lesogorsk, S.S.S.R.	80	55.06 N	43.56 E
Lesogorsk, S.S.S.R.	88	56.03 N	99.33 E
Lesogorsk, S.S.S.R.	89	49.27 N	142.08 E
Lesogorskij	24	61.02 N	28.53 E
Lesopil'noje	89	46.44 N	134.20 E
Lesotho □[1]	138		
	158	29.30 S	28.30 E
Lesovščina	78	50.47 N	28.35 E
Lesozavodsk	89	45.28 N	133.27 E
Lesozavodskij	24	66.44 N	32.49 E
Lesparre-Médoc	32	45.18 N	0.56 W
Les Pavillons-sous-Bois	261	48.55 N	2.30 E
Les Pieux	32	49.31 N	1.48 W
Les Planches-en-Montagne	58	46.40 N	6.01 E
Les Ponts-de-Martel	58	46.54 N	6.41 E
Les Praz-de-Chamonix	58	45.56 N	6.52 E
Lesquin	50	50.35 N	3.07 E
Les Riceys	50	47.59 N	4.22 E
Les Roches-l'Evêque	50	47.47 N	0.53 E
Les Rousses	58	46.29 N	6.04 E
Les Ruelles	261	48.40 N	1.37 E
Les Sables-d'Olonne	32	46.30 N	1.47 W
Lessach	64	47.11 N	13.49 E
Les Salles-sur-Verdon	62	43.46 N	6.12 E
Lessay	32	49.13 N	1.32 W
Les Scaffarels	62	43.57 N	6.41 E
Lesse ≃	56	50.14 N	4.54 E
Lessebo	26	56.45 N	15.16 E
Lessen → Lessines	50	50.43 N	3.50 E
Lesser Antilles ❙❙	238	15.00 N	61.00 W
Lesser Khingan Mountains → Xiaoxing'anling-shanmai ⛰	89	50.00 N	126.25 E
Lesser Slave ≃	182	55.10 N	114.03 W
Lesser Slave Lake ⊜	182	55.25 N	115.30 W
Lesser Sunda Islands → Nusa Tenggara ❙❙	108	9.00 S	120.00 E
Lessines (Lessen)	50	50.43 N	3.50 E
Lessini, Monti ⛰	64	45.41 N	11.13 E
L'Estaque	62	43.22 N	5.20 E
Leste ≃	250	6.20 S	57.46 W
Lester, Pa., U.S.	285	39.52 N	75.17 W
Lester, Wash., U.S.	224	47.12 N	121.29 W
Les Thilliers-en-Vexin	50	49.14 N	1.36 E
Lestijärvi	26	63.32 N	24.39 E
Lestijoki ≃	26	64.04 N	23.38 E
Lestkov	60	49.54 N	12.52 E
Lestock	184	51.18 N	104.00 W
L'Estréchure	62	44.06 N	3.47 E
Les Trois Lacs ⊜	206	45.48 N	71.54 W
Le Sueur	190	44.27 N	93.54 W
Le Sueur ≃	190	44.07 N	94.03 W
Lešukonskoje	24	64.54 N	45.40 E
Lesung, Tanjung ≻	115a	6.28 S	105.40 E
Lesunovo	80	55.40 N	43.07 E
Les Vans	62	44.24 N	4.08 E
Les Verrières	58	46.54 N	6.30 E
Lésvos ❙	38	39.10 N	26.20 E
Leszno	30	51.51 N	16.35 E
Letälven ≃	40	59.05 N	14.20 E
L'Étang-la-Ville	261	48.52 N	2.05 E
Letcher	198	43.54 N	98.08 W
Letchmore Heath	260	51.40 N	0.20 W
Letchworth	42	51.58 N	0.14 W
Letchworth State Park ♠	210	42.42 N	77.56 W
Letea, Ostrovul ❙	38	45.20 N	29.20 E
Le Teil	62	44.33 N	4.41 E
Le Temple	261	49.00 N	1.58 E
Letenye	30	46.26 N	16.43 E
Le Tertre-Saint-Denis	261	48.56 N	1.36 E
Lethbridge, Austl.	274a	33.44 S	150.48 E
Lethbridge, Alta., Can.	182	49.42 N	112.50 W
Lethbridge, Newf., Can.	186	48.21 N	53.52 W
Le Theil-sur-Huisne	50	48.16 N	0.42 E
Lethem	246	3.23 N	59.48 W
Le Thillot	58	47.53 N	6.46 E
Le Tholy	58	48.05 N	6.45 E
Le Thor	62	43.56 N	5.00 E
Le Thoronet	62	43.27 N	6.18 E
Leti, Kepulauan ❙❙	164	8.13 S	127.50 E
Leti, Pulau ❙	112	8.12 S	127.41 E
Letiahau ≃	156	21.16 S	24.00 E
Letičev	78	49.23 N	27.37 E
Leticia	246	4.09 S	69.57 W
Leting	98	39.27 N	118.53 E
Letino	68	41.26 N	14.17 E
Letjiesbos	158	32.34 S	22.16 E
Letka	24	59.36 N	49.22 E
Letlhakane	156	21.27 S	25.30 E
Letlhakeng	156	24.08 S	25.02 E
Letmathe	56	51.22 N	7.37 E
Letn'aja Zolotica	24	64.57 N	36.50 E
Letnerečenskij	24	64.17 N	34.23 E
Letong	112	2.58 N	105.42 E
Le Touquet-Paris-Plage	50	50.31 N	1.35 E
Le Touvet	62	45.21 N	5.57 E
Letovo	265b	55.34 N	37.24 E
Letpadan	110	17.47 N	95.45 E
Le Trait	50	49.28 N	0.49 E
Le Trayas	62	43.28 N	6.55 E
Le Tremblay-sur-Mauldre	261	48.47 N	1.53 E
Le Tréport	50	50.04 N	1.22 E
Letschin	54	52.39 N	14.21 E
Letsôk-aw Kyun ❙	110	11.37 N	98.15 E
Letter	52	52.24 N	9.38 E
Letterfrack	48	53.33 N	10.00 W
Letterkenny	48	54.57 N	7.44 W
Lettermullen	48	53.13 N	9.42 W
Letterston	42	51.56 N	5.00 W
Lettonie → Latvijskaja Sovetskaja Socialističeskaja Respublika □[3]	76	57.00 N	25.00 E
Letts	218	39.14 N	85.35 W
Letzlingen	54	52.26 N	11.29 E
Leu	38	44.11 N	24.00 E
Léua	152	11.34 S	20.32 E
Leubnitz	54	50.43 N	12.21 E
Leubsdorf	54	50.48 N	13.08 E
Leuca	68	39.48 N	18.21 E
Leucadia	228	33.04 N	117.18 W
Leucate, Étang de C	32	42.51 N	3.00 E
Leuchars	46	56.23 N	2.53 W
Leuchtenberg	60	49.36 N	12.15 E
Leudeville	261	48.34 N	2.20 E
Leuenberger Forst ↞[3]	264a	52.40 N	13.53 E
Leuglay	58	47.49 N	4.48 E
Leuk	58	46.19 N	7.38 E
Leukerbad	58	46.23 N	7.38 E
Leulumoega	175a	13.49 S	171.55 W
Leumeah	274a	34.03 S	150.50 E
Leuna	54	51.19 N	12.01 E
Leupoldsgrün	54	50.17 N	11.47 E
Leupoldstein	60	49.42 N	11.23 E
Leura	170	33.43 S	150.20 E
Leura, Mount ∧[2]	169	38.15 S	143.09 E
Leuser, Gunung ∧	114	3.45 N	97.11 E
Leušinskij Tuman, Ozero ⊜	86	59.42 N	65.35 E
Leutenberg	54	50.34 N	11.28 E
Leutersdorf	54	50.57 N	14.40 E
Leutershausen	56	49.18 N	10.24 E
Leutesdorf	56	50.27 N	7.23 E
Leutkirch	58	47.49 N	10.01 E
Leuven (Louvain)	56	50.53 N	4.42 E
Leuville-sur-Orge	261	48.37 N	2.16 E
Leuwiliang	115a	6.34 S	106.37 E
Leuze, Bel.	50	50.36 N	3.36 E
Leuze, Bel.	56	50.34 N	4.54 E
Levack	190	46.38 N	81.23 W
Levádhia	38	38.25 N	22.54 E
Levaja Mama ≃	88	57.10 N	111.54 E
Le Val-d'Ajol	58	47.55 N	6.29 E
Le Val-d'Albian	261	48.45 N	2.11 E
Levallois-Perret	261	48.54 N	2.18 E
Le Val-Saint-Germain	261	48.34 N	2.04 E
Levan	200	39.33 N	111.52 W
Levanger	26	63.45 N	11.18 E
Levanna, Monte ∧	62	45.24 N	7.12 E
Levant, Île du ❙	62	43.03 N	6.28 E
Levante, Riviera di •[2]	62	44.15 N	9.30 E
Levanto	62	44.10 N	9.38 E
Levanzo	70	37.59 N	12.20 E
Levanzo, Isola di ❙	70	38.00 N	12.20 E
Levaši	84	42.27 N	47.20 E
Le Vauclin	240e	14.33 N	60.51 W
Levdym	86	60.29 N	66.19 E
Leveaux Mountain ∧[2]	190	47.37 N	90.47 W
Level, Isla ❙	254	44.29 S	74.23 W
Level Green	279b	40.24 N	79.43 W
Levelland	196	33.35 N	102.23 W
Levelock	180	59.07 N	156.52 W

Symbol	English	Deutsch	Español	Français	Português
≃	River	Fluss	Río	Rivière	Rio
☰	Canal	Kanal	Canal	Canal	Canal
⌊	Waterfall, Rapids	Wasserfall, Stromschnellen	Cascada, Rápidos	Chute d'eau, Rapides	Cascata, Rápidos
⋓	Strait	Meeresstrasse	Estrecho	Détroit	Estreito
C	Bay, Gulf	Bucht, Golf	Bahía, Golfo	Baie, Golfe	Baía, Golfo
⊜	Lake, Lakes	See, Seen	Lago, Lagos	Lac, Lacs	Lago, Lagos
≚	Swamp	Sumpf	Pantano	Marais	Pântano
⍓	Ice Features, Glacier	Eis- und Gletscherformen	Accidentes Glaciales	Formes glaciaires	Acidentes Glaciares
⍑	Other Hydrographic Features	Andere Hydrographische Objekte	Otros Elementos Hidrográficos	Autres données hydrographiques	Outros Elementos Hidrográficos
⤓	Submarine Features	Untermeerische Objekte	Accidentes Submarinos	Formes de relief sous-marin	Acidentes Submarinos
□	Political Unit	Politische Einheit	Unidad Politica	Entité politique	Unidade Política
ʊ	Cultural Institution	Kulturelle Institution	Institución Cultural	Institution culturelle	Instituição Cultural
⊥	Historical Site	Historische Stätte	Sitio Histórico	Site historique	Sitio Histórico
♠	Recreational Site	Erholungs- und Ferienort	Sitio de Recreo	Centre de loisirs	Sítio de Lazer
⊠	Airport	Flughafen	Aeropuerto	Aéroport	Aeroporto
▪	Military Installation	Militäranlage	Instalación Militar	Installation militaire	Instalação Militar
↞	Miscellaneous	Verschiedenes	Misceláneo	Divers	Miscelânea

ENGLISH — Name · Page · Lat.°′ · Long.°′

DEUTSCH — Name · Seite · Breite°′ · Länge°′ E=Ost

Name	Page	Lat.°′	Long.°′
Level Park	216	42.22 N	85.18 W
Leven	46	56.12 N	3.00 W
Leven ≃, Eng., U.K.	44	54.14 N	3.01 W
Leven ≃, Eng., U.K.	44	54.31 N	1.21 W
Leven, Loch ⊜, Scot., U.K.	46	56.12 N	3.22 W
Leven, Loch ⊜, Scot., U.K.	46	56.41 N	5.07 W
Leven Point ≻	158	27.55 S	32.35 E
Levens	62	43.52 N	7.13 E
Levenshulme ◆[8]	262	53.27 N	2.10 W
Levent	130	38.27 N	37.52 E
Leventina, Valle ∨	58	46.25 N	9.52 E
L'Evêque	50	49.18 N	0.11 E
Leveque, Cape ≻	68	16.24 S	122.56 E
Leverano	68	40.17 N	18.00 E
Leverburgh	46	57.45 N	7.00 W
Leverett Glacier ⛆	9	85.30 S	150.00 W
Leveretts Chapel	222	32.19 N	94.55 W
Levering	190	45.38 N	84.47 W
Leverkusen	56	51.03 N	6.59 E
Levern	52	52.22 N	8.26 E
Lever Park ♠	262	53.37 N	2.34 W
Le Vésinet	261	48.54 N	2.08 E
Le Vésuve → Vesuvio ∧[1]	66	40.49 N	14.26 E
Leviathan Peak ∧	226	38.41 N	119.37 W
Levice	30	48.13 N	18.37 E
Levicha	86	57.36 N	59.55 E
Levick, Mount ∧	9	74.08 S	163.12 E
Levico	64	46.01 N	11.18 E
Levie	36	41.42 N	9.07 E
Levier	58	46.57 N	6.08 E
Le Vigan	32	43.59 N	3.35 E
Levin	172	40.37 S	175.17 E
Levino	76	60.29 N	37.30 E
Lévis	206	46.48 N	71.11 W
Lévis □[6]	206	46.40 N	71.15 W
Lévis-Saint Nom	261	48.43 N	1.58 E
Levítha I	38	37.00 N	26.28 E
Levittown → Willingboro, N.J., U.S.	208	40.03 N	74.53 W
Levittown, N.Y., U.S.	210	40.41 N	73.31 W
Levittown, Pa., U.S.	208	40.09 N	74.50 W
Levittown Shop-A-Rama ◆[9]	285	40.09 N	74.49 W
Lévka	130	35.07 N	32.51 E
Lévka Óri ⋀	38	35.18 N	24.01 E
Levkás	38	38.50 N	20.41 E
Levkás I	38	38.39 N	20.27 E
Levkímmi	38	39.25 N	20.04 E
Levkónoikon	130	35.15 N	33.45 E
Levkosía (Nicosia)	130	35.10 N	33.22 E
Levoča	30	49.02 N	20.36 E
Levokumskoje	84	44.48 N	44.39 E
Levroux	32	46.59 N	1.37 E
Levski	38	43.22 N	25.08 E
Lev Tolstoj	76	53.13 N	39.27 E
Levuka	175g	17.41 S	178.50 E
Lévuo ≃	76	56.04 N	24.23 E
Levyj Tuzlov ≃	83	47.35 N	39.23 E
Lewapaku	115b	9.43 S	119.55 E
Lewbeach	210	42.00 N	74.47 W
Lewe	110	19.38 N	96.07 E
Lewedorp	52	51.30 N	3.45 E
Lewellen	198	41.20 N	102.09 W
Lewer ≃	156	25.30 S	17.45 E
Lewes, Eng., U.K.	42	50.52 N	0.01 E
Lewes, Del., U.S.	208	38.47 N	75.08 W
Lewin Brzeski	30	50.46 N	17.37 E
Lewis, Iowa, U.S.	198	41.18 N	95.05 W
Lewis, Kans., U.S.	198	37.56 N	99.15 W
Lewis □[6], Ky., U.S.	218	38.32 N	83.21 W
Lewis □[6], Mo., U.S.	219	40.08 N	91.45 W
Lewis □[6], N.Y., U.S.	212	43.47 N	75.29 W
Lewis □[6], Wash., U.S.	224	46.35 N	122.22 W
Lewis ≃	224	45.51 N	122.48 W
Lewis, Butt of ≻	46	58.31 N	6.16 W
Lewis, East Fork ≃	224	45.52 N	122.43 W
Lewis, Isle of I	46	58.20 N	6.35 W
Lewis, Mount ∧	204	40.24 N	116.51 W
Lewis and Clark ≃	224	46.10 N	123.52 W
Lewis and Clark Caverns State Park ♠	202	45.49 N	111.13 W
Lewis and Clark Lake ⊜[1]	198	42.50 N	97.45 W
Lewisberry	208	40.08 N	76.52 W
Lewisburg, Ky., U.S.	194	36.59 N	86.57 W
Lewisburg, Ohio, U.S.	218	39.51 N	84.33 W
Lewisburg, Pa., U.S.	210	40.58 N	76.53 W
Lewisburg, Tenn., U.S.	194	35.27 N	86.48 W
Lewisburg, W. Va., U.S.	188	37.48 N	80.27 W
Lewis Center	214	40.12 N	83.01 W
Lewis Creek ≃, Calif., U.S.	226	35.17 N	120.58 W
Lewis Creek ≃, Ind., U.S.	218	39.22 N	85.51 W
Lewisdale	284c	38.58 N	76.58 W
Lewisetta	208	38.01 N	76.28 W
Lewis Gut C	276	41.09 N	73.09 W
Lewisham	273d	26.07 S	27.49 E
Lewisham ◆[8]	42	51.27 N	0.01 E
Lewis Hills ⋀[2]	186	48.48 N	58.30 W
Lewis Island I	220	27.44 N	82.38 W
Lewis-Lockport Airport ⊠	278	41.36 N	88.05 W
Lewis Pass ⅄	172	42.23 S	172.24 E
Lewisport	194	37.56 N	86.54 W
Lewisporte	186	49.15 N	55.03 W
Lewis Range ⋀, Austl.	162	20.20 S	128.40 E
Lewis Range ⋀, N.A.	202	48.30 N	113.15 W
Lewis Run	214	41.52 N	78.40 W
Lewis Run ≃	279b	40.17 N	79.55 W
Lewis Smith Lake ⊜[1]	194	34.05 N	87.07 W
Lewiston, Calif., U.S.	204	40.43 N	122.48 W
Lewiston, Idaho, U.S.	202	46.25 N	117.01 W
Lewiston, Maine, U.S.	188	44.06 N	70.13 W
Lewiston, Mich., U.S.	190	44.53 N	84.18 W
Lewiston, Minn., U.S.	190	44.00 N	91.49 W
Lewiston, N.Y., U.S.	210	43.10 N	79.03 W
Lewiston, Utah, U.S.	200	41.58 N	111.51 W
Lewiston Orchards	202	46.23 N	116.59 W
Lewistown, Ill., U.S.	194	40.24 N	90.09 W
Lewistown, Md., U.S.	208	39.32 N	77.25 W
Lewistown, Mo., U.S.	219	40.05 N	91.49 W
Lewistown, Mont., U.S.	202	47.04 N	109.26 W
Lewistown, Ohio, U.S.	216	40.25 N	83.53 W
Lewistown, Pa., U.S.	208	40.36 N	77.31 W
Lewisville, N.B., Can.	186	45.06 N	64.46 W
Lewisville, Ark., U.S.	194	33.22 N	93.35 W
Lewisville, Ind., U.S.	218	39.48 N	85.21 W
Lewisville, Pa., U.S.	208	39.43 N	75.53 W
Lewisville, Tex., U.S.	222	33.03 N	97.00 W
Lewisville Dam ◆[6]	222	33.05 N	96.55 W
Lewoleba	112	8.23 S	123.24 E
Lewotobi Lakilaki, Ili ∧	115b	8.32 S	122.46 E
Lewvan	184	50.00 N	104.06 W
Lexa	194	34.36 N	90.45 W
Lexington, Ga., U.S.	192	33.52 N	83.07 W
Lexington, Ill., U.S.	216	40.39 N	88.47 W
Lexington, Ind., U.S.	218	38.39 N	85.37 W
Lexington, Ky., U.S.	218	38.03 N	84.30 W
Lexington, Mass., U.S.	207	42.27 N	71.14 W
Lexington, Mich., U.S.	190	43.16 N	82.32 W
Lexington, Miss., U.S.	194	33.07 N	90.03 W
Lexington, Mo., U.S.	194	39.11 N	93.52 W
Lexington, Nebr., U.S.	198	40.47 N	99.45 W
Lexington, N.C., U.S.	192	35.49 N	80.15 W
Lexington, N.Y., U.S.	210	42.15 N	74.22 W
Lexington, Ohio, U.S.	214	40.41 N	82.35 W
Lexington, Okla., U.S.	196	35.01 N	97.20 W
Lexington, Oreg., U.S.	202	45.27 N	119.41 W
Lexington, S.C., U.S.	192	34.00 N	81.14 W
Lexington, Tenn., U.S.	194	35.39 N	88.24 W
Lexington, Tex., U.S.	222	30.25 N	97.01 W
Lexington, Va., U.S.	192	37.47 N	79.27 W
Lexington Park	188	38.16 N	76.27 W
Lexington Reservoir ⊜[1]	226	37.12 N	121.59 W
Lexton	169	37.17 S	143.31 E
Leybourne	260	51.18 N	0.25 E
Leyburn	44	54.19 N	1.49 W
Leyden → Leiden	52	52.09 N	4.30 E
Leyland	44	53.42 N	2.42 W
Leyne	130	37.22 N	28.02 E
Leyond ≃	184	51.40 N	96.32 W
Leyou ≃	152	1.07 S	13.08 E
Leyre ≃	32	44.39 N	1.01 W
Leysdown-on-Sea	42	51.24 N	0.55 E
Leysin	58	46.21 N	7.01 E
Leyte	116	11.23 N	124.29 E
Leyte □[4]	116	10.50 N	124.55 E
Leyte I	116	10.50 N	124.50 E
Leyte Gulf C	116	10.50 N	125.25 E
Leyu	106	31.55 N	120.43 E
Lèz ≃	62	44.13 N	4.43 E
Lèz ≊	62	43.31 N	3.55 E
Leža	76	58.56 N	40.45 E
Leža ≃	76	59.15 N	40.10 E
Leżajsk	30	50.16 N	22.24 E
Lezama	246	9.43 N	66.24 W
Lézard, Pointe à ≻	241o	16.08 N	61.47 W
Lézarde ≃	240e	14.36 N	61.01 W
Lézat	58	46.30 N	5.56 E
Lèze ≃	62	43.40 N	5.28 E
Lezhë	38	41.47 N	19.39 E
Lezhi	107	30.17 N	105.02 E
Ležn'ovo	80	56.46 N	40.53 E
Lezzeno	58	45.56 N	9.11 E
L'gov	78	51.43 N	35.17 E
Lhanbryde	46	57.37 N	3.13 W
Lhasa → Lasa	120	29.40 N	91.09 E
L'Hautil	261	49.00 N	2.01 E
L'Hermite, Isla I	254	55.52 S	67.20 W
Lhokkruet	114	4.52 N	95.24 E
Lhoknga	114	5.29 N	95.15 E
Lhokseumawe	114	5.10 N	97.08 E
Lhoksukon	114	5.03 N	97.19 E
L'Hôpital	56	49.10 N	6.44 E
L'Hôpital-sous-Rochefort	62	45.46 N	3.56 E
Lhuis	62	45.45 N	5.32 E
Lhuntsi Dzong	120	27.39 N	91.09 E
Lhut ≃	144	10.25 N	51.05 E
Li	110	17.48 N	98.57 E
Li ≃	110	18.26 N	98.42 E
Liancheng	100	25.44 N	116.46 E
Lianchipu	107	29.45 N	104.55 E
Liancourt	50	49.20 N	2.28 E
Liandao	98	36.59 N	121.31 E
Liane ≃	50	50.43 N	1.36 E
Lianfu	89	53.28 N	123.51 E
Liang	164	3.30 S	128.19 E
Lianga	116	8.38 N	126.06 E
Lianga Bay C	116	8.37 N	126.12 E
Liangbingbao	89	45.48 N	128.19 E
Liangbingtai	89	43.12 N	128.47 E
Liangbuaya	112	0.05 N	116.46 E
Liangchahe	107	29.03 N	106.18 E
Liangcheng	98	35.35 N	119.35 E
Liangcun	100	26.36 N	115.34 E
Liangdang	102	33.57 N	106.23 E
Liangdongmiao	107	28.59 N	106.13 E
Liangfengwu	107	30.11 N	105.22 E
Lianghe, Zhg.	89	45.09 N	128.45 E
Lianghe, Zhg.	102	24.51 N	98.25 E
Liangheguan	102	32.52 N	109.19 E
Lianghekou, Zhg.	102	33.29 N	104.41 E
Lianghekou, Zhg.	102	29.14 N	108.40 E
Lianghekou, Zhg.	102	31.38 N	102.32 E
Lianghekou, Zhg.	107	28.55 N	106.03 E
Liangjia	107	29.29 N	105.33 E
Liangjiadian	98	39.10 N	121.54 E
Liangjiafang	98	41.04 N	117.18 E
Liangjianfang	105	40.45 N	117.20 E
Liangjiang	102	23.23 N	108.22 E
Liangjiangkou	98	42.38 N	128.05 E
Liangjiawazi	104	40.40 N	120.42 E
Liangjiazi	104	42.13 N	122.31 E
Liangkou	100	23.43 N	113.43 E
Lianglukou, Zhg.	107	29.18 N	106.15 E
Lianglukou, Zhg.	107	29.43 N	106.37 E
Liangmen	98	35.34 N	114.54 E
Liangmentou	100	28.58 N	121.12 E
Liangmushi	106	30.46 N	119.35 E
Liangpa	102	24.10 N	106.13 E
Liangpengting	106	30.47 N	119.38 E
Liangping	102	30.41 N	107.49 E
Liangqiu	98	35.12 N	117.47 E
Liangshan ∧, Zhg.	102	23.45 N	99.45 E
Liangshan ∧, Zhg.	102	24.05 N	99.02 E
Liangtinghe	100	30.20 N	116.12 E
Liangtoumen	100	29.31 N	120.45 E
Liangtun	98	40.14 N	122.34 E
Liangwangzhuang	105	39.01 N	116.58 E
Liangxiang	105	39.44 N	116.08 E
Liangying	100	23.14 N	116.21 E
Liangyuan	100	32.00 N	117.34 E
Liangzhu	106	30.23 N	120.03 E
Liangzihu ⊜	100	30.16 N	114.34 E
Lianhe	98	42.36 N	125.37 E
Lianhu ⊜	106	32.02 N	119.32 E
Lianhua	100	27.07 N	113.57 E
Lianhuachi	105	40.28 N	116.33 E
Lianhuapao	89	45.32 N	129.50 E
Lianhuashan ⋀	100	23.40 N	116.00 E
Lianjiang, Zhg.	100	26.12 N	119.31 E
Lianjiang, Zhg.	102	21.38 N	110.15 E
Lianjiang ≃, Zhg.	100	23.16 N	116.32 E
Lianjiang ≃, Zhg.	100	25.46 N	115.38 E
Lianjiang ≃, Zhg.	100	24.02 N	113.18 E
Lianjiechang	107	29.41 N	104.30 E
Liannan (Sanjiang)	102	24.38 N	112.10 E
Lianozovo ◆[8]	265b	55.54 N	37.35 E
Lianping	100	24.22 N	114.31 E
Lianpu	100	26.02 N	118.38 E
Lianshanguan	104	40.58 N	123.46 E
Lianshi	106	30.42 N	120.26 E
Lianshui	100	33.47 N	119.16 E
Lianshui ≃	100	25.07 N	116.24 E
Liansiji	98	33.58 N	114.24 E
Lianxian	102	24.41 N	112.21 E
Lianyuan (Lantian)	102	27.42 N	111.19 E
Lianyun'gang	98	34.44 N	119.30 E
Lianyunshan ∧	100	28.32 N	113.50 E
Lianzhou → Hepu	102	21.39 N	109.11 E
Liaobinta	104	42.08 N	123.04 E
Liaocheng	98	36.30 N	115.59 E
Liaodongbandao ≻[1]	98	40.00 N	122.20 E
Liaodongwan C	98	40.30 N	121.30 E
Liaohe ≃	104	40.40 N	122.09 E
Liaohekou C[1]	104	40.42 N	122.05 E
Liaojiangshi	100	26.05 N	113.17 E
Liaoning □[4]	90	41.00 N	123.00 E
Liaoshui ≃	100	29.11 N	116.00 E
Liaotung, Gulf of → Liaodongwan C	98	40.30 N	121.30 E
Liaotung Peninsula → Liaodongbandao ≻[1]	98	40.00 N	122.20 E
Liaoyang	104	41.17 N	123.11 E
Liaoyangwobao	89	43.00 N	123.28 E
Liaoyuan	89	42.54 N	125.07 E
Liaozhong	104	41.31 N	122.44 E
Liapádhes	38	39.40 N	19.44 E
Liāquatpur	123	28.56 N	70.57 E
Liard ≃	176	61.52 N	121.18 W
Liāri	120	25.41 N	66.29 E
Liart	50	49.46 N	4.20 E
Liat, Pulau I	112	2.53 S	107.05 E
Liathach ∧	46	57.35 N	5.29 W
Lib I	14	8.19 N	167.25 E
Liban → Lebanon □[1]	128	33.50 N	35.50 E
Libanga	152	0.19 N	18.41 E
Líbano	246	4.55 N	75.04 W
Libano → Lebanon □[1]	128	33.50 N	35.50 E
Libanon → Lebanon □[1]	128	33.50 N	35.50 E
Libau → Liepāja	76	56.31 N	21.01 E
Libby	202	48.23 N	115.33 W
Libby Dam ◆[6]	202	48.24 N	115.20 W
Libčeves	54	50.26 N	13.50 E
Libčice nad Vltavou	54	50.10 N	14.20 E
Liběchov	54	50.20 N	14.28 E
Libenge	152	3.39 N	18.38 E
Liberal, Kans., U.S.	198	37.02 N	100.55 W
Liberal, Mo., U.S.	194	37.34 N	94.31 W
Liberdade	256	22.01 S	44.19 W
Liberdade ◆[8]	287b	23.35 S	46.37 W
Liberdade ≃	250	9.40 S	52.17 W
Liberdade, Riozinho da ≃	248	7.10 S	71.51 W
Liberec	30	50.46 N	15.03 E
Liberia	236	10.38 N	85.27 W
Liberia □[1]	134		
	150	6.30 N	9.30 W
Liberta	240c	17.02 N	61.47 W
Libertad, Arg.	258	34.42 S	58.41 W
Libertad, Ur.	258	34.38 S	56.39 W
Libertad, Ven.	246	9.23 N	68.44 W
Libertad, Ven.	246	8.20 N	69.37 W
Libertador □[5]	286c	10.27 N	66.57 W
Libertador General Bernardo O'Higgins □[4]	252	34.30 S	71.00 W
Libertador General San Martín, Arg.	252	26.48 S	55.02 W
Libertador General San Martín (Ledesma), Arg.	252	23.48 S	64.48 W
Liberty, Ill., U.S.	219	39.53 N	91.06 W
Liberty, Ind., U.S.	218	39.38 N	84.56 W
Liberty, Ky., U.S.	194	37.19 N	84.56 W
Liberty, Miss., U.S.	194	31.09 N	90.48 W
Liberty, Mo., U.S.	194	39.15 N	94.25 W
Liberty, Nebr., U.S.	198	40.05 N	96.29 W
Liberty, N.C., U.S.	192	35.51 N	79.34 W
Liberty, N.Y., U.S.	210	41.48 N	74.45 W
Liberty, Pa., U.S.	210	41.34 N	77.06 W
Liberty, Pa., U.S.	279b	40.20 N	79.51 W
Liberty, S.C., U.S.	192	34.48 N	82.42 W
Liberty, Tex., U.S.	222	30.03 N	94.47 W
Liberty □[6]	222	30.12 N	94.50 W
Liberty Acres	280	33.56 N	118.22 W
Liberty Bell Park Race Track ♠	285	40.05 N	74.58 W
Liberty Center, Ind., U.S.	216	40.42 N	85.17 W
Liberty Center, Ohio, U.S.	216	41.27 N	84.07 W
Liberty City	222	32.27 N	94.57 W
Liberty Corner	276	40.40 N	74.35 W
Liberty Ditch ≊	226	36.31 N	120.02 W
Liberty Farms	226	38.19 N	121.42 W
Liberty Hill	196	30.40 N	97.55 W
Liberty Island I	276	40.41 N	74.03 W
Liberty Lake ⊜[1]	208	39.25 N	76.53 W
Liberty Manor	284b	39.21 N	76.47 W
Liberty Mills	216	41.02 N	85.44 W
Liberty Park	216	41.26 N	87.22 W
Liberty Tunnel ◆[5]	279b	40.26 N	80.01 W
Libertyville	216	42.17 N	87.57 W
Líbeznice	54	50.10 N	14.30 E
Libia → Libya □[1]	146	27.00 N	17.00 E
Libibi	152	14.42 S	17.44 E
Libishan	106	30.45 N	119.20 E
Lībiyā → Libya □[1]	146	27.00 N	17.00 E
Liblar	56	50.49 N	6.49 E
Liblín	60	49.55 N	13.32 E
Libni, Jabal ∧[2]	132	30.44 N	33.50 E
Libo	102	25.28 N	107.53 E
Libobo, Tanjung ≻	164	0.54 S	128.28 E
Liboc ≃	54	50.10 N	13.31 E
Libochovice	54	50.22 N	14.03 E
Libode	158	31.33 S	29.02 E
Liboi	154	0.24 N	40.57 E
Liboka ≃[1]	152	0.27 S	16.36 E
Liboko	152	2.43 N	21.28 E
Libona	116	8.20 N	124.44 E
Liboumba ≃	152	0.38 N	12.54 E
Libourne	32	44.55 N	0.14 W
Libramont	56	49.55 N	5.23 E
Library	214	40.18 N	80.02 W
Librazhd	38	41.11 N	20.19 E
Libreville	152	0.23 N	9.27 E
Librizzi	70	38.06 N	14.57 E
Libro Point ≻	116	11.26 N	119.29 E
Libu	102	23.41 N	111.30 E
Libucan Island I	116	11.54 N	124.39 E
Libunga	154	1.49 N	26.35 E
Liburung	112	3.55 S	120.09 E
Libušín	54	50.09 N	14.04 E
Libya □[1]	136		
	146	27.00 N	17.00 E
Libyan Desert → Aṣ-Ṣaḥrā' al-Lībīyah ◆[2]	136	24.00 N	25.00 E
Libyan Plateau → Aḍ-Ḍiffah ⋀[1]	140	30.30 N	25.30 E
Libye → Libya □[1]	146	27.00 N	17.00 E
Libyen → Libya □[1]	146	27.00 N	17.00 E
Libysche Wüste → Aṣ-Ṣaḥrā' al-Lībīyah ◆[2]	136	24.00 N	25.00 E
Licantén	252	34.59 S	72.00 W
Licata	70	37.06 N	13.56 E
Licciana Nardi	64	44.16 N	10.02 E
Lice	130	38.28 N	40.39 E
Lich	56	50.33 N	8.50 E
Lichačova, Mys ≻	89	42.44 N	132.51 E
Lichaja ≃	83	48.08 N	40.15 E
Lichang	107	28.53 N	104.26 E
Licheng, Zhg.	98	36.44 N	117.12 E
Licheng, Zhg.	100	33.00 N	119.02 E
Licheng, Zhg.	102	36.30 N	113.21 E
Lichères-près-Aigremont	50	47.43 N	3.51 E
Lichfield	42	52.42 N	1.48 W
Lich-hoi-thuong	110	9.26 N	106.08 E
Lichiang	100	22.44 N	120.30 E
Lichitiseni	38	46.23 N	27.17 E
Lichoborka ≃	265b	55.50 N	37.38 E
Lichoslavl'	76	57.07 N	35.28 E
Lichovka	78	48.41 N	33.55 E
Lichovskoj	83	48.07 N	40.12 E
Lichtaart	56	51.14 N	4.54 E
Lichte	54	50.31 N	11.10 E
Lichtenau	56	48.43 N	8.01 E
Lichtenberg, B.R.D.	54	50.23 N	11.40 E
Lichtenberg, D.D.R.	54	50.50 N	13.25 E
Lichtenberg, Fr.	56	48.55 N	7.29 E
Lichtenburg	158	26.08 S	26.08 E
Lichtendorf	263	51.28 N	7.37 E
Lichtenfels	56	50.09 N	11.04 E
Lichtenplatz ◆[8]	263	51.15 N	7.12 E
Lichtenrade ◆[8]	264a	52.23 N	13.25 E
Lichtensee	54	51.23 N	13.22 E
Lichtensteig	58	47.19 N	9.05 E
Lichtenstein	54	50.45 N	12.37 E
Lichtenstein, Schloss ʊ	58	48.24 N	9.15 E
Lichtentanne	54	50.42 N	12.25 E
Lichtenvoorde	52	51.59 N	6.34 E
Lichterfelde ◆[8]	264a	52.26 N	13.19 E
Lichtervelde	50	51.02 N	3.09 E
Lichuan, Zhg.	100	27.18 N	116.53 E
Lichuan, Zhg.	102	30.18 N	108.51 E
Lick Creek ≃, Ill., U.S.	219	39.42 N	89.41 W
Lick Creek ≃, Ind., U.S.	218	38.33 N	86.31 W
Lick Creek ≃, Mo., U.S.	219	39.31 N	91.39 W
Lick Creek ≃, Ohio, U.S.	216	41.21 N	84.25 W
Lick Creek ≃, Tenn., U.S.	192	36.11 N	83.10 W
Lickershamn	26	57.50 N	18.31 E
Licking	194	37.30 N	91.51 W
Licking □[6]	214	40.10 N	82.30 W
Licking ≃	188	39.06 N	84.30 W
Licking, North Fork ≃, Ky., U.S.	218	38.35 N	84.13 W
Licking, North Fork ≃, Ohio, U.S.	214	40.03 N	82.23 W
Licking, South Fork ≃	218	38.41 N	84.20 W
Lick Observatory ʊ[3]	226	37.22 N	121.37 W
Ličko Polje ═	36	44.35 N	15.25 E
Lick Run ≃, Pa., U.S.	210	41.12 N	77.32 W
Lick Run ≃, Pa., U.S.	279b	40.17 N	79.57 W
Licodia Eubea	70	37.09 N	14.42 E
Licosa, Punta ≻	68	40.15 N	14.54 E
Licun	98	38.32 N	117.08 E
Licungó ≃	154	17.40 S	37.15 E
Lid'	76	59.39 N	35.05 E
Lida	76	53.53 N	25.18 E
Lidan ≃	26	58.31 N	13.09 E
Lidao	98	37.15 N	122.32 E
Lidarentuncun	104	41.32 N	123.12 E
Lidcombe	274a	33.52 S	151.03 E
Liddel Water ≃	44	55.04 N	2.57 W
Liddesdale ∨	44	55.12 N	2.46 W
Liddon Gulf C	176	75.03 N	113.00 W
Liden	26	62.42 N	16.48 E
Lidgerwood	198	46.05 N	97.09 W
Lidgetton	158	29.25 S	30.05 E
Lidian	107	28.57 N	103.44 E
Lídice, Bra.	256	22.51 S	44.12 W
Lídice, Pan.	236	8.45 N	79.54 W
Lidice ⊥	54	50.03 N	14.08 E
Lidingö	40	59.22 N	18.08 E
Lidköping	26	58.30 N	13.10 E
Lido	64	45.25 N	12.22 E
Lido, Litorale di ✦[2]	64	45.23 N	12.21 E
Lido, Porto di C	64	45.26 N	12.25 E
Lido Beach	276	40.35 N	73.38 W
Lido di Camaiore	64	43.54 N	10.13 E
Lido di Castel Fusano ◆[8]	66	41.43 N	12.20 E
Lido di Iesolo	64	45.30 N	12.39 E
Lido di Metaponto	68	40.22 N	16.50 E
Lido di Ostia ◆[8]	66	41.44 N	12.14 E
Lido di Pomposa	66	44.45 N	12.14 E
Lido di Siponto	68	41.37 N	15.55 E
Lido Key I	220	27.19 N	82.35 W
Lidsjön ⊜	40	58.55 N	16.51 E
Lidu	107	30.35 N	106.04 E
Lidzbark	30	53.17 N	19.49 E
Lidzbark Warmiński	30	54.09 N	20.35 E
Liebenau	52	52.36 N	9.05 E
Liebenburg	52	52.01 N	10.26 E
Liebenthal → Lubomierz	30	51.01 N	15.30 E
Liebenwalde	54	52.52 N	13.23 E
Lieberhausen	56	51.03 N	7.40 E
Lieberose	54	51.59 N	14.17 E
Liebertwolkwitz	54	51.17 N	12.28 E
Liebstadt	54	50.52 N	13.51 E
Liechtenstein □[1]	22		
	58	47.09 N	9.35 E
Liedberg	263	51.10 N	6.32 E
Liedekerke	50	50.52 N	4.05 E
Liège (Luik)	56	50.38 N	5.34 E
Liège □[4]	56	50.30 N	5.30 E
Liège, Aéroport ⊠	56	50.39 N	5.30 E
Liegnitz → Legnica	30	51.13 N	16.09 E
Lieja → Liège	56	50.38 N	5.34 E
Lieksa	26	63.19 N	30.01 E
Lielais Liepu Kalns ∧[2]	76	56.25 N	27.50 E
Lielupe ≃	76	57.01 N	23.56 E
Lielvārde	76	56.43 N	24.51 E
Liemianxi	107	30.29 N	106.05 E
Lienart	154	3.04 N	25.31 E
Lienchou → Hepu	102	21.39 N	109.11 E
Lienen	52	52.09 N	7.58 E
Lien-huong	110	11.13 N	108.44 E
Lienz	64	46.50 N	12.47 E
Liepāja	76	56.31 N	21.01 E
Liepājas Ezers ⊜	76	56.27 N	21.03 E
Liepe	54	53.58 N	13.56 E
Liepna	76	57.25 N	27.25 E
Liepnitzsee ⊜	264a	52.45 N	13.30 E
Lièpvre	58	48.16 N	7.17 E
Lier (Lierre)	50	51.08 N	4.34 E
Lierenfeld ◆[8]	263	51.13 N	6.51 E
Lierna	58	45.57 N	9.18 E
Liernais	50	47.12 N	4.17 E
Lierneux	56	50.18 N	5.48 E
Liershizhai	104	41.49 N	123.43 E
Liesborn	52	51.43 N	8.15 E
Lieser ≃, B.R.D.	56	49.55 N	7.01 E
Lieser ≃, Öst.	64	46.47 N	13.39 E
Lieshout	52	51.32 N	5.35 E
Liesing ◆[8]	264b	48.08 N	16.17 E
Liesing ≃	264b	48.08 N	16.28 E
Liesingbach ≃	61	47.20 N	15.02 E
Liesjärven Kansallispuisto ♠	26	60.40 N	23.54 E
Lieskau	54	51.37 N	13.48 E
Liesse	50	49.37 N	3.48 E
Liessies	50	50.07 N	4.05 E
Liestal	58	47.29 N	7.44 E
Lieşti	38	45.38 N	27.32 E
Lietzow	54	54.29 N	13.30 E
Lieurey	50	49.14 N	0.29 E
Lieusaint	261	48.38 N	2.33 E
Lieutel, Ruisseau le ≃	261	48.49 N	1.52 E
Lieutenant Robert J. Palenscar Memorial Airport ⊠	285	39.51 N	75.03 W
Liévin	50	50.25 N	2.46 E
Lièvre, Rivière du ≃	176	45.31 N	75.26 W
Liezen	61	47.35 N	14.15 E
Lifanga	152	0.19 N	21.57 E
Liffey ≃	44	53.21 N	6.16 W
Liffol-le-Grand	58	48.19 N	5.35 E
Lifford	48	54.50 N	7.29 W
Liffré	32	48.13 N	1.30 W
Lifjell ∧	26	59.30 N	8.52 E
Lifoku	152	0.04 S	21.18 E
Lifou, Île I	175f	20.53 S	167.13 E
Lifoula	273b	4.06 S	15.25 E
Lifton	42	50.39 N	4.17 W
Liftwood	285	39.47 N	75.31 W
Lifudzin	89	44.21 N	134.58 E
Lifune ≃	152	8.21 S	13.22 E
Ligačovo	265b	55.56 N	37.15 E
Ligang	100	30.04 N	121.52 E
Ligao, Pil.	116	6.17 N	124.09 E
Ligao, Pil.	116	13.14 N	123.32 E
Ligasa	152	0.42 N	23.45 E
Līgatne	76	57.14 N	25.02 E
Ligezhuang, Zhg.	105	39.49 N	115.56 E
Ligezhuang, Zhg.	105	39.42 N	118.12 E
Light ≃	168b	34.35 S	138.22 E
Lightfoot	208	37.20 N	76.45 W
Lighthouse Point	220	26.17 N	80.07 W
Lighthouse Point ≻, Ont., Can.	214	41.50 N	82.38 W
Lighthouse Point ≻, Fla., U.S.	192	29.54 N	84.21 W
Lighthouse Point ≻, Mich., U.S.	190	45.13 N	85.32 W
Lighthouse Reef ✢[2]	232	17.20 N	87.32 W
Lightning Creek ≃, Sask., Can.	184	49.12 N	101.43 W
Lightning Creek ≃, N.A.	224	48.50 N	121.03 W
Lightning Creek ≃, Wyo., U.S.	198	43.11 N	104.44 W
Lightstreet	210	41.02 N	76.25 W
Lightsville	216	40.18 N	84.42 W
Lignano Pineta	64	45.40 N	13.07 E
Lignano Sabbiadoro	64	45.42 N	13.09 E
Lignières	32	46.45 N	2.11 E
Lignite	198	48.53 N	102.34 W
Lignon ≃	62	45.44 N	4.08 E
Lignumvitae Key I	220	24.55 N	80.42 W
Ligny-en-Barrois	58	48.41 N	5.20 E
Ligny-en-Cambrésis	50	50.06 N	3.22 E
Ligny-le-Châtel	50	47.54 N	3.45 E
Ligny-le-Ribault	50	47.41 N	1.47 E
Ligonha ≃	154	16.54 S	39.09 E
Ligonier, Ind., U.S.	216	41.28 N	85.35 W
Ligonier, Pa., U.S.	214	40.15 N	79.14 W
Ligovka	78	49.08 N	36.03 E
Ligovo	76	60.13 N	31.48 E
Ligovo ◆[8]	265a	59.50 N	30.12 E
Ligovskij Kanal ≊	265a	59.47 N	30.10 E
Liguancun	98	40.01 N	121.59 E
Ligueil	32	47.03 N	0.49 E
Ligui	232	25.43 N	111.16 W
Ligure, Mar → Ligurian Sea ▾[2]	36	43.30 N	9.00 E
Liguria □[4]	62	44.30 N	8.50 E
Liguria, Mar de → Ligurian Sea ▾[2]	36	43.30 N	9.00 E
Ligurian Sea ▾[2]	36	43.30 N	9.00 E
Ligurisches Meer → Ligurian Sea ▾[2]	36	43.30 N	9.00 E
Lihir Group II	164	3.05 S	152.40 E
Lihir Island I	164	3.05 S	152.35 E
Lihou Reef and Cays ✢[2]	166	17.25 S	151.40 E
Lihu	100	23.23 N	116.03 E
Lihue	229b	21.59 N	159.22 W
Lihue Airport ⊠	229b	21.59 N	159.21 W
Lihula	76	58.41 N	23.50 E
Lijia, Zhg.	104	41.43 N	122.20 E
Lijia, Zhg.	106	31.38 N	120.00 E
Lijiaba	107	29.37 N	105.33 E
Lijiadian	104	42.07 N	121.14 E
Lijiaji	100	31.59 N	115.51 E
Lijiajie	107	29.49 N	105.30 E
Lijiakou	105	39.12 N	116.29 E
Lijiang	102	26.57 N	100.15 E
Lijiang ≃	100	24.16 N	115.12 E
Lijiapuzi	104	40.59 N	123.38 E
Lijiaqiao, Zhg.	105	40.03 N	116.40 E
Lijiaqiao, Zhg.	105	39.47 N	117.47 E
Lijiaqiao, Zhg.	106	32.12 N	120.41 E
Lijiatun, Zhg.	98	39.24 N	122.20 E
Lijiatun, Zhg.	104	41.19 N	121.23 E
Lijiatuo	107	29.28 N	106.33 E
Lijiawobao	104	41.00 N	122.26 E
Lijiaxiang	106	30.57 N	119.59 E
Lijiazao	105	39.17 N	118.19 E
Lijin, Zhg.	98	37.29 N	118.16 E
Lijin, Zhg.	104	41.40 N	121.20 E
Lik ≃	110	18.31 N	102.31 E
Likako	152	0.15 N	21.00 E
Likasi (Jadotville)	154	10.59 S	26.44 E
Likati	152	3.21 N	23.53 E
Likati ≃	152	2.53 N	24.03 E
Likely	182	52.37 N	121.34 W
Likėnai	76	56.12 N	24.37 E
Likete	152	0.43 S	21.25 E
Likhu ≃	124	27.15 N	86.12 E
Liki	112	1.36 S	101.11 E
Likimi	152	2.50 N	20.45 E
Likino	82	55.38 N	37.08 E
Likino-Dulevo	82	55.43 N	38.58 E
Liknes	26	58.19 N	6.59 E
Likokou	152	0.12 S	12.48 E
Likoma Island I	154	12.05 S	34.45 E
Likou, Zhg.	98	34.16 N	115.37 E
Likou, Zhg.	100	33.51 N	113.20 E
Likou, Zhg.	100	29.53 N	117.28 E
Likou, Zhg.	106	31.24 N	120.37 E
Likouala □[5]	152	2.00 N	17.30 E
Likouala ≃	152	1.13 S	16.48 E
Likouala-aux-Herbes ≃	152	0.50 S	17.11 E
Likova ≃	265b	55.34 N	37.21 E
Likstammen ⊜	40	58.58 N	17.12 E
Liku	174v	19.02 S	169.47 W
Likupang	112	1.41 N	125.04 E
Likuyu	154	10.20 S	36.14 E
Lilanchengzhen	105	39.12 N	116.43 E
Lilanga	152	0.34 S	23.55 E
Lilasi	124	29.22 N	84.30 E
Lilbert	222	31.44 N	94.54 W
L'Île-Bouchard	32	47.07 N	0.25 E
Lilenga	152	0.54 N	22.06 E
L'Île-Rousse	32	42.38 N	8.56 E
Lili	106	31.00 N	120.42 E
Lilian Point ≻	174d	0.53 S	169.35 E
Lilienfeld	61	48.03 N	15.36 E
Lilienthal	52	53.08 N	8.55 E
Liling	100	27.40 N	113.30 E
Lilio	116	14.08 N	121.26 E
Liljendal	40	60.08 N	14.04 E
Lilla Edet	26	58.08 N	12.08 E
Lillafüred ♠	38	48.07 N	20.38 E
Lillah Bharwanah	123	32.34 N	72.45 E
Lillån	40	59.19 N	15.13 E
Lillby	26	63.28 N	23.00 E
Lille	50	50.38 N	3.04 E
Lille Bælt ⊔	41	55.20 N	9.45 E
Lillebonne	50	49.31 N	0.33 E
Lillehammer	26	61.08 N	10.30 E
Lillerød	41	55.52 N	12.22 E
Lillers	50	50.34 N	2.29 E
Lillesand	26	58.15 N	8.24 E
Lilleshall	42	52.44 N	2.21 W
Lillestrøm	26	59.57 N	11.05 E
Lille Værløse	41	55.47 N	12.23 E
Lillhärdal	26	61.51 N	14.04 E
Lillian	222	32.30 N	97.11 W
Lillington	192	35.24 N	78.49 W
Lillinonah Lake ⊜[1]	207	41.28 N	73.21 W
Lilli Pilli	274a	34.04 S	151.07 E
Lillo	34	39.43 N	3.18 W
Lillooet	182	50.42 N	121.56 W
Lillooet ≃	182	49.45 N	122.08 W
Lillooet Lake ⊜	182	50.13 N	122.29 W
Lilly	214	40.25 N	78.33 W
Lilly Creek ≃	222	32.47 N	94.56 W
Liloan	116	10.09 N	125.07 E
Lilongwe	154	13.59 S	33.44 E
Lilo Viejo	252	26.56 S	62.58 W
Liloy	116	8.08 N	122.40 E
Liluāh	272b	22.35 N	88.23 E
Lily	192	37.02 N	84.17 W
Lily Cache Creek ≃	278	41.41 N	88.07 W
Lilydale, Austl.	166	41.15 S	147.13 E
Lilydale, Austl.	169	37.45 S	145.21 E
Lily Dale, N.Y., U.S.	214	42.21 N	79.19 W
Lilyfield	274a	33.52 S	151.10 E
Lim ≃, Afr.	152	7.54 N	15.46 E
Lim ≃, Jugo.	38	43.45 N	19.13 E
Lima, Arg.	258	34.03 S	59.12 W
Lima, Para.	252	23.54 S	56.20 W
Lima, Perú	248		
	286d	12.03 S	77.03 W
Lima, Sve.	26	60.56 N	13.26 E
Lima, Ill., U.S.	219	40.11 N	91.23 W
Lima, Mont., U.S.	202	44.38 N	112.36 W
Lima, N.Y., U.S.	210	42.54 N	77.37 W
Lima, Ohio, U.S.	216	40.46 N	84.06 W
Lima, Pa., U.S.	285	39.55 N	75.26 W
Lima □[5]	248	12.00 S	76.35 W
Lima (Limia) ≃, Eur.	34	41.41 N	8.50 W
Lima ≃, It.	64	44.00 N	10.35 E
Lima, Punta ≻	240m	18.11 N	65.41 W
Lima-Callao, Aeropuerto Internacional ⊠	286d	12.02 S	77.07 W
Lima Center	216	42.47 N	88.49 W
Limache	252	33.01 S	71.16 W
Lima Duarte	256	21.51 S	43.48 W
Lima Duarte, Serra de ⋀[2]	256	21.54 S	43.52 W
Liman, S.S.S.R.	78	49.36 N	36.27 E
Liman, S.S.S.R.	78	45.41 N	29.45 E
Liman, S.S.S.R.	80	45.47 N	47.14 E
Liman, S.S.S.R.	83	49.21 N	38.57 E
Liman, Yis.	132	33.03 N	35.06 E
Liman ≃	115a	6.29 S	105.48 E
Limanowa	30	49.43 N	20.26 E
Limanskoje	78	46.38 N	30.00 E
Lima Nueva	236	15.23 N	87.56 W
Limão ◆[8]	287b	23.30 S	46.40 W
Limapuluh	114	3.10 N	99.26 E
Lima Reservoir ⊜[1]	202	44.38 N	112.17 W
Limarí ≃	252	30.44 S	71.43 W
Limas	112	0.14 N	104.31 E
Limasawa Island I	116	9.56 N	125.05 E
Limassa	152	4.14 N	22.02 E
Limassol → Lemesós	130	34.40 N	33.02 E
Limavady	48	55.03 N	6.57 W
Limaville	214	40.59 N	81.09 W
Limay, Fr.	50	49.00 N	1.44 E
Limay, Pil.	116	14.34 N	120.36 E
Limay ≃	254	38.59 S	68.00 W
Limay Mahuida	252	37.12 S	66.42 W
Limbach-Oberfrohna	54	50.51 N	12.45 E
Limbadi	68	38.33 N	15.58 E
Limbang	108	4.45 N	115.00 E
Limbani	248	14.08 S	69.42 W
Limbara, Monte ∧	71	40.51 N	9.10 E
Limbaži	76	57.31 N	24.42 E
Limbdi	120	22.34 N	71.48 E
Limbe	154	15.49 S	35.03 E
Limbiate	62	45.36 N	9.07 E
Limboto	112	0.37 N	122.57 E
Limbourg	56	50.37 N	5.56 E
Limbrick	262	53.38 N	2.36 W
Limbueta	152	12.30 S	18.42 E
Limbunya	164	17.14 S	129.50 E
Limburg □[4], Bel.	56	51.00 N	5.30 E
Limburg □[4], Ned.	52	51.14 N	5.50 E
Limburg an der Lahn	56	50.23 N	8.04 E
Limburgerhof	56	49.25 N	8.24 E
Limecrest	218	39.54 N	83.48 W
Limefield	262	53.37 N	2.18 W
Limeira	255	22.34 S	47.24 W
Limekiln Canyon ∨	280	34.18 N	118.33 W
Lime Lake	210	42.26 N	78.29 W
Limen	100	27.07 N	119.19 E
Limena	64	45.29 N	11.50 E
Limentra ≃	64	44.14 N	11.03 E
Limerick, Sask., Can.	184	49.40 N	106.15 W
Limerick, Eire	48	52.40 N	8.38 W
Limerick, Pa., U.S.	285	40.14 N	75.32 W
Limerick □[6]	48	52.30 N	9.00 W
Limerick Lake ⊜	212	44.54 N	77.37 W
Limerock	207	41.55 N	71.28 W
Lime Springs	190	43.27 N	92.17 W
Limestone, Austl.	162	21.11 S	119.50 E
Limestone, Fla., U.S.	220	27.22 N	81.54 W
Limestone, Maine, U.S.	186	46.55 N	67.50 W
Limestone, N.Y., U.S.	210	42.02 N	78.38 W
Limestone, Pa., U.S.	214	41.08 N	79.20 W
Limestone □[6]	222	31.35 N	96.35 W
Limestone Bay C	184	53.50 N	98.50 W
Limestone Canyon ∨	280	33.45 N	117.41 W
Limestone Creek ≃	210	43.06 N	75.58 W
Limestone Lake ⊜, Man., Can.	184	56.35 N	96.00 W
Limestone Lake ⊜, Sask., Can.	184	54.36 N	103.18 W
Limestone Point ≻[1]	184	53.50 N	98.50 W
Limestone Point Lake ⊜	184	55.07 N	100.32 W
Lime Street Station ◆[5]	262	53.25 N	2.59 W
Lime Village	180	61.21 N	155.28 W
Limfjorden ⊔	26	56.55 N	9.10 E
Limhamn ◆[8]	41	55.35 N	12.54 E
Limia (Lima) ≃	34	41.41 N	8.50 W
Limina	70	37.56 N	15.17 E
Liminka	26	64.49 N	25.24 E
Liminzhen	98	34.31 N	115.56 E
Limit Brook ≃	283	42.42 N	71.25 W
Limmared	26	57.32 N	13.21 E
Limmaren ⊜	40	59.44 N	18.43 E
Limmen	52	52.34 N	4.41 E
Limmen Bight C[3]	164	14.45 S	135.40 E
Límnos I	38	39.54 N	25.21 E
Limoeiro	250	7.52 S	35.27 W
Limoeiro do Norte	250	5.08 S	38.05 W
Limoges, Ont., Can.	212	45.20 N	75.15 W
Limoges, Fr.	32	45.50 N	1.16 E
Limoges-Fourches	261	48.38 N	2.40 E
Limogne	32	44.24 N	1.46 E
Limón, C.R.	236	10.00 N	83.02 W
Limón, Hond.	236	15.52 N	85.33 W
Limon, Colo., U.S.	198	39.16 N	103.41 W
Limón □[4]	236	10.00 N	83.15 W
Limonar	240p	22.57 N	81.24 W
Limón de Ramos	232	24.43 N	107.08 W
Limone Piemonte	62	44.12 N	7.34 E
Limonest	62	45.50 N	4.46 E
Limone sul Garda	64	45.49 N	10.47 E
Limours	50	48.39 N	2.05 E
Limousins, Plateau du ⋀[1]	32	45.30 N	1.15 E
Limoux	32	43.04 N	2.14 E
Limpopo ≃	156	25.15 S	33.30 E
Limpsfield	42	51.16 N	0.01 E
Limski kanal C	64	45.07 N	13.38 E
Limu	102	25.02 N	110.51 E
Limuling ⋀	110	19.10 N	109.30 E
Limuru	154	1.06 S	36.39 E
Linachamari	24	69.40 N	31.20 E
Līnah	128	28.42 N	43.48 E
Lin'an	106	30.14 N	119.43 E
Linanäs	40	59.28 N	18.31 E
Linao Bay C	116	6.45 N	124.00 E
Linapacan Island I	116	11.27 N	119.49 E
Linapacan Strait ⊔	116	11.37 N	119.56 E
Linares, Chile	252	35.51 S	71.36 W
Linares, Col.	246	1.23 N	77.31 W
Linares, Esp.	34	38.05 N	3.38 W
Linares, Méx.	232	24.52 N	99.34 W
Linariá	38	37.24 N	24.57 E
Linaro, Capo ≻	66	42.02 N	11.50 E
Linas	261	48.38 N	2.16 E
Linas, Monte ∧	71	39.27 N	8.37 E
Linas-montlhery, Domaine Militaire de ▪	261	48.37 N	2.13 E
Linatchyrvavaam ≃	180	67.18 N	175.20 W
Linate, Aeroporto di ⊠	62	45.27 N	9.16 E
Lincai	100	33.50 N	114.56 E
Lincang	102	23.45 N	102.20 E

Symbols in the index entries represent the broad categories identified in the key at the right. Symbols with superior numbers (⋀[2]) identify subcategories (see complete key on page *I · 30*).

Kartensymbole in dem Registerverzeichnis stellen die rechts in Schlüssel erklärten Kategorien dar. Symbole mit hochgestellten Ziffern (⋀[2]) bezeichnen Unterabteilungen einer Kategorie (vgl. vollständiger Schlüssel auf Seite *I · 30*).

Los símbolos incluídos en el texto del índice representan las grandes categorias identificadas con la clave a la derecha. Los símbolos con numeros en su parte superior (⋀[2]) identifican las subcategorias (véase la clave completa en la página *I · 30*).

Les symboles de l'index représentent les catégories indiquées dans la légende à droite. Les symboles suivis d'un indice (⋀[2]) représentent des sous-catégories (voir légende complète à la page *I · 30*).

Os símbolos incluídos no texto do índice representam as grandes categorias identificadas com a chave à direita. Os símbolos com números em sua parte superior (⋀[2]) identificam as subcategorias (veja-se a chave completa à página *I · 30*).

	English	Deutsch	Español	Français	Português
∧	Mountain	Berg	Montaña	Montagne	Montanha
⋀	Mountains	Berge	Montañas	Montagnes	Montanhas
⅄	Pass	Pass	Paso	Col	Passo
∨	Valley, Canyon	Tal, Cañon	Valle, Cañón	Vallée, Canyon	Vale, Canhão
═	Plain	Ebene	Llano	Plaine	Planície
≻	Cape	Kap	Cabo	Cap	Cabo
I	Island	Insel	Isla	Île	Ilha
II	Islands	Inseln	Islas	Îles	Ilhas
✦	Other Topographic Features	Andere Topographische Objekte	Otros Elementos Topográficos	Autres données topographiques	Outros Elementos Topográficos

ESPAÑOL Nombre / FRANÇAIS Nom / PORTUGUÊS Nome	Página / Page / Página	Lat.°′	Long.°′ W=Oeste / W=Ouest / W=Oeste
Lince	286d	12.06 S	77.03 W
Linch	200	43.37 N	106.12 W
Lincheng	98	37.27 N	114.29 E
Linchengqiao	106	30.55 N	119.47 E
Linch'ing → Linqing	98	36.53 N	115.41 E
Lincluden	44	55.05 N	3.38 W
Lincoln, Arg.	252	34.52 S	61.32 W
Lincoln, Ont., Can.	212	43.10 N	79.29 W
Lincoln, N.Z.	172	43.39 S	172.29 E
Lincoln, Eng., U.K.	44	53.14 N	0.33 W
Lincoln, Ark., U.S.	194	35.57 N	94.25 W
Lincoln, Calif., U.S.	226	38.54 N	121.17 W
Lincoln, Del., U.S.	208	38.52 N	75.25 W
Lincoln, Ill., U.S.	219	40.09 N	89.22 W
Lincoln, Ind., U.S.	216	40.37 N	86.12 W
Lincoln, Kans., U.S.	198	39.02 N	98.09 W
Lincoln, Maine, U.S.	188	45.22 N	68.30 W
Lincoln, Mass., U.S.	207	42.26 N	71.18 W
Lincoln, Mich., U.S.	190	44.41 N	83.25 W
Lincoln, Mo., U.S.	194	38.23 N	93.20 W
Lincoln, Mont., U.S.	202	46.58 N	112.41 W
Lincoln, Nebr., U.S.	198	40.48 N	96.42 W
Lincoln, N.H., U.S.	188	44.03 N	71.40 W
Lincoln, Pa., U.S.	208	40.12 N	76.12 W
Lincoln, Pa., U.S.	279b	40.18 N	79.51 W
Lincoln, R.I., U.S.	207	41.54 N	71.25 W
Lincoln, Tex., U.S.	222	30.17 N	96.52 W
Lincoln □6, Mo., U.S.	219	33.19 N	90.57 W
Lincoln □6, Oreg., U.S.	224	44.59 N	123.52 W
Lincoln, Mount ∧	200	39.21 N	106.07 W
Lincoln Acres	228	32.40 N	117.04 W
Lincoln Boyhood National Memorial ⊥	194	38.10 N	86.58 W
Lincoln Cathedral ✝1	44	53.14 N	0.33 W
Lincoln Center ✝	276	40.46 N	73.59 W
Lincoln City	224	44.59 N	123.59 W
Lincoln Creek ≃, Nebr., U.S.	198	40.54 N	97.06 W
Lincoln Creek ≃, Wash., U.S.	224	46.45 N	123.02 W
Lincolndale	210	41.19 N	73.43 W
Lincoln Estates	278	41.31 N	87.49 W
Lincoln Gap	166	32.37 S	137.35 E
Lincoln Heath ⩘2	44	53.15 N	0.32 W
Lincoln Heights, Ohio, U.S.	214	40.47 N	82.30 W
Lincoln Heights, Ohio, U.S.	218	39.15 N	84.28 W
Lincoln Heights, Pa., U.S.	279b	40.19 N	79.37 W
Lincoln Home National Historical Site ⊥	219	39.47 N	89.38 W
Lincolnia Heights	284c	38.50 N	77.09 W
Lincoln Marsh ≡	44	53.17 N	0.12 E
Lincoln National Park ♠	166	34.50 S	135.35 E
Lincoln Park, Ga., U.S.	192	32.52 N	84.19 W
Lincoln Park, Mich., U.S.	216	42.14 N	83.09 W
Lincoln Park, N.Y., U.S.	210	41.57 N	74.00 W
Lincoln Park ♠, Calif., U.S.	282	37.46 N	122.30 W
Lincoln Park ♠, Ill., U.S.	278	41.56 N	87.38 W
Lincoln Park Airport ⊠	276	40.57 N	74.19 W
Lincoln Place ♦8	279b	40.22 N	79.55 W
Lincoln Sea ⫪2	16	83.00 N	56.00 W
Lincolnshire	216	42.11 N	87.54 W
Lincolnshire □6	42	52.55 N	0.22 W
Lincolnshire Wolds ⩘2	44	53.20 N	0.10 W
Lincoln's New Salem State Park ♠	219	39.58 N	89.52 W
Lincoln Tomb State Memorial ⊥	219	39.50 N	89.39 W
Lincolnton, Ga., U.S.	192	33.48 N	82.28 W
Lincolnton, N.C., U.S.	192	35.29 N	81.14 W
Lincoln Tunnel ♦5	276	40.46 N	74.01 W
Lincoln University	208	39.48 N	75.55 W
Lincoln Village, Calif., U.S.	226	38.01 N	121.19 W
Lincoln Village, Ohio, U.S.	218	39.58 N	83.08 W
Lincolnville	214	41.47 N	79.51 W
Lincolnwood	278	42.00 N	87.46 W
Lincolnwood Hills	278	41.31 N	87.54 W
Linconia	285	40.08 N	74.59 W
Lincroft	208	40.20 N	74.07 W
Linda, S.S.S.R.	80	56.37 N	44.07 E
Linda, Calif., U.S.	226	39.08 N	121.34 W
Linda-a-Velha	266c	38.43 N	9.14 W
Lindale, Ga., U.S.	192	34.11 N	85.11 W
Lindale, Tex., U.S.	222	32.31 N	95.25 W
Lindau, B.R.D.	41	54.36 N	9.47 E
Lindau, B.R.D.	52	51.39 N	10.07 E
Lindau, B.R.D.	58	47.33 N	9.41 E
Lindau, D.D.R.	54	52.02 N	12.06 E
Lindbergh	219	39.02 N	92.08 W
Lindbergh Field ⊠	228	32.44 N	117.11 W
Lind Coulee ≃	202	47.00 N	119.10 W
Linde ≃	74	64.57 N	124.36 E
Lindelse	41	54.52 N	10.44 E
Linden, Ala., U.S.	194	32.18 N	87.47 W
Linden, Calif., U.S.	226	38.01 N	121.05 W
Linden, Mich., U.S.	216	42.49 N	83.47 W
Linden, N.J., U.S.	210	40.38 N	74.15 W
Linden, Pa., U.S.	210	41.14 N	77.08 W
Linden, Pa., U.S.	279b	40.14 N	80.08 W
Linden, Tenn., U.S.	194	35.37 N	87.50 W
Linden, Tex., U.S.	194	33.01 N	94.22 W
Linden ♦8	273d	26.08 S	28.00 E
Linden Airport ⊠	276	40.37 N	74.15 W
Lindenberg, D.D.R.	54	53.02 N	12.07 E
Lindenberg, D.D.R.	54	52.12 N	14.07 E
Lindenberg, D.D.R.	54	52.36 N	13.31 E
Lindenberg im Allgäu	58	47.36 N	9.53 E
Linden-dahlhausen ♦8	263	51.26 N	7.09 E
Lindenfels	56	49.41 N	8.47 E
Lindenhorst ♦8	263	51.33 N	7.27 E
Lindenhurst, Ill., U.S.	216	42.25 N	88.02 W
Lindenhurst, N.Y., U.S.	210	40.41 N	73.22 W
Lindenhurst, Pa., U.S.	285	40.14 N	74.54 W
Lindenows Fjord C2	176	60.45 N	43.30 W
Linden Park	216	40.13 N	85.23 W
Lindenthal	54	51.24 N	12.20 E
Lindenwold	208	39.49 N	74.59 W
Lindenwood, Ill., U.S.	216	42.03 N	89.02 W
Lindenwood, Ind., U.S.	218	39.41 N	86.09 W
Linderhausen	263	51.18 N	7.17 E
Linderhof, Schloss ⊥	64	47.34 N	10.57 E
Lindern	52	52.50 N	7.46 E
Linderöd	41	55.56 N	13.49 E
Linderödsåsen ⩘2	26	55.53 N	13.56 E
Lindesay, Mount ∧	162	34.49 S	117.18 E
Lindesberg	40	59.35 N	15.15 E
Lindesnäs	40	60.20 N	14.32 E
Lindesnes ≻	26	58.00 N	7.02 E
Lindfield, Austl.	274a	33.47 S	151.10 E
Lindfield, Eng., U.K.	42	51.01 N	0.05 W
Lindfors	40	59.36 N	13.49 E
Lindholmen	40	59.35 N	18.06 E
Lindhorst	52	52.21 N	9.17 E
Lindhos	38	36.06 N	28.04 E
Lindhos ⊥	38	36.06 N	28.05 E
Lindi	154	10.00 S	39.43 E
Lindi ≃	154	0.33 N	25.05 E
Lindian	89	47.11 N	124.52 E
Lindis Pass)(	172	44.36 S	169.38 E
Lindkirchen	60	48.40 N	11.47 E
Lindlar	56	51.01 N	7.23 E
Lindley, S. Afr.	158	28.00 S	27.57 E
Lindley, N.Y., U.S.	210	42.02 N	77.08 W
Lind National Park ♠	166	37.35 S	149.05 E
Lindö	40	58.37 N	16.15 E
Lindóia	256	22.31 S	46.39 W
Lindome	26	57.34 N	12.05 E
Lindon	198	39.44 N	103.24 W
Lindong, Zhg.	100	26.03 N	118.49 E
Lindong, Zhg.	105	39.51 N	117.41 E
Lindow	54	52.58 N	13.00 E
Lind Point ≻	240m	18.20 N	64.48 W
Lindsay, Ont., Can.	212	44.21 N	78.44 W
Lindsay, Calif., U.S.	204	36.12 N	119.05 W
Lindsay, Nebr., U.S.	198	41.42 N	97.42 W
Lindsay, Okla., U.S.	196	34.50 N	97.38 W
Lindsborg	198	38.35 N	97.40 W
Lindsey	214	41.25 N	83.13 W
Lindstrom	190	45.23 N	92.52 W
Lindved	41	55.47 N	9.35 E
Lindy Lake	276	41.05 N	74.22 W
Lineboro	208	39.43 N	76.51 W
Line Creek ≃	194	33.34 N	88.42 W
Line Islands II	14	0.05 N	157.00 W
Line Lexington	208	40.17 N	75.16 W
Line Mountain ∧	210	40.45 N	76.37 W
Linesville	214	41.39 N	80.26 W
Lineville, Ala., U.S.	194	33.19 N	85.45 W
Lineville, Iowa, U.S.	190	40.35 N	93.32 W
Linfa	287b	23.44 S	46.56 W
Linfen	102	36.05 N	111.32 E
Linfield	208	40.13 N	75.34 W
Linford	260	51.29 N	0.25 E
Ling ≃	46	57.19 N	5.27 W
Ling'an	106	30.36 N	120.30 E
Linganamakki Reservoir ⊛1	122	14.04 N	74.54 E
Lingao	102	20.00 N	109.40 E
Lingayen	116	16.01 N	120.14 E
Lingayen Gulf C	116	16.15 N	120.14 E
Lingbi	100	33.33 N	117.33 E
Lingbo	26	61.03 N	16.41 E
Lingchuan, Zhg.	102	25.26 N	110.15 E
Lingchuan, Zhg.	102	33.45 N	113.15 E
Lingda	106	31.12 N	119.18 E
Lingdian	106	31.51 N	121.25 E
Lingdou	100	26.22 N	118.56 E
Lingekeke	120	29.59 N	87.33 E
Lingen	52	52.31 N	7.19 E
Lingesestausee ⊛1	263	51.06 N	7.32 E
Lingfengwei	100	24.44 N	115.35 E
Lingfield	42	51.11 N	0.01 W
Lingga, Kepulauan II	112	0.05 S	104.35 E
Lingga, Pulau I	112	0.12 S	104.35 E
Lingham Lake ⊛	212	44.46 N	77.25 W
Linghe	98	36.23 N	119.03 E
Linghu	106	30.44 N	120.10 E
Lingig	116	8.02 N	126.24 E
Lingjiachang	107	29.27 N	104.53 E
Lingjiao	106	30.09 N	120.04 E
Lingkar Dzong	124	28.45 N	90.36 E
Lingkou, Zhg.	100	29.16 N	120.38 E
Lingkou, Zhg.	106	31.57 N	119.38 E
Lingle	200	42.08 N	104.21 W
Linglestown	208	40.21 N	76.48 W
Lingling	102	26.11 N	111.29 E
Linglongta	98	40.54 N	119.59 E
Lingma	102	23.22 N	107.53 E
Lingolsheim	58	48.34 N	7.41 E
Lingomo	152	0.38 N	21.59 E
Lingqiu, Zhg.	98	39.24 N	114.13 E
Lingqiu, Zhg.	98	39.28 N	113.40 E
Lingshan, Zhg.	98	36.33 N	120.27 E
Lingshan, Zhg.	102	22.28 N	109.17 E
Lingshanwei	98	35.58 N	120.13 E
Lingshi	98	36.54 N	111.43 E
Lingshou	98	38.18 N	114.24 E
Lingshui	110	18.31 N	110.01 E
Lingtangqiao	100	32.43 N	119.14 E
Lingu	120	29.26 N	87.36 E
Linguaglossa	70	37.50 N	15.08 E
Linguère	150	15.24 N	15.07 W
Lingwu	102	38.06 N	106.21 E
Lingxian, Zhg.	98	37.21 N	116.34 E
Lingxian, Zhg.	102	26.30 N	113.46 E
Lingxiazhu	100	29.03 N	119.46 E
Lingyuan	98	41.15 N	119.16 E
Lingzhuangzi	105	39.04 N	117.09 E
Lingzinan	105	39.29 N	115.15 E
Linh, Ngoc ∧	110	15.04 N	107.59 E
Linhai	100	28.51 N	121.07 E
Linhares	255	19.25 S	40.04 W
Linh-cam	110	18.31 N	105.34 E
Linhe	102	40.51 N	107.30 E
Linhezhuang	105	40.04 N	117.39 E
Linhó	266c	38.46 N	9.23 W
Linhsia → Linxia	102	35.34 N	103.08 E
Linhuaiguan	100	32.55 N	117.40 E
Linhuanji	100	33.42 N	116.33 E
Lini → Linyi	98	35.04 N	118.22 E
Linjiang, Zhg.	98	41.49 N	126.54 E
Linjiang, Zhg.	100	28.04 N	115.21 E
Linjiang, Zhg.	100	27.50 N	118.26 E
Linjiang, Zhg.	102	33.01 N	105.01 E
Linjiangchang	107	29.14 N	105.58 E
Linjianghu	100	28.40 N	118.01 E
Linjiangsi, Zhg.	102	29.42 N	104.01 E
Linjiangsi, Zhg.	107	30.15 N	104.37 E
Linjiatai	104	40.43 N	123.58 E
Linkenheim	56	49.07 N	8.24 E
Linköping	26	58.25 N	15.37 E
Linkou	89	45.15 N	130.16 E
Linksfield ♦8	273d	26.10 S	28.06 E
Linksmakalnis	76	54.45 N	23.55 E
Linkuva	76	56.05 N	23.59 E
Linkwood	208	38.32 N	75.57 W
Linli	102	29.18 N	111.30 E
Linlithgow	46	55.59 N	3.37 W
Linmeyer	273d	26.16 S	28.04 E
Linmingguan	98	36.47 N	114.30 E
Linn, Kans., U.S.	198	39.41 N	97.05 W
Linn, Mo., U.S.	219	38.29 N	91.51 W
Linn ♦8	263	51.20 N	6.38 E
Linnancang	105	39.50 N	117.37 E
Linnansaaren Kansallispuisto ♠	26	62.07 N	28.31 E
Linndale	279a	41.27 N	81.46 W
Linne	52	51.10 N	5.57 E
Linnell	226	36.21 N	119.11 W
Linnés Hammarby ⊥	40	59.49 N	17.46 E
Linney Head ≻	42	51.38 N	5.04 W
Linn Grove	216	40.39 N	85.02 W
Linnhe, Loch C	46	56.39 N	5.21 W
Linnich	56	50.59 N	6.16 E
Linntown	210	40.58 N	76.54 W
Linnville Bayou ≃	222	28.57 N	95.42 W
Linosa	71a	35.51 N	12.52 E
Linosa, Isola di I	71a	35.51 N	12.52 E
Linovica	78	50.28 N	32.22 E
Lin'ovo	80	50.53 N	44.51 E
Linow	54	53.06 N	12.49 E
Linpu	100	30.03 N	120.15 E
Linqi, Zhg.	98	35.48 N	113.53 E
Linqi, Zhg.	100	29.51 N	119.56 E
Linqing	98	36.53 N	115.41 E
Linqu	98	36.32 N	118.31 E
Linquan	100	33.06 N	115.13 E
Linru	100	34.11 N	112.49 E
Linruzhen	100	34.17 N	112.35 E
Lins	255	21.40 S	49.45 W
Linshanhe	100	30.44 N	114.52 E
Linshanwei	100	30.09 N	120.59 E
Linshui	102	30.21 N	106.59 E
Linshui ≃	102	40.20 N	99.30 E
Linslade	42	51.55 N	0.41 W
Linstead	241q	18.08 N	77.02 W
Lintan	102	34.37 N	103.40 E
Lintao	102	35.27 N	103.46 E
Linté	152	5.24 N	11.42 E
Linth ≃	58	47.07 N	9.07 E
Linthal, Fr.	58	47.56 N	7.08 E
Linthal, Schw.	58	46.55 N	9.00 E
Linthicum Heights	284b	39.12 N	76.39 W
Linthkanal ≡	58	47.13 N	8.57 E
Linthwaite	262	53.37 N	1.51 W
Lintingkou	105	39.39 N	117.30 E
Linton, Austl.	169	37.41 S	143.34 E
Linton, N.Z.	172	40.26 S	175.33 E
Linton, Eng., U.K.	42	52.06 N	0.17 E
Linton, Eng., U.K.	260	51.13 N	0.31 E
Linton, Ind., U.S.	194	39.02 N	87.10 W
Linton, N. Dak., U.S.	198	46.16 N	100.14 W
Lintong	102	34.21 N	109.11 E
Linton Park ♠	260	51.13 N	0.31 E
Lintorf	56	51.20 N	6.49 E
Linum	264a	52.46 N	12.53 E
Linville, Austl.	171a	26.51 S	152.16 E
Linville, N.C., U.S.	192	36.04 N	81.52 W
Linwood, Austl.	168b	34.21 S	138.46 E
Linwood, Ind., U.S.	218	40.12 N	85.41 W
Linwood, Mass., U.S.	207	42.06 N	71.39 W
Linwood, N.J., U.S.	208	39.21 N	74.34 W
Linwood, Pa., U.S.	285	39.49 N	75.24 W
Linwood, Wash., U.S.	202	47.42 N	117.23 W
Linworth	214	40.06 N	83.04 W
Linwu, Zhg.	98	36.14 N	119.17 E
Linwu, Zhg.	102	25.16 N	112.20 E
Linxi	90	43.30 N	118.00 E
Linxia	102	35.34 N	103.08 E
Linxian, Zhg.	98	36.04 N	113.50 E
Linxian, Zhg.	102	37.58 N	110.59 E
Linxiang	100	29.28 N	113.30 E
Linyanti	156	18.04 S	24.01 E
Linyanti (Chobe) ≃	156	17.50 S	25.05 E
Linyi, Zhg.	98	35.04 N	118.22 E
Linyi, Zhg.	98	37.13 N	116.51 E
Linyi, Zhg.	102	35.15 N	110.59 E
Linying	100	33.50 N	113.57 E
Linyü → Shanhaiguan	98	40.01 N	119.44 E
Linyüan	100	22.30 N	120.25 E
Linz, B.R.D.	56	50.34 N	7.17 E
Linz, Öst.	61	48.18 N	14.18 E
Linze	102	39.19 N	100.17 E
Linzgau ♦1	58	47.45 N	9.16 E
Linzhai	100	24.18 N	115.03 E
Linzhang	98	36.21 N	114.36 E
Linzhi	120	29.25 N	94.22 E
Linzi, Zhg.	98	36.52 N	118.21 E
Linzi, Zhg.	100	33.03 N	119.38 E
Linzikou	100	28.42 N	112.46 E
Linzolo	152	4.25 S	15.07 E
Lioko, Zaïre	152	1.25 N	23.07 E
Lioko, Zaïre	152	0.02 N	22.04 E
Lio Matoh	112	3.10 N	115.14 E
Liomer	50	49.51 N	1.49 E
Lion, Golfe du C	32	43.00 N	4.00 E
Lionel Town	241q	17.48 N	77.14 W
Lioni	68	40.52 N	15.11 E
Lion Rock Tunnel ♦5	271d	22.21 N	114.09 E
Lions Den	154	17.16 S	30.02 E
Lion's Head	212	44.59 N	81.15 W
Lionville	208	40.03 N	75.39 W
Lioppa	112	7.40 S	126.00 E
Liouesso	152	1.02 N	15.43 E
Liozno	76	55.02 N	30.48 E
Lipa	116	13.57 N	121.10 E
Lipan	196	32.31 N	98.03 W
Lipany	30	49.10 N	20.58 E
Lipari	70	38.28 N	14.57 E
Lipari, Isola I	70	38.29 N	14.56 E
Lipatkain	112	0.01 S	101.13 E
Lipayan	104	42.13 N	123.23 E
Lipcy	78	50.13 N	36.25 E
Lipeck	80	52.37 N	39.35 E
Lipeck □4	80	52.15 N	40.30 E
Lipeckoje Vtoroje	78	47.46 N	29.41 E
Liperi	26	62.32 N	29.22 E
Lipetsk → Lipeck	76	52.37 N	39.35 E
Lipez, Cerro ∧	248	21.53 S	66.52 W
Liphook	42	51.05 N	0.49 W
Lipiany	30	53.00 N	14.59 E
Lipicy	76	53.22 N	37.51 E
Lipin Bor	76	60.16 N	37.57 E
Liping	102	26.17 N	109.00 E
Lipis ≃	114	4.10 N	102.04 E
Lipiyu	104	41.09 N	123.36 E
Lipka ≃	265b	55.45 N	37.11 E
Lipkany	78	48.16 N	26.48 E
Lipki	78	53.58 N	37.42 E
Lipník nad Bečvou	30	49.31 N	17.35 E
Lipniški	76	54.00 N	25.37 E
Lipno	30	52.51 N	19.10 E
Lipno, údolní nádrž ⊛1	30	48.43 N	14.04 E
Lipoa Point ≻	229a	21.02 N	156.38 W
Lipova	38	46.05 N	21.40 E
Lipovaja Dolina	78	50.35 N	33.48 E
Lipovcy	89	44.11 N	131.44 E
Lipovec	78	49.14 N	29.03 E
Lipovka, S.S.S.R.	78	50.52 N	40.02 E
Lipovka, S.S.S.R.	80	52.26 N	46.11 E
Lipovka, S.S.S.R.	80	49.46 N	44.56 E
Lippborg	52	51.40 N	8.02 E
Lippe ≃	52	51.39 N	6.38 E
Lipperode	52	51.41 N	8.22 E
Lippoldsberg	52	51.37 N	9.33 E
Lippolthausen ♦8	263	51.37 N	7.29 E
Lippstadt	52	51.40 N	8.19 E
Lipscomb	196	36.14 N	100.16 W
Lipsko	30	51.09 N	21.39 E
Lipsoí I	38	37.20 N	26.45 E
Lipsós I	130	37.20 N	26.45 E
Lipton	184	50.54 N	103.50 W
Liptovská Teplička	30	48.59 N	20.06 E
Liptovský Mikuláš	30	49.06 N	19.37 E
Liptrap, Cape ≻	166	38.54 S	145.55 E
Lipu	102	24.25 N	110.29 E
Lipu La)(	124	30.21 N	81.03 E
Liqi	100	27.39 N	116.19 E
Liqiao	107	29.03 N	104.48 E
Lira, Ug.	154	2.15 N	32.54 E
Lira, Ven.	286c	10.26 N	66.46 W
Liranga	152	0.40 S	17.36 E
Lirangdian	105	39.14 N	116.14 E
Lircay	248	12.56 S	74.43 W
Liren	100	33.55 N	118.47 E
Lirentuncun	104	41.24 N	122.59 E
Liri ≃	66	41.25 N	13.52 E
Liria	34	39.38 N	0.36 W
Liro ≃	58	46.18 N	9.23 E
Lisa, Punta ≻	236	8.00 N	80.22 W
Lisala	152	2.09 N	21.31 E
Lisavy	82	56.33 N	38.32 E
Lisboa	34	38.43 N	9.08 W
Lisboa	266c	38.43 N	9.08 W
Lisboa □5	266c	38.48 N	9.16 W
Lisboa, Universidade de ✝2	266c	38.45 N	9.09 W
Lisbon → Lisboa, Port.	34	38.43 N	9.08 W
Lisbon, Ill., U.S.	216	41.29 N	88.29 W
Lisbon, Maine, U.S.	188	44.02 N	70.06 W
Lisbon, Md., U.S.	208	39.20 N	77.04 W
Lisbon, N.H., U.S.	188	44.13 N	71.55 W
Lisbon, N. Dak., U.S.	198	46.27 N	97.41 W
Lisbon, Ohio, U.S.	214	40.47 N	80.46 W
Lisbon Falls	188	44.03 N	70.03 W
Lisbonne → Lisboa	34	38.43 N	9.08 W
Lisburn	48	54.31 N	6.03 W
Lisburne, Cape ≻, N. Heb.	175f	15.40 S	166.43 E
Lisburne, Cape ≻, Alaska, U.S.	180	68.52 N	166.14 W
Liscannor Bay C	48	52.55 N	9.25 W
Liscarney	48	53.43 N	9.35 W
Liscia	71	41.11 N	9.19 E
Liscia ≃	36	41.11 N	9.19 E
Liscia, Lago di ⊛	71	41.00 N	9.16 E
Lisdoonvarna	48	53.01 N	9.15 W
Lisec	78	48.52 N	24.36 E
Liseleje	41	56.01 N	11.59 E
Lishan, Zhg.	100	31.50 N	113.16 E
Lishan, Zhg.	104	41.10 N	123.00 E
Lishangzhuang	105	39.35 N	118.11 E
Lishanke	98	40.41 N	119.53 E
Lishe	100	29.48 N	121.28 E
Lishehe ≃	102	24.18 N	101.32 E
Lishi, Zhg.	102	37.32 N	111.09 E
Lishi, Zhg.	106	31.14 N	120.37 E
Lishi, Zhg.	107	29.20 N	105.24 E
Lishiba	107	29.04 N	106.15 E
Lishichang	107	29.10 N	105.42 E
Lishu	89	43.21 N	124.37 E
Lishui (Yunhe), Zhg.	100	28.06 N	119.34 E
Lishui, Zhg.	100	28.27 N	119.54 E
Lishui, Zhg.	105	40.03 N	115.51 E
Lishui, Zhg.	106	31.39 N	119.01 E
Lishuzhen	89	45.05 N	130.41 E
Lisi	130	35.06 N	33.41 E
Lisianski Island I	14	26.02 N	174.00 W
Lisica ≃	86	58.34 N	85.11 E
Lisičansk	83	48.55 N	38.26 E
Lisichansk → Lisičansk	83	48.55 N	38.26 E
Lisicy	82	56.47 N	36.21 E
Lisieux, Sask., Can.	184	49.17 N	105.59 W
Lisieux, Fr.	50	49.09 N	0.14 E
Lisij Nos	265a	60.01 N	30.00 E
Lišina	60	49.37 N	13.10 E
Lisitu	154	9.39 S	34.39 E
Lisizhuang	105	38.55 N	115.07 E
Lisja	80	57.15 N	54.22 E
Liska ≃	80	48.32 N	43.08 E
Liskeard	42	50.28 N	4.28 W
Liski, S.S.S.R.	78	50.56 N	39.29 E
Liski → Georgiu-Dež, S.S.S.R.	78	50.59 N	39.30 E
Lísková	60	49.25 N	12.43 E
L'Isle, Fr.	50	47.35 N	4.00 E
L'Isle, Schw.	58	46.37 N	6.25 E
Lisle, Ill., U.S.	216	41.48 N	88.05 W
Lisle, N.Y., U.S.	210	42.21 N	76.00 W
L'Isle Adam	50	49.07 N	2.14 E
L'Isle-Jourdain, Fr.	32	46.14 N	0.41 E
L'Isle-Jourdain, Fr.	32	43.37 N	1.05 E
L'Isle-sur-la-Sorgue	62	43.55 N	5.03 E
L'Isle-sur-le-Doubs	58	47.27 N	6.35 E
Lisman	194	32.05 N	88.17 W
Lismore, Austl.	166	28.48 S	153.17 E
Lismore, Austl.	169	37.58 S	143.20 E
Lismore, N.S., Can.	186	45.42 N	62.16 W
Lismore, Eire	48	52.08 N	7.55 W
Lismore Castle ⊥	48	52.08 N	7.52 W
Lismore Island I	46	56.29 N	5.33 W
Lisnaskea	48	54.15 N	7.27 W
Lišn'ovka	78	51.28 N	25.25 E
Lisö ♦1	40	58.55 N	17.45 E
Lišov	61	49.01 N	14.37 E
Liss	42	51.03 N	0.55 W
Lissabon → Lisboa	34	38.43 N	9.08 W
Lissberg	56	50.22 N	9.05 E
Lisse	52	52.15 N	4.33 E
Lisses	261	48.36 N	2.26 E
Lissewege	50	51.18 N	3.11 E
Lissie	222	29.33 N	96.13 W
Lissingen	56	50.14 N	6.38 E
Lissone	62	45.37 N	9.14 E
Lissy	261	48.38 N	2.42 E
Lista	80	47.44 N	45.54 E
Lista ≻1	26	58.07 N	6.40 E
Lister ≃	263	51.05 N	7.45 E
Lištica	36	43.23 N	17.36 E
Listowel, Ont., Can.	212	43.44 N	80.57 W
Listowel, Eire	48	52.27 N	9.29 W
Listv'anka	88	51.52 N	104.51 E
Listv'anskij	86	54.27 N	83.29 E
Lisui	105	40.05 N	116.44 E
Lit	26	63.19 N	14.49 E
Lita	100	27.22 N	116.34 E
Litang, Malay.	112	5.20 N	118.31 E
Litang, Zhg.	102	23.11 N	109.05 E
Litang, Zhg.	102	29.59 N	100.19 E
Litanghe ≃	102	28.04 N	101.30 E
Litani (Itany) ≃	250	3.40 N	54.00 W
Līṭānī, Nahr al- ≃	132	33.20 N	35.14 E
Litava ≃	61	49.02 N	16.36 E
Litcham	42	52.44 N	0.47 E
Litchfield, Conn., U.S.	207	41.45 N	73.11 W
Litchfield, Ill., U.S.	219	39.11 N	89.39 W
Litchfield, Mich., U.S.	216	42.03 N	84.46 W
Litchfield, Minn., U.S.	190	45.08 N	94.31 W
Litchfield, Nebr., U.S.	198	41.09 N	99.09 W
Litchfield, Ohio, U.S.	214	41.10 N	82.02 W
Litchfield □6	207	41.45 N	73.11 W
Litchfield Park	200	33.30 N	112.22 W
Litchville	198	46.39 N	98.11 W
Literberry	219	39.51 N	90.12 W
Lith, Wādī al- ≃	144	20.40 N	40.35 E
Litherland	44	53.28 N	2.59 W
Lithgow	170	33.29 S	150.09 E
Lithia	220	27.51 N	82.10 W
Lithinon, Akra ≻	38	34.55 N	24.44 E
Lithonia	192	33.43 N	84.06 W
Lithuanian Soviet Socialist Republic → Litovskaja Sovetskaja Socialističeskaja Respublika □3	76	56.00 N	24.00 E
Litian	100	26.58 N	114.10 E
Litija	36	46.03 N	14.50 E
Litin	78	49.20 N	28.05 E
Litipāra	124	24.42 N	87.37 E
Lititz	208	40.09 N	76.18 W
Litke	89	53.57 N	140.15 E
Litókhoron	38	40.06 N	22.30 E
Litoko	154	1.13 S	24.47 E
Litoměřice	54	50.35 N	14.09 E
Litomyšl	30	49.52 N	16.19 E
Litoo	154	9.54 S	38.24 E
Litoral, Cordillera del ⩘	286c	10.33 N	66.52 W
Litouqiao	106	31.15 N	118.54 E
Litovel	30	49.42 N	17.05 E
Litovko	89	49.15 N	135.11 E
Litovskaja Sovetskaja Socialističeskaja Respublika □3	76	56.00 N	24.00 E
Littau	58	47.03 N	8.16 E
Little ≃, Austl.	169	38.01 S	144.35 E
Little ≃, Ont., Can.	281	42.20 N	82.56 W
Little ≃, U.S.	194	33.37 N	93.52 W
Little ≃, Ala., U.S.	194	31.18 N	87.46 W
Little ≃, Ala., U.S.	194	34.16 N	85.40 W
Little ≃, Conn., U.S.	207	41.36 N	72.03 W
Little ≃, Ga., U.S.	192	30.51 N	83.21 W
Little ≃, Ga., U.S.	192	33.39 N	82.32 W
Little ≃, Ind., U.S.	216	40.53 N	85.32 W
Little ≃, Ky., U.S.	194	36.51 N	87.58 W
Little ≃, Mass., U.S.	283	42.37 N	70.42 W
Little ≃, Mass., U.S.	283	42.46 N	70.51 W
Little ≃, N.C., U.S.	192	35.21 N	78.02 W
Little ≃, N.C., U.S.	192	35.15 N	78.42 W
Little ≃, N.Y., U.S.	210	43.18 N	75.43 W
Little ≃, Okla., U.S.	196	35.00 N	96.25 W
Little ≃, S.C., U.S.	192	34.11 N	81.45 W
Little ≃, S.C., U.S.	192	33.56 N	82.25 W
Little ≃, S.C., U.S.	192	34.10 N	81.11 W
Little ≃, Tenn., U.S.	192	35.51 N	83.57 W
Little ≃, Tex., U.S.	222	30.51 N	96.41 W
Little ≃, Va., U.S.	192	37.05 N	80.32 W
Little ≃, Va., U.S.	208	37.49 N	77.26 W
Little, Middle Fork ≃	194	33.57 N	94.34 W
Little Abaco Island I	238	26.53 N	77.43 W
Little Amwell	260	51.47 N	0.02 W
Little Andaman I	110	10.45 N	92.30 E
Little Arkansas ≃	198	37.43 N	97.22 W
Little Auglaize ≃	216	41.07 N	84.25 W
Little Averill Lake ⊛	206	44.57 N	71.44 W
Little Avon ≃	42	51.42 N	2.28 W
Little Baddow	260	51.44 N	0.35 E
Littlebark Bay C	212	45.27 N	77.47 W
Little Barrier Island I	172	36.12 S	175.05 E
Little Bay Islands	186	49.39 N	55.47 W
Little Bear Creek ≃	196	37.43 N	101.43 W
Little Beaver Creek ≃, U.S.	198	46.17 N	103.56 W
Little Beaver Creek ≃, U.S.	198	39.49 N	101.03 W
Little Beaver Creek ≃, U.S.	214	40.38 N	80.31 W
Little Beaver Creek ≃, Wash., U.S.	224	48.54 N	121.06 W
Little Beaver Creek, Middle Fork ≃	214	40.43 N	80.37 W
Little Beaver Creek, West Fork ≃	214	40.43 N	80.37 W
Little Belt Mountains ⩘	202	46.45 N	110.35 W
Little Berkhamsted	260	51.45 N	0.08 W
Little Bighorn ≃	202	45.44 N	107.34 W
Little Billabong	171b	35.35 S	147.32 E
Little Bitterroot ≃	202	47.30 N	114.19 W
Little Black ≃	194	36.25 N	90.45 W
Little Black Bear Indian Reserve ♦4	184	51.00 N	103.12 W
Little Blackfoot ≃	202	46.31 N	112.48 W
Little Blue ≃, U.S.	198	39.41 N	96.40 W
Little Blue ≃, Ind., U.S.	218	39.32 N	85.46 W
Littleborough	44	53.39 N	2.05 W
Little Bow ≃	182	49.53 N	112.29 W
Little Bow Lake ⊛	182	50.12 N	112.41 W
Little Brazos ≃	222	30.38 N	96.31 W
Little Brokenstraw Creek ≃	214	41.50 N	79.23 W
Little Brosna ≃	48	53.10 N	8.05 W
Little Buffalo ≃	176	61.00 N	113.46 W
Little Bullhead	184	51.40 N	96.51 W
Little Burstead	260	51.36 N	0.24 E
Little Calumet ≃	278	41.39 N	87.34 W
Little Catalina	186	48.33 N	53.02 W
Little Cayman I	238	19.41 N	80.03 W
Little Cedar ≃	190	42.57 N	92.31 W
Little Chalfont	260	51.40 N	0.34 W
Little Chariton, East Fork ≃	194	39.20 N	92.50 W
Little Chartiers Creek ≃	279b	40.17 N	80.08 W
Little Choptank River C	208	38.32 N	76.13 W
Little Churchill ≃	184	57.15 N	95.21 W
Little Chute	190	44.17 N	88.16 W
Little Coco Island I	110	14.00 N	93.13 E
Little Colorado ≃	200	36.11 N	111.48 W
Little Compton	207	41.30 N	71.10 W
Little Cooley ≃	214	41.44 N	79.53 W
Little Cottonwood ≃	198	44.15 N	94.20 W
Little Creek	208	39.10 N	75.27 W
Little Creek ≃, Ga., U.S.	192	33.13 N	83.24 W
Little Creek ≃, N.J., U.S.	285	39.56 N	74.48 W
Little Creek Naval Amphibious Base ■	208	36.55 N	76.10 W
Little Cumbrae Island I	46	55.43 N	4.57 W
Little Current	190	45.58 N	81.56 W
Little Current ≃	176	50.57 N	84.36 W
Little Cypress Bayou ≃	194	32.41 N	94.15 W
Little Cypress Creek ≃	222	32.39 N	94.42 W
Little Darby Creek ≃, Ohio, U.S.	218	39.53 N	83.13 W
Little Darby Creek ≃, Pa., U.S.	285	40.01 N	75.22 W
Little Dart ≃	42	50.54 N	3.51 W
Little Deer Creek ≃, Ind., U.S.	216	40.36 N	86.28 W
Little Deer Creek ≃, Pa., U.S.	279b	40.33 N	79.50 W
Little Deschutes ≃	202	43.51 N	121.27 W
Little Diomede Island I	180	65.45 N	168.57 W
Little Don ≃	212	43.42 N	79.20 W
Little Dry Creek ≃, Calif., U.S.	226	39.22 N	121.52 W
Little Dry Creek ≃, Mont., U.S.	202	47.21 N	106.22 W
Little Ease Run ≃	285	39.39 N	75.04 W
Little Eau Pleine ≃	190	44.40 N	89.41 W
Little Egg Harbor C	208	39.35 N	74.18 W
Little Elkhart ≃	216	41.43 N	85.49 W
Little End	260	51.41 N	0.14 E
Little Etobicoke Creek ≃	275b	43.37 N	79.34 W
Little Fabius ≃	219	39.59 N	91.59 W
Little Falls, Minn., U.S.	190	45.59 N	94.21 W
Little Falls, N.J., U.S.	276	40.53 N	74.14 W
Little Falls, N.Y., U.S.	210	43.03 N	74.52 W
Little Falls ≃	208	39.36 N	76.38 W
Little Falls Dam ♦6	284c	38.57 N	77.08 W
Little Farms	218	39.57 N	83.10 W
Little Ferry	276	40.51 N	74.03 W
Littlefield	196	33.55 N	102.20 W
Little Flatrock ≃	218	39.26 N	85.33 W
Littlefork	190	48.24 N	93.33 W
Little Fork ≃	190	48.31 N	93.35 W
Little Fort	182	51.25 N	120.12 W
Little Genesee	210	42.02 N	78.13 W
Little Gold ≃	162	18.01 S	126.29 E
Little Gunpowder Falls ≃	208	39.23 N	76.22 W
Littlehampton	42	50.48 N	0.33 W
Little Harbour Deep	186	50.15 N	56.33 W
Little Haw Creek ≃	192	29.23 N	81.24 W
Little Hawk Lake ⊛	212	45.10 N	78.42 W
Little Hoosic ≃	210	42.49 N	73.20 W
Little Hope	214	42.06 N	79.49 W
Little Hulton	262	53.32 N	2.25 W
Little Humboldt ≃	204	41.00 N	117.43 W
Little Humboldt, North Fork ≃	204	41.24 N	117.10 W
Little Humboldt, South Fork ≃	204	41.24 N	117.10 W
Little Hurricane Creek ≃	192	31.23 N	82.19 W
Little Inagua I	238	21.30 N	73.00 W
Little Indian Creek ≃, Ill., U.S.	216	41.31 N	88.46 W
Little Indian Creek ≃, Ind., U.S.	218	38.12 N	86.08 W
Little Island Pond ⊛	283	42.43 N	71.17 W
Littlejohns Creek ≃	226	37.52 N	121.14 W
Little Juniata ≃	208	40.34 N	78.03 W
Little Juniata Creek ≃	208	40.23 N	77.02 W
Little Kanawha ≃	188	39.16 N	81.34 W
Little Kanawha, West Fork ≃	188	38.57 N	81.16 W
Little Karroo (Klein Karroo) ⩘1	158	33.45 S	21.20 E
Little Kentucky ≃	218	38.41 N	85.12 W
Little Klickitat ≃	224	45.51 N	121.04 W
Little Koniuji Island I	180	55.01 N	159.26 W
Little Lake	228	33.45 N	116.56 W
Little Lake ⊛, Ont., Can.	212	44.26 N	79.40 W
Little Lake ⊛, La., U.S.	194	29.30 N	90.10 W
Little Laramie ≃	200	41.28 N	105.44 W
Little Laver	260	51.46 N	0.14 E
Little Leigh	262	53.17 N	2.35 W
Little Lever	262	53.34 N	2.22 W
Little Limestone Lake ⊛	184	53.46 N	99.18 W
Little London	241q	18.15 N	78.13 W
Little Lost ≃	202	43.46 N	112.58 W
Little Lun ≃	116	6.02 N	125.17 E
Little Mahoning Creek ≃	214	40.49 N	79.00 W
Little Maitland ≃	212	43.52 N	81.18 W
Little Malad ≃	202	42.05 N	112.17 W
Little Manatee ≃	220	27.42 N	82.28 W
Little Manatee, South Fork ≃	220	27.39 N	82.18 W
Little Marco Pass C	220	26.01 N	81.46 W
Little Marsh	210	41.53 N	77.24 W
Little Meadows	210	41.59 N	76.08 W
Little Mecatina ≃	176	50.28 N	59.35 W
Little Medicine Bow ≃	200	41.58 N	106.18 W
Little Miami ≃	218	39.05 N	84.26 W
Little Miami, North Fork ≃	218	39.48 N	83.47 W
Little Miami, Todd Fork ≃	218	39.21 N	84.08 W
Little Miami, Todd Fork, East Fork ≃	218	39.09 N	84.18 W
Littlemill	46	57.32 N	3.49 W
Little Minch ⊔	46	57.35 N	6.55 W
Little Mississippi ≃	212	45.17 N	77.35 W
Little Missouri ≃, U.S.	198	47.30 N	102.25 W
Little Missouri ≃, Ark., U.S.	194	33.49 N	92.54 W
Little Mountain ∧	208	40.47 N	76.40 W
Little Muddy ≃, Ill., U.S.	194	37.50 N	89.11 W
Little Muddy ≃, N. Dak., U.S.	198	48.12 N	103.36 W
Little Mulberry Creek ≃	194	32.26 N	86.51 W
Little Muskegon ≃	188	43.26 N	85.37 W
Little Nahant	283	42.25 N	70.56 W
Little Namaqualand □9	156	29.00 S	17.00 E
Little Neck ♦8	276	40.46 N	73.44 W
Little Neck Bay C	276	40.47 N	73.46 W
Little Nemaha ≃	198	40.19 N	95.40 W
Little Neshaminy Creek ≃	285	40.15 N	75.02 W
Little Niangua ≃	194	38.04 N	92.54 W
Little Nicobar I	110	7.20 N	93.40 E
Little Ohoopee ≃	192	32.27 N	82.24 W
Little Osage ≃	194	38.02 N	94.14 W
Little Otter Creek ≃	212	42.44 N	80.51 W
Little Ouse ≃	42	52.30 N	0.22 E
Little Owyhee ≃	202	42.28 N	117.15 W
Little Panoche Creek ≃	226	36.50 N	120.42 W
Little Patuxent ≃	284b	39.11 N	76.52 W
Little Peconic Bay C	207	40.59 N	72.24 W
Little Pee Dee ≃	192	33.42 N	79.11 W
Little Pic ≃	190	48.48 N	86.37 W
Little Pine and Lucky Man Indian Reserve ♦4	184	52.56 N	109.05 W
Little Pine Creek ≃, Pa., U.S.	210	41.18 N	77.22 W
Little Pine Creek ≃, Pa., U.S.	279b	40.31 N	79.57 W
Little Pine Island I	220	26.36 N	82.05 W
Little Pine Key I	220	24.44 N	81.19 W
Little Pine State Park ♠	210	41.22 N	77.20 W
Little Pipe Creek ≃	208	39.36 N	77.16 W
Little Platte ≃	194	39.24 N	94.41 W
Little Plum Creek ≃	279b	40.30 N	79.51 W
Little Popo Aggie ≃	202	42.54 N	108.35 W
Little Porcupine Creek ≃, Mont., U.S.	202	48.02 N	106.04 W
Little Porcupine Creek ≃, Mont., U.S.	202	46.18 N	106.34 W
Littleport	42	52.28 N	0.19 E
Little Portage Creek ≃	216	42.00 N	85.27 W
Little Powder ≃	198	45.28 N	105.20 W
Little Pucketa Creek ≃	279b	40.33 N	79.45 W
Little Quill Lake ⊛	184	51.55 N	104.05 W
Little Rann of Kutch ≡	120	23.25 N	71.15 E
Little Red ≃	194	35.11 N	91.27 W
Little Red, Middle Fork ≃	194	35.37 N	92.11 W
Little Red Deer ≃	182	52.04 N	114.09 W
Little Red River Indian Reserve ♦4	184	53.30 N	105.58 W
Little Redstone Lake ⊛	212	45.13 N	78.34 W
Little River, Austl.	169	37.58 S	144.30 E
Little River, N.Z.	172	43.46 S	172.47 E
Little River, Kans., U.S.	198	38.24 N	98.01 W
Little River, Tex., U.S.	222	30.59 N	97.22 W
Little Rock, Ark., U.S.	194	34.44 N	92.15 W
Littlerock, Calif., U.S.	228	34.31 N	117.59 W
Little Rock, Ill., U.S.	216	41.43 N	88.34 W
Littlerock, Wash., U.S.	224	46.54 N	123.01 W
Little Rock ≃	198	43.16 N	96.15 W
Little Rock Air Force Base ■	194	34.55 N	92.10 W
Little Rock Creek ≃	228	34.28 N	118.01 W
Little Rock Wash ∨	228	34.42 N	118.02 W
Little Rocky Mountains ⩘	202	47.50 N	108.10 W
Little Rouge Creek ≃	212	43.48 N	79.08 W
Little Sable Point ≻	190	43.38 N	86.32 W
Little Sac ≃	194	37.39 N	93.46 W
Little Sachigo Lake ⊛	184	54.09 N	92.11 W
Little Saint Bernard Pass → Petit-Saint-Bernard, Col du)(	62	45.41 N	6.53 E
Little Salkehatchie ≃	192	32.37 N	80.53 W
Little Salmon ≃, Idaho, U.S.	202	45.25 N	116.19 W
Little Salmon ≃, N.Y., U.S.	212	43.32 N	76.16 W
Little Salmon, North Branch ≃	212	43.24 N	76.04 W
Little Salmon, South Branch ≃	212	43.24 N	76.09 W
Little Salmon Lake ⊛	180	62.12 N	134.45 W
Little Salt Lake ⊛	200	37.55 N	112.53 W
Little Sandy ≃	188	38.35 N	82.51 W
Little Sandy, East Fork ≃	188	38.30 N	82.50 W
Little Sandy Creek ≃	200	42.06 N	109.27 W
Little Scarcies ≃	150	8.51 N	13.09 W
Little Scioto ≃, Ohio, U.S.	214	40.31 N	83.12 W

≃ River	Fluss	Río	Rivière	Rio
≡ Canal	Kanal	Canal	Canal	Canal
⌐ Waterfall, Rapids	Wasserfall, Stromschnellen	Cascada, Rápidos	Chute d'eau, Rapides	Cascata, Rápidos
⊔ Strait	Meeresstrasse	Estrecho	Détroit	Estreito
C Bay, Gulf	Bucht, Golf	Bahía, Golfo	Baie, Golfe	Baía, Golfo
⊛ Lake, Lakes	See, Seen	Lago, Lagos	Lac, Lacs	Lago, Lagos
≡ Swamp	Sumpf	Pantano	Marais	Pântano
⊓ Ice Features, Glacier	Eis- und Gletscherformen	Accidentes Glaciales	Formes glaciaires	Acidentes Glaciares
⫪ Other Hydrographic Features	Andere Hydrographische Objekte	Otros Elementos Hidrográficos	Autres données hydrographiques	Outros Elementos Hidrográficos
✢ Submarine Features	Untermeerische Objekte	Accidentes Submarinos	Formes de relief sous-marin	Acidentes Submarinos
□ Political Unit	Politische Einheit	Unidad Política	Entité politique	Unidade Política
✝ Cultural Institution	Kulturelle Institution	Institución Cultural	Institution culturelle	Instituição Cultural
⊥ Historical Site	Historische Stätte	Sitio Histórico	Site historique	Sitio Histórico
♠ Recreational Site	Erholungs- und Ferienort	Sitio de Recreo	Centre de loisirs	Sitio de Lazer
⊠ Airport	Flughafen	Aeropuerto	Aéroport	Aeroporto
■ Military Installation	Militäranlage	Instalación Militar	Installation militaire	Instalação Militar
♦ Miscellaneous	Verschiedenes	Misceláneo	Divers	Miscelânea

ENGLISH Name	Page	Lat.°′	Long.°′	DEUTSCH Name	Seite	Breite°′	Länge°′ E=Ost

Little Scioto ≐, Ohio, U.S. 218 38.46 N 82.53 W
Little Sewickley Creek ≐, Pa., U.S. 279b 40.33 N 80.12 W
Little Sewickley Creek ≐, Pa., U.S. 279b 40.15 N 79.45 W
Little Silver 276 40.20 N 74.03 W
Little Sioux ≐ 198 41.49 N 96.04 W
Little Sioux, West Fork ≐ 198 42.04 N 96.00 W
Little Sitkin Island I 181a 51.55 N 178.30 E
Little Smoky ≐ 182 55.42 N 117.38 W
Little Snake ≐ 200 40.27 N 108.26 W
Little Sodus Bay C 210 43.20 N 76.43 W
Little Southwest Miramichi ≐ 186 46.57 N 65.50 W
Little Stanney 262 53.15 N 2.53 W
Little Stony Creek ≐ 226 39.20 N 122.31 W
Little Stour ≐ 42 51.19 N 1.15 E
Littlestown 208 39.45 N 77.05 W
Little Sugarloaf ▲2 274b 37.41 S 145.19 E
Little Sur ≐ 226 36.20 N 121.54 W
Little Sutton 262 53.17 N 2.57 W
Little Swatara Creek ≐ 208 40.24 N 76.29 W
Little Tallapoosa ≐ 192 33.18 N 85.34 W
Little Tanaga Island I 180 51.48 N 176.10 W
Little Tennessee ≐ 192 35.47 N 84.15 W
Little Thurrock 260 51.28 N 0.21 E
Little Timber Creek ≐ 285 39.53 N 75.08 W
Little Tinicum Island I 285 39.51 N 75.17 W
Little Tobago I, Br. Vir. Is. 240m 18.26 N 64.51 W
Little Tobago I, Trin. 241r 11.18 N 60.30 W
Little Toby Creek ≐ 214 41.22 N 78.49 W
Littleton, Eng., U.K. 260 51.24 N 0.28 W
Littleton, Colo., U.S. 200 39.37 N 105.01 W
Littleton, Mass., U.S. 207 42.32 N 71.31 W
Littleton, N.H., U.S. 188 44.18 N 71.46 W
Littleton, N.C., U.S. 192 36.26 N 77.54 W
Littleton, W. Va., U.S. 188 39.42 N 80.31 W
Little Traverse Bay C 190 45.24 N 85.03 W
Little Truckee ≐ 226 39.25 N 120.05 W
Little Turtle ≐ 184 48.46 N 92.36 W
Little Turtle State Recreation Area ♦ 216 40.50 N 85.26 W
Little Valley 210 42.15 N 78.48 W
Little Valley Creek ≐ 285 40.04 N 75.28 W
Little Vermilion ≐ 216 41.20 N 89.05 W
Little Vermillion Lake @ 184 51.16 N 93.50 W
Little Wabash ≐ 194 37.54 N 88.05 W
Little Walsingham 42 52.54 N 0.51 E
Little Waltham 260 51.47 N 0.29 E
Little Warley 260 51.35 N 0.19 E
Little Washita ≐ 196 34.58 N 97.51 W
Little White ≐ 198 43.44 N 100.40 W
Little White Salmon ≐ 224 45.43 N 121.38 W
Little Wichita ≐ 196 33.54 N 97.59 W
Little Wichita, East Fork ≐ 196 33.52 N 98.07 W
Little Wind ≐ 202 42.57 N 108.29 W
Little Wind, North Fork ≐ 202 43.01 N 108.53 W
Little Wind, South Fork ≐ 202 43.01 N 108.53 W
Little Wolf ≐ 190 44.23 N 88.48 W
Little Wood ≐ 202 42.57 N 114.21 W
Little York, Ind., U.S. 218 38.42 N 85.54 W
Little York, N.Y., U.S. 210 42.42 N 76.10 W
Little Zab (Zāb-e Kūchek) (Az-Zāb as-Saghīr) ≐ 128 35.12 N 43.25 E
Litunga 152 13.17 S 16.43 E
Litvinov 54 50.37 N 13.36 E
Litvinovka, S.S.S.R. 80 48.24 N 40.53 E
Litvinovka, S.S.S.R. 83 49.18 N 39.27 E
Litvinovo 76 59.34 N 38.01 E
Litvinskoje 86 50.42 N 72.42 E
Litzmannstadt → Łódź 30 51.46 N 19.30 E
Liuan 100 31.44 N 116.31 E
Liuanzhuang 105 39.14 N 117.11 E
Liuba 102 33.32 N 107.07 E
Liubotong 100 31.26 N 116.00 E
Liucao 106 31.07 N 121.41 E
Liuchen 102 23.09 N 110.29 E
Liucheng, Zhg. 100 24.03 N 115.08 E
Liucheng, Zhg. 102 24.32 N 109.21 E
Liuchengba 102 27.27 N 102.53 E
Liuch'iu Hsü I 100 22.20 N 120.22 E
Liuch'iut'ai 100 23.12 N 120.48 E
Liuchonghe ≐ 102 29.40 N 107.25 E
Liuchow → Liuzhou 102 24.22 N 109.32 E
Liucun 106 30.44 N 119.23 E
Liucura 252 38.39 S 71.05 W
Liudaogou 98 41.34 N 127.12 E
Liudaohe 105 40.39 N 116.12 E
Liudiquan 98 34.25 N 116.06 E
Liudongqiao 106 31.03 N 119.32 E
Liudu 100 26.44 N 119.33 E
Liuduo 100 34.01 N 120.17 E
Liuduzhuang 105 39.27 N 117.50 E
Liuerbao 104 41.13 N 122.55 E
Liufang 100 27.56 N 116.22 E
Liufentzu 269d 24.57 N 121.35 E
Liugezhuang, Zhg. 98 38.33 N 116.30 E
Liugezhuang, Zhg. 105 40.03 N 118.16 E
Liugonghe 100 30.20 N 115.36 E
Liugou 105 40.57 N 118.14 E
Liuguan, Zhg. 100 29.56 N 113.08 E
Liuguan, Zhg. 105 39.22 N 116.16 E
Liuguantun 104 41.20 N 121.21 E
Liuhe, Zhg. 98 42.15 N 125.43 E
Liuhe, Zhg. 100 33.20 N 112.48 E
Liuhe, Zhg. 100 30.46 N 113.12 E
Liuhe, Zhg. 105 39.31 N 118.17 E
Liuhe, Zhg. 106 31.30 N 121.15 E
Liuhe ≐, Zhg. 98 42.45 N 126.04 E
Liuhe ≐, Zhg. 98 40.38 N 118.09 E
Liuhe ≐, Zhg. 106 31.31 N 121.18 E
Liuhegou, Zhg. 98 36.18 N 114.06 E
Liuhegou, Zhg. 104 41.56 N 122.44 E
Liuheita 104 42.09 N 123.56 E
Liuhejie 102 24.26 N 101.35 E
Liuhekou 105 40.39 N 118.09 E
Liuhekou C1 106 31.31 N 121.18 E
Liuhengdao I 106 30.02 N 122.12 E
Liuhuang 100 29.43 N 116.08 E
Liuhudang 104 42.31 N 122.22 E
Liujia, Zhg. 102 24.54 N 107.49 E
Liujia, Zhg. 106 32.04 N 121.30 E
Liujiachang 107 29.46 N 103.49 E
Liujiachuan 105 40.07 N 114.47 E
Liujiadai 106 31.57 N 120.23 E
Liujiadian 89 50.07 N 124.17 E
Liujiadu 106 32.15 N 120.33 E
Liujiafen 105 39.58 N 115.47 E
Liujiagangzi 104 41.28 N 122.33 E
Liujiagou 98 37.47 N 120.53 E
Liujiahang 106 31.21 N 121.22 E
Liujiahe, Zhg. 106 31.12 N 121.24 E
Liujiahe, Zhg. 104 40.40 N 123.58 E
Liujiahe, Zhg. 98 40.04 N 119.34 E
Liujiashan 105 40.14 N 114.49 E
Liujiatun, Zhg. 104 42.08 N 122.44 E
Liujiatun, Zhg. 104 41.52 N 122.44 E
Liujiatun, Zhg. 104 41.51 N 122.05 E
Liujiawopeng 104 42.49 N 123.01 E
Liujiazi, Zhg. 98 41.00 N 120.13 E
Liujiazi, Zhg. 104 41.48 N 123.47 E
Liujiazi, Zhg. 104 42.22 N 122.41 E
Liujiazi, Zhg. 104 42.36 N 122.15 E
Liujingcun 105 39.27 N 115.26 E
Liujisu 105 40.01 N 117.13 E
Liukang Tenggaya, Kepulauan II 112 6.45 S 118.50 E
Liukedao I 100 22.34 N 114.52 E
Liukeshu 86 44.59 N 90.12 E
Liuku 102 25.48 N 98.52 E
Liuli 154 11.05 S 34.38 E
Liulicun 105 39.56 N 116.28 E
Liulidian 106 31.31 N 119.17 E
Liuligou 104 41.24 N 121.29 E
Liulihe 105 39.36 N 116.01 E
Liulin 98 36.41 N 115.42 E
Liulindian 100 31.34 N 114.52 E
Liuliwei 100 24.20 N 114.03 E
Liulongtai 104 41.32 N 120.56 E
Liumachang 107 29.51 N 104.54 E
Liumaogou 89 48.12 N 127.13 E
Liupangtun 104 41.36 N 123.28 E
Liupowu 98 37.38 N 117.25 E
Liuqianhutun 104 42.01 N 123.41 E
Liuquan 98 34.27 N 117.20 E
Liurenba 100 29.57 N 114.49 E
Liusheng 100 32.12 N 112.55 E
Liushi, Zhg. 98 38.33 N 115.44 E
Liushi, Zhg. 100 28.03 N 120.51 E
Liushilipu 100 32.45 N 115.58 E
Liushishan ▲ 120 36.15 N 82.05 E
Liushudian 98 35.54 N 119.30 E
Liushudixia 104 42.26 N 121.14 E
Liushuigou 100 31.34 N 112.27 E
Liushuituo 89 44.17 N 124.15 E
Liushuquan 105 39.21 N 118.06 E
Liusiqiao 100 29.47 N 116.21 E
Liusong 105 39.40 N 117.06 E
Liuta 98 35.52 N 115.18 E
Liutai 98 41.20 N 113.43 E
Liutaizi 104 41.46 N 122.39 E
Liutang 102 24.58 N 110.21 E
Liutiaozhaicun 104 41.29 N 123.12 E
Liutuan 98 36.56 N 119.22 E
Liutuhutun 104 40.44 N 120.32 E
Liuwangliou 98 34.48 N 116.28 E
Liuwa Plain ≐ 152 14.30 S 22.40 E
Liuwei 106 32.16 N 119.25 E
Liuwudian 100 24.36 N 118.13 E
Liuxia 106 30.15 N 120.03 E
Liuxiaoshuihang 106 31.45 N 121.48 E
Liuxihe ≐ 100 23.22 N 112.54 E
Liuyang 100 28.09 N 113.38 E
Liuyanghe ≐ 100 28.13 N 112.58 E
Liuyuan 98 36.10 N 114.34 E
Liuyuankou 98 34.54 N 114.20 E
Liuzhai 102 25.15 N 107.20 E
Liuzhou 102 24.22 N 109.32 E
Liuzhuang 106 33.10 N 120.19 E
Liuzong 106 32.12 N 121.19 E
Livada 38 47.52 N 23.07 E
Livadija 89 42.50 N 132.39 E
Livanátai 38 38.42 N 23.03 E
Līvāni 76 56.22 N 26.11 E
Livanjsko Polje ≐ 36 43.55 N 16.45 E
Livanovka 86 52.06 N 61.59 E
Livarot 50 49.01 N 0.09 E
Lively, Ont., Can. 190 46.26 N 81.09 W
Lively, Va., U.S. 208 37.47 N 76.31 W
Lively Island I 254 52.02 S 58.30 W
Livengood 180 65.32 N 148.33 W
Livenka, S.S.S.R. 78 50.44 N 40.14 E
Livenka, S.S.S.R. 78 50.26 N 38.18 E
Livenza ≐ 64 45.35 N 12.51 E
Live Oak, Calif., U.S. 226 39.17 N 121.40 W
Live Oak, Fla., U.S. 192 30.18 N 82.59 W
Live Oak Creek ≐ 196 30.39 N 101.42 W
Liverdun 56 48.45 N 6.03 E
Liverdy-en-Brie 261 48.42 N 2.47 E
Livergnano 66 44.19 N 11.21 E
Liveringa 162 18.03 S 124.10 E
Livermore, Calif., U.S. 226 37.41 N 121.46 W
Livermore, Iowa, U.S. 190 42.52 N 94.10 W
Livermore, Ky., U.S. 194 37.29 N 87.08 W
Livermore Falls 188 44.28 N 70.11 W
Liverpool, Austl. 170 33.55 S 150.56 E
Liverpool, N.S., Can. 186 44.02 N 64.43 W
Liverpool, Eng., U.K. 44
262 53.25 N 2.55 W
Liverpool, Ind., U.S. 216 41.34 N 87.18 W
Liverpool, N.Y., U.S. 210 43.06 N 76.13 W
Liverpool, Pa., U.S. 208 40.34 N 77.00 W
Liverpool, Tex., U.S. 222 29.18 N 95.17 W
Liverpool □8 262 53.25 N 2.55 W
Liverpool (Speke) Airport ⊠ 44 53.21 N 2.52 W
Liverpool, Cape ≻ 176 73.38 N 78.06 W
Liverpool, University of ✐2 262 53.24 N 2.58 W
Liverpool Bay C, N.W. Ter., Can. 180 69.45 N 130.00 W
Liverpool Bay C, N.S., Can. 186 44.02 N 64.41 W
Liverpool Bay C, Eng., U.K. 44 53.30 N 3.16 W
Liverpool Football Ground ♦ 262 53.26 N 2.57 W
Liverpool Heights 210 43.07 N 76.13 W
Liverpool Range ⛰ 166 31.40 S 150.30 E
Liverpool Street Station ♦5 260 51.31 N 0.05 W
Livet-et-Gavet 62 45.06 N 5.56 E
Livigno 64 46.32 N 10.04 E
Livilliers 261 49.06 N 2.06 E
Livingston, Guat. 236 15.50 N 88.45 W
Livingston, Scot., U.K. 46 55.53 N 3.32 W
Livingston, Ala., U.S. 194 32.35 N 88.11 W
Livingston, Calif., U.S. 226 37.23 N 120.43 W
Livingston, Ill., U.S. 194 38.58 N 89.46 W
Livingston, Ky., U.S. 192 37.18 N 84.13 W
Livingston, La., U.S. 194 30.30 N 90.45 W
Livingston, Mont., U.S. 202 45.40 N 110.34 W
Livingston, N.J., U.S. 210 40.48 N 74.19 W
Livingston, N.Y., U.S. 210 42.09 N 73.47 W
Livingston, Tenn., U.S. 194 36.23 N 85.19 W
Livingston, Tex., U.S. 222 30.43 N 94.56 W
Livingston, Wis., U.S. 190 42.54 N 90.26 W
Livingston □6, Ill., U.S. 216 40.53 N 88.38 W
Livingston □6, Mich., U.S. 216 42.38 N 83.50 W
Livingston □6, N.Y., U.S. 210 42.48 N 77.49 W
Livingstone 154 17.50 S 25.53 E
Livingstone, Chutes de (Livingstone Falls) ⌄ 152 4.50 S 14.30 E
Livingstone, Lake @1 222 30.50 N 95.30 W
Livingstone Falls → Livingstone, Chutes de ⌄ 152 4.50 S 14.30 E
Livingstone Lake @ 212 45.22 N 78.43 W
Livingstone Mountains ⛰ 154 9.45 S 34.20 E
Livingstonia 154 10.36 S 34.07 E
Livingston Island I 9 62.35 S 60.30 W
Livingston Mall ♦9 276 40.47 N 74.21 W
Livingston Manor 210 41.54 N 74.50 W
Livno 36 43.50 N 17.01 E
Livny 76 52.25 N 37.37 E
Livojoki ≐ 26 65.24 N 26.48 E
Livonia, Ind., U.S. 218 38.34 N 86.17 W
Livonia, La., U.S. 194 30.33 N 91.33 W
Livonia, Mich., U.S. 216 42.25 N 83.23 W
Livonia, N.Y., U.S. 210 42.49 N 77.40 W
Livonia Center 210 42.49 N 77.38 W
Livonia Mall ♦9 281 42.26 N 83.20 W
Livorno (Leghorn) 66 43.33 N 10.19 E
Livorno □4 66 43.14 N 10.35 E
Livorno Ferraris 62 45.17 N 8.05 E
Livourne → Livorno 66 43.33 N 10.19 E
Livramento → Santana do Livramento 252 30.53 S 55.31 W
Livramento do Brumado 255 13.39 S 41.50 W
Livron-sur-Drôme 62 44.46 N 4.51 E
Livry-Gargan 261 48.56 N 2.33 E
Livry-sur-Seine 261 48.31 N 2.41 E
Liwa 112 5.04 S 104.06 E
Liwale 154 9.46 S 37.56 E
Liwale Chini 154 9.41 S 38.01 E
Liwan 154 4.54 N 35.40 E
Liwonde 154 14.52 S 35.28 E
Liwung ≐ 269e 6.08 S 106.49 E
Lixi 100 29.15 N 114.46 E
Lixian, Zhg. 98 38.29 N 115.34 E
Lixian, Zhg. 105 39.33 N 116.26 E
Lixianjiang → Black ≐ 110 21.15 N 105.20 E
Lixin 100 26.52 N 116.42 E
Lixingji, Zhg. 98 34.38 N 115.54 E
Lixingji, Zhg. 100 33.28 N 115.28 E
Lixingzhuang 105 39.25 N 117.56 E
Lixoúrion 38 38.12 N 20.26 E
Lixus ⊥ 148 35.15 N 6.13 W
Liyang 106 31.26 N 119.29 E
Liyangzhen 102 29.30 N 111.37 E
Liyuanbao 100 25.16 N 112.55 E
Lizard 42 49.58 N 5.12 W
Lizarda 250 9.36 S 46.41 W
Lizard Head Peak ▲ 200 42.47 N 109.11 W
Lizard Point ≻ 42 49.56 N 5.13 W
Lizard Point Indian Reserve ♦4 184 50.40 N 100.57 W
Lizechang 107 30.10 N 106.10 E
Lizhai 106 31.34 N 121.45 E
Lizhou 102 28.08 N 102.10 E
Lizhu 100 29.56 N 120.30 E
Lizhuang 107 28.47 N 104.46 E
Lizhuangqiao 106 31.48 N 119.37 E
Lizino 83 49.33 N 38.51 E
Lizinovka 78 50.08 N 39.28 E
Liziwei 107 30.19 N 106.39 E
Lizy-sur-Ourcq 50 49.01 N 3.02 E
Lizzana 64 45.51 N 11.03 E
Lizzanello 68 40.18 N 18.13 E
Lizzano 68 40.23 N 17.27 E
Lizzano in Belvedere 64 44.10 N 10.53 E
Ljalovo 82 56.03 N 37.14 E
Ljan 26 59.51 N 10.48 E
Ljubelj (Loibl Pass))(61 46.26 N 14.16 E
Ljubija 36 44.56 N 16.37 E
Ljubimec 38 41.50 N 26.05 E
Ljubinje 38 42.57 N 18.05 E
Ljubljana 36 46.03 N 14.31 E
Ljubovija 38 44.11 N 19.22 E
Ljubuški 36 43.12 N 17.33 E
Ljugarn 26 57.19 N 18.42 E
Ljunga 40 58.31 N 16.21 E
Ljungan ≐ 26 62.19 N 17.23 E
Ljungaverk 26 62.29 N 16.03 E
Ljungby 26 56.50 N 13.56 E
Ljungbyhed 41 56.04 N 13.12 E
Ljungbyholm 26 56.38 N 16.10 E
Ljungdalen 26 62.51 N 12.47 E
Ljungsbro 26 58.31 N 15.30 E
Ljungskile 26 58.14 N 11.55 E
Ljusdal 26 61.50 N 16.05 E
Ljusfallshammar 40 58.47 N 15.29 E
Ljusnan ≐ 26 61.12 N 17.08 E
Ljusnaren @ 40 59.51 N 14.56 E
Ljusne 26 61.13 N 17.08 E
Ljusterö I 40 59.31 N 18.37 E
Ljutomer 61 46.31 N 16.12 E
Llagas Creek ≐ 226 36.58 N 121.31 W
Llaima, Volcán ▲1 252 38.43 S 71.43 W
Llallagua 248 18.25 S 66.38 W
Llanaber 42 52.45 N 4.05 W
Llanaelhaiarn 42 52.59 N 4.24 W
Llanarth 42 52.12 N 4.18 W
Llanarthney 42 51.52 N 4.09 W
Llanbedrog 42 52.52 N 4.29 W
Llanberis, Pass of V 42 53.06 N 4.04 W
Llanbister 42 52.21 N 3.19 W
Llanboidy 42 51.54 N 4.36 W
Llanbrynmair 42 52.37 N 3.57 W
Llanbyther 42 52.04 N 4.09 W
Llancanelo, Laguna @ 252 35.35 S 69.09 W
Llandaff 42 51.30 N 3.14 W
Llandaff Cathedral ♦1 42 51.29 N 3.15 W
Llanddewi Brefi 42 52.10 N 3.57 W
Llandeilo 42 51.52 N 3.59 W
L.L. Anderson Reservoir @1 226 39.07 N 120.25 W
Llandilo 274a 33.43 S 150.45 E
Llandinam 42 52.29 N 3.26 W
Llandissilio 42 51.53 N 4.44 W
Llandovery 42 51.59 N 3.48 W
Llandrindod Wells 42 52.15 N 3.23 W
Llandudno 44 53.19 N 3.49 W
Llandybie 42 51.50 N 4.00 W
Llandyssul 42 52.02 N 4.19 W
Llanelli 42 51.42 N 4.10 W
Llanelltyd 42 52.45 N 3.54 W
Llanelly 169 36.44 S 143.51 E
Llanenddwyn 42 52.49 N 4.06 W
Llanerchymedd 44 53.20 N 4.22 W
Llanes 34 43.25 N 4.45 W
Llanfaethlu 44 53.21 N 4.32 W
Llanfair Caereinion 42 52.39 N 3.20 W
Llanfairfechan 44 53.15 N 3.58 W
Llanfairpwllgwyngyll 44 53.13 N 4.12 W
Llanfrynach 42 51.56 N 3.21 W
Llanfyllin 42 52.46 N 3.17 W
Llanfynydd 42 51.56 N 4.06 W
Llanfyrnach 42 51.57 N 4.35 W
Llangadog 42 51.56 N 3.53 W
Llangefni 44 53.16 N 4.18 W
Llangennech 42 51.41 N 4.04 W
Llangollen 42 52.58 N 3.10 W
Llangollen Estates 208 39.39 N 75.37 W
Llangranog 42 52.09 N 4.28 W
Llangurig 42 52.25 N 3.36 W
Llangwryfon 42 52.19 N 4.03 W
Llanharan 42 51.33 N 3.25 W
Llanidloes 42 52.27 N 3.32 W
Llanilar 42 52.21 N 4.01 W
Llanllyfni 42 53.03 N 4.17 W
Llano 196 30.45 N 98.41 W
Llano ≐ 196 30.35 N 98.25 W
Llano Colorado 204 31.38 N 115.55 W
Llano Grande 234 20.28 N 105.37 W
Llanon 42 52.17 N 4.10 W
Llanos ≐ 246 5.00 N 70.00 W
Llanpumsaint 42 51.56 N 4.18 W
Llanquera 248 18.06 S 67.47 W
Llanquihue 254 41.15 S 73.01 W
Llanquihue, Lago @ 254 41.08 S 72.48 W
Llanrhaeadr-ym-Mochnant 42 52.51 N 3.17 W
Llanrhidian 42 51.37 N 4.11 W
Llanrhystyd 42 52.18 N 4.09 W
Llanrwst 44 53.08 N 3.48 W
Llansá 34 42.22 N 3.09 E
Llansantffraid-ym-Mechain 42 52.47 N 3.08 W
Llansawel 42 52.01 N 4.00 W
Llanta 252 26.20 S 69.49 W
Llantrisant 42 51.33 N 3.23 W
Llantwit Major 42 51.25 N 3.30 W
Llanuwchllyn 42 52.52 N 3.41 W
Llanwenog 42 52.06 N 4.12 W
Llanwrda 42 51.58 N 3.53 W
Llanwrtyd Wells 42 52.07 N 3.38 W
Llata 248 9.25 S 76.47 W
Llavallol ♦8 288 34.48 S 58.28 W
Llay 42 53.06 N 2.59 W
Llentrisca, Cabo de ≻ 34 38.51 N 1.14 E
Llera 234 23.19 N 99.01 W
Llerena 34 38.14 N 6.01 W
Lleulleu, Lago @ 252 38.09 S 73.20 W
Lleyn Peninsula ≻1 42 52.54 N 4.30 W
Llica 248 19.52 S 68.16 W
Llico 252 34.46 S 72.05 W
Llivia 32 42.28 N 1.59 E
Llijić 85 40.52 N 68.31 E
Llobregat ≐ 34 41.19 N 2.09 E
Llobregat, Delta del ≐2 266d 41.17 N 2.08 E
Llorente 116 11.25 N 125.33 E
Llorente ≐ 116 11.25 N 125.33 E
Lloyd 218 38.37 N 82.52 W
Lloyd Harbor 210 40.54 N 73.28 W
Lloyd Harbor C 276 40.55 N 73.27 W
Lloydminster 184 53.17 N 110.00 W
Lloyd Neck ≻1 276 40.56 N 73.28 W
Lloyd Point ≻ 210 40.57 N 73.29 W
Lloyds ≐ 186 48.33 N 57.08 W
Lluchmayor 34 39.29 N 2.54 E
Llullaillaco, Volcán ▲1 252 24.43 S 68.33 W
Llusco 248 14.21 S 72.07 W
Llyswen 42 52.02 N 3.17 W
Lnáře 60 49.28 N 13.47 E
I-n-Azaoua ≐4 148 20.49 N 7.30 E
Lo ≐ 110 21.18 N 105.25 E
Loa 200 38.24 N 111.38 W
Loa ≐ 248 21.26 S 70.04 W
Loa ≐, Chile 248 21.26 S 70.04 W
Loa ≐, Congo 273b 4.30 S 15.10 E
Loami 194 39.40 N 89.51 W
Loanatit 175f 19.22 S 169.14 E
Loanda → Luanda, Ang. 152 8.48 S 13.14 E
Loanda, Bra. 255 22.54 S 53.10 W
Loanda, Gabon 152 0.55 S 9.00 E
Loande ≐ 152 8.41 S 17.56 E
Loange (Luangue) ≐ 152 4.17 S 20.02 E
Loango Buele 152 5.10 S 12.59 E
Loanhead 46 55.53 N 3.09 W
Loanja ≐ 154 17.22 S 24.48 E
Loano 62 44.08 N 8.15 E
Loantaka Brook ≐ 276 40.43 N 74.28 W
Lo Aranguiz 286e 33.23 S 70.40 W
Loay 116 9.36 N 124.01 E
Lob' ≐ 82 56.29 N 35.51 E
Lobamba 158 26.27 S 31.12 E
Loban 24 65.44 N 45.25 E
Loban' ≐ 80 56.58 N 51.12 E
Lobanovo 76 53.04 N 38.14 E
Lobanovskije Vyselki 82 54.18 N 38.58 E
Lo Barnechea 286e 33.21 S 70.31 W
Lobaski 80 54.38 N 45.09 E
Lobatos 234 22.49 N 103.24 W
Lobatse 156 25.11 S 25.40 E
Löbau 54 51.05 N 14.40 E
Lobau ≐ 264b 48.10 N 16.32 E
Lobaye □5 152 4.00 N 18.00 E
Lobaye ≐ 152 3.41 N 18.35 E
Lobbes 50 50.21 N 4.15 E
Lobbs Run ≐ 279b 40.15 N 79.55 W
Lobdell Lake @ 216 42.48 N 83.48 W
Löbejün 54 51.38 N 11.53 E
Lo Benitez 286e 33.34 S 70.42 W
Lobenstein 54 50.26 N 11.38 E
Loberia 252 38.09 S 58.47 W
Lo Bernales 286e 33.34 S 70.34 W
Löberöd 41 55.47 N 13.30 E
Lobethal 168b 34.54 S 138.52 E
Łobez 30 53.39 N 15.36 E
Lobito 152 12.20 S 13.34 E
Lobitos 248 4.26 S 81.17 W
Lobitos Creek ≐ 282 37.22 N 122.24 W
Lobkoviči 76 53.50 N 31.45 E
Lobn'a 82 56.01 N 37.30 E
Löbnitz, D.D.R. 54 51.35 N 12.28 E
Löbnitz, D.D.R. 54 54.17 N 12.43 E
Lobo, Indon. 164 3.45 S 134.05 E
Lobo, Pil. 116 13.39 N 121.13 E
Lobo ≐ 150 6.02 N 6.47 W
Loboko 152 0.45 S 16.38 E
Lobos, Arg. 258 35.11 S 59.06 W
Lobos, Méx. 234 20.29 N 105.03 W
Lobos, Cabo ≻ 232 29.55 N 112.46 W
Lobos, Estero de C 232 27.22 N 110.33 W
Lobos, Isla de I, Esp. 148 28.45 N 13.49 W
Lobos, Isla de I, Méx. 234 21.27 N 97.13 W
Lobos, Point ≻ 226 37.47 N 122.31 W
Lobos, Puerto de C 234 21.12 N 97.25 W
Lobos, Punta ≻, Chile 248 21.01 S 70.11 W
Lobos, Punta ≻, Ur. 258 34.54 S 56.15 W
Lobos de Afuera, Islas II 248 6.57 S 80.42 W
Lobos de Tierra, Isla I 248 6.27 S 80.52 W
Lo Boza 286e 33.23 S 70.46 W
Lobskoje 24 62.45 N 35.16 E
Lobstädt 54 51.08 N 12.29 E
Lobstick Lake @ 176 54.00 N 64.50 W
Löbtau ♦8 264 51.03 N 13.42 E
Loburg 54 52.07 N 12.05 E
Lobva 86 59.12 N 60.32 E
Łobżenica 30 53.16 N 17.15 E
Locana 62 45.25 N 7.27 E
Locana, Val di V 62 45.25 N 7.27 E
Locarno 58 46.10 N 8.48 E
Lo Castillo, Aeropuerto ⊠ 286e 33.23 S 70.36 W
Locate Triulzi 62 45.21 N 9.13 E
Loccum 52 52.27 N 9.08 E
Loceri 71 39.51 N 9.35 E
Loch 169 38.22 S 145.43 E
Lochaber ♦1 46 56.57 N 5.06 W
Lochailort 46 56.53 N 5.40 W
Lochaline 46 56.32 N 5.47 W
Lochar Water ≐ 44 54.59 N 3.27 W
Lochau 60 49.55 N 11.59 E
Lo Chau I 271d 22.11 N 114.15 E
Lochboisdale 46 57.09 N 7.19 W
Lochbuie 46 56.21 N 5.52 W
Lochcarron 46 57.24 N 5.30 W
Lochdonhead 46 56.26 N 5.41 W
Lochearn 284b 39.21 N 76.43 W
Lochearnhead 46 56.23 N 4.17 W
Lochem 52 52.09 N 6.25 E
Loches 50 47.08 N 1.00 E
Lochgair 46 56.03 N 5.20 W
Loch Garman → Wexford 48 52.20 N 6.27 W
Lochgelly 46 56.08 N 3.19 W
Lochgilphead 46 56.03 N 5.26 W
Lochgoilhead 46 56.10 N 4.54 W
Lochiel 168b 33.56 S 138.10 E
Lochindorb @ 46 57.24 N 3.43 W
Lochino 265b 55.42 N 37.19 E
Lochinver 46 58.09 N 5.15 W
Lochmaben 44 55.08 N 3.27 W
Lochnagar ▲ 46 56.57 N 3.16 W
Lochovice 60 49.51 N 13.59 E
Lochranza 46 55.42 N 5.18 W
Loch Raven Dam ♦6 284b 39.26 N 76.33 W
Loch Raven Reservoir @1 208 39.27 N 76.34 W
Lochristi 50 51.06 N 3.50 E
Lochsa ≐ 202 46.08 N 115.36 W
Loch Sheldrake 210 41.46 N 74.39 W
Lochvica 78 50.22 N 33.16 E
Lochwinnoch 46 55.48 N 4.38 W
Lochy, Loch @ 46 56.57 N 4.53 W
Lock 166 33.34 S 135.46 E
Locke, Calif., U.S. 226 38.15 N 121.31 W
Locke, Ind., U.S. 216 41.28 N 86.00 W
Locke, N.Y., U.S. 210 42.40 N 76.26 W
Lockeford 226 38.10 N 121.09 W
Lockeport 186 43.42 N 65.07 W
Lockerbie 44 55.07 N 3.22 W
Lockesburg 194 33.58 N 94.10 W
Lockhart, Austl. 166 35.14 S 146.43 E
Lockhart, Fla., U.S. 220 28.37 N 81.26 W
Lockhart, Tex., U.S. 222 29.53 N 97.41 W
Lock Haven 210 41.08 N 77.27 W
Lockheed Aircraft Corporation ✐3, Calif., U.S. 280 34.12 N 118.22 W
Lockheed Aircraft Corporation ✐3, Calif., U.S. 282 37.25 N 122.02 W
Lockington 216 40.12 N 84.13 W
Lockney 196 34.07 N 101.27 W
Löcknitz 54 53.27 N 14.12 E
Löcknitz ≐, D.D.R. 54 53.07 N 11.16 E
Löcknitz ≐, D.D.R. 264a 52.25 N 13.49 E
Lockport, Man., Can. 184 50.05 N 96.56 W
Lockport, Ill., U.S. 216 41.36 N 88.03 W
Lockport, La., U.S. 194 29.38 N 90.32 W
Lockport, N.Y., U.S. 210 43.10 N 78.42 W
Lockport Lock ♦5 278 41.35 N 88.04 W
Locksley Park 210 42.45 N 78.52 W
Lockvattnet @ 40 59.03 N 17.05 E
Lockview 279b 40.10 N 79.55 W
Lockwillow 273d 26.17 S 27.50 E
Lockwood, Calif., U.S. 226 35.56 N 121.05 W
Lockwood, Mo., U.S. 194 37.23 N 93.57 W
Lockwood Corners 214 41.00 N 81.34 W
Lockyer Creek ≐ 171a 27.25 S 152.36 E
Locminé 50 47.53 N 2.50 W
Loc-ninh 110 11.51 N 106.36 E
Loco, Bayou ≐ 222 31.28 N 94.44 W
Locon 50 50.34 N 2.40 E
Locorotondo 68 40.45 N 17.20 E
Locri 68 38.14 N 16.16 E
Locri Epizefiri ⊥ 68 38.12 N 16.13 E
Locroja 248 12.41 S 74.26 W
Locsin 116 13.09 N 123.43 E
Locumba 248 17.36 S 70.46 W
Locumba ≐ 248 17.54 S 70.57 W
Locust 208 40.24 N 74.01 W
Locust Creek ≐ 194 39.40 N 93.17 W
Locust Fork ≐ 194 33.33 N 87.11 W
Locust Grove, N.Y., U.S. 276 40.48 N 73.30 W
Locust Grove, Okla., U.S. 196 36.12 N 95.10 W
Locust Lake State Park ♦ 208 40.46 N 76.08 W
Locust Point ≻ 276 40.49 N 73.48 W
Locust Valley 210 40.53 N 73.36 W
Lod (Lydda) 132 31.58 N 34.54 E
Lod, Nemel-Te'ufa ⊠ 132 31.59 N 34.53 E
Loda 216 40.31 N 88.04 W
Lodal Creek ≐ 285 40.14 N 75.27 W
Löddeköpinge 41 55.46 N 13.01 E
Loddenhøj ▲2 41 56.13 N 9.48 E
Loddon 42 52.32 N 1.29 E
Loddon ≐, Austl. 169 35.41 S 143.55 E
Loddon ≐, Eng., U.K. 42 51.30 N 0.53 W
Lodè 71 40.35 N 9.32 E
Lodejnoje Polje 26 60.44 N 33.30 E
Lodenau 54 51.24 N 14.57 E
Löderburg 54 51.52 N 11.32 E
Lodève 32 43.43 N 3.19 E
Lodge Creek ≐ 202 48.36 N 109.15 W
Lodge Grass 202 45.19 N 107.22 W
Lodgepole, Alta., Can. 182 53.06 N 115.19 W
Lodgepole, Nebr., U.S. 198 41.09 N 102.38 W
Lodgepole Creek ≐ 198 41.02 N 102.10 W
Lodhāsuli 126 22.19 N 87.03 E
Lodhrān 123 29.32 N 71.38 E
Lodi, It. 62 45.19 N 9.30 E
Lodi, Calif., U.S. 226 38.08 N 121.16 W
Lodi, N.J., U.S. 210 40.53 N 74.05 W
Lodi, N.Y., U.S. 210 42.37 N 76.50 W
Lodi, Ohio, U.S. 214 41.03 N 82.01 W
Lodi, Wis., U.S. 190 43.19 N 89.32 W
Lodi Park ♦ 272a 28.36 N 77.13 E
Lodi Vecchio 62 45.18 N 9.24 E
Lodja 152 3.29 S 23.26 E
Lodosa 34 42.25 N 2.05 W
Lodoyo 115a 8.10 S 112.13 E
Lodrone 64 45.50 N 10.32 E
Lods 58 47.03 N 6.15 E
Lodsch → Łódź 30 51.46 N 19.30 E
Lodwar 154 3.07 N 35.36 E
Łódź 30 51.46 N 19.30 E
Loe Agra 123 34.35 N 71.43 E
Loei 110 17.29 N 101.35 E
Loei ≐ 110 17.51 N 101.37 E
Loen 26 61.52 N 6.52 E
Loenen 52 52.07 N 6.01 E
Loengo 152 4.45 S 26.27 E
Loeriesfontein 158 30.56 S 19.26 E
Lo Espejo 286e 33.32 S 70.43 W
Lofer 64 47.35 N 12.41 E
Loffa □6 150 7.40 N 10.00 W
Loffa ≐ 150 6.36 N 11.08 W
Löffingen 58 47.53 N 8.20 E
Lofoten II 24 68.30 N 15.00 E
Lofoten Basin ≐1 10 71.00 N 5.00 E
Lofthus 26 60.20 N 6.40 E
Loftus, Austl. 274a 34.03 S 151.03 E
Loftus, Eng., U.K. 44 54.33 N 0.53 W
Lofty, Mount ▲, Austl. 168b 34.59 S 138.42 E
Lofty, Mount ▲, Austl. 274b 37.43 S 145.17 E
Log 80 49.29 N 43.52 E
Loga, B.R.D. 52 53.14 N 7.29 E
Loga, Niger 150 13.37 N 3.14 E
Logačovka 80 52.23 N 52.21 E
Logan, Iowa, U.S. 198 41.39 N 95.47 W
Logan, Kans., U.S. 198 39.40 N 99.34 W
Logan, N. Mex., U.S. 196 35.22 N 103.25 W
Logan, Ohio, U.S. 188 39.32 N 82.25 W
Logan, Utah, U.S. 200 41.44 N 111.50 W
Logan, W. Va., U.S. 188 37.51 N 81.59 W
Logan □6, Ill., U.S. 219 40.09 N 89.22 W
Logan □6, Ohio, U.S. 216 40.22 N 83.46 W
Logan ♦8 285 40.02 N 75.09 W
Logan ≐, Austl. 171a 27.43 S 153.18 E
Logan ≐, Alta., Can. 182 55.09 N 111.42 W
Logan ≐, Utah, U.S. 200 41.44 N 111.57 W
Logan, Mount ▲, Yukon, Can. 180 60.34 N 140.24 W
Logan, Mount ▲, Wash., U.S. 224 48.32 N 120.57 W
Logan Creek ≐, Calif., U.S. 226 39.22 N 122.06 W
Logan Creek ≐, Mo., U.S. 194 37.11 N 90.49 W
Logan Creek ≐, Nebr., U.S. 198 41.37 N 96.29 W
Logandale 204 36.36 N 114.29 W
Logan International Airport ⊠ 283 42.22 N 71.00 W
Logan Lake @ 212 44.52 N 78.59 W
Logan Martin Lake @1 194 33.40 N 86.15 W
Logan Mountains ⛰ 180 61.30 N 129.00 W
Logan Pass)(202 48.42 N 113.43 W
Logansport, Ind., U.S. 216 40.45 N 86.21 W
Logansport, La., U.S. 194 31.58 N 93.58 W
Logan Square ♦8 278 41.56 N 87.42 W
Loganton 210 41.02 N 77.18 W
Loganville, Ga., U.S. 192 33.50 N 83.54 W
Loganville, Pa., U.S. 208 39.52 N 76.42 W
Logården @ 40 60.37 N 16.00 E
Lögdeälven ≐ 26 63.33 N 19.25 E
Logduz 76 60.00 N 44.41 E
Loge ≐, Ang. 152 10.12 S 17.00 E
Loge ≐, Ang. 152 7.49 S 13.06 E
Logia 164 2.55 S 151.27 E
Loginovo 82 55.42 N 38.44 E
Logirim 154 4.43 N 33.14 E
Logišin 76 52.20 N 25.59 E
Lognes 261 48.50 N 2.38 E
Lognes-Émerainville, Aérodrome de ⊠ 261 48.49 N 2.37 E
Logo 154 5.20 N 30.18 E
Logojsk 76 54.12 N 27.49 E
Logone ≐ 146 12.06 N 15.02 E
Logone Birni 146 11.47 N 15.06 E
Logone Gana 146 11.33 N 15.09 E
Logone Occidental □5 146 8.50 N 16.00 E
Logone Occidental ≐ 146 9.07 N 16.26 E
Logone Oriental □5 146 8.15 N 16.20 E
Logone Oriental ≐ 146 9.07 N 16.26 E
Logovskij 80 48.26 N 43.23 E
Log pod Mangartom 64 46.24 N 13.36 E
Logroño 34 42.28 N 2.27 W
Logrosán 34 39.20 N 5.29 W
Løgstør 26 56.58 N 9.15 E
Løgten 41 56.17 N 10.19 E
Logudoro ♦1 71 40.35 N 8.40 E
Logue Brook Dam ♦6 168a 33.00 S 115.57 E
Løgumgårde 41 55.05 N 8.57 E
Løgumkloster 41 55.03 N 8.57 E
Logumukum 154 0.27 N 36.05 E
Logy Creek ≐ 224 46.11 N 120.35 W
Loh I 175f 13.21 S 166.38 E
Lohāgara 126 23.11 N 89.39 E
Lohals 41 55.08 N 10.55 E
Lohārdaga 124 23.26 N 84.41 E
Lohāru 120 28.27 N 75.49 E
Lohatlha 158 28.02 S 23.04 E
Lohausen ♦8 263 51.16 N 6.44 E
Lohauserholz ♦8 263 51.39 N 7.48 E
Lohberg 263 51.35 N 6.46 E
Löhdorf ♦8 263 51.09 N 7.01 E
Lo Hermida 286e 33.29 S 70.33 W
Lohfelden 56 51.16 N 9.32 E
Lohheide 263 51.30 N 6.40 E
Lohiān 123 31.10 N 75.11 E
Lohiniva 24 67.10 N 24.58 E
Lohja 26 60.15 N 24.05 E
Lohjan harju ▲ 26 60.15 N 24.30 E
Lohjanjärvi @ 26 60.15 N 23.55 E
Löhlbach 56 51.04 N 8.58 E
Lohma 60 49.37 N 12.26 E
Lohmar 56 50.50 N 7.13 E
Lohme, D.D.R. 54 54.35 N 13.37 E
Löhme, D.D.R. 264a 52.37 N 13.40 E
Lohmen, D.D.R. 54 50.59 N 13.59 E
Lohmen, D.D.R. 54 53.41 N 12.05 E
Lohmühle 263 51.31 N 6.40 E
Lohne, B.R.D. 52 52.42 N 8.12 E
Löhne, B.R.D. 52 52.11 N 8.41 E
Löhnen 263 51.36 N 6.39 E
Loho → Luohe 100 33.35 N 114.01 E
Lohr am Main 56 50.00 N 9.34 E
Lohrville 198 42.17 N 94.33 W
Lohsa 54 51.23 N 14.24 E
Loi, Phou ▲ 110 20.16 N 103.12 E
Loiano 66 44.16 N 11.19 E
Loibl Pass (Ljubelj))(61 46.26 N 14.16 E
Loiborsoit 154 3.52 S 36.26 E
Loi-kaw 110 19.41 N 97.13 E
Loile ≐ 152 0.52 S 20.12 E
Loimaa 26 60.51 N 23.03 E
Loimijoki ≐ 26 61.13 N 22.38 E
Loi Mwe 110 21.11 N 99.46 E
Loing ≐ 50 48.23 N 2.48 E
Loing, Canal du ≡ 50 48.22 N 2.50 E
Loir ≐ 32 47.33 N 0.32 W
Loira → Loire ≐ 32 47.16 N 2.11 W
Loire 62 45.33 N 4.48 E
Loire □5 62 45.30 N 4.00 E
Loire ≐ 32 47.16 N 2.11 W
Loire, Canal latéral à la ≡ 50 47.37 N 2.44 E
Loire-Atlantique □5 32 47.20 N 1.35 W
Loiret □5 50 47.55 N 2.20 E
Loiret ≐ 50 47.52 N 1.48 E
Loir-et-Cher □5 50 47.30 N 1.30 E
Loïs, Lac @ 190 48.34 N 78.44 W
Loisach ≐ 64 47.56 N 11.27 E
Loisia 58 46.29 N 5.27 E
Loison ≐ 56 49.30 N 5.17 E
Loitz 54 53.58 N 13.07 E
Loíza, Embalse de @1 240m 18.17 N 66.00 W
Loíza Aldea 240m 18.26 N 65.53 W
Loja, Ec. 246 4.00 S 79.13 W
Loja, Esp. 34 37.10 N 4.09 W
Loja □4 246 4.10 S 79.30 W
Lojang → Luoyang 102 34.41 N 112.28 E
Lojev 78 51.56 N 30.46 E
Lojga 24 61.05 N 44.37 E
Lojno 24 59.44 N 52.39 E
Løjt Kirkeby 41 55.05 N 9.28 E
Loka, Süd. 154 4.16 N 31.01 E
Loka, Zaïre 152 0.20 N 17.57 E
Loka brunn 40 59.36 N 14.28 E
Lokači 78 50.44 N 24.39 E
Lokako 152 2.14 S 21.45 E
Lokalema 152 1.59 N 22.17 E
Lokan ≐ 116 5.25 N 117.44 E
Lokandu 154 2.31 S 25.47 E
Lokbatan 84 40.20 N 49.43 E
Løken 26 59.48 N 11.29 E
Loken tekojärvi @1 24 67.55 N 27.40 E
Lokeren 50 51.06 N 4.00 E
Loket 54 50.09 N 12.45 E
Lokichar 154 2.23 N 35.39 E
Lokichokio 154 4.12 N 34.21 E
Lokitaung 154 4.16 N 35.45 E
Lokka 24 67.49 N 27.44 E
Løkken 26 57.22 N 9.43 E
Løkken verk 26 63.08 N 9.42 E
Lokn'a 76 56.50 N 30.09 E
Loknaš ≐ 82 56.11 N 36.04 E
Loko 150 8.02 N 7.49 E
Lokofa-Bokolongo 152 0.12 N 19.22 E
Lokoja 150 7.47 N 6.45 E
Lokolama 152 2.34 S 19.53 E
Lokolenge 152 1.11 N 22.40 E
Lokolo ≐ 152 0.43 S 19.40 E
Lokomo 152 2.41 N 15.19 E
Lokoro ≐ 152 1.43 S 18.23 E
Lokossa 150 6.38 N 1.43 E
Lokosso 150 10.19 N 3.40 W
Lokot', S.S.S.R. 76 52.34 N 34.34 E
Lokot', S.S.S.R. 86 51.11 N 81.11 E
Lokoua ≐ 273b 4.06 S 15.16 E
Loksa 76 59.35 N 25.45 E
Loks Land I 176 62.26 N 64.38 W
Loktyši 76 52.50 N 26.43 E
Lokve 64 46.01 N 13.49 E
Loky ≐ 157b 12.47 S 49.39 E
Lokyang 271c 1.20 N 103.41 E
Lol 140 6.26 N 29.37 E
Lol ≐ 140 9.13 N 28.59 E
Lóla, Ang. 152 14.22 S 13.42 E
Lola, Guinée 150 7.48 N 8.32 W
Lola, Mount ▲ 226 39.26 N 120.22 W
Lolenge 152 0.07 N 20.59 E
Loleta 204 40.38 N 124.13 W
Lolingo 152 0.55 N 22.38 E
Loliondo 154 2.03 S 35.37 E
Lolita 222 28.50 N 96.32 W
Lolland I 41 54.46 N 11.30 E
Lollar 56 50.39 N 8.42 E

Symbols in the index entries represent the broad categories identified in the key at the right. Symbols with superior numbers (⛰2) identify subcategories (see complete key on page *I · 30*).

Kartensymbole in dem Registerverzeichnis stellen die rechts in Schlüssel erklärten Kategorien dar. Symbole mit hochgestellten Ziffern (⛰2) bezeichnen Unterabteilungen einer Kategorie (vgl. vollständiger Schlüssel auf Seite *I · 30*).

Los símbolos incluidos en el texto del índice representan las grandes categorías identificadas con la clave a la derecha. Los símbolos con números en su parte superior (⛰2) identifican las subcategorías (véase la clave completa en la página *I · 30*).

Les symboles de l'index représentent les catégories indiquées dans la légende à droite. Les symboles suivis d'un indice (⛰2) représentent des sous-catégories (voir légende complète à la page *I · 30*).

Os símbolos incluídos no texto do índice representam as grandes categorias identificadas com a chave à direita. Os símbolos com números em sua parte superior (⛰2) identificam as subcategorias (veja-se a chave completa à página *I · 30*).

	English	Deutsch	Español	Français	Português
▲	Mountain	Berg	Montaña	Montagne	Montanha
⛰	Mountains	Berge	Montañas	Montagnes	Montanhas
)(	Pass	Pass	Paso	Col	Passo
V	Valley, Canyon	Tal, Cañon	Valle, Cañón	Vallée, Canyon	Vale, Canhão
≐	Plain	Ebene	Llano	Plaine	Planície
≻	Cape	Kap	Cabo	Cap	Cabo
I	Island	Insel	Isla	Île	Ilha
II	Islands	Inseln	Islas	Îles	Ilhas
♦	Other Topographic Features	Andere Topographische Objekte	Otros Elementos Topográficos	Autres données topographiques	Outros Elementos Topográficos

ESPAÑOL: Nombre / Página / Lat.°′ / Long.°′ W=Oeste — FRANÇAIS: Nom / Page / Lat.°′ / Long.°′ W=Ouest — PORTUGUÊS: Nome / Página / Lat.°′ / Long.°′ W=Oeste

Lolo, Mont., U.S. 202 46.45 N 114.05 W
Lolo, Zaïre 152 2.13 N 23.00 E
Lolo ≃ 152 1.07 S 12.28 E
Lolobau Island I 164 4.55 S 151.10 E
Lolo Creek ≃, Idaho, U.S. 202 46.45 N 116.10 W
Lolo Creek ≃, Mont., U.S. 202 46.45 N 114.03 W
Lolodorf 152 3.14 N 10.44 E
Lolo Pass)(202 46.38 N 114.35 W
Lolotique 236 13.33 N 88.21 W
Lolowai 175f 15.18 S 168.00 E
Lolui Island I 154 0.07 S 33.42 E
Lolwa 154 1.22 N 29.31 E
Lolworth Range Λ 166 20.20 S 145.15 E
Lom, Blg. 38 43.49 N 23.14 E
Lom, Česko. 54 50.37 N 13.40 E
Lom, Nor. 26 61.50 N 8.33 E
Lom, S.S.S.R. 80 57.54 N 39.12 E
Lom Λ 60 49.54 N 13.12 E
Lom ≃, Afr. 152 5.20 N 13.24 E
Lom ≃, Blg. 38 43.50 N 23.15 E
Loma 144 6.55 N 37.34 E
Loma, Point ≻ 228 32.41 N 117.14 W
Loma Blanca, Chile 286e 33.30 S 70.47 W
Loma Blanca, Méx. 200 31.35 N 106.17 W
Loma Bonita 234 18.07 N 95.53 W
Lomakino 85 40.05 N 68.10 E
Lomako ≃ 152 0.50 N 20.50 E
Loma Linda, Méx. 286a 19.28 N 99.14 W
Loma Linda, Calif., U.S. 228 34.04 N 117.16 W
Lomaloma 175g 17.17 S 178.59 W
Loma Mansa Λ 150 9.13 N 11.07 W
Lomami ≃ 138 0.46 N 24.16 E
Loma Mountains Λ 150 9.10 N 11.07 W
Loma Ridge Λ 280 33.45 N 117.43 W
Lomas 248 15.34 S 74.50 W
Lomas, Bahía C 254 52.35 S 69.05 W
Lomas Alegres 234 17.38 N 92.36 W
Lomas Chapultepec ◆8 286a 19.26 N 99.13 W
Lomas del Real 234 22.30 N 97.54 W
Lomas de Monreal 200 31.17 N 110.56 W
Lomas de Zamora 258 34.46 S 58.24 W
Lomas de Zamora □5 288 34.45 S 58.24 W
Loma Verde 258 35.16 S 58.24 W
Lomax, Ill., U.S. 190 40.41 N 91.04 W
Lomax, Tex., U.S. 222 29.41 N 95.04 W
Łomazy 30 51.55 N 23.10 E
Lomazzo 62 45.42 N 9.02 E
Lomba ≃ 152 15.36 S 21.32 E
Lombagin 112 0.55 N 124.04 E
Lombard 216 41.53 N 88.01 W
Lombarda, Serra Λ1 250 2.50 N 51.50 W
Lombardia □4 36 45.40 N 9.30 E
Lombardy 273d 26.07 S 28.08 E
Lombe 152 9.27 S 16.13 E
Lomblen, Pulau I 112 8.25 S 123.30 E
Lombo do Tejo, Mouchão do I 266c 38.52 N 9.00 W
Lombok 115b 8.30 S 116.40 E
Lombok I 115b 8.45 S 116.30 E
Lombok, Selat Ʉ 115b 8.30 S 115.50 E
Lombong 114 1.48 N 103.51 E
Lomé 150 6.08 N 1.13 E
Lomela 152 2.18 S 23.17 E
Lomela ≃ 152 0.14 S 20.42 E
Lomellina □9 62 45.15 N 8.45 E
Lomello 62 45.07 N 8.47 E
Lometa 196 31.13 N 98.24 W
Lomi 24 67.05 N 16.09 E
Lomié 152 3.10 N 13.37 E
Lomira 190 43.35 N 88.27 W
Lo Miranda 252 34.11 S 70.54 W
Lomita 228 33.48 N 118.19 W
Lom Kao 110 16.53 N 101.14 E
Lomma 41 55.41 N 13.05 E
Lommabukten C 41 55.40 N 12.58 E
Lommatzsch 54 51.12 N 13.18 E
Lomme 50 50.39 N 2.59 E
Lomme ≃ 56 50.08 N 5.10 E
Lommel 56 51.14 N 5.18 E
Lomnice nad Popelkou 30 50.32 N 15.22 E
Lomond 182 50.21 N 112.39 W
Lomond, Loch @, N.S., Can. 186 45.46 N 60.35 W
Lomond, Loch @, Ont., Can. 190 48.26 N 89.19 W
Lomond, Loch @, Scot., U.K. 46 56.05 N 4.36 W
Lomond, Loch @, Ill., U.S. 278 42.17 N 88.01 W
Lomonosov 265a 59.55 N 29.46 E
Lomonosovskij 86 52.50 N 66.28 E
Lomovatka 83 48.27 N 38.34 E
Lomovoje 24 64.01 N 40.40 E
Lompobatang, Gunung Λ 112 5.20 S 119.55 E
Lompoc 204 34.38 N 120.27 W
Lom Sak 110 16.47 N 101.15 E
Lomy 88 52.17 N 117.59 E
Łomża 30 53.11 N 22.05 E
Lonaconing 188 39.34 N 78.59 W
Lonate Pozzolo 62 45.36 N 8.45 E
Lonato 64 45.27 N 10.29 E
Lonāvale 122 18.45 N 73.25 E
Lončakovo 89 47.05 N 134.10 E
Loncoche 254 39.22 S 72.38 W
Loncon ≃ 64 45.42 N 12.47 E
Loncopué 252 38.04 S 70.37 W
Londa 126 22.06 N 90.25 E
Londela-Kaye 152 4.51 S 13.24 E
Londerzeel 50 51.00 N 4.18 E
Londinières 50 49.50 N 1.24 E
Londo 154 2.03 N 25.43 E
Londoko 89 49.02 N 131.59 E
London, Ont., Can. 212 42.59 N 81.14 W
London, Kiribati 174o 1.58 N 157.28 W
London, Eng., U.K. 42 / 260 51.30 N 0.10 W
London, Calif., U.S. 226 36.30 N 119.25 W
London, Ky., U.S. 192 37.08 N 84.05 W
London, Ohio, U.S. 218 39.53 N 83.27 W
London, Tex., U.S. 196 30.41 N 99.35 W
London, Wis., U.S. 216 43.03 N 89.01 W
London (Stansted) Airport ⊠, Eng., U.K. 42 51.40 N 0.15 E
London (Gatwick) Airport ⊠, Eng., U.K. 42 51.09 N 0.21 W
London (Heathrow) Airport ⊠, Eng., U.K. 260 51.27 N 0.28 W
London Bridge Station ◆5 260 51.30 N 0.05 W
London Colney 260 51.43 N 0.18 W
Londonderry, N.S., Can. 186 45.29 N 63.36 W
Londonderry, N. Ire., U.K. 48 55.00 N 7.19 W
Londonderry, N.H., U.S. 207 42.51 N 71.22 W
Londonderry, Ohio, U.S. 214 39.16 N 82.47 W
Londonderry, Cape ≻ 164 13.45 S 126.55 E
Londonderry, Isla I 254 55.03 S 70.35 W
Londontowne 208 38.55 N 76.33 W
London Zoo ♠ 260 51.32 N 0.09 W
Londres, Arg. 252 27.43 S 67.07 W
Londres → London, Eng., U.K. 42 51.30 N 0.10 W
Londrina 255 23.18 S 51.09 W
Lonedell 219 38.18 N 90.50 W
Lonely Lake @ 184 51.09 N 99.05 W
Lonelyville 276 40.39 N 73.11 W
Lone Mountain Λ, Nev., U.S. 204 38.02 N 117.29 W
Lone Mountain Λ, S. Dak., U.S. 198 45.23 N 103.44 W
Lone Oak, Ky., U.S. 194 37.02 N 88.40 W
Lone Oak, Tex., U.S. 222 33.01 N 95.57 W
Lone Pine 204 36.36 N 118.04 W
Lone Rock 190 43.11 N 90.12 W
Lone Star 222 32.56 N 94.43 W
Lone Tree 190 41.29 N 91.26 W
Lone Tree Creek ≃, U.S. 200 40.25 N 104.35 W
Lone Tree Creek ≃, Calif., U.S. 226 37.53 N 121.14 W
Lone Wolf 196 34.59 N 99.15 W
Long 110 18.05 N 99.50 E
Long ≃ 50 47.41 N 0.28 E
Long, Loch C 44 56.04 N 4.50 W
Longa 152 14.42 S 18.32 E
Longa ≃, Ang. 152 10.15 S 13.30 E
Longa ≃, Ang. 152 16.25 N 19.04 E
Longá ≃, Bra. 250 3.09 S 41.56 W
Longa, Proliv Ʉ 74 70.20 N 178.00 E
Longairo 154 4.30 N 32.17 E
Long Akah 112 3.19 N 114.47 E
Long'an 102 25.03 N 109.00 E
Longanqiao 89 47.31 N 124.27 E
Longare 64 45.29 N 11.36 E
Longarone 64 46.16 N 12.18 E
Longasy 60 51.58 N 35.09 E
Longaví 252 35.58 S 71.41 W
Longbangun 112 0.36 N 115.11 E
Long Barn 226 38.05 N 120.08 W
Long Bay C, Austl. 274a 33.58 S 151.16 E
Long Bay C, Barb. 241g 13.04 N 59.29 W
Long Bay C, Jam. 241q 17.51 N 77.27 W
Long Bay C, U.S. 192 33.35 N 78.45 W
Long Beach, Calif., U.S. 228 / 280 33.46 N 118.11 W
Long Beach, Miss., U.S. 194 30.22 N 89.07 W
Long Beach, N.Y., U.S. 210 40.35 N 73.41 W
Long Beach, Wash., U.S. 224 46.21 N 124.03 W
Long Beach Breakwater ◆5 280 33.43 N 118.09 W
Long Beach Middle Harbor C 280 33.45 N 118.13 W
Long Beach Municipal Airport ⊠ 280 33.49 N 118.09 W
Long Beach Naval Station ■ 280 33.45 N 118.14 W
Longbeleh 112 0.16 N 116.11 E
Longbelepai 112 2.45 N 114.04 E
Longbenton 44 55.02 N 1.35 W
Longboat Key 220 27.24 N 82.39 W
Longboat Key I 220 27.23 N 82.39 W
Long Branch, N.J., U.S. 208 40.18 N 74.00 W
Longbranch, Wash., U.S. 224 47.13 N 122.46 W
Long Branch ≃ 219 39.23 N 91.49 W
Long Buckby 42 52.19 N 1.04 W
Longbuwei 100 25.32 N 115.24 E
Long Cane Creek ≃ 192 33.57 N 82.24 W
Long Canyon V 226 38.59 N 120.41 W
Longchamp, Hippodrome de ♠ 261 48.51 N 2.14 E
Longchamps, Arg. 258 34.52 S 58.23 W
Longchamps, Bel. 56 50.03 N 5.42 E
Longchang, Zhg. 104 40.53 N 123.08 E
Longchang, Zhg. 107 29.21 N 105.17 E
Longchaumois 58 46.27 N 5.56 E
Longchêne 261 48.38 N 2.00 E
Longchuan, Zhg. 100 24.07 N 115.17 E
Longchuan, Zhg. 102 24.14 N 97.45 E
Long Creek, Ill., U.S. 219 39.48 N 88.50 W
Long Creek, Oreg., U.S. 202 44.43 N 119.06 W
Long Creek ≃ 184 49.07 N 103.00 W
Long Crendon 42 51.47 N 1.01 W
Longcun 100 23.34 N 115.33 E
Longde 102 35.28 N 106.22 E
Longdendale V 262 53.29 N 1.56 W
Long Ditton 260 51.23 N 0.20 W
Longdongtuo 107 29.59 N 106.21 E
Longdou 100 27.25 N 117.24 E
Longdu 106 31.51 N 118.56 E
Long Eaton 42 52.54 N 1.15 W
Longeau 58 47.46 N 5.18 E
Long Eddy 210 41.51 N 75.08 W
Longeville-lès-Saint-Avold 56 49.07 N 6.38 E
Longfengchang 107 30.26 N 105.38 E
Longfengkan 104 41.51 N 124.01 E
Longfengyutun 104 40.39 N 122.57 E
Longfield 260 51.24 N 0.18 E
Longford, Austl. 166 38.10 S 147.05 E
Longford, Eire 48 53.44 N 7.47 W
Longford □6 48 53.40 N 7.40 W
Longford Park ♠ 262 53.27 N 2.17 W
Longframlington 44 55.18 N 1.47 W
Longgang, Zhg. 100 29.38 N 114.57 E
Longgang, Zhg. 100 33.22 N 120.04 E
Longgang, Zhg. 100 22.42 N 113.59 E
Longgang, Zhg. 102 24.41 N 101.09 E
Longgangzi 104 42.09 N 123.26 E
Long Green 208 39.28 N 76.31 W
Long Grove 216 42.11 N 88.00 W
Longguan 105 40.47 N 115.34 E
Longgudu 100 27.45 N 116.14 E
Longguntur 112 0.13 N 112.12 E
Long Harbour 186 47.26 N 53.48 W
Long Harbour C, Newf., Can. 186 47.44 N 55.01 W
Long Harbour C, H.K. 271d 22.27 N 114.20 E
Longhe ≃ 105 39.23 N 116.49 E
Longhorn Cavern State Park ♠ 196 30.20 N 98.30 W
Longhorsley 44 55.15 N 1.46 W
Longhoughton 44 55.26 N 1.36 W
Longhua, Zhg. 98 41.17 N 117.37 E
Longhua, Zhg. 100 23.37 N 114.14 E
Longhua, Zhg. 106 31.09 N 121.26 E
Longhua Airport ⊠ 106 31.09 N 121.26 E
Longhuasi 107 28.47 N 104.08 E
Longhui (Taohuaping), Zhg. 102 27.00 N 110.59 E
Longhui, Zhg. 107 29.32 N 104.48 E
Longhuiwei 100 25.32 N 114.47 E
Longhutang 106 31.52 N 119.59 E
Longi 70 38.01 N 14.45 E
Longido 154 2.44 S 36.41 E
Longiram 112 0.02 S 115.38 E
Long Island I, Antig. 240c 17.08 N 61.45 W
Long Island I, Austl. 166 22.09 S 149.54 E
Long Island I, Ba. 238 23.15 N 75.07 W
Long Island I, Newf., Can. 186 47.35 N 54.05 W
Long Island I, N.W. Ter., Can. 176 54.50 N 79.20 W
Long Island I, N.S., Can. 186 44.20 N 66.15 W
Long Island I, Pap. N. Gui. 164 5.20 S 147.05 E
Long Island I, Alaska, U.S. 182 54.54 N 132.45 W
Long Island I, Mass., U.S. 283 42.19 N 70.58 W
Long Island I, N.Y., U.S. 188 40.50 N 73.00 W
Long Island I, Wash., U.S. 224 46.27 N 123.58 W
Long Island City ◆8 276 40.45 N 73.56 W
Long Island Sound Ʉ 188 41.05 N 72.58 W
Long Island University (C.W. Post Center) ʋ2, N.Y., U.S. 276 40.49 N 73.36 W
Long Island University ʋ2, N.Y., U.S. 276 40.41 N 73.59 W
Longitudinal, Valle V 252 36.00 S 72.00 W
Long Jetty 170 33.22 S 151.29 E
Longji 107 29.23 N 106.04 E
Longjiadian 104 42.10 N 120.47 E
Longjiang, Zhg. 89 47.19 N 123.12 E
Longjiang, Zhg. 100 22.53 N 113.04 E
Longjiang, Zhg. 100 22.59 N 116.13 E
Longjiang ≃, Zhg. 100 23.26 N 114.38 E
Longjiang ≃, Zhg. 100 22.59 N 116.18 E
Longjie Λ 102 25.15 N 98.25 E
Longjiezhen 107 29.53 N 104.32 E
Longjin 100 22.38 N 116.37 E
Longjing 100 23.53 N 112.52 E
Longjingguan)(105 40.23 N 118.08 E
Longjohn Slough ≃ 278 41.43 N 87.53 W
Longjuchang 107 30.00 N 103.59 E
Longjumeau 50 48.42 N 2.18 E
Longka, Zhg. 120 33.12 N 79.47 E
Longka, Zhg. 120 31.10 N 84.00 E
Longkamp 56 49.53 N 7.07 E
Longkang 100 33.09 N 116.54 E
Long Ke 271d 22.23 N 114.22 E
Long Key I, Fla., U.S. 220 24.49 N 80.49 W
Long Key I, Fla., U.S. 220 27.44 N 82.45 W
Long King Creek ≃ 222 30.34 N 94.58 W
Longkou, Zhg. 98 37.38 N 120.18 E
Longkou, Zhg. 100 26.11 N 115.15 E
Longkou, Zhg. 100 29.57 N 113.47 E
Longkou, Zhg. 100 32.55 N 114.59 E
Longkouqiao 85 39.40 N 77.09 E
Long Lake, Ill., U.S. 216 42.22 N 88.08 W
Long Lake, N.Y., U.S. 188 43.58 N 74.25 W
Long Lake, Tex., U.S. 222 31.39 N 95.47 W
Long Lake @, Ont., Can. 212 44.41 N 76.45 W
Long Lake @, Ont., Can. 212 45.00 N 79.36 W
Long Lake @, Mich., U.S. 190 45.12 N 83.30 W
Long Lake @, Mich., U.S. 281 42.37 N 83.44 W
Long Lake @, Mich., U.S. 281 42.36 N 83.28 W
Long Lake @, N. Dak., U.S. 198 46.43 N 100.07 W
Long Lake @, N.Y., U.S. 188 44.00 N 74.20 W
Long Lake @, Wash., U.S. 224 47.03 N 122.47 W
Long Lake Creek ≃ 198 46.40 N 100.13 W
Long Lake Shores 281 42.35 N 83.19 W
Long Lama 112 3.46 N 114.24 E
Longlangshan Λ 100 21.50 N 100.30 E
Longlaville 56 49.32 N 5.48 E
Longleaf 194 31.00 N 92.34 W
Long Leaf Park 192 34.12 N 77.56 W
Longleat ʋ 42 51.12 N 2.17 W
Long-legged Lake @ 184 50.46 N 94.08 W
Longli 102 26.26 N 106.58 E
Longlin 102 24.49 N 105.31 E
Longling 102 24.39 N 98.40 E
Longmeadow 207 42.03 N 72.34 W
Long Melford 42 52.05 N 0.43 E
Longmen, Zhg. 89 48.55 N 126.54 E
Longmen, Zhg. 100 23.44 N 114.15 E
Longmen, Zhg. 100 25.06 N 116.58 E
Longmen, Zhg. 100 24.56 N 118.04 E
Longmen, Zhg. 100 29.53 N 119.57 E
Longmen, Zhg. 100 28.14 N 114.15 E
Longmen, Zhg. 107 29.27 N 104.53 E
Longmenchang 107 30.53 N 106.10 E
Longmensuo 98 40.56 N 115.54 E
Longmentan 107 29.12 N 106.13 E
Longmiaozhen 98 40.03 N 123.42 E
Longming 102 22.59 N 107.11 E
Longmire 224 46.45 N 121.49 W
Longmont 198 40.10 N 105.06 W
Longmorn 46 57.36 N 3.17 W
Long Mountain Λ 194 36.41 N 92.26 W
Long Mountain Λ2 42 52.39 N 3.09 W
Longmu 100 24.08 N 113.12 E
Longnan 100 24.54 N 114.48 E
Longnawan 112 1.54 N 114.53 E
Long Neck ≻1 276 41.03 N 73.29 W
Long Neck Point ≻ 276 41.02 N 73.29 W
Longnüsi 107 30.23 N 106.11 E
Longny-au-Perche 50 48.32 N 0.45 E
Longobucco 68 39.27 N 16.37 E
Longperrier 261 49.03 N 2.40 E
Long Pine 198 42.32 N 99.42 W
Longping 100 29.53 N 115.41 E
Long Plains 168b 34.21 S 138.22 E
Long Point, Austl. 274a 34.01 S 150.54 E
Long Point, Ill., U.S. 216 41.00 N 88.54 W
Long Point ≻, Ba. 240b 25.01 N 77.20 W
Long Point ≻, Man., Can. 184 53.02 N 98.40 W
Long Point ≻, Newf., Can. 186 48.48 N 58.46 W
Long Point ≻, Ont., Can. 212 44.06 N 76.29 W
Long Point ≻, Pil. 116 9.39 N 118.20 E
Long Point ≻, Calif., U.S. 280 33.44 N 118.23 W
Long Point ≻, Vir. Is., U.S. 240m 18.18 N 64.53 W
Long Point ≻, Vir. Is., U.S. 241n 17.41 N 64.50 W
Long Point ≻1 214 42.34 N 80.15 W
Long Point ≻ 212 44.32 N 80.18 W
Long Point Bay C 212 42.40 N 80.14 W
Long Point Creek ≃ 216 41.02 N 88.48 W
Long Point Provincial Park ♠ 214 42.35 N 80.35 W
Long Pond @, U.S. 283 42.41 N 71.21 W
Long Pond @, Mass., U.S. 207 41.43 N 70.04 W
Long Pond @, Mass., U.S. 207 41.48 N 70.57 W
Longpont 50 49.16 N 3.13 E
Longport 208 39.19 N 74.32 W
Long Prairie 198 45.59 N 94.52 W
Long Prairie ≃ 198 46.20 N 94.36 W
Longpré-les-Corps-Saints 50 50.01 N 1.59 E
Long Preston 44 54.02 N 2.15 W
Longqiantai 104 41.23 N 120.52 E
Longqu, Zhg. 98 34.16 N 114.49 E
Longqu, Zhg. 98 34.54 N 116.47 E
Longquan 100 28.04 N 119.07 E
Longquanguan 98 38.55 N 113.51 E
Longquanshan Λ 107 30.00 N 104.10 E
Longquansi 107 30.21 N 104.39 E
Longquanyi 107 30.34 N 104.16 E
Long Range Mountains Λ 186 49.20 N 57.30 W
Longreach 166 23.26 S 144.15 E
Long Reach C 186 45.26 N 66.09 W
Long Reach Ʉ 212 44.07 N 77.04 W
Long Reef ✢2 164 11.11 S 151.40 E
Long Reef Point ≻ 274a 33.45 S 151.19 E
Longridge 44 53.51 N 2.36 W
Long Run ≃, Ill., U.S. 278 41.37 N 88.03 W
Long Run ≃, Pa., U.S. 279b 40.20 N 79.48 W
Long Sault Dam ◆6 206 45.00 N 74.45 W
Long Sault Islands II 206 45.00 N 74.55 W
Longsegah 112 2.15 N 116.42 E
Longshan, Zhg. 100 22.59 N 113.17 E
Longshan, Zhg. 100 33.36 N 116.18 E
Longshan, Zhg. 102 29.28 N 109.20 E
Longshansuo 100 30.05 N 121.33 E
Longsheng 102 25.42 N 110.01 E
Longshengchang 107 30.36 N 105.21 E
Longshengzhuang 98 40.40 N 113.21 E
Longshizhen, Zhg. 107 30.12 N 106.26 E
Longshizhen, Zhg. 107 29.23 N 105.10 E
Longshuizhen 107 29.33 N 105.45 E
Longs Peak Λ 200 40.15 N 105.37 W
Long Sutton 42 52.47 N 0.08 E
Longtaichang 107 30.04 N 105.34 E
Longtan, Zhg. 100 23.40 N 113.24 E
Longtan, Zhg. 102 28.20 N 108.52 E
Longtan, Zhg. 106 31.20 N 118.45 E
Longtan, Zhg. 106 32.11 N 119.04 E
Longtan, Zhg. 107 29.19 N 104.35 E
Longtansi 107 30.42 N 104.10 E
Long Teru 112 3.52 N 114.15 E
Long-thanh 110 10.47 N 106.57 E
Longtian 100 25.38 N 119.28 E
Longtian'an 106 31.10 N 120.49 E
Long Tom ≃ 202 44.23 N 123.15 W
Longton, Eng., U.K. 42 53.00 N 2.09 W
Longton, Eng., U.K. 262 53.44 N 2.48 W
Longton, Kans., U.S. 198 37.23 N 96.05 W
Longtou 98 38.51 N 121.18 E
Longtoupu 100 27.54 N 113.12 E
Longtouwei 100 25.14 N 115.24 E
Longtown 44 55.01 N 2.58 W
Long-truong 269c 10.49 N 106.49 E
Longué 32 47.23 N 0.06 W
Longueau 50 49.52 N 2.21 E
Longuesse 261 49.04 N 1.56 E
Longueuil 206 45.32 N 73.30 W
Longueville, Austl. 274a 33.50 S 151.10 E
Longueville, Fr. 50 48.31 N 3.15 E
Longueville-sur-Scie 50 49.48 N 1.06 E
Longuyon 56 49.26 N 5.36 E
Long Valley 210 40.47 N 74.47 W
Long Valley Creek ≃, Calif., U.S. 226 39.03 N 122.34 W
Long Valley Creek ≃, Nev., U.S. 226 39.31 N 119.39 W
Long Valley Wash V 204 39.56 N 116.39 W
Longvic 58 47.17 N 5.04 E
Longview, Alta., Can. 182 50.32 N 114.14 W
Longview, N.C., U.S. 192 35.44 N 81.23 W
Longview, Tex., U.S. 222 32.30 N 94.44 W
Longview, Wash., U.S. 224 46.08 N 122.57 W
Longview Heights 222 32.30 N 94.41 W
Longvilliers 261 48.35 N 2.00 E
Longvilly 56 50.01 N 5.50 E
Longwai 112 0.42 N 116.39 E
Longwan 105 38.57 N 116.10 E
Longwangmiao, Zhg. 98 36.12 N 115.13 E
Longwangmiao, Zhg. 102 40.36 N 95.52 E
Longwangmiao, Zhg. 104 42.35 N 123.42 E
Longwangmiao, Zhg. 104 41.38 N 121.04 E
Longwarry 169 38.07 S 145.46 E
Longwen 100 24.36 N 116.21 E
Longwo 100 23.28 N 115.17 E
Longwokou 106 32.18 N 119.52 E
Longwood 220 28.42 N 81.21 W
Longwood Gardens ♠ 285 39.52 N 75.40 W
Longwood Lake 276 40.59 N 74.52 W
Longwood Park 192 34.55 N 79.42 W
Longworth 182 53.55 N 121.28 W
Longwy 56 49.31 N 5.46 E
Longxi → Zhangzhou, Zhg. 100 24.33 N 117.39 E
Longxi, Zhg. 102 34.56 N 104.47 E
Longxi, Zhg. 107 29.59 N 106.09 E
Longxi ≃, Zhg. 100 26.24 N 118.26 E
Longxi ≃, Zhg. 106 30.49 N 120.06 E
Longxian, Zhg. 102 34.51 N 106.59 E
Longxian, Zhg. 107 29.09 N 105.50 E
Longxumen 98 40.37 N 118.31 E
Long-xuyen 110 10.23 N 105.25 E
Longyan 100 25.08 N 117.02 E
Longyou 100 29.02 N 119.10 E
Longyouhe ≃ 106 32.08 N 120.38 E
Longyuan 100 24.56 N 114.27 E
Longzhen 89 48.41 N 126.42 E
Longzhou 102 22.22 N 106.52 E
Longzhu 100 28.25 N 92.31 E
Loni 272a 28.45 N 77.17 E
Lonigo 64 45.23 N 11.23 E
Löningen 52 52.44 N 7.46 E
Lonkala 152 4.37 S 23.14 E
Lönnewitz 54 51.34 N 13.11 E
Lonny 56 49.49 N 4.35 E
Lonoke 194 34.47 N 91.54 W
Lönsboda 26 56.24 N 14.19 E
Lønsdal 24 66.44 N 15.28 E
Lonsdale 190 44.29 N 93.25 W
Lonsdale, Point ≻ 169 38.17 S 144.37 E
Lons-le-Saunier 58 46.40 N 5.33 E
Lonton 110 25.06 N 96.17 E
Lontra ≃ 250 6.37 S 48.39 W
Lontra, Ribeirão ≃ 255 21.28 S 53.37 W
Lonua ≃ 152 1.16 S 22.36 E
Loo 84 43.43 N 39.36 E
Looc 116 12.16 N 121.59 E
Loogootee 194 38.41 N 86.55 W
Looking Glass ≃ 216 42.52 N 84.54 W
Lookout 210 41.47 N 75.11 W
Lookout, Cape ≻, N.C., U.S. 192 34.35 N 76.32 W
Lookout, Cape ≻, Oreg., U.S. 224 45.20 N 124.00 W
Lookout, Point ≻, Austl. 171a 27.26 S 153.33 E
Lookout, Point ≻, Md., U.S. 208 38.02 N 76.19 W
Lookout Mountain Λ, U.S. 194 34.25 N 85.40 W
Lookout Mountain Λ, Oreg., U.S. 202 44.20 N 120.22 W
Lookout Mountain Λ, Oreg., U.S. 224 45.21 N 121.31 W
Lookout Mountain Λ, Wash., U.S. 224 48.40 N 122.22 W
Lookout Pass)(202 47.27 N 115.42 W
Lookout Point Lake @1 202 43.52 N 122.40 W
Lookout Ridge Λ 180 69.07 N 158.36 W
Loolmalassin Λ1 154 3.03 S 35.49 E
Loomis, Calif., U.S. 226 38.49 N 121.12 W
Loomis, Nebr., U.S. 198 40.29 N 99.31 W
Loon 116 9.48 N 123.47 E
Loon ≃ 184 55.50 N 101.59 W
Loon Creek ≃ 202 44.49 N 114.49 W
Loongana 162 30.57 S 127.02 E
Loon Lake @, Can. 184 55.51 N 102.00 W
Loon Lake @, Mich., U.S. 281 42.41 N 83.22 W
Loon Lake @1 226 39.00 N 120.18 W
Loon op Zand 52 51.38 N 5.04 E
Loop 196 32.55 N 102.25 W
Loop ◆8 278 41.53 N 87.38 W
Loop Head ≻ 48 52.34 N 9.56 W
Lo Ortuzar 286e 33.28 S 70.45 W
Loos 50 50.37 N 3.01 E
Loosduinen ◆8 52 52.04 N 4.13 E
Loose, B.R.D. 54 54.31 N 9.53 E
Loose, Eng., U.K. 260 51.14 N 0.31 E
Loose Creek 219 38.30 N 91.57 W
Lop 110 13.18 N 107.37 E
Lopandino 76 52.28 N 34.49 E
Lopanka 80 46.24 N 40.59 E
Lopar'ovo 80 58.20 N 42.41 E
Lopasn'a ≃ 82 54.51 N 37.52 E
Lopatiči 76 53.34 N 30.53 E
Lopatin, S.S.S.R. 78 50.13 N 24.50 E
Lopatin, S.S.S.R. 84 43.53 N 47.41 E
Lopatina, Gora Λ 89 50.52 N 143.10 E
Lopatino, S.S.S.R. 80 52.37 N 45.47 E
Lopatino, S.S.S.R. 82 54.45 N 37.00 E
Lopatino, S.S.S.R. 89 48.24 N 142.15 E
Lopatinskij 82 55.21 N 38.34 E
Lopatka, Mys ≻ 74 50.52 N 156.40 E
Lopatovo 76 56.08 N 29.12 E
Lop Buri 110 14.48 N 100.37 E
Lopevi I 175f 16.30 S 168.21 E
Lopez, Pa., U.S. 210 41.27 N 76.20 W
Lopez, Wash., U.S. 224 48.31 N 122.54 W
López, Arroyo de ≃ 258 35.26 S 57.35 W
Lopez, Cap ≻ 152 0.37 S 8.43 E
Lopez Bay C 116 13.56 N 122.12 E
López Collada 232 31.45 N 113.55 W
Lopez Dam ◆6 226 35.12 N 120.29 W
Lopez Island I 224 48.30 N 122.54 W
Lopik 52 51.58 N 4.56 E
Lop Nor → Luobubo @ 90 40.20 N 90.15 E
Lopori ≃ 152 1.14 N 19.49 E
Lopotovo 82 56.04 N 36.49 E
Loppersum 52 53.19 N 6.45 E
Loppi 26 60.43 N 24.27 E
Lo Prado Arriba 286e 33.26 S 70.45 W
Lopšen'ga 24 64.58 N 37.41 E
L'Opton Ruisseau ≃ 261 48.52 N 1.29 E
Lopt'uga 24 63.16 N 47.56 E
Lopuchovka, S.S.S.R. 80 51.59 N 44.42 E
Lopuchovka, S.S.S.R. 80 50.37 N 44.29 E
Łopuszno 30 50.57 N 20.15 E
Lora 123 33.53 N 73.17 E
Lora ≃ 246 9.25 N 72.25 W
Lora, Hāmūn-i- @ 128 29.20 N 64.50 E
Lora Creek ≃ 162 28.10 S 135.22 E
Lora del Río 34 37.39 N 5.32 W
Lorain 214 / 279a 41.28 N 82.10 W
Lorain □6 214 41.22 N 82.06 W
Lorain County Regional Airport ⊠ 279a 41.20 N 82.11 W
Loraine, Calif., U.S. 228 35.19 N 118.25 W
Loraine, Ill., U.S. 219 40.09 N 91.13 W
Loraine, Tex., U.S. 196 32.25 N 100.43 W
Loralai 120 30.22 N 68.36 E
Loramie, Lake @1 216 40.23 N 84.18 W
Loramie Creek ≃ 216 40.11 N 84.14 W
Lorca 34 37.40 N 1.42 W
Lorch, B.R.D. 56 50.02 N 7.48 E
Lorch, B.R.D. 56 48.49 N 9.40 E
Lorchhausen 56 50.03 N 7.47 E
Lord Howe Island I 160 31.33 S 159.05 E
Lord Howe Rise ✢3 14 29.00 S 162.30 E
Lord Mayor Bay C 176 69.44 N 92.00 W
Lordsburg 200 32.21 N 108.43 W
Lord's Cricket Ground ♠ 260 51.32 N 0.10 W
Lordstown 214 41.09 N 80.53 W
Lords Valley 210 41.23 N 75.04 W
Loreauville 194 30.03 N 91.44 W
Loreley ♠ 56 50.08 N 7.44 E
Lorena, Bra. 256 22.44 S 45.08 W
Lorena, Tex., U.S. 222 31.23 N 97.13 W
Lorengau 164 2.00 S 147.15 E
Lorentz ≃ 164 5.23 S 138.04 E
Lorentzen 56 48.57 N 7.10 E
Lorenzago di Cadore 64 46.29 N 12.28 E
Lorenzo 196 33.40 N 101.32 W
Lorenzo Geyres (Queguay) 252 32.05 S 57.55 W
Loreo 64 45.04 N 12.11 E
Lorestān □8 128 33.30 N 48.30 E
Loreto, Arg. 252 27.46 S 57.17 W
Loreto, Bol. 248 15.13 S 64.40 W
Loreto, Bra. 250 7.05 S 45.09 W
Loreto, Col. 246 3.48 S 70.15 W
Loreto, It. 66 43.26 N 13.36 E
Loreto, Méx. 232 26.01 N 111.21 W
Loreto, Méx. 234 22.16 N 101.58 W
Loreto, Para. 252 23.16 S 57.11 W
Loreto, Pil. 116 10.21 N 125.34 E
Loreto, Pil. 116 8.12 N 125.45 E
Loreto □5 246 3.00 S 75.00 W
Loreto Aprutino 66 42.26 N 13.59 E
Lorette, Man., Can. 184 49.44 N 96.52 W
Lorette, Fr. 62 45.31 N 4.35 E
Loretteville 206 46.51 N 71.21 W
Loretto → Loreto, It. 66 43.26 N 13.36 E
Loretto, Pa., U.S. 214 40.31 N 78.38 W
Loretto, Tenn., U.S. 194 35.05 N 87.26 W
Lorgues 62 43.29 N 6.22 E
Lorian Swamp ☷ 154 0.40 N 39.35 E
Lorica 246 9.14 N 75.49 W
Lorida 220 27.27 N 81.15 W
Lorient 32 47.45 N 3.22 W
L'Orignal 206 45.37 N 74.42 W
Lorimor 194 41.07 N 94.03 W
Loring, Aeródromo de ⊠ 266a 40.22 N 3.47 W
Loring Air Force Base ■ 186 46.57 N 67.54 W
Lorino 180 65.30 N 171.43 W
Loriol-sur-Drôme 62 44.45 N 4.49 E
Loris 192 34.04 N 78.53 W
Lorman 194 31.49 N 91.03 W
L'Orme 261 48.39 N 1.41 E
Lormes 50 47.17 N 3.49 E
Lorn, Firth of C1 46 56.20 N 5.45 W
Lorna Glen 162 26.14 S 121.33 E
Lorne, Austl. 169 38.33 S 143.59 E
Lorne, N.B., Can. 186 47.53 N 66.08 W
Loro Ciuffenna 66 43.35 N 11.38 E
Loronyo 154 4.39 N 32.38 E
Lorquin 58 48.40 N 7.00 E
Lörrach 58 47.37 N 7.40 E
Lorrain, Rivière du ≃ 240e 14.50 N 61.03 W
Lorraine □9 32 49.00 N 6.00 E
Lorrez-le-Bocage 50 48.14 N 2.54 E
Lorris 50 47.53 N 2.31 E
Lorsch 56 49.39 N 8.34 E
Lorsica 62 44.26 N 9.16 E
Lorup 52 52.55 N 7.38 E
Lorze ≃ 58 47.15 N 8.25 E
Los 26 61.44 N 15.10 E
Los, Îles de II 150 9.30 N 13.48 W
Losa, Nuraghe ⊥ 71 40.07 N 8.46 E
Losada ≃ 246 2.12 N 73.55 W
Los Aguacates 286c 10.35 N 66.48 W
Los Alamitos 280 33.48 N 118.04 W
Los Alamitos Naval Air Station ■ 228 33.47 N 118.03 W
Los Alamitos Race Course ♠ 280 33.48 N 118.03 W
Los Alamos, Méx. 232 28.40 N 103.30 W
Los Alamos, Calif., U.S. 204 34.44 N 120.17 W
Los Alamos, N. Mex., U.S. 200 35.53 N 106.19 W
Los Aldamas 232 26.03 N 99.11 W
Los Altos, Méx. 196 26.14 N 98.28 W
Los Altos, Calif., U.S. 226 37.23 N 122.06 W
Los Altos Hills 226 37.21 N 122.08 W
Los Amates, Guat. 236 15.16 N 89.06 W
Los Amates, Méx. 234 18.08 N 102.15 W
Los Andes 252 32.50 S 70.37 W
Los Angeles, Chile 252 37.28 S 72.21 W
Los Angeles, Calif., U.S. 228 / 280 34.03 N 118.15 W
Los Angeles □6 228 34.20 N 118.10 W
Los Angeles ≃ 228 33.46 N 118.12 W
Los Angeles Aqueduct ≅1 204 35.22 N 118.05 W
Los Angeles County Art Museum ʋ 280 34.05 N 118.22 W
Los Angeles County Fairgrounds ♠ 280 34.05 N 117.46 W
Los Angeles Harbor C 280 33.42 N 118.16 W
Los Angeles International Airport ⊠ 228 33.56 N 118.24 W
Los Antiguos 254 46.33 S 71.37 W
Losantville 218 40.02 N 85.11 W
Losap I1 14 6.54 N 152.44 E
Los Arabos 240p 22.44 N 80.43 W
Losarang 115a 6.24 S 108.10 E
Los Arroyos, Laguna de @ 248 12.38 S 65.00 W
Los Banos 226 37.04 N 120.51 W
Los Banos Creek ≃ 226 37.20 N 120.57 W
Los Banos Creek, North Fork ≃ 226 36.57 N 121.07 W
Los Banos Creek, South Fork ≃ 226 36.57 N 121.07 W
Los Berros 252 31.57 S 68.39 W
Los Blancos 252 23.36 S 62.36 W
Los Burros 232 25.03 N 110.50 W
Los Cardales 258 34.20 S 58.59 W
Los Cerrillos, Arg. 252 31.57 S 65.28 W
Los Cerrillos, Ur. 258 34.37 S 56.22 W
Los Cerrillos, Aeropuerto ⊠ 286e 33.30 S 70.43 W
Los Cerritos Center ◆9 280 33.52 N 118.05 W
Los Chacos 248 14.33 S 62.11 W
Löschenrod 56 50.30 N 9.41 E
Los Chiles 236 11.02 N 84.43 W
Los Conquistadores 252 30.36 S 58.28 W
Los Coronados, Islas II 204 32.25 N 117.15 W
Los Coyotes Indian Reservation ◆4 204 33.20 N 116.35 W
Los Cuatro Álamos 286e 33.32 S 70.44 W
Los Dos Caminos 286c 10.31 N 66.50 W
Los Ebanos, Méx. 232 24.40 N 97.45 W
Los Ebanos, Tex., U.S. 196 26.14 N 98.34 W
Loseley House ⊥ 260 51.13 N 0.36 W
Los Esclavos ≃ 236 13.50 N 90.20 W
Losevo 78 50.40 N 40.02 E
Los Flamencos, Laguna @ 258 35.36 S 58.42 W
Los Frentones 252 26.25 S 61.25 W
Los Fresnos 196 26.04 N 97.29 W
Los Garzas 196 26.23 N 99.46 W
Los Gatos 226 37.14 N 121.59 W
Los Gatos Creek ≃, Calif., U.S. 226 37.20 N 121.54 W
Los Gatos Creek ≃, Calif., U.S. 226 36.13 N 120.08 W
Los Glaciares, Parque Nacional ♠ 254 49.52 S 73.05 W
Los Guerras 196 26.25 N 99.05 W
Loshan → Leshan 107 29.34 N 103.45 E
Los Haros 234 22.46 N 102.57 W
Losheim 56 49.30 N 6.44 E
Los Hermanos, Islas II 246 11.45 N 64.25 W
Los Herreras, Méx. 196 25.55 N 99.24 W
Los Herreras, Méx. 232 25.10 N 105.31 W
Losi 273a 6.40 N 3.31 E
Losice 30 52.14 N 22.43 E
Los Indios, Canal de Ʉ 240p 21.56 N 83.16 W
Lošinj, Otok I 36 44.36 N 14.24 E
Losinoborskaja 86 58.27 N 89.28 E
Losino-Petrovskij 82 55.52 N 38.12 E
Losinovka 78 50.51 N 31.54 E
Los Jazmines, Presa @1 286a 19.25 N 99.16 W
Los Juríes 252 28.28 S 62.06 W
Loškar'ovka 78 47.57 N 34.12 E
Loskopdam ◆6 156 25.23 S 29.20 E
Loskop Game Reserve ◆4 156 25.23 S 29.20 E
Los Lagos 254 39.51 S 72.50 W
Los Llanos 240m 18.03 N 66.24 W
Los Llanos [de Aridane] 148 28.39 N 17.54 W
Los López 196 26.15 N 99.05 W
Los Lunas 200 34.48 N 106.44 W
Los Mármoles, Parque Nacional ♠ 234 20.55 N 99.12 W
Los Médanos, Istmo de •3 241s 11.35 N 69.45 W
Los Menucos 254 40.50 S 68.08 W
Los Metates 234 23.46 N 106.02 W
Los Micos, Laguna de C 236 15.45 N 87.36 W
Los'mino 76 55.04 N 34.24 E
Los Mochis 232 25.45 N 108.57 W
Los Molinos 204 40.03 N 122.06 W
Los Muermos 254 41.24 S 73.29 W
Los Naranjos 286c 10.27 N 66.48 W
Los Navalmorales 34 39.43 N 4.38 W
Lošnica 76 54.17 N 28.46 E
Los Nietos 280 33.58 N 118.04 W
Løsning 41 55.48 N 9.42 E
Los Nogales 196 26.16 N 99.43 W
Los Olmos Creek ≃, Tex., U.S. 196 26.21 N 98.48 W
Los Olmos Creek ≃, Tex., U.S. 196 27.20 N 97.40 W
Los Osos 226 35.19 N 120.50 W
Los Palacios, Arg. 252 29.22 S 68.11 W
Los Palacios, Cuba 240p 22.35 N 83.15 W
Los Palacios y Villafranca 34 37.10 N 5.56 W
Los Perros, Arroyo ≃ 288 34.37 S 58.46 W
Los Pinos ◆8 286b 23.04 N 82.23 W
Los Pinos ≃ 200 36.56 N 107.36 W
Los Placeres 234 18.13 N 100.54 W
Los Polvorines 288 34.30 S 58.41 W
Los Quillayes 286e 33.34 S 70.37 W
Los Quirquinchos 252 33.22 S 61.43 W
Los Rábanos 240m 18.11 N 66.50 W
Los Ramones 196 25.42 N 99.37 W
≃S Remedios 286a 19.31 N 99.05
Los Reyes de Salgado 234 19.35 N 102.29 W
Los Reyes la Paz 286a 19.21 N 98.58 W
Los Ríos □4 246 1.30 S 79.25 W
Los Rodríguez 232 27.11 N 101.21 W
Los Roques, Islas II 246 11.50 N 66.45 W
Lossa 54 51.13 N 11.25 E
Lossa ≃ 54 51.18 N 11.10 E
Los Santos 246 7.56 N 80.25 W
Los Santos □4 236 7.55 N 80.25 W
Los Santos de Maimona 34 38.27 N 6.23 W
Los Sauces 252 37.58 S 72.50 W
Lossburg 58 48.25 N 8.27 E
Lössel 263 51.21 N 7.39 E
Losser 52 52.15 N 7.00 E
Los Serranos 228 33.59 N 117.42 W
Lossie ≃ 46 57.43 N 3.16 W
Lossiemouth 46 57.43 N 3.18 W
Lössnitz 54 50.37 N 12.43 E
Lost ≃, U.S. 202 41.56 N 121.30 W
Lost ≃, Ind., U.S. 194 38.33 N 86.49 W
Lost ≃, Minn., U.S. 198 47.51 N 96.02 W
Lost ≃, W. Va., U.S. 188 39.05 N 78.34 W
Lostant 216 41.09 N 89.04 W
Los Taques 246 11.50 N 70.16 W
Lost Bridge State Recreation Area ♠ 216 40.45 N 85.37 W
Lost Creek ≃, Ala., U.S. 194 33.38 N 87.14 W
Lost Creek ≃, Ark., U.S. 194 34.10 N 92.31 W
Lost Creek ≃, Ohio, U.S. 218 39.58 N 84.09 W

Symbol	English	Deutsch	Español	Français	Português
≃	River	Fluss	Río	Rivière	Rio
≅	Canal	Kanal	Canal	Canal	Canal
⅃	Waterfall, Rapids	Wasserfall, Stromschnellen	Cascada, Rápidos	Chute d'eau, Rapides	Cascata, Rápidos
Ʉ	Strait	Meeresstrasse	Estrecho	Détroit	Estreito
C	Bay, Gulf	Bucht, Golf	Bahía, Golfo	Baie, Golfe	Baía, Golfo
@	Lake, Lakes	See, Seen	Lago, Lagos	Lac, Lacs	Lago, Lagos
☷	Swamp	Sumpf	Pantano	Marais	Pântano
⍓	Ice Features, Glacier	Eis- und Gletscherformen	Accidentes Glaciales	Formes glaciaires	Acidentes Glaciares
Ŧ	Other Hydrographic Features	Andere Hydrographische Objekte	Otros Elementos Hidrográficos	Autres données hydrographiques	Outros Elementos Hidrográficos
✢	Submarine Features	Untermeerische Objekte	Accidentes Submarinos	Formes de relief sous-marin	Acidentes Submarinos
□	Political Unit	Politische Einheit	Unidad Política	Entité politique	Unidade Política
ʋ	Cultural Institution	Kulturelle Institution	Institución Cultural	Institution culturelle	Instituição Cultural
⊥	Historical Site	Historische Stätte	Sitio Histórico	Site historique	Sitio Histórico
♠	Recreational Site	Erholungs- und Ferienort	Sitio de Recreo	Centre de loisirs	Sítio de Lazer
⊠	Airport	Flughafen	Aeropuerto	Aéroport	Aeroporto
■	Military Installation	Militäranlage	Instalación Militar	Installation militaire	Instalação Militar
◆	Miscellaneous	Verschiedenes	Misceláneo	Divers	Miscelânea

Lost Creek ≃, Utah, U.S. 200 41.04 N 111.32 W
Lost Creek ≃, Wyo., U.S. 200 42.01 N 108.11 W
Lost Draw ∨ 196 32.58 N 102.02 W
Los Telares 252 28.59 S 63.26 W
Los Teques 246 10.21 N 67.02 W
Los Testigos, Islas II 246 11.22 N 63.06 W
Lost Hills 204 35.37 N 119.41 W
Lostine ≃ 202 45.33 N 117.29 W
Lost Lake ⊜, Oreg., U.S. 224 45.29 N 121.49 W
Lost Lake ⊜, Wash., U.S. 224 47.20 N 121.24 W
Lost Nation 190 41.58 N 90.49 W
Lostock ≃ 262 53.40 N 2.48 W
Lostock Gralam 262 53.16 N 2.28 W
Los Trancos Creek ≃ 282 37.25 N 122.12 W
Los Trancos Woods 282 37.21 N 122.12 W
Los Tres Palos 232 24.33 N 98.18 W
Lost River Range ⋀ 202 44.10 N 113.35 W
Lost Trail Pass)(202 45.41 N 113.57 W
Lostwithiel 42 50.25 N 4.40 W
Losuia 164 8.32 S 151.04 E
Los Vidrios 232 31.59 N 113.28 W
Los Vilos 252 31.55 S 71.31 W
Los Yébenes 34 39.34 N 3.53 W
Lot 174r 6.49 N 158.18 E
Lot □5 32 44.35 N 1.40 E
Lot ≃ 32 44.18 N 0.20 E
Lota 252 37.05 S 73.10 W
Lotagipi Swamp (Lotikipi Plain) ≚ 144 4.36 N 34.55 E
Lotak 112 0.11 S 115.54 E
Lotbinière □6 206 46.30 N 71.40 W
Lotela, Lake ⊜ 220 27.34 N 81.29 W
Løten 26 60.49 N 11.19 E
Lot-et-Garonne □5 32 44.20 N 0.20 E
Loṭfābād 128 37.32 N 59.20 E
Lothair, S. Afr. 158 26.26 S 30.27 E
Lothair, Ky., U.S. 192 37.15 N 83.10 W
Lot Harbor C 174r 6.48 N 158.19 E
Lothian □4 46 55.55 N 3.05 W
Lothian Region □4 46 55.50 N 3.15 W
Lothringen → Lorraine □9 32 49.00 N 6.00 E
Lotikipi Plain (Lotagipi Swamp) ≚ 144 4.36 N 34.55 E
Loto 152 2.49 S 22.29 E
Loto ≃ 152 6.49 N 24.14 E
Lotofaga 175a 13.59 S 171.50 W
Lotoi ≃ 152 1.35 S 18.30 E
Lotorp 40 58.44 N 15.50 E
Lotošino 76 56.14 N 35.38 E
Lotrului, Munţii ⋀ 38 45.30 N 23.52 E
Lotsane ≃ 156 22.41 S 28.11 E
Lötschberg Tunnel ↔5 58 46.25 N 7.45 E
Lötschental ∨ 58 46.25 N 7.50 E
Lotseninsel I 41 54.40 N 10.01 E
Lott 222 31.12 N 97.02 W
Lotta ≃ 24 68.36 N 31.06 E
Lottaville 278 41.31 N 87.22 W
Lottivue 214 42.40 N 83.46 W
Löttringhausen ↔8 263 51.27 N 7.27 E
Lottsburg 208 37.57 N 76.31 W
Lotts Creek ≃ 192 32.09 N 81.47 W
Lottsford Branch ≃ 284c 38.55 N 76.49 W
Lottstetten 58 47.38 N 8.34 E
Lotuke, Jabal ∧ 154 4.07 N 33.48 E
Lotung 100 24.41 N 121.46 E
Lötzen → Giżycko 30 54.03 N 21.47 E
Lotzorai 71 39.58 N 9.39 E
Louame ≃ 152 0.49 N 15.47 E
Louang Namtha 110 20.57 N 101.25 E
Louangphrabang 110 19.52 N 102.08 E
Louangphrabang □4 102 20.30 N 102.30 E
L'Ouarsenis, Massif de ⋀ 34 35.40 N 1.50 E
Loubaresse 62 44.36 N 4.03 E
Loube, Montagne de la ∧ 62 43.22 N 5.59 E
Loubetsi 152 3.12 S 12.10 E
Louchi 24 66.04 N 33.00 E
Loučim 60 49.22 N 13.07 E
Loučná ∧ 54 50.39 N 13.37 E
Loude 98 35.54 N 117.18 E
Loudéac 32 48.10 N 2.45 W
Louden Cove C 276 41.05 N 73.43 W
Loudes 62 45.05 N 3.45 E
Loudi 102 27.47 N 111.37 E
Loudima Poste 152 4.07 S 13.04 E
Loudon 192 35.44 N 84.20 W
Loudonville, N.Y., U.S. 210 42.42 N 73.47 W
Loudonville, Ohio, U.S. 214 40.38 N 82.14 W
Loudoun □6 208 39.05 N 77.30 W
Loudun 32 47.01 N 0.05 E
Loué 32 48.00 N 0.09 W
Loue ≃ 58 47.01 N 5.27 E
Louga 150 15.37 N 16.13 W
Louge 252 36.57 S 61.40 W
Louge ≃ 32 43.27 N 1.20 E
Loughborough 42 52.47 N 1.11 W
Loughborough Lake ⊜ 212 44.23 N 76.30 W
Loughermore ∧2 44 54.59 N 7.05 W
Loughman 220 28.14 N 81.34 W
Loughor 42 51.40 N 4.04 W
Loughor ≃ 42 51.40 N 4.04 W
Loughrea 48 53.12 N 8.34 W
Loughros More Bay C 48 54.47 N 8.35 W
Loughton 260 51.39 N 0.03 E
Louhans 58 46.38 N 5.13 E
Louin 194 31.59 N 89.16 W
Louisa, Ky., U.S. 192 38.07 N 82.36 W
Louisa, Va., U.S. 192 38.01 N 78.01 W
Louisa, Lac ⊜ 206 45.46 N 74.25 W
Louisa, Lake ⊜, Ont., Can. 212 45.28 N 78.30 W
Louisa, Lake ⊜, Fla., U.S. 220 28.29 N 81.44 W
Louisbourg 186 45.55 N 59.58 W
Louis Bull Indian Reserve ↔4 182 52.53 N 113.31 W
Louisburg, Kans., U.S. 198 38.37 N 94.41 W
Louisburg, N.C., U.S. 192 36.06 N 78.18 W
Louisburgh 48 53.46 N 9.51 W
Louisdale 186 45.36 N 61.04 W
Louise, Miss., U.S. 194 32.59 N 90.35 W
Louise, Tex., U.S. 222 29.06 N 96.25 W
Louise, Lake ⊜ 180 62.20 N 146.30 W
Louise Island I 182 52.58 N 131.50 W
Louiseville 206 46.15 N 72.57 W
Louis Gentil → Youssoufia 148 32.16 N 8.33 W
Louisiade Archipelago II 160 11.00 S 153.00 E
Louisiade Rise ↔3 14 13.00 S 158.00 E
Louisiana 219 39.27 N 91.03 W
Louisiana □3 178
194 31.15 N 92.15 W
Louisiana ♦ 41 55.58 N 12.33 E
Lou Island I 164 2.25 S 147.20 E
Louis Trichardt 156 23.01 S 29.43 E
Louisvale 158 28.33 S 21.12 E
Louisville, Ont., Can. 214 42.28 N 82.07 W
Louisville, Ala., U.S. 194 31.47 N 85.33 W
Louisville, Ga., U.S. 192 33.00 N 82.24 W
Louisville, Ill., U.S. 194 38.46 N 88.30 W
Louisville, Ky., U.S. 218 38.16 N 85.45 W
Louisville, Miss., U.S. 194 33.07 N 89.03 W
Louisville, Nebr., U.S. 198 41.00 N 96.10 W
Louisville, Ohio, U.S. 214 40.50 N 81.16 W
Louisville Ridge ↔3 14 31.30 S 173.30 W
Louisville Seamount ↔3 14 31.15 S 172.20 W
Louis-XIV, Pointe > 176 54.37 N 79.45 W
Loujiaying 98 42.04 N 116.04 E
Loukanga 273b 4.20 S 15.09 E
Loukoua ≃ 273b 4.07 S 15.10 E
Loulé 34 37.08 N 8.02 W
Loum 152 4.43 N 9.44 E
Loumou 273b 4.08 S 15.09 E
Lount Lake ⊜ 184 50.10 N 94.20 W
Louny 54 50.19 N 13.46 E
Loup ≃, Fr. 62 43.38 N 7.09 E
Loup ≃, Nebr., U.S. 198 41.24 N 97.19 W
Loup, Gorge du ∨ 56 49.47 N 6.23 E
Loup, Rivière du ≃ 206 46.13 N 72.55 W
Loup City 198 41.17 N 98.58 W
Lourches 50 50.19 N 3.21 E
Lourdes, Newf., Can. 186 48.39 N 59.00 W
Lourdes, Fr. 32 43.06 N 0.03 W
Lourel de Baixo 266c 38.49 N 9.22 W
Lourenço 250 2.30 N 51.40 W
Lourenço Marques → Maputo 156 25.58 S 32.35 E
Lourenço Marques → Maputo □5 156 26.00 S 32.25 E
Lourenço Velho 256 22.22 S 45.19 W
Lourenço Velho ≃, Bra. 256 23.26 S 45.35 W
Lourenço Velho ≃, Bra. 256 22.22 S 45.31 W
Loures 34 38.50 N 9.10 W
Loures ≃ 266c 38.50 N 9.08 W
Lourinhã 34 39.14 N 9.19 W
Lourmarin 62 43.46 N 5.22 E
Lourosa 34 40.19 N 7.56 W
Loury 50 48.00 N 2.05 E
Lousã, Port. 34 40.07 N 8.15 W
Lousa, Port. 266c 38.53 N 9.12 W
Louse Creek ≃ 198 46.22 N 100.57 W
Loushan ∧ 89 45.15 N 128.58 E
Louta 150 13.30 N 3.10 W
Loutang 106 31.26 N 121.12 E
Loutézou, Île de I 273b 4.22 S 15.10 E
Louth, Austl. 166 30.32 S 145.07 E
Louth, Eire 44 53.57 N 6.33 W
Louth, Eire 48 53.37 N 6.53 W
Louth, Eng., U.K. 44 53.22 N 0.01 W
Louth □6 48 53.55 N 6.30 W
Louth Bay C 166 34.34 S 136.02 E
Louti, Mayo ≃ 146 9.38 N 13.56 E
Loutit Bay C 169 38.33 S 144.00 E
Loutrá Aidhipsoú 38 38.51 N 23.02 E
Loutre ≃ 219 38.42 N 91.25 W
Loutre, Bayou de ≃ 194 32.41 N 92.08 W
Loutrópirgos 267c 38.02 N 23.28 E
Louvain → Leuven 56 50.53 N 4.42 E
Louveciennes 261 48.52 N 2.07 E
Louveigné 56 50.32 N 5.42 E
Louveira 256 23.04 S 46.58 W
Louviers, Fr. 50 49.13 N 1.10 E
Louviers, Colo., U.S. 200 39.28 N 105.01 W
Louvigné-du-Désert 32 48.29 N 1.08 W
Louvre ♦ 261 48.52 N 2.20 E
Louvres 50 49.02 N 2.30 E
Louvroil 50 50.16 N 3.58 E
Louwsburg 158 27.37 S 31.07 E
Lou Yaeger, Lake ⊜1 219 39.10 N 89.37 W
Lövånger 26 64.22 N 21.18 E
Lovászi 61 46.33 N 16.34 E
Lovat' ≃ 76 58.14 N 31.28 E
Lovcy 82 55.00 N 39.15 E
Love 184 53.29 N 104.09 W
Loveč 38 43.08 N 24.43 E
Love Clough 262 53.44 N 2.17 W
Lovedale 279b 40.17 N 79.52 W
Lovejoy 219 38.39 N 90.10 W
Lovelady 222 31.08 N 95.27 W
Loveland, Colo., U.S. 200 40.24 N 105.05 W
Loveland, Ohio, U.S. 218 39.16 N 84.16 W
Lovell 202 44.50 N 108.24 W
Lovell Island I 283 42.20 N 70.56 W
Lovelock 204 40.11 N 118.28 W
Lovely 192 37.50 N 82.24 W
Love Point > 208 39.02 N 76.18 W
Lovere 64 45.49 N 10.04 E
Lovering Lake ⊜ 206 45.10 N 72.09 W
Lovero 64 46.14 N 10.14 E
Loves Green 260 51.43 N 0.24 E
Loves Park 216 42.19 N 89.03 W
Loviisa → Lovisa 26 60.27 N 26.14 E
Lovilia 190 41.08 N 92.55 W
Loving, N. Mex., U.S. 196 32.17 N 104.06 W
Loving, Tex., U.S. 196 33.16 N 98.31 W
Lovingston 192 37.46 N 78.52 W
Lovington, Ill., U.S. 219 39.43 N 88.38 W
Lovington, N. Mex., U.S. 196 32.57 N 103.21 W
Lovisa (Loviisa) 26 60.27 N 26.14 E
Lövő 61 47.30 N 16.47 E
Lovö I 40 59.20 N 17.50 E
Lovosice 54 50.31 N 14.03 E
Lovozero 24 68.00 N 35.00 E
Lovozero, Ozero ⊜ 24 67.54 N 35.12 E
Lövstabruk 40 60.24 N 17.53 E
Lövstabukten C 40 60.35 N 17.45 E
Lövstads slott ⊥ 40 58.33 N 16.02 E
Lóvua, Ang. 152 7.20 S 20.16 E
Lóvua, Ang. 152 11.36 S 23.53 E
Lovua (Lóvua) ≃ 152 6.07 S 20.35 E
Low 188 45.48 N 75.57 W
Low, Cape > 176 63.07 N 85.18 W
Lowa 154 1.24 S 25.51 E
Lowa ≃ 154 1.24 S 25.51 E
Lowāda 126 22.27 N 87.37 E
Lowat → Lovat' ≃ 76 58.14 N 31.28 E
Lowber 279b 40.15 N 79.46 W
Lowden 190 41.52 N 90.56 W
Lowder Brook ≃ 283 43.14 N 71.11 W
Lowell, Ind., U.S. 216 41.18 N 87.25 W
Lowell, Mass., U.S. 207
283 42.39 N 71.18 W
Lowell, Mich., U.S. 216 42.56 N 85.20 W
Lowell, Oreg., U.S. 202 43.55 N 122.47 W
Lowell, Lake ⊜1 202 43.33 N 116.40 W
Lowell, University of ♦2 283 42.39 N 71.20 W
Lowell-Dracut State Forest ♠ 283 42.40 N 71.22 W
Lowelli 140 5.59 N 33.45 E
Lowellville 214 41.02 N 80.32 W
Löwen → Leuven, Bel. 56 50.53 N 4.42 E
Löwen → Lewin Brzeski, Pol. 30 50.46 N 17.37 E
Löwenberg, D.D.R. 54 52.54 N 13.08 E
Löwenberg → Lwówek Śląski, Pol. 30 51.07 N 15.35 E
Löwenbruch 264a 52.18 N 13.19 E
Löwenstein 56 49.06 N 9.22 E
Lowe Pine ♠ 171a 27.32 S 152.57 E
Lowe Pond ⊜ 283 42.41 N 70.59 W
Lower Arrow Lake ⊜ 182 49.40 N 118.08 W
Lower Bear River Reservoir ⊜1 226 38.33 N 120.14 W
Lower Bershire Valley 276 40.54 N 74.37 W
Lower Beverly Lake ⊜ 212 44.36 N 76.09 W
Lower Broughton ↔8 262 53.29 N 2.15 W
Lower Brule Indian Reservation ↔4 198 44.05 N 99.44 W
Lower Buckhorn Lake ⊜ 212 44.33 N 78.17 W
Lower Burrell 214 40.35 N 79.44 W
Lower Chittering 168a 31.34 S 116.06 E
Lower Crystal Springs Reservoir ⊜1 226 37.32 N 122.22 W
Lower Darwen 262 53.43 N 2.28 W
Lower Eltham Park ♠ 274b 37.45 S 145.09 E
Lower Elwha Indian Reservation ↔4 224 48.09 N 123.33 W
Lower Fort Garry National Historic Park ♠ 184 50.07 N 96.55 W
Lower Ganga Canal ≍ 124 26.27 N 80.17 E
Lower Gap C 212 44.10 N 76.35 W
Lower Halstow 260 51.22 N 0.40 E
Lower Hay Lake ⊜ 212 45.25 N 78.13 W
Lower Higham 260 51.26 N 0.28 E
Lower Highland Creek Park ♠ 275b 43.47 N 79.10 W
Lower Huron Metropolitan Park ♠ 281 42.12 N 83.25 W
Lower Hutt 172 41.13 S 174.55 E
Lower Juba □4 144 0.15 S 42.10 E
Lower Kalskag 180 61.31 N 160.22 W
Lower Keechi Creek ≃ 222 31.08 N 95.46 W
Lower Klamath Lake ⊜ 204 41.55 N 121.42 W
Lower Lake 226 38.55 N 122.36 W
Lower Lake ⊜ 204 41.15 N 120.02 W
Lower Loteni 158 29.32 S 29.36 E
Lower Manitou Lake ⊜ 184 49.15 N 93.00 W
Lower Matecumbe Key I 220 24.51 N 80.43 W
Lower Montville 276 40.54 N 74.22 W
Lower Mystic Lake ⊜ 283 42.26 N 71.09 W
Lower Nazeing 260 51.44 N 0.01 E
Lower New York Bay C 276 40.33 N 74.02 W
Lower Otay Reservoir ⊜1 228 32.37 N 116.55 W
Lower Paia 229a 20.55 N 156.23 W
Lower Paudash Lake ⊜ 212 44.58 N 78.01 W
Lower Peover 262 53.16 N 2.23 W
Lower Place 262 53.36 N 2.09 W
Lower Plenty 274b 37.44 S 145.06 E
Lower Portland 170 33.27 S 150.53 E
Lower Post 176 59.55 N 128.30 W
Lower Red Lake ⊜ 198 48.00 N 94.50 W
Lower River Rouge ≃ 281 42.18 N 83.14 W
Lower Rouge Parkway ♠ 281 42.18 N 83.20 W
Lower Stoke 260 51.27 N 0.38 E
Lower Ugashik Lake ⊜ 180 57.30 N 156.56 W
Lower Van Norman Lake ⊜1 280 34.17 N 118.29 W
Lower West Pubnico 186 43.38 N 65.48 W
Lower Whitley 262 53.18 N 2.35 W
Lower Wood's Harbour 186 43.31 N 65.44 W
Lowery, Lake ⊜ 220 28.07 N 81.41 W
Lowestoft 42 52.29 N 1.45 E
Lowgar □4 120 33.50 N 69.00 E
Lowick 44 55.38 N 2.00 W
Łowicz 30 52.07 N 19.56 E
Lowman 210 42.02 N 76.44 W
Lowmoor 192 37.47 N 79.53 W
Lowood 171a 27.28 S 152.35 E
Lowries Run ≃ 279b 40.30 N 80.05 W
Low Rocky Point > 166 43.00 S 145.30 E
Lowry City 194 38.08 N 93.44 W
Lowther ≃ 44 54.39 N 2.44 W
Lowther Hills ⋀2 44 55.19 N 3.38 W
Lowton 262 53.28 N 2.35 W
Lowton Common 262 53.29 N 2.33 W
Lowville, N.Y., U.S. 212 43.47 N 75.29 W
Lowville, Pa., U.S. 214 42.01 N 79.49 W
Loxahatchee 220 26.49 N 80.13 W
Loxley 194 30.37 N 87.45 W
Loxstedt 52 53.28 N 8.38 E
Loxten 52 52.03 N 8.08 E
Loxton, Austl. 166 34.27 S 140.35 E
Loxton, S. Afr. 158 31.30 S 22.22 E
Loyal 190 44.44 N 90.30 W
Loyal, Loch ⊜ 46 58.23 N 4.22 W
Loyalhanna 214 40.19 N 79.21 W
Loyalhanna Creek ≃ 214 40.28 N 79.27 W
Loyalhanna Lake ⊜1 214 40.25 N 79.28 W
Loyalsock Creek ≃ 210 41.14 N 76.56 W
Loyalton 204 39.41 N 120.14 W
Loyalty Islands → Loyauté, Îles II 175f 21.00 S 167.00 E
Loyalty Ridge ↔3 14 21.30 S 168.00 E
Loyang → Luoyang 102 34.41 N 112.28 E
Loyauté, Îles (Loyality Islands) II 175f 21.00 S 167.00 E
Loyne, Loch ⊜ 46 57.06 N 5.00 W
Loyola Marymount University ♦2 280 33.58 N 118.25 W
Loyola University ♦2 278 42.00 N 87.39 W
Loyoro 154 3.21 N 34.16 E
Loysburg 214 40.10 N 78.23 W
Loysville 208 40.22 N 77.21 W
Loza 60 49.53 N 13.18 E
Lozano 258 34.51 S 59.03 W
Lozère □5 32 44.30 N 3.30 E
Lozère, Mont ∧ 62 44.25 N 3.46 E
Loznica 38 44.32 N 19.13 E
Ložnikovo, S.S.S.R. 86 56.54 N 73.56 E
Ložnikovo, S.S.S.R. 88 51.22 N 117.03 E
Lozno-Aleksandrovka 78 49.50 N 38.44 E
Loznoje 80 49.17 N 44.26 E
Lozovaja, S.S.S.R. 78 48.54 N 36.20 E
Lozovaja, S.S.S.R. 83 49.28 N 37.54 E
Lozovaja, S.S.S.R. 86 53.17 N 77.45 E
Lozovoje, S.S.S.R. 78 49.18 N 27.18 E
Lozovoje, S.S.S.R. 83 49.13 N 37.36 E
Lozovskij 83 48.33 N 38.54 E
Lozoyuela 34 40.55 N 3.37 W
Loz'va ≃ 86 59.36 N 62.20 E
Lozzo di Cadore 64 46.29 N 12.27 E
Lterh, Oued ∨ 148 21.39 N 2.30 E
Lu 62 45.00 N 8.29 E
Lua 152 5.18 S 16.06 E
Lua ≃ 152 2.46 N 18.26 E
Luabo 156 18.30 S 36.10 E
Luabu ≃ 152 2.46 S 18.19 E
Luachimo ≃ 152 6.33 S 20.59 E
Luaha-sibuha 110 0.31 S 98.28 E
Luala ≃ 154 17.57 S 36.30 E
Lualaba ≃ 154 0.26 N 25.20 E
Luali 152 5.06 S 12.29 E
Lualoje ≃ 152 12.18 S 21.38 E
Luama ≃ 154 4.46 S 26.53 E
Lua Makika ⊥6 229a 20.34 N 156.34 W
Luambe Game Reserve ↔4 154 12.25 S 32.15 E
Luambimba ≃ 152 15.00 S 22.48 E
Luampa 154 15.03 S 24.28 E
Luampa ≃ 154 14.33 S 24.10 E
Luana ≃ 152 7.56 S 21.06 E
Luana Point > 241q 18.02 N 77.52 W
Luan Balu 114 2.38 N 96.13 E
Luancheng, Zhg. 98 37.53 N 114.39 E
Luancheng, Zhg. 102 22.45 N 108.51 E
Luanchuan 102 33.51 N 111.36 E
Luancundo ≃ 152 16.25 S 21.27 E
Luanda 152 8.48 S 13.14 E
Luanda □5 152 8.30 S 13.20 E
Luanda ≃ 152 7.16 S 16.00 E
Luando ≃ 152 10.19 S 16.40 E
Luando, Reserva Natural Integral do ↔4 152 10.50 S 18.00 E
Luang ≃ 110 18.01 N 103.04 E
Luang, Khao ∧ 110 8.31 N 99.47 E
Luang, Thale C 110 7.30 N 100.15 E
Luang Chiang Dao, Doi ∧ 110 19.23 N 98.54 E
Luanginga (Luanguinga) ≃ 152 15.11 S 22.56 E
Luang Prabang → Louangphrabang 110 19.52 N 102.08 E
Luang Prabang Range ⋀ 110 18.30 N 101.15 E
Luangue 152 7.19 S 19.38 E
Luangue (Loange) ≃ 152 4.17 S 20.02 E
Luanguinga (Luanginga) ≃ 152 15.11 S 22.56 E
Luangwa (Aruângua) ≃, Afr. 138
154 15.36 S 30.25 E
Luangwa Valley Game Reserve (South) ↔4, Zam. 154 12.50 S 31.45 E
Luangwa Valley Game Reserve (North) ↔4, Zam. 154 11.50 S 32.15 E
Luanhe 105 40.57 N 117.44 E
Luanhe ≃ 98 40.32 N 118.15 E
Luanping 98 40.57 N 117.20 E
Luanshishan 104 42.10 N 123.41 E
Luanshya 154 13.08 S 28.24 E
Luán Toro 252 36.12 S 65.06 W
Luanxian 98 39.45 N 118.44 E
Luanza 154 8.42 S 28.42 E
Luapula □4 154 10.55 S 29.00 E
Luapula ≃ 154 9.26 S 28.33 E
Luar, Danau ⊜ 112 0.55 N 111.59 E
Luarca 34 43.32 N 6.32 W
Luashi 152 10.56 S 23.37 E
Luashi ≃ 152 10.41 S 22.55 E
Luassinga ≃ 152 15.47 S 18.50 E
Luati 152 14.35 S 21.13 E
Luatira 152 12.52 S 17.14 E
Lua-Vindu ≃ 152 3.38 N 19.16 E
Lubaantum ⊥ 232 16.17 N 88.58 W
Lubaczów 30 50.10 N 23.07 E
Lubalo 152 9.12 S 19.16 E
Lubalo ≃ 152 7.22 S 19.20 E
Lubamiti 152 2.29 S 17.47 E
Lubań, Pol. 30 51.08 N 15.18 E
L'uban', S.S.S.R. 76 59.21 N 31.13 E
L'uban', S.S.S.R. 76 52.48 N 27.59 E
L'uban', S.S.S.R. 76 52.37 N 29.08 E
Lubāna 76 56.54 N 26.43 E
Lubānas Ezers ⊜ 76 56.46 N 26.53 E
Lubang 116 13.52 N 120.07 E
Lubang Islands II 116 13.46 N 120.15 E
Lubango 152 14.55 S 13.30 E
Lubanowo 54 53.09 N 14.36 E
Lubansenshi ≃ 154 11.21 S 30.35 E
Lub'any 80 56.02 N 51.24 E
Lubao 100 23.22 N 112.55 E
L'ubar 78 49.55 N 27.44 E
Lübars, D.D.R. 54 52.10 N 12.09 E
Lübars, D.D.R. 54 52.39 N 12.02 E
Lübars ↔8 264a 52.37 N 13.22 E
Lubartów 30 51.28 N 22.38 E
L'ubašovka 78 47.51 N 30.15 E
Lubawa 30 53.30 N 19.45 E
Lubaynī, Baḩr al- ≍ 273c 29.56 N 31.11 E
Lübbecke 52 52.18 N 8.36 E
Lübben 54 51.56 N 13.53 E
Lübbenau 54 51.52 N 13.57 E
Lubber Brook ≃ 283 42.33 N 71.09 W
Lubbers Run ≃ 276 40.56 N 74.43 W
Lübbesee ⊜ 54 53.05 N 13.34 E
Lubbock 196 33.35 N 101.51 W
Lübbow 54 52.54 N 11.10 E
Lubbub Creek ≃ 194 33.04 N 88.10 W
L'ubča 76 53.45 N 26.03 E
L'ubčany 82 55.15 N 37.33 E
L'ubeč, S.S.S.R. 78 51.42 N 30.39 E
Lubec, Maine, U.S. 188 44.52 N 66.59 W
Lübeck 52 53.52 N 10.40 E
Lubefu 152 4.43 S 24.25 E
Lubefu ≃ 152 4.10 S 23.00 E
Lubelska, Wyżyna ⋀2 30 51.00 N 23.00 E
Lubembe (Luembe) ≃ 152 6.37 S 21.05 E
Lüben → Lubin 30 51.24 N 16.13 E
Lubenec 54 50.06 N 13.20 E
L'ubercy 82 55.41 N 37.53 E
Lubéron, Montagne du ⋀ 62 43.48 N 5.22 E
Lubersac 32 45.27 N 1.24 E
L'ubešov 78 51.46 N 25.31 E
Lübesse 54 53.29 N 11.28 E
Lubi ≃ 152 4.58 S 23.26 E
Lubiana → Ljubljana 36 46.03 N 14.31 E
Lubic Island I 116 10.58 N 120.44 E
L'ubickoje 80 51.46 N 49.19 E
Lubień Kujawski 30 52.25 N 19.10 E
Lubilash ≃ 152 6.02 S 23.45 E
Lubile 154 2.55 S 26.45 E
L'ubim 80 58.22 N 40.41 E
L'ubimovka, S.S.S.R. 78 51.31 N 35.37 E
L'ubimovka, S.S.S.R. 78 46.47 N 33.34 E
L'ubimovka, S.S.S.R. 86 52.15 N 66.45 E
L'ubimyj 83 47.53 N 39.28 E
Lubin, Pol. 30 51.24 N 16.13 E
Lubin, Pol. 54 53.50 N 14.25 E
L'ubino 86 56.32 N 88.46 E
L'ubinskij 86 55.09 N 72.42 E
Lubishi ≃ 152 6.54 S 24.09 E
Lubja ≃ 265a 59.58 N 30.30 E
Lublin 30 51.15 N 22.35 E
Lubliniec 30 50.40 N 18.41 E
L'ublino ↔8 265b 55.41 N 37.44 E
Lubmin 54 54.08 N 13.37 E
Lubná 60 50.04 N 13.42 E
Lubnān, Jabal (Lebanon Mountains) ⋀ 132 34.00 N 36.00 E
L'ubnica 76 57.58 N 32.42 E
Lubny 78 50.01 N 33.00 E
L'ubochna 76 53.31 N 34.23 E
Lubok China 114 2.27 N 102.04 E
Lubomierz 30 51.01 N 15.30 E
L'uboml' 78 51.14 N 24.01 E
Luboń 30 52.23 N 16.54 E
Lubondai 152 6.34 S 22.39 E
Lubondoi 154 8.02 S 26.31 E
L'ubostan' 78 51.19 N 35.44 E
L'ubotin 78 49.57 N 35.57 E
Lubraniec 30 52.33 N 18.50 E
Lubsko 30 51.46 N 14.59 E
Lübtheen 54 53.18 N 11.04 E
Lubu, Indon. 112 0.46 S 122.30 E
Lubu, Zhg. 102 23.09 N 112.13 E
Lubuagan 116 17.21 N 121.10 E
Lubudi, Zaïre 152 6.51 S 21.18 E
Lubudi, Zaïre 154 9.57 S 25.58 E
Lubudi ≃, Zaïre 152 4.03 S 21.23 E
Lubudi ≃, Zaïre 154 9.13 S 25.38 E
Lubue 152 4.09 S 19.52 E
Lubue ≃ 152 4.10 S 19.53 E
Lubukambacang 112 0.37 S 101.25 E
Lubukbatang 112 4.03 S 104.12 E
Lubukbertubung 112 0.02 N 102.08 E
Lubuklinggau 112 3.18 S 102.52 E
Lubukpakam 114 3.33 N 98.52 E
Lubukraya, Dolok ∧ 114 1.29 N 99.13 E
Lubuksikaping 112 0.08 N 100.10 E
Lubumbaschi → Lubumbashi 154 11.40 S 27.28 E
Lubumbashi (Élisabethville) 154 11.40 S 27.28 E
Lubunda 154 5.10 S 26.40 E
Lubutu 154 0.44 S 26.35 E
Luby 54 50.12 N 12.25 E
L'ubytino 76 58.49 N 33.23 E
Lübz 54 53.27 N 12.01 E
Lučak 85 38.23 N 67.25 E
Lucala 152 9.16 S 15.15 E
Lucala ≃ 152 6.38 S 12.34 E
Lucan, Ont., Can. 190 43.11 N 81.24 W
Lucan, Eire 48 53.22 N 6.27 W
Lucanas 248 14.36 S 74.15 W
Lucania □9 68 40.30 N 16.00 E
Lucania, Mount ∧ 180 61.01 N 140.28 W
Lucano 152 11.16 S 21.38 E
Lucaogou 102 42.26 N 96.55 E
L'uca-Ongokton, Gora ∧ 74 67.52 N 106.24 E
Lucas, Iowa, U.S. 190 41.02 N 93.28 W
Lucas, Kans., U.S. 198 39.04 N 98.32 W
Lucas, Ohio, U.S. 214 40.42 N 82.25 W
Lucas, Tex., U.S. 222 33.05 N 96.35 W
Lucas □6 214 41.39 N 83.32 W
Lucas González 252 32.24 S 59.33 W
Lucas Valley 282 38.03 N 122.35 W
Lucasville 218 38.53 N 83.00 W
Lucban 116 14.06 N 121.33 E
Lucca 66 43.50 N 10.29 E
Lucca □4 64 44.02 N 10.27 E
Lucca Sicula 70 37.35 N 13.18 E
Luce, Water of ≃ 44 54.52 N 4.48 W
Lucea 241q 18.27 N 78.10 W
Luce Bay C 44 54.47 N 4.50 W
Luce Bayou ≃ 222 30.03 N 95.07 W
Lucedale 194 30.55 N 88.35 W
Lucena, Esp. 34 37.24 N 4.29 W
Lucena, Pil. 116 13.56 N 121.37 E
Lucena del Cid 34 40.08 N 0.17 W
Lucenay-l'Évêque 32 47.05 N 4.15 E
Luc-en-Diois 62 44.37 N 5.27 E
Lučenec 30 48.20 N 19.40 E
Lucens 58 46.42 N 6.50 E
Luceque 152 14.41 S 15.04 E
Lucera 68 41.30 N 15.20 E
Lucéram 62 43.53 N 7.22 E
Lucerne → Luzern, Schw. 58 47.03 N 8.18 E
Lucerne, Calif., U.S. 204 39.06 N 122.48 W
Lucerne, Ind., U.S. 216 40.52 N 86.24 W
Lucerne, Lake → Vierwaldstätter See ⊜ 58 47.00 N 8.28 E
Lucerne Lake ⊜ 228 34.31 N 57.00 W
Lucernemines 214 40.34 N 79.09 W
Lucerne Valley 228 34.27 N 116.57 W
Lucero 200 30.49 N 106.30 W
Lucero, Lake ⊜ 200 32.42 N 106.25 W
Lučesa ≃ 76 55.10 N 30.11 E
Luch 80 57.01 N 42.15 E
Luch ≃ 80 56.14 N 42.25 E
Luchena ≃ 34 37.44 N 1.50 W
Lucheng, Zhg. 102 24.21 N 106.00 E
Lücheng, Zhg. 106 31.55 N 119.44 E
Lucheng, Zhg. 106 31.47 N 120.02 E
Luché-Pringé 50 47.42 N 0.05 E
Lucheringo ≃ 154 11.43 S 36.17 E
Luchiang 100 24.04 N 120.26 E
Luchibe ≃ 152 12.07 S 21.13 E
Luchico (Lushiko) ≃ 152 6.13 S 19.40 E
Luchou 269d 25.05 N 121.28 E
Luchovicy 82 54.59 N 39.03 E
Lüchow, B.R.D. 54 52.58 N 11.10 E
Luchow → Luzhou, Zhg. 107 28.54 N 105.27 E
Lüchtringen 52 51.47 N 9.25 E
Luchuan 102 22.19 N 110.11 E
Luci 100 29.52 N 119.47 E
L'učicheza, Gora ∧ 89 45.10 N 135.48 E
Lucie ≃ 250 3.35 N 57.38 W
Lucikou 100 28.56 N 116.04 E
Lučin 76 53.01 N 30.01 E
Lucinda 214 41.19 N 79.22 W
Lucindale 166 36.59 S 140.22 E
Lucipara, Kepulauan II 164 5.30 S 127.33 E
Lucira 152 13.51 S 12.31 E
Lucito 66 41.44 N 14.41 E
Luciyu I 100 25.07 N 119.22 E
Luck, S.S.S.R. 78 50.44 N 25.20 E
Luck, Wis., U.S. 190 45.34 N 92.28 W
Luck, Mount ∧2 162 28.47 S 123.33 E
Lucka 54 51.06 N 12.20 E
Luckau 54 51.51 N 13.43 E
Luckeesarai 124 25.11 N 86.05 E
Luckenwalde 54 52.05 N 13.10 E
Luckey 214 41.27 N 83.29 W
Luckhoff 158 29.44 S 24.43 E
Luckiamute ≃ 202 44.45 N 123.09 W
Luck Lake ⊜ 184 51.05 N 107.07 W
Lucknow, Bhārat 124 26.51 N 80.55 E
Lucknow, Ont., Can. 190 43.57 N 81.31 W
Lucknow, Pa., U.S. 208 40.20 N 76.54 W
Lucky Lake 184 51.00 N 107.10 W
Lucky Peak Lake ⊜1 202 43.33 N 116.00 W
Luco dei Marsi 66 41.58 N 13.28 E
Lucomagno, Passo del)(58 46.33 N 8.49 E
Luçon, Fr. 32 46.27 N 1.10 W
Lucon, Pa., U.S. 285 40.14 N 75.25 W
Luconha ≃ 152 12.54 S 21.15 E
Lucun, Zhg. 98 36.12 N 118.01 E
Lucun, Zhg. 106 30.49 N 119.26 E
Lucunga ≃ 152 6.57 S 12.48 E
Lucungu ≃ 152 6.41 S 14.26 E
Lucusse 152 12.32 S 20.48 E
Lucy Creek 166 22.25 S 136.20 E
Lüda (Dairen) 98 38.53 N 121.35 E
Luda Kamčija ≃ 38 43.03 N 27.29 E
Ludanli 106 31.37 N 119.20 E
Ludao 89 43.51 N 129.19 E
Ludao I 98 39.44 N 123.45 E
Ludbreg 36 46.15 N 16.37 E
Luddan 123 29.54 N 72.34 E
Luddenden 262 53.44 N 1.56 W
Luddenham 274a 33.53 S 150.41 E
Luddesdown 260 51.22 N 0.24 E
Lüdenscheid 56 51.13 N 7.38 E
Lüdenscheid □8 263 51.09 N 7.33 E
Lüder ≃ 56 50.31 N 9.27 E
Lüderitz, D.D.R. 54 52.30 N 11.44 E
Lüderitz, Namibia 156 26.38 S 15.10 E
Lüderitz □5 156 26.30 S 15.45 E
Lüdersdorf 54 53.47 N 10.46 E
Ludgershall 42 51.16 N 1.37 W
Ludgo 40 58.55 N 17.08 E
Ludhiāna 123 30.54 N 75.51 E
Ludian 102 27.11 N 103.33 E
Luding 102 29.55 N 102.15 E
Lüdinghausen 52 51.46 N 7.26 E
Lüdinghausen □8 263 51.41 N 7.30 E
Ludington 190 43.57 N 86.27 W
Ludingtonville 210 41.29 N 73.39 W
L'udinovo 76 53.52 N 34.27 E
L'udkovo 76 54.36 N 34.43 E
Ludlam Bay C 208 39.10 N 74.42 W
Ludlow, Eng., U.K. 42 52.22 N 2.43 W
Ludlow, Colo., U.S. 198 37.20 N 104.35 W
Ludlow, Ill., U.S. 216 40.23 N 88.08 W
Ludlow, Ky., U.S. 218 39.05 N 84.33 W
Ludlow, Mass., U.S. 207 42.10 N 72.29 W
Ludlow, Pa., U.S. 214 41.44 N 78.57 W
Ludlow, Vt., U.S. 188 43.24 N 72.42 W
Ludlow Falls 218 40.00 N 84.20 W
Ludlowville 210 42.33 N 76.32 W
Ludonghe 102 25.53 N 103.33 E
Ludoni 76 58.12 N 29.21 E
Ludowici 192 31.43 N 81.45 W
Luduqiao 106 31.28 N 121.11 E
Luduș 38 46.29 N 24.05 E
Ludvika 40 60.09 N 15.11 E
Ludwag 60 49.57 N 11.05 E
Ludwigsburg 56 48.53 N 9.11 E
Ludwigsfelde 54 52.17 N 13.16 E
Ludwigsfelder-Heide ↔3 264a 52.18 N 13.14 E
Ludwigshafen 56 49.29 N 8.26 E
Ludwigshafen am Bodensee 58 47.49 N 9.03 E
Ludwigslust 54 53.19 N 11.30 E
Ludwigsort → Laduškin 76 54.36 N 20.11 E
Ludwigsstadt 54 50.30 N 11.23 E
Ludwigstein, Burg ⊥ 56 51.20 N 9.55 E
Ludza 76 56.33 N 27.43 E
Lue 170 32.39 S 149.51 E
Luebo 152 5.21 S 21.25 E
Lueders 196 32.48 N 99.37 W
Lueg, Pass)(64 47.34 N 13.12 E
Lueki 154 3.22 S 25.51 E
Luele ≃ 152 7.55 S 20.09 E
Luemba 154 3.42 S 28.40 E
Luembe (Lubembe) ≃ 152 6.37 S 21.05 E
Luena 154 9.27 S 25.47 E
Luena ≃, Ang. 152 12.31 S 22.34 E
Luena ≃, Zam. 152 14.45 S 23.25 E
Luena Flats ≡ 152 14.50 S 23.20 E
Luengué ≃ 152 16.54 S 21.52 E
Luenha (Ruenya) ≃ 154 16.24 S 33.48 E
Lueo ≃ 152 9.06 S 23.51 E
Luepa 246 5.43 N 61.31 W
Lueta 152 7.19 S 22.06 E
Lueta ≃ 152 7.04 S 21.40 E
Lueti ≃ 152 16.14 S 23.13 E
Lueyang 102 33.19 N 106.19 E
Lüfangsicun 104 41.25 N 123.22 E
Lufeng, Zhg. 100 22.57 N 115.38 E
Lufeng, Zhg. 102 25.07 N 102.07 E
Lüfeng, Zhg. 107 29.51 N 105.58 E
Lufico 152 6.24 S 13.23 E
Lufira ≃ 154 8.16 S 26.27 E
Lufkin 222 31.20 N 94.44 W
Lufubu ≃ 154 8.36 S 30.47 E
Lufuidje ≃ 152 12.52 S 22.47 E
Lufupa 154 10.37 S 24.56 E
Lufupa ≃ 154 14.37 S 26.12 E
Luga 76 58.44 N 29.52 E
Luga ≃ 76 59.40 N 28.18 E
Lugagnano Val d'Arda 62 44.49 N 9.50 E
Lugan' ≃ 83 48.37 N 39.27 E
Lugančik ≃ 83 48.35 N 39.32 E
Lugang, Zhg. 100 27.23 N 115.36 E
Lugang, Zhg. 100 31.17 N 118.22 E
Luganga 154 7.31 S 35.32 E
Lugano 58 46.01 N 8.58 E
Lugano, Lago di ⊜ 58 46.00 N 9.00 E
Lugansk → Vorošilovgrad 83 48.34 N 39.20 E
Luganskoje 83 48.26 N 38.15 E
Luganville 175f 15.32 S 167.08 E
Lugards Falls L 154 3.03 S 38.42 E
Lugareño 240p 21.33 N 77.28 W
Lugarno 274a 33.59 S 151.03 E
Lugau 54 50.44 N 12.44 E
Lügde 52 51.57 N 9.15 E
Lugela 154 16.25 S 36.43 E
Lugenda 154 12.30 S 37.43 E
Lugenda ≃ 154 11.25 S 38.33 E
Lugg ≃ 42 52.02 N 2.38 W
Luggarus → Locarno 58 46.10 N 8.48 E
Lugh Ganane 144 3.56 N 42.32 E
Luginino 76 57.43 N 35.17 E
Luginy 78 51.04 N 28.24 E
Lugnano in Teverina 66 42.34 N 12.20 E
Lugnaquillia ∧ 48 52.58 N 6.27 W
Lugnås 40 58.39 N 13.42 E
Lugny 58 46.28 N 4.49 E
Lugo, Esp. 34 43.00 N 7.34 W
Lugo, It. 66 44.25 N 11.54 E
Lugoj 38 45.41 N 21.54 E
Lugongshi 106 31.38 N 121.12 E
Lugos → Lugoj 38 45.41 N 21.54 E
Lugouqiao 105 39.51 N 116.13 E
Lugovaja Subbota 86 59.52 N 69.45 E
Lugovoj, S.S.S.R. 85 42.56 N 72.45 E
Lugovoj, S.S.S.R. 86 59.44 N 65.55 E
Lugovoje 85 42.55 N 72.43 E
Lugovskij 88 58.02 N 112.54 E
Lugovskoje 80 50.38 N 46.28 E
Lugu 102 28.21 N 102.09 E
Lugufu ≃ 154 5.10 S 30.14 E
Lugunga ∧ 154 6.47 S 36.19 E
Luguru 154 2.55 S 33.58 E
Lugus Island I 116 5.41 N 120.50 E
Luhanka 26 61.47 N 25.42 E
Luhe 60 49.35 N 12.09 E
Luhe ≃ 52 53.18 N 10.11 E
Lühedian 100 32.33 N 114.28 E
Luhit ≃ 120 27.48 N 95.28 E
Lühmannsdorf 54 54.00 N 13.38 E
Luhombero ≃ 154 8.24 S 37.12 E
Luhsien → Luzhou 107 28.54 N 105.27 E
Luhuo 102 31.26 N 100.48 E
Lui ≃, Ang. 152 8.41 S 17.56 E
Lui ≃, Zam. 152 16.21 S 23.18 E
Lui, Beinn ∧ 46 56.24 N 4.49 W
Luia 152 8.26 S 21.45 E
Luia (Ruya) ≃, Afr. 154 16.35 S 33.13 E
Luia ≃, Ang. 152 8.24 S 21.42 E
Lúia ≃, Moç. 154 15.34 S 32.58 E
Luiana 152 17.23 S 23.03 E
Luiana ≃ 152 17.27 S 23.14 E
Luichart, Loch ⊜ 46 57.37 N 4.46 W
Luido 156 21.31 S 34.41 E
Luie ≃ 152 4.33 S 17.41 E
Luik → Liège 56 50.38 N 5.34 E
Luilaka ≃ 152 0.52 S 20.12 E
Luilu ≃ 152 6.22 S 23.50 E
Luimbale 152 12.15 S 15.99 E
Luimneach → Limerick 48 52.40 N 8.38 W
Luing I 46 56.13 N 5.40 W
Luino 58 46.00 N 8.44 E
Luio ≃ 152 13.15 S 21.39 E
Luipaardsvlei 273d 26.16 S 27.42 E
Luís Alves 252 26.44 S 48.57 W
Luisant 50 48.25 N 1.29 E
Luís Correia 250 2.53 S 41.40 W
Luisen-Berg ∧2 264a 52.27 N 13.07 E
Luisenthal 54 50.47 N 10.43 E
Luís Gomes 250 6.25 S 38.23 W
Luis Guillón 288 34.48 S 58.27 W
Luishia 154 11.10 S 27.02 E
Luisiânia 255 21.41 S 50.17 W
Luis Moya, Méx. 234 22.25 N 102.15 W
Luis Moya, Méx. 234 23.05 N 103.56 W
Luis Peña, Cayo de I 240m 18.18 N 65.20 W
Luis Pereira, Arroyo ≃ 258 34.33 S 57.02 W
Luita 152 8.04 S 19.25 E
Luitpold Coast ⊥2 9 78.30 S 32.00 W
Luiza 152 7.12 S 22.25 E
Luiza ≃ 152 7.35 S 22.40 E
Luizavo ≃ 152 11.42 S 23.12 E
Luizi 154 6.03 S 27.28 E
Luján, Arg. 252 33.03 S 68.52 W
Luján, Arg. 252 32.22 S 65.57 W
Luján, Arg. 258 34.34 S 59.07 W
Luján ≃ 288 34.26 S 58.32 W
Lujia 106 31.15 N 121.37 E
Lujiabang 106 31.20 N 121.03 E

Symbols in the index entries represent the broad categories identified in the key at the right. Symbols with superior numbers (⋀2) identify subcategories (see complete key on page I · 30).

Kartensymbole in dem Registerverzeichnis stellen die rechts in Schlüssel erklärten Kategorien dar. Symbole mit hochgestellten Ziffern (⋀2) bezeichnen Unterabteilungen einer Kategorie (vgl. vollständiger Schlüssel auf Seite I · 30).

Los símbolos incluidos en el texto del índice representan las grandes categorías identificadas con la clave a la derecha. Los símbolos con numeros en su parte superior (⋀2) identifican las subcategorías (véase la clave completa en la página I · 30).

Les symboles de l'index représentent les catégories indiquées dans la légende à droite. Les symboles suivis d'un indice (⋀2) représentent des sous-catégories (voir légende complète à la page I · 30).

Os símbolos incluídos no texto do índice representam as grandes categorias identificadas com a chave à direita. Os símbolos com números em sua parte superior (⋀2) identificam as subcategorias (veja-se a chave completa à página I · 30).

Symbol	English	Deutsch	Español	Français	Português
∧	Mountain	Berg	Montaña	Montagne	Montanha
⋀	Mountains	Berge	Montañas	Montagnes	Montanhas
)(	Pass	Pass	Paso	Col	Passo
∨	Valley, Canyon	Tal, Cañon	Valle, Cañón	Vallée, Canyon	Vale, Canhão
≚	Plain	Ebene	Llano	Plaine	Planície
>	Cape	Kap	Cabo	Cap	Cabo
I	Island	Insel	Isla	Île	Ilha
II	Islands	Inseln	Islas	Îles	Ilhas
⊥	Other Topographic Features	Andere Topographische Objekte	Otros Elementos Topográficos	Autres données topographiques	Outros Elementos Topográficos

ESPAÑOL — Nombre / Página / Lat.°′ / Long.°′ W=Oeste
FRANÇAIS — Nom / Page / Lat.°′ / Long.°′ W=Ouest
PORTUGUÊS — Nome / Página / Lat.°′ / Long.°′ W=Oeste

Nombre / Nom / Nome	Página / Page	Lat.°′	Long.°′
Lujiachang	107	30.14 N	105.34 E
Lujiagangzi	104	42.05 N	122.59 E
Lujiang	100	31.14 N	117.17 E
Lujiang ≃	100	27.02 N	115.03 E
Lujiao	100	29.10 N	112.52 E
Lujiaoxi	107	28.55 N	105.48 E
Lujiaqiao, Zhg.	106	31.47 N	120.27 E
Lujiaqiao, Zhg.	107	28.50 N	106.21 E
Lujiaqiao, Zhg.	107	30.16 N	104.25 E
Lujiatun, Zhg.	98	40.14 N	122.11 E
Lujiatun, Zhg.	104	41.10 N	121.56 E
Lujiatun, Zhg.	104	41.58 N	122.38 E
Lujiatun, Zhg.	104	42.18 N	124.15 E
Lujiazhou	100	28.16 N	114.35 E
L'uk	80	56.55 N	52.48 E
Lukachukai Wash V	200	36.39 N	109.36 W
Lukačok	89	53.03 N	132.16 E
Lukala	152	5.31 S	14.32 E
Lukanga, Zaïre	152	1.41 S	18.09 E
Lukanga, Zaïre	152	1.00 S	18.08 E
Lukanga Swamp ☰	154	14.25 S	27.45 E
Luk'anovo	82	54.52 N	37.25 E
Lukašin	84	40.12 N	44.01 E
Lukaškin Jar	86	60.20 N	78.24 E
Lukašovka	78	51.38 N	35.35 E
Luke, Mount ▲	162	27.13 S	116.48 E
Lukenie ≃	152	2.44 S	18.09 E
Lukens, Mount ▲	280	34.16 N	118.14 W
Lukeqin	86	42.44 N	89.42 E
Lukeville	200	31.53 N	112.49 W
Luki	76	53.29 N	26.15 E
Lukino, S.S.S.R.	82	55.26 N	37.04 E
Lukino, S.S.S.R.	82	55.50 N	36.49 E
Lukk	146	32.01 N	24.45 E
Lukka	140	14.33 N	23.42 E
Luk Kang	271d	22.27 N	114.02 E
Luknovo	80	56.12 N	42.03 E
Lukojanov	80	55.02 N	44.30 E
Lukolela, Zaïre	152	5.23 S	24.32 E
Lukolela, Zaïre	152	1.03 S	17.12 E
Lukong	107	29.31 N	105.39 E
Lukop	174r	6.54 N	158.19 E
Lukose ≃	154	7.28 S	36.31 E
Lukoshi ≃	152	10.05 S	22.59 E
Lukosi	154	18.30 S	26.30 E
Lukoškino	82	55.19 N	37.16 E
Lukou, Zhg.	100	27.42 N	113.08 E
Lukou, Zhg.	100	29.30 N	113.26 E
Lukou, Zhg.	100	27.14 N	114.04 E
Lukou, Zhg.	106	31.48 N	118.52 E
Lukouyu	100	28.24 N	113.18 E
Lukov	78	51.13 N	24.19 E
Lukovit	38	43.12 N	24.10 E
Lukovskaja	80	50.35 N	41.52 E
Łuków	30	51.56 N	22.23 E
Lukuga ≃	154	5.40 S	26.55 E
Lukula	152	5.23 S	12.57 E
Lukula ≃	152	5.08 S	12.28 E
Lukulu	152	14.25 S	23.12 E
Lukulu ≃	154	10.56 S	31.05 E
Lukumburu	154	9.45 S	35.09 E
Lukunga ≃	273b	4.25 S	15.14 E
Lukuni	152	5.52 S	17.11 E
Lukusashi ≃	154	14.38 S	30.00 E
Lukusuzi Game Reserve ◆[4]	154	12.50 S	32.35 E
Lula, It.	71	40.28 N	9.29 E
Lula, Miss., U.S.	194	34.27 N	90.29 W
Lula, Zaïre	152	5.22 S	16.02 E
Luleå	26	65.34 N	22.10 E
Luleälven ≃	24	65.35 N	22.03 E
Lüleburgaz	130	41.24 N	27.21 E
Lules	252	26.56 S	65.21 W
Luliang	102	25.05 N	103.36 E
Lüliangshan ⩚	102	37.25 N	111.20 E
Luliāni	123	31.15 N	74.25 E
Luliao	269d	25.07 N	121.39 E
Luling	222	29.41 N	97.39 W
Lullingstone Castle ⊥	260	51.21 N	0.12 E
Lulo ≃	152	9.25 S	18.14 E
Lulong	98	39.54 N	118.50 E
Lulonga	152	0.37 N	18.23 E
Lulonga ≃	152	0.43 N	18.23 E
Lulu ≃	152	1.18 N	23.42 E
Lulua ≃	152	5.02 S	21.07 E
Luluabourg → Kananga	152	5.54 S	22.25 E
Lulu Island I, B.C., Can.	224	49.09 N	123.05 W
Lulu Island I, Alaska, U.S.	182	55.28 N	133.30 W
Luluozhen	98	37.06 N	113.58 E
Lulworth, Mount ▲	162	26.53 S	117.42 E
Luma	174y	14.14 S	169.32 W
Lumai	152	13.31 S	21.21 E
Lumajang	115a	8.08 S	113.13 E
Lumaling	120	29.53 N	92.37 E
Lumb	262	53.42 N	1.58 W
Lumbala	152	12.39 S	22.34 E
Lumbala ≃	152	12.38 S	22.34 E
Lumban	116	14.18 N	121.27 E
Lumbanganjang	114	2.22 N	98.43 E
Lumbangaraga	114	1.53 N	99.04 E
Lumbanlobu	114	2.31 N	99.08 E
Lumbe ≃	152	16.42 S	23.42 E
Lumber ≃	192	34.12 N	79.10 W
Lumber City	192	31.56 N	82.41 W
Lumberport	188	39.23 N	80.21 W
Lumberton, Miss., U.S.	194	31.00 N	89.27 W
Lumberton, N.C., U.S.	192	34.37 N	79.00 W
Lumbis	112	4.18 N	116.15 E
Lumbo	154	15.00 S	40.44 E
Lumbovka	24	67.44 N	40.30 E
Lumbrales	34	40.56 N	6.43 W
Lumbrein	58	46.41 N	9.08 E
Lumbres	50	50.42 N	2.08 E
Lumbwa	154	0.12 S	35.28 E
Lumby	182	50.15 N	118.58 W
Lumding	120	25.45 N	93.10 E
Lumege ≃	152	11.55 S	20.58 E
Lumerau ≃	116	5.21 N	118.53 E
Lumiei ≃	64	46.24 N	12.51 E
Luminárias	256	21.30 S	44.54 W
Luminosa	256	22.35 S	45.38 W
Lumintao ≃	116	12.43 N	120.55 E
Lummen	56	50.59 N	5.12 E
Lummi Bay C	224	48.46 N	122.41 W
Lummi Indian Reservation ◆[4]	224	48.48 N	122.38 W
Lummi Island	224	48.42 N	122.40 W
Lummi Island I	224	48.42 N	122.40 W
Lumphanan	46	57.07 N	2.41 W
Lumphăt	110	13.30 N	106.59 E
Lumpini Park ♠	269a	13.44 N	100.33 E
Lumpkin	192	32.03 N	84.48 W
Lumpun ≃	80	57.01 N	51.22 E
Lumsån ≃	40	59.59 N	15.26 E
Lumsås	41	55.57 N	11.31 E
Lumsden, N.B., Can.	186	49.19 N	53.37 W
Lumsden, Sask., Can.	184	50.34 N	104.53 W
Lumsden, N.Z.	172	45.44 S	168.27 E
Lumsden, Scot., U.K.	46	57.15 N	2.52 W
Lumsheden	40	60.43 N	16.15 E
Lums Pond State Park ♠	208	39.34 N	75.43 W
Lumu, Indon.	112	2.11 S	119.09 E
Lumu, Zhg.	106	31.22 N	120.37 E
Lumuhu ⊚	120	33.45 N	79.30 E
Lumuna	154	3.46 S	26.24 E
Lumuna ≃	152	16.59 S	21.25 E
Lumut	114	4.14 N	100.38 E
Lumut, Tanjung >	112	3.50 S	105.57 E
Lumwana	154	11.50 S	25.10 E
Lün, Mong.	88	47.24 N	102.52 E
Lün, Mong.	88	47.52 N	105.15 E
Luna, Pil.	116	18.18 N	121.21 E
Luna, Pil.	116	16.51 N	120.23 E
Luna ≃	246	4.32 S	60.41 W
Lunada Bay C	280	33.46 N	118.25 W
Lunain ≃	50	48.20 N	2.47 E
Lunamatrona	71	39.39 N	8.54 E
Lunan	102	24.49 N	103.16 E
Lunan Bay C	46	56.39 N	2.28 W
Lunano	66	43.44 N	12.26 E
Luna Pier	216	41.48 N	83.27 W
Lūnāvāda	120	23.08 N	73.37 E
Luncarty	46	56.27 N	3.28 W
Lund, B.C., Can.	182	49.58 N	124.44 W
Lund, Sve.	41	55.42 N	13.11 E
Lund, Nev., U.S.	204	38.52 N	115.00 W
Lunda □[5]	152	9.00 S	20.00 E
Lunda ≃, Ang.	152	6.07 S	13.52 E
L'unda ≃, S.S.S.R.	80	56.32 N	46.03 E
Lundåkrabukten C	41	55.48 N	12.53 E
Lundale	188	37.48 N	81.45 W
Lundar	184	50.42 N	98.02 W
Lundazi	154	12.19 S	33.13 E
Lundby	41	55.07 N	11.53 E
Lunde	41	55.29 N	10.21 E
Lundeborg	41	55.08 N	10.47 E
Lunden	41	54.20 N	9.01 E
Lunderskov	41	55.29 N	9.18 E
Lundevatn ⊚	26	58.22 N	6.36 E
Lundi ≃	154	21.43 S	32.34 E
Lundsberg	40	59.30 N	14.10 E
Lundsfjärden ⊚	40	59.38 N	14.41 E
Lundy I	42	51.10 N	4.40 W
Lundys Lane	214	41.53 N	80.21 W
Lune ≃	44	54.02 N	2.50 W
Lüneburg	52	53.15 N	10.23 E
Lüneburg □[6]	52	53.00 N	10.15 E
Lüneburger Heide ◆[1]	52	53.10 N	10.20 E
Lüneburger Heide, Naturpark ♠	52	53.10 N	9.55 E
Lunel	62	43.41 N	4.08 E
Lünen	52	51.36 N	7.32 E
Lunenburg, N.S., Can.	186	44.23 N	64.19 W
Lunenburg, Mass., U.S.	207	42.36 N	71.44 W
Lunenburg, Va., U.S.	192	36.58 N	78.16 W
Luneray	50	49.50 N	0.55 E
Lünern	263	51.33 N	7.46 E
Lunéville	56	48.36 N	6.30 E
Lunga I	46	56.13 N	5.42 W
Lunga ≃, Ang.	152	5.59 S	16.20 E
Lunga ≃, Zam.	154	14.34 S	26.25 E
Lunga Game Reserve ◆[4]	154	12.55 S	25.10 E
Lungälven ≃	40	59.34 N	14.10 E
Lunga Reservoir ⊚[1]	208	38.32 N	77.28 W
Lungau ◆[1]	64	47.07 N	13.39 E
Lungavilla	62	45.02 N	9.04 E
Lungch'i → Zhangzhou	100	24.33 N	117.39 E
Lunge	152	12.12 S	16.05 E
Lunge'nake	120	31.45 N	85.55 E
Lungern	58	46.47 N	8.10 E
Lunghezza ◆[8]	267a	41.55 N	12.35 E
Lunghua Pagoda ⊕[1]	269b	31.09 N	121.25 E
Lungi	150	8.38 N	13.13 W
Lungleh	120	22.53 N	92.44 E
Lungro	68	39.44 N	16.07 E
Lung Shun Wan Chau I	271d	22.22 N	114.21 E
Lungt'an	100	24.52 N	121.12 E
Lungué-Bungo (Lungwebungu) ≃	152	14.19 S	23.14 E
Lunguya	154	3.23 S	32.24 E
Lungwebungu (Lungué-Bungo) ≃	152	14.19 S	23.14 E
Lūni	120	26.00 N	73.00 E
Lūni ≃	120	24.41 N	71.15 E
Luni ⊥	64	44.04 N	10.01 E
Lunia-Bubi	154	7.30 S	24.49 E
Lunigiana ◆[1]	64	44.15 N	9.50 E
Lunin	76	52.18 N	26.38 E
Luninec	76	52.15 N	26.48 E
Lunino, S.S.S.R.	80	53.35 N	45.14 E
Lunino, S.S.S.R.	82	54.09 N	38.29 E
Lunjiao	100	22.53 N	113.13 E
Lunnaja, Gora ▲	180	68.14 N	174.20 E
Lunndörrsfjällen ▲	26	63.00 N	13.00 E
Lunno	76	53.27 N	24.16 E
Lunongzha	106	31.59 N	120.55 E
Lunsar	150	8.41 N	12.32 W
Lunsemfwa ≃	154	14.54 S	30.12 E
Lunt	262	53.31 N	2.59 W
Lunteren	52	52.05 N	5.37 E
Lunyuk	115b	8.57 S	117.14 E
Lunz am See	61	47.51 N	15.03 E
Lunzenau	54	50.58 N	12.45 E
Lunzhen	98	36.47 N	116.34 E
Luoba, Zhg.	100	24.51 N	114.13 E
Luoba, Zhg.	107	29.08 N	106.11 E
Luobei (Fengxiangzhen)	89	47.34 N	130.50 E
Luobo	102	28.22 N	101.38 E
Luobu	102	24.30 N	109.40 E
Luobubo (Lop Nor) ⊚	90	40.20 N	90.15 E
Luobumiao	102	40.19 N	107.30 E
Luobuqiongzi	124	29.02 N	89.15 E
Luochanghe	100	31.01 N	117.18 E
Luocheng	102	24.51 N	108.59 E
Luochengpu	107	29.23 N	104.01 E
Luochuan	102	35.55 N	109.26 E
Luoci	102	25.19 N	102.18 E
Luodian, Zhg.	102	22.47 N	111.31 E
Luodian, Zhg.	106	31.25 N	121.20 E
Luoding	110	22.47 N	111.31 E
Luoduoke	120	33.28 N	79.40 E
Luoduxi	107	30.22 N	106.35 E
Luofa	105	39.25 N	116.50 E
Luofang, Zhg.	100	28.40 N	115.04 E
Luofang, Zhg.	100	27.52 N	115.06 E
Luofu, Zaïre	154	0.10 S	29.14 E
Luofu, Zhg.	100	24.32 N	115.35 E
Luofushan ⩚	100	23.28 N	114.10 E
Luogang, Zhg.	100	23.11 N	113.30 E
Luogang, Zhg.	100	24.25 N	115.38 E
Luogosanto	71	41.03 N	9.13 E
Luoguhe	89	53.18 N	121.30 E
Luohanchang	107	28.55 N	105.29 E
Luohanshan ▲	100	25.51 N	119.13 E
Luohe	100	33.35 N	114.01 E
Luohe ≃	102	34.42 N	110.15 E
Luohua	100	26.35 N	118.43 E
Luoji	100	32.06 N	117.16 E
Luojiachang	107	30.49 N	106.32 E
Luojiangzhen	102	31.21 N	104.28 E
Luojiatang	106	30.18 N	120.13 E
Luojiatun, Zhg.	98	40.11 N	118.34 E
Luojiatun, Zhg.	104	42.06 N	122.44 E
Luojiatun, Zhg.	104	40.55 N	122.04 E
Luojiawei	100	26.55 N	115.02 E
Luoke	100	24.07 N	114.28 E
Luokeng	100	24.32 N	113.23 E
Luokou, Zhg.	100	26.46 N	115.59 E
Luokou, Zhg.	100	25.39 N	112.46 E
Luokou, Zhg.	100	25.46 N	115.39 E
Luokou, Zhg.	100	28.54 N	117.24 E
Luolong	102	30.45 N	96.09 E
Luolongchang	107	28.49 N	104.57 E
Luomizhuang	98	35.46 N	118.54 E
Luonan	102	34.05 N	110.04 E
Luoning	102	34.25 N	111.42 E
Luoping	102	24.59 N	104.21 E
Luopu	120	37.02 N	80.15 E
Luoqi	102	29.48 N	106.56 E
Luoqiao	100	26.28 N	119.01 E
Luoquanjing	107	29.50 N	104.31 E
Luoshan, Zhg.	100	29.41 N	113.18 E
Luoshan, Zhg.	100	32.13 N	114.32 E
Luoshan, Zhg.	105	39.55 N	117.33 E
Luoshe, Zhg.	106	30.41 N	120.04 E
Luoshe, Zhg.	106	31.39 N	120.11 E
Luossa ≃	152	8.24 S	17.03 E
Luosuojiang ≃	102	21.51 N	101.13 E
Luotian	100	30.48 N	115.22 E
Luotuodian	100	32.13 N	113.49 E
Luotuoqiao	100	29.56 N	121.32 E
Luotuoshan	89	43.43 N	129.28 E
Luowenba	102	31.48 N	107.48 E
Luowenyu	105	40.16 N	117.57 E
Luoxi	100	29.05 N	114.58 E
Luoxiaoshan ⩚	100	26.00 N	114.00 E
Luoyang (Loyang)	102	34.41 N	112.28 E
Luoyangqiao	106	31.39 N	120.05 E
Luoyuan	100	26.31 N	119.32 E
Luozha	120	28.24 N	90.49 E
Luozhexi	107	29.02 N	103.54 E
Luozi	152	4.57 S	14.08 E
Lupala	156	17.50 S	19.06 E
Lupani	154	18.54 S	27.44 E
Lupao	116	15.53 N	120.54 E
Lupar ≃	112	1.30 N	111.00 E
Łupawa	30	54.26 N	17.24 E
Lupberg	60	49.09 N	11.45 E
Lupembe	154	9.15 S	35.15 E
Lupeni	38	45.22 N	23.13 E
Lupire	152	14.36 S	19.29 E
Lupiro	154	8.23 S	36.40 E
Lupon	116	6.54 N	126.00 E
Lupow → Łupawa	30	54.26 N	17.24 E
Luppa	54	51.20 N	12.57 E
Luputa	152	7.10 S	23.42 E
Luqiao, Zhg.	100	32.34 N	117.14 E
Luqiao, Zhg.	100	28.35 N	121.22 E
Luqu	102	34.41 N	102.22 E
Luque	34	37.33 N	4.16 W
Luquillo	240m	18.22 N	65.43 W
Luquillo, Sierra de ⩚	240m	18.17 N	65.47 W
Lūrah ≃	120	31.33 N	66.33 E
Luray	188	38.40 N	78.28 W
Lure	58	47.41 N	6.30 E
Lure, Montagne de ⩚	62	44.07 N	5.47 E
Luremo	152	8.31 S	17.50 E
Lurgan	48	54.28 N	6.20 W
Luribay	248	17.06 S	67.39 W
Lurigancho	286d	12.02 S	77.01 W
Lurín	248	12.17 S	76.52 W
Lúrio	154	13.35 S	40.30 E
Lúrio ≃, Moç.	154	13.35 S	40.32 E
Lurio ≃, Suomi	24	67.08 N	27.29 E
Lurisia	62	44.18 N	7.42 E
Lurnea	274a	33.56 S	150.54 E
Lurö I	26	58.48 N	13.14 E
Lürrip ◆[8]	263	51.12 N	6.28 E
Lusahunga	154	2.52 S	31.15 E
Lusaka, Zaïre	154	7.10 S	29.27 E
Lusaka, Zam.	154	15.25 S	28.17 E
Lusakert	84	40.23 N	44.36 E
Lusambo	152	4.58 S	23.27 E
Lusancay Islands and Reefs II	164	8.25 S	150.20 E
Lusanga	152	4.50 S	18.44 E
Lusangaye	154	4.54 S	26.00 E
Lusangi	154	4.37 S	27.08 E
Luscar	182	53.04 N	117.24 W
Luseke	152	2.51 S	23.08 E
Luseland	184	52.05 N	109.30 W
Lusen ▲	60	48.56 N	13.31 E
Lusenga Plain Game Reserve ◆[4]	154	9.30 S	29.10 E
Lusengo	152	1.46 N	19.29 E
Luserna San Giovanni	62	44.48 N	7.15 E
Lush, Mount ▲	164	17.02 S	127.30 E
Lushan, Zhg.	100	33.45 N	112.53 E
Lushan, Zhg.	102	30.15 N	102.58 E
Lushan ▲	100	29.31 N	115.58 E
Lushanguanliju	100	29.33 N	115.58 E
Lushi	102	34.05 N	111.01 E
Lushiko (Luchico) ≃	152	6.13 S	19.40 E
Lushnje	38	40.56 N	19.42 E
Lushoto	154	4.47 S	38.17 E
Lushui (Luzhang)	102	26.00 N	98.51 E
Lushui ≃	100	27.04 N	115.00 E
Lüshun (Port Arthur)	98	38.48 N	121.16 E
Lüsi	106	32.03 N	121.36 E
Lusi ≃	115a	7.05 S	110.55 E
Lusiana	64	45.47 N	11.34 E
Lusignan	32	46.26 N	0.07 E
Lusignan, Lac ⊚	206	46.40 N	74.09 W
Lusigny-sur-Barse	50	48.15 N	4.16 E
Lusikisiki	158	31.25 S	29.30 E
L'usino	76	52.38 N	26.31 E
Lusk, Eire	48	53.32 N	6.10 W
Lusk, Wyo., U.S.	200	42.46 N	104.27 W
Lus-la-Croix-Haute	62	44.40 N	5.42 E
Luso	152	11.47 S	19.52 E
Lusongwa	152	12.58 S	24.16 E
Luspebryggan	24	67.01 N	19.51 E
Lussac-les-Châteaux	32	46.24 N	0.44 E
Lussan	62	44.09 N	4.22 E
Lustenau	58	47.26 N	9.39 E
Luster	26	61.26 N	7.24 E
Lustin	56	50.23 N	4.53 E
Lustrafjorden C[2]	26	61.20 N	7.22 E
Lüstringen	52	52.16 N	8.08 E
Luswishi ≃	154	13.55 S	27.24 E
Lūt, Dasht-e ◆[2]	128	33.00 N	57.00 E
Lü-ta → Lüda	98	38.53 N	121.35 E
L'uta ≃	76	58.37 N	28.40 E
Lutago (Luttach)	64	46.57 N	11.55 E
Lutaiji	100	33.32 N	115.03 E
Lütan, Zhg.	98	34.07 N	114.27 E
Lütan, Zhg.	100	28.57 N	119.46 E
Lutao	116	10.00 N	124.04 E
Lu Tassu, Serra di ▲	71	41.01 N	9.08 E
Lutcher	194	30.02 N	90.42 W
Lutembo	152	13.26 S	21.16 E
Lutembo ≃	152	12.03 S	22.15 E
L'uten'ka	78	50.13 N	34.02 E
Lutesville	194	37.18 N	89.59 W
Lutéte ≃	152	9.21 S	15.14 E
Lutexu ≃	273b	4.24 S	15.12 E
Lütgendortmund ◆[8]	263	51.30 N	7.21 E
Luthe	52	52.26 N	9.28 E
Luther, Mich., U.S.	190	44.02 N	85.41 W
Luther, Okla., U.S.	196	35.40 N	97.12 W
Luther Lake ⊚	212	43.55 N	80.26 W
Luthersburg	214	41.03 N	78.43 W
Lutherville-timonium	284b	39.25 N	76.37 W
Luthrie	46	56.21 N	3.05 W
Luti	175e	7.14 S	156.59 E
Lütian, Zhg.	100	23.48 N	113.56 E
Lutian, Zhg.	100	26.33 N	114.38 E
Lütjenburg	54	54.17 N	10.35 E
Lütjensee	52	53.39 N	10.22 E
Luton, Eng., U.K.	42	51.53 N	0.25 W
Luton, Eng., U.K.	260	51.22 N	0.32 E
Lutong	112	4.28 N	114.00 E
Lutosn'a ≃	82	56.26 N	36.52 E
Lutouzhen	100	32.16 N	112.53 E
Lutry	58	46.30 N	6.41 E
Lutshi	154	4.09 S	26.30 E
Lutshima ≃	152	5.22 S	18.59 E
Lutsk → Luck	78	50.44 N	25.20 E
Luttach → Lutago	64	46.57 N	11.55 E
Lutter am Barenberge	52	51.59 N	10.16 E
Lutterbach	58	47.46 N	7.17 E
Lutterworth	42	52.28 N	1.10 W
Lüttich → Liège	56	50.38 N	5.34 E
Luttrell	192	36.12 N	83.44 W
Lüttringhausen ◆[8]	263	51.13 N	7.14 E
Lutuai ≃	152	12.33 S	20.16 E
Lutugino	83	48.24 N	39.13 E
Lutz	220	28.09 N	82.28 W
Lützel	56	50.58 N	8.10 E
Lutzelbourg	56	48.44 N	7.15 E
Lützelflüh	58	47.00 N	7.41 E
Lützen	54	51.15 N	12.08 E
Lutzerath	56	50.07 N	7.00 E
Lützow	54	53.40 N	11.11 E
Lützow-Holm Bay C	9	69.10 S	37.30 E
Lutzputs	158	28.03 S	20.40 E
Lützschena	54	51.23 N	12.16 E
Lutzville	158	31.33 S	18.22 E
Luus	102	45.12 N	105.42 E
Luverne, Ala., U.S.	194	31.43 N	86.16 W
Lu Verne, Iowa, U.S.	190	42.55 N	94.05 W
Luverne, Minn., U.S.	198	43.39 N	96.13 W
Luvo	152	5.51 S	14.05 E
Luvo ≃	152	10.18 S	17.08 E
Luvua	154	8.48 S	25.19 E
Lúvua ≃, Ang.	152	11.57 S	22.30 E
Luvua ≃, Zaïre	154	6.46 S	26.58 E
Luvuvhu ≃	156	22.40 S	30.55 E
Luwegu ≃	154	8.31 S	37.23 E
Luwei	106	31.02 N	120.49 E
Luwingu	154	10.15 S	29.55 E
Luwuk, Indon.	112	0.56 S	122.47 E
Luwuk → Banggai, Indon.	112	1.34 S	123.30 E
Luxana Bay C	182	52.03 N	131.00 W
Luxapallila Creek ≃	194	33.28 N	88.26 W
Luxembourg	56	49.36 N	6.09 E
Luxembourg □[4]	56	50.00 N	5.30 E
Luxembourg □[1]	22		
	56	49.45 N	6.05 E
Luxembourg, Jardin du ♠	261	48.51 N	2.19 E
Luxemburg	190	44.32 N	87.42 W
Luxemburg → Luxembourg □[1]	56	49.45 N	6.05 E
Luxemburgo → Luxembourg □[1]	56	49.45 N	6.05 E
Luxeuil-les-Bains	58	47.49 N	6.23 E
Luxi, Zhg.	102	24.32 N	103.41 E
Luxi (Mangshi), Zhg.	102	24.20 N	98.25 E
Luxi ≃	100	28.11 N	116.48 E
Lüxia	100	26.41 N	120.06 E
Luxiang, Zhg.	106	31.32 N	120.45 E
Lüxiang, Zhg.	106	30.50 N	121.10 E
Luxikou	100	29.54 N	113.42 E
Luxmanor	284c	39.02 N	77.07 W
Luxor → Al-Uqşur, Mişr	140	25.41 N	32.39 E
Luxor, Pa., U.S.	214	40.20 N	79.28 W
Luxora	194	35.45 N	89.56 W
Lu Xun Museum ⊕	269b	31.16 N	121.28 E
Lüxuqiao	106	31.50 N	119.31 E
Luy ≃	32	43.39 N	1.08 W
Luyan	106	30.25 N	120.53 E
Lüyangyi	104	41.23 N	121.40 E
Luyanó ≃	286b	23.07 N	82.21 W
Luyashan ⩚	102	38.45 N	111.50 E
Luyeh	100	22.55 N	121.08 E
Luyi	100	33.53 N	115.28 E
Luyu	106	31.34 N	121.41 E
Luyuan, Zhg.	106	31.51 N	120.38 E
Luyuan, Zhg.	271a	39.54 N	116.27 E
Luz, Bra.	255	19.48 S	45.40 W
Luz, Bra.	287a	22.48 S	43.05 W
Luz ◆[8]	266c	38.46 N	9.10 W
Luz, Estação da ◆[5]	287b	23.32 S	46.38 W
Luz, Isla I	254	45.30 S	73.59 W
Luz, Ponta da >	287a	22.47 S	43.05 W
Luza, S.S.S.R.	24	60.39 N	47.10 E
Luza, S.S.S.R.	24	62.42 N	37.06 E
Luža, S.S.S.R.	76	59.58 N	31.56 E
Luža ≃	82	55.03 N	36.35 E
Luzarches	50	49.07 N	2.25 E
Luzern	58	47.03 N	8.18 E
Luzern □[3]	58	47.05 N	8.05 E
Luzerne	210	41.17 N	75.54 W
Luzerne □[6]	210	41.14 N	75.53 W
Luzhai, Zhg.	100	29.16 N	120.17 E
Luzhai, Zhg.	102	24.31 N	109.50 E
Luzhi	106	31.16 N	120.52 E
Luzhou	107	28.54 N	105.27 E
Luziânia	255	16.15 S	47.56 W
Lužické hory ⩚	54	50.48 N	14.40 E
Luzilândia	250	3.28 S	42.22 W
Lužki, S.S.S.R.	76	55.21 N	27.52 E
Lužki, S.S.S.R.	82	54.51 N	37.36 E
Lužná	54	50.06 N	13.45 E
Lužniki ◆[8]	265b	55.43 N	37.33 E
Luzon	236	9.25 N	82.32 W
Luzon I	116	16.00 N	121.00 E
Luzon Strait U	108	20.30 N	121.00 E
Luzy	32	46.48 N	3.58 E
Luzzara	64	44.58 N	10.41 E
Luzzi	68	39.27 N	16.17 E
L'va ≃	78	52.00 N	27.36 E
L'va Tolstogo	82	54.37 N	36.03 E
L'vov	78	49.50 N	24.00 E
L'vovskij	82	55.19 N	37.31 E
Lwów → L'vov	78	49.50 N	24.00 E
Lwówek	30	52.28 N	16.10 E
Lwówek Śląski	30	51.07 N	15.35 E
Lyall, Mount ▲	172	45.17 S	167.34 E
Lyallpur	123	31.25 N	73.05 E
Lyantonde	154	0.24 S	31.09 E
Lybster	46	58.18 N	3.13 W
Lychen	54	53.12 N	13.19 E
Lyck → Ełk	30	53.50 N	22.22 E
Lyckeby	26	56.12 N	15.39 E
Lyčkovo, S.S.S.R.	76	57.55 N	32.24 E
Lyčkovo, S.S.S.R.	78	49.06 N	35.12 E
Lycksele	26	64.36 N	18.40 E
Lycoming □[6]	210	41.14 N	77.00 W
Lycoming Creek ≃	210	41.13 N	77.02 W
Lydd	42	50.57 N	0.55 E
Lydda → Lod	132	31.58 N	34.54 E
Lydden V	42	50.56 N	2.22 W
Lydenburg	156	25.10 S	30.29 E
Lydford	42	50.39 N	4.06 W
Lydgate	262	53.44 N	2.07 W
Lydham	42	52.31 N	2.58 W
Lydia Mills	192	34.28 N	81.55 W
Lydiate	262	53.32 N	2.57 W
Lydick	216	41.42 N	86.22 W
Lydney	42	51.44 N	2.32 W
Lye Green	260	51.43 N	0.35 W
Lyell, Mount ▲, Can.	182	51.57 N	117.06 W
Lyell, Mount ▲, Calif., U.S.	226	37.44 N	119.16 W
Lyell Brown, Mount ▲	162	23.21 S	130.24 E
Lyell Island I	182	52.40 N	131.30 W
Lyford	196	26.24 N	97.48 W
Lygnern ⊚	26	57.29 N	12.20 E
Lykens	208	40.34 N	76.43 W
Lykošino	76	58.07 N	33.43 E
Lyle, Minn., U.S.	190	43.30 N	92.57 W
Lyle, Wash., U.S.	224	45.42 N	121.17 W
Lyles	194	35.55 N	87.21 W
Lyman, Nebr., U.S.	198	41.55 N	104.02 W
Lyman, S.C., U.S.	192	34.56 N	82.09 W
Lyman, Wash., U.S.	224	48.31 N	122.04 W
Lyman, Wyo., U.S.	200	41.20 N	110.18 W
Lymbel'karamo	86	60.15 N	83.32 E
Lyme	207	41.19 N	72.10 W
Lyme Bay C	42	50.38 N	3.00 W
Lyme Hall ⊥	262	53.20 N	2.03 W
Lyme Park ♠	262	53.21 N	2.04 W
Lyme Regis	42	50.44 N	2.57 W
Lyminge	42	51.08 N	1.05 E
Lymington	42	50.46 N	1.33 W
Lymkoj	86	59.31 N	70.22 E
Lymm	262	53.23 N	2.29 W
Lympne	42	51.05 N	1.02 E
Lyn	212	44.35 N	75.47 W
Łyna (Lava) ≃	76	54.37 N	21.14 E
Lynæs	41	55.57 N	11.52 E
Lynbrook	276	40.39 N	73.41 W
Lynch, Ky., U.S.	192	36.58 N	82.55 W
Lynch, Nebr., U.S.	198	42.50 N	98.28 W
Lynch, Lac ⊚	190	46.25 N	77.05 W
Lynchburg, Ohio, U.S.	218	39.14 N	83.48 W
Lynchburg, S.C., U.S.	192	34.04 N	80.04 W
Lynchburg, Tenn., U.S.	194	35.17 N	86.22 W
Lynchburg, Va., U.S.	192	37.24 N	79.10 W
Lynches ≃	192	33.50 N	79.22 W
Lynchville	214	41.26 N	78.34 W
Lynd ≃	164	16.28 S	143.18 E
Lynde Creek ≃	212	43.51 N	78.57 W
Lynden, Ont., Can.	212	43.14 N	80.09 W
Lynden, Wash., U.S.	224	48.57 N	122.27 W
Lyndhurst, Austl.	166	19.12 S	144.23 E
Lyndhurst, Austl.	166	30.17 S	138.21 E
Lyndhurst, Austl.	274b	38.03 S	145.15 E
Lyndhurst, Eng., U.K.	42	50.52 N	1.34 W
Lyndhurst, N.J., U.S.	276	40.49 N	74.07 W
Lyndhurst, Ohio, U.S.	214	41.31 N	81.30 W
Lyndoch	168b	34.37 S	138.53 E
Lyndon, Austl.	162	23.37 S	115.15 E
Lyndon, Kans., U.S.	198	38.36 N	95.41 W
Lyndon, Ky., U.S.	218	38.16 N	85.34 W
Lyndon ≃	162	23.29 S	114.06 E
Lyndon B. Johnson Space Center ⊕[3]	222	29.34 N	95.05 W
Lyndonville, N.Y., U.S.	210	43.19 N	78.23 W
Lyndonville, Vt., U.S.	188	44.32 N	72.01 W
Lyndora	214	40.51 N	79.55 W
Lyne	260	51.23 N	0.33 W
Lyne ≃	44	54.58 N	3.01 W
Lyneham	42	51.31 N	1.58 W
Lynemouth	44	55.12 N	1.31 W
Lyne Water ≃	46	54.39 N	3.16 W
Lynga	80	57.17 N	53.04 E
Lyngdal	26	58.08 N	7.05 E
Lynge	41	55.51 N	12.17 E
Lyngen	24	69.34 N	20.10 E
Lyngen C[2]	24	69.58 N	20.30 E
Lyngør	26	58.38 N	9.10 E
Lynher ≃	42	50.28 N	4.12 W
Lynmouth	42	51.15 N	3.50 W
Lynn, Ala., U.S.	194	34.03 N	87.33 W
Lynn, Ind., U.S.	218	40.03 N	84.56 W
Lynn, Mass., U.S.	207	42.28 N	70.57 W
Lynn ≃	212	42.47 N	80.12 W
Lynn Canal C	180	58.50 N	135.15 W
Lynndyl	200	39.31 N	112.22 W
Lynne Acres	284b	39.21 N	76.45 W
Lynnfield	207	42.32 N	71.03 W
Lynn Garden	192	36.35 N	82.34 W
Lynn Harbor C	283	42.27 N	70.57 W
Lynn Haven	194	30.15 N	85.39 W
Lynn Lake	184	56.51 N	101.03 W
Lynnville	190	41.35 N	92.47 W
Lynnwood, Pa., U.S.	210	41.14 N	75.56 W
Lynnwood, Pa., U.S.	214	40.07 N	79.51 W
Lynnwood, Wash., U.S.	224	47.49 N	122.19 W
Lynton	42	51.15 N	3.50 W
Lyntupy	76	55.03 N	26.19 E
Lynwood, Calif., U.S.	228	33.55 N	118.12 W
Lynwood, Ill., U.S.	278	41.32 N	87.32 W
Lynx Lake ⊚	176	62.25 N	106.15 W
Lyø I	41	55.02 N	10.10 E
Lyon	62	45.45 N	4.51 E
Lyon □[6]	226	39.00 N	119.15 W
Lyon ≃	46	56.37 N	4.01 W
Lyon ◆[5]	261	48.51 N	2.23 E
Lyon, Glen V	46	56.35 N	4.20 W
Lyon, Loch ⊚	46	56.32 N	4.36 W
Lyon Inlet C	176	66.32 N	83.53 W
Lyon Mountain	188	44.43 N	73.55 W
Lyon Mountain ▲	188	44.41 N	73.53 W
Lyonnais □[9]	62	45.45 N	4.30 E
Lyonnais, Monts du ⩚	62	45.40 N	4.30 E
Lyons, Colo., U.S.	200	40.13 N	105.16 W
Lyons, Ga., U.S.	192	32.12 N	82.19 W
Lyons, Ill., U.S.	216	41.49 N	87.50 W
Lyons, Ind., U.S.	194	38.59 N	87.05 W
Lyons, Kans., U.S.	198	38.21 N	98.12 W
Lyons, Mich., U.S.	216	42.59 N	84.57 W
Lyons, Nebr., U.S.	198	41.56 N	96.28 W
Lyons, N.Y., U.S.	210	43.04 N	77.00 W
Lyons, Ohio, U.S.	216	41.42 N	84.04 W
Lyons, Tex., U.S.	222	30.23 N	96.34 W
Lyons, Wis., U.S.	216	42.39 N	88.21 W
Lyons ≃	162	25.02 S	115.09 E
Lyon Satolas, Aérodrome de ⊠	62	45.43 N	5.04 E
Lyons Creek ≃	284a	43.03 N	79.04 W
Lyons Falls	212	43.37 N	75.22 W
Lyons-la-Forêt	50	49.24 N	1.28 E
Lyons Plains	207	41.13 N	73.21 W
Lyons Run ≃	279b	40.25 N	79.43 W
Lyon Station	208	40.28 N	75.45 W
Lyonsville	276	40.57 N	74.25 W
Lyracrumpane	48	52.20 N	9.30 W
Lyrestad	40	58.48 N	14.04 E
Lys (Leie) ≃, Eur.	50	51.03 N	3.43 E
Lys ≃, It.	62	45.36 N	7.47 E
Lysá ▲	60	49.29 N	12.42 E
Lysaja Gora	78	48.11 N	31.06 E
Lysaker	26	59.54 N	10.36 E
Lys'anka	78	49.16 N	30.50 E
Lysá pod Makytou	30	49.12 N	18.13 E
Lysefjorden C[2]	26	59.00 N	6.14 E
Lysekil	26	58.16 N	11.26 E
Łysica ▲	30	50.54 N	20.55 E
Lysjön ⊚	40	60.07 N	14.18 E
Lyskovo	80	56.04 N	45.02 E
Lysogorka	83	47.42 N	39.12 E
Lyss	58	47.04 N	7.18 E
Lysterfield	274b	37.56 S	145.18 E
Lysterfield Hills ⩚[2]	274b	37.56 S	145.16 E
Lysterfield Reservoir ⊚[1]	274b	37.58 S	145.18 E
Lyster Station	206	46.22 N	71.37 W
Lys'va	86	58.07 N	57.47 E
Lys'va ≃	80	58.15 N	54.47 E
Lysyje Gory	80	51.32 N	44.46 E
Lytham Saint Anne's	44	53.45 N	2.57 W
Lytkarino	82	55.35 N	37.54 E
Lytle	196	29.14 N	98.48 W
Lytle Creek ≃	228	34.09 N	117.23 W
Lyttelton, N.Z.	172	43.35 S	172.42 E
Lyttelton, S. Afr.	158	25.50 S	28.11 E
Lytton	182	50.14 N	121.34 W
Lytton Springs	222	30.00 N	97.37 W
Lyubertsy → L'ubercy	82	55.41 N	37.53 E

M

Nombre / Nom / Nome	Página / Page	Lat.°′	Long.°′
Ma ≃	110	19.47 N	105.56 E
Ma, Oued el V, Alg.	148	27.45 N	7.45 W
Ma, Oued el- V, Maur.	148	24.03 N	9.10 W
Maad, Djebel bou ▲	34	36.26 N	2.08 E
Maadid, Djebel ▲	34	35.52 N	4.46 E
Maalaea Bay C	229a	20.47 N	156.29 W
Ma'alot-Tarshiḥa	132	33.01 N	35.17 E
Maam Cross	48	53.27 N	9.31 W
Maan, Tür.	130	36.51 N	38.50 E
Ma'ān, Urd.	132	30.12 N	35.44 E
Ma'ān □[8]	132	30.20 N	36.30 E
Maaninka	26	63.09 N	27.18 E
Maanshan, Zhg.	100	31.42 N	118.30 E
Maanshan, Zhg.	107	29.52 N	104.59 E
Ma-ao	116	10.29 N	122.59 E
Maar	140	6.54 N	31.33 E
Maardu	76	59.28 N	25.02 E
Maarianhamina → Mariehamn	26	60.06 N	19.57 E
Ma'ārik, Qārat al- ▲[2]	142	29.59 N	30.52 E
Ma'arrat an-Nu'mān	130	35.38 N	36.40 E
Ma'arrat Mişrīn	130	36.01 N	36.40 E
Ma'arrat Şaydnāyā	132	33.41 N	36.23 E
Maarssen	52	52.08 N	5.08 E
Maas	48	54.50 N	8.22 W
Maas (Meuse) ≃	30	51.49 N	5.01 E
Maasbracht	52	51.08 N	5.53 E
Maasdam	52	51.47 N	4.32 E
Maaseik	56	51.06 N	5.48 E
Maasholm	41	54.41 N	9.59 E
Maasin	116	10.08 N	124.50 E
Ma'āṣir ash-Shūf	132	33.40 N	35.40 E
Maasniel	52	51.13 N	6.01 E
Maassluis	52	51.55 N	4.15 E
Maastricht	56	50.52 N	5.43 E
Maave	156	21.03 S	34.47 E
Ma-ayon ≃	116	11.25 N	122.46 E
Maba, Zhg.	100	32.59 N	118.48 E
Maba, Zhg.	100	24.41 N	113.35 E
Maba, Ouadi V	146	15.10 N	21.00 E
Mababe Depression •[7]	156	18.50 S	24.15 E
Mabaduan	164	9.16 S	142.44 E
Mabaho, Mount ▲	116	9.15 N	125.42 E
Mabaia	152	7.13 S	14.03 E
Mabalane	156	23.37 S	32.31 E
Mabana	224	48.06 N	122.25 W
Mabanga	152	1.30 N	19.06 E
Mabank	222	32.22 N	96.06 W
Mabaoquan	105	40.09 N	115.53 E
Ma'barot	132	32.22 N	34.54 E
Mabaruma	246	8.12 N	59.47 W
Mabashi	268	35.49 N	139.55 E
Mabau	112	2.14 S	111.54 E
Mabay	240p	20.16 N	76.40 W
Mabber, Ras >	144	9.28 N	50.53 E
Mabel Creek	162	29.01 S	134.17 E
Mabeleapodi	156	20.58 S	22.36 E
Mabel Lake ⊚	182	50.35 N	118.44 W
Maben	194	33.33 N	89.05 W
Mabenga-Cité	152	3.39 S	18.40 E
Mabenge	152	4.14 N	24.09 E
Maberry, Loch ⊚	44	55.02 N	4.41 W
Mabeul	36	36.27 N	10.46 E
Mabi, Nihon	96	34.38 N	133.41 E
Mabi, Zhg.	100	26.21 N	119.36 E
Mabian	107	28.48 N	103.41 E
Mabian ≃	107	29.04 N	103.43 E
Mabicun	102	35.59 N	112.15 E
Mablethorpe	44	53.21 N	0.15 E
Mableton	192	33.49 N	84.35 W
Mabole ≃	150	9.01 N	12.44 W
Maboma	154	2.32 N	28.13 E
Mabonto	150	8.52 N	11.49 W
Mabote	156	22.03 S	34.09 E
Mabou	186	46.05 N	61.22 W
Mabrak, Jabal ▲	132	30.13 N	35.29 E
Mabrous Tafidinga ⊤[4]	146	21.13 N	13.38 E
Mabrūk, Lībīya	146	29.50 N	17.10 E
Mabrūk, Sūd.	140	8.07 N	29.25 E
Mabton	202	46.13 N	120.00 W
Mabu	100	31.33 N	116.04 E
Mabuguai	100	29.49 N	112.42 E
Mabuki	154	2.59 S	33.11 E
Mabuni	174m	26.05 N	127.43 E
Mabwe	154	8.39 S	26.31 E
Mc → Mac			
Mača, S.S.S.R.	74	59.54 N	117.35 E
Maca, Ven.	286c	10.28 N	66.48 W
Macá, Cerro ▲	254	45.06 S	73.12 W
Macachín	252	37.09 S	63.39 W
Macaco, Morro do ▲[2]	287a	22.56 S	43.07 W
Macacos, Ilha dos I	250	1.20 S	50.35 W
Macacu ≃	256	22.42 S	43.02 W
McAdam	186	45.36 N	67.20 W
McAdams Peak ▲[2]	219	38.58 N	90.32 W
McAdoo	210	40.55 N	76.00 W
McAdoo Heights	210	40.54 N	76.01 W
Macaé	255	22.23 S	41.47 W
McAfee	210	41.11 N	74.33 W
Macaíba	250	5.51 S	35.21 W
Macajalar Bay C	116	8.37 N	124.38 E
Macajuba	255	12.09 S	40.22 W
Macalaya	116	12.53 N	123.46 E
Macalelon	116	13.45 N	122.08 E
McAlester	196	34.56 N	95.46 W
Macalister	182	52.27 N	122.24 W
Macalister ≃	166	38.02 S	146.59 E
Macalister, Mount ▲	170	34.27 S	149.45 E
McAlisterville	208	40.38 N	77.16 W
McAllen	196	26.12 N	98.15 W
McAlpine	208	39.16 N	76.50 W
McAlpine Dam ◆[6]	218	38.16 N	85.47 W
MacAlpine Lake ⊚	176	66.40 N	103.15 W
McAlveys Fort	214	40.39 N	77.50 W
Macambira	250	10.40 S	37.32 W
Macamic, Lac ⊚	190	48.48 N	78.59 W
Macão	34	39.33 N	8.00 W
Macao → Macau □[2]	100	22.10 N	113.33 E
Macapá	250	0.02 N	51.03 W
Macar	130	37.06 N	30.56 E
Macará	246	4.23 S	79.57 W
Macarani	255	15.33 S	40.24 W
Macarao	286c	10.26 N	67.02 W
Macarao ≃	286c	10.26 N	67.01 W
Macareo, Caño ≃[1]	246	9.47 N	61.37 W
Macari ≃	250	1.52 N	50.31 W
MacArthur, Pil.	116	10.50 N	125.00 E
MacArthur, Ill., U.S.	278	41.39 N	87.44 W
McArthur	188	39.15 N	82.29 W
McArthur ≃	164	15.54 S	136.40 E
McArthur River	164	16.27 S	136.07 E
Macas	246	2.19 S	78.07 W
Macatawa ≃	216	42.48 N	86.05 W
Macatawa, Lake C	216	42.47 N	86.10 W
Macaterick, Loch ⊚	44	55.12 N	4.26 W
Macau, Bra.	250	5.07 S	36.38 W
Macau (Aomen), Macau	100	22.14 N	113.35 E
Macau □[2]	90		
	100	22.10 N	113.33 E
Macau, Ilha I	156	20.55 S	35.05 E
Macauã ≃	248	9.13 S	68.44 W
Macaúbas	255	13.02 S	42.42 W
McAuley	184	50.16 N	101.23 W
Macaya, Pic de ▲	238	18.25 N	74.00 W
Macaza ≃	206	46.21 N	74.47 W
McBain	190	44.12 N	85.13 W
McBee	192	34.28 N	80.15 W
McBeth	222	29.11 N	95.30 W
McBeth Fjord C[2]	176	69.38 N	68.30 W
McBride	182	53.18 N	120.10 W
McCall	202	44.55 N	116.06 W
McCall Creek	194	31.31 N	90.42 W
McCallum	186	47.38 N	56.15 W
McCallum Creek ≃	169	37.03 S	143.49 E
McCamey	196	31.08 N	102.13 W
McCammon	202	42.39 N	112.12 W
Maccarese ◆[8]	267a	41.53 N	12.13 E
Maccarese, Bonifica di ◆[1]	267a	41.51 N	12.13 E
McCarteney Creek ≃	202	47.13 N	120.05 W
Mccarthy	180	61.26 N	142.55 W
McCauley Island I	182	53.40 N	130.15 W
McCaysville	192	34.59 N	84.23 W
Macchiagodena	66	41.33 N	14.24 E

English	Deutsch	Español	Français	Português
≃ River	Fluss	Río	Rivière	Rio
Ξ Canal	Kanal	Canal	Canal	Canal
L Waterfall, Rapids	Wasserfall, Stromschnellen	Cascada, Rápidos	Chute d'eau, Rapides	Cascata, Rápidos
U Strait	Meeresstrasse	Estrecho	Détroit	Estreito
C Bay, Gulf	Bucht, Golf	Bahía, Golfo	Baie, Golfe	Baía, Golfo
⊚ Lake, Lakes	See, Seen	Lago, Lagos	Lac, Lacs	Lago, Lagos
☰ Swamp	Sumpf	Pantano	Marais	Pântano
⊓ Ice Features, Glacier	Eis- und Gletscherformen	Accidentes Glaciales	Formes glaciaires	Acidentes Glaciares
⊤ Other Hydrographic Features	Andere Hydrographische Objekte	Otros Elementos Hidrográficos	Autres données hydrographiques	Outros Elementos Hidrográficos
✣ Submarine Features	Untermeerische Objekte	Accidentes Submarinos	Formes de relief sous-marin	Acidentes Submarinos
□ Political Unit	Politische Einheit	Unidad Politica	Entité politique	Unidade Política
⊕ Cultural Institution	Kulturelle Institution	Institución Cultural	Institution culturelle	Instituição Cultural
⊥ Historical Site	Historische Stätte	Sitio Histórico	Site historique	Sitio Histórico
♠ Recreational Site	Erholungs- und Ferienort	Sitio de Recreo	Centre de loisirs	Sítio de Lazer
⊠ Airport	Flughafen	Aeropuerto	Aéroport	Aeroporto
■ Military Installation	Militäranlage	Instalación Militar	Installation militaire	Instalação Militar
◆ Miscellaneous	Verschiedenes	Misceláneo	Divers	Miscelânea

McChord Air Force Base ■ 224 47.08 N 122.29 W
McClarens Run ≃ 279b 40.27 N 80.12 W
McClarty Lake @ 184 54.28 N 100.20 W
McCleary 224 47.03 N 123.16 W
McClees Creek ≃ 276 40.22 N 74.03 W
McClellan Air Force Base ■ 226 38.39 N 121.23 W
McClellan Creek ≃ 196 35.22 N 100.34 W
McClellanville 192 33.05 N 79.28 W
Macclenny 192 30.18 N 82.07 W
Macclesfield, Austl. 168b 35.10 S 138.50 E
Macclesfield, Eng., U.K. 44 53.16 N 2.07 W
Macclesfield □[8] 262 53.17 N 2.15 W
Macclesfield Canal ≡ 262 53.24 N 2.03 W
Macclesfield Forest ◆[3] 262 53.15 N 2.03 W
McClintock, Mount ∧ 9 80.13 S 157.26 E
McCloud 204 41.15 N 122.08 W
McCloud ≃ 204 40.46 N 122.18 W
McClure, Ill., U.S. 194 37.19 N 89.26 W
McClure, Ohio, U.S. 216 41.22 N 83.57 W
McClure, Pa., U.S. 210 40.42 N 77.19 W
McClure, Lake @[1] 226 37.37 N 120.16 W
McClusky 198 47.29 N 100.27 W
McColl 192 34.40 N 79.33 W
McComas 192 37.23 N 81.17 W
McComb, Miss., U.S. 194 31.14 N 90.27 W
McComb, Ohio, U.S. 216 41.06 N 83.48 W
McConaughy, Lake @[1] 198 41.15 N 101.50 W
McConnell Air Force Base ■ 198 37.38 N 97.15 W
McConnell Range ⋀ 180 64.00 N 123.50 W
McConnellsburg 188 39.56 N 77.59 W
McConnells Mill 279b 40.15 N 80.15 W
McConnells Mill State Park ♦ 214 40.57 N 80.11 W
McConnellstown 214 40.27 N 78.05 W
McConnellsville 210 43.16 N 75.42 W
McConnelsville 188 39.39 N 81.51 W
McCook, Ill., U.S. 278 41.48 N 87.50 W
McCook, Nebr., U.S. 198 40.12 N 100.38 W
McCordsville 218 39.54 N 85.55 W
McCormick 192 33.55 N 82.17 W
McCormick Place ψ 278 41.51 N 87.37 W
McCoy 224 45.03 N 123.13 W
McCoy Lake @ 184 52.35 N 92.19 W
McCrae Lake @ 212 44.55 N 79.48 W
McCraney Creek ≃ 219 39.39 N 91.12 W
McCreary 184 50.46 N 99.30 W
McCrory 194 35.16 N 91.12 W
Mcculloch, Mount ∧ 162 25.10 S 129.52 E
McCullom Lake 216 42.22 N 88.18 W
Mccullough 279b 40.22 N 79.38 W
McCullough Mountain ∧ 204 35.36 N 115.11 W
McCune 198 37.21 N 95.01 W
McCurtain 196 35.09 N 94.58 W
McCusker ≃ 184 55.32 N 108.40 W
McCutchenville 214 40.59 N 83.16 W
McDade 222 30.17 N 97.15 W
McDavid 194 30.52 N 87.19 W
McDermitt 204 41.59 N 117.36 W
McDermott 218 38.50 N 83.04 W
Macdhui, Ben ∧ 158 30.39 S 27.58 E
MacDill Air Force Base ■ 220 27.51 N 82.29 W
McDonald, Kans., U.S. 198 39.47 N 101.22 W
McDonald, Pa., U.S. 214 40.22 N 80.14 W
Macdonald ≃ 170 33.23 S 150.59 E
McDonald, Lac @ 206 45.52 N 74.35 W
Macdonald, Lake @ 162 23.30 S 129.00 E
McDonald, Lake @ 202 48.35 N 113.55 W
Macdonald, Mount ∧ 175f 17.36 S 168.23 E
McDonald Creek ≃ 202 47.01 N 108.09 W
MacDonald Downs 162 22.27 S 135.13 E
McDonald Islands II 6 53.02 S 72.36 E
Macdonald Lake @ 212 45.14 N 78.34 W
McDonald Park ♦ 282 37.18 N 122.17 W
MacDonald Pass)(202 46.34 N 112.18 W
Macdonald Range ⋀ 182 49.12 N 114.46 W
Macdonnell Ranges ⋀ 162 23.45 S 133.20 E
McDonogh 284c 39.24 N 76.46 W
McDonough, Ga., U.S. 192 33.27 N 84.09 W
McDonough, N.Y., U.S. 210 42.30 N 75.46 W
McDouall Peak 162 29.51 S 134.55 E
McDougall, Mount ∧ 200 42.54 N 110.36 W
MacDowell Lake @ 184 52.15 N 92.45 W
McDowell Peak ∧ 200 33.40 N 111.50 W
Macduff 46 57.40 N 2.29 W
Macdui, Ben ∧ 46 57.05 N 3.38 W
Mačecha 80 50.48 N 43.17 E
Mačechi 78 49.31 N 34.26 E
Maceday Lake @ 281 42.42 N 83.26 W
Macedo de Cavaleiros 34 41.32 N 6.58 W
Macedon 210 43.04 N 77.18 W
Macedon, Mount ∧ 169 37.23 S 144.35 E
Macedonia, Conn., U.S. 207 41.47 N 73.30 W
Macedonia, Ohio, U.S. 214 41.19 N 81.31 W
Macedonia → Makedonija □[3] 38 41.50 N 22.00 E
Macedonia □[9] 38 41.00 N 23.00 E
Macedonia Brook State Park ♦ 207 41.47 N 73.29 W
Macedonio Alcalá 234 17.52 N 96.02 W
Maceió 250 9.40 S 35.43 W
Maceira 266c 38.52 N 9.19 W
McElhattan 210 41.09 N 77.22 W
McElmo Creek ≃ 200 37.13 N 109.12 W
Mc Ennen Airport ⊠ 281 42.12 N 83.37 W
Mcensk 76 53.17 N 36.35 E
Macenta 150 8.33 N 9.28 W
Macenta □[4] 150 8.30 N 9.25 W
Maceo 246 6.33 N 74.47 W
Macerata 66 43.18 N 13.27 E
Macerata □[4] 66 43.12 N 13.10 E
Macerata Feltria 66 43.48 N 12.26 E
McEwen 194 36.06 N 87.38 W
McEwensville 210 41.05 N 76.49 W
McFadden 200 41.39 N 106.08 W
McFarland, Calif., U.S. 226 35.41 N 119.14 W
McFarland, Wis., U.S. 216 43.01 N 89.17 W
MacFarlane ≃ 176 59.12 N 107.58 W
Macfarlane, Lake @ 166 31.55 S 136.42 E
Macfarlane, Mount ∧ 172 43.56 S 169.23 E
McGavock Lake @ 184 56.32 N 101.25 W
McGehee 194 33.38 N 91.24 W
McGill 204 39.23 N 114.47 W
McGillivray, Lac @ 190 46.04 N 77.06 W
McGill University ψ[2] 275a 45.30 N 73.35 W
Macgillycuddy's Reeks ⋀ 48 51.55 N 9.45 W
McGinnis Slough Wildlife Refuge ◆[4] 278 41.39 N 87.52 W
McGovern 214 40.14 N 80.13 W
Mcgrann 214 40.47 N 79.31 W
Mcgrath 180 62.58 N 155.38 W
McGraw 210 42.36 N 76.06 W
MacGregor 184 49.57 N 98.49 W
McGregor, Ont., Can. 214 42.09 N 82.58 W
McGregor, S. Afr. 158 33.57 S 19.50 E
McGregor, Iowa, U.S. 190 43.01 N 91.11 W
McGregor, Tex., U.S. 222 31.26 N 97.24 W
McGregor ≃ 182 54.11 N 122.00 W
McGregor Creek ≃ 214 42.24 N 82.11 W
McGregor Lake @ 182 50.31 N 112.53 W
McGregor Range ⋀ 166 26.40 S 142.45 E
McGuffey 216 40.42 N 83.47 W
McGuire, Mount ∧ 202 45.10 N 114.36 W
McGuire Air Force Base ■ 208 40.02 N 74.35 W
Macha 248 18.49 S 66.05 W
Machacamarca 248 18.10 S 67.02 W
Machache ∧ 158 29.21 S 27.55 E
Machachi 246 0.30 S 78.34 W
Machačkala 84 42.58 N 47.30 E
Machada, Mata Nacional da ♦ 266c 38.36 N 9.02 W
Machadinho ≃ 248 9.00 S 61.52 W
Machado 256 21.41 S 45.56 W
Machado ≃ 256 21.38 S 45.52 W
Machadodorp 156 25.40 S 30.14 E
Machados 256 22.30 S 46.25 W
Machærus ⊥ 132 31.34 N 35.38 E
Machagai 252 26.56 S 60.03 W
Machaila 156 22.15 S 32.55 E
Machakos 154 1.31 S 37.16 E
Machala 246 3.16 S 79.58 W
Machalí 252 34.11 S 70.40 W
Machalino 80 53.05 N 46.14 E
Māchalpur 124 24.08 N 76.18 E
Machaneng 156 23.10 S 27.26 E
Machang, Malay. 114 5.46 N 102.13 E
Machang, Zhg. 98 34.06 N 119.02 E
Machang, Zhg. 98 42.02 N 119.43 E
Machanga 156 20.58 S 34.59 E
Machangcun 105 38.54 N 115.26 E
Machangfu 102 25.14 N 103.45 E
Machangjianhe ≃ 105 39.00 N 117.40 E
Machaquilá ≃ 236 16.13 N 90.01 W
Macharadze 84 41.56 N 42.01 E
Machattie, Lake @ 166 24.50 S 139.48 E
Machault 50 49.21 N 4.30 E
Machava 156 25.54 S 32.29 E
Machaze 156 20.51 S 33.26 E
Machebu 100 29.25 N 119.32 E
Machece 156 19.17 S 35.33 E
Machecoul 32 47.00 N 1.50 W
Macheke 154 18.05 S 31.51 E
Machelen 50 50.55 N 4.26 E
Macheng 100 31.13 N 115.00 E
McHenry, Ill., U.S. 216 42.21 N 88.16 W
McHenry, Miss., U.S. 194 30.42 N 89.08 W
Mc Henry □[6] 216 42.19 N 88.27 W
McHenry Dam and Lake Defiance State Park ♦ 216 42.18 N 88.15 W
Macherio 266b 45.38 N 9.16 E
Mācherla 122 16.29 N 79.26 E
Machern 54 51.21 N 12.37 E
Mcherrah ◆[1] 148 27.00 N 4.40 W
Machery 261 48.36 N 2.05 E
Machesna Mountain ∧ 226 35.17 N 120.14 W
Machhīwara 123 30.55 N 76.12 E
Machhlīshahr 124 25.41 N 82.25 E
Machhuakhali 126 22.05 N 90.21 E
Machias, Maine, U.S. 188 44.43 N 67.28 W
Machias, N.Y., U.S. 210 42.25 N 78.30 W
Machias ≃ 186 44.43 N 67.22 W
Machias Bay C 186 44.40 N 67.20 W
Machichaco, Cabo ≻ 34 43.27 N 2.45 W
Machichi ≃ 184 57.03 N 92.06 W
Machico 148 32.42 N 16.46 W
Machida 94 35.32 N 139.27 E
Machili ≃ 154 17.26 S 25.02 E
Machilīpatnam (Bandar) 122 16.10 N 81.08 E
Machindžauri 84 41.40 N 41.43 E
Mchinga 154 9.44 S 39.42 E
Mchinji 154 13.41 S 32.55 E
Machiques 246 10.04 N 72.34 W
Machiya ≃ 94 35.01 N 136.42 E
Machkund @[1] 122 18.26 N 82.35 E
Machmud-Mekteb 84 44.26 N 45.13 E
Machn'ovo 86 58.27 N 61.42 E
Macho, Arroyo del ∨ 196 33.36 N 104.28 W
Machočen, Porog ⌊ 88 57.23 N 121.29 E
Machona, Laguna C 234 18.20 N 93.40 W
Machorovka 86 54.17 N 69.41 E
Machtaly 85 41.22 N 68.02 E
Mchungo 154 7.42 S 39.17 E
Machupicchu 248 13.07 S 72.34 W
Machu Picchu ⊥ 248 13.07 S 72.34 W
Machupo ≃ 248 12.34 S 64.25 W
Machynlleth 42 52.35 N 3.51 W
Maciá, Arg. 252 32.10 S 59.23 W
Macia, Moç. 156 25.03 S 33.10 E
Macías Nguema Biyogo → Bioko I 152 3.30 N 8.40 E
Maciel, Arroyo ≃ 258 33.42 S 57.59 W
Măcin 38 45.15 N 28.08 E
Macina ◆[1] 150 14.30 N 5.00 W
McInnes Lake @ 184 52.12 N 93.45 W
McIntosh, Ala., U.S. 194 31.16 N 88.02 W
McIntosh, Ill., U.S. 216 42.03 N 88.23 W
McIntosh, Minn., U.S. 198 47.38 N 95.53 W
McIntosh, S. Dak., U.S. 198 45.55 N 101.21 W
McIntosh Lake @ 184 55.45 N 105.08 W
McIntyre 214 40.34 N 79.18 W
Macintyre ≃, Austl. 166 29.25 S 148.45 E
Macintyre ≃, Austl. 166 28.38 S 150.47 E
McIntyre Bay C 182 54.05 N 131.55 W
Mačkassy 80 52.46 N 45.34 E
Mackay, Austl. 166 21.09 S 149.11 E
Mackay, Idaho, U.S. 202 43.55 N 113.37 W
MacKay ≃ 184 57.03 N 111.55 W
Mackay, Lake @ 162 22.30 S 129.00 E
McKay, Mount ∧ 162 22.26 S 120.01 E
McKay Creek ≃ 202 45.40 N 118.50 W
MacKay Lake @ 176 63.55 N 110.25 W
McKean 214 41.59 N 80.09 W
McKean □[6] 214 41.49 N 78.27 W
McKeand ≃ 176 65.26 N 68.10 W
McKee 192 37.25 N 84.01 W
McKee City 208 39.26 N 74.37 W
McKee Creek ≃ 219 39.46 N 90.36 W
McKeesport 214 40.21 N 79.52 W
McKees Rocks 214 40.28 N 80.10 W
McKenna 224 46.56 N 122.33 W
Mackenrode 54 51.33 N 10.33 E
Mackenzie 246 6.00 N 58.17 W
McKenzie, Ala., U.S. 194 31.33 N 86.43 W
McKenzie, Tenn., U.S. 194 36.08 N 88.31 W
Mackenzie □[5] 176 65.00 N 115.00 W
Mackenzie ≃ 176 69.15 N 134.08 W
McKenzie ≃ 202 44.07 N 123.06 W
MacKenzie Bay C, Ant. 9 68.20 S 71.15 E
Mackenzie Bay C, Can. 180 69.00 N 136.30 W
McKenzie Bridge 202 44.05 N 123.04 W
McKenzie Creek ≃ 212 43.02 N 79.53 W
McKenzie Island 184 51.05 N 93.48 W
McKenzie Lake @, Ont., Can. 212 45.22 N 78.02 W
McKenzie Lake @, Sask., Can. 184 54.12 N 102.30 W
Mackenzie Mountains ⋀ 180 64.00 N 130.00 W
McKerrow, Lake @ 172 44.26 S 168.03 E
Mackeyville 210 41.03 N 77.28 W
McKillip Ditch ≡ 216 40.50 N 86.51 W
Mackinac, Straits of U 190 45.49 N 84.42 W
Mackinac Bridge ◆[5] 190 45.50 N 84.45 W
Mackinac Island 190 45.51 N 84.37 W
Mackinac Island I 190 45.51 N 84.38 W
Mackinac Island State Park ♦ 190 45.52 N 84.40 W
Mackinaw 190 40.32 N 89.21 W
Mackinaw ≃ 194 40.33 N 89.44 W
Mackinaw City 190 45.47 N 84.44 W
McKinlay 166 21.16 S 141.17 E
McKinlay ≃ 166 20.50 S 141.28 E
McKinley, Mount ∧ 180 63.30 N 151.00 W
McKinley Airport ⊠ 281 42.33 N 82.58 W
Mc Kinley Park 180 63.44 N 148.54 W
McKinley Park ♦ 279b 40.25 N 80.00 W
McKinleyville, Calif., U.S. 204 40.57 N 124.06 W
McKinleyville, W. Va., U.S. 214 40.15 N 80.36 W
McKinney 222 33.12 N 96.37 W
Mackinnon Road 154 3.44 S 39.03 E
McKittrick, Calif., U.S. 226 35.18 N 119.37 W
McKittrick, Mo., U.S. 219 38.44 N 91.27 W
McKittrick Summit ∧ 226 35.18 N 119.46 W
Macklin 184 52.20 N 109.56 W
McKnight Lake @ 184 56.03 N 101.08 W
McKnightstown 208 39.52 N 77.20 W
McKnight Village 279b 40.31 N 80.00 W
M'ačkovo, S.S.S.R. 82 55.13 N 38.40 E
M'ačkovo, S.S.S.R. 82 56.21 N 39.03 E
McKownville 210 42.41 N 73.50 W
Macksville, Austl. 166 30.43 S 152.55 E
Macksville, Kans., U.S. 198 37.58 N 98.56 W
McLarty Hills ⋀[2] 162 19.29 S 123.33 E
McLaughlin 198 45.49 N 100.49 W
McLaughlin ≃ 184 53.46 N 97.38 W
McLaughlin Run ≃ 279b 40.22 N 80.07 W
McLaurin 194 31.10 N 89.13 W
Maclean 166 29.28 S 153.13 E
McLean, Sask., Can. 184 50.30 N 104.04 W
McLean, Ill., U.S. 194 40.19 N 89.10 W
McLean, N.Y., U.S. 210 42.33 N 76.17 W
McLean, Tex., U.S. 196 35.14 N 100.36 W
McLean, Va., U.S. 208 38.56 N 77.11 W
Mc Lean □[6] 216 40.29 N 88.45 W
McLean Lake @ 184 56.27 N 109.15 W
McLean Mountain ∧ 186 47.07 N 68.50 W
McLeansboro 194 38.06 N 88.32 W
Macleantown 158 32.47 S 27.45 E
Maclear 158 31.02 S 28.23 E
Macleay ≃ 166 30.52 S 153.01 E
McLennan 182 55.42 N 116.54 W
McLennan □[6] 222 31.35 N 97.13 W
Macleod 274b 37.43 S 145.04 E
McLeod ≃ 182 54.08 N 115.42 W
Macleod, Lake @ 162 24.00 S 113.35 E
McLeod Bay C 176 62.53 N 110.00 W
McLeodganj 123 30.15 N 73.42 E
McLeodganj Road 123 30.09 N 73.44 E
McLeod Lake 182 54.59 N 123.02 W
McLoughlin, Mount ∧ 202 42.27 N 122.19 W
McLoughlin Bay C 176 67.50 N 99.00 W
McLoughlin House National Historic Site ⊥ 224 45.20 N 122.33 W
Maclovio Herrera 232 29.05 N 105.08 W
McLure 182 51.03 N 120.14 W
McMahan 222 29.51 N 97.31 W
McMahon 184 50.05 N 107.32 W
McMasterville 206 45.33 N 73.15 W
MacMillan ≃ 180 62.52 N 135.55 W
McMillan, Lake @[1] 196 32.40 N 104.20 W
McMinnville, Oreg., U.S. 224 45.13 N 123.12 W
McMinnville, Tenn., U.S. 194 35.41 N 85.46 W
McMurdo ψ[3] 9 77.50 S 166.25 E
McMurdo Sound U 9 77.30 S 165.00 E
McMurray 214 40.17 N 80.05 W
McNair 222 29.48 N 95.02 W
McNary 200 34.04 N 109.51 W
McNeil, Ark., U.S. 194 33.21 N 93.13 W
McNeil, Tex., U.S. 222 30.27 N 97.43 W
McNeil, Mount ∧ 182 54.35 N 130.14 W
McNeil Island I 224 47.13 N 122.41 W
McNeill 194 30.40 N 89.38 W
McNulty 224 45.50 N 122.51 W
Macocha ∨ 30 49.23 N 16.45 E
Macocolo 152 6.47 S 16.08 E
Macolin 58 47.09 N 7.14 E
Macolla, Punta ≻ 241s 12.06 N 70.13 W
Macolo 152 7.05 S 16.48 E
Macomb 190 40.27 N 90.40 W
Macomb □[6] 214 42.40 N 82.54 W
Macomb Mall ◆[9] 281 42.32 N 82.55 W
Macomer 71 40.16 N 8.47 E
Macon, Bel. 50 50.03 N 4.13 E
Mâcon, Fr. 58 46.18 N 4.50 E
Macon, Ga., U.S. 192 32.50 N 83.38 W
Macon, Ill., U.S. 219 39.43 N 89.00 W
Macon, Miss., U.S. 194 33.07 N 88.34 W
Macon, Mo., U.S. 194 39.44 N 92.28 W
Macon □[6], Ill., U.S. 219 39.51 N 89.32 W
Macon □[6], Mo., U.S. 219 39.50 N 92.20 W
Macon, Bayou ≃ 194 31.55 N 91.33 W
Macon Creek ≃ 216 41.58 N 83.38 W
Macondo 152 12.35 S 23.44 E
Macondo ≃ 152 13.23 S 23.03 E
Mâconnais, Monts du ⋀ 58 46.18 N 4.45 E
Macorís, Cabo ≻ 238 19.47 N 70.28 W
Macosquin 44 55.06 N 6.43 W
Macossa 156 17.52 S 33.56 E
Macouba, Pointe de ≻ 240e 14.53 N 61.09 W
Macoun Lake @ 184 56.32 N 103.50 W
Macoupin □[6] 219 39.17 N 89.53 W
Macoupin Creek ≃ 219 39.11 N 90.36 W
Macouria 250 4.55 N 52.22 W
Macovane 156 21.28 S 35.04 E
McPhail ≃ 184 52.44 N 96.31 W
McPhee Bay C 212 44.35 N 79.19 W
McPherson 198 38.22 N 97.40 W
Macpherson, Mount ∧[2] 162 21.49 S 121.35 E
McPherson Range ⋀ 166 28.20 S 153.00 E
Macquarie ≃, Austl. 166 30.07 S 147.24 E
Macquarie ≃, Austl. 166 41.44 S 147.08 E
Macquarie, Lake @ 170 33.05 S 151.35 E
Macquarie Fields 274a 33.59 S 150.53 E
Macquarie Harbour C 166 42.19 S 145.23 E
Macquarie Marshes ☷ 166 30.50 S 147.32 E
Macquarie Ridge ⊹[3] 9 57.00 S 159.00 E
Macquarie Rise ⊹[3] 4 55.00 S 150.00 E
Macquarie University ψ[2] 274a 33.46 S 151.06 E
McQueeney 196 29.35 N 98.02 W
McRae, Ark., U.S. 194 35.07 N 91.49 W
McRae, Ga., U.S. 192 32.04 N 82.53 W
McRae, Mount ∧ 162 22.17 S 117.35 E
Macritchie Reservoir @[1] 271c 1.21 N 103.50 E
McRoberts 192 37.12 N 82.40 W
Mac Robertson Coast •[2] 9 68.10 S 65.00 E
Macrohon 116 10.05 N 124.56 E
Macroom 48 51.54 N 8.57 W
McSherrystown 208 39.48 N 77.02 W
Mactan Airfield ■ 116 10.18 N 123.58 E
Mactan Island I 116 10.18 N 123.58 E
MacTier 212 45.08 N 79.47 W
Macuelizo 236 15.18 N 88.31 W
Macugnaga 58 45.58 N 7.58 E
Macujer 246 0.23 N 72.55 W
Macul 286e 33.30 S 70.34 W
Macúl, Parque de ♦ 286e 33.30 S 70.35 W
Maculabo Island I 116 14.24 N 122.49 E
Macumba ≃ 162 27.45 S 136.50 E
Macun 130 36.58 N 30.50 E
Macungie 208 40.31 N 75.34 W
Macunqiao 100 33.50 N 116.13 E
Macuro 246 10.39 N 61.56 W
Maçururé ≃ 250 8.47 S 38.59 W
Macusani 248 14.05 S 70.26 W
Macuspana 234 17.46 N 92.36 W
Macusse 152 17.51 S 20.21 E
Macuto 286c 10.37 N 66.53 W
Macuze 156 17.42 S 37.11 E
McVeigh 192 37.32 N 82.15 W
McVeytown 214 40.30 N 77.44 W
McVickers Brook ≃ 276 40.45 N 74.38 W
McVille 198 47.46 N 98.11 W
McWilliams 194 31.50 N 87.06 W
Macy 216 40.58 N 86.08 W
Mad ≃, Ont., Can. 212 44.25 N 79.54 W
Mad ≃, Calif., U.S. 204 40.57 N 124.07 W
Mad ≃, N.Y., U.S. 212 43.20 N 75.44 W
Mad ≃, Ohio, U.S. 188 39.46 N 84.11 W
Mad ≃, Vt., U.S. 188 44.18 N 72.41 W
Mada ≃ 150 7.59 N 7.55 E
Madaba, Tan. 154 8.40 S 37.47 E
Ma'dabā, Urd. 132 31.43 N 35.48 E
Madadi 146 18.28 N 20.45 E
Madagascar □[1] 138
157b 19.00 S 46.00 E
Madagascar Basin ⊹[1] 10 26.00 S 55.00 E
Madagascar Ridge ⊹[3] 10 31.00 S 45.00 E
Madagasikara → Madagascar □[1] 157b 19.00 S 46.00 E
Madagaskar → Madagascar □[1] 157b 19.00 S 46.00 E
Madagiz 84 40.19 N 46.44 E
Madā'in Şāliḩ 128 26.48 N 37.53 E
Madajevo 80 54.48 N 44.31 E
Madam 150 7.58 N 3.32 W
Madama 146 21.58 N 13.39 E
Madamarodi 144 2.37 N 44.37 E
Madame, Isle I 186 45.33 N 61.02 W
Madan 38 41.30 N 24.57 E
Madanapalle 122 13.33 N 78.30 E
Madang, Pap. N. Gui. 164 5.15 S 145.50 E
Madang, Zhg. 100 29.58 N 116.40 E
Madang □[5] 164 5.00 S 145.30 E
Madanpur 272b 22.40 N 88.32 E
Madanpur Dabās ◆[8] 272a 28.43 N 77.02 E
Madaoua 150 14.06 N 6.26 E
Mādār Gāng ≃[1] 126 22.12 N 89.04 E
Mādāri Hāt 124 26.42 N 89.17 E
Mādārīpur 124 23.10 N 90.12 E
Mādārpur 272b 22.54 N 88.27 E
Madawaska, Ont., Can. 212 45.30 N 77.59 W
Madawaska, Maine, U.S. 186 47.21 N 68.20 W
Madawaska ≃ 212 45.27 N 76.21 W
Madawaska Highlands ⋀[1] 212 45.15 N 77.35 W
Madawaska Lake @ 212 45.20 N 78.23 W
Madaya, Mya. 110 22.13 N 96.07 E
Maḑāyā, Sūrīy. 132 33.41 N 36.06 E
Madbar 140 6.19 N 30.40 E
Maddalena, Colle della (Col de Larche))(62 44.25 N 6.53 E
Maddalena, Isola I 71 41.14 N 9.25 E
Maddaloni 68 41.02 N 14.22 E
Maddela 116 16.21 N 121.41 E
Madden, Mount ∧ 162 33.12 S 119.51 E
Maddington 168a 32.03 S 115.59 E
Maddock 198 47.58 N 99.32 W
Maddy, Loch C 46 57.36 N 7.08 W
Made 52 51.41 N 4.46 E
Madeir 140 7.50 N 29.12 E
Madeira 218 39.11 N 84.22 W
Madeira I 148 32.44 N 17.00 W
Madeira ≃ 242 3.22 S 58.45 W
Madeira, Arquipélago da II 148 32.40 N 16.45 W
Madeira Beach 220 27.48 N 82.48 W
Madeirinha ≃ 248 8.31 S 60.46 W
Madeirinha, Paraná ≃[1] 246 3.25 S 58.51 W
M'adel' 76 54.53 N 26.57 E
Mädelegabel ∧ 58 47.18 N 10.18 E
Madeleine, Îles de la II 186 47.30 N 61.45 W
Madeleine, Pointe ≻ 275a 45.27 N 73.57 W
Madeleine-Centre 186 49.15 N 65.21 W
Madeley, Eng., U.K. 42 52.39 N 2.28 W
Madeley, Eng., U.K. 42 52.59 N 2.20 W
Madelia 190 44.03 N 94.25 W
Madeline Island I 190 46.50 N 90.40 W
Maden 130 38.23 N 39.40 E
Maden ◆[8] 267b 40.52 N 29.08 E
Madenhanları 130 40.11 N 40.25 E
Madenijet 86 47.53 N 78.37 E
Madera, Méx. 232 29.12 N 108.07 W
Madera, Calif., U.S. 226 36.57 N 120.03 W
Madera, Pa., U.S. 214 40.50 N 78.26 W
Madera □[6] 226 37.15 N 119.45 W
Madera Canal ≡ 226 37.05 N 119.59 W
Madera Lake @[1] 226 37.02 N 119.59 W
Madera Peak ∧ 226 37.32 N 119.23 W
Maderas, Islas → Madeira, Arquipélago da II 148 32.40 N 16.45 W
Maderas, Volcán ∧[1] 236 11.27 N 85.31 W
Maderno 64 45.38 N 10.35 E
Madgaon (Margao) 122 15.18 N 73.57 E
Madh ◆[8] 272c 19.08 N 72.47 E
Madhipura 124 25.55 N 86.47 E
Madhkūr, Bi'r ⊤[4] 142 30.42 N 32.32 E
Mādhopur 123 32.22 N 75.36 E
Madhubani 124 26.22 N 86.05 E
Madhudaha 272b 22.31 N 88.25 E
Madhugiri 122 13.40 N 77.12 E
Madhukhāli 126 23.33 N 89.38 E
Madhumati ≃[1] 126 22.53 N 89.52 E
Madhupar 126 22.54 N 86.28 E
Madhupur 126 24.16 N 86.39 E
Madhya Bhārat Pathār ◆[1] 124 25.00 N 77.00 E
Madhyamgrām 272b 22.42 N 88.27 E
Madhya Pradesh □[4] 120 23.00 N 79.00 E
Madi □[5] 154 3.15 N 31.45 E
Mādi ≃ 124 27.49 N 84.27 E
Madia 154 7.08 S 26.00 E
Madian 106 32.15 N 119.58 E
Madianzi 105 39.39 N 117.15 E
Madibi 152 4.18 S 18.24 E
Madibira 154 8.12 S 34.49 E
Madibogo 158 26.25 S 25.10 E
Madida 98 42.57 N 130.48 E
Madidi ≃ 248 12.32 S 66.52 W
Madill 196 34.06 N 96.46 W
Madimba, Ang. 152 6.31 S 14.21 E
Madimba, Zaïre 152 4.58 S 15.08 E
Madina 150 13.24 N 8.51 W
Madina do Boé 150 11.45 N 14.13 W
Madinani 150 9.37 N 6.57 W
Madīnat ash-Sha'b 144 12.50 N 44.56 E
Madingo 152 4.07 S 11.22 E
Madingou 152 4.09 S 13.34 E
Madingzi 104 42.08 N 120.52 E
Madi Opei 154 3.37 N 33.05 E
Madirobe 157b 16.04 S 46.15 E
Madirovalo 157b 16.26 S 46.30 E
Madison, Ala., U.S. 194 34.42 N 86.45 W
Madison, Calif., U.S. 226 38.41 N 121.58 W
Madison, Conn., U.S. 207 41.17 N 72.36 W
Madison, Fla., U.S. 192 30.28 N 83.25 W
Madison, Ga., U.S. 192 33.36 N 83.28 W
Madison, Ill., U.S. 219 38.41 N 90.10 W
Madison, Ind., U.S. 218 38.44 N 85.23 W
Madison, Kans., U.S. 198 38.08 N 96.08 W
Madison, Maine, U.S. 188 44.48 N 69.53 W
Madison, Md., U.S. 208 38.31 N 76.13 W
Madison, Minn., U.S. 198 45.01 N 96.11 W
Madison, Mo., U.S. 219 39.28 N 92.13 W
Madison, Nebr., U.S. 198 41.50 N 97.27 W
Madison, N.J., U.S. 210 40.46 N 74.25 W
Madison, N.C., U.S. 192 36.23 N 79.58 W
Madison, N.Y., U.S. 210 42.54 N 75.31 W
Madison, Pa., U.S. 279b 40.15 N 79.41 W
Madison, S. Dak., U.S. 198 44.00 N 97.07 W
Madison, Va., U.S. 188 38.23 N 78.15 W
Madison, W. Va., U.S. 188 38.04 N 81.49 W
Madison, Wis., U.S. 216 43.05 N 89.22 W
Madison □[6], Ill., U.S. 219 38.49 N 89.58 W
Madison □[6], Ind., U.S. 218 40.10 N 85.41 W
Madison □[6], N.Y., U.S. 210 43.05 N 75.42 W
Madison □[6], Ohio, U.S. 218 39.53 N 83.27 W
Madison □[6], Tex., U.S. 222 30.58 N 95.55 W
Madison ≃ 202 45.56 N 111.30 W
Madison, West Fork ≃ 202 44.55 N 111.35 W
Madisonburg, Ohio, U.S. 214 40.51 N 81.55 W
Madisonburg, Pa., U.S. 210 40.55 N 77.31 W
Madison Heights, Mich., U.S. 216 42.30 N 83.06 W
Madison Heights, Va., U.S. 192 37.25 N 79.08 W
Madison Mills 218 39.40 N 83.20 W
Madison-on-the-lake 214 41.42 N 81.24 W
Madison Park 276 40.26 N 74.19 W
Madison Range ⋀ 202 45.15 N 111.20 W
Madison Square Garden ♦ 276 40.45 N 74.00 W
Madisonville, Ky., U.S. 194 37.20 N 87.30 W
Madisonville, La., U.S. 194 30.24 N 90.09 W
Madisonville, Tenn., U.S. 192 35.31 N 84.22 W
Madisonville, Tex., U.S. 222 30.57 N 95.55 W
Madiun 115a 7.37 S 111.31 E
Madiun ≃ 115a 7.23 S 111.27 E
Madiyi 102 28.14 N 110.30 E
Madjingo, Congo 152 1.23 N 14.06 E
Madjingo, Gabon 152 1.22 N 14.04 E
Madjori 150 11.26 N 1.15 E
Madlangampisiberg ∧ 158 27.12 S 30.28 E
Madley, Mount ∧ 162 24.31 S 123.58 E
Madoc 212 44.30 N 77.28 W
Mado Gashi 154 0.44 N 39.10 E
Madol 140 9.02 N 27.46 E
Madon ≃ 58 48.36 N 6.06 E
Madona 76 56.51 N 26.13 E
Madonna (Unserfrau) 64 46.43 N 10.52 E
Madonna della Guardia ψ[1] 62 44.29 N 8.51 E
Madonna della Quercia ψ[1] 66 42.25 N 12.06 E
Madonna dell'Olmo 62 44.25 N 7.32 E
Madonna del Sasso ψ[1] 58 46.11 N 8.33 E
Madonna di Campiglio 64 46.14 N 10.49 E
Madonna di Tirano 64 46.13 N 10.09 E
Madora 76 53.09 N 30.11 E
Madougou 150 14.24 N 3.05 W
Madrakah 144 21.59 N 39.59 E
Madras, Bhārat 122 13.05 N 80.17 E
Madras, Oreg., U.S. 202 44.38 N 121.08 W
Madras → Tamil Nadu □[3] 122 11.00 N 78.15 E
Madre, Laguna C, Méx. 232 25.00 N 97.40 W
Madre, Laguna C, Tex., U.S. 196 27.00 N 97.35 W
Madre, Sierra ⋀, N.A. 236 15.20 N 92.20 W
Madre, Sierra ⋀, Pil. 116 16.20 N 122.00 E
Madre de Deus de Minas 256 21.29 S 44.20 W
Madre de Dios □[5] 248 12.00 S 70.15 W
Madre de Dios ≃ 248 10.59 S 66.08 W
Madre de Dios, Isla I 254 50.15 S 75.05 W
Madre del Sur, Sierra ⋀ 234 17.00 N 100.00 W
Madre Occidental, Sierra ⋀ 232 25.00 N 105.00 W
Madre Oriental, Sierra ⋀ 232 22.00 N 99.30 W
Madre Vieja ≃ 236 14.01 N 91.26 W
Madrid, Col. 246 4.44 N 74.16 W
Madrid, Esp. 34
266a 40.24 N 3.41 W
Madrid, Pil. 116 9.15 N 126.00 E
Madrid, Ala., U.S. 194 31.01 N 85.24 W
Madrid, Iowa, U.S. 190 41.53 N 93.49 W
Madrid, Nebr., U.S. 198 40.51 N 101.33 W
Madridejos, Esp. 34 39.28 N 3.32 W
Madridejos, Pil. 116 11.18 N 123.44 E
Madrigalejo 34 39.09 N 5.37 W
Madrillon 284c 38.55 N 77.14 W
Madriz □[5] 236 13.30 N 86.30 W
Madroñera 34 39.26 N 5.46 W
Madruga 240p 22.55 N 81.51 W
Madrūsah 146 24.48 N 14.32 E
Madsen 184 50.58 N 93.55 W
Madsūs, Bi'r ⊤[4] 142 29.15 N 32.19 E
Maducang Island I 116 10.42 N 120.15 E
Maduda 152 4.55 S 13.06 E
Maduo, Zaïre 152 1.24 S 20.44 E
Maduo (Huangheyan), Zhg. 102 34.53 N 98.24 E
Madura, Austl. 162 31.55 S 127.00 E
Madura → Madurai, Bhārat 122 9.56 N 78.07 E
Madura I 115a 7.00 S 113.30 E
Madura, Selat U 115a 7.25 S 113.25 E
Madurai 122 9.56 N 78.07 E
Madurāntakam 122 12.31 N 79.54 E
Madureira, Serra de ⋀ 287a 22.49 S 43.31 W
Madurerira ◆[8] 287a 22.53 S 43.21 W
Maduru ≃ 122 7.52 N 81.31 E
Madwar al-Bighāl ∧[2] 142 29.09 N 29.54 E
Madyan ◆[1] 128 27.40 N 35.35 E
Madžalis 84 42.08 N 47.50 E
Mãe, Ilha da I 287a 22.59 S 43.04 W
Maeander Reef ⊹[2] 116 8.05 N 119.18 E
Maebaru 92 33.33 N 130.12 E
Maebashi 94 36.23 N 139.04 E
Maeda 270 34.55 N 135.08 E
Mãe dos Homens 256 22.52 S 46.37 W
Maegye-ri 98 34.45 N 126.18 E
Mae Hong Son 110 19.16 N 97.56 E
Mae Klong ≃ 110 13.21 N 100.00 E
Mae Nam Khong → Mekong ≃ 12 10.33 N 105.24 E
Maenclochog 42 51.54 N 4.48 W
Maengsan 98 39.40 N 126.30 E
Maeno ◆[8] 268 35.46 N 139.42 E
Maenza 66 41.31 N 13.11 E
Mae Ramat 110 16.58 N 98.31 E
Mae Rim 110 18.54 N 98.57 E
Maerkang 102 31.50 N 102.40 E
Maerkansu 85 39.19 N 73.53 E
Ma'erna 102 31.13 N 102.02 E
Maershan ∧ 102 26.18 N 100.20 E
Mae Sariang 110 18.10 N 97.56 E
Maeser 200 40.28 N 109.32 W
Mae Sot 110 16.43 N 98.34 E
Maesteg 42 51.37 N 3.40 W
Maestra, Sierra ⋀ 240p 20.00 N 76.45 W
Maestre de Campo Island I 116 12.56 N 121.42 E
Maestu 34 42.44 N 2.27 W
Mae Tha 110 18.28 N 99.08 E
Maevarano ≃ 157b 14.35 S 47.58 E
Maevatanana 157b 16.56 S 46.49 E
Maewo I 175f 15.10 S 168.10 E
Ma'fan 146 25.55 N 14.29 E
Mafang 105 40.03 N 116.59 E
Mafangchang 107 29.24 N 106.06 E
Mafangcun 105 40.09 N 116.24 E
Ma Faro ⊹[2] 122 5.50 N 73.26 E
Mafeking, Man., Can. 184 52.41 N 101.06 W
Mafeking, S. Afr. 156 25.53 S 25.39 E
Mafembage 152 14.32 S 21.42 E
Mafengtun 104 40.49 N 122.54 E
Mafeteng 158 29.51 S 27.15 E
Maffliers 261 49.05 N 2.19 E
Maffra 166 37.58 S 146.59 E
Mafia Island I 154 7.50 S 39.50 E
Mafou ≃ 150 10.32 N 10.08 W
Mafra, Bra. 252 26.07 S 49.49 W
Mafra, Port. 34 38.56 N 9.20 W
Magadan 74 59.34 N 150.48 E
Magadi 154 1.54 S 36.17 E
Magadi, Lake @ 154 1.52 S 36.17 E
Magaguadavic Lake @ 186 45.43 N 67.12 W
Magai-butsu ψ[1] 96 33.05 N 131.45 E
Magalhães Bastos ◆[8] 287a 22.53 S 43.23 W
Magalhães de Almeida 250 3.24 S 42.12 W
Magaliesberg ∧ 158 25.50 S 27.30 E
Magallanes → Punta Arenas, Chile 254 53.09 S 70.55 W
Magallanes, Pil. 116 12.50 N 123.50 E
Magallanes, Estrecho de (Strait of Magellan) U 254 54.00 S 71.00 W
Magallanes y Antártica Chilena □[4] 254 51.30 S 73.30 W
Maganga 154 0.51 N 26.22 E
Magangué 246 9.14 N 74.45 W
Maganoy ≃ 116 6.55 N 124.30 E
Magansk 88 55.52 N 93.15 E
Magara, Bhārat 126 22.34 N 87.34 E
Mağara, Tür. 130 36.43 N 33.52 E
Magaramkent 84 41.37 N 48.21 E
Magaria 150 13.00 N 8.54 E
Magat ≃ 116 17.02 N 121.49 E
Magazine Mountain ∧ 194 35.10 N 93.38 W
Magazzolo ≃ 70 37.25 N 13.15 E
Magboro 273a 6.43 N 3.24 E
Magburaka 150 8.43 N 11.57 W
Magdagači 89 53.27 N 125.48 E
Magdalena, Arg. 258 35.04 S 57.32 W
Magdalena, Bol. 248 13.20 S 64.08 W
Magdalena, Méx. 234 20.55 N 103.57 W
Magdalena, Perú 248 6.21 S 77.49 W
Magdalena, N. Mex., U.S. 200 34.07 N 107.14 W
Magdalena □[5] 246 10.00 N 74.00 W
Magdalena ≃, Col. 246 11.06 N 74.51 W
Magdalena ≃, Méx. 232 30.48 N 112.32 W
Magdalena, Bahía C 232 24.35 N 112.00 W
Magdalena, Isla I 254 44.40 S 73.10 W
Magdalena, Punta ≻ 246 3.56 N 77.21 W
Magdalena Contreras ◆[8] 286a 19.18 N 99.17 W
Magdalena de Kino 232 30.38 N 110.57 W
Magdalena Nueva 286d 12.06 S 77.05 W
Magdalena Peñasco 234 17.14 N 97.34 W
Magdalena Tequisistlán 234 16.22 N 95.15 W
Magdalen Laver 260 51.45 N 0.11 E
Magdalinovka 78 48.55 N 34.54 E
Magdeborn 54 51.14 N 12.26 E
Magdeburg 54 52.07 N 11.38 E
Magdeburg □[5] 54 52.15 N 11.30 E
Magdeburger Börde ⌣ 54 52.00 N 11.30 E
Magdeburgo → Magdeburg 54 52.07 N 11.38 E
Magdiwang 116 12.30 N 122.31 E
Magdonskij, Porog ⌊ 88 57.45 N 100.55 E
Magé, Bra. 256 22.39 S 43.02 W
Măge, Mya. 110 26.33 N 98.33 E
Magé □[7] 287a 22.41 S 43.07 W
Magé ≃ 256 22.41 S 43.03 W
Magee 194 31.52 N 89.44 W
Magee, Island ≻[1] 48 54.49 N 5.42 W
Magelang 115a 7.28 S 110.13 E
Magellan, Strait of → Magallanes, Estrecho de U 254 54.00 S 71.00 W
Magellan-Strasse → Magallanes, Estrecho de U 254 54.00 S 71.00 W
Magé-Mirim 287a 22.40 S 43.01 W
Magen 132 31.18 N 34.26 E
Magenta 62 45.28 N 8.53 E
Magenta, Lake @ 162 33.26 S 119.10 E
Magerov 78 50.08 N 23.43 E
Magerøya I 24 71.03 N 25.45 E
Magetan 115a 7.39 S 111.20 E
Magezhuang 105 40.08 N 117.59 E
Maggia 58 46.15 N 8.42 E
Maggia ≃ 58 46.09 N 8.48 E
Maggia, Valle ∨ 58 46.17 N 8.40 E
Maggie Creek ≃ 204 40.43 N 116.05 W
Maggieville 166 17.27 S 141.10 E
Maggiorasca, Monte ∧ 62 44.33 N 9.29 E
Maggiore ≃ 267a 43.43 N 13.06 E
Maggiore, Fosso ≃ 267a 41.54 N 12.16 E
Maggiore, Lago @ 36 46.00 N 8.40 E
Maggiore, Monte ∧ 68 41.14 N 14.12 E
Maghāghah 142 28.39 N 30.50 E
Maghama 150 15.31 N 12.51 W
Maghār 132 32.53 N 35.24 E
Maghdūshah 132 33.31 N 35.23 E
Maghera 48 54.51 N 6.40 W
Magherafelt 48 54.45 N 6.36 W
Maghnia 148 34.50 N 1.50 W
Magholpur ◆[8] 272a 28.42 N 77.06 E
Maghull 44 53.32 N 2.57 W
Magician Lake @ 216 42.04 N 86.10 W
Magicienne Bay C 174n 15.08 N 145.46 E
Magic Mountain ♦ 228 34.26 N 118.36 W
Magill Heights 279b 40.37 N 79.52 W
Magill Lake @, Man., Can. 184 54.45 N 94.58 W
Magill Lake @, Qué., Can. 206 45.35 N 71.17 W
Magina ∧ 34 37.43 N 3.28 W
Maginu 268 35.35 N 139.36 E
Magiolobo Bay C 116 11.07 N 125.21 E
Magione 66 43.08 N 12.12 E
Magisano 68 39.01 N 16.27 E
Magiscatzin 234 22.48 N 98.42 W
Magiss Lake @ 184 52.59 N 91.40 W
Maglaj 38 44.33 N 18.06 E
Magliana ◆[8] 267a 41.50 N 12.25 E
Magliana, Fosso ≃ 267a 41.49 N 12.25 E
Magliano dei Marsi 66 42.05 N 13.22 E
Magliano in Toscana 66 42.36 N 11.17 E
Magliano Sabina 66 42.22 N 12.29 E
Maglie 68 40.07 N 18.19 E

Symbols in the index entries represent the broad categories identified in the key at the right. Symbols with superior numbers (⋀[2]) identify subcategories (see complete key on page I · 30).

Kartensymbole in dem Registerverzeichnis stellen die rechts in Schlüssel erklärten Kategorien dar. Symbole mit hochgestellten Ziffern (⋀[2]) bezeichnen Unterabteilungen einer Kategorie (vgl. vollständiger Schlüssel auf Seite I · 30).

Los símbolos incluídos en el texto del índice representan las grandes categorías identificadas con la clave a la derecha. Los símbolos con numeros en su parte superior (⋀[2]) identifican las subcategorías (véase la clave completa en la página I · 30).

Les symboles de l'index représentent les catégories indiquées dans la légende à droite. Les symboles suivis d'un indice (⋀[2]) représentent des sous-catégories (voir légende complète à la page I · 30).

Os símbolos incluídos no texto do índice representam as grandes categorias identificadas com a chave à direita. Os símbolos com números em sua parte superior (⋀[2]) identificam as subcategorias (veja-se a chave completa à página I · 30).

	English	Deutsch	Español	Français	Português
∧	Mountain	Berg	Montaña	Montagne	Montanha
⋀	Mountains	Berge	Montañas	Montagnes	Montanhas
)(	Pass	Pass	Paso	Col	Passo
∨	Valley, Canyon	Tal, Cañon	Valle, Cañón	Vallée, Canyon	Vale, Canhão
⌣	Plain	Ebene	Llano	Plaine	Planície
≻	Cape	Kap	Cabo	Cap	Cabo
I	Island	Insel	Isla	Île	Ilha
II	Islands	Inseln	Islas	Îles	Ilhas
•	Other Topographic Features	Andere Topographische Objekte	Otros Elementos Topográficos	Autres données topographiques	Outros Elementos Topográficos

ESPAÑOL — Nombre | Página | Lat.°′ | Long.°′ W=Oeste

Maglód 264c 47.27 N 19.21 E
M'aglovo 265a 59.53 N 30.41 E
Magna 200 40.42 N 112.06 W
Magnago 266b 45.35 N 8.48 E
Magnanville 261 48.58 N 1.41 E
Magnet 184 51.19 N 99.30 W
Magnetawan ≃ 190 45.46 N 80.37 W
Magnetic Island I 166 19.08 S 146.50 E
Magnetic Springs 214 40.21 N 83.16 W
Magnetischer Nordpol → North Magnetic Pole ⬥ 16 76.02 N 101.00 W
Magnetischer Südpol → South Magnetic Pole ⬥ 9 66.40 S 140.10 E
Magnières 58 48.27 N 6.34 E
Magnitka 86 55.21 N 59.43 E
Magnitogorsk 86 53.27 N 59.04 E
Magnitostroj 80 51.43 N 53.05 E
Magnolia, Ark., U.S. 194 33.16 N 93.14 W
Magnolia, Del., U.S. 208 39.04 N 75.29 W
Magnolia, Mass., U.S. 283 42.35 N 70.43 W
Magnolia, Minn., U.S. 198 43.39 N 96.05 W
Magnolia, Miss., U.S. 194 31.09 N 90.28 W
Magnolia, N.J., U.S. 285 39.51 N 75.02 W
Magnolia, N.C., U.S. 192 34.54 N 78.03 W
Magnolia, Ohio, U.S. 214 40.39 N 81.18 W
Magnolia, Tex., U.S. 222 30.13 N 95.45 W
Magnor 26 59.57 N 12.12 E
Magny-en-Vexin 50 49.09 N 1.47 E
Magny-le-Hongre 261 48.52 N 2.49 E
Magny-les-Hameaux 261 48.44 N 2.04 E
Mago 89 53.15 N 140.13 E
Màgoé 154 15.48 S 31.43 E
Magog 206 45.16 N 72.09 W
Magog ≃ 206 45.24 N 71.54 W
Magog, Lake @ 206 45.18 N 72.03 W
Magoito 266c 38.52 N 9.26 W
Magome ⬥[8] 268 35.35 N 139.43 E
Magongdang @ 106 31.27 N 119.43 E
Magoro 154 1.44 N 34.06 E
Magothy Bay C 208 37.10 N 75.55 W
Magothy River C 208 39.04 N 76.28 W
Magoúla 267c 38.04 N 23.32 E
Magoye 154 16.00 S 27.37 E
M'agozero 76 60.21 N 34.50 E
Magpie 186 50.19 N 64.30 W
Magpie ≃, Ont., Can. 190 47.56 N 84.50 W
Magpie ≃, Qué., Can. 186 50.19 N 64.27 W
Magpie, Lac @ 186 51.00 N 64.41 W
Magpie-Ouest ≃ 186 51.02 N 64.42 W
Magra 126 22.59 N 88.22 E
Magra ≃ 64 44.03 N 9.58 E
Magra Hāt 126 22.14 N 88.23 E
Magrath 182 49.25 N 112.52 W
Magrè (Margreid) 64 46.17 N 11.12 E
Magro ≃ 34 39.11 N 0.25 W
Magruder Mountain ∧ 204 37.25 N 117.33 W
Magsaysay (Linugos) 116 9.01 N 125.11 E
Magsingal 116 17.41 N 120.25 E
Magu ≃ 250 2.56 S 41.55 W
Maguan 102 22.59 N 104.19 E
Maguanying 271a 39.52 N 116.17 E
Magude 156 25.02 S 32.40 E
Magudu 158 27.31 S 31.40 E
Magumeri 146 12.08 N 12.50 E
Māgura 124 23.29 N 89.25 E
Maguru 150 12.28 N 6.35 E
Maguse Lake @ 176 61.40 N 95.10 W
Maguzhan 120 31.15 N 88.00 E
Magwe, Mya. 110 20.09 N 94.55 E
Magwe, Sūd. 154 4.08 N 32.17 E
Magwe □[8] 110 23.00 N 95.00 E
Magwood Park ♠ 275b 43.39 N 79.30 W
Magyarország → Hungary □[1] 30 47.00 N 20.00 E
Mahābād 128 36.45 N 45.43 E
Mahābaleshwar 122 17.55 N 73.40 E
Mahābalipuram 122 12.37 N 80.12 E
Mahabe 157b 17.05 S 45.20 E
Mahābhārat Range ⩕ 124 27.40 N 84.30 E
Mahabo, Madag. 157b 23.40 S 46.08 E
Mahabo, Madag. 157b 20.23 S 44.40 E
Mahād 122 18.05 N 73.25 E
Mahadday Weyne 144 3.00 N 45.32 E
Mahādebpur 126 23.51 N 89.53 E
Mahādeo Hills ⩕[2] 122 22.22 N 78.34 E
Mahādeo Range ⩕ 122 17.50 N 74.15 E
Mahaena, Passe de ⩌ 174s 17.33 S 149.19 W
Mahaffey 214 40.53 N 78.44 W
Mahagi 154 2.18 N 30.59 E
Mahagi Port 154 2.09 N 31.14 E
Mahai 102 38.17 N 94.13 E
Mahaicony Village 246 6.36 N 57.48 W
Mahajamba ≃ 157b 15.33 S 47.08 E
Mahajamba, Baie de la C 157b 15.24 S 47.05 E
Mahājan 123 28.47 N 73.50 E
Mahajilo ≃ 157b 19.42 S 45.22 E
Maḥajjah 132 32.57 N 36.14 E
Mahakam ≃ 112 0.35 S 117.17 E
Mahālandi 126 24.04 N 88.07 E
Mahalatswe 156 23.05 S 26.51 E
Mahali Mountains ⩕ 154 6.12 S 29.50 E
Mahalla el-Kubra → Al-Maḥallah al-Kubrā 142 30.58 N 31.10 E
Maḥallāt 128 33.55 N 50.27 E
Maḥallat Kayl 142 31.01 N 30.17 E
Maḥallat Marḥūm 142 30.48 N 30.57 E
Maḥallat Minūf 142 30.53 N 30.58 E
Maḥallat Zayyād 142 31.02 N 31.14 E
Maham 124 28.59 N 76.18 E
Mahamba 158 27.07 S 31.10 E
Mahānadi ≃ 118 20.19 N 86.45 E
Mahānadpati 126 23.00 N 88.16 E
Mahānanda ≃ 124 24.29 N 88.18 E
Mahanay Island I 116 10.12 N 124.14 E
Mahanoro 157b 19.54 S 48.48 E
Mahanoy City 208 40.49 N 76.08 W
Mahanoy Creek ≃ 208 40.42 N 76.51 W
Mahantango Creek ≃ 208 40.47 N 76.56 W
Mahantango Mountain ∧ 208 40.40 N 76.45 W
Mahao 89 43.09 N 127.55 E
Mahape 272c 19.07 N 73.01 E
Mahārājganj, Bhārat 124 26.07 N 84.29 E
Mahārājganj, Bhārat 124 27.09 N 83.34 E
Mahārājpur, Bhārat 124 25.01 N 79.44 E
Mahārājpur, Bhārat 272a 28.39 N 77.20 E
Mahārāshtra □[3] 122 19.00 N 76.00 E
Maḥārīq, Wādī ∨ 142 27.48 N 31.47 E
Mahārlū, Daryācheh-ye @ 128 29.25 N 52.50 E
Mahāsamund 120 21.06 N 82.06 E
Maha Sarakham 110 16.11 N 103.18 E
Maha Sawat, Khlong ≋ 269a 13.47 N 100.28 E
Mahasoa 157b 22.12 S 46.06 E
Mahasolo 157b 19.07 S 46.22 E
Mahāsu □[5] 123 31.10 N 77.10 E
Mahates 246 10.14 N 75.12 W
Mahatsinjo 157b 21.26 S 45.51 E
Maḥaṭṭat Abū al-Lasan 132 30.05 N 35.31 E
Maḥaṭṭat Abū Jirdhān 132 30.20 N 35.46 E
Maḥaṭṭat Abū Ṭarafah 132 30.00 N 35.56 E
Maḥaṭṭat al-Furayfirah 132 30.54 N 35.59 E
Maḥaṭṭat al-Ḥasā 132 30.49 N 35.59 E
Maḥaṭṭat al-Jīzah 132 31.43 N 35.58 E
Maḥaṭṭat al-Manzil 132 31.03 N 36.01 E
Maḥaṭṭat al-Qaṣr 132 31.54 N 35.56 E
Maḥaṭṭat al-Qaṭrānah 132 31.15 N 36.03 E

FRANÇAIS — Nom | Page | Lat.°′ | Long.°′ W=Ouest

Maḥaṭṭat 'aqabat al-Ḥijāzīyah 132 29.44 N 35.52 E
Maḥaṭṭat ash-Shīdīyah 132 29.56 N 35.56 E
Maḥaṭṭat as-Suwāqah 132 31.22 N 36.07 E
Maḥaṭṭat Bḥamdūn 132 33.48 N 35.39 E
Maḥaṭṭat Ḍab'ah 132 31.36 N 36.04 E
Maḥaṭṭat Faṣṣū'ah 132 29.46 N 35.54 E
Maḥaṭṭat Jurf ad-Darāwīsh 132 30.42 N 35.52 E
Maḥaṭṭat Muṣawwal 132 30.05 N 35.52 E
Maḥaṭṭat Samnah 132 30.09 N 35.39 E
Maḥaṭṭat 'Unayzah 132 30.29 N 35.48 E
Mahaut 240d 15.21 N 61.25 W
Mahavavy ≃, Madag. 157b 15.57 S 45.54 E
Mahavavy ≃, Madag. 157b 13.00 S 48.55 E
Mahaweli ≃ 122 8.27 N 81.13 E
Mahaxai 110 17.25 N 105.12 E
Maḥbas, Wādī al- ∨ 140 15.50 N 29.45 E
Mahbés 148 27.13 N 9.44 W
Mahbūbābād 122 17.37 N 80.01 E
Mahbūbnagar 122 16.44 N 77.59 E
Mahd adh-Dhahab 128 23.30 N 40.52 E
Mahdāt, Bi'r al- ⫪[4] 142 30.44 N 32.32 E
Mahe 122 11.42 N 75.32 E
Mahébourg 157c 20.24 S 57.42 E
Mahé Island I 138 4.40 S 55.28 E
Mahendraganj 120 25.20 N 89.45 E
Mahendragarh 124 28.17 N 76.09 E
Mahendragarh □[5] 124 28.20 N 76.10 E
Mahendra Giri ∧ 122 18.58 N 84.21 E
Mahenge, Tan. 154 8.41 S 36.43 E
Mahenge, Tan. 154 7.38 S 36.16 E
Maheno 172 45.10 S 170.50 E
Mahesgādi 272b 22.39 N 88.33 E
Maheshmunda 126 24.13 N 86.24 E
Maheshtala 272b 22.30 N 88.15 E
Maheshwar 120 22.11 N 75.35 E
Mahespur 124 23.21 N 88.55 E
Mahgawān 124 26.29 N 78.37 E
Mahi ≃ 120 22.16 N 72.58 E
Mahia Peninsula ≻[1] 172 39.10 S 177.53 E
Mahiāri 272b 22.35 N 88.14 E
Māhikpur 272b 22.32 N 88.14 E
Mahilāra 126 22.56 N 90.16 E
Māhīm ⬥[8] 272c 19.03 N 72.49 E
Māhīm ≃ 272c 19.03 N 72.51 E
Māhīm Bay C 272c 19.02 N 72.50 E
Mahina 150 13.46 N 10.51 W
Mahinerangi, Lake @ 172 45.51 S 170.03 E
Mahinog 116 9.09 N 124.47 E
Mahīshādal 126 22.11 N 87.59 E
Mahishdānga 272b 22.54 N 88.11 E
Mahlabatini, S. Afr. 158 27.37 S 31.42 E
Mahlabatini, S. Afr. 158 28.14 S 31.30 E
Mahlberg 58 48.17 N 7.48 E
Mahlow 54 52.22 N 13.24 E
Mahlsdorf 54 52.47 N 11.13 E
Mahlsdorf ⬥[8] 264a 52.31 N 13.37 E
Mahlsdorf-Süd ⬥[8] 264a 52.29 N 13.36 E
Maḥmūdābād, Bhārat 124 27.18 N 81.07 E
Maḥmūdābād, Īrān 128 36.38 N 52.15 E
Maḥmūd-e 'Erāqī 120 35.01 N 69.20 E
Maḥmūdīyah, Tur'at al- ≋ 142 31.11 N 29.53 E
Mahmudiye 130 39.30 N 31.00 E
Mahmūdpur, Bhārat 272a 28.46 N 77.22 E
Mahmudpur, Bhārat 272b 22.41 N 88.09 E
Mahmut Bendi ⬥[6] 267b 41.10 N 28.57 E
Mahmutbey 267b 41.03 N 28.49 E
Mahmutşevketpaşa 267b 41.09 N 29.11 E
Mahnomen 198 47.19 N 96.01 W
Mahoba 124 25.17 N 79.52 E
Mahogany Mountain ∧ 202 43.14 N 117.16 W
Mahomet 216 40.12 N 88.24 W
Mahón 34 39.53 N 4.15 E
Mahone Bay 186 44.27 N 64.23 W
Mahone Bay C 186 44.30 N 64.15 W
Mahoning □[6] 214 41.06 N 80.39 W
Mahoning ≃ 214 40.58 N 80.23 W
Mahoning, West Branch ≃ 214 41.12 N 80.57 W
Mahoning Creek ≃ 214 40.55 N 79.27 W
Mahoning Creek Lake @[1] 214 40.50 N 79.10 W
Mahony Lake @ 180 65.30 N 125.20 W
Mahood Falls 182 51.50 N 120.39 W
Mahood Lake @ 182 51.55 N 120.24 W
Mahopac 210 41.22 N 73.45 W
Mahopac Falls 210 41.22 N 73.46 W
Mahora 34 39.13 N 1.44 W
Mahoras Brook ≃ 276 40.25 N 74.08 W
Mahrāt, Jabal ⩕ 144 17.05 N 51.30 E
Mahrauli ⬥[8] 272a 28.31 N 77.11 E
Mähren → Morava □[9] 30 49.20 N 17.00 E
Mähring 60 49.55 N 12.32 E
Mahroni 124 24.35 N 78.43 E
Mahtomedi 190 45.04 N 92.57 W
Mahuiling 100 29.24 N 115.48 E
Māhul ⬥[8] 272c 19.01 N 72.53 E
Mahulia 126 22.39 N 86.24 E
Mahur Island I 164 2.50 S 152.40 E
Mahuta 154 10.52 S 39.27 E
Mahuva 120 21.05 N 71.48 E
Mahwah, Bhārat 124 27.03 N 76.56 E
Mahwah, N.J., U.S. 276 41.06 N 74.09 W
Mahwah ≃ 276 41.06 N 74.10 W
Mai, Île de I 275a 45.36 N 73.50 W
Maia, Am. Sam. 174y 14.13 S 169.28 W
Maia, Port. 34 41.14 N 8.37 W
Mai Aché 146 12.00 N 15.44 E
Maianga 152 14.12 S 21.45 E
Maiano 64 46.11 N 13.04 E
Maiauatá 250 1.51 S 49.02 W
Maibara 94 35.19 N 136.17 E
Maicao 246 11.23 N 72.13 W
Maîche 58 47.15 N 6.48 E
Maichen 102 20.29 N 109.59 E
Maici ≃ 248 6.30 S 61.43 W
Maicurú ≃ 250 2.14 S 54.17 W
Maida 68 38.51 N 16.22 E
Maidan ♠ 272b 22.33 N 88.21 E
Maiden 192 35.35 N 81.13 W
Maidenhead 42 51.32 N 0.44 W
Maiden Newton 42 50.46 N 2.35 W
Maidens Choice Run ≃ 284b 39.17 N 76.40 W
Maidstone, Austl. 274b 37.47 S 144.52 E
Maidstone, Ont., Can. 214 42.13 N 82.53 W
Maidstone, Sask., Can. 184 53.06 N 109.18 W
Maidstone, Eng., U.K. 42 51.17 N 0.32 E
Maidstone □[8] 260 51.17 N 0.35 E
Maiduguri 146 11.51 N 13.10 E
Maie 154 2.46 N 30.34 E
Maiella, Montagna della ⩕ 66 42.05 N 14.07 E
Maienfeld 58 47.00 N 9.32 E
Maierato 68 38.42 N 16.11 E
Maifeld □[9] 56 50.20 N 7.20 E
Maigaiti 85 38.55 N 77.38 E
Maigatari 150 12.46 N 9.27 E
Maignelay 50 49.33 N 2.31 E
Maigudo, Mount ∧ 144 7.33 N 37.15 E
Maihar 124 24.16 N 80.45 E
Maijdi 124 22.52 N 91.06 E
Maijoma 196 28.55 N 104.21 W
Maikala Plateau ⩕[1] 124 22.30 N 81.00 E
Maikala Range ⩕ 122 22.30 N 81.30 E
Maikammer 56 49.18 N 9.07 E
Maiko ≃ 154 0.14 N 25.33 E
Maikoor, Pulau I 164 6.15 S 134.15 E
Mailand → Milano 62 45.28 N 9.12 E
Mailāni 124 28.17 N 80.21 E
Maili 229c 21.25 N 158.11 W
Mailiao 100 23.45 N 120.15 E
Maillane 62 43.50 N 4.47 E

PORTUGUÊS — Nome | Página | Lat.°′ | Long.°′ W=Oeste

Mailley-et-Chazelot 58 47.32 N 6.03 E
Maillezais 32 46.22 N 0.44 W
Mailly-le-Camp 50 48.40 N 4.13 E
Mailly-le-Château 50 47.36 N 3.38 E
Mailly-Maillet 50 50.04 N 2.36 E
Mailsi 123 29.48 N 72.11 E
Maimbung 116 5.56 N 121.02 E
Mā'īn 132 31.41 N 35.44 E
Main ≃, B.R.D. 30 50.00 N 8.18 E
Main ≃, N. Ire., U.K. 44 54.43 N 6.18 W
Maināguri 124 26.34 N 88.49 E
Mainart ≃ 255 20.27 S 43.17 W
Mainau 58 47.42 N 9.11 E
Mainburg 60 48.38 N 11.47 E
Main Canal ≋, Calif., U.S. 226 37.23 N 120.26 W
Main Canal ≋, Calif., U.S. 226 37.25 N 121.05 W
Main Canal ≋, Wash., U.S. 224 47.07 N 120.44 W
Main Canal Extension ≋ 224 46.24 N 120.41 W
Main Channel ⩌ 190 45.22 N 81.50 W
Maincourt-sur-Yvette 261 48.43 N 1.58 E
Main Creek ≃ 276 40.34 N 74.11 W
Maincy 261 48.33 N 2.42 E
Mai-Ndome, Lac @ 152 2.00 S 18.20 E
Main Duck Island I 212 43.56 N 76.37 W
Maine 210 42.12 N 76.04 W
Maine □[9] 32 48.15 N 0.05 W
Maine □[3] 178 45.15 N 69.15 W
Maine ≃ 48 52.09 N 9.45 W
Mainebene □[9] 56 50.00 N 8.45 E
Maine-et-Loire □[5] 32 47.25 N 0.30 W
Mainesburg 210 41.47 N 77.07 W
Maïné-Soroa 146 13.12 N 12.02 E
Maineville 218 39.18 N 84.13 W
Mainguerin 261 48.32 N 1.51 E
Mainhardt 56 49.04 N 9.33 E
Mainit 116 9.32 N 125.32 E
Mainit, Lake @ 116 9.26 N 125.32 E
Mainland 285 40.15 N 75.22 W
Mainland I, Scot., U.K. 46 59.00 N 3.15 W
Mainland I, Scot., U.K. 46a 60.16 N 1.16 W
Mainleus 54 50.06 N 11.22 E
Mainoru 164 14.02 S 134.05 E
Mainpuri 124 27.14 N 79.01 E
Mainpuri □[5] 124 27.10 N 79.00 E
Maintenon 50 48.35 N 1.35 E
Maintirano 157b 18.03 S 44.01 E
Main Topsail ∧ 186 49.08 N 56.33 W
Mainvilliers 50 48.27 N 1.28 E
Mainz 56 50.01 N 8.16 E
Maio I 150a 15.15 N 23.10 W
Maiolati Spontini 66 43.28 N 13.06 E
Maiori 68 40.39 N 14.38 E
Maiori, Nuraghe ⊥ 71 40.56 N 9.06 E
Maipa 164 8.21 S 146.33 E
Maipo ≃ 252 33.37 S 71.39 W
Maipo, Volcán ∧[1] 252 34.10 S 69.50 W
Maipú, Arg. 252 36.52 S 57.52 W
Maipú, Arg. 252 32.58 S 68.47 W
Maipú, Chile 252 33.31 S 70.46 W
Maiqihamiao 89 43.22 N 120.46 E
Maiquetía 246 10.36 N 66.57 W
Maiquetía, Aeropuerto ⊠ 286c 10.37 N 66.59 W
Maira ≃ 62 44.49 N 7.38 E
Maira, Valle ∨ 62 44.30 N 7.08 E
Mairabāri 120 26.28 N 92.26 E
Mairi 250 11.43 S 40.08 W
Mairinque 256 23.33 S 47.10 W
Mairiporã 256 23.19 S 46.35 W
Mairiporã □[7] 287b 23.24 S 46.37 W
Mairipotaba 255 17.18 S 49.28 W
Maisach 60 48.13 N 11.16 E
Maisaka 94 34.41 N 137.37 E
Maishi 100 29.11 N 113.58 E
Maišiagala 76 54.52 N 25.04 E
Maiskhāl Island I 120 21.36 N 91.56 E
Maison de Pierre, Lac de la @ 206 46.53 N 74.42 W
Maisonneuve, Parc ♠ 275a 45.33 N 73.34 W
Maisons-Alfort 261 48.48 N 2.26 E
Maisons-Laffitte 50 48.57 N 2.09 E
Maisons-Laffitte, Château de ⊥ 261 48.57 N 2.09 E
Maisse 50 48.24 N 2.23 E
Maissin 56 49.58 N 5.11 E
Mait 144 10.57 N 47.06 E
Maitani 270 34.49 N 135.22 E
Maitengwe 156 20.06 S 27.13 E
Maitengwe ≃ 156 19.59 S 26.26 E
Maithon Reservoir @[1] 126 23.50 N 86.43 E
Maitland, Austl. 168b 34.22 S 137.40 E
Maitland, Austl. 170 32.44 S 151.33 E
Maitland, N.S., Can. 186 45.19 N 63.30 W
Maitland, Ont., Can. 212 44.38 N 75.37 W
Maitland, Fla., U.S. 220 28.38 N 81.22 W
Maitland ≃ 190 43.45 N 81.43 W
Maitland, Lake @ 162 27.11 S 121.03 E
Maixie 100 27.38 N 115.29 E
Maíz ≃ 236 11.17 N 83.52 W
Maíz, Islas del II 236 12.15 N 83.00 W
Maizefield 158 26.28 S 29.31 E
Maizières-lès-Metz 56 49.13 N 6.09 E
Maizières-lès-Vic 58 48.43 N 6.46 E
Maizuru 96 35.27 N 135.20 E
Maja ≃ 89 54.31 N 134.41 E
Majābirah, Minqār al- ▪[4] 142 30.16 N 29.49 E
Majačka ≃ 83 48.44 N 37.33 E
Majačnyj 86 52.41 N 55.44 E
Majadahonda 266a 40.29 N 3.52 W
Majagua 240p 21.55 N 79.00 W
Majagual 246 8.33 N 74.38 W
Majaki, S.S.S.R. 78 46.25 N 30.16 E
Majaki, S.S.S.R. 83 48.57 N 37.37 E
Majakovskij 84 42.06 N 42.48 E
Majalengka 115a 6.50 S 108.13 E
Majana, Ensenada de C 240p 22.41 N 82.45 W
Majari ≃ 246 3.29 N 60.58 W
Majchura 85 39.02 N 68.35 E
Majdal 'Anjar 132 33.42 N 35.54 E
Majdantal 85 43.41 N 68.02 E
Majd el Kurūm 132 32.55 N 35.15 E
Majeigha 140 11.33 N 24.40 E
Majenang 115a 7.18 S 108.45 E
Majene 112 3.33 S 118.57 E
Majenica 216 40.46 N 85.27 W
Majevica ⩕ 38 44.30 N 18.55 E
Maji 144 6.11 N 35.38 E
Majiacun 106 30.08 N 119.58 E
Majiahe 102 35.20 N 104.46 E
Majiahe ≃ 98 38.09 N 117.53 E
Majiahu 104 41.13 N 121.30 E
Majiaji 100 32.32 N 118.50 E
Majian, Zhg. 100 29.43 N 120.00 E
Majian, Zhg. 100 29.19 N 119.36 E
Majiang, Zhg. 102 23.48 N 111.09 E
Majiang, Zhg. 110 26.28 N 107.28 E
Majiangzong 120 30.27 N 90.03 E
Majiaoba 102 32.14 N 104.35 E
Majiaping 102 36.31 N 103.20 E
Majiasi 105 39.03 N 117.05 E
Majiawopu 104 41.46 N 121.06 E
Majiayan 100 27.26 N 112.56 E
Majiazhai 104 42.22 N 124.04 E
Majiazhou 100 26.46 N 114.47 E
Majidun Creek ≃ 273a 6.38 N 3.28 E
Majie, Zhg. 102 23.50 N 105.07 E
Majie, Zhg. 102 25.03 N 103.45 E
Majijo 174r 6.55 N 158.19 E
Majin 100 29.18 N 118.24 E
Majinxi ≃ 100 29.00 N 118.21 E
Majinzhuangzi 104 41.55 N 123.53 E

Majishan I 106 31.26 N 120.06 E
Majītha 123 31.46 N 74.57 E
Majja 74 61.44 N 130.18 E
Majkain 86 51.27 N 75.52 E
Majkop 84 44.35 N 40.07 E
Majkor 86 59.01 N 55.54 E
Majlibaš 86 45.49 N 62.39 E
Majli-Saj 85 41.17 N 72.29 E
Majlispur 126 24.13 N 90.53 E
Majma'ah 128 25.54 N 45.20 E
Majmak 85 42.40 N 71.15 E
Majna, S.S.S.R. 80 54.07 N 47.37 E
Majna, S.S.S.R. 86 53.00 N 91.28 E
Majnan 272b 22.59 N 88.09 E
Majnic, Ozero @ 180 63.15 N 176.40 E
Majno-Gytkino 180 63.36 N 176.30 E
Majno-Pyl'gino 74 62.32 N 177.02 E
Majŏn-ni, C.M.I.K. 98 39.06 N 127.07 E
Majŏn-ni, Taehan 271b 37.36 N 126.41 E
Major, Puig ∧ 34 39.48 N 2.48 E
Majorca → Mallorca I 34 39.30 N 3.00 E
Major Isidoro 250 9.32 S 37.00 W
Majorque, Île → Mallorca I 34 39.30 N 3.00 E
Majrūr 140 14.01 N 30.27 E
Majrūr, Wādī ∨ 140 15.44 N 26.26 E
Majsk 86 57.49 N 77.16 E
Majskij, S.S.S.R. 83 47.43 N 40.03 E
Majskij, S.S.S.R. 84 43.38 N 44.04 E
Majskij, S.S.S.R. 89 52.18 N 129.38 E
Majskij, S.S.S.R. 89 49.00 N 140.10 E
Majskoje, S.S.S.R. 82 56.08 N 37.55 E
Majskoje, S.S.S.R. 86 50.55 N 78.15 E
Majtan 86 45.46 N 74.20 E
Majtobe 85 43.01 N 70.35 E
Māju 126 22.37 N 88.05 E
Majuba Hill ⬥[1] 158 27.28 S 29.51 E
Majunga 157b 15.43 S 46.19 E
Majunga □[4] 157b 17.00 S 46.00 E
Majuqiao 105 39.46 N 116.32 E
Majuro I[1] 14 7.09 N 171.12 E
Majuzigou 104 41.49 N 121.38 E
Maka 150 13.40 N 14.17 W
Makabana 152 2.48 S 12.29 E
Makabe 94 36.16 N 140.06 E
Makadasa ≃ 116 7.22 N 124.36 E
Makaha, Haw., U.S. 229c 21.28 N 158.13 W
Makaha, Zimb. 154 17.17 S 32.37 E
Makaha Point ≻ 229b 22.08 N 159.44 W
Makah Indian Reservation ⬥[4] 224 48.20 N 124.41 W
Makahuena Point ≻ 229b 21.52 N 159.27 W
Makaising 124 27.53 N 84.41 E
Makak 152 3.33 N 11.02 E
Makalamabedi 156 20.19 S 23.51 E
Makale 112 3.06 S 119.51 E
Makallé 252 27.13 S 59.17 W
Makālu ≃ 124 27.54 N 87.06 E
Makamba 154 4.08 S 29.49 E
Makanapur 272a 28.38 N 77.21 E
Makanči 86 46.48 N 82.00 E
Makanya 154 4.20 S 37.51 E
Makanza 152 1.36 N 19.07 E
Makaoo Indian Reserve ⬥[4] 184 53.40 N 110.02 W
Makapu Point ≻ 174v 18.59 S 169.56 W
Makapuu Head ≻ 229c 21.19 N 157.39 W
Makarakskij 86 55.36 N 88.03 E
Makarewa 172 46.20 S 168.21 E
Makari 146 12.35 N 14.28 E
Makar-Ib 24 63.39 N 49.24 E
Makaricha 24 66.15 N 58.20 E
Makarje 80 58.35 N 48.11 E
Makarjev 80 57.52 N 43.48 E
Makarjevo 80 56.06 N 45.06 E
Makarov, S.S.S.R. 78 50.28 N 29.49 E
Makarov, S.S.S.R. 89 48.38 N 142.48 E
Makarovo, S.S.S.R. 80 52.18 N 43.20 E
Makarovo, S.S.S.R. 82 54.22 N 36.40 E
Makarovo, S.S.S.R. 88 57.29 N 107.52 E
Makarska 36 43.18 N 17.02 E
Makasar → Ujung Pandang 112 5.07 S 119.24 E
Makasar, Selat (Makassar Strait) ⩌ 112 2.00 S 117.30 E
Makaševka 80 51.30 N 42.36 E
Makassar Strait → Makasar, Selat ⩌ 112 2.00 S 117.30 E
Makasuko 154 6.00 S 34.56 E
Makat 80 47.39 N 53.19 E
Makatea I 14 15.50 S 148.15 W
Makati 269f 14.34 N 121.02 E
Makaw, Mya. 110 26.27 N 96.42 E
Makaw, Zaïre 152 3.29 S 18.19 E
Makawao 229a 20.52 N 156.19 W
Makaweli 229b 21.55 N 159.38 W
Makay, Massif du ⩕ 157b 21.15 S 45.15 E
Makaya 152 3.22 S 18.02 E
Makaza)(38 41.16 N 25.26 E
Makedonija □[3] 38 41.50 N 22.00 E
Makefu 174v 18.59 S 169.55 W
Makehahu @ 120 35.00 N 83.03 E
Makejevka, S.S.S.R. 78 50.40 N 31.50 E
Makejevka, S.S.S.R. 83 48.02 N 37.58 E
Makejevka, S.S.S.R. 83 49.14 N 37.59 E
Makemie Park 208 37.55 N 75.34 W
Makemo I[1] 14 16.35 S 143.40 W
Makena 229a 20.39 N 156.27 W
Makeni 150 8.53 N 12.03 W
Makere 154 4.17 S 30.25 E
Maketu 172 37.46 S 176.27 E
Makeyevka → Makejevka 83 48.02 N 37.58 E
Makgadikgadi Pans ☷ 156 20.45 S 25.30 E
Makhachkala → Machačkala 84 42.58 N 47.30 E
Makhad 123 33.08 N 71.44 E
Makhaleng ≃ 158 30.20 S 27.23 E
Mākhālpur 272b 22.56 N 88.10 E
Makham 110 12.40 N 102.12 E
Makhdūmnagar 124 26.28 N 82.46 E
Makhfar al-Quwayrah 132 29.48 N 35.19 E
Makhrūq, Wādī al- ∨ 132 31.30 N 37.10 E
Makhyah, Wādī ∨ 144 16.55 N 48.41 E
Maki, Indon. 164 3.11 S 134.14 E
Maki, Nihon 92 37.45 N 138.53 E
Maki, Nihon 270 34.52 N 135.04 E
Makikihi 172 44.38 S 171.09 E
Makilala 116 6.55 N 125.05 E
Makin I[1] 14 3.07 N 172.48 E
Makindu 154 2.17 S 37.49 E
Makino, Nihon 94 35.28 N 136.05 E
M'akino, S.S.S.R. 265b 55.48 N 37.22 E
Makinsk 86 52.37 N 70.26 E
Makio-dam ⬥[6] 94 35.50 N 137.36 E
Makioka 94 35.45 N 138.43 E
Makira Bay C 175e 10.25 S 161.29 E
M'akiševo 76 56.34 N 28.53 E
M'akit 74 61.24 N 152.09 E
Makkah (Mecca) 144 21.27 N 39.49 E
Makkavejevo 88 51.44 N 113.58 E
Makkum 52 53.04 N 5.24 E
Maklakovo 86 58.16 N 92.29 E
Makó, Magy. 30 46.13 N 20.29 E
Mako, Sén. 150 12.52 N 12.21 W
Makobe Lake @ 190 47.27 N 80.25 W
Makoka 154 2.34 S 25.29 E
Makok-ni 271b 37.43 N 126.38 E
Makokou 152 0.34 N 12.52 E
Makoli 154 17.27 S 26.05 E
Makongai I 175g 17.27 S 178.58 E
Makongo 154 3.25 N 26.22 E
Makongolosi 154 8.24 S 33.09 E
Makopse 84 43.59 N 39.13 E
Makorako ∧ 172 39.09 S 176.02 E
Makoro 154 3.08 N 29.44 E

Makošino 78 51.27 N 32.18 E
Makotuku 172 40.07 S 176.14 E
Makoua 152 0.01 N 15.39 E
Makov 30 49.23 N 18.30 E
Makovskoje 86 58.12 N 90.52 E
Maków Mazowiecki 30 52.52 N 21.06 E
Maków Podhalański 30 49.44 N 19.41 E
Makrai 124 22.04 N 77.06 E
Makrampur 126 22.44 N 90.14 E
Makrāna 120 27.03 N 74.43 E
M'aksa 76 58.54 N 38.12 E
Maksaticha 76 57.48 N 35.53 E
Maksimicha 88 53.15 N 108.43 E
Maksimkin Jar 86 58.42 N 86.48 E
Maksimoviči 78 51.13 N 29.37 E
Maksimovka, S.S.S.R. 80 52.59 N 51.10 E
Maksimovka, S.S.S.R. 83 47.38 N 37.34 E
Maksimovo 82 56.20 N 35.58 E
Maksudangarh 124 24.03 N 77.15 E
Maktau 154 3.24 S 38.08 E
Makteïr ⫪[4] 148 22.10 N 10.50 W
Makthar 148 35.51 N 9.12 E
Mākū, Īrān 128 39.17 N 44.31 E
Maku, Zhg. 105 39.33 N 114.46 E
Makuhari 268 35.39 N 140.03 E
Makuliro 154 9.35 S 37.26 E
Mākum 102 27.30 N 95.27 E
Makumbako 154 8.51 S 34.50 E
Makumbi 152 5.51 S 20.41 E
Makunudu I 122 6.25 N 72.41 E
Makunudu Atoll I[1] 122 6.20 N 72.36 E
Makura I 175f 17.08 S 168.27 E
Makuragi-san ∧ 96 35.32 N 133.08 E
Makurazaki 92 31.16 N 130.19 E
Makurdi 150 7.45 N 8.32 E
Makushin Volcano ∧[1] 180 53.53 N 166.50 W
Makušino 86 55.13 N 67.13 E
Makuyuni 154 3.33 S 36.06 E
Makwa Lake @ 184 54.04 N 109.15 W
Makwānpur Garhi 124 27.25 N 85.08 E
Makwassie 158 27.26 S 26.00 E
Makwende-Bayo 154 7.08 S 28.06 E
Makwiro 154 17.58 S 30.28 E
Māl, Bhārat 124 26.52 N 88.44 E
Mal, Maur. 150 16.58 N 13.23 W
Mala, Perú 248 12.39 S 76.38 W
Malå, Sve. 26 65.11 N 18.44 E
Mala ≃ 248 12.40 S 76.41 W
Mala, Punta ≻ 246 7.28 N 80.00 W
Malabadi 130 38.09 N 41.12 E
Malabang 116 7.38 N 124.03 E
Malabar, Austl. 274a 33.58 S 151.15 E
Malabar, Fla., U.S. 220 28.00 N 80.34 W
Malabar Coast ▪[2] 122 10.00 N 76.15 E
Malabar Farm ⊥ 214 40.38 N 82.25 W
Malabar Hill ∧[2] 272c 18.57 N 72.48 E
Malabar Point ≻ 272c 18.57 N 72.47 E
Malabo 152 3.45 N 8.47 E
Malabon 116 14.39 N 120.57 E
Mal Abrigo 258 34.09 S 56.57 W
Malabrigo Point ≻ 116 13.36 N 121.15 E
Malabuyoc 116 9.39 N 123.19 E
Malaca, Estrecho de → Malacca, Strait of ⩌ 110 2.30 N 101.20 E
Malacacheta 255 17.50 S 42.05 W
Malacca, Strait of ⩌ 110 2.30 N 101.20 E
Malachovka 82 55.39 N 38.00 E
Malachovo, S.S.S.R. 82 54.45 N 37.27 E
Malachovo, S.S.S.R. 82 54.22 N 37.31 E
Malachovskij 80 49.08 N 41.43 E
Malacky 30 48.27 N 17.00 E
Mālād ⬥[8] 272c 19.11 N 72.51 E
Malad ≃ 200 41.35 N 112.07 W
Malad City 202 42.12 N 112.15 W
Malafede ≃ 267a 41.47 N 12.24 E
Málaga, Col. 246 6.42 N 72.44 W
Málaga, Esp. 34 36.43 N 4.25 W
Malaga, Calif., U.S. 226 36.42 N 119.46 W
Malaga, N.J., U.S. 208 39.34 N 75.02 W
Malaga, N. Mex., U.S. 196 32.14 N 104.04 W
Malagarasi 154 5.06 S 30.50 E
Malagarasi ≃ 154 5.12 S 29.47 E
Malagash 186 45.46 N 63.23 W
Malagasy Republic → Madagascar □[1] 157b 19.00 S 46.00 E
Malago ≃ 116 10.55 N 123.02 E
Malagón 34 39.10 N 3.51 W
Malagón ≃ 34 37.35 N 7.29 W
Malagrotta ⬥[8] 66 41.53 N 12.20 E
Malahat 224 48.32 N 123.34 W
Malahide 48 57.27 N 6.09 W
Malaimbandy 157b 20.20 S 45.36 E
Malaisie → Malaysia □[1] 112 2.30 N 112.30 E
Malaita □[8] 175e 9.00 S 161.00 E
Malaita I 175e 9.00 S 161.00 E
Malaita Division □[5] 175e 9.00 S 161.00 E
Malaja Belaja ≃ 88 52.52 N 103.05 E
Malaja Beloz'orka 78 47.14 N 34.56 E
Malaja Bessergenovka 83 47.09 N 38.36 E
Malaja Bira ≃ 89 48.07 N 133.14 E
Malaja Borščovka 82 56.33 N 36.53 E
Malaja Bykovka 80 51.54 N 47.45 E
Malaja Čuja ≃ 88 58.56 N 112.13 E
Malaja Devica 78 50.41 N 32.10 E
Malaja Doroginka 82 54.06 N 38.56 E
Malaja Dubna 82 55.52 N 38.58 E
Malaja Istra ≃ 82 55.54 N 36.50 E
Malaja Ižmora 80 53.33 N 42.50 E
Malaja Janisol' 83 47.22 N 37.20 E
Malaja Jekaterinovka 80 51.26 N 44.17 E
Malaja Ket' ≃ 86 57.53 N 91.14 E
Malaja Kinel' ≃ 80 53.29 N 51.30 E
Malaja Kokšaga ≃ 80 56.09 N 47.53 E
Malaja Konkudera ≃ 88 57.26 N 112.37 E
Malaja Kuberle ≃ 80 47.22 N 42.17 E
Malaja Kuril'skaja Gr'ada (Habomai-shotō) II 92a 43.30 N 146.10 E
Malaja Laba ≃ 84 44.16 N 40.53 E
Malaja Neva ≃[1] 265a 59.57 N 30.15 E
Malaja Ochta ⬥[8] 265a 59.56 N 30.24 E
Malaja Orlovka 80 47.18 N 41.24 E
Malaja Pera 24 64.11 N 54.47 E
Malaja Serdoba 80 52.28 N 44.56 E
Malaja Sestra ≃ 82 56.17 N 35.57 E
Malaja Tokmačevka 78 47.32 N 35.54 E
Malaja Višera 76 58.51 N 32.14 E
Malaja Viska 78 48.39 N 31.38 E
Malaka → Melaka 114 2.12 N 102.15 E
Malaka, Sempitan ⩌ 114 5.44 N 95.30 E
Malakāl 140 9.31 N 31.39 E
Malākand 123 34.34 N 71.56 E
Mala Kapela ⩕ 36 44.50 N 15.30 E
Malakka, Strasse von → Malacca, Strait of ⩌ 110 2.30 N 101.20 E
Malakoff, Fr. 261 48.49 N 2.19 E
Malakoff, Tex., U.S. 222 32.10 N 96.01 W
Malakpur ⬥[8] 272a 28.42 N 77.12 E
Malakwāl 123 32.34 N 73.13 E
Malala 164 5.15 S 147.10 E
Malalag 116 6.36 N 125.24 E
Malalbergo 64 44.43 N 11.32 E
Malam 146 11.27 N 20.59 E
Malamala 112 3.21 S 120.55 E
Malamaui Island I 116 6.44 N 121.58 E
Malambo, Arroyo ≃ 258 33.43 S 58.46 W
Malambunga 116 9.02 N 117.38 E
Malamocco 64 45.22 N 12.20 E
Malampaya Sound ⩌ 116 10.51 N 119.20 E
Malān 110 25.37 N 96.21 E

Malān, Rās ≻ 128 25.18 N 65.11 E
Malanao Island I 116 9.27 N 118.37 E
Malanas ≃ 116 17.41 N 120.43 E
Mālancha 272b 22.55 N 88.26 E
Mālancha ≃[1] 126 21.40 N 89.20 E
Mālandighi 126 23.33 N 87.24 E
Malandji 152 5.56 S 22.18 E
Malang 115a 7.59 S 112.37 E
Malang, Gunung ∧ 115a 7.02 S 107.01 E
Malangali 154 8.34 S 34.51 E
Malangas 116 7.37 N 123.01 E
Malanguan)(105 40.16 N 117.39 E
Malangwa 124 26.52 N 85.34 E
Malanipa Island I 116 6.53 N 122.16 E
Malanje 152 9.32 S 16.20 E
Malanje □[5] 152 9.30 S 16.30 E
Malanut Bay C 116 9.16 N 117.59 E
Malanville 150 11.52 N 3.23 E
Malanyu 105 40.14 N 117.39 E
Malanzán 252 30.48 S 66.37 W
Malapa I 175e 9.48 S 160.52 E
Malapane → Ozimek 30 50.41 N 18.13 E
Mała Panew ≃ 30 50.44 N 17.52 E
Malapantao, Mount ∧ 116 9.54 N 122.37 E
Malapardis Brook ≃ 276 40.49 N 74.25 W
Mala Pascua, Cabo ≻ 240m 17.59 N 65.55 W
Malapascua Island I 116 11.20 N 124.07 E
Mälaren @ 40 59.30 N 17.12 E
Malargüe 252 35.28 S 69.35 W
Mälar-See → Mälaren @ 40 59.30 N 17.12 E
Malartic 190 48.08 N 78.08 W
Malartic, Lac @ 190 48.15 N 78.07 W
Malasia → Malaysia □[1] 112 2.30 N 112.30 E
Malasiqui 116 15.55 N 120.25 E
Malaspina 254 44.56 S 66.54 W
Malaspina Glacier ⍓ 180 59.50 N 140.30 W
Malaspina Strait ⩌ 182 49.44 N 124.20 W
Malassis 261 48.38 N 2.03 E
Malāṭīyah 142 28.42 N 30.51 E
Malatya 130 38.21 N 38.19 E
Malatya □[4] 130 38.30 N 38.10 E
Malaucène 62 44.10 N 5.08 E
Malaunay 50 49.32 N 1.02 E
Malaut 123 30.13 N 74.29 E
Malavalli 122 12.23 N 77.05 E
Malawali, Pulau I 112 7.03 N 117.18 E
Malawi □[1] 138; 154 13.30 S 34.00 E
Malawi, Lake → Nyasa, Lake @ 154 12.00 S 34.30 E
Malawiya 140 15.16 N 36.12 E
Malaya □[9] 114 4.00 N 102.00 E
Malayal 116 7.12 N 121.57 E
Malaybalay 116 8.09 N 125.05 E
Malāyer 128 34.17 N 48.50 E
Malay Peninsula ≻[1] 110 6.00 N 101.00 E
Malay Reef ⊹[2] 166 17.59 S 149.18 E
Malaysia □[1] 108; 112 2.30 N 112.30 E
Malazgirt 130 39.09 N 42.31 E
Malbaie ≃ 186 47.39 N 70.09 W
Malbaie, Baie de C 186 48.35 N 64.14 W
Malbon 166 21.04 S 140.18 E
Malbooma 162 30.41 S 134.11 E
Malborghetto Valbruna 64 46.30 N 13.26 E
Malbork 30 54.02 N 19.01 E
Malbrán 252 29.21 S 62.27 W
Malbuisson 58 46.48 N 6.18 E
Malbun 58 47.35 N 9.33 E
Malcesine 64 45.46 N 10.48 E
Mal'cevo 82 55.56 N 37.57 E
Mal'čevskaja 78 49.04 N 40.21 E
Mal'čevsko-Polnenskaja 83 48.58 N 40.12 E
Malchanskij Chrebet ⩕ 88 50.45 N 109.30 E
Malchin 54 53.44 N 12.46 E
Malchiner See @ 54 53.43 N 12.38 E
Malching 60 48.19 N 13.12 E
Malchow 54 53.28 N 12.25 E
Malchow ⬥[8] 264a 52.35 N 13.29 E
Malčin 88 49.44 N 93.18 E
Malcolm 162 28.56 S 121.30 E
Malcolm, Point ≻ 162 33.48 S 123.45 E
Malcom 190 41.43 N 92.33 W
Malcompeth → Mahābaleshwar 122 17.55 N 73.40 E
Malcontenta 64 45.25 N 12.13 E
Malczyce 30 51.14 N 16.29 E
Mālda 124 25.02 N 88.09 E
Mālda □[5] 124 25.00 N 88.10 E
Maldegem 50 51.13 N 3.27 E
Malden, Mass., U.S. 207 42.26 N 71.04 W
Malden, Mo., U.S. 194 36.34 N 89.57 W
Malden ≃ 283 42.24 N 71.05 W
Malden Bridge 210 42.28 N 73.35 W
Malden Island I 14 4.03 S 154.59 W
Malden on Hudson 210 42.06 N 73.56 W
Maldivas → Maldives □[1] 12 3.15 N 73.00 E
Maldive Islands → Maldives □[1] 12 3.15 N 73.00 E
Maldive Islands II 12 3.15 N 73.00 E
Maldives □[1] 12 3.15 N 73.00 E
Mal di Ventre, Isola di I 71 39.59 N 8.18 E
Maldon, Austl. 169 37.00 S 144.04 E
Maldon, Eng., U.K. 42 51.45 N 0.40 E
Maldon □[8] 260 51.43 N 0.40 E
Maldonado 252 34.54 S 54.57 W
Maldonado, Punta ≻ 234 16.20 N 98.35 W
Male, It. 64 46.21 N 10.55 E
Male, Mald. 12 4.10 N 73.30 E
Male, Mya. 110 23.02 N 95.58 E
Maléa, Ákra ≻ 38 36.26 N 23.12 E
Malea, Dolok ∧ 114 0.56 N 99.38 E
Malediven → Maldives □[1] 12 3.15 N 73.00 E
Mālegaon 122 20.33 N 74.32 E
Malegno, It. 64 46.40 N 11.08 E
Malegno, It. 64 45.56 N 10.14 E
Malehra 124 24.34 N 79.19 E
Maleit, Lake @ 140 7.55 N 28.35 E
Malejevka 78 47.29 N 32.43 E
Malek, S.S.S.R. 85 40.47 N 68.37 E
Malek, Sūd. 140 6.04 N 31.36 E
Malek Dīn 120 32.25 N 68.04 E
Malek Kandī 128 37.09 N 46.06 E
Malekula I 175f 16.15 S 167.30 E
Malela, Zaïre 154 4.22 S 26.08 E
Malela, Zaïre 154 2.28 S 26.09 E
Malen'ga 24 63.50 N 36.25 E
Malengoya 154 3.32 N 25.25 E
Malente 54 54.10 N 10.33 E
Maleo 62 45.10 N 9.46 E
Māler Kotla 124 30.31 N 75.53 E
Malesco 58 46.08 N 8.30 E
Malesherbes 50 48.18 N 2.25 E
Malestroit 32 47.49 N 2.23 W
Maleta 88 50.50 N 108.25 E
Maletto 70 37.49 N 14.52 E
Malfa 70 38.35 N 14.50 E
Malgas 158 34.18 S 20.35 E
Malgersdorf 60 48.32 N 12.45 E
Malgobek 84 43.32 N 44.34 E
Malgomaj @ 26 64.47 N 16.12 E
Malha Wells 140 15.08 N 26.12 E
Malheur ≃ 202 44.03 N 116.59 W
Malheur, North Fork ≃ 202 43.45 N 118.04 W

Symbol	English	Deutsch	Español	Français	Português
≃	River	Fluss	Río	Rivière	Rio
≋	Canal	Kanal	Canal	Canal	Canal
ʟ	Waterfall, Rapids	Wasserfall, Stromschnellen	Cascada, Rápidos	Chute d'eau, Rapides	Cascata, Rápidos
⩌	Strait	Meeresstrasse	Estrecho	Détroit	Estreito
C	Bay, Gulf	Bucht, Golf	Bahía, Golfo	Baie, Golfe	Baía, Golfo
@	Lake, Lakes	See, Seen	Lago, Lagos	Lac, Lacs	Lago, Lagos
☷	Swamp	Sumpf	Pantano	Marais	Pântano
⍓	Ice Features, Glacier	Eis- und Gletscherformen	Accidentes Glaciales	Formes glaciaires	Acidentes Glaciares
⫪	Other Hydrographic Features	Andere Hydrographische Objekte	Otros Elementos Hidrográficos	Autres données hydrographiques	Outros Elementos Hidrográficos
⊹	Submarine Features	Untermeerische Objekte	Accidentes Submarinos	Formes de relief sous-marin	Acidentes Submarinos
□	Political Unit	Politische Einheit	Unidad Política	Entité politique	Unidade Política
ʊ	Cultural Institution	Kulturelle Institution	Institución Cultural	Institution culturelle	Instituição Cultural
⊥	Historical Site	Historische Stätte	Sitio Histórico	Site historique	Sitio Histórico
♠	Recreational Site	Erholungs- und Ferienort	Sitio de Recreo	Centre de loisirs	Sítio de Lazer
⊠	Airport	Flughafen	Aeropuerto	Aéroport	Aeroporto
▪	Military Installation	Militäranlage	Instalación Militar	Installation militaire	Instalação Militar
⬥	Miscellaneous	Verschiedenes	Misceláneo	Divers	Miscelânea

Malheur, South Fork ≃ 202 43.33 N 118.10 W
Malheur Lake ⊜ 202 43.20 N 118.45 W
Mali, Cam. 146 8.28 N 12.35 E
Mali, Guinée 150 12.05 N 12.18 W
Mali, Zaïre 154 2.48 S 26.08 E
Mali □[4] 150 12.05 N 12.05 W
Mali □[1] 134 17.00 N 4.00 W
Mali I 175g 16.20 S 179.21 E
Mali ≃ 102 25.43 N 97.29 E
Maliangping 102 31.29 N 111.20 E
Malianjingzi 102 41.32 N 95.23 E
Malibamatso ≃ 158 29.20 S 29.28 E
Malibu 228 34.02 N 118.42 W
Malibu Lake ⊜[1] 228 34.07 N 118.45 W
Malienkang 269d 25.10 N 121.39 E
Maligay Bay C 116 7.30 N 123.14 E
Malighati 126 22.33 N 87.40 E
Maligne ≃ 182 52.56 N 118.02 W
Maligne Lake ⊜ 182 52.40 N 117.31 W
Malīhābād 124 26.55 N 80.43 E
Māliḥah, Wādī ∨ 142 29.21 N 32.35 E
Malik 112 0.34 S 123.14 E
Malik, Wādī al- ∨ 140 18.02 N 30.58 E
Malik Sīāh, Kūh-i- ∧ 128 29.51 N 60.52 E
Mali Kyun I 110 13.06 N 98.16 E
Malili 112 2.38 S 121.06 E
Målilla 26 57.23 N 15.48 E
Malimba, Monts ⛰ 154 7.32 S 29.30 E
Malim Nawar 114 4.21 N 101.07 E
Malimono 116 9.34 N 125.25 E
Malin, Eire 48 55.18 N 7.15 W
Malin, S.S.S.R. 78 50.46 N 29.15 E
Malin, Oreg., U.S. 202 42.01 N 121.24 W
Malinalco ⏊ 234 18.57 N 99.30 W
Malinaltepec 234 17.03 N 98.40 W
Malinau 112 3.35 N 116.38 E
Malin Beg 48 54.40 N 8.48 E
Malindang, Mount ∧ 116 8.13 N 123.38 E
Malindi 154 3.13 S 40.07 E
Malindi Marinee National Park ♠ 154 3.15 S 40.10 E
Malines → Mechelen 50 51.02 N 4.28 E
Malinga 152 2.25 S 12.14 E
Malingguan)(98 37.20 N 114.00 E
Malingping 115a 6.46 S 106.01 E
Malingsbosjön ⊜ 40 59.55 N 15.27 E
Malin Head ≻ 48 55.23 N 7.24 W
Malinki 82 54.05 N 38.59 E
Malinniki 82 56.17 N 38.24 E
Malino, Indon. 112 5.15 S 119.51 E
Malino, S.S.S.R. 82 55.06 N 38.11 E
Malino, S.S.S.R. 265b 55.58 N 37.13 E
Malino, Bukit ∧ 112 0.45 N 120.47 E
Malinoa I 174w 21.02 S 175.08 W
Malinovka, S.S.S.R. 78 49.47 N 36.43 E
Malinovka, S.S.S.R. 80 51.47 N 43.26 E
Malinovka, S.S.S.R. 86 53.24 N 87.17 E
Malinta 216 41.19 N 84.02 W
Malinyi 154 8.56 S 36.08 E
Malipara 272b 22.57 N 88.14 E
Mali Rajinac ∧ 36 44.48 N 15.02 E
Malita 116 6.25 N 125.36 E
Malitbog 116 10.10 N 125.00 E
Maliuchang 107 29.05 N 104.07 E
Maliuping 107 29.55 N 106.23 E
Ma-Liu Shui 271d 22.25 N 114.12 E
Malivo 82 55.07 N 39.02 E
Maliwun 110 10.14 N 98.37 E
Māliya 120 23.05 N 70.46 E
Malizhen 102 23.10 N 104.35 E
Maljamar 196 32.51 N 103.46 W
Malka, S.S.S.R. 74 53.20 N 157.30 E
Malka, S.S.S.R. 84 43.47 N 43.21 E
Malka ≃ 84 43.44 N 44.15 E
Malkāpur 120 20.53 N 76.12 E
Malkapuram 122 17.42 N 83.16 E
Malkara 130 40.53 N 26.54 E
Malkerns 158 26.32 S 31.11 E
Malko Tărnovo 38 41.59 N 27.32 E
Mallacoota National Park ♠ 166 37.30 S 149.50 E
Mallāḥ 132 32.30 N 36.51 E
Mallaig, Alta., Can. 182 54.13 N 111.22 W
Mallaig, Scot., U.K. 46 57.00 N 5.50 W
Mallala 168b 34.26 S 138.30 E
Mallamalla Range ⛰ 122 15.30 N 78.50 E
Mallaoua 150 13.02 N 9.36 E
Mallapunyah 164 16.59 S 135.49 E
Mallaranny 48 53.54 N 9.49 W
Mallard Reservoir ⊜[1] 282 38.01 N 122.03 W
Mallawī 142 27.44 N 30.50 E
Mallémbé 152 3.32 S 10.53 E
Mallemort 62 43.44 N 5.11 E
Mallersdrof 60 48.47 N 12.16 E
Mallery Lake ⊜ 176 63.55 N 98.25 W
Malles Venosta (Mals) 64 46.41 N 10.32 E
Mallet 252 25.55 S 50.50 W
Mallig 116 17.08 N 121.41 E
Malligasta 252 29.11 S 67.26 W
Mallina 162 20.53 S 118.02 E
Malling 41 56.02 N 10.10 E
Mallnitz 64 46.59 N 13.10 E
Mallorca I 34 39.30 N 3.00 E
Mallorquinas 266d 41.28 N 2.16 E
Mallorytown 212 44.29 N 75.53 W
Mallow 48 52.08 N 8.39 W
Mallwitz → Małowice 30 51.34 N 15.27 E
Mallwood 216 42.51 N 89.02 W
Malm 26 64.04 N 11.13 E
Malmbäck 26 57.35 N 14.28 E
Malmberget 24 67.10 N 20.40 E
Malmédy 56 50.25 N 6.02 E
Malmesbury, S. Afr. 158 33.28 S 18.44 E
Malmesbury, Eng., U.K. 42 51.36 N 2.06 W
Malmesbury, Vale of ∨ 42 51.22 N 2.10 W
Malmköping 40 59.08 N 16.44 E
Malmö 41 55.36 N 13.00 E
Malmöhus Län □[6] 26 55.45 N 13.30 E
Malmsbury 169 37.12 S 144.23 E
Malmsbury Reservoir ⊜[1] 169 37.13 S 144.22 E
Malmslätt 26 58.25 N 15.30 E
Malmstrom Air Force Base ▪ 202 47.30 N 111.10 W
Malmyž 80 56.31 N 50.41 E
Malna 116 8.08 N 124.27 E
Malnate 62 45.48 N 8.53 E
Malnoue 261 48.50 N 2.36 E
Malo 64 45.39 N 11.24 E
Malo I 175f 15.40 S 167.11 E
Malo, Arroyo ≃ 258 33.43 S 58.52 W
Maloarchangel'sk 76 52.24 N 36.30 E
Maloarchangel'skoje 88 50.24 N 108.50 E
Maloba 154 6.18 S 27.39 E
Malodel'skaja 80 50.11 N 43.53 E
Maloduša 78 52.09 N 30.14 E
Maloelap I[1] 14 8.45 N 171.03 E
Malo-Iljinovka ◆[8] 83 48.38 N 37.59 E
Maloja 58 46.24 N 9.41 E
Malojapass)(58 46.24 N 9.41 E
Malojaroslavec 82 55.01 N 36.28 E
Malojaz 86 55.13 N 58.09 E
Maloje Goloustnoje 88 52.18 N 105.18 E
Maloje Jeravnoje, Ozero ⊜ 88 52.40 N 111.36 E
Malojekaterinovka 78 47.39 N 35.16 E
Maloje Kozino 80 56.26 N 43.41 E
Maloje More, Proliv Ա 88 53.20 N 107.25 E
Maloje Polesje ◆[1] 78 50.10 N 25.00 E
Maloje-Ščerbedino 80 51.59 N 42.50 E
Maloje Skuratovo 76 53.33 N 37.00 E
Malokirsanovka 83 47.28 N 38.31 E
Malokrasnojarka 86 56.28 N 76.01 E
Malo-les-Bains 50 51.03 N 2.24 E
Malolo 154 7.18 S 36.35 E
Malolos, Guam 174p 13.18 N 144.46 E
Malolos, Pil. 116 14.51 N 120.49 E
Malom 164 3.10 S 151.50 E
Maloma 158 27.00 S 31.40 E
Maloma ≃ 24 58.20 N 48.28 E
Malombe, Lake ⊜ 154 14.38 S 35.12 E
Malomichajlovka 78 48.06 N 36.23 E
Malonabatovskij 80 48.57 N 43.40 E
Malone, Fla., U.S. 192 30.57 N 85.10 W
Malone, N.Y., U.S. 188 44.51 N 74.17 W
Malone, Tex., U.S. 222 31.55 N 96.54 W
Malone, Wash., U.S. 224 46.58 N 123.20 W
Malonga 152 10.24 S 23.10 E
Malonno 64 46.07 N 10.18 E
Małopolska ◆[1] 30 50.10 N 21.30 E
Malor'azancevo 83 48.53 N 38.23 E
Malorita 78 51.47 N 24.05 E
Malorossijskij 86 53.12 N 62.30 E
Malo Strait Ա 175f 15.50 S 167.10 E
Malošujka 24 63.45 N 37.22 E
Maloti Mountains ⛰ 158 29.05 S 28.20 E
Måløv 41 55.45 N 12.20 E
Małowice 30 51.34 N 15.27 E
Måløy 26 61.56 N 5.07 E
Malozemel'skaja Tundra ◆[1] 24 67.50 N 51.00 E
Malpaisillo 236 12.35 N 86.41 W
Malpartida de Plasencia 34 39.59 N 6.02 W
Malpas, Austl. 166 34.43 S 140.37 E
Malpas, Eng., U.K. 42 53.01 N 2.46 W
Malpaso 234 22.37 N 102.46 W
Malpe 122 13.21 N 74.43 E
Malpelo, Isla de I 242 3.59 N 81.35 W
Malpensa, Aeroporto di ⊠ 62 45.38 N 8.44 E
Malpeque Bay C 186 46.30 N 63.47 W
Malprabha ≃ 122 16.12 N 76.03 E
Mālpura 120 26.17 N 75.23 E
Mals → Malles Venosta 64 46.41 N 10.32 E
Mälsåkers slott ⏊ 40 59.23 N 17.18 E
Malsch 56 48.53 N 8.19 E
Malše ≃ 61 48.58 N 14.28 E
Målselva ≃ 24 69.14 N 18.30 E
Malta, Bra. 250 6.54 S 37.31 W
Malta, Öst. 64 46.57 N 13.30 E
Malta, S.S.S.R. 76 56.21 N 27.10 E
Malta, Ill., U.S. 216 41.56 N 88.52 W
Malta, Mont., U.S. 202 48.21 N 107.52 W
Malta, Ohio, U.S. 188 39.39 N 81.52 W
Malta □[1] 22
36 35.50 N 14.35 E
Malta I 36 35.53 N 14.27 E
Malta ≃ 76 56.44 N 26.53 E
Maltahöhe 156 24.50 S 17.00 E
Maltahöhe □[5] 156 25.00 S 16.30 E
Malta-Tal ∨ 64 47.03 N 13.24 E
Maltby 44 53.26 N 1.11 W
Malte → Malta □[1] 36 35.50 N 14.35 E
Malte Brun, Mount ∧ 172 43.34 S 170.18 E
Maltepe, Tür. 130 40.02 N 27.58 E
Maltepe, Tür. 267b 40.55 N 29.08 E
Malton 44 54.08 N 0.48 W
Malton ◆[8] 275b 43.42 N 79.38 W
Maltrata 234 18.48 N 97.16 W
Maltsch → Malczyce 30 51.14 N 16.29 E
Malugou 89 43.39 N 128.27 E
Maluku □[4] 164 5.00 S 130.00 E
Maluku (Moluccas) II 108 2.00 S 128.00 E
Maluku, Laut (Molucca Sea) ⊤[2] 108 0.00 S 125.00 E
Maluku-Maes 152 4.06 S 15.31 E
Ma'lūlā 130 33.50 N 36.33 E
Ma'lūlā, Jabal ∧ 132 33.54 N 36.36 E
Malu Mare 38 44.15 N 23.51 E
Malumfashi 150 11.47 N 7.37 E
Malunda 112 3.00 S 118.50 E
Malung 26 60.40 N 13.44 E
Maluso 116 6.33 N 121.53 E
Malūṭ 140 10.26 N 32.12 E
Maluti 126 24.09 N 87.41 E
Maluwe 150 8.40 N 2.17 W
Maluzhen 106 31.20 N 121.16 E
Malvaglia 58 46.25 N 8.59 E
Malvaglio 266b 45.31 N 8.47 E
Malvagna 70 37.55 N 15.04 E
Mālvan 122 16.04 N 73.28 E
Malveira 266c 38.45 N 9.27 W
Malvern, Austl. 274b 37.52 S 145.02 E
Malvern, Ark., U.S. 194 34.22 N 92.49 W
Malvern, Iowa, U.S. 198 41.00 N 95.35 W
Malvern, Ohio, U.S. 214 40.41 N 81.11 W
Malvern, Pa., U.S. 285 40.02 N 75.31 W
Malvern ◆[8] 273d 26.12 S 28.06 E
Malverne 276 40.40 N 73.40 W
Malvern East 273d 26.12 S 28.08 E
Malvern Hills 166 24.29 S 145.10 E
Malvern Hills ⛰[2] 42 52.05 N 2.21 W
Malvern Link 42 52.08 N 2.18 W
Malvinas 252 29.37 S 58.59 W
Malvito 68 39.36 N 16.03 E
Malwal 140 9.19 N 31.35 E
Mālwa Plateau ⛰[1] 124 23.50 N 77.30 E
Malybaj 85 43.30 N 78.25 E
Malý Dunaj ≃ 30 48.08 N 17.09 E
Malyi Nesvetaj ≃ 83 47.32 N 39.49 E
Malyj, Ostrov I 76 60.02 N 28.02 E
Malyj An'uj ≃ 74 68.30 N 160.49 E
Malyj Barmamyt, Gora ∧ 84 43.41 N 42.27 E
Malyj Čeremšan ≃ 80 54.18 N 50.01 E
Malyj Chamar-Daban, Chrebet ⛰ 88 51.00 N 105.00 E
Malyj Civil' ≃ 80 55.54 N 47.28 E
Malyje Alabuchi 80 51.33 N 42.10 E
Malyje Čany, Ozero ⊜ 86 54.33 N 78.02 E
Malyje Derbety 80 47.56 N 44.41 E
Malyje Gorod'atiči 76 52.33 N 28.20 E
Malyje Jagury 80 45.26 N 43.01 E
Malyje Kamkaly 86 44.44 N 71.31 E
Malyje Karmakuly 72 72.23 N 52.44 E
Malyje Porogi 265a 59.47 N 30.42 E
Malyj Irgiz ≃ 80 52.12 N 47.58 E
Malyj Jenisej (Ka-Chem) ≃ 88 51.43 N 94.26 E
Malyj Jugan ≃ 86 60.40 N 73.54 E
Malyj Kavkaz ⛰ 84 41.00 N 44.35 E
Malyj Kemčug ≃ 86 56.55 N 91.49 E
Malyj Kundyš ≃ 80 56.22 N 47.53 E
Malyj L'achovskij, Ostrov I 74 74.07 N 140.36 E
Malyj Šantar, Ostrov I 89 54.30 N 137.36 E
Malyj Sarybulak 86 52.10 N 72.35 E
Malyj Tagul ≃ 88 54.50 N 97.23 E
Malyj Tajmyr, Ostrov I 74 78.08 N 107.12 E
Malyj T'uters, Ostrov I 76 59.49 N 26.56 E
Malyj Uran ≃ 80 52.30 N 53.01 E
Malyj Uzen' ≃ 80 48.50 N 49.39 E
Malyj Zelenčuk ≃ 84 44.24 N 41.56 E
Malyn' 82 54.36 N 38.40 E
Malyševo 76 57.50 N 35.36 E
Malzéville 58 48.43 N 6.12 E
Mama 88 58.18 N 112.54 E
Mama ≃ 88 58.18 N 112.55 E
Ma Ma Creek ≃ 171a 27.35 S 152.13 E
Mamadyš 80 55.44 N 51.25 E
Mamagota 175e 6.46 S 155.24 E
Mamahuolang 104 42.24 N 124.12 E
Mamaia 38 44.15 N 28.37 E
Mamajiecun 104 41.26 N 122.51 E
Mamakan 88 57.48 N 114.01 E
Mamaku 172 38.06 S 176.05 E
Mamakula 174v 18.57 S 169.54 W
Mamakwash Lake ⊜ 184 51.38 N 92.56 W
Mamala Bay C 229a 21.18 N 157.57 W
Mamalu Bay C 229a 20.37 N 156.09 W
Mamanguape 250 6.50 S 35.07 W
Mamanutha Group II 175g 17.34 S 177.04 E
Mamao, Hakau ⊤[2] 174w 21.00 S 175.12 W
Mamara 248 14.14 S 72.35 W
Mamaregu 175e 6.32 S 155.12 E
Mamaroneck 210 40.57 N 73.44 W
Mamaroneck ≃ 276 40.57 N 73.44 W
Mamaroneck Harbor C 276 40.56 N 73.43 W
Mamasa 112 2.56 S 119.22 E
Mamasa ≃ 112 3.30 S 119.42 E
Mamba 94 36.07 N 138.55 E
Mambaí 255 14.28 S 46.07 W
Mambajao 116 9.15 N 124.43 E
Mambajao, Mount ∧ 116 9.10 N 124.44 E
Mambali 154 4.33 S 32.41 E
Mambalot 116 8.51 N 117.55 E
Mambare ≃ 164 8.20 S 147.55 E
Mambasa 154 1.21 N 29.03 E
Mambéllé 152 3.51 N 16.42 E
Mamberamo ≃ 164 1.26 S 137.53 E
Mambéré ≃ 152 3.31 N 16.03 E
Mambili ≃ 152 0.07 N 16.08 E
Mambrui 154 3.07 S 40.09 E
Mambucaba 256 23.01 S 44.31 W
Mambucaba ≃ 256 23.02 S 44.32 W
Mamburao 116 13.14 N 120.35 E
Mambusao ≃ 116 11.24 N 122.41 E
Mamdūḥ, Rujm ∧ 132 32.14 N 36.15 E
Mamedkala 84 42.10 N 48.06 E
Mamehaktebo 112 0.08 N 115.32 E
Ma-Me-O Beach 182 52.58 N 113.59 W
Mamera 286c 10.27 N 66.59 W
Mamera, Quebrada ≃ 286c 10.27 N 66.59 W
Mamers 50 48.21 N 0.23 E
Mamfe 152 5.46 N 9.17 E
Mamiá ≃ 250 1.55 S 55.07 W
Mamiá, Lago ⊜ 246 4.15 S 63.03 W
Mamie 192 36.08 N 75.50 W
Mamiña 248 20.05 S 69.14 W
Maminigui 150 7.24 N 5.50 W
Mamirolle 58 47.12 N 6.10 E
Mamisonskij, Pereval)(84 42.43 N 43.48 E
Maml'utka 86 54.57 N 68.35 E
Mammendorf 60 48.12 N 11.09 E
Mammola 68 38.22 N 16.15 E
Mammoth, Ariz., U.S. 200 32.43 N 110.38 W
Mammoth, W. Va., U.S. 188 38.16 N 81.22 W
Mammoth Cave National Park ♠ 194 37.08 N 86.13 W
Mammoth Lakes 204 37.38 N 118.58 W
Mammoth Pool Reservoir ⊜[1] 226 37.20 N 119.20 W
Mammoth Spring 194 36.30 N 91.33 W
Mamoiada 71 40.13 N 9.17 E
Mamonovo, S.S.S.R. 76 54.28 N 19.57 E
Mamonovo, S.S.S.R. 265b 55.41 N 37.19 E
Mamont 279b 40.29 N 79.36 W
Mamontovo, S.S.S.R. 86 52.43 N 81.37 E
Mamontovo, S.S.S.R. 86 51.45 N 81.25 E
Mamoré ≃ 248 10.23 S 65.53 W
Mamori, Lago ⊜ 246 3.38 S 60.07 W
Mamoriá ≃ 248 7.30 S 66.21 W
Mamoritanas ≃ 246 1.39 S 67.22 W
Mamou, Guinée 150 10.23 N 12.05 W
Mamou, La., U.S. 194 30.38 N 92.25 W
Mamou □[4] 150 10.30 N 12.00 W
Mamoutzou 157a 12.47 S 45.14 E
Mampikony 157b 16.06 S 47.38 E
Mampong 150 7.04 N 1.24 W
Mamraš 84 41.44 N 48.19 E
Mamre 158 33.30 S 18.29 E
Mamry, Jezioro ⊜ 30 54.08 N 21.42 E
Mamué 152 13.35 S 13.13 E
Mamuju 112 2.41 S 118.54 E
Mamulique 196 26.08 N 100.20 W
Ma'mūn 140 12.15 N 22.41 E
Mamuno 156 22.16 S 20.01 E
Mamure 130 40.08 N 35.18 E
Mamuru ≃ 250 2.42 S 56.44 W
Mamykovo 80 54.38 N 50.37 E
Mamyl' 24 61.57 N 56.41 E
Man, Bhārat 120 33.51 N 78.32 E
Man, C. Iv. 150 7.24 N 7.33 W
Man, W. Va., U.S. 192 37.45 N 81.53 W
Man □[5] 150 7.15 N 7.30 W
Man (Île de) → Isle of Man □[2] 44 54.15 N 4.30 W
Man, Isle of → Isle of Man □[2] 44 54.15 N 4.30 W
Mana 229b 22.02 N 159.46 W
Mana ≃, Guy. fr. 250 5.44 N 53.54 W
Mana ≃, S.S.S.R. 86 55.57 N 92.28 E
Manabí □[4] 246 0.40 S 80.05 W
Manabique, Punta de ≻ 236 15.56 N 88.37 W
Manacá ≃ 246 2.52 S 61.50 W
Manacacías ≃ 246 4.23 N 72.04 W
Manacapuru 246 3.18 S 60.37 W
Manacle Point ≻ 42 50.03 N 5.03 W
Manacor 34 39.34 N 3.12 E
Manado 112 1.29 N 124.51 E
Managua 236 12.09 N 86.17 W
Managua □[5] 236 12.00 N 86.25 W
Managua, Aeropuerto ⊠ 286b 23.00 N 82.17 W
Managua, Lago de ⊜ 236 12.20 N 86.20 W
Manahawkin 208 39.42 N 74.16 W
Manahawkin Bay C 208 39.40 N 74.12 W
Manaia 172 39.33 S 174.08 E
Manā'if, Bi'r al- ⊤[4] 142 30.31 N 32.12 E
Manajenki 76 53.42 N 36.27 E
Manakalampona ∧ 157b 15.23 S 48.50 E
Manakara 157b 22.08 S 48.01 E
Manakau 172 40.43 S 175.13 E
Manakau ∧ 172 42.14 S 173.37 E
Manākhah 144 15.07 N 43.44 E
Manalapan Brook ≃ 276 40.24 N 74.23 W
Manāli 123 32.16 N 77.10 E
Manama → Al-Manāmah 128 26.13 N 50.35 E
Manambaroa ≃ 157b 17.41 S 44.04 E
Manambato, Madag. 157b 13.14 S 49.54 E
Manambato, Madag. 157b 13.43 S 49.07 E
Manambolo ≃ 157b 19.18 S 44.24 E
Manambolosy 157b 16.02 S 49.40 E
Manam Island I 164 4.05 S 145.05 E
Mánamo, Caño ≃[1] 246 9.55 N 62.16 W
Manamoc Island I 116 11.19 N 120.41 E
Manampatrana 157b 21.40 S 47.35 E
Manana I 229c 21.20 N 157.40 W
Mananantanana ≃ 157b 21.25 S 45.33 E
Mananao 116 13.30 N 120.34 E
Mananara 157b 16.10 S 49.46 E
Mananara ≃ 157b 23.21 S 47.42 E
Manandaza 157b 19.19 S 45.23 E
Mananjary 157b 21.13 S 48.20 E
Manankoro 150 10.28 N 7.27 W
Manantenina 157b 24.17 S 47.19 E
Manantiales Behr 254 45.41 S 67.31 W
Manantico Creek ≃ 208 39.20 N 75.00 W
Mānānwala 123 31.38 N 74.18 E
Manaoag 116 16.03 N 120.29 E
Manaoba I 175e 8.18 S 160.47 E
Manáos → Manaus 246 3.08 S 60.01 W
Manapiare ≃ 246 5.04 N 66.30 W
Manapire ≃ 246 7.42 N 66.07 W
Manapla 116 10.58 N 123.07 E
Manapouri 172 45.34 S 167.36 E
Manapouri, Lake ⊜ 172 45.30 S 167.30 E
Manappārai 122 10.36 N 78.25 E
Manaquiri, Lago ⊜ 246 3.29 S 60.31 W
Manār ≃ 122 18.39 N 77.44 E
Manaravolo 157b 23.59 S 45.39 E
Manas 144 2.52 N 43.26 E
Manās ≃ 120 26.13 N 90.38 E
Manas, Gora ∧ 85 42.18 N 71.01 E
Ma'nasaluowochi ⊜ 120 30.42 N 81.27 E
Ma'nasi 86 44.18 N 86.13 E
Ma'nasihu ⊜ 86 45.45 N 85.55 E
Manāslu ∧ 124 28.33 N 84.33 E
Manasota Key I 220 26.58 N 82.23 W
Manasquan 208 40.07 N 74.03 W
Manasquan ≃ 208 40.06 N 74.02 W
Manassa 200 37.11 N 105.56 W
Manassas 208 38.45 N 77.28 W
Manassas National Battlefield Park ♠ 208 38.50 N 77.32 W
Manassas Park 208 38.47 N 77.28 W
Manastash Creek ≃ 224 46.59 N 120.35 W
Manastash Creek, North Fork ≃ 224 46.57 N 120.44 W
Manastash Creek, South Fork ≃ 224 46.57 N 120.44 W
Manastash Ridge ∧ 224 46.55 N 120.30 W
Manastırbükü 130 40.48 N 38.56 E
Manatang 112 8.26 S 124.28 E
Manatawny 208 40.17 N 75.41 W
Manatawny Creek ≃ 208 40.14 N 75.39 W
Manatee □[6] 220 27.26 N 82.25 W
Manatee ≃ 220 27.32 N 82.38 W
Manatee, Lake ⊜[1] 220 27.29 N 82.20 W
Manatí, Col. 246 10.27 N 74.58 W
Manatí, Cuba 240p 21.19 N 76.56 W
Manatí, P.R. 240m 18.26 N 66.29 W
Manatí ≃ 240p 21.40 N 79.50 W
Manatí, Bahía de C 240p 21.24 N 76.48 W
Manaul 116 12.27 N 121.25 E
Manaung 110 18.51 N 93.44 E
Manaus 246 3.08 S 60.01 W
Manavgat 130 36.47 N 31.26 E
Manawa 190 44.28 N 88.55 W
Manawai 175e 9.05 S 161.11 E
Manawan Lake ⊜ 184 55.24 N 103.14 W
Manāwar 120 22.14 N 75.05 E
Manawatu ≃ 172 40.28 S 175.13 E
Manawoka, Pulau I 164 4.05 S 131.20 E
Manay 116 7.13 N 126.32 E
Manayunk ◆[8] 285 40.01 N 75.13 W
Manazuru 94 35.09 N 139.08 E
Manazuru-misaki ≻ 94 35.08 N 139.10 E
Manban 102 23.04 N 103.11 E
Mānbāzār 126 23.04 N 86.39 E
Manbian 102 24.19 N 100.32 E
Manbij 130 36.31 N 37.57 E
Mancelona 190 44.54 N 85.04 W
Mancenillier, Anse du C 241o 16.15 N 61.15 W
Mancha Blanca 254 40.47 S 65.27 W
Mancha Real 34 37.47 N 3.37 W
Manchaug 207 42.06 N 71.45 W
Manche □[5] 32 49.00 N 1.10 W
Mancheng 105 38.56 N 115.20 E
Mancherāl 122 18.52 N 79.26 E
Manchester, Eng., U.K. 44
262 53.30 N 2.15 W
Manchester, Conn., U.S. 207 41.47 N 72.31 W
Manchester, Ga., U.S. 192 32.51 N 84.37 W
Manchester, Ill., U.S. 219 39.33 N 90.20 W
Manchester, Iowa, U.S. 190 42.29 N 91.27 W
Manchester, Ky., U.S. 192 37.09 N 83.46 W
Manchester, Mass., U.S. 207 42.34 N 70.46 W
Manchester, Mich., U.S. 216 42.09 N 84.02 W
Manchester, N.H., U.S. 188 42.59 N 71.28 W
Manchester, N.Y., U.S. 210 42.58 N 77.14 W
Manchester, Ohio, U.S. 218 38.41 N 83.36 W
Manchester, Pa., U.S. 208 40.04 N 76.43 W
Manchester, Tenn., U.S. 194 35.29 N 86.05 W
Manchester, Vt., U.S. 188 43.10 N 73.05 W
Manchester, Wash., U.S. 224 47.33 N 122.33 W
Manchester □[8] 262 53.27 N 2.13 W
Manchester Airport ⊠ 44 53.21 N 2.15 W
Manchester Bridge 210 41.41 N 73.52 W
Manchester City Football Ground ♠ 262 53.27 N 2.14 W
Manchester Docks ◆[5] 262 53.28 N 2.17 W
Manchester Race Course ♠ 262 53.30 N 2.16 W
Manchester Ship Canal ≚ 262 53.19 N 2.57 W
Manchester United Football Ground ♠ 262 53.28 N 2.18 W
Manching 60 48.43 N 11.30 E
Manchioneal 241q 18.02 N 76.17 W
Manchouli → Manzhouli 88 49.35 N 117.22 E
Manchuria ◆[1] 90 47.00 N 125.00 E
Manciano 66 42.35 N 11.31 E
Mancieulles 56 49.17 N 5.53 E
Máncora 246 4.06 S 81.05 W
Mancos 200 37.21 N 108.18 W
Mancos ≃ 200 36.59 N 108.59 W
Mand 128 26.07 N 62.03 E
Mānd ≃, Bhārat 120 21.42 N 83.15 E
Mand ≃, Bhārat 124 21.58 N 83.13 E
Mand ≃, Īrān 128 28.11 N 51.17 E
Manda, Bhārat 126 22.06 N 86.14 E
Manda, Tan. 154 8.30 S 32.44 E
Manda, Tan. 154 10.28 S 34.35 E
Manda, Tan. 154 7.58 S 32.26 E
Manda, Jabal ∧ 140 8.39 N 24.27 E
Mandabe, Madag. 157b 20.55 S 45.49 E
Mandabe, Madag. 157b 21.03 S 44.55 E
Mandach 102 44.27 N 108.20 E
Mandaguaçu 255 23.20 S 52.05 W
Mandaguari 255 23.32 S 51.42 W
Mandai 271c 1.25 N 103.45 E
Manda Island I 154 2.15 S 40.57 E
Mandal 26 58.02 N 7.27 E
Mandal, Jibāl ∧[2] 140 12.09 N 29.31 E
Mandala, Puncak ∧ 164 4.44 S 140.20 E
Mandalay 110 22.00 N 96.05 E
Mandalay □[5] 110 22.00 N 96.00 E
Mandale 216 41.01 N 84.20 W
Mandale Station ◆[5] 272c 19.03 N 72.56 E
Mandalgov' 102 45.45 N 106.20 E
Mandalī 128 33.45 N 45.32 E
Mandalkia 272b 22.43 N 88.08 E
Mandal-Ovoo 102 44.22 N 104.20 E
Mandalselva ≃ 26 58.02 N 7.28 E
Mandaluyong 269f 14.35 N 121.02 E
Mandalya Körfezi C 130 37.12 N 27.20 E
Mandan 198 46.50 N 100.54 W
Mandanici 70 38.00 N 15.19 E
Mandāoli ◆[8] 272a 28.38 N 77.18 E
Mandaon 116 12.14 N 123.17 E
Mandaoua Gadaoulé 146 14.14 N 11.01 E
Mandapeta 122 16.52 N 81.56 E
Mandapur 126 23.00 N 88.29 E
Mandar, Tanjung ≻ 112 3.33 S 118.56 E
Mandar, Teluk C 112 3.40 S 119.15 E
Mandara Mountains (Monts Mandara) ⛰ 146 10.45 N 13.40 E
Mandas 71 39.38 N 9.07 E
Mandasor 120 24.04 N 75.04 E
Mandatoriccio 68 39.28 N 16.50 E
Mandaue 116 10.20 N 123.56 E
Mandāwar 124 29.30 N 78.08 E
Mandeb, Bāb el- Ա 144 12.40 N 43.20 E
Mandehu 104 42.07 N 121.33 E
Mandel 128 33.17 N 61.52 E
Mandélia 146 11.43 N 15.15 E
Mandelieu 62 43.33 N 6.56 E
Mandello del Lario 58 45.54 N 9.19 E
Mandera 154 3.56 N 41.52 E
Manderfeld 56 50.20 N 6.20 E
Manderscheid 56 50.05 N 6.49 E
Manderson 202 44.16 N 107.58 W
Mandeure 58 47.27 N 6.48 E
Mandeville, Qué., Can. 206 46.22 N 73.22 W
Mandeville, Jam. 241q 18.02 N 77.30 W
Mandeville, N.Z. 172 46.00 S 168.49 E
Mandeville, La., U.S. 194 30.22 N 90.04 W
Mandi 123 31.43 N 76.55 E
Mandiana 150 10.38 N 8.41 W
Mandiangin 112 2.01 S 102.58 E
Mandi Angin, Gunong ∧ 114 4.42 N 102.52 E
Mandi Bahāuddīn 123 32.35 N 73.30 E
Mandi Būrewāla 123 31.29 N 72.39 E
Mandi Dabwāli 123 29.58 N 74.42 E
Mandié 154 16.30 S 33.30 E
Mandimba 154 14.21 S 35.39 E
Mandinga 246 9.27 N 79.04 W
Mandioli, Pulau I 108 0.44 S 127.14 E
Mandioré, Lagoa ⊜ 248 18.08 S 57.33 W
Mandira ⊜[1] 124 22.20 N 84.35 E
Mandiri ≃ 115a 7.02 S 106.32 E
Mandi Sādiqganj 123 30.20 N 73.44 E
Mandjafa 146 11.11 N 15.25 E
Mandjé, Lac ⊜ 152 1.01 S 9.31 E
Mandji-Kili 152 1.36 S 10.26 E
Mandla 124 22.36 N 80.23 E
Mandla □[5] 124 22.50 N 80.50 E
Mandling 64 47.24 N 13.34 E
Mandora 162 19.44 S 120.51 E
Mandoto 157b 19.34 S 46.17 E
Mandoul ≃ 146 8.56 N 17.58 E
Mandouri 150 10.51 N 0.49 E
Māndrā, Bhārat 272b 22.55 N 88.07 E
Mándra, Ellás 267c 38.04 N 23.30 E
Mandra, Pāk. 123 33.22 N 73.14 E
Mandrare ≃ 157b 25.10 S 46.27 E
Mandres-les-Roses 261 48.42 N 2.33 E
Mandriola ◆[8] 267a 41.45 N 12.30 E
Mandriole 64 44.33 N 12.14 E
Mandrioli, Passo dei)(64 43.48 N 11.55 E
Mandritsara 157b 15.50 S 48.49 E
Mandronarivo 157b 21.07 S 45.38 E
Māndu 122 22.22 N 75.23 E
Mandu, Ribeirão do ≃ 256 22.14 S 45.55 W
Manduba, Ponta ≻ 256 24.05 S 46.18 W
Manduhu 104 41.36 N 122.38 E
Mandun 102 22.17 N 100.05 E
Mandurah 168a 32.32 S 115.43 E
Manduri 255 23.01 S 49.19 W
Manduria 68 40.24 N 17.38 E
Māndvi, Bhārat 120 22.50 N 69.22 E
Māndvi, Bhārat 120 21.15 N 73.18 E
Mandvi ◆[8] 272c 18.57 N 72.50 E
Mandya 122 12.33 N 76.54 E
Mané 150 12.59 N 1.21 W
Måne ≃ 26 59.00 N 9.40 E
Manea 42 52.30 N 0.11 E
Manebach 54 50.41 N 10.51 E
Mānebhanjyāng 124 27.12 N 86.26 E
Manek Urai 114 5.23 N 102.14 E
Manele Bay C 229a 20.45 N 156.53 W
Manendragarh 124 23.13 N 82.13 E
Manera 157b 22.55 S 44.20 E
Manerbio 64 45.21 N 10.08 E
Manětin 60 49.59 N 13.14 E
Maneviči 78 51.17 N 25.33 E
Manfalūṭ 142 27.19 N 30.58 E
Manfredonia 68 41.38 N 15.55 E
Manfredonia, Golfo di C 68 41.35 N 16.05 E
Manga, Bra. 255 14.46 S 43.56 W
Manga, H. Vol. 150 11.40 N 1.04 W
Manga, Ur. 258 34.49 S 56.06 W
Manga ◆[1] 146 15.00 N 14.00 E
Mangabeiras, Chapada das ⛰[2] 250 10.00 S 46.30 W
Mangagoy 116 8.11 N 126.21 E
Mangahao ≃ 172 40.23 S 175.50 E
Mangai 164 2.45 S 151.05 E
Mangaia I 14 21.55 S 157.55 W
Mangakino 172 38.22 S 175.47 E
Mangala 152 1.02 N 23.50 E
Mangalagiri 122 16.26 N 80.33 E
Mangaldai 120 26.26 N 92.02 E
Mangalia 38 43.50 N 28.35 E
Mangalkot 126 23.33 N 87.54 E
Mangalmé 146 12.21 N 19.37 E
Mangalore 122 12.52 N 74.53 E
Mangalpaita 126 23.19 N 89.11 E
Mangalvedha 122 17.31 N 75.28 E
Mangamahu 172 39.49 S 175.22 E
Manganji 268 35.40 N 139.26 E
Mangaoka 157b 12.19 S 49.07 E
Mangapehi 172 38.31 S 175.18 E
Mangaratiba 256 22.57 S 44.02 W
Mangart, Monte (Mangrt) ∧ 64 46.25 N 13.40 E
Mangatarem 116 15.47 N 120.17 E
Mangawān 124 24.41 N 81.33 E
Mangaweka 172 39.48 S 175.47 E
Mangaweka ∧ 172 39.49 S 176.05 E
Mangcao Point ≻ 116 11.02 N 123.54 E
Mangchang 102 25.08 N 107.31 E
Mangde ≃ 124 27.35 N 90.28 E
Mange, S.L. 150 8.55 N 12.51 W
Mange, Zaïre 152 0.54 N 20.30 E
Mange, Zhg. 120 32.25 N 83.35 E
Mangeigne 146 10.31 N 21.19 E
Mangela, Mount ∧ 175e 8.16 S 157.43 E
Mangerton Mountain ∧ 48 51.57 N 9.29 W
Mangfall ≃ 64 47.51 N 12.08 E
Manggar 112 2.53 S 108.16 E
Manggeng 114 3.36 N 96.55 E
Manggonggri 164 3.30 S 133.19 E
Mangguar, Tanjung ≻ 164 2.53 S 134.51 E
Mangham 194 32.19 N 91.47 W
Mangichu ≃ 126 23.24 N 90.48 E
Mangindrano 157b 14.17 S 48.58 E
Mangin Range ⛰ 110 24.20 N 95.42 E
Mangkalihat, Tanjung ≻ 112 1.02 N 118.59 E
Mangkutana 112 2.24 S 120.48 E
Mangla 123 33.08 N 73.38 E
Mangla Dam ◆[6] 123 33.09 N 73.44 E
Manglares, Cabo ≻ 246 1.36 N 79.02 W
Manglaur 124 29.48 N 77.52 E
Manglisi 84 41.43 N 44.24 E
Mangnuiyingzi 104 41.37 N 120.43 E
Mango 220 28.00 N 82.19 W
Mango I 175g 17.27 S 179.09 W
Mangoche 154 14.28 S 35.16 E
Mangoky ≃, Madag. 157b 21.29 S 43.41 E
Mangoky ≃, Madag. 157b 23.27 S 45.13 E
Mangolding 60 48.57 N 12.13 E
Mangole, Pulau I 112 1.53 S 125.50 E
Mangombe 154 1.25 S 26.54 E
Mangone 68 39.12 N 16.20 E
Mangonia Park 220 26.46 N 80.05 W
Mangonui 172 34.59 S 173.32 E
Mangoplah 171b 35.23 S 147.15 E
Mangoro ≃ 157b 20.00 S 48.45 E
Mangotsfield 42 51.28 N 2.28 W
Mangoupa 140 5.53 N 24.40 E
Māngrol 120 21.07 N 70.07 E
Mangrove Cay I 238 24.10 N 77.45 W
Mangrove Creek ≃ 170 33.28 S 151.10 E
Mangrove Mountain 170 33.19 S 151.14 E
Mangrove Point ≻ 220 26.56 N 82.08 W
Mangrt (Monte Mangart) ∧ 64 46.25 N 13.40 E
Mangrullo, Cuchilla ⛰[2] 258 34.34 S 56.42 W
Mangrūl Pīr 122 20.19 N 77.21 E
Mångsälven ≃ 40 59.59 N 14.36 E
Mangsang 112 2.10 S 104.00 E
Mangualde 34 40.36 N 7.46 W
Mangueira, Lagoa C 252 33.06 S 52.48 W
Mangueirinha 252 25.57 S 52.09 W
Mangueni, Plateau de ⛰[1] 146 22.35 N 12.40 E
Mangues ≃ 250 10.21 S 48.27 W
Manguinho, Aeroporto de ⊠ 287a 22.52 S 43.15 W
Manguito 240p 22.35 N 80.55 W
Mangulile 236 15.03 N 86.49 W
Mangum 196 34.53 N 99.30 W
Mangungu 152 5.13 S 19.35 E
Mangut, S.S.S.R. 86 55.47 N 70.46 E
Mangut, S.S.S.R. 88 49.46 N 112.38 E
Mangya 90 37.40 N 90.50 E
Man'gyŏng 98 35.52 N 126.48 E
Manhan ≃ 207 42.17 N 72.38 W
Manhartsberg ∧ 61 48.32 N 15.44 E
Manhasset 276 40.48 N 73.42 W
Manhasset Bay C 276 40.50 N 73.43 W
Manhasset Hills 276 40.46 N 73.41 W
Manhasset Neck ≻[1] 276 40.50 N 73.42 W
Manhattan, Ill., U.S. 216 41.25 N 87.59 W
Manhattan, Kans., U.S. 198 39.11 N 96.35 W
Manhattan, Mont., U.S. 202 45.52 N 111.20 W
Manhattan □[8] 276 40.46 N 73.55 W
Manhattan Beach 228 33.54 N 118.24 W
Manhattan Bridge ◆[5] 276 40.42 N 73.59 W
Manhattan College ᵾ[2] 276 40.53 N 73.54 W
Manhattan State Beach ♠ 280 33.54 N 118.25 W
Manheim 208 40.10 N 76.24 W
Manhiça 156 25.24 S 32.48 E
Mān Hpāng 110 22.41 N 98.36 E
Manhuaçu 255 20.15 S 42.02 W
Manhuaçu ≃ 255 19.30 S 41.06 W
Manhumirim 255 20.22 S 41.57 W
Maní, P.R. 240m 18.15 N 67.10 W
Mani, Zaïre 154 6.27 S 25.20 E
Māni', Jabal al- ∧ 132 33.19 N 36.17 E
Mania ≃ 157b 19.42 S 45.22 E
Maniago 64 46.10 N 12.43 E
Maniamba 154 12.43 S 35.00 E
Manianga 273b 4.08 S 15.17 E
Manica e Sofala □[5] 156 19.00 S 34.00 E
Manicahan 116 7.01 N 122.12 E
Manicaland □[4] 154 19.30 S 32.15 E
Manicani Island I 116 10.59 N 125.38 E
Manicaragua 240p 22.09 N 79.58 W
Maniçauá-Miçu ≃ 250 10.58 S 53.20 W
Manicoré 248 5.49 S 61.17 W
Manicoré ≃ 248 5.51 S 61.19 W
Manicouagan ≃ 186 49.11 N 68.13 W
Manicouagan, Réservoir ⊜[1] 186 51.30 N 68.19 W
≃Nifold 44 53.03 N 1.47
Manigan'ge 102 32.01 N 99.11 E
Manigotagan 184 51.06 N 96.18 W
Manigotagan ≃ 184 51.07 N 96.20 W
Maniguin Island I 116 11.36 N 121.45 E
Manihari 124 25.21 N 87.38 E
Manihiki I[1] 14 10.24 S 161.01 W
Manika, Plateau de la ⛰[1] 154 10.00 S 26.00 E
Manikanāli 126 23.19 N 87.03 E
Mānikganj 124 23.52 N 90.00 E
Mānikpur 124 25.04 N 81.07 E
Manila, Pil. 116
269f 14.35 N 121.00 E
Manila, Ark., U.S. 194 35.53 N 90.10 W
Manila, Utah, U.S. 200 40.59 N 109.43 W
Manila □[7] 269f 14.37 N 120.58 E
Manila Bay C 116 14.30 N 120.45 E
Manila Cathedral ᵾ[1] 269f 14.35 N 120.59 E
Manilaid I 76 58.13 N 24.08 E
Manila International Airport ⊠ 269f 14.31 N 121.01 E
Manilla, Austl. 166 30.45 S 150.43 E
Manilla, Ind., U.S. 218 39.35 N 85.37 W
Manilla, Iowa, U.S. 198 41.53 N 95.14 W
Manille → Manila 116 14.35 N 121.00 E
Manily 74 62.29 N 165.36 E
Mani Majra 123 30.43 N 76.50 E
Manimpé 150 14.09 N 5.31 W
Maningory ≃ 157b 17.13 S 49.28 E
Maningrida 164 12.03 S 134.13 E
Maninian 150 10.00 N 7.50 W
Maninjau, Danau ⊜ 112 0.20 S 100.11 E
Manino 76 53.58 N 34.20 E
Manipa, Pulau I 164 3.17 S 127.35 E
Manipa, Selat Ա 164 3.20 S 127.23 E
Manipur □[8] 120 25.00 N 94.00 E
Manique de Baixo 266c 38.44 N 9.22 W
Manirāmpur 126 23.01 N 89.14 E
Manisa 130 38.36 N 27.26 E
Manisa □[4] 130 38.50 N 28.10 E
Manistee 190 44.15 N 86.19 W
Manistee ≃ 190 44.15 N 86.21 W
Manistique 190 45.57 N 86.15 W
Manistique ≃ 190 45.57 N 86.15 W
Manistique, West Branch ≃ 190 46.02 N 86.09 W
Manistique Lake ⊜ 190 46.15 N 85.45 W
Manito 194 40.25 N 89.47 W
Manitoba □[4] 184
176 54.00 N 97.00 W
Manitoba, Lake ⊜ 184 51.00 N 98.45 W
Manito Lake ⊜ 184 52.45 N 109.45 W
Manitou 184 49.15 N 98.31 W
Manitou ≃ 184 48.58 N 93.20 W
Manitou, Lac ⊜, Qué., Can. 186 50.54 N 65.18 W
Manitou, Lac ⊜, Qué., Can. 186 50.29 N 63.54 W
Manitou, Lac ⊜, Qué., Can. 206 46.03 N 74.23 W
Manitou, Lake ⊜ 216 41.03 N 86.11 W
Manitou Beach, Sask., Can. 184 51.43 N 105.26 W
Manitou Beach, Mich., U.S. 216 41.58 N 84.19 W
Manitou Lake ⊜ 190 45.48 N 82.00 W
Manitoulin Island I 190 45.45 N 82.30 W
Manitou Springs 200 38.52 N 104.55 W
Manitouwabing Lake ⊜ 212 45.29 N 79.54 W
Manitowaning 190 45.45 N 81.49 W
Manitowish Waters 190 46.09 N 89.53 W
Manitowoc 190 44.06 N 87.40 W
Manitowoc ≃ 190 44.05 N 87.39 W
Maniwaki 188 46.23 N 75.58 W
Ma'nīyā 142 30.50 N 30.39 E
Manizales 246 5.05 N 75.32 W
Manja, Madag. 157b 21.26 S 44.20 E
Manjā, Urd. 132 31.45 N 35.51 E
Manjacaze 156 24.44 S 33.53 E

Symbols in the index entries represent the broad categories identified in the key at the right. Symbols with superior numbers (⛰[2]) identify subcategories (see complete key on page I · 30).

Kartensymbole in dem Registerverzeichnis stellen die rechts in Schlüssel erklärten Kategorien dar. Symbole mit hochgestellten Ziffern (⛰[2]) bezeichnen Unterabteilungen einer Kategorie (vgl. vollständiger Schlüssel auf Seite I · 30).

Los símbolos incluídos en el texto del índice representan las grandes categorias identificadas con la clave a la derecha. Los símbolos con numeros en su parte superior (⛰[2]) identifican las subcategorías (véase la clave completa en la página I · 30).

Les symboles de l'index représentent les catégories indiquées dans la légende à droite. Les symboles suivis d'un indice (⛰[2]) représentent des sous-catégories (voir légende complète à la page I · 30).

Os símbolos incluídos no texto do índice representam as grandes categorias identificadas com a chave à direita. Os símbolos com números em sua parte superior (⛰[2]) identificam as subcategorias (veja-se a chave completa à página I · 30).

	English	Deutsch	Español	Français	Português
∧	Mountain	Berg	Montaña	Montagne	Montanha
⛰	Mountains	Berge	Montañas	Montagnes	Montanhas
)(	Pass	Pass	Paso	Col	Passo
∨	Valley, Canyon	Tal, Cañon	Valle, Cañón	Vallée, Canyon	Vale, Canhão
≚	Plain	Ebene	Llano	Plaine	Planície
≻	Cape	Kap	Cabo	Cap	Cabo
I	Island	Insel	Isla	Île	Ilha
II	Islands	Inseln	Islas	Îles	Ilhas
⏊	Other Topographic Features	Andere Topographische Objekte	Otros Elementos Topográficos	Autres données topographiques	Outros Elementos Topográficos

ESPAÑOL Nombre / FRANÇAIS Nom / PORTUGUÊS Nome	Página / Page / Página	Lat.°′	Long.°′ W=Oeste / W=Ouest / W=Oeste
Manjakandriana	157b	18.55 S	47.47 E
Manjeri	122	11.07 N	76.07 E
Manjeshwara	122	12.42 N	74.53 E
Manjiang	98	41.57 N	127.36 E
Manjimup	162	34.14 S	116.09 E
Mānjra ≃	122	18.49 N	77.52 E
Manjuyod	116	9.41 N	123.09 E
Mank	61	48.06 N	15.20 E
Mankaiana	158	26.42 S	31.00 E
Mankanaj	86	48.58 N	60.58 E
Månkarbo	40	60.14 N	17.28 E
Mān Kāt	110	22.05 N	98.01 E
Mankato, Kans., U.S.	198	39.47 N	98.12 W
Mankato, Minn., U.S.	190	44.10 N	94.01 W
Mankent	85	42.25 N	69.50 E
Mankera	123	31.23 N	71.26 E
Mankim	152	5.01 N	12.00 E
Mankinholes	262	53.42 N	2.03 W
Mankono	150	8.04 N	6.12 W
Mankota	184	49.25 N	107.04 W
Man'kovka, S.S.S.R.	78	48.58 N	30.20 E
Man'kovka, S.S.S.R.	83	49.34 N	38.27 E
Man'kovo	83	49.24 N	40.17 E
Man'kovo-Ber'ozovskaja	80	48.47 N	41.33 E
Mankoya	154	14.47 S	24.48 E
Mānkundu	272b	22.50 N	88.22 E
Mānkur, Bhārat	126	23.20 N	87.33 E
Mānkur, Bhārat	126	22.30 N	87.54 E
Manlaj	102	44.06 N	107.01 E
Manley	262	53.14 N	2.45 W
Manley Hot Springs	180	65.00 N	150.37 W
Manleys Corner	283	42.03 N	71.04 W
Manlius	210	43.00 N	75.59 W
Manlléu	34	42.00 N	2.17 E
Manly, Austl.	170	33.48 S	151.17 E
Manly, Iowa, U.S.	190	43.17 N	93.12 W
Manly Warringah War Memorial Park ♠	274a	33.46 S	151.15 E
Manmād	122	20.15 N	74.27 E
Mann ≃	164	12.20 S	134.07 E
Mann, Mount ∧	162	25.59 S	129.42 E
Manna, Indon.	112	4.27 S	102.55 E
Mān Na, Mya.	110	23.27 N	97.14 E
Mannahill	166	32.26 S	139.59 E
Mannar	122	8.59 N	79.54 E
Mannar, Gulf of C	122	8.30 N	79.00 E
Mannārgudi	122	10.40 N	79.26 E
Mannar Island I	122	9.03 N	79.50 E
Mann Creek ≃	281	42.32 N	83.44 W
Männedorf	58	47.15 N	8.42 E
Mannersdorf am Leithagebirge	61	47.58 N	16.36 E
Mannersdorf an der Rabnitz	61	47.25 N	16.31 E
Mannheim	56	49.29 N	8.29 E
Manni	120	34.48 N	87.15 E
Manning, Iowa, U.S.	198	41.55 N	95.03 W
Manning, N. Dak., U.S.	198	47.14 N	102.47 W
Manning, S.C., U.S.	192	33.42 N	80.13 W
Manning, Cape ≻	174o	2.02 N	157.26 W
Manning Provincial Park ♠	182	49.07 N	120.54 W
Manning Strait ⊔	175e	7.24 S	158.00 E
Mannington	188	39.32 N	80.20 W
Manningtree	42	51.57 N	1.04 E
Mannō	96	34.11 N	133.51 E
Mann Ranges ⛰	162	26.00 S	129.30 E
Mannsville	212	43.43 N	76.04 W
Mannswörth ◆[8]	264b	48.09 N	16.31 E
Mannu	71	39.18 N	8.58 E
Mannu ∧	71	40.50 N	8.23 E
Mannu, Capo ≻	71	40.47 N	8.09 E
Mannus	171b	35.48 S	147.57 E
Mannus Creek ≃	171b	35.58 S	148.03 E
Mannville	182	53.20 N	111.10 W
Mano	150	8.02 N	12.06 W
Mano ≃	150	6.56 N	11.31 W
Manoa	248	9.40 S	65.27 W
Manohardi	126	24.08 N	90.43 E
Manoharpur, Bhārat	124	22.23 N	85.12 E
Manoharpur, Bhārat	126	21.59 N	87.18 E
Manokin ≃	208	38.05 N	75.55 W
Manokotak	180	58.40 N	159.09 W
Manokwari	164	0.52 S	134.05 E
Manolo Fortich (Maluko)	116	8.25 N	124.58 E
Manoma ≃	89	49.18 N	136.37 E
Manombo	157b	22.57 S	43.28 E
Manomet	207	41.55 N	70.34 W
Manomet Hill ∧[2]	207	41.55 N	70.36 W
Manong	114	4.36 N	100.53 E
Manonga ≃	154	4.08 S	34.12 E
Manono	154	7.18 S	27.25 E
Manono I	175a	13.50 S	172.05 W
Manoora	168b	34.00 S	138.49 E
Manoppello	66	42.15 N	14.03 E
Manor, Sask., Can.	184	49.36 N	102.05 W
Manor, Pa., U.S.	214	40.20 N	79.40 W
Manor, Tex., U.S.	222	30.20 N	97.33 W
Manorbier	42	51.39 N	4.48 W
Manorhamilton	48	54.18 N	8.10 W
Manorhaven	276	40.50 N	73.42 W
Manor Hill	214	40.38 N	77.55 W
Manori ◆[8]	272c	19.12 N	72.47 E
Manori Creek C	272c	19.12 N	72.48 E
Manori Point ≻	272c	19.11 N	72.47 E
Manoron	110	11.38 N	99.04 E
Manorville	214	40.48 N	79.31 W
Manosque	62	43.50 N	5.47 E
Manotick	212	45.13 N	75.41 W
Manouane ≃	186	49.30 N	71.11 W
Manouane, Lac @	186	50.41 N	70.45 W
Manouanis ≃	186	50.28 N	70.08 W
Manouanis, Lac @	186	50.51 N	70.20 W
Manouba	36	36.50 N	10.06 E
Manovo ≃	146	9.12 N	20.29 E
Manown	279b	40.13 N	79.54 W
Manpaka	273b	4.18 S	15.12 E
Manpitou	100	22.17 N	112.52 E
Mānpur, Bhārat	122	20.22 N	80.43 E
Mānpur, Bhārat	124	23.46 N	81.08 E
Manqabād	142	27.12 N	31.07 E
Manqaṭīn	142	28.20 N	30.40 E
Manquehue, Cerro ∧	286e	33.21 S	70.36 W
Manresa	34	41.44 N	1.50 E
Manresa Island I	276	41.04 N	73.25 W
Mānsa, Bhārat	120	23.26 N	72.40 E
Mānsa, Bhārat	123	29.59 N	75.23 E
Mansa (Fort Rosebery), Zam.	154	11.12 S	28.53 E
Mansabá	150	12.18 N	15.15 W
Mansafīs	142	28.00 N	30.49 E
Mansalay	116	12.31 N	121.26 E
Mānsar	123	33.54 N	72.19 E
Mansara	150	13.20 N	4.39 W
Manse ≃	50	47.08 N	0.25 E
Manseau	206	46.22 N	72.00 W
Mānsehra	123	34.20 N	73.12 E
Mansein	110	25.12 N	95.58 E
Mansel Island I	176	62.00 N	79.50 W
Mansfeld	54	51.35 N	11.27 E
Mansfield, Austl.	169	37.03 S	146.05 E
Mansfield, Eng., U.K.	44	53.09 N	1.11 W
Mansfield, Ark., U.S.	194	35.04 N	94.13 W
Mansfield, Ga., U.S.	192	33.31 N	83.44 W
Mansfield, Ill., U.S.	216	40.13 N	88.31 W
Mansfield, La., U.S.	194	32.02 N	93.43 W
Mansfield, Mass., U.S.	207	42.02 N	71.13 W
Mansfield, Mo., U.S.	194	37.06 N	92.35 W
Mansfield, N.J., U.S.	285	40.05 N	74.43 W
Mansfield, Ohio, U.S.	214	40.46 N	82.31 W
Mansfield, Pa., U.S.	210	41.48 N	77.05 W
Mansfield, Tex., U.S.	222	32.34 N	97.09 W
Mansfield, Mount ∧	188	44.33 N	72.49 W
Mansfield Center	207	41.50 N	72.16 W
Mansfield Hollow Lake @[1]	207	41.45 N	72.11 W
Mansfield Hollow State Park ♠	207	41.46 N	72.10 W
Mansfield Municipal Airport ⊠	283	42.00 N	71.12 W
Mansfield Woodhouse	44	53.11 N	1.12 W
Manshan I	106	31.14 N	120.17 E
Manshuijing	107	29.55 N	104.07 E
Mansieville Location	273d	26.05 S	27.45 E
Mānsinhapur	272b	22.39 N	88.09 E
Manskoje Belogorje ⛰	88	54.35 N	94.00 E
Mansle	32	45.53 N	0.11 E
Manso ≃, Bra.	248	14.42 S	56.16 W
Manso ≃, Bra.	255	13.18 S	46.51 W
Mansôa	150	12.10 N	14.36 W
Manson	198	42.32 N	94.32 W
Manson ≃	182	55.42 N	123.47 W
Mansonville	206	45.03 N	72.23 W
Mansourah	34	36.04 N	4.28 E
Mansura → Al-Manṣūrah, Miṣr	142	31.03 N	31.23 E
Mansura, La., U.S.	194	31.04 N	92.03 W
Manṣūrah	132	33.08 N	35.48 E
Manṣūrīyah, Tur'at al- ☰	142	31.03 N	31.24 E
Mansurovo	82	55.52 N	36.36 E
Manta, Ec.	246	0.57 S	80.44 W
Manta, It.	62	44.37 N	7.29 E
Manta, Bahía de C	246	0.54 S	80.42 W
Mantabuan Island I	116	5.02 N	120.13 E
Mantagao ≃	184	51.50 N	97.48 W
Mantalingajan, Mount ∧	116	8.48 N	117.40 E
Mantalingajan Range ⛰	116	8.46 N	117.40 E
Mantanani Besar, Pulau I	112	6.45 N	116.17 E
Mantangule Island I	116	8.10 N	117.10 E
Mantantale	152	2.10 S	20.06 E
Mantare	154	2.43 S	33.13 E
Mantaro ≃	248	12.15 S	73.58 W
Manteca	226	37.48 N	121.13 W
Mantecal	246	7.33 N	69.09 W
Mantekamuhu @	120	34.30 N	89.15 E
Mantel	60	49.39 N	12.03 E
Manteno	216	41.14 N	88.12 W
Manteo	192	35.55 N	75.40 W
Mantes-Chérence, Aérodrome de ⊠	261	49.05 N	1.41 E
Mantes-Gassicourt, Aérodrome de ⊠	261	49.00 N	1.41 E
Mantes-la-Jolie	50	48.59 N	1.43 E
Manteswar	126	23.26 N	88.06 E
Manthelan	50	47.08 N	0.47 E
Manti	200	39.16 N	111.38 W
Manticao	116	8.24 N	124.17 E
Mantilla ◆[8]	286b	23.04 N	82.20 W
Mantin	114	2.49 N	101.54 E
Mantiqueira, Serra da ⛰	256	22.00 S	45.45 W
Mant Islands II	174r	7.00 N	158.17 E
Mantok	112	1.09 S	123.14 E
Manton	190	44.24 N	85.24 W
Mantorville	190	44.05 N	92.45 W
Mantos Blancos	252	23.25 S	70.05 W
Mantou	104	42.27 N	122.26 E
Mantova	64	45.09 N	10.48 E
Mantova □[4]	64	45.10 N	10.47 E
Mant Passage ⊔	174r	7.02 N	158.18 E
Māntri	126	21.39 N	86.49 E
Mänttä	26	62.02 N	24.38 E
Mantua, Cuba	240p	22.17 N	84.17 W
Mantua → Mantova, It.	64	45.09 N	10.48 E
Mantua, N.J., U.S.	208	39.48 N	75.10 W
Mantua, Ohio, U.S.	214	41.17 N	81.14 W
Mantua, Va., U.S.	284c	38.51 N	77.15 W
Mantua ≃	240p	22.12 N	84.25 W
Mantua Creek ≃	285	39.51 N	75.14 W
Mantua Creek, Bees Branch ≃	285	39.46 N	75.08 W
Mantua Creek, Chestnut Branch ≃	285	39.47 N	75.10 W
Mantua Creek, Porch Branch ≃	285	39.46 N	75.07 W
Mantua Terrace	285	39.48 N	75.10 W
Manturovo, S.S.S.R.	78	51.28 N	37.07 E
Manturovo, S.S.S.R.	80	58.20 N	44.46 E
Mäntyharju	26	61.25 N	26.53 E
Mäntyluoto	26	61.35 N	21.29 E
Manu	248	12.15 S	70.50 W
Manú ≃	248	12.16 S	70.51 W
Manuae I[1]	14	19.21 S	158.56 W
Manua Islands II	174y	14.13 S	169.35 W
Manuel	234	22.44 N	98.19 W
Manuel Alves ≃	250	11.19 S	48.28 W
Manuel Alves Grande ≃	250	7.27 S	47.35 W
Manuel Benavides	232	29.05 N	103.55 W
Manuel Derqui	252	27.50 S	58.48 W
Manuel Duarte	256	22.06 S	43.34 W
Manuel M. Diéguez	234	19.34 N	102.55 W
Manuel Ribas	252	24.31 S	51.39 W
Manuel Rodríguez, Isla I	254	52.35 S	73.50 W
Manuel Urbano	248	8.53 S	69.18 W
Manués-Açu ≃	250	3.22 S	57.44 W
Manuhangi I[1]	14	19.12 S	141.16 W
Manuherikia ≃	172	45.16 S	169.24 E
Manui, Pulau I	112	3.35 S	123.08 E
Manuilovskaja	76	60.29 N	40.40 E
Manu Island I	164	1.17 S	143.35 E
Manūjān	128	27.24 N	57.32 E
Manuk ≃	115a	6.14 S	108.13 E
Manuk, Pulau I	164	5.33 S	130.18 E
Manukan	116	8.31 N	123.06 E
Manukau	172	37.02 S	174.54 E
Manukau Harbour C	172	37.01 S	174.44 E
Manulla ≃	48	53.57 N	9.12 W
Manulu Lagoon C	174o	1.56 N	157.20 W
Manumuskin ≃	208	39.18 N	75.00 W
Manundi, Tanjung ≻	164	0.38 S	135.22 E
Manunui	172	38.53 S	175.20 E
Manupari ≃	248	11.50 S	67.16 W
Manurimi ≃	248	11.42 S	67.16 W
Manuripe (Manuripi) ≃	248	11.06 S	67.36 W
Manuro Point ≻	175f	17.41 S	168.36 E
Manursing Island I	276	40.58 N	73.40 W
Manursing Island Park ♠	276	40.58 N	73.40 W
Manus □[5]	164	2.00 S	147.00 E
Mānushmuria	126	22.22 N	86.47 E
Manus Island I	164	2.05 S	147.00 E
Manutahi	172	39.40 S	174.24 E
Manutuke	172	38.41 S	177.55 E
Manvel, N. Dak., U.S.	198	48.04 N	97.10 W
Manvel, Tex., U.S.	222	29.28 N	95.22 W
Manville, N.J., U.S.	210	40.32 N	74.36 W
Manville, R.I., U.S.	207	41.58 N	71.28 W
Manwakh	144	16.50 N	48.05 E
Mānwat	122	19.18 N	76.30 E
Many	194	31.34 N	93.29 W
Manyal Shīḥah	273c	29.57 N	31.14 E
Manyana	156	23.23 S	21.44 E
Manyani	154	3.05 S	38.30 E
Manyara, Lake @	154	3.35 S	35.50 E
Manyberries	184	49.24 N	110.42 W
Manyč ≃	72	47.15 N	40.00 E
Manyč Gudilo, Ozero @	80	46.24 N	42.38 E
Many Island Lake @	184	50.08 N	110.03 W
Manyoni	154	5.45 S	34.50 E
Many Peaks	166	24.33 S	151.23 E
Manytsch → Manyč ≃	72	47.15 N	40.00 E
Manz'a	86	58.29 N	96.15 E
Mānzai	120	30.07 N	68.52 E
Manzanares	34	39.00 N	3.22 W
Manzanares ≃	34	40.19 N	3.32 W
Manzanares, Canal del ☰	266a	40.23 N	3.41 W
Manzanillo, Cuba	240p	20.21 N	77.07 W
Manzanillo, Méx.	234	19.03 N	104.20 W
Manzanillo, Bahía C	234	19.04 N	104.22 W
Manzanillo, Punta ≻, Pan.	236	9.38 N	79.32 W
Manzanillo, Punta ≻, Ven.	241s	11.32 N	69.17 W
Manzanillo Bay ≃	238	19.45 N	71.46 W
Manzanita, Oreg., U.S.	224	45.43 N	123.56 W
Manzanita, Wash., U.S.	224	47.42 N	122.33 W
Manzano, It.	64	45.59 N	13.23 E
Manzano, N. Mex., U.S.	200	34.39 N	106.21 W
Manzanola	198	38.06 N	103.52 W
Manzano Peak ∧	200	34.35 N	106.26 W
Manželija	78	49.19 N	33.38 E
Manzhouli	88	49.35 N	117.22 E
Manziana	66	42.08 N	12.08 E
Manzil	120	29.15 N	63.05 E
Manzilah, Birkat al- @	142	31.08 N	31.56 E
Manzilah, Buḥayrat al- @	142	31.15 N	32.00 E
Manzini	158	26.30 S	31.25 E
Manzone	258	34.29 S	58.52 W
Manzovka	89	44.12 N	132.26 E
Manzurka	88	53.30 N	106.04 E
Mao, Rep. Dom.	238	19.34 N	71.05 W
Mao, Tchad	146	14.07 N	15.19 E
Maoba	102	30.02 N	108.59 E
Maocifan	100	31.40 N	112.53 E
Maocun	98	34.25 N	117.16 E
Maodianzi	107	30.42 N	104.25 E
Maodun'emuqi	89	48.50 N	118.51 E
Maoertuo	107	29.19 N	106.24 E
Mao Hsü I	100	23.19 N	119.19 E
Maojia	107	29.10 N	104.08 E
Maojiagou	104	40.58 N	120.51 E
Maojiaji	100	31.32 N	114.16 E
Maojiakou	100	29.53 N	112.58 E
Maojiaping	105	40.34 N	114.43 E
Maojiapuzi	104	41.10 N	123.32 E
Maojiashi	106	31.30 N	121.05 E
Maojiatun	104	41.05 N	121.58 E
Maojiazao	98	39.53 N	113.26 E
Maoke, Pegunungan ⛰	164	4.00 S	138.00 E
Maolin, Zhg.	89	43.58 N	123.24 E
Maolin, Zhg.	100	30.32 N	118.14 E
Maoming	102	21.55 N	110.52 E
Maomu	102	40.18 N	99.28 E
Ma On Shan ∧	271d	22.25 N	114.15 E
Ma On Shan Tsuen	271d	22.25 N	114.14 E
Maoping	102	30.23 N	110.33 E
Maopora, Pulau I	112	7.35 S	127.35 E
Maoshi	100	26.57 N	113.05 E
Maospati	115a	7.36 S	111.26 E
Maouri, Dallol ∨	150	12.05 N	3.32 E
Maowen	102	31.30 N	103.39 E
Maoxing	89	45.32 N	124.33 E
Maozhou	105	38.51 N	116.06 E
Map I	174q	9.35 N	138.11 E
Mapaga	112	0.06 S	119.48 E
Mapai	158	25.51 S	31.58 E
Mapan	112	2.21 S	111.10 E
Mapanda	152	9.32 S	24.16 E
Mapane	112	1.24 S	120.40 E
Mapanza Mission	154	16.15 S	26.55 E
Mapaochang	107	29.38 N	105.50 E
Mapaoni ≃	250	1.55 N	54.13 W
Mapastepec	234	15.26 N	92.54 W
Mapaville	219	38.15 N	90.28 W
Mapfongui	152	1.15 S	12.59 E
Mapi	164	7.07 S	139.23 E
Mapi ≃	164	7.00 S	139.16 E
Mapia, Kepulauan II	108	0.50 N	134.20 E
Mapida	112	0.33 S	119.46 E
Mapimí	232	25.49 N	103.51 W
Mapimí, Bolsón de ◆[2]	232	27.30 N	103.30 W
Mapimí, Bufa de ∧	196	25.47 N	103.48 W
Maping	100	24.16 N	117.54 E
Mapinga	154	6.36 S	39.04 E
Mapinggang	100	31.36 N	113.32 E
Mapinhane	156	22.19 S	35.03 E
Mapire	246	7.45 N	64.42 W
Mapiri	248	15.15 S	68.10 W
Mapiri ≃	248	9.52 S	66.21 W
Mapixari, Ilha I	246	2.10 S	65.08 W
Maple ◆[8]	275b	43.51 N	79.31 W
Maple ≃, U.S.	198	45.47 N	98.33 W
Maple ≃, Iowa, U.S.	198	42.00 N	95.59 W
Maple ≃, Mich., U.S.	190	42.59 N	84.57 W
Maple ≃, Minn., U.S.	190	44.05 N	94.00 W
Maple ≃, N. Dak., U.S.	198	46.56 N	96.55 W
Maple Airfield ⊠	275b	43.51 N	79.32 W
Maple Bay	224	48.49 N	123.36 W
Maple Bluff	216	43.07 N	89.22 W
Maple Creek	184	49.55 N	109.27 W
Maple Creek ≃	198	41.33 N	96.27 W
Maplecrest	210	42.17 N	74.11 W
Maple Cross	260	51.37 N	0.30 W
Mapledale	214	41.23 N	79.51 W
Maple Falls	224	48.56 N	122.05 W
Maple Glen	285	40.11 N	75.11 W
Maple Grove, Ont., Can.	212	43.55 N	78.44 W
Maple Grove, Qué., Can.	206	45.19 N	73.50 W
Maple Heights	214	41.25 N	81.34 W
Maple Lake	190	45.14 N	94.00 W
Maple Lake @	212	45.06 N	78.40 W
Maple Lane	216	41.45 N	86.14 W
Maple Leaf Gardens ♠	275b	43.40 N	79.23 W
Maple Meadow Brook ≃	283	42.33 N	71.09 W
Maple Mount	194	37.42 N	87.26 W
Maple Park	216	41.55 N	88.36 W
Maples	216	41.01 N	84.58 W
Maple Springs	214	42.12 N	79.25 W
Maplesville	194	32.47 N	86.52 W
Mapleton, S. Afr.	158	26.20 S	28.14 E
Mapleton, Iowa, U.S.	198	42.10 N	95.47 W
Mapleton, Minn., U.S.	190	43.56 N	93.57 W
Mapleton, Oreg., U.S.	202	44.02 N	123.52 W
Mapleton, Utah, U.S.	200	40.08 N	111.36 W
Mapleton Depot	214	40.24 N	77.57 W
Maple Valley	224	47.25 N	122.03 W
Mapleville	207	41.57 N	71.39 W
Maplewood, Mo., U.S.	219	38.37 N	90.19 W
Maplewood, N.J., U.S.	276	40.44 N	74.17 W
Maplewood, Ohio, U.S.	216	40.23 N	84.02 W
Maplewood, Wash., U.S.	224	47.30 N	122.07 W
Maplewood Terrace	279b	40.17 N	79.32 W
Mapocho ≃	286e	33.25 S	70.47 W
Mapocho, Estación ◆[5]	286e	33.26 S	70.40 W
Mapoi	154	5.28 N	27.40 E
Mappsville	208	37.51 N	75.34 W
Maprik	164	3.40 S	143.05 E
Mapuera ≃	250	1.05 S	57.02 W
Mapujiang	105	40.24 N	114.56 E
Mapulanguene	156	24.29 S	32.06 E
Mapulau ≃	246	1.23 N	63.24 W
Mapumulo	158	29.11 S	31.02 E
Maputa	158	26.59 S	32.46 E
Maputo (Lourenço Marques)	156	25.58 S	32.35 E
Maputo (Lourenço Marques) □[5]	156	26.00 S	32.25 E
Maputo (Great Usutu) ≃	158	26.11 S	32.42 E
Ma'qalā'	128	26.31 N	47.19 E
Maqiangou	105	39.30 N	115.02 E
Maqiao, Zhg.	100	29.48 N	114.22 E
Maqiao, Zhg.	106	30.28 N	120.42 E
Maquanhe ≃	124	29.35 N	84.10 E
Maqueda	34	40.04 N	4.22 W
Maqueda Bay C	116	11.44 N	124.58 E
Maqueda Channel ⊔	116	13.42 N	124.01 E
Maquela do Zombo	152	6.03 S	15.07 E
Maquereau, Pointe au ≻	186	48.12 N	64.47 W
Maquiling, Mount ∧	116	14.08 N	121.12 E
Maquinchao	254	41.15 S	68.44 W
Maquoketa	190	42.04 N	90.40 W
Maquoketa ≃	190	42.11 N	90.19 W
Maquoketa, North Fork ≃	190	42.05 N	90.40 W
Mara, Bhārat	120	28.11 N	94.06 E
Mara, Perú	248	14.06 S	72.07 W
Mara, Zhg.	120	28.11 N	94.08 E
Mara □[4]	154	1.45 S	34.00 E
Mara ≃, Afr.	154	1.31 S	33.56 E
Mara ≃, S.S.S.R.	88	58.06 N	104.06 E
Maraã, Bra.	246	1.50 S	65.22 W
Maraa, Poly. fr.	174s	17.46 S	149.34 W
Maraa, Passe de ⊔	174s	17.44 S	149.34 W
Marabá	250	5.21 S	49.07 W
Marabahan	112	3.00 S	114.45 E
Marabut	116	11.07 N	125.13 E
Maracá ≃	250	0.26 S	51.26 W
Maracá, Ilha de I, Bra.	246	3.25 N	61.40 W
Maracá, Ilha de I, Bra.	250	2.05 N	50.25 W
Maracaçumé ≃	250	1.23 S	45.42 W
Maracaí	255	22.36 S	50.39 W
Maracaibo	246	10.40 N	71.37 W
Maracaibo, Lago de @	246	9.50 N	71.30 W
Maracaju	255	21.38 S	55.09 W
Maracaju, Serra de ⛰[2]	255	23.57 S	55.01 W
Maracalagonis	71	39.17 N	9.13 E
Maracanã	250	0.46 S	47.27 W
Maracanã ◆[8]	287a	22.54 S	43.14 W
Maracanã ≃	248	8.22 S	59.41 W
Maracanã, Estádio Municipal ♠	287a	22.55 S	43.14 W
Maracanaú	250	3.52 S	38.38 W
Maracás	255	13.26 S	40.27 W
Maracay	246	10.15 N	67.36 W
Maracossic Creek ≃	208	37.53 N	77.11 W
Marādah	146	29.14 N	19.13 E
Maradi	150	13.29 N	7.06 E
Maradi □[5]	150	14.00 N	7.00 E
Marae	174s	17.32 S	149.54 W
Marāghah, Sabkhat al- @	130	35.39 N	37.39 E
Marāgheh	128	37.23 N	46.13 E
Maragini	164	3.33 S	141.34 E
Maragogi	250	9.01 S	35.13 W
Maragogipe	255	12.46 S	38.55 W
Mārahra	124	27.44 N	78.35 E
Marahuaca, Cerro ∧	246	3.34 N	65.27 W
Maraial	250	8.47 S	35.50 W
Maraiche Lake @	184	54.28 N	102.01 W
Marainviller	58	48.35 N	6.36 E
Maraisburg	273d	26.11 S	27.56 E
Marais des Cygnes ≃	194	38.02 N	94.14 W
Marais Temps Clair @	219	38.54 N	90.24 W
Marajó, Baía de C	250	1.00 S	48.30 W
Marajó, Ilha de I	250	1.00 S	49.30 W
Marakabei	158	29.32 S	28.09 E
Ma'rakah	132	33.16 N	35.18 E
Mārākand	84	38.52 N	45.14 E
Maralal	154	1.06 N	36.42 E
Maralaleng	156	25.47 S	22.45 E
Maraldy	86	52.26 N	77.45 E
Marali	152	6.01 N	18.24 E
Maralik	84	40.35 N	43.52 E
Maram	120	25.25 N	94.06 E
Maramag	116	7.46 N	125.00 E
Maramasike I	175e	9.32 S	161.27 E
Marambaia ≃	256	21.44 S	46.25 W
Marambaia, Ilha da I	256	23.04 S	43.58 W
Marambaia, Pico da ∧	256	23.04 S	43.59 W
Marampa	150	8.41 N	12.28 W
Maramsilli Reservoir @[1]	122	20.32 N	81.41 E
Maramureș □[4]	38	47.40 N	24.00 E
Maramureșului, Munții ⛰	38	47.50 N	24.45 E
Maran	114	3.35 N	102.46 E
Mārān, Koh-i- ∧	120	29.26 N	66.49 E
Marana, Mali	150	14.38 N	11.55 W
Marana, Ariz., U.S.	200	32.27 N	111.13 W
Maranalgo	162	29.23 S	117.48 E
Maranboy	164	14.30 S	132.45 E
Maranchón	34	41.03 N	2.12 W
Marand	128	38.26 N	45.46 E
Marandellas	154	18.10 S	31.36 E
Maranello	64	44.32 N	10.52 E
Maranenuka	174t	1.29 N	173.02 E
Marang, Malay.	114	5.12 N	103.13 E
Marang, Mya.	110	10.27 N	98.47 E
Marangá ≃	287a	22.51 S	43.23 W
Marangani	248	14.22 S	71.10 W
Marangas	116	8.40 N	117.38 E
Marange-Zondrange	56	49.07 N	6.32 E
Maranguape	250	3.53 S	38.40 W
Maranhão □[3]	250	5.00 S	45.00 W
Maranhão ≃	255	14.34 S	49.02 W
Maranhão, Cachoeira L	250	4.49 S	56.18 W
Marano	266b	45.38 N	8.38 E
Marano, Laguna di C	64	45.44 N	13.10 E
Maranoa ≃	166	27.50 S	148.37 E
Marano di Napoli	68	40.54 N	14.11 E
Marano Lagunare	64	45.46 N	13.10 E
Marañón ≃	242	4.30 S	73.27 W
Marano sul Panaro	64	44.27 N	10.58 E
Marano Vicentino	64	45.41 N	11.25 E
Marans	32	46.19 N	1.00 W
Maraoli ◆[8]	272c	19.03 N	72.54 E
Maraoné, Massif du ⛰	146	14.40 N	21.33 E
Marapanim	250	0.42 S	47.42 W
Marapendi, Lagoa de C	287a	23.01 S	43.24 W
Marapi ≃	250	0.37 N	55.58 W
Marapicu	256	22.48 S	43.35 W
Marapicu, Morro do ∧	287a	22.50 S	43.36 W
Mararoa ≃	172	45.34 S	167.36 E
Mararui	154	1.56 S	41.18 E
Maras, Perú	248	13.20 S	72.09 W
Maraș, Tür.	130	37.36 N	36.55 E
Maraș □[4]	130	38.00 N	37.05 E
Marasany	80	57.27 N	54.25 E
Maraș Dağları ⛰	130	37.40 N	37.00 E
Marasende, Pulau I	112	5.08 S	118.09 E
Mărășești	38	45.52 N	27.14 E
Maratasã ≃	250	4.14 S	42.15 W
Maratea	68	39.59 N	15.45 E
Marathon, Austl.	166	20.49 S	143.34 E
Marathon, Ont., Can.	190	48.40 N	86.25 W
Marathón, Ellás	38	38.10 N	23.58 E
Marathon, Fla., U.S.	220	24.43 N	81.05 W
Marathon, N.Y., U.S.	210	42.26 N	76.02 W
Marathon, Tex., U.S.	196	30.12 N	103.15 W
Marathon, Wis., U.S.	190	44.56 N	89.50 W
Marathóvounon	130	35.13 N	33.37 E
Maratua, Pulau I	112	2.15 N	118.36 E
Marau, Bra.	252	28.27 S	52.12 W
Maraú, Bra.	255	14.06 S	39.00 W
Marauiá ≃	246	0.23 S	65.13 W
Marausa	70	37.56 N	12.30 E
Maravari	175e	7.51 S	156.42 E
Maravatío de Ocampo	234	19.54 N	100.27 W
Marāveh Tappeh	128	37.55 N	55.57 E
Maravilha, Bra.	250	9.14 S	37.21 W
Maravilha, Bra.	252	26.47 S	53.09 W
Maravillas	232	27.22 N	104.29 W
Maravillas Creek ≃	196	29.34 N	102.47 W
Mara Vista	207	41.33 N	70.34 W
Marav Lake @	120	29.04 N	69.18 E
Maravovo	175e	9.17 S	159.38 E
Marāwah	146	32.29 N	21.25 E
Marawi, Pil.	116	8.01 N	124.18 E
Marawī, Sūd.	140	18.29 N	31.49 E
Maraye-en-Othe	50	48.10 N	3.51 E
Marayes	252	31.29 S	67.20 W
Marayong	274a	33.45 S	150.54 E
Maraza	84	40.33 N	48.56 E
Marbach, B.R.D.	56	50.37 N	9.43 E
Marbach, D.D.R.	54	51.02 N	13.13 E
Marbach, Schw.	58	46.52 N	7.55 E
Marbach am Neckar	56	48.56 N	9.14 E
Marbache	56	48.48 N	6.05 E
Marbais	50	50.33 N	4.31 E
Marbeck	52	51.49 N	6.52 E
Marbella	34	36.31 N	4.53 W
Marble, Minn., U.S.	190	47.19 N	93.18 W
Marble, N.C., U.S.	192	35.10 N	83.55 W
Marble, Pa., U.S.	214	41.20 N	79.26 W
Marble Arch ⊥	146	30.29 N	18.35 E
Marble Bar	162	21.11 S	119.44 E
Marble Canyon ∨	200	36.30 N	111.50 W
Marble Falls	196	30.34 N	98.17 W
Marble Hall	156	24.57 S	29.13 E
Marblehead, Ill., U.S.	219	39.50 N	91.22 W
Marblehead, Mass., U.S.	207	42.30 N	70.51 W
Marblehead, Ohio, U.S.	214	41.32 N	82.44 W
Marblehead Neck ≻[1]	283	42.29 N	70.51 W
Marble Hill	194	37.18 N	89.58 W
Marble Lake @	216	41.54 N	84.54 W
Marblemount	224	48.32 N	121.26 W
Marble Rock	190	42.58 N	92.52 W
Marbleton	206	45.37 N	71.35 W
Marburg, Austl.	171a	27.34 S	152.35 E
Marburg, S. Afr.	158	30.44 S	30.26 E
Marburg, Lake @[1]	208	39.48 N	76.53 W
Marburg an der Drau → Maribor	36	46.33 N	15.39 E
Marburg an der Lahn	56	50.49 N	8.46 E
Marca, Ponta da ≻	152	16.31 S	11.42 E
Marcaconga	248	13.59 S	71.34 W
Marcal ≃	30	47.41 N	17.32 E
Marcala	236	14.07 N	88.00 W
Marcali	30	46.35 N	17.25 E
Marcallo con Casone	266b	45.29 N	8.52 E
Marcaria	64	45.07 N	10.32 E
Marceau, Lac @	186	51.25 N	66.41 W
Marcedusa	68	39.02 N	16.50 E
Marcelin	184	52.55 N	106.47 W
Marceline	194	39.43 N	92.57 W
Marcelino Ramos	252	27.28 S	51.54 W
Marcella	276	40.59 N	74.28 W
Marcellina	66	42.01 N	12.48 E
Marcellus, Mich., U.S.	216	42.03 N	85.49 W
Marcellus, N.Y., U.S.	210	42.59 N	76.20 W
Marcellus Falls	210	43.00 N	76.20 W
Marcevo	83	47.15 N	38.53 E
March	42	52.33 N	0.06 E
March (Morava) ≃	30	48.10 N	16.59 E
Marcha	74	61.49 N	122.20 E
March Air Force Base ■	228	33.54 N	117.15 W
Marchais	261	48.31 N	2.03 E
Marchal	152	5.16 S	14.58 E
Marchamat	85	40.30 N	72.19 E
Marchand	214	40.51 N	79.02 W
Marchaux	58	47.19 N	6.08 E
Marche □[4]	66	43.30 N	13.15 E
Marche □[9]	32	46.05 N	2.10 E
Marche-en-Famenne	56	50.12 N	5.20 E
Marchegg	61	48.17 N	16.55 E
Marche-les-Dames	56	50.29 N	4.58 E
Marchémoret	261	49.03 N	2.46 E
Marchena	34	37.20 N	5.24 W
Marchena, Isla I	246a	0.21 N	90.29 W
Marchenoir	50	47.49 N	1.24 E
Marchesa Bay C	116	6.35 N	117.40 E
Marchesato	68	39.07 N	16.58 E
Marchfeld ◆[1]	264b	48.17 N	16.31 E
Marchienne-au-Pont	50	50.24 N	4.23 E
Marchiennes	50	50.24 N	3.17 E
Marching	60	48.49 N	11.43 E
Mar Chiquita, Laguna C	252	37.37 S	57.24 W
Mar Chiquita, Laguna @	252	30.42 S	62.36 W
Marchtrenk	61	48.11 N	14.07 E
Marciana	66	42.47 N	10.10 E
Marciana Marina	66	42.48 N	10.12 E
Marcianise	68	41.02 N	14.17 E
Marciano della Chiana	66	43.18 N	11.47 E
Marčichina Buda	78	51.58 N	34.03 E
Marcigny	32	46.17 N	4.02 E
Marcillac-Vallon	32	44.29 N	2.28 E
Marcilloles	62	45.20 N	5.11 E
Marcilly	261	49.02 N	2.53 E
Marcilly-la-Campagne	50	48.50 N	1.13 E
Marcilly-le-Hayer	50	48.21 N	3.38 E
Marcilly-sur-Eure	50	48.49 N	1.21 E
Marck	50	50.57 N	1.57 E
Marckolsheim	58	48.10 N	7.33 E
Marco, Bra.	250	3.08 S	40.09 W
Marco, It.	64	45.51 N	11.01 E
Marco, Fla., U.S.	220	25.58 N	81.44 W
Marcoing	50	50.07 N	3.11 E
Marco Island I	220	25.55 N	81.45 W
Marcola	202	44.10 N	122.52 W
Marcolino, Igarapé ≃	250	11.03 S	58.35 W
Marcona	248	15.03 S	75.01 W
Marco Polo Bridge ◆[5]	271a	39.52 N	116.12 E
Marco Polo di Tessera, Aeroporto ⊠	64	45.30 N	12.21 E
Marcos Juárez	252	32.42 S	62.06 W
Marcos Paz	258	34.46 S	58.50 W
Marcos Paz □[5]	288	34.49 S	58.49 W
Marcotte, Lac @	206	46.47 N	73.12 W
Marcounda	152	7.37 N	16.59 E
Marcoussis	261	48.39 N	2.14 E
Marcq	261	48.52 N	1.49 E
Marcq-en-Baroeul	50	50.40 N	3.05 E
Marčugi	82	55.21 N	38.33 E
Marcus	198	42.50 N	95.48 W
Marcus Baker, Mount ∧	180	61.26 N	147.45 W
Marcus Hook	208	39.49 N	75.25 W
Marcus Hook Creek ≃	285	39.49 N	75.25 W
Marcus Island → Minami-Tori-shima I	14	24.18 N	153.58 E
Marcy, Mount ∧	188	44.07 N	73.56 W
Marda	162	30.13 S	119.17 E
Mardakert	84	40.12 N	46.48 E
Mardalsfossen L	26	62.30 N	8.07 E
Mardān	123	34.12 N	72.02 E
Mardarovka	78	47.32 N	29.44 E
Mar de Cães, Vala de ☰	266c	38.51 N	8.59 W
Mar de Espanha	256	21.52 S	43.00 W
Mardela Springs	208	38.28 N	75.45 W
Mar del Plata	252	38.00 S	57.33 W
Mardi, Hadjer ∧	146	14.49 N	22.04 E
Mardie	162	21.11 S	115.57 E
Mardin	130	37.18 N	40.44 E
Mardin □[4]	130	37.25 N	41.00 E
Mar Dyke ≃	260	51.29 N	0.14 E
Mare	164	9.10 S	141.40 E
Maré, Île I	175f	21.30 S	168.00 E
Mare, Muntele ∧	38	46.29 N	23.14 E
Marecchia ≃	66	44.04 N	12.34 E
Marechal Cândido Rondon	252	24.34 S	54.04 W
Marechal Deodoro	250	9.43 S	35.54 W
Maree, Loch @	46	57.42 N	5.30 W
Mareeba	166	17.00 S	145.26 E
Mareetsane	158	26.09 S	25.25 E
Mareg	144	3.47 N	47.18 E
Mareil-en-France	261	49.04 N	2.26 E
Mareil-le-Guyon	261	48.47 N	1.51 E
Mareil-Marly	261	48.53 N	2.05 E
Mare Island I	226	38.06 N	122.16 W
Mare Island Naval Shipyard ■	226	38.06 N	122.17 W
Mare Island Strait ⊔	282	38.06 N	122.17 W
Mareje, Gunung ∧	115b	8.46 S	116.08 E
Marek	112	4.48 S	120.21 E
Maremma ◆[1]	66	42.30 N	11.30 E
Marene	62	44.39 N	7.44 E
Marengo, Ill., U.S.	216	42.15 N	88.37 W
Marengo, Ind., U.S.	218	38.22 N	86.21 W
Marengo, Iowa, U.S.	190	41.48 N	92.04 W
Marengo, Mich., U.S.	216	42.17 N	84.51 W
Marengo, Ohio, U.S.	214	40.24 N	82.49 W
Marengo ◆[1]	62	44.55 N	8.40 E
Marengo ⊥	62	44.49 N	8.40 E
Marengo Cave ◆[5]	218	38.23 N	86.21 W
Marenisco	190	46.23 N	90.30 W
Marennes	32	45.50 N	1.06 W
Marerano	157b	21.23 S	44.52 E
Mareșalçakmak	130	39.22 N	39.13 E
Maresias	256	23.48 S	45.33 W
Marettimo	70	37.58 N	12.04 E
Marettimo, Isola I	70	37.58 N	12.03 E
Mareuil-en-Brie	50	48.57 N	3.45 E
Mareuil-lès-Meaux	261	48.56 N	2.52 E
Mareuil-sur-Aÿ	50	49.03 N	4.02 E
Mareuil-sur-Belle	32	45.28 N	0.28 E
Marevo	76	57.19 N	32.05 E
Marey-sur-Tille	58	47.35 N	5.03 E
Marfa	196	30.18 N	104.01 W
Marfinka	83	47.36 N	38.32 E
Marfino	80	46.25 N	48.44 E
Marfleet	44	53.45 N	0.17 W
Mar Forest ◆[3]	46	57.00 N	3.35 W
Margam, Īrān	84	39.09 N	44.57 E
Margam, Wales, U.K.	42	51.34 N	3.44 W
Marganec	78	47.38 N	34.40 E
Margao → Madgaon	122	15.18 N	73.57 E
Margaree	186	46.24 N	61.05 W
Margaree Harbour	186	46.26 N	61.07 W
Margaret ≃	162	18.10 S	125.37 E
Margaret, Mount ∧	224	46.18 N	122.08 W
Margaret Bay	182	51.20 N	127.29 W
Margaret Creek ≃	166	29.26 S	137.07 E
Margarethenhöhe ◆[8]	263	51.26 N	6.58 E
Margaret River, Austl.	162	18.38 S	126.52 E
Margaret River, Austl.	162	33.57 S	115.04 E
Margaret Roding	260	51.47 N	0.19 E
Margaretting	260	51.41 N	0.25 E
Margarettsville	208	36.32 N	77.21 W
Margaretville	210	42.09 N	74.39 W
Margarita, Bahía → Marguerite Bay C	9	68.30 S	68.30 W
Margarita, Isla I	246	9.05 N	74.30 W
Margarita, Isla de I	246	11.00 N	64.00 W
Margarita Belén	252	27.16 S	58.58 W
Margarita Peak ∧	228	33.26 N	117.23 W
Margaritovka	83	46.55 N	38.52 E
Margate, S. Afr.	158	30.55 S	30.15 E
Margate, Eng., U.K.	42	51.24 N	1.24 E
Margate, Fla., U.S.	220	26.18 N	80.12 W
Margate City	208	39.20 N	74.31 W
Margater ∧	123	35.14 N	72.35 E
Margecany	30	48.54 N	21.01 E
Margelan → Margilan	85	40.28 N	71.44 E
Margeride, Monts de la ⛰	32	44.50 N	3.30 E
Margès	62	45.09 N	5.03 E
Mārgherita, Bhārat	120	27.17 N	95.41 E
Margherita → Jamame, Som.	144	0.04 N	42.46 E
Margherita di Savoia	68	41.23 N	16.09 E
Margherita Peak ∧	154	0.22 N	29.51 E
Marghī	120	34.58 N	66.31 E
Marghita	38	47.21 N	22.21 E
Marghūb, Kūh-e ∧	128	33.06 N	57.30 E
Margi ≃	70	37.16 N	14.58 E
Margilan	85	40.28 N	71.44 E
Margit Híd ◆[5]	264c	47.31 N	19.02 E
Margit-sziget I	264c	47.32 N	19.03 E
Margny-lès-Compiègne	50	49.26 N	2.49 E
Margone	62	45.13 N	7.11 E
Margonin	30	52.59 N	17.05 E
Margos	248	10.04 S	76.26 W
Margosatubig	116	7.34 N	123.10 E
Margot Lake @	184	52.28 N	93.10 W
Mārgow, Dasht-e ◆[2]	128	30.45 N	63.10 E
Margreid → Magrè	64	46.17 N	11.12 E
Margua ≃	246	7.03 N	72.05 W
Marguerite, Pic → Margherita Peak ∧	154	0.22 N	29.51 E
Marguerite Bay C	9	68.30 S	68.30 W
Marguerittes	62	43.51 N	4.27 E
Margut	56	49.35 N	5.16 E
Mārī'	130	36.28 N	37.11 E
Mari ≃	248	7.05 S	64.34 W
Maria	116	9.12 N	123.39 E
Maria I[1]	14	21.48 S	154.41 W
Mariabrunn ◆[8]	264b	48.12 N	16.14 E
María Cleofas, Isla I	234	21.16 N	106.14 W
Maria da Fé	256	22.18 S	45.23 W
María Elena	252	22.21 S	69.40 W
Maria Enzersdorf	264b	48.06 N	16.17 E
Maria Gail	64	46.36 N	13.52 E
Mariager	26	56.39 N	10.00 E
Mariāhu	124	25.37 N	82.37 E
María Ignacia (Vela)	252	37.24 S	59.30 W
Maria Island I, Austl.	164	14.52 S	135.40 E
Maria Island I, Austl.	166	42.39 S	148.04 E
Mariakani	154	3.52 S	39.28 E
Maria Laach ɤ[1]	56	50.24 N	7.14 E
María la Baja	246	9.59 N	75.17 W
Maria Lanzendorf	264b	48.06 N	16.25 E
Maria Luggau	64	46.42 N	12.45 E
María Madre, Isla I	234	21.35 N	106.33 W
María Magdalena, Isla I	234	21.25 N	106.24 W

English	Deutsch	Español	Français	Português
≃ River	Fluss	Río	Rivière	Rio
☰ Canal	Kanal	Canal	Canal	Canal
L Waterfall, Rapids	Wasserfall, Stromschnellen	Cascada, Rápidos	Chute d'eau, Rapides	Cascata, Rápidos
⊔ Strait	Meeresstrasse	Estrecho	Détroit	Estreito
C Bay, Gulf	Bucht, Golf	Bahía, Golfo	Baie, Golfe	Baía, Golfo
@ Lake, Lakes	See, Seen	Lago, Lagos	Lac, Lacs	Lago, Lagos
☷ Swamp	Sumpf	Pantano	Marais	Pântano
⍓ Ice Features, Glacier	Eis- und Gletscherformen	Accidentes Glaciales	Formes glaciaires	Acidentes Glaciares
⍑ Other Hydrographic Features	Andere Hydrographische Objekte	Otros Elementos Hidrográficos	Autres données hydrographiques	Outros Elementos Hidrográficos
✢ Submarine Features	Untermeerische Objekte	Accidentes Submarinos	Formes de relief sous-marin	Acidentes Submarinos
□ Political Unit	Politische Einheit	Unidad Política	Entité politique	Unidade Política
ɤ Cultural Institution	Kulturelle Institution	Institución Cultural	Institution culturelle	Instituição Cultural
⊥ Historical Site	Historische Stätte	Sitio Histórico	Site historique	Sítio Histórico
♠ Recreational Site	Erholungs- und Ferienort	Sitio de Recreo	Centre de loisirs	Sítio de Lazer
⊠ Airport	Flughafen	Aeropuerto	Aéroport	Aeroporto
■ Military Installation	Militäranlage	Instalación Militar	Installation militaire	Instalação Militar
◆ Miscellaneous	Verschiedenes	Misceláneo	Divers	Miscelânea

Marian, Lake ⊜ 220 27.52 N 81.06 W
Mariana 255 20.23 S 43.25 W
Mariana Basin ⊹[1] 14 12.00 N 154.00 E
Mariana Islands II 108 16.00 N 145.30 E
Mariana Ridge ⊹[3] 14 17.00 N 146.00 E
Mariana Trench ⊹[1] 14 16.00 N 148.00 E
Marianhill 158 29.52 S 30.50 E
Mariāni 120 26.40 N 94.20 E
Marian Lake ⊜ 176 63.00 N 116.10 W
Marianna, Ark., U.S. 194 34.46 N 90.46 W
Marianna, Fla., U.S. 192 30.47 N 85.14 W
Mariannelund 26 57.37 N 15.34 E
Mariano Acosta 258 34.43 S 58.48 W
Mariano Comense 62 45.42 N 9.11 E
Mariano del Friuli 64 45.55 N 13.27 E
Mariano I. Loza 252 29.22 S 58.12 W
Mariano J. Haedo 288 34.38 S 58.36 W
Mariano Machado 152 13.02 S 14.40 E
Mariano Moreno, Arg. 252 38.44 S 70.01 W
Mariano Moreno → Moreno, Arg. 258 34.39 S 58.48 W
Marianopoli 70 37.36 N 13.55 E
Marianópolis 250 4.47 S 44.38 W
Mariánské Lázně 60 49.59 N 12.43 E
Maria Paula 287a 22.54 S 43.02 W
Mariar 164 2.48 S 132.50 E
Mariarano 157b 15.29 S 46.42 E
Marias ≃ 202 47.56 N 110.30 W
Marías, Islas II 234 21.25 N 106.28 W
Marias Pass)(202 48.19 N 113.21 W
Maria Stein 216 40.24 N 84.28 W
María Teresa 252 34.01 S 61.54 W
Maria Theresa Reef ⊹[2] 14 37.00 S 151.15 W
Maria-Theresiopel → Subotica 38 46.06 N 19.39 E
Mariato, Punta ≻ 246 7.13 N 80.53 W
Maria Van Diemen, Cape ≻ 172 34.28 S 172.39 E
Mariaville 210 42.49 N 74.08 W
Mariazell 61 47.47 N 15.19 E
Ma'rib 144 15.30 N 45.20 E
Maribios, Cordillera de los ⋀ 236 12.35 N 86.50 W
Maribo 41 54.46 N 11.31 E
Maribojoc Bay C 116 9.42 N 123.50 E
Maribor 61 46.33 N 15.39 E
Maribyrnong 274b 37.46 S 144.54 E
Maribyrnong ≃ 169 37.49 S 144.55 E
Marica, Blg. 38 42.02 N 25.50 E
Maricá, Bra. 256 22.55 S 42.49 W
Marica, S.S.S.R. 78 51.45 N 35.16 E
Maricá □[7] 287a 22.57 S 42.59 W
Marica (Évros) (Meriç) ≃ 38 40.52 N 26.12 E
Maricá, Lagoa de C 256 22.56 S 42.50 W
Maricaban Island I 116 13.39 N 120.53 E
Maricao 240m 18.11 N 66.59 W
Maricás, Ilhas II 256 23.01 S 42.55 W
Maricha Bil ⊜ 272b 22.55 N 88.31 E
Marico ≃ 156 24.12 S 26.52 E
Maricopa, Ariz., U.S. 200 33.04 N 112.03 W
Maricopa, Calif., U.S. 204 35.03 N 119.24 W
Maricourt (Wakeham Bay) 176 61.36 N 71.58 W
Maricunga, Salar de ≚ 252 26.55 S 69.05 W
Maridagao ≃ 116 7.13 N 124.41 E
Marīdī 154 4.55 N 29.28 E
Marié ≃ 246 0.27 S 66.26 W
Mariec 80 56.32 N 49.50 E
Marie Curtis Park ♠ 275b 43.35 N 79.33 W
Mariedamm 40 58.51 N 15.09 E
Mariefred 40 59.16 N 17.13 E
Marie-Galante I 241o 15.56 N 61.16 W
Mariehamn 26 60.06 N 19.57 E
Marieholm 41 55.52 N 13.09 E
Mariel 240p 22.59 N 82.45 W
Marie Lake ⊜ 184 54.37 N 110.18 W
Marie-Lefranc, Lac ⊜ 206 46.08 N 75.00 W
Mariembourg 50 50.06 N 4.31 E
Marienbad → Mariánské Lázně 60 49.59 N 12.43 E
Marienbaum 52 51.41 N 6.22 E
Marienberg, B.R.D. 56 50.39 N 7.57 E
Marienberg, D.D.R. 54 50.39 N 13.10 E
Marienberg, Pap. N. Gui. 164 3.55 S 144.15 E
Marien-Berg ∧[2] 264a 52.22 N 13.32 E
Marienborn 54 52.12 N 11.08 E
Marienburg → Malbork 30 54.02 N 19.01 E
Mariendorf ◆[8] 264a 52.26 N 13.23 E
Marienfelde ◆[8] 264a 52.25 N 13.22 E
Marienhafe 52 53.31 N 7.16 E
Marienheide 56 51.05 N 7.32 E
Mariental, B.R.D. 54 52.16 N 10.59 E
Mariental, Namibia 156 24.36 S 17.59 E
Marienville 214 41.28 N 79.07 W
Maries □[6] 219 38.15 N 91.56 W
Maries ≃ 194 38.30 N 92.01 W
Mariestad 40 58.43 N 13.51 E
Marieta ≃ 246 5.02 N 66.38 W
Marietta, Fla., U.S. 192 30.19 N 81.47 W
Marietta, Ga., U.S. 192 33.57 N 84.33 W
Marietta, Ind., U.S. 218 39.27 N 85.53 W
Marietta, Minn., U.S. 198 45.01 N 96.25 W
Marietta, Ohio, U.S. 188 39.25 N 81.27 W
Marietta, Okla., U.S. 196 33.56 N 97.07 W
Marietta, Pa., U.S. 208 40.04 N 76.35 W
Marietta, Tex., U.S. 222 33.10 N 94.33 W
Marietta, Wash., U.S. 224 48.47 N 122.36 W
Marieville 206 45.26 N 73.10 W
Mariga ≃ 150 9.40 N 5.55 E
Marigliano 66 40.56 N 14.27 E
Marignane 62 43.25 N 5.13 E
Marignier 58 46.06 N 6.31 E
Marigny-le-Châtel 50 48.24 N 3.44 E
Marigny-L'église 50 47.22 N 3.56 E
Marigot, Dom. 240d 15.32 N 61.18 W
Marigot, Guad. 238 18.04 N 63.06 W
Marihatag 116 8.48 N 126.18 E
Mariinsk 86 56.13 N 87.45 E
Mariinskoje 89 51.43 N 140.13 E
Marijskaja Avtonomnaja Sovetskaja Socialističeskaja Respublika □[3] 80 56.30 N 48.00 E
Marijskaja Nizina ≚ 80 56.30 N 46.35 E
Marikana 158 25.42 S 27.30 E
Marikina 269f 14.38 N 121.06 E
Marikina ≃ 269f 14.33 N 121.04 E
Marília 255 22.13 S 49.56 W
Marilla 210 42.50 N 78.33 W
Mari-Malmyž 80 56.30 N 50.52 E
Marimari ≃ 246 3.58 S 58.49 W
Marimba 152 8.28 S 17.08 E
Marín, Esp. 34 42.23 N 8.42 W
Marín, Méx. 232 25.52 N 100.03 W
Marin □[6] 226 38.03 N 122.33 W
Marina 226 36.41 N 121.48 W
Marina ◆[8] 282 37.47 N 122.27 W
Marina del Rey 280 33.59 N 118.28 W
Marina del Rey C 280 33.58 N 118.27 W
Marina di Andora 62 43.57 N 8.08 E
Marina di Campo 66 42.44 N 10.14 E
Marina di Caronia 70 38.02 N 14.28 E
Marina di Carrara 64 44.02 N 10.02 E
Marina di Cecina 66 43.18 N 10.29 E
Marina di Gioiosa Ionica 68 38.18 N 16.20 E
Marina di Grosseto 66 42.43 N 10.59 E
Marina di Massa 64 44.00 N 10.06 E
Marina di Minturno 66 41.16 N 13.45 E
Marina di Orosei 71 40.22 N 9.43 E
Marina di Palma ◆[8] 70 37.10 N 13.43 E
Marina di Pietrasanta 64 43.56 N 10.12 E
Marina di Pisa 66 43.40 N 10.16 E
Marina di Ragusa 70 36.47 N 14.33 E
Marina di Ravenna 66 44.29 N 12.17 E
Marina Fall ∟ 246 5.22 N 59.29 W
Marin City 282 37.52 N 122.21 W
Marinduque □[4] 116 13.25 N 121.55 E
Marinduque Island I 116 13.24 N 121.58 E
Marine 219 38.47 N 89.47 W
Marine City 214 42.43 N 82.30 W
Marine-Ehrenmal ⊥ 54 54.23 N 10.15 E
Marineland of the Pacific ʊ[3] 228 33.44 N 118.24 W
Marinella 70 37.35 N 12.50 E
Marine Museum ʊ 280 33.43 N 118.17 W
Marineo 70 37.57 N 13.25 E
Marine Park ♠ 283 42.20 N 71.01 W
Marine Parkway Bridge ◆[5] 276 40.34 N 73.53 W
Mariners Museum ʊ 208 37.03 N 76.30 W
Marines 50 49.09 N 1.59 E
Marinette 190 45.06 N 87.38 W
Marine World / Africa USA ♠ 282 37.32 N 122.16 W
Maringá 255 23.25 S 51.55 W
Maringa ≃ 152 1.14 N 19.48 E
Maringe Lagoon C 175e 8.07 S 159.34 E
Maringouin 194 30.29 N 91.31 W
Marinha Grande 34 39.45 N 8.56 W
Marin Headlands State Park ♠ 282 37.49 N 122.30 W
Marin Mall ◆[9] 282 37.56 N 122.31 W
Marino 66 41.46 N 12.39 E
Marinovka, S.S.S.R. 78 47.46 N 30.53 E
Marinovka, S.S.S.R. 80 48.41 N 43.49 E
Marinovka, S.S.S.R. 83 47.54 N 38.51 E
Marin Peninsula ≻[1] 282 37.51 N 122.31 W
Marins 256 22.27 S 45.08 W
Marinskij Posad 80 56.07 N 47.43 E
Marintu 112 0.34 N 110.00 E
Marinwood 226 38.02 N 122.32 W
Mario, Monte ∧[2] 267a 41.55 N 12.27 E
Marion, Austl. 168b 35.01 S 138.34 E
Marion, Ala., U.S. 194 32.32 N 87.26 W
Marion, Ark., U.S. 194 35.13 N 90.12 W
Marion, Conn., U.S. 207 41.34 N 72.56 W
Marion, Ill., U.S. 194 37.44 N 88.56 W
Marion, Ind., U.S. 216 40.33 N 85.40 W
Marion, Iowa, U.S. 190 42.02 N 91.36 W
Marion, Kans., U.S. 198 38.21 N 97.01 W
Marion, Ky., U.S. 194 37.20 N 88.05 W
Marion, La., U.S. 194 32.54 N 92.15 W
Marion, Mass., U.S. 207 41.42 N 70.46 W
Marion, Mich., U.S. 190 44.06 N 85.09 W
Marion, Miss., U.S. 194 32.25 N 88.39 W
Marion, N.C., U.S. 192 35.41 N 82.01 W
Marion, N. Dak., U.S. 198 46.37 N 98.20 W
Marion, N.Y., U.S. 210 43.08 N 77.11 W
Marion, Ohio, U.S. 214 40.35 N 83.08 W
Marion, S.C., U.S. 192 34.11 N 79.24 W
Marion, S. Dak., U.S. 198 43.25 N 97.16 W
Marion, Va., U.S. 192 36.50 N 81.31 W
Marion, Wis., U.S. 190 44.21 N 89.05 W
Marion □[6], Fla., U.S. 220 29.00 N 82.03 W
Marion □[6], Ill., U.S. 219 38.38 N 88.57 W
Marion □[6], Ind., U.S. 218 39.46 N 86.09 W
Marion □[6], Mo., U.S. 219 39.50 N 91.37 W
Marion □[6], Ohio, U.S. 214 40.35 N 83.08 W
Marion □[6], Oreg., U.S. 224 45.06 N 122.47 W
Marion □[6], Tex., U.S. 222 32.48 N 94.33 W
Marion, Lake ⊜ 220 28.05 N 81.32 W
Marion, Lake ⊜[1] 192 33.30 N 80.25 W
Marion Bay C 166 42.48 S 147.55 E
Marion Center 214 40.46 N 79.03 W
Marion Downs 166 23.22 S 139.39 E
Marion Heights 210 40.48 N 76.28 W
Marion Hill 214 40.44 N 80.18 W
Marion Hills 278 41.45 N 87.57 W
Marion Junction 194 32.26 N 87.14 W
Marion Reef ⊹[2] 166 19.10 S 152.17 E
Marion Station 208 38.02 N 75.46 W
Marionville 194 37.00 N 93.38 W
Marióppolis 252 26.20 S 52.33 W
Maripa 246 7.26 N 65.09 W
Maripá de Minas 256 21.48 S 42.58 W
Maripipi Island I 116 11.47 N 124.19 E
Mariposa 226 37.29 N 119.58 W
Mariposa □[6] 226 37.29 N 119.58 W
Mariposa Creek ≃ 226 37.14 N 120.26 W
Mariposa Slough ≃ 226 37.12 N 120.46 W
Mariquita 246 5.12 N 74.54 W
Mariquita, Cerro ∧ 234 23.13 N 98.22 W
Marisa 112 0.28 N 121.56 E
Marisa ≃ 112 0.28 N 121.56 E
Mariscal Estigarribia 252 22.02 S 60.38 W
Marisco, Ponta do ≻ 287a 23.01 S 43.17 W
Mariškino 82 55.21 N 38.37 E
Marissa 219 38.15 N 89.45 W
Maritime Alps (Alpes Maritimes) (Alpi Marittime) ⋀ 62 44.15 N 7.10 E
Maritimes, Alpes → Maritime Alps ⋀ 62 44.15 N 7.10 E
Marittime, Alpi → Maritime Alps ⋀ 62 44.15 N 7.10 E
Mari-Turek 80 56.47 N 49.36 E
Maritzburg → Pietermaritzburg 158 29.37 S 30.16 E
Mariupol' → Ždanov 83 47.06 N 37.33 E
Mariusa, Caño ≃[1] 246 9.43 N 61.26 W
Mariusa, Isla I 241r 9.39 N 61.19 W
Mariveles 116 14.26 N 120.29 E
Märjamaa 76 58.54 N 24.26 E
Marjanovka, S.S.S.R. 78 50.28 N 24.48 E
Marjanovka, S.S.S.R. 86 54.58 N 72.38 E
Marjanskaja 78 45.06 N 38.38 E
Marjevka 86 53.46 N 67.24 E
Marjina Gorka 76 53.31 N 28.09 E
Marjinka 83 47.56 N 37.31 E
Marjino, S.S.S.R. 82 54.28 N 37.12 E
Marjino, S.S.S.R. 89 48.31 N 130.38 E
Marjino, S.S.S.R. 265a 59.50 N 29.56 E
Marjino, S.S.S.R. 265b 55.52 N 37.18 E
Marjinskaja 84 43.53 N 43.29 E
Marjinsko 76 58.49 N 28.32 E
Mārjirjis, Jūn C 132 33.54 N 35.33 E
Marj 'Uyūn 132 33.22 N 35.35 E
Mark ≃ 50 50.43 N 3.50 E
Marka, Som. 144 1.47 N 44.52 E
Mārkā, Urd. 132 31.59 N 35.59 E
Mark Acres 279b 40.21 N 79.42 W
Markakol', Ozero ⊜ 86 48.45 N 85.48 E
Markala 150 13.41 N 6.05 W
Markansu 85 39.18 N 73.20 E
Mārkāpur 122 15.44 N 79.17 E
Markaryd 26 56.26 N 13.36 E
Markdale 212 44.19 N 80.39 W
Markdorf 58 47.43 N 9.23 E
Marked Tree 194 35.32 N 90.25 W
Markelo 52 52.14 N 6.30 E
Markelovo 86 56.42 N 83.33 E
Marken I 52 52.28 N 5.03 E
Markendorf 54 51.59 N 13.10 E
Markerwaard ◆[1] 52 52.33 N 5.15 E
Markesan 190 43.42 N 88.59 W
Market Bosworth 42 52.37 N 1.24 W
Market Deeping 42 52.41 N 0.19 W
Market Drayton 42 52.54 N 2.29 W
Market Harborough 42 52.29 N 0.55 W
Markethill 44 54.18 N 6.31 W
Market Lavington 42 51.18 N 1.59 W
Market Rasen 44 53.24 N 0.21 W
Market Weighton 44 53.52 N 0.40 W
Markgröningen 56 48.54 N 9.05 E
Markham, Ont., Can. 212 43.52 N 79.16 W
Markham, Tex., U.S. 222 28.57 N 96.04 W
Markham ≃ 164 6.35 S 146.25 E
Markham, Mount ∧ 9 82.51 S 161.21 E
Markham Bay C 176 63.30 N 71.48 W
Markinch 46 56.12 N 3.08 W
Märkisch Buchholz 54 52.07 N 13.46 E
Märkisch Friedland → Mirosławiec 30 53.21 N 16.05 E
Markkleeberg 54 51.17 N 12.23 E
Markland Dam ◆[6] 218 38.47 N 84.58 W
Markle, Ind., U.S. 216 40.50 N 85.20 W
Markle, Pa., U.S. 279b 40.34 N 79.39 W
Markleeville 226 38.41 N 119.47 W
Markleville 218 39.59 N 85.37 W
Markley Canyon V 282 38.00 N 121.50 W
Marklissa → Leśna 30 51.02 N 15.16 E
Marknesse 52 52.43 N 5.52 E
Markneukirchen 54 50.18 N 12.19 E
Markoldendorf 52 51.48 N 9.46 E
Markópoulon 267c 37.54 N 23.54 E
Markovka 83 49.31 N 39.34 E
Markovo, S.S.S.R. 74 64.40 N 170.25 E
Markovo, S.S.S.R. 80 57.01 N 40.30 E
Markovo, S.S.S.R. 82 55.52 N 39.17 E
Markovo, S.S.S.R. 88 57.20 N 107.04 E
Markoye 150 14.39 N 0.02 E
Markranstädt 54 51.18 N 12.13 E
Marks, S.S.S.R. 80 51.42 N 46.46 E
Marks, Miss., U.S. 194 34.16 N 90.16 W
Marksuhl 56 50.55 N 10.11 E
Marksville 194 31.08 N 92.04 W
Markt Bibart 56 49.39 N 10.26 E
Marktbreit 56 49.40 N 10.08 E
Markt Erlbach 56 49.29 N 10.38 E
Marktheidenfeld 56 49.50 N 9.36 E
Markt Indersdorf 60 48.22 N 11.23 E
Marktl 60 48.15 N 12.51 E
Marktleugast 54 50.10 N 11.38 E
Marktleuthen 54 50.08 N 12.00 E
Marktoberdorf 58 47.47 N 10.37 E
Marktredwitz 30 50.00 N 12.06 E
Markt Rettenbach 58 47.57 N 10.23 E
Marktschellenberg 64 47.42 N 13.02 E
Markt Schwaben 60 48.11 N 11.51 E
Mark Twain Cave •[5] 219 39.42 N 91.21 W
Mark Twain State Park ♠ 219 39.29 N 91.48 W
Markulešty 78 47.52 N 28.14 E
Markundi 140 11.33 N 23.49 E
Markvue Manor 279b 40.20 N 79.46 W
Mark West Creek ≃ 226 38.30 N 122.42 W
Marl 52 51.38 N 7.05 E
Marlasi 164 5.30 S 134.38 E
Marlboro, Alta., Can. 182 53.33 N 116.45 W
Marlboro, N.J., U.S. 208 40.19 N 74.15 W
Marlboro, N.Y., U.S. 210 41.36 N 73.58 W
Marlboro, Ohio, U.S. 214 40.53 N 81.12 W
Marlboro, Pa., U.S. 285 39.54 N 75.42 W
Marlborough, Austl. 166 22.49 S 149.53 E
Marlborough, Guy. 246 7.29 N 58.38 W
Marlborough, Eng., U.K. 42 51.26 N 1.43 W
Marlborough, Conn., U.S. 207 41.38 N 72.28 W
Marlborough, Mass., U.S. 207 42.21 N 71.33 W
Marlborough Downs ⋀[1] 42 51.30 N 1.45 W
Marle 50 49.44 N 3.46 E
Marlenheim 58 48.37 N 7.30 E
Marles-en-Brie 261 48.44 N 2.53 E
Marles-les-Mines 50 50.30 N 2.31 E
Marlette 190 43.20 N 83.05 W
Marlette Lake ⊜ 226 39.10 N 119.54 W
Marley 278 41.33 N 87.55 W
Marley Creek ≃ 278 41.31 N 87.57 W
Marlieux 58 46.04 N 5.04 E
Marlin 222 31.18 N 96.53 W
Marlinton 188 38.13 N 80.06 W
Marl-Loemühle, Flughafen ⊠ 263 51.39 N 7.10 E
Marlow, D.D.R. 54 54.09 N 12.34 E
Marlow, Eng., U.K. 42 51.35 N 0.48 W
Marlow, Okla., U.S. 196 34.39 N 97.57 W
Marlpit Hill 260 51.13 N 0.04 E
Marlton 208 39.54 N 74.55 W
Marlton Heights 285 39.40 N 75.21 W
Marly, Forêt de ♠ 261 48.50 N 2.00 E
Marly-la-Ville 261 49.05 N 2.30 E
Marly-le-Roi 50 48.52 N 2.05 E
Marma, Sve. 26 61.16 N 16.52 E
Marma, Sve. 40 60.30 N 17.25 E
Marmaduke 194 36.11 N 90.23 W
Marmagne 58 46.50 N 4.21 E
Marmande 32 44.30 N 0.10 E
Marmara, Sea of → Marmara Denizi ▿[2] 130 40.40 N 28.15 E
Marmara Adası I 130 40.38 N 27.37 E
Marmara Denizi (Sea of Marmara) ▿[2] 130 40.40 N 28.15 E
Marmara Ereğlisi 130 40.58 N 27.57 E
Marmara Gölü ⊜ 130 38.37 N 28.02 E
Marmaris 130 36.51 N 28.16 E
Marmarītā 130 34.47 N 36.15 E
Marmarth 198 46.18 N 103.54 W
Marmaton ≃ 194 38.00 N 94.19 W
Marmelos 248 6.08 S 61.50 W
Marmelos, Rio dos ≃ 248 6.06 S 61.46 W
Marmet 188 38.15 N 81.04 W
Marmion Lake ⊜[1] 190 48.54 N 91.30 W
Marmirolo 64 45.13 N 10.45 E
Marmolada ∧ 64 46.26 N 11.51 E
Marmora, Ont., Can. 212 44.29 N 77.41 W
Marmora, N.J., U.S. 208 39.16 N 74.39 W
Marmora, Punta la ∧ 71 39.59 N 9.20 E
Marmore 66 42.33 N 12.43 E
Marmore ≃ 62 45.44 N 7.37 E
Marmore, Cascàta delle ∟ 66 42.33 N 12.43 E
Marmot Bay C 180 58.00 N 152.20 W
Marmot Island I 180 58.13 N 151.51 W
Marmoutier 58 48.41 N 7.23 E
Marnate 266b 45.38 N 8.54 E
Marnay 58 47.17 N 5.46 E
Marnaz 58 46.04 N 6.32 E
Marne, B.R.D. 52 53.57 N 9.00 E
Marne, Mich., U.S. 216 43.02 N 85.50 W
Marne □[5] 32 48.55 N 4.10 E
Marne ≃ 32 48.49 N 2.24 E
Marne à la Saône, Canal de la ≍ 58 48.44 N 4.36 E
Marne au Rhin, Canal de la ≍ 56 48.35 N 7.47 E
Marneuli 84 41.28 N 44.50 E
Marnhull 42 50.58 N 2.18 W
Marnitz 54 53.19 N 11.56 E
Maroa, Ill., U.S. 219 40.02 N 88.57 W
Maroa, Ven. 246 2.43 N 67.33 W
Maroala 157b 15.23 S 47.59 E
Maroantsetra 157b 15.26 S 49.44 E
Maroc → Morocco □[1] 148 32.00 N 5.00 W
Maroelaboom 156 19.15 S 18.53 E
Marofandilia 157b 20.07 S 44.34 E
Maroglio ≃ 70 37.03 N 14.15 E
Marokko → Morocco □[1] 148 32.00 N 5.00 W
Marol ◆[8] 272c 19.07 N 72.53 E
Marolambo 157b 20.02 S 48.07 E
Maroldsweisach 56 50.12 N 10.39 E
Marolles-en-Brie 261 48.44 N 2.33 E
Marolles-en-Hurepoix 261 48.34 N 2.18 E
Marolles-les-Braults 50 48.15 N 0.19 E
Maromandia 157b 14.13 S 48.08 E
Maromme 50 49.28 N 1.02 E
Maromokotro ∧ 157b 14.01 S 48.59 E
Marone 64 45.44 N 10.05 E
Marong 102 31.07 N 99.20 E
Maronghi Creek ≃ 171a 26.58 S 152.22 E
Maroni (Marowijne) ≃ 250 5.45 N 53.58 W
Maroon 171a 28.10 S 152.44 E
Maroondah Aqueduct ≍[1] 274b 37.42 S 145.01 E
Maros 112 5.00 S 119.34 E
Maros (Mureș) ≃ 38 46.15 N 20.13 E
Maroseranana 157b 18.32 S 48.51 E
Marostica 64 45.45 N 11.39 E
Marosvásárhely → Tîrgu Mureș 38 46.33 N 24.33 E
Marotandrano 157b 16.10 S 48.50 E
Marotolana 157b 14.01 S 48.37 E
Marotta 66 43.46 N 13.08 E
Maroua 146 10.36 N 14.20 E
Maroubra 274a 33.57 S 151.16 E
Maroubra Bay C 274a 33.57 S 151.16 E
Marouini ≃ 250 3.18 N 54.04 W
Marovato, Madag. 157b 15.48 S 48.05 E
Marovato, Madag. 157b 16.28 S 48.25 E
Marovoay 157b 16.06 S 46.39 E
Marovoay Nord 157b 16.57 S 44.34 E
Marovo Lagoon C 175e 8.29 S 158.04 E
Marowijne □[5] 250 4.15 N 54.35 W
Marowijne (Maroni) ≃ 250 5.45 N 53.58 W
Marpent 50 50.18 N 4.05 E
Marpi Point ≻ 174n 15.17 N 145.49 E
Marple 44 53.24 N 2.03 W
Marpo Point ≻ 174n 14.57 N 145.40 E
Marqa I 144 18.13 N 41.19 E
Marquam 224 45.04 N 122.41 W
Marquand 194 37.26 N 90.10 W
Marquard 158 28.54 S 27.28 E
Marquardt 54 52.27 N 12.57 E
Marquartstein 64 47.45 N 12.28 E
Marquesas Islands → Marquises, Îles II 6 9.00 S 139.30 W
Marquesas Keys II 220 24.34 N 82.08 W
Marquette, Kans., U.S. 198 38.33 N 97.50 W
Marquette, Mich., U.S. 190 46.33 N 87.24 W
Marquette Park ♠ 278 41.46 N 87.42 W
Márquez, Perú 286d 11.57 S 77.08 W
Marquez, Tex., U.S. 222 31.14 N 96.15 W
Marquina-Jemein 34 43.16 N 2.30 W
Marquion 50 50.13 N 3.05 E
Marquis 241k 12.06 N 61.37 W
Marquis, Cape ≻ 241f 14.03 N 60.54 W
Marquise 50 50.49 N 1.42 E
Marquises, Îles (Marquesas Islands) II 6 9.00 S 139.30 W
Marrabel 168b 34.08 S 138.53 E
Marra Creek ≃ 166 30.05 S 147.05 E
Marradi 66 44.04 N 11.37 E
Marradong 168a 32.52 S 116.27 E
Marrah, Jabal ∧ 140 13.04 N 24.21 E
Marra Hills ⋀[2] 140 6.05 N 27.33 E
Marrakech 148 31.38 N 8.00 W
Marrawah 166 40.56 S 144.41 E
Marree 166 29.39 S 138.04 E
Marrero 194 29.54 N 90.07 W
Marrickville 274a 33.55 S 151.09 E
Marromeu 156 18.20 S 35.56 E
Marrowstone Island I 224 48.04 N 122.41 W
Marrubiu 71 39.45 N 8.38 E
Marruecos → Morocco □[1] 148 32.00 N 5.00 W
Marrupa 154 13.08 S 37.30 E
Mars 214 40.42 N 80.06 W
Marsabit 154 2.20 N 37.59 E
Marsabit National Park ♠ 154 2.20 N 38.00 E
Marsac-en-Livradois 62 45.29 N 3.44 E
Marṣafā wa Kafr Aḥmad Ḥashīsh 142 30.25 N 31.15 E
Marsal 56 48.48 N 6.36 E
Marsala 70 37.48 N 12.26 E
Marsangue, Ruisseau la ≃ 261 48.43 N 2.45 E
Marsannay-la-Côte 58 47.16 N 4.59 E
Marsanne 62 44.39 N 4.52 E
Marsā Sūsah 146 32.54 N 21.58 E
Mars'aty 86 60.05 N 60.29 E
Marscheid ◆[8] 263 51.14 N 7.14 E
Marsciano 66 42.54 N 12.20 E
Marsden, Austl. 166 33.45 S 147.32 E
Marsden, Eng., U.K. 262 53.36 N 1.56 W
Marsden, Point ≻ 168b 35.35 S 137.38 E
Marsden Park 274a 33.42 S 150.50 E
Marsdiep ⊔ 52 52.59 N 4.45 E
Marseille 62 43.18 N 5.24 E
Marseille-en-Beauvaisis 50 49.35 N 1.57 E
Marseille-Marignane, Aéroport de ⊠ 62 43.27 N 5.13 E
Marseilles, Ill., U.S. 216 41.20 N 88.43 W
Marseilles, Ohio, U.S. 214 40.42 N 83.23 W
Marsella → Marseille 62 43.18 N 5.24 E
Marsfield 274a 33.47 S 151.07 E
Marsfjället ∧ 24 65.05 N 15.28 E
Marshakala ∧ 123 35.25 N 75.35 E
Marshall, Liber. 150 6.10 N 10.23 W
Marshall, Ark., U.S. 194 35.55 N 92.38 W
Marshall, Ill., U.S. 194 39.23 N 87.42 W
Marshall, Mich., U.S. 216 42.16 N 84.58 W
Marshall, Minn., U.S. 198 44.27 N 95.47 W
Marshall, Mo., U.S. 194 39.07 N 93.12 W
Marshall, N.C., U.S. 192 35.48 N 82.41 W
Marshall, Tex., U.S. 194 32.33 N 94.23 W
Marshall, Va., U.S. 188 38.52 N 77.52 W
Marshall, Wis., U.S. 216 43.10 N 89.04 W
Marshall □[6], Ill., U.S. 216 41.02 N 89.24 W
Marshall □[6], Ind., U.S. 216 41.21 N 86.19 W
Marshall ≃ 162 22.59 S 136.59 E
Marshall Bennett Islands II 164 8.50 S 151.50 E
Marshallberg 192 34.44 N 76.31 W
Marshall Canyon Regional Park ♠ 280 34.09 N 117.43 W
Marshall Gold Discovery State Historical Park ♠ 226 38.48 N 120.53 W
Marshall Hall 208 38.41 N 77.06 W
Marshall Islands II 14 9.00 N 168.00 E
Marshalls Creek 210 41.03 N 75.08 W
Marshallton, Del., U.S. 208 39.45 N 75.39 W
Marshallton, Pa., U.S. 285 39.57 N 75.41 W
Marshalltown 190 42.03 N 92.55 W
Marshallville, Ga., U.S. 192 32.27 N 89.56 W
Marshallville, Ohio, U.S. 214 40.54 N 81.44 W
Marshbank Metropolitan Park ♠ 281 42.36 N 83.23 W
Marshbrook 154 18.34 S 31.03 E
Marsh Creek ≃, Calif., U.S. 282 37.53 N 121.49 W
Marsh Creek ≃, Mich., U.S. 281 42.06 N 83.13 W
Marsh Creek ≃, Pa., U.S. 214 41.03 N 77.36 W
Marsh Creek ≃, Pa., U.S. 285 40.03 N 75.43 W
Marsh Creek ≃, Wis., U.S. 216 42.13 N 89.04 W
Marshes Creek ≃ 276 40.36 N 74.13 W
Marshfield, Eng., U.K. 42 51.28 N 2.19 W
Marshfield, Mass., U.S. 207 42.07 N 70.43 W
Marshfield, Mo., U.S. 194 37.15 N 92.54 W
Marshfield, Wis., U.S. 190 44.40 N 90.10 W
Marshfield Airport ⊠ 283 42.06 N 70.40 W
Marshfield Center 283 42.07 N 70.43 W
Marshfield Hills 207 42.09 N 70.44 W
Marsh Harbour 238 26.33 N 77.03 W
Marsh Hill 210 41.29 N 76.58 W
Mars Hill, Ind., U.S. 218 39.43 N 86.09 W
Mars Hill, Maine, U.S. 186 46.31 N 67.52 W
Mars Hill, N.C., U.S. 192 35.47 N 82.29 W
Marsh Island I 194 29.35 N 91.53 W
Marsh Lake ⊜ 180 60.25 N 134.18 W
Marsh Peak ∧ 200 40.43 N 109.50 W
Marshside 262 53.40 N 2.58 W
Marshville 192 34.59 N 80.26 W
Marshyhope Creek ≃ 208 38.32 N 75.45 W
Marsica ◆[1] 66 41.50 N 13.45 E
Marsico Nuovo 68 40.25 N 15.44 E
Marsico Vetere 68 40.23 N 15.49 E
Marsillargues 62 43.40 N 4.11 E
Marsing 202 43.33 N 116.48 W
Marske-by-the-Sea 44 54.36 N 1.01 W
Mars-la-Tour 56 49.06 N 5.54 E
Marson 56 48.55 N 4.32 E
Marssassoum 150 12.50 N 16.00 W
Marssum 52 53.12 N 5.42 E
Märsta 40 59.37 N 17.51 E
Marstal 41 54.51 N 10.31 E
Marsteller 214 40.39 N 78.47 W
Märstetten 58 47.36 N 9.04 E
Marston 262 53.16 N 2.30 W
Marston Moor ≚ 44 53.57 N 1.17 W
Marston Moor Battlesite (1644) ⊥ 44 53.57 N 1.17 W
Marstons Mills 207 41.39 N 70.25 W
Marstrand 26 57.53 N 11.35 E
Marsyandi ≃ 124 28.05 N 84.28 E
Mart 222 31.33 N 96.50 W
Marta 66 42.32 N 11.55 E
Marta ≃ 66 42.14 N 11.42 E
Martaban 110 16.32 N 97.37 E
Martaban, Gulf of C 110 16.30 N 97.00 E
Martano 68 40.12 N 18.18 E
Martap 152 6.54 N 13.03 E
Martapura, Indon. 112 3.25 S 114.51 E
Martapura, Indon. 112 4.19 S 104.22 E
Marte 146 12.22 N 13.51 E
Marteg ≃ 42 52.20 N 3.33 W
Martel, Fr. 32 44.56 N 1.37 E
Martel, Ohio, U.S. 214 40.40 N 82.55 W
Martelange 56 49.50 N 5.44 E
Martell 226 38.22 N 120.48 W
Martello 64 46.34 N 10.47 E
Martello, Val V 64 46.31 N 10.45 E
Martemjanovskij 86 55.54 N 80.22 E
Marten ◆[8] 263 51.31 N 7.23 E
Marten Lake ⊜ 190 46.42 N 79.41 W
Marten Mountain ∧ 182 55.28 N 114.43 W
Marte R. Gomez, Presa ⊜[1] 232 26.10 N 99.00 W
Martfeld 52 52.52 N 9.04 E
Marthaguy Creek ≃ 166 30.16 S 147.35 E
Martha Lake 224 47.51 N 122.20 W
Marthall 262 53.17 N 2.18 W
Marthasville 219 38.38 N 91.04 W
Martha's Vineyard I 207 41.25 N 70.40 W
Martí, Cuba 240p 22.57 N 80.55 W
Martí, Cuba 240p 21.09 N 77.27 W
Martignacco 64 46.05 N 13.08 E
Martignat 58 46.13 N 5.36 E
Martigny 58 46.06 N 7.04 E
Martigny-les-Bains 58 48.06 N 5.49 E
Martigues 62 43.24 N 5.03 E
Martil 34 35.37 N 5.17 W
Martim Francisco 256 22.31 S 46.57 W
Martin, Česko. 30 49.05 N 18.55 E
Martin, Ky., U.S. 192 37.34 N 82.45 W
Martin, Mich., U.S. 216 42.37 N 85.39 W
Martin, N. Dak., U.S. 198 47.50 N 100.07 W
Martin, Ohio, U.S. 214 41.33 N 83.20 W
Martin, S. Dak., U.S. 198 43.10 N 101.44 W
Martin, Tenn., U.S. 194 36.21 N 88.51 W
Martin □[6] 220 27.07 N 80.31 W
Martín ≃ 34 41.18 N 0.19 W
Martín, Arroyo ≃ 288 34.51 S 58.04 W
Martin, Isle I 46 57.55 N 5.14 W
Martina 58 46.53 N 10.30 E
Martina Franca 68 40.42 N 17.21 E
Martin Airport ⊠ 284b 39.20 N 76.25 W
Martinborough 172 41.13 S 175.28 E
Martín Chico, Punta ≻ 258 34.10 S 58.13 W
Martindale 196 29.50 N 97.51 W
Martindale Creek ≃ 218 39.48 N 85.09 W
Martindale Pond ⊜ 284a 43.11 N 79.16 W
Martin-Église 50 49.54 N 1.09 E
Martinengo 62 45.34 N 9.46 E
Mărtinești 38 45.30 N 27.18 E
Martinez 226 37.55 N 121.55 W
Martínez ◆[8] 258 34.29 S 58.30 W
Martínez de la Torre 234 20.04 N 97.03 W
Martín García, Isla I 258 34.13 S 58.15 W
Martinho Campos 255 19.20 S 45.13 W
Martinica → Martinique □[2] 240e 14.40 N 61.00 W
Martini Creek ≃ 282 37.33 N 122.31 W
Martinique □[2] 230; 240e 14.40 N 61.00 W
Martin Lake ⊜[1] 194 32.50 N 85.55 W
Martinniemi 26 65.13 N 25.18 E
Martinópole 250 3.15 S 40.41 W
Martin Peninsula ≻[1] 9 74.25 S 114.10 W
Martín Pérez ≃ 286b 23.07 N 82.20 W
Martin Point ≻ 180 70.08 N 143.16 W
Martin Run ≃ 279a 41.27 N 82.12 W
Martins 250 6.05 S 37.55 W
Martinsberg 61 48.22 N 15.09 E
Martins Brook ≃ 283 42.34 N 71.06 W
Martinsbuch 60 48.45 N 12.25 E
Martinsburg, Mo., U.S. 219 39.06 N 91.39 W
Martinsburg, N.Y., U.S. 212 43.44 N 75.28 W
Martinsburg, Ohio, U.S. 214 40.16 N 82.21 W
Martinsburg, Pa., U.S. 214 40.19 N 78.20 W
Martinsburg, W. Va., U.S. 188 39.27 N 77.58 W
Martins Creek 208 40.47 N 75.11 W
Martins Creek ≃ 210 41.37 N 75.46 W
Martinscroft 262 53.24 N 2.31 W
Martins Ferry 214 40.06 N 80.44 W
Martinshaun 60 48.40 N 12.13 E
Martins Mills 222 32.25 N 95.47 W
Martins Pond ⊜ 283 42.36 N 71.08 W
Martinstein 56 49.48 N 7.32 E
Martinsthal 56 50.03 N 8.07 E
Martinsville, Austl. 170 33.03 S 151.25 E
Martinsville, Ill., U.S. 194 39.20 N 87.53 W
Martinsville, Ind., U.S. 218 39.26 N 86.25 W
Martinsville, N.J., U.S. 276 40.36 N 74.34 W
Martinsville, Ohio, U.S. 218 39.19 N 83.49 W
Martinsville, Va., U.S. 192 36.41 N 79.52 W
Martinton 216 40.55 N 87.44 W
Martintown 206 45.09 N 74.42 W
Martin Van Buren National Historic Site ⊥ 210 42.22 N 73.43 W
Martin Vaz, Ilhas II 244 20.30 S 28.51 W
Martis 71 40.47 N 8.49 E
Martisovo 76 56.34 N 31.55 E
Martock 42 50.59 N 2.46 W
Martofte 41 55.33 N 10.40 E
Marton, N.Z. 172 40.05 S 175.23 E
Marton, Eng., U.K. 262 53.12 N 2.13 W
Martorell 266d 41.29 N 1.56 E
Martorellas 266d 41.32 N 2.14 E
Martos 34 37.43 N 3.58 W
Martovaja 78 49.57 N 36.57 E
Martre, Lac la ⊜ 176 63.15 N 116.55 W
Martti 24 67.28 N 28.28 E
Martūbah 146 32.35 N 22.46 E
Martuk 86 50.46 N 56.31 E
Martuni, S.S.S.R. 84 40.08 N 45.19 E
Martuni, S.S.S.R. 84 39.48 N 47.06 E
Martville 210 43.17 N 76.38 W
Martynoviči 78 51.17 N 29.37 E
Martynovka 78 49.38 N 31.18 E
Martynovo 80 50.43 N 50.23 E
Martynovskij 80 50.29 N 42.18 E
Maru 150 12.22 N 6.22 E
Marua 164 9.30 S 149.20 E
Marudi 112 4.11 N 114.19 E
Marudu, Teluk C 112 6.45 N 116.55 E
Marugame 96 34.17 N 133.47 E
Maruggio 68 40.19 N 17.34 E
Marui 164 4.05 S 143.00 E
Maruia 172 42.11 S 172.13 E
Maruia ≃ 172 41.47 S 172.12 E
Maruim 250 10.45 S 37.05 W
Maruko 94 36.19 N 138.16 E
Marula 154 20.26 S 28.06 E
Marulan 170 34.43 S 150.00 E
Marulan South 170 34.46 S 150.02 E
Marum 52 53.08 N 6.16 E
Marum, Mount ∧ 175f 16.15 S 168.07 E
Marunga 152 17.27 S 20.02 E
Marungu 154 3.44 S 30.48 E
Marungu ⋀ 154 7.42 S 30.00 E
Maruoka 94 36.09 N 136.16 E
Mårup 41 55.57 N 10.35 E
Marusino 265b 55.42 N 37.59 E
Maruškino 82 55.36 N 37.12 E
Ma'rūt 120 31.34 N 67.03 E
Marutea I[1] 14 17.00 S 143.10 W
Maruyama 94 35.01 N 139.58 E
Maruyama ≃ 96 35.39 N 134.50 E
Marv Dasht 128 29.50 N 52.40 E
Marve ◆[8] 272c 19.12 N 72.49 E
Marvejols 32 44.33 N 3.18 E
Marvell 194 34.33 N 90.55 W
Marvel Loch 162 31.28 S 119.28 E
Marviken 40 58.34 N 16.51 E
Marvila ◆[8] 266c 38.44 N 9.06 W
Marville 56 49.27 N 5.27 E
Marvin Creek ≃ 214 41.48 N 78.26 W
Marvine, Mount ∧ 200 38.40 N 111.39 W
Mar Vista ◆[8] 280 34.00 N 118.27 W
Mārwār 120 25.44 N 73.36 E
Marwayne 184 53.32 N 110.20 W
Marwitz 264a 52.41 N 13.09 E
Marwitzer Heide ◆[3] 264a 52.40 N 13.06 E
Marwood 214 40.48 N 79.47 W
Marxhagen 54 53.37 N 12.36 E
Marxloh ◆[8] 263 51.31 N 6.46 E
Mary 128 37.36 N 61.50 E
Mary □[4] 128 37.36 N 61.50 E
Mary ≃ 164 12.53 S 131.38 E
Mary Anne Group II 162 21.13 S 115.32 E
Maryborough, Austl. 166 25.32 S 152.42 E
Maryborough, Austl. 169 37.03 S 143.45 E
Maryborough → Portlaoighise, Eire 48 53.02 N 71.17 W
Mary D 208 40.45 N 76.04 W
Marydale 158 29.23 S 22.05 E
Marydel 208 39.07 N 75.45 W
Maryfield 184 49.48 N 101.32 W
Maryhill 224 45.41 N 120.49 W
Mary Jane, Lake ⊜ 220 28.22 N 81.11 W
Mary Kathleen 166 20.49 S 139.58 E
Maryknoll 210 41.11 N 73.50 W
Mary Lake ⊜ 212 45.15 N 79.15 W
Maryland, N.Y., U.S. 210 42.32 N 74.53 W
Maryland, Zimb. 154 17.39 S 30.29 E
Maryland □[6] 150 4.40 N 8.00 W
Maryland □[3] 178; 188 39.00 N 76.45 W
Maryland, University of (Baltimore County Campus) ʊ[2], Md., U.S. 284b 39.15 N 76.43 W
Maryland, University of ʊ[2], Md., U.S. 284c 38.59 N 76.57 W
Maryland City 208 39.06 N 76.50 W
Maryland Gardens Park ♠ 275b 43.47 N 79.32 W
Maryland Heights 219 38.44 N 90.27 W
Maryland Line 208 39.43 N 76.40 W
Maryland Park 284c 38.53 N 76.54 W
Marylebone 262 53.34 N 2.38 W
Maryneal 196 32.14 N 100.27 W
Marypark 46 57.26 N 3.21 W
Maryport 44 54.43 N 3.30 W
Marys ≃, Ill., U.S. 194 37.53 N 89.47 W
Marys ≃, Nev., U.S. 204 41.04 N 115.16 W
Marys Creek ≃ 202 42.18 N 115.48 W
Mary's Igloo 180 65.09 N 165.04 W
Marys Peak ∧ 202 44.30 N 123.33 W
Marystown 186 47.10 N 55.09 W
Marysvale 200 38.27 N 112.11 W
Marysville, Austl. 169 37.31 S 145.45 E
Marysville, B.C., Can. 182 49.38 N 115.57 W
Marysville, N.B., Can. 186 45.59 N 66.35 W
Marysville, Calif., U.S. 226 39.09 N 121.35 W
Marysville, Kans., U.S. 198 39.51 N 96.39 W
Marysville, Mich., U.S. 214 42.54 N 82.29 W
Marysville, Ohio, U.S. 214 40.14 N 83.22 W
Marysville, Pa., U.S. 208 40.20 N 76.56 W
Marysville, Wash., U.S. 224 48.03 N 122.11 W
Mār Yūsuf 132 33.53 N 35.33 E
Maryūt, Buḥayrat ⊜ 142 31.08 N 29.54 E
Maryvale 171a 28.05 S 152.15 E
Maryvale ◆[8] 275b 43.46 N 79.18 W
Maryville, Mo., U.S. 194 40.21 N 94.52 W
Maryville, Tenn., U.S. 192 35.46 N 83.58 W
Marywell 46 57.02 N 2.42 W
Marywood 216 41.48 N 88.18 W
Marzabotto 64 44.20 N 11.12 E
Marzagão 255 17.59 S 48.39 W
Marzahn ◆[8] 264a 52.33 N 13.33 E
Marzahna 54 52.00 N 12.46 E
Marzahne 54 52.31 N 12.31 E
Marzal, Aven de •[5] 62 44.22 N 4.31 E
Marzo, Punta ≻ 246 6.50 N 77.42 W
Marzolara 64 44.38 N 10.10 E
Marzūq 146 25.55 N 13.55 E
Marzūq, Ḥammādat ◆[2] 146 26.10 N 12.45 E
Marzūq, Idehan •[8] 146 24.30 N 13.00 E
Masa 152 3.45 S 15.29 E
Masachapa 236 11.47 N 86.31 W
Mas'adah (Cæsarea Philippi) 132 33.14 N 35.45 E
Masada Landing Ground ⊠ 132 31.19 N 35.21 E
Más Afuera, Isla → Alejandro Selkirk, Isla I 244 33.45 S 80.46 W
Masagua 236 14.12 N 90.51 W
Masaguisi 116 12.41 N 121.32 E
Masai 114 1.29 N 103.53 E
Masai-Amboseli Game Reserve ♠ 154 2.30 S 37.00 E
Masai-Mara Game Reserve ♠ 154 1.15 S 35.15 E

Symbols in the index entries represent the broad categories identified in the key at the right. Symbols with superior numbers (⋀[2]) identify subcategories (see complete key on page I · 30).

Kartensymbole in dem Registerverzeichnis stellen die rechts in Schlüssel erklärten Kategorien dar. Symbole mit hochgestellten Ziffern (⋀[2]) bezeichnen Unterabteilungen einer Kategorie (vgl. vollständiger Schlüssel auf Seite I · 30).

Los símbolos incluídos en el texto del índice representan las grandes categorias identificadas con la clave a la derecha. Los símbolos con numeros en su parte superior (⋀[2]) identifican las subcategorías (véase la clave completa en la página I · 30).

Les symboles de l'index représentent les catégories indiquées dans la légende à droite. Les symboles suivis d'un indice (⋀[2]) représentent des sous-catégories (voir légende complète à la page I · 30).

Os símbolos incluídos no texto do índice representam as grandes categorias identificadas com a chave à direita. Os símbolos com números em sua parte superior (⋀[2]) identificam as subcategorias (veja-se a chave completa à página I · 30).

	English	Deutsch	Español	Français	Português
∧	Mountain	Berg	Montaña	Montagne	Montanha
⋀	Mountains	Berge	Montañas	Montagnes	Montanhas
)(	Pass	Pass	Paso	Col	Passo
V	Valley, Canyon	Tal, Cañon	Valle, Cañón	Vallée, Canyon	Vale, Canhão
≚	Plain	Ebene	Llano	Plaine	Planície
≻	Cape	Kap	Cabo	Cap	Cabo
I	Island	Insel	Isla	Île	Ilha
II	Islands	Inseln	Islas	Îles	Ilhas
•	Other Topographic Features	Andere Topographische Objekte	Otros Elementos Topográficos	Autres données topographiques	Outros Elementos Topográficos

ESPAÑOL | Nombre | Página | Lat.° ′ | Long.° ′ W = Oeste
FRANÇAIS | Nom | Page | Lat.° ′ | Long.° ′ W = Ouest
PORTUGUÊS | Nome | Página | Lat.° ′ | Long.° ′ W = Oeste

Masai Steppe ≃ 154 4.45 S 37.00 E
Masak 85 43.37 N 78.18 E
Masaka 154 0.20 S 31.44 E
Masaka □5 154 0.30 S 31.35 E
Masaki, Nihon 96 33.47 N 132.42 E
Masaki, Nihon 268 35.13 N 140.02 E
Masalasef 146 11.43 N 17.08 E
Masalembo-besar I 112 5.34 S 114.26 E
Masally 84 39.03 N 48.40 E
Masalog Point ➤ 174n 15.01 N 145.41 E
Masamba 112 2.32 S 120.20 E
Masan 98 35.11 N 128.32 E
Masangwe ∧ 154 5.28 S 30.05 E
Masānjor 126 24.07 N 87.19 E
Masapelid Island I 116 9.42 N 125.39 E
Masapun 112 7.47 S 126.38 E
Masarah 142 27.29 N 30.50 E
Masaran 115a 7.28 S 110.55 E
Maʻṣarat Samālūṭ 142 28.19 N 30.43 E
Masaryktown 220 28.27 N 82.28 W
Masasi 154 10.43 S 38.48 E
Masatepe 236 11.55 N 86.09 W
Más a Tierra, Isla → Robinson Crusoe, Isla I 244 33.38 S 78.52 W
Masaya 236 11.58 N 86.06 W
Masaya □5 236 12.00 N 86.10 W
Masayama 150 8.15 N 10.49 W
Masba 146 11.30 N 13.00 E
Masbate 116 12.22 N 123.36 E
Masbate □4 116 12.20 N 123.30 E
Masbate Island I 116 12.15 N 123.30 E
Masbate Pass ⋃ 116 12.30 N 123.35 E
Mascali 70 37.45 N 15.12 E
Mascalucia 70 37.34 N 15.03 E
Mascara 148 35.45 N 0.01 E
Mascarene Basin ✢1 12 27.00 S 55.00 E
Mascarene Islands II 157c 21.00 S 57.00 E
Mascasin 252 31.22 S 66.59 W
Maschen 52 53.24 N 10.02 E
Maschito 68 40.54 N 15.50 E
Mascot, Austl. 274a 33.56 S 151.12 E
Mascot, Tenn., U.S. 192 36.04 N 83.44 W
Mascota 234 20.32 N 104.49 W
Mascota ≃ 234 20.38 N 104.59 W
Mascotte 220 28.35 N 81.53 W
Mascouche 206 45.45 N 73.36 W
Mascouche ≃ 206 45.41 N 73.40 W
Mascoutah 219 38.29 N 89.48 W
Mascuppic Lake ⊛ 283 42.41 N 71.23 W
Mase 102 27.16 N 104.08 E
Mase ≃ 94 35.40 N 137.10 E
Masefield 184 49.09 N 107.48 W
Masela, Pulau I 164 8.09 S 129.50 E
Masenberg ∧ 61 47.21 N 15.53 E
Maser 64 45.48 N 11.59 E
Maserada sul Piave 64 45.45 N 12.17 E
Maserti 130 37.24 N 40.58 E
Maseru 158 29.28 S 27.30 E
Masevaux 58 47.47 N 7.00 E
Maševka 78 49.26 N 34.52 E
Maševo 78 52.06 N 32.48 E
Masha 100 27.26 N 117.50 E
Mashaba 154 20.02 S 30.29 E
Mashaba Mountains ∧ 154 18.45 S 30.32 E
Mashʻabbe Sade 132 31.00 N 34.47 E
Mashābih I 128 25.37 N 36.29 E
Mashai Pass)(158 29.42 S 29.10 E
Mashalah 142 30.44 N 31.08 E
Masham 44 54.13 N 1.40 W
Mashan, Zhg. 89 45.13 N 130.35 E
Mashan, Zhg. 100 27.33 N 113.46 E
Mashan, Zhg. 102 23.50 N 108.16 E
Mashar 140 9.14 N 26.52 E
Mashbury 260 51.47 N 0.24 E
Mashel ≃ 224 46.51 N 122.20 W
Mashenqiao 105 40.04 N 117.36 E
Masherbrum ∧ 123 35.38 N 76.18 E
Mashgharah 132 33.32 N 35.39 E
Mashhad, Īrān 128 36.18 N 59.36 E
Mashhad, Yis. 132 32.44 N 35.19 E
Mashi, Nig. 150 13.00 N 7.54 E
Mashi, Zhg. 100 25.01 N 114.09 E
Mashi, Zhg. 100 29.05 N 114.22 E
Mashike 92a 43.51 N 141.31 E
Mashiko 94 36.28 N 140.06 E
Mashita ≃ 94 35.40 N 137.10 E
Mashīz 128 29.56 N 56.37 E
Mashkai ≃ 128 26.02 N 65.19 E
Māshkel (Māshkīd) ≃ 128 28.02 N 63.25 E
Māshkel, Hāmūn-i- ⊛ 128 28.15 N 63.00 E
Mashki Chāh 128 29.01 N 62.27 E
Māshkīd (Māshkel) ≃ 128 28.02 N 63.25 E
Mashonaland North □4 154 16.30 S 30.00 E
Mashonaland South □4 154 18.15 S 30.45 E
Mashpee 207 41.39 N 70.29 W
Mashraʻar-Raqq 140 8.25 N 29.16 E
Mashtūl as-Sūq 142 30.22 N 31.22 E
Mashuikou 105 39.48 N 115.16 E
Mashū-ko ⊛ 92a 43.35 N 144.32 E
Mashūray 120 32.12 N 68.21 E
Masibi 152 11.08 S 22.42 E
Masihi 114 2.47 N 99.40 E
Masīlah, Wādī ∨ 144 15.10 N 51.05 E
Masi-Manimba 152 4.46 S 17.55 E
Masin 164 6.15 S 139.19 E
Masina 272b 22.55 N 88.32 E
Masina 154 1.41 N 31.43 E
Masindi 116 15.32 N 119.57 E
Masinloc 142 31.03 N 31.00 E
Maṣīrah, Khalīj al- C 118 20.10 N 58.15 E
Masisea 248 8.36 S 74.19 W
Masisi 154 1.24 S 28.49 E
Masiwang, Tanjung ➤ 164 3.27 S 130.49 E
Masjed Soleymān 128 31.58 N 49.18 E
Masjid Tanah 114 2.21 N 102.07 E
Mask, Lough ⊛ 48 53.35 N 9.20 W
Maska 150 11.20 N 7.20 E
Maskanah 130 36.01 N 38.05 E
Maskelyne Islands II 175f 16.32 S 167.49 E
Maskharah, Jabal al- ∧ 142 29.44 N 31.34 E
Maskin 128 23.35 N 56.39 E
Maškino 82 54.53 N 36.08 E
Maskinongé □6 206 46.35 N 73.30 W
Maskinongé ≃, Qué., Can. 206 46.10 N 73.01 W
Maskinongé ≃, Qué., Can. 206 45.49 N 74.40 W
Maskinongé, Lac ⊛ 206 46.19 N 73.23 W
Maškoviči 82 54.11 N 36.17 E
Masku 26 60.34 N 22.06 E
Maskun, Ras ➤ 144 11.12 N 43.25 E
Maskūtān 128 26.51 N 59.49 E
Maskwa ≃ 184 50.33 N 96.08 W
Maslʻanino 86 54.20 N 84.13 E
Maslʻanskaja 86 55.56 N 70.08 E
Maslova 265a 59.47 N 30.48 E
Maslovka 78 51.33 N 39.14 E
Maslovo 86 60.13 N 60.10 E
Masnières 50 50.07 N 3.13 E
Masnou 266d 41.29 N 2.19 E
Maso 150 7.14 N 2.53 W
Masoala 157b 15.59 S 50.10 E
Masoala, Cap ➤ 157b 15.59 S 50.13 E
Masoala, Presquʼile ➤1 157b 15.40 S 50.12 E
Masoarivo 157b 19.03 S 44.19 E
Masomeloka 157b 20.17 S 48.37 E
Mason, Mich., U.S. 216 42.35 N 84.26 W
Mason, Ohio, U.S. 218 39.17 N 84.19 W
Mason, Tenn., U.S. 194 35.25 N 89.33 W
Mason, Tex., U.S. 196 30.45 N 99.14 W
Mason, W. Va., U.S. 188 39.01 N 82.01 W
Mason □6, Ill., U.S. 219 40.18 N 90.04 W
Mason □6, Ky., U.S. 218 38.35 N 83.48 W
Mason □6, Wash., U.S. 224 47.20 N 123.09 W
Mason, Lake ⊛ 162 27.39 S 119.34 E
Mason Bay C 172 46.56 S 167.44 E
Mason City, Ill., U.S. 219 40.12 N 89.42 W
Mason City, Iowa, U.S. 190 43.09 N 93.12 W
Mason City, Nebr., U.S. 198 41.13 N 99.18 W
Mason Creek 182 55.40 N 124.29 W
Masone 62 44.30 N 8.42 E
Masonicus Brook ≃ 276 41.06 N 74.09 W
Mason Lake ⊛ 224 47.20 N 122.57 W
Masons Creek ≃ 285 39.59 N 74.51 W
Masontown 188 39.51 N 79.54 W
Mason Valley ∨ 226 39.07 N 119.10 W
Masonville, N.J., U.S. 285 39.59 N 74.52 W
Masonville, N.Y., U.S. 210 42.15 N 75.23 W
Maspalomas 148 27.45 N 15.34 W
Maspeth ✦8 276 40.43 N 73.55 W
Masqaṭ (Muscat) 128 23.37 N 58.35 E
Maṣraʻ 142 27.14 N 31.02 E
Massa 64 44.01 N 10.09 E
Massa-Carrara □4 64 44.15 N 10.03 E
Massachusetts □3 207
Massachusetts ≃ 178 42.15 N 71.50 W
Massachusetts Bay C 207 42.20 N 70.50 W
Massachusetts Institute of Technology ✿2 283 42.21 N 71.06 W
Massaciuccoli, Lago di ⊛ 66 43.50 N 10.20 E
Massacre Lake ⊛ 204 41.39 N 119.35 W
Massa Fermana 66 43.09 N 13.28 E
Massa Fiscaglia 66 44.48 N 12.01 E
Massafra 68 40.35 N 17.07 E
Massaguet 146 12.28 N 15.26 E
Massakory 146 13.00 N 15.44 E
Massa Lombarda 66 44.27 N 11.49 E
Massa Lubrense 68 40.36 N 14.20 E
Massa Marittima 66 43.03 N 10.53 E
Massa Martana 66 42.46 N 12.31 E
Massandra 78 44.32 N 34.12 E
Massangano 152 9.37 S 14.15 E
Massangena 156 21.32 S 32.57 E
Massapê 250 3.31 S 40.19 W
Massapequa 210 40.40 N 73.29 W
Massapequa Park 276 40.40 N 73.28 W
Massapequa State Park ♠ 276 40.42 N 73.27 W
Massapoag Brook ≃ 283 42.09 N 71.09 W
Massapoag Lake ⊛ 283 42.06 N 71.11 W
Massara 156 18.20 S 34.09 E
Massarosa 66 43.52 N 10.20 E
Massasoit State Park ♠ 207 41.53 N 71.01 W
Massaua → Mesewa 144 15.38 N 39.28 E
Massawa → Mesewa 144 15.38 N 39.28 E
Massawippi ≃ 206 45.22 N 71.51 W
Massawippi, Lake ⊛ 206 45.14 N 72.00 W
Massay 50 47.09 N 2.00 E
Massé, Ruisseau ≃ 275a 45.28 N 73.17 W
Massello 62 44.57 N 7.04 E
Massen 52 51.32 N 7.38 E
Massena, Iowa, U.S. 198 41.15 N 94.46 W
Massena, N.Y., U.S. 206 44.56 N 74.53 W
Massenya 146 11.24 N 16.10 E
Masset 182 54.02 N 132.09 W
Masset Inlet C 182 53.42 N 132.20 W
Masseube 32 43.26 N 0.35 E
Massey 190 46.12 N 82.05 W
Massey Creek ≃ 275b 43.42 N 79.20 W
Massiac 32 45.15 N 3.12 E
Massiaru 76 58.00 N 24.35 E
Massico, Monte ∧ 68 41.10 N 13.55 E
Massieville 218 39.16 N 82.58 W
Massif Central → Central, Massif ∧ 32 45.00 N 3.10 E
Massillon 214 40.48 N 81.32 W
Massima 152 1.27 S 11.42 E
Massina 273b 4.08 S 15.19 E
Massinga 156 23.20 S 35.25 E
Massingir 156 23.51 S 32.04 E
Massive, Mount ∧ 200 39.12 N 106.28 W
Masson, Lac ⊛ 206 46.03 N 74.02 W
Masson Island I 9 66.08 S 96.34 E
Massy 261 48.44 N 2.17 E
Mastābah 144 20.49 N 39.20 E
Mastabat ar-Ruwayān ✧2 142 29.06 N 30.08 E
Maštaga 84 40.32 N 50.00 E
Masterson 196 35.38 N 101.58 W
Masterton 172 40.57 S 175.40 E
Mas-Thibert 62 43.34 N 4.44 E
Mastic Point 192 25.03 N 77.57 W
Mastigouche ≃ 206 46.20 N 73.24 W
Mastigouche-Nord ≃ 206 46.24 N 73.25 W
Mastūj 120 36.17 N 72.31 E
Mastūj ≃ 123 35.54 N 71.49 E
Mastung 120 29.48 N 66.51 E
Mastūrah 128 23.06 N 38.50 E
Masu 146 12.10 N 13.19 E
Masua 126 24.16 N 90.46 E
Masuda 96 34.40 N 131.51 E
Masuho 94 35.34 N 138.28 E
Masuie 154 18.05 S 25.45 E
Masuika 152 7.37 S 22.32 E
Masuku 154 17.12 S 27.07 E
Maṣūleh 128 37.10 N 48.59 E
Masulipatam → Machilīpatnam 122 16.10 N 81.08 E
Masura 126 23.16 N 90.24 E
Masurai, Gunung ∧ 112 2.30 S 101.51 E
Masury 214 41.13 N 80.33 W
Masyāf 130 35.03 N 36.21 E
Maszewo, Pol. 30 53.29 N 15.02 E
Maszewo, Pol. 54 52.06 N 14.55 E
Mat ≃ 38 41.39 N 19.34 E
Mata, Indon. 115b 8.12 S 122.56 E
Mata, Zaïre 152 7.53 S 21.58 E
Mata Amarilla 254 49.36 S 71.13 W
Mataba, Mount ∧ 269f 14.42 N 121.10 E
Matabeleland ✧1 156 19.30 S 28.00 E
Matabeleland North □4 154 19.00 S 27.15 E
Matabeleland South □4 154 21.00 S 29.15 E
Matābhānga 124 26.20 N 89.13 E
Matabuena 34 41.10 N 3.40 W
Matachel ≃ 34 38.50 N 6.17 W
Matachewan 190 47.56 N 80.39 W
Matad 88 47.12 N 115.35 E
Mata de Plátano, Quebrada ≃ 286c 10.35 N 66.46 W
Matadero Creek ≃ 282 37.26 N 122.08 W
Mata de São João 255 12.31 S 38.17 W
Matadi 152 5.49 S 13.27 E
Matador 196 34.01 N 100.49 W
Matagalpa 236 12.55 N 85.55 W
Matagalpa □5 236 13.00 N 85.30 W
Matag-ob 116 11.20 N 124.29 E
Matagorda 196 28.41 N 95.58 W
Matagorda □6 222 28.57 N 96.00 W
Matagorda Bay C 196 28.35 N 96.20 W
Matagorda Island I 196 28.15 N 96.30 W
Matagorda Peninsula ➤1 196 28.32 N 96.07 W
Mata Grande 250 9.07 S 37.44 W
Matahiae, Pointe ➤ 174s 17.49 S 149.17 W
Mataiva I1 14 14.53 S 148.40 W
Mataj 86 45.53 N 78.43 E
Matajing 107 29.32 N 104.00 E
Matak, Pulau I 112 3.18 N 106.16 E
Matakana, Austl. 166 33.00 S 145.54 E
Matakana, N.Z. 172 36.21 S 174.43 E
Matakana Island I 172 37.35 S 176.05 E
Matakitaki ≃ 172 41.48 S 172.19 E
Matala 152 14.46 S 15.04 E
Matale 122 7.28 N 80.37 E
Matam 150 15.40 N 13.15 W
Matama 96 33.36 N 131.28 E
Matama, Cerro ∧ 236 9.47 N 83.15 W
Matamata 172 37.49 S 175.47 E
Matameye 150 13.26 N 8.28 E
Matamoros 210 41.22 N 74.42 W
Matamoros 232 25.53 N 97.30 W
Matamoros de la Laguna 232 25.32 N 103.15 W
Matan 112 1.52 S 110.00 E
Matana 154 3.46 S 29.41 E
Matang, Danau ⊛ 112 2.28 S 121.20 E
Matanalem, Cape ➤ 164 2.28 S 149.57 E
Matandu ≃ 154 8.45 S 39.19 E
Matane 186 48.51 N 67.32 W
Matane, Parc de ♠ 186 48.45 N 67.00 W
Matang, Malay. 114 4.49 N 100.41 E
Matang, Zhg. 100 29.17 N 113.05 E
Matang, Zhg. 100 32.20 N 121.04 E
Matangi 172 37.49 S 175.25 E
Matani 84 42.06 N 45.13 E
Matanuska 123 33.48 N 71.34 E
Matanuska ≃ 180 61.30 N 149.15 W
Matanza → San Justo 258 34.40 S 58.33 W
Matanza □5 288 34.46 S 58.37 W
Matanza ≃ 258 34.42 S 58.28 W
Matanza, Aeródromo ⊠ 288 34.44 S 58.30 W
Matanzas, Cuba 240p 23.03 N 81.35 W
Matanzas, Méx. 234 21.37 N 101.38 W
Matanzas □4 240p 22.40 N 81.20 W
Matanzas, Bahía de C 240p 23.04 N 81.30 W
Mata Ortiz 232 30.08 N 108.03 W
Matapa 156 23.11 S 24.39 E
Matapalo, Cabo ➤ 236 8.23 N 83.19 W
Matape ≃ 232 28.17 N 110.41 W
Matapédia 186 47.58 N 66.57 W
Matapédia, Lac ⊛ 186 48.33 N 67.33 W
Matapi ≃ 250 0.03 S 51.12 W
Matapu 172 39.29 S 174.14 E
Mataquito ≃ 252 34.59 S 72.12 W
Matará, Perú 248 7.16 S 78.16 W
Matara, S. Lan. 122 5.56 N 80.33 E
Mataram 115b 8.35 S 116.07 E
Matarani 248 17.00 S 72.06 W
Mataranka 164 14.56 S 133.07 E
Matarca 246 0.30 S 72.38 W
Matārimah, Raʼs ➤ 142 29.27 N 32.42 E
Matarinao Bay C 116 11.14 N 125.34 E
Mataró 34 41.32 N 2.27 E
Matarraña ≃ 34 41.14 N 0.22 E
Matas ≃ 266d 41.30 N 2.16 E
Matasango 286d 12.05 S 76.58 W
Matasiri, Pulau I 112 4.48 S 115.48 E
Mataso I 175f 17.14 S 168.26 E
Mätäsvaara 26 63.26 N 29.36 E
Matata 172 37.53 S 176.45 E
Matatamane Point ➤ 174v 19.07 S 169.51 W
Matatepai, Pointe ➤ 174x 9.43 S 139.02 W
Matatiele 158 30.24 S 28.43 E
Matatindoc Point ➤ 116 9.43 N 122.23 E
Matatula, Cape ➤ 174u 14.15 S 170.34 W
Mataura 172 46.11 S 168.52 E
Mataurá ≃, Bra. 248 5.30 S 60.45 W
Mataura ≃, N.Z. 172 46.34 S 168.43 E
Matautu 175a 13.57 S 171.56 W
Matauvau, Passe ⋃ 174s 17.34 S 149.23 W
Matavai 175a 13.28 S 172.35 W
Matavai, Baie de C 174s 17.30 S 149.30 W
Matavera 174k 21.13 S 159.44 W
Matawai 172 38.21 S 177.32 E
Matawan 208 40.25 N 74.14 W
Matawin ≃ 206 46.54 N 72.56 W
Matāy 142 28.25 N 30.46 E
Matbari 126 22.18 N 89.57 E
Matbūl 142 31.05 N 31.02 E
Matča 85 39.27 N 69.39 E
Matchaponix Brook ≃ 276 40.23 N 74.23 W
Matchi-Manitou, Lac ⊛ 190 48.00 N 77.04 W
Matching 260 51.47 N 0.13 E
Matching Green 260 51.47 N 0.14 E
Matching Tye 260 51.47 N 0.12 E
Mateare 236 12.14 N 86.26 W
Mateba, Île de I 152 5.54 S 12.50 E
Matehuala 234 23.39 N 100.39 W
Mateke Hills ✧2 154 21.48 S 31.00 E
Matelica 66 43.15 N 13.00 E
Matemo, Ilha I 154 12.13 S 40.36 E
Matera 68 40.40 N 16.37 E
Matera □4 68 40.30 N 16.25 E
Materborn 52 51.46 N 6.06 E
Matese, Lago del ⊛ 68 41.25 N 14.25 E
Matese, Monti del ∧ 66 41.27 N 14.22 E
Mátészalka 30 47.57 N 22.19 E
Matete ≃ 273b 4.24 S 15.20 E
Matetsi 154 18.16 S 25.56 E
Mateur 148 37.03 N 9.40 E
Matewan 192 37.37 N 82.10 W
Matfield 207 42.02 N 71.00 W
Matfors 154 18.05 S 25.45 E
Matha 32 45.52 N 0.19 W
Mathematicians Seamount Group ✢3 16 16.00 N 112.00 W
Mather, Man., Can. 184 49.06 N 99.07 W
Mather, Calif., U.S. 226 37.53 N 119.52 W
Mather, Pa., U.S. 188 39.56 N 80.05 W
Mather Air Force Base ■ 226 38.34 N 121.18 W
Mather Gorge ∨ 284c 38.59 N 77.15 W
Matheson 190 48.32 N 80.28 W
Matheson Island 184 51.44 N 96.56 W
Matheu 258 34.22 S 58.50 W
Mathews 208 37.26 N 76.19 W
Mathews □6 208 37.25 N 76.20 W
Mathews, Lake ⊛ 228 33.51 N 117.26 W
Mathi 62 45.15 N 7.32 E
Mathis 196 28.06 N 97.50 W
Mathle 272b 22.35 N 88.14 E
Mathry 42 51.57 N 5.05 W
Mathura, Bhārat 122 10.57 N 78.27 E
Mathura, Bhārat 124 27.30 N 77.41 E
Mathura □5 124 27.35 N 77.35 E
Mathura Bil ⊛ 272b 22.56 N 88.31 E
Mathurai → Madurai 122 9.56 N 78.07 E
Mathurāpur, Bngl. 126 24.02 N 88.47 E
Mathurāpur, Bngl. 126 23.17 N 89.15 E
Mati 116 6.57 N 126.13 E
Matiakhola 126 23.16 N 86.56 E
Matiakoali 150 12.22 N 1.02 E
Matiāli 124 26.56 N 88.49 E
Matiāri 126 23.48 N 88.27 E
Matias Barbosa 256 21.53 S 43.20 W
Matias Romero 234 16.53 N 95.02 W
Matibhānga 126 23.29 N 89.56 E
Maticora ≃ 246 11.03 N 71.09 W
Matiere 172 38.35 S 175.06 E
Matignon 32 48.36 N 2.18 W
Matiguás 236 12.50 N 85.28 W
Matillas, Laguna ⊛ 234 18.02 N 92.42 W
Matinecock 276 40.53 N 73.38 W
Matinenda Lake ⊛ 190 46.22 N 82.57 W
Matinha 250 3.06 S 45.02 W
Matinicock Point ➤ 276 40.54 N 73.38 W
Matinicus Island I 188 43.54 N 68.55 W
Matino 68 40.02 N 18.08 E
Matipó 255 20.17 S 42.21 W
Matipó ≃ 255 19.53 S 42.33 W
Matīr Ṭāris 142 29.22 N 30.54 E
Matiyure ≃ 246 7.36 N 67.39 W
Mātla ≃1 126 22.04 N 88.38 E
Matlab Bāzār 126 23.20 N 90.43 E
Matlacha 220 26.37 N 81.53 W
Matlacha Pass ⋃ 220 26.37 N 82.04 W
Matlamanyane 156 19.33 S 25.57 E
Matlapa 234 21.15 N 98.50 W
Matlevo 76 54.54 N 35.39 E
Mātli 120 25.02 N 68.39 E
Matlock, Eng., U.K. 44 53.08 N 1.32 W
Matlock, Wash., U.S. 224 47.14 N 123.25 W
Matmata 148 33.33 N 9.58 E
Matnog 116 12.35 N 124.05 E
Mato 154 8.01 S 24.55 E
Mato ≃ 246 7.09 N 65.07 W
Mato, Cerro ∧ 246 7.15 N 65.14 W
Matoaca 208 37.14 N 77.29 W
Matobe 112 2.42 S 100.11 E
Matočkin Šar 72 73.16 N 56.27 E
Matočkin Šar, Proliv ⋃ 72 73.20 N 55.21 E
Mato do Gado 256 23.42 S 47.07 W
Mato Grosso 248 15.00 S 59.57 W
Mato Grosso □3 248 12.00 S 57.00 W
Mato Grosso, Planalto do ✧1 242 15.30 S 56.00 W
Mato Grosso do Sul □3 248 20.00 S 56.00 W
Matola 156 25.59 S 32.29 E
Matola-Rio 156 25.58 S 32.26 E
Matombo 154 7.03 S 37.46 E
Mato Mole, Serra do ✧2 256 23.00 S 46.12 W
Matong 164 5.35 S 151.45 E
Matonipi ≃ 186 51.21 N 69.45 W
Matope 154 15.20 S 34.59 E
Matopo Hills ✧2 154 20.36 S 28.28 E
Matopos 154 20.24 S 28.28 E
Matopos National Park ♠ 154 20.33 S 28.20 E
Matos ≃ 248 14.07 S 65.25 W
Matosinhos 34 41.11 N 8.42 W
Matoso, Ponta do ➤ 287a 22.50 S 43.11 W
Matou, Tʼaiwan 100 23.11 N 120.16 E
Matou, Zhg. 98 36.29 N 114.26 E
Matou, Zhg. 100 29.49 N 115.35 E
Matou, Zhg. 100 25.14 N 118.22 E
Matou, Zhg. 105 39.18 N 116.45 E
Matou, Zhg. 105 39.46 N 116.49 E
Matouji 98 35.02 N 115.07 E
Matour 58 46.18 N 4.29 E
Matoury 250 4.51 N 52.20 W
Matouxi 107 30.15 N 106.31 E
Matouying 98 39.18 N 118.47 E
Matouzhen, Zhg. 98 34.39 N 118.18 E
Matouzhen, Zhg. 100 33.32 N 116.56 E
Matouzhen, Zhg. 100 30.48 N 118.29 E
Matouzhen, Zhg. 105 39.33 N 116.07 E
Mato Verde 255 15.23 S 42.52 W
Matozinhos 255 19.35 S 44.07 W
Mātra ✧ 30 47.55 N 20.00 E
Maṭraḥ 128 23.38 N 58.34 E
Mattraville 274a 33.54 S 151.18 E
Matrei am Brenner 64 47.08 N 11.27 E
Matrei in Osttirol 64 47.00 N 12.32 E
Matru 150 7.36 N 12.11 W
Maṭrūḥ 140 31.21 N 27.14 E
Matsap 158 28.38 S 22.47 E
Matsapa 158 26.29 S 31.23 E
Matsari 152 5.21 N 12.14 E
Matsena 150 13.05 N 10.05 E
Matsiatra ≃ 157b 21.25 S 45.33 E
Matsieng 158 29.36 S 27.32 E
Matsknutsgårdarna 40 60.28 N 15.22 E
Matsqui 224 49.12 N 122.25 W
Matsu → Matsu Shan I 100 26.09 N 119.56 E
Matsubara 96 34.34 N 135.33 E
Matsubushi 268 35.55 N 139.49 E
Matsuda 94 35.21 N 139.09 E
Matsudai 94 37.08 N 138.37 E
Matsudaira 94 35.03 N 137.13 E
Matsudo 94 35.47 N 139.54 E
Matsudo Race Track ♠ 268 35.48 N 139.55 E
Matsue 96 35.28 N 133.04 E
Matsugasaki 268 35.53 N 139.58 E
Matsuida 94 36.19 N 138.48 E
Matsukawa, Nihon 94 36.25 N 137.51 E
Matsukawa, Nihon 94 35.36 N 137.55 E
Matsumae 92a 41.26 N 140.07 E
Matsumoto 94 36.14 N 137.58 E
Matsuno 96 33.13 N 132.42 E
Matsunoyama 94 37.05 N 138.37 E
Matsuo 94 35.38 N 140.28 E
Matsuōji 268 35.08 N 140.01 E
Matsuoka 94 36.05 N 136.18 E
Matsuo-san ∧2 270 34.38 N 135.44 E
Matsusaka 94 34.34 N 136.32 E
Matsu Shan I 100 26.09 N 119.56 E
Matsushima 92 38.22 N 141.04 E
Matsutō 94 36.31 N 136.34 E
Matsuura 96 33.20 N 129.42 E
Matsuyama 96 33.50 N 132.45 E
Matsuzaka 94 34.34 N 136.32 E
Matsuzaki 94 34.45 N 138.47 E
Matta ≃ 208 38.07 N 77.26 W
Mattagami ≃ 176 50.43 N 81.29 W
Mattagami Heights 190 48.29 N 81.22 W
Mattagami Lake ⊛ 190 47.54 N 81.35 W
Mattamuskeet, Lake ⊛ 192 35.30 N 76.11 W
Mattāncheri 122 9.59 N 76.16 E
Mattapan ✦8 283 42.16 N 71.06 W
Mattapoisett 207 41.40 N 70.49 W
Mattaponi 208 37.32 N 76.47 W
Mattaponi ≃ 208 37.31 N 76.47 W
Mattarana 62 44.15 N 9.37 E
Mattarello 64 46.00 N 11.07 E
Mattawa, Ont., Can. 190 46.19 N 78.42 W
Mattawa, Wash., U.S. 202 46.44 N 119.54 W
Mattawa ≃ 190 46.19 N 78.43 W
Mattawamkeag 188 45.31 N 68.21 W
Mattawamkeag ≃ 188 45.30 N 68.24 W
Mattawan 216 42.12 N 85.47 W
Mattawoman Creek ≃ 208 38.34 N 77.12 W
Matterhorn ∧, Eur. 58 45.59 N 7.43 E
Matterhorn ∧, Nev., U.S. 204 41.49 N 115.23 W
Mattersburg 61 47.44 N 16.25 E
Mattertal ∨ 58 46.10 N 7.49 E
Matteson 216 41.30 N 87.40 W
Matteson Lake ⊛ 216 41.56 N 85.12 W
Matthew Flinders Memorial ✧ 169 38.19 S 145.04 E
Matthews 216 40.23 N 85.30 W
Matthews Mountain ∧ 194 37.29 N 90.21 W
Matthews Ridge 246 7.30 N 60.10 W
Matthew Town 238 20.57 N 73.40 W
Matthiessen State Park ♠ 216 41.17 N 89.01 W
Maṭṭī, Sabkhat ⊛ 128 23.51 N 52.00 E
Mattie, Lake ⊛ 220 28.08 N 81.46 W
Mattig ≃ 60 48.10 N 13.07 E
Mattighofen 60 48.06 N 13.09 E
Mattinata 68 41.42 N 16.03 E
Mattituck 207 40.59 N 72.32 W
Mattole ≃ 204 40.18 N 124.21 W
Mattoon, Ill., U.S. 194 39.29 N 88.22 W
Mattoon, Wis., U.S. 190 45.01 N 89.02 W
Mattox Creek ≃ 208 38.12 N 76.58 W
Mattox Draw ∨ 198 38.03 N 101.11 W
Mattsee 64 47.58 N 13.06 E
Mattydale 210 43.06 N 76.09 W
Matu 112 2.41 N 111.32 E
Matua 112 2.59 S 110.45 E
Matuba 156 24.27 S 32.55 E
Matucana 248 11.51 S 76.24 W
Matudo → Matsudo 94 35.47 N 139.54 E
Matue → Matsue 96 35.28 N 133.04 E
Matuku I 175g 19.10 S 179.46 E
Matumoto → Matsumoto 94 36.14 N 137.58 E
Matungo ≃ 152 16.25 S 21.27 E
Matunuck 207 41.23 N 71.32 W
Matura Bay C 241r 10.38 N 61.01 W
Maturín 246 9.45 N 63.11 W
Maturino 76 59.06 N 37.55 E
Matusevich Glacier ⊼ 9 69.11 S 157.20 E
Matusov 78 49.03 N 31.34 E
Matutina 255 19.13 S 45.58 W
Matuto 154 14.46 S 35.59 E
Matutum, Mount ∧ 116 6.22 N 125.05 E
Matuzaka → Matsuzaka 94 34.34 N 136.32 E
Matvejevka 80 53.32 N 53.29 E
Matvejev-Kurgan 83 47.35 N 38.52 E
Matvejevo, S.S.S.R. 76 58.38 N 43.30 E
Matvejevo, S.S.S.R. 86 57.47 N 57.51 E
Mâtyásföld ✦8 264c 47.31 N 19.13 E
Mátyás-Templom ✿1 264c 47.30 N 19.02 E
Matyra ≃ 76 52.38 N 39.38 E
Matyševo 80 50.49 N 44.12 E
Mau 124 25.17 N 81.23 E
Mau (Ireng) ≃ 246 3.33 N 59.51 W
Mauá, Bra. 256 23.40 S 46.27 W
Maúa, Moç. 154 13.51 S 37.10 E
Mauá □7 287b 23.40 S 46.27 W
Mau Aimma 124 25.42 N 81.55 E
Mauban 116 14.12 N 121.44 E
Maubara 112 8.37 S 125.12 E
Maubeuge 50 50.17 N 3.58 E
Ma-ubin 110 16.44 N 95.39 E
Mauchamps 261 48.32 N 2.12 E
Mauchline 46 55.31 N 4.24 W
Maud, Scot., U.K. 46 57.31 N 2.06 W
Maud, Mo., U.S. 219 39.37 N 92.15 W
Maud, Ohio, U.S. 218 39.21 N 84.23 W
Maud, Okla., U.S. 196 35.08 N 96.46 W
Maud, Tex., U.S. 194 33.20 N 94.21 W
Maud, Point ➤ 162 23.06 S 113.45 E
Maudaha 124 25.41 N 80.07 E
Maude 166 34.28 S 144.18 E
Maudétour-en-Vexin 261 49.06 N 1.47 E
Mau-é-ele 156 24.21 S 34.07 E
Mauensee 58 47.10 N 8.04 E
Mauer ✦8 264b 48.09 N 16.16 E
Mauerbach 264b 48.15 N 16.10 E
Mauerbach ≃ 264b 48.12 N 16.14 E
Mauerkirchen 60 48.11 N 13.08 E
Mauès 250 3.24 S 57.42 W
Mau Escarpment ✧4 154 0.40 S 36.02 E
Maug ≃ 116 8.20 N 125.53 E
Mauganj 124 24.41 N 81.53 E
Mauga Silisili ∧ 175a 13.35 S 172.27 W
Mauger, Île I 186 51.05 N 58.45 W
Maug Islands II 108 20.01 N 145.13 E
Mauguio 62 43.37 N 4.01 E
Mauguio, Étang de C 62 43.35 N 4.02 E
Maui □6 229a 20.53 N 156.30 W
Maui I 229a 20.45 N 156.15 W
Mauk 115a 6.04 S 106.30 E
Mauke I 14 20.09 S 157.23 W
Maulbach 56 50.43 N 9.04 E
Maulbronn 56 49.00 N 8.49 E
Maulde 50 50.30 N 3.26 E
Mauldin 192 34.47 N 82.19 W
Mauldre ≃ 261 48.58 N 1.49 E
Maule 50 48.55 N 1.51 E
Maule □4 252 35.19 S 72.25 W
Maule ≃ 252 35.30 S 71.30 W
Maule, Laguna del ⊛ 252 36.04 S 70.30 W
Mauléon 32 46.56 N 0.45 W
Maulette 261 48.48 N 1.37 E
Maullin 254 41.38 S 73.37 W
Maulvi Bāzār 120 24.29 N 91.47 E
Maumee 214 41.34 N 83.39 W
Maumee ≃ 216 41.42 N 83.28 W
Maumee Bay C 216 41.43 N 83.26 W
Maumelle, Lake ⊛1 194 34.55 N 92.40 W
Maumere 115b 8.37 S 122.14 E
Maun 156 20.00 S 23.25 E
Maunabo 240m 18.01 N 65.54 W
Mauna Kea ∧1 229d 19.50 N 155.28 W
Maunaloa 229a 21.08 N 157.13 W
Mauna Loa ∧1 229d 19.29 N 155.36 W
Maunalua Bay C 229c 21.17 N 157.44 W
Maunath Bhanjan 124 25.57 N 83.33 E
Maunatlala 156 22.32 S 27.28 E
Maunesha ≃ 216 43.13 N 88.57 W
Maunga Roa ∧ 174k 21.13 S 159.48 W
Maungatapere 172 35.45 S 174.12 E
Maungaturoto 172 36.06 S 174.22 E
Maungdaw 110 20.50 N 92.21 E
Maungmagan 110 14.09 N 98.06 E
Maungu 154 3.33 S 38.45 E
Maunoir, Lac ⊛ 180 67.30 N 125.00 W
Maupin 224 45.11 N 121.05 W
Maur 123 30.05 N 75.15 E
Mau Rānīpur 124 25.15 N 79.08 E
Maurecourt 261 49.00 N 2.04 E
Maure-de-Bretagne 32 47.54 N 1.59 W
Mauregard 261 49.02 N 2.35 E
Maurentanien → Mauritania □1 134 20.00 N 12.00 W
Maurepas, Lake ⊛ 194 30.15 N 90.30 W
Maures ✧ 62 43.16 N 6.23 E
Mauriac 248 17.18 S 68.41 W
Mauria, Passo della)(64 46.27 N 12.31 E
Mauriac 32 45.13 N 2.20 E
Maurice (Île) → Mauritius □2 157c 20.17 S 57.33 E
Maurice ≃ 208 39.13 N 75.02 W
Maurice, Lake ⊛ 162 29.28 S 130.58 E
Maurice K. Goddard State Park ♠ 214 41.23 N 81.10 W
Mauricetown 208 39.17 N 74.58 W
Mauriceville 172 40.47 S 175.42 E
Mauricio → Mauritius □2 157c 20.17 S 57.33 E
Maurienne ∨ 62 45.13 N 6.30 E
Mauritania □1 134 20.00 N 12.00 W
Mauritanie → Mauritania □1 134 20.00 N 12.00 W
Mauriti 250 7.23 S 38.46 W
Mauritius □1 138
Mauritius I 157c 20.17 S 57.33 E
Mauritius □2 157c 20.17 S 57.33 E
Mauron 32 48.05 N 2.18 W
Maurs 32 44.43 N 2.11 E
Maurui 154 5.07 S 38.23 E
Maury ≃ 188 37.50 N 79.25 W
Maury Channel ⋃ 176 75.44 N 94.40 W
Maury Island ➤1 224 47.20 N 122.24 W
Maussane 62 43.43 N 4.48 E
Mauston 190 43.48 N 90.05 W
Mautalade 126 22.25 N 89.05 E
Mautau, Pointe ➤ 174x 9.42 S 138.58 W
Mautern 61 47.24 N 14.50 E
Mauterndorf 64 47.08 N 13.40 E
Mauth 60 48.53 N 13.35 E
Mauthausen 61 48.14 N 14.32 E
Mauthen 64 46.40 N 13.00 E
Mauvais Coulee ∨ 198 48.21 N 99.06 W
Mauvaise Terre Creek ≃ 219 39.43 N 90.38 W
Mauvaise Terre Lake ⊛1 219 39.42 N 90.12 W
Mauvezin 32 43.44 N 0.55 E
Mauzé-sur-le-Mignon 32 46.12 N 0.40 W
Mava 164 6.50 S 141.25 E
Mavá ≃ 246 0.44 N 69.30 W
Mavaca ≃ 246 2.31 N 65.11 W
Mavanza 156 22.43 S 35.08 E
Māvelikara 122 9.16 N 76.33 E
Mavinga 152 15.50 S 20.21 E
Mavita 156 19.33 S 33.10 E
Mavonde 156 18.32 S 33.02 E
Mavrovoúni ∧, Ellás 267c 37.55 N 23.30 E
Mavrovoúni ∧, Ellás 267c 37.54 N 23.48 E
Mavuradona Mountains ✧ 154 16.30 S 31.20 E
Mawa 154 2.43 N 26.42 E
Mawai 114 1.52 N 103.57 E
Mawan 98 37.24 N 118.14 E
Mawāna 124 29.06 N 77.55 E
Mawangkanlishan ∧ 120 34.19 N 80.03 E
Mawangtang 106 30.43 N 120.41 E
Ma Wan Island I 271d 22.21 N 114.03 E
Mawasangka 112 5.17 S 122.18 E
Mawchi 110 18.49 N 97.09 E
Maw-daung Pass)(110 11.47 N 99.39 E
Mawdesley 262 53.38 N 2.46 W
Mawdesley Lake ⊛ 184 54.01 N 100.39 W
Maweigang 100 29.21 N 116.45 E
Mawgan 42 50.06 N 5.06 W
Mawi 272a 28.39 N 77.25 E
Mawiwi 154 3.06 N 27.40 E
Māwiyah 144 13.35 N 44.21 E
Mawjib, Wādī al- ∨ 132 31.28 N 35.34 E
Mawkhi 110 16.17 N 98.53 E
Mawlaik 110 23.38 N 94.24 E
Mawlamyaing → Moulmein 110 16.30 N 97.38 E
Mawr, Wādī ∨ 144 15.41 N 42.42 E
Mawshij 144 13.43 N 43.17 E
Mawson Escarpment ✧4 9 73.05 S 68.10 E
Mawson Peninsula ➤1 9 68.35 S 154.11 E
Maw Taung ∧ 110 11.39 N 99.35 E
Mawuba 102 29.50 N 108.11 E
Max 198 47.49 N 101.18 W
Maxaranguape 250 5.31 S 35.16 W
Maxatawny 208 40.33 N 75.41 W
Maxcanú 232 20.35 N 89.59 W
Maxéville 58 48.43 N 6.10 E
Maxglan, Flughafen ⊠ 64 47.48 N 13.02 E
Maxhütte Haidhof 60 49.12 N 12.05 E
Maxiang 100 24.41 N 118.15 E
Maximo 214 40.53 N 81.11 W
Maximo Paz 258 34.56 S 58.37 W
Maxinkuckee, Lake ⊛ 216 41.12 N 86.24 W
Maxixe 156 23.51 S 35.21 E
Maxon Creek ≃ 196 29.53 N 102.24 W
Maxton 192 34.44 N 79.21 W
Maxville 206 45.17 N 74.51 W
Maxwell, Calif., U.S. 226 39.17 N 122.11 W
Maxwell, Ind., U.S. 218 39.51 N 85.46 W
Maxwell, Iowa, U.S. 190 41.53 N 93.24 W
Maxwell, Nebr., U.S. 198 41.05 N 100.31 W
Maxwell, N. Mex., U.S. 196 36.32 N 104.33 W
Maxwell, Tex., U.S. 222 29.53 N 97.48 W
Maxwell Air Force Base ■ 194 32.23 N 86.21 W
Maxwell Bay C 176 74.35 N 89.00 W
Maxwelltown 44 55.04 N 3.38 W
May 196 31.59 N 98.55 W
May ≃, Atlan., Can. 182 55.43 N 111.22 W
May ≃, Pap. N. Gui. 164 4.35 S 141.35 E
May, Cape ➤ 208 38.58 N 74.55 W
May, Isle of I 46 56.11 N 2.34 W
May, Mount ∧ 182 54.02 N 119.58 W
Maya, Pulau I 112 1.10 S 109.35 E
Mayaguana I 238 22.23 N 72.57 W
Mayaguana Passage ⋃ 238 22.32 N 73.15 W
Mayagüez 240m 18.12 N 67.09 W
Mayagüez, Aeropuerto ⊠ 240m 18.15 N 67.09 W
Mayagüez, Bahía de C 240m 18.12 N 67.10 W
Mayahi 150 13.58 N 7.40 E
Mayajigua 240p 22.14 N 79.04 W
Mayaka 152 5.17 S 16.52 E
Mayala 273b 4.21 S 15.09 E
Mayales, Punta ➤ 236 11.52 N 85.26 W
Mayama 152 3.51 S 14.54 E
Mayamba 152 4.46 S 16.52 E
Mayamey 128 36.24 N 55.42 E
Maya Mountains ∧ 232 16.40 N 88.50 W
Mayang (Gaocun) 102 27.41 N 109.35 E
Mayantoc 116 15.37 N 120.23 E
Mayao 106 30.50 N 120.23 E
Mayapan ⊥ 232 20.38 N 89.27 W
Mayapur 272b 22.27 N 88.08 E
Mayari 240p 20.40 N 75.41 W
Mayari Arriba 240p 20.25 N 75.32 W
Mayaro Bay C 241r 10.15 N 60.58 W
Maya-san ∧ 96 34.44 N 135.12 E
May Ayini 144 14.46 N 39.10 E
Maybee 216 42.00 N 83.31 W
Mayberry 192 37.22 N 81.22 W
Maybole 44 55.21 N 4.41 W
Maybrook 210 41.29 N 74.13 W
Maychew 144 13.02 N 39.34 E
Maydelle 222 31.48 N 95.18 W
Maydena 166 42.55 S 146.30 E
Maydī 144 16.20 N 42.46 E
Maydolong 116 11.30 N 125.30 E
Maydūm 142 29.22 N 31.10 E
Mayen 56 50.19 N 7.13 E
Mayence → Mainz 56 50.01 N 8.16 E
Mayenne 32 48.18 N 0.37 W
Mayenne □5 32 48.05 N 0.40 W
Mayenne ≃ 32 47.30 N 0.33 W
Mayer 200 34.24 N 112.14 W
Mayerling 61 48.03 N 16.06 E
Mayersville 194 32.54 N 91.03 W
Mayerthorpe 182 53.57 N 115.08 W
Mayet 50 47.46 N 0.17 E
Mayfair ✦8, S. Afr. 273d 26.12 S 28.01 E
Mayfair ✦8, Pa., U.S. 285 40.02 N 75.03 W
Mayfield 172 43.49 S 171.25 E
Mayfield, Eng., U.K. 42 53.01 N 1.45 W
Mayfield, Ind., U.S. 218 40.11 N 85.21 W
Mayfield, Ky., U.S. 194 36.44 N 88.38 W
Mayfield, N.Y., U.S. 210 43.06 N 74.16 W
Mayfield, Ohio, U.S. 279a 41.33 N 81.26 W
Mayfield, Utah, U.S. 200 39.07 N 111.42 W
Mayfield Creek ≃ 194 36.57 N 89.05 W
Mayfield Dam ✦6 224 46.30 N 122.35 W
Mayfield Heights 214 41.31 N 81.27 W
Mayfield Lake ⊛1 224 46.31 N 122.32 W
Mayford 260 51.18 N 0.34 W
May Inlet C 176 76.15 N 100.45 W
Māyir 130 36.23 N 37.02 E
May Jirgui 150 13.44 N 8.08 E
Maykop → Majkop 84 44.35 N 40.07 E
Maymont 184 52.33 N 107.40 W
Maymūn, Wādī ∨ 146 30.10 N 10.27 E
Maymyo 110 22.02 N 96.28 E
Mayna 126 22.14 N 87.47 E
Maynāmati 126 23.29 N 91.07 E
Maynard, Iowa, U.S. 190 42.46 N 91.53 W
Maynard, Mass., U.S. 207 42.30 N 71.33 W
Maynard, Ohio, U.S. 214 40.07 N 80.53 W
Maynardville 192 36.15 N 83.48 W

≃ River | Fluss | Río | Rivière | Rio
≃ Canal | Kanal | Canal | Canal | Canal
⋎ Waterfall, Rapids | Wasserfall, Stromschnellen | Cascada, Rápidos | Chute d'eau, Rapides | Cascata, Rápidos
⋃ Strait | Meeresstrasse | Estrecho | Détroit | Estreito
C Bay, Gulf | Bucht, Golf | Bahía, Golfo | Baie, Golfe | Baía, Golfo
⊛ Lake, Lakes | See, Seen | Lago, Lagos | Lac, Lacs | Lago, Lagos
≣ Swamp | Sumpf | Pantano | Marais | Pântano
⊼ Ice Features, Glacier | Eis- und Gletscherformen | Accidentes Glaciales | Formes glaciaires | Acidentes Glaciares
✢ Other Hydrographic Features | Andere Hydrographische Objekte | Otros Elementos Hidrográficos | Autres données hydrographiques | Outros Elementos Hidrográficos

✢ Submarine Features | Untermeerische Objekte | Accidentes Submarinos | Formes de relief sous-marin | Acidentes Submarinos
□ Political Unit | Politische Einheit | Unidad Política | Entité politique | Unidade Política
✿ Cultural Institution | Kulturelle Institution | Institución Cultural | Institution culturelle | Instituição Cultural
⊥ Historical Site | Historische Stätte | Sitio Histórico | Site historique | Sitio Histórico
♠ Recreational Site | Erholungs- und Ferienort | Sitio de Recreo | Centre de loisirs | Sitio de Lazer
⊠ Airport | Flughafen | Aeropuerto | Aéroport | Aeroporto
■ Military Installation | Militäranlage | Instalación Militar | Installation militaire | Instalação Militar
✦ Miscellaneous | Verschiedenes | Misceláneo | Divers | Miscelânea

Mayne 224 48.51 N 123.18 W
Mayne ≃ 166 23.34 S 141.18 E
May Nefalis 144 14.57 N 38.23 E
Mayne Island I 224 48.51 N 123.17 W
Maynooth 48 53.23 N 6.35 W
Mayo, Yukon, Can. 180 63.35 N 135.54 W
Mayo, Tchad 146 9.07 N 18.11 E
Mayo, Fla., U.S. 192 30.03 N 83.10 W
Mayo, Md., U.S. 208 38.53 N 76.31 W
Mayo □[6] 48 53.50 N 9.30 W
Mayo ≃, Arg. 254 45.46 S 69.43 W
Mayo ≃, Col. 246 1.40 N 77.21 W
Mayo ≃, Méx. 232 26.45 N 109.47 W
Mayo ≃, Perú 248 6.37 S 76.16 W
Mayoba 154 17.13 S 26.16 E
Mayo Bay C 116 6.56 N 126.22 E
Mayodan 192 36.25 N 79.58 W
Mayo-Kebbi □[5] 146 10.00 N 15.30 E
Mayoko, Congo 152 2.18 S 12.49 E
Mayoko, Zaïre 152 1.05 S 23.49 E
Mayola ≃ 44 54.45 N 6.31 W
Mayo Lake @ 180 63.46 N 135.10 W
Mayo Ndaga 146 6.54 N 11.25 E
Mayon Volcano ∧[1] 116 13.15 N 123.41 E
Mayor Buratovich 252 39.15 S 62.37 W
Mayor Island I 172 37.18 S 176.16 E
Mayor Pablo Lagerenza 248 19.58 S 60.45 W
Mayotte □[2] 138
 157a 12.50 S 45.10 E
Mayotte I 157a 12.50 S 45.10 E
Mayoyao 116 16.59 N 121.14 E
Maypearl 222 32.19 N 97.01 W
May Pen 241q 17.58 N 77.14 W
Mayraira Point ≻ 116 18.39 N 120.51 E
Mayrán, Laguna de ≡ 196 25.45 N 102.45 W
Mayres 62 44.40 N 4.07 E
Mayrhofen 64 47.10 N 11.52 E
Mays 218 39.45 N 85.26 W
Maysah, Tall al- ∧ 132 31.08 N 35.40 E
Maysfield 222 30.54 N 96.51 W
Mays Landing 208 39.27 N 74.44 W
Mays Lick 218 38.31 N 83.50 W
Maysville, Ky., U.S. 218 38.39 N 83.46 W
Maysville, Mo., U.S. 194 39.48 N 94.35 W
Maysville, N.C., U.S. 192 34.59 N 77.14 W
Maysville, Okla., U.S. 196 34.49 N 97.24 W
Maythalūn 132 32.21 N 35.16 E
Maytiguid Island I 116 11.03 N 119.36 E
Maytown 208 40.04 N 76.35 W
Mayu 100 27.48 N 120.26 E
Mayumba 152 3.25 S 10.39 E
Mayūrākshi Dam ⬩[6] 126 24.03 N 86.29 E
Māyūram 122 11.06 N 79.40 E
Mayūrbhanj □[5] 126 21.50 N 86.30 E
Mayville, Mich., U.S. 190 43.20 N 83.21 W
Mayville, N. Dak., U.S. 198 47.30 N 97.19 W
Mayville, N.Y., U.S. 214 42.15 N 79.30 W
Mayville, Wis., U.S. 190 43.30 N 88.33 W
Maywood, Calif., U.S. 280 33.59 N 118.11 W
Maywood, Ill., U.S. 216 41.53 N 87.51 W
Maywood, Mo., U.S. 219 39.57 N 91.36 W
Maywood, Nebr., U.S. 198 40.39 N 100.37 W
Maywood, N.J., U.S. 276 40.56 N 74.04 W
Maywood, N.Y., U.S. 210 42.42 N 73.52 W
Maywood Race Track ♣ 278 41.44 N 87.50 W
Maza, Arg. 252 36.50 S 63.19 W
Maza, S.S.S.R. 80 57.14 N 44.13 E
Mazabuka 154 15.51 S 27.46 E
Mazagan → El-Jadida 148 33.16 N 8.30 W
Mazagão 250 0.07 S 51.17 W
Mazagaon ⬩[8] 272c 18.57 N 72.50 E
Mazagão Velho 250 0.13 S 51.25 W
Ma'zah, Jabal ∧ 130 35.51 N 40.38 E
Mazamet 32 43.30 N 2.24 E
Mazamitla 234 19.55 N 103.02 W
Mazamitote, Arroyo de ≃ 232 24.51 N 103.12 W
Mazán ≃ 246 3.28 S 73.11 W
Māzandarān □[4] 128 36.30 N 53.30 E
Mazanovo 89 51.40 N 128.52 E
Mazār, Jabal ∧ 132 33.34 N 36.03 E
Mazar, Oued ∨ 148 31.50 N 1.36 E
Mazara, Val di ⬩[1] 70 37.50 N 13.00 E
Mazara del Vallo 70 37.39 N 12.35 E
Mazār-e Sharīf 120 36.42 N 67.06 E
Mazargues 62 43.15 N 5.24 E
Mazaro ≃ 70 37.39 N 12.35 E
Mazarredo 254 47.05 S 66.42 W
Mazarrón 34 37.36 N 1.19 W
Mazarrón, Golfo de C 34 37.30 N 1.18 W
Mazarsu 85 41.56 N 72.40 E
Mazaruni ≃ 246 6.25 N 58.38 W
Mazaruni-Potaro □[5] 246 6.00 N 60.00 W
Mazatenango 236 14.32 N 91.30 W
Mazatlán 234 23.13 N 106.25 W
Mazatlán de Flores 234 18.02 N 96.54 W
Mazatzal Mountains ∧∧ 200 34.00 N 111.55 W
Mazatzal Peak ∧ 200 34.03 N 111.28 W
Maze 94 35.52 N 137.10 E
Mažeikiai 76 56.19 N 22.20 E
Mazenod 184 49.53 N 106.14 W
Mazeppa, Minn., U.S. 190 44.17 N 92.32 W
Mazeppa, Pa., U.S. 210 40.59 N 76.59 W
Mazha 100 23.27 N 114.00 E
Māzhān, Īrān 128 32.35 N 59.01 E
Mazhan, Zhg. 98 36.04 N 118.45 E
Mazhangfang 104 42.23 N 122.26 E
Mazhuang, Zhg. 98 37.47 N 115.17 E
Mazhuang, Zhg. 100 32.54 N 114.03 E
Mazhuang, Zhg. 105 39.11 N 116.15 E
Mazhūr, Khubb al- •[8] 128 27.45 N 43.55 E
Mazigou 105 40.28 N 114.48 E
Mazilovo ⬩[8] 265b 55.44 N 37.26 E
Mazīnān 128 36.18 N 56.46 E
Mazinaw Lake @ 212 44.55 N 77.12 W
Mazirbe 76 57.41 N 22.21 E
Mazoco 154 11.40 S 35.48 E
Mazoe ≃ 154 16.32 S 33.25 E
Mazomanie 190 43.11 N 89.48 W
Mazomba ≃ 256 22.53 S 43.45 W
Mazon 216 41.14 N 88.25 W
Mazon ≃ 216 41.21 N 88.25 W
Mazon, East Fork ≃ 216 41.11 N 88.18 W
Mazon, West Fork ≃ 216 41.15 N 88.21 W
Mazongshan ∧ 102 41.27 N 97.00 E
Mazorra ⬩[8] 286b 23.01 N 82.24 W
Mazou ≃ 50 47.15 N 2.59 E
Mazoul Ŧ[4] 148 28.20 N 7.50 E
Mazoula 148 28.20 N 7.50 E
Mazowsze ⬩[1] 30 52.30 N 20.40 E
Mazra'at-Bayt Jinn 132 33.19 N 35.55 E
Mazsalaca 76 57.52 N 25.03 E
Mazul'skij 86 56.16 N 90.28 E
Mazunga 154 21.45 S 29.52 E
Mazury ⬩[1] 30 53.45 N 21.00 E
Mazzarino 70 37.18 N 14.13 E
Mazzarrà Sant'andrea 70 38.05 N 15.08 E
Mazzin 64 46.27 N 11.42 E
Mba 175g 17.33 S 177.41 E
Mba ≃ 175g 17.29 S 177.40 E
Mbabala Island I 154 11.18 S 29.44 E
Mbabane 158 26.18 S 31.06 E
Mbabo, Tchabal ∧ 152 7.16 N 12.09 E
Mbacké 150 14.48 N 15.55 W
Mbaéré ≃ 152 3.47 N 17.31 E
Mbage 140 5.30 N 25.13 E
Mbahiakro 150 7.27 N 4.20 W
Mbaïki 152 3.53 N 18.00 E
Mbakana, Montagne de ∧ 152 7.58 N 15.06 E
Mbakaou, Barrage de ⬩[5] 152 6.25 N 12.55 E
Mbala, Centraf. 152 7.48 N 20.51 E
Mbala (Abercorn), Zam. 154 8.50 S 31.22 E
Mbalam 152 2.13 N 13.49 E
Mbale 154 1.05 N 34.10 E
Mbali 152 2.50 S 16.12 E
Mbali, Kaga ∧∧ 152 7.14 N 21.30 E
Mbali Lim ≃ 152 4.26 N 18.20 E
Mbalizi 154 8.56 S 33.22 E
Mbalmayo 152 3.31 N 11.30 E
Mbalouro 273b 4.09 S 15.21 E
Mbalouro ≃ 273b 4.09 S 15.21 E
Mbam ≃ 152 4.24 N 11.17 E
Mbamba Bay 154 11.17 S 34.46 E
Mbamou, Île I 273b 4.13 S 15.25 E
Mbamou, Pointe ≻ 273b 4.16 S 15.19 E
Mbandaka (Coquilhatville) 152 0.04 N 18.16 E
Mbanga 152 3.52 N 10.49 E
Mbanio, Lagune C 152 3.35 S 11.00 E
Mbanza-Ngungu 138 5.15 S 14.52 E
Mbar 150 14.32 N 15.46 W
Mbarangandu ≃ 154 8.57 S 37.24 E
Mbarara 154 0.37 S 30.39 E
Mbari ≃ 152 4.34 N 22.43 E
Mbasay 146 7.39 N 15.40 E
Mbate 154 8.52 S 39.10 E
Mbatto 150 6.28 N 4.22 W
Mbé 152 3.18 N 15.54 E
Mbé ≃ 152 0.27 N 9.41 E
Mbemba 154 10.03 S 38.36 E
Mbengga I 175g 18.23 S 178.08 E
Mbéré ≃ 152 7.45 N 15.36 E
Mbereshi Mission 154 9.45 S 28.46 E
Mberubu 150 6.10 N 7.38 E
Mbeya 154 8.54 S 33.27 E
Mbeya □[4] 154 8.30 S 33.00 E
Mbia 140 6.15 N 29.19 E
Mbigou 152 1.53 S 11.56 E
Mbinda 152 2.00 S 12.55 E
Mbindawina 152 15.57 S 23.18 E
Mbinga 154 10.56 S 35.01 E
Mbingué 150 10.00 N 5.54 W
Mbirira 154 4.21 S 30.10 E
Mbirizi 154 0.23 S 31.27 E
Mbissa 152 0.41 N 10.59 E
Mbogo 154 7.26 S 33.26 E
Mboie 152 6.56 S 21.54 E
Mboli 152 4.08 N 23.09 E
Mbomou □[5] 152 5.00 N 23.30 E
Mbomou (Bomu) ≃ 136 4.08 N 22.26 E
Mbonge 152 4.33 N 9.05 E
Mbor 152 6.24 N 11.19 E
Mboro, Sén. 150 15.09 N 16.54 W
Mboro, Sūd. 140 6.18 N 28.45 E
Mborong 115b 8.49 S 120.37 E
Mboté 152 3.56 S 12.43 E
Mbouda 152 5.38 N 10.15 E
Mboula 152 4.27 N 16.29 E
Mbour 150 14.24 N 16.58 W
Mbout 150 16.02 N 12.35 W
Mbrés 152 6.40 N 19.48 E
M'bridge ≃ 152 7.14 S 12.52 E
Mbua 175g 16.48 S 178.37 E
Mbua Bay C 175g 16.49 S 178.35 E
Mbuji-Mayi (Bakwanga) 152 6.09 S 23.38 E
Mbulo I 175e 8.46 S 158.17 E
Mbulu 154 3.51 S 35.32 E
Mbulula 154 5.26 S 27.26 E
Mbuma 154 3.32 N 24.50 E
Mburucuyá 252 28.03 S 58.14 W
Mbutha 175g 16.39 S 179.50 E
Mbwemburu ≃ 154 9.29 S 39.39 E
M'Chedallah 34 36.21 N 4.16 E
Mchinga 154 9.44 S 39.42 E
Mchinji 154 13.41 S 32.55 E
Mchungo 154 7.42 S 39.17 E
M'Clintock Channel ⵡ 176 71.00 N 101.00 W
M'Clure, Cape ≻ 176 74.35 N 121.08 W
M'Clure Strait ⵡ 176 74.30 N 116.00 W
Mdandu 154 9.09 S 34.42 E
M'Daourouch 36 36.05 N 7.49 E
Meacham 184 52.08 N 105.45 W
Mead, Lake @[1] 200 36.05 N 114.25 W
Meade, Kans., U.S. 198 37.17 N 100.20 W
Meade, Mich., U.S. 214 42.43 N 82.52 W
Meade ≃ 180 70.50 N 156.25 W
Meaden Peak ∧ 200 40.46 N 107.03 W
Meade Peak ∧ 202 42.30 N 111.15 W
Meadie, Loch @ 46 58.20 N 4.33 W
Meadow, Tex., U.S. 196 33.20 N 102.12 W
Meadow, Utah, U.S. 200 38.53 N 112.24 W
Meadowbank Park ♣ 274a 33.49 S 151.06 E
Meadowbrook, Ill., U.S. 219 38.54 N 90.01 W
Meadowbrook, Ind., U.S. 216 41.03 N 85.03 W
Meadow Brook ≃, Mass., U.S. 283 42.03 N 70.58 W
Meadow Brook ≃, Pa., U.S. 285 40.07 N 75.04 W
Meadow Creek ≃ 202 46.03 N 115.18 W
Meadowdale 278 41.32 N 87.21 W
Meadow Flat 170 33.26 S 149.56 E
Meadow Island I 276 40.36 N 73.33 W
Meadow Lake 184 54.08 N 108.26 W
Meadow Lake @, Sask., Can. 184 54.07 N 108.20 W
Meadow Lake @, N.Y., U.S. 276 40.44 N 73.50 W
Meadow Lake @, Oreg., U.S. 224 45.19 N 123.26 W
Meadow Lake Provincial Park ♣ 184 54.28 N 109.10 W
Meadowlands, S. Afr. 273d 26.13 S 27.54 E
Meadow Lands, Pa., U.S. 214 40.15 N 80.13 W
Meadowlark Airport ⊠ 280 33.43 N 118.02 W
Meadowood, Del., U.S. 285 39.42 N 75.42 W
Meadowood, Md., U.S. 284c 39.04 N 77.00 W
Meadows 168b 35.11 S 138.46 E
Meadows, Island of I 276 40.34 N 74.12 W
Meadows Field ⊠ 226 35.26 N 119.03 W
Meadowvale ⬩[8] 275b 43.37 N 79.43 W
Meadow Valley Wash ∨ 204 36.39 N 114.35 W
Meadowview 192 36.46 N 81.52 W
Meadow Vista 226 39.06 N 121.01 W
Meads Creek ≃ 210 42.10 N 77.07 W
Meadville, Miss., U.S. 194 31.28 N 90.54 W
Meadville, Mo., U.S. 194 39.47 N 93.18 W
Meadville, Pa., U.S. 214 41.38 N 80.09 W
Meaford 212 44.36 N 80.35 W
Meaghers Grant 186 44.55 N 63.15 W
Me-akan-dake ∧ 92a 43.23 N 144.01 E
Meakerville 180 60.32 N 145.00 W
Mealasta Isle I 46 58.05 N 7.08 W
Mealhada 34 40.22 N 8.27 W
Méan 56 50.22 N 5.20 E
Meana 128 36.55 N 60.30 E
Meana Sardo 71 39.57 N 9.04 E
Meandarra 166 27.20 S 149.53 E
Meander Creek Reservoir @[1] 214 41.09 N 80.47 W
Meander River 176 59.02 N 117.42 W
Mearim ≃ 250 3.04 S 44.35 W
Measham 42 52.43 N 1.29 W
Meath □[6] 48 53.35 N 6.40 W
Meath □[9] 48 53.36 N 6.54 W
Meaux 50 48.57 N 2.52 E
Meaux-Esbly, Aérodrome de ⊠ 261 48.55 N 2.50 E
Mebane 192 36.06 N 79.16 W
Mebisere 273a 6.42 N 3.31 E
Mebtoûh, Oued el ≃ 34 35.16 N 0.32 W
Meča ≃ 82 54.50 N 39.10 E
Meca, La → Makkah 144 21.27 N 39.49 E
Mecanhelas 154 15.12 S 35.54 E
Mecatán 234 21.32 N 105.08 W
Mecatlán 234 20.13 N 97.41 W
Mecaya ≃ 246 0.29 N 75.11 W
Mecca → Makkah 144 21.27 N 39.49 E
Mečebilovo 78 49.04 N 36.41 E
Mečetinskaja 78 46.46 N 40.27 E
Mečetka 78 50.54 N 40.05 E
Mechanic Falls 188 44.07 N 70.24 W
Mechanicsburg, Ill., U.S. 219 39.48 N 89.24 W
Mechanicsburg, Ind., U.S. 218 40.09 N 86.28 W
Mechanicsburg, Ohio, U.S. 218 40.04 N 83.34 W
Mechanicsburg, Pa., U.S. 188 40.13 N 77.01 W
Mechanicstown, N.Y., U.S. 210 41.27 N 74.24 W
Mechanicstown, Ohio, U.S. 214 40.37 N 80.57 W
Mechanicsville, Iowa, U.S. 190 41.54 N 91.15 W
Mechanicsville, Md., U.S. 208 38.26 N 76.44 W
Mechanicsville, Va., U.S. 192 37.36 N 77.22 W
Mechanicville 210 42.54 N 73.42 W
Mechara 144 8.32 N 40.22 E
Mechelen (Malines) 50 51.02 N 4.28 E
Mechel'ta 84 42.48 N 46.30 E
Méchéria 148 33.35 N 0.18 W
Mechernich 56 50.35 N 6.38 E
Mechita 252 35.04 S 60.24 W
Mechlin → Mechelen 50 51.02 N 4.28 E
Mechol 174q 9.37 N 138.10 E
Mechonskoje 86 56.09 N 64.34 E
Mechra Safsaf 34 34.52 N 2.36 W
Mechren'ga 24 61.46 N 40.57 E
Mechrenga ≃ 24 63.15 N 41.20 E
Mechroha 36 36.21 N 7.51 E
Mecidiye, Tür. 130 38.53 N 27.42 E
Mecidiye, Tür. 130 40.38 N 26.32 E
Mečigmen 180 65.28 N 172.05 W
Mečigmeskij Zaliv C 180 65.25 N 172.00 W
Měčín 60 49.29 N 13.25 E
Meçitözü 130 40.31 N 35.19 E
Meckelfeld 52 53.25 N 10.01 E
Meckenbeuren 58 47.42 N 9.34 E
Meckenheim 56 50.37 N 7.07 E
Meckering 162 31.38 S 117.01 E
Meckesheim 56 49.19 N 8.49 E
Meckinghoven 263 51.37 N 7.19 E
Mecklenburg, D.D.R. 54 53.47 N 11.28 E
Mecklenburg, N.Y., U.S. 210 42.27 N 76.43 W
Mecklenburg □[9] 54 53.30 N 13.00 E
Mecklenburger Bucht C 54 54.20 N 11.40 E
Mecklenburgische Seenplatte ⬩[1] 54 53.30 N 12.00 E
Meclov 60 49.31 N 12.52 E
Meco 210 43.03 N 74.23 W
Mecoacán 234 18.23 N 93.07 W
Mecoacán, Laguna C 234 18.22 N 93.09 W
Meconta 154 14.49 S 39.50 E
Mecox Bay C 207 40.54 N 72.20 W
Mecque, La → Makkah 144 21.27 N 39.49 E
Mecrihan 130 37.08 N 39.03 E
Mecsek ∧∧ 30 46.15 N 18.05 E
Mecúfi 154 13.17 S 40.30 E
Mecula 154 12.04 S 37.40 E
Meda, It. 62 45.40 N 9.09 E
Meda, Port. 34 40.58 N 7.16 W
Medak 122 18.02 N 78.16 E
Medākul 126 23.03 N 90.11 E
Médan, Fr. 261 48.57 N 2.00 E
Medan, Indon. 114 3.35 N 98.40 E
Medang 114 2.06 N 101.38 E
Medang, Pulau I 115b 8.09 S 117.23 E
Medang, Tanjung ≻ 114 2.08 N 101.39 E
Médanos 252 38.50 S 62.41 W
Medanosa, Punta ≻ 254 48.06 S 65.55 W
Medaryville 216 41.05 N 86.55 W
Meddahia, 'Assâbet el ∧ 148 22.08 N 11.58 W
Mede 62 45.06 N 8.44 E
Médéa 148 36.12 N 2.50 E
Medebach 56 51.12 N 8.42 E
Medeiros Neto 255 17.20 S 40.14 W
Medel, Val ∨ 58 46.37 N 8.50 E
Medellín, Col. 246 6.15 N 75.35 W
Medellin, Pil. 116 11.08 N 123.58 E
Medelpad □[9] 26 62.40 N 16.15 E
Medemblik 52 52.46 N 5.06 E
Měděnec 54 50.25 N 13.05 E
Medenica 78 49.26 N 23.45 E
Médenine 148 33.21 N 10.30 E
Médenine □[5] 148 32.00 N 10.00 E
Mederdra 150 16.55 N 15.39 W
Medesano 64 44.45 N 10.08 E
Medevi 40 58.40 N 14.57 E
Medfield 207 42.11 N 71.18 W
Medford, Mass., U.S. 207 42.25 N 71.07 W
Medford, N.J., U.S. 208 39.54 N 74.49 W
Medford, N.Y., U.S. 210 40.49 N 73.00 W
Medford, Okla., U.S. 196 36.48 N 97.44 W
Medford, Oreg., U.S. 202 42.19 N 122.52 W
Medford, Wis., U.S. 190 45.09 N 90.20 W
Medford Farms 285 39.52 N 74.45 W
Medford Lakes 285 39.52 N 74.49 W
Medfra 180 63.06 N 154.44 W
Medgidia 38 44.15 N 28.16 E
Medgyes → Mediaș 38 46.10 N 24.21 E
Medi 154 5.04 N 30.44 E
Media 208 39.54 N 75.23 W
Media Agua 252 31.59 S 68.25 W
Mediapolis 190 41.00 N 91.10 W
Mediaș 38 46.10 N 24.21 E
Medical Lake 202 47.34 N 117.41 W
Medicina 66 44.28 N 11.38 E
Medicine Bow 200 41.54 N 106.12 W
Medicine Bow ≃ 200 42.00 N 106.40 W
Medicine Bow Mountains ∧∧ 200 41.10 N 106.10 W
Medicine Bow Peak ∧ 200 41.21 N 106.19 W
Medicine Creek ≃, Mo., U.S. 194 39.43 N 93.24 W
Medicine Creek ≃, Nebr., U.S. 198 40.17 N 100.10 W
Medicine Creek ≃, S. Dak., U.S. 198 44.06 N 99.42 W
Medicine Hat 184 50.03 N 110.40 W
Medicine Knoll Creek ≃ 198 44.19 N 100.05 W
Medicine Lake 198 48.30 N 104.30 W
Medicine Lake @ 198 48.28 N 104.24 W
Medicine Lodge 198 37.17 N 98.35 W
Medicine Lodge ≃ 196 36.49 N 98.20 W
Medina → Al-Madīnah, Ar. Sa. 128 24.28 N 39.36 E
Medina, Bra. 255 16.15 S 41.29 W
Medina, Pil. 116 8.55 N 125.01 E
Medina, N. Dak., U.S. 198 46.54 N 99.18 W
Medina, N.Y., U.S. 210 43.13 N 78.23 W
Medina, Ohio, U.S. 214 41.08 N 81.52 W
Medina, Tex., U.S. 196 29.48 N 99.15 W
Medina □[6] 214 41.08 N 81.52 W
Medina ≃ 196 29.12 N 98.20 W
Medinaceli 34 41.10 N 2.26 W
Medina del Campo 34 41.18 N 4.55 W
Medina de Ríoseco 34 41.53 N 5.02 W
Médina Gonassé 150 13.08 N 13.45 W
Medinah 278 41.59 N 88.01 W
Médina Saback 150 13.36 N 15.35 W
Medina-Sidonia 34 36.27 N 5.55 W
Medinat al-Faiyum → Al-Fayyūm 142 29.19 N 30.50 E
Medininkai 76 54.32 N 25.40 E
Medino 164 9.40 S 149.40 E
Medio, Arroyo del ≃ 258 33.49 S 57.43 W
Medio Creek ≃ 196 28.19 N 97.19 W
Mediterranean Sea Ŧ[2] 10 35.00 N 20.00 E
Mediterraneo, Mare → Mediterranean Sea Ŧ[2] 10 35.00 N 20.00 E
Mediterráneo, Mare → Mediterranean Sea Ŧ[2] 10 35.00 N 20.00 E
Medjana 34 36.08 N 4.41 E
Medje 154 2.25 N 27.18 E
Medjerda, Monts de la ∧∧ 36 36.35 N 8.15 E
Medjerda, Oued ≃ 148 37.07 N 10.13 E
Medjez el Bab 148 36.39 N 9.37 E
Medkovec 38 43.37 N 23.10 E
Mednogorsk 86 51.24 N 57.37 E
Mednoje 76 56.56 N 35.29 E
Mednyj, Ostrov I 74 54.45 N 167.35 E
Médoc ⬩[1] 32 45.20 N 1.00 W
Medolla 64 44.51 N 11.04 E
Medora, Ill., U.S. 219 39.11 N 90.09 W
Medora, Ind., U.S. 218 38.49 N 86.10 W
Medora, N. Dak., U.S. 198 46.55 N 103.31 W
Médouneu 152 0.57 N 10.47 E
Medow 54 53.50 N 13.32 E
Medstead, Sask., Can. 184 53.19 N 108.02 W
Medstead, Eng., U.K. 42 51.08 N 1.04 W
Medua 126 22.38 N 90.44 E
Meductic 186 46.00 N 67.29 W
Medulla 220 27.58 N 81.58 W
Međumurje ⬩[1] 61 46.25 N 16.30 E
Meduna ≃ 64 45.49 N 12.34 E
Medveđa 38 42.50 N 21.35 E
Medvedevo, S.S.S.R. 76 60.02 N 43.01 E
Medvedevo, S.S.S.R. 80 56.37 N 47.47 E
Medvedevo, S.S.S.R. 86 60.37 N 77.21 E
Medvedevskoje 76 58.58 N 35.58 E
Medvedica ≃, S.S.S.R. 76 57.05 N 37.32 E
Medvedica ≃, S.S.S.R. 80 49.35 N 42.41 E
Medvedickij 80 50.47 N 44.43 E
Medvědí hora ∧ 60 48.59 N 13.25 E
Medvedkovo ⬩[8] 265b 55.53 N 37.38 E
Medvedok 80 57.23 N 50.05 E
Medvedovskaja 78 45.27 N 39.01 E
Medvėgalis ∧ 76 55.38 N 22.45 E
Medvenka 82 54.15 N 37.42 E
Medvežij, Ostrov I 89 54.41 N 136.18 E
Medvežinka 83 48.10 N 39.31 E
Medvežje, Ozero @ 86 55.07 N 68.00 E
Medvežjegorsk 24 62.55 N 34.23 E
Medvežji Ostrova II, S.S.S.R. 74 70.52 N 161.26 E
Medvežji Ostrova II, S.S.S.R. 89 54.41 N 136.18 E
Medvežji Ozera @ 265b 55.52 N 38.00 E
Medvežji Oz'ora 265b 55.52 N 37.59 E
Medvežskaja 24 64.57 N 57.34 E
Medvin 78 49.23 N 30.47 E
Medv'onka 78 51.26 N 36.07 E
Medv'onka ≃ 265b 55.44 N 37.12 E
Medway, Maine, U.S. 188 45.37 N 68.35 W
Medway, Mass., U.S. 207 42.08 N 71.24 W
Medway, Ohio, U.S. 218 39.53 N 83.59 W
Medway □[8] 260 51.24 N 0.31 E
Medway ≃, N.S., Can. 186 44.08 N 64.36 W
Medway ≃, Eng., U.K. 42 51.27 N 0.44 E
Medyn' 82 54.58 N 35.52 E
Medynka ≃ 82 54.44 N 36.02 E
Medynskij Zavorot, Mys ≻ 24 68.58 N 59.17 E
Medžibož 78 49.26 N 27.25 E
Medzilaborce 30 49.16 N 21.55 E
Meeberrie 162 26.58 S 115.58 E
Meekatharra 162 26.36 S 118.29 E
Meeker, Colo., U.S. 200 40.02 N 107.55 W
Meeker, Ohio, U.S. 214 40.39 N 83.18 W
Meeks Bay 226 39.02 N 120.08 W
Meelpaeg Lake @[1] 186 48.16 N 56.35 W
Meenaar 168a 31.38 S 116.53 E
Meentheena 162 21.17 S 120.28 E
Meer 52 51.27 N 4.44 E
Meeralpen → Maritime Alps ∧∧ 62 44.15 N 7.10 E
Meerane 54 50.51 N 12.28 E
Meerbeck 263 51.28 N 6.39 E
Meerbeke 50 50.50 N 4.02 E
Meerhout 56 51.08 N 5.05 E
Meerhusener Moor ⬩[3] 52 53.35 N 7.30 E
Meerkerk 52 51.45 N 5.00 E
Meerle 52 51.28 N 4.48 E
Meersburg 58 47.41 N 9.16 E
Meerseen 56 50.53 N 5.45 E
Meerut 124 28.59 N 77.42 E
Meerut □[5] 124 29.00 N 77.35 E
Meese ≃ 42 52.40 N 2.39 W
Meeteetse 202 44.09 N 108.52 W
Meetinghouse Branch ≃ 284c 38.47 N 76.55 W
Mega, Indon. 164 0.41 S 131.53 E
Mega, Yai. 144 4.07 N 38.16 E
Mega, Pulau I 112 4.00 S 101.02 E
Megalo 144 6.55 N 41.48 E
Megálon Khorion 38 36.27 N 27.21 E
Megalópolis 38 37.24 N 22.08 E
Meganom, Mys ≻ 78 44.48 N 35.05 E
Mégantic □[6] 206 46.10 N 71.30 W
Mégantic, Lac @ 188 45.32 N 70.53 W
Mégantic, Mont ∧ 206 45.28 N 71.09 W
Mégara 38 38.01 N 23.21 E
Megargel 196 33.27 N 98.56 W
Mégaron, Kólpos C 267c 37.56 N 23.20 E
Megasini ∧ 120 21.38 N 86.21 E
Meget 88 52.24 N 104.03 E
Megève 62 45.52 N 6.37 E
Mégevette 58 46.12 N 6.30 E
Megezez, Mount ∧ 144 9.13 N 37.37 E
Meghalaya □[3] 120 25.30 N 91.15 E
Meghna ≃ 124 22.50 N 90.50 E
Mégiscane ≃ 190 48.29 N 77.08 W
Mégiscane, Lac @ 190 48.35 N 75.55 W
Megi-shima I 96 34.24 N 134.03 E
Megorskaja Gr'ada ∧ 76 60.30 N 36.00 E
Megra, S.S.S.R. 24 66.09 N 41.37 E
Megra, S.S.S.R. 76 60.10 N 37.13 E
Megrel'skij Chrebet ∧∧ 84 42.49 N 42.24 E
Megri 84 38.56 N 46.16 E
Meguro ⬩[8] 268 35.38 N 139.42 E
Meguro ≃ 268 35.37 N 139.45 E
Mehadia 38 44.55 N 22.22 E
Méhaigne ≃ 56 50.32 N 5.13 E
Mehaïguêne, Oued ∨ 148 32.15 N 2.59 E
Mehakit 112 2.51 S 115.57 E
Mehar 120 27.11 N 67.49 E

ENGLISH

Name | Page | Lat.°′ | Long.°′

Mehdia 148 35.26 N 1.40 E
Mehede 40 60.27 N 17.24 E
Mehedinți □[4] 38 44.30 N 22.50 E
Meheisa 140 19.37 N 32.57 E
Mehekar 122 20.09 N 76.34 E
Mehendiganj 126 22.49 N 90.32 E
Meherpur 124 23.46 N 88.38 E
Meherrin ≃ 192 36.26 N 76.57 W
Mehetia I 14 17.52 S 148.03 W
Mehidpur 120 23.49 N 75.40 E
Mehikoorma 76 58.14 N 27.28 E
Mehlem 56 50.39 N 7.11 E
Mehlsack → Pieniężno 30 54.15 N 20.08 E
Mehlteuer 54 50.32 N 12.02 E
Mehlville 219 38.31 N 90.19 W
Mehmetkân 130 38.26 N 41.17 E
Mehnagar 124 25.53 N 83.07 E
Mehndāwal 124 26.59 N 83.07 E
Mehoopany 210 41.34 N 76.04 W
Mehoopany Creek ≃ 210 41.34 N 76.03 W
Mehpālpur ⬩[8] 272a 28.33 N 77.08 E
Mehr 52 51.43 N 6.29 E
Mehrābād, Īrān 128 36.53 N 47.55 E
Mehrābād, Īrān 267d 35.40 N 51.20 E
Mehrābād Airport ⊠ 267d 35.41 N 51.19 E
Mehram Nagar ⬩[8] 272a 28.34 N 77.07 E
Mehrān 128 33.07 N 46.10 E
Mehring 56 49.48 N 6.49 E
Mehrīz 128 31.35 N 54.28 E
Mehrow 264a 52.34 N 13.37 E
Mehrum 263 51.35 N 6.37 E
Mehsāna 120 23.36 N 72.24 E
Mè-hsa-tè 110 19.33 N 97.38 E
Mehtar Lām 120 34.39 N 70.10 E
Mehun-sur-Yèvre 50 47.09 N 2.13 E
Meia Meia 154 5.49 S 35.48 E
Meia Ponte ≃ 255 18.32 S 49.36 W
Meichang 105 39.22 N 117.10 E
Meichuan 100 30.10 N 115.36 E
Meicun, Zhg. 100 25.30 N 116.56 E
Meicun, Zhg. 106 30.22 N 119.01 E
Meicun, Zhg. 106 30.40 N 119.04 E
Meicun, Zhg. 106 31.33 N 120.24 E
Meide 263 51.11 N 6.55 E
Meiderich ⬩[8] 263 51.28 N 6.46 E
Meidling ⬩[8] 264b 48.11 N 16.20 E
Méier ⬩[8] 287a 22.54 S 43.16 W
Meierij ⬩[1] 52 51.35 N 5.40 E
Meierkaisong 120 30.54 N 84.31 E
Meiersberg 263 51.17 N 6.57 E
Meig ≃ 46 57.34 N 4.41 W
Meiganga 152 6.31 N 14.11 E
Meigle 46 56.35 N 3.09 W
Meigs 192 31.04 N 83.06 W
Meihe ≃ 105 39.21 N 117.50 E
Meihekou 98 42.27 N 125.33 E
Meihern 60 49.00 N 11.38 E
Meihsien → Meixian 100 24.21 N 116.08 E
Meihua 100 26.02 N 119.40 E
Meihuajie 100 25.14 N 113.05 E
Meijel 52 51.21 N 5.53 E
Meijiadang @ 106 30.56 N 120.43 E
Meijiang ≃, Zhg. 100 26.00 N 115.23 E
Meijiang ≃, Zhg. 100 24.24 N 116.34 E
Meijino-mori-minō-kokutei-kōen ♣ 94 34.51 N 135.29 E
Meiji Shrine ❦[1] 268 35.41 N 139.42 E
Meiji University ❦[2] 268 35.41 N 139.45 E
Meikeng 100 23.59 N 114.05 E
Meikle Millyea ∧ 44 55.07 N 4.19 W
Meikle Says Law ∧ 46 55.55 N 2.40 W
Meiktila 110 20.52 N 95.52 E
Meila 54 51.09 N 13.13 E
Meilap 174r 6.54 N 158.09 E
Meilen 58 47.16 N 8.38 E
Meili 106 31.42 N 120.53 E
Meilie 100 26.18 N 117.38 E
Meilin, Zhg. 100 23.18 N 115.58 E
Meilin, Zhg. 106 30.35 N 119.04 E
Meillerie 58 46.24 N 6.43 E
Meilong 100 22.56 N 115.17 E
Meilunyingzi 104 42.18 N 122.10 E
Meina 62 45.47 N 8.32 E
Meine 52 52.23 N 10.32 E
Meiners Oaks 228 34.30 N 119.17 W
Meinerzhagen 56 51.06 N 7.38 E
Meiningen 54 50.34 N 10.25 E
Meinung 100 22.54 N 120.32 E
Meio, Ilha do I 287a 23.02 S 43.17 W
Meio, Rio do ≃ 255 17.47 S 39.47 W
Meiqi 106 30.48 N 119.45 E
Meiringen 58 46.43 N 8.12 E
Meisburg 56 50.06 N 6.41 E
Meisenheim 56 49.42 N 7.40 E
Meishan, Zhg. 100 28.52 N 113.38 E
Meishan, Zhg. 107 30.02 N 103.49 E
Meissen 54 51.10 N 13.28 E
Meissendorf 52 52.43 N 9.50 E
Meiss Lake @ 204 41.52 N 122.04 W
Meissner ∧ 56 51.12 N 9.50 E
Meissner-Kaufunger Wald, Naturpark ♣ 56 51.15 N 9.45 E
Meitan 102 27.46 N 107.35 E
Meitian 100 25.21 N 112.47 E
Meitik 174r 6.57 N 158.14 E
Meitingen 56 48.32 N 10.50 E
Meiwa 94 34.33 N 136.39 E
Meixian 100 24.21 N 116.08 E
Meiyao 89 49.37 N 124.30 E
Meiyino 140 6.12 N 34.40 E
Meizhai 102 25.30 N 108.50 E
Meizhou 100 23.50 N 117.20 E
Meizhoudao I 100 25.06 N 119.07 E
Meizhouwan C 100 25.06 N 119.00 E
Meizhu 106 31.16 N 119.13 E
Mejia 126 23.34 N 87.06 E
Mejillones 252 23.06 S 70.27 W
Mejillones del Sur, Bahía de C 252 23.03 S 70.27 W
Mejorada del Campo 266a 40.24 N 3.29 W
Meka 162 27.26 S 116.48 E
Mekambo 152 1.01 N 13.56 E
Mekdela 144 11.28 N 39.23 E
Mekele 144 13.33 N 39.30 E
Mekerra, Oued ≃ 34 35.00 N 0.45 W
Mekerrhane, Sebkha ═ 148 26.19 N 1.20 E
Mékhé 150 15.07 N 16.38 W
Mekhliganj 124 26.21 N 88.55 E
Mekhtar 120 30.29 N 69.22 E
Mékinac ≃ 206 46.51 N 72.46 W
Mekka → Makkah 144 21.27 N 39.49 E
Meknès 148 33.53 N 5.37 W
Mekong ≃ 12 10.33 N 105.24 E
Mekongga, Gunung ∧ 112 3.38 S 121.15 E
Mekongga, Pegunungan ∧∧ 112 3.35 S 121.15 E
Mékôngk → Mekong ≃ 12 10.33 N 105.24 E
Mekoryuk 180 60.23 N 166.12 W
Mékrou ≃ 150 12.24 N 2.49 E
Mel 64 46.04 N 12.05 E
Melado ≃ 252 35.43 S 71.05 W
Melah, Oued ≃ 148 33.42 N 7.26 W
Melah, Oued el ∨, Alg. 148 28.21 N 6.00 E
Melah, Oued el ∨, Tun. 148 34.03 N 8.06 E
Melah, Sebkhet el @ 148 29.05 N 1.10 W
Melaka 114 2.12 N 102.15 E
Melaka □[3] 114 2.15 N 102.15 E
Melalap 112 5.14 N 116.00 E
Melandro ≃ 68 40.37 N 15.27 E

DEUTSCH

Name | Seite | Breite°′ | Länge°′ E=Ost

Melanesia II 14 13.00 S 164.00 E
Melanesian Border Plateau ✢[3] 14 11.00 S 179.00 E
Melanesian Mission Station ❦[1] 174c 29.02 S 167.55 E
Melappālaiyam 122 8.42 N 77.43 E
Melara 64 45.03 N 11.11 E
Melaune 54 51.11 N 14.44 E
Melawi ≃ 112 0.05 N 111.29 E
Melayu ≃ 271c 1.27 N 103.42 E
Melbern 216 41.28 N 84.39 W
Melbost 46 58.15 N 6.22 W
Melbourn 42 52.05 N 0.01 E
Melbourne, Austl. 169
 274b 37.49 S 144.58 E
Melbourne, Ont., Can. 214 42.49 N 81.33 W
Melbourne, Eng., U.K. 42 52.49 N 1.25 W
Melbourne, Ark., U.S. 194 36.04 N 91.54 W
Melbourne, Fla., U.S. 220 28.05 N 80.37 W
Melbourne, Iowa, U.S. 190 41.57 N 93.06 W
Melbourne, University of ❦[2] 274b 37.48 S 144.58 E
Melbourne Beach 220 28.05 N 80.34 W
Melbourne Island I 176 68.30 N 104.45 W
Melbourne Regional Airport ⊠ 220 28.06 N 80.38 W
Melby House 46 60.18 N 1.39 W
Mel'cany 80 54.28 N 44.43 E
Melcher 190 41.13 N 93.14 W
Melchor, Isla I 254 45.08 S 73.57 W
Melchor Ocampo 196 26.03 N 99.33 W
Melchor Romero ⬩[8] 258 34.56 S 58.03 W
Melchtal 58 46.50 N 8.17 E
Melcombe Regis 42 50.38 N 2.28 W
Melcroft 214 40.03 N 79.24 W
Melderskin ∧ 26 60.01 N 6.05 E
Meldola 66 44.07 N 12.05 E
Meldorf 30 54.05 N 9.05 E
Meldrum Bay 190 45.56 N 83.07 W
Meldrum Creek 182 52.07 N 122.20 W
Mele, Bhārat 272b 22.49 N 88.09 E
Mélé, Centraf. 146 9.46 N 21.33 E
Mele, It. 62 44.27 N 8.45 E
Mele, Capo ≻ 62 43.57 N 8.10 E
Mele Bay C 175f 17.43 S 168.15 E
Melechovo 80 56.17 N 41.17 E
Meleck 86 57.25 N 90.12 E
Meledin 144 10.25 N 49.52 E
Melefan 130 38.11 N 41.34 E
Melegnano 62 45.21 N 9.19 E
Meleješt' 78 46.59 N 29.33 E
Melekeiok 175b 7.29 N 134.38 E
Melekess 80 54.14 N 49.39 E
Melena del Sur 240p 22.47 N 82.09 W
Melendiz Dağı ∧ 130 38.07 N 34.25 E
Melendugno 68 40.16 N 18.20 E
Melenki 80 55.20 N 41.38 E
Meleškoviči 78 51.56 N 28.59 E
Meleuz 86 52.58 N 55.55 E
Mélèzes, Rivière aux ≃ 176 57.40 N 69.29 W
Melfa 208 37.39 N 75.45 W
Melfa ≃ 66 41.30 N 13.35 E
Melfi, It. 68 41.00 N 15.39 E
Melfi, Tchad 146 11.04 N 17.56 E
Melfort, Sask., Can. 184 52.52 N 104.36 W
Melfort, Zimb. 154 17.59 S 31.19 E
Melfort, Loch C 46 56.15 N 5.31 W
Melgaço, Bra. 250 1.47 S 50.44 W
Melgaço, Port. 34 42.07 N 8.16 W
Melgar 246 4.12 N 74.39 W
Mel'guny 80 52.09 N 40.52 E
Melhus 26 63.17 N 10.16 E
Meli ≃ 150 8.17 N 10.41 W
Meliau 112 0.08 S 110.18 E
Melibocus ∧ 56 49.42 N 8.40 E
Melichovo, S.S.S.R. 78 50.42 N 36.48 E
Melichovo, S.S.S.R. 82 55.07 N 37.39 E
Melicuccà 68 38.18 N 15.53 E
Melide 58 45.57 N 8.57 E
Meligalás 38 37.13 N 21.59 E
Melilla 34 35.19 N 2.58 W
Melilli 70 37.11 N 15.07 E
Melimoyu, Cerro ∧ 254 44.05 S 72.52 W
Melincué 252 33.39 S 61.27 W
Melipilla 252 33.42 S 71.13 W
Mélisey 58 47.45 N 6.35 E
Melissa 68 39.18 N 17.01 E
Melissano 68 39.58 N 18.07 E
Melíssia 267c 38.03 N 23.50 E
Melita 184 49.16 N 101.00 W
Melito di Porto Salvo 68 37.55 N 15.47 E
Melitopol' 78 46.50 N 35.22 E
Melívoia 38 39.45 N 22.48 E
Melk 61 48.14 N 15.20 E
Melk ≃ 61 48.14 N 15.19 E
Melka Teka 144 6.05 N 43.08 E
Melkbosstrand 158 33.43 S 18.27 E
Melksham 42 51.23 N 2.09 W
Mella ≃ 64 45.13 N 10.13 E
Mellansel 26 63.26 N 18.19 E
Mellau 58 47.21 N 9.53 E
Melle, B.R.D. 52 52.12 N 8.20 E
Melle, Fr. 32 46.13 N 0.09 W
Melleck 64 47.40 N 12.45 E
Mellègue, Oued ≃ 36 36.32 N 8.51 E
Mellen 190 46.20 N 90.40 W
Mellendorf 52 52.33 N 9.43 E
Mellenville 210 42.15 N 73.40 W
Mellerud 26 58.42 N 12.28 E
Mellette 198 45.09 N 98.30 W
Mellid 34 42.55 N 8.00 W
Mellier ≃ 56 49.43 N 5.32 E
Melling 262 53.30 N 2.56 W
Mellingen 54 50.56 N 11.23 E
Mellish Reef I[1] 160 17.25 S 155.50 E
Mellish Rise ✢[3] 14 17.00 S 156.00 E
Mellit 140 14.08 N 25.33 E
Mellone, Monte ∧ 267a 41.50 N 12.43 E
Mellong Range ∧∧ 170 33.06 S 150.43 E
Mellon Udrigle 46 57.55 N 5.39 W
Mellor 262 53.46 N 2.32 W
Mellor Brook 262 53.47 N 2.33 W
Mellor Glacier ⌂ 9 73.30 S 66.30 E
Mellösa 40 59.06 N 16.33 E
Melloulou, Oued ≃ 148 34.13 N 3.21 W
Mellrichstadt 56 50.26 N 10.18 E
Mellum I 52 53.40 N 8.10 E
Melmerby 44 54.44 N 2.35 W
Melmore 214 41.02 N 83.07 W
Melmoth 158 28.38 S 31.24 E
Mel'nica-Podol'skaja 78 48.37 N 26.10 E
Mělník 54 50.20 N 14.29 E
Mel'nikovo, S.S.S.R. 85 40.19 N 70.19 E
Mel'nikovo, S.S.S.R. 86 56.34 N 84.05 E
Melo 252 32.22 S 54.11 W
Melo, Ilha de I 150 11.02 N 15.13 W
Melocheville 206 45.19 N 73.56 W
Meloco 154 13.25 S 39.08 E
Melolo 115b 9.53 S 120.40 E
Melolo ≃ 115b 9.52 S 120.41 E
Melong 152 5.07 N 9.57 E
Melos → Mílos I 38 36.41 N 24.15 E
Melovaja ≃ 83 49.23 N 40.16 E
Melovatka 83 49.21 N 38.11 E
Melovoje 83 49.22 N 40.06 E
Melovoj Syrt ∧ 80 52.15 N 52.35 E
Melozitna ≃ 180 64.46 N 155.29 W
Melrhir, Chott @ 148 34.20 N 6.20 E
Melrose, Austl. 162 27.56 S 121.19 E
Melrose, Austl. 166 32.42 S 146.58 E
Melrose, Scot., U.K. 46 55.36 N 2.44 W
Melrose, Mass., U.S. 207 42.27 N 71.04 W
Melrose, Minn., U.S. 198 45.40 N 94.49 W
Melrose, N. Mex., U.S. 196 34.26 N 103.38 W

Symbols in the index entries represent the broad categories identified in the key at the right. Symbols with superior numbers (∧∧[2]) identify subcategories (see complete key on page I · 30).

Kartensymbole in dem Registerverzeichnis stellen die rechts im Schlüssel erklärten Kategorien dar. Symbole mit hochgestellten Ziffern (∧∧[2]) bezeichnen Unterabteilungen einer Kategorie (vgl. vollständiger Schlüssel auf Seite I · 30).

Los símbolos incluídos en el texto del índice representan las grandes categorias identificadas con la clave a la derecha. Los símbolos con numeros en su parte superior (∧∧[2]) identifican las subcategorías (véase la clave completa en la página I · 30).

Les symboles de l'index représentent les catégories indiquées dans la légende à droite. Les symboles suivis d'un indice (∧∧[2]) représentent des sous-catégories (voir légende complète à la page I · 30).

Os símbolos incluídos no texto do índice representam as grandes categorias identificadas com a chave à direita. Os símbolos com números em sua parte superior (∧∧[2]) identificam as subcategorias (veja-se a chave completa à página I · 30).

Symbol	English	Deutsch	Español	Français	Português
∧	Mountain	Berg	Montaña	Montagne	Montanha
∧∧	Mountains	Berge	Montañas	Montagnes	Montanhas
)(	Pass	Pass	Paso	Col	Passo
∨	Valley, Canyon	Tal, Cañon	Valle, Cañón	Vallée, Canyon	Vale, Canhão
═	Plain	Ebene	Llano	Plaine	Planície
≻	Cape	Kap	Cabo	Cap	Cabo
I	Island	Insel	Isla	Île	Ilha
II	Islands	Inseln	Islas	Îles	Ilhas
•	Other Topographic Features	Andere Topographische Objekte	Otros Elementos Topográficos	Autres données topographiques	Outros Elementos Topográficos

ESPAÑOL

Nombre	Página	Lat.°′	Long.°′ W=Oeste
Melrose, N.Y., U.S.	210	42.50 N	73.37 W
Melrose, Ohio, U.S.	216	41.05 N	84.25 W
Melrose, Wis., U.S.	190	44.08 N	91.01 W
Melrose ◆[8]	276	40.49 N	73.55 W
Melrose Abbey ⊽[1]	46	55.37 N	2.45 W
Melrose Park, Fla., U.S.	220	26.06 N	80.12 W
Melrose Park, Ill., U.S.	216	41.54 N	87.51 W
Melrose Park, Pa., U.S.	285	40.04 N	75.08 W
Mels	58	47.03 N	9.25 E
Melsetter	154	19.48 S	32.50 E
Melstone	202	46.36 N	107.52 W
Melsungen	56	51.08 N	9.32 E
Melta, Mount Λ	116	5.41 N	117.20 E
Meltaus	24	66.54 N	25.22 E
Meltham	262	53.36 N	1.51 W
Melton, Austl.	168b	34.05 S	137.59 E
Melton, Austl.	169	37.41 S	144.35 E
Melton Constable	42	52.53 N	1.01 E
Melton Hill Lake @[1]	192	36.00 N	84.15 W
Melton Mowbray	42	52.46 N	0.53 W
Melúa	246	3.55 N	72.50 W
Meluan	112	1.52 N	111.56 E
Meluco	154	12.36 S	39.38 E
Melúli ≃	154	16.28 S	39.44 E
Melun, Fr.	50	48.32 N	2.40 E
Melun, Mya.	110	20.14 N	93.24 E
Melunga	152	17.16 S	16.24 E
Melun-Villaroche, Aérodrome de ⊠	261	48.37 N	2.40 E
Melūr	122	10.03 N	78.20 E
Melvern	198	38.30 N	95.38 W
Melviag	46	57.48 N	5.49 W
Melvich	46	58.33 N	3.55 W
Melville, Austl.	168a	32.03 S	115.49 E
Melville, Sask., Can.	184	50.55 N	102.48 W
Melville, La., U.S.	194	30.42 N	91.45 W
Melville, N.Y., U.S.	276	40.48 N	73.25 W
Melville ◆[8]	273d	26.11 S	28.00 E
Melville, Cape ≻, Austl.	164	14.11 S	144.30 E
Melville, Cape ≻, Pil.	116	7.49 N	117.01 E
Melville, Détroit de → Viscount Melville Sound ⋓	176	74.10 N	113.00 W
Melville, Lake @	176	53.45 N	59.30 W
Melville Bugt C	16	75.30 N	63.00 W
Melville Hall Airport ⊠	240d	15.33 N	61.18 W
Melville Hills ⋀[2]	176	69.20 N	122.00 W
Melville Island I, Austl.	164	11.40 S	131.00 E
Melville Island I, N.W. Ter., Can.	16	75.15 N	110.00 W
Melville Peninsula ≻[1]	176	68.00 N	84.00 W
Melville Sound ⋓, N.W. Ter., Can.	176	68.05 N	107.30 W
Melville Sound ⋓, Ont., Can.	212	44.57 N	81.05 W
Melvin, Ill., U.S.	216	40.34 N	88.15 W
Melvin, Tex., U.S.	196	31.13 N	99.35 W
Melvin, Lough @, Eur.	48	54.26 N	8.10 W
Melvin, Lough @, N. Ire., U.K.	28	54.26 N	8.10 W
Melvindale	214	42.17 N	83.11 W
Melvin Lake @	184	57.08 N	100.15 W
Mélykút	30	46.13 N	19.24 E
Melzo	62	45.30 N	9.25 E
Memala	112	1.44 S	112.36 E
Memāri	126	23.12 N	88.07 E
Memba	154	14.11 S	40.30 E
Membalong	112	3.09 S	107.38 E
Memboro	115b	9.22 S	119.32 E
Membre	56	49.52 N	4.54 E
Même ≃	50	48.11 N	0.39 E
Memel, S. Afr.	158	27.43 S	29.30 E
Memel → Klaipėda, S.S.S.R.	76	55.43 N	21.07 E
Memel → Nemunas ≃	76	55.18 N	21.23 E
Mēmele ≃	76	56.24 N	24.10 E
Memewin, Lac @	190	46.29 N	78.42 W
Memmelsdorf	60	49.56 N	10.57 E
Memmert I	52	53.39 N	6.53 E
Memmingen	58	47.59 N	10.11 E
Memo ≃	246	9.16 N	66.40 W
Memori, Tanjung ≻	164	0.52 S	134.08 E
Memorial Bridge ◆[5]	269a	13.44 N	100.30 E
Memorial Coliseum and Sports Arena ♠	280	34.01 N	118.17 W
Mémót	110	11.49 N	106.11 E
Mempawah	112	0.22 N	108.58 E
Memphis, Fla., U.S.	220	27.32 N	82.34 W
Memphis, Ind., U.S.	218	38.29 N	85.46 W
Memphis, Mich., U.S.	214	42.54 N	82.46 W
Memphis, Mo., U.S.	194	40.28 N	92.10 W
Memphis, Tenn., U.S.	194	35.08 N	90.03 W
Memphis, Tex., U.S.	196	34.44 N	100.32 W
Memphis Naval Air Station ■	194	35.21 N	89.52 W
Memphremagog, Lake @	206	45.05 N	72.15 W
Memsie	46	57.39 N	2.02 W
Mena, S.S.S.R.	78	51.31 N	32.13 E
Mena, Ark., U.S.	194	34.35 N	94.15 W
Menado → Manado	112	1.29 N	124.51 E
Menaggio	58	46.01 N	9.14 E
Menahga	198	46.45 N	95.06 W
Menai	274a	34.01 S	151.01 E
Menai Bridge	44	53.14 N	4.10 W
Menai Strait ⋓	44	53.12 N	4.12 W
Ménaka	150	15.55 N	2.24 E
Menaldum	52	53.12 N	5.39 E
Mènam Khong → Mekong ≃	12	10.33 N	105.24 E
Menan	202	43.43 N	112.00 W
Menands	210	42.42 N	73.45 W
Menangina	162	29.50 S	121.54 E
Menarandra ≃	157b	25.17 S	44.30 E
Menard	196	30.55 N	99.47 W
Menard □[6]	219	40.01 N	89.51 W
Menard Creek ≃	222	30.29 N	94.50 W
Menars	50	47.38 N	1.24 E
Menasha	190	44.13 N	88.26 W
Menate	112	0.14 S	113.02 E
Menawashei	140	12.40 N	24.59 E
Menchang	105	38.54 N	117.01 E
Menčikury	78	47.04 N	34.48 E
Mencué	254	40.25 S	69.38 W
Menda	89	43.40 N	123.08 E
Mendanau, Pulau I	112	2.51 S	107.26 E
Mendarik, Pulau I	112	1.18 N	107.02 E
Mendatai	102	38.51 N	94.39 E
Mendatica	62	44.05 N	7.49 E
Mendawai	112	2.59 S	113.16 E
Mendawai ≃	112	3.17 S	113.21 E
Mendaya	115a	8.23 S	114.42 E
Mende	32	44.30 N	3.30 E
Mendebo Mountains ⋀	144	6.50 N	39.20 E
Mendel' ≃	86	58.13 N	90.08 E
Menden	56	51.26 N	7.47 E
Menden ◆[8]	263	51.24 N	6.54 E
Mendenhall, Miss., U.S.	194	31.58 N	89.52 W
Mendenhall, Pa., U.S.	285	39.51 N	75.38 W
Mendenhall, Cape ≻	180	59.51 N	166.15 W
Mendes	256	22.32 S	43.44 W
Méndez	246	2.43 S	78.19 W
Mendez-Nuñez	116	14.08 N	120.54 E
Mendham	210	40.46 N	74.36 W
Mendi, Pap. N. Gui.	164	6.10 S	143.40 E

FRANÇAIS

Nom	Page	Lat.°′	Long.°′ W=Ouest
Mendi, Yai.	144	9.50 N	35.06 E
Mendip Hills ⋀[2]	42	51.15 N	2.40 W
Mendlesham	42	52.16 N	1.05 E
Mendocino	204	39.19 N	123.48 W
Mendocino, Cape ≻	204	40.25 N	124.25 W
Mendocino Fracture Zone ✧	16	40.00 N	140.00 W
Mendola ≃	70	37.44 N	13.32 E
Mendon, Ill., U.S.	219	40.05 N	91.17 W
Mendon, Mass., U.S.	207	42.06 N	71.33 W
Mendon, Mich., U.S.	216	42.00 N	85.27 W
Mendon, N.Y., U.S.	210	43.00 N	77.34 W
Mendon, Ohio, U.S.	216	40.40 N	84.31 W
Mendon, Pa., U.S.	279b	40.11 N	79.41 W
Mendorf	60	48.52 N	11.36 E
Mendota, Calif., U.S.	226	36.45 N	120.23 W
Mendota, Ill., U.S.	216	41.33 N	89.07 W
Mendota, Lake @	216	43.05 N	89.25 W
Mendoza, Arg.	252	32.53 S	68.49 W
Mendoza, Perú	248	6.20 S	77.24 W
Mendoza, Perú	286d	12.06 S	76.59 W
Mendoza, Ur.	258	34.17 S	56.13 W
Mendoza □[4]	252	34.30 S	68.30 W
Mendoza, Arroyo de ≃	258	34.21 S	56.18 W
Mendrisio	58	45.52 N	8.59 E
Mend'ukino	82	54.47 N	38.51 E
Mendung	112	0.31 N	103.13 E
Ménéac	32	48.09 N	2.28 W
Mene de Mauroa	246	10.43 N	71.01 W
Mene Grande	246	9.49 N	70.56 W
Menemen	130	38.36 N	27.04 E
Menen	50	50.48 N	3.07 E
Meneng Point ≻	174b	0.32 S	166.57 E
Menes	115a	6.23 S	105.55 E
Menfi	70	37.36 N	12.58 E
Mengalum, Pulau I	112	6.16 N	115.12 E
Mengban	102	23.08 N	101.19 E
Mengbang	102	21.28 N	101.19 E
Mengcheng	100	33.17 N	116.33 E
Mengchihe ≃	107	29.47 N	104.56 E
Mengcun	98	38.06 N	117.05 E
Mengdapu	104	41.35 N	123.12 E
Mengede ◆[8]	263	51.34 N	7.23 E
Mengeh Jek	120	37.02 N	66.07 E
Mengen, B.R.D.	58	48.03 N	9.20 E
Mengen, Tür.	130	40.59 N	31.37 E
Mengeringhausen	56	51.22 N	8.59 E
Mengersgereuth-Hämmern	54	50.24 N	11.07 E
Menges Mills	208	39.52 N	76.54 W
Menggala	112	4.28 S	105.17 E
Menggu	102	26.34 N	102.57 E
Menggubao	104	42.27 N	122.23 E
Menggudai	102	38.10 N	108.15 E
Menghai	102	22.00 N	100.26 E
Menghe	106	32.03 N	119.47 E
Mengheyi	98	35.51 N	115.04 E
Mengisor, Ozero @	86	54.33 N	67.57 E
Mengjiacun	106	31.33 N	118.46 E
Mengjiagang	89	46.22 N	130.40 E
Mengjiatai	104	42.06 N	123.21 E
Mengjiawan	102	38.35 N	109.25 E
Mengjiawopeng	104	41.22 N	121.51 E
Mengjiayuanjia	105	40.52 N	118.08 E
Mengka	102	25.10 N	98.01 E
Mengkibol	114	1.58 N	103.20 E
Mengkuang	114	3.11 N	102.24 E
Mengli	106	31.39 N	120.13 E
Menglian	102	22.20 N	99.38 E
Menglinghausen ◆[8]	263	51.28 N	7.25 E
Menglong	102	21.44 N	100.23 E
Mengluchang	107	29.19 N	103.35 E
Mengmucun	106	31.59 N	119.01 E
Mengo □[5]	154	0.30 N	32.15 E
Mengong	152	2.56 N	11.25 E
Mengqigou	104	42.00 N	121.08 E
Mengshan	102	24.07 N	110.33 E
Mengtong	107	30.44 N	105.53 E
Mengulek, Gora Λ	86	50.58 N	89.30 E
Mengwang	102	22.26 N	100.34 E
Mengyin	98	35.45 N	117.57 E
Mengyinzhai	98	36.04 N	117.47 E
Mengzhe	102	22.02 N	100.16 E
Mengzhi	102	24.10 N	99.46 E
Mengzi	102	23.22 N	103.20 E
Menihek Lakes @	176	54.00 N	66.35 W
Ménil-la-Tour	56	48.46 N	5.52 E
Menindee	166	32.24 S	142.26 E
Menindee Lake @	166	32.21 S	142.20 E
Meningie	166	35.42 S	139.20 E
Menjiaqiangzi	104	42.29 N	121.19 E
Menkoutang	106	31.01 N	119.27 E
Menlo	224	46.38 N	123.39 W
Menlo Park	226	37.28 N	122.13 W
Menlo Park Mall ◆[9]	276	40.32 N	74.20 W
Menlo Park Terrace	276	40.32 N	74.20 W
Mennecy	261	48.34 N	2.26 E
Mennetou-sur-Cher	50	47.16 N	1.53 E
Mennighüffen	52	52.13 N	8.43 E
Menno	198	43.14 N	97.34 W
Meno, Indon.	164	3.52 S	135.31 E
Meno, Okla., U.S.	196	36.24 N	98.11 W
Menominee	190	45.06 N	87.37 W
Menominee ≃	190	45.05 N	87.36 W
Menomonee ≃	216	43.02 N	87.54 W
Menomonee Falls	216	43.11 N	88.07 W
Menomonie	190	44.53 N	91.55 W
Menongue	152	14.36 S	17.48 E
Menor, Mar C	34	37.43 N	0.48 W
Menorca I	34	40.00 N	4.00 E
Mens	62	44.49 N	5.45 E
Menslage	52	52.41 N	7.49 E
Menstrup	41	55.13 N	11.36 E
Mentana	66	42.02 N	12.38 E
Mentasta Lake	180	62.55 N	143.45 W
Mentasta Mountains ⋀	180	62.40 N	143.07 W
Mentawai, Kepulauan II	108	2.00 S	99.30 E
Mentawai, Selat ⋓	112	1.56 S	100.12 E
Mentekab	114	3.29 N	102.21 E
Menteke, Peski ◆[2]	80	47.20 N	50.40 E
Menteng ◆[8]	269e	6.12 S	106.50 E
Menteroda	54	51.18 N	10.33 E
Menteşpiri	130	41.41 N	32.39 E
Menthon-Saint-Bernard	62	45.51 N	6.12 E
Menton	62	43.47 N	7.30 E
Mentone → Menton, Fr.	62	43.47 N	7.30 E
Mentone, Calif., U.S.	228	34.05 N	117.08 W
Mentone, Ind., U.S.	216	41.10 N	86.02 W
Mentone, Tex., U.S.	196	31.42 N	103.36 W
Mentor, Ky., U.S.	218	38.53 N	84.16 W
Mentor, Ohio, U.S.	214	41.40 N	81.20 W
Mentor-on-the-lake	214	41.43 N	81.21 W
Mentougou	105	39.56 N	116.03 E
Mentzdam ◆[6]	158	33.10 S	25.09 E
Menucourt	261	49.02 N	1.59 E
Menuma	94	36.13 N	139.23 E
Men'uša	76	58.23 N	30.42 E
Menyamya	164	7.10 S	146.00 E
Menyapa, Gunung Λ	112	1.05 N	116.05 E
Menyuan	102	37.27 N	101.48 E
Menza ≃	88	50.14 N	108.38 E
Menzel Bourguiba	148	37.10 N	9.48 E
Menzel Bou Zelfa	36	36.41 N	10.36 E
Menzel Djemil	36	37.14 N	9.55 E
Menzelen	52	51.37 N	6.32 E
Menzelerheide	263	51.37 N	6.31 E
Menzelinsk	80	55.43 N	53.08 E
Menzel Temime	148	36.47 N	10.59 E
Menzenschwand	58	47.49 N	8.04 E
Menzies	162	29.41 S	121.02 E
Menzies, Mount Λ	9	73.30 S	61.50 E
Menziken	58	47.14 N	8.12 E
Meob Bay C	156	24.25 S	14.34 E

PORTUGUÊS

Nome	Página	Lat.°′	Long.°′ W=Oeste
Meola Āgri	272a	28.42 N	77.23 E
Meolo	64	45.37 N	12.27 E
Meon ≃	42	50.48 N	1.15 W
Meopham	260	51.22 N	0.22 E
Meopham Station	260	51.23 N	0.21 E
Meoqui	232	28.17 N	105.29 W
Meota	184	53.02 N	108.27 W
Méouge ≃	62	44.16 N	5.50 E
Méounes-lès-Montrieux	62	43.17 N	5.58 E
Mepal	42	52.24 N	0.07 E
Mepisckaro, Gora Λ	84	41.50 N	42.40 E
Meppel	52	52.42 N	6.11 E
Meppen	52	52.41 N	7.17 E
Mequon	216	43.13 N	87.58 W
Mer	50	47.42 N	1.30 E
Mera ≃	58	46.11 N	9.25 E
Merah	112	0.50 N	116.48 E
Merai	164	4.50 S	152.20 E
Meråker	26	63.26 N	11.45 E
Merakurak	115a	6.53 S	111.59 E
Mera Lava I	175f	14.25 S	168.03 E
Meram	130	37.50 N	32.27 E
Meramangye, Lake @	162	28.25 S	132.13 E
Merambéllou, Kólpos C	38	35.14 N	25.47 E
Meramec ≃	194	38.23 N	90.21 W
Meramec Caverns ●[5]	219	38.15 N	91.06 W
Meramec State Park ♠	219	38.14 N	91.05 W
Meran → Merano, It.	64	46.40 N	11.09 E
Meran, Nig.	273a	6.38 N	3.16 E
Meranggau	112	0.12 S	110.17 E
Merangin ≃	112	2.09 S	102.47 E
Merano (Meran)	64	46.40 N	11.09 E
Merapi, Gunung Λ	115a	8.03 S	114.15 E
Merapoh	114	4.41 N	101.59 E
Merasheen	186	47.25 N	54.21 W
Merasheen Island I	186	47.30 N	54.15 W
Merate	62	45.42 N	9.25 E
Meratus, Pegunungan ⋀	112	2.45 S	115.40 E
Merauke	164	8.28 S	140.20 E
Merauke ≃	164	8.30 S	140.24 E
Merawang, Pulau I	271c	1.20 N	103.38 E
Merbabu, Gunung Λ	115a	7.33 S	110.26 E
Merbau	114	1.07 N	102.33 E
Merbein	166	34.11 S	142.04 E
Mer Bleue Peat Bog ☷	212	45.24 N	75.30 W
Merca → Marka	144	1.47 N	44.52 E
Mercaderes	246	1.47 N	77.10 W
Mercader y Millás	266d	41.21 N	2.05 E
Mercan Dağları ⋀	84	39.34 N	39.33 E
Mercāra	122	12.25 N	75.44 E
Mercatale	66	43.15 N	12.08 E
Mercato San Severino	68	40.47 N	14.46 E
Mercato Saraceno	66	43.57 N	12.12 E
Merced	226	37.18 N	120.29 W
Merced □[6]	226	37.15 N	120.40 W
Merced ≃	226	37.21 N	120.58 W
Merced, Lake @	282	37.43 N	122.29 W
Merced, North Fork ≃	226	37.37 N	120.03 W
Merced, South Fork ≃	226	37.39 N	119.53 W
Merced Airport ⊠	226	37.17 N	120.31 W
Mercedario, Cerro Λ	252	31.59 S	70.07 W
Mercedes, Arg.	252	33.40 S	65.28 W
Mercedes, Arg.	252	29.12 S	58.05 W
Mercedes, Arg.	258	34.39 S	59.27 W
Mercedes, Pil.	116	14.07 N	123.01 E
Mercedes, Tex., U.S.	196	26.09 N	97.55 W
Mercedes, Ur.	252	33.16 S	58.01 W
Mercedita, Aeropuerto ⊠	240m	18.01 N	66.34 W
Mercer, N.Z.	172	37.16 S	175.03 E
Mercer, Mo., U.S.	194	40.31 N	93.32 W
Mercer, Ohio, U.S.	216	40.40 N	84.35 W
Mercer, Pa., U.S.	214	41.14 N	80.15 W
Mercer, Wis., U.S.	190	46.10 N	90.04 W
Mercer □[6], N.J., U.S.	208	40.13 N	74.45 W
Mercer □[6], Ohio, U.S.	216	40.33 N	84.34 W
Mercer □[6], Pa., U.S.	214	41.14 N	80.15 W
Mercer Island	224	47.35 N	122.15 W
Mercersburg	188	39.50 N	77.54 W
Mercerville	208	40.14 N	74.41 W
Mercês, Bra.	256	21.12 S	43.21 W
Mercês, Port.	266c	38.47 N	9.19 W
Merchants Bay C	176	67.10 N	62.50 W
Merchants Millpond @	208	36.26 N	76.41 W
Merchantville	285	39.57 N	75.03 W
Merchong ≃	114	3.03 N	103.27 E
Merchtem	50	50.58 N	4.14 E
Mercier (Saint-Philomène)	275a	45.19 N	73.45 W
Mercier, Pont ◆[5]	275a	45.25 N	73.39 W
Mercoal	182	53.10 N	117.05 W
Mercogliano	68	40.55 N	14.44 E
Mercümüt	130	38.25 N	39.04 E
Mercury	204	36.40 N	115.59 W
Mercury Islands II	172	36.35 S	175.55 E
Mercy Bay C	176	74.05 N	119.00 W
Mercy-le-Bas	56	49.23 N	5.45 E
Merdeka Bridge ◆[5]	271c	1.18 N	103.53 E
Merdeka Palace ⊽	269e	6.10 S	106.49 E
Merdinik	130	40.48 N	42.36 E
Méré, Fr.	261	48.47 N	1.49 E
Mere, Eng., U.K.	42	51.06 N	2.16 W
Mere, Eng., U.K.	262	53.20 N	2.25 W
Mere Brow	262	53.40 N	2.53 W
Mereckij	85	43.48 N	74.42 E
Mereclough	262	53.46 N	2.11 W
Meredale	273d	26.17 S	27.59 E
Meredith, Austl.	169	37.51 S	144.04 E
Meredith, N.H., U.S.	188	43.39 N	71.30 W
Meredith, Cape ≻	254	52.15 S	60.39 W
Meredith, Lake @[1]	196	35.36 N	101.42 W
Meredosia	219	39.50 N	90.34 W
Meredosia Lake @	219	39.52 N	90.33 W
Merefa	78	49.49 N	36.03 E
Merelbeke	50	51.00 N	3.45 E
Merenkurkku (Norra Kvarken) ⋓	26	63.36 N	20.43 E
Merevari ≃	246	4.28 N	63.57 W
Méréville	50	48.19 N	2.05 E
Merewa	144	7.40 N	37.00 E
Merewether	170	32.57 S	151.46 E
Mereworth	260	51.15 N	0.23 E
Mergenevo	80	49.56 N	51.17 E
Mergozzo	58	45.58 N	8.26 E
Mergui (Myeik)	110	12.26 N	98.36 E
Mergui Archipelago II	110	12.00 N	98.00 E
Merḥavya	132	32.36 N	35.19 E
Meria	272b	22.59 N	88.20 E
Meribah	166	34.42 S	140.51 E
Méribel	62	45.25 N	6.34 E
Meriç (Marica) (Évros) ≃	38	40.52 N	26.12 E
Méricourt	50	50.24 N	2.52 E
Mérida, Esp.	34	38.55 N	6.20 W
Mérida, Méx.	200	32.39 N	114.58 W
Mérida, Méx.	232	20.58 N	89.37 W
Merida, Pil.	116	10.55 N	124.32 E
Mérida, Ven.	246	8.36 N	71.08 W
Mérida □[3]	246	8.30 N	71.10 W
Mérida, Cordillera de ⋀	246	8.40 N	71.00 W
Meridale	210	42.22 N	74.57 W
Meriden, Eng., U.K.	42	52.26 N	1.37 W
Meriden, Conn., U.S.	207	41.32 N	72.48 W
Meriden, N.J., U.S.	276	40.57 N	74.28 W
Meridian, Calif., U.S.	226	39.09 N	121.55 W
Meridian, Ga., U.S.	192	31.27 N	81.23 W
Meridian, Idaho, U.S.	202	43.37 N	116.24 W
Meridian, Miss., U.S.	194	32.22 N	88.42 W
Meridian, N.Y., U.S.	210	43.10 N	76.32 W
Meridian, Pa., U.S.	214	40.51 N	79.58 W
Meridian, Tex., U.S.	222	31.55 N	97.39 W
Meridian Hills	218	39.53 N	86.09 W
Mériel	261	49.05 N	2.12 E
Mérignac	32	44.50 N	0.42 W
Merigold	194	33.50 N	90.50 W
Merikarvia	26	61.51 N	21.30 E
Merille ≃	144	1.25 N	38.26 E
Merimbula	166	36.53 S	149.54 E
Merín, Laguna (Lagoa Mirim) C	252	32.45 S	52.50 W
Merinda	166	20.01 S	148.10 E
Mering	60	48.16 N	10.59 E
Merin Gubai	144	1.27 N	44.23 E
Merino	198	40.29 N	103.21 W
Merinos	252	32.24 S	56.54 W
Merion Station	285	40.00 N	75.15 W
Merir I	108	4.19 N	132.19 E
Merishausen	58	47.45 N	8.37 E
Merit	222	33.13 N	96.17 W
Meriti ≃	287a	22.48 S	43.20 W
Merivale Gardens	212	45.19 N	75.44 W
Merizo	174p	13.16 N	144.40 E
Merke	85	42.52 N	73.11 E
Merkel	196	32.28 N	100.01 W
Merkem	50	50.57 N	2.51 E
Merkendorf	56	49.12 N	10.42 E
Merkinė	76	54.10 N	24.10 E
Merklin	60	49.34 N	13.07 E
Merklingen	58	48.30 N	9.44 E
Merksem	50	51.15 N	4.27 E
Merksplas	56	51.22 N	4.52 E
Merkuloviči	76	52.58 N	30.36 E
Merkys ≃	76	54.10 N	24.11 E
Merlara	64	45.10 N	11.26 E
Merlebach	56	49.09 N	6.48 E
Merlejevo	82	55.05 N	37.13 E
Merlimau, Pulau I	271c	1.17 N	103.42 E
Merlimont-Plage	50	50.28 N	1.35 E
Merlin, Ont., Can.	214	42.14 N	82.14 W
Merlin, Oreg., U.S.	202	42.31 N	123.25 W
Merlin Seamount ✧[3]	14	8.20 S	150.25 W
Merlo, Arg.	252	32.21 S	65.02 W
Merlo, Arg.	258	34.40 S	58.45 W
Merlo □[5]	288	34.40 S	58.45 W
Merlo, Aeródromo ⊠	288	34.41 S	58.45 W
Merlynston	274b	37.43 S	144.58 E
Mermaid Beach	171a	28.03 S	153.27 E
Mern	41	55.03 N	12.04 E
Merna	198	41.29 N	99.46 W
Mernye	30	46.30 N	17.50 E
Meron	132	32.59 N	35.26 E
Meron, Hare Λ	132	32.58 N	35.25 E
Meros, Ponta dos ≻	256	23.13 S	44.21 W
Merotai Besar	112	4.26 N	117.46 E
Merouana	34	35.38 N	5.55 E
Merouane, Chott @	148	34.00 N	6.02 E
Mer'oža	76	59.02 N	36.23 E
Merredin	162	31.29 S	118.16 E
Merrick	276	40.40 N	73.33 W
Merrick Λ	44	55.08 N	4.29 W
Merrick Bay C	276	40.38 N	73.33 W
Merrickville	212	44.55 N	75.50 W
Merri Creek ≃	169	37.48 S	145.01 E
Merriewold Lake	210	41.22 N	74.12 W
Merrifield	284c	38.52 N	77.14 W
Merrill, Iowa, U.S.	198	42.43 N	96.15 W
Merrill, Mich., U.S.	190	43.25 N	84.20 W
Merrill, Oreg., U.S.	202	42.01 N	121.36 W
Merrill, Wis., U.S.	190	45.11 N	89.41 W
Merrillan	190	44.27 N	90.50 W
Merrill C. Meigs Field ⊠	278	41.52 N	87.37 W
Merrill Lake @	212	44.55 N	77.24 W
Merrillville	216	41.29 N	87.20 W
Merrimac	207	42.50 N	71.00 W
Merrimack ≃	207	42.49 N	70.49 W
Merrimac Terrace	283	42.49 N	71.00 W
Merriman, S. Afr.	158	31.13 S	23.38 E
Merriman, Nebr., U.S.	198	42.55 N	101.42 W
Merrin, Mount Λ	175f	19.35 S	169.22 E
Merrionette Park	278	41.41 N	87.42 W
Merriott	42	50.54 N	2.48 W
Merritt, B.C., Can.	182	50.07 N	120.47 W
Merritt, Wash., U.S.	224	47.47 N	120.51 W
Merritt, Lake @[1]	282	37.48 N	122.16 W
Merritt Island	220	28.21 N	80.42 W
Merritt Island I	220	28.33 N	80.40 W
Merritt Reservoir @[1]	198	42.35 N	100.55 W
Merriwa	166	32.08 S	150.21 E
Mer Rouge	194	32.47 N	91.48 W
Merrow	207	41.49 N	72.19 W
Merrygoen	166	31.50 S	149.14 E
Merrylands	274a	33.50 S	150.59 E
Merrymount Park ♠	283	42.16 N	71.01 W
Merryville	194	30.45 N	93.33 W
Mersa Fatma	144	14.55 N	40.20 E
Mersa Matruh → Maṭrūḥ	140	31.21 N	27.14 E
Mersch	56	49.46 N	6.06 E
Merscheid ◆[8]	263	51.10 N	7.01 E
Merse V	46	55.39 N	2.15 W
Merse ≃	66	43.05 N	11.22 E
Mersea Island I	42	51.47 N	0.55 E
Merseburg	54	51.21 N	11.59 E
Mers el Kébir	148	35.45 N	0.43 W
Mersey ≃, Austl.	166	41.10 S	146.22 E
Mersey ≃, N.S., Can.	186	44.02 N	64.43 W
Mersey ≃, Eng., U.K.	262	53.26 N	3.01 W
Merseyside □[6]	262	53.29 N	2.59 W
Mersey Tunnel ◆[5]	262	53.24 N	3.00 W
Mersin	130	36.48 N	34.38 E
Mersing	114	2.26 N	103.50 E
Mers-les-Bains	50	50.04 N	1.23 E
Mērsrags	76	57.21 N	23.07 E
Mersthaw	260	51.16 N	0.09 W
Merta	120	26.39 N	74.02 E
Merta Road	120	26.43 N	73.55 E
Merthyr Tydfil	42	51.46 N	3.23 W
Merti	154	1.04 N	38.40 E
Mertingen	56	48.39 N	10.47 E
Mértola	34	37.38 N	7.40 W
Merton, Austl.	169	36.59 S	145.42 E
Merton, Wis., U.S.	216	43.09 N	88.18 W
Merton ◆[8]	42	51.25 N	0.12 W
Mertz Glacier Tongue ⊓	9	67.40 S	144.45 E
Mertzon	196	31.16 N	100.49 W
Mertztown	208	40.30 N	75.40 W
Méru, Fr.	50	49.14 N	2.08 E
Meru, Kenya	154	0.03 N	37.39 E
Meru, Mount Λ	154	3.14 S	36.40 E
Meruoca	250	3.28 S	40.28 W
Merv → Mary	128	37.36 N	61.50 E
Mervans	58	46.48 N	5.11 E
Merville	50	50.38 N	2.38 E
Mervin	184	53.20 N	108.53 W
Merwede	158	31.38 S	23.48 E
Merweville	158	32.40 S	21.31 E
Merwin, Lake @[1]	224	45.59 N	122.26 W
Merxleben	54	51.07 N	10.40 E
Mery	82	55.49 N	36.36 E
Méry-la-Bataille	50	49.33 N	2.38 E
Méry-sur-Oise	261	49.04 N	2.11 E
Méry-sur-Seine	50	48.30 N	3.53 E
Merzdorf	54	51.23 N	14.32 E
Merzhausen	58	47.58 N	7.49 E
Merzifon	130	40.53 N	35.29 E
Merzig	56	49.27 N	6.36 E
Mesa, Moç.	154	13.00 S	39.33 E
Mesa, S. Afr.	158	26.29 S	26.59 E
Mesa, Ariz., U.S.	200	33.25 N	111.50 W
Mesa ≃	34	41.15 N	1.48 W
Mesa, Cerro Λ	254	48.46 S	71.29 W
Mesabi Range ⋀[2]	190	47.30 N	92.50 W
Mesachie Lake	224	48.49 N	124.07 W
Mesa del Nayar	234	22.16 N	104.35 W
Mesa de Santa Rita	234	23.04 N	105.31 W
Mesagne	68	40.33 N	17.49 E
Mes'agutovo	86	55.35 N	58.20 E
Mesaména	152	3.44 N	12.50 E
Mesa Mountain Λ	200	37.55 N	106.38 W
Mesarás, Kólpos C	38	34.58 N	24.36 E
Mesa Verde National Park ♠	200	37.13 N	108.30 W
Mescalero	200	33.09 N	105.46 W
Mescalero Indian Reservation ◆[4]	200	33.12 N	105.40 W
Meščerino, S.S.S.R.	76	53.37 N	37.23 E
Meščerino, S.S.S.R.	82	55.11 N	38.21 E
Meščerskij	265b	55.40 N	37.25 E
Meščerskoje	82	55.17 N	37.38 E
Meschede	56	51.20 N	8.17 E
Meschetskij Chrebet ⋀	84	41.48 N	42.30 E
Mescit Dağı Λ	130	40.22 N	41.11 E
Meščovsk	76	54.19 N	35.17 E
Meščura	24	63.20 N	50.52 E
Mese	58	46.17 N	9.21 E
Mèsè Atet	110	18.38 N	97.39 E
Mesen-Bucht → Mezenskaja Guba C	24	66.40 N	43.45 E
Meseritz → Międzyrzecz	30	52.28 N	15.35 E
Mesero	266b	45.30 N	8.51 E
Mesewa (Massaua)	144	15.38 N	39.28 E
Mesewa Channel ⋓	144	15.30 N	40.00 E
Mesfinto	144	13.20 N	37.19 E
Mesgarābād	267d	35.37 N	51.31 E
Mesgouez, Lac @	176	51.24 N	75.05 W
Meshed → Mashhad	128	36.18 N	59.36 E
Meshomasic Mountain Λ	207	41.38 N	72.32 W
Meshoppen	210	41.34 N	76.03 W
Meshoppen Creek ≃	210	41.37 N	76.03 W
Mesick	190	44.24 N	85.43 W
Mesilinka ≃	182	56.09 N	124.28 W
Mesilla	200	32.16 N	106.48 W
Mesillas, Méx.	234	23.33 N	103.35 W
Mesillas, Méx.	234	23.14 N	106.03 W
Mesima ≃	68	38.30 N	16.15 E
Meskiana	148	35.39 N	7.41 E
Meskiana, Oued ≃	36	35.49 N	7.53 E
Meşkinan	130	37.18 N	40.22 E
Meskine	146	11.25 N	15.21 E
Meškuičiai	76	56.05 N	23.28 E
Meskum	114	1.34 N	102.01 E
Meslay-du-Maine	32	47.57 N	0.33 W
Meslay-le-Grenet	50	48.22 N	1.23 E
Meslo	144	6.27 N	39.50 E
Mesnil-Val-Plage	50	50.03 N	1.20 E
Mesocco	58	46.23 N	9.14 E
Mesola	66	44.55 N	12.14 E
Mesolcina, Valle V	58	46.20 N	9.10 E
Mesolóngion	38	38.21 N	21.17 E
Mésondo	152	3.43 N	10.28 E
Mesopotamia	214	41.27 N	80.57 W
Mesopotamia ◆[1]	128	34.00 N	44.00 E
Mesoraca	68	39.05 N	16.48 E
Mesóyia □[9]	267c	37.56 N	23.53 E
Mespelbrunn ⊥	56	49.54 N	9.19 E
Mesquita, Bra.	255	19.13 S	42.35 W
Mesquita, Bra.	256	22.48 S	43.26 W
Mesquite, Nev., U.S.	204	36.48 N	114.04 W
Mesquite, Tex., U.S.	222	32.46 N	96.36 W
Messaad, Oued V	148	33.45 N	2.51 E
Messach Mellet ⋀[2]	146	24.30 N	11.35 E
Messalo ≃	154	11.40 S	40.26 E
Messaoud, Oued V	148	27.28 N	0.21 W
Messdorf	54	52.43 N	11.33 E
Messent National Park ♠	166	36.05 S	139.50 E
Messina, It.	70	38.11 N	15.34 E
Messina, S. Afr.	156	22.23 S	30.00 E
Messina □[4]	70	38.03 N	14.52 E
Messina, Stretto di ⋓	70	38.15 N	15.35 E
Messíni	38	37.04 N	22.00 E
Messíni ⊥	38	37.11 N	21.57 E
Messiniakós Kólpos C	38	36.58 N	22.00 E
Messix Peak Λ	202	41.29 N	112.31 W
Messkirch	58	47.59 N	9.07 E
Messojacha ≃	74	67.52 N	77.27 E
Messtetten	58	48.11 N	8.58 E
Messy	261	48.58 N	2.42 E
Mestá	38	38.15 N	25.55 E
Mesta (Néstos) ≃	38	40.41 N	24.44 E
Mestasa	148	35.07 N	4.25 W
Městečko	60	50.03 N	13.52 E
Mestia	84	43.03 N	42.43 E
Mestlin	54	53.35 N	11.56 E
Město Touškov	60	49.46 N	13.15 E
Mestre	64	45.29 N	12.15 E
Mestrino	64	45.26 N	11.45 E
Mesudiye	130	40.28 N	37.46 E
Mesum	52	52.13 N	7.29 E
Meszah Peak Λ	180	58.28 N	131.26 W
Meta, It.	68	40.39 N	14.24 E
Meta, Mo., U.S.	219	38.19 N	92.10 W
Meta □[5]	246	3.30 N	73.00 W
Meta ≃	246	6.12 N	67.28 W
Métabief	58	46.47 N	6.21 E
Metagācha	272b	22.38 N	88.31 E
Metairie	194	29.59 N	90.09 W
Metalanim	174r	6.53 N	158.16 E
Metaline Falls	202	48.52 N	117.22 W
Metallifere, Colline ⋀	66	43.15 N	11.00 E
Metallostroj	265a	59.47 N	30.33 E
Metamora, Ill., U.S.	190	40.47 N	89.22 W
Metamora, Ind., U.S.	218	39.27 N	85.08 W
Metamora, Mich., U.S.	216	42.57 N	83.17 W
Metamora, Ohio, U.S.	216	41.43 N	83.55 W
Metán	252	25.29 S	64.57 W
Metapán	236	14.20 N	89.27 W
Metapontum ⊥	68	40.23 N	16.50 E
Metarica	154	14.20 S	36.48 E
Metaurilia	66	43.49 N	13.03 E
Metauro ≃	66	43.50 N	13.03 E
Metcalfe	212	45.14 N	75.28 W
Metchosin	224	48.22 N	123.33 W
Metechi	84	41.55 N	44.21 E
Metedeconk, South Branch ≃	208	40.04 N	74.09 W
Meteghan	186	44.11 N	66.10 W
Metehara	144	8.55 N	39.57 E
Metelen	52	52.08 N	7.12 E
Metema	144	12.57 N	36.12 E
Metéora ⊽[1]	38	39.46 N	21.36 E
Meteor Seamount ✧[3]	8	47.50 S	8.55 E
Metepec, Méx.	234	19.15 N	99.36 W
Metepec, Méx.	234	18.56 N	98.28 W
Metharaw	110	16.12 N	98.08 E
Methil	46	56.10 N	3.01 W
Methler	263	51.35 N	7.37 E
Methlick	46	57.25 N	2.14 W
Methóni	38	36.50 N	21.43 E
Methow	182	48.08 N	120.00 W
Methow ≃	224	48.40 N	120.32 W
Methuen	207	42.44 N	71.11 W
Methven	172	43.38 S	171.39 E
Methwold	42	52.31 N	0.33 E
Methyen	46	56.25 N	3.34 W
Metiskow	184	52.24 N	110.38 W
Metković	36	43.03 N	17.39 E
Metlakatla, B.C., Can.	182	54.20 N	130.27 W
Metlakatla, Alaska, U.S.	180	55.08 N	131.35 W
Metlatonoc	234	17.11 N	98.20 W
Metlika	36	45.39 N	15.19 E
Metlili, Oued V	148	31.54 N	4.53 E
Metlili Chaamba	148	32.18 N	3.40 E
Metmahu @	120	34.15 N	82.20 E
Metnitz	61	46.59 N	14.13 E
Metnitz ≃	61	46.53 N	14.27 E
Meto, Bayou ≃	194	34.05 N	91.26 W
Metolius ≃	202	44.36 N	121.17 W
Metomkin Bay C	208	37.43 N	75.35 W
Metomkin Inlet C	208	37.41 N	75.35 W
Metomkin Island I	208	37.43 N	75.33 W
Metro	115a	5.05 S	105.20 E
Metropolis	194	37.09 N	88.44 W
Metropolitan	190	46.00 N	87.53 W
Metropolitan Beach ♠	281	42.35 N	82.48 W
Metropolitan Museum of Art ⊽	276	40.47 N	73.58 W
Metropolitan Oakland International Airport ⊠	226	37.43 N	122.13 W
Metschow	54	53.49 N	12.58 E
Metsematluku	156	24.01 S	24.40 E
Metsera	154	2.35 S	26.07 E
Métsovon	38	39.46 N	21.11 E
Mettawa	278	42.14 N	87.56 W
Metten	60	48.52 N	12.55 E
Mettendorf	56	49.57 N	6.19 E
Metter	192	32.24 N	82.03 W
Mettet	56	50.19 N	4.40 E
Mettetal Airport ⊠	281	42.21 N	83.27 W
Mettingen	52	52.18 N	7.46 E
Mettlach	56	49.30 N	6.36 E
Mettmach	60	48.10 N	13.21 E
Mettmann	56	51.15 N	6.58 E
Mettray	50	47.27 N	0.39 E
Mettuppālaiyam	122	11.18 N	76.57 E
Mettūr	122	11.48 N	77.48 E
Metu	144	8.20 N	35.36 E
Metuchen	210	40.33 N	74.22 W
Metuge	154	12.58 S	40.20 E
Metulla	132	33.16 N	35.35 E
Metundo, Ilha I	154	11.10 S	40.41 E
Metz	56	49.08 N	6.10 E
Metzervisse	56	49.19 N	6.17 E
Metzger	224	45.26 N	122.44 W
Metzingen	56	48.32 N	9.17 E
Metzkausen	263	51.16 N	6.57 E
Metztitlán, Laguna @	234	20.40 N	98.50 W
Meu ≃	32	48.02 N	1.47 W
Meuban	152	2.27 N	12.41 E
Meudon	261	48.48 N	2.14 E
Meudon, Bois de ♠	261	48.47 N	2.12 E
Meulaboh	114	4.09 N	96.08 E
Meulan	50	49.01 N	1.54 E
Meulebeke	50	50.57 N	3.17 E
Meung-sur-Loire	50	47.50 N	1.42 E
Meureubo ≃	114	4.09 N	96.09 E
Meureudu	114	5.16 N	96.16 E
Meursault	58	46.59 N	4.46 E
Meurthe ≃	32	48.47 N	6.09 E
Meurthe-et-Moselle □[5]	32	48.35 N	6.10 E
Meuse	58	47.59 N	5.33 E
Meuse □[5]	56	49.00 N	5.30 E
Meuse (Maas) ≃	30	51.49 N	5.01 E
Meuselwitz	54	51.02 N	12.17 E
Meux Creek ≃	212	44.07 N	81.02 W
Mevagissey	42	50.16 N	4.48 W
Mewāt Plain ≚	124	27.40 N	76.15 E
Mexborough	44	53.30 N	1.17 W
Mexia	222	31.41 N	96.29 W
Mexiana, Ilha I	250	0.02 S	49.35 W
Mexicali	232	32.40 N	115.29 W
Mexican Hat	200	37.09 N	109.52 W
Mexico, Ind., U.S.	216	40.49 N	86.07 W
Mexico, Maine, U.S.	188	44.34 N	70.33 W
Mexico, Mo., U.S.	219	39.10 N	91.53 W
Mexico, N.Y., U.S.	212	43.28 N	76.14 W
Mexico, Pa., U.S.	208	40.32 N	77.21 W
México □[3]	234	19.20 N	99.45 W
Mexico □[1]	230	23.00 N	102.00 W
Mexico (México) □[1], N.A.	232	23.00 N	102.00 W
México, Golfo de → Mexico, Gulf of C	230	25.00 N	90.00 W
Mexico, Gulf of C	230	25.00 N	90.00 W
Mexico Basin ✧[1]	16	25.00 N	91.00 W
Mexico Bay C	212	43.31 N	76.17 W
Mexico City → Ciudad de México	234	19.24 N	99.09 W
Mexiko → Ciudad de México	234	19.24 N	99.09 W
Mexiko → Mexico □[1]	232	23.00 N	102.00 W
Mexiko, Golf von → Mexico, Gulf of C	230	25.00 N	90.00 W
Meximieux	58	45.54 N	5.12 E
Mexique → Mexico □[1]	230	23.00 N	102.00 W
Mexique, Golfe du → Mexico, Gulf of C	230	25.00 N	90.00 W
Mexticacán	234	21.13 N	102.43 W
Mey, Castle of ⊥	46	58.38 N	3.14 W
Meyanodas	164	7.38 S	131.38 E
Meycauayan	116	14.44 N	120.58 E
Meydan	130	38.21 N	41.47 E
Meydancık	130	41.25 N	42.14 E
Meydān-e Gel ≚	128	29.04 N	54.50 E
Meydān Kalay	120	32.25 N	66.44 E
Meydān Khvolah	120	33.36 N	69.51 E
Meyenburg	54	53.18 N	12.14 E
Meyers Chuck	180	55.44 N	132.12 W
Meyersdale	188	39.45 N	79.05 W
Meyers Lake	214	40.52 N	81.24 W
Meyersville	222	28.55 N	97.21 W
Meyerton	158	26.33 S	28.01 E
Meyísti I	130	36.08 N	29.34 E
Meymac	32	45.32 N	2.09 E
Meymaneh	120	35.55 N	64.47 E
Meymeh	128	33.27 N	51.10 E
Meymeh ≃	128	32.05 N	47.16 E
Meyo-Centre	152	2.33 N	11.02 E
Meyrargues	62	43.38 N	5.32 E
Meyrin	58	46.14 N	6.05 E
Meyronne	184	49.39 N	106.50 W
Meyrueis	32	44.10 N	3.26 E
Meža ≃	61	46.35 N	15.02 E
Meẓada, Ḥorvot (Masada) ⊥	132	31.19 N	35.21 E
Mezapa	236	15.33 N	87.23 W
Mezdra	38	43.09 N	23.42 E
Meždurečensk	86	53.42 N	88.03 E
Meždurečenskij	86	59.36 N	65.53 E
Mèze	32	43.25 N	3.36 E
Mézel	62	43.59 N	6.12 E
Mezen'	24	65.50 N	44.13 E
Mezen' ≃	24	66.11 N	43.59 E
Mézenc, Mont Λ	62	44.55 N	4.11 E
Mezenskaja Guba C	24	66.40 N	43.45 E
Meževaja	78	48.16 N	36.44 E
Mežgorje	78	48.32 N	23.30 E
Meziadin Lake @	182	56.04 N	129.18 W
Mézières-en-Brenne	32	46.49 N	1.13 E
Mézières-sur-Seine	261	48.58 N	1.48 E
Mézilhac	62	44.48 N	4.21 E
Mézin	32	44.03 N	0.16 E
Mezinovskij	76	55.30 N	40.21 E
Mežirič	78	50.43 N	34.29 E
Mezőberény	30	46.50 N	21.02 E
Mezőcsát	30	47.49 N	20.55 E

Symbol	English	Deutsch	Español	Français	Português
≃	River	Fluss	Río	Rivière	Rio
Ξ	Canal	Kanal	Canal	Canal	Canal
↳	Waterfall, Rapids	Wasserfall, Stromschnellen	Cascada, Rápidos	Chute d'eau, Rapides	Cascata, Rápidos
⋓	Strait	Meeresstrasse	Estrecho	Détroit	Estreito
C	Bay, Gulf	Bucht, Golf	Bahía, Golfo	Baie, Golfe	Baía, Golfo
@	Lake, Lakes	See, Seen	Lago, Lagos	Lac, Lacs	Lago, Lagos
☷	Swamp	Sumpf	Pantano	Marais	Pântano
⊓	Ice Features, Glacier	Eis- und Gletscherformen	Accidentes Glaciales	Formes glaciaires	Acidentes Glaciares
⊤	Other Hydrographic Features	Andere Hydrographische Objekte	Otros Elementos Hidrográficos	Autres données hydrographiques	Outros Elementos Hidrográficos

Symbol	English	Deutsch	Español	Français	Português
✧	Submarine Features	Untermeerische Objekte	Accidentes Submarinos	Formes de relief sous-marin	Acidentes Submarinos
□	Political Unit	Politische Einheit	Unidad Politica	Entité politique	Unidade Política
⊽	Cultural Institution	Kulturelle Institution	Institución Cultural	Institution culturelle	Instituição Cultural
⊥	Historical Site	Historische Stätte	Sitio Histórico	Site historique	Sitio Histórico
♠	Recreational Site	Erholungs- und Ferienort	Sitio de Recreo	Centre de loisirs	Sítio de Lazer
⊠	Airport	Flughafen	Aeropuerto	Aéroport	Aeroporto
■	Military Installation	Militäranlage	Instalación Militar	Installation militaire	Instalação Militar
◆	Miscellaneous	Verschiedenes	Misceláneo	Divers	Miscelânea

Name	Page	Lat.°′	Long.°′
Mezőkovácsháza	30	46.25 N	20.55 E
Mezőkövesd	30	47.50 N	20.34 E
Mezőtúr	30	47.00 N	20.38 E
Mezquital	234	23.29 N	104.23 W
Mezquital ≃	232	22.54 N	104.54 W
Mezquital del Oro	234	21.10 N	103.23 W
Mezquitic	234	22.23 N	103.41 W
Mezraa	130	41.12 N	35.08 E
Mézy	261	49.00 N	1.53 E
Mezzana	64	46.19 N	10.48 E
Mezzano	64	46.09 N	11.48 E
Mezzenile	62	45.17 N	7.23 E
Mezzocorona	64	46.13 N	11.07 E
Mezzoiuso	70	37.52 N	13.28 E
Mezzola, Lago di ⊜	58	46.12 N	9.26 E
Mezzoldo	58	46.01 N	9.40 E
Mezzolombardo	64	46.13 N	11.05 E
Mezzomerico	266b	45.37 N	8.36 E
Mfangano Island I	154	0.28 S	34.01 E
Mfou	152	3.43 N	11.38 E
Mgači	89	51.05 N	142.17 E
Mgeni ≃	158	29.48 S	31.02 E
Mgeta	154	8.19 S	36.08 E
Mglin	76	53.04 N	32.51 E
M'goun, Irhil ʌ	148	31.31 N	6.25 W
M'hai, B'nom ʌ	110	11.21 N	107.50 E
Mhasvād	122	17.38 N	74.47 E
Mhlume	158	26.02 S	31.50 E
Mholach, Beinn ʌ[2]	46	56.45 N	4.18 W
Mhòr, Beinn ʌ	46	57.17 N	7.19 W
Mhòr, Loch ⊜	46	57.14 N	4.26 W
Mhow	120	22.33 N	75.46 E
Miacatlán	234	18.46 N	99.22 W
Mia-dong ⊸[8]	271b	37.37 N	127.01 E
Miagao	116	10.39 N	122.14 E
Miahuatlán de Porfirio Díaz	234	16.20 N	96.36 W
Miajadas	34	39.09 N	5.54 W
Miājlar	120	26.15 N	70.23 E
Miaméré	146	8.52 N	19.50 E
Miami, Man., Can.	184	49.21 N	98.11 W
Miami, Ariz., U.S.	200	33.24 N	110.52 W
Miami, Fla., U.S.	220	25.46 N	80.12 W
Miami, Ind., U.S.	216	40.37 N	86.06 W
Miami, Okla., U.S.	194	36.53 N	94.53 W
Miami, Tex., U.S.	196	35.42 N	100.38 W
Miami, Zimb.	154	16.40 S	29.46 E
Miami □[6], Ind., U.S.	216	40.45 N	86.04 W
Miami □[6], Ohio, U.S.	218	40.02 N	84.13 W
Miami ≃	224	45.33 N	123.53 W
Miami Beach, Ont., Can.	212	44.13 N	79.29 W
Miami Beach, Fla., U.S.	220	25.47 N	80.08 W
Miami Canal ≋	220	25.47 N	80.15 W
Miami Creek ≃	226	37.21 N	119.44 W
Miami International Airport ⊠	220	25.48 N	80.17 W
Miami Lakes	220	25.53 N	80.18 W
Miamisburg	218	39.38 N	84.17 W
Miamisburg Mound State Memorial ⊥	218	39.38 N	84.17 W
Miami Shores	220	25.51 N	80.11 W
Miami Springs	220	25.49 N	80.17 W
Miami State Recreation Area ♠	216	40.40 N	85.55 W
Miamiville	218	39.13 N	84.18 W
Mīānābād	128	37.02 N	57.27 E
Miān Channūn	123	30.27 N	72.22 E
Mianchi	102	34.48 N	111.49 E
Mīāndowāb	128	36.58 N	46.06 E
Miandrivazo	157b	19.31 S	45.28 E
Mianduhe	89	49.05 N	121.06 E
Miane	64	45.57 N	12.06 E
Mīāneh	128	37.26 N	47.42 E
Miang, Phu ʌ	110	17.42 N	101.01 E
Miangas, Pulau I	108	5.35 N	126.35 E
Mianhu	100	23.28 N	116.09 E
Mianhuadi	104	41.15 N	120.49 E
Miāni, Bhārat	120	21.51 N	69.23 E
Miāni, Pāk.	123	32.32 N	73.04 E
Miāni Hōr C	120	25.34 N	66.19 E
Mianning	102	28.39 N	102.09 E
Mianus ≃	207	41.03 N	73.35 W
Mianus Reservoir ⊜[1]	276	41.08 N	73.37 W
Miānwāli	123	32.35 N	71.33 E
Mianxian	102	33.09 N	106.48 E
Mianyang, Zhg.	100	30.23 N	113.25 E
Mianyang, Zhg.	102	31.30 N	104.49 E
Mianzhu, Zhg.	102	32.17 N	110.02 E
Mianzhu, Zhg.	102	31.20 N	104.09 E
Miaodaoqundao II	98	37.56 N	120.40 E
Miaoergou	86	45.32 N	83.52 E
Miaofengshan	105	40.04 N	116.13 E
Miaogou	104	41.12 N	120.40 E
Miaojiagou	104	42.16 N	123.22 E
Miaojiatun	104	40.54 N	120.55 E
Miaokou	98	35.48 N	114.09 E
Miaoli	100	24.34 N	120.48 E
Miaoling ʌʌ	102	26.15 N	107.26 E
Miaopu	106	31.00 N	118.44 E
Miaoqian	100	30.33 N	117.44 E
Miaotou	106	30.58 N	120.33 E
Miaowan	100	33.07 N	114.41 E
Miaowan I	100	21.54 N	114.00 E
Miaoyang	98	40.49 N	124.24 E
Miaozhen	106	31.43 N	121.21 E
Miarayon	116	8.04 N	124.50 E
Miarinarivo, Madag.	157b	18.57 S	46.55 E
Miarinarivo, Madag.	157b	16.38 S	48.15 E
Miarinavaratra	157b	20.13 S	47.31 E
Miasa	94	36.34 N	137.53 E
Miass	86	54.59 N	60.06 E
Miass ≃	86	56.06 N	64.30 E
Miasteczko Krajeńskie	30	53.06 N	17.01 E
Miastko	30	54.01 N	17.00 E
Miboro-dam ⊸[6]	94	36.08 N	136.55 E
Mibu	94	36.25 N	139.48 E
Mibu ≃	94	35.49 N	137.57 E
Mica	156	24.10 S	30.48 E
Mica Mountain ʌ	200	32.13 N	110.33 W
Micangshan ʌʌ	102	32.32 N	107.49 E
Micanopy	192	29.30 N	82.17 W
Micaúne	156	18.18 S	36.35 E
Mičavičevnik	24	64.14 N	57.58 E
Micha-cchakaja	84	42.17 N	42.04 E
Michael, Mount ʌ	164	6.25 S	145.20 E
Michael J. Kirwan Reservoir ⊜[1]	214	41.10 N	81.10 W
Michajlo-Koc'ubinskoje	78	51.27 N	31.04 E
Michajlov	82	54.14 N	39.02 E
Michajlovka, S.S.S.R.	78	47.16 N	35.14 E
Michajlovka, S.S.S.R.	78	49.53 N	39.38 E
Michajlovka, S.S.S.R.	78	49.19 N	36.28 E
Michajlovka, S.S.S.R.	80	47.38 N	46.54 E
Michajlovka, S.S.S.R.	80	50.05 N	43.15 E
Michajlovka, S.S.S.R.	83	48.30 N	38.54 E
Michajlovka, S.S.S.R.	83	48.44 N	37.16 E
Michajlovka, S.S.S.R.	83	48.09 N	37.22 E
Michajlovka, S.S.S.R.	85	42.37 N	78.20 E
Michajlovka, S.S.S.R.	85	42.50 N	75.42 E
Michajlovka, S.S.S.R.	85	43.06 N	71.36 E
Michajlovka, S.S.S.R.	86	51.49 N	79.45 E
Michajlovka, S.S.S.R.	86	53.51 N	76.32 E
Michajlovka, S.S.S.R.	86	56.26 N	78.53 E
Michajlovka, S.S.S.R.	88	51.07 N	119.20 E
Michajlovka, S.S.S.R.	88	50.26 N	104.10 E
Michajlovka, S.S.S.R.	88	52.57 N	103.18 E
Michajlovka, S.S.S.R.	88	55.30 N	114.09 E
Michajlovka, S.S.S.R.	88	51.53 N	110.28 E
Michajlovka, S.S.S.R.	89	49.13 N	129.56 E
Michajlovka, S.S.S.R.	89	43.56 N	132.00 E
Michajlovka, S.S.S.R.	265a	59.43 N	30.01 E
Michajlovka, S.S.S.R.	265a	60.04 N	30.14 E
Michajlovo	80	56.56 N	45.04 E
Michajlovo-Aleksandrovskij	83	49.13 N	40.15 E
Michajlovskaja	80	50.58 N	41.52 E
Michajlovskij, S.S.S.R.	76	60.05 N	43.29 E
Michajlovskij, S.S.S.R.	80	56.11 N	45.47 E
Michajlovskij, S.S.S.R.	86	51.41 N	79.47 E
Michajlovskij, S.S.S.R.	86	50.17 N	55.23 E
Michajlovskoje, S.S.S.R.	76	58.23 N	37.40 E
Michajlovskoje, S.S.S.R.	82	55.50 N	36.20 E
Michajlovskoje, S.S.S.R.	265b	55.35 N	37.35 E
Michalevo	82	55.27 N	38.26 E
Michali	82	55.17 N	39.05 E
Michalkovo	82	54.11 N	37.33 E
Michalovce	30	48.45 N	21.55 E
Michalovy Hory	60	49.55 N	12.47 E
Michanoviči	76	53.45 N	27.40 E
Michaud Point ≻	186	45.34 N	60.40 W
Michejevo	88	57.10 N	104.53 E
Michel	182	49.43 N	114.49 W
Michelago	171b	35.43 S	149.10 E
Michelau	56	50.10 N	11.06 E
Micheldever	42	51.09 N	1.15 W
Micheldorf	61	47.52 N	14.08 E
Michelfeld	60	49.42 N	11.35 E
Michel Peak ʌ	182	53.35 N	126.26 W
Michelsneukirchen	60	49.08 N	12.33 E
Michelson, Mount ʌ	180	69.19 N	144.17 W
Michel'sona	265b	55.42 N	37.54 E
Michelstadt	56	49.41 N	9.00 E
Michendorf	54	52.18 N	13.01 E
Miches	238	18.59 N	69.03 W
Micheta	84	41.52 N	44.44 E
Michiana	216	41.46 N	86.48 W
Michiana Regional Airport ⊠	216	41.42 N	86.19 W
Michigamee ≃	190	46.04 N	88.13 W
Michigan	198	48.07 N	98.07 W
Michigan □[3]	178; 190	44.00 N	85.00 W
Michigan, Lake ⊜	190	44.00 N	87.00 W
Michigan, University of (North Campus) ♁[2], Mich., U.S.	281	42.17 N	83.43 W
Michigan, University of ♁[2], Mich., U.S.	281	42.17 N	83.44 W
Michigan Center	190	42.14 N	84.20 W
Michigan City	216	41.43 N	86.54 W
Michigan International Speedway ♠	216	42.03 N	84.15 W
Michigan State Fair Grounds ♠	281	42.27 N	83.07 W
Michigantown	216	40.20 N	86.23 W
Michika	146	10.38 N	13.24 E
Michikamau Lake ⊜	176	54.00 N	64.00 W
Michillinda	280	34.07 N	118.05 W
Michipicoten Bay C	190	47.55 N	84.56 W
Michipicoten Island I	190	47.45 N	85.45 W
Michnevo	82	55.07 N	37.58 E
Michninskaja	24	60.26 N	46.14 E
Michoacán	204	32.28 N	115.20 W
Michoacán □[3]	234	19.10 N	101.50 W
Michoacanejo	234	21.33 N	102.36 W
Michów	30	51.32 N	22.19 E
Michurinsk → Mičurinsk	80	52.54 N	40.30 E
Mickle Fell ʌ	44	54.37 N	2.18 W
Mickleham	260	51.16 N	0.19 W
Mickleover	42	52.24 N	1.34 W
Mickleton	285	39.47 N	75.14 W
Mickle Trafford	262	53.13 N	2.50 W
Mickleyville	218	39.45 N	86.16 W
Mico ≃	236	12.11 N	84.16 W
Mico, Montañas del ʌʌ	236	15.30 N	88.55 W
Miconge	152	4.26 S	12.51 E
Micoud	241f	13.50 N	60.54 W
Micronesia II	14	11.00 N	159.00 E
Mičurin	38	42.10 N	27.51 E
Mičurinsk	80	52.54 N	40.30 E
Midai, Pulau I	112	3.00 N	107.47 E
Midale	184	49.22 N	103.27 W
Midar	148	34.58 N	3.30 W
Mid-Atlantic Ridge ⊹[3]	8	0.00	25.00 W
Midbar Yehuda → Wilderness of Judæa ⊸[2]	132	31.30 N	35.18 E
Middalya	162	23.55 S	114.45 E
Middelburg, Ned.	52	51.30 N	3.37 E
Middelburg, S. Afr.	156	25.47 S	29.28 E
Middelburg, S. Afr.	158	31.30 S	25.00 E
Middelfart	41	55.30 N	9.45 E
Middelharnis	52	51.45 N	4.11 E
Middelkerke	50	51.11 N	2.49 E
Middelkerke, Vliegveld ⊠	50	51.12 N	2.52 E
Middelpos	158	31.55 S	20.13 E
Middelstum	52	53.20 N	6.38 E
Middelvlei	273d	26.14 S	27.38 E
Middelwit	156	24.58 S	27.00 E
Middenbeemster	52	52.33 N	4.55 E
Middenin	158	27.43 S	28.02 E
Middenmeer	52	52.47 N	5.00 E
Middle ≃, B.C., Can.	182	54.50 N	125.08 W
Middle ≃, Calif., U.S.	226	38.03 N	121.31 W
Middle ≃, Iowa, U.S.	194	41.29 N	93.24 W
Middle ≃, Minn., U.S.	198	48.22 N	97.04 W
Middle ≃, Mo., U.S.	219	38.39 N	91.53 W
Middle Alkali Lake ⊜	204	41.28 N	120.04 W
Middle America Trench ⊹[1]	16	15.00 N	95.00 W
Middle Andaman I	110	12.30 N	92.50 E
Middle Bass	214	41.41 N	82.50 W
Middle Bass Island I	214	41.41 N	82.49 W
Middle Bay	186	51.28 N	57.30 W
Middle Bay C	276	40.37 N	73.36 W
Middleboro	207	41.49 N	70.55 W
Middle Bosque ≃	222	31.31 N	97.16 W
Middlebourne	188	39.30 N	80.54 W
Middlebranch	214	40.54 N	81.20 W
Middle Breakwater ⊸[5]	280	33.43 N	118.13 W
Middlebro	184	49.01 N	95.21 W
Middle Brook	186	48.45 N	54.13 W
Middle Brook ≃, N.J., U.S.	276	40.39 N	74.41 W
Middle Brook ≃, N.J., U.S.	276	40.33 N	74.33 W
Middle Brook, East Branch ≃	276	40.35 N	74.33 W
Middle Brook, West Branch ≃	276	40.35 N	74.33 W
Middleburg, Md., U.S.	208	39.36 N	77.16 W
Middleburg, N.Y., U.S.	210	42.36 N	74.20 W
Middleburg, Ohio, U.S.	216	40.18 N	83.35 W
Middleburg, Pa., U.S.	208	40.47 N	77.03 W
Middleburg, Va., U.S.	188	38.58 N	77.44 W
Middleburgh Heights	214	41.22 N	81.48 W
Middlebury, Conn., U.S.	207	41.32 N	73.07 W
Middlebury, Ind., U.S.	216	41.41 N	85.42 W
Middlebury, Vt., U.S.	188	44.01 N	73.10 W
Middlebush	276	40.29 N	74.32 W
Middle Caicos I	238	21.47 N	71.43 W
Middle Cape ≻	220	25.09 N	81.09 W
Middle Castor ≃	212	45.16 N	75.24 W
Middle Channel ≃[1], N.W. Ter., Can.	180	69.05 N	136.00 W
Middle Channel ≃[1], Mich., U.S.	281	42.33 N	82.42 W
Middle Concho ≃	196	31.27 N	100.25 W
Middle Creek ≃, U.S.	208	39.41 N	76.18 W
Middle Creek ≃, Pa., U.S.	210	40.46 N	76.52 W
Middle Creek ≃, Pa., U.S.	210	41.28 N	75.11 W
Middle Fabius ≃	194	39.58 N	91.35 W
Middle Falls	210	43.07 N	73.32 W
Middlefield, Conn., U.S.	207	41.31 N	72.43 W
Middlefield, N.Y., U.S.	210	42.41 N	74.50 W
Middlefield, Ohio, U.S.	214	41.28 N	81.05 W
Middle Fork Reservoir ⊜[1]	218	39.51 N	84.51 W
Middle Ground I	272c	18.55 N	72.51 E
Middle Ground ⊹[2]	174g	28.15 N	177.25 W
Middle Grove, Mo., U.S.	219	39.24 N	92.16 W
Middle Grove, N.Y., U.S.	210	43.05 N	73.55 W
Middle Haddam	207	41.33 N	72.33 W
Middleham	44	54.17 N	1.49 W
Middle Harbour C	274a	33.48 S	151.14 E
Middle Head ≻	274a	33.50 S	151.16 E
Middle Hope	210	41.34 N	74.01 W
Middle Island	210	40.53 N	72.56 W
Middle Island I	162	34.07 S	123.12 E
Middle Level Main Drain ≋	42	52.43 N	0.22 E
Middle Loup ≃	198	41.17 N	98.23 W
Middle Maitland ≃	212	43.53 N	81.19 W
Middlemarch	172	45.31 S	170.07 E
Middle Musquodoboit	186	45.03 N	63.09 W
Middle Oakville Creek ≃	275b	43.32 N	79.47 W
Middle Pease ≃	196	34.15 N	100.07 W
Middle Point	216	40.51 N	84.27 W
Middle Popo Aggie ≃	202	42.51 N	108.42 W
Middleport, N.Y., U.S.	210	43.13 N	78.29 W
Middleport, Ohio, U.S.	188	39.00 N	82.03 W
Middleport, Pa., U.S.	208	40.44 N	76.05 W
Middle Raccoon ≃	198	41.34 N	94.12 W
Middle Reservoir ⊜[1]	283	42.27 N	71.07 W
Middle River	208	39.19 N	76.27 W
Middle River C	208	39.19 N	76.25 W
Middle River Rouge ≃	281	42.20 N	83.15 W
Middle Rouge Parkway ♠	281	42.21 N	83.21 W
Middle Run ≃	285	39.41 N	75.43 W
Middle Rush Creek ≃	198	38.52 N	103.29 W
Middlesboro	192	36.36 N	83.43 W
Middlesbrough	44	54.35 N	1.14 W
Middlesex, Belize	232	17.02 N	88.31 W
Middlesex, N.C., U.S.	192	35.47 N	78.12 W
Middlesex, N.Y., U.S.	210	42.42 N	77.16 W
Middlesex □[6], Ont., Can.	212	43.00 N	81.08 W
Middlesex □[6], Conn., U.S.	207	41.33 N	72.39 W
Middlesex □[6], Mass., U.S.	207	42.22 N	71.06 W
Middlesex □[6], N.J., U.S.	208	40.29 N	74.27 W
Middlesex □[6], Va., U.S.	208	37.40 N	76.35 W
Middlesex Fells Reservation ♠	283	42.27 N	71.07 W
Middlesex Reservoir ⊜[1]	276	40.37 N	74.19 W
Middle Stewiacke	186	45.13 N	63.08 W
Middle Swan	168a	31.52 S	116.00 E
Middle Thames ≃	212	42.59 N	80.58 W
Middleton, Austl.	166	22.22 S	141.32 E
Middleton, N.S., Can.	186	44.57 N	65.04 W
Middleton, Eng., U.K.	42	52.43 N	0.28 E
Middleton, Eng., U.K.	44	53.45 N	1.32 W
Middleton, Eng., U.K.	44	53.33 N	2.13 W
Middleton, Mass., U.S.	207	42.36 N	71.01 W
Middleton, Mich., U.S.	190	43.11 N	84.43 W
Middleton, Tenn., U.S.	194	35.04 N	88.54 W
Middleton, Wis., U.S.	216	43.06 N	89.30 W
Middleton ≃	166	22.35 S	141.51 E
Middleton in Teesdale	44	54.38 N	2.04 W
Middleton Island I	180	59.25 N	146.25 W
Middleton-on-the-Wolds	44	53.56 N	0.33 W
Middleton Pond ⊜	283	42.36 N	71.02 W
Middleton Reef I[1]	160	29.28 S	159.06 E
Middletown, N. Ire., U.K.	48	54.18 N	6.50 W
Middletown, Calif., U.S.	226	38.45 N	122.37 W
Middletown, Conn., U.S.	207	41.33 N	72.39 W
Middletown, Del., U.S.	208	39.25 N	75.47 W
Middletown, Ill., U.S.	219	40.11 N	89.35 W
Middletown, Ind., U.S.	218	40.03 N	85.32 W
Middletown, Ky., U.S.	218	38.15 N	85.32 W
Middletown, Md., U.S.	188	39.27 N	77.33 W
Middletown, Mo., U.S.	219	39.08 N	91.25 W
Middletown, N.J., U.S.	276	40.24 N	74.07 W
Middletown, N.Y., U.S.	210	41.27 N	74.25 W
Middletown, Ohio, U.S.	218	39.29 N	84.25 W
Middletown, Pa., U.S.	188	40.12 N	76.44 W
Middletown, Pa., U.S.	279b	40.16 N	79.37 W
Middletown, R.I., U.S.	207	41.32 N	71.17 W
Middletown, Va., U.S.	188	39.02 N	78.17 W
Middletown Park	218	40.09 N	85.26 W
Middle Tuolumne ≃	226	37.50 N	120.01 W
Middleville, Mich., U.S.	216	42.43 N	85.28 W
Middleville, N.Y., U.S.	210	43.08 N	74.58 W
Middleville, N.Y., U.S.	276	41.54 N	73.17 W
Middlewich	44	53.11 N	2.27 W
Middle Yegua Creek ≃	222	30.19 N	96.47 W
Middle Yuba ≃	226	39.22 N	121.12 W
Midelt	148	32.41 N	4.43 W
Midfield	222	28.56 N	96.13 W
Midge Hall	262	53.42 N	2.45 W
Midgic	186	45.59 N	64.18 W
Mid Glamorgan □[6]	42	51.40 N	3.30 W
Midgley	262	53.44 N	1.58 W
Midhurst, Ont., Can.	212	44.27 N	79.44 W
Midhurst, Eng., U.K.	42	50.59 N	0.45 W
Midi, Aiguille du ʌ	62	45.52 N	6.53 E
Midi, Canal du ≋	32	43.26 N	1.58 E
Midi de Bigorre, Pic du ʌ	32	42.56 N	0.08 E
Mid Illovo	158	29.59 S	30.25 E
Mid-Indian Basin ⊹[1]	12	10.00 S	80.00 E
Mid-Indian Ridge ⊹[3]	6	20.00 S	67.00 E
Mid-Island Plaza ⊸[9]	276	40.46 N	73.32 W
Midland, Austl.	168a	31.53 S	116.00 E
Midland, Ont., Can.	212	44.45 N	79.53 W
Midland, Calif., U.S.	204	33.52 N	114.48 W
Midland, Mich., U.S.	190	43.37 N	84.14 W
Midland, N.C., U.S.	192	35.14 N	80.30 W
Midland, Ohio, U.S.	218	39.18 N	83.55 W
Midland, Pa., U.S.	214	40.15 N	80.13 W
Midland, Pa., U.S.	214	40.38 N	80.27 W
Midland, S. Dak., U.S.	198	44.04 N	101.10 W
Midland, Tex., U.S.	196	32.00 N	102.05 W
Midland, Wash., U.S.	224	47.10 N	122.24 W
Midland Bay C	212	44.47 N	79.52 W
Midland Beach ⊸[8]	276	40.34 N	74.05 W
Midland City	219	40.09 N	89.08 W
Midland Park, Mich., U.S.	216	42.23 N	85.22 W
Midland Park, N.J., U.S.	276	41.00 N	74.09 W
Midland Park Lake ⊜	212	44.44 N	79.53 W
Midlands □[4]	154	19.00 S	29.45 E
Midleton	48	51.55 N	8.10 W
Midlothian, Ill., U.S.	216	41.38 N	87.42 W
Midlothian, Tex., U.S.	222	32.29 N	97.00 W
Midlothian Creek ≃	278	41.39 N	87.40 W
Midlum	52	53.43 N	8.37 E
Midnapore, Bhārat	126	22.26 N	87.20 E
Midnapore, Alta., Can.	182	50.55 N	114.05 W
Midnapore □[5]	126	22.25 N	87.20 E
Midnapore Canal ≋	126	22.25 N	87.53 E
Midnapore Plain ⊻	126	22.00 N	87.45 E
Midocean Ridge ⊹[3]	10	68.00 N	10.00 W
Mid-Ohio Race Course ♠	214	40.40 N	82.38 W
Midongy Nord	157b	20.45 S	46.13 E
Midongy Sud	157b	23.35 S	47.01 E
Midori	96	34.43 N	132.37 E
Midou ≃	32	43.54 N	0.30 W
Mid-Pacific Mountains ⊹[3]	14	20.00 N	179.00 E
Midpines	226	37.33 N	119.56 W
Midsayap	116	7.12 N	124.32 E
Midshipman Point ≻	282	38.07 N	122.27 W
Midsland	52	53.22 N	5.16 E
Midsomer Norton	42	51.18 N	2.28 W
Miduzhen	102	25.22 N	100.31 E
Midvale, Del., U.S.	285	39.39 N	75.37 W
Midvale, Idaho, U.S.	202	44.28 N	116.44 W
Midvale, Ohio, U.S.	214	40.26 N	81.23 W
Midville	192	32.49 N	88.14 W
Midway, S. Afr.	273d	26.18 S	27.51 E
Midway, Ala., U.S.	194	32.05 N	85.31 W
Midway, Ind., U.S.	216	41.37 N	85.55 W
Midway, Ky., U.S.	218	38.09 N	84.41 W
Midway, Pa., U.S.	279b	40.16 N	79.34 W
Midway, Tex., U.S.	222	31.02 N	95.45 W
Midway, Utah, U.S.	200	40.31 N	111.28 W
Midway City	280	33.45 N	118.00 W
Midway Islands □[2]	6; 174g	28.13 N	177.22 W
Midway Mall ⊸[9]	279a	41.24 N	82.07 W
Midway Naval Station ■	174g	28.13 N	177.26 W
Midway Park	192	34.43 N	77.21 W
Midwest	200	43.25 N	106.16 W
Midwest City	196	35.27 N	97.24 W
Mid-Western □[3]	150	6.00 N	6.00 E
Midwolda	52	53.12 N	7.00 E
Midyat	130	37.25 N	41.23 E
Midžor (Midžur) ʌ	38	43.23 N	22.42 E
Mie	96	32.58 N	131.35 E
Mie □[5]	92	34.30 N	136.30 E
Miechów	30	50.23 N	20.01 E
Miedwie, Jezioro ⊜	54	53.17 N	14.52 E
Międzybórz	30	51.24 N	17.40 E
Międzychód	30	52.36 N	15.55 E
Międzylesie	30	50.10 N	16.40 E
Międzyrzec Podlaski	30	52.00 N	22.47 E
Międzyrzecz	30	52.28 N	15.35 E
Międzyzdroje	30	53.55 N	14.28 E
Miehuapu	105	39.11 N	117.44 E
Miejska Górka	30	51.40 N	16.58 E
Miélan	32	43.26 N	0.19 E
Mielec	30	50.18 N	21.25 E
Mielno	30	54.16 N	16.01 E
Mien ⊜	26	56.25 N	14.51 E
Mienga	152	17.17 S	19.48 E
Mienhua Hsü I	100	25.29 N	122.06 E
Mient'ienhuo Shan ʌ	269d	25.11 N	121.30 E
Miercurea-Ciuc	38	46.22 N	25.48 E
Mieres	34	43.15 N	5.46 W
Mierlo	52	51.27 N	5.37 E
Mieroszów	30	50.41 N	16.10 E
Miersdorf	264a	52.20 N	13.37 E
Miersig	38	46.53 N	21.51 E
Mier y Noriega	234	23.25 N	100.07 W
Miesaituo	120	35.52 N	94.20 E
Miesau	56	49.24 N	7.26 E
Miesbach	64	47.47 N	11.50 E
Mieso	144	9.15 N	40.48 E
Mieste	54	52.28 N	11.11 E
Miesterhorst	54	52.27 N	11.09 E
Mieszkowice	30	52.46 N	14.30 E
Mifflin, Ohio, U.S.	214	40.47 N	82.22 W
Mifflin, Pa., U.S.	208	40.34 N	77.24 W
Mifflin □[6]	210	40.40 N	77.33 W
Mifflinburg	210	40.55 N	77.03 W
Mifflintown	208	40.34 N	77.24 W
Mifflinville	210	41.03 N	76.19 W
Miftāḥ, Wādī V	142	30.15 N	31.46 E
Migdal	132	32.50 N	35.30 E
Migdal Ha'Emeq	132	32.41 N	35.15 E
Migdol	158	26.54 S	25.27 E
Migennes	50	47.58 N	3.31 E
Mīghān	128	31.49 N	59.28 E
Mıgırtepe ʌ	130	36.50 N	36.22 E
Migiurtinia □[4]	144	10.00 N	50.00 E
Migliarino	66	44.46 N	11.56 E
Migliaro	64	44.48 N	11.58 E
Miglionico	68	40.34 N	16.30 E
Mignano Monte Lungo	68	41.23 N	13.58 E
Mignone ≃	66	42.11 N	11.44 E
Mignoviči	76	54.16 N	31.34 E
Mignovillard	58	46.48 N	6.08 E
Migori ≃	154	0.59 S	34.15 E
Miguel Alemán, Presa ⊜[1]	234	18.13 N	96.32 W
Miguel Alves	250	4.10 S	42.54 W
Miguel Auza	232	24.18 N	103.25 W
Miguel Calmon	250	11.26 S	40.36 W
Miguel Couto	287a	22.43 S	43.27 W
Miguel de la Borda	236	9.09 N	80.19 W
Migueles, Arroyo de los ≃	266a	40.20 N	3.32 W
Miguelete	258	34.01 S	57.39 W
Miguelete, Arroyo ≃	258	34.14 S	57.54 W
Miguel Hidalgo □[7]	286a	19.26 N	99.11 W
Miguel Hidalgo, Presa ⊜[1]	232	26.30 N	108.35 W
Miguelópolis	255	20.12 S	48.03 W
Miguel Pereira	256	22.27 S	43.22 W
Miguel Riglos	252	36.51 S	63.42 W
Migulinskaja	80	49.42 N	41.16 E
Migvie	46	57.08 N	2.56 W
Migyaunglaung	110	14.40 N	98.09 E
Mihăeşti	38	45.07 N	25.00 E
Mihai Viteazu	38	44.39 N	28.41 E
Mihajlovgrad	38	43.25 N	23.13 E
Mihalıççık	130	39.52 N	31.30 E
Mihama, Nihon	94	35.36 N	135.56 E
Mihama, Nihon	94	34.46 N	136.54 E
Mihama, Nihon	96	33.54 N	135.08 E
Mihara, Nihon	96	34.17 N	134.46 E
Mihara, Nihon	96	34.32 N	135.34 E
Mihara, Nihon	96	34.24 N	133.05 E
Mihara-yama ʌ	94	34.43 N	139.23 E
Mihe ≃	98	37.12 N	119.10 E
Mihla	54	51.04 N	10.20 E
Mihmandar	130	36.52 N	35.18 E
Miho	94	36.00 N	140.18 E
Mihonoseki	96	35.34 N	133.19 E
Miho-wan C	96	35.30 N	133.23 E
Mihuangzhuang	105	39.07 N	116.12 E
Mijaly	86	48.57 N	53.42 E
Mijares ≃	34	39.55 N	0.01 W
Mijdaḥah	144	14.00 N	48.26 E
Mijdrecht	52	52.13 N	4.52 E
Mijiang	98	43.01 N	130.08 E
Mijoux	58	46.22 N	6.00 E
Mikabo-yama ʌ	94	36.09 N	138.55 E
Mikame	96	33.25 N	132.27 E
Mikamo	96	35.09 N	133.37 E
Mikasa	92a	43.20 N	141.40 E
Mikaševiči	78	52.13 N	27.28 E
Mikata	94	35.33 N	135.55 E
Mikata-ko ⊜	94	35.34 N	135.53 E
Mikatou	273b	4.16 S	15.08 E
Mikawa, Nihon	94	36.29 N	136.29 E
Mikawa, Nihon	96	33.37 N	132.58 E
Mikawa-wan-kokutei-kōen ♠	94	34.42 N	137.10 E
Mikazuki	96	34.58 N	134.27 E
Mikese	154	6.46 S	37.54 E
Mikhaylov, Cape ≻	9	66.51 S	118.33 E
Miki, Nihon	96	34.17 N	134.05 E
Miki, Nihon	96	34.48 N	134.59 E
Mikínai ⊥	38	37.44 N	22.45 E
Mikindani	154	10.17 S	40.07 E
Mikinduri	154	0.07 N	37.50 E
Mikkabi	94	34.48 N	137.33 E
Mikkaichi	270	34.26 N	135.35 E
Mikkeli	26	61.41 N	27.15 E
Mikkelin lääni □[4]	26	62.00 N	27.30 E
Mikkwa ≃	176	58.25 N	114.45 W
Mikołajki	30	53.49 N	21.36 E
Mikołów	30	50.11 N	18.55 E
Mikomeseng	152	2.08 N	10.37 E
Mikomoto-jima I	94	34.34 N	138.56 E
Mikongo, Monts ʌʌ	152	0.15 N	10.55 E
Míkonos	38	37.26 N	25.20 E
Míkonos I	38	37.29 N	25.25 E
Mikope	152	5.03 S	20.48 E
Mikre	38	43.02 N	24.31 E
Mikrí Préspa, Límni ⊜	38	40.46 N	21.04 E
Miksimil	126	22.52 N	89.23 E
Mikšino	76	57.15 N	35.43 E
Mikstat	30	51.32 N	17.59 E
Mikulášovice	54	50.58 N	14.20 E
Mikulino	76	55.02 N	31.07 E
Mikulkin, Mys ≻	24	67.48 N	46.40 E
Mikulov	61	48.49 N	16.39 E
Mikumi	154	7.24 S	36.59 E
Mikumi National Park ♠	154	7.12 S	37.05 E
Mikun'	24	62.21 N	50.06 E
Mikuni	94	36.13 N	136.09 E
Mikuni-sammyaku ʌʌ	94	36.50 N	138.40 E
Mikuni-tōge)(	94	36.46 N	138.50 E
Mikuni-yama ʌ	94	35.59 N	138.43 E
Mikura-jima I	92	33.52 N	139.36 E
Mila	34	36.27 N	6.16 E
Milaca	190	45.45 N	93.39 W
Miladummadulu Atoll I[1]	122	6.15 N	73.15 E
Milagre	256	21.18 S	47.00 W
Milagres	250	7.17 S	38.57 W
Milagro	246	2.07 S	79.36 W
Milagros	116	12.13 N	123.30 E
Milam □[6]	222	30.47 N	96.57 W
Milan → Milano, It.	62	45.28 N	9.12 E
Milan, Ga., U.S.	192	32.01 N	83.04 W
Milan, Ind., U.S.	218	39.07 N	85.08 W
Milan, Mich., U.S.	216	42.05 N	83.40 W
Milan, Minn., U.S.	198	45.07 N	95.55 W
Milan, Mo., U.S.	194	40.12 N	93.07 W
Milan, N. Mex., U.S.	200	35.09 N	107.54 W
Milan, Ohio, U.S.	214	41.18 N	82.36 W
Milan, Pa., U.S.	210	41.54 N	76.32 W
Milan, Tenn., U.S.	194	35.55 N	88.46 W
Milando	152	8.45 S	17.36 E
Milan Federal Correctional Institution ♁	281	42.06 N	83.40 W
Milang	168b	35.25 S	138.58 E
Milano (Milan), It.	62; 266b	45.28 N	9.12 E
Milano, Tex., U.S.	222	30.43 N	96.52 W
Milano □[4]	62	45.30 N	9.30 E
Milanoa	157b	13.35 S	49.47 E
Milano Marittima	66	44.16 N	12.21 E
Milanville	210	41.40 N	75.04 W
Milâs	130	37.19 N	27.47 E
Milaševiči	78	51.39 N	27.56 E
Mil'atino, S.S.S.R.	76	54.29 N	34.18 E
Mil'atino, S.S.S.R.	82	55.41 N	35.48 E
Milazzo	70	38.13 N	15.14 E
Milazzo, Capo di ≻	70	38.16 N	15.14 E
Milazzo, Golfo di C	70	38.15 N	15.20 E
Milbank	198	45.13 N	96.38 W
Milbanke Sound U	182	52.18 N	128.33 W
Milborne Port	42	50.58 N	2.27 W
Milbridge	188	44.32 N	67.53 W
Milbuk	116	6.10 N	124.16 E
Milburn	196	34.14 N	96.33 W
Milburn Creek ≃	276	40.38 N	73.36 W
Milden	184	51.30 N	107.31 W
Mildenau	54	50.35 N	13.04 E
Mildenhall	42	52.21 N	0.30 E
Milders	64	47.06 N	11.16 E
Mildmay	212	44.03 N	81.07 W
Mildred, Ill., U.S.	219	39.46 N	89.38 W
Mildred, Pa., U.S.	210	41.29 N	76.23 W
Mildura	166	34.12 S	142.09 E
Mile	102	24.26 N	103.26 E
Miléai	38	39.20 N	23.09 E
Milena	70	37.28 N	13.44 E
Milepa	154	11.43 S	36.20 E
Mile Run ≃	276	40.31 N	74.28 W
Miles, Austl.	166	26.40 S	150.11 E
Miles, Tex., U.S.	196	31.36 N	100.11 W
Miles ≃	283	42.40 N	70.51 W
Milesburg	214	40.56 N	77.47 W
Miles City	202	46.25 N	105.51 W
Miles Creek C	208	38.46 N	76.12 W
Miles Creek ≃	226	37.12 N	120.21 W
Mile Seven Hundred Thirty Three	180	60.03 N	131.07 W
Milešovka ʌ	54	50.33 N	13.56 E
Milestone	184	50.00 N	104.30 W
Milesville	279b	40.12 N	79.52 W
Mileto	68	38.36 N	16.04 E
Miletto, Monte ʌ	68	41.27 N	14.22 E
Miletus ⊥	130	37.28 N	27.15 E
Mileura	162	26.23 S	117.20 E
Milevsko	30	49.27 N	14.22 E
Milford, Eng., U.K.	42	51.11 N	1.38 W
Milford, Conn., U.S.	207	41.13 N	73.04 W
Milford, Del., U.S.	208	38.55 N	75.25 W
Milford, Ill., U.S.	216	40.38 N	87.42 W
Milford, Ind., U.S.	216	41.25 N	85.51 W
Milford, Iowa, U.S.	198	43.20 N	95.09 W
Milford, Ky., U.S.	218	38.35 N	84.10 W
Milford, Maine, U.S.	188	44.57 N	68.39 W
Milford, Md., U.S.	284b	39.21 N	76.44 W
Milford, Mass., U.S.	207	42.08 N	71.32 W
Milford, Mich., U.S.	216	42.35 N	83.36 W
Milford, N.H., U.S.	188	42.50 N	71.39 W
Milford, N.J., U.S.	210	40.34 N	75.06 W
Milford, N.Y., U.S.	210	42.35 N	74.57 W
Milford, Ohio, U.S.	218	39.11 N	84.18 W
Milford, Pa., U.S.	210	41.19 N	74.48 W
Milford, Tex., U.S.	222	32.07 N	96.57 W
Milford, Utah, U.S.	200	38.24 N	113.01 W
Milford, Va., U.S.	208	38.01 N	77.22 W
Milford Brook ≃	276	40.19 N	74.17 W
Milford Center	218	40.11 N	83.26 W
Milford Cross Roads	285	39.43 N	75.44 W
Milford Dam ⊸[6]	198	39.02 N	96.54 W
Milford Haven	42	51.40 N	5.02 W
Milford Haven C	42	51.42 N	5.03 W
Milford Lake ⊜[1]	198	39.15 N	97.00 W
Milford-on-Sea	42	50.44 N	1.36 W
Milford Sound	172	44.40 S	167.54 E
Milford Sound U	172	44.35 S	167.47 E
Milford Station	186	45.03 N	63.26 W
Milgis ≃	154	1.48 N	38.06 E
Milgoo ʌ	162	28.51 S	118.07 E
Mil'guvejem ≃	180	68.22 N	171.30 E
Milḥ, Baḥr al- ⊜	128	32.40 N	43.35 E
Milḥ, Ra's al- ≻	146	32.19 N	23.08 E
Milḥat Ashqar ⊜	128	35.18 N	41.55 E
Milhaud	62	43.47 N	4.18 E
Mili I[1]	14	6.08 N	171.55 E
Miliana	148	36.15 N	2.15 E
Miliane, Oued ≃	36	36.46 N	10.18 E
Milibangalala, Ponta ≻	158	26.26 S	32.56 E
Milicia ≃	70	38.04 N	13.33 E
Milicz	30	51.32 N	17.17 E
Milieu, Rivière du ≃	206	46.47 N	73.56 W
Milīj	142	30.36 N	31.03 E
Miling	162	30.30 S	116.21 E
Milis	71	40.03 N	8.38 E
Militello in Val di Catania	70	37.16 N	14.48 E
Militello Rosmarino	70	38.03 N	14.41 E
Militsch → Milicz	30	51.32 N	17.17 E
Milk ≃	202	48.05 N	106.15 W
Milk Creek ≃, Colo., U.S.	200	40.24 N	107.45 W
Milk Creek ≃, Oreg., U.S.	224	45.15 N	122.41 W
Milk Hill ʌ[2]	42	51.23 N	1.51 W
Mil'kovo	74	54.43 N	158.37 E
Milk River	182	49.09 N	112.05 W
Milk River Ridge ʌ	182	49.15 N	112.30 W
Milk River Ridge Reservoir ⊜[1]	182	49.15 N	112.17 W
Mill	52	51.41 N	5.47 E
Mill ≃, Conn., U.S.	276	41.08 N	73.16 W
Mill ≃, Mass., U.S.	207	42.18 N	72.37 W
Mill ≃, Mass., U.S.	283	42.38 N	70.41 W
Mill ≃, Mass., U.S.	283	42.08 N	71.21 W
Mill ≃, Mass., U.S.	283	42.44 N	70.52 W
Mill ≃, Mass., U.S.	283	42.12 N	70.57 W
Mill ≃, N.Y., U.S.	276	40.38 N	73.39 W
Millard	198	41.13 N	96.07 W
Millau	32	44.06 N	3.05 E
Mill Bay	224	48.39 N	123.34 W
Millboro	192	37.59 N	79.36 W
Millbourne	285	39.58 N	75.15 W
Millbrae	226	37.36 N	122.24 W
Millbrook, Ont., Can.	212	44.09 N	78.27 W
Millbrook, Eng., U.K.	42	50.20 N	4.13 W
Millbrook, Mass., U.S.	283	42.03 N	70.41 W
Millbrook, N.J., U.S.	276	40.52 N	74.33 W
Millbrook, N.Y., U.S.	210	41.47 N	73.42 W
Mill Brook ≃, Mass., U.S.	283	42.31 N	71.18 W
Mill Brook ≃, N.J., U.S.	276	40.53 N	74.32 W
Mill Brook ≃, N.J., U.S.	276	40.25 N	74.06 W
Mill Brook ≃, N.J., U.S.	276	40.29 N	74.23 W
Millburn	276	40.44 N	74.20 W
Millbury, Mass., U.S.	207	42.11 N	71.46 W
Millbury, Ohio, U.S.	214	41.34 N	83.25 W
Mill City	202	44.45 N	122.29 W
Mill Creek, Pa., U.S.	214	40.26 N	77.56 W
Millcreek, Utah, U.S.	200	40.43 N	111.51 W
Mill Creek, W. Va., U.S.	188	38.44 N	79.58 W
Mill Creek ≃, U.S.	216	42.23 N	87.54 W
Mill Creek ≃, Calif., U.S.	226	36.49 N	119.21 W
Mill Creek ≃, Calif., U.S.	228	34.05 N	117.06 W
Mill Creek ≃, Del., U.S.	285	39.42 N	75.39 W
Mill Creek ≃, Ill., U.S.	219	39.50 N	91.24 W
Mill Creek ≃, Ind., U.S.	194	39.30 N	86.57 W
Mill Creek ≃, Ind., U.S.	216	41.01 N	86.36 W
Mill Creek ≃, Iowa, U.S.	198	42.47 N	95.31 W
Mill Creek ≃, Kans., U.S.	198	39.55 N	96.56 W
Mill Creek ≃, Ky., U.S.	218	38.28 N	84.20 W
Mill Creek ≃, N.J., U.S.	276	40.48 N	74.03 W
Mill Creek ≃, N.J., U.S.	285	40.02 N	74.55 W
Mill Creek ≃, N.Y., U.S.	212	43.57 N	76.08 W
Mill Creek ≃, N.Y., U.S.	276	40.31 N	74.14 W
Mill Creek ≃, Ohio, U.S.	214	41.06 N	80.40 W
Mill Creek ≃, Ohio, U.S.	214	40.14 N	83.09 W
Mill Creek ≃, Ohio, U.S.	218	39.06 N	84.32 W
Mill Creek ≃, Ohio, U.S.	279a	41.25 N	81.38 W
Mill Creek ≃, Pa., U.S.	210	41.53 N	77.08 W
Mill Creek ≃, Pa., U.S.	214	41.09 N	79.03 W
Mill Creek ≃, Pa., U.S.	285	40.03 N	75.16 W
Mill Creek ≃, Pa., U.S.	285	40.08 N	74.52 W
Mill Creek ≃, Tex., U.S.	222	32.46 N	95.46 W
Mill Creek ≃, Tex., U.S.	222	29.50 N	96.07 W
Mill Creek ≃, Tex., U.S.	222	30.08 N	95.37 W
Mill Creek ≃, Va., U.S.	208	38.09 N	77.10 W
Mill Creek, East Fork ≃	222	29.55 N	96.17 W
Mill Creek, North Fork ≃	224	45.33 N	121.18 W
Mill Creek, South Fork ≃	224	45.36 N	121.12 W
Mill Creek, West Fork ≃	222	29.55 N	96.17 W
Millcreek Township	214	42.05 N	80.10 W
Milldale	207	41.34 N	72.53 W
Milledgeville, Ga., U.S.	192	33.04 N	83.14 W
Milledgeville, Ill., U.S.	190	41.58 N	89.46 W
Milledgeville, Ohio, U.S.	218	39.36 N	83.35 W
Mille Îles, Rivière des ≃	206	45.42 N	73.32 W
Mille Lacs, Lac des ⊜	190	48.50 N	90.30 W
Mille Lacs Kathio State Park ♠	190	46.08 N	93.43 W
Mille Lacs Lake ⊜	190	46.15 N	93.40 W
Millemont	261	48.49 N	1.45 E
Millen	192	32.48 N	81.57 W
Millendon	168a	31.48 S	116.02 E
Miller, Mo., U.S.	194	37.13 N	93.50 W
Miller, S. Dak., U.S.	198	44.31 N	98.59 W
Miller □[6]	219	38.15 N	92.15 W
Miller, Mount ʌ	180	60.25 N	142.23 W
Miller City	216	41.06 N	84.08 W
Miller Creek ≃, Ont., Can.	284a	42.57 N	78.58 W
Miller Creek ≃, Calif., U.S.	282	38.02 N	122.30 W
Miller House	180	65.32 N	145.11 W
Miller Mountain ʌ	204	38.03 N	118.12 W

Symbols in the index entries represent the broad categories identified in the key at the right. Symbols with superior numbers (ʌʌ[2]) identify subcategories (see complete key on page *I* · *30*).

Kartensymbole in dem Registerverzeichnis stellen die rechts in Schlüssel erklärten Kategorien dar. Symbole mit hochgestellten Ziffern (ʌʌ[2]) bezeichnen Unterabteilungen einer Kategorie (vgl. vollständiger Schlüssel auf Seite *I* · *30*).

Los símbolos incluídos en el texto del índice representan las grandes categorias identificadas con la clave a la derecha. Los símbolos con numeros en su parte superior (ʌʌ[2]) identifican las subcategorías (véase la clave completa en la página *I* · *30*).

Les symboles de l'index représentent les catégories indiquées dans la légende à droite. Les symboles suivis d'un indice (ʌʌ[2]) représentent des sous-catégories (voir légende complète à la page *I* · *30*).

Os símbolos incluídos no texto do índice representam as grandes categorias identificadas com a chave à direita. Os símbolos com números em sua parte superior (ʌʌ[2]) identificam as subcategorias (veja-se a chave completa à página *I* · *30*).

Symbol	English	Deutsch	Español	Français	Português
ʌ	Mountain	Berg	Montaña	Montagne	Montanha
ʌʌ	Mountains	Berge	Montañas	Montagnes	Montanhas
)(	Pass	Pass	Paso	Col	Passo
V	Valley, Canyon	Tal, Cañon	Valle, Cañón	Vallée, Canyon	Vale, Canhão
⊻	Plain	Ebene	Llano	Plaine	Planície
≻	Cape	Kap	Cabo	Cap	Cabo
I	Island	Insel	Isla	Île	Ilha
II	Islands	Inseln	Islas	Îles	Ilhas
⊥	Other Topographic Features	Andere Topographische Objekte	Otros Elementos Topográficos	Autres données topographiques	Outros Elementos Topográficos

ESPAÑOL

Nombre	Página	Lat. °′	Long. °′ W=Oeste
Millerovo, S.S.S.R.	78	48.55 N	40.25 E
Millerovo, S.S.S.R.	83	47.49 N	39.15 E
Miller Peak ∧	200	31.23 N	110.17 W
Miller Place	210	40.58 N	73.00 W
Millers ≃	207	42.35 N	72.30 W
Millersburg, Ind., U.S.	216	41.32 N	85.42 W
Millersburg, Ind., U.S.	218	38.34 N	86.20 W
Millersburg, Ky., U.S.	218	38.18 N	84.10 W
Millersburg, Mich., U.S.	190	45.20 N	84.04 W
Millersburg, Ohio, U.S.	214	40.33 N	81.55 W
Millersburg, Pa., U.S.	208	40.33 N	76.58 W
Millers Creek ≃	196	33.27 N	99.14 W
Miller Seamount ✢[3]	16	53.30 N	144.20 W
Millers Falls	207	42.35 N	72.30 W
Millers Ferry	194	32.06 N	87.22 W
Millers Flat	172	45.40 S	169.25 E
Millers Island	284b	39.14 N	76.24 W
Millers Pond ⊜	276	40.51 N	73.12 W
Millersport	188	39.54 N	82.32 W
Millers Run ≃	279b	40.22 N	80.07 W
Millerstown	210	40.33 N	77.09 W
Millersville, Ohio, U.S.	214	41.19 N	83.17 W
Millersville, Pa., U.S.	208	40.00 N	76.22 W
Millerton, N.Y., U.S.	210	41.57 N	73.31 W
Millerton, Pa., U.S.	210	41.59 N	76.56 W
Millerton Lake ⊜[1]	226	37.01 N	119.41 W
Millerton Lake State Recreation Area ♠	226	37.02 N	119.37 W
Millertown	186	48.49 N	56.33 W
Millertown Junction	186	49.01 N	56.21 W
Millesimo	62	44.22 N	8.12 E
Millet	182	53.06 N	113.28 W
Millett, Mich., U.S.	216	42.42 N	84.38 W
Millett, Tex., U.S.	196	28.35 N	99.12 W
Milleur Point ≻	44	55.01 N	5.06 W
Millevaches, Plateau de ⋏[1]	32	45.30 N	2.10 E
Millford	48	55.07 N	7.43 W
Mill Green	260	51.41 N	0.22 E
Mill Grove	216	40.25 N	85.17 W
Mill Hall	210	41.06 N	77.29 W
Mill Hill ◆[8]	260	51.37 N	0.13 W
Mill Hill ∧[2]	262	53.25 N	1.54 W
Millhousen	218	39.13 N	85.26 W
Millican	222	30.28 N	96.12 W
Millicent	166	37.36 S	140.22 E
Milligan, Fla., U.S.	194	30.45 N	86.38 W
Milligan, Nebr., U.S.	198	40.30 N	97.23 W
Milligantown	279b	40.33 N	79.41 W
Milliken	275b	43.49 N	79.18 W
Millingen aan de Rijn	52	51.52 N	6.02 E
Millington, Ill., U.S.	216	41.34 N	88.36 W
Millington, Md., U.S.	208	39.16 N	75.50 W
Millington, Mich., U.S.	190	43.17 N	83.32 W
Millington, N.J., U.S.	210	40.40 N	74.31 W
Millington, Tenn., U.S.	194	35.21 N	89.54 W
Millinocket	188	45.39 N	68.43 W
Millionnyj	89	54.30 N	126.19 E
Millis	207	42.10 N	71.22 W
Mill Island I, Ant.	9	65.30 S	100.40 E
Mill Island I, N.W. Ter., Can.	176	64.00 N	78.00 W
Mill Lake ⊜	212	45.22 N	80.00 W
Millmerran	166	27.52 S	151.16 E
Millmont	210	40.53 N	77.08 W
Mill Neck	276	40.52 N	73.34 W
Mill Neck ≻[1]	276	40.53 N	73.33 W
Mill Neck Creek C	276	40.54 N	73.33 W
Millom	44	54.13 N	3.18 W
Mill Pond ⊜	276	40.53 N	73.22 W
Millport, Scot., U.K.	46	55.46 N	4.55 W
Millport, Ala., U.S.	194	33.34 N	88.05 W
Millport, N.Y., U.S.	210	42.16 N	76.50 W
Millport, Pa., U.S.	214	41.55 N	78.07 W
Millrift	210	41.25 N	74.45 W
Mill River	207	42.07 N	73.16 W
Millry	194	31.33 N	88.19 W
Mills, Pa., U.S.	214	41.57 N	77.41 W
Mills, Wyo., U.S.	202	42.50 N	106.22 W
Mills, Lake ⊜[1]	224	47.59 N	123.36 W
Millsboro	208	38.36 N	75.17 W
Mills Creek ≃, Austl.	166	22.23 S	143.05 E
Mills Creek ≃, Calif., U.S.	282	37.27 N	122.25 W
Mills Lake ⊜	176	61.30 N	118.10 W
Mills/Norrie State Park ♠	210	41.52 N	73.57 W
Millstadt	219	38.28 N	90.06 W
Millstatt	64	46.48 N	13.35 E
Millstätter See ⊜	64	46.47 N	13.35 E
Millstone	276	40.30 N	74.35 W
Millstone ≃	276	40.33 N	74.34 W
Millstream, Austl.	162	21.35 S	117.04 E
Millstream, B.C., Can.	224	48.30 N	123.31 W
Millstreet	48	52.03 N	9.04 W
Milltown, Ind., U.S.	218	38.21 N	86.17 W
Milltown, Mont., U.S.	202	46.53 N	113.52 W
Milltown, N.J., U.S.	208	40.27 N	74.27 W
Milltown, Wis., U.S.	190	45.32 N	92.30 W
Millvale	279b	40.29 N	79.58 W
Mill Valley	226	37.54 N	122.32 W
Mill Village	214	41.53 N	79.58 W
Millville, Mass., U.S.	207	42.02 N	71.35 W
Millville, N.J., U.S.	208	39.24 N	75.02 W
Millville, Ohio, U.S.	218	39.24 N	84.40 W
Millville, Pa., U.S.	210	41.07 N	76.32 W
Millville Lake	283	42.48 N	71.13 W
Millville Lake ⊜	283	42.48 N	71.13 W
Millwood, N.Y., U.S.	210	41.11 N	73.48 W
Millwood, Va., U.S.	188	39.04 N	78.02 W
Millwood Lake ⊜[1]	194	33.45 N	94.00 W
Milly-la-Forêt	50	48.24 N	2.28 E
Milly-Lamartine	58	46.21 N	4.42 E
Milmay	208	39.26 N	74.52 W
Milmersdorf	54	53.06 N	13.38 E
Milmine	219	39.54 N	88.39 W
Milmont Park	285	39.53 N	75.20 W
Milne Bay □[5]	164	10.00 S	152.30 E
Milne Bay C	164	10.22 S	150.30 E
Milner	224	49.20 N	122.42 W
Milnesville	210	40.59 N	75.59 W
Milngavie	46	55.57 N	4.20 W
Milnor	198	46.16 N	97.27 W
Milnrow	44	53.37 N	2.06 W
Milnthorpe	44	54.14 N	2.46 W
Milo, Alta., Can.	182	50.34 N	112.53 W
Milo, Iowa, U.S.	190	41.17 N	93.27 W
Milo, Maine, U.S.	188	45.15 N	68.59 W
Milo ≃	150	11.04 N	9.14 W
Milon-la-Chapelle	261	48.44 N	2.03 E
Mílos	38	36.45 N	24.27 E
Mílos I	38	36.41 N	24.15 E
Miloslaviči	76	53.41 N	32.15 E
Miloslavskoje	76	53.34 N	39.24 E
Miłosław	30	52.13 N	17.29 E
Milow, D.D.R.	54	52.31 N	12.18 E
Milow, D.D.R.	54	53.11 N	11.32 E
Milpa Alta □[7]	286a	19.11 N	99.02 W
Milpa Alta ◆[8]	286a	19.11 N	99.01 W
Milparinka	166	29.44 S	141.53 E
Milpitas	226	37.26 N	121.54 W
Milpitas Wash ∨	204	33.18 N	114.44 W
Milroy, Ind., U.S.	218	39.30 N	85.28 W
Milroy, Pa., U.S.	208	40.43 N	77.35 W
Milseburg ∧	56	50.32 N	9.53 E
Mil'skaja Step' ⊻	84	40.00 N	48.00 E
Milspe	263	51.18 N	7.21 E
Miltach	60	49.09 N	12.46 E
Miltenberg	56	49.42 N	9.15 E
Miltitz	54	51.19 N	12.16 E
Milton, Austl.	170	35.19 S	150.26 E
Milton, Ont., Can.	212	43.31 N	79.53 W
Milton, N.Z.	172	46.07 S	169.58 E
Milton, Del., U.S.	208	38.47 N	75.19 W
Milton, Fla., U.S.	194	30.38 N	87.03 W

FRANÇAIS

Nom	Page	Lat. °′	Long. °′ W=Ouest
Milton, Ill., U.S.	219	39.34 N	90.39 W
Milton, Ind., U.S.	218	38.58 N	85.01 W
Milton, Ind., U.S.	218	39.47 N	85.09 W
Milton, Iowa, U.S.	190	40.41 N	92.10 W
Milton, Ky., U.S.	218	38.43 N	85.22 W
Milton, Mass., U.S.	207	42.15 N	71.05 W
Milton, N.J., U.S.	276	41.02 N	74.32 W
Milton, N. Dak., U.S.	198	48.38 N	98.03 W
Milton, N.Y., U.S.	210	41.39 N	73.57 W
Milton, Pa., U.S.	210	41.01 N	76.51 W
Milton, Vt., U.S.	188	44.38 N	73.07 W
Milton, Wash., U.S.	224	47.15 N	122.19 W
Milton, W. Va., U.S.	188	38.26 N	82.08 W
Milton, Wis., U.S.	216	42.47 N	88.56 W
Milton, Lake ⊜	214	41.06 N	80.58 W
Milton Abbot	42	50.35 N	4.15 W
Milton-freewater	202	45.56 N	118.23 W
Milton Harbor C	276	40.57 N	73.42 W
Milton Point ≻	276	40.57 N	73.42 W
Miltonvale	198	39.21 N	97.27 W
Miltou	146	10.14 N	17.26 E
Miltown Malbay	48	52.50 N	9.23 W
Miltzow	54	54.12 N	13.13 E
Milumba	154	7.06 S	31.04 E
Miluo	100	28.50 N	113.04 E
Mil'utinskaja	80	48.38 N	41.40 E
Mil'utke, Gora ∧	180	65.42 N	178.03 W
Milverton, Ont., Can.	212	43.34 N	80.55 W
Milverton, Eng., U.K.	42	51.02 N	3.16 W
Milwaukee	216	43.02 N	87.55 W
Milwaukee □[6]	216	43.02 N	87.58 W
Milwaukee ≃	190	43.02 N	87.54 W
Milwaukee Bay C	216	43.02 N	87.53 W
Milwaukie	224	45.27 N	122.38 W
Mim	150	6.54 N	2.34 W
Mima	96	33.17 N	132.36 E
Mimasaka	96	35.00 N	134.10 E
Mimbres ≃	200	32.13 N	107.28 W
Mimbres Mountains ⋏	200	32.45 N	107.45 W
Mimi ≃	92	32.20 N	131.37 E
Mimico ◆[8]	275b	43.37 N	79.30 W
Mimico Creek ≃	275b	43.37 N	79.29 W
Mimizan	32	44.12 N	1.14 W
Mimmaya	92	41.12 N	140.26 E
Mimoň	54	50.40 N	14.44 E
Mimongo	152	1.11 S	11.36 E
Mimoso, Bra.	248	16.17 S	55.48 W
Mimoso, Bra.	255	15.10 S	48.05 W
Mimoso do Sul	255	21.04 S	41.22 W
Mims	220	28.40 N	80.51 W
Mimuro-yama ∧	96	35.14 N	134.28 E
Minā, Ar. Sa.	144	21.25 N	39.52 E
Mina, Méx.	196	26.01 N	100.32 W
Mina, Nev., U.S.	204	38.24 N	118.07 W
Mina ≃	112	10.09 S	124.12 E
Mîna, Oued ≃	34	35.47 N	0.30 E
Mīnā' al-Aḥmadī	128	29.04 N	48.08 E
Mīnāb	128	27.09 N	57.05 E
Mīnāb ≃	128	27.01 N	56.53 E
Minabe	96	33.46 N	135.19 E
Minabegawa	96	33.47 N	135.20 E
Mina el Limón	236	12.45 N	86.44 W
Minago ≃	184	54.34 N	98.08 W
Minahasa ≻[1]	112	1.00 N	124.35 E
Mināj ≃[1]	126	22.31 N	89.22 E
Minakami	94	36.46 N	138.58 E
Minakuchi	94	34.58 N	136.10 E
Minam ≃	202	45.37 N	117.43 W
Minamata	92	32.13 N	130.24 E
Minami	94	35.39 N	136.57 E
Minami ◆[8], Nihon	268	35.24 N	139.36 E
Minami ◆[8], Nihon	270	34.40 N	135.31 E
Minami ◆[8], Nihon	270	34.58 N	135.45 E
Minamiaiki	94	36.02 N	138.33 E
Minami-alps-kokuritsu-kōen ♠	94	35.40 N	138.13 E
Minamiashigara	94	35.19 N	139.07 E
Minami-bōsō-kokutei-kōen ♠	94	35.10 N	140.05 E
Minamichita	94	34.44 N	136.52 E
Minami-Daitō-jima I	90	25.50 N	131.15 E
Minami-iō-jima I	14	24.14 N	141.28 E
Minamiizu	94	34.39 N	138.50 E
Minamimaki	94	36.00 N	138.30 E
Minaminasu	94	36.39 N	140.06 E
Minamisenju ◆[8]	268	35.44 N	139.48 E
Minamishinano	94	35.19 N	137.56 E
Minami-Tori-shima (Marcus Island) I	14	24.18 N	153.58 E
Minano	94	36.04 N	139.06 E
Mina Pirquitas	252	22.41 S	66.31 W
Minard, S. Afr.	158	31.17 S	27.35 E
Minard, Scot., U.K.	46	56.07 N	5.15 W
Minas, Cuba	240p	21.29 N	77.37 W
Minas, Indon.	114	0.50 N	101.29 E
Minas, Ur.	252	34.23 S	55.14 W
Minas, Sierra de las ⋏	236	15.10 N	89.40 W
Minas Basin C	186	45.20 N	64.00 W
Minas Channel ʯ	186	45.15 N	64.45 W
Minas de Barroterán	232	27.40 N	101.20 W
Minas de Corrales	252	31.35 S	55.28 W
Minas de Matahambre	240p	22.35 N	83.57 W
Minas de Oro	236	14.46 N	87.20 W
Minas de Ríotinto	34	37.40 N	6.39 W
Minas Gerais □[3]	255	18.00 S	44.00 W
Minas Novas	255	17.15 S	42.36 W
Mînăstirea	38	44.13 N	26.54 E
Minatitlán	234	17.59 N	94.31 W
Minato ◆[8], Nihon	268	35.39 N	139.45 E
Minato ◆[8], Nihon	270	34.39 N	135.26 E
Minato ≃	268	35.13 N	139.52 E
Minbāl	142	28.24 N	30.41 E
Minbu	110	20.11 N	94.52 E
Minbulak	85	41.30 N	75.53 E
Minbya	110	20.22 N	93.15 E
Minbyin	110	19.17 N	93.32 E
Minchinābād	123	30.10 N	73.34 E
Minchinhampton	42	51.42 N	2.10 W
Minchinmávida, Volcán ∧[1]	254	42.49 S	72.28 W
Minchumina, Lake ⊜	180	63.52 N	152.15 W
Mincio ≃	64	45.04 N	10.59 E
Minco	196	35.19 N	97.57 W
Minčol ∧	30	49.15 N	20.59 E
Mind'ak	86	54.02 N	58.48 E
Mindanao I	116	8.00 N	125.00 E
Mindanao ≃	116	7.07 N	124.24 E
Mindanao Sea ⊤[2]	116	9.10 N	124.25 E
Mindego Creek ≃	282	37.18 N	122.15 W
Mindego Hill ∧[2]	282	37.18 N	122.13 W
Mindel ≃	58	48.31 N	10.23 E
Mindelheim	58	48.03 N	10.29 E
Mindelo	150a	16.53 N	25.00 W
Mindemoya	190	45.44 N	82.10 W
Minden, B.R.D.	52	52.17 N	8.55 E
Minden, Ont., Can.	212	44.55 N	78.43 W
Minden, La., U.S.	194	32.37 N	93.17 W
Minden, Nebr., U.S.	198	40.30 N	98.57 W
Minden, Nev., U.S.	226	38.57 N	119.45 W
Minden, W. Va., U.S.	188	37.59 N	81.07 W
Minden City	190	43.40 N	82.47 W
Mindenmines	194	37.28 N	94.35 W
Minderoo	162	22.00 S	115.02 E
Mindif	146	10.24 N	14.26 E
Mindiptana	164	5.45 S	140.42 E
Mindjik, Bahr ≃	146	10.01 N	20.41 E
Mindon	110	19.21 N	94.44 E
Mindoro I	116	12.50 N	121.05 E
Mindoro Occidental □[4]	116	13.00 N	121.00 E
Mindoro Oriental □[4]	116	13.00 N	121.20 E
Mindoro Strait ʯ	116	12.20 N	120.40 E
Mindouli	152	4.17 S	14.21 E
Mindourou	152	4.06 N	14.34 E
Minduri	256	21.41 S	44.37 W
Mindživan	84	39.03 N	46.42 E

PORTUGUÊS

Nome	Página	Lat. °′	Long. °′ W=Oeste
Mine, Nihon	96	34.10 N	131.13 E
Mine, Nihon	96	33.17 N	130.26 E
Mine, Yai.	144	8.20 N	40.09 E
Minear Lake ⊜	278	42.17 N	87.57 W
Minebank Run ≃	284b	39.25 N	76.32 W
Mine Brook ≃, Mass., U.S.	283	42.09 N	71.15 W
Mine Brook ≃, Mass., U.S.	283	42.08 N	71.26 W
Mine Brook ≃, N.J., U.S.	276	40.41 N	74.38 W
Mine Centre	190	48.45 N	92.37 W
Minehead	42	51.13 N	3.29 W
Mine Hill	210	40.53 N	74.36 W
Mineiros	255	17.34 S	52.34 W
Mineo	70	37.16 N	14.42 E
Mineola, N.Y., U.S.	210	40.45 N	73.38 W
Mineola, Tex., U.S.	222	32.40 N	95.29 W
Mineral	224	46.43 N	122.11 W
Mineral City	214	40.36 N	81.25 W
Mineral Creek ≃	224	46.45 N	122.08 W
Mineral del Monte	234	20.08 N	98.40 W
Mineral del Oro	234	19.48 N	100.08 W
Mineral'nyje Vody	84	44.12 N	43.08 E
Mineral Point, Pa., U.S.	214	40.23 N	78.50 W
Mineral Point, Wis., U.S.	190	42.52 N	90.11 W
Mineral Ridge	214	41.08 N	80.46 W
Mineral Springs, Ark., U.S.	194	33.53 N	93.55 W
Mineral Springs, Pa., U.S.	214	41.00 N	78.22 W
Mineral Wells	196	32.48 N	98.07 W
Minerbe	64	45.14 N	11.20 E
Minerbio	64	44.37 N	11.29 E
Minersville, Pa., U.S.	208	40.41 N	76.16 W
Minersville, Utah, U.S.	200	38.13 N	112.55 W
Mine Run ≃	285	40.15 N	75.28 W
Minerva, Ky., U.S.	218	38.42 N	83.55 W
Minerva, Ohio, U.S.	214	40.44 N	81.06 W
Minerva, Tex., U.S.	222	30.46 N	96.59 W
Minerva Park	214	40.04 N	83.00 W
Minervino Murge	68	41.05 N	16.05 E
Minesing Swamp ☷	212	44.23 N	79.51 W
Minetto	210	43.24 N	76.29 W
Mineville	188	44.05 N	73.31 W
Mineyama	96	35.37 N	135.04 E
Minfeng	120	37.05 N	82.40 E
Minga	154	11.08 S	27.57 E
Mingala	152	5.06 N	21.49 E
Mingan	186	50.18 N	64.02 W
Mingan, Îles de ǁ	186	50.12 N	63.35 W
Mingan Mountains ⋏	116	15.29 N	121.24 E
Mingāora	123	34.47 N	72.22 E
Mingardo ≃	68	40.02 N	15.18 E
Mingary	166	32.08 S	140.44 E
Mingcheng	89	43.11 N	125.59 E
Mingečaur	84	40.45 N	47.03 E
Mingečaurskoje Vodochranilišče ⊜[1]	84	40.50 N	46.50 E
Mingela	166	19.53 S	146.38 E
Mingenew	162	29.11 S	115.26 E
Mingera Creek ≃	166	20.38 S	138.10 E
Mingfankuangqu	100	27.21 N	120.24 E
Minggang	100	32.29 N	114.03 E
Minggao	100	34.20 N	112.15 E
Minggugong (Ming Palace) ʊ	106	32.01 N	118.46 E
Minghuang	106	31.41 N	119.56 E
Mingin	110	22.52 N	94.39 E
Mingjiaqiao	100	32.53 N	119.13 E
Mingjuesi	106	31.34 N	118.53 E
Minglanilla	34	39.32 N	1.36 W
Mingling (Ming Tombs) ⊥	105	40.22 N	116.12 E
Mingo, Congo	152	1.55 S	14.59 E
Mingo, Ohio, U.S.	216	40.13 N	83.38 W
Mingo Creek ≃, Pa., U.S.	279b	40.13 N	79.57 W
Mingo Creek ≃, Pa., U.S.	285	40.10 N	75.32 W
Mingo Junction	214	40.19 N	80.37 W
Mingo Lake ⊜	176	64.35 N	72.10 W
Mingorría	34	40.45 N	4.40 W
Mingoville	214	40.56 N	77.39 W
Mingoyo	154	10.06 S	39.38 E
Mingrel'skaja	78	45.01 N	38.20 E
Mingshantou	100	29.18 N	112.33 E
Mingshui, Zhg.	89	47.10 N	125.55 E
Mingshui, Zhg.	102	42.06 N	96.04 E
Mingulay I	46	56.49 N	7.38 W
Mingwan	106	31.04 N	120.17 E
Mingxi	100	26.24 N	117.13 E
Mingyuelu	85	39.34 N	75.26 E
Minhla, Mya.	110	17.59 N	95.43 E
Minhla, Mya.	110	19.58 N	95.03 E
Minho □[9]	34	41.40 N	8.30 W
Minho (Miño) ≃	34	41.52 N	8.51 W
Minhou	100	25.59 N	119.18 E
Minianko	150	9.58 N	8.22 W
Minićevo	38	43.41 N	22.18 E
Minicoy Island I	122	8.17 N	73.02 E
Minier	194	40.26 N	89.19 W
Minigwal, Lake ⊜	162	29.35 S	123.12 E
Minija ≃	76	55.21 N	21.17 E
Minilulan Point ≻	116	9.08 N	123.42 E
Minilya	162	23.51 S	113.58 E
Minilya ≃	162	23.56 S	113.51 E
Minimarg	123	34.47 N	75.05 E
Minīn	132	33.39 N	36.18 E
Miniota	184	50.08 N	101.00 W
Minirodo, Baie de C	157b	25.10 S	44.15 E
Minisinakwa Lake ⊜	190	47.40 N	81.43 W
Ministikwan Lake ⊜	184	54.01 N	109.39 W
Ministro Ramos Mexía	254	40.30 S	67.17 W
Ministro Rivadavia	288	34.51 S	58.22 W
Minitonas	184	52.07 N	101.00 W
Minj	164	5.54 S	144.39 E
Minjar	86	55.04 N	57.33 E
Minjary, Mount ∧	171b	35.14 S	148.08 E
Minjiadianzi	104	41.35 N	121.41 E
Minjiaji	100	31.08 N	115.01 E
Minjiang ≃, Zhg.	100	26.05 N	119.32 E
Minjiang ≃, Zhg.	102	28.54 N	105.28 E
Minjiangkou ≃[1]	100	26.06 N	119.40 E
Minkamman	140	6.03 N	31.32 E
Min'kovo	76	59.42 N	43.28 E
Minkulincy	78	49.24 N	25.38 E
Min-Kuš	85	41.41 N	74.28 E
Minlaton	168b	34.46 S	137.36 E
Minle, Zhg.	100	22.59 N	112.58 E
Minle, Zhg.	102	38.27 N	100.56 E
Minna	150	9.37 N	6.33 E
Minna Bluff ≻[1]	9	78.32 S	166.30 E
Minna-jima I	175d	24.45 N	124.42 E
Minna-shima I	174m	26.39 N	127.49 E
Minneapolis, Kans., U.S.	198	39.08 N	97.42 W
Minneapolis, Minn., U.S.	190	44.59 N	93.13 W
Minnechaduza Creek ≃	198	42.54 N	100.29 W
Minnedosa	184	50.14 N	99.51 W
Minnedosa ≃	184	49.53 N	100.08 W
Minnehaha	224	45.39 N	122.37 W
Minnehaha, Lake ⊜	220	28.31 N	81.46 W
Minneola, Fla., U.S.	220	28.35 N	81.45 W
Minneola, Kans., U.S.	198	37.26 N	100.01 W
Minneola, Lake ⊜	220	28.34 N	81.46 W
Minneota	198	44.58 N	93.12 W
Minnertsga	52	53.15 N	5.35 E
Minnesota □[3]	178	46.00 N	94.15 W
Minnesota ≃	190	44.54 N	93.10 W
Minnesota Lake	190	43.51 N	93.50 W
Minnewanka, Lake ⊜	182	51.15 N	115.20 W
Minnewaukan	198	48.04 N	99.15 W
Minnie Creek	162	24.02 S	115.42 E
Minnigaff	44	54.58 N	4.30 W
Minnipa	162	32.51 S	135.09 E
Minnitaki Lake ⊜	184	49.58 N	92.00 W
Minnoch, Water of ≃	44	55.02 N	4.33 W
Mino, Nihon	94	35.32 N	136.55 E
Minō, Nihon	96	34.50 N	135.30 E
Miño (Minho) ≃, Eur.	34	41.52 N	8.51 W
Minō ≃, Nihon	270	34.47 N	134.57 E
Minoa	210	43.04 N	76.00 W
Minobu	94	35.22 N	138.26 E
Minobu-san ∧	94	35.24 N	138.25 E
Minobu-sanchi ⋏	94	35.14 N	138.20 E
Minocqua	190	45.52 N	89.43 W
Mino-kamo	94	35.26 N	137.01 E
Mino-mikawa-kōgen ⋏[1]	94	35.11 N	137.23 E
Minong	190	46.06 N	91.49 W
Minonk	190	40.54 N	89.02 W
Minōnoshō	270	34.39 N	135.59 E
Minooka	216	41.27 N	88.16 W
Minorca → Menorca I	34	40.00 N	4.00 E
Minori	94	36.14 N	140.21 E
Minorsville	218	38.20 N	84.42 W
Minot, Mass., U.S.	283	42.14 N	70.46 W
Minot, N. Dak., U.S.	198	48.14 N	101.18 W
Minot Air Force Base ■	198	48.26 N	101.21 W
Minowa	94	35.55 N	137.59 E
Minqin	102	39.03 N	103.38 E
Minqing	100	26.12 N	118.51 E
Minquadale	285	39.42 N	75.34 W
Minquan	98	34.41 N	115.11 E
Minsen	52	53.42 N	7.58 E
Minshan ⋏	102	33.15 N	103.15 E
Minshāt Adh Dhahab	142	28.00 N	30.42 E
Minshat al-Amir Muhammad 'Ali	142	29.10 N	30.38 E
Minshāt al-Bakkārī	273c	30.01 N	31.08 E
Minshāt al-Ikhwah	142	30.56 N	31.21 E
Minshāt al-Mughālaqah	142	27.44 N	30.47 E
Minshāt Būlīn	142	31.11 N	30.10 E
Minshāt Sulṭān	142	30.32 N	30.55 E
Minsk	76	53.54 N	27.34 E
Minsk □[4]	24	54.30 N	28.00 E
Minskaja Vozvyšennost' ⋏[1]	76	54.00 N	27.10 E
Mińsk Mazowiecki	30	52.11 N	21.34 E
Minster, Eng., U.K.	42	51.20 N	1.19 E
Minster, Eng., U.K.	42	51.26 N	0.49 E
Minster, Ohio, U.S.	216	40.24 N	84.23 W
Minsterley	42	52.39 N	2.55 W
Minta	152	4.35 N	12.48 E
Mintaka Pass)(	123	36.58 N	74.54 E
Mintard	263	51.22 N	6.54 E
Mintaro	168b	33.55 S	138.43 E
Mint Canyon	228	34.26 N	118.25 W
Mintlaw	46	57.31 N	2.00 W
Minto, Austl.	274a	34.01 S	150.51 E
Minto, Man., Can.	184	49.25 N	100.01 W
Minto, N.B., Can.	186	46.05 N	66.05 W
Minto, Yukon, Can.	180	62.34 N	136.51 W
Minto, Alaska, U.S.	180	64.53 N	149.11 W
Minto, N. Dak., U.S.	198	48.17 N	97.15 W
Minto, Lac ⊜	176	51.00 N	73.37 W
Minto Inlet C	176	71.20 N	117.00 W
Mintom	152	2.42 N	13.17 E
Minton	184	49.05 N	105.35 W
Mintoum	152	0.27 N	12.16 E
Minturn	200	39.35 N	106.26 W
Minturnae ⊥	68	41.14 N	13.45 E
Minturno	66	41.15 N	13.45 E
Minūf	142	30.28 N	30.56 E
Minulovo	265a	60.03 N	30.45 E
Minumadai-yōsui ≊	268	35.50 N	139.42 E
Minur'uk	85	40.56 N	73.22 E
Minusinsk	86	53.43 N	91.42 E
Minutang	120	28.13 N	96.32 E
Minute Man National Historical Park ♠	207	42.27 N	71.17 W
Minvoul	152	2.09 N	12.08 E
Minxian	102	34.22 N	104.08 E
Minya → Al-Minyā	142	28.06 N	30.45 E
Minyā al-Qamḥ	142	30.31 N	31.21 E
Minya Konka → Gonggashan ∧	102	29.35 N	101.51 E
Minyat an-Naṣr	142	31.07 N	31.39 E
Minyat as-Sīrij ◆[8]	273c	30.05 N	31.15 E
Minyat Sandūb	142	31.00 N	31.23 E
Minžir	78	46.40 N	28.19 E
Minzow	54	53.23 N	12.30 E
Mio	190	44.39 N	84.08 W
Mioglia	62	44.29 N	8.25 E
Mionica	38	44.15 N	20.05 E
Miory	76	55.37 N	27.38 E
Mipi	120	28.57 N	95.48 E
Miquan	86	44.06 N	87.35 E
Miquelon I	186	47.03 N	56.20 W
Miquihuana	234	23.34 N	99.47 W
Miquon	285	40.04 N	75.16 W
Mīr, Miṣr	142	27.27 N	30.44 E
Mir, Niger	146	14.05 N	11.59 E
Mir, S.S.S.R.	76	53.27 N	26.28 E
Mira, It.	64	45.26 N	12.08 E
Mira, Port.	34	40.26 N	8.44 W
Mira ≃, N.S., Can.	186	46.03 N	60.00 W
Mira ≃, Col.	246	1.36 N	79.01 W
Mira ≃, Port.	34	37.43 N	8.47 W
Mīrābād	128	30.25 N	61.50 E
Mira Bay C	186	46.02 N	59.56 W
Mirabeau	62	43.42 N	5.39 E
Mirabella Eclano	68	41.02 N	14.59 E
Mirabella Imbaccari	70	37.19 N	14.27 E
Mirabello, Ippodromo ♠	266b	45.36 N	9.17 E
Mirabello Monferrato	62	45.02 N	8.31 E
Miracema do Norte	250	9.33 S	48.24 W
Mirada Hills → La Mirada	228	33.54 N	118.01 W
Mirador	250	6.22 S	44.22 W
Mirador, Cerro ∧	286d	11.57 S	77.02 W
Miradouro	255	20.53 S	42.21 W
Miraflores, Arg.	252	28.36 S	65.55 W
Miraflores, Col.	246	5.12 N	73.12 W
Miraflores, Col.	246	1.25 N	72.13 W
Miraflores, Perú	286d	12.07 S	77.02 W
Miraflores, Palacio ʊ	286c	10.31 N	66.55 W
Mīrah, Wādī al- ∨	128	32.26 N	41.42 E
Miraí	256	21.12 S	42.37 W
Miraj	122	16.50 N	74.38 E
Miraki	85	39.02 N	67.10 E
Miraleste	228	33.46 N	118.19 W
Mira Loma	228	34.01 N	117.31 W
Miramar, Arg.	252	30.54 S	62.40 W
Miramar, Arg.	252	38.16 S	57.51 W
Miramar, C.R.	236	10.06 N	84.44 W
Miramar, Fr.	62	43.30 N	6.57 E
Miramar, Moç.	156	23.50 S	35.34 E
Miramar, Fla., U.S.	220	25.59 N	80.11 W
Miramar ◆[8]	286b	23.07 N	82.25 W
Miramar, Laguna ⊜	236	16.23 N	91.16 W
Miramare	66	44.02 N	12.38 E
Miramare, Aeroporto di ⊠	66	44.02 N	12.35 E
Miramare, Castello di ⊥	64	45.42 N	13.43 E
Miramar Naval Air Station ■	228	32.52 N	117.07 W
Miramas	62	43.35 N	5.00 E
Mirambeau	32	45.23 N	0.34 W
Miramichi Bay C	186	47.08 N	65.08 W
Mira Monte	228	36.42 N	119.03 W
Mīram Shāh	120	33.00 N	70.04 E
Mīrān	123	31.24 N	70.43 E
Miranda, Austl.	274a	34.02 S	151.06 E
Miranda, Bra.	248	20.14 S	56.22 W
Miranda, Col.	246	3.15 N	76.14 W
Miranda, Moç.	154	12.30 S	35.28 E
Miranda, Calif., U.S.	204	40.14 N	123.49 W
Miranda □[3]	246	10.15 N	66.25 W
Miranda ≃	248	19.25 S	57.20 W
Miranda de Ebro	34	42.41 N	2.57 W
Miranda do Douro	34	41.30 N	6.16 W
Mirande	32	43.31 N	0.25 E
Mirandela	34	41.29 N	7.11 W
Mirando City	196	27.26 N	99.00 W
Mirandola	64	44.53 N	11.04 E
Mirano	64	45.30 N	12.07 E
Mirantão	256	22.15 S	44.30 W
Mirante do Paranapanema	255	22.17 S	51.54 W
Mirapuxi ≃	255	13.06 S	51.10 W
Mirasaka	96	34.46 N	132.58 E
Miravalles, Volcán ∧[1]	236	10.45 N	85.10 W
Miravete, Puerto de)(	34	39.43 N	5.43 W
Mīr Bachcheh Kūt	120	34.45 N	69.08 E
Mir-Bašir	84	40.20 N	46.55 E
Mirbāṭ	118	17.00 N	54.45 E
Mirboo North	169	38.24 S	146.10 E
Mirebeau-sur-Bèze	58	47.24 N	5.19 E
Mirecourt	58	48.18 N	6.08 E
Miren	64	45.54 N	13.37 E
Mireny	78	46.58 N	29.04 E
Mirfield	44	53.40 N	1.41 W
Mirgorod	78	49.58 N	33.36 E
Mirgorodka	80	50.58 N	53.33 E
Miri	112	4.23 N	113.59 E
Miriam Vale	166	24.20 S	151.34 E
Miribel	62	45.49 N	4.57 E
Mirim, Lagoa (Laguna Merín) C	252	32.45 S	52.50 W
Mirimichi, Lake ⊜	283	42.02 N	71.18 W
Mírina	38	39.52 N	25.04 E
Miriñay ≃	252	30.10 S	57.39 W
Mirinzal	250	2.01 S	44.43 W
Miriti	248	6.15 S	59.00 W
Miritiparaná ≃	246	1.11 S	70.02 W
Miriyama	164	3.57 S	141.45 E
Mīrjāveh	128	29.01 N	61.28 E
Mirke ◆[8]	263	51.16 N	7.09 E
Mirna ≃	64	45.19 N	13.36 E
Mirnock ∧	64	46.46 N	13.43 E
Mirnoje Ozero	86	57.44 N	78.45 E
Mirnyj, S.S.S.R.	74	62.33 N	113.53 E
Mirnyj, S.S.S.R.	78	50.57 N	28.34 E
Mirnyj, S.S.S.R.	80	53.30 N	50.18 E
Mirnyy ʊ[3]	9	66.33 S	93.00 E
Mirond Lake ⊜	184	55.06 N	102.47 W
Mironeasa	38	46.58 N	27.25 E
Mironovka	78	49.39 N	30.59 E
Mironovo	88	58.19 N	109.38 E
Mironovskij	83	48.29 N	38.17 E
Miropol'	78	50.07 N	27.41 E
Miropolje	78	51.02 N	35.16 E
Miroslav	61	48.57 N	16.18 E
Mirosławiec	30	53.21 N	16.05 E
Mirošov	60	49.41 N	13.40 E
Mirovoje	78	47.45 N	34.45 E
Mirovskoje	78	48.05 N	33.23 E
Mirow	54	53.16 N	12.49 E
Mīrpur, Bngl.	126	23.56 N	88.59 E
Mīrpur, Bngl.	126	23.47 N	90.21 E
Mīrpur, Pāk.	123	33.11 N	73.46 E
Mīrpur Batoro	120	24.44 N	68.16 E
Mīrpur Bībīwāri	120	28.32 N	67.44 E
Mīrpur Khās	120	25.32 N	69.00 E
Mīrpur Sakro	120	24.33 N	67.37 E
Mirria	150	13.43 N	9.07 E
Mirror	182	52.28 N	113.07 W
Mirror Lake ⊜, Mass., U.S.	283	42.05 N	71.20 W
Mirror Lake ⊜, N.J., U.S.	276	40.29 N	74.22 W
Mirs Bay C	100	22.30 N	114.24 E
Mirskoj Chrebet ⋏	86	52.24 N	92.48 E
Mirtağ	130	38.23 N	41.56 E
Mirto	70	38.05 N	14.45 E
Mirtóön Pélagos ⊤[2]	38	36.51 N	23.18 E
Mirvan	130	38.33 N	39.48 E
Miryang	98	35.31 N	128.44 E
Miry Run ≃	285	40.15 N	74.49 W
Mirza-Aki	85	40.45 N	73.25 E
Mirzaani	84	41.23 N	46.09 E
Mirzāganj	126	22.21 N	90.14 E
Mīrzakālu	126	22.29 N	90.48 E
Mirzāpur, Bhārat	124	25.09 N	82.35 E
Mirzāpur, Bhārat	272b	22.50 N	88.24 E
Mirzāpur, Bngl.	126	24.06 N	90.06 E
Mirzāpur □[5]	124	24.55 N	82.50 E
Mis	64	46.12 N	11.57 E
Misa ≃	66	43.43 N	13.14 E
Misāḥah, Bi'r ⊤[4]	140	22.12 N	27.57 E
Misailovo	265b	55.34 N	37.49 E
Misaka	94	35.38 N	138.40 E
Misaka-tōge)(	96	33.42 N	132.52 E
Misaki, Nihon	94	35.18 N	140.22 E
Misaki → Miura, Nihon	94	35.08 N	139.37 E
Misaki, Nihon	96	34.19 N	135.09 E
Misaki, Nihon	96	33.23 N	132.07 E
Mi-saki ≻	93b	30.50 N	131.04 E
Misakubo	94	35.09 N	137.52 E
Misallah, Ra's ≻	142	29.50 N	32.36 E
Misamis Occidental □[4]	116	8.20 N	123.42 E
Misamis Oriental □[4]	116	8.45 N	125.00 E
Misano Adriatico	66	43.57 N	12.39 E
Misantla	234	19.56 N	96.50 W
Misasa	96	35.24 N	133.54 E
Misasagi → Fujiidera	96	34.34 N	135.36 E
Misato, Nihon	94	36.23 N	138.57 E
Misato, Nihon	94	36.15 N	137.54 E
Misato, Nihon	94	34.43 N	136.24 E
Misato, Nihon	96	34.09 N	135.22 E
Misato, Nihon	268	35.50 N	139.53 E
Misawa	92	40.41 N	141.24 E
Misawa Air Base (United States) ■	92	40.45 N	141.23 E
Misbourne ≃	260	51.34 N	0.29 W
Misburg	52	52.23 N	9.51 E
Miscou Centre	186	47.57 N	64.34 W
Miscou Island I	186	47.57 N	64.33 W
Miscou Point ≻	186	48.03 N	64.32 W
Mišelevka	88	52.51 N	103.09 E
Misema ≃	190	47.54 N	79.53 W
Mi-sen ∧	96	34.16 N	132.19 E
Misenheimer	192	35.29 N	80.17 W
Miseno	68	40.47 N	14.05 E
Misericórdia, Serra da ∧	287a	22.51 S	43.17 W
Misgār	123	36.47 N	74.47 E
Mish'āb, Ra's al- ≻	128	28.12 N	48.39 E
Mishan (Dongan)	89	45.33 N	131.52 E
Mishansha ≃	248	11.13 S	72.59 W
Mishawaka	216	41.40 N	86.11 W
Mishawum Lake ⊜	283	42.30 N	71.08 W
Mishbiḥ, Jabal ∧	140	22.38 N	34.44 E
Misheguk Mountain ∧	180	68.15 N	161.03 W
Misheiti, Jabal al- ∧	132	30.47 N	34.18 E
Mishe-Mokwa, Lake ⊜	285	39.52 N	74.48 W
Mishibishu Lake ⊜	190	48.05 N	85.25 W
Mishicot	190	44.14 N	87.38 W
Mishima, Nihon	94	35.07 N	138.55 E
Mishima → Settsu, Nihon	96	34.46 N	135.33 E
Mi-shima I	96	34.46 N	131.09 E
Mishmar HaNegev	132	31.21 N	34.43 E
Mishmar HaYarden	132	33.00 N	35.36 E
Mishmi Hills ⋏[2]	120	29.00 N	96.00 E
Mishō	96	32.57 N	132.34 E
Mishqal, Jabal al- ∧	132	31.53 N	36.08 E
Mishui ≃, Zhg.	100	27.09 N	112.51 E
Mishui ≃, Zhg.	100	28.50 N	113.06 E
Mišicha	88	51.38 N	105.35 E
Misikan	120	35.45 N	89.25 E
Misilmeri	70	38.02 N	13.27 E
Misima Island I	164	10.40 S	152.45 E
Misinto	266b	45.40 N	9.05 E
Misiones □[4]	252	27.00 S	55.00 W
Misiones □[5]	252	27.00 S	57.00 W
Misión San Francisco de Laishí	252	26.14 S	58.38 W
Misirevo	82	56.16 N	36.45 E
Misk	130	38.48 N	42.13 E
Miskī	140	14.51 N	24.13 E
Miski, Enneri ∨	146	20.00 N	17.55 E
Miškino, S.S.S.R.	86	55.20 N	63.55 E
Miškino, S.S.S.R.	265a	59.42 N	30.45 E
Miskito Channel ʯ	236	14.20 N	83.08 W
Miskitos, Cayos ǁ	236	14.23 N	82.46 W
Miskitos Reef ✢[2]	236	14.28 N	82.42 W
Miskolc	30	48.06 N	20.47 E
Misli	130	38.10 N	34.52 E
Mislinja	61	46.28 N	15.14 E
Mislinja ≃	61	46.35 N	15.02 E
Mislippi	146	10.00 N	15.37 E
Mislivna ∧	61	48.40 N	14.44 E
Mismār	140	18.13 N	35.38 E
Mismār, Jabal ∧	140	18.06 N	35.42 E
Mišn'ovo	76	53.58 N	36.21 E
Misoke	154	1.06 S	28.38 E
Misool, Pulau I	164	1.52 S	130.10 E
Mispillion ≃	208	38.57 N	75.20 W
Misquamaebin Lake ⊜	184	53.30 N	91.05 W
Misquamicut	207	41.20 N	71.49 W
Miṣr → Egypt □[1]	140	27.00 N	30.00 E
Miṣr al-Jadīdah (Heliopolis) ◆[8]	273c	30.06 N	31.20 E
Miṣr al-Qadīmah (Old Cairo) ◆[8]	273c	30.00 N	31.14 E
Misrātah	146	32.23 N	15.06 E
Misrātah □[4]	146	30.00 N	16.30 E
Misrikh	124	27.27 N	80.31 E
Missanello	68	40.17 N	16.10 E
Missão Santa Cruz	152	16.14 S	21.57 E
Missão Velha	250	7.15 S	39.08 W
Misserghin	34	35.37 N	0.45 W
Missinaibi ≃	176	50.44 N	81.29 W
Missinaibi Lake ⊜	190	48.23 N	83.40 W
Mission, S. Dak., U.S.	198	43.18 N	100.40 W
Mission, Tex., U.S.	196	26.13 N	98.20 W
Mission ◆[8]	282	37.45 N	122.25 W
Mission Bay C	228	32.47 N	117.15 W
Mission City	182	49.08 N	122.18 W
Mission Creek ≃	282	37.32 N	121.55 W
Mission Hills ◆[8]	280	34.16 N	118.27 W
Mission Indian Reservation ◆[4]	228	33.22 N	116.58 W
Mission Mountain ∧	194	34.15 N	94.33 W
Mission Peak ∧	282	37.31 N	121.53 W
Mission Range ⋏	202	47.30 N	113.55 W
Mission Texas State Historic Park ♠	222	31.33 N	95.15 W
Mission Valley	222	28.54 N	97.12 W
Mission Viejo	228	33.36 N	117.40 W
Missisquoi □[6]	206	45.10 N	72.55 W
Missisquoi ≃	206	45.00 N	73.08 W
Missisquoi Bay C	206	45.05 N	73.10 W
Missisquoi-Nord ≃	206	45.02 N	72.26 W
Mississagagon Lake ⊜	212	44.52 N	77.05 W
Mississagi ≃	190	46.10 N	83.01 W
Mississagi Provincial Park ♠	190	46.35 N	82.30 W
Mississagua ≃	212	44.34 N	78.20 W
Mississagua Lake ⊜	212	44.42 N	78.19 W
Mississauga	212	43.35 N	79.37 W
Mississinewa ≃	216	40.46 N	86.02 W
Mississinewa Lake ⊜[1]	216	40.42 N	85.52 W
Mississippi □[3]	178		
	194	32.50 N	89.30 W
Mississippi ≃, Ont., Can.	212	45.26 N	76.16 W
Mississippi ≃, U.S.	178	29.00 N	89.15 W
Mississippi Bay C	162	34.00 S	122.17 E
Mississippi Delta ⊻[2]	194	29.10 N	89.15 W
Mississippi Lake ⊜	212	45.05 N	76.12 W
Mississippi Sound ʯ	194	30.15 N	88.40 W
Missolonghi → Mesolóngion	38	38.21 N	21.17 E
Missoula	202	46.52 N	114.01 W
Missouri □[3]	178		
	194	38.30 N	93.30 W
Missouri ≃	178	38.50 N	90.08 W
Missouri, Coteau du ⋏[2]	198	46.00 N	99.30 W
Missouri Buttes ∧	198	44.37 N	104.47 W
Missouri City	222	29.37 N	95.32 W
Missouri Creek ≃	219	40.07 N	90.43 W
Missouri Valley	198	41.33 N	95.53 W
Mistake, Mount ∧	171a	27.52 S	152.20 E
Mistake Creek	164	17.06 S	129.04 E
Mistake Creek ≃	166	21.38 S	146.50 E
Mistake Mountains ⋏	171a	27.52 S	152.22 E
Mistaken Point ≻	186	46.38 N	53.10 W
Mistanipisipou ≃	186	51.32 N	61.50 W
Mistassibi ≃	176	48.53 N	72.13 W
Mistassibi-Nord-Est ≃	186	49.50 N	71.56 W
Mistassini, Lac ⊜	176	51.00 N	73.37 W
Mistatim	184	52.52 N	103.22 W
Mistawasis Indian Reserve ◆[4]	184	53.06 N	106.48 W
Mistelbach	60	49.55 N	11.31 E
Mistelbach an de Zaya	61	48.34 N	16.35 E
Mistelgau	60	49.55 N	11.28 E
Misteln ⊜	40	59.07 N	16.57 E
Misterbianco	70	37.31 N	15.00 E
Misterei	140	13.07 N	22.09 E
Misterton, Eng., U.K.	42	50.52 N	2.47 W
Misterton, Eng., U.K.	44	53.27 N	0.51 W
Misti, Volcán ∧[1]	248	16.18 S	71.24 W
Mistikokan ≃	184	57.00 N	91.27 W
Mistrás ⊥	38	37.04 N	22.21 E
Mistretta	70	37.56 N	14.22 E
Misugi	94	34.33 N	136.16 E
Misumi, Nihon	92	32.37 N	130.27 E
Misumi, Nihon	96	34.46 N	131.58 E
Misumi, Nihon	96	34.22 N	131.15 E
Misumi ≃	96	34.47 N	131.56 E
Misurina	64	46.35 N	12.15 E
Mišurin Rog	78	48.50 N	33.58 E
Mišutino, S.S.S.R.	76	59.31 N	36.01 E
Mišutino, S.S.S.R.	82	56.23 N	38.06 E
Mita, Punta ≻	234	20.47 N	105.33 W
Mīt Abū Ghālib	142	31.17 N	31.40 E
Mit'ajevo, S.S.S.R.	82	55.16 N	36.32 E
Mit'ajevo, S.S.S.R.	86	60.17 N	61.06 E
Mitaka	94	35.40 N	139.33 E
Mitake, Nihon	94	35.25 N	137.08 E
Mitake, Nihon	94	35.51 N	137.37 E
Mit'akinka ≃	83	48.35 N	39.50 E
Mit'akino	82	54.24 N	38.50 E
Mit'akinskaja	83	48.36 N	39.47 E
Mīt al-'Āmil	142	30.54 N	31.21 E
Mitatib	140	16.03 N	36.11 E
Mitau → Jelgava	76	56.39 N	23.42 E
Mīt Badr Ḥalāwah	142	30.51 N	31.14 E

English	Deutsch	Español	Français	Português
≃ River	Fluss	Río	Rivière	Rio
≊ Canal	Kanal	Canal	Canal	Canal
ʟ Waterfall, Rapids	Wasserfall, Stromschnellen	Cascada, Rápidos	Chute d'eau, Rapides	Cascata, Rápidos
ʯ Strait	Meeresstrasse	Estrecho	Détroit	Estreito
C Bay, Gulf	Bucht, Golf	Bahía, Golfo	Baie, Golfe	Baía, Golfo
⊜ Lake, Lakes	See, Seen	Lago, Lagos	Lac, Lacs	Lago, Lagos
☷ Swamp	Sumpf	Pantano	Marais	Pântano
⊼ Ice Features, Glacier	Eis- und Gletscherformen	Accidentes Glaciales	Formes glaciaires	Acidentes Glaciares
⊤ Other Hydrographic Features	Andere Hydrographische Objekte	Otros Elementos Hidrográficos	Autres données hydrographiques	Outros Elementos Hidrográficos

English	Deutsch	Español	Français	Português
✢ Submarine Features	Untermeerische Objekte	Accidentes Submarinos	Formes de relief sous-marin	Acidentes Submarinos
□ Political Unit	Politische Einheit	Unidad Politica	Entité politique	Unidade Política
ʊ Cultural Institution	Kulturelle Institution	Institución Cultural	Institution culturelle	Instituição Cultural
⊥ Historical Site	Historische Stätte	Sitio Histórico	Site historique	Sitio Histórico
♠ Recreational Site	Erholungs- und Ferienort	Sitio de Recreo	Centre de loisirs	Sítio de Lazer
⊠ Airport	Flughafen	Aeropuerto	Aéroport	Aeroporto
■ Military Installation	Militäranlage	Instalación Militar	Installation militaire	Instalação Militar
◆ Miscellaneous	Verschiedenes	Misceláneo	Divers	Miscelânea

Mīt Bashshār 142 30.31 N 31.24 E
Mitcham, Austl. 168b 34.59 S 138.36 E
Mitcham, Austl. 274b 37.49 S 145.12 E
Mitcham ⬥[8] 260 51.24 N 0.10 W
Mitcheldean 42 51.53 N 2.30 W
Mitchell, Austl. 166 26.29 S 147.58 E
Mitchell, Ont., Can. 212 43.28 N 81.12 W
Mitchell, Ill., U.S. 219 38.46 N 90.06 W
Mitchell, Ind., U.S. 218 38.44 N 86.28 W
Mitchell, Nebr., U.S. 198 41.57 N 103.48 W
Mitchell, Oreg., U.S. 202 44.34 N 120.09 W
Mitchell, S. Dak., U.S. 198 43.43 N 104.01 W
Mitchell ≃, Austl. 164 15.12 S 141.35 E
Mitchell ≃, Austl. 166 37.53 S 147.41 E
Mitchell, Lake ⊜[1] 194 32.50 N 86.30 W
Mitchell, Mount ∧ 192 35.46 N 82.16 W
Mitchell Bay C 214 42.28 N 82.26 W
Mitchell Corners 212 43.57 N 78.48 W
Mitchell Field ⊠ 278 41.55 N 88.15 W
Mitchell Lake ⊜, B.C., Can. 182 52.53 N 120.36 W
Mitchell Lake ⊜, Ont., Can. 212 44.34 N 78.58 W
Mitchell Point ≻ 214 42.26 N 82.26 W
Mitchell River Mission 164 15.28 S 141.44 E
Mitchellville 190 41.40 N 93.22 W
Mitchelstown 48 52.16 N 8.16 W
Mīt Fāris 142 31.02 N 31.36 E
Mīt Ghamr 142 30.43 N 31.16 E
Mīt Ḥalfah 273c 30.10 N 31.14 E
Mīt Ḥamal 142 30.26 N 31.32 E
Mithapur 120 22.25 N 69.00 E
Mitha Tiwāna 123 32.14 N 72.07 E
Mithi 120 24.44 N 69.48 E
Míthimna 38 39.22 N 26.10 E
Mitiaro I 14 19.49 S 157.43 W
Mitidja, Plaine de la ⌣ 34 36.45 N 3.00 E
Mitilíni 38 39.06 N 26.32 E
Mitino 265b 55.51 N 37.21 E
Mitis, Lac ⊜ 186 48.17 N 67.45 W
Mitishto ≃ 184 54.50 N 98.58 W
Mitiškovo 76 54.40 N 33.31 E
Mitiwanga 214 41.22 N 82.27 W
Mīt Kinānah 142 30.23 N 31.16 E
Mitkof Island I 180 56.45 N 132.50 W
Mitla ⊥ 234 16.55 N 96.17 W
Mitla, Laguna C 234 17.03 N 100.25 W
Mitla, Mamarr Mitla Pass)(142 30.00 N 32.53 E
Mito, Nihon 94 36.22 N 140.28 E
Mito, Nihon 94 34.49 N 137.19 E
Mitō, Nihon 96 34.13 N 131.21 E
Mito, Nihon 96 34.40 N 131.59 E
Mito, Nihon 268 35.10 N 139.37 E
Mito, Tchad 146 10.49 N 15.44 E
Mitomi 94 35.47 N 138.44 E
Mitoya 96 35.17 N 132.52 E
Mitra, Monte ∧ 152 1.23 N 9.57 E
Mitra do Bispo ∧ 256 22.10 S 44.34 W
Mitre ∧ 172 40.48 S 175.27 E
Mitre, Península ≻[1] 254 54.48 S 65.40 W
Mitre Peak ∧ 172 44.38 S 167.50 E
Mitrofania Island I 180 55.51 N 158.49 W
Mitrofanovka 78 49.58 N 39.42 E
Mitrofanovo 24 63.13 N 56.00 E
Mīt Ruhaynah 273c 29.51 N 31.15 E
Mīt Ruhaynah (Memphis) ⊥ 142 29.51 N 31.15 E
Mitry-le-Neuf 261 48.57 N 2.36 E
Mitry-Mory 261 48.59 N 2.37 E
Mitsamiouli 157a 11.23 S 43.18 E
Mitsinjo 157b 16.01 S 45.52 E
Mitsio, Nosy I 157b 12.54 S 48.36 E
Mitsu, Nihon 96 34.48 N 133.56 E
Mitsu, Nihon 96 34.47 N 134.33 E
Mitsubori 268 35.56 N 139.56 E
Mitsue 94 34.29 N 136.10 E
Mitsugi 96 34.30 N 133.09 E
Mitsuishi 96 34.48 N 134.16 E
Mitsukaidō, Nihon 94 36.01 N 139.59 E
Mitsuke 92 37.32 N 138.56 E
Mitsumarenge-dake ∧ 94 36.23 N 137.35 E
Mitsusawa Park Race Track ♠ 268 35.28 N 139.37 E
Mitsuzaku 268 35.25 N 140.00 E
Mitta, Oued el ∨ 148 34.20 N 6.44 E
Mittagong 170 34.27 S 150.27 E
Mittagskogel ∧ 61 46.31 N 13.57 E
Mittainville 261 48.40 N 1.39 E
Mitta Mitta ≃ 171b 36.12 S 147.11 E
Mitte ⬥[8] 264a 52.31 N 13.24 E
Mittelberg, B.R.D. 58 47.38 N 10.25 E
Mittelberg, Öst. 58 47.20 N 10.10 E
Mitteldorf → Międzychód 30 52.36 N 15.55 E
Mittelfischach 56 49.02 N 9.52 E
Mittelfranken □[5] 56 49.20 N 10.40 E
Mittellandkanal ≈ 30 52.16 N 11.41 E
Mittelmeer → Mediterranean Sea ⊤[2] 10 35.00 N 20.00 E
Mittelsaida 54 50.46 N 13.18 E
Mittelstetten 60 48.15 N 11.06 E
Mittenwald 64 47.27 N 11.15 E
Mittenwalde, D.D.R. 54 53.11 N 13.39 E
Mittenwalde, D.D.R. 54 52.16 N 13.32 E
Mitterding 60 48.22 N 13.24 E
Mitterndorf 64 47.33 N 13.55 E
Mittersill 64 47.16 N 12.29 E
Mitterskirchen 60 48.21 N 12.44 E
Mitterteich 60 49.57 N 12.15 E
Mittewald an der Drau 64 46.46 N 12.36 E
Mittwalde → Międzylesie 30 50.10 N 16.40 E
Mittweida 54 50.59 N 12.59 E
Mitú 246 1.08 N 70.03 W
Mitumba, Monts ⋀ 154 6.00 S 29.00 E
Mituochang 107 28.53 N 105.37 E
Mitwaba 154 8.38 S 27.20 E
Mitwitz 56 50.15 N 11.12 E
Mityana 154 0.24 N 32.03 E
Mīt Yazīd 142 30.30 N 31.20 E
Mitzic 152 0.47 N 11.34 E
Miura 94 35.08 N 139.37 E
Miura-chosuichi ⊜[1] 94 35.49 N 137.23 E
Miura-dam ⬥[6] 94 35.49 N 137.24 E
Miura-hantō ≻[1] 94 35.15 N 139.39 E
Mius 80 51.26 N 47.56 E
Mius ≃ 83 47.18 N 38.49 E
Miusinsk 83 48.05 N 38.53 E
Miusskij Liman C[1] 83 47.15 N 38.40 E
Miwa, Nihon 94 35.11 N 136.47 E
Miwa, Nihon 94 36.39 N 140.18 E
Miwa, Nihon 94 36.12 N 139.49 E
Miwa, Nihon 96 35.12 N 135.14 E
Miwa, Nihon 96 34.13 N 132.06 E
Miwa, Nihon 270 34.31 N 135.51 E
Mi-Wuk Village 226 38.05 N 120.13 W
Mixcoac ⬥[8] 286a 19.23 N 99.12 W
Mixcoac, Presa de ⊜[1] 286a 19.22 N 99.14 W
Mixco Viejo ⊥ 236 14.52 N 90.40 W
Mixian 100 34.31 N 113.22 E
Mixin 107 30.23 N 105.46 E
Mixquiahuala 234 20.14 N 99.13 W
Mixtán 234 17.55 N 95.51 W
Mixteco ≃ 234 18.11 N 98.30 W
Mixtlán 234 20.26 N 104.25 W
Miya 94 36.05 N 137.15 E
Miya ≃, Nihon 94 34.32 N 136.44 E
Miya ≃, Nihon 94 36.28 N 137.15 E
Miyagawa, Nihon 94 36.19 N 137.09 E
Miyagawa, Nihon 94 34.22 N 136.21 E
Miyagi □[5] 92 38.22 N 140.52 E
Miyāh, Wādī al- ∨ 140 25.00 N 33.23 E
Miyahara 268 35.56 N 139.37 E
Miyajima 96 34.18 N 132.19 E
Miyake 270 34.35 N 135.47 E
Miyake-jima I 92 34.05 N 139.32 E
Miyako 92 39.38 N 141.57 E
Miyakojima ⬥[8] 270 34.43 N 135.33 E
Miyako-jima I 175d 24.47 N 125.20 E
Miyakonojō 92 31.44 N 131.04 E
Miyako-rettō II 175d 24.24 N 125.00 E
Miyama, Nihon 92 34.06 N 136.14 E
Miyama, Nihon 94 35.33 N 136.45 E
Miyama, Nihon 94 36.01 N 136.20 E
Miyama, Nihon 96 35.16 N 135.33 E
Miyama, Nihon 96 33.59 N 135.22 E
Miyamaki 270 34.49 N 135.47 E
Miyanojō 92 31.54 N 130.27 E
Miyanoura-dake ∧ 93b 30.20 N 130.31 E
Miyara 175d 24.20 N 124.14 E
Miyata 96 33.32 N 130.34 E
Miyazaki, Nihon 92 31.54 N 131.26 E
Miyazaki, Nihon 94 35.56 N 136.05 E
Miyazakino-hana ≻ 96 34.04 N 135.05 E
Miyazu 96 35.32 N 135.11 E
Miyi 102 27.00 N 102.08 E
Miyoshi, Nihon 96 34.48 N 132.51 E
Miyoshi, Nihon 96 34.02 N 133.52 E
Miyoshi, Nihon 96 33.57 N 133.03 E
Miyoshi, Nihon 268 35.50 N 139.31 E
Miyota 94 36.18 N 138.30 E
Miyun 105 40.22 N 116.50 E
Mizan Teferi 144 6.53 N 35.28 E
Mizar 130 37.26 N 39.26 E
Mizdah 146 31.26 N 12.59 E
Mize 194 31.52 N 89.34 W
Mizen Head ≻, Eire 48 52.51 N 6.01 W
Mizen Head ≻, Eire 48 51.27 N 9.49 W
Miževiči 76 52.59 N 25.05 E
Mizhi 102 37.49 N 110.02 E
Mizil 38 45.00 N 26.26 E
Mizoč 78 50.24 N 26.09 E
Mizoguchi 96 35.21 N 133.26 E
Mizo Hills ⋀[2] 120 22.50 N 93.00 E
Mizonokuchi 268 35.36 N 139.37 E
Mizonuma 268 35.48 N 139.36 E
Mizoram □[8] 120 23.30 N 93.00 E
Mizpah 208 39.29 N 74.50 W
Mizpah Creek ≃ 198 46.16 N 105.17 W
Mizpe Ramon 132 30.36 N 34.48 E
Mizque 248 17.56 S 65.19 W
Mizue ⬥[8] 268 35.41 N 139.54 E
Mizuho, Nihon 94 35.46 N 139.21 E
Mizuho, Nihon 96 35.10 N 135.22 E
Mizuho, Nihon 96 34.51 N 132.31 E
Mizuko 268 35.50 N 139.34 E
Mizumaki 96 33.51 N 130.42 E
Mizunami 94 35.22 N 137.15 E
Mizunoko-jima I 96 33.02 N 132.11 E
Mizusawa 92 39.08 N 141.08 E
Mizushima-nada C 96 34.25 N 133.40 E
Mizutori 270 34.47 N 135.45 E
Mizuwake-tōge)(96 33.15 N 131.17 E
Mjälgen 40 60.33 N 15.07 E
Mjällom 26 62.59 N 18.26 E
Mjangad 86 48.15 N 91.57 E
Mjanji 154 0.15 N 33.59 E
Mjanyana 158 31.50 S 28.10 E
Mjölby 26 58.19 N 15.08 E
Mjøndalen 26 59.45 N 10.01 E
Mjörn ⊜ 26 57.54 N 12.25 E
Mjøsa ⊜ 26 60.40 N 11.00 E
Mkalama 154 4.07 S 34.38 E
Mkata 154 5.47 S 38.17 E
Mkhada, Garaet el ☲ 36 36.48 N 8.00 E
Mkokotoni 154 5.52 S 39.15 E
Mkomazi ≃ 158 30.12 S 30.50 E
Mkomazi Game Reserve ⬥[4] 154 4.10 S 38.10 E
Mkondo ≃ 158 26.39 S 31.25 E
Mkulwe 154 8.35 S 32.19 E
Mkumvura ≃ 154 15.55 S 31.07 E
Mkunumbi 154 2.18 S 40.42 E
Mkushi 154 13.40 S 29.20 E
Mkushi ≃ 154 14.40 S 29.07 E
Mkushi River 154 13.32 S 29.45 E
Mkuze 158 27.10 S 32.00 E
Mkuze ≃ 158 27.53 S 32.29 E
Mkuze Game Reserve ⬥[4] 158 27.40 S 32.15 E
Mkwaja 154 5.47 S 38.51 E
Mkwaya 154 10.06 S 39.40 E
Mladá Boleslav 54 50.23 N 14.59 E
Mladenovac 38 44.26 N 20.42 E
Mladotice 60 49.58 N 13.18 E
Mlala Hills ⋀[2] 154 6.47 S 31.45 E
M'Lang 116 6.55 N 124.53 E
M'Lang ≃ 116 6.52 N 124.45 E
Mlanje Peak → Sapitwa ∧ 154 15.57 S 35.36 E
Mlava ≃ 38 44.45 N 21.13 E
Mława 30 53.06 N 20.23 E
Mlawula 158 26.11 S 32.01 E
Mliba 158 26.14 S 31.36 E
Mlinov 78 50.31 N 25.37 E
Mljet, Otok I 36 42.45 N 17.30 E
Mljetski Kanal)(36 42.48 N 17.35 E
Mmadinare 156 21.57 S 27.52 E
Mmanford 42 51.48 N 3.59 W
Mnazi 154 8.54 S 39.06 E
Mncwasa Point ≻ 158 32.05 S 29.05 E
Mneni 154 20.38 S 30.03 E
Mnevniki ⬥[8] 265b 55.45 N 37.28 E
Mnichov 60 50.03 N 12.49 E
Mníšek pod Brdy 30 49.52 N 14.16 E
Mo 24 66.15 N 14.08 E
Mo ≃ 150 8.45 N 11.36 W
Moa ≃, Afr. 150 6.59 N 11.36 W
Moa ≃, Bra. 248 7.39 S 72.41 W
Moa, Pulau I 164 8.10 S 127.56 E
Moab 200 38.35 N 109.33 W
Moabi 152 2.15 S 11.00 E
Moaco ≃ 248 7.41 S 68.18 W
Moa Island I 164 10.12 S 142.16 E
Moala I 175g 18.36 S 179.53 E
Moalboal 116 9.56 N 123.23 E
Moama 166 36.07 S 144.47 E
Moamba 156 25.35 S 32.13 E
Moana 168b 35.13 S 138.29 E
Moanda 152 1.34 S 13.11 E
Moanza 152 5.25 S 17.30 E
Moar Lake ⊜ 184 52.00 N 95.09 W
Moate 48 53.24 N 7.58 W
Moatize 154 16.08 S 33.45 E
Moawhango 172 39.35 S 175.52 E
Moba, Nig. 273a 6.27 N 3.28 E
Moba, Zaïre 154 7.03 S 29.47 E
Mobara 94 35.25 N 140.18 E
Mobārakpur 126 22.58 N 89.10 E
Mobaye 152 4.19 N 21.11 E
Mobayi-Mbongo 152 4.18 N 21.11 E
Mobberley 262 53.19 N 2.20 W
Mobeetie 196 35.31 N 100.26 W
Mobeka 152 1.53 N 19.46 E
Mobenzélé 152 0.54 N 17.51 E
Moberly 194 39.25 N 92.26 W
Moberly ≃ 182 56.12 N 120.55 W
Moberly Lake 182 55.48 N 121.45 W
Mobile, Ala., U.S. 194 30.42 N 88.05 W
Mobile, Ariz., U.S. 200 33.03 N 112.16 W
Mobile Bay C 194 30.25 N 88.00 W
Mobjack 208 37.23 N 76.21 W
Mobjack Bay C 208 37.19 N 76.21 W
Mobridge 198 45.32 N 100.26 W
Mobu 100 26.50 N 117.42 E
Moca, P.R. 240m 18.24 N 67.07 W
Moca, Rep. Dom. 238 19.24 N 70.31 W
Moča ≃ 82 55.25 N 37.28 E
Mocajuba 250 2.35 S 49.30 W
Močalejevka 80 53.38 N 51.46 E
Močališče 80 56.21 N 48.23 E
Moçambique 154 15.03 S 40.42 E
Moçambique □[5] 154 15.00 S 39.00 E
Moçambique → Mozambique □[1] 138 18.15 S 35.00 E
Moçâmedes 152 15.10 S 12.09 E
Moçâmedes □[5] 152 15.20 S 12.30 E
Mocanaqua 210 41.08 N 76.08 W
Mocanguê Grande, Ilha I 287a 22.52 S 43.08 W
Mocassins, Lac des ⊜ 206 46.35 N 74.25 W
Mo-cay 110 10.08 N 106.20 E
Moccasin, Calif., U.S. 226 37.49 N 120.18 W
Moccasin, Ill., U.S. 219 39.09 N 88.45 W
Moc-chau 110 20.51 N 104.37 E
Mocha → Al-Mukhā 144 13.19 N 43.15 E
Mocha, Isla I 252 38.22 S 73.56 W
Mocheng 106 31.35 N 120.43 E
Mochh 123 32.45 N 71.31 E
Mochigase 96 35.20 N 134.12 E
Mochitlán 234 17.30 N 99.18 W
Mochizuki 94 36.16 N 138.22 E
Mocho, Arroyo ≃ 226 37.41 N 121.55 W
Mochov 54 50.08 N 14.50 E
Mochovoje 76 52.57 N 36.34 E
Mochtín 60 49.22 N 13.21 E
Mochudi 156 24.28 S 26.05 E
Močily 82 54.20 N 38.41 E
Mocímboa da Praia 154 11.20 S 40.21 E
Mocímboa do Rovuma 154 11.20 S 39.18 E
Möckeln ⊜, Sve. 26 56.40 N 14.10 E
Möckeln ⊜, Sve. 40 59.18 N 14.30 E
Möckern 54 52.08 N 11.57 E
Mockfjärd 40 60.30 N 14.58 E
Mockhorn Island I 208 37.13 N 75.53 W
Möckmühl 56 49.19 N 9.22 E
Mockrehna 54 51.30 N 12.49 E
Mocksville 192 35.54 N 80.34 W
Moclips 224 47.14 N 124.13 W
Mocó ≃ 246 1.49 S 66.48 W
Môco, Serra ∧ 152 12.28 S 15.10 E
Mocoa 246 1.09 N 76.37 W
Mococa 256 21.28 S 47.01 W
Mocoduene 156 23.40 S 35.10 E
Mocomoco 248 15.22 S 68.59 W
Mocoretá 252 30.38 S 57.58 W
Mocorito 232 25.29 N 107.55 W
Moctezuma, Méx. 232 29.48 N 109.42 W
Moctezuma, Méx. 234 22.45 N 101.05 W
Moctezuma ≃, Méx. 232 29.09 N 109.40 W
Moctezuma ≃, Méx. 234 21.59 N 98.34 W
Mocuba 154 16.50 S 36.59 E
Mocubúri 154 14.39 S 38.54 E
Mocubúri ≃ 154 14.10 S 40.31 E
Močurica ≃ 38 42.31 N 26.32 E
Modane 62 45.12 N 6.40 E
Modaomen C 100 22.08 N 113.24 E
Modāsa 120 23.28 N 73.18 E
Modbury 42 50.21 N 3.53 W
Modder ≃ 158 29.02 S 24.37 E
Modderbee 273d 26.10 S 28.24 E
Modderfontein 158 26.05 S 28.10 E
Modderfontein ≃ 273d 26.13 S 28.10 E
Modderrivier 158 29.02 S 24.38 E
Model City 284a 43.11 N 78.59 W
Modena, It. 64 44.40 N 10.55 E
Modena, N.Y., U.S. 210 41.40 N 74.07 W
Modena □[4] 64 44.30 N 10.54 E
Moder ≃ 56 48.49 N 8.06 E
Möderath 56 50.53 N 6.43 E
Möderbrugg 61 47.17 N 14.29 E
Modern Art, Museum of ❦ 276 40.46 N 73.58 W
Modeste, Mount ∧ 224 48.37 N 124.06 W
Modesto, Calif., U.S. 226 37.39 N 121.00 W
Modesto, Ill., U.S. 219 39.29 N 89.59 W
Modesto City-County Airport ⊠ 226 37.39 N 120.57 W
Modesto Main Canal ≈ 226 37.39 N 120.27 W
Modesto Reservoir ⊜[1] 226 37.26 N 121.58 W
Modica 70 36.52 N 14.46 E
Modigliana 66 44.09 N 11.47 E
Modione ≃ 70 37.34 N 12.49 E
Modjamboli 152 2.28 N 22.06 E
Modjeska 280 33.43 N 117.37 W
Mödling 264b 48.05 N 16.17 E
Mödling ≃ 264b 48.04 N 16.22 E
Modo 140 5.29 N 30.38 E
Modoc 218 40.03 N 85.08 W
Modon ≃ 50 47.16 N 1.27 E
Modowi 164 4.05 S 134.39 E
Modra, Česko. 30 48.21 N 17.17 E
Modra, Tchad 146 20.43 N 17.42 E
Modra Špilja •[5] 36 43.00 N 16.02 E
Modriča 38 44.57 N 18.18 E
Modřice 61 49.07 N 16.37 E
Mo-duc 110 14.57 N 108.53 E
Modugno 68 41.05 N 16.47 E
Moe 169 38.10 S 146.15 E
Moe ≃, Austl. 169 38.08 S 146.17 E
Moe ≃, Qué., Can. 206 45.19 N 71.49 W
Moecherville 216 41.44 N 88.17 W
Moeda 255 20.20 S 44.03 W
Moehau ∧ 172 36.35 S 175.24 E
Moel Fferna ∧ 42 52.57 N 3.18 W
Moelv 26 60.56 N 10.42 E
Moema 255 19.50 S 45.24 W
Moen 50 50.46 N 3.24 E
Moen I 175c 7.26 N 151.52 E
Moena 64 46.22 N 11.39 E
Moengo 250 5.37 N 54.24 W
Moenkopi 200 36.07 N 111.13 W
Moenkopi Wash ∨ 200 36.54 N 111.26 W
Moeraki Point ≻ 172 45.22 S 170.52 E
Moeranyah Lake ⊜ 166 33.02 S 143.58 E
Moerbeke, Bel. 50 50.45 N 3.55 E
Moerbeke, Bel. 50 51.10 N 3.56 E
Moerdijk 52 51.43 N 4.38 E
Moerewa 172 35.23 S 174.02 E
Moergestel 52 51.33 N 5.11 E
Moero, Lago → Mweru, Lake ⊜ 154 9.00 S 28.45 E
Moers 56 51.27 N 6.37 E
Moers □[8] 263 51.32 N 6.36 E
Moersbach ≃ 263 51.33 N 6.36 E
Moesa ≃ 58 46.13 N 9.03 E
Moffat 44 55.20 N 3.27 W
Moffat Peak ∧ 172 45.02 S 168.07 E
Moffatt 222 31.12 N 97.28 W
Moffatt Lake ⊜ 206 45.34 N 71.19 W
Moffat Water ≃ 44 55.18 N 3.25 W
Moffet Point ≻ 180 55.26 N 162.32 W
Moffett Field Naval Air Station ■ 226 37.24 N 122.03 W
Moffit 198 46.41 N 100.18 W
Mofolo 273d 26.14 S 27.53 E
Mofoluku 273a 6.33 N 3.20 E
Moga 123 30.48 N 75.10 E
Mogadiscio → Mogadisho 144 2.01 N 45.20 E
Mogadisho 144 2.01 N 45.20 E
Mogadishu → Mogadisho 144 2.01 N 45.20 E
Mogador → Essaouira 148 31.30 N 9.47 W
Mogadore 214 41.03 N 81.24 W
Mogadore Reservoir ⊜[1] 214 41.04 N 81.21 W
Mogadouro 34 41.20 N 6.39 W
Mogalakwena ≃ 156 23.00 S 28.40 E
Mogalo 152 3.10 N 19.04 E
Mogami ≃ 92 38.55 N 139.48 E
Moganshan ∧ 106 30.36 N 119.52 E
Moganshan ⋀ 106 30.34 N 119.50 E
Mogapinyana 156 22.19 S 27.27 E
Mogaung 110 25.18 N 96.56 E
Mogdy 89 50.35 N 133.51 E
Mogees 285 40.06 N 75.19 W
Møgeltønder 41 54.56 N 8.49 E
Mogenstrup 41 55.11 N 11.53 E
Mogent ≃ 266d 41.33 N 2.15 E
Moggio Udinese 64 46.25 N 13.12 E
Mogi, Serra do ⋀ 287b 23.47 S 46.20 W
Mongibello → Etna, Monte ∧[1] 70 37.46 N 14.55 E
Mogi das Cruzes 256 23.31 S 46.11 W
Mogielnica 30 51.42 N 20.43 E
Mogi-Guaçu 256 22.22 S 46.57 W
Mogi-Guaçu ≃ 255 20.53 S 48.10 W
Mogila-Bel'mak, Gora ∧[2] 78 47.20 N 36.35 E
Mogila-Mečetnaja, Gora ∧[2] 83 48.16 N 38.53 E
Mogilev → Mogil'ov 76 53.54 N 30.21 E
Mogilno 30 52.40 N 17.58 E
Mogil'ov, S.S.S.R. 76 53.54 N 30.21 E
Mogil'ov, S.S.S.R. 78 48.52 N 34.29 E
Mogil'ov-Podol'skij 78 48.27 N 27.48 E
Mogi-Mirim 256 22.26 S 46.57 W
Mogincual 154 15.35 S 40.25 E
Moglal, Wādī ∨ 140 19.18 N 34.29 E
Moglia 64 44.56 N 10.55 E
Mogliano Veneto 64 45.33 N 12.14 E
Mogoča 88 53.44 N 119.44 E
Mogoča ≃ 76 58.00 N 36.26 E
Mogočin 86 57.43 N 83.34 E
Mogod 88 48.15 N 103.05 E
Mogogh 140 8.26 N 31.19 E
Mogojto 88 54.25 N 110.27 E
Mogojtuj 88 51.17 N 114.55 E
Mogok 110 22.55 N 96.30 E
Mogollon Mountains ⋀ 200 33.25 N 108.40 W
Mogollon Rim •[4] 200 32.30 N 111.00 W
Mogor 120 32.52 N 67.47 E
Mogorella 71 39.52 N 8.51 E
Mogoro 71 39.41 N 8.47 E
Mogotes 246 6.30 N 72.58 W
Mogotón, Pico ∧ 236 13.45 N 86.23 W
Mograt Island I 140 19.30 N 33.15 E
Mogroum 146 11.06 N 15.25 E
Moguer 34 37.16 N 6.50 W
Mogyoród 264c 47.36 N 19.15 E
Mogyoródi-patak ≃ 264c 47.36 N 19.05 E
Mogzon 88 51.45 N 111.58 E
Mohács 30 45.59 N 18.42 E
Mohaka 172 39.07 S 177.11 E
Mohaka ≃ 172 39.07 S 177.12 E
Mohale's Hoek 158 30.07 S 27.26 E
Mohall 198 48.46 N 101.31 W
Moḥammadābād 128 30.53 N 61.28 E
Mohammadia 148 35.33 N 0.03 E
Mohammedia (Fedala) 148 33.44 N 7.24 W
Mohana 124 25.54 N 77.45 E
Mohangi 154 0.03 N 29.05 E
Mohania 124 25.11 N 83.37 E
Mohanpur, Bhārat 126 21.51 N 87.26 E
Mohanpur, Bhārat 272a 28.44 N 77.10 E
Mohanpur, Bngl. 126 23.24 N 90.36 E
Mohave, Lake ⊜[1] 204 35.25 N 114.38 W
Mohawk, Mich., U.S. 190 47.18 N 88.26 W
Mohawk, N.Y., U.S. 210 43.00 N 75.00 W
Mohawk ≃ 210 42.47 N 73.42 W
Mohawk, East Branch ≃ 212 43.22 N 75.28 W
Mohawk, Lake ⊜ 210 41.02 N 74.41 W
Mohawk Mountain ∧ 207 41.49 N 73.17 W
Mohawk Point ≻ 212 42.51 N 79.29 W
Mohe 89 53.29 N 122.19 E
Moheda 26 57.00 N 14.34 E
Mohegan 207 41.28 N 72.06 W
Mohegan Lake 210 41.19 N 73.51 W
Moheli I 157a 12.15 S 43.45 E
Mohelnice 30 49.46 N 16.55 E
Mohican ≃ 214 40.22 N 82.09 W
Mohican, Black Fork ≃ 214 40.35 N 82.17 W
Mohican, Cape ≻ 180 60.12 N 167.28 W
Mohican, Clear Fork ≃ 214 40.35 N 82.12 W
Mohican, Jerome Fork ≃ 214 40.45 N 82.23 W
Mohican, Lake Fork ≃ 214 40.27 N 82.12 W
Mohican, Muddy Fork ≃ 214 40.45 N 82.08 W
Mohican State Park ♠ 214 40.37 N 82.16 W
Mohicanville Dam ⬥[6] 214 40.44 N 82.09 W
Mohicanville Reservoir ⊜[1] 214 40.45 N 82.00 W
Mohili ⬥[8] 272c 19.06 N 72.53 E
Mohill 48 53.54 N 7.52 W
Mohinora, Cerro ∧ 232 26.06 N 107.04 W
Möhlau 54 51.44 N 12.21 E
Mohlesi Pass)(158 29.29 S 29.21 E
Möhlin 58 47.34 N 7.51 E
Mohmand □[8] 123 34.30 N 71.20 E
Möhne ≃ 52 51.27 N 7.57 E
Möhnestausee ⊜[1] 52 51.29 N 8.08 E
Mohns Ridge ⬥[3] 10 73.00 N 5.00 E
Mohnton 208 40.17 N 75.59 W
Mohnyin 110 24.47 N 96.22 E
Moho ≃ 236 16.04 N 88.52 W
Moholm 40 58.37 N 14.02 E
Mohon 56 49.45 N 4.44 E
Mohorn 54 51.00 N 13.28 E
Mohoro 154 8.08 S 39.10 E
Mohoru 154 1.01 S 34.07 E
Möhringen 58 47.57 N 8.46 E
Mohrsville 208 40.28 N 75.59 W
Mohrungen → Morąg 30 53.56 N 19.56 E
Moi 26 58.28 N 6.32 E
Moiano, It. 68 40.39 N 14.28 E
Moiano, It. 68 41.05 N 14.32 E
Moindou 175f 21.42 S 165.41 E
Moinești 38 46.28 N 26.29 E
Moingbi 140 5.46 N 28.49 E
Moinhos 256 22.43 S 46.20 W
Moinkum 85 43.48 N 73.41 E
Mointy 86 47.13 N 73.21 E
Moio Alcantara 70 37.54 N 15.03 E
Moiporá 255 16.34 S 50.42 W
Moira 48 54.30 N 6.17 W
Moira ≃ 212 44.09 N 77.23 W
Moiraba 250 2.27 S 49.25 W
Moira Lake ⊜ 212 44.29 N 77.27 W
Moirans 62 45.20 N 5.34 E
Moirans-en-Montagne 58 46.26 N 5.44 E
Mõisaküla 76 58.06 N 25.11 E
Moisdon 32 47.37 N 1.22 W
Moisejeviči 76 53.13 N 28.17 E
Moisejevka, S.S.S.R. 83 49.14 N 39.51 E
Moisejevka, S.S.S.R. 86 58.05 N 76.16 E
Moisejevo Alabuška 76 51.54 N 42.06 E
Moisenay 261 48.34 N 2.44 E
Moisés Ville 252 30.43 S 61.29 W
Moisie 186 50.11 N 66.05 W
Moisie, Baie C 186 50.16 N 65.56 W
Moisling ⬥[8] 52 53.50 N 10.38 E
Moison Creek ≃ 281 42.18 N 82.40 W
Moissac 32 44.06 N 1.05 E
Moïssala 146 8.21 N 17.46 E
Moisselles 261 49.03 N 2.20 E
Moisson 261 49.05 N 1.40 E
Moisson, Forêt de ♠ 261 49.03 N 1.39 E
Moissy-Cramayel 261 48.38 N 2.36 E
Moita 34 38.39 N 8.59 W
Moitaco 246 8.01 N 64.21 W
Moivre ≃ 56 48.52 N 4.28 E
Möja I 26 59.26 N 18.55 E

ENGLISH — Name / Page / Lat.°′ / Long.°′

Mojácar 34 37.08 N 1.51 W
Mojana, Caño ≃[1] 246 9.02 N 74.46 W
Mojave 228 35.03 N 118.10 W
Mojave ≃ 204 35.06 N 116.04 W
Mojave Desert ⬥[2] 204 35.00 N 117.00 W
Mojave River Forks Reservoir ⊜[1] 228 34.20 N 117.15 W
Moji 85 38.59 N 74.24 E
Mojiang 102 23.28 N 101.39 E
Mojjero ≃ 74 68.44 N 103.42 E
Mojnalyk 88 51.18 N 95.33 E
Mojo 144 8.38 N 39.07 E
Mojoagung 115a 7.34 S 112.21 E
Mojokerto 115a 7.28 S 112.26 E
Mojosari 115a 7.31 S 112.33 E
Mojstrana 64 46.27 N 13.56 E
Moju 250 1.53 S 48.46 W
Moju ≃ 250 1.40 S 48.25 W
Mōka 94 36.26 N 140.01 E
Mokai 172 38.32 S 175.54 E
Mokambo 154 12.25 S 28.21 E
Mokameh 124 25.24 N 85.55 E
Mokane 219 38.41 N 91.53 W
Mokapu Peninsula ≻[1] 229c 21.27 N 157.45 W
Mokaria 152 2.00 N 23.20 E
Mokarta, Castello di ⊥ 70 37.48 N 12.45 E
Mokau 172 38.41 S 174.37 E
Mokau ≃ 172 38.42 S 174.37 E
Moke 102 30.14 N 100.01 E
Mokelumne ≃ 226 38.13 N 121.28 W
Mokelumne, Middle Fork ≃ 226 38.22 N 120.37 W
Mokelumne, North Fork ≃ 226 38.22 N 120.37 W
Mokelumne, South Fork ≃ 226 38.23 N 120.35 W
Mokelumne Aqueduct ≈[1] 226 37.54 N 122.07 W
Mokelumne Hill 226 38.18 N 120.42 W
Mokena 216 41.32 N 87.53 W
Mokhotlong 158 29.22 S 29.02 E
Mokil I[1] 14 6.40 N 159.47 E
Mokimbo 154 6.20 S 28.42 E
Mokino 80 57.27 N 49.11 E
Mokkoidumis 144 1.40 N 44.32 E
Moklakan 88 54.56 N 118.56 E
Möklinta 40 60.05 N 16.32 E
Mokochu, Khao ∧ 110 15.56 N 99.06 E
Mokokchūng 120 26.20 N 94.32 E
Mokolo, Cam. 146 10.45 N 13.48 E
Mokolo, Zaïre 152 1.57 N 18.05 E
Mokombe 152 0.14 S 23.48 E
Mokoreta ≃ 172 46.21 S 168.51 E
Mokou 273b 4.13 S 15.13 E
Mokpalin 110 17.26 N 96.53 E
Mokp'o 98 34.48 N 126.22 E
Mokraja Jel'muta 80 46.51 N 41.41 E
Mokraja Ol'chovka 80 50.28 N 44.59 E
Mokraja Sura ≃ 78 48.19 N 35.09 E
Mokraja Volnovacha ≃ 83 47.30 N 37.15 E
Mokrany 78 51.50 N 24.14 E
Mokrisset 34 34.59 N 5.20 W
Mokro-Jelančik 83 47.42 N 38.31 E
Mokrous 80 51.14 N 47.37 E
Mokrousovo 86 55.48 N 66.45 E
Mokrušinskoje 86 57.31 N 93.11 E
Mokryje Jaly ≃ 78 48.05 N 36.44 E
Mokryj Gašun 80 46.53 N 42.45 E
Mokryj Jelančik ≃ 83 47.08 N 38.20 E
Mokryj Kor 82 54.34 N 37.58 E
Mokša ≃ 80 54.44 N 41.53 E
Mokšan 80 53.26 N 44.37 E
Moku 154 2.57 N 29.22 E
Mokuleia 229c 21.35 N 158.09 W
Mokumbusu 152 1.44 N 21.04 E
Mokvin 78 50.57 N 26.48 E
Mokwa 150 9.20 N 5.02 E
Mol 56 51.11 N 5.06 E
Mola di Bari 68 41.04 N 17.05 E
Molale 144 10.08 N 39.42 E
Molalla 224 45.09 N 122.35 W
Molalla ≃ 224 45.18 N 122.43 W
Molalla, North Fork ≃ 224 45.05 N 122.29 W
Molanda 152 2.28 N 20.48 E
Molanosa 184 54.30 N 105.33 W
Moláoi 38 36.48 N 22.52 E
Molara, Isola I 71 40.52 N 9.43 E
Molaretto 62 45.10 N 7.00 E
Molat, Otok I 36 44.15 N 14.49 E
Molbergen 52 52.51 N 7.55 E
Molčanovka 83 46.52 N 38.37 E
Molčanovo 86 57.35 N 83.48 E
Mold 44 53.10 N 3.08 W
Moldary 86 50.47 N 78.29 E
Moldau → Vltava ≃ 30 50.21 N 14.30 E
Moldavia □[9] 38 46.30 N 27.00 E
Moldavian Soviet Socialist Republic → Moldavskaja Sovetskaja Socialističeskaja Respublika □[3] 78 47.00 N 29.00 E
Moldavskaja Sovetskaja Socialističeskaja Respublika □[3] 78 47.00 N 29.00 E
Molde 26 62.44 N 7.11 E
Moldotau, Chrebet ⋀ 85 41.35 N 74.40 E
Moldova ≃ 38 46.54 N 26.58 E
Moldova-Nouă 38 44.44 N 21.40 E
Moldoveanu ∧ 38 45.36 N 24.44 E
Môle ≃, Fr. 62 43.15 N 6.32 E
Mole ≃, Eng., U.K. 42 51.24 N 0.21 W
Mole ≃, Eng., U.K. 42 50.57 N 3.54 W
Môle, Cap du ≻ 238 19.50 N 73.25 W
Mole Creek 166 41.33 S 146.24 E
Molega Lake ⊜ 186 44.22 N 64.53 W
Mole Game Reserve ⬥[4] 150 9.30 N 2.00 W
Molegbe 152 4.14 N 20.53 E
Molenbeek-St.-Jean 50 50.51 N 4.19 E
Molepolole 156 24.25 S 25.30 E
Moléson ∧ 58 46.33 N 7.01 E
Molėtai 76 55.14 N 25.25 E
Mole Valley □[8] 260 51.16 N 0.18 W
Molfetta 68 41.12 N 16.36 E
Molibagu 112 0.23 N 123.59 E
Molidawadawoerzuzizhiqi (Buxi) 89 48.28 N 124.27 E
Molières-sur-Cèze 62 44.15 N 4.09 E
Molimiao 89 44.34 N 121.54 E
Molina 252 35.07 S 71.17 W
Molina de Aragón 34 40.51 N 1.53 W
Molina de Segura 34 38.03 N 1.12 W
Molina di Ledro 64 45.56 N 10.46 E
Molinara 68 41.18 N 14.54 E
Moline, Ill., U.S. 190 41.30 N 90.31 W
Moline, Kans., U.S. 198 37.22 N 96.18 W
Moline, Mich., U.S. 216 42.44 N 85.40 W
Molinella 64 44.37 N 11.40 E
Molinges 58 46.21 N 5.46 E
Molingguan 106 31.50 N 118.50 E
Molini, Capo ≻ 70 37.34 N 15.10 E
Molini di Tures (Mühlen) 64 46.54 N 11.56 E
Moliniere Point ≻ 241k 12.05 N 61.45 W
Molino 194 30.43 N 87.20 W
Molino de Rosas ⬥[8] 286a 19.22 N 99.13 W
Molinos 252 25.25 S 66.19 W
Molins de Rey 34 41.25 N 2.01 E
Moliro 154 8.13 S 30.34 E
Molise □[4] 66 41.35 N 14.30 E
Moliterno 68 40.14 N 50.52 E
Molkābād 128 34.32 N 52.35 E
Mölkau 54 51.20 N 12.26 E

DEUTSCH — Name / Seite / Breite°′ / Länge°′ E=Ost

Molkom 40 59.36 N 13.43 E
Möll ≃ 64 46.50 N 13.26 E
Mollahasan 130 39.22 N 42.37 E
Mollāhāt 126 22.56 N 89.48 E
Mollakendi 130 38.36 N 39.20 E
Mollaro 64 46.16 N 11.05 E
Möllbrücke 64 46.50 N 13.22 E
Mölle 41 56.17 N 12.29 E
Möllen 263 51.35 N 6.42 E
Möllenbeck, D.D.R. 54 53.17 N 11.44 E
Möllenbeck, D.D.R. 54 53.23 N 13.20 E
Mollendo 248 17.02 S 72.01 W
Möllensee ⊜ 264a 52.26 N 13.51 E
Mollepata 248 13.31 S 72.32 W
Moller, Port C 180 55.51 N 160.25 W
Möllersdorf 264b 48.02 N 16.18 E
Mollet 266d 41.33 N 2.13 E
Mollia 62 45.49 N 8.02 E
Molliens-Vidame 50 49.53 N 2.01 E
Mollington 262 53.13 N 2.55 W
Mollis 58 47.05 N 9.04 E
Mölln, B.R.D. 54 53.37 N 10.41 E
Molln, Öst. 61 47.53 N 14.15 E
Mollösund 26 58.04 N 11.28 E
Mollusk 208 37.44 N 76.32 W
Molly Ann Brook ≃ 276 40.55 N 74.11 W
Mölnbo 40 59.03 N 17.25 E
Mölndal 26 57.39 N 12.01 E
Mölnlycke 26 57.39 N 12.09 E
Mölntorp 40 59.33 N 16.15 E
Molocaboc Island I 116 10.58 N 123.34 E
Moločansk 78 47.12 N 35.36 E
Molochio 68 38.18 N 16.02 E
Moločnaja ≃ 78 46.42 N 35.20 E
Moločnoje 76 59.17 N 39.41 E
Moločnoje, Ozero ⊜ 78 46.30 N 35.20 E
Molócuè ≃ 154 17.03 S 38.52 E
Molodečno 76 54.19 N 26.49 E
Molodežnaja ❦[3] 9 67.35 S 46.35 E
Molodi 82 55.17 N 37.31 E
Molodo 150 14.14 N 6.02 W
Molodogvardejsk 83 48.20 N 39.40 E
Molodoj Tud 76 56.26 N 33.36 E
Molod'ožnyj 89 50.23 N 136.48 E
Mologa ≃ 76 58.50 N 37.11 E
Molokai I 229a 21.07 N 157.00 W
Molokča ≃ 82 56.15 N 38.45 E
Molokini I 229a 20.38 N 156.30 W
Molokovo, S.S.S.R. 76 58.10 N 36.45 E
Molokovo, S.S.S.R. 82 55.34 N 37.52 E
Molong 166 33.06 S 148.52 E
Molonglo ≃ 171b 35.15 S 148.58 E
Molopo ≃ 156 28.30 S 20.13 E
Molotkoviči 78 52.07 N 25.56 E
Molotov → Perm' 86 58.00 N 56.15 E
Molotovsk → Severodvinsk 24 64.34 N 39.50 E
Molou 146 13.42 N 21.44 E
Moloundou 152 2.03 N 15.10 E
Molowaie 152 5.47 S 23.20 E
Moloy 58 47.32 N 4.55 E
Mols Bjerge ∧[2] 41 56.13 N 10.32 E
Molsheim 58 48.32 N 7.29 E
Molson Lake ⊜ 184 54.12 N 96.45 W
Molteno 158 31.22 S 26.22 E
Moltke, Cape ≻ 175e 6.03 S 154.52 E
Molu, Pulau I 164 6.45 S 131.33 E
Moluca, Mar de la → Maluku, Laut ⊤[2] 108 0.00 S 125.00 E
Molucas, Islas → Maluku II 108 2.00 S 128.00 E
Moluccas → Maluku II 108 2.00 S 128.00 E
Molucca Sea → Maluku, Laut ⊤[2] 108 0.00 S 125.00 E
Molukken → Maluku II 108 2.00 S 128.00 E
Molumbo 154 15.27 S 30.15 E
Molundo 116 7.56 N 124.23 E
Moluques → Maluku II 108 2.00 S 128.00 E
Molveno, Lago di ⊜ 64 46.08 N 10.57 E
Molvoticy 76 57.25 N 32.20 E
Molžaninovo 82 55.56 N 37.22 E
Moma, Moç. 154 16.44 S 39.14 E
Moma, Zaïre 152 1.36 S 23.57 E
Moma ≃ 74 66.26 N 143.06 E
Momanga 152 18.12 S 21.42 E
Momats ≃ 164 5.20 S 137.47 E
Momax 234 21.56 N 103.19 W
Momba ≃ 154 8.28 S 32.40 E
Mombaça 250 5.45 S 39.38 W
Mombachito, Cerro ∧ 236 12.24 N 85.34 W
Mombacho, Volcán ∧[1] 236 11.50 N 85.58 W
Mombango 152 1.45 N 24.26 E
Mombaruzzo 62 44.46 N 8.27 E
Mombasa 154 4.03 S 39.40 E
Mombetsu 92a 44.21 N 143.22 E
Mombo 154 4.53 S 38.17 E
Mombongo 152 1.39 N 23.09 E
Momboyo ≃ 152 0.16 S 19.00 E
Mombuey 34 42.02 N 6.20 W
Mombum 164 8.23 S 138.51 E
Momčilgrad 38 41.32 N 25.25 E
Momence 216 41.10 N 87.40 W
Momfafa, Tanjung ≻ 164 0.18 S 131.20 E
Momi 175g 17.55 S 177.17 E
Momignies 50 50.02 N 4.10 E
Mommark 41 54.55 N 10.03 E
Mommenheim 56 48.45 N 7.39 E
Momo 152 1.52 N 11.48 E
Momotombo, Volcán ∧[1] 236 12.26 N 86.33 W
Momozaka 270 34.51 N 135.02 E
Mompog Island I 116 13.31 N 122.11 E
Mompog Pass)(116 13.34 N 122.13 E
Mompono 152 0.04 N 21.48 E
Mompós 246 9.14 N 74.26 W
Momskij Chrebet ⋀ 74 66.00 N 146.00 E
Mon 110 18.31 N 96.38 E
Møn I 41 55.00 N 12.20 E
Mon ≃ 110 20.20 N 94.54 E
Mona 200 39.49 N 111.51 W
Mona, Canal de la)(238 18.30 N 67.45 W
Mona, Isla de I 238 18.05 N 67.54 W
Mona, Punta ≻ 236 9.38 N 82.37 W
Monaca 214 40.41 N 80.17 W
Monach, Sound of)(46 57.34 N 7.35 W
Monachovo 83 48.09 N 38.07 E
Monaci, Fiume dei ≃ 70 37.24 N 14.48 E
Monaco 62 43.42 N 7.23 E
Monaco □[1] 22 / 62 43.45 N 7.25 E
Monadhliath Mountains ⋀ 46 57.10 N 4.00 W
Monadnock, Mount ∧ 207 42.52 N 72.07 W
Monagas □[3] 246 9.20 N 63.00 W
Monaghan 48 54.15 N 6.58 W
Monaghan □[6] 48 54.10 N 7.00 W
Monagrillo 236 7.59 N 80.26 W
Monahans 196 31.36 N 102.54 W
Monahans Draw ∨ 196 31.55 N 101.46 W
Monahans Sandhills State Park ♠ 196 31.38 N 102.50 W
Monakino 89 43.24 N 133.29 E
Mona Lake ⊜ 216 43.11 N 86.17 W
Monamolin 48 52.33 N 6.20 W
Monango 198 46.10 N 98.43 W
Monapo 154 14.57 S 40.17 E

Symbols in the index entries represent the broad categories identified in the key at the right. Symbols with superior numbers (⋀[2]) identify subcategories (see complete key on page *I* · 30).

Kartensymbole in dem Registerverzeichnis stellen die rechts in Schlüssel erklärten Kategorien dar. Symbole mit hochgestellten Ziffern (⋀[2]) bezeichnen Unterabteilungen einer Kategorie (vgl. vollständiger Schlüssel auf Seite *I* · 30).

Los símbolos incluídos en el texto del índice representan las grandes categorías identificadas con la clave a la derecha. Los símbolos con numeros en su parte superior (⋀[2]) identifican las subcategorías (véase la clave completa en la página *I* · 30).

Les symboles de l'index représentent les catégories indiquées dans la légende à droite. Les symboles suivis d'un indice (⋀[2]) représentent des sous-catégories (voir légende complète à la page *I* · 30).

Os símbolos incluídos no texto do índice representam as grandes categorias identificadas com a chave à direita. Os símbolos com números em sua parte superior (⋀[2]) identificam as subcategorias (veja-se a chave completa à página *I* · 30).

Symbol	English	Deutsch	Español	Français	Português
∧	Mountain	Berg	Montaña	Montagne	Montanha
⋀	Mountains	Berge	Montañas	Montagnes	Montanhas
)(	Pass	Pass	Paso	Col	Passo
∨	Valley, Canyon	Tal, Cañon	Valle, Cañón	Vallée, Canyon	Vale, Canhão
⌣	Plain	Ebene	Llano	Plaine	Planície
≻	Cape	Kap	Cabo	Cap	Cabo
I	Island	Insel	Isla	Île	Ilha
II	Islands	Inseln	Islas	Îles	Ilhas
•	Other Topographic Features	Andere Topographische Objekte	Otros Elementos Topográficos	Autres données topographiques	Outros Elementos Topográficos

ESPAÑOL · FRANÇAIS · PORTUGUÊS

Nombre / Nom / Nome	Página / Page / Página	Lat.°′	Long.°′ W=Oeste / W=Ouest / W=Oeste
Monapo ≃	154	15.07 S	40.33 E
Mona Quimbundo	152	9.55 S	19.58 E
Monar, Loch ⊜	46	57.25 N	5.06 W
Monarch	192	34.43 N	81.35 W
Monarch Mountain ∧	182	51.54 N	125.53 W
Monarch Pass)(	200	38.30 N	106.19 W
Monarto South	168b	35.08 S	139.08 E
Monaš	80	46.58 N	50.36 E
Monashee Mountains ⩕	182	50.30 N	118.30 W
Monashee Provincial Park ♠	182	50.28 N	118.11 W
Monash University ʊ[2]	274b	37.55 S	145.08 E
Monasterace	68	38.27 N	16.33 E
Monasterevin	48	53.07 N	7.02 W
Monasterolo di Savigliano	62	44.40 N	7.37 E
Monastir, It.	71	39.23 N	9.02 E
Monastir → Bitola, Jugo.	38	41.01 N	21.20 E
Monastir, Tun.	148	35.47 N	10.50 E
Monastyrišče	78	49.00 N	29.49 E
Monastyriska	78	49.06 N	25.11 E
Monastyrščina	76	54.21 N	31.50 E
Monatélé	152	4.16 N	11.12 E
Mona Vale	170	33.41 S	151.18 E
Monbulk	274b	37.52 S	145.25 E
Monbulk Creek ≃	274b	37.54 S	145.15 E
Moncada, Esp.	266d	41.29 N	2.11 E
Moncada, Pil.	116	15.44 N	120.34 E
Moncalieri	62	45.00 N	7.41 E
Moncalvo	62	45.03 N	8.16 E
Monção, Bra.	250	3.30 S	45.15 W
Moncão, Port.	34	42.05 N	8.29 W
Moncata Fenicia ⊥	70	37.33 N	14.57 E
Monceau-sur-Sambre	50	50.25 N	4.22 E
Mončegorsk	24	67.54 N	32.58 E
Mönchdorf	61	48.21 N	14.48 E
Mönchengladbach	56		
	263	51.12 N	6.28 E
Mönchengladbach, Flughafen ⊠	263	51.14 N	6.29 E
Mönchhof	61	47.52 N	16.56 E
Monchique	34	37.19 N	8.33 W
Mönchröden	56	50.18 N	11.03 E
Mönchweiler	58	48.06 N	8.25 E
Moncks Corner	192	33.12 N	80.01 W
Monclova	232	26.54 N	101.25 W
Moncontour	32	48.21 N	2.39 W
Moncoutant	32	46.43 N	0.35 W
Moncton	186	46.06 N	64.47 W
Mondaí	252	27.05 S	53.25 W
Mondaino	66	43.51 N	12.41 E
Mondavio	66	43.40 N	12.58 E
Monday ≃	252	25.33 S	54.41 W
Mondego ≃	34	40.09 N	8.52 W
Mondego, Cabo ≻	34	40.11 N	8.55 W
Mondello	70	38.13 N	13.20 E
Mondeodo	112	3.33 S	122.12 E
Mondeor	273d	26.17 S	28.00 E
Mondfeld	56	49.47 N	9.25 E
Mondimbi	152	1.43 N	22.58 E
Mondo, Tan.	154	4.59 S	35.54 E
Mondo, Tchad	146	13.47 N	15.32 E
Mondolè, Monte ∧	62	44.13 N	7.46 E
Mondolfo	66	43.45 N	13.06 E
Mondombe	152	0.53 S	22.45 E
Mondoñedo	34	43.26 N	7.22 W
Mondorf-les-Bains	56	49.31 N	6.16 E
Mondoro	150	14.40 N	1.57 W
Mondoubleau	50	47.59 N	0.54 E
Mondovì, It.	62	44.23 N	7.49 E
Mondovi, Wis., U.S.	190	44.34 N	91.40 W
Mondragon, Fr.	62	44.14 N	4.43 E
Mondragon, Pil.	116	12.31 N	124.45 E
Mondragone	68	41.07 N	13.53 E
Mondrain Island I	162	34.08 S	122.15 E
Mondsee	64	47.52 N	13.21 E
Mondsee ⊜	64	47.49 N	13.23 E
Monds Island I	285	39.50 N	75.19 W
Mondy	88	51.40 N	100.59 E
Monee	216	41.25 N	87.45 W
Moneglia	62	44.14 N	9.30 E
Monemvasía	38	36.41 N	23.03 E
Monero	200	36.54 N	106.52 W
Moneron, Ostrov I	89	46.17 N	141.15 E
Monesiglio	62	44.28 N	8.07 E
Monessen	214	40.09 N	79.53 W
Monesterio	34	38.05 N	6.16 W
Monestier-de-Clermont	62	44.54 N	5.38 E
Monetnyj	86	57.03 N	60.53 E
Monett	194	36.55 N	93.55 W
Monette	194	35.53 N	90.21 W
Money Creek ≃	216	40.40 N	88.58 W
Moneygall	48	52.53 N	7.57 W
Moneymore	48	54.42 N	6.41 W
Monfalcone	64	45.49 N	13.32 E
Monferrato □[9]	62	44.55 N	8.05 E
Monflanquin	32	44.32 N	0.46 E
Monforte	34	39.03 N	7.26 W
Monforte de Lemos	34	42.31 N	7.30 W
Monforte San Giorgio	70	38.09 N	15.23 E
Monfort Heights	218	39.12 N	84.37 W
Monga	152	4.12 N	22.49 E
Mongaguá	256	24.06 S	46.37 W
Mongai-Musenge	152	4.04 S	19.34 E
Mongala ≃	152	1.53 N	19.46 E
Mongalla	154	5.12 N	31.46 E
Mongandjo	152	1.21 N	24.20 E
Mongat	266d	41.28 N	2.17 E
Mongaup ≃	210	41.25 N	74.45 W
Mongaup Valley	210	41.40 N	74.47 W
Mongbwalu	154	1.57 N	30.02 E
Mongbyŏn-ni	271b	37.40 N	126.44 E
Mong-cai	110	21.32 N	107.58 E
Monge ∧	266c	38.46 N	9.26 W
Mongerbino, Capo ≻	70	38.06 N	13.30 E
Mongeri	150	8.19 N	11.44 W
Mongers Lake ⊜	162	29.15 S	117.05 E
Monggŭmp'o	98	38.09 N	124.47 E
Möng Hai	110	20.46 N	99.49 E
Möng Hawm	110	23.51 N	98.20 E
Monghidoro	66	44.13 N	11.19 E
Möng Hpāyak	110	20.53 N	99.54 E
Möng Hsat	110	20.32 N	99.15 E
Monghyr	124	25.23 N	86.28 E
Monghyr □[5]	124	25.10 N	86.10 E
Mongi ≃	164	6.35 S	147.35 E
Mongiana	68	38.31 N	16.19 E
Mongiuffi	70	37.55 N	15.17 E
Möng Küng	110	21.36 N	97.32 E
Möng Ma	110	21.37 N	99.54 E
Möng Mit	110	23.07 N	96.41 E
Möng Nai	110	20.31 N	97.52 E
Möng Nawng	110	21.39 N	98.08 E
Mongo, Tchad	146	12.11 N	18.42 E
Mongo, Ind., U.S.	216	41.41 N	85.17 W
Mongo ≃	150	9.34 N	12.11 W
Mongoj	88	53.57 N	113.50 E
Mongol Altajn Nuruu ⩕	90	47.00 N	92.00 E
Mongol Ard Uls → Mongolia □[1]	90	46.00 N	105.00 E
Mongolei → Mongolia □[1]	90	46.00 N	105.00 E
Mongol Els ➛[2]	88	47.45 N	94.30 E
Mongolia □[1]	90	46.00 N	105.00 E
Mongolie → Mongolia □[1]	90	46.00 N	105.00 E
Mongomo	152	1.38 N	11.19 E
Möngönmor't	88	48.11 N	108.29 E
Mongororo	146	12.01 N	22.28 E
Mongoumba	152	3.38 N	18.36 E
Möng Pai	110	19.44 N	97.05 E
Möng Pan	110	20.19 N	98.22 E
Möng Pawn	110	20.49 N	97.28 E
Möng Ping	110	22.22 N	99.02 E
Mongpong ≃	116	12.44 N	120.48 E
Mongrando	62	45.31 N	8.00 E
Mongrove, Punta ≻	234	17.56 N	102.11 W
Möng Si	110	23.40 N	98.23 E
Mongu	152	15.15 S	23.09 E
Mongu ≃	273b	4.24 S	15.24 E
Môngua	152	16.43 S	15.23 E
Monguè	154	16.22 S	35.35 E
Monguelfo (Welsberg)	64	46.45 N	12.06 E
Monguno	146	12.40 N	13.38 E
Möng Yai	110	22.25 N	98.02 E
Möng Yawng	110	21.11 N	100.22 E
Monheim, B.R.D.	56	48.50 N	10.51 E
Monheim, B.R.D.	56	51.05 N	6.52 E
Moniaive	44	55.12 N	3.55 W
Mönichkirchen	61	47.31 N	16.02 E
Monico	190	45.35 N	89.09 W
Monida Pass)(	202	44.33 N	112.18 W
Mon Idée	50	49.53 N	4.23 E
Monie	152	4.00 S	17.22 E
Monie Bay C	208	38.13 N	75.51 W
Monie Creek ≃	208	38.14 N	75.50 W
Monifieth	46	56.29 N	2.49 W
Monimail	46	56.18 N	3.08 W
Moninger	214	40.14 N	80.13 W
Monino	82	55.50 N	38.11 E
Moniquirá	246	5.52 N	73.36 W
Mõniste	76	57.35 N	26.33 E
Monistrol-d'Allier	62	44.57 N	3.38 E
Monistrol-sur-Loire	62	45.17 N	4.10 E
Monitor Range ⩕	204	38.45 N	116.30 W
Monitor Valley ∨	204	39.00 N	116.40 W
Monivea	48	53.23 N	8.43 W
Monjolo	256	22.49 S	42.57 W
Monk, Pointe ≻	275a	45.29 N	73.57 W
Monkayo	116	7.50 N	126.03 E
Mönkebude	54	53.46 N	13.57 E
Monken Hadley ➛[8]	260	51.40 N	0.11 W
Monkey Bay	154	14.05 S	34.55 E
Monkey Point ≻	236	11.36 N	83.39 W
Monkey River	236	16.22 N	88.29 W
Mońki	30	53.24 N	22.49 E
Monkira	166	24.49 S	140.34 E
Monkoto	152	1.38 S	20.39 E
Monks Heath	262	53.16 N	2.14 W
Monkton	212	43.35 N	81.05 W
Monmouth, Wales, U.K.	42	51.50 N	2.43 W
Monmouth, Ill., U.S.	190	40.55 N	90.39 W
Monmouth, Ind., U.S.	216	40.52 N	84.57 W
Monmouth, Oreg., U.S.	202	44.51 N	123.14 W
Monmouth □[6]	208	40.16 N	74.17 W
Monmouth Beach	276	40.20 N	73.59 W
Monmouth Hills	276	40.24 N	74.00 W
Monmouth Junction	208	40.20 N	74.36 W
Monmouth Mountain ∧	182	51.00 N	123.47 W
Monmouth Peak ∧	202	44.48 N	123.33 W
Monnickendam	52	52.27 N	5.02 E
Monnow ≃, U.K.	42	51.48 N	2.42 W
Monnow ≃, Wales, U.K.	42	51.48 N	2.42 W
Mono □[5]	150	6.45 N	1.50 E
Mono □[6]	226	38.18 N	119.22 W
Mono I	175e	7.21 S	155.34 E
Mono ≃	150	6.17 N	1.51 E
Monobe	96	33.42 N	133.53 E
Monobe ≃	96	33.32 N	133.41 E
Monocacy ≃, Md., U.S.	208	39.13 N	77.27 W
Monocacy ≃, Pa., U.S.	208	39.13 N	77.27 W
Monocacy Station	208	40.16 N	75.46 W
Monogarovo	82	54.42 N	38.45 E
Mono Lake ⊜	204	38.00 N	119.00 W
Monolith	228	35.07 N	118.22 W
Monomoy Island I	207	41.35 N	69.59 W
Monomoy Point ≻	207	41.33 N	70.02 W
Monon	216	40.52 N	86.53 W
Monona, Iowa, U.S.	190	43.03 N	91.23 W
Monona, Wis., U.S.	216	43.04 N	89.20 W
Monona, Lake ⊜	216	43.03 N	89.22 W
Monongahela	214	40.11 N	79.56 W
Monongahela ≃	214	40.27 N	80.00 W
Monongahela Brook ≃	285	39.47 N	75.09 W
Monongahela Seamount ✢[3]	14	26.30 S	179.05 W
Monopoli	68	40.57 N	17.19 E
Monor	30	47.21 N	19.27 E
Mono Road Station	275b	43.51 N	79.51 W
Monos ⊥	232	18.27 N	89.02 W
Monóvar	34	38.25 N	0.47 W
Monowai, Lake ⊜	172	45.52 S	167.27 E
Monponsett	207	42.01 N	70.51 W
Monponsett Pond ⊜	283	42.01 N	70.51 W
Monreal	34	42.42 N	1.30 W
Monreal del Campo	34	40.47 N	1.21 W
Monreale	70	38.05 N	13.17 E
Monreale, Castello di ⊥	71	39.38 N	8.49 E
Monroe, Conn., U.S.	207	41.18 N	73.16 W
Monroe, Fla., U.S.	220	30.28 N	84.17 W
Monroe, Ga., U.S.	192	33.47 N	83.43 W
Monroe, Ind., U.S.	216	40.45 N	84.56 W
Monroe, Iowa, U.S.	190	41.31 N	93.06 W
Monroe, La., U.S.	194	32.33 N	92.07 W
Monroe, Mich., U.S.	214	41.55 N	83.24 W
Monroe, Nebr., U.S.	198	41.28 N	97.36 W
Monroe, N.J., U.S.	276	41.07 N	74.38 W
Monroe, N.C., U.S.	192	34.59 N	80.33 W
Monroe, N.Y., U.S.	210	41.20 N	74.11 W
Monroe, Ohio, U.S.	218	39.27 N	84.22 W
Monroe, Oreg., U.S.	202	44.19 N	123.18 W
Monroe, Utah, U.S.	200	38.38 N	112.07 W
Monroe, Va., U.S.	192	37.30 N	79.08 W
Monroe, Wash., U.S.	224	47.51 N	121.58 W
Monroe, Wis., U.S.	190	42.36 N	89.38 W
Monroe □[6], Fla., U.S.	220	25.10 N	81.10 W
Monroe □[6], Ill., U.S.	219	38.20 N	90.09 W
Monroe □[6], Ind., U.S.	218	39.10 N	86.26 W
Monroe □[6], Mich., U.S.	216	41.55 N	83.26 W
Monroe □[6], Mo., U.S.	219	39.30 N	92.00 W
Monroe □[6], N.Y., U.S.	210	43.10 N	77.36 W
Monroe □[6], Pa., U.S.	210	40.59 N	75.12 W
Monroe, Lake ⊜	220	28.52 N	81.16 W
Monroe Bridge	207	42.43 N	72.57 W
Monroe Center, Conn., U.S.	207	41.20 N	73.12 W
Monroe Center, Ill., U.S.	216	42.06 N	89.00 W
Monroe City, Ind., U.S.	194	38.37 N	87.21 W
Monroe City, Mo., U.S.	219	39.39 N	91.44 W
Monroe City, Tex., U.S.	222	29.47 N	94.35 W
Monroe Lake ⊜[1]	218	39.05 N	86.25 W
Monroe Manor	216	41.36 N	86.40 W
Monroeton	210	41.43 N	76.30 W
Monroeville, Ala., U.S.	194	31.31 N	87.20 W
Monroeville, Ind., U.S.	216	40.58 N	84.52 W
Monroeville, N.J., U.S.	208	39.38 N	75.10 W
Monroeville, Ohio, U.S.	214	41.15 N	82.42 W
Monroeville, Pa., U.S.	214	40.26 N	79.47 W
Monroeville Mall ➛[9]	279b	40.26 N	79.48 W
Monrovia, Liber.	150	6.18 N	10.47 W
Monrovia, Calif., U.S.	228	34.09 N	118.03 W
Monrovia, Ind., U.S.	218	39.35 N	86.29 W
Monrovia Mountain Park ♠	280	34.10 N	118.10 W
Monrovia Peak ∧	280	34.13 N	117.58 W
Mons (Bergen), Bel.	50	50.27 N	3.56 E
Mons, Fr.	62	43.41 N	6.43 E
Monsanto, Parque Florestal de ♠	266c	38.43 N	9.11 W
Monsarás, Ponta do ≻	255	19.35 S	39.45 W
Monschau	56	50.33 N	6.14 E
Monse	112	4.07 S	123.15 E
Monsefú	248	6.52 S	79.52 W
Monselice	64	45.14 N	11.45 E
Monsenhor Hipólito	250	6.59 S	41.07 W
Monsenhor Paulo	256	21.46 S	45.33 W
Monsenhor Tabosa	250	4.47 S	40.04 W
Monserrato	71	39.15 N	9.08 E
Monsey	210	41.07 N	74.04 W
Monsheim, B.R.D.	56	49.38 N	8.12 E
Mönsheim, B.R.D.	56	48.52 N	8.52 E
Møns Klint •[4]	41	54.58 N	12.33 E
Monsols	58	46.13 N	4.31 E
Monson, Maine, U.S.	188	45.17 N	69.30 W
Monson, Mass., U.S.	207	42.06 N	72.19 W
Monster	52	52.02 N	4.10 E
Mönsterås	26	57.02 N	16.26 E
Monsummano Terme	66	43.52 N	10.49 E
Montà	62	44.48 N	7.57 E
Montabaur	56	50.26 N	7.50 E
Montabaur □[5]	56	50.30 N	7.40 E
Montafon ∨	58	47.02 N	9.57 E
Montagano	66	41.39 N	14.40 E
Montagnana	64	45.14 N	11.28 E
Montagnareale	70	38.07 N	14.57 E
Montagnola ⩕	66	43.17 N	11.11 E
Montagrier	32	45.16 N	0.29 E
Montagu	158	33.45 S	20.08 E
Montague, P.E.I., Can.	186	46.10 N	62.39 W
Montague, Calif., U.S.	204	41.44 N	122.32 W
Montague, Mass., U.S.	207	42.32 N	72.32 W
Montague, Mich., U.S.	190	43.25 N	86.22 W
Montague, Tex., U.S.	196	33.40 N	97.43 W
Montague, Isla I	232	31.45 N	114.48 W
Montague City	207	42.35 N	72.35 W
Montague Island I	180	60.00 N	147.30 W
Montague Peak ∧	180	60.15 N	147.01 W
Montagu Island I	18	58.25 S	26.20 W
Montaigle, Château de ⊥	56	50.18 N	4.49 E
Montaigu	32	46.59 N	1.19 W
Montaigut-en-Combraille	32	46.11 N	2.38 E
Montainville	261	48.53 N	1.56 E
Montaione	66	43.33 N	10.55 E
Montaj-Taš	85	42.06 N	68.58 E
Montalba	222	31.53 N	95.38 W
Montalbán	34	40.50 N	0.48 W
Montalbancito	286c	10.28 N	66.59 W
Montalbano Elicona	70	38.02 N	15.01 E
Montalbano Ionico	68	40.17 N	16.34 E
Montalcino	66	43.03 N	11.29 E
Montaldo di Cosola	62	44.40 N	9.11 E
Montale	66	43.56 N	11.01 E
Montalegre	34	41.49 N	7.48 W
Montalet-le-Bois	261	49.03 N	1.50 E
Montalieu-Vercieu	62	45.49 N	5.24 E
Montallegro	70	37.23 N	13.21 E
Mont Alto	208	39.50 N	77.34 W
Montalto ∧	68	38.10 N	15.55 E
Montalto delle Marche	66	42.59 N	13.36 E
Montalto di Castro	66	42.21 N	11.37 E
Montalto Ligure	62	43.56 N	7.51 E
Montalto Uffugo	68	39.25 N	16.10 E
Montalvin Manor	226	37.59 N	122.21 W
Montalvo	228	34.15 N	119.12 W
Montana, Schw.	58	46.18 N	7.29 E
Montana, Alaska, U.S.	180	62.05 N	150.04 W
Montana □[3]	178		
	202	47.00 N	110.00 W
Montana de Oro State Park ♠	226	35.15 N	120.50 W
Montana Indian Reserve ➛[4]	182	52.43 N	113.25 W
Montanaro	62	45.14 N	7.51 E
Montánchez	34	39.13 N	6.09 W
Montandon	210	40.58 N	76.51 W
Montano Antilia	68	40.10 N	15.22 E
Montara	226	37.33 N	122.31 W
Montara Beach ♠	282	37.33 N	122.31 W
Montara Mountain ⩕	282	37.32 N	122.27 W
Montargil	34	39.05 N	8.10 W
Montargis	50	48.00 N	2.45 E
Montataire	50	49.16 N	2.26 E
Montauban	32	44.01 N	1.21 E
Montauban, Lac ⊜	206	46.52 N	72.10 W
Montauban-les-Mines	206	46.50 N	72.20 W
Montauk	188	41.03 N	71.57 W
Montauk Harbor C	207	41.04 N	71.55 W
Montauk Point ≻	207	41.04 N	71.52 W
Montauroux	62	43.37 N	6.46 E
Monta Vista	226	37.19 N	122.03 W
Montazzoli	66	41.57 N	14.26 E
Montbard	50	47.37 N	4.20 E
Montbarrey	58	47.01 N	5.39 E
Montbazon	50	47.17 N	0.43 E
Montbéliard	58	47.31 N	6.48 E
Mont Belvieu	222	29.51 N	94.54 W
Montbenoît	58	46.59 N	6.28 E
Mont Blanc, Tunnel du ➛[5]	58	45.50 N	6.53 E
Montblanch	34	41.22 N	1.10 E
Mont-Bonvillers	56	49.20 N	5.51 E
Montbovon	58	46.29 N	7.03 E
Montbozon	58	47.28 N	6.16 E
Montbrison	62	45.36 N	4.03 E
Montbron	32	45.40 N	0.30 E
Montbronn	56	48.59 N	7.19 E
Montcalm □[6]	206	46.20 N	74.20 W
Montceau-les-Mines	58	46.40 N	4.22 E
Montcenis	58	46.47 N	4.23 E
Mont Cenis, Col du)(	62	45.15 N	6.54 E
Mont Cenis, Lac du ⊜	62	45.14 N	6.55 E
Montcevelles, Lac ⊜	186	51.07 N	60.38 W
Montchanin, Fr.	58	46.45 N	4.27 E
Montchanin, Del., U.S.	285	39.47 N	75.35 W
Montchauvet	261	48.54 N	1.38 E
Montclair, Calif., U.S.	228	34.06 N	117.41 W
Montclair, N.J., U.S.	210	40.49 N	74.13 W
Montclair State College ʊ[2]	276	40.51 N	74.12 W
Montcornet	50	49.41 N	4.01 E
Montdale	210	41.32 N	75.37 W
Mont-de-Marsan	32	43.53 N	0.30 W
Montdidier	50	49.39 N	2.34 E
Mont Dore	175f	22.16 S	166.34 E
Monte, Castel del ⊥	68	41.05 N	16.16 E
Monte, Laguna del ⊜	252	37.00 S	62.28 W
Monte Adone, Galleria di ➛[5]	64	44.21 N	11.25 E
Monteagle	194	35.15 N	85.50 W
Monteagudo	248	19.49 S	63.59 W
Monte Albán ⊥	234	17.02 N	96.45 W
Monte Alegre, Bra.	250	6.04 S	35.20 W
Monte Alegre, Bra.	250	2.01 S	54.04 W
Monte Alegre de Goiás	255	13.14 S	47.10 W
Monte Alegre de Minas	255	18.52 S	48.52 W
Monte Alegre de Sergipe	250	10.02 S	37.33 W
Monte Alegre do Piauí	250	9.46 S	45.18 W
Monte Alegre do Sul	256	22.40 S	46.41 W
Monte Azul	255	15.09 S	42.53 W
Monte Azul Paulista	255	20.55 S	48.38 W
Montebello, Qué., Can.	206	45.39 N	74.56 W
Montebello, It.	62	45.00 N	9.06 E
Montebello, P.R.	240m	18.22 N	66.31 W
Montebello, Calif., U.S.	228	34.01 N	118.06 W
Montebello Iónico	68	37.59 N	15.45 E
Montebello Islands II	162	20.25 S	115.32 E
Montebello Vicentino	64	45.27 N	11.23 E
Montebelluna	64	45.47 N	12.03 E
Monte Belo	256	21.20 S	46.23 W
Montebruno	62	44.31 N	9.15 E
Monte Buey	252	32.55 S	62.27 W
Montecalvo Irpino	68	41.11 N	15.02 E
Monte Campatri	267a	41.48 N	12.44 E
Montecarlo	252	26.34 S	54.47 W
Monte Carlo □[8]	62	43.44 N	7.25 E
Montecarotto	66	43.31 N	13.04 E
Monte Caseros	252	30.15 S	57.39 W
Montecassiano	66	43.21 N	13.26 E
Montecassino, Abbazia di ʊ[1]	66	41.29 N	13.48 E
Montecastrilli	66	42.39 N	12.29 E
Montecatini Terme	66	43.53 N	10.46 E
Monte Cavallo	66	42.59 N	13.00 E
Montecchio	66	43.51 N	12.46 E
Montecchio Emilia	64	44.42 N	10.27 E
Montecchio Maggiore	64	45.30 N	11.24 E
Montecelio	66	42.01 N	12.44 E
Montechiaro d'Asti	62	45.01 N	8.07 E
Montechiarugolo	64	44.42 N	10.25 E
Monte Chingolo ➛[8]	288	34.45 S	58.20 W
Monteciccardo	66	43.49 N	12.48 E
Montecilfone	66	41.54 N	14.50 E
Montecillos, Cordillera de ⩕	236	14.25 N	87.51 W
Montecito	204	34.26 N	119.39 W
Monte Comán	252	34.36 S	67.54 W
Montecorice	68	40.14 N	14.59 E
Montecorvino Pugliano	68	40.41 N	14.57 E
Montecorvino Rovella	68	40.42 N	14.59 E
Montecosaro	66	43.19 N	13.37 E
Monte Creek	182	50.39 N	119.57 W
Montecreto	64	44.14 N	10.41 E
Montecristi	246	1.03 S	80.40 W
Monte Cristo	248	14.43 S	61.14 W
Monte Cristo, Cerro ∧	236	14.25 N	89.21 W
Montecristo, Isola di I	36	42.20 N	10.19 E
Montecuccolo ʊ[1]	64	44.19 N	10.50 E
Montedinove	66	42.58 N	13.35 E
Monte di Procida	68	40.48 N	14.03 E
Monte do Carmo	250	10.45 S	48.07 W
Montedoro	70	37.27 N	13.49 E
Monte Escobedo	234	22.18 N	103.35 W
Monte Estoril	266c	38.42 N	9.24 W
Montefalcione	68	40.58 N	14.53 E
Montefalco	66	42.54 N	12.39 E
Montefalcone di Val Fortore	68	41.20 N	15.00 E
Montefano	66	43.25 N	13.26 E
Montefeltro ➛[1]	66	43.50 N	12.30 E
Montefiascone	66	42.32 N	12.02 E
Montefiorino	64	44.22 N	10.37 E
Monteforte d'Alpone	64	45.25 N	11.17 E
Monteforte Irpino	68	40.54 N	14.42 E
Montefrío	34	37.19 N	4.01 W
Montegallo	66	42.50 N	13.19 E
Montegiordano	68	40.02 N	16.32 E
Montegiorgio	66	43.08 N	13.32 E
Monte Giovi, Passo di (Jaufen Pass))(	64	46.50 N	11.19 E
Montego Bay	241q	18.28 N	77.55 W
Montegranaro	66	43.14 N	13.38 E
Monte Grande	252	30.06 S	70.31 W
Monte Grande, Aeródromo ⊠	288	34.48 S	58.28 W
Monte Grimano	66	43.52 N	12.29 E
Montegrotto Terme	64	45.19 N	11.46 E
Montegut	194	29.29 N	90.33 W
Monteiasi	68	40.30 N	17.23 E
Monteiro	250	7.53 S	37.07 W
Monteiro Lobato	256	22.58 S	45.50 W
Monteith, Mount ∧	182	55.45 N	122.30 W
Montejicar	34	37.34 N	3.30 W
Montejinni	164	16.40 S	131.45 E
Montelavar	266c	38.51 N	9.20 W
Monteleone di Puglia	68	41.10 N	15.15 E
Monteleone di Spoleto	66	42.39 N	12.58 E
Monteleone Rocco Doria	71	40.29 N	8.34 E
Monteleone Sabino	66	42.14 N	12.51 E
Montelepre	70	38.05 N	13.10 E
Montelíbano	246	8.05 N	75.29 W
Montélimar	62	44.34 N	4.45 E
Montelindo ≃	252	23.56 S	57.12 W
Montella	68	40.51 N	15.01 E
Montellano	34	37.00 N	5.34 W
Montello, Nev., U.S.	204	41.16 N	114.12 W
Montello, Wis., U.S.	190	43.48 N	89.20 W
Monteluco ʊ[1]	66	42.43 N	12.45 E
Montelungo	64	44.24 N	9.54 E
Montelupo Fiorentino	66	43.44 N	11.01 E
Montemaggiore Belsito	70	37.51 N	13.46 E
Montemagno	62	44.59 N	8.20 E
Monte Maíz	252	33.12 S	62.36 W
Montemarano	68	40.55 N	15.00 E
Montemarciano	66	43.38 N	13.19 E
Montemayor, Meseta de ⩕[1]	254	44.20 S	66.10 W
Montemesola	68	40.34 N	17.20 E
Montemiletto	68	41.01 N	14.54 E
Montemilone	68	41.02 N	15.38 E
Montemor	266c	38.49 N	9.12 W
Montemor ∧	266c	38.49 N	9.12 W
Montemorelos	232	25.12 N	99.49 W
Montemor-o-Novo	34	38.39 N	8.13 W
Montemor-o-Velho	34	40.10 N	8.41 W
Montemurro	68	40.18 N	15.59 E
Montendre	32	45.17 N	0.24 W
Montenegro	252	29.42 S	51.28 W
Montenegro → Crna Gora □[3]	38	42.30 N	19.18 E
Montenero	66	43.30 N	10.21 E
Montenero ∧	68	39.13 N	16.35 E
Montenero di Bisaccia	66	41.57 N	14.47 E
Monteodorisio	66	42.05 N	14.39 E
Monte Oliveto Maggiore, Abbazia del ʊ[1]	66	43.12 N	11.32 E
Monte Pascoal, Parque Nacional de ♠	255	16.54 S	39.24 W
Monte Patria	252	30.42 S	70.58 W
Montepescali	66	42.53 N	11.05 E
Monte Porzio Catone	267a	41.49 N	12.43 E
Monteprandone	66	42.55 N	13.50 E
Montepuez	154	13.07 S	39.00 E
Montepuez ≃	154	12.32 S	40.27 E
Montepulciano	66	43.05 N	11.47 E
Monte Quemado	252	25.48 S	62.52 W
Monterado	112	0.45 N	109.08 E
Monterchi	66	43.29 N	12.07 E
Montereale	66	42.31 N	13.15 E
Montereale Valcellina	64	46.10 N	12.39 E
Montereau	50	47.51 N	2.34 E
Montereau-faut-Yonne	50	48.23 N	2.57 E
Montereau-sur-le-Jard	261	48.35 N	2.40 E
Monterey, Calif., U.S.	226	36.37 N	121.55 W
Monterey, Ind., U.S.	216	41.09 N	86.29 W
Monterey, Ky., U.S.	218	38.25 N	84.52 W
Monterey, Mass., U.S.	207	42.11 N	73.13 W
Monterey, N.Y., U.S.	210	42.18 N	77.03 W
Monterey, Tenn., U.S.	194	36.09 N	85.16 W
Monterey, Va., U.S.	188	38.25 N	79.35 W
Monterey □[6]	226	36.40 N	121.38 W
Monterey Bay C	226	36.45 N	121.55 W
Monterey Park	228	34.04 N	118.07 W
Monterey Peninsula Airport ⊠	226	36.35 N	121.51 W
Montería	246	8.46 N	75.53 W
Monteriggioni	66	43.23 N	11.13 E
Montero	248	17.20 S	63.15 W
Monte Romano	66	42.16 N	11.54 E
Monteroni d'Arbia	66	43.14 N	11.25 E
Monteroni di Lecce	68	40.19 N	18.06 E
Monteros	252	27.10 S	65.30 W
Monterosso al Mare	62	44.09 N	9.39 E
Monterosso Almo	70	37.05 N	14.46 E
Monterosso Calabro	68	38.43 N	16.17 E
Monterotondo	66	42.03 N	12.37 E
Monterotondo Marittimo	66	43.09 N	10.51 E
Monterrey, Méx.	232	25.40 N	100.19 W
Monterrey, Méx.	234	16.05 N	93.23 W
Monterrico, Hipódromo de ♠	286d	12.06 S	76.59 W
Monterubbiano	66	43.05 N	13.43 E
Montes Altos	250	5.50 S	47.04 W
Monte San Biagio	66	41.21 N	13.21 E
Monte San Giovanni Campano	66	41.38 N	13.31 E
Montesano, It.	36	40.16 N	15.43 E
Montesano, Wash., U.S.	224	46.59 N	123.36 W
Montesano sulla Marcellana	68	40.16 N	15.42 E
Monte San Savino	66	43.20 N	11.43 E
Monte Santa Maria Tiberina	66	43.26 N	12.09 E
Monte Sant'Angelo	68	41.42 N	15.57 E
Monte Santo, Bra.	250	9.54 S	49.03 W
Monte Santo, Bra.	250	10.26 S	39.20 W
Monte Santo de Minas	256	21.12 S	46.59 W
Monte Santu, Capo di ≻	71	40.05 N	9.44 E
Montesarchio	68	41.04 N	14.38 E
Montescaglioso	68	40.33 N	16.40 E
Montes Claros	255	16.43 S	43.52 W
Montescudaio	66	43.18 N	10.40 E
Montese	64	44.16 N	10.56 E
Monte Sereno	226	37.15 N	122.01 W
Monte Sião	256	22.26 S	46.34 W
Montesilvano	66	42.29 N	14.08 E
Montespaccato ➛[8]	267a	41.54 N	12.23 E
Montespertoli	66	43.38 N	11.04 E
Montespluga	58	46.30 N	9.21 E
Montesson	261	48.55 N	2.09 E
Montets, Col des)(	58	46.00 N	6.55 E
Monteux	62	44.02 N	5.00 E
Montevago	70	37.42 N	12.58 E
Montevallo	194	33.06 N	86.52 W
Montevarchi	66	43.31 N	11.34 E
Monte Verde, Ang.	152	8.43 S	16.51 E
Monteverde, It.	68	41.00 N	15.32 E
Monte Verde ≃	256	21.55 S	43.33 W
Monteverde Nuovo ➛[8]	267a	41.51 N	12.27 E
Montevergine, Santuario di ʊ[1]	68	40.55 N	14.45 E
Montevideo, Ur.	242	34.53 S	56.11 W
Montevideo, Minn., U.S.	198	44.57 N	95.43 W
Montevideo □[5]	258	34.50 S	56.12 W
Monte Vista	200	37.35 N	106.09 W
Montévrain	261	48.53 N	2.45 E
Montezemolo	62	44.22 N	8.08 E
Montezuma, Ga., U.S.	192	32.18 N	84.02 W
Montezuma, Ind., U.S.	194	39.48 N	87.22 W
Montezuma, Iowa, U.S.	190	41.35 N	92.32 W
Montezuma, Kans., U.S.	198	37.36 N	100.27 W
Montezuma, N.Y., U.S.	210	43.00 N	76.42 W
Montezuma, Ohio, U.S.	216	40.29 N	84.33 W
Montezuma Castle National Monument ♠	200	34.30 N	112.00 W
Montezuma Creek ≃	200	37.17 N	109.20 W
Montezuma Hills ⩕[2]	282	38.07 N	121.51 W
Montezuma Slough ≃	226	38.04 N	121.52 W
Montfaucon, Fr.	56	49.17 N	5.08 E
Montfaucon, Fr.	62	45.10 N	4.18 E
Montfaucon, Schw.	58	47.17 N	7.03 E
Montfermeil	261	48.54 N	2.34 E
Montfleur	58	46.19 N	5.26 E
Montflorit	266d	41.29 N	2.08 E
Montfoort	52	52.03 N	4.57 E
Montfort, Fr.	32	48.08 N	1.58 W
Montfort, Wis., U.S.	190	42.58 N	90.26 W
Montfort-l'Amaury	261	48.47 N	1.49 E
Montfort-le-Rotrou	50	48.03 N	0.25 E
Montfort-sur-Risle	50	49.18 N	0.40 E
Mont Fouari, Réserve du ➛[4]	152	2.45 S	11.35 E
Montfrin	62	43.53 N	4.36 E
Montgé	261	49.02 N	2.45 E
Montgenèvre	62	44.56 N	6.43 E
Montgenèvre, Col de)(	62	44.56 N	6.44 E
Montgeron	261	48.42 N	2.27 E
Montgeroult	261	49.05 N	2.00 E
Montgesoye	58	47.05 N	6.12 E
Montgomery → Sāhīwāl, Pāk.	123	30.40 N	73.06 E
Montgomery, Wales, U.K.	42	52.33 N	3.03 W
Montgomery, Ala., U.S.	194	32.23 N	86.18 W
Montgomery, Ill., U.S.	216	41.44 N	88.21 W
Montgomery, La., U.S.	194	31.40 N	92.53 W
Montgomery, Mich., U.S.	216	41.47 N	84.48 W
Montgomery, Minn., U.S.	190	44.26 N	93.35 W
Montgomery, N.Y., U.S.	210	41.32 N	74.14 W
Montgomery, Pa., U.S.	210	41.10 N	76.52 W
Montgomery, Tex., U.S.	222	30.23 N	95.42 W
Montgomery, W. Va., U.S.	188	38.11 N	81.19 W
Montgomery □[6], Ill., U.S.	219	39.09 N	89.29 W
Montgomery □[6], Md., U.S.	208	39.05 N	77.09 W
Montgomery □[6], Mo., U.S.	219	38.57 N	91.27 W
Montgomery □[6], N.Y., U.S.	210	42.57 N	74.22 W
Montgomery □[6], Ohio, U.S.	218	39.45 N	84.15 W
Montgomery □[6], Pa., U.S.	208	40.07 N	75.21 W
Montgomery □[6], Tex., U.S.	222	30.18 N	95.30 W
Montgomery City	219	38.59 N	91.30 W
Montgomery Dam ➛[6]	214	40.39 N	80.24 W
Montgomery Knolls	284b	39.14 N	76.48 W
Montgomery Mall ➛[9]	284c	39.01 N	77.09 W
Montgomeryville	285	40.15 N	75.15 W
Montgomeryville Airport ⊠	285	40.15 N	75.14 W
Montguyon	32	45.13 N	0.11 W
Monthermé	56	49.53 N	4.44 E
Monthey	58	46.15 N	6.57 E
Monthois	56	49.19 N	4.43 E
Monthureux-sur-Saône	58	48.02 N	5.58 E
Monthyon	261	49.00 N	2.50 E
Monti	71	40.49 N	9.19 E
Monticelli d'Ongina	64	45.05 N	9.56 E
Monticello, Ark., U.S.	194	33.38 N	91.47 W
Monticello, Fla., U.S.	192	30.33 N	83.52 W
Monticello, Ga., U.S.	192	33.18 N	83.40 W
Monticello, Ill., U.S.	194	40.01 N	88.34 W
Monticello, Ind., U.S.	216	40.45 N	86.46 W
Monticello, Iowa, U.S.	190	42.15 N	91.12 W
Monticello, Ky., U.S.	194	36.50 N	84.51 W
Monticello, Minn., U.S.	190	45.18 N	93.48 W
Monticello, Miss., U.S.	194	31.33 N	90.07 W
Monticello, Mo., U.S.	219	40.07 N	91.43 W
Monticello, N.Y., U.S.	210	41.39 N	74.42 W
Monticello, Utah, U.S.	200	37.52 N	109.21 W
Monticello, Wis., U.S.	190	42.45 N	89.35 W
Monticello ⊥	188	38.00 N	78.30 W
Monticello Conte Otto	64	45.35 N	11.35 E
Monticello Dam ➛[6]	226	38.30 N	122.07 W
Montichiari	64	45.25 N	10.23 E
Monticiano	66	43.08 N	11.11 E
Montiel, Campo de ≚	34	38.46 N	2.44 W
Montier-en-Der	58	48.29 N	4.46 E
Montieri	66	43.08 N	11.01 E
Montieri, Poggio di ∧	66	43.08 N	11.00 E
Montiers-sur-Saulx	58	48.32 N	5.16 E
Montignac	32	45.04 N	1.10 E
Montigny	58	48.31 N	6.48 E
Montigny-devant-Sassey	56	49.26 N	5.09 E
Montigny-le-Bretonneux	261	48.46 N	2.02 E
Montigny-le-Roi	58	48.00 N	5.30 E
Montigny-lès-Cormeilles	261	48.59 N	2.12 E
Montigny-sur-Aube	58	47.57 N	4.46 E
Montijo, Esp.	34	38.55 N	6.37 W
Montijo, Pan.	236	7.59 N	81.03 W
Montijo, Port.	34	38.42 N	8.58 W
Montijo, Aeroporto ⊠	266c	38.42 N	9.02 W
Montijo, Golfo de C	246	7.40 N	81.07 W
Montilla	34	37.35 N	4.38 W
Montividiu	255	17.24 S	51.14 W
Montivilliers	50	49.33 N	0.12 E
Montjay-la-Tour	261	48.55 N	2.40 E
Montjoie, Lac ⊜, Qué., Can.	206	45.25 N	72.06 W
Montjoie, Lac ⊜, Qué., Can.	206	46.17 N	75.08 W
Mont-Joli	186	48.35 N	68.11 W
Montjovet	62	45.43 N	7.40 E
Montjuich, Castillo de ⊥	266d	41.22 N	2.10 E
Montjuich, Estadio de ♠	266d	41.22 N	2.09 E
Montjuich, Faro de ➛[5]	266d	41.21 N	2.11 E
Montjuich, Parque de ♠	266d	41.21 N	2.09 E
Mont-Laurier	176	46.33 N	75.30 W
Montlebon	58	47.02 N	6.37 E
Montlhéry	50	48.38 N	2.16 E
Montlhéry, Tour de ʊ	261	48.38 N	2.16 E
Montlignon	261	49.01 N	2.17 E
Montlouet	261	48.31 N	1.43 E
Mont-Louis	32	42.31 N	2.07 E
Montlouis-sur-Loire	50	47.23 N	0.50 E
Montluçon	32	46.21 N	2.36 E
Montluel	62	45.51 N	5.03 E
Montmagny, Qué., Can.	186	46.59 N	70.33 W
Montmagny, Fr.	261	48.58 N	2.21 E
Montmajour, Abbaye de ʊ[1]	62	43.43 N	4.40 E
Montmartre ➛[8]	261	48.53 N	2.21 E
Montmédy	56	49.31 N	5.22 E
Montmélian	62	45.30 N	6.04 E
Montmeló	266d	41.33 N	2.15 E
Montmerle-sur-Saône	58	46.05 N	4.46 E
Montmin	62	45.48 N	6.16 E
Montmirail, Fr.	50	48.06 N	0.48 E
Montmirail, Fr.	50	48.52 N	3.32 E
Montmirey-le-Château	58	47.13 N	5.32 E
Montmoreau-Saint-Cybard	32	45.24 N	0.08 E
Montmorenci	216	40.28 N	87.02 W
Montmorency	274b	37.43 S	145.07 E
Montmorency ≃	186	46.53 N	71.07 W
Montmorency, Forêt de ♠	261	49.02 N	2.16 E
Montmorillon	32	46.26 N	0.52 E
Montmort	50	48.55 N	3.49 E
Monto	166	24.52 S	151.07 E
Montodine	62	45.17 N	9.42 E
Montoggio	62	44.31 N	9.03 E
Montoire-sur-le-Loir	50	47.45 N	0.52 E
Montone	66	43.22 N	12.20 E
Montone ≃, It.	64	44.24 N	12.14 E
Montone ≃, It.	66	43.22 N	12.20 E
Montopoli in Val d'Arno	66	43.40 N	10.45 E
Mont Orford, Parc du ♠	206	45.22 N	72.05 W
Montorio al Vomano	66	42.35 N	13.38 E
Montorio nei Frentani	66	41.46 N	14.55 E
Montorio Veronese	64	45.27 N	11.04 E
Montornés del Vallés	266d	41.33 N	2.16 E
Montoro	34	38.01 N	4.23 W
Mont'Orso, Galleria di ➛[5]	66	41.20 N	13.15 E
Montour □[6]	210	40.58 N	76.37 W
Montour Falls	210	42.21 N	76.51 W
Montour Run ≃, Pa., U.S.	279b	40.36 N	79.57 W
Montour Run ≃, Pa., U.S.	279b	40.31 N	80.08 W
Montoursville	210	41.15 N	76.55 W
Mont Park	274b	37.43 S	145.04 E
Montparnasse ➛[5]	261	48.51 N	2.19 E
Montpelier, Jam.	241q	18.22 N	77.56 W
Montpelier, Idaho, U.S.	202	42.19 N	111.18 W
Montpelier, Ind., U.S.	216	40.33 N	85.17 W
Montpelier, Miss., U.S.	194	33.43 N	88.57 W
Montpelier, Ohio, U.S.	216	41.35 N	84.36 W
Montpelier, Vt., U.S.	188	44.16 N	72.35 W
Montpellier	62	43.36 N	3.53 E
Montpezat-sous-Bauzon	62	44.43 N	4.12 E
Mont-Pichet	261	48.53 N	2.54 E
Montpon-Ménesterol	32	45.00 N	0.10 E
Montpont-en-Bresse	58	46.33 N	5.09 E
Montréal, Qué., Can.	206		
	275a	45.31 N	73.34 W
Montréal, Fr.	50	47.32 N	4.02 E
Montreal, Wis., U.S.	190	46.26 N	90.14 W

	English	Deutsch	Español	Français	Português
≃	River	Fluss	Río	Rivière	Rio
≍	Canal	Kanal	Canal	Canal	Canal
ⱡ	Waterfall, Rapids	Wasserfall, Stromschnellen	Cascada, Rápidos	Chute d'eau, Rapides	Cascata, Rápidos
)(	Strait	Meeresstrasse	Estrecho	Détroit	Estreito
C	Bay, Gulf	Bucht, Golf	Bahía, Golfo	Baie, Golfe	Baía, Golfo
⊜	Lake, Lakes	See, Seen	Lago, Lagos	Lac, Lacs	Lago, Lagos
☰	Swamp	Sumpf	Pantano	Marais	Pântano
⛋	Ice Features, Glacier	Eis- und Gletscherformen	Accidentes Glaciales	Formes glaciaires	Acidentes Glaciares
⫧	Other Hydrographic Features	Andere Hydrographische Objekte	Otros Elementos Hidrográficos	Autres données hydrographiques	Outros Elementos Hidrográficos

	English	Deutsch	Español	Français	Português
✢	Submarine Features	Untermeerische Objekte	Accidentes Submarinos	Formes de relief sous-marin	Acidentes Submarinos
□	Political Unit	Politische Einheit	Unidad Politica	Entité politique	Unidade Política
ʊ	Cultural Institution	Kulturelle Institution	Institución Cultural	Institution culturelle	Instituição Cultural
⊥	Historical Site	Historische Stätte	Sitio Histórico	Site historique	Sitio Histórico
♠	Recreational Site	Erholungs- und Ferienort	Sitio de Recreo	Centre de loisirs	Sítio de Lazer
⊠	Airport	Flughafen	Aeropuerto	Aéroport	Aeroporto
■	Military Installation	Militäranlage	Instalación Militar	Installation militaire	Instalação Militar
➛	Miscellaneous	Verschiedenes	Misceláneo	Divers	Miscelânea

ENGLISH / DEUTSCH

Name	Page / Seite	Lat. / Breite	Long. / Länge (E=Ost)
Montreal ≃, Ont., Can.	190	47.14 N	84.39 W
Montreal ≃, Ont., Can.	190	47.08 N	79.27 W
Montreal ≃, Sask., Can.	184	55.06 N	105.19 W
Montreal ≃, U.S.	190	46.44 N	90.25 W
Montréal, Île de I	206	45.30 N	73.40 W
Montréal, Université de ⊛[2]	275a	45.30 N	73.37 W
Montréal-Est	206	45.38 N	73.31 W
Montreal International Airport ⊠	275a	45.28 N	73.45 W
Montreal Lake	184	54.03 N	105.46 W
Montreal Lake @	184	54.20 N	105.40 W
Montreal Lake Indian Reserve ◆[4]	184	54.00 N	105.45 W
Montréal-Nord	206	45.36 N	73.38 W
Montreal Water Works Aqueduct ⊔[1]	275a	45.26 N	73.36 W
Montrésor	50	47.09 N	1.12 E
Montresta	71	40.22 N	8.30 E
Montret	58	46.41 N	5.07 E
Montreuil	261	48.52 N	2.27 E
Montreuil-Bellay	32	47.08 N	0.09 W
Montreuil-sous-Bois	50	48.52 N	2.26 E
Montreuil-sur-Mer	50	50.28 N	1.46 E
Montreux	58	46.26 N	6.55 E
Montrevel-en-Bresse	58	46.20 N	5.08 E
Montrichard	50	47.21 N	1.11 E
Montriond	58	46.12 N	6.41 E
Montrond-les-Bains	62	45.38 N	4.14 E
Montrose, Austl.	274b	37.49 S	145.21 E
Montrose, Scot., U.K.	46	56.43 N	2.29 W
Montrose, Calif., U.S.	228	34.12 N	118.13 W
Montrose, Colo., U.S.	200	38.29 N	107.53 W
Montrose, Iowa, U.S.	190	40.31 N	91.25 W
Montrose, Mich., U.S.	190	43.11 N	83.54 W
Montrose, N.Y., U.S.	210	41.15 N	73.56 W
Montrose, Ohio, U.S.	214	41.08 N	81.37 W
Montrose, Pa., U.S.	210	41.50 N	75.53 W
Montrose, S. Dak., U.S.	198	43.42 N	97.11 W
Montrose Harbor C	278	41.58 N	87.38 W
Montrose Hill	279b	40.30 N	79.51 W
Montross	208	38.06 N	76.50 W
Montrouge	261	48.49 N	2.19 E
Mont-Royal	206	45.31 N	73.39 W
Mont Royal, Parc ♠	275a	45.31 N	73.35 W
Mont Royal Tunnel ◆[5]	275a	45.31 N	73.38 W
Montry	261	48.53 N	2.50 E
Monts	50	47.17 N	0.37 E
Monts, Pointe des ≻	186	49.20 N	67.23 W
Mont-Saint-Aignan	50	47.16 N	1.23 E
Mont-Sainte-Anne, Parc du ♠	186	47.08 N	70.55 W
Mont-Saint-Hilaire	206	45.34 N	73.12 W
Mont-Saint-Martin	56	49.32 N	5.47 E
Mont-Saint-Michel → Le Mont Saint-Michel ⊛[1]	32	48.38 N	1.32 W
Mont-Saint-Vincent	58	46.38 N	4.29 E
Montsauche	50	47.13 N	4.01 E
Montsec	56	48.53 N	5.43 E
Montserrado □[6]	150	6.40 N	10.40 W
Montserrat □[2]	230		
	238	16.45 N	62.12 W
Montserrat, Monasterio de ⊛[1]	34	41.36 N	1.49 E
Montsoult	261	49.04 N	2.19 E
Mont-sur-Vaudrey	58	46.58 N	5.36 E
Mont Tremblant, Parc du ♠	206	46.42 N	74.20 W
Montuenga	34	41.03 N	4.37 W
Montvale, N.J., U.S.	276	41.03 N	74.02 W
Montvale, Va., U.S.	192	37.23 N	79.43 W
Montverde	220	28.36 N	81.41 W
Montville, Conn., U.S.	207	41.27 N	72.08 W
Montville, N.J., U.S.	276	40.52 N	74.22 W
Montville, Ohio, U.S.	214	41.36 N	81.03 W
Montville Airpark ⊠	276	40.56 N	74.20 W
Monument, S. Afr.	273d	26.06 S	27.43 E
Monument, Oreg., U.S.	202	44.49 N	119.25 W
Monument, Pa., U.S.	214	41.07 N	77.42 W
Monument Beach	207	41.43 N	70.37 W
Monument Draw ∨, U.S.	196	32.26 N	102.10 W
Monument Draw ∨, Tex., U.S.	196	30.51 N	102.33 W
Monument Hill State Historic Site ⊥	222	29.53 N	96.54 W
Monumento	256	22.44 S	43.51 W
Monument Peak ∧, Colo., U.S.	200	39.43 N	107.55 W
Monument Peak ∧, Idaho, U.S.	202	42.07 N	114.14 W
Monument Valley ∨	200	37.05 N	110.20 W
Monveda	152	2.57 N	21.27 E
Monymusk	46	57.13 N	2.31 W
Monyo	110	17.59 N	95 30 E
Monywa	110	22.05 N	95.08 E
Monza	62	45.35 N	9.16 E
Monze	154	16.16 S	27.28 E
Monzen	92	37.17 N	136.46 E
Monzie	46	56.24 N	3.48 W
Monzón, Esp.	34	41.55 N	0.12 E
Monzón, Perú	248	9.10 S	76.23 W
Moóca ◆[8]	287b	23.33 S	46.35 W
Moóca, Ribeirão da ≃	287b	23.36 S	46.35 W
Moodie Island I	176	64.37 N	65.30 W
Moodus	207	41.30 N	72.27 W
Moodus Reservoir @[1]	207	41.30 N	72.24 W
Moody	222	31.19 N	97.21 W
Moody Air Force Base ■	192	30.59 N	83.11 W
Moody Wood Dale Airport ⊠	278	41.59 N	87.58 W
Mooers	206	44.58 N	73.35 W
Mooi ≃	158	28.45 S	30.34 E
Mooirivier	158	29.13 S	29.50 E
Mook	52	51.45 N	5.54 E
Mookane	156	24.59 S	24.33 E
Mooketsi	156	23.35 S	30.05 E
Moolalloo Point ≻	168a	31.48 S	115.44 E
Moolawatana	166	29.55 S	139.43 E
Moolman	158	27.10 S	30.53 E
Mooloogool	162	26.06 S	119.05 E
Moon	214	40.31 N	80.14 W
Moon ≃	212	45.07 N	79.55 W
Moon, Mountains of the → Ruwenzori ⋀	154	0.23 N	29.54 E
Moonachie	276	40.50 N	74.03 W
Moonachie Creek ≃	276	40.48 N	74.03 W
Moonah Creek ≃	166	22.03 S	138.33 E
Moon Crest	279b	40.32 N	80.11 W
Moondarra Reservoir @[1]	169	38.04 S	146.22 E
Moonee Valley Racecourse ♠	274b	37.46 S	144.56 E
Moonie ≃	166	29.19 S	148.43 E
Moon Island I, Ont., Can.	212	45.09 N	80.01 W
Moon Island I, Mass., U.S.	283	42.18 N	71.00 W
Moon Run	214	40.30 N	80.14 W
Moonta	168b	34.04 S	137.35 E
Moonyoonooka	162	28.47 S	114.43 E
Moor, Kepulauan II	164	2.57 S	135.45 E
Moora	162	30.39 S	116.00 E
Moorabbin	169	37.56 S	145.02 E
Moorabbin Airport ⊠	274b	37.59 S	145.09 E
Mooraberree	166	25.14 S	140.59 E
Moorabool ≃	169	38.09 S	144.19 E
Moorarie	162	25.56 S	117.35 E
Moorburg	52	53.17 N	7.53 E
Moorcroft	198	44.16 N	104.57 W
Moordorf	52	53.28 N	7.23 E
Moordrecht	52	51.59 N	4.40 E
Moore, Austl.	171a	26.53 S	152.18 E
Moore, Eng., U.K.	262	53.21 N	2.38 W
Moore, Idaho, U.S.	202	43.44 N	113.22 W
Moore, Mont., U.S.	202	46.59 N	109.42 W
Moore, Okla., U.S.	196	35.20 N	97.29 W
Moore, Tex., U.S.	196	29.03 N	99.01 W
Moore ≃	162	31.22 S	115.29 E
Moore, Lake @	162	29.50 S	117.35 E
Moorea I	174s	17.32 S	149.50 W
Moorebank	274a	33.56 S	150.56 E
Moore Creek ≃	212	45.29 N	77.58 W
Moorefield, Ky., U.S.	218	38.16 N	83.56 W
Moorefield, Ohio, U.S.	214	40.12 N	81.10 W
Moorefield, W. Va., U.S.	188	39.04 N	78.58 W
Moore Haven	220	26.50 N	81.05 W
Moore Haven Lock ◆[5]	220	26.51 N	81.05 W
Moore Lake @, Ont., Can.	212	44.48 N	78.48 W
Moore Lake @, Ont., Can.	212	45.26 N	78.01 W
Moore Lake @, Mich., U.S.	281	42.37 N	83.36 W
Mooreland, Ind., U.S.	218	39.60 N	85.15 W
Mooreland, Okla., U.S.	196	36.26 N	99.12 W
Moore Park ♠	274a	33.54 S	151.13 E
Moore Point ≻	275b	43.48 N	79.03 W
Moore Reservoir @[1]	188	44.25 N	71.50 W
Mooresburg	210	40.59 N	76.43 W
Moores Creek National Military Park ♠	192	34.24 N	78.08 W
Moores Hill	218	39.07 N	85.05 W
Moore Station	222	32.11 N	95.35 W
Moorestown	208	39.58 N	74.57 W
Moorestown Airport ⊠	285	39.59 N	74.56 W
Moorestown Mall ◆[9]	285	39.56 N	74.58 W
Mooresville, Ind., U.S.	218	39.37 N	86.22 W
Mooresville, N.C., U.S.	192	35.35 N	80.48 W
Mooreville	281	42.06 N	83.44 W
Moorfoot Hills ⋀[2]	46	55.45 N	3.02 W
Moorhead, Minn., U.S.	198	46.53 N	96.45 W
Moorhead, Miss., U.S.	194	33.27 N	90.30 W
Mooring	222	30.41 N	96.33 W
Mooringsport	194	32.41 N	93.58 W
Moorooka	171a	27.32 S	153.02 E
Mooroolbark	274b	37.47 S	145.19 E
Moorpark	228	34.17 N	118.53 W
Moorreesburg	158	33.08 S	18.40 E
Moorrege	52	53.40 N	9.39 E
Moorriem	52	53.15 N	8.19 E
Moorsburg an der Isar	60	48.29 N	11.57 E
Moorsel	50	50.57 N	4.06 E
Moorside	262	53.34 N	2.04 W
Moorslede	50	50.53 N	3.04 E
Moos → Moso in Passiria, It.	64	46.50 N	11.10 E
Moos → Moso, It.	64	46.41 N	12.23 E
Moosach ◆[8]	60	48.11 N	11.31 E
Moosbrunn	264b	48.01 N	16.28 E
Moosburg	30	48.29 N	11.57 E
Moose ≃	212	43.37 N	75.22 W
Moose Creek	206	45.15 N	74.58 W
Moose Creek ≃	206	45.23 N	75.04 W
Moosehead Lake @	188	45.40 N	69.40 W
Mooseheart	216	41.49 N	88.20 W
Moose Heights	182	53.05 N	122.30 W
Moose Hill ∧[2]	283	42.07 N	71.13 W
Moose Island I	184	51.42 N	97.10 W
Moose Jaw	184	50.23 N	105.32 W
Moose Jaw ≃	184	50.34 N	105.17 W
Moose Lake, Man., Can.	184	53.43 N	100.20 W
Moose Lake, Minn., U.S.	190	46.26 N	92.45 W
Moose Lake @, Alta., Can.	182	54.15 N	110.55 W
Moose Lake @, Man., Can.	184	56.30 N	95.15 W
Moose Lake @, Ont., Can.	212	45.09 N	78.28 W
Mooselookmeguntic Lake @	188	44.53 N	70.48 W
Moose Mountain ∧	184	49.45 N	102.37 W
Moose Mountain Creek ≃	184	49.12 N	102.10 W
Moose Mountain Provincial Park ♠	184	49.48 N	102.25 W
Moose Pass	180	60.29 N	149.22 W
Moosham	60	48.56 N	12.16 E
Moosomin	184	50.07 N	101.40 W
Moosomin Indian Reserve ◆[4]	184	53.06 N	108.14 W
Moosonee	176	51.17 N	80.39 W
Moosup	207	41.43 N	71.53 W
Mooti	144	0.40 N	41.58 E
Moots Creek ≃	216	40.32 N	86.47 W
Mopane	156	22.37 S	29.52 E
Mopanyang ⊔	100	29.32 N	122.16 E
Mopeia Velha	156	17.59 S	35.44 E
Mopelia I[1]	14	16.50 S	153.55 W
Mopipi	156	21.07 S	24.55 E
Mopo	100	33.07 N	113.02 E
Mopoï	154	5.08 N	26.55 E
Moppo → Mokp'o	98	34.48 N	126.22 E
Mopti	150	14.30 N	4.12 W
Mopti □[4]	150	14.40 N	4.15 W
Moqokorei	144	4.03 N	46.08 E
Moquegua	248	17.12 S	70.56 W
Moquegua □[5]	248	16.50 S	70.55 W
Mór	30	47.23 N	18.12 E
Mor ≃	126	24.01 N	88.03 E
Mòr, Glen ∨	46	57.10 N	4.40 W
Mor, Sgurr ∧	46	57.42 N	5.03 W
Mora, Bhārat	272c	18.54 N	72.56 E
Mora, Cam.	146	11.03 N	14.09 E
Mora, Esp.	34	39.41 N	3.46 W
Mora, Port.	34	38.56 N	8.10 W
Mora, Sve.	26	61.00 N	14.33 E
Mora, Minn., U.S.	190	45.53 N	93.18 W
Mora, N. Mex., U.S.	200	35.58 N	105.20 W
Mora ≃	196	35.44 N	104.23 W
Moraby	40	60.23 N	15.35 E
Morača, Manastir ⊛[1]	38	42.44 N	19.20 E
Morada	226	38.01 N	121.15 W
Morādābād	124	28.50 N	78.47 E
Morada Nova	250	5.07 S	38.23 W
Morada Nova de Minas	255	18.37 S	45.22 W
Mora de Rubielos	34	40.15 N	0.45 W
Morado Primero, Cerro ∧	252	22.49 S	65.26 W
Moraduccio	66	44.10 N	11.29 E
Morafenobe	157b	17.49 S	44.55 E
Morag	30	53.56 N	19.56 E
Moraga	226	37.50 N	122.08 W
Mórahalom	30	46.13 N	19.54 E
Moraine	218	39.40 N	84.15 W
Moraine State Park ♠	214	40.56 N	80.07 W
Morainvilliers	261	48.56 N	1.56 E
Morākhi ≃	126	24.01 N	88.10 E
Mor'akovskij Zaton	86	56.45 N	84.41 E
Moral de Calatrava	34	38.50 N	3.35 W
Moraleda, Canal de ⊔	254	44.30 S	73.30 W
Morales, Guat.	236	15.29 N	88.49 W
Morales, Perú	248	6.28 S	76.28 W
Morales, Arroyo ≃	258	34.48 S	58.36 W
Morales, Laguna de C	234	23.35 N	97.47 W
Moramanga	157b	18.56 S	48.12 E
Moran, Kans., U.S.	198	37.55 N	95.10 W
Moran, Mich., U.S.	190	46.00 N	84.50 W
Moran, Tex., U.S.	196	32.33 N	99.10 W
Morangis	261	48.42 N	2.20 E
Morangup Hill ∧[2]	168a	31.41 S	116.19 E
Morann	214	40.48 N	78.21 W
Morano Calabro	68	39.50 N	16.08 E
Morano sul Po	62	45.10 N	8.22 E
Moran State Park ♠	224	48.41 N	122.52 W
Morant Bay	241q	17.53 N	76.25 W
Morant Cays II	238	17.24 N	75.59 W
Morant Point ≻	241q	17.55 N	76.10 W
Morar, Loch @	46	56.57 N	5.43 W
Mörarp	41	56.04 N	12.52 E
Morasverdes	34	40.36 N	6.16 W
Morat, Lac de (Murtensee) @	58	46.55 N	7.05 E
Moratalla	34	38.12 N	1.53 W
Morattico	208	37.47 N	76.38 W
Moratuwa	122	6.46 N	79.53 E
Morava □[9]	30	49.20 N	17.00 E
Morava (March) ≃	30	48.10 N	16.59 E
Moravia, C.R.	236	9.51 N	83.26 W
Moravia, Iowa, U.S.	190	40.53 N	92.49 W
Moravia, N.Y., U.S.	210	42.43 N	76.25 W
Moravia → Morava □[9]	30	49.20 N	17.00 E
Moravian Indian Reserve ◆[4]	214	42.34 N	81.53 W
Moravská Dyje ≃	61	48.51 N	15.30 E
Moravská Ostrava → Ostrava	30	49.50 N	18.17 E
Moravská Třebová	30	49.45 N	16.40 E
Moravské Budějovice	61	49.03 N	15.49 E
Moravsky Krumlov	61	49.03 N	16.19 E
Morawa	162	29.13 S	116.00 E
Morawhanna	246	8.16 N	59.45 W
Moraya	248	21.45 S	65.32 W
Morayfield	171a	27.07 S	152.57 E
Moray Firth C[1]	46	57.45 N	3.30 W
Morazán, Guat.	236	14.56 N	90.09 W
Morazán, Hond.	236	15.17 N	87.34 W
Morbach	56	49.48 N	7.07 E
Morbegno	36	46.08 N	9.34 E
Morbihan □[5]	32	47.55 N	2.50 W
Mörbisch	61	47.45 N	16.40 E
Mörbylånga	26	56.31 N	16.23 E
Morcenx	32	44.02 N	0.55 W
Morciano di Romagna	66	43.55 N	12.38 E
Morcone	68	41.20 N	14.40 E
Morcote	58	45.56 N	8.55 E
Morcy	80	51.18 N	47.51 E
Morden	184	49.11 N	98.05 W
Morden ◆[8]	260	51.24 N	0.12 W
Mordialloc	169	38.00 S	145.05 E
Mordino	24	61.21 N	51.52 E
Mordoğan	130	38.30 N	26.37 E
Mordovo, S.S.S.R.	80	52.05 N	40.46 E
Mordovo, S.S.S.R.	80	51.07 N	45.48 E
Mordovo-Adel'akovo	80	53.47 N	51.36 E
Mordovskaja Avtonomnaja Sovetskaja Socialističeskaja Respublika □[3]	80	54.30 N	44.00 E
Mordovskij Buguruslan	80	53.48 N	52.31 E
Mordovskij Zapovednik ◆[4]	80	54.48 N	43.20 E
Mordves	82	54.34 N	38.13 E
Mordy	30	52.13 N	22.31 E
More, Ben ∧, Scot., U.K.	46	56.25 N	6.01 W
More, Ben ∧, Scot., U.K.	46	56.21 N	4.35 W
More, Loch @	46	58.17 N	4.52 W
More Assynt, Ben ∧	46	58.08 N	4.53 W
Moreau ≃, Mo., U.S.	219	38.33 N	92.06 W
Moreau ≃, S. Dak., U.S.	198	45.18 N	100.43 W
Moreau, North Fork ≃	198	45.09 N	102.50 W
Moreau, South Fork ≃	198	45.09 N	102.50 W
Morec	80	51.03 N	44.03 E
Morecambe	44	54.04 N	2.53 W
Morecambe Bay C	44	54.07 N	3.00 W
Moree, Austl.	166	29.28 S	149.51 E
Morée, Fr.	50	47.54 N	1.14 E
Morehead	218	38.11 N	83.25 W
Morehead ≃	164	9.00 S	141.25 E
Morehead City	192	34.43 N	76.43 W
Morehouse	194	36.51 N	89.41 W
Moreland, Ga., U.S.	192	33.17 N	84.46 W
Moreland, Ky., U.S.	194	37.30 N	84.49 W
Moreland Hills	279a	41.27 N	81.29 W
Morelia	234	19.42 N	101.07 W
Morell	186	46.25 N	62.42 W
Morella, Austl.	166	22.59 S	143.52 E
Morella, Esp.	34	40.37 N	0.06 W
Morello ≃	70	37.29 N	14.08 E
Morelos, Méx.	196	28.25 N	100.53 W
Morelos, Méx.	232	26.42 N	107.40 W
Morelos, Méx.	234	22.53 N	102.37 W
Morelos □[3]	234	18.45 N	99.00 W
Morelos ◆[8]	286a	19.27 N	99.07 W
Morena	124	26.30 N	78.09 E
Morena □[5]	124	26.00 N	77.20 E
Morena, Sierra ∧	282	37.25 N	122.18 W
Morena, Sierra ⋀	34	38.00 N	5.00 W
Morenci, Ariz., U.S.	200	33.05 N	109.22 W
Morenci, Mich., U.S.	216	41.43 N	84.13 W
Moreni	38	45.00 N	25.39 E
Moreno, Arg.	258	34.39 S	58.48 W
Moreno, Calif., U.S.	228	33.55 N	117.09 W
Moreno □[5]	288	34.36 S	58.48 W
Moreno ≃	234	18.32 N	96.01 W
Moreno, Bahía C	252	23.35 S	70.30 W
Møre og Romsdal □[6]	26	62.40 N	7.50 E
Mores	71	40.33 N	8.50 E
Moresby Island I, B.C., Can.	182	52.50 N	131.55 W
Moresby Island I, B.C., Can.	224	48.40 N	123.20 W
Mores Island I	238	26.18 N	77.33 W
Moresnet	56	50.43 N	5.59 E
Morestel	62	45.40 N	5.28 E
Moreton, Austl.	164	12.28 S	142.38 E
Moreton, Eng., U.K.	260	51.44 N	0.14 E
Moreton, Eng., U.K.	262	53.24 N	3.07 W
Moreton, Cape ≻	171a	27.02 S	153.28 E
Moreton Bay C	171a	27.20 S	153.15 E
Moretonhampstead	42	50.40 N	3.45 W
Moreton-in-Marsh	42	51.59 N	1.42 W
Moreton Island I	171a	27.10 S	153.25 E
Moret-sur-Loing	50	48.22 N	2.49 E
Moretta	62	44.46 N	7.32 E
Moreuil	50	49.46 N	2.29 E
Morey Park	210	42.33 N	73.43 W
Morey Peak ∧	204	38.37 N	116.17 W
Morez	58	46.31 N	6.02 E
Morfa Nefyn	42	52.56 N	4.33 W
Mörfelden	56	49.58 N	8.34 E
Mórfou	130	35.12 N	32.59 E
Mórfou, Kólpos C	130	35.10 N	32.50 E
Morga	80	54.26 N	46.29 E
Morgan, Austl.	166	34.02 S	139.40 E
Morgan, Ga., U.S.	192	31.32 N	84.36 W
Morgan, Ky., U.S.	218	38.36 N	84.24 W
Morgan, Minn., U.S.	198	44.25 N	94.56 W
Morgan, Pa., U.S.	279b	40.22 N	80.08 W
Morgan, Tex., U.S.	222	32.01 N	97.37 W
Morgan, Utah, U.S.	200	41.02 N	111.41 W
Morgan □[6], Ill., U.S.	219	39.44 N	90.14 W
Morgan □[6], Ind., U.S.	218	39.30 N	86.25 W
Morgan, Mount ∧	171b	35.44 S	148.47 E
Morgan City, Ala., U.S.	194	34.28 N	86.34 W
Morgan City, La., U.S.	194	29.42 N	91.12 W
Morgan Creek ≃	196	32.19 N	100.55 W
Morganfield	194	37.41 N	87.55 W
Morgan Hill	226	37.08 N	121.39 W
Morganito	246	5.04 N	67.44 W
Morgan Park ◆[8]	278	41.42 N	87.40 W
Morgan's Bay	158	32.43 S	28.20 E
Morgan's Point	222	29.41 N	94.59 W
Morgans Point ≻	212	42.52 N	79.21 W
Morgan State College ⊛[2]	284b	39.21 N	76.35 W
Morgantina ⊥	70	37.25 N	14.29 E
Morganton	192	35.45 N	81.41 W
Morgantown, Ind., U.S.	218	39.22 N	86.16 W
Morgantown, Ky., U.S.	194	37.14 N	86.41 W
Morgantown, Md., U.S.	208	38.21 N	76.58 W
Morgantown, Miss., U.S.	194	31.19 N	89.55 W
Morgantown, Ohio, U.S.	218	39.08 N	83.13 W
Morgantown, Pa., U.S.	208	40.09 N	75.54 W
Morgantown, W. Va., U.S.	188	39.38 N	79.57 W
Morganville	208	40.23 N	74.15 W
Morganza	194	30.44 N	91.36 W
Morgårdshammar	40	60.09 N	15.23 E
Morgauši	80	55.58 N	46.47 E
Morgenzon	158	26.45 S	29.36 E
Morges	58	46.31 N	6.30 E
Morgex	62	45.45 N	7.02 E
Morghāb (Murgab) ≃	128	38.18 N	61.12 E
Morghar	126	23.40 N	89.37 E
Morgongåva	40	59.56 N	16.57 E
Morgongiori	71	39.45 N	8.46 E
Morguilla, Punta ≻	252	37.46 S	73.40 W
Morhange	56	48.55 N	6.38 E
Mori, It.	64	45.51 N	10.59 E
Mori, Nihon	92a	42.06 N	140.35 E
Mori, Nihon	94	34.50 N	137.56 E
Mori, Nihon	270	34.32 N	135.00 E
Mori ≃	164	10.00 S	148.30 E
Moriah	241r	11.15 N	60.43 W
Moriah, Mount ∧	204	39.17 N	114.12 W
Morialta Falls Reserve ♠	168b	34.55 S	138.40 E
Moriarty	200	34.59 N	106.03 W
Moriarty, Mount ∧	224	49.08 N	124.26 W
Morib	114	2.45 N	101.26 E
Moribaya	150	9.53 N	9.33 W
Morice ≃	182	54.24 N	126.45 W
Morice Lake @	182	54.00 N	127.37 W
Morichal Largo ≃	246	9.27 N	62.25 W
Moricsala ♠	76	57.17 N	22.11 E
Morie, Loch @	46	57.44 N	4.28 W
Morienval	50	49.18 N	2.56 E
Morigerati	68	40.08 N	15.33 E
Moriguchi	96	34.44 N	135.34 E
Morija	158	29.34 S	27.31 E
Moriki	150	12.52 N	6.30 E
Moringen	52	51.42 N	9.52 E
Morino, It.	66	41.53 N	13.25 E
Morino, S.S.S.R.	76	57.54 N	30.22 E
Morinville	182	53.48 N	113.39 W
Morioka	92	39.42 N	141.09 E
Morīri, Tso @	120	32.54 N	78.20 E
Morisset	170	33.06 S	151.29 E
Moriston ≃	46	57.12 N	4.36 W
Moritzburg ⊥	54	51.09 N	13.40 E
Morivione ◆[8]	266b	45.26 N	9.12 E
Moriya	94	35.56 N	140.00 E
Moriyama	94	35.04 N	135.59 E
Moriyoshi-zan ∧	92	39.58 N	140.33 E
Morki	80	56.25 N	49.01 E
Morkill ≃	182	53.42 N	120.30 W
Morkiny Gory	76	57.33 N	36.18 E
Mörkö I	40	58.59 N	17.40 E
Morkoka ≃	74	65.10 N	115.52 E
Mørkøv	41	55.40 N	11.32 E
Morlaix	32	48.35 N	3.50 W
Morlanwelz	50	50.27 N	4.14 E
Morles	56	50.38 N	9.51 E
Morley, Eng., U.K.	44	53.46 N	1.36 W
Morley, Mich., U.S.	190	43.29 N	85.27 W
Morley, N.Y., U.S.	212	44.40 N	75.12 W
Morley Green	262	53.20 N	2.16 W
Mörlunda	26	57.19 N	15.51 E
Mormal'	76	52.45 N	29.53 E
Mormanno	68	39.53 N	16.00 E
Mormant	50	48.36 N	2.53 E
Mormoiron	62	44.04 N	5.11 E
Mormon Bar	226	37.28 N	119.57 W
Mormon Lake @	200	34.57 N	111.27 W
Mormon Peak ∧	204	36.57 N	114.30 W
Mormon Reservoir @[1]	202	43.16 N	114.49 W
Mormon Slough ≃	226	37.57 N	121.18 W
Mormon Station Historical State Monument ♠	226	39.00 N	119.50 W
Morna	272a	28.35 N	77.22 E
Mornant	62	45.37 N	4.40 E
Mornas	62	44.12 N	4.44 E
Morne, Pointe ≻	241o	16.20 N	61.18 W
Morne-à-l'Eau	241o	16.21 N	61.31 W
Morne-Rouge	240e	14.46 N	61.08 W
Morney	166	25.22 S	141.28 E
Morningdale	207	42.19 N	71.41 W
Morningside	284c	38.50 N	76.53 W
Morningstar ≃	48	52.27 N	8.41 W
Morning Sun	190	41.05 N	91.15 W
Mornington	169	38.13 S	145.03 E
Mornington, Isla I	254	49.45 S	75.23 W
Mornington Island I	164	16.33 S	139.24 E
Mornington Peninsula ≻[1]	169	38.20 S	145.05 E
Morno	150	8.41 N	1.31 W
Mornou, Hadjer ∧	146	17.12 N	23.08 E
Moro, Pāk.	120	26.40 N	68.00 E
Moro, Oreg., U.S.	224	45.29 N	120.44 W
Moro ≃	150	7.25 N	11.03 W
Morobe	164	7.45 S	147.35 E
Morobe □[5]	164	7.00 S	146.30 E
Moroč'	76	52.34 N	27.36 E
Moroč' ≃	76	52.35 N	27.35 E
Morocco	216	40.57 N	87.27 W
Morocco □[1]	134		
	148	32.00 N	5.00 W
Morococala	248	18.10 S	66.44 W
Morococha	248	11.37 S	76.09 W
Moro Creek ≃	194	33.18 N	92.22 W
Morogoro	154	6.49 S	37.40 E
Morogoro □[4]	154	8.00 S	37.00 E
Moro Gulf C	116	6.51 N	123.00 E
Moroka	273d	26.16 S	27.52 E
Morokweng	158	26.12 S	23.45 E
Moroleón	234	20.08 N	101.12 W
Morombe	157b	21.45 S	43.22 E
Morón, Arg.	258	34.39 S	58.37 W
Morón, Cuba	240p	22.06 N	78.38 W
Mörön, Mong.	88	47.27 N	110.14 E
Mörön, Mong.	88	49.38 N	100.10 E
Mörön, Mong.	88	48.15 N	100.23 E
Morón, Ven.	246	10.29 N	68.11 W
Morón □[5]	288	34.37 S	58.37 W
Mörön ≃	88	47.14 N	110.37 E
Morón, Aeródromo ⊠	288	34.41 S	58.38 W
Morón, Arroyo ≃	288	34.33 S	58.37 W
Morona ≃	246	4.45 S	77.04 W
Morona-Santiago □[4]	246	2.30 S	78.00 W
Morondava	157b	20.17 S	44.17 E
Morón de Almazán	34	41.25 N	2.25 W
Morón de la Frontera	34	37.08 N	5.27 W
Morones, Sierra ⋀	234	21.45 N	103.10 W
Morong	116	14.41 N	120.16 E
Morongo Indian Reservation ◆[4]	204	33.59 N	116.50 W
Moroni, Comores	157a	11.41 S	43.16 E
Moroni, Utah, U.S.	200	39.32 N	111.35 W
Moros ≃	34	40.03 N	5.31 W
Morošečnoje	74	56.24 N	156.12 E
Morotai I	108	2.20 N	128.25 E
Moroto	154	2.32 N	34.39 E
Moroto ∧	154	2.32 N	34.46 E
Morovis	240m	18.20 N	66.24 W
Morovsk	78	51.06 N	30.50 E
Morowali	112	1.52 S	121.30 E
Moroyama	94	35.56 N	139.19 E
Morozkovo	86	59.29 N	61.01 E
Morozovka, S.S.S.R.	78	50.09 N	39.38 E
Morozovka, S.S.S.R.	83	49.28 N	39.54 E
Morozovsk	80	48.22 N	41.50 E
Morozovskaja	24	61.10 N	50.18 E
Morpeth, Ont., Can.	214	42.23 N	81.51 W
Morpeth, Eng., U.K.	44	55.10 N	1.41 W
Morphett Vale	168b	35.07 S	138.31 E
Morra, Monte ∧	267a	42.02 N	12.50 E
Morral	214	40.41 N	83.13 W
Morral, Arroyo del ≃	266d	41.29 N	2.03 E
Morrelganj	126	22.28 N	89.51 E
Morretes	252	25.28 S	48.49 W
Morrice	216	42.50 N	84.11 W
Morrill	198	41.58 N	103.56 W
Morrilton	194	35.09 N	92.45 W
Morrin	182	51.40 N	112.47 W
Morrinhos, Bra.	250	3.14 S	40.07 W
Morrinhos, Bra.	255	17.44 S	49.07 W
Morrinsville	172	37.39 S	175.32 E
Morris, Man., Can.	184	49.21 N	97.22 W
Morris, Conn., U.S.	207	41.43 N	73.15 W
Morris, Ill., U.S.	216	41.22 N	88.26 W
Morris, Ind., U.S.	218	39.17 N	85.11 W
Morris, Minn., U.S.	198	45.35 N	95.55 W
Morris, N.Y., U.S.	210	42.33 N	75.15 W
Morris, Okla., U.S.	196	35.36 N	95.51 W
Morris, Pa., U.S.	210	41.36 N	77.18 W
Morris □[6], N.J., U.S.	210	40.48 N	74.29 W
Morris □[6], Tex., U.S.	222	33.05 N	94.45 W
Morris ≃	184	49.21 N	97.22 W
Morris, Mount ∧	162	26.09 S	131.04 E
Morrisburg	212	44.54 N	75.11 W
Morrisdale	214	40.57 N	78.14 W
Morris Dam ◆[6]	280	34.11 N	117.53 W
Morris Jesup, Kap ≻	16	83.38 N	33.52 W
Morris Lake @	276	41.03 N	74.37 W
Morrison, Arg.	252	32.36 S	62.50 W
Morrison, Ill., U.S.	190	41.49 N	89.58 W
Morrison, Mo., U.S.	219	38.40 N	91.38 W
Morrison Creek ≃	275b	43.28 N	79.39 W
Morrison Lake @, Ont., Can.	212	44.52 N	79.28 W
Morrison Lake @, Mich., U.S.	216	42.53 N	85.13 W
Morrisonville	219	39.25 N	89.27 W
Morris Park ♠	285	39.59 N	75.15 W
Morris Plains	210	40.49 N	74.29 W
Morris Reservoir @[1]	228	34.12 N	117.52 W
Morris Run	210	41.41 N	77.01 W
Morristown, Ariz., U.S.	200	33.51 N	112.37 W
Morristown, Ill., U.S.	216	42.10 N	89.03 W
Morristown, Ind., U.S.	218	39.40 N	85.42 W
Morristown, Minn., U.S.	190	44.14 N	93.26 W
Morristown, N.J., U.S.	210	40.48 N	74.29 W
Morristown, N.Y., U.S.	212	44.35 N	75.39 W
Morristown, Ohio, U.S.	214	40.04 N	81.05 W
Morristown, S. Dak., U.S.	198	45.56 N	101.43 W
Morristown, Tenn., U.S.	192	36.13 N	83.18 W
Morristown Airport ⊠	276	40.48 N	74.25 W
Morristown National Historical Park ♠	210	40.46 N	74.32 W
Morrisville, N.Y., U.S.	210	42.54 N	75.39 W
Morrisville, Pa., U.S.	285	40.13 N	74.47 W
Morrisville, Vt., U.S.	188	44.34 N	72.44 W
Morro	246	2.39 S	80.19 W
Morro, Castillo del (Morro Castle) ⊥	286b	23.09 N	82.21 W
Morro, Punta ≻	252	27.07 S	70.57 W
Morro, Punta del ≻	234	19.51 N	96.27 W
Morro Agudo	287a	22.45 S	43.29 W
Morro Bay	226	35.22 N	120.51 W
Morro Bay C	226	35.20 N	120.51 W
Morro Bay State Park ♠	226	35.20 N	120.52 W
Morro Creek ≃	226	35.23 N	120.52 W
Morro de Mazatán	234	16.07 N	95.27 W
Morro do Chapéu	250	11.33 S	41.09 W
Morro do Pilar	255	19.12 S	43.23 W
Morro d'Oro	66	42.39 N	13.54 E
Morrone del Sannio	66	41.43 N	14.47 E
Morropón	248	5.15 S	80.00 W
Morros	250	2.52 S	44.03 W
Morrosquillo, Golfo de C	246	9.35 N	75.40 W
Morrow, La., U.S.	194	30.50 N	92.05 W
Morrow, Ohio, U.S.	218	39.21 N	84.08 W
Morrow □[6]	214	40.33 N	82.50 W
Morrow Island I	282	38.07 N	122.05 W
Morrow Point Reservoir @[1]	200	38.25 N	107.30 W
Mörrum	26	56.11 N	14.45 E
Morrumbala	154	17.22 S	35.36 E
Morrumbene	156	23.39 S	35.20 E
Mörrumsån ≃	26	56.09 N	14.44 E
Mors I	26	56.50 N	8.45 E
Morsains	50	48.48 N	3.32 E
Morsang-sur-Orge	261	48.40 N	2.21 E
Moršansk	80	53.26 N	41.49 E
Morsbach	56	50.52 N	7.43 E
Mörsch	56	48.58 N	8.17 E
Morschwiller-le-Bas	58	47.45 N	7.16 E
Morščichino	265b	55.56 N	37.20 E
Morse, Sask., Can.	184	50.25 N	107.03 W
Morse, La., U.S.	194	30.08 N	92.30 W
Morse, Tex., U.S.	196	36.04 N	101.29 W
Morse Mill	219	38.17 N	90.40 W
Mörsenbroich ◆[8]	263	51.15 N	6.48 E
Morse Reservoir @[1]	218	40.06 N	86.02 W
Morses Pond @	283	42.18 N	71.19 W
Morsi	120	21.21 N	78.00 E
Morskaja Masel'ga	24	63.06 N	34.54 E
Morskaja Pristan' ◆[5]	265a	59.53 N	30.11 E
Morskoj Bir'uček, Ostrov I	84	44.42 N	47.02 E
Morskoj Passažirskij Port ◆[5]	265a	59.55 N	30.14 E
Morskoj Vokzal ◆[5]	265a	59.57 N	30.17 E
Morson	184	49.03 N	94.18 W
Morsott	36	35.40 N	8.01 E
Morstein	285	40.01 N	75.35 W
Mort	272a	28.43 N	77.25 E
Morta	272a	28.44 N	77.27 E
Mortagne	32	48.31 N	0.33 E
Mortagne ≃	58	48.33 N	6.27 E
Mortagne-au-Perche	50	48.31 N	0.33 E
Mortagne-sur-Sèvre	32	47.00 N	0.57 W
Mortain	32	48.39 N	0.56 W
Mortana	162	33.02 S	134.07 E
Mortara	62	45.15 N	8.44 E
Mortcho ◆[1]	146	16.00 N	21.10 E
Morteau	58	47.04 N	6.37 E
Mortefontaine	50	49.07 N	2.36 E
Mortegliano	64	45.57 N	13.10 E
Morte Point ≻	42	51.11 N	4.13 W
Morteratsch, Piz ∧	58	46.22 N	9.51 E
Morteros	252	30.42 S	62.00 W
Mortes, Rio das ≃	256	21.18 S	43.58 W
Mortesoro	140	10.12 N	34.09 E
Mort-Homme, Forêt du ◆[3]	56	49.15 N	5.15 E
Mortlach	184	50.28 N	106.03 W
Mortlake, Austl.	166	38.05 S	142.48 E
Mortlake, Austl.	274a	33.51 S	151.07 E
Mortlake ◆[8]	260	51.28 N	0.16 W
Mortola Inferiore	62	43.47 N	7.33 E
Morton, Ill., U.S.	190	40.37 N	89.28 W
Morton, Minn., U.S.	198	44.33 N	94.59 W
Morton, Miss., U.S.	194	32.21 N	89.40 W
Morton, N.Y., U.S.	210	43.20 N	78.00 W
Morton, Pa., U.S.	285	39.55 N	75.20 W
Morton, Tex., U.S.	196	33.44 N	102.46 W
Morton, Wash., U.S.	224	46.33 N	122.17 W
Morton, Mount ∧[2]	274b	37.56 S	145.20 E
Morton Arboretum ◆[4]	278	41.49 N	88.04 W
Morton Craig Range ⋀	162	28.12 S	124.41 E
Morton Grove	216	42.02 N	87.47 W
Mortons Gap	194	37.14 N	87.28 W
Mortorio, Isola I	71	41.05 N	9.36 E
Mortrée	50	48.38 N	0.05 E
Mörtschach	64	46.55 N	12.55 E
Mortsel	50	51.10 N	4.28 E
M'ortvyj Donec ≃	83	47.15 N	39.14 E
Morty	80	55.49 N	51.44 E
Morumbi, Estádio do ♠	287b	23.37 S	46.43 W
Morungaba	256	22.52 S	46.48 W
Morungole ∧	154	3.49 N	34.02 E
Moruya	166	35.55 S	150.05 E
Morvan ⋀	32	47.05 N	4.00 E
Morven, Austl.	166	26.25 S	147.07 E
Morven, N.Z.	172	44.50 S	171.07 E
Morven, Ga., U.S.	192	30.56 N	83.30 W
Morven, N.C., U.S.	192	34.52 N	80.01 W
Morven ∧, Scot., U.K.	46	58.14 N	3.42 W
Morven ∧, Scot., U.K.	46	57.07 N	3.02 W
Morvi	120	22.49 N	70.50 E
Morwell	169	38.14 S	146.24 E
Morwell ≃	169	38.10 S	146.23 E
Morwenstow	42	50.54 N	4.33 W
Moryń	30	52.49 N	14.13 E
Morženga	76	59.37 N	40.12 E
Morzhovoi	180	54.55 N	163.18 W
Morzine	58	46.11 N	6.43 E
Moržovec, Ostrov I	24	66.44 N	42.35 E
Moša ≃, S.S.S.R.	24	62.25 N	39.46 E
M'oša ≃, S.S.S.R.	80	55.25 N	49.22 E
Mosal'sk	76	54.29 N	34.59 E
Mosambik → Mozambique □[1]	138	18.15 S	35.00 E
Mošanicy	82	54.56 N	38.23 E
Mosås	40	59.12 N	15.08 E
Mosbach	56	49.21 N	9.08 E
Mosby	26	58.14 N	7.54 E
Moscavide	266c	38.47 N	9.06 W
Mosciano Sant'Angelo	66	42.45 N	13.53 E
Moščnyj, Ostrov I	76	60.01 N	27.50 E
Moscos Islands II	110	14.00 N	97.45 E
Moscou → Moskva	82	55.45 N	37.35 E
Moscow → Moskva, S.S.S.R.	82	55.45 N	37.35 E
Moscow, Idaho, U.S.	202	46.44 N	117.00 W
Moscow, Ind., U.S.	218	39.29 N	85.34 W
Moscow, Ohio, U.S.	218	38.52 N	84.14 W
Moscow, Pa., U.S.	210	41.20 N	75.31 W
Moscow, Tex., U.S.	222	30.55 N	94.50 W
Moscow → Moskva ≃	76	55.05 N	38.50 E
Moscow Mills	219	38.57 N	90.55 W
Moscú → Moskva	82	55.45 N	37.35 E
Moscufo	66	42.25 N	14.03 E
Mosel	54	50.47 N	12.28 E
Mosel (Moselle) ≃	32	50.22 N	7.36 E
Moselebe ≃	156	25.03 S	23.13 E
Moselle, Miss., U.S.	194	31.30 N	89.17 W
Moselle, Mo., U.S.	219	38.23 N	90.54 W
Moselle □[5]	56	49.00 N	6.30 E
Moselle (Mosel) ≃	32	50.22 N	7.36 E
Moselotte ≃	58	48.01 N	6.38 E
Mošenskoje	76	58.31 N	34.35 E
Mosermandl ∧	64	47.12 N	13.24 E
Mosers River	186	44.59 N	62.15 W
Moses Lake	202	47.08 N	119.17 W
Moses Point	180	64.42 N	162.03 W
Moses Power Plant ◆[6]	284a	43.09 N	79.02 W
Mosetse	156	20.37 S	26.32 E
Mosgiel	172	45.53 S	170.21 E
Moshannon	214	41.02 N	78.00 W
Moshannon Creek ≃	214	41.04 N	78.06 W
Moshanpu	100	29.34 N	112.41 E
Mosheim, Tenn., U.S.	192	36.11 N	82.57 W
Mosheim, Tex., U.S.	222	31.38 N	97.36 W
Moshi	154	3.21 S	37.20 E
Moshiyu	104	41.15 N	124.05 E
Moshupa	156	24.50 S	25.31 E
Mosier	224	45.41 N	121.24 W
Mosina	30	52.16 N	16.51 E
Mosinee	190	44.47 N	89.43 W
Mosjøen	24	65.50 N	13.10 E
Moskal'vo	89	53.35 N	142.30 E
Moskau → Moskva	82	55.45 N	37.35 E
Moskenesøya I	24	67.59 N	13.00 E
Moskháton	267c	37.57 N	23.41 E
Moškino	80	57.45 N	45.20 E
Moskito-Golf → Mosquitos, Golfo de los C	236	9.00 N	81.15 W
Moškovo	86	55.18 N	83.37 E
Moskovskaja Slav'anka	265a	59.45 N	30.30 E
Moskovskij	85	40.44 N	72.03 E
Moskovskij Aerovokzal ⊛	265b	55.48 N	37.32 E
Moskovskij Park Pobedy ♠	265a	59.52 N	30.20 E
Moskovskij Vokzal ◆[5]	265a	59.56 N	30.22 E
Moskva	82		
	265b	55.45 N	37.35 E
Moskva □[4]	82	55.45 N	37.30 E
Moskva ≃	76	55.05 N	38.50 E
Moskva, Gorod □[7]	265b	55.45 N	37.35 E
Moskva, Pik ∧	85	38.57 N	71.49 E
Mosman	170	33.49 S	151.14 E
Mosman Park	168a	32.01 S	115.46 E
Mošny	78	49.32 N	31.44 E
Moso (Moos)	64	46.41 N	12.23 E
Moso in Passiria (Moos)	64	46.50 N	11.10 E
Mošok	80	55.48 N	41.17 E
Mosolovo	80	54.17 N	40.32 E
Mosomane	156	24.04 S	26.15 E
Moson-Duna ≃	61	47.54 N	17.17 E
Mosonmagyaróvár	30	47.51 N	17.17 E
Mosonszentjános	61	47.47 N	17.08 E
Mospino	83	47.53 N	38.03 E

Symbols in the index entries represent the broad categories identified in the key at the right. Symbols with superior numbers (⋀[2]) identify subcategories (see complete key on page *I · 30*).

Kartensymbole in dem Registerverzeichnis stellen die rechts in Schlüssel erklärten Kategorien dar. Symbole mit hochgestellten Ziffern (⋀[2]) bezeichnen Unterabteilungen einer Kategorie (vgl. vollständiger Schlüssel auf Seite *I · 30*).

Los símbolos incluídos en el texto del índice representan las grandes categorias identificadas con la clave a la derecha. Los símbolos con numeros en su parte superior (⋀[2]) identifican las subcategorías (véase la clave completa en la página *I · 30*).

Les symboles de l'index représentent les catégories indiquées dans la légende à droite. Les symboles suivis d'un indice (⋀[2]) représentent des sous-catégories (voir légende complète à la page *I · 30*).

Os símbolos incluídos no texto do índice representam as grandes categorias identificadas com a chave à direita. Os símbolos com números em sua parte superior (⋀[2]) identificam as subcategorias (veja-se a chave completa à página *I · 30*).

Symbol	English	Deutsch	Español	Français	Português
∧	Mountain	Berg	Montaña	Montagne	Montanha
⋀	Mountains	Berge	Montañas	Montagnes	Montanhas
)(	Pass	Pass	Paso	Col	Passo
∨	Valley, Canyon	Tal, Cañon	Valle, Cañón	Vallée, Canyon	Vale, Canhão
⁼	Plain	Ebene	Llano	Plaine	Planície
≻	Cape	Kap	Cabo	Cap	Cabo
I	Island	Insel	Isla	Île	Ilha
II	Islands	Inseln	Islas	Îles	Ilhas
⊥	Other Topographic Features	Andere Topographische Objekte	Otros Elementos Topográficos	Autres données topographiques	Outros Elementos Topográficos

ESPAÑOL

Nombre	Página	Lat.°′	Long.°′ W=Oeste
Mosqueiro	250	1.10 S	48.28 W
Mosquera	246	2.30 N	78.29 W
Mosquero	196	35.47 N	103.58 W
Mosquic, Lac ⊜	206	46.39 N	74.28 W
Mosquito, Punta ➤	246	9.07 N	77.53 W
Mosquito, Riacho ≃	252	22.02 S	57.57 W
Mosquito Brook ≃	283	42.40 N	71.02 W
Mosquito Creek ≃, Iowa, U.S.	198	41.11 N	95.50 W
Mosquito Creek ≃, Ohio, U.S.	214	41.10 N	80.45 W
Mosquito Creek ≃, Pa., U.S.	214	41.07 N	78.07 W
Mosquito Creek Lake ⊜[1]	214	41.22 N	80.45 W
Mosquito Indian Reserve ➛[4]	184	52.30 N	108.15 W
Mosquito Lagoon C	220	28.45 N	80.45 W
Mosquitos, Costa de □[9]	236	13.00 N	83.45 W
Mosquitos, Golfo de los C	236	9.00 N	81.15 W
Mosquito State Park ♠	214	41.09 N	80.46 W
Moss	26	59.26 N	10.42 E
Mossaka	152	1.13 S	16.48 E
Mossâmedes	255	16.07 S	50.11 W
Mossbank, Sask., Can.	184	49.55 N	105.59 W
Moss Bank, Eng., U.K.	262	53.29 N	2.44 W
Mossbank, Scot., U.K.	46	60.27 N	1.12 W
Moss Bank Park ♠	262	53.36 N	2.28 W
Moss Beach	282	37.32 N	122.31 W
Mossburn	172	45.40 S	168.15 E
Mosselbaai (Mossel Bay)	158	34.11 S	22.08 E
Mosselbaai C	158	34.06 S	22.20 E
Mossendjo	152	2.57 S	12.44 E
Mosses, Col des)(	58	46.24 N	7.06 E
Mossgiel	166	33.15 S	144.34 E
Moss Hill	222	30.15 N	94.45 W
Mössingen	58	48.24 N	9.03 E
Moss Landing	226	36.48 N	121.47 W
Mossleigh	182	50.43 N	113.20 W
Mossley	44	53.32 N	2.02 W
Mossley Hill ➛[8]	262	53.23 N	2.55 W
Mossman	164	16.28 S	145.22 E
Mossmans Brook ≃	276	41.03 N	74.27 W
Moss Moor ➛[3]	262	53.37 N	2.00 W
Moss Mountain Λ	194	34.50 N	92.40 W
Mossø ⊜	41	56.02 N	9.48 E
Mosson ≃	62	43.33 N	3.54 E
Mossoró	250	5.11 S	37.20 W
Mosso Santa Maria	62	45.38 N	8.08 E
Moss Point	194	30.25 N	88.29 W
Moss Point ➤	279a	41.37 N	81.32 W
Moss Side	262	53.46 N	2.57 W
Mossuril	154	14.58 S	40.42 E
Moss Vale	170	34.33 S	150.22 E
Mossy ≃	184	54.05 N	103.00 W
Mossyrock	224	46.32 N	122.29 W
Mossyrock Dam ➛[6]	224	46.32 N	122.25 W
Most	54	50.32 N	13.39 E
Mosta	80	56.32 N	42.10 E
Mostaganem	148	35.51 N	0.07 E
Mostar	36	43.20 N	17.49 E
Mostardas	252	31.06 S	50.57 W
Møsting, Kap ➤	176	64.00 N	41.00 W
Mostiska	78	49.48 N	23.09 E
Mostiștea ≃	38	44.15 N	27.10 E
Mostizzolo	64	46.24 N	11.01 E
Mostki	83	49.19 N	38.30 E
Most na Soči	64	46.09 N	13.44 E
Mostok	76	53.59 N	30.28 E
Móstoles	266a	40.19 N	3.52 W
Mostoos Hills ⩕[2]	184	54.50 N	108.45 W
Mostovaja	76	56.13 N	33.08 E
Mostovoje	78	47.24 N	30.59 E
Mostovskoj	84	44.25 N	40.48 E
Mostovskoje	86	55.46 N	66.22 E
Mosty	76	53.25 N	24.32 E
Mostyn, Malay.	112	4.40 N	118.11 E
Mostyn, Wales, U.K.	44	53.19 N	3.16 W
Mosul → Al-Mawṣil	128	36.20 N	43.08 E
Møsvatnet ⊜	26	59.52 N	8.05 E
Mota	144	11.02 N	37.52 E
Mota I	175f	13.49 S	167.42 E
Motaba ≃	152	2.03 N	18.03 E
Mota del Cuervo	34	39.30 N	2.52 W
Mota del Marqués	34	41.38 N	5.10 W
Motagua ≃	236	15.44 N	88.14 W
Motala	26	58.33 N	15.03 E
Motala ström ≃	40	58.38 N	16.10 E
Motane I	174x	9.59 S	138.49 W
Motatán	246	9.24 N	70.36 W
Motaze	156	24.48 S	32.52 E
Motegi	94	36.32 N	140.11 E
Mote Park ♠	260	51.17 N	0.34 E
Moteve, Cap ➤	174x	9.58 S	139.02 W
Moth	124	25.43 N	78.57 E
Mothe I	175g	18.40 S	178.30 W
Mother Brook ☲	283	42.15 N	71.10 W
Motherwell	46	55.48 N	4.00 W
Motīhāri	124	26.39 N	84.55 E
Motilla del Palancar	34	39.34 N	1.53 W
Motiong	116	11.47 N	125.00 E
Motiti Island I	172	37.38 S	176.26 E
Motjärnshyttan	40	59.56 N	13.58 E
Motloutse	156	21.28 S	27.24 E
Motloutse ≃	156	22.15 S	29.00 E
Moto-ara ≃	94	35.53 N	139.50 E
Motol'	76	52.19 N	25.36 E
Motomachi	92	34.45 N	139.21 E
Motomura	94	34.45 N	139.22 E
Motopu	174x	9.55 S	139.03 W
Motor Island I	284a	42.58 N	78.56 W
Motorki	80	56.53 N	51.29 E
Motorovo	86	56.31 N	71.10 E
Motosu	94	35.29 N	136.40 E
Motosu-ko ⊜	94	35.28 N	138.35 E
Motou	106	32.18 N	120.34 E
Motovilovo	80	55.36 N	43.51 E
Motovun	64	45.20 N	13.50 E
Motoyama	96	33.45 N	133.35 E
Moto-yama Λ[2]	174f	24.48 N	141.20 E
Motozintla de Mendoza	232	15.22 N	92.14 W
Motril	34	36.45 N	3.31 W
Motrone	64	43.54 N	10.12 E
Motru	38	44.50 N	23.00 E
Mott	198	46.22 N	102.20 W
Motta	64	45.36 N	11.29 E
Motta Camastra	70	37.54 N	15.10 E
Motta d'Affermo	70	37.59 N	14.18 E
Motta di Livenza	64	45.47 N	12.36 E
Mottafollone	68	39.39 N	16.04 E
Motta Montecorvino	68	41.30 N	15.07 E
Motta San Giovanni	70	38.00 N	15.41 E
Motta Sant'Anastasia	70	37.31 N	14.58 E
Motta Visconti	62	45.17 N	8.59 E
Möttingen	56	48.48 N	10.35 E
Mottingham ➛[8]	260	51.26 N	0.03 E
Mottisfont	42	51.02 N	1.32 W
Mottola	68	40.38 N	17.03 E
Mottram in Longdendale	262	53.27 N	2.01 W
Motts Creek ≃	276	40.38 N	73.45 W
Mottville, Mich., U.S.	216	41.48 N	85.45 W
Mottville, N.Y., U.S.	210	42.59 N	76.27 W
Motu ≃	172	37.51 S	177.35 E
Motueka	172	41.07 S	173.00 E
Motueka ≃	172	41.05 S	173.01 E
Motuo	120	29.20 N	95.15 E
Motupe	248	6.09 S	79.44 W
Motupena Point ➤	175e	6.32 S	155.09 E
Moturiki I	175g	17.46 S	178.45 E

FRANÇAIS

Nom	Page	Lat.°′	Long.°′ W=Ouest
Motutapu	174v	19.02 S	169.52 W
Motutapu I	174k	21.14 S	159.43 W
Motygino	86	58.11 N	94.40 E
Motyklejka	74	59.26 N	148.38 E
Motyžin	78	50.23 N	29.55 E
Motyzlej	80	54.54 N	42.54 E
Mou	175f	21.05 S	165.26 E
Mouangko	152	3.39 N	9.49 E
Mouans-Sartoux	62	43.37 N	6.58 E
Mouchard	58	46.58 N	5.48 E
Mouchoir Bank ✣[4]	238	20.55 N	70.45 W
Mouchoir Passage ⋓	238	21.10 N	71.00 W
Moúdhros	38	39.52 N	25.16 E
Mouding	102	25.24 N	101.35 E
Moudjéria	150	17.53 N	12.20 W
Moudon	58	46.40 N	6.48 E
Moudongouma ≃	152	1.36 N	17.24 E
Mougdi	146	11.30 N	17.34 E
Mouila	152	1.52 S	11.01 E
Mouit	150	16.35 N	13.05 W
Mouka	152	7.16 N	21.52 E
Moukden → Shenyang	104	41.48 N	123.27 E
Moulamein	166	35.05 S	144.02 E
Moulay-bou-Selham	34	34.53 N	6.15 W
Moulay-Idriss	148	34.02 N	5.27 W
Mouldsworth	262	53.14 N	2.44 W
Moule à Chique, Cap ➤	241f	13.43 N	60.57 W
Moulhoulé	144	12.36 N	43.12 E
Moulin, Île du I	275a	45.41 N	73.32 W
Moulin-des-Ponts	58	46.20 N	5.19 E
Moulineaux	50	49.21 N	0.58 E
Moulinet	62	43.57 N	7.25 E
Moulins	32	46.34 N	3.20 E
Moulins-la-Marche	50	48.39 N	0.29 E
Moulmein	110	16.30 N	97.38 E
Moulmeingyun	110	16.23 N	95.16 E
Moulouya, Oued ≃	148	35.05 N	2.25 W
Moulton, Eng., U.K.	262	53.13 N	2.31 W
Moulton, Ala., U.S.	194	34.29 N	87.18 W
Moulton, Iowa, U.S.	190	40.41 N	92.41 W
Moulton, Tex., U.S.	222	29.34 N	97.09 W
Moultrie	192	31.11 N	83.47 W
Moultrie □[6]	219	39.36 N	88.37 W
Moultrie, Lake ⊜[1]	192	33.20 N	80.05 W
Mound	222	31.21 N	97.38 W
Mound City, Ill., U.S.	194	37.05 N	89.10 W
Mound City, Kans., U.S.	198	38.08 N	94.49 W
Mound City, Mo., U.S.	194	40.07 N	95.14 W
Mound City, S. Dak., U.S.	198	45.44 N	100.04 W
Mound City Group National Monument ♠	218	39.23 N	83.00 W
Mound Lake ⊜	219	40.05 N	90.17 W
Moundou	146	8.34 N	16.05 E
Moundridge	198	38.12 N	97.31 W
Mounds, Ill., U.S.	194	37.07 N	89.12 W
Mounds, Okla., U.S.	196	35.53 N	96.04 W
Mounds State Park ♠	218	40.07 N	85.37 W
Mounds State Recreation Area ♠	218	39.30 N	84.59 W
Moundsville	188	39.55 N	80.44 W
Moundville	194	32.59 N	87.38 W
Moungahaumi Λ	172	38.18 S	177.40 E
Moung Roessei	110	12.46 N	103.27 E
Mounianghi ≃	152	0.32 N	12.52 E
Mounier, Mont Λ	62	44.09 N	6.58 E
Mounimangqishan ⩕	102	32.35 N	100.35 E
Mounlapamôk	110	14.20 N	105.52 E
Mount, Cape ➤	150	6.47 N	11.20 W
Mount Aetna	208	40.25 N	76.18 W
Mountain	190	45.11 N	88.28 W
Mountain □[4]	116	17.20 N	121.10 E
Mountain ≃	180	65.41 N	128.50 W
Mountainair	200	34.31 N	106.15 W
Mountain Ash	42	51.42 N	3.24 W
Mountain Brook	194	33.29 N	86.46 W
Mountain Chute Dam ➛[6]	212	45.11 N	76.54 W
Mountain City, Ga., U.S.	192	34.55 N	83.23 W
Mountain City, Nev., U.S.	204	41.50 N	115.58 W
Mountain City, Tenn., U.S.	192	36.28 N	81.48 W
Mountain Creek	194	32.43 N	86.29 W
Mountain Creek ≃, Pa., U.S.	208	40.09 N	77.11 W
Mountain Creek ≃, Tex., U.S.	222	32.42 N	96.58 W
Mountain Creek Lake ⊜[1]	222	32.43 N	96.58 W
Mountain Dale	210	41.41 N	74.32 W
Mountain Grove	194	37.08 N	92.16 W
Mountain Home, Ark., U.S.	194	36.20 N	92.23 W
Mountain Home, Idaho, U.S.	202	43.08 N	115.41 W
Mountainhome, Pa., U.S.	210	41.11 N	75.17 W
Mountain Home Air Force Base ■	202	43.03 N	115.52 W
Mountain Iron	190	47.32 N	92.37 W
Mountain Lake, Fla., U.S.	220	27.57 N	81.36 W
Mountain Lake, Minn., U.S.	198	43.57 N	94.56 W
Mountain Lake ⊜, Ont., Can.	212	44.59 N	78.43 W
Mountain Lake ⊜, Ont., Can.	212	44.42 N	81.03 W
Mountain Lake ⊜, N.J., U.S.	276	40.53 N	74.27 W
Mountain Lakes	210	40.54 N	74.27 W
Mountain Lodge	210	41.23 N	74.09 W
Mountain Nile (Baḥr al-Jabal) ≃	136	9.30 N	30.30 E
Mountain Park	182	52.55 N	117.14 W
Mountain Pine	194	34.34 N	93.10 W
Mountain Point	180	55.18 N	131.32 W
Mountain Ranch	226	38.14 N	120.33 W
Mountainside	208	40.40 N	74.21 W
Mountain Spring Lakes	276	41.02 N	74.23 W
Mountain Valley Lake ⊜	279b	40.18 N	79.35 W
Mountain View, Ark., U.S.	194	35.52 N	92.07 W
Mountain View, Calif., U.S.	226	37.23 N	122.04 W
Mountain View, Mo., U.S.	194	36.59 N	91.42 W
Mountain View, Okla., U.S.	196	35.06 N	98.45 W
Mountain View, Wyo., U.S.	200	41.16 N	110.20 W
Mountain View, Wyo., U.S.	200	42.52 N	106.55 W
Mountain View Acres	228	34.31 N	117.24 W
Mountain Village	180	62.05 N	163.44 W
Mountain Zebra National Park ♠	158	32.16 S	25.29 E
Mount Airy, Md., U.S.	188	39.23 N	77.09 W
Mount Airy, N.C., U.S.	192	36.31 N	80.37 W
Mount Airy ➛[8]	285	40.04 N	75.12 W
Mount Albert	212	44.08 N	79.19 W
Mount Alford	171a	28.04 S	152.36 E
Mount Alida	158	29.09 S	30.18 E
Mount Alverno	285	39.53 N	75.25 W
Mount Angel	224	45.04 N	122.48 W
Mount Ann Park ♠	283	42.37 N	70.44 W
Mount Apo National Park ♠	116	6.57 N	125.16 E

PORTUGUÊS

Nome	Página	Lat.°′	Long.°′ W=Oeste
Mount Arayat National Park ♠	116	15.13 N	120.46 E
Mount Arlington	210	40.56 N	74.38 W
Mount Assiniboine Provincial Park ♠	182	50.54 N	115.40 W
Mount Auburn	219	39.46 N	89.16 W
Mount Augustus	162	24.19 S	116.54 E
Mount Ayliff	158	30.54 S	29.20 E
Mount Ayr, Ind., U.S.	216	40.57 N	87.18 W
Mount Ayr, Iowa, U.S.	198	40.43 N	94.14 W
Mount Baldy	280	34.14 N	117.40 W
Mount Barker, Austl.	162	34.38 S	117.40 E
Mount Barker, Austl.	168b	35.04 S	138.52 E
Mount Bellew Bridge	48	53.28 N	8.29 W
Mount Bethel	210	40.54 N	75.07 W
Mount Blanchard	216	40.54 N	83.33 W
Mount Bold Reservoir ⊜[1]	168b	35.07 S	138.42 E
Mount Brydges	214	42.54 N	81.29 W
Mount Buller	169	37.10 S	146.27 E
Mount Calm	222	31.45 N	96.53 W
Mount Carmel, Newf., Can.	186	47.09 N	53.29 W
Mount Carmel, Ill., U.S.	194	38.25 N	87.46 W
Mount Carmel, Ky., U.S.	218	38.29 N	83.38 W
Mount Carmel, Ohio, U.S.	218	39.06 N	84.21 W
Mount Carmel, Pa., U.S.	208	40.48 N	76.25 W
Mount Carmel Heights	218	39.07 N	84.18 W
Mount Carroll	190	42.06 N	89.58 W
Mount Cavenagh	162	25.58 S	133.15 E
Mount Charles	275b	43.41 N	79.40 W
Mount Clare	188	39.13 N	80.21 W
Mount Clemens	214	42.36 N	82.53 W
Mount Colah	274a	33.41 S	151.07 E
Mount Compass	168b	35.22 S	138.37 E
Mount Cook National Park ♠	172	43.35 S	170.15 E
Mount Cory	216	40.56 N	83.50 W
Mount Crawford	168b	34.40 S	138.57 E
Mount Crosby	171a	27.32 S	152.48 E
Mount Dandenong	274b	37.50 S	145.22 E
Mount Dennis ➛[8]	275b	43.42 N	79.30 W
Mount Desert Island I	188	44.20 N	68.20 W
Mount Diablo Creek ≃	282	38.02 N	122.02 W
Mount Diablo State Park ♠	226	37.51 N	121.55 W
Mount Dora	220	28.48 N	81.38 W
Mount Doreen	162	22.03 S	131.18 E
Mount Druitt	274a	33.46 S	150.49 E
Mount Dutton	162	27.50 S	135.43 E
Mount Eaton	214	40.42 N	81.42 W
Mount Eba	166	30.12 S	135.40 E
Mount Eden	226	37.38 N	122.06 W
Mount Eden Creek ≃	282	37.36 N	122.09 W
Mount Edgecumbe	180	57.03 N	135.21 W
Mount Edwards	171a	28.01 S	152.31 E
Mount Elgon National Park ♠	154	1.07 N	34.44 E
Mount Emu Creek ≃	169	38.18 S	142.55 E
Mount Enterprise	222	31.55 N	94.41 W
Mount Ephraim	285	39.53 N	75.06 W
Mount Evelyn	274b	37.47 S	145.23 E
Mount Fern	276	40.52 N	74.34 W
Mount Field National Park ♠	166	43.10 S	146.45 E
Mount Fletcher	158	30.40 S	28.30 E
Mount Forest	212	43.59 N	80.44 W
Mount Freedom	210	40.50 N	74.34 W
Mount Frere	158	31.00 S	28.58 E
Mount Gambier	166	37.50 S	140.46 E
Mount Garnet	166	17.41 S	145.07 E
Mount Gay	188	37.51 N	82.00 W
Mount Gilead, N.C., U.S.	192	35.10 N	79.56 W
Mount Gilead, Ohio, U.S.	214	40.33 N	82.50 W
Mount Glorious National Park ♠	171a	27.19 S	152.47 E
Mount Gravatt	171a	27.33 S	153.06 E
Mount Greenwood ➛[8]	278	41.42 N	87.43 W
Mount Hagen	164	5.50 S	144.15 E
Mount Hawthorn	168a	31.55 S	115.50 E
Mount Healthy	218	39.14 N	84.33 W
Mount Hebron	284b	39.18 N	76.50 W
Mount Helena	168a	31.53 S	116.13 E
Mount Hermon, Calif., U.S.	226	37.03 N	122.04 W
Mount Hermon, Mass., U.S.	207	42.40 N	72.29 W
Mount Holly, N.J., U.S.	208	39.59 N	74.47 W
Mount Holly, N.C., U.S.	192	35.18 N	81.01 W
Mount Holly Springs	208	40.07 N	77.11 W
Mount Hope, Austl.	166	34.07 S	135.23 E
Mount Hope, Ont., Can.	212	43.09 N	79.55 W
Mount Hope, Kans., U.S.	198	37.52 N	97.40 W
Mount Hope, N.J., U.S.	276	40.56 N	74.33 W
Mount Hope, Ohio, U.S.	214	40.38 N	81.47 W
Mount Hope, W. Va., U.S.	188	37.54 N	81.10 W
Mount Hope Lake ⊜	276	40.56 N	74.32 W
Mount Horeb	190	43.00 N	89.44 W
Mount Houston	222	29.54 N	95.18 W
Mount Howitt	166	26.31 S	142.16 E
Mount Hunter Rivulet ≃	274a	34.02 S	150.40 E
Mount Ida	194	34.34 N	93.38 W
Mount Isa	166	20.44 S	139.30 E
Mount Jackson, Pa., U.S.	214	40.58 N	80.26 W
Mount Jackson, Va., U.S.	188	38.45 N	78.39 W
Mount Jewett	214	41.44 N	78.38 W
Mount Juliet	194	36.12 N	86.31 W
Mount Kenya National Park ♠	154	0.09 S	37.19 E
Mount Kisco	210	41.12 N	73.44 W
Mount Kokeby	168a	32.13 S	116.58 E
Mountlake Terrace	224	47.47 N	122.18 W
Mount Laurel	285	39.56 N	74.54 W
Mount Lebanon	214	40.23 N	80.03 W
Mount Liberty	214	40.21 N	82.38 W
Mount Lofty Ranges ⩕, Austl.	168b	35.15 S	138.50 E
Mount Lofty Ranges ⩕, Austl.	168b	34.45 S	139.00 E
Mount Magnet	162	28.04 S	117.49 E
Mount Manara	166	32.29 S	143.56 E
Mount Margaret	166	26.54 S	143.21 E
Mount Marion	210	42.02 N	73.59 W
Mount Martha	169	38.17 S	145.01 E
Mount Maunganui	172	37.37 S	176.11 E
Mount Mayon National Park ♠	116	13.16 N	123.39 E
Mount McKinley National Park ♠	180	63.30 N	150.00 W
Mount Mee	171a	27.04 S	152.46 E
Mountmellick	48	53.07 N	7.20 W
Mount Misery Point ➤	276	40.58 N	73.05 W
Mount Molloy	164	16.41 S	145.20 E
Mount Monger	162	30.59 S	121.53 E
Mount Morgan	166	23.39 S	150.23 E
Mount Morris, Ill., U.S.	190	42.03 N	89.26 W
Mount Morris, Mich., U.S.	190	43.07 N	83.42 W
Mount Morris, N.Y., U.S.	210	42.44 N	77.53 W
Mount Mulligan	166	16.51 S	144.52 E
Mount Nebo	279b	40.33 N	80.06 W
Mount Nebo National Park ♠	171a	27.22 S	152.43 E
Mountnessing	260	51.39 N	0.21 E
Mount Nimba National Park ♠	150	7.40 N	8.27 W
Mount Olive, Ill., U.S.	219	39.04 N	89.43 W
Mount Olive, Miss., U.S.	194	31.46 N	89.39 W
Mount Olive, N.C., U.S.	192	35.12 N	78.04 W
Mount Oliver	279b	40.28 N	79.59 W
Mount Olivet	218	38.32 N	84.02 W
Mount Orab	218	39.02 N	83.56 W
Mount Penn	208	40.20 N	75.54 W
Mount Perry	166	25.11 S	151.39 E
Mount Pilchuck State Park ♠	224	48.04 N	121.48 W
Mount Pleasant, Austl.	168b	34.47 S	139.02 E
Mount Pleasant, Ont., Can.	212	43.05 N	80.19 W
Mount Pleasant, Ind., U.S.	218	38.07 N	86.31 W
Mount Pleasant, Iowa, U.S.	190	40.58 N	91.33 W
Mount Pleasant, Mich., U.S.	190	43.35 N	84.47 W
Mount Pleasant, N.C., U.S.	192	35.24 N	80.26 W
Mount Pleasant, Ohio, U.S.	214	40.11 N	80.48 W
Mount Pleasant, Pa., U.S.	214	40.09 N	79.33 W
Mount Pleasant, S.C., U.S.	192	32.47 N	79.52 W
Mount Pleasant, Tenn., U.S.	194	35.32 N	87.13 W
Mount Pleasant, Tex., U.S.	222	33.09 N	94.58 W
Mount Pleasant, Utah, U.S.	200	39.33 N	111.27 W
Mount Pleasant Mills	208	40.43 N	77.01 W
Mount Pleasant Park ♠	284b	39.22 N	76.35 W
Mount Pocono	210	41.08 N	75.22 W
Mount Pritchard	274a	33.54 S	150.54 E
Mount Prospect, S. Afr.	158	27.29 S	29.53 E
Mount Prospect, Ill., U.S.	216	42.04 N	87.56 W
Mount Pulaski	219	40.01 N	89.17 W
Mount Rainier	284c	38.56 N	76.58 W
Mount Rainier National Park ♠	224	46.52 N	121.43 W
Mountrath	48	53.00 N	7.27 W
Mount Rebecca	162	26.48 S	135.10 E
Mount Repose	218	39.10 N	84.14 W
Mount Revelstoke National Park ♠	182	51.06 N	118.00 W
Mount Riddock	162	23.03 S	134.40 E
Mount Robson Provincial Park ♠	182	52.58 N	118.50 W
Mount Roskill	172	36.55 S	174.45 E
Mount Royal	285	39.49 N	75.13 W
Mount Rushmore National Memorial ⊥	198	43.50 N	103.24 W
Mount Sandiman	162	24.24 S	115.23 E
Mount Sarah	162	26.57 S	135.22 E
Mount Savage	188	39.42 N	78.53 W
Mount's Bay C	42	50.03 N	5.25 W
Mount Selinda	154	20.25 S	32.43 E
Mount Selman	222	32.04 N	95.17 W
Mount Seymour Provincial Park ➛[4]	182	49.23 N	122.57 W
Mount Shasta	204	41.19 N	122.19 W
Mount Sinai	276	40.57 N	73.02 W
Mount Sinai Harbor C	276	40.57 N	73.02 W
Mount Sinai Ridge Λ	218	39.04 N	84.58 W
Mount Somers	172	43.43 S	171.24 E
Mountsorrel	42	52.44 N	1.07 W
Mount Spokane State Park ♠	202	47.58 N	117.13 W
Mount Sterling, Ill., U.S.	219	39.59 N	90.45 W
Mount Sterling, Ky., U.S.	192	38.04 N	83.56 W
Mount Sterling, Mo., U.S.	219	38.28 N	91.38 W
Mount Sterling, Ohio, U.S.	218	39.43 N	83.16 W
Mount Stewart, P.E.I., Can.	186	46.22 N	62.52 W
Mount Stewart, S. Afr.	158	33.10 S	24.26 E
Mount Stromlo Observatory ʋ[3]	171b	35.20 S	149.00 E
Mount Summit	218	40.00 N	85.23 W
Mount Surprise	166	18.09 S	144.19 E
Mount Sylvia	171a	27.44 S	152.14 E
Mount Tamalpais State Park ♠	226	37.54 N	122.34 W
Mount Torrens	168b	34.52 S	138.57 E
Mount Tremper	210	42.03 N	74.17 W
Mount Uniacke	186	44.54 N	63.50 W
Mount Union	214	40.23 N	77.53 W
Mount Upton	210	42.26 N	75.23 W
Mount Vernon, Austl.	162	24.13 S	118.14 E
Mount Vernon, Ala., U.S.	194	31.05 N	88.01 W
Mount Vernon, Ga., U.S.	192	32.11 N	82.36 W
Mount Vernon, Ill., U.S.	219	38.19 N	88.55 W
Mount Vernon, Ind., U.S.	194	37.56 N	87.54 W
Mount Vernon, Iowa, U.S.	190	41.55 N	91.23 W
Mount Vernon, Ky., U.S.	192	37.21 N	84.20 W
Mount Vernon, Mo., U.S.	194	37.06 N	93.49 W
Mount Vernon, N.Y., U.S.	210	40.54 N	73.50 W
Mount Vernon, N.Y., U.S.	210	42.45 N	78.53 W
Mount Vernon, Ohio, U.S.	214	40.23 N	82.29 W
Mount Vernon, Oreg., U.S.	202	44.25 N	119.07 W
Mount Vernon, Pa., U.S.	279b	40.17 N	79.48 W
Mount Vernon, S. Dak., U.S.	198	43.43 N	104.16 W
Mount Vernon, Tex., U.S.	222	33.11 N	95.13 W
Mount Vernon, Wash., U.S.	224	48.25 N	122.20 W
Mount Vernon ⊥	208	38.47 N	77.06 W
Mount Victoria	170	33.35 S	150.15 E
Mount Victory	216	40.32 N	83.31 W
Mount View	207	41.39 N	71.25 W
Mountville	208	40.02 N	76.26 W
Mount Vision	210	42.35 N	75.04 W
Mount Washington ➛[8]	284b	39.22 N	76.40 W
Mount Waverley	274b	37.53 S	145.08 E
Mount Wedge, Austl.	162	22.45 S	132.09 E
Mount Wedge, Austl.	162	33.29 S	135.10 E
Mount Wellington	172	36.54 S	174.51 E
Mount Willoughby	162	27.58 S	134.08 E
Mount Wilson Observatory ʋ[3]	228	34.14 N	118.03 W
Mount Wolf	208	40.04 N	76.43 W
Mount Zion	219	39.46 N	88.53 W
Mounyaz	146	10.41 N	21.18 E
Mouping	98	37.24 N	121.35 E
Moura, Bra.	246	1.27 S	61.38 W
Moura, Port.	34	38.08 N	7.27 W
Moura, Tchad	146	13.47 N	21.13 E
Mourdi, Dépression du •[7]	146	18.10 N	23.00 E
Mourdiah	150	14.28 N	7.28 W
Mouriès	62	43.41 N	4.52 E
Mourmelon-le-Grand	50	49.08 N	4.22 E
Mourne ≃	48	54.49 N	7.28 W
Mourne Beg ≃	48	54.41 N	7.39 W
Mourne Mountains ⩕	48	54.10 N	6.05 W
Mousa I	46	60.00 N	1.11 W
Mouscron	50	50.44 N	3.13 E
Mousgougou	146	10.47 N	16.09 E
Moussa Ali Λ	144	12.28 N	42.24 E
Mousseaux-sur-Seine	261	49.03 N	1.39 E
Moussey	58	48.40 N	6.47 E
Moussoro	146	13.39 N	16.29 E
Moussy-le-Neuf	261	49.04 N	2.36 E
Moussy-le-Vieux	261	49.03 N	2.38 E
Moustiers-Sainte-Marie	62	43.51 N	6.13 E
Mouthe	58	46.43 N	6.12 E
Mouthier-Haute-Pierre	58	47.02 N	6.16 E
Moutier	58	47.17 N	7.23 E
Moûtiers	62	45.29 N	6.32 E
Moutiers-au-Perche	50	48.29 N	0.51 E
Moutnice	61	49.02 N	16.46 E
Moutohora	172	38.17 S	177.32 E
Moutomoukadi	152	4.41 S	13.15 E
Moutong	112	0.28 N	121.13 E
Mouton Island I	186	43.54 N	64.46 W
Moux	50	47.10 N	4.09 E
Mouy	50	49.19 N	2.19 E
Mouydir, Monts du ⩕	148	24.45 N	4.05 E
Mouyombi-Tali	152	2.32 S	10.48 E
Mouyondzi	152	3.58 S	13.57 E
Mouzákion	38	39.26 N	21.40 E
Mouzon	56	49.36 N	5.05 E
Mouzon ≃	58	48.21 N	5.41 E
Móvano	232	26.42 N	103.39 W
Moville, Eire	48	55.11 N	7.03 W
Moville, Iowa, U.S.	198	42.29 N	96.04 W
Mowangzui	100	30.31 N	113.34 E
Moweaqua	219	39.38 N	89.01 W
Mowein	140	7.36 N	28.11 E
Mowry Slough ≃	282	37.29 N	122.03 W
Mowrystown	218	39.02 N	83.45 W
Mowshera	123	34.01 N	71.59 E
Moxhe	56	50.38 N	5.05 E
Moxi	107	30.18 N	105.41 E
Moxico □[5]	152	13.00 S	20.30 E
Moxotó ≃	250	9.19 S	38.14 W
Moy	48	54.27 N	6.42 W
Moy ≃	48	54.12 N	9.08 W
Moya, Comores	157a	12.18 S	44.27 E
Moya, Perú	248	12.24 S	75.10 W
Moyagee	162	27.45 S	117.54 E
Moyahua	234	21.16 N	103.10 W
Moyale, Kenya	154	3.32 N	39.03 E
Moyale, Yai.	144	3.30 N	39.07 E
Moyamba	150	8.10 N	12.26 W
Moycullen	48	53.21 N	9.09 W
Moydans	62	44.24 N	5.30 E
Moÿ-de-l'aisne	50	49.45 N	3.22 E
Moyedao I	98	36.55 N	122.32 E
Moyen Atlas ⩕	148	33.30 N	5.00 W
Moyen-Chari □[5]	146	9.00 N	18.00 E
Moyenmoutier	58	48.23 N	6.55 E
Moyenneville	50	50.04 N	1.45 E
Moyen-Ogooué □[4]	152	0.30 S	10.30 E
Moyenvic	56	48.47 N	6.33 E
Moyeuvre-Grande	56	49.15 N	6.02 E
Moyie	182	49.17 N	115.50 W
Moyie ≃	182	48.42 N	116.11 W
Moyie Springs	202	48.43 N	116.11 W
Moylan	285	39.54 N	75.23 W
Moyle ≃	48	52.24 N	7.39 W
Moyo	154	3.39 N	31.43 E
Moyo ≃	115b	8.26 S	117.28 E
Moyo, Pulau I	115b	8.15 S	117.34 E
Moyobamba	248	6.03 S	76.58 W
Moyock	208	36.32 N	76.11 W
Moyogalpa	236	11.32 N	85.42 W
Moyu	120	37.17 N	79.44 E
Moyuta, Volcán Λ[1]	236	14.02 N	90.06 W
Moza	132	31.47 N	35.09 E
M'oža ≃, S.S.S.R.	76	55.27 N	30.43 E
M'oža ≃, S.S.S.R.	80	58.23 N	44.54 E
Možajevka	83	48.44 N	39.45 E
Možajsk	82	55.30 N	36.01 E
Možajskij	265a	59.43 N	30.07 E
Možajskoje Vodochranilišče ⊜[1]	82	55.35 N	35.50 E
Mozambique → Moçambique	154	15.03 S	40.42 E
Mozambique □[1]	138	18.15 S	35.00 E
Mozambique ✣[3]	10	32.00 S	35.00 E
Mozambique Channel ⋓	138	19.00 S	41.00 E
Mozarlândia	255	14.47 S	50.35 W
Možarovka	86	51.09 N	59.05 E
Možarov Majdan	80	55.37 N	45.53 E
Možary	80	53.53 N	41.02 E
Mozdok	84	43.44 N	44.38 E
Možga	80	56.23 N	52.17 E
Mozhabong Lake ⊜	190	46.57 N	82.05 W
Mozhugongka	120	29.50 N	91.45 E
Mozia ⊥	70	37.52 N	12.28 E
Mozichang	107	29.20 N	103.53 E
Mozolevo	76	59.19 N	33.51 E
Mozu	270	34.34 N	134.29 E
Mozuli	76	56.36 N	28.11 E
Mozyr'	78	52.03 N	29.14 E
Mozzanica	62	45.29 N	9.41 E
Mozzano	66	42.50 N	13.31 E
Mozzate	266b	45.41 N	8.57 E
Mpaka	158	26.26 S	31.47 E
Mpala	154	6.45 S	29.31 E
Mpama ≃	152	0.57 S	15.39 E
Mpanda	154	6.22 S	31.02 E
Mpé	152	2.54 S	14.43 E
Mpelé, Mont Λ	152	3.15 S	11.14 E
Mpese	152	5.14 S	15.33 E
Mpessoba	150	12.40 N	5.43 W
Mphoengs	154	21.10 S	27.51 E
Mpigi	154	0.13 N	32.42 E
Mpika	154	11.54 S	31.26 E
Mpila	273b	4.14 S	15.18 E
Mpimbe	154	15.18 S	35.04 E
Mpoka	152	1.26 S	17.02 E
Mponela	154	13.21 S	33.43 E
Mporokoso	154	9.23 S	30.05 E
Mpouya	152	2.37 S	16.13 E
Mpraeso	150	6.35 N	0.44 W
Mpui	154	8.21 S	31.50 E
Mpulungu	154	8.46 S	31.07 E
Mpwapwa	154	6.21 S	36.29 E
Mqanduli	158	31.48 S	28.46 E
Mrągowo	30	53.52 N	21.19 E
Mrakovo	86	52.43 N	56.38 E
Mranggen	115a	7.01 S	110.31 E
Mras-su ≃	86	53.45 N	87.49 E
Mrewa	154	17.39 S	31.47 E
Mrhila, Djebel Λ	148	35.25 N	9.14 E
Mrijo	154	5.10 S	36.15 E
Mrkonjić Grad	36	44.25 N	17.05 E
Mrkopalj	36	45.19 N	14.51 E
Mrocza	30	53.14 N	17.36 E
Msagali	154	6.21 S	36.18 E
Msaken	148	35.44 N	10.35 E
Msata	154	6.20 S	38.23 E
Mšec	54	50.10 N	13.54 E
Mšeno	54	50.27 N	14.38 E
M'Sila	148	35.46 N	4.31 E
Mšinskaja	76	59.01 N	29.57 E
Msoro Mission	154	13.36 S	31.55 E
Msta	76	57.55 N	34.29 E
Msta ≃	76	58.25 N	31.20 E
Mstera	80	56.23 N	41.56 E
Mstislavl'	76	54.02 N	31.42 E
Mstiž	76	54.34 N	28.10 E
Mszana Dolna	30	49.42 N	20.05 E
Mszczonów	30	51.58 N	20.31 E
Mtakataka	154	14.12 S	34.32 E
Mtakuja	154	7.22 S	30.37 E
Mtama	154	10.18 S	39.22 E
Mtamvuna ≃	158	31.06 S	30.12 E
Mtelo Λ	154	1.39 N	35.23 E
Mtilikwe ≃	154	21.09 S	31.30 E
Mtito Andei	154	2.41 S	38.10 E
Mtoko	154	17.24 S	32.13 E
Mtowabaga	154	2.30 S	35.53 E
Mtubatuba	158	28.30 S	32.08 E
Mtunzini	158	28.57 S	31.46 E
Mtwara	154	10.16 S	40.11 E
Mtwara □[4]	154	10.00 S	39.00 E
Mtyangimbori	154	10.16 S	35.31 E
Mu ≃, Mya.	110	21.56 N	95.38 E
Mu ≃, Nihon	92a	42.33 N	141.56 E
Mu, Cerro Λ	246	9.29 N	73.07 W
Mua	174w	21.11 S	175.07 W
Muacandala	152	10.02 S	19.40 E
Mualama	154	16.53 S	38.17 E
Mualang	112	0.42 N	111.18 E
Mu'allaqah	140	13.28 N	23.57 E
Muan	98	34.58 N	126.26 E
Muaná	250	1.32 S	49.13 W
Muanda	152	5.56 S	12.21 E
Muangai	152	12.32 S	19.51 E
Muang Bèng	110	20.22 N	101.44 E
Muang Hay	110	21.03 N	101.49 E
Muang Hinboun	110	17.35 N	104.36 E
Muang Hôngsa	110	19.43 N	101.20 E
Muang Houn	110	20.09 N	101.27 E
Muang Hounxianghoung	110	21.37 N	102.18 E
Muang Huang	110	18.45 N	103.42 E
Muang Khammouan	110	17.24 N	104.48 E
Muang Khao	110	19.47 N	103.29 E
Muang Khi	110	18.27 N	101.46 E
Muang Không	110	14.07 N	105.51 E
Muang Khôngxédôn	110	15.34 N	105.49 E
Muang Khoua	110	21.05 N	102.31 E
Muang La	110	20.52 N	102.07 E
Muang Liap	110	18.29 N	101.40 E
Muang Long	110	20.57 N	100.48 E
Muang Meung	110	20.43 N	100.28 E
Muang Ngoy	110	20.43 N	102.41 E
Muang Nong	110	16.22 N	106.30 E
Muang Ou Nua	110	22.18 N	101.48 E
Muang Ou Tai	110	22.07 N	101.48 E
Muang Pakbèng	110	19.54 N	101.08 E
Muang Pak-Lay	110	18.12 N	101.25 E
Muang Paktha	110	20.06 N	100.36 E
Muang Pakxan	110	18.22 N	103.39 E
Muang Peun	110	20.13 N	103.52 E
Muang Phalan	110	16.39 N	105.34 E
Muang Phiang	110	19.06 N	101.32 E
Muang Phônthong	110	15.05 N	105.39 E
Muang Phoun	110	19.07 N	102.43 E
Muang Sam Sip	110	15.31 N	104.44 E
Muang Sing	110	21.11 N	101.09 E
Muang Soum	110	18.45 N	102.36 E
Muang Souvannakhili	110	15.23 N	105.49 E
Muang Souy	110	19.33 N	102.52 E
Muang Sung	110	20.19 N	102.27 E
Muang Thadua	110	19.26 N	101.50 E
Muang Thatèng	110	15.26 N	106.23 E
Muang Thathôm	110	19.00 N	103.36 E
Muang Va	110	21.53 N	102.19 E
Muang Vangviang	110	18.56 N	102.27 E
Muang Vapi	110	15.40 N	105.55 E
Muang Xaignabouri	110	19.15 N	101.45 E
Muang Xamtong	110	19.51 N	103.51 E
Muang Xay	110	20.42 N	101.59 E
Muang Xépôn	110	16.41 N	106.14 E
Muang Xon	110	20.27 N	103.19 E
Muang Yo	110	21.31 N	101.51 E
Muang You	110	19.49 N	102.50 E
Muanza	156	18.59 S	34.48 E
Muar (Bandar Maharani)	114	2.02 N	102.34 E
Muar ≃	114	2.03 N	102.35 E
Muara	112	5.02 N	115.02 E
Muaraaman	112	3.07 S	102.12 E
Muaraancalung	112	0.27 N	116.41 E
Muarabeliti	112	3.15 S	103.02 E
Muarabenangin	112	0.58 S	115.19 E
Muarabinuangeun	115a	6.50 S	105.53 E
Muarabulian	112	1.43 S	103.15 E
Muarabungo	112	1.28 S	102.07 E
Muaradua	112	4.32 S	104.05 E
Muaraenim	112	3.39 S	103.48 E
Muaragusung	112	1.35 N	117.17 E
Muarajuloi	112	0.12 S	114.03 E
Muarakaman	112	0.09 S	116.43 E
Muarakelingi	112	3.05 S	103.14 E
Muarakumpe	112	1.24 S	104.00 E
Muaralabuh	112	1.29 S	101.03 E
Muaralakitan	112	2.51 S	103.19 E
Muaralasan	112	1.48 N	117.12 E
Muaralembu	112	0.24 S	101.21 E
Muaramawai	112	0.37 N	116.49 E
Muarapangean	112	2.38 N	116.41 E
Muarapantai	112	0.45 S	101.43 E
Muarapayang	112	1.32 S	115.48 E
Muararupit	112	2.44 S	102.54 E
Muarasabak	112	1.08 S	103.51 E
Muarasiberut	108	1.36 S	99.11 E
Muarasipongi	112	0.37 N	99.51 E
Muaratebo	112	1.30 S	102.26 E
Muarateladang	112	2.50 S	103.58 E
Muaratembesi	112	1.42 S	103.07 E
Muaratewe	112	0.57 S	114.53 E
Muaratuhup	112	0.37 S	114.50 E
Muaratunan	112	1.24 S	116.39 E
Muarawahau	112	1.02 N	116.52 E
Muāri, Rās ➤	120	24.49 N	66.40 E
Muasdale	46	55.36 N	5.41 W
Muá Ximica	152	9.50 S	18.41 E
Mubārakpur	124	26.05 N	83.18 E
Mubārakpur Dabās ➛[8]	272a	28.43 N	77.03 E
Mubayyad ⊤[4]	142	30.55 N	32.48 E
Mubende	154	0.35 N	31.23 E
Mubende □[5]	154	0.45 N	31.10 E
Mubi	146	10.18 N	13.20 E
Mubian	102	23.16 N	105.54 E
Mubur, Pulau I	112	3.20 N	106.12 E
Mucacata	154	13.20 S	39.59 E
Mucaitá ≃	250	6.59 S	42.40 W
Mucajaí ≃	246	2.25 N	60.52 W
Mucambo	250	3.54 S	40.44 W
Mucári	152	9.30 S	16.54 E
Muccan	162	20.38 S	120.04 E
Muccia	66	43.05 N	13.02 E
Much	56	50.54 N	7.25 E
Mucha	269d	24.59 N	121.34 E
Muchangfu	100	31.55 N	116.35 E
Muchanovo	82	56.31 N	38.20 E
Muchavec ≃	76	52.05 N	23.39 E
Much Dewchurch	42	51.59 N	2.46 W
Muchea	168a	31.35 S	115.59 E
Mücheln	54	51.18 N	11.48 E
Muchen	89	48.10 N	136.13 E
Muchengjie	107	29.47 N	103.29 E
Much Hoole	262	53.42 N	2.48 W
Muchinga Escarpment •[4]	154	13.40 S	31.00 E
Muchinga Mountains ⩕	154	12.00 S	31.45 E
Muchino, S.S.S.R.	80	58.11 N	51.02 E

≃	River	Fluss	Río	Rivière	Rio
☲	Canal	Kanal	Canal	Canal	Canal
ᒪ	Waterfall, Rapids	Wasserfall, Stromschnellen	Cascada, Rápidos	Chute d'eau, Rapides	Cascata, Rápidos
⋓	Strait	Meeresstrasse	Estrecho	Détroit	Estreito
C	Bay, Gulf	Bucht, Golf	Bahía, Golfo	Baie, Golfe	Baía, Golfo
⊜	Lake, Lakes	See, Seen	Lago, Lagos	Lac, Lacs	Lago, Lagos
☷	Swamp	Sumpf	Pantano	Marais	Pântano
⍓	Ice Features, Glacier	Eis- und Gletscherformen	Accidentes Glaciales	Formes glaciaires	Acidentes Glaciares
⊤	Other Hydrographic Features	Andere Hydrographische Objekte	Otros Elementos Hidrográficos	Autres données hydrographiques	Outros Elementos Hidrográficos

✣	Submarine Features	Untermeerische Objekte	Accidentes Submarinos	Formes de relief sous-marin	Acidentes Submarinos
□	Political Unit	Politische Einheit	Unidad Politica	Entité politique	Unidade Política
ʋ	Cultural Institution	Kulturelle Institution	Institución Cultural	Institution culturelle	Instituição Cultural
⊥	Historical Site	Historische Stätte	Sitio Histórico	Site historique	Sitio Histórico
♠	Recreational Site	Erholungs- und Ferienort	Sitio de Recreo	Centre de loisirs	Sítio de Lazer
⊠	Airport	Flughafen	Aeropuerto	Aéroport	Aeroporto
■	Military Installation	Militäranlage	Instalación Militar	Installation militaire	Instalação Militar
➛	Miscellaneous	Verschiedenes	Misceláneo	Divers	Miscelânea

Muchino, S.S.S.R. 89 52.16 N 127.14 E
Muchor-Konduj 88 52.25 N 113.16 E
Muchoršibir' 88 51.03 N 107.50 E
Muchrani 84 41.56 N 44.35 E
Muchtadir 84 41.41 N 48.46 E
Muchtolovo 80 55.27 N 43.13 E
Muchuan 107 28.55 N 103.58 E
Much Wenlock 42 52.36 N 2.34 W
Mucifal 266c 38.48 N 9.26 W
Mučikan 88 53.02 N 120.27 E
Muck I 46 56.50 N 6.15 W
Mücka 54 51.18 N 14.40 E
Muckadilla 166 26.35 S 148.23 E
Muckalee Creek ≃ 192 31.38 N 84.09 W
Mučkapskij 80 51.52 N 42.28 E
Mučkas 24 64.02 N 48.27 E
Mücke 56 50.38 N 9.03 E
Muckendorf an der Donau 264b 48.20 N 16.09 E
Mucking 260 51.30 N 0.26 E
Muckle Roe I 46a 60.22 N 1.27 W
Muckleshoot Indian Reservation ◆[4] 224 47.16 N 122.09 W
Mucoma 152 15.18 S 13.39 E
Mucope, Ang. 152 16.24 S 14.53 E
Mucope, Ang. 152 8.42 S 21.43 E
Mucrone, Monte ∧ 62 45.36 N 7.56 E
Mucubela 154 16.55 S 37.52 E
Mucuchíes 246 8.45 N 70.55 W
M'uc'ucl'u 84 40.28 N 47.55 E
Mucugê 255 13.00 S 41.23 W
Mucuim ≃ 248 6.33 S 64.18 W
Muculo 152 16.47 S 14.51 E
Muçum 252 29.10 S 51.53 W
Mucumbura 154 16.09 S 31.31 E
Mucun 100 26.44 N 114.00 E
Mucupia 156 18.01 S 36.48 E
Mucupina, Monte ∧ 236 15.08 N 86.38 W
Mucur 130 39.04 N 34.23 E
Mucuri 255 18.05 S 39.34 W
Mucuri ≃ 255 18.05 S 39.34 W
Mucusso 152 17.51 S 20.21 E
Mud ≃, Ky., U.S. 194 37.13 N 86.54 W
Mud ≃, W. Va., U.S. 188 38.25 N 82.17 W
Muda ≃ 114 5.33 N 100.22 E
Mudanjiang 89 44.35 N 129.36 E
Mudanjiang ≃ 89 46.22 N 129.33 E
Mudanya 130 40.22 N 28.52 E
Mudau 56 49.32 N 9.11 E
Mudaysīsāt, Jabal ∧ 132 31.39 N 36.14 E
Mud Creek ≃, U.S. 198 43.17 N 96.15 W
Mud Creek ≃, Ill., U.S. 219 38.21 N 89.48 W
Mud Creek ≃, Ind., U.S. 216 41.06 N 86.21 W
Mud Creek ≃, Ind., U.S. 216 40.26 N 85.55 W
Mud Creek ≃, Nebr., U.S. 198 41.01 N 98.54 W
Mud Creek ≃, N.Y., U.S. 210 43.05 N 78.43 W
Mud Creek ≃, N.Y., U.S. 210 42.17 N 77.13 W
Mud Creek ≃, N.Y., U.S. 210 42.59 N 77.23 W
Mud Creek ≃, Okla., U.S. 196 33.55 N 97.28 W
Mud Creek ≃, S. Dak., U.S. 198 45.11 N 98.24 W
Mud Creek ≃, Tex., U.S. 222 31.48 N 94.58 W
Mud Creek ≃, Vt., U.S. 206 45.02 N 72.12 W
Muddus Nationalpark ♦ 24 67.00 N 20.16 E
Muddy ≃, Nev., U.S. 204 36.27 N 114.22 W
Muddy ≃, Wash., U.S. 224 46.04 N 122.01 W
Muddy Boggy Creek ≃ 196 34.03 N 95.47 W
Muddy Branch ≃ 284c 39.03 N 77.18 W
Muddy Brook ≃ 276 41.07 N 73.20 W
Muddy Creek ≃, U.S. 276 41.03 N 74.02 W
Muddy Creek ≃, Mo., U.S. 194 38.51 N 93.03 W
Muddy Creek ≃, Mont., U.S. 202 47.56 N 111.46 W
Muddy Creek ≃, Ohio, U.S. 214 41.27 N 83.03 W
Muddy Creek ≃, Pa., U.S. 208 39.47 N 76.18 W
Muddy Creek ≃, Utah, U.S. 200 38.24 N 110.42 W
Muddy Creek ≃, Wyo., U.S. 198 42.35 N 104.57 W
Muddy Creek ≃, Wyo., U.S. 200 41.59 N 106.08 W
Muddy Creek ≃, Wyo., U.S. 200 41.32 N 110.13 W
Muddy Creek ≃, Wyo., U.S. 200 41.01 N 107.42 W
Muddy Creek ≃, Wyo., U.S. 202 43.17 N 108.14 W
Muddy Fork ≃ 224 46.22 N 121.34 W
Muddy Gut C 284b 39.17 N 76.26 W
Muddy Peak ∧ 204 36.18 N 114.42 W
Müden, B.R.D. 52 52.52 N 10.07 E
Müden, B.R.D. 54 52.31 N 10.22 E
Mudersbach 56 50.49 N 7.56 E
Mudgee 166 32.36 S 149.35 E
Mudgeeraba 171a 28.04 S 153.22 E
Mudhol 122 16.21 N 75.17 E
Mud Island I 171a 27.20 S 153.15 E
Mud Islands II 169 38.17 S 144.45 E
Mudjatik ≃ 184 56.02 N 107.36 W
Mudjuga 24 63.46 N 39.15 E
Mud Lake ⊜, Idaho, U.S. 202 43.53 N 112.24 W
Mud Lake ⊜, Minn., U.S. 198 48.20 N 95.58 W
Mud Lake ⊜, Nev., U.S. 204 37.52 N 117.04 W
Mud Lake ⊜, N.Y., U.S. 212 44.30 N 75.28 W
Mud Lake Reservoir ⊜[1] 198 45.50 N 98.10 W
Mudon 110 16.15 N 97.44 E
Mudongzhen 102 29.35 N 106.51 E
Mudu 106 31.15 N 120.30 E
Mudugh □[4] 144 5.50 N 47.10 E
Mudurnu 130 40.28 N 31.13 E
Mudurnu ≃ 130 40.49 N 30.33 E
M'ud'ur'um ≃ 85 40.53 N 76.36 E
Mueda 154 11.39 S 39.33 E
Muelle de los Bueyes 236 12.04 N 84.32 W
Mueller, Mount ∧ 162 19.54 S 127.51 E
Muenster 196 33.39 N 97.23 W
Muerchang 107 29.48 N 106.37 E
Muerte, Valle de la → Death Valley ∨ 204 36.30 N 117.00 W
Muerto, Mar C 234 16.10 N 94.10 W
Muerto, Mar → Dead Sea ⊜ 132 31.30 N 35.30 E
Mufulira 154 12.33 S 28.14 E
Mufuma 152 9.04 S 17.06 E
Mufushan ∧ 100 29.02 N 113.54 E
Mufushan ∧∧ 100 29.00 N 114.00 E
Muganskaja Step' ⌣ 84 39.40 N 48.15 E
Mugazine 158 26.07 S 32.30 E
Mugegawa 94 35.31 N 136.51 E
Mugello ∨ 66 43.55 N 11.30 E
Mügeln 54 51.14 N 13.02 E
Muger ≃ 144 9.54 N 37.57 E
Müggelberge ∧∧[2] 264a 52.25 N 13.39 E
Müggelheim ◆[8] 264a 52.25 N 13.40 E
Muggendorf 60 49.48 N 11.16 E
Muggia 64 45.36 N 13.46 E
Muggio 266b 45.36 N 9.14 E
Mughalsarai 124 25.18 N 83.07 E
Mughr 132 33.05 N 35.43 E
Mugi, Nihon 94 35.33 N 136.59 E
Mugi, Nihon 96 33.40 N 134.25 E
Mu Gia, Deo)(110 17.40 N 105.47 E
Muginga 152 8.20 S 17.37 E
Muğla 130 37.12 N 28.22 E
Muğla □[4] 130 37.10 N 28.30 E
Mugodžarskaja 86 48.36 N 58.27 E
Mugodžary ∧∧[2] 86 49.00 N 58.40 E
Mugombazi 154 5.50 S 30.14 E
Mugo-ri 98 38.58 N 126.31 E
Mugrejevskij 80 56.36 N 42.21 E
Mugron 32 43.45 N 0.45 W
Mūgu Karnāli ≃ 124 29.38 N 81.52 E
Mugur-Aksy 86 50.21 N 90.30 E
Mūḥ, Sabkhat ⊜ 130 34.30 N 38.20 E
Muhala 154 5.40 S 28.43 E
Muhamdi 124 27.57 N 80.13 E
Muḥammad, Ra's ≻ 140 27.44 N 34.15 E
Muhammadābād 124 26.02 N 83.23 E
Muhammadpur 126 23.24 N 89.36 E
Muḥammad Qawl 140 20.54 N 37.05 E
Muḥayshir, Birkat ⊜ 142 30.43 N 31.56 E
Muheza 154 5.10 S 38.47 E
Muḥīṭ, Maṣrif al- ≡ 273c 30.07 N 31.06 E
Mühl ≃ 60 48.25 N 13.59 E
Mühlacker 56 48.57 N 8.50 E
Mühlau 54 50.54 N 12.45 E
Mühlbach am Hochkönig 64 47.22 N 13.08 E
Muhlbach-sur-Munster 58 48.02 N 7.05 E
Mühlberg 54 51.26 N 13.13 E
Mühldorf 61 48.22 N 15.21 E
Mühldorf am Inn 60 48.15 N 12.32 E
Mühlen → Molini de Tures 64 46.54 N 11.56 E
Mühlenbeck 54 52.40 N 13.22 E
Mühlenbecker See ⊜ 264a 52.41 N 13.24 E
Muhlenberg 210 41.14 N 76.09 W
Mühlen-Berg ∧[2] 264a 52.23 N 13.15 E
Mühlen Eichsen 54 53.45 N 11.15 E
Mühlenfliess ≃ 264a 52.26 N 13.41 E
Mühlenrahmede 263 51.16 N 7.40 E
Mühlhausen, B.R.D. 263 51.33 N 7.44 E
Mühlhausen, D.D.R. 54 51.12 N 10.27 E
Mühlhausen im Täle 56 48.34 N 9.39 E
Mühlheim, B.R.D. 56 50.07 N 8.50 E
Mühlheim, B.R.D. 56 49.54 N 7.01 E
Mühlheim an der Donau 58 48.01 N 8.53 E
Mühlig-Hofmann Mountains ∧∧ 9 72.00 S 5.20 E
Mühlleiten 264b 48.10 N 16.34 E
Mühltroff 54 50.32 N 11.55 E
Mühlviertel ◆[1] 30 48.25 N 14.10 E
Muhola 26 63.20 N 25.05 E
Muhos 26 64.48 N 25.59 E
Muḥradah 130 35.15 N 36.35 E
Mühringen 58 48.25 N 8.46 E
Muhu I 76 58.38 N 23.15 E
Muhula 154 13.53 S 39.30 E
Muhulu 154 1.03 S 27.17 E
Muhushan 104 40.42 N 120.36 E
Muhutwe 154 1.33 S 31.42 E
Muhu Väin ʯ 76 58.45 N 23.20 E
Muhuwesi ≃ 154 11.16 S 37.58 E
Mui ≃ 152 17.51 S 15.41 E
Muick, Loch ⊜ 46 56.55 N 3.10 W
Muiden 52 52.19 N 5.04 E
Muiderslot ⊥ 52 52.20 N 5.10 E
Muides-sur-Loire 50 47.40 N 1.31 E
Muié 152 14.25 S 20.36 E
Muikaichi 96 34.21 N 131.56 E
Muikamachi 94 37.04 N 138.53 E
Muine Bheag 48 52.41 N 6.58 W
Muir, Mich., U.S. 216 43.00 N 84.56 W
Muir, Pa., U.S. 208 40.36 N 76.31 W
Muir, Mount ∧ 180 61.06 N 148.24 W
Muir Beach 282 37.52 N 122.35 W
Muirdrum 46 56.31 N 2.42 W
Muir Gorge ∨ 226 37.57 N 119.32 W
Muirkirk, Scot., U.K. 46 55.31 N 4.04 W
Muirkirk, Md., U.S. 284c 39.04 N 76.53 W
Muir of Ord 46 57.31 N 4.27 W
Muiron Islands II 162 21.35 S 114.20 E
Muir Seamount ⊹[3] 16 33.30 N 62.30 W
Muirtown 46 56.16 N 3.45 W
Muir Woods 282 37.53 N 122.34 W
Muir Woods National Monument ♦ 226 37.54 N 122.33 W
Muiskraal 158 33.56 S 21.13 E
Muisne 246 0.36 N 80.02 W
Muite 154 14.02 S 39.00 E
Mui Wo 271d 22.16 N 113.59 E
Muizen 50 51.01 N 4.31 E
Muja, S.S.S.R. 88 56.24 N 115.39 E
Muja, Yai. 144 12.02 N 39.29 E
Muja ≃ 88 56.24 N 115.39 E
Mujāhidpur ◆[8] 272a 28.34 N 77.13 E
Mujang-ni 98 35.26 N 126.32 E
Mujezerskij 24 63.57 N 31.55 E
Mujiapucun 104 41.06 N 122.48 E
Mujiayu 105 40.24 N 116.55 E
Mujimbeji Mission 154 12.11 S 24.57 E
Mujnak 86 43.48 N 59.02 E
Muju 98 36.02 N 127.40 E
Mujunkum, Peski ◆[2], S.S.S.R. 85 44.00 N 71.40 E
Mujunkum, Peski ◆[2], S.S.S.R. 86 44.20 N 71.00 E
Muka 88 56.42 N 104.41 E
Mukačevo 78 48.27 N 22.45 E
Mukah 112 2.54 N 112.06 E
Mukaishima 96 34.20 N 133.10 E
Mukalla → Al-Mukallā 144 14.32 N 49.08 E
Mukandpur ◆[8] 272a 28.44 N 77.11 E
Mukandwara 120 24.49 N 75.59 E
Mukawa 94 35.47 N 138.23 E
Mukāwir 132 31.34 N 35.38 E
Mukawwar I 140 20.48 N 37.13 E
Mukdahan 110 16.32 N 104.43 E
Mukden → Shenyang 104 41.48 N 123.27 E
Mukebo 154 6.49 S 28.03 E
Mukeriān 123 31.57 N 75.37 E
Mukeru 175b 7.25 N 134.30 E
Mukharram al-Fawqānī 130 34.49 N 37.04 E
Mukhmās 132 31.52 N 35.17 E
Mukho 98 37.33 N 129.06 E
Mukilteo 224 47.57 N 122.18 W
Mukinbudin 162 30.54 S 118.13 E
Mukinge Hill 154 13.29 S 25.52 E
Mukō 96 34.56 N 135.42 E
Muko ≃ 96 34.41 N 135.23 E
Mukomuko 112 2.35 S 101.07 E
Mukomwenze 154 6.52 S 27.16 E
Mukoshima-rettō II 14 27.37 N 142.10 E
Mukry 128 37.36 N 65.44 E
Muksi-ri 98 39.52 N 125.54 E
Muksu ≃ 85 39.15 N 71.23 E
Muksūdpur 126 23.18 N 89.51 E
Muktāgācha 124 24.46 N 90.14 E
Muktsar 123 30.29 N 74.31 E
Mukuku 154 12.09 S 29.49 E
Mukuleshi ≃ 152 10.21 S 24.30 E
Mukur 86 48.03 N 54.30 E
Mukusaki 115b 8.33 S 121.37 E
Mukutan 154 0.38 N 36.16 E
Mukutawa ≃ 184 53.10 N 97.28 W
Mukwela 154 17.02 S 26.39 E
Mukwonago 216 42.52 N 88.20 W
Mūl 122 20.04 N 79.40 E
Mula 34 38.03 N 1.30 W
Mula ≃, Bhārat 122 18.34 N 74.20 E
Mūla ≃, Pāk. 120 27.57 N 67.36 E
Mulādi 126 22.54 N 90.25 E
Muladu I 122 7.01 N 72.59 E
Mulaly 86 45.27 N 78.19 E
Mulan 89 45.57 N 128.03 E
Muland ◆[8] 272c 19.10 N 72.57 E
Mulanda 152 14.41 S 21.48 E
Mulanje, Malawi 154 16.03 S 35.31 E
Mulanje, Moç. 154 16.03 S 35.45 E
Mulanje Mountains ∧∧ 154 15.58 S 35.38 E
Mulargia, Lago di ⊜ 71 39.37 N 9.14 E
Mulas, Punta ≻ 240m 18.09 N 65.27 W
Mulas, Punta de ≻ 240p 21.01 N 75.35 W
Mulashi 102 29.40 N 100.39 E
Mulatos 232 28.39 N 108.51 W
Mulatupo 246 8.57 N 77.45 W
Mulayit Taung ∧ 110 16.11 N 98.32 E
Mulazzo 64 44.19 N 9.53 E
Mulbāgal 122 13.10 N 78.24 E
Mulben 46 57.31 N 3.06 W
Mulberry, Ark., U.S. 194 35.30 N 94.03 W
Mulberry, Fla., U.S. 220 27.54 N 81.59 W
Mulberry, Ind., U.S. 216 40.21 N 86.40 W
Mulberry, Ohio, U.S. 218 39.11 N 84.15 W
Mulberry ≃ 194 35.28 N 94.03 W
Mulberry Creek ≃, Ala., U.S. 194 32.27 N 86.52 W
Mulberry Creek ≃, Tex., U.S. 196 34.37 N 100.55 W
Mulberry Fork ≃ 194 33.33 N 87.11 W
Mulberry Grove 219 38.56 N 89.16 W
Mulberry Mountain ∧ 194 35.42 N 92.56 W
Mulchatna ≃ 180 59.39 N 157.08 W
Mulchén 252 37.43 S 72.14 W
Mulda, D.D.R. 54 50.48 N 13.25 E
Mul'da, S.S.S.R. 24 67.28 N 63.34 E
Mulde ≃ 54 51.10 N 12.48 E
Muldenstein 54 51.40 N 12.19 E
Muldersdrifseloop ≃ 273d 26.06 S 27.51 E
Muldersvlei 158 30.41 S 22.13 E
Muldoon 222 29.49 N 97.04 W
Muldraugh 194 37.56 N 85.59 W
Muldrow 194 35.24 N 94.36 W
Muleba 154 1.49 S 31.40 E
Mule Creek ≃ 198 37.05 N 99.00 W
Mulegé 232 26.53 N 112.01 W
Mulegns 58 46.33 N 9.37 E
Mulei 86 43.49 N 90.11 E
Muleng 89 44.56 N 130.31 E
Mulengzhen 89 44.31 N 130.13 E
Mules (Mauls) 64 46.51 N 11.31 E
Mules, Pulau I 115b 8.54 S 120.17 E
Muleshoe 196 34.13 N 102.43 W
Mulevala 154 16.30 S 37.30 E
Mulga Downs 162 22.08 S 118.26 E
Mulgathing 162 30.15 S 134.00 E
Mulgathing Rocks ∧ 162 30.14 S 133.58 E
Mulghar 126 22.46 N 89.45 E
Mulgoa 170 33.50 S 150.40 E
Mulgoa Creek ≃ 274a 33.46 S 150.39 E
Mulgowie 171a 27.43 S 152.22 E
Mulgrave, Austl. 274b 37.56 S 145.12 E
Mulgrave, N.S., Can. 186 45.37 N 61.23 W
Mulgrave Hills ∧∧[2] 180 67.42 N 163.24 W
Mulgul 162 24.49 S 118.26 E
Mulhacén ∧ 34 37.03 N 3.19 W
Mulhall 196 36.04 N 97.24 W
Mülhausen → Mulhouse 58 47.45 N 7.20 E
Mülheim an der Ruhr 56 51.24 N 6.54 E
Mülheimer Ruhrtalbrüke ◆[5] 263 51.23 N 6.54 E
Mulhouse (Mülhausen) 58 47.45 N 7.20 E
Muli, N. Cal. 175f 20.42 S 166.25 E
Muli, Zhg. 102 28.10 N 100.47 E
Mulinhe ≃ 102 42.20 N 100.20 E
Mulino 224 45.13 N 122.35 W
Mulita ≃ 116 7.18 N 124.52 E
Mulkear ≃ 48 52.40 N 8.33 W
Mūlki 122 13.06 N 74.48 E
Mull, Island of I 46 56.25 N 5.54 W
Mull, Sound of ʯ 46 56.32 N 5.50 W
Mullagh 48 53.49 N 6.57 W
Mullaghareirk Mountains ∧∧ 48 52.20 N 9.10 W
Mullaghcleevaun ∧ 48 53.06 N 6.23 W
Mullaghmore ∧ 48 54.52 N 6.50 W
Mullan 202 47.28 N 115.48 W
Mullen 198 42.03 N 101.01 W
Müllenbach 56 50.19 N 6.55 E
Mullengudgery 166 31.41 S 147.26 E
Mullens 192 37.35 N 81.23 W
Muller, Pegunungan ∧∧ 112 0.40 N 113.50 E
Muller Creek ≃ 162 22.29 S 134.30 E
Muller Range ∧∧ 164 5.35 S 142.15 E
Mullerup 41 55.30 N 11.13 E
Mullet Key I 220 27.37 N 82.44 W
Mullet Peninsula ≻[1] 48 54.12 N 10.00 W
Mullett Lake ⊜ 190 45.30 N 84.30 W
Mullewa 162 28.33 S 115.31 E
Mull Head ≻, Scot., U.K. 46 59.23 N 2.54 W
Mull Head ≻, Scot., U.K. 46 58.58 N 2.43 W
Müllheim 58 47.48 N 7.38 E
Mullhyttan 40 59.09 N 14.41 E
Mullica ≃ 208 39.33 N 74.25 W
Mullica, Alquatka Branch ≃ 285 39.47 N 74.48 W
Mullica Hill 208 39.44 N 75.13 W
Mulligan ≃ 166 25.00 S 138.30 E
Mulliken 216 42.46 N 84.54 W
Mullin 196 31.33 N 98.40 W
Mullinahone 48 52.30 N 7.30 W
Mullinavat 48 52.21 N 7.10 W
Mullingar 48 53.32 N 7.20 W
Mullins 192 34.12 N 79.15 W
Mullinville 198 37.35 N 99.29 W
Mullion 42 50.01 N 5.15 W
Mullovka 80 54.13 N 49.25 E
Müllrose 54 52.14 N 14.25 E
Mullsjö 26 57.55 N 13.53 E
Mullumbimby 166 28.33 S 153.30 E
Mulobezi 154 16.48 S 25.09 E
Mulonda Funda 154 11.06 S 25.28 E
Mulondo 152 15.39 S 15.14 E
Mulongo 154 7.50 S 27.00 E
Mulshi Lake ⊜ 122 18.30 N 73.30 E
Multai 120 21.46 N 78.15 E
Multān 123 30.11 N 71.29 E
Multé 232 17.41 N 91.24 W
Multeen ≃ 48 52.31 N 8.01 W
Multen ⊜ 40 59.10 N 14.37 E
Multia 26 62.25 N 24.47 E
Multnomah □[6] 224 45.30 N 122.22 W
Multnomah Channel ≃[1] 224 45.51 N 122.52 W
Multnomah Falls L 224 45.35 N 122.07 W
Mulu, Gunong ∧ 112 4.04 N 114.56 E
Mulumbe, Monts ∧∧ 154 8.16 S 28.16 E
Mulungu 250 7.02 S 35.28 W
Mulungushi 154 14.40 S 28.50 E
Mulungushi Dam ◆[6] 154 14.40 S 28.50 E
Muluwusuhe ≃ 120 34.40 N 95.00 E
Mulvane 198 37.29 N 97.14 W
Mulwad 140 18.39 N 30.35 E
Mulyah Mountain ∧ 166 30.37 S 144.31 E
Muma 152 3.24 N 23.15 E
Mumbles Head ≻ 42 51.35 N 3.59 W
Mumbwa 154 14.59 S 27.04 E
Mumcular 130 37.05 N 27.40 E
Mume 154 9.40 S 27.26 E
Mumen 102 32.09 N 106.28 E
Mumeng 164 7.00 S 146.35 E
Mumford, N.Y., U.S. 210 42.59 N 77.52 W
Mumford, Tex., U.S. 222 30.44 N 96.34 W
Mumias 154 0.20 N 34.29 E
Muminabad 85 38.06 N 70.01 E
Mümling ≃ 56 49.50 N 9.09 E
Mumoni ∧ 154 0.31 S 38.01 E
Mumra 80 45.47 N 47.41 E
Mumser Knob ∧[2] 214 40.40 N 81.54 W
Mumu 140 12.06 N 23.42 E
Mumungwe 156 21.59 S 26.24 E
Mun ≃ 110 15.19 N 105.30 E
Mun, Jabal ∧ 140 14.08 N 22.42 E
Muna 232 20.29 N 89.43 W
Muna ≃ 74 67.52 N 123.06 E
Muna, Pulau I 112 5.00 S 122.30 E
Muna, Selat ʯ 112 5.15 S 122.10 E
Munā al-Amīr 142 29.54 N 31.15 E
Munābāo 120 25.45 N 70.17 E
Munajly 86 46.47 N 54.31 E
Munakata 96 33.50 N 130.35 E
Munamägi ∧[2] 76 57.43 N 27.04 E
Munam-ni 98 38.41 N 126.54 E
Munbong-ni 271b 37.43 N 126.49 E
Muncar 115a 8.26 S 114.20 E
Münchberg 54 50.11 N 11.47 E
Müncheberg 54 52.30 N 14.08 E
Münchehofe 264a 52.30 N 13.40 E
München 60 48.08 N 11.34 E
Münchenbernsdorf 54 50.49 N 11.56 E
Münchenbuchsee 58 47.01 N 7.27 E
Münchendorf 264b 48.02 N 16.23 E
München-Gladbach → Mönchengladbach 56 51.12 N 6.28 E
München-Riem, Flughafen ⊠ 60 48.08 N 11.41 E
Münchenstein 58 47.31 N 7.37 E
Münchhausen 56 50.57 N 8.43 E
Munchique, Cerro ∧ 246 2.32 N 76.57 W
Münchnerau 60 48.32 N 12.05 E
Munch'ŏn 98 39.16 N 127.15 E
Muncie 216 40.11 N 85.23 W
Muncusun 130 38.54 N 35.38 E
Muncy 210 41.12 N 76.47 W
Muncy Creek ≃ 210 41.13 N 76.48 W
Muncy Valley 210 41.21 N 76.35 W
Mundare 182 53.36 N 112.20 W
Mundaring 168a 31.54 S 116.10 E
Munday 196 33.27 N 99.38 W
Mundelein 216 42.16 N 88.00 W
Mündelheim ◆[8] 263 51.21 N 6.41 E
Münden 56 51.25 N 9.39 E
Münden, Naturpark ♦ 56 51.20 N 9.40 E
Munderfing 60 48.05 N 13.11 E
Munderkingen 58 48.14 N 9.38 E
Munderoo ∧ 171b 35.48 S 147.47 E
Mundesley 42 52.53 N 1.26 E
Mundijong 168a 32.18 S 115.59 E
Mundiwindi 162 23.52 S 120.09 E
Mūndka ◆[8] 272a 28.41 N 77.02 E
Mundo ≃ 34 38.19 N 1.40 W
Mundolsheim 58 48.39 N 7.42 E
Mundon Hill 260 51.41 N 0.42 E
Mundo Novo 255 11.52 S 40.28 W
Mundra 120 22.51 N 69.44 E
Mundrabilla 162 31.52 S 127.51 E
Mundubbera 166 25.36 S 151.18 E
Mundybaš 86 53.14 N 87.19 E
Mundytau, Gora ∧ 85 38.00 N 68.27 E
Munenga 152 10.02 S 14.41 E
Munera 34 39.02 N 2.28 W
Munford 194 35.27 N 89.47 W
Munfordville 194 37.16 N 85.54 W
Mungallala 166 26.27 S 147.33 E
Mungallala Creek ≃ 166 28.05 S 147.15 E
Mungana 166 17.07 S 144.24 E
Mungaoli 124 24.25 N 78.06 E
Mungári 154 17.12 S 33.31 E
Mungar Junction 166 25.36 S 152.36 E
Mungau 152 13.56 S 21.55 E
Mungbere 154 2.38 N 28.30 E
Mungeli 124 22.04 N 81.41 E
Mungeranie 162 28.00 S 138.36 E
Mungindi 166 28.58 S 148.59 E
Mungla 126 22.19 N 89.36 E
Mungra Badshāhpur 124 25.40 N 82.11 E
Mungun-Tajga, Gora ∧ 86 50.16 N 90.05 E
Mun'gyŏng 98 36.44 N 128.07 E
Munhall 214 40.24 N 79.53 W
Munhamade 154 16.37 S 36.58 E
Munhango 152 12.12 S 18.42 E
Munhango ≃ 152 11.20 S 19.50 E
Munhoz 256 22.37 S 46.22 W
Munhye-ri 98 38.10 N 127.19 E
Munich → München 60 48.08 N 11.34 E
Muniesa 34 41.02 N 0.48 W
Munim ≃ 250 2.45 S 44.04 W
Munirka ◆[8] 272a 28.34 N 77.10 E
Munising 190 46.25 N 86.40 W
Munith 216 42.23 N 84.16 W
Muñiz 258 34.33 S 58.42 W
Muniz Freire 255 20.28 S 41.25 W
Munkács → Mukačevo 78 48.27 N 22.45 E
Munka-Ljungby 41 56.15 N 12.58 E
Munkebjerg ∧[2] 41 55.41 N 9.37 E
Munkebo 41 55.27 N 10.34 E
Munkedal 26 58.29 N 11.41 E
Munkerud 40 59.50 N 13.31 E
Munkfors 40 59.50 N 13.32 E
Munksund 26 65.17 N 21.29 E
Munktorp 40 59.32 N 16.08 E
Munku-Sardyk, Gora ∧ 88 51.45 N 100.32 E
Munlochy 46 57.32 N 4.15 W
Münnerstadt 56 50.15 N 10.11 E
Munnsville 210 42.59 N 75.35 W
Munntown 279b 40.14 N 80.05 W
Muñoz 116 15.43 N 120.54 E
Muñoz ≃ 240p 21.22 N 78.32 W
Munozero 24 67.05 N 34.12 E
Muñoz Gamero, Península ≻[1] 254 52.30 S 73.10 W
Munpal-li 271b 37.45 N 126.43 E
Munro ◆[8] 288 34.32 S 58.31 W
Munroe Falls 214 41.08 N 81.26 W
Munro Lake ⊜ 184 54.38 N 95.16 W
Munsan 98 37.51 N 126.48 E
Munsarpur 126 24.18 N 88.26 E
Munsey Park 276 40.48 N 73.41 W
Munshiganj 124 23.33 N 90.32 E
Münsing 64 47.54 N 11.22 E
Münsingen, B.R.D. 58 48.25 N 9.29 E
Münsingen, Schw. 58 46.53 N 7.34 E
Munsö I 40 59.23 N 17.35 E
Munson, Alta., Can. 182 51.34 N 112.45 W
Munson, Pa., U.S. 214 40.57 N 78.10 W
Munsons Corners 210 42.35 N 76.13 W
Münster, B.R.D. 52 51.57 N 7.37 E
Munster, B.R.D. 52 52.59 N 10.05 E
Munster, Fr. 56 48.55 N 6.54 E
Munster, Fr. 58 48.03 N 7.08 E
Münster, Schw. 58 46.29 N 8.16 E
Munster, Ind., U.S. 216 41.34 N 87.30 W
Münster □[6] 52 51.50 N 7.25 E
Munster □[9] 48 52.25 N 8.20 W
Munster ≃ 48 52.33 N 7.12 W
Münsterberg → Ziębice 30 50.37 N 17.00 E
Münsterkirche ✝[1] 263 51.27 N 7.01 E
Münsterland ◆[1] 52 52.00 N 7.30 E
Münsterlingen 58 47.38 N 9.14 E
Münstermaifeld 56 50.15 N 7.22 E
Muntadgin 162 31.45 S 118.34 E
Muntahak ∧ 114 1.52 N 103.47 E
Munte 112 0.30 N 119.55 E
Muntendam 52 53.07 N 6.53 E
Muntok 112 2.04 S 105.11 E
Mununzi 154 0.36 N 29.15 E
Munuscong Lake ⊜ 190 46.10 N 84.08 W
Münzenberg 56 50.27 N 8.46 E
Münzkirchen 60 48.29 N 13.34 E
Munzur Silsilesi ∧∧ 130 39.30 N 39.10 E
Muojärvi ⊜ 26 65.56 N 29.36 E
Muolea Point ≻ 229a 20.41 N 156.01 W
Muong Het 110 20.49 N 104.01 E
Muong-hinh 110 19.49 N 105.03 E
Muong Luong Nam Tha 102 20.57 N 101.25 E
Muong Saiapoun 110 18.24 N 101.31 E
Muong-sen 110 19.24 N 104.08 E
Muong-te 110 22.28 N 102.37 E
Muonio 24 67.57 N 23.42 E
Muoro 36 40.20 N 9.20 E
Muotathal 58 46.59 N 8.46 E
Mupa 152 16.10 S 15.44 E
Mupa, Parque Nacional da ◆[4] 152 16.00 S 15.35 E
Mupa Game Reserve ◆[4] 152 15.35 S 14.40 E
Mupini 156 17.50 S 19.40 E
Mup'ungjang 98 35.58 N 127.49 E
Muqaddam, Wādī ∨ 140 18.04 N 31.30 E
Muqaṭṭa' 140 14.40 N 35.51 E
Muqaybirah, Bi'r al- ⊤[4] 142 30.53 N 32.50 E
Muqayshiṭ I 128 24.12 N 53.42 E
Muqi 98 41.46 N 124.39 E
Muqsam, Jabal ∧ 140 13.38 N 27.42 E
Muquequete 152 14.50 S 14.16 E
Muqui 255 20.57 S 41.20 W
Mur (Mura) ≃ 30 46.18 N 16.53 E
Mura (Mur) ≃, Eur. 30 46.18 N 16.53 E
Mura ≃, S.S.S.R. 88 58.27 N 98.34 E
Muradiye, Tür. 128 38.59 N 43.46 E
Muradiye, Tür. 130 38.39 N 27.21 E
Murādnagar 124 28.47 N 77.30 E
Murafa ≃ 78 48.13 N 28.14 E
Murāgācha 126 23.32 N 88.24 E
Muraglione, Passo del)(66 43.56 N 11.39 E
Murajá 250 0.47 S 47.57 W
Murakami 92 38.14 N 139.29 E
Murallón, Cerro ∧ 254 49.48 S 73.25 W
Muramvya 154 3.16 S 29.37 E
Murán 30 48.46 N 20.02 E
Murana 164 3.33 S 133.49 E
Murano, Isola di I 64 45.28 N 12.21 E
Muranskij Porog L 88 58.02 N 112.16 E
Muraoka 96 35.28 N 134.35 E
Murarai 124 24.27 N 87.52 E
Muraši 24 59.24 N 48.55 E
Muraški 265b 55.59 N 37.45 E
Murat 32 45.07 N 2.52 E
Murat ≃ 130 38.39 N 39.50 E
Muratbaşı ∧ 84 39.24 N 43.21 E
Muratdağı ∧ 130 38.55 N 29.43 E
Muratkovo 86 58.26 N 62.23 E
Muratlı 130 41.10 N 27.30 E
Muratovo 83 48.48 N 38.45 E
Muratpur 272b 22.59 N 88.27 E
Murau 61 47.07 N 14.01 E
Murauaú ≃ 246 0.09 N 60.40 W
Muravera 71 39.25 N 9.34 E
Muravjevka 89 49.50 N 127.44 E
Muravjovo 76 56.14 N 34.14 E
Murayama, Nihon 92 38.28 N 140.22 E
Murayama, Nihon 268 35.45 N 139.23 E
Murayama-chosuichi ⊜[1] 268 35.45 N 139.25 E
Murayr, Jabal ∧[2] 142 30.31 N 30.36 E
Murča 34 41.24 N 7.27 W
Mūrcheh Khvort 128 33.06 N 51.30 E
Murchin 54 53.54 N 13.44 E
Murchison, Austl. 166 36.37 S 145.14 E
Murchison, N.Z. 172 41.48 S 172.20 E
Murchison, Tex., U.S. 222 32.17 N 95.45 W
Murchison ≃ 162 27.42 S 114.09 E
Murchison, Mount ∧, Austl. 162 26.46 S 116.25 E
Murchison, Mount ∧, N.Z. 172 43.01 S 171.22 E
Murchison Falls L, Malawi 154 15.54 S 34.44 E
Murchison Falls L, Ug. 154 2.17 N 31.41 E
Murchison Falls National Park ♦ 154 2.15 N 31.50 E
Murchison Range ∧∧ 162 20.11 S 134.26 E
Murcia, Esp. 34 37.59 N 1.07 W
Murcia, Pil. 116 10.36 N 123.02 E
Murcia □[9] 34 38.30 N 1.45 W
Murciélago 236 10.55 N 85.44 W
Murciélago, Islas II 236 10.51 N 85.57 W
Murcielagos Bay C 116 8.39 N 123.33 E
Mur-de-Barrez 32 44.51 N 2.39 E
Murdeduke, Lake ⊜ 169 38.11 S 143.53 E
Murder Creek ≃, Ala., U.S. 194 31.04 N 87.06 W
Murder Creek ≃, N.Y., U.S. 210 43.05 N 78.31 W
Murderkill ≃ 208 39.03 N 75.24 W
Murdo 198 43.53 N 100.43 W
Murdock 220 27.01 N 82.09 W
Mure 94 36.45 N 138.14 E
Mureaux, Aérodrome des ⊠ 261 49.00 N 1.57 E
Mureck 61 46.42 N 15.46 E
Mürefte 130 40.40 N 27.14 E
Mureş □[4] 38 46.35 N 24.40 E
Mureş (Maros) ≃ 38 46.15 N 20.13 E
Muret 32 43.28 N 1.21 E
Murfreesboro, Ark., U.S. 194 34.04 N 93.41 W
Murfreesboro, N.C., U.S. 192 36.27 N 77.06 W
Murfreesboro, Tenn., U.S. 194 35.51 N 86.23 W
Murg 58 47.33 N 8.01 E
Murg ≃ 56 48.55 N 8.10 E
Murgab 85 38.10 N 73.59 E
Murgab (Morghāb) ≃, As. 128 38.18 N 61.12 E
Murgab ≃, S.S.S.R. 85 38.20 N 72.30 E
Murgeni 38 46.12 N 28.01 E
Murgenthal 58 47.16 N 7.50 E
Murgha Faqīrzai 120 31.03 N 67.46 E
Murgha Kibzai 120 30.44 N 69.25 E
Murgon 166 26.15 S 151.57 E
Murguía 34 42.57 N 2.49 W
Murgul 130 41.17 N 41.46 E
Muri, Cook Is. 174k 21.14 S 159.43 W
Muri, Schw. 58 46.56 N 7.29 E
Muri, Schw. 58 47.16 N 8.21 E
Muria, Gunung ∧ 112 6.36 S 110.53 E
Muriaé ≃ 255 21.43 S 41.22 W
Murias de Paredes 34 42.51 N 6.11 W
Muribeca 250 10.26 S 36.59 W
Muribeca dos Guararapes 250 8.10 S 35.01 W
Murici 250 9.19 S 35.56 W
Muricizal ≃ 250 6.40 S 48.40 W
Murīdke 123 31.48 N 74.16 E
Muriége 152 9.58 S 21.11 E
Muriel Lake ⊜ 182 54.10 N 110.40 W
Murih, Pulau I 112 1.54 N 108.38 E
Murila 152 10.44 S 20.20 E
Murilo I[1] 14 8.40 N 152.11 E
Mūrinda 123 30.47 N 76.29 E
Murinéli 256 22.07 S 42.39 W
Murinja 88 54.47 N 107.21 E
Murino, S.S.S.R. 88 51.30 N 104.23 E
Murino, S.S.S.R. 265a 60.03 N 30.27 E
Murinskij ≃ 265a 60.01 N 30.28 E
Muriqui ≃ 287a 22.52 S 43.02 W
Murisengo 62 45.05 N 8.08 E
Muritiba 255 12.39 S 38.59 W
Müritz ⊜ 54 53.25 N 12.43 E
Muriwai 172 38.46 S 177.55 E
Murkong Selek 120 27.49 N 95.16 E
Murliganj 124 25.54 N 86.59 E
Murlo 66 43.09 N 11.23 E
Murmansk 24 68.58 N 33.05 E
Murmansk Rise ⊹[3] 10 74.00 N 37.00 E
Murmaši 24 68.47 N 32.42 E
Murmerwoude 52 53.16 N 6.00 E
Murmino 80 54.36 N 40.03 E
Murnau 64 47.40 N 11.12 E
Murnei 140 12.57 N 22.52 E
Murō 94 34.34 N 136.02 E
Muro, Capo di ≻ 36 41.44 N 8.40 E
Muro Lucano 68 40.45 N 15.29 E
Murom 80 55.34 N 42.02 E
Muromcevo 86 56.23 N 75.14 E
Muroran 92a 42.18 N 140.59 E
Muros 34 42.47 N 9.02 W
Muros y Noya, Ría de C[1] 34 42.45 N 9.00 W
Muroto 96 33.18 N 134.09 E
Muroto-anan-kaigan-kokutei-kōen ♦ 96 33.41 N 134.32 E
Muroto-zaki ≻ 96 33.15 N 134.11 E
Murovanyje Kurilovcy 78 48.43 N 27.31 E
Murowana Goślina 30 52.35 N 17.01 E
Murphy, Idaho, U.S. 202 43.13 N 116.33 W
Murphy, Mo., U.S. 219 38.27 N 90.28 W
Murphy, N.C., U.S. 192 35.05 N 84.01 W
Murphy Lake ⊜ 182 52.00 N 121.00 W
Murphys 226 38.08 N 120.28 W
Murphysboro 194 37.46 N 89.20 W
Murphy Slough ≃ 226 36.28 N 120.00 W
Murr ≃ 56 48.57 N 9.16 E
Murr, Wādī ∨ 142 28.27 N 32.18 E
Murrah, Qārat al- ∧[2] 142 30.00 N 32.41 E
Murra Murra 166 28.16 S 146.48 E
Murrāt, Ābār ⊤[4] 140 21.03 N 32.55 E
Murray, Iowa, U.S. 190 41.03 N 93.57 W
Murray, Ky., U.S. 194 36.37 N 88.19 W
Murray, Utah, U.S. 200 40.40 N 111.53 W
Murray ≃, Austl. 166 35.22 S 139.22 E
Murray ≃, Austl. 168a 32.35 S 115.46 E
Murray ≃, B.C., Can. 182 55.40 N 121.10 W
Murray, Lake ⊜ 164 7.00 S 141.30 E
Murray, Lake ⊜[1] 192 34.04 N 81.23 W
Murray, Mount ∧ 180 60.54 N 128.49 W
Murray Bay → La Malbaie 186 47.39 N 70.10 W
Murray Bridge 168b 35.07 S 139.17 E
Murray Canal ≡ 212 44.04 N 77.35 W
Murray City 188 39.31 N 82.10 W
Murray Downs 162 21.04 S 134.40 E
Murray Fracture Zone ⊹ 16 34.00 N 133.00 W
Murray Harbour 186 46.00 N 62.31 W
Murray Head ≻ 186 46.00 N 62.28 W
Murray Maxwell Bay C 176 70.00 N 80.00 W
Murray Mouth ≃[1] 168b 35.34 S 138.54 E
Murraysburg 158 31.58 S 23.47 E
Murrayville, B.C., Can. 224 49.10 N 122.36 W
Murrayville, Ill., U.S. 194 39.35 N 90.15 W
Murrébuè 154 13.02 S 40.30 E
Murree 123 33.54 N 73.24 E
Mürren 58 46.34 N 7.54 E
Murrhardt 56 48.59 N 9.34 E
Murrí ≃ 246 6.33 N 76.52 W
Murrieta 228 33.33 N 117.13 W
Murrin Murrin 162 28.55 S 121.49 E
Murro di Porca, Capo ≻ 70 37.00 N 15.20 E
Murrumbidgee ≃ 166 34.43 S 143.12 E
Murrumburrah 166 34.33 S 148.21 E
Murrupula 154 15.27 S 38.47 E
Murrurundi 166 31.46 S 150.50 E
Murry Hill 279b 40.17 N 80.09 W
Murrysville 279b 40.26 N 79.42 W
Mursala, Pulau I 114 1.38 N 98.32 E
Mürsel 130 39.11 N 37.59 E
Murshidābād 126 24.11 N 88.16 E
Murshidābād □[5] 126 24.05 N 88.10 E
Mürşitpınar 130 36.54 N 38.19 E
Murska Sobota 61 46.40 N 16.10 E
Murskij, Porog L 88 58.27 N 98.30 E
Mursko središče 61 46.31 N 16.27 E
Murtajāpur 122 20.44 N 77.23 E
Murtal 266c 38.42 N 9.22 W
Murtee 166 31.35 S 143.30 E
Murten 58 46.56 N 7.07 E
Murtensee → Morat, Lac de ⊜ 58 46.55 N 7.05 E
Murter, Otok I 36 43.48 N 15.37 E
Murtle Lake ⊜ 182 52.08 N 119.38 W
Murtoa 166 36.37 S 142.28 E
Murton 44 54.49 N 1.24 W
Murtosa 34 40.44 N 8.38 W
Muru 140 6.36 N 29.15 E
Muru ≃ 248 8.09 S 70.45 W
Muruasigar ∧ 154 3.08 N 35.02 E
Murud 122 18.19 N 72.58 E
Murud, Gunong ∧ 112 3.52 N 115.30 E
Murukta 74 67.46 N 102.01 E
Murung ≃ 112 0.12 S 114.03 E
Murupara 172 38.28 S 176.42 E
Murutinga 246 3.26 S 59.12 W
Murvaul, Lake ⊜[1] 222 32.03 N 94.28 W
Murvaul Creek ≃ 194 32.05 N 94.12 W
Murwāra 124 23.51 N 80.24 E
Murwillumbah 166 28.19 S 153.24 E
Mürz ≃ 61 47.24 N 15.17 E
Mürzsteg 61 47.40 N 15.29 E
Mürzzuschlag 61 47.36 N 15.41 E
Muş 130 38.44 N 41.30 E
Muş □[4] 130 39.00 N 42.00 E
Musa 152 2.40 N 19.18 E
Musa ≃, Pap. N. Gui. 164 9.25 S 148.50 E
Mūša (Mūša) ≃, S.S.S.R. 76 56.24 N 24.10 E
Mūsā, Jabal (Mount Sinai) ∧ 140 28.32 N 33.59 E
Mūsā, 'Uyūn (Springs of Moses) ⊤[4] 142 29.52 N 32.39 E
Musabeyli 130 39.51 N 34.37 E
Musadi 152 2.34 S 22.47 E
Mūsa Khel 123 32.38 N 71.44 E
Mūsa Khel Bāzār 120 30.52 N 69.49 E
Musala ∧ 38 42.11 N 23.34 E
Musan 98 42.14 N 129.13 E
Musao 154 7.43 S 26.17 E
Mūsá Qal'eh 120 32.22 N 64.46 E
Mūsā Qal'eh ≃ 128 32.05 N 64.51 E
Musar 272b 22.54 N 88.14 E
Musara 164 10.00 S 149.50 E
Musasa 154 3.21 S 31.33 E
Musashi → Iruma, Nihon 94 35.50 N 139.28 E
Musashi, Nihon 96 33.30 N 131.43 E
Musashino 94 35.42 N 139.34 E
Musashino-daichi ∧∧[1] 268 35.44 N 139.28 E
Musau 58 47.32 N 10.40 E
Musay'īd 128 24.59 N 51.32 E
Musaymīr 144 13.27 N 44.37 E
Musazade 130 41.22 N 41.16 E
Mūsāzai 120 30.23 N 66.32 E
Muscat → Masqaṭ 128 23.37 N 58.35 E
Muscat and Oman → Oman □[1] 118 22.00 N 58.00 E
Muscatatuck ≃ 218 38.46 N 86.10 W
Muscatatuck, Grassy Fork ≃ 218 39.45 N 85.07 W
Muscatatuck, Vernon Fork ≃ 218 38.46 N 85.54 W
Muscatine 190 41.25 N 91.03 W
Müsch 56 50.23 N 6.49 E
Mus-Chaja, Gora ∧ 74 62.35 N 140.50 E
Muschwitz 54 51.11 N 12.07 E

Symbols in the index entries represent the broad categories identified in the key at the right. Symbols with superior numbers (∧∧[2]) identify subcategories (see complete key on page I · 30).

Kartensymbole in dem Registerverzeichnis stellen die rechts in Schlüssel erklärten Kategorien dar. Symbole mit hochgestellten Ziffern (∧∧[2]) bezeichnen Unterabteilungen einer Kategorie (vgl. vollständiger Schlüssel auf Seite I · 30).

Los símbolos incluídos en el texto del índice representan las grandes categorias identificadas con la clave a la derecha. Los símbolos con numeros en su parte superior (∧∧[2]) identifican las subcategorías (véase la clave completa en la página I · 30).

Les symboles de l'index représentent les catégories indiquées dans la légende à droite. Les symboles suivis d'un indice (∧∧[2]) représentent des sous-catégories (voir légende complète à la page I · 30).

Os símbolos incluídos no texto do índice representam as grandes categorias identificadas com a chave à direita. Os símbolos com números em sua parte superior (∧∧[2]) identificam as subcategorias (veja-se a chave completa à página I · 30).

Symbol	English	Deutsch	Español	Français	Português
∧	Mountain	Berg	Montaña	Montagne	Montanha
∧∧	Mountains	Berge	Montañas	Montagnes	Montanhas
)(	Pass	Pass	Paso	Col	Passo
∨	Valley, Canyon	Tal, Cañon	Valle, Cañón	Vallée, Canyon	Vale, Canhão
⌣	Plain	Ebene	Llano	Plaine	Planície
≻	Cape	Kap	Cabo	Cap	Cabo
I	Island	Insel	Isla	Île	Ilha
II	Islands	Inseln	Islas	Îles	Ilhas
⊥	Other Topographic Features	Andere Topographische Objekte	Otros Elementos Topográficos	Autres données topographiques	Outros Elementos Topográficos

ESPAÑOL — Nombre, Página, Lat.°′, Long.°′ W=Oeste
FRANÇAIS — Nom, Page, Lat.°′, Long.°′ W=Ouest
PORTUGUÊS — Nome, Página, Lat.°′, Long.°′ W=Oeste

Nombre	Página	Lat.°′	Long.°′ W=Oeste
Muscle Shoals	194	34.45 N	87.40 W
Musclow, Mount ∧	182	53.17 N	127.09 W
Musclow Lake ⊜	184	51.25 N	94.56 W
Muscoda	190	43.11 N	90.27 W
Musconetcong ≃	210	40.36 N	75.11 W
Musconetcong, Lake ⊜	276	40.54 N	74.42 W
Muscongus Bay ⊂	186	43.55 N	69.20 W
Muscooten Bay ⊜	219	40.05 N	90.25 W
Muscote Bay ⊂	212	44.06 N	77.18 W
Muscoy	228	34.09 N	117.19 W
Muse	214	40.18 N	80.12 W
Musengezi ≃	154	15.43 S	31.14 E
Museo Nacional de Antropologia ʊ	286a	19.25 N	99.11 W
Müsgebi	130	37.02 N	27.21 E
Musgrave, Austl.	164	14.47 S	143.30 E
Musgrave, B.C., Can.	224	48.45 N	123.32 W
Musgrave, Mount ∧	172	43.48 S	170.43 E
Musgrave Ranges ⩕	162	26.10 S	131.50 E
Musgravetown	186	48.24 N	53.53 W
Mūshā	142	27.08 N	31.18 E
Mushābani	126	22.31 N	86.27 E
Mushandike National Park ♠	154	20.10 S	30.38 E
Mushāsh, Jabal al- ∧[2]	142	28.54 N	31.11 E
Mushenge	152	4.32 S	21.21 E
Mushie	152	3.01 S	16.54 E
Mushigang	100	29.44 N	115.14 E
Mushilin	100	23.36 N	117.06 E
Mushima	154	14.13 S	25.05 E
Mushin	150	6.32 N	3.22 E
Mushitageshan ∧	120	38.17 N	75.11 E
Mushui ≃	100	27.00 N	119.41 E
Mushu Island ▮	164	3.25 S	143.35 E
Mūsi ≃, Bhārat	122	16.41 N	79.40 E
Musi ≃, Indon.	112	2.20 S	104.56 E
Musishan ∧	120	36.03 N	80.07 E
Muskauer Heide ◆[3]	54	51.25 N	14.40 E
Muskeg ≃	182	54.01 N	119.03 W
Muskeget Channel ⩊	207	41.25 N	70.20 W
Muskeget Island ▮	207	41.20 N	70.18 W
Muskeg Lake Indian Reserve ◆[4]	184	52.58 N	106.57 W
Muskego	216	42.54 N	88.08 W
Muskego Lake ⊜	216	42.53 N	88.07 W
Muskegon	216	43.14 N	86.16 W
Muskegon ≃	190	43.14 N	86.20 W
Muskegon County Airport ⊠	216	43.10 N	86.14 W
Muskegon Heights	216	43.12 N	86.12 W
Muskegon Lake ⊜	216	43.14 N	86.17 W
Muskegon State Park ♠	216	43.14 N	86.20 W
Mušketova, Gora ∧	88	53.35 N	113.32 E
Muskingum □[6]	214	40.06 N	81.51 W
Muskingum ≃	214	40.03 N	81.59 W
Muskingum Brook ≃	285	39.48 N	74.44 W
Muskira	124	25.40 N	79.48 E
Muskö ▮	40	59.00 N	18.06 E
Muskoday Indian Reserve ◆[4]	184	53.06 N	105.30 W
Muskogee	196	35.45 N	95.22 W
Muskoka □[6]	212	45.05 N	79.03 W
Muskoka, Lake ⊜	212	45.00 N	79.25 W
Muskoka, North Branch ≃	212	45.02 N	79.19 W
Muskoka, South Branch ≃	212	45.02 N	79.19 W
Muskosh Channel ⩊	212	44.55 N	79.53 W
Muskowekwan Indian Reserve ◆[4]	184	51.19 N	104.06 W
Muskrat Creek ≃	202	43.09 N	108.11 W
Muskratdam Lake ⊜	184	53.25 N	91.40 W
Muskrat Lake ⊜	190	45.40 N	76.55 W
Muskwa ≃	176	58.45 N	122.35 W
Muskwa Lake ⊜	182	56.09 N	114.38 W
Musl'umovo	80	55.18 N	53.12 E
Muşmuş	132	32.32 N	35.09 E
Musocco ◆[8]	266b	45.30 N	9.08 E
Musofu Mission	154	13.31 S	29.02 E
Musoma	154	1.30 S	33.48 E
Musone ≃, It.	64	45.50 N	11.55 E
Musone ≃, It.	66	43.28 N	13.38 E
Musoshi	154	11.54 S	27.46 E
Musquanousse, Lac ⊜	186	50.22 N	61.05 W
Musquapsink Brook ≃	276	40.59 N	74.01 W
Musquaro, Lac ⊜	186	50.38 N	61.05 W
Musquash ≃	212	44.57 N	79.52 W
Musquash Brook ≃	283	42.42 N	71.26 W
Musquashcut Pond ⊜	283	42.13 N	70.46 W
Musquodoboit Harbour	186	44.47 N	63.09 W
Mussau Island ▮	164	1.30 S	149.40 E
Musselburgh	46	55.57 N	3.04 W
Musselkanaal	52	52.56 N	7.00 E
Musselshell ≃	202	47.21 N	107.58 W
Mussel Slough ≃	226	36.11 N	119.47 W
Mussende	152	10.32 S	16.05 E
Mussidan	32	45.02 N	0.22 E
Mussolo	152	9.59 S	17.19 E
Mussomeli	70	37.35 N	13.45 E
Mussoorie	124	30.27 N	78.05 E
Mussuco	152	17.08 S	19.05 E
Mussum	52	51.48 N	6.34 E
Mussuma	152	14.14 S	21.59 E
Mussy-sur-Seine	58	47.58 N	4.30 E
Mustafakemalpaşa	130	40.02 N	28.24 E
Mustafino	80	55.01 N	53.38 E
Mustahil	144	5.12 N	44.17 E
Müstair	58	46.37 N	10.27 E
Mustajevo	80	51.48 N	53.25 E
Mustajõe	76	57.59 N	26.58 E
Mustāng	124	29.11 N	83.58 E
Mustang Draw ∨	196	32.12 N	101.36 W
Mustang Island ▮	196	28.00 N	96.55 W
Mustāy	142	30.37 N	31.09 E
Musters, Lago ⊜	254	45.27 S	69.13 W
Mustinka ≃	198	45.45 N	96.38 W
Mustjala	76	58.28 N	22.14 E
Mustla	76	58.14 N	25.52 E
Musţurud	273c	30.08 N	31.17 E
Mustvee	76	58.51 N	26.56 E
Musu-dan ≻	98	40.50 N	129.43 E
Musun	84	39.42 N	43.49 E
Muswellbrook	166	32.16 S	150.53 E
Muszyna	30	49.21 N	20.54 E
Mūt, Mişr	140	25.29 N	28.59 E
Mut, Tür.	130	36.39 N	33.27 E
Muta	61	46.37 N	15.10 E
Mutá, Ponta do ≻	255	13.52 S	38.56 W
Mu'tah	132	31.06 N	35.42 E
Mutalau	174v	18.56 S	169.50 W
Mutambara	154	19.36 S	32.33 E
Mutanchiang → Mudanjiang	89	44.35 N	129.36 E
Mutanda, Moç.	156	21.02 S	33.31 E
Mutanda, Zaïre	152	5.17 S	16.34 E
Mutanda Mission	154	12.24 S	26.16 E
Mutankiang → Mudanjiang	89	44.35 N	129.36 E
Mutarammil, Jabal al- ∧	132	31.04 N	36.06 E
Mutayyin	144	15.59 N	43.04 E
Mutbīn	132	33.09 N	36.15 E
Mutějovice	54	50.09 N	13.41 E
Mutha	154	1.48 S	38.26 E
Muthill	46	56.19 N	3.50 W
Mutiko	154	1.39 S	28.12 E
Muting	164	7.23 S	140.20 E
Mutis, Gunung ∧	112	9.34 S	124.14 E
Mutmur	130	38.51 N	38.31 E
Mutok Harbor ⊂	174r	6.48 N	158.16 E
Mutombo-Mukulu	152	7.58 S	24.00 E
Mutoraj	74	61.20 N	100.30 E
Mutoto	152	5.42 S	22.42 E
Mutouchengzi	98	41.20 N	119.59 E
Mutouhao	107	28.49 N	105.04 E
Mutquín	252	28.19 S	66.10 W
Mutsamudu	157a	12.09 S	44.25 E
Mutshatsha	152	10.39 S	24.27 E
Mutsu	92	41.17 N	141.10 E
Mutsuai	268	35.08 N	139.38 E
Mutsumi	96	34.26 N	131.34 E
Mutsuura ◆[8]	268	35.19 N	139.37 E
Mutsu-wan ⊂	92	41.05 N	140.55 E
Muttaburra	166	22.36 S	144.33 E
Mutte Kopf ∧	58	47.16 N	10.39 E
Muttenz	58	47.32 N	7.39 E
Mutters	64	47.14 N	11.23 E
Mutterstadt	56	49.26 N	8.21 E
Mutton Bay	186	50.47 N	59.02 W
Muttontown	276	40.49 N	73.33 W
Muttra → Mathura	124	27.30 N	77.41 E
Muttyāluppettai	122	11.57 N	79.50 E
Mutual, Ohio, U.S.	218	40.05 N	83.38 W
Mutual, Pa., U.S.	279b	40.14 N	79.30 W
Muţūbis	142	31.18 N	30.31 E
Mutuca, Ribeirão da ≃	256	21.36 S	45.39 W
Mutucu, Lago ⊜	250	1.21 N	50.24 W
Mutuípe	255	13.15 S	39.31 W
Mutum	255	19.49 S	41.26 W
Mutum ≃	246	4.25 S	68.03 W
Mutumbo	152	13.14 S	17.17 E
Mutunópolis	255	13.40 S	49.15 W
Mutu-Nui, Islote ▮	174z	27.12 S	109.28 W
Muturi	164	2.06 S	133.43 E
Muturi ≃	164	2.13 S	133.40 E
Mututi, Ilha ▮	250	0.45 S	51.00 W
Mutzig	58	48.32 N	7.28 E
Mutzschen	54	51.16 N	12.53 E
Mūvattupula	122	9.58 N	76.35 E
Muvukoni	154	0.24 S	38.14 E
Muwan	106	30.44 N	118.43 E
Muwopu	104	41.03 N	121.12 E
Muxaluando	152	8.07 S	14.17 E
Muxihe	100	31.06 N	115.22 E
Muxima	152	9.31 S	13.56 E
Muyaga	154	3.14 S	30.33 E
Muyang	100	27.06 N	119.34 E
Muyinga	154	2.51 S	30.20 E
Muymanu ≃	248	11.27 S	69.03 W
Muy Muy	236	12.46 N	85.38 W
Muyuka	152	4.17 N	9.25 E
Muyumba	154	7.15 S	26.59 E
Mužač'	82	54.22 N	36.21 E
Muzaffarābād	123	34.22 N	73.28 E
Muzaffargarh	123	30.04 N	71.12 E
Muzaffarnagar	124	29.28 N	77.41 E
Muzaffarnagar □[5]	124	29.30 N	77.30 E
Muzaffarpur	124	26.07 N	85.24 E
Muzaffarpur □[5]	124	26.00 N	85.20 E
Muzambinho	256	21.22 S	46.32 W
Muzambinho ≃	256	21.15 S	46.26 W
Muzambo ≃	256	21.27 S	46.05 W
Muzayrīb	132	32.42 N	36.01 E
Muzbek, Gora ∧	85	40.23 N	69.39 E
Muzbel' ◆[1]	86	50.15 N	70.50 E
Muzeze	152	15.03 S	17.43 E
Muzhen	100	30.43 N	117.56 E
Muži	74	65.22 N	64.40 E
Mužiči	84	43.03 N	44.59 E
Mužiksu	86	47.42 N	84.58 E
Muzillac	32	47.33 N	2.29 W
Muzkol, Chrebet ⩕	85	38.25 N	73.30 E
Muzoka	154	16.41 S	27.19 E
Muzon, Cape ≻	180	54.41 N	132.44 W
Muz Tau ∧	86	43.50 N	85.40 E
Muzūrah	142	28.53 N	30.48 E
Muzzana del Turgnano	64	45.49 N	13.08 E
Mvadhi-Ousyé	152	1.13 N	13.12 E
Mvam	152	0.13 S	9.39 E
Mvangane	152	2.38 N	11.44 E
Mvela	154	14.46 S	35.16 E
Mvengué	152	3.17 N	11.01 E
Mvolo	140	6.03 N	29.56 E
Mvomero	154	6.20 S	37.25 E
Mvoung ≃	152	0.04 N	12.18 E
Mvouti	152	4.15 S	12.29 E
Mvuha	154	7.12 S	37.51 E
Mwadi-Kalumba	152	7.53 S	18.46 E
Mwadui	154	3.33 S	33.36 E
Mwanangumune	152	15.31 S	23.30 E
Mwango	152	6.51 S	24.13 E
Mwanza, Malawi	154	15.37 S	34.31 E
Mwanza, Tan.	154	2.31 S	32.54 E
Mwanza, Zaïre	154	7.54 S	26.45 E
Mwanza, Zam.	152	17.02 S	24.27 E
Mwanza □[4]	154	2.45 S	32.45 E
Mwaya, Tan.	154	9.33 S	33.57 E
Mwaya, Tan.	154	8.55 S	36.50 E
Mweelrea ∧	48	53.38 N	9.50 W
Mwehu	154	5.44 S	26.40 E
Mweka	152	4.51 S	21.34 E
Mwemena	154	10.19 S	27.28 E
Mwenda	154	12.01 S	28.44 E
Mwendjila	152	7.12 S	18.51 E
Mwene-Ditu	152	7.03 S	23.27 E
Mwenga	154	3.02 S	28.26 E
Mwepo	154	11.56 S	26.11 E
Mwerasandu	154	0.59 S	30.23 E
Mwereni	154	4.20 S	39.08 E
Mweru, Lake ⊜	154	9.00 S	28.45 E
Mweru Marsh Game Reserve ◆[4]	154	8.45 S	29.30 E
Mweru Wantipa, Lake ⊜	154	8.45 S	29.40 E
Mwetshi	152	4.42 S	22.39 E
Mwilambwe	154	8.07 S	25.00 E
Mwimbi	154	8.39 S	31.40 E
Mwingi	154	0.56 S	38.04 E
Mwinilunga	152	11.44 S	24.26 E
Mwitikira	154	6.31 S	35.39 E
Mwombezhi ≃	154	12.52 S	25.00 E
Mya, Oued ∨	148	30.47 N	4.54 E
Myaing	110	21.37 N	94.51 E
Myakka ≃	220	26.56 N	82.11 W
Myakka, Lake ⊜	220	27.16 N	82.17 W
Myakka City	220	27.21 N	82.10 W
Myakka River State Park ♠	220	27.15 N	82.17 W
Myall Range ⩕	170	32.58 S	151.22 E
Myanaung	110	18.17 N	95.19 E
Myanma → Burma □[1]	110	22.00 N	98.00 E
Myaungmya	110	16.36 N	94.56 E
Myawadi	110	16.41 N	98.31 E
Mybster	46	58.27 N	3.25 W
Myckelgensjö	26	63.34 N	17.37 E
Myebon	110	20.03 N	93.22 E
Myeik → Mergui	110	12.26 N	98.36 E
Myers, Ky., U.S.	218	38.21 N	83.57 W
Myers, N.Y., U.S.	210	42.32 N	76.32 W
Myerstown	208	40.22 N	76.19 W
Myingyan	110	21.28 N	95.23 E
Myinmoletkat Taung ∧	110	13.28 N	98.48 E
Myitkyinā	110	25.23 N	97.24 E
Myitta	110	14.10 N	98.31 E
Myittha	110	21.25 N	96.08 E
Myittha ≃	110	23.12 N	94.17 E
Myjava	30	48.45 N	17.34 E
Myjeldino	24	61.46 N	54.48 E
Myjlybulak	86	48.57 N	75.13 E
Myk	85	39.39 N	68.25 E
Myla	24	65.25 N	50.48 E
Mylau	54	50.37 N	12.16 E
Myl'džino	86	59.03 N	78.29 E
Myllendonk, Schloss ⊥	263	51.13 N	6.29 E
Myllykoski	26	60.47 N	26.48 E
Myllymäki	26	62.32 N	24.17 E
Mylor	168b	35.03 S	138.45 E
Mynämäki	26	60.40 N	22.00 E
Mynaral	86	45.25 N	73.41 E
Mynbulak, Gora ∧	85	41.43 N	69.49 E
Mynfontein	158	30.55 S	23.57 E
Mynydd Bach ∧[2]	42	52.15 N	4.05 W
Mynydd Eppynt ∧	42	52.05 N	3.30 W
Mynydd Hiraethog ∧	42	53.05 N	3.33 W
Mynydd Pencarreg ∧[2]	42	52.04 N	4.04 W
Mynydd Prescelly ∧	42	51.58 N	4.42 W
Mynžilgi, Gora ∧	85	43.49 N	68.40 E
Myōgi	94	36.17 N	138.49 E
Myōgi-san ∧	94	36.17 N	138.44 E
Myo-gyi	110	21.27 N	96.22 E
Myohaung	110	20.36 N	93.10 E
Myohyang-san ⩕	98	40.02 N	126.17 E
Myohyang-sanmaek ⩕	98	40.30 N	127.00 E
Myojin-dake ∧	270	34.57 N	135.36 E
Myōjin-ga-take ∧	94	35.17 N	139.03 E
Myōjin-san ∧	96	33.34 N	133.04 E
Myōken-san ∧	96	35.24 N	134.39 E
Myōken-zan ∧[2]	270	34.30 N	134.57 E
Myōkō	94	36.56 N	138.13 E
Myōkō-kōgen	94	36.52 N	138.12 E
Myōkō-zan ∧	94	36.52 N	138.07 E
Myŏnmong-ni ◆[8]	271b	37.35 N	127.05 E
Myponga	168b	35.24 S	138.28 E
Myra ⊥	130	36.15 N	29.54 E
Mýrdalsjökull ⊼	24a	63.40 N	19.05 W
Myrnam	182	53.40 N	111.14 W
Myroodah	162	18.08 S	124.16 E
Myrskylä (Mörskom)	26	60.40 N	25.51 E
Myrtle Beach	192	33.42 N	78.52 W
Myrtle Beach Air Force Base ■	192	33.41 N	78.56 W
Myrtle Creek	202	43.01 N	123.17 W
Myrtle Grove	194	30.25 N	87.18 W
Myrtle Point	202	43.04 N	124.08 W
Myrtle Springs	222	32.37 N	95.56 W
Myrtletowne	204	40.47 N	124.04 W
Myrtleville	170	34.29 S	149.49 E
Myšega	82	54.31 N	37.02 E
Mysen	26	59.33 N	11.20 E
Mysingen ⩊	40	59.00 N	18.15 E
Myski	86	53.42 N	87.48 E
Myškino	76	57.47 N	38.27 E
Myśla ≃	54	52.40 N	14.29 E
Myślenice	30	49.51 N	19.56 E
Myślibórz	30	52.55 N	14.52 E
Mysłowice	30	50.15 N	19.07 E
Mysore	122	12.18 N	76.39 E
Mysore □[3]	122	14.00 N	76.00 E
Mys Šmidta	180	68.56 N	179.26 W
Mystic, Conn., U.S.	207	41.21 N	71.58 W
Mystic, Iowa, U.S.	190	40.47 N	92.57 W
Mystic ≃	283	42.23 N	71.03 W
Mystic Seaport ʊ	207	41.22 N	71.58 W
Mys Vchodnoj	74	73.53 N	86.43 E
Mysy	24	60.34 N	53.57 E
Mys Želanija	72	76.56 N	68.35 E
Myszków	30	50.36 N	19.20 E
Myszyniec	30	53.24 N	21.21 E
Myt	80	56.48 N	42.21 E
My-tho	110	10.21 N	106.21 E
Mytholm	262	53.44 N	2.01 W
Mytholmroyd	262	53.44 N	1.59 W
Mytilene → Mitilíni	38	39.06 N	26.32 E
Mytišči	82	55.55 N	37.46 E
Mytishchi → Mytišči	82	55.55 N	37.46 E
Mýto	60	49.47 N	13.44 E
Myton	200	40.12 N	110.04 W
Mývatn ⊜	24a	65.37 N	16.58 W
Myzovo	78	51.22 N	24.31 E
Mzab, Oued ∨	148	32.19 N	5.24 E
Mže ≃	60	49.46 N	13.24 E
Mzenga	154	6.56 S	38.43 E
Mziha	154	5.54 S	37.47 E
Mzimba	154	11.52 S	33.34 E
Mzimkulu ≃	158	30.44 S	30.28 E
Mzimvubu ≃	158	31.38 S	29.32 E
Mzuzu	154	11.27 S	33.55 E
Mzymta ≃	84	43.27 N	39.56 E
N			
Na ▮	174r	6.52 N	158.22 E
Naab ≃	60	49.01 N	12.02 E
Naach, Jbel ∧	34	34.53 N	3.22 W
Naachtpunkt Brook ≃	276	40.54 N	74.15 W
Naaldwijk	52	52.00 N	4.12 E
Naalehu	229d	19.04 N	155.35 W
Na'ām	140	9.42 N	28.27 E
Naama, Sebkret en ☷	148	33.20 N	0.16 W
Naaman Creek ≃	285	39.48 N	75.27 W
Naantali	26	60.27 N	22.02 E
Naarden	52	52.17 N	5.09 E
Naarn ≃	61	48.11 N	14.49 E
Naas	48	53.13 N	6.39 W
Naas ≃	171b	35.36 S	149.04 E
Naast	50	50.33 N	4.05 E
Na'azuz, Har ∧	132	30.01 N	35.00 E
Nabā, Jabal an- (Mount Nebo) ∧	132	31.46 N	35.45 E
Nababiep	156	29.36 S	17.46 E
Nabābpur	272b	22.42 N	88.12 E
Nabadid	144	9.39 N	43.28 E
Nabadwīp	126	23.25 N	88.22 E
Nabaganga ≃[1]	126	22.59 N	89.34 E
Nabagram	126	24.12 N	88.06 E
Nabalat al-Ḥajanah	140	13.13 N	29.02 E
Nabari	94	34.37 N	136.05 E
Nabari ≃	94	34.45 N	136.01 E
Nabarūh	142	31.06 N	31.18 E
Nabas	116	11.50 N	122.05 E
Nabasta	126	23.15 N	88.01 E
Nabb	218	38.36 N	85.38 W
Nabberu, Lake ⊜	162	25.36 S	120.30 E
Nabburg	60	49.28 N	12.11 E
Nabeina	174t	1.26 N	173.05 E
Naberera	154	4.12 S	36.56 E
Nabereżnoje	265b	55.57 N	37.58 E
Nabereżnyje Čelny	80	55.42 N	52.19 E
Nabesna	180	62.22 N	143.00 W
Nabesna ≃	180	63.03 N	141.52 W
Nabeul	148	36.27 N	10.44 E
Nabeul □[8]	36	36.35 N	10.45 E
Nābha	123	30.22 N	76.09 E
Nab Hill ∧[2]	262	53.47 N	1.57 W
Nabī Hārūn, Jabal an- ∧	132	30.19 N	35.24 E
Nabileque ≃	248	20.55 S	57.49 W
Nabire	164	3.22 S	135.29 E
Nabisipi ≃	186	50.14 N	62.13 W
Nabiswera	154	1.28 N	32.16 E
Nabī Yūnus, Ra's an- ≻	132	33.39 N	35.24 E
Nabnasset	207	42.37 N	71.25 W
Nabnasset Pond ⊜	283	42.37 N	71.26 W
Nabogame	232	26.14 N	106.57 W
Naboomspruit	156	24.32 S	28.36 E
Nabordo	150	10.10 N	9.20 E
Nabou	150	11.27 N	2.43 W
Nabq	140	28.04 N	34.25 E
Nabua	116	13.24 N	123.22 E
Nabudalin	89	50.14 N	120.10 E
Nabula	120	31.55 N	80.10 E
Nābulus	132	32.13 N	35.16 E
Nābulus □[8]	132	32.18 N	35.17 E
Nabunturan	116	7.35 N	125.58 E
Nacajuca	234	18.08 N	93.01 W
Nacala	154	14.34 S	40.41 E
Nacala-Velha	154	14.32 S	40.37 E
Načalovo	80	46.20 N	48.11 E
Nacaome	236	13.31 N	87.30 W
Nacastillo	234	19.35 N	104.55 W
Nacereddine	34	36.08 N	3.26 E
Nachabinka ≃	265b	55.51 N	37.12 E
Nachabino	82	55.51 N	37.11 E
Naches	224	46.44 N	120.42 W
Naches ≃	202	46.38 N	120.31 W
Nachičevan'	84	39.13 N	45.24 E
Nachičevanskaja Avtonomnaja Sovetskaja Socialističeskaja Respublika □[3]	84	39.20 N	45.30 E
Nachi-katsuura	92	33.30 N	135.55 E
Nāchinda	126	21.53 N	87.46 E
Nachingwea	154	10.23 S	38.46 E
Nāchna	120	27.30 N	71.43 E
Náchod	30	50.25 N	16.10 E
Nachodka	89	42.48 N	132.52 E
Nachrodt-Wiblingwerde	56	51.19 N	7.37 E
Nächstebreck ◆[8]	263	51.18 N	7.14 E
Nachterstedt	54	51.49 N	11.20 E
Nachuge	110	10.45 N	92.22 E
Nachvak Fiord ⊂[2]	176	59.03 N	63.45 W
Naci	116	6.19 N	124.46 E
Nacimiento	252	37.30 S	72.40 W
Nacimiento ≃	226	35.49 N	120.45 W
Nacimiento Reservoir ⊜[1]	226	35.45 N	121.00 W
Nacka	40	59.18 N	18.10 E
Naco, Méx.	232	31.20 N	109.56 W
Naco, Ariz., U.S.	200	31.20 N	109.57 W
Nacogdoches	222	31.36 N	94.39 W
Nacogdoches □[6]	222	31.40 N	94.45 W
Nácori Chico	232	29.39 N	109.01 W
Nacozari [de García]	232	30.24 N	109.39 W
Ñacunday	252	26.01 S	54.46 W
Nada	222	29.24 N	96.23 W
Nada ◆[8]	270	34.44 N	135.14 E
Nadābhānga	272b	22.24 N	88.14 E
Nadachi	94	37.09 N	138.06 E
Nadasaki	96	34.32 N	133.52 E
Nadbai	124	27.14 N	77.12 E
Nadder ≃	42	51.03 N	1.48 W
Nadedinskoje	89	48.21 N	133.08 E
Nadela	34	42.58 N	7.30 W
Nadelkap → Agulhas, Cape ≻	158	34.52 S	20.00 E
Naden Harbour ⊂	182	54.00 N	132.35 W
Nadi	140	18.40 N	33.42 E
Nadia □[5]	126	23.30 N	88.30 E
Nadiād	120	22.42 N	72.52 E
Nādir, Mişr	142	30.33 N	30.51 E
Nadir, Vir. Is., U.S.	240m	18.19 N	64.53 W
Nădlac	38	46.10 N	20.45 E
Nador	148	35.12 N	2.55 W
Nadporožje	76	60.28 N	34.17 E
Nadrin	56	50.10 N	5.41 E
Nadterečnaja	84	43.37 N	45.22 E
Nadvoicy	24	63.52 N	34.15 E
Nadvornaja	78	48.38 N	24.34 E
Nadym	72	65.35 N	72.42 E
Nadym ≃	74	66.12 N	72.00 E
Nadyrovo	80	54.53 N	52.28 E
Naeba-san ∧	94	36.51 N	138.41 E
Nae-dong	98	37.16 N	126.27 E
Naenwa	120	25.46 N	75.51 E
Nærbø	26	58.40 N	5.39 E
Næsby	41	55.25 N	10.22 E
Næstved	41	55.14 N	11.46 E
Nafada	146	11.08 N	11.20 E
Nafadji	150	12.37 N	11.37 W
Nafarros	266c	38.49 N	9.25 W
Nafāzah, 'Alam ∧[2]	142	30.30 N	29.42 E
Näfels	58	47.06 N	9.04 E
Nafīshah	142	30.34 N	32.15 E
Nafoora	146	29.20 N	21.20 E
Naftalan	84	40.31 N	46.50 E
Nafūsah, Jabal ⩕[2]	146	31.50 N	12.00 E
Nafutan Point ≻	174n	15.05 N	145.45 E
Nāg	120	27.24 N	65.08 E
Naga, Nihon	96	34.16 N	135.26 E
Naga, Pil.	116	10.13 N	123.45 E
Naga, Pil.	116	13.37 N	123.11 E
Nâga, Kreb en ◆[4]	148	24.00 N	6.00 W
Naga, Oued en ∨	148	27.53 N	7.10 W
Nagaga	154	10.54 S	39.07 E
Nagahama, Nihon	94	35.23 N	136.16 E
Nagahama, Nihon	96	33.36 N	132.29 E
Nagai, Nihon	92	38.06 N	140.02 E
Nagai, Nihon	268	35.12 N	139.37 E
Nagai Island ▮	180	55.11 N	159.55 W
Nāgāland □[3]	120	26.00 N	95.00 E
Nagambie	169	36.47 S	145.10 E
Nagannu-shima ▮	174m	26.16 N	127.33 E
Nagano	94	36.39 N	138.11 E
Nagano □[5]	94	36.00 N	138.00 E
Nagano-dam ◆[6]	94	35.50 N	136.33 E
Naganohara	94	36.33 N	138.38 E
Nagao, Nihon	96	34.16 N	134.10 E
Nagao, Nihon	270	34.50 N	135.43 E
Nagao-hana ≻	96	35.32 N	134.01 E
Nagaoka, Nihon	92	37.27 N	138.51 E
Nagaoka, Nihon	94	34.55 N	135.42 E
Nāgappattinam	122	10.46 N	79.50 E
Nagar, Bhārat	123	32.07 N	77.10 E
Nagar, Bhārat	124	27.26 N	77.06 E
Nagara	270	34.26 N	135.44 E
Nagara ≃	94	35.01 N	136.43 E
Nagareyama	94	35.51 N	139.54 E
Nāgārjuna Sāgar ⊜[1]	122	16.35 N	79.21 E
Nagarote	236	12.16 N	86.34 W
Nagar Pārkar	120	24.22 N	70.45 E
Nāgarpur	124	24.03 N	89.53 E
Nagar Untāri	124	24.17 N	83.30 E
Nagas	116	13.06 N	123.18 E
Nagasa	94	35.08 N	140.02 E
Nagasaka	94	35.49 N	138.22 E
Nagasaki	92	32.48 N	129.55 E
Nagasawa	268	35.12 N	139.41 E
Nagashima, Nihon	92	34.12 N	136.20 E
Nagashima, Nihon	94	35.05 N	136.42 E
Naga-shima ▮, Nihon	96	34.41 N	134.15 E
Naga-shima ▮, Nihon	96	33.49 N	132.05 E
Nagashino ⊥	94	34.56 N	137.32 E
Nagasin Lake ⊜	190	47.44 N	83.37 W
Nagasu → Usa, Nihon	96	33.31 N	131.22 E
Nagasu, Nihon	96	32.56 N	130.27 E
Nagata ◆[8]	270	34.40 N	135.09 E
Nagataki	270	34.23 N	135.20 E
Nagatino ◆[8]	265b	55.41 N	37.41 E
Nagato, Nihon	94	36.15 N	138.16 E
Nagato, Nihon	96	34.21 N	131.10 E
Nagatsuta ◆[8]	268	35.32 N	139.30 E
Nāgaur	120	27.12 N	73.44 E
Nāgāvali ≃	122	18.13 N	83.56 E
Nagavskaja	80	47.47 N	42.50 E
Nagawa	94	36.05 N	137.41 E
Nagawicka Lake ⊜	216	43.05 N	88.23 W
Nagcarlan	116	14.08 N	121.25 E
Nāgda	120	23.27 N	75.25 E
Nagele	52	52.37 N	5.44 E
Nāgercoil	122	8.10 N	77.26 E
Nagi	96	35.07 N	134.11 E
Nagiba	116	13.41 N	120.53 E
Nagibino	86	55.46 N	72.43 E
Nagichot	154	4.16 N	33.34 E
Nagīna	124	29.27 N	78.27 E
Nāgirāt	126	23.38 N	89.18 E
Nagi-san ∧	96	35.10 N	134.11 E
Nagiso	94	35.36 N	137.37 E
Nagla	272a	28.31 N	77.22 E
Naglarby	40	60.25 N	15.34 E
Nagles Mountains ⩕	48	52.05 N	8.30 W
Nagłowice	30	50.41 N	20.06 E
Nago, It.	64	45.53 N	10.53 E
Nago, Nihon	174m	26.35 N	127.59 E
Nāgod	124	24.34 N	80.36 E
Nagog Pond ⊜	283	42.31 N	71.26 W
Nagoja → Nagoya	94	35.10 N	136.55 E
Nagold	56	48.33 N	8.43 E
Nagold ≃	56	48.52 N	8.42 E
Nagol'naja ≃	83	47.57 N	38.58 E
Nagol'no-Tarasovka	83	48.00 N	39.29 E
Nagorje	76	56.55 N	38.16 E
Nagornoje	78	45.26 N	28.27 E
Nagorno-Karabachskaja Avtonomnaja Oblast' □[4]	84	40.00 N	46.40 E
Nagornyj, S.S.S.R.	74	55.58 N	124.57 E
Nagornyj, S.S.S.R.	265a	59.43 N	30.16 E
Nagorsk	24	59.18 N	50.48 E
Nagorskoje	82	56.54 N	38.06 E
Nago-wan ⊂	174m	26.34 N	127.57 E
Nagoya	94	35.10 N	136.55 E
Nagoya-kūkō ⊠	94	35.15 N	136.55 E
Nāgpur	120	21.09 N	79.06 E
Nagrai	123	34.23 N	72.41 E
Nāgrākata	124	26.54 N	88.55 E
Nagrota	123	32.03 N	76.05 E
Nagu ▮	26	60.10 N	21.48 E
Nagua	238	19.23 N	69.50 W
Naguabo	240m	18.13 N	65.44 W
Naguilian	116	17.01 N	121.50 E
Nagumbuaya Point ≻	116	13.34 N	124.21 E
Naguri	94	35.53 N	139.11 E
Naguri ▮	122	6.39 N	72.55 E
Nagyatád	30	46.14 N	17.22 E
Nagybajom	30	46.23 N	17.31 E
Nagybánya → Baia-Mare	38	47.40 N	23.35 E
Nagycenk	61	47.36 N	16.42 E
Nagyecsed	30	47.52 N	22.24 E
Nagykálló	78	47.53 N	21.51 E
Nagykanizsa	30	46.27 N	17.00 E
Nagykáta	30	47.25 N	19.45 E
Nagy-Kevély ∧	264c	47.37 N	18.59 E
Nagykőrös	30	47.02 N	19.43 E
Nagy-Milic ∧	30	48.35 N	21.28 E
Nagytarcsa	264c	47.32 N	19.17 E
Nagytétény ◆[8]	264c	47.24 N	18.58 E
Nagyvarad → Oradea	38	47.03 N	21.57 E
Naha	174m	26.13 N	127.40 E
Naha Airfield ⊠	174m	26.13 N	127.40 E
Nahabuan	112	0.49 N	114.05 E
Nahakki	123	34.25 N	71.20 E
Nahalal	132	32.41 N	35.12 E
Naḥal 'Oz	132	31.28 N	34.30 E
Nāhan	124	30.33 N	77.18 E
Nahang (Nihing) ≃	128	26.00 N	62.44 E
Nahant	207	42.25 N	70.55 W
Nahant Bay ⊂	207	42.27 N	70.55 W
Nahari	96	33.25 N	134.01 E
Nahari ≃	96	33.25 N	134.01 E
Nahariyya	132	33.00 N	35.05 E
Nahar Ouassel, Oued ≃	148	35.42 N	2.33 E
Naharpur ◆[8]	272a	28.42 N	77.07 E
Nahāta	126	23.20 N	89.31 E
Nahāvand	128	34.12 N	48.22 E
Nahcotta	224	46.30 N	124.02 W
Nahe	89	48.28 N	124.52 E
Nahe ≃	56	49.58 N	7.57 E
Naḥf	132	32.56 N	35.19 E
Nahma	190	45.50 N	86.40 W
Nahmer	263	51.20 N	7.35 E
Nahmer ≃	263	51.21 N	7.35 E
Nahoe	174x	9.45 S	138.55 W
Nahon ≃	50	47.14 N	1.39 E
Nahuala, Laguna ⊂	234	16.46 N	99.44 W
Nahualate ≃	236	14.03 N	91.32 W
Nahuatzén	234	19.42 N	101.50 W
Nahuel Huapí	254	41.03 S	71.09 W
Nahuel Huapí, Lago ⊜	254	40.58 S	71.30 W
Nahuel Huapí, Parque Nacional ♠	254	41.00 S	71.48 W
Nahuel Niyeu	254	40.30 S	66.33 W
Nahuizalco	236	13.46 N	89.45 W
Nahunta	192	31.12 N	81.59 W
Nāhyā	142	30.03 N	31.07 E
Naia ≃	66	42.46 N	12.22 E
Naic	116	14.19 N	120.46 E
Naicá	232	27.53 N	105.31 W
Naicam	184	52.25 N	104.30 W
Naidong	120	29.14 N	31.46 E
Naiguatá, Pico ∧	286c	10.33 N	66.46 W
Naihāti, Bhārat	126	22.54 N	88.25 E
Naihāti, Bngl.	126	22.49 N	89.37 E
Naikliu	112	9.30 S	123.50 E
Naila	54	50.19 N	11.42 E
Nailin	98	41.53 N	119.15 E
Nails Creek ≃	222	30.16 N	96.44 W
Nailsea	42	51.26 N	2.43 W
Nailsworth	42	51.42 N	2.14 W
Nā'im, Jabal an- ∧	132	31.04 N	35.55 E
Naimanqi	89	42.55 N	120.43 E
Nain, Newf., Can.	176	56.32 N	61.41 W
Nā'īn, Īrān	128	32.52 N	53.05 E
Nain ⊜	40	60.14 N	13.50 E
Naini Tāl	124	29.23 N	79.27 E
Naini Tāl □[5]	124	29.20 N	79.30 E
Nainpur	124	22.26 N	80.07 E
Naipli, Tür.	130	40.19 N	38.07 E
Naipli, Tür.	130	39.48 N	27.13 E
Naiqiguolehe ≃	120	35.58 N	95.00 E
Nairai ▮	175g	17.49 S	179.24 E
Nairn	46	57.35 N	3.53 W
Nairn ≃	46	57.35 N	3.52 W
Nairne	168b	35.02 S	138.54 E
Nairobi	154	1.17 S	36.49 E
Nairobi Airport ⊠	276	41.08 N	74.21 W
Nairobi National Park ♠	154	1.24 S	36.50 E
Naissaar ▮	76	59.33 N	24.32 E
Naita, Mount ∧	154	5.32 N	35.19 E
Naitaumba ▮	175g	17.31 S	179.17 W
Naivasha	154	0.43 S	36.26 E
Naivasha, Lake ⊜	154	0.46 S	36.21 E
Naivos	114	2.30 N	96.10 E
Naizifang	105	39.36 N	116.47 E
Najac	32	44.17 N	2.00 E
Najafābād	128	32.37 N	51.21 E
Najafgarh ◆[8]	272a	28.37 N	76.59 E
Najafgarh Drain ☰	272a	28.43 N	77.14 E
Najasa ≃	240p	20.42 N	77.55 W
Najd □[8]	144	21.00 N	46.00 E
Nájera	34	42.25 N	2.44 W
Najhā	132	33.23 N	36.22 E
Naj'Ḥammādī	140	26.03 N	32.15 E
Najiajie	104	41.37 N	123.47 E
Najībābād	124	29.38 N	78.20 E
Najin	98	42.15 N	130.18 E
Najinkouzi	89	50.23 N	126.57 E
Najio	270	34.50 N	135.18 E
Najramdal Uul ∧	86	49.10 N	87.52 E
Najstenjarvi	24	62.16 N	32.38 E
Naju	98	35.03 N	126.43 E
Najza, Gora ∧	86	49.24 N	70.42 E
Naka, Nihon	94	36.25 N	140.28 E
Naka, Nihon	96	35.02 N	134.55 E
Naka, Nihon	268	35.49 N	140.03 E
Naka, Nihon	270	34.42 N	135.45 E
Naka, Nihon	270	34.50 N	135.48 E
Naka ◆[8]	268	35.27 N	139.39 E
Naka ≃, Nihon	94	36.20 N	140.36 E
Naka ≃, Nihon	94	35.39 N	139.51 E
Naka ≃, Nihon	96	33.56 N	134.42 E
Nakadōri-shima ▮	92	32.57 N	129.04 E
Nakagami	268	35.49 N	139.21 E
Nakagawa	94	35.38 N	137.56 E
Nakagawa ◆[8]	268	35.33 N	139.35 E
Nakagō	94	36.58 N	138.14 E
Nakagusuku-wan ⊂	174m	26.14 N	127.53 E
Nakagyō ◆[8]	270	35.01 N	135.45 E
Nakaheji	96	33.47 N	135.31 E
Nakai	94	35.20 N	139.14 E
Nakaizu	94	34.57 N	139.00 E
Nakajima, Nihon	94	37.07 N	136.51 E
Nakajima, Nihon	96	33.58 N	132.07 E
Nakajima, Nihon	268	35.18 N	139.58 E
Nakajima, Nihon	268	35.26 N	139.56 E
Naka-jima ▮	96	33.58 N	132.37 E
Nakajō, Nihon	92	38.03 N	139.24 E
Nakajō, Nihon	94	36.36 N	138.02 E
Nakakawane	94	35.03 N	138.05 E
Nāka Khārari	120	25.15 N	66.44 E
Nakalele Point ≻	229a	21.02 N	156.35 W
Nākālia	126	24.02 N	89.40 E
Nakama	96	33.50 N	130.43 E
Nakaminato	94	36.21 N	140.36 E
Nakamura	96	32.59 N	132.56 E
Nakanai Mountains ⩕	164	5.35 S	151.10 E
Nakano, Nihon	94	36.45 N	138.22 E
Nakano, Nihon	268	35.20 N	139.54 E
Nakano, Nihon	270	34.58 N	135.58 E
Nakano ◆[8]	268	35.42 N	139.42 E
Nakanobu ◆[8]	268	35.36 N	139.43 E
Nakanojō	94	36.35 N	138.51 E
Nakano-shima ▮	93b	29.49 N	129.52 E
Nakanoshima-suidō ▮	93b	29.44 N	129.49 E
Nakaosu	174m	26.37 N	128.02 E
Nakaōzō ◆[8]	270	34.51 N	135.11 E
Nakape	140	5.47 N	28.37 E
Nakashibetsu	92a	43.33 N	144.59 E
Nākāsipāra	126	23.35 N	88.21 E
Nakasongola	154	1.19 N	32.28 E
Nakatō	268	35.45 N	139.24 E
Nakatomi, Nihon	94	35.28 N	138.26 E
Nakatomi, Nihon	268	35.49 N	139.30 E
Nakatosa	96	33.20 N	133.14 E
Nakatsu, Nihon	96	33.34 N	131.13 E
Nakatsu, Nihon	96	33.57 N	135.18 E
Nakatsu, Nihon	268	35.30 N	139.20 E
Nakatsu ≃	94	37.00 N	138.39 E
Nakatsue	96	33.08 N	130.56 E
Nakatsugawa	94	35.29 N	137.30 E
Nakatsumine-yama ∧	96	33.58 N	134.31 E
Nakauchigami	270	34.56 N	135.10 E
Naka-umi ⊂	96	35.28 N	133.12 E
Nakayama, Nihon	96	35.31 N	133.35 E
Nakayama, Nihon	96	33.38 N	132.42 E
Nakayama ◆[8]	268	35.31 N	139.33 E
Nakayama ≃	96	33.55 N	133.08 E
Nakazato, Nihon	94	37.03 N	138.42 E
Nakazato, Nihon	94	36.05 N	138.50 E
Nakazuma	268	35.58 N	139.35 E
Nakechake	120	30.11 N	83.09 E
Nakehe ≃	120	31.29 N	93.51 E
Nakéty	175f	21.33 S	166.03 E
Nakfa	144	16.43 N	38.32 E
Nakhola	120	26.07 N	92.11 E
Nakhon Nayok	110	14.12 N	101.13 E
Nakhon Pathom	110	13.49 N	100.03 E
Nakhon Phanom	110	17.24 N	104.47 E
Nakhon Ratchasima	110	14.58 N	102.07 E
Nakhon Sawan	110	15.41 N	100.07 E
Nakhon Si Thammarat	110	8.26 N	99.58 E
Nakhon Thai	110	17.07 N	100.50 E
Nakhtarana	120	23.20 N	69.15 E
Nakina	176	50.10 N	86.42 W
Nakkaş ≃	267b	41.00 N	28.45 E
Nakło nad Notecią	30	53.08 N	17.35 E
Naknek	180	58.44 N	157.02 W
Naknek Lake ⊜	180	58.40 N	156.15 W
Nako	150	10.38 N	3.04 W
Nakodar	123	31.07 N	75.29 E
Nakonde	154	9.20 S	32.42 E
Nakosono-seki ⊥	94	36.53 N	140.46 E
Nakou	100	27.09 N	117.38 E
Nakskov	41	54.50 N	11.09 E
Nakskov Fjord ⊂	41	54.50 N	11.02 E
Näkten ⊜	26	62.52 N	14.38 E
Naktong-gang ≃	98	35.07 N	128.57 E
Nakūr	124	29.55 N	77.18 E
Nakuru	154	0.17 S	36.04 E
Nakuru, Lake ⊜	154	0.22 S	36.05 E
Nakusp	182	50.15 N	117.48 W
Nāl ≃	120	26.02 N	65.19 E
Nālāgarh	123	31.03 N	76.43 E
Nalajch	88	47.45 N	107.13 E
Nālanda	124	25.07 N	85.25 E
Nalao	102	24.22 N	105.23 E
Nalázi	156	24.03 S	33.20 E
Nalbāri	120	26.25 N	91.26 E
Nalcayec, Isla ▮	254	46.06 S	73.49 W
Nalchik → Nal'čik	84	43.29 N	43.37 E
Nālchiti	124	22.38 N	90.17 E
Nal'čik	84	43.29 N	43.37 E
Naldānga	126	23.26 N	89.11 E
Nāldera	123	31.11 N	77.11 E
Näldsjön ⊜	26	63.23 N	14.17 E
Nałęczów	30	51.18 N	22.11 E
Nalgonda	122	17.03 N	79.16 E
Nalgora	126	22.52 N	90.39 E
Nalhāti	126	24.18 N	87.49 E
Naliagrām	126	23.36 N	89.37 E
Naliang	102	21.43 N	107.51 E
Nalige	86	43.28 N	83.44 E
Nālikul	272b	22.49 N	88.11 E
Nalinhe ≃	102	42.10 N	101.00 E
Nalinnes	50	50.19 N	4.26 E
Nalisan	104	42.06 N	122.12 E
Nallamalla Range ⩕	122	15.30 N	78.45 E
Nalles (Nals)	64	46.32 N	11.12 E
Nallıhan	130	40.11 N	31.21 E
Na Logu	64	46.23 N	13.45 E
Nalolo	152	15.35 S	23.07 E
Nalón ≃	34	43.32 N	6.04 W
Nalong	102	23.35 N	106.05 E
Nalusa	152	14.55 S	22.13 E
Nālūt	146	31.52 N	10.59 E
Nalžovské Hory	60	49.20 N	13.33 E
Namaacha	156	25.58 S	32.05 E
Namachire	152	11.26 S	22.43 E
Namacunde	152	17.18 S	15.50 E
Namacurra	154	17.29 S	37.01 E
Namai Bay ⊂	175b	7.32 N	134.39 E
Namak, Daryācheh-ye ⊜	128	34.45 N	51.36 E
Namak, Kavīr-e ◆[2]	128	34.30 N	52.40 E
Namakan Lake ⊜	190	48.27 N	92.35 W
Namakat ⊜	154	2.14 N	36.34 E
Nāmakkal	122	11.14 N	78.10 E
Namakzār, Daryācheh-ye ⊜	128	34.00 N	60.30 E
Namamugi ◆[8]	268	35.29 N	139.41 E
Namanga	154	2.33 S	36.46 E
Namangan	85	41.00 N	71.40 E
Namanyere	154	7.31 S	31.03 E
Namapa	154	13.43 S	39.50 E
Namaqualand ◆[1]	158	29.43 S	19.05 E
Namari	150	15.05 N	13.39 W
Namarodu, Cape ≻	164	3.38 S	152.30 E
Namarrói	154	15.58 S	36.55 E
Namasagali	154	1.01 N	32.57 E
Namatanai	164	3.40 S	152.25 E
Namber	164	1.04 S	134.49 E
Nambi	162	28.54 S	121.41 E
Nambling	164	5.10 S	152.00 E
Nambour	166	26.38 S	152.58 E
Nambouwalu	175g	16.59 S	178.42 E
Nambuangongo	152	8.01 S	14.12 E
Nambucca Heads	166	30.39 S	153.00 E

English	Deutsch	Español	Français	Português
≃ River	Fluss	Río	Rivière	Rio
☰ Canal	Kanal	Canal	Canal	Canal
↳ Waterfall, Rapids	Wasserfall, Stromschnellen	Cascada, Rápidos	Chute d'eau, Rapides	Cascata, Rápidos
⩊ Strait	Meeresstrasse	Estrecho	Détroit	Estreito
⊂ Bay, Gulf	Bucht, Golf	Bahía, Golfo	Baie, Golfe	Baía, Golfo
⊜ Lake, Lakes	See, Seen	Lago, Lagos	Lac, Lacs	Lago, Lagos
☷ Swamp	Sumpf	Pantano	Marais	Pântano
⊼ Ice Features, Glacier	Eis- und Gletscherformen	Accidentes Glaciales	Formes glaciaires	Acidentes Glaciares
⊤ Other Hydrographic Features	Andere Hydrographische Objekte	Otros Elementos Hidrográficos	Autres données hydrographiques	Outros Elementos Hidrográficos
✣ Submarine Features	Untermeerische Objekte	Accidentes Submarinos	Formes de relief sous-marin	Acidentes Submarinos
□ Political Unit	Politische Einheit	Unidad Politica	Entité politique	Unidade Política
ʊ Cultural Institution	Kulturelle Institution	Institución Cultural	Institution culturelle	Instituição Cultural
⊥ Historical Site	Historische Stätte	Sitio Histórico	Site historique	Sitio Histórico
♠ Recreational Site	Erholungs- und Ferienort	Sitio de Recreo	Centre de loisirs	Sítio de Lazer
⊠ Airport	Flughafen	Aeropuerto	Aéroport	Aeroporto
■ Military Installation	Militäranlage	Instalación Militar	Installation militaire	Instalação Militar
◆ Miscellaneous	Verschiedenes	Misceláneo	Divers	Miscelânea

Nam-can 110 8.46 N 104.59 E
Namcha Barwa → Namuchabawashan ∧ 102 29.38 N 95.04 E
Namch'ang 98 35.26 N 129.16 E
Namdae-ch'ŏn ≃ 98 40.46 N 129.22 E
Namdanak 85 41.11 N 69.42 E
Nam-dinh 110 20.25 N 106.10 E
Nämdö I 40 59.12 N 18.41 E
Nämdöfjärden ⋃ 40 59.12 N 18.34 E
Namegawa 94 36.04 N 139.22 E
Nameh 112 2.34 N 116.21 E
Nameigos Lake ⊜ 190 48.46 N 84.43 W
Namekagon ≃ 190 46.05 N 92.06 W
Namelakl Passage ⋃ 175b 7.24 N 134.38 E
Namen → Namur 56 50.28 N 4.52 E
Namerikawa 94 36.46 N 137.20 E
Námestovo 30 49.25 N 19.30 E
Nametil 154 15.43 S 39.21 E
Namew Lake ⊜ 184 54.13 N 101.56 W
Nam-gang ≃ 98 39.03 N 125.52 E
Namhae 98 34.50 N 127.54 E
Namhan-gang ≃ 98 37.31 N 127.18 E
Namhkam 110 23.50 N 97.41 E
Namho-ri 98 38.07 N 125.10 E
Namhsan 110 22.58 N 97.10 E
Namiai 94 35.22 N 137.41 E
Namib Desert ✦2 156 23.00 S 15.00 E
Nambia □2 138
156 22.00 S 17.00 E
Namibie → Namibia □2 156 22.00 S 17.00 E
Namie 92 37.29 N 141.00 E
Namies 158 29.18 S 19.13 E
Namīn 128 38.25 N 48.30 E
Naminga 88 56.33 N 118.41 E
Nāmja La)(124 29.27 N 82.34 E
Namji-ri 98 35.23 N 128.29 E
Nāmkhāna 126 21.46 N 88.14 E
Namlan 110 22.15 N 97.24 E
Namlea 164 3.18 S 127.06 E
Namlos 58 47.21 N 10.40 E
Namnoi, Khao ∧ 110 10.36 N 98.38 E
Namo 112 1.24 S 119.57 E
Namoerhe ≃ 89 48.23 N 124.32 E
Namoi ≃ 166 30.00 S 148.07 E
Namoi Islands II 14 5.27 N 153.40 E
Namoluk I[1] 14 5.55 N 153.08 E
Namonuito I[1] 14 8.46 N 150.02 E
Namorik I[1] 14 5.36 N 168.07 E
Namoruputh 154 4.34 N 35.57 E
Namounou 150 11.52 N 1.42 E
Namous, Oued en V 148 31.00 N 0.15 W
Namoya 154 4.01 S 27.34 E
Nampa, Alta., Can. 182 56.02 N 117.08 W
Nampa, Idaho, U.S. 202 43.34 N 116.34 W
Nampala 150 15.17 N 5.33 W
Nam Pat 110 17.43 N 100.41 E
Nampawng 110 22.45 N 97.52 E
Nam Phong 110 16.42 N 102.52 E
Nampicuan 116 15.44 N 120.38 E
Namp'o 98 38.45 N 125.23 E
Nampont-Saint-Martin 50 50.21 N 1.45 E
Namp'ot'ae-san ∧ 98 41.44 N 128.24 E
Nampuecha 154 13.59 S 40.18 E
Nampula 154 15.07 S 39.15 E
Namrun 130 37.09 N 34.36 E
Namsan Park ♠ 271b 37.34 N 126.59 E
Namsanyŏng-ni 98 38.59 N 127.26 E
Namsen ≃ 24 64.27 N 11.28 E
Namsi 98 39.54 N 124.36 E
Namslau → Namysłów 30 51.05 N 17.42 E
Namsos 24 64.29 N 11.30 E
Nam Tok 110 14.14 N 99.04 E
Namtu 110 23.05 N 97.24 E
Namu 182 51.49 N 127.52 W
Namu I[1] 14 8.00 N 168.10 E
Namuchabawashan ∧ 102 29.38 N 95.04 E
Namuhu ⊜ 120 30.42 N 90.30 E
Namuka-i-Lau I 175g 18.51 S 178.38 W
Namúli, Serra ⩕ 154 15.15 S 37.08 E
Namur, Bel. 56 50.28 N 4.52 E
Namur, Qué., Can. 206 45.54 N 74.56 W
Namur □4 56 50.20 N 4.50 E
Nāmūs, Jabal an- ∧2 146 25.00 N 17.35 E
Namutoni 156 18.49 S 16.55 E
Namwala 154 15.45 S 26.26 E
Namwera 154 14.22 S 35.30 E
Namwŏn 98 35.25 N 127.21 E
Namyang, C.M.I.K. 98 42.57 N 129.53 E
Namyang, Taehan 98 37.14 N 126.44 E
Namysłów 30 51.05 N 17.42 E
Nan 110 18.47 N 100.47 E
Nan ≃ 110 15.42 N 100.09 E
Nana ≃ 152 5.00 N 15.50 E
Nānā, Wādī V 146 30.02 N 15.22 E
Nana Barya ≃ 146 7.59 N 17.43 E
Nanacamilpa 234 19.29 N 98.33 W
Nana Candundo 152 11.31 S 23.03 E
Nanaimo 182 49.10 N 123.56 W
Nanaimo ≃ 224 49.08 N 123.54 W
Nanaimo Lakes ⊜ 224 49.07 N 124.11 W
Nānakheri ✦8 272a 28.31 N 76.59 E
Nana Kru 150 4.50 N 8.44 W
Nanakuli 229c 21.23 N 158.09 W
Nanam 98 41.43 N 129.41 E
Nan'an 100 24.58 N 118.23 E
Nana Nambéré □5 152 6.00 N 16.00 E
Nan'anba 107 28.46 N 104.38 E
Nanango 166 26.40 S 152.00 E
Nanango Point ≻ 175e 6.51 S 156.59 E
Nanantun 110 24.45 N 95.41 E
Nanao, Nihon 94 37.03 N 136.58 E
Nanao, T'aiwan 100 24.28 N 121.47 E
Nan'ao, Zhg. 100 23.27 N 117.02 E
Nan'aodao I 100 23.26 N 117.03 E
Nanao-wan C 94 37.06 N 137.00 E
Nanas Channel ⋃ 271c 1.25 N 103.58 E
Nanatsuka 94 36.34 N 136.41 E
Nanatsu-shima II 94 37.36 N 136.53 E
Nanawan ≃ 184 53.13 N 97.13 W
Nanay ≃ 246 3.42 S 73.16 W
Nanba 102 32.20 N 104.58 E
Nanbaita 105 38.58 N 115.39 E
Nanbaixia 98 35.45 N 117.23 E
Nanbao 106 31.32 N 121.37 E
Nanbu, Nihon 94 35.17 N 138.27 E
Nanbu, Zhg. 102 31.23 N 106.02 E
Nancefield 273d 26.17 S 27.53 E
Nancha 89 47.08 N 129.19 E
Nanchang, Zhg. 100 28.41 N 115.53 E
Nanchang (Liantang), Zhg. 100 28.34 N 115.56 E
Nancheng, Zhg. 100 25.39 N 118.26 E
Nancheng, Zhg. 100 27.35 N 116.40 E
Nancheng → Hanzhong, Zhg. 102 32.59 N 107.11 E
Nanching → Nanjing 106 32.03 N 118.47 E
Nanchital 234 18.04 N 94.24 W
Nanchong (Nanchung) 107 30.48 N 106.04 E
Nanchuan 102 29.08 N 107.07 E
Nanchuang 100 24.38 N 121.00 E
Nanch'ung → Nanchong 107 30.48 N 106.04 E
Nancowry Island I 110 7.59 N 93.32 E
Nancroix 62 45.32 N 6.46 E
Nancun, Zhg. 98 39.46 N 114.07 E
Nancun, Zhg. 98 36.32 N 120.06 E
Nancy 58 48.41 N 6.12 E
Nanda Devi ∧ 124 30.23 N 79.59 E
Nāndāha 272b 22.50 N 88.17 E
Nandaime 236 11.46 N 86.03 W
Nandan 96 34.15 N 134.43 E
Nandarivatu 175g 17.34 S 177.58 E
Nandashan 100 29.59 N 112.44 E
Nānded 122 19.09 N 77.20 E
Nāndgaon, Bhārat 122 20.19 N 74.39 E
Nāndgaon, Bhārat 272c 18.58 N 73.08 E
Nandi 175g 17.48 S 177.25 E
Nandi Bay C 175g 17.44 S 177.25 E
Nandi Drug ∧ 122 13.25 N 77.42 E
Nandigrām 126 22.01 N 87.58 E
Nandikotkūr 122 15.52 N 78.16 E
Nandinghe ≃ 102 23.25 N 98.41 E
Nandlstadt 60 48.32 N 11.48 E
Nandom 150 10.51 N 2.45 W
N'andoma 24 61.40 N 40.12 E
Nandu 106 31.27 N 119.19 E
Nanduhe ≃ 110 20.04 N 110.22 E
Nanduluohe 105 40.11 N 117.13 E
Nāndūra 122 20.50 N 76.27 E
Nandurbār 122 21.22 N 74.15 E
Nanduri 175g 16.27 S 179.09 E
Nandy 261 48.35 N 2.34 E
Nandyāl 122 15.29 N 78.29 E
Nanfangquan 106 31.26 N 120.16 E
Nanfen 104 41.06 N 123.44 E
Nanfeng, Zhg. 100 27.15 N 116.32 E
Nanfeng, Zhg. 100 29.16 N 116.32 E
Nangabadau 112 1.02 N 111.54 E
Nangade 154 11.05 S 39.36 E
Nanga-Eboko 152 4.41 N 12.22 E
Nangahale 115b 8.34 S 122.32 E
Nangakelawit 112 0.23 N 112.26 E
Nangalangki 112 1.15 S 111.40 E
Nangalao Island I 116 11.27 N 120.11 E
Nangal Dewat ✦8 272a 28.33 N 77.06 E
Nangamau 112 0.06 S 111.55 E
Nangamesi, Teluk C 115b 9.37 S 120.20 E
Nangamuntatai 112 0.22 S 112.23 E
Nangang, Zhg. 100 31.22 N 116.59 E
Nangang, Zhg. 100 23.05 N 113.32 E
Nangang C 100 23.30 N 117.00 E
Nan'gangwa 105 39.46 N 116.09 E
Nangaobat 112 0.57 N 113.13 E
Nan'gaodian 105 39.25 N 115.58 E
Nānga Parbat ∧ 123 35.15 N 74.36 E
Nangapinoh 112 0.20 S 111.44 E
Nangaraun 112 0.38 N 113.11 E
Nangarhār □4 120 34.15 N 70.30 E
Nangatayap 112 1.32 S 110.34 E
Nangezhuang 105 39.31 N 116.23 E
Nanggulan 115a 7.46 S 110.12 E
Nangi 272b 22.31 N 88.13 E
Nangin 110 10.31 N 98.31 E
Nangis 50 48.33 N 3.00 E
Nangjiangqiao 100 28.58 N 113.44 E
Nangka ≃ 269f 14.41 N 121.06 E
Nanglai ≃ 126 24.20 N 90.04 E
Nāngloi ✦8 272a 28.40 N 77.02 E
Nangloi Jat ✦8 272a 28.41 N 77.04 E
Nangō, Nihon 92 31.30 N 131.30 E
Nangō, Nihon 94 37.13 N 139.33 E
Nangola 150 12.40 N 6.36 W
Nangoma 152 15.30 S 23.08 E
Nangong 98 37.24 N 115.22 E
Nangou 89 43.17 N 128.37 E
Nangō-yama-tunnel ✦6 94 35.12 N 139.10 E
Nangqian (Xiangda) 102 32.22 N 96.21 E
Nang Rong 110 14.38 N 102.48 E
Nanguan 102 37.00 N 112.31 E
Nangweshi 152 16.26 S 23.17 E
Nanhai → Foshan 100 23.03 N 113.09 E
Nanhai → South China Sea ▾2 108 10.00 N 113.00 E
Nanhe 98 37.01 N 114.41 E
Nanhedian 100 33.23 N 112.25 E
Nanhekan 107 30.24 N 103.27 E
Nanhezhao 105 39.05 N 115.56 E
Nanhsi 100 23.11 N 120.30 E
Nanhu 102 39.57 N 94.13 E
Nanhua 102 25.14 N 101.13 E
Nanhualou 104 42.30 N 123.53 E
Nanhuang 98 36.58 N 121.47 E
Nanhui 106 31.03 N 121.45 E
Nanhuta Shan ∧ 100 24.22 N 121.26 E
Nanhutou 89 43.44 N 128.55 E
Nanika Lake ⊜ 182 53.45 N 127.40 W
Naniwa ✦8 270 34.39 N 135.30 E
Nanjangūd 122 12.06 N 76.42 E
Nanjemoy 208 38.27 N 77.13 W
Nanjemoy Creek C 208 38.25 N 77.07 W
Nanjiang 100 32.44 N 120.52 E
Nanjiaohe ≃ 98 36.15 N 120.06 E
Nanjie 107 29.11 N 105.00 E
Nanjing (Shancheng), Zhg. 100 24.32 N 117.22 E
Nanjing, Zhg. 100 24.41 N 114.25 E
Nanjing (Nanking), Zhg. 106 32.03 N 118.47 E
Nanjing, Zhg. 107 28.49 N 105.12 E
Nanjinyi 107 30.02 N 104.42 E
Nanjirinji 154 9.39 S 39.04 E
Nanjishan I 100 27.28 N 121.04 E
Nanjiushan I 100 29.26 N 122.12 E
Nanjō 94 35.50 N 136.13 E
Nanjumahe ≃ 105 39.24 N 115.43 E
Nankai 96 34.21 N 135.15 E
Nankan 96 33.03 N 130.32 E
Nankāna Sāhib 123 31.27 N 73.42 E
Nankang, T'aiwan 269d 25.03 N 121.36 E
Nankang, Zhg. 100 25.42 N 114.44 E
Nankin 214 40.55 N 82.17 W
Nanking → Nanjing 106 32.03 N 118.47 E
Nankō-kōen ♠ 94 37.05 N 140.14 E
Nankoku 96 33.39 N 133.44 E
Nankou, Zhg. 100 26.38 N 117.24 E
Nankou, Zhg. 105 40.14 N 116.07 E
Nankouquian 98 41.59 N 124.30 E
Nanku 106 31.06 N 120.37 E
Nankye 110 14.20 N 98.11 E
Nanle 98 36.04 N 115.10 E
Nanling, Zhg. 100 25.59 N 119.14 E
Nanling, Zhg. 100 30.56 N 118.20 E
Nanling ⩕ 90 25.00 N 112.00 E
Nanlingqiao 100 29.35 N 114.19 E
Nanliucun 105 40.10 N 116.04 E
Nanliyang 98 37.28 N 113.37 E
Nanlongba 102 28.02 N 107.31 E
Nanlushan ∧ 89 43.27 N 126.42 E
Nanma 102 24.17 N 101.03 E
Nanmatang 106 32.18 N 120.38 E
Nanmeng 105 39.11 N 116.22 E
Nanmoku 94 36.10 N 138.44 E
Nanmatol Islands II 174r 6.52 N 158.21 E
Nanmulin 120 29.41 N 89.04 E
Nannerch 262 53.13 N 3.15 W
Nannine 162 26.53 S 118.20 E
Nanning 102 22.48 N 108.20 E
Nanniwan 102 36.29 N 109.40 E
Nannup 162 33.59 S 115.45 E
Nanny ≃ 44 53.40 N 6.14 W
Na Noi 110 18.19 N 100.43 E
Nanokele ✦8 272c 19.01 N 72.55 E
Nanomea I[1] 14 5.39 S 176.08 E
Nanoose Bay 224 49.16 N 124.12 W
Nanoose Harbour C 224 49.20 N 124.10 W
Nanoshi 272c 18.56 N 73.05 E
Nanpanjiang ≃, Zhg. 102 24.34 N 103.04 E
Nanpanjiang ≃, Zhg. 102 25.07 N 106.00 E
Nanpāra 124 27.52 N 81.30 E
Nanpengchang 107 29.21 N 106.38 E
Nanpi 98 38.02 N 116.42 E
Nanping, Zhg. 89 43.24 N 129.05 E
Nanping, Zhg. 98 42.16 N 129.09 E
Nanping, Zhg. 100 26.38 N 118.10 E
Nanping, Zhg. 100 33.30 N 116.51 E
Nanping, Zhg. 102 21.50 N 107.28 E
Nanping, Zhg. 102 33.07 N 104.20 E
Nanpuxi ≃ 100 27.02 N 118.18 E
Nanqiaotou 106 31.36 N 119.14 E
Nanqingtuo 105 39.37 N 117.53 E
Nanqu 104 40.44 N 122.08 E
Nanquan 98 36.24 N 120.17 E
Nanridao I 100 25.13 N 119.30 E
Nanruhe ≃ 100 32.43 N 115.01 E
Nansa ≃ 34 43.22 N 4.29 W
Nansei 92 34.22 N 136.41 E
Nansei-shotō (Ryukyu Islands) II 90 26.30 N 128.00 E
Nansemond □6 208 36.43 N 76.40 W
Nansen, Lago ⊜ 254 47.57 S 72.21 W
Nansha I 106 31.36 N 121.22 E
Nanshahe 98 35.03 N 117.12 E
Nanshan, Zhg. 100 26.38 N 118.20 E
Nanshan, Zhg. 105 39.21 N 115.34 E
Nanshan → Qilianshanmai ⩕ 102 39.06 N 98.40 E
Nanshanba 100 25.34 N 116.32 E
Nanshanchengzi 98 42.09 N 125.19 E
Nanshankou 102 43.09 N 93.41 E
Nanshanlingcun 105 39.09 N 117.26 E
Nanshui 100 22.02 N 113.16 E
Nansifa 105 39.27 N 116.27 E
Nansio 154 2.08 S 33.03 E
Nans-les-Pins 62 43.22 N 5.47 E
Nanson 162 28.34 S 114.46 E
Nant 32 44.01 N 3.18 E
Nant ≃ 50 47.30 N 1.14 E
Nantai 104 40.56 N 122.50 E
Nantais, Lac ⊜ 176 60.59 N 74.00 W
Nantai-san ∧, Nihon 94 36.46 N 139.29 E
Nantai-san ∧, Nihon 94 36.43 N 140.26 E
Nantai-zan ∧ 92 36.46 N 139.29 E
Nantang 100 26.08 N 115.12 E
Nantangdun 106 31.15 N 120.56 E
Nantangmei 105 38.51 N 114.56 E
Nantasket Beach 283 42.16 N 70.52 W
Nantawarra 168b 34.00 S 138.14 E
Nant Bran ≃ 42 51.57 N 3.28 W
Nanterre 50 48.53 N 2.12 E
Nantes 32 47.13 N 1.33 W
Nanteuil-le-Haudouin 50 49.08 N 2.48 E
Nanteuil-lès-Meaux 261 48.56 N 2.54 E
Nantian, Zhg. 100 27.57 N 119.56 E
Nantian, Zhg. 100 29.08 N 121.56 E
Nantianmen 104 40.56 N 123.04 E
Nanticoke 210 41.12 N 76.00 W
Nanticoke ≃ 208 38.16 N 75.56 W
Nanticoke Creek ≃, Ont., Can. 212 42.48 N 80.04 W
Nanticoke Creek ≃, N.Y., U.S. 210 42.05 N 76.05 W
Nanto 92 34.20 N 136.31 E
Nanton 182 50.21 N 113.46 W
Nantong (Nantung) 106 32.02 N 120.53 E
Nant'ou, T'aiwan 100 23.54 N 120.41 E
Nantou, Zhg. 100 22.33 N 113.55 E
Nantouillet 261 49.00 N 2.42 E
Nantschang → Nanchang 100 28.41 N 115.53 E
Nantua 58 46.09 N 5.37 E
Nantuantingzhuang 105 40.17 N 118.17 E
Nantucket 207 41.17 N 70.06 W
Nantucket □6 207 41.17 N 70.06 W
Nantucket Island I 207 41.16 N 70.03 W
Nantucket Sound ⋃ 207 41.30 N 70.15 W
Nantuego 154 11.21 S 38.24 E
Nantulo 154 12.17 S 39.03 E
Nantung → Nantong 106 32.02 N 120.53 E
Nantwich 42 53.04 N 2.32 W
Nanty Glo 214 40.28 N 78.50 W
Nant-y-moch Reservoir ⊜1 42 52.27 N 3.50 W
Nanu 164 8.50 S 142.40 E
Nanue I 174r 6.52 N 158.19 E
Nanuet 210 41.05 N 74.01 W
Nanuet Mall ✦9 276 41.06 N 74.01 W
Nanuku Passage ⋃ 175g 16.45 S 179.15 W
Nanumanga I 14 6.18 S 176.20 E
Nanuque 255 17.50 S 40.21 W
Nānūr 126 23.42 N 87.52 E
Nanusa, Pulau-pulau II 108 4.42 N 127.06 E
Nanushuk ≃ 180 69.18 N 151.00 W
Nanwan 100 32.09 N 113.57 E
Nan Wan C 100 21.53 N 120.48 E
Nanwengkouzi 89 51.10 N 125.25 E
Nanwenquan 107 29.26 N 106.35 E
Nanxi, Zhg. 100 31.31 N 115.38 E
Nanxi, Zhg. 100 26.24 N 118.24 E
Nanxi, Zhg. 107 28.51 N 104.58 E
Nanxi ≃, Zhg. 100 24.29 N 117.48 E
Nanxi ≃, Zhg. 100 28.15 N 120.43 E
Nanxian 102 29.20 N 112.19 E
Nanxiang 106 31.17 N 121.18 E
Nanxikou 107 30.43 N 106.07 E
Nanxin, Zhg. 98 35.33 N 117.12 E
Nanxin, Zhg. 105 39.11 N 115.38 E
Nanxinghu ⊜ 106 31.08 N 120.48 E
Nanxinzhuang 98 36.39 N 115.15 E
Nanxiong 100 25.10 N 114.20 E
Nanxun 106 30.53 N 120.26 E
Nanya 100 26.52 N 118.19 E
Nanyandangshan ∧ 100 27.36 N 120.24 E
Nanyang, Zhg. 100 27.24 N 119.39 E
Nanyang, Zhg. 100 33.00 N 112.32 E
Nanyang'an 100 33.25 N 120.13 E
Nanyangcun 106 31.53 N 121.43 E
Nanyanggangzi 89 48.43 N 125.27 E
Nanyanghu ⊜ 98 35.12 N 116.41 E
Nanyangshan ∧ 106 31.20 N 120.28 E
Nanyang University ♥2 271c 1.21 N 103.41 E
Nanyihu ⊜ 106 31.07 N 118.57 E
Nanyō, Nihon 98 38.03 N 140.10 E
Nanyō, Nihon 96 34.04 N 131.47 E
Nanyuan 105 39.48 N 116.23 E
Nanyuan Airport ⊠ 271a 38.47 N 116.23 E
Nanyue 100 27.14 N 112.42 E
Nanyuki 154 0.01 N 37.04 E
Nanyulin 105 40.09 N 115.23 E
Nanyunhe ≃ 105 39.10 N 117.10 E
Nanzamu 98 41.56 N 124.23 E
Nanzha 106 31.51 N 120.12 E
Nanzhai 106 31.34 N 120.02 E
Nanzhang 100 31.50 N 111.41 E
Nanzhangcun 105 39.03 N 115.46 E
Nanzhao 100 33.30 N 112.27 E
Nanzhaoji 100 32.38 N 115.58 E
Nanzhen 100 30.51 N 117.20 E
Nanzhenjie 106 31.48 N 119.17 E
Nanzhuang, Zhg. 105 40.43 N 116.14 E
Nanzhuang, Zhg. 100 40.22 N 116.21 E
Nanzila 154 16.05 S 26.07 E
Nao 152 4.35 N 15.09 E
Nao, Cabo de la ≻ 34 38.44 N 0.14 E
Naoābād 272b 22.28 N 88.27 E
Naoābād [illegible]
Naococane, Lac ⊜ 176 52.52 N 70.40 W
Naoetsu 94 37.11 N 138.15 E
Naogaon 124 24.47 N 88.56 E
Naohekou 89 47.20 N 134.10 E
Naoiri 96 33.04 N 131.23 E
Naokot 120 24.51 N 69.27 E
Naolihe ≃ 89 47.20 N 134.10 E
Naolinco de Victoria 234 19.39 N 96.51 W
Não-me-Toque 252 28.28 S 52.49 W
Naopāra 126 24.09 N 88.54 E
Naopukuria 272b 22.55 N 88.16 E
Naos 156 22.46 S 16.42 E
Naosap Lake ⊜ 184 54.51 N 101.24 W
Naoshima 96 34.30 N 133.59 E
Naours 50 50.02 N 2.17 E
Náousa 38 40.37 N 22.05 E
Naozhoudao I 102 20.57 N 110.34 E
Napa 226 38.18 N 122.17 W
Napa □6 226 38.18 N 122.17 W
Napa ≃ 226 38.07 N 122.18 W
Napacao Point ≻ 116 9.43 N 124.31 E
Napajedla 30 49.10 N 17.31 E
Napakiak 180 60.42 N 161.57 W
Napaku 112 2.32 N 115.58 E
Napali I 174r 6.53 N 158.22 E
Na Pali Coast State Park ♠ 229b 22.05 N 159.45 W
Napalkovo 74 70.03 N 73.47 E
Napamute 180 61.33 N 158.42 W
Napanee 212 44.15 N 76.57 W
Napanee ≃ 212 44.12 N 77.02 W
Napanoch 210 41.44 N 74.22 W
Napareuli 84 42.03 N 45.31 E
Napas 86 59.53 N 81.58 E
Napaskiak 180 60.42 N 161.54 W
Napa Valley V 226 38.18 N 122.18 W
Napavine 224 46.35 N 122.54 W
Napayauan Island I 116 12.22 N 123.14 E
Napè 110 18.18 N 105.06 E
Napenay 252 26.44 S 60.37 W
Naperville 216 41.47 N 88.09 W
Napetipi ≃ 186 51.21 N 58.08 W
Napf ∧ 58 47.00 N 7.56 E
Napido 164 0.41 S 135.23 E
Napiéolédougou 150 9.18 N 5.35 W
Napier, N.Z. 172 39.29 S 176.55 E
Napier, S. Afr. 158 34.29 S 19.53 E
Napier, Mount ∧ 162 17.32 S 129.10 E
Napier Mountains ⩕ 9 66.30 S 53.40 E
Napierville 206 45.11 N 73.25 W
Napierville □6 206 45.10 N 73.35 W
Napinka 184 49.17 N 100.50 W
Naplate 216 41.20 N 88.54 W
Naples → Napoli, It. 68 40.51 N 14.17 E
Naples, Fla., U.S. 220 26.08 N 81.48 W
Naples, Idaho, U.S. 202 48.34 N 116.24 W
Naples, Ill., U.S. 219 39.45 N 90.36 W
Naples, N.Y., U.S. 210 42.37 N 77.25 W
Naples, Tex., U.S. 222 33.12 N 94.41 W
Naples Park 220 26.16 N 81.48 W
Napo □4 246 0.20 S 76.50 W
Napo ≃ 246 3.20 S 72.40 W
Napola 70 37.59 N 12.38 E
Napoleon, Ind., U.S. 218 39.12 N 85.20 W
Napoleon, Ky., U.S. 218 38.46 N 84.47 W
Napoleon, Mich., U.S. 216 42.10 N 84.15 W
Napoleon, N. Dak., U.S. 198 46.30 N 99.46 W
Napoleon, Ohio, U.S. 216 41.23 N 84.08 W
Napoleonville 194 29.57 N 91.01 W
Nápoles → Napoli 68 40.51 N 14.17 E
Napoli (Naples) 68 40.51 N 14.17 E
Napoli □4 68 40.53 N 14.25 E
Napoli, Golfo di C 68 40.43 N 14.10 E
Napopo 154 4.12 N 28.02 E
Nappamerry 166 27.36 S 141.07 E
Nappanee 216 41.27 N 86.00 W
Nappan Island I 212 44.23 N 77.49 W
Napton on the Hill 42 52.15 N 1.24 W
Napu 115b 9.24 S 119.56 E
Napudalutaishan ∧ 89 51.06 N 122.13 E
Naqādah 140 25.54 N 32.43 E
Naqadeh 128 36.57 N 45.23 E
Naqb, Ra's an- ∧ 132 29.50 N 35.40 E
Naquhe ≃ 120 31.15 N 94.37 E
Nar ≃ 42 52.45 N 0.24 E
Nara, Mali 150 15.10 N 7.17 W
Nara, Nihon 96
270 34.41 N 135.50 E
Nara □5 96 34.30 N 135.50 E
Nāra ≃, Pāk. 120 24.07 N 69.07 E
Nara ≃, S.S.S.R. 82 54.53 N 37.26 E
Nara-bonchi ⌣1 270 34.38 N 135.50 E
Naracoorte 166 36.58 S 140.44 E
Naradhan 166 33.37 S 146.19 E
Narai ≃ 94 36.20 N 137.55 E
Naraina ✦8 272a 28.37 N 77.08 E
Naraini 124 25.11 N 80.29 E
Narainpur 126 24.03 N 86.36 E
Narakawa 94 35.59 N 137.50 E
Narāl 126 23.10 N 89.30 E
Naramata 182 49.36 N 119.35 W
Naran 88 48.32 N 98.17 E
Naranbulag 86 49.22 N 92.33 E
Nārang 123 31.54 N 74.31 E
Narangba 171a 27.12 S 152.58 E
Naranja 220 25.31 N 80.25 W
Naranjal, Ec. 246 2.42 S 79.37 W
Naranjal, Perú 286d 11.58 S 77.06 W
Naranjal, Ven. 286c 10.28 N 67.02 W
Naranjito, Hond. 236 14.57 N 88.41 W
Naranjito, P.R. 240m 18.18 N 66.15 W
Naranjo 236 10.06 N 84.22 W
Naranjo ≃ 236 14.30 N 92.11 W
Naranjo, Río del ≃ 234 18.54 N 103.37 W
Naranjo Islands II 116 12.23 N 124.03 E
Naranjos 234 21.21 N 97.41 W
Narao 92 32.50 N 129.04 E
Narasannapeta 122 18.25 N 84.03 E
Narasapur 122 16.27 N 81.40 E
Narasaraopet 122 16.15 N 80.04 E
Narashino 94 35.41 N 140.02 E
Narasinhapur 126 23.10 N 90.36 E
Narasun 88 50.06 N 112.58 E
Narathiwat 110 6.26 N 101.50 E
Nara Visa 196 35.37 N 103.06 W
Nara Women's University ♥2 270 34.42 N 135.49 E
Nārāyanganj 124 23.37 N 90.30 E
Nārāyani (Gandak) ≃ 124 25.39 N 85.13 E
Nārāyanpāra 272b 22.54 N 88.19 E
Nārāyanpet 122 16.44 N 77.30 E
Nārāyanpur 272b 22.29 N 88.24 E
Narazeni 84 42.27 N 41.57 E
Narberth, Wales, U.K. 42 51.48 N 4.45 W
Narberth, Pa., U.S. 285 40.01 N 75.18 W
Narbonne 32 43.11 N 3.00 E
Narcao 71 39.10 N 8.40 E
Narcea ≃ 34 43.28 N 6.06 W
Nardò 68 40.11 N 18.02 E
Nare 246 6.12 N 74.35 W
Narellan 170 34.02 S 150.44 E
Narembeen 162 32.04 S 118.24 E
Naren 89 49.52 N 120.23 E
Narendranagar 124 30.10 N 78.18 E
Naretha 162 31.00 S 124.50 E
Narew ≃ 30 52.26 N 20.42 E
Nargund 122 15.43 N 75.23 E
Narhan 272c 19.08 N 73.07 E
Nāri ≃ 120 28.35 N 67.50 E
Nārī, Jabal an- ⩕2 146 24.30 N 22.28 E
Naria 124 23.18 N 90.25 E
Nariai 270 34.53 N 135.38 E
Narial [illegible]
Narijn ≃ 88 50.21 N 93.23 E
Nārikelbāria 126 23.17 N 89.21 E
Nariman 102 45.57 N 101.32 E
Narimanabad 84 38.53 N 48.52 E
Narimba, Her Majesty's Air Station (Royal Australian Navy Airfield) ■ 274a 33.43 S 150.53 E
Narinca 130 37.52 N 38.46 E
Narinda, Baie de C 157b 14.55 S 47.30 E
Nārīn Ghar 120 36.01 N 69.06 E
Nariño □5 246 1.30 N 78.00 W
Narita 94 35.47 N 140.19 E

ENGLISH

Name	Page	Lat.°′	Long.°′

Nariwa 96 34.47 N 133.33 E
Nariwa ≃ 96 34.46 N 133.36 E
Narizón, Punta ≻ 232 27.52 N 110.54 W
Narjan-Mar 24 67.39 N 53.00 E
Nārkanda 123 31.16 N 77.27 E
Narkatiāganj 124 27.06 N 84.28 E
Närke □9 40 59.06 N 15.03 E
Närkes Marieberg 40 59.12 N 15.10 E
Narlı 130 37.27 N 37.09 E
Narma 80 54.46 N 42.01 E
Narmada ≃ 118 21.38 N 72.36 E
Narmada Valley V 124 22.30 N 77.00 E
Narmak ✦8 267d 35.43 N 51.29 E
Narman 130 40.21 N 41.52 E
Narmušad' 80 54.40 N 41.07 E
Nar-Nar-Goon 169 38.05 S 145.34 E
Nārnaul 124 28.03 N 76.06 E
Narni 66 42.31 N 12.31 E
Naro ≃ 70 37.14 N 13.37 E
Naroč' ≃ 76 54.26 N 26.39 E
Naroč', Ozero ⊜ 76 54.52 N 26.45 E
Narodiči 78 51.13 N 29.03 E
Naro-Fominsk 82 55.23 N 36.43 E
Naro Island I 116 11.53 N 123.40 E
Narok 154 1.05 S 35.52 E
Narol 30 50.22 N 23.21 E
Narón 34 43.32 N 8.10 W
Narooma 166 36.14 S 150.03 E
Naro-Osakovo 82 55.33 N 36.33 E
Narovčat 80 53.52 N 43.41 E
Narovl'a 78 51.48 N 29.29 E
Narovorovo 175f 15.13 S 168.09 E
Nārowāl 123 32.07 N 73.25 E
Närpes (Närpiö) 26 62.28 N 21.20 E
Närpiö → Närpes 26 62.28 N 21.20 E
Narrabeen 170 33.43 S 151.18 E
Narrabeen Lagoon C 274a 33.43 S 151.17 E
Narrabri 166 30.19 S 149.47 E
Narragansett 207 41.26 N 71.27 W
Narragansett Bay C 207 41.40 N 71.20 W
Narran ≃ 166 29.45 S 147.20 E
Narra Narra ∧ 171b 35.50 S 147.27 E
Narrandera 166 34.45 S 146.33 E
Narraway ≃ 182 54.48 N 119.56 W
Narraweena 274a 33.45 S 151.16 E
Narre Warren 274b 38.02 S 145.19 E
Narre Warren North 274b 37.59 S 145.19 E
Narrogin 162 32.56 S 117.10 E
Narromine 166 32.14 S 148.15 E
Narrows, Md., U.S. 208 38.58 N 76.15 W
Narrows, Va., U.S. 192 37.20 N 80.48 W
Narrowsburg 210 41.36 N 75.04 W
Närsen ⊜ 40 60.17 N 14.23 E
Narsimhapur 124 22.57 N 79.12 E
Narsingdi 124 23.55 N 90.43 E
Narsinghgarh 124 23.42 N 77.06 E
Narsinghpur □5 124 23.00 N 79.00 E
Narsīpatnam 122 17.40 N 82.37 E
Narskije Prudy, Ozero ⊜1 82 55.32 N 36.36 E
Narssag 176 60.54 N 46.00 W
Nartuby ≃ 62 43.28 N 6.34 E
Naru 92 32.49 N 128.56 E
Narubis, Namibia 158 26.55 S 18.35 E
Narubis, Namibia 158 27.10 S 19.05 E
Naruko 92 38.44 N 140.43 E
Naruksovo 80 54.37 N 44.33 E
Naruo 270 34.43 N 135.23 E
Narusawa 94 35.45 N 138.44 E
Naruto, Nihon 92 34.11 N 134.37 E
Narutō, Nihon 94 35.36 N 140.25 E
Naruto, Nihon 96 34.11 N 134.37 E
Naruto-kaikyō ⋃ 96 34.14 N 134.39 E
Narva, S.S.S.R. 76 59.23 N 28.12 E
Narva, S.S.S.R. 86 55.25 N 93.39 E
Narva ≃ 76 59.27 N 28.02 E
Narvacan 116 17.25 N 120.28 E
Narva-Jõesuu 76 59.27 N 28.03 E
Narvan 85 40.15 N 67.12 E
Narvik 24 68.26 N 17.25 E
Narvskij Zaliv C 76 59.30 N 27.40 E
Narvskoje Vodochranilišče ⊜1 76 59.18 N 28.14 E
Narwāna 124 29.37 N 76.07 E
Narwietooma 162 23.15 S 132.35 E
Narym 86 58.58 N 81.30 E
Naryn, S.S.S.R. 85 41.26 N 75.59 E
Naryn, S.S.S.R. 88 50.13 N 96.27 E
Naryn ≃ 85 40.54 N 71.45 E
Narynkol 72 42.43 N 80.12 E
Naryntau, Gory ⩕ 85 41.25 N 76.50 E
Naryškino, S.S.S.R. 76 52.58 N 35.44 E
Naryškino, S.S.S.R. 80 52.27 N 43.41 E
Naryū-zaki ≻ 96 35.36 N 135.28 E
Narzole 62 44.35 N 7.52 E
Nås, Sve. 40 60.27 N 14.29 E
Näs, Sve. 40 58.41 N 15.50 E
Nasadkino 82 56.29 N 37.21 E
Näsåker 26 63.26 N 16.54 E
Na-san 110 21.12 N 104.02 E
Nasarawa 150 8.30 N 7.40 E
Năsăud 38 47.17 N 24.24 E
Nasa Wallops Station ♥3 208 37.52 N 75.28 W
Nasbinals 32 44.40 N 3.03 E
Naschel 252 32.55 S 65.23 W
Nase → Naze 93b 28.23 N 129.30 E
Naseby, N.Z. 172 45.02 S 170.09 E
Naseby, Eng., U.K. 42 52.25 N 0.58 W
Naselle 224 46.22 N 123.49 W
Naselle ≃ 224 46.25 N 123.55 W
Nash 193 33.27 N 94.08 W
Nashawena Island I 207 41.26 N 70.53 W
Nashoba Brook ≃ 283 42.28 N 71.24 W
Nashport 214 40.04 N 82.09 W
Nashū', Wādī an- V 146 26.25 N 14.15 E
Nashua, Iowa, U.S. 190 42.57 N 92.32 W
Nashua, Mont., U.S. 202 48.08 N 106.22 W
Nashua, N.H., U.S. 188 42.46 N 71.27 W
Nashua ≃ 207 42.30 N 71.43 W
Nashuixi 102 30.09 N 108.40 E
Nashultasjön ⊜ 40 59.14 N 16.21 E
Nashville, Ont., Can. 275b 43.50 N 79.40 W
Nashville, Ark., U.S. 194 33.57 N 93.51 W
Nashville, Ga., U.S. 192 31.12 N 83.15 W
Nashville, Ill., U.S. 219 38.21 N 89.23 W
Nashville, Ind., U.S. 218 39.12 N 86.15 W
Nashville, Mich., U.S. 216 42.36 N 85.05 W
Nashville, N.C., U.S. 192 35.58 N 77.58 W
Nashville, Ohio, U.S. 214 40.36 N 82.07 W
Nashville, Tenn., U.S. 194 36.09 N 86.48 W
Nashwaak ≃ 186 45.57 N 66.37 W
Nashwaaksis 186 45.59 N 66.39 W
Nashwah 142 30.30 N 31.29 E
Nashwauk 190 47.23 N 93.10 W
Našice 38 45.29 N 18.06 E
Nasielsk 30 52.36 N 20.48 E
Näsijärvi ⊜ 26 61.37 N 23.42 E
Nāsik 122 19.59 N 73.48 E
Nāsir 140 8.36 N 33.04 E
Nasīrābād, Bhārat 120 26.18 N 74.44 E
Nasīrābād, Bngl. 124 24.45 N 90.24 E
Nasīrābād, Pāk. 120 28.23 N 68.24 E
Naskaftym 80 52.57 N 45.38 E
Naskaupi ≃ 176 53.45 N 60.50 W
Näsnaren ⊜ 40 58.51 N 16.19 E
Naso 70 38.07 N 14.47 E
Nasondoye 154 10.22 S 25.06 E
Nasorolevu ∧ 175g 16.38 S 178.42 E
Nasosnyj 84 40.37 N 49.34 E
Nasrābād 128 34.08 N 51.26 E
Nasrānī, Jabal an- ∧ 130 34.06 N 37.24 E
Nasriddinbek 85 40.41 N 71.55 E

DEUTSCH

Name	Seite	Breite°′	Länge°′ E=Ost

Nāsriganj 124 25.03 N 84.20 E
Nass ≃ 182 55.00 N 129.50 W
Nassau, Ba. 240b 25.05 N 77.21 W
Nassau, B.R.D. 56 50.19 N 7.47 E
Nassau, D.D.R. 54 50.46 N 13.32 E
Nassau, N.Y., U.S. 210 42.31 N 73.37 W
Nassau □6 210 40.45 N 73.38 W
Nassau, Bahía C 254 55.25 S 67.40 W
Nassau, Naturpark ♠ 56 50.20 N 7.45 E
Nassau Bay 222 29.32 N 95.05 W
Nassau Coliseum ♠ 276 40.43 N 73.36 W
Nassau International Airport ⊠ 240b 25.02 N 77.28 W
Nassau Island I 14 11.33 S 165.25 W
Nassau Shores 276 40.39 N 73.27 W
Nassawadox 208 37.28 N 75.51 W
Nassawango Creek ≃ 208 38.10 N 75.25 W
Nassenfels 60 48.48 N 11.16 E
Nassenheide 54 52.49 N 13.12 E
Nasser, Lake ⊜1 140 22.40 N 32.00 E
Nassereith 58 47.19 N 10.50 E
Nassian 150 8.27 N 3.29 W
Nässjö 26 57.39 N 14.41 E
Nastapoca ≃ 176 56.55 N 76.33 W
Nastapoka Islands II 176 57.00 N 76.50 W
Nastasjino 82 54.28 N 38.16 E
Nastaška 78 49.39 N 30.19 E
Nastätten 56 50.12 N 7.51 E
Nastauli 272a 28.43 N 77.22 E
Nastf, Bi'r ▾4 142 30.18 N 30.28 E
Nasu 94 37.01 N 140.07 E
Nasu-dake ∧ 92 37.07 N 139.58 E
Nasugbu 116 14.05 N 120.38 E
Nasukoin Mountain ∧ 202 48.48 N 114.35 W
Nasva 76 56.35 N 30.10 E
Nat ≃ 190 48.48 N 82.07 W
Nata, Bots. 156 20.12 S 26.12 E
Natá, Pan. 236 8.20 N 80.31 W
Nata ≃ 156 20.14 S 26.10 E
Natagaima 246 3.37 N 75.06 W
Nātāgarh 272b 22.42 N 88.25 E
Natal, Bra. 250 5.47 S 35.13 W
Natal, B.C., Can. 182 49.44 N 114.50 W
Natal, Indon. 110 0.33 N 99.07 E
Natal □3 158 28.40 S 30.40 E
Natal Basin ✧1 10 29.00 N 40.00 E
Natalia 196 29.11 N 98.52 W
Nataljevka 83 47.10 N 38.29 E
Nataljin Jar 80 51.46 N 50.35 E
Nataljino 80 52.56 N 49.02 E
Natalkuz Lake ⊜ 182 53.26 N 125.20 W
Natalspruit 273d 26.19 S 28.09 E
Natalspruit ≃ 273d 26.19 S 28.10 E
Natanes Plateau ⩕1 200 33.35 N 110.15 W
Natash, Wādī V 140 24.25 N 33.26 E
Natashō 96 35.24 N 135.38 E
Natashquan 186 50.12 N 61.49 W
Natashquan ≃ 176 50.06 N 61.49 W
Natashquan, Pointe de ≻ 186 50.06 N 61.44 W
Natashquan-Est ≃ 186 51.20 N 61.40 W
Natchez 194 31.34 N 91.23 W
Natchez Trace National Parkway ♠ 194 36.08 N 86.49 W
Natchitoches 194 31.46 N 93.05 W
Natco Lake ⊜ 276 40.26 N 74.09 W
Natércia 256 22.07 S 45.30 W
Naters 58 46.20 N 7.59 E
Natewa Bay C 175g 16.35 S 179.40 E
Na Thawi 110 6.45 N 100.42 E
Nāthdwāra 120 24.56 N 73.49 E
Nathia Gali 123 34.04 N 73.24 E
Nathula I 175g 16.53 S 177.25 E
Natick 207 42.17 N 71.21 W
Natick Laboratories ■ 283 42.17 N 71.22 W
Natimuk 166 36.45 S 141.57 E
Nation ≃ 182 55.28 N 125.35 W
National Accelerator Laboratory ♥3 216 41.50 N 88.15 W
National Agricultural Research Center ♥3 284c 39.02 N 76.52 W
National Airport ⊠ 281 42.19 N 83.25 W
National Arboretum ♠ 284c 38.54 N 76.58 W
National Art Gallery ♥ 269d 25.02 N 121.30 E
National Assembly ♥ 269a 13.46 N 100.31 E
National Baseball Hall of Fame and Museum ♥ 210 42.42 N 74.57 W
National City 228 32.40 N 117.06 W
National Gallery ♥ 260 51.31 N 0.08 W
National Institute of Health ♥ 284c 39.00 N 77.06 W
National Maritime Museum ♥ 260 51.29 N 0.00
National Park 285 39.51 N 75.12 W
National Taiwan Normal University ♥2 269d 25.02 N 121.31 E
National Taiwan University ♥2 269d 25.01 N 121.32 E
National Zoological Park ♥ 284c 38.56 N 77.03 W
Nation Lakes ⊜ 182 55.10 N 125.00 W
Natipi, Lac ⊜ 186 51.27 N 71.23 W
Natisone ≃ 64 45.57 N 13.22 E
Natitingou 150 10.19 N 1.22 E
Native Bay C 176 63.52 N 82.30 W
Natividade 250 11.43 S 47.47 W
Natividade da Serra 256 23.24 S 45.26 W
Natívitas ✦8 286a 19.14 N 99.05 W
Natkyizin 110 14.55 N 97.57 E
Natl 132 31.39 N 35.52 E
Natoma 198 39.11 N 99.01 W
Natong 102 23.01 N 107.50 E
Nator 124 24.25 N 88.59 E
Natori 92 38.08 N 140.55 E
Natorp 263 51.30 N 7.38 E
Natron, Lake ⊜ 154 2.25 S 36.00 E
Natrona Heights 214 40.38 N 79.44 W
Natrūn, Wādī an- ✦7 142 30.25 N 30.13 E
Natsui ≃ 94 37.03 N 140.59 E
Nattai ≃ 170 34.05 S 150.25 E
Nattai River 170 34.05 S 150.27 E
Nattam 122 10.14 N 78.14 E
Nattarö I 40 58.51 N 18.07 E
Nattastunturit ∧ 24 68.12 N 27.20 E
Nattaung ∧ 110 18.48 N 97.02 E
Natternberg 60 48.50 N 12.55 E
Natters 64 47.14 N 11.22 E
Nattwerder 264a 52.26 N 12.56 E
Natuchajevskaja 78 44.54 N 37.34 E
Natudaha 126 23.39 N 88.41 E
Natukanaoka Pan ⊜ 156 18.40 S 15.45 E
Natu La)(124 27.23 N 88.51 E
Natuna Besar I 112 4.00 N 108.15 E
Natural Arch And Cave ♠ 171a 28.10 S 153.14 E
Natural Bridge 212 44.04 N 75.30 W
Natural Bridges National Monument ♠ 200 37.30 N 110.08 W
Natural Bridge State Park ♠ 192 37.47 N 83.42 W
Naturaliste, Cape ≻ 162 33.32 S 115.01 E
Naturaliste Channel ⋃ 162 25.25 S 113.00 E
Naturita 200 38.14 N 108.34 W
Naturita Creek ≃ 200 38.13 N 108.32 W
Naturno (Naturns) 64 46.39 N 11.00 E
Natzungen 52 51.36 N 9.14 E

Symbols in the index entries represent the broad categories identified in the key at the right. Symbols with superior numbers (⩕²) identify subcategories (see complete key on page I · 30).

Kartensymbole in dem Registerverzeichnis stellen die rechts in Schlüssel erklärten Kategorien dar. Symbole mit hochgestellten Ziffern (⩕²) bezeichnen Unterabteilungen einer Kategorie (vgl. vollständiger Schlüssel auf Seite I · 30).

Los símbolos incluidos en el texto del índice representan las grandes categorías identificadas con la clave a la derecha. Los símbolos con números en su parte superior (⩕²) identifican las subcategorías (véase la clave completa en la página I · 30).

Les symboles de l'index représentent les catégories indiquées dans la légende à droite. Les symboles suivis d'un indice (⩕²) représentent des sous-catégories (voir légende complète à la page I · 30).

Os símbolos incluídos no texto do índice representam as grandes categorias identificadas com a chave à direita. Os símbolos com números em sua parte superior (⩕²) identificam as subcategorias (veja-se a chave completa à página I · 30).

∧ Mountain	Berg	Montaña	Montagne	Montanha
⩕ Mountains	Berge	Montañas	Montagnes	Montanhas
)(Pass	Pass	Paso	Col	Passo
V Valley, Canyon	Tal, Cañon	Valle, Cañón	Vallée, Canyon	Vale, Canhão
— Plain	Ebene	Llano	Plaine	Planície
≻ Cape	Kap	Cabo	Cap	Cabo
I Island	Insel	Isla	Île	Ilha
II Islands	Inseln	Islas	Îles	Ilhas
✦ Other Topographic Features	Andere Topographische Objekte	Otros Elementos Topográficos	Autres données topographiques	Outros Elementos Topográficos

ESPAÑOL — Nombre | Página | Lat.°′ | Long.°′ W=Oeste
FRANÇAIS — Nom | Page | Lat.°′ | Long.°′ W=Ouest
PORTUGUÊS — Nome | Página | Lat.°′ | Long.°′ W=Oeste

Nombre / Nom / Nome	Página / Page	Lat.°′	Long.°′ W=Oeste
Nau	85	40.09 N	69.22 E
Naucalpan → Ciudad de Naucalpan de Juárez	286a	19.28 N	99.14 W
Naucalpan □[7]	286a	19.26 N	99.17 W
Naucelle	32	44.12 N	2.20 E
Naučnyj	78	44.44 N	34.01 E
Naude	272c	19.03 N	73.06 E
Nauders	58	46.53 N	10.30 E
Nauen	54	52.36 N	12.52 E
Nauener Luch ☷	264a	52.37 N	12.55 E
Nauener Stadtforst ♣	264a	52.38 N	12.58 E
Naugachhia	124	25.24 N	87.06 E
Naugatuck	207	41.30 N	73.04 W
Naugatuck ≃	207	41.19 N	73.05 W
Naughton	190	46.24 N	81.12 W
Naugol'noje	82	56.22 N	38.11 E
Naui	140	18.28 N	30.43 E
Naujamiestis	76	55.44 N	23.10 E
Naujan	116	13.20 N	121.18 E
Naujan, Lake ⊜	116	13.10 N	121.21 E
Naujoji Akmenė	76	56.19 N	22.55 E
Naukan	180	66.01 N	169.43 W
Naulavaara ∧[2]	26	63.53 N	28.13 E
Naulila	152	17.12 S	14.42 E
Naumburg, B.R.D.	56	51.15 N	9.10 E
Naumburg, D.D.R.	54	51.09 N	11.48 E
Naumburg am Queiss → Nowogrodziec	30	51.12 N	15.25 E
Naumovščina	76	58.23 N	28.20 E
Naunak	86	59.00 N	80.13 E
Naundorf	54	50.56 N	13.25 E
Naunglon	110	16.48 N	97.45 E
Naungpale	110	19.33 N	97.08 E
Naunhof	54	51.16 N	12.35 E
Naupada ⬥[8]	272c	19.04 N	72.50 E
Ñaupe	248	5.36 S	79.54 W
Nā'ūr	132	31.53 N	35.50 E
Nauraushaun Brook ≃	276	41.03 N	73.59 W
Nauroth	56	50.42 N	7.52 E
Nauroz Kalāt	128	28.47 N	65.38 E
Naurskaja	84	43.38 N	45.19 E
Nauru □[1]	14		
	174b	0.32 S	166.55 E
Naushahra	123	33.09 N	74.14 E
Naushahro Fīroz	120	26.50 N	68.07 E
Naushon Island I	207	41.29 N	70.45 W
Nauški	88	50.28 N	106.07 E
Nausori	175g	18.02 S	175.32 E
Naust	46	57.47 N	5.39 W
Naustdal	26	61.31 N	5.43 E
Nauta	246	4.32 S	73.33 W
Nautanwa	124	27.26 N	83.25 E
Nautilus Park	207	41.22 N	72.05 W
Nautla	234	20.13 N	96.47 W
Nautla ≃	234	20.15 N	96.47 W
Nauvoo	190	40.33 N	91.23 W
Nava	232	28.25 N	100.46 W
Nava, Arroyo de la ≃	266a	40.31 N	3.46 W
Nava, Colle di)(	62	44.05 N	7.53 E
Nava del Rey	34	41.20 N	5.05 W
Navahermosa	34	39.38 N	4.28 W
Navajo ≃	200	37.01 N	107.10 W
Navajo Creek ≃	200	36.59 N	111.24 W
Navajo Indian Reservation ⬥[4]	200	36.25 N	110.00 W
Navajo Mountain ∧	200	37.02 N	110.52 W
Navajo National Monument ♣	200	36.40 N	110.33 W
Navajo Reservoir ⊜[1]	200	36.55 N	107.30 W
Naval	116	11.34 N	124.23 E
Navalcarnero	34	40.18 N	4.00 W
Navalmoral de la Mata	34	39.54 N	5.32 W
Naval Ordnance Test Station ▪	228	35.32 N	117.05 W
Navalvillar de Pela	34	39.06 N	5.28 W
Navan	48	53.39 N	6.41 W
Navāpur ≃	120	21.10 N	73.48 E
Navarin, Mys ≻	180	62.16 N	179.10 E
Navarino → Pílos	38	36.55 N	21.43 E
Navarino, Isla I	254	55.05 S	67.40 W
Navarra □[4]	34	42.40 N	1.30 W
Navarre, Austl.	169	36.54 S	143.07 E
Navarre, Ohio, U.S.	214	40.43 N	81.32 W
Navarro	258	35.01 S	59.16 W
Navarro □[6]	222	32.05 N	96.30 W
Navarro ≃	204	39.11 N	123.45 W
Navarro, Cañada ≃	258	35.00 S	59.18 W
Navarro Mills Lake ⊜[1]	222	31.56 N	96.45 W
Navašino	80	55.32 N	42.12 E
Navasota	222	30.23 N	96.05 W
Navasota ≃	222	30.20 N	96.09 W
Navassa	192	34.16 N	77.58 W
Navassa Island I	238	18.24 N	75.01 W
Nave	64	45.35 N	10.17 E
Nävekvarn	40	58.38 N	16.49 E
Navenne	58	47.36 N	6.10 E
Naver ≃	46	58.32 N	4.15 W
Naver, Loch ⊜	46	58.17 N	4.23 W
Navesink	276	40.24 N	74.02 W
Navesink River C	276	40.23 N	73.58 W
Navesnoje	76	52.17 N	37.57 E
Nâves-Parmelan	58	45.56 N	6.11 E
Navesti ≃	76	58.30 N	24.54 E
Navestock	260	51.39 N	0.13 E
Navestock Side	260	51.39 N	0.16 E
Navia, Arg.	252	34.47 S	66.35 W
Navia, Esp.	34	43.32 N	6.43 W
Navia ≃	34	43.33 N	6.44 W
Navibandar	120	21.26 N	69.48 E
Navidad, Chile	252	33.57 S	71.50 W
Navidad, Méx.	234	20.35 N	104.42 W
Navidad ≃	196	28.41 N	96.35 W
Navidad, Bahía C	234	19.12 N	104.43 W
Navio, Riacho do ≃	250	8.39 S	38.36 W
Naviraí	255	23.08 S	54.13 W
Navis	64	47.07 N	11.32 E
Naviti I	175g	17.07 S	177.15 E
Navl'a	76	52.51 N	34.30 E
Navl'a ≃	76	52.42 N	34.01 E
Navoi	72	40.15 N	65.15 E
Navojoa	232	27.06 N	109.26 W
Navolato	232	24.47 N	107.42 W
Navoloki	80	57.28 N	41.59 E
Navotas	269f	14.40 N	120.57 E
Návpaktos	38	38.23 N	21.50 E
Návplion	38	37.34 N	22.48 E
Navrongo	150	10.54 N	1.06 W
Navşar	128	37.18 N	44.35 E
Navsāri	120	20.51 N	72.55 E
Navua	175g	18.14 S	178.10 E
Navua ≃	175g	18.15 S	178.09 E
Navy Island I	284a	43.04 N	79.01 W
Navy Pier ⬥[5]	278	41.53 N	87.36 W
Navy Yard City	224	47.32 N	122.41 W
Nawa, Nihon	96	35.26 N	133.30 E
Nawa → Naha, Nihon	174m	26.13 N	127.40 E
Nawá, Sūrīy.	132	32.53 N	36.03 E
Nawābganj, Bhārat	124	26.56 N	81.13 E
Nawābganj, Bhārat	124	28.33 N	79.38 E
Nawābganj, Bhārat	124	26.52 N	82.08 E
Nawābganj, Bngl.	124	24.36 N	88.17 E
Nawābganj, Bngl.	126	23.40 N	90.10 E
Nawābshāh	120	26.15 N	68.25 E
Nawāda	124	24.53 N	85.32 E
Nawāh	120	32.19 N	67.53 E
Nawākot, Nepāl	124	27.55 N	85.10 E
Nawa Kot, Pāk.	120	28.20 N	71.22 E
Nawalapitiya	122	7.03 N	80.32 E
Nawalgarh	120	27.51 N	75.16 E
Nawān Kot	123	31.06 N	71.32 E
Nawāpāra, Bhārat	122	20.58 N	81.51 E
Nawapārā, Bhārat	126	23.29 N	88.15 E
Nawāpāra, Bngl.	126	23.02 N	89.23 E
Nawasā al-Ghayṭ	142	30.58 N	31.19 E
Nawāshahr, Bhārat	123	31.07 N	76.08 E
Nawāshahr, Pāk.	123	34.10 N	73.16 E
Nawāṣif, Ḥarrat •[9]	144	21.20 N	42.10 E
Nawāy	142	27.47 N	30.46 E
Nawiliwili Bay C	229b	21.57 N	159.21 W
Nawinda Kuta	152	16.25 S	24.28 E
Nawŏn-ni	98	36.25 N	126.40 E
Naxera	208	37.20 N	76.27 W
Naxi	107	28.47 N	105.22 E
Náxos	38	37.06 N	25.23 E
Náxos I	38	37.02 N	25.35 E
Naxos ⊥	70	37.49 N	15.17 E
Naxuebiruzong	120	31.30 N	93.51 E
Nayābās	272a	28.35 N	77.19 E
Nayāgaon	126	23.32 N	90.46 E
Nayāgarh	120	20.08 N	85.06 E
Nayāgrām	126	22.02 N	87.11 E
Nayak	120	34.44 N	66.57 E
Nayāpāra	126	21.35 N	87.01 E
Nayarit	204	32.20 N	115.19 W
Nayarit □[3]	234	22.00 N	105.00 W
Nayau I	175g	17.58 S	179.03 W
Nāy Band, Īrān	128	32.20 N	57.34 E
Nāy Band, Īrān	128	27.23 N	52.38 E
Nāy Band, Kūh-e ∧	128	32.27 N	57.23 E
Nayé	150	14.25 N	12.12 W
Nayland	42	51.59 N	0.52 E
Naylor	194	36.34 N	90.36 W
Nayong	102	26.50 N	105.13 E
Nayoro	92a	44.21 N	142.28 E
Nayyāl, Wādī ∨	128	28.40 N	39.26 E
Nazālī Ṭāḥā'	142	28.11 N	30.42 E
Nazaré, Bra.	250	6.23 S	47.40 W
Nazaré, Bra.	255	13.02 S	39.00 W
Nazaré, Port.	34	39.36 N	9.04 W
Nazaré da Mata	250	7.44 S	35.14 W
Nazaré do Piauí	250	6.59 S	42.40 W
Nazareno	256	21.13 S	44.37 W
Nazaré Paulista	256	23.11 S	46.24 W
Nazareth, Bel.	50	50.58 N	3.36 E
Nazareth, Pa., U.S.	208	40.44 N	75.19 W
Nazareth → Nazerat, Yis.	132	32.42 N	35.18 E
Nazareth Bank ⊹[4]	12	14.30 S	60.45 E
Nazário	255	16.36 S	49.54 W
Nazarjevo, S.S.S.R.	82	55.22 N	36.24 E
Nazarjevo, S.S.S.R.	265b	55.59 N	37.16 E
Nazarovo	86	56.01 N	90.26 E
Nazarovskij	78	49.33 N	40.56 E
Nazas	232	25.14 N	104.08 W
Nazas ≃	232	25.35 N	105.00 W
Nazca	248	14.50 S	74.57 W
Naze	93b	28.23 N	129.30 E
Nazeing	260	51.44 N	0.03 E
Nazerat (Nazareth)	132	32.42 N	35.18 E
Nazerat 'Illit	132	32.42 N	35.19 E
Nazeret	144	8.32 N	39.22 E
Nazija	76	59.50 N	31.35 E
Nazik Gölü ⊜	130	38.53 N	42.16 E
Nazilli	130	37.55 N	28.21 E
Nazimicha	265b	55.59 N	38.08 E
Nazımiye	130	39.11 N	39.50 E
Nazimovo	86	59.30 N	90.58 E
Nazina	86	60.07 N	78.52 E
Nāzira	120	26.55 N	94.44 E
Nāzir Hāt	120	22.38 N	91.47 E
Nāzirpur	126	22.43 N	89.58 E
Nazko ≃	182	53.07 N	123.34 W
Nazlat al-'Amūdayn	142	28.14 N	30.42 E
Nazlat al-Badramān	142	27.40 N	30.44 E
Nazlat as-Sammān	273c	29.59 N	31.08 E
Nazlat Khalīfah	273c	30.01 N	31.10 E
Nazlat Quftan Bāshā	142	28.57 N	30.49 E
Nazlat Thābit	142	28.25 N	30.47 E
Nazran'	84	43.13 N	44.46 E
Nazwā	128	22.56 N	57.32 E
Nazyvajevsk	86	55.34 N	71.21 E
N. B. C. Studios ⊛[3]	280	34.09 N	118.20 W
Nchanga	154	12.30 S	27.53 E
Nchelenge	154	9.20 S	28.50 E
Ncheu	154	14.49 S	34.38 E
Ncue	152	2.01 N	10.28 E
Ndabala	154	13.28 S	29.50 E
Ndai I	175e	7.57 S	160.37 E
Ndala	154	4.46 S	33.16 E
Ndali	150	9.51 N	2.43 E
Ndande	150	15.16 N	16.30 W
Ndélé	146	8.24 N	20.39 E
Ndélélé	152	4.02 N	14.56 E
Ndemba	152	0.11 N	14.19 E
Ndendé	152	2.23 S	11.23 E
Ndikiniméki	152	4.46 N	10.50 E
Ndjamena	146	12.07 N	15.03 E
Ndjili ⬥[8]	273b	4.20 S	15.22 E
Ndjili ≃	273b	4.19 S	15.24 E
Ndjim ≃	152	4.38 N	11.24 E
Ndjo	152	1.15 S	14.30 E
Ndjolé	152	0.11 S	10.45 E
Ndogo, Lagune C	152	2.35 S	10.00 E
Ndola	154	12.58 S	28.38 E
Ndolo ⬥[8]	273b	4.19 S	15.19 E
Ndomayop	152	1.21 N	10.18 E
Ndona	115b	8.46 S	121.45 E
Ndongo	152	2.19 S	13.38 E
Ndoro Hills ∧∧[2]	146	7.15 N	11.00 E
Ndoto Mountains ∧∧	154	1.45 N	37.07 E
Ndouba	152	0.11 S	14.09 E
Ndouci	150	5.52 N	4.46 W
Ndougou	152	1.39 S	9.40 E
Ndreketi ≃	175g	16.34 S	178.53 E
Ndrhamcha, Sebkha de ⊜	150	18.45 N	15.48 W
Ndu	152	4.41 N	22.49 E
Nduguti	154	4.18 S	34.42 E
Ndumbwe	154	10.14 S	39.58 E
Ndumo Game Reserve ⬥[4]	158	26.53 S	32.15 E
Ndundure, Île I	175f	21.20 S	167.44 E
Nduye	154	1.50 N	29.01 E
Ne	268	35.47 N	140.03 E
Nea ≃	26	63.13 N	11.02 E
Neabul Creek ≃	166	27.45 S	147.32 E
Néa Erithraía	267c	38.05 N	23.49 E
Néa Filadhélfia	267c	38.02 N	23.44 E
Neagari	94	36.27 N	136.27 E
Neagh, Lough ⊜	48	54.37 N	6.25 W
Neah Bay	224	48.22 N	124.37 W
Néa Ionía	267c	38.02 N	23.45 E
Neajlov ≃	38	44.11 N	26.12 E
Néa Khalkidhón	267c	38.02 N	23.43 E
Neale, Lake ⊜	162	24.22 S	130.00 E
Neales ≃	162	28.08 S	136.47 E
Neales Flat	168b	34.15 S	139.10 E
Néa Liósia	267c	38.02 N	23.42 E
Neamț □[4]	38	47.00 N	26.30 E
Neandertal, Naturschutzgebiet ♣	263	51.15 N	7.00 E
Néa Páfos (Paphos)	130	34.45 N	32.25 E
Neapel → Napoli	68	40.51 N	14.17 E
Néa Pendéli	267c	38.04 N	23.52 E
Néa Péramos	267c	38.00 N	23.26 E
Neápolis, Ellás	38	36.30 N	23.04 E
Neápolis, Ellás	38	35.15 N	25.37 E
Neapolis, Ohio, U.S.	216	41.29 N	83.52 W
Néa Psará	38	38.23 N	23.48 E
Near Islands II	181a	52.40 N	173.30 E
Near North Side ⬥[8]	278	41.54 N	87.38 W
Néa Smírni	267c	37.57 N	23.43 E
Neasons Hill	214	41.37 N	80.08 W
Neatahwanta, Lake ⊜	210	43.18 N	76.27 W
Neath	42	51.40 N	3.48 W
Neath ≃	42	51.37 N	3.50 W
Neauphle-le-Château	50	48.49 N	1.54 E
Neauphle-le-Vieux	261	48.49 N	1.52 E
Neavitt	208	38.44 N	76.17 W
Neba	94	35.15 N	137.35 E
Néba, Île I	175f	20.09 S	163.56 E
Nebaj	236	15.24 N	91.08 W
Nebbou	150	11.18 N	1.53 W
Nebelhorn ∧	58	47.25 N	10.20 E
Nebeur	36	36.17 N	8.47 E
Nebine Creek ≃	166	29.07 S	146.56 E
Nebit-Dag	128	39.30 N	54.22 E
Neblina, Pico da ∧	246	0.48 N	66.02 W
Nebo	194	39.27 N	90.47 W
Nebo, Mount ∧, Utah, U.S.	200	39.49 N	111.46 W
Nebo, Mount → Nabā, Jabal an- ∧, Urd.	132	31.46 N	35.45 E
Nebolči	76	59.08 N	33.18 E
Nebra	54	51.17 N	11.34 E
Nebraska	218	39.04 N	85.28 W
Nebraska □[3]	178		
	198	41.30 N	100.00 W
Nebraska City	198	40.41 N	95.52 W
Nebrodi ∧∧	70	37.54 N	14.35 E
Nebyloje	80	56.22 N	39.59 E
Nečajannoje	78	46.57 N	31.33 E
Nečajevka	80	53.17 N	44.27 E
Nečajevo	82	54.42 N	37.23 E
Nečatka, Ozero ⊜	88	57.45 N	117.30 E
Necaxa ≃	234	20.16 N	97.27 W
Necedah	190	44.02 N	90.05 W
Nechajevskaja	80	50.25 N	41.44 E
Nechako ≃	182	53.56 N	122.42 W
Nechako Plateau ∧∧[1]	182	54.00 N	124.30 W
Nechako Range ∧∧	182	53.20 N	124.30 W
Nechako Reservoir ⊜[1]	182	53.25 N	125.10 W
Neche	198	48.59 N	97.33 W
Neches	222	31.52 N	95.30 W
Neches ≃	194	29.55 N	93.52 W
Nechí	246	8.07 N	74.46 W
Nechí ≃	246	8.08 N	74.46 W
Nechmeya	36	36.36 N	7.31 E
Nechranická Přehradová Nádrž ⊜[1]	54	50.20 N	13.20 E
Nechvorošča	78	49.09 N	34.44 E
Neckar ≃	30	49.31 N	8.26 E
Neckarailfingen	56	48.36 N	9.16 E
Neckarbischofsheim	56	49.17 N	8.57 E
Neckarelz	56	49.20 N	9.06 E
Neckargemünd	56	49.23 N	8.47 E
Neckarsteinach	56	49.25 N	8.53 E
Neckarsulm	56	49.12 N	9.13 E
Neckartenzlingen	56	48.35 N	9.14 E
Neck Creek ≃	276	40.36 N	74.12 W
Necker	284b	39.23 N	76.29 W
Necker Island I	14	23.35 N	164.42 W
Necker Ridge ⊹[3]	14	21.00 N	170.00 W
Necochea	252	38.33 S	58.45 W
Necropoli Anghelu Ruiu ⊥	71	40.38 N	8.20 E
Necropoli di Spina ⊥	66	44.43 N	12.08 E
Necrópolis ⬥	266a	40.25 N	3.38 W
Nedančiči	78	51.30 N	30.37 E
Ned Brown Preserve ♣	278	42.02 N	88.01 W
Nedel'noje	82	54.50 N	36.39 E
Nederbrakel	50	50.48 N	3.46 E
Nederland	194	29.58 N	93.60 W
Nederland → Netherlands □[1]	30	52.15 N	5.30 E
Nederlandse Antillen → Netherlands Antilles □[2]	241s	12.15 N	69.00 W
Neder-Rijn ≃[1]	52	51.59 N	6.20 E
Nederweert	52	51.17 N	5.45 E
Nederzwalm-Hermelgem	50	50.53 N	3.41 E
Nedlands	168a	31.59 S	115.49 E
Nedlitz	54	52.04 N	12.14 E
Nedlitz ⬥[8]	264a	52.26 N	13.03 E
Nedre Soppero	24	68.01 N	21.44 E
Nedre Vättern ⊜	40	59.49 N	15.40 E
Nedrigajlov	78	50.50 N	33.53 E
Nédroma	148	35.01 N	1.45 W
Nedrow	210	42.59 N	76.09 W
Nedstrand	26	59.21 N	5.51 E
Neebish Island I	190	46.16 N	84.09 W
Neede	52	52.08 N	6.36 E
Needham, Ind., U.S.	218	39.32 N	85.58 W
Needham, Mass., U.S.	207	42.17 N	71.14 W
Needham Market	42	52.09 N	1.03 E
Needhams Point ≻	241g	13.05 N	59.36 W
Needle Mountain ∧	202	44.05 N	109.37 W
Needles	204	34.51 N	114.37 W
Needville	222	29.24 N	95.51 W
Neelyton	214	40.10 N	77.50 W
Ñeembucú □[5]	252	27.00 S	58.00 W
Neenah	190	44.11 N	88.28 W
Neepawa	184	50.13 N	99.29 W
Neerim South	169	38.01 S	145.58 E
Neermoor	52	53.18 N	7.26 E
Neeroeteren	56	51.05 N	5.42 E
Neerpelt	56	51.13 N	5.25 E
Neersen	263	51.15 N	6.29 E
Nee Soon	271c	1.24 N	103.49 E
Neetze	52	53.15 N	10.39 E
Neetze ≃	54	53.20 N	10.28 E
Nefedjevo	82	54.39 N	37.56 E
Nefern ≃	42	52.02 N	4.50 W
Neffs	208	40.42 N	75.37 W
Neffsville	208	40.06 N	76.18 W
Nef'odovo	86	58.48 N	72.34 E
Nefta	148	33.52 N	7.33 E
Nefteabad	85	40.12 N	70.34 E
Neftečala	84	39.23 N	49.16 E
Neftegorsk	84	44.22 N	39.42 E
Neftekamsk	80	56.06 N	54.17 E
Neftekumsk	84	44.45 N	44.48 E
Nefyn	42	52.57 N	4.31 W
Negage	152	7.45 S	15.16 E
Négala	150	12.52 N	8.27 W
Negapatam → Nāgappattinam	122	10.46 N	79.50 E
Negara, Indon.	112	2.37 S	115.06 E
Negara, Indon.	115a	8.22 S	114.37 E
Negara ≃	112	3.00 S	114.45 E
Negast	54	54.15 N	13.01 E
Negaunee	190	46.30 N	87.36 W
Negba	132	31.40 N	34.41 E
Negele	144	5.20 N	39.36 E
Negenborn	52	51.53 N	9.34 E
Negeribatin	112	4.35 S	104.32 E
Negeri Sembilan □[3]	114	2.45 N	102.10 E
Negev → HaNegev ⬥[1]	132	30.30 N	34.55 E
Negishi	268	35.51 N	139.23 E
Negley	214	40.48 N	80.32 W
Negola	152	14.10 S	14.30 E
Negomano	154	11.27 S	38.31 E
Negombo	122	7.13 N	79.50 E
Negoreloje	76	53.36 N	27.04 E
Negotin	38	44.14 N	22.32 E
Negra, Laguna ⊜	252	34.03 S	53.40 W
Negra, Ponta ≻	256	22.58 S	42.42 W
Negra, Punta ≻, Belize	232	16.17 N	88.34 W
Negra, Punta ≻, Perú	248	6.06 S	81.09 W
Negra, Puntilla ≻	148	22.54 N	16.18 W
Negra, Serra ∧, Bra.	250	6.30 S	46.15 W
Negra, Serra ∧, Bra.	256	21.58 S	43.54 W
Negrais	266c	38.53 N	9.17 W
Negras, Lomas ∧[2]	286d	11.55 S	77.06 W
Negreira	34	42.54 N	8.44 W
Nègres, Pointe des ≻	240e	14.36 N	61.06 W
Negrești	38	46.50 N	27.27 E
Negrești-Oaș	38	47.52 N	23.25 E
Negrine	148	34.30 N	7.30 E
Negritos	246	4.38 S	81.19 W
Negro ≃, Arg.	254	41.02 S	62.47 W
Negro ≃, Bol.	248	9.49 S	65.42 W
Negro ≃, Bol.	248	14.11 S	63.07 W
Negro ≃, Bra.	248	19.13 S	57.17 W
Negro ≃, Bra.	248	5.15 S	70.53 W
Negro ≃, Bra.	250	9.15 S	47.34 W
Negro ≃, Bra.	252	26.01 S	50.30 W
Negro ≃, Col.	246	5.44 N	74.39 W
Negro ≃, N.A.	236	13.02 N	87.17 W
Negro ≃, Para.	252	24.23 S	57.11 W
Negro ≃, S.A.	246	3.08 S	59.55 W
Negro ≃, S.A.	252	33.24 S	58.22 W
Negro ≃, Ven.	246	9.36 N	72.15 W
Negro, Cerro ∧, Arg.	254	46.55 S	70.12 W
Negro, Cerro ∧, Arg.	254	44.09 S	69.30 W
Negro, Mar → Black Sea ⊤[2]	22	43.00 N	35.00 E
Negro Bay C	144	7.52 N	49.50 E
Negros I	116	10.00 N	123.00 E
Negros Occidental □[4]	116	10.20 N	123.00 E
Negros Oriental □[4]	116	9.40 N	123.00 E
Negru-Vodă	38	43.50 N	28.12 E
Neguac	186	47.15 N	65.05 W
Nehalem	224	45.43 N	123.54 W
Nehalem ≃	224	45.40 N	123.56 W
Nehawka	198	40.50 N	95.59 W
Nehbandān	128	31.32 N	60.02 E
Neheim-Hüsten	56	51.27 N	7.57 E
Nehonsey Brook ≃	285	39.49 N	75.18 W
Néhoué, Baie de C	175f	20.21 S	164.09 E
Neiba	238	18.28 N	71.25 W
Neiba, Bahía de C	238	18.15 N	71.02 W
Neichiang → Neijiang	107	29.35 N	105.03 E
Neidenburg → Nidzica	30	53.22 N	20.26 E
Neidpath	184	50.08 N	107.15 W
Neige, Crêt de la ∧	58	46.16 N	5.56 E
Neiges, Piton des ∧	157c	21.05 S	55.29 E
Neihart	202	46.56 N	110.44 W
Neiheshui ≃	100	22.54 N	115.38 E
Neihu	269d	25.05 N	121.35 E
Neihuang	98	35.59 N	114.55 E
Neijiang	107	29.35 N	105.03 E
Neikiang → Neijiang	107	29.35 N	105.03 E
Neilburg	184	52.50 N	109.38 W
Neillsville	190	44.34 N	90.36 W
Neilston	46	55.47 N	4.27 W
Neimen	263	51.29 N	7.48 E
Neimenggu Zizhiqu (Inner Mongolia) □[4]	90	43.00 N	115.00 E
Nein	132	32.38 N	35.21 E
Neindorf	54	52.20 N	10.50 E
Neinstedt	54	51.45 N	11.05 E
Neiqiu	98	37.17 N	114.31 E
Neira	246	5.10 N	75.32 W
Neirone	62	44.27 N	9.11 E
Neishuishan	269d	25.09 N	121.43 E
Neisse → Nysa	30	50.29 N	17.20 E
Neisse (Nysa Łużycka) (Nisa) ≃	30	52.04 N	14.46 E
Neiva	246	2.56 N	75.18 W
Neiwufuquan	105	40.11 N	117.39 E
Neixiang	102	33.12 N	111.57 E
Neizengshan ∧	100	24.02 N	117.32 E
Neja	80	58.18 N	43.54 E
Neja ≃	80	57.48 N	43.42 E
Nejapa de Madero	234	16.37 N	95.59 W
Nejdek	54	50.17 N	12.42 E
Nejo	144	9.30 N	35.30 E
Nejva ≃	86	57.54 N	62.18 E
Nekalagba	154	2.50 N	28.01 E
Nekemte	144	9.02 N	36.31 E
Nekhab ⊥	140	25.10 N	32.48 E
Nekoosa	190	44.19 N	89.54 W
Neko-zaki ≻	96	35.40 N	134.46 E
Nekrasino	82	56.18 N	36.33 E
Nekrasovka	265b	55.41 N	37.56 E
Nekrasovo, S.S.S.R.	80	51.10 N	45.18 E
Nekrasovo, S.S.S.R.	82	54.30 N	38.57 E
Nekrasovskoje	80	57.41 N	40.22 E
Nekselø I	41	55.47 N	11.18 E
Neksø	26	55.04 N	15.09 E
Nela Park ♣	279a	41.33 N	81.33 W
Nel'aty	88	56.29 N	115.41 E
Nelichu ∧	140	6.08 N	34.25 E
Nelidovo	76	56.13 N	32.46 E
Neligh	198	42.08 N	98.02 W
Nel'kan	74	57.40 N	136.13 E
Nellie	214	40.20 N	82.04 W
Nellikuppam	122	11.46 N	79.41 E
Nellingen, B.R.D.	56	48.44 N	9.18 E
Nellingen, B.R.D.	56	48.33 N	9.47 E
Nellis Air Force Base ▪	204	36.14 N	115.02 W
Nelliston	210	42.56 N	74.37 W
Nellore	122	14.26 N	79.58 E
Nel'ma	89	47.39 N	139.09 E
Nelson, B.C., Can.	182	49.29 N	117.17 W
Nelson, N.Z.	172	41.17 S	173.17 E
Nelson, Eng., U.K.	44	53.51 N	2.13 W
Nelson, Nebr., U.S.	198	40.12 N	98.04 W
Nelson, Pa., U.S.	210	41.59 N	77.14 W
Nelson ≃	184	57.04 N	92.30 W
Nelson, Cape ≻, Austl.	166	38.26 S	141.33 E
Nelson, Cape ≻, Pap. N. Gui.	164	9.00 S	149.15 E
Nelson, Estrecho ⋈	254	51.37 S	75.00 W
Nelson Creek ≃, Nev., U.S.	204	40.36 N	114.28 W
Nelson Creek ≃, Tex., U.S.	222	30.56 N	95.31 W
Nelson House	184	55.47 N	98.51 W
Nelson Island I	180	60.35 N	164.45 W
Nelson-Kennedy Ledges State Park ♣	214	41.18 N	81.04 W
Nelson Lake ⊜	184	55.44 N	100.00 W
Nelson Lakes National Park ♣	172	41.50 S	172.40 E
Nelson Reservoir ⊜[1]	202	48.30 N	107.34 W
Nelsons Dockyard ⊥	240c	17.00 N	61.46 W
Nelsonville, N.Y., U.S.	210	41.25 N	73.57 W
Nelsonville, Ohio, U.S.	188	39.27 N	82.14 W
Nelspoort	158	32.07 S	23.00 E
Nelspoortjie	158	29.58 S	22.25 E
Nelspruit	156	25.30 S	30.58 E
Néma, Maur.	150	16.37 N	7.15 W
Nema, S.S.S.R.	80	57.31 N	50.31 E
Néma, Dhar •[4]	150	16.40 N	7.13 W
Nemacolin	188	39.52 N	79.56 W
Nemadji ≃	190	46.41 N	92.02 W
Nemaha	198	40.20 N	95.40 W
Nemam	122	8.27 N	77.01 E
Neman (Ragnit)	76	55.02 N	22.02 E
Neman (Nemunas) ≃	76	55.18 N	21.23 E
Nematābād	267d	35.38 N	51.21 E
Nembe	150	4.35 N	6.26 E
Nembrala	112	10.53 S	122.50 E
Nembro	62	45.45 N	9.45 E
Něměice	60	49.26 N	13.05 E
Nemčinovka	265b	55.43 N	37.23 E
Nemda ≃, S.S.S.R.	80	57.35 N	48.56 E
Nemda ≃, S.S.S.R.	80	57.21 N	43.08 E
Nemegosenda ≃	190	48.31 N	82.53 W
Nemegt Uul ∧∧	102	43.40 N	101.10 E
Nemeiben Lake ⊜	184	55.20 N	105.20 W
Nemenčinė	76	54.51 N	25.29 E
Nemeriči	76	53.51 N	33.59 E
Nemi	66	41.43 N	12.43 E
Nemi, Lago di ⊜	267a	41.43 N	12.42 E
Nemira ∧	38	46.15 N	26.19 E
Nemirov, S.S.S.R.	78	48.58 N	28.50 E
Nemirov, S.S.S.R.	78	50.07 N	23.25 E
Nemirovo	82	55.54 N	36.12 E
Nemo	222	32.16 N	97.39 W
Nemoli	68	40.04 N	15.48 E
Nemours	50	48.16 N	2.42 E
Nemoviči	78	51.16 N	26.38 E
Nemrut Gölü ⊜	130	38.37 N	42.12 E
Nemuna, Bjeshkët e ∧∧	38	42.27 N	19.47 E
Nemunas (Neman) ≃	76	55.18 N	21.23 E
Nemuro	92a	43.20 N	145.35 E
Nemuro-hantō ≻[1]	92a	43.21 N	145.42 E
Nemuro Strait ⋈	92a	44.00 N	145.20 E
Nemzeti Múzeum ⊛	264c	47.29 N	19.05 E
Nena Creek ≃	224	45.07 N	121.07 W
Nenagh	48	52.52 N	8.12 W
Nenagh ≃	48	52.56 N	8.17 W
Nenana	180	64.34 N	149.07 W
Nenana ≃	180	64.30 N	149.00 W
Nenaševo	82	54.34 N	37.28 E
Nenasi	114	3.08 N	103.27 E
Nendaz	58	46.11 N	7.18 E
Nendeln	58	47.12 N	9.32 E
Nendö I	14	10.45 S	165.54 E
Nene ≃	42	52.48 N	0.13 E
Neneckij Nacionalnyj Okrug □[8]	24	67.30 N	54.00 E
Nenggiri ≃	114	4.53 N	101.48 E
Nengjia	104	41.38 N	120.46 E
Nengo ≃	152	14.27 S	22.09 E
Nengonengo I[1]	14	18.47 S	141.48 W
Nenndorf	52	53.23 N	9.53 E
Nenneper ≃	263	51.32 N	6.26 E
Neno	154	15.24 S	34.39 E
Nentón ≃	236	15.48 N	91.52 W
Nenzing	58	47.11 N	9.42 E
Neo	94	35.38 N	136.37 E
Neo ≃	94	35.24 N	136.34 E
Neodesha	198	37.25 N	95.41 W
Neoga	194	39.19 N	88.27 W
Neola, Iowa, U.S.	198	41.27 N	95.37 W
Neola, Utah, U.S.	200	40.26 N	110.02 W
Neon	192	37.12 N	82.43 W
Neoneli	71	40.04 N	8.57 E
Néon Fáliron	267c	37.57 N	23.40 E
Néon Karlovásion	38	37.48 N	26.44 E
Néon Psikhikón	267c	38.00 N	23.47 E
Neopit	190	44.59 N	88.50 W
Neopmuk	60	49.29 N	13.35 E
Neópolis	250	10.18 S	36.35 W
Neosho	194	36.52 N	94.22 W
Neosho ≃	194	35.48 N	95.18 W
Neotsu	224	45.00 N	123.59 W
Nepa	88	59.14 N	108.14 E
Nepa ≃	88	59.16 N	108.16 E
Nepal (Nepāl) □[1]	118		
	124	28.00 N	84.00 E
Nepālganj	124	28.03 N	81.37 E
Nepa Nagar	120	21.28 N	76.23 E
Nepaug Reservoir ⊜[1]	207	41.48 N	72.57 W
Nepean ≃	170	33.27 S	150.53 E
Nepean, Point ≻	169	38.18 S	144.39 E
Nepean Bay C	168b	35.42 S	137.44 E
Nepean Island I	174c	29.04 S	167.58 E
Nepean Reservoir ⊜[1]	170	34.22 S	150.35 E
Nepecino	82	55.12 N	38.37 E
Nepeña	248	9.10 S	78.23 W
Nepewassi Lake ⊜	190	46.20 N	80.40 W
Nephi	200	39.43 N	111.50 W
Nephin ∧	48	54.01 N	9.22 W
Nephin Beg Range ∧∧	48	54.00 N	9.35 W
Nepi	66	42.14 N	12.21 E
Nepisiguit ≃	186	47.37 N	65.38 W
Nepisiguit Bay C	186	47.46 N	65.32 W
Népliget ♣	264c	47.29 N	19.07 E
Nepoko ≃	154	1.40 N	27.01 E
Nepomuceno	256	21.14 S	45.15 W
Nepomuk	30	49.29 N	13.36 E
Neponset ≃	283	42.17 N	71.02 W
Neponset Reservoir ⊜[1]	283	42.05 N	71.15 W
Neponset River Reservation ♣	283	42.13 N	71.08 W
Neppermin	54	53.56 N	14.02 E
Nepr'adva ≃	76	53.40 N	38.39 E
Népstadion ♣	264c	47.30 N	19.06 E
Nép-sziget I	264c	47.34 N	19.05 E
Neptune, N.J., U.S.	208	40.12 N	74.02 W
Neptune, Ohio, U.S.	216	40.36 N	84.30 W
Neptune Beach	192	30.19 N	81.24 W
Neptune City	208	40.12 N	74.03 W
Neqarot, Naḥal ∨	132	30.40 N	35.15 E
Nera ≃, Eur.	38	44.49 N	21.22 E
Nera ≃, It.	66	42.26 N	12.24 E
Nérac	32	44.08 N	0.20 E
Nerákion	267c	38.01 N	23.27 E
Nerang	171a	28.00 S	153.20 E
Nerang ≃	171a	28.03 S	153.17 E
Nerastro, Sarīr ⬥[2]	146	24.20 N	20.37 E
Neratovice	54	50.14 N	14.31 E
Nerča ≃	88	51.56 N	116.40 E
Nerchau	54	51.16 N	12.47 E
Nerčinsk	88	51.58 N	116.35 E
Nerčinskij Chrebet ∧∧	88	50.50 N	117.50 E
Nerčinskij Zavod	88	51.19 N	119.36 E
Nerčugan ≃	88	53.26 N	116.38 E
Nère ≃	50	47.34 N	2.18 E
Nerechta	80	57.28 N	40.34 E
Nerenstetten	56	48.31 N	10.06 E
Neresheim	56	48.45 N	10.15 E
Nereta	76	56.13 N	25.18 E
Nereto	66	42.49 N	13.49 E
Neretva ≃	36	43.01 N	17.27 E
Nerevoznoje	80	56.53 N	53.54 E
Nerima ⬥[8]	268	35.44 N	139.42 E
Nerima, Camp ▪	268	35.45 N	139.39 E
Neringa	76	55.18 N	21.01 E
Neriquinha	152	15.45 S	21.42 E
Neris ≃	76	54.54 N	23.53 E
Nerito	66	42.32 N	13.28 E
Nerja	34	36.44 N	3.52 W
Nerka, Lake ⊜	180	59.30 N	158.45 W
Nerl', S.S.S.R.	76	57.03 N	37.59 E
Nerl', S.S.S.R.	80	56.40 N	40.24 E
Nerl' ≃, S.S.S.R.	76	57.07 N	37.39 E
Nerl' ≃, S.S.S.R.	80	56.11 N	40.34 E
Nero, Ozero ⊜	80	57.07 N	39.27 E
Neroj	88	54.28 N	97.49 E
Néronde	62	45.50 N	4.14 E
Nérondes	32	47.00 N	2.49 E
Nerópolis	255	16.25 S	49.14 W
Nerriga	170	35.07 S	150.05 E
Nerrima	162	18.24 S	124.29 E
Nerrimunga Creek ≃	170	34.57 S	150.04 E
Nersingen	58	48.25 N	10.07 E
Nerskaja ≃	82	55.23 N	38.35 E
Nerul	272c	19.02 N	73.01 E
Nerus ≃	114	5.20 N	103.05 E
Nerussa ≃	76	52.33 N	33.47 E
Nerva	34	37.42 N	6.32 W
Nervi	62	44.23 N	9.02 E
Nervia ≃	62	43.47 N	7.38 E
Nerviano	62	45.33 N	8.58 E
Nerville-la-Forêt	261	49.05 N	2.17 E
Nes, Ned.	52	53.26 N	5.45 E
Nes, Ned.	52	53.04 N	5.51 E
Nes, Nor.	26	60.34 N	9.59 E
Nes', S.S.S.R.	24	66.37 N	44.36 E
Nes, Har ∧	132	30.22 N	34.47 E
Nesbyen	26	60.34 N	9.09 E
Neščerdo, Ozero ⊜	76	55.54 N	29.04 E
Neščeretovo	83	49.24 N	38.48 E
Nesco	208	39.38 N	74.42 W
Nescochague Creek ≃	285	39.39 N	74.41 W
Nescochague Creek, Great Swamp Branch ≃	285	39.41 N	74.43 W
Nesconset	276	40.50 N	73.09 W
Nescopeck	210	41.03 N	76.13 W
Nescopeck Creek ≃	210	41.03 N	76.14 W
Nescopeck Mountain ∧	210	41.03 N	76.05 W
Nesebâr	38	42.39 N	27.44 E
Neshaminy Creek ≃	208	40.04 N	74.55 W
Neshaminy Hills	285	40.10 N	74.57 W
Neshannock Creek ≃	214	40.59 N	80.21 W
Nesher	132	32.46 N	35.03 E
Neškan	180	67.03 N	173.01 W
Neškanpil'gun, Laguna C	180	66.57 N	172.45 W
Neskaupstaður	24a	65.10 N	13.43 W
Neskowin	224	45.05 N	123.59 W
Nesle	50	49.46 N	2.55 E
Nesna	24	66.12 N	13.02 E
Nesque ≃	62	43.59 N	4.59 E
Nesquehoning	210	40.52 N	75.49 W
Ness	262	53.17 N	3.03 W
Ness, Loch ⊜	46	57.18 N	4.27 W
Ness City	198	38.27 N	99.54 W
Nesse ≃	54	50.59 N	10.32 E
Nesselrode, Mount ∧	180	58.58 N	134.18 W
Nesselwang	58	47.37 N	10.30 E
Nesselwängle	58	47.29 N	10.37 E
Nesslau	58	47.13 N	9.13 E
Nessmersiel	52	53.40 N	7.21 E
Nesso	58	45.55 N	9.08 E
Neštěmice	54	50.40 N	14.07 E
Nesterkovo	76	59.10 N	30.33 E
Nesterov, S.S.S.R.	76	54.38 N	22.34 E
Nesterov, S.S.S.R.	78	50.04 N	23.58 E
Nesterovka	80	52.26 N	53.42 E
Nesterovo, S.S.S.R.	80	54.31 N	41.49 E
Nesterovo, S.S.S.R.	82	56.45 N	36.30 E
Nesterovo, S.S.S.R.	88	52.22 N	107.53 E
Nestiary	80	56.34 N	45.21 E
Nestoita	78	47.47 N	29.21 E
Neston	44	53.18 N	3.04 W
Nestore ≃	66	43.21 N	12.15 E
Néstos (Mesta) ≃	38	40.41 N	24.44 E
Nesttun	26	60.19 N	5.20 E
Nestucca ≃	224	45.12 N	123.57 W
Nesvetaj	83	47.27 N	39.40 E
Nesviž	76	53.13 N	26.40 E
Nes Ẕiyyona	132	31.55 N	34.48 E
Netanya	132	32.20 N	34.51 E
Netarhāt	124	23.29 N	84.16 E
Netarts	224	45.26 N	123.57 W
Netarts Bay C	224	45.24 N	123.56 W
Netcong	210	40.54 N	74.42 W
Nethan ≃	46	55.42 N	3.52 W
Nether Alderley	262	53.17 N	2.14 W
Netherdale	166	21.08 S	148.32 E
Netherlands □[1]	22		
	30	52.15 N	5.30 E
Netherlands Antilles □[2]	230		
	241s	12.15 N	69.00 W
Netherton	262	53.30 N	2.58 W
Nethy Bridge	46	57.16 N	3.38 W
Netia	154	14.48 S	39.59 E
Netley Marsh	42	50.53 N	1.21 W
Neto ≃	68	39.13 N	17.08 E
Netolice	61	49.03 N	14.12 E
Netra	56	51.06 N	10.05 E
Netrakona	124	24.53 N	90.43 E
Netstal	58	47.03 N	9.03 E
Nettancourt	56	48.52 N	4.57 E
Nette	52	52.02 N	10.05 E
Nette ⬥[8]	263	51.33 N	7.25 E
Nettelstedt	52	52.18 N	8.41 E
Nettetal	56	51.18 N	6.16 E
Nettilling Fiord C[2]	176	66.02 N	68.12 W
Nettilling Lake ⊜	176	66.30 N	70.40 W
Nett Lake ⊜	190	48.10 N	93.10 W
Nett Lake Indian Reservation ⬥[4]	190	48.06 N	93.10 W
Nettlebed	42	51.35 N	1.00 W
Nettle Creek ≃	218	40.03 N	83.48 W
Nettleden	260	51.47 N	0.32 W
Nettlestead	260	51.14 N	0.25 E
Nettlestead Green	260	51.14 N	0.25 E
Nettleton	194	34.05 N	88.44 W
Nettuno	66	41.27 N	12.39 E
Nettuno, Grotta di •[5]	71	40.34 N	8.09 E
Netze → Noteć ≃	30	52.44 N	15.26 E
Netzschkau	54	50.36 N	12.14 E
Neualbenreuth	60	49.59 N	12.27 E
Neuastenberg	56	51.10 N	8.29 E
Neubeckum	52	51.48 N	8.01 E
Neu Bentschen → Zbąszynek	30	52.15 N	15.50 E
Neubrandenburg	54	53.33 N	13.15 E
Neubrandenburg □[5]	54	53.30 N	13.15 E
Neubraunschweig → New Brunswick □[4]	186	46.30 N	66.15 W
Neubritannien → New Britain I	164	6.00 S	150.00 E
Neu Büddenstedt	54	52.10 N	10.31 E
Neubukow	54	54.02 N	11.40 E
Neuburg am Inn	60	48.30 N	13.27 E
Neuburg an der Donau	60	48.44 N	11.11 E
Neuchâtel	58	46.59 N	6.56 E
Neuchâtel □[3]	58	47.00 N	6.55 E
Neuchâtel, Lac de ⊜	58	46.52 N	6.50 E
Neudamm → Dębno	30	52.45 N	14.40 E
Neu-Delhi → New Delhi	124	28.36 N	77.12 E
Neudenau	56	49.17 N	9.16 E
Neudietendorf	54	50.55 N	10.55 E
Neudorf, B.R.D.	56	49.10 N	8.29 E
Neudorf, Sask., Can.	184	50.44 N	102.59 W
Neudorf, D.D.R.	54	50.29 N	12.58 E
Neudorf ⬥[8]	263	51.25 N	6.47 E
Neue Hebriden → New Hebrides □[2]	175f	16.00 S	167.00 E
Neuemühle	264a	52.18 N	13.39 E
Neuenburg, B.R.D.	52	53.23 N	7.57 E
Neuenbürg, B.R.D.	56	48.50 N	8.35 E
Neuenburg, B.R.D.	58	47.49 N	7.35 E
Neuenburg → Neuchâtel, Schw.	58	46.59 N	6.56 E
Neuendettelsau	56	49.17 N	10.47 E
Neuendorf	54	54.31 N	13.05 E
Neuendorfer See ⊜	54	52.07 N	13.55 E
Neuenegg	58	46.54 N	7.18 E
Neuenhagen bei Berlin	54	52.32 N	13.41 E
Neuenhaus	52	52.30 N	6.59 E
Neuenhof ⬥[8]	263	51.10 N	7.13 E
Neuenhoven	263	51.08 N	6.31 E
Neue Niers ≃	263	51.16 N	6.26 E
Neuenkamp ⬥[8]	263	51.26 N	6.44 E
Neuenkirchen, B.R.D.	52	51.50 N	8.26 E
Neuenkirchen, B.R.D.	52	53.46 N	8.53 E
Neuenkirchen, B.R.D.	52	52.30 N	8.04 E
Neuenkirchen, B.R.D.	52	52.14 N	7.22 E
Neuenkirchen, B.R.D.	52	53.14 N	8.31 E
Neuenkirchen, B.R.D.	52	53.02 N	9.42 E
Neuenkirchen, D.D.R.	54	53.32 N	13.20 E
Neuenland, Flughafen ⊠	52	53.03 N	8.46 E
Neuenrade	56	51.17 N	7.47 E
Neuensalz	54	50.30 N	12.13 E

Symbol	English	Deutsch	Español	Français	Português
≃	River	Fluss	Rio	Rivière	Rio
	Canal	Kanal	Canal	Canal	Canal
	Waterfall, Rapids	Wasserfall, Stromschnellen	Cascada, Rápidos	Chute d'eau, Rapides	Cascata, Rápidos
⋈	Strait	Meeresstrasse	Estrecho	Détroit	Estreito
C	Bay, Gulf	Bucht, Golf	Bahía, Golfo	Baie, Golfe	Baía, Golfo
⊜	Lake, Lakes	See, Seen	Lago, Lagos	Lac, Lacs	Lago, Lagos
☷	Swamp	Sumpf	Pantano	Marais	Pântano
	Ice Features, Glacier	Eis- und Gletscherformen	Accidentes Glaciales	Formes glaciaires	Acidentes Glaciares
⊤	Other Hydrographic Features	Andere Hydrographische Objekte	Otros Elementos Hidrográficos	Autres données hydrographiques	Outros Elementos Hidrográficos
⊹	Submarine Features	Untermeerische Objekte	Accidentes Submarinos	Formes de relief sous-marin	Acidentes Submarinos
□	Political Unit	Politische Einheit	Unidad Política	Entité politique	Unidade Política
⊛	Cultural Institution	Kulturelle Institution	Institución Cultural	Institution culturelle	Instituição Cultural
⊥	Historical Site	Historische Stätte	Sitio Histórico	Site historique	Sítio Histórico
♣	Recreational Site	Erholungs- und Ferienort	Sitio de Recreo	Centre de loisirs	Sítio de Lazer
⊠	Airport	Flughafen	Aeropuerto	Aéroport	Aeroporto
▪	Military Installation	Militäranlage	Instalación Militar	Installation militaire	Instalação Militar
⬥	Miscellaneous	Verschiedenes	Misceláneo	Divers	Miscelânea

Name	Page	Lat.°′	Long.°′
Neuenstadt am Kocher	56	49.14 N	9.20 E
Neuenwalde	52	53.40 N	8.40 E
Neuerburg	56	50.00 N	6.17 E
Neu-Erlaa ◆[8]	264b	48.08 N	16.19 E
Neues Palais ⊥	264a	52.24 N	13.01 E
Neu Fahrland	264a	52.26 N	13.03 E
Neufahrn bei Freising	60	48.19 N	11.40 E
Neufahrn in Niederbayern	60	48.44 N	12.11 E
Neuf-Brisach	58	48.01 N	7.32 E
Neufchâteau, Bel.	56	49.50 N	5.26 E
Neufchâteau, Fr.	58	48.21 N	5.42 E
Neufchâtel-en-Bray	50	49.44 N	1.27 E
Neufchâtel-sur-Aisne	50	49.26 N	4.02 E
Neufelden	61	48.29 N	14.00 E
Neuffen	56	48.33 N	9.22 E
Neuffossé, Canal de ≍	50	50.45 N	2.15 E
Neufmanil	56	49.49 N	4.48 E
Neuf-Marché	50	49.25 N	1.43 E
Neufmontiers-lès-Meaux	261	48.58 N	2.50 E
Neufundland → Newfoundland □[4]	176	52.00 N	56.00 W
Neufvilles	50	50.34 N	4.00 E
Neugersdorf	54	50.59 N	14.36 E
Neuglobsow	54	53.09 N	13.02 E
Neugraben-Fischbek ◆[8]	52	53.28 N	9.52 E
Neuguinea → New Guinea I	164	5.00 S	140.00 E
Neuharlingersiel	52	53.42 N	7.42 E
Neu-Hartmannsdorf	264a	52.22 N	13.51 E
Neuhaus, B.R.D.	58	47.48 N	8.34 E
Neuhaus, D.D.R.	54	53.17 N	10.55 E
Neuhaus, D.D.R.	54	50.30 N	11.08 E
Neuhaus, Öst.	61	47.47 N	15.11 E
Neuhaus an der Oste	52	53.48 N	9.02 E
Neuhausen, B.R.D.	58	47.58 N	8.55 E
Neuhausen, D.D.R.	54	50.41 N	13.28 E
Neuhausen, Schw.	58	47.41 N	8.37 E
Neuhausen → Gurjevsk, S.S.S.R.	76	54.47 N	20.38 E
Neuhausen auf den Fildern	56	48.41 N	9.16 E
Neuhaus im Solling	52	51.45 N	9.31 E
Neuhaus-Schierschnitz	54	50.19 N	11.14 E
Neuheum	114	5.34 N	95.32 E
Neuhof	56	50.27 N	9.40 E
Neuhof an der Zenn	56	49.27 N	10.38 E
Neuillé-Pont-Pierre	50	47.33 N	0.33 E
Neuilly-en-Thelle	50	49.13 N	2.17 E
Neuilly-l'Évêque	58	47.55 N	5.26 E
Neuilly-Saint-Front	50	49.10 N	3.16 E
Neuilly-sur-Marne	261	48.51 N	2.32 E
Neuilly-sur-Seine	50	48.53 N	2.16 E
Neuirland → New Ireland I	164	3.20 S	152.00 E
Neu-Isenburg	56	50.03 N	8.41 E
Neukagran ◆[8]	264b	48.14 N	16.27 E
Neu-Kaledonien → New Caledonia □[2]	175f	21.30 S	165.30 E
Neukalen	54	53.49 N	12.47 E
Neu Kaliss	54	53.10 N	11.17 E
Neukieritzsch	54	51.10 N	12.25 E
Neukirch, B.R.D.	58	47.39 N	9.41 E
Neukirch, D.D.R.	54	51.05 N	14.20 E
Neukirch, D.D.R.	54	51.17 N	13.58 E
Neukirchen, B.R.D.	41	54.52 N	8.44 E
Neukirchen, B.R.D.	54	54.19 N	11.01 E
Neukirchen, B.R.D.	56	50.46 N	9.41 E
Neukirchen, B.R.D.	56	49.29 N	6.50 E
Neukirchen, B.R.D.	60	49.05 N	11.45 E
Neukirchen, B.R.D.	263	51.07 N	6.41 E
Neukirchen, D.D.R.	54	50.46 N	12.52 E
Neukirchen, D.D.R.	54	51.05 N	12.32 E
Neukirchen, D.D.R.	54	50.47 N	12.22 E
Neukirchen, Öst.	64	47.15 N	12.17 E
Neukirchen, Öst.	64	47.52 N	13.42 E
Neukirchen am Walde	60	48.24 N	13.46 E
Neukirchen bei Sulzbach-Rosenberg	60	49.32 N	11.38 E
Neukirchen-Vluyn	56	51.27 N	6.33 E
Neukloster	54	53.52 N	11.41 E
Neukölln ◆[8]	264a	52.29 N	13.27 E
Neukuhren → Pionerskij	76	54.57 N	20.20 E
Neulangerwisch	264a	52.19 N	13.04 E
Neulienken	54	53.27 N	14.22 E
Neu Lübbenau	54	52.04 N	13.53 E
Neulussheim	56	49.17 N	8.31 E
Neumagen	56	49.51 N	6.53 E
Neuman Creek ≃	284a	42.42 N	78.48 W
Neumark	54	50.39 N	12.21 E
Neumarkt → Środa Śląska, Pol.	30	51.10 N	16.36 E
Neumarkt → Tîrgu-Secuiesc, Rom.	38	46.00 N	26.08 E
Neumarkt → Tîrgu Mureș, Rom.	38	46.33 N	24.33 E
Neumarkt am Wallersee	64	47.57 N	13.14 E
Neumarkt im Hansruckkreis	60	48.16 N	13.45 E
Neumarkt in der Oberpfalz	60	49.16 N	11.28 E
Neumarkt in Steiermark	61	47.04 N	14.25 E
Neumarkt-Sankt Veit	60	48.22 N	12.30 E
Neumittelwalde → Międzybórz	30	51.24 N	17.40 E
Neumühle	60	49.28 N	11.50 E
Neumünster	30	54.04 N	9.59 E
Neun ≃	110	19.42 N	104.03 E
Neunburg vorm Wald	60	49.21 N	12.24 E
Neundorf	54	51.49 N	11.34 E
Neung-sur-Beuvron	50	47.32 N	1.48 E
Neunkirchen, B.R.D.	56	50.32 N	8.06 E
Neunkirchen, Öst.	61	47.43 N	16.05 E
Neunkirchen am Brand	60	49.37 N	11.08 E
Neunkirchen am Potzberg	56	49.30 N	7.29 E
Neunkirchen/saar	56	49.20 N	7.10 E
Neuötting	60	48.14 N	12.42 E
Neupetershain	54	51.36 N	14.09 E
Neuquén	252	38.57 S	68.04 W
Neuquén □[4]	254	39.00 S	70.00 W
Neuquén ≃	252	38.59 S	68.00 W
Neurara	252	24.10 S	68.29 W
Neuravensburg	58	47.38 N	9.46 E
Neureisenberg	264b	48.01 N	16.30 E
Neurode → Nowa Ruda	30	50.35 N	16.31 E
Neuruppin	54	52.55 N	12.48 E
Neusalz → Nowa Sól	30	51.48 N	15.44 E
Neusalza-Spremberg	54	51.02 N	14.32 E
Neu Sankt Johann	58	47.14 N	9.12 E
Neusatz → Novi Sad	38	45.15 N	19.50 E
Neuschottland → Nova Scotia □[4]	186	45.00 N	63.00 W
Neuschwanstein, Schloss ⊻	58	47.35 N	10.44 E
Neuse ≃	192	35.06 N	76.30 W
Neuseddin	264a	52.18 N	12.59 E
Neuseeland → New Zealand □[1]	172	41.00 S	174.00 E
Neusibirische Inseln → Novosibirskije Ostrova II	74	75.00 N	142.00 E
Neusiedl am See	61	47.57 N	16.51 E
Neusiedler See (Fertő) ⊜	61	47.50 N	16.45 E
Neusohl → Banská Bystrica	30	48.44 N	19.07 E
Neusorg	60	49.56 N	11.58 E
Neuss	56	51.12 N	6.41 E
Neusserweyhe ◆[8]	263	51.13 N	6.39 E
Neustadt, B.R.D.	56	50.51 N	9.07 E
Neustadt, Ont., Can.	212	44.05 N	81.00 W
Neustadt, D.D.R.	54	51.01 N	14.13 E
Neustadt, D.D.R.	54	50.44 N	11.44 E
Neustadt, D.D.R.	54	52.52 N	12.25 E
Neustadt ◆[8]	52	53.04 N	8.47 E
Neustadt am Rübenberge	52	52.30 N	9.28 E
Neustadt an der Aisch	56	49.34 N	10.37 E
Neustadt an der Donau	60	48.48 N	11.46 E
Neustadt an der Waldnaab	60	49.44 N	12.11 E
Neustadt an der Weinstrasse	56	49.21 N	8.08 E
Neustadt bei Coburg	56	50.19 N	11.07 E
Neustädtel → Nowe Miasteczko	30	51.42 N	15.45 E
Neustädter Bucht C	54	54.02 N	10.50 E
Neustadt-Glewe	54	53.25 N	11.36 E
Neustadt in Holstein	54	54.06 N	10.48 E
Neustadt in Oberschlesien → Prudnik	30	50.19 N	17.34 E
Neustettin → Szczecinek	30	53.43 N	16.42 E
Neustift am Walde ◆[8]	264b	48.15 N	16.18 E
Neustift im Stubaital	64	47.07 N	11.19 E
Neustrelitz	54	53.21 N	13.04 E
Neuteich → Nowy Staw	30	54.09 N	19.00 E
Neu Töplitz	264a	52.27 N	12.54 E
Neutral Hills ▲[2]	184	52.10 N	110.50 W
Neutral Zone □[2]	128	29.10 N	45.30 E
Neutraubling	60	48.59 N	12.12 E
Neutrebbin	54	52.40 N	14.13 E
Neu-Ulm	58	48.23 N	10.01 E
Neuve-Chapelle	50	50.35 N	2.47 E
Neuves-Maisons	58	48.37 N	6.06 E
Neuvic	32	45.23 N	2.16 E
Neuville-aux-Bois	50	48.04 N	2.03 E
Neuville-de-Poitou	32	46.41 N	0.15 E
Neuville-en-Condroz	56	50.32 N	5.27 E
Neuville-lès-Dieppe	50	49.55 N	1.06 E
Neuville-sur-Oise	261	49.01 N	2.04 E
Neuville-sur-Saône	62	45.52 N	4.51 E
Neuvy-le-Roi	50	47.36 N	0.36 E
Neuvy-sur-Barangeon	50	47.19 N	2.15 E
Neuvy-sur-Loire	50	47.31 N	2.53 E
Neuwaldegg ◆[8]	264b	48.14 N	16.17 E
Neuwarp → Nowe Warpno	30	53.44 N	14.16 E
Neuwedell → Drawno	30	53.13 N	15.45 E
Neuwerk ◆[8]	263	51.13 N	6.28 E
Neuwerk I	52	53.55 N	8.30 E
Neuwied	56	50.25 N	7.27 E
Neuwiller-lès-Saverne	56	48.49 N	7.24 E
Neuwirtshaus	56	50.11 N	9.50 E
Neu Wulmstorf	52	53.28 N	9.48 E
Neuzelle	54	52.05 N	14.38 E
Neu Zittau	54	52.23 N	13.44 E
Neva ≃	265a	59.55 N	30.15 E
Névache	62	45.01 N	6.37 E
Nevada, Iowa, U.S.	190	42.01 N	93.27 W
Nevada, Mo., U.S.	194	37.51 N	94.22 W
Nevada, Ohio, U.S.	214	40.49 N	83.08 W
Nevada, Tex., U.S.	222	33.02 N	96.22 W
Nevada □[6]	226	39.16 N	121.01 W
Nevada □[3]	178		
	204	39.00 N	117.00 W
Nevada, Sierra ▲, Esp.	34	37.05 N	3.10 W
Nevada, Sierra ▲, Calif., U.S.	204	38.00 N	119.15 W
Nevada City	226	39.16 N	121.01 W
Nevada Creek ≃	202	46.54 N	113.02 W
Nevado de Toluca, Parque Nacional ♠	234	19.10 N	99.50 W
Neval'cevo	86	58.38 N	81.53 E
Nevali	272c	19.01 N	73.07 E
Nevanka	88	56.30 N	98.54 E
Neve, Serra da ▲	152	13.52 S	13.26 E
Nevel'	76	56.02 N	29.55 E
Nevel'sk	89	46.40 N	141.53 E
Nevel'skogo, Proliv ⋃	89	52.05 N	141.35 E
Nevendon	260	51.36 N	0.30 E
Never	89	53.58 N	124.05 E
Neverkino	80	52.47 N	46.44 E
Neverovo	80	55.07 N	44.24 E
Nevers	32	47.00 N	3.09 E
Neversink ≃	210	41.21 N	74.42 W
Neversink Reservoir ⊜[1]	210	41.48 N	74.42 W
Nevertire	166	31.52 S	147.39 E
Neves	256	22.51 S	43.06 W
Nevesinje	38	43.15 N	18.07 E
Nevėžis ≃	76	54.56 N	23.46 E
Nevežkino	80	53.07 N	43.19 E
Neviano	68	40.06 N	18.06 E
Neviano degli Arduini	64	44.35 N	10.19 E
Neviges	56	51.19 N	7.05 E
Neville Island	279b	40.31 N	80.08 W
Neville Island I	279b	40.31 N	80.08 W
Nevinnomyssk	84	44.38 N	41.56 E
Nevis I	238	17.10 N	62.34 W
Nevis ≃	46	56.50 N	5.00 W
Nevis, Ben ∧	46	56.48 N	4.59 W
Nevis, Loch C	46	57.01 N	5.43 W
Nevjansk	86	57.32 N	60.13 E
Nevlunghamn	26	58.58 N	9.52 E
Nevon	88	58.07 N	102.49 E
Nevşehir	130	38.38 N	34.43 E
Nevşehir □[4]	130	38.50 N	34.40 E
Nevskoje	76	58.08 N	30.26 E
New ≃, Belize	232	18.22 N	88.24 W
New ≃, Guy.	246	3.23 N	57.36 W
New ≃, N.A.	204	33.08 N	115.44 W
New ≃, Eng., U.K.	260	51.40 N	0.01 W
New ≃, U.S.	192	38.10 N	81.12 W
New ≃, Ariz., U.S.	200	33.31 N	112.18 W
New ≃, Fla., U.S.	192	29.50 N	84.40 W
New ≃, Fla., U.S.	192	29.55 N	82.25 W
New ≃, N.C., U.S.	192	34.32 N	77.20 W
New ≃, S.C., U.S.	192	32.09 N	80.50 W
New ≃, Tenn., U.S.	192	36.25 N	84.38 W
Newabāgam	272b	22.48 N	88.24 E
New Abbey	44	54.59 N	3.38 W
New Addington ◆[8]	260	51.21 N	0.01 W
Newala	154	10.56 S	39.18 E
New Albany, Ind., U.S.	218	38.18 N	85.49 W
New Albany, Miss., U.S.	194	34.29 N	89.00 W
New Albany, Ohio, U.S.	214	40.05 N	82.49 W
New Albany, Pa., U.S.	210	41.36 N	76.27 W
New Albin	190	43.30 N	91.17 W
New Alexandria, Ohio, U.S.	214	40.17 N	80.40 W
New Alexandria, Pa., U.S.	214	40.24 N	79.25 W
New Alexandria, Va., U.S.	284c	38.47 N	77.03 W
New Alfa	140	15.10 N	35.40 E
New Almaden	226	37.11 N	121.49 W
New Alresford	42	51.06 N	1.10 W
New Amsterdam	246	6.15 N	57.31 W
New Angledool	166	29.07 S	147.57 E
Newark, Ark., U.S.	194	35.42 N	91.27 W
Newark, Calif., U.S.	226	37.32 N	122.02 W
Newark, Del., U.S.	208	39.41 N	75.45 W
Newark, Ill., U.S.	216	41.32 N	88.35 W
Newark, Md., U.S.	208	38.15 N	75.17 W
Newark, Mo., U.S.	219	39.60 N	91.59 W
Newark, N.J., U.S.	210		
	276	40.44 N	74.10 W
Newark, N.Y., U.S.	210	43.03 N	77.06 W
Newark, Ohio, U.S.	214	40.04 N	82.24 W
Newark, Tex., U.S.	222	33.00 N	97.29 W
Newark, Port C	276	40.42 N	74.08 W
Newark Airport ⊠	210	40.42 N	74.10 W
Newark Bay C	276	40.39 N	74.09 W
Newark Bay Bridge ◆[5]	276	40.42 N	74.07 W
Newark Lake ⊜	204	39.41 N	115.44 W
Newark Slough ≃	282	37.31 N	122.05 W
Newark-upon-Trent	42	53.05 N	0.49 W
Newark Valley	210	42.14 N	76.11 W
New Athens, Ill., U.S.	219	38.19 N	89.53 W
New Athens, Ohio, U.S.	214	40.11 N	81.00 W
New Augusta	194	31.12 N	89.02 W
Newaukum, North Fork ≃	224	46.36 N	122.51 W
Newaukum, South Fork ≃	224	46.36 N	122.51 W
Newaygo	190	43.25 N	85.48 W
New Baden, Ill., U.S.	219	38.32 N	89.42 W
New Baden, Tex., U.S.	222	31.03 N	96.26 W
New Baltimore, Mich., U.S.	214	42.41 N	82.44 W
New Baltimore, N.Y., U.S.	210	42.27 N	73.47 W
New Bavaria	216	41.12 N	84.10 W
New Bedford, Mass., U.S.	207	41.38 N	70.56 W
New Bedford, Pa., U.S.	214	41.06 N	80.30 W
New Bedford ≃	42	52.35 N	0.20 E
Newberg	224	45.18 N	122.58 W
New Berlin, Ill., U.S.	219	39.44 N	89.55 W
New Berlin, N.Y., U.S.	210	42.38 N	75.20 W
New Berlin, Pa., U.S.	210	40.53 N	76.59 W
New Berlin, Wis., U.S.	216	42.58 N	88.07 W
New Berlinville	208	40.20 N	75.38 W
Newbern, Ala., U.S.	194	32.36 N	87.38 W
Newbern, Ill., U.S.	219	39.01 N	90.20 W
New Bern, N.C., U.S.	192	35.07 N	77.03 W
Newberry, Fla., U.S.	192	29.39 N	82.37 W
Newberry, Mich., U.S.	190	46.21 N	85.30 W
Newberry, S.C., U.S.	192	34.17 N	81.37 W
New Bethlehem	214	41.00 N	79.20 W
Newbiggin-by-the-Sea	44	55.11 N	1.30 W
New Bloomfield, Mo., U.S.	219	38.43 N	92.05 W
New Bloomfield, Pa., U.S.	208	40.25 N	77.11 W
New Bloomington	214	40.35 N	83.19 W
Newbold Island I	285	40.08 N	74.45 W
Newboro	212	44.39 N	76.19 W
Newboro Lake ⊜	212	44.38 N	76.20 W
Newborough, Austl.	169	38.11 S	146.17 E
Newborough, Wales, U.K.	44	53.09 N	4.22 W
New Boston, Ill., U.S.	190	41.10 N	91.00 W
New Boston, Mich., U.S.	216	42.10 N	83.24 W
New Boston, Ohio, U.S.	218	38.45 N	82.56 W
New Boston, Tex., U.S.	194	33.28 N	94.25 W
New Braintree	207	42.19 N	72.07 W
New Braunfels	196	29.42 N	98.08 W
New Bremen	216	40.26 N	84.23 W
Newbridge → Droichead Nua	48	53.11 N	6.48 W
Newbridge on Wye	42	52.13 N	3.27 W
New Brighton, N.Z.	172	43.31 S	172.44 E
New Brighton, Eng., U.K.	262	53.26 N	3.03 W
New Brighton, Pa., U.S.	214	40.44 N	80.19 W
New Brighton ◆[8]	276	40.38 N	74.06 W
New Britain, Conn., U.S.	207	41.40 N	72.47 W
New Britain, Pa., U.S.	208	40.18 N	75.11 W
New Britain I	164	6.00 S	150.00 E
New Britain Trench ✢[1]	14	6.00 S	152.30 E
New Brockton	194	31.23 N	85.57 W
Newbrook	182	54.19 N	112.57 W
New Brunswick, Ind., U.S.	218	39.57 N	86.31 W
New Brunswick, N.J., U.S.	208	40.29 N	74.27 W
New Brunswick □[4]	176		
	186	46.30 N	66.15 W
New Buffalo, Mich., U.S.	216	41.47 N	86.45 W
New Buffalo, Pa., U.S.	208	40.27 N	76.58 W
New Bullards Bar Reservoir ⊜[1]	226	39.25 N	121.08 W
Newburg, Mo., U.S.	194	37.55 N	91.54 W
Newburg, Pa., U.S.	208	40.08 N	77.32 W
Newburg, Pa., U.S.	214	40.31 N	78.25 W
Newburgh, Ont., Can.	212	44.19 N	76.52 W
Newburgh, Eng., U.K.	262	53.35 N	2.47 W
Newburgh, Scot., U.K.	46	56.20 N	3.15 W
Newburgh, Scot., U.K.	46	57.18 N	2.00 W
Newburgh, Ind., U.S.	194	37.57 N	87.24 W
Newburgh, N.Y., U.S.	210	41.30 N	74.01 W
Newburgh Heights	279a	41.27 N	81.40 W
Newburn	44	54.59 N	1.43 W
Newbury, Ont., Can.	214	42.41 N	81.48 W
Newbury, Eng., U.K.	42	51.25 N	1.20 W
Newbury, Mass., U.S.	207	42.48 N	70.52 W
Newbury Old Town	207	42.46 N	70.51 W
Newbury Park	228	34.11 N	118.53 W
Newburyport	207	42.49 N	70.53 W
Newby	44	54.20 N	0.28 W
Newby Bridge	44	54.16 N	2.58 W
New Caledonia □[2]	14		
	175f	21.30 S	165.30 E
New Canaan	207	41.09 N	73.30 W
New Caney	222	30.09 N	95.13 W
New Canton	219	39.38 N	91.06 W
New Carlisle, Qué., Can.	186	48.01 N	65.20 W
New Carlisle, Ind., U.S.	216	41.42 N	86.31 W
New Carlisle, Ohio, U.S.	218	39.56 N	84.02 W
New Carrollton	284c	38.58 N	76.53 W
New Cassel	276	40.44 N	73.36 W
Newcastle, Austl.	170	32.56 S	151.46 E
Newcastle, N.B., Can.	186	47.00 N	65.34 W
Newcastle, Ont., Can.	212	43.55 N	78.35 W
Newcastle, Eire	48	52.16 N	7.48 W
Newcastle, S. Afr.	158	27.49 S	29.55 E
Newcastle, Eng., U.K.	42	52.26 N	3.06 W
Newcastle, N. Ire., U.K.	48	54.12 N	5.54 W
Newcastle, Calif., U.S.	226	38.53 N	121.08 W
New Castle, Colo., U.S.	200	39.34 N	107.32 W
New Castle, Del., U.S.	208	39.40 N	75.34 W
New Castle, Ind., U.S.	218	39.55 N	85.22 W
New Castle, Ky., U.S.	218	38.26 N	85.10 W
Newcastle, Maine, U.S.	188	44.02 N	69.33 W
Newcastle, Nebr., U.S.	198	42.39 N	96.53 W
Newcastle, Ohio, U.S.	214	40.20 N	82.10 W
New Castle, Pa., U.S.	214	41.00 N	80.20 W
Newcastle, Tex., U.S.	196	33.12 N	98.44 W
New Castle, Va., U.S.	192	37.30 N	80.07 W
Newcastle, Wyo., U.S.	198	43.50 N	104.11 W
New Castle □[6]	208	39.44 N	75.33 W
Newcastle (Ouston) Airport ⊠	44	55.01 N	1.53 W
Newcastle Bay C	164	10.50 S	142.37 E
Newcastle Bight C[3]	170	32.51 S	151.54 E
Newcastle Creek ≃	164	17.20 S	133.23 E
Newcastle Emlyn	42	52.02 N	4.28 W
Newcastle Mine	182	51.28 N	112.46 W
Newcastleton	44	55.11 N	2.49 W
Newcastle-under-Lyme	44	53.00 N	2.14 W
Newcastle upon Tyne	44	54.59 N	1.35 W
Newcastle Waters	162	17.24 S	133.24 E
Newcastle West	48	52.27 N	9.03 W
New Centerville	285	40.04 N	75.26 W
Newcestown	48	51.47 N	8.51 W
New Chicago	216	41.34 N	87.16 W
Newchurch, Wales, U.K.	42	52.09 N	3.08 W
New Church, Va., U.S.	208	37.59 N	75.32 W
New City	210	41.09 N	73.59 W
Newclare ◆[8]	273d	26.11 S	27.58 E
New Columbia	210	41.02 N	76.52 W
New Columbus	210	41.10 N	76.18 W
Newcomerstown	214	40.16 N	81.36 W
New Concord	188	40.00 N	81.44 W
New Corydon	216	40.34 N	84.51 W
New Croton Aqueduct ≍[1]	276	41.11 N	73.49 W
New Croton Reservoir ⊜[1]	210	41.14 N	73.46 W
New Cumberland, Pa., U.S.	208	40.14 N	76.53 W
New Cumberland, W. Va., U.S.	214	40.30 N	80.36 W
New Cumberland Dam ◆[6]	214	40.32 N	80.37 W
New Cumnock	44	55.24 N	4.12 W
New Dayton	182	49.25 N	112.23 W
New Deer	46	57.30 N	2.12 W
Newdegate	162	33.06 S	119.01 E
New Delhi	124		
	272a	28.36 N	77.12 E
New Delhi Railroad Station ◆[5]	272a	28.39 N	77.13 E
New Denver	182	49.59 N	117.22 W
New Derry	214	40.21 N	79.19 W
New Don Pedro Reservoir ⊜[1]	226	37.43 N	120.23 W
New Dundee	212	43.21 N	80.31 W
New Dungeness Bay C	224	48.10 N	123.07 W
New Eagle	214	40.12 N	79.56 W
New Edinburg	194	33.46 N	92.14 W
New Effington	198	45.51 N	96.55 W
New Egypt	208	40.04 N	74.32 W
Newell, Iowa, U.S.	198	42.36 N	95.00 W
Newell, S. Dak., U.S.	198	44.43 N	103.25 W
Newell, W. Va., U.S.	214	40.36 N	80.36 W
Newell, Lake ⊜, Austl.	162	24.50 S	126.10 E
Newell, Lake ⊜, Alta., Can.	182	50.25 N	111.56 W
New Ellenton	192	33.24 N	81.42 W
Newellton	194	32.10 N	91.14 W
New Eltham ◆[8]	260	51.26 N	0.04 E
New Empire	226	40.35 N	119.21 W
New England	198	46.32 N	102.52 W
New England National Park ♠	166	30.30 S	152.15 E
New England Range ▲	166	30.00 S	151.50 E
Newenham, Cape ≻	180	58.37 N	162.12 W
Newent	42	51.56 N	2.24 W
New Enterprise	214	40.10 N	78.25 W
New Ermelo	158	26.32 S	30.02 E
Newfane, N.Y., U.S.	210	43.17 N	78.43 W
Newfane, Vt., U.S.	188	42.59 N	72.39 W
New Ferry	262	53.22 N	2.59 W
Newfield, N.J., U.S.	208	39.33 N	75.01 W
Newfield, N.Y., U.S.	210	42.22 N	76.35 W
Newfield Pond ⊜	283	42.38 N	71.22 W
New Field Workshops ⊻[3]	174b	0.31 S	166.56 E
New Florence, Mo., U.S.	219	38.54 N	91.27 W
New Florence, Pa., U.S.	214	40.23 N	79.05 W
New Forest ◆[3]	42	50.53 N	1.35 W
New Fork ≃	200	42.33 N	109.58 W
Newfound Gap)(	192	35.37 N	83.25 W
Newfoundland, N.J., U.S.	276	41.03 N	74.26 W
Newfoundland, Pa., U.S.	210	41.19 N	75.19 W
Newfoundland □[4]	176	52.00 N	56.00 W
Newfoundland I	186	48.30 N	56.00 W
Newfoundland Basin ✢[1]	16	43.00 N	43.00 W
New Franklin	194	39.01 N	92.44 W
New Freedom	208	39.44 N	76.42 W
New Galilee	214	40.50 N	80.24 W
New Galloway	44	55.05 N	4.10 W
New Garden	285	39.49 N	75.45 W
Newgate	182	49.00 N	115.10 W
Newgate Street	260	51.44 N	0.07 W
New Georgia I	175e	8.15 S	157.30 E
New Georgia Group II	175e	8.30 S	157.20 E
New Germantown	208	40.18 N	77.34 W
New Germany	186	44.33 N	64.43 W
New Glarus	190	42.49 N	89.38 W
New Glasgow	186	45.35 N	62.39 W
New Gretna	208	39.35 N	74.28 W
New Guinea I	164	5.00 S	140.00 E
New Guinea, Territory of → Papua New Guinea □[1]	164	6.00 S	150.00 E
Newgulf	222	29.16 N	95.54 W
Newhalem	224	48.41 N	121.16 W
Newhalen	180	59.43 N	154.54 W
Newhall, Eng., U.K.	42	52.48 N	1.34 W
Newhall, Calif., U.S.	228	34.23 N	118.31 W
Newham ◆[8]	42	51.32 N	0.03 E
New Hamburg, Ont., Can.	212	43.23 N	80.42 W
New Hamburg, N.Y., U.S.	210	41.35 N	73.57 W
New Hampshire	216	40.33 N	83.57 W
New Hampshire □[3]	178		
	188	43.35 N	71.40 W
New Hampton, Iowa, U.S.	190	43.03 N	92.19 W
New Hampton, N.Y., U.S.	210	41.25 N	74.24 W
New Hanover, S. Afr.	158	29.28 S	30.28 E
New Hanover, Ill., U.S.	219	38.23 N	90.13 W
New Hanover I	164	2.30 S	150.15 E
New Harmony	194	38.08 N	87.56 W
New Hartford, Conn., U.S.	207	41.53 N	72.59 W
New Hartford, Iowa, U.S.	190	42.34 N	92.37 W
New Hartford, Mo., U.S.	219	39.12 N	91.16 W
New Hartford, N.Y., U.S.	210	43.04 N	75.18 W
Newhaven, Eng., U.K.	42	50.47 N	0.03 E
New Haven, Conn., U.S.	207	41.18 N	72.56 W
New Haven, Ill., U.S.	194	37.55 N	88.08 W
New Haven, Ind., U.S.	216	41.04 N	85.01 W
New Haven, Ky., U.S.	194	37.39 N	85.36 W
New Haven, Mich., U.S.	214	42.44 N	82.48 W
New Haven, Mo., U.S.	219	38.37 N	91.13 W
New Haven, N.Y., U.S.	212	43.29 N	76.19 W
New Haven, Ohio, U.S.	214	41.02 N	82.41 W
New Haven, W. Va., U.S.	188	38.59 N	81.58 W
New Haven □[6]	207	41.18 N	72.56 W
New Hazelton	182	55.15 N	127.35 W
New Hebrides □[2]	14		
	175f	16.00 S	167.00 E
New Hebrides (Nouvelles-Hébrides) II	175f	16.00 S	167.00 E
New Hebrides Basin ✢[1]	14	16.00 S	162.00 E
New Hebrides Trench ✢[1]	14	19.00 S	168.00 E
Newhebron	194	31.44 N	83.58 W
New Hempstead	276	41.08 N	74.03 W
New Hey	262	53.36 N	2.06 W
New Hogan Lake ⊜[1]	226	38.09 N	120.48 W
New Holland, Eng., U.K.	44	53.42 N	0.22 W
New Holland, Ill., U.S.	219	40.11 N	89.36 W
New Holland, Ohio, U.S.	218	39.33 N	83.15 W
New Holland, Pa., U.S.	208	40.06 N	76.05 W
New Holstein	190	43.57 N	88.05 W
New Hope, Ala., U.S.	194	34.32 N	86.24 W
New Hope, Pa., U.S.	208	40.22 N	74.57 W
New Hudson	281	42.31 N	83.37 W
New Hudson Airport ⊠	281	42.30 N	83.37 W
New Hyde Park	276	40.44 N	73.41 W
New Hythe	260	51.19 N	0.27 E
New Iberia	194	30.00 N	91.49 W
Newington, Eng., U.K.	42	51.05 N	1.08 E
Newington, Eng., U.K.	260	51.21 N	0.40 E
Newington, Conn., U.S.	207	41.43 N	72.45 W
New Inn	48	52.26 N	7.53 W
New Ipswich	207	42.46 N	71.51 W
New Ireland □[5]	164	3.00 S	151.30 E
New Ireland I	164	3.20 S	152.00 E
New Island I	126	21.31 N	88.12 E
New Jersey □[3]	178		
	188	40.15 N	74.30 W
New Jersey Institute of Technology ⊻[2]	276	40.45 N	74.11 W
New Jersey Sports Center ♠	276	40.49 N	74.05 W
New Kensington	214	40.34 N	79.46 W
New Kent	208	37.31 N	76.59 W
New Kent □[6]	208	37.30 N	77.00 W
New Kingstown	208	40.13 N	77.07 W
Newkirk	196	36.53 N	97.03 W
Newkirk Estates	285	39.42 N	75.42 W
New Knoxville	216	40.30 N	84.19 W
New Kowloon (Xinjiulong)	271d	22.20 N	114.10 E
New Lagos ◆[8]	273a	6.30 N	3.22 E
New Lake ⊜	192	35.38 N	76.20 W
Newland	192	36.05 N	81.56 W
Newland Head ≻	168b	35.39 S	138.31 E
Newland Range ▲	162	27.53 S	123.58 E
Newlands ◆[8]	273d	26.11 S	27.58 E
New Lane	262	53.37 N	2.52 W
New Lebanon, N.Y., U.S.	210	42.28 N	73.24 W
New Lebanon, Ohio, U.S.	218	39.45 N	84.23 W
New Lebanon, Pa., U.S.	214	41.25 N	80.04 W
New Lebanon Center	210	42.28 N	73.25 W
New Leipzig	198	46.22 N	101.57 W
New Lenox	216	41.31 N	87.58 W
New Lexington	188	39.43 N	82.13 W
New Liberty	218	38.37 N	84.54 W
New Lisbon	190	43.53 N	90.10 W
New Liskeard	190	47.30 N	79.40 W
New London, Conn., U.S.	207	41.21 N	72.07 W
New London, Iowa, U.S.	190	40.55 N	91.24 W
New London, Minn., U.S.	198	45.18 N	94.56 W
New London, Mo., U.S.	219	39.35 N	91.24 W
New London, N.H., U.S.	188	43.25 N	71.59 W
New London, Ohio, U.S.	214	41.05 N	82.24 W
New London, Pa., U.S.	208	39.47 N	75.52 W
New London, Tex., U.S.	222	32.15 N	94.56 W
New London, Wis., U.S.	190	44.23 N	88.45 W
New London □[6]	207	41.21 N	72.07 W
New London Submarine Base ■	207	41.24 N	72.05 W
New Longton	262	53.44 N	2.45 W
Newlonsburg	279b	40.25 N	79.40 W
New Lyme	214	41.36 N	80.47 W
Newlyn	169	37.25 S	143.59 E
Newlyn East	42	50.22 N	5.03 W
Newmachar	46	57.16 N	2.11 W
New Machavie	158	26.48 S	26.57 E
New Madison	218	39.58 N	84.43 W
New Madrid	194	36.36 N	89.32 W
Newmains	44	55.47 N	3.53 W
Newman, Calif., U.S.	226	37.19 N	121.01 W
Newman, Ill., U.S.	194	39.48 N	87.59 W
Newman, Mount ∧	162	23.16 S	119.33 E
New Manchester	214	40.31 N	80.35 W
Newman Grove	198	41.45 N	97.47 W
Newmanstown	208	40.21 N	76.13 W
Newmansville	219	40.00 N	90.01 W
New Marion	218	39.00 N	85.22 W
Newmarket, Austl.	171a	27.25 S	153.01 E
Newmarket, Ont., Can.	212	44.03 N	79.28 W
Newmarket, Eire	48	52.13 N	9.00 W
Newmarket, S. Afr.	273d	26.17 S	28.08 E
Newmarket, Eng., U.K.	42	52.15 N	0.25 E
New Market, Ala., U.S.	194	34.55 N	86.26 W
New Market, Iowa, U.S.	198	40.44 N	94.54 W
New Market, Md., U.S.	208	39.23 N	77.16 W
Newmarket, N.H., U.S.	188	43.05 N	70.56 W
New Market, N.J., U.S.	276	40.34 N	74.27 W
New Market, Va., U.S.	188	38.39 N	78.40 W
Newmarket-on-Fergus	48	52.45 N	8.53 W
Newmarket Race Course ♠	273d	26.17 S	28.08 E
New Martinsville	188	39.39 N	80.52 W
New Meadows	202	44.58 N	116.32 W
New Melle	219	38.43 N	90.53 W
New Melones Lake ⊜[1]	226	38.00 N	120.32 W
New Memphis	219	38.29 N	89.41 W
New Mexico □[3]	178	34.30 N	106.00 W
New Miami	218	39.26 N	84.32 W
New Middletown	214	40.58 N	80.34 W
New Milford, Conn., U.S.	207	41.35 N	73.25 W
New Milford, Ill., U.S.	216	42.11 N	89.04 W
New Milford, N.J., U.S.	276	40.56 N	74.01 W
New Milford, Pa., U.S.	210	41.52 N	75.44 W
New Millpond ⊜	276	40.50 N	73.13 W
New Millport	214	40.54 N	78.32 W
New Mills	44	53.23 N	2.00 W
Newmilns	46	55.37 N	4.20 W
New Milton	42	50.44 N	1.40 W
New Minden	219	38.26 N	89.22 W
New Munster	216	42.35 N	88.14 W
Newnan	192	33.23 N	84.48 W
Newnans Lake ⊜	192	29.39 N	82.13 W
Newnham	42	51.49 N	2.27 W
New Norcia	162	30.58 S	116.13 E
New Norfolk	166	42.47 S	147.03 E
New Norway	182	52.53 N	112.58 W
New Orleans	194	29.58 N	90.07 W
New Oxford	208	39.52 N	77.04 W
New Palestine	218	39.43 N	85.53 W
New Paltz	210	41.45 N	74.05 W
New Paris, Ind., U.S.	216	41.30 N	85.50 W
New Paris, Ohio, U.S.	218	39.51 N	84.48 W
New Paris, Pa., U.S.	214	40.06 N	78.39 W
New Philadelphia, Ohio, U.S.	214	40.30 N	81.27 W
New Philadelphia, Pa., U.S.	208	40.43 N	76.07 W
New Pine Creek	202	42.01 N	120.18 W
New Pittsburg	214	40.50 N	82.06 W
New Plymouth, N.Z.	172	39.04 S	174.05 E
New Plymouth, Idaho, U.S.	202	43.58 N	116.49 W
New Point	218	39.19 N	85.20 W
New Point Comfort ≻	208	37.18 N	76.17 W
Newport, Austl.	274a	33.40 S	151.19 E
Newport, Austl.	274b	37.51 S	144.53 E
Newport, Qué., Can.	186	48.16 N	64.45 W
Newport, Eire	48	52.42 N	8.24 W
Newport, Eire	48	53.53 N	9.34 W
New Port, Ned. Ant.	241s	12.03 N	68.49 W
Newport, Eng., U.K.	42	52.47 N	2.22 W
Newport, Eng., U.K.	42	50.42 N	1.18 W
Newport, Wales, U.K.	42	52.01 N	4.51 W
Newport, Wales, U.K.	42	51.35 N	3.00 W
Newport, Ark., U.S.	194	35.37 N	91.17 W
Newport, Del., U.S.	208	39.43 N	75.37 W
Newport, Ind., U.S.	194	39.53 N	87.24 W
Newport, Ky., U.S.	218	39.06 N	84.29 W
Newport, Maine, U.S.	188	44.50 N	69.17 W
Newport, Md., U.S.	208	38.25 N	76.54 W
Newport, Mich., U.S.	216	42.00 N	83.18 W
Newport, N.H., U.S.	188	43.21 N	72.09 W
Newport, N.J., U.S.	208	39.18 N	75.11 W
Newport, N.Y., U.S.	210	43.11 N	75.01 W
Newport, Ohio, U.S.	216	39.23 N	81.14 W
Newport, Oreg., U.S.	202	44.38 N	124.03 W
Newport, Pa., U.S.	188	40.29 N	77.08 W
Newport, R.I., U.S.	207	41.13 N	71.18 W
Newport, Tenn., U.S.	192	35.58 N	83.11 W
Newport, Vt., U.S.	188	44.57 N	72.12 W
Newport, Wash., U.S.	202	48.11 N	117.03 W
Newport □[6]	207	41.35 N	71.15 W
Newport Bay C	208	38.14 N	75.13 W
Newport Beach	228	33.37 N	117.56 W
Newport Center	206	44.57 N	72.19 W
Newport Hills	224	47.33 N	122.10 W
Newport News	208	37.04 N	76.28 W
Newport-on-Tay	46	56.26 N	2.55 W
Newport Pagnell	42	52.05 N	0.44 W
New Port Richey	220	28.16 N	82.43 W
Newportville	285	40.09 N	74.53 W
Newportville Terrace	285	40.07 N	74.54 W
New Prague	190	44.32 N	93.34 W
New Preston	207	41.40 N	73.21 W
New Providence, N.J., U.S.	210	40.42 N	74.24 W
New Providence, Pa., U.S.	208	39.56 N	76.12 W
New Providence, Tenn., U.S.	194	36.32 N	87.23 W
New Providence I	240b	25.02 N	77.24 W
Newquay, Eng., U.K.	42	50.25 N	5.05 W
New Quay, Wales, U.K.	42	52.13 N	4.22 W
New Redruth	273d	26.16 S	28.07 E
New Richland	190	43.54 N	93.30 W
New Richmond, Qué., Can.	186	48.10 N	65.52 W
New Richmond, Ohio, U.S.	218	38.57 N	84.17 W
New Richmond, Wis., U.S.	190	45.07 N	92.32 W
New Riegel	214	41.03 N	83.19 W
New Rim Ditch ≍	228	35.08 N	118.58 W
New Ringgold	208	40.41 N	76.00 W
New Road	186	44.45 N	63.28 W
New Roads	194	30.42 N	91.26 W
New Rochelle	188	40.55 N	73.47 W
New Rockford	198	47.41 N	99.15 W
New Romney	42	50.59 N	0.57 E
New Ross, N.S., Can.	186	44.44 N	64.27 W
New Ross, Eire	48	52.24 N	6.56 W
New Rossington	44	53.29 N	1.04 W
Newry, N. Ire., U.K.	48	54.11 N	6.20 W
Newry, Pa., U.S.	214	40.24 N	78.26 W
Newry, S.C., U.S.	192	34.43 N	82.55 W
New Salem, Ind., U.S.	218	39.32 N	85.22 W
New Salem, N. Dak., U.S.	198	46.51 N	101.25 W
New Salisbury	218	38.19 N	86.06 W
New Sarum → Salisbury	42	51.05 N	1.48 W
New Schwabenland ◆[1]	9	72.30 S	1.00 E
Newsham Park ♠	262	53.25 N	2.56 W
New Sharon	190	41.28 N	92.39 W
New Sheffield	214	40.36 N	80.17 W
New Shrewsbury	276	40.19 N	74.04 W
New Smyrna Beach	220	29.02 N	80.56 W
Newsome	222	32.59 N	95.08 W
Newsoms	208	36.37 N	77.14 W
New South Wales □[3]	166	33.00 S	146.00 E
New South Wales, University of ⊻[2]	274a	33.55 S	151.14 E
New South Wales Lawn Tennis Association Courts ♠	274a	33.53 S	151.14 E
New Springfield	214	40.55 N	80.36 W
New Square	276	41.08 N	74.02 W
New Stanton	214	40.13 N	79.37 W
Newstead	169	37.07 S	144.04 E
New Stuyahok	180	59.29 N	157.20 W
New Suffolk	207	41.00 N	72.28 W
New Summerfield	222	31.59 N	95.06 W
New Terrell City Lake ⊜[1]	222	32.44 N	96.14 W
New Territories □[8]	271d	22.24 N	114.10 E
New Thunderchild Indian Reserve ◆[4]	184	53.30 N	108.50 W
Newtok	180	60.56 N	164.38 W
Newton, Eng., U.K.	44	53.57 N	2.27 W
Newton, Eng., U.K.	262	53.16 N	2.43 W
Newton, Ga., U.S.	192	31.19 N	84.20 W
Newton, Ill., U.S.	194	38.59 N	88.10 W
Newton, Iowa, U.S.	190	41.42 N	93.03 W
Newton, Kans., U.S.	198	38.03 N	97.21 W
Newton, Mass., U.S.	207	42.21 N	71.11 W
Newton, Miss., U.S.	194	32.19 N	89.10 W
Newton, N.J., U.S.	210	41.03 N	74.45 W
Newton, N.C., U.S.	192	35.40 N	81.13 W
Newton, Tex., U.S.	194	30.51 N	93.46 W
Newton □[6]	216	40.46 N	87.27 W
Newton Abbot	42	50.32 N	3.36 W
Newton Arlosh	44	54.53 N	3.15 W
Newton Aycliffe	44	54.36 N	1.32 W
Newton Brook ◆[8]	275b	43.48 N	79.24 W
Newton Center	283	42.20 N	71.12 W

Symbols in the index entries represent the broad categories identified in the key at the right. Symbols with superior numbers (▲[2]) identify subcategories (see complete key on page *I* · 30).

Kartensymbole in dem Registerverzeichnis stellen die rechts in Schlüssel erklärten Kategorien dar. Symbole mit hochgestellten Ziffern (▲[2]) bezeichnen Unterabteilungen einer Kategorie (vgl. vollständiger Schlüssel auf Seite *I* · 30).

Los símbolos incluídos en el texto del índice representan las grandes categorias identificadas con la clave a la derecha. Los símbolos con numeros en su parte superior (▲[2]) identifican las subcategorías (véase la clave completa en la página *I* · 30).

Les symboles de l'index représentent les catégories indiquées dans la légende à droite. Les symboles suivis d'un indice (▲[2]) représentent des sous-catégories (voir légende complète à la page *I* · 30).

Os símbolos incluídos no texto do índice representam as grandes categorias identificadas com a chave à direita. Os símbolos com números em sua parte superior (▲[2]) identificam as subcategorias (veja-se a chave completa à página *I* · 30).

	English	Deutsch	Español	Français	Português
∧	Mountain	Berg	Montaña	Montagne	Montanha
▲	Mountains	Berge	Montañas	Montagnes	Montanhas
)(	Pass	Pass	Paso	Col	Passo
∨	Valley, Canyon	Tal, Cañon	Valle, Cañón	Vallée, Canyon	Vale, Canhão
≚	Plain	Ebene	Llano	Plaine	Planície
≻	Cape	Kap	Cabo	Cap	Cabo
I	Island	Insel	Isla	Île	Ilha
II	Islands	Inseln	Islas	Îles	Ilhas
⊥	Other Topographic Features	Andere Topographische Objekte	Otros Elementos Topográficos	Autres données topographiques	Outros Elementos Topográficos

ESPAÑOL Nombre	Página	Lat.°'	Long.°' W=Oeste
FRANÇAIS Nom	Page	Lat.°'	Long.°' W=Ouest
PORTUGUÊS Nome	Página	Lat.°'	Long.°' W=Oeste

Newton Falls, N.Y., U.S. 188 44.13 N 74.59 W
Newton Falls, Ohio, U.S. 214 41.11 N 80.59 W
Newton Ferrers 42 50.18 N 4.02 W
Newton Flotman 42 52.32 N 1.16 E
Newtongrange 46 55.52 N 3.04 W
Newton Hamilton 214 40.24 N 77.51 W
Newton Highlands 283 42.19 N 71.13 W
Newton-le-Willows 44 53.28 N 2.37 W
Newton Lower Falls 283 42.19 N 71.23 W
Newtonmore 46 57.04 N 4.08 W
Newton Stewart 44 54.57 N 4.29 W
Newtonsville 218 39.11 N 84.05 W
Newton Upper Falls 283 42.19 N 71.13 W
Newtonville, Ont., Can. 212 43.56 N 78.30 W
Newtonville, Mass., U.S. 283 42.21 N 71.13 W
Newtonville, N.J., U.S. 208 39.34 N 74.52 W
Newtown, Austl. 169 38.09 S 144.20 E
Newtown, Newf., Can. 186 49.12 N 53.31 W
Newtown, Eng., U.K. 262 53.21 N 2.00 W
Newtown, Wales, U.K. 42 52.32 N 3.19 W
Newtown, Conn., U.S. 207 41.25 N 73.19 W
Newtown, Ind., U.S. 216 40.12 N 87.09 W
Newtown, Ky., U.S. 218 38.13 N 84.57 W
New Town, N. Dak., U.S. 198 47.59 N 102.30 W
Newtown, Pa., U.S. 208 40.14 N 74.56 W
Newtown ⁺⁸ 274a 33.54 S 151.11 E
Newtownabbey 48 54.36 N 5.54 W
Newtownards 48 54.36 N 5.41 W
Newtownbutler 48 54.12 N 7.23 W
Newtown Creek ≃, N.Y., U.S. 276 40.44 N 73.58 W
Newtown Creek ≃, Pa., U.S. 285 40.13 N 74.56 W
Newtown Crommelin 48 54.59 N 6.13 W
Newtown Forbes 48 53.46 N 7.50 W
Newtownhamilton 48 54.11 N 6.35 W
Newtown Saint Boswells 46 55.34 N 2.40 W
Newtown Square 208 39.59 N 75.24 W
Newtownstewart 48 54.43 N 7.24 W
New Tredegar 42 51.43 N 3.14 W
New Tripoli 208 40.41 N 75.45 W
New Troy 216 41.53 N 86.33 W
New Truxton 219 38.58 N 91.15 W
New Ulm, Minn., U.S. 190 44.19 N 94.28 W
New Ulm, Tex., U.S. 222 29.53 N 96.29 W
New Uosenow 54 53.47 N 13.46 E
New Utrecht ⁺⁸ 276 40.36 N 73.59 W
New Vernon 276 40.45 N 74.30 W
New Vienna 218 39.19 N 83.42 W
Newville, Ind., U.S. 216 41.21 N 84.51 W
Newville, Pa., U.S. 208 40.10 N 77.24 W
New Vineyard 188 44.48 N 70.07 W
New Washington, Pil. 116 11.39 N 122.26 E
New Washington, Ind., U.S. 218 38.34 N 85.33 W
New Washington, Ohio, U.S. 214 40.58 N 82.51 W
New Waterford, N.S., Can. 186 46.15 N 60.05 W
New Waterford, Ohio, U.S. 214 40.51 N 80.37 W
New Waverly, Ind., U.S. 216 40.46 N 86.12 W
New Waverly, Tex., U.S. 222 30.32 N 95.29 W
New Westminster 182 49.12 N 122.55 W
New Whiteland 218 39.33 N 86.05 W
New Wilmington 214 41.07 N 80.20 W
New Windsor → Windsor, Eng., U.K. 42 51.29 N 0.38 W
New Windsor, N.Y., U.S. 210 41.29 N 74.02 W
New Woodbine Racetrack ♦ 275b 43.43 N 79.36 W
New Woodstock 210 42.51 N 75.51 W
New World Island I 186 49.35 N 54.40 W
New Year Creek ≃ 222 30.08 N 96.12 W
New York 210
New York ▢⁶ 276 40.43 N 74.01 W
New York ▢³ 276 40.43 N 74.01 W
New York 178
New York 188 43.00 N 75.00 W
New York, City College of ʋ² 276 40.49 N 73.57 W
New York, Polytechnic Institute of ʋ² 276 40.42 N 73.59 W
New York, State University of (Stony Brook) ʋ², N.Y., U.S. 276 40.55 N 73.08 W
New York, State University of (Buffalo) ʋ², N.Y., U.S. 284a 42.57 N 78.49 W
New York, State University of, College at Buffalo ʋ² 284a 42.56 N 78.53 W
New York Mills, Minn., U.S. 198 46.31 N 95.22 W
New York Mills, N.Y., U.S. 210 43.06 N 75.18 W
New York State Barge Canal ≚ 210 43.05 N 78.43 W
New York Stock Exchange ʋ 276 40.42 N 74.01 W
New York University ʋ² 276 40.51 N 73.55 W
New Zealand ▢¹ 14
New Zealand 172 41.00 S 174.00 E
New Zealand Plateau ⁺³ 9 51.00 S 170.00 E
Nexapa ≃ 234 18.07 N 98.46 W
Nexon 32 45.41 N 1.11 E
Nexpa ≃ 234 18.05 N 102.46 W
Ney 216 41.23 N 84.32 W
Neyagawa 96 34.46 N 135.38 E
Neye 263 51.07 N 7.22 E
Neyestausee @¹ 263 51.08 N 7.24 E
Ney Lake @ 184 54.38 N 92.25 W
Neyland 42 51.43 N 4.57 W
Neylandville 222 33.12 N 96.00 W
Neyrīz 128 29.12 N 54.19 E
Neyshābūr 128 36.12 N 58.50 E
Neyyāttinkara 122 8.24 N 77.05 E
Nezahualcóyotl, Presa @¹ 234 17.10 N 93.40 W
Nezamajevskaja 78 46.09 N 40.16 E
Nezameno-toko ♦ 94 35.46 N 137.42 E
Nežárka ≃ 61 49.11 N 14.41 E
Nezavertajlovka 78 46.37 N 29.56 E
Nežin 78 51.03 N 31.54 E
Nezlobnaja 84 44.08 N 43.23 E
Neznanka ≃ 265b 55.34 N 37.21 E
Neznanovo 80 54.02 N 40.06 E
Nezperce 202 46.14 N 116.14 W
Nez Perce Indian Reservation ⁺⁴ 202 46.20 N 116.30 W
Nez Perce National Historical Park ♦ 202 45.50 N 116.15 W
Nezvěstice 60 49.39 N 13.32 E
Ngabang 112 0.23 N 109.57 E
Ngabé 152 3.12 S 16.11 E
Ngabordamlu, Tanjung ≻ 164 6.56 S 134.11 E
Ngadirojo 115a 8.13 S 111.19 E
Ngadza 152 5.10 N 20.12 E
Ngahere 172 42.24 S 171.27 E
Ngala 146 12.20 N 14.10 E
Ngale 152 2.56 N 21.20 E
Ngali 152 2.27 S 19.20 E
Ngalipaeng 112 3.24 N 125.37 E
Ngaloa Harbour C 175g 19.06 S 178.11 E
Ngamakoussou ≃ 273b 4.10 S 15.19 E
Ngamba 273b 4.15 S 15.18 E
Ngambé 152 4.14 N 10.37 E
Ngamdu 146 11.48 N 12.18 E
Ngamegei Passage ⅋ 175b 7.44 N 134.34 E
Ngami, Lake @ 156 20.37 S 22.40 E
Ngamiland ▢⁵ 156 19.09 S 22.47 E
Ngamo 154 19.08 S 27.32 E
Ngamouéri 273b 4.14 S 15.14 E
Ngangala 154 4.42 N 31.55 E
Ngangerabeli Plain ≚ 154 1.30 S 40.15 E
Ngang Kong C 271d 22.16 N 114.00 E
Nganjuk 115a 7.36 S 111.55 E
Ngao 110 18.46 N 99.59 E
Ngaoundéré 152 7.19 N 13.35 E
Ngapara 172 44.57 S 170.45 E
Ngape 110 20.04 N 94.38 E
Ngaputaw 110 16.32 N 94.42 E
Ngara 154 2.28 S 30.39 E
Ngardmau 175b 7.37 N 134.35 E
Ngardmau Bay C 175b 7.39 N 134.35 E
Ngarimbi 154 8.28 S 38.36 E
Ngaruawahia 172 37.40 S 175.09 E
Ngaruroro ≃ 172 39.34 S 176.56 E
Ngasamo 154 2.33 S 33.53 E
Ngat ≃ 110 19.09 N 99.01 E
Ngatangiia 174k 21.14 S 159.43 W
Ngatangiia Harbour C 174k 21.14 S 159.45 W
Ngatea 172 37.17 S 175.30 E
Ngathainggyaung 110 17.24 N 95.05 E
Ngatik I¹ 14 5.51 N 157.16 E
Ngau I 175g 18.02 S 179.18 E
Ngauruhoe, Mount A 172 39.09 S 175.38 E
Ngau Tau Kok → Tai Wan Tsun 271d 22.19 N 114.12 E
Ngawen 115a 7.00 S 111.18 E
Ngawi 115a 7.24 S 111.26 E
Ngaya A 140 9.18 N 23.28 E
Ngay Nua 110 21.50 N 101.54 E
Ngebel 115a 7.46 S 111.37 E
Ngele 152 0.29 S 20.25 E
Ngele 158 30.35 S 29.35 E
Ngemelis Islands II 175b 7.07 N 134.15 E
Ngerengere 154 6.45 S 38.07 E
Ngetera 146 12.31 N 12.38 E
Ngezi National Park ♦ 154 18.40 S 30.28 E
Nggamea I 175g 16.46 S 179.46 W
Nggela Group II 175e 9.00 S 160.10 E
Nggele Levu I 175g 16.05 S 179.09 W
Nghabe ≃ 156 20.22 S 22.28 E
Nghia-hanh 110 15.03 N 108.47 E
Nghia-hung 110 19.18 N 105.26 E
Nghia-lo 110 21.36 N 104.31 E
Ngiap ≃ 110 18.24 N 103.36 E
Ngidinga 152 5.37 S 15.17 E
Ngila 152 4.43 N 11.41 E
Ngimbang 115a 7.17 S 112.12 E
Ng'iro, Ewaso ≃, Kenya 154 2.04 S 36.07 E
Ng'iro, Ewaso ≃, Kenya 154 0.28 N 39.55 E
Ngo 152 2.29 S 15.45 E
Ngoap 152 4.09 N 12.51 E
Ngobé, Lagune C 152 1.55 S 9.25 E
Ngoboli 154 4.57 N 32.37 E
Ngo Ki 271d 22.18 N 113.58 E
Ngoko ≃ 152 1.40 N 16.03 E
Ngol-Kedju Hill A² 152 6.20 N 9.45 E
Ngolo 146 9.56 N 22.16 E
Ngoma 154 2.11 S 29.18 E
Ngomahuru 154 20.26 S 30.43 E
Ngomba 154 8.23 S 32.53 E
Ngomba A 154 5.43 S 35.52 E
Ngombe, Zaïre 152 6.35 S 20.42 E
Ngombe, Zaïre 273b 4.24 S 15.11 E
Ngome 158 27.46 S 31.28 E
Ngomedzap 152 3.15 N 11.12 E
Ngomeni, Ras ≻ 154 2.59 S 40.14 E
Ngong 154 1.22 S 36.39 E
Ngongotaha 172 38.05 S 176.12 E
Ngono ≃ 154 1.08 S 31.35 E
Ngon Shun Chau I 271d 22.19 N 114.08 E
Ngonye Falls ⌊ 152 16.40 S 23.35 E
Ngop 140 6.16 N 30.12 E
Ngora 154 1.27 N 33.46 E
Ngorengore 154 1.02 S 35.30 E
Ngoro 115a 7.41 S 112.16 E
Ngorongoro Crater ⁺⁶ 154 3.10 S 35.35 E
Ngosa Farm 154 12.18 S 27.28 E
Ngote 154 2.14 N 30.48 E
Ngotto 152 4.00 N 17.21 E
Ngoui 150 16.09 N 13.55 W
Ngoulémakong 152 3.07 N 11.25 E
Ngouma 150 15.38 N 3.22 W
Ngounié ▢⁴ 152 2.00 S 11.00 E
Ngounié ≃ 152 0.37 S 10.18 E
Ngouo, Mont A 140 7.55 N 24.38 E
Ngouri 146 13.38 N 15.22 E
Ngoywa 154 5.56 S 32.48 E
Ngozi 154 2.54 S 29.50 E
Ngqeleni 158 31.40 S 29.02 E
Ngudiabaka ≃ 273b 4.25 S 15.11 E
Nguélémendouka 152 4.23 N 12.55 E
Nguigmi 146 14.15 N 13.07 E
Nguiroungou 152 6.27 N 22.37 E
Ngulu I¹ 108 8.27 N 137.29 E
Ngum ≃ 110 18.09 N 103.06 E
Nguna I 175f 17.26 S 168.21 E
Ngunga 154 3.41 S 33.34 E
Ngunju, Tanjung ≻ 115b 10.19 S 120.28 E
Ngunut 115a 8.06 S 112.01 E
Ngurore 146 9.18 N 12.14 E
Nguru 146 12.52 N 10.27 E
Nguru Mountains ⋀ 154 6.00 S 37.30 E
Ngwakets ▢⁵ 156 24.45 S 24.00 E
Ngweni 158 27.56 S 32.15 E
Ngwenya A 158 26.11 S 31.02 E
Ngwerere 154 15.18 S 28.20 E
Ngwezi ≃ 154 17.40 S 25.07 E
Nha-be 269c 10.42 N 106.44 E
Nha-be ≃ 269c 10.39 N 106.44 E
Nhacoongo 156 24.18 S 35.14 E
Nhamacolomo 156 18.05 S 34.26 E
Nhamundá 250 2.14 S 56.43 W
Nhamundá ≃ 246 2.12 S 56.41 W
Nha-nam 110 21.27 N 106.06 E
Nhandeara 255 20.40 S 50.02 W
Nhareia 152 11.25 S 17.03 E
Nha-trang 110 12.15 N 109.11 E
Nhecolândia 248 19.16 S 57.04 W
Nhia 152 10.15 S 14.12 E
Nhill 166 36.20 S 141.39 E
Nhlazatshe 158 28.10 S 31.14 E
Nhon-trach 269c 10.43 N 106.51 E
Nhundo 152 14.25 S 21.23 E
Nhunguaçu 256 22.21 S 42.53 W
Niabembe 154 2.14 S 27.44 E
Niafounké 150 15.56 N 4.00 W
Niagara 190 45.46 N 88.02 W
Niagara ▢⁶, Ont., Can. 212 43.05 N 79.20 W
Niagara ▢⁶, N.Y., U.S. 210 43.10 N 78.42 W
Niagara ≃ 212 43.15 N 79.04 W
Niagara County Historical Center ʋ 284a 43.10 N 78.43 W
Niagara Falls, Ont., Can. 212
Niagara Falls 284a 43.06 N 79.04 W
Niagara Falls, N.Y., U.S. 210
Niagara Falls 284a 43.06 N 79.02 W
Niagara Falls ⌊ 212 43.05 N 79.04 W
Niagara Falls Airport ⊠ 284a 43.02 N 79.08 W
Niagara Falls International Airport ⊠ 284a 43.06 N 78.56 W
Niagara-on-the-Lake 212 43.15 N 79.04 W
Niagara University ʋ² 284a 43.08 N 79.02 W
Niagassola 150 12.19 N 9.07 W
Niah 112 3.52 N 113.44 E
Niakaramandougou 150 8.40 N 5.17 W
Niamey 150 13.31 N 2.07 E
Niamey ▢⁵ 150 14.00 N 2.00 E
Niamtougou 150 9.46 N 1.06 E
Nianbadu 100 28.17 N 118.28 E
Niandan Koro 150 11.05 N 9.15 W
Nianforando 150 9.32 N 10.31 W
Niangara 154 3.42 N 27.52 E
Niangay, Lac @ 150 15.50 N 3.00 W
Niangmake 102 30.14 N 99.40 E
Niangnianggong 104 41.00 N 121.13 E
Niangniangmiao 98 42.34 N 118.05 E
Niangniangwa 105 40.33 N 117.30 E
Niangoloko 150 10.17 N 4.55 W
Niangua ≃ 194 37.58 N 92.48 W
Niangzizhuang 105 40.02 N 118.05 E
Nia-Nia 154 1.24 N 27.36 E
Nianpan 104 41.48 N 124.02 E
Nianqingtanggula-shanmai ⋀ 120 30.00 N 90.00 E
Niantan ≃ 150 10.30 N 10.26 W
Niantic, Conn., U.S. 207 41.19 N 72.12 W
Niantic, Ill., U.S. 219 39.51 N 89.10 W
Nianyugou 104 42.00 N 123.59 E
Nianyushan 100 29.11 N 117.04 E
Nianzhuang 98 34.19 N 117.47 E
Nianzigang 100 31.03 N 114.18 E
Nianzishan 89 47.32 N 122.52 E
Niapu 154 2.25 N 26.28 E
Niari ▢⁵ 152 3.15 S 12.30 E
Niari ≃ 152 3.56 S 12.12 E
Niaro 140 10.38 N 31.31 E
Nias, Pulau I 114 1.05 N 97.35 E
Niassa ▢⁵ 154 13.30 S 36.00 E
Nibbiano 62 44.54 N 9.19 E
Nibe 26 56.59 N 9.38 E
Nibong Tebal 114 5.10 N 100.29 E
Nibria 272b 22.36 N 88.16 E
Nīca 76 56.19 N 21.04 E
Nica ≃ 86 57.29 N 64.33 E
Nicaragua ▢¹ 230
Nicaragua 236 13.00 N 85.00 W
Nicaragua, Lago de @ 236 11.30 N 85.30 W
Nicaro 240p 20.42 N 75.33 W
Nicastro 68 38.59 N 16.20 E
Nice 62 43.42 N 7.15 E
Nice-Côte d'Azur, Aéroport de ⊠ 62 43.40 N 7.14 E
Niceville 194 30.31 N 86.29 W
Nichelino 62 44.59 N 7.38 E
Nichengjiao 106 30.55 N 121.49 E
Nichihara 96 34.30 N 131.50 E
Nichinan, Nihon 92 31.36 N 131.23 E
Nichinan, Nihon 96 35.09 N 133.16 E
Nicholas ▢⁶ 218 38.20 N 84.02 W
Nicholas Channel ⅋ 238 23.25 N 80.05 W
Nicholas Research Institute ʋ³ 274b 37.53 S 145.21 E
Nicholasville 192 37.53 N 84.34 W
Nicholls 192 31.31 N 82.38 W
Nichols, Calif., U.S. 282 38.02 N 121.59 W
Nichols, Fla., U.S. 220 27.54 N 82.02 W
Nichols, N.Y., U.S. 210 42.01 N 76.22 W
Nichols Brook ≃ 283 42.37 N 70.59 W
Nicholson, Austl. 162 18.02 S 128.54 E
Nicholson, Ky., U.S. 218 38.54 N 84.33 W
Nicholson, Miss., U.S. 194 30.29 N 89.42 W
Nicholson, Pa., U.S. 210 41.38 N 75.47 W
Nicholson ≃, Austl. 162 17.34 S 128.38 E
Nicholson ≃, Austl. 166 17.31 S 139.36 E
Nicholson Island I 212 43.56 N 77.31 W
Nicholson Range ⋀ 162 27.15 S 116.45 E
Nichols Run ≃ 284b 39.03 N 77.18 W
Nickerie ▢⁵ 250 4.00 N 57.30 W
Nickerie ≃ 250 5.59 N 57.00 W
Nickerson 198 38.08 N 98.05 W
Nickol Bay C 162 20.39 S 116.52 E
Nicktown 214 40.37 N 78.48 W
Nicobar Basin ⁺¹ 12 5.00 N 92.00 E
Nicobar Islands II 110 8.00 N 93.30 E
Nicola 182 50.10 N 120.40 W
Nicola ≃ 182 50.25 N 121.18 W
Nicolae Bălcescu 38 47.34 N 26.52 E
Nicolai Mountain A 224 46.05 N 123.28 W
Nicola Lake @ 182 50.10 N 120.25 W
Nicola Mameet Indian Reserve ⁺⁴ 182 50.11 N 120.49 W
Nicolás Bravo 234 18.21 N 93.10 W
Nicolás Pérez, Sierra de ⋀ 234 22.27 N 99.08 W
Nicolás Romero ▢⁷ 286a 19.37 N 99.17 W
Nicolaus 226 38.54 N 121.35 W
Nicolet 206 46.13 N 72.37 W
Nicolet ▢⁶ 206 46.15 N 72.20 W
Nicolet ≃ 206 46.14 N 72.39 W
Nicolet, Lac @ 206 45.50 N 71.33 W
Nicolet-Centre ≃ 206 45.46 N 71.50 W
Nicolet-Sud-Ouest ≃ 206 46.13 N 72.36 W
Nicoll Bay C 276 40.43 N 73.07 W
Nicollet 190 44.17 N 94.11 W
Nicoll Point ≻ 276 40.42 N 73.03 W
Nicolls Town 238 25.08 N 78.00 W
Nicolosi 70 37.37 N 15.01 E
Nicosia, It. 70 37.45 N 14.24 E
Nicosia → Levkosía, Kípros 130 35.10 N 33.22 E
Nicotera 68 38.34 N 15.57 E
Nicoya 236 10.09 N 85.27 W
Nicoya, Golfo de C 236 9.47 N 84.48 W
Nicoya, Península de ≻¹ 236 10.00 N 85.25 W
Nictheroy → Niterói 256 22.53 S 43.07 W
Nida ≃ 30 50.18 N 20.52 E
Nidadavole 122 16.55 N 81.40 E
Nidau 58 47.07 N 7.14 E
Nidd ≃ 44 54.01 N 1.12 W
Nidda 56 50.24 N 9.00 E
Nidda ≃ 56 50.06 N 8.34 E
Nidder ≃ 56 50.12 N 8.47 E
Nide 102 31.51 N 96.19 E
Nideck, Château et Cascade du ⊥ 58 48.34 N 7.16 E
Nideggen 56 50.47 N 6.29 E
Nidelva ≃ 26 58.24 N 8.48 E
Nidwalden ▢³ 58 46.55 N 8.28 E
Nidže (Nitse Óros) ⋀ 38 40.58 N 21.49 E
Nidzica 30 53.22 N 20.26 E
Niebüll 41 54.48 N 8.50 E
Nied ≃ 56 49.23 N 6.40 E
Nieddu, Monte A 71 40.45 N 9.34 E
Niederaden ⁺⁸ 263 51.36 N 7.34 E
Niederanven 56 49.39 N 6.15 E
Niederaschau 64 47.47 N 12.19 E
Niederau 54 51.10 N 13.32 E
Niederaula 56 50.48 N 9.36 E
Niederbayern ▢⁵ 60 48.45 N 12.45 E
Niederbipp 58 47.16 N 7.39 E
Niederbobritzsch 54 50.54 N 13.26 E
Niederbonsfeld 263 51.23 N 7.08 E
Niederbronn-les-Bains 56 48.57 N 7.38 E
Niederdonk 263 51.14 N 6.41 E
Niederelfringhausen 263 51.21 N 7.10 E
Niedere Tauern ⋀ 61 47.18 N 14.00 E
Niederfinow 54 52.50 N 13.55 E
Niederfrohna 54 50.53 N 12.43 E
Niederhaverbeck 52 53.09 N 9.54 E
Niederheimbach 56 50.02 N 7.48 E
Niederhohne 56 51.13 N 10.06 E
Nieder-Kassel ⁺⁸ 263 51.14 N 6.45 E
Niederkrüchten 56 51.12 N 6.13 E
Nieder-Lahnstein 56 50.19 N 7.36 E
Niederlande → Netherlands ▢¹ 30 52.15 N 5.30 E
Niederländische Antillen → Netherlands Antilles ▢² 241s 12.15 N 69.00 W
Niederlausitz ▢⁹ 54 51.40 N 14.15 E
Niederlehme 54 52.19 N 13.39 E
Niedermarsberg 56 51.28 N 8.50 E
Niedermarschacht 52 53.25 N 10.21 E
Nieder-Mörlen 56 50.23 N 8.43 E
Niederndodeleben 54 52.08 N 11.30 E
Nieder-Neuendorf 264a 52.37 N 13.12 E
Niedernhall 56 49.17 N 9.36 E
Niedernwöhren 52 52.21 N 9.08 E
Niederoderwitz 54 50.57 N 14.44 E
Nieder-Ohmen 56 50.38 N 9.02 E
Nieder-Olm 56 49.55 N 8.11 E
Niederorschel 54 51.22 N 10.25 E
Niederösterreich ▢³ 61 48.20 N 15.50 E
Niedersachsen ▢³ 30 52.00 N 10.00 E
Niedersachswerfen 54 51.33 N 10.46 E
Niederschöneweide ⁺⁸ 264a 52.27 N 13.31 E
Niederschönhausen ⁺⁸ 54 52.35 N 13.23 E
Niedersee → Ruciane-Nida 30 53.39 N 21.35 E
Niederselters 56 50.20 N 8.14 E
Niedersonthofen 58 47.38 N 10.13 E
Niederstetten 56 49.24 N 9.55 E
Niederstotzingen 56 48.32 N 10.14 E
Niedersulz 61 48.29 N 16.40 E
Niedertrumer See @ 60 47.59 N 13.07 E
Niederurnen 58 47.07 N 9.03 E
Niederwald 58 46.26 N 8.12 E
Niederwalgern 56 50.44 N 8.41 E
Niederweningen 58 47.30 N 8.23 E
Niederwiesa 54 50.51 N 13.01 E
Nieder-Wöllstadt 56 50.16 N 8.46 E
Niederwürschnitz 54 50.43 N 12.45 E
Niedu 100 25.28 N 114.08 E
Niefang 152 1.50 N 10.14 E
Nieheim 52 51.48 N 9.06 E
Niekerkshoop 158 29.19 S 22.51 E
Niel 50 51.07 N 4.20 E
Niélé 150 10.12 N 5.38 W
Niellim 146 9.42 N 17.49 E
Nielson Airport ⊠ 269f 14.34 N 121.01 E
Niem 152 6.12 N 15.14 E
Niemba 154 5.57 S 28.26 E
Niemegk 54 52.04 N 12.41 E
Niemeyer ⁺⁸ 287a 23.00 S 43.15 W
Niemodlin 30 50.39 N 17.37 E
Niéna 150 11.26 N 6.21 W
Nienberge 52 52.00 N 7.34 E
Nienborg-Wigbold 52 52.08 N 7.06 E
Nienburg, B.R.D. 52 52.38 N 9.13 E
Nienburg, D.D.R. 54 51.50 N 11.46 E
Niendorf 54 53.59 N 10.50 E
Nienhagen, B.R.D. 52 52.33 N 10.05 E
Nienhagen, D.D.R. 54 51.57 N 11.09 E
Niénokoué, Mont A 150 5.26 N 7.10 W
Niepkuhlen ≃ 263 51.29 N 6.31 E
Niepołomice 30 50.03 N 20.13 E
Nieppe 50 50.42 N 2.50 E
Nier ≃ 48 52.17 N 7.48 W
Niéré 146 14.30 N 21.09 E
Niéri Ko ≃ 150 13.21 N 13.23 W
Nierong 120 32.09 N 92.11 E
Niers ≃, B.R.D. 263 51.10 N 6.28 E
Niers ≃, Eur. 52 51.43 N 5.57 E
Nierst 263 51.19 N 6.43 E
Nierstein 56 49.52 N 8.20 E
Niesen A 58 46.39 N 7.39 E
Niesky 54 51.17 N 14.49 E
Nieszawa 30 52.50 N 18.55 E
Nieto, Cañada de ≃ 258 34.00 S 58.15 W
Nieu Bethesda 158 31.51 S 24.34 E
Nieuw-Amsterdam, Ned. 52 52.44 N 6.51 E
Nieuw Amsterdam, Sur. 250 5.53 N 55.05 W
Nieuw-Buinen 52 52.57 N 6.55 E
Nieuwefontein 158 28.01 S 19.06 E
Nieuwe-Niedorp 52 52.45 N 4.54 E
Nieuwe-Pekela 52 53.04 N 6.58 E
Nieuweschans 52 53.11 N 7.12 E
Nieuwkoop 52 52.08 N 4.47 E
Nieuw Nickerie 250 5.57 N 56.59 W
Nieuwolda 52 53.14 N 6.59 E
Nieuwoudtville 158 31.23 S 19.07 E
Nieuwpoort 50 51.08 N 2.45 E
Nieuwpoort-Bad 50 51.09 N 2.42 E
Nieuw-Schoonebeek 52 52.38 N 6.59 E
Nieuw-Vennep 52 52.16 N 4.38 E
Nieuw-Weerdinge 52 52.52 N 6.59 E
Nieva ≃ 246 4.35 S 77.53 W
Nievenheim 56 51.07 N 6.46 E
Nieveria 286d 11.59 S 76.55 W
Nieves 234 24.00 N 103.01 W
Nièvre ▢⁵ 32 47.05 N 3.30 E
Nièvre ≃ 50 47.10 N 3.13 E
Nif 174q 9.28 N 138.04 E
Nīf Ya'qūb 132 31.50 N 35.14 E
Niğde 130 13.38 N 5.27 W
Nigan 126 23.30 N 87.59 E
Niğde 130 37.59 N 34.42 E
Niğde ▢⁴ 130 38.15 N 34.15 E
Nigel 158 26.30 S 28.28 E
Niger ▢¹ 134 16.00 N 8.00 E
Niger ▢⁵ 150 5.33 N 6.33 E
Niger ≃ 150 4.50 N 6.00 E
Niger Delta ≃² 150 4.50 N 6.00 E
Nigeria ▢¹ 134 10.00 N 8.00 E
Nigerian Museum ʋ 273a 6.20 N 3.24 E
Nigg 46 57.43 N 4.00 W
Nighāsan 124 28.14 N 80.52 E
Nightcaps 172 45.58 S 168.02 E
Night Hawk Lake @ 190 48.28 N 81.00 W
Nightingale Island I 10 37.24 S 12.28 W
Nightmute 180 60.29 N 164.00 W
Nigi 98 34.43 N 117.41 E
Nigrita 38 40.55 N 23.30 E
Nigwar 144 13.54 N 36.33 E
Nihe 104 41.27 N 121.13 E
Nihing (Nahang) ≃ 128 26.00 N 62.44 E
Nihoa I 14 23.06 N 161.58 W
Nihommatsu 92 37.35 N 140.26 E
Nihon → Japan ▢¹ 92 36.00 N 138.00 E
Nihonbashi ⁺⁸ 268 35.41 N 139.47 E
Nihon-kai → Japan, Sea ≃² 90 40.00 N 135.00 E
Nihon University ʋ² 268 35.42 N 139.45 E
Nihtaur 124 29.20 N 78.23 E
Nihuil 252 35.02 S 68.40 W
Nihuil, Embalse del @¹ 252 35.05 S 68.45 W
Niida ≃ 96 33.11 N 132.58 E
Niigata 92 37.55 N 139.03 E
Niigata ▢⁵ 94 37.08 N 138.30 E
Niigata-heiya ≚ 92 37.45 N 139.00 E
Niihama 96 33.58 N 133.16 E
Niihari 94 36.07 N 140.09 E
Niiharu 94 36.41 N 138.55 E
Niihau I 229b 21.55 N 160.10 W
Nii-jima I 94 34.22 N 139.16 E
Niimi 96 34.59 N 133.28 E
Niinisalo 26 61.50 N 22.29 E
Nii-shima I 92 34.22 N 139.16 E
Niitsu 92 37.48 N 139.07 E
Niiza 94 35.48 N 139.34 E
Nijar 34 36.58 N 2.12 W
Nijil 132 30.31 N 35.33 E
Nijkerk 52 52.13 N 5.30 E
Nijlen 56 51.10 N 4.39 E
Nijmegen 52 51.50 N 5.50 E
Nijo Castle ⊥ 270 35.01 N 135.45 E
Nijvel → Nivelles 50 50.36 N 4.20 E
Nijverdal 52 52.22 N 6.27 E
Nikaia 267c 37.58 N 23.39 E
Nike 150 6.26 N 7.29 E
Nikel' 24 69.24 N 30.12 E
Nikel'tau 86 50.23 N 58.13 E
Nikiforovo 265b 55.50 N 38.05 E
Nikiniki 112 9.49 S 124.28 E
Nikip Lake @ 184 52.53 N 91.53 W
Nikishka 180 60.44 N 151.19 W
Nikitovka, S.S.S.R. 78 50.23 N 38.25 E
Nikitovka, S.S.S.R. 83 48.21 N 38.02 E
Nikitskoje, S.S.S.R. 82 55.18 N 38.28 E
Nikitskoje, S.S.S.R. 82 55.13 N 35.46 E
Nikki 150 9.56 N 3.12 E
Nikkō 94 36.45 N 139.37 E
Nikks → -kokuritsu-kōen 94 36.49 N 139.33 E
Niklā al-'Inab 142 30.55 N 30.46 E
Nikobaren → Nicobar Islands II 110 8.00 N 93.30 E
Nikolai 180 62.58 N 154.09 W
Nikolaiken → Mikołajki 30 53.49 N 21.36 E
Nikolajev, S.S.S.R. 78 49.32 N 23.58 E
Nikolajev, S.S.S.R. 78 46.58 N 32.00 E
Nikolajevka, S.S.S.R. 78 47.06 N 34.14 E
Nikolajevka, S.S.S.R. 78 47.33 N 40.44 E
Nikolajevka, S.S.S.R. 78 47.38 N 33.12 E
Nikolajevka, S.S.S.R. 78 46.23 N 29.24 E
Nikolajevka, S.S.S.R. 78 51.04 N 34.02 E
Nikolajevka, S.S.S.R. 78 44.58 N 33.37 E
Nikolajevka, S.S.S.R. 80 52.11 N 48.04 E
Nikolajevka, S.S.S.R. 80 46.21 N 47.44 E
Nikolajevka, S.S.S.R. 80 52.28 N 49.14 E
Nikolajevka, S.S.S.R. 80 53.08 N 47.12 E
Nikolajevka, S.S.S.R. 83 48.51 N 37.46 E
Nikolajevka, S.S.S.R. 83 47.18 N 38.50 E
Nikolajevka, S.S.S.R. 83 48.46 N 38.20 E
Nikolajevka, S.S.S.R. 83 47.39 N 37.41 E
Nikolajevka, S.S.S.R. 86 56.29 N 95.06 E
Nikolajevka, S.S.S.R. 86 54.57 N 75.44 E
Nikolajevka, S.S.S.R. 86 49.10 N 81.59 E
Nikolajevka, S.S.S.R. 88 55.46 N 98.10 E
Nikolajevka, S.S.S.R. 88 46.34 N 134.47 E
Nikolajevo 76 58.16 N 29.29 E
Nikolajevo-Kozlovskij 83 47.13 N 38.21 E
Nikolajevskaja 80 47.37 N 41.29 E
Nikolajevskij 80 50.01 N 45.28 E
Nikolajevsk-na-Amure 89 53.08 N 140.44 E
Nikolajevskoje, S.S.S.R. 78 45.08 N 39.36 E
Nikolajevskoje, S.S.S.R. 88 51.04 N 111.48 E
Nikolajevskoje, S.S.S.R. 88 52.21 N 117.00 E
Nikolassee ⁺⁸ 264a 52.26 N 13.12 E
Nikolayev → Nikolajev 78 46.58 N 32.00 E
Nikolo-Berezovec 76 58.38 N 42.17 E
Nikolo-Ber'ozovka 80 56.08 N 54.09 E
Nikolo-Chovanskoje 265b 55.36 N 37.27 E
Nikologory 80 56.09 N 41.59 E
Nikolo-Kropotki 82 56.44 N 37.55 E
Nikolo-L'vovsk 89 43.54 N 131.23 E
Nikolo-Makarovo 80 57.38 N 43.34 E
Nikolsdorf 64 46.47 N 12.55 E
Nikol'sk, S.S.S.R. 24 59.30 N 45.27 E
Nikol'sk, S.S.S.R. 80 53.45 N 46.05 E
Nikolski 180 53.15 N 168.22 W
Nikol'skij, S.S.S.R. 24 60.55 N 34.00 E
Nikol'skij, S.S.S.R. 86 47.55 N 67.28 E
Nikol'skij, S.S.S.R. 86 56.18 N 68.58 E
Nikol'skij Toržok 76 59.53 N 38.46 E
Nikol'skoje, S.S.S.R. 74 55.12 N 166.00 E
Nikol'skoje, S.S.S.R. 76 52.39 N 36.04 E
Nikol'skoje, S.S.S.R. 76 55.26 N 35.04 E
Nikol'skoje, S.S.S.R. 76 59.30 N 42.32 E
Nikol'skoje, S.S.S.R. 76 59.23 N 44.36 E
Nikol'skoje, S.S.S.R. 78 50.35 N 41.10 E
Nikol'skoje, S.S.S.R. 80 47.46 N 46.24 E
Nikol'skoje, S.S.S.R. 80 52.37 N 43.49 E
Nikol'skoje, S.S.S.R. 82 54.27 N 36.24 E
Nikol'skoje, S.S.S.R. 82 54.18 N 35.53 E
Nikol'skoje, S.S.S.R. 82 54.51 N 36.35 E
Nikol'skoje, S.S.S.R. 82 54.30 N 36.50 E
Nikol'skoje, S.S.S.R. 82 56.09 N 36.43 E
Nikol'skoje, S.S.S.R. 82 54.03 N 37.10 E
Nikol'skoje, S.S.S.R. 82 55.53 N 36.26 E
Nikol'skoje, S.S.S.R. 82 55.37 N 36.41 E
Nikol'skoje, S.S.S.R. 82 55.15 N 36.04 E
Nikol'skoje, S.S.S.R. 83 47.46 N 37.18 E
Nikol'skoje, S.S.S.R. 86 57.12 N 84.21 E
Nikol'skoje, S.S.S.R. 86 52.02 N 55.43 E
Nikol'skoje, S.S.S.R. 265a 59.41 N 30.47 E
Nikol'skoje, S.S.S.R. 265b 55.46 N 37.54 E
Nikol'skoje-na-Čeremšane 80 54.03 N 49.14 E
Nikol'skoje-na-Dnepre 78 48.12 N 35.12 E
Nikol'skoje-Ur'upino 265b 55.48 N 37.13 E
Nikonorovka 83 49.07 N 39.59 E
Nikonova Gora 76 60.22 N 36.07 E
Nikonovskoje 82 55.17 N 38.10 E
Nikopol, Blg. 38 43.42 N 24.54 E
Nikopol', S.S.S.R. 78 47.35 N 34.25 E
Niksar 130 40.36 N 36.58 E
Nīkshahr 128 26.13 N 60.12 E
Nikšić 38 42.46 N 18.56 E
Nikulino, S.S.S.R. 76 55.16 N 33.46 E
Nikulino, S.S.S.R. 80 58.05 N 44.41 E
Nikulino, S.S.S.R. 82 56.48 N 35.50 E
Nikulino ⁺⁸ 265b 55.40 N 37.28 E
Nikulkino 82 56.07 N 38.38 E
Nikul'skoje 82 55.10 N 38.41 E
Nikunau I 14 1.23 S 176.26 E
Nil → Nile ≃ 140 30.10 N 31.06 E
Nīl, Nahr an- → Nile ≃ 140 30.10 N 31.06 E
Nila, Pulau I 164 6.44 S 129.31 E
Nilakka @ 26 63.07 N 26.33 E
Niland 204 33.14 N 115.31 W
Nil Blanc → White Nile ≃ 140 15.38 N 32.31 E
Nīl el-Abyad (Bahr an-Nīl) 140 30.10 N 31.06 E
Nīleh, Kūh-e A 128 32.59 N 50.32 E
Nileke 86 43.47 N 82.41 E
Niles, Ill., U.S. 278 42.01 N 87.49 W
Niles, Mich., U.S. 216 41.50 N 86.15 W
Niles, Ohio, U.S. 214 41.11 N 80.45 W
Nileshwar 122 12.15 N 75.06 E
Niles Pond @ 283 42.35 N 70.40 W
Nilgani 272b 22.46 N 88.26 E
Nilgaut, Lac @ 190 46.36 N 77.15 W
Nilgiri 126 21.28 N 86.46 E
Nilo → Nile ≃ 140 30.10 N 31.06 E
Nilo Azul → Blue Nile ≃ 140 15.38 N 32.31 E
Nilo Blanco → White Nile ≃ 140 15.38 N 32.31 E
Nilópolis 256 22.49 S 43.25 W
Nilópolis ▢⁷ 287a 22.49 S 43.25 W
Nilphāmāri 124 25.56 N 88.51 E
Nilsiä 26 63.12 N 28.05 E
Niltepec 234 16.34 N 94.37 W
Nīlwāl ⁺⁸ 272a 28.40 N 76.59 E
Nilwood 219 39.24 N 89.49 W
Nima 96 35.09 N 132.24 E
Nimach 120 24.28 N 74.52 E
Niman ≃ 89 51.24 N 132.45 E
Nimančik 89 52.09 N 133.47 E
Nimba ▢⁶ 150 7.40 N 8.50 W
Nimbahera 120 24.37 N 74.41 E
Nimba Mountains ⋀ 150 7.30 N 8.30 W
Nimelen ≃ 89 52.27 N 136.32 E
Nîmes 62 43.50 N 4.21 E
Nimis 64 46.12 N 13.16 E
Nimishillen Creek ≃ 214 40.38 N 81.22 W
Nimisila 214 40.56 N 81.34 W
Nimisila Reservoir @¹ 214 40.57 N 81.31 W
Nim Ka Thāna 120 27.44 N 75.48 E
Nimmitabel 166 36.31 S 149.16 E
Nimmonsburg 210 42.09 N 75.55 W
Nimpkish Lake @ 182 50.25 N 126.59 W
Nimrod Glacier ⊓ 9 82.27 S 161.00 E
Nimrod Lake @¹ 194 34.55 N 93.20 W
Nimrūz ▢⁴ 128 30.30 N 62.00 E
Nims ≃ 56 49.51 N 6.28 E
Nimta 272b 22.40 N 88.25 E
Nimule 154 3.36 N 32.03 E
Nimy 50 50.28 N 3.57 E
Nina Bang Lake @ 176 70.51 N 79.07 W
Nin Bay C 116 12.13 N 123.15 E
Ninda 152 14.47 S 21.24 E
Nindigully 166 28.21 S 148.49 E
Nindiri 236 12.00 N 86.08 W
Nine Ashes 260 51.42 N 0.18 E
Nine Degree Channel ⅋, As. 122 9.00 N 73.00 E
Nine Degree Channel ⅋, Bhārat 122 9.00 N 73.00 E
Ninemile Creek ≃, N.Y., U.S. 210 43.11 N 75.20 W
Ninemile Creek ≃, N.Y., U.S. 210 43.24 N 76.38 W
Ninemile Creek ≃, N.Y., U.S. 210 43.06 N 76.14 W
Nine Mile Creek ≃, Utah, U.S. 200 39.50 N 109.53 W
Ninemile Island I 279b 40.29 N 79.52 W
Nine Mile Lake @ 212 44.57 N 79.34 W
Nine Mile Point ≻ 212 44.09 N 76.34 W
Ninepin Group II 271d 22.16 N 114.21 E
Ninette 184 49.22 N 99.43 W
Ninety East Ridge ⁺³ 12 15.00 S 88.00 E
Ninety Mile Beach ≚², Austl. 166 38.13 S 147.23 E
Ninety Mile Beach ≚², N.Z. 172 34.48 S 173.00 E
Ninety Six 192 34.11 N 82.01 W
Nineveh, Ind., U.S. 218 39.22 N 86.05 W
Nineveh, N.Y., U.S. 210 42.12 N 75.36 W
Nineveh ⊥ 128 36.25 N 43.10 E
Ninfa ⊥ 66 41.36 N 12.58 E
Ninfas, Punta ≻ 254 42.56 S 64.20 W
Ninfield 42 50.53 N 0.25 E
Ninga 184 49.13 N 99.51 W
Ningan 89 44.22 N 129.25 E
Ningari 150 14.40 N 3.16 W
Ningbo 100 29.52 N 121.31 E
Ningcheng (Tianyi) 98 41.33 N 119.20 E
Ningde 100 26.43 N 119.33 E
Ningdu 100 26.31 N 115.58 E
Ninggang 100 26.50 N 114.02 E
Ningguo 106 30.38 N 118.58 E
Ninghai 100 29.17 N 121.25 E
Ninghe (Lutai) 105 39.20 N 117.48 E
Ninghepu 105 40.43 N 116.07 E
Ninghua 100 26.15 N 116.38 E
Ningi 150 11.04 N 9.32 E
Ningjin, Zhg. 98 37.37 N 114.55 E
Ningjin, Zhg. 98 37.39 N 116.48 E
Ningjing 102 29.40 N 98.30 E
Ningjingshan ⋀ 102 30.41 N 98.12 E
Ningling 98 34.27 N 115.21 E
Ningming 102 22.07 N 107.09 E
Ningnan 102 27.11 N 102.36 E
Ningpo → Ningbo 100 29.52 N 121.31 E
Ningqiang 102 32.44 N 106.19 E
Ningshan (Guankou) 102 33.04 N 108.39 E
Ningshuo (Xiaobabao) 102 37.58 N 106.02 E
Ningsia → Yinchuan 102 38.30 N 106.18 E
Ningsia Hut Autonomous Region → Ningxia Huizu Zizhiqu ▢⁴ 102 37.00 N 106.00 E
Ningwu 102 39.01 N 112.21 E
Ningxi 100 28.35 N 121.00 E
Ningxia Huizu Zizhiqu ▢⁴ 102 37.00 N 106.00 E
Ningxian 102 35.31 N 108.01 E
Ningxiang 100 28.15 N 112.33 E
Ningyang 98 35.47 N 116.49 E
Ningyō-tōge ✕ 96 35.19 N 133.56 E
Ningyuan 102 25.37 N 111.46 E
Ningyuanbao 102 38.38 N 102.30 E
Ningyuanpu 105 40.44 N 114.54 E
Ninh-binh 110 20.15 N 105.59 E
Ninh-hoa 110 12.29 N 109.08 E
Ninhue 252 36.24 S 72.24 W
Ninigo Group II 164 1.15 S 144.15 E
Ninilchik 180 60.03 N 151.41 W
Ninnescah ≃ 198 37.20 N 97.10 W
Ninnescah, North Fork ≃ 198 37.34 N 97.42 W
Ninnescah, South Fork ≃ 198 37.34 N 97.42 W
Ninnis Glacier Tongue ⊓ 9 68.12 S 147.12 E
Ninomiya, Nihon 94 36.22 N 139.58 E
Ninomiya, Nihon 94 35.18 N 139.16 E
Ninove 50 50.50 N 4.01 E
Niny 84 44.29 N 43.57 E
Nio 96 34.12 N 133.29 E
Nioaque 248 21.08 S 55.48 W
Nioaque ≃ 248 20.46 S 56.04 W
Niobe 214 42.01 N 79.27 W
Niobrara 198 42.45 N 98.02 W
Niobrara ≃ 198 42.45 N 98.00 W
Nioka 154 2.10 N 30.39 E
Nioki 152 2.43 S 17.41 E
Niokolo Koba 150 13.04 N 12.43 W
Niokolo Koba, Parc National du ♦ 150 13.00 N 13.00 W
Niono 150 14.15 N 6.00 W
Nionsamoridougou 150 8.43 N 8.50 W
Niordenskiold ≃ 180 62.05 N 136.18 W
Nioro du Rip 150 13.45 N 15.48 W
Nioro du Sahel 150 15.15 N 9.35 W
Niort 32 46.19 N 0.27 W
Niota 192 35.31 N 84.33 W
Niout ≃ 150 16.03 N 6.52 W
Nipan 166 24.47 S 150.01 E
Nipāni 122 16.24 N 74.23 E
Nipawin 184 53.22 N 104.00 W
Nipawin Provincial Park ♦ 184 54.00 N 104.40 W
Nipe, Bahía de C 240p 20.47 N 75.42 W
Nipe, Sierra de ⋀ 240p 20.28 N 75.49 W
Nipekamew Lake @ 184 54.24 N 104.58 W
Nipepe 154 14.01 S 37.55 E
Nipigon 190 49.01 N 88.16 W
Nipigon, Lake @ 176 49.50 N 88.30 W
Nipigon Bay C 190 48.53 N 87.50 W
Nipin ≃ 184 55.45 N 109.02 W
Nipisi Lake @ 182 55.47 N 114.57 W
Nipissing ▢⁶ 212 45.30 N 78.50 W
Nipissing, Lake @ 190 46.17 N 80.00 W

≃ River	Fluss	Rio	Rivière	Rio
≚ Canal	Kanal	Canal	Canal	Canal
⌊ Waterfall, Rapids	Wasserfall, Stromschnellen	Cascada, Rápidos	Chute d'eau, Rapides	Cascata, Rápidos
⅋ Strait	Meeresstrasse	Estrecho	Détroit	Estreito
C Bay, Gulf	Bucht, Golf	Bahía, Golfo	Baie, Golfe	Baía, Golfo
@ Lake, Lakes	See, Seen	Lago, Lagos	Lac, Lacs	Lago, Lagos
≡ Swamp	Sumpf	Pantano	Marais	Pântano
⊓ Ice Features, Glacier	Eis- und Gletscherformen	Accidentes Glaciales	Formes glaciaires	Acidentes Glaciares
⁺ Other Hydrographic Features	Andere Hydrographische Objekte	Otros Elementos Hidrográficos	Autres données hydrographiques	Outros Elementos Hidrográficos

Symbol	Deutsch	Español	Français	Português
⁺ Submarine Features	Untermeerische Objekte	Accidentes Submarinos	Formes de relief sous-marin	Acidentes Submarinos
▢ Political Unit	Politische Einheit	Unidad Política	Entité politique	Unidade Política
ʋ Cultural Institution	Kulturelle Institution	Institución Cultural	Institution culturelle	Instituição Cultural
⊥ Historical Site	Historische Stätte	Sitio Histórico	Site historique	Sítio Histórico
♦ Recreational Site	Erholungs- und Ferienort	Sitio de Recreo	Centre de loisirs	Sítio de Lazer
⊠ Airport	Flughafen	Aeropuerto	Aéroport	Aeroporto
▪ Military Installation	Militäranlage	Instalación Militar	Installation militaire	Instalação Militar
⁺ Miscellaneous	Verschiedenes	Misceláneo	Divers	Miscelânea

ENGLISH — Name | Page | Lat.°′ | Long.°′

DEUTSCH — Name | Seite | Breite°′ | Länge°′ E=Ost

Nipissis, Lac ⊜ **186** 51.02 N 66.10 W
Nipisso, Lac ⊜ **186** 50.52 N 65.50 W
Nipomo **204** 35.03 N 120.29 W
Nippenicket, Lake ⊜ **283** 41.58 N 71.03 W
Nippers Harbour **186** 49.48 N 55.52 W
Nippersink Creek ≃ **216** 42.23 N 88.22 W
Niqichang **107** 29.02 N 104.16 E
Niqiuji **100** 33.25 N 115.38 E
Niquelândia **255** 14.27 S 48.27 W
Niquero **240p** 20.03 N 77.35 W
Niquivil **252** 30.25 S 68.42 W
Nīr **128** 38.02 N 47.59 E
Nīr, Jabal an- ⋀[2] **128** 24.10 N 43.20 E
Nīra ≃ **122** 17.59 N 75.07 E
Nir'am **132** 31.31 N 34.35 E
Nirasaki **94** 35.42 N 138.27 E
Nirayama **94** 35.03 N 138.57 E
Nirgua **246** 10.09 N 68.34 W
Nirim **132** 31.20 N 34.24 E
Nirmal **122** 19.06 N 78.21 E
Nirmali **124** 26.19 N 86.35 E
Nirsa **126** 23.47 N 86.43 E
Nirwāno **128** 26.22 N 62.43 E
Niš **38** 43.19 N 21.54 E
Nisa **34** 39.31 N 7.39 W
Nisa (Neisse) (Nysa Łużycka) ≃ **30** 52.04 N 14.46 E
Nišava ≃ **38** 43.22 N 21.46 E
Nisbet **210** 41.13 N 77.07 W
Niscemi **70** 37.09 N 14.23 E
Nischintāpur **272b** 22.26 N 88.22 E
Nişf Thānī Bashbīsh **142** 31.07 N 31.11 E
Nish → Niš **38** 43.19 N 21.54 E
Nishan **120** 32.17 N 83.30 E
Nishi ↞[8], Nihon **268** 35.27 N 139.38 E
Nishi ↞[8], Nihon **270** 34.41 N 135.30 E
Nishiarai ↞[8] **268** 35.47 N 139.47 E
Nishiazai **94** 35.31 N 136.10 E
Nishibetsuin **270** 34.58 N 135.31 E
Nishigō **94** 37.09 N 140.10 E
Nishiiyayama **96** 33.53 N 133.49 E
Nishiizu **94** 34.46 N 138.47 E
Nishi-jima I **96** 34.39 N 134.29 E
Nishikata **94** 36.28 N 139.45 E
Nishikatsura **94** 35.31 N 138.51 E
Nishiki **96** 34.16 N 131.57 E
Nishiki ≃ **96** 34.09 N 132.15 E
Nishikiori **270** 34.29 N 135.34 E
Nishimori ↞[8] **270** 34.45 N 135.01 E
Nishinari ↞[8] **270** 34.38 N 135.28 E
Nishinasuno **94** 36.53 N 139.59 E
Nishinomiya **96** 34.43 N 135.20 E
Nishinoomote **93b** 30.44 N 131.00 E
Nishio **94** 34.52 N 137.03 E
Nishitani **94** 35.52 N 136.30 E
Nishitoda ↞[8] **270** 34.43 N 135.00 E
Nishitosa **96** 33.09 N 132.47 E
Nishiwaki **96** 34.59 N 134.58 E
Nishiyodogawa ↞[8] **270** 34.42 N 135.27 E
Nisi **102** 28.06 N 99.33 E
Nisinomiya → Nishinomiya **96** 34.43 N 135.20 E
Nísiros I **38** 36.35 N 27.10 E
Niska Lake ⊜ **184** 55.35 N 108.38 W
Niskayuna **210** 42.46 N 73.50 W
Nisling ≃ **180** 62.27 N 139.30 W
Nismes **56** 50.05 N 4.33 E
Nispen **52** 51.29 N 4.28 E
Nisporeny **78** 47.06 N 28.11 E
Nisqually ≃ **224** 47.06 N 122.42 W
Nisqually Indian Reservation ↞[4] **224** 47.02 N 122.42 W
Nisqually Reach ⊂ **224** 47.07 N 122.45 W
Nissan ≃ **26** 56.40 N 12.51 E
Nissequogue **276** 40.54 N 73.12 W
Nissequogue ≃ **276** 40.54 N 73.13 W
Nissequogue, Northeast Branch ≃ **276** 40.50 N 73.13 W
Nissequogue River State Park ♠ **276** 40.51 N 73.13 W
Nisser ⊜ **26** 59.10 N 8.30 E
Nisshin **94** 35.08 N 137.02 E
Nissoria **70** 37.39 N 14.27 E
Nissum Bredning ⊂ **26** 56.38 N 8.22 E
Nissum Fjord ⊂[2] **26** 56.21 N 8.14 E
Nisswa **190** 46.31 N 94.17 W
Nistelrode **52** 51.43 N 5.33 E
Nisutlin ≃ **180** 60.10 N 132.30 W
Nita, Indon. **115b** 8.40 S 122.11 E
Nita, Nihon **96** 35.12 N 133.01 E
Nitalas **272c** 19.06 N 73.08 E
Nītaure **76** 57.10 N 25.10 E
Niterói **256** / **287a** 22.53 S 43.07 W
Niterói □[7] **287a** 22.56 S 43.04 W
Nith ≃, Ont., Can. **212** 43.12 N 80.22 W
Nith ≃, Scot., U.K. **44** 55.00 N 3.35 W
Nithāri **272a** 28.35 N 77.21 E
Nithāri ↞[8] **272a** 28.42 N 77.03 E
Nithi River **182** 54.01 N 125.01 W
Nithsdale ∨ **44** 55.14 N 3.46 W
Nitibe **112** 9.19 S 124.12 E
Nitinat **224** 48.55 N 124.29 W
Nitinat ≃ **224** 48.49 N 124.37 W
Nitinat Lake ⊜ **182** 48.45 N 124.45 W
Niton **42** 50.35 N 1.16 W
Nitra **30** 48.20 N 18.05 E
Nitra ≃ **30** 47.46 N 18.10 E
Nitro **188** 38.25 N 81.50 W
Nitry **50** 47.40 N 3.53 E
Nítse Óros (Nidže) ∧ **38** 40.58 N 21.49 E
Nitta **94** 36.17 N 139.18 E
Nittälven ≃ **40** 59.51 N 14.50 E
Nittany Mountain ∧ **210** 41.00 N 77.25 W
Nittedal **26** 60.04 N 10.53 E
Nittenau **60** 49.12 N 12.16 E
Nittendorf **60** 49.02 N 11.58 E
Niuaunofo ≻ **174w** 21.04 S 175.20 W
Niubaotun **105** 39.46 N 116.41 E
Niubu **100** 31.02 N 117.39 E
Niuchutuncun **104** 41.28 N 122.58 E
Niudouguang **100** 24.51 N 115.44 E
Niue □[2] **14** 19.02 S 169.52 W
Nive □[2] **174v** 9.02 S 169.52 W
Niuerhe ≃ **89** 52.04 N 120.48 E
Niufentai **89** 47.05 N 120.02 E
Niufodu **107** 29.23 N 105.02 E
Niuhang **100** 28.44 N 115.51 E
Niujiazhuang **98** 37.21 N 118.29 E
Niujingjie **110** 25.46 N 100.33 E
Niujouch'i **100** 23.17 N 120.24 E
Niuke **120** 30.41 N 82.01 E
Niulake **102** 28.10 N 94.49 E
Niulanjiang ≃ **102** 27.28 N 103.10 E
Niulanshan **105** 40.13 N 116.39 E
Niulongxi **107** 29.29 N 103.48 E
Niumaowu **98** 40.58 N 124.59 E
Niupeng **106** 31.32 N 121.50 E
Niupichang **107** 30.35 N 103.40 E
Niuquanzi **98** 41.39 N 116.26 E
Niushan **98** 34.30 N 118.47 E
Niushandao I **100** 25.26 N 119.56 E
Niushitun **98** 35.18 N 114.24 E
Niut, Gunung ∧ **112** 1.00 N 109.55 E
Niutanchang **107** 29.05 N 105.21 E
Niutao I **14** 6.06 S 177.17 E
Niuti **100** 32.58 N 113.35 E
Niutianwei **100** 27.17 N 115.44 E
Niutoushan **89** 45.09 N 126.45 E
Niutuozhen **105** 39.15 N 116.20 E
Niuxichang **107** 28.47 N 104.31 E
Niuxintai **104** 41.21 N 123.53 E
Niuxintun **104** 41.56 N 121.21 E
Niuyuanzi **105** 40.20 N 117.47 E
Niuzhuang **104** 40.58 N 122.32 E
Nivå **41** 55.56 N 12.31 E
Nivala **26** 63.55 N 24.58 E
Nive ≃, Austl. **166** 26.02 S 146.25 E
Nive ≃, Fr. **32** 43.30 N 1.29 W
Nive Downs **166** 25.30 S 146.32 E
Nivelles (Nijvel) **50** 50.36 N 4.20 E
Nivernais □[9] **32** 47.00 N 3.30 E
Nivernais, Canal du ≍ **50** 47.40 N 3.40 E
Niverville, Man., Can. **184** 49.37 N 97.01 W
Niverville, N.Y., U.S. **210** 42.26 N 73.40 W
Nivillers **50** 49.28 N 2.10 E
Nivnoje **76** 53.11 N 32.35 E
Nivskij **24** 67.16 N 32.23 E
Nixa **194** 37.03 N 93.18 W
Nixichang **102** 29.09 N 104.08 E
Nixon, Nev., U.S. **204** 39.50 N 119.21 W
Nixon, Pa., U.S. **214** 40.45 N 79.56 W
Nixon, Tex., U.S. **222** 29.16 N 97.46 W
Niyodo **96** 33.32 N 133.08 E
Niyodo ≃ **96** 33.27 N 133.29 E
Niyor **114** 2.05 N 103.17 E
Niža **24** 66.20 N 43.16 E
Nizam ↞[8] **267b** 40.52 N 29.07 E
Nizāmābād **122** 18.40 N 78.07 E
Nizamghāt **120** 28.16 N 95.42 E
Nizām Sāgar ⊜[1] **122** 18.10 N 77.55 E
Nižankoviči **78** 49.40 N 22.47 E
Nīzgān ≃ **128** 33.13 N 63.40 E
Nizhniy Tagil → Nižnij Tagil **86** 57.55 N 59.57 E
Nizhny Novgorod → Gor'kij **80** 56.20 N 44.00 E
Nižin **76** 52.38 N 28.10 E
Nizino **265a** 59.50 N 29.53 E
Nizip **130** 37.01 N 37.46 E
Nízke Beskydy ⋀ **30** 49.20 N 21.30 E
Nízke Tatry ⋀ **30** 48.54 N 19.40 E
Nižn'aja **80** 56.34 N 49.07 E
Nižn'aja Čvorovaja **86** 59.11 N 77.31 E
Nižnaja Dobrinka **80** 50.18 N 45.42 E
Nižn'aja Duvanka **78** 49.35 N 38.10 E
Nižn'aja-Gerasimovka **83** 48.46 N 39.44 E
Nižn'aja Grajvoronka **78** 51.47 N 37.45 E
Nižn'aja Irga **86** 56.51 N 57.26 E
Nižn'aja Ivanovka ↞[8] **83** 48.09 N 38.46 E
Nižn'aja Karelina **88** 57.55 N 107.44 E
Nižn'aja Keul'skaja, Šivera ∟ **88** 58.25 N 102.46 E
Nižn'aja Krynka **83** 48.07 N 38.11 E
Nižnaja Matrenka **80** 52.16 N 40.06 E
Nižn'aja-Ol'chovaja **83** 48.44 N 39.35 E
Nižn'aja Omka **86** 55.26 N 74.55 E
Nižn'aja Omra **24** 62.46 N 55.46 E
Nižn'aja Ošma **80** 55.44 N 51.18 E
Nižn'aja Ouvanka **83** 49.35 N 38.10 E
Nižn'aja Peša **24** 66.43 N 47.36 E
Nižn'aja Pojma **88** 56.11 N 97.13 E
Nižn'aja Pokrovka **80** 51.40 N 50.07 E
Nižn'aja Šachtama **88** 51.24 N 117.40 E
Nižn'aja Salda **86** 58.05 N 60.43 E
Nižn'aja Syzran **80** 53.04 N 48.34 E
Nižn'aja Tavda **86** 57.40 N 66.12 E
Nižn'aja Tojma **24** 62.24 N 44.10 E
Nižn'aja Tunguska ≃ **74** 65.48 N 88.04 E
Nižn'aja Tura **86** 58.37 N 59.49 E
Nižn'aja Vol'dža **86** 58.19 N 79.20 E
Nižn'aja Zaimka **88** 56.09 N 98.14 E
Nižneangarsk **88** 55.47 N 109.33 E
Nižnebakanskij **78** 44.52 N 37.52 E
Nižne-Baranikovka **83** 49.05 N 39.51 E
Nižnečujskij **85** 43.12 N 74.21 E
Nižnedevick **78** 51.33 N 38.20 E
Nižne-Gnilovskoj ↞[8] **83** 47.11 N 39.36 E
Nižnegnutov **80** 48.02 N 42.22 E
Nižnegorskij **78** 45.27 N 34.44 E
Nižneilimsk **88** 57.11 N 103.16 E
Nižneje **83** 48.46 N 38.37 E
Nižneje Al'kejevo **80** 54.46 N 50.03 E
Nižn'eje Gir'unino **88** 51.12 N 116.58 E
Nižneje Kučukovo **80** 56.13 N 52.57 E
Nižneje Kujto, Ozero ⊜ **24** 64.58 N 31.38 E
Nižneje M'ačkovo **82** 55.33 N 37.59 E
Nižneje Platino **83** 48.48 N 39.30 E
Nižnejepravalje ≃ **83** 48.17 N 39.57 E
Nižneje Romanovo **86** 59.47 N 69.35 E
Nižneje Sančelejevo **80** 53.40 N 49.27 E
Nižnekamskij **80** 55.32 N 51.58 E
Nižnekundr'učenskaja **80** 47.45 N 40.57 E
Nižnelemskij **24** 64.01 N 56.16 E
Nižne Mit'akin Pervyj **83** 48.41 N 40.02 E
Nižnenagol'naja **83** 49.00 N 39.59 E
Nižneoz'ornoje **80** 51.37 N 53.56 E
Nižne-Podpol'nyj **83** 47.12 N 40.01 E
Nižne-Pokrovka **83** 49.13 N 38.38 E
Nižnetambovskoje **89** 50.54 N 138.13 E
Nižne-T'oploje **83** 48.48 N 39.23 E
Nižnetroickij **80** 54.20 N 53.41 E
Nižneudinsk **88** 54.54 N 99.03 E
Nižnij Baskunčak **80** 48.13 N 46.50 E
Nižnij Časučej **88** 50.31 N 115.08 E
Nižnij Čir **80** 48.22 N 43.03 E
Nižnij Čulym **86** 54.37 N 78.56 E
Nižnije Černi **80** 47.41 N 43.26 E
Nižnije Čeršely **80** 54.40 N 52.08 E
Nižnije Sergi **86** 56.40 N 59.18 E
Nižnije Serogozy **78** 46.49 N 33.24 E
Nižnije Timers'any **80** 54.34 N 47.45 E
Nižnije V'azovyje **80** 55.49 N 48.32 E
Nižnij Ingaš **88** 56.12 N 96.31 E
Nižnij Kisl'aj **78** 50.50 N 40.11 E
Nižnij Kuranach **74** 58.49 N 125.32 E
Nižnij Lomov **80** 53.32 N 43.41 E
Nižnij Mamon **78** 50.11 N 40.30 E
Nižnij Odec **24** 63.40 N 54.52 E
Nižnij Ol'šan **78** 50.45 N 38.55 E
Nižnij Oseredok, Ostrov I **80** 45.45 N 48.35 E
Nižnij P'andž **120** 37.08 N 68.32 E
Nižnij Paramonov **80** 47.57 N 41.55 E
Nižnij Rogačik **78** 47.21 N 34.02 E
Nižnij Serebr'akov **80** 47.58 N 41.02 E
Nižnij Škaft **80** 53.36 N 45.40 E
Nižnij Stan **88** 52.18 N 115.44 E
Nižnij Tagil **86** 57.55 N 59.57 E
Nižnij Takanyš **80** 55.57 N 51.04 E
Nižnij Trojanov Val ⊥ **78** 45.40 N 28.30 E
Nižnij Ufalej **86** 55.55 N 59.59 E
Nižnij V'aloz'orskij **24** 66.44 N 35.10 E
Nižnyj Nagol'čik **83** 48.01 N 39.04 E
Nizy **78** 50.47 N 34.46 E
Nizy-le-Comte **50** 49.34 N 4.03 E
Nizza Monferrato **62** 44.46 N 8.21 E
Nizzana, Nahal ∨ **132** 30.57 N 34.23 E
Nizzanim **132** 31.43 N 34.38 E
Njassa-See → Nyasa, Lake ⊜ **154** 12.00 S 34.30 E
Njinjo **154** 8.48 S 38.54 E
Njoko ≃ **152** 17.10 S 24.05 E
Njombe **154** 9.20 S 34.46 E
Njombe ≃ **154** 6.56 S 35.06 E
Njupeskär ∟ **26** 61.38 N 12.41 E
Njurunda **26** 62.16 N 17.22 E
Nkai **154** 19.00 S 28.54 E
Nkala Mission **154** 15.55 S 26.00 E
Nkambe **152** 6.38 N 10.40 E
Nkandla **158** 28.37 S 31.05 E
Nkawkaw **150** 6.33 N 0.47 W
Nkhata Bay **154** 11.33 S 34.18 E
Nkhota Kota **154** 12.57 S 34.17 E
Nkolabona **152** 1.14 N 11.43 E
Nkomi, Lagune ⊂ **152** 1.35 S 9.17 E
Nkongsamba **152** 4.57 N 9.56 E
Nkonko **154** 6.20 S 34.58 E
Nkoso **152** 2.42 S 22.39 E
Nkoto **152** 1.56 S 19.41 E
Nkunga **152** 4.41 S 18.34 E
Nkwalini **158** 28.45 S 31.33 E
Nmai ≃ **102** 25.42 N 97.30 E
Nnewi **150** 6.00 N 6.59 E
Nō **94** 37.06 N 137.59 E
Noābād **272b** 22.34 N 88.31 E
Noailles **50** 49.20 N 2.12 E
Noākhāli **124** 22.49 N 91.06 E
Noak Hill ↞[8] **260** 51.37 N 0.14 E
Noale **64** 45.32 N 12.04 E
Noamundi **124** 22.09 N 85.32 E
Noank **207** 41.19 N 72.01 W
Noarlunga **168b** 35.11 S 138.30 E
Noasca **62** 45.27 N 7.19 E
Noatak **180** 67.34 N 162.59 W
Noatak ≃ **180** 67.00 N 162.30 W
Nobby **171a** 27.51 S 151.54 E
Nobel **212** 45.25 N 80.06 W
Nobeoka **92** 32.35 N 131.40 E
Nobéré **150** 11.33 N 1.12 W
Nobidome **268** 35.48 N 139.34 E
Nobidome-yōsui ≍[1] **268** 35.44 N 139.27 E
Nōbi-heiya ≚ **94** 35.15 N 136.45 E
Nobitz **54** 50.58 N 12.29 E
Noble, Ill., U.S. **194** 38.42 N 88.13 W
Noble, Okla., U.S. **196** 35.08 N 97.24 W
Noble □[6] **216** 41.24 N 85.25 W
Noble Park **274b** 37.58 S 145.10 E
Noblestown **279b** 40.24 N 80.12 W
Noblesville **218** 40.03 N 86.01 W
Nobleton, Ont., Can. **212** 43.54 N 79.40 W
Nobleton, Fla., U.S. **220** 28.39 N 82.16 W
Noboribetsu **92a** 42.27 N 141.11 E
Noborito **268** 35.37 N 139.34 E
Nobres **248** 14.44 S 56.20 W
Nobsa **246** 5.46 N 72.57 W
Nocatee **220** 27.09 N 81.53 W
Noccundra **166** 27.50 S 142.36 E
Nocé **50** 48.22 N 0.42 E
Noce ≃ **64** 46.09 N 11.04 E
Nocera Inferiore **68** 40.44 N 14.38 E
Nocera Superiore **68** 40.44 N 14.40 E
Nocera Tirinese **68** 39.02 N 16.09 E
Nocera Umbra **66** 43.05 N 12.47 E
Noceto **64** 44.48 N 10.11 E
Nochistlán **234** 21.22 N 102.51 W
Nochten **54** 51.26 N 14.36 E
Noci **68** 40.48 N 17.08 E
Nociara ≃ **70** 37.15 N 14.17 E
Nociglia **68** 40.02 N 18.20 E
Nockamixon Lake ⊜[1] **208** 40.28 N 75.14 W
Nockamixon State Park ♠ **208** 40.27 N 75.16 W
Nockatunga **166** 27.43 S 142.43 E
Nocona **196** 33.47 N 97.44 W
Nocupétaro **234** 18.48 N 101.04 W
Noda **94** 35.56 N 139.52 E
Nodagawa **96** 35.31 N 135.06 E
Noda-sogo Baseball Ground ♠ **268** 35.57 N 139.52 E
Nodaway ≃ **194** 39.54 N 94.58 W
Nodera **270** 34.45 N 134.56 E
Nodier, Lac ⊜ **190** 47.38 N 78.26 W
Nodol' ≃ **82** 56.07 N 36.42 E
Nods **58** 47.06 N 6.20 E
Noé, Ouadi ∨ **146** 15.39 N 21.19 E
Noel **194** 36.33 N 94.29 W
Noenieput **158** 27.29 S 20.06 E
Noepoli **68** 40.05 N 16.20 E
Noer **41** 54.27 N 10.00 E
Noetinger **252** 32.22 S 62.19 W
Nœux-les-Mines **50** 50.29 N 2.40 E
Nofels **58** 47.15 N 9.34 E
Nogajsk **78** 46.44 N 36.20 E
Nogajskaja Step' ≚ **84** 44.17 N 46.05 E
Nogal ≃ **144** 7.58 N 49.52 E
Nogales, Chile **252** 32.44 S 71.15 W
Nogales, Méx. **234** 18.49 N 97.10 W
Nogales, Ariz., U.S. **200** 31.20 N 110.56 W
Nogal Valley ∨ **144** 8.35 N 48.35 E
Nogami **94** 36.07 N 139.07 E
Nogangjin **98** 39.30 N 125.23 E
Nogara **64** 45.11 N 11.04 E
Nogaro **32** 43.46 N 0.02 W
Nōgata **96** 33.44 N 130.44 E
Nogent-en-Bassigny **58** 48.02 N 5.21 E
Nogent-le-Roi **50** 48.39 N 1.32 E
Nogent-le-Rotrou **50** 48.19 N 0.50 E
Nogent-sur-Marne **50** 48.50 N 2.29 E
Nogent-sur-Oise **50** 49.16 N 2.28 E
Nogent-sur-Seine **50** 48.29 N 3.30 E
Nogent-sur-Vernisson **50** 47.51 N 2.45 E
Nogi **94** 36.14 N 139.44 E
Noginsk **82** 55.51 N 38.27 E
Nogisaki **268** 35.57 N 139.58 E
Nogles Creek ≃ **212** 44.35 N 78.31 W
Nogliki **89** 51.48 N 143.10 E
Nogoa ≃ **166** 23.33 S 148.32 E
Nōgohaku-san ∧ **94** 35.46 N 136.31 E
Nogoonnuur **86** 49.33 N 90.17 E
Nogoyá **252** 32.24 S 59.48 W
Nógrád □[6] **30** 48.00 N 19.35 E
Noguera Pallarese ≃ **34** 42.15 N 0.54 E
Noguera Ribagorzana ≃ **34** 41.40 N 0.43 E
Nohain ≃ **50** 47.24 N 2.55 E
Nohar **123** 29.11 N 74.46 E
Noheji **92** 40.52 N 141.08 E
Nohili Point ≻ **229b** 22.04 N 159.47 W
Nohjhīl **124** 27.51 N 77.39 E
Nohta **124** 23.40 N 79.34 E
Noicattaro **68** 41.02 N 16.59 E
Noichi **96** 33.33 N 133.42 E
Noir, Causse ⋀[1] **32** 44.10 N 3.15 E
Noir, Isla I **254** 54.29 S 73.02 W
Noir, Montagne ⋀ **32** 43.28 N 2.18 E
Noire ≃, Qué., Can. **190** 45.54 N 76.57 W
Noire ≃, Qué., Can. **206** 46.39 N 72.08 W
Noire ≃, Qué., Can. **206** 45.33 N 72.58 W
Noire, Mer du → Black Sea ⊽[2] **22** 43.00 N 35.00 E
Noire, Montagne ∧ **206** 46.14 N 74.18 W
Noirétable **62** 45.49 N 3.46 E
Noirmoutier **32** 47.00 N 2.14 W
Noirmoutier, Île de I **32** 47.00 N 2.15 W
Noiseau **261** 48.47 N 2.33 E
Noisiel **261** 48.51 N 2.37 E
Noisy ≃ **212** 44.19 N 80.08 W
Noisy-le-Grand **261** 48.51 N 2.33 E
Noisy-le-Roi **261** 48.51 N 2.04 E
Nojember'an **84** 41.12 N 45.01 E
Nojima-zaki ≻ **94** 34.56 N 139.53 E
Nojiri-ko ⊜ **94** 36.49 N 138.13 E
Nojon **102** 43.10 N 102.12 E
Nojon Uul ⋀ **102** 43.10 N 101.30 E
Nokami **96** 34.15 N 135.20 E
Nokaneng **156** 19.40 S 22.16 E
Nōke **270** 34.26 N 135.29 E
Nokha **120** 27.35 N 73.29 E
Nokia **26** 61.28 N 23.30 E
Nokilalaki, Bulu ∧ **112** 1.13 S 120.08 E
Nok Kundi **120** 28.48 N 62.46 E
Nokogiri-yama ∧ **268** 35.09 N 139.51 E
Nokomis, Sask., Can. **184** 51.30 N 105.00 W
Nokomis, Fla., U.S. **220** 27.07 N 82.27 W
Nokomis, Ill., U.S. **219** 39.18 N 89.18 W
Nokomis Lake ⊜ **184** 56.58 N 103.02 W
Nokou **146** 14.35 N 14.47 E
Nokrek ∧ **124** 25.27 N 90.20 E
Nola, Centraf. **152** 3.32 N 16.04 E
Nola, It. **68** 40.55 N 14.33 E
Nolan ≃ **222** 32.07 N 97.26 W
Nolan Creek ≃ **222** 31.02 N 97.26 W
Nolanville **222** 31.05 N 97.36 W
Nolay **58** 46.57 N 4.38 E
Nole **62** 45.15 N 7.35 E
Noli **62** 44.12 N 8.26 E
Noli, Capo di ≻ **62** 44.12 N 8.25 E
Nolichucky ≃ **192** 36.07 N 83.14 W
Nolin ≃ **194** 37.13 N 86.15 W
Nolin Lake ⊜[1] **194** 37.20 N 86.10 W
Nolinsk **80** 57.33 N 49.57 E
Nomahegan Brook ≃ **276** 40.41 N 74.18 W
Nomans Land I **207** 41.15 N 70.49 W
Noma Omuramba ≃ **156** 18.52 S 20.53 E
Nombre de Dios, Méx. **232** 28.41 N 106.05 W
Nombre de Dios, Méx. **234** 23.51 N 104.14 W
Nombre de Dios, Pan. **236** 9.35 N 79.28 W
Nombre de Dios, Cordillera ⋀ **236** 15.35 N 86.55 W
Nome **180** 64.30 N 165.24 W
Nomény **56** 48.54 N 6.14 E
Nomexy **58** 48.18 N 6.23 E
Nomgon, Mong. **102** 42.57 N 104.55 E
Nomgon, Mong. **102** 45.27 N 105.05 E
Nomgon Uul ⋀ **102** 43.00 N 104.50 E
Nomini Bay ⊂ **208** 38.09 N 76.43 W
Nominingue **206** 46.24 N 75.02 W
Nominingue, Lac ⊜ **206** 46.26 N 74.59 W
Nomozaki **92** 32.35 N 129.45 E
Nomtsas **156** 24.22 S 16.47 E
Nomura **96** 33.22 N 132.38 E
Nonacho Lake ⊜ **176** 61.42 N 109.40 W
Nonancourt **50** 48.46 N 1.12 E
Nonant-le-Pin **50** 48.42 N 0.13 E
Nonantola **64** 44.41 N 11.02 E
Nonburg **24** 65.34 N 50.32 E
Nonceveux **56** 50.28 N 5.44 E
Nondalton **180** 60.00 N 154.49 W
Nondwa **154** 6.26 S 35.20 E
Nondweni **158** 28.11 S 30.49 E
None **62** 44.56 N 7.32 E
Nonette ≃ **50** 49.12 N 2.24 E
None-yama ∧ **96** 33.29 N 134.10 E
Nong'an, Zhg. **89** 44.22 N 124.36 E
Nong'an, Zhg. **89** 44.25 N 125.10 E
Nong Bua Lamphu **110** 17.11 N 102.25 E
Nong Han **110** 17.21 N 103.07 E
Nong Hèt **110** 19.29 N 103.59 E
Nong Khai **110** 17.52 N 102.44 E
Nongoma **158** 27.58 S 31.35 E
Nongpoh **120** 25.54 N 91.53 E
Nongstoin **120** 25.31 N 91.16 E
Nonnenhorn **58** 47.34 N 9.36 E
Nonnevitz **54** 54.39 N 13.17 E
Nonning **166** 32.30 S 136.30 E
Nonnweiler **56** 49.36 N 6.58 E
Nonoai **252** 27.21 S 52.47 W
Nonoava **232** 27.28 N 106.44 W
Nonoc Island I **116** 9.51 N 125.37 E
Nono de Julho, Túnel ↞[5] **287b** 23.34 S 46.39 W
Nonogasta **252** 29.18 S 67.30 W
Nonoichi **94** 36.32 N 136.37 E
Nonouti I[1] **14** 0.40 S 174.21 E
Nonsan **98** 36.12 N 127.05 E
Nonsuch Bay ⊂ **240c** 17.03 N 61.42 W
Nonthaburi **110** 13.50 N 100.29 E
Nonthaburi □[4] **269a** 13.52 N 100.27 E
Non Thai **110** 15.12 N 102.19 E
Nontron **32** 45.32 N 0.40 E
Nonvianuk Lake ⊜ **180** 59.00 N 155.15 W
Noojee **169** 37.55 S 146.00 E
Nookawarra **162** 26.19 S 116.52 E
Nooksack **224** 48.55 N 122.19 W
Nooksack ≃ **224** 48.46 N 122.35 W
Nooksack, Middle Fork ≃ **224** 48.50 N 122.08 W
Nooksack, North Fork ≃ **224** 48.50 N 122.11 W
Nooksack, South Fork ≃ **224** 48.50 N 122.11 W
Noonamah **164** 12.38 S 131.04 E
Noonan **198** 48.54 N 103.01 W
Noon Hill ∧[2] **283** 42.09 N 71.19 W
Noonkanbah **162** 18.30 S 124.50 E
Noorat **169** 38.12 S 142.56 E
Noord-Beveland I **52** 51.35 N 3.45 E
Noord-Brabant □[4] **52** 51.30 N 5.00 E
Noord-Holland □[4] **52** 52.40 N 4.50 E
Noordhorn **52** 53.16 N 6.24 E
Noordoewer **156** 28.45 S 17.37 E
Noordoost Polder ↞[1] **52** 52.42 N 5.45 E
Noordpunt ≻ **241s** 12.23 N 69.10 W
Noord-Scharwoude **52** 52.43 N 4.47 E
Noordwijk aan Zee **52** 52.14 N 4.26 E
Noordwijk-Binnen **52** 52.13 N 4.27 E
Noordwijkerhout **52** 52.15 N 4.30 E
Noordwolde **52** 52.54 N 6.09 E
Noormarkku **26** 61.35 N 21.52 E
Noorvik **180** 66.50 N 161.12 W
Noosaville **166** 26.24 S 153.04 E
Nootka Island I **182** 49.32 N 126.42 W
Nootka Sound ⋓ **182** 49.33 N 126.38 W
Nopaltepec **234** 18.17 N 95.59 W
No Point, Point ≻ **276** 41.09 N 73.08 W
Nóqui **152** 5.51 S 13.25 E
Nora, Sve. **40** 59.31 N 15.02 E
Nora, Ind., U.S. **218** 39.55 N 86.08 W
Nora ≃ **89** 52.26 N 129.58 E
Nora ⊥ **71** 39.00 N 9.01 E
Nor Ačin **84** 40.19 N 44.35 E
Norah Head ≻ **170** 33.17 S 151.35 E
Nora Islands II **144** 16.02 N 39.58 E
Norala **116** 6.28 N 124.38 E
Noralee **182** 53.59 N 126.26 W
Noranda **190** 48.15 N 79.02 W
Noraskög ⋀ **40** 59.39 N 14.50 E
Nora Springs **190** 43.09 N 93.01 W
Norberg **40** 60.04 N 15.56 E
Norberto de la Riestra **252** 35.16 S 59.46 W
Norborne **194** 39.18 N 93.40 W
Norbottens Län □[6] **24** 66.00 N 20.00 E
Norcan Lake ⊜ **212** 45.10 N 76.53 W
Norcatur **198** 39.50 N 100.11 W
Norchia ⊥ **66** 42.20 N 11.57 E
Norcia **66** 42.48 N 13.05 E
Norco **228** 33.56 N 117.33 W
Norcott, Mount ∧ **162** 32.07 S 121.59 E
Norcross **192** 33.57 N 84.13 W
Nord □[4] **146** 9.00 N 13.30 E
Nord □[5] **50** 50.20 N 3.40 E
Nord ↞[5] **261** 48.53 N 2.21 E
Nord, Canal du ≍ **50** 47.14 N 2.27 E
Nord, Cap → Nordkapp ≻ **24** 71.11 N 25.48 E
Nord, Rivière du ≃ **206** 45.31 N 74.20 W
Nordamerika → North America ⊥[1] **16** 45.00 N 100.00 W
Nordanholen **40** 60.30 N 14.57 E
Nordausques **50** 50.49 N 2.05 E
Nordaustlandet I **12** 79.48 N 22.24 E
Nordbögge **263** 51.37 N 7.44 E
Nordborg **41** 55.03 N 9.45 E
Nordby **41** 55.58 N 10.34 E
Nord Dakota → North Dakota □[3] **198** 47.30 N 100.15 W
Norddeich **52** 53.37 N 7.09 E
Nordegg **182** 52.28 N 116.04 W
Nordegg ≃ **182** 52.53 N 115.18 W
Nordeifel, Naturpark ♠ **56** 50.40 N 6.20 E
Norden, B.R.D. **52** 53.36 N 7.12 E
Norden, Eng., U.K. **262** 53.38 N 2.13 W
Norden, Calif., U.S. **226** 39.20 N 120.22 W
Nordendorf **56** 48.36 N 10.50 E
Nordenham **52** 53.29 N 8.28 E
Nordenšel'da, Archipelag II **74** 76.45 N 96.00 E
Norderney **52** 53.42 N 7.08 E
Norderney I **52** 53.42 N 7.10 E
Norderstapel **41** 54.21 N 9.14 E
Norderstedt **52** 53.43 N 10.00 E
Nordfjord ⊂[2] **26** 61.54 N 5.12 E
Nordfjordeid **26** 61.54 N 6.00 E
Nordfold **24** 67.46 N 15.12 E
Nordfriesische Inseln → North Frisian Islands II **24** 54.50 N 8.12 E
Nordgermersleben **54** 52.13 N 11.20 E
Nordhalben **54** 50.22 N 11.30 E
Nordhausen **54** 51.30 N 10.47 E
Nordheim **222** 28.55 N 97.36 W
Nordheim von der Rhön **56** 50.28 N 10.11 E
Nordhelle ∧[2] **263** 51.09 N 7.46 E
Nordhorn **52** 52.27 N 7.05 E
Nordic Park **278** 41.57 N 88.02 W
Nordingrå **26** 62.56 N 18.16 E
Nordirland → Northern Ireland □[8] **28** 54.40 N 6.45 W
Nordiyya **132** 32.19 N 34.54 E
Nordkanal ≍ **263** 51.10 N 6.42 E
Nordkapp ≻ **24** 71.11 N 25.48 E
Nordkinnhalvøya ≻[1] **24** 70.55 N 27.45 E
Nordkirchen **52** 51.44 N 7.31 E
Nordkjosbotn **24** 69.13 N 19.30 E
Nord-Korea → Korea, North □[1] **98** 40.00 N 127.00 E
Nordland **224** 48.03 N 122.41 W
Nordland □[6] **24** 67.00 N 14.40 E
Nördliche Dwina → Severnaja Dvina ≃ **24** 64.32 N 40.30 E
Nördlicher Teutoburger Wald-Wiehengebirge, Naturpark ♠ **52** 52.20 N 8.05 E
Nördliches Eismeer → Arctic Ocean ⊽[1] **16** 85.00 N 170.00 E
Nördlingen **56** 48.51 N 10.30 E
Nordmaling **26** 63.34 N 19.30 E
Nordmark **40** 59.50 N 14.06 E
Nordmarka ↞[1] **26** 60.00 N 10.25 E
Nordostrundingen ≻ **16** 81.36 N 12.09 W
Nord-Ostsee-Kanal ≍ **30** 53.53 N 9.08 E
Nordpfälzer Bergland ⋀ **56** 49.40 N 7.40 E
Nordradde ≃ **52** 52.43 N 7.17 E
Nordreisa **24** 69.46 N 21.03 E
Nordre Strømfjord ⊂[2] **176** 67.50 N 52.00 W
Nordrhein-Westfalen □[3] **30** 51.30 N 7.30 E
Nordsee → North Sea ⊽[2] **22** 55.20 N 3.00 E
Nordstemmen **52** 52.09 N 9.46 E
Nordstrand I **41** 54.30 N 8.53 E
Nordstrandischmoor I **41** 54.33 N 8.48 E
Nord-Trøndelag □[6] **24** 64.25 N 12.00 E
Nordvik **74** 74.02 N 111.32 E
Nordwalde **52** 52.05 N 7.28 E
Nordwest-Kap → North West Cape ≻ **162** 21.45 S 114.10 E
Nore **26** 60.10 N 9.01 E
Nore ≃ **48** 52.25 N 6.58 W
Noremberg → Nürnberg **60** 49.27 N 11.04 E
Nörenberg → Ińsko **30** 53.27 N 15.33 E
Norf **263** 51.09 N 6.43 E
Norfbach ≃ **263** 51.11 N 6.44 E
Norfolk, Conn., U.S. **207** 41.59 N 73.12 W
Norfolk, Mass., U.S. **283** 42.07 N 71.19 W
Norfolk, Nebr., U.S. **198** 42.02 N 97.25 W
Norfolk, Va., U.S. **208** 36.40 N 76.14 W
Norfolk □[6], Ont., Can. **214** 42.48 N 80.25 W
Norfolk □[6], Eng., U.K. **42** 52.35 N 1.00 E
Norfolk □[6], Mass., U.S. **207** 42.15 N 71.10 W
Norfolk Broads ↞[1] **42** 52.40 N 1.30 E
Norfolk-Insel → Norfolk Island □[2] **174c** 29.02 S 167.57 E
Norfolk Island □[2] **14** / **174c** 29.02 S 167.57 E
Norfolk Island Aerodome ⊠ **174c** 29.03 S 167.56 E
Norfolk Island Trough ÷[1] **14** 30.00 S 165.00 E
Norfolk Naval Base ■ **208** 36.57 N 76.18 W
Norfolk Naval Shipyard ■ **208** 36.49 N 76.18 W
Norfolk Regional Airport ⊠ **208** 36.54 N 76.12 W
Norfolk Ridge ÷[3] **14** 29.00 S 167.00 E
Norfork Lake ⊜[1] **194** 36.25 N 92.10 W
Norg **52** 53.04 N 6.27 E
Norge **208** 37.22 N 76.46 W
Norge → Norway □[1] **24** 62.00 N 10.00 E
Norham **44** 55.43 N 2.10 W
Norheimsund **26** 60.22 N 6.08 E
Norikura-dake ∧ **94** 36.06 N 137.33 E
Noril'sk **74** 69.20 N 88.06 E
Noring, Gunong ∧ **114** 5.24 N 101.44 E
Norland, Ont., Can. **212** 44.43 N 78.49 W
Norland, Fla., U.S. **220** 25.57 N 80.12 W
Norlane **169** 38.06 S 144.21 E
Norley **262** 53.15 N 2.39 W
Norlina **192** 36.27 N 78.12 W
Norma, It. **66** 41.35 N 12.58 E
Norma, N.J., U.S. **208** 39.29 N 75.05 W
Normal, Ala., U.S. **194** 34.47 N 86.34 W
Normal, Ill., U.S. **216** 40.31 N 88.59 W
Norman, Ark., U.S. **194** 34.27 N 93.41 W
Norman, Ind., U.S. **218** 38.57 N 86.16 W
Norman, Okla., U.S. **196** 35.13 N 97.26 W
Norman ≃ **166** 17.28 S 140.49 E
Norman, Lake ⊜[1] **192** 35.35 N 80.55 W
Normanby, Austl. **171a** 27.28 S 153.01 E
Normanby, N.Z. **172** 39.32 S 174.17 E
Normanby ≃ **164** 14.25 S 144.08 E
Normanby Island I **164** 10.05 S 151.05 E
Norman Creek ⊂ **284b** 39.18 N 76.25 W
Normandie □[9] **32** 49.00 N 0.05 W
Normandien **158** 27.57 S 29.47 E
Normandy → Normandie □[9] **32** 49.00 N 0.05 W
Normandy Heights **284b** 39.17 N 76.48 W
Normandy Park **224** 47.27 N 122.21 W
Normangee **222** 31.02 N 96.07 W
Normanhurst **274a** 33.43 S 151.06 E
Normanhurst, Mount ∧ **162** 25.04 S 122.32 E
Norman Island I **240m** 18.20 N 64.37 W
Normannische Inseln → Channel Islands II **28** 49.20 N 2.20 W
Norman Park **192** 31.16 N 83.38 W
Normans Kill ≃ **210** 42.36 N 73.44 W
Normanton, Austl. **166** 17.40 S 141.05 E
Normanton, Eng., U.K. **44** 53.41 N 1.27 W
Normanville **168b** 35.27 S 138.19 E
Norman Wells **180** 65.17 N 126.51 W
Nor Marsh ≋ **260** 51.24 N 0.38 E
Nornalup **162** 35.00 S 116.49 E
Norogachic **232** 27.15 N 107.07 W
Noroton ≃ **276** 41.03 N 73.31 W
Noroton Point ≻ **276** 41.03 N 73.26 W
Norovlin **88** 48.44 N 112.59 E
Noroy-le-Bourg **58** 47.37 N 6.18 E
Norphlet **194** 33.19 N 92.40 W
Norquay **184** 51.53 N 102.05 W
Ñorquincó **254** 41.51 S 70.54 W
Norra Björkfjärden ⊂ **40** 59.27 N 17.28 E
Norrahammar **26** 57.42 N 14.06 E
Norra Hörken ⊜ **40** 60.04 N 14.53 E
Norra Kvarken (Merenkurkku) ⋓ **26** 63.36 N 20.43 E
Norra Kvills Nationalpark ♠ **26** 57.44 N 15.37 E
Norrälgen ⊜ **40** 59.50 N 14.34 E
Norra Rörum **41** 56.01 N 13.30 E
Norra Storfjället ∧ **24** 65.52 N 15.18 E
Norrboda **40** 60.28 N 18.25 E
Norrbotten □[9] **26** 66.45 N 23.00 E
Nørre Åby **41** 55.27 N 9.54 E
Nørre Alslev **41** 54.54 N 11.54 E
Nørre Broby **41** 55.15 N 10.14 E
Nørre Nærå **41** 55.34 N 10.17 E
Norrent-Fontes **50** 50.35 N 2.24 E
Nørre Snede **41** 55.58 N 9.25 E
Nørresundby **26** 57.04 N 9.55 E
Nørre Vejrup **41** 55.31 N 8.47 E
Norrfjärden **26** 65.25 N 21.27 E
Norridge **216** 41.57 N 87.49 W
Norridgewock **188** 44.43 N 69.48 W
Norris **192** 36.12 N 84.04 W
Norris, Lake ⊜ **220** 28.57 N 81.32 W
Norris Arm **186** 49.05 N 55.15 W
Norris Bridge ↞[5] **208** 37.37 N 76.26 W
Norris City **194** 37.59 N 88.20 W
Norrish Creek ≃ **224** 49.10 N 122.08 W
Norris Lake ⊜[1] **192** 36.20 N 83.55 W
Norris Point **186** 49.31 N 57.53 W
Norristown **208** 40.07 N 75.21 W
Norrköping **40** 58.36 N 16.11 E
Norroway Brook ≃ **283** 42.11 N 71.03 W
Norrskedika **40** 60.17 N 18.17 E
Norrsundet **26** 60.56 N 17.08 E
Norrtälje **40** 59.46 N 18.42 E
Norrtäljeviken ⊂ **40** 59.47 N 18.53 E
Norseman **162** 32.12 S 121.46 E
Norsewood **172** 40.04 S 176.13 E
Norsjå ⊜ **26** 59.18 N 9.20 E
Norsjö **26** 64.55 N 19.29 E
Norsk **89** 52.20 N 129.55 E
Norsminde **41** 56.01 N 10.16 E
Norte □[4] **148** 26.50 N 11.15 W
Norte, Cabo ≻, Bra. **250** 1.40 N 49.55 W
Norte, Cabo ≻, Chile **174z** 27.03 S 109.24 W
Norte, Canal do ⋓ **250** 0.30 N 50.30 W
Norte, Cayo I **240m** 18.20 N 65.15 W
Norte, Estación del ↞[5], Esp. **266a** 40.25 N 3.43 W
Norte, Estación del ↞[5], Esp. **266d** 41.24 N 2.02 E
Norte, Mar del → North Sea ⊽[2] **22** 55.20 N 3.00 E
Norte, Punta ≻, Arg. **252** 36.17 S 56.47 W
Norte, Punta ≻, Arg. **254** 42.04 S 63.45 W
Norte, Serra do ⋀[1] **248** 11.20 S 59.00 W
Norte Cabo → Nordkapp ≻ **24** 71.11 N 25.48 E
Norte de Santander □[5] **246** 8.00 N 73.00 W
Nortelândia **248** 14.25 S 56.48 W
Nörten-Hardenberg **52** 51.38 N 9.56 E
North, S.C., U.S. **192** 33.37 N 81.06 W
North, Va., U.S. **208** 37.27 N 76.25 W
North ≃, Newf., Can. **176** 57.30 N 62.05 W
North ≃, Ont., Can. **212** 44.44 N 79.39 W
North ≃, Ala., U.S. **194** 33.15 N 87.30 W
North ≃, Iowa, U.S. **194** 41.31 N 93.27 W
North ≃, Mass., U.S. **283** 42.10 N 70.43 W
North ≃, Mo., U.S. **219** 39.52 N 91.27 W
North ≃, Wash., U.S. **224** 46.45 N 123.53 W
North, Cape ⊥[2] **186** 47.02 N 60.25 W
North Abington **207** 42.08 N 70.57 W
North Adams, Mass., U.S. **207** 42.42 N 73.07 W
North Adams, Mich., U.S. **216** 41.58 N 84.32 W
North Albany **202** 44.39 N 123.06 W
Northallerton **44** 54.20 N 1.26 W
Northam, Austl. **168a** 31.39 S 116.40 E
Northam, S. Afr. **156** 25.03 S 27.11 E
Northam, Eng., U.K. **42** 51.02 N 4.12 W
North America ⊥[1] **4** / **16** 45.00 N 100.00 W
North American Basin ÷[1] **8** 31.00 N 62.00 W
North Amherst **207** 42.25 N 72.32 W
North Amityville **276** 40.42 N 73.26 W
Northampton, Austl. **162** 28.21 S 114.37 E
Northampton, Eng., U.K. **42** 52.14 N 0.54 W
Northampton, Mass., U.S. **207** 42.19 N 72.38 W
Northampton, N.Y., U.S. **207** 40.54 N 72.40 W
Northampton, Pa., U.S. **208** 40.41 N 75.30 W
Northampton □[6], N.C., U.S. **208** 36.28 N 77.21 W
Northampton □[6], Pa., U.S. **210** 40.45 N 75.18 W
Northampton □[6], Va., U.S. **208** 37.20 N 75.50 W
Northamptonshire □[6] **42** 52.20 N 0.50 W
North Andaman I **110** 13.15 N 92.55 E
North Andover **207** 42.42 N 71.08 W
North Andrews Gardens **220** 26.12 N 80.07 W
North Anna ≃ **192** 37.48 N 77.25 W
North Anson **188** 44.52 N 69.54 W
North Apollo **214** 40.35 N 79.34 W
North Arlington **276** 40.47 N 74.08 W
North Arm ≃[1] **224** 49.12 N 123.10 W
North Atlanta **192** 33.51 N 84.21 W
North Attleboro **207** 41.59 N 71.20 W
North Attleboro National Fish Hatchery ♠ **283** 42.00 N 71.17 W
North Auburn **274a** 33.50 S 151.02 E
North Augusta **192** 33.30 N 81.58 W
North Aulatsivik Island I **176** 59.50 N 64.00 W
North Aurora **216** 41.48 N 88.20 W
Northaw **260** 51.42 N 0.09 W
North Babylon **276** 40.44 N 73.19 W
North Balabac Strait ⋓ **116** 8.10 N 117.04 E
North Baltimore **216** 41.11 N 83.41 W
North Balwyn **274b** 37.48 S 145.05 E
North Bannister **168a** 32.35 S 116.26 E
North Barrackpore **126** 22.46 N 88.22 E
North Bass Island I **214** 41.43 N 82.49 W
North Battleford **184** 52.47 N 108.17 W
North Bay, Ont., Can. **190** 46.19 N 79.28 W
North Bay, N.Y., U.S. **210** 43.14 N 75.45 W
North Bay, Wis., U.S. **216** 42.46 N 87.47 W
North Bay ⊂, Ont., Can. **212** 44.53 N 79.48 W
North Bay ⊂, Wash., U.S. **224** 46.59 N 124.04 W
North Bay Village **220** 25.51 N 80.08 W
North Beach **168a** 31.52 S 115.45 E
North Beach ↞[8] **282** 37.48 N 122.25 W
North Belle Vernon **214** 40.08 N 79.52 W
North Bellmore **276** 40.41 N 73.32 W
North Bend, B.C., Can. **182** 49.53 N 121.27 W
North Bend, Nebr., U.S. **198** 41.28 N 96.47 W
North Bend, Ohio, U.S. **218** 39.09 N 84.45 W
North Bend, Oreg., U.S. **202** 43.24 N 124.14 W

Symbols in the index entries represent the broad categories identified in the key at the right. Symbols with superior numbers (⋀[2]) identify subcategories (see complete key on page *I* · *30*).

Kartensymbole in dem Registerverzeichnis stellen die rechts in Schlüssel erklärten Kategorien dar. Symbole mit hochgestellten Ziffern (⋀[2]) bezeichnen Unterabteilungen einer Kategorie (vgl. vollständiger Schlüssel auf Seite *I* · *30*).

Los símbolos incluídos en el texto del índice representan las grandes categorias identificadas con la clave a la derecha. Los símbolos con numeros en su parte superior (⋀[2]) identifican las subcategorias (véase la clave completa en la página *I* · *30*).

Les symboles de l'index représentent les catégories indiquées dans la légende à droite. Les symboles suivis d'un indice (⋀[2]) représentent des sous-catégories (voir légende complète à la page *I* · *30*).

Os símbolos incluídos no texto do índice representam as grandes categorias identificadas com a chave à direita. Os símbolos com números em sua parte superior (⋀[2]) identificam as subcategorias (veja-se a chave completa à página *I* · *30*).

	English	Deutsch	Español	Français	Português
∧	Mountain	Berg	Montaña	Montagne	Montanha
⋀	Mountains	Berge	Montañas	Montagnes	Montanhas
)(	Pass	Pass	Paso	Col	Passo
∨	Valley, Canyon	Tal, Cañon	Valle, Cañón	Vallée, Canyon	Vale, Canhão
≚	Plain	Ebene	Llano	Plaine	Planície
≻	Cape	Kap	Cabo	Cap	Cabo
I	Island	Insel	Isla	Île	Ilha
II	Islands	Inseln	Islas	Îles	Ilhas
⊥	Other Topographic Features	Andere Topographische Objekte	Otros Elementos Topográficos	Autres données topographiques	Outros Elementos Topográficos

ESPAÑOL: Nombre · Página · Lat.°′ · Long.°′ W=Oeste
FRANÇAIS: Nom · Page · Lat.°′ · Long.°′ W=Ouest
PORTUGUÊS: Nome · Página · Lat.°′ · Long.°′ W=Oeste

North Bend, Pa., U.S. 214 41.21 N 77.42 W
North Bend, Wash., U.S. 224 47.30 N 121.47 W
North Benfleet 260 51.35 N 0.32 E
North Bengal Plains ≅ 124 26.20 N 88.30 E
North Bennington 188 42.56 N 73.15 W
North Bergen 276 40.48 N 74.01 W
North Berwick, Scot., U.K. 46 56.04 N 2.44 W
North Berwick, Maine, U.S. 188 43.17 N 70.45 W
North Bethlehem 210 42.40 N 73.50 W
North Bihar Plains ≅ 124 26.20 N 86.00 E
North Billerica 207 42.35 N 71.17 W
North Bloomfield 214 41.28 N 80.52 W
North Boggy Creek ≃ 196 34.23 N 96.04 W
North Bonneville 224 45.39 N 121.57 W
Northborough 207 42.19 N 71.39 W
North Bosque ≃ 196 31.40 N 97.24 W
North Boston 210 42.41 N 78.47 W
North Bourke 166 30.03 S 145.57 E
North Box Hill 274b 37.48 S 145.07 E
North Braddock 279b 40.24 N 79.52 W
North Branch, Mich., U.S. 190 43.14 N 83.12 W
North Branch, Minn., U.S. 190 45.31 N 92.58 W
North Branch, N.J., U.S. 276 40.35 N 74.41 W
North Branch Canal ≡ 224 47.12 N 120.40 W
North Branford 207 41.20 N 72.46 W
North Breakers ➝2 174g 28.14 N 177.25 W
Northbridge, Austl. 274a 33.49 S 151.13 E
Northbridge, Mass., U.S. 207 42.09 N 71.39 W
North Bristol 214 41.24 N 80.52 W
Northbrook, Ont., Can. 212 44.44 N 77.10 W
Northbrook, Ill., U.S. 216 42.08 N 87.50 W
Northbrook, Pa., U.S. 285 39.55 N 75.41 W
North Brookfield, Mass., U.S. 207 42.16 N 72.05 W
North Brookfield, N.Y., U.S. 210 42.51 N 75.24 W
North Brunswick 208 40.28 N 74.28 W
North Caicos I 238 21.56 N 71.59 W
North Caldwell 276 40.52 N 74.16 W
North Canton, Conn., U.S. 207 41.54 N 72.54 W
North Canton, Ga., U.S. 192 34.15 N 84.29 W
North Canton, Ohio, U.S. 214 40.53 N 81.24 W
North Cape 216 42.47 N 88.05 W
North Cape ≻, N.Z. 172 34.25 S 173.02 E
North Cape → Nordkapp ≻, Nor. 24 71.11 N 25.48 E
North Cape ≻, Pap. N. Gui. 164 2.32 S 150.49 E
North Cape May 208 38.59 N 74.57 W
North Captiva Island I 220 26.35 N 82.13 W
North Caribou Lake ⊜ 176 52.50 N 90.40 W
North Carlsbad 228 33.11 N 117.21 W
North Carolina □3 178
192 35.30 N 80.00 W
North Carver 207 41.55 N 70.48 W
North Cascades National Park ♠, Wash., U.S. 182 48.45 N 121.14 W
North Cascades National Park ♠, Wash., U.S. 224 48.30 N 121.00 W
North Castor ≃ 212 45.16 N 75.24 W
North Catasauqua 208 40.40 N 75.29 W
North Cemetery ✝ 269l 14.38 N 120.59 E
North-Central □3 150 11.00 N 7.45 E
North Chagrin Reservation ♠ 279a 41.34 N 81.26 W
North Channel 𝕌, Ont., Can. 190 46.02 N 82.50 W
North Channel 𝕌, Ont., Can. 212 44.10 N 76.45 W
North Channel 𝕌, U.K. 44 55.10 N 5.40 W
North Channel ≃1 281 42.38 N 82.40 W
North Charleroi 214 40.09 N 79.54 W
North Charleston 192 32.53 N 80.00 W
North Chatham 210 42.29 N 73.38 W
North Chelmsford 207 42.38 N 71.23 W
North Chicago 216 42.20 N 87.51 W
North Chili 210 43.06 N 77.45 W
Northchurch 260 51.46 N 0.36 W
North City 224 47.30 N 121.47 W
North Cleveland 222 30.21 N 95.06 W
Northcliff ➝8 273d 26.09 S 27.58 E
Northcliffe 162 34.36 S 116.07 E
North Clymer 214 42.04 N 79.34 W
North Cohasset 283 42.16 N 70.51 W
North Cohocton 210 42.34 N 77.28 W
North College Hill 218 39.12 N 84.32 W
North Collins 210 42.36 N 78.56 W
North Concho ≃ 196 31.27 N 100.25 W
North Conway 188 44.03 N 71.08 W
Northcote 274b 37.46 S 145.00 E
North Cray ➝8 260 51.26 N 0.08 E
North Creek 188 43.42 N 73.59 W
North Creek ≃ 278 41.33 N 87.37 W
Northcrest 222 31.38 N 97.06 W
North Crosswicks 285 40.10 N 74.39 W
North Dakota □3 178
198 47.30 N 100.15 W
North Dandalup 168a 32.31 S 115.58 E
North Dartmouth 207 41.38 N 70.59 W
North Dighton 207 41.52 N 71.08 W
North Dorset Downs ⋀1 42 50.47 N 2.30 W
North Down Cbangor 48 54.40 N 5.40 W
North Downs ⋀1 42 50.12 N 0.10 E
North Dum-Dum 126 22.38 N 88.23 E
North East, Md., U.S. 188 39.36 N 75.56 W
North East, Pa., U.S. 214 42.13 N 79.50 W
North East □5 156 21.00 S 27.30 E
Northeast Cape 180 63.18 N 168.42 W
Northeast Cape ≻ 180 63.17 N 168.45 W
Northeast Cape Fear ≃ 192 34.11 N 77.57 W
Northeast Creek ≃ 284b 39.18 N 76.29 W
North-Eastern □3 146 11.00 N 12.00 E
North Eastern □4 154 1.00 N 40.15 E
Northeastern University ✌2 283 42.20 N 71.05 W
North Eastham 207 41.52 N 69.59 W
Northeast Harbor 188 44.18 N 68.17 W
Northeast Henrietta 210 43.04 N 77.36 W
Northeast Islands II 175c 7.36 N 151.57 E
North Easton 207 42.04 N 71.06 W
Northeast Pass 𝕌 175c 7.30 N 151.59 E
Northeast Point ≻, Ba. 238 21.20 N 73.01 W
Northeast Point ≻, Ba. 238 22.43 N 73.50 W
North East Point ≻, Kiribati 174o 1.57 N 157.16 W
Northeast Point ≻, St. Vin. 241h 13.03 N 61.13 W
Northeast Providence Channel 𝕌 238 25.40 N 77.09 W
North Edwards 228 35.01 N 117.44 W
North Egmont 207 42.12 N 73.26 W
Northeim 52 51.42 N 10.00 E
North Elkhorn Creek ≃ 218 38.13 N 84.48 W
North Elm Creek ≃ 222 30.53 N 97.00 W
North English 190 41.31 N 92.05 W
Northern □4, Ghana 150 9.30 N 1.00 W
Northern □4, Malawi 154 11.00 S 34.00 E
Northern □4, S.L. 150 9.15 N 11.45 W
Northern □4, Zam. 154 11.00 S 31.00 E
Northern □5 164 9.00 S 148.30 E
Northern Aire Estates 278 42.08 N 88.02 W
Northern Arm 186 49.10 N 55.23 W
Northern Cheyenne Indian Reservation ➝4 202 45.31 N 106.45 W
Northern Circārs ⋀2 122 18.00 N 83.15 E
Northern Division □5, Fiji 175g 16.30 S 179.30 E
Northern Division □5, N. Heb. 175f 14.30 S 167.00 E
Northern Dvina → Severnaja Dvina ≃ 24 64.32 N 40.30 E
Northern Indian Lake ⊜ 176 57.20 N 97.20 W
Northern Ireland □8 28 54.40 N 6.45 W
Northern Light Lake ⊜ 190 48.15 N 90.38 W
Northern Territory □8 160 20.00 S 134.00 E
North Esk ≃, Scot., U.K. 46 55.54 N 3.04 W
North Esk ≃, Scot., U.K. 46 56.44 N 2.28 W
North Essendon 274b 37.45 S 144.54 E
North Evans 210 42.42 N 78.56 W
Northey Island I 260 51.44 N 0.43 E
North Fabius ≃ 194 39.54 N 91.30 W
North Fairfield 214 41.06 N 82.37 W
North Fair Oaks 282 37.28 N 122.12 W
North Falmouth 207 41.39 N 70.37 W
Northfield, B.C., Can. 224 49.11 N 123.59 W
Northfield, Conn., U.S. 207 41.42 N 73.07 W
Northfield, Ill., U.S. 278 42.06 N 87.46 W
Northfield, Mass., U.S. 207 42.42 N 72.27 W
Northfield, Minn., U.S. 190 44.27 N 93.09 W
Northfield, N.J., U.S. 208 39.22 N 74.33 W
Northfield, Ohio, U.S. 214 41.20 N 81.32 W
Northfield, Vt., U.S. 188 44.09 N 72.40 W
Northfield Airport ⊠ 279a 41.17 N 81.31 W
Northfield Center 279a 41.19 N 81.32 W
Northfield Park Race Track ♠ 279a 41.21 N 81.31 W
Northfield Village 279a 41.21 N 81.31 W
Northfield Woods 278 42.05 N 87.52 W
North Fillmore 228 34.24 N 118.56 W
North Fitzroy 274b 37.47 S 144.59 E
Northfleet 42 51.27 N 0.21 E
North Flinders Range ⋀ 166 31.00 S 139.00 E
North Fond du Lac 190 43.38 N 88.28 W
Northford 207 41.24 N 72.48 W
North Foreland ≻ 42 51.23 N 1.27 E
North Fork 226 37.14 N 119.31 W
North Fork ≃ 194 36.13 N 92.17 W
North Fork Lake ⊜1 226 38.56 N 121.00 W
North Fork Reservoir ⊜1 224 45.13 N 122.15 W
North Fork Village 218 39.21 N 83.02 W
North Fort Myers 220 26.40 N 81.54 W
North Freedom 190 43.27 N 89.52 W
North Frisian Islands II 24 54.50 N 8.12 E
Northgate 216 43.01 N 85.36 W
Northgate ➝9 282 38.00 N 122.33 W
North Georgetown 214 40.51 N 80.59 W
North Germiston 273d 26.14 S 28.09 E
North Glanford 212 43.11 N 79.54 W
North Glen Ellyn 278 41.54 N 88.04 W
North Gower 212 45.08 N 75.43 W
North Grafton 207 42.14 N 71.42 W
North Granby 207 41.59 N 72.50 W
North Grand Island Bridge ➝5 284a 43.04 N 78.59 W
North Great River 206 40.45 N 73.11 W
North Grosvenordale 207 41.59 N 71.54 W
North Grove 216 40.37 N 85.58 W
North Hadley 207 42.23 N 72.36 W
North Haledon 276 40.58 N 74.11 W
North Hampton 218 39.59 N 83.56 W
North Hanover 283 42.09 N 70.52 W
North Haven 207 41.23 N 72.52 W
North Havre 202 48.36 N 109.41 W
North Hawaiian Seamount Range ➝3 6 29.00 N 163.00 W
North Head ≻ 274a 33.49 S 151.18 E
North Henik Lake ⊜ 176 61.45 N 97.40 W
North Hero 188 44.49 N 73.18 W
North Highlands 226 38.40 N 121.23 W
North Hill 42 50.34 N 4.25 W
North Hills, Del., U.S. 285 39.46 N 75.30 W
North Hills, Ill., U.S. 278 42.18 N 88.01 W
North Hills, N.Y., U.S. 276 40.47 N 73.41 W
North Hinksey 42 51.45 N 1.16 W
North Hogan Creek ≃ 218 39.03 N 84.54 W
North Hollywood ➝8 280 34.10 N 118.23 W
North Holmwood 260 51.13 N 0.20 W
North Honcut Creek ≃ 226 39.19 N 121.36 W
North Hoosick 210 42.56 N 73.21 W
North Hornell 210 42.21 N 77.40 W
North Horr 154 3.19 N 37.04 E
North Houston 222 29.54 N 95.31 W
North Hudson 190 44.59 N 92.46 W
North Industry 214 40.45 N 81.22 W
North Irwin 279b 40.20 N 79.43 W
North Island I, Bhārat 122 10.08 N 72.20 E
North Island I, Kenya 154 4.04 N 36.03 E
North Island I, N.Z. 172 39.00 S 176.00 E
North Islet I 116 8.56 N 120.02 E
North Jackson 214 41.06 N 80.52 W
North Java 210 42.41 N 78.20 W
North Judson 216 41.13 N 86.46 W
North Kingstown 207 41.34 N 71.27 W
North Kingsville 214 41.54 N 80.42 W
North Knife Lake ⊜ 176 58.05 N 97.05 W
North Knob ⋀ 214 41.43 N 75.33 W
North Korea → Korea, North □1 98 40.00 N 127.00 E
Northlake, Ill., U.S. 278 41.55 N 87.54 W
North Lake, Wis., U.S. 216 43.10 N 88.22 W
North Lake ⊜, Ill., U.S. 276 41.09 N 73.41 W
North Lake ⊜, Tex., U.S. 222 32.57 N 96.58 W
North Lakhimpur 120 27.14 N 94.07 E
Northland ➝9 281 42.27 N 83.13 W
North Landing ≃ 208 36.31 N 76.01 W
North Lansing 216 42.08 N 104.56 W
North Las Vegas 204 36.12 N 115.07 W
North La Veta Pass)(200 37.37 N 105.11 W
North Lawrence 214 40.51 N 81.38 W
Northleach 42 51.51 N 1.50 W
North Lewisburg 216 40.13 N 83.33 W
North Liberty 216 41.32 N 86.26 W
North Lima 214 40.57 N 80.40 W
North Lindenhurst 276 40.43 N 73.23 W
Northline Terrace 222 29.55 N 95.25 W
North Little Rock 194 34.46 N 92.14 W
North Llano ≃ 196 30.30 N 99.46 W
North Logan 202 41.45 N 111.49 W
North Loma Linda 228 34.02 N 117.05 W
North Loon Mountain ⋀ 202 45.07 N 115.52 W
North Loup 198 41.30 N 98.46 W
North Loup ≃ 198 41.17 N 98.23 W
North MacMillan ≃ 180 63.03 N 133.18 W
North Madison 214 41.48 N 81.03 W
North Magnetic Pole ✦ 16 76.02 N 101.00 W
North Malosmadulu Atoll I1 122 5.35 N 72.55 E
North Mamm Peak ⋀ 200 39.23 N 107.52 W
North Manchester 216 41.00 N 85.46 W
North Manitou Island I 190 45.06 N 86.01 W
North Mankato 190 44.10 N 94.00 W
North Manly 274a 33.46 S 151.16 E
North Maroota 170 33.29 S 150.56 E
North Marshfield 283 42.09 N 70.47 W
North Massapequa 276 40.43 N 73.28 W
Northmead, Austl. 274a 33.47 S 151.00 E
Northmead, S. Afr. 273d 26.10 S 28.20 E
North Merrick 276 40.41 N 73.34 W
North Miami 220 25.54 N 80.11 W
North Miami Beach 220 25.56 N 80.09 W
North Middleboro 207 41.53 N 70.55 W
North Milk ≃ 202 49.08 N 112.23 W
North Mokelumne ≃ 226 38.08 N 121.35 W
North Moose Lake ⊜ 184 54.08 N 100.13 W
North Moreau Creek ≃ 194 38.30 N 92.18 W
North Muskegon 216 43.15 N 86.17 W
North Myrtle Beach 192 33.48 N 78.42 W
North Nahanni ≃ 180 62.05 N 124.30 W
North Naples 220 26.12 N 81.48 W
North Narrabeen 274a 33.42 S 151.18 E
North Nemah ≃ 224 46.30 N 123.53 W
North New Hyde Park 276 40.45 N 73.41 W
North New River Canal ≡ 220 26.05 N 80.12 W
North Niles 216 41.52 N 86.15 W
North Ninepin Island I 271d 22.16 N 114.20 E
North Norwich 210 42.37 N 75.32 W
North Oaks 222 30.22 N 97.41 W
North Ockendon ➝8 260 51.32 N 0.18 E
North Ogden 200 41.18 N 112.00 W
North Olmsted 214 41.25 N 81.56 W
Northolt Aerodrome ⊠ 260 51.33 N 0.23 W
Northome 190 47.52 N 94.17 W
Northop 262 53.12 N 3.08 W
North Ore Creek ≃ 281 42.43 N 83.47 W
North Orwell 210 41.55 N 76.19 W
Northowram 262 53.44 N 1.50 W
North Oxford 207 42.10 N 71.53 W
North Palisade ⋀ 204 37.06 N 118.31 W
North Palm Beach 220 26.49 N 80.04 W
North Para ≃ 168b 34.36 S 138.45 E
North Park 216 42.20 N 89.02 W
North Park ➝8 278 41.59 N 87.43 W
North Park ♠ 279b 40.36 N 80.00 W
North Park Lake ⊜ 279b 40.36 N 80.00 W
North Parramatta 274a 33.48 S 151.00 E
North Pass 𝕌 175c 7.41 N 151.48 E
North Patchogue 276 40.47 N 73.01 W
North Peak ⋀, Alaska, U.S. 180 62.34 N 162.23 W
North Peak ⋀, Calif., U.S. 282 37.33 N 122.28 W
North Pease ≃ 196 34.15 N 100.07 W
North Pelham, N.H., U.S. 283 42.47 N 71.21 W
North Pelham, N.Y., U.S. 276 40.55 N 73.48 W
North Pembroke 207 42.05 N 70.47 W
North Pender Island I 224 48.49 N 123.17 W
North Perry 214 41.47 N 81.07 W
North Petherton 42 51.06 N 3.01 W
North Philadelphia ➝8 285 39.58 N 75.09 W
North Philadelphia Airport ⊠ 285 40.05 N 75.01 W
North Pine Grove 214 41.24 N 79.13 W
North Piney Creek ≃ 202 42.31 N 110.05 W
North Pitcher 210 42.37 N 75.49 W
North Plainfield 210 40.37 N 74.25 W
North Plains 224 45.36 N 123.00 W
North Platte 198 41.08 N 100.46 W
North Platte ≃ 178 41.15 N 100.45 W
North Pleasureville 218 38.22 N 85.07 W
North Plympton 283 41.59 N 70.48 W
North Point, H.K. 271d 22.17 N 114.12 E
Northpoint, Pa., U.S. 214 40.54 N 79.08 W
North Point ≻ 271d 22.17 N 114.11 E
North Point ≻, Barb. 241g 13.20 N 59.36 W
North Point ≻, P.E.I., Can. 186 47.05 N 64.00 W
North Point ≻, Mich., U.S. 190 45.02 N 83.16 W
North Pole 180 64.40 N 147.07 W
North Pole ✦ 16 90.00 N 0.00
North Popo Aggie ≃ 202 42.51 N 108.42 W
Northport, Ala., U.S. 194 33.14 N 87.35 W
Northport, Fla., U.S. 220 27.01 N 82.10 W
Northport, Mich., U.S. 190 45.08 N 85.37 W
Northport, N.Y., U.S. 210 40.53 N 73.20 W
Northport, Wash., U.S. 202 48.55 N 117.48 W
North Portal 184 49.00 N 102.33 W
Northport Harbor C 276 40.53 N 73.22 W
North Powder 202 45.13 N 117.55 W
North Pownal 207 42.48 N 73.16 W
North Prairie 216 42.56 N 88.24 W
North Providence 207 41.50 N 71.26 W
North Puyallup 224 47.12 N 122.17 W
North Queensferry 46 56.01 N 3.25 W
North Quincy 219 39.58 N 91.24 W
North Raisin ≃ 206 45.09 N 74.43 W
North Ram ≃ 182 52.16 N 115.38 W
North Randall 279a 41.27 N 81.32 W
North Reading 207 42.34 N 71.05 W
North Reservoir ⊜1 283 42.28 N 71.07 W
North Richland Hills 222 32.51 N 97.12 W
North Richmond 282 37.57 N 122.22 W
Northridge, Ohio, U.S. 218 39.49 N 84.12 W
Northridge, Ohio, U.S. 218 39.59 N 83.47 W
Northridge ➝8 280 34.14 N 118.33 W
Northridge Fashion Center ➝9 280 34.13 N 118.33 W
North Ridge Village 218 39.57 N 86.09 W
North Ridgeville 214 41.23 N 82.01 W
North Rim 200 36.12 N 112.03 W
North River C 208 37.25 N 76.25 W
North Riverside 278 41.51 N 87.49 W
North Robinson 214 40.48 N 82.51 W
North Rocks 274a 33.46 S 151.02 E
North Ronaldsay I 46 59.22 N 2.26 W
North Ronaldsay Firth 𝕌 46 59.20 N 2.25 W
North Rose 210 43.11 N 76.54 W
North Royalton 214 41.19 N 81.44 W
North Rustico 186 46.27 N 63.19 W
North Ryde 274a 33.48 S 151.07 E
North Salem 214 40.09 N 81.33 W
North Salt Lake 200 40.50 N 111.55 W
North San Juan 226 39.22 N 121.06 W
North Santiam ≃ 202 44.41 N 123.00 W
North Saskatchewan ≃ 176 53.15 N 105.06 W
North Saugeen ≃ 212 44.19 N 81.17 W
North Scituate, Mass., U.S. 207 42.14 N 70.47 W
North Scituate, R.I., U.S. 207 41.50 N 71.35 W
North Sea ➝2 22 55.20 N 3.00 E
North Seaton Colliery 44 55.11 N 1.32 W
North Seven ≃ 196 32.35 N 104.23 W
North Shafter 226 35.31 N 119.18 W
Norths Highland ⋀1 9 66.40 S 126.00 E
North Shoal Lake ⊜ 184 50.29 N 97.40 W
North Shore 216 42.16 N 88.23 W
Northshore Center ➝9 283 42.32 N 70.57 W
North Shore Channel ≡ 278 42.05 N 87.41 W
North Shores 216 41.50 N 83.25 W
North Shoshone Peak ⋀ 204 39.09 N 117.29 W
North Siberian Lowland → Severo-Sibirskaja Nizmennost' ≅ 74 73.00 N 100.00 E
Northside 174h 2.47 S 171.43 W
North Side ➝8 279b 40.28 N 80.01 W
North Skunk ≃ 194 41.15 N 92.02 W
North Somercotes 44 53.28 N 0.08 E
North Sound 𝕌, Antig. 240c 17.07 N 61.45 W
North Sound 𝕌, Eire 48 53.11 N 9.43 W
North Sound 𝕌, Scot., U.K. 46 59.18 N 2.46 W
North Spicer Island I 176 68.30 N 78.55 W
North Spirit Lake ⊜ 184 52.30 N 92.53 W
North Spot I 236 16.15 N 88.11 W
North Springfield, Pa., U.S. 214 41.59 N 80.26 W
North Springfield, Va., U.S. 284c 38.48 N 77.13 W
North Stamford Reservoir ⊜1 276 41.08 N 73.32 W
North Star 216 40.19 N 84.34 W
North Stradbroke Island I 171a 27.35 S 153.28 E
North Sudbury 283 42.23 N 71.24 W
North Sulphur ≃ 196 33.23 N 95.18 W
North Sunday Creek ≃ 202 46.27 N 105.54 W
North Sunderland 44 55.34 N 1.39 W
North Swansea 207 41.47 N 71.16 W
North Sydenham ≃ 281 42.35 N 82.23 W
North Sydney, Austl. 274a 33.50 S 151.13 E
North Sydney, N.S., Can. 186 46.13 N 60.15 W
North Syracuse 210 43.08 N 76.08 W
North Tamborine 171a 27.56 S 153.11 E
North Taranaki Bight C3 172 38.42 S 174.15 E
North Tarrytown 276 41.05 N 73.52 W
North Tawton 42 50.48 N 3.53 W
North Terre Haute 194 39.31 N 87.22 W
North Tewksbury 283 42.38 N 71.15 W
North Thames ≃ 212 42.59 N 81.16 W
North Thompson ≃ 182 50.41 N 120.21 W
North Tidworth 42 51.16 N 1.40 W
North Toe ≃ 192 36.00 N 82.16 W
North Tokelau Trough ➝1 14 4.00 S 168.00 W
North Tolsta 46 58.20 N 6.13 W
North Tonawanda 210 43.02 N 78.53 W
North Towanda 210 41.47 N 76.28 W
North Troy 188 45.00 N 72.24 W
North Truro 207 42.02 N 70.06 W
North Tule Draw ∨ 196 34.30 N 101.36 W
North Turlock 226 37.31 N 120.51 W
North Turramurra 274a 33.43 S 150.09 E
North Twin Lake ⊜ 186 49.16 N 55.56 W
North Tyne ≃ 44 54.59 N 2.08 W
North Ubian Island I 116 6.09 N 120.27 E
North Uist I 46 57.36 N 7.18 W
Northumberland 210 40.54 N 76.48 W
Northumberland □6, Ont., Can. 212 44.10 N 78.00 W
Northumberland □6, Eng., U.K. 44 55.15 N 2.05 W
Northumberland □6, Pa., U.S. 210 40.49 N 76.39 W
Northumberland □6, Va., U.S. 208 37.50 N 76.25 W
Northumberland Isles II 166 21.40 S 150.00 E
Northumberland National Park ♠ 44 55.15 N 2.20 W
Northumberland Strait 𝕌 186 46.00 N 63.30 W
North Umpqua ≃ 202 43.16 N 123.27 W
North Uxbridge 207 42.06 N 71.39 W
Northvale 276 41.00 N 73.57 W
North Valley Stream 276 40.41 N 73.41 W
North Vancouver 182 49.19 N 123.04 W
North Vassalboro 188 44.29 N 69.37 W
North Vernon 218 39.00 N 85.38 W
North Versailles 279b 40.22 N 79.48 W
North Vietnam → Vietnam □1 108 16.00 N 108.00 E
North Vijayapuri 122 16.52 N 79.35 E
Northville, Mich., U.S. 216 42.26 N 83.29 W
Northville, N.Y., U.S. 210 43.13 N 74.11 W
Northville Downs ♠ 281 42.26 N 83.29 W
Northvue 214 40.54 N 79.56 W
Northwaa 46 59.16 N 2.17 W
North Wabasca Lake ⊜ 182 56.00 N 113.55 W
North Wales 208 40.13 N 75.17 W
North Walsham 42 52.50 N 1.24 E
North Wantagh 276 40.41 N 73.30 W
North Warren 214 41.38 N 79.09 W
North Washington, Pa., U.S. 214 41.03 N 79.49 W
North Washington, Pa., U.S. 279b 40.32 N 79.36 W
Northway 180 62.59 N 141.43 W
North Wazīristān □5 123 33.05 N 70.40 E
North Weald Bassett 42 51.43 N 0.10 E
North Webster 216 41.19 N 85.42 W
North Weissport 210 40.50 N 75.41 W
North West □5 246 7.45 N 59.30 W
Northwest ≃ 208 36.31 N 76.05 W
North West Cape ≻, Austl. 162 21.45 S 114.10 E
Northwest Cape ≻, Alaska, U.S. 180 63.46 N 171.45 W
Northwest Cape ≻, Fla., U.S. 220 25.13 N 81.11 W
North Westchester 207 41.35 N 72.24 W
North Western 210 43.20 N 75.22 W
North-Western □3 150 11.00 N 5.30 E
North-Western □4 154 13.00 S 25.00 E
Northwestern University ✌2, Ill., U.S. 278 42.04 N 87.40 W
Northwestern University (Chicago Campus) ✌2, Ill., U.S. 278 41.54 N 87.37 W
Northwest Frontier □4 120 33.30 N 71.30 E
Northwest Gander ≃ 186 48.50 N 55.00 W
Northwest Harbor C 284b 39.16 N 76.35 W
Northwest Head ≻ 116 10.08 N 118.45 E
Northwest Miramichi ≃ 186 46.58 N 65.35 W
North West Point ≻ 174o 2.02 N 157.29 W
Northwest Providence Channel 𝕌 238 26.10 N 78.20 W
North West River 176 53.32 N 60.08 W
Northwest Territories □4 176 70.00 N 100.00 W
North Weymouth 283 42.15 N 70.57 W
Northwich 44 53.16 N 2.32 W
North Wichita ≃ 196 33.43 N 99.29 W
North Wilbraham 207 42.09 N 72.25 W
North Wildwood 208 39.00 N 74.48 W
North Wilkesboro 192 36.10 N 81.09 W
North Willow Creek ≃ 202 46.51 N 107.54 W
North Wilmington 283 42.34 N 71.10 W
North Windham, Conn., U.S. 207 41.45 N 72.09 W
North Windham, Maine, U.S. 188 43.50 N 70.26 W
Northwold 42 52.33 N 0.35 E
Northwood, Iowa, U.S. 190 43.27 N 93.13 W
Northwood, Mich., U.S. 216 42.19 N 85.38 W
Northwood, N. Dak., U.S. 198 47.44 N 97.34 W
Northwood, Ohio, U.S. 214 41.37 N 83.30 W
Northwood ➝8 260 51.37 N 0.25 W
North Woodslee 281 42.13 N 82.43 W
North Yamhill ≃ 224 45.13 N 123.08 W
North Yelta 168b 34.03 S 137.37 E
North York 212 43.46 N 79.25 W
North York Moors ⋀2 44 54.24 N 0.53 W
North York Moors National Park ♠ 44 54.23 N 0.50 W
North Yorkshire □6 44 54.15 N 1.30 W
North Yuba ≃ 226 39.22 N 121.08 W
North Zulch 222 30.55 N 96.07 W
Norton, N.B., Can. 186 45.38 N 65.42 W
Norton, Eng., U.K. 44 54.09 N 0.47 W
Norton, Eng., U.K. 262 53.20 N 2.40 W
Norton, Kans., U.S. 198 39.50 N 99.53 W
Norton, Mass., U.S. 207 41.58 N 71.11 W
Norton, Ohio, U.S. 214 41.01 N 81.39 W
Norton, Vt., U.S. 206 45.00 N 71.48 W
Norton, Va., U.S. 192 36.56 N 82.38 W
Norton Air Force Base ■ 228 34.06 N 117.14 W
Norton Basin C 276 40.36 N 73.47 W
Norton Bay C 180 64.45 N 161.15 W
Norton Canes 42 52.41 N 1.59 W
Norton Creek ≃ 281 42.34 N 83.34 W
Norton de Matos 152 12.21 S 14.46 E
Norton Fitzwarren 42 51.02 N 3.09 W
Norton Grove 207 42.00 N 71.12 W
Norton Heath 260 51.43 N 0.19 E
Norton Hill 210 42.25 N 74.04 W
Norton Pond ⊜ 206 44.56 N 71.51 W
Norton Reservoir ⊜1 283 41.59 N 71.12 W
Norton Shores 216 43.10 N 86.14 W
Norton Sound 𝕌 180 63.50 N 164.00 W
Nortonville, Ont., Can. 275b 43.43 N 79.44 W
Nortonville, Kans., U.S. 198 39.25 N 95.20 W
Nortorf 52 53.55 N 9.16 E
Nort-sur-Erdre 32 47.26 N 1.30 W
Noruega → Norway □1 24 62.00 N 10.00 E
Noruega, Mar de → Norwegian Sea ➝2 10 70.00 N 2.00 E
Norumbega Reservoir ⊜1 283 42.20 N 71.18 W
Nørup 41 55.43 N 9.19 E
Norval 212 43.39 N 79.51 W
Norvalspont 158 30.38 S 25.27 E
Norvège → Norway □1 24 62.00 N 10.00 E
Norvegia, Cape ≻ 9 71.25 S 12.18 W
Norvell 216 42.10 N 84.11 W
Norvelt 214 40.12 N 79.32 W
Norvin Green State Forest ♠ 276 41.03 N 74.20 W
Norwalk, Calif., U.S. 228 33.54 N 118.05 W
Norwalk, Conn., U.S. 207 41.07 N 73.27 W
Norwalk, Iowa, U.S. 190 41.29 N 93.41 W
Norwalk, Ohio, U.S. 214 41.15 N 82.37 W
Norwalk ≃ 207 41.06 N 73.25 W
Norwalk Harbor C 276 41.06 N 73.24 W
Norwalk Islands II 276 41.03 N 73.23 W
Norway, Ind., U.S. 216 40.47 N 86.46 W
Norway, Iowa, U.S. 190 41.54 N 91.55 W
Norway, Maine, U.S. 188 44.13 N 70.32 W
Norway, Mich., U.S. 190 45.47 N 87.55 W
Norway □1 22
24 62.00 N 10.00 E
Norway Bay C 176 71.08 N 104.35 W
Norway House 184 53.59 N 97.50 W
Norway Lake ⊜ 212 45.20 N 76.43 W
Norwegen → Norway □1 24 62.00 N 10.00 E
Norwegian Basin ➝1 10 69.00 N 5.00 W
Norwegian Sea ➝2 10 70.00 N 2.00 E
Norwell 283 42.10 N 70.48 W
Norwich, Ont., Can. 212 42.59 N 80.36 W
Norwich, Eng., U.K. 42 52.38 N 1.18 E
Norwich, Conn., U.S. 207 41.32 N 72.05 W
Norwich, Kans., U.S. 198 37.27 N 97.51 W
Norwich, N.Y., U.S. 210 42.32 N 75.31 W
Norwich Airport ⊠ 42 52.31 N 1.15 E
Norwin Heights 279b 40.20 N 79.44 W
Norwood, Ont., Can. 212 44.23 N 77.59 W
Norwood, Colo., U.S. 200 38.08 N 108.20 W
Norwood, Mass., U.S. 207 42.11 N 71.12 W
Norwood, Minn., U.S. 190 44.46 N 93.55 W
Norwood, N.J., U.S. 276 40.60 N 73.57 W
Norwood, N.C., U.S. 192 35.14 N 80.07 W
Norwood, N.Y., U.S. 188 44.45 N 75.00 W
Norwood, Ohio, U.S. 218 39.10 N 84.28 W
Norwood, Pa., U.S. 285 39.53 N 75.18 W
Norwood ➝8 273d 26.10 S 28.04 E
Norwood Memorial Airport ⊠ 283 42.11 N 71.10 W
Norwood Park ➝8 278 41.59 N 87.48 W
Norwood Pond ⊜ 283 42.35 N 70.52 W
Norwoodville 190 41.39 N 93.33 W
Noryang 98 34.56 N 127.52 E
Norzagaray 116 14.54 N 121.02 E
Nosaka 94 35.39 N 140.34 E
Nosate 266b 45.33 N 8.43 E
Nosbonsing, Lake ⊜ 190 46.12 N 79.13 W
Nose 96 34.58 N 135.24 E
Nose ≻ 270 34.49 N 135.09 E
Nose Creek ≃ 182 54.53 N 119.28 W
Noshiro 92 40.12 N 140.02 E
Noska ≃ 86 58.53 N 68.40 E
Nosova 86 59.30 N 63.13 E
Nosovaja, S.S.S.R. 24 68.15 N 54.35 E
Nosovaja, S.S.S.R. 80 57.15 N 45.35 E
Nosovka 78 50.55 N 31.35 E
Nosovo, S.S.S.R. 76 57.07 N 27.50 E
Nosovo, S.S.S.R. 83 47.16 N 38.40 E
Nosovščina 24 62.56 N 37.03 E
Nosratābād 128 29.54 N 59.59 E
Noss, Isle of I 46a 60.09 N 1.01 W
Nossa Senhora da Aparecida 256 22.02 S 42.48 W
Nossa Senhora das Dores 250 10.29 S 37.13 W
Nossa Senhora do Amparo 256 22.22 S 44.05 W
Nossa Senhora do Livramento 248 15.48 S 56.22 W
Nossa Senhora do Ó ➝8 287b 23.30 S 46.41 W
Nossebro 26 58.11 N 12.43 E
Nossen 54 51.03 N 13.17 E
Nossentiner Heide ➝3 54 53.35 N 12.25 E
Noss Head ≻ 46 58.28 N 3.04 W
Nossi-Bé I 157b 13.20 S 48.15 E
Nossob 156 22.18 S 17.10 E
Nossob (Nossop) ≃ 156 26.55 S 20.37 E
Nossombougou 150 13.06 N 7.56 W
Nošul' 24 60.09 N 49.28 E
Nosy Varika 157b 20.35 S 48.32 E
Notasulga 194 32.34 N 85.40 W
Notch Cliff 284b 39.27 N 76.28 W
Notch Peak ⋀ 200 39.08 N 113.24 W
Noteć ≃ 30 52.44 N 15.26 E
Notengo, Laguna de C 234 16.12 N 98.07 W
Notigi Lake ⊜ 184 55.57 N 99.18 W
Notikewin ≃ 176 57.15 N 117.05 W
Noto, It. 70 36.53 N 15.04 E
Noto, Nihon 92 37.18 N 137.09 E
Noto ≃ 89 44.41 N 134.04 E
Noto, Golfo di C 70 36.50 N 15.12 E
Noto, Val di ➝1 70 37.05 N 14.35 E
Noto Antica ⊥ 70 36.56 N 15.02 E
Notodden 26 59.34 N 9.17 E
Notogawa 94 35.10 N 136.10 E
Noto-hantō ≻1 92 37.20 N 137.00 E
Noto-hantō-kokutei-kōen ♠ 94 37.10 N 136.50 E
Notojima 94 37.08 N 137.00 E
Nōtori-dake ⋀ 94 35.37 N 138.15 E
Notoro-ko ⊜ 92a 44.05 N 144.10 E
Notozero, Ozero ⊜ 24 66.28 N 32.05 E
Notre-Dame, N.B., Can. 186 46.19 N 64.43 W
Notre Dame, Ind., U.S. 216 41.42 N 86.14 W
Notre-Dame ✌1 261 48.51 N 2.21 E
Notre-Dame, Bois ♠ 261 48.45 N 2.35 E
Notre Dame, Monts ⋀ 186 48.10 N 68.00 W
Notre-Dame, Ruisseau ≃ 275a 45.41 N 73.26 W
Notre Dame Bay C 186 49.45 N 55.15 W
Notre-Dame-de-Bellecombe 62 45.48 N 6.31 E
Notre-Dame-de-Lorette ✌1 50 50.25 N 2.42 E
Notre-Dame-de-Lourdes 184 49.32 N 98.33 W
Notre-Dame-de-Pierreville 206 46.06 N 72.53 W
Notre-Dame-des-Victoires ➝8 275a 45.35 N 73.34 W
Notre-Dame-du-Haut ✌1 32 47.43 N 6.37 E
Notre-Dame-du-Laus 188 46.05 N 75.37 W
Notre-Dame-du-Nord 190 47.36 N 79.30 W
Notrees 196 31.55 N 102.45 W
Notreure ≃ 50 47.41 N 2.36 E
Notsu 96 33.02 N 131.42 E
Notsuharu 96 33.09 N 131.32 E
Nottawa 216 41.55 N 85.27 W
Nottawa Creek ≃ 216 42.01 N 85.24 W
Nottawasaga ≃ 212 44.32 N 80.01 W
Nottawasaga Bay C 212 44.40 N 80.30 W
Nottaway ≃ 176 51.22 N 79.55 W
Nottingham, Eng., U.K. 42 52.58 N 1.10 W
Nottingham, Pa., U.S. 208 39.45 N 76.01 W
Nottingham, Pa., U.S. 285 40.07 N 74.58 W
Nottingham Island I 176 63.20 N 77.55 W
Nottingham Park 278 41.46 N 87.48 W
Nottingham Road 158 29.22 S 30.00 E
Nottinghamshire □6 44 53.00 N 1.00 W
Notting Hill 274b 37.54 S 145.08 E
Nottleben 54 50.58 N 10.50 E
Nottoway 192 37.08 N 78.05 W
Nottoway ≃ 192 36.33 N 76.55 W
Nottuln 52 51.55 N 7.22 E
Notukeu Creek ≃ 184 49.55 N 106.30 W
Notwani ≃ 156 23.35 S 26.58 E
Nouadhibou 148 20.54 N 17.04 W
Nouakchott 150 18.06 N 15.57 W
Nouâmrhar 150 19.22 N 16.31 W
Nouan-le-Fuzelier 50 47.32 N 2.02 E
Nouans-les-Fontaines 50 47.08 N 1.18 E
Nouméa 175f 22.16 S 166.27 E
Noun ≃ 152 4.55 N 11.06 E
Nouna 150 12.44 N 3.52 W
Nounsley 260 51.46 N 0.36 E
Noupoort 158 31.10 S 24.57 E
Nous 158 28.44 S 19.52 E
Nouveau Brunswick → New Brunswick □4 186 46.30 N 66.15 W
Nouveau Mexique → New Mexico □3 178 34.30 N 106.00 W
Nouveau-Québec, Cratère du ⚬6 176 61.17 N 73.40 W
Nouvelle 186 48.08 N 66.19 W
Nouvelle ≃ 186 48.07 N 66.18 W
Nouvelle-Calédonie → New Caledonia □2 175f 21.30 S 165.30 E
Nouvelle-Calédonie I 175f 21.30 S 165.30 E
Nouvelle Écosse → Nova Scotia □4 186 45.00 N 63.00 W
Nouvelle-France, Cap de ≻ 176 62.27 N 73.42 W
Nouvelle Galles du Sud → New South Wales □3 166 33.00 S 146.00 E
Nouvelle-Orléans → New Orleans 194 29.58 N 90.07 W
Nouvelles-Hébrides → New Hebrides □2 175f 16.00 S 167.00 E
Nouvelle Zélande → New Zealand □1 172 41.00 S 174.00 E
Nouvelle Zemble → Novaja Zeml'a II 72 74.00 N 57.00 E
Nouvion-en-Ponthieu 50 50.12 N 1.47 E
Nouvion-sur-Meuse 56 49.42 N 4.48 E
Nouzonville 56 49.49 N 4.45 E
Nova, Magy. 61 46.41 N 16.41 E
Nova, Ohio, U.S. 214 41.02 N 82.18 W
Nova, Ilha I 250 0.20 N 49.40 W
Nova América 255 15.01 S 49.56 W
Nova Anadia 112 8.56 S 125.52 E
Nova Andradina 255 22.10 S 53.15 W
Nova Aurora 255 18.04 S 48.16 W
Novabad, S.S.S.R. 85 39.01 N 70.09 E
Novabad, S.S.S.R. 85 38.37 N 68.45 E
Nová Baňa 30 48.26 N 18.39 E
Nová Bystřice 61 49.01 N 15.06 E
Nova Cachoeirinha ➝8 287b 23.28 S 46.40 W
Nova Caipemba 152 7.26 S 14.38 E
Novacella ✌1 64 46.44 N 11.39 E
Nova Chaves 152 10.34 S 21.17 E
Nova Cintra 256 22.13 S 46.46 W
Nova Era 255 19.45 S 43.03 W
Nova Esperança 255 23.08 S 52.13 W
Nova Fátima 255 23.29 S 50.33 W
Novafeltria 66 43.53 N 12.17 E
Nova Freixo 154 14.49 S 36.33 E
Nova Friburgo 256 22.16 S 42.32 W
Nova Gaia 152 10.09 S 17.31 E
Nova Goa → Panaji 122 15.29 N 73.50 E
Nova Gorica 64 45.57 N 13.39 E
Nova Gradiška 36 45.16 N 17.23 E
Nova Granada 255 20.29 S 49.19 W
Nova Iguaçu 256 22.45 S 43.27 W
Nova Iguaçu □7 287a 22.45 S 43.29 W
Novaja, S.S.S.R. 82 55.13 N 38.54 E
Novaja, S.S.S.R. 265b 55.48 N 38.03 E
Novaja ➝8 265a 60.02 N 30.28 E
Novaja Astrachan' 83 49.07 N 38.36 E
Novaja Belaja 78 49.46 N 39.11 E
Novaja Binaradka 80 53.48 N 49.56 E
Novaja Borovaja 78 50.42 N 28.39 E
Novaja Čigla 78 51.13 N 40.28 E
Novaja Derevn'a, S.S.S.R. 82 54.01 N 38.53 E
Novaja Derevn'a, S.S.S.R. 88 57.15 N 103.08 E

Symbol	English	Deutsch	Español	Français	Português
≃	River	Fluss	Río	Rivière	Rio
≡	Canal	Kanal	Canal	Canal	Canal
L	Waterfall, Rapids	Wasserfall, Stromschnellen	Cascada, Rápidos	Chute d'eau, Rapides	Cascata, Rápidos
𝕌	Strait	Meeresstrasse	Estrecho	Détroit	Estreito
C	Bay, Gulf	Bucht, Golf	Bahía, Golfo	Baie, Golfe	Baía, Golfo
⊜	Lake, Lakes	See, Seen	Lago, Lagos	Lac, Lacs	Lago, Lagos
≚	Swamp	Sumpf	Pantano	Marais	Pântano
⊼	Ice Features, Glacier	Eis- und Gletscherformen	Accidentes Glaciales	Formes glaciaires	Acidentes Glaciares
➝2	Other Hydrographic Features	Andere Hydrographische Objekte	Otros Elementos Hidrográficos	Autres données hydrographiques	Outros Elementos Hidrográficos
➝1	Submarine Features	Untermeerische Objekte	Accidentes Submarinos	Formes de relief sous-marin	Acidentes Submarinos
□	Political Unit	Politische Einheit	Unidad Política	Entité politique	Unidade Política
✌	Cultural Institution	Kulturelle Institution	Institución Cultural	Institution culturelle	Instituição Cultural
⊥	Historical Site	Historische Stätte	Sitio Histórico	Site historique	Sítio Histórico
♠	Recreational Site	Erholungs- und Ferienort	Sitio de Recreo	Centre de loisirs	Sítio de Lazer
⊠	Airport	Flughafen	Aeropuerto	Aéroport	Aeroporto
■	Military Installation	Militäranlage	Instalación Militar	Installation militaire	Instalação Militar
➝	Miscellaneous	Verschiedenes	Misceláneo	Divers	Miscelânea

Name (ENGLISH) / Name (DEUTSCH)	Page / Seite	Lat.°′ / Breite°′	Long.°′ / Länge°′ E=Ost
Novaja Ivanovka	78	45.55 N	29.05 E
Novaja Janisol'	83	47.17 N	37.16 E
Novaja Kachovka	78	46.45 N	33.23 E
Novaja Kalitva	78	50.06 N	40.01 E
Novaja Kazanka	80	48.57 N	49.36 E
Novaja Kazmaska	80	56.49 N	53.31 E
Novaja Kriuša	78	50.16 N	41.16 E
Novaja Ladoga	76	60.05 N	32.16 E
Novaja L'al'a	86	59.03 N	60.36 E
Novaja Majačka	78	46.36 N	33.14 E
Novaja Maluksa	76	59.39 N	31.21 E
Novaja Malykla	80	54.13 N	49.57 E
Novaja Mojgora	82	54.27 N	38.32 E
Novaja Odessa	78	47.19 N	31.47 E
Novaja Porubežka	80	51.45 N	49.40 E
Novaja Praga	78	48.33 N	32.54 E
Novaja Ropša	265a	59.45 N	29.53 E
Novaja Sibir' Ostrov I	74	75.00 N	149.00 E
Novaja Sloboda	78	51.23 N	34.08 E
Novaja Slobodka	82	54.56 N	36.47 E
Novaja Šul'ba	86	50.33 N	81.20 E
Novaja Uda	88	54.07 N	103.33 E
Novaja Ušica	78	48.49 N	27.16 E
Novaja Usman'	78	51.37 N	39.24 E
Novaja Vodolaga	78	49.43 N	35.52 E
Novaja Zburjevka	78	46.28 N	32.24 E
Novaja Zeml'a II	72	74.00 N	57.00 E
Nováky	30	48.43 N	18.34 E
Nova Lamego	150	12.19 N	14.11 W
Novalesa	62	45.11 N	7.01 E
Novaliches Watershed Reservation ⊜[1]	269f	14.43 N	121.05 E
Nova Lima	255	19.59 S	43.51 W
Nova Lisboa → Huambo	152	12.44 S	15.47 E
Nova Lusitânia	156	19.54 S	34.35 E
Nova Mambone	156	20.59 S	35.01 E
Nova Milanese	266b	45.35 N	9.12 E
Nova Nabúri	154	16.46 S	38.57 E
Nova Olinda	250	7.06 S	39.40 W
Nova Olinda, Riacho ≃	250	8.05 S	42.34 W
Nova Olinda do Norte	246	3.45 S	59.03 W
Nová Paka	30	50.29 N	15.31 E
Nova Ponente (Deutschnofen)	64	46.25 N	11.25 E
Nova Ponte	255	19.08 S	47.41 W
Nova Prata	252	28.47 S	51.36 W
Novar	212	45.27 N	79.15 W
Novara, It.	62		
	266b	45.28 N	8.38 E
Novara □[4]	58	46.00 N	8.25 E
Novara ≃	70	38.03 N	15.06 E
Novara di Sicilia	70	38.01 N	15.08 E
Nova Resende	255	21.08 S	46.25 W
Nová Role	54	50.15 N	12.47 E
Nova Roma	255	13.51 S	46.57 W
Nova Russas	250	4.42 S	40.34 W
Nova Sagres	112	8.24 S	127.15 E
Nova Scotia □[4]	176		
	186	45.00 N	63.00 W
Nova Sintra	152	12.09 S	17.16 E
Nova Siri	68	40.09 N	16.32 E
Nova Sofala	156	20.09 S	34.42 E
Nova Soure	250	11.14 S	38.29 W
Novate Mezzola	58	46.15 N	9.27 E
Novate Milanese	266b	45.32 N	9.08 E
Nova Timboteua	250	1.12 S	47.24 W
Novato	226	38.06 N	122.34 W
Novato Creek ≃	282	38.06 N	122.29 W
Nova Varoš	38	43.28 N	19.48 E
Nova Venécia	255	18.43 S	40.24 W
Nova Veneza	252	28.39 S	49.30 W
Nova Vida	248	10.11 S	62.47 W
Nova Vida, Cachoeira ᒪ	248	9.25 S	63.36 W
Novaya Zemlya Ridge ✧[3]	10	73.00 N	51.00 E
Nova Zagora	38	42.29 N	26.01 E
Nova Zembla Island I	176	72.10 N	74.50 W
Nove	64	45.43 N	11.40 E
Nové Hardy	61	48.47 N	14.37 E
Novelda	34	38.23 N	0.46 W
Novellara	64	44.51 N	10.44 E
Novelty	219	40.01 N	92.12 W
Nové Město	30	50.21 N	16.09 E
Nové Město nad Váhom	30	48.46 N	17.49 E
Nové Město na Moravě	30	49.34 N	16.04 E
Noventa di Piave	64	45.39 N	12.31 E
Noventa Padovana	64	45.24 N	11.58 E
Noventa Vicentina	64	45.17 N	11.32 E
Noves	62	43.52 N	4.54 E
Nové Sedlo	54	50.10 N	12.42 E
Nové Strašecí	54	50.07 N	13.53 E
Nové Údoli	60	48.48 N	13.48 E
Nové Zámky	30	47.59 N	18.11 E
Novgorod	76	58.31 N	31.17 E
Novgorodka	78	48.21 N	32.39 E
Novgorod-Severskij	78	51.59 N	33.16 E
Novgorodskoje	83	48.20 N	37.50 E
Novi	216	42.29 N	83.28 W
Novi Bečej	38	45.36 N	20.08 E
Novice	196	31.59 N	99.37 W
Novičicha	86	52.13 N	81.24 E
Novi di Modena	64	44.54 N	10.54 E
Novigrad, Jugo.	36	45.19 N	13.34 E
Novigrad, Jugo.	36	44.11 N	15.33 E
Novikovo, S.S.S.R.	86	58.15 N	80.39 E
Novikovo, S.S.S.R.	89	46.23 N	143.20 E
Novi Ligure	62	44.46 N	8.47 E
Noville	56	50.40 N	5.23 E
Novi Lyon Drain ≖	281	42.30 N	83.38 W
Novinger	194	40.19 N	92.42 W
Novinka	76	59.49 N	33.20 E
Novion-Porcien	50	49.36 N	4.25 E
Novi Pazar, Blg.	38	43.21 N	27.12 E
Novi Pazar, Jugo.	38	43.08 N	20.31 E
Novi Sad	38	45.15 N	19.50 E
Novi Vinodolski	36	45.08 N	14.48 E
Novka	76	55.27 N	30.24 E
Novki	80	56.22 N	41.06 E
Novl'anka	80	55.48 N	41.44 E
Novlenskoje	76	59.37 N	39.20 E
Nôvo ≃, Bra.	248	4.55 S	70.33 W
Nôvo ≃, Bra.	250	4.30 S	53.50 W
Novo ≃, Bra.	256	21.23 S	42.44 W
Novo, Lago ⊜	250	1.30 N	50.40 W
Novoachtyrka	83	48.55 N	38.49 E
Nôvo Acôrdo	255	13.10 S	46.48 W
Novoajdar	83	48.57 N	39.00 E
Novoaleksandrovka, S.S.S.R.	80	51.56 N	52.26 E
Novoaleksandrovka, S.S.S.R.	83	48.17 N	39.37 E
Novoaleksandrovka, S.S.S.R.	83	49.08 N	39.17 E
Novoaleksandrovka, S.S.S.R.	86	51.47 N	68.49 E
Novoaleksandrovo	265b	55.59 N	37.33 E
Novoaleksandrovskaja	80	45.29 N	41.16 E
Novoaleksejevka, S.S.S.R.	78	46.13 N	34.39 E
Novoaleksejevka, S.S.S.R.	78	46.06 N	32.30 E
Novoaleksejevka, S.S.S.R.	86	50.08 N	55.39 E
Novoaleksejevka, S.S.S.R.	86	52.56 N	64.41 E
Novoaleksejevka, S.S.S.R.	86	52.47 N	74.54 E
Novoaltajsk	86	53.24 N	83.58 E
Novoamvrosijevskoje	83	47.49 N	38.29 E
Novoanninskij	80	50.32 N	42.41 E
Novoarchangel'sk	78	48.39 N	30.48 E
Novoarchangel'skoje	265b	55.55 N	37.33 E
Novo Aripuanã	246	5.08 S	60.22 W
Novoasbest	86	57.44 N	60.45 E
Novoazorskoje	83	47.08 N	38.05 E
Novobachmutovka	83	48.15 N	37.48 E
Novobatajsk	83	46.54 N	39.47 E
Novobelaja	78	49.49 N	39.18 E
Novobessergenovka	83	47.11 N	38.51 E
Novobogatinskoje	80	47.22 N	51.11 E
Novobogdanovka	78	47.06 N	35.29 E
Novobogorodskoje	80	53.11 N	53.56 E
Novoborovaja	83	49.15 N	38.33 E
Novo Brasil	255	16.11 S	50.38 W
Novobratcevskij	82	55.51 N	37.23 E
Novoburejskij	89	49.49 N	129.54 E
Novo Čeremšansk	80	54.21 N	50.10 E
Novočerkassk	83	47.25 N	40.06 E
Novočernorečenskij	86	56.16 N	91.06 E
Novocharitonovo	82	55.35 N	38.30 E
Novocherkassk → Novočerkassk	83	47.25 N	40.06 E
Novochop'orsk	80	51.07 N	41.37 E
Novochop'orskij	80	51.06 N	41.33 E
Novochovrino ◆[8]	265b	55.52 N	37.30 E
Novociml'anskaja	80	47.59 N	42.17 E
Nôvo Cruzeiro	255	17.29 S	41.53 W
Novodanilovka	78	46.38 N	35.00 E
Novoderev'ankovskaja	78	46.19 N	38.45 E
Novoderkul	83	49.08 N	39.38 E
Novodevičje	80	53.37 N	48.52 E
Novodolinka	86	51.12 N	72.33 E
Novodolinskij	86	49.44 N	72.45 E
Novodoroninskoje	88	51.08 N	112.08 E
Novodružesk	83	48.58 N	38.21 E
Novodubovoje	76	52.19 N	39.13 E
Novodugino	76	55.38 N	34.18 E
Novodžerelijevskaja	78	45.46 N	38.41 E
Novoekonomičeskoje	83	48.18 N	37.15 E
Novofetinino	82	56.14 N	39.17 E
Novogaritovo	80	52.47 N	40.07 E
Novogirejevo ◆[8]	265b	55.45 N	37.49 E
Novogorbovo	82	55.43 N	36.29 E
Novogornyj	86	55.37 N	60.47 E
Novograd-Volynskij	78	50.36 N	27.36 E
Novogrigorjevka	78	46.24 N	34.59 E
Novogrigorjevskaja	80	49.26 N	43.37 E
Novogrigorjevskoje	84	44.25 N	43.51 E
Novogrodovka	83	48.13 N	37.20 E
Novogroznenskij	84	43.15 N	46.15 E
Novogrudok	76	53.36 N	25.50 E
Novogupalovka	78	48.02 N	35.26 E
Nôvo Hamburgo	252	29.41 S	51.08 W
Novo Horizonte	255	21.28 S	49.13 W
Novoignatjevka	83	47.38 N	37.41 E
Novoiljinsk	88	51.42 N	108.41 E
Novoiljinskij	86	57.54 N	55.30 E
Novoivanovka, S.S.S.R.	78	49.44 N	33.28 E
Novoivanovka, S.S.S.R.	83	47.41 N	38.23 E
Novoivanovka, S.S.S.R.	85	43.08 N	71.26 E
Novoivanovskoje	265b	55.43 N	37.22 E
Novoizborsk	76	57.50 N	27.59 E
Novojampol'	89	52.55 N	127.38 E
Novojamskoje	76	52.14 N	34.28 E
Novoje, S.S.S.R.	82	55.38 N	38.55 E
Novoje, S.S.S.R.	86	58.53 N	68.40 E
Novoje Alechnovo	82	56.02 N	36.49 E
Novojegorjevskoje	86	51.46 N	80.53 E
Novojekaterinovka	83	47.43 N	38.07 E
Novoje Koval'ovo	265a	59.59 N	30.34 E
Novoje Leušino	80	56.48 N	40.32 E
Novojel'n'a	76	53.28 N	25.35 E
Novojenisejsk	86	58.16 N	92.24 E
Novoje Pavšino	82	54.15 N	37.07 E
Novoje Zarečje	76	57.43 N	34.22 E
Novokadinsk	88	54.46 N	101.24 E
Novokamala	88	55.58 N	94.58 E
Novokarasuk	86	56.16 N	71.46 E
Novokaširovo	80	54.58 N	52.32 E
Novokaširsk	82	54.51 N	38.15 E
Novokazalinsk	86	45.50 N	62.10 E
Novokijevskij	80	50.27 N	43.08 E
Novokorsunskaja	78	45.38 N	39.09 E
Novokrasn'anka	83	49.08 N	38.18 E
Novokrasnoje	78	48.01 N	31.21 E
Novokručininskij	88	51.46 N	113.48 E
Novokubanka	86	51.40 N	70.44 E
Novokujbyševsk	80	53.07 N	49.58 E
Novokurovka	89	48.51 N	134.20 E
Novokuzneck	86	53.45 N	87.06 E
Novokuznetsk → Novokuzneck	86	53.45 N	87.06 E
Novoladožskij Kanal ≖	265a	60.26 N	32.48 E
Novolakskoje	84	43.07 N	46.29 E
Novolazarevskaja ʊ[3]	9	70.45 S	11.50 E
Novoleuškovskaja	78	45.59 N	39.58 E
Novoli	68	40.23 N	18.03 E
Novolimarevka	83	49.17 N	39.36 E
Novolukoml'	76	54.40 N	29.08 E
Novol'vovsk	76	53.55 N	38.47 E
Novomalorossijskaja	78	45.38 N	39.53 E
Novomansurkino	80	53.52 N	51.52 E
Novomargaritovka	83	46.54 N	38.50 E
Novomariinka	88	55.27 N	96.01 E
Novomarkovka	86	51.44 N	72.17 E
Novomel'nikov	84	43.56 N	45.09 E
Novomelovatka	78	50.27 N	40.46 E
Novomelovoje	78	51.23 N	38.13 E
Novo Mesto	36	45.48 N	15.10 E
Novomichajlovka, S.S.S.R.	83	47.51 N	37.29 E
Novomichajlovka, S.S.S.R.	86	55.13 N	81.57 E
Novomichajlovskij	86	53.55 N	54.36 E
Novomichajlovskoje, S.S.S.R.	78	44.15 N	38.51 E
Novomichajlovskoje, S.S.S.R.	82	55.25 N	37.10 E
Novominskaja	78	46.19 N	38.57 E
Novomirgorod	78	48.47 N	31.39 E
Novomoskovsk, S.S.S.R.	78	48.37 N	35.12 E
Novomoskovsk, S.S.S.R.	82	54.05 N	38.13 E
Novomyšastovskaja	78	45.12 N	38.35 E
Novonagajevo	80	55.56 N	54.15 E
Novonikolajevka, S.S.S.R.	78	46.13 N	32.45 E
Novonikolajevka, S.S.S.R.	78	47.59 N	35.55 E
Novonikolajevka, S.S.S.R.	83	46.59 N	39.36 E
Novonikolajevka, S.S.S.R.	85	42.26 N	70.28 E
Novonikolajevskij	80	50.58 N	42.22 E
Novonikolayevsk → Novosibirsk	86	55.02 N	82.55 E
Novonikol'skoje, S.S.S.R.	76	59.25 N	33.13 E
Novonikol'skoje, S.S.S.R.	80	49.09 N	45.00 E
Novonikol'skoje, S.S.S.R.	83	49.21 N	39.51 E
Novonikol'skoje, S.S.S.R.	86	59.46 N	79.12 E
Novonikol'skoje, S.S.S.R.	265b	55.50 N	37.15 E
Novoomel'kovo	83	49.08 N	39.05 E
Novo Oriente	250	5.32 S	40.42 W
Novoorsk	86	51.23 N	58.58 E
Novopavlovka, S.S.S.R.	88	50.49 N	106.30 E
Novopavlovka, S.S.S.R.	88	51.13 N	109.14 E
Novopavlovskaja	84	43.58 N	43.38 E
Novopavlovskoje	88	50.56 N	111.35 E
Novopetrovo	86	57.11 N	69.10 E
Novopetrovskoje	82	55.59 N	36.28 E
Novopiscovo	76	57.19 N	41.54 E
Novopodrezkovo	82	55.57 N	37.21 E
Novopokrovka, S.S.S.R.	78	48.03 N	34.37 E
Novopokrovka, S.S.S.R.	85	42.52 N	74.45 E
Novopokrovka, S.S.S.R.	86	50.41 N	80.28 E
Novopokrovka, S.S.S.R.	86	53.43 N	67.45 E
Novopokrovka, S.S.S.R.	89	45.52 N	134.28 E
Novopokrovskoje	80	51.35 N	43.36 E
Novopolevodino	80	51.46 N	47.29 E
Novopolock	76	55.31 N	28.38 E
Novopskov	83	49.33 N	39.05 E
Novorajčichinsk	89	49.47 N	129.38 E
Novor'ažsk	80	53.44 N	40.07 E
Novo Redondo	152	11.13 S	13.50 E
Novorepnoje	80	51.06 N	48.24 E
Novorossijka	85	42.44 N	76.07 E
Novorossijsk	78	44.45 N	37.45 E
Novorossijskoje	86	50.13 N	58.00 E
Novorossiysk → Novorossijsk	78	44.45 N	37.45 E
Novorossoš'	83	49.32 N	39.15 E
Novorudnyj	86	51.30 N	58.10 E
Novorybinka	86	51.51 N	71.14 E
Novorybnoje	74	72.50 N	105.50 E
Novoržev	76	57.02 N	29.20 E
Novošachtinsk	83	47.47 N	39.56 E
Novosaratovka	265a	59.50 N	30.32 E
Novoščerbinovskaja	78	46.28 N	38.38 E
Novosel'e	86	54.10 N	76.53 E
Novoselenginsk	88	51.06 N	106.37 E
Novoselica	78	48.14 N	26.17 E
Novoselickoje	84	44.45 N	43.26 E
Novoselišče	78	49.48 N	25.03 E
Novoselje	265a	59.48 N	30.05 E
Novoselki, S.S.S.R.	82	54.49 N	38.55 E
Novoselki, S.S.S.R.	82	55.08 N	37.33 E
Novosel'nyj	86	50.00 N	54.38 E
Novoselovka Pervaja	83	48.12 N	37.31 E
Novoselovo, S.S.S.R.	82	56.04 N	39.04 E
Novoselovo, S.S.S.R.	86	55.04 N	91.07 E
Novoselovo, S.S.S.R.	88	56.04 N	107.42 E
Novosel'skoje	78	45.20 N	28.33 E
Novosemejkino	80	53.23 N	50.22 E
Novosergijevka, S.S.S.R.	80	52.06 N	53.39 E
Novosergijevka, S.S.S.R.	265a	59.54 N	30.34 E
Novoseslavino	80	53.21 N	40.26 E
Novošešminsk	80	55.04 N	51.15 E
Novoshakhtinsk → Novošachtinsk	83	47.47 N	39.56 E
Novosibirsk	86	55.02 N	82.55 E
Novosibirskije Ostrova II	74	75.00 N	142.00 E
Novosibirskoje Vodochranilišče ⊜[1]	86	54.35 N	82.35 E
Novosil'	76	52.58 N	37.03 E
Novosil'skoje	78	51.56 N	38.31 E
Novosokol'niki	76	56.21 N	30.10 E
Novos'olki, S.S.S.R.	76	52.24 N	28.33 E
Novos'olki, S.S.S.R.	76	56.01 N	33.37 E
Novos'olki, S.S.S.R.	78	52.02 N	24.21 E
Novos'olki, S.S.S.R.	80	55.48 N	42.41 E
Novos'olki, S.S.S.R.	80	54.50 N	39.46 E
Novos'olki, S.S.S.R.	265a	59.42 N	30.17 E
Novos'olovka	83	49.04 N	37.42 E
Novos'olovskoje	78	45.26 N	33.34 E
Novospasovka	83	47.42 N	39.04 E
Novospasskoje	80	53.08 N	47.45 E
Novostrel'covka	83	49.20 N	39.55 E
Novostrojevo	76	54.27 N	21.50 E
Novosvetlovka	83	48.30 N	39.30 E
Novotavolžanka	78	50.22 N	36.50 E
Novotitarovskaja	78	45.14 N	39.00 E
Novotroick	86	51.12 N	58.20 E
Novotroickoje, S.S.S.R.	78	46.22 N	34.20 E
Novotroickoje, S.S.S.R.	80	58.28 N	47.06 E
Novotroickoje, S.S.S.R.	83	47.43 N	37.35 E
Novotroickoje, S.S.S.R.	85	43.42 N	73.46 E
Novotroickoje, S.S.S.R.	86	56.11 N	78.41 E
Novo-Troitsk → Novotroick	86	51.12 N	58.20 E
Novotulka, S.S.S.R.	80	50.50 N	47.34 E
Novotulka, S.S.S.R.	80	52.38 N	48.45 E
Novotul'skij	82	54.10 N	37.43 E
Novoukolovo	78	51.02 N	38.25 E
Novoukrainka	78	48.19 N	31.32 E
Novouljanovsk	80	54.08 N	48.24 E
Novoural'sk	86	51.15 N	57.16 E
Novouzensk	80	50.28 N	48.08 E
Novovaršavka	86	54.11 N	74.42 E
Novovasiljevka, S.S.S.R.	78	46.51 N	36.46 E
Novovasiljevka, S.S.S.R.	78	46.48 N	35.44 E
Novov'atsk	80	58.29 N	49.44 E
Novov'azniki	80	56.12 N	42.10 E
Novovolynsk	78	50.50 N	24.05 E
Novovoroncovka	78	47.29 N	33.54 E
Novovoronežskij	78	51.16 N	39.11 E
Novovoskresenovka	85	42.50 N	73.32 E
Novovoskresenskoje	78	47.21 N	33.37 E
Novozacharkino	80	52.11 N	48.29 E
Novozagorje	82	55.39 N	38.38 E
Novozavidovskij	82	56.33 N	36.26 E
Novožilovskaja	24	64.50 N	51.20 E
Novozizevka	80	50.48 N	49.08 E
Novozybkov	76	52.32 N	31.56 E
Novska	36	45.21 N	16.59 E
Nový Bohumín	30	49.56 N	18.20 E
Nový Bor	54	50.45 N	14.33 E
Novyj	86	55.39 N	86.39 E
Novyj Afon	84	43.06 N	40.48 E
Novyj Bor	24	66.43 N	52.16 E
Novyj Bug	78	47.41 N	32.30 E
Novyj Bujan	80	53.41 N	50.04 E
Novyj Bykov	78	50.36 N	31.39 E
Novyj Donbass ◆[8]	83	48.05 N	38.46 E
Novyj Dvor	76	52.50 N	24.21 E
Novyje Ajbesi	80	54.49 N	47.02 E
Novyje Aneny	78	46.52 N	29.14 E
Novyje Basy	78	50.53 N	34.51 E
Novyje Burasy	80	52.08 N	46.06 E
Novyje Denisoviči	76	54.12 N	29.13 E
Novyje Gorki	80	56.42 N	41.06 E
Novyje Maty	80	55.15 N	54.04 E
Novyje Salty	80	54.06 N	53.26 E
Novyje Senžary	78	49.21 N	34.19 E
Novyje Z'atcy	80	57.27 N	52.36 E
Nový Jičín	30	49.36 N	18.00 E
Novyj Jaryčev	78	49.55 N	24.18 E
Novyj Jegorlyk	80	46.24 N	41.54 E
Novyj Karačaj	84	43.49 N	41.56 E
Novyj Karamass	80	56.11 N	48.58 E
Novyj Kiner	80	56.24 N	49.44 E
Novyj Multan	80	57.09 N	52.19 E
Novyj Nekouz	76	57.54 N	38.04 E
Novyj Oskol	78	50.46 N	37.53 E
Novyj Pogost	76	55.30 N	27.29 E
Novyj Port	74	67.40 N	72.52 E
Novyj Put'	85	43.29 N	73.52 E
Novyj Ropsk	76	52.18 N	32.19 E
Novyj Stan	82	56.18 N	37.00 E
Novyj Svet	83	47.48 N	38.00 E
Novyj Tap	86	57.04 N	67.49 E
Novyj Terek ≃	84	43.37 N	47.25 E
Novyj Tevriz	86	59.04 N	78.08 E
Novyj Torjal	80	57.00 N	48.44 E
Novyj Vas'ugan	86	58.34 N	76.29 E
Nowa Dęba	30	50.26 N	21.46 E
Nowaja Semlja → Novaja Zeml'a II	72	74.00 N	57.00 E
Nowa Ruda	30	50.35 N	16.31 E
Nowa Sól (Neusalz)	30	51.48 N	15.44 E
Nowata	196	36.42 N	95.38 W
Nowater Creek ≃	202	43.57 N	108.00 W
Nowbarān	128	35.08 N	48.42 E
Nowe	30	53.40 N	18.43 E
Nowe Miasteczko	30	51.42 N	15.45 E
Nowe Miasto Lubawskie	30	53.27 N	19.35 E
Nowe Miasto nad Pilicą	30	51.38 N	20.35 E
Nowendoc	166	31.32 S	151.43 E
Nowe Warpno	30	53.44 N	14.16 E
Nowgong, Bhārat	120	26.21 N	92.40 E
Nowgong, Bhārat	124	25.04 N	79.27 E
Nowingi	166	34.36 S	142.14 E
Nowitna ≃	180	65.55 N	154.17 W
Nowogard	30	53.40 N	15.08 E
Nowogród	30	53.15 N	21.53 E
Nowogrodziec	30	51.12 N	15.25 E
Nowokusnezk → Novokuzneck	86	53.45 N	87.06 E
Nowood ≃	202	44.17 N	107.58 W
Nowosibirsk → Novosibirsk	86	55.02 N	82.55 E
Nowra	170	34.53 S	150.36 E
Nowrangapur	122	19.14 N	82.33 E
Nowshāk ∧	123	36.26 N	71.50 E
Nowshera	120	34.01 N	71.59 E
Nowy Dwór Gdański	30	54.13 N	19.06 E
Nowy Dwór Mazowiecki	30	52.26 N	20.43 E
Nowy Sącz	30	49.38 N	20.42 E
Nowy Staw	30	54.09 N	19.00 E
Nowy Targ	30	49.29 N	20.02 E
Nowy Tomyśl	30	52.20 N	16.07 E
Now Zād	120	32.24 N	64.28 E
Noxapater	194	33.00 N	89.04 W
Noxe ≃	50	48.33 N	3.35 E
Noxen	210	41.25 N	76.03 W
Noxon	202	48.01 N	115.47 W
Noxon Reservoir ⊜[1]	202	47.54 N	115.40 W
Noy ≃	110	17.05 N	105.02 E
Noya	34	42.47 N	8.53 W
Noya ≃, Esp.	34	41.28 N	1.56 E
Noya ≃, Gabon	152	0.58 N	9.48 E
Noyant	50	47.31 N	0.08 E
Noye ≃	50	49.51 N	2.20 E
Noyelles-sur Mer	50	50.11 N	1.43 E
Noyers	50	47.42 N	4.00 E
Noyers, Ruisseau des ≃	275a	45.21 N	73.22 W
Noyes Island I	180	55.30 N	133.40 W
Noyon	50	49.35 N	3.00 E
Nožaj-Jurt	84	43.05 N	46.24 E
Nozawa-onsen	94	36.55 N	138.27 E
Nozay, Fr.	32	47.34 N	1.38 W
Nozay, Fr.	261	48.40 N	2.14 E
Nozeroy	58	46.47 N	6.02 E
Nozori-dam ◆[6]	94	36.43 N	138.39 E
Nozori-ko ⊜	94	36.42 N	138.39 E
Nozuta	268	35.35 N	139.27 E
Nozza	64	45.42 N	10.23 E
Nqamakwe	158	32.12 S	27.56 E
Nqutu	158	28.13 S	30.32 E
N'Rougas	158	29.07 S	21.09 E
Nsa, Oued en ∨	148	32.28 N	5.24 E
Nsaba	150	5.39 N	0.45 W
Nsah	152	2.22 S	15.19 E
Nsang	152	2.02 N	10.56 E
Nsanje	154	16.55 S	35.12 E
Nsawam	150	5.50 N	0.20 W
Nsefu Game Reserve ◆[4]	154	13.07 S	32.10 E
Nsele ≃	152	4.14 S	15.33 E
Nseleni	158	28.33 S	31.39 E
Nsok	152	1.08 N	11.16 E
Nsoko	158	27.02 S	31.57 E
Nsontin	152	3.09 S	18.00 E
Nsouélé	273b	4.12 S	15.11 E
Nsukka	150	6.52 N	7.24 E
Nsuta	150	5.17 N	1.58 W
Ntakat ⊤[4]	150	16.49 N	11.43 W
Ntambanana	158	28.36 S	31.45 E
Ntandembele	152	2.11 S	17.08 E
Ntchisi	154	13.19 S	33.58 E
Ntem ≃	152	2.15 N	9.45 E
Ntoum	152	0.23 N	9.47 E
Ntsama	152	0.32 S	14.38 E
Ntui	152	4.27 N	11.38 E
Ntumba	154	8.20 S	32.05 E
Ntusi	154	0.03 N	31.13 E
Ntwetwe Pan ⊻	156	20.30 S	25.20 E
Nuala	154	13.27 S	28.16 E
Nuanchitang	104	41.02 N	120.41 E
Nuanetsi	154	21.22 S	30.45 E
Nuanetsi ≃	156	22.40 S	31.50 E
Nuangola	210	41.09 N	75.58 W
Nuanli	102	23.26 N	100.51 E
Nuannuan	269d	25.06 N	121.44 E
Nuanshui	100	28.53 N	117.51 E
Nuanzhouying	100	25.22 N	117.22 E
Nuasjärvi ⊜	26	64.10 N	28.05 E
Nuatabu	174t	1.33 N	172.59 E
Nuatja	150	6.57 N	1.10 E
Nu'aymah	132	32.38 N	36.10 E
Nūbah	142	30.29 N	31.33 E
Nūbah, Jibāl an- ∧∧	140	12.00 N	30.45 E
Nūbārīyah, Tur'at an- ≖	142	30.43 N	30.46 E
Nubian Desert ◆[2]	140	20.30 N	33.00 E
Ñuble ≃	252	36.39 S	72.27 W
Nubra ≃	123	34.39 N	77.36 E
Nucet	38	46.28 N	22.35 E
Nucetto	62	44.20 N	8.04 E
Nucha → Šeki	84	41.12 N	47.12 E
Nuchatlitz Inlet C	182	49.45 N	126.55 W
N'uchča	24	63.27 N	46.28 E
Nuch'ŏn-ni	98	38.14 N	126.16 E
Nucla	200	38.16 N	108.33 W
Núcleo Colonial São Bento	287a	22.44 S	43.18 W
N'učpas	24	60.51 N	51.18 E
Nucuray ≃	246	5.02 S	75.34 W
Nuda, Monte la ∧	64	44.17 N	10.15 E
Nudaybah	142	30.59 N	30.22 E
Nudlung Fiord C[2]	176	68.21 N	67.22 W
Nudol'-Šarino	82	56.06 N	36.31 E
Nudow	264a	52.20 N	13.10 E
Nudž	84	40.56 N	47.41 E
Nueces ≃	196	27.50 N	97.30 W
Nueces Plains ⊻	196	28.30 N	99.15 W
Nueltin Lake ⊜	176	60.20 N	99.50 W
Nuenen	52	51.29 N	5.33 E
Nüerhe	104	41.04 N	121.00 E
Nüerhe ≃	98	40.57 N	121.19 E
Nuestra Señora de las Lajas ʊ[1]	246	0.49 N	77.36 W
Nuestra Señora de Talavera	252	25.26 S	63.48 W
Nueva, Isla I	254	55.13 S	66.30 W
Nueva Antioquia	246	6.05 N	69.26 W
Nueva Asunción □[5]	248	21.00 S	61.00 W
Nueva Atzacoalco ◆[8]	286a	19.29 N	99.05 W
Nueva Brunswick → New Brunswick □[4]	186	46.30 N	66.15 W
Nueva Caledonia → New Caledonia □[2]	175f	21.30 S	165.30 E
Nueva California	252	32.45 S	68.20 W
Nueva Casas Grandes	232	30.25 N	107.55 W
Nueva Chicago ◆[8]	288	34.40 S	58.30 W
Nueva Ciudad Guerrero	232	26.35 N	99.15 W
Nueva Concepción	236	14.08 N	89.18 W
Nueva Cuadrilla	234	18.04 N	101.33 W
Nueva Ecija □[4]	116	15.35 N	121.00 E
Nueva Escocia → Nova Scotia □[4]	186	45.00 N	63.00 W
Nueva Esparta □[3]	246	11.00 N	64.00 W
Nueva Francia	252	28.11 S	64.12 W
Nueva Galia	252	35.07 S	65.15 W
Nueva Germania	252	23.54 S	56.45 W
Nueva Gerona	240p	21.53 N	82.48 W
Nueva Guinea, Isla → New Guinea I	164	5.00 S	140.00 E
Nueva Hébridas → New Hebrides □[2]	175f	16.00 S	167.00 E
Nueva Helvecia	258	34.19 S	57.13 W
Nueva Imperial	252	38.44 S	72.57 W
Nueva Italia de Ruiz	234	19.01 N	102.06 W
Nueva Lubecka	254	44.32 S	70.24 W
Nueva Ocotepeque	236	14.24 N	89.13 W
Nueva Palmira	258	33.53 S	58.25 W
Nueva Paz	240p	22.46 N	81.45 W
Nueva Pompeya ◆[8]	288	34.39 S	58.25 W
Nueva Rosita	232	27.57 N	101.13 W
Nueva San Salvador	236	13.41 N	89.17 W
Nueva Segovia □[5]	236	13.40 N	86.10 W
Nueva Siberia, Islas → Novosibirskije Ostrova II	74	75.00 N	142.00 E
Nueva Venecia	236	14.03 N	91.33 W
Nueva Vizcaya □[4]	116	16.20 N	121.20 E
Nueva Zelandia → New Zealand □[1]	172	41.00 S	174.00 E
Nueva Zembla, Isla de → Novaja Zeml'a II	72	74.00 N	57.00 E
Nueve de Julio	252	35.27 S	60.52 W
Nuevitas	240p	21.33 N	77.16 W
Nuevitas, Bahía de C	240p	21.30 N	77.12 W
Nuevo	228	33.48 N	117.09 W
Nuevo, Golfo C	254	42.42 S	64.36 W
Nuevo Berlín	252	32.59 S	58.03 W
Nuevo Camarón	196	27.05 N	99.55 W
Nuevo Chagres	236	9.14 N	80.05 W
Nuevo Laredo	232	27.30 N	99.31 W
Nuevo Léon	204	32.20 N	115.12 W
Nuevo León □[3]	232	25.40 N	100.00 W
Nuevo Morelos	234	17.31 N	95.02 W
Nuevo Necaxa	234	20.13 N	98.00 W
Nuevo Poblado el Oro	196	26.50 N	101.19 W
Nuevo Primero de Mayo	196	26.01 N	98.02 W
Nuevo Progreso	232	18.38 N	92.18 W
Nuevo Rocafuerte	246	0.56 S	75.24 W
Nuevo Saucillo	196	27.20 N	104.54 W
Nugget Point ≻	172	46.27 S	169.49 E
Nûgssuaq ≻[1]	176	71.45 N	53.00 W
Nugu ⊜[1]	122	11.58 N	76.28 E
Nuguria Islands II	14	3.20 S	154.45 E
Nūh	124	28.07 N	77.01 E
Nūh, Rās ≻	128	25.05 N	62.24 E
Nuhaka	172	39.03 S	177.45 E
Nuhaydāt as-Sūd, Jabal an- ∧	142	28.01 N	32.21 E
Nuhūd, Jabal an- ∧	140	14.50 N	29.53 E
Nui I[1]	14	7.15 S	177.10 E
Nuia	76	58.04 N	25.33 E
Nuits-Saint-Georges	58	47.08 N	4.57 E
Nuits-sur-Armançon	50	47.44 N	4.12 E
N'uja	74	60.32 N	116.14 E
N'uja ≃	74	60.32 N	116.20 E
Nujiang	102	29.58 N	97.25 E
N'uk, Ozero ⊜	24	64.27 N	31.45 E
Nuka Island I	180	59.21 N	150.42 W
Nukata	94	34.55 N	137.17 E
Nukey Bluff ⊥[4]	166	32.33 S	135.40 E
Nukhayb	128	32.02 N	42.15 E
Nukhaylah ⊤[4]	140	19.03 N	26.19 E
Nukiki	175e	6.46 S	156.28 E
N'uksenica	24	60.25 N	44.13 E
Nuktal', Chrebet ∧∧	84	42.15 N	46.35 E
Nukualofa	174w	21.08 S	175.12 W
Nukufetau I[1]	14	8.00 S	178.22 E
Nukuhu	164	5.35 S	149.25 E
Nukulailai I[1]	14	9.23 S	179.52 E
Nukumanu Islands II	14	4.30 S	159.30 E
Nukunonu I	14	9.12 S	171.54 W
Nukunuku	174w	21.08 S	175.18 W
Nukuoro I[1]	14	3.51 N	154.58 E
Nukus	72	42.50 N	59.29 E
Nulato	180	64.43 N	158.06 W
Nules	34	39.51 N	0.09 W
Nullagine	162	21.53 S	120.06 E
Nullagine ≃	162	20.43 S	120.33 E
Nullarbor	162	31.26 S	130.55 E
Nullarbor Plain ⊻	162	31.00 S	129.00 E
Nulltown	218	39.35 N	85.10 W
Nuluerhushan ∧∧	104	42.20 N	120.35 E
Nul'vand	85	38.16 N	70.32 E
Nulvi	71	40.47 N	8.45 E
Num, Pulau I	164	1.30 S	135.13 E
Numabin Bay C	184	56.30 N	103.08 W
Numakuma	96	34.20 N	133.20 E
Numana	66	43.31 N	13.37 E
Numancia	116	9.52 N	125.58 E
Numancia ⊥	34	41.48 N	2.25 W
Numansdorp	52	51.44 N	4.26 E
Numara I	122	6.26 N	73.03 E
Numarán	234	20.15 N	101.56 W
Numata, Nihon	92a	43.48 N	141.57 E
Numata, Nihon	94	36.38 N	139.03 E
Numata, Nihon	96	34.27 N	132.24 E
Numatinna ≃	140	7.14 N	27.37 E
Numazu	94	35.06 N	138.52 E
Numbargulme, Mount ∧	164	14.56 S	145.03 E
Number 5 Mine	214	41.08 N	80.11 W
Numedal ∨	26	60.06 N	9.06 E
Numeralla	171b	36.11 S	149.20 E
Numfoor, Pulau I	164	1.03 S	134.54 E
Numidia	210	40.53 N	76.24 W
Numila	229b	21.54 N	159.34 W
Nu Mine	214	40.48 N	79.18 W
Numto	74	63.40 N	71.20 E
Numurkah	166	36.06 S	145.26 E
Nun ≃[1]	150	4.20 N	6.00 E
Nun'amo	180	65.37 N	170.40 W
Nunapitchuk	180	60.54 N	162.29 W
Nunawading	169	37.49 S	145.10 E
Nünchritz	54	51.18 N	13.23 E
Nunda	210	42.35 N	77.57 W
Nundah	171a	27.24 S	153.04 E
Nundu	154	3.49 S	29.05 E
Nuneaton	42	52.32 N	1.28 W
Núñez ◆[8]	288	34.33 S	58.27 W
Nunez ≃	150	10.36 N	14.40 W
Núñez, Isla I	254	53.31 S	73.48 W
Nungarin	162	31.11 S	118.06 E
Nungesser Lake ⊜	184	51.28 N	93.35 W
Nungwe	154	2.46 S	32.01 E
Nunica	216	43.10 N	86.04 W
Nunivak Island I	180	60.00 N	166.30 W
Nunjiang	89	49.10 N	125.11 E
Nunjiang ≃	89	45.25 N	124.40 E
Nunjikompita	162	32.16 S	134.19 E
Nunkini	232	20.20 N	90.11 W
Nunkun ∧	123	33.59 N	76.01 E
Nunligran	180	64.48 N	175.24 W
Nunnelly	194	35.52 N	87.28 W
Ñuñoa	286e	33.28 S	70.36 W
Nunshan	89	48.59 N	125.14 E
Nunspeet	52	52.23 N	5.46 E
Nuomindashan ∧	89	50.15 N	122.46 E
Nuominhe ≃	89	48.06 N	124.26 E
Nuorang	120	27.36 N	92.59 E
Nuoro	71	40.19 N	9.20 E
Nuoro □[4]	71	40.10 N	9.20 E
Nuqruş, Jabal ∧	140	24.49 N	34.36 E
Nuquí	246	5.42 N	77.17 W
Nura	86	48.53 N	62.20 E
Nura ≃	86	50.30 N	69.59 E
Nurakita I	14	10.45 S	179.30 E
Nurallao	71	39.47 N	9.05 E
Nuraminis	71	39.26 N	9.01 E
Nuratau, Chrebet ∧∧	85	40.20 N	67.15 E
Nuraxi, Nuraghe su ⊥	71	39.42 N	9.00 E
N'urba	74	63.17 N	118.20 E
Nürburg	56	50.21 N	6.57 E
Nürburgring ♠	56	50.21 N	6.58 E
Nur Dağları ∧∧	130	36.45 N	36.20 E
Nure ≃	62	45.03 N	9.49 E
Nurek	85	38.23 N	69.19 E
Nurekskoje Vodochranilišče ⊜[1]	85	38.30 N	69.30 E
Nuremberg → Nürnberg, B.R.D.	60	49.27 N	11.04 E
Nuremberg, Pa., U.S.	210	40.56 N	76.10 W
Nürenbei	107	30.11 N	106.04 E
Nurettin	130	39.14 N	42.25 E
Nurhak	130	37.58 N	37.25 E
Nuri	232	28.02 N	109.22 W
Nuria, Monte ∧	66	42.21 N	13.05 E
Nuriootpa	168b	34.29 S	139.00 E
Nurlat	80	54.26 N	50.46 E
Nurlaty	80	55.37 N	48.18 E
Nūrmahal	123	31.06 N	75.36 E
Nurmes	26	63.33 N	29.07 E
Nurmijärvi	26	60.28 N	24.48 E
Nurnagar	126	22.20 N	89.03 E
Nürnberg	60	49.27 N	11.04 E
Nürnberg, Flughafen ⊠	60	49.30 N	11.06 E
Nūrpur, Bhārat	123	31.10 N	76.29 E
Nūrpur, Bhārat	123	32.18 N	75.54 E
Nurpur, Bhārat	126	22.13 N	88.05 E
Nūrpur, Pāk.	123	31.53 N	71.54 E
Nurra ◆[1]	36	40.45 N	8.15 E
Nurrari Lakes ⊜	162	29.01 S	130.05 E
Nurri	71	39.43 N	9.14 E
Nurri, Mount ∧	166	31.42 S	146.02 E
Nursery	222	28.56 N	97.06 W
Nürtingen	56	48.38 N	9.20 E
Nuruhak Dağı ∧	130	38.04 N	37.29 E
Nus	62	45.45 N	7.28 E
Nūsa	144	14.00 N	46.43 E
Nusa Barung, Pulau I	115a	8.28 S	113.20 E
Nusa Tenggara (Lesser Sunda Islands) II	108	9.00 S	120.00 E
Nusa Tenggara Barat (Lesser Sunda Islands) □[4]	115b	8.50 S	117.30 E
Nusa Tenggara Timur □[4]	112	9.30 S	122.00 E
Nusaybin	130	37.03 N	41.13 E
Nusco	68	40.53 N	15.05 E
Nushagak ≃	180	59.00 N	158.30 W
Nushagak Bay C	180	58.40 N	158.40 W
Nushagak Peninsula ≻[1]	180	58.30 N	159.00 W
Nushan ∧∧	102	28.41 N	98.24 E
Nu-shima I	96	34.10 N	134.50 E
Nushki	120	29.33 N	66.01 E
Nusplingen	58	48.08 N	8.53 E
Nušpoly	82	56.39 N	37.44 E
Nussdorf ◆[8]	264b	48.15 N	16.22 E
Nussdorf am Attersee	64	47.53 N	13.31 E
Nuta ≃	96	34.23 N	133.04 E
Nutae	174s	17.44 S	149.15 W
Nutauge, Laguna C	180	67.55 N	176.45 W
Nutepelmen, S.S.S.R.	180	65.31 N	178.30 W
Nutepel'men, S.S.S.R.	180	67.26 N	174.56 W
Nutfield	260	51.14 N	0.07 W
Nuth	56	50.55 N	5.54 E
Nuthe ≃, D.D.R.	54	51.58 N	11.53 E
Nuthe ≃, D.D.R.	54	52.23 N	13.04 E
Nut Lake Indian Reserve ◆[4]	184	52.20 N	103.30 W
Nutley	210	40.49 N	74.10 W
Nutrioso	200	33.57 N	109.13 W
Nut Swamp Brook ≃	276	40.21 N	74.06 W
Nuttby Mountain ∧[2]	186	45.33 N	63.13 W
Nutter Fort	188	39.20 N	80.19 W
Nutting Lake	207	42.32 N	71.16 W
Nutting Lake ⊜	283	42.32 N	71.16 W
Nutwood	219	39.05 N	90.39 W
Nutwood Downs	164	15.49 S	134.10 E
Nutzotin Mountains ∧∧	180	62.10 N	141.40 W
Nu'ūmīyah, Wādī an- ∨	142	29.31 N	31.17 E
Nuupere, Pointe ≻	174s	17.36 S	149.47 W
Nuuuli	174u	14.18 S	170.42 W
N'uvčim	24	61.22 N	50.42 E
Nuwa-jima I	96	33.58 N	132.38 E
Nuwākot	124	28.08 N	83.53 E
Nuwara-Eliya	122	6.58 N	80.46 E
Nuwaybi' al-Muzayyinah	140	28.58 N	34.39 E
Nuwerus	158	31.08 S	18.24 E
Nuweveldberge ∧∧	158	32.13 S	21.40 E
Nuxis	71	39.09 N	8.44 E
Nuyakuk Lake ⊜	180	60.00 N	158.40 W
Nuyts, Point ≻	162	35.04 S	116.37 E
Nuyts Archipelago II	162	32.35 S	133.17 E
Nūzvīd	122	16.47 N	80.51 E
N'Vinda	152	13.04 S	18.57 E
Nwa	152	6.30 N	11.00 E
Nxainxai	156	19.50 S	21.13 E
Nxaunxau	156	18.19 S	21.04 E
Nyaake	150	4.52 N	7.37 W
Nyabéssan	152	2.24 N	10.24 E
Nyabing	162	33.32 S	118.09 E
Nyac	180	61.01 N	159.57 W
Nyack	210	41.05 N	73.55 W
Nyack Beach State Park ♠	276	41.07 N	73.55 W
Nyadiri ≃	154	16.44 S	32.33 E
Nyahanga	154	2.23 S	33.33 E
Nyahua	154	5.24 S	33.19 E
Nyah West	166	35.11 S	143.22 E
Nyakabindi	154	2.38 S	33.59 E
Nyakakiri	154	2.15 S	31.28 E
Nyakanazi	154	3.00 S	31.15 E
Nyakrom	150	5.37 N	0.48 W
Nyakulenga	152	13.03 S	23.29 E
Nyala	140	12.03 N	24.53 E
Nyalas	114	2.26 N	102.28 E
Nyamandhlovu	154	19.50 S	28.16 E
Nyamina	150	13.19 N	6.59 W
Nyamlell	140	9.07 N	26.58 E
Nyamtumbo	154	10.29 S	36.02 E
Nyamwage	154	8.08 S	39.00 E
Nyandekwa	154	3.55 S	32.30 E
Nyanding, Khawr ∨	140	8.40 N	32.41 E
Nyanga □[4]	152	3.00 S	11.00 E
Nyanga ≃	152	2.58 S	10.15 E
Nyanga, Lake ⊜	162	29.57 S	126.10 E
Nyanga, Réserve de la ◆[4]	152	3.00 S	11.45 E
Nyangana	152	18.00 S	20.41 E
Nyangui ∧	154	17.53 S	32.44 E
Nyanji Mission	154	14.23 S	31.48 E
Nyanza	154	2.21 S	29.45 E
Nyanza □[4]	154	0.30 S	34.30 E
Nyanza-Lac	154	4.21 S	29.36 E
Nyasa, Lake (Lake Malawi) ⊜	154	12.00 S	34.30 E
Nyaunglebin	110	17.57 N	96.44 E
Nyavikungu	154	11.26 S	25.54 E
Nyazvidzi ≃	154	20.00 S	32.17 E

Symbols in the index entries represent the broad categories identified in the key at the right. Symbols with superior numbers (∧∧[2]) identify subcategories (see complete key on page *I* · *30*).

Kartensymbole in dem Registerverzeichnis stellen die rechts in Schlüssel erklärten Kategorien dar. Symbole mit hochgestellten Ziffern (∧∧[2]) bezeichnen Unterabteilungen einer Kategorie (vgl. vollständiger Schlüssel auf Seite *I* · *30*).

Los símbolos incluídos en el texto del índice representan las grandes categorias identificadas con la clave a la derecha. Los símbolos con numeros en su parte superior (∧∧[2]) identifican las subcategorías (véase la clave completa en la página *I* · *30*).

Les symboles de l'index représentent les catégories indiquées dans la légende à droite. Les symboles suivis d'un indice (∧∧[2]) représentent des sous-catégories (voir légende complète à la page *I* · *30*).

Os símbolos incluídos no texto do índice representam as grandes categorias identificadas com a chave à direita. Os símbolos com números em sua parte superior (∧∧[2]) identificam as subcategorias (veja-se a chave completa à página *I* · *30*).

	English	Deutsch	Español	Français	Português
∧	Mountain	Berg	Montaña	Montagne	Montanha
∧∧	Mountains	Berge	Montañas	Montagnes	Montanhas
)(	Pass	Pass	Paso	Col	Passo
∨	Valley, Canyon	Tal, Cañon	Valle, Cañón	Vallée, Canyon	Vale, Canhão
⊻	Plain	Ebene	Llano	Plaine	Planície
≻	Cape	Kap	Cabo	Cap	Cabo
I	Island	Insel	Isla	Île	Ilha
II	Islands	Inseln	Islas	Îles	Ilhas
⊥	Other Topographic Features	Andere Topographische Objekte	Otros Elementos Topográficos	Autres données topographiques	Outros Elementos Topográficos

ESPAÑOL

Nombre	Página	Lat.°′	Long.°′ W=Oeste
Nybergsund	26	61.15 N	12.19 E
Nyborg	41	55.19 N	10.48 E
Nybro	26	56.45 N	15.54 E
Nyda	74	66.36 N	72.54 E
Nyenchentangiha ∧	124	30.22 N	90.35 E
Nyengo Swamp ☷	152	14.51 S	22.07 E
Nyenyam	120	28.11 N	85.58 E
Nyeri	154	0.25 S	36.57 E
Nyerol	140	8.41 N	32.02 E
Nyfer ≏	42	52.02 N	4.50 W
Nygligan, Mys ≻	180	65.05 N	172.06 W
Nyhammar	40	60.17 N	14.58 E
Nyhyttan	40	59.40 N	14.48 E
Nyiel	140	6.06 N	31.13 E
Nyika Plateau ⛰[1]	154	10.40 S	33.50 E
Nyilumba	154	10.29 S	40.20 E
Nyimba	154	14.35 S	30.52 E
Nyíradony	30	47.41 N	21.55 E
Nyírbátor	30	47.50 N	22.08 E
Nyíregyháza	30	47.59 N	21.43 E
Nyiri Desert ➜[2]	154	2.25 S	37.20 E
Nyiru, Mount ∧	154	2.08 N	36.51 E
Nykøbing, Dan.	26	56.48 N	8.52 E
Nykøbing, Dan.	41	54.46 N	11.53 E
Nykøbing, Dan.	41	55.55 N	11.41 E
Nyköping	40	58.45 N	17.00 E
Nykroppa	40	59.38 N	14.18 E
Nykvarn	40	59.11 N	17.26 E
Nyland	26	63.00 N	17.46 E
Nyland Acres	228	34.14 N	119.09 W
Nylga, S.S.S.R.	80	56.46 N	52.22 E
Nylga, S.S.S.R.	89	51.38 N	127.35 E
Nylstroom	156	24.42 S	28.20 E
Nymagee	166	32.04 S	146.20 E
Nymboida ≏	166	29.39 S	152.30 E
Nymburk	30	50.11 N	15.03 E
Nymphenburg ➜[8]	60	48.09 N	11.30 E
Nynäshamn	40	58.54 N	17.57 E
Nyngan	166	31.34 S	147.11 E
Nyoma	120	33.11 N	78.38 E
Nyon	58	46.23 N	6.14 E
Nyong ≏	152	3.17 N	9.54 E
Nyons, Fr.	62	44.10 N	5.50 E
Nyons, Fr.	62	44.22 N	5.08 E
Nyord I	41	55.03 N	12.13 E
Nyou	150	12.46 N	1.56 W
Nýřany	60	49.43 N	13.12 E
Nyrov	24	60.42 N	56.40 E
Nýrsko	60	49.18 N	13.09 E
Nyš	89	51.31 N	142.46 E
Nysa, Pol.	30	50.29 N	17.20 E
Nyša, S.S.S.R.	80	56.23 N	51.51 E
Nysa Kłodzka ≏	30	50.49 N	17.50 E
Nysa Łużycka (Neisse) (Nisa) ≏	30	52.04 N	14.46 E
Nyslott → Savonlinna	26	61.52 N	28.53 E
Nysø	41	55.08 N	12.02 E
Nyssa	202	43.53 N	117.00 W
Nysted	41	54.40 N	11.45 E
Nytva	86	57.56 N	55.20 E
Nyūdō-zaki ≻	92	40.00 N	139.42 E
Nyugati Pályaudvar ➜[5]	264c	47.31 N	19.04 E
Nyūgawa	96	33.56 N	133.05 E
Nyūkawa	94	36.10 N	137.19 E
Nyungwe	154	10.16 S	34.07 E
Nyunzu	154	5.57 S	28.01 E
Nyuri	120	27.42 N	92.13 E
Nyūzen	94	36.56 N	137.30 E
Nyvång	41	56.08 N	12.54 E
Nyvrovo	89	54.19 N	142.36 E
Nzébéla	150	8.05 N	9.06 W
Nzega	154	4.13 S	33.11 E
Nzéla	152	1.25 S	12.39 E
Nzérékoré	150	7.45 N	8.49 W
Nzérékoré □[4]	150	7.50 N	8.45 W
Nzheleledam ➜[6]	156	22.44 S	30.06 E
Nzi ≏	150	5.57 N	4.50 W
Nzima	154	3.03 S	32.48 E
Nziro	152	3.17 N	24.06 E
Nzo ≏	150	6.16 N	7.03 W
Nzoia ≏	154	0.03 N	33.57 E
Nzubuka	154	4.45 S	32.50 E
O			
Oa, Mull of ≻	46	55.35 N	6.19 W
Oacoma	198	43.48 N	99.24 W
Oadby	42	52.36 N	1.04 W
Oad Street	260	51.20 N	0.41 E
Oahe, Lake @[1]	198	45.30 N	100.25 W
Oahe Dam ➜[6]	198	44.21 N	100.23 W
Oahu I	229c	21.30 N	158.00 W
Oak ≏	184	49.51 N	100.28 W
O-akan-dake ∧	92a	43.27 N	144.10 E
Oakbank	168b	34.59 S	138.51 E
Oak Bay	182	48.27 N	123.18 W
Oak Beach	276	40.38 N	73.17 W
Oak Bluffs	207	41.27 N	70.34 W
Oakboro	192	35.13 N	80.20 W
Oak Brook	278	41.50 N	87.57 W
Oakbrook Center ➜[9]	278	41.52 N	87.57 W
Oakbrook Terrace	278	41.52 N	87.58 W
Oakburn	184	50.35 N	100.32 W
Oak City, N.C., U.S.	192	35.58 N	77.18 W
Oak City, Utah, U.S.	200	39.22 N	112.20 W
Oak Creek, Colo., U.S.	200	40.16 N	106.57 W
Oak Creek, Wis., U.S.	216	42.53 N	87.55 W
Oak Creek ≏, U.S.	198	45.39 N	100.31 W
Oak Creek ≏, Colo., U.S.	200	40.25 N	106.50 W
Oak Creek ≏, Kans., U.S.	198	39.29 N	98.28 W
Oak Creek ≏, N. Dak., U.S.	198	48.38 N	100.24 W
Oak Creek ≏, Tex., U.S.	196	31.48 N	100.13 W
Oakdale, Austl.	162	34.26 S	119.00 E
Oakdale, Calif., U.S.	226	37.46 N	120.51 W
Oakdale, Conn., U.S.	207	41.28 N	72.10 W
Oakdale, Ill., U.S.	219	38.16 N	89.30 W
Oakdale, La., U.S.	194	30.49 N	92.40 W
Oakdale, Mass., U.S.	207	42.23 N	71.48 W
Oakdale, Nebr., U.S.	198	42.04 N	97.58 W
Oakdale, N.J., U.S.	285	39.59 N	74.49 W
Oakdale, N.Y., U.S.	210	40.44 N	73.07 W
Oakdale, Pa., U.S.	214	40.24 N	80.11 W
Oakdale, Tenn., U.S.	192	35.59 N	84.33 W
Oakdale Woods	278	41.56 N	87.58 W
Oakengates	42	52.42 N	2.28 W
Oakes	198	46.08 N	98.06 W
Oakesdale	202	47.08 N	117.15 W
Oakey	171a	27.26 S	151.43 E
Oakeys Brook ≏	276	40.25 N	74.30 W
Oakfield, Maine, U.S.	188	46.06 N	68.10 W
Oakfield, N.Y., U.S.	210	43.04 N	78.16 W
Oakfield, Wis., U.S.	190	43.41 N	88.34 W
Oakford, Ind., U.S.	216	40.25 N	86.06 W
Oakford, Pa., U.S.	208	40.09 N	74.58 W
Oakford Park	279b	40.20 N	79.35 W
Oak Forest	216	41.36 N	87.45 W
Oakgrove, Eng., U.K.	262	53.13 N	2.07 W
Oak Grove, La., U.S.	194	32.52 N	91.23 W
Oak Grove, Oreg., U.S.	224	45.26 N	122.38 W
Oak Hall	208	37.56 N	75.33 W
Oakham	42	52.40 N	0.43 W
Oak Harbor, Ohio, U.S.	214	41.30 N	83.09 W
Oak Harbor, Wash., U.S.	224	48.18 N	122.39 W
Oak Hill, Fla., U.S.	220	28.52 N	80.51 W
Oak Hill, Mich., U.S.	190	44.13 N	86.19 W
Oak Hill, N.Y., U.S.	210	42.25 N	74.09 W
Oak Hill, Ohio, U.S.	188	38.54 N	82.34 W
Oak Hill, W. Va., U.S.	188	37.59 N	81.09 W
Oakhurst, Calif., U.S.	226	37.19 N	119.40 W
Oakhurst, N.J., U.S.	208	40.16 N	74.01 W

FRANÇAIS

Nom	Page	Lat.°′	Long.°′ W=Ouest
Oakhurst, Tex., U.S.	222	30.44 N	95.19 W
Oak Island I	276	40.39 N	73.18 W
Oak Knolls	204	34.51 N	120.27 W
Oak Lake	184	49.47 N	100.38 W
Oak Lake @, Man., Can.	184	49.40 N	100.45 W
Oak Lake @, Ont., Can.	184	50.26 N	93.50 W
Oak Lake @, Ont., Can.	212	44.36 N	77.55 W
Oakland, Ont., Can.	214	42.09 N	82.36 W
Oakland, Calif., U.S.	226		
	282	37.47 N	122.13 W
Oakland, Fla., U.S.	220	28.33 N	81.38 W
Oakland, Ill., U.S.	194	39.39 N	88.02 W
Oakland, Iowa, U.S.	198	41.19 N	95.23 W
Oakland, Maine, U.S.	188	44.33 N	69.43 W
Oakland, Md., U.S.	188	39.25 N	79.24 W
Oakland, Md., U.S.	284c	38.52 N	76.55 W
Oakland, Miss., U.S.	194	34.03 N	89.55 W
Oakland, Nebr., U.S.	198	41.50 N	96.28 W
Oakland, N.J., U.S.	210	41.02 N	74.15 W
Oakland, Oreg., U.S.	202	43.25 N	123.18 W
Oakland, Pa., U.S.	210	41.57 N	75.37 W
Oakland, Pa., U.S.	214	40.26 N	79.58 W
Oakland, Tex., U.S.	222	29.36 N	96.50 W
Oakland □[6]	216	42.40 N	83.23 W
Oakland ➜[8]	279b	40.26 N	79.58 W
Oakland-Alameda County Coliseum ♠	282	37.45 N	122.12 W
Oakland Army Base ■	282	37.49 N	122.19 W
Oakland Beach	214	41.37 N	80.18 W
Oakland City	194	38.20 N	87.21 W
Oakland Gardens ➜[8]	276	40.45 N	73.45 W
Oakland Mall ➜[9]	281	42.32 N	83.07 W
Oakland Park	220	26.12 N	80.07 W
Oakland-Pontiac Airport ⊠	281	42.40 N	83.24 W
Oaklands	168b	35.00 S	137.41 E
Oaklands ➜[8]	273d	26.09 S	28.04 E
Oakland University ʊ[2]	281	42.41 N	83.13 W
Oak Lawn, Ill., U.S.	216	41.43 N	87.45 W
Oaklawn, Kans., U.S.	198	37.36 N	97.18 W
Oaklawn, Md., U.S.	284c	38.47 N	76.57 W
Oakleigh	169	37.54 S	145.06 E
Oakleigh South	274b	37.56 S	145.05 E
Oakley, Calif., U.S.	226	37.58 N	121.43 W
Oakley, Idaho, U.S.	202	42.15 N	113.53 W
Oakley, Ill., U.S.	219	39.53 N	88.48 W
Oakley, Kans., U.S.	198	39.08 N	100.51 W
Oakley Park	216	42.34 N	83.30 W
Oaklyn	285	39.54 N	75.05 W
Oakman	194	33.37 N	87.23 W
Oakmont	214	40.31 N	79.50 W
Oak Mountain State Park ♠	194	33.22 N	86.41 W
Oakmulgee Creek ≏	194	32.28 N	87.09 W
Oak Neck ≻[1]	276	40.54 N	73.34 W
Oak Neck Point ≻	276	40.55 N	73.34 W
Oakohay Creek ≏	194	31.44 N	89.25 W
Oak Orchard Creek ≏	210	43.22 N	78.12 W
Oak Orchard Swamp ☷	210	43.07 N	78.18 W
Oakover ≏	162	20.43 S	120.33 E
Oak Park, Austl.	274b	37.43 S	144.55 E
Oak Park, Ill., U.S.	216	41.53 N	87.48 W
Oak Park, Mich., U.S.	216	42.28 N	83.11 W
Oak Park, Pa., U.S.	285	40.15 N	75.18 W
Oak Point	184	50.30 N	98.00 W
Oakridge, Calif., U.S.	226	38.03 N	121.20 W
Oak Ridge, N.J., U.S.	210	41.03 N	74.29 W
Oakridge, Oreg., U.S.	202	43.45 N	122.28 W
Oak Ridge, Pa., U.S.	214	41.00 N	79.18 W
Oak Ridge, Tenn., U.S.	192	36.01 N	84.16 W
Oak Ridge Lake	276	41.00 N	74.32 W
Oak Ridge Reservoir @[1]	276	41.03 N	74.30 W
Oaks	285	40.08 N	81.28 W
Oaks Corners	210	42.56 N	77.01 W
Oak Shades	276	40.26 N	74.13 W
Oakton	284c	38.53 N	77.18 W
Oaktown	194	38.52 N	87.26 W
Oakura	172	39.07 S	173.57 E
Oak Valley, Calif., U.S.	228	34.11 N	118.45 W
Oak Valley, N.J., U.S.	208	39.49 N	75.10 W
Oak View, Calif., U.S.	228	34.24 N	119.18 W
Oak View, Md., U.S.	284c	39.01 N	76.59 W
Oakview, N.J., U.S.	285	39.51 N	75.09 W
Oakview Beach	212	44.29 N	80.03 W
Oakville, Man., Can.	184	49.56 N	97.58 W
Oakville, Ont., Can.	212	43.27 N	79.41 W
Oakville, Conn., U.S.	207	41.36 N	73.05 W
Oakville, Ind., U.S.	218	40.05 N	85.23 W
Oakville, Mo., U.S.	219	38.27 N	90.19 W
Oakville, Wash., U.S.	224	46.50 N	123.14 W
Oakville Creek ≏	212	43.27 N	79.40 W
Oakwood, Ont., Can.	212	44.20 N	78.53 W
Oakwood, Ohio, U.S.	188	41.06 N	84.23 W
Oakwood, Ohio, U.S.	214	41.22 N	81.30 W
Oakwood, Ohio, U.S.	218	39.44 N	84.10 W
Oakwood, Tex., U.S.	222	31.35 N	95.51 W
Oakwood Beach	208	39.33 N	75.31 W
Oakwood Park ♠	279a	41.26 N	82.06 W
Oamaru	172	45.06 S	170.58 E
Ōamishirasato	94	35.31 N	140.19 E
Ōana	268	35.45 N	140.04 E
Oancea	38	45.55 N	28.06 E
Ōarai	94	36.18 N	140.34 E
Oaro	172	42.31 S	173.30 E
Oasis □[5]	148	26.30 N	5.00 E
Oat Creek ≏	226	38.50 N	121.56 W
Oates Coast •[2]	9	70.00 S	160.00 E
Oatka Creek ≏	210	43.01 N	77.44 W
Oatlands	166	42.18 S	147.21 E
Oatley	274a	33.59 S	151.05 E
Oatley Park ♠	274a	33.59 S	151.04 E
Oatman	200	35.02 N	114.23 W
Oaxaca □[3]	234	17.00 N	96.30 W
Oaxaca [de Juárez]	234	17.03 N	96.43 W
Ob' ≏	72	66.45 N	69.30 E
Oba	94	35.58 N	136.04 E
Oba I	175f	15.25 S	167.50 E
Oba ≏	190	48.55 N	84.17 W
Obaba	152	2.00 S	16.10 E
Obabika Lake @	190	47.05 N	80.17 W
Obala	152	4.10 N	11.32 E
Oba Lake @	190	48.38 N	84.18 W
Obama, Nihon	92	32.43 N	130.13 E
Obama, Nihon	94	35.30 N	135.45 E
Obama-jima I	175d	24.19 N	123.59 E
Obama-wan C	94	35.30 N	135.42 E
Oban, Austl.	166	21.14 S	139.03 E
Oban, Nig.	150	5.17 N	8.35 E
Oban, Scot., U.K.	46	56.25 N	5.29 W
Obanazawa	92	38.36 N	140.24 E
Obando	269f	14.43 N	120.56 E
Oban Hills ⛰[2]	150	5.35 N	8.35 E
Obata	94	34.30 N	136.40 E
Ob' Bay C	9	70.35 S	163.22 E
Obbia	144	5.20 N	48.38 E
Obbola	26	63.42 N	20.19 E
Občuga	76	54.30 N	29.22 E
Obdam	52	52.41 N	4.41 E
Obed	182	53.33 N	117.12 W
Obed ≏	192	36.04 N	84.39 W
Obeliai	76	55.56 N	25.48 E
Oberá	252	27.29 S	55.08 W
Ober-Abtsteinach	56	49.33 N	8.47 E
Oberägeri	58	47.08 N	8.37 E
Oberalppass)(	58	46.39 N	8.40 E
Oberalteich	60	48.55 N	12.40 E
Oberammergau	64	47.35 N	11.04 E
Oberau	64	47.33 N	11.08 E
Oberaudorf	64	47.39 N	12.10 E

PORTUGUÊS

Nome	Página	Lat.°′	Long.°′ W=Oeste
Oberaurach	64	47.24 N	12.26 E
Oberbauer	263	51.17 N	7.26 E
Oberbayern □[5]	60	48.15 N	11.45 E
Oberbieber	56	50.28 N	7.29 E
Oberbonsfeld	263	51.22 N	7.08 E
Oberbrügge	263	51.11 N	7.34 E
Obercunnersdorf	54	51.02 N	14.40 E
Oberdiessbach	58	46.51 N	7.38 E
Oberdolling	60	48.50 N	11.35 E
Oberdorla	54	51.10 N	10.25 E
Oberdrauburg	64	46.45 N	12.58 E
Oberelfringhausen	263	51.20 N	7.11 E
Ober Engadin V	58	46.37 N	9.58 E
Oberengstringen	58	47.25 N	8.28 E
Ober Ennstal V	30	47.28 N	14.10 E
Oberer See → Superior, Lake @	190	48.00 N	88.00 W
Oberfranken □[5]	60	49.50 N	11.20 E
Obergeis	56	50.54 N	9.35 E
Oberglogau → Głogówek	30	50.22 N	17.51 E
Obergum	52	53.20 N	6.31 E
Obergünzburg	58	47.51 N	10.25 E
Obergurgl	64	46.52 N	11.01 E
Obergurig	54	51.07 N	14.24 E
Oberhaan	263	51.13 N	7.02 E
Oberhaching	60	48.02 N	11.37 E
Oberharmersbach	58	48.22 N	8.07 E
Oberhaslach	58	48.33 N	7.20 E
Oberhausen	56	51.28 N	6.50 E
Oberhof	54	50.41 N	10.44 E
Oberhofen	58	46.44 N	7.40 E
Oberhollerau	60	48.41 N	12.27 E
Oberinntal V	64	47.13 N	10.45 E
Oberjettingen	56	48.34 N	8.46 E
Oberjoch	58	47.31 N	10.23 E
Ober-Kassel ➜[8]	263	51.14 N	6.46 E
Oberkaufungen	56	51.17 N	9.38 E
Oberkirch	58	48.31 N	8.05 E
Ober-kirchbach	264b	48.17 N	16.12 E
Oberkirchen	56	51.09 N	8.22 E
Oberkochen	56	48.47 N	10.06 E
Oberkotzau	54	50.16 N	11.56 E
Oberlaa ➜[8]	264b	48.08 N	16.24 E
Oberlausitz □[9]	54	51.15 N	14.30 E
Oberlin, Kans., U.S.	198	39.49 N	100.32 W
Oberlin, La., U.S.	194	30.37 N	92.46 W
Oberlin, Ohio, U.S.	214	41.18 N	82.13 W
Oberlin, Pa., U.S.	208	40.14 N	76.49 W
Oberlungwitz	54	50.47 N	12.44 E
Obermarchtal	58	48.14 N	9.34 E
Obermeiser	56	51.26 N	9.19 E
Obermieming	64	47.18 N	10.59 E
Obermodern	56	48.51 N	7.32 E
Obermoschel	56	49.44 N	7.46 E
Obermühl	60	48.27 N	13.55 E
Obermünstertal	58	47.52 N	7.49 E
Obernai	58	48.28 N	7.29 E
Obernbeck	52	52.12 N	8.41 E
Obernberg am Inn	60	48.19 N	13.20 E
Obernburg am Main	56	49.50 N	9.08 E
Oberndorf	52	53.45 N	9.08 E
Oberndorf am Neckar	58	48.18 N	8.34 E
Oberndorf bei Salzburg	64	47.57 N	12.56 E
Oberndorf in Tirol	64	47.30 N	12.23 E
Oberne	171b	35.24 S	147.50 E
Oberne Hill ∧[2]	171b	35.26 S	147.53 E
Obernhausen	56	50.29 N	9.56 E
Obernkirchen	52	52.16 N	9.07 E
Obernsees	60	49.55 N	11.23 E
Obernzell	60	48.34 N	13.39 E
Oberoderwitz	54	50.58 N	14.42 E
Oberon	170	33.43 S	149.52 E
Oberösterreich □[3]	30	48.15 N	14.00 E
Oberpettnau	64	47.18 N	11.08 E
Oberpfalz □[5]	60	49.30 N	12.10 E
Oberpleis	56	50.43 N	7.16 E
Oberpullendorf	61	47.31 N	16.31 E
Ober-Ramstadt	56	49.49 N	8.44 E
Oberried, B.R.D.	60	49.06 N	13.03 E
Oberried, Schw.	58	46.44 N	7.58 E
Oberriet	58	47.19 N	9.33 E
Oberröblingen	54	51.26 N	11.18 E
Ober-Roden	56	49.59 N	8.50 E
Ober Sankt Veit ➜[8]	264b	48.11 N	16.16 E
Oberscheidental	56	49.30 N	9.09 E
Oberscheinfeld	56	49.42 N	10.26 E
Oberscheld	56	50.44 N	8.20 E
Oberschleissheim	60	48.15 N	11.34 E
Oberschöneweide ➜[8]	264a	52.28 N	13.31 E
Obersee @	64	47.31 N	12.59 E
Oberseebach	56	48.58 N	7.59 E
Obersickte	54	52.13 N	10.38 E
Oberspier	54	51.19 N	10.51 E
Oberspreewald ➜[1]	54	51.50 N	14.05 E
Oberstadtfeld	56	50.10 N	6.46 E
Oberstaufen	58	47.33 N	10.01 E
Oberstdorf	58	47.24 N	10.16 E
Obersteinbach	56	49.02 N	7.41 E
Oberstreu	56	50.24 N	10.17 E
Obersuhl	56	50.56 N	10.02 E
Obertheres	56	50.01 N	10.26 E
Obertilliach	64	46.42 N	12.37 E
Obertin	78	48.42 N	25.11 E
Obertraubling	60	48.58 N	12.10 E
Obertraun	64	47.33 N	13.41 E
Obertrum	64	47.56 N	13.05 E
Obertürken	60	48.19 N	12.50 E
Oberueckersee @	54	53.12 N	13.52 E
Oberursel	56	50.11 N	8.35 E
Oberuzwil	58	47.26 N	9.08 E
Obervellach	64	46.56 N	13.12 E
Oberviechtach	60	49.28 N	12.25 E
Obervolta → Upper Volta □[1]	150	13.00 N	2.00 W
Oberwald	58	46.32 N	8.21 E
Oberwart	61	47.17 N	16.13 E
Oberweissbach	54	50.35 N	11.08 E
Oberweissenbrunn	56	50.24 N	9.57 E
Oberwengern	263	51.23 N	7.22 E
Oberwesel	56	50.06 N	7.43 E
Oberwiesenthal	54	50.25 N	12.59 E
Ober-Wilden	56	50.48 N	8.05 E
Oberwolfach	58	48.19 N	8.12 E
Oberwölz Stadt	61	47.13 N	14.17 E
Oberzeiring	61	47.15 N	14.29 E
Obetz	218	39.54 N	82.58 W
Obey ≏	192	36.34 N	85.31 W
Obey, East Fork ≏	192	36.27 N	85.07 W
Obey, West Fork ≏	192	36.27 N	85.09 W
Obgruiten	263	51.13 N	7.01 E
Obhausen	54	51.23 N	11.39 E
Obi	150	8.22 N	8.46 E
Obi, Kepulauan II	164	1.30 S	127.45 E
Obi, Pulau I	164	1.30 S	127.45 E
Obi, Selat ⊔	164	0.52 S	127.33 E
Obiaruku	150	5.51 N	6.09 E
Obichingou ≏	85	38.53 N	70.01 E
Obichody	78	51.02 N	28.59 E
Óbidos	250	1.55 S	55.31 W
Obi-Garm	85	38.43 N	69.42 E
Obihiro	92a	42.55 N	143.12 E
Obikanda	85	39.10 N	67.10 E
Obilatu, Pulau I	108	1.25 S	127.20 E
Obil'noje, S.S.S.R.	80	47.31 N	44.25 E
Obil'noje, S.S.S.R.	84	44.15 N	43.33 E
Obing	60	48.00 N	12.24 E
Obion	194	36.16 N	89.12 W
Obion ≏	194	35.55 N	89.39 W
Obion, Middle Fork ≏	194	36.13 N	88.56 W
Obion, Rutherford Fork ≏	194	36.17 N	89.01 W
Obion, South Fork ≏	194	36.17 N	89.03 W
Obion Creek ≏	194	36.35 N	89.11 W
Obira	92a	44.00 N	141.35 E
Obitočnaja Kosa ≻[2]	78	46.33 N	36.13 E
Obitočnyj Zaliv C	78	46.35 N	36.00 E
Obi Trough ✢[1]	14	33.00 S	98.00 E
Obitsu	268	35.20 N	140.04 E
Obitsu ≏	94	35.24 N	139.54 E
Objačevo	24	60.20 N	49.34 E
Oblačnaja, Gora ∧	89	43.45 N	134.10 E
Öblarn	61	47.27 N	13.59 E
Oblastnaja	80	56.59 N	52.37 E
Oblivnoj, Ostrov I	84	39.39 N	49.27 E
Oblivskaja	80	48.32 N	42.30 E
Oblong	194	39.00 N	87.55 W
Oblučje	89	49.03 N	131.04 E
Obninsk	82	55.05 N	36.37 E
Obnora ≏	76	58.14 N	40.58 E
Obnova	38	43.26 N	24.59 E
Obo, Centraf.	154	5.24 N	26.30 E
Obo, Yai.	144	3.46 N	38.50 E
Oboa ∧	154	1.50 N	34.47 E
Obobogorap	158	27.18 S	20.04 E
Obock	144	11.59 N	43.16 E
Obojan'	78	51.13 N	36.16 E
Ō-boke ♠	96	33.55 N	133.46 E
Obokote	154	0.52 S	26.19 E
Obol'	76	55.22 N	29.17 E
Obol' ≏	76	55.24 N	29.02 E
Oboldino	265b	55.53 N	37.56 E
Obolon'	78	49.36 N	32.52 E
Oborniki	30	52.39 N	16.51 E
Obot	144	4.30 N	37.20 E
Obout	152	3.28 N	11.44 E
Obouya	152	0.56 S	15.43 E
Oboz'orskij	24	63.28 N	40.18 E
Obra ≏	30	52.36 N	15.28 E
Obrazcovo-Travino	80	45.58 N	48.02 E
Obree, Mount ∧	164	9.30 S	148.05 E
Obrenovac	38	44.39 N	20.12 E
O'brien	202	42.04 N	123.42 W
O'Brien Coulee V	202	48.48 N	110.22 W
Obrighoven-Lackhausen	52	51.40 N	6.38 E
Obrovac	36	44.12 N	15.41 E
Obrovo	76	52.30 N	25.34 E
Obručeva, Gora ∧	88	53.36 N	113.52 E
Obručevka	85	42.30 N	69.05 E
Obručevo	85	40.07 N	68.30 E
Obruk	130	38.10 N	33.12 E
Obryta	54	53.13 N	14.59 E
Obryvistoje	89	48.46 N	144.40 E
Obša ≏	76	55.55 N	32.32 E
Obšarovka	80	53.07 N	48.52 E
Obščij Syrt ∧	80	52.00 N	51.30 E
Observation Peak ∧	204	40.46 N	120.10 W
Observatoire, Caye de l' I	160	21.25 S	158.50 E
Observatory Inlet ⊔	182	55.10 N	129.54 W
Obskaja Guba C	72	69.00 N	73.00 E
Obsteig	64	47.18 N	10.56 E
Obtovo	78	51.37 N	33.13 E
Ōbu	94	35.00 N	136.58 E
Obu ➜[8]	270	34.44 N	135.09 E
Obuasi	150	6.14 N	1.39 W
Obubra	150	6.05 N	8.21 E
Obuchov	78	50.08 N	30.37 E
Obuchova	76	56.06 N	32.22 E
Obuchoviči	78	51.00 N	29.46 E
Obuchovka	86	46.13 N	81.05 E
Obuchovo, S.S.S.R.	82	55.50 N	38.16 E
Obuchovo, S.S.S.R.	82	56.09 N	36.55 E
Óbuda ➜[8]	264c	47.33 N	19.02 E
Óbudai-sziget I	264c	47.33 N	19.04 E
Obudu	150	6.40 N	9.09 E
Obusa ≏	88	53.45 N	103.50 E
Obuse	94	36.42 N	138.19 E
Obuškovo	82	55.47 N	37.02 E
Obu-tōge)(	270	34.44 N	135.10 E
Obva ≏	86	58.32 N	55.18 E
Obvinsk	86	58.29 N	54.51 E
Obwalden □[3]	58	46.50 N	8.14 E
Obžericha	80	57.11 N	42.58 E
Očakov	78	46.37 N	31.33 E
Očakovo ➜[8]	265b	55.41 N	37.27 E
Ocala	192	29.11 N	82.07 W
Ocallí	248	6.09 S	78.18 W
Očamčire	84	42.44 N	41.28 E
Ocamo ≏	246	2.48 N	65.14 W
Ocampo, Méx.	232	27.20 N	102.21 W
Ocampo, Méx.	232	28.11 N	108.23 W
Ocampo, Méx.	234	21.39 N	101.30 W
Ocaña, Col.	246	8.15 N	73.20 W
Ocaña, Esp.	34	39.56 N	3.31 W
Ocate Creek ≏	196	36.17 N	104.30 W
Occaquan ≏	208	38.40 N	77.14 W
Occaquan Reservoir @[1]	208	38.43 N	77.22 W
Očchamuri	84	41.52 N	41.50 E
Occhieppo Inferiore	62	45.33 N	8.01 E
Occhiobello	64	44.55 N	11.35 E
Occidental, Cordillera ⛰, Col.	246	5.00 N	76.00 W
Occidental, Cordillera ⛰, Perú	248	10.00 S	77.00 W
Occidental College ʊ[2]	280	34.08 N	118.13 W
Occidental de Zapata, Ciénaga ☷	240p	22.25 N	81.20 W
Occimiano	62	45.03 N	8.30 E
Occoquan	208	38.41 N	77.16 W
Occoquan Bay C	208	38.37 N	77.13 W
Ocean □[6]	208	39.58 N	74.12 W
Oceana	192	37.42 N	81.38 W
Oceana Naval Air Station ■	208	36.50 N	76.02 W
Ocean Bay Park	276	40.39 N	73.08 W
Ocean Beach	276	40.38 N	73.18 W
Ocean Bluff	207	42.06 N	70.39 W
Ocean Breeze Park	220	27.15 N	80.14 W
Ocean Cape ≻	176	59.30 N	139.45 W
Ocean City, Md., U.S.	188	38.20 N	75.05 W
Ocean City, N.J., U.S.	208	39.16 N	74.36 W
Ocean City, Wash., U.S.	224	47.04 N	124.10 W
Ocean Falls	182	52.21 N	127.40 W
Ocean Gate	208	39.39 N	74.08 W
Ocean Grove	207	41.44 N	71.12 W
Ocean Heights	207	41.25 N	70.33 W
Ocean Island I	174d	0.52 S	169.35 E
Ocean Lake @[1]	202	43.11 N	108.36 W
Oceano	204	35.06 N	120.37 W
Ocean Park, B.C., Can.	224	49.02 N	122.53 W
Ocean Park, Wash., U.S.	224	46.30 N	124.03 W
Ocean Port	276	40.19 N	74.01 W
Ocean Shores	224	47.01 N	124.09 W
Oceanside, Calif., U.S.	228	33.12 N	117.23 W
Oceanside, N.Y., U.S.	210	40.38 N	73.38 W
Ocean Springs	194	30.25 N	88.50 W
Ocean View, Del., U.S.	208	38.33 N	75.05 W
Ocean View, N.J., U.S.	208	39.10 N	74.44 W
Oceanville	208	39.28 N	74.28 W
Oceanway	192	30.28 N	81.38 W
Oceola	214	40.51 N	83.06 W
Očer	80	57.53 N	54.42 E
Očeretino	83	48.14 N	37.36 E
O. C. Fisher Lake @[1]	196	31.30 N	100.30 W
Ocha	89	53.34 N	142.56 E
Ochagavía, Canal de Ξ	286e	33.30 S	70.49 W
Ochanomizu Women's University ʊ[2]	268	35.43 N	139.44 E
Ochansk	86	57.43 N	55.23 E
Ochapowace Indian Reserve ➜[4]	184	50.30 N	102.24 W
Ocheyedan	198	43.25 N	95.32 W
Ocheyedan ≏	198	43.08 N	95.09 W
Ōchi, Nihon	96	35.04 N	132.36 E
Ochi, Nihon	96	33.32 N	133.15 E
Ochiai	96	35.01 N	133.45 E
Ochiai ➜[8]	268	35.43 N	139.42 E
O'chiese Indian Reserve ➜[4]	182	52.50 N	115.28 W
Ochil Hills ⛰[2]	46	56.14 N	3.40 W
Ochiltree	44	55.28 N	4.23 W
Ōchise ≏	94	35.03 N	137.46 E
Ochlocknee	192	30.59 N	84.05 W
Ochlockonee ≏	192	29.58 N	84.21 W
Ochoco Creek ≏	202	44.19 N	120.53 W
Ochoco Mountains ⛰	202	44.30 N	120.35 W
Ochopee	220	25.54 N	81.17 W
Ocho Rios	241q	18.25 N	77.07 W
Ochota ≏	74	59.20 N	143.04 E
Ochotsk	74	59.23 N	143.18 E
Ochotskisches Meer → Okhotsk, Sea of ⍑[2]	74	53.00 N	150.00 E
Ochotskoje More → Okhotsk, Sea of ⍑[2]	74	53.00 N	150.00 E
Ochre River	184	51.03 N	99.47 W
Ochsenfurt	56	49.40 N	10.03 E
Ochsenhausen	58	48.04 N	9.56 E
Ochsenwerder ➜[8]	52	53.28 N	10.05 E
Ochta ≏	265a	59.57 N	30.24 E
Ochtendung	56	50.21 N	7.23 E
Ochtrup	52	52.13 N	7.11 E
Ochvat	76	56.46 N	32.27 E
Oci ≏	152	15.14 S	15.16 E
Ocilla	192	31.36 N	83.15 W
Ock ≏	42	51.39 N	1.17 W
Ockelbo	26	60.53 N	16.43 E
Öckerö	26	57.43 N	11.39 E
Ockham	260	51.18 N	0.27 W
Ockholm	41	54.40 N	8.49 E
Ockies	158	31.31 S	21.41 E
Ocmulgee ≏	192	31.58 N	82.32 W
Ocmulgee National Monument ♠	192	32.43 N	83.38 W
Ocna Mureș	38	46.23 N	23.51 E
Ocoa, Bahía de C	238	18.22 N	70.39 W
Ocoee	220	28.35 N	81.33 W
Ocoee ≏	192	35.12 N	84.40 W
Ocoña	248	16.26 S	73.07 W
Ocoña ≏	248	16.28 S	73.07 W
Oconee	219	39.17 N	89.07 W
Oconee ≏	192	31.58 N	82.32 W
Ocongate	248	13.38 S	71.24 W
O'Connell	170	33.32 S	149.44 E
Oconomowoc	216	43.07 N	88.30 W
Oconomowoc ≏	216	43.07 N	88.37 W
Oconomowoc Lake	216	42.37 N	88.28 W
Oconomowoc Lake @	216	43.06 N	88.27 W
Oconto	190	44.43 N	87.52 W
Oconto ≏	190	44.53 N	87.50 W
Oconto, North Branch ≏	190	45.00 N	88.23 W
Oconto Falls	190	44.42 N	88.08 W
Ocós	236	14.31 N	92.11 W
Ocotal	236	13.38 N	86.29 W
Ocotepec	234	17.13 N	93.09 W
Ocotepeque □[5]	236	14.30 N	89.00 W
Ocotlán	234	20.21 N	102.46 W
Ocotlán de Morelos	234	16.48 N	96.40 W
Ocoyoacac	234	19.16 N	99.26 W
Ocozingo	232	16.54 N	92.07 W
Ocozocoautla [de Espinosa]	234	16.46 N	93.22 W
Ocracoke	192	35.07 N	75.58 W
Ocracoke Island I	192	35.09 N	75.53 W
Ocre, Monte ∧	66	42.15 N	13.26 E
Ocreza, Ribeira da ≏	34	39.32 N	7.50 W
Ocros	248	10.24 S	77.24 W
Octoraro Creek ≏	208	39.39 N	76.09 W
Octoraro Creek, East Branch ≏	208	39.49 N	76.02 W
Octoraro Creek, West Branch ≏	208	39.49 N	76.05 W
Ocú	236	7.57 N	80.47 W
Ocuilán de Arteaga	234	18.58 N	99.25 W
Ocumare del Tuy	246	10.07 N	66.46 W
Ocurí	248	18.50 S	65.50 W
Ocussi	112	9.12 S	124.21 E
Oda, Ghana	150	5.55 N	0.59 W
Oda, Nihon	96	33.34 N	132.48 E
Ōda, Nihon	96	35.11 N	132.30 E
Oda ≏	96	34.37 N	133.44 E
Oda, Jabal ∧	140	20.21 N	36.39 E
Ŏdaejin	98	41.34 N	129.40 E
Ōdai	94	34.24 N	136.25 E
Ōdaigahara-san ∧	92	34.11 N	136.05 E
Odaka	92	37.34 N	141.00 E
Ödåkra	41	56.06 N	12.44 E
Odanakumadona	156	20.53 S	24.45 E
Ōdate	92	40.16 N	140.34 E
Odawara	94	35.15 N	139.10 E
Odayeri	267b	41.14 N	28.51 E
Odda	26	60.04 N	6.33 E
Odden	41	55.58 N	11.22 E
Odder	41	55.58 N	10.10 E
Oddur	144	4.10 N	43.53 E
Oddville	218	38.27 N	84.15 W
Odebolt	198	42.19 N	95.15 W
Ödeby	40	59.24 N	15.25 E
Odei ≏	184	56.06 N	96.55 W
Odeleite, Ribeira de ≏	34	37.21 N	7.27 W
Odell, Ill., U.S.	216	41.00 N	88.31 W
Odell, Nebr., U.S.	198	40.03 N	96.48 W
Odell, Oreg., U.S.	224	45.38 N	121.32 W
Odell, Tex., U.S.	196	34.21 N	99.25 W
Odell Lake @	202	43.34 N	122.00 W
Odelzhausen	60	48.19 N	11.12 E
Odem	196	27.57 N	97.35 W
Odemira	34	37.36 N	8.38 W
Ödemiş	130	38.13 N	27.59 E
Ödenburg → Sopron	61	47.41 N	16.36 E
Odendaalsrus	158	27.48 S	26.45 E
Odenkirchen ➜[8]	263	51.08 N	6.27 E
Odensbacken	40	59.10 N	15.32 E
Odense	41	55.24 N	10.23 E
Odense Å ≏	41	55.26 N	10.26 E
Odense Fjord C	41	55.30 N	10.34 E
Odenthal	56	51.02 N	7.07 E
Odenwald ⛰	56	49.40 N	9.00 E
Oder (Odra) ≏	30	53.32 N	14.38 E
Oderberg	54	52.52 N	14.02 E
Oderbruch ➜[1]	54	52.40 N	14.15 E
Oderen	58	47.55 N	6.59 E
Oderhaff (Zalew Szczeciński) C	54	53.46 N	14.14 E
Oder-Havel-Kanal Ξ	54	52.52 N	14.02 E
Oder-Spree-Kanal Ξ	54	52.23 N	13.41 E
Odertalsperre ➜[6]	54	51.38 N	10.30 E
Oderzo	64	45.47 N	12.29 E
Odesa → Odessa	78	46.28 N	30.44 E
Ödeshög	26	58.14 N	14.39 E
Odessa, Ont., Can.	212	44.17 N	76.43 W
Odessa, S.S.S.R.	78	46.28 N	30.44 E
Odessa, Del., U.S.	208	39.27 N	75.40 W
Odessa, Fla., U.S.	220	28.11 N	82.36 W
Odessa, Mo., U.S.	194	39.00 N	93.57 W
Odessa, N.Y., U.S.	210	42.20 N	76.48 W
Odessa, Tex., U.S.	196	31.51 N	102.22 W
Odessa, Wash., U.S.	202	47.20 N	118.41 W
Odessa □[4]	38	46.00 N	30.00 E
Odessa Lake @	212	44.19 N	76.41 W
Odesskoje	86	54.13 N	72.58 E
Odiakwe	156	20.01 S	25.17 E
Odib, Wādī V	140	22.38 N	36.06 E
Odiel ≏	34	37.10 N	6.54 W
Odienné	150	9.30 N	7.34 W
Odienné □[5]	150	9.30 N	7.20 W
Odiham	42	51.15 N	0.57 W
Odin	219	38.37 N	89.03 W
Odin, Mount ∧	182	50.33 N	118.08 W
Odincovo, S.S.S.R.	82	54.40 N	38.00 E
Odincovo, S.S.S.R.	82	55.41 N	37.17 E
Odiongan	116	12.24 N	121.59 E
Odiongan Bay C	116	12.25 N	121.58 E
Odivelas	266c	38.47 N	9.11 W
Odobești	38	45.45 N	27.04 E
Odojev	76	53.56 N	36.41 E
Odolanów	30	51.35 N	17.39 E
Ōdomari-chosuichi @	96	34.43 N	132.18 E
Odon	194	38.51 N	86.59 W
Ŏdŏngk	110	11.48 N	104.45 E
O'Donnell	196	32.58 N	101.50 W
O'Donnell ≏	162	18.22 S	126.36 E
Odoorn	52	52.51 N	6.51 E
Odorheiu Secuiesc	38	46.18 N	25.18 E
Odra Port	54	53.52 N	14.14 E
Odrinhas	266c	38.53 N	9.22 W
Odry	30	49.39 N	17.50 E
Odrzywół	30	51.32 N	20.33 E
Odsherred ➜[1]	41	55.52 N	11.37 E
Ødsted	41	55.39 N	9.25 E
Odum	192	31.40 N	82.02 W
Odweina	144	9.23 N	45.04 E
Odžaci	38	45.30 N	19.16 E
Odzi	154	18.58 S	32.23 E
Odzi ≏	154	19.45 S	32.24 E
Odziba	152	3.35 S	15.31 E
Ōe	96	35.23 N	135.09 E
Oebisfelde	54	52.25 N	10.59 E
Oedelem	50	51.10 N	3.20 E
Oederan	54	50.52 N	13.09 E
Oeding	52	51.56 N	6.49 E
Oedt	56	51.19 N	6.22 E
Oegstgeest	52	52.10 N	4.29 E
Oeiras, Bra.	250	7.01 S	42.08 W
Oeiras, Port.	266c	38.41 N	9.21 W
Oeiras do Pará	250	1.58 S	49.51 W
Oelde	52	51.49 N	8.08 E
Oelemari ≏	250	3.13 N	54.09 W
Oella	284b	39.16 N	76.47 W
Oels → Oleśnica	30	51.13 N	17.23 E
Oelsig	54	51.41 N	13.22 E
Oelsnitz, D.D.R.	54	50.43 N	12.41 E
Oelsnitz, D.D.R.	54	50.24 N	12.10 E
Oelwein	190	42.41 N	91.55 W
Oenpelli Mission	164	12.20 S	133.04 E
Oensingen	58	47.17 N	7.44 E
Oepping	60	48.36 N	13.56 E
Oer-Erkenschwick	52	51.39 N	7.15 E
Oerlinghausen	52	51.57 N	8.39 E
Oermten	263	51.29 N	6.27 E
Oesede	52	52.12 N	8.04 E
Oeslau	56	50.17 N	11.01 E
Oespel ➜[8]	263	51.30 N	7.23 E
Oeste, Parque del ♠	266a	40.26 N	3.44 W
Oestrich	263	51.22 N	7.38 E
Oestrich ➜[8]	263	51.34 N	7.22 E
Oestrum	263	51.25 N	6.40 E
Ōetaka-yama ∧	96	35.04 N	132.26 E
Oettingen in Bayern	56	48.57 N	10.36 E
Oetz	58	47.12 N	10.54 E
Oeuf ≏	50	48.11 N	2.21 E
Oeventrop	56	51.23 N	8.08 E
Oeversee	41	54.42 N	9.26 E
Ōe-yama ∧	96	35.27 N	135.07 E
Of	130	40.57 N	40.18 E
O'Fallon, Ill., U.S.	219	38.35 N	89.55 W
O'Fallon, Mo., U.S.	219	38.49 N	90.42 W
O'Fallon Creek ≏	198	46.50 N	105.09 W
Ofanto ≏	68	41.22 N	16.13 E
Ofaqim	132	31.17 N	34.37 E
Ofenpass → Fuorn, pass dal)(	58	46.37 N	10.15 E
Offa	150	8.09 N	4.44 E
Offaly □[6]	48	53.20 N	7.30 W
Offanengo	62	45.22 N	9.44 E
Offemont	58	47.40 N	6.53 E
Offenbach	56	50.08 N	8.47 E
Offenburg	58	48.28 N	7.57 E
Offendorf	58	48.43 N	7.55 E
Offerdal	26	63.28 N	14.00 E
Offham	260	51.17 N	0.23 E
Officer	274b	38.04 S	145.25 E
Officer Creek ≏	162	27.45 S	132.24 E
Offida	66	42.56 N	13.41 E
Offingen	58	48.29 N	10.21 E
Offranville	50	49.52 N	1.03 E
Offutt Air Force Base ■	198	41.08 N	95.56 W
Oficina Alianza	248	20.46 S	69.42 W
Oficina Chile	252	25.09 S	69.54 W
Oficina Pedro de Valdivia	252	22.36 S	69.40 W
Oficina Victoria	248	20.44 S	69.42 W
Ofin	273a	6.33 N	3.30 E
Öflingen	58	47.35 N	7.55 E
O'Flynn, Lough @	48	53.46 N	8.40 W
Ofotfjorden C[2]	24	68.23 N	16.10 E
Oftringen	58	47.19 N	7.56 E
Ofu	174y	14.10 S	169.42 W
Ofu I	174y	14.11 S	169.42 W
Ōfukuroshinden	268	35.53 N	139.27 E
Ōfuna	268	35.21 N	139.32 E
Ōfunato	92	39.04 N	141.43 E
Oga	92	39.53 N	139.51 E
Oga-hantō ≻[1]	92	39.55 N	139.50 E
Ōgaki, Nihon	94	35.21 N	136.37 E
Ōgaki, Nihon	96	34.06 N	132.30 E
Ogallala	198	41.08 N	101.43 W
Ogan ≏	112	3.01 S	104.44 E
Ogano	94	36.01 N	139.00 E
Ogasa	94	34.41 N	138.06 E
Ogasawara-guntō (Bonin Islands) II	14	27.00 N	142.10 E
Ōgata, Nihon	94	37.13 N	138.20 E
Ōgata, Nihon	96	33.01 N	133.01 E
Ogata, Nihon	96	32.58 N	131.29 E
Ōga-tō ∧	94	36.13 N	138.06 E
Ogatsu	92	38.41 N	141.28 E
Ogawa, Nihon	92	32.35 N	130.43 E
Ogawa, Nihon	94	36.37 N	137.58 E
Ogawa, Nihon	94	36.03 N	139.16 E
Ogawa, Nihon	94	36.10 N	140.21 E
Ogawa, Nihon	94	36.45 N	140.08 E
Ogawa, Nihon	268	35.44 N	139.28 E
Ogawara-ko @	92	40.47 N	141.20 E
Ogbomosho	150	8.08 N	4.15 E
Ogden, Iowa, U.S.	190	42.02 N	94.02 W
Ogden, Kans., U.S.	198	39.07 N	96.43 W
Ogden, Pa., U.S.	208	39.49 N	75.27 W
Ogden, Utah, U.S.	200	41.14 N	111.58 W
Ogden, Mount ∧	180	58.26 N	133.23 W
Ogden Dunes	216	41.38 N	87.12 W
Ogden Island I	212	44.52 N	75.12 W
Ogden Point ≻	212	43.58 N	77.53 W
Ogden Reservoir @[1]	262	53.42 N	2.22 W
Ogdensburg, N.J., U.S.	210	41.05 N	74.36 W
Ogdensburg, N.Y., U.S.	212	44.42 N	75.29 W
Ogeechee ≏	192	31.51 N	81.06 W
Ogeechee Creek ≏	192	32.20 N	81.33 W
Ogema	184	49.35 N	104.55 W
Ōge-shima I	96	34.12 N	134.38 E
Oggersheim	56	49.29 N	8.22 E
Oghi	123	34.31 N	73.01 E
Ogibalovo	76	60.34 N	39.40 E
Ogidaki Mountain ∧[2]	190	46.58 N	83.58 W
Ogies	158	26.02 S	29.04 E
Ögij Nuur @	88	47.47 N	102.48 E
Ogijo	273a	6.42 N	3.31 E
Ogilvie, Austl.	162	28.09 S	114.38 E

Symbol	English	Deutsch	Español	Français	Português
≏	River	Fluss	Río	Rivière	Rio
Ξ	Canal	Kanal	Canal	Canal	Canal
ᒪ	Waterfall, Rapids	Wasserfall, Stromschnellen	Cascada, Rápidos	Chute d'eau, Rapides	Cascata, Rápidos
⊔	Strait	Meeresstrasse	Estrecho	Détroit	Estreito
C	Bay, Gulf	Bucht, Golf	Bahía, Golfo	Baie, Golfe	Baía, Golfo
@	Lake, Lakes	See, Seen	Lago, Lagos	Lac, Lacs	Lago, Lagos
☷	Swamp	Sumpf	Pantano	Marais	Pântano
⍓	Ice Features, Glacier	Eis- und Gletscherformen	Accidentes Glaciales	Formes glaciaires	Acidentes Glaciares
⍑	Other Hydrographic Features	Andere Hydrographische Objekte	Otros Elementos Hidrográficos	Autres données hydrographiques	Outros Elementos Hidrográficos
✢	Submarine Features	Untermeerische Objekte	Accidentes Submarinos	Formes de relief sous-marin	Acidentes Submarinos
□	Political Unit	Politische Einheit	Unidad Política	Entité politique	Unidade Política
ʊ	Cultural Institution	Kulturelle Institution	Institución Cultural	Institution culturelle	Instituição Cultural
⊥	Historical Site	Historische Stätte	Sitio Histórico	Site historique	Sítio Histórico
♠	Recreational Site	Erholungs- und Ferienort	Sitio de Recreo	Centre de loisirs	Sítio de Lazer
⊠	Airport	Flughafen	Aeropuerto	Aéroport	Aeroporto
■	Military Installation	Militäranlage	Instalación Militar	Installation militaire	Instalação Militar
➜	Miscellaneous	Verschiedenes	Misceláneo	Divers	Miscelânea

Name	Page	Lat.	Long.
Ogilvie, Minn., U.S.	190	45.50 N	93.26 W
Ogilvie ≃	180	65.52 N	137.16 W
Ogilvie Mountains ⛰	180	65.00 N	139.30 W
Ogilville	218	39.08 N	86.01 W
Ōgino-sen ∧	96	35.26 N	134.36 E
Ogi-shima I	96	34.26 N	134.04 E
Ogle □[6]	216	42.01 N	89.20 W
Oglesby, Ill., U.S.	216	41.18 N	89.04 W
Oglesby, Tex., U.S.	222	31.25 N	97.31 W
Oglethorpe	192	32.18 N	84.04 W
Ogliastra ⊸[1]	71	39.56 N	9.37 E
Ogliastro Cilento	68	40.21 N	15.03 E
Oglio ≃	64	45.02 N	10.39 E
Ogmore	166	22.37 S	149.40 E
Ogmore ≃	42	51.28 N	3.38 W
Ogmore Vale	42	51.38 N	3.31 W
Ogni	86	51.54 N	83.31 E
Ognica	54	53.07 N	14.27 E
Ognon ≃	58	47.20 N	5.29 E
Ogn'ov Jar	86	58.23 N	76.29 E
Ogn'ovka	86	49.36 N	83.25 E
Oğnut	130	39.08 N	40.53 E
Ōgo	94	36.25 N	139.10 E
Ōgo ⊸[8]	270	34.49 N	135.06 E
Ōgo ≃	270	34.47 N	135.04 E
Ogōchi-dam ⊸[6]	94	35.47 N	139.04 E
Ogodža	89	52.44 N	132.31 E
Ogoja	150	6.40 N	8.48 E
Ogoki ≃	176	51.38 N	85.57 W
Ogooué ≃	152	0.49 S	9.00 E
Ogooué-Ivindo □[4]	152	0.30 N	13.00 E
Ogooué-Lolo □[4]	152	1.00 S	13.00 E
Ogooué-Maritime □[4]	152	2.00 S	9.30 E
Ogōri, Nihon	96	34.06 N	131.24 E
Ogōri, Nihon	96	33.22 N	130.32 E
Ogorodnoje	78	45.53 N	28.50 E
Ogose	94	35.58 N	139.18 E
Ogosta ≃	38	43.45 N	23.51 E
Ogou ≃	150	7.50 N	1.19 E
Ogoyo	273a	6.26 N	3.29 E
Ogr	140	12.02 N	27.06 E
Ogre	76	56.51 N	24.36 E
Ogre ≃	76	56.48 N	24.36 E
Ogrodzieniec	30	50.27 N	19.31 E
Ogrosen	54	51.42 N	14.02 E
Ōguchi	94	35.20 N	136.55 E
Ŏgu-dong	98	38.57 N	126.56 E
Ogudu	273a	6.34 N	3.24 E
Ogulin	36	45.16 N	15.14 E
Ogun ≃	273a	6.37 N	3.27 E
Ogun Forest Reserve ♠	273a	6.37 N	3.26 E
Oguni, Nihon	92	38.04 N	139.45 E
Oguni, Nihon	96	33.07 N	131.04 E
Ogunlogun	273a	6.41 N	3.28 E
Ogunquit	188	43.16 N	70.36 W
Ogura-san ∧	94	36.02 N	138.37 E
Ogurčinskij, Ostrov I	128	38.55 N	53.02 E
Oguri-tōge)(	96	33.06 N	130.39 E
Oguta	150	5.44 N	6.44 E
Oğuz	130	39.32 N	38.51 E
Oğuzeli	130	36.59 N	37.30 E
Ogwashi-Uku	150	6.10 N	6.31 E
Ohai	172	45.55 S	167.57 E
Ohakune	172	39.25 S	175.24 E
Ohanapecosh ≃	224	46.38 N	121.37 W
Ohanet	148	28.45 N	8.55 E
Ōhara, Nihon	94	35.15 N	140.23 E
Ōhara, Nihon	96	35.07 N	134.20 E
Ōharano ⊸[8]	270	34.58 N	135.40 E
Ōhara-tunnel ⊸[5]	94	35.12 N	137.50 E
Ōhata	92	41.24 N	141.10 E
Ōhatake	268	35.57 N	139.46 E
Ohau, Lake ⊜	172	44.15 S	169.51 E
Ohaupo	172	37.55 S	175.19 E
Ohey	56	50.26 N	5.08 E
O'Higgins, Cabo ≻	174z	27.05 S	109.15 W
O'Higgins, Cerro ∧	254	48.48 S	73.11 W
O'Higgins, Lago (Lago San Martín) ⊜	254	49.00 S	72.40 W
Ohingaiti	172	39.52 S	175.43 E
Ohio	190	41.34 N	89.28 W
Ohio □[6], Ind., U.S.	218	38.57 N	84.51 W
Ohio □[6], W. Va., U.S.	214	40.09 N	80.35 W
Ohio □[3]	178		
	188	40.15 N	82.45 W
Ohio ≃	178	36.59 N	89.08 W
Ohio Brush Creek ≃	218	38.41 N	83.27 W
Ohio Brush Creek, Baker Fork ≃	218	39.02 N	83.26 W
Ohio Brush Creek, Little West Fork ≃	218	38.58 N	83.34 W
Ohio Brush Creek, West Fork ≃	218	38.56 N	83.28 W
Ohio Caverns ⊥[5]	216	40.14 N	83.43 W
Ohio City	216	40.46 N	84.37 W
Ohio Peak ∧	200	38.49 N	107.07 W
Ohiopyle State Park ♠	188	39.50 N	79.31 W
Ohioville, N.Y., U.S.	210	41.45 N	74.03 W
Ohioville, Pa., U.S.	214	40.41 N	80.30 W
Ōhira	94	36.20 N	139.42 E
Ōhira-yama ∧	96	34.20 N	133.57 E
Ōhito	94	34.59 N	138.56 E
Ohlau → Oława	30	50.57 N	17.17 E
Ohligs ⊸[8]	263	51.09 N	7.00 E
Ohlman	219	39.21 N	89.13 W
Ohlsdorf	64	47.57 N	13.47 E
Ohm ≃	56	50.51 N	8.48 E
Ōho	94	36.08 N	140.06 E
Ohoitom	164	5.56 S	132.41 E
Ohonua	174w	21.20 S	174.57 W
Ohoopee ≃	192	31.54 N	82.07 W
Ohopoho	152	18.03 S	13.45 E
Ōhori	268	35.20 N	139.52 E
Ohorn	54	51.10 N	14.02 E
Ohra Stausee ⊜[1]	54	50.46 N	10.42 E
Ohrdruf	54	50.50 N	10.44 E
Ohre ≃, Eur.	54	52.18 N	11.47 E
Ohře (Eger) ≃, Eur.	54	50.32 N	14.08 E
Ohrid	38	41.07 N	20.47 E
Ohrid, Lake ⊜	38	41.02 N	20.43 E
Ohrigstad	156	24.49 S	30.33 E
Öhringen	56	49.12 N	9.29 E
Ohrnberg	56	49.15 N	9.27 E
Ohu	60	48.36 N	12.14 E
Ohuira, Bahía de C	232	25.38 N	108.58 W
Ohura	172	38.50 S	174.59 E
Ōi, Nihon	96	35.28 N	135.37 E
Ōi, Nihon	268	35.51 N	139.30 E
Ōi ≃, Nihon	94	34.46 N	138.18 E
Ōi ≃, Nihon	96	35.01 N	135.39 E
Oiapoque	250	3.50 N	51.50 W
Oiapoque (Oyapock) ≃	250	4.08 N	51.40 W
Oies, Île aux I	186	47.07 N	70.30 W
Ōigawa	94	34.48 N	138.17 E
Oignies	50	50.28 N	2.59 E
Oik	85	43.46 N	70.58 E
Oil Center	196	32.30 N	103.16 W
Oil City, La., U.S.	194	32.45 N	93.58 W
Oil City, Pa., U.S.	214	41.26 N	79.42 W
Oil Creek ≃	214	41.26 N	79.42 W
Oil Creek State Park ♠	214	41.33 N	79.40 W
Oildale	226	35.25 N	119.01 W
Oil Springs	214	42.47 N	82.07 W
Oilton, Okla., U.S.	196	36.05 N	96.35 W
Oilton, Tex., U.S.	196	27.33 N	98.59 W
Oinville-sur-Montcient	261	49.02 N	1.51 E
Oir, Beinn an ∧	46	55.54 N	6.00 W
Oirschot	52	51.30 N	5.18 E
Oise □[5]	50	49.30 N	2.30 E
Oise ≃	50	49.00 N	2.04 E
Oise à l'Aisne, Canal de l' ☲	50	49.36 N	3.11 E
Oisemont	50	49.57 N	1.46 E
Ōiso, Nihon	94	35.18 N	139.19 E
Ōiso, Nihon	270	34.33 N	135.01 E
Oissel	50	49.20 N	1.06 E
Oissery	261	49.04 N	2.49 E
Oisterwijk	52	51.35 N	5.12 E
Oistins	241g	13.04 N	59.32 W
Oistins Bay C	241g	13.03 N	59.33 W
Ōita	96	33.14 N	131.36 E
Ōita □[5]	96	33.15 N	131.30 E
Ōita ≃	96	33.15 N	131.37 E
Oiticica	250	5.03 S	41.05 W
Oituz, Pasul)(	38	46.03 N	26.23 E
Ōiwa	270	34.53 N	135.33 E
Ōizumi, Nihon	94	36.15 N	139.25 E
Ōizumi, Nihon	94	35.52 N	138.23 E
Oizuruga-take ∧	94	36.18 N	136.47 E
Öja I	40	58.45 N	17.52 E
Oja ≃	86	53.26 N	91.55 E
Ojai	228	34.27 N	119.15 W
Öjaren ⊜	40	60.43 N	16.50 E
Ojat' ≃	76	60.31 N	33.00 E
Ojcowski Park Narodowy ♠	30	50.15 N	19.50 E
Öje	26	60.49 N	13.51 E
Ojek	88	52.35 N	104.27 E
Ojgon Nuur ⊜	88	49.10 N	96.36 E
Ojgor	86	49.10 N	89.17 E
Ōji	96	34.35 N	135.42 E
Ojika-hantō ≻[1]	92	38.20 N	141.30 E
Ōjima	94	36.15 N	139.20 E
Ojinaga	232	29.34 N	104.25 W
Ojitlán	234	18.04 N	96.23 W
Ojiya	92	37.18 N	138.48 E
Ojm'akon	74	63.28 N	142.49 E
Ojocaliente	234	22.34 N	102.15 W
Ojo de Agua de Alférez	234	22.51 N	99.42 W
Ojo de la Casa	200	31.23 N	106.32 W
Ojo de Liebre, Laguna C	232	27.45 N	114.15 W
Ojos del Salado, Nevado ∧	252	27.06 S	68.32 W
Ojota	273a	6.35 N	3.23 E
Ojtal, S.S.S.R.	85	42.55 N	73.17 E
Ojtal, S.S.S.R.	85	40.24 N	74.06 E
Oju	150	6.53 N	8.26 E
Ojuelos de Jalisco	234	21.52 N	101.35 W
Ojus	220	25.57 N	80.09 W
Oka	150	7.29 N	5.49 E
Oka ≃, S.S.S.R.	80	56.20 N	43.59 E
Oka ≃, S.S.S.R.	88	55.15 N	102.10 E
Okaba	164	8.06 S	139.42 E
Okabe, Nihon	94	36.12 N	139.15 E
Okabe, Nihon	94	34.55 N	138.17 E
Okagaki	96	33.50 N	130.38 E
Okahandja	156	21.59 S	16.58 E
Okahandja □[5]	156	21.30 S	17.00 E
Okahukura	172	38.47 S	175.13 E
Okahumpka	220	28.45 N	81.54 W
Okaihau	172	35.19 S	173.47 E
Okalataka	152	0.20 S	14.59 E
Okaloacoochee Slough ≃	220	26.16 N	81.17 W
Okam	130	40.53 N	42.36 E
Okamoto	270	34.59 N	135.58 E
Okamoto ⊸[8]	270	34.44 N	135.16 E
Okanagan (Okanogan) ≃	182	48.06 N	119.43 W
Okanagan Centre	182	50.03 N	119.27 W
Okanagan Falls	182	49.21 N	119.34 W
Okanagan Indian Reserve ⊸[4]	182	50.21 N	119.17 W
Okanagan Lake ⊜	182	50.00 N	119.28 W
Okanagan Landing	182	50.14 N	119.22 W
Okanagan Range ⛰	202	48.40 N	119.45 W
Okanda, Parc National de l' ♠	152	0.30 S	11.40 E
Okanogan	202	48.22 N	119.35 W
Okanogan □[6]	224	48.39 N	120.41 W
Okanogan Range (Okanagan Range) ⛰	182	49.00 N	120.00 W
Okapilco Creek ≃	192	30.45 N	83.30 W
Okaputa	156	20.09 S	16.56 E
Okāra	123	30.49 N	73.27 E
Okarche	196	35.44 N	97.58 W
Okarito	172	43.14 S	170.11 E
Okasaki	270	34.46 N	135.52 E
Okato	172	39.12 S	173.53 E
Okau	174q	9.32 N	138.06 E
Okauchee	216	43.07 N	88.26 W
Okauchee Lake ⊜	216	43.07 N	88.26 W
Okaukuejo	156	19.10 S	15.54 E
Okavango (Cubango) ≃	138	18.50 S	22.25 E
Okavango Swamp ☷	156	18.45 S	22.45 E
Ōkawa, Nihon	92	33.12 N	130.23 E
Ōkawa, Nihon	94	35.05 N	138.15 E
Ōkawa, Nihon	96	33.47 N	133.26 E
Ōkawachi	96	35.04 N	134.45 E
Ōkawado	268	35.56 N	139.49 E
Okawville	219	38.26 N	89.33 W
Okaya	94	36.03 N	138.03 E
Okayama	96	34.39 N	133.55 E
Okayama □[5]	96	35.00 N	134.00 E
Okayama-heiya ≚	92	34.35 N	133.51 E
Okazaki	94	34.57 N	137.10 E
Okch'ŏn	98	36.20 N	127.34 E
Oke-Aro	273a	6.41 N	3.19 E
Okeechobee	220	27.15 N	80.50 W
Okeechobee □[6]	220	27.25 N	80.52 W
Okeechobee, Lake ⊜	220	26.55 N	80.45 W
O'Keefe Centre ☩	275b	43.37 N	79.22 W
Okeene	196	36.07 N	98.19 W
Okefenokee Swamp ☷	192	30.42 N	82.20 W
Okegawa	94	36.00 N	139.35 E
Okehampton	42	50.44 N	4.00 W
Oke-Igbo	150	7.09 N	4.43 E
Okemah	196	35.26 N	96.19 W
Okemasis and Beardy Indian Reserve ⊸[4]	184	52.48 N	106.20 W
Okement ≃	42	50.50 N	4.01 W
Okemos	216	42.43 N	84.26 W
Okene	150	7.33 N	6.15 E
Oke-Ode	150	8.33 N	5.02 E
Oke Ogbe	273a	6.24 N	3.23 E
Oker	52	51.54 N	10.29 E
Oker ≃	54	52.30 N	10.22 E
Okere ≃	154	2.07 N	33.55 E
Oker Talsperre ⊸[6]	52	51.48 N	10.27 E
Okhaldhunga	124	27.19 N	86.30 E
Okhla ⊸[8]	272a	28.34 N	77.18 E
Okhotsk, Sea of (Ochotskoje More) ⊤[2]	74	53.00 N	150.00 E
Okhotsk Basin ✢[1]	12	53.00 N	148.00 E
Okiep	156	29.39 S	17.53 E
Oki-guntō II	92	36.15 N	133.15 E
Okinawa □[5]	93b	26.31 N	127.59 E
Okinawa-jima I	174m	26.30 N	128.00 E
Okino-Daitō-jima I	90	24.28 N	131.11 E
Okino-Erabu-shima I	93b	27.22 N	128.35 E
Okinokami-shima I	175d	24.11 N	123.33 E
Okino-Kl'uči	88	50.36 N	107.06 E
Okino-shima I, Nihon	94	35.12 N	136.04 E
Okino-shima I, Nihon	96	34.07 N	135.06 E
Okino-Tori-Shima I	90	20.25 N	136.00 E
Okinskij Chrebet ⛰	88	53.10 N	99.50 E
Okitipupa	150	6.29 N	4.46 E
Okitsu-zaki ≻	96	33.09 N	133.14 E
Okkang-ni	98	40.18 N	124.42 E
Okkerbil' ≃	265a	59.56 N	30.26 E
Okladnevo	76	58.36 N	33.39 E
Oklahoma, Pa., U.S.	214	41.07 N	78.44 W
Oklahoma, Pa., U.S.	279b	40.35 N	79.35 W
Oklahoma □[3]	178		
	196	35.30 N	98.00 W
Oklahoma City	196	35.28 N	97.32 W
Oklawaha	220	29.03 N	81.56 W
Oklawaha ≃	192	29.28 N	81.41 W
Oklee	198	47.50 N	95.51 W
Okmulgee	196	35.37 N	95.58 W
Oknica	78	48.24 N	27.29 E
Okno	78	48.34 N	25.58 E
Oko, Wādī ∨	140	21.15 N	35.56 E
Okobojo Creek ≃	198	44.38 N	100.28 W
Ōkōchi	94	35.09 N	138.22 E
Okok ≃	154	2.06 N	33.53 E
Okoka	152	2.57 S	23.27 E
Okola	152	4.01 N	11.23 E
Okollo	154	2.40 N	31.08 E
Okolo	152	3.46 S	23.55 E
Okolona, Ark., U.S.	194	34.00 N	93.20 W
Okolona, Ky., U.S.	194	38.08 N	85.41 W
Okolona, Miss., U.S.	194	34.00 N	88.45 W
Okombahe	156	21.23 S	15.22 E
Okondja	152	0.41 S	13.47 E
Okonek	30	53.33 N	16.50 E
Okonešnikovo	86	54.50 N	75.05 E
Okorokovo	82	54.02 N	36.40 E
Okotoks	182	50.44 N	113.59 W
Okoyo	152	1.28 S	15.04 E
Okpara ≃	150	7.40 N	2.35 E
Okrika	150	4.47 N	7.04 E
Oksbøl	26	55.38 N	8.17 E
Okskij Zapovednik ⊸[4]	80	54.45 N	40.45 E
Oksko-Donskaja Ravnina ≚	80	53.00 N	40.30 E
Oksovskij	24	62.37 N	39.55 E
Oksskolten ∧	24	65.59 N	14.15 E
Oksu ≃, S.S.S.R.	85	40.12 N	69.16 E
Oksu ≃, S.S.S.R.	85	38.09 N	73.57 E
Okt'abr', S.S.S.R.	76	57.50 N	37.26 E
Okt'abr', S.S.S.R.	85	43.41 N	77.12 E
Okt'abr', S.S.S.R.	86	45.45 N	61.34 E
Okt'abr'sk	80	53.11 N	48.40 E
Okt'abr'skij, S.S.S.R.	24	61.04 N	43.08 E
Okt'abr'skij, S.S.S.R.	24	59.29 N	48.50 E
Okt'abr'skij, S.S.S.R.	76	52.38 N	28.53 E
Okt'abr'skij, S.S.S.R.	76	53.47 N	39.29 E
Okt'abr'skij, S.S.S.R.	78	44.56 N	39.00 E
Okt'abr'skij, S.S.S.R.	78	50.26 N	36.22 E
Okt'abr'skij, S.S.S.R.	80	54.28 N	53.28 E
Okt'abr'skij, S.S.S.R.	80	57.08 N	40.20 E
Okt'abr'skij, S.S.S.R.	80	56.17 N	44.12 E
Okt'abr'skij, S.S.S.R.	80	47.58 N	43.38 E
Okt'abr'skij, S.S.S.R.	80	58.19 N	44.19 E
Okt'abr'skij, S.S.S.R.	80	56.35 N	53.58 E
Okt'abr'skij, S.S.S.R.	82	54.14 N	38.54 E
Okt'abr'skij, S.S.S.R.	82	55.37 N	37.58 E
Okt'abr'skij, S.S.S.R.	83	47.28 N	40.04 E
Okt'abr'skij, S.S.S.R.	85	38.33 N	68.22 E
Okt'abr'skij, S.S.S.R.	86	49.38 N	83.35 E
Okt'abr'skij, S.S.S.R.	86	56.31 N	57.12 E
Okt'abr'skij, S.S.S.R.	86	52.35 N	62.40 E
Okt'abr'skij, S.S.S.R.	88	50.04 N	118.04 E
Okt'abr'skij, S.S.S.R.	88	56.05 N	99.26 E
Okt'abr'skij, S.S.S.R.	89	53.01 N	128.37 E
Okt'abr'skij, S.S.S.R.	89	49.02 N	140.11 E
Okt'abr'skoje, S.S.S.R.	74	62.28 N	66.03 E
Okt'abr'skoje, S.S.S.R.	76	52.18 N	39.44 E
Okt'abr'skoje, S.S.S.R.	78	45.18 N	34.09 E
Okt'abr'skoje, S.S.S.R.	78	48.38 N	33.04 E
Okt'abr'skoje, S.S.S.R.	80	45.37 N	42.49 E
Okt'abr'skoje, S.S.S.R.	80	52.54 N	46.30 E
Okt'abr'skoje, S.S.S.R.	83	48.28 N	37.22 E
Okt'abr'skoje, S.S.S.R.	86	52.07 N	65.40 E
Okt'abr'skoje, S.S.S.R.	86	54.26 N	62.44 E
Okt'abr'skoje, S.S.S.R.	86	52.20 N	55.30 E
Okt'abr'skoj Revol'ucii, Ostrov I	74	79.30 N	97.00 E
Oktember'an	84	40.09 N	44.02 E
Oktong-ni	98	38.27 N	127.07 E
Oktwin	110	18.49 N	96.26 E
Oktyabr'skiy → Okt'abr'skij	80	54.28 N	53.28 E
Oku	96	34.40 N	134.05 E
Ōkubo, Nihon	268	35.21 N	139.56 E
Ōkubo, Nihon	270	34.41 N	134.47 E
Ōkubo ⊸[8]	268	35.24 N	139.35 E
Okučani	36	45.16 N	17.12 E
Ōkuchi, Nihon	92	32.04 N	130.37 E
Okuchi, Nihon	94	36.17 N	136.39 E
Okuku ≃	172	43.16 S	172.28 E
Okulovka	76	58.26 N	33.18 E
Okuma Bay C	9	77.48 S	158.35 W
Okumi	84	42.43 N	41.45 E
Okumyōgata	94	35.51 N	137.02 E
Okundi	150	6.22 N	8.44 E
Okun'ov Nos	24	66.15 N	52.28 E
Ōkura-yama ∧	96	35.08 N	133.22 E
Okusawa ⊸[8]	268	35.36 N	139.40 E
Okushiri	92a	42.10 N	139.31 E
Okushiri-tō I	92a	42.10 N	139.27 E
Ōkusu-yama ∧	268	35.15 N	139.38 E
Okuta	150	9.14 N	3.15 E
Okutadami Dam ⊸[6]	94	37.09 N	139.15 E
Okutama-ko ⊜	94	35.47 N	139.02 E
Okutango-hantō ≻[1]	96	35.40 N	135.10 E
Okutsu	96	35.14 N	133.56 E
Ōkuwa	94	35.41 N	137.40 E
Okwa ≃	156	22.30 S	23.00 E
Okwoga	150	7.01 N	7.50 E
Olá, Pan.	236	8.25 N	80.39 W
Ola, S.S.S.R.	74	59.35 N	151.17 E
Ola, Ark., U.S.	194	35.02 N	93.13 W
Ola ≃	76	52.41 N	29.39 E
Ólafsfjörður	24a	66.06 N	18.38 W
Olancha	204	36.17 N	118.01 W
Olancha Peak ∧	204	36.16 N	118.07 W
Olanchito	236	15.30 N	86.35 W
Olancho □[5]	236	14.45 N	86.00 W
Öland I	26	56.45 N	16.38 E
Olandsån ≃	40	60.20 N	18.14 E
Olango Island I	116	10.16 N	124.03 E
Olanta	192	33.58 N	79.56 W
Olar	192	33.11 N	81.11 W
Olarevo	76	59.22 N	40.04 E
Olaria, Bra.	256	21.52 S	43.56 W
Olaria, Bra.	287a	22.41 S	43.08 W
Olaria ⊸[8]	287a	22.52 S	43.15 W
Olary	166	32.17 S	140.19 E
Olascoaga	252	35.12 S	60.36 W
Olasore	273a	6.40 N	3.17 E
Olathe, Colo., U.S.	200	38.36 N	107.59 W
Olathe, Kans., U.S.	198	38.53 N	94.49 W
Olavarría	252	36.54 S	60.17 W
Olavinlinna ⊥	26	61.52 N	29.00 E
Oława	30	50.57 N	17.17 E
Olbernhau	54	50.39 N	13.20 E
Olbersdorf	54	50.52 N	14.46 E
Olbersleben	54	51.09 N	11.20 E
Olbia	71	40.55 N	9.31 E
Olbia, Golfo di C	71	40.55 N	9.39 E
Ølby Lyng	41	55.29 N	12.09 E
Olca, Volcán ∧[1]	248	20.57 S	68.30 W
Ol'chi	80	53.53 N	41.28 E
Ol'chon, Ostrov I	88	53.09 N	107.24 E
Ol'chovaja ≃, S.S.S.R.	80	48.47 N	40.51 E
Ol'chovaja ≃, S.S.S.R.	83	48.35 N	39.17 E
Ol'chovatka, S.S.S.R.	78	50.18 N	39.17 E
Ol'chovatka, S.S.S.R.	83	48.15 N	38.25 E
Ol'chovčik ⊸[8]	83	48.04 N	38.31 E
Ol'chovka, S.S.S.R.	80	49.52 N	44.34 E
Ol'chovka, S.S.S.R.	86	56.22 N	63.46 E
Ol'chovka ⊸[8]	83	48.24 N	39.07 E
Ol'chovoje	83	48.40 N	39.34 E
Olcott	210	43.20 N	78.43 W
Old ≃, Calif., U.S.	226	38.04 N	121.35 W
Old ≃, Tex., U.S.	222	30.25 N	96.19 W
Old Bahama Channel ⋓	238	22.30 N	78.50 W
Old Bedford ≃	42	52.35 N	0.20 E
Old Bennington	210	42.52 N	73.13 W
Old Bethpage	276	40.45 N	73.28 W
Old Bethpage Village ⊥	276	40.47 N	73.28 W
Old Bight	238	24.15 N	75.21 W
Old Brazoria	222	29.04 N	95.34 W
Old Bridge	276	40.25 N	74.22 W
Old Brookville	276	40.49 N	73.36 W
Oldbury	42	52.30 N	2.00 W
Old Cairo → Miṣr al-Qadīmah ⊸[8]	273c	30.00 N	31.14 E
Oldcastle	48	53.46 N	7.10 W
Old Colwyn	44	53.18 N	3.43 W
Old Cork	166	22.56 S	141.52 E
Old Crow	180	67.35 N	139.50 W
Old Crow ≃	180	67.35 N	139.50 W
Oldeani	154	3.21 S	35.33 E
Oldebroek	52	52.26 N	5.54 E
Old Economy ⊥	279b	40.36 N	80.14 W
Olden, Nor.	26	61.50 N	6.49 E
Olden, Tex., U.S.	196	32.25 N	98.45 W
Oldenbrok	52	53.17 N	8.23 E
Oldenburg, B.R.D.	52	53.08 N	8.13 E
Oldenburg, Ind., U.S.	218	39.20 N	85.12 W
Oldenburg □[6]	52	53.10 N	8.10 E
Oldenburg in Holstein	54	54.17 N	10.52 E
Oldendorf	52	53.35 N	9.14 E
Oldenstadt	52	52.58 N	10.35 E
Oldenswort	41	54.22 N	8.56 E
Oldenzaal	52	52.19 N	6.56 E
Oldersum	52	53.20 N	7.20 E
Old Faithful Geyser ⊤[4]	202	44.30 N	110.45 W
Old Farm	284c	39.03 N	77.09 W
Old Field	276	40.57 N	73.08 W
Old Field Point ≻	276	40.58 N	73.07 W
Old Fletton	42	52.33 N	0.15 W
Old Ford Mountain ∧	182	55.05 N	126.30 W
Old Forge, N.Y., U.S.	188	43.43 N	74.58 W
Old Forge, Pa., U.S.	210	41.22 N	75.44 W
Old Forge Village	276	40.49 N	74.29 W
Old Fort	214	41.15 N	83.09 W
Old Fort Bay	186	51.26 N	57.49 W
Old Fort Erie ⊥	284a	42.53 N	78.56 W
Old Fort Henry ⊥	212	44.14 N	76.28 W
Old Fort Niagara ⊥	210	43.16 N	79.03 W
Old Fort Parker State Historic Site ⊥	222	31.34 N	96.34 W
Old Fort Point ≻	240b	25.03 N	77.29 W
Old Greenwich	276	41.02 N	73.34 W
Oldham, Eng., U.K.	44	53.33 N	2.07 W
Oldham, S. Dak., U.S.	198	44.14 N	97.19 W
Oldham □[6]	218	38.23 N	85.27 W
Oldham □[8]	262	53.34 N	2.03 W
Oldham Pines	283	42.05 N	70.50 W
Oldham Pond ⊜	283	42.03 N	70.51 W
Oldham Village	207	42.04 N	70.50 W
Old Harbor	180	57.12 N	153.19 W
Old Harbour	241q	17.56 N	77.07 W
Old Hickory Lake ⊜[1]	194	36.18 N	86.30 W
Old Howe ≃	44	53.57 N	0.21 W
Oldisleben	54	51.18 N	11.10 E
Old Lyme	207	41.19 N	72.20 W
Old Malden ⊸[8]	260	51.23 N	0.15 W
Oldman ≃	182	49.56 N	111.42 W
Old Man House ⊥	224	47.43 N	122.34 W
Old Man Mountain ∧	186	49.08 N	57.43 W
Old Manor	276	40.24 N	74.11 W
Oldmans Creek ≃	208	39.47 N	75.27 W
Oldmeldrum	46	57.20 N	2.20 W
Old Mkushi	154	14.22 S	29.22 E
Old Monroe	219	38.56 N	90.45 W
Old Mystic	207	41.23 N	71.58 W
Old Nene ≃	42	52.40 N	0.10 E
Old Noranside	166	22.13 S	140.04 E
Old North Church ☩[1]	283	42.22 N	71.03 W
Old Ocean	222	29.05 N	95.45 W
Ol Doinyo National Park ♠	154	1.09 S	37.12 E
Ol'doj ≃	89	53.33 N	123.21 E
Old Orchard ⊸[9]	278	42.04 N	87.45 W
Old Orchard Beach	188	43.31 N	70.23 W
Old Perlican	186	48.05 N	53.01 W
Old Place Creek ≃	276	40.38 N	74.12 W
Old Point Comfort ≻	208	37.00 N	76.19 W
Old Rhodes Key I	220	25.22 N	80.14 W
Old Ripley	219	38.54 N	89.34 W
Old Road	240c	17.01 N	61.50 W
Old Road Bay C	284b	39.12 N	76.27 W
Old Road Bluff ≻	240c	16.59 N	61.50 W
Old Round Rock	222	30.31 N	97.42 W
Olds	182	51.47 N	114.06 W
Old Saybrook	207	41.18 N	72.23 W
Oldsmar	220	28.02 N	82.40 W
Old Speck Mountain ∧	188	44.34 N	70.57 W
Old Sturbridge Village ⊥	207	42.07 N	72.07 W
Old Swamp ≃	283	42.11 N	70.57 W
Old Swedes Church ☩[1]	285	39.44 N	75.32 W
Old Tampa Bay C	220	27.56 N	82.35 W
Old Tappan	276	41.01 N	73.59 W
Old Tate	156	21.22 S	27.46 E
Old Town	188	44.56 N	68.39 W
Old Trafford Cricket Ground ♠	262	53.28 N	2.17 W
Old Trap	192	36.15 N	76.02 W
Olduvai Gorge ∨	154	2.58 S	35.22 E
Old Westbury	276	40.47 N	73.37 W
Old Westbury Gardens ♠	276	40.46 N	73.36 W
Oldwick	210	40.40 N	74.45 W
Old Windsor	260	51.28 N	0.35 W
Old Wives Lake ⊜	184	50.06 N	106.00 W
Old Woman Creek ≃	198	43.19 N	104.21 W
Öldzijt, Mong.	88	48.10 N	102.34 E
Öldzijt, Mong.	102	45.20 N	106.20 E
Old Zoinsville	208	40.29 N	75.31 W
Olean	210	42.05 N	78.26 W
Olean Creek ≃	210	42.04 N	78.25 W
O'Leary	186	46.42 N	64.13 W
Olecko	30	54.03 N	22.30 E
Olegário Maciel	256	22.19 S	45.35 W
Oleggio	62	45.36 N	8.38 E
Olekma → Ol'okma ≃	74	60.22 N	120.42 E
Olema	24	64.30 N	46.08 E
Olen, Bel.	56	51.09 N	4.51 E
Ølen, Nor.	26	59.36 N	5.48 E
Ölen ⊜	40	59.13 N	14.31 E
Olenegorsk	24	68.09 N	33.15 E
Olenevka	78	45.23 N	32.32 E
Olenguj ≃	88	51.46 N	113.46 E
Olenica	24	66.29 N	35.20 E
Olenij, Ostrov I	74	72.25 N	77.45 E
Olenino	76	56.12 N	33.29 E
Olenja Rečka	86	52.48 N	93.14 E
Olen'kovo	82	54.34 N	38.06 E
Olen'ok	74	68.33 N	112.18 E
Olen'ok ≃	74	73.00 N	119.55 E
Olen'okskij Zaliv C	74	73.20 N	121.00 E
Olentangy ≃	214	39.58 N	83.06 W
Olenty	80	50.02 N	52.07 E
Olenty ≃	80	49.50 N	52.03 E
Oleopolis	214	41.27 N	79.37 W
Oléron, Île d' I	32	45.56 N	1.15 W
Olesko	78	49.58 N	24.53 E
Olešná	60	49.46 N	13.48 E
Oleśnica	30	51.13 N	17.23 E
Olesno	30	50.53 N	18.25 E
Olevano Romano	66	41.52 N	13.02 E
Olevano sul Tusciano	68	40.40 N	15.01 E
Olevsk	78	51.13 N	27.39 E
Olevuga I	175e	8.58 S	160.05 E
Oley	208	40.23 N	75.47 W
Olfen	52	51.42 N	7.23 E
Ol'ga, S.S.S.R.	89	43.45 N	135.18 E
Olga, Wash., U.S.	224	48.37 N	122.50 W
Olga, Mount ∧, Austl.	162	25.19 S	130.46 E
Olga, Mount ∧, Vt., U.S.	207	42.51 N	72.48 W
Olgiata	267a	42.02 N	12.22 E
Olgiate Comasco	62	45.48 N	8.58 E
Olgiate Olona	62	45.38 N	8.53 E
Ölgij, Mong.	86	48.59 N	92.01 E
Ölgij, Mong.	86	48.56 N	89.57 E
Olginate	62	45.48 N	9.24 E
Ol'ginka, S.S.S.R.	78	44.14 N	38.53 E
Ol'ginka, S.S.S.R.	83	47.42 N	37.31 E
Ol'gino, S.S.S.R.	86	54.59 N	71.54 E
Ol'gino, S.S.S.R.	89	52.53 N	125.47 E
Ol'gino ⊸[8]	265a	60.00 N	30.09 E
Ol'ginskaja, S.S.S.R.	78	45.57 N	38.34 E
Ol'ginskaja, S.S.S.R.	83	47.11 N	39.56 E
Ølgod	26	55.49 N	8.37 E
Ol'gopol'	78	48.12 N	29.29 E
Ol'govo	82	56.16 N	37.21 E
Olhão	34	37.02 N	8.50 W
Ôlho d'Água das Cunhãs	250	4.43 S	44.34 W
Ôlho-d'Água das Flores	250	9.33 S	37.17 W
Oli ≃	150	9.45 N	4.38 E
Olib, Otok I	36	44.22 N	14.48 E
Oliden	258	35.11 S	57.57 W
Oliena	71	40.16 N	9.24 E
Olifants (Rio dos Elefantes) ≃, Afr.	156	24.10 S	32.40 E
Olifants ≃, Namibia	156	25.30 S	19.30 E
Olifants ≃, S. Afr.	158	31.42 S	18.12 E
Olifants ≃, S. Afr.	158	33.41 S	21.42 E
Olifantshoek	158	27.57 S	22.42 E
Olifantsrivierberge ⛰	158	32.40 S	19.00 E
Oliki	265a	59.46 N	29.55 E
Olimarao I[1]	108	7.41 N	145.52 E
Olimbía ⊥	38	37.38 N	21.41 E
Ólimbos	38	35.44 N	27.11 E
Ólimbos ∧, Ellás	38	40.05 N	22.21 E
Ólimbos ∧, Kípros	130	34.56 N	32.52 E
Olímpia	255	20.44 S	48.54 W
Olímpico, Estadio ♠	286a	19.20 N	99.12 W
Olímpio Noronha	256	22.04 S	45.16 W
Olimpo → Ólimbos ∧	38	40.05 N	22.21 E
Olin	190	42.00 N	91.09 W
Olinalá	234	17.50 N	98.51 W
Olinda, Austl.	170	32.50 S	150.08 E
Olinda, Austl.	274b	37.51 S	145.22 E
Olinda, Bra.	250	8.01 S	34.51 W
Olinda, Bra.	256	22.49 S	43.25 W
Olinda, Mount ∧	274b	37.52 S	145.21 E
Olinda Creek ≃	274b	37.41 S	145.21 E
Olindina	250	11.22 S	38.21 W
Olinsk	88	52.24 N	116.13 E
Olio	166	21.54 S	143.13 E
Olišovka	78	51.13 N	31.18 E
Olite	34	42.29 N	1.39 W
Oliva, Arg.	252	32.03 S	63.34 W
Oliva, Esp.	34	38.55 N	0.07 W
Oliva de la Frontera	34	38.16 N	6.55 W
Olivais ⊸[8]	266c	38.46 N	9.06 E
Olival Basto	266c	38.47 N	9.10 W
Olive Branch	194	34.58 N	89.50 W
Olivebridge	210	41.55 N	74.13 W
Olive Hill	218	38.16 N	83.10 W
Olivehurst	226	39.06 N	121.34 W
Oliveira	255	20.41 S	44.49 W
Oliveira dos Brejinhos	255	12.19 S	42.54 W
Oliveira Fortes	256	21.20 S	43.27 W
Oliveira Salazar, Barragem ⊸[6]	156	19.08 S	33.00 E
Olivelifuri I	122	5.17 N	73.35 E
Olive Mount ⊸[8]	262	53.24 N	2.55 W
Olivença	154	11.47 S	35.13 E
Olivenza	34	38.41 N	7.06 W
Oliver	182	49.11 N	119.33 W
Olivera	258	34.38 S	59.15 W
Oliver Creek ≃	222	33.06 N	97.17 W
Oliver Ditch ☲	216	41.00 N	87.10 W
Oliverea	210	42.04 N	74.28 W
Oliveri	70	38.07 N	15.03 E
Oliver Lake ⊜	184	56.56 N	103.22 W
Oliver Springs	192	36.03 N	84.20 W
Olivet, Fr.	50	47.52 N	1.54 E
Olivet, Mich., U.S.	216	42.27 N	84.56 W
Olivet, S. Dak., U.S.	198	43.14 N	97.40 W
Oliveto Citra	68	40.41 N	15.14 E
Oliveto Lucano	68	40.32 N	16.11 E
Olivette	219	38.40 N	90.24 W
Olivia	198	44.46 N	94.59 W
Olivine Range ⛰	172	44.18 S	168.30 E
Olivo	116	10.52 N	123.53 E
Olivo ≃	70	37.22 N	14.15 E
Olivone	58	46.32 N	8.57 E
Olivos ⊸[8]	258	34.32 S	58.29 W
Öljaren ⊜	40	59.08 N	16.02 E
Olla	194	31.54 N	92.14 W
Ollagüe	248	21.14 S	68.16 W
Ollagüe, Volcán ∧[1]	248	21.18 S	68.12 W
Ollainville	261	48.35 N	2.13 E
Ollantaytambo	248	13.16 S	72.16 W
Ollatrim ≃	48	52.52 N	8.13 W
Ollerton, Eng., U.K.	44	53.12 N	1.00 W
Ollerton, Eng., U.K.	262	53.17 N	2.20 W
Ollerup	41	55.04 N	10.30 E
Olliergues	62	45.40 N	3.38 E
Ollioules	62	43.08 N	5.51 E
Ollomont	62	45.50 N	7.22 E
Ollon	58	46.18 N	7.00 E
Olloua	152	0.56 S	14.34 E
Olmedillo de Roa	34	41.47 N	3.56 W
Olmedo, Esp.	34	41.23 N	4.41 W
Olmedo, It.	71	40.39 N	8.23 E
Olmo al Brembo	58	45.58 N	9.39 E
Olmos	248	5.59 S	79.46 W
Olmsted	214	41.24 N	81.44 W
Olmsted Falls	279a	41.22 N	81.55 W
Olmütz → Olomouc	30	49.36 N	17.16 E
Olney, Eng., U.K.	42	52.81 N	0.43 W
Olney, Ill., U.S.	194	38.44 N	88.05 W
Olney, Mo., U.S.	219	39.05 N	91.15 W
Olney, Tex., U.S.	196	33.22 N	98.45 W
Olney ⊸[8]	285	40.02 N	75.08 W
Olofström	26	56.16 N	14.30 E
Oloj ≃	74	66.29 N	159.29 E
Ol'okma ≃	74	60.22 N	120.42 E
Ol'okminsk	74	60.24 N	120.24 E
Ol'okminskij Stanovik ⛰	88	54.30 N	120.00 E
Olokui ∧	229a	21.08 N	156.51 W
Olomane ≃	186	50.14 N	60.37 W
Olombo	152	1.18 S	15.53 E
Olomega, Laguna de ⊜	236	13.19 N	88.04 W
Olomouc	30	49.36 N	17.16 E
Olona ≃	62	45.06 N	9.21 E
Olonec	24	61.00 N	32.57 E
Olongapo	116	14.50 N	120.16 E
Olonki	88	52.54 N	103.45 E
Olorgasailie National Monument ♠	154	1.40 S	36.22 E
Oloron, Gave d' ≃	32	43.33 N	1.05 W
Oloron-Sainte-Marie	32	43.12 N	0.36 W
Olosega	174y	14.11 S	169.39 W
Olosega I	174y	14.11 S	169.39 W
Olot	34	42.11 N	2.29 E
Olov'annaja, S.S.S.R.	88	50.56 N	115.35 E
Olov'annaja, S.S.S.R.	180	66.10 N	178.59 W
Oloví	54	50.11 N	12.33 E
Olpe, B.R.D.	56	51.02 N	7.52 E
Olpe, Kans., U.S.	198	38.16 N	96.10 W
Olperer ∧	64	47.03 N	11.39 E
Ol'ša	76	54.51 N	31.52 E
Olsabach ≃	61	46.56 N	14.25 E
Ol'šana, S.S.S.R.	78	49.13 N	31.13 E
Ol'šana, S.S.S.R.	78	49.47 N	37.46 E
Ol'šana, S.S.S.R.	78	50.48 N	34.02 E
Ol'šanka, S.S.S.R.	78	48.14 N	30.52 E
Ol'šanka, S.S.S.R.	78	51.46 N	35.25 E
Olšany, Česko.	60	49.24 N	13.38 E
Ol'šany, S.S.S.R.	78	52.05 N	27.20 E
Ol'šany, S.S.S.R.	78	50.03 N	35.53 E
Olsberg	56	51.21 N	8.29 E
Ølsemagle	41	55.30 N	12.10 E
Olshammar	40	58.45 N	14.48 E
Olst	52	52.20 N	6.06 E
Ølstykke	41	55.47 N	12.11 E
Olsufjevo	76	53.36 N	33.40 E
Olsztyn (Allenstein)	30	53.48 N	20.29 E
Olsztynek	30	53.36 N	20.17 E
Olt □[4]	38	44.20 N	24.30 E
Olt ≃	38	43.43 N	24.51 E
Olta	252	30.37 S	66.16 W
Olten	58	47.21 N	7.54 E
Olteni	38	44.10 N	25.18 E
Oltenița	38	44.05 N	26.39 E
Olteț ≃	38	44.14 N	24.27 E
Olton	196	34.11 N	102.08 W
Oltre il Colle	64	45.54 N	9.46 E
Oltu	130	40.33 N	41.59 E
Oltu ≃	130	40.50 N	41.40 E
Oluan Pi ≻	100	21.54 N	120.51 E
Olukonda	156	18.03 S	16.00 E
Olu Malau Islands II	175e	10.10 S	161.57 E
Olur	130	40.50 N	42.08 E
Olustee, Fla., U.S.	192	30.12 N	82.26 W
Olustee, Okla., U.S.	196	34.33 N	99.25 W
Olustee Creek ≃	192	29.57 N	82.32 W
Oluta	234	17.55 N	94.54 W
Olutanga (Suba Nipa)	116	7.26 N	122.54 E
Olutanga Island I	116	7.22 N	122.52 E
Olutaya Island I	116	11.39 N	122.50 E
Olute	273a	6.28 N	3.16 E
Ol'utorskij, Mys ≻	74	59.55 N	170.27 E
Ol'utorskij Zaliv C	74	59.55 N	170.27 E
Oluwo	273a	6.42 N	3.18 E
Olvenstedt	54	52.09 N	11.34 E
Olvera	34	36.56 N	5.16 W
Olychovatka	78	50.12 N	37.31 E
Olyka	78	50.42 N	25.51 E
Olym	78	51.42 N	38.10 E
Olymp → Ólimbos ∧	38	40.05 N	22.21 E
Olympe, Mont → Ólimbos ∧	38	40.05 N	22.21 E
Olympia	224	47.03 N	122.53 W
Olympia → Olimbía ⊥	38	37.38 N	21.41 E
Olympia Fields	216	41.32 N	87.42 W
Olympia Heights	220	25.43 N	80.17 W
Olympia-Stadion ♠	264a	52.31 N	13.14 E
Olympia Stadium ♠	281	42.21 N	83.06 W
Olympic Mountains ⛰	224	47.50 N	123.45 W
Olympic National Park ♠	224	47.48 N	123.30 W
Olympic Park ♠	274b	37.49 S	144.59 E
Olympic Valley	226	39.13 N	120.14 W
Olympic View	224	47.43 N	122.45 W
Olympieion ⊥	267c	37.58 N	23.44 E
Olympus, Mount → Ólimbos ∧, Ellás	38	40.05 N	22.21 E
Olympus, Mount ∧, Ky., U.S.	192	38.03 N	83.39 W
Olympus, Mount ∧, Wash., U.S.	224	47.48 N	123.43 W
Olyphant	210	41.28 N	75.37 W
Olzai	71	40.11 N	9.09 E
Ol'zony	88	52.57 N	105.15 E
Om' ≃	86	54.59 N	73.22 E
Ōmachi, Nihon	94	36.30 N	137.52 E
Ōmachi, Nihon	270	34.28 N	135.25 E
Omaezaki	94	34.35 N	138.13 E
Omae-zaki ≻	94	34.36 N	138.14 E
Ōmagari	92	39.27 N	140.29 E
Omagh, Ont., Can.	275b	43.30 N	79.49 W
Omagh, N. Ire., U.K.	48	54.36 N	7.18 W
Ōmagi	268	35.52 N	139.42 E
Omaguas	246	4.08 S	73.15 W
Omaha, Nebr., U.S.	198	41.16 N	95.57 W
Omaha, Tex., U.S.	222	33.11 N	94.45 W
Omaha Indian Reservation ⊸[4]	198	42.08 N	96.22 W
Omak	202	48.24 N	119.31 W
Omakau	172	45.05 S	169.36 E
Omak Lake ⊜	202	48.16 N	119.23 W
Omalo	84	42.23 N	45.38 E
Omal'skij Chrebet ⛰	89	52.47 N	137.30 E
Ōmama	94	36.26 N	139.17 E
Oman □[1]	118	22.00 N	58.00 E
Oman, Gulf of C	118	24.30 N	58.30 E
Omar	192	37.46 N	82.00 W
Omarama	172	44.29 S	169.58 E
'Omar Gambon	144	3.12 N	45.50 E
Omaruru	156	21.28 S	15.56 E
Omaruru □[5]	156	21.00 S	15.45 E
Omaruru ≃	156	22.07 S	14.15 E
Omas	248	12.31 S	76.17 W
Omatako ∧	156	21.07 S	16.43 E
Omate	248	16.41 S	70.59 W
Omatena	115b	9.53 S	119.47 E
Ōma-zaki ≻	92a	41.32 N	140.55 E
Ombella-Mpoko □[5]	152	5.00 N	18.00 E
Omberg ∧[2]	26	58.20 N	14.39 E
Ombersley	42	52.17 N	2.13 W
Ombombo	156	18.43 S	13.53 E
Omboué	152	1.34 S	9.15 E
Ombrone ≃	66	42.39 N	11.00 E
Ombúes de Lavalle	258	33.55 S	57.47 W
Ombutosu ∧	156	21.22 S	16.50 E
Ombwe	154	4.22 S	25.35 E
Omčak	74	61.38 N	147.55 E
Omčaly	128	40.47 N	53.43 E
Omdraaisvlei	158	30.08 S	23.08 E
Omdurman → Umm Durmān	140	15.38 N	32.30 E
Ōme	94	35.47 N	139.15 E
Omega, Ga., U.S.	192	31.21 N	83.36 W
Omega, Ohio, U.S.	218	39.09 N	82.55 W
Omegna	62	45.53 N	8.24 E
Omel'nik	78	49.12 N	33.32 E
Omemee	212	44.18 N	78.33 W
Omeo	166	37.06 S	147.36 E
Ömerin	130	37.18 N	42.04 E
Ömerköy	130	39.48 N	28.03 E
Ömerli	130	41.05 N	29.19 E
Omerville	206	45.17 N	72.07 W
Ometepe, Isla de I	236	11.30 N	85.35 W
Ometepec	234	16.41 N	98.25 W
Ometepec ≃	234	16.30 N	98.45 W

Symbols in the index entries represent the broad categories identified in the key at the right. Symbols with superior numbers (⛰[2]) identify subcategories (see complete key on page I · 30).

Kartensymbole in dem Registerverzeichnis stellen die rechts in Schlüssel erklärten Kategorien dar. Symbole mit hochgestellten Ziffern (⛰[2]) bezeichnen Unterabteilungen einer Kategorie (vgl. vollständiger Schlüssel auf Seite I · 30).

Los símbolos incluídos en el texto del índice representan las grandes categorias identificadas con la clave a la derecha. Los símbolos con numeros en su parte superior (⛰[2]) identifican las subcategorías (véase la clave completa en la página I · 30).

Les symboles de l'index représentent les catégories indiquées dans la légende à droite. Les symboles suivis d'un indice (⛰[2]) représentent des sous-catégories (voir légende complète à la page I · 30).

Os símbolos incluídos no texto do índice representam as grandes categorias identificadas com a chave à direita. Os símbolos com números em sua parte superior (⛰[2]) identificam as subcategorias (veja-se a chave completa à página I · 30).

	English	Deutsch	Español	Français	Português
∧	Mountain	Berg	Montaña	Montagne	Montanha
⛰	Mountains	Berge	Montañas	Montagnes	Montanhas
)(	Pass	Pass	Paso	Col	Passo
∨	Valley, Canyon	Tal, Cañon	Valle, Cañón	Vallée, Canyon	Vale, Canhão
≚	Plain	Ebene	Llano	Plaine	Planície
≻	Cape	Kap	Cabo	Cap	Cabo
I	Island	Insel	Isla	Île	Ilha
II	Islands	Inseln	Islas	Îles	Ilhas
⊥	Other Topographic Features	Andere Topographische Objekte	Otros Elementos Topográficos	Autres données topographiques	Outros Elementos Topográficos

ESPAÑOL — Nombre, Página, Lat.°′, Long.°′ W=Oeste
FRANÇAIS — Nom, Page, Lat.°′, Long.°′ W=Ouest
PORTUGUÊS — Nome, Página, Lat.°′, Long.°′ W=Oeste

Om Hajer 144 14.24 N 36.46 E
Omi, Nihon 94 36.27 N 138.03 E
Ōmi, Nihon 94 37.01 N 137.48 E
Ōmi, Nihon 94 35.20 N 136.24 E
Omigawa 94 35.51 N 140.37 E
Ōmi-hachiman 94 35.08 N 136.06 E
Omin 174q 9.36 N 138.10 E
Ōminato → Mutsu 92 41.17 N 141.10 E
Omineca ≃ 182 56.05 N 124.30 W
Omineca Mountains ∧∧ 182 56.00 N 125.00 W
Omin-ni ◂[8] 271b 37.27 N 127.01 E
Ōmino 270 34.32 N 135.33 E
Omišalj 36 45.13 N 14.34 E
Ōmi-shima I 96 34.25 N 131.13 E
Omitara 156 22.18 S 18.01 E
Omitlán ≃ 234 17.06 N 99.34 W
Ōmiya, Nihon 94 35.54 N 139.38 E
Ōmiya, Nihon 94 36.33 N 140.25 E
Ōmiya, Nihon 96 35.35 N 135.06 E
Ōmiya-daichi ∧∧[1] 268 35.56 N 139.38 E
Omiya Park Race Track ♠ 268 35.55 N 139.38 E
Øm Kloster ⊥ 41 56.03 N 9.45 E
Ommaney, Cape ≻ 180 56.10 N 134.39 W
Ommanney Bay C 176 73.07 N 100.11 W
Omme Å ≃ 41 55.53 N 8.40 E
Ommen 52 52.32 N 6.25 E
Ömnödelger 88 47.58 N 109.53 E
Ömnögov' 86 49.08 N 91.43 E
Ömnögov' □[4] 102 43.00 N 104.00 E
Omø I 41 55.09 N 11.10 E
Omo ≃ 144 4.51 N 36.55 E
Omoa, Bahía de C 236 15.45 N 88.10 W
Omodeo, Lago ⊜ 71 40.08 N 8.55 E
Omogo 96 33.41 N 133.02 E
Omoi ≃ 94 36.09 N 139.41 E
Omoko 150 5.20 N 6.39 E
Omole 273a 6.38 N 3.22 E
Omoloj ≃ 74 71.10 N 132.08 E
Omolon ≃ 74 68.42 N 158.36 E
Omono ≃ 92 39.46 N 140.03 E
Omont 56 49.36 N 4.44 E
Omo Ranch 226 38.35 N 120.35 W
Ōmori ◂[8] 268 35.34 N 139.44 E
Omotegō 94 37.03 N 140.18 E
Omrel'kaj ≃ 180 68.34 N 170.30 E
Omro 190 44.02 N 88.44 W
Omsino 80 58.36 N 50.28 E
Omsk 86 55.00 N 73.24 E
Omsukčan 74 62.32 N 155.48 E
O-mu, Mya. 110 22.58 N 99.18 E
Ōmu, Nihon 92a 44.34 N 142.58 E
Omu-Aran 150 8.09 N 5.07 E
Ōmuda → Ōmuta 96 33.02 N 130.27 E
Omul ∧ 38 45.26 N 25.26 E
Omulew ≃ 30 53.05 N 21.32 E
Ōmura 92 32.54 N 129.57 E
Omuramba Omatako ≃ 156 17.59 S 20.30 E
Ōmuro 268 35.54 N 139.58 E
Omurtag 38 43.06 N 26.25 E
Ōmuta 96 33.02 N 130.27 E
Omutinskij 86 56.31 N 67.41 E
Omutninsk 86 58.40 N 52.12 E
Ŏmyŏnbo 98 41.16 N 127.36 E
On 110 21.40 N 106.35 E
Ona, Nor. 26 62.52 N 6.34 E
Ona, Fla., U.S. 220 27.29 N 81.55 W
Ona ≃, S.S.S.R. 86 52.34 N 89.50 E
Ona → Bir'usa ≃, S.S.S.R. 88 57.43 N 95.24 E
Onadikondo 152 3.52 S 24.10 E
Onaga 198 39.29 N 96.10 W
Onagawa 92 38.26 N 141.27 E
Onalaska, Tex., U.S. 222 30.48 N 95.07 W
Onalaska, Wash., U.S. 224 46.35 N 122.42 W
Onalaska, Wis., U.S. 190 43.53 N 91.14 W
Onamia 190 46.04 N 93.40 W
Onancock 208 37.43 N 75.45 W
Onangué, Lac ⊜ 152 0.57 S 10.04 E
Onaping ≃ 190 46.37 N 81.18 W
Onaping Lake ⊜ 190 46.57 N 81.30 W
Onarga 216 40.43 N 88.01 W
Ōnari 268 35.55 N 139.37 E
Onatchiway, Lac ⊜ 186 49.00 N 71.03 W
Onawa 198 42.02 N 96.06 W
Onaway 190 45.21 N 84.14 W
Oncativo 252 31.55 S 63.40 W
Once ◂[8] 288 34.36 S 58.24 W
Onchāi 272b 22.57 N 88.19 E
Onchi 270 34.37 N 135.38 E
Onch'ŏn-dong 98 40.51 N 129.07 E
Oncócua 152 16.34 S 13.28 E
Onda, Bhārat 126 23.08 N 87.12 E
Onda, Esp. 34 39.58 N 0.15 W
Ondangua 156 17.55 S 16.00 E
Ondas, Rio das ≃ 255 12.08 S 45.00 W
Ondava ≃ 30 48.27 N 21.48 E
Onderdijk 52 52.45 N 5.07 E
Onder-Sneeuberg ∧∧ 158 32.10 S 23.47 E
Onderstedorings 158 30.13 S 20.37 E
Ondo, Nig. 150 7.04 N 4.47 E
Ondo, Nihon 96 34.11 N 132.32 E
Ondo-ōhashi ◂[5] 96 34.12 N 132.33 E
Öndörchaan (Cecer Chaan) 88 47.19 N 110.39 E
Öndörchangaj 88 49.20 N 94.50 E
Öndör-Önc 102 45.51 N 103.11 E
Öndöršireet 88 47.27 N 104.50 E
Öndör-Ulaan 88 48.06 N 100.27 E
O'Neals 226 37.08 N 119.42 W
One Arrow Indian Reserve ◂[4] 184 52.48 N 106.03 W
Oneata I 175g 18.27 S 178.29 W
Oneco, Conn., U.S. 207 41.42 N 71.48 W
Oneco, Fla., U.S. 220 27.27 N 82.33 W
Onega 24 63.55 N 38.05 E
Onega ≃ 24 63.58 N 37.55 E
Onega, Lake → Onežskoje Ozero ⊜ 24 61.30 N 35.45 E
Oneglia 62 43.53 N 8.02 E
One Hundred and Two ≃ 194 39.44 N 94.43 W
One Hundred and Two, West Fork ≃ 194 40.26 N 94.49 W
One Hundred Fifty Mile House 182 52.07 N 121.56 W
One Hundred Mile House 182 51.39 N 121.18 W
Oneida, Ill., U.S. 190 41.04 N 90.13 W
Oneida, Ky., U.S. 192 37.16 N 83.39 W
Oneida, N.Y., U.S. 210 43.06 N 75.39 W
Oneida, Ohio, U.S. 218 40.42 N 81.09 W
Oneida, Pa., U.S. 210 40.54 N 76.08 W
Oneida, Tenn., U.S. 192 36.30 N 84.31 W
Oneida □[6] 210 43.10 N 75.20 W
Oneida ≃ 210 43.12 N 76.17 W
Oneida Castle 210 43.05 N 75.40 W
Oneida County Airport ⊠ 210 43.09 N 75.23 W
Oneida Creek ≃ 210 43.10 N 75.44 W
Oneida Indian Reservation ◂[4] 190 44.30 N 88.10 W
Oneida Indian Reserve ◂[4] 214 42.49 N 81.24 W
Oneida Lake ⊜ 210 43.13 N 76.00 W
O'Neil Forebay ⊜[1] 226 37.05 N 121.03 W
O'Neill 198 42.27 N 98.39 W
Onekama 190 44.22 N 86.12 W
Onekotan, Ostrov I 74 49.25 N 154.45 E
Onema 152 4.33 S 24.31 E
Oneman Lake ⊜ 184 50.20 N 94.45 W
Onemen, Zaliv C 180 64.45 N 176.35 E
Oneonta, Ala., U.S. 194 33.57 N 86.29 W
Oneonta, N.Y., U.S. 210 42.27 N 75.04 W
Oneroa I 174k 21.15 S 159.43 W
One Tree Hill 168b 34.43 S 138.46 E
One Tree Hill ∧[2] 274b 37.52 S 145.19 E
One Tree Hill Lookout ♠ 169 36.48 S 144.18 E
Onevai I 174w 21.05 S 175.07 W
Onežskaja Guba C 24 64.20 N 36.30 E
Onežskij Poluostrov ≻[1] 24 64.35 N 38.00 E
Onežskoje Ozero (Lake Onega) ⊜ 24 61.30 N 35.45 E
Onga ≃ 96 33.54 N 130.39 E
Ongaonga 172 39.55 S 176.25 E
Ongarue 172 38.43 S 175.17 E
Ong-con, Cu-lao I 269c 10.45 N 106.50 E
Ongea Levu I 175g 19.08 S 178.24 W
Ongers ≃ 158 31.04 S 23.13 E
Ongerup 162 33.58 S 118.29 E
Ongijn Gol ≃ 102 44.30 N 103.40 E
Ongjin 98 37.57 N 125.21 E
Ongoka 154 1.23 S 26.02 E
Ongole 122 15.31 N 80.04 E
Ongon 102 45.41 N 113.05 E
Ongudaj 86 50.45 N 86.09 E
Oni 84 42.34 N 43.27 E
Onich 46 56.42 N 5.13 W
Onida 198 44.42 N 100.04 W
Onifai 71 40.24 N 9.39 E
Oniferi 71 40.16 N 9.10 E
Onigajō-yama ∧ 96 33.07 N 132.41 E
Onilahy ≃ 157b 23.34 S 43.45 E
Onin, Jazirah ≻[1] 164 2.50 S 132.05 E
Onion Creek ≃ 222 30.12 N 97.35 W
Onion Peak ∧ 224 45.49 N 123.53 W
Onishi 94 36.09 N 139.04 E
Onistagane, Lac ⊜ 186 50.42 N 71.19 W
Onitsha 150 6.09 N 6.47 E
Onjuku 94 35.11 N 140.22 E
Onkaparinga ≃ 168b 35.10 S 138.28 E
Onkivesi ⊜ 26 63.18 N 27.18 E
Onko 152 4.07 S 19.59 E
Onley 208 37.41 N 75.43 W
Onna 174m 26.30 N 127.51 E
Onnaing 50 50.23 N 3.36 E
Onno 58 45.55 N 9.17 E
Onny ≃ 42 52.23 N 2.45 W
Ōno, Nihon 94 35.28 N 136.38 E
Ōno, Nihon 94 35.59 N 136.29 E
Ōno, Nihon 96 33.02 N 131.30 E
Ōno, Nihon 96 34.18 N 132.17 E
Ono, Nihon 96 34.51 N 134.56 E
Ono, Nihon 270 34.57 N 135.14 E
Ono, Pa., U.S. 208 40.24 N 76.32 W
Ono I 175g 18.55 S 178.29 E
Ōno ≃ 96 33.15 N 131.43 E
Onochoj 88 51.58 N 108.01 E
Onoda 96 33.59 N 131.11 E
Ōno-dam ◂[6] 96 35.15 N 135.27 E
Onogami 94 36.33 N 138.56 E
Onohara 96 34.05 N 133.40 E
Ono-i-lau I 14 20.39 S 178.42 W
Ōnomi 96 33.21 N 133.09 E
Onomichi 96 34.25 N 133.12 E
Onon 88 49.09 N 112.35 E
Onon ≃ 88 51.42 N 115.50 E
Onondaga, Mich., U.S. 216 42.27 N 84.34 W
Onondaga, N.Y., U.S. 210 43.00 N 76.11 W
Onondaga □[6] 210 43.03 N 76.09 W
Onondaga Creek ≃ 210 43.04 N 76.11 W
Onondaga Indian Reservation ◂[4] 210 42.55 N 76.09 W
Onor 89 50.11 N 142.40 E
Onota Lake ⊜ 207 42.28 N 73.17 W
Onoto 246 9.36 N 65.12 W
Onotoa I[1] 14 1.52 S 175.34 E
Onoway 182 53.42 N 114.12 W
Ons, Isla de I 34 42.23 N 8.56 W
Onsbjerg 41 55.51 N 10.35 E
Onseepkans 158 28.46 S 19.14 E
Onsen 96 35.33 N 134.29 E
Onset 207 41.45 N 70.39 W
Onslow 162 21.39 S 115.06 E
Onslow Bay C 192 34.20 N 77.20 W
Onslow Village 260 51.14 N 0.36 W
Onsted 216 42.00 N 84.11 W
Onstmettingen 58 48.17 N 9.00 E
Onstwedde 52 53.02 N 7.02 E
Ontake-san ∧ 94 35.53 N 137.29 E
Ontario, Calif., U.S. 228 34.04 N 117.39 W
Ontario, Ind., U.S. 216 41.43 N 85.23 W
Ontario, N.Y., U.S. 210 43.13 N 77.17 W
Ontario, Ohio, U.S. 214 40.46 N 82.39 W
Ontario, Oreg., U.S. 202 44.02 N 116.58 W
Ontario □[6], Ont., Can. 212 44.15 N 79.05 W
Ontario □[6], N.Y., U.S. 210 42.54 N 77.17 W
Ontario □[4] 176 51.00 N 85.00 W
Ontario, Lake ⊜ 190 43.45 N 78.00 W
Ontario Center 210 43.14 N 77.19 W
Ontario International Airport ⊠ 228 34.04 N 117.36 W
Ontario Place ♠ 275b 43.38 N 79.25 W
Ontario Science Centre ⊽ 275b 43.43 N 79.21 W
Ontelaunee, Lake ⊜ 208 40.27 N 75.55 W
Onteniente 34 38.49 N 0.37 W
Ontojärvi ⊜ 26 64.08 N 29.09 E
Ontonagon 190 46.52 N 89.19 W
Ontonagon ≃ 190 46.52 N 89.20 W
Ontonagon, East Branch ≃ 190 46.42 N 89.11 W
Ontonagon, Middle Branch ≃ 190 46.42 N 89.10 W
Ontonagon, West Branch ≃ 190 46.42 N 89.11 W
Ontong Java Atoll I[1] 175e 5.20 S 159.30 E
Ontong Java Rise ✢[3] 14 7.00 S 160.00 E
Onufrijevka 78 48.54 N 33.26 E
Onufrijevo 82 55.51 N 36.31 E
Ōnuma 268 35.32 N 139.25 E
Onverwacht 250 5.36 N 55.12 W
Onward 216 40.42 N 86.12 W
Ŏnyang 98 35.34 N 129.07 E
Onzain 50 47.30 N 1.11 E
Onzo ≃ 152 8.12 S 13.16 E
Oodnadatta 162 27.33 S 135.28 E
Oog van Wonderfontein ≃ 273d 26.16 S 27.42 E
Ōoka 94 36.30 N 137.59 E
Ooldea 162 30.27 S 131.50 E
Oolitic 218 38.54 N 86.31 W
Oologah Lake ⊜[1] 196 36.33 N 95.36 W
Ooma 174d 0.53 S 169.36 E
Oombergen 50 50.54 N 3.50 E
Oona River 182 53.57 N 130.18 W
Ooratippra 162 22.00 S 136.00 E
Ooratippra Creek ≃ 162 21.55 S 136.05 E
Oos 56 48.47 N 8.11 E
Oos-Londen → East London 158 33.00 S 27.55 E
Oostakker 50 51.06 N 3.46 E
Oostburg, Ned. 52 51.20 N 3.30 E
Oostburg, Wis., U.S. 190 43.37 N 87.48 W
Oost-Cappel 50 50.55 N 2.36 E
Oostduinkerke 50 51.07 N 2.41 E
Oostelijk Flevoland ◂[1] 52 52.30 N 5.45 E
Oostende (Ostende) 50 51.13 N 2.55 E
Oosterbeek 52 52.00 N 5.50 E
Oosterend 52 53.05 N 4.52 E
Oosterhout 52 51.38 N 4.51 E
Ooster Schelde C 52 51.30 N 4.00 E
Oosterwolde 52 52.59 N 6.17 E
Oosterzele 50 50.57 N 3.48 E
Oosthuizen 52 52.35 N 5.00 E
Oostkamp 50 51.09 N 3.14 E
Oostmahorn 52 53.24 N 6.09 E
Oostmalle 56 51.18 N 4.44 E
Oostpunt ≻ 241s 12.02 N 68.45 W
Oostrozebeke 50 50.55 N 3.20 E
Oost-Souburg 52 51.27 N 3.35 E
Oost-Vlaanderen □[4] 50 51.00 N 3.45 E
Oostvleteren 50 50.56 N 2.44 E
Oost-Vlieland 52 53.17 N 5.04 E
Oostvoorne 52 51.55 N 4.06 E
Ootacamund 122 11.24 N 76.42 E
Ootmarsum 52 52.25 N 6.54 E
Ootsa Lake 182 53.47 N 126.03 W
Ootsa Lake ⊜ 182 53.49 N 126.18 W
Ootse 156 25.02 S 25.45 E
Ootua, Mont ∧ 174x 9.47 S 138.58 W
Opaka 38 43.27 N 26.10 E
Opala 152 0.37 S 24.21 E
Opalaca, Cordillera ∧∧ 236 14.30 N 88.20 W
Opal Cliffs 226 36.58 N 121.58 W
Opale, Côte d' •[2] 50 50.40 N 1.35 E
Opalenica 30 52.19 N 16.23 E
Opalicha 265b 55.49 N 37.15 E
Opa Locka 220 25.54 N 80.15 W
Opari 154 3.56 N 32.03 E
Oparino 24 59.52 N 48.17 E
Opasatica, Lac ⊜ 190 48.05 N 79.18 W
Opasatika Lake ⊜ 190 49.04 N 83.08 W
Opasquia 184 53.16 N 93.35 W
Opasquia Lake ⊜ 184 53.18 N 93.34 W
Opatija 36 45.21 N 14.19 E
Opatów 30 50.49 N 21.26 E
Opava 30 49.56 N 17.54 E
Opečenskij Posad 76 58.16 N 34.07 E
Opeepeesway Lake ⊜ 190 47.38 N 82.14 W
Opeilu 273a 6.42 N 3.18 E
Opelika 194 32.39 N 85.23 W
Opelousas 194 30.32 N 92.05 W
Open Bay C 164 4.50 S 151.20 E
Open Door 258 34.30 S 59.05 W
Opeongo Lake ⊜ 190 45.42 N 78.23 W
Opequon Creek ≃ 188 39.35 N 77.52 W
Operaház ⊽ 264c 47.30 N 19.04 E
Ophain-Bois-Seigneur-Isaac 50 50.40 N 4.21 E
Ophasselt 50 50.49 N 3.53 E
Opheim 202 48.51 N 106.24 W
Opherdicke 263 51.29 N 7.38 E
Opheusden 52 51.56 N 5.38 E
Ophir, Alaska, U.S. 180 63.10 N 156.31 W
Ophir, Oreg., U.S. 202 42.34 N 124.23 W
Ophirton ◂[8] 273d 26.14 S 28.01 E
Ophthalmia Range ∧∧ 162 23.17 S 119.30 E
Opi 66 41.47 N 13.50 E
Opienge 154 0.12 N 27.30 E
Opihikao 229d 19.26 N 154.53 W
Opinaca ≃ 176 52.15 N 78.02 W
Opinan 46 57.43 N 5.47 W
Opinicon Lake ⊜ 212 44.33 N 76.20 W
Opiscotéo, Lac ⊜ 176 53.10 N 68.10 W
Opladen 56 51.04 N 7.00 E
Opmeer 52 52.43 N 4.56 E
Opobo 150 4.34 N 7.27 E
Opobo Town 150 4.30 N 7.30 E
Opočka 76 56.43 N 28.38 E
Opoczno 30 51.23 N 20.17 E
Opol 116 8.31 N 124.34 E
Opole (Oppeln) 30 50.41 N 17.55 E
Opole Lubelskie 30 51.09 N 21.58 E
Opon → Lapu-Lapu 116 10.19 N 123.57 E
Oponono Lake ⊜ 156 18.08 S 15.45 E
Opopeo 234 19.24 N 101.36 W
Oporto → Porto 34 41.11 N 8.36 W
Opošn'a 78 49.58 N 34.37 E
Opotiki 172 38.00 S 177.17 E
Opp 194 31.17 N 86.22 W
Oppach 54 51.03 N 14.30 E
Oppdal 26 62.36 N 9.40 E
Oppelhain 54 51.33 N 13.35 E
Oppeln → Opole 30 50.41 N 17.55 E
Oppenau 58 48.28 N 8.10 E
Oppenberg 61 47.29 N 14.16 E
Oppenheim, B.R.D. 56 49.51 N 8.21 E
Oppenheim, N.Y., U.S. 210 43.04 N 74.42 W
Oppenhuizen 52 53.00 N 5.42 E
Oppido Lucano 68 40.47 N 16.00 E
Oppido Mamertina 68 38.16 N 16.00 E
Oppio 66 44.03 N 10.50 E
Oppland □[6] 26 61.10 N 9.40 E
Opportunity, Mont., U.S. 202 46.07 N 112.49 W
Opportunity, Wash., U.S. 202 47.39 N 117.15 W
Oppum ◂[8] 263 51.19 N 6.37 E
Opsa 76 55.32 N 26.47 E
Opsaheden 40 60.28 N 13.59 E
Optic Lake 184 54.46 N 101.13 W
Opua 172 35.19 S 174.07 E
Opunake 172 39.27 S 173.51 E
Opwijk 50 50.58 N 4.11 E
Oquawka 190 40.56 N 90.57 W
Oquendo, Perú 286d 11.58 S 77.08 W
Oquendo, Pil. 116 12.08 N 124.32 E
O'Quinn 222 29.50 N 96.58 W
Or' ≃ 86 51.12 N 58.30 E
Or, Côte d' ∧ 58 47.10 N 4.50 E
Or, Étang d' ⊜ 261 48.38 N 1.51 E
Ora (Auer), It. 64 46.21 N 11.18 E
Ora, Lībīya 146 28.33 N 19.24 E
Ōra, Nihon 174m 26.33 N 128.02 E
Ora Banda 162 30.22 S 121.04 E
Oracle 200 32.37 N 110.46 W
Oradea 38 47.03 N 21.57 E
Oradell 276 40.57 N 74.02 W
Oradell Reservoir ⊜[1] 276 40.58 N 74.01 W
Öræfajökull ⍓ 24a 64.03 N 16.38 W
Orahovica 38 45.31 N 17.53 E
Orai 124 25.59 N 79.28 E
Oraibi 200 35.53 N 110.37 W
Oraibi Wash ∨ 200 35.26 N 110.49 W
Oraison 62 43.55 N 5.55 E
Oran (Ouahran), Alg. 148 35.43 N 0.43 W
Oran, Mo., U.S. 194 37.05 N 89.39 W
Oran, Sebkra d' ⊜ 148 35.30 N 1.00 W
Orange, Austl. 166 33.17 S 149.06 E
Orange, Fr. 62 44.08 N 4.48 E
Orange, Calif., U.S. 228 33.47 N 117.51 W
Orange, Conn., U.S. 207 41.17 N 73.02 W
Orange, Mass., U.S. 207 42.35 N 72.19 W
Orange, Ohio, U.S. 279a 41.26 N 81.29 W
Orange, Tex., U.S. 194 30.01 N 93.44 W
Orange, Va., U.S. 188 38.15 N 78.07 W
Orange □[6], Calif., U.S. 228 33.43 N 117.54 W
Orange □[6], Fla., U.S. 220 28.32 N 81.16 W
Orange □[6], Ind., U.S. 218 38.33 N 86.28 W
Orange □[6], N.Y., U.S. 210 41.24 N 74.20 W
Orange (Oranje) ≃ 156 28.41 S 16.28 E
Orange, Cabo ≻ 250 4.24 N 51.33 W
Orange Bowl ♠ 220 25.46 N 80.14 W
Orangeburg, Ky., U.S. 218 38.35 N 83.39 W
Orangeburg, N.Y., U.S. 210 41.03 N 73.57 W
Orangeburg, S.C., U.S. 192 33.30 N 80.52 W
Orange City, Fla., U.S. 220 28.57 N 81.17 W
Orange City, Iowa, U.S. 198 43.00 N 96.03 W
Orange County Airport ⊠ 228 33.40 N 117.51 W
Orange Cove 226 36.37 N 119.19 W
Orange Free State (Oranje-Vrystaat) □[3] 158 28.30 S 27.00 E
Orange Grove 196 27.58 N 97.56 W
Orange Grove ◂[8] 273d 26.10 S 28.05 E
Orange Lake, Fla., U.S. 192 29.25 N 82.13 W
Orange Lake, N.Y., U.S. 210 41.33 N 74.06 W
Orange Lake ⊜ 192 29.29 N 82.10 W
Orangemouth → Oranjemund 156 28.38 S 16.24 E
Orange Park 192 30.10 N 81.42 W
Orange Park Acres 280 33.48 N 117.47 W
Orangevale 226 38.41 N 121.13 W
Orangeville, Ont., Can. 212 43.55 N 80.06 W
Orangeville, S. Afr. 158 27.00 S 28.15 E
Orangeville, Ohio, U.S. 214 41.20 N 80.31 W
Orangeville, Pa., U.S. 210 41.05 N 76.25 W
Orangeville, Utah, U.S. 200 39.13 N 111.03 W
Orange Walk 232 18.06 N 88.33 W
Orango, Ilha de I 150 11.10 N 16.08 W
Orani, It. 71 40.15 N 9.11 E
Orani, Pil. 116 14.49 N 120.32 E
Oranienbaum 54 51.48 N 12.24 E
Oranienburg 54 52.45 N 13.14 E
Oraniye ◂[8] 267b 41.03 N 29.01 E
Oranje 52 52.55 N 6.28 E
Oranje → Orange ≃ 156 28.41 S 16.28 E
Oranjefontein 156 23.25 S 27.41 E
Oranje Gebergte ∧∧ 250 3.00 N 55.05 W
Oranjemund 156 28.38 S 16.24 E
Oranjerivier 158 29.40 S 24.12 E
Oranjestad 241s 12.33 N 70.06 W
Oranki 80 55.53 N 43.44 E
Oranmore 48 53.16 N 8.54 W
Ŏran-ni 98 34.22 N 126.29 E
Oranžerei 80 45.50 N 47.36 E
Oraparinna 166 31.22 S 138.43 E
Or 'Aqiva 132 32.30 N 34.55 E
Orarak 140 6.15 N 32.23 E
Orari ≃ 172 44.15 S 171.25 E
Oras 116 12.09 N 125.26 E
Oras ≃ 116 12.08 N 125.26 E
Oras Bay C 116 12.07 N 125.28 E
Orăștie 38 45.50 N 23.12 E
Orașul Stalin → Brașov 38 45.39 N 25.37 E
Oratório, Ribeirão do ≃ 287b 23.37 S 46.32 W
Oratov 78 49.12 N 29.32 E
Oravais (Oravainen) 26 63.18 N 22.23 E
Oravița 38 45.02 N 21.41 E
Orawia 172 46.03 S 167.49 E
Orb ≃ 32 43.15 N 3.18 E
Orba ≃ 62 44.53 N 8.37 E
Orbassano 62 45.01 N 7.32 E
Orbe 58 46.43 N 6.32 E
Orbe ≃ 58 46.47 N 6.39 E
Orbec-en-Auge 50 49.01 N 0.25 E
Orbetello 66 42.27 N 11.13 E
Orbetello, Laguna di C 66 42.27 N 11.14 E
Orbey 58 48.08 N 7.10 E
Orbieu ≃ 32 43.14 N 2.54 E
Orbigny 50 47.12 N 1.14 E
Orbigo ≃ 34 41.58 N 5.40 W
Orbiquet ≃ 50 49.09 N 0.14 E
Orbisonia 214 40.15 N 77.54 W
Orbost 166 37.42 S 148.27 E
Örbyhus 40 60.14 N 17.42 E
Orcadas, Islas → Orkney Islands II 46 59.00 N 3.00 W
Orcadas del Sur, Islas → South Orkney Islands II 9 60.35 S 45.30 W
Orcades du Sud, Îles → South Orkney Islands II 9 60.35 S 45.30 W
Orcas 224 48.36 N 122.57 W
Orcas Island I 224 48.39 N 122.55 W
Orce ≃ 34 37.44 N 2.28 W
Orcemont 261 48.35 N 1.49 E
Orcera 34 38.19 N 2.39 W
Orchamps 58 47.09 N 5.40 E
Orchard, Nebr., U.S. 198 42.20 N 98.14 W
Orchard, Tex., U.S. 222 29.36 N 95.58 W
Orchard City 200 38.51 N 107.58 W
Orchard Hills, Austl. 274a 33.47 S 150.43 E
Orchard Hills, Pa., U.S. 279b 40.35 N 79.32 W
Orchard Homes 202 46.55 N 114.04 W
Orchard Island 216 40.28 N 83.53 W
Orchard Lake ⊜ 281 42.35 N 83.22 W
Orchard Park 210 42.43 N 78.45 W
Orchard Park Airport ⊠ 284a 42.48 N 78.45 W
Orchard Peak ∧ 226 35.44 N 120.08 W
Orchards 224 45.40 N 122.34 W
Orchard Valley 200 41.06 N 104.19 W
Orchard View 285 40.04 N 74.53 W
Orchha 124 25.21 N 78.39 E
Orchies 50 50.28 N 3.14 E
Orchila, Isla I 246 11.48 N 66.09 W
Orchon 88 49.09 N 105.21 E
Orchon ≃ 88 50.21 N 106.05 E
Orchontuul 88 48.58 N 104.59 E
Orcia ≃ 66 42.58 N 11.21 E
Orcières 62 44.41 N 6.20 E
Orčik ≃ 78 49.10 N 35.04 E
Orco ≃ 62 45.10 N 7.52 E
Orcotuna 248 11.58 S 75.20 W
Ord 198 41.36 N 98.56 W
Ord ≃ 164 15.30 S 128.21 E
Ord, Mount ∧ 160 17.20 S 125.34 E
Orda 86 57.12 N 56.54 E
Ordenes 34 43.04 N 8.24 W
Orderville 200 37.16 N 112.38 W
Ordesa, Parque Nacional de ♠ 34 42.39 N 0.02 E
Ordine di Malta, Sovrano Internazionale Militare (S.M.O.M.) ⊽ 267a 41.55 N 12.29 E
Ord Mountain ∧ 204 34.40 N 116.49 W
Ord Mountains ∧∧ 228 34.42 N 117.10 W
Ordoqui 252 35.54 S 61.10 W
Ord River 162 17.23 S 128.51 E
Ordu, Tür. 130 41.00 N 37.53 E
Ordu, Tür. 130 35.56 N 36.01 E
Ordu □[4] 130 37.45 N 37.30 E
Ordubad 84 38.56 N 46.02 E
Ordway 198 38.13 N 103.46 W
Ordynskoje 86 54.22 N 81.56 E
Ordzhonikidze → Jenakijevo, S.S.S.R. 83 48.14 N 38.13 E
Ordzhonikidze → Ordžonikidze, S.S.S.R. 84 43.03 N 44.40 E
Ordžonikidze, S.S.S.R. 78 44.57 N 35.22 E
Ordžonikidze, S.S.S.R. 78 47.40 N 34.04 E
Ordžonikidze, S.S.S.R. 84 43.03 N 44.40 E
Ordžonikidze, S.S.S.R. 84 40.53 N 47.23 E
Ordžonikidze, S.S.S.R. 84 42.01 N 43.12 E
Ordžonikidze, S.S.S.R. 85 41.21 N 69.22 E
Ordžonikidzeabad 85 38.34 N 69.01 E
Ordžonikidzevskaja 84 43.18 N 45.03 E
Ordžonikidzevskij, S.S.S.R. 84 43.51 N 41.54 E
Ordžonikidzevskij, S.S.S.R. 86 54.46 N 88.59 E
Ore 150 6.44 N 4.52 E
Ore ≃ 46 56.10 N 3.15 W
Öreälven ≃ 26 63.32 N 19.44 E
Oreana 219 39.56 N 88.52 W
Örebro 40 59.17 N 15.13 E
Örebro Län □[6] 40 59.30 N 15.00 E
Orechov 78 47.34 N 35.47 E
Orechovka, S.S.S.R. 80 52.56 N 48.14 E
Orechovka, S.S.S.R. 83 48.17 N 39.13 E
Orechovo 80 58.28 N 41.58 E
Orechovo-Zujevo 82 55.49 N 38.59 E
Orechovsk 76 54.41 N 30.30 E
Orechov'skij ◂[8] 83 48.01 N 38.42 E
Ore City 222 32.48 N 94.43 W
Oredež 76 58.49 N 30.20 E
Oredež ≃ 76 58.49 N 30.00 E
Orefield 208 40.38 N 75.35 W
Oregon, Ill., U.S. 190 42.01 N 89.20 W
Oregon, Mo., U.S. 194 39.59 N 95.09 W
Oregon, Ohio, U.S. 214 41.38 N 83.28 W
Oregon, Wis., U.S. 216 42.56 N 89.23 W
Oregon □[3] 178, 202 44.00 N 121.00 W
Oregon Caves National Monument ♠ 202 42.06 N 123.24 W
Oregon City 224 45.21 N 122.36 W
Oregon Creek ≃ 226 39.23 N 121.05 W
Oregon Dunes National Recreation Area ♠ 202 43.45 N 124.12 W
Oregon House 226 39.21 N 121.17 W
Öregrund 40 60.20 N 18.26 E
Öregrundsgrepen C 40 60.27 N 18.18 E
Orehoved 41 54.57 N 11.52 E
Orekhovo-Zuyevo → Orechovo-Zujevo 82 55.49 N 38.59 E
Orel → Or'ol 76 52.59 N 36.05 E
Orel', Ozero ⊜ 89 53.30 N 139.42 E
Oreland 285 40.07 N 75.11 W
Orellana 248 6.54 S 75.04 W
Orellana, Embalse de ⊜[1] 34 39.00 N 5.25 W
Orem 200 40.19 N 111.42 W
Orenburg 86 51.54 N 55.06 E
Orenburg □[4] 80 52.38 N 53.00 E
Örencik 130 39.16 N 29.33 E
Oreng 114 4.03 N 97.28 E
Orense, Arg. 252 38.40 S 59.47 W
Orense, Esp. 34 42.20 N 7.51 W
Orepuki 172 46.17 S 167.44 E
Oreški 82 55.43 N 36.21 E
Oressa ≃ 76 52.33 N 28.45 E
Orestes 216 40.16 N 85.44 W
Orestiás 38 41.30 N 26.31 E
Orestimba Creek ≃ 226 37.25 N 121.00 W
Øresund → The Sound ⊔ 41 55.50 N 12.40 E
Oreti ≃ 172 46.28 S 168.17 E
Oreto ≃ 70 38.06 N 13.24 E
Orewa 172 36.34 S 174.42 E
Oreye 56 50.44 N 5.22 E
Orfanoú, Kólpos C 38 40.40 N 23.50 E
Orford, Eng., U.K. 42 52.06 N 1.31 E
Orford, Eng., U.K. 262 53.25 N 2.35 W
Orford Ness ≻ 42 52.05 N 1.34 E
Orfordville 190 42.38 N 89.16 W
Organ Needle ∧ 200 32.21 N 106.33 W
Organ Pipe Cactus National Monument ♠ 200 32.00 N 112.55 W
Órgãos, Serra dos ∧∧ 256 22.22 S 42.45 W
Orgaz 34 39.39 N 3.54 W
Orge ≃ 50 48.42 N 2.24 E
Orgejev 78 47.23 N 28.48 E
Orgelet 58 46.31 N 5.37 E
Orgères-en-Beauce 50 48.09 N 1.42 E
Orgerus 261 48.50 N 1.42 E
Orgeval 50 48.55 N 1.59 E
Orgiano 64 45.21 N 11.28 E
Orgnac, Aven d' •[5] 62 44.19 N 4.27 E
Orgnac-l'Aven 62 44.19 N 4.27 E
Orgof 144 3.03 N 43.44 E
Orgon 62 43.47 N 5.02 E
Orgosolo 71 40.12 N 9.21 E
Orgtrud 80 56.12 N 40.37 E
Orgūn 120 32.51 N 69.07 E
Orhangazi 130 40.30 N 29.18 E
Orhanlar 130 39.54 N 27.37 E
Oria, It. 68 40.30 N 17.38 E
Oria, Zaïre 154 3.17 N 30.41 E
Orica 236 14.41 N 86.56 W
Oriçanga, Rio do ≃ 256 22.18 S 47.03 W
Oriči 80 58.24 N 49.05 E
Orick 204 41.17 N 124.04 W
Oricola 66 42.02 N 13.02 E
Orient, Iowa, U.S. 198 41.12 N 94.25 W
Orient, N.Y., U.S. 207 41.08 N 72.18 W
Orient, Ohio, U.S. 218 39.48 N 83.09 W
Oriental, Méx. 234 19.22 N 97.37 W
Oriental, N.C., U.S. 192 35.02 N 76.42 W
Oriental, Cordillera ∧∧, Col. 246 6.00 N 73.00 W
Oriental, Cordillera ∧∧, Perú 248 11.00 S 74.00 W
Oriental, Pico ∧ 286c 10.32 N 66.50 W
Oriental de Zapata, Ciénaga ☰ 240p 22.15 N 80.50 W
Orientaliă, Poarta)(38 45.06 N 22.18 E
Oriental Park 214 42.09 N 79.22 W
Oriente 252 38.44 S 60.37 W
Orientos 166 28.05 S 141.14 E
Origgio 266b 45.36 N 9.01 E
Origny-en-Thiérache 50 49.54 N 4.01 E
Origny-Sainte-Benoite 50 49.50 N 3.30 E
Orihuela 34 38.05 N 0.57 W
Orillia 212 44.37 N 79.25 W
Orimattila 26 60.48 N 25.45 E
Orinda 226 37.53 N 122.11 W
Orinduik 246 4.42 N 60.01 W
Orini 172 37.34 S 175.18 E
Orinin 78 48.46 N 26.24 E
Orinoco ≃ 246 8.37 N 62.15 W
Orinoco, Delta del ≃[2] 246 9.15 N 61.30 W
Oriole, Md., U.S. 208 38.10 N 75.49 W
Oriole, Pa., U.S. 210 41.08 N 77.13 W
Oriolo 68 40.03 N 16.27 E
Oriomo 164 8.50 S 143.15 E
Orion, Pil. 116 14.37 N 120.34 E
Orion, Ill., U.S. 190 41.21 N 90.23 W
Oripää 26 60.51 N 22.41 E
Oriskany 210 43.09 N 75.20 W
Oriskany Battle Monument ⊥ 210 43.11 N 75.23 W
Oriskany Creek ≃ 210 43.10 N 75.20 W
Oriskany Falls 210 42.56 N 75.28 W
Orissa □[3] 122 20.00 N 84.00 E
Orissaare 76 58.34 N 23.05 E
Orissa Coast Canal ≍ 126 21.51 N 87.41 E
Oristano 71 39.54 N 8.36 E
Oristano □[4] 71 39.55 N 8.40 E
Oristano, Golfo di C 71 39.50 N 8.29 E
Öriszentpéter 61 46.51 N 16.25 E
Orituco ≃ 246 8.45 N 67.27 W
Orivesi 26 61.41 N 24.21 E
Orivesi ⊜ 26 62.16 N 29.24 E
Oriximiná 250 1.45 S 55.52 W
Orizaba 234 18.51 N 97.06 W
Orizaba, Pico de → Citlaltépetl, Volcán ∧[1] 234 19.01 N 97.16 W
Orizona 255 17.03 S 48.18 W
Orjahovo 38 43.45 N 23.57 E
Ørje 26 59.29 N 11.39 E
Orjen ∧ 38 42.30 N 18.38 E
Orjiva 34 36.54 N 3.25 W
Ork, Ness of ≻ 46 59.05 N 2.48 W
Orkanger 26 63.19 N 9.52 E
Örkelljunga 41 56.17 N 13.17 E
Orken 263 51.06 N 6.34 E
Örkenez 130 38.12 N 31.17 E
Orkla ≃ 26 63.18 N 9.50 E
Orkney, Sask., Can. 184 49.08 N 107.55 W
Orkney, S. Afr. 158 27.00 S 26.39 E
Orkney Islands □[4] 46 59.00 N 3.00 W
Orkney Islands II 46 59.00 N 3.00 W
Orl'a 76 53.30 N 24.59 E
Orla ≃ 54 50.46 N 11.31 E
Orlamünde 54 50.47 N 11.31 E
Orland, Calif., U.S. 204 39.45 N 122.11 W
Orland, Ind., U.S. 216 41.44 N 85.10 W
Orlândia 255 20.43 S 47.53 W
Orland Lake ⊜ 278 41.38 N 87.52 W
Orlando, S. Afr. 273d 26.14 S 27.55 E
Orlando, Fla., U.S. 220 28.32 N 81.23 W
Orlando, Capo d' ≻ 70 38.10 N 14.45 E
Orlando Jetport ⊠ 220 28.26 N 81.19 W
Orlando Naval Training Center ▪ 220 28.34 N 81.20 W
Orlando West Extension 273d 26.15 S 27.54 E
Orland Park 216 41.38 N 87.52 W
Orleães 252 28.21 S 49.18 W
Orléanais □[9] 50 47.50 N 2.00 E
Orléans, Ont., Can. 212 45.28 N 75.31 W
Orléans, Fr. 50 47.55 N 1.54 E
Orleans, Calif., U.S. 204 41.18 N 123.32 W
Orleans, Ind., U.S. 218 38.40 N 86.27 W
Orleans, Mass., U.S. 207 41.47 N 70.00 W
Orleans, Nebr., U.S. 198 40.08 N 99.27 W
Orleans, Vt., U.S. 188 44.49 N 72.12 W
Orleans □[6], N.Y., U.S. 210 43.15 N 78.12 W
Orleans □[6], Vt., U.S. 206 44.57 N 72.12 W
Orléans, Canal d' ≍ 50 47.54 N 1.55 E
Orléans, Île d' I 186 46.55 N 70.58 W
Orléansville → El Asnam 148 36.10 N 1.20 E
Orlenga ≃ 88 56.03 N 105.53 E
Orlik, S.S.S.R. 80 48.17 N 51.32 E
Orlik, S.S.S.R. 88 52.30 N 99.55 E
Orlinga 88 56.03 N 105.53 E
Orlinnaja, Gora ∧ 180 62.35 N 178.30 E
Orlová 30 49.50 N 18.24 E
Orlov Gaj 80 50.57 N 48.12 E
Orlovista 220 28.32 N 81.28 W
Orlovka, S.S.S.R. 78 51.02 N 40.32 E
Orlovka, S.S.S.R. 78 51.54 N 32.47 E
Orlovka, S.S.S.R. 78 45.40 N 33.21 E
Orlovka, S.S.S.R. 83 48.10 N 37.39 E
Orlovka, S.S.S.R. 86 59.03 N 85.59 E
Orlovka ≃ 86 58.40 N 86.08 E
Orlovo, S.S.S.R. 78 51.45 N 39.35 E
Orlovo, S.S.S.R. 265b 55.38 N 37.23 E
Orlovskij 80 46.52 N 42.03 E
Orlu 150 5.47 N 7.02 E
Orly 261 48.45 N 2.24 E
Ormanlı 130 41.10 N 31.39 E
Ormāra 128 25.12 N 64.38 E
Ormāra, Rās ≻ 120 25.09 N 64.35 E
Orme, Rivière à l ≃ 275a 45.27 N 73.56 W
Ormea 62 44.09 N 7.54 E
Ormesby 44 54.33 N 1.11 W
Ormesby Saint Margaret 42 52.40 N 1.42 E
Ormiston 184 49.45 N 105.22 W
Ormoc 116 11.00 N 124.37 E
Ormoc Bay C 116 10.58 N 124.35 E
Ormond 274b 37.54 S 145.03 E
Ormond Beach 192 29.17 N 81.02 W
Ormož 61 46.25 N 16.09 E
Ormsby 214 41.48 N 78.33 W
Ormsby □[6] 226 39.11 N 119.46 W
Ormsjön ⊜ 26 64.23 N 16.03 E
Ormskirk 44 53.35 N 2.54 W
Ormstown 206 45.08 N 74.00 W
Ormtjernkampen Nasjonalpark ♠ 26 61.12 N 9.48 E
Ornain ≃ 58 48.46 N 4.47 E
Ornans 58 47.06 N 6.09 E
Ornäs 40 60.31 N 15.32 E
Ornavasso 58 45.58 N 8.24 E
Orne □[5] 32 48.40 N 0.05 E
Orne ≃, Fr. 50 48.08 N 0.11 E
Orne ≃, Fr. 50 48.39 N 0.14 E
Orne ≃, Fr. 56 49.17 N 6.11 E
Ornes 26 61.18 N 7.22 E
Orneta 30 54.08 N 20.08 E
Ornö I 40 59.04 N 18.24 E
Örnsköldsvik 26 63.18 N 18.43 E
Oro 98 40.02 N 127.26 E
Orø I 41 55.46 N 11.49 E
Oro, Río del ≃, Méx. 232 25.35 N 105.03 W
Oro, Río del ≃, Méx. 234 18.27 N 100.57 W
Orobie, Alpi ∧∧ 64 46.00 N 10.00 E
Oročanskij Golec, Gora ∧ 88 53.29 N 114.18 E
Oročen 74 58.28 N 125.26 E
Orocovis 240m 18.14 N 66.23 W
Orocué 246 4.48 N 71.20 W
Orocuina 236 13.26 N 87.06 W
Orodara 150 10.59 N 4.55 W
Orofino 202 46.29 N 116.15 W
Örög Nuur ⊜, Mong. 86 50.10 N 91.00 E
Orog Nuur ⊜, Mong. 102 45.03 N 100.42 E
Oro Grande 228 34.36 N 117.20 W
Orohena, Mont ∧ 174s 17.37 S 149.28 W
Orok, Ol Doinyo ∧ 154 2.29 S 36.46 E
Oroku 174m 26.12 N 127.39 E
Or'ol, S.S.S.R. 76 52.59 N 36.05 E
Or'ol, S.S.S.R. 86 59.21 N 56.35 E
Or'ol □[4] 78 52.00 N 38.00 E
Or'ol' ≃ 78 48.30 N 34.54 E
Oroluk I[1] 14 7.32 N 155.18 E
Oromocto 186 45.51 N 66.29 W
Oromocto Lake ⊜ 186 45.36 N 67.00 W
Oron, Nig. 150 4.48 N 8.14 E
Oron, S.S.S.R. 88 57.11 N 116.28 E
Oron, Ozero ⊜ 88 57.06 N 116.30 E
Oron-la-Ville 58 46.34 N 6.50 E
Orono, Ont., Can. 212 43.59 N 78.37 W
Orono, Maine, U.S. 188 44.53 N 68.40 W
Orono Lake ⊜ 184 52.13 N 94.55 W
Oronoque ≃ 246 2.45 N 57.25 W
Oronsay I 46 56.01 N 6.16 W
Orontes → Asi ≃ 130 36.02 N 35.58 E
Oropeo 234 18.50 N 101.48 W
Oroquieta 116 8.29 N 123.48 E
Oroquieta ≃ 116 8.29 N 123.48 E
Orós 250 6.15 S 38.55 W
Orós, Açude ⊜[1] 250 6.15 S 39.05 W
Orosei 71 40.23 N 9.42 E
Orosei, Golfo di C 71 40.15 N 9.44 E
Orosháza 30 46.34 N 20.40 E
Orosi 226 36.33 N 119.17 W
Orosí, Volcán ∧[1] 236 10.59 N 85.29 W
Oroszlány 30 47.30 N 18.19 E
Orotelli 71 40.18 N 9.07 E
Orote Peninsula ≻[1] 174p 13.26 N 144.38 E
Orotina 236 9.54 N 84.31 W
Oroville, Calif., U.S. 226 39.31 N 121.33 W
Oroville, Wash., U.S. 202 48.56 N 119.26 W
Oroville, Lake ⊜[1] 204 39.32 N 121.25 W
Orowoc Creek ≃ 276 40.43 N 73.13 W
Orphin 261 48.35 N 1.47 E
Orpierre 62 44.19 N 5.41 E
Orpington ◂[8] 260 51.23 N 0.06 E

≃ River — Fluss — Río — Rivière — Rio
≍ Canal — Kanal — Canal — Canal — Canal
↳ Waterfall, Rapids — Wasserfall, Stromschnellen — Cascada, Rápidos — Chute d'eau, Rapides — Cascata, Rápidos
⊔ Strait — Meeresstrasse — Estrecho — Détroit — Estreito
C Bay, Gulf — Bucht, Golf — Bahía, Golfo — Baie, Golfe — Baía, Golfo
⊜ Lake, Lakes — See, Seen — Lago, Lagos — Lac, Lacs — Lago, Lagos
☰ Swamp — Sumpf — Pantano — Marais — Pântano
⍓ Ice Features, Glacier — Eis- und Gletscherformen — Accidentes Glaciales — Formes glaciaires — Acidentes Glaciares
∨ Other Hydrographic Features — Andere Hydrographische Objekte — Otros Elementos Hidrográficos — Autres données hydrographiques — Outros Elementos Hidrográficos

✢ Submarine Features — Untermeerische Objekte — Accidentes Submarinos — Formes de relief sous-marin — Acidentes Submarinos
□ Political Unit — Politische Einheit — Unidad Politica — Entité politique — Unidade Política
⊽ Cultural Institution — Kulturelle Institution — Institución Cultural — Institution culturelle — Instituição Cultural
⊥ Historical Site — Historische Stätte — Sitio Histórico — Site historique — Sitio Histórico
♠ Recreational Site — Erholungs- und Ferienort — Sitio de Recreo — Centre de loisirs — Sítio de Lazer
⊠ Airport — Flughafen — Aeropuerto — Aéroport — Aeroporto
▪ Military Installation — Militäranlage — Instalación Militar — Installation militaire — Instalação Militar
◂ Miscellaneous — Verschiedenes — Misceláneo — Divers — Miscelânea

Orrefors 26 56.50 N 15.45 E
Orrell 262 53.32 N 2.43 W
Orrick 194 39.13 N 94.07 W
Orrin 198 48.05 N 100.10 W
Orrin, Glen ∨ 46 57.30 N 4.46 W
Orrin, Loch ⊜ 46 57.30 N 4.45 W
Orrius 266d 41.33 N 2.21 E
Orr Lake ⊜, Man., Can. 184 56.07 N 97.11 W
Orr Lake ⊜, Ont., Can. 212 44.37 N 79.47 W
Orroroo 166 32.44 S 138.37 E
Orrs Island 188 43.46 N 69.59 W
Orrtanna 208 39.51 N 77.22 W
Orrville, Ala., U.S. 194 32.18 N 87.15 W
Orrville, Ohio, U.S. 214 40.50 N 81.46 W
Orrville, Pa., U.S. 279b 40.33 N 79.47 W
Orša, S.S.S.R. 76 54.30 N 30.24 E
Orsa, Sve. 26 61.07 N 14.37 E
Orša ≐ 82 56.48 N 36.11 E
Orsago 64 45.56 N 12.25 E
Orsan 62 44.08 N 4.40 E
Oršanka 80 56.55 N 47.53 E
Orsara di Puglia 68 41.17 N 15.16 E
Orsasjön ⊜ 26 61.07 N 14.34 E
Orsay 50 48.48 N 2.11 E
Orsett 260 51.31 N 0.22 E
Orsières 58 46.02 N 7.09 E
Orsjön ⊜ 26 61.35 N 16.20 E
Orsk 86 51.12 N 58.34 E
Orskär I 40 60.31 N 18.23 E
Ørslev 41 55.02 N 11.59 E
Orsogna 66 42.13 N 14.17 E
Orsomarso 68 39.48 N 15.55 E
Orson 210 41.49 N 75.27 W
Orșova 38 44.42 N 22.24 E
Orsoy 52 51.31 N 6.41 E
Ørsta 26 62.12 N 6.09 E
Ørsted 41 55.20 N 10.04 E
Orsundaån ≐ 40 59.44 N 17.21 E
Örsundsbro 40 59.44 N 17.18 E
Országház ⊠ 264c 47.31 N 19.03 E
Orta 130 40.38 N 33.06 E
Orta, Lago d' ⊜ 62 45.49 N 8.24 E
Ortaca 130 36.49 N 28.47 E
Ortaklar 130 37.53 N 27.30 E
Ortaköy, Tür. 130 38.00 N 34.23 E
Ortaköy, Tür. 130 40.17 N 35.16 E
Ortaköy, Tür. 130 40.27 N 38.02 E
Ortaköy, Tür. 130 38.44 N 34.03 E
Ortaköy ✦8 267b 41.03 N 29.01 E
Orta Nova 68 41.19 N 15.42 E
Orta San Giulio 62 45.48 N 8.25 E
Orte 66 42.27 N 12.23 E
Ortega 246 3.56 N 75.13 W
Ortega Channel ⊔ 175e 8.22 S 159.37 E
Ortegal, Cabo ≻ 34 43.45 N 7.53 W
Orteguaza ≐ 246 0.43 N 75.16 W
Ortelsburg → Szczytno 30 53.34 N 21.00 E
Ortenberg, B.R.D. 56 50.21 N 9.02 E
Ortenberg, B.R.D. 58 48.27 N 7.58 E
Ortenburg 60 48.33 N 13.14 E
Orth 54 54.27 N 11.03 E
Orthez 32 43.29 N 0.46 W
Orthon ≐ 248 10.50 S 66.04 W
Ortigalita Creek ≐ 226 36.57 N 120.52 W
Ortigalita Peak ▲ 226 36.48 N 120.55 W
Ortigara, Monte ▲ 64 46.00 N 11.29 E
Ortigueira, Bra. 252 24.12 S 50.55 W
Ortigueira, Esp. 34 43.41 N 7.51 W
Ortigueira, Ría de C1 34 43.42 N 7.51 W
Orting 224 47.06 N 122.12 W
Ortisei (Sankt Ulrich) 64 46.34 N 11.40 E
Ortiz, Méx. 232 28.17 N 110.43 W
Ortiz, Ven. 246 9.37 N 67.17 W
Ortles (Ortler) ▲ 64 46.31 N 10.33 E
Ortofta 41 55.47 N 13.14 E
Ortona 66 42.21 N 14.24 E
Ortona Lock ✦5 220 26.47 N 81.18 W
Orton Park ♠ 275b 43.46 N 79.12 W
Ortonura 85 41.29 N 76.12 E
Ortonville, Mich., U.S. 216 42.51 N 83.27 W
Ortonville, Minn., U.S. 198 45.19 N 96.27 W
Ortonville State Recreation Area ♠ 216 42.52 N 83.26 W
Ortoterek 85 41.56 N 71.21 E
Orto-Tokoj 85 42.21 N 76.01 E
Ortovero 62 44.03 N 8.07 E
Ortrand 54 51.22 N 13.45 E
Orträsk 26 64.08 N 18.59 E
Ortueri 71 40.02 N 8.59 E
Ortúzar, Canal de ≅ 286e 33.33 S 70.47 W
Örtze ≐ 52 52.40 N 9.57 E
Oruanui 172 38.35 S 176.02 E
Oruba 273a 6.35 N 3.25 E
Orubskoje Gorodišče ⊥ 82 55.12 N 36.45 E
Orudjevo 82 56.26 N 37.32 E
Orune 71 40.24 N 9.22 E
Oruro 248 17.59 S 67.09 W
Oruro □5 248 18.40 S 67.30 W
Or'us-Mijele ≐ 88 58.35 N 121.30 E
Orust I 26 58.10 N 11.38 E
Orūzgān (Qala-i-Hazār Qadam) 120 32.56 N 66.38 E
Orūzgān □4 120 33.15 N 66.00 E
Orval, Abbaye d' ⊎1 56 49.38 N 5.22 E
Orvanne ≐ 50 48.22 N 2.50 E
Orvieto 66 42.43 N 12.07 E
Orvilla 208 40.16 N 75.17 W
Orvilliers 261 48.52 N 1.39 E
Orvin ≐ 50 48.28 N 3.23 E
Orvinio 66 42.08 N 12.56 E
Orviston 214 41.06 N 77.45 W
Orvyn, Gora ▲ 180 65.14 N 175.20 W
Orwell, Ont., Can. 214 42.46 N 81.02 W
Orwell, N.Y., U.S. 212 43.35 N 76.00 W
Orwell, Ohio, U.S. 214 41.32 N 80.52 W
Orwell ≐ 42 51.57 N 1.17 E
Orwigsburg 208 40.39 N 76.06 W
Orwin 208 40.35 N 76.31 W
Or Yehuda 132 32.01 N 34.51 E
Oryu-dong ✦8 271b 37.29 N 126.51 E
Orževo 78 50.45 N 26.07 E
Orževka 80 52.43 N 42.55 E
Oržica 78 49.48 N 32.42 E
Orzinuovi 62 45.24 N 9.55 E
Orzyc ≐ 30 52.47 N 21.13 E
Orzysz 30 53.49 N 21.56 E
Os, Nor. 26 62.30 N 11.12 E
Oš, S.S.S.R. 85 40.33 N 72.48 E
Ōsa, Nihon 96 35.05 N 133.34 E
Osa, S.S.S.R. 86 57.17 N 55.26 E
Osa, S.S.S.R. 88 53.24 N 103.53 E
Osa, Península de ≻1 236 8.34 N 83.31 W
Osage, Iowa, U.S. 190 43.17 N 92.49 W
Osage, Mo., U.S. 219 38.25 N 92.02 W
Osage, N.J., U.S. 285 39.51 N 75.01 W
Osage, Wyo., U.S. 198 43.59 N 104.25 W
Osage □6 219 38.27 N 91.50 W
Osage ≐ 194 38.35 N 91.57 W
Osage Beach 194 38.09 N 92.37 W
Osage City 198 38.38 N 95.50 W
Ōsaka 96, 270 34.40 N 135.30 E
Ōsaka □5 96 34.30 N 135.30 E
Osaka Castle ⊥ 270 34.41 N 135.32 E
Ōsaka-hana ≻ 96 35.11 N 132.25 E
Ōsaka-heiya ≚ 94 34.42 N 135.35 E
Osaka International Airport ⊠ 270 34.47 N 135.26 E
Ōsaka-kō C 270 34.38 N 135.26 E
Ōsaka-kokusai-kūkō ⊠ 96 34.47 N 135.26 E
Osakarovka 86 50.32 N 72.39 E
Ōsaka-tōge)(, Nihon 96 33.49 N 135.36 E
Ōsaka-tōge)(, Nihon 270 34.56 N 135.18 E
Osaka University ⊎2 270 34.42 N 135.30 E
Ōsaka-wan C 96 34.30 N 135.18 E
Ōsaki-bana ≻ 96 33.19 N 132.23 E
Ōsaki-gahana ≻ 96 35.11 N 132.25 E
Ōsaki-kami-shima I 96 34.14 N 132.54 E
Osakis 198 45.52 N 95.09 W
Ōsaki-shimo-jima I 96 34.10 N 132.50 E
Osăm ≐ 38 43.42 N 24.51 E
Osan 98 37.11 N 127.04 E
Osanovo 82 54.12 N 38.41 E
Osasco 256 23.32 S 46.46 W
Osasco □7 287b 23.32 S 46.46 W
Ōsawa 94 35.15 N 139.51 E
Ōsawano 94 36.34 N 137.12 E
Osawatomie 198 38.31 N 94.57 W
Ōsa-yama ▲ 96 34.45 N 132.12 E
Osbaldeston 262 53.47 N 2.32 W
Osborne, Kans., U.S. 198 39.26 N 98.42 W
Osborne, Pa., U.S. 279b 40.32 N 80.10 W
Osburger Hochwald ✦3 56 49.40 N 6.50 E
Osburn 202 47.30 N 116.00 W
Osby 26 56.22 N 13.59 E
Osbyholm 41 55.51 N 13.36 E
Oscar Peak ▲ 182 54.51 N 129.07 W
Oscarville 180 60.43 N 161.46 W
Oscawana Lake 210 41.23 N 73.52 W
Osceola, Ark., U.S. 194 35.42 N 89.58 W
Osceola, Ind., U.S. 216 41.40 N 86.04 W
Osceola, Iowa, U.S. 190 41.02 N 93.46 W
Osceola, Mo., U.S. 194 38.03 N 93.42 W
Osceola, Nebr., U.S. 198 41.11 N 97.33 W
Osceola, Pa., U.S. 210 41.59 N 77.21 W
Osceola, Tex., U.S. 222 32.08 N 97.14 W
Osceola, Wis., U.S. 190 45.19 N 92.42 W
Osceola □6 220 28.00 N 81.15 W
Osceola Mills 214 40.51 N 78.16 W
Oščepkovo 86 56.29 N 70.42 E
Os Césares 256 22.47 S 46.49 W
Oschatz 54 51.17 N 13.07 E
Oschersleben 54 52.01 N 11.13 E
Oschiri 70 40.43 N 9.06 E
Oscoda 190 44.26 N 83.20 W
Öse ≐ 263 51.26 N 7.49 E
Osečenka 76 57.33 N 34.48 E
Osečina 38 44.23 N 19.36 E
Osejevskaja 82 55.53 N 38.10 E
Osejkino 82 56.15 N 35.54 E
Osek 54 50.37 N 13.40 E
Ösel → Saaremaa I 76 58.25 N 22.30 E
Oselce 60 49.26 N 13.40 E
Osen 24 64.17 N 10.30 E
Osetrovo 88 56.47 N 105.47 E
Ōse-zaki ≻ 94 35.02 N 138.47 E
Osgood, Ind., U.S. 218 39.08 N 85.17 W
Osgood, Ohio, U.S. 216 40.20 N 84.30 W
Osgoode 212 45.08 N 75.36 W
Osh → Oš 85 40.33 N 72.48 E
Oshamambe 92a 42.30 N 140.22 E
O'Shanassy ≐ 166 18.59 S 138.46 E
O'Shaughnessy Dam ✦6 226 37.57 N 119.47 W
O'Shaughnessy Reservoir ⊜1 214 40.12 N 83.09 W
Oshawa 212 43.54 N 78.51 W
Oshawa Creek ≐ 212 43.52 N 78.49 W
Oshibe ✦8 270 34.45 N 135.04 E
Oshigambo 156 17.47 S 16.05 E
Oshika, Nihon 92 38.16 N 141.32 E
Ōshika, Nihon 94 35.34 N 138.02 E
Oshikango 156 17.25 S 15.56 E
Ōshima, Nihon 92 33.03 N 129.33 E
Ōshima, Nihon 94 37.07 N 138.30 E
Ōshima, Nihon 96 33.55 N 132.15 E
Ōshima, Nihon 96 34.13 N 132.01 E
Ō-shima I, Nihon 92 33.28 N 135.50 E
Ō-shima I, Nihon 92a 41.30 N 139.22 E
Ō-shima I, Nihon 94 34.43 N 139.24 E
Ō-shima I, Nihon 94 36.15 N 136.07 E
Ō-shima I, Nihon 96 33.38 N 134.30 E
Ō-shima I, Nihon 96 34.00 N 133.22 E
Ō-shima I, Nihon 96 33.54 N 130.26 E
Ō-shima I, Nihon 96 34.09 N 133.04 E
Ō-shima I, Nihon 96 34.30 N 131.25 E
Oshima-hantō ≻1 92a 42.00 N 140.30 E
Oshimizu 94 36.49 N 136.46 E
Oshino 94 35.28 N 138.51 E
Oshivre ✦8 272c 19.09 N 72.51 E
Oshkosh, Nebr., U.S. 198 41.24 N 102.21 W
Oshkosh, Wis., U.S. 190 44.01 N 88.33 W
Oshnovīyeh 128 37.02 N 45.06 E
Oshodi 273a 6.34 N 3.21 E
Oshoek 158 26.13 S 30.59 E
Oshogbo 150 7.47 N 4.34 E
Oshtemo 216 42.15 N 85.41 W
Oshtorān Kūh ▲ 128 33.20 N 49.16 E
Oshtorīnān 128 34.01 N 48.38 E
Oshwe 152 3.24 S 19.30 E
Osi 150 8.08 N 5.14 E
Osiān 120 26.43 N 72.55 E
Osica de Jos 38 44.15 N 24.17 E
Osich'ŏn-ni 98 41.25 N 128.16 E
Osiek 30 50.31 N 21.28 E
Osiglia 62 44.17 N 8.12 E
Osijek 38 45.33 N 18.41 E
Osilinka ≐ 182 56.05 N 124.29 W
Osilo 71 40.45 N 8.40 E
Osimo 66 43.29 N 13.29 E
Osini 71 39.50 N 9.29 E
Osinki 80 52.51 N 49.30 E
Osinniki, S.S.S.R. 80 58.03 N 47.02 E
Osinniki, S.S.S.R. 86 53.37 N 87.21 E
Osinovka, S.S.S.R. 83 49.34 N 39.05 E
Osinovka, S.S.S.R. 88 50.34 N 109.27 E
Osinovka, S.S.S.R. 88 56.19 N 101.56 E
Osinovskij Chrebet ⛰ 180 67.10 N 175.00 E
Ośnów Dolny 54 52.48 N 14.10 E
Osintorf 76 54.42 N 30.39 E
Osio Sotto 62 45.36 N 9.35 E
Osipaonica 38 44.33 N 21.04 E
Osipenko → Berd'ansk 78 46.45 N 36.49 E
Osipoviči 76 53.18 N 28.38 E
Osipovo Selo 76 56.51 N 30.30 E
Osire 156 20.59 S 17.19 E
Oskaloosa, Iowa, U.S. 190 41.18 N 92.39 W
Oskaloosa, Kans., U.S. 198 39.13 N 95.19 W
Oskar-Fredriksborg 40 59.24 N 18.26 E
Oskarshamn 26 57.16 N 16.26 E
Oskarström 26 56.48 N 12.58 E
Os'kino 78 51.14 N 39.02 E
Oskol ≐ 78 49.06 N 37.25 E
Oskolkovo 24 67.58 N 53.42 E
Oskū 128 37.55 N 46.06 E
Oskuj 76 59.17 N 32.05 E
Oskuja ≐ 76 59.14 N 31.54 E
Oslava ≐ 61 49.05 N 16.22 E
Osling ≐ 56 49.55 N 6.00 E
Oslo 26 59.55 N 10.45 E
Oslob 116 9.31 N 123.26 E
Oslofjorden C2 26 59.20 N 10.35 E
Os'ma ≐ 76 54.55 N 33.24 E
Osmānābād 122 18.10 N 76.02 E
Osmancık 130 40.59 N 34.49 E
Osmaneli 130 40.22 N 30.01 E
Osmaniye 130 37.05 N 36.14 E
Osmanlı 130 41.52 N 34.37 E
Osmanpaşa 130 39.38 N 34.58 E
Osm'anskaja Vozvyšennost' ✦1 76 54.20 N 26.00 E
Osm'any 76 54.25 N 25.56 E
Osmeña 116 10.11 N 125.31 E
Osmington 42 50.38 N 2.22 W
Os'mino 76 59.01 N 29.06 E
Osminog, Gora ▲ 180 67.54 N 176.50 E
Ösmo 40 58.59 N 17.54 E
Osmond 198 42.22 N 97.36 W
Osmore, Río de ≐ 248 17.33 S 71.12 W
Osmoy 261 48.52 N 1.43 E
Osmussaar I 76 59.18 N 23.22 E
Osnabrück 52 52.16 N 8.02 E
Osnabrück □6 52 52.30 N 7.40 E
Ośno 30 52.28 N 14.50 E
Osny 261 49.04 N 2.04 E
Oso 224 48.16 N 121.56 W
Oso ≐ 154 1.09 S 27.22 E
Oso, Gran Lago del → Great Bear Lake ⊜ 176 66.00 N 120.00 W
Osoba 85 40.44 N 70.26 E
Osogna 58 46.18 N 9.00 E
Osoppo 64 46.15 N 13.05 E
Osorakan-zan ▲ 96 34.36 N 132.08 E
Osore-san ▲ 92 41.18 N 141.05 E
Osorio, Quebrada ≐ 286c 10.36 N 66.56 W
Osório Fonseca 250 3.40 S 58.13 W
Osorno, Chile 254 40.34 S 73.09 W
Osorno, Esp. 34 42.24 N 4.22 W
Osorun 273a 6.33 N 3.29 E
Os'otr ≐ 82 54.58 N 38.46 E
Osoyoos 182 49.02 N 119.28 W
Osoyoos Indian Reserve ✦4 182 49.08 N 119.30 W
Osoyoos Lake ⊜ 182 49.00 N 119.26 W
Osøyra 26 60.11 N 5.28 E
Ospedaletti 62 43.48 N 7.43 E
Ospedaletto, It. 64 46.17 N 13.07 E
Ospedaletto, It. 64 46.03 N 11.33 E
Ospino 246 9.18 N 69.27 W
Ospitale di Cadore 64 46.20 N 12.19 E
Ospitaletto 64 45.33 N 10.04 E
Osprey 220 27.12 N 82.29 W
Osprey Reef ✦2 164 13.55 S 146.38 E
Ospwagan Lake ⊜ 184 55.35 N 98.03 W
Os Ribeiros 256 22.06 S 46.49 W
Oss 52 51.46 N 5.31 E
Ossa, Mount ▲ 166 41.54 S 146.01 E
Ossabaw Island I 192 31.47 N 81.06 W
Osse ≐, Fr. 32 44.07 N 0.17 E
Osse ≐, Nig. 150 6.10 N 5.20 E
Ossenberg 263 51.34 N 6.35 E
Ossendrecht 52 51.24 N 4.19 E
Osseo, Mich., U.S. 216 41.53 N 84.33 W
Osseo, Wis., U.S. 190 44.35 N 91.12 W
Ossett 44 53.41 N 1.35 W
Ossi 71 40.40 N 8.35 E
Ossiacher See ⊜ 64 46.40 N 13.55 E
Ossian, Ind., U.S. 216 40.53 N 85.10 W
Ossian, Iowa, U.S. 190 43.09 N 91.46 W
Ossian, Loch ⊜ 46 56.46 N 4.38 W
Ossining 210 41.10 N 73.52 W
Ossipee ≐ 188 43.41 N 71.07 W
Ossjøen ⊜ 26 61.13 N 11.53 E
Ossling 54 51.21 N 14.09 E
Ossokmanuan Lake ⊜ 176 53.25 N 65.00 W
Ossona 266b 45.30 N 8.54 E
Ossora 74 59.20 N 163.13 E
Ossum-Bösinghoven 263 51.18 N 6.39 E
Ošta 24 60.49 N 35.32 E
Ostaboningue, Lac ⊜ 190 47.09 N 78.53 W
Östanå, Sve. 40 60.38 N 16.48 E
Östanå, Sve. 40 59.33 N 18.35 E
Östanbyn 40 60.39 N 16.48 E
Ostankino ✦8 265b 55.49 N 37.37 E
Östansjö 40 59.03 N 14.59 E
Ostapje 78 49.33 N 33.46 E
Ostaškov 76 57.09 N 33.06 E
Ostašovo 82 55.52 N 35.52 E
Ost-Berlin → Berlin (Ost) 264a 52.30 N 13.25 E
Ostbevern 52 52.02 N 7.50 E
Østbirk 41 55.58 N 9.46 E
Ostbüren 263 51.31 N 7.46 E
Østby 26 61.15 N 12.32 E
Ostchinesisches Meer → East China Sea ✦2 90 30.00 N 126.00 E
Oste ≐ 52 53.33 N 9.10 E
Osted 41 55.34 N 11.58 E
Osteen 220 28.51 N 81.10 W
Ostellato 66 44.45 N 11.56 E
Ostende → Oostende 50 51.13 N 2.55 E
Ostenfelde 52 51.52 N 8.04 E
Oster, S.S.S.R. 76 54.01 N 32.48 E
Oster, S.S.S.R. 78 50.57 N 30.53 E
Oster ≐, B.R.D. 60 48.33 N 13.29 E
Oster ≐, S.S.S.R. 76 53.47 N 31.46 E
Osterath 263 51.16 N 6.37 E
Osterbönen 263 51.37 N 7.48 E
Osterburg, D.D.R. 54 52.47 N 11.44 E
Osterburg, Pa., U.S. 214 40.16 N 78.31 W
Osterburken 56 49.26 N 9.26 E
Österbybruk 40 60.12 N 17.54 E
Österbymo 26 57.50 N 15.16 E
Ostercappeln 52 52.20 N 8.13 E
Österdalälven ≐ 26 60.33 N 15.08 E
Østerdalen ∨ 26 61.15 N 11.10 E
Österfärnebo 40 60.18 N 16.48 E
Osterfeld 54 51.05 N 11.56 E
Osterfeld ✦8 263 51.30 N 6.53 E
Östergötland □9 26 58.24 N 15.34 E
Östergötlands Län □6 26 58.25 N 15.45 E
Österhaninge 40 59.08 N 18.12 E
Osterhofen 60 48.42 N 13.01 E
Øster Højst 41 55.00 N 9.03 E
Osterholz-Scharmbeck 52 53.14 N 8.47 E
Osterley Park ♠ 260 51.30 N 0.21 W
Österlövsta 40 60.26 N 17.47 E
Ostermundigen 58 46.58 N 7.29 E
Osternienburg 54 51.48 N 12.01 E
Osterode, B.R.D. 52 51.44 N 10.11 E
Osterode → Ostróda, Pol. 30 53.43 N 19.59 E
Østerøya I 26 60.33 N 5.35 E
Österreich → Austria □1 30 47.20 N 13.20 E
Österreichische Alpen ⛰ 30 47.40 N 15.10 E
Österreichisches Freilichtmuseum ♠ 61 47.10 N 15.19 E
Östersjön → Baltic Sea ✦2 24 57.00 N 19.00 E
Österskär 40 59.28 N 18.18 E
Östersund 26 63.11 N 14.39 E
Östervåla 40 60.11 N 17.11 E
Osterville 207 41.38 N 70.22 W
Osterwick 52 52.01 N 7.13 E
Osterwieck 54 51.58 N 10.42 E
Ostfeld 263 51.30 N 7.45 E
Østfold □6 26 59.20 N 11.30 E
Ostfriesische Inseln II 52 53.44 N 7.25 E
Ostfriesland □9 52 53.20 N 7.40 E
Ost-Ghats → Eastern Ghāts ⛰ 122 14.00 N 78.50 E
Ostgrossefehn 52 53.24 N 7.36 E
Östhammar 40 60.15 N 18.22 E
Ostheim vor der Rhön 56 50.28 N 10.13 E
Osthofen 56 49.42 N 8.19 E
Ostia, Bonifica di ✦1 267a 41.46 N 12.18 E
Ostia Antica ⊥ 66 41.45 N 12.18 E
Ostiano 64 45.13 N 10.15 E
Ostiglia 64 45.04 N 11.08 E
Ostki 78 51.16 N 27.22 E
Östliche Sierra Madre → Madre Oriental, Sierra ⛰ 232 22.00 N 99.30 W
Östmark 26 60.17 N 12.45 E
Ost'or ≐ 78 50.56 N 30.52 E
Ostpeene ≐ 54 53.43 N 12.46 E
Ostra 66 43.37 N 13.09 E
Östraby 41 55.46 N 13.41 E
Ostrach 58 47.57 N 9.23 E
Ostrach ≐ 58 48.04 N 9.24 E
Östra Grevie 41 55.28 N 13.08 E
Östra Husby 40 58.35 N 16.33 E
Östra Laxsjön ⊜ 40 58.54 N 14.42 E
Östra Ljungby 41 56.11 N 13.04 E
Ostrander 214 40.16 N 83.13 W
Ostrau → Ostrava, Česko. 30 49.50 N 18.17 E
Ostrau, D.D.R. 54 51.12 N 13.09 E
Ostrava 30 49.50 N 18.17 E
Ostra Vetere 66 43.36 N 13.03 E
Ostredok ▲ 30 48.55 N 19.04 E
Ostrhauderfehn 52 53.08 N 7.37 E
Östrich 263 51.40 N 6.55 E
Ostricourt 50 50.27 N 3.02 E
Östringen 56 49.13 N 8.43 E
Ostritz 54 51.01 N 14.56 E
Ostróda 30 53.43 N 19.59 E
Ostrog 78 50.20 N 26.31 E
Ostrog, Manastir ⊎1 38 42.39 N 19.00 E
Ostrogožsk 78 50.52 N 39.05 E
Ostrokonje 76 59.52 N 42.02 E
Ostrołęka 30 53.06 N 21.34 E
Ostromeč 60 49.37 N 12.58 E
Ostroróg 30 52.39 N 16.27 E
Ostrošickij Gorodok 76 54.04 N 27.42 E
Ostrov, Česko. 54 50.17 N 12.57 E
Ostrov, Rom. 38 44.06 N 27.22 E
Ostrov, S.S.S.R. 76 60.34 N 37.55 E
Ostrov, S.S.S.R. 76 57.20 N 28.22 E
Ostrov, S.S.S.R. 76 52.53 N 25.59 E
Ostrov, S.S.S.R. 265b 55.35 N 37.51 E
Ostrov ✦1 30 47.55 N 17.35 E
Ostrov'anskij 80 46.45 N 42.13 E
Ostrovcy 82 55.35 N 38.01 E
Ostrovec 76 54.37 N 25.57 E
Ostrovki 265a 59.48 N 30.50 E
Ostrovno 76 55.08 N 29.53 E
Ostrovskaja 80 50.26 N 44.27 E
Ostrovskoje 80 57.48 N 42.15 E
Ostrov-Zalit 76 58.01 N 28.04 E
Ostrowiec Świętokrzyski 30 50.57 N 21.23 E
Ostrów Lubelski 30 51.30 N 22.52 E
Ostrów Mazowiecka 30 52.49 N 21.54 E
Ostrów Wielkopolski 30 51.39 N 17.49 E
Ostryna 76 53.44 N 24.32 E
Ostrzeszów 30 51.25 N 17.57 E
Ostsee → Baltic Sea ✦2 24 57.00 N 19.00 E
Ostseebad Ahrenshoop 54 54.23 N 12.25 E
Ostseebad Boltenhagen 54 54.00 N 11.12 E
Ostseebad Dierhagen 41 54.17 N 12.22 E
Ostseebad Graal-Müritz 54 54.15 N 12.12 E
Ostseebad Nienhagen 54 54.09 N 11.58 E
Ostseebad Rerik 54 54.06 N 11.37 E
Ostseebad Wustrow 54 54.21 N 12.23 E
Ost-Sümmern 263 51.26 N 7.44 E
Osttirol ✦1 64 46.55 N 12.30 E
Ostuacán 234 17.25 N 93.18 W
Ostula 234 18.30 N 103.28 W
Ostuni 68 40.44 N 17.35 E
Ostwald 58 48.33 N 7.43 E
Osuga 76 56.02 N 34.18 E
Osuga ≐ 76 57.16 N 34.49 E
Osuka 94 34.41 N 137.59 E
Osum ≐ 38 40.48 N 19.52 E
Ōsumi 270 34.50 N 135.45 E
Ōsumi-hantō ≻1 92 31.20 N 130.55 E
Ōsumi-kaikyō ⊔ 92 31.00 N 131.00 E
Ōsumi-shotō II 93b 30.30 N 130.00 E
Osuna 34 37.14 N 5.07 W
Osu-ri 98 35.31 N 127.18 E
Osvaldo Cruz 255 21.47 S 50.50 W
Osveja 76 56.01 N 28.06 E
Osvejskoje, Ozero ⊜ 76 56.03 N 28.08 E
Ošvor 24 66.58 N 62.53 E
Oswaldtwistle 44 53.43 N 2.26 W
Oswaldtwistle Moor ✦3 262 53.43 N 2.23 W
Oswald West State Park ♠ 224 45.45 N 123.58 W
Oswayo 214 41.55 N 78.01 W
Oswayo Creek ≐ 210 42.02 N 78.21 W
Oswegatchie ≐ 212 44.42 N 75.30 W
Oswego, Ill., U.S. 216 41.41 N 88.21 W
Oswego, Ind., U.S. 216 41.19 N 85.47 W
Oswego, Kans., U.S. 198 37.10 N 95.06 W
Oswego, N.Y., U.S. 212 43.27 N 76.31 W
Oswego □6 212 43.22 N 76.15 W
Oswego ≐, N.J., U.S. 208 39.40 N 74.32 W
Oswego ≐, N.Y., U.S. 212 43.28 N 76.31 W
Oswestry 42 52.52 N 3.04 W
Oświęcim 30 50.03 N 19.12 E
Osyka 194 31.00 N 90.28 W
Ōta, Nihon 94 36.18 N 139.22 E
Ōta, Nihon 96 33.31 N 131.33 E
Ōta ✦8 268 35.35 N 139.44 E
Ōta ≐, Nihon 94 34.40 N 137.54 E
Ōta ≐, Nihon 96 34.22 N 132.25 E
Otago Peninsula ≻1 172 45.52 S 170.40 E
Otahuhu 172 36.57 S 174.51 E
Ōtake 96 34.12 N 132.13 E
Otaki, N.Z. 172 40.45 S 175.09 E
Ōtaki, Nihon 94 35.17 N 140.15 E
Ōtaki, Nihon 94 35.57 N 138.56 E
Ōtaki, Nihon 94 35.48 N 137.33 E
Ōtaki, Nihon 94 35.49 N 137.40 E
Ōtaki-yama ▲ 96 34.07 N 134.08 E
Otane 172 39.53 S 176.38 E
Otanmäki 26 64.07 N 27.06 E
Otar 85 43.33 N 75.13 E
Otaru 92a 43.13 N 141.00 E
Otatara 172 46.26 S 168.18 E
Otatitlán 234 18.12 N 96.02 W
Otautau 172 46.09 S 168.00 E
Otava 26 61.39 N 27.04 E
Otavalo 246 0.14 N 78.16 W
Otavi 156 19.39 S 17.20 E
Ōtawara 94 36.52 N 140.02 E
Otawa-yama ▲ 270 34.28 N 135.53 E
Otay 228 32.36 N 117.04 W
Otchinjau 156 16.30 S 13.57 E
Oteapan 234 18.00 N 94.39 W
Otego 210 42.23 N 75.10 W
Otego Creek ≐ 210 42.24 N 75.11 W
Otélé 152 3.55 N 11.15 E
Otematata 172 44.37 S 170.16 E
Otepää 76 58.03 N 26.30 E
Oteros ≐ 232 26.55 N 108.22 W
Otěšice 60 49.33 N 13.07 E
Otford, Austl. 170 34.12 S 151.01 E
Otford, Eng., U.K. 260 51.19 N 0.12 E
Otgon 88 47.16 N 97.33 E
Otgon Tenger Uul ▲ 88 47.35 N 97.35 E
Otham 260 51.15 N 0.35 E
Othello 224 46.50 N 119.10 W
Othery 42 51.05 N 2.53 W
Othfresen 52 52.00 N 10.23 E
Othis 261 49.04 N 2.41 E
Othonoi I 38 39.50 N 19.26 E
Oti ≐ 150 8.40 N 0.13 E
Otibanda 164 7.15 S 146.30 E
Otinapa 232 24.11 N 105.02 W
Otira 172 42.50 S 171.33 E

ENGLISH Name	Page	Lat.°′	Long.°′

Otis, Colo., U.S. 198 40.09 N 102.58 W
Otis, Ind., U.S. 216 41.36 N 86.54 W
Otis, Kans., U.S. 198 38.32 N 99.03 W
Otis, Mass., U.S. 207 42.12 N 73.06 W
Otisco 218 38.33 N 85.40 W
Otisco Lake ⊜ 210 42.52 N 76.18 W
Otish, Monts ⛰ 176 52.22 N 70.30 W
Otis Reservoir ⊜1 207 42.09 N 73.02 W
Otisville 210 41.28 N 74.32 W
Otjassy 80 53.14 N 41.39 E
Otjikondo 156 19.50 S 15.23 E
Otjimbingue 156 22.19 S 16.10 E
Otjimbingwe Game Reserve ✦4 156 22.20 S 16.05 E
Otjinene 156 21.13 S 18.42 E
Otjituuo 156 19.40 S 18.32 E
Otjiwarongo 156 20.29 S 16.36 E
Otjiwarongo □5 156 21.45 S 17.00 E
Otjiwero 156 17.59 S 13.22 E
Otjosondjou ≐ 156 19.30 S 20.04 E
Otju 156 18.15 S 13.18 E
Otju □5 156 20.00 S 15.00 E
Otley 44 53.54 N 1.41 W
Otm'ok, Pereval)(85 42.20 N 73.10 E
Otmuchów 30 50.28 N 17.10 E
Otnes 26 61.45 N 11.14 E
Ōtō 96 33.41 N 135.35 E
Otočac 36 44.52 N 15.14 E
Oton 116 10.42 N 122.29 E
Otonabee ≐ 212 44.08 N 78.14 W
Otoque, Isla I 236 8.36 N 79.36 W
Ōtori-kita 270 34.33 N 135.27 E
Otorma 80 53.32 N 42.32 E
Otoro ≐ 236 15.00 N 88.16 W
Otorohanga 172 38.11 S 175.12 E
Otoskwin ≐ 176 52.13 N 88.06 W
Otowa 94 34.51 N 137.18 E
Otowa-yama ▲ 270 34.58 N 135.51 E
Otowa-yama-tunnel ✦5 94 34.58 N 135.51 E
Ōtoyo 96 33.46 N 133.40 E
Otra ≐ 26 58.09 N 8.00 E
Otradnaja 84 44.23 N 41.31 E
Otradnoje 265a 59.47 N 30.49 E
Otradnyj 80 53.22 N 51.21 E
Otranto 68 40.09 N 18.30 E
Otranto, Capo d' ≻ 68 40.06 N 18.31 E
Otranto, Strait of ≐1 38 40.00 N 19.00 E
Otricoli 66 42.25 N 12.29 E
Otrokovice 30 49.13 N 17.31 E
Ötscher ▲ 61 47.52 N 15.12 E
Otsego 216 42.27 N 85.42 W
Otsego □6 210 42.42 N 74.56 W
Otsego Lake ⊜ 210 42.45 N 74.52 W
Otselic ≐ 210 42.20 N 75.58 W
Ōtsu, Nihon 96 35.00 N 135.52 E
Ōtsu, Nihon 268 35.16 N 139.42 E
Ōtsu ≐ 270 34.30 N 135.24 E
Ōtsuchi 92 39.21 N 141.54 E
Ōtsuki 94 35.36 N 138.57 E
Ōtsu-shima I 96 34.00 N 131.42 E
Otta, Nig. 150 6.42 N 3.10 E
Otta, Nor. 26 61.46 N 9.32 E
Otta ≐ 26 61.46 N 9.31 E
Ottakring ✦8 264b 48.12 N 16.19 E
Ottana 71 40.14 N 9.02 E
Otta Pass ⊔ 175c 7.09 N 151.53 E
Ottarnic Pond ⊜ 283 42.46 N 71.25 W
Ottati 68 40.28 N 15.19 E
Ottavia ✦8 267a 41.58 N 12.24 E
Ottaviao 68 40.51 N 14.28 E
Ottawa, Ont., Can. 212 45.25 N 75.42 W
Ottawa, Ill., U.S. 216 41.21 N 88.51 W
Ottawa, Kans., U.S. 198 38.37 N 95.16 W
Ottawa, Ohio, U.S. 216 41.01 N 84.03 W
Ottawa □6, Mich., U.S. 216 42.57 N 86.02 W
Ottawa □6, Ohio, U.S. 214 41.31 N 82.56 W
Ottawa ≐, Can. 176 45.20 N 73.58 W
Ottawa ≐, Ohio, U.S. 214 41.44 N 83.28 W
Ottawa ≐, Ohio, U.S. 216 41.00 N 84.15 W
Ottawa-Carleton □6 212 45.15 N 75.45 W
Ottawa Hills 214 41.40 N 83.39 W
Ottawa International Airport ⊠ 212 45.19 N 75.40 W
Ottawa Islands II 176 59.30 N 80.10 W
Ottbergen 52 51.42 N 9.18 E
Ottenby 26 56.14 N 16.25 E
Ottendorf-Okrilla 54 51.11 N 13.50 E
Ottenhöfen 58 48.34 N 8.09 E
Ottenschlag 61 48.25 N 15.13 E
Ottenstein Stausee ⊜1 61 48.37 N 15.17 E
Otter ≐ 42 50.46 N 3.17 W
Otterbach ≐ 56 49.07 N 8.21 E
Otterbäcken 40 58.57 N 14.02 E
Otterbein 216 40.29 N 87.06 W
Otterberg 56 49.30 N 7.46 E
Otterburn 44 55.14 N 2.10 W
Otterburne 184 49.30 N 97.03 W
Otterburn Park 206 45.33 N 73.13 W
Otter Creek 192 29.19 N 82.48 W
Otter Creek ≐, Ont., Can. 212 42.44 N 80.51 W
Otter Creek ≐, Ont., Can. 212 44.06 N 81.07 W
Otter Creek ≐, Ind., U.S. 218 38.58 N 85.37 W
Otter Creek ≐, Iowa, U.S. 194 41.20 N 93.30 W
Otter Creek ≐, Mo., U.S. 219 39.31 N 91.51 W
Otter Creek ≐, Mont., U.S. 202 45.36 N 106.17 W
Otter Creek ≐, N.Y., U.S. 212 43.43 N 75.23 W
Otter Creek ≐, Utah, U.S. 200 38.10 N 112.02 W
Otter Creek ≐, Vt., U.S. 188 44.13 N 73.17 W
Otter Creek Reservoir ⊜1 200 38.12 N 111.59 W
Otterhöfen 56 48.33 N 8.12 E
Otter Lake, Qué., Can. 188 45.51 N 76.26 W
Otter Lake, Mich., U.S. 190 43.13 N 83.28 W
Otter Lake ⊜, Ont., Can. 212 44.47 N 76.07 W
Otter Lake ⊜, Ont., Can. 212 45.17 N 79.56 W
Otter Lake ⊜, Sask., Can. 184 55.35 N 104.39 W
Otterlo 52 52.06 N 5.45 E
Otterndorf 52 53.48 N 8.53 E
Otterøya I 26 62.42 N 6.48 E
Otter River 207 42.36 N 72.03 W
Ottersberg 52 53.06 N 9.08 E
Ottershaw 260 51.22 N 0.32 W
Ottersleben ✦8 54 52.05 N 11.34 E
Otter Tail Lake ≐ 198 46.16 N 96.36 W
Otterup 41 55.31 N 10.24 E
Otterville, Ont., Can. 212 42.55 N 80.36 W
Otterville, Ill., U.S. 219 39.03 N 90.24 W
Otterville, Mo., U.S. 194 38.42 N 93.00 W
Ottery ≐ 42 50.39 N 4.20 W
Ottery Saint Mary 42 50.45 N 3.17 W
Ottignies 56 50.40 N 4.34 E
Ottine 222 29.36 N 97.35 W
Ottleben 54 52.05 N 11.07 E
Ottmachau → Otmuchów 30 50.28 N 17.10 E
Ottmarsbocholt 52 51.49 N 7.32 E
Ottnang 60 48.06 N 13.40 E
Ottnaren ⊜ 40 60.29 N 16.37 E
Otto, N.Y., U.S. 210 42.21 N 78.50 W
Otto, Tex., U.S. 222 31.27 N 96.49 W
Ottobeuren 58 47.56 N 10.18 E
Ottobeuren, Klosterkirche ⊎1 58 48.01 N 10.28 E

DEUTSCH Name	Seite	Breite°′	Länge°′ E=Ost

Ottobiano 62 45.09 N 8.50 E
Ottobrunn 60 48.04 N 11.40 E
Ottone 62 44.37 N 9.20 E
Ottoschwanden 58 48.12 N 7.52 E
Ottosdal 158 26.58 S 26.00 E
Ottoshoop 156 25.45 S 25.59 E
Ottoville 216 40.54 N 84.18 W
Ottuk, S.S.S.R. 85 41.38 N 75.51 E
Ottuk, S.S.S.R. 85 42.18 N 76.18 E
Ottumwa 190 41.01 N 92.25 W
Ottweiler 56 49.24 N 7.09 E
Otty Lake ⊜ 212 44.50 N 76.13 W
Otu, Nig. 150 8.14 N 3.24 E
Otu → Ōtsu, Nihon 96 35.00 N 135.52 E
Otukpa 150 7.09 N 7.41 E
Otumpa 252 27.19 S 62.13 W
Otun 273a 6.42 N 3.22 E
Oturkpo 150 7.14 N 8.08 E
Otuzco 248 7.54 S 78.35 W
Otway, Bahía ⊔ 254 53.20 S 74.00 W
Otway, Cape ≻ 166 38.52 S 143.31 E
Otway, Seno C 254 53.05 S 71.30 W
Otway Range ⛰ 169 38.30 S 143.50 E
Otwock 30 52.07 N 21.16 E
Otyn'a 78 48.44 N 24.51 E
Ötztal ∨ 64 47.05 N 10.55 E
Ötztaler Ache ≐ 64 47.14 N 10.50 E
Ötztaler Alpen (Alpi Venoste) ⛰ 64 46.45 N 10.55 E
Ou ≐ 110 20.04 N 102.13 E
Ouachita ≐ 194 31.38 N 91.49 W
Ouachita, Lake ⊜1 194 34.40 N 93.25 W
Ouachita Mountains ⛰ 194 34.40 N 94.25 W
Ouaco 175f 20.50 S 164.29 E
Ouada, Djebel ▲ 146 8.56 N 23.26 E
Ouadane 148 20.56 N 11.37 W
Ouadda 152 8.04 N 22.24 E
Ouaddai □5 146 13.00 N 21.00 E
Ouadey, Ouadi el ∨ 146 13.34 N 18.03 E
Ouadou ∨ 150 15.40 N 9.53 W
Ouagadougou 150 12.22 N 1.31 W
Ouah ≐ 152 0.43 N 12.55 E
Ouahigouya 150 13.35 N 2.25 W
Ouahran → Oran 148 35.43 N 0.43 W
Ouak 152 7.43 N 13.30 E
Ouaka □5 152 6.00 N 21.00 E
Ouaka ≐ 152 4.59 N 19.56 E
Oualâta 150 17.18 N 7.02 W
Oualâta, Dhar ✦4 150 17.48 N 7.24 W
Oualidia 148 32.44 N 9.08 W
Ouallam 150 14.19 N 2.05 E
Ouallene 148 24.37 N 1.14 E
Oualto 150 9.01 N 10.06 W
Ouamiri 152 6.12 N 20.45 E
Ouanary 250 4.13 N 51.40 W
Ouanda Djallé 146 8.54 N 22.48 E
Ouandjia ≐ 146 9.35 N 21.43 E
Ouango 152 4.19 N 22.33 E
Ouani 150 16.46 N 0.17 W
Ouanne ≐ 50 47.57 N 2.47 E
Ouan Taredert 148 27.33 N 9.32 E
Ouaquaga 210 42.08 N 75.39 W
Ouarane ✦1 134 21.00 N 10.30 W
Ouararda, Passe de)(148 21.01 N 13.03 W
Ouareau ≐ 206 45.56 N 73.25 W
Ouareau, Lac ⊜1 206 46.17 N 74.09 W
Ouargaye 150 11.32 N 0.01 E
Ouargla 148 31.59 N 5.25 E
Ouarkoye 150 12.05 N 3.40 W
Ouarkziz, Jbel ⛰ 148 28.50 N 9.00 W
Ouarra ≐ 154 5.05 N 24.26 E
Ouarsenis, Djebel ▲ 34 35.53 N 1.38 E
Ouarville 50 48.21 N 1.46 E
Ouarzazate 148 30.57 N 6.50 W
Ouassoulou ≐ 150 11.35 N 8.11 W
Ouatcha 150 13.22 N 9.18 E
Oubangui (Ubangi) ≐ 152 0.30 S 17.42 E
Ouche ≐ 58 47.06 N 5.16 E
Ōuchi 96 34.16 N 134.18 E
Oucques 50 47.49 N 1.18 E
Ōuda 94 34.28 N 135.56 E
Oudaze Lake ⊜ 212 45.27 N 79.11 W
Oud-Beijerland 52 51.49 N 4.25 E
Ouddorp 52 51.18 N 3.56 E
Oude IJssel (Issel) ≐ 52 52.00 N 6.10 E
Oudenaarde 50 50.51 N 3.36 E
Oudenbosch 52 51.35 N 4.31 E
Oudenburg 50 50.46 N 3.53 E
Oude-Pekela 52 53.04 N 6.58 E
Oude Rijn ≐ 52 52.05 N 4.20 E
Oudeschild 52 53.02 N 4.50 E
Oude-Tonge 52 51.41 N 4.12 E
Oudewater 52 52.02 N 4.52 E
Oud-Gastel 52 51.35 N 4.27 E
Oudjda → Oujda 148 34.41 N 1.45 W
Oud-Loosdrecht 52 52.13 N 5.04 E
Oudtshoorn 158 33.35 S 22.14 E
Oudyoumoudi 150 14.04 N 0.28 W
Oued Athmenia 34 36.15 N 6.17 E
Oued Cheham 36 36.23 N 7.46 E
Oued Fodda 34 36.11 N 1.32 E
Oued Meliz 36 36.27 N 8.34 E
Oued Rhiou 34 35.58 N 0.55 E
Oued Tlelat 34 35.34 N 0.27 W
Oued Zarga 36 36.40 N 9.25 E
Oued-Zem 148 32.55 N 6.33 W
Ouellé 150 7.18 N 4.01 W
Ouémé □5 150 7.00 N 2.35 E
Ouémé ≐ 150 6.29 N 2.32 E
Ouen, Île I 175f 22.26 S 166.49 E
Ouenkoro 150 13.23 N 3.50 W
Ouenza 148 35.57 N 8.04 E
Ouenza, Djebel ▲ 36 35.57 N 8.05 E
Ouenzé ✦8 273b 4.14 S 15.17 E
Ouergayo 150 6.19 N 5.56 W
Ouessa 150 11.03 N 2.47 W
Ouessant, Île d' I 32 48.28 N 5.05 W
Ouesso 152 1.37 N 16.04 E
Ouest, Pointe de l' ≻ 186 49.52 N 64.31 W
Ouest, Rivière de l' ≐ 206 45.39 N 74.21 W
Ouezzane 148 34.52 N 5.35 W
Ouffet 56 50.26 N 5.28 E
Ouganda → Uganda □1 154 1.00 N 32.00 E
Ougarou 150 12.09 N 0.56 E
Oughter, Lough ⊜ 48 54.00 N 7.30 W
Oughterard 48 53.25 N 9.17 W
Ouham □5 152 7.00 N 18.00 E
Ouham-Pendé □5 152 7.00 N 16.00 E
Ouidah 150 6.22 N 2.05 E
Ouistreham 32 49.17 N 0.15 W
Oujda 148 34.41 N 1.45 W
Oujiamiao 102 31.55 N 112.09 E
Oujiang ≐ 100 28.04 N 120.35 E
Oulainen 26 64.16 N 24.48 E
Oulangan Kansallispuisto ♠ 24 66.12 N 29.30 E
Oulchy-le-Château 50 49.12 N 3.21 E
Oule ≐ 62 44.25 N 5.21 E
Ouled Agla 34 35.58 N 4.45 E
Ouled Djellal 148 34.28 N 5.02 E
Ouled-Naïl, Monts des ⛰ 148 34.33 N 3.28 E
Ouleout Creek ≐ 210 42.20 N 75.18 W
Oulins 50 48.52 N 1.28 E
Oullins 62 45.43 N 4.48 E
Oulou, Bahr ≐ 146 9.48 N 21.32 E
Oulton Broad 42 52.31 N 1.42 E
Oulu 26 65.01 N 25.28 E
Oulujärvi ⊜ 26 64.20 N 27.15 E
Oulujoki ≐ 26 65.01 N 25.25 E

Symbols in the index entries represent the broad categories identified in the key at the right. Symbols with superior numbers (⛰²) identify subcategories (see complete key on page *I · 30*).

Kartensymbole in dem Registerverzeichnis stellen die rechts in Schlüssel erklärten Kategorien dar. Symbole mit hochgestellten Ziffern (⛰²) bezeichnen Unterabteilungen einer Kategorie (vgl. vollständiger Schlüssel auf Seite *I · 30*).

Los símbolos incluídos en el texto del índice representan las grandes categorías identificadas con la clave a la derecha. Los símbolos con numeros en su parte superior (⛰²) identifican las subcategorías (véase la clave completa en la página *I · 30*).

Les symboles de l'index représentent les catégories indiquées dans la légende à droite. Les symboles suivis d'un indice (⛰²) représentent des sous-catégories (voir légende complète à la page *I · 30*).

Os símbolos incluídos no texto do índice representam as grandes categorias identificadas com a chave à direita. Os símbolos com números em sua parte superior (⛰²) identificam as subcategorias (veja-se a chave completa à página *I · 30*).

▲ Mountain — Berg — Montaña — Montagne — Montanha
⛰ Mountains — Berge — Montañas — Montagnes — Montanhas
)(Pass — Pass — Paso — Col — Passo
∨ Valley, Canyon — Tal, Cañon — Valle, Cañón — Vallée, Canyon — Vale, Canhão
≚ Plain — Ebene — Llano — Plaine — Planície
≻ Cape — Kap — Cabo — Cap — Cabo
I Island — Insel — Isla — Île — Ilha
II Islands — Inseln — Islas — Îles — Ilhas
✦ Other Topographic Features — Andere Topographische Objekte — Otros Elementos Topográficos — Autres données topographiques — Outros Elementos Topográficos

ESPAÑOL — Nombre · Página · Lat.°′ · Long.°′ W=Oeste
FRANÇAIS — Nom · Page · Lat.°′ · Long.°′ W=Ouest
PORTUGUÊS — Nome · Página · Lat.°′ · Long.°′ W=Oeste

Oulun lääni □4 24 65.00 N 27.00 E
Oulx 62 45.02 N 6.50 E
Oum Chalouba 146 15.48 N 20.46 E
Oumé 150 6.23 N 5.25 W
Oum er Rbia, Oued ≃ 148 33.19 N 8.21 W
Oum Hadjer 146 13.18 N 19.41 E
Oum Hadjer, Ouadi V 146 16.38 N 20.14 E
Oumm ed Droûs Guebli, Sebkhet ⊜ 148 24.03 N 11.45 W
Oumm ed Drous Telli, Sebkhet ⊜ 148 24.20 N 11.30 W
Ounara 148 31.33 N 9.28 W
Ounasjoki ≃ 24 66.30 N 25.45 E
Oundle 42 52.29 N 0.29 W
Ounianga Kébir 146 19.04 N 20.29 E
Ouolossébougou 150 12.00 N 7.55 W
Our ≃ 56 49.53 N 6.18 E
Oura-wan C 174m 26.32 N 128.04 E
Ouray 200 38.01 N 107.40 W
Ouray, Mount ∧ 200 38.25 N 106.14 W
Ource ≃ 58 48.06 N 4.23 E
Ourcq ≃ 50 49.01 N 3.01 E
Ourcq, Canal de l' ⊏ 50 48.51 N 2.22 E
Ourém 250 1.33 S 47.06 W
Ouri 146 21.34 N 19.13 E
Ouri, Tarso ∧ 146 21.25 N 18.56 E
Ouricuri 250 7.53 S 40.05 W
Ourimbah 170 33.22 S 151.23 E
Ourinhos 255 22.59 S 49.52 W
Ourique 34 37.39 N 8.13 W
Ournie 171b 35.56 S 147.51 E
Ouro, Paraná do ≃ 248 8.29 S 70.30 W
Ouro, Ponta do ≻ 158 26.51 S 32.54 E
Ouro, Rio d' ≃ 287a 22.42 S 43.35 W
Ouro Branco 250 6.42 S 36.57 W
Ouro Fino 256 22.17 S 46.22 W
Ouro Prêto 255 20.23 S 43.30 W
Ouro Prêto ≃ 248 11.02 S 65.13 W
Ouroufa, Vallée d' V 150 14.42 N 7.00 E
Ouroux 50 47.11 N 3.57 E
Ours, Grand Lac de l' → Great Bear Lake ⊜ 176 66.00 N 120.00 W
Oursi 150 14.41 N 0.27 W
Ourthe ≃ 56 50.38 N 5.35 E
Ourville-en-Caux 50 49.44 N 0.36 E
Ou-sammyaku ⋀ 92 38.45 N 140.50 E
Ouse 166 42.29 S 146.42 E
Ouse ≃, Ont., Can. 212 44.17 N 78.03 W
Ouse ≃, Eng., U.K. 42 50.47 N 0.03 E
Ouse ≃, Eng., U.K. 44 53.42 N 0.41 W
Oust ≃ 32 47.39 N 2.06 W
Outardes, Baie aux C 186 49.02 N 68.30 W
Outardes, Rivière aux ≃ 176 49.04 N 68.28 W
Outardes Est, Rivière aux ≃ 206 45.06 N 74.04 W
Outarville 50 48.13 N 2.01 E
Outcalt 276 40.23 N 74.24 W
Outeniekwaberge ⋀ 158 33.53 S 22.35 E
Outerbridge Crossing ⇝5 276 40.31 N 74.15 W
Outer Harbour 168b 34.47 S 138.30 E
Outer Hebrides II 46 57.45 N 7.00 W
Outer Island I 190 47.03 N 90.30 W
Outer Santa Barbara Passage ⊔ 228 33.10 N 118.30 W
Outjo 156 20.08 S 16.08 E
Outlane 262 53.39 N 1.53 W
Outlet Bay C 208 37.22 N 75.49 W
Outlook, Sask., Can. 184 51.30 N 107.03 W
Outlook, Mont., U.S. 198 48.53 N 104.47 W
Outokumpu 26 62.44 N 29.01 E
Outpost Mountain ∧ 180 69.08 N 151.12 W
Outreau 50 50.42 N 1.35 E
Outremont 206 45.31 N 73.38 W
Outside Canal ⊏ 226 37.13 N 121.02 W
Out Skerries II 46a 60.25 N 0.42 W
Outwell 42 52.37 N 0.14 E
Outwood 44 53.42 N 1.30 W
Ouvèze ≃ 62 43.59 N 4.51 E
Ouvidor 255 18.14 S 47.50 W
Ouye, Forêt de l' ♠ 261 48.32 N 2.00 E
Ouyen 166 35.04 S 142.20 E
Ouzinkie 180 57.55 N 152.30 W
Ouzouer-le-Marché 50 47.55 N 1.32 E
Ouzouer-sur-Loire 50 47.46 N 2.29 E
Ovacık 130 41.05 N 32.55 E
Ovada 62 44.38 N 8.38 E
Oval 210 41.09 N 77.11 W
Ovalau I 175g 17.40 S 178.48 E
Ovalle 252 30.36 S 71.12 W
Ovamboland □5 156 18.00 S 16.00 E
Ovamboland □9 156 17.45 S 16.30 E
Ovar 34 40.52 N 8.38 W
Ovaro 64 46.29 N 12.52 E
Ovau I 175e 6.47 S 156.01 E
Ovčinino 82 56.02 N 39.03 E
Ovcyno 265a 59.48 N 30.37 E
Övedskloster 41 55.41 N 13.38 E
Ovejas 246 9.32 N 75.14 W
Ovelgönne 52 53.20 N 8.25 E
Ovenden 262 53.44 N 1.53 W
Oveng 152 2.25 N 12.16 E
Overath 56 50.55 N 7.14 E
Overberge 263 51.37 N 7.41 E
Overbrook 184 48.37 N 95.33 W
Overbrook ⇝8, Pa., U.S. 279b 40.24 N 79.59 W
Overbrook ⇝8, Pa., U.S. 285 39.58 N 75.16 W
Overdinkel 52 52.14 N 7.01 E
Overflakkee I 52 51.45 N 4.10 E
Overflowing ≃ 184 53.10 N 101.05 W
Overhalla 24 64.30 N 11.57 E
Overijse 56 50.46 N 4.32 E
Overijssel □4 52 52.25 N 6.30 E
Över Jerstal 41 55.12 N 9.18 E
Överkalix 24 66.21 N 22.56 E
Overland 219 38.42 N 90.21 W
Overland Park 198 38.59 N 94.40 W
Overlea 208 39.22 N 76.31 W
Overloon 52 51.35 N 5.57 E
Övermark (Ylimarkku) 26 62.38 N 21.30 E
Overpeck Creek ≃ 276 40.51 N 74.02 W
Overpelt 56 51.13 N 5.25 E
Overseal 42 52.44 N 1.34 W
Overstrand 42 52.56 N 1.20 E
Overton, Eng., U.K. 42 51.15 N 1.15 W
Overton, Nebr., U.S. 198 40.44 N 99.32 W
Overton, Nev., U.S. 204 36.33 N 114.27 W
Overton, Tex., U.S. 222 32.16 N 94.59 W
Overton Arm C 204 36.20 N 114.25 W
Övertorneå 24 66.23 N 23.40 E
Overum 26 57.59 N 16.19 E
Over Wallop 42 51.09 N 1.35 W
Ovett 194 31.29 N 89.02 W
Ovid, Mich., U.S. 216 43.01 N 84.22 W
Ovid, N.Y., U.S. 210 42.41 N 76.49 W
Ovidiopol' 78 46.17 N 30.27 E
Oviedo, Esp. 34 43.22 N 5.50 W
Oviedo, Fla., U.S. 220 28.40 N 81.13 W
Oviglio 62 44.52 N 8.29 E
Oviken 26 62.59 N 14.24 E
Oviksfjällen ⋀ 26 63.02 N 13.51 E
Ovilla 222 32.32 N 96.53 W
Ovindoli 66 42.08 N 13.31 E
Oviniśče 76 58.22 N 37.02 E
Ovino 76 59.41 N 33.11 E
Oviši 76 57.34 N 21.45 E
Övörchangaj □4 102 46.00 N 102.30 E
Øvre Anarjokka Nasjonalpark ♠ 24 69.00 N 25.00 E
Øvre Årdal 26 61.19 N 7.48 E
Øvre Dividalen Nasjonalpark ♠ 24 68.39 N 19.45 E
Øvre Pasvik Nasjonalpark ♠ 24 69.06 N 28.55 E
Øvre Rendal 26 61.53 N 11.05 E
Övre Vättern ⊜ 40 59.52 N 15.40 E
Ovruč 78 51.21 N 28.49 E
Ovs'anikovo 76 60.09 N 45.16 E
Ovs'anka, S.S.S.R. 86 55.57 N 92.33 E
Ovs'anka, S.S.S.R. 89 53.35 N 126.57 E
Ovs'annikovo 82 56.54 N 37.33 E
Ovstug 76 53.24 N 33.52 E
Owada 268 35.49 N 139.33 E
Owaka 172 46.27 S 169.40 E
Owando 152 0.29 S 15.55 E
Owaneco 219 39.29 N 89.12 W
Owasco 210 42.51 N 76.28 W
Owasco Inlet ≃ 210 42.45 N 76.28 W
Owasco Lake ⊜ 210 42.52 N 76.32 W
Owasco Outlet ≃ 210 43.04 N 76.39 W
Owase 92 34.04 N 136.12 E
Owasso 196 36.16 N 95.51 W
Owatonna 190 44.05 N 93.14 W
Owbeh 128 34.22 N 63.10 E
Owe 272c 19.04 N 73.04 E
Owego 210 42.06 N 76.16 W
Owego Creek, East Branch ≃ 210 42.10 N 76.15 W
Owel, Lough ⊜ 48 53.34 N 7.25 W
Owen, Austl. 168b 34.16 S 138.33 E
Owen, B.R.D. 56 48.35 N 9.27 E
Owen, Ind., U.S. 218 38.27 N 85.34 W
Owen, Wis., U.S. 190 44.57 N 90.33 W
Owen □6 218 38.33 N 84.49 W
Owen, Mount ∧ 172 41.33 S 172.32 E
Owenboy ≃ 48 51.48 N 8.18 W
Owenea ≃ 48 54.47 N 8.26 W
Owen Falls Dam ⇝6 154 0.27 N 33.11 E
Owenkillew ≃ 48 54.44 N 7.18 W
Owenmore ≃ 48 54.07 N 9.50 W
Owen River 172 41.39 S 172.27 E
Owens ≃ 204 36.31 N 117.57 W
Owensboro 194 37.46 N 87.07 W
Owens Creek ≃ 226 37.13 N 120.42 W
Owens Lake ⊜ 204 36.25 N 117.56 W
Owen Sound 212 44.34 N 80.56 W
Owen Sound C 212 44.40 N 80.55 W
Owen Stanley Range ⋀ 164 9.20 S 147.55 E
Owensville, Ind., U.S. 194 38.16 N 87.41 W
Owensville, Mo., U.S. 219 38.21 N 91.29 W
Owensville, Ohio, U.S. 218 39.07 N 84.08 W
Owenton, Ky., U.S. 218 38.32 N 84.50 W
Owenton, Va., U.S. 208 37.53 N 77.06 W
Owentown 222 32.26 N 95.12 W
Owerri 150 5.29 N 7.02 E
Owhango 172 39.00 S 175.23 E
Owikeno Lake ⊜ 182 51.41 N 127.00 W
Owings 208 38.43 N 76.36 W
Owings Mills 284b 39.25 N 76.47 W
Owingsville 188 38.09 N 83.46 W
Owl ≃, Alta., Can. 182 54.54 N 111.57 W
Owl ≃, Man., Can. 176 57.51 N 92.44 W
Owl Creek ≃, U.S. 198 44.41 N 103.29 W
Owl Creek ≃, Mont., U.S. 202 45.18 N 107.21 W
Owl Creek ≃, Wyo., U.S. 202 43.41 N 108.11 W
Owl Creek, South Fork ≃ 202 43.43 N 108.32 W
Owl Creek Mountains ⋀ 202 43.30 N 108.35 W
Owo 150 7.15 N 5.37 E
Oworonsoki 273a 6.33 N 3.24 E
Owosso 216 43.00 N 84.10 W
Owyhee 204 41.57 N 116.06 W
Owyhee ≃ 202 43.46 N 117.02 W
Owyhee, Lake ⊜1 202 43.28 N 117.20 W
Owyhee, South Fork ≃ 202 42.26 N 116.53 W
Oxapampa 248 10.34 S 75.24 W
Oxbow, Sask., Can. 184 49.14 N 102.11 W
Oxbow, Mich., U.S. 281 42.38 N 83.28 W
Oxbow, N.Y., U.S. 212 44.17 N 75.37 W
Oxbow Lake ⊜ 281 42.38 N 83.28 W
Ox Creek ≃ 198 48.37 N 100.17 W
Oxelösund 40 58.40 N 17.06 E
Oxford, N.S., Can. 186 45.44 N 63.52 W
Oxford, N.Z. 172 43.18 S 172.11 E
Oxford, Eng., U.K. 42 51.46 N 1.15 W
Oxford, Ala., U.S. 194 33.37 N 85.50 W
Oxford, Conn., U.S. 207 41.20 N 73.07 W
Oxford, Fla., U.S. 220 28.56 N 82.02 W
Oxford, Ind., U.S. 216 40.31 N 87.15 W
Oxford, Iowa, U.S. 190 41.43 N 91.47 W
Oxford, Kans., U.S. 198 37.16 N 97.10 W
Oxford, Ky., U.S. 218 38.16 N 84.30 W
Oxford, Maine, U.S. 188 44.08 N 70.30 W
Oxford, Md., U.S. 208 38.42 N 76.10 W
Oxford, Mass., U.S. 207 42.07 N 71.52 W
Oxford, Mich., U.S. 216 42.49 N 83.16 W
Oxford, Miss., U.S. 194 34.22 N 89.32 W
Oxford, Nebr., U.S. 198 40.15 N 99.38 W
Oxford, N.J., U.S. 210 40.48 N 75.00 W
Oxford, N.C., U.S. 192 36.19 N 78.35 W
Oxford, N.Y., U.S. 210 42.27 N 75.36 W
Oxford, Ohio, U.S. 218 39.30 N 84.44 W
Oxford, Pa., U.S. 208 39.47 N 75.59 W
Oxford, Wis., U.S. 190 43.47 N 89.34 W
Oxford □6 212 43.08 N 80.50 W
Oxford Falls 274a 33.44 S 151.15 E
Oxford House 184 54.56 N 95.16 W
Oxford House Indian Reserve ⇝4 184 54.54 N 95.15 W
Oxford Junction 190 41.59 N 90.57 W
Oxford Lake ⊜ 184 54.51 N 95.37 W
Oxford Peak ∧ 202 42.16 N 112.06 W
Oxfordshire □6 42 51.50 N 1.15 W
Oxhey 260 51.39 N 0.23 W
Oxie 41 55.33 N 13.04 E
Oxley 166 34.12 S 144.06 E
Oxley Creek ≃ 171a 27.32 S 153.00 E
Oxnard 228 34.12 N 119.11 W
Oxnard Beach 228 34.09 N 119.13 W
Oxon Hill 284c 38.48 N 76.59 W
Oxon Run ≃ 284c 38.49 N 77.00 W
Ox Pasture Brook ≃ 283 42.45 N 70.54 W
Oxshott 260 51.20 N 0.21 W
Oxted 42 51.16 N 0.01 W
Oxtongue ≃ 212 45.19 N 79.01 W
Oxtongue Lake ⊜ 212 45.22 N 78.55 W
Oxus → Amu Darya ≃ 72 43.40 N 59.01 E
Oy 58 47.38 N 10.28 E
Oya, Malay. 112 2.52 N 111.53 E
Oya, Nihon 96 35.20 N 134.40 E
Oya ≃ 112 2.52 N 111.52 E
Oyabe 94 36.40 N 136.52 E
Oyabe ≃ 94 36.48 N 137.04 E
Oyake-yama ∧2 270 34.56 N 135.19 E
Oyama, B.C., Can. 182 50.07 N 119.22 W
Oyama, Nihon 94 36.18 N 139.48 E
Oyama, Nihon 94 36.36 N 137.18 E
Oyama, Nihon 94 35.21 N 139.00 E
Oyama, Nihon 268 35.36 N 139.22 E
Oyamada 94 34.46 N 136.13 E
Oya-magaibutsu ❖1 94 36.36 N 139.50 E
Oyamazaki 270 34.54 N 135.42 E
Oyameles 234 19.43 N 97.32 W
Oyano 92 32.35 N 130.30 E
Oyapock (Oiapoque) ≃ 250 4.08 N 51.40 W
Oyashirazu ♠ 94 36.59 N 137.40 E
Oybin 54 50.50 N 14.44 E
Oye-et-Pallet 58 46.51 N 6.20 E
Oyem 152 1.37 N 11.35 E
Oyen 184 51.22 N 110.28 W
Øyeren ⊜ 26 59.48 N 11.14 E
Oykel ≃ 46 57.56 N 4.25 W
Oykel Bridge 46 57.58 N 4.43 W
Oymyakon → Ojm'akon 74 63.28 N 142.49 E
Oyo, Congo 152 0.01 N 15.54 E
Oyo, Nig. 150 7.51 N 3.56 E
Oyo ≃ 115a 7.57 S 110.22 E
Ōyodo 92 34.23 N 135.48 E
Ōyodo ⇝8 270 34.43 N 135.30 E
Ōyodo ≃ 92 31.53 N 131.28 E
Oyón 248 10.39 S 76.47 W
Oyonnax 58 46.15 N 5.40 E
Ōyorogi-san ∧ 96 35.05 N 132.51 E
Oyotún 248 6.51 S 79.19 W
Oyster 208 37.17 N 75.55 W
Oyster Bay 210 40.52 N 73.32 W
Oyster Bay C, Austl. 168b 34.54 S 137.48 E
Oyster Bay C, Austl. 274a 34.00 S 151.06 E
Oyster Bay Cove 276 40.52 N 73.31 W
Oyster Bay Harbor C 276 40.53 N 73.32 W
Oyster Creek 222 29.00 N 95.20 W
Oyster Creek ≃ 222 29.59 N 95.18 W
Oyster Point ∧ 282 37.50 N 121.52 W
Oyster Point ≻ 168b 34.55 S 137.48 E
Oyster Rock I2 272c 18.54 N 72.50 E
Oysterville 224 46.33 N 124.02 W
Øystese 26 60.23 N 6.13 E
Oyten 52 53.04 N 9.01 E
Ozaki 268 35.59 N 139.51 E
Ozala, Parc National d' ♠ 152 1.00 S 15.00 E
Ozamiz 116 8.08 N 123.50 E
Ozanne ≃ 50 48.11 N 1.22 E
Ozariči 76 52.28 N 29.16 E
Ozark, Ala., U.S. 194 31.28 N 85.38 W
Ozark, Ark., U.S. 194 35.29 N 93.50 W
Ozark, Mo., U.S. 194 37.01 N 93.12 W
Ozark Escarpment ⊥4 194 36.15 N 91.15 W
Ozark Plateau ⋀1 194 37.00 N 93.00 W
Ozarks, Lake of the ⊜1 194 38.10 N 92.50 W
Ozaukee □6 216 44.14 N 88.00 W
Ozbourn Seamount ⟡3 14 25.55 S 174.50 W
Ózd 30 48.14 N 20.18 E
Ozd'atiči 76 54.06 N 28.50 E
Oze ≃ 96 34.12 N 132.14 E
Ozeblin ∧ 36 44.35 N 15.53 E
Ozek 86 46.35 N 60.41 E
Ozereckoje 82 56.04 N 37.23 E
Ožerelje 82 54.48 N 38.17 E
Ožerelki 82 55.51 N 38.52 E
Ozerišče 76 54.48 N 33.13 E
Ozerki, S.S.S.R. 80 51.13 N 53.56 E
Ozerki, S.S.S.R. 80 51.32 N 45.16 E
Ozerki, S.S.S.R. 80 52.01 N 45.29 E
Ozerki, S.S.S.R. 86 53.38 N 83.44 E
Ozerki, S.S.S.R. 265a 59.54 N 30.44 E
Ozerna ≃ 82 55.44 N 36.08 E
Ozernoje 78 50.11 N 28.42 E
Ozernovskij 74 51.30 N 156.31 E
Ozernyj 180 66.24 N 179.06 W
Ozero 80 56.58 N 44.43 E
Ozero Stambovskoje ♠ 82 56.42 N 35.53 E
Ozery 82 54.51 N 38.34 E
Ozette Lake ⊜ 224 48.06 N 124.38 W
Ozgol 267d 35.47 N 51.30 E
Ozgoryš 85 41.15 N 74.45 E
Ozieri 71 40.35 N 9.00 E
Ozimek 30 50.41 N 18.13 E
Ozinki 80 51.12 N 49.45 E
Ožogino, Ozero ⊜ 74 69.16 N 146.36 E
Ozoir-la-Ferrière 261 48.46 N 2.40 E
Ozona, Fla., U.S. 220 28.04 N 82.47 W
Ozona, Tex., U.S. 196 30.43 N 101.12 W
Ozone Park ⇝8 276 40.40 N 73.51 W
Ozorków 30 51.58 N 19.19 E
Oz'ornaja 86 53.25 N 63.15 E
Oz'ornoje, S.S.S.R. 80 51.46 N 51.28 E
Oz'ornoje, S.S.S.R. 86 56.48 N 71.15 E
Oz'ornyj, S.S.S.R. 80 57.10 N 40.59 E
Oz'ornyj, S.S.S.R. 86 51.08 N 60.50 E
Oz'orsk, S.S.S.R. 76 54.25 N 22.01 E
Oz'orsk, S.S.S.R. 78 51.43 N 26.24 E
Oz'orskij 89 46.36 N 143.08 E
Oz'ory 76 53.43 N 24.11 E
Ozouer-le-Voulgis 261 48.40 N 2.47 E
Ōzu, Nihon 92 32.52 N 130.52 E
Ōzu, Nihon 96 33.30 N 132.33 E
Ozubulu 150 5.57 N 6.51 E
Ozuluama 234 21.40 N 97.51 W
Ozumba de Alzate 234 19.03 N 98.48 W

P

Pâ 150 11.33 N 3.15 W
Paadekraal Monument ⊥ 273d 26.06 S 27.47 E
Paagoumène 175f 20.29 S 164.11 E
Paal 56 51.02 N 5.11 E
Paama I 175f 16.28 S 168.14 E
Pa-an 110 16.53 N 97.38 E
Paar ≃ 60 48.45 N 11.33 E
Paaren 264a 52.39 N 12.59 E
Paarl 158 33.45 S 18.56 E
Paarlshoop ⇝8 273d 26.13 S 27.59 E
Paasbach ≃ 263 51.25 N 7.11 E
Paauilo 229d 20.02 N 155.22 W
Pabarabuk 164 6.05 S 144.05 E
Pabbay I, Scot., U.K. 46 56.51 N 7.35 W
Pabbay I, Scot., U.K. 46 57.46 N 7.15 W
Pabbi 123 34.01 N 71.47 E
Pabbiring, Kepulauan II 112 4.55 S 119.25 E
Pabean 112 6.50 S 115.19 E
Pabellón, Ensenada del C 232 24.27 N 107.36 W
Pabellón, Punta ≻ 254 43.14 S 74.23 W
Pabellon de Arteaga 234 22.10 N 102.21 W
Pabianice 30 51.40 N 19.22 E
Pabillonis 71 39.35 N 8.43 E
Pablo 202 47.36 N 114.07 W
Pābna 124 24.00 N 89.15 E
Pabo 154 3.00 N 32.09 E
Pabradė 76 54.59 N 25.44 E
Paca 115b 8.29 S 120.11 E
Pacaás Novos ≃ 248 10.51 S 65.20 W
Pacaás Novos, Serra dos ⋀ 248 10.45 S 64.15 W
Pacaembu 255 21.34 S 51.17 W
Pacaembú, Estádio do ♠ 287b 23.33 S 46.39 W
Pacahuaras ≃ 248 10.04 S 65.46 W
Pacajá ≃ 250 1.56 S 50.50 W
Pacajus 250 4.10 S 38.28 W
Pacaltsdorp 158 34.00 S 22.28 E
Pacaraima, Sierra de → Pakaraima Mountains ⋀ 246 5.30 N 60.40 W
Pacarán 248 12.52 S 76.03 W
Pacaraos 248 11.11 S 76.44 W
Pacasmayo 248 7.24 S 79.34 W
Pacatuba 250 3.58 S 38.37 W
Paccha ≃ 248 9.05 S 76.54 W
Pace 194 33.42 N 90.52 W
Paceco 70 37.59 N 12.33 E
Pačelma, S.S.S.R. 80 53.20 N 43.20 E
Pačelma, S.S.S.R. 80 53.15 N 43.21 E
Pacet 115a 6.45 S 107.03 E
Pachača 74 60.34 N 169.03 E
Pachacamac 248 12.14 S 76.53 W
Pachacamac ⊥ 248 12.14 S 76.52 W
Pachāgarh 124 26.20 N 88.34 E
Pachamba 126 24.12 N 86.16 E
Pachaug Pond ⊜ 207 41.34 N 71.54 W
Pacheco 226 37.59 N 122.04 W
Pacheco Creek ≃ 226 36.58 N 121.28 W
Pacheco Pass)(226 37.03 N 121.13 W
Pachecos 256 22.48 S 42.50 W
Pāchh Elāsin 126 24.08 N 89.54 E
Páchi I 267c 37.58 N 23.22 E
Pachino 70 36.43 N 15.05 E
Pachitea ≃ 248 8.46 S 74.32 W
Pachiza 248 7.16 S 76.46 W
Pachkoli ⇝8 272c 19.08 N 72.54 E
Pachmarhi 124 22.28 N 78.26 E
Pacho 246 5.08 N 74.10 W
Pachomovo 82 54.38 N 37.33 E
Pachor 124 23.42 N 76.44 E
Pāchora 122 20.40 N 75.21 E
Pachotnyj Ugol 80 52.58 N 41.56 E
Pachra ≃ 82 55.32 N 37.59 E
Pachtaabad 85 38.28 N 68.10 E
Pachuca [de Soto] 234 20.07 N 98.44 W
Paciência ⇝8 256 22.55 S 43.38 W
Pacific, B.C., Can. 182 54.46 N 128.17 W
Pacific, Mo., U.S. 219 38.29 N 90.45 W
Pacific, Wash., U.S. 224 47.16 N 122.15 W
Pacific □6 224 46.30 N 123.39 W
Pacifica 226 37.38 N 122.29 W
Pacific Beach 224 47.13 N 124.12 W
Pacific City 224 45.12 N 123.57 W
Pacific Creek ≃ 200 42.08 N 109.24 W
Pacific Gardens 226 37.58 N 121.20 W
Pacific Grove 226 36.38 N 121.56 W
Pacific Islands Trust Territory □2 14 10.00 N 155.00 E
Pacífico, Océano → Pacific Ocean ⊤1 6 10.00 S 150.00 W
Pacific Ocean ⊤1 4
6 10.00 S 150.00 W
Pacifico Mountain ∧ 228 34.23 N 118.02 W
Pacific Palisades ⇝8 280 34.03 N 118.32 W
Pacific Ranges ⋀ 182 50.45 N 125.30 W
Pacific Rim National Park ♠ 224 48.35 N 124.40 W
Pacifique, Océan → Pacific Ocean ⊤1 6 10.00 S 150.00 W
Pacijan Island I 116 10.39 N 124.20 E
Paciran 115a 6.52 S 112.20 E
Pacitan 115a 8.12 S 111.07 E
Pack 61 46.58 N 14.59 E
Packanack Brook ≃ 276 40.55 N 74.17 W
Packanack Lake ⊜ 276 40.56 N 74.15 W
Packard Mountain ∧2 207 42.28 N 72.21 W
Pack Monadnock Mountain ∧ 207 42.52 N 71.52 W
Packsattel)(61 46.58 N 14.58 E
Packwood 224 46.36 N 121.40 W
Packwood Lake ⊜ 224 46.35 N 121.34 W
Pacllón 248 10.18 S 77.07 W
Pacock Brook ≃ 276 41.05 N 74.31 W
Paço de Arcos 266c 38.42 N 9.17 W
Paço do Lumiar 250 2.31 S 44.07 W
Pacoima ⇝8 280 34.16 N 118.26 W
Pacolet ≃ 192 34.50 N 81.27 W
Pacolet Mills 192 34.55 N 81.45 W
Pácora, Col. 246 5.31 N 75.27 W
Pacora, Pan. 246 9.05 N 79.17 W
Pacoti 250 4.13 S 38.56 W
Pacov 30 49.28 N 15.00 E
Pacquet 186 49.59 N 55.53 W
Pacuare ≃ 236 10.14 N 83.17 W
Pacuí ≃ 255 16.46 S 45.01 W
Pacuneiro ≃ 255 13.02 S 53.25 W
Pacy-sur-Eure 50 49.01 N 1.23 E
Paczkow 30 50.27 N 17.00 E
Padada 116 6.42 N 125.22 E
Padada ≃ 116 6.42 N 125.23 E
Padaido, Kepulauan II 164 1.15 S 136.30 E
Padam 123 33.28 N 76.53 E
Padamarang, Pulau I 112 4.07 S 121.24 E
Padamo ≃ 246 2.54 N 65.17 W
Padampur 120 20.59 N 83.04 E
Padang, Indon. 112 2.59 N 105.40 E
Padang, Indon. 112 6.11 S 120.26 E
Padang, Indon. 112 1.39 S 108.55 E
Padang, Indon. 112 0.57 S 100.21 E
Padang, Pulau I 114 1.10 N 102.20 E
Padang Besar 114 6.40 N 100.19 E
Padangbetuah 112 3.39 S 102.13 E
Padang Endau 114 2.40 N 103.37 E
Padangpanjang 112 0.27 S 100.25 E
Padangsidempuan 114 1.22 N 99.16 E
Padangtiji 114 5.22 N 95.50 E
Padangtikar, Pulau I 112 0.50 S 109.30 E
Padang Tungku 114 4.14 N 101.59 E
Padany 24 63.17 N 33.22 E
Padas 115a 7.25 S 111.32 E
Padas ≃ 112 5.14 N 115.34 E
Padasjoki 26 61.21 N 25.17 E
Padauiri ≃ 246 0.15 S 64.05 W
Padborg 41 54.49 N 9.22 E
Padcaya 248 21.52 S 64.48 W
Paddington ⇝8 260 51.31 N 0.10 W
Paddington Station ⇝5 260 51.31 N 0.11 W
Paddle ≃ 182 54.05 N 114.15 W
Paddle Prairie 176 57.57 N 117.29 W
Paddock Lake 216 42.34 N 88.07 W
Paddock Wood 42 51.11 N 0.23 E
Padea 38 44.01 N 23.52 E
Padea-besar I 112 3.30 S 123.05 E
Padeghar 272c 18.58 N 73.03 E
Paden City 188 39.36 N 80.56 W
Paderborn 52 51.43 N 8.45 E
Paderno Dugnano 266b 45.34 N 9.10 E
Paderno Ponchielli 64 45.14 N 9.55 E
Padghe 272c 19.03 N 73.07 E
Padibe 154 3.28 N 32.50 E
Padiham 44 53.49 N 2.19 W
Padilla 248 19.19 S 64.20 W
Padilla Bay C 224 48.35 N 122.32 W
Padingge 120 32.52 N 88.39 E
Padirac, Gouffre de ⊥5 32 44.44 N 1.27 E
Padjelanta Nationalpark ♠ 24 67.28 N 16.41 E
Padle 272c 19.09 N 73.03 E
Padloping Island I 176 67.07 N 62.35 W
Padma → Ganges ≃ 124 23.22 N 90.32 E
Padmanābhapuram 122 8.14 N 77.20 E
Padola 64 46.36 N 12.28 E
Padoue → Padova 64 45.25 N 11.53 E
Padova 64 45.25 N 11.53 E
Padova □4 64 45.21 N 11.49 E
Padovka 80 52.28 N 49.31 E
Pādra 120 22.14 N 73.05 E
Padrão, Ponta do ≻ 152 6.03 S 12.18 E
Padrauna 124 26.55 N 83.59 E
Padre Bernardo 255 15.21 S 48.30 W
Padre Brito 256 21.18 S 43.59 W
Padre Burgos 116 10.02 N 125.01 E
Padre Island I 196 27.00 N 97.15 W
Padre Island National Seashore ♠ 196 26.26 N 27.43 W
Padre Miguel ⇝8 287a 22.53 S 43.26 W
Padre Paraíso 255 17.06 S 41.31 W
Padria 71 40.24 N 8.38 E
Padrón 34 42.44 N 8.40 W
Padrone, Cape ≻ 158 33.46 S 26.30 E
Padrt' 60 49.40 N 13.46 E
Padstow, Austl. 274a 33.57 S 151.02 E
Padstow, Eng., U.K. 42 50.33 N 4.56 W
Padua → Padova 64 45.25 N 11.53 E
Paduari ≃ 246 2.08 S 61.15 W
Paducah, Ky., U.S. 194 37.05 N 88.36 W
Paducah, Tex., U.S. 196 34.01 N 100.18 W
Padula 68 40.20 N 15.39 E
Paduli 68 41.10 N 14.53 E
Padunskaja 86 55.02 N 85.02 E
Pădurea Craiului, Munții ⋀ 38 46.55 N 22.20 E
Paea 174s 17.41 S 149.35 W
Paedun 98 35.03 N 128.21 E
Paekakariki 172 40.59 S 174.57 E
Paektu-san ∧ 98 42.00 N 128.03 E
Paengaroa 172 37.49 S 176.25 E
Paerdegat Basin C 276 40.37 N 73.54 W
Paeroa 172 37.23 S 175.40 E
Paesana 62 44.41 N 7.16 E
Paese 64 45.40 N 12.10 E
Paestum ⊥ 68 40.25 N 15.00 E
Paete 116 14.23 N 121.29 E
Páez ≃ 246 2.28 N 75.34 W
Pafúri 156 22.27 S 31.21 E
Pag 36 44.27 N 15.04 E
Pag, Otok I 36 44.30 N 15.00 E
Paga 150 10.58 N 1.06 W
Pagadenbaru 115a 6.28 S 107.48 E
Pagadian 116 7.49 N 123.25 E
Pagadian Bay C 116 7.48 N 123.31 E
Pagai Selatan, Pulau I 112 3.00 S 100.20 E
Pagai Utara, Pulau I 112 2.42 S 100.07 E
Pagalu I 138 1.25 S 5.36 E
Pagalungan 116 7.04 N 124.41 E
Pagan 110 21.10 N 94.51 E
Pagan I 108 18.07 N 145.46 E
Pagancillo 252 29.34 S 68.03 W
Paganella ∧ 64 46.08 N 11.02 E
Pagani 68 40.45 N 14.37 E
Paganica 66 42.21 N 13.28 E
Paganico 66 42.56 N 11.16 E
Pagaralam 112 4.01 S 103.16 E
Pagaran Tonga 114 1.14 N 99.46 E
Pagasitikós Kólpos C 38 39.15 N 22.51 E
Pagatan 112 3.36 S 115.56 E
Pagato ≃ 184 55.49 N 102.05 W
Pagato Lake ⊜ 184 56.08 N 102.30 W
Pagbilao 116 13.58 N 121.41 E
Pagbilao Grande Island I 116 13.55 N 121.46 E
Pagdanan Bay C 116 10.31 N 119.15 E
Page, Ariz., U.S. 200 36.57 N 111.27 W
Page, N. Dak., U.S. 198 47.09 N 97.34 W
Page Field ⊠ 220 26.35 N 81.52 W
Pagėgiai 76 55.09 N 21.54 E
Pageland 192 34.46 N 80.24 W
Page Manor 218 39.45 N 84.07 W
Pagerdewa 112 3.46 S 105.18 E
Paget, Mount ∧ 244 54.26 S 36.33 W
Paghmān 120 34.36 N 68.57 E
Paglia ≃ 66 42.42 N 12.11 E
Pagliara 70 37.59 N 15.22 E
Paglieta 66 42.10 N 14.30 E
Pagliete, Bonifica delle ⇝1 267a 41.53 N 12.12 E
Pagny-sur-Moselle 56 48.59 N 6.01 E
Pago Bay C 174p 13.25 N 144.48 E
Pagoda Peak ∧ 200 40.10 N 107.20 W
Pagoda Point ≻ 110 15.57 N 94.15 E
Pago Pago 174u 14.16 S 170.42 W
Pago Pago Harbor C 174u 14.17 S 170.40 W
Pagosa Springs 200 37.16 N 107.01 W
Pagote 272c 18.54 N 72.59 E
Pagouda 150 9.45 N 1.19 E
Pagsangahan 116 13.13 N 122.33 E
Pagsanjan 116 14.15 N 121.25 E
Pagua Bay C 240d 15.32 N 61.17 W
Paguate 200 35.08 N 107.23 W
Pagudpud 116 18.34 N 120.47 E
Pagueras, Torrente de ≃ 266d 41.28 N 1.58 E
Paguilou 152 1.12 S 9.31 E
Paguyaman ≃ 112 0.31 N 122.38 E
Pah, Tür. 84 39.08 N 39.40 E
Pah, Tür. 130 39.08 N 30.10 E
Pahādi ⇝8 272c 19.10 N 72.51 E
Pahala 229d 19.12 N 155.29 W
Pahang □3 114 3.30 N 102.45 E
Pahang ≃ 114 3.32 N 103.28 E
Páhara, Laguna C 236 14.18 N 83.15 W
Pahāsu 124 28.11 N 78.03 E
Pahau Point ≻ 229b 21.49 N 160.15 W
Pahi 114 5.28 N 102.13 E
Pahia Point ≻ 172 46.19 S 167.41 E
Pahiatua 172 40.27 S 175.50 E
Pahlād Garhi 272a 28.40 N 77.21 E
Pahlavī → Bandar-e Pahlavī 128 37.28 N 49.27 E
Pahlavī Dezh, Īrān 128 37.01 N 54.30 E
Pahlavī Dezh, Īrān 128 35.51 N 46.02 E
Pahlevi → Bandar-e Pahlavī 128 37.28 N 49.27 E
Pahlgām 123 34.02 N 75.20 E
Pahoa 229d 19.28 N 154.51 W
Pahokee 220 26.49 N 80.40 W
Pahrump 204 36.12 N 115.59 W
Pahsimeroi ≃ 202 44.41 N 114.03 W
Pahuatlán de Valle 234 20.17 N 98.09 W
Pai 110 19.19 N 98.27 E
Pai ≃ 110 19.09 N 97.33 E
Pai, Ilha do I 287a 22.59 S 43.05 W
Paia 229a 20.54 N 156.22 W
Paianía 267c 37.57 N 23.51 E
Paicines 226 36.44 N 121.17 W
Paico 248 14.02 S 73.39 W
Paide 76 58.54 N 25.33 E
Paifangchang 107 30.31 N 106.38 E
Paige 222 30.13 N 97.07 W
Paignton 42 50.26 N 3.34 W
Paiguano 252 30.01 S 70.32 W
Paiho 100 23.21 N 120.25 E
Paiján 248 7.44 S 79.19 W
Päijänne ⊜ 26 61.35 N 25.30 E
Pāikgācha 126 22.35 N 89.20 E
Pail, Bhārat 123 30.43 N 76.03 E
Pail, Pāk. 123 32.38 N 72.27 E
Paila ≃ 248 16.02 S 64.12 W
Pailĭn 110 12.51 N 102.36 E
Pailitas 246 8.58 N 73.38 W
Pailolo Channel ⊔ 229a 21.05 N 156.42 W
Pailoutou 106 30.56 N 121.16 E
Pailoutun 104 40.44 N 122.49 E
Paimboeuf 32 47.17 N 2.02 W
Paimio 26 60.27 N 22.42 E
Paimpol 32 48.46 N 3.03 W
Painan 112 1.21 S 100.34 E
Paincourt 214 42.23 N 82.17 W
Painesdale 190 47.02 N 88.41 W
Painesville 214 41.43 N 81.15 W
Pains 255 20.22 S 45.40 W
Painscastle 42 52.07 N 3.12 W
Painswick 42 51.48 N 2.11 W
Paint ≃ 190 45.58 N 88.15 W
Paint Creek ≃, Mich., U.S. 281 42.06 N 83.36 W
Paint Creek ≃, Ohio, U.S. 218 39.18 N 82.56 W
Paint Creek ≃, Pa., U.S. 214 41.10 N 79.28 W
Paint Creek ≃, Tex., U.S. 196 30.18 N 99.54 W
Paint Creek, East Fork ≃ 218 39.32 N 83.25 W
Paint Creek, North Fork ≃ 218 39.18 N 83.02 W
Paint Creek Lake ⊜1 218 39.15 N 83.22 W
Painted Desert ⇝2 200 36.00 N 111.20 W
Painted Post 210 42.07 N 77.08 W
Painter 208 37.34 N 75.44 W
Painter Creek ≃ 218 40.05 N 84.21 W
Paintertown 279b 40.21 N 79.42 W
Paint Lake ⊜ 184 55.28 N 97.57 W
Paint Rock 196 31.30 N 99.55 W
Paint Rock ≃ 194 34.28 N 86.28 W
Paintsville 192 37.49 N 82.48 W
Paiol da Vargem 256 22.41 S 46.26 W
Paiolinho 256 21.52 S 45.54 W
Paisco 64 46.04 N 10.17 E
Paisha 100 23.37 N 119.35 E
Paisley, Austl. 274b 37.51 S 144.51 E
Paisley, Ont., Can. 212 44.18 N 81.16 W
Paisley, Scot., U.K. 46 55.50 N 4.26 W
Paisley, Fla., U.S. 220 28.60 N 81.32 W
Paisley, Oreg., U.S. 202 42.42 N 120.32 W
Païta, N. Cal. 175f 22.08 S 166.22 E
Paita, Perú 248 5.06 S 81.07 W
Paita, Bahía de C 248 5.04 S 81.05 W
Paitan 100 23.31 N 113.46 E
Paitan ≃ 116 6.30 N 117.30 E
Paitan Bay C 116 6.45 N 117.20 E
Paiton 115a 7.43 S 113.30 E
Paiva 256 21.18 S 43.25 W
Paiva ≃ 34 41.04 N 8.16 W
Paiva Couceiro 152 14.51 S 14.30 E
Paizhou 100 30.13 N 113.56 E
Paj 24 61.13 N 34.24 E
Pajacuarán 234 20.07 N 102.34 W
Pajala 24 67.11 N 23.22 E
Paján 246 1.34 S 80.25 W
Pajapan 234 18.15 N 94.42 W
Pajares, Puerto de)(34 43.00 N 5.46 W
Pajaro 226 36.54 N 121.39 W
Pajaro ≃ 226 36.51 N 121.48 W
Pajaros Point ≻ 240m 18.31 N 64.18 W
Paj-Choj ⋀2 72 69.00 N 63.00 E
Pajdugina ≃ 86 58.50 N 81.47 E
Pajęczno 30 51.09 N 19.00 E
Pajeú ≃ 250 8.55 S 38.42 W
Pajiangkou 100 23.46 N 113.14 E
Pajjer, Gora ∧ 72 66.42 N 64.25 E
Pajtok 85 40.53 N 72.15 E
Pak ≃ 110 21.05 N 102.31 E
Paka 114 4.39 N 103.26 E
Paka ≃ 114 4.40 N 103.27 E
Pākāla 122 13.28 N 79.07 E
Pakanbaru 112 0.32 N 101.27 E
Pakaraima Mountains ⋀ 246 5.30 N 60.40 W
Pakaur 124 24.38 N 87.51 E
Pak Ban 110 21.14 N 102.28 E
Pakch'ŏn 98 39.45 N 125.35 E
Pakeng 140 6.55 N 30.40 E
Pakenham, Austl. 169 38.04 S 145.29 E
Pakenham, Ont., Can. 212 45.20 N 76.17 W
Pākhāl ⊜1 122 17.57 N 79.59 E
Pákhi 267c 37.59 N 23.22 E
Pákhna 130 34.46 N 32.48 E
Pakhoi → Beihai 102 21.29 N 109.05 E
Pakin I1 14 7.04 N 157.48 E
Pakipaki 172 39.41 S 176.48 E
Pakistan (Pākistān) □1 118 30.00 N 70.00 E
Pakistan, East → Bangladesh □1 120 24.00 N 90.00 E
Pak Kong Tsun 271d 22.23 N 114.15 E
Pak Kret 269a 13.55 N 100.30 E
Pakokku 110 21.20 N 95.05 E
Pakość 30 52.49 N 18.05 E
Pakouabo 150 7.10 N 5.48 W
Pakowki Lake ⊜ 184 49.22 N 110.57 W
Pākpattan 123 30.21 N 73.24 E
Pak Phanang 110 8.21 N 100.12 E
Pak Phayun 110 7.21 N 100.19 E
Pakrac 36 45.26 N 17.12 E
Pākrāganj 126 24.00 N 90.41 E
Pakruojis 76 55.58 N 23.52 E
Paks 30 46.39 N 18.53 E
Pak Sane → Muang Pakxan 110 18.22 N 103.39 E
Pāksey 126 24.05 N 89.03 E
Pak Thong Chai 110 14.43 N 102.01 E
Paktīā □4 120 33.30 N 69.30 E
Pākundia 126 24.20 N 90.42 E
P'akupur ≃ 74 65.00 N 77.48 E
Pakwach 154 2.28 N 31.30 E
Pakwash Lake ⊜ 184 50.45 N 93.30 W
Pakxé 110 15.07 N 105.47 E
Pala, Mya. 110 12.51 N 98.40 E
Pala, Tchad 146 9.22 N 14.54 E
Pala, Calif., U.S. 228 33.22 N 117.05 W
Palaau State Park ♠ 229a 21.11 N 157.00 W
Palabek 154 3.26 N 32.34 E
Palacios 196 28.42 N 96.13 W
Palacios ≃ 248 16.36 S 64.18 W
Paladru 62 45.28 N 5.33 E
Palagano 64 44.20 N 10.39 E
Palagianello 68 40.37 N 16.58 E
Palagiano 68 40.35 N 17.02 E
Palagonia 70 37.19 N 14.45 E
Palagruža, Otoci II 68 42.24 N 16.15 E
Palai 122 9.44 N 76.41 E
Palai, Punta ∧ 71 40.20 N 8.55 E
Palaia 66 43.36 N 10.46 E
Palaiá Epídhavros 38 37.38 N 23.09 E
Palaia Kórinthos ⊥ 38 37.54 N 22.56 E
Palaiá Psará 38 38.46 N 25.36 E
Palaikhóri 130 34.55 N 33.05 E
Pala Indian Reservation ⇝4 228 33.21 N 117.04 W
Palaiokhóra 38 35.14 N 23.41 E
Palaión Fáliron 267c 37.55 N 23.41 E
Palaiseau 50 48.43 N 2.15 E
Pālakollu 122 16.32 N 81.44 E
Pālam ⇝8 272a 28.35 N 77.05 E
Palam Airport ⊠ 123 28.35 N 77.07 E
Palamás 38 39.28 N 22.05 E
Palāmau □5 124 24.00 N 84.00 E
Pālam International Airport ⊠ 272a 28.35 N 77.07 E
Palamós 34 41.51 N 3.08 E
Pālampur 123 32.07 N 76.32 E
Palamuse 76 58.41 N 26.35 E
Palamut 130 38.59 N 27.41 E
Palana 74 59.07 N 159.58 E
Palanan, Mount ∧ 116 17.03 N 122.15 E
Palanan Bay C 116 17.09 N 122.27 E
Palanan Point ≻ 116 17.09 N 122.30 E
Palanas 116 12.09 N 123.55 E
Palandöken Dağları ⋀ 130 39.47 N 41.15 E
Pālang 126 23.13 N 90.21 E
Pālang ≃1 126 23.15 N 90.21 E
Palanga 76 55.55 N 21.03 E
Palanganene 152 6.26 S 18.50 E
Palangkaraya 112 2.16 S 113.56 E
Pālanpur 120 24.10 N 72.26 E
Palanquinos 34 42.27 N 5.31 W
Palanzano 64 44.26 N 10.11 E
Palaoa Point ≻ 229a 20.44 N 156.58 W
Palapag 116 12.33 N 125.07 E
Palapye 156 22.37 S 27.06 E
Pālār ≃ 122 12.28 N 80.10 E
Palasan Island I 116 14.52 N 122.03 E
Palas del Rey 34 42.52 N 7.52 W
Palāshdānga 126 23.24 N 87.22 E
Palāspol 126 22.43 N 89.05 E
Palāstha 126 23.51 N 87.03 E
Palata 66 41.53 N 14.47 E
Palatcy 86 49.09 N 83.43 E
Palatine 216 42.07 N 88.03 W
Palatine Bridge 210 42.55 N 74.35 W
Palatka, S.S.S.R. 74 60.06 N 150.54 E
Palatka, Fla., U.S. 192 29.39 N 81.38 W
Palau, It. 71 41.11 N 9.23 E
Palau, Méx. 196 27.54 N 101.26 W
Palau □5 175b 7.30 N 134.30 E

Symbol	English	Deutsch	Español	Français	Português
≃	River	Fluss	Rio	Rivière	Rio
⊏	Canal	Kanal	Canal	Canal	Canal
⊥	Waterfall, Rapids	Wasserfall, Stromschnellen	Cascada, Rápidos	Chute d'eau, Rapides	Cascata, Rápidos
⊔	Strait	Meeresstrasse	Estrecho	Détroit	Estreito
C	Bay, Gulf	Bucht, Golf	Bahía, Golfo	Baie, Golfe	Baía, Golfo
⊜	Lake, Lakes	See, Seen	Lago, Lagos	Lac, Lacs	Lago, Lagos
⩯	Swamp	Sumpf	Pantano	Marais	Pântano
⋔	Ice Features, Glacier	Eis- und Gletscherformen	Accidentes Glaciales	Formes glaciaires	Acidentes Glaciares
⊤	Other Hydrographic Features	Andere Hydrographische Objekte	Otros Elementos Hidrográficos	Autres données hydrographiques	Outros Acidentes Hidrográficos
⟡	Submarine Features	Untermeerische Objekte	Accidentes Submarinos	Formes de relief sous-marin	Acidentes Submarinos
□	Political Unit	Politische Einheit	Unidad Politica	Entité politique	Unidade Política
❖	Cultural Institution	Kulturelle Institution	Institución Cultural	Institution culturelle	Instituição Cultural
⊥	Historical Site	Historische Stätte	Sitio Histórico	Site historique	Sítio Histórico
♠	Recreational Site	Erholungs- und Ferienort	Sitio de Recreo	Centre de loisirs	Sítio de Lazer
⊠	Airport	Flughafen	Aeropuerto	Aéroport	Aeroporto
⊕	Military Installation	Militäranlage	Instalación Militar	Installation militaire	Instalação Militar
⇝	Miscellaneous	Verschiedenes	Misceláneo	Divers	Miscelânea

Name	Page	Lat.°′	Long.°′
Palauig	116	15.26 N	119.54 E
Palaui Island I	116	18.33 N	122.08 E
Palau Islands II	175b	7.30 N	134.30 E
Palauk	110	13.16 N	98.38 E
Pal'avaam ≃	180	68.50 N	170.45 E
Pal'avaamskij Chrebet ⛰	180	68.20 N	177.00 E
Palavas-les-Flots	62	43.32 N	3.56 E
Palaw	110	12.58 N	98.39 E
Palawai Basin ≚[1]	229a	20.47 N	156.55 W
Palawan I	116	9.30 N	118.30 E
Palawan Passage ⋓	116	10.00 N	118.00 E
Palayan	116	15.33 N	121.06 E
Pālayankottai	122	8.43 N	77.44 E
Palazzo Adriano	70	37.41 N	13.23 E
Palazzolo Acreide	70	37.04 N	14.54 E
Palazzolo dello Stella	64	45.48 N	13.05 E
Palazzolo sull'Oglio	62	45.36 N	9.53 E
Palazzolo Vercellese	62	45.11 N	8.14 E
Palazzo San Gervasio	68	40.56 N	16.00 E
Palazzuolo sul Senio	66	44.07 N	11.33 E
P'albong-san ∧	98	40.16 N	127.57 E
Palca, Bol.	248	16.34 S	67.59 W
Palca, Perú	248	11.21 S	75.31 W
Palcamayo	248	11.18 S	75.46 W
Pal'co	76	53.17 N	34.56 E
Paldi	224	48.48 N	123.51 W
Paldiski	76	59.20 N	24.06 E
Pāldor ∧	124	28.16 N	85.11 E
Palech	80	56.48 N	41.51 E
Palel	120	24.27 N	94.02 E
Paleleh	112	1.04 N	121.57 E
Palembang	112	2.55 S	104.45 E
Palena	66	41.59 N	14.08 E
Palena ≃	254	43.50 S	72.59 W
Palena, Lago (Lago General Vintter) ⊜	254	43.55 S	71.40 W
Palencia	34	42.01 N	4.32 W
Palen Dry Lake ⊜	204	33.46 N	115.12 W
Palenque	232	17.31 N	91.58 W
Palenque ⊥	232	17.30 N	92.00 W
Palenque, Punta ≻	238	18.14 N	70.09 W
Palenville	210	42.10 N	74.01 W
Palermo, Col.	246	2.54 N	75.26 W
Palermo, It.	70	38.07 N	13.22 E
Palermo, Calif., U.S.	226	39.26 N	121.33 W
Palermo, Ur.	252	33.48 S	55.59 W
Palermo □[4]	70	37.49 N	13.35 E
Palermo ⬥[8]	288	34.35 S	58.25 W
Palermo, Golfo di C	70	38.08 N	13.26 E
Palese, Aeroporto di ⊠	68	41.10 N	16.47 E
Palestina, Bra.	255	20.23 S	49.25 W
Palestina, Méx.	196	29.10 N	100.55 W
Palestine, Ill., U.S.	194	39.00 N	87.37 W
Palestine, Ohio, U.S.	218	40.03 N	84.45 W
Palestine, Tex., U.S.	222	31.46 N	95.38 W
Palestine □[1]	132	31.25 N	34.20 E
Palestine, Lake ⊜[1]	222	32.06 N	95.27 W
Palestrina	66	41.50 N	12.53 E
Paletwa	110	21.18 N	92.51 E
Palézieux	58	46.33 N	6.50 E
Palfau	61	47.42 N	14.48 E
Pālghāt	122	10.47 N	76.39 E
Palgrave, Mount ∧	162	23.22 S	115.58 E
Palgrave Point ≻	156	20.45 S	13.20 E
Palhais	266c	38.37 N	9.03 W
Palhano	250	4.44 S	37.57 W
Palhano ≃	250	4.33 S	37.42 W
Pāli, Bhārat	120	25.46 N	73.20 E
Pali, Bhārat	124	25.51 N	76.33 E
Paliano	66	41.48 N	13.03 E
Palikea ∧	229c	21.26 N	158.06 W
Palikir Passage ⋓	174r	6.59 N	158.08 E
Palima	112	4.20 S	120.22 E
Palimanan	115a	6.42 S	108.26 E
Palimbang	116	6.12 N	124.12 E
Palimé	150	6.54 N	0.38 E
Palín	236	14.24 N	90.42 W
Palin, Mount ∧	116	6.21 N	117.08 E
Palinges	32	46.33 N	4.13 E
Palinuro	68	40.02 N	15.17 E
Palinuro, Capo ≻	68	40.02 N	15.16 E
Palisade, Colo., U.S.	200	39.07 N	108.21 W
Palisade, Nebr., U.S.	198	40.21 N	101.07 W
Palisades, Idaho, U.S.	202	43.21 N	111.13 W
Palisades, N.Y., U.S.	276	41.01 N	73.55 W
Palisades Amusement Park ♠	276	40.50 N	73.59 W
Palisades Interstate Park ♠	210	40.56 N	73.55 W
Palisades Park, Mich., U.S.	216	42.18 N	86.19 W
Palisades Park, N.J., U.S.	276	40.51 N	74.00 W
Palisades Reservoir ⊜[1]	202	43.15 N	111.05 W
Paliseul	56	49.54 N	5.08 E
Palit, Kep i ≻	38	41.24 N	19.24 E
Pālitāna	120	21.31 N	71.50 E
Palivere	76	58.59 N	23.52 E
Palizada	232	18.15 N	92.05 W
Palizzi	68	37.58 N	15.59 E
Paljakka ∧[2]	26	64.41 N	28.08 E
Pälkäne	26	61.20 N	24.16 E
Palk Bay C	122	9.30 N	79.15 E
Palkino, S.S.S.R.	76	57.32 N	28.01 E
Palkino, S.S.S.R.	80	58.15 N	42.56 E
Pālkonda	122	18.36 N	83.45 E
Pālkonda Hills ⛰[2]	122	14.05 N	79.05 E
Palk Strait ⋓	122	10.00 N	79.45 E
Palla Bianca (Weisskugel) ∧	64	46.48 N	10.44 E
Pallagorio	68	39.18 N	16.54 E
Pallamana	168b	35.02 S	139.12 E
Pallasca	248	8.15 S	78.01 W
Pallas Grean	48	52.33 N	8.22 W
Pallaskenry	48	52.39 N	8.52 W
Pallas-Ounastunturin Kansallispuisto ♠	24	68.06 N	24.00 E
Pallasovka	80	50.03 N	46.53 E
Pallastunturi ∧	24	68.06 N	24.00 E
Pallejá	266d	41.25 N	2.00 E
Pallier	175f	14.53 S	166.35 E
Palling	182	54.21 N	125.55 W
Pallíni	267c	38.00 N	23.53 E
Pallinup ≃	162	34.29 S	118.54 E
Pallisa	154	1.10 N	33.42 E
Palliser, Cape ≻	172	41.37 S	175.17 E
Palliser Bay C	172	41.25 S	175.05 E
Pallu	123	28.56 N	74.13 E
Palluau	32	46.48 N	1.37 W
Palma, Bra.	255	21.22 S	42.19 W
Palma, Moç.	154	10.46 S	40.29 E
P'al'ma, S.S.S.R.	24	62.26 N	35.53 E
Palma ≃, Bra.	255	12.33 S	47.52 W
Palma ≃, It.	70	37.09 N	13.43 E
Palma, Bahía de C	34	39.27 N	2.35 E
Palma, Sierra de la ⛰	196	25.50 N	101.30 W
Palma Campania	68	40.52 N	14.33 E
Palmácia	250	4.08 S	38.50 W
Palma del Río	34	37.42 N	5.17 W
Palma [de Mallorca]	34	39.34 N	2.39 E
Palma di Montechiaro	70	37.11 N	13.46 E
Palmaḥim	132	31.56 N	34.42 E
Palmanova	64	45.54 N	13.19 E
Palma Pegada	234	22.42 N	101.48 W
Palmar ≃	246	10.10 N	71.50 W
Palmar Camp	232	16.26 N	88.53 W
Palmar de Cariaco	286c	10.34 N	66.55 W
Palmar de Sepúlveda	232	25.43 N	107.55 W
Palmar de Varela	246	10.45 N	74.45 W
Palmarejo	240m	18.03 N	67.05 W
Palmares, Bra.	250	8.41 S	35.36 W
Palmares, C.R.	236	10.03 N	84.26 W
Palmares, C.R.	236	9.21 N	83.40 W
Palmares do Sul	252	30.16 S	50.31 W
Palmaria, Isola I	62	44.02 N	9.51 E
Palmarito	246	7.37 N	70.10 W
Palmarito [Tochapan]	234	18.54 N	97.37 W
Palmarola, Isola I	66	40.56 N	12.51 E
Palmar Sur	236	8.58 N	83.29 W
Palmas	252	26.30 S	52.00 W
Palmas, Canal de las ☰	288	34.36 S	58.18 W
Palmas, Cape ≻	150	4.22 N	7.44 W
Palmas, Golfo di C	71	39.02 N	8.31 E
Palmas, Ilha das I	287a	23.02 S	43.12 W
Palmas Bellas	236	9.14 N	80.05 W
Palmas de Monte Alto	255	14.16 S	43.10 W
Palma Sola	220	27.31 N	82.38 W
Palma Soriano	240p	20.13 N	76.00 W
Palm Bay	220	28.02 N	80.35 W
Palm Beach, Austl.	170	33.36 S	151.19 E
Palm Beach, Austl.	171a	28.08 S	153.28 E
Palm Beach, Fla., U.S.	220	26.42 N	80.02 W
Palm Beach □[6]	220	26.38 N	80.27 W
Palm Beach Gardens	220	26.49 N	80.06 W
Palm Beach International Airport ⊠	220	26.41 N	80.05 W
Palm City	220	27.09 N	80.16 W
Palmdale, Calif., U.S.	228	34.35 N	118.07 W
Palmdale, Fla., U.S.	220	26.57 N	81.19 W
Palmdale, Pa., U.S.	208	40.18 N	76.37 W
Palmdale, Lake ⊜[1]	228	34.33 N	118.07 W
Palm Desert	204	33.43 N	116.22 W
Palmeira, Bra.	252	25.25 S	50.00 W
Palmeira, C.V.	150a	16.46 N	22.59 W
Palmeira das Missões	252	27.55 S	53.17 W
Palmeira d'Oeste	255	20.23 S	50.47 W
Palmeira dos Indios	250	9.25 S	36.37 W
Palmeirais	250	5.58 S	43.04 W
Palmeiral	256	21.38 S	46.31 W
Palmeirante	250	7.49 S	48.09 W
Palmeiras	255	12.31 S	41.34 W
Palmeiras ≃, Bra.	250	12.22 S	47.08 W
Palmeiras ≃, Bra.	255	15.25 S	51.10 W
Palmeirina	250	8.56 S	36.17 W
Palmeirinhas, Ponta das ≻	152	9.05 S	13.00 E
Palmela ≃	256	21.38 S	45.23 W
Palmelo	255	17.20 S	48.27 W
Palmer, Austl.	168b	34.51 S	139.10 E
Palmer, P.R.	240m	18.22 N	65.46 W
Palmer, Alaska, U.S.	180	61.36 N	149.07 W
Palmer, Ill., U.S.	219	39.27 N	89.24 W
Palmer, Mass., U.S.	207	42.09 N	72.20 W
Palmer, Mich., U.S.	190	46.27 N	87.35 W
Palmer, Nebr., U.S.	198	41.13 N	98.15 W
Palmer, Tenn., U.S.	194	35.21 N	85.34 W
Palmer, Tex., U.S.	222	32.26 N	96.40 W
Palmer ≃, Austl.	162	24.46 S	133.25 E
Palmer ≃, Austl.	164	15.34 S	142.26 E
Palmer ≃, Qué., Can.	206	46.19 N	71.27 W
Palmerah ⬥[8]	269e	6.12 S	106.47 E
Palmer Heights	208	40.42 N	75.16 W
Palmer Lake	200	39.07 N	104.55 W
Palmer Land ⬥[1]	9	71.30 S	65.00 W
Palmer Mill Brook ≃	283	41.58 N	70.52 W
Palmer Park	284c	38.55 N	76.52 W
Palmer Park ♠	281	42.26 N	83.07 W
Palmers Crossing	194	31.16 N	89.15 W
Palmerston, Ont., Can.	212	43.50 N	80.51 W
Palmerston, N.Z.	172	45.29 S	170.43 E
Palmerston I[1]	14	18.04 S	163.10 W
Palmerston, Cape ≻	166	21.32 S	149.29 E
Palmerston Lake ⊜	212	45.01 N	76.50 W
Palmerston North	172	40.21 S	175.37 E
Palmerton	210	40.48 N	75.37 W
Palmerville	164	15.59 S	144.05 E
Palmetto, Fla., U.S.	220	27.31 N	82.35 W
Palmetto, Ga., U.S.	192	33.31 N	84.40 W
Palmetto, La., U.S.	194	30.43 N	91.55 W
Palmford	158	27.11 S	29.42 E
Palm Harbor	220	28.05 N	82.46 W
Palmi	68	38.21 N	15.51 E
Palminópolis	255	16.47 S	50.08 W
Palmira, Arg.	252	33.03 S	68.34 W
Palmira, Col.	246	3.32 N	76.16 W
Palmira, Cuba	240p	22.14 N	80.23 W
Palmira, Ec.	246	2.05 S	78.43 W
Palmira, Méx.	196	28.58 N	100.47 W
Palmitas	252	33.31 S	57.49 W
Palmitos	252	27.05 S	53.08 W
Palmnicken → Jantarnyj	76	54.52 N	19.57 E
Palmoli	66	41.56 N	14.32 E
Palm River	220	27.56 N	82.23 W
Palms ⬥[8]	280	34.02 N	118.25 W
Palm Shores	220	28.11 N	80.35 W
Palm Springs, Calif., U.S.	204	33.50 N	116.33 W
Palm Springs, Fla., U.S.	220	26.39 N	80.06 W
Palmyra → Tudmur, Sūrīy.	130	34.33 N	38.17 E
Palmyra, Ill., U.S.	219	39.26 N	89.60 W
Palmyra, Ind., U.S.	218	38.24 N	86.07 W
Palmyra, Mich., U.S.	216	41.52 N	83.56 W
Palmyra, Mo., U.S.	219	39.48 N	91.31 W
Palmyra, N.J., U.S.	208	40.00 N	75.01 W
Palmyra, N.Y., U.S.	210	43.04 N	77.14 W
Palmyra, Ohio, U.S.	214	41.07 N	81.02 W
Palmyra, Pa., U.S.	208	40.18 N	76.36 W
Palmyra, Va., U.S.	192	37.51 N	78.16 W
Palmyra, Wis., U.S.	216	42.53 N	88.35 W
Palmyra ⊥	130	34.33 N	38.17 E
Palmyra Atoll I[1]	14	5.52 N	162.06 W
Palni	122	10.28 N	77.32 E
Palo, It.	66	41.56 N	12.06 E
Palo, Pil.	116	11.10 N	124.59 E
Palo Alto, Méx.	196	26.32 N	99.45 W
Palo Alto, Calif., U.S.	226	37.27 N	122.09 W
Palo Alto, Pa., U.S.	208	40.41 N	76.11 W
Palo Alto Airport ⊠	282	37.28 N	122.07 W
Palo Blanco, Méx.	196	26.45 N	101.32 W
Palo Blanco, P.R.	240m	18.26 N	66.39 W
Palo Blanco Creek ≃	196	27.10 N	97.52 W
Paločka	86	58.25 N	84.32 E
Palo del Colle	68	41.03 N	16.42 E
Palo Duro Canyon State Park ♠	196	34.55 N	101.42 W
Palo Duro Creek ≃, U.S.	196	36.39 N	100.58 W
Palo Duro Creek ≃, Tex., U.S.	196	35.00 N	101.55 W
Paloemeu ≃	250	3.21 N	55.26 W
Palo Flechado Pass)(	200	36.30 N	105.30 W
Paloh, Indon.	112	1.43 N	109.18 E
Paloh, Malay.	112	2.25 N	111.15 E
Paloh, Malay.	114	2.11 N	103.12 E
Paloich, Sūd.	140	10.28 N	32.32 E
Paloich, Sūd.	140	6.45 N	30.08 E
Palojoensuu	24	68.17 N	23.05 E
Paloma Creek ≃	226	36.15 N	121.26 W
Palomares	286d	12.00 S	77.01 W
Palomares Creek ≃	282	37.42 N	122.02 W
Palomar Mountain ∧	204	33.22 N	116.50 W
Palomar Mountain State Park ♠	228	33.19 N	116.53 W
Palomar Park	282	37.29 N	122.16 W
Palomas, Méx.	196	28.43 N	103.45 W
Palomas, Méx.	232	31.44 N	107.37 W
Palomas, Mesa de ∧	232	28.46 N	103.41 W
Palomas Creek ≃	200	33.03 N	107.16 W
Palombara Sabina	66	42.04 N	12.46 E
Palominos, Isla I	240m	18.21 N	65.34 W
Palomonte	68	40.40 N	15.17 E
Palompon	116	11.03 N	124.23 E
Palo Negro	246	10.11 N	67.33 W
Palo Pinto	196	32.46 N	98.18 W
Palo Pinto Reservoir ⊜[1]	196	32.38 N	98.18 W
Palopo	112	3.00 S	120.12 E
Palora ≃	246	1.51 S	77.49 W
Palos	240p	22.48 N	81.44 W
Palos, Cabo de ≻	34	37.38 N	0.41 W
Palo Santo	252	25.34 S	59.21 W
Palo Seco	240m	18.28 N	66.09 W
Palos Gardens	278	41.40 N	87.48 W
Palos Heights	216	41.40 N	87.48 W
Palos Hills	278	41.41 N	87.49 W
Palos Hills ♠	278	41.42 N	87.53 W
Palos Park	278	41.40 N	87.50 W
Palos Verdes Estates	228	33.48 N	118.24 W
Palos Verdes Hills ⛰[2]	280	33.46 N	118.21 W
Palos Verdes Point ≻	228	33.47 N	118.26 W
Palotai-sziget I	264c	47.35 N	19.05 E
Paloúkia	267c	37.58 N	23.31 E
Palouse	202	46.55 N	117.04 W
Palouse ≃	202	46.35 N	118.13 W
Palo Verde	204	33.26 N	114.44 W
P'alovskoje Vodochranilišče ⊜[1]	82	56.03 N	37.40 E
Palpa	248	14.32 S	75.11 W
Palpalá	252	24.15 S	65.12 W
Pålsboda	40	59.04 N	15.20 E
Pālsit	126	23.12 N	88.03 E
Paltamo	26	64.25 N	27.50 E
Paltenbach ≃	61	47.34 N	14.20 E
Palu, Indon.	112	0.53 S	119.53 E
Palu, Tür.	130	38.42 N	39.57 E
Palu ≃	112	0.52 S	119.51 E
Palu, Pulau I	115b	8.20 S	121.43 E
Palu, Teluk C	112	0.40 S	119.45 E
Paluan	116	13.25 N	120.28 E
Paluan Bay C	116	13.23 N	120.25 E
Palù del Fersina	64	46.08 N	11.21 E
Paludi	68	39.32 N	16.41 E
Paluga	24	65.16 N	45.11 E
Paluke	150	5.02 N	8.06 W
Paluška ∧	61	48.45 N	14.24 E
Paluxy ≃	196	32.15 N	97.43 W
Paluzza	64	46.32 N	13.01 E
Palvantaš	85	40.34 N	72.12 E
Palvart	128	38.11 N	64.34 E
Palwal	124	28.09 N	77.20 E
Pal-Waukee Airport ⊠	278	42.07 N	87.54 W
Pam	175f	20.16 S	164.19 E
Pama	150	11.15 N	0.42 E
Pama ≃	152	4.23 N	18.27 E
Pama, Réserve de ⬥[4]	150	11.30 N	1.00 E
Pamaluan	112	1.04 S	116.39 E
Pamangkat	112	1.10 N	108.58 E
Pamanukan	115a	6.16 S	107.49 E
Pamarayan	115a	6.16 S	106.17 E
Pam'ati 13 Borcov	86	56.13 N	92.20 E
Pam'atnaja	86	56.01 N	65.42 E
Pam'at' Parižskoj Kommuny	80	56.06 N	44.31 E
Pāmban Channel ⋓	122	9.17 N	79.10 E
Pāmban Island I	122	9.15 N	79.20 E
Pambegua	150	10.40 N	8.19 E
Pambuhan	116	13.59 N	123.05 E
Pambujan	116	12.34 N	124.56 E
Pambunan ≃	116	12.34 N	124.55 E
Pamekasan	115a	7.10 S	113.28 E
Pamel	50	50.50 N	4.04 E
Pamenang	112	2.07 S	102.31 E
Pameungpeuk	115a	7.38 S	107.43 E
Pamiers	32	43.07 N	1.36 E
Pamir ⛰	85	38.00 N	73.00 E
Pamlico ≃	192	35.20 N	76.30 W
Pamlico Sound ⋓	192	35.20 N	75.55 W
Pamotan	115a	6.46 S	111.29 E
Pampa	196	35.32 N	100.58 W
Pampã ≃	255	17.43 S	40.36 W
Pampa ⬥[1]	252	35.00 S	63.00 W
Pampa Almirón	252	26.42 S	59.08 W
Pampacolca	248	15.43 S	72.33 W
Pampa del Castillo	254	45.48 S	68.05 W
Pampa del Chañar	252	30.11 S	68.43 W
Pampa del Indio	252	26.02 S	59.55 W
Pampa del Infierno	252	26.31 S	61.10 W
Pampa de los Guanacos	252	26.14 S	61.51 W
Pampa Grande	248	18.05 S	64.06 W
Pampana ≃	150	8.24 N	12.00 W
Pampanga □[4]	116	15.05 N	120.40 E
Pampanga ≃	116	14.47 N	120.39 E
Pampanua	112	4.14 S	120.08 E
Pamparato	62	44.17 N	7.55 E
Pampas	248	12.24 S	74.54 W
Pampas ≃	248	13.23 S	73.15 W
Pampeluna → Pamplona	34	42.49 N	1.38 W
Pamplico	192	34.00 N	79.34 W
Pamplona, Col.	246	7.23 N	72.39 W
Pamplona, Esp.	34	42.49 N	1.38 W
Pampoenpoort	158	31.03 S	22.40 E
Pampow	54	53.32 N	14.15 E
Pāmpur	123	34.01 N	74.56 E
Pamukova	130	40.31 N	30.09 E
Pamunkey ≃	208	37.32 N	76.48 W
Pana	219	39.23 N	89.05 W
Panabá	232	21.17 N	88.16 W
Panabo	116	7.19 N	125.42 E
Panaca	204	37.47 N	114.23 W
Panacachi	248	18.23 S	66.21 W
Panacan	116	9.16 N	118.25 E
Panacea	192	30.02 N	84.23 W
Panache, Lake ⊜	190	46.15 N	81.20 W
Panadura	122	6.43 N	79.54 E
Panaete Island I	164	10.40 S	152.20 E
Panāgar	124	23.18 N	79.59 E
Panagjurište	38	42.30 N	24.11 E
Panagtaran Point ≻	116	9.41 N	118.45 E
Panahan	112	1.44 S	111.49 E
Panaitan, Pulau I	115a	6.36 S	105.12 E
Panaitan, Selat ⋓	115a	6.40 S	105.16 E
Panaji (Panjim)	122	15.29 N	73.50 E
Pānākua	272b	22.23 N	88.21 E
Panakudi	122	8.19 N	77.36 E
Panamá, Bra.	255	18.11 S	49.21 W
Panamá, Pan.	236	8.58 N	79.32 W
Panama, Ill., U.S.	219	39.02 N	89.32 W
Panama, N.Y., U.S.	214	42.05 N	79.29 W
Panama, Okla., U.S.	194	35.10 N	94.40 W
Panamá □[4]	236	8.48 N	79.55 W
Panama □[1]	230		
	246	9.00 N	80.00 W
Panama Canal ☰	236	9.20 N	79.55 W
Panama City	194	30.10 N	85.41 W
Panamá La Vieja ⊥	236	9.00 N	79.29 W
Panambi	252	28.18 S	53.30 W
Panamint Range ⛰	204	36.30 N	117.20 W
Panamint Valley ∨	204	36.15 N	117.20 W
Pan'an	100	29.06 N	120.27 E
Panao, Perú	248	9.49 S	76.00 W
Pan'ao, Zhg.	107	30.09 N	103.37 E
Panaon Island I	116	10.03 N	125.13 E
Panarea, Isola I	70	38.38 N	15.04 E
Panaro ≃	64	44.55 N	11.25 E
Panarukan	115a	7.42 S	113.56 E
Panasoffkee, Lake ⊜	220	28.47 N	82.08 W
Pana Tinai Island I	164	11.15 S	153.10 E
Panay I	116	11.15 N	122.30 E
Panay ≃	116	11.35 N	122.43 E
Panay Gulf C	116	10.15 N	122.15 E
Panayía	38	39.56 N	25.20 E
Panay Island I	116	13.58 N	124.20 E
Pancalieri	62	44.50 N	7.35 E
Pancas	266c	38.48 N	8.55 W
Pančevo, Jugo.	38	44.52 N	20.39 E
Pančevo, S.S.S.R.	78	48.44 N	31.51 E
Pānchāl	126	23.15 N	87.18 E
Pānchet Hill ∧[2]	126	23.37 N	86.47 E
Pānchet Hill Reservoir ⊜[1]	126	23.42 N	86.35 E
Pānchghara	272b	22.44 N	88.16 E
Panchgram	126	24.12 N	88.01 E
Panch'iao	269d	25.01 N	121.27 E
Panchla	126	22.32 N	88.09 E
Panchor	114	2.10 N	102.43 E
Pancho Simón, Arroyo ≃	286b	23.03 N	82.21 W
Pānchur	272b	22.32 N	88.16 E
Pānchuria	272b	22.33 N	88.29 E
Panciu	38	45.55 N	27.05 E
Panda	156	24.02 S	34.45 E
Panda Gongoue	157a	11.50 S	43.24 E
Pandakan	115a	7.39 S	112.41 E
Pandalāyini	122	11.28 N	75.43 E
Pandamatenga	156	18.35 S	25.42 E
Pandan, Malay.	112	3.09 N	113.22 E
Pandan, Pil.	116	11.43 N	122.06 E
Pandan, Pil.	116	14.03 N	124.10 E
Pandan, Selat ⋓	271c	1.15 N	103.44 E
Pandanan Island I	116	8.17 N	117.13 E
Pandan Bay C	116	11.43 N	122.04 E
Pandaria	124	22.14 N	81.25 E
Pandarochan Bay C	116	12.12 N	121.10 E
Pandasan	112	6.28 N	116.32 E
Pandaveswar	126	23.43 N	87.17 E
Pan de Azúcar	252	34.48 S	55.14 W
Pan de Azucar Island I	116	11.17 N	123.10 E
Pandeglang	115a	6.18 S	106.06 E
Pandėlys	76	56.01 N	25.13 E
Pāndharkawada	122	20.01 N	78.32 E
Pandharpur	122	17.40 N	75.20 E
Pāndhurna	122	21.36 N	78.31 E
Pandino	62	45.24 N	9.33 E
Pando	252	34.43 S	55.57 W
Pando □[5]	248	11.20 S	67.40 W
Pando, Cerro ∧	236	8.55 N	82.43 W
Pandora	216	40.57 N	83.58 W
Pandua, Bhārat	124	25.08 N	88.10 E
Pandua, Bhārat	126	23.05 N	88.17 E
P'andž (Panj) ≃	120	37.06 N	68.20 E
Panebianco ≃	70	37.24 N	15.04 E
Panelas	250	8.40 S	36.01 W
Panerzhuang	105	39.20 N	117.28 E
Paneveggio	64	46.18 N	11.44 E
Panevėžys	76	55.44 N	24.21 E
Panfang	100	27.54 N	115.57 E
Panfilov	86	44.10 N	80.01 E
Panfilovo	80	50.26 N	42.55 E
Pang	64	47.49 N	12.05 E
Panga	154	1.51 N	26.25 E
Pangaduni Island I	126	21.35 N	88.52 E
Pangala	152	3.19 S	14.34 E
Pangalanes, Canal des ☰	157b	22.40 S	47.50 E
Pangandaran	115a	7.41 S	108.39 E
Pangani	154	5.26 S	38.58 E
Pangani ≃	154	5.26 S	38.58 E
Panganiran	116	13.02 N	123.26 E
Pangantocan	116	7.50 N	124.49 E
Panganuran	116	7.24 N	122.03 E
Pangasinan □[4]	116	16.00 N	120.20 E
Pangbourne	42	51.29 N	1.05 W
Pangburn	194	35.15 N	91.51 W
Pange	56	49.05 N	6.22 E
Pangfou → Bangbu	100	32.58 N	117.24 E
Pangga, Tanjung ≻	115b	8.55 S	116.02 E
Panggezhuang, Zhg.	105	39.38 N	116.19 E
Panggezhuang, Zhg.	105	39.16 N	115.49 E
Panghkam	110	23.53 N	97.37 E
Pangi	154	3.11 S	26.38 E
Pangian	112	1.06 S	119.24 E
Pangjiabao	105	40.42 N	115.23 E
Pangkah	115a	6.58 S	109.10 E
Pangkajene	112	4.50 S	119.32 E
Pangkalanberandan	114	4.01 N	98.17 E
Pangkalanbuun	112	2.41 S	111.37 E
Pangkalansusu	114	4.06 N	98.14 E
Pangkalaseang, Tanjung ≻	112	0.42 S	123.26 E
Pangkalpinang	112	2.08 S	106.08 E
Pangkatan	114	2.09 N	100.00 E
Pangkor, Pulau I	114	4.13 N	100.33 E
Panglao	116	9.35 N	123.45 E
Panglao Island I	116	9.35 N	123.48 E
Pangman	184	49.39 N	104.38 W
Pangnirtung	176	66.08 N	65.44 W
Pangnirtung Fiord C[2]	176	66.06 N	65.58 W
Pango Aluquém	152	8.43 S	14.27 E
Pangong Tso ⊜	120	33.45 N	78.43 W
Pangŏ-ri	98	35.29 N	129.26 E
Pangp'u → Bangbu	100	32.58 N	117.24 E
Pangsa	126	23.47 N	89.25 E
Pangtara	110	20.57 N	96.40 E
Pangubatan	116	6.57 N	125.47 E
Panguil Bay C	116	8.01 N	123.43 E
Panguipulli, Lago ⊜	254	39.43 S	72.13 W
Panguiranan	116	12.04 N	123.19 E
Panguitch	200	37.49 N	112.26 W
Pangururan	114	2.37 N	98.42 E
Pangushan	100	25.46 N	115.30 E
Pangutaran	116	6.18 N	120.35 E
Pangutaran Group II	116	6.15 N	120.30 E
Pangutaran Island I	116	6.18 N	120.34 E
Pangutaran Passage ⋓	116	6.13 N	120.30 E
Pangyan	116	5.42 N	125.17 E
Pangzidian	107	30.38 N	105.04 E
Panhame (Hunyani) ≃	154	15.37 S	30.39 E
Panhandle	196	35.21 N	101.23 W
Panhe ≃	100	33.11 N	115.07 E
Paniai, Danau ⊜	164	3.50 S	136.15 E
Pania-Mutombo	152	5.11 S	23.51 E
Panian I	174r	6.47 N	158.16 E
Paniau ∧	229b	21.57 N	160.05 W
Panié, Mont ∧	175f	20.36 S	164.46 E
Pānihāti	126	22.42 N	88.22 E
Panika	80	50.59 N	50.11 E
Panikoviči	76	57.41 N	27.34 E
Panindícuaro	234	19.59 N	101.46 W
Panino, S.S.S.R.	76	56.25 N	34.34 E
Panino, S.S.S.R.	78	51.38 N	40.08 E
Panino-Nesterovo	82	55.23 N	38.11 E
Panīpāt	124	29.23 N	76.58 E
Paniqui	116	15.40 N	120.35 E
Panissières	62	45.47 N	4.20 E
Panitian	116	9.05 N	118.05 E
Panj (P'andž) ≃	120	37.06 N	68.20 E
Panjāb	120	34.22 N	67.01 E
Panjang	115a	5.28 S	105.18 E
Pānjāng ≃	124	29.28 N	82.50 E
Panjang, Pulau I	112	2.44 N	108.55 E
Panje	272c	18.54 N	72.57 E
Panjgūr	128	26.58 N	64.06 E
Panji	114	2.34 N	97.50 E
Panjiadian	98	36.38 N	116.27 E
Panjiapie	100	32.54 N	120.42 E
Panjiasha I	106	31.25 N	121.38 E
Panjiatun	104	41.04 N	121.38 E
Panjim → Panaji	122	15.29 N	73.50 E
Pānjkora ≃	123	34.39 N	71.44 E
Panjnad ≃	123	28.57 N	70.30 E
Panjpāi	120	29.55 N	66.30 E
Pankakoski	26	63.19 N	30.09 E
Panke ≃	264a	52.32 N	13.22 E
Panker	54	54.20 N	10.34 E
Pānkhāli	126	22.37 N	89.31 E

ENGLISH

Name	Page	Lat.°′	Long.°′
Pankof, Cape ≻	180	54.40 N	163.04 W
Pankow ⬥[8]	54	52.34 N	13.25 E
Pankratovo	76	59.10 N	43.30 E
Pankshin	150	9.20 N	9.24 E
Panlı	130	38.52 N	33.56 E
Panlong, Zhg.	100	25.52 N	114.52 E
Panlong, Zhg.	106	31.11 N	121.16 E
Panlong, Zhg.	106	31.58 N	121.35 E
Panlong, Zhg.	107	29.31 N	105.17 E
P'anmunjŏm	98	37.57 N	126.40 E
Panna	124	24.43 N	80.12 E
Panna □[5]	124	24.30 N	80.10 E
Panni	68	41.13 N	15.16 E
Panningen	52	51.20 N	5.59 E
Pannonhalma ʋ[1]	30	47.28 N	17.50 E
Panoche Creek ≃	226	36.44 N	120.31 W
Panola	194	32.57 N	88.16 W
Panola □[6]	222	32.07 N	94.30 W
Panopah	112	1.56 S	111.11 E
Páno Panayiá	130	34.55 N	32.38 E
Páno Plátres	130	34.53 N	32.52 E
Panora	198	41.42 N	94.22 W
Panorama	255	21.21 S	51.51 W
Pánormos	38	37.38 N	25.02 E
Panovo, S.S.S.R.	24	59.48 N	46.27 E
Panovo, S.S.S.R.	88	58.58 N	101.58 E
P'anp'yŏng-ni	98	40.28 N	125.49 E
Panruti	122	11.46 N	79.33 E
Pansfelde	54	51.39 N	11.16 E
Panshan	104	41.12 N	122.04 E
Panshanger Aerodrome ⊠	260	51.48 N	0.08 W
Pansik, Rápido ᒪ	236	14.30 N	85.15 W
Pansionat	265b	55.59 N	37.41 E
Pānskura	126	22.25 N	87.42 E
Pantabañgan	116	15.50 N	121.09 E
Pantajevka	78	48.41 N	32.53 E
Pantalica, Necropoli di ⊥	70	37.08 N	15.01 E
Pantanaw	110	16.59 N	95.28 E
Pântano	256	22.23 S	46.01 W
Pântano, Ribeirão do ≃	256	22.15 S	45.59 W
Pantar, Pulau I	112	8.25 S	124.07 E
Pantelejmonovka	83	48.12 N	37.59 E
Pantelleria	70	36.50 N	11.57 E
Pantelleria, Isola di I	70	36.47 N	12.00 E
Panteón Nacional ⊥	286c	10.31 N	66.55 W
Pantepec ≃	234	20.56 N	97.44 W
Pantha	110	23.49 N	94.33 E
Pantheon ⊥	267a	41.55 N	12.29 E
Panther Creek ≃, Idaho, U.S.	202	45.19 N	114.24 W
Panther Creek ≃, Ky., U.S.	194	37.45 N	87.19 W
Panther Creek, South Fork ≃	194	37.42 N	87.05 W
Panther Lake	210	43.19 N	75.54 W
Pantin	50	48.54 N	2.24 E
Pantitlán ⬥[8]	286a	19.25 N	99.05 W
Panto, Tanjung ≻	115a	6.51 S	105.54 E
Panton, Mount ∧	162	17.21 S	129.13 E
Pantonlabu	114	5.08 N	97.28 E
Pantry Brook ≃	283	42.24 N	71.22 W
Panu	152	3.48 S	19.07 E
Pánuco	234	22.03 N	98.10 W
Pánuco ≃	234	22.16 N	97.47 W
Panukulan	116	14.56 N	121.49 E
Pānuria	126	23.49 N	86.58 E
Pan'utino	78	48.56 N	36.17 E
Panvel	122	18.59 N	73.06 E
Panvel ≃	272c	19.01 N	73.04 W
Panvel Creek ≃	272c	18.59 N	73.00 E
Panwāri	124	25.27 N	79.29 E
Panxi	106	30.35 N	119.20 E
Panxian	102	25.50 N	104.36 E
Panxidu	98	35.39 N	115.52 E
Panyabungan	114	0.51 N	99.33 E
Panyam	150	9.25 N	9.13 E
Panyang	140	10.04 N	29.58 E
Panyčevo	86	57.05 N	81.49 E
Panyu	100	22.57 N	113.20 E
Panzerstausee ⊜[1]	263	51.11 N	7.16 E
Panzi	152	7.13 S	17.58 E
Panzós	236	15.24 N	89.40 W
Pao ≃, Thai	110	16.13 N	103.43 E
Pao ≃, Ven.	246	8.33 N	68.01 W
Pao ≃, Ven.	246	8.06 N	64.17 W
Paochi → Baoji	102	34.22 N	107.14 E
Pão de Açúcar	250	9.45 S	37.26 W
Pão de Açúcar (Sugar Loaf) ∧	287a	22.57 S	43.09 W
Paoki → Baoji	102	34.22 N	107.14 E
Paola, It.	68	39.22 N	16.03 E
Paola, Kans., U.S.	198	38.35 N	94.53 W
Paoli, Ind., U.S.	218	38.33 N	86.28 W
Paoli, Pa., U.S.	208	40.02 N	75.29 W
Paoli, Wis., U.S.	216	42.56 N	89.32 W
Paonia	200	38.52 N	107.36 W
Paonta	124	30.27 N	77.37 E
Paoshenmiao	98	41.12 N	118.17 E
Paotaiyingzi	98	41.48 N	115.12 E
Paoting → Baoding	105	38.52 N	115.29 E
Paotow → Baotou	102	40.40 N	109.59 E
Paoua	152	7.15 N	16.26 E
Paoying → Baoying	100	33.16 N	119.20 E
Paôy Pêt	110	13.39 N	102.33 E
P'aozero, Ozero ⊜	24	66.05 N	30.58 E
Paozi	104	42.17 N	122.20 E
Pap	85	40.53 N	71.07 E
Pápa	30	47.19 N	17.28 E
Papa, Sound of ⋓	46a	60.18 N	1.41 W
Papagaio	250	6.01 S	45.21 W
Papagaio ≃	246	1.53 S	62.35 W
Papagayo ≃	234	16.46 N	99.43 W
Papagayo, Golfo de C	236	10.42 N	85.50 W
Papago Indian Reservation ⬥[4]	200	32.20 N	112.00 W
Papai I	271d	22.15 N	114.02 E
Papaikou	229d	19.47 N	155.06 W
Papakating Creek ≃	276	41.11 N	74.38 W
Papakura	172	37.04 S	174.57 E
Papale, Palazzo ʋ	267a	41.45 N	12.39 E
Papalia	112	5.58 S	124.01 E
Papaloapan ≃	234	18.42 N	95.38 W
Papanoa	234	17.21 N	101.02 W
Papantla [de Olarte]	234	20.27 N	97.19 W
Papar, Indon.	115a	7.41 S	112.04 E
Papar, Malay.	112	5.44 N	115.56 E
Paparoa	172	36.06 S	174.14 E
Paparoa Range ⛰	172	42.00 S	171.35 E
Papasidero	68	39.52 N	15.54 E
Papa Stour I	46a	60.20 N	1.42 W
Papatoetoe	172	36.58 S	174.52 E
Papawai Point ≻	229a	20.47 N	156.33 W
Papa Westray I	46	59.21 N	2.54 W
Papayacu, Lago ⊜	248	5.03 S	76.25 W
Papeete	174s	17.32 S	149.34 W
Papelón	286c	10.27 N	66.47 W
Papenburg	52	53.05 N	7.23 E
Papendrecht	52	51.50 N	4.40 E
Papenoo	174s	17.30 S	149.25 W
Papenoo ≃	174s	17.30 S	149.25 W
Papetoai	174s	17.29 S	149.52 W
Papetoai, Baie de C	174s	17.30 S	149.51 W
Papey I	24a	64.37 N	14.11 W
Paphos → Néa Páfos	130	34.45 N	32.25 E
Papigochic ≃	232	29.09 N	109.40 W
Papilė	76	56.09 N	22.48 E
Papillion	198	41.09 N	96.03 W
Papineau	216	40.58 N	87.43 W

DEUTSCH

Name	Seite	Breite°′	Länge°′ E=Ost
Papineau □[6]	206	45.50 N	75.00 W
Papineau, Lac ⊜	206	45.48 N	74.46 W
Papineau, Parc de ♠	188	45.55 N	75.20 W
Papineau Creek ≃	212	45.13 N	77.43 W
Papineau Lake ⊜	212	45.20 N	77.50 W
Papineauville	206	45.37 N	75.01 W
Papiol	266d	41.26 N	2.01 E
Paposo	252	25.01 S	70.28 W
Papouasie Nouvelle-Guinée → Papua New Guinea □[1]	164	6.00 S	150.00 E
Papozze	64	44.59 N	12.02 E
Pappenheim, B.R.D.	56	48.56 N	10.58 E
Pappenheim, D.D.R.	54	50.47 N	10.27 E
Paps of Jura ∧	46	55.55 N	6.00 W
Papua, Gulf of C	164	8.30 S	145.00 E
Papua Neuguinea → Papua New Guinea □[1]	164	6.00 S	150.00 E
Papua New Guinea □[1]	14		
	164	6.00 S	150.00 E
Papua Passage ⋓	174k	21.15 S	159.47 W
Papuasia Nueva Guinea → Papua New Guinea □[1]	164	6.00 S	150.00 E
Papudo	252	32.31 S	71.27 W
Papulovo	24	60.34 N	48.00 E
Papun	110	18.04 N	97.27 E
Papunava ≃	246	2.09 N	70.32 W
Papunya	162	23.16 S	131.54 E
Papurí ≃	246	0.36 N	69.11 W
Paquequer ≃	256	22.12 S	42.54 W
Paquequer, Serra do ⛰	256	22.12 S	42.48 W
Paquequer Pequeno	256	22.20 S	43.02 W
Paquera	236	9.50 N	84.56 W
Paquetá, Ilha de I	287a	22.46 S	43.06 W
Paquica, Cabo ≻	252	21.54 S	70.12 W
Par	42	50.21 N	4.43 W
Pará → Belém	250	1.27 S	48.29 W
Pará □[3]	250	4.00 S	53.00 W
Para □[5]	250	5.30 N	55.15 W
Pará ≃, Bra.	250	1.30 S	48.55 W
Pará ≃, Bra.	255	19.13 S	45.07 W
Para ≃, S.S.S.R.	80	54.23 N	40.52 E
Pará, Ilha do I	250	0.18 S	51.15 W
Para, Pulau I	112	3.05 N	125.30 E
Parabel'	86	58.43 N	81.31 E
Parabel' ≃	86	58.44 N	81.35 E
Parabiago	62	45.33 N	8.57 E
Parabita	68	40.03 N	18.08 E
Paracale	116	14.17 N	122.48 E
Paracambi	256	22.37 S	43.43 W
Paracari ≃	250	4.36 S	57.47 W
Paracas, Bahía de C	248	13.50 S	76.17 W
Paracas, Península ≻[1]	248	13.48 S	76.24 W
Paracatu	255	17.13 S	46.52 W
Paracatu ≃, Bra.	255	16.35 S	45.06 W
Paracatu ≃, Bra.	255	16.30 S	45.04 W
Paracel Islands II	108	16.30 N	112.15 E
Parachilna	166	31.08 S	138.23 E
Pārachinār	120	33.54 N	70.06 E
Paracho [de Verduzco]	234	19.39 N	102.04 W
Paraćin	38	43.52 N	21.24 E
Parácuaro	234	20.09 N	100.46 W
Paracuellos de Jarama	266a	40.30 N	3.32 W
Paracuru	250	3.24 S	39.04 W
Parád	30	47.55 N	20.02 E
Parada, Punta ≻	248	15.22 S	75.12 W
Paradas	34	37.18 N	5.30 W
Paradino	76	53.59 N	31.51 E
Paradise, Calif., U.S.	204	39.46 N	121.37 W
Paradise, Mont., U.S.	202	47.23 N	114.48 W
Paradise, Nev., U.S.	204	36.09 N	115.10 W
Paradise, Pa., U.S.	208	40.01 N	76.08 W
Paradise, Tex., U.S.	222	33.09 N	97.41 W
Paradise Hill, Sask., Can.	184	53.32 N	109.28 W
Paradise Hill, S. Afr.	273d	26.18 S	28.00 E
Paradise Hill, Alaska, U.S.	180	62.25 N	160.03 W
Paradise Island I	240b	25.05 N	77.19 W
Paradise Mountain ∧	171a	27.45 S	152.02 E
Paradise Valley, Ariz., U.S.	200	33.32 N	111.57 W
Paradise Valley, Nev., U.S.	204	41.30 N	117.32 W
Parado	115b	8.45 S	118.36 E
Parado ≃	250	10.17 S	55.39 W
Parafield	168b	34.47 S	138.38 E
Parafijevka	78	50.53 N	32.38 E
Paragačaj	84	39.07 N	45.56 E
Paragon	218	39.24 N	86.34 W
Paragonah	200	37.53 N	112.46 W
Paragould	194	36.03 N	90.29 W
Paraguá ≃, Bol.	248	13.34 S	61.53 W
Paragua ≃, Ven.	246	6.55 N	62.55 W
Paraguaçu	256	21.33 S	45.44 W
Paraguaçu ≃	255	12.45 S	38.54 W
Paraguaçu Paulista	255	22.25 S	50.34 W
Paraguaipoa	246	11.21 N	71.57 W
Paraguaná, Península de ≻[1]	246	11.55 N	70.00 W
Paraguarí	252	25.38 S	57.09 W
Paraguarí □[5]	252	26.00 S	57.10 W
Paraguay □[1]	18	23.00 S	58.00 W
Paraguay (Paraguai) ≃, S.A.	18	27.18 S	58.38 W
Paraguay ≃, S.A.	244	27.18 S	58.38 W
Parahi	150	11.09 N	13.07 W
Parahyba → João Pessoa	250	7.07 S	34.52 W
Paraíba □[3]	250	7.15 S	36.30 W
Paraíba do Sul	256	22.09 S	43.17 W
Paraíba do Sul ≃	255	21.37 S	41.03 W
Paraibano	250	6.30 S	44.01 W
Paraibuna	256	23.23 S	45.39 W
Paraibuna ≃, Bra.	256	22.06 S	43.08 W
Paraibuna ≃, Bra.	256	23.22 S	45.40 W
Paraíso, Bra.	255	19.03 S	52.59 W
Paraíso, Bra.	256	22.19 S	45.42 W
Paraíso, C.R.	236	9.50 N	83.51 W
Paraíso, Méx.	234	18.24 N	93.14 W
Paraiso, Pan.	236	9.02 N	79.38 W
Paraíso do Norte	255	23.13 S	52.38 W
Paraíso Garcia	256	21.32 S	43.53 W
Paraíso Novillero	234	18.16 N	95.59 W
Paraisópolis	256	22.33 S	45.47 W
Paraitinga ≃, Bra.	256	23.22 S	45.40 W
Paraitinga ≃, Bra.	256	23.34 S	46.02 W
Parakan	115a	7.17 S	110.06 E
Parakou	150	9.21 N	2.37 E
Paralía Aspropírgos	267c	38.02 N	23.35 E
Paralímni	130	35.02 N	33.59 E
Param I	174r	7.01 N	158.15 E
Paramagudi	122	9.33 N	78.36 E
Parama Island I	164	9.00 S	143.25 E
Paramaribo	250	5.50 N	55.10 W
Parambu	250	6.13 S	40.43 W
Paramillo, Nudo de ∧	246	7.04 N	75.55 W
Paramirim	255	13.26 S	42.15 W
Paramirim ≃	250	11.34 S	43.18 W
Paramithiá	38	39.28 N	20.30 E
Paramonga	248	10.40 S	77.50 W
Paramoti	250	4.06 S	39.15 W
Paramount	228	33.53 N	118.09 W
Paramus	210	40.57 N	74.04 W
Paramušir, Ostrov I	74	50.25 N	155.50 E
Paramus Park ⬥[9]	276	40.57 N	74.04 W
Paran, Naḥal (Wādī al-Jirāfī) ∨	132	30.24 N	35.10 E

Symbols in the index entries represent the broad categories identified in the key at the right. Symbols with superior numbers (⛰[2]) identify subcategories (see complete key on page I · 30).

Kartensymbole in dem Registerverzeichnis stellen die rechts in Schlüssel erklärten Kategorien dar. Symbole mit hochgestellten Ziffern (⛰[2]) bezeichnen Unterabteilungen einer Kategorie (vgl. vollständiger Schlüssel auf Seite I · 30).

Los símbolos incluidos en el texto del índice representan las grandes categorias identificadas con la clave a la derecha. Los símbolos con numeros en su parte superior (⛰[2]) identifican las subcategorias (véase la clave completa en la página I · 30).

Les symboles de l'index représentent les catégories indiquées dans la légende à droite. Les symboles suivis d'un indice (⛰[2]) représentent des sous-catégories (voir légende complète à la page I · 30).

Os símbolos incluídos no texto do índice representam as grandes categorias identificadas com a chave à direita. Os símbolos com números em sua parte superior (⛰[2]) identificam as subcategorias (veja-se a chave completa à página I · 30).

	English	Deutsch	Español	Français	Português
∧	Mountain	Berg	Montaña	Montagne	Montanha
⛰	Mountains	Berge	Montañas	Montagnes	Montanhas
)(	Pass	Pass	Paso	Col	Passo
∨	Valley, Canyon	Tal, Cañon	Valle, Cañón	Vallée, Canyon	Vale, Canhão
⌴	Plain	Ebene	Llano	Plaine	Planície
≻	Cape	Kap	Cabo	Cap	Cabo
I	Island	Insel	Isla	Île	Ilha
II	Islands	Inseln	Islas	Îles	Ilhas
⊥	Other Topographic Features	Andere Topographische Objekte	Otros Elementos Topográficos	Autres données topographiques	Outros Elementos Topográficos

ESPAÑOL

Nombre	Página	Lat.°′	Long.°′ W=Oeste
Paraná, Arg.	252	31.44 S	60.32 W
Paranã, Bra.	255	12.33 S	47.52 W
Paraná □[3]	252	24.00 S	51.00 W
Paranã ≃, Bra.	255	12.30 S	48.14 W
Paraná ≃, S.A.	18	33.43 S	59.15 W
Paranabi	256	23.54 S	45.14 W
Paraná Bravo ≃[1]	258	33.53 S	58.27 W
Paraná de las Palmas ≃[1]	258	34.18 S	58.33 W
Paranaguá	252	25.31 S	48.30 W
Paranaguá, Baía C	252	25.29 S	48.33 W
Paraná Guazú ≃[1]	258	34.00 S	58.25 W
Paranaíba	255	19.40 S	51.11 W
Paranaíba ≃	255	20.07 S	51.05 W
Paraná Ibicuy ≃[1]	258	33.48 S	59.10 W
Paranaidji	250	6.33 S	47.27 W
Paranaíta ≃	250	9.28 S	56.43 W
Paranam	250	5.37 N	55.06 W
Paraná Miní ≃[1]	258	34.13 S	58.25 W
Paranapanema ≃	255	22.40 S	53.09 W
Paranapiacaba	256	23.47 S	46.19 W
Paranapiacaba, Serra do ⩕	252	24.20 S	49.00 W
Parañaque	269f	14.30 N	120.59 E
Paranavaí	255	23.04 S	52.28 W
Parang, Pil.	116	7.23 N	124.16 E
Parang, Pil.	116	5.55 N	120.54 E
Parang, Pulau ❙	115a	5.45 S	110.14 E
Paran'ga	80	56.43 N	49.24 E
Paranhos	255	23.55 S	55.25 W
Paranjang	98	37.08 N	126.55 E
Paraopeba	255	19.18 S	44.25 W
Parapara	246	9.44 N	67.18 W
Paraparaumu	172	40.55 S	175.01 E
Paraparaumu Beach	172	40.54 S	174.59 E
Parapayè	58	45.55 N	7.32 E
Parapetí ≃	248	18.58 S	62.21 W
Parara	112	2.37 S	120.07 E
Parás, Méx.	196	26.30 N	99.31 W
Paras, Perú	248	13.30 S	74.35 W
Parasan	116	8.05 N	123.33 E
Parāsi	124	27.32 N	83.40 E
Parāsia	124	22.12 N	78.46 E
Parasida	126	23.46 N	87.20 E
Parasnāth	124	23.59 N	86.02 E
Parasnath Jain Temple ʋ[1]	272b	22.36 N	88.23 E
Paratei	256	23.14 S	46.00 W
Parateí ≃	256	23.12 S	46.00 W
Parati	256	23.13 S	44.43 W
Paratico	64	45.39 N	9.57 E
Parati-Mirim	256	23.14 S	44.38 W
Paratinga	255	12.42 S	43.10 W
Paratoo	166	32.42 S	139.22 E
Parauapebas ≃	250	5.35 S	49.41 W
Parauari ≃	250	4.36 S	57.47 W
Paraúna	255	17.02 S	50.26 W
Paravani, Ozero ◎	84	41.26 N	43.48 E
Paray-le-Monial	32	46.27 N	4.07 E
Parbakalan	114	2.38 N	98.27 E
Pārbati ≃	124	25.51 N	76.36 E
Pārbatipur	124	25.39 N	88.55 E
Parbhani	122	19.16 N	76.47 E
Parbig	86	57.14 N	81.24 E
Parbig ≃	86	57.37 N	82.18 E
Parbold	262	53.36 N	2.46 W
Parburuan	114	1.52 N	99.55 E
Parchen	54	52.21 N	12.05 E
Parchim	54	53.25 N	11.51 E
Parchment	216	42.19 N	85.33 W
Parchomenko	83	48.34 N	39.43 E
Parchomovka	78	50.08 N	35.01 E
Parchwitz → Prochowice	30	51.17 N	16.22 E
Parcines (Partschins)	64	46.41 N	11.04 E
Parczew	30	51.39 N	22.54 E
Pardee Reservoir ◎[1]	226	38.16 N	120.51 W
Pardeeville	190	43.32 N	89.18 W
Pardes Ḥanna	132	32.28 N	34.58 E
Pārdi	122	20.31 N	72.57 E
Pardo ≃, Bra.	250	5.21 S	52.53 W
Pardo ≃, Bra.	252	29.59 S	52.23 W
Pardo ≃, Bra.	255	15.48 S	44.48 W
Pardo ≃, Bra.	255	22.55 S	49.58 W
Pardo ≃, Bra.	255	15.39 S	38.57 W
Pardo ≃, Bra.	255	20.10 S	48.38 W
Pardo ≃, Bra.	255	21.46 S	52.09 W
Pardo ≃, Bra.	256	21.25 S	42.39 W
Pardo ≃, Bra.	256	23.32 S	45.30 W
Pardomuan	114	2.06 N	98.20 E
Pardubice	30	50.02 N	15.47 E
Pare	115a	7.46 S	112.11 E
Parece Vela → Okino-Tori-Shima ❙	90	20.25 N	136.00 E
Parecis	248	14.09 S	56.56 W
Parecis ≃	248	12.56 S	56.43 W
Parecis, Chapada dos ⩕	248	13.00 S	60.00 W
Parede	266c	38.41 N	9.21 W
Paredes de Nava	34	42.09 N	4.41 W
Paredes do Sapucaí	256	21.48 S	45.43 W
Paredón	232	25.56 N	100.58 W
Parelhas	250	6.41 S	36.39 W
Parelheiros ◂[8]	256	23.51 S	46.44 W
Pareloup, Lac de ◎	32	44.15 N	2.45 E
Paremata	172	41.07 S	174.52 E
Paren'	74	62.28 N	163.05 E
Paren' ≃	74	62.25 N	163.10 E
Parengarenga Harbour C	172	34.31 S	172.57 E
Parent	176	47.55 N	74.37 W
Parent, Lac ◎	190	48.38 N	77.03 W
Parentis-en-Born	32	44.21 N	1.05 W
Pareora	172	44.30 S	171.12 E
Parepare	112	4.01 S	119.38 E
Parera	252	35.08 S	64.32 W
Parey	54	52.22 N	11.59 E
Parfenjevo, S.S.S.R.	24	61.21 N	42.43 E
Parfenjevo, S.S.S.R.	80	58.29 N	43.25 E
Parfentevo	82	55.06 N	38.49 E
Parfino	76	57.58 N	31.41 E
Parforce-Heide ◂[3]	264a	52.22 N	13.10 E
Párga	38	39.17 N	20.23 E
Pārgaon	272c	18.59 N	73.05 E
Pargarutan	114	1.28 N	99.20 E
Pargas (Parainen)	26	60.18 N	22.18 E
Pargey Creek ≃	285	39.49 N	75.18 W
Pargny-sur-Saulx	56	48.46 N	4.50 E
Pargolovo	76	60.04 N	30.18 E
Parham	240c	17.05 N	61.46 W
Parhebangan	114	2.15 N	98.45 E
Pari	124	27.44 N	89.09 E
Pari ◂[8]	287b	23.32 S	46.37 W
Paria ≃	200	36.52 N	111.36 W
Paria, Gulf of C	246	10.20 N	62.00 W
Paria, Península de ≻[1]	241r	10.40 N	62.10 W
Pariaguán	246	8.51 N	64.43 W
Pariaman	112	0.38 S	100.08 E
Pariamanu ≃	248	12.26 S	69.16 W
Paricá, Lago ◎	246	1.53 S	65.45 W
Pariči	76	52.48 N	29.25 E
Paricutín ∧[1]	234	19.28 N	102.15 W
Parida, Isla ❙	236	8.07 N	82.20 W
Pariette Draw ∨	200	40.02 N	109.45 W
Parigi, Indon.	112	0.48 S	120.10 E
Parigi, Indon.	115a	6.12 S	106.22 E
Parigné-l'Évêque	50	47.56 N	0.22 E
Parika	246	6.52 N	58.25 W
Parikkala	26	61.33 N	29.30 E
Parima ≃	246	3.34 N	63.47 W
Parima, Sierra ⩕	246	2.30 N	64.00 W
Pariñas, Punta ≻	246	4.40 S	81.20 W
Parîngul ∧	38	45.22 N	23.33 E
Parintins	250	2.36 S	56.44 W
Paripiranga	250	10.41 S	37.52 W
Pariquera-Açu	252	24.43 S	47.53 W
Paris, Ont., Can.	212	43.12 N	80.23 W
Paris, Fr.	50		
	261	48.52 N	2.20 E

FRANÇAIS

Nom	Page	Lat.°′	Long.°′ W=Ouest
Paris, Kiribati	174o	1.56 N	157.29 W
Paris, Ark., U.S.	194	35.18 N	93.44 W
Paris, Idaho, U.S.	202	42.14 N	111.24 W
Paris, Ill., U.S.	194	39.36 N	87.42 W
Paris, Ky., U.S.	218	38.13 N	84.14 W
Paris, Maine, U.S.	188	44.16 N	70.30 W
Paris, Mo., U.S.	219	39.29 N	92.00 W
Paris, Ohio, U.S.	214	40.48 N	81.10 W
Paris, Pa., U.S.	214	40.24 N	80.31 W
Paris, Tenn., U.S.	194	36.19 N	88.20 W
Paris, Tex., U.S.	196	33.40 N	95.33 W
Paris □[5]	261	48.52 N	2.20 E
Paris, Port de C	261	48.57 N	2.17 E
Parish	210	43.24 N	76.08 W
Parisien de Pantin, Cimetière ◂	261	48.54 N	2.23 E
Paris-le-Bourget, Aéroport de ⊠	261	49.00 N	2.25 E
Parismina	236	10.12 N	83.38 W
Parismina ≃	236	10.19 N	83.21 W
Paris-Orly, Aeroport de ⊠	50	48.43 N	2.22 E
Paris-Plage, Aéroport ⊠	50	50.31 N	1.38 E
Parit	112	3.10 S	104.38 E
Parita, Bahía de C	236	8.08 N	80.24 W
Parit Bunga	114	2.04 N	102.33 E
Parit Buntar	114	5.07 N	100.30 E
Pariti	112	10.01 S	123.43 E
Parit Jawa	114	1.57 N	102.39 E
Parižskaja Kommuna ◂[8]	83	48.26 N	38.49 E
Park ≃	198	48.28 N	97.09 W
Park, North Branch ≃	198	48.26 N	97.27 W
Park, South Branch ≃	198	48.26 N	97.27 W
Parka	154	4.31 N	27.20 E
Parkano	26	62.01 N	23.01 E
Parkany	78	46.49 N	29.31 E
Parkchester	285	40.00 N	75.35 W
Park City, Ill., U.S.	216	42.21 N	87.53 W
Park City, Kans., U.S.	198	37.46 N	97.19 W
Park City, Mont., U.S.	202	45.38 N	108.55 W
Park City, Utah, U.S.	200	40.39 N	111.30 W
Park Creek ≃	285	40.13 N	75.08 W
Parkdale, P.E.I., Can.	186	46.15 N	63.07 W
Parkdale, Mo., U.S.	219	38.29 N	90.32 W
Parkdale, Oreg., U.S.	224	45.31 N	121.36 W
Parkdene	273d	26.14 S	28.16 E
Parkent	85	41.18 N	69.40 E
Parker, Ariz., U.S.	200	34.09 N	114.17 W
Parker, Fla., U.S.	194	30.08 N	85.36 W
Parker, Pa., U.S.	214	41.06 N	79.41 W
Parker, S. Dak., U.S.	198	43.24 N	97.08 W
Parker □[6]	222	32.48 N	97.42 W
Parker ≃	207	42.45 N	70.49 W
Parker, Cape ≻	176	75.04 N	79.40 W
Parker, Lake ◎	220	28.04 N	81.56 W
Parker City	218	40.11 N	85.12 W
Parker Dam	204	34.17 N	114.09 W
Parker Dam ◂[6]	200	34.18 N	114.10 W
Parker Ford	285	40.12 N	75.35 W
Parker Peak ∧	198	43.24 N	103.41 W
Parker Range	162	31.38 S	119.35 E
Parker River National Wildlife Refuge ◂[4]	283	42.45 N	70.48 W
Parkersburg, Ill., U.S.	194	38.36 N	88.03 W
Parkersburg, Iowa, U.S.	190	42.35 N	92.47 W
Parkersburg, W. Va., U.S.	188	39.17 N	81.32 W
Parkers Creek ≃	285	40.00 N	74.53 W
Parkers Prairie	198	46.09 N	95.20 W
Parkerville	168a	31.53 S	116.09 E
Parker Volcano ∧[1]	116	6.07 N	124.54 E
Parkes	166	33.08 S	148.11 E
Parkesburg	208	39.58 N	75.55 W
Park Falls	190	45.56 N	90.32 W
Park Forest	216	41.28 N	87.38 W
Park Forest South	216	41.36 N	87.39 W
Parkgate, Eng., U.K.	262	53.16 N	2.20 W
Parkgate, Eng., U.K.	262	53.18 N	3.05 W
Park Hall	208	38.13 N	76.26 W
Parkhill, Ont., Can.	190	43.09 N	81.41 W
Parkhill, Pa., U.S.	214	40.22 N	78.52 W
Parkhill Gardens	273d	26.14 S	28.11 E
Parkin	194	35.16 N	90.34 W
Parkitapo	154	1.29 S	35.34 E
Park Lake	216	42.48 N	84.27 W
Parkland, Pa., U.S.	285	40.09 N	74.56 W
Parkland, Wash., U.S.	224	47.09 N	122.26 W
Parklawn	284c	38.50 N	77.09 W
Park Layne	218	39.53 N	84.03 W
Parklea	274a	33.44 S	150.57 E
Parkman	214	41.22 N	81.04 W
Park Meadows	279b	40.18 N	79.44 W
Parkmore	44	55.02 N	6.06 W
Park Orchards	274b	37.46 S	145.13 E
Park Plateau ⩕[1]	198	37.15 N	104.45 W
Park Range ⩕	200	40.00 N	106.30 W
Park Rapids	198	46.55 N	95.04 W
Park Ridge, Ill., U.S.	216	42.01 N	87.50 W
Park Ridge, N.J., U.S.	276	41.02 N	74.02 W
Park Ridge Farms	285	40.10 N	74.42 W
Park Ridge Manor	278	42.02 N	87.50 W
Park River	198	48.24 N	97.45 W
Parkrose	224	45.34 N	122.33 W
Park Rynie	158	30.25 S	30.35 E
Parks Creek ≃	212	44.17 N	77.21 W
Park Shore Resort	216	41.55 N	85.59 W
Parkside, Md., U.S.	284c	39.02 N	77.06 W
Parkside, Pa., U.S.	285	39.52 N	75.23 W
Parksley	208	37.47 N	75.39 W
Park Station ◂[5]	273d	26.12 S	28.03 E
Parkstein	60	49.44 N	12.04 E
Parkstetten	60	48.55 N	12.36 E
Parkston	198	43.24 N	97.59 W
Parksville, B.C., Can.	182	49.19 N	124.19 W
Parksville, N.Y., U.S.	210	41.52 N	74.46 W
Parkview	279b	40.30 N	79.56 W
Parkville, Md., U.S.	208	39.23 N	76.32 W
Parkville, Mo., U.S.	198	39.11 N	94.41 W
Parkwater	202	47.40 N	117.18 W
Parkway, Calif., U.S.	226	38.30 N	121.27 W
Parkway, Mo., U.S.	219	38.20 N	90.57 W
Parkwood	284c	39.01 N	77.05 W
Parlākimidi	122	18.46 N	84.05 E
Parlament ʋ	264b	48.12 N	16.22 E
Parliament, Houses of ʋ	260	51.30 N	0.07 W
Parlier	226	36.37 N	119.32 W
Parma, It.	64	44.48 N	10.20 E
Parma, Idaho, U.S.	202	43.47 N	116.57 W
Parma, Mich., U.S.	216	42.15 N	84.36 W
Parma, Mo., U.S.	194	36.37 N	89.48 W
Parma, Ohio, U.S.	214	41.22 N	81.43 W
Parma □[4]	64	44.40 N	10.10 E
Parma ≃	64	44.56 N	10.26 E
Parma Heights	214	41.23 N	81.45 W
Parmain	261	49.07 N	2.12 E
Parmatown Center ◂[9]	279a	41.23 N	81.44 W
Parnaguá	250	10.13 S	44.38 W
Parnahyba → Parnaíba	250	2.54 S	41.47 W
Parnaíba	250	2.54 S	41.47 W
Parnaíba ≃	250	3.00 S	41.50 W
Parnaibinha ≃	250	9.17 S	45.55 W
Parnamirim, Bra.	250	5.55 S	35.15 W
Parnamirim, Bra.	250	8.05 S	39.34 W
Parnarama	250	5.41 S	43.06 W
Parnassós ∧	38	38.32 N	22.35 E
Parnassus	172	42.43 S	173.18 E
Parndorf	61	47.59 N	16.51 E
Parnell	216	40.14 N	88.42 W
Párnis ∧	38	38.11 N	23.42 E
Párnis Óros ⩕	267c	38.07 N	23.41 E
Parnon ⩕	38	37.18 N	22.35 E
Pärnu	76	58.24 N	24.32 E
Pärnu ≃	76	58.23 N	24.29 E

PORTUGUÊS

Nome	Página	Lat.°′	Long.°′ W=Oeste
Pärnu-Jaagupi	76	58.37 N	24.30 E
Pärnu Laht C	76	58.15 N	24.25 E
Paro	124	27.26 N	89.25 E
Pārola	120	20.53 N	75.07 E
Paromaj	89	52.50 N	143.02 E
Parona	130	37.31 N	41.58 E
Paroo	162	26.16 S	119.46 E
Paroo ≃	166	31.28 S	143.32 E
Parorā	272b	22.48 N	68.09 E
Páros	38	37.04 N	25.08 E
Páros ❙	38	37.08 N	25.12 E
Parow	158	33.53 S	18.37 E
Parowan	200	37.51 N	112.57 W
Parpaillon ⩕	62	44.30 N	6.40 E
Parpan	58	46.46 N	9.33 E
Parpik Pass)(	123	36.58 N	75.25 E
Parr	216	41.02 N	87.13 W
Parral, Chile	252	36.09 S	71.50 W
Parral → Hidalgo del Parral, Méx.	232	26.56 N	105.40 W
Parral, Ohio, U.S.	214	40.33 N	81.30 W
Parramatta	170	33.49 S	151.00 E
Parramatta ≃	274a	33.51 S	151.14 E
Parramatta Park ♠	274a	33.49 S	151.00 E
Parramore Island ❙	208	37.32 N	75.38 W
Parras de la Fuente	232	25.25 N	102.11 W
Parrett ≃	42	51.13 N	3.01 W
Parrish, Ala., U.S.	194	33.44 N	87.17 W
Parrish, Fla., U.S.	220	27.35 N	82.25 W
Parris Island Marine Corps Recruit Depot ▪	192	32.21 N	80.41 W
Parrita	236	9.30 N	84.19 W
Parrsboro	186	45.24 N	64.20 W
Parry, Cape ≻	176	70.08 N	124.24 W
Parry, Mount ∧	182	52.53 N	128.45 W
Parry Bay C	176	68.07 N	82.00 W
Parry Island ❙	212	45.18 N	80.10 W
Parry Island Indian Reserve ◂[4]	212	45.18 N	80.10 W
Parry Peninsula ≻[1]	180	69.45 N	124.30 W
Parry Sound	212	45.21 N	80.02 W
Parry Sound □[6]	212	45.25 N	79.55 W
Parry Sound ⋓	212	45.21 N	80.06 W
Parryville	208	40.49 N	75.40 W
Parsad	120	24.11 N	73.42 E
Parsberg	60	49.09 N	11.43 E
Parsdorf	60	48.09 N	11.47 E
Parseier Spitze ∧	58	47.10 N	10.28 E
Parsęta ≃	30	54.12 N	15.33 E
Parshall	198	47.57 N	102.08 W
Parshallville	281	42.41 N	83.46 W
Paršino	88	59.10 N	111.48 E
Parsippany	210	40.52 N	74.26 W
Parsippany, Lake ◎	276	40.51 N	74.26 W
Parsnāth ∧	124	23.53 N	86.08 E
Parsnip ≃	182	55.10 N	123.00 W
Parsoburan	114	2.19 N	99.20 E
Parsonage Island ❙	276	40.37 N	73.37 W
Parsons, Kans., U.S.	198	37.20 N	95.16 W
Parsons, Tenn., U.S.	194	35.39 N	88.07 W
Parsons, W. Va., U.S.	188	39.06 N	79.41 W
Parson's Pond	186	50.02 N	57.43 W
Parsons Pond ◎	186	50.00 N	57.35 W
Parsons Range ⩕	164	13.30 S	135.15 E
Parsteiner See ◎	54	52.55 N	13.59 E
Pärsti	76	58.25 N	25.32 E
Partābpur	124	23.29 N	83.13 E
Partanna	70	37.43 N	12.53 E
Partāppur	126	21.48 N	86.44 E
Partenen	58	46.58 N	10.03 E
Parthala	272a	28.36 N	77.24 E
Parthe ≃	54	51.22 N	12.21 E
Parthenay	32	46.39 N	0.15 W
Partille	26	57.44 N	12.07 E
Partington	262	53.25 N	2.26 W
Partinico	70	38.03 N	13.07 E
Partizánske	30	48.39 N	18.23 E
Partizanskoje	86	55.30 N	94.24 E
Parton	44	54.34 N	3.35 W
Partree	48	53.41 N	9.19 W
Partridge, Point ≻	224	48.13 N	122.46 W
Partridge Creek ≃	212	44.44 N	77.13 W
Partridge Crop Lake ◎	184	55.38 N	97.27 W
Partridge Point ≻	186	50.09 N	56.10 W
Partschins → Parcines	64	46.41 N	11.04 E
Paru ≃, Bra.	250	1.33 S	52.38 W
Parú ≃, Ven.	246	4.20 N	66.27 W
Parubcan	116	13.43 N	123.45 E
Parucito ≃	246	5.18 N	65.59 W
Paru de Este ≃	250	1.10 N	54.40 W
Paru de Oeste ≃	250	1.30 S	56.00 W
Parung	115a	6.25 S	106.42 E
Pårup, Dan.	41	56.08 N	9.21 E
Pårup, Dan.	41	55.24 N	10.20 E
Parūr	122	10.09 N	76.14 E
Paruro	248	13.46 S	71.51 W
Parutino	78	46.43 N	31.53 E
Parvān □[4]	120	35.15 N	69.30 E
Pārvatīpuram	122	18.47 N	83.26 E
Parvin State Park ♠	208	39.30 N	75.09 W
Pârvomaj	38	42.06 N	25.13 E
Påryd	26	56.34 N	15.55 E
Parys	158	27.04 S	27.16 E
Paša ≃	76	60.29 N	32.55 E
Paşabahçe ◂[8]	267b	41.06 N	29.05 E
Pasacao	116	13.31 N	123.03 E
Pasaco	236	13.59 N	90.12 W
Pasadena, Newf., Can.	186	49.01 N	57.36 W
Pasadena, Calif., U.S.	228	34.09 N	118.09 W
Pasadena, Tex., U.S.	222	29.42 N	95.13 W
Pasado, Cabo ≻	246	0.22 S	80.30 W
Pasaje	246	3.20 S	79.49 W
Pasaje ≃	252	25.35 S	63.57 W
Pasaje Talavera ≃[1]	258	33.53 S	58.55 W
Pa Sak ≃	110	14.21 N	100.35 E
Pasaleng Bay C	116	18.36 N	120.56 E
Paşalimanı Adası ❙	130	40.28 N	27.37 E
Pasān	124	22.51 N	82.12 E
Pasanauri	84	42.21 N	44.41 E
Pasangkayu	112	1.10 S	119.20 E
Pasarbantal	112	2.45 S	101.20 E
Pasarseluma	112	4.09 S	102.32 E
Pasar Senen Station ◂[5]	269e	6.10 S	106.50 E
Pasarwajo	112	5.29 S	122.50 E
Pasatiempo	226	37.02 N	122.02 W
Pasaunda	272a	28.42 N	77.21 E
Paşavenk	130	38.53 N	39.29 E
Pasawng	110	18.52 N	97.18 E
Pasay	269f	14.33 N	121.00 E
Pasayten, Middle Fork ≃	224	48.53 N	120.37 W
Pasayten, West Fork ≃	224	48.53 N	120.37 W
Pascack Brook ≃	276	40.59 N	73.59 W
Pascagama, Lac ◎	190	48.34 N	75.36 W
Pascagoula	194	30.23 N	88.31 W
Pascagoula ≃	194	30.21 N	88.34 W
Pascalis, Lac ◎	190	48.16 N	77.24 W
Paşcani	38	47.15 N	26.44 E
Pasco, Fla., U.S.	220	28.20 N	82.22 W
Pasco, Wash., U.S.	202	46.14 N	119.06 W
Pasco □[5]	248	10.30 S	75.15 W
Pasco □[6]	220	28.20 N	82.27 W
Pascoag	207	41.57 N	71.42 W
Pascoe Vale	274b	37.44 S	144.56 E
Pasco Seamount ⊹[3]	14	13.00 S	174.30 W
Pascua, Isla de (Easter Island) ❙	174z	27.07 S	109.22 W
Pascuales, Boca ≃[1]	234	18.52 N	103.58 W
Pas-de-Calais □[5]	50	50.30 N	2.20 E
Pas-en-Artois	50	50.09 N	2.30 E
Pasewalk	54	53.30 N	14.00 E
Pasian di Prato	64	46.03 N	13.11 E
Pasiano di Pordenone	64	45.51 N	12.37 E
Pasig	116	14.35 N	121.05 E
Pasig ≃	269f	14.36 N	120.58 E
Pāsighāt	120	28.04 N	95.20 E
Pašija	86	58.26 N	58.16 E
P'asina ≃	74	73.50 N	87.10 E
Pasinler (Hasankale)	130	39.59 N	41.41 E
Pašino	86	55.11 N	83.00 E
P'asino, Ozero ◎	74	69.45 N	87.45 E
P'asinskij Zaliv C	74	74.00 N	86.00 E
Pasión, Rió de la ≃	232	16.28 N	90.33 W
Pasirganting	112	2.02 S	100.53 E
Pasir Gudang	271c	1.27 N	103.53 E
Pasirian	115a	8.13 S	113.06 E
Pasir Mas	114	6.02 N	102.08 E
Pasir Panjang	271c	1.17 N	103.47 E
Pasirpengarayan	114	0.51 N	100.16 E
Pasir Puteh, Malay.	114	5.50 N	102.24 E
Pasir Puteh, Malay.	271c	1.26 N	103.56 E
Påskallavik	26	57.10 N	16.27 E
Paskeville	168b	34.02 S	137.54 E
Paškovo, S.S.S.R.	80	53.39 N	42.25 E
Paškovo, S.S.S.R.	89	48.54 N	130.42 E
Paškovskij	78	45.02 N	39.06 E
Pasłęk	30	54.05 N	19.39 E
Pasłęka ≃	30	54.26 N	19.45 E
Pasley, Cape ≻	162	33.57 S	123.31 E
Pasley Bay C	176	70.40 N	96.27 W
Pašman, Otok ❙	36	43.58 N	15.21 E
Pasmore ≃	166	31.07 S	139.48 E
Pašn'a	24	63.21 N	56.28 E
Pasni	128	25.16 N	63.28 E
Paso de Indios	254	43.52 S	69.06 W
Paso del Cerro	252	31.29 S	55.50 W
Paso del Macho	234	18.58 N	96.43 W
Paso de los Libres	252	29.43 S	57.05 W
Paso de los Toros	252	32.49 S	56.31 W
Paso del Rey	288	34.39 S	58.46 W
Paso del Toro	234	19.02 N	96.07 W
Paso de Ovejas	234	19.17 N	96.26 W
Paso de Patria	252	27.13 S	58.35 W
Paso de San Antonio	196	29.05 N	103.55 W
Paso Hondo	232	15.49 N	92.02 W
Paso Limay	254	40.33 S	70.26 W
Pasorapa	248	18.16 S	64.37 W
Paso Real de Sarabia	234	17.03 N	95.01 W
Paso Robles	226	35.38 N	120.41 W
Paso Seco	240m	17.59 N	66.23 W
Pašozero	76	60.02 N	34.37 E
Pasqua Indian Reserve ◂[4]	184	50.45 N	104.02 W
Pasque Island ❙	207	41.27 N	70.50 W
Pasquia Hills ⩕[2]	184	53.13 N	102.37 W
Pasquia Lake ◎	184	53.37 N	101.20 W
Pasquotank □[6]	208	36.26 N	76.26 W
Pasquotank ≃	192	36.10 N	76.03 W
Pasrūr	123	32.16 N	74.40 E
Passa-Cinco, Corredeira ⌞	256	21.19 S	43.08 W
Passadumkeag	188	45.11 N	68.37 W
Passadumkeag Mountain ∧	188	45.10 N	68.20 W
Passage East	48	52.13 N	6.59 W
Passagem Franca	250	6.10 S	43.47 W
Passage West	48	51.52 N	8.20 W
Passaic	210	40.51 N	74.08 W
Passaic □[6]	210	40.55 N	74.10 W
Passaic ≃	276	40.43 N	74.07 W
Passamaquoddy Bay C	186	45.06 N	66.59 W
Passa Quatro	256	22.23 S	44.58 W
Passa Três	256	22.42 S	44.00 W
Passau	60	48.35 N	13.28 E
Passa Vinte	256	22.13 S	44.15 W
Pass Creek ≃	198	43.45 N	101.28 W
Passero, Capo ≻	70	36.41 N	15.10 E
Passignano sul Trasimeno	66	43.11 N	12.08 E
Passing ◂[8]	60	48.08 N	11.27 E
Passirio (Passer) ≃	64	46.41 N	11.10 E
Pass Island	186	47.29 N	56.11 W
Pašskij Perevoz	76	60.24 N	32.59 E
Passo Corese	66	42.09 N	12.39 E
Passo de Camaragibe	250	9.14 S	35.29 W
Passo Fundo	252	28.15 S	52.24 W
Passo Fundo ≃	252	27.16 S	52.42 W
Passopisciaro	70	37.52 N	15.02 E
Passos	255	20.43 S	46.37 W
Passow	54	53.08 N	14.06 E
Passy	58	45.55 N	6.41 E
Passy ◂[8]	32	48.52 N	2.17 E
Pastaza □[4]	246	1.45 S	76.50 W
Pastaza ≃	246	4.50 S	76.25 W
Pastecho ≃	182	56.07 N	114.15 W
Pasteur, Lac ◎	186	50.13 N	66.58 W
Pastillo	240m	17.59 N	66.29 W
Pasto	246	1.13 N	77.17 W
Pastol Bay C	180	63.07 N	163.15 W
Pastora Peak ∧	200	36.47 N	109.10 W
Pastoría, Laguna de C	234	15.59 N	97.40 W
Pastoria Creek ≃	228	35.01 N	118.51 W
Pastos Bons	250	6.36 S	44.05 W
Pastrana	34	40.25 N	2.55 W
Pastrengo	64	45.29 N	10.48 E
Pašukovo	82	55.55 N	38.16 E
Pasuquin	116	18.20 N	120.37 E
Pasur	130	38.30 N	41.02 E
Pasuruan	115a	7.38 S	112.54 E
Pasvalys	76	56.04 N	24.24 E
Pásztó	30	47.55 N	19.42 E
Pata	116	5.51 N	121.10 E
Patacamaya	248	17.14 S	67.55 W
Pātāchārkuchi	120	26.31 N	91.16 E
Patagonia	200	31.33 N	110.45 W
Patagonia ◂[1]	254	44.00 S	68.00 W
Pataha Creek ≃	202	46.31 N	117.59 W
Pata Island ❙	116	5.49 N	121.10 E
Patamban	234	19.48 N	102.18 W
Pātan, Bhārat	120	23.50 N	72.07 E
Pātan, Bhārat	124	23.18 N	79.42 E
Patan → Lalitpur, Nepāl	124	27.41 N	85.20 E
Patapsco	208	39.32 N	76.54 W
Patapsco ≃	208	39.09 N	76.27 W
Patapsco, Cooks Branch ≃	284b	39.27 N	76.53 W
Patapsco, Davis Branch ≃	284b	39.19 N	76.51 W
Patapsco, North Branch ≃	208	39.21 N	76.53 W
Patapsco, Rockburn Branch ≃	284b	39.14 N	76.43 W
Patapsco, Soapstone Branch ≃	284b	39.13 N	76.43 W
Patapsco River Neck ≻[1]	284b	39.14 N	76.27 W
Patapsco State Park ♠	208	39.20 N	76.55 W
Patargān, Daqq-e ☷	128	33.30 N	60.40 E
Pataudi	124	28.19 N	76.47 E
Pataula Creek ≃	192	31.46 N	85.02 W
Patay	50	48.03 N	1.42 E
Pataz	248	7.44 S	77.37 W
Patcham	42	50.52 N	0.08 W
Patchewollock	166	35.23 S	142.11 E
Patchogue	210	40.46 N	73.00 W
Patchogue Bay C	276	40.44 N	73.01 W
Patchway	42	51.32 N	2.34 W
Pat Cleburne, Lake ◎[1]	222	32.25 N	97.30 W
Pate	154	2.08 S	41.00 E
Patea	172	39.45 S	174.28 E
Patea ≃	172	39.46 S	174.29 E
Patearoa	172	45.16 S	170.03 E
Pategi	150	8.44 N	5.44 E
Pate Island ❙	154	2.07 S	41.03 E
Pateley Bridge	44	54.05 N	1.45 W
Patel Nagar ◂[8]	272a	28.39 N	77.10 E
Patensie	158	33.46 S	24.49 E
Patéras Óros ∧	267c	38.07 N	23.25 E
Patergassen	64	46.49 N	13.52 E
Paterna	34	39.30 N	0.26 W
Paternion	64	46.43 N	13.38 E
Paternò	70	37.34 N	14.54 E
Pateros, Pil.	269f	14.33 N	121.04 E
Pateros, Wash., U.S.	202	48.03 N	119.54 W
Patersdorf	60	49.01 N	12.59 E
Paterson, Austl.	170	32.36 S	151.37 E
Paterson, S. Afr.	158	33.26 S	25.58 E
Paterson, N.J., U.S.	210		
	276	40.55 N	74.10 W
Paterson, Cape ≻	169	38.40 S	145.36 E
Paterswolde	52	53.08 N	6.35 E
Pātghāti	126	22.53 N	89.55 E
Pathalgaon	124	22.34 N	83.28 E
Pathānkot	123	32.17 N	75.39 E
Pathānkot Airport ⊠	123	32.15 N	75.37 E
Pātharghāra	272b	22.34 N	88.35 E
Pātharghāta	126	22.02 N	89.58 E
Patharia	124	23.54 N	79.12 E
Pathfinder Reservoir ◎[1]	200	42.30 N	106.50 W
Pathfinder Seamount ⊹[3]	16	50.55 N	143.20 W
Pathiong	140	6.46 N	30.54 E
Pathiu	110	10.42 N	99.19 E
Path of Condie	46	56.15 N	3.30 W
Pāthrāil	126	24.12 N	89.56 E
Pathro ≃	126	24.12 N	86.48 E
Pathum Thani	110	14.01 N	100.32 E
Pati, Indon.	112	0.33 S	111.19 E
Pati, Indon.	115a	6.45 S	111.01 E
Pati ≃	246	3.41 S	67.37 W
Patía	246	2.04 N	77.04 W
Patía ≃	246	2.13 N	78.40 W
Patiāla	123	30.19 N	76.24 E
Patiāla □[5]	124	30.20 N	76.20 E
Patiāla ∧	123	32.32 N	72.11 E
P'atichatki	78	48.24 N	33.42 E
Pati do Alferes	256	22.25 S	43.25 W
P'atigorsk	84	44.03 N	43.04 E
Pātihāl	272b	22.39 N	88.08 E
Patikul	116	6.04 N	121.06 E
Patillas	240m	18.00 N	66.01 W
P'atimar	80	49.31 N	50.32 E
Patinti, Selat ⋓	164	0.30 S	127.45 E
Patipāda	272c	19.04 N	73.05 E
Pati Point ≻	174p	13.36 N	144.57 E
Pātiram	124	25.19 N	88.45 E
Patire, Convento del ʋ[1]	68	39.34 N	16.35 E
Pătîrlagele	38	45.19 N	26.22 E
Pativilca	248	10.42 S	77.47 W
Pativilca ≃	248	10.44 S	77.48 W
Pātkai Range ⩕	120	27.00 N	96.00 E
Patman	222	32.57 N	94.34 W
Pátmos ❙	130	37.20 N	26.33 E
Patna, Bhārat	124	25.36 N	85.07 E
Patna, Bhārat	126	21.56 N	87.52 E
Pātna, Bhārat	272b	22.59 N	88.18 E
Patna □[5]	124	25.20 N	85.30 E
Patnāgarh	122	20.43 N	83.09 E
Patnanongan Island ❙	116	14.48 N	122.11 E
P'atnica, S.S.S.R.	82	54.46 N	38.09 E
P'atnica, S.S.S.R.	82	56.05 N	36.48 E
P'atnickoje, S.S.S.R.	78	50.25 N	37.51 E
P'atnickoje, S.S.S.R.	82	54.20 N	35.53 E
Pātnoli	272c	18.57 N	73.05 E
Patnoñgon	116	10.55 N	122.00 E
Patnos	84	39.14 N	42.52 E
Pato Branco	252	26.13 S	52.40 W
Patoka	219	38.45 N	89.06 W
Patoka ≃	194	38.25 N	87.44 W
Patokino	82	56.27 N	39.06 E
Patomskoje Nagorje ⩕[1]	88	59.00 N	114.00 E
Patonga	154	2.46 N	33.18 E
Patos	250	7.01 S	37.16 W
Patos, Cachoeira dos ⌞	248	9.20 S	60.15 W
Patos, Lagoa dos C	252	31.06 S	51.15 W
Patos, Río de los ≃	252	31.18 S	69.25 W
Patos, Rio dos ≃, Bra.	248	13.33 S	56.29 W
Patos, Rio dos ≃, Bra.	255	14.59 S	48.46 W
Patos de Minas	255	18.35 S	46.32 W
Patos Island ❙	224	48.47 N	122.56 W
P'atovskij	82	54.41 N	36.04 E
Patquía	252	30.03 S	66.53 W
Pátrai	38	38.15 N	21.44 E
Patraïkós Kólpos C	38	38.14 N	21.15 E
Patras → Pátrai	38	38.15 N	21.44 E
Pātrasāer	124	23.13 N	87.31 E
Patricio Lynch, Isla ❙	254	48.37 S	75.26 W
Patrick Air Force Base ▪	220	28.15 N	80.36 W
Patrick Henry International Airport ⊠	208	37.08 N	76.30 W
Patrick Point ≻	214	42.35 N	81.28 W
Patrington	44	53.41 N	0.02 W
Patriot	218	38.50 N	84.49 W
Patrocínio	255	18.57 S	46.59 W
Patrocínio Paulista	255	20.38 S	47.17 W
Patsaliga Creek ≃	194	31.22 N	86.31 W
Patscherkofel ∧	64	47.13 N	11.28 E
Pattada	71	40.35 N	9.06 E
Pattani	110	6.52 N	101.16 E
Pattani ≃	114	6.45 N	101.18 E
Patten	188	46.01 N	68.27 W
Pattenburg	210	40.38 N	75.01 W
Pattensen	52	52.15 N	9.46 E
Pattenville	283	42.35 N	71.14 W
Patterdale	44	54.32 N	2.56 W
Patterson, Calif., U.S.	226	37.28 N	121.07 W
Patterson, Ga., U.S.	192	31.23 N	82.08 W
Patterson, Ill., U.S.	219	39.29 N	90.29 W
Patterson, La., U.S.	194	29.42 N	91.18 W
Patterson, N.Y., U.S.	210	41.31 N	73.36 W
Patterson, Ohio, U.S.	216	40.47 N	83.32 W
Patterson, Mount ∧	180	64.04 N	134.39 W
Patterson Creek ≃	188	39.34 N	78.23 W
Patterson Gardens	216	41.56 N	83.25 W
Patterson Heights	214	40.45 N	80.19 W
Patterson Island ❙	190	48.39 N	87.00 W
Patterson Park ♠	284b	39.17 N	76.35 W
Pattersonville	210	42.53 N	74.05 W
Patteson, Port C	175f	13.49 S	167.34 E
Patteson Passage ⋓	175f	15.26 S	168.12 E
Patti, Bhārat	123	31.17 N	74.51 E
Patti, Bhārat	124	25.55 N	82.12 E
Patti, It.	70	38.08 N	14.58 E
Patti, Golfo di C	36	38.12 N	15.05 E
Pattison, Miss., U.S.	194	31.53 N	90.53 W
Pattison, Tex., U.S.	222	29.49 N	95.60 W
Pattoki	123	31.01 N	73.51 E
Patton	214	40.38 N	78.39 W
Patton, Cape ≻	169	38.42 S	143.50 E
Patton Park ♠	281	42.19 N	83.10 W
Pattonsburg	194	40.03 N	94.08 W
Patton Seamount Group ⊹[3]	16	55.30 N	149.30 W
Pattscheid	263	51.05 N	7.03 E
Pattukkottai	122	10.26 N	79.19 E
Pattullo, Mount ∧	180	56.14 N	129.39 W
Patu	250	6.06 S	37.38 W
Pātua	126	22.06 N	90.23 E
Patuākhāli	124	22.21 N	90.21 E
Patuca ≃	236	15.50 N	84.17 W
Patuca, Punta ≻	236	15.51 N	84.18 W
Patuha, Gunung ∧	115a	7.10 S	107.23 E
Pātul	272b	22.45 N	88.10 E
Pātuli, Bhārat	126	23.33 N	88.15 E
Pātuli, Bngl.	126	24.13 N	89.54 E
Patulul	236	14.25 N	91.10 W
Patumahoe	172	37.11 S	174.50 E
Pat'ung Kuan)(	100	23.30 N	121.01 E
Pātūr	122	20.27 N	76.56 E
Patusi	164	2.10 S	147.10 E
Patutu ∧	172	39.15 S	175.51 E
Patuxent ≃	208	38.18 N	76.25 W
Patuxent, Western Branch ≃	208	38.47 N	76.43 W
Patuxent River Naval Air Test Center ▪	208	38.17 N	76.25 W
Patwāri	272a	28.35 N	77.27 E
Pátzcuaro	234	19.31 N	101.36 W
Pátzcuaro, Lago de ◎	234	19.35 N	101.35 W
Patzicía	236	14.38 N	90.56 W
Patzig	54	54.28 N	13.24 E
Patzún	236	14.41 N	91.01 W
Pau	32	43.18 N	0.22 W
Pau, Gave de ≃	32	43.33 N	1.12 W
Pau Brasil	255	15.27 S	39.39 W
Paucarbamba	248	12.25 S	74.36 W
Paucarpata	248	16.26 S	71.30 W
Paucartambo	248	13.18 S	71.40 W
Pau d'Arco	250	7.30 S	49.22 W
Paudash Lake ◎	212	44.58 N	78.04 W
Pau dos Ferros	250	6.07 S	38.10 W
Pauh	112	2.08 S	102.48 E
Pauhunri ∧	124	27.58 N	88.50 E
Pauini	248	7.40 S	66.58 W
Pauini ≃, Bra.	246	1.42 S	62.50 W
Pauini ≃, Bra.	248	7.47 S	67.05 W
Pauk	110	21.27 N	94.27 E
Pauksa Taung ∧	110	19.55 N	94.18 E
Paul	202	42.40 N	113.36 W
Paul, Lac à ◎	186	49.52 N	70.46 W
Paula Lima	256	21.35 S	43.29 W
Paularo	64	46.32 N	13.07 E
Paulaya ≃	236	15.51 N	85.06 W
Paulding, Miss., U.S.	194	32.02 N	89.02 W
Paulding, Ohio, U.S.	216	41.08 N	84.35 W
Paulding □[6]	216	41.08 N	84.35 W
Paulding Bay C	9	66.35 S	123.00 E
Paulhan	32	43.32 N	3.27 E
Paulicéia	255	21.17 S	51.51 W
Paulilatino	71	40.05 N	8.46 E
Paulina Peak ∧	202	43.41 N	121.15 W
Pauline, Mount ∧	182	53.33 N	119.54 W
Paulinenaue	54	52.40 N	12.43 E
Paulínia	256	22.45 S	47.10 W
Paulino Neves	250	2.43 S	42.33 W
Paulins Kill	210	41.03 N	74.49 W
Paulins Kill ≃	210	40.55 N	75.05 W
Paulinzella ⊥	54	50.42 N	11.06 E
Paulis → Isiro	154	2.47 N	27.37 E
Paulista	250	7.57 S	34.53 W
Paulistana	250	8.09 S	41.09 W
Paulistas	255	18.25 S	42.52 W
Paullina	198	42.59 N	95.41 W
Paull Lake ◎	184	56.08 N	104.50 W
Paullo	62	45.25 N	9.24 E
Paulo Afonso	250	9.21 S	38.14 W
Paulo Afonso, Parque Nacional de ♠	250	9.20 S	38.12 W
Paulo de Faria	255	20.02 S	49.24 W
Paulo e Virginia, Gruta ⍛[5]	287a	22.57 S	43.18 W
Pauloff Harbor (Pavlof Harbor)	180	54.27 N	162.42 W
Paulpietersburg	158	27.30 S	30.51 E
Paul Roux	158	28.18 S	27.59 E
Paulsboro	208	39.50 N	75.15 W
Pauls Cross Roads	208	37.52 N	76.53 W
Paul Seamount ⊹[3]	14	18.30 N	172.30 W
Paulstown	48	52.41 N	7.01 W
Pauls Valley	196	34.44 N	97.13 W
Paulton	279b	40.34 N	79.34 W
Paulushofen	60	49.01 N	11.30 E
Pāunān	272b	22.57 N	88.17 E
Paung	110	16.37 N	97.28 E
Paungbyin	110	24.16 N	94.49 E
Paungde	110	18.29 N	95.30 E
Paunggyi	110	17.19 N	96.11 E
Pauni	122	20.47 N	79.38 E
Paup	164	3.15 S	142.35 E
Paupack	210	41.24 N	75.14 W
Pauri, Bhārat	124	30.09 N	78.47 E
Pauri, Bhārat	124	25.32 N	77.21 E
Pausa, D.D.R.	54	50.35 N	12.00 E
Pausa, Perú	248	15.16 S	73.20 W
Pausania	36	40.55 N	9.06 E
Pausin	264a	52.38 N	13.03 E
Paute	246	2.47 S	78.50 W
Paute ≃	246	2.46 S	78.16 W
Pauto ≃	246	5.09 N	70.55 W
Pautou → Baotou	102	40.40 N	109.59 E
Pauwalu Point ≻	229a	20.52 N	156.08 W
Pauwela	229a	20.56 N	156.19 W
Pauwela Point ≻	229a	20.57 N	156.19 W
Pavai ◂[8]	272c	19.07 N	72.55 E
Pavai Lake ◎	272c	19.07 N	72.55 E
Pavant Range ⩕	200	38.45 N	112.15 W
Pavda	86	59.15 N	59.30 E
Pāveh	128	35.03 N	46.22 E
Pavel'cevo	82	56.15 N	36.26 E
Pavelec	76	53.50 N	39.16 E
Paveleckij Vokzal ◂[5]	265b	55.44 N	37.38 E
Pavia	62	45.10 N	9.10 E
Pavia □[4]	62	45.07 N	9.08 E
Pavia, Naviglio di ☰	266b	45.27 N	9.11 E
Pavia di Udine	64	45.59 N	13.17 E
Pavilion, B.C., Can.	182	50.52 N	121.50 W
Pavilion, N.Y., U.S.	210	42.53 N	78.01 W
Pavilion Key ❙	220	25.42 N	81.22 W
Pavillion	200	43.15 N	108.42 W
Pavilly	50	49.34 N	0.58 E
Pāvilosta	76	56.53 N	21.14 E
Pavino	24	59.07 N	46.07 E
Pavione, Monte ∧	64	46.07 N	11.50 E
Pavlice	61	48.59 N	15.53 E
Pavlikeni	38	43.14 N	25.18 E
Pavliščevo, S.S.S.R.	82	55.11 N	35.59 E
Pavliščevo, S.S.S.R.	82	55.34 N	35.59 E
Pavlodar	86	52.18 N	76.57 E
Pavlof Bay C	180	55.30 N	161.32 W
Pavlof Volcano ∧[1]	180	55.24 N	161.52 W
Pavlograd	78	48.32 N	35.53 E
Pavlogradka	86	54.12 N	73.33 E
Pavlopol'	83	47.16 N	37.47 E
Pavlovka, S.S.S.R.	78	47.45 N	37.14 E
Pavlovka, S.S.S.R.	80	52.41 N	47.09 E
Pavlovka, S.S.S.R.	83	49.36 N	38.42 E
Pavlovka, S.S.S.R.	83	48.08 N	39.33 E
Pavlovka, S.S.S.R.	86	55.25 N	56.33 E
Pavlovka, S.S.S.R.	86	51.55 N	54.47 E
Pavlovo, S.S.S.R.	76	60.05 N	45.17 E
Pavlovo, S.S.S.R.	80	55.58 N	43.04 E
Pavlovo, S.S.S.R.	265a	59.56 N	30.40 E
Pavlovo, S.S.S.R.	265a	59.49 N	30.54 E
Pavlovsk, S.S.S.R.	76	59.41 N	30.27 E
Pavlovsk, S.S.S.R.	78	50.27 N	40.08 E
Pavlovsk, S.S.S.R.	86	53.20 N	82.59 E
Pavlovskaja	78	46.08 N	39.48 E
Pavlovskaja Sloboda	82	55.49 N	37.05 E
Pavlovskij, S.S.S.R.	80	57.50 N	54.51 E
Pavlovskij, S.S.S.R.	86	52.32 N	63.06 E
Pavlovskij Posad	82	55.47 N	38.40 E
Pavlyš	78	48.55 N	33.21 E
Pavne	272c	19.05 N	73.01 E
Pavo	192	30.57 N	83.45 W
Pavón, Arg.	258	34.23 S	59.03 W
Pavón, Col.	246	3.37 N	72.15 W
Pavón, Arroyo ≃	258	34.30 S	57.05 W
Pavona	267a	41.43 N	12.37 E
Pavonia	214	40.49 N	82.26 W
Pavšino	265b	55.49 N	37.21 E
Pavšozero	76	60.38 N	35.34 E
Pavullo nel Frignano	64	44.20 N	10.50 E
Pavuna, Arroio ≃	287a	22.58 S	43.23 W
Pavuvu ❙	175e	9.03 S	159.06 E

≃ River	Fluss	Río	Rivière	Rio
☰ Canal	Kanal	Canal	Canal	Canal
⌞ Waterfall, Rapids	Wasserfall, Stromschnellen	Cascada, Rápidos	Chute d'eau, Rapides	Cascata, Rápidos
⋓ Strait	Meeresstrasse	Estrecho	Détroit	Estreito
C Bay, Gulf	Bucht, Golf	Bahía, Golfo	Baie, Golfe	Baía, Golfo
◎ Lake, Lakes	See, Seen	Lago, Lagos	Lac, Lacs	Lago, Lagos
☷ Swamp	Sumpf	Pantano	Marais	Pântano
⛉ Ice Features, Glacier	Eis- und Gletscherformen	Accidentes Glaciales	Formes glaciaires	Acidentes Glaciares
⍑ Other Hydrographic Features	Andere Hydrographische Objekte	Otros Elementos Hidrográficos	Autres données hydrographiques	Outros Elementos Hidrográficos

⊹ Submarine Features	Untermeerische Objekte	Accidentes Submarinos	Formes de relief sous-marin	Acidentes Submarinos
□ Political Unit	Politische Einheit	Unidad Politica	Entité politique	Unidade Política
ʋ Cultural Institution	Kulturelle Institution	Institución Cultural	Institution culturelle	Instituição Cultural
⊥ Historical Site	Historische Stätte	Sitio Histórico	Site historique	Sitio Histórico
♠ Recreational Site	Erholungs- und Ferienort	Sitio de Recreo	Centre de loisirs	Sítio de Lazer
⊠ Airport	Flughafen	Aeropuerto	Aéroport	Aeroporto
▪ Military Installation	Militäranlage	Instalación Militar	Installation militaire	Instalação Militar
◂ Miscellaneous	Verschiedenes	Misceláneo	Divers	Miscelânea

Name	Page / Seite	Lat. / Breite	Long. / Länge E=Ost
Pavy	76	58.03 N	29.30 E
Pawai, Pulau I	271c	1.12 N	103.43 E
Pawan ≃	112	1.51 S	109.57 E
Pawāyan	124	28.04 N	80.06 E
Pawcatuck	207	41.22 N	71.52 W
Paw Creek	192	35.17 N	80.56 W
Päwesin	54	52.31 N	12.42 E
Pawhuska	196	36.40 N	96.20 W
Pawling	210	41.34 N	73.36 W
Pawnee, Ill., U.S.	219	39.35 N	89.35 W
Pawnee, Okla., U.S.	196	36.20 N	96.48 W
Pawnee ≃	198	38.10 N	99.06 W
Pawnee City	198	40.07 N	96.09 W
Pawnee Creek ≃	198	40.34 N	103.14 W
Pawnee Rock	198	38.16 N	99.01 W
Pawota	110	17.46 N	97.17 E
Pawpaw, Ill., U.S.	216	41.41 N	88.59 W
Paw Paw, Mich., U.S.	216	42.13 N	85.53 W
Paw Paw, W. Va., U.S.	188	39.32 N	78.27 W
Paw Paw ≃	216	42.07 N	86.29 W
Paw Paw Creek ≃	216	40.52 N	85.58 W
Paw Paw Lake	216	42.12 N	86.15 W
Paw Paw Lake ⊜	216	42.12 N	86.16 W
Pawtucket	207	41.53 N	71.23 W
Pawtucket Falls L	207	42.39 N	71.20 W
Paxoí I	38	39.12 N	20.12 E
Paxson	180	63.02 N	145.30 W
Paxton, Austl.	170	32.54 S	151.16 E
Paxton, Ill., U.S.	216	40.27 N	88.06 W
Paxton, Mass., U.S.	207	42.19 N	71.56 W
Paxton, Nebr., U.S.	198	41.07 N	101.21 W
Paxtonia	208	40.19 N	76.48 W
Paxtonville	208	40.46 N	77.05 W
Paya	236	15.37 N	85.17 W
Paya Besar	114	3.47 N	103.16 E
Payadapu	114	3.05 N	97.23 E
Payāgpur	124	27.25 N	81.48 E
Payagyi	110	17.29 N	96.32 E
Payakumbuh	112	0.14 S	100.38 E
Paya Lebar	271c	1.22 N	103.53 E
Paya Lebar Airport ⊠	271c	1.21 N	103.54 E
Payamlı	130	37.01 N	38.35 E
Payangan	115b	8.26 S	115.15 E
Payas	130	36.47 N	36.10 E
Payas, Cerro ∧	236	15.50 N	85.00 W
Payerne	58	46.49 N	6.56 E
Payeti	115b	9.41 S	120.20 E
Payette	202	44.05 N	116.56 W
Payette ≃	202	44.05 N	116.57 W
Payette, Middle Fork ≃	202	44.05 N	116.07 W
Payette, North Fork ≃	202	44.05 N	116.07 W
Payette, South Fork ≃	202	44.06 N	116.00 W
Payette Lake ⊜[1]	202	44.57 N	116.05 W
Paylampur	272b	22.47 N	88.16 E
Payne	216	41.05 N	84.44 W
Payne ≃	206	45.14 N	75.08 W
Payne, Bassin C	176	60.00 N	70.00 W
Payne, Lac ⊜	176	59.25 N	74.00 W
Payneham	168b	34.53 S	138.38 E
Paynes Creek ≃	204	40.16 N	122.11 W
Paynes Find	162	29.15 S	117.41 E
Paynesville, S. Afr.	273d	26.14 S	28.28 E
Paynesville, Minn., U.S.	198	45.23 N	94.43 W
Paynesville, Mo., U.S.	219	39.16 N	90.54 W
Paynetown State Recreation Area ♠	218	39.05 N	86.27 W
Paynton	184	53.01 N	108.56 W
Paysandú	252	32.19 S	58.05 W
Pays-Bas → Netherlands □[1]	30	52.15 N	5.30 E
Payson, Ariz., U.S.	200	34.14 N	111.20 W
Payson, Ill., U.S.	219	39.49 N	73.14 W
Payson, Utah, U.S.	200	40.03 N	111.44 W
Payún, Cerro ∧	252	36.30 S	69.18 W
Paz ≃	236	13.45 N	90.08 W
Paz, Cañada de la ≃	288	34.53 S	58.38 W
Paz, Ribeirão da ≃	250	9.14 S	52.01 W
Pazanji	122	10.41 N	76.04 E
Pazar, Tür.	130	40.17 N	36.18 E
Pazar, Tür.	130	41.11 N	40.53 E
Pazarcık, Tür.	130	37.31 N	37.19 E
Pazarcık, Tür.	130	40.00 N	29.54 E
Pazardžik	38	42.12 N	24.20 E
Pazarköy, Tür.	130	40.55 N	32.11 E
Pazarköy, Tür.	130	39.51 N	27.24 E
Pazarviran	130	38.41 N	36.11 E
Pazaryeri, Tür.	130	41.57 N	34.01 E
Pazaryeri, Tür.	130	38.05 N	28.14 E
Paz de Ariporo	246	5.53 N	71.54 W
Paz de Río	246	5.59 N	72.47 W
Pazifischer Ozean → Pacific Ocean ▾[1]	6	10.00 S	150.00 W
P'ažijeva Sel'ga	24	61.29 N	34.29 E
Pazin	36	45.14 N	13.56 E
Pazña	248	18.36 S	66.55 W
Paznaun ∨	58	47.03 N	10.20 E
Pčevža	76	59.23 N	32.20 E
Pčevža ≃	76	59.21 N	31.54 E
Pchery	54	50.10 N	14.08 E
Pe	110	13.28 N	98.31 E
Pea	174w	21.10 S	175.14 W
Pea ≃	194	31.01 N	85.51 W
Peabody, Kans., U.S.	198	38.10 N	97.07 W
Peabody, Mass., U.S.	207	42.32 N	70.55 W
Peace ≃, Can.	176	59.00 N	111.25 W
Peace ≃, Fla., U.S.	220	26.55 N	82.05 W
Peace Arch ⊥	224	49.00 N	122.45 W
Peace Bridge ◆[5]	284a	42.54 N	78.55 W
Peace Dale	207	41.27 N	71.30 W
Peacehaven	42	50.47 N	0.01 E
Peace River	182	56.14 N	117.17 W
Peach Creek	188	37.53 N	81.59 W
Peach Creek ≃, Tex., U.S.	222	29.24 N	97.19 W
Peach Creek ≃, Tex., U.S.	222	30.07 N	95.10 W
Peach Creek, Sandy Fork ≃	222	29.34 N	97.19 W
Peachdale	158	26.30 S	24.42 E
Peachland	182	49.46 N	119.44 W
Peach Springs	200	35.32 N	113.25 W
Peacock Hills ⋀[2]	176	66.05 N	110.45 W
Peacock Point ≻, Ont., Can.	212	42.47 N	79.59 W
Peacock Point ≻, Wake I.	174a	19.16 N	166.37 E
Peacock Sound ⊔	9	72.55 S	100.00 W
Pea Hill Branch ≃	284c	38.45 N	76.57 W
Peak Crossing	171a	27.47 S	152.44 E
Peak Dale	262	53.17 N	1.52 W
Peak District National Park ♠	44	53.17 N	1.45 W
Peake Creek ≃	162	28.05 S	136.07 E
Peaked Mountain ∧	186	46.34 N	68.49 W
Peak Forest	262	53.19 N	1.50 W
Peak Forest Canal ≍	262	53.29 N	2.06 W
Peak Hill, Austl.	162	25.38 S	118.43 E
Peak Hill, Austl.	166	32.44 S	148.12 E
Peakhurst	274a	33.58 S	151.04 E
Peakview	171b	36.04 S	149.24 E
Peäldoaivi ∧	24	69.11 N	26.36 E
Peale, Mount ∧	200	38.26 N	109.14 W
Peale Island I	174a	19.19 N	166.35 E
Peapack Brook ≃	276	40.41 N	74.39 W
Pearblossom	228	34.30 N	117.55 W
Pearce	200	31.54 N	109.49 W
Peard Bay C	180	70.51 N	159.10 W
Pea Ridge ∧	218	38.25 N	83.36 W
Pea Ridge National Military Park ♠	194	36.29 N	94.06 W
Pearisburg	192	37.20 N	80.44 W
Pearl, Ill., U.S.	194	39.28 N	90.38 W
Pearl, Miss., U.S.	194	32.18 N	90.12 W
Pearl ≃	194	30.11 N	89.32 W
Pearl, Lake ⊜	283	42.04 N	71.21 W
Pearland	222	29.34 N	95.17 W
Pearl and Hermes Reef ✦[2]	14	27.55 N	175.45 W
Pearl Bank ✦[4]	116	5.49 N	119.42 E
Pearl Beach	214	42.37 N	82.35 W
Pearl City	229c	21.24 N	157.59 W
Pearl Creek ≃	198	44.15 N	98.08 W
Pearl Harbor C	229c	21.22 N	157.58 W
Pearl Harbor Naval Base ■	229c	21.21 N	157.57 W
Pearl Peak ∧	204	40.14 N	115.32 W
Pearl River, La., U.S.	194	30.23 N	89.45 W
Pearl River, N.Y., U.S.	210	41.04 N	74.02 W
Pearls Airport ⊠	241k	12.09 N	61.37 W
Pearns Point ≻	240c	17.05 N	61.54 W
Pearsall	196	28.53 N	99.06 W
Pearse Island I	182	54.51 N	130.21 W
Pearsoll Peak ∧	202	42.18 N	123.50 W
Pearson	192	31.18 N	82.51 W
Pearson Lake ⊜	184	56.15 N	97.15 W
Pearston	158	32.35 S	25.08 E
Peary Land ◆[1]	16	83.00 N	35.00 W
Pease ≃	196	34.12 N	99.07 W
Pease Air Force Base ■	188	43.06 N	70.49 W
Peaster	222	32.52 N	97.52 W
Peat Inn	46	56.17 N	2.53 W
Pebane	154	17.10 S	38.08 E
Pebas	246	3.20 S	71.49 W
Pebble Beach	226	36.34 N	121.57 W
Pebble Island I	254	51.18 S	59.35 W
Peć	38	42.40 N	20.19 E
Pecan Bayou ≃	196	31.28 N	98.43 W
Pecangakan	115a	6.41 S	110.42 E
Pecan Gap	196	33.26 N	95.51 W
Peçanha	255	18.33 S	42.34 W
Peças, Ilha das I	252	25.26 S	48.19 W
Pecatonica	190	42.19 N	89.22 W
Pecatonica ≃	190	42.27 N	89.05 W
Pecatu	115b	8.50 S	115.07 E
Peccioli	66	43.33 N	10.43 E
Pécel	264c	47.29 N	19.21 E
Pečenegi	78	49.52 N	36.55 E
Peçenek	130	40.25 N	32.19 E
Pečeneżin	78	48.32 N	24.54 E
Pečenga	24	69.33 N	31.07 E
Pečerniki	82	54.39 N	39.14 E
Pečernikovskije Vyselki	82	54.10 N	39.10 E
Pechanga Indian Reservation ◆[4]	228	33.27 N	117.04 W
Peche Isle I	281	42.21 N	82.56 W
Pechincha ◆[8]	287a	22.56 S	43.21 W
Pechora → Pečora ≃	24	68.13 N	54.15 E
Pechorka ≃	265b	55.35 N	38.03 E
Pechra-Jakovlevskaja	265b	55.48 N	37.58 E
Pechra-Pokrovskoje	265b	55.50 N	37.57 E
Pechu	84	43.24 N	40.49 E
Peči	80	54.48 N	44.19 E
Pecica	38	46.10 N	21.05 E
Pečicy	82	55.36 N	38.27 E
Peck	190	43.16 N	82.49 W
Peck Bay C	208	39.16 N	74.37 W
Peck-Berge ⋀[2]	264a	52.36 N	13.34 E
Peckeloh	52	52.01 N	8.07 E
Peckelsheim	52	51.36 N	9.07 E
Pecket Well	262	53.46 N	2.00 W
Peck Lake ⊜	210	43.07 N	74.25 W
Peckman ≃	276	40.53 N	74.13 W
Peconic ≃	207	40.55 N	72.37 W
Pečora, S.S.S.R.	24	65.10 N	57.11 E
Pečora, S.S.S.R.	78	48.52 N	28.42 E
Pečora ≃	24	68.13 N	54.15 E
Pecoraro, Monte ∧	68	38.32 N	16.20 E
Pečoro-Ilyčskij Zapovednik ◆[4]	24	62.20 N	59.00 E
Pečorskaja Guba C	24	68.40 N	54.45 E
Pečorskoje More ▾[2]	24	70.00 N	54.00 E
Pečory	76	57.49 N	27.36 E
Pecos, N. Mex., U.S.	200	35.29 N	105.41 W
Pecos, Tex., U.S.	196	31.25 N	103.30 W
Pecos ≃	196	29.42 N	101.22 W
Pecos National Monument ♠	200	35.26 N	105.56 W
Pecos Plains ⊻	196	33.20 N	104.30 W
Pecq	50	50.41 N	3.20 E
Pecquencourt	50	50.23 N	3.13 E
Pecqueuse	261	48.39 N	2.03 E
Pécs	30	46.05 N	18.13 E
Pedana	122	16.16 N	81.10 E
Pedas	114	2.37 N	102.04 E
Pedasí	246	7.32 N	80.02 W
Pedaso	66	43.06 N	13.50 E
Peddāpuram	122	17.05 N	82.08 E
Peddie	158	33.14 S	27.07 E
Peddocks Island I	283	42.17 N	70.56 W
Pededze ≃	76	56.56 N	26.54 E
Pedernales, Arg.	252	35.15 S	59.39 W
Pedernales, Méx.	234	19.08 N	101.28 W
Pedernales, Rep. Dom.	238	18.02 N	71.45 W
Pedernales, Ven.	246	9.58 N	62.16 W
Pedernales ≃	196	30.26 N	98.04 W
Pedernales, Salar de ⊻	252	26.15 S	69.10 W
Pederobba	64	45.53 N	11.58 E
Pedersborg	41	55.27 N	11.34 E
Pederstrup	41	54.54 N	11.16 E
Pedesina	58	46.05 N	9.33 E
Pedirka	162	26.40 S	135.14 E
Pedja ≃	76	58.25 N	26.11 E
Pedley	228	33.59 N	117.28 W
Pé do Morro	256	22.20 S	44.57 W
Pedra	250	8.30 S	36.57 W
Pedra Azul	255	16.01 S	41.16 W
Pedra Bela	256	22.47 S	46.27 W
Pedra Branca	250	5.27 S	39.43 W
Pedra Branca ∧	256	22.56 S	43.28 W
Pedra da Gávea ∧	287a	23.00 S	43.17 W
Pedra de Guaratiba ◆[8]	256	23.00 S	43.39 W
Pedra do Sino ∧	256	22.30 S	43.03 W
Pedra Grande, Recifes da ✦[2]	255	17.45 S	38.58 W
Pedra Lume	150a	16.46 N	22.54 W
Pedralva	256	22.14 S	45.28 W
Pedras	250	2.48 S	57.16 W
Pedras, Rio das ≃, Bra.	255	12.13 S	45.15 W
Pedras, Rio das ≃, Bra.	287a	22.51 S	43.01 W
Pedras de Fogo	250	7.23 S	35.07 W
Pedra Selada	256	22.21 S	44.26 W
Pedras Negras	248	12.51 S	62.54 W
Pedras Salgadas	34	41.32 N	7.36 W
Pedraza	246	10.11 N	74.55 W
Pedregal, Pan.	236	8.22 N	82.26 W
Pedregal, Ven.	246	11.01 N	70.08 W
Pedregulho	255	20.16 S	47.29 W
Pedreira	256	22.43 S	46.55 W
Pedreira ≃	250	0.12 N	50.47 W
Pedreiras	250	4.34 S	44.39 W
Pedreros	286d	12.01 S	76.57 W
Pedriceña	232	25.06 N	103.47 W
Pedricktown	208	39.46 N	75.24 W
Pedrinhas	250	11.12 S	37.41 W
Pedro, Point ≻	122	9.50 N	80.14 E
Pedro Afonso	250	8.59 S	48.11 W
Pedro Avelino	250	5.31 S	36.23 W
Pedro Bay	180	59.47 N	154.07 W
Pedro Betancourt	240p	22.44 N	81.17 W
Pedro do Rio	256	22.20 S	43.09 W
Pedrógão Grande	34	39.55 N	8.09 W
Pedro Gomes	255	18.04 S	54.32 W
Pedro González, Isla I	246	8.24 N	79.06 W
Pedro II	250	4.25 S	41.28 W
Pedro Juan Caballero	252	22.34 S	55.37 W
Pedro Leopoldo	255	19.38 S	44.03 W
Pedro Luro	252	39.29 S	62.41 W
Pedro Muñoz	34	39.24 N	2.58 W
Pedro Osório	252	31.51 S	52.45 W
Pedro R. Fernández	252	28.45 S	58.39 W
Pedro Teixeira	256	21.43 S	43.44 W
Pedro Velho	250	6.26 S	35.14 W
Peebinga	166	34.56 S	140.55 E
Peebles, Scot., U.K.	46	55.39 N	3.12 W
Peebles, Ohio, U.S.	218	38.57 N	83.24 W
Peedamullah	162	21.50 S	115.38 E
Pee Dee ≃	192	33.21 N	79.16 W
Peekaboo Mountain ∧[2]	188	45.45 N	67.53 W
Peekskill	210	41.17 N	73.55 W
Peel, Austl.	170	33.19 S	149.38 E
Peel, I. of Man	44	54.13 N	4.40 W
Peel □[6]	212	43.45 N	79.47 W
Peel ≃	180	67.37 N	134.40 W
Peel Channel ≃[1]	180	68.13 N	135.00 W
Peel Fell ∧	44	55.17 N	2.35 W
Peel Inlet C	168a	32.35 S	115.44 E
Peel Island I	171a	27.30 S	153.22 E
Pe Ell	224	46.34 N	123.18 W
Peel Point ≻	176	73.22 N	114.35 W
Peel Sound ⊔	176	73.15 N	96.30 W
Peene ≃	54	54.09 N	13.46 E
Peenemünde	54	54.08 N	13.46 E
Peepeekeesis Indian Reserve ◆[4]	184	50.52 N	103.24 W
Peer	56	51.08 N	5.28 E
Peerless	202	48.47 N	105.50 W
Peers	182	53.40 N	116.00 W
Peesane	184	52.52 N	103.36 W
Peetz	198	40.58 N	103.07 W
Peetzsee ⊜	264a	52.26 N	13.50 E
Pefferlaw	212	44.19 N	79.12 W
Pefferlaw Brook ≃	212	44.15 N	79.13 W
Pegasus, Port C	172	47.12 S	167.41 E
Pegasus Bay C	172	43.20 S	173.00 E
Pegau	54	51.10 N	12.14 E
Pegli	62	44.26 N	8.48 E
Peglia, Monte ∧	66	42.49 N	12.13 E
Pegnitz	60	49.45 N	11.33 E
Pegnitz ≃	60	49.29 N	11.00 E
Pego	34	38.51 N	0.07 W
Pegolotte	64	45.12 N	12.02 E
Pegswood	44	55.11 N	1.38 W
Pegtymel' ≃	180	69.25 N	174.35 E
Pegtymel'skij Chrebet ⋀	180	68.30 N	175.00 E
Pegu	110	17.20 N	96.29 E
Pegu □[8]	110	18.00 N	96.00 E
Pegu ≃	110	16.47 N	96.13 E
Pegueros	234	20.57 N	102.40 W
Peguis Indian Reserve ◆[4]	184	51.20 N	97.35 W
Pegu Yoma ⋀	110	19.00 N	95.50 E
Pegwell Bay C	42	51.18 N	1.26 E
Pegyš	24	63.26 N	50.30 E
Pehčevo	38	41.46 N	22.54 E
Pehladpur ◆[8]	272a	28.35 N	77.06 E
Pehlivanköy	130	41.21 N	26.55 E
Pehowa	124	29.59 N	76.35 E
Pehuajó	252	35.48 S	61.53 W
Pehula	26	61.17 N	22.42 E
Peian → Beian	89	48.15 N	126.30 E
Peichiang Ch'i ≃	100	23.32 N	120.09 E
Peiching → Beijing	105	39.55 N	116.25 E
Peigan Indian Reserve ◆[4]	182	49.35 N	113.40 W
Peihai → Beihai	102	21.29 N	109.05 E
Peij	52	51.06 N	5.53 E
Peijiatun	98	39.19 N	121.41 E
Peikang	100	23.35 N	120.19 E
Peilstein im Mühlviertel	60	48.37 N	13.53 E
Peinan	100	22.48 N	121.06 E
Peinanta Ch'i ≃	100	22.46 N	121.10 E
Peine	52	52.19 N	10.13 E
Peine, Pointe à ≻	240d	15.23 N	61.15 W
Peinnechaung I	110	19.59 N	93.04 E
Peio	64	46.22 N	10.40 E
Peip'ing → Beijing	105	39.55 N	116.25 E
Peipsi Järv → Čudskoje Ozero ⊜	76	58.45 N	27.30 E
Peipus, Lake → Čudskoje Ozero ⊜	76	58.45 N	27.30 E
Peïra-Cava	62	43.56 N	7.22 E
Peirce, Cape ≻	180	58.35 N	161.47 W
Peirce Reservoir ⊜[1]	271c	1.22 N	103.49 E
Peisey-Nancroix	62	45.33 N	6.45 E
Peiskretscham → Pyskowice	30	50.24 N	18.38 E
Peissenberg	64	47.48 N	11.04 E
Peissenberg ∧	64	47.48 N	11.01 E
Peiting	58	47.47 N	10.55 E
Peit'ou	269d	25.08 N	121.29 E
Peitz	54	51.51 N	14.24 E
Peixe	255	12.03 S	48.32 W
Peixe, Rio do ≃, Bra.	255	14.06 S	50.51 W
Peixe, Rio do ≃, Bra.	255	21.31 S	51.58 W
Peixe, Rio do ≃, Bra.	256	22.23 S	46.51 W
Peixe, Rio do ≃, Bra.	256	23.24 S	45.28 W
Peixe, Rio do ≃, Bra.	256	21.38 S	45.11 W
Peixe, Rio do ≃, Bra.	256	23.12 S	46.06 W
Peixe, Rio do ≃, Bra.	256	21.55 S	43.21 W
Peixe-Boi	250	1.12 S	47.18 W
Peixes, Rio dos ≃	250	10.42 S	57.56 W
Peixian, Zhg.	98	34.44 N	116.59 E
Peixian, Zhg.	98	34.21 N	117.59 E
Peixoto de Azevedo ≃	250	10.06 S	55.31 W
Peiziyan	98	35.07 N	115.01 E
Pejantan, Pulau I	112	0.07 N	107.14 E
Pejelagartero	234	18.04 N	93.45 W
Pek ≃	38	44.46 N	21.33 E
Pekalongan	115a	6.53 S	109.40 E
Pekan	114	3.30 N	103.25 E
Pekanheran	112	0.21 S	102.26 E
Pekin, Ill., U.S.	190	40.35 N	89.40 W
Pekin, Ind., U.S.	218	38.30 N	86.00 W
Pekin, N.Y., U.S.	284a	43.10 N	78.53 W
Pekin, Ohio, U.S.	214	40.43 N	81.07 W
Pékin → Beijing, Zhg.	105	39.55 N	116.25 E
Peking → Beijing	105	39.55 N	116.25 E
Peking National Library ʊ	271a	39.56 N	116.22 E
Peking Shih → Beijing Shih □[7]	105	40.15 N	116.30 E
Peking Sports Field ♠	271a	39.52 N	116.23 E
Peking University ʊ[2]	271a	39.59 N	116.18 E
Peking Workers' Stadium ♠	271a	39.55 N	116.27 E
Peking Zoo ♠	271a	39.56 N	116.19 E
Peklino	76	53.33 N	33.32 E
Pekša ≃	80	55.53 N	39.40 E
Pektubajevo	80	57.02 N	48.23 E
Pekul'nej, Chrebet ⋀	180	66.00 N	175.00 E
Péla	150	7.37 N	9.07 W
Pelabuhandagaung	112	1.08 S	103.05 E
Pelabuhan Kelang	114	3.00 N	101.24 E
Pelabuhanratu	115a	6.59 S	106.33 E
Pelabuhan Ratu, Teluk C	115a	7.03 S	106.27 E
Pel'a-Chovanskaja	80	54.36 N	44.56 E
Pelado, Cerro ∧	286a	19.09 N	99.13 W
Pelagejevka	83	48.06 N	38.36 E
Pelagie, Isole II	71a	35.40 N	12.40 E
Pelago	66	43.46 N	11.30 E
Pelahatchie	194	32.19 N	89.48 W
Pelaihari	112	3.48 S	114.45 E
Pelalawan	112	0.27 N	102.05 E
Pelat, Mont ∧	62	44.16 N	6.42 E
Pelawan	114	2.47 N	102.55 E
Pełczyce	30	53.03 N	15.18 E
Peleaga, Vîrful ∧	38	45.22 N	22.54 E
Pelechuco	248	14.48 S	69.04 W
Peleduj	74	59.36 N	112.45 E
Pelée, Montagne ∧	240e	14.48 N	61.10 W
Pelee, Point ≻	214	41.54 N	82.30 W
Pelee Island I	214	41.46 N	82.39 W
Pelee Passage ⊔	214	41.52 N	82.37 W
Pelekech ∧	154	3.48 N	35.04 E
Peleliu I	175b	7.01 N	134.15 E
Peleng, Pulau I	112	1.20 S	123.10 E
Peleng, Selat ⊔	112	1.10 S	122.45 E
Pelenija	78	47.53 N	27.50 E
Pelf, Monte ∧	64	46.14 N	12.12 E
Pelham, Ont., Can.	212	43.02 N	79.17 W
Pelham, Ga., U.S.	192	31.08 N	84.09 W
Pelham, Mass., U.S.	207	42.24 N	72.24 W
Pelham, N.H., U.S.	207	42.44 N	71.19 W
Pelham, N.Y., U.S.	276	40.55 N	73.49 W
Pelham Bay C	276	40.52 N	73.47 W
Pelham Bay Park ♠	276	40.52 N	73.49 W
Pelham Manor	276	40.54 N	73.48 W
Pelhřimov	30	49.26 N	15.13 E
Pelican	180	57.57 N	136.14 W
Pelican ≃	198	46.17 N	96.08 W
Pelican Bay C	184	52.45 N	100.20 W
Pelican Island I, Mo., U.S.	219	38.52 N	90.18 W
Pelican Island I, Tex., U.S.	222	29.20 N	94.48 W
Pelican Lake	190	45.30 N	89.10 W
Pelican Lake ⊜, Alta., Can.	182	55.47 N	113.15 W
Pelican Lake ⊜, Man., Can.	184	49.20 N	99.35 W
Pelican Lake ⊜, Man., Can.	184	53.50 N	96.08 W
Pelican Lake ⊜, Man., Can.	184	52.30 N	100.20 W
Pelican Lake ⊜, Sask., Can.	184	55.08 N	103.00 W
Pelican Lake ⊜, S. Dak., U.S.	198	44.52 N	97.11 W
Pelican Lake ⊜, Tex., U.S.	222	28.53 N	95.27 W
Pelican Mountain ∧	182	55.35 N	113.40 W
Pelican Narrows	184	55.10 N	102.56 W
Pelican Rapids, Man., Can.	184	52.45 N	100.42 W
Pelican Rapids, Minn., U.S.	198	46.34 N	96.05 W
Pelileo	246	1.19 S	78.32 W
Pelister ∧	38	41.00 N	21.12 E
Peljekajse Nationalpark ♠	24	66.18 N	16.58 E
Pelješac, Poluotok ≻[1]	36	42.58 N	17.20 E
Pelkosenniemi	24	67.07 N	27.30 E
Pelkum, B.R.D.	263	51.39 N	7.45 E
Pelkum, B.R.D.	263	51.40 N	7.24 E
Pella, S. Afr.	158	29.01 S	19.06 E
Pella, Iowa, U.S.	190	41.25 N	92.55 W
Pélla ⊥	38	40.45 N	22.33 E
Pellaro	68	38.01 N	15.39 E
Pell City	194	33.35 N	86.17 W
Pellechia, Monte ∧	66	42.07 N	12.52 E
Pellegrini	252	36.16 S	63.09 W
Pellegrini, Lago ⊜	252	38.40 S	68.00 W
Pellegrino, Cozzo ∧	68	39.45 N	16.03 E
Pellegrino, Monte ∧	70	38.10 N	13.21 E
Pellegrino Parmense	64	44.44 N	9.55 E
Pellendorf	264b	48.06 N	16.27 E
Peller, Monte ∧	64	46.18 N	10.57 E
Pellestrina, Litorale di ●[2]	64	45.16 N	12.18 E
Pelletier Lake ⊜	184	56.30 N	97.00 W
Pellice ≃	62	44.50 N	7.38 E
Pellingen	56	49.40 N	6.40 E
Pell Lake	216	42.32 N	88.21 W
Pello	24	66.47 N	24.00 E
Pellston	190	45.33 N	84.47 W
Pellworm I	30	54.31 N	8.38 E
Pelly	184	51.52 N	101.55 W
Pelly ≃	180	62.47 N	137.19 W
Pelly Bay C	176	68.53 N	89.51 W
Pelly Crossing	180	62.50 N	136.35 W
Pelly Lake ⊜	176	65.59 N	101.12 W
Pelly Mountains ⋀	180	62.00 N	133.00 W
Pelón de Ñado, Cerro ∧	234	20.05 N	99.55 W
Pelopónnisos ◆[1]	38	37.30 N	22.00 E
Peloritani, Monti ⋀	70	38.03 N	15.20 E
Pelotas	252	31.46 S	52.20 W
Pelotas ≃	252	27.28 S	51.55 W
Pelplin	30	53.56 N	18.42 E
Pelque ≃	254	51.03 S	70.58 W
Pelsin	54	53.48 N	13.40 E
Pelusium Bay → Ţīnah, Khalīj aţ- C	140	31.08 N	32.40 E
Pel'ušn'a	76	58.56 N	32.52 E
Pélussin	62	45.25 N	4.41 E
Pelvo d'Elva ∧	62	44.33 N	9.15 E
Pelvoux, Massif du ⋀[1]	62	44.55 N	6.20 E
Pelym	86	59.38 N	63.05 E
Pemadumcook Lake ⊜	188	45.40 N	68.55 W
Pemalang	115a	6.54 S	109.22 E
Pemali ≃	115a	6.47 S	109.01 E
Pematang	112	0.12 S	102.04 E
Pematangsiantar	114	2.57 N	99.03 E
Pematangtanahjawa	114	2.53 N	99.12 E
Pemba	154	16.31 S	27.22 E
Pemba □[4]	154	5.10 S	39.48 E
Pemba Channel ⊔	154	5.10 S	39.20 E
Pemba Island I	154	7.31 S	39.25 E
Pembarisan, Pegunungan ⋀	115a	7.13 S	108.45 E
Pemberton, Austl.	162	34.28 S	116.01 E
Pemberton, B.C., Can.	182	50.20 N	122.48 W
Pemberton, Eng., U.K.	262	53.32 N	2.41 W
Pemberton, N.J., U.S.	208	39.58 N	74.41 W
Pemberton, Ohio, U.S.	216	40.18 N	84.02 W
Pemberton Airport ⊠	285	39.59 N	74.41 W
Pemberton Indian Reserve ◆[4]	182	50.19 N	122.42 W
Pemberville	214	41.25 N	83.28 W
Pembina	198	48.58 N	97.15 W
Pembina ≃, Alta., Can.	182	54.45 N	114.15 W
Pembina ≃, N.A.	184	48.56 N	97.15 W
Pembina Mountains ⋀[2]	198	49.00 N	98.05 W
Pembine	190	45.38 N	87.59 W
Pembrey	42	51.42 N	4.16 W
Pembroke, Ont., Can.	190	45.49 N	77.07 W
Pembroke, Wales, U.K.	42	51.41 N	4.55 W
Pembroke, Ga., U.S.	192	32.08 N	81.37 W
Pembroke, Ky., U.S.	194	36.47 N	87.21 W
Pembroke, Maine, U.S.	188	44.57 N	67.10 W
Pembroke, N.C., U.S.	192	34.41 N	79.12 W
Pembroke, N.Y., U.S.	210	43.00 N	78.27 W
Pembroke, Va., U.S.	192	37.19 N	80.38 W
Pembroke, Cape ≻	176	62.56 N	81.55 W
Pembroke Castle ⊥	42	51.41 N	4.56 W
Pembroke Dock	42	51.42 N	4.56 W
Pembroke Pines	220	26.01 N	80.11 W
Pembrokeshire Coast National Park ♠	42	51.47 N	5.06 W
Pembuang	112	2.34 S	112.19 E
Pembuang ≃	112	3.24 S	112.33 E
Pembury	42	51.09 N	0.20 E
Pemfling	60	49.16 N	12.37 E
Pemichigamau Lake ⊜	184	56.16 N	99.33 W
Pemigewasset ≃	188	43.26 N	71.40 W
Pemmican Portage	184	53.56 N	102.17 W
Pemuco	252	36.58 S	72.06 W
Pemynoos Indian Reserve ◆[4]	182	50.29 N	121.15 W
Pemzašen	84	40.35 N	43.57 E
Peña Blanca	236	8.27 N	81.40 W
Peña Blanca, Macizos de ∧	236	13.15 N	85.41 W
Peñafiel, Esp.	34	41.36 N	4.07 W
Penafiel, Port.	34	41.12 N	8.17 W
Pen'agino	265b	55.50 N	37.21 E
Peñagolosa ∧	34	40.13 N	0.21 W
Peña Gorda, Cerro ∧	234	20.44 N	104.50 W
Peña Grande ◆[8]	266a	40.29 N	3.44 W
Pen'akša	80	56.22 N	44.56 E
Peñalara ∧	34	40.51 N	3.57 W
Peñalolén	286e	33.29 S	70.32 W
Pena-Lunanga	154	4.16 S	28.10 E
Penalva	250	3.18 S	45.10 W
Penambulai, Pulau I	164	6.24 S	134.48 E
Peña Negra, Punta ≻	246	4.17 S	81.15 W
Peña Nevada, Cerro ∧	234	23.46 N	99.52 W
Penang → Georgetown	114	5.25 N	100.20 E
Penanjung, Teluk C	115a	7.45 S	108.37 E
Penápolis	255	21.24 S	50.04 W
Peñaranda de Bracamonte	34	40.54 N	5.12 W
Pen Argyl	210	40.52 N	75.16 W
Peñarroya-Pueblonuevo	34	38.18 N	5.16 W
Penarth	42	51.27 N	3.11 W
Peñas, Cabo de ≻	34	43.39 N	5.51 W
Penas, Golfo de C	254	47.22 S	74.50 W
Penasco	200	36.10 N	105.41 W
Peñasco, Rio ≃	196	32.45 N	104.19 W
Penataquit Creek ≃	276	40.43 N	73.14 W
Penbrook	208	40.17 N	76.51 W
Pencader	42	52.01 N	4.16 W
Pencahue	252	35.24 S	71.49 W
Pence	190	46.25 N	90.16 W
Penchard	261	48.59 N	2.52 E
Penck Trough ∨	9	73.00 S	2.45 W
Pencoed	42	51.32 N	3.30 W
Pendang	112	1.28 S	114.51 E
Pendéli	267c	38.03 N	23.52 E
Pendelikón Óros ∧	267c	38.06 N	23.54 E
Pendembu, S.L.	150	9.06 N	12.12 W
Pendembu, S.L.	150	8.06 N	10.42 W
Pendências	250	5.15 S	36.43 W
Pendeng	114	4.06 N	97.36 E
Pender	198	42.07 N	96.43 W
Pender Bay C	162	16.45 S	122.42 E
Pendhar	272c	19.04 N	73.06 E
Pendik	267b	40.53 N	29.13 E
Pendjari ≃	150	10.54 N	0.51 E
Pendjari, Parc National de la ♠	150	11.20 N	1.15 E
Pendlebury	262	53.31 N	2.20 W
Pendle Hill	274a	33.48 S	150.57 E
Pendle Hill ∧[2]	44	53.52 N	2.17 W
Pendleton, Ind., U.S.	218	39.60 N	85.45 W
Pendleton, N.Y., U.S.	284a	43.05 N	78.44 W
Pendleton, Oreg., U.S.	202	45.40 N	118.47 W
Pendleton, S.C., U.S.	192	34.39 N	82.47 W
Pendleton □[6]	218	38.42 N	84.22 W
Pendolo	112	2.05 S	120.42 E
Pendopo	112	3.17 S	103.52 E
Pend Oreille ≃	202	49.04 N	117.37 W
Pend Oreille, Lake ⊜	202	48.10 N	116.11 W
Pend Oreille, Mount ∧	202	48.25 N	116.10 W
Pendotiba ≃	287a	22.53 S	43.02 W
Pendžikent	85	39.29 N	67.35 E
Penebel	115b	8.25 S	115.09 E
Penedo	250	10.17 S	36.36 W
Penedono	34	40.59 N	7.24 W
Penela	34	40.02 N	8.23 W
Penelope	222	31.52 N	96.56 W
Penetang Harbour C	212	44.47 N	79.57 W
Penetanguishene	212	44.47 N	79.55 W
Penfield, Ill., U.S.	216	40.18 N	87.57 W
Penfield, N.Y., U.S.	210	43.08 N	77.29 W
Penfield, Ohio, U.S.	214	41.10 N	82.08 W
Penfield, Pa., U.S.	214	41.13 N	78.34 W
Penganga ≃	122	19.53 N	79.09 E
Pengastulan	115b	8.11 S	114.55 E
P'engchia Hsü I	100	25.38 N	122.04 E
Pengdian	100	32.30 N	114.40 E
Penge, S. Afr.	156	24.22 S	30.13 E
Penge, Zaïre	154	5.31 S	24.37 E
Penge ◆[8]	260	51.25 N	0.04 W
Penggong	106	30.27 N	119.57 E
Penggongmiao	100	26.07 N	113.34 E
P'enghu, T'aiwan	100	23.34 N	119.34 E
Penghu, Zhg.	100	25.24 N	118.11 E
P'enghu Liehtao II	100	23.30 N	119.30 E
P'enghu Shuitao ⊔	100	23.30 N	119.50 E
Pengiki, Pulau I	112	0.15 N	108.03 E
Pengjiachang, Zhg.	100	30.15 N	113.31 E
Pengjiachang, Zhg.	107	30.36 N	103.53 E
Pengjialouzi	104	41.56 N	123.40 E
Pengjiawan	100	32.16 N	114.04 E
Pengjiawu	105	39.41 N	117.10 E
Pengkalan Baharu	114	4.28 N	100.38 E
Pengkou	100	25.32 N	116.42 E
Penglai	98	37.48 N	120.42 E
Penglang	106	31.23 N	121.05 E
Pengnanchang	107	30.25 N	105.53 E
Pengpu → Bangbu	100	32.58 N	117.24 E
Pengshan	107	30.13 N	103.52 E
Pengshihe	100	30.28 N	113.10 E
Pengshui	102	29.18 N	108.09 E
Penguin	166	41.07 S	146.04 E
Pengxi	102	30.49 N	105.40 E
Pengxian	102	31.00 N	103.50 E
Pengze	100	29.53 N	116.33 E
Pengzhai	100	24.23 N	115.06 E
Pengzhuangzi	105	40.06 N	114.51 E
Penha	252	26.46 S	48.39 W
Penha ◆[8]	287a	22.49 S	43.17 W
Penha, Ribeirão da ≃	256	22.24 S	46.50 W
Penha de França ◆[8]	287b	23.32 S	46.32 W
Penha Longa, Bra.	256	22.04 S	43.05 W
Penhalonga, Zimb.	154	18.54 S	32.40 E
Penhold	182	52.08 N	113.52 W
Penhorn Creek ≃	276	40.45 N	74.05 W
Penhsi → Benxi	104	41.18 N	123.45 E
Peniche	34	39.21 N	9.23 W
Penicuik	46	55.50 N	3.14 W
Penida, Nusa I	115b	8.44 S	115.32 E
Penig	54	50.56 N	12.41 E
Peningo Neck ≻[1]	276	40.57 N	73.41 W
Peninjai	112	1.26 S	101.50 E
Peninsula Lake ⊜	212	45.20 N	79.05 W
Peninsula State Park ♠	190	45.09 N	87.14 W
Peñíscola	34	40.21 N	0.25 E
Penistone	44	53.32 N	1.37 W
Penitas	196	26.17 N	98.27 W
Penitencia Creek ≃	282	37.27 N	121.55 W
Penitente, Serra do ⋀[2]	250	8.45 S	46.20 W
Penjamillo [de Degollado]	234	20.06 N	101.54 W
Pénjamo	234	20.26 N	101.44 W
Penketh	262	53.23 N	2.40 W
Penki → Benxi	104	41.18 N	123.45 E
Penkino	82	54.50 N	38.53 E
Penkun	54	53.17 N	14.14 E
Pen Lake ⊜	212	45.28 N	78.23 W
Penllyn	285	40.10 N	75.15 W
Penmaenmawr	44	53.16 N	3.54 W
Penmarc'h, Pointe de ≻	32	47.48 N	4.22 W
Penn	279b	40.20 N	79.38 W
Penna, Punta della ≻	66	42.10 N	14.43 E
Pennabilli	66	43.49 N	12.16 E
Pennant Hills	274a	33.44 S	151.04 E
Pennant Hills Park ♠	274a	33.45 S	151.06 E
Pennant Point ≻	186	44.26 N	63.39 W
Pennant Station	184	50.33 N	108.12 W
Pennask Lake ⊜	182	50.00 N	120.05 W
Pennask Mountain ∧	182	49.53 N	120.07 W
Penn Brook ≃	283	42.44 N	70.59 W
Penn Cove C	224	48.14 N	122.41 W
Penn Cove Park	224	48.14 N	122.41 W
Penndel	285	40.09 N	74.55 W
Penne	66	42.27 N	13.55 E
Penne, Punta ≻	68	40.41 N	17.56 E
Penne-d'Agenais	32	44.23 N	0.49 E
Pennedepie	50	49.25 N	0.11 E
Pennel Creek ≃	198	46.34 N	104.52 W
Penner ≃	122	14.35 N	80.10 E
Pennes (Pens)	64	46.47 N	11.25 E
Pennes, Val di ∨	64	46.47 N	11.25 E
Penneshaw	168b	35.44 S	137.56 E
Penngrove	226	38.18 N	122.40 W
Penn Hills	214	40.28 N	79.53 W
Penn Hills Center ◆[9]	279b	40.28 N	79.50 W
Pennines ⋀	44	54.10 N	2.05 W
Pennines, Alpes ⋀	58	46.05 N	7.50 E
Penningby	40	59.41 N	18.40 E
Penningby slott ⊥	40	59.41 N	18.40 E
Pennington, N.J., U.S.	208	40.19 N	74.48 W
Pennington, Tex., U.S.	222	31.11 N	95.14 W
Pennington ≃[1]	150	4.45 N	5.35 E
Pennington Gap	192	36.41 N	83.02 W
Pennino, Monte ∧	66	43.06 N	12.53 E
Penn Run	214	40.37 N	79.01 W
Pennsauken	208	39.58 N	75.04 W
Pennsauken Creek ≃	285	39.59 N	75.03 W
Pennsauken Creek, North Branch ≃	285	39.58 N	75.01 W
Pennsauken Creek, South Branch ≃	285	39.58 N	75.01 W
Pennsauken Merchandise Mart ◆[9]	285	39.59 N	75.01 W
Pennsboro	188	39.17 N	80.58 W
Penns Brook ≃	276	40.43 N	74.32 W
Pennsburg	208	40.23 N	75.30 W
Pennsbury Heights	285	40.12 N	74.49 W
Pennsbury Manor ⊥	285	40.08 N	74.46 W
Penn's Cave ●[5]	210	40.53 N	77.36 W
Penns Creek	210	40.52 N	77.04 W
Penns Creek ≃	210	40.48 N	76.51 W
Pennsdale	210	41.15 N	76.48 W
Penns Grove	208	39.43 N	75.28 W
Pennside	208	40.20 N	75.53 W
Penns Neck	276	40.20 N	74.38 W
Pennsuco	220	25.56 N	80.25 W
Pennsville	208	39.39 N	75.31 W
Penns Woods	279b	40.21 N	79.46 W
Pennsylvania □[3]	178		
	188	40.45 N	77.30 W
Pennsylvania, University of ʊ[2]	285	39.57 N	75.12 W
Pennsylvania Canal ≍	285	40.13 N	74.47 W
Pennsylvania Station ◆[5]	276	40.45 N	74.00 W
Penn Valley, Calif., U.S.	226	39.12 N	121.11 W
Penn Valley, Pa., U.S.	285	40.01 N	75.16 W
Penn Valley Terrace	285	40.11 N	74.47 W
Pennville	216	40.30 N	85.09 W
Penn Wynne	285	39.59 N	75.16 W
Penny	182	53.50 N	121.17 W
Penn Yan	210	42.40 N	77.03 W
Pennycutaway ≃	184	56.43 N	92.44 W
Penny Hill	285	39.46 N	75.31 W
Pennypack Creek ≃	285	40.02 N	75.00 W
Pennypack Park ♠	285	40.04 N	75.03 W
Penny Strait ⊔	176	76.30 N	97.00 W
Peno	76	56.55 N	32.45 E
Penobscot	210	41.10 N	75.52 W
Penobscot ≃	188	44.30 N	68.50 W
Penobscot, East Branch ≃	186	45.35 N	68.32 W
Penobscot, West Branch ≃	186	45.35 N	68.32 W
Penobscot Bay C	188	44.15 N	68.52 W
Peno Creek ≃	219	39.32 N	91.16 W
Pen'ok	86	55.30 N	81.34 E
Penola	166	37.23 S	140.50 E
Peñoles	196	25.39 N	104.30 W
Peñon, Cerro ∧	286a	19.19 N	99.00 W
Peñón Blanco	232	24.47 N	104.02 W
Peñón de Ifach ♠	34	38.38 N	0.05 E
Peñón del Rosario, Cerro ∧	234	19.40 N	98.11 W
Penong	162	31.55 S	133.01 E
Penonomé	236	8.31 N	80.22 W
Penot, Mount ∧	175f	16.20 S	167.31 E
Penrhyn I[1]	14	9.00 S	158.00 W
Penrhyn Bay	44	53.19 N	3.45 W
Penrhyndeudraeth	42	52.56 N	4.04 W
Penrith, Austl.	170	33.45 S	150.42 E
Penrith, Eng., U.K.	44	54.40 N	2.44 W
Penryn, Eng., U.K.	42	50.09 N	5.06 W
Penryn, Calif., U.S.	226	38.51 N	121.10 W
Penryn, Pa., U.S.	208	40.12 N	76.22 W
Pens → Pennes	64	46.47 N	11.25 E
Pensacola	194	30.25 N	87.13 W
Pensacola Bay C	194	30.25 N	87.06 W
Pensacola Mountains ⋀	9	83.45 S	55.00 W
Pensacola Naval Air Station ■	194	30.21 N	87.19 W
Pensacola Seamount ✦[3]	14	17.35 N	157.35 W
Pensaukee ≃	190	44.49 N	87.55 W
Pensby	262	53.21 N	3.06 W
Pense	184	50.25 N	105.00 W
Penshaw	44	54.53 N	1.29 W
Pensiangan	112	4.33 N	116.19 E
Pensilvania	246	5.31 N	75.05 W
Pentagna	256	22.09 S	43.45 W
Pentagon ʊ	284c	38.52 N	77.03 W
Pentagon Mountain ∧	202	47.56 N	113.07 W
Pentecoste	250	3.48 S	39.17 W
Pentecost Island I	175f	15.42 S	168.10 E
Pentecôte, Lac ⊜	186	49.53 N	67.20 W

Symbols in the index entries represent the broad categories identified in the key at the right. Symbols with superior numbers (⋀[2]) identify subcategories (see complete key on page *I · 30*).

Kartensymbole in dem Registerverzeichnis stellen die rechts in Schlüssel erklärten Kategorien dar. Symbole mit hochgestellten Ziffern (⋀[2]) bezeichnen Unterabteilungen einer Kategorie (vgl. vollständiger Schlüssel auf Seite *I · 30*).

Los símbolos incluídos en el texto del índice representan las grandes categorias identificadas con la clave a la derecha. Los símbolos con numeros en su parte superior (⋀[2]) identifican las subcategorías (véase la clave completa en la página *I · 30*).

Les symboles de l'index représentent les catégories indiquées dans la légende à droite. Les symboles suivis d'un indice (⋀[2]) représentent des sous-catégories (voir légende complète à la page *I · 30*).

Os símbolos incluídos no texto do índice representam as grandes categorias identificadas com a chave à direita. Os símbolos com números em sua parte superior (⋀[2]) identificam as subcategorias (veja-se a chave completa à página *I · 30*).

∧ Mountain	Berg	Montaña	Montagne	Montanha
⋀ Mountains	Berge	Montañas	Montagnes	Montanhas
)(Pass	Pass	Paso	Col	Passo
∨ Valley, Canyon	Tal, Cañon	Valle, Cañón	Vallée, Canyon	Vale, Canhão
⊻ Plain	Ebene	Llano	Plaine	Planície
≻ Cape	Kap	Cabo	Cap	Cabo
I Island	Insel	Isla	Île	Ilha
II Islands	Inseln	Islas	Îles	Ilhas
● Other Topographic Features	Andere Topographische Objekte	Otros Elementos Topográficos	Autres données topographiques	Outros Elementos Topográficos

ESPAÑOL

Nombre	Página	Lat.°′	Long.°′ W=Oeste
Penticton	182	49.30 N	119.35 W
Penticton Indian Reserve ⬩[4]	182	49.30 N	119.40 W
Pentire Point ≻	42	50.36 N	4.55 W
Pentland	166	20.32 S	145.24 E
Pentland Firth ⋓	46	58.44 N	3.07 W
Pentland Hills ⛰[2]	46	55.46 N	3.25 W
Pentraeth	44	53.17 N	4.12 W
Pentre Halkyn	262	53.15 N	3.12 W
Pentucket, Lake ⊜	283	42.47 N	71.05 W
Pentucket Pond ⊜	283	42.44 N	71.00 W
Pentwater	190	43.47 N	86.26 W
Penuba	112	0.20 S	104.28 E
Peñuelas	240m	18.03 N	66.43 W
Penugonda	122	16.40 N	81.44 E
Penuguan	112	2.27 S	104.31 E
Penukonda	122	14.05 N	77.35 E
Penunjok, Tanjong ≻	114	4.22 N	103.29 E
Pènwègon	110	18.13 N	96.34 E
Penwell	196	31.44 N	102.35 W
Peny	78	51.04 N	35.54 E
Pen-y-Ghent ∧	44	54.09 N	2.14 W
Penygroes, Wales, U.K.	42	51.49 N	4.02 W
Penygroes, Wales, U.K.	44	53.04 N	4.17 W
Penyu, Kepulauan ▮▮	164	5.22 S	127.46 E
Penyu, Teluk C	115a	7.45 S	109.15 E
Penza	80	53.13 N	45.00 E
Penza □[4]	76	53.30 N	43.00 E
Penzance	42	50.07 N	5.33 W
Penzberg	64	47.45 N	11.23 E
Penzig → Pieńsk	30	51.15 N	15.03 E
Penžina ≃	74	62.28 N	165.18 E
Penzing ⬩[8]	264b	48.12 N	16.18 E
Penzino	80	52.07 N	50.27 E
Penžinskaja Guba C	74	61.00 N	162.00 E
Penžinskij Chrebet ⛰	74	62.30 N	167.00 E
Penzlin	54	53.30 N	13.05 E
Péone	62	44.07 N	6.54 E
Peonias, Quebrada ≃	286c	10.32 N	67.01 W
Peoples Creek ≃	202	48.24 N	108.19 W
Peoples Ditch ≊	226	36.15 N	119.41 W
People's University of China ℧[2]	271a	39.58 N	116.18 E
Peoria, Ariz., U.S.	200	33.35 N	112.14 W
Peoria, Ill., U.S.	190	40.42 N	89.36 W
Peoria, Ohio, U.S.	216	40.19 N	83.27 W
Peotillos	234	22.30 N	100.37 W
Peotone	216	41.20 N	87.47 W
Peover Eye ≃	262	53.15 N	2.31 W
Peover Heath	262	53.15 N	2.19 W
Pepa	154	7.42 S	29.47 E
Pepacton Reservoir ⊜[1]	210	42.06 N	74.54 W
Pepaw ≃	184	52.40 N	102.23 W
Pepel	150	8.35 N	13.03 W
Peper	140	7.04 N	33.00 E
Pepin	190	44.27 N	92.09 W
Pepin, Lake ⊜	190	44.30 N	92.15 W
Pepinster	56	50.34 N	5.49 E
Péplos	130	40.58 N	26.16 E
Pepperdine University ℧[2]	280	33.58 N	118.18 W
Pepperell	207	42.40 N	71.35 W
Pepper Park State Recreation Area ♠	220	27.30 N	80.18 W
Pepper Pike	279a	41.29 N	81.28 W
Peqi'in Hadasha	132	32.59 N	35.20 E
Peqin	38	41.03 N	19.45 E
Pequannock	210	40.57 N	74.18 W
Pequannock ≃	276	40.58 N	74.17 W
Pequanticut Brook ≃	283	42.01 N	71.08 W
Pequea Creek ≃	208	39.53 N	76.22 W
Pequena ≃	287a	22.55 S	43.25 W
Pequeri	256	21.50 S	43.06 W
Pequeri ≃	248	17.23 S	55.38 W
Pequest ≃	210	40.50 N	75.05 W
Pequez	208	39.53 N	76.22 W
Pequizeiro	250	8.32 S	48.58 W
Pequop Mountains ⛰	204	40.45 N	114.40 W
Pequot Lakes	190	46.36 N	94.19 W
Perabumulih	112	3.27 S	104.15 E
Perak □[3]	114	5.00 N	101.00 E
Perak ≃	114	3.58 N	100.53 E
Perak, Kuala C	114	4.00 N	100.47 E
Peralba, Monte ∧	64	46.37 N	12.43 E
Perales de Alfambra	34	40.38 N	1.00 W
Perales del Rio	266a	40.19 N	3.38 W
Peralillo	252	34.29 S	71.29 W
Peralta	200	34.50 N	106.41 W
Pérama	267c	37.58 N	23.34 E
Perambalūr	122	11.14 N	78.53 E
Perämeri (Bottenviken) C	26	65.00 N	23.00 E
Peranāmbattu	122	12.56 N	78.43 E
Perarolo di Cadore	64	46.24 N	12.21 E
Peräseinäjoki	26	62.34 N	23.04 E
Percé	186	48.31 N	64.13 W
Percée, Pointe ∧	58	45.57 N	6.33 E
Perch ≃	212	44.00 N	76.05 W
Perchas	240m	18.19 N	66.59 W
Perchau	61	47.06 N	14.27 E
Perche, Collines du ⛰[2]	50	48.25 N	0.40 E
Perche Creek ≃	194	38.49 N	92.24 W
Perch Lake ⊜	212	44.07 N	75.54 W
Perchtoldsdorf	264b	48.07 N	16.17 E
Perchuškovo	265b	55.41 N	37.10 E
Percival Lakes ⊜	162	21.25 S	125.00 E
Percy Creek ≃	212	44.15 N	77.49 W
Percy Isles ▮▮	166	21.39 S	150.16 E
Percy Lake ⊜	212	45.13 N	78.22 W
Percy Reach ⊜	212	44.15 N	77.45 W
Perdasdefogu	71	39.41 N	9.26 E
Perdekop	158	27.13 S	29.38 E
Perdices, Arroyo de las ≃	288	34.41 S	58.22 W
Perdida ≃	250	9.13 S	47.59 W
Perdido	194	31.00 N	87.37 W
Perdido ≃, Bra.	248	22.10 S	57.33 W
Perdido ≃, U.S.	194	30.29 N	87.26 W
Perdido, Arroyo ≃	254	42.55 S	67.00 W
Perdido, Arroyo del ≃	258	33.37 S	57.23 W
Perdido, Cuchilla del ⛰[2]	258	33.43 S	57.17 W
Perdido, Monte ∧	34	42.40 N	0.05 E
Perdido Bay C	194	30.21 N	87.27 W
Perdifumo	68	40.16 N	15.01 E
Perdix	208	40.22 N	76.57 W
Perdizes	255	19.21 S	47.17 W
Perdreauville	261	48.58 N	1.38 E
Perdu, Lac ⊜	186	50.44 N	70.14 W
Perdue	184	52.04 N	107.32 W
Perebrody	78	51.43 N	27.00 E
Perečin	78	48.44 N	22.26 E
Peredel	76	55.12 N	35.41 E
Peredel'cy	82	55.36 N	37.21 E
Peredelkino	265b	55.39 N	37.21 E
Peregino	76	57.27 N	31.21 E
Pereginskoje	78	48.49 N	24.12 E
Peregonovka	78	48.32 N	30.31 E
Pereira	246	4.49 N	75.43 W
Pereira, Cachoeira ↳	250	4.25 S	56.17 W
Pereira Barreto	255	20.38 S	51.07 W
Pereira de Eça	152	17.03 S	15.47 E
Pereiras	256	22.42 S	46.24 W
Pereiro	250	6.03 S	38.28 W
Perejaslav-Chmel'nickij	78	50.06 N	31.30 E

FRANÇAIS

Nom	Page	Lat.°′	Long.°′ W=Ouest
Perejaslavka	89	47.58 N	135.06 E
Perejaslavskaja	78	45.51 N	39.02 E
Perejezdnoje	83	48.47 N	38.04 E
Perejež'na	24	59.43 N	48.12 E
Perekopnoje	80	51.13 N	48.04 E
Perekopovka	78	50.37 N	33.25 E
Perekopskaja	80	49.21 N	43.20 E
Père-Lachaise, Cimetière du ⬩	261	48.51 N	2.25 E
Perelazi	76	53.02 N	31.28 E
Perelazovskij	80	49.09 N	42.33 E
Perelešino	78	51.44 N	40.07 E
Perel'ub	80	51.52 N	50.22 E
Pere Marquette ≃	190	43.57 N	86.27 W
Pere Marquette, Big South Branch ≃	190	43.56 N	86.10 W
Pere Marquette State Park ♠	219	39.00 N	90.30 W
Perem'otnoje	80	51.11 N	50.49 E
Peremul Par ▮[1]	122	11.10 N	72.04 E
Peremyšl'	82	54.16 N	36.10 E
Peremyšl'any	78	49.41 N	24.33 E
Perené ≃	248	11.09 S	74.18 W
Perenjori	162	29.26 S	116.17 E
Pererov	78	52.04 N	28.00 E
Pereščepino	78	49.01 N	35.22 E
Pereščepnoje	80	50.32 N	45.06 E
Pereslavl'-Zalesskij	82	56.44 N	38.51 E
Peresypkino Pervoje	80	52.55 N	42.55 E
Peretrusovo	82	56.51 N	36.53 E
Pereval'sk	83	48.26 N	38.47 E
Perevolockij	86	51.32 N	55.06 E
Perevoz, S.S.S.R.	80	55.36 N	44.32 E
Perevoz, S.S.S.R.	88	59.00 N	116.57 E
Perevoz, S.S.S.R.	265a	59.43 N	30.47 E
Pereyra, Arroyo ≃	288	34.47 S	58.08 W
Pereyra, Punta ≻	258	34.14 S	58.04 W
Pérez	252	33.00 S	60.46 W
Perfugas	71	40.50 N	8.53 E
Perg	61	48.15 N	14.37 E
Pergam, Pulau ▮	271c	1.24 N	103.40 E
Pergamino	252	33.53 S	60.35 W
Pergamum ⊥	130	39.10 N	27.13 E
Pergau ≃	114	5.23 N	102.02 E
Pergine Valdarno	66	43.28 N	11.41 E
Pergine Valsugana	64	46.04 N	11.14 E
Pergola	66	43.34 N	12.50 E
Pergusa, Lago di ⊜	70	37.31 N	14.18 E
Perham	198	46.36 N	95.34 W
Perho	26	63.13 N	24.25 E
Peri	64	45.39 N	10.54 E
Peribán de Ramos	234	19.32 N	102.28 W
Péribonca ≃	176	48.45 N	72.05 W
Péribonca, Lac ⊜	186	50.04 N	71.15 W
Perico, Arg.	252	24.23 S	65.06 W
Perico, Cuba	240p	22.46 N	81.01 W
Pericos	232	25.03 N	107.42 W
Pericumã ≃	250	2.17 S	44.42 W
Peridot	200	33.18 N	110.28 W
Périers	32	49.11 N	1.25 W
Perigiraja	112	0.16 S	103.30 E
Périgord □[9]	32	45.20 N	1.00 E
Perigoso, Canal ⋓	250	0.05 N	49.40 W
Périgueux	32	45.11 N	0.43 E
Perijá, Sierra de ⛰	246	10.00 N	73.00 W
Perim → Barīm ▮	144	12.40 N	43.25 E
Peri-Mirim	250	2.38 S	44.54 W
Perinaldo	62	43.52 N	7.40 E
Peringat	114	6.02 N	102.17 E
Periprava	38	45.24 N	29.32 E
Peristérion	267c	38.01 N	23.42 E
Perito	68	40.18 N	15.09 E
Perito Moreno	254	46.36 S	70.56 W
Peritoró	250	4.20 S	44.18 W
Perivale ⬩[8]	260	51.32 N	0.19 W
Periyakulam	122	10.07 N	77.33 E
Periyār ≃	122	10.11 N	76.13 E
Periyār Lake ⊜	122	9.32 N	77.12 E
Perkam, Tanjung ≻	164	1.28 S	137.54 E
Perkasie	208	40.22 N	75.18 W
Perkins	196	35.58 N	97.02 W
Perkinsfield	212	44.42 N	79.57 W
Perkins Observatory ℧[3]	214	40.14 N	83.02 W
Perkinston	194	30.47 N	89.08 W
Perkinsville, Ind., U.S.	218	40.09 N	85.52 W
Perkinsville, N.Y., U.S.	210	42.32 N	77.38 W
Perkiomen Creek ≃	208	40.07 N	75.28 W
Perkiomen Creek, East Branch ≃	208	40.15 N	75.27 W
Perkiomen Junction Pawling	285	40.21 N	75.28 W
Perkiomen Valley Airport ⊠	285	40.12 N	75.25 W
Perl	56	49.28 N	6.36 E
Perlas, Archipiélago de las ▮▮	246	8.25 N	79.00 W
Perlas, Laguna de C	236	12.30 N	83.40 W
Perlas, Punta ≻	236	12.23 N	83.30 W
Perleberg	54	53.04 N	11.51 E
Perlez	38	45.12 N	20.24 E
Perlis □[3]	114	6.30 N	100.15 E
Perl'ovka	78	51.51 N	38.51 E
Perm'	86	58.00 N	56.15 E
Perm' □[4]	80	59.00 N	56.00 E
Permanente Creek ≃	282	37.25 N	122.05 W
Permas	24	59.20 N	45.34 E
Përmet	38	40.14 N	20.21 E
Permisi	80	54.06 N	45.48 E
Permskaja Oblast' □[4]	24	59.00 N	56.00 E
Pernambuco → Recife	250	8.03 S	34.54 W
Pernambuco □[3]	250	8.00 S	37.00 W
Pernate	266b	45.27 N	8.41 E
Pernatty Lagoon ⊜	166	31.31 S	137.14 E
Pernay	50	47.27 N	0.30 E
Pernes-les-Fontaines	62	44.00 N	5.03 E
Pernik	38	42.36 N	23.02 E
Pernink	54	50.20 N	12.45 E
Perniö	26	60.12 N	23.08 E
Pernitz	61	47.54 N	15.58 E
Pernovo	82	55.58 N	39.10 E
Pero	266b	45.31 N	9.05 E
Peroba, Ribeirão do ≃	287b	23.27 S	46.22 W
Pérols, Étang de C	62	43.33 N	3.56 E
Peron, Cape ≻	168a	32.17 S	115.41 E
Péronne	50	49.56 N	2.56 E
Péronnes	50	50.26 N	4.08 E
Peron Peninsula ≻[1]	162	24.50 S	113.30 E
Pero Pinheiro	266c	38.51 N	9.20 W
Perosa Argentina	62	44.58 N	7.10 E
Perote	234	19.34 N	97.14 W
Perotó	248	14.50 S	64.31 W
Pérou → Peru □[1]	242	10.00 S	76.00 W
Pérouges	58	45.54 N	5.11 E
Peroulaz	62	45.42 N	7.19 E
Perovo ⬩[8]	265b	55.44 N	37.46 E
Perow	182	54.31 N	126.26 W
Perpendicular, Point ≻	170	35.06 S	150.48 E
Perpignan	32	42.41 N	2.53 E
Perranporth	42	50.20 N	5.09 W
Perrault Falls	184	50.19 N	93.11 W
Perray ≃	261	48.31 N	1.42 E
Perrero	62	44.56 N	7.05 E
Perriers-sur-Andelle	50	49.25 N	1.22 E
Perrignier	58	46.18 N	6.27 E
Perrigny	58	46.40 N	5.35 E
Perrin	196	33.02 N	98.04 W
Perrine	220	25.36 N	80.21 W
Perrineville	208	40.14 N	74.27 W
Perris	228	33.47 N	117.14 W
Perris, Lake ⊜[1]	228	33.50 N	117.10 W

PORTUGUÊS

Nome	Página	Lat.°′	Long.°′ W=Oeste
Perro, Laguna del ⊜	200	34.40 N	105.57 W
Perro, Punta del ≻	34	36.45 N	6.25 W
Perros ≃	234	16.20 N	94.59 W
Perros, Bahía de los C	240p	22.25 N	78.30 W
Perros-Guirec	32	48.49 N	3.27 W
Perrot, Île ▮	206	45.22 N	73.57 W
Perry, Fla., U.S.	192	30.07 N	83.35 W
Perry, Ga., U.S.	192	32.27 N	83.44 W
Perry, Ill., U.S.	219	39.47 N	90.45 W
Perry, Iowa, U.S.	190	41.50 N	94.06 W
Perry, Kans., U.S.	198	39.05 N	95.24 W
Perry, Mich., U.S.	216	42.50 N	84.13 W
Perry, Mo., U.S.	219	39.26 N	91.40 W
Perry, N.Y., U.S.	210	42.43 N	78.00 W
Perry, Ohio, U.S.	214	41.46 N	81.09 W
Perry, Okla., U.S.	196	36.17 N	97.17 W
Perry, Tex., U.S.	222	31.25 N	96.55 W
Perry, Utah, U.S.	200	35.18 N	105.22 W
Perry □[6]	208	40.25 N	77.11 W
Perrydale	224	45.03 N	123.16 W
Perry Hall	208	39.25 N	76.28 W
Perry Heights	214	40.48 N	81.24 W
Perry-jōriku-kinenhi ⊥	94	35.14 N	139.43 E
Perry Lake ⊜[1]	198	39.20 N	95.30 W
Perrymont	279b	40.33 N	80.02 W
Perryopolis	214	40.05 N	79.45 W
Perry Park	218	38.33 N	85.00 W
Perrysburg, N.Y., U.S.	210	42.27 N	79.00 W
Perrysburg, Ohio, U.S.	214	41.33 N	83.38 W
Perry's Landing Monument ⊥	268	35.14 N	139.43 E
Perry's Victory and International Peace Memorial ⊥	214	41.33 N	82.50 W
Perrysville, Ohio, U.S.	214	40.40 N	82.19 W
Perrysville, Pa., U.S.	214	40.32 N	80.02 W
Perrysville, Pa., U.S.	279b	40.31 N	79.32 W
Perryton	196	36.24 N	100.48 W
Perryville, Alaska, U.S.	180	55.54 N	159.10 W
Perryville, Ark., U.S.	194	35.00 N	92.48 W
Perryville, Mo., U.S.	194	37.43 N	89.52 W
Perryville, N.Y., U.S.	210	43.01 N	75.48 W
Peršaj	76	54.02 N	26.41 E
Persan	50	49.09 N	2.16 E
Perşani, Munţii ⛰	38	45.40 N	25.15 E
Persberg	40	59.45 N	14.15 E
Perschling ≃	61	48.20 N	15.58 E
Perşembe	130	41.04 N	37.46 E
Persepolis → Takht-e Jamshīd ⊥	128	29.57 N	52.52 E
Perseverance, Mount ∧	171a	27.25 S	152.10 E
Perseverancia	248	14.44 S	62.48 W
Pershagen	40	59.10 N	17.39 E
Pershing	218	39.49 N	85.08 W
Pershore	42	52.07 N	2.05 W
Pershyttan	40	59.30 N	15.00 E
Persia	198	41.34 N	95.35 W
Persia → Iran □[1]	128	32.00 N	53.00 E
Persian Gulf C	128	27.00 N	51.00 E
Pérsico, Golfo → Persian Gulf C	128	27.00 N	51.00 E
Persimmon Creek ≃	194	31.31 N	86.50 W
Persique, Golfe → Persian Gulf C	128	27.00 N	51.00 E
Persischer Golf → Persian Gulf C	128	27.00 N	51.00 E
Peršotravensk	78	50.12 N	27.39 E
Peršotravnevoje, S.S.S.R.	78	48.22 N	36.24 E
Peršotravnevoje, S.S.S.R.	78	51.24 N	28.53 E
Peršotravnevoje, S.S.S.R.	83	47.03 N	37.18 E
Perštejn	54	50.23 N	13.08 E
Perstorp	41	56.08 N	13.23 E
Pertandangan, Tanjung ≻	114	2.41 N	100.14 E
Pertang ≃	114	3.14 N	102.19 E
Pertek	130	38.50 N	39.22 E
Perth, Austl.	168a	31.56 S	115.50 E
Perth, Ont., Can.	212	44.54 N	76.15 W
Perth, Scot., U.K.	46	56.24 N	3.28 W
Perth, N.Y., U.S.	210	43.03 N	74.12 W
Perth □[6]	212	43.30 N	81.05 W
Perth Amboy	210	40.31 N	74.16 W
Perth-Andover	186	46.45 N	67.42 W
Perthes	58	48.39 N	4.49 E
Perth International Airport ⊠	168a	31.57 S	115.58 E
Perthois ⬩[1]	58	48.40 N	4.45 E
Pertisau	64	47.26 N	11.42 E
Pertovo	80	54.22 N	41.31 E
Pertuis	62	43.41 N	5.30 E
Peru, Ill., U.S.	216	41.20 N	89.08 W
Peru, Ind., U.S.	216	40.45 N	86.04 W
Peru, Nebr., U.S.	198	40.29 N	95.44 W
Peru, N.Y., U.S.	188	44.35 N	73.32 W
Peru □[1]	242	10.00 S	76.00 W
Peruaçu ≃	255	15.11 S	44.07 W
Peru Basin ⊹[1]	18	25.00 S	90.00 W
Peruc	54	50.19 N	13.59 E
Peru-Chile Trench ⊹[1]	18	21.00 S	72.00 W
Perugia	66	43.08 N	12.22 E
Perugia □[4]	66	43.03 N	12.33 E
Perugorría	252	29.20 S	58.37 W
Peruíbe	252	24.19 S	47.00 W
Peruípe ≃	255	17.43 S	39.16 W
Peruque Creek ≃	219	38.53 N	90.39 W
Perus ⬩[8]	256	23.25 S	46.45 W
Perus ≃	287b	23.23 S	46.46 W
Perušić	36	44.39 N	15.23 E
Péruwelz	50	50.31 N	3.35 E
Pervaja Maja	86	48.55 N	67.25 E
Pervenchères	50	48.26 N	0.26 E
Pervesinka	80	52.13 N	43.15 E
Pervijze	50	51.05 N	2.47 E
Pervoavgustovskij	76	52.14 N	35.03 E
Pervoje Pole	180	63.05 N	179.19 W
Pervomajka, S.S.S.R.	83	49.09 N	37.58 E
Pervomajka, S.S.S.R.	86	51.17 N	70.08 E
Pervomajka ⬩[8]	83	48.17 N	39.50 E
Pervomajsk, S.S.S.R.	78	48.04 N	30.52 E
Pervomajsk, S.S.S.R.	80	54.53 N	43.49 E
Pervomajsk, S.S.S.R.	83	48.37 N	38.35 E
Pervomajsk, S.S.S.R.	83	49.05 N	39.37 E
Pervomajsk, S.S.S.R.	86	57.59 N	94.12 E
Pervomajsk, S.S.S.R.	88	58.01 N	94.10 E
Pervomajskij, S.S.S.R.	24	64.26 N	40.47 E
Pervomajskij, S.S.S.R.	76	54.04 N	32.29 E
Pervomajskij, S.S.S.R.	76	53.54 N	25.23 E
Pervomajskij, S.S.S.R.	78	49.24 N	36.12 E
Pervomajskij, S.S.S.R.	80	53.15 N	40.18 E
Pervomajskij, S.S.S.R.	80	53.22 N	51.38 E
Pervomajskij, S.S.S.R.	80	51.22 N	48.54 E
Pervomajskij, S.S.S.R.	82	55.57 N	37.52 E
Pervomajskij, S.S.S.R.	82	54.03 N	37.32 E
Pervomajskij, S.S.S.R.	82	55.32 N	37.09 E
Pervomajskij, S.S.S.R.	83	47.58 N	38.47 E
Pervomajskij, S.S.S.R.	85	42.51 N	74.04 E
Pervomajskij, S.S.S.R.	86	53.43 N	55.43 E
Pervomajskij, S.S.S.R.	86	54.52 N	61.08 E
Pervomajskij, S.S.S.R.	86	59.29 N	61.24 E
Pervomajskij, S.S.S.R.	88	51.44 N	115.39 E
Pervomajskoje, S.S.S.R.	76	52.56 N	33.36 E
Pervomajskoje, S.S.S.R.	78	45.43 N	33.51 E
Pervomajskoje, S.S.S.R.	80	55.05 N	47.22 E
Pervomajskoje, S.S.S.R.	80	46.03 N	42.13 E
Pervomajskoje, S.S.S.R.	80	51.28 N	47.37 E
Pervomajskoje, S.S.S.R.	80	46.21 N	43.37 E
Pervomajskoje, S.S.S.R.	80	48.50 N	41.14 E
Pervomajskoje, S.S.S.R.	80	50.56 N	46.46 E
Pervomajskoje, S.S.S.R.	85	42.05 N	69.53 E
Pervomajskoje, S.S.S.R.	86	53.45 N	84.08 E
Pervomajskoje, S.S.S.R.	86	57.06 N	86.12 E
Pervoural'sk	86	56.54 N	59.58 E
Pervušino	80	58.02 N	41.56 E
Pervyj Kuril'skij Proliv ⋓	74	50.50 N	156.36 E
Perwenitz	264a	52.40 N	13.01 E
Pes'	76	58.55 N	34.19 E
Pes' ≃	76	59.08 N	35.18 E
Pesa ≃	66	43.44 N	11.01 E
Pes'akov, Ostrov ▮	24	68.47 N	57.35 E
Pesangrohan ≃	269e	6.11 S	106.45 E
Pesaro	66	43.54 N	12.55 E
Pesaro e Urbino □[4]	66	43.40 N	12.38 E
Pesca	246	5.33 N	73.03 W
Pescadero	226	37.15 N	122.23 W
Pescadero, Laguna C	234	22.12 N	105.20 W
Pescadero Creek ≃, Calif., U.S.	226	37.16 N	122.25 W
Pescadero Creek ≃, Calif., U.S.	226	36.42 N	121.17 W
Pescadores → P'enghu Liehtao ▮▮	100	23.30 N	119.30 E
Pescadores, Punta ≻, Méx.	232	23.46 N	109.43 W
Pescadores, Punta ≻, Perú	248	16.21 S	73.15 W
Pescaglia	66	43.58 N	10.25 E
Pesčanaja	78	48.08 N	29.44 E
Pesčanka, S.S.S.R.	78	48.12 N	28.53 E
Pesčanka, S.S.S.R.	80	51.18 N	43.40 E
Pesčanoje, S.S.S.R.	24	62.12 N	35.45 E
Pesčanoje, S.S.S.R.	78	49.44 N	31.50 E
Pesčanoje, S.S.S.R.	83	49.34 N	37.51 E
Pesčanoje, S.S.S.R.	86	53.01 N	76.19 E
Pesčanokopskoje	80	46.12 N	41.04 E
Pescantina	64	45.29 N	10.51 E
Pesčanyj	83	47.02 N	37.28 E
Pesčanyje, Ostrova ▮▮	83	46.52 N	38.17 E
Pescara	66	42.28 N	14.13 E
Pescara □[4]	66	42.20 N	13.57 E
Pescara ≃	66	42.28 N	14.13 E
Pescasseroli	66	41.48 N	13.47 E
Pesch	263	51.11 N	6.32 E
Pesch, Schloss ⊥	263	51.18 N	6.39 E
Peschici	68	41.57 N	16.01 E
Peschiera del Garda	64	45.26 N	10.42 E
Peschio, Monte ∧	267a	41.43 N	12.46 E
Pescia	66	43.54 N	10.41 E
Pescina	66	42.02 N	13.39 E
Pescocostanzo	66	41.53 N	14.04 E
Pescolanciano	66	41.41 N	14.20 E
Pescopagano	68	40.50 N	15.24 E
Pescorocchiano	66	42.12 N	13.09 E
Pesco Sannita	68	41.14 N	14.49 E
Pesé	236	7.54 N	80.37 W
Pesek, Pulau ▮	271c	1.17 N	103.41 E
Peseux	58	46.59 N	6.53 E
Peshastin	224	47.34 N	120.36 W
Peshastin Creek ≃	224	47.33 N	120.35 W
Peshāwar	123	34.01 N	71.33 E
Peshīn Jān	128	33.25 N	61.28 E
Peshkopi	38	41.41 N	20.26 E
Peshmāl	123	35.26 N	72.36 E
Peshtigo	190	45.03 N	87.45 W
Peshtigo ≃	190	44.58 N	87.40 W
Pesio ≃	62	44.28 N	7.53 E
Pesjane	82	56.01 N	38.48 E
Peski, S.S.S.R.	76	53.21 N	24.38 E
Peski, S.S.S.R.	78	50.23 N	33.27 E
Peski, S.S.S.R.	80	51.16 N	42.27 E
Peški, S.S.S.R.	82	56.08 N	37.04 E
Peski, S.S.S.R.	82	55.13 N	38.46 E
Peski, S.S.S.R.	83	49.26 N	38.59 E
Peski-Rad'kovskije	83	49.17 N	37.36 E
Peskovatskoje	82	54.03 N	36.16 E
Peskovka, S.S.S.R.	78	50.42 N	29.38 E
Peskovka, S.S.S.R.	86	59.04 N	52.22 E
Peškovo	83	47.02 N	39.24 E
Peškovo Grecovo	82	54.26 N	37.36 E
Peškovskoje	86	53.45 N	62.23 E
Pesmes	58	47.17 N	5.34 E
Pesnica	61	46.36 N	15.41 E
Pesnica ≃	61	46.24 N	16.05 E
Pesočenskij	82	54.10 N	36.06 E
Pesočin	78	49.57 N	36.06 E
Pesočn'a	80	54.07 N	40.50 E
Pesočnoje, S.S.S.R.	76	53.20 N	27.06 E
Pesočnoje, S.S.S.R.	80	58.01 N	39.10 E
Pesočnyj	76	60.07 N	30.08 E
Peso da Régua	34	41.10 N	7.47 W
Pespire	236	13.35 N	87.22 W
Pesqueira	250	8.22 S	36.42 W
Pesquería	196	25.47 N	100.03 W
Pessac	32	44.48 N	0.38 W
Pessáni	130	41.05 N	26.06 E
Pessin	54	52.38 N	12.40 E
Pessinetto	62	45.17 N	7.24 E
Pest □[6]	30	47.25 N	19.20 E
Pest'aki	80	56.43 N	42.40 E
Peštera	38	42.02 N	24.18 E
Pesterzsébet ⬩[8]	264c	47.26 N	19.07 E
Pesthidegkút ⬩[8]	264c	47.34 N	18.58 E
Pestimre ⬩[8]	264c	47.24 N	19.12 E
Pestlőrinc ⬩[8]	264c	47.26 N	19.12 E
Pestovo, S.S.S.R.	76	58.36 N	35.48 E
Pestovo, S.S.S.R.	80	57.12 N	46.44 E
Pestovskoje Vodochranilišče ⊜[1]	82	56.06 N	37.40 E
Pestravka	80	52.24 N	49.58 E
Pestrecy	80	55.46 N	49.39 E
Pestrikovo	82	55.05 N	38.53 E
Pestújhely ⬩[8]	264c	47.32 N	19.07 E
Petacalco, Bahía de C	234	17.57 N	102.05 W
Petah Tiqwa	132	32.05 N	34.53 E
Petäjävesi	26	62.15 N	25.12 E
Petal	194	31.21 N	89.17 W
Petalcingo	232	17.17 N	92.27 W
Petaling Jaya	114	3.05 N	101.39 E
Petalión, Kólpos C	38	37.59 N	24.02 E
Petaluma	226	38.14 N	122.39 W
Petaluma ≃	226	38.06 N	122.30 W
Pétange	56	49.34 N	5.52 E
Petare	246	10.29 N	66.49 W
Petatlán	234	17.31 N	101.16 W
Petauke	154	14.15 S	31.20 E
Petawawa	190	45.54 N	77.17 W
Petawawa ≃	190	45.55 N	77.15 W
Pété	146	10.58 N	14.30 E
Petegem	50	50.58 N	3.32 E
Petén □[5]	236	16.15 N	89.50 W
Peteń Itzá, Lago ⊜	232	16.59 N	89.50 W
Petenwell Dam ⬩[6]	190	44.01 N	90.02 W
Petenwell Lake ⊜[1]	190	44.10 N	89.57 W
Peterboro	210	42.58 N	75.41 W
Peterborough, Austl.	166	32.58 S	138.50 E
Peterborough, Ont., Can.	212	44.18 N	78.19 W
Peterborough, Eng., U.K.	42	52.35 N	0.15 W
Peterborough, N.H., U.S.	188	42.53 N	71.57 W
Peterborough □[6]	212	44.33 N	78.15 W
Peterculter	46	57.05 N	2.16 W
Peterhead	46	57.30 N	1.49 W
Peter Hill ∧	46	56.58 N	2.42 W
Peter I Island ▮	9	68.47 S	90.35 W
Peter Island ▮	240m	18.22 N	64.35 W
Peter Lake ⊜, N.W. Ter., Can.	176	63.08 N	92.48 W
Peter Lake ⊜, Sask., Can.	184	57.15 N	103.53 W
Peterlee	44	54.46 N	1.19 W
Petermann Ranges ⛰	162	25.00 S	129.46 E
Peter Pond Lake ⊜	184	55.55 N	108.44 W
Peter Pond Lake Indian Reserve ⬩[4]	184	55.55 N	109.00 W
Petersberg	56	50.33 N	9.43 E
Peters Brook ≃	276	40.33 N	74.37 W
Petersburg, Alaska, U.S.	180	56.50 N	132.59 W
Petersburg, Ill., U.S.	219	40.01 N	89.51 W
Petersburg, Mich., U.S.	216	41.54 N	83.43 W
Petersburg, Nebr., U.S.	198	41.51 N	98.05 W
Petersburg, N.J., U.S.	208	39.15 N	74.43 W
Petersburg, N.Y., U.S.	210	42.45 N	73.21 W
Petersburg, Ohio, U.S.	214	40.55 N	80.32 W
Petersburg, Pa., U.S.	214	40.34 N	78.03 W
Petersburg, Tenn., U.S.	194	35.19 N	86.38 W
Petersburg, Tex., U.S.	196	33.52 N	101.36 W
Petersburg, Va., U.S.	208	37.13 N	77.24 W
Petersburg, W. Va., U.S.	188	39.00 N	79.07 W
Petersburg National Battlefield ♠	208	37.14 N	77.22 W
Peters Canyon Reservoir ⊜[1]	280	33.47 N	117.45 W
Peters Creek ≃, Calif., U.S.	282	37.15 N	122.13 W
Peters Creek ≃, Pa., U.S.	279b	40.18 N	79.52 W
Peters Creek, Piney Fork ≃	279b	40.16 N	79.58 W
Petersdorf, B.R.D.	54	54.29 N	11.04 E
Petersdorf, B.R.D.	60	48.31 N	11.02 E
Petersfield	42	51.00 N	0.56 W
Petershagen, B.R.D.	52	52.23 N	8.58 E
Petershagen, D.D.R.	54	52.24 N	14.20 E
Petershagen bei Berlin	54	52.31 N	13.46 E
Petersham, Austl.	274a	33.54 S	151.09 E
Petersham, Mass., U.S.	207	42.29 N	72.11 W
Petershausen	60	48.24 N	11.28 E
Peterskirchen	60	48.05 N	12.29 E
Peterson	198	42.55 N	95.21 W
Peters Pond ⊜	283	42.43 N	71.16 W
Peterswald Hill ∧[2]	162	26.43 S	123.39 E
Peter the Great Bay → Petra Velikogo, Zaliv C	89	42.40 N	132.00 E
Pétervására	30	48.01 N	20.06 E
Petilia Policastro	68	39.07 N	16.47 E
Pétionville	238	18.31 N	72.17 W
Petit	273d	26.06 S	28.22 E
Petit Bois Island ▮	194	30.12 N	88.26 W
Petit-Bourg	241o	16.12 N	61.36 W
Petit-Canal	241o	16.23 N	61.29 W
Petitcodiac	186	45.56 N	65.10 W
Petitcodiac ≃	186	45.50 N	64.33 W
Petit Cul-de-Sac Marin C	241o	16.12 N	61.33 W
Petite-Cascapedia, Parc de la ♠	186	48.30 N	65.50 W
Petite-Nation, Rivière de la ≃	206	45.35 N	75.06 W
Petite Rivière de La Baleine ≃	176	56.00 N	76.45 W
Petite Rivière du Chêne ≃	206	46.34 N	72.02 W
Petite Rivière Noire, Piton de la ∧	157c	20.24 S	57.24 E
Petite Rivière Rouge ≃	206	45.45 N	75.00 W
Petite Sauldre ≃	50	47.27 N	2.05 E
Petite-Synthe	50	51.01 N	2.19 E
Petite Terre, Îles de la ▮▮	241o	16.10 N	61.07 W
Petit-Fort-Philippe	50	51.00 N	2.07 E
Petit-Goâve	238	18.26 N	72.52 W
Petit Jean ≃	194	35.10 N	92.56 W
Petit Jean State Park ♠	194	35.06 N	92.57 W
Petit Lac du Nord ⊜	186	50.50 N	67.10 W
Petit Lac Nominingue ⊜	206	46.21 N	75.00 W
Petit Loango	152	2.16 S	9.35 E
Petit Loango, Parc National du ♠	152	2.15 S	9.36 E
Petit Mécatina, Île du ▮	186	50.33 N	59.20 W
Petit-Mecatina, Rivière du ≃	176	50.28 N	59.35 W
Petit Morin ≃	50	48.56 N	3.07 E
Petitot ≃	176	60.14 N	123.29 W
Petit Rhône ≃	62	43.27 N	4.24 E
Petit-Saint-Bernard, Col du)(	62	45.41 N	6.53 E
Petitsikapau Lake ⊜	176	54.45 N	66.25 W
Petkeljärven Kansallispuisto ♠	24	62.35 N	31.12 E
Petkus	54	51.59 N	13.21 E
Petlād	120	22.28 N	72.48 E
Petlalcingo	234	18.05 N	97.54 W
Petnahor	267b	41.11 N	28.53 E
Petnjička Pećina •[5]	38	44.15 N	19.54 E
Peto	232	20.08 N	88.55 W
Petoh	114	2.53 N	103.15 E
Petőháza ⊥	61	47.36 N	16.54 E
Petone	172	41.13 S	174.52 E
Petorca	252	32.15 S	70.56 W
Petoskey	190	45.22 N	84.57 W
Petownikip Lake ⊜	184	52.56 N	92.02 W
Petra ⊥	132	30.20 N	35.26 E
Petralia Soprana	70	37.47 N	14.06 E
Petralia Sottana	70	37.48 N	14.05 E
Petras, Mount ∧	9	75.52 S	128.38 W
Petra Velikogo, Zaliv C	89	42.40 N	132.00 E
Petre, Point ≻	212	43.50 N	77.09 W
Petrecovo	24	61.18 N	57.07 E
Petrella, Monte ∧	66	41.18 N	13.40 E
Petrella Salto	66	42.18 N	13.04 E
Petrella Tifernina	66	41.41 N	14.42 E
Petrič	38	41.24 N	23.13 E
Petrie	171a	27.16 S	152.59 E
Petrified Forest National Park ♠	200	34.55 N	109.49 W
Petrikov	78	52.08 N	28.30 E
Petrikovka	78	48.43 N	34.37 E
Petrila	38	45.27 N	23.25 E
Petrinja	36	45.26 N	16.17 E
Petriščevo, S.S.S.R.	82	54.37 N	36.57 E
Petriščevo, S.S.S.R.	82	55.30 N	36.18 E
Petrodvorec	76	59.53 N	29.54 E
Petrograd → Leningrad	76	59.55 N	30.15 E
Petrogrado-Doneckoje ⬩[8]	83	48.42 N	38.41 E
Petrohanski prohod)(	38	43.08 N	23.08 E
Petrohué	254	41.08 S	72.25 W
Petrokrepost'	76	59.57 N	31.02 E
Petrolândia	250	9.05 S	38.18 W
Petrólea	246	8.30 N	72.35 W
Petroleum	216	40.37 N	85.09 W
Petrolia, Ont., Can.	214	42.52 N	82.09 W
Petrolia, Pa., U.S.	214	41.01 N	79.43 W
Petrolia, Tex., U.S.	196	34.01 N	98.14 W
Petrolina	250	9.24 S	40.30 W
Petrolina de Goiás	255	16.06 S	49.20 W
Petrominsk	24	64.47 N	38.25 E
Petronà	68	39.03 N	16.45 E
Petrona, Punta ≻	240m	17.56 N	66.23 W
Petronila Creek ≃	196	27.32 N	97.32 W
Petropavlovka, S.S.S.R.	78	50.06 N	40.54 E
Petropavlovka, S.S.S.R.	78	48.27 N	36.26 E
Petropavlovka, S.S.S.R.	83	49.43 N	37.42 E
Petropavlovka, S.S.S.R.	88	50.38 N	105.19 E
Petropavlovsk, S.S.S.R.	86	54.54 N	69.06 E
Petropavlovsk, S.S.S.R.	86	56.20 N	57.09 E
Petropavlovskaja Krepost' ⊥	265a	59.57 N	30.19 E
Petropavlovsk-Kamčatskij	74	53.01 N	158.39 E
Petropavlovskoje, S.S.S.R.	86	52.06 N	85.06 E
Petropavlovskoje, S.S.S.R.	88	58.13 N	108.59 E
Petrópolis	256	22.31 S	43.10 W
Petros	192	36.06 N	84.26 W
Petroşani	38	45.25 N	23.22 E
Petrosino	70	37.43 N	12.29 E
Petro-Slav'anka	265a	59.48 N	30.31 E
Petroso, Monte ∧	66	41.44 N	13.55 E
Petroúpolis	267c	38.03 N	23.41 E
Petrovac	38	44.22 N	21.27 E
Petrovgrad → Zrenjanin	38	45.23 N	20.24 E
Petrovka, S.S.S.R.	78	46.54 N	30.44 E
Petrovka, S.S.S.R.	80	53.13 N	51.58 E
Petrovka, S.S.S.R.	83	48.53 N	39.52 E
Petrovka, S.S.S.R.	83	48.48 N	39.16 E
Petrovo, S.S.S.R.	76	58.22 N	35.09 E
Petrovo, S.S.S.R.	78	48.20 N	33.16 E
Petrovo, S.S.S.R.	82	55.00 N	38.08 E
Petrovo, S.S.S.R.	88	54.30 N	105.15 E
Petrovo-Dal'neje	265b	55.45 N	37.11 E
Petrovo-Krasnoselje ⬩[8]	83	48.18 N	38.52 E
Petrovsk	80	52.19 N	45.23 E
Petrovskaja	78	45.25 N	37.57 E
Petrovskij, S.S.S.R.	80	50.45 N	41.59 E
Petrovskij, S.S.S.R.	80	56.39 N	40.19 E
Petrovskij, S.S.S.R.	82	54.29 N	36.59 E
Petrovskoje, S.S.S.R.	78	49.10 N	36.54 E
Petrovskoje, S.S.S.R.	80	57.01 N	39.16 E
Petrovskoje, S.S.S.R.	80	52.39 N	40.15 E
Petrovskoje, S.S.S.R.	82	55.32 N	36.59 E
Petrovskoje, S.S.S.R.	82	55.27 N	38.21 E
Petrovskoje, S.S.S.R.	83	48.18 N	38.52 E
Petrovskoje, S.S.S.R.	265b	55.36 N	37.53 E
Petrovsko-Razumovskoje ⬩[8]	265b	55.50 N	37.34 E
Petrovsk-Zabajkal'skij	88	51.17 N	108.50 E
Petrov Val	80	50.09 N	45.12 E
Petrozavodsk	24	61.47 N	34.20 E
Petrozsény → Petroşani	38	45.25 N	23.22 E
Petru I, Pam'atnik ⊥	265a	59.56 N	30.18 E
Petrun'	24	66.28 N	60.43 E
Petrusburg	158	29.08 S	25.27 E
Petrušino	265a	59.48 N	30.50 E
Petrus Steyn	158	27.38 S	28.08 E
Petrusville	158	30.05 S	24.41 E
Petschora → Pečora ≃	24	68.13 N	54.15 E
Petten	52	52.45 N	4.39 E
Pettenbach	61	47.57 N	14.01 E
Petteril ≃	44	54.54 N	2.55 W
Petticoat Creek ≃	275b	43.48 N	79.06 W
Pettigo	48	54.33 N	7.50 W
Pettineo	70	37.58 N	14.17 E
Pettisville	216	41.32 N	84.14 W
Pettneu am Arlberg	58	47.09 N	10.20 E
Pettus	196	28.37 N	97.48 W
Petty Harbour	186	47.28 N	52.43 W
Petty Island ▮	285	39.58 N	75.07 W
Petua	272b	22.25 N	88.27 E
Petuchovo	86	55.06 N	67.58 E
Petuški	80	55.55 N	39.28 E
Petworth	42	50.59 N	0.38 W
Petzen ∧	61	46.31 N	14.45 E
Petzow	264a	52.21 N	12.56 E
Peudada	114	5.12 N	96.35 E
Peuerbach	60	48.21 N	13.56 E
Peuetsagoe, Gunung ∧	114	4.55 N	96.20 E
Peureulak	114	4.48 N	97.53 E
Peureulak ≃	114	4.54 N	97.53 E
Peureulak, Ujung ≻	114	4.54 N	97.54 E
Peusangan ≃	114	5.16 N	96.51 E
Peusangan, Ujung ≻	114	5.18 N	96.50 E
Pevek	74	69.42 N	170.17 E
Pevely	219	38.17 N	90.24 W
Pevensey	42	50.49 N	0.20 E
Pevensey Levels ≚	42	50.50 N	0.20 E
Peveragno	62	44.20 N	7.37 E
Pewamo	216	43.00 N	84.51 W
Pewaukee	216	43.05 N	88.16 W
Pewaukee Lake ⊜	216	43.04 N	88.19 W
Pewee Valley	218	38.19 N	85.29 W
Pews Creek ≃	276	40.27 N	74.06 W
Pewsey	42	51.21 N	1.46 W
Pewsey, Vale of ∨	42	51.20 N	1.48 W
Pewsum	52	53.26 N	7.05 E
Péyia	130	34.53 N	32.23 E
Peykjahlid	24a	65.40 N	16.50 W
Peyrolles-en-Provence	62	43.39 N	5.35 E
Peyruis	62	44.02 N	5.56 E
Peza ≃	24	65.36 N	44.35 E
Pezas	86	54.39 N	87.46 E
Pezawa Taung ∧	110	19.33 N	94.31 E
Pézenas	32	43.27 N	3.25 E
Pežženga	76	59.10 N	44.16 E
Pezinok	30	48.18 N	17.17 E
Pezu	123	32.19 N	70.44 E
Pezzana	62	45.16 N	8.29 E
Pfäfers	58	46.59 N	9.30 E
Pfaffenhausen	58	48.07 N	10.27 E
Pfaffenhofen an der Ilm	60	48.31 N	11.30 E
Pfaffenhoffen	56	48.51 N	7.37 E
Pfaffenöden ∧[2]	264b	48.04 N	16.33 E
Pfäffikersee ⊜	58	47.21 N	8.48 E
Pfäffikon, Schw.	58	47.12 N	8.46 E
Pfäffikon, Schw.	58	47.22 N	8.47 E
Pfaffnau	58	47.14 N	7.54 E
Pfaffstätten	264b	48.01 N	16.16 E
Pfalz □[5]	56	49.20 N	8.00 E
Pfalzdorf	52	51.42 N	6.11 E
Pfalzel	56	49.47 N	6.41 E

≃ River	Fluss	Río	Rivière	Rio
≊ Canal	Kanal	Canal	Canal	Canal
↳ Waterfall, Rapids	Wasserfall, Stromschnellen	Cascada, Rápidos	Chute d'eau, Rapides	Cascata, Rápidos
⋓ Strait	Meeresstrasse	Estrecho	Détroit	Estreito
C Bay, Gulf	Bucht, Golf	Bahía, Golfo	Baie, Golfe	Baía, Golfo
⊜ Lake, Lakes	See, Seen	Lago, Lagos	Lac, Lacs	Lago, Lagos
☷ Swamp	Sumpf	Pantano	Marais	Pântano
⍌ Ice Features, Glacier	Eis- und Gletscherformen	Accidentes Glaciales	Formes glaciaires	Acidentes Glaciares
⍑ Other Hydrographic Features	Andere Hydrographische Objekte	Otros Elementos Hidrográficos	Autres données hydrographiques	Outros Elementos Hidrográficos
⊹ Submarine Features	Untermeerische Objekte	Accidentes Submarinos	Formes de relief sous-marin	Acidentes Submarinos
□ Political Unit	Politische Einheit	Unidad Politica	Entité politique	Unidade Política
℧ Cultural Institution	Kulturelle Institution	Institución Cultural	Institution culturelle	Instituição Cultural
⊥ Historical Site	Historische Stätte	Sitio Histórico	Site historique	Sitio Histórico
♠ Recreational Site	Erholungs- und Ferienort	Sitio de Recreo	Centre de loisirs	Sítio de Lazer
⊠ Airport	Flughafen	Aeropuerto	Aéroport	Aeroporto
▪ Military Installation	Militäranlage	Instalación Militar	Installation militaire	Instalação Militar
⬩ Miscellaneous	Verschiedenes	Misceláneo	Divers	Miscelânea

Pfälzer Wald, Naturpark ♠ 56 49.15 N 7.50 E
Pfänder ∧ 58 47.30 N 9.47 E
Pfarrkirchen 60 48.27 N 12.56 E
Pfarrweisach 56 50.09 N 10.44 E
Pfastatt 58 47.47 N 7.18 E
Pfatter 60 48.58 N 12.23 E
Pfaueninsel, Schloss ⊥ 264a 52.26 N 13.07 E
Pfeddersheim 56 49.38 N 8.16 E
Pfeffenhausen 60 48.40 N 11.58 E
Pfeiffer-Big Sur State Park ♠ 226 36.15 N 121.47 W
Pferderennbahn ♠ 263 51.31 N 7.32 E
Pflugerville 222 30.26 N 97.37 W
Pförten → Brody 30 51.45 N 14.45 E
Pforzen 58 47.55 N 10.37 E
Pforzheim 56 48.54 N 8.42 E
Pfreimd 60 49.30 N 12.11 E
Pfreimd ≃ 60 49.29 N 12.11 E
Pfrimm ≃ 56 49.39 N 8.22 E
Pfronten 58 47.34 N 10.33 E
Pfuhl 58 48.24 N 10.02 E
Pfullendorf 58 47.55 N 9.15 E
Pfullingen 58 48.28 N 9.13 E
Pfunds 58 46.58 N 10.33 E
Pfungstadt 56 49.48 N 8.36 E
Pfünz 60 48.53 N 11.16 E
Pfyn 58 47.36 N 8.57 E
Phachi ≃ 110 13.56 N 99.24 E
Phaéton, Port ⊂ 174s 17.44 S 149.21 W
Phagwāra 123 31.14 N 75.46 E
Phala 156 23.45 S 26.57 E
Phalaborwa 156 23.55 S 31.13 E
Phalanx 214 41.15 N 80.58 W
Phalempin 50 50.31 N 3.01 E
Phālia 123 32.26 N 73.35 E
Phalodi 120 27.08 N 72.22 E
Phalsbourg 56 48.46 N 7.16 E
Phaltan 122 17.59 N 74.26 E
Phalti 272b 22.46 N 88.34 E
Phan 110 19.28 N 99.43 E
Phanat Nikhom 110 13.27 N 101.11 E
Phangan, Ko ❙ 110 9.45 N 100.04 E
Phang Hoei, Khao ∧ 110 15.15 N 101.23 E
Phangnga 110 8.28 N 98.32 E
Phaniang ≃ 110 16.49 N 102.24 E
Phanom Dongrak, Thiu Khao ⛰ 110 14.25 N 103.30 E
Phanom Thuan 110 14.07 N 99.42 E
Phan-rang 110 11.34 N 108.59 E
Phan-thiet 110 10.56 N 108.06 E
Phan Thong 110 13.28 N 101.06 E
Phantom Lake 216 42.52 N 88.21 W
Pharenda 124 27.06 N 83.17 E
Phariāro 120 27.12 N 68.59 E
Pharr 196 26.12 N 98.11 W
Phasi Charoen 269a 13.43 N 100.26 E
Phasi Charoen, Khlong ≋ 269a 13.44 N 100.30 E
Phat-diem 110 20.06 N 106.06 E
Phato 110 9.48 N 98.48 E
Phatthalung 110 7.37 N 100.05 E
Phayao 110 19.10 N 99.55 E
Pheasant Creek ≃ 184 50.35 N 103.28 W
Pheba 194 33.35 N 88.57 W
Phelan 228 34.25 N 117.34 W
Phelps, N.Y., U.S. 210 42.57 N 77.03 W
Phelps, Tex., U.S. 222 30.42 N 95.27 W
Phelps, Wis., U.S. 190 46.04 N 89.05 W
Phelps Lake ⊜ 192 35.46 N 76.27 W
Phenix City 192 32.29 N 85.01 W
Phet Buri 110 13.06 N 99.57 E
Phet Buri ≃ 110 13.13 N 99.59 E
Phetchabun 110 16.25 N 101.08 E
Phetchabun, Thiu Khao ⛰ 110 16.20 N 100.55 E
Phibun Mangsahan 110 15.14 N 105.14 E
Phichai 110 17.17 N 100.05 E
Phichit 110 16.26 N 100.22 E
Philadelphia, S. Afr. 158 33.40 S 18.36 E
Philadelphia, Ill., U.S. 219 39.58 N 90.07 W
Philadelphia, Miss., U.S. 194 32.46 N 89.07 W
Philadelphia, Mo., U.S. 219 39.50 N 91.44 W
Philadelphia, N.Y., U.S. 212 44.09 N 75.43 W
Philadelphia, Pa., U.S. 208
285 39.57 N 75.07 W
Philadelphia, Tenn., U.S. 192 35.41 N 84.24 W
Philadelphia □^{6} 285 39.57 N 75.07 W
Philadelphia International Airport ⊠ 208 39.53 N 75.14 W
Philadelphia Naval Shipyard ■ 285 39.53 N 75.11 W
Philae ⊥ 140 24.01 N 32.53 E
Phil Campbell 194 34.21 N 87.42 W
Philip 198 44.02 N 101.40 W
Philipp 194 33.45 N 90.12 W
Philippeville → Skikda, Alg. 148 36.50 N 6.58 E
Philippeville, Bel. 50 50.12 N 4.32 E
Philippi 188 39.09 N 80.02 W
Philippi, Lake ⊜ 166 24.22 S 139.00 E
Philippi Glacier ◪ 9 66.45 S 88.20 E
Philippine Basin ⊹^{1} 14 18.00 N 133.00 E
Philippinen → Philippines □^{1} 116 13.00 N 122.00 E
Philippines □^{1} 108
116 13.00 N 122.00 E
Philippines, University of the ⊸^{2} 269f 14.39 N 121.04 E
Philippine Sea ⊤^{2} 14 20.00 N 135.00 E
Philippine Trench ⊹^{1} 14 9.00 N 127.00 E
Philippolis 158 30.19 S 25.13 E
Philippopolis → Plovdiv 38 42.09 N 24.45 E
Philippsreut 60 48.52 N 13.41 E
Philippsthal 264a 52.20 N 13.09 E
Philipsburg, Qué., Can. 206 45.02 N 73.05 W
Philipsburg, Ned. Ant. 238 17.59 N 63.10 W
Philipsburg, Mont., U.S. 202 46.20 N 113.18 W
Philipsburg, Pa., U.S. 214 40.53 N 78.05 W
Philipsburg Manor ⊥ 276 41.05 N 73.52 W
Philipse Manor ⊥ 276 40.56 N 73.54 W
Philip Smith Mountains ⛰ 180 68.30 N 148.00 W
Philipstown 158 30.26 S 24.29 E
Phillaur 123 31.01 N 75.47 E
Phillip Island ❙ 169 38.29 S 145.14 E
Phillips, Maine, U.S. 188 44.49 N 70.21 W
Phillips, Tex., U.S. 196 35.42 N 101.22 W
Phillips, Wis., U.S. 190 45.41 N 90.24 W
Phillipsburg, Kans., U.S. 198 39.45 N 99.19 W
Phillipsburg, N.J., U.S. 210 40.42 N 75.12 W
Philmont 210 42.15 N 73.39 W
Philo, Ill., U.S. 194 40.01 N 88.09 W
Philo, Ohio, U.S. 188 39.52 N 81.55 W
Philomath 202 44.32 N 123.22 W
Philpots Island ❙ 176 74.48 N 80.00 W
Phimai 110 15.13 N 102.30 E
Phinga 272b 22.41 N 88.25 E
Phitsanulok 110 16.50 N 100.15 E
Phnom Penh → Phnum Pénh 110 11.33 N 104.55 E
Phnum Pénh 110 11.33 N 104.55 E
Phnum Tbêng Méanchey 110 13.49 N 104.58 E
Pho ≃ 124 27.41 N 89.53 E
Phoenicia 210 42.05 N 74.19 W
Phoenix, Ariz., U.S. 200 33.27 N 112.05 W
Phoenix, Ill., U.S. 278 41.37 N 87.38 W
Phoenix, Md., U.S. 208 39.31 N 76.37 W
Phoenix, N.Y., U.S. 210 43.14 N 76.18 W
Phoenix ❙^{1} 14 3.43 S 170.43 W
Phoenix Islands ❙❙ 14 4.00 S 172.00 W
Phoenix Lake ⊜^{1} 282 37.57 N 122.35 W
Phoenix Trough ⊹^{1} 14 6.00 S 172.30 W
Phoenixville 208 40.08 N 75.31 W
Phon 110 15.49 N 102.36 E
Phong ≃ 110 16.23 N 102.56 E
Phôngsali 110 21.41 N 102.06 E
Phong Saly □^{4} 102 21.40 N 102.05 E
Phong-tho 110 22.32 N 103.21 E
Phon Phisai 110 18.01 N 103.05 E
Phrae 110 18.09 N 100.08 E
Phra Khanong ⊸^{8} 269a 13.42 N 100.35 E
Phra Nakhon → Krung Thep 110 13.45 N 100.31 E
Phra Nakhon Si Ayutthaya 110 14.21 N 100.33 E
Phran Kratai 110 16.40 N 99.36 E
Phrao 110 19.22 N 99.13 E
Phra Phutthabat 110 14.43 N 100.48 E
Phra Pradaeng 269a 13.40 N 100.32 E
Phra Rop, Khao ∧ 110 13.11 N 99.31 E
Phrom Phiram 110 17.02 N 100.12 E
Phsar Réam 110 10.30 N 103.37 E
Phu-cat 110 14.01 N 109.03 E
Phu-cuong 110 10.58 N 106.39 E
Phu-huu, Viet. 110 18.58 N 105.31 E
Phu-huu, Viet. 269c 10.43 N 106.47 E
Phuket 110 7.53 N 98.24 E
Phuket, Ko ❙ 110 8.00 N 98.22 E
Phularwān 123 32.22 N 73.00 E
Phulbari 126 21.52 N 88.08 E
Phulbāria 126 23.22 N 89.50 E
Phuljhuri 126 22.12 N 90.04 E
Phulkusma 126 22.43 N 86.52 E
Phu-loc 110 16.16 N 107.53 E
Phūlpur 124 25.33 N 82.06 E
Phulra 123 34.20 N 73.03 E
Phultala 126 22.59 N 89.28 E
Phu-ly 110 20.32 N 105.56 E
Phum Duang ≃ 110 9.10 N 99.20 E
Phumĭ Bâ Khăm 110 13.51 N 107.22 E
Phumĭ Banam 110 11.19 N 105.18 E
Phumĭ Béng 110 13.05 N 104.18 E
Phumĭ Châmbák 110 11.14 N 104.49 E
Phumĭ Chângho Ândêng 110 12.39 N 104.35 E
Phumĭ Chhuk 110 10.50 N 104.28 E
Phumĭ Chruŏy Slêng 110 13.14 N 105.57 E
Phumĭ Dăk Dăm 110 12.20 N 107.21 E
Phumĭ Kâmpóng Srâlau 110 14.05 N 105.46 E
Phumĭ Kâmpóng Trâbâk 110 13.06 N 105.14 E
Phumĭ Kântuŏt Sâmraông 110 14.12 N 104.37 E
Phumĭ Kaôh Kért 110 13.47 N 104.32 E
Phumĭ Kaôh Kŏng 110 11.26 N 103.11 E
Phumĭ Khpôb 110 11.02 N 105.12 E
Phumĭ Krêk 110 11.46 N 105.56 E
Phumĭ Lvéa Kraôm 110 13.21 N 102.54 E
Phumĭ Moŭng 110 13.45 N 103.33 E
Phumĭ Narŭng 110 13.53 N 105.34 E
Phumĭ Phnum Srâlau 110 11.03 N 103.42 E
Phumĭ Prêk Kák 110 12.15 N 105.32 E
Phumĭ Prêk Sândêk 110 11.51 N 105.22 E
Phumĭ Prey Toch 110 12.54 N 103.23 E
Phumĭ Puŏk Chăs 110 13.26 N 103.44 E
Phumĭ Rôluŏs Chăs 110 13.19 N 104.00 E
Phumĭ Sâmraông 110 14.11 N 103.31 E
Phumĭ Spœ Tbong 110 12.20 N 105.19 E
Phumĭ Srê Kôkir 110 13.08 N 106.04 E
Phumĭ Srê Rônéam 110 12.16 N 106.25 E
Phumĭ Tbêng 110 13.35 N 104.55 E
Phumĭ Thalabârĭvăt 110 13.33 N 105.57 E
Phumĭ Thmâ Pôk 110 13.57 N 103.04 E
Phumĭ Tnaôt 110 12.56 N 104.34 E
Phumĭ Tœk Choŭ 110 13.36 N 103.24 E
Phu-my 110 14.10 N 109.03 E
Phung-hiep 110 9.49 N 105.50 E
Phuntsholing 124 26.53 N 89.23 E
Phuoc-binh 110 11.50 N 106.58 E
Phuoc Khanh 269c 10.40 N 106.48 E
Phuoc-le 108 10.30 N 107.10 E
Phuoc-long 110 9.26 N 105.28 E
Phuoc-long-xa 269c 10.49 N 106.46 E
Phuoc-luong 269c 10.45 N 106.48 E
Phu-quoc, Dao ❙ 110 10.12 N 104.00 E
Phurphura 272b 22.44 N 88.08 E
Phu-tho 110 21.24 N 105.13 E
Phu-tho-hoa 269c 10.46 N 106.38 E
Phu Tho Race Track ♠ 269c 10.46 N 106.40 E
Phutthaisong 110 15.32 N 103.01 E
Phu-vang 110 16.31 N 107.37 E
Phu-vinh 110 9.56 N 106.20 E
Phu-yen 110 21.16 N 104.39 E
Pia 154 4.00 N 26.17 E
Piaanu Pass ⋃ 175c 7.20 N 151.26 E
Piabas 250 1.12 S 46.54 W
Piabetá 256 22.37 S 43.10 W
Piacá 250 7.42 S 47.18 W
Piaçabuçu 250 10.24 S 36.25 W
Piacatu 255 21.38 S 50.30 W
Piacatuba 256 21.29 S 42.47 W
Piacenza 62 45.01 N 9.40 E
Piacenza □^{4} 62 44.53 N 9.35 E
Piacouadie, Lac ⊜ 186 51.16 N 70.54 W
Piadena 64 45.08 N 10.22 E
Piaggine 68 40.21 N 15.23 E
Piako ≃ 172 37.12 S 175.30 E
Pialba 166 25.17 S 152.51 E
Pian, Lac ⊜ 190 47.50 N 79.08 W
Piana 36 42.14 N 8.38 E
Piana, Isola ❙ 71 40.58 N 8.13 E
Piana Crixia 62 44.29 N 8.18 E
Piana degli Albanesi 70 38.00 N 13.17 E
Piana degli Albanesi, Lago di ⊜ 70 37.58 N 13.18 E
Piana Mwanga 154 7.40 S 28.10 E
Piancastagnaio 66 42.51 N 11.41 E
Piancó 250 7.12 S 37.57 W
Pian Creek ≃ 166 30.02 S 148.12 E
Piandian 98 36.38 N 113.47 E
Pian di Sco 66 43.38 N 11.33 E
Pianella 66 42.24 N 14.02 E
Pianello Val Tidone 62 44.57 N 9.24 E
Pianezza 62 45.06 N 7.33 E
Pianguan 102 39.35 N 111.59 E
Pianjiaojie 102 26.01 N 100.32 E
Piankatank ≃ 208 37.32 N 76.18 W
Pianlingpuzi 104 41.24 N 123.58 E
Piano 64 45.46 N 11.08 E
Piano d'Arta 64 46.29 N 13.01 E
Piano del Voglio 66 44.10 N 11.13 E
Pianoro 64 44.22 N 11.20 E
Pianosa, Isola ❙ 68 42.13 N 15.45 E
Pianosinatico 66 44.07 N 10.44 E
Pians 58 47.08 N 10.30 E
Pianyanchang 107 29.59 N 106.36 E
Piapot 184 50.00 N 109.11 W
Piapot Indian Reserve ⊸^{4} 184 50.45 N 104.26 W
Piares, Punta ≻ 234 16.49 N 99.55 W
Piasa 219 39.07 N 90.07 W
Piasa Creek ≃ 219 38.56 N 90.17 W
Piaseczno 30 52.05 N 21.01 E
Piashti, Lac ⊜ 186 50.29 N 62.52 W
Piaski 30 51.08 N 22.51 E
Piat 116 17.48 N 121.29 E
Piatã 255 13.09 S 41.48 W
Piatra-Neamț 38 46.56 N 26.22 E
Piatra Olt 38 44.24 N 24.16 E
Piatt □^{6} 219 40.00 N 88.35 W
Piau 256 21.31 S 43.19 W
Piauí □^{3} 250 7.00 S 43.00 W
Piauí ≃, Bra. 250 6.38 S 42.42 W
Piauí ≃, Bra. 255 16.41 S 41.53 W
Piaus, Rio dos ≃ 255 12.27 S 49.32 W
Piave ≃ 64 45.32 N 12.44 E
Piawaning 162 30.51 S 116.22 E
Piaxtla ≃ 232 23.42 N 106.49 W
Piazza Armerina 70 37.23 N 14.22 E
Piazzola sul Brenta 64 45.32 N 11.47 E
Piberegg 61 47.05 N 15.05 E
Pibor ≃ 140 8.26 N 33.13 E
Pibor Post 140 6.48 N 33.08 E
Pibroch 182 54.16 N 113.52 W
Pic ≃ 190 48.36 N 86.18 W
Pica 248 20.30 S 69.21 W
Picacho 200 32.43 N 111.30 W
Picacho, Cerro del ∧ 286a 19.35 N 99.06 W
Pičajevo 80 53.15 N 42.12 E
Picanoc ≃ 190 46.05 N 76.03 W
Picardie □^{9} 50 50.00 N 3.30 E
Picatinny Arsenal ■ 276 40.57 N 74.33 W
Picatinny Lake ⊜ 276 40.57 N 74.33 W
Picayune 194 30.26 N 89.41 W
Piccadilly 186 48.34 N 58.55 W
Piccadilly Circus 154 13.56 S 29.24 E
Piccadilly Station ⊸^{5} 262 53.28 N 2.14 W
Piccione 66 43.11 N 12.31 E
Piccolo, Mar (Taranto) ⊤^{2} 68 40.29 N 17.16 E
Piccotts End 260 51.46 N 0.28 W
Pic de Tio ∧ 150 8.52 N 8.54 W
Piceance Creek ≃ 200 40.05 N 108.14 W
Picentini, Monti ∧ 68 40.45 N 15.00 E
Picerno 68 40.38 N 15.38 E
Pičeury 80 54.19 N 45.50 E
Pīch ≃ 123 34.52 N 71.09 E
Pichana ≃ 246 3.31 S 71.43 W
Pichanal 252 23.19 S 64.13 W
Picháturo 234 19.30 N 101.46 W
Picheng 106 32.07 N 119.42 E
Picher 196 36.59 N 94.50 W
Pichhor 124 25.58 N 78.24 E
Pichilemu 252 34.23 S 72.00 W
Pichileufú, Arroyo ≃ 254 40.35 S 70.39 W
Pichimá 246 4.24 N 77.21 W
Pichi-Mahuida 252 38.50 S 64.57 W
Pichinango, Arroyo ≃ 258 34.10 S 57.15 W
Pichincha □^{4} 246 0.10 S 78.40 W
Pichis ≃ 248 9.59 S 74.59 W
Pichl bei Wels 60 48.11 N 13.54 E
Pichor 124 25.11 N 78.11 E
Pichtovka 86 56.00 N 82.42 E
Pichucalco 234 17.31 N 93.09 W
Pichucalco ≃ 234 17.57 N 92.55 W
Picinguaba 256 23.22 S 44.50 W
Picinisco 66 41.39 N 13.52 E
Pic Island ❙ 190 48.43 N 86.38 W
Pickardville 182 54.03 N 113.53 W
Pickaway □^{6} 218 39.36 N 82.57 W
Pickens, Miss., U.S. 194 32.53 N 89.58 W
Pickens, S.C., U.S. 192 34.53 N 82.42 W
Pickens, W. Va., U.S. 188 38.39 N 80.13 W
Pickensville 194 33.14 N 88.16 W
Pickerel ≃ 190 45.55 N 80.50 W
Pickerel Lake ⊜ 184 52.36 N 99.30 W
Pickering, Ont., Can. 212 43.52 N 79.02 W
Pickering, Eng., U.K. 44 54.14 N 0.46 W
Pickering, Vale of ∨ 44 54.12 N 0.45 W
Pickering Beach 212 43.50 N 78.59 W
Pickering Brook 168a 32.03 S 116.08 E
Pickering Creek ≃ 285 40.08 N 75.30 W
Pickering Creek Reservoir ⊜^{1} 285 40.07 N 75.30 W
Pickett, Lake ⊜ 220 28.36 N 81.07 W
Pickford 190 46.10 N 84.22 W
Pičkir'ajevo 80 54.12 N 42.27 E
Pickle Crow 176 51.30 N 90.04 W
Pickmere 262 53.17 N 2.28 W
Pick Mere ⊜ 262 53.17 N 2.29 W
Pickstown 198 43.04 N 98.32 W
Pickton 222 33.02 N 95.24 W
Pickwick Lake ⊜^{1} 194 34.55 N 88.10 W
Pickwick Landing Dam ⊸^{6} 194 35.00 N 88.21 W
Picnic Point ≻ 274b 37.57 S 145.00 E
Pico 66 41.27 N 13.34 E
Pico ∧ 150a 14.56 N 24.21 W
Pico ❙ 148a 38.28 N 28.20 W
Pico, Ponta do ∧ 148a 38.28 N 28.25 W
Pico de Orizaba, Parque Nacional ♠ 234 19.05 N 97.16 W
Pico de Oro 234 18.01 N 93.37 W
Pico de Tancítaro, Parque Nacional ♠ 234 19.27 N 102.22 W
Pico Rivera 228 33.58 N 118.07 W
Picos 250 7.05 S 41.28 W
Picos, Riacho dos ≃ 255 12.46 S 41.47 W
Picota 248 6.55 S 76.20 W
Pico Truncado 254 46.48 S 67.58 W
Picquigny 50 49.57 N 2.09 E
Picton, Austl. 170 34.11 S 150.36 E
Picton, Ont., Can. 212 44.00 N 77.08 W
Picton, N.Z. 172 41.18 S 174.01 E
Picton, Eng., U.K. 262 53.14 N 2.51 W
Picton, Isla ❙ 254 55.02 S 66.57 W
Picton Bay ⊂ 212 44.03 N 77.08 W
Picton Junction 168a 33.21 S 115.41 E
Pictou 186 45.41 N 62.43 W
Pictou Island ❙ 186 45.50 N 62.34 W
Picture Butte 182 49.53 N 112.47 W
Pictured Rocks National Lakeshore ♠ 190 46.35 N 86.20 W
Picture Rocks 210 41.17 N 76.43 W
Picúa, Punta ≻ 240m 18.25 N 65.46 W
Picuí 250 6.31 S 36.21 W
Picunda 84 43.12 N 40.21 E
Picún Leufú 254 39.31 S 69.15 W
Picún Leufú, Arroyo ≃ 254 39.31 S 69.08 W
Pidálion, Akrotírion ≻ 130 34.56 N 34.05 E
Pidarak 128 25.51 N 63.14 E
Piddle ≃ 42 50.42 N 2.04 W
Piddletrenthide 42 50.48 N 2.25 W
Pide Adası ❙ 267b 40.53 N 29.04 E
Pidie, Ujung ≻ 114 5.30 N 95.53 E
Piding 64 47.46 N 12.55 E
Pidurutalagala ∧ 122 7.00 N 80.46 E
Piedade 287a 22.41 S 43.05 W
Piedade ⊸^{8} 287a 22.53 S 43.19 W
Piedade do Baruel 287b 23.37 S 46.18 W
Piedade do Rio Grande 256 21.28 S 44.12 W
Piedecuesta 246 6.59 N 73.03 W
Piedicavallo 62 45.42 N 7.57 E
Piedicroce 32 42.23 N 9.23 E
Piediluco 66 42.32 N 12.45 E
Piedimonte Etneo 70 37.48 N 15.12 E
Piedimonte Matese 68 41.21 N 14.22 E
Piedimonte San Germano 66 41.30 N 13.45 E
Piedimulera 58 46.01 N 8.16 E
Piè di Ripa 66 43.15 N 13.29 E
Piedmont, Ala., U.S. 194 33.55 N 85.37 W
Piedmont, Calif., U.S. 226 37.50 N 122.15 W
Piedmont, Mo., U.S. 194 37.09 N 90.42 W
Piedmont, Ohio, U.S. 214 40.11 N 81.12 W
Piedmont, S.C., U.S. 192 34.42 N 82.28 W
Piedmont Lake ⊜^{1} 214 40.08 N 81.11 W
Piedra 226 36.47 N 119.25 W
Piedra ≃ 200 37.01 N 107.24 W
Piedra, Cerro ∧ 252 37.41 S 73.07 W
Piedra Azul, Quebrada ≃ 286c 10.36 N 66.57 W
Piedra Blanca 232 29.05 N 102.19 W
Piedrabuena 34 39.02 N 4.10 W
Piedra del Águila 254 40.03 S 70.05 W
Piedrafita, Puerto de)(34 42.40 N 7.01 W
Piedrahita 34 40.28 N 5.19 W
Piedra Roja 236 8.38 N 81.48 W
Piedras, Arroyo de las ≃ 288 34.43 S 58.19 W
Piedras, Punta ≻, Arg. 258 35.25 S 57.08 W
Piedras, Punta ≻, Ur. 258 33.59 S 58.17 W
Piedras, Punta ≻, Ven. 246 10.40 N 61.40 W
Piedras, Punta de ≻ 234 20.50 N 97.14 W
Piedras Blancas 252 31.11 S 59.56 W
Piedras Blancas, Point ≻ 226 35.40 N 121.17 W
Piedras Coloradas 252 32.23 S 57.36 W
Piedras de Tunja ♠ 246 4.49 N 74.20 W
Piedras Negras, Guat. 232 17.11 N 91.15 W
Piedras Negras, Méx. 232 28.42 N 100.31 W
Piedras Negras ⊥ 232 17.12 N 91.15 W
Piedra Sola 252 32.04 S 56.21 W
Piegaro 66 42.58 N 12.05 E
Pie Island ❙ 190 48.15 N 89.05 W
Pieksämäki 26 62.18 N 27.08 E
Piéla 150 12.42 N 0.08 W
Pielach ≃ 61 48.15 N 15.22 E
Pielavesi 26 63.14 N 26.45 E
Pielavesi ⊜ 26 63.18 N 26.35 E
Pielinen ⊜ 26 63.15 N 29.40 E
Piemonte □^{4} 62 45.00 N 8.00 E
Pienaarsrivier 156 25.15 S 28.18 E
Piendamó 246 2.38 N 76.30 W
Pieniężno 30 54.15 N 20.08 E
Pieniński Park Narodowy ♠ 30 49.25 N 20.25 E
Pieni-Salpausselkä ∧ 26 61.08 N 27.20 E
Piennes 56 49.19 N 5.47 E
Pieńsk 30 51.15 N 15.03 E
Pienza 66 43.04 N 11.41 E
Pierce, Colo., U.S. 200 40.38 N 104.45 W
Pierce, Idaho, U.S. 202 46.29 N 115.48 W
Pierce, Nebr., U.S. 198 42.12 N 97.32 W
Pierce, Tex., U.S. 222 29.14 N 96.12 W
Pierce □^{6} 224 47.04 N 122.07 W
Pierce, Lake ⊜ 220 27.58 N 81.31 W
Pierce City 194 36.57 N 94.01 W
Pierce Lake ⊜, Can. 184 54.10 N 92.56 W
Pierce Lake ⊜, Sask., Can. 184 54.30 N 109.42 W
Pierceton 216 41.12 N 85.42 W
Piermont 210 41.03 N 73.55 W
Pierowall 46 59.20 N 2.59 W
Pierpont, Ohio, U.S. 214 41.45 N 80.34 W
Pierpont, S. Dak., U.S. 198 45.30 N 97.50 W
Pierre 198 44.22 N 100.21 W
Pierre, Bayou ≃, La., U.S. 194 31.51 N 93.06 W
Pierre, Bayou ≃, Miss., U.S. 194 31.55 N 91.11 W
Pierre-Buffière 32 45.42 N 1.21 E
Pierreclos 58 46.20 N 4.41 E
Pierre-de-Bresse 58 46.53 N 5.15 E
Pierrefeu-du-Var 62 43.13 N 6.08 E
Pierrefitte-sur-Aire 56 48.54 N 5.20 E
Pierrefitte-sur-Sauldre 50 47.30 N 2.09 E
Pierrefitte-sur-Seine 261 48.58 N 2.22 E
Pierrefonds, Qué., Can. 206 45.29 N 73.52 W
Pierrefonds, Fr. 50 49.21 N 2.59 E
Pierrefontaine-les-Varans 58 47.13 N 6.33 E
Pierrelatte 62 44.23 N 4.42 E
Pierrelaye 261 49.01 N 2.09 E
Pierre Pertuis, Col de)(58 47.12 N 7.11 E
Pierrepont Manor 212 43.44 N 76.04 W
Pierre-sur-Haute ∧ 62 45.39 N 3.49 E
Pierreville, Qué., Can. 206 46.04 N 72.49 W
Pierreville, Trin. 241r 10.18 N 61.01 W
Pierron 219 38.47 N 89.36 W
Pierron, Lac ⊜ 206 46.53 N 74.20 W
Pierry 50 49.01 N 3.56 E
Pierson 192 29.14 N 81.28 W
Piersonville 285 40.10 N 74.42 W
Pierz 190 45.59 N 94.06 W
Piesendorf 64 47.17 N 12.43 E
Piešťany 30 48.36 N 17.50 E
Piesting ≃ 61 48.02 N 16.30 E
Pietarsaari → Jakobstad 26 63.40 N 22.42 E
Pieterburen 52 53.24 N 6.27 E
Pieterlen 58 47.11 N 7.20 E
Pietermaritzburg 158 29.37 S 30.16 E
Pietersburg 156 23.54 S 29.25 E
Pietersfield 273d 26.14 S 28.26 E
Pietrabbondante 66 41.45 N 14.23 E
Pietracamela 66 42.31 N 13.33 E
Pietracatella 66 41.35 N 14.52 E
Pietra del Pertusillo, Lago di ⊜ 68 40.17 N 15.58 E
Pietragalla 68 40.45 N 15.53 E
Pietra Ligure 62 44.09 N 8.17 E
Pietralunga 66 43.26 N 12.26 E
Pietramala 66 44.10 N 11.20 E
Pietramelara 68 41.16 N 14.11 E
Pietramontecorvino 68 41.32 N 15.07 E
Pietrapaola 68 39.29 N 16.49 E
Pietrapertosa 68 40.31 N 16.04 E
Pietraperzia 70 37.25 N 14.08 E
Pietrarossa ≃ 70 37.22 N 14.35 E
Pietrasanta 64 43.57 N 10.14 E
Pietrelcina 68 41.12 N 14.51 E
Piet Retief 158 27.01 S 30.50 E
Pietrosu, Vîrful ∧ 38 47.36 N 24.38 E
Pietrosul ∧ 38 47.08 N 25.11 E
Pieve 64 45.46 N 10.45 E
Pieve d'Alpago 64 46.10 N 12.21 E
Pieve del Cairo 62 45.03 N 8.48 E
Pieve di Cadore 64 46.26 N 12.22 E
Pieve di Cento 64 44.43 N 11.18 E
Pieve di Soligo 64 45.53 N 12.10 E
Pieve di Teco 62 44.03 N 7.56 E
Pieve Fosciana 64 44.08 N 10.25 E
Pievepelago 64 44.12 N 10.37 E
Pieve Porto Morone 62 45.07 N 9.26 E
Pieve Santo Stefano 66 43.40 N 12.02 E
Piffard 210 42.50 N 77.51 W
Piffgal 123 36.10 N 73.10 E
Pigádhia 130 35.31 N 27.12 E
Pigari 80 51.24 N 49.42 E
Pigeon, Mich., U.S. 190 43.50 N 83.16 W
Pigeon, Pa., U.S. 214 41.32 N 79.03 W
Pigeon ≃, Man., Can. 184 52.15 N 97.00 W
Pigeon ≃, Ont., Can. 212 44.22 N 78.31 W
Pigeon ≃, N.A. 190 48.00 N 89.34 W
Pigeon ≃, U.S. 192 36.00 N 83.11 W
Pigeon ≃, U.S. 216 41.46 N 85.47 W
Pigeon ≃, Mich., U.S. 190 45.27 N 84.33 W
Pigeon ≃, Mich., U.S. 190 43.56 N 83.17 W
Pigeon ≃, Mich., U.S. 216 42.54 N 86.11 W
Pigeon Bay ⊂ 214 42.01 N 82.40 W
Pigeon Cove 207 42.41 N 70.38 W
Pigeon Creek ≃, Ala., U.S. 194 31.20 N 86.42 W
Pigeon Creek ≃, Ind., U.S. 194 37.59 N 87.35 W
Pigeon Creek ≃, Ind., U.S. 216 41.41 N 85.17 W
Pigeon Creek ≃, Pa., U.S. 279b 40.12 N 79.55 W
Pigeon Creek ≃, Pa., U.S. 285 40.12 N 75.35 W
Pigeon Forge 192 35.47 N 83.33 W
Pigeon Lake ⊜, Alta., Can. 182 53.00 N 114.00 W
Pigeon Lake ⊜, Ont., Can. 212 44.30 N 78.30 W
Pigeon Run ≃ 285 40.06 N 75.35 W
Pigeon Swamp ≋ 276 40.23 N 74.29 W
Pigezhuang 105 39.39 N 116.15 E
Pigg ≃ 192 37.00 N 79.29 W
Piggott 194 36.23 N 90.11 W
Piggs Peak 158 25.38 S 31.15 E
Pigkawagan 116 7.12 N 124.32 E
Piglio 66 41.49 N 13.08 E
Pigna 62 43.56 N 7.40 E
Pignans 62 43.18 N 6.13 E
Pignataro Maggiore 68 41.11 N 14.10 E
Pignola 68 40.34 N 15.47 E
Pigs, Bay of → Cochinos, Bahía de ⊂ 240p 22.07 N 81.10 W
Pigüé 252 37.37 S 62.25 W
Pihama 172 39.30 S 173.56 E
Pihāni 124 27.38 N 80.12 E
Piha Passage ⋃ 174w 21.07 S 175.05 W
Pihlajavesi ⊜ 26 61.45 N 28.50 E
Pihlava 26 61.33 N 21.36 E
Pihtipudas 26 63.23 N 25.34 E
Pihuamo 234 19.15 N 103.23 W
P'ihyŏn 98 40.01 N 124.37 E
Piikkiö 26 60.26 N 22.31 E
Piippola 26 64.10 N 25.58 E
Pijijiapan 234 15.42 N 93.14 W
Pijnacker 52 52.02 N 4.27 E
Pijol, Pico ∧ 236 15.06 N 87.35 W
Pikal'ovo 76 59.31 N 34.06 E
Pikangikum 184 51.49 N 94.00 W
Pikangikum Lake ⊜ 184 51.48 N 94.00 W
Pike 210 42.33 N 78.09 W
Pike □^{6}, Ill., U.S. 219 39.36 N 90.48 W
Pike □^{6}, Mo., U.S. 219 39.21 N 91.10 W
Pike □^{6}, Ohio, U.S. 218 39.05 N 83.06 W
Pike □^{6}, Pa., U.S. 210 41.19 N 74.48 W
Pike ≃, N.A. 206 45.04 N 73.06 W
Pike ≃, Minn., U.S. 190 47.48 N 92.22 W
Pike ≃, Wis., U.S. 190 45.26 N 87.52 W
Pike, North Branch ≃ 190 45.30 N 88.01 W
Pike, South Branch ≃ 190 45.30 N 88.01 W
Pike Creek ≃, Ont., Can. 281 42.19 N 82.51 W
Pike Creek ≃, Del., U.S. 285 39.42 N 75.42 W
Pike Lake ⊜ 212 44.46 N 76.21 W
Pikelot ❙ 14 8.05 N 147.38 E
Pike Lowe ∧^{2} 262 53.42 N 2.34 W
Pike Run ≃ 276 40.25 N 74.38 W
Pikes Peak 218 39.08 N 86.09 W
Pikes Peak ∧ 200 38.51 N 105.03 W
Pikes Rock ∧^{2} 214 41.56 N 79.24 W
Pikesville 284b 39.23 N 76.44 W
Piketberg 158 32.54 S 18.46 E
Piketon 218 39.04 N 83.01 W
Piketown 208 40.23 N 76.45 W
Pikeville, Ky., U.S. 192 37.29 N 82.31 W
Pikeville, Tenn., U.S. 194 35.36 N 85.11 W
Pikkola 265a 59.42 N 30.08 E
Pikounda 152 0.33 N 16.42 E
Pikwitonei 184 55.35 N 97.09 W
Pila, Arg. 252 36.01 S 58.08 W
Pila, It. 62 45.41 N 7.18 E
Piła (Schneidemühl), Pol. 30 53.10 N 16.44 E
Pilamedu 122 11.01 N 77.01 E
Pilanesberg ∧ 156 25.14 S 27.04 E
Pilão Arcado 250 10.09 S 42.26 W
Pilar, Arg. 252 31.27 S 61.15 W
Pilar, Arg. 252 31.41 S 63.54 W
Pilar, Arg. 258 34.27 S 58.54 W
Pilar, Bra. 250 9.36 S 35.56 W
Pilar, Bra. 287a 22.42 S 43.19 W
Pilar, Para. 252 26.52 S 58.23 W
Pilar, Pil. 116 11.29 N 123.00 E
Pilar, Pil. 116 9.52 N 126.06 E
Pilar □^{5} 288 34.28 S 58.52 W
Pilar Bay ⊂ 116 11.34 N 123.00 E
Pilarcitos Creek ≃ 282 37.28 N 122.27 W
Pilarcitos Lake ⊜ 282 37.33 N 122.25 W
Pilar de Goiás 255 14.41 S 49.27 W
Pilar do Sul 255 23.49 S 47.42 W
Pilares 196 30.24 N 104.52 W
Pilas Group ❙❙ 116 6.45 N 121.35 E
Pilas Island ❙ 116 6.38 N 121.37 E
Pilatus ∧ 58 46.59 N 8.15 E
Pilawa 30 51.58 N 21.31 E
Pilaya ≃ 248 20.55 S 64.04 W
Pilbarra Point ≻ 175f 18.59 S 169.14 E
Pilcher Park ♠ 278 41.32 N 88.01 W
Pilchuck ≃ 224 47.55 N 122.02 W
Pilchuck Creek ≃ 224 48.12 N 122.13 W
Pilcomayo ≃ 18 25.21 S 57.42 W
Pil'dozero 24 65.43 N 33.28 E
Piles Creek ≃ 276 40.37 N 74.12 W
Pilga 162 21.29 S 119.25 E
Pilger 198 42.00 N 97.03 W
Pilgrim Gardens 285 39.57 N 75.19 W
Pilgrim Memorial Monument ⊥ 207 42.04 N 70.12 W
Pilgrims Hatch 260 51.38 N 0.17 E
Pilgrim's Rest 156 24.55 S 30.44 E
Pil'gyn 180 69.18 N 179.08 W
Pili 116 13.33 N 123.16 E
Pīlībhīt 124 28.38 N 79.48 E
Pīlībhīt □^{5} 124 28.40 N 80.00 E
Pilica ≃ 30 51.52 N 21.17 E
Pilipinas → Philippines □^{1} 116 13.00 N 122.00 E
Pilis ⛰ 264c 47.37 N 18.59 E
Pilisborosjenő 264c 47.36 N 19.00 E
Pilkhua 124 28.43 N 77.39 E
Píllaro 246 1.10 S 78.32 W
Pillar Point ≻ 282 37.30 N 122.30 W
Pillar Point ≻^{1} 212 43.59 N 76.09 W
Pillau → Baltijsk 76 54.39 N 19.55 E
Pilley's Island 186 49.31 N 55.44 W
Pilliga 166 30.21 S 148.54 E
Pillings Pond ⊜ 283 42.32 N 71.02 W
Pillnitz ⊸^{8} 54 51.00 N 13.52 E
Pillon, Col du)(58 46.22 N 7.13 E
Pillow 208 40.38 N 76.48 W
Pillsbury Sound ⋃ 240m 18.20 N 64.49 W
Pil'na 80 55.33 N 45.55 E
Pilón ≃ 232 25.22 N 99.32 W
Pílos 38 36.55 N 21.43 E
Pilot Butte 184 50.28 N 104.25 W
Pilot Grove 194 38.53 N 92.55 W
Pilot Hill 226 38.50 N 121.02 W
Pilot Knob ∧, Ark., U.S. 194 35.42 N 93.57 W
Pilot Knob ∧, Idaho, U.S. 202 45.54 N 115.42 W
Pilot Mound 184 49.16 N 98.55 W
Pilot Mountain 192 36.23 N 80.28 W
Pilot Peak ∧, Nev., U.S. 204 41.02 N 114.06 W
Pilot Peak ∧, Nev., U.S. 204 38.21 N 117.58 W
Pilot Peak ∧, Wyo., U.S. 202 44.58 N 109.53 W
Pilot Point, Alaska, U.S. 180 57.34 N 157.35 W
Pilot Point, Tex., U.S. 196 33.24 N 96.58 W
Pilot Rock 202 45.29 N 118.50 W
Pilot Station 180 61.56 N 162.54 W
Pilpah Range ⛰ 166 20.23 S 138.34 E
Pilsen → Plzeň 60 49.45 N 13.23 E
Pilsensee ⊜ 60 48.01 N 11.11 E
Pilsum 52 53.29 N 7.04 E
Piltene 76 57.13 N 21.40 E
Piluchang 107 29.13 N 105.37 E
Pil'ugino 80 53.25 N 52.26 E
Pilusi 106 32.05 N 120.05 E
Pilzno 30 49.59 N 21.17 E
Pim ≃ 74 61.18 N 71.57 E
Pima 200 32.54 N 109.50 W
Pimah 110 15.36 N 107.25 E
Pimba 166 31.15 S 136.47 E
Pimelles 50 47.50 N 4.10 E
Pimenteira, Vereda ≃ 250 10.04 S 42.25 W
Pimenteiras 250 6.14 S 41.25 W
Pimentel, Bra. 250 3.43 S 45.30 W
Pimentel, Perú 248 6.50 S 79.57 W
Pimlico Race Course ♠ 284b 39.21 N 76.40 W
Pimmit Hills 284c 38.55 N 77.12 W
Pimmit Run ≃ 284c 38.55 N 77.07 W
Pimu-Lendo 152 1.46 N 20.54 E
Pimville 158 26.18 S 27.54 E
Pina, Cuba 240p 22.01 N 78.43 W
Pina, Esp. 34 41.29 N 0.32 W
Pina ≃ 78 52.07 N 26.04 E
Pinacanauan ≃ 116 17.37 N 121.44 E
Pinamalayan 116 13.02 N 121.29 E
Pinamungajan 116 10.16 N 123.35 E
Pinang → George Town 114 5.25 N 100.20 E
Pinang □^{3} 114 5.20 N 100.25 E
Pinang, Pulau ❙ 114 5.23 N 100.15 E
Pinangah 112 5.12 N 116.50 E
Pınar 130 37.02 N 27.57 E
Pınarbaşı, Tür. 130 38.44 N 36.24 E
Pınarbaşı, Tür. 130 41.36 N 33.07 E
Pinar del Río 240p 22.25 N 83.42 W
Pinar del Río □^{4} 240p 22.30 N 83.45 W
Pinardville 188 42.59 N 71.33 W
Pınarhisar 130 41.37 N 27.30 E
Pinas, Arg. 252 31.09 S 65.29 W
Piñas, Ec. 246 3.42 S 79.42 W
Piñas, Cerro ∧ 236 15.25 N 85.47 W
Pinatubo, Mount ∧ 116 15.08 N 120.21 E
Pinazo, Arroyo ≃ 288 34.24 S 58.48 W
Pincher Creek 182 49.29 N 113.57 W
Pinchi Lake ⊜ 182 54.35 N 124.20 W
Pinckney 216 42.27 N 83.57 W
Pinckney State Recreation Area ♠ 216 42.25 N 84.04 W
Pinckneyville 194 38.05 N 89.23 W
Pincourt 206 45.23 N 74.00 W
Pinčuga 86 58.23 N 96.59 E
Pińczów 30 50.32 N 20.35 E
Pindaíba, Ribeirão ≃ 255 14.18 S 51.45 W
Pindale 110 21.11 N 95.51 E
Pindamonhangaba 256 22.55 S 45.28 W
Pindar 162 28.29 S 115.48 E
Pindaré ≃ 250 3.17 S 44.47 W
Pind Dādan Khān 123 32.35 N 73.03 E
Pinde → Píndhos Óros ⛰ 38 39.49 N 21.14 E
Pinder Point ≻ 192 26.28 N 78.39 W
Píndhos Óros ⛰ 38 39.49 N 21.14 E
Pindi Bhattiān 123 31.54 N 73.16 E
Pindiga 146 9.59 N 10.54 E
Pindi Gheb 123 33.14 N 72.16 E
Pindo → Píndhos Óros ⛰ 38 39.49 N 21.14 E
Pindobaçu 250 10.44 S 40.21 W
Pindorama de Goiás 250 10.55 S 47.40 W
Pindoyacu ≃ 246 2.07 S 76.03 W
Pinduši 24 62.56 N 34.35 E
Pindus Mountains → Píndhos Óros ⛰ 38 39.49 N 21.14 E
Pindwāra 120 24.48 N 73.04 E
Pine ≃, Austl. 171a 27.17 S 153.04 E
Pine ≃, B.C., Can. 182 56.08 N 120.41 W
Pine ≃, Man., Can. 184 52.00 N 100.09 W
Pine ≃, Ont., Can. 212 44.20 N 79.52 W
Pine ≃, Mich., U.S. 190 43.35 N 84.08 W
Pine ≃, Mich., U.S. 190 44.15 N 85.55 W
Pine ≃, Mich., U.S. 190 46.03 N 84.40 W
Pine ≃, Mich., U.S. 190 44.26 N 83.21 W
Pine ≃, Mich., U.S. 214 42.49 N 82.29 W
Pine ≃, Wis., U.S. 190 45.50 N 88.08 W
Pine ≃, Wis., U.S. 190 43.12 N 90.18 W
Pine ≃, Wis., U.S. 190 44.08 N 88.54 W
Pine Apple 194 31.52 N 86.59 W
Pine Barrens ⊸^{1} 208 39.48 N 74.35 W
Pine Beach 206 45.32 N 73.57 W
Pine Bluff 194 34.13 N 92.01 W
Pine Bluffs 198 41.11 N 104.04 W
Pine Bluff Southeast 194 34.12 N 92.00 W
Pine Brook 276 40.52 N 74.20 W
Pine Brook ≃, U.S. 276 41.04 N 74.05 W
Pine Brook ≃, Mass., U.S. 283 42.00 N 70.47 W
Pine Brook ≃, N.J., U.S. 276 40.19 N 74.20 W
Pine Bush 210 41.37 N 74.18 W
Pine Castle 220 28.28 N 81.22 W
Pine City, Minn., U.S. 190 45.50 N 92.59 W
Pine City, N.Y., U.S. 210 42.02 N 76.52 W
Pinecliff Lake ⊜ 276 41.08 N 74.23 W
Pinecraft 220 27.19 N 82.30 W
Pine Creek 164 13.49 S 131.49 E
Pine Creek ≃, Alta., Can. 182 54.56 N 112.31 W
Pine Creek ≃, Calif., U.S. 282 37.58 N 122.02 W
Pine Creek ≃, Nev., U.S. 204 40.36 N 116.10 W
Pine Creek ≃, Pa., U.S. 210 41.10 N 77.16 W
Pine Creek ≃, Pa., U.S. 279b 40.30 N 79.57 W
Pine Creek ≃, Pa., U.S. 285 40.05 N 75.37 W
Pine Creek, West Branch ≃ 210 41.43 N 77.38 W
Pine Creek Indian Reserve ⊸^{4} 184 52.03 N 100.14 W
Pine Creek Point ≻ 276 41.07 N 73.16 W
Pine Crest, Fla., U.S. 220 28.01 N 82.32 W
Pinecrest, Va., U.S. 208 38.50 N 77.09 W
Pinecrest Lake ⊜ 226 38.12 N 119.58 W
Pine Crest Point ≻ 284a 42.52 N 79.11 W
Pinedale, Calif., U.S. 226 36.50 N 119.48 W
Pinedale, Wyo., U.S. 200 42.52 N 109.52 W
Pine Falls 184 50.35 N 96.15 W
Pine Flat Lake ⊜^{1} 226 36.52 N 119.18 W
Pinega 24 64.42 N 43.19 E
Pinega ≃ 24 64.08 N 41.54 E
Pine Glen 212 45.19 N 75.43 W
Pine Grove, Calif., U.S. 226 38.25 N 120.39 W
Pine Grove, Fla., U.S. 220 28.16 N 81.11 W
Pine Grove, N.J., U.S. 285 39.53 N 74.52 W
Pine Grove, Pa., U.S. 208 40.33 N 76.23 W
Pine Grove, W. Va., U.S. 188 39.34 N 80.41 W
Pine Grove Mills 214 40.44 N 77.53 W
Pine Hill, Austl. 166 23.39 S 146.58 E
Pine Hill, Ala., U.S. 194 31.59 N 87.35 W
Pine Hill, N.J., U.S. 208 39.47 N 74.59 W
Pine Hill, N.Y., U.S. 210 42.08 N 74.29 W
Pinehill, Tex., U.S. 222 32.06 N 94.36 W
Pine Hills 220 28.35 N 81.27 W
Pinehouse Lake 184 55.31 N 106.36 W
Pinehouse Lake ⊜ 184 55.32 N 106.35 W
Pinehurst, Ga., U.S. 192 32.12 N 83.46 W

Symbols in the index entries represent the broad categories identified in the key at the right. Symbols with superior numbers (⛰^{2}) identify subcategories (see complete key on page *I · 30*).

Kartensymbole in dem Registerverzeichnis stellen die rechts in Schlüssel erklärten Kategorien dar. Symbole mit hochgestellten Ziffern (⛰^{2}) bezeichnen Unterabteilungen einer Kategorie (vgl. vollständiger Schlüssel auf Seite *I · 30*).

Los símbolos incluídos en el texto del índice representan las grandes categorías identificadas con la clave a la derecha. Los símbolos con numeros en su parte superior (⛰^{2}) identifican las subcategorías (véase la clave completa en la página *I · 30*).

Les symboles de l'index représentent les catégories indiquées dans la légende à droite. Les symboles suivis d'un indice (⛰^{2}) représentent des sous-catégories (voir légende complète à la page *I · 30*).

Os símbolos incluídos no texto do índice representam as grandes categorias identificadas com a chave à direita. Os símbolos com números em sua parte superior (⛰^{2}) identificam as subcategorias (veja-se a chave completa à página *I · 30*).

	English	Deutsch	Español	Français	Português
∧	Mountain	Berg	Montaña	Montagne	Montanha
⛰	Mountains	Berge	Montañas	Montagnes	Montanhas
)(	Pass	Pass	Paso	Col	Passo
∨	Valley, Canyon	Tal, Cañon	Valle, Cañón	Vallée, Canyon	Vale, Canhão
≚	Plain	Ebene	Llano	Plaine	Planície
≻	Cape	Kap	Cabo	Cap	Cabo
❙	Island	Insel	Isla	Île	Ilha
❙❙	Islands	Inseln	Islas	Îles	Ilhas
⊥	Other Topographic Features	Andere Topographische Objekte	Otros Elementos Topográficos	Autres données topographiques	Outros Elementos Topográficos

ESPAÑOL — Nombre | Página | Lat.°′ | Long.°′ W=Oeste
FRANÇAIS — Nom | Page | Lat.°′ | Long.°′ W=Ouest
PORTUGUÊS — Nome | Página | Lat.°′ | Long.°′ W=Oeste

Pinehurst, Idaho, U.S. 202 47.32 N 116.14 W
Pinehurst, Mass., U.S. 207 42.32 N 71.14 W
Pinehurst, N.C., U.S. 192 35.12 N 79.28 W
Pinehurst, Tex., U.S. 222 30.10 N 95.41 W
Pinehurst Lake ⊜ 182 54.39 N 111.25 W
Pine Island, Minn., U.S. 190 44.12 N 92.38 W
Pine Island, N.Y., U.S. 210 41.18 N 74.28 W
Pine Island I 220 26.35 N 82.06 W
Pine Island Bay C 9 74.50 S 102.05 W
Pine Island Bayou ≃ 194 30.10 N 94.07 W
Pine Island Creek ≃ 283 42.47 N 70.48 W
Pine Island Dam ⟵[6] 214 40.08 N 80.43 W
Pine Island Sound Ⲩ 220 26.33 N 82.10 W
Pine Lake, Ind., U.S. 216 41.38 N 86.45 W
Pine Lake, Mass., U.S. 283 42.24 N 71.27 W
Pine Lake ⊜, Ont., Can. 212 44.57 N 79.27 W
Pine Lake ⊜, Mich., U.S. 281 42.35 N 83.20 W
Pine Lake ⊜, N.Y., U.S. 210 43.12 N 74.31 W
Pineland 194 31.15 N 93.58 W
Pine Lawn 219 38.42 N 90.18 W
Pinellas □[6] 220 27.53 N 82.43 W
Pinellas, Point ≻ 220 27.42 N 82.38 W
Pinellas Park 220 27.51 N 82.43 W
Pine Marsh ☷ 276 40.37 N 73.34 W
Pine Meadow Lake ⊜ 276 41.11 N 74.07 W
Pine Mountain ∧, U.S. 192 36.55 N 83.20 W
Pine Mountain ∧, Calif., U.S. 226 35.41 N 121.05 W
Pine Mountain ∧, Calif., U.S. 280 34.13 N 117.54 W
Pine Mountain ∧, Conn., U.S. 207 41.58 N 72.56 W
Pine Mountain ∧, Ga., U.S. 192 32.51 N 84.47 W
Pine Mountain ∧, Oreg., U.S. 202 43.47 N 120.54 W
Pine Mountain ∧, Wyo., U.S. 200 41.02 N 109.01 W
Pine Nut Mountains ∧∧ 226 39.00 N 119.25 W
Pine Orchard Meadows 284b 39.17 N 76.52 W
Pine Pass)(182 55.22 N 122.40 W
Pine Plains 210 41.59 N 73.40 W
Pine Point, Austl. 168b 34.34 S 137.52 E
Pine Point, N.W. Ter., Can. 176 61.01 N 114.15 W
Pine Point Park ♠ 275b 43.43 N 79.33 W
Pine Portage Dam ⟵[6] 190 49.18 N 88.19 W
Piner 218 38.50 N 84.32 W
Pine Rest 283 42.24 N 71.26 W
Pine Ridge, Pa., U.S. 285 39.55 N 75.22 W
Pine Ridge, S. Dak., U.S. 198 43.02 N 102.33 W
Pine Ridge, Va., U.S. 284c 38.52 N 77.14 W
Pine Ridge ∧ 198 42.40 N 103.00 W
Pine Ridge Estates 276 41.02 N 73.41 W
Pine Ridge Indian Reservation ⟵[4] 198 43.25 N 102.21 W
Pine River, Man., Can. 184 51.47 N 100.32 W
Pine River, Minn., U.S. 190 46.43 N 94.24 W
Piñero 258 34.32 S 58.45 W
Pinerolo 62 44.53 N 7.21 E
Piñeros, Isla I 240m 18.15 N 65.35 W
Pinerovka 80 51.34 N 43.04 E
Pine Run ≃ 279b 40.37 N 79.35 W
Pines ≃ 283 42.27 N 70.58 W
Pines, Isle of → Juventud, Isla de la I 240p 21.40 N 82.50 W
Pines, Lake o' the ⊜[1] 222 32.46 N 94.35 W
Pines, Point of ≻ 283 42.26 N 70.58 W
Pine Shores 220 27.17 N 82.32 W
Pines Lake ⊜ 276 41.00 N 74.16 W
Pines Run ≃ 285 39.50 N 75.05 W
Pine Swamp Knob ∧ 188 39.33 N 79.31 W
Pineto 66 42.36 N 14.04 E
Pinetop 200 34.08 N 109.56 W
Pinetops 192 35.46 N 77.38 W
Pinetown 158 29.52 S 30.46 E
Pine Tree Hill ∧ 114 3.43 N 101.42 E
Pine Valley 210 42.14 N 76.51 W
Pine Valley ∨ 204 38.25 N 113.40 W
Pine Village 216 40.27 N 87.15 W
Pineville, Ky., U.S. 192 36.46 N 83.42 W
Pineville, La., U.S. 194 31.19 N 92.26 W
Pineville, Mo., U.S. 194 36.36 N 94.23 W
Pineville, N.C., U.S. 192 35.05 N 80.53 W
Pineville, Pa., U.S. 208 40.18 N 75.00 W
Pineville, W. Va., U.S. 192 37.35 N 81.32 W
Pinewood, Fla., U.S. 220 25.53 N 80.14 W
Pinewood, S.C., U.S. 192 33.44 N 80.27 W
Piney 50 48.22 N 4.20 E
Piney ≃ 194 35.49 N 87.33 W
Piney Branch ≃ 284c 38.56 N 77.18 W
Piney Buttes ∧ 202 47.30 N 107.00 W
Piney Creek ≃, Tex., U.S. 222 31.03 N 94.34 W
Piney Creek ≃, Wyo., U.S. 202 44.34 N 106.32 W
Piney Fork 214 40.15 N 80.50 W
Piney Point 222 29.46 N 95.31 W
Piney Point ≻ 208 38.08 N 76.32 W
Piney Run ≃ 284c 38.58 N 77.17 W
Pinfold 262 53.36 N 2.55 W
Ping ≃ 110 15.42 N 100.09 E
Pinga 154 1.01 S 28.42 E
Ping'an, Zhg. 104 41.11 N 123.26 E
Ping'an, Zhg. 107 30.36 N 104.42 E
Ping'anbao 98 41.48 N 116.07 E
Ping'ancheng 105 40.03 N 117.48 E
Ping'andi 104 42.34 N 121.52 E
Ping'anzhen 89 45.20 N 123.42 E
Pingaring 162 32.45 S 118.37 E
Pingba, Zhg. 100 31.19 N 113.18 E
Pingba, Zhg. 102 26.22 N 106.09 E
Pingchang 102 31.35 N 107.03 E
Pingchaoshi 106 32.07 N 120.45 E
Ping Chau I 271d 22.17 N 114.02 E
Pingdeng 107 29.35 N 105.59 E
Pingding 98 37.48 N 113.37 E
Pingdingbao 104 42.22 N 123.35 E
Pingdingshan 98 41.26 N 124.45 E
Pingdu 98 36.47 N 119.54 E
Pingelap I[1] 14 6.13 N 160.42 E
Pingelly 162 32.32 S 117.05 E
Pingfang, Zhg. 100 30.07 N 113.48 E
Pingfang, Zhg. 104 42.27 N 120.38 E
Pingfang, Zhg. 104 42.14 N 120.38 E
Pingfang, Zhg. 104 41.17 N 120.40 E
Pingfang, Zhg. 104 41.28 N 120.48 E
Pingfang, Zhg. 271a 39.56 N 116.33 E
Pingfangdu 104 41.45 N 121.12 E
Pingfangzi 104 41.31 N 121.21 E
Pinggu 105 40.09 N 117.07 E
Pingguo 102 23.19 N 107.39 E
Pinghai, Zhg. 100 25.14 N 119.15 E
Pinghai, Zhg. 100 22.39 N 114.53 E
Pinghaiwan C 100 25.10 N 119.20 E
Pinghe, Zhg. 100 24.25 N 117.22 E
Pinghe, Zhg. 102 22.51 N 102.30 E
Pingheshui ≃ 100 24.25 N 116.36 E
P'inghsiang → Pingxiang 102 22.09 N 106.43 E
Pinghu, Zhg. 100 30.56 N 115.22 E
Pinghu, Zhg. 100 22.42 N 114.08 E
Pinghu, Zhg. 100 26.46 N 118.48 E
Pinghu, Zhg. 106 30.42 N 121.01 E
Pingjiang 100 28.44 N 113.34 E
Pingjiang ≃ 100 25.59 N 115.07 E
Pingjing 105 39.20 N 116.06 E
Pinglan 100 22.22 N 113.27 E
Pingle, Zhg. 102 24.37 N 110.40 E
Pingle, Zhg. 102 24.31 N 106.59 E
Pingli 102 32.19 N 109.21 E
Pingliang 102 35.27 N 107.10 E
Pinglidian 98 37.17 N 119.59 E
Pingling 100 23.39 N 114.23 E
Pinglucheng 102 39.50 N 112.19 E
Pingluo 102 38.57 N 106.35 E
Pingluopu 104 41.56 N 123.20 E
Pingnan, Zhg. 100 26.56 N 119.02 E
Pingnan, Zhg. 102 23.30 N 110.30 E
Pingqiao 100 33.24 N 119.13 E
Pingquan 98 40.59 N 118.34 E
Pingrup 162 33.32 S 118.31 E
Ping Shan, H.K. 271d 22.27 N 114.00 E
Pingshan, Zhg. 100 22.43 N 114.22 E
Pingshan, Zhg. 100 23.26 N 113.15 E
Pingshan, Zhg. 100 22.59 N 114.43 E
Pingshan, Zhg. 100 25.36 N 117.52 E
Pingshan, Zhg. 102 38.15 N 114.10 E
Pingshang 98 35.11 N 119.07 E
Pingshi, Zhg. 100 32.32 N 113.03 E
Pingshi, Zhg. 100 25.20 N 113.02 E
Pingshui 100 29.53 N 120.38 E
Pingtaizi 105 40.44 N 116.25 E
Pingtan, Zhg. 100 23.04 N 114.38 E
Pingtan, Zhg. 100 25.31 N 119.47 E
Pingtan, Zhg. 107 29.38 N 105.16 E
Pingtanchang 107 30.29 N 106.12 E
Pingtang 102 25.55 N 107.15 E
Pingtian 100 25.19 N 113.31 E
Pingtoushan I 100 27.59 N 121.11 E
P'ingtung 100 22.40 N 120.29 E
Pingües, Cayos II 240p 20.47 N 78.15 W
Pingüicas, Cerro ∧ 234 21.10 N 99.42 W
Pingwang 106 30.59 N 120.38 E
Pingwu 102 32.29 N 104.37 E
Pingxiang, Zhg. 100 27.38 N 113.50 E
Pingxiang, Zhg. 102 22.09 N 106.43 E
Pingyang, Zhg. 89 48.13 N 124.23 E
Pingyang, Zhg. 100 27.41 N 120.33 E
Pingyao, Zhg. 102 37.16 N 112.09 E
Pingyao, Zhg. 106 30.24 N 119.58 E
Pingyi 98 35.34 N 117.37 E
Pingyin 98 36.19 N 116.22 E
Pingyu 100 32.57 N 114.41 E
Pingyuan, Zhg. 98 37.11 N 116.25 E
Pingyuan, Zhg. 100 24.36 N 115.54 E
Pingzhai 102 24.07 N 104.22 E
Pingzhuang 98 42.03 N 119.22 E
Pinhal 256 22.12 S 46.45 W
Pinhal, Ribeirão do ≃ 256 22.42 S 46.42 W
Pinhal Novo 34 38.38 N 8.55 W
Pinhalzinho 256 22.46 S 46.36 W
Pinhão 250 10.34 S 37.44 W
Pinheiral 256 22.31 S 43.59 W
Pinheirinhos 256 22.26 S 44.59 W
Pinheiro 250 2.31 S 45.05 W
Pinheiro de Loures 266c 38.50 N 9.12 W
Pinheiro Machado 252 31.34 S 53.23 W
Pinheiros 256 22.32 S 44.54 W
Pinheiros ≃ 287b 23.32 S 46.44 W
Pinhel 34 40.46 N 7.04 W
Pinhoe 42 50.44 N 3.27 W
Pinhuã ≃ 248 6.21 S 65.00 W
Pini, Pulau I 110 0.08 N 98.40 E
Pinillos 246 8.55 N 74.28 W
Piniós ≃ 38 39.54 N 22.45 E
Pinitos, Sierra de ∧∧ 200 31.08 N 110.50 W
Pinjar, Lake ⊜ 168a 31.38 S 115.49 E
Pinjarra 168a 32.37 S 115.53 E
Pinjor Garden ♠ 123 30.47 N 76.47 E
Pinka ≃ 61 47.00 N 16.35 E
Pinkafeld 61 47.22 N 16.07 E
Pinkiang → Haerbin 89 45.45 N 126.41 E
Pinlaung 110 20.08 N 96.47 E
Pinlebu 110 24.05 N 95.21 E
Pinn ≃ 260 51.31 N 0.29 W
Pinnacle ∧, N.Z. 172 41.49 S 173.17 E
Pinnacle ∧, N.Y., U.S. 188 43.13 N 74.23 W
Pinnacle Buttes ∧ 202 43.44 N 109.57 W
Pinnacle Island I 180 60.12 N 172.46 W
Pinnacle Peak ∧ 224 46.45 N 121.43 W
Pinnacles National Monument ♠ 226 36.28 N 121.19 W
Pinnaroo 166 35.16 S 140.55 E
Pinneberg 52 53.40 N 9.47 E
Pinner ⟵[8] 260 51.36 N 0.23 W
Pino, Sierra del ∧∧ 196 28.15 N 103.03 W
Pin Oak Creek ≃ 222 31.57 N 96.28 W
Pinocchio 66 43.35 N 13.30 E
Pinochle Peak ∧ 224 45.43 N 123.36 W
Pinole 226 38.00 N 122.17 W
Pinole Creek ≃ 282 38.01 N 122.18 W
Pinole Point ≻ 282 38.01 N 122.22 W
Pinole Ridge ∧ 282 37.59 N 122.15 W
Pinos 234 22.18 N 101.34 W
Pinos, Mount ∧ 228 34.50 N 119.09 W
Pinos, Point ≻ 226 36.38 N 121.56 W
Pinos-Puente 34 37.15 N 3.45 W
Pinotepa de Don Luis 234 16.25 N 97.55 W
Pinotepa Nacional 234 16.19 N 98.01 W
Pinrang 112 3.48 S 119.38 E
Pins, Île de → Juventud, Isla de la I 240p 21.40 N 82.50 W
Pins, Île des I 175f 22.37 S 167.30 E
Pins, Pointe aux ≻ 214 42.15 N 81.51 W
Pins, Rivière des ≃ 206 46.01 N 72.03 W
Pinsk 78 52.07 N 26.04 E
Pinson 194 33.41 N 86.41 W
Pinsot 62 45.21 N 6.06 E
Pinta, Isla I 246a 0.35 N 90.44 W
Pintada Arroyo ∨ 196 34.53 N 104.39 W
Pintado 258 33.50 S 56.18 W
Pintado ≃ 255 13.33 S 50.16 W
Pintado, Arroyo de ≃ 258 34.08 S 56.14 W
Pintado, Cuchilla del ∧∧[2] 258 34.12 S 56.25 W
Pintados 248 20.37 S 69.38 W
Pintasan 112 5.26 N 117.43 E
Pinteus 266c 38.52 N 9.09 W
Pintlalla Creek ≃ 194 32.21 N 86.30 W
Pinto 252 29.09 S 62.39 W
Pinto Butte ∧ 184 49.22 N 107.25 W
Pinto Creek ≃, Alta., Can. 182 53.51 N 117.35 W
Pinto Creek ≃, Sask., Can. 184 49.40 N 106.42 W
Pintos, Arroyo de ≃ 258 33.55 S 56.51 W
Pintos Negreiros 256 22.18 S 45.13 W
Pintoyacu ≃ 246 3.35 S 73.55 W
Pinturas ≃ 254 46.35 S 70.18 W
Pintuyan 116 9.57 N 125.15 E
Pin'ug 24 60.15 N 47.48 E
Pinukpuk 116 17.35 N 121.22 E
Pinwherry 44 55.09 N 4.50 W
Pinxton 42 53.06 N 1.19 W
Pinzano al Tagliamento 64 46.11 N 12.57 E
Pinzgau ∨ 64 47.15 N 12.40 E
Pinzón, Isla I 246a 0.36 S 90.40 W
Piobbico 66 43.35 N 12.31 E
Pioche 204 37.56 N 114.27 W
Pio IX 250 6.50 S 40.37 W
Piolenc 62 44.11 N 4.46 E
Piombino 66 42.55 N 10.32 E
Piombino, Canale di Ⲩ 66 42.53 N 10.30 E
Pioneer, Austl. 162 31.48 S 121.43 E
Pioneer, Calif., U.S. 226 38.25 N 120.33 W
Pioneer, Ohio, U.S. 216 41.41 N 84.33 W
Pioneer Mine 182 50.46 N 122.46 W
Pioneer Mountains ∧∧ 202 45.40 N 113.00 W
Pioneer Park ♠ 273d 26.10 S 28.04 E
Pioner, Ostrov I 74 79.50 N 92.30 E
Pionerskij [Neukuhren] 76 54.57 N 20.20 E
Pionierbivak 164 2.16 S 138.02 E
Pionki 30 51.30 N 21.27 E
Pio Pico State Historical Park ♠ 280 33.59 N 118.04 W
Piopio 172 38.28 S 175.01 E
Pioppo 70 38.03 N 13.14 E
Piora, Mount ∧ 164 6.45 S 146.00 E
Pioraco 66 43.11 N 12.59 E
Piorini ≃ 246 3.23 S 63.30 W
Piorini, Lago ⊜ 246 3.34 S 63.15 W
Piotrków Trybunalski 30 51.25 N 19.42 E
Piotta 58 46.31 N 8.40 E
Pio V. Corpus (Limbujan) 116 11.53 N 124.03 E
Piove di Sacco 64 45.18 N 12.02 E
Piovene-Rocchette 64 45.45 N 11.25 E
Pio XII 250 3.53 S 45.17 W
Pipa 107 29.07 N 105.05 E
Pipalkoti 124 30.26 N 79.27 E
Pīpār 120 26.23 N 73.32 E
Piparia 124 22.45 N 78.21 E
Pīpar Road 120 26.27 N 73.27 E
Pipas 152 14.56 S 12.12 E
Pipe Creek ≃, Ind., U.S. 194 40.08 N 85.52 W
Pipe Creek ≃, Ind., U.S. 216 40.45 N 86.13 W
Pipe Creek ≃, Ind., U.S. 218 39.26 N 85.06 W
Piper City 216 40.45 N 88.11 W
Pipe Spring National Monument ♠ 200 36.43 N 112.33 W
Pipestem Creek ≃ 198 46.54 N 98.43 W
Pipestone 198 43.58 N 96.19 W
Pipestone ≃ 176 52.53 N 89.23 W
Pipestone Creek ≃, Can. 184 49.42 N 100.45 W
Pipestone Creek ≃, Mich., U.S. 216 42.04 N 86.24 W
Pipestone National Monument ♠ 198 44.00 N 96.18 W
Pipi ≃ 146 7.27 N 22.48 E
Pipinas 258 35.32 S 57.20 W
Piping Brook ≃ 276 41.08 N 73.37 W
Pipiriki 172 39.29 S 175.03 E
Piplān 123 32.17 N 71.21 E
Piplūn 126 23.21 N 88.07 E
Pipmouacane, Réservoir ⊜[1] 186 49.35 N 70.30 W
Pipri 124 23.58 N 82.40 E
Pipriac 28 47.49 N 1.57 W
Piqiang 85 40.20 N 77.38 E
Piqiao 106 31.34 N 119.27 E
Piqua 218 40.09 N 84.15 W
Piquet Carneiro 250 5.48 S 39.25 W
Piquete 256 22.36 S 45.11 W
Piquete, Ribeirão ≃ 256 22.36 S 45.01 W
Piquiri ≃ 252 24.03 S 54.14 W
Pira 150 8.30 N 1.44 E
Piracaia 256 23.03 S 46.21 W
Piracanjuba 255 17.18 S 49.01 W
Piracanjuba ≃, Bra. 255 17.18 S 48.13 W
Piracanjuba ≃, Bra. 255 18.14 S 48.48 W
Piracão ≃ 287a 23.02 S 43.36 W
Piracicaba 255 22.43 S 47.38 W
Piracicaba ≃ 255 22.36 S 48.19 W
Piracuruca 250 3.56 S 41.42 W
Piraeus → Piraiévs 38 37.57 N 23.38 E
Pirahmet 130 38.11 N 39.51 E
Piraí 256 22.38 S 43.54 W
Piraí ≃ 256 22.28 S 43.50 W
Piraí do Sul 252 24.31 S 49.56 W
Piraiévs (Piraeus) 38 / 267c 37.57 N 23.38 E
Piraino 70 38.10 N 14.52 E
Piraju 255 23.12 S 49.23 W
Pirajuba 255 19.54 S 48.42 W
Pirajucara, Ribeirão ≃ 287b 23.34 S 46.43 W
Pirajuí 255 21.59 S 49.29 W
Pirakata 126 22.34 N 87.11 E
Piramida, Gora ∧ 88 54.15 N 95.45 E
Piramidal'nyj, Pik ∧ 85 39.34 N 69.57 E
Pirámide de Cuicuilco ⊥ 286a 19.18 N 99.11 W
Pirámide de Santa Cecilia ⊥ 286a 19.35 N 99.11 W
Pirámide de Tenayuca ⊥ 286a 19.32 N 99.11 W
Pirámide Xochicalco ⊥ 234 18.48 N 99.19 W
Piram Island I 120 21.36 N 72.41 E
Piran, Jugo. 36 45.32 N 13.34 E
Piran, Tür. 130 38.22 N 40.04 E
Piraña, Arroyo ≃ 288 34.24 S 58.30 W
Pirané 252 25.43 S 59.06 W
Piranga 255 20.41 S 43.18 W
Pirangaí 256 22.34 S 44.37 W
Piranguinho 256 22.24 S 45.32 W
Piranha ≃ 250 5.56 S 48.15 W
Piranhas, Bra. 250 9.27 S 37.46 W
Piranhas, Bra. 255 16.31 S 51.51 W
Piranhas ≃, Bra. 250 5.15 S 36.45 W
Piranhas ≃, Bra. 250 8.40 S 49.28 W
Piranji ≃ 250 4.23 S 37.48 W
Pīrān Shahr 128 36.41 N 45.08 E
Pirapemas 250 3.43 S 44.14 W
Pirapetinga 256 21.54 S 43.40 W
Pirapetinga ≃ 256 21.37 S 42.32 W
Pirapetinga, Ribeirão ≃ 256 21.49 S 43.36 W
Pirapó ≃ 255 22.30 S 52.01 W
Pirapora 255 17.21 S 44.56 W
Pirapora do Bom Jesus □[7] 287b 23.24 S 46.56 W
Piraputanga 255 20.26 S 55.32 W
Piraquara 252 25.26 S 49.04 W
Piraquê ≃ 287a 23.01 S 43.37 W
Pirarajá 252 33.44 S 54.45 W
Piraras, Cachoeira de ⌊ 255 14.02 S 53.25 W
Pirassununga 255 21.59 S 47.25 W
Pirata, Monte ∧[2] 240m 18.06 N 65.33 W
Pirate Creek ≃ 282 37.33 N 121.52 W
Pir'atin 78 50.15 N 32.30 E
Piratinga ≃ 255 15.41 S 46.07 W
Piratini 252 31.27 S 53.06 W
Piratini ≃ 252 28.06 S 55.27 W
Piratininga 287a 22.57 S 43.04 W
Piratininga, Lagoa de C 256 22.57 S 43.05 W
Piratuba 252 27.27 S 51.48 W
Piratuba, Lago C 250 1.37 N 50.10 W
Piratucu ≃ 250 1.59 S 56.58 W
Piraúba 256 21.17 S 43.02 W
Piraube, Lac ⊜ 186 50.33 N 71.42 W
Piray ≃ 248 16.32 S 63.45 W
Pirbright 260 51.18 N 0.39 W
Pirdop 38 42.42 N 24.11 E
Pirenópolis 255 15.51 S 48.57 W
Pires, Ribeirão ≃ 287b 23.43 S 46.25 W
Pires do Rio 255 17.18 S 48.17 W
Pírgos 38 37.41 N 21.28 E
Piriá 250 1.40 S 50.02 W
Piriápolis 252 34.54 S 55.17 W
Piribebuy 252 25.29 S 57.03 W
Pirin ∧∧ 38 41.40 N 23.30 E
Pirinççiköy 267b 41.10 N 28.50 E
Pirineos → Pyrenees ∧∧ 34 42.40 N 1.00 E
Piripiri 250 4.16 S 41.47 W
Piritiba 250 11.44 S 40.34 W
Píritu, Ven. 246 11.22 N 69.08 W
Píritu, Ven. 246 9.23 N 69.12 W
Pirituba ⟵[8] 287b 23.29 S 46.43 W
Pīr Jo Goth 120 27.36 N 68.37 E
Pirk 54 50.25 N 12.04 E
Pirlerkondu 130 36.55 N 32.31 E
Pīr Mahal 123 30.46 N 72.26 E
Pirmasens 56 49.12 N 7.36 E
Pirna 54 50.58 N 13.56 E
Piroči 82 55.04 N 38.57 E
Pirogovka 78 51.54 N 33.18 E
Pirogovskij 265b 55.59 N 37.44 E
Pirogovskoje Vodochranilišče ⊜[1] 82 55.58 N 37.40 E
Pirojpur 126 22.34 N 89.59 E
Pirón ≃ 34 41.23 N 4.31 W
Pirongia 172 38.00 S 175.12 E
Pirot 38 43.09 N 22.35 E
Pirovano 252 36.30 S 61.34 W
Pirovskoje 86 57.37 N 92.16 E
Pirpirituba 250 6.46 S 35.30 W
Pirraşit Dağı ∧ 84 38.56 N 43.51 E
Pirris ≃ 236 9.29 N 84.19 W
Pirsagat 84 39.54 N 49.24 E
Pirsagat ≃ 84 39.53 N 49.19 E
Pirtleville 200 31.22 N 109.34 W
Piru, Indon. 164 3.04 S 128.12 E
Piru, Calif., U.S. 228 34.25 N 118.48 W
Piru, Lake ⊜[1] 228 34.30 N 118.45 W
Piru Creek ≃ 228 34.23 N 118.47 W
Pisa 66 43.43 N 10.23 E
Pisa □[4] 66 43.25 N 10.43 E
Pisa ∧[2] 26 63.13 N 28.18 E
Pisa ≃ 30 53.15 N 21.52 E
Pisa, Certosa di ⛊[1] 66 43.45 N 10.31 E
Pisa, Mount ∧ 172 44.52 S 169.11 E
Pisac ⊥ 248 13.25 S 71.53 W
Pisagua 248 19.36 S 70.13 W
Pisam-bong ∧ 98 40.41 N 126.34 E
Pisang, Pulau I 164 1.23 S 128.55 E
Pisarevka 78 49.53 N 40.12 E
Pisarve 272c 19.06 N 73.05 E
Pisau, Tanjong ≻ 112 6.04 N 118.03 E
Piščalje 80 58.14 N 48.42 E
Piscasaw Creek ≃ 216 42.16 N 88.49 W
Piscataway 210 40.34 N 74.27 W
Piscataway Creek ≃, Md., U.S. 208 38.42 N 77.02 W
Piscataway Creek ≃, Va., U.S. 208 37.54 N 76.50 W
Pişchia 38 45.55 N 21.20 E
Pisciotta 68 40.06 N 15.14 E
Pisco 248 13.42 S 76.13 W
Pisco ≃ 248 13.42 S 76.15 W
Pişcolt 38 47.35 N 22.18 E
Piscovo 80 57.11 N 40.32 E
Piseco Lake ⊜ 210 43.23 N 74.36 W
Písek 30 49.19 N 14.10 E
Pisgah 218 39.19 N 84.22 W
Pishan 120 37.37 N 78.18 E
Pishan I 100 28.06 N 121.30 E
Pishīn 120 30.35 N 67.00 E
Pishīn Lora (Lowrah) ≃ 120 29.09 N 64.55 E
Pisinemo 200 32.02 N 112.19 W
Pising 112 5.05 S 121.54 E
Pis'mennoje 78 48.13 N 35.48 E
Pismo Beach 226 35.09 N 120.38 W
Pišnur 80 57.47 N 47.58 E
Piso, Lake ⊜ 150 6.48 N 11.17 W
Pisogne 64 45.48 N 10.06 E
Pisqui ≃ 248 7.45 S 75.01 W
Pissila 150 13.10 N 0.49 W
Pissos 32 44.19 N 0.47 W
Pistakee 216 42.25 N 88.11 W
Pistakee Lake ⊜ 216 42.23 N 88.12 W
Pisticci 68 40.23 N 16.34 E
Pistoia 66 43.55 N 10.54 E
Pistoia □[4] 64 43.58 N 10.50 E
Pistolet Bay C 186 51.32 N 55.50 W
Pistuk Peak ∧ 180 59.43 N 159.42 W
Pisuerga ≃ 34 41.33 N 4.52 W
Pisz 30 53.38 N 21.49 E
Pit ≃ 204 40.45 N 122.22 W
Pit, North Fork ≃ 204 41.28 N 120.33 W
Pit, South Fork ≃ 204 41.28 N 120.33 W
Pita 150 11.05 N 12.24 W
Pita □[4] 150 11.00 N 12.45 W
Pital 246 2.16 N 75.49 W
Pitalito 246 1.51 N 76.02 W
Pitampura Kālan ⟵[8] 272a 28.42 N 77.08 E
Pitanga 252 24.46 S 51.44 W
Pitangueiras 255 21.02 S 48.13 W
Pitangueiras, Ribeirão das ≃ 256 21.27 S 44.27 W
Pitangui 255 19.40 S 44.54 W
Pitcairn 279b 40.24 N 79.47 W
Pitcairn □[2] 6 / 174e 25.04 S 130.05 W
Pitcairn Island I 6 25.04 S 130.06 W
Pitcher 210 42.35 N 75.52 W
Pitch Place 260 51.16 N 0.36 W
Piteå 26 65.20 N 21.30 E
Piteälven ≃ 24 65.14 N 21.32 E
Piteglio 66 44.01 N 10.46 E
Pitelino 80 54.34 N 41.49 E
Piterka 80 50.42 N 47.27 E
Piteşti 38 44.52 N 24.52 E
Pithāpuram 122 17.07 N 82.16 E
Pithara 162 30.24 S 116.40 E
Pithiviers 50 48.10 N 2.15 E
Pithoragarh 124 29.35 N 80.13 E
Pithoragarh □[5] 124 30.10 N 80.30 E
Piti 174p 13.28 N 144.41 E
Piti, Lagoa ⊜ 158 26.34 S 32.53 E
Pitigliano 66 42.38 N 11.40 E
Pitillal del Norte 234 20.40 N 105.01 W
Pitim 80 53.12 N 42.21 E
Pitiquito 232 30.42 N 112.02 W
Pitk'aranta 24 61.34 N 31.27 E
Pitkas Point 180 62.02 N 163.17 W
Pitlochry 46 56.43 N 3.45 W
Pitman 208 39.44 N 75.08 W
Pitman Airport ⊠ 285 39.45 N 75.08 W
Pitner Ditch ⌶ 216 41.14 N 86.53 W
Pitogo 116 10.08 N 124.33 E
Pitomača 36 45.57 N 17.14 E
Pitou, Zhg. 100 25.01 N 114.35 E
Pitou, Zhg. 100 23.34 N 116.05 E
Pitou, Zhg. 100 24.26 N 114.22 E
Pitrufquén 254 38.59 S 72.39 W
Pitsani 156 25.30 S 25.35 E
Pitschen → Byczyna 30 51.07 N 18.11 E
Pitsea 260 51.34 N 0.31 E
Pitseng 158 28.58 S 28.16 E
Pitsford Reservoir ⊜[1] 42 52.20 N 0.52 W
Pitt ≃ 224 49.12 N 122.47 W
Pitt, Mount ∧ 174c 29.01 S 167.56 E
Pittem 50 51.00 N 3.16 E
Pitten ≃ 61 47.44 N 16.14 E
Pittenweem 46 56.12 N 2.44 W
Pitti Island I 122 10.50 N 72.38 E
Pitt Island I 182 53.35 N 129.45 W
Pitt Lake ⊜ 182 49.25 N 122.32 W
Pittsboro, Ind., U.S. 218 39.52 N 86.28 W
Pittsboro, Miss., U.S. 194 33.56 N 89.20 W
Pittsboro, N.C., U.S. 192 35.43 N 79.11 W
Pittsburg, Calif., U.S. 226 38.02 N 121.53 W
Pittsburg, Kans., U.S. 198 37.25 N 94.42 W
Pittsburg, N.H., U.S. 206 45.03 N 71.21 W
Pittsburg, Tex., U.S. 222 32.60 N 94.58 W
Pittsburgh, Pa., U.S. 214 / 279b 40.26 N 80.00 W
Pittsburgh, University of ⛊[2] 279b 40.27 N 79.58 W
Pittsburgh-Monroeville Airport ⊠ 279b 40.27 N 79.46 W
Pittsfield, Ill., U.S. 219 39.36 N 90.48 W
Pittsfield, Maine, U.S. 188 44.47 N 69.23 W
Pittsfield, Mass., U.S. 207 42.27 N 73.15 W
Pittsfield, N.H., U.S. 188 43.18 N 71.19 W
Pittsfield, Pa., U.S. 214 41.50 N 79.23 W
Pittsford, Mich., U.S. 216 41.52 N 84.28 W
Pittsford, N.Y., U.S. 210 43.05 N 77.31 W
Pitt Stadium ♠ 279b 40.27 N 79.58 W
Pittston 210 41.19 N 75.47 W
Pittsview 194 32.11 N 85.10 W
Pittsville 208 38.24 N 75.52 W
Pittsworth 166 27.43 S 151.38 E
Pituil 252 28.34 S 67.27 W
Pitumarca 248 13.59 S 71.25 W
Pituri Creek ≃ 166 22.58 S 138.50 E
Pitz Bach ≃ 64 47.13 N 10.46 E
Pitztal ∨ 58 47.07 N 10.47 E
Pium 250 10.27 S 49.11 W
Pium ≃ 250 10.12 S 49.57 W
Piumafua ∧ 174y 14.10 S 169.39 W
Piura 248 5.12 S 80.38 W
Piura □[5] 248 5.10 S 80.00 W
Piura ≃ 248 5.32 S 80.53 W
Piute Peak ∧ 204 35.27 N 118.24 W
Piute Reservoir ⊜[1] 200 38.17 N 112.12 W
Piuthān 124 28.06 N 82.54 E
Piva ≃ 38 43.21 N 18.51 E
Pivan' 89 50.29 N 137.06 E
Piverone 62 45.27 N 8.00 E
Pivijay 246 10.28 N 74.37 W
Piwniczna 30 49.27 N 20.42 E
Pixian 102 30.49 N 103.49 E
Pixley 226 35.58 N 119.17 W
Piyadin 130 37.01 N 29.58 E
Pižanka 80 57.28 N 48.33 E
Pizarro 246 4.58 N 77.22 W
Pižma 80 57.52 N 47.06 E
Pižma ≃ 80 57.37 N 48.58 E
Pizzighettone 62 45.11 N 9.47 E
Pizzillo, Monte ∧ 70 37.48 N 15.01 E
Pizzo 68 38.44 N 16.10 E
Pizzoferrato 66 41.55 N 14.14 E
Pizzoli 66 42.26 N 13.18 E
Pizzone 66 41.40 N 14.02 E
Pjalka 24 66.43 N 40.59 E
Pjana ≃ 80 55.40 N 45.57 E
Pjöngjang → P'yŏngyang 98 39.01 N 125.45 E
Placanica 68 38.25 N 16.27 E
Place Bonaventure ⟵[9] 275a 45.30 N 73.34 W
Placentia, Newf., Can. 186 47.14 N 53.58 W
Placentia, Calif., U.S. 228 33.52 N 117.46 W
Placentia Bay C 186 47.15 N 54.30 W
Placer, Pil. 116 11.52 N 123.55 E
Placer, Pil. 116 9.39 N 125.36 E
Placer □[6] 226 38.54 N 121.04 W
Placeres de Picacho 234 23.11 N 105.42 W
Placerville 226 38.43 N 120.48 W
Placetas 240p 22.19 N 79.40 W
Place Versailles ⟵[9] 275a 45.35 N 73.32 W
Plachino 76 54.28 N 39.20 E
Plachtejevka 78 46.07 N 29.43 E
Placid, Lake ⊜ 220 27.14 N 81.22 W
Placida 220 26.50 N 82.16 W
Plácido de Castro 248 10.20 S 67.11 W
Plácido Rosas 252 32.45 S 53.44 W
Plačkovica ∧∧ 38 41.45 N 22.35 E
Plaffeien 58 46.44 N 7.17 E
Plages, Lac des ⊜ 206 45.59 N 74.54 W
Plage-Sainte-Cécile 50 50.34 N 1.35 E
Plailly 261 49.06 N 2.35 E
Plai Mat ≃ 110 15.22 N 102.45 E
Plain 224 47.46 N 120.39 W
Plain City, Ohio, U.S. 214 40.06 N 83.16 W
Plain City, Utah, U.S. 200 41.18 N 112.06 W
Plain Dealing 194 32.54 N 93.42 W
Plaines, Île aux I 275a 45.21 N 73.50 W
Plainfield, Conn., U.S. 207 41.41 N 71.55 W
Plainfield, Ill., U.S. 216 41.37 N 88.12 W
Plainfield, Ind., U.S. 218 39.42 N 86.24 W
Plainfield, Mass., U.S. 207 42.31 N 72.55 W
Plainfield, N.J., U.S. 210 40.37 N 74.26 W
Plainfield, Ohio, U.S. 214 40.13 N 81.43 W
Plainfield, Pa., U.S. 208 40.12 N 77.17 W
Plainfield, Wis., U.S. 190 44.13 N 89.30 W
Plainfield Heights 216 43.01 N 85.37 W
Plains, Ga., U.S. 192 32.02 N 84.24 W
Plains, Kans., U.S. 198 37.16 N 100.35 W
Plains, Mont., U.S. 202 47.27 N 114.53 W
Plains, Tex., U.S. 196 33.11 N 102.50 W
Plainsboro 208 40.20 N 74.36 W
Plainview, Ark., U.S. 194 34.60 N 93.18 W
Plainview, Calif., U.S. 226 36.08 N 119.08 W
Plainview, Ill., U.S. 219 39.10 N 89.59 W
Plainview, Minn., U.S. 190 44.10 N 92.10 W
Plainview, Nebr., U.S. 198 42.21 N 97.47 W
Plainview, N.Y., U.S. 210 40.46 N 73.28 W
Plainview, Tex., U.S. 196 34.11 N 101.43 W
Plainville, Conn., U.S. 207 41.41 N 72.51 W
Plainville, Ill., U.S. 219 39.47 N 91.11 W
Plainville, Ind., U.S. 194 38.48 N 87.09 W
Plainville, Kans., U.S. 198 39.14 N 99.18 W
Plainville, Mass., U.S. 207 42.00 N 71.20 W
Plainville, N.Y., U.S. 210 43.10 N 76.27 W
Plainwell 216 42.27 N 85.38 W
Plaisance, Baie de C 186 47.18 N 61.53 W
Plaisir 261 48.49 N 1.57 E
Plaistow 188 42.50 N 71.06 W
Plaksino 76 56.11 N 30.42 E
Plamondon 182 54.51 N 112.19 W
Plampang 115b 8.48 S 117.48 E
Planá 60 49.52 N 12.44 E
Plana, Isla I 34 38.10 N 0.28 W
Planada 226 37.18 N 120.19 W
Planalto, Bra. 252 27.20 S 53.03 W
Planalto, Bra. 255 14.39 S 40.29 W
Planches 50 48.42 N 0.22 E
Plandome 276 40.48 N 73.42 W
Plandome Heights 276 40.48 N 73.42 W
Plandome Manor 276 40.49 N 73.42 W
Plan-d'Orgon 62 43.48 N 5.00 E
Plane ≃ 54 52.23 N 12.30 E
Planegg 60 48.06 N 11.25 E
Planerskoje 78 44.57 N 35.14 E
Planeta Rica 246 8.25 N 75.36 W
Plangeross 58 46.59 N 10.52 E
Plánice 60 49.24 N 13.29 E
Plankenfels 60 49.53 N 11.20 E
Plankinton 198 43.43 N 98.29 W
Plano, Ill., U.S. 216 41.40 N 88.32 W
Plano, Tex., U.S. 222 33.01 N 96.42 W
Plansee ⊜ 64 47.28 N 10.48 E
Planta de Evaporación ⛊[3] 286a 19.35 N 99.00 W
Plantagenet 206 45.32 N 75.00 W
Plantation, Fla., U.S. 220 26.05 N 80.14 W
Plantation, Fla., U.S. 220 24.59 N 80.33 W
Plantation, Ky., U.S. 218 38.17 N 85.36 W
Plantation Key I 220 24.58 N 80.33 W
Plant City 220 28.01 N 82.08 W
Plantersville, Ala., U.S. 194 32.40 N 86.55 W
Plantersville, Miss., U.S. 194 34.12 N 88.40 W
Plantersville, Tex., U.S. 222 30.20 N 95.52 W
Planting Fields Arboretum ♠ 276 40.52 N 73.33 W
Plantsite 200 33.02 N 109.21 W
Plantsville 207 41.35 N 72.54 W
Plaquemine 194 30.17 N 91.14 W
Plaridel, Pil. 116 10.32 N 124.46 E
Plaridel, Pil. 116 8.37 N 123.43 E
Plasencia 34 40.02 N 6.05 W
Plaški 36 45.05 N 15.22 E
Plassenburg ⊥ 60 50.06 N 11.28 E
Plassey 126 23.47 N 88.15 E
Plast 86 54.22 N 60.50 E
Plaster Rock 186 46.54 N 67.24 W
Plastovo 82 54.17 N 37.03 E
Plastun 89 44.45 N 136.19 E
Plastunovskaja 78 45.18 N 39.16 E
Plasy 60 49.56 N 13.24 E
Plata, Río de la C[1] 258 35.00 S 57.00 W
Plata, Río de la ≃ 240m 18.29 N 66.15 W
Platani ≃ 70 37.24 N 13.16 E
Platania ≃ 68 39.00 N 16.19 E
Plátanos 288 34.47 S 58.11 W
Plátanos, Arroyo ≃ 288 34.45 S 58.08 W
Plate, Île I 275a 45.22 N 73.48 W
Platea 214 41.57 N 80.20 W
Plateau Creek ≃ 200 39.11 N 108.18 W
Plateaux □[5] 152 2.15 S 15.30 E
Plathe → Płoty 30 53.49 N 15.16 E
Platì 68 38.13 N 16.03 E
Platinum 180 59.01 N 161.49 W
Platnirovskaja 78 45.23 N 39.23 E
Plato 246 9.47 N 74.47 W
Platono-Petrovka 83 46.59 N 39.28 E
Platonovka 80 52.43 N 41.57 E
Platón Sánchez 234 21.17 N 98.22 W
Platovo 83 48.05 N 39.53 E
Platrand 158 27.08 S 29.29 E
Platt 260 51.17 N 0.20 E
Platta 58 46.40 N 8.51 E
Platte 198 43.23 N 98.51 W
Platte ≃, U.S. 194 39.16 N 94.50 W
Platte ≃, Minn., U.S. 190 45.47 N 94.17 W
Platte ≃, Nebr., U.S. 198 41.04 N 95.53 W
Platte ≃, Wis., U.S. 190 42.37 N 90.40 W
Platte Center 198 41.32 N 97.29 W
Platte City 194 39.22 N 94.47 W
Platte Creek ≃ 198 43.19 N 99.00 W
Platte Island I 138 5.52 S 55.23 E
Plattekill 210 41.37 N 74.05 W
Platteville, Colo., U.S. 200 40.13 N 104.49 W
Platteville, Wis., U.S. 190 42.44 N 90.29 W
Platt Hall ⊥ 262 53.27 N 2.13 W
Plattling 60 48.47 N 12.53 E
Plattsburg 194 39.34 N 94.27 W
Plattsburgh 188 44.42 N 73.28 W
Plattsburgh Air Force Base ■ 188 44.40 N 73.28 W
Plattsmouth 198 41.01 N 95.53 W
Plattsville 212 43.18 N 80.37 W
Platveld 156 19.58 S 17.07 E
Plau 54 53.27 N 12.16 E
Plaue, D.D.R. 54 52.24 N 12.25 E
Plaue, D.D.R. 54 50.47 N 10.54 E
Plauen 54 50.30 N 12.08 E
Plauer See ⊜ 54 53.30 N 12.20 E
Plav 38 42.36 N 19.56 E
Plave 64 46.02 N 13.36 E
Pļaviņas 76 56.37 N 25.43 E
Plavsk 76 53.43 N 37.18 E
Plaxtol 260 51.15 N 0.18 E
Playa Azul 234 17.59 N 102.24 W
Playa Baracoa 286b 23.03 N 82.34 W
Playa Bonita 236 9.39 N 84.27 W
Playa de Fajardo 240m 18.20 N 65.38 W
Playa de Guayanés 240m 18.04 N 65.49 W
Playa de Guayanilla 240m 18.01 N 66.46 W
Playa del Carmen 238 20.36 N 87.06 W
Playa del Rey ⟵[8] 280 33.58 N 118.26 W
Playa de Naguabo 240m 18.12 N 65.43 W
Playa de Ponce 240m 17.59 N 66.37 W
Playa Noriega, Laguna ⊜ 232 29.10 N 111.50 W
Playas Lake ⊜ 200 31.50 N 108.34 W
Playa Vicente 234 17.50 N 95.49 W
Playa Vicente ≃ 234 18.31 N 95.42 W
Playford ≃ 162 19.03 S 135.35 E
Playgreen Lake ⊜ 184 54.00 N 98.10 W
Playland ♠ 276 40.58 N 73.41 W
Playon Grande 246 9.21 N 78.20 W
Plaza 198 48.01 N 101.58 W
Plaza Caisan 236 8.46 N 82.45 W
Plaza de Mayo ♠ 288 34.36 S 58.23 W
Plaza de Toros ♠ 266a 40.26 N 3.39 W
Plaza de Toros Las Arenas ♠ 266d 41.23 N 2.09 W
Plaza de Toros Monumental ♠ 266d 41.24 N 2.11 E
Plaza Huincul 252 38.55 S 69.09 W
Plaza Park 285 40.04 N 74.53 W
Plazas de Soberanía en el Norte de África → Spanish North Africa □[2] 34 35.53 N 5.19 W
Pleasant 275b 43.41 N 79.49 W
Pleasant, Lake ⊜[1] 200 33.53 N 112.16 W
Pleasant, Mount ∧ 192 37.44 N 79.10 W
Pleasant Bay 186 46.49 N 60.48 W
Pleasantdale, Sask., Can. 184 52.35 N 104.30 W
Pleasantdale, N.Y., U.S. 210 42.47 N 73.40 W
Pleasant Gap 214 40.52 N 77.45 W
Pleasant Garden 192 35.58 N 79.46 W
Pleasant Grove, Calif., U.S. 226 38.49 N 121.29 W
Pleasant Grove, Utah, U.S. 200 40.22 N 111.44 W
Pleasant Grove Creek ≃ 226 38.48 N 121.32 W
Pleasant Hill, Calif., U.S. 226 37.56 N 122.04 W
Pleasant Hill, Ill., U.S. 219 39.27 N 90.52 W
Pleasant Hill, La., U.S. 194 31.49 N 93.31 W
Pleasant Hill, Mo., U.S. 194 38.47 N 94.16 W
Pleasant Hill, N.C., U.S. 208 36.32 N 77.32 W
Pleasant Hill, Ohio, U.S. 218 40.03 N 84.20 W
Pleasant Hill Lake ⊜[1] 214 40.38 N 82.21 W
Pleasant Hills 214 40.20 N 79.58 W
Pleasant Home 224 45.28 N 122.20 W
Pleasant Lake, Ind., U.S. 216 41.35 N 85.01 W
Pleasant Lake, Mich., U.S. 216 42.23 N 84.22 W
Pleasant Lake ⊜ 216 42.13 N 83.56 W
Pleasant Mills 216 40.47 N 84.51 W
Pleasant Mount 210 41.44 N 75.26 W
Pleasant Mountain ∧[2] 186 45.26 N 66.49 W
Pleasanton, Calif., U.S. 226 37.40 N 121.53 W
Pleasanton, Kans., U.S. 198 38.11 N 94.43 W
Pleasanton, Tex., U.S. 196 28.58 N 98.29 W
Pleasanton Ridge ∧ 282 37.40 N 121.55 W
Pleasant Plains, Ill., U.S. 219 39.52 N 89.55 W
Pleasant Plains, N.J., U.S. 208 40.00 N 74.13 W
Pleasant Point 172 44.16 S 171.08 E
Pleasant Prairie 216 42.33 N 87.57 W
Pleasant Ridge 281 42.31 N 83.10 W
Pleasant Unity 214 40.15 N 79.28 W
Pleasant Valley, N.Y., U.S. 210 41.45 N 73.50 W
Pleasant Valley, Ohio, U.S. 218 39.22 N 83.03 W
Pleasant Valley, Pa., U.S. 279b 40.31 N 75.18 W
Pleasantville, Iowa, U.S. 190 41.23 N 93.18 W

Symbol	English	Deutsch	Español	Français	Português
≃	River	Fluss	Río	Rivière	Rio
⌶	Canal	Kanal	Canal	Canal	Canal
⌊	Waterfall, Rapids	Wasserfall, Stromschnellen	Cascada, Rápidos	Chute d'eau, Rapides	Cascata, Rápidos
Ⲩ	Strait	Meeresstrasse	Estrecho	Détroit	Estreito
C	Bay, Gulf	Bucht, Golf	Bahía, Golfo	Baie, Golfe	Baía, Golfo
⊜	Lake, Lakes	See, Seen	Lago, Lagos	Lac, Lacs	Lago, Lagos
☷	Swamp	Sumpf	Pantano	Marais	Pântano
⊼	Ice Features, Glacier	Eis- und Gletscherformen	Accidentes Glaciales	Formes glaciaires	Acidentes Glaciares
⫪	Other Hydrographic Features	Andere Hydrographische Objekte	Otros Elementos Hidrográficos	Autres données hydrographiques	Outros Elementos Hidrográficos
⤙	Submarine Features	Untermeerische Objekte	Accidentes Submarinos	Formes de relief sous-marin	Acidentes Submarinos
□	Political Unit	Politische Einheit	Unidad Politica	Entité politique	Unidade Política
⛊	Cultural Institution	Kulturelle Institution	Institución Cultural	Institution culturelle	Instituição Cultural
⊥	Historical Site	Historische Stätte	Sitio Histórico	Site historique	Sitio Histórico
♠	Recreational Site	Erholungs- und Ferienort	Sitio de Recreo	Centre de loisirs	Sítio de Lazer
⊠	Airport	Flughafen	Aeropuerto	Aéroport	Aeroporto
■	Military Installation	Militäranlage	Instalación Militar	Installation militaire	Instalação Militar
⟵	Miscellaneous	Verschiedenes	Misceláneo	Divers	Miscelânea

ENGLISH Name	Page	Lat.°′	Long.°′

DEUTSCH Name	Seite	Breite°′	Länge°′ E=Ost

Pleasantville, Md., U.S. 284b 39.11 N 76.38 W
Pleasantville, N.J., U.S. 208 39.23 N 74.32 W
Pleasantville, N.Y., U.S. 210 41.08 N 73.48 W
Pleasantville, Pa., U.S. 214 41.36 N 79.35 W
Pleasington 262 53.44 N 2.34 W
Pleasure Beach 207 41.18 N 72.08 W
Pleasure Ridge Park 218 38.10 N 85.50 W
Pleasureville 218 38.21 N 85.07 W
Pléaux 32 45.08 N 2.14 E
Plechanovo 82 54.14 N 37.33 E
Plechanovskoje 76 52.39 N 39.50 E
Plechovo 78 51.07 N 35.18 E
Plecký (Plöckenstein) ∧ 60 48.46 N 13.51 E
Pledger 222 29.11 N 95.55 W
Pleebo 150 4.35 N 7.40 W
Pleiku 110 13.59 N 108.00 E
Pleine d'Aleria ↼[1] 36 42.05 N 9.25 E
Pleinfeld 56 49.06 N 10.59 E
Pleissa 54 50.50 N 12.46 E
Pleisse ≃ 54 51.20 N 12.22 E
Pléneuf 32 48.36 N 2.33 W
Plenty 184 51.47 N 108.36 W
Plenty ≃, Austl. 162 23.25 S 136.31 E
Plenty ≃, Austl. 274b 37.45 S 145.07 E
Plenty, Bay of C 172 37.40 S 177.00 E
Plentywood 198 48.47 N 104.34 W
Plered 115a 6.38 S 107.23 E
Pleščejevo, Ozero ⊜ 82 56.46 N 38.47 E
Pleščenicy 76 54.25 N 27.50 E
Pleseck 24 62.43 N 40.20 E
Plešivka 82 54.23 N 37.09 E
Plesna ≃ 54 50.07 N 12.28 E
Pless, B.R.D. 58 48.05 N 10.08 E
Pless → Pszczyna, Pol. 30 49.59 N 18.57 E
Plessa 54 51.28 N 13.37 E
Plessisville 206 46.14 N 71.47 W
Pleszew 30 51.54 N 17.48 E
Pletenevka 82 54.31 N 36.06 E
Pleternica 38 45.17 N 17.48 E
Plétipi, Lac ⊜ 176 51.44 N 70.06 W
Plet'onyj Tašlyk 78 48.29 N 31.40 E
Plettenberg 56 51.13 N 7.52 E
Plettenbergbaai 158 34.04 S 23.22 E
Pleurs 50 48.41 N 3.52 E
Pleven 38 43.25 N 24.37 E
Plevna, Mo., U.S. 219 39.58 N 92.05 W
Plevna, Mont., U.S. 198 46.25 N 104.31 W
Pleyben 28 48.14 N 3.58 W
Pleystein 60 49.39 N 12.25 E
Pliening 60 48.12 N 11.48 E
Pliezhausen 56 48.33 N 9.12 E
Plimmerton 172 41.05 S 174.52 E
Plimoth Plantation ⊥ 207 41.57 N 70.38 W
Plintovka 265a 60.01 N 30.46 E
Pliski 78 51.07 N 32.24 E
Pliskov 78 49.23 N 29.18 E
Plitvička Jezera ⊜ 36 44.53 N 15.38 E
Plješevica ⩕ 36 44.40 N 15.45 E
Pljevlja 38 43.21 N 19.21 E
Ploaghe 71 40.40 N 8.45 E
Ploče 36 43.04 N 17.26 E
Plochingen 56 48.42 N 9.25 E
Płock 30 52.33 N 19.43 E
Plöckenpass)(64 46.36 N 12.58 E
Plöckenstein (Plecký) ∧ 60 48.46 N 13.51 E
Pločno ∧ 36 43.23 N 17.57 E
Plodorodnoje 80 46.44 N 41.06 E
Ploegsteert 50 50.43 N 2.53 E
Ploërmel 32 47.56 N 2.24 W
Ploeşti → Ploieşti 38 44.56 N 26.02 E
Ploieşti 38 44.56 N 26.02 E
Plomàrion 38 38.59 N 26.22 E
Plomb du Cantal ∧ 32 45.03 N 2.46 E
Plombières-les-Bains 58 47.58 N 6.29 E
Plombières-lès-Dijon 58 47.20 N 4.58 E
Plomer 258 34.48 S 59.02 W
Plomer, Point ≻ 166 31.19 S 152.58 E
Plön 54 54.09 N 10.25 E
Plonge, Lac la ⊜ 184 55.08 N 107.25 W
Płońsk 30 52.38 N 20.23 E
Pl'os 80 57.27 N 41.31 E
Plose, Cima delle ∧ 64 46.42 N 11.44 E
Ploskij 78 46.17 N 40.15 E
Ploskoje 76 52.45 N 38.21 E
Ploskoš' 76 56.46 N 31.16 E
Pl'oso 76 59.47 N 35.43 E
Plotbišče 80 56.50 N 50.35 E
Plotina 83 48.33 N 40.05 E
Plotnica 78 52.03 N 26.39 E
Plottier 252 38.58 S 68.14 W
Płoty 30 53.49 N 15.16 E
Plötz 54 51.38 N 11.56 E
Plouay 32 47.55 N 3.20 W
Ploučnice ≃ 54 50.47 N 14.13 E
Ploudalmézeau 32 48.32 N 4.39 W
Plouescat 32 48.40 N 4.10 W
Plouguenast 32 48.17 N 2.43 W
Plouha 32 48.41 N 2.56 W
Plovdiv 38 42.09 N 24.45 E
Plover ≃ 190 44.29 N 89.35 W
Plover Islands II 180 71.15 N 155.30 W
Pluckemin 276 40.39 N 74.39 W
Plum, Pa., U.S. 214 41.35 N 79.51 W
Plum, Pa., U.S. 214 40.28 N 79.44 W
Plum, Tex., U.S. 222 29.56 N 96.58 W
Pluma Hidalgo 234 15.55 N 96.25 W
Plumas 184 50.25 N 99.02 W
Plumbon 115a 6.42 S 108.28 E
Plumbridge 48 54.46 N 7.15 W
Plum Brook ≃ 281 42.34 N 82.58 W
Plum Creek ≃, Ill., U.S. 278 41.33 N 87.29 W
Plum Creek ≃, Nebr., U.S. 198 40.41 N 99.40 W
Plum Creek ≃, S. Dak., U.S. 198 44.13 N 100.43 W
Plum Creek ≃, Tex., U.S. 196 29.38 N 97.36 W
Plum Creek, Clear Fork ≃ 222 29.45 N 97.37 W
Plumerville 194 35.10 N 92.38 W
Plum Grove 222 30.15 N 95.05 W
Plum Grove Estates 278 42.04 N 88.02 W
Plum Island 283 42.49 N 70.59 W
Plum Island I, Mass., U.S. 207 42.45 N 70.48 W
Plum Island I, N.Y., U.S. 207 41.11 N 72.12 W
Plum Island Airport ⊠ 283 42.48 N 70.50 W
Plum Island Sound Ʉ 283 42.45 N 70.48 W
Plumley 262 53.17 N 2.25 W
Plummer 202 47.20 N 116.53 W
Plummers Landing 218 38.19 N 83.33 W
Plumper Sound Ʉ 224 48.47 N 123.13 W
Plum Point ≻ 276 40.50 N 40.43 W
Plumpton 274a 33.45 S 150.50 E
Plumridge Lakes ⊜ 162 29.30 S 125.25 E
Plum Run ≃ 279b 40.15 N 80.13 W
Plumsteadville 208 40.23 N 75.09 W
Plumtree 154 20.30 S 27.50 E
Plumville 214 40.48 N 79.11 W
Plumwood 218 40.01 N 83.23 W
Plungė 76 55.55 N 21.51 E
Pl'usa 76 58.26 N 29.21 E
Pl'uskovo 76 52.46 N 33.49 E
Pl'ussa ≃ 76 59.19 N 28.11 E
Plym ≃ 42 50.12 N 4.07 W
Plymouth, Monts. 238 16.42 N 62.13 W
Plymouth, Trin. 241r 11.13 N 60.47 W
Plymouth, Eng., U.K. 42 50.23 N 4.10 W
Plymouth, Calif., U.S. 226 38.29 N 120.51 W
Plymouth, Conn., U.S. 207 41.40 N 73.03 W
Plymouth, Ill., U.S. 194 40.29 N 90.58 W
Plymouth, Ind., U.S. 216 41.21 N 86.19 W
Plymouth, Mass., U.S. 207 41.58 N 70.41 W
Plymouth, Mich., U.S. 216 42.22 N 83.28 W
Plymouth, Nebr., U.S. 198 40.18 N 97.00 W
Plymouth, N.H., U.S. 188 43.45 N 71.41 W
Plymouth, N.C., U.S. 192 35.52 N 76.43 W
Plymouth, N.Y., U.S. 210 42.37 N 75.36 W
Plymouth, Ohio, U.S. 214 40.59 N 82.40 W
Plymouth, Pa., U.S. 210 41.14 N 75.58 W
Plymouth, Wis., U.S. 190 43.45 N 87.58 W
Plymouth □[6] 207 41.58 N 70.41 W
Plymouth ≃ 283 42.12 N 70.54 W
Plymouth Bay C 207 41.57 N 70.37 W
Plymouth Harbor C 283 41.58 N 70.39 W
Plymouth Meeting 285 40.06 N 75.15 W
Plymouth Rock ⊥ 207 41.57 N 70.39 W
Plympton, Eng., U.K. 42 50.23 N 4.03 W
Plympton, Mass., U.S. 207 41.57 N 70.49 W
Plymptonville 214 41.03 N 78.28 W
Plymstock 42 50.22 N 4.04 W
Plynlimon ∧ 42 52.28 N 3.47 W
Plzeň 60 49.45 N 13.23 E
Pniewy 30 52.31 N 16.15 E
Pô 150 11.10 N 1.09 W
Po ≃ 36 44.57 N 12.04 E
Po, Foci del ≃[1] 64 44.52 N 12.30 E
Poá 256 23.32 S 46.20 W
Poá ≃ 287b 23.37 S 46.45 W
Poana ≃ 250 0.56 N 57.03 W
Poané, Baie de C 175f 21.24 S 168.02 E
Poás, Volcán ∧[1] 236 10.11 N 84.13 W
Pobé, Benin 150 6.58 N 2.41 E
Pobé, H. Vol. 150 13.53 N 1.45 W
Pobeda, Gora ∧ 74 65.12 N 146.12 E
Pobeda Ice Island I 9 64.30 S 97.00 E
Pobedino 74 49.51 N 142.49 E
Pobedy, Pik ∧ 72 42.02 N 80.05 E
Pobershau 54 50.38 N 13.13 E
Poběžovice 60 49.31 N 12.48 E
Poblado Cerro Gordo 240m 18.29 N 66.20 W
Poblado Jacaguas 240m 18.03 N 66.32 W
Poblado Mediania Alta 240m 18.26 N 65.50 W
Poblado Sábalos 240m 18.11 N 67.09 W
Poblado Santana 240m 18.27 N 66.40 W
Poblet 258 35.04 S 57.57 W
Pocahontas, Ark., U.S. 194 36.16 N 90.58 W
Pocahontas, Ill., U.S. 219 38.50 N 89.33 W
Pocahontas, Iowa, U.S. 198 42.44 N 94.40 W
Pocahontas State Park ♠ 208 37.23 N 77.34 W
Počajev 78 50.01 N 25.31 E
Pocantico Hills 276 41.06 N 73.50 W
Pocantico Lake ⊜ 276 41.07 N 73.50 W
Poção 250 8.11 S 36.42 W
Pocasset 207 41.41 N 70.37 W
Pocatalico ≃ 188 38.29 N 81.49 W
Pocatello 202 42.52 N 112.27 W
Počegda 24 62.42 N 43.23 E
Počep 76 52.56 N 33.27 E
Počepy 76 53.17 N 31.20 E
Pocé-sur-Cisse 50 47.26 N 0.59 E
Počet 88 57.10 N 96.30 E
Pöchlarn 61 48.12 N 15.13 E
Pochutla 234 15.44 N 96.28 W
Pochvistnevo 80 53.38 N 52.08 E
Pocinhos 250 7.04 S 36.03 W
Pocinhos do Rio Verde 256 21.56 S 46.25 W
Počinki 80 54.42 N 44.51 E
Počinnaja Sopka 76 58.25 N 34.22 E
Počinok 76 54.25 N 32.27 E
Pockau 54 50.40 N 13.27 E
Pocking, B.R.D. 60 48.24 N 13.19 E
Pöcking, B.R.D. 64 47.58 N 11.17 E
Pocklington 44 53.56 N 0.46 W
Pocoata 248 18.41 S 66.11 W
Poço Do Bispo ↼[8] 266c 38.44 N 9.06 W
Poções 255 14.31 S 40.21 W
Poço Fundo 256 21.48 S 45.58 W
Poço Fundo, Cachoeira do ∟ 256 22.10 S 44.13 W
Pocol 64 46.31 N 12.07 E
Pocomoke ≃ 208 37.58 N 75.39 W
Pocomoke City 188 38.05 N 75.34 W
Pocomoke Sound Ʉ 208 37.52 N 75.49 W
Pocona 248 17.39 S 65.24 W
Poconé 248 16.15 S 56.37 W
Pocono International Raceway ♠ 210 41.03 N 75.31 W
Pocono Lake 210 41.06 N 75.31 W
Pocono Manor 210 41.06 N 75.22 W
Pocono Mountains ⩕[2] 210 41.10 N 75.20 W
Pocono Pines 210 41.05 N 75.29 W
Pocono Summit 210 41.07 N 75.25 W
Pocopson 285 39.54 N 75.37 W
Pocopson Creek ≃ 285 39.54 N 75.37 W
Poço Redondo 250 9.49 S 37.41 W
Poços de Caldas 256 21.48 S 46.34 W
Poço Verde 250 10.42 S 38.11 W
Pocrane 255 19.37 S 41.37 W
Pocrí 236 8.16 N 80.33 W
Podbel'skaja 80 53.37 N 51.50 E
Podberezje, S.S.S.R. 76 56.57 N 30.38 E
Podberezje, S.S.S.R. 82 56.46 N 37.10 E
Podbořany 54 50.11 N 13.25 E
Podborki 82 54.11 N 35.56 E
Podborovje 76 59.28 N 34.43 E
Podbuž 78 49.22 N 23.15 E
Podbužje 76 53.30 N 34.56 E
Podčerje 24 63.53 N 57.57 E
Podchožeje 82 54.19 N 38.34 E
Podčinnyj 80 50.52 N 45.13 E
Poddębice 30 51.53 N 18.58 E
Poddemjur 24 64.05 N 53.26 E
Poddolgoje 76 53.12 N 38.04 E
Poddorje 76 57.28 N 31.07 E
Poděbrady 30 50.08 N 15.07 E
Podejuch → Podjuchy ↼[8] 54 53.20 N 14.36 E
Po della Donzella ≃ 64 44.48 N 12.25 E
Po delle Tolle ≃ 64 44.50 N 12.28 E
Podensac 32 44.39 N 0.22 W
Podenzano 62 44.57 N 9.41 E
Podersdorf am See 61 47.51 N 16.50 E
Podgajcy 78 49.16 N 25.08 E
Podgorenskij 78 50.24 N 39.39 E
Podgorica → Titograd 38 42.26 N 19.14 E
Podgornaja 78 50.28 N 41.10 E
Podgornoje, S.S.S.R. 78 50.27 N 39.37 E
Podgornoje, S.S.S.R. 78 51.43 N 39.07 E
Podgornoje, S.S.S.R. 80 46.33 N 43.07 E
Podgornoje, S.S.S.R. 85 42.55 N 72.25 E
Podgornoje, S.S.S.R. 86 57.47 N 82.36 E
Podgorodnaja 78 48.07 N 30.51 E
Podgorodnoje 78 48.34 N 35.08 E
Podhale ⩕[2] 30 49.25 N 20.00 E
Podhůří 60 49.28 N 13.40 E
Podi 112 1.08 S 121.16 E
Po di Goro ≃ 64 44.48 N 12.27 E
Po di Volano ≃ 64 44.49 N 12.15 E
Podjom-Michajlovka 80 52.49 N 50.32 E
Podjuchy ↼[8] 54 53.20 N 14.36 E
Podkamen' 78 49.57 N 25.19 E
Podkamennaja Tunguska 74 61.36 N 90.09 E
Podkamennaja Tunguska ≃ 74 61.36 N 90.18 E
Podkoren 64 46.30 N 13.45 E
Podkumok ≃ 84 44.14 N 43.36 E
Podlasie ↼[1] 30 52.30 N 23.00 E
Podlesnoje, S.S.S.R. 78 48.47 N 32.15 E
Podlesnoje, S.S.S.R. 80 51.50 N 47.03 E
Podlopatki 88 50.55 N 107.05 E
Podmošje 82 56.23 N 37.24 E
Podol'sk 82 55.26 N 37.33 E
Podol'skaja Vozvyšennost' ⩕[1] 78 49.00 N 27.00 E
Podor, Maur. 150 16.40 N 15.00 W
Podor, Sén. 150 16.40 N 14.57 W
Podora 24 62.22 N 54.19 E
Podosinovec 24 60.17 N 47.04 E
Podoz'orskij 80 57.14 N 40.20 E
Podporožje 24 60.53 N 34.07 E
Podravina ↼[1] 38 45.40 N 17.40 E
Podravska Slatina 38 45.42 N 17.42 E
Podrezčicha 24 59.22 N 51.28 E
Podstepnyj 80 51.08 N 51.28 E
Podsvilje 76 55.09 N 27.58 E
Podt'osovo 88 58.36 N 92.06 E
Pod'uga 24 61.06 N 40.53 E
Podujevo 38 42.55 N 21.11 E
Poduškino 265b 55.43 N 37.17 E
Podu Turcului 38 46.12 N 27.23 E
Podvoločisk 78 49.33 N 26.09 E
Podvousy 60 49.32 N 13.08 E
Podymachino 88 56.59 N 106.11 E
Podyvotje 78 52.03 N 34.08 E
Poe 216 40.56 N 85.05 W
Poel I 54 54.00 N 11.26 E
Poeldijk 52 52.01 N 4.12 E
Poelela, Lagoa ⊜ 156 24.38 S 35.00 E
Poelkapelle 50 50.55 N 2.57 E
Poestenkill 210 42.41 N 73.34 W
Poesten Kill ≃ 210 42.43 N 73.42 W
Poetto 71 39.12 N 9.10 E
Pofadder 158 29.10 S 19.22 E
Pogamasing Lake ⊜ 190 46.57 N 81.50 W
Pogan, Zhg. 100 27.40 N 116.46 E
Pogan, Zhg. 100 28.18 N 116.46 E
Pogăniş ≃ 38 45.41 N 21.22 E
Pogar 76 52.33 N 33.16 E
Poge, Cape ≻ 207 41.25 N 70.27 W
Poggendorf 54 54.03 N 13.07 E
Poggiardo 68 40.03 N 18.23 E
Poggibonsi 66 43.28 N 11.09 E
Poggio 64 44.30 N 10.00 E
Poggio Berni 66 44.02 N 12.24 E
Poggio Bustone 66 42.30 N 12.53 E
Poggio Imperiale 68 41.49 N 15.22 E
Poggiomarino 68 40.48 N 14.32 E
Poggio Mirteto 66 42.16 N 12.41 E
Poggio Moiano 66 42.12 N 12.53 E
Poggioreale 70 37.47 N 13.01 E
Poggio Renatico 64 44.46 N 11.29 E
Poggiorsini 68 40.55 N 16.15 E
Poggio Rusco 64 44.59 N 11.07 E
Poggio Sannita 66 41.47 N 14.25 E
Pogibi 89 52.12 N 141.42 E
Pogliano 266b 45.32 N 8.59 E
Pogny 56 48.52 N 4.29 E
Pogoanele 38 44.54 N 27.00 E
Pogodajev 80 51.37 N 51.04 E
Pogoniani 38 40.00 N 20.25 E
Pogoreloje Gorodišče 76 56.08 N 34.56 E
Pogoso 152 6.46 S 17.12 E
Pogost, S.S.S.R. 76 53.51 N 29.09 E
Pogost, S.S.S.R. 76 52.51 N 27.39 E
Pogost, S.S.S.R. 80 57.39 N 42.33 E
Pogost, S.S.S.R. 82 56.52 N 39.04 E
Pogožeje 78 51.36 N 37.16 E
Pogradec 38 40.54 N 20.39 E
Po Grande ≃ 64 44.57 N 12.26 E
Pograničnoje 80 50.32 N 48.38 E
Pograničnyj, S.S.S.R. 80 46.57 N 45.46 E
Pograničnyj, S.S.S.R. 89 44.25 N 131.24 E
Pogrebišče 78 49.29 N 29.16 E
Pogromni Volcano ∧[1] 180 54.33 N 164.45 W
Pogromnoje 80 52.35 N 52.32 E
Pogruznaja 80 54.14 N 50.29 E
Poh 112 0.46 S 122.49 E
P'ohang 98 36.03 N 129.20 E
Pohatcong Creek ≃ 210 40.37 N 75.11 W
Pohick Creek ≃ 284c 38.46 N 77.14 W
Pohick Creek, Rabbit Branch ≃ 284c 38.48 N 77.17 W
Pohick Creek, Sideburn Branch ≃ 284c 38.48 N 77.17 W
Pohjanmaa ↼[1] 26 64.00 N 25.00 E
Pohjois-Karjalan lääni □[4] 24 63.00 N 30.00 E
Pöhl, Talsperre ↼[6] 54 50.33 N 12.12 E
Pöhla 54 50.31 N 12.49 E
Pöhlde 52 51.37 N 10.18 E
Pohl-Göns 56 50.28 N 8.39 E
Pohopoco Creek ≃ 210 40.49 N 75.40 W
Pohořelice 61 48.59 N 16.32 E
Pohorje ⩕ 36 46.30 N 15.20 E
Pohsien → Boxian 100 33.53 N 115.45 E
Pohue Bay C 229d 19.00 N 155.48 W
Poiana Mare 38 43.55 N 23.04 E
Poiana Ruşcăi, Munţii ⩕ 38 45.41 N 22.30 E
Pöide 76 58.31 N 23.03 E
Poigny-la-Forêt 261 48.41 N 1.45 E
Poim 80 53.01 N 43.11 E
Poing 60 48.10 N 11.49 E
Poinsett, Cape ≻ 9 65.42 S 113.18 E
Poinsett, Lake ⊜, Fla., U.S. 220 28.20 N 80.50 W
Poinsett, Lake ⊜, S. Dak., U.S. 198 44.34 N 97.05 W
Point 222 32.56 N 95.52 W
Point Arena 204 38.55 N 123.41 W
Point Au Fer Island I 194 29.15 N 91.15 W
Point Baker 180 56.21 N 133.37 W
Pointblank 222 30.45 N 95.13 W
Point Chautauqua 214 42.14 N 79.28 W
Point Cloates 162 22.35 S 113.41 E
Point Comfort 196 28.41 N 96.33 W
Point Cook 274b 37.56 S 144.45 E
Point Cook Royal Australian Air Force Station ■ 169 37.56 S 144.45 E
Point du Jour, Ruisseau du ≃ 206 45.50 N 73.25 W
Pointe-à-la-Frégate 186 49.12 N 64.55 W
Pointe-à-la-Garde 186 48.05 N 66.32 W
Pointe a la Hache 194 29.35 N 89.48 W
Pointe-à-Maurier 186 50.20 N 59.48 W
Pointe-à-Pitre 241o 16.14 N 61.32 W
Pointe-à-Pitre-le Raizet, Aérodrome de ⊠ 241o 16.17 N 61.32 W
Pointe-au-Chêne 206 45.38 N 74.45 W
Pointe Aux Peaux Farms 216 41.57 N 83.16 W
Pointe-aux-Trembles 206 45.39 N 73.30 W
Pointe-Calumet 275a 45.30 N 73.58 W
Pointe-Claire 206 45.26 N 73.50 W
Pointe-des-Cascades 275a 45.20 N 73.58 W
Pointe-des-galets → Le Port 157c 20.55 S 55.18 E
Pointe-du-Moulin 275a 45.22 N 73.52 W
Point Edward 214 43.00 N 82.24 W
Pointe-Gatineau 212 45.28 N 75.42 W
Pointe-Noire, Congo 152 4.48 S 11.51 E
Pointe-Noire, Guad. 241o 16.14 N 61.47 W
Point Enterprise 222 31.40 N 96.26 W
Pointers 208 39.36 N 75.28 W
Point Fortin 241r 10.11 N 61.41 W
Point Hope 180 68.21 N 166.41 W
Point Imperial ∧ 200 36.16 N 111.58 W
Point Independence 207 41.44 N 70.39 W
Point Lake ⊜ 176 65.15 N 113.04 W
Point Leamington 186 49.20 N 55.24 W
Point Lookout 276 40.35 N 73.35 W
Point Marion 188 39.44 N 79.53 W
Point McLeay 168b 35.32 S 139.06 E
Point Mugu Naval Air Station ■ 228 34.07 N 119.07 W
Point of Rocks 208 39.17 N 77.32 W
Point O'Woods 276 40.39 N 73.08 W
Point Pass 168b 34.05 S 139.03 E
Point Pelee National Park ♠ 214 41.57 N 82.30 W
Point Peninsula ≻[1] 212 44.01 N 76.15 W
Point Pleasant, Md., U.S. 284b 39.11 N 76.35 W
Point Pleasant, N.J., U.S. 208 40.05 N 74.04 W
Point Pleasant, Ohio, U.S. 218 38.54 N 84.14 W
Point Pleasant, Pa., U.S. 208 40.25 N 75.04 W
Point Pleasant, W. Va., U.S. 188 38.52 N 82.08 W
Point Pleasant Beach 208 40.05 N 74.03 W
Point Reyes National Seashore ♠ 204 38.00 N 122.58 W
Point Roberts 224 48.59 N 123.13 W
Point Samson 162 20.36 S 117.12 E
Point Sapin 186 46.58 N 64.50 W
Point View Reservoir ⊜[1] 276 40.58 N 74.15 W
Point Whiteshed 180 60.28 N 145.57 W
Poirino 62 44.55 N 7.51 E
Poiseevo 80 55.32 N 53.30 E
Poison Creek ≃ 202 43.15 N 108.09 W
Poison Spider Creek ≃ 200 42.46 N 106.31 W
Poisson Blanc, Réservoir du ⊜[1] 188 46.00 N 75.45 W
Poissonnier Point ≻ 162 19.57 S 119.11 E
Poissons 58 48.25 N 5.13 E
Poissy 50 48.56 N 2.03 E
Poitiers 32 46.35 N 0.20 E
Poitou □[9] 32 46.20 N 0.30 W
Poix 50 49.47 N 1.59 E
Poix-Terron 56 49.39 N 4.39 E
Pojarkovo 89 49.38 N 128.38 E
Pojiang ≃ 100 28.57 N 116.39 E
Pojma ≃ 88 56.54 N 97.48 E
Pojo 248 17.45 S 64.49 W
Pojoaque Valley 200 35.53 N 105.59 W
Pojuca 255 12.21 S 38.20 W
Pojuca ≃ 255 12.34 S 38.03 W
Pok 174r 6.49 N 158.12 E
Pokagon State Park ♠ 216 41.43 N 85.01 W
Pokaran 120 26.55 N 71.55 E
Pokataroo 166 29.35 S 148.42 E
Pokatejeva 88 56.59 N 97.25 E
Pokatilovka, S.S.S.R. 80 51.06 N 51.53 E
Pokatilovka, S.S.S.R. 86 45.23 N 80.10 E
Poke Run ≃ 279b 40.30 N 79.33 W
Pokhara 124 28.14 N 83.59 E
Pokharia 126 23.55 N 86.37 E
Pok Liu Chau I 271d 22.12 N 114.07 E
Poko, Sūd. 140 5.38 N 31.50 E
Poko, Zaïre 154 3.09 N 26.53 E
Pokojnoje 84 44.48 N 44.16 E
Pokok Sena 114 6.10 N 100.32 E
Pokol'ubiči 76 52.30 N 31.02 E
Pokrov 82 55.55 N 39.10 E
Pokrovka, S.S.S.R. 78 47.59 N 36.14 E
Pokrovka, S.S.S.R. 80 48.22 N 46.04 E
Pokrovka, S.S.S.R. 80 53.47 N 53.19 E
Pokrovka, S.S.S.R. 85 42.20 N 78.01 E
Pokrovka, S.S.S.R. 85 42.45 N 71.36 E
Pokrovka, S.S.S.R. 86 49.28 N 81.28 E
Pokrovka, S.S.S.R. 86 54.17 N 68.15 E
Pokrovka, S.S.S.R. 89 43.57 N 131.39 E
Pokrov-Konopl'anskaja Gr'ada ∧ 76 58.25 N 36.30 E
Pokrovo-Kirejevo 83 47.38 N 38.16 E
Pokrovsk 74 61.29 N 129.06 E
Pokrovskaja Arčada 80 52.56 N 44.13 E
Pokrovskij 78 46.32 N 31.38 E
Pokrovskoje, S.S.S.R. 76 52.38 N 36.51 E
Pokrovskoje, S.S.S.R. 78 49.44 N 38.13 E
Pokrovskoje, S.S.S.R. 80 53.54 N 40.26 E
Pokrovskoje, S.S.S.R. 80 54.04 N 43.37 E
Pokrovskoje, S.S.S.R. 82 55.53 N 36.19 E
Pokrovskoje, S.S.S.R. 82 56.25 N 37.03 E
Pokrovskoje, S.S.S.R. 83 47.25 N 38.54 E
Pokrovskoje, S.S.S.R. 83 48.37 N 38.09 E
Pokrovskoje, S.S.S.R. 86 57.14 N 66.48 E
Pokrovskoje, S.S.S.R. 265a 59.44 N 30.46 E
Pokrovskoje ↼[8] 265b 55.37 N 37.37 E
Pokrovsko-Strešnevo ↼[8] 265b 55.49 N 37.29 E
Pokrovsk-Ural'skij 86 60.10 N 59.49 E
Pokur 74 61.02 N 75.26 E
Pola → Pula, Jugo. 64 44.52 N 13.50 E
Pola, Pil. 116 13.09 N 121.26 E
Pola, S.S.S.R. 76 57.56 N 31.50 E
Pola ≃ 76 58.04 N 31.37 E
Pola Bay C 116 13.10 N 121.28 E
Polacca 200 35.50 N 110.23 W
Polacca Wash ∨ 200 35.22 N 110.50 W
Pola de Laviana 34 43.15 N 5.34 W
Pola de Lena 34 43.10 N 5.49 W
Pola de Siero 34 43.23 N 5.40 W
Polān 128 25.35 N 61.12 E
Polanco 252 33.54 S 55.09 W
Poland, Kiribati 174o 1.59 N 157.32 W
Poland, Ohio, U.S. 214 41.01 N 80.37 W
Poland □[1] 22
 30 52.00 N 19.00 E
Polangui 116 13.17 N 123.29 E
Polanów 30 54.08 N 16.39 E
Polapare ≃ 115b 9.43 S 119.06 E
Pol'arnik 180 67.00 N 179.15 W
Pol'arnyj 24 69.12 N 33.22 E
Pol'arnyj Ural ⩕ 24 66.55 N 64.30 E
Polar Record Glacier ⊓ 9 69.49 S 75.30 E
Polatlı 130 39.36 N 32.09 E
Polba 272b 22.57 N 88.18 E
Polbain 46 58.02 N 5.23 W
Polch 56 50.18 N 7.18 E
Polcirkeln 24 66.34 N 21.05 E
Polcura 252 37.17 S 71.43 W
Połczyn Zdrój 30 53.46 N 16.06 E
Polden Hills ⩕[2] 42 51.08 N 2.50 W
Poldnevica 80 58.37 N 46.38 E
Pol'dorak 85 39.25 N 69.56 E
Poleang 112 4.42 S 121.46 E
Polecat Creek ≃ 196 36.00 N 95.57 W
Poledník ∧ 60 49.04 N 13.24 E
Polee, Pulau I 164 2.12 S 130.15 E
Polegate 42 50.49 N 0.15 E
Pol-e Khomrī 120 35.56 N 68.43 E
Pole Moor 262 53.39 N 1.54 W
Pole Mountain ∧ 200 41.14 N 105.23 W
Polen → Poland □[1] 30 52.00 N 19.00 E
Polenezköy 267b 41.07 N 29.12 E
Polenia Bay C 175f 18.43 S 169.11 E
Pol-e Safīd 128 36.06 N 53.01 E
Polesden Lacey ⊥ 260 51.15 N 0.22 W
Polesella 64 44.58 N 11.45 E
Polesine □[9] 64 45.00 N 11.45 E
Polesine Parmense 64 45.01 N 10.04 E
Polesje 76 53.05 N 31.17 E
Polesje ↼[1] 72 52.30 N 27.30 E
Polessk [Labiau] 76 54.52 N 21.05 E
Polesskoje 78 51.14 N 29.22 E
Polesworth 42 52.37 N 1.36 W
Polevaja 78 51.37 N 36.30 E
Polevskoj 86 56.26 N 60.11 E
Polewali 112 3.25 S 119.20 E
Polgár 30 47.52 N 21.08 E
Pŏlgyo 98 34.52 N 127.21 E
Poli 146 8.29 N 13.15 E
Polia 68 38.45 N 16.19 E
Políaigos I 38 36.46 N 24.38 E
Policastro, Golfo di C 68 40.00 N 15.30 E
Policastro Bussentino 68 40.09 N 15.32 E
Police 30 53.35 N 14.33 E
Polička 30 49.43 N 16.16 E
Policoro 68 40.13 N 16.41 E
Polignac 62 45.04 N 3.52 E
Polignano a Mare 68 41.00 N 17.13 E
Poligny 58 46.50 N 5.43 E
Polikastron 38 41.00 N 22.34 E
Polikhnítos 38 39.05 N 26.11 E
Polillo 116 14.43 N 121.56 E
Polillo Island I 116 14.50 N 121.57 E
Polillo Islands II 116 14.50 N 122.05 E
Polillo Strait Ʉ 116 14.44 N 121.51 E
Polinesia Francesa → French Polynesia □[2] 14 15.00 S 140.00 W
Polinik ∧ 64 46.54 N 13.09 E
Polinyá 266d 41.33 N 2.10 E
Pólis 130 35.02 N 32.25 E
Polist' ≃ 76 58.06 N 31.31 E
Polistena 68 38.25 N 16.05 E
Politécnico Nacional, Instituto ɤ[2] 286a 19.30 N 99.08 W
Politotdel'skoje 83 47.33 N 39.05 E
Pölitz → Police 30 53.35 N 14.33 E
Polivanovo 80 53.36 N 47.23 E
Políyiros 38 40.23 N 23.27 E
Polizzi Generosa 70 37.49 N 14.00 E
Polk, Nebr., U.S. 198 41.05 N 97.46 W
Polk, Ohio, U.S. 214 40.57 N 82.13 W
Polk, Pa., U.S. 214 41.22 N 79.56 W
Polk □[6], Fla., U.S. 220 28.01 N 81.37 W
Polk □[6], Oreg., U.S. 224 45.00 N 123.23 W
Polk □[6], Tex., U.S. 222 30.45 N 94.48 W
Polk City 220 28.11 N 81.50 W
Pol'kino 74 71.10 N 99.13 E
Polkton 192 35.00 N 80.12 W
Polla 68 40.30 N 15.30 E
Pollāchi 122 10.40 N 77.01 E
Pollanten 60 49.09 N 11.28 E
Pollaphuca Reservoir ⊜[1] 48 53.08 N 6.31 W
Pöllau 61 47.18 N 15.51 E
Polleben 54 51.34 N 11.36 E
Pollenfeld 60 48.57 N 11.12 E
Pollenza 66 43.16 N 13.21 E
Pollica 68 40.11 N 15.03 E
Pollina 70 37.59 N 14.09 E
Polling 64 47.48 N 11.09 E
Pollino, Monte ∧ 68 39.55 N 16.11 E
Pollnow → Polanów 30 54.08 N 16.39 E
Polloc Harbor C 116 7.23 N 124.12 E
Pollock, La., U.S. 194 31.31 N 92.24 W
Pollock, S. Dak., U.S. 198 45.55 N 100.17 W
Pollock Pines 226 38.46 N 120.34 W
Pollock Run ≃ 279b 40.14 N 79.47 W
Pollok 222 31.27 N 94.52 W
Pollutri 66 42.08 N 14.35 E
Pollux ∧ 172 44.14 S 168.53 E
Polmak 24 70.04 N 28.00 E
Polná 30 49.29 N 15.43 E
Polnaja ≃ 83 48.54 N 39.50 E
Pol'noje-Jaltunovo 80 53.59 N 41.52 E
Polnovo-Seliger 76 57.32 N 32.55 E
Polo, Pil. 269f 14.42 N 120.57 E
Polo, Ill., U.S. 190 41.59 N 89.35 W
Polo, Mo., U.S. 194 39.33 N 94.03 W
Polochic ≃ 236 15.28 N 89.22 W
Polock, S.S.S.R. 76 55.31 N 28.46 E
Polock, S.S.S.R. 86 52.46 N 59.42 E
Pologi 78 47.29 N 36.15 E
Pologne → Poland □[1] 30 52.00 N 19.00 E
Pologoje Zajmišče 80 48.29 N 45.57 E
Pologrudovo 86 57.07 N 74.13 E
Polom, S.S.S.R. 24 59.13 N 50.50 E
Polom, S.S.S.R. 80 57.47 N 53.29 E
Polo Magnético del Sur → South Magnetic Pole ↼ 9 66.40 S 140.10 E
Pölömäki ∧[2] 26 63.21 N 27.03 E
Polomet' ≃ 76 57.41 N 32.12 E
Polonia → Poland □[1] 30 52.00 N 19.00 E
Poloninskij Chrebet ⩕ 78 48.40 N 23.20 E
Polonio, Cabo ≻ 252 34.24 S 53.46 W
Polonio Pass)(226 35.37 N 120.11 W
Polonnaruwa 122 7.56 N 81.00 E
Polonnaruwa ⊥ 122 7.56 N 81.00 E
Polonnoje 78 50.07 N 27.30 E
Polos 130 41.50 N 27.04 E
Pološkovo 82 54.08 N 35.53 E
Polo Sur → South Pole ↼ 9 90.00 S 0.00
Polotn'anyj 82 55.44 N 36.00 E
Polotsk → Polock 76 55.31 N 28.46 E
Polovinkino 83 49.14 N 38.55 E
Polovinnoje, S.S.S.R. 86 53.46 N 79.15 E
Polovinnoje, S.S.S.R. 86 54.43 N 63.50 E
Polovo 76 57.03 N 32.27 E
Polperro 42 50.19 N 4.31 W
Polruan 42 50.19 N 4.36 W
Pölsbach ≃ 61 47.11 N 14.45 E
Polska → Poland □[1] 30 52.00 N 19.00 E
Polski Trâmbeš 38 43.22 N 25.38 E
Polson 202 47.41 N 114.09 W
Polster ∧ 61 47.32 N 14.58 E
Polsum 52 51.37 N 7.03 E
Poltava 78 49.35 N 34.34 E
Poltavka 86 54.22 N 71.45 E
Poltevy Pen'ki 80 54.35 N 42.06 E
Poltimore 188 45.47 N 75.43 W
Põltsamaa 76 58.38 N 25.58 E
Põltsamaa ≃ 76 58.27 N 26.09 E
Poludino 86 54.51 N 69.55 E
Poluj ≃ 74 66.31 N 66.33 E
Polunočnoje 72 60.52 N 60.25 E
Poluokenushan ⩕ 86 44.06 N 83.10 E
Polūr 122 12.30 N 79.08 E
Polur'adinki 82 54.51 N 38.41 E
Poluškino 265b 55.41 N 38.05 E
Pol'ustrovo ↼[8] 265a 59.58 N 30.25 E
Põlva 76 58.03 N 27.03 E
Polvaredas 258 35.35 S 59.30 W
Polverigi 66 43.31 N 13.23 E
Polvijärvi 26 62.51 N 29.22 E
Polvoranca 266a 40.19 N 3.48 W
Polynesia II 14 4.00 S 156.00 W
Polynésie française → French Polynesia □[2] 14 15.00 S 140.00 W
Polynnoje 80 46.51 N 46.56 E
Polysajevo 86 54.35 N 86.14 E
Pölzig 54 50.57 N 12.11 E
Pomabamba 248 8.50 S 77.28 W
Pomacanchi 248 14.02 S 71.34 W
Pomahaka ≃ 172 46.09 S 169.34 E
Pomán 252 28.24 S 66.13 W
Pomarance 66 43.18 N 10.52 E
Pomarico 68 40.31 N 16.33 E
Pomarkku 26 61.42 N 22.00 E
Pomaro 234 18.20 N 103.18 W
Pomata 248 16.16 S 69.18 W
Pomáz 264c 47.39 N 19.02 E
Pomba ≃ 256 21.24 S 42.32 W
Pombais, Ribeira de ≃ 266c 38.48 N 9.07 W
Pombal, Bra. 250 6.46 S 37.47 W
Pombal, Port. 34 39.55 N 8.38 W
Pombas, Rio das ≃ 248 6.27 S 60.18 W
Pombia 266b 45.39 N 8.38 E
Pomellen 54 53.20 N 14.23 E
Pomene 156 22.53 S 35.33 E
Pomerania □[9] 30 54.00 N 16.00 E
Pomeranian Bay C 54 54.00 N 14.15 E
Pomerene 200 32.01 N 110.17 W
Pomerode 252 26.45 S 49.11 W
Pomeroon ≃ 246 7.37 N 58.45 W
Pomeroy, S. Afr. 158 28.33 S 30.26 E
Pomeroy, N. Ire., U.K. 48 54.36 N 6.56 W
Pomeroy, Iowa, U.S. 198 42.33 N 94.41 W
Pomeroy, Ohio, U.S. 188 39.02 N 82.02 W
Pomeroy, Pa., U.S. 208 39.58 N 75.53 W
Pomeroy, Wash., U.S. 202 46.28 N 117.36 W
Pomezia 66 41.40 N 12.30 E
Pomfret, S. Afr. 156 25.50 S 23.32 E
Pomfret, Conn., U.S. 207 41.54 N 71.58 W
Pomfret, Md., U.S. 208 38.35 N 77.02 W
Pomi 38 47.42 N 23.19 E
Pomigliano d'Arco 66 40.54 N 14.23 E
Pominovo 82 55.26 N 39.11 E
Pomio 164 5.30 S 151.30 E
Pommard 58 47.01 N 4.47 E
Pomme de Terre ≃, Minn., U.S. 198 45.10 N 96.05 W
Pomme de Terre ≃, Mo., U.S. 194 38.11 N 93.24 W
Pomme de Terre Reservoir ⊜[1] 194 37.51 N 93.19 W
Pommera 50 50.10 N 2.26 E
Pommern → Pomerania □[9] 30 54.00 N 16.00 E
Pommersche Bucht → Pomeranian Bay C 54 54.00 N 14.15 E
Pommersfelden 56 49.46 N 10.49 E
Pomona, Namibia 156 27.09 S 15.18 E
Pomona, Calif., U.S. 228 34.04 N 117.45 W
Pomona, Kans., U.S. 198 38.36 N 95.27 W
Pomona, N.J., U.S. 208 39.29 N 74.35 W
Pomona, N.Y., U.S. 276 41.10 N 74.02 W
Pomona Estates 273d 26.06 S 28.15 E
Pomona Lake ⊜[1] 198 38.40 N 95.35 W
Pomona Park 192 29.30 N 81.36 W
Pomongo 152 5.00 S 19.08 E
Pomor'any 78 49.38 N 24.56 E
Pomorie 38 42.33 N 27.39 E
Pomorze → Pomerania □[9] 30 54.00 N 16.00 E
Pomošnaja 78 48.14 N 31.26 E
Pomozdino 24 62.12 N 54.06 E
Pompano Beach 220 26.15 N 80.07 W
Pompano Beach Highlands 220 26.18 N 80.11 W
Pompei 68 40.45 N 14.30 E
Pompei ⊥ 68 40.45 N 14.30 E
Pompéia 255 22.08 S 50.10 W
Pompejevka 89 48.23 N 130.46 E
Pompeston Creek ≃ 285 40.01 N 75.01 W
Pompéu 255 19.12 S 44.59 W
Pompey, Fr. 56 48.46 N 6.07 E
Pompey, N.Y., U.S. 210 42.54 N 76.01 W
Pomponio Beach ♠ 282 37.17 N 122.24 W
Pomponio Creek ≃ 282 37.18 N 122.25 W
Pomponne 261 48.53 N 2.41 E
Pompon-yama ∧ 270 34.56 N 135.37 E
Pomposa 66 44.49 N 12.11 E
Pompton ≃ 276 40.54 N 74.16 W
Pompton Lakes 210 41.00 N 74.17 W
Pompton Lakes ⊜ 276 41.00 N 74.17 W
Pompton Plains 276 40.58 N 74.18 W
Pomquet 186 45.38 N 61.51 W
Pomssen 54 51.14 N 12.37 E
Ponape 174r 6.58 N 158.13 E
Ponape □[5] 174r 6.52 N 158.15 E
Ponape I 174r 6.55 N 158.15 E
Ponape Harbor C 174r 7.00 N 158.13 E
Ponask Lake ⊜ 184 54.00 N 92.41 W
Ponass Lake ⊜ 184 52.18 N 103.58 W
Ponazyrevo 80 58.21 N 46.19 E
Ponca 198 42.34 N 96.43 W
Ponca City 196 36.42 N 97.05 W
Ponca Creek ≃ 198 42.48 N 98.05 W
Ponce 240m 18.01 N 66.37 W
Ponce de Leon 194 30.44 N 85.56 W
Ponce de Leon Bay C 220 25.21 N 81.07 W
Ponce de Leon Inlet C 192 29.04 N 80.55 W
Poncé-sur-le-Loir 50 47.46 N 0.40 E
Poncha Pass)(200 38.25 N 106.05 W
Ponchatoula 194 30.26 N 90.26 W
Poncin 58 46.05 N 5.24 E
Poncitlán 234 20.22 N 102.55 W
Pond Brook ≃, N.J., U.S. 276 41.02 N 74.15 W
Pond Brook ≃, Ohio, U.S. 279a 41.17 N 81.24 W
Pondcreek 196 36.40 N 97.48 W
Pond Creek ≃, Colo., U.S. 198 38.17 N 103.40 W
Pond Creek ≃, Tex., U.S. 222 31.02 N 96.46 W
Pond Eddy 210 41.27 N 74.49 W
Ponder 222 33.11 N 97.17 W
Pondera Coulee ∨ 202 48.16 N 111.03 W
Ponders End ↼[8] 260 51.39 N 0.03 W
Pondicherry 122 11.56 N 79.53 E
Pondicherry □[8] 122 11.56 N 79.50 E
Pond Inlet 176 72.41 N 78.00 W
Pond Inlet C 176 72.46 N 77.00 W
Pondok Tanjong 114 5.00 N 100.44 E
Pondoland ↼[1] 158 31.10 S 29.30 E
Pondorf 60 48.57 N 11.34 E
Pondosa 204 41.12 N 121.41 W
Pond Run ≃ 285 40.13 N 74.44 W
Poneas Island I 116 9.55 N 125.57 E
Ponente, Capo ≻ 71a 35.31 N 12.31 E
Ponente, Punta ≻ 71a 35.52 N 12.51 E
Ponente, Riviera di ≗[2] 62 44.10 N 8.20 E
Ponérihouen 175f 21.05 S 165.24 E
Poneto 216 40.39 N 85.13 W
Ponežukaj 78 44.53 N 39.22 E
Ponferrada 34 42.33 N 6.35 W
Pong 110 19.10 N 100.17 E
Pongani 164 9.05 S 148.35 E
Pongara, Pointe ≻ 152 0.21 N 9.21 E
Pongaroa 172 40.33 S 176.11 E
Pongau ∨ 64 47.21 N 13.14 E
Ponghyŏn 98 37.49 N 125.36 E
Pongo ≃ 140 8.42 N 27.40 E
Pongola ≃ 158 26.57 S 32.17 E
Pon'goma 24 65.21 N 34.25 E
Pong Tamale 150 9.41 N 0.49 W
Ponhook Lake ⊜ 186 44.18 N 64.54 W
Poni ≃ 208 38.07 N 77.26 W
Poniatowa 30 51.11 N 22.05 E
Poniec 30 51.47 N 16.50 E
Ponil Creek ≃ 196 36.29 N 104.48 W
Poninka 78 50.12 N 27.32 E
Ponino 80 58.16 N 52.49 E
Pönitz, B.R.D. 54 54.03 N 10.40 E
Ponitz, D.D.R. 54 50.51 N 12.25 E
Ponizovje 76 55.17 N 31.04 E
Ponkapog Pond ⊜ 283 42.12 N 71.06 W
Pônley 110 12.26 N 104.27 E
Ponnaiyār ≃ 122 11.46 N 79.47 E
Ponnāni 122 10.46 N 75.54 E
Ponnūru Nidubrolu 122 16.04 N 80.34 E
Pono 164 6.22 S 134.36 E
Ponoj 24 67.05 N 41.07 E
Ponoj ≃ 24 66.59 N 41.17 E
Ponoka 182 52.42 N 113.35 W
Ponomar'ovka, S.S.S.R. 80 53.19 N 54.08 E
Ponomar'ovka, S.S.S.R. 86 56.08 N 82.23 E
Ponornica 78 51.43 N 32.49 E

Symbols in the index entries represent the broad categories identified in the key at the right. Symbols with superior numbers (⩕[2]) identify subcategories (see complete key on page *I · 30*).

Kartensymbole in dem Registerverzeichnis stellen die rechts in Schlüssel erklärten Kategorien dar. Symbole mit hochgestellten Ziffern (⩕[2]) bezeichnen Unterabteilungen einer Kategorie (vgl. vollständiger Schlüssel auf Seite *I · 30*).

Los símbolos incluídos en el texto del índice representan las grandes categorías identificadas con la clave a la derecha. Los símbolos con numeros en su parte superior (⩕[2]) identifican las subcategorías (véase la clave completa en la página *I · 30*).

Les symboles de l'index représentent les catégories indiquées dans la légende à droite. Les symboles suivis d'un indice (⩕[2]) représentent des sous-catégories (voir légende complète à la page *I · 30*).

Os símbolos incluídos no texto do índice representam as grandes categorias identificadas com a chave à direita. Os símbolos com números em sua parte superior (⩕[2]) identificam as subcategorias (veja-se a chave completa à página *I · 30*).

Symbol	English	Deutsch	Español	Français	Português
∧	Mountain	Berg	Montaña	Montagne	Montanha
⩕	Mountains	Berge	Montañas	Montagnes	Montanhas
)(	Pass	Pass	Paso	Col	Passo
∨	Valley, Canyon	Tal, Cañon	Valle, Cañón	Vallée, Canyon	Vale, Canhão
≚	Plain	Ebene	Llano	Plaine	Planície
≻	Cape	Kap	Cabo	Cap	Cabo
I	Island	Insel	Isla	Île	Ilha
II	Islands	Inseln	Islas	Îles	Ilhas
≗	Other Topographic Features	Andere Topographische Objekte	Otros Elementos Topográficos	Autres données topographiques	Outros Elementos Topográficos

ESPAÑOL

Nombre	Página	Lat.°′	Long.°′ W=Oeste
Ponorogo	115a	7.52 S	111.27 E
Ponpāj	272b	22.56 N	88.15 E
Pons, Esp.	34	41.55 N	1.12 E
Pons, Fr.	32	45.35 N	0.33 W
Ponsacco	66	43.37 N	10.38 E
Ponson Island I	116	10.46 N	124.32 E
Ponsul ≃	34	39.40 N	7.31 W
Pont	62	45.34 N	7.07 E
Pont-à-Celles	50	50.30 N	4.21 E
Ponta Delgada	148a	37.44 N	25.40 W
Ponta de Pedras	250	1.23 S	48.52 W
Ponta Grossa	252	25.05 S	50.09 W
Pontal ≃	250	9.08 S	40.12 W
Pontalete	256	21.27 S	45.40 W
Pontalina	255	17.31 S	49.27 W
Pontallier-sur-Saône	58	47.18 N	5.25 E
Pont-à-Marcq	50	50.31 N	3.07 E
Pont-à-Mousson	56	48.54 N	6.04 E
Pontão	34	39.55 N	8.22 W
Ponta Porã	255	22.32 S	55.43 W
Pontardawe	42	51.44 N	3.51 W
Pontardulais	42	51.43 N	4.03 W
Pontarlier	58	46.54 N	6.22 E
Pontas de Pedra	250	7.38 S	34.48 W
Pontassieve	66	43.46 N	11.26 E
Pontaubert	50	47.29 N	3.52 E
Pont-Audemer	50	49.21 N	0.31 E
Pontault-Combault	261	48.47 N	2.36 E
Pontaumur	32	45.52 N	2.40 E
Pont-Aven	32	47.51 N	3.45 W
Pontbriand	206	46.09 N	71.15 W
Pont Canavese	62	45.25 N	7.36 E
Pontcarré	261	48.48 N	2.42 E
Pontcharra	62	45.26 N	6.01 E
Pontchartrain	261	48.48 N	1.54 E
Pontchartrain, Lake @	194	30.10 N	90.10 W
Pontchâteau	32	47.26 N	2.05 W
Pont-Croix	32	48.02 N	4.29 W
Pont-d'Ain	58	46.03 N	5.20 E
Pont-de-Bonne	56	50.27 N	5.17 E
Pont-de-Chéruy	62	45.45 N	5.11 E
Pont-de-l'Arche	50	49.18 N	1.10 E
Pont-de-Pany	58	47.18 N	4.49 E
Pont-de-Poitte	58	46.35 N	5.41 E
Pont-de-Roide	58	47.23 N	6.46 E
Pont-de-Ruan	50	47.15 N	0.35 E
Pont-de-Salars	32	44.17 N	2.44 E
Pont de Suert	34	42.24 N	0.45 E
Pont-de-Vaux	58	46.26 N	4.56 E
Pont-de-Veyle	58	46.16 N	4.53 E
Ponte a Elsa	66	43.41 N	10.54 E
Ponte Alta	256	22.26 S	47.06 W
Ponte Alta do Bom Jesus	255	12.06 S	46.29 W
Ponte Alta do Norte	250	10.45 S	47.34 W
Ponte a Moriano	66	43.54 N	10.31 E
Ponte 13 Archi	68	41.31 N	14.56 E
Pontebba	64	46.30 N	13.18 E
Ponte Branca	255	16.27 S	52.40 W
Ponte Caffaro	64	45.50 N	10.32 E
Pontecagnano	68	40.39 N	14.52 E
Pontecchio Marconi	64	44.25 N	11.15 E
Pontecchio Polesine	64	45.01 N	11.49 E
Pontecorvo	66	41.27 N	13.40 E
Pontecurone	62	44.57 N	8.56 E
Ponte da Barca	34	41.48 N	8.25 W
Ponte d'Arbia	66	43.10 N	11.28 E
Ponte delle Arche	64	46.02 N	10.52 E
Ponte dell'Olio	62	44.52 N	9.39 E
Pontedera	66	43.40 N	10.38 E
Ponte de Sor	34	39.15 N	8.01 W
Ponte di Barbarano	64	45.23 N	11.34 E
Ponte di Legno	64	46.16 N	10.31 E
Ponte di Nava	62	44.08 N	7.53 E
Ponte di Piave	64	45.43 N	12.28 E
Ponte do Lima	34	41.46 N	8.35 W
Ponte do Púngoè	156	19.30 S	34.32 E
Pontefract	44	53.42 N	1.18 W
Ponte Galeria ◆[8]	267a	41.49 N	12.21 E
Ponte Gardena (Waidbruck)	64	46.36 N	11.32 E
Ponte Ghiereto	66	43.59 N	11.15 E
Pontegrande	58	45.59 N	8.09 E
Ponte in Valtellina	64	46.12 N	9.59 E
Ponteix	184	49.49 N	107.30 W
Pontelagoscuro	64	44.53 N	11.36 E
Ponteland	44	55.03 N	1.44 W
Pontelandolfo	68	41.17 N	14.41 E
Pontelongo	64	45.15 N	12.02 E
Ponte nell'Alpi	64	46.11 N	12.16 E
Ponte Nova	255	20.24 S	42.54 W
Pont-en-Royans	62	45.04 N	5.21 E
Ponte Nuovo	66	43.01 N	12.28 E
Pontenure	62	44.59 N	9.47 E
Pontepetri	66	44.02 N	10.53 E
Pontericcioli	66	43.26 N	12.38 E
Ponte Rocchetta	64	46.14 N	11.04 E
Ponterwyd	42	52.25 N	3.50 W
Pontes	256	22.26 S	46.28 W
Ponte San Giovanni	66	43.05 N	12.26 E
Ponte San Pietro	62	45.42 N	9.35 E
Pontesbury	42	52.39 N	2.54 W
Ponte Selva	64	45.52 N	9.54 E
Ponte Serrada	252	26.52 S	51.58 W
Pontestura	62	45.08 N	8.20 E
Ponte Tresa	58	45.58 N	8.52 E
Pontevedra, Arg.	258	34.45 S	58.42 W
Pontevedra, Esp.	34	42.26 N	8.38 W
Pontevedra, Pil.	116	10.22 N	122.52 E
Pontevedra, Ría de C[1]	34	42.22 N	8.45 W
Pont-Évêque	62	45.32 N	4.55 E
Pontevico	64	45.16 N	10.05 E
Pontfaverger-Moronvilliers	50	49.18 N	4.19 E
Pontgibaud	32	46.50 N	2.51 E
Ponthévrard	261	48.33 N	1.55 E
Ponthierry	261	48.32 N	2.33 E
Ponthierville → Ubundu	154	0.21 S	25.29 E
Pontiac, Ill., U.S.	190	40.53 N	88.38 W
Pontiac, Mich., U.S.	216	42.37 N	83.18 W
Pontiac □[6]	212	46.30 N	77.00 W
Pontiac, Parc de ♠	190	46.25 N	76.35 W
Pontiac Lake	281	42.40 N	83.28 W
Pontiac Lake @	281	42.40 N	83.28 W
Pontiac Lake State Recreation Area ♠	216	42.41 N	83.28 W
Pontiac Mall ◆[9]	281	42.39 N	83.20 W
Pontiac Metropolitan Stadium ♠	281	42.39 N	83.15 W
Pontianak	112	0.02 S	109.20 E
Pontian Kechil	114	1.29 N	103.23 E
Pontida	62	45.43 N	9.30 E
Pontigny	50	47.55 N	3.43 E
Pontinha ◆[8]	266c	38.46 N	9.11 W
Pontinia	66	41.24 N	13.02 E
Pontivy	32	48.04 N	2.59 W
Pont-l'Abbé	32	47.52 N	4.13 W
Pont-lès-Moulins	58	47.19 N	6.22 E
Pont-l'évêque	50	49.18 N	0.11 E
Pontlevoy	50	47.23 N	1.15 E
Pontoise	50	49.03 N	2.06 E
Pontoise-Cormeilles-en-Vexin, Aérodrome ⊠	261	49.06 N	2.02 E
Ponton Creek ≃	162	31.10 S	124.25 E
Pontonnyj	265a	59.47 N	30.38 E
Pontoon Beach	219	38.43 N	90.04 W
Pontorson	32	48.33 N	1.31 W
Pontotoc, Miss., U.S.	194	34.15 N	89.00 W
Pontotoc, Tex., U.S.	196	30.54 N	98.59 W
Pontremoli	62	44.22 N	9.53 E
Pont-Remy	50	50.03 N	1.55 E
Pontresina	58	46.28 N	9.53 E
Pontrhydfendigaid	42	52.17 N	3.51 W
Pont-Rouge	206	46.45 N	71.42 W
Pont-Royal	62	43.43 N	5.11 E
Pont-Sainte-Marie	50	48.19 N	4.06 E

FRANÇAIS

Nom	Page	Lat.°′	Long.°′ W=Ouest
Pont-Sainte-Maxence	50	49.18 N	2.36 E
Pont-Saint-Esprit	62	44.15 N	4.39 E
Pont-Saint-Martin	62	45.36 N	7.48 E
Pont-Saint-Vincent	58	48.36 N	6.06 E
Pont-Scorff	28	47.50 N	3.24 W
Ponts Quentin, Ruisseau des ≃	261	48.44 N	1.48 E
Pont-sur-Yonne	50	48.17 N	3.12 E
Pontuda, Ilha I	287a	23.02 S	43.18 W
Pontvallain	50	47.45 N	0.12 E
Pont-Viau ◆[8]	275a	45.34 N	73.41 W
Pontyberem	42	51.17 N	4.09 W
Pontycymmer	42	51.37 N	3.34 W
Pontypool	42	51.43 N	3.02 W
Pontypridd	42	51.37 N	3.22 W
Pony	202	45.40 N	111.54 W
Ponyri	76	52.19 N	36.20 E
Ponza	66	40.54 N	12.58 E
Ponziane, Isole I	66	40.55 N	12.57 E
Ponziane, Isole II	66	40.55 N	12.57 E
Ponzone	62	44.35 N	8.27 E
Poochera	162	32.43 S	134.51 E
Pool □[5]	152	3.30 S	15.00 E
Poole	42	50.43 N	1.59 W
Poole, Mount ∧	166	29.37 S	141.46 E
Poole Bay C	42	50.42 N	1.52 W
Pooler	192	32.07 N	81.15 W
Poole's Cavern ◆[5]	262	53.14 N	1.56 W
Pooles Island I	208	39.17 N	76.16 W
Poolesville	208	39.09 N	77.25 W
Poolewe	46	57.45 N	5.37 W
Pooley Island I	182	52.44 N	128.16 W
Poolville	222	32.58 N	97.52 W
Poona → Pune	122	18.32 N	73.52 E
Poona-Bayabo (Gata)	116	7.51 N	124.22 E
Pooncarie	166	33.23 S	142.34 E
Poondinna, Mount ∧	162	27.20 S	129.59 E
Poopó	248	18.23 S	66.59 W
Poopó, Lago @	248	18.45 S	67.07 W
Pooraka	168b	34.50 S	138.37 E
Poor Knights Islands II	172	35.30 S	174.45 E
Poor Man Indian Reserve ◆[4]	184	51.30 N	104.23 W
Poor Meadow Brook ≃	283	42.01 N	70.55 W
Poortjie	158	30.13 S	22.44 E
Poowong	169	38.21 S	145.46 E
Popa, Isla I	236	9.11 N	82.07 W
Popasnaja	83	48.37 N	38.20 E
Popasnoje	78	48.48 N	35.31 E
Popayán	246	2.27 N	76.36 W
Pope	194	34.13 N	89.57 W
Pope Creek ≃	226	38.37 N	122.17 W
Popel'n'a	78	49.57 N	29.27 E
Popel'nastoje	78	48.39 N	33.43 E
Poperečnoje	88	52.23 N	110.42 E
Poperinge	50	50.51 N	2.43 E
Popești-Leordeni	38	44.23 N	26.10 E
Pope Valley	226	38.37 N	122.26 W
Popham Bay C	176	64.10 N	65.10 W
Popigaj	74	71.55 N	110.47 E
Popigaj ≃	74	72.54 N	106.36 E
Popilta Lake @	166	33.10 S	141.43 E
Popinci	38	42.25 N	24.17 E
Popki	80	50.11 N	44.30 E
Popkum	224	49.12 N	121.44 W
Poplar, Calif., U.S.	226	36.03 N	119.08 W
Poplar, Mont., U.S.	198	48.07 N	105.12 W
Poplar, Wis., U.S.	190	46.35 N	91.48 W
Poplar ◆[8]	260	51.31 N	0.01 W
Poplar ≃, Can.	184	53.00 N	97.24 W
Poplar ≃, N.A.	198	48.05 N	105.11 W
Poplar ≃, Minn., U.S.	198	47.51 N	96.04 W
Poplar, West Fork ≃	198	48.31 N	105.22 W
Poplar Bluff	194	36.45 N	90.24 W
Poplar Grove	216	42.22 N	88.49 W
Poplar Heights	284c	38.53 N	77.12 W
Poplar Hill	184	52.05 N	94.18 W
Poplar Mountain ∧	194	36.43 N	85.03 W
Poplar Point	184	50.04 N	97.57 W
Poplar Ridge	210	42.44 N	76.37 W
Poplar Springs	208	39.21 N	77.06 W
Poplarville	194	30.51 N	89.32 W
Poplevinskij	76	53.41 N	39.33 E
Popo Aggie ≃	202	43.01 N	108.21 W
Popocatépetl, Volcán ∧[1]	234	19.02 N	98.38 W
Popof Island I	180	55.17 N	160.25 W
Popoh	115a	8.15 S	111.48 E
Popokabaka	152	5.42 S	16.35 E
Popoli	66	42.10 N	13.50 E
Popomanasiu, Mount ∧	175e	9.42 S	160.04 E
Popondetta	164	8.46 S	148.14 E
Popova	89	42.58 N	131.42 E
Popovka, S.S.S.R.	76	60.08 N	39.21 E
Popovka, S.S.S.R.	80	49.14 N	41.12 E
Popovkino	82	56.07 N	36.01 E
Popovo	38	43.21 N	26.13 E
Poppberg ∧	60	49.25 N	11.35 E
Poppel	56	51.27 N	5.02 E
Poppenbüttel ◆[8]	52	53.39 N	10.04 E
Poppenhausen	56	50.06 N	10.08 E
Poppi	66	43.43 N	11.46 E
Popple ≃	190	45.50 N	88.21 W
Poprad	30	49.03 N	20.18 E
Poprad ≃	30	49.38 N	20.42 E
Popricani	38	47.18 N	27.31 E
Pŏpsŏng	98	35.22 N	126.27 E
Pŏptong	98	38.59 N	127.05 E
Poptún	236	16.21 N	89.26 W
Populonia	66	42.59 N	10.29 E
Poputnaja	84	44.31 N	41.27 E
Poqinshumu	104	42.24 N	121.36 E
Poquessing Creek ≃	285	40.03 N	74.58 W
Poquetanuck	207	41.29 N	72.03 W
Poquonock	207	41.54 N	72.41 W
Poquonock Bridge	207	41.19 N	72.11 W
Poquoson	208	37.07 N	76.21 W
Poquoson ≃	208	37.10 N	76.24 W
Poquott	276	40.57 N	73.05 W
Porādaha	126	23.51 N	89.01 E
Porādiha	126	21.33 N	86.26 E
Porāli Nai ≃	120	25.58 N	66.26 E
Poranga	250	4.44 S	40.55 W
Porangahau	172	40.18 S	176.37 E
Porangatu	255	13.26 S	49.10 W
Porbandar	120	21.38 N	69.36 E
Porce ≃	246	7.28 N	74.53 W
Porcelette	56	49.09 N	6.36 E
Por Chaman	128	33.08 N	63.51 E
Porcher Island I	182	53.57 N	130.30 W
Porcheville	261	48.58 N	1.47 E
Porchov	76	57.46 N	29.34 E
Porcia	64	45.57 N	12.36 E
Porciúncula	255	20.58 S	42.02 W
Porco	248	19.50 S	65.59 W
Porcos, Rio dos ≃	255	12.42 S	45.07 W
Porcuna	34	37.52 N	4.11 W
Porcupine ≃	180	66.35 N	145.15 W
Porcupine Brook ≃	283	42.46 N	71.13 W
Porcupine Dome ∧	180	65.31 N	145.31 W
Porcupine Hills ∧∧[2]	184	52.30 N	101.45 W
Porcupine Mountains ∧∧	190	46.40 N	89.40 W
Porcupine Mountains State Park ♠	190	46.47 N	89.50 W
Porcupine Point ≻	180	60.45 N	146.44 W
Pordenone	64	45.57 N	12.39 E
Pordenone □[4]	64	46.00 N	12.45 E
Pordim	38	43.23 N	24.51 E
Poreč	36	45.13 N	13.37 E
Porecatu	255	22.43 S	51.24 W
Porečje, S.S.S.R.	76	55.43 N	35.33 E
Porečje, S.S.S.R.	76	56.06 N	30.29 E
Porečje, S.S.S.R.	76	53.55 N	24.07 E

PORTUGUÊS

Nome	Página	Lat.°′	Long.°′ W=Oeste
Porečje Rybnoje	80	57.06 N	39.23 E
Poreckoje	80	55.12 N	46.20 E
Porez	80	57.40 N	51.10 E
Pori	26	61.29 N	21.47 E
Poricy Brook ≃	276	40.21 N	74.05 W
Porirua	172	41.08 S	174.51 E
Porjaguba	24	66.47 N	33.45 E
Porkkala	26	59.59 N	24.26 E
Porlamar	246	10.57 N	63.51 W
Porlezza	58	46.03 N	9.07 E
Porlock	42	51.14 N	3.36 W
Porma ≃	34	42.29 N	5.28 W
Pornassio	62	44.04 N	7.52 E
Pörnbach	60	48.37 N	11.28 E
Pornic	32	47.07 N	2.06 W
Porog, S.S.S.R.	24	63.50 N	38.29 E
Porog, S.S.S.R.	76	59.16 N	33.24 E
Porogi	265a	59.46 N	30.47 E
Poro Island I	116	10.40 N	124.27 E
Porokylä	26	63.33 N	29.06 E
Poroma	248	18.29 S	65.30 W
Poronaj ≃	89	49.14 N	143.06 E
Poronajsk	89	49.14 N	143.04 E
Porong	115a	7.32 S	112.41 E
Porong ≃	115a	7.32 S	112.51 E
Poropotank ≃	208	37.27 N	76.42 W
Poror ∧	154	1.14 N	36.37 E
Poroškovo	78	48.41 N	22.45 E
Porosozero	24	62.43 N	32.42 E
Poroto Mountains ∧∧	154	9.00 S	33.45 E
Porozovo	76	52.56 N	24.22 E
Porožskij	88	56.04 N	101.46 E
Porpoise Bay C	9	66.30 S	128.30 E
Porpoise Channel ⊔	276	40.55 N	73.09 W
Porquerolles	62	43.00 N	6.12 E
Porquerolles, Île de I	62	43.00 N	6.13 E
Porrentruy	58	47.25 N	7.05 E
Porretta Terme	64	44.09 N	10.59 E
Porsangen C[2]	24	70.58 N	27.00 E
Porsangerhalvøya ≻[1]	24	70.50 N	25.00 E
Porsea	114	2.27 N	99.09 E
Porsgrunn	26	59.09 N	9.40 E
Porsuk ≃	130	39.42 N	31.59 E
Port → Le Port	157c	20.55 S	55.18 E
Portachuelo	248	17.21 S	63.24 W
Portacloy	48	54.19 N	9.48 W
Port Adelaide	168b	34.51 S	138.30 E
Porta di Roma, Necropoli del ⊥	267a	41.46 N	12.16 E
Portadown	48	54.26 N	6.27 W
Portaferry	48	54.23 N	5.33 W
Portage, Alaska, U.S.	180	60.50 N	148.58 W
Portage, Ind., U.S.	216	41.34 N	87.14 W
Portage, Mich., U.S.	216	42.12 N	85.41 W
Portage, Ohio, U.S.	216	41.20 N	83.39 W
Portage, Pa., U.S.	214	40.23 N	78.41 W
Portage, Utah, U.S.	200	41.59 N	112.14 W
Portage, Wis., U.S.	190	43.33 N	89.28 W
Portage □[6]	214	41.09 N	81.15 W
Portage ≃, Mich., U.S.	216	41.57 N	85.38 W
Portage ≃, Ohio, U.S.	214	41.31 N	83.05 W
Portage, East Branch ≃	216	41.17 N	83.31 W
Portage, Middle Branch ≃	216	41.22 N	83.28 W
Portage, North Branch ≃	216	41.25 N	83.27 W
Portage, South Branch ≃	216	41.22 N	83.30 W
Portage Bay C	184	51.33 N	98.50 W
Portage Des Sioux	219	38.55 N	90.21 W
Portage Lake @, Mich., U.S.	216	42.25 N	83.54 W
Portage Lake @, Mich., U.S.	216	42.03 N	85.31 W
Portage Lakes	214	40.59 N	81.32 W
Portage Lakes @	214	40.59 N	81.32 W
Portage Lakes State Park ♠	214	40.57 N	81.32 W
Portage-la-Prairie	184	49.59 N	98.18 W
Portage Park ◆[8]	278	41.57 N	87.46 W
Portageville, Mo., U.S.	194	36.26 N	89.42 W
Portageville, N.Y., U.S.	210	42.34 N	78.02 W
Portal, Ga., U.S.	192	32.33 N	81.56 W
Portal, N. Dak., U.S.	198	48.59 N	102.33 W
Port Alberni	182	49.14 N	124.48 W
Portal del Infierno ⌊	236	14.22 N	85.38 W
Portalegre, Bra.	250	6.02 S	38.00 W
Portalegre, Port.	34	39.17 N	7.26 W
Portales	196	34.11 N	103.20 W
Port Alexander	180	56.15 N	134.39 W
Port Alfred (Kowie)	158	33.36 S	26.55 E
Port Alice	182	50.23 N	127.27 W
Port Allegany	214	41.49 N	78.17 W
Port Allen	194	30.27 N	91.12 W
Port Alma, Austl.	166	23.35 S	150.51 E
Port Alma, Ont., Can.	214	42.11 N	82.15 W
Port Alsworth	180	60.12 N	154.20 W
Port Angeles	224	48.07 N	123.27 W
Port Angeles Harbor C	224	48.07 N	123.24 W
Port Anson	186	49.32 N	55.50 W
Port Antonio	241q	18.11 N	76.28 W
Port Aransas	196	27.50 N	97.04 W
Portarlington, Austl.	169	38.07 S	144.39 E
Portarlington, Eire	48	53.10 N	7.11 W
Port Arthur, Austl.	166	43.09 S	147.51 E
Port Arthur → Thunder Bay, Ont., Can.	190	48.23 N	89.15 W
Port Arthur, Tex., U.S.	194	29.55 N	93.55 W
Port Arthur → Lüshun, Zhg.	98	38.48 N	121.16 E
Port Ashton	180	60.04 N	148.01 W
Port Askaig	46	55.51 N	6.07 W
Port Augusta	166	32.30 S	137.46 E
Port au Port	186	48.33 N	58.44 W
Port au Port Bay C	186	48.40 N	58.45 W
Port au Port Peninsula ≻[1]	186	48.35 N	59.00 W
Port-au-Prince	238	18.32 N	72.20 W
Port-au-Prince, Baie de C	238	18.40 N	72.30 W
Port Austin	190	44.03 N	83.01 W
Port aux Basques → Channel-Port-aux-Basques	186	47.34 N	59.09 W
Porta Westfalica	52	52.14 N	8.55 E
Porta Westfalica ♠	52	52.14 N	8.55 E
Port Bannatyne	46	55.52 N	5.05 W
Port Barre	194	30.34 N	91.57 W
Port Bell	154	0.17 N	32.39 E
Port-Bergé	157b	15.33 S	47.40 E
Port Blair	110	11.40 N	92.45 E
Port Blakely	224	47.37 N	122.28 W
Port Blandford	186	48.21 N	54.10 W
Port Bolivar	222	29.23 N	94.46 W
Port Borden	186	46.15 N	63.42 W
Port-Bouët	150	5.15 N	3.58 W
Port Broughton	166	33.36 S	137.56 E
Port Burwell	212	42.39 N	80.49 W
Port Byron, Ill., U.S.	190	41.36 N	90.20 W
Port Byron, N.Y., U.S.	210	43.02 N	76.38 W
Port Campbell	169	38.37 S	143.00 E
Port Campbell National Park ♠	169	38.38 S	142.55 E
Port Canning	126	22.18 N	88.40 E
Port Carbon	208	40.42 N	76.10 W
Port Carling	212	45.07 N	79.35 W
Port-Cartier-Ouest	186	50.01 N	66.52 W

Nome	Página	Lat.°′	Long.°′ W=Oeste
Port-Cartier-Sept-Îles, Parc de ♠	186	50.35 N	67.10 W
Port Chalmers	172	45.49 S	170.37 E
Port Charlotte	220	26.59 N	82.06 W
Port Chester	210	41.00 N	73.40 W
Port Chester Harbor C	276	40.59 N	73.40 W
Port Chicago	226	38.03 N	122.01 W
Port Clements	182	53.42 N	132.11 W
Port Clinton, Austl.	168b	34.14 S	138.01 E
Port Clinton, Ohio, U.S.	214	41.31 N	82.56 W
Port Clinton, Pa., U.S.	208	40.35 N	76.02 W
Port Clyde	188	43.56 N	69.15 W
Port Colborne	212	42.53 N	79.14 W
Port Colden	210	40.46 N	74.57 W
Port Columbus International Airport ⊠	218	40.00 N	82.53 W
Port Coquitlam	182	49.16 N	122.46 W
Port Costa	226	38.03 N	122.11 W
Port Crane	210	42.10 N	75.50 W
Port Credit	212	43.33 N	79.35 W
Port-Cros	62	43.00 N	6.23 E
Port-Cros, Île de I	62	43.00 N	6.24 E
Port-Daniel, Parc de ♠	186	48.18 N	64.55 W
Port-Daniel, Rśerve (Port Daniel Reserve) ♠	186	48.18 N	64.55 W
Port-de-Bouc	62	43.24 N	4.59 E
Port-de-Paix	238	19.57 N	72.50 W
Port Dickinson	210	42.08 N	75.53 W
Port Dickson	114	2.31 N	101.48 E
Port Dover	212	42.47 N	80.12 W
Porte Crayon, Mount ∧	188	38.56 N	79.27 W
Port Edward, B.C., Can.	182	54.14 N	130.18 W
Port Edward, S. Afr.	158	31.02 S	30.13 E
Port Edward → Weihai, Zhg.	98	37.28 N	122.07 E
Port Edwards	190	44.21 N	90.05 W
Portegolpe	236	10.20 N	85.46 W
Porteiras	250	7.31 S	39.07 W
Porteirinha	255	15.44 S	43.02 W
Portel, Bra.	250	1.57 S	50.49 W
Portel, Port.	34	38.18 N	7.42 W
Portela ≃	287a	23.00 S	43.27 W
Portela, Aeroporto da ⊠	266c	38.46 N	9.08 W
Port Elgin, N.B., Can.	186	46.03 N	64.05 W
Port Elgin, Ont., Can.	190	44.26 N	81.24 W
Port Elizabeth, St. Vin.	241h	13.03 N	61.13 W
Port Elizabeth, S. Afr.	158	33.58 S	25.40 E
Port Elizabeth, N.J., U.S.	208	39.19 N	74.59 W
Port Ellen	46	55.39 N	6.12 W
Port Elliot	168b	35.32 S	138.41 E
Porteña	252	31.01 S	62.04 W
Port-en-Bessin	32	49.21 N	0.45 W
Porter, Ind., U.S.	216	41.37 N	87.04 W
Porter, Okla., U.S.	196	35.52 N	95.31 W
Porter, Tex., U.S.	222	30.06 N	95.14 W
Porter, Wash., U.S.	224	46.56 N	123.18 W
Porter □[6]	216	41.28 N	87.04 W
Port'Ercole	66	42.23 N	11.12 E
Porter Corners	210	43.09 N	73.53 W
Porter Creek ≃	279a	41.41 N	81.56 W
Port Erin	44	54.06 N	4.44 W
Porter Lake @	184	56.21 N	107.20 W
Porter Springs	222	31.16 N	95.36 W
Porters Retreat	170	34.00 S	149.48 E
Porters Run ≃	279b	40.27 N	79.33 W
Portersville	214	40.56 N	80.09 W
Porterville, S. Afr.	158	33.00 S	19.00 E
Porterville, Calif., U.S.	204	36.04 N	119.01 W
Porterville, Miss., U.S.	194	32.41 N	88.28 W
Portes-lés-Valence	62	44.52 N	4.53 E
Port Essington	182	54.09 N	129.57 W
Portete, Bahía de C	246	12.13 N	71.55 W
Port-Étienne → Nouadhibou	148	20.54 N	17.04 W
Port Ewen	210	41.54 N	73.59 W
Porteynon	42	51.33 N	4.13 W
Porteynon Point ≻	42	51.32 N	4.12 W
Portezuelo	234	20.25 N	102.31 W
Port Fairy	166	38.23 S	142.14 E
Port Fitzroy	172	36.10 S	175.21 E
Port Gamble	224	47.51 N	122.35 W
Port Gamble Indian Reservation ◆[4]	224	47.53 N	122.34 W
Port-Gentil	152	0.43 S	8.47 E
Port Germein	166	33.01 S	138.00 E
Port Gibson, Miss., U.S.	194	31.58 N	90.58 W
Port Gibson, N.Y., U.S.	210	43.02 N	77.09 W
Port Glasgow	46	55.57 N	4.41 W
Portglenone	48	54.53 N	6.27 W
Port Graham	180	59.21 N	151.50 W
Port Greville	186	45.24 N	64.33 W
Porth	42	51.38 N	3.25 W
Port Hacking	274a	34.04 S	151.08 E
Port Hacking Point ≻	274a	34.05 S	151.10 E
Port Hammond	224	49.13 N	122.39 W
Port Harcourt	150	4.43 N	7.05 E
Port Hardy	182	50.43 N	127.29 W
Port Hawkesbury	186	45.37 N	61.21 W
Porthcawl	42	51.29 N	3.43 W
Port Hedland	162	20.19 S	118.34 E
Port Heiden	180	56.55 N	158.41 W
Port Henry	188	44.03 N	73.28 W
Port Hill	186	46.35 N	63.53 W
Porth Neigwl C	42	52.48 N	4.34 W
Port Hood	186	46.01 N	61.32 W
Port Hope, Ont., Can.	212	43.57 N	78.18 W
Port Hope, Mich., U.S.	190	43.57 N	82.43 W
Port Hueneme	228	34.09 N	119.12 W
Port Hughes	168b	34.04 S	137.32 E
Port Huron	214	42.58 N	82.27 W
Portici	68	40.49 N	14.20 E
Portico di Romagna	66	44.01 N	11.47 E
Portigliola	68	38.14 N	16.13 E
Port-Il'ič	84	38.53 N	48.48 E
Portillo	240p	19.55 N	77.11 W
Portimão	34	37.08 N	8.32 W
Portinho, Rio do ≃	287a	23.03 S	43.35 W
Port Isaac	42	50.35 N	4.49 W
Port Isabel	196	26.04 N	97.13 W
Portishead	42	51.30 N	2.46 W
Port Jefferson, N.Y., U.S.	210	40.57 N	73.04 W
Port Jefferson, Ohio, U.S.	216	40.20 N	84.06 W
Port Jefferson Harbor C	276	40.58 N	73.05 W
Port Jefferson Station	210	40.56 N	73.03 W
Port Jervis	210	41.22 N	74.41 W
Port-Katon	83	46.52 N	38.46 E
Port Keats Mission	164	14.13 S	129.32 E
Port Kembla	170	34.29 S	150.54 E
Port Kennedy	285	40.06 N	75.25 W
Port Kenny	162	33.10 S	134.42 E
Portknockie	46	57.41 N	2.51 W
Port Láirghe → Waterford	48	52.15 N	7.06 W
Port Lambton	214	42.39 N	82.30 W
Portland, Austl.	166	38.21 S	141.36 E
Portland, Austl.	170	33.22 S	150.00 E
Portland, N.Z.	172	35.48 S	174.19 E
Portland, Ark., U.S.	194	33.14 N	91.30 W
Portland, Conn., U.S.	207	41.34 N	72.38 W
Portland, Ind., U.S.	216	40.26 N	84.59 W
Portland, Maine, U.S.	188	43.39 N	70.17 W

Nome	Página	Lat.°′	Long.°′ W=Oeste
Portland, Mich., U.S.	216	42.52 N	84.54 W
Portland, Mo., U.S.	219	38.43 N	91.43 W
Portland, N. Dak., U.S.	198	47.30 N	97.22 W
Portland, N.Y., U.S.	214	42.23 N	79.28 W
Portland, Oreg., U.S.	224	45.33 N	122.36 W
Portland, Pa., U.S.	210	40.55 N	75.06 W
Portland, Tenn., U.S.	194	36.35 N	86.31 W
Portland, Tex., U.S.	196	27.53 N	97.20 W
Portland, Wis., U.S.	216	43.12 N	88.58 W
Portland, Bill of ≻	42	50.31 N	2.27 W
Portland, Cape ≻	166	40.45 S	147.57 E
Portland, Isle of I	42	50.33 N	2.27 W
Portland Bay C	166	38.19 S	141.47 E
Portland Bight C[3]	241q	17.53 N	77.08 W
Portland Canal C	180	55.10 N	130.08 W
Portland Creek Pond @	186	50.12 N	57.34 W
Portland Inlet C	182	54.50 N	130.15 W
Portland International Airport ⊠	224	45.35 N	122.36 W
Portland Island I	172	39.17 S	177.52 E
Portland Mills	214	41.23 N	78.50 W
Portland Point ≻	241q	17.42 N	77.11 W
Portlandville	210	42.32 N	74.58 W
Portlaoghise	48	53.02 N	7.17 W
Port Lavaca	196	28.37 N	96.38 W
Portlaw	48	52.17 N	7.19 W
Port-Lesney	58	47.00 N	5.49 E
Port Leyden	212	43.35 N	75.21 W
Port Lincoln	166	34.44 S	135.52 E
Port Lions	180	57.52 N	152.53 W
Portlock Reefs ✢[2]	164	9.30 S	144.45 E
Port Lockroy ʊ[3]	9	64.48 S	63.30 W
Port Logan	44	54.43 N	4.56 W
Port Loko	150	8.46 N	12.47 W
Port-Louis, Fr.	32	47.43 N	3.21 W
Port-Louis, Guad.	241o	16.25 N	61.32 W
Port Louis, Maus.	157c	20.10 S	57.30 E
Port Ludlow	224	47.56 N	122.41 W
Port-Lyautey → Kenitra	148	34.16 N	6.40 W
Port MacDonnell	166	38.03 S	140.42 E
Port Macquarie	166	31.26 S	152.55 E
Port Madison Indian Reservation ◆[4]	224	47.45 N	122.35 W
Portmadoc	42	52.55 N	4.08 W
Portmahomack	46	57.49 N	3.50 W
Port Maitland, N.S., Can.	186	43.59 N	66.09 W
Port Maitland, Ont., Can.	214	42.52 N	79.34 W
Port Maria	241q	18.22 N	76.54 W
Port Matilda	214	40.48 N	78.03 W
Port Mayaca	220	26.59 N	80.36 W
Port McNeill	182	50.35 N	127.06 W
Port McNicoll	212	44.45 N	79.49 W
Port Melbourne	274b	37.51 S	144.56 E
Port Mellon	182	49.32 N	123.29 W
Port-Menier	186	49.48 N	64.20 W
Port Moller	180	55.59 N	160.34 W
Port Monmouth	276	40.26 N	74.07 W
Port Moody	182	49.17 N	122.51 W
Port Morant	241q	17.54 N	76.19 W
Port Moresby	164	9.30 S	147.10 E
Port Morien	186	46.08 N	59.52 W
Port Morris	276	40.54 N	74.41 W
Port Mouton	186	43.56 N	64.51 W
Port Murray	210	40.47 N	74.55 W
Portnaguiran	46	58.17 N	6.13 W
Portnahaven	46	55.41 N	6.31 W
Port Neches	194	29.59 N	93.58 W
Port Neill	166	34.07 S	136.20 E
Port Nelson	184	57.03 N	92.36 W
Portneuf	206	46.42 N	71.53 W
Portneuf □[6]	206	46.45 N	72.00 W
Portneuf ≃, Qué., Can.	186	48.38 N	69.05 W
Portneuf ≃, Qué., Can.	206	46.42 N	71.53 W
Portneuf ≃, Idaho, U.S.	202	42.58 N	112.35 W
Portneuf, Lac @	186	49.08 N	79.18 W
Portneuf-Station	206	46.43 N	71.54 W
Portneuf-sur-Mer	186	48.37 N	69.06 W
Port Neville	182	50.29 N	126.05 W
Port Noarlunga	168b	35.09 S	138.28 E
Port Nolloth	156	29.17 S	16.51 E
Port Norris	208	39.15 N	75.02 W
Port-Nouveau-Québec	176	58.32 N	65.54 W
Pôrto, Bra.	250	3.54 S	42.42 W
Porto, Port.	34	41.11 N	8.36 W
Porto, Bonifica di ◆[1]	267a	41.48 N	12.16 E
Pôrto Acre	248	9.34 S	67.31 W
Pôrto Alegre, Bra.	252	30.04 S	51.11 W
Porto Alegre, S. Tom./P.	152	0.02 N	6.32 E
Porto Alexandre	152	15.49 S	11.53 E
Pôrto Amazonas	252	25.33 S	49.53 W
Porto Amboim	152	10.44 S	13.44 E
Porto Amélia	154	12.58 S	40.30 E
Porto Azzurro	66	42.46 N	10.24 E
Portobello	46	55.58 N	3.07 W
Pôrto Belo, Bra.	252	27.10 S	48.33 W
Portobelo, Pan.	236	9.33 N	79.39 W
Pôrto Calvo	250	9.04 S	35.24 W
Porto Ceresio	58	45.54 N	8.55 E
Pôrto das Caixas	256	22.42 S	42.53 W
Porto d'Ascoli	66	42.55 N	13.53 E
Pôrto das Flôres	256	22.05 S	43.34 W
Pôrto das Gabarras	250	3.07 S	44.34 W
Pôrto de Mós	34	39.36 N	8.39 W
Pôrto de Moz	250	1.45 S	52.14 W
Pôrto de Pedras	250	9.10 S	35.17 W
Porto di Potenza Picena	66	43.21 N	13.42 E
Porto Empedocle	70	37.17 N	13.32 E
Pôrto Esperança	248	19.37 S	57.27 W
Pôrto Esperidião	248	15.51 S	58.28 W
Porto Farina	36	37.10 N	10.12 E
Pôrto Feliz	255	23.13 S	47.32 W
Portoferraio	66	42.49 N	10.19 E
Pôrto Ferreira	255	21.51 S	47.28 W
Portofino	62	44.18 N	9.12 E
Port of Ness	46	58.29 N	6.13 W
Pôrto Franco	250	6.20 S	47.24 W
Port of Spain	241r	10.39 N	61.31 W
Porto Garibaldi	66	44.41 N	12.14 E
Pôrto Grande	250	0.42 N	51.24 W
Portogruaro	64	45.47 N	12.50 E
Porto Inglês	150a	15.08 N	23.13 W
Portola	204	39.48 N	120.28 W
Portola State Park ♠	226	37.15 N	122.13 W
Portola Valley	226	37.23 N	122.13 W
Pôrto Lucena	252	27.51 S	55.01 W
Pörtom (Pirttikylä)	26	62.42 N	21.37 E
Portomaggiore	64	44.42 N	11.48 E
Porto Maurizio	62	43.52 N	8.01 E
Pôrto Mendes	252	24.30 S	54.20 W
Pôrto Murtinho	248	21.42 S	57.52 W
Pôrto Nacional	250	10.42 S	48.25 W
Porto-Novo, Benin	150	6.29 N	2.37 E
Porto Novo, Bhārat	122	11.29 N	79.46 E
Porto Novo Creek C	273a	6.26 N	3.20 E
Portopalo, It.	70	36.41 N	15.08 E
Porto Palo, It.	70	37.34 N	12.54 E
Port Orange	192	29.09 N	80.59 W
Port Orchard	224	47.32 N	122.38 W
Pôrto Real	256	22.25 S	44.20 W
Pôrto Real do Colégio	250	10.11 S	36.49 W
Porto Recanati	66	43.26 N	13.40 E
Port Orford	202	42.45 N	124.30 W
Porto Rico	152	6.08 S	12.30 E
Porto Rico → Puerto Rico □[2]	240m	18.15 N	66.30 W
Portorož	64	45.31 N	13.36 E

Nome	Página	Lat.°′	Long.°′ W=Oeste
Porto Salvo	266c	38.43 N	9.18 W
Porto San Giorgio	66	43.11 N	13.48 E
Porto Sant'Elpidio	66	43.15 N	13.45 E
Porto Santo I	148	33.04 N	16.20 W
Porto Santo Stefano	66	42.26 N	11.07 E
Pôrto São José	255	22.43 S	53.10 W
Portoscuso	71	39.12 N	8.23 E
Pôrto Seguro, Bra.	255	16.26 S	39.05 W
Porto-Séguro, Togo	150	6.12 N	1.29 E
Porto Tolle	66	44.56 N	12.22 E
Porto Torres	71	40.50 N	8.24 E
Pôrto União	252	26.15 S	51.05 W
Pôrto Válter	248	8.15 S	72.45 W
Porto Valtravaglia	58	45.58 N	8.41 E
Porto-Vecchio	36	41.35 N	9.16 E
Pôrto Velho	248	8.46 S	63.54 W
Pôrto Velho do Cunha	256	21.50 S	42.32 W
Portovenere	62	44.03 N	9.51 E
Portoviejo	246	1.03 S	80.27 W
Portpatrick	44	54.51 N	5.07 W
Port Penn	208	39.31 N	75.35 W
Port Perry	212	44.06 N	78.57 W
Port Phillip Bay C	169	38.07 S	144.48 E
Port Pirie	166	33.11 S	138.01 E
Port Providence	285	40.08 N	75.30 W
Port Radium	176	66.05 N	118.02 W
Port Reading	276	40.34 N	74.16 W
Portree	46	57.24 N	6.12 W
Port Renfrew	182	48.33 N	124.25 W
Port Republic	208	39.31 N	74.29 W
Port Rexton	186	48.23 N	53.20 W
Port Richey	220	28.16 N	82.44 W
Port Richmond	208	37.33 N	76.49 W
Port Rowan	214	42.37 N	80.28 W
Port Royal, Jam.	241q	17.56 N	76.51 W
Port Royal, Ky., U.S.	218	38.33 N	85.05 W
Port Royal, Pa., U.S.	208	40.32 N	77.23 W
Port Royal, Va., U.S.	208	38.10 N	77.12 W
Port-Royal-des-Champs, Abbaye de ʊ[1]	261	48.45 N	2.01 E
Port Royal National Historic Park ♠	186	44.44 N	65.40 W
Portrush	48	55.12 N	6.40 W
Port Said → Būr Sa'īd	142	31.16 N	32.18 E
Port-Sainte-Marie	32	44.15 N	0.24 E
Port Saint Joe	192	29.49 N	85.18 W
Port Saint Johns	158	31.38 S	29.33 E
Port-Saint-Louis	62	43.23 N	4.48 E
Port Saint Lucie	220	27.20 N	80.20 W
Port-Saint-Servan	186	51.19 N	58.02 W
Port Salerno	220	27.09 N	80.12 W
Portsalon	48	55.13 N	7.37 W
Port Sanilac	190	43.26 N	82.33 W
Port Saunders	186	50.39 N	57.18 W
Pörtschach	61	46.37 N	14.08 E
Portsea	169	38.19 S	144.43 E
Port Seton	46	55.58 N	2.57 W
Port Shepstone	158	30.46 S	30.22 E
Port Simpson	182	54.33 N	130.25 W
Portslade	42	50.50 N	0.11 W
Portsmouth, Dom.	240d	15.35 N	61.28 W
Portsmouth, Eng., U.K.	42	50.48 N	1.05 W
Portsmouth, N.H., U.S.	188	43.04 N	70.46 W
Portsmouth, Ohio, U.S.	218	38.45 N	82.59 W
Portsmouth, R.I., U.S.	207	41.36 N	71.15 W
Portsmouth, Va., U.S.	208	36.52 N	76.24 W
Portsmouth Naval Shipyard ■	188	43.05 N	70.45 W
Portsoy	46	57.41 N	2.41 W
Port Stanley, Ont., Can.	214	42.40 N	81.13 W
Port Stanley → Stanley, Falk. Is.	254	51.42 S	57.51 W
Portstewart	48	55.11 N	6.43 W
Port Sudan → Būr Sūdān	140	19.37 N	37.14 E
Port Sulphur	194	29.29 N	89.42 W
Port Sunlight	262	53.21 N	2.59 W
Port-sur-Saône	58	47.41 N	6.03 E
Port Talbot	42	51.36 N	3.47 W
Port Taufiq → Būr Tawfīq	128	29.57 N	32.34 E
Porttipahdan tekojärvi @[1]	24	68.08 N	26.40 E
Port Tobacco River C	208	38.27 N	77.02 W
Port Townsend	224	48.07 N	122.46 W
Port Trevorton	208	40.42 N	76.52 W
Portugal □[1]	22		
	34	39.30 N	8.00 W
Portugal, Cachoeira ⌊	248	9.55 S	64.16 W
Portugal Cove South	186	46.42 N	53.15 W
Portugalete	34	43.19 N	3.01 W
Portugália	152	7.20 S	20.47 E
Portuguesa □[3]	246	9.10 N	69.15 W
Portuguesa ≃	246	7.57 N	67.32 W
Portuguese Guinea → Guinea-Bissau □[1]	150	12.00 N	15.00 W
Portumna	48	53.06 N	8.13 W
Port Union, Newf., Can.	186	48.30 N	53.05 W
Port Union, Ont., Can.	275b	43.47 N	79.08 W
Port-Vendres	32	42.31 N	3.07 E
Port Victoria → Victoria	138	4.38 S	55.27 E
Portville	210	42.02 N	78.20 W
Port Vincent	168b	34.47 S	137.51 E
Port-Vladimir	24	69.25 N	33.06 E
Port Vue	279b	40.20 N	79.52 W
Port Wakefield, Austl.	168b	34.11 S	138.09 E
Port Wakefield, Alaska, U.S.	180	57.52 N	152.51 W
Port Washington, B.C., Can.	224	48.49 N	123.19 W
Port Washington, N.Y., U.S.	210	40.49 N	73.41 W
Port Washington, Ohio, U.S.	214	40.20 N	81.31 W
Port Washington, Wis., U.S.	190	43.23 N	87.53 W
Port Weld	114	4.50 N	100.38 E
Port Wentworth	192	32.09 N	81.10 W
Port William, Scot., U.K.	44	54.46 N	4.35 W
Port William, Ohio, U.S.	218	39.33 N	83.47 W
Port Wing	190	46.47 N	91.23 W
Porum	196	35.22 N	95.16 W
Porus	241q	18.02 N	77.25 W
Porvenir	254	53.18 S	70.22 W
Porvoo → Borgå	26	60.24 N	25.40 E
Porvoonjoki ≃	26	60.23 N	25.40 E
Porz	56	50.53 N	7.03 E
Porzdni	80	57.00 N	42.33 E
Porzuna	34	39.09 N	4.09 W
Posada	71	40.38 N	9.43 E
Posada ≃	71	40.39 N	9.45 E
Posadas, Arg.	252	27.23 S	55.53 W
Posadas, Esp.	34	37.48 N	5.06 W
Posavina ∨	36	45.10 N	17.20 E
Poščharv	85	38.24 N	71.10 E
Poschiavino ≃	58	46.12 N	10.10 E
Poschiavo	58	46.18 N	10.04 E
Pošechonje-Volodarsk	76	58.30 N	39.07 E
Posen → Poznań, Pol.	30	52.25 N	16.55 E
Posen, Ill., U.S.	278	41.38 N	87.41 W
Posen, Mich., U.S.	190	45.16 N	83.42 W
Poseritz	54	54.18 N	13.16 E
Posesión, Bahía C	254	52.17 S	69.14 W

Symbol	English	Deutsch	Español	Français	Português
≃	River	Fluss	Río	Rivière	Rio
≊	Canal	Kanal	Canal	Canal	Canal
⌊	Waterfall, Rapids	Wasserfall, Stromschnellen	Cascada, Rápidos	Chute d'eau, Rapides	Cascata, Rápidos
⊔	Strait	Meeresstrasse	Estrecho	Détroit	Estreito
C	Bay, Gulf	Bucht, Golf	Bahía, Golfo	Baie, Golfe	Baía, Golfo
@	Lake, Lakes	See, Seen	Lago, Lagos	Lac, Lacs	Lago, Lagos
≋	Swamp	Sumpf	Pantano	Marais	Pântano
⊓	Ice Features, Glacier	Eis- und Gletscherformen	Accidentes Glaciales	Formes glaciaires	Acidentes Glaciares
⊤	Other Hydrographic Features	Andere Hydrographische Objekte	Otros Elementos Hidrográficos	Autres données hydrographiques	Outros Elementos Hidrográficos
✢	Submarine Features	Untermeerische Objekte	Accidentes Submarinos	Formes de relief sous-marin	Acidentes Submarinos
□	Political Unit	Politische Einheit	Unidad Política	Entité politique	Unidade Política
ʊ	Cultural Institution	Kulturelle Institution	Institución Cultural	Institution culturelle	Instituição Cultural
⊥	Historical Site	Historische Stätte	Sitio Histórico	Site historique	Sítio Histórico
♠	Recreational Site	Erholungs- und Ferienort	Sitio de Recreo	Centre de loisirs	Sítio de Lazer
⊠	Airport	Flughafen	Aeropuerto	Aéroport	Aeroporto
■	Military Installation	Militäranlage	Instalación Militar	Installation militaire	Instalação Militar
◆	Miscellaneous	Verschiedenes	Misceláneo	Divers	Miscelânea

ENGLISH: Name | Page | Lat.°′ | Long.°′ — DEUTSCH: Name | Seite | Breite°′ | Länge°′ E=Ost

Name	Page	Lat.	Long.
Posets, Pico de ∧	34	42.39 N	0.25 E
Posevnaja	86	54.18 N	83.20 E
Poshan → Boshan	98	36.29 N	117.50 E
Poshiwu	106	30.22 N	119.36 E
Posieux	58	46.46 N	7.06 E
Posina	64	45.47 N	11.15 E
Pösing	60	49.14 N	12.33 E
Posio	26	66.06 N	28.09 E
Positano	68	40.38 N	14.29 E
Posjet	89	42.39 N	130.50 E
Poso	112	1.23 S	120.44 E
Poso, Danau ⊜	112	1.52 S	120.35 E
Poso, Teluk C	112	1.15 S	120.55 E
Poso Creek ≃	226	35.41 N	119.22 W
Pos'olki	80	53.08 N	46.29 E
Pos'olok	265a	59.43 N	30.12 E
Posŏng	98	34.47 N	127.04 E
Posooy, Mount ∧	116	17.21 N	120.48 E
Pospelicha	86	51.57 N	81.46 E
Possagno	64	45.51 N	11.51 E
Posse	255	14.05 S	46.22 W
Posse dos Coutinhos	256	22.49 S	42.45 W
Possendorf	54	50.57 N	13.42 E
Posses	256	21.43 S	46.08 W
Possession Sound Ʉ	224	48.00 N	122.20 W
Possidhonia ⊥	38	37.40 N	24.00 E
Pössneck	54	50.42 N	11.37 E
Possruck (Kozjak) ⛰	61	46.37 N	15.28 E
Possum Kingdom Lake ⊜[1]	196	32.55 N	98.28 W
Post	196	33.12 N	101.23 W
Posta	66	42.31 N	13.06 E
Postal (Burgstall)	64	46.36 N	11.11 E
Postau	60	48.39 N	12.20 E
Postavy	76	55.07 N	26.50 E
Postbauer	60	49.19 N	11.21 E
Post Creek ≃	210	42.09 N	77.02 W
Poste-de-la-Baleine	176	55.17 N	77.45 W
Poste-Mistassini	176	50.25 N	73.52 W
Poste Ramartina	157b	19.38 S	45.58 E
Posterholt	52	51.07 N	6.03 E
Poste Weygand	148	24.28 N	0.39 E
Post Falls	202	47.43 N	116.57 W
Postiglione	68	40.33 N	15.13 E
Postmasburg	158	28.18 S	23.05 E
Post Maurice Cortier (Bidon Cinq)	148	22.18 N	1.05 E
Pôsto do Registro	256	22.23 S	42.35 W
Postojna	36	45.47 N	14.13 E
Postojnska Jama •[7]	36	45.47 N	14.12 E
Postoloprty	54	50.20 N	13.40 E
P'ostraja Dresva	74	61.34 N	156.41 E
Postrevalle	248	18.29 S	63.51 W
Postsee ⊜	54	54.13 N	10.13 E
Poststadion ♠	264a	52.32 N	13.21 E
Postville	190	43.05 N	91.34 W
Pota	115b	8.20 S	120.46 E
Potaizi	104	41.34 N	121.08 E
Potake Pond ⊜	276	41.08 N	74.13 W
Pótam	232	27.36 N	110.23 W
Potanino	76	60.16 N	32.47 E
Potapovo Vtoroje	265b	55.56 N	37.58 E
Potaro ≃	246	5.22 N	58.54 W
Potaro Landing	246	5.23 N	59.08 W
Potato Creek ≃, Ga., U.S.	192	32.47 N	84.21 W
Potato Creek ≃, Pa., U.S.	214	41.53 N	78.23 W
Potawatomie Woods ♠	278	42.08 N	87.53 W
Potawatomi Indian Reservation ⇁[4]	198	39.20 N	95.50 W
Potchefstroom	158	26.46 S	27.01 E
Poté	255	17.49 S	41.49 W
Poteau	194	35.03 N	94.37 W
Poteau ≃	194	35.23 N	94.26 W
Potechino	89	54.33 N	127.46 E
Poteet	196	29.02 N	98.34 W
Potengi	250	7.06 S	40.00 W
Potengi ≃	250	5.47 S	35.16 W
Pötenitz	54	53.57 N	10.58 E
Pötenitzer Wiek C	54	53.55 N	10.55 E
Potenza	68	40.38 N	15.49 E
Potenza □[4]	68	40.30 N	15.50 E
Potenza ≃	66	43.25 N	13.40 E
Potenza Picena	66	43.22 N	13.37 E
Poteriteri, Lake ⊜	172	46.06 S	167.08 E
Potes	34	43.09 N	4.37 W
Potfontein	158	30.12 S	24.08 E
Potgietersrus	156	24.15 S	28.55 E
Poth	196	29.04 N	98.05 W
Potholes Reservoir ⊜[1]	202	47.01 N	119.19 W
Poti	84	42.09 N	41.40 E
Poti ≃	250	5.02 S	42.50 W
Potic Creek ≃	210	42.16 N	73.55 W
Potijevka	78	50.37 N	28.58 E
Potiraguá	255	15.36 S	39.53 W
Potirendaba	255	21.08 S	49.08 W
Potiská nížina ≚	30	48.40 N	22.00 E
Potiskum	146	11.43 N	11.05 E
Potlatch	202	46.55 N	116.54 W
Potlatch ≃	202	46.28 N	116.46 W
Po Toi Group II	271d	22.11 N	114.16 E
Po Toi Island I	271d	22.10 N	114.15 E
Potol Point ≻	116	11.56 N	121.57 E
Potomac, Ill., U.S.	216	40.18 N	87.48 W
Potomac, Md., U.S.	284c	39.01 N	77.12 W
Potomac ≃	188	38.00 N	76.18 W
Potomac, South Branch, South Fork ≃	188	39.04 N	78.59 W
Potomac Creek ≃	208	38.21 N	77.18 W
Potomac Creek, Long Branch ≃	208	38.23 N	77.29 W
Potomac Heights	188	38.36 N	77.08 W
Poto Poto ⇁[8]	273b	4.15 S	15.18 E
Potosí, Bol.	248	19.35 S	65.45 W
Potosi, Mo., U.S.	194	37.56 N	90.47 W
Potosí □[5]	248	20.40 S	67.00 W
Potosí, Bahía C	234	17.34 N	101.30 W
Potosí, Cerro ∧	232	24.52 N	100.13 W
Pototan	116	10.55 N	122.40 E
Potrerillos, Chile	252	26.26 S	69.29 W
Potrerillos, Hond.	236	15.11 N	87.58 W
Potrerillos Arriba	236	8.41 N	82.30 W
Potrero ⇁[8]	282	37.48 N	122.24 W
Potrero de Gallegos	234	22.38 N	103.41 W
Potrero del Llano	196	29.12 N	104.28 W
Potrero Grande, C.R.	236	9.00 N	83.11 W
Potrero Grande, Méx.	232	24.59 N	106.26 W
Potsdam, D.D.R.	54	52.24 N	13.04 E
Potsdam, S. Afr.	158	32.56 S	27.42 E
Potsdam, N.Y., U.S.	188	44.40 N	74.59 W
Potsdam, Ohio, U.S.	218	39.58 N	84.25 W
Potsdam □[5]	54	52.30 N	12.45 E
Potsdam, Staatsforst ♠	264a	52.26 N	13.04 E
Potshausen	52	53.11 N	7.37 E
Pott, Île I	175f	19.35 S	163.36 E
Pottawatomie Creek ≃	194	38.29 N	94.55 W
Potten End	260	51.46 N	0.31 W
Pottenstein	60	49.46 N	11.25 E
Potter	198	41.13 N	103.19 W
Potter □[6]	214	41.47 N	78.01 W
Potter Heigham	42	52.44 N	1.33 E
Potter Hollow	210	42.25 N	74.13 W
Potter Lake	216	44.07 N	88.06 W
Potter Point ≻	274a	34.03 S	151.13 E
Potters Bar	42	51.42 N	0.11 W
Potters Mills	208	40.48 N	77.32 W
Potter Street	42	51.46 N	0.08 E
Pottersville	276	40.43 N	74.44 W
Potterville	216	42.38 N	84.45 W
Pöttmes	60	48.35 N	11.06 E
Potton	42	52.08 N	0.14 W
Potts Camp	194	34.39 N	89.18 W
Potts Creek ≃	192	37.45 N	80.00 W
Potts Grove	210	40.60 N	76.48 W
Potts Hill Reservoirs ⊜[1]	274a	33.54 S	151.02 E
Pott Shrigley	262	53.19 N	2.05 W
Pottstown	208	40.15 N	75.38 W
Pottstown Limerick Airport ⊠	285	40.14 N	75.34 W
Pottsville	208	40.41 N	76.12 W
Potwin	198	37.56 N	97.01 W
Pötzleinsdorf ⇁[8]	264b	48.15 N	16.19 E
Pötzleinsdorfer Park ♠	264b	48.14 N	16.18 E
P'otzu	100	23.29 N	120.16 E
Pouancé	32	47.44 N	1.11 W
Pouce-Coupe	182	55.43 N	120.08 W
Pouce Coupé ≃	182	56.08 N	119.52 W
Pouch	54	51.37 N	12.24 E
Pouch Cove	186	47.46 N	52.46 W
Pouembout	175f	21.08 S	164.53 E
Poughkeepsie	210	41.42 N	73.56 W
Poughquag	210	41.37 N	73.41 W
Pouilly-en-Auxois	58	47.16 N	4.33 E
Pouilly-sur-Loire	50	47.17 N	2.57 E
Pouilly-sur-Meuse	56	49.32 N	5.07 E
Poulain, Étang ⊜	261	48.43 N	1.44 E
Poulan	192	31.31 N	83.47 W
Poulin-de-Courval, Lac ⊜	186	48.52 N	70.27 W
Poulsbo	224	47.44 N	122.39 W
Poulter, Lac ⊜	190	47.07 N	76.45 W
Poultney	188	43.31 N	73.14 W
Poulton-le-Fylde	44	53.51 N	2.59 W
Poume	175f	20.14 S	164.02 E
Poŭn	98	36.29 N	127.43 E
Pound	192	37.07 N	82.36 W
Poundmaker Indian Reserve ⇁[4]	184	52.51 N	109.00 W
Poundstock	42	50.46 N	4.33 W
Pouoanuu, Mont ∧	174x	9.49 S	139.07 W
Pourri, Mont ∧	62	45.32 N	6.52 E
Pouru-Saint-Rémy	56	49.41 N	5.05 E
Pourville-sur-Mer	50	49.55 N	1.02 E
Pouso Alegre	256	22.13 S	45.56 W
Pouso Alto	256	22.11 S	44.58 W
Pouso Redondo	252	27.15 S	49.57 W
Pouso Sêco	256	22.41 S	44.10 W
Pouss	146	10.51 N	15.03 E
Poutasi	175a	14.01 S	171.41 W
Poŭthĭsăt	110	12.32 N	103.55 E
Poŭthĭsăt ≃	110	12.41 N	104.09 E
Pouxeux	58	48.06 N	6.34 E
Pouzauges	32	46.47 N	0.50 W
Považská Bystrica	30	49.08 N	18.27 E
Povenec	24	62.51 N	34.45 E
Poverello, Monte ∧	70	38.05 N	15.22 E
Poverennyj	80	46.45 N	43.12 E
Poverty Bay C	172	38.42 S	177.58 E
Povetkino	82	54.20 N	38.23 E
Poviglio	64	44.51 N	10.32 E
Povljen ⛰	38	43.55 N	19.30 E
Póvoa, Mouchão da I	266c	38.51 N	9.03 W
Povoação	148a	37.45 N	25.15 W
Póvoa de Santa Iria	266c	38.52 N	9.04 W
Póvoa de Santo Adrião	266c	38.48 N	9.10 W
Póvoa de Varzim	34	41.23 N	8.46 W
Povorino	80	51.12 N	42.14 E
Povorotnyj, Mys ≻	89	42.42 N	133.04 E
Povorsk	78	51.16 N	25.07 E
Povrly	54	50.40 N	14.10 E
Povungnituk	176	60.02 N	77.10 W
Povungnituk, Rivière de ≃	176	60.03 N	77.15 W
Powassan	190	46.05 N	79.22 W
Poway	228	32.58 N	117.02 W
Poway Creek ≃	228	32.56 N	117.15 W
Powder ≃, U.S.	178	46.44 N	105.26 W
Powder ≃, Oreg., U.S.	202	44.45 N	117.03 W
Powder, Dry Fork ≃	200	43.47 N	106.15 W
Powder, Middle Fork ≃	200	43.42 N	106.33 W
Powder, North Fork ≃	202	43.42 N	106.33 W
Powder, Red Fork ≃	202	43.39 N	106.47 W
Powder, South Fork ≃	202	43.40 N	106.30 W
Powder Horn Lake ⊜	278	41.38 N	87.32 W
Powderly	196	33.49 N	95.31 W
Powdermaker Ditch ≍	279a	41.30 N	82.02 W
Powder River Pass)(	202	44.09 N	107.04 W
Powell, Ohio, U.S.	214	40.09 N	83.05 W
Powell, Pa., U.S.	210	41.42 N	76.31 W
Powell, Tex., U.S.	222	32.07 N	96.20 W
Powell, Wyo., U.S.	202	44.45 N	108.46 W
Powell ≃	192	36.29 N	83.42 W
Powell, Lake ⊜[1]	200	37.25 N	110.45 W
Powell, Mount ∧	200	39.46 N	106.20 W
Powell Creek ≃, Austl.	166	25.02 S	143.40 E
Powell Creek ≃, Ohio, U.S.	216	41.17 N	84.21 W
Powellhurst	224	45.31 N	122.31 W
Powell Lake ⊜	182	50.11 N	124.24 W
Powell River	182	49.52 N	124.33 W
Powells Valley	208	40.26 N	76.56 W
Powellton	188	38.05 N	81.19 W
Powers, Mich., U.S.	190	45.39 N	87.32 W
Powers, Oreg., U.S.	202	42.53 N	124.04 W
Powers Lake, N. Dak., U.S.	198	48.34 N	102.39 W
Powers Lake, Wis., U.S.	216	42.33 N	88.17 W
Powers Lookout ♠	169	36.50 S	146.22 E
Powhatan, La., U.S.	194	31.52 N	93.12 W
Powhatan, Va., U.S.	192	37.29 N	77.55 W
Powhatan Point	188	39.52 N	80.49 W
Powis, Vale of ∨	42	52.38 N	3.08 W
Powissett Brook ≃	283	42.16 N	71.14 W
Powlett ≃	169	38.35 S	145.32 E
Pownal	210	42.46 N	73.14 W
Powys □[6]	42	52.17 N	3.20 W
Poxau	60	48.34 N	12.33 E
Poxoréo	255	15.50 S	54.23 W
Poya	175f	21.19 S	165.07 E
Poyang	100	28.59 N	116.40 E
Poyanghu ⊜	100	29.00 N	116.25 E
Poyen	194	34.19 N	92.38 W
Poygan, Lake ⊜	190	44.19 N	88.50 W
Poyle	260	51.28 N	0.31 W
Poynette	190	43.24 N	89.24 W
Poynor	222	32.04 N	95.36 W
Poynton	262	53.21 N	2.07 W
Poyntzpass	48	54.18 N	6.23 W
Poyraz	267b	41.12 N	29.07 E
Poyraz Burnu ≻	267b	41.12 N	29.09 E
Poysdorf	61	48.40 N	16.38 E
Poza Grande	232	25.50 N	112.05 W
Pozantı	130	37.25 N	34.52 E
Požarevac	38	44.37 N	21.11 E
Poza Rica de Hidalgo	234	20.33 N	97.27 W
Požarskoje	89	46.16 N	134.04 E
Pozdejevka	89	50.36 N	128.56 E
Požega	38	43.50 N	20.02 E
Poznań	30	52.25 N	16.55 E
Pozo Alcón	34	37.42 N	2.56 W
Pozo Almonte	248	20.16 S	69.48 W
Pozoblanco	34	38.22 N	4.51 W
Pozo-Cañada	34	38.48 N	1.45 W
Pozo Colorado	252	23.28 S	58.51 W
Pozo del Molle	252	32.02 S	62.55 W
Pozo del Tigre	252	24.54 S	60.19 W
Pozo Hondo	252	27.10 S	64.30 W
Pozos	234	21.14 N	100.29 W
Pozos, Arroyo de los ≃	288	34.57 S	58.45 W
Pozos, Punta ≻	254	47.57 S	65.47 W
Pozsony → Bratislava	30	48.09 N	17.07 E
Pozuelo de Alarcón	34	40.26 N	3.49 W
Pozuelo de Alarcón ⇁[8]	266a	40.26 N	3.49 W
Pozuelos	246	10.11 N	64.39 W
Pozuelos, Laguna de ⊜	252	22.22 S	66.01 W
Pozuzo	248	10.04 S	75.32 W
Pozuzo ≃	248	9.52 S	75.12 W
Požva	86	59.05 N	56.05 E
Pozzallo	70	36.43 N	14.51 E
Pozzillo, Lago di ⊜	70	37.40 N	14.35 E
Pozzolo Formigaro	62	44.48 N	8.47 E
Pozzomaggiore	71	40.24 N	8.39 E
Pozzuoli	68	40.49 N	14.07 E
Pozzuolo del Friuli	64	45.59 N	13.12 E
Pra ≃, Ghana	150	5.01 N	1.37 W
Pra ≃, S.S.S.R.	80	54.45 N	41.01 E
Prabuty	30	53.46 N	19.10 E
Pracai ≃	250	2.26 S	51.19 W
Praça Sêca ⇁[8]	287a	22.54 S	43.21 W
Prachantakham	110	14.04 N	101.31 E
Prachatice	30	49.01 N	14.00 E
Prachin Buri	110	14.03 N	101.22 E
Prachuap Khiri Khan	110	11.49 N	99.48 E
Prackenbach	60	49.06 N	12.50 E
Pracupi ≃	250	2.06 S	51.30 W
Pradelles	62	44.46 N	3.53 E
Pradera	246	3.25 N	76.15 W
Pradleves	62	44.25 N	7.17 E
Prado	255	17.21 S	39.13 W
Prado, Museo del ⚲	266a	40.25 N	3.41 W
Prado Dam ⇁[6]	280	33.54 N	117.39 W
Prado Flood Control Basin ≚[1]	280	33.54 N	117.38 W
Prados	255	21.03 S	44.05 W
Pr'adovka	78	48.55 N	34.41 E
Prads	62	44.13 N	6.27 E
Præstø	41	55.07 N	12.03 E
Prag → Praha	54	50.05 N	14.26 E
Praga → Praha	54	50.05 N	14.26 E
Pragelato	62	45.01 N	6.57 E
Pragersko	61	46.23 N	15.40 E
Praglia, Monastero di ⚲[1]	64	45.23 N	11.45 E
Prägraten	64	47.01 N	12.23 E
Prague → Praha, Česko.	54	50.05 N	14.26 E
Prague, Nebr., U.S.	198	41.19 N	96.48 W
Prague, Okla., U.S.	196	35.29 N	96.41 W
Praha (Prague)	54	50.05 N	14.26 E
Praha ∧	60	49.40 N	13.49 E
Prahova □[4]	38	45.00 N	26.00 E
Prahova ≃	38	44.43 N	26.27 E
Prahran	274b	37.51 S	144.59 E
Praia	150a	14.55 N	23.31 W
Praia a Mare	68	39.54 N	15.47 E
Praia da Cruz Quebrada	266c	38.42 N	9.14 W
Praia das Maçãs	266c	38.50 N	9.28 W
Praia da Vitória	148a	38.44 N	27.04 W
Praia de Araçatiba	256	23.06 S	44.15 W
Praia Funda, Ponta da ≻	287a	23.05 S	43.33 W
Praia Grande, Bra.	252	29.12 S	49.57 W
Praia Grande, Bra.	256	24.01 S	46.25 W
Praikalogu	115b	9.45 S	119.25 E
Prainha, Bra.	248	7.16 S	60.23 W
Prainha, Bra.	250	1.48 S	53.29 W
Praino	68	40.37 N	14.32 E
Prairie	166	20.52 S	144.36 E
Prairie ≃, Mich., U.S.	216	41.55 N	85.38 W
Prairie ≃, Minn., U.S.	190	47.18 N	93.29 W
Prairie ≃, Wis., U.S.	190	45.10 N	89.42 W
Prairie City, Ill., U.S.	190	40.37 N	90.28 W
Prairie City, Iowa, U.S.	190	41.36 N	93.14 W
Prairie City, Oreg., U.S.	202	44.28 N	118.43 W
Prairie Creek ≃, Fla., U.S.	220	26.59 N	81.56 W
Prairie Creek ≃, Ill., U.S.	216	40.55 N	87.49 W
Prairie Creek ≃, Ill., U.S.	216	41.21 N	88.12 W
Prairie Creek ≃, Ill., U.S.	216	40.24 N	88.01 W
Prairie Creek ≃, Mich., U.S.	216	42.59 N	85.01 W
Prairie Creek ≃, Nebr., U.S.	198	41.22 N	97.32 W
Prairie Creek Reservoir ⊜[1]	218	40.08 N	85.17 W
Prairie Dog Creek ≃	198	40.00 N	99.23 W
Prairie du Chien	190	43.03 N	91.09 W
Prairie du Sac	190	43.17 N	89.43 W
Prairie Elk Creek ≃	198	48.00 N	105.51 W
Prairie Grove	194	35.59 N	94.19 W
Prairie Hill	222	31.39 N	96.47 W
Prairie Lea	222	29.44 N	97.45 W
Prairie River	184	52.52 N	103.00 W
Prairies, Coteau des ⛰[2]	198	44.30 N	96.45 W
Prairies, Rivière des ≃	275a	45.42 N	73.29 W
Prairie View, Ill., U.S.	278	42.12 N	87.57 W
Prairie View, Tex., U.S.	222	30.04 N	96.00 W
Prairie Village	198	39.01 N	94.38 W
Prajekan	115a	7.47 S	113.59 E
Prakhon Chai	110	14.37 N	103.05 E
Pralboino	64	45.16 N	10.13 E
Prali	62	44.54 N	7.03 E
Pralls Island I	276	40.37 N	74.12 W
Pralognan-la-Vanoise	62	45.23 N	6.43 E
Pram	60	48.14 N	13.37 E
Pram ≃	60	48.28 N	13.26 E
Pramaggiore, Monte ∧	64	46.22 N	12.33 E
Prambachkirchen	60	48.19 N	13.55 E
Prambanan	115a	7.45 S	110.30 E
Prameny	60	50.03 N	12.46 E
Pr'amicyno	78	51.39 N	35.56 E
Pramort	54	54.26 N	12.55 E
Prampram	150	5.42 N	0.07 E
Pran Buri	110	12.23 N	99.55 E
Pran Buri ≃	110	12.24 N	100.00 E
Prang	150	7.59 N	0.53 W
Prangli I	76	59.38 N	25.02 E
Pranzo	64	45.55 N	10.48 E
Prapa, Khlong ≍	269a	13.46 N	100.32 E
Prapat	114	2.40 N	98.56 E
Praraye	58	45.55 N	7.32 E
Prärien → Great Plains ≚	16	42.00 N	100.00 W
Praskovejevka	83	48.40 N	38.00 E
Praslin, Lac ⊜	186	50.03 N	69.48 W
Praslin, Port C	241f	13.53 N	60.54 W
Praslin Island I	138	4.19 S	55.44 E
Prasónisi, Ákra ≻	38	35.42 N	27.46 E
Praszka	30	51.04 N	18.26 E
Prat, Isla I	254	48.15 S	75.00 W
Prata, Bra.	250	7.41 S	37.06 W
Prata, Bra.	255	19.18 S	48.55 W
Prata, Bra.	287a	22.45 S	43.25 W
Prata, Rio da ≃, Bra.	255	17.28 S	46.35 W
Prata, Rio da ≃, Bra.	255	18.49 S	49.54 W
Prata, Rio da ≃, Bra.	255	18.50 S	52.11 W
Prata, Rio da ≃, Bra.	287a	22.56 S	43.34 W
Pratāpgarh	120	24.02 N	74.47 E
Pratapgarh □[5]	124	25.55 N	82.00 E
Pratāpnagar	126	22.23 N	89.13 E
Pratápolis	255	20.45 S	46.52 W
Pratas Islands → Dongshaqundao II	90	20.42 N	116.43 E
Pratau	54	51.50 N	12.38 E
Prat de Llobregat	34	41.20 N	2.06 E
Pratella	68	41.24 N	14.11 E
Prater ♠	264b	48.12 N	16.25 E
Prathet Thai → Thailand □[1]	110	15.00 N	100.00 E
Pratinha	255	19.46 S	46.24 W
Prato	66	43.53 N	11.06 E
Prato allo Stelvio	64	46.37 N	10.35 E
Pratola Peligna	66	42.06 N	13.52 E
Pratola Serra	68	40.59 N	14.51 E
Pratolino	66	43.52 N	11.18 E
Pratomagno ⛰	66	43.39 N	11.39 E
Pratt	198	37.39 N	98.44 W
Pratteln	58	47.31 N	7.42 E
Prättigau ∨	58	46.55 N	9.45 E
Pratt's Bottom ⇁[8]	260	51.20 N	0.07 E
Prattsburg	210	42.32 N	77.17 W
Prattsville	210	42.19 N	74.26 W
Prattville	194	32.28 N	86.29 W
Pratudão ≃	255	13.56 S	44.55 W
Prauthoy	58	47.40 N	5.17 E
Pravaja Mama ≃	88	57.10 N	111.54 E
Pravda	89	47.00 N	142.01 E
Pravdinsk, S.S.S.R.	76	54.27 N	21.01 E
Pravdinsk, S.S.S.R.	80	56.32 N	43.34 E
Pravdinskij	82	56.04 N	37.51 E
Pravia	34	43.29 N	6.07 W
Prawet Buri Rom, Khlong ≍	269a	13.42 N	100.35 E
Prawle Point ≻	42	50.13 N	3.42 W
Praya	115b	8.42 S	116.17 E
Pr'aža	24	61.42 N	33.35 E
Praz-sur-Arly	62	45.50 N	6.34 E
Prazzo	62	44.29 N	7.03 E
Preakness Brook ≃	276	40.54 N	74.15 W
Preakness Mountain ∧	276	40.58 N	74.13 W
Preakness Valley Park ♠	276	40.55 N	74.14 W
Preble, Ind., U.S.	216	40.50 N	85.01 W
Preble, N.Y., U.S.	210	42.44 N	76.09 W
Preble □[6]	218	39.45 N	84.38 W
Preci	66	42.53 N	13.02 E
Prečistoje, S.S.S.R.	76	55.41 N	34.56 E
Prečistoje, S.S.S.R.	76	55.31 N	32.22 E
Prečistoje, S.S.S.R.	80	58.27 N	40.19 E
Précy-sous-Thil	50	47.23 N	4.19 E
Précy-sur-Marne	261	48.56 N	2.47 E
Précy-sur-Oise	50	49.12 N	2.22 E
Preda	58	46.36 N	9.46 E
Predappio	66	44.06 N	11.58 E
Predazzo	64	46.19 N	11.36 E
Predeal	38	45.30 N	25.35 E
Prédecelle ≃	261	48.35 N	2.07 E
Predești	38	44.21 N	23.36 E
Predgornoje	86	47.10 N	81.02 E
Predigtstuhl ∧	61	48.48 N	15.22 E
Predivinsk	86	57.04 N	93.27 E
Predkarpatje ⛰[1]	78	49.00 N	24.30 E
Predlitz	64	47.04 N	13.55 E
Predmostnoje	78	45.57 N	34.37 E
Predoi (Prettau)	64	47.02 N	12.06 E
Predore	64	45.40 N	10.01 E
Preeceville	184	51.58 N	102.40 W
Pré-en-Pail	32	48.27 N	0.12 W
Preetz	54	54.14 N	10.16 E
Pregarten	61	48.12 N	14.32 E
Pregel → Pregol'a ≃	76	54.41 N	20.22 E
Pregnana	266b	45.31 N	9.00 E
Pregol'a ≃	76	54.41 N	20.22 E
Pregonero	246	8.01 N	71.46 W
Pregos	256	21.46 S	42.54 W
Pregradnaja	84	43.58 N	41.12 E
Pregradnoje	80	45.49 N	41.45 E
Preguiças ≃	250	2.34 S	42.44 W
Preila	76	55.22 N	21.04 E
Preiļi	76	56.18 N	26.43 E
Preissac, Lac ⊜	190	48.20 N	78.20 W
Prekestolen ♠	26	59.00 N	6.01 E
Preko	36	44.05 N	15.11 E
Prekomurje ⇁[1]	61	46.40 N	16.10 E
Prĕk Poŭthĭ	110	11.51 N	105.07 E
Prelate	184	50.51 N	109.23 W
Přelouč	30	50.02 N	15.34 E
Premana	58	46.03 N	9.25 E
Prembun	115a	7.43 S	109.48 E
Prémery	50	47.10 N	3.20 E
Premiá de Mar	266d	41.29 N	2.21 E
Premier Grand Ruisseau ≃	275a	45.39 N	73.12 W
Premnitz	54	52.32 N	12.19 E
Prémont, Qué., Can.	206	46.22 N	73.03 W
Premont, Tex., U.S.	196	27.22 N	98.08 W
Prémontré	50	49.33 N	3.24 E
Premosello	58	46.00 N	8.20 E
Premuda, Otok I	36	44.20 N	14.37 E
Prenestini, Monti ⛰	66	41.50 N	12.55 E
Prenjas	38	41.04 N	20.32 E
Prentice	190	45.33 N	90.17 W
Prentiss	194	31.36 N	89.52 W
Prenton	262	53.22 N	3.03 W
Prenzlau	54	53.19 N	13.52 E
Prenzlauer Berg ⇁[8]	264a	52.32 N	13.26 E
Preobražennoje	83	49.32 N	38.10 E
Preobraženovka	89	48.04 N	131.55 E
Preparis Island I	110	14.52 N	93.41 E
Preparis North Channel Ʉ	110	15.27 N	94.05 E
Preparis South Channel Ʉ	110	14.40 N	94.00 E
Přerov	30	49.27 N	17.27 E
Prerow	54	54.26 N	12.35 E
Pré-Saint-Didier	62	45.46 N	6.59 E
Presanella, Cima ∧	64	46.13 N	10.40 E
Prescot	44	53.26 N	2.48 W
Prescott, Ont., Can.	212	44.43 N	75.31 W
Prescott, Ariz., U.S.	200	34.33 N	112.28 W
Prescott, Ark., U.S.	194	33.48 N	93.23 W
Prescott, Oreg., U.S.	224	46.03 N	122.54 W
Prescott, Wis., U.S.	190	44.45 N	92.48 W
Prescott □[6]	206	45.30 N	74.45 W
Prescott Island I	176	73.01 N	96.50 W
Preseglie	64	45.40 N	10.24 E
Preševo	38	42.18 N	21.39 E
Presho	198	43.54 N	100.04 W
Presicce	68	39.54 N	18.16 E
Presidencia de la Plaza	252	27.01 S	59.51 W
Presidencia Roca	252	26.08 S	59.36 W
Presidencia Roque Sáenz Peña	252	26.47 S	60.27 W
Presidente Costa e Silva, Ponte ⇁[5]	287a	22.53 S	43.10 W
Presidente Derqui	258	34.29 S	58.51 W
Presidente Dutra	250	5.15 S	44.30 W
Presidente Epitácio	255	21.46 S	52.06 W
Presidente Getúlio	252	27.03 S	49.37 W
Presidente Hayes □[5]	252	24.00 S	59.00 W
Presidente Nicolás Avellaneda, Parque ♠	288	34.39 S	58.29 W
Presidente Olegário	255	18.25 S	46.25 W
Presidente Prudente	255	22.07 S	51.22 W
Presidente Ríos, Lago ⊜	254	46.28 S	74.25 W
Presidente Roosevelt, Estação ⇁[5]	287b	23.33 S	46.36 W
Presidente Venceslau	255	21.52 S	51.50 W
Presidential Heights	279b	40.34 N	80.03 W
President Roxas	116	11.26 N	122.56 E
Presidio	196	29.33 N	104.23 W
Presidio, Río del ≃	234	23.06 N	106.17 W
Presidio of San Francisco ▪	226	37.48 N	122.28 W
Presles	56	50.23 N	4.35 E
Presles-en-Brie	261	48.43 N	2.45 E
Presnogor'kovka	86	54.30 N	65.45 E
Presnovka	86	54.40 N	67.09 E
Presolana, Passo della)(	64	45.55 N	10.06 E
Prešov	30	49.00 N	21.15 E
Prespa, Lake ⊜	38	40.55 N	21.00 E
Prespansko Jezero → Prespa, Lake ⊜	38	40.55 N	21.00 E
Presque Isle	186	46.41 N	68.01 W
Presque Isle ≻[1]	214	42.09 N	80.06 W
Presque Isle ≃	190	46.43 N	89.59 W
Presque Isle State Park ♠	214	42.09 N	80.06 W
Presqu'ile Bay C	212	44.01 N	77.43 W
Presqu'ile Point ≻, Ont., Can.	212	44.42 N	80.54 W
Presqu'ile Point ≻, Ont., Can.	212	44.00 N	77.41 W
Presqu'ile Provincial Park ♠	212	44.00 N	77.42 W
Pressana	64	45.17 N	11.24 E
Pressath	60	49.46 N	11.56 E
Pressbaum	61	48.11 N	16.05 E
Pressburg → Bratislava	30	48.09 N	17.07 E
Pressel	54	51.34 N	12.41 E
Prestatyn	44	53.20 N	3.24 W
Prestbury	262	53.17 N	2.09 W
Prestea	150	5.27 N	2.08 W
Presteigne	42	52.17 N	3.00 W
Přeštice	60	49.34 N	13.20 E
Presto, Bol.	248	18.55 S	64.56 W
Presto, Pa., U.S.	279b	40.23 N	80.07 W
Preston, Austl.	169	37.45 S	145.01 E
Preston, Cuba	240p	20.46 N	75.39 W
Preston, Eng., U.K.	44		
	262	53.46 N	2.42 W
Preston, Ga., U.S.	192	31.59 N	84.37 W
Preston, Idaho, U.S.	202	42.06 N	111.53 W
Preston, Iowa, U.S.	190	42.03 N	90.24 W
Preston, Kans., U.S.	198	37.46 N	98.33 W
Preston, Md., U.S.	208	38.43 N	75.54 W
Preston, Minn., U.S.	190	43.40 N	92.05 W
Preston, Wash., U.S.	224	47.31 N	121.56 W
Preston □[8]	262	53.48 N	2.42 W
Preston ≃, Austl.	168a	33.20 S	115.40 E
Preston ≃, Qué., Can.	206	46.05 N	75.04 W
Preston, Cape ≻	162	20.51 S	116.12 E
Preston, Lac ⊜	206	46.05 N	75.04 W
Preston, Lake ⊜, Austl.	168a	32.59 S	115.42 E
Preston, Lake ⊜, Fla., U.S.	220	28.18 N	81.08 W
Preston Airport ⊠	276	40.22 N	74.15 W
Preston Brook	262	53.19 N	2.39 W
Preston Brook Canal Tunnel ⇁[5]	262	53.19 N	2.38 W
Preston Heights	216	41.28 N	88.08 W
Preston Hollow	210	42.27 N	74.13 W
Preston North End Football Ground ♠	262	53.47 N	2.42 W
Prestonpans	46	55.57 N	3.00 W
Preston Peak ∧	204	41.50 N	123.37 W
Prestonsburg	192	37.40 N	82.46 W
Prestrud Inlet C	9	78.18 S	156.00 W
Preststranda	26	59.06 N	9.04 E
Prestville	182	55.45 N	118.06 W
Prestwich	44	53.32 N	2.17 W
Prestwick	46	55.30 N	4.37 W
Prestwick Airport ⊠	46	55.30 N	4.36 W
Prêto ≃, Bra.	246	1.41 S	63.48 W
Prêto ≃, Bra.	248	8.03 S	62.54 W
Prêto ≃, Bra.	250	3.32 S	43.46 W
Prêto ≃, Bra.	250	11.21 S	43.52 W
Prêto ≃, Bra.	255	18.25 S	39.47 W
Prêto ≃, Bra.	255	20.08 S	49.38 W
Prêto ≃, Bra.	255	18.44 S	50.23 W
Prêto ≃, Bra.	255	17.00 S	46.12 W
Prêto ≃, Bra.	255	19.22 S	41.56 W
Prêto ≃, Bra.	255	13.37 S	48.06 W
Preto ≃, Bra.	256	22.01 S	43.20 W
Preto ≃, Bra.	256	22.14 S	43.07 W
Prêto, Igarapé ≃	246	4.10 S	68.57 W
Prêto do Igapó-Açu ≃	246	4.26 S	59.48 W
Pretoria	158	25.45 S	28.10 E
Pretoriusvlei	158	28.30 S	22.59 E
Prettau → Predoi	64	47.02 N	12.06 E
Prettin	54	51.39 N	12.55 E
Prettyboy Reservoir ⊜[1]	208	39.38 N	76.45 W
Pretty Prairie	198	37.47 N	98.01 W
Pretzfeld	60	49.45 N	11.11 E
Pretzier	54	52.49 N	11.15 E
Pretzsch	54	51.42 N	12.48 E
Preussisch Eylau → Bagrationovsk	76	54.23 N	20.39 E
Preussisch Friedland → Debrzno	30	53.33 N	17.14 E
Preussisch Holland → Pasłęk	30	54.05 N	19.39 E
Preussisch Königsdorf → Olesno	30	50.53 N	18.25 E
Preussisch-Oldendorf	52	52.18 N	8.30 E
Preussisch-Ströhen	52	52.29 N	8.40 E
Préveza	38	38.57 N	20.44 E
Prevost Island I	224	48.50 N	123.22 W
Prey Lvéa	110	11.10 N	104.57 E
Prey Nŏb	110	10.38 N	103.47 E
Prey Vêng	110	11.29 N	105.19 E
Prezza, Monte ∧	66	42.02 N	13.49 E
Priaral'skije Karakumy ⇁[2]	86	47.00 N	63.30 E
Priargunsk	88	50.27 N	119.00 E
Priay	58	46.00 N	5.17 E
Priazovskaja Vozvyšennost' ⛰[1]	83	47.30 N	37.30 E
Priazovskoje	78	46.43 N	35.38 E
Pribel'skij, Zapovednik ♠	86	53.01 N	56.53 E
Pribilof Islands II	180	57.00 N	170.00 W
Priboj	38	43.35 N	19.31 E
Příbor	30	49.39 N	18.10 E
Příbram	30	49.42 N	14.01 E
Pribylovo	76	60.26 N	28.40 E
Priccio, Cozzo ∧	70	37.01 N	14.46 E
Price, Austl.	168b	34.17 S	138.00 E
Price, Tex., U.S.	222	32.08 N	94.57 W
Price, Utah, U.S.	200	39.36 N	110.48 W
Price ≃	200	39.10 N	110.06 W
Price, Cape ≻	110	13.34 N	93.03 E
Price Bend C	276	40.55 N	73.24 W
Price Island I	182	52.23 N	128.36 W
Prichard	194	30.44 N	88.07 W
Prickly Point ≻	241k	11.59 N	61.45 W
Pričornomorskaja Nizmennost' ≚	78	47.00 N	33.00 E
Priddy	196	31.40 N	98.31 W
Pridneprovsk	78	48.24 N	35.09 E
Pridneprovskaja Nizmennost' ≚	78	50.00 N	32.00 E
Pridneprovskaja Vozvyšennost' ⛰[1]	78	49.00 N	32.00 E
Priego	34	40.27 N	2.18 W
Priego de Córdoba	34	37.26 N	4.11 W
Priekulė, S.S.S.R.	76	55.33 N	21.19 E
Priekule, S.S.S.R.	76	56.26 N	21.35 E
Prienai	76	54.38 N	23.57 E
Prien am Chiemsee	64	47.51 N	12.20 E
Prieros	54	52.13 N	13.46 E
Prieska	158	29.40 S	22.42 E
Priest ≃	202	48.11 N	116.53 W
Priestewitz	54	51.15 N	13.30 E
Priest Island I	46	57.58 N	5.30 W
Priest Lake ⊜	202	48.34 N	116.52 W
Priestley, Mount ∧	182	55.13 N	128.53 W
Priest River	202	48.11 N	116.55 W
Prieta, Loma ∧	226	37.07 N	121.51 W
Prieta, Peña ∧	34	43.01 N	4.44 W
Prieto ≃	240m	18.15 N	66.54 W
Prieto Diaz	116	13.02 N	124.12 E
Prievidza	30	48.47 N	18.37 E
Prignitz ⇁[1]	54	53.05 N	12.15 E
Priirtyšskaja Ravnina ≚	86	52.30 N	76.15 E
Priiskovyj, S.S.S.R.	86	54.39 N	88.42 E
Priiskovyj, S.S.S.R.	88	51.57 N	116.39 E
Prijedor	36	44.59 N	16.43 E
Prijepolje	38	43.23 N	19.39 E
Prijutnoje	80	46.06 N	43.31 E
Prijutovo	80	53.54 N	53.56 E
Prikaspijskaja Nizmennost' ≚	80	48.00 N	52.00 E
Prikolotnoje	78	50.09 N	37.21 E
Prikubanskaja Nizmennost' ≚	78	46.00 N	39.30 E
Prikumsk	84	44.46 N	44.09 E
Prilep	38	41.20 N	21.33 E
Prilepy	82	54.03 N	37.42 E
Prilly	58	46.32 N	6.36 E
Priluki, S.S.S.R.	76	59.16 N	39.53 E
Priluki, S.S.S.R.	78	50.36 N	32.24 E
Priluki, S.S.S.R.	82	54.51 N	37.53 E
Prima Porta ⇁[8]	267a	42.00 N	12.29 E
Primavera	250	0.56 S	47.06 W
Přimda	60	49.41 N	12.41 E
Primeira Cruz	250	2.30 S	43.26 W
Primeiro de Maio	255	22.48 S	51.01 W
Primera	196	26.14 N	97.43 W
Primero de Mayo	196	27.12 N	101.15 W
Primghar	198	43.05 N	95.38 W
Primkenau → Przemków	30	51.32 N	15.48 E
Primolano	64	45.58 N	11.42 E
Primorje [Warnicken]	76	54.57 N	20.02 E
Primorka	83	47.16 N	39.03 E
Primorsk, S.S.S.R.	76	60.22 N	28.36 E
Primorsk, S.S.S.R.	76	54.44 N	20.01 E
Primorsk, S.S.S.R.	80	49.16 N	45.03 E
Primorsk, S.S.S.R.	84	40.13 N	49.33 E
Primorskij, S.S.S.R.	78	45.07 N	35.29 E
Primorskij, S.S.S.R.	89	43.07 N	131.38 E
Primorskij Chrebet ⛰	88	52.30 N	106.00 E
Primorskij Kraj □[4]	89	45.25 N	135.25 E
Primorsko	38	42.16 N	27.46 E
Primorsko-Achtarsk	78	46.03 N	38.11 E
Primorskoje	83	47.11 N	37.42 E
Primos	285	39.55 N	75.18 W
Primrose, S. Afr.	273d	26.12 S	28.10 E
Primrose, Pa., U.S.	210	40.42 N	76.17 W
Primrose, Pa., U.S.	279b	40.21 N	80.16 W
Primrose Brook ≃	276	40.43 N	74.31 W
Primrose Lake ⊜	184	54.55 N	109.45 W
Prims ≃	56	49.20 N	6.44 E
Primstal	56	49.32 N	6.58 E
Prince, Lake ⊜[1]	208	36.48 N	76.38 W
Prince Albert, Ont., Can.	212	44.05 N	78.58 W
Prince Albert, Sask., Can.	184	53.12 N	105.46 W
Prince Albert, S. Afr.	158	33.13 S	22.02 E
Prince Albert Mountains ⛰	9	76.00 S	161.30 E
Prince Albert National Park ♠	184	54.00 N	106.25 W
Prince Albert Road	158	33.01 S	21.40 E
Prince Albert Sound Ʉ	176	70.25 N	115.00 W
Prince Alexander Mountains ⛰	164	3.30 S	142.50 E
Prince Alfred Hamlet	158	33.18 S	19.20 E
Prince Charles Island I	176	67.50 N	76.00 W
Prince Charles Mountains ⛰	9	72.00 S	67.00 E
Prince-de-Galles, Cap du ≻	176	61.36 N	71.30 W
Prince-de-Galles, Île du → Prince of Wales Island I, Austl.	164	10.40 S	142.10 E
Prince-de-Galles, Île du → Prince of Wales Island I, N.W. Ter., Can.	176	72.40 N	99.00 W
Prince Edward □[6]	212	44.00 N	77.15 W
Prince Edward Bay C	212	43.57 N	76.57 W
Prince Edward Island □[4]	176		
	186	46.20 N	63.20 W
Prince Edward Island National Park ♠	186	46.31 N	63.26 W
Prince Edward Islands II	6	46.35 S	37.56 E
Prince Edward Park ♠	274a	34.02 S	151.03 E
Prince Edward Point ≻	212	44.56 N	76.52 W
Prince Frederick	188	38.33 N	76.35 W
Prince Gallitzin State Park ♠	214	40.40 N	78.32 W
Prince George, B.C., Can.	182	53.55 N	122.45 W
Prince George, Va., U.S.	208	37.13 N	77.17 W
Prince George □[6]	208	37.13 N	77.10 W
Prince Georges □[6]	208	38.49 N	76.45 W
Prince Kemal el Din's Monument ⊥	140	22.51 N	25.48 E
Prince Leopold Island I	176	74.02 N	89.55 W
Prince of Wales, Cape ≻	180	65.40 N	168.05 W
Prince of Wales Island I, Austl.	164	10.40 S	142.10 E
Prince of Wales Island I, N.W. Ter., Can.	176	72.40 N	99.00 W
Prince of Wales Island I, Alaska, U.S.	180	55.47 N	132.50 W
Prince of Wales Strait Ʉ	176	73.00 N	117.00 W
Prince Olav Coast •[2]	9	68.30 S	42.30 E
Prince Patrick Island I	16	76.45 N	119.30 W
Prince Regent Inlet C	176	73.00 N	90.30 W
Prince Rupert	182	54.19 N	130.19 W
Prince Rupert Bay C	240d	15.34 N	61.29 W
Prince Rupert Bluff Point ≻	240d	15.35 N	61.29 W
Princesa, Puerto C	116	9.45 N	118.43 E
Princesa Astrid, Costa → Princess Astrid Coast •[2]	9	70.45 S	12.30 E
Princesa Carlota, Bahía → Princess Charlotte Bay C	164	14.25 S	144.00 E
Princesa Isabel	250	7.44 S	38.00 W
Princesa Marta, Costa → Princess Martha Coast •[2]	9	72.00 S	7.30 W
Princesa Ragnhild, Costa → Princess Ragnhild Coast •[2]	9	70.15 S	27.30 E
Princes Bay C	276	40.31 N	74.12 W
Princes Risborough	42	51.44 N	0.51 W
Princess Anne	188	38.12 N	75.41 W

Symbols in the index entries represent the broad categories identified in the key at the right. Symbols with superior numbers (⛰[2]) identify subcategories (see complete key on page *I · 30*).

Kartensymbole in dem Registerverzeichnis stellen die rechts in Schlüssel erklärten Kategorien dar. Symbole mit hochgestellten Ziffern (⛰[2]) bezeichnen Unterabteilungen einer Kategorie (vgl. vollständiger Schlüssel auf Seite *I · 30*).

Los símbolos incluídos en el texto del índice representan las grandes categorias identificadas con la clave a la derecha. Los símbolos con numeros en su parte superior (⛰[2]) identifican las subcategorías (véase la clave completa en la página *I · 30*).

Les symboles de l'index représentent les catégories indiquées dans la légende à droite. Les symboles suivis d'un indice (⛰[2]) représentent des sous-catégories (voir légende complète à la page *I · 30*).

Os símbolos incluídos no texto do índice representam as grandes categorias identificadas com a chave à direita. Os símbolos com números em sua parte superior (⛰[2]) identificam as subcategorias (veja-se a chave completa à página *I · 30*).

Symbol	English	Deutsch	Español	Français	Português
∧	Mountain	Berg	Montaña	Montagne	Montanha
⛰	Mountains	Berge	Montañas	Montagnes	Montanhas
)(	Pass	Pass	Paso	Col	Passo
∨	Valley, Canyon	Tal, Cañon	Valle, Cañón	Vallée, Canyon	Vale, Canhão
≚	Plain	Ebene	Llano	Plaine	Planície
≻	Cape	Kap	Cabo	Cap	Cabo
I	Island	Insel	Isla	Île	Ilha
II	Islands	Inseln	Islas	Îles	Ilhas
•	Other Topographic Features	Andere Topographische Objekte	Otros Elementos Topográficos	Autres données topographiques	Outros Elementos Topográficos

ESPAÑOL

Nombre	Página	Lat.°′	Long.°′ W=Oeste
Princess Astrid Coast	9	70.45 S	12.30 E
Princess Charlotte Bay	164	14.25 S	144.00 E
Princess Martha Coast	9	72.00 S	7.30 W
Princess Ragnhild Coast	9	70.15 S	27.30 E
Princess Ranges	162	26.08 S	121.55 E
Princess Royal Channel	182	53.10 N	128.37 W
Princess Royal Island	182	52.57 N	128.49 W
Princes Town	241r	10.16 N	61.23 W
Princeton, B.C., Can.	182	49.27 N	120.31 W
Princeton, Newf., Can.	186	48.25 N	53.36 W
Princeton, Ont., Can.	212	43.10 N	80.32 W
Princeton, Calif., U.S.	226	39.24 N	122.01 W
Princeton, Fla., U.S.	220	25.32 N	80.25 W
Princeton, Ill., U.S.	190	41.23 N	89.28 W
Princeton, Ind., U.S.	194	38.21 N	87.34 W
Princeton, Ky., U.S.	194	37.07 N	87.53 W
Princeton, Maine, U.S.	188	45.13 N	67.34 W
Princeton, Mich., U.S.	190	46.17 N	87.29 W
Princeton, Minn., U.S.	190	45.34 N	93.35 W
Princeton, Mo., U.S.	194	40.24 N	93.35 W
Princeton, N.J., U.S.	208	40.21 N	74.40 W
Princeton, N.C., U.S.	192	35.28 N	78.10 W
Princeton, Tex., U.S.	222	33.11 N	96.30 W
Princeton, W. Va., U.S.	192	37.22 N	81.06 W
Princeton, Wis., U.S.	190	43.51 N	89.08 W
Princeton Airfield	276	40.24 N	74.39 W
Princeton Battlefield Park	276	40.20 N	74.41 W
Princeton Junction	208	40.19 N	74.37 W
Princeton Township	276	40.22 N	74.40 W
Princeton University	276	40.21 N	74.39 W
Princetown	42	50.33 N	4.00 W
Princeville, Qué., Can.	206	46.10 N	71.53 W
Princeville, Ill., U.S.	190	40.45 N	89.45 W
Princeville, N.C., U.S.	192	35.53 N	77.82 W
Prince William	208	38.42 N	77.27 W
Prince William Forest Park	208	38.36 N	77.23 W
Prince William Sound	180	60.40 N	147.00 W
Príncipe	152	1.37 N	7.25 E
Príncipe Alberto, Montes → Prince Albert Mountains	9	76.00 S	161.30 E
Príncipe Carlos, Montes → Prince Charles Mountains	9	72.00 S	67.00 E
Príncipe Channel	182	53.28 N	130.00 W
Príncipe da Beira	248	12.25 S	64.25 W
Príncipe de Gales, Isla → Prince of Wales Island, Austl.	164	10.40 S	142.10 E
Príncipe de Gales, Isla → Prince of Wales Island, N.W. Ter., Can.	176	72.40 N	99.00 W
Príncipe Eduardo, Isla → Prince Edward Island	186	46.20 N	63.20 W
Príncipe Olav, Costa → Prince Olav Coast	9	68.30 S	42.30 E
Príncipe Patricio, Isla → Prince Patrick Island	16	76.45 N	119.30 W
Prineville	202	44.18 N	120.51 W
Prineville Reservoir	202	44.08 N	120.42 W
Prineville Southeast	202	44.17 N	120.53 W
Pringgabaja	115b	8.34 S	116.37 E
Pringy	261	48.31 N	2.34 E
Prinsenbeek	52	51.36 N	4.42 E
Prinses Margrietkanaal	52	53.10 N	5.55 E
Prinskof	158	32.06 S	20.53 E
Prinzapolka	236	13.24 N	83.34 W
Prinzapolka	236	13.24 N	83.34 W
Prinzessin Astrid-Küste → Princess Astrid Coast	9	70.45 S	12.30 E
Prinzessin Charlotte Bucht → Princess Charlotte Bay	164	14.25 S	144.00 E
Prinzessin Martha-Küste → Princess Martha Coast	9	72.00 S	7.30 W
Prinzessin Ragnhild-Küste → Princess Ragnhild Coast	9	70.15 S	27.30 E
Priobskoje Plato	86	52.40 N	83.00 E
Prioksko-Terrasnyj Zapovednik	82	54.51 N	37.36 E
Priolo Gargallo	70	37.09 N	15.11 E
Prior, Cabo	34	43.34 N	8.19 W
Priort	264a	52.31 N	12.58 E
Priozernyj	80	47.23 N	45.14 E
Prioz'ornyj	86	47.50 N	84.13 E
Prioz'orsk	24	61.02 N	30.04 E
Prip'at'	78	51.21 N	30.09 E
Pripet → Prip'at'	78	51.21 N	30.09 E
Pripet Marshes → Polesje	72	52.30 N	27.30 E
Pripjat → Prip'at'	78	51.21 N	30.09 E
Pripjet → Prip'at'	78	51.21 N	30.09 E
Pripol'arnyj Ural	24	65.00 N	60.00 E
Priputni	78	50.57 N	32.14 E
Prirečje	88	55.07 N	101.03 E
Prirečnyj	80	51.03 N	52.26 E
Přísečnice	54	50.27 N	13.06 E
Priselje	76	55.09 N	32.49 E
Prišib, S.S.S.R.	78	47.16 N	35.21 E
Prišib, S.S.S.R.	84	39.08 N	48.36 E
Prislon	82	56.48 N	37.16 E
Pristan'-Prževal'sk	85	42.34 N	78.18 E
Pristen', S.S.S.R.	78	51.15 N	36.41 E
Pristen', S.S.S.R.	83	49.36 N	37.38 E
Priština	38	42.39 N	21.10 E
Pritchett	198	37.22 N	102.52 W
Pritzerbe	54	52.30 N	12.27 E
Pritzier	54	53.22 N	11.04 E
Pritzwalk	54	53.09 N	12.10 E
Priural'nyj	80	51.29 N	53.06 E
Privas	62	44.44 N	4.36 E
Priverno	66	41.28 N	13.11 E
Privetnoje	78	44.50 N	34.41 E
Privodino	24	61.05 N	46.28 E
Privokzal'nyj, S.S.S.R.	82	55.59 N	35.56 E
Privokzal'nyj, S.S.S.R.	86	58.53 N	60.43 E
Privolje, S.S.S.R.	83	49.01 N	38.18 E
Privolje, S.S.S.R.	83	48.52 N	37.16 E
Privol'naja	78	46.09 N	38.42 E
Privol'n'anskij	83	48.41 N	38.28 E
Privol'noje, S.S.S.R.	78	47.29 N	32.17 E
Privol'noje, S.S.S.R.	80	50.57 N	46.06 E
Privolžje	80	52.52 N	48.37 E
Privolžsk	80	57.23 N	41.17 E
Privolžskaja Vozvyšennost'	80	52.00 N	46.00 E
Privolžskij, S.S.S.R.	80	46.24 N	48.00 E
Privolžskij, S.S.S.R.	80	51.24 N	46.02 E

FRANÇAIS

Nom	Page	Lat.°′	Long.°′ W=Ouest
Privolžskoje	80	51.06 N	45.57 E
Prizren	38	42.12 N	20.44 E
Prizzi	70	37.43 N	13.26 E
Prizzi, Lago di	70	37.44 N	13.25 E
Prnjavor	36	44.52 N	17.40 E
Pro	286d	11.57 S	77.05 W
Probolinggo	115a	7.45 S	113.13 E
Proboštov	54	50.39 N	13.50 E
Probstzella	54	50.32 N	11.22 E
Probus	42	50.17 N	4.57 W
Procchio	66	42.47 N	10.15 E
Prochladnoje	86	48.30 N	82.41 E
Prochladnyj	84	43.46 N	44.00 E
Prochorkino	86	59.34 N	79.26 E
Prochorovka	82	54.07 N	38.11 E
Prochowice	30	51.17 N	16.22 E
Procida	68	40.46 N	14.02 E
Procida, Isola di	68	40.45 N	14.01 E
Procter	182	49.37 N	116.57 W
Proctor, Minn., U.S.	190	46.45 N	92.13 W
Proctor, Vt., U.S.	188	43.40 N	73.02 W
Proctor Brook	283	42.32 N	70.54 W
Proctor Lake	228	35.07 N	118.21 W
Proctor Lake	196	32.02 N	98.32 W
Proddatūr	122	14.44 N	78.33 E
Proença-a-Nova	34	39.45 N	7.55 W
Profen	54	51.07 N	12.13 E
Pro Football Hall of Fame	214	40.49 N	81.25 W
Prognoj	83	48.45 N	39.51 E
Progreso, Méx.	196	27.28 N	100.59 W
Progreso, Méx.	232	21.17 N	89.40 W
Progreso, Ur.	258	34.40 S	56.13 W
Progreso Industrial	234	19.38 N	99.21 W
Progress, S.S.S.R.	89	49.42 N	129.39 E
Progress, Oreg., U.S.	224	45.28 N	122.47 W
Progress, Pa., U.S.	208	40.08 N	76.34 W
Project City	204	40.41 N	122.21 W
Prokopjeva	88	58.03 N	100.39 E
Prokopjevsk	86	53.53 N	86.45 E
Prokopyevsk → Prokopjevsk	86	53.53 N	86.45 E
Prokuplje	38	43.14 N	21.36 E
Prokuševo	76	59.55 N	34.56 E
Prokutskoje	86	56.19 N	69.46 E
Proletarij	76	58.26 N	31.44 E
Proletarsk, S.S.S.R.	78	48.56 N	38.23 E
Proletarsk, S.S.S.R.	85	40.10 N	69.30 E
Proletarsk	83	48.56 N	38.23 E
Proletarskaja	80	46.42 N	41.44 E
Proletarskij, S.S.S.R.	78	50.47 N	35.47 E
Proletarskij, S.S.S.R.	82	55.01 N	37.23 E
Proletarskij	83	48.08 N	39.18 E
Prolysovo	76	52.54 N	34.09 E
Prome (Pyè)	110	18.49 N	95.13 E
Promised Land State Park	210	41.18 N	75.11 W
Promissão	255	21.32 S	49.52 W
Promitorio	267a	42.03 N	12.39 E
Promontogno	58	46.21 N	9.34 E
Prompton	210	41.35 N	75.19 W
Prompton Lake	210	41.36 N	75.20 W
Prompton State Park	210	41.37 N	75.22 W
Promyšlennaja	86	54.55 N	85.40 E
Promyšlennovskij	86	55.29 N	86.12 E
Promyšlennyj	24	67.35 N	63.55 E
Promyslovka, S.S.S.R.	80	45.44 N	47.10 E
Promyslovka, S.S.S.R.	89	43.00 N	132.24 E
Pron'a, S.S.S.R.	76	53.25 N	31.01 E
Pron'a, S.S.S.R.	80	54.21 N	40.24 E
Pron'a Gorodišče	82	54.15 N	38.43 E
Pronin	80	49.12 N	42.11 E
Pronsfeld	56	50.10 N	6.20 E
Pronsk	76	54.07 N	39.37 E
Prony, Baie du	175f	22.22 S	166.53 E
Prophet	176	58.45 N	122.45 W
Prophetstown	194	41.40 N	89.56 W
Propriá	250	10.13 S	36.51 W
Propriano	36	41.40 N	8.55 E
Prorer Wiek	54	54.27 N	13.38 E
Prorva	86	46.03 N	53.15 E
Proryvnoje	86	54.23 N	64.26 E
Pros'anaja	78	48.07 N	36.23 E
Pros'anov	78	49.42 N	35.47 E
Prösen	54	51.25 N	13.30 E
Proserpine	166	20.24 S	148.34 E
Prosigk	54	51.42 N	12.03 E
Proskoveja	84	44.43 N	44.12 E
Proskurov → Chmel'nickij	78	49.25 N	27.00 E
Prosna	30	52.10 N	17.39 E
Prosnica	80	58.26 N	50.15 E
Prosotsáni	38	41.10 N	23.59 E
Prospect, Austl.	168b	34.54 S	138.35 E
Prospect, Austl.	274a	33.48 S	150.56 E
Prospect, Conn., U.S.	207	41.30 N	72.59 W
Prospect, N.Y., U.S.	210	43.18 N	75.09 W
Prospect, Ohio, U.S.	214	40.27 N	83.11 W
Prospect, Pa., U.S.	214	40.54 N	80.03 W
Prospect Bay	208	38.56 N	76.14 W
Prospect Heights	278	42.06 N	87.56 W
Prospect Hill	168b	35.13 S	138.44 E
Prospect Hill, Mass., U.S.	207	41.21 N	70.45 W
Prospect Hill, Mass., U.S.	283	42.23 N	71.15 W
Prospect Hill Park	283	42.23 N	71.15 W
Prospect Meadows	278	42.05 N	87.57 W
Prospect Park, N.J., U.S.	276	40.56 N	74.10 W
Prospect Park, Pa., U.S.	214	41.31 N	78.13 W
Prospect Park, Pa., U.S.	285	39.53 N	75.19 W
Prospect Park	276	40.40 N	73.58 W
Prospect Park Lake	276	40.39 N	73.57 W
Prospect Plains	276	40.19 N	74.28 W
Prospect Point	276	40.58 N	74.38 W
Prospect Point	276	40.52 N	73.43 W
Prospect Reservoir	274a	33.49 S	150.54 E
Prospectville	285	40.13 N	75.11 W
Prosper	222	33.14 N	96.48 W
Prosperi Airport	278	41.33 N	87.47 W
Prosperidad	116	8.34 N	125.52 E
Prosser	202	46.12 N	119.46 W
Prosser Creek	226	39.22 N	120.07 W
Prosser Creek Reservoir	226	39.22 N	120.08 W
Prostějov	30	49.29 N	17.07 E
Prostiboř	60	49.40 N	12.54 E
Prostken → Prostki	30	53.43 N	22.26 E
Prostki	30	53.43 N	22.26 E
Proston	166	26.10 S	151.36 E
Proszowice	30	50.12 N	20.18 E
Protasovo, S.S.S.R.	82	56.08 N	37.36 E
Protasovo, S.S.S.R.	82	54.11 N	37.00 E
Protasovo, S.S.S.R.	82	54.48 N	38.35 E
Protasy	76	52.47 N	29.05 E
Protea	273d	26.17 S	27.51 E
Protection	198	37.12 N	99.29 W
Protection Island	224	48.07 N	122.55 W
Protem	158	34.16 S	20.05 E
Protestantes	256	22.44 S	46.18 W
Protoka	78	45.43 N	37.46 E
Protva	82	55.01 N	36.41 E
Protva	82	54.51 N	37.16 E
Protville	36	36.54 N	10.01 E
Prötzel	54	52.38 N	13.59 E
Proud Lake State Recreational Area	281	42.35 N	83.29 W

PORTUGUÊS

Nome	Página	Lat.°′	Long.°′ W=Oeste
Proud Lake State Recreation Area	281	42.34 N	83.33 W
Proulxville	206	46.40 N	72.30 W
Provadija	38	43.11 N	27.26 E
Proval, Zaliv	88	52.21 N	106.45 E
Provence	62	44.00 N	6.00 E
Provence, Alpes de	62	43.40 N	6.00 E
Provenchères-sur-Fave	58	48.19 N	7.05 E
Providence, Ky., U.S.	194	37.24 N	87.39 W
Providence, R.I., U.S.	207	41.50 N	71.25 W
Providence, Utah, U.S.	200	41.43 N	111.49 W
Providence	207	41.52 N	71.36 W
Providence	207	41.43 N	71.21 W
Providence Forge	208	37.27 N	77.02 W
Providence Island	138	9.14 S	51.02 E
Providência, Bra.	256	21.40 S	42.35 W
Providencia, Chile	286e	33.26 S	70.37 W
Providencia, Méx.	196	27.06 N	103.32 W
Providencia, Isla de	236	13.21 N	81.22 W
Providenciales	238	21.47 N	72.17 W
Providenija	74	64.23 N	173.18 W
Providenija, Buchta	180	64.30 N	173.20 W
Provincetown	207	42.03 N	70.11 W
Provincia, Cerro de la	286e	33.25 S	70.26 W
Provincial Capital	269f	14.35 N	121.04 E
Provins	50	48.33 N	3.18 E
Provo	200	40.14 N	111.39 W
Provo	200	40.14 N	111.44 W
Provost	184	52.21 N	110.16 W
Prozor	36	43.49 N	17.37 E
Prud'anka	78	50.14 N	36.09 E
Prudence Island	207	41.37 N	71.19 W
Prudentópolis	252	25.12 S	50.57 W
Prudentov	80	49.39 N	46.19 E
Prudhoe	44	54.58 N	1.51 W
Prudhoe Bay	180	70.20 N	148.20 W
Prudhoe Island	166	21.19 S	149.40 E
Prudišči	82	54.24 N	38.26 E
Prudki	82	54.46 N	36.29 E
Prudnik	30	50.19 N	17.34 E
Prudy	76	53.47 N	26.32 E
Pruggern	64	47.25 N	13.52 E
Prüm	56	50.12 N	6.25 E
Prüm	56	49.49 N	6.28 E
Prunay-le-Temple	261	48.52 N	1.40 E
Prunay-sous-Ablis	261	48.32 N	1.48 E
Prunedale	226	36.47 N	121.40 W
Prunéřov	54	50.25 N	13.16 E
Prunières	62	44.33 N	6.20 E
Prunn	60	48.57 N	11.44 E
Prunn, Schloss	60	48.57 N	11.44 E
Pruszków	30	52.11 N	20.48 E
Prut (Prutul)	78	45.28 N	28.12 E
Pruth → Prut	78	45.28 N	28.12 E
Prutting	64	47.53 N	12.11 E
Prutul (Prut)	78	45.28 N	28.12 E
Prutz	58	47.05 N	10.40 E
Pružany	76	52.33 N	24.28 E
Prydz Bay	9	69.00 S	76.00 E
Pryor	196	36.19 N	95.19 W
Pryor Creek	202	45.54 N	108.19 W
Pryor Mountain	222	31.43 N	95.12 W
Prysor	42	52.56 N	4.00 W
Przasnysz	30	53.01 N	20.55 E
Przedbórz	30	51.06 N	19.53 E
Przemków	30	51.32 N	15.48 E
Przemocze	54	53.27 N	14.55 E
Przemyśl	30	49.47 N	22.47 E
Prževal'sk	85	42.29 N	78.24 E
Przeworsk	30	50.05 N	22.29 E
Przewóz	54	51.29 N	14.59 E
Przybiernów	54	53.46 N	14.46 E
Przysucha	30	51.22 N	20.38 E
Pšagar	85	39.58 N	68.08 E
Psakhná	38	38.35 N	23.38 E
Psará	38	38.35 N	25.37 E
Psárion	38	37.20 N	21.51 E
Psebaj	84	44.07 N	40.47 E
Pšecha	78	44.47 N	39.48 E
Psekups	78	45.00 N	39.09 E
Pselec	78	51.17 N	36.32 E
Psikhikón	267c	38.01 N	23.46 E
Pšiš	78	45.01 N	39.18 E
Pšiš, Gora	84	43.24 N	41.12 E
Psittália	267c	37.56 N	23.35 E
Pskem	85	41.56 N	70.22 E
Pskem	85	41.38 N	70.01 E
Pskent	85	40.54 N	69.20 E
Pskov	76	57.50 N	28.20 E
Pskovskoje Ozero	76	58.00 N	28.00 E
Pskowsee → Pskovskoje Ozero	76	58.00 N	28.00 E
Ps'ol	78	49.02 N	33.33 E
Pšov	54	50.10 N	13.29 E
Pszczyna	30	49.59 N	18.57 E
Pszów	30	50.03 N	18.24 E
Ptič'	78	52.09 N	28.52 E
Ptič'	76	52.09 N	28.52 E
Ptolemaís	38	40.31 N	21.41 E
Ptolemais	146	32.43 N	20.57 E
Ptuj	61	46.25 N	15.52 E
Pua-a, Cape	175a	13.26 S	172.43 W
Puah, Pulau	112	0.30 S	122.34 E
Puamau, Baie	174x	9.46 S	138.52 W
Puán, Arg.	252	37.33 S	62.43 W
Puan, Taehan	98	35.45 N	126.44 E
Puapua	175a	13.34 S	172.09 W
Pubāil	126	23.56 N	90.29 E
Pubnico	186	43.42 N	65.47 W
Pucallpa	248	8.23 S	74.32 W
Pucará	248	18.43 S	64.11 W
Pucarani	248	16.23 S	68.30 W
Puce	214	42.18 N	82.47 W
Puces, Rivière aux	281	42.18 N	82.47 W
Pučevejem	180	68.48 N	170.30 E
Pučež	80	56.59 N	43.11 E
Puchberg am Schneeberg	61	47.47 N	15.54 E
Pucheng, Zhg.	100	27.55 N	118.31 E
Pucheng, Zhg.	102	34.59 N	109.29 E
Pucheta	252	29.54 S	57.34 W
Puchhausen	60	48.45 N	12.30 E
Puchheim	60	48.09 N	11.20 E
Púchov	30	49.08 N	18.20 E
Puchoviči	76	53.32 N	28.15 E
Pucioasa	38	45.04 N	25.26 E
Pucio Point	116	11.46 N	121.51 E
Pučišća	36	43.21 N	16.44 E
Puck	30	54.44 N	18.27 E
Pucketa Creek	279b	40.33 N	79.45 W
Pudahuel, Aeropuerto de	286e	33.23 S	70.49 W
Pudding	224	45.18 N	122.43 W
Puddingstone Reservoir State Recreation Area	280	34.05 N	117.49 W
Puddington	262	53.15 N	3.00 W
Puddletown	42	50.45 N	2.21 W
Pūdeh Tal	128	31.03 N	62.15 E
Pudem	80	58.18 N	52.10 E
Pudi	102	27.58 N	99.05 E
Pudimoe	158	27.26 S	24.44 E
Puding	102	26.21 N	105.40 E
Pudino	86	57.34 N	79.24 E
Pudops Dam	186	48.09 N	56.50 W
Pudož	24	61.48 N	36.32 E
Pudsey	44	53.48 N	1.40 W
Puduhe	102	25.39 N	102.39 E
Puduhe	102	26.19 N	102.45 E
Pudukkottai	122	10.23 N	78.49 E
Puebla	234	18.50 N	98.00 W
Puebla de Alcocer	34	38.59 N	5.15 W
Puebla de Don Fadrique	34	37.58 N	2.26 W
Puebla de Don Rodrigo	34	39.05 N	4.37 W
Puebla de Sanabria	34	42.03 N	6.38 W
Puebla de Trives	34	42.20 N	7.15 W
Puebla [de Zaragoza]	234	19.03 N	98.12 W
Pueblito de Ponce	240m	18.26 N	66.58 W
Pueblo	198	38.16 N	104.37 W
Pueblo Hundido	252	26.23 S	70.03 W
Pueblo Ledesma	252	23.50 S	64.46 W
Pueblo Libertador	252	30.13 S	59.23 W
Pueblo Libre	286d	12.05 S	77.04 W
Pueblo Mountain	202	42.06 N	118.39 W
Pueblonuevo, Col.	246	8.31 N	75.15 W
Pueblo Nuevo, Méx.	234	20.31 N	101.22 W
Pueblo Nuevo, Nic.	236	13.23 N	86.29 W
Pueblo Nuevo, P.R.	240m	18.28 N	66.51 W
Pueblo Nuevo, Ur.	258	34.26 S	56.29 W
Pueblo Nuevo, Ven.	246	11.58 N	69.55 W
Pueblo Nuevo	266a	40.26 N	3.39 W
Puebloviejo, Ec.	246	1.34 S	79.30 W
Pueblo Viejo, Méx.	234	17.24 N	93.47 W
Pueblo Viejo, Méx.	234	17.33 N	100.05 W
Pueblo Viejo, Laguna de	234	22.10 N	97.53 W
Puelches	252	38.09 S	65.55 W
Puente Alto	252	33.37 S	70.35 W
Puenteareas	34	42.11 N	8.30 W
Puente-Caldelas	34	42.23 N	8.30 W
Puente de Arganda	266a	40.19 N	3.31 W
Puente de Camotlán	234	21.32 N	104.12 W
Puente de Ixtla	234	18.37 N	99.20 W
Puentedeume	34	43.24 N	8.10 W
Puente-Genil	34	37.23 N	4.47 W
Puente Hills	280	34.00 N	117.55 W
Puente Hills Mall	280	33.59 N	117.56 W
Puente la Reina	34	42.40 N	1.49 W
Puente Negro	196	27.55 N	101.01 W
Puente Nuevo, Embalse de	34	38.00 N	5.00 W
Pueo Point	229b	21.54 N	160.04 W
Puer	102	23.07 N	101.00 E
Puerca, Punta	240m	18.14 N	65.36 W
Puerco, Rio	200	34.22 N	107.50 W
Puerdu	102	28.08 N	104.24 E
Puerto Acosta	248	15.32 S	69.15 W
Puerto Adela	252	24.33 S	54.22 W
Puerto Aisén	254	45.24 S	72.42 W
Puerto Alegre	248	13.53 S	61.36 W
Puerto Alfonso	246	2.11 S	71.01 W
Puerto Ángel	234	15.40 N	96.29 W
Puerto Armuelles	236	8.17 N	82.52 W
Puerto Asís	246	0.30 N	76.31 W
Puerto Ayacucho	246	5.40 N	67.35 W
Puerto Bahía Negra	248	20.15 S	58.12 W
Puerto Baquerizo Moreno	246a	0.54 S	89.36 W
Puerto Barrios	236	15.43 N	88.36 W
Puerto Belgrano	252	38.54 S	62.06 W
Puerto Bermejo	252	26.56 S	58.30 W
Puerto Bermúdez	248	10.20 S	74.54 W
Puerto Berrío	246	6.29 N	74.24 W
Puerto Bolívar	246	3.16 S	79.59 W
Puerto Boyacá	246	5.45 N	74.39 W
Puerto Cabello	246	10.28 N	68.01 W
Puerto Cabezas	236	14.02 N	83.23 W
Puerto Carreño	246	6.12 N	67.22 W
Puerto Casado	252	22.20 S	57.55 W
Puerto Castilla	236	16.01 N	86.01 W
Puerto Chicama	248	7.42 S	79.27 W
Puerto Colombia	246	10.59 N	74.58 W
Puerto Constanza	258	33.50 S	59.03 W
Puerto Cortés, C.R.	236	8.58 N	83.32 W
Puerto Cortés, Hond.	236	15.48 N	87.56 W
Puerto Cumarebo	246	11.29 N	69.21 W
Puerto de Lajas, Cerro	232	28.59 N	107.02 W
Puerto Delicia	252	26.12 S	54.35 W
Puerto Delón	236	14.22 N	85.53 W
Puerto del Rosario	148	28.30 N	13.52 W
Puerto de Nutrias	246	8.05 N	69.18 W
Puerto de Pollensa	34	39.55 N	3.05 E
Puerto de San José	236	13.55 N	90.49 W
Puerto de San Juan de Dios	234	22.19 N	99.33 W
Puerto Deseado	254	47.45 S	65.54 W
Puerto El Triunfo	236	13.17 N	88.33 W
Puerto Escondido	234	15.50 N	97.10 W
Puerto Espãna → Port of Spain	241r	10.39 N	61.31 W
Puerto Esperanza	252	26.01 S	54.39 W
Puerto Felipe, Bahía → Port Phillip Bay	169	38.07 S	144.48 E
Puerto Fonciere	252	22.29 S	57.48 W
Puerto Guaraní	248	21.18 S	57.55 W
Puerto Heath	248	12.30 S	68.40 W
Puerto Iguazú	252	25.34 S	54.34 W
Puerto Ingeniero Ibáñez	254	46.18 S	71.56 W
Puerto Jiménez	236	8.33 N	83.19 W
Puerto Juárez	232	21.11 N	86.49 W
Puerto la Cruz	246	10.13 N	64.38 W
Puerto la Plata, Zona Nacional	288	34.52 S	57.52 W
Puerto Leda	248	20.41 S	58.02 W
Puerto Leguízamo	246	0.12 S	74.46 W
Puerto Lempira	236	15.13 N	83.47 W
Puerto Libertad, Arg.	252	25.55 S	54.36 W
Puerto Libertad, Méx.	232	29.55 N	112.43 W
Puerto Limón, Col.	246	3.23 N	73.30 W
Puerto Limón → Limón, C.R.	236	10.00 N	83.02 W
Puertollano	34	38.41 N	4.07 W
Puerto Lobos	254	42.00 S	65.06 W
Puerto López	246	4.05 N	72.58 W
Puerto Madryn	254	42.46 S	65.03 W
Puerto Maldonado	248	12.36 S	69.11 W
Puerto Manatí	240p	21.22 N	76.50 W
Puerto Mihanovich	248	20.52 S	57.59 W
Puerto Montt	254	41.28 S	72.57 W
Puerto Morazán	236	12.51 N	87.11 W
Puerto Morelos	232	20.50 N	86.52 W
Puerto Morrito	236	11.37 N	85.05 W
Puerto Nariño	246	4.56 N	67.48 W
Puerto Natales	254	51.44 S	72.31 W
Puerto Nuevo, Punta	240m	18.30 N	66.24 W
Puerto Octay	254	40.58 S	72.54 W
Puerto Ordaz → Ciudad Guayana	246	8.22 N	62.40 W
Puerto Padre	240p	21.12 N	76.36 W
Puerto Páez	246	6.13 N	67.28 W
Puerto Palmer, Pico	196	27.08 N	101.47 W
Puerto Peñasco	232	31.20 N	113.33 W
Puerto Pilón	236	9.22 N	79.48 W
Puerto Pinasco	252	22.43 S	57.50 W
Puerto Pirámides	254	42.34 S	64.17 W
Puerto Piray	252	26.28 S	54.42 W
Puerto Píritu	246	10.04 N	65.03 W
Puerto Plata	238	19.48 N	70.41 W
Puerto Portillo	248	9.46 S	72.45 W
Puerto Potrero	236	10.28 N	85.47 W
Puerto Presidente Stroessner	252	25.30 S	54.36 W
Puerto Princesa, Pil.	116	9.44 N	118.44 E
Puerto Princesa, Pil.	116	10.06 N	125.29 E
Puerto Real, Esp.	34	36.32 N	6.11 W
Puerto Real, P.R.	240m	18.05 N	67.11 W
Puerto Reyes	246	0.59 S	73.17 W
Puerto Rico, Bol.	248	11.05 S	67.38 W
Puerto Rico, Col.	246	1.54 N	75.10 W
Puerto Rico	230		
	240m	18.15 N	66.30 W
Puerto Rico, International Airport Of	240m	18.27 N	66.00 W
Puerto Rico Trench	16	19.30 N	64.00 W
Puerto Rondón	246	6.17 N	71.06 W
Puerto Saavedra	252	38.47 S	73.24 W
Puerto Salgar	246	5.28 N	74.39 W
Puerto Sastre	252	22.06 S	57.59 W
Puerto Siles	248	12.48 S	65.05 W
Puerto Somoza	236	12.12 N	86.46 W
Puerto Suárez	248	18.57 S	57.51 W
Puerto Supe	248	10.49 S	77.45 W
Puerto Tejada	246	3.14 N	76.24 W
Puerto Toledo	246	0.59 S	74.09 W
Puerto Umbría	246	0.52 N	76.33 W
Puerto Vallarta	234	20.37 N	105.15 W
Puerto Varas	254	41.19 S	72.59 W
Puerto Victoria, Arg.	252	26.20 S	54.39 W
Puerto Victoria, Perú	248	9.54 S	74.58 W
Puerto Viejo, C.R.	236	10.26 N	83.59 W
Puerto Viejo, C.R.	236	9.39 N	82.45 W
Puerto Villamizar	246	8.19 N	72.26 W
Puerto Visser	254	45.24 S	67.08 W
Puerto Wilches	246	7.21 N	73.54 W
Puerto Ybapobó	252	23.42 S	57.12 W
Pueyrredón, Lago (Lago Cochrane)	254	47.20 S	72.00 W
Puffendorf	56	50.56 N	6.13 E
Puffing Billy	274b	37.55 S	145.21 E
Pugačov	80	52.01 N	48.50 E
Pugač'ovo	80	56.35 N	53.02 E
Puge, Tan.	154	4.45 S	33.07 E
Puge, Zhg.	102	27.28 N	102.31 E
Puget, Cape	180	59.52 N	148.26 W
Puget Island	224	46.10 N	123.23 W
Puget Sound	224	47.50 N	122.30 W
Puget Sound Naval Shipyard	224	47.33 N	122.38 W
Puget-sur-Argens	62	43.27 N	6.41 E
Puget-Théniers	62	43.57 N	6.54 E
Puget-Ville	62	43.17 N	6.08 E
Pugh Mountain	224	48.08 N	121.22 W
Pughtown	285	40.10 N	75.40 W
Puglia	68	41.00 N	16.45 E
Pugong-ni	271b	37.43 N	126.58 E
Pugŏ-ri	98	42.01 N	129.59 E
Pugwash	186	45.51 N	63.40 W
Puhe	104	41.57 N	123.36 E
Puhi	229b	21.58 N	159.24 W
Puhja	76	58.20 N	26.19 E
Puhos	26	62.05 N	29.54 E
Puhosjärvi	26	65.19 N	27.55 E
Puica	248	15.04 S	72.42 W
Puiești	38	46.25 N	27.33 E
Puigcerdá	34	42.26 N	1.56 E
Puigmal	34	42.23 N	2.07 E
Puimoisson	62	43.52 N	6.08 E
Puinahua, Canal de	248	5.20 S	74.13 W
Puinān	272b	22.56 N	88.13 E
Puir	89	53.10 N	141.25 E
Puiseaux	50	48.12 N	2.28 E
Puiseaux	50	48.00 N	2.44 E
Puiseux-en-France	261	49.04 N	2.29 E
Puiseux-Pontoise	261	49.03 N	2.01 E
Puisieux	50	50.07 N	2.42 E
Puits	50	48.31 N	4.15 E
Pujada Bay	116	6.51 N	126.14 E
Pujehun	150	7.21 N	11.42 W
Puji, Zhg.	98	36.42 N	117.37 E
Puji, Zhg.	100	30.01 N	112.33 E
Puji, Zhg.	100	27.59 N	113.25 E
Pujiang, Zhg.	100	29.28 N	119.53 E
Pujiang, Zhg.	107	30.12 N	103.30 E
Pujilí	246	0.57 S	78.41 W
Pujon	115a	7.50 S	112.28 E
Pujun	112	1.20 S	114.20 E
Pujut	114	1.25 N	100.39 E
Pukaki, Lake	172	44.07 S	170.10 E
Pukalani	229a	20.51 N	156.20 W
Pukaskwa	190	48.00 N	85.53 W
Pukaskwa National Park	190	48.20 N	85.50 W
Pukch'ang	98	39.36 N	126.17 E
Pukchin	98	40.10 N	125.43 E
Pukch'ŏn	98	36.13 N	126.45 E
Pukch'ŏng	98	40.15 N	128.20 E
Pukë	38	42.03 N	19.54 E
Pukeashun Mountain	182	51.12 N	119.14 W
Pukekohe	172	37.12 S	174.55 E
Puketeraki Range	172	42.58 S	172.12 E
Puketoi Range	172	40.30 S	176.05 E
Pukeuri Junction	172	45.02 S	171.02 E
Pukhan-gang	98	37.31 N	127.18 E
Pukhan-san	271b	37.41 N	127.00 E
Pukhrāyān	124	26.14 N	79.51 E
Pukoo	229d	21.04 N	156.48 W
Pukou, Zhg.	100	26.16 N	119.35 E
Pukou, Zhg.	106	32.07 N	118.43 E
Puksoozero	24	62.38 N	40.36 E
Puksubaek-san	98	40.42 N	127.44 E
Puktae-ch'ŏn	98	40.28 N	129.00 E
Pula, It.	71	39.01 N	9.00 E
Pula, Jugo.	64	44.52 N	13.50 E
Pulacayo	248	20.25 S	66.41 W
Pulan	120	30.16 N	81.14 E
Pulanduta Point	116	11.54 N	123.10 E
Pulangi	116	7.18 N	124.50 E
Pulangpisau	112	2.46 S	114.14 E
Pulap	14	7.35 N	149.24 E
Pulaski, Ind., U.S.	216	40.59 N	86.40 W
Pulaski, Mich., U.S.	216	42.07 N	84.40 W
Pulaski, N.Y., U.S.	212	43.34 N	76.08 W
Pulaski, Ohio, U.S.	216	41.30 N	84.26 W
Pulaski, Pa., U.S.	214	41.07 N	80.26 W
Pulaski, Tenn., U.S.	194	35.12 N	87.02 W
Pulaski, Va., U.S.	192	37.03 N	80.47 W
Pulaski, Wis., U.S.	190	44.41 N	88.14 W
Pulaski	216	41.03 N	86.36 W
Pulathane	130	41.01 N	39.34 E
Pulau	164	5.50 S	138.15 E
Pulaukida	112	2.44 S	102.34 E
Pulaukijang	112	0.42 S	103.12 E
Pulaumerak	115a	5.56 S	106.00 E
Pulautelo	110	0.03 N	98.16 E
Puławy	30	51.25 N	21.57 E
Pulborough	42	50.58 N	0.30 W
Pul'chakim	85	38.10 N	67.21 E
Pulehu Gulch	229a	20.50 N	156.28 W
Pulfero	64	46.11 N	13.29 E
Pulga	123	31.59 N	77.26 E
Pulgaon	122	20.44 N	78.20 E
Pulham Market	42	52.26 N	1.14 E
Pulheim	56	51.00 N	6.47 E
Puli	100	23.58 N	120.57 E
Pulicat	122	13.25 N	80.19 E
Pulicat Lake	122	13.40 N	80.10 E
Pulichatum	128	35.57 N	61.07 E
Puliciano	66	43.23 N	11.51 E
Puliyangudi	122	9.10 N	77.25 E
Pulizhuang	98	35.57 N	118.17 E
Pulj → Pula	64	44.52 N	13.50 E
Pulkau	61	48.42 N	15.51 E
Pulkaubach	61	48.43 N	16.21 E
Pulkkila	26	64.16 N	25.52 E
Pulkovo	265a	59.46 N	30.20 E
Pullach im Isarta	60	48.03 N	11.31 E
Pullman, Mich., U.S.	216	42.29 N	86.05 W
Pullman, Wash., U.S.	202	46.44 N	117.10 W
Pullman	278	41.43 N	87.36 W
Pullo	248	15.14 S	73.50 W
Pully	58	46.31 N	6.39 E
Pul'mo	78	51.31 N	23.47 E
Pulo	68	41.12 N	16.34 E
Pulo Anna	108	4.40 N	131.58 E
Pulog, Mount	116	16.36 N	120.54 E
Pulogadung	269e	6.11 S	106.54 E
Pulon'ga	24	66.17 N	40.02 E
Púlpito, Punta	232	26.31 N	111.28 W
Púlpito do Sul	152	15.46 S	12.00 E
Pulsano	68	40.23 N	17.22 E
Pulsen	54	51.23 N	13.26 E
Pulsnitz	54	51.11 N	14.01 E
Pulsnitz	54	51.27 N	13.30 E
Pulteney	210	42.31 N	77.10 W
Pultneyville	210	43.17 N	77.11 W
Pułtusk	30	52.43 N	21.05 E
Pulü	107	29.50 N	106.11 E
Pülümür Geçidi	130	39.31 N	39.54 E
Puluo	120	36.11 N	81.30 E
Pulupandan	116	10.31 N	122.48 E
Pulur	130	40.10 N	39.53 E
Pulusuk	14	6.42 N	149.19 E
Pulversheim	58	47.51 N	7.18 E
Pumbi	152	3.26 N	22.11 E
Pumei	102	23.28 N	105.15 E
Pumen	100	27.16 N	120.25 E
Pumphrey	284b	39.13 N	76.38 W
Pumpkin Buttes	200	43.44 N	105.54 W
Pumpkin Center	228	35.18 N	119.05 W
Pumpkin Creek, Mont., U.S.	198	46.15 N	105.45 W
Pumpkin Creek, Nebr., U.S.	198	41.38 N	103.01 W
Pumpkin Creek, Lawrence Fork	198	41.36 N	103.14 W
Pumpsaint	42	52.03 N	3.58 W
Pumsi	80	57.12 N	51.39 E
Puna	248	19.46 S	65.28 W
Puná, Isla	246	2.50 S	80.08 W
Punaauia	174s	17.38 S	149.36 W
Punaauia, Pointe	174s	17.38 S	149.36 W
Punakha	124	27.37 N	89.52 E
Punaluu	229c	21.35 N	157.53 W
Punan, Indon.	112	1.20 N	115.34 E
Punan, Indon.	112	3.24 N	116.16 E
Punan, Zhg.	100	24.39 N	117.41 E
Punata	248	17.32 S	65.50 W
Pūnch	123	33.46 N	74.06 E
Punch	123	33.30 N	74.30 E
Pūnch	123	33.13 N	73.40 E
Puncha	126	23.10 N	86.39 E
Punchaw	182	53.28 N	123.13 W
Punchbowl	274a	33.56 S	151.03 E
Pundaguitan	116	6.22 N	126.10 E
Punda Milia	156	22.40 S	31.05 E
Pünderich	56	50.02 N	7.08 E
Pūndri	124	29.45 N	76.33 E
Punduga	76	60.08 N	40.12 E
Pune (Poona)	122	18.32 N	73.52 E
Punga	85	40.45 N	70.49 E
P'ungam-ni	98	37.43 N	128.11 E
Punganūru	122	13.22 N	78.35 E
Pungești	38	46.42 N	27.20 E
Punggol	271c	1.25 N	103.55 E
Punggol	271c	1.25 N	103.54 E
Pungo	192	35.23 N	76.33 W
Pungo Andongo	152	9.40 S	15.35 E
P'ungsan	98	38.28 N	125.01 E
P'ungsong-ni	98	39.56 N	127.11 E
Púnguè	154	19.50 S	34.48 E
Punia	154	1.28 S	26.27 E
Puning	100	23.18 N	116.12 E
Punitaqui	252	30.50 S	71.16 W
Punjab	123	31.00 N	75.30 E
Punjab	120	31.00 N	72.30 E
Punkaharju	26	61.47 N	29.20 E
Punkalaidun	26	61.07 N	23.06 E
Punnichy	184	51.23 N	104.18 W
Puno	248	15.50 S	70.02 W
Puno	248	15.00 S	70.00 W
Punta, Castillo de la	286b	23.09 N	82.21 W
Punta, Cerro de	240m	18.10 N	66.36 W
Punta Alegre	240p	22.23 N	78.49 W
Punta Alta	254	38.53 S	62.05 W
Punta Arenas	254	53.09 S	70.55 W
Punta Banda, Cabo	232	31.45 N	116.45 W
Punta Brava	286b	23.01 N	82.30 W
Punta de Agua Creek	196	35.32 N	102.27 W
Punta de Bombón	248	17.11 S	71.48 W
Punta de Díaz	252	28.03 S	70.37 W
Punta del Cobre	252	27.30 S	70.16 W
Punta del Este	252	34.58 S	54.57 W
Punta Delgada	254	42.46 S	63.38 W
Punta de los Llanos	252	30.09 S	66.33 W
Punta de Mata	246	9.43 N	63.38 W
Punta Flecha	116	7.23 N	123.25 E
Punta Gorda, Belize	232	16.07 N	88.48 W
Punta Gorda, Fla., U.S.	220	26.56 N	82.03 W
Punta Gorda, Bahía de	236	11.15 N	83.45 W
Punta Indio, Canal	258	34.36 S	58.16 W
Punta Moreno	248	7.36 S	78.54 W
Punta Negra, Salar de	252	24.35 S	69.00 W
Punta Piedras	246	10.54 N	64.06 W
Punta Porá	252	25.13 S	58.31 W
Punta Prieta	232	28.58 N	114.17 W
Punta Raisi, Aeroporto di	70	38.11 N	13.06 E
Puntarenas	236	9.58 N	84.50 W
Puntarenas	236	9.00 N	83.15 W
Punta Santiago	240m	18.10 N	65.45 W
Puntas del Sauce	258	33.51 S	57.01 W
Punto Fijo	246	11.42 N	70.13 W
Puntzi Lake	182	52.12 N	124.02 W
Punung	115a	8.08 S	111.01 E
Punxsutawney	214	40.57 N	78.59 W
Puolanka	26	64.52 N	27.40 E
Puolo Point	229b	21.54 N	159.36 W
Puper	164	0.10 S	131.18 E
Pup'yŏng	271b	37.30 N	126.43 E
Puqi, Zhg.	100	28.11 N	121.01 E
Puqi, Zhg.	100	29.43 N	113.53 E
Puqian	100	23.34 N	114.38 E
Puquio	248	14.42 S	74.08 W
Pur	74	67.31 N	77.55 E
Purabiya Plain	124	25.50 N	82.30 E
Puracé, Volcán	246	2.21 N	76.23 W
Purandarpur	126	23.51 N	87.36 E
Pūranpur	124	28.31 N	80.09 E
Purari	164	7.25 S	145.05 E
Purba	114	2.54 N	98.42 E
Purbashthāli	126	23.28 N	88.21 E
Purbeck, Isle of	42	50.38 N	2.00 W
Purbolinggo	115a	7.24 S	109.22 E
Purcell	196	35.01 N	97.22 W
Purcell Mountains	182	50.00 N	116.30 W
Purcellville	188	39.08 N	77.43 W
Purchase	276	41.02 N	73.43 W
Purchena	34	37.21 N	2.22 W
Purdon	222	31.57 N	96.37 W
Purdoški	80	54.40 N	43.32 E
Purdy	194	36.49 N	93.55 W
Purdy Islands	164	2.50 S	146.20 E
Purech	80	56.39 N	43.05 E
Pureora, Mount	172	38.33 S	175.38 E
Purépero	234	19.55 N	102.01 W
Purfleet	42	51.29 N	0.15 E
Purga	171a	27.43 S	152.44 E
Purga Creek	171a	27.42 S	152.45 E
Purgatoire	198	38.04 N	103.10 W
Purgatory Brook	283	42.11 N	71.11 W
Purgg	61	47.32 N	14.04 E
Purgstall	61	48.03 N	15.08 E
Puri	120	19.48 N	85.51 E
Purial, Sierra del	240p	20.12 N	74.42 W
Purificación, Col.	246	3.51 N	74.55 W
Purificación, Méx.	234	19.43 N	104.38 W
Purificación, Méx.	232	23.58 N	98.42 W
Purificación, Méx.	234	19.18 N	104.54 W

River	Fluss	Río	Rivière	Rio
Canal	Kanal	Canal	Canal	Canal
Waterfall, Rapids	Wasserfall, Stromschnellen	Cascada, Rápidos	Chute d'eau, Rapides	Cascata, Rápidos
Strait	Meeresstrasse	Estrecho	Détroit	Estreito
Bay, Gulf	Bucht, Golf	Bahía, Golfo	Baie, Golfe	Baía, Golfo
Lake, Lakes	See, Seen	Lago, Lagos	Lac, Lacs	Lago, Lagos
Swamp	Sumpf	Pantano	Marais	Pântano
Ice Features, Glacier	Eis- und Gletscherformen	Accidentes Glaciales	Formes glaciaires	Acidentes Glaciares
Other Hydrographic Features	Andere Hydrographische Objekte	Otros Elementos Hidrográficos	Autres données hydrographiques	Outros Elementos Hidrográficos
Submarine Features	Untermeerische Objekte	Accidentes Submarinos	Formes de relief sous-marin	Acidentes Submarinos
Political Unit	Politische Einheit	Unidad Política	Entité politique	Unidade Política
Cultural Institution	Kulturelle Institution	Institución Cultural	Institution culturelle	Instituição Cultural
Historical Site	Historische Stätte	Sitio Histórico	Site historique	Sítio Histórico
Recreational Site	Erholungs- und Ferienort	Sitio de Recreo	Centre de loisirs	Sítio de Lazer
Airport	Flughafen	Aeropuerto	Aéroport	Aeroporto
Military Installation	Militäranlage	Instalación Militar	Installation militaire	Instalação Militar
Miscellaneous	Verschiedenes	Misceláneo	Divers	Miscelânea

Purikari Neem ≻ 76 59.40 N 25.43 E
Purísima, Méx. 196 29.09 N 100.46 W
Purísima, Méx. 232 25.25 N 105.26 W
Purísima, Sierra de la ⛰ 196 26.30 N 101.44 W
Purisima Creek ≃ 282 37.24 N 122.26 W
Purísima de Bustos 234 21.02 N 101.52 W
Purkersdorf 264b 48.12 N 16.11 E
Purleigh 260 51.41 N 0.40 E
Purley 222 33.05 N 95.16 W
Purley ◆[8] 260 51.20 N 0.07 W
Purli 122 18.51 N 76.32 E
Purling 210 42.17 N 74.00 W
Purmerend 52 52.31 N 4.57 E
Pūrna ≃, Bhārat 122 21.05 N 76.00 E
Pūrna ≃, Bhārat 122 19.07 N 77.02 E
Purnea 124 25.47 N 87.31 E
Puronga 76 60.09 N 40.54 E
Purranque 254 40.55 S 73.10 W
Purros 156 18.38 S 12.59 E
Pursat
→ Poŭthĭsăt 110 12.32 N 103.55 E
Purton 42 51.36 N 1.52 W
Puruándiro 234 20.05 N 101.30 W
Puruarán 234 19.06 N 101.32 W
Puruchuca 286d 12.04 S 76.57 W
Puruê ≃ 246 1.40 S 68.08 W
Purukcahu 112 0.35 S 114.35 E
Purūlia 126 23.20 N 86.22 E
Purūlia □[5] 124 23.20 N 86.25 E
Puruni ≃ 246 6.00 N 59.12 W
Purus (Purús) ≃ 242 3.42 S 61.28 W
Puruvesi ⊜ 26 61.50 N 29.27 E
Purvis 194 31.09 N 89.25 W
Purwakarta 115a 6.34 S 107.26 E
Purwantoro 115a 7.51 S 111.15 E
Purwareja 115a 7.28 S 109.25 E
Purwodadi, Indon. 115a 7.05 S 110.54 E
Purwodadi, Indon. 115a 7.49 S 110.00 E
Purwokerto 115a 7.25 S 109.14 E
Purworejo 115a 7.43 S 110.01 E
Pusa, Bhārat 124 25.59 N 85.41 E
Pusa, Malay. 112 1.36 N 111.17 E
Pusad 122 19.54 N 77.35 E
Pusan 98 35.06 N 129.03 E
Pusan □[8] 98 35.10 N 129.05 E
Pusat Gayo, Pegunungan ⛰ 114 4.15 N 97.05 E
Puščino 82 54.50 N 37.36 E
Pusei 175f 15.22 S 166.36 E
Pusgo Point ≻ 116 13.31 N 122.38 E
Pushang 98 36.08 N 119.42 E
Pushkar 120 26.30 N 74.33 E
Pushkin
→ Puškin 76 59.43 N 30.25 E
Pushthrough 186 47.39 N 56.10 W
Pushui ≃ 107 30.25 N 103.49 E
Puškar'ovka 78 48.40 N 34.16 E
Puskiakiwenin Indian Reserve ◆[4] 184 53.57 N 110.26 W
Puškin 76 59.43 N 30.25 E
Puškin, Aeroport ⊠ 265a 59.41 N 30.21 E
Puškino, S.S.S.R. 80 51.14 N 46.59 E
Puškino, S.S.S.R. 82 56.36 N 35.46 E
Puškino, S.S.S.R. 82 56.01 N 37.51 E
Puškino, S.S.S.R. 84 39.27 N 48.33 E
Puškinskaja, Gora ∧ 89 47.03 N 142.50 E
Puškinskij 265a 59.43 N 30.18 E
Puškinskije Gory 76 57.01 N 28.54 E
Puskwaskau ≃ 182 55.29 N 118.10 W
Puslinch Lake ⊜ 212 43.25 N 80.16 W
Pusŏng-ni 98 40.19 N 127.19 E
Püspökladány 30 47.19 N 21.07 E
Pussay 50 48.21 N 2.00 E
Püssi 76 59.24 N 27.01 E
Puster-Tal ∨ 64 46.45 N 12.20 E
Pustin' 76 59.54 N 35.32 E
Pustomyty 78 49.42 N 23.56 E
Pustoš' 76 60.07 N 42.45 E
Pustoška 76 56.20 N 29.22 E
Pustozersk 24 67.33 N 52.27 E
Pusur ≃[1] 126 21.45 N 89.30 E
Puszczykowo 30 52.17 N 16.52 E
Putaendo 252 32.38 S 70.44 W
Putah Creek ≃ 226 38.35 N 122.16 W
Putai 100 23.23 N 120.09 E
Putang 106 31.34 N 118.59 E
Putang ≃ 269e 6.13 S 106.54 E
Putao 102 27.21 N 97.24 E
Putaruru 172 38.03 S 175.47 E
Put'atin 89 42.52 N 132.25 E
Put'atino 80 54.10 N 41.07 E
Putbus 54 54.21 N 13.28 E
Puteaux 261 48.53 N 2.14 E
Puteran, Pulau ▮ 115a 7.05 S 114.00 E
Putfontein 273d 26.08 S 28.24 E
Putgarten 54 54.40 N 13.25 E
Puth Kalān ◆[8] 272a 28.43 N 77.05 E
Putian, Zhg. 100 25.28 N 119.02 E
Putian, Zhg. 102 20.03 N 110.36 E
Putifigari 71 40.34 N 8.27 E
Putignano 68 40.51 N 17.07 E
Putila 78 48.01 N 25.03 E
Putilkovo 265b 55.52 N 37.23 E
Putina 248 14.55 S 69.52 W
Put-in-Bay 214 41.39 N 82.49 W
Putincevo 86 49.50 N 84.22 E
Puting, Tanjung ≻ 112 3.31 S 111.46 E
Putivl' 78 51.21 N 33.52 E
Putla de Guerrero 234 17.02 N 97.56 W
Putlitz 54 53.15 N 12.02 E
Putnam, Conn., U.S. 207 41.55 N 71.55 W
Putnam, Tex., U.S. 196 32.22 N 99.12 W
Putnam □[6], N.Y., U.S. 210 41.26 N 73.41 W
Putnam □[6], Ohio, U.S. 216 41.01 N 84.03 W
Putnam Lake 210 41.28 N 73.35 W
Putnam Lake ⊜ 276 41.05 N 73.38 W
Putnam Valley 210 41.20 N 73.52 W
Putnamville Reservoir ⊜[1] 283 42.36 N 70.57 W
Putney, Ga., U.S. 192 31.29 N 84.07 W
Putney, Vt., U.S. 188 42.59 N 72.31 W
Putney ◆[8] 260 51.28 N 0.13 W
Puto 175e 5.41 S 154.43 E
Putorana, Gory ⛰ 12 69.00 N 95.00 E
Putorana, Plato ⛰[1] 74 69.00 N 95.00 E
Putorino 172 39.08 S 177.00 E
Putre 248 18.12 S 69.35 W
Putri Narrows ⊔ 271c 1.27 N 103.42 E
Putsonderwater 158 29.09 S 21.51 E
Pütt 263 51.11 N 6.59 E
Puttalam 122 8.02 N 79.49 E
Puttalam Lagoon ⊂ 122 8.07 N 79.47 E
Putte, Bel. 56 51.04 N 4.38 E
Putte, Ned. 52 51.22 N 4.23 E
Puttelange-lès-Farschviller 56 49.03 N 6.56 E
Putten 52 52.15 N 5.36 E
Putten ▮ 52 51.50 N 4.15 E
Puttgarden 41 54.30 N 11.13 E
Püttlingen 56 49.17 N 6.53 E
Puttūr 122 13.27 N 79.33 E
Putty 170 32.57 S 150.40 E
Putú 252 35.13 S 72.17 W
Putumayo □[8] 246 0.30 N 76.00 W
Putumayo (Içá) ≃ 246 3.07 S 67.58 W
Putu Range ⛰ 150 5.30 N 8.10 W
Putussibau 112 0.50 N 112.56 E
Putzkau 54 51.06 N 14.13 E
Putzu Idu 71 40.02 N 8.25 E
Puu Kaaumakua ∧ 229c 21.30 N 157.54 W
Puu Keahiakahoe ∧ 229c 21.23 N 157.49 W
Puukolii 229a 20.56 N 156.41 W
Puu Kukui ∧ 229a 20.52 N 156.35 W
Puulavesi ⊜ 26 61.50 N 26.42 E
Puumala 26 61.32 N 28.11 E
Puunene 229a 20.52 N 156.28 W
Puurmani 76 58.34 N 26.17 E
Puurs 50 51.05 N 4.17 E
Puuwai 229b 21.54 N 160.12 W
Puxcatán ≃ 234 17.37 N 92.34 W
Puxi 100 25.10 N 119.08 E
Puxian 102 36.30 N 111.02 E
Puxico 194 36.57 N 90.10 W
Puxingchang 107 30.41 N 105.06 E
Puxmetacán ≃ 234 17.22 N 95.36 W
Puyallup 224 47.11 N 122.18 W
Puyallup ≃ 224 47.15 N 122.24 W
Puyang 98 35.43 N 115.01 E
Puyangjiang ≃ 100 30.05 N 120.11 E
Puy-de-Dôme □[5] 32 45.45 N 3.05 E
Puy de Dôme ∧ 32 45.47 N 2.58 E
Puy de Sancy ∧ 32 45.32 N 2.49 E
Puyehue 254 40.40 S 72.37 W
Puylaurens 32 43.34 N 2.01 E
Puy l'Évêque 32 44.30 N 1.08 E
Puyloubier 62 43.31 N 5.41 E
Puymorens, Col de)(32 42.30 N 1.50 E
Puyo, Ec. 246 1.28 S 77.59 W
Puyŏ, Taehan 98 36.18 N 126.54 E
Puysegur Point ≻ 172 46.09 S 166.36 E
Puyuan 106 30.41 N 120.38 E
Puyuguapi, Canal ⊔ 254 44.45 S 72.48 W
Puyun-dong 98 41.55 N 129.30 E
Pūzak, Jehīl-e ⊜ 128 31.30 N 61.45 E
Puzhen 106 32.09 N 118.41 E
Puzzle Creek ≃ 162 17.58 S 135.41 E
Puzzle Lake ⊜, Ont., Can. 212 44.36 N 76.58 W
Puzzle Lake ⊜, Fla., U.S. 220 28.41 N 81.02 W
Pwalagu 150 10.35 N 0.50 W
Pweto 154 8.28 S 28.54 E
Pwinbyu 110 20.22 N 94.40 E
Pwllheli 42 52.53 N 4.25 W
Pyalo 110 19.09 N 95.11 E
Pyalong 169 37.07 S 144.54 E
Pyamalaw ≃[1] 110 15.49 N 94.42 E
Pyapon 110 16.17 N 95.41 E
Pyatigorsk
→ P'atigorsk 84 44.03 N 43.04 E
Pyawbwe 110 20.35 N 96.04 E
Pyaye 110 19.15 N 95.06 E
Pyčas 80 56.29 N 52.28 E
Pye Islands ▮▮ 180 59.22 N 150.25 W
Pyhäjärvi ⊜, Suomi 26 61.28 N 23.35 E
Pyhäjärvi ⊜, Suomi 26 61.53 N 30.00 E
Pyhäjärvi ⊜, Suomi 26 62.46 N 25.30 E
Pyhäjärvi ⊜, Suomi 26 63.35 N 25.57 E
Pyhäjoki 26 64.28 N 24.14 E
Pyhäjoki ≃ 26 64.28 N 24.13 E
Pyhämaa ▮ 26 60.57 N 21.20 E
Pyhän-Häkin kansallispuisto ♠ 26 62.52 N 25.30 E
Pyhäsalmi 26 63.41 N 25.59 E
Pyhäselkä 26 62.26 N 29.58 E
Pyhäselkä ⊜ 26 62.26 N 29.58 E
Pyhätunturi ∧ 24 67.01 N 27.09 E
Pyhätunturin Kansallispuisto ♠ 24 67.01 N 27.10 E
Pyhtää (Pyttis) 26 60.29 N 26.32 E
Pyinbongyi 110 17.34 N 96.34 E
Pyingaing 110 23.09 N 94.51 E
Pyinkayaing 110 15.58 N 94.24 E
Pyinmana 110 19.44 N 96.13 E
Pyle 42 51.32 N 3.42 W
Pylos
→ Pílos 38 36.55 N 21.43 E
Pymatuning Creek ≃ 214 41.18 N 80.27 W
Pymatuning Reservoir ⊜[1] 214 41.37 N 80.30 W
Pymatuning State Park ♠, Ohio, U.S. 214 41.38 N 80.33 W
Pymatuning State Park ♠, Pa., U.S. 214 41.30 N 80.27 W
Pymble 274a 33.45 S 151.09 E
Pyngopil'gyn, Laguna ⊂ 180 67.24 N 175.10 W
Pyŏlch'ang-ni 98 39.17 N 126.26 E
P'yŏngan Namdo □[4] 98 39.20 N 126.00 E
P'yŏngan-pukdo □[4] 98 40.10 N 125.20 E
P'yŏngch'ang 98 37.23 N 128.22 E
P'yŏngdong-ni 98 37.10 N 128.02 E
P'yŏnggang 98 38.26 N 127.16 E
P'yonghae 98 36.46 N 129.28 E
P'yŏngt'aek 98 37.00 N 127.05 E
P'yŏngyang 98 39.01 N 125.45 E
P'yŏngyang □[4] 98 39.05 N 125.50 E
Pyŏrha-ri 98 40.48 N 126.32 E
Pyote 196 31.32 N 103.08 W
Pyramid Head ≻ 228 32.49 N 118.21 W
Pyramid Lake ⊜ 204 40.00 N 119.35 W
Pyramid Lake ⊜[1] 228 34.39 N 118.47 W
Pyramid Lake Indian Reservation ◆[4] 204 40.20 N 119.35 W
Pyramid Peak ∧, Calif., U.S. 226 38.50 N 120.19 W
Pyramid Peak ∧, Wash., U.S. 224 47.07 N 121.24 W
Pyramid Peak ∧, Wyo., U.S. 200 43.27 N 110.28 W
Pyramid Point ≻ 174h 2.52 S 171.37 W
Pyrenäen
→ Pyrenees ⛰ 34 42.40 N 1.00 E
Pyrenees ⛰ 34 42.40 N 1.00 E
Pyrénées-Atlantiques □[5] 32 43.15 N 0.50 W
Pyre Peak ∧ 180 52.20 N 172.31 W
Pyrford 260 51.19 N 0.30 W
Pyrgi ⊥ 66 42.01 N 11.58 E
Pyrgos
→ Pírgos 38 37.41 N 21.28 E
Pyritz
→ Pyrzyce 30 53.10 N 14.55 E
Pyrkanajan, Gora ∧ 180 69.14 N 175.50 E
Pyrkino 80 53.29 N 45.07 E
Pyrmont 216 40.28 N 86.41 W
Pyrzyce 30 53.10 N 14.55 E
Pyskowice 30 50.24 N 18.38 E
Pyšma 86 56.56 N 63.13 E
Pyšma ≃ 86 57.08 N 66.18 E
Pytalovo 76 57.04 N 27.56 E
Pythonga, Lac ⊜ 190 46.23 N 76.25 W
Pyu 110 18.29 N 96.26 E
Pyuntaza 110 17.52 N 96.44 E
Pyvėsa ≃ 76 56.06 N 24.27 E
Pyzdry 30 52.11 N 17.41 E

Q

Qabātiyah 132 32.25 N 35.17 E
Qabbāsīn 130 36.25 N 37.34 E
Qabb Ilyās 132 33.48 N 35.49 E
Qabr al-Jamal, 'Alāmat ∧[2] 142 30.44 N 30.17 E
Qabr Hūd 144 16.08 N 49.37 E
Qacha's Nek 158 30.06 S 28.42 E
Qaddīs Anṭūn, Dayr al- (Monastery of Saint Anthony) ✝[1] 142 28.55 N 32.21 E
Qaddīs Būlus, Dayr al- (Monastery of Saint Paul) ✝[1] 142 28.52 N 32.33 E
Qāderābād 128 30.17 N 53.16 E
Qādiān 123 31.49 N 75.23 E
Qafarah 128 23.59 N 45.11 E
Qāfilah 142 31.04 N 30.16 E
Qahā 142 30.17 N 31.12 E
Qahbūna 142 30.48 N 31.54 E
Qāhirah / Almāza, Al- Military Base ■ 142 30.06 N 31.21 E
Qāhirah West, Al- Military Base ■ 142 30.06 N 30.56 E
Qala' an-Naḥl 140 13.38 N 34.57 E
Qalabshū 142 31.26 N 31.19 E
Qalamshāh 142 29.10 N 30.50 E
Qalamūn, Jabal al- ∧[2] 142 28.56 N 30.30 E
Qalandūl 142 27.49 N 30.50 E
Qalāt 120 32.07 N 66.54 E
Qal'at al-Akhḍar 128 28.06 N 37.07 E
Qal'at al-Mu'aẓẓam 128 27.43 N 37.27 E
Qal'at Bīshah 144 20.01 N 42.36 E
Qal'at Ṣāliḥ 128 31.31 N 47.16 E
Qal'at Sukkar 128 31.51 N 46.05 E
Qal'eh Kāh 128 32.18 N 61.31 E
Qaleh Murgeh Airfield ⊠ 267d 35.39 N 51.23 E
Qal'eh Shahr 120 35.33 N 65.34 E
Qal'eh-ye Now, Afg. 120 35.27 N 67.08 E
Qal'eh-ye Now, Afg. 128 34.59 N 63.08 E
Qal'eh-ye Panjeh 123 37.00 N 72.36 E
Qal'eh-ye Sāber 120 34.02 N 69.01 E
Qal'eh-ye Sarkārī 120 35.54 N 67.17 E
Qallābāt, Sūd. 140 12.58 N 36.09 E
Qallābāt, Sūd. 140 12.43 N 23.26 E
Qallīn 142 31.03 N 30.51 E
Qalqilīya 132 32.11 N 34.58 E
Qalyūb 142 30.11 N 31.12 E
Qamar, Ghubbat al- ⊂ 118 16.00 N 52.30 E
Qamata 158 32.00 S 27.21 E
Qamīnis 146 31.39 N 20.03 E
Qamr-ud-dīn Kārez 120 31.39 N 68.25 E
Qamṣar 128 33.45 N 51.26 E
Qanā, Ar. Sa. 128 27.47 N 41.25 E
Qānā, Lubnān 132 33.13 N 35.18 E
Qan'abah 132 33.08 N 35.40 E
Qanāyah 132 33.01 N 36.11 E
Qandahār 120 31.32 N 65.30 E
Qandahār □[4] 120 31.00 N 65.45 E
Qandala 144 11.23 N 49.53 E
Qanṭarah, Jabal ∧[2] 142 30.09 N 30.15 E
Qantur 140 9.45 N 25.52 E
Qārā 130 34.09 N 36.44 E
Qaradog 144 9.30 N 46.57 E
Qarah Bāgh 128 34.56 N 61.46 E
Qarārah, Jabal ∧[2] 142 28.39 N 30.54 E
Qarāvol 120 37.14 N 68.46 E
Qareh Sū ≃, Īrān 128 34.52 N 51.25 E
Qareh Sū ≃, Īrān 128 36.10 N 56.25 E
Qareh Sū ≃, Īrān 128 39.27 N 47.24 E
Qareh Ẕīā' od Dīn 84 38.54 N 45.02 E
Qarqīn 120 37.25 N 66.03 E
Qarrit, Qaf' e)(38 40.29 N 20.40 E
Qarṭabā 130 34.06 N 35.51 E
Qārūn, Birkat ⊜ 142 29.28 N 30.40 E
Qaṣa-e Qand 128 26.12 N 60.45 E
Qāsemābād 267d 35.46 N 51.31 E
Qāsh, Nahr al- (Gash) ≃ 140 16.48 N 35.51 E
Qāsim 132 32.59 N 36.05 E
Qāsimwāla 123 30.09 N 73.50 E
Qasr Abā as-Sa'ūd 144 17.29 N 44.08 E
Qaṣr ad-Dayr, Jabal ∧ 132 30.48 N 35.34 E
Qaṣr al-Azraq ⊥ 132 31.53 N 36.49 E
Qaṣr al-Burayqah 146 30.25 N 19.34 E
Qaṣr al-Farāfirah 140 27.03 N 27.58 E
Qaṣr al-Jibālī 142 29.20 N 30.38 E
Qaṣr al-Kharānah ⊥ 132 31.44 N 36.28 E
Qaṣr al-Mushāsh ⊥ 132 31.49 N 36.19 E
Qaṣr al-Mushattā ⊥ 132 31.44 N 36.01 E
Qaṣr al-Qarahbullī 146 32.45 N 13.43 E
Qaṣr 'Amrah ⊥ 132 31.48 N 36.35 E
Qaṣr aṣ-Ṣaḥabi 146 30.01 N 20.48 E
Qaṣr aṭ-Ṭūbah ⊥ 132 31.20 N 36.34 E
Qaṣr Baghdād 142 30.44 N 30.53 E
Qaṣr Banī Walīd 146 31.45 N 14.01 E
Qaṣr Bū-Hādī 146 31.03 N 16.40 E
Qaṣr Ḍab'ah ⊥ 132 31.36 N 36.03 E
Qaṣr-e Fīrūzeh 267d 35.40 N 51.32 E
Qaṣr-e Shīrīn 128 34.31 N 45.35 E
Qaṣr Qārūn 142 29.25 N 30.25 E
Qa'ṭabah 144 13.51 N 44.42 E
Qaṭanā 132 33.26 N 36.05 E
Qatar □[1] 118
128 25.00 N 51.10 E
Qaṭia, Bi'r ⊤[4] 142 30.58 N 32.45 E
Qaṭmā 130 36.36 N 36.57 E
Qaṭrānī, Jabal ∧[2] 142 29.41 N 30.35 E
Qattāntyah, Ghurd al- •[8] 142 29.50 N 30.17 E
Qattara Depression
→ Qaṭṭārah, Munkhafaḍ al- •[7] 140 30.00 N 27.30 E
Qaṭṭārah, Munkhafaḍ al- (Qattara Depression) •[7] 140 30.00 N 27.30 E
Qawz Rajab 140 16.04 N 35.34 E
Qāy 142 29.09 N 30.57 E
Qāyen 128 33.44 N 59.11 E
Qayṭah 132 33.04 N 36.08 E
Qāzigund 123 33.38 N 75.09 E
Qazvīn 128 36.16 N 50.00 E
Qena
→ Qinā 140 26.10 N 32.43 E
Qeqertaq ▮ 176 71.55 N 55.30 W
Qesari, Ḥorbat (Cæsarea) ⊥ 132 32.30 N 34.53 E
Qeshm 128 26.58 N 56.16 E
Qeshm ▮ 128 26.45 N 55.45 E
Qeydār 128 36.07 N 48.35 E
Qeys, Jazīreh-ye ▮ 128 26.32 N 53.56 E
Qeyṣār 120 35.41 N 64.17 E
Qezel Owzan ≃ 128 36.45 N 49.22 E
Qezel Qeshlāq 84 39.08 N 45.21 E
Qeẕi'ot 132 30.53 N 34.27 E
Qiakemake 85 40.05 N 75.24 E
Qialima 104 41.32 N 122.40 E
Qi'an 106 32.11 N 121.03 E
Qian'an, Zhg. 89 45.00 N 124.01 E
Qian'an, Zhg. 98 39.59 N 118.40 E
Qiancaijiatun 104 41.14 N 121.38 E
Qiandiwu 105 39.16 N 116.38 E
Qiandong 100 23.41 N 116.55 E
Qiandun 106 31.16 N 121.00 E
Qianertaizi 104 42.04 N 122.42 E
Qianfang 100 28.32 N 116.13 E
Qianguoerluosi 89 45.08 N 124.47 E
Qiangzilu 105 40.26 N 117.13 E
Qianhonghepu 104 41.23 N 123.07 E
Qianhuang 106 31.36 N 119.58 E
Qianji 100 33.55 N 118.56 E
Qianjiadian 89 43.42 N 122.35 E
Qianjiang, Zhg. 100 30.25 N 112.51 E
Qianjiang, Zhg. 102 23.37 N 109.00 E
Qianjian'gangzi 104 41.34 N 122.26 E
Qianjiangtai 104 41.46 N 122.03 E
Qianjiaqiao 106 30.53 N 121.31 E
Qianjiaying 105 39.35 N 118.21 E
Qianjiazhai 104 41.28 N 122.02 E
Qianjiazhuang 106 32.16 N 120.17 E
Qianjing 106 31.33 N 121.15 E
Qianjinmiao 100 25.09 N 118.20 E
Qiankeng 106 30.43 N 119.47 E
Qiankoutou 105 39.42 N 117.01 E
Qianlijiazhuang 105 39.25 N 118.17 E
Qianluanshanzi 104 42.17 N 122.27 E
Qianmajiagushanzi 104 42.23 N 123.33 E
Qianmen Station ◆[5] 271a 39.54 N 116.23 E
Qianmintun 104 41.49 N 123.15 E
Qianning 102 30.30 N 101.31 E
Qianpai 102 22.22 N 111.11 E
Qianqi 100 27.20 N 120.20 E
Qianqianjianglugou 104 41.59 N 120.58 E
Qiansandaoliangzi 104 42.06 N 120.44 E
Qianshahezi 104 41.46 N 123.01 E
Qianshan, Zhg. 100 30.38 N 116.33 E
Qianshan, Zhg. 100 22.16 N 113.33 E
Qianshan (Hekou), Zhg. 100 28.18 N 117.41 E
Qianshan, Zhg. 106 31.06 N 120.24 E
Qianshanyang ⊜ 106 30.50 N 120.08 E
Qianshuangshanzi 104 41.22 N 121.13 E
Qiansongshu-lianggou 104 41.47 N 120.59 E
Qiansuo 100 28.44 N 121.27 E
Qiantangjiang ≃ 106 30.23 N 120.33 E
Qiantangzhen 107 30.12 N 106.18 E
Qianwei 98 40.12 N 120.06 E
Qianxi, Zhg. 102 26.57 N 106.00 E
Qianxi (Xingcheng), Zhg. 105 40.09 N 118.19 E
Qianxiatazi 104 42.23 N 123.53 E
Qianyamen 104 42.04 N 121.26 E
Qianyao 106 30.54 N 120.54 E
Qianyaopu 104 42.02 N 123.37 E
Qianzhou 106 31.44 N 120.13 E
Qiaodunmen 100 27.29 N 120.18 E
Qiaoershan ⛰ 102 31.48 N 99.10 E
Qiaogou 100 32.26 N 115.45 E
Qiaohengjin 102 29.30 N 99.50 E
Qiaojia 102 26.57 N 102.52 E
Qiaokou 100 25.55 N 113.10 E
Qiaolima 120 34.35 N 81.00 E
Qiaolin 100 31.57 N 118.32 E
Qiaomu 98 39.34 N 114.27 E
Qiaopurikebazha 85 38.48 N 76.19 E
Qiaoqi 106 31.49 N 120.18 E
Qiaoshe 100 28.48 N 115.58 E
Qiaosi 106 30.21 N 120.18 E
Qiaotou, Zhg. 100 33.05 N 112.46 E
Qiaotou, Zhg. 102 28.17 N 99.22 E
Qiaotou, Zhg. 104 41.13 N 123.44 E
Qiaotou, Zhg. 106 32.11 N 119.14 E
Qiaotou, Zhg. 107 29.18 N 104.39 E
Qiaotoucun 106 30.36 N 119.08 E
Qiaotouji 100 31.45 N 117.34 E
Qiaotouyi 100 28.24 N 112.58 E
Qiaotouzhen, Zhg. 106 30.49 N 119.13 E
Qiaotouzhen, Zhg. 106 30.33 N 118.50 E
Qiaowei 102 22.51 N 109.50 E
Qiaoxia 106 31.09 N 119.35 E
Qiaoxiajie 100 28.10 N 120.34 E
Qiaozhen 106 31.39 N 121.24 E
Qibao 106 31.09 N 121.20 E
Qibyā 132 31.59 N 35.01 E
Qichun (Caohe) 100 30.17 N 115.26 E
Qidong, Zhg. 98 37.04 N 117.29 E
Qidong, Zhg. 102 26.44 N 112.04 E
Qidong, Zhg. 106 31.49 N 121.40 E
Qidu 100 30.16 N 117.46 E
Qiemo 120 38.08 N 85.32 E
Qiesanglinzi 104 41.42 N 123.30 E
Qieshikou 271a 39.59 N 116.24 E
Qiezixi 107 29.25 N 106.30 E
Qifṭ (Coptos) 140 26.00 N 32.49 E
Qiganka 89 53.02 N 120.33 E
Qigong 102 28.38 N 100.38 E
Qigongtai 104 41.50 N 123.08 E
Qihe 98 36.42 N 116.47 E
Qiji 98 37.16 N 115.21 E
Qijiadian 89 46.48 N 125.36 E
Qijiang 107 29.02 N 106.39 E
Qijiang ≃, Zhg. 107 30.38 N 105.26 E
Qijiang ≃, Zhg. 107 29.01 N 106.36 E
Qijiapuzi 104 40.54 N 122.31 E
Qijiawan 100 30.53 N 114.13 E
Qijiawopeng 104 41.02 N 121.26 E
Qijiazi 104 41.54 N 122.58 E
Qijizhen 98 36.17 N 116.03 E
Qika 89 50.35 N 119.16 E
Qikou 98 38.35 N 117.31 E
Qila Abdullāh 120 30.43 N 66.38 E
Qila Dīdār Singh 123 32.08 N 74.01 E
Qilagugannishan ∧ 120 28.46 N 87.38 E
Qila Lādgasht 128 27.54 N 62.57 E
Qila Saifullāh 120 30.43 N 68.21 E
Qila Sobha Singh 123 32.14 N 74.46 E
Qili 100 30.13 N 117.27 E
Qilianshanmai (Nanshan) ⛰ 102 39.06 N 98.40 E
Qilihai ⊜ 105 39.19 N 117.33 E
Qilihe, Zhg. 104 41.21 N 121.16 E
Qilihe, Zhg. 104 41.30 N 121.15 E
Qilihezi 104 40.56 N 121.02 E
Qilin 106 31.56 N 121.21 E
Qiling 100 24.05 N 115.27 E
Qilingzicun 104 41.05 N 123.06 E
Qilinhu ⊜ 120 31.50 N 89.00 E
Qilinmen 106 32.04 N 118.55 E
Qiliping 100 31.27 N 114.39 E
Qiliqiao 106 31.35 N 120.48 E
Qilizhen, Zhg. 102 35.43 N 108.59 E
Qilizhen, Zhg. 106 32.19 N 121.05 E
Qilṭ, 'Ayn al- ⊤[4] 132 31.50 N 35.23 E
Qimafang 98 40.48 N 114.31 E
Qiman al-'Arūs 142 29.18 N 31.10 E
Qimen, Zhg. 100 25.18 N 113.15 E
Qimen, Zhg. 100 29.52 N 117.42 E
Qimoudi 105 39.35 N 115.32 E
Qinā 140 26.10 N 32.43 E
Qinā, Wādī ∨, Miṣr 140 26.12 N 32.44 E
Qinā, Wādī ∨, Miṣr 142 29.39 N 31.53 E
Qincaigou 104 40.38 N 120.37 E
Qing'an 89 46.52 N 128.30 E
Qingbaikou 105 40.01 N 115.50 E
Qingcao'ai)(100 27.40 N 119.34 E
Qingcaoge 100 30.50 N 116.46 E
Qingcaohu ⊜ 106 31.06 N 118.48 E
Qingchengzi 104 40.44 N 123.36 E
Qingcungang 106 30.56 N 121.34 E
Qingdao (Tsingtao) 98 36.06 N 120.19 E
Qingdian 105 39.51 N 117.22 E
Qingduizi, Zhg. 98 39.50 N 123.18 E
Qingduizi, Zhg. 104 41.28 N 121.53 E
Qingfengtuo 98 40.59 N 116.04 E
Qingfu 102 28.29 N 104.35 E
Qinggang 89 46.43 N 126.07 E
Qingguang 105 39.11 N 117.02 E
Qingguji 98 34.45 N 115.47 E
Qinghai □[4] 90 36.00 N 96.00 E
Qinghai ⊜ 102 36.50 N 100.20 E
Qinghe, Zhg. 86 46.36 N 90.39 E
Qinghe, Zhg. 98 40.02 N 122.35 E
Qinghe, Zhg. 105 40.01 N 116.20 E
Qinghecheng 104 41.28 N 124.15 E
Qinghechengzi 104 41.44 N 121.25 E
Qinghemen 104 41.45 N 121.25 E
Qinghetou 98 35.51 N 115.41 E
Qinghezhen 98 37.16 N 117.39 E
Qinghu 100 28.40 N 118.34 E
Qinghua 100 29.24 N 117.46 E
Qinghuashui ≃ 100 25.00 N 114.00 E
Qinghuayuan 105 40.00 N 116.19 E
Qinghuazhen 100 32.55 N 112.19 E
Qingjian 102 37.10 N 110.00 E
Qingjiang, Zhg. 100 28.05 N 115.29 E
Qingjiang, Zhg. 107 29.17 N 105.34 E
Qingjiang ≃ 102 30.22 N 111.20 E
Qingjiangdu 100 28.16 N 121.06 E
Qingjujie 107 30.42 N 106.07 E
Qinglian 100 24.27 N 112.45 E
Qingliu 100 26.12 N 116.52 E
Qingliuzhen 107 29.56 N 105.19 E
Qinglong, Zhg. 98 40.24 N 118.54 E
Qinglong, Zhg. 102 25.50 N 105.10 E
Qinglongchang, Zhg. 107 29.28 N 103.27 E
Qinglongchang, Zhg. 107 29.51 N 105.40 E
Qinglongchang, Zhg. 107 30.20 N 103.51 E
Qinglongchang, Zhg. 107 28.50 N 106.31 E
Qinglonggang 106 31.51 N 121.15 E
Qinglongguan 107 30.25 N 104.48 E
Qinglonghe ≃ 105 39.35 N 117.46 E
Qinglongji 98 34.05 N 116.37 E
Qinglongwanhe ≃ 105 38.51 N 117.19 E
Qinglongwei 100 25.28 N 114.28 E
Qingmuguan 107 29.41 N 106.18 E
Qingningsi 106 31.16 N 121.33 E
Qingong 100 33.38 N 119.12 E
Qingping, Zhg. 98 36.47 N 116.06 E
Qingping, Zhg. 107 29.00 N 106.21 E
Qingpu 106 31.09 N 121.06 E
Qingshan, Zhg. 100 31.33 N 116.22 E
Qingshan, Zhg. 100 30.38 N 114.23 E
Qingshan, Zhg. 106 30.16 N 119.48 E
Qingshan, Zhg. 106 30.36 N 119.41 E
Qingshan ⛰ 102 35.20 N 97.50 E
Qingshanpu 100 29.27 N 114.01 E
Qingshanshi 100 28.31 N 113.08 E
Qingshen 107 29.50 N 103.50 E
Qingshui 102 34.42 N 106.21 E
Qingshuibao 102 39.23 N 99.09 E
Qingshuihe ≃, Zhg. 102 37.30 N 105.30 E
Qingshuihe ≃, Zhg. 107 29.09 N 104.00 E
Qingshuijian 105 39.59 N 115.58 E
Qingshuilangshan ⛰ 102 26.15 N 99.35 E
Qingshuipu 107 30.11 N 103.57 E
Qingshuixi 107 29.09 N 103.55 E
Qingtan 100 31.48 N 112.48 E
Qingtang, Zhg. 100 26.28 N 115.48 E
Qingtang, Zhg. 100 24.14 N 113.51 E
Qingtian 100 28.10 N 120.17 E
Qingtuosi 98 35.29 N 118.20 E
Qingtuozi, Zhg. 104 41.05 N 121.28 E
Qingtuozi, Zhg. 105 39.08 N 117.45 E
Qingxi, Zhg. 89 49.19 N 127.10 E
Qingxi, Zhg. 100 31.40 N 118.00 E
Qingxi, Zhg. 107 30.40 N 106.14 E
Qingxian 98 38.34 N 116.46 E
Qingyang, Zhg. 89 45.20 N 128.47 E
Qingyang, Zhg. 100 30.38 N 117.48 E
Qingyang, Zhg. 102 36.06 N 107.47 E
Qingyang, Zhg. 106 31.46 N 120.15 E
Qingyihu ⊜ 98 34.22 N 118.54 E
Qingyijiang 100 30.55 N 118.28 E
Qingyijiang ≃ 107 29.34 N 103.42 E
Qingyuan, Zhg. 98 42.13 N 124.56 E
Qingyuan, Zhg. 100 27.38 N 119.04 E
Qingyuan, Zhg. 100 23.43 N 113.01 E
Qingyuan, Zhg. 102 24.35 N 108.45 E
Qingyuan
→ Baoding, Zhg. 105 38.52 N 115.29 E
Qingyun 98 37.52 N 117.21 E
Qingyunbao 104 42.34 N 123.50 E
Qingzhen, Zhg. 102 26.29 N 106.22 E
Qingzhen, Zhg. 106 30.45 N 120.30 E
Qingzhou 100 23.39 N 116.57 E
Qinhuaihe ≃ 106 32.01 N 118.50 E
Qinhuangdao (Chinwangtao) 98 39.56 N 119.36 E
Qinjia 89 46.47 N 127.00 E
Qinjiang ≃, Zhg. 100 23.58 N 115.47 E
Qinjiang ≃, Zhg. 100 26.16 N 115.52 E
Qinlanzhen 100 32.37 N 119.08 E
Qinlingshanmai ⛰ 102 34.00 N 108.00 E
Qinnancang 100 33.16 N 119.55 E
Qinshui 102 35.41 N 112.11 E
Qinshui ≃ 102 27.08 N 109.36 E
Qinxian, Zhg. 102 36.48 N 112.41 E
Qinxian (Qinzhou), Zhg. 102 21.59 N 108.36 E
Qinyang 102 35.06 N 112.57 E
Qinyuan 102 36.30 N 112.15 E
Qionghai (Jiaji) 110 19.20 N 110.30 E
Qionglai 107 30.25 N 103.27 E
Qionglaishan ⛰ 102 31.21 N 102.50 E
Qionglongshan ∧ 106 31.15 N 120.25 E
Qiongzhouhaixia ⊔ 102 20.10 N 110.15 E
Qipandi 105 39.46 N 115.12 E
Qipanshan 98 42.05 N 117.30 E
Qiqihaer (Tsitsihar) 89 47.19 N 123.55 E
Qiryat 132 32.49 N 35.06 E
Qiryat 'Anavim 132 31.48 N 35.07 E
Qiryat Bialik 132 32.50 N 35.05 E
Qiryat Binyamin 132 32.48 N 35.05 E
Qiryat Gat 132 31.36 N 34.46 E
Qiryat Ḥayyim 132 32.49 N 35.04 E
Qiryat Mal'akhi 132 31.44 N 34.44 E
Qiryat Motzkin 132 32.50 N 35.04 E
Qiryat Ono 132 32.04 N 34.51 E
Qiryat Shemona 132 33.13 N 35.34 E
Qiryat Tiv'on 132 32.43 N 35.08 E
Qiryat Yam 132 32.51 N 35.04 E
Qirzah, Wādī ∨ 146 30.56 N 14.31 E
Qiseqishan ∧ 89 48.37 N 122.32 E
Qishn 144 15.26 N 51.40 E
Qishon ≃ 132 32.49 N 35.02 E
Qishrān ▮ 144 20.14 N 40.05 E
Qishudang 107 29.13 N 104.39 E
Qishui ≃ 100 30.09 N 115.20 E
Qishuyan 106 31.44 N 120.04 E
Qiṣrāyā 130 34.53 N 36.26 E
Qitaizi 104 41.33 N 122.11 E
Qitamu 89 44.22 N 126.20 E
Qitangzhen 107 29.47 N 106.16 E
Qitao 98 34.12 N 119.52 E
Qiting 100 31.02 N 114.44 E
Qitingqiao 106 31.26 N 119.52 E
Qitou 100 24.54 N 117.29 E
Qiubei 102 24.07 N 104.12 E
Qiuchang 107 28.59 N 104.42 E
Qiuji 100 33.51 N 118.01 E
Qiujia 106 31.49 N 121.51 E
Qiujiatun 104 41.20 N 121.00 E
Qiujin 100 29.10 N 115.42 E
Qiuxian 98 36.49 N 115.10 E
Qiuxihe 102 29.59 N 104.33 E
Qiuxihe ≃ 107 29.58 N 104.40 E
Qiweigang 106 32.01 N 119.59 E
Qixia 98 37.17 N 120.48 E
Qixian, Zhg. 100 34.33 N 114.47 E
Qixian, Zhg. 100 33.28 N 117.01 E
Qixiashan 106 32.10 N 118.57 E
Qixiasi Temple ✝[1] 106 32.12 N 118.58 E
Qixinglizi ∧ 89 46.35 N 130.52 E
Qixingqiao 106 30.49 N 120.51 E
Qiyang 102 26.29 N 111.43 E
Qiyi 100 32.30 N 112.54 E
Qiying 102 36.38 N 106.25 E
Qīzān 144 16.54 N 42.29 E
Qizhou 100 30.04 N 115.20 E
Qizil Jilga 120 35.21 N 78.52 E
Qizil Langar 120 35.13 N 77.59 E
Qizimei ▮ 106 30.17 N 121.36 E
Qolhak 267d 35.47 N 51.26 E
Qom 128 34.39 N 50.54 E
Qom ≃ 128 34.48 N 51.02 E
Qondūz 120 37.45 N 68.51 E
Qondūz □[4] 120 36.45 N 68.30 E
Qondūz ≃ 120 37.00 N 68.16 E
Qorveh 128 35.10 N 47.48 E
Qoṭbābād 128 28.42 N 53.34 E
Qoṭūr 128 38.28 N 44.25 E
Quabbin Reservoir ⊜[1] 207 42.22 N 72.18 W
Quaddick Reservoir ⊜[1] 207 41.57 N 71.49 W
Quadra Island ▮ 182 50.08 N 125.16 W
Quadraro ◆[8] 267a 41.51 N 12.33 E
Quadrath-Ichendorf 56 50.56 N 6.41 E
Quadros, Lagoa dos ⊂ 252 29.42 S 50.05 W
Quail Valley 228 33.43 N 117.15 W
Quairading 162 32.01 S 117.25 E
Quakake 210 40.51 N 76.02 W
Quakenbrück 52 52.40 N 7.57 E
Quaker Hill, Conn., U.S. 207 41.24 N 72.07 W
Quaker Hill, N.Y., U.S. 210 41.35 N 73.33 W
Quakers Hill 170 33.43 S 150.53 E
Quakers Knob ∧[2] 214 40.21 N 80.24 W
Quaker Street 210 42.44 N 74.11 W
Quakertown, N.J., U.S. 210 40.34 N 74.57 W
Quakertown, Pa., U.S. 208 40.26 N 75.21 W
Qualicum Beach 182 49.21 N 124.27 W
Quambatook 166 35.51 S 143.31 E
Quanah 196 34.18 N 99.44 W
Quanery, Anse ⊂ 240d 15.26 N 61.15 W
Quangang 100 28.10 N 115.34 E
Quang-ngai 110 15.07 N 108.48 E
Quanjiangyan 100 27.43 N 113.59 E
Quanjiao 100 32.06 N 118.16 E
Quan-long (Ca-mau) 110 9.11 N 105.08 E
Quanmian 104 42.02 N 122.13 E
Quannan 100 24.44 N 114.31 E
Quannapowitt, Lake ⊜ 283 42.31 N 71.05 W
Quanshang 100 26.25 N 116.55 E
Quanshengpu 104 41.59 N 123.22 E
Quanshui 104 41.18 N 124.11 E
Quanshuitou 105 40.24 N 116.39 E
Quantico, Md., U.S. 208 38.23 N 75.44 W
Quantico, Va., U.S. 208 38.31 N 77.17 W
Quantico Marine Corps Air Station ■ 208 38.31 N 77.19 W
Quantock Hills ⛰[2] 42 51.07 N 3.10 W
Quantou 89 42.52 N 124.07 E
Quanxishi 100 26.51 N 112.45 E
Quanyanhezi 104 40.52 N 123.26 E
Quanzhou 100 24.54 N 118.35 E
Quanzhougang ⊂ 100 24.52 N 118.37 E
Qu'Appelle 184 50.33 N 103.52 W
Qu'Appelle ≃ 184 50.25 N 101.20 W
Qu'Appelle Dam ◆[6] 184 51.00 N 106.25 W
Quaraí 252 30.23 S 56.27 W
Quaraí (Guareim) ≃ 252 30.12 S 57.36 W
Quaregnon 50 50.26 N 3.51 E
Quarles, Pegunungan ⛰ 112 2.55 S 119.30 E
Quarrata 66 43.51 N 10.58 E
Quarré-les-Tombes 50 47.22 N 3.59 E
Quarry 222 30.18 N 96.30 W
Quarry Heights 276 41.04 N 73.45 W
Quarryville, Conn., U.S. 207 41.32 N 72.42 W
Quarryville, Pa., U.S. 208 39.54 N 76.10 W
Quartu Sant'elena 71 39.14 N 9.11 E
Quartz Hill 228 34.39 N 118.13 W
Quartz Lake ⊜ 176 70.55 N 80.33 W
Quartz Mountain ∧ 202 43.10 N 122.40 W
Quartzsite 200 33.40 N 114.13 W
Quatá 255 22.16 S 50.42 W
Quatis 256 22.25 S 44.16 W
Quatre, Isle ▮ 241h 12.57 N 61.15 W
Quatre Piliers, Forêt des ◆[3] 261 48.49 N 1.42 E
Quatsino Sound ⊔ 182 50.25 N 127.55 W
Qubei 124 28.18 N 86.53 E
Qūchān 128 37.06 N 58.30 E
Quchijie 102 28.03 N 111.53 E
Qudaym 130 35.03 N 38.25 E
Qudi 98 37.06 N 117.15 E
Qudsia Gardens ♠ 272a 28.40 N 77.13 E
Qué ≃ 152 14.45 S 14.45 E
Queanbeyan 171b 35.21 S 149.14 E
Queanbeyan ≃ 171b 35.20 S 149.14 E
Québec 206 46.49 N 71.14 W
Québec □[6] 206 46.50 N 71.20 W
Quebec (Québec) □[4] 176 52.00 N 72.00 W
Quebec Airport ⊠ 206 46.47 N 71.23 W
Quebec House ⊥ 260 51.14 N 0.05 E
Quebeck 194 35.49 N 85.34 W
Quebra-Anzol ≃ 255 19.09 S 47.38 W
Quebra-Cangalha, Serra do ⛰ 256 22.55 S 45.10 W
Quebracho 252 31.57 S 57.53 W
Quebrada Seca 240m 18.14 N 65.40 W
Quebradillas 240m 18.29 N 66.56 W
Quebrangulo 250 9.20 S 36.29 W
Quecholac 234 18.57 N 97.40 W
Quechultenango 234 17.25 N 99.13 W
Quecreek 214 40.06 N 79.05 W
Quedal, Cabo ≻ 254 40.59 S 73.59 W
Quedas 156 19.30 S 33.29 E
Quedlinburg 54 51.48 N 11.09 E
Queen 214 40.16 N 78.31 W
Queen Alexandra Range ⛰ 9 84.00 S 168.00 E
Queen Anne 208 38.55 N 75.57 W
Queen Anne Creek ≃ 285 40.08 N 74.53 W
Queen Annes □[6] 208 39.03 N 76.04 W
Queen Bess, Mount ∧ 182 51.16 N 124.34 W
Queenborough 42 51.26 N 0.45 E
Queen Charlotte 182 53.16 N 132.05 W
Queen Charlotte Bay ⊂ 254 51.50 S 60.40 W
Queen Charlotte Islands ▮▮ 182 53.00 N 132.00 W
Queen Charlotte Mountains ⛰ 182 53.00 N 132.00 W
Queen Charlotte Sound ⊔ 182 51.30 N 129.30 W
Queen Charlotte Strait ⊔ 182 50.50 N 127.25 W
Queen City, Mo., U.S. 194 40.25 N 92.34 W
Queen City, Tex., U.S. 194 33.09 N 94.09 W
Queen Elizabeth II Reservoir ⊜[1] 260 51.23 N 0.24 W
Queen Elizabeth Islands ▮▮ 16 78.00 N 95.00 W
Queen Elizabeth National Park ♠ 154 0.15 S 30.00 E
Queen Fabiola Mountains ⛰ 9 71.30 S 35.40 E
Queen Mary ◆ 280 33.45 N 118.12 W
Queen Mary Coast •[2] 9 67.00 S 96.00 E
Queen Mary Reservoir ⊜[1] 260 51.25 N 0.28 W
Queen Maud Gulf ⊂ 176 68.25 N 102.30 W
Queen Maud Land ◆[1] 9 72.30 S 12.00 E
Queen Maud Mountains ⛰ 9 86.00 S 160.00 W
Queens □[6] 210 40.34 N 73.52 W
Queensbury 44 53.46 N 1.50 W
Queens Channel ▮▮ 176 76.11 N 96.00 W
Queens Channel ⊔ 164 14.46 S 129.24 E
Queenscliff 169 38.16 S 144.40 E
Queens College ✝[2] 276 40.44 N 73.49 W
Queensferry, Scot., U.K. 46 55.59 N 3.25 W
Queensferry, Wales, U.K. 44 53.12 N 3.01 W
Queensland □[3] 160 22.00 S 145.00 E
Queens Park ♠, Austl. 274a 33.54 S 151.16 E
Queens Park ♠, Ont., Can. 275b 43.40 N 79.24 W
Queen's Park ♠, Eng., U.K. 262 53.44 N 2.28 W
Queens Park ♠, Eng., U.K. 262 53.30 N 2.13 W
Queens Park ♠, Eng., U.K. 262 53.35 N 2.27 W
Queensport 186 45.20 N 61.16 W
Queens Sound ⊔ 182 51.55 N 128.11 W
Queenston Chippawa Power Canal ≂ 284a 43.08 N 79.03 W
Queenstown, Austl. 166 42.05 S 145.33 E
Queenstown
→ Cobh, Eire 48 51.51 N 8.17 W
Queenstown, Guy. 246 7.12 N 58.29 W
Queenstown, N.Z. 172 45.02 S 168.40 E
Queenstown, S. Afr. 158 31.52 S 26.52 E
Queenstown, Md., U.S. 208 38.59 N 76.09 W
Queensville 212 44.08 N 79.28 W
Queen Victoria Park ♠ 284a 43.05 N 79.05 W
Queerhe 104 40.57 N 121.35 E
Queets 224 47.32 N 124.20 W
Queets ≃ 224 47.33 N 124.21 W
Queguay Grande ≃ 252 32.09 S 58.09 W
Queige 62 45.43 N 6.28 E
Queimada, Ilha ▮ 250 0.10 S 50.50 W
Queimada Nova 250 8.35 S 41.25 W
Queimadas 250 10.58 S 39.38 W
Queimados 256 22.42 S 43.34 W
Quela 152 9.16 S 17.02 E

Symbols in the index entries represent the broad categories identified in the key at the right. Symbols with superior numbers (⛰[2]) identify subcategories (see complete key on page *I · 30*).

Kartensymbole in dem Registerverzeichnis stellen die rechts in Schlüssel erklärten Kategorien dar. Symbole mit hochgestellten Ziffern (⛰[2]) bezeichnen Unterabteilungen einer Kategorie (vgl. vollständiger Schlüssel auf Seite *I · 30*).

Los símbolos incluídos en el texto del índice representan las grandes categorias identificadas con la clave a la derecha. Los símbolos con numeros en su parte superior (⛰[2]) identifican las subcategorías (véase la clave completa en la página *I · 30*).

Les symboles de l'index représentent les catégories indiquées dans la légende à droite. Les symboles suivis d'un indice (⛰[2]) représentent des sous-catégories (voir légende complète à la page *I · 30*).

Os símbolos incluídos no texto do índice representam as grandes categorias identificadas com a chave à direita. Os símbolos com números em sua parte superior (⛰[2]) identificam as subcategorias (veja-se a chave completa à página *I · 30*).

	English	Deutsch	Español	Français	Português
∧	Mountain	Berg	Montaña	Montagne	Montanha
⛰	Mountains	Berge	Montañas	Montagnes	Montanhas
)(	Pass	Pass	Paso	Col	Passo
∨	Valley, Canyon	Tal, Cañon	Valle, Cañón	Vallée, Canyon	Vale, Canhão
≚	Plain	Ebene	Llano	Plaine	Planície
≻	Cape	Kap	Cabo	Cap	Cabo
▮	Island	Insel	Isla	Île	Ilha
▮▮	Islands	Inseln	Islas	Îles	Ilhas
•	Other Topographic Features	Andere Topographische Objekte	Otros Elementos Topográficos	Autres données topographiques	Outros Elementos Topográficos

ESPAÑOL

Nombre	Página	Lat.°′	Long.°′ W=Oeste
Quelimane	156	17.53 S	36.51 E
Quelizhen	106	30.54 N	121.26 E
Quelle	52	52.00 N	8.29 E
Quellendorf	54	51.45 N	12.07 E
Quelo	152	6.27 S	12.48 E
Quelpart Island → Cheju-do I	90	33.20 N	126.30 E
Queluz → Conselheiro Lafaiete, Bra.	255	20.40 S	43.48 W
Queluz, Bra.	256	22.32 S	44.46 W
Queluz, Port.	266c	38.45 N	9.15 W
Quemado, N. Mex., U.S.	200	34.20 N	108.30 W
Quemado, Tex., U.S.	196	28.56 N	100.38 W
Quemado de Güines	240p	22.48 N	80.15 W
Quemahoning Reservoir ⊜[1]	214	40.09 N	78.57 W
Quembo ≃	152	14.57 S	20.22 E
Quemchi	254	42.09 S	73.29 W
Quemoy → Chinmen Tao I	100	24.27 N	118.23 E
Quemú Quemú	252	36.03 S	63.33 W
Quend	50	50.19 N	1.38 E
Quend Plage	50	50.19 N	1.33 E
Queñi, Nevado de ∧	254	40.14 S	71.49 W
Quenouilles, Lac aux ⊜	206	46.10 N	74.23 W
Quentin	208	40.17 N	76.26 W
Quepos	236	9.27 N	84.09 W
Que Que	154	18.55 S	29.49 E
Quequén	252	38.32 S	58.42 W
Quequén Salado ≃	254	38.56 S	60.31 W
Quercianella	66	43.27 N	10.22 E
Quercy □[9]	32	44.30 N	1.25 E
Querecotillo	248	4.50 S	80.40 W
Querenburg ⬥[8]	263	51.27 N	7.16 E
Querência do Norte	255	23.00 S	53.28 W
Querenhorst	54	52.20 N	10.57 E
Querétaro	234	20.36 N	100.23 W
Querétaro □[3]	234	21.00 N	99.55 W
Querfurt	54	51.23 N	11.36 E
Quero	64	45.55 N	11.56 E
Querobabi	232	30.03 N	111.01 W
Querobamba	248	13.52 S	73.50 W
Quesada, C.R.	236	10.19 N	84.26 W
Quesada, Esp.	34	37.51 N	3.04 W
Queset Brook ≃	283	42.02 N	71.04 W
Queshan	100	32.48 N	114.01 E
Quesnel	182	52.59 N	122.30 W
Quesnel ≃	182	53.00 N	122.30 W
Quesnel Lake ⊜	182	52.32 N	121.05 W
Quesnoy	50	50.43 N	3.00 E
Que-son	110	15.40 N	108.14 E
Questa	200	36.42 N	105.36 W
Questembert	32	47.40 N	2.27 W
Quetena	248	22.10 S	67.25 W
Quetico Lake ⊜	190	48.34 N	91.52 W
Quetico Provincial Park ♠	190	48.30 N	91.30 W
Quetta	120	30.12 N	67.00 E
Quettehou	32	49.36 N	1.18 W
Quetzala ≃	234	16.35 N	98.30 W
Quevedo	246	1.02 S	79.29 W
Quevedo ≃	246	1.02 S	79.28 W
Quezaltenango	236	14.50 N	91.31 W
Quezaltenango □[5]	236	14.45 N	91.40 W
Quezaltepeque, El Sal.	236	13.50 N	89.17 W
Quezaltepeque, Guat.	236	14.38 N	89.27 W
Quezon, Pil.	116	14.01 N	122.11 E
Quezon, Pil.	116	15.34 N	120.49 E
Quezon □[4]	116	13.58 N	122.02 E
Quezon □[7]	269f	14.38 N	121.03 E
Quezon City, Pil.	116		
	269f	14.38 N	121.00 E
Quezon Memorial ⊥	269f	14.39 N	121.03 E
Quezon National Park ♠	116	14.01 N	121.51 E
Qufu	98	35.36 N	117.02 E
Qugou, Zhg.	102	36.10 N	100.56 E
Qugou, Zhg.	105	39.17 N	116.15 E
Quiabaya	248	15.37 S	68.46 W
Quibala	152	10.46 S	14.59 E
Quibaxi	152	8.29 S	14.36 E
Quibdó	246	5.42 N	76.40 W
Quiberon	32	47.29 N	3.07 W
Quiberville	50	49.54 N	0.55 E
Quíbor	246	9.56 N	69.37 W
Quibray Bay C	274a	34.01 S	151.11 E
Quibú ≃	286b	23.05 N	82.27 W
Quiçama, Parque Nacional de ♠	152	9.45 S	13.30 E
Qui-chau	110	19.33 N	105.06 E
Quiches	248	8.25 S	77.27 W
Quickborn	52	53.44 N	9.53 E
Quicksand Creek ≃	192	37.32 N	83.21 W
Quiculungo	152	8.31 S	15.19 E
Quidapil Point ≻	116	6.49 N	123.57 E
Quidnessett	207	41.39 N	71.26 W
Quidnick	207	41.42 N	71.33 W
Quien Sabe Creek ≃	226	36.43 N	121.09 W
Quiévrain	50	50.24 N	3.41 E
Quiévy	50	50.10 N	3.25 E
Quiindy	252	25.58 S	57.16 W
Quijiang ≃	107	29.59 N	106.16 E
Quilá	232	24.23 N	107.13 W
Quilalí	236	13.34 N	86.02 W
Quilates, Cap ≻	34	35.20 N	3.45 W
Quilcene	224	47.49 N	122.53 W
Quilenda	152	10.33 S	14.22 E
Quilengues	152	14.05 S	14.04 E
Quileute Indian Reservation ⬥[4]	224	47.55 N	124.38 W
Quilicura	286e	33.22 S	70.45 W
Quilicura, Canal de ≍	286e	33.22 S	70.47 W
Quilimarí	252	32.07 S	71.30 W
Quilino	252	30.12 S	64.29 W
Quillabamba	248	12.49 S	72.43 W
Quillacas	248	19.14 S	66.58 W
Quillacollo	248	17.26 S	66.17 W
Quillagua	248	21.39 S	69.33 W
Quillan	32	42.52 N	2.11 E
Quillebeuf-sur-Seine	50	49.29 N	0.31 E
Quill Lake	184	52.05 N	104.15 W
Quillota	252	32.53 S	71.16 W
Quilmes	258	34.44 S	58.16 W
Quilmes □[5]	288	34.44 S	58.16 W
Quilmes, Aeródromo ⊠	288	34.42 S	58.15 W
Quilombo ≃	256	23.52 S	46.21 W
Quilon	122	8.53 N	76.36 E
Quilotosa Wash V	200	32.56 N	112.46 W
Quilpie	166	26.37 S	144.15 E
Quilpué	252	33.03 S	71.27 W
Quilty	48	52.47 N	9.26 W
Quimarí, Alto de ∧	246	8.07 N	76.23 W
Quimbango	152	11.01 S	17.26 E
Quimbaya	246	4.38 N	75.47 W
Quimbele	152	6.28 S	16.13 E
Quimbo	152	13.59 S	16.05 E
Quimbonge	152	8.36 S	18.30 E
Quimbumbe	152	7.50 S	14.03 E
Quimby	198	42.38 N	95.38 W
Quime	248	17.02 S	67.15 W
Quimichis	234	22.21 N	105.32 W
Quimili	252	27.38 S	62.25 W
Quimper	32	48.00 N	4.06 W
Quimperlé	32	47.52 N	3.33 W
Quimpitirique	248	12.15 S	73.52 W
Quinalasag Island I	116	13.56 N	123.38 E
Quinault	224	47.28 N	123.50 W
Quinault ≃	224	47.23 N	124.18 W

FRANÇAIS

Nom	Page	Lat.°′	Long.°′ W=Ouest
Quinault, North Fork ≃	224	47.32 N	123.40 W
Quinault Indian Reservation ⬥[4]	224	47.24 N	124.10 W
Quinault Lake ⊜	224	47.28 N	123.52 W
Quinby Inlet C	208	37.28 N	75.40 W
Quincampoix	50	49.32 N	1.11 E
Quincemil	248	13.16 S	70.38 W
Quinches	248	12.13 S	76.05 W
Quincy, Calif., U.S.	204	39.56 N	120.57 W
Quincy, Ill., U.S.	219	39.56 N	91.23 W
Quincy, Ky., U.S.	218	38.37 N	83.07 W
Quincy, Mass., U.S.	207	42.15 N	71.01 W
Quincy, Mich., U.S.	216	41.57 N	84.53 W
Quincy, Ohio, U.S.	216	40.18 N	83.58 W
Quincy, Oreg., U.S.	224	46.04 N	123.05 W
Quincy, Pa., U.S.	208	39.48 N	77.35 W
Quincy, Wash., U.S.	202	47.14 N	119.51 W
Quincy Bay C	283	42.17 N	70.58 W
Quincy Hills ⩘[2]	194	39.55 N	91.15 W
Quincy-sous-Sénart	261	48.40 N	2.33 E
Quincy-Voisins	261	48.54 N	2.53 E
Quindanning	168a	33.03 S	116.34 E
Quindío □[5]	246	4.30 N	75.40 W
Quinebaug	207	42.01 N	71.57 W
Quinebaug ≃	207	41.33 N	72.03 W
Quines	252	32.13 S	65.48 W
Quinga	154	15.49 S	40.15 E
Quingey	58	47.06 N	5.53 E
Quinhagak	180	59.45 N	161.43 W
Quinh-luu	110	19.10 N	105.42 E
Qui-nhon	110	13.46 N	109.14 E
Quiniluban Group II	116	11.27 N	120.48 E
Quinjenje	152	12.49 S	14.55 E
Quinlan	222	32.55 N	96.08 W
Quinn ≃	204	40.58 N	119.05 W
Quiñones, Arroyo de los ≃	266a	40.33 N	3.34 W
Quinson	62	43.42 N	6.02 E
Quinta da Boa Vista ♠	287a	22.54 S	43.15 W
Quintanar de la Orden	34	39.34 N	3.03 W
Quintana Roo □[3]	232	19.40 N	88.30 W
Quinta Normal	286e	33.27 S	70.42 W
Quinta Normal de Agricultura ⚜[2]	286e	33.27 S	70.42 W
Quinte, Bay of C	212	44.07 N	77.15 W
Quinter	198	39.04 N	100.14 W
Quintero	252	32.47 S	71.32 W
Quintin	32	48.24 N	2.55 W
Quintino Sella, Canale ≍	266b	45.29 N	8.38 E
Quinto	34	41.25 N	0.29 W
Quinto Creek ≃	226	37.11 N	121.02 W
Quinto de Noviembre, Presa ⬥[6]	236	13.59 N	88.44 W
Quinton, Sask., Can.	184	51.23 N	104.24 W
Quinton, N.J., U.S.	208	39.33 N	75.25 E
Quinton, Okla., U.S.	196	35.07 N	95.22 W
Quinto Romano ⬥[8]	266b	45.29 N	9.05 E
Quinzano d'Oglio	64	45.19 N	10.00 E
Quinzáu	152	6.51 S	12.46 E
Quinze, Lac des ⊜	190	47.35 N	79.05 W
Quionga	154	10.37 S	40.30 E
Quiotepec ≃	234	17.35 N	97.00 W
Quiotepec ⊥	234	17.54 N	96.58 W
Quipapá	250	8.50 S	36.02 W
Quipar ≃	34	38.14 N	1.36 W
Quipeio	152	12.26 S	15.30 E
Quipemba	152	7.12 S	15.06 E
Quipit ≃	116	8.04 N	122.29 E
Quirauk Mountain ∧	208	39.42 N	77.31 W
Quiriguá ⊥	236	15.17 N	89.04 W
Quirihue	252	36.17 S	72.32 W
Quirima	152	10.48 S	18.09 E
Quirimbo	152	10.36 S	14.12 E
Quirindi	166	31.31 S	150.41 E
Quirinópolis	255	18.32 S	50.30 W
Quiriquire	246	9.59 N	63.13 W
Quiriri ≃	152	15.13 S	18.47 E
Quiririm	256	23.02 S	45.38 W
Quirke Lake ⊜	190	46.28 N	82.33 W
Quiroga, Esp.	34	42.29 N	7.16 W
Quiroga, Méx.	234	19.40 N	101.32 W
Quirós	252	28.47 S	65.07 W
Quiros, Cape ≻	175f	14.55 S	167.01 E
Quirpon Island I	186	51.35 N	55.25 W
Quiruvilca	248	8.00 S	78.19 W
Quissac	62	43.55 N	4.00 E
Quissanga	154	12.25 S	40.29 E
Quissico	156	24.42 S	34.44 E
Quissongo	152	10.01 S	15.07 E
Quistello	64	45.00 N	10.59 E
Quitapa	152	10.23 S	18.14 E
Quitaque	196	34.22 N	101.04 W
Quita Sueño Bank ✣[4]	236	14.20 N	81.15 W
Quitaúna	287b	23.31 S	46.47 W
Quiterajo	154	11.48 S	40.25 E
Quitéria ≃	255	20.16 S	51.08 W
Quitexe	152	7.56 S	15.02 E
Quitilipi	252	26.52 S	60.13 W
Quitman, Ga., U.S.	192	30.47 N	83.33 W
Quitman, Miss., U.S.	194	32.03 N	88.43 W
Quitman, Tex., U.S.	222	32.48 N	95.27 W
Quito	246	0.13 S	78.30 W
Quivilla	248	9.32 S	76.41 W
Quixadá	250	4.58 S	39.01 W
Quixeramobim	250	5.12 S	39.17 W
Quixeré	250	5.05 S	37.59 W
Quixico	152	7.59 S	14.25 E
Quixinge	152	9.52 S	14.23 E
Quixito ≃	246	4.29 S	70.18 W
Quizenga	152	9.21 S	15.28 E
Qujiadian	89	43.13 N	123.53 E
Qujiang, Zhg.	100	28.15 N	115.45 E
Qujiang, Zhg.	100	24.48 N	113.17 E
Qujing	102	25.32 N	103.41 E
Qujiu	102	22.28 N	107.40 E
Quke	120	28.16 N	87.24 E
Qukou	105	39.46 N	117.07 E
Qulay'ah, Ra's al- ≻	128	28.53 N	48.18 E
Qulbān al-'Īsāwīyah	128	30.38 N	37.53 E
Qulin	194	36.36 N	90.15 W
Qulubbā	142	27.45 N	30.50 E
Qulūd, Jabal ∧[2]	140	11.41 N	29.31 E
Qulūṣanā	142	28.21 N	30.44 E
Qulzum, Baḥr al- C	142	29.55 N	32.31 E
Qumalai (Sewugou)	102	34.35 N	95.27 E
Qumbu	158	31.10 S	28.48 E
Qumo	98	36.54 N	114.43 E
Qunaytirah, Khirbat ⊥	132	31.44 N	35.27 E
Qunayfidhah, Nafūd ≃	128	24.45 N	45.30 E
Qunbush al-Ḥamrā'	142	29.00 N	30.59 E
Qunshen'guan	105	39.49 N	117.59 E
Quobba, Point ≻	162	24.23 S	113.24 E
Quoich ≃	176	64.00 N	93.30 W
Quoich, Loch ⊜	46	57.04 N	5.17 W
Quoile ≃	48	54.21 N	5.42 W
Quoin Point ≻	158	34.46 S	19.37 E
Quonochontaug	207	41.21 N	71.43 W
Quorn	166	32.21 S	138.03 E
Quorndon	42	52.45 N	1.09 W
Quoyness	46	58.54 N	3.18 W
Qurayn, Kawlat al- ∧	142	29.25 N	31.55 E
Qurayyah, Wādī V	132	30.26 N	34.01 E
Qurayyāt, Al- □[4]	132	31.28 N	37.05 E
Qurdūd	140	10.17 N	29.56 E
Qurrāṣah	140	14.38 N	32.12 E
Qurūn Harḥash ∧[2]	142	28.09 N	31.42 E
Qūṣ	142	25.55 N	32.45 E
Quṣayr ad-Daffah ⊥	146	30.20 N	37.03 E
Qushan I	100	30.27 N	122.20 E
Qūshchī	128	37.59 N	45.03 E
Qushui	120	29.22 N	90.43 E
Qushuichang	107	30.41 N	106.02 E

PORTUGUÊS

Nome	Página	Lat.°′	Long.°′ W=Oeste
Qutang	100	32.30 N	120.21 E
Qutbapur ⬥[8]	272a	28.35 N	77.01 E
Qutb Minar ⚜[1]	272a	28.32 N	77.11 E
Qutdligssat	176	70.04 N	53.01 W
Quthing	158	30.30 S	27.36 E
Quṭūr	142	30.59 N	30.57 E
Quwaysinā	142	30.34 N	31.09 E
Quxi, Zhg.	100	28.00 N	120.31 E
Quxi, Zhg.	100	23.36 N	116.26 E
Quxia	106	32.06 N	120.09 E
Quxian, Zhg.	100	28.58 N	118.52 E
Quxian, Zhg.	102	30.51 N	106.59 E
Quxingji	98	34.52 N	114.39 E
Quxiong	102	31.09 N	96.00 E
Quyang	98	38.34 N	114.42 E
Qūyjāq-e-Bālā	84	39.16 N	47.07 E
Quyon	188	45.31 N	76.14 W
Quyquyó	252	26.14 S	57.01 W
Quzaymah, Jabal ∧	132	30.34 N	36.21 E
Quzhou	98	36.46 N	114.57 E
Quzong	102	30.08 N	96.00 E
R			
Råå	41	56.00 N	12.44 E
Raab → Győr, Magy.	30	47.42 N	17.38 E
Raab, Öst.	60	48.21 N	13.39 E
Raab (Rába) ≃	30	47.42 N	17.38 E
Raabs an der Thaya	61	48.51 N	15.30 E
Raadt ⬥[8]	263	51.24 N	6.56 E
Raahe	26	64.41 N	24.29 E
Rääkkylä	26	62.19 N	29.37 E
Raalte	52	52.24 N	6.16 E
Raamsdonksveer	52	51.42 N	4.56 E
Ra'ananna	132	32.11 N	34.53 E
Raas, Pulau I	115a	7.09 S	114.32 E
Raasay I	46	57.23 N	6.04 W
Raasay, Sound of U	46	57.27 N	6.06 W
Raasdorf	264b	48.15 N	16.34 E
Raasiku	76	59.22 N	25.11 E
Rab	36	44.46 N	14.46 E
Rab, Otok I	36	44.47 N	14.45 E
Raba	115b	8.27 S	118.46 E
Rába (Raab) ≃, Eur.	30	47.42 N	17.38 E
Raba ≃, Pol.	30	50.09 N	20.30 E
Rabableh	144	8.14 N	48.18 E
Rabaçal ≃	34	41.30 N	7.12 W
Rábade	34	43.07 N	7.37 W
Rábahidvég	61	47.04 N	16.45 E
Rabai	154	3.58 S	39.37 E
Rabak	140	13.09 N	32.44 E
Rabal	164	6.22 S	134.52 E
Rabat, Magreb	148	34.02 N	6.51 W
Rabat (Victoria), Malta	36	36.02 N	14.14 E
Rabat, Malta	36	35.52 N	14.25 E
Rabaul	164	4.12 S	152.12 E
Rabbit ≃	216	42.38 N	86.06 W
Rabbit, Lac ⊜	190	47.30 N	78.22 W
Rabbit Creek ≃, S. Dak., U.S.	198	45.13 N	102.10 W
Rabbit Creek ≃, Tex., U.S.	222	32.26 N	94.47 W
Rabbit Ears Pass)(	200	40.23 N	106.37 W
Rabbit Lake ⊜, Ont., Can.	190	47.00 N	79.37 W
Rabbit Lake ⊜, Calif., U.S.	228	34.27 N	117.01 W
Rabbs Creek ≃	222	29.59 N	96.55 W
Rábca ≃	61	47.43 N	17.17 E
R'abcevo	76	54.39 N	32.19 E
Rabeira, Ponta da ≻	287a	22.49 S	43.10 W
Rabenau	54	50.57 N	13.38 E
Rabette, Ruisseau la ≃	261	48.35 N	2.00 E
Rābigh	128	22.48 N	39.01 E
Rabinal	236	15.06 N	90.27 W
Rabiusa ≃	58	46.48 N	9.20 E
Rabka	30	49.36 N	19.56 E
Rabkavi Banhatti	122	16.28 N	75.06 E
Rabnābād Channel U	126	21.50 N	90.19 E
Rabočeostrovsk	24	64.02 N	34.46 E
Rabočij	86	59.07 N	79.00 E
Rabong, Gunong ∧	114	4.48 N	102.07 E
Rabotki	80	56.03 N	44.38 E
R'abovskij	80	50.01 N	41.53 E
Rabun Bald ∧	192	34.58 N	83.18 W
Raby	262	53.19 N	3.02 W
Racale	68	39.57 N	18.06 E
Racalmuto	70	37.24 N	13.44 E
Răcari	38	44.38 N	25.45 E
Racconigi	62	44.46 N	7.46 E
Raccoon ≃	194	41.35 N	93.37 W
Raccoon Creek ≃, N.J., U.S.	208	39.48 N	75.23 W
Raccoon Creek ≃, Ohio, U.S.	214	40.02 N	82.24 W
Raccoon Creek ≃, Pa., U.S.	214	40.38 N	80.22 W
Raccoon Creek ≃, Pa., U.S.	285	39.48 N	75.23 W
Raccoon Creek ≃, Va., U.S.	208	36.48 N	77.10 W
Raccoon Creek State Park ♠	214	40.30 N	80.27 W
Raccoon Island I	285	39.49 N	75.22 W
Raccoon Lake ⊜[1]	219	38.32 N	89.08 W
Raccuia	70	38.03 N	14.54 E
Race, Cape ≻	186	46.40 N	53.10 W
Raceland	194	29.48 N	90.40 W
Race Point ≻	207	42.04 N	70.14 W
Racette, Lac ⊜	206	46.34 N	74.03 W
Racette, Ruisseau ≃	206	46.36 N	74.04 W
Raceview	273d	26.17 S	28.08 E
Rach'a	76	60.05 N	30.49 E
Rach-gia	110	10.01 N	105.05 E
Rach-gia, Vinh C	110	10.00 N	105.00 E
Rachmanovka, S.S.S.R.	78	47.48 N	33.13 E
Rachmanovka, S.S.S.R.	80	51.57 N	49.29 E
Rachmanovo	82	55.44 N	38.37 E
Rachny Lesovyje	78	48.47 N	28.29 E
Rachov	78	48.03 N	24.12 E
Raciąż	30	52.47 N	20.06 E
Racibórz (Ratibor)	30	50.06 N	18.13 E
Racine, Pa., U.S.	214	40.49 N	80.20 W
Racine, Wis., U.S.	216	42.43 N	87.48 W
Racine □[6]	216	42.45 N	88.05 W
Racines	64	46.52 N	11.18 E
Račinskij Chrebet ∧	84	42.30 N	43.30 E
Rackerby	226	39.26 N	121.20 W
Ráckeve	30	47.10 N	18.56 E
Rackwick	46	58.52 N	3.23 W
R'ad	76	57.56 N	35.04 E
Råda	40	60.00 N	13.36 E
Radama, Îles II	157b	14.00 S	47.47 E
Radama, Presqu'île ≻[1]	157b	14.16 S	47.53 E
Rådasjön ⊜	40	59.58 N	13.38 E
Radaur	124	30.02 N	77.09 E
Rădăuți	38	47.51 N	25.55 E
Radbuza ≃	60	49.46 N	13.24 E
Radčenskoje	78	49.48 N	40.32 E
Radcliff	194	37.51 N	85.57 W
Radcliffe	44	53.34 N	2.20 W
Radcliffe-on-Trent	42	52.57 N	1.03 W
Radda in Chianti	66	43.29 N	11.22 E
Raddusa	70	37.28 N	14.32 E
Råde	26	59.21 N	10.51 E
Radebaugh	279b	40.19 N	79.35 W
Radeberg	54	51.07 N	13.55 E
Radebeul	54	51.06 N	13.40 E
Radeburg	54	51.13 N	13.43 E
Radeče	36	46.04 N	15.11 E
Radechov	78	50.18 N	24.37 E
Radegast	54	51.39 N	12.05 E
Radenci	61	46.38 N	16.03 E
Radenthein	64	46.48 N	13.43 E
Radevormwald	56	51.12 N	7.21 E
Radford	192	37.08 N	80.34 W
Rādhānagar, Bhārat	126	23.09 N	87.19 E
Rādhānagar, Bhārat	272b	22.27 N	88.28 E
Rādhanpur	120	23.50 N	71.36 E
Radici, Foce delle)(	64	44.12 N	10.31 E
Radicofani	66	42.54 N	11.46 E
Radicondoli	66	43.16 N	11.02 E
Rădinești	38	44.48 N	23.46 E
Radiščevo	80	52.51 N	47.53 E
Radisson	184	52.27 N	107.23 W
Radiumbad Brambach	54	50.13 N	12.19 E
Radium Hot Springs	182	50.38 N	116.03 W
Radix, Point ≻	241r	10.20 N	60.59 W
Radkersburg	61	46.41 N	15.59 E
Rad'kovka	78	51.06 N	36.58 E
Radldorf	60	48.53 N	12.27 E
Radlett	42	51.42 N	0.20 W
Radlett Aerodrome ⊠	260	51.43 N	0.19 W
Radley Run ≃	285	39.54 N	75.37 W
Radlje ob Dravi	61	46.37 N	15.13 E
Rådmansö ≻[1]	40	59.45 N	18.55 E
Radnevo	38	42.18 N	25.56 E
Radnice	60	49.51 N	13.37 E
Radnor, Ohio, U.S.	214	40.23 N	83.09 W
Radnor, Pa., U.S.	285	40.02 N	75.21 W
Radnor Forest ∧	42	52.18 N	3.10 W
Radnor Mere ⊜	262	53.17 N	2.14 W
Radofinnikovo	76	59.09 N	30.55 E
Radogošča	76	59.47 N	34.51 E
Radoj'a	78	47.44 N	28.09 E
Radolfzell	58	47.44 N	8.58 E
Radom, Pol.	30	51.25 N	21.10 E
Radom, Ill., U.S.	219	38.17 N	89.12 W
Radomicko	54	52.10 N	14.58 E
Radomir	38	42.33 N	22.58 E
Radomka	78	51.56 N	32.32 E
Radomka ≃	30	51.43 N	21.26 E
Radomsko	30	51.05 N	19.25 E
Radomyšl'	78	50.30 N	29.14 E
Radomyśl Wielki	30	50.12 N	21.16 E
Radošice	60	49.33 N	13.39 E
Radoškoviči	76	54.09 N	27.14 E
Radotín	30	50.00 N	14.22 E
Radovicy	80	55.06 N	39.32 E
Radoviš	38	41.38 N	22.28 E
Radovljica	36	46.21 N	14.11 E
Radstadt	64	47.23 N	13.27 E
Radstädter Tauern)(	64	47.15 N	13.24 E
Radstock	42	51.18 N	2.28 W
Raduha ∧	61	46.25 N	14.45 E
Radul'	78	51.49 N	30.42 E
Radun'	76	54.03 N	25.00 E
Radušnoje	78	47.49 N	33.29 E
Radutino	76	52.39 N	33.57 E
Radvaniči	78	52.02 N	24.02 E
Radviliškis	76	55.50 N	23.31 E
Radville	184	49.27 N	104.17 W
Raḍwā, Jabal ∧	128	24.34 N	38.18 E
Radway	182	54.04 N	112.57 W
Radykovskoje	80	45.56 N	41.57 E
Radymno	30	49.57 N	22.48 E
Radziejów	30	52.38 N	18.32 E
Radzyń Chełmiński	30	53.24 N	18.56 E
Radzyń Podlaski	30	51.48 N	22.38 E
Rae	176	62.50 N	116.03 W
Rae ≃	176	67.55 N	115.30 W
Rāe Bareli	124	26.13 N	81.14 E
Rāe Bareli □[5]	124	26.20 N	81.20 E
Raeford	192	34.59 N	79.14 W
Rae Isthmus •[3]	176	66.55 N	86.10 W
Rāenda	126	22.18 N	89.51 E
Raeren	56	50.41 N	6.07 E
Raesfeld	52	51.46 N	6.50 E
Raeside, Lake ⊜	162	29.30 S	122.00 E
Rae Strait U	176	68.45 N	95.00 W
Raetihi	172	39.26 S	175.17 E
Raevavae I	14	23.52 S	147.40 W
Rafael, Cachoeira do L	248	10.25 S	63.15 W
Rafaela	252	31.16 S	61.29 W
Rafael Calzada	258	34.48 S	58.22 W
Rafael Castillo	288	34.43 S	58.37 W
Rafael Perazza	258	34.32 S	56.47 W
Rafaḥ	132	31.18 N	34.15 E
Rafaï	152	4.58 N	23.56 E
Rafalovka	78	51.22 N	25.52 E
Raffadali	70	37.24 N	13.32 E
Raffelberg, Rennbahn ♠	263	51.26 N	6.50 E
Raffili Mission	140	6.53 N	27.58 E
Rafḥā'	128	29.42 N	43.30 E
Rafinesque, Mount ∧	210	42.47 N	73.37 W
Rafsanjān	128	30.24 N	56.01 E
Raft ≃	202	42.37 N	113.15 W
Raft River Mountains ⩘	200	41.55 N	113.25 W
Rafz	58	47.37 N	8.32 E
Raga	140	8.28 N	25.41 E
Ragada	64	46.10 N	10.38 E
Ragang, Mount ∧	116	7.43 N	124.32 E
Ragay	116	13.49 N	122.47 E
Ragay Gulf C	116	13.30 N	122.45 E
Rågeleje	41	56.06 N	12.10 E
Rägelin	54	53.01 N	12.38 E
Ragewitz	54	51.14 N	12.51 E
Ragged, Mount ∧	162	33.27 S	123.25 E
Ragged Island I	238	22.12 N	75.44 W
Ragged Lake ⊜	212	45.28 N	78.38 W
Ragged Top Mountain ∧	200	41.27 N	105.20 W
Raghabpur	272b	22.25 N	88.21 E
Rāghogarh	124	24.27 N	77.12 E
Raghumāthbāri	126	22.22 N	87.47 E
Raghunāthpur, Bhārat	126	23.33 N	86.40 E
Raghunāthpur, Bngl.	126	23.12 N	89.31 E
Raglan, Austl.	170	33.26 S	149.36 E
Raglan, N.Z.	172	37.48 S	174.53 E
Raglan, Wales, U.K.	42	51.47 N	2.51 W
Ragland	194	33.45 N	86.09 W
Ragnit → Neman	76	55.02 N	22.02 E
Ragnitz	61	46.50 N	15.35 E
Ragoleto, Lago ⊜	70	37.08 N	14.42 E
Ragow	264a	52.17 N	13.33 E
Ragozino	86	59.15 N	77.52 E
Ragsveden	40	60.29 N	14.05 E
Raguhn	54	51.42 N	12.17 E
Raguli	80	45.38 N	43.42 E
Ragusa, It.	70	36.55 N	14.44 E
Ragusa → Dubrovnik, Jugo.	38	42.38 N	18.07 E
Ragusa □[4]	70	36.55 N	14.36 E
Raguva	76	55.34 N	24.36 E
Raha	112	4.51 S	122.43 E
Raḥā, Harrat ar- ∧[9]	140	27.40 N	36.35 E
Rahad, Nahr ar- (Rahad) ≃	140	14.28 N	33.31 E
Rahad al-Baraī	140	11.18 N	23.53 E
Rahat, Harrat ∧[9]	144	22.20 N	40.05 E
Rāhatgaon	124	22.15 N	77.14 E
Rāhatgarh	124	23.47 N	78.22 E
Raḥbah	130	34.30 N	36.09 E
Rahden	52	52.26 N	8.37 E
Rahimatpur	122	17.36 N	74.12 E
Rahīm ki Bāzār	120	24.19 N	69.10 E
Rahīmyār Khān	120	28.25 N	70.18 E
Rahīmyār Khān □[5]	123	28.50 N	70.50 E
Rahlstedt ⬥[8]	263	53.36 N	10.09 E
Rahm	263	51.26 N	6.26 E
Rahm ⬥[8], B.R.D.	263	51.32 N	7.23 E
Rahm ⬥[8], B.R.D.	263	51.21 N	6.47 E
Rahmer See ⊜	264a	52.45 N	13.25 E
Rahns	285	40.12 N	75.27 W
Rahnsdorf ⬥[8]	264a	52.26 N	13.42 E
Rāhon	123	31.03 N	76.07 E
Rahotu	172	39.20 S	173.48 E
Rahouia	34	35.32 N	1.01 E
Rāhwāli	123	32.15 N	74.10 E
Rahway	210	40.37 N	74.17 W
Rahway ≃	276	40.35 N	74.12 W
Rahway, East Branch ≃	276	40.42 N	74.18 W
Rahway, Robinsons Branch ≃	276	40.37 N	74.17 W
Rahway, South Branch ≃	276	40.36 N	74.17 W
Rahway, West Branch ≃	276	40.42 N	74.18 W
Rahway River Parkway ♠	276	40.41 N	74.19 W
Raiano	66	42.06 N	13.49 E
Raiatea I	14	16.50 S	151.25 W
Rāichūr	122	16.12 N	77.22 E
Raidak ≃	124	26.22 N	89.45 E
Rāidighi	126	22.00 N	88.26 E
Raiding	61	47.34 N	16.32 E
Raiford	192	30.04 N	82.14 W
Raiganj	124	25.37 N	88.07 E
Raigarh	122	21.54 N	83.24 E
Raigarh □[5]	124	22.20 N	83.30 E
Raijua, Pulau I	112	10.37 S	121.36 E
Rāikot	123	30.39 N	75.36 E
Railroad	208	39.46 N	76.42 W
Railroad Canyon Reservoir ⊜[1]	228	33.42 N	117.16 W
Railroad Creek ≃	224	48.12 N	120.36 W
Rail Road Flat	226	38.20 N	120.30 W
Railroad Valley V	204	38.25 N	115.40 W
Railton	166	41.21 S	146.25 E
Raimangal ≃[1]	126	21.47 N	89.08 E
Rain	56	48.41 N	10.55 E
Rainbach im Innkreis	60	48.27 N	13.32 E
Rainbow	228	33.24 N	117.10 W
Rainbow Bridge ⬥[5]	284a	43.05 N	79.04 W
Rainbow Bridge National Monument ♠	200	36.58 N	110.56 W
Rainbow City	236	9.21 N	79.53 W
Rainbow Falls L	182	52.23 N	119.59 W
Rainbow Lakes	276	40.52 N	74.28 W
Rainbow Park ♠	278	41.46 N	87.33 W
Rainbow Shores	212	43.37 N	76.12 W
Rainelle	188	37.58 N	80.47 W
Rainford	44	53.30 N	2.48 W
Rainham	42	51.23 N	0.36 E
Rainham ⬥[8]	42	51.31 N	0.11 E
Rainhill	44	53.26 N	2.46 W
Rainhill Stoops	262	53.24 N	2.45 W
Rainier, Oreg., U.S.	224	46.06 N	122.56 W
Rainier, Wash., U.S.	224	46.53 N	122.41 W
Rainier, Mount ∧	224	46.52 N	121.46 W
Rainow	262	53.17 N	2.04 W
Rains → Riva di Tures	64	46.57 N	12.04 E
Rains □[6]	222	32.50 N	95.47 W
Rainsboro	218	39.13 N	83.25 W
Rainsford Island I	283	42.18 N	70.57 W
Rainworth	44	53.07 N	1.08 W
Rainy ≃, N.A.	184	48.50 N	94.41 W
Rainy ≃, Mich., U.S.	190	45.27 N	84.13 W
Rainy Lake ⊜, Ont., Can.	212	45.32 N	79.30 W
Rainy Lake ⊜, N.A.	184	48.42 N	93.10 W
Rainy River	190	48.43 N	94.29 W
Raipur, Bhārat	122	21.14 N	81.38 E
Raipur, Bhārat	124	30.19 N	78.06 E
Raipur, Bhārat	126	22.48 N	86.57 E
Raipur, Bhārat	272a	28.32 N	77.20 E
Raipur, Bhārat	272b	22.24 N	88.09 E
Rāipur, Bngl.	126	23.03 N	90.46 E
Rāipura	126	23.59 N	90.53 E
Raipur Uplands ⩘[1]	122	21.00 N	82.20 E
Rairākhol	120	21.04 N	84.21 E
Ra'īs	128	23.34 N	38.36 E
Raisdorf	54	54.17 N	10.16 E
Raisen	124	23.20 N	77.48 E
Raisen □[5]	124	23.10 N	78.10 E
Raisin	226	36.36 N	119.54 W
Raisin ≃, Ont., Can.	206	45.08 N	74.29 W
Raisin ≃, Mich., U.S.	216	41.53 N	83.20 W
Raisinghnagar	123	29.32 N	73.27 E
Raismes	50	50.23 N	3.29 E
Raita	126	24.07 N	88.57 E
Raitenbuch	60	49.01 N	11.08 E
Raiti	236	14.35 N	85.02 W
Rāiwind	123	31.15 N	74.13 E
Raizeux	261	48.37 N	1.41 E
Raja, Gili I	115a	7.14 S	113.47 E
Raja, Ujung ≻	114	3.45 N	96.33 E
Rājābari	126	23.23 N	90.28 E
Rajabasa	112	5.25 S	104.24 E
Rājābhāt Khāwa	124	26.37 N	89.32 E
Rājābhita	126	23.52 N	86.20 E
Rājahmundry	122	16.59 N	81.47 E
Rajāj	140	10.55 N	24.43 E
Rāja Jang	123	31.13 N	74.16 E
Raja-Jooseppi	24	68.28 N	28.21 E
Rājākhera	124	26.55 N	78.11 E
Rājaldesar	120	28.02 N	74.28 E
Raj-Aleksandrovka	83	48.48 N	37.51 E
Rājāluka	126	22.09 N	86.38 E
Rajamäki	26	60.32 N	24.45 E
Rājampet	122	14.11 N	79.10 E
Rajang ≃	112	2.04 N	111.12 E
Rājanpur	120	29.06 N	70.19 E
Rājapālaiyam	122	9.27 N	77.34 E
Rājāpur, Bhārat	122	16.40 N	73.31 E
Rājāpur, Bhārat	124	25.23 N	81.09 E
Rājāpur, Bhārat	272b	22.39 N	88.11 E
Rājāpur, Bngl.	126	22.34 N	90.09 E
Rājasthān □[4]	120	27.00 N	74.00 E
Rājasthān Canal ≍	120	31.10 N	75.00 E
Rājauri	123	33.23 N	74.18 E
Rājbāri, Bhārat	126	22.25 N	88.48 E
Rājbāri, Bngl.	124	23.46 N	89.39 E
Raj Bhawan ⚜	272b	22.34 N	88.21 E
Rajčichinsk	89	49.46 N	129.25 E
Rājendrapur	126	24.06 N	90.27 E
Rajevskij	86	54.04 N	54.56 E
Raj Gāngpur	124	22.11 N	84.35 E
Rājganj ≃[1]	126	27.20 N	90.18 E
Rājgarh, Bhārat	123	28.38 N	75.23 E
Rājgarh, Bhārat	124	23.56 N	76.58 E
Rājgarh, Bhārat	124	27.14 N	76.38 E
Rājgarh, Bhārat	124	23.45 N	76.50 E
Rajghat ⚜[1]	272a	28.39 N	77.15 E
Rājgīr	124	25.02 N	85.25 E
Rajgorod	83	49.22 N	37.57 E
Rajgorodok, S.S.S.R.	80	48.48 N	52.53 E
Rajgorodok, S.S.S.R.	83	48.54 N	37.43 E
Rajgród	30	53.44 N	22.42 E
Rājhāt	124	22.56 N	88.21 E
Rājibpur	272b	22.49 N	88.34 E
Rajik	112	2.36 S	105.56 E
Rajka	61	48.02 N	17.11 E
Rājkot	120	22.18 N	70.47 E
Rajkuzi	265a	59.47 N	29.57 E
Rājmahal	124	25.03 N	87.50 E
Rājmahal Hills ⩘[2]	124	24.50 N	87.35 E
Rājnagar	126	23.57 N	87.19 E
Rāj-Nāndgaon	120	21.06 N	81.02 E
Rajokri ⬥[8]	272a	28.31 N	77.07 E
Rājpīpla	120	21.47 N	73.34 E
Rājpur, Bhārat	120	21.56 N	75.08 E
Rājpur, Bhārat	120	22.24 N	74.22 E
Rājpur, Bhārat	126	22.25 N	88.25 E
Rājpur ⬥[8]	272a	28.41 N	77.12 E
Rājpura	124	30.29 N	76.36 E
Rājshāhi	124	24.22 N	88.36 E
Rajskoje	83	48.34 N	37.25 E
Rajula	122	21.03 N	71.26 E
Rakaia	172	43.45 S	172.01 E
Rakaia ≃	172	43.56 S	172.13 E
Rakamaz	30	48.08 N	21.30 E
Rakaposhi ∧	123	36.10 N	74.30 E
Rakata, Pulau I	115a	6.10 S	105.26 E
Rakha La)(	124	27.53 N	87.34 E
Rakhawt, Wādī V	144	17.40 N	51.40 E
Rakhneh	128	31.39 N	59.13 E
Rakhni	120	30.03 N	69.55 E
Rakhshān ≃	128	27.00 N	64.08 E
Rākīn	132	31.14 N	35.42 E
Rakitnoje, S.S.S.R.	78	50.51 N	35.50 E
Rakitnoje, S.S.S.R.	78	49.42 N	30.27 E
Rakitnoje, S.S.S.R.	78	51.17 N	27.14 E
Rakitnoje, S.S.S.R.	89	45.36 N	134.17 E
Rakke	76	58.59 N	26.15 E
Rakkestad	26	59.26 N	11.21 E
Rakoniewice	30	52.10 N	16.16 E
Rakops	156	21.00 S	24.32 E
Rákoscsaba ⬥[8]	264c	47.29 N	19.17 E
Rákoshegy ⬥[8]	264c	47.28 N	19.14 E
Rákoskeresztúr ⬥[8]	264c	47.29 N	19.15 E
Rákoskert ⬥[8]	264c	47.28 N	19.19 E
Rákosliget ⬥[8]	264c	47.30 N	19.16 E
Rákospalota ⬥[8]	264c	47.34 N	19.08 E
Rákos-patak ≃	264c	47.33 N	19.04 E
Rákosszentmihály ⬥[8]	264c	47.32 N	19.11 E
Rakovnická plošina ⩘[1]	54	50.08 N	13.47 E
Rakovník	54	50.05 N	13.43 E
Rakovski	38	42.18 N	24.58 E
Rakša	80	53.33 N	41.37 E
Raksakiny	86	60.37 N	73.52 E
Rakuša	80	47.03 N	52.47 E
Råkvåg	26	63.46 N	10.05 E
Rakvere	76	59.22 N	26.20 E
Rakwa	164	2.42 S	134.30 E
Raleigh, Newf., Can.	186	51.34 N	55.44 W
Raleigh, Miss., U.S.	194	32.02 N	89.30 W
Raleigh, N.C., U.S.	192	35.47 N	78.39 W
Raleigh Hills	224	45.29 N	122.46 W
Ralls	196	33.41 N	101.23 W
Ralls □[6]	219	39.34 N	91.30 W
Ralsko ∧	54	50.42 N	14.47 E
Ralston, Nebr., U.S.	198	41.12 N	96.03 W
Ralston, Pa., U.S.	210	41.31 N	76.57 W
Ram ≃	182	52.23 N	115.25 W
Rama, Nic.	236	12.09 N	84.15 W
Rama, Yis.	132	32.56 N	35.22 E
Rama ≃	236	12.08 N	84.13 W
Ramacca	70	37.23 N	14.42 E
Ramachandrapuram	122	16.51 N	82.01 E
Ramādah	144	13.38 N	43.56 E
Ramah	200	35.08 N	108.30 W
Rama Indian Reserve ⬥[4]	212	44.41 N	79.15 W
Ramales de la Victoria	34	43.15 N	3.27 W
Ramalho, Serra do ⩘	255	13.45 S	44.00 W
Rām Allāh	132	31.54 N	35.12 E
Raman	123	29.58 N	74.58 E
Rāmanagaram	122	12.43 N	77.18 E
Rāmanāthapuram	122	9.23 N	78.50 E
Ramānāthpur	272b	22.41 N	88.14 E
Ramanbāti	272b	22.47 N	88.08 E
Ramanetaka, Baie C	157b	14.13 S	47.52 E
Rāmānuj Ganj	124	23.48 N	83.42 E
Ramapo	276	41.08 N	74.10 W
Ramapo ≃	276	40.58 N	74.17 W
Ramapo Lake ⊜	276	41.02 N	74.16 W
Ramapo Mountains ⩘	276	41.08 N	74.12 W
Ramapo Valley Airport ⊠	276	41.06 N	74.02 W
Ramas, Cape ≻	122	15.07 N	73.55 E
Ramasaig	46	57.24 N	6.44 W
Ramasucha	76	52.46 N	33.33 E
Ramat Gan	132	32.05 N	34.49 E
Ramat HaSharon	132	32.09 N	34.50 E
Ramat HaShofet	132	32.37 N	35.06 E
Ramathlabama	156	25.40 S	25.35 E
Ramatuelle	62	43.13 N	6.37 E
Ramat Yoḥanan	132	32.47 N	35.07 E
Rama VI Bridge ⬥[5]	269a	13.48 N	100.31 E
Rāmban	123	33.15 N	75.15 E
Rambervillers	58	48.21 N	6.38 E
Rambi I	175g	16.30 S	179.59 E
Rambipuji	115a	8.13 S	113.36 E
Rambleton Acres	208	39.39 N	75.38 W
Rambouillet	50	48.39 N	1.50 E
Rambouillet, Château de ⊥	261	48.39 N	1.49 E
Rambouillet, Forêt de ♠	261	48.40 N	1.50 E
Rambutyo Island I	164	2.20 S	147.50 E
Rām Dās	123	31.58 N	74.54 E
Rāmdia	126	23.42 N	89.32 E
Rāmdurg	122	15.57 N	75.18 E
Ramea	186	47.31 N	57.23 W
Ramea Islands II	186	47.31 N	57.21 W
Rāmechhāp	124	27.20 N	86.05 E
Rame Head ≻, S. Afr.	158	31.48 S	29.22 E
Rame Head ≻, Eng., U.K.	42	50.19 N	4.13 W
Rämen ⊜	40	60.18 N	15.10 E
Ramenje, S.S.S.R.	76	60.17 N	43.46 E
Ramenje, S.S.S.R.	82	56.34 N	37.13 E
Ramenka ⬥[8]	265b	55.41 N	37.30 E
Ramenskoje	82	55.34 N	38.14 E
Ramer	194	32.03 N	86.13 W
Ramerupt	50	48.31 N	4.18 E
Rameški	76	57.21 N	36.03 E
Rāmeswaram	122	9.17 N	79.18 E
Ramey	214	40.48 N	78.24 W
Ramey Air Force Base ■	240m	18.30 N	67.08 W
Rāmganj	126	23.06 N	90.51 E
Rāmgarh, Bhārat	120	27.15 N	75.11 E
Rāmgarh, Bhārat	120	27.22 N	70.30 E
Rāmgarh, Bhārat	124	24.34 N	87.15 E
Rāmgarh, Bhārat	124	23.38 N	85.31 E
Rāmgarh, Bhārat	126	22.42 N	87.04 E
Rāmgarh, Bngl.	126	22.59 N	91.44 E
Rāmgarh Hills ⩘[2]	124	22.50 N	83.10 E
Ram Head ≻	240m	18.11 N	64.42 W
Rāmhormoz	128	31.16 N	49.36 E
Ramingstein	64	47.04 N	13.50 E
Ramírez, Méx.	196	25.57 N	97.46 W
Ramírez, Méx.	196	27.20 N	100.58 W
Ramiriquí	246	5.24 N	73.20 W
Ramis ≃	144	7.59 N	41.34 E
Ramit	85	38.44 N	69.17 E
Ramit Zapovednik ⬥[4]	85	38.52 N	69.20 E
Rāmjībanpur	126	22.50 N	87.37 E
Rāmkānāli	126	23.35 N	86.45 E
Ramla, Qārat ar- ∧[2]	142	30.02 N	30.39 E
Ramla	132	31.55 N	34.52 E
Ramla ≃	144	13.20 N	41.45 E
Ramm, Jabal ∧	132	29.35 N	35.24 E
Rämmen	40	60.07 N	14.08 E
Rāmnagar, Bhārat	123	32.49 N	75.19 E
Rāmnagar, Bhārat	124	29.24 N	79.07 E
Rāmnagar, Bhārat	124	25.17 N	83.02 E
Rāmnagar, Bhārat	126	21.41 N	87.33 E
Rāmnagar, Bhārat	272b	22.23 N	88.19 E
Ramnäs	40	59.46 N	16.12 E
Ramon'	78	51.54 N	39.20 E
Ramon, Har ∧	132	30.30 N	34.38 E
Ramon, Makhtesh ⬥	132	30.36 N	34.49 E
Ramon, Naḥal V	132	30.36 N	34.55 E
Ramona, Calif., U.S.	228	33.08 N	116.52 W
Ramona, Okla., U.S.	196	36.32 N	95.55 W

Symbol	English	Deutsch	Español	Français	Português
≃	River	Fluss	Río	Rivière	Rio
≍	Canal	Kanal	Canal	Canal	Canal
L	Waterfall, Rapids	Wasserfall, Stromschnellen	Cascada, Rápidos	Chute d'eau, Rapides	Cascata, Rápidos
U	Strait	Meeresstrasse	Estrecho	Détroit	Estreito
C	Bay, Gulf	Bucht, Golf	Bahía, Golfo	Baie, Golfe	Baía, Golfo
⊜	Lake, Lakes	See, Seen	Lago, Lagos	Lac, Lacs	Lago, Lagos
	Swamp	Sumpf	Pantano	Marais	Pântano
	Ice Features, Glacier	Eis- und Gletscherformen	Accidentes Glaciales	Formes glaciaires	Acidentes Glaciares
	Other Hydrographic Features	Andere Hydrographische Objekte	Otros Elementos Hidrográficos	Autres données hydrographiques	Outros Elementos Hidrográficos
✣	Submarine Features	Untermeerische Objekte	Accidentes Submarinos	Formes de relief sous-marin	Acidentes Submarinos
□	Political Unit	Politische Einheit	Unidad Política	Entité politique	Unidade Política
⚜	Cultural Institution	Kulturelle Institution	Institución Cultural	Institution culturelle	Instituição Cultural
⊥	Historical Site	Historische Stätte	Sitio Histórico	Site historique	Sítio Histórico
♠	Recreational Site	Erholungs- und Ferienort	Sitio de Recreo	Centre de loisirs	Sítio de Lazer
⊠	Airport	Flughafen	Aeropuerto	Aéroport	Aeroporto
■	Military Installation	Militäranlage	Instalación Militar	Installation militaire	Instalação Militar
⬥	Miscellaneous	Verschiedenes	Misceláneo	Divers	Miscelânea

Name	Page	Lat.°′	Long.°′
Ramona, S. Dak., U.S.	198	44.07 N	97.13 W
Ramor, Lough ⊜	48	53.49 N	7.05 W
Ramos	234	22.50 N	101.55 W
Ramos •[8]	287a	22.51 S	43.15 W
Ramos ≃[1]	150	5.08 N	5.22 E
Ramos Arizpe	232	25.33 N	100.58 W
Ramosch	58	46.50 N	10.22 E
Ramos Island I, Pil.	116	8.06 N	117.02 E
Ramos Island I, Sol.is.	175e	8.15 S	160.11 E
Ramos Mejía	258	34.38 S	58.34 W
Ramotswa	156	24.56 S	25.50 E
Rāmpāl	126	22.34 N	89.39 E
Rampart	180	65.30 N	150.10 W
Ramparts ≃	180	66.11 N	129.03 W
Rampillon	50	48.33 N	3.04 E
Rampside	44	54.05 N	3.10 W
Rāmpur, Bhārat	120	31.27 N	77.38 E
Rāmpur, Bhārat	123	29.49 N	77.27 E
Rāmpur, Bhārat	124	28.49 N	79.02 E
Rāmpur □[5]	124	28.50 N	79.05 E
Rāmpura	120	24.28 N	75.26 E
Rāmpura Phūl	123	30.17 N	75.14 E
Rampur Boalia → Rājshāhi	124	24.22 N	88.36 E
Rāmpur Hāt	126	24.10 N	87.47 E
Ramrath	263	51.06 N	6.41 E
Ramree Island I	110	19.06 N	93.48 E
Rāmsāgar	126	23.05 N	87.17 E
Rāmsar	128	36.53 N	50.41 E
Ramsau	64	47.36 N	12.54 E
Ramsay Range ⛰	162	18.31 S	127.03 E
Ramsbeck	56	51.18 N	8.24 E
Ramsberg	40	59.46 N	15.17 E
Ramsbottom	44	53.40 N	2.19 W
Ramsden Bellhouse	260	51.37 N	0.29 E
Ramsden Heath	260	51.38 N	0.28 E
Ramsdorf	52	51.54 N	6.55 E
Ramsele	26	63.33 N	16.29 E
Ramseur	192	35.44 N	79.39 W
Ramsey, I. of Man	44	54.20 N	4.21 W
Ramsey, Eng., U.K.	42	51.56 N	1.14 E
Ramsey, Eng., U.K.	42	52.27 N	0.07 W
Ramsey, Ill., U.S.	219	39.08 N	89.06 W
Ramsey, N.J., U.S.	210	41.03 N	74.09 W
Ramsey Brook ≃	276	41.02 N	74.08 W
Ramsey Creek ≃	219	39.03 N	89.04 W
Ramsey Island I	42	51.52 N	5.10 W
Ramsey Lake ⊜	190	47.15 N	82.16 W
Ramsey Lake State Park ♠	219	39.10 N	89.08 W
Ramsgate, Austl.	274a	33.59 S	151.08 E
Ramsgate, Eng., U.K.	42	51.20 N	1.25 E
Rāmshai	124	26.44 N	88.51 E
Rāmshīr	128	30.54 N	49.24 E
Ramshorn Peak ∧	202	45.09 N	111.06 W
Rämshyttan	40	60.18 N	15.13 E
Ramsjö	26	62.11 N	15.39 E
Ramsloh	52	53.06 N	7.40 E
Ramstein	56	49.27 N	7.33 E
Rāmtek	120	21.24 N	79.20 E
Rāmu, Bngl.	120	21.25 N	92.07 E
Ramu, Kenya	154	3.56 N	41.13 E
Ramu ≃	164	5.00 S	144.40 E
Ramuševo	76	57.50 N	31.37 E
Ramvik	26	62.49 N	17.51 E
Ramville, Îlet I	240e	14.42 N	60.53 W
Ramygala	76	55.31 N	24.18 E
Ramzaj	80	53.18 N	44.44 E
Rānāghāt	126	23.11 N	88.35 E
Rana Kao, Volcán ∧[1]	174z	27.11 S	109.27 W
Ranalt	64	47.02 N	11.13 E
Rana Roi, Volcán ∧[1]	174z	27.05 S	109.23 W
Rana Roraka, Volcán ∧[1]	174z	27.07 S	109.18 W
Rånäs	40	59.48 N	18.17 E
Ranau	112	5.58 N	116.41 E
Ranau, Danau ⊜	112	4.50 S	103.55 E
Ranbīrsinghpura	123	32.38 N	74.44 E
Ranburne	194	33.31 N	85.21 W
Ranburn Woods	278	41.33 N	87.22 W
Rancabali	115a	7.08 S	107.21 E
Rancagua	252	34.10 S	70.45 W
Rancah	115a	7.12 S	108.30 E
Rance ≃	32	48.31 N	1.59 W
Rancevo, S.S.S.R.	76	56.56 N	34.03 E
Rancevo, S.S.S.R.	76	56.40 N	33.02 E
Rancharia	255	22.15 S	50.55 W
Rancheria	180	60.05 N	130.40 W
Ranchería ≃	246	11.34 N	72.54 W
Rancheria Rock ∧	202	44.53 N	120.08 W
Ranches of Taos	200	36.22 N	105.37 W
Ranchester	202	44.54 N	107.16 W
Rānchī	124	23.21 N	85.20 E
Rānchi □[5]	124	23.00 N	85.00 E
Ranchillos	252	26.57 S	65.03 W
Rānchi Plateau ⛰[1]	124	23.20 N	84.50 E
Rancho Colorado, Presa de ⊜[1]	286a	19.29 N	99.17 W
Rancho Cordova	226	38.36 N	121.17 W
Rancho Del Mar	226	38.10 N	122.15 W
Rancho Nuevo, Méx.	196	26.22 N	99.54 W
Rancho Nuevo, Méx.	234	23.12 N	97.48 W
Rancho Palos Verdes	228	33.45 N	118.24 W
Rancho Rinconado	226	37.18 N	122.01 W
Rancho Santa Fe	228	33.01 N	117.12 W
Rancho Veloz	240p	22.53 N	80.23 W
Ranchuelo	240p	22.23 N	80.09 W
Ranco, Lago ⊜	254	40.14 S	72.24 W
Rancocas	208	40.01 N	74.52 W
Rancocas Creek, North Branch ≃	208	40.00 N	74.52 W
Rancocas Creek,south Branch ≃	208	40.00 N	74.52 W
Rancocas Creek, Southwest Branch ≃	285	39.57 N	74.48 W
Rancocas Heights	285	39.59 N	74.51 W
Rancocas Woods	285	39.59 N	74.52 W
Rancul	252	35.03 S	64.42 W
Rand	166	35.36 S	146.35 E
Rand (Germiston) Airport ⊠	273d	26.15 S	28.09 E
Randa	58	46.07 N	7.47 E
Randall Lake ⊜	216	41.57 N	85.02 W
Randall Park •[9]	279a	41.26 N	81.32 W
Randalls Island I	276	40.48 N	73.55 W
Randallstown	284b	39.22 N	76.48 W
Randalstown	48	54.45 N	6.18 W
Randan	32	46.01 N	3.21 E
Randazzo	70	37.53 N	14.57 E
Randbøl	41	55.42 N	9.16 E
Randburg	273d	26.06 S	27.59 E
Rānder	120	21.14 N	72.47 E
Randers	26	56.28 N	10.03 E
Randfontein	158	26.11 S	27.42 E
Randgate	273d	26.11 S	27.41 E
Randhurst •[9]	278	42.05 N	87.56 W
Randle	224	46.32 N	121.57 W
Randleman	192	35.49 N	79.48 W
Randlett	196	34.11 N	98.28 W
Randolph, Ariz., U.S.	200	32.55 N	111.31 W
Randolph, Maine, U.S.	188	44.19 N	69.46 W
Randolph, Mass., U.S.	207	42.10 N	71.03 W
Randolph, Nebr., U.S.	198	42.23 N	97.21 W
Randolph, N.Y., U.S.	210	42.10 N	78.59 W
Randolph, Ohio, U.S.	214	41.02 N	81.15 W
Randolph, Utah, U.S.	200	41.40 N	111.11 W
Randolph, Vt., U.S.	188	43.55 N	72.40 W
Randolph, Wis., U.S.	190	43.35 N	89.00 W
Randolph □[6], Ind., U.S.	218	40.10 N	85.00 W
Randolph □[6], Mo., U.S.	219	39.22 N	92.20 W
Randolph Air Force Base ■	196	29.32 N	98.16 W
Randolph Hills	284c	39.03 N	77.06 W
Randolph Village	284c	38.53 N	76.52 W
Random Island I	186	48.08 N	53.45 W
Random Lake	190	43.33 N	87.57 W
Randow ≃	54	53.41 N	14.04 E
Randowaya	164	1.52 S	136.31 E
Randowbruch ☷	54	53.15 N	14.10 E
Randsburg	228	35.22 N	117.39 W
Randsfjorden ⊜	26	60.25 N	10.24 E
Rand Stadium ♠	273d	26.14 S	28.03 E
Randublatung	115a	7.12 S	111.23 E
Randudongkal	115a	7.06 S	109.19 E
Randwick	170	33.55 S	151.15 E
Randwick Racecourse ♠	274a	33.54 S	151.14 E
Råneå	26	65.52 N	22.18 E
Ranelagh	258	34.48 S	58.12 W
Rāner	123	28.53 N	73.17 E
Ranérou	150	15.18 N	13.58 W
Rāneswar	126	24.02 N	87.25 E
Raneue	114	5.03 N	95.20 E
Ranford	168a	32.48 S	116.31 E
Ranfurly, N.Z.	172	45.08 S	170.06 E
Ranfurly, Scot., U.K.	46	55.52 N	4.33 W
Rangae	114	6.17 N	101.44 E
Rāngāmāti	120	22.38 N	92.12 E
Rangantemiang	112	0.35 S	113.19 E
Rangasa, Tanjung ≻	112	2.38 S	118.49 E
Rangaunu Bay C	172	34.50 S	173.15 E
Range Creek ≃	200	39.18 N	110.04 W
Range Indian Reserve •[4]	182	49.09 N	119.50 W
Rangeley	188	44.58 N	70.39 W
Rangely	200	40.05 N	108.48 W
Ranger	196	32.28 N	98.41 W
Ranger Lake ⊜	190	46.54 N	83.35 W
Rangersdorf	64	46.51 N	12.58 E
Ranghezhen	100	33.43 N	112.51 E
Rangia	120	26.28 N	91.38 E
Rangiora	172	43.18 S	172.36 E
Rangitaiki ≃	172	37.54 S	176.53 E
Rangitata ≃	172	44.12 S	171.30 E
Rangitikei ≃	172	40.18 S	175.14 E
Rangitukia	172	37.46 S	178.27 E
Rangkasbitung	115a	6.21 S	106.15 E
Rangkul'	85	38.29 N	74.22 E
Rangoon	110	16.47 N	96.10 E
Rangoon ≃	110	16.29 N	96.21 E
Rangpo	124	27.11 N	88.32 E
Rangpur, Bngl.	124	25.45 N	89.15 E
Rangpur, Pāk.	123	30.31 N	71.34 E
Rangpuri ⊥	272a	28.33 N	77.08 E
Rangsang, Pulau I	114	1.00 N	102.55 E
Rangsdorf	54	52.17 N	13.25 E
Rangsdorfer See ⊜	264a	52.17 N	13.24 E
Ranguana Cay I	236	16.20 N	88.09 W
Ranguana Entrance ʊ	236	16.19 N	88.09 W
Rangun → Rangoon	110	16.47 N	96.10 E
Ranholas	266c	38.47 N	9.22 W
Rānibāndh	126	22.52 N	86.47 E
Rānībennur	122	14.37 N	75.37 E
Rānīganj	126	23.37 N	87.08 E
Rānīkhet	124	29.39 N	79.25 E
Ranino	80	52.58 N	40.15 E
Rānipet	122	12.56 N	79.20 E
Ranis	54	50.39 N	11.34 E
Rāniwāra	120	24.45 N	72.13 E
Rāniyah	128	36.15 N	44.53 E
Ranken ≃	166	20.31 S	137.36 E
Ranken Store	166	19.35 S	136.55 E
Rankin, Ill., U.S.	216	40.28 N	87.54 W
Rankin, Mich., U.S.	216	42.55 N	83.46 W
Rankin, Pa., U.S.	279b	40.25 N	79.53 W
Rankin, Tex., U.S.	196	31.13 N	101.56 W
Rankin Inlet	176	62.45 N	92.10 W
Rankins Springs	166	33.50 S	146.16 E
Rānkūs	132	33.45 N	36.23 E
Rankweil	58	47.17 N	9.39 E
Ranlo	192	35.17 N	81.07 W
Rannersdorf	264b	48.08 N	16.28 E
Rannij	80	51.29 N	52.37 E
Rannoch, Loch ⊜[1]	46	56.41 N	4.18 W
Rannoch Moor •[3]	46	56.38 N	4.40 W
Rann of Kutch ≚	120	24.00 N	70.00 E
Ranobe ≃	157b	17.10 S	44.08 E
Ranohira	157b	22.29 S	45.24 E
Ranomafana, Madag.	157b	24.36 S	46.58 E
Ranomafana, Madag.	157b	18.57 S	48.50 E
Ranomena	157b	23.25 S	47.17 E
Ranong	110	9.58 N	98.38 E
Ranopiso	157b	25.03 S	46.40 E
Ranot	110	7.46 N	100.19 E
Ranotsara Nord	157b	22.48 S	46.36 E
Rānsai	272c	18.53 N	73.05 E
Ransäter	40	59.46 N	13.26 E
Ransbach	60	49.19 N	11.45 E
Ranshaw	208	40.47 N	76.31 W
Ransiki	164	1.30 S	134.10 E
Ransom, Ill., U.S.	216	41.09 N	88.39 W
Ransom, Kans., U.S.	198	38.38 N	99.56 W
Ransom, Pa., U.S.	210	41.24 N	75.50 W
Ransom Creek ≃	284a	43.04 N	78.45 W
Ransomville	210	43.14 N	78.55 W
Ranson	188	39.18 N	77.52 W
Ransta	40	59.48 N	16.38 E
Ranstadt	56	50.21 N	8.59 E
Rantabe	157b	15.42 S	49.39 E
Rantasalmi	26	62.04 N	28.18 E
Rantau, Indon.	112	2.56 S	115.09 E
Rantau, Malay.	114	2.35 N	101.58 E
Rantaukampar	114	1.24 N	100.59 E
Rantaupanjang, Indon.	112	1.51 S	102.19 E
Rantaupanjang, Indon.	112	1.16 S	101.49 E
Rantaupanjang, Indon.	114	0.58 N	99.13 E
Rantauprapat	114	2.06 N	99.50 E
Rantekombola, Bulu ∧	112	3.21 S	120.01 E
Ranten	61	47.09 N	14.05 E
Rantepao	112	2.59 S	119.54 E
Rantigny	50	49.20 N	2.26 E
Rantoul	216	40.19 N	88.09 W
Rantsila	26	64.31 N	25.39 E
Rantzau	54	54.15 N	10.30 E
Ranua	26	65.55 N	26.32 E
Rānvād	272c	18.53 N	72.55 E
Ranwanlenau	156	19.35 S	22.47 E
Råö	26	57.24 N	11.56 E
Raoerdun	100	28.48 N	117.40 E
Raohe	89	46.47 N	134.00 E
Raon-l'Étape	58	48.24 N	6.51 E
Raon-sur-Plaine	58	48.31 N	7.06 E
Raoping	100	23.43 N	117.01 E
Raoui, Erg er •[2]	148	29.17 N	2.20 W
Raoul Island I	14	29.16 S	177.54 W
Raowu	102	29.30 N	96.46 E
Raoyang	98	38.16 N	115.44 E
Raoyanghe	104	41.46 N	122.26 E
Raoyanghe ≃	104	41.11 N	122.02 E
Rapa I	14	27.36 S	144.20 W
Rapa, Ponta do ≻	252	27.22 S	48.26 W
Rapallo	62	44.21 N	9.14 E
Rapang	112	3.50 S	119.48 E
Rāpar	120	23.34 N	70.38 E
Rapatovo	80	55.04 N	54.37 E
Rāpch ≃	128	25.28 N	59.21 E
Rapel ≃	252	33.55 S	71.51 W
Rapelli	252	26.24 S	64.29 W
Raphoe	48	54.52 N	7.36 W
Rapid ≃, Mich., U.S.	190	45.55 N	86.58 W
Rapid ≃, Minn., U.S.	198	48.42 N	94.26 W
Rapid ≃, Wash., U.S.	224	47.48 N	121.18 W
Rapidan ≃	188	38.22 N	77.37 W
Rapid Bay	168b	35.32 S	138.12 E
Rapid City, Man., Can.	184	50.08 N	100.02 W
Rapid City, Mich., U.S.	190	44.50 N	85.17 W
Rapid City, S. Dak., U.S.	198	44.05 N	103.14 W
Rapid Creek ≃	198	43.54 N	102.37 W
Rapide Taureau, Barrage du •[6]	206	46.52 N	73.39 W
Rapid River	190	45.56 N	86.58 W
Räpina	76	58.06 N	27.27 E
Rapkan	85	40.22 N	70.40 E
Rapla	76	59.01 N	24.47 E
Rapness	46	59.14 N	2.51 W
Rapolano Terme	66	43.17 N	11.36 E
Rapolla	68	40.58 N	15.41 E
Rapone	68	40.51 N	15.30 E
Raposo ∧[2]	266c	38.40 N	9.11 W
Rappahannock ≃	208	37.34 N	76.18 W
Rappbodestausee ⊜[1]	54	51.09 N	10.58 E
Rappenlochschlucht ∨	58	47.23 N	9.47 E
Rapperswil	58	47.14 N	8.50 E
Rāpti ≃, As.	124	26.17 N	83.41 E
Rāpti ≃, Nepāl	124	27.33 N	84.07 E
Rápulo ≃	248	13.43 S	65.32 W
Rapu-Rapu	116	13.11 N	124.08 E
Rapu-Rapu Island I	116	13.12 N	124.09 E
Raqabah, Khashm ar- ∧[2]	142	28.18 N	31.43 E
Rāqūbah	146	29.04 N	19.08 E
Raquette ≃	206	45.00 N	74.42 W
Raraka I[1]	14	16.10 S	144.54 W
Rāribahāl	126	24.05 N	87.21 E
Raritan	210	40.34 N	74.38 W
Raritan ≃	208	40.29 N	74.17 W
Raritan, North Branch ≃	210	40.33 N	74.41 W
Raritan, South Branch ≃	210	40.33 N	74.41 W
Raritan Bay C	208	40.28 N	74.12 W
Raroia I	14	16.01 S	142.27 W
Raron	58	46.19 N	7.48 E
Rarotonga I	174k	21.14 S	159.46 W
Rarz	85	39.23 N	68.44 E
Rasa, Ilha I	287a	23.04 S	43.09 W
Rasa, Punta ≻	254	40.51 S	62.19 W
Rašaant	88	49.13 N	101.26 E
Rasa da Guaratiba, Ilha I	256	23.05 S	43.34 W
Rasa Island I	116	9.14 N	118.27 E
Ra's al-'Ayn	130	36.51 N	40.04 E
Ra's al-Barr	142	31.31 N	31.50 E
Ra's al-Khalīj	142	31.15 N	31.39 E
Ra's al-Khaymah	128	25.47 N	55.57 E
Ra's al-Ushsh •[8]	142	31.08 N	32.18 E
Ra's an-Naqb, Mișr	132	29.36 N	34.51 E
Ra's an-Naqb, Urd.	132	30.00 N	35.29 E
Rasawi	164	2.04 S	134.01 E
Ra's Ba'labakk	130	34.15 N	36.25 E
Rasbo	40	59.57 N	17.53 E
Raschau	54	50.32 N	12.50 E
Ras Dashen ∧	144	13.10 N	38.26 E
Ras Djebel	36	37.13 N	10.09 E
Rasdorf	56	50.43 N	9.53 E
Raseborg	26	59.59 N	23.39 E
Raseiniai	76	55.24 N	23.07 E
Râs el Aïoun	36	35.30 N	8.18 E
Ras el Ma, Alg.	148	34.31 N	0.46 W
Râs el Mâ, Mali	150	16.37 N	4.28 W
Ras el Oued	148	35.57 N	5.03 E
Rasen-Antholz → Anterselva di Sopra	64	46.52 N	12.08 E
Raševka	78	50.14 N	33.54 E
Rashād	140	11.51 N	31.04 E
Rāshayyā	132	33.30 N	35.51 E
Rashīd (Rosetta)	142	31.24 N	30.25 E
Rashīd, Far' ≃	142	31.30 N	30.21 E
Rashīd, Mașabb (Rosetta Mouth) ≃[1]	142	31.30 N	30.21 E
Rashīd Qal'eh	120	31.31 N	67.31 E
Rashin → Najin	98	42.15 N	130.18 E
Rasht	128	37.16 N	49.36 E
Rashtrapati Bhawan ʋ	272a	28.37 N	77.12 E
Rasiga 'Alula ≻	144	11.59 N	50.50 E
Rasina ≃	38	43.37 N	21.22 E
Rāsipuram	122	11.28 N	78.10 E
Rasi Salai	110	15.20 N	104.09 E
Rāsk	128	26.13 N	61.25 E
Raška	38	43.17 N	20.37 E
Rask Mølle	41	55.52 N	9.37 E
Rās Koh ∧	128	28.50 N	65.12 E
Raškov	78	47.57 N	28.50 E
Raskunda	126	22.48 N	87.26 E
Rasm al-Arwām, Sabkhat ⊜	130	35.53 N	37.40 E
R'asna	76	54.01 N	31.12 E
R'asnopol'	78	47.04 N	31.12 E
Raso, Cabo ≻	266c	38.43 N	9.29 W
Raso, Ilhéu I	150a	16.37 N	24.36 W
Rasocolmo, Capo ≻	70	38.18 N	15.31 E
Rason Lake ⊜	162	28.46 S	124.20 E
Raspberry Peak ∧	194	34.23 N	94.01 W
Raspopinskaja	80	49.24 N	42.52 E
Rasra	124	25.51 N	83.51 E
Rasskazovka	265b	55.38 N	37.20 E
Rasskazovo	80	52.40 N	41.53 E
Rasšua, Ostrov I	74	47.45 N	153.01 E
Rassudovo	82	55.29 N	36.54 E
Rassvet	84	43.58 N	46.44 E
Rassypnaja	80	51.35 N	53.37 E
Rassypnoje	83	48.08 N	38.34 E
Rast	38	43.53 N	23.17 E
Rastälven ≃	40	59.37 N	14.56 E
Rastatt	56	48.51 N	8.12 E
Rastavica ≃	78	49.44 N	30.01 E
Rastede	52	53.15 N	8.11 E
Rastegai'sa ∧	24	70.00 N	26.18 E
Rastenberg	54	51.10 N	11.25 E
Rastenburg → Kętrzyn	30	54.06 N	21.23 E
Rastorf	54	54.16 N	10.19 E
Rastorgujevo	82	55.33 N	37.41 E
Rastovcy	82	56.39 N	37.35 E
Rastunovo	82	55.16 N	37.50 E
Rasu, Monte ∧	71	40.25 N	9.00 E
Rasūl	123	32.42 N	73.34 E
Rasūlnagar	123	32.20 N	73.47 E
Rasulpur	272a	28.37 N	77.22 E
Rasulpur •[8]	272a	28.42 N	77.01 E
Rasun di sopra	64	46.48 N	12.03 E
Rasun di sotto	64	46.47 N	12.02 E
Rasura	58	46.06 N	9.33 E
Råsvalen ⊜	40	59.40 N	15.10 E
Răsvani	38	44.25 N	26.53 E
Rat ≃, Man., Can.	184	55.41 N	99.04 W
Rat ≃, Man., Can.	184	49.35 N	97.08 W
Ratahan	112	1.04 N	124.48 E
Ratangarh	120	28.05 N	74.36 E
Ratanpur, Bhārat	126	23.07 N	87.04 E
Ratanpur, Bhārat	272b	22.50 N	88.14 E
Rätansbyn	26	62.29 N	14.32 E
Rat Burana	269a	13.41 N	100.30 E
Ratčino, S.S.S.R.	80	53.02 N	39.55 E
Ratčino, S.S.S.R.	82	55.16 N	38.39 E
Ratcliff	222	31.24 N	95.08 W
Rateče	64	46.30 N	13.43 E
Ratekau	54	53.57 N	10.44 E
Rāth	124	25.35 N	79.34 E
Rath •[8]	263	51.17 N	6.49 E
Rathangan	48	53.12 N	6.59 W
Rathbone	210	42.08 N	77.19 W
Rathbun Lake ⊜	212	44.47 N	78.12 W
Rathbun Lake ⊜[1]	190	40.54 N	93.05 W
Rathcormack	48	52.54 N	8.17 W
Rathdowney, Austl.	171a	28.12 S	152.52 E
Rathdowney, Eire	48	52.50 N	7.34 W
Rathdrum, Eire	48	52.56 N	6.13 W
Rathdrum, Idaho, U.S.	202	47.49 N	116.54 W
Rathebur	54	53.44 N	13.46 E
Ratheim	52	51.04 N	6.10 E
Rathen	46	57.38 N	2.02 W
Rathenow	54	52.36 N	12.20 E
Rathfriland	48	54.14 N	6.10 W
Rathkeale	48	52.32 N	8.56 W
Rathlin Island I	48	55.18 N	6.13 W
Rathlin Sound ʊ	48	55.16 N	6.17 W
Ráth Luirc	48	52.21 N	8.41 W
Rathmecke	263	51.15 N	7.38 E
Rathmelton	48	55.02 N	7.38 W
Rathmore	48	52.03 N	9.13 W
Rathmullen	48	55.06 N	7.33 W
Rathnew	48	53.00 N	6.05 W
Rathowen	48	53.40 N	7.31 W
Rathstock	54	52.31 N	14.32 E
Rathwell	184	49.40 N	98.32 W
Ratibor → Racibórz	30	50.06 N	18.13 E
Raticosa, Passo della)(	66	44.10 N	11.20 E
Rätikon ⛰	58	47.03 N	9.40 E
Ratingen	56	51.18 N	6.51 E
Ratisbon → Regensburg	60	49.01 N	12.06 E
Rätische Alpen → Rhaetian Alps ⛰	58	46.30 N	10.00 E
Rat Island I	181a	51.55 N	178.20 E
Rat Islands II	181a	52.00 N	178.00 E
Rat'kovo	82	56.01 N	38.38 E
Rat Lake ⊜	184	56.10 N	99.40 W
Ratlām	120	23.19 N	75.04 E
Ratmanova, Ostrov I	180	65.46 N	169.02 W
Ratnāgiri	122	16.59 N	73.18 E
Ratnapura	122	6.41 N	80.24 E
Ratno	78	51.40 N	24.31 E
Ratodero	120	27.48 N	68.18 E
Ratomka	76	53.56 N	27.21 E
Raton	196	36.54 N	104.24 W
Ratt ≃	224	47.27 N	124.21 W
Rattanaburi	110	15.19 N	103.51 E
Rattaphum	110	7.08 N	100.16 E
Rattenberg	64	47.26 N	11.54 E
Rattlesnake	202	46.56 N	113.59 W
Rattlesnake Creek ≃, Kans., U.S.	198	38.13 N	98.22 W
Rattlesnake Creek ≃, Ohio, U.S.	218	39.16 N	83.23 W
Rattlesnake Creek ≃, Oreg., U.S.	202	42.44 N	117.47 W
Rattlesnake Creek ≃, Wash., U.S.	224	46.45 N	120.55 W
Rattlesnake Creek ≃, Wash., U.S.	224	45.48 N	121.29 W
Rattlesnake Hills ⛰[2]	200	42.45 N	107.10 W
Rattlesnake Mountain ∧	207	41.42 N	72.50 W
Rattlesnake Peak ∧	280	34.16 N	117.47 W
Rattling Brook	186	49.38 N	56.10 W
Rattling Run ≃	279b	40.33 N	79.32 W
Rattray Head ≻	46	57.37 N	1.49 W
Rattu	123	35.08 N	74.48 E
Rättvik	26	60.53 N	15.06 E
Ratz, Mount ∧	180	57.23 N	132.19 W
Ratzebuhr → Okonek	30	53.33 N	16.50 E
Ratzeburg	54	53.42 N	10.46 E
Ratzeburger See ⊜	54	53.45 N	10.47 E
Rätzlingen	54	52.23 N	11.08 E
Rau	112	0.34 N	100.01 E
Raub, Malay.	114	3.48 N	101.52 E
Raub, Ind., U.S.	216	40.44 N	87.29 W
Raubsville	208	40.38 N	75.12 W
Rauch	252	36.46 S	59.06 W
Rauchenwarth	264b	48.05 N	16.32 E
Rauchtown	210	41.07 N	77.14 W
Raucourt-et-Flaba	56	49.36 N	4.57 E
Rauen	54	52.20 N	14.01 E
Rauenstein	54	50.24 N	11.03 E
Raufarhöfn	24a	66.30 N	15.57 W
Raufoss	26	60.43 N	10.37 E
Rauhe Ebrach ≃	56	49.50 N	10.56 E
Raukumara Range ⛰	172	37.47 S	178.02 E
Raul Soares	255	20.05 S	42.22 W
Rauma	26	61.08 N	21.30 E
Rauma ≃	26	62.33 N	7.43 E
Raumünzach	56	48.38 N	8.21 E
Rauna	76	57.20 N	25.43 E
Raunds	42	52.21 N	0.33 W
Raung, Gunung ∧	115a	8.08 S	114.03 E
Raunheim	56	50.01 N	8.28 E
Raupal'an	180	65.28 N	171.59 W
Raurimu	172	39.07 S	175.24 E
Rauris	64	47.13 N	13.00 E
Raurkela	124	22.13 N	84.53 E
Rauschenberg	56	50.53 N	8.55 E
Rausu	92a	44.01 N	145.12 E
Rautalampi	26	62.38 N	26.50 E
Rāutara	272b	22.51 N	88.28 E
Rautavaara	26	63.29 N	28.18 E
Ravahere I[1]	14	18.14 S	142.09 W
Ravalgaon	122	20.38 N	74.25 E
Ravanica, Manastir ʋ[1]	38	43.58 N	21.26 E
Ravānsar	128	34.43 N	46.40 E
Ravanusa	70	37.16 N	13.58 E
Rāvar	128	31.15 N	56.53 E
Ravarano	64	44.35 N	10.04 E
Ravarino	64	44.44 N	11.06 E
Rava-Russkaja	78	50.14 N	23.37 E
Ravascletto	64	46.32 N	12.57 E
Ravat	85	39.54 N	70.10 E
Ravelo	248	18.48 S	65.32 W
Ravena	210	42.29 N	73.49 W
Ravenglass	44	54.21 N	3.24 W
Raven Lake ⊜	212	45.13 N	78.51 W
Ravenna, It.	66	44.25 N	12.12 E
Ravenna, Ky., U.S.	192	37.41 N	83.57 W
Ravenna, Mich., U.S.	216	43.11 N	85.56 W
Ravenna, Nebr., U.S.	198	41.02 N	98.55 W
Ravenna, Ohio, U.S.	214	41.09 N	81.15 W
Ravenna □[4]	66	44.25 N	11.59 E
Ravensbourne	171a	27.22 S	152.10 E
Ravensbourne National Park ♠	171a	27.21 S	152.15 E
Ravensburg	58	47.47 N	9.37 E
Ravenscrag	184	49.30 N	109.05 W
Ravensdale	224	47.21 N	121.59 W
Ravenshoe	166	17.37 S	145.29 E
Ravensthorpe, Austl.	162	33.35 S	120.02 E
Ravensthorpe, Eng., U.K.	44	53.42 N	1.35 W
Ravenswood, S. Afr.	273d	26.11 S	28.15 E
Ravenswood, Mich., U.S.	216	42.45 N	84.36 W
Ravenswood, W. Va., U.S.	188	38.57 N	81.46 W
Ravenswood Park ♠	283	42.36 N	70.42 W
Ravenswood Point ≻	282	37.30 N	122.08 W
Ravensworth	284c	38.48 N	77.13 W
Rāver	120	21.15 N	76.02 E
Ravernet ≃	44	54.30 N	6.04 W
Rāvi ≃	123	30.35 N	71.48 E
Ravières	50	47.45 N	4.17 E
Ravine	208	40.34 N	76.24 W
Ravine Lake ⊜[1]	276	40.43 N	74.38 W
Ravinia Park ♠	278	42.09 N	87.46 W
Ravlı	130	40.08 N	33.06 E
Ravna Gora	36	45.23 N	14.57 E
Ravnina	128	37.57 N	62.40 E
Ravsted	41	55.01 N	9.08 E
Rāwah	128	34.28 N	41.55 E
Rāwala Kot	123	33.52 N	73.46 E
Rāwalpindi	123	33.36 N	73.04 E
Rawa Mazowiecka	30	51.46 N	20.16 E
Rāwāndūz	128	36.37 N	44.31 E
Rawang	114	3.19 N	101.35 E
Rawas ≃	112	2.42 S	103.24 E
Rawḍah ⊜	130	35.15 N	41.05 E
Rawḍah, Wādī ar- ∨	130	34.22 N	37.21 E
Rawd al-Faraj •[8]	273c	30.05 N	31.14 E
Rawdon	206	46.03 N	73.44 W
Rawene	172	35.24 S	173.30 E
Rawḥah	144	19.28 N	41.48 E
Rawhide Creek ≃	198	42.06 N	104.20 W
Rawhide Lake ⊜	190	46.39 N	82.37 W
Rawhide Mountain ∧	204	38.17 N	116.25 W
Rawi, Ko I	114	6.33 N	99.14 E
Rawicz	30	51.37 N	16.52 E
Rawlinna	162	31.01 S	125.20 E
Rawlins	200	41.47 N	107.14 W
Rawlinson, Mount ∧	162	25.58 S	127.28 E
Rawlinson Range ⛰	162	24.51 S	128.00 E
Rawmarsh	44	53.27 N	1.21 W
Rawreth	260	51.37 N	0.35 E
Rawson, Arg.	252	34.36 S	60.04 W
Rawson, Arg.	254	43.18 S	65.06 W
Rawson, Ohio, U.S.	216	40.57 N	83.47 W
Rawsonville, S. Afr.	158	33.41 S	19.20 E
Rawsonville, Mich., U.S.	281	42.13 N	83.32 W
Rawtenstall	44	53.42 N	2.18 W
Raxalpe •[1]	61	47.42 N	15.43 E
Raxaul	124	26.59 N	84.51 E
Ray, Ill., U.S.	219	40.12 N	90.29 W
Ray, Ind., U.S.	216	41.45 N	84.53 W
Ray, N. Dak., U.S.	198	48.21 N	103.10 W
Ray ≃, Eng., U.K.	42	51.38 N	1.49 W
Ray ≃, Eng., U.K.	42	51.48 N	1.15 W
Ray, Cape ≻	186	47.40 N	59.18 W
Raya	112	1.05 N	118.32 E
Raya, Bukit ∧	112	0.40 S	112.41 E
Raya, Pulau I	114	4.52 N	95.22 E
Rāyachoti	122	14.03 N	78.45 E
Rāyadrug	122	14.42 N	76.52 E
Rāyagada	122	19.10 N	83.25 E
Rayburn	222	30.25 N	94.56 W
Rayello	68	40.39 N	14.37 E
Rayen, B.R.D.	263	51.28 N	6.32 E
Rāyen, Īrān	128	29.34 N	57.26 E
Ray Hubbard, Lake ⊜[1]	222	32.53 N	96.35 W
Rayland	214	40.11 N	80.41 W
Rayleigh	42	51.36 N	0.36 E
Raymond, Alta., Can.	182	49.27 N	112.39 W
Raymond, Calif., U.S.	226	37.13 N	119.54 W
Raymond, Ill., U.S.	219	39.19 N	89.34 W
Raymond, Minn., U.S.	198	45.01 N	95.14 W
Raymond, Miss., U.S.	194	32.15 N	90.25 W
Raymond, Ohio, U.S.	216	40.20 N	83.28 W
Raymond, Wash., U.S.	224	46.41 N	123.44 W
Raymond Terrace	170	32.46 S	151.44 E
Raymondville	196	26.29 N	97.47 W
Raymore	184	50.25 N	104.31 W
Ray Mountains ⛰	180	65.45 N	151.30 W
Rāyna	126	23.05 N	87.54 E
Rayne	194	30.14 N	92.16 W
Rayner Glacier ◪	9	67.40 S	48.30 E
Raynham	207	41.57 N	71.04 W
Raynham Dog Track ♠	283	41.59 N	71.04 W
Rayón, Méx.	232	29.43 N	110.35 W
Rayón, Méx.	234	21.51 N	99.40 W
Rayón, Méx.	234	17.12 N	93.00 W
Rayón, Parque Nacional ♠	234	19.54 N	100.10 W
Rayones	232	25.01 N	100.05 W
Rayong	110	12.40 N	101.17 E
Rāypur	272b	22.25 N	88.31 E
Rayrah ⊤[4]	140	15.21 N	34.41 E
Rayse Creek ≃	219	38.13 N	89.00 W
Rayton	158	25.45 S	28.32 E
Raytown	194	39.00 N	94.28 W
Rayville	194	32.28 N	91.45 W
Raywood	222	30.02 N	94.40 W
Rayyikhah I	128	26.12 N	36.21 E
Raz, Pointe du ≻	32	48.02 N	4.44 W
Raza, Punta ≻	234	21.02 N	105.20 W
Razan, Īrān	128	35.23 N	49.02 E
R'azan', S.S.S.R.	80	54.38 N	39.44 E
R'azan □[4]	82	54.15 N	39.00 E
R'azancevo	82	56.42 N	39.12 E
Ražanj	38	43.40 N	21.33 E
R'azanovo	82	55.29 N	37.31 E
Razāq, Kūh-e ⛰	267d	35.42 N	51.35 E
Razbegaj	265a	59.47 N	29.56 E
Războeni	38	47.05 N	26.32 E
Razdan	84	40.30 N	44.46 E
Razdan ≃	84	39.58 N	44.27 E
Razdel'naja	78	46.51 N	30.05 E
Razdolinsk	86	58.25 N	94.38 E
Razdolje	88	52.27 N	103.13 E
Razdol'noje, S.S.S.R.	78	45.47 N	33.29 E
Razdol'noje, S.S.S.R.	83	47.37 N	38.01 E
Razdol'noje, S.S.S.R.	89	43.30 N	131.52 E
Razdol'nyj	80	46.38 N	42.57 E
Razdorskaja	78	47.33 N	40.38 E
Razdory, S.S.S.R.	78	48.21 N	35.42 E
Razdory, S.S.S.R.	265b	55.45 N	37.18 E
Razelm, Lacul ⊜	38	44.54 N	28.57 E
R'aženoje	83	47.31 N	38.52 E
Raževo	86	56.09 N	68.25 E
Razgrad	38	43.32 N	26.31 E
Razlog	38	41.53 N	23.28 E
Razmachnino	88	51.47 N	115.28 E
Razmitelevo	265a	59.54 N	30.41 E
Raznočinovka	80	46.37 N	47.57 E
Raznomojka	86	52.29 N	55.52 E
Razorback Mountain ∧	182	51.35 N	124.42 W
R'ažsk	80	53.43 N	40.04 E
Razvil'noje	80	46.14 N	41.18 E
Razzoli, Isola I	71	41.18 N	9.21 E
Ré, Île de I	32	46.12 N	1.25 W
Rea ≃, Eng., U.K.	42	52.30 N	1.51 W
Rea ≃, Eng., U.K.	42	52.18 N	2.32 W
Read	262	53.49 N	2.21 W
Reading, Eng., U.K.	42	51.28 N	0.59 W
Reading, Ill., U.S.	216	41.05 N	88.51 W
Reading, Kans., U.S.	198	38.31 N	95.58 W
Reading, Mass., U.S.	207	42.31 N	71.07 W
Reading, Mich., U.S.	216	41.50 N	84.45 W
Reading, Ohio, U.S.	218	39.14 N	84.27 W
Reading, Pa., U.S.	208	40.20 N	75.56 W
Reading Center	210	42.26 N	76.56 W
Reading Station •[5]	285	39.57 N	75.10 W
Readington	210	40.34 N	74.44 W
Readlyn	190	42.42 N	92.13 W
Readsboro	207	42.46 N	72.57 W
Readstown	190	43.27 N	90.45 W
Reagan	222	31.13 N	96.47 W
Real	116	14.40 N	121.36 E
Real ≃	250	11.27 S	37.22 W
Real, Estero ≃	236	12.55 N	87.23 W
Real del Castillo	232	31.58 N	116.19 W
Real del Padre	252	34.50 S	67.46 W
Real de San Carlos	258	34.26 S	57.53 W
Realengo •[8]	256	22.53 S	43.25 W
Real Felipe, Castillo ⊥	286d	12.04 S	77.09 W
Realicó	252	35.02 S	64.15 W
Realitos	196	27.27 N	98.32 W
Réalmont	32	43.47 N	2.12 E
Realmonte	70	37.18 N	13.28 E
Reamstown	208	40.13 N	76.08 W
Reana del Roiale	64	46.12 N	13.13 E
Reardan	202	47.40 N	117.53 W
Reata	232	26.08 N	101.05 W
Reatini, Monti ⛰	66	42.28 N	13.00 E
Réau	261	48.37 N	2.38 E
Reay	46	58.33 N	3.47 W
Reay Forest •[3]	46	58.19 N	4.47 W
Rebais	50	48.51 N	3.14 E
Rebecca, Lake ⊜	162	29.53 S	122.10 E
Rebecq-Rognon	50	50.40 N	4.08 E
Rebeida, Wādī ∨	140	20.45 N	34.06 E
Rebel Hill	285	40.04 N	75.20 W
Rebersburg	210	40.57 N	77.27 W
Rebi	164	6.23 S	134.06 E
Rebiana ⊤[4]	146	24.15 N	22.00 E
Rebiana Sand Sea → Nerastro, Sarīr •[2]	146	24.20 N	20.37 E
Rebild ʋ	26	56.50 N	9.51 E
Reboly	24	63.50 N	30.47 E
Rebouças	252	25.36 S	50.42 W
Rebricha	86	53.05 N	82.20 E
Rebun-jima I	92a	45.23 N	141.02 E
Recalde	252	36.39 S	61.05 W
Recanati	66	43.24 N	13.32 E
Rečane	76	56.25 N	31.39 E
Recco	62	44.22 N	9.09 E
Recey-sur-Ource	58	47.47 N	4.52 E
Rechāh Lām	120	34.58 N	70.51 E
Rechberghausen	56	48.44 N	9.38 E
Recherche, Archipelago of the II	162	34.05 S	122.45 E
Recherche, Cape ≻	175e	10.11 S	161.19 E
Réchicourt-le-Château	58	48.40 N	6.51 E
Rechlin	54	53.21 N	12.43 E
Rechna Doāb ⛰[1]	123	31.35 N	73.30 E
Rečica, S.S.S.R.	76	52.22 N	30.25 E
Rečica, S.S.S.R.	78	51.52 N	26.48 E
Recife	250	8.03 S	34.54 W
Recife, Kaap ≻	158	34.02 S	25.44 E
Recinto	252	36.48 S	71.44 W
Recke	52	52.22 N	7.43 E
Rečki	78	51.07 N	34.30 E
Recklinghausen	52	51.36 N	7.13 E
Recklinghausen □[8]	263	51.38 N	7.02 E
Recklinghausen-Süd •[8]	263	51.34 N	7.13 E
Recknitz ≃	54	54.14 N	12.28 E
Recoaro Terme	64	45.42 N	11.13 E
Recogne	56	49.55 N	5.22 E
Recologne	58	47.16 N	5.50 E
Reconquista	252	29.09 S	59.39 W
Reconquista ≃	288	34.25 S	58.35 W
Recovery Glacier ◪	9	81.10 S	28.00 W
Recreio, Bra.	248	8.11 S	58.14 W
Recreio, Bra.	255	21.32 S	42.28 W
Recreo	252	29.16 S	65.04 W
Rector	194	36.16 N	90.17 W
Rectorville	218	38.34 N	83.39 W
Recuay	248	9.43 S	77.28 W
Recz	30	53.16 N	15.33 E
Red (Hong-ha) (Yuanjiang) ≃, As.	110	20.17 N	106.34 E
Red ≃, Qué., Can.	206	45.38 N	71.22 W
Red ≃, N.A.	178	50.24 N	96.48 W
Red ≃, U.S.	178	31.00 N	91.40 W
Red ≃, U.S.	194	36.32 N	87.22 W
Red ≃, Idaho, U.S.	202	45.48 N	115.28 W
Red ≃, Ky., U.S.	192	37.51 N	84.05 W
Red ≃, N. Mex., U.S.	200	36.39 N	105.42 W
Red ≃, Wis., U.S.	190	44.49 N	88.38 W
Red, Elm Fork ≃	196	34.53 N	99.19 W
Red, North Fork ≃	196	34.24 N	99.14 W
Red, Salt Fork ≃	196	34.27 N	99.22 W
Red, South Fork ≃	194	36.41 N	86.56 W
Reda	30	54.37 N	18.21 E
Redang, Pulau I	114	5.47 N	103.00 E
Redange	56	49.46 N	5.54 E
Redang Panjang	114	5.07 N	100.47 E
Red Bank, N.J., U.S.	276	40.21 N	74.03 W
Red Bank, Tenn., U.S.	194	35.07 N	85.17 W
Red Bank Battle Monument ⊥	285	39.52 N	75.11 W
Redbank Creek ≃	214	40.58 N	79.33 W
Red Banks	194	34.50 N	89.34 W
Red Bay, Newf., Can.	186	51.44 N	56.25 W
Red Bay, Ala., U.S.	194	34.27 N	88.09 W
Redbay, Fla., U.S.	194	30.35 N	85.57 W
Red Bay C	44	55.04 N	6.02 W
Redberry Lake ⊜	184	52.40 N	107.10 W
Redbird	214	41.48 N	81.06 W
Red Bird ≃	192	37.16 N	83.38 W
Red Bluff	204	40.11 N	122.15 W
Red Bluff Reservoir ⊜[1]	196	31.57 N	103.56 W
Red Boiling Springs	194	36.32 N	85.51 W
Redbourn	42	51.48 N	0.24 W
Redbridge •[8]	42	51.34 N	0.05 E
Red Bud	219	38.13 N	89.59 W
Red Canyon ∨	198	43.18 N	103.49 W
Redcar	44	54.37 N	1.04 W
Red Cedar ≃, Mich., U.S.	216	42.43 N	84.33 W
Red Cedar ≃, Wis., U.S.	190	44.42 N	91.53 W
Red Cedar Lake ⊜	190	46.45 N	79.54 W
Red Clay Creek ≃	285	39.43 N	75.39 W
Red Clay Creek, East Branch ≃	285	39.49 N	75.42 W
Red Clay Creek, West Branch ≃	285	39.49 N	75.42 W
Redcliff, Alta., Can.	184	50.05 N	110.47 W
Redcliff, Colo., U.S.	200	39.31 N	106.22 W
Redcliff, Zimb.	154	19.02 S	29.50 E
Redcliffe	171a	27.14 S	153.07 E
Redcliffe, Mount ∧	162	28.25 S	121.32 E
Red Cliff Indian Reservation •[4]	190	46.50 N	90.47 W
Red Cliffs	166	34.19 S	142.11 E
Red Cloud	198	40.05 N	98.32 W
Red Creek	210	43.15 N	76.43 W
Red Creek ≃	194	30.41 N	88.40 W
Red Cross Lake ⊜	184	55.05 N	92.55 W
Red Deer	182	52.16 N	113.48 W
Red Deer ≃, Can.	176	50.56 N	109.54 W
Red Deer ≃, Can.	184	52.53 N	101.01 W
Red Deer Lake ⊜, Alta., Can.	182	52.43 N	113.02 W
Red Deer Lake ⊜, Man., Can.	184	52.56 N	101.20 W
Reddersburg	158	29.38 S	26.07 E
Red Devil	180	61.46 N	157.18 W
Red Dial	44	54.48 N	3.10 W
Reddick	216	41.06 N	88.15 W
Redding, Calif., U.S.	204	40.35 N	122.24 W
Redding, Conn., U.S.	207	41.18 N	73.23 W
Redding Ridge	207	41.19 N	73.21 W
Reddish	262	53.26 N	2.09 W
Redditch	42	52.19 N	1.56 W
Rede ≃	44	55.08 N	2.13 W
Redefin	54	53.21 N	11.11 E
Redelinghuys	158	32.30 S	18.33 E
Redenção	250	4.13 S	38.43 W
Redenção da Serra	256	23.16 S	45.33 W
Redesdale ∨	44	55.17 N	2.16 W
Redes Mere ⊜	262	53.15 N	2.14 W
Redeye ≃	198	46.26 N	94.49 W
Redfield, Iowa, U.S.	198	41.35 N	94.12 W
Redfield, N.Y., U.S.	212	43.32 N	75.49 W
Redfield, S. Dak., U.S.	198	44.53 N	98.31 W
Redfish Lake ⊜	202	44.07 N	114.56 W
Redford	196	29.47 N	104.10 W
Redford •[8]	281	42.25 N	83.16 W
Redford Township	216	42.25 N	83.16 W
Red Fort ⊥	272a	28.40 N	77.14 E
Redhead	241r	10.47 N	60.57 W
Red Hill, Austl.	162	21.59 S	116.03 E
Redhill, Eng., U.K.	42	51.14 N	0.11 W
Red Hill, Calif., U.S.	280	33.45 N	117.48 W
Red Hill, Pa., U.S.	208	40.22 N	75.29 W

Symbols in the index entries represent the broad categories identified in the key at the right. Symbols with superior numbers (⛰[2]) identify subcategories (see complete key on page *I* · *30*).

Kartensymbole in dem Registerverzeichnis stellen die rechts in Schlüssel erklärten Kategorien dar. Symbole mit hochgestellten Ziffern (⛰[2]) bezeichnen Unterabteilungen einer Kategorie (vgl. vollständiger Schlüssel auf Seite *I* · *30*).

Los símbolos incluídos en el texto del índice representan las grandes categorias identificadas con la clave a la derecha. Los símbolos con numeros en su parte superior (⛰[2]) identifican las subcategorías (véase la clave completa en la página *I* · *30*).

Les symboles de l'index représentent les catégories indiquées dans la légende à droite. Les symboles suivis d'un indice (⛰[2]) représentent des sous-catégories (voir légende complète à la page *I* · *30*).

Os símbolos incluídos no texto do índice representam as grandes categorias identificadas com a chave à direita. Os símbolos com números em sua parte superior (⛰[2]) identificam as subcategorias (veja-se a chave completa à página *I* · *30*).

	English	Deutsch	Español	Français	Português
∧	Mountain	Berg	Montaña	Montagne	Montanha
⛰	Mountains	Berge	Montañas	Montagnes	Montanhas
)(	Pass	Pass	Paso	Col	Passo
∨	Valley, Canyon	Tal, Cañon	Valle, Cañón	Vallée, Canyon	Vale, Canhão
≚	Plain	Ebene	Llano	Plaine	Planície
≻	Cape	Kap	Cabo	Cap	Cabo
I	Island	Insel	Isla	Île	Ilha
II	Islands	Inseln	Islas	Îles	Ilhas
⊥	Other Topographic Features	Andere Topographische Objekte	Otros Elementos Topográficos	Autres données topographiques	Outros Elementos Topográficos

ESPAÑOL — Nombre · Página · Lat.°′ · Long.°′ W=Oeste
FRANÇAIS — Nom · Page · Lat.°′ · Long.°′ W=Ouest
PORTUGUÊS — Nome · Página · Lat.°′ · Long.°′ W=Oeste

Red Hill ∧ 172 41.38 S 173.04 E
Redhill Aerodrome ⊠ 260 51.12 N 0.07 W
Red Hill Branch ≃ 284b 39.14 N 76.51 W
Red Hook 210 41.55 N 73.53 W
Redhouse Creek ≃ 284b 39.18 N 76.31 W
Rédics 61 46.36 N 16.30 E
Red Indian Lake ⊜ 186 48.40 N 56.50 W
Redington Beach 220 27.49 N 82.49 W
Redington Shores 220 27.50 N 82.50 W
Red Island I 186 47.23 N 54.11 W
Redja ≃ 76 58.05 N 31.33 E
Redkey 216 40.21 N 85.09 W
Redkino 82 56.38 N 36.17 E
Red Lake 184 51.03 N 93.49 W
Red Lake ⊜, Ont., Can. 184 51.01 N 94.05 W
Red Lake ⊜, Ariz., U.S. 200 35.40 N 114.04 W
Red Lake ⊜, Fla., U.S. 220 28.24 N 81.15 W
Red Lake ⊜, S. Dak., U.S. 198 43.44 N 99.13 W
Red Lake ⊜1 222 31.40 N 95.58 W
Red Lake ≃ 198 47.55 N 97.01 W
Red Lake Falls 198 47.53 N 96.16 W
Red Lake Indian Reservation ♦4 190 48.05 N 95.05 W
Red Lake Road 184 49.58 N 93.22 W
Redland, Scot., U.K. 46 59.05 N 3.05 W
Redland, Tex., U.S. 222 31.25 N 94.43 W
Redland Bay 171a 27.37 S 153.18 E
Redlands 228 34.03 N 117.11 W
Red Level 194 31.24 N 86.36 W
Red Lick 194 31.48 N 90.59 W
Redlin 54 53.22 N 12.01 E
Red Lion, Pa., U.S. 188 39.54 N 76.36 W
Red Lion, Pa., U.S. 285 39.53 N 75.41 W
Red Lodge 202 45.11 N 109.15 W
Red Mill • 206 46.25 N 72.28 W
Redmond, Oreg., U.S. 202 44.17 N 121.11 W
Redmond, Utah, U.S. 200 39.00 N 111.52 W
Redmond, Wash., U.S. 224 47.40 N 122.07 W
Red Mountain 228 35.21 N 117.37 W
Red Mountain ∧, Calif., U.S. 204 41.35 N 123.06 W
Red Mountain ∧, Calif., U.S. 228 35.21 N 117.36 W
Red Mountain ∧, Mont., U.S. 202 47.07 N 112.44 W
Red Mountain Pass)(200 37.54 N 107.43 W
Rednitz ≃ 56 49.28 N 10.59 E
Red Oak, Iowa, U.S. 198 41.01 N 95.14 W
Red Oak, Okla., U.S. 196 34.57 N 95.05 W
Red Oak, Tex., U.S. 222 32.31 N 96.48 W
Red Oak Creek ≃ 222 32.28 N 96.30 W
Red Oaks Mill 210 41.40 N 73.53 W
Redon 32 47.39 N 2.05 W
Redonda I 238 16.55 N 62.19 W
Redonda, Ilha I 256 23.04 S 43.12 W
Redonda, Isla I 241r 9.52 N 61.35 W
Redonda Islands II 182 50.13 N 124.48 W
Redondela 34 42.17 N 8.36 W
Redondo, Port. 34 38.39 N 7.33 W
Redondo, Wash., U.S. 224 47.21 N 122.19 W
Redondo, Mount ∧ 116 10.21 N 125.38 E
Redondo Beach 228 33.51 N 118.23 W
Redondo State Beach ♦ 280 33.50 N 118.24 W
Redoubt, Mount ∧ 224 48.57 N 121.18 W
Redoubt Volcano ∧1 180 60.29 N 152.45 W
Red Pass 182 52.59 N 118.59 W
Red Pheasant Indian Reserve ♦4 184 52.30 N 108.07 W
Red Pine Lake ⊜ 212 45.12 N 78.42 W
Red Point ⟩ 170 34.29 S 150.55 E
Red Rock, B.C., Can. 182 53.39 N 122.41 W
Red Rock, Ont., Can. 190 48.58 N 88.15 W
Red Rock, Tex., U.S. 222 29.58 N 97.27 W
Red Rock I 282 37.56 N 122.26 W
Red Rock ≃ 202 44.59 N 112.52 W
Red Rock, Lake ⊜1 190 41.30 N 93.20 W
Red Rock Canyon Park ♦ 228 35.23 N 118.00 W
Red Rock Creek ≃ 196 36.36 N 97.03 W
Red Rocks Point ⟩ 162 32.13 S 127.32 E
Red Root Creek ≃ 276 40.30 N 74.19 W
Red Run ≃, Md., U.S. 284b 39.24 N 76.47 W
Red Run ≃, Mich., U.S. 281 42.34 N 82.58 W
Redruth 42 50.13 N 5.14 W
Red Sea ⊤2 136 20.00 N 38.00 E
Red Springs 192 34.49 N 79.11 W
Redstone 182 52.08 N 123.42 W
Redstone ≃, N.W. Ter., Can. 180 64.17 N 124.33 W
Redstone ≃, Ont., Can. 190 48.27 N 81.03 W
Redstone Creek ≃ 198 44.04 N 98.05 W
Redstone Lake ⊜ 212 45.11 N 78.32 W
Red Sucker ≃ 184 55.19 N 92.31 W
Red Sucker Lake ⊜ 184 54.09 N 93.40 W
Reduction 279b 40.11 N 79.46 W
Redut 80 47.22 N 51.53 E
Redvers 184 49.33 N 101.39 W
Redwater 182 53.57 N 113.06 W
Redwater ≃, U.S. 198 44.40 N 103.51 W
Redwater ≃, Mont., U.S. 198 48.03 N 105.13 W
Red Wharf Bay C 44 53.18 N 4.10 W
Redwillow ≃ 182 55.04 N 119.21 W
Red Willow Creek ≃ 198 40.13 N 100.29 W
Red Wing 190 44.34 N 92.31 W
Redwood 212 44.18 N 75.48 W
Redwood ≃ 198 44.34 N 95.05 W
Redwood City 226 37.29 N 122.13 W
Redwood Creek ≃, Calif., U.S. 204 41.18 N 124.05 W
Redwood Creek ≃, Calif., U.S. 226 38.18 N 122.18 W
Redwood Creek ≃, Calif., U.S. 282 37.31 N 122.12 W
Redwood Creek ≃, Calif., U.S. 282 37.52 N 122.35 W
Redwood Estates 226 37.10 N 121.59 W
Redwood Falls 198 44.32 N 95.07 W
Redwood National Park ♦ 204 41.30 N 124.05 W
Redwood Point ⟩ 282 37.32 N 122.12 W
Redwood Regional Park ♦ 282 37.38 N 122.10 W
Redwood Terrace 282 37.19 N 122.18 W
Redwood Valley 204 39.16 N 123.12 W
Ree, Lough ⊜ 48 53.35 N 8.00 W
Reed City 190 43.53 N 85.31 W
Reeder 198 46.06 N 102.57 W
Reeders 210 41.01 N 75.20 W
Reeders Point ⟩ 171a 27.22 S 153.55 E
Reed Lake ⊜, Man., Can. 184 54.37 N 100.30 W
Reed Lake ⊜, Sask., Can. 184 50.24 N 107.05 W
Reedley 226 36.36 N 119.27 W
Reedsburg, Ohio, U.S. 214 40.49 N 82.07 W
Reedsburg, Wis., U.S. 190 43.32 N 90.00 W
Reeds Peak ∧ 200 33.09 N 107.51 W
Reedsport 202 43.42 N 124.06 W
Reedsville, Pa., U.S. 208 40.40 N 77.36 W
Reedsville, Wis., U.S. 190 44.09 N 87.57 W
Reedurban 214 40.47 N 81.22 W
Reedville 208 37.51 N 76.17 W
Reedy Creek ≃ 220 28.04 N 81.21 W
Reedy Creek Swamp ☰ 220 28.17 N 81.31 W
Reedy Lake ⊜ 220 27.44 N 81.22 W
Reef Islets II 175f 13.36 S 167.32 E
Reef Point ⟩ 158 34.11 S 24.36 E
Reefton 172 42.07 S 171.52 E
Reelfoot Lake ⊜ 194 36.25 N 89.22 W
Reepham 42 52.46 N 1.07 E
Reersø ⟩1 41 55.31 N 11.06 E
Rees 52 51.45 N 6.23 E
Rees □8 263 51.41 N 6.45 E
Reese 190 43.27 N 83.42 W
Reese ≃ 204 40.39 N 116.54 W
Reese Air Force Base ■ 196 33.36 N 102.02 W
Reese Village 196 33.36 N 102.01 W
Reeseville 190 43.18 N 88.51 W
Reesville 218 39.29 N 83.41 W
Reetz 54 53.11 N 11.52 E
Reetz in der Neumark → Recz 30 53.16 N 15.33 E
Refaa, Djebel ∧ 34 35.34 N 5.52 E
Refahiye 130 39.54 N 38.46 E
Reform 194 33.23 N 88.01 W
Reforma de Pineda 234 16.24 N 94.28 W
Refton 208 39.57 N 76.14 W
Refuge Cove 182 50.07 N 124.50 W
Refugio 196 28.18 N 97.17 W
Refugio, Isla I 254 43.58 S 73.12 W
Refugio Creek ≃ 282 38.01 N 122.17 W
Refugio Island I 116 10.28 N 123.21 E
Rega ≃ 30 54.10 N 15.18 E
Regaïa 34 35.38 N 5.46 W
Regalbuto 70 37.39 N 14.38 E
Regar 85 38.32 N 68.13 E
Regau 64 47.59 N 13.41 E
Regen 60 48.59 N 13.07 E
Regen ≃ 60 49.01 N 12.06 E
Regency Estates 284c 39.03 N 77.10 W
Regeneração 250 6.15 S 42.41 W
Regensburg 60 49.01 N 12.06 E
Regensdorf 58 47.26 N 8.28 E
Regenstauf 60 49.08 N 12.08 E
Regent, Austl. 274b 37.44 S 145.00 E
Regent, N. Dak., U.S. 198 46.25 N 102.33 W
Regents Park 274a 33.53 S 151.02 E
Regents Park ♣8 273d 26.15 S 28.04 E
Regent's Park ♦ 260 51.32 N 0.09 W
Regentville 274a 33.47 S 150.40 E
Reggane 148 26.42 N 0.10 E
Regge ≃ 52 52.31 N 6.22 E
Reggello 66 43.41 N 11.32 E
Reggio di Calabria 68 38.06 N 15.39 E
Reggio di Calabria □4 68 38.10 N 16.00 E
Reggiolo 64 44.55 N 10.48 E
Reggio nell'Emilia 64 44.43 N 10.36 E
Reggio nell'Emilia □4 64 44.37 N 10.37 E
Regharen ⊜ 40 58.54 N 15.46 E
Reghin 38 46.47 N 24.42 E
Regina, Sask., Can. 184 50.25 N 104.39 W
Regina, Guy. fr. 250 4.19 N 52.08 W
Regina, S. Afr. 158 27.02 S 26.30 E
Regina Beach 184 50.47 N 105.00 W
Regina Elena, Canale ☰ 266b 45.41 N 8.39 E
Regis-Breitingen 54 51.05 N 12.26 E
Registro 252 24.30 S 47.50 W
Registro do Araguaia 255 15.44 S 51.50 W
Regiwar 120 25.57 N 65.44 E
Regnéville 32 49.01 N 1.33 W
Regnitz ≃ 56 49.54 N 10.49 E
Rego Park ♣8 276 40.44 N 73.52 W
Regozero 24 65.28 N 31.10 E
Regresso, Cachoeira do ⌐ 250 0.58 S 54.51 W
Regstrup 41 55.40 N 11.37 E
Reguengos de Monsaraz 34 38.25 N 7.32 W
Reh 263 51.22 N 7.33 E
Rehau 54 50.15 N 12.02 E
Rehberg 54 52.43 N 12.10 E
Reh-Berge ✗2 54 52.35 N 13.11 E
Rehberge, Volkspark ♦ 264a 52.33 N 13.20 E
Rehburg 52 52.28 N 9.13 E
Rehden 52 52.37 N 8.29 E
Rehe 56 50.38 N 8.07 E
Rehe ≃ 105 40.54 N 117.55 E
Rehefeld-Zaunhaus 54 50.43 N 13.42 E
Rehfelde 54 52.30 N 13.54 E
Rehli 124 23.38 N 79.05 E
Rehme 52 52.12 N 8.49 E
Rehna 54 53.47 N 11.03 E
Rehoboth 156 23.18 S 17.03 E
Rehoboth □5 156 23.30 S 17.30 E
Rehoboth Bay C 208 38.40 N 75.06 W
Rehoboth Beach 208 38.43 N 75.05 W
Rehoboth Seamount ♣3 16 37.35 N 59.55 W
Rèhon 56 49.30 N 5.45 E
Rehovot 132 31.54 N 34.49 E
Rehti 124 22.44 N 77.26 E
Reiche Ebrach ≃ 56 49.49 N 10.58 E
Reiche Liesing ≃ 264b 48.08 N 16.16 E
Reichelsheim 56 49.43 N 8.50 E
Reichenau, B.R.D. 58 47.41 N 9.03 E
Reichenau, Öst. 61 47.42 N 15.50 E
Reichenau → Bogatynia, Pol. 54 50.53 N 15.00 E
Reichenau, Schw. 58 46.49 N 9.24 E
Reichenbach, D.D.R. 54 50.37 N 12.18 E
Reichenbach, D.D.R. 54 51.08 N 14.48 E
Reichenbach → Dzierżoniów, Pol. 30 50.44 N 16.39 E
Reichenbach, Schw. 58 46.38 N 7.42 E
Reichenberg → Liberec 30 50.46 N 15.03 E
Reichenhofen 58 47.50 N 9.58 E
Reichensachsen 56 51.09 N 9.59 E
Reichen Spitze ∧ 64 47.09 N 12.07 E
Reichertshausen 60 48.28 N 11.31 E
Reichertsheim 60 48.12 N 12.17 E
Reichertshofen 60 48.40 N 11.28 E
Reichraming 61 47.53 N 14.27 E
Reichsbrücke ♣5 264b 48.14 N 16.25 E
Reichshoffen 56 48.56 N 7.40 E
Reid 162 30.49 S 128.26 E
Reid, Mount ∧, Austl. 162 17.58 S 130.38 E
Reid, Mount ∧, Alaska, U.S. 180 55.42 N 131.15 W
Reid Lake ⊜1 184 50.02 N 108.05 W
Reidsville, Ga., U.S. 192 32.06 N 82.07 W
Reidsville, N.C., U.S. 192 36.21 N 79.40 W
Reiffton 208 40.19 N 75.53 W
Reigate 42 51.14 N 0.13 W
Reigate and Banstead □8 260 51.17 N 0.12 W
Reignac-sur-Indre 50 47.13 N 0.55 E
Reignier 58 46.08 N 6.16 E
Reigoldswil 58 47.24 N 7.41 E
Reihoku 92 32.31 N 130.02 E
Reillanne 62 43.53 N 5.40 E
Reims 50 49.15 N 4.02 E
Reims, Montagne de ✗2 50 49.08 N 4.00 E
Reina Adelaida, Archipiélago II 254 52.10 S 74.25 W
Reina Alejandra → Queen Alexandra Range ✗ 9 84.00 S 168.00 E
Reina Carlota, Estrecho de la → Queen Charlotte Sound ⱺ 182 51.30 N 129.30 W
Reinach, Schw. 58 47.15 N 8.11 E
Reinach, Schw. 58 47.30 N 7.35 E
Reina Fabiola → Queen Fabiola Mountains ✗ 9 71.30 S 35.40 E
Reina Maria, Costa de la → Queen Mary Coast ♣2 9 67.00 S 96.00 E
Reina Maud, Tierras de la → Queen Maud Land ♣1 9 72.30 S 12.00 E
Reinbeck 190 42.19 N 92.36 W
Reinbek 52 53.31 N 10.14 E
Reinberg 54 54.12 N 13.15 E
Reindeer ≃ 184 55.36 N 103.11 W
Reindeer Island I 184 52.25 N 98.00 W
Reindeer Lake ⊜ 176 57.15 N 102.40 W
Reindeer Station 180 68.42 N 134.06 W
Reine Charlotte, Détroit de la → Queen Charlotte Sound ⱺ 182 51.30 N 129.30 W
Reineck 58 47.28 N 9.34 E
Reinerton 208 40.36 N 76.34 W
Reinfeld 52 53.49 N 10.28 E
Reinga, Cape ⟩ 172 34.25 S 172.41 E
Reinhardswald ♣3 52 51.30 N 9.30 E
Reinhardtsdorf 54 50.53 N 14.11 E
Reinheim 56 49.49 N 8.50 E
Reinickendorf ♣8 264a 52.35 N 13.21 E
Reinosa 34 43.00 N 4.08 W
Reino Unido → United Kingdom □1 28 54.00 N 2.00 W
Reinsdorf, D.D.R. 54 50.42 N 12.33 E
Reinsdorf, D.D.R. 54 51.54 N 12.37 E
Reinshagen ♣8 263 51.10 N 7.09 E
Reinstorf 54 53.50 N 11.38 E
Reis 130 38.16 N 31.35 E
Reisach 64 46.39 N 13.09 E
Reisaelva ≃ 24 69.48 N 21.00 E
Reischach 60 48.17 N 12.44 E
Reisdorf 56 49.53 N 6.15 E
Reisholz ♣8 263 51.11 N 6.52 E
Reisjärvi 26 63.37 N 24.54 E
Reiss 46 58.28 N 3.10 W
Reisterstown 188 39.28 N 76.50 W
Reisterstown Plaza ♣9 284b 39.02 N 76.42 W
Reitano 70 37.58 N 14.20 E
Reitdiep ☰ 52 53.20 N 6.18 E
Reiteralpe ✗ 64 47.37 N 12.47 E
Reith bei Seefeld 64 47.18 N 11.12 E
Reit im Winkl 64 47.40 N 12.28 E
Reitmehring 60 48.03 N 12.12 E
Reitz 158 27.53 S 28.31 E
Reitzenhain 54 50.33 N 13.13 E
Reivilo 158 27.36 S 24.08 E
Reixach 266d 41.30 N 2.12 E
Rejinagar 126 23.53 N 88.15 E
Rejmyra 40 58.50 N 15.55 E
Rejowiec Fabryczny 30 51.08 N 23.13 E
Rejštejn 60 49.09 N 13.31 E
Rekarne 40 59.26 N 16.20 E
Rekarne □9 40 59.17 N 16.25 E
Reken 52 51.50 N 7.02 E
Rekjoäni 272b 22.37 N 88.28 E
Rela 120 29.27 N 89.45 E
Reliance 200 41.40 N 109.12 W
Relief Reservoir ⊜1 226 38.16 N 119.44 W
Religione, Punta ⟩ 70 36.42 N 14.46 E
Reliz Creek ≃ 226 36.19 N 121.18 W
Rellingen 52 53.39 N 9.49 E
Rellinghausen ♣8 263 51.25 N 7.04 E
Reloncaví, Seno C 254 41.40 S 72.35 W
Remada 148 32.19 N 10.24 E
Remagen 56 50.34 N 7.13 E
Rémalard 50 48.26 N 0.47 E
Remansão 250 4.25 S 49.34 W
Remanso 250 9.41 S 42.04 W
Remarde ≃ 261 48.35 N 2.15 E
Remarkable, Mount ∧ 162 32.48 S 138.10 E
Rembang 115a 6.42 S 111.20 E
Rembau 114 2.35 N 102.06 E
Rembia 114 2.20 N 102.13 E
Remchi 34 35.04 N 1.26 W
Remecó 252 37.38 S 63.39 W
Remedios, Col. 246 7.02 N 74.41 W
Remedios, Cuba 240p 22.30 N 79.33 W
Remedios, Pan. 236 8.14 N 81.51 W
Remedios, Punta ⟩ 236 13.31 N 89.49 W
Remedios, Santuario de los ✝1 286a 19.28 N 99.15 W
Remedios de Escalada ♣8 258 34.43 S 58.23 W
Remels 52 53.18 N 7.44 E
Remennicy 82 56.43 N 36.36 E
Remer 190 47.03 N 93.55 W
Remeshk 128 26.50 N 58.49 E
Remhoogte 158 29.33 S 23.01 E
Remich 56 49.33 N 6.22 E
Remich Airport ⊠ 279b 40.36 N 79.49 W
Rémigny, Lac ⊜ 190 47.51 N 79.12 W
Remilly 56 49.01 N 6.24 E
Remingtonville 214 41.20 N 81.29 W
Remington, Ind., U.S. 216 40.46 N 87.09 W
Remington, Va., U.S. 188 38.32 N 77.49 W
Rémire 250 4.53 N 52.17 W
Remiremont 58 48.01 N 6.35 E
Remo 144 6.50 N 41.15 E
Remo □8 273a 6.42 N 3.29 E
Remolà, Laguna del C 266d 41.17 N 2.04 E
Remollon 62 44.28 N 6.10 E
Remontnoje 80 46.33 N 43.39 E
Remoray 58 46.46 N 6.14 E
Remoulins 62 43.56 N 4.34 E
Removka ♣8 265a 47.59 N 38.43 E
Rempang, Pulau I 114 0.51 N 104.10 E
Remptendorf 54 50.31 N 11.39 E
Rems ≃ 56 48.52 N 9.16 E
Remscheid 263 51.11 N 7.11 E
Remscheider-Stausee ⊜1 263 51.10 N 7.14 E
Remsen, Iowa, U.S. 198 42.49 N 95.58 W
Remsen, N.Y., U.S. 210 43.19 N 75.11 W
Remsfeld 56 51.00 N 9.29 E
Remuna 126 21.33 N 86.54 E
Remus 190 43.36 N 85.09 W
Rémuzat 62 44.24 N 5.21 E
Rena 26 61.08 N 11.22 E
Renaix → Ronse 50 50.45 N 3.36 E
Renāla Khurd 123 30.53 N 73.36 E
Rena Point ⟩ 116 16.10 N 119.45 E
Renard Islands II 164 10.50 S 153.05 E
Renascença 246 3.50 S 66.21 W
Renata 182 49.26 N 118.06 W
Renaud Island I 9 65.40 S 66.00 W
Renbu 124 29.10 N 89.59 E
Renca 286e 33.24 S 70.44 W
Renca, Cerro ∧ 286e 33.23 S 70.43 W
Renčeni 76 57.44 N 25.26 E
Renchen 58 48.35 N 8.01 E
Rencontre East 186 47.38 N 55.12 W
Rencun 98 36.19 N 113.50 E
Renda, S.S.S.R. 76 57.09 N 22.22 E
Renda, Yai. 144 14.30 N 39.53 E
Rende 68 39.19 N 16.11 E
Rendena, Valle ∨ 58 46.08 N 10.42 E
Rend Lake ⊜1 194 38.05 N 88.58 W
Rendova I 175e 8.32 S 157.20 E
Rendsburg 41 54.18 N 9.40 E
Renens 58 46.32 N 6.35 E
Rene Reef ♣2 14 16.20 N 178.50 E
Renesse 52 51.44 N 3.46 E
Renews 186 46.56 N 52.56 W
Renfrew, Ont., Can. 212 45.28 N 76.41 W
Renfrew, Scot., U.K. 46 55.53 N 4.24 W
Renfrew, Pa., U.S. 214 40.46 N 79.58 W
Renfrew □6 212 45.25 N 77.05 W
Rengam 114 1.53 N 103.24 E
Ren'gang 106 32.01 N 120.50 E
Rengasdengklok 115a 6.09 S 107.17 E
Rengat 112 0.24 S 102.33 E
Rengel 115a 7.04 S 112.00 E
Rengen ⊜ 26 64.05 N 14.03 E
Ren'gezhuang 105 39.45 N 118.10 E
Rengit 114 1.41 N 103.09 E
Rengkang 112 1.07 N 112.10 E
Rengo 252 34.25 S 70.52 W
Rengsdorf 56 50.30 N 7.29 E
Reng Tlāng ∧ 120 21.59 N 92.36 E
Renhe, Zhg. 100 33.32 N 114.02 E
Renhe, Zhg. 100 27.41 N 115.15 E
Renhechang 107 30.05 N 105.56 E
Renheji 100 31.56 N 115.07 E
Renhua 100 25.06 N 113.44 E
Renhuai 102 27.48 N 106.18 E
Reni, Bhārat 123 28.41 N 75.02 E
Reni, S.S.S.R. 78 45.27 N 28.17 E
Renick 188 38.00 N 80.22 W
Renish Point ⟩ 46 57.44 N 6.59 W
Renjiawopeng 104 41.27 N 122.18 E
Renjiaxu 100 30.49 N 121.00 E
Renju 100 24.51 N 115.24 E
Renko 26 60.54 N 24.17 E
Renkum 52 51.58 N 5.45 E
Renliuchang 107 29.13 N 106.39 E
Renlongchang 107 30.32 N 105.47 E
Renmark 166 34.11 S 140.45 E
Renmei 100 25.50 N 117.56 E
Renmin 89 46.37 N 125.32 E
Renminshenliqu ☰ 98 35.10 N 113.55 E
Renna, Monte ∧ 70 36.52 N 14.41 E
Rennau 54 52.17 N 10.55 E
Renne, Lac du → Reindeer Lake ⊜ 176 57.15 N 102.40 W
Rennell I 160 11.40 S 160.10 E
Rennell, Isla I 254 52.00 S 74.00 W
Rennell Ridge ♣3 14 11.30 S 158.00 E
Renner 222 32.59 N 96.47 W
Rennerdale 279b 40.24 N 80.08 W
Rennerod 56 50.36 N 8.04 E
Renner Springs 162 18.20 S 133.48 E
Rennertshofen 60 48.45 N 11.02 E
Rennes 32 48.05 N 1.41 W
Rennick Bay C 9 70.18 S 161.45 E
Rennick Glacier ⩍ 9 70.30 S 161.45 E
Rennie 184 49.51 N 95.33 W
Renningen 56 48.46 N 8.56 E
Renntier-See → Reindeer Lake ⊜ 176 57.15 N 102.40 W
Rennweg 64 47.01 N 13.37 E
Reno, Nev., U.S. 226 39.31 N 119.48 W
Reno, Pa., U.S. 214 41.25 N 79.45 W
Reno, Tex., U.S. 222 32.56 N 97.05 W
Reno ≃ 64 44.37 N 12.17 E
Reno Beach 214 41.40 N 83.15 W
Reno Hill ∧ 200 42.35 N 106.03 W
Reno International Airport ⊠ 226 39.30 N 119.46 W
Renous 186 46.49 N 65.48 W
Renous ≃ 186 46.50 N 65.50 W
Renovo 214 41.20 N 77.38 W
Renqiao 100 33.27 N 117.16 E
Renqiu 98 38.43 N 116.05 E
Rens 41 54.54 N 9.06 E
Renshan 100 22.50 N 114.48 E
Renshou 100 27.08 N 117.51 E
Rensjön 26 68.05 N 19.49 E
Rensselaer, Ind., U.S. 216 40.57 N 87.09 W
Rensselaer, Mo., U.S. 219 39.40 N 91.33 W
Rensselaer, N.Y., U.S. 210 42.39 N 73.44 W
Rensselaer □6 210 42.43 N 73.40 W
Rensselaer Falls 212 44.35 N 75.19 W
Rensselaerville 210 42.31 N 74.08 W
Renteria 34 43.19 N 1.54 W
Rentfort ♣8 263 51.35 N 6.57 E
Renton 224 47.30 N 122.11 W
Rentuo 107 29.14 N 106.23 E
Rentweinsdorf 56 50.04 N 10.47 E
Renun ≃ 114 3.05 N 97.55 E
Renville 198 44.48 N 95.13 W
Renwez 56 49.50 N 4.36 E
Renwick, N.Z. 172 41.30 S 173.50 E
Renwick, Iowa, U.S. 190 42.50 N 93.59 W
Renyizhen 107 29.29 N 105.28 E
Renziehausen Park ♦ 279b 40.21 N 79.50 W
Réo, H. Vol. 150 12.19 N 2.28 W
Reo, Indon. 115b 8.19 S 120.30 E
Reola ♣8 272a 28.34 N 76.59 E
Repartición 286d 12.00 S 77.04 W
Repartimento ≃ 250 6.06 S 50.40 W
Repaupo 285 39.48 N 75.18 W
Repbäcken 40 60.26 N 15.20 E
Répce ≃ 30 47.41 N 17.03 E
Repentigny 206 45.44 N 73.28 W
Repetek 128 38.34 N 63.11 E
Repetekskij Zapovednik ♣4 128 38.28 N 63.18 E
Repino 76 60.10 N 29.52 E
Repjovka, S.S.S.R. 78 51.05 N 38.39 E
Repjovka, S.S.S.R. 80 53.09 N 48.06 E
Repki 78 51.48 N 31.05 E
Repolka 76 59.16 N 29.34 E
Repolovo 86 60.40 N 69.50 E
Reporoa 172 38.26 S 176.21 E
Reposaari 26 61.37 N 21.27 E
Reppen → Rzepin 54 52.22 N 14.50 E
Repton 194 31.25 N 87.14 W
Republic, Kans., U.S. 198 39.55 N 97.49 W
Republic, Mich., U.S. 190 46.22 N 87.59 W
Republic, Mo., U.S. 194 37.07 N 93.29 W
Republic, Ohio, U.S. 214 41.07 N 83.01 W
Republic, Wash., U.S. 202 48.39 N 118.44 W
República Centroafricana → Central African Republic □1 136 7.00 N 21.00 E
Republic Airport ⊠ 276 40.44 N 73.25 W
Republican ≃ 198 39.03 N 96.48 W
Republican, South Fork ≃ 198 40.03 N 101.31 W
Republic Observatory ✝3 273d 26.11 S 28.05 E
Republic Steel Corporation ✝3 279a 41.28 N 81.40 W
Republik Kongo → Zaire □1 10 0.00 25.00 E
République centrafricaine → Central African Republic □1 136 7.00 N 21.00 E
République démocratique du Congo → Zaire □1 10 0.00 25.00 E
Repueblo de Oriente 196 25.51 N 99.39 W
Repulse Bay 176 66.32 N 86.15 W
Repulse Bay C 166 20.36 S 148.43 E
Repvåg 24 70.45 N 25.41 E
Requena, Esp. 34 39.29 N 1.06 W
Requena, Perú 248 4.58 S 73.50 W
Réquista 62 44.02 N 2.32 E
Rère ≃ 50 47.22 N 1.50 E
Reriutaba 250 4.10 S 40.35 W
Reşadiye, Tür. 130 40.24 N 37.21 E
Reşadiye, Tür. 267b 41.05 N 29.15 E
Reşadiye Yarımadası ⟩1 130 36.40 N 27.45 E
Resang, Tanjong ⟩ 114 2.35 N 103.51 E
Resarö 40 59.26 N 18.20 E
Rescalda 266b 45.38 N 8.56 E
Rescaldina 266b 45.37 N 8.57 E
Reschenpass (Passo di Resia))(64 46.50 N 10.30 E
Reschenscheideck)(64 46.51 N 10.31 E
Rescue 208 36.59 N 76.34 W
Research 274b 37.42 S 145.11 E
Reseda ♣8 280 34.12 N 118.31 W
Resen 38 41.05 N 21.00 E
Resende 256 22.28 S 44.27 W
Reserva 252 24.38 S 50.52 W
Reserve, La., U.S. 194 30.04 N 90.34 W
Reserve, N. Mex., U.S. 200 33.43 N 108.45 W
Reserve Township 279b 40.29 N 79.59 W
Reservoir 274b 37.43 S 145.00 E
Reservoir Pond ⊜ 283 42.10 N 71.07 W
Rešetilovka 78 49.34 N 34.04 E
Rešetnikovo 82 56.27 N 36.34 E
Reshou 107 30.00 N 104.08 E
Reshui 98 42.09 N 119.18 E
Reshuitang 102 24.10 N 103.09 E
Resipol, Beinn ∧ 46 56.43 N 5.39 W
Resistencia 252 27.27 S 58.59 W
Reşiţa 38 45.17 N 21.53 E
Resiutta 64 46.23 N 13.13 E
Resko 30 53.47 N 15.25 E
Resma 80 57.24 N 42.34 E
Resn'ovka 78 49.47 N 27.25 E
Resolute 176 74.41 N 94.54 W
Resolution Island I, N.W. Ter., Can. 176 61.30 N 65.00 W
Resolution Island I, N.Z. 172 45.40 S 166.40 E
Resolven 42 51.42 N 3.42 W
Resort, Loch C 46 58.03 N 7.06 W
Resoty 76 57.09 N 28.30 E
Resplandes 250 6.17 S 45.13 W
Resplendor 255 19.20 S 41.15 W
Ressa ≃ 76 54.45 N 35.10 E
Ressaca, Ribeirão ≃ 287b 23.38 S 46.51 W
Resse ♣8 263 51.34 N 7.07 E
Resseta ≃ 76 53.49 N 35.15 E
Ressons-sur-Matz 50 49.33 N 2.45 E
Resta ≃ 76 53.36 N 30.56 E
Resthaven 216 41.16 N 88.09 W
Restigouche ≃ 186 48.04 N 66.20 W
Restinga 34 35.42 N 5.23 W
Restinga Sêca 252 29.49 S 53.23 W
Reston, Man., Can. 184 49.35 N 101.02 W
Reston, Scot., U.K. 46 55.51 N 2.11 W
Reston, Va., U.S. 208 38.58 N 77.21 W
Restoule Lake ⊜ 190 46.03 N 79.47 W
Restrepo, Col. 246 3.48 N 76.31 W
Restrepo, Col. 246 4.15 N 73.33 W
Resülhınzır ⟩ 130 36.22 N 35.45 E
Resurrección 234 19.06 N 98.07 W
Resuttano 70 37.41 N 14.02 E
Retalhuleu 236 14.32 N 91.41 W
Retalhuleu □5 236 14.20 N 91.50 W
Retamosa 252 33.35 S 54.44 W
Retelimba 175f 16.06 S 167.25 E
Retem, Oued er ∨ 148 33.30 N 5.41 E
Řetenice 54 50.38 N 13.46 E
Retezat, Munţii ✗ 38 45.25 N 23.00 E
Rethel 50 49.31 N 4.22 E
Rethem 52 52.45 N 9.23 E
Réthimnon 38 35.22 N 24.29 E
Retiche, Alpi → Rhaetian Alps ✗ 58 46.30 N 10.00 E
Retie 56 51.16 N 5.04 E
Retiers 28 47.55 N 1.23 W
Retiro, Estacion ♣5 288 34.36 S 58.22 W
Retiro, Parque del ♦ 266a 40.25 N 3.41 W
Retournac 62 45.12 N 4.02 E
Retreat 222 32.03 N 96.29 W
Retsof 210 42.50 N 77.53 W
Rettenberg 58 47.35 N 10.17 E
Rettendon 260 51.39 N 0.33 E
Rettendon Place 260 51.38 N 0.34 E
Rettichovka 89 44.10 N 132.47 E
Rettin 54 54.06 N 10.53 E
Return Creek ≃ 226 37.56 N 119.28 W
Retz 61 48.45 N 15.57 E
Retzow 54 52.37 N 12.41 E
Reu 174r 6.49 S 158.16 E
Reuden 54 52.04 N 12.18 E
Reungeut 114 4.34 N 96.22 E
Reunion □2 138, 157c 21.06 S 55.36 E
Reus 34 41.09 N 1.07 E
Reuschenberg ♣8 263 51.10 N 6.42 E
Reusel 52 51.21 N 5.22 E
Reusrath 263 51.06 N 6.57 E
Reuss ≃ 58 47.28 N 8.14 E
Reut ≃ 78 47.15 N 29.09 E
Reuterstadt Stavenhagen 54 53.42 N 12.53 E
Reutlingen 58 48.29 N 9.11 E
Reutov 82 55.46 N 37.52 E
Reutte 58 47.29 N 10.43 E
Reuver 52 51.17 N 6.05 E
Rev'akino 82 54.22 N 37.40 E
Reval → Tallinn 76 59.25 N 24.45 E
Revda, S.S.S.R. 24 67.55 N 34.30 E
Revda, S.S.S.R. 86 56.48 N 59.57 E
Réveillon, Ruisseau le ≃ 261 48.42 N 2.30 E
Revel 62 45.11 N 5.52 E
Revelganj 124 25.47 N 84.40 E
Revelstoke 182 50.59 N 118.12 W
Reventazón 248 6.10 S 80.58 W
Reventazón ≃ 236 10.17 N 83.24 W
Revere, It. 64 45.03 N 11.08 E
Revere, Mass., U.S. 207 42.24 N 71.01 W
Revere, Pa., U.S. 208 40.31 N 75.10 W
Revermont ✗2 58 46.27 N 5.25 E
Revesby 274a 33.57 S 151.01 E
Revest-du-Bion 62 44.05 N 5.33 E
Révia 154 13.23 S 36.31 E
Reviga 38 44.42 N 27.06 E
Revigny-sur-Ornain 56 48.50 N 4.59 E
Revilla del Campo 34 42.13 N 3.32 W
Revillagigedo, Islas II 232 19.00 N 111.30 W
Revillagigedo Channel ⱺ 182 55.10 N 131.13 W
Revillagigedo Island I 182 55.35 N 131.23 W
Revillo 198 45.01 N 96.34 W
Revin 56 49.56 N 4.38 E
Revloc 214 40.29 N 78.46 W
Revničov 54 50.08 N 13.45 E
Revò 64 46.23 N 11.03 E
Revol'ucii, Muzej ✝ 265b 55.46 N 37.36 E
Revol'ucii, Pik ∧ 85 38.31 N 72.21 E
Revsundssjön ⊜ 26 62.49 N 15.17 E
Revúboè ≃ 154 16.13 S 33.37 E
Revué ≃ 156 19.49 S 34.00 E
Revuelto Creek ≃ 196 35.02 N 103.26 W
Rew 124 21.54 N 78.32 E
Rewa 124 24.32 N 81.18 E
Rewa □5 124 24.45 N 81.30 E
Rewa ≃, Fiji 175g 18.08 S 178.33 E
Rewa ≃, Guy. 246 3.53 N 58.45 W
Rewāri 124 28.11 N 76.37 E
Rewataya, Taka ♣2 112 6.05 S 118.55 E
Rex, Mount ∧ 9 74.57 S 76.00 W
Rexburg 202 43.49 N 111.47 W
Rexdale ♣8 275b 43.43 N 79.35 W
Rexford, Kans., U.S. 198 39.28 N 100.45 W
Rexford, Mont., U.S. 202 48.53 N 115.13 W
Rexhame 283 42.07 N 70.41 W
Rexton 186 46.39 N 64.52 W
Rexville, Ind., U.S. 278 41.31 N 87.21 W
Rexville, N.Y., U.S. 210 42.05 N 77.40 W
Rey 128 35.35 N 51.25 E
Rey, Arroyo del ≃ 288 34.46 S 58.27 W
Rey, Estrecho de → King Sound ⱺ 162 17.00 S 123.30 E
Rey, Isla del I 236 8.22 N 78.55 W
Rey, Laguna del ⊜ 196 27.01 N 103.26 W
Rey Bouba 146 8.40 N 14.11 E
Reyes 248 14.19 S 67.23 W
Reyes, Point ⟩ 204 38.00 N 123.01 W
Reyes Peak ∧ 228 34.38 N 119.17 W
Reyhanlı 130 36.18 N 36.32 E
Rey Jorge, Estrecho → King George Sound ⱺ 162 35.03 S 117.57 E
Rey Jorge, Isla → King George Island I 9 62.00 S 58.15 W
Reykjanes ⟩1 24a 63.49 N 22.43 W
Reykjanes Ridge ♣3 10 60.00 N 28.00 W
Reykjavík 24a 64.09 N 21.51 W
Reynaldo Cullen 252 31.19 S 60.39 W
Reynella 168b 35.06 S 138.32 E
Reynolds, Ga., U.S. 192 32.34 N 84.06 W
Reynolds, Ind., U.S. 216 40.45 N 86.52 W
Reynolds, N. Dak., U.S. 198 47.40 N 97.07 W
Reynolds Channel ⱺ 276 40.36 N 73.40 W
Reynolds Creek ≃, Austl. 171a 27.56 S 152.36 E
Reynolds Creek ≃, Ont., Can. 212 42.59 N 80.58 W
Reynoldsville 214 41.06 N 78.53 W
Reynosa 232 26.07 N 98.18 W
Reyssouze ≃ 58 46.27 N 4.54 E
Rež 86 57.23 N 61.24 E
Rež ≃ 86 57.54 N 62.18 E
Reza, Gora (Kūh-e Rīzeh) ∧ 128 37.47 N 58.05 E
Rezā'īyeh 128 37.33 N 45.04 E
Rezā'īyeh, Daryācheh-ye ⊜ 128 37.40 N 45.30 E
Rezé 32 47.12 N 1.34 W
Rēzekne 76 56.30 N 27.19 E
Rēzekne ≃ 76 56.46 N 26.58 E
Rezeny 78 46.46 N 28.54 E
Rezina 78 47.44 N 28.58 E
Rezino 86 55.51 N 75.18 E
Rēznas Ezers ⊜ 76 56.20 N 27.27 E
Rezonville 56 49.06 N 6.00 E
Rezovo 38 41.59 N 28.02 E
Rezovska (Rezve) ≃ 130 41.59 N 28.01 E
Rezvāndeh 128 37.33 N 49.09 E
Rezve (Rezovska) ≃ 130 41.59 N 28.01 E
Rezzato 64 45.31 N 10.19 E
Rezzoaglio 62 44.32 N 9.23 E
Rezzonico 58 46.04 N 9.16 E
Rhade 52 53.19 N 9.07 E
Rhadeswood Reservoir ⊜1 262 53.29 N 1.56 W
Rhaetian Alps (Rätische Alpen) (Alpi Retiche) ✗ 58 46.30 N 10.00 E
Rhallamane, Sebkha de ≃ 148 23.41 N 9.50 W
Rhame 198 46.14 N 103.39 W
Rharbi, Chott ⊜ 148 33.50 N 1.30 W
Rharbi, Oued el ∨ 148 31.50 N 0.51 E
Rharbi, Zahrez ⊜ 148 34.50 N 2.50 E
Rharsa, Chott el ⊜ 148 34.06 N 7.50 E
Rhaunen 56 49.52 N 7.20 E
Rhayader 42 52.18 N 3.30 W
Rhdsneigr 44 53.14 N 4.31 W
Rhea Creek ≃ 202 45.30 N 119.46 W
Rheda-Wiedenbrück 52 51.50 N 8.18 E
Rhede, B.R.D. 52 51.50 N 6.11 E
Rhede, B.R.D. 52 53.03 N 7.16 E
Rheden 52 52.01 N 6.02 E
Rheems 208 40.08 N 76.34 W
Rheem Valley 226 37.52 N 122.07 W
Rheidol ≃ 42 52.25 N 4.05 W
Rheims → Reims 50 49.15 N 4.02 E
Rhein, Sask., Can. 184 51.22 N 102.10 W
Rhein → Ryn, Pol. 30 53.56 N 21.33 E
Rhein → Rhine ≃ 30 51.52 N 6.02 E
Rheinbach 56 50.37 N 6.57 E
Rheinberg 52 51.33 N 6.35 E
Rheinbischofsheim 56 48.39 N 7.55 E
Rheinböllen 56 50.00 N 7.40 E
Rheinbrohl 56 50.30 N 7.19 E
Rheinbrücke ♣5 263 51.12 N 6.44 E
Rheindürkheim 56 49.42 N 8.21 E
Rheine 52 52.17 N 7.26 E
Rheinen 263 51.27 N 7.38 E
Rheinfall ⌐ 58 47.41 N 8.38 E
Rheinfelden, B.R.D. 58 47.33 N 7.47 E
Rheinfelden, Schw. 58 47.33 N 7.48 E
Rheinhausen 52 51.24 N 6.44 E
Rhein-Herne-Kanal ☰ 263 51.27 N 6.47 E
Rheinhessen □5 56 49.40 N 8.40 E
Rheinisch-Bergischer Kreis □8 263 51.06 N 7.25 E
Rheinkamp 52 51.30 N 6.37 E
Rheinland-Pfalz □3 56 50.00 N 7.00 E
Rhein-Main-Donau Kanal ☰ 60 49.45 N 11.00 E
Rheinpark ♦ 263 51.15 N 6.46 E
Rheinsberg 54 53.06 N 12.53 E
Rheinstadion ♦ 263 51.16 N 6.44 E
Rheinstein, Burg ⊥ 56 50.00 N 7.50 E
Rheinwald ∨ 58 46.32 N 9.17 E
Rheinwaldhorn ∧ 58 46.30 N 9.02 E
Rhein-Westerwald, Naturpark ♦ 56 50.35 N 7.20 E
Rhein-Wupper-Kreis □8 263 51.07 N 7.06 E
Rheinzabern 56 49.07 N 8.16 E
Rhêmes-Notre-Dame 62 45.34 N 7.07 E
Rhenen 52 51.57 N 5.34 E
Rhens 56 50.17 N 7.37 E
Rheurdt 263 51.28 N 6.28 E
Rheydt 56, 263 51.10 N 6.25 E
Rheydt, Schloss ⊥ 263 51.11 N 6.29 E
Rhin ≃, D.D.R. 54 52.59 N 12.55 E
Rhin → Rhine ≃, Eur. 30 51.52 N 6.02 E
Rhinau 58 48.19 N 7.42 E
Rhine 192 31.59 N 83.12 W
Rhine (Rhein) (Rhin) ≃ 30 51.52 N 6.02 E
Rhinebeck 210 41.56 N 73.55 W
Rhinecliff 210 41.55 N 73.57 W
Rhineland 219 38.43 N 91.31 W
Rhinelander 190 45.38 N 89.25 W
Rhin Kanal ☰ 54 52.47 N 12.24 E
Rhinluch ☰ 54 52.50 N 12.50 E
Rhinns of Kells ✗ 44 55.07 N 4.22 W
Rhino Camp 154 2.58 N 31.24 E
Rhinow 54 52.45 N 12.20 E
Rhiou, Oued ≃ 34 36.00 N 0.55 E
Rhir, Cap ⟩ 148 30.38 N 9.55 W
Rhis, Oued ≃ 34 35.14 N 3.57 W
Rhiw ✗ 42 52.36 N 3.11 W
Rho, It. 62 45.32 N 9.02 E
Rho, N. Cal. 175f 21.22 S 167.50 E
Rhode Island □3 207, 178 41.40 N 71.30 W
Rhode Island I 207 41.33 N 71.15 W
Rhode Island Sound ⱺ 207 41.25 N 71.15 W
Rhoden 52 51.28 N 9.00 E
Rhodes, Austl. 274a 33.50 S 151.05 E
Rhodes → Ródhos, Ellás 38 36.26 N 28.13 E
Rhodes, S. Afr. 158 30.47 S 27.59 E
Rhodes, Eng., U.K. 262 53.33 N 2.14 W
Rhodes → Ródhos I 38 36.10 N 28.00 E
Rhodesia → Zimbabwe □1 138 20.00 S 30.00 E
Rhodes Inyanga National Park ♦ 154 18.12 S 32.45 E
Rhodes Park ♦ 273d 26.12 S 28.06 E

≃ River	Fluss	Rio	Rivière	Rio
☰ Canal	Kanal	Canal	Canal	Canal
⌐ Waterfall, Rapids	Wasserfall, Stromschnellen	Cascada, Rápidos	Chute d'eau, Rapides	Cascata, Rápidos
ⱺ Strait	Meeresstrasse	Estrecho	Détroit	Estreito
C Bay, Gulf	Bucht, Golf	Bahía, Golfo	Baie, Golfe	Baía, Golfo
⊜ Lake, Lakes	See, Seen	Lago, Lagos	Lac, Lacs	Lago, Lagos
☰ Swamp	Sumpf	Pantano	Marais	Pântano
⩍ Ice Features, Glacier	Eis- und Gletscherformen	Accidentes Glaciales	Formes glaciaires	Acidentes Glaciares
⊤ Other Hydrographic Features	Andere Hydrographische Objekte	Otros Elementos Hidrográficos	Autres données hydrographiques	Outros Acidentes Hidrográficos

♣ Submarine Features	Untermeerische Objekte	Accidentes Submarinos	Formes de relief sous-marin	Acidentes Submarinos
□ Political Unit	Politische Einheit	Unidad Politica	Entité politique	Unidade Politica
✝ Cultural Institution	Kulturelle Institution	Institución Cultural	Institution culturelle	Instituição Cultural
⊥ Historical Site	Historische Stätte	Sitio Histórico	Site historique	Sitio Histórico
♦ Recreational Site	Erholungs- und Ferienort	Sitio de Recreo	Centre de loisirs	Sitio de Lazer
⊠ Airport	Flughafen	Aeropuerto	Aéroport	Aeroporto
■ Military Installation	Militäranlage	Instalación Militar	Installation militaire	Instalação Militar
♣ Miscellaneous	Verschiedenes	Misceláneo	Divers	Miscelânea

Name	Page	Lat.	Long.
Rhodes Peak ∧	202	46.41 N	114.47 W
Rhodes Salt Marsh ☷	204	38.17 N	118.06 W
Rhodes' Tomb ♠	154	20.30 S	28.30 E
Rhododendron	224	45.20 N	121.55 W
Rhododendron State Park ♠	207	42.47 N	72.12 W
Rhodon	261	48.43 N	2.04 E
Rhodon, Ruisseau le ≃	261	48.42 N	2.04 E
Rhodope Mountains ⩘	38	41.30 N	24.30 E
Rhodt	56	49.16 N	8.07 E
Rhome	222	33.03 N	97.28 W
Rhondda	42	51.40 N	3.27 W
Rhône ≃	32	43.20 N	4.50 E
Rhône à Sète, Canal du ≋	62	43.25 N	3.42 E
Rhône au Rhin, Canal du ≋	58	47.06 N	5.19 E
Rhosesmor	262	53.12 N	3.10 W
Rhosllanerchrugog	42	53.00 N	3.03 W
Rhos-on-Sea	44	53.19 N	3.45 W
Rhossilli	42	51.34 N	4.17 W
Rhuddlan	44	53.18 N	3.27 W
Rhue ≃	32	45.23 N	2.29 E
Rhum I	46	57.00 N	6.20 W
Rhum, Sound of Ц	46	56.56 N	6.14 W
Rhyl	44	53.19 N	3.29 W
Rhymney	42	51.46 N	3.18 W
Rhymney ≃	42	51.28 N	3.10 W
Rhynie	46	57.19 N	2.50 W
Riace	68	38.25 N	16.29 E
Riachão	250	7.22 S	46.37 W
Riachão do Dantas	250	11.04 S	37.44 W
Riachão do Jacuípe	250	11.48 S	39.21 W
Riacho de Santana	255	13.37 S	42.57 W
Riacho Grande	256	23.48 S	46.35 W
Riachos, Islas de los II	254	40.10 S	62.08 W
Riachuelo, Bra.	250	10.44 S	37.11 W
Riachuelo, Chile	254	40.49 S	73.21 W
Riachuelo, Ur.	258	34.28 S	57.43 W
Riachuelo, Arroyo ≃	258	34.27 S	57.44 W
Rialma	255	15.18 S	49.34 W
Rialto, Bra.	256	22.35 S	44.16 W
Rialto, Calif., U.S.	228	34.06 N	117.22 W
Rianápolis	255	15.29 S	49.28 W
Riāng	120	27.32 N	92.56 E
Riangnom	140	9.55 N	30.01 E
Riaño	34	42.58 N	5.01 W
Rians	62	43.37 N	5.45 E
Riánsares ≃	34	39.32 N	3.18 W
Riāsi	123	33.05 N	74.50 E
Riau □[4]	112	1.00 N	102.00 E
Riau, Kepulauan II	112	1.00 N	104.30 E
Riaz	58	46.38 N	7.04 E
Riaza	34	41.17 N	3.28 W
Riaza ≃	34	41.42 N	3.55 W
Rib ≃	42	51.48 N	0.04 W
Ribadavia	34	42.17 N	8.08 W
Ribadeo	34	43.32 N	7.02 W
Ribadesella	34	43.28 N	5.04 W
Ribagorza ◂[1]	34	42.15 N	0.30 E
Ribamar	250	2.33 S	44.03 W
Ribarroja, Embalse de ⊜[1]	34	41.12 N	0.20 E
Ribas de Jarama	266a	40.23 N	3.31 W
Ribas do Rio Pardo	255	20.27 S	53.46 W
Ribauè	154	14.57 S	38.17 E
Ribble ≃	44	53.44 N	2.50 W
Ribbleton	262	53.46 N	2.40 W
Ribble Valley □[8]	262	53.48 N	2.31 W
Ribbon Fall L	226	37.44 N	119.39 W
Ribchester	262	53.49 N	2.32 W
Ribe	41	55.21 N	8.46 E
Ribe □[6]	41	55.35 N	8.50 E
Ribe Å ≃	41	55.21 N	8.40 E
Ribeauvillé	58	48.12 N	7.19 E
Ribécourt	50	49.31 N	2.55 E
Ribeira	252	24.40 S	49.01 W
Ribeira de Iguape ≃	252	24.40 S	47.24 W
Ribeira do Amparo	250	11.03 S	38.26 W
Ribeira do Pombal	250	10.50 S	38.32 W
Ribeira Grande, C.V.	150a	17.11 N	25.04 W
Ribeira Grande, Port.	148a	37.49 N	25.31 W
Ribeirão, Bra.	250	8.31 S	35.23 W
Ribeirão, Bra.	256	23.17 S	45.36 W
Ribeirão, Bra.	287b	23.35 S	46.55 W
Ribeirão das Lajes, Représa do ⊜[1]	256	22.45 S	43.55 W
Ribeirão de São Joaquim	256	22.17 S	44.11 W
Ribeirão do Pinhal	255	23.24 S	50.18 W
Ribeirão do Pote	256	23.36 S	45.50 W
Ribeirão Fundo	256	22.40 S	46.15 W
Ribeirão Grande	256	22.48 S	45.27 W
Ribeirão Pires	256	23.43 S	46.25 W
Ribeirão Prêto	255	21.10 S	47.48 W
Ribeirao Vermelho	255	21.11 S	45.03 W
Ribeirãozinho	255	16.27 S	52.35 W
Ribeiro Gonçalves	250	7.32 S	45.14 W
Ribeiro Junqueira	256	21.28 S	42.31 W
Ribemont	50	49.48 N	3.28 E
Ribera	70	37.30 N	13.16 E
Ribérac	32	45.15 N	0.20 E
Riberalta	248	10.59 S	66.06 W
Riberão Pires □[7]	287b	23.43 S	46.21 W
Ribiers	62	44.14 N	5.52 E
Rib Lake	190	45.20 N	90.12 W
Ribnica	36	45.44 N	14.44 E
Ribnitz-Damgarten	54	54.15 N	12.28 E
Ribstone Creek ≃	184	52.51 N	110.05 W
Ricadi	68	38.37 N	15.52 E
Ricarda, Laguna de la C	266d	41.18 N	2.07 E
Ricardo Flores Magón	232	29.58 N	106.58 W
Ricaurte	246	1.13 N	77.59 W
Riccall	44	53.50 N	1.04 W
Riccarton	172	43.32 S	172.36 E
Riccia	66	41.29 N	14.50 E
Riccione	66	43.59 N	12.39 E
Rice	222	32.15 N	96.30 W
Rice Creek ≃	216	42.16 N	84.57 W
Rice Lake	190	45.30 N	91.44 W
Rice Lake ⊜, Ont., Can.	190	47.42 N	82.08 W
Rice Lake ⊜, Ont., Can.	212	44.08 N	78.13 W
Rice Lake Indian Reserve ◂[4]	212	44.10 N	78.12 W
Riceville, Iowa, U.S.	190	43.22 N	92.33 W
Riceville, Pa., U.S.	214	41.47 N	79.48 W
Riceville, Tenn., U.S.	192	35.23 N	84.42 W
Rich, Cape ≻	212	44.43 N	80.38 W
Richan	184	49.59 N	92.49 W
Richard Collinson Inlet C	176	72.45 N	113.45 W
Richards	222	30.32 N	95.51 W
Richard's Bay	158	28.47 S	32.06 E
Richard's Bay C	158	28.50 S	32.02 E
Richard's Bay Game Reserve ◂[4]	158	28.48 S	32.05 E
Richards-Gebaur Air Force Base ■	194	38.51 N	94.33 W
Richard's Harbour	186	47.37 N	56.24 W
Richards Island I	180	69.20 N	134.30 W
Richardson, Tex., U.S.	222	32.57 N	96.44 W
Richardson, Wash., U.S.	224	48.27 N	122.54 W
Richardson ≃	176	58.30 N	111.30 W
Richardson, Mount ∧	162	28.49 S	119.59 E
Richardson Bay C	282	37.52 N	122.29 W
Richardson Lakes ⊜	188	44.50 N	70.52 W
Richardson Mountains ⩘, Can.	180	67.15 N	136.30 W
Richardson Mountains ⩘, N.Z.	172	44.45 S	168.31 E
Richardsville	214	41.14 N	79.01 W
Richard-Toll	150	16.28 N	15.41 W
Richardton	198	46.53 N	102.19 W
Rîchât, Guelb er ∧	148	21.07 N	11.24 W
Richboro	208	40.13 N	75.01 W
Richburg	210	42.05 N	78.09 W
Riche, Pointe ≻	186	50.42 N	57.25 W
Richebourg	261	48.49 N	1.38 E
Richelieu, Qué., Can.	206	45.27 N	73.15 W
Richelieu, Fr.	32	47.01 N	0.19 E
Richelieu □[6]	206	45.55 N	73.00 W
Richelieu ≃	206	46.03 N	73.07 W
Richer	184	49.39 N	96.28 W
Richey	198	47.39 N	105.04 W
Richfield, Idaho, U.S.	202	43.03 N	114.09 W
Richfield, Minn., U.S.	190	44.53 N	93.17 W
Richfield, Ohio, U.S.	214	41.14 N	81.39 W
Richfield, Pa., U.S.	208	40.41 N	77.07 W
Richfield, Utah, U.S.	200	38.46 N	112.05 W
Richfield Springs	210	42.51 N	74.59 W
Richford, N.Y., U.S.	210	42.21 N	76.12 W
Richford, Vt., U.S.	188	45.00 N	72.40 W
Rich Fountain	219	38.24 N	91.53 W
Richgrove	226	35.48 N	119.07 W
Rich Hill	194	38.06 N	94.22 W
Richibucto	186	46.41 N	64.52 W
Richisau	58	47.02 N	8.54 E
Richland, Ga., U.S.	192	32.06 N	84.39 W
Richland, Mich., U.S.	216	42.22 N	85.31 W
Richland, Mo., U.S.	194	37.51 N	92.26 W
Richland, N.J., U.S.	208	39.30 N	74.52 W
Richland, N.Y., U.S.	212	43.34 N	76.03 W
Richland, Pa., U.S.	208	40.21 N	76.16 W
Richland, Tex., U.S.	222	31.56 N	96.26 W
Richland, Tex., U.S.	222	32.57 N	95.49 W
Richland, Wash., U.S.	202	46.17 N	119.18 W
Richland □[6]	214	40.46 N	82.31 W
Richland Center	190	43.20 N	90.23 W
Richland Creek ≃, Ill., U.S.	219	38.14 N	89.54 W
Richland Creek ≃, Mo., U.S.	219	38.53 N	91.53 W
Richland Creek ≃, Tenn., U.S.	194	35.02 N	86.55 W
Richland Creek ≃, Tex., U.S.	222	31.58 N	96.03 W
Richland Hills	222	32.49 N	97.14 W
Richlands, N.C., U.S.	192	34.54 N	77.34 W
Richlands, Va., U.S.	192	37.06 N	81.48 W
Richland Springs	196	31.16 N	98.57 W
Richmond, Austl.	166	20.44 S	143.08 E
Richmond, Austl.	170	33.36 S	150.46 E
Richmond, Austl.	274b	37.49 S	145.00 E
Richmond, B.C., Can.	182	49.10 N	123.10 W
Richmond, Ont., Can.	212	45.11 N	75.50 W
Richmond, Qué., Can.	206	45.40 N	72.09 W
Richmond, N.Z.	172	41.20 S	173.11 E
Richmond, S. Afr.	158	31.23 S	23.56 E
Richmond, S. Afr.	158	29.54 S	30.08 E
Richmond, S. Afr.	273d	26.19 S	28.13 E
Richmond, Eng., U.K.	44	54.24 N	1.44 W
Richmond, Calif., U.S.	226	37.57 N	122.22 W
Richmond, Ill., U.S.	216	42.28 N	88.18 W
Richmond, Ind., U.S.	218	39.50 N	84.54 W
Richmond, Kans., U.S.	198	38.24 N	95.15 W
Richmond, Ky., U.S.	192	37.45 N	84.18 W
Richmond, Maine, U.S.	188	44.05 N	69.48 W
Richmond, Mass., U.S.	207	42.23 N	73.22 W
Richmond, Mich., U.S.	214	42.49 N	82.45 W
Richmond, Minn., U.S.	190	45.27 N	94.31 W
Richmond, Mo., U.S.	194	39.17 N	93.58 W
Richmond, Ohio, U.S.	214	40.26 N	80.46 W
Richmond, Tex., U.S.	222	29.35 N	95.46 W
Richmond, Utah, U.S.	200	41.55 N	111.48 W
Richmond, Vt., U.S.	188	44.24 N	72.59 W
Richmond, Va., U.S.	208	37.30 N	77.28 W
Richmond □[6], Qué., Can.	206	45.40 N	72.00 W
Richmond □[6], N.Y., U.S.	210	40.38 N	74.05 W
Richmond □[6], Va., U.S.	208	37.32 N	77.28 W
Richmond ◂[8], Eng., U.K.	42	51.28 N	0.18 W
Richmond ◂[8], Calif., U.S.	282	37.46 N	122.29 W
Richmond ◂[8], Pa., U.S.	285	39.59 N	75.06 W
Richmond, Mount ∧	172	41.29 S	173.24 E
Richmond, Point ≻	282	37.55 N	122.23 W
Richmond Beach	224	47.46 N	122.23 W
Richmond College ♥[2]	276	40.38 N	74.05 W
Richmond Creek ≃	276	40.34 N	74.11 W
Richmond Heights, Fla., U.S.	220	25.58 N	80.22 W
Richmond Heights, Mo., U.S.	219	38.38 N	90.19 W
Richmond Heights, Ohio, U.S.	214	41.33 N	81.29 W
Richmond Highlands	224	47.46 N	122.22 W
Richmond Hill, Ont., Can.	212	43.52 N	79.27 W
Richmond Hill, Ga., U.S.	192	31.56 N	81.18 W
Richmond Hill ◂[8]	276	40.42 N	73.49 W
Richmond Mall ◂[9]	279a	41.32 N	81.30 W
Richmond National Battlefield Park ♠	208	37.25 N	77.23 W
Richmond Park ♠	260	51.26 N	0.16 W
Richmond Peak ∧	241h	13.17 N	61.13 W
Richmond Range ⩘	172	41.27 S	173.30 E
Richmond Royal Australian Air Force Base ■	170	33.37 S	150.48 E
Richmond-San Rafael Bridge ◂[5]	282	37.56 N	122.27 W
Richmondtown Restoration ⊥	276	40.34 N	74.09 W
Richmond Valley ◂[8]	276	40.31 N	74.13 W
Richmondville	210	42.38 N	74.34 W
Richrath	263	51.08 N	6.56 E
Rich Square	192	36.16 N	77.17 W
Richtenberg	54	54.12 N	12.53 E
Richterswil	58	47.13 N	8.42 E
Richton	194	31.16 N	88.56 W
Richton Park	216	41.29 N	87.43 W
Richvale, Ont., Can.	212	43.51 N	79.26 W
Richvale, Calif., U.S.	226	39.30 N	121.45 W
Richview	219	38.23 N	89.11 W
Richville, N.Y., U.S.	212	44.25 N	75.23 E
Richville, Ohio, U.S.	214	40.45 N	81.27 W
Richwood, N.J., U.S.	285	39.43 N	75.10 W
Richwood, Ohio, U.S.	214	40.26 N	83.18 W
Richwood, W. Va., U.S.	188	38.14 N	80.32 W
Richwood Village	222	29.04 N	95.25 W
Rickenbacker Air Force Base ■	218	39.48 N	82.56 W
Rickenpass)(	58	47.14 N	9.02 E
Ricken Tunnel ◂[5]	58	47.12 N	9.05 E
Ricketts Glen State Park ♠	210	41.20 N	76.18 W
Ricketts Point ≻	274b	38.00 S	145.02 E
Rickleån ≃	26	64.05 N	20.56 E
Rickling	54	54.01 N	10.13 E
Rickmansworth	42	51.39 N	0.29 W
Rico	200	37.41 N	108.02 W
Ricoa ≃	241s	11.30 N	69.12 W
Ricobayo, Embalse de ⊜[1]	34	41.30 N	5.55 W
Ricupe	152	14.37 S	21.25 E
Ridā'	144	14.38 N	44.54 E
Ridanna (Ridnaun)	64	46.55 N	11.15 E
Riddarhyttan	40	59.48 N	15.33 E
Ridderkerk	52	51.52 N	4.36 E
Riddes	58	46.10 N	7.13 E
Riddle	202	42.57 N	123.22 W
Riddle Mountain ∧	202	43.07 N	118.30 W
Riddlesburg	214	40.10 N	78.15 W
Riddlewood	285	39.54 N	75.26 W
Riddon, Loch C	46	55.58 N	5.12 W
Rideau ≃	212	45.27 N	75.42 W
Ridge, Eng., U.K.	260	51.41 N	0.15 W
Ridge, N.Y., U.S.	207	40.54 N	72.53 W
Ridge, Tex., U.S.	222	31.09 N	96.19 W
Ridge Acres	276	40.41 N	74.32 W
Ridgecrest, Calif., U.S.	204	35.38 N	117.36 W
Ridgecrest, Wash., U.S.	224	47.45 N	122.21 W
Ridgedale	184	53.04 N	104.09 W
Ridge Farm	194	39.54 N	87.39 W
Ridgefield, Conn., U.S.	207	41.17 N	73.30 W
Ridgefield, Ill., U.S.	216	42.16 N	88.22 W
Ridgefield, N.J., U.S.	210	40.50 N	74.00 W
Ridgefield, Wash., U.S.	224	45.49 N	122.45 W
Ridgefield Park	276	40.51 N	74.01 W
Ridgeland	192	32.29 N	80.59 W
Ridgely	194	36.16 N	89.29 W
Ridge Manor	220	28.31 N	82.10 W
Ridgemont	210	43.13 N	77.43 W
Ridgetown	214	42.26 N	81.54 W
Ridgeville, Man., Can.	184	49.04 N	97.01 W
Ridgeville, Ind., U.S.	216	40.18 N	85.02 W
Ridgeville, Md., U.S.	208	39.22 N	77.10 W
Ridgeville, S.C., U.S.	192	33.06 N	80.19 W
Ridgeville Corners	216	41.26 N	84.16 W
Ridgeway, Mich., U.S.	216	41.59 N	83.52 W
Ridgeway, Mo., U.S.	194	40.23 N	93.56 W
Ridgeway, N.J., U.S.	208	40.02 N	74.17 W
Ridgeway, Ohio, U.S.	216	40.31 N	83.34 W
Ridgeway, Tex., U.S.	222	33.11 N	95.46 W
Ridgeway, Wis., U.S.	190	43.01 N	90.01 W
Ridgeway Ditch ≋	279a	41.25 N	82.05 W
Ridgewood, Ill., U.S.	278	41.48 N	87.54 W
Ridgewood, N.J., U.S.	210	40.59 N	74.07 W
Ridgewood ◂[8]	276	40.42 N	73.53 W
Ridgewood Reservoir ⊜[1]	276	40.41 N	73.53 W
Ridgway, Colo., U.S.	200	38.09 N	107.46 W
Ridgway, Ill., U.S.	194	37.48 N	88.16 W
Ridgway, Pa., U.S.	214	41.26 N	78.44 W
Riding Mountain ∧	184	50.37 N	99.37 W
Riding Mountain National Park ♠	184	50.55 N	100.25 W
Ridley Creek ≃	285	39.51 N	75.21 W
Ridley Park	285	39.53 N	75.19 W
Ridnaun → Ridanna	64	46.55 N	11.15 E
Ridotta Capuzzo	146	31.35 N	25.03 E
Riebeek-Kasteel	158	33.23 S	18.53 E
Riebeek-Oos	158	33.10 S	26.10 E
Riebeek-Wes	158	33.21 S	18.52 E
Riecawr, Loch ⊜	44	55.13 N	4.27 W
Riedau	60	48.18 N	13.38 E
Riedelbach	56	50.18 N	8.23 E
Rieden	60	49.19 N	11.57 E
Riedenburg	60	48.58 N	11.41 E
Rieder	54	51.44 N	11.10 E
Riederalp	58	46.23 N	8.01 E
Riedern	56	49.40 N	9.23 E
Ried im Innkreis	60	48.13 N	13.30 E
Ried im Oberinntal	58	47.03 N	10.39 E
Riedisheim	58	47.45 N	7.22 E
Riedlingen	58	48.09 N	9.28 E
Riegel	58	48.09 N	7.45 E
Riegelsville, N.J., U.S.	210	40.36 N	75.11 W
Riegelsville, Pa., U.S.	208	40.36 N	75.12 W
Riegersburg, Schloss ⊥	61	47.01 N	15.56 E
Riegersdorf	64	46.33 N	13.47 E
Riehen	58	47.35 N	7.39 E
Rieka → Rijeka	36	45.20 N	14.27 E
Rielasingen	58	47.44 N	8.50 E
Riemke ◂[8]	263	51.30 N	7.13 E
Riemst	56	50.48 N	5.36 E
Rieneck	56	50.05 N	9.38 E
Rienza (Rienz) ≃	64	46.43 N	11.39 E
Rienzi	194	34.46 N	88.38 W
Riesa	54	51.18 N	13.17 E
Riesco, Isla I	254	53.00 S	72.30 W
Rieseby	41	54.32 N	9.48 E
Riesel	222	31.28 N	96.56 W
Riesenbeck	52	52.16 N	7.37 E
Riesenburg → Prabuty	30	53.46 N	19.10 E
Riese Pio X	64	45.44 N	11.55 E
Riesi	70	37.17 N	14.05 E
Riestedt	54	51.29 N	11.21 E
Riet ≃	158	29.00 S	23.54 E
Rietavas	76	55.44 N	21.56 E
Rietberg	52	51.47 N	8.25 E
Rietbron	158	32.54 S	23.10 E
Rietfontein, Namibia	156	21.58 S	20.58 E
Rietfontein, S. Afr.	158	26.44 S	20.01 E
Riethuiskraal	158	34.20 S	21.22 E
Rieti	66	42.24 N	12.51 E
Rieti □[4]	66	42.18 N	12.52 E
Rietschen	54	51.23 N	14.47 E
Rietspruit ≃	273d	26.06 S	27.39 E
Rietvlei	158	30.29 S	29.51 E
Rietzer See ⊜	54	52.22 N	12.39 E
Riez	62	43.49 N	6.06 E
Riezlern	58	47.21 N	10.11 E
Rif ⩘	148	35.00 N	4.00 W
Rifflart	273b	4.25 S	15.21 E
Rifiano (Riffian)	64	46.42 N	11.11 E
Rifle	200	39.32 N	107.47 W
Rifle ≃	190	44.00 N	83.45 W
Rifstangi ≻	24a	66.35 N	16.10 W
Rifton	210	41.50 N	74.03 W
Rift Valley □[4]	154	0.30 N	36.00 E
Rift Valley ∨	10	3.00 S	29.00 E
Rīga, S.S.S.R.	76	56.57 N	24.06 E
Riga, S.S.S.R.	88	56.36 N	106.17 E
Riga, Mich., U.S.	216	41.49 N	83.50 W
Riga, Gulf of → Rižskij Zaliv C	76	57.30 N	23.35 E
Riga, Mount ∧	162	21.59 S	116.25 E
Rigacikun	150	10.40 N	7.28 E
Rigaih	114	4.40 N	95.34 E
Rīgān	128	28.37 N	58.58 E
Rīgas Jūras Līcis → Rižskij Zaliv C	76	57.30 N	23.35 E
Rigaud	206	45.29 N	74.18 W
Rigaud ≃	206	45.29 N	74.18 W
Rigby	202	43.40 N	111.55 W
Rīgestān ◂[1]	128	31.00 N	65.00 E
Riggins	202	45.25 N	116.19 W
Riggisberg	58	46.48 N	7.29 E
Riggston	219	39.42 N	90.25 W
Righedo, Passo del)(	64	44.27 N	9.55 E
Rigi ∧	58	47.05 N	8.30 E
Rignano Flaminio	66	42.12 N	12.29 E
Rignano Garganico	68	41.40 N	15.35 E
Rignano sull'Arno	66	43.43 N	11.27 E
Rigney	58	47.23 N	6.11 E
Rigney Bluff	210	43.19 N	77.38 W
Rigny-Ussé	50	47.15 N	0.18 E
Rigo	164	9.47 S	147.34 E
Rigolet	176	54.20 N	58.35 W
Rig-Rig	146	14.16 N	14.21 E
Riguldi	76	59.08 N	23.33 E
Rīḥ, Jazīrat ar- I	140	18.10 N	38.27 E
Riḥāb	132	32.19 N	36.06 E
Rihand ≃	124	24.33 N	82.59 E
Rihand Dam ◂[6]	124	24.05 N	82.45 E
Rihand Reservoir ◂[6]	120	24.05 N	82.45 E
Riihimäki	26	60.45 N	24.46 E
Riiser-Larsen Peninsula ≻[1]	9	68.55 S	34.00 E
Rijau	150	11.07 N	5.14 E
Riječki Zaljev C	36	45.15 N	14.25 E
Rijeka	36	45.20 N	14.27 E
Rijen	52	51.35 N	4.55 E
Rijkevorsel	56	51.21 N	4.46 E
Rijksdorp	52	52.09 N	4.25 E
Rijn → Rhine ≃	30	51.52 N	6.02 E
Rijnsburg	52	52.12 N	4.27 E
Rijssel → Lille	50	50.38 N	3.04 E
Rijssen	52	52.18 N	6.30 E
Rijswijk	52	52.04 N	4.20 E
Rikaze	120	29.17 N	88.53 E
Rike	144	10.42 N	39.55 E
Rikers Island I	276	40.47 N	73.53 W
Rikers Island Channel Ц	276	40.47 N	73.52 W
Rikkavesi ⊜	26	62.50 N	28.44 E
Riksgränsen	24	68.24 N	18.12 E
Rikuchūkaigan-kokuritsu-kōen ♠	92	39.25 N	141.57 E
Rikujō-jieitai-asahikawa-chūtonchi ■	92a	43.49 N	142.25 E
Rikujō-jieitai-chitose-chūtonchi ■	92a	42.46 N	141.40 E
Rikujō-jieitai-fukuoka-chūtonchi ■	96	33.32 N	130.28 E
Rikujō-jieitai-kaitaichi-chūtonchi ■	96	34.21 N	132.32 E
Rikujō-jieitai-kengun-chūtonchi ■	92	32.46 N	130.45 E
Rikujō-jieitai-sōmahara-chūtonchi ■	94	36.23 N	139.58 E
Rikuzen-takata	92	39.01 N	141.38 E
Rila ⩘	38	42.08 N	23.33 E
Riley	198	39.18 N	96.50 W
Riley Creek ≃	216	41.02 N	84.00 W
Riley Lake ⊜	212	44.50 N	79.11 W
Rileys Range ⩘	170	34.21 S	150.10 E
Rilievo	70	37.55 N	12.33 E
Rillieux	62	45.49 N	4.54 E
Rillington	44	54.09 N	0.42 W
Rillito	200	32.25 N	111.09 W
Rillton	214	40.17 N	79.44 W
Rilly-la-Montagne	50	49.10 N	4.03 E
Rilski manastir ♥[1]	38	42.08 N	23.20 E
Rima ≃	150	13.04 N	5.10 E
Rímac	286d	12.03 S	77.03 W
Rímac ≃	248	12.02 S	77.09 W
Rímachi, Lago ⊜	246	4.25 S	76.43 W
Rimāḥ, Jabal ar- ∧	132	32.19 N	36.52 E
Rima San Giuseppe	62	45.52 N	8.00 E
Rimatara I	14	22.38 S	152.51 W
Rimavská Sobota	30	48.23 N	20.02 E
Rimbey	182	52.38 N	114.14 W
Rimbo	40	59.45 N	18.22 E
Rimé, Ouadi ∨	146	14.02 N	18.03 E
Rimersburg	214	41.02 N	79.30 W
Rimforsa	26	58.08 N	15.40 E
Rimi	150	12.58 N	7.43 E
Rimini	66	44.04 N	12.34 E
Rîmna ≃	38	45.39 N	27.19 E
Rîmnicu-Sărat	38	45.23 N	27.03 E
Rîmnicu-Vîlcea	38	45.06 N	24.22 E
Rimo Glacier ⊓	123	35.25 N	77.30 E
Rimogne	56	49.50 N	4.33 E
Rimouski	186	48.26 N	68.33 W
Rimouski ≃	186	48.27 N	68.32 W
Rimouski, Parc de ♠	186	48.07 N	68.10 W
Rimpar	56	49.51 N	9.57 E
Rimrock Lake ⊜[1]	224	46.38 N	121.12 W
Rimsko-Korsakovka	80	51.34 N	48.31 E
Rin → Rhine ≃	30	51.52 N	6.02 E
Rinca	115b	8.37 S	119.48 E
Rinca, Pulau I	115b	8.41 S	119.42 E
Rinchnach	60	48.57 N	13.12 E
Rinčinlchümbe	88	51.07 N	99.40 E
Rincón, C.R.	236	8.42 N	83.29 W
Rincon, Ned. Ant.	241s	12.15 N	68.20 W
Rincón, P.R.	240m	18.20 N	67.15 W
Rincon, Ga., U.S.	192	32.18 N	81.14 W
Rincon, N. Mex., U.S.	200	32.40 N	107.04 W
Rincón, Bahía de C	240m	17.58 N	66.20 W
Rinconada, Arg.	252	22.26 S	66.10 W
Rinconada, Méx.	196	25.42 N	100.43 W
Rinconada, Hipódromo de la ♠	286c	10.26 N	66.56 W
Rincón del Bonete, Lago Artificial ⊜[1]	252	32.45 S	56.00 W
Rincón del Ocote, Cerro ∧	236	13.36 N	87.10 W
Rincón de Romos	234	22.14 N	102.18 W
Rincón de Tamayo	234	20.25 N	100.45 W
Rincon Indian Reservation ◂[4]	228	33.15 N	116.57 W
Rincon Valley	226	38.28 N	122.39 W
Rindal	26	63.03 N	9.13 E
Rindown Castle ⊥	48	53.32 N	7.59 W
Ringe	41	55.14 N	10.29 E
Ringebu	26	61.31 N	10.10 E
Ringenwalde	54	53.03 N	13.42 E
Ringertown	279b	40.25 N	79.36 W
Ringford	44	54.54 N	4.03 W
Ringgau ◂[1]	56	51.04 N	10.04 E
Ringgit, Gunung ∧	115a	7.43 S	113.50 E
Ringgold, Ga., U.S.	192	34.55 N	85.07 W
Ringgold, La., U.S.	194	32.20 N	93.17 W
Ringgold, Pa., U.S.	214	41.00 N	79.10 W
Ringgold Isles II	175g	16.15 S	179.25 W
Ringim	150	12.08 N	9.10 E
Ringkøbing	26	56.05 N	8.15 E
Ringkøbing □[6]	41	56.10 N	8.50 E
Ringkøbing Fjord C[2]	26	56.00 N	8.15 E
Ringlet	114	4.25 N	101.23 E
Ringling	196	34.10 N	97.36 W
Ringling Museums ♥	220	27.23 N	82.34 W
Ringmer	42	50.53 N	0.04 E
Ringoes	208	40.26 N	74.52 W
Rings Island	283	42.49 N	70.52 W
Ringsjön ⊜	41	55.52 N	13.32 E
Ringsted, Dan.	41	55.27 N	11.49 E
Ringsted, Iowa, U.S.	198	43.18 N	94.31 W
Ringtown	210	40.51 N	76.14 W
Rīngus	120	27.21 N	75.34 E
Ringvassøya I	24	69.55 N	19.15 E
Ringville	48	52.02 N	7.34 W
Ringwood, Austl.	169	37.49 S	145.14 E
Ringwood, Eng., U.K.	42	50.51 N	1.47 W
Ringwood, N.J., U.S.	210	41.08 N	74.16 W
Ringwood Manor ⊥	276	41.08 N	74.15 W
Ringwood North	274b	37.48 S	145.14 E
Ringwood State Park ♠	210	41.08 N	74.16 W
Riñihue	254	39.49 S	72.27 W
Riñihue, Lago ⊜	254	39.50 S	72.18 W
Rinjani, Gunung ∧	115b	8.24 S	116.28 E
Rinkenæs	41	54.54 N	9.34 E
Rinkerode	52	51.50 N	7.41 E
Rinnes, Ben ∧	46	57.23 N	3.15 W
Rinns of Islay ⩘	46	55.45 N	6.25 W
Rinns Point ≻	46	55.41 N	6.30 W
Rinnthal	56	49.13 N	7.55 E

ENGLISH

Name	Page	Lat.°′	Long.°′
Rinsumageest	52	53.18 N	5.57 E
Rinteln	52	52.11 N	9.04 E
Rinxent	50	50.48 N	1.44 E
Rio, Fla., U.S.	220	27.15 N	80.14 W
Rio, Wis., U.S.	190	43.27 N	89.14 W
Rio Azul	252	25.43 S	50.47 W
Río Balsas	234	17.59 N	99.47 W
Riobamba	246	1.40 S	78.38 W
Río Benito	152	1.35 N	9.37 E
Río Blanco, Chile	252	32.55 S	70.19 W
Río Blanco (Tenango de Rio Blanco), Méx.	234	18.50 N	97.09 W
Rio Bonito	256	22.43 S	42.37 W
Rio Bonito ◂[8]	287b	23.43 S	46.41 W
Rio Branco, Bra.	248	9.58 S	67.48 W
Río Branco, Ur.	252	32.34 S	53.25 W
Río Bravo, Méx.	196	28.17 N	100.55 W
Río Bravo, Méx.	232	25.59 N	98.06 W
Rio Brilhante	255	21.48 S	54.33 W
Río Bueno	254	40.19 S	72.58 W
Río Caribe	246	10.42 N	63.07 W
Rio Casca	255	20.13 S	42.39 W
Río Cauto	240p	20.33 N	76.55 W
Río Ceballos	252	31.10 S	64.20 W
Río Chico	254	41.43 S	70.30 W
Rio Claro, Bra.	255	22.24 S	47.33 W
Rio Claro, Bra.	256	22.43 S	44.09 W
Rio Claro, Trin.	241r	10.18 N	61.11 W
Rio Claro, Représa do ⊜[1]	256	23.39 S	45.54 W
Río Colorado	252	39.01 S	64.05 W
Rio Comprido ◂[8]	287a	22.55 S	43.12 W
Río Cuarto	252	33.08 S	64.21 W
Rio da Conceição	250	11.24 S	46.54 W
Rio das Antas	252	26.55 S	51.04 W
Rio das Flores	256	22.10 S	43.35 W
Rio das Pedras	156	23.12 S	35.23 E
Rio de Contas	255	13.36 S	41.48 W
Rio de Janeiro	256		
	287a	22.54 S	43.14 W
Rio de Janeiro □[3]	255	22.00 S	42.30 W
Rio de Janeiro □[7]	287a	22.55 S	43.30 W
Río de Jesús	236	7.59 N	81.10 W
Río de las Playas	234	17.51 N	94.02 W
Rio Dell	204	40.30 N	124.07 W
Rio-del-Rey C[1]	152	4.31 N	8.45 E
Rio de Mouro	266c	38.46 N	9.20 W
Río de Oro	246	8.17 N	73.23 W
Río de Oro, Bahía de C	148	23.45 N	15.47 W
Rio d'Oeste	252	27.12 S	49.48 W
Rio do Ouro	256	22.51 S	42.59 W
Rio do Prado	255	16.35 S	40.34 W
Rio do Sul	252	27.13 S	49.39 W
Rio d'Ouro	287a	22.39 S	43.32 W
Rio Espera	255	20.51 S	43.29 W
Rio Fortuna	252	28.06 S	49.07 W
Río Gallegos	254	51.38 S	69.13 W
Río Grande, Arg.	254	53.47 S	67.42 W
Rio Grande, Bra.	252	32.02 S	52.05 W
Río Grande, Méx.	234	23.50 N	103.02 W
Río Grande, Méx.	234	15.59 N	97.27 W
Río Grande, Pan.	236	8.37 N	81.17 W
Río Grande, P.R.	240m	18.23 N	65.50 W
Rio Grande, N.J., U.S.	208	39.01 N	74.53 W
Río Grande, Ven.	286c	10.35 N	66.57 W
Rio Grande, Barragem do ◂[6]	287b	23.42 S	46.40 W
Rio Grande, Ponte do ◂[5]	287b	23.46 S	46.31 W
Rio Grande, Reservatório do ⊜[1]	256	23.47 S	46.37 W
Rio Grande City	196	26.23 N	98.49 W
Rio Grande da Serra □[7]	287b	23.45 S	46.23 W
Rio Grande do Norte □[3]	250	5.45 S	36.00 W
Rio Grande do Sul → Rio Grande	252	32.02 S	52.05 W
Rio Grande do Sul □[3]	252	30.00 S	54.00 W
Riograndina	256	22.11 S	42.30 W
Ríohacha	246	11.33 N	72.55 W
Río Hato	236	8.23 N	80.10 W
Río Hondo, Méx.	286a	19.25 N	99.16 W
Rio Hondo, Tex., U.S.	196	26.14 N	97.35 W
Rioja	248	6.05 S	77.09 W
Río Jueyes	240m	18.01 N	66.20 W
Riola	64	44.16 N	11.04 E
Río Lagartos	232	21.36 N	88.10 W
Riolândia	255	19.59 S	49.40 W
Rio Largo	250	9.29 S	35.51 W
Riola Sardo	71	39.59 N	8.32 E
Rio Linda	226	38.41 N	121.27 W
Riolo Terme	66	44.16 N	11.43 E
Río Luján	258	34.17 S	58.54 W
Riom	32	45.54 N	3.07 E
Riomaggiore	62	44.06 N	9.44 E
Rio Marina	66	42.49 N	10.25 E
Río Mayo	254	45.41 S	70.16 W
Río Mulatos	248	19.42 S	66.47 W
Río Muni □[4]	152	1.30 N	10.30 E
Rional Reef ✣[2]	14	17.00 N	177.50 E
Riondel	182	49.46 N	116.52 W
Rio Negrinho	252	26.15 S	49.31 W
Rio Negro, Bra.	252	26.06 S	49.48 W
Rio Negro, Bra.	255	19.27 S	54.58 W
Río Negro, Chile	254	40.47 S	73.14 W
Rionegro, Col.	246	6.09 N	75.22 W
Rionegro, Col.	246	7.16 N	73.09 W
Río Negro □[4]	254	40.00 S	67.00 W
Rio Negro, Pantanal do ☷	248	19.00 S	56.00 W
Rionero in Vulture	68	40.56 N	15.41 E
Rionero Sannitico	66	41.42 N	14.08 E
Rioni ≃	84	42.08 N	41.39 E
Rio Novo	256	21.29 S	43.08 W
Rio Novo do Sul	255	20.52 S	40.56 W
Riópar	34	38.30 N	2.27 W
Rio Pardo	252	29.59 S	52.22 W
Rio Pardo de Minas	255	15.37 S	42.33 W
Rio Pequeno, Reservatório do ⊜[1]	287b	23.46 S	46.30 W
Río Pico	254	44.13 S	71.21 W
Río Piedras, Arg.	252	25.18 S	64.54 W
Río Piedras, P.R.	240m	18.24 N	66.03 W
Río Pilcomayo, Parque Nacional ♠	252	25.10 S	58.00 W
Rio Piracicaba	255	19.55 S	43.11 W
Rio Pomba	256	21.17 S	43.11 W
Rio Prêto, Bra.	256	22.06 S	43.50 W
Rio Prêto, Bra.	256	22.48 S	45.46 W
Rio Prêto → São José do Rio Prêto, Bra.	256	22.10 S	42.57 W
Rio Real	250	11.28 S	37.56 W
Rio Saliceto	64	44.49 N	10.49 E
Río San Juan □[5]	236	11.10 N	84.30 W
Rio Sêco	256	22.46 S	42.40 W
Río Segundo	252	31.40 S	63.55 W
Rio Sorocaba, Représa do ⊜[1]	256	23.37 S	47.16 W
Río Sucio, Col.	246	5.25 N	75.42 W
Ríosucio, Col.	246	7.27 N	77.07 W
Río Tercero	252	32.11 S	64.06 W
Rio Tinto	250	6.48 S	35.05 W
Riotord	62	45.14 N	4.24 E
Rio Tuba	116	8.30 N	117.25 E
Riou, Île de I	62	43.11 N	5.24 E
Rioveggio	64	44.17 N	11.14 E
Rio Verde, Bra.	255	17.43 S	50.56 W
Ríoverde, Méx.	234	21.56 N	99.59 W
Rio Verde de Mato Grosso	255	18.56 S	54.52 W
Rio Vermelho	255	18.18 S	43.00 W
Rio Vista, Calif., U.S.	226	38.10 N	121.42 W
Rio Vista, Tex., U.S.	222	32.14 N	97.23 W

DEUTSCH

Name	Seite	Breite°′	Länge°′ E=Ost
Rioz	58	47.25 N	6.04 E
Riozinho ≃, Bra.	246	2.55 S	67.07 W
Riozinho ≃, Bra.	250	8.25 S	45.43 W
Riozinho ≃, Bra.	250	10.22 S	49.50 W
Říp ∧	54	50.24 N	14.18 E
Ripacandida	68	40.55 N	15.43 E
Ripalti, Punta dei ≻	66	42.42 N	10.25 E
Ripatransone	66	43.00 N	13.46 E
Ripley, Eng., U.K.	42	53.03 N	1.24 W
Ripley, Eng., U.K.	260	51.18 N	0.29 W
Ripley, Ill., U.S.	219	40.01 N	90.38 W
Ripley, Ind., U.S.	216	41.06 N	86.39 W
Ripley, Miss., U.S.	194	34.44 N	88.57 W
Ripley, N.Y., U.S.	214	42.16 N	79.43 W
Ripley, Ohio, U.S.	218	38.45 N	83.51 W
Ripley, Tenn., U.S.	194	35.45 N	89.32 W
Ripley, W. Va., U.S.	188	38.49 N	81.43 W
Ripley □[6]	218	39.04 N	85.15 W
Ripoll	34	42.12 N	2.12 E
Ripoll ≃	266d	41.29 N	2.12 E
Ripollet	266d	41.30 N	2.10 E
Ripon, Qué., Can.	206	45.47 N	75.06 W
Ripon, Eng., U.K.	44	54.08 N	1.31 W
Ripon, Calif., U.S.	226	37.44 N	121.07 W
Ripon, Wis., U.S.	190	43.51 N	88.50 W
Riposto	70	37.44 N	15.12 E
Rippling Ridge	284b	39.11 N	76.37 W
Ripponden	44	53.41 N	1.57 W
Rippowam ≃	276	41.03 N	73.33 W
Riquewihr	58	48.10 N	7.18 E
Ririba, Laga ≃	154	3.34 N	37.15 E
Riri Bāzār	124	27.57 N	83.26 E
Ririe	202	43.38 N	111.46 W
Risālpur Cantonment	123	34.04 N	72.00 E
Risaralda □[5]	246	5.00 N	76.00 W
Risasi	154	0.25 S	25.44 E
Risbäck	26	64.42 N	15.32 E
Risca	42	51.37 N	3.07 W
Rischenau	52	51.53 N	9.17 E
Risción, Punta de la ≻	232	25.10 N	108.22 W
Riscle	32	43.40 N	0.05 W
Rī Shahr	128	28.55 N	50.50 E
Rishīkesh	124	30.07 N	78.42 E
Rishiri-suidō Ц	92a	45.10 N	141.25 E
Rishiri-tō I	92a	45.11 N	141.15 E
Rishiri-zan ∧	92a	45.11 N	141.15 E
Rishmayyā	132	33.44 N	35.36 E
Rishon leẔiyyon	132	31.58 N	34.48 E
Rishpon	132	32.12 N	34.49 E
Rishra	272b	22.43 N	88.21 E
Rishrāsh, Wādī ∨	142	29.29 N	31.16 E
Rishton	262	53.46 N	2.25 W
Rishworth	262	53.40 N	1.57 W
Rishworth Moor ◂[3]	262	53.39 N	2.01 W
Risinge	40	58.42 N	15.51 E
Rising Star	196	32.06 N	98.58 W
Rising Sun, Ind., U.S.	218	38.57 N	84.51 W
Rising Sun, Md., U.S.	188	39.42 N	76.04 W
Risingsun, Ohio, U.S.	214	41.16 N	83.25 W
Risle ≃	50	49.26 N	0.23 E
Risnjak ∧	36	45.26 N	14.37 E
Rîşnov	38	45.36 N	25.28 E
Risø	41	55.42 N	12.06 E
Rison, Ark., U.S.	194	33.58 N	92.11 W
Rison, Md., U.S.	208	38.33 N	77.11 W
Risør	26	58.43 N	9.14 E
Ris-Orangis	50	48.39 N	2.25 E
Riss ≃	58	48.17 N	9.49 E
Rissani	148	31.23 N	4.09 W
Risskov ◂[8]	41	56.11 N	10.14 E
Risstissen	58	48.16 N	9.49 E
Rişşū, Jabal ∧[2]	142	29.53 N	30.25 E
Risti	76	58.59 N	24.03 E
Ristiina	26	61.30 N	27.16 E
Ristijärvi	26	64.44 N	28.24 E
Ristinge	41	54.50 N	10.38 E
Ristna	76	58.56 N	22.05 E
Risum-lindholm	41	54.45 N	8.53 E
Rita Blanca Creek ≃	196	35.40 N	102.29 W
Ritchie, S. Afr.	158	29.02 S	24.38 E
Ritchie, Md., U.S.	284c	38.52 N	76.52 W
Ritchie Branch ≃	284c	38.53 N	76.52 W
Rithāla ◂[8]	272a	28.43 N	77.06 E
Ritidian Point ≻	174p	13.39 N	144.51 E
Ritscher Upland ⩘[1]	9	73.20 S	9.30 W
Ritsumeikan University ♥[2]	270	35.01 N	135.46 E
Ritsurin-kōen ♠	96	34.21 N	134.02 E
Ritta Island I	220	26.44 N	80.48 W
Ritter, Mount ∧	226	37.42 N	119.12 W
Ritterhude	52	53.11 N	8.45 E
Rittersgrün	54	50.29 N	12.47 E
Rittman	214	40.58 N	81.47 W
Rittō	94	35.01 N	136.00 E
Ritzleben	54	52.50 N	11.21 E
Ritzville	202	47.08 N	118.23 W
Riu	120	28.19 N	95.03 E
Riva, It.	64	45.53 N	10.50 E
Riva, Md., U.S.	208	38.57 N	76.35 W
Rivadavia, Arg.	252	31.33 S	68.37 W
Rivadavia, Arg.	252	33.11 S	68.28 W
Rivadavia, Arg.	252	35.28 S	62.57 W
Rivadavia, Arg.	252	24.11 S	62.53 W
Rivadavia, Chile	252	29.58 S	70.34 W
Riva del Sole	66	42.46 N	10.52 E
Riva Deresi ≃	267b	41.14 N	29.12 E
Riva di Tures (Rain)	64	46.57 N	12.04 E
Rivaköy	267b	41.13 N	29.12 E
Rivanazzano	62	44.56 N	9.01 E
Rivanna ≃	192	37.45 N	78.10 W
Rivare	216	40.49 N	84.50 W
Rivarolo Canavese	62	45.19 N	7.43 E
Rivarolo Mantovano	64	45.04 N	10.26 E
Rivas	236	11.26 N	85.50 W
Rivas □[5]	236	11.25 N	85.50 W
Rivasdale	273d	26.17 S	27.56 E
Rīvash	128	35.26 N	58.26 E
Rivas-Vaciamadrid	266a	40.20 N	3.31 W
Riva Trigoso	62	44.16 N	9.26 E
Rive, Île de la I	273b	4.21 S	15.26 E
Rive d'Arcano	64	46.08 N	13.02 E
Rive-de-Gier	62	45.32 N	4.37 E
Rivello	68	40.04 N	15.45 E
Rivera, Arg.	252	37.12 S	63.14 W
Rivera, Col.	246	2.47 N	75.15 W
Rivera, Ur.	252	30.54 S	55.31 W
Riverbank	226	37.44 N	120.56 W
River Cess	150	5.28 N	9.32 W
Riverdale, Calif., U.S.	226	36.26 N	119.52 W
Riverdale, Ill., U.S.	278	41.38 N	87.38 W
Riverdale, Md., U.S.	284c	38.58 N	76.55 W
Riverdale, N.J., U.S.	276	40.59 N	74.32 W
Riverdale, N. Dak., U.S.	198	47.30 N	101.22 W
Riverdale, Oreg., U.S.	224	45.27 N	122.41 W
Riverdale ◂[8]	276	40.54 N	73.54 W
Riverdale Park ♠	275b	43.40 N	79.21 W
River Drive Park	212	44.08 N	79.31 W
River Edge, N.J., U.S.	276	40.56 N	74.02 W
River Edge, Ohio, U.S.	279a	41.25 N	81.51 W
River Falls, Ala., U.S.	194	31.21 N	86.33 W
River Falls, Wis., U.S.	190	44.52 N	92.38 W
River Forest	278	41.53 N	87.49 W
Rivergaro	62	44.55 N	9.36 E
River Grove	278	41.56 N	87.50 W
River Haven	216	41.05 N	85.02 W
Riverhead, Eng., U.K.	260	51.17 N	0.10 E
Riverhead, N.Y., U.S.	207	40.55 N	72.40 W
River Hébert	186	45.42 N	64.23 W
River Hill	279b	40.12 N	79.54 W
River Hills	216	43.12 N	87.57 W
Riverhurst	184	50.53 N	106.52 W
Riverina ◂[1]	166	35.30 S	145.30 E
River John	186	45.45 N	63.03 W
River Jordan	182	48.25 N	124.03 W
Riverlea	214	40.05 N	83.02 W

Symbols in the index entries represent the broad categories identified in the key at the right. Symbols with superior numbers (⩘[2]) identify subcategories (see complete key on page *I · 30*).

Kartensymbole in dem Registerverzeichnis stellen die rechts in Schlüssel erklärten Kategorien dar. Symbole mit hochgestellten Ziffern (⩘[2]) bezeichnen Unterabteilungen einer Kategorie (vgl. vollständiger Schlüssel auf Seite *I · 30*).

Los símbolos incluídos en el texto del índice representan las grandes categorias identificadas con la clave a la derecha. Los símbolos con numeros en su parte superior (⩘[2]) identifican las subcategorías (véase la clave completa en la página *I · 30*).

Les symboles de l'index représentent les catégories indiquées dans la légende à droite. Les symboles suivis d'un indice (⩘[2]) représentent des sous-catégories (voir légende complète à la page *I · 30*).

Os símbolos incluídos no texto do índice representam as grandes categorias identificadas com a chave à direita. Os símbolos com números em sua parte superior (⩘[2]) identificam as subcategorias (veja-se a chave completa à página *I · 30*).

	English	Deutsch	Español	Français	Português
∧	Mountain	Berg	Montaña	Montagne	Montanha
⩘	Mountains	Berge	Montañas	Montagnes	Montanhas
)(	Pass	Pass	Paso	Col	Passo
∨	Valley, Canyon	Tal, Cañon	Valle, Cañón	Vallée, Canyon	Vale, Canhão
═	Plain	Ebene	Llano	Plaine	Planície
≻	Cape	Kap	Cabo	Cap	Cabo
I	Island	Insel	Isla	Île	Ilha
II	Islands	Inseln	Islas	Îles	Ilhas
♦	Other Topographic Features	Andere Topographische Objekte	Otros Elementos Topográficos	Autres données topographiques	Outros Elementos Topográficos

ESPAÑOL — Nombre / Página / Lat.°′ / Long.°′ W=Oeste
FRANÇAIS — Nom / Page / Lat.°′ / Long.°′ W=Ouest
PORTUGUÊS — Nome / Página / Lat.°′ / Long.°′ W=Oeste

River Lea Navigation ≍ 260 51.32 N 0.02 W
River Meadow Brook ≃ 283 42.38 N 71.17 W
Rivero, Isla I 254 45.37 S 74.20 W
River of Ponds 186 50.32 N 57.24 W
River Pines, Calif., U.S. 226 38.33 N 120.45 W
River Pines, Mass., U.S. 207 42.34 N 71.17 W
River Plaza 208 40.21 N 74.05 W
River Road 202 44.03 N 123.05 W
River Rouge 216 42.16 N 83.08 W
River Rouge Park ♠ 281 42.22 N 83.15 W
Rivers 184 50.02 N 100.12 W
Rivers □[3] 150 4.30 N 6.30 E
Rivers, Lake of the ⊜ 184 49.45 N 105.45 W
Riversdale, N.Z. 172 45.54 S 168.45 E
Riversdale, S. Afr. 158 34.07 S 21.15 E
Riverside, Calif., U.S. 228 33.59 N 117.22 W
Riverside, Conn., U.S. 276 41.02 N 73.35 W
Riverside, Ill., U.S. 278 41.50 N 87.49 W
Riverside, Iowa, U.S. 190 41.29 N 91.35 W
Riverside, Mich., U.S. 216 42.17 N 84.29 W
Riverside, Mich., U.S. 216 42.11 N 86.23 W
Riverside, N.J., U.S. 208 40.02 N 74.58 W
Riverside, N.Y., U.S. 210 42.55 N 73.40 W
Riverside, N.Y., U.S. 210 42.08 N 77.01 W
Riverside, Pa., U.S. 210 40.57 N 76.38 W
Riverside, Tex., U.S. 222 30.57 N 95.24 W
Riverside □[6] 228 33.45 N 117.10 W
Riverside ⬥[8] 281 42.20 N 82.57 W
Riverside International Raceway ♠ 228 33.57 N 117.17 W
Riverside Park ♠, Mich., U.S. 281 42.22 N 83.26 W
Riverside Park ♠, N.Y., U.S. 284a 42.57 N 78.54 W
Rivers Inlet 182 51.41 N 127.15 W
Rivers Inlet C 182 51.39 N 127.30 W
Riversleigh 166 19.02 S 138.44 E
Riverstone 170 33.40 S 150.52 E
Riverton, Austl. 168b 34.09 S 138.45 E
Riverton, Man., Can. 184 50.59 N 96.59 W
Riverton, N.Z. 172 46.21 S 168.01 E
Riverton, Ill., U.S. 219 39.51 N 89.33 W
Riverton, Nebr., U.S. 198 40.05 N 98.46 W
Riverton, N.J., U.S. 208 40.01 N 75.01 W
Riverton, Utah, U.S. 200 40.31 N 111.56 W
Riverton, Va., U.S. 188 38.57 N 78.12 W
Riverton, Wyo., U.S. 200 43.02 N 108.23 W
Riverton Heights 224 47.28 N 122.17 W
River Vale 276 40.59 N 74.01 W
River View, S. Afr. 158 28.27 S 32.10 E
River View, Ala., U.S. 194 32.47 N 85.09 W
Riverview, Fla., U.S. 220 27.52 N 82.20 W
Riverview, Mich., U.S. 216 42.11 N 83.10 W
Riverview Park ♠ 279b 40.29 N 80.01 W
Riverwood, Austl. 274a 33.57 S 151.03 E
Riverwood, Ind., U.S. 218 40.06 N 85.58 W
Riverwoods 278 42.10 N 87.54 W
Rives, Fr. 62 45.21 N 5.30 E
Rives, Tenn., U.S. 194 36.21 N 89.04 W
Rivesaltes 32 42.46 N 2.52 E
Rives Junction 216 42.23 N 84.28 W
Rive Sud, Canal de la ≍ 275a 45.25 N 73.41 W
Rivesville 188 39.32 N 80.07 W
Riviera, Ariz., U.S. 204 35.04 N 114.35 W
Riviera, Tex., U.S. 196 27.18 N 97.49 W
Riviera ∨ 58 46.15 N 8.58 E
Riviera Beach 220 26.47 N 80.04 W
Rivière-à-Claude 186 49.13 N 65.54 W
Rivière à Goyaves, Pointe de la ≻ 241o 16.11 N 61.35 W
Rivière-au-Tonnerre 186 50.16 N 64.47 W
Rivière-Bleue 186 47.26 N 69.03 W
Rivière-Bois-Clair 206 46.34 N 71.50 W
Rivière-de-la-Chaloupe 186 49.08 N 62.32 W
Rivière-du-Loup 186 47.50 N 69.32 W
Rivière du Rempart 157c 20.06 S 57.41 E
Rivière-Matane 186 48.39 N 67.20 W
Rivière-Mékinac 206 46.47 N 72.48 W
Rivière-Pentecôte 186 49.47 N 67.10 W
Rivière-Pilote 240e 14.29 N 60.54 W
Rivière-Salée 240e 14.32 N 60.59 W
Rivière-Trois-Pistoles 186 48.07 N 69.10 W
Riviersonderend 158 34.09 S 19.55 E
Rivignano 64 45.52 N 13.03 E
Rivington 262 53.37 N 2.34 W
Rivington Reservoirs ⊜[1] 262 53.37 N 2.34 W
Rivisondoli 66 41.52 N 14.04 E
Rivoli 62 45.04 N 7.31 E
Rivoli Bay C 166 37.32 S 140.04 E
Rivolta d'Adda 62 45.28 N 9.31 E
Rivoltella 64 45.27 N 10.33 E
Riwaka 172 41.05 S 173.00 E
Rixford 214 41.55 N 78.30 W
Rixheim 58 47.46 N 7.24 E
Riyadh → Ar-Riyāḍ 128 24.38 N 46.43 E
Rīyāq 132 33.51 N 36.00 E
Rīz 128 32.23 N 51.20 E
Rizal, Pil. 116 15.43 N 121.06 E
Rizal → Pasay, Pil. 269f 14.33 N 121.00 E
Rizal □[4] 116 14.35 N 121.10 E
Rizal Memorial Stadium ♠ 269f 14.34 N 120.59 E
Rize 130 41.02 N 40.31 E
Rize □[4] 130 40.55 N 40.55 E
Rīzeh, Kūh-e (Gora Reza) ∧ 128 37.47 N 58.05 E
Rizhao 98 35.27 N 119.29 E
Rizokárpason 130 35.36 N 34.23 E
Rižskij Vokzal ⬥[5] 265b 55.48 N 37.38 E
Rižskij Zaliv C 76 57.30 N 23.35 E
Rizziconi 68 38.25 N 15.57 E
Rizzuto, Capo ≻ 68 38.54 N 17.06 E
Rjukan 26 59.52 N 8.34 E
Roa, Esp. 34 41.42 N 3.55 W
Roa, N.Z. 172 42.21 S 171.23 E
Roa, Nor. 26 60.17 N 10.37 E
Roa, Zaïre 154 3.49 N 24.56 E
Roachdale 194 39.51 N 86.48 W
Roadhead 44 55.04 N 2.46 W
Roadknight, Point ≻ 169 38.26 S 144.11 E
Roadside 158 27.31 S 28.52 E
Road Town 240m 18.27 N 64.37 W
Roana 64 45.52 N 11.28 E
Roan Cliffs ⩦[4] 200 39.20 N 109.40 W
Roan Creek ≃ 200 39.20 N 108.13 W
Roan Fell ∧ 44 55.13 N 2.52 W
Roan Mountain 192 36.12 N 82.05 W
Roann 216 40.55 N 85.55 W
Roanne 32 46.02 N 4.04 E
Roanoke, Ala., U.S. 194 33.09 N 85.22 W
Roanoke, Ill., U.S. 190 40.48 N 89.12 W
Roanoke, Ind., U.S. 216 40.58 N 85.22 W
Roanoke, Tex., U.S. 222 32.60 N 97.14 W
Roanoke, Va., U.S. 192 37.16 N 79.57 W
Roanoke (Staunton) ≃ 192 35.56 N 76.43 W
Roanoke Island I 192 35.53 N 75.39 W
Roanoke Rapids 192 36.28 N 77.40 W
Roanoke Rapids Dam ⬥[6] 192 36.24 N 77.40 W
Roanoke Rapids Lake ⊜[1] 192 36.30 N 77.45 W
Roans Prairie 222 30.35 N 95.57 W
Roaring ≃ 224 45.13 N 122.12 W
Roaring Branch 210 41.34 N 76.57 W
Roaring Brook ≃ 212 43.44 N 75.24 W
Roaring Fork ≃ 200 39.33 N 107.20 W
Roaring River Slough ≃ 282 38.05 N 121.55 W
Roaring Run ≃ 279b 40.33 N 79.32 W
Roaring Spring 214 40.20 N 78.24 W
Roaring Springs 196 33.54 N 100.52 W
Roaringwater Bay C 48 51.25 N 9.35 W
Roatán 236 16.18 N 86.35 W
Roatán, Isla de I 236 16.23 N 86.30 W
Robâa Oued Yahia 36 36.05 N 9.35 E
Robāṭ 128 30.04 N 54.49 E
Robāṭ Karīm 128 35.28 N 51.05 E
Robbeneiland I 158 33.49 S 18.22 E
Robbers Cave State Park ♠ 196 35.01 N 95.27 W
Robbins, Calif., U.S. 226 38.53 N 121.42 W
Robbins, Ill., U.S. 216 41.39 N 87.42 W
Robbins, N.C., U.S. 192 35.26 N 79.35 W
Robbins, Tenn., U.S. 192 36.21 N 84.35 W
Robbins Airport ⊠ 283 42.34 N 70.58 W
Robbins Ditch ≍ 216 41.21 N 86.43 W
Robbins Island I 166 40.41 S 144.57 E
Robbins Pond ⊜ 283 42.00 N 70.55 W
Robbins Rest 276 40.39 N 73.10 W
Robbinston 188 45.05 N 67.07 W
Robbinsville, N.J., U.S. 208 40.13 N 74.37 W
Robbinsville, N.C., U.S. 192 35.19 N 83.48 W
Robbio 62 45.17 N 8.35 E
Robe 166 37.11 S 139.45 E
Robe ≃, Austl. 162 21.19 S 115.40 E
Robe ≃, Eire 48 53.37 N 9.16 W
Robe, Mount ∧ 166 31.40 S 141.20 E
Robecchetto con Induno 266b 45.32 N 8.46 E
Robecco d'Oglio 64 45.15 N 10.04 E
Robecco sul Naviglio 266b 45.26 N 8.53 E
Röbel 54 53.23 N 12.35 E
Robeline 194 31.41 N 93.18 W
Röberget ∧[2] 40 59.45 N 14.54 E
Robersonville 192 35.50 N 77.15 W
Robert, Havre du C 240e 14.40 N 60.55 W
Roberta 192 32.43 N 84.01 W
Roberta Mills 192 35.22 N 80.38 W
Robert College ʊ[2] 267b 41.04 N 29.02 E
Robert E. Lee Memorial Park ♠ 284b 39.23 N 76.39 W
Robert-Espagne 56 48.45 N 5.02 E
Robert F. Kennedy Memorial Stadium ♠ 284c 38.53 N 76.58 W
Robert H. Treman State Park ♠ 210 42.24 N 76.35 W
Robert Lee 196 31.54 N 100.29 W
Robert Louis Stevenson Memorial State Park ♠ 226 38.40 N 122.36 W
Robert Louis Stevenson's Tomb ⊥ 175a 13.50 S 171.44 W
Robert McIlwaine National Park ♠ 154 17.55 S 30.50 E
Robert Morse College ʊ[2] 279b 40.31 N 80.12 W
Robert Moses State Park ♠ 210 40.37 N 73.16 W
Robert Mueller Municipal Airport ⊠ 222 30.18 N 97.42 W
Roberto Payró 258 35.10 S 57.39 W
Robert Point ≻ 168a 32.31 S 115.42 E
Roberts, Idaho, U.S. 202 43.43 N 112.08 W
Roberts, Ill., U.S. 216 40.37 N 88.11 W
Roberts, Mont., U.S. 202 45.22 N 109.10 W
Roberts, Mount ∧ 171a 28.13 S 152.28 E
Roberts, Point ≻ 224 49.00 N 123.06 W
Robert's Arm 186 49.29 N 55.49 W
Robertsbridge 42 50.59 N 0.29 E
Roberts Canyon ∨ 280 34.11 N 117.54 W
Roberts Creek Mountain ∧ 204 39.52 N 116.18 W
Robertsdale, Ala., U.S. 194 30.33 N 87.43 W
Robertsdale, Pa., U.S. 214 40.11 N 78.07 W
Robertsfield 150 6.15 N 10.24 W
Robertsfors 26 64.11 N 20.51 E
Robertsganj 124 24.42 N 83.04 E
Robertsham ⬥[8] 273d 26.15 S 28.00 E
Robertsholm 40 60.35 N 76.16 E
Robert S. Kerr Lake ⊜[1] 194 35.25 N 95.00 W
Roberts Mountain ∧ 180 60.03 N 166.16 W
Robertson, Austl. 170 34.35 S 150.35 E
Robertson, S. Afr. 158 33.46 S 19.50 E
Robertson □[6], Ky., U.S. 218 38.32 N 84.04 W
Robertson □[6], Tex., U.S. 222 31.00 N 96.30 W
Robertson, Lac ⊜ 186 51.00 N 59.10 W
Robertson Bay C 9 71.25 S 170.00 E
Robertson Range ⩕ 162 23.10 S 121.00 E
Robertsonville 206 46.09 N 71.13 W
Roberts Park 278 41.44 N 87.49 W
Roberts Peak ∧ 182 52.57 N 120.32 W
Robertsport 150 6.45 N 11.22 W
Robertstown, Austl. 168b 34.00 S 139.05 E
Robertstown, Eire 48 53.15 N 6.59 W
Robertsville 214 40.46 N 81.11 W
Robertville 56 50.27 N 6.07 E
Robert Williams 152 12.51 S 15.33 E
Roberval 176 48.31 N 72.13 W
Robi 144 7.51 N 39.46 E
Robin Hood's Bay 44 54.25 N 0.33 W
Robins Air Force Base ■ 192 32.38 N 83.35 W
Robins Island I 207 40.58 N 72.28 W
Robinson, S. Afr. 273d 26.09 S 27.43 E
Robinson, Ill., U.S. 194 39.00 N 87.44 W
Robinson, Tex., U.S. 222 31.31 N 97.06 W
Robinson ≃ 164 16.03 S 137.16 E
Robinson Brook ≃ 283 43.02 N 71.13 W
Robinson Creek ≃ 226 38.16 N 119.15 W
Róbinson Crusoe, Isla (Isla Más A Tierra) I 244 33.38 S 78.52 W
Robinson Gorge National Park ♠ 166 25.15 S 149.10 E
Robinson Lake ⊜ 222 29.35 N 94.36 W
Robinson Pond ⊜ 283 42.48 N 71.23 W
Robinson Range ⩕ 162 25.45 S 119.00 E
Robinson Run ≃ 279b 40.23 N 80.06 W
Robinson Run, North Branch ≃ 279b 40.23 N 80.11 W
Robinsons 186 48.15 N 58.48 W
Robinvale 166 34.36 S 142.46 E
Robleda 34 40.23 N 6.36 W
Robledo 34 38.46 N 2.26 W
Roblin 184 51.14 N 101.21 W
Röblingen 54 51.28 N 11.40 E
Roboré 248 18.20 S 59.45 W
Röbrinken 40 58.36 N 15.53 E
Rob Roy Island I 175e 7.25 S 157.35 E
Robson, Mount ∧ 182 53.07 N 119.09 W
Robstown 196 27.47 N 97.40 W
Roby, Eng., U.K. 262 53.25 N 2.51 W
Roby, Ill., U.S. 219 39.44 N 89.24 W
Roby, Tex., U.S. 196 32.45 N 100.23 W
Roby Mill 262 53.34 N 2.44 W
Roca, Cabo da ≻ 34 38.47 N 9.30 W
Roçadas 152 16.43 S 15.01 E
Roca del Toro, Punta ≻ 200 31.19 N 113.43 W
Roçado 250 6.40 S 44.19 W
Rocafuerte 246 0.55 S 80.28 W
Roça Grande 256 21.36 S 42.58 W
Rocanville 184 50.24 N 101.43 W
Roca Partida, Isla I 232 19.01 N 112.02 W
Roca Partida, Punta ≻ 234 18.42 N 95.10 W
Rocas, Atol das I[1] 250 3.52 S 33.59 W
Roccabernarda 68 39.08 N 16.52 E
Roccacasale 66 42.07 N 13.53 E
Roccadaspide 68 40.26 N 15.12 E
Rocca di Cambio 66 42.14 N 13.29 E
Rocca di Mezzo 66 42.12 N 13.31 E
Rocca di Neto 68 39.11 N 17.00 E
Rocca di Papa 66 41.46 N 12.42 E
Roccafluvione 66 42.51 N 13.29 E
Roccagloriosa 68 40.06 N 15.26 E
Roccalbegna 66 42.47 N 11.30 E
Roccalumera 70 37.58 N 15.24 E
Rocca Massima 66 41.41 N 12.55 E
Roccamena 70 37.50 N 13.09 E
Roccamonfina 68 41.17 N 13.59 E
Roccanova 68 40.13 N 16.12 E
Roccapalumba 70 37.48 N 13.39 E
Rocca Pia 66 41.56 N 13.59 E
Rocca Pietore 64 46.26 N 11.59 E
Roccaprebalza 64 44.31 N 9.57 E
Rocca Priora 267a 41.48 N 12.45 E
Roccaraso 66 41.51 N 14.05 E
Rocca San Casciano 66 44.03 N 11.50 E
Rocca Santa Maria 66 42.41 N 13.30 E
Roccasecca 66 41.33 N 13.40 E
Roccasecca dei Volsci 66 41.29 N 13.13 E
Roccastrada 66 43.00 N 11.10 E
Roccavione 62 44.19 N 7.29 E
Roccavivara 66 41.50 N 14.36 E
Roccelito, Monte ∧ 70 37.50 N 13.47 E
Roccella Ionica 68 38.19 N 16.24 E
Roccella Valdemone 70 37.56 N 15.00 E
Rocchetta Sant'Antonio 68 41.06 N 15.27 E
Rocciamelone ∧ 62 45.12 N 7.05 E
Roch ≃ 44 53.34 N 2.18 W
Rocha, Bra. 256 21.28 S 45.49 W
Rocha, Ur. 252 34.29 S 54.20 W
Rocha da Gale, Barragem ⬥[6] 34 37.42 N 7.35 W
Rocha Miranda ⬥[8] 287a 22.52 S 43.22 W
Rocha Sobrinho 287a 22.47 S 43.25 W
Rochdale, Eng., U.K. 44 53.38 N 2.09 W
Rochdale, Mass., U.S. 207 42.12 N 71.54 W
Rochdale, N.Y., U.S. 210 41.43 N 73.50 W
Rochdale □[8] 262 53.37 N 2.08 W
Rochdale Canal ≍ 262 53.43 N 1.54 W
Roche 42 50.24 N 4.48 W
Rochebrune, Pic de ∧ 62 44.49 N 6.51 E
Rochechouart 32 45.50 N 0.50 E
Rochedinho 255 20.14 S 54.33 W
Rochedo 255 19.57 S 54.52 W
Rochedo de Minas 256 21.38 S 43.01 W
Rochefort, Bel. 56 50.10 N 5.13 E
Rochefort, Fr. 32 45.57 N 0.58 W
Rochefort-en-Yvelines 50 48.35 N 1.59 E
Rochefort-Montagne 32 45.41 N 2.48 E
Rochefort-sur-Nenon 58 47.07 N 5.34 E
Roche Harbor 224 48.36 N 123.09 W
Rochehaut 56 49.51 N 5.00 E
Roche-la-Molière 62 45.26 N 4.19 E
Roche-lez-Beaupré 58 47.17 N 6.07 E
Rochelle, Ga., U.S. 192 31.57 N 83.27 W
Rochelle, Ill., U.S. 216 41.56 N 89.04 W
Rochelle, Tex., U.S. 196 31.13 N 99.13 W
Rochelle Park 276 40.55 N 74.04 W
Rochemaure 62 44.35 N 4.42 E
Roche-Percée 184 49.03 N 102.45 W
Rochepot, Château de la ⊥ 58 46.57 N 4.40 E
Rochester, Austl. 166 36.22 S 144.42 E
Rochester, Eng., U.K. 42 51.24 N 0.30 E
Rochester, Eng., U.K. 44 55.16 N 2.16 W
Rochester, Ill., U.S. 219 39.45 N 89.32 W
Rochester, Ind., U.S. 216 41.04 N 86.13 W
Rochester, Mass., U.S. 207 41.44 N 70.49 W
Rochester, Mich., U.S. 214 42.41 N 83.08 W
Rochester, Minn., U.S. 190 44.02 N 92.29 W
Rochester, N.H., U.S. 188 43.18 N 70.59 W
Rochester, N.Y., U.S. 210 43.10 N 77.36 W
Rochester, Ohio, U.S. 214 41.07 N 82.18 W
Rochester, Pa., U.S. 214 40.43 N 80.17 W
Rochester, Tex., U.S. 196 33.19 N 99.51 W
Rochester, Wash., U.S. 224 46.49 N 123.06 W
Rochester, Wis., U.S. 216 42.45 N 88.14 W
Rochester City Airport ⊠ 260 51.21 N 0.30 E
Rochester Mills 214 40.49 N 78.59 W
Rochester-Monroe County Airport ⊠ 210 43.07 N 77.40 W
Rochester-Utica State Recreation Area ♠ 214 42.39 N 83.04 W
Rochetaillée 62 45.25 N 4.27 E
Rocheuses → Rocky Mountains ⩕ 16 48.00 N 116.00 W
Rochford 42 51.36 N 0.43 E
Rochford □[8] 260 51.36 N 0.39 E
Rochfort Bridge 48 53.23 N 7.17 W
Rochlitz 54 51.03 N 12.47 E
Rochon, Lacs ⊜ 206 46.43 N 75.14 W
Rock 190 46.04 N 87.10 W
Rock □[6] 216 42.41 N 89.05 W
Rock ≃, U.S. 190 41.29 N 90.37 W
Rock ≃, U.S. 198 43.05 N 96.27 W
Rockall I 22 57.35 N 13.48 W
Rockall Rise ✢[3] 10 59.00 N 14.00 W
Rockanje 52 51.53 N 4.05 E
Rockaway, N.J., U.S. 210 40.54 N 74.31 W
Rockaway, Oreg., U.S. 224 45.37 N 123.57 W
Rockaway ≃ 210 40.51 N 74.21 W
Rockaway Inlet C 276 40.34 N 73.55 W
Rockaway Neck 276 40.51 N 74.21 W
Rockaway Park ⬥[8] 276 40.35 N 73.50 W
Rockaway Point ⬥[8] 276 40.33 N 73.55 W
Rockaway Point ≻ 276 40.33 N 73.56 W
Rockaways' Playland ♠ 276 40.35 N 73.49 W
Rockbank 274b 37.43 S 144.39 E
Rock Bay 182 50.20 N 125.29 W
Rockbridge 219 39.16 N 90.12 W
Rock Bridge State Park ♠ 219 38.53 N 92.19 W
Rock Brook ≃ 276 40.25 N 74.40 W
Rock Candy Mountain ∧ 224 47.01 N 123.07 W
Rockcastle ≃ 192 36.58 N 84.21 W
Rock City Falls 210 43.04 N 73.55 W
Rockcliffe Park 212 45.27 N 75.41 W
Rockcorry 48 54.07 N 7.01 W
Rock Creek, B.C., Can. 182 49.06 N 118.58 W
Rock Creek, Ohio, U.S. 214 41.40 N 80.52 W
Rock Creek ≃, N.A. 202 48.25 N 107.05 W
Rock Creek ≃, U.S. 208 38.54 N 77.04 W
Rock Creek ≃, Calif., U.S. 226 37.55 N 120.58 W
Rock Creek ≃, Idaho, U.S. 202 42.39 N 113.01 W
Rock Creek ≃, Ill., U.S. 216 41.12 N 87.59 W
Rock Creek ≃, Ind., U.S. 216 40.49 N 85.23 W
Rock Creek ≃, Ind., U.S. 216 40.42 N 86.35 W
Rock Creek ≃, Mont., U.S. 202 46.43 N 113.40 W
Rock Creek ≃, Mont., U.S. 202 45.31 N 108.49 W
Rock Creek ≃, Nev., U.S. 204 40.39 N 116.54 W
Rock Creek ≃, Oreg., U.S. 202 42.39 N 119.08 W
Rock Creek ≃, Oreg., U.S. 202 45.34 N 120.25 W
Rock Creek ≃, Oreg., U.S. 224 45.51 N 123.12 W
Rock Creek ≃, S. Dak., U.S. 198 43.44 N 97.58 W
Rock Creek ≃, Utah, U.S. 200 40.17 N 110.30 W
Rock Creek ≃, Wash., U.S. 202 45.42 N 120.29 W
Rock Creek ≃, Wash., U.S. 202 46.55 N 117.56 W
Rock Creek ≃, Wyo., U.S. 200 41.54 N 106.08 W
Rock Creek Butte ∧ 202 44.49 N 118.07 W
Rock Creek Park ♠ 284c 38.58 N 77.03 W
Rock Cut State Park ♠ 216 42.20 N 89.00 W
Rockdale, Austl. 170 33.57 S 151.08 E
Rockdale, Ill., U.S. 216 41.30 N 88.06 W
Rockdale, Md., U.S. 284b 39.21 N 76.46 W
Rockdale, Pa., U.S. 285 39.53 N 75.26 W
Rockdale, Tex., U.S. 222 30.39 N 97.00 W
Rockdale, W. Va., U.S. 214 40.18 N 80.35 W
Rockefeller Center ʊ 276 40.45 N 74.00 W
Rockefeller Park ♠ 279a 41.32 N 81.38 W
Rockefeller Plateau ⩕[1] 9 80.00 S 135.00 W
Rockenhausen 56 49.38 N 7.49 E
Rockensüss 56 51.03 N 9.50 E
Rockfall 207 41.28 N 72.44 W
Rock Falls 190 41.47 N 89.41 W
Rock Ferry 262 53.22 N 3.00 W
Rockfield 216 40.39 N 86.34 W
Rock Flat 171b 36.21 S 149.12 E
Rockford, Ala., U.S. 194 32.53 N 86.13 W
Rockford, Ill., U.S. 216 42.17 N 89.06 W
Rockford, Ind., U.S. 218 38.59 N 85.54 W
Rockford, Iowa, U.S. 190 43.03 N 92.57 W
Rockford, Mich., U.S. 190 43.07 N 85.33 W
Rockford, Ohio, U.S. 216 40.42 N 84.39 W
Rockford, Tenn., U.S. 192 35.49 N 83.56 W
Rock Forest 206 45.20 N 71.59 W
Rockglen, Sask., Can. 184 49.10 N 105.57 W
Rock Glen, N.Y., U.S. 210 42.41 N 78.07 W
Rock Hall 188 39.08 N 76.14 W
Rockhammar 40 59.32 N 15.26 E
Rockhampton 166 23.23 S 150.31 E
Rockhampton Downs 162 18.57 S 135.01 E
Rock Hill, N.Y., U.S. 210 41.38 N 74.36 W
Rock Hill, S.C., U.S. 192 34.56 N 81.01 W
Rockhill Furnace 214 40.15 N 77.54 W
Rockingham, Austl. 168a 32.17 S 115.44 E
Rockingham, N.C., U.S. 192 34.56 N 79.46 W
Rockingham □[6] 207 42.50 N 71.15 W
Rockingham ⊥ 276 40.24 N 74.37 W
Rockingham Bay C 166 18.10 S 146.05 E
Rockingham Forest ⬥[3] 42 52.30 N 0.37 W
Rockingham Park ♠ 283 42.45 N 71.14 W
Rock Island, Qué., Can. 206 45.01 N 72.06 W
Rock Island, Ill., U.S. 190 41.30 N 90.34 W
Rock Island, Tex., U.S. 222 29.32 N 96.35 W
Rocklake 198 48.47 N 99.15 W
Rock Lake ⊜, Man., Can. 184 49.11 N 99.12 W
Rock Lake ⊜, Ont., Can. 212 45.30 N 78.23 W
Rock Lake ⊜, Ill., U.S. 278 41.40 N 88.03 W
Rock Lake ⊜, Wis., U.S. 216 43.04 N 88.56 W
Rockland, Del., U.S. 285 39.48 N 75.34 W
Rockland, Idaho, U.S. 202 42.34 N 112.53 W
Rockland, Maine, U.S. 188 44.06 N 69.06 W
Rockland, Mass., U.S. 207 42.08 N 70.55 W
Rockland, Mich., U.S. 190 46.41 N 89.11 W
Rockland, N.Y., U.S. 210 41.58 N 74.54 W
Rockland □[6] 210 41.09 N 73.59 W
Rockland Lake 276 41.09 N 73.55 W
Rockland Lake ⊜ 276 41.08 N 73.55 W
Rockland Lake State Park ♠ 276 41.08 N 73.55 W
Rocklands Reservoir ⊜[1] 166 37.15 S 142.00 E
Rockledge, Fla., U.S. 220 28.20 N 80.43 W
Rockledge, Pa., U.S. 285 40.03 N 75.05 W
Rockleigh 276 41.00 N 73.56 W
Rocklin 226 38.48 N 121.14 W
Rockmart 192 34.00 N 85.02 W
Rock Meadow Brook ≃ 283 42.16 N 71.13 W
Rock of Cashel ⊥ 48 52.31 N 7.53 W
Rock Point 208 38.16 N 76.50 W
Rock Point ≻ 175f 15.55 S 168.17 E
Rock Pond ⊜ 283 42.44 N 71.00 W
Rockport, Ill., U.S. 219 39.32 N 91.00 W
Rockport, Ky., U.S. 194 37.20 N 86.59 W
Rockport, Maine, U.S. 188 44.11 N 69.06 W
Rockport, Mass., U.S. 207 42.39 N 70.36 W
Rock Port, Mo., U.S. 194 40.25 N 95.31 W
Rockport, Tex., U.S. 196 28.01 N 97.04 W
Rock Rapids 198 43.26 N 96.10 W
Rock River 200 41.44 N 105.58 W
Rock Run 208 39.59 N 75.50 W
Rock Run ≃ 284c 38.58 N 77.11 W
Rock Sound 238 24.54 N 76.12 W
Rocksprings, Tex., U.S. 196 30.01 N 100.13 W
Rock Springs, Wyo., U.S. 200 41.35 N 109.13 W
Rockstone 246 5.59 N 58.33 W
Rock Stream 210 42.28 N 76.56 W
Rockton, Ill., U.S. 216 42.27 N 89.04 W
Rockton, Pa., U.S. 214 41.05 N 78.39 W
Rock Valley 198 43.12 N 96.18 W
Rockville, N.Z. 172 40.44 S 172.38 E
Rockville, Conn., U.S. 207 41.52 N 72.27 W
Rockville, Ind., U.S. 194 39.46 N 87.14 W
Rockville, Md., U.S. 284c 39.05 N 77.09 W
Rockville, Mass., U.S. 283 42.08 N 71.22 W
Rockville, Pa., U.S. 208 40.20 N 76.54 W
Rockville, R.I., U.S. 207 41.31 N 71.46 W
Rockville Centre 210 40.40 N 73.37 W
Rockwall 222 32.56 N 96.28 W
Rockwall □[6] 222 32.55 N 96.23 W
Rockwell, Iowa, U.S. 190 42.59 N 93.11 W
Rockwell, N.C., U.S. 192 35.33 N 80.25 W
Rockwell, Lake ⊜ 214 41.12 N 81.19 W
Rockwell City 198 42.24 N 94.38 W
Rockwell International Corporation ʊ[3] 280 33.52 N 117.51 W
Rockwood, Ont., Can. 212 43.37 N 80.08 W
Rockwood, Maine, U.S. 188 45.41 N 69.44 W
Rockwood, Mich., U.S. 216 42.10 N 83.15 W
Rockwood, Oreg., U.S. 224 45.31 N 122.28 W
Rockwood, Pa., U.S. 188 39.54 N 79.09 W
Rockwood, Tenn., U.S. 192 35.52 N 84.41 W
Rockwood Lake ⊜ 276 41.06 N 73.38 W
Rockwood Lake Brook ≃ 276 41.03 N 73.36 W
Rocky 196 35.09 N 99.04 W
Rocky ≃, Alta., Can. 182 53.08 N 117.59 W
Rocky ≃, Mich., U.S. 216 41.57 N 85.39 W
Rocky ≃, N.C., U.S. 192 35.37 N 79.09 W
Rocky ≃, Ohio, U.S. 214 41.30 N 81.49 W
Rocky, East Branch ≃ 279a 41.24 N 81.53 W
Rocky, West Branch ≃ 214 41.24 N 81.53 W
Rocky Arroyo ∨ 196 32.32 N 104.21 W
Rocky Boys Indian Reservation ⬥[4] 202 48.18 N 109.45 W
Rocky Branch ≃ 284c 38.53 N 77.19 W
Rocky Comfort Creek ≃ 192 32.59 N 82.25 W
Rocky Coulee ∨ 202 47.10 N 119.16 W
Rocky Creek ≃ 192 35.53 N 80.47 W
Rockyford, Alta., Can. 182 51.13 N 113.08 W
Rocky Ford, Colo., U.S. 198 38.03 N 103.43 W
Rocky Ford Creek ≃ 216 41.19 N 83.37 W
Rocky Fork Lake ⊜ 218 39.11 N 83.28 W
Rocky Fork State Park ♠ 218 39.11 N 83.30 W
Rocky Gorge Reservoir ⊜[1] 208 39.07 N 77.54 W
Rocky Grove 214 41.25 N 79.49 W
Rocky Gully 162 34.30 S 116.48 E
Rocky Harbour 186 49.36 N 57.55 W
Rocky Harbour C 271d 22.20 N 114.19 E
Rocky Hill, Conn., U.S. 207 41.40 N 72.39 W
Rocky Hill, N.J., U.S. 276 40.24 N 74.38 W
Rocky Island Lake ⊜[1] 190 46.56 N 83.04 W
Rocky Lake ⊜ 184 54.08 N 101.30 W
Rocky Mount, N.C., U.S. 192 35.56 N 77.48 W
Rocky Mount, Va., U.S. 192 37.00 N 79.54 W
Rocky Mountain ∧ 202 47.49 N 112.49 W
Rocky Mountain House 182 52.22 N 114.55 W
Rocky Mountain National Park ♠ 200 40.19 N 105.42 W
Rocky Mountains ⩕ 16 48.00 N 116.00 W
Rocky Point, N.Y., U.S. 207 40.57 N 72.56 W
Rocky Point, Wash., U.S. 224 47.35 N 122.41 W
Rocky Point ≻, Ba. 192 26.00 N 77.25 W
Rocky Point ≻, Namibia 156 19.03 S 12.30 E
Rocky Point ≻, Norf. I. 174c 29.03 S 167.55 E
Rocky Point ≻, Alaska, U.S. 180 64.25 N 163.10 W
Rocky Point ≻, Mass., U.S. 207 41.57 N 70.35 W
Rocky Point ≻, N.Y., U.S. 276 40.55 N 73.32 W
Rocky Ridge 214 41.32 N 83.13 W
Rocky Ridge ∧ 282 37.48 N 122.03 W
Rocky River 214 41.30 N 81.40 W
Rocky River Reservation ♠ 279a 41.27 N 81.50 W
Rocky Run ≃, N. Dak., U.S. 198 47.38 N 99.02 W
Rocky Run ≃, Pa., U.S. 285 39.54 N 75.28 W
Rocky Run ≃, Va., U.S. 284c 38.58 N 77.15 W
Rocky Saugeen ≃ 212 44.13 N 80.53 W
Rocky Top ∧ 202 44.47 N 122.17 W
Roclenge-sur-Geer 56 50.45 N 5.36 E
Rocosas, Montañas → Rocky Mountains ⩕ 16 48.00 N 116.00 W
Rocquencourt 261 48.50 N 2.07 E
Rocroi 50 49.55 N 4.31 E
Roda 192 36.58 N 82.50 W
Roda ≃ 54 50.52 N 11.44 E
Rodach 56 50.20 N 10.46 E
Rodach ≃ 56 50.08 N 10.52 E
Rodakovo 83 48.33 N 39.02 E
Rodalben 56 49.14 N 7.38 E
Rodalquilar 34 37.40 N 2.08 W
Rodas 240p 22.20 N 80.33 W
Rodas,, Isla de → Ródhos I 38 36.10 N 28.00 E
Rodaun ⬥[8] 264b 48.08 N 16.16 E
Rødberg 26 60.16 N 8.58 E
Rødby 41 54.42 N 11.24 E
Rødbyhavn 41 54.39 N 11.21 E
Roddickton 186 50.52 N 56.08 W
Rødding 41 55.23 N 9.06 E
Rodeio 252 26.57 S 49.23 W
Rodeiro 256 21.12 S 42.52 W
Rødekro 41 55.04 N 9.21 E
Rodel 46 57.41 N 7.05 W
Roden 52 53.07 N 6.26 E
Roden ≃ 42 52.43 N 2.36 W
Rodenberg 52 52.18 N 9.21 E
Rodenkirchen, B.R.D. 52 53.24 N 8.26 E
Rodenkirchen, B.R.D. 56 50.54 N 6.59 E
Rodeo, Arg. 252 30.12 S 69.06 W
Rodeo, Méx. 232 25.11 N 104.34 W
Rodeo, Calif., U.S. 226 38.02 N 122.09 W
Rodeo, N. Mex., U.S. 200 31.50 N 109.02 W
Röderau 54 51.19 N 13.19 E
Roderick ≃ 162 26.57 S 116.13 E
Roderick Island I 182 52.40 N 128.22 W
Rodewisch 54 50.32 N 12.24 E
Rodez 32 44.21 N 2.35 E
Rodheim-Bieber 56 50.37 N 8.35 E
Rodhópis, Orosirá → Rhodope Mountains ⩕ 38 41.30 N 24.30 E
Ródhos (Rhodes) 38 36.26 N 28.13 E
Ródhos I 38 36.10 N 28.00 E
Rodi Garganico 68 41.55 N 15.53 E
Rodina 88 57.44 N 95.14 E
Roding 60 49.12 N 12.32 E
Roding ≃ 42 51.31 N 0.06 E
Rodinga 162 24.34 S 134.05 E
Rodinka 80 57.24 N 43.34 E
Rodino, S.S.S.R. 76 58.57 N 44.59 E
Rodino, S.S.S.R. 86 52.30 N 80.15 E
Rodionovo-Nesvetajskoje 83 47.36 N 39.42 E
Rodman 180 57.28 N 135.21 W
Rodman Naval Station ■ 236 8.56 N 79.36 W
Rodn'a 76 56.22 N 34.55 E
Rodnei, Munţii ⩕ 38 47.35 N 24.40 E
Rodney, Ont., Can. 214 42.34 N 81.41 W
Rodney, Miss., U.S. 194 31.52 N 91.12 W
Rodney, Cape ≻, N.Z. 172 36.17 S 174.49 E
Rodney, Cape ≻, Alaska, U.S. 180 64.39 N 166.24 W
Rodney Village 208 39.08 N 75.31 W
Rodničok 80 51.26 N 42.54 E
Rodniki, S.S.S.R. 80 57.06 N 41.44 E
Rodniki, S.S.S.R. 265b 55.39 N 38.04 E
Rodnikovskij 86 50.39 N 57.12 E
Rodolfo, Lago → Rudolf, Lake ⊜ 144 3.30 N 36.05 E
Rodolfo Iselín 252 34.39 S 68.01 W
Rodonit, Kep i ≻ 38 41.35 N 19.27 E
Rodostov 78 51.58 N 24.57 E
Rødovre 41 55.41 N 12.29 E
Rodrigo de Freitas, Lagoa C 287a 22.58 S 43.13 W
Rodrigues I 12 19.42 S 63.25 E
Rodríguez, Méx. 196 27.10 N 100.01 W
Rodríguez, Ur. 258 34.23 S 56.33 W
Rodríguez, Arroyo ≃ 288 34.52 S 58.02 W
Rodstock, Cape ≻ 162 33.12 S 134.20 E
Roduco 208 36.28 N 76.49 W
Rødven 26 62.38 N 7.33 E
Rødvig 41 55.15 N 12.23 E
Roe ≃ 44 55.07 N 6.59 W
Roebling 208 40.07 N 74.47 W
Roebourne 162 20.47 S 117.09 E
Roebuck Bay C 162 19.04 S 122.17 E
Roehampton ⬥[8] 260 51.27 N 0.14 W
Roe Island I 282 38.04 N 122.02 W
Roeland Park 198 39.02 N 94.37 W
Roelands 168a 33.18 S 115.50 E
Roeliff Jansen Kill ≃ 210 42.11 N 73.52 W
Roelofarendsveen 52 52.12 N 4.38 E
Roelofskamp 158 26.10 S 24.24 E
Roen, Monte ∧ 64 46.22 N 11.11 E
Roer (Rur) ≃ 56 51.12 N 5.59 E
Roermond 52 51.12 N 6.00 E
Roesbrugge-Haringe 50 50.55 N 2.37 E
Roeselare (Roulers) 50 50.57 N 3.08 E
Roesinger, Lake ⊜ 224 47.58 N 121.55 W
Roessleville 210 42.42 N 73.49 W
Roes Welcome Sound Ʉ 176 64.00 N 88.00 W
Roetgen 56 50.39 N 6.12 E
Rœulx 50 50.30 N 4.06 E
Rofan Spitze ∧ 64 47.27 N 11.46 E
Roff 196 34.38 N 96.50 W
Röfors 40 58.57 N 14.37 E
Rofrano 68 40.12 N 15.25 E
Rogačevo 82 56.26 N 37.10 E
Rogačov 76 53.05 N 30.03 E
Rogačovka 78 51.30 N 39.34 E
Rogagua, Laguna ⊜ 248 13.43 S 66.54 W
Rogaguado, Laguna ⊜ 248 12.52 S 65.43 W
Rogaland □[6] 26 59.00 N 6.15 E
Rogalik 83 48.56 N 40.03 E
Rogan' 78 49.54 N 36.29 E
Rogans Hill 274a 33.44 S 151.01 E
Rogan's Seat ∧ 44 54.25 N 2.07 W
Rogart 46 58.00 N 4.08 W
Rogäsen 54 52.19 N 12.20 E
Rogaška Slatina 36 46.14 N 15.38 E
Rogatica 38 43.48 N 19.00 E
Rogatin 78 49.25 N 24.37 E
Rogätz 54 52.19 N 11.46 E
Rogen ⊜ 26 62.19 N 12.23 E
Roger, Lac ⊜ 190 47.50 N 78.51 W
Roger Island I 283 42.43 N 70.50 W
Rogers, Ark., U.S. 194 36.20 N 94.07 W
Rogers, Conn., U.S. 207 41.50 N 71.54 W
Rogers, Ohio, U.S. 214 40.48 N 80.38 W
Rogers, Tex., U.S. 222 30.56 N 97.14 W
Rogers, Mount ∧ 192 36.39 N 81.33 W
Rogers City 190 45.25 N 83.49 W
Rogers Lake ⊜ 228 34.52 N 117.51 W
Rogers Park ⬥[8] 278 42.01 N 87.40 W
Rogersville, N.B., Can. 186 46.44 N 65.26 W
Rogersville, Ala., U.S. 194 34.50 N 87.17 W
Rogersville, Tenn., U.S. 192 36.25 N 83.02 W
Roggeveldberge ⩕ 158 32.17 S 20.08 E
Roggewein, Cabo ≻ 174z 27.07 S 109.15 W
Roggiano Gravina 68 39.37 N 16.09 E
Roghudi 68 38.03 N 15.55 E
Rogliano, Fr. 62 42.57 N 9.25 E
Rogliano, It. 68 39.11 N 16.20 E
Rognac 62 43.29 N 5.14 E
Rognedino 76 53.48 N 33.33 E
Rögnitz ≃ 54 53.19 N 10.57 E
Rognon ≃ 58 48.23 N 5.10 E
Rogny 50 47.45 N 2.53 E
Rogojampi 115a 8.19 S 114.17 E
Rogovatoje 78 51.14 N 38.22 E
Rogovo 82 55.13 N 37.05 E
Rogovskaja 78 45.44 N 38.44 E
Rogovskoje 80 58.33 N 50.43 E
Rogožkino 83 47.10 N 39.21 E
Rogoźno 30 52.46 N 17.00 E
Rogozov 78 50.14 N 31.03 E
Rogue ≃, Mich., U.S. 190 43.04 N 85.35 W
Rogue ≃, Oreg., U.S. 202 42.26 N 124.25 W
Rogue River 202 42.26 N 123.10 W
Rohdenhaus 263 51.18 N 7.01 E
Rohilkhand Plains ⌣ 124 28.20 N 79.30 E
Rohinjan 272c 19.06 N 73.04 E
Rohitpur 126 23.42 N 90.19 E
Rohl ≃ 140 6.22 N 29.46 E
Röhlinghausen ⬥[8] 263 51.36 N 7.14 E
Rohnert Park 226 38.21 N 122.42 W
Rohr 60 48.46 N 11.58 E
Rohrbach in Oberösterreich 60 48.34 N 13.59 E
Rohrbach-lès-Bitche 56 49.03 N 7.16 E
Rohrbeck 264a 52.32 N 13.02 E
Rohrberg 54 52.42 N 11.02 E
Rohrbrunn 56 49.54 N 9.23 E
Röhrenfurth 56 51.09 N 9.32 E
Rohri 120 27.41 N 68.54 E
Röhrsdorf 54 50.51 N 12.50 E
Rohtak 123 28.54 N 76.34 E
Roi 174r 6.56 N 158.17 E
Roi, Île du → King Island I 166 39.50 S 144.00 E
Roia (Roya) ≃ 62 43.48 N 7.35 E
Roi Baudouin ʊ[3] 9 70.25 S 24.20 E
Roi Et 110 16.03 N 103.40 E
Roi Georges, Îles du II 14 14.32 S 145.08 W
Roi Léopold, Monts du → King Leopold Ranges ⩕ 160 17.30 S 125.45 E
Roine ⊜ 26 61.24 N 24.06 E
Roinville 261 48.32 N 2.03 E
Roisel 50 49.57 N 3.06 E
Roissy 261 48.47 N 2.39 E
Roissy-en-France 261 49.00 N 2.31 E
Roitzsch 54 51.34 N 12.16 E
Roja, S.S.S.R. 76 57.30 N 22.49 E
Roja, S.S.S.R. 83 47.59 N 37.20 E
Rojas 252 34.12 S 60.44 W
Rojl'anka 78 46.17 N 29.46 E
Rojo → Red ≃ 178 31.00 N 91.40 W
Rojo, Cabo ≻, Méx. 234 21.33 N 97.20 W
Rojo, Cabo ≻, P.R. 240m 17.56 N 67.11 W
Rojo, Mar → Red Sea ⊤[2] 136 20.00 N 38.00 E
Rokan 112 0.34 N 100.25 E
Rokan ≃ 114 2.00 N 100.52 E
Rokan-kanan ≃ 114 1.23 N 100.56 E
Rokan-kiri ≃ 114 1.23 N 100.56 E
Röke 41 56.14 N 13.30 E
Rokel ≃ 150 8.33 N 12.48 W
Rokewood 169 37.54 S 143.43 E
Rokewood Junction 169 37.51 S 143.41 E
Rokheh 120 35.16 N 69.28 E
Rokiškis 76 55.58 N 25.35 E
Rokkō-sanchi ⩕ 270 34.45 N 135.13 E
Rokkō-zan ∧ 96 34.46 N 135.16 E
Roklum 54 52.04 N 10.44 E
Roksana 273d 26.07 S 28.04 E
Rokuan Kansallispuisto ♠ 26 64.32 N 26.33 E
Rokugō 94 35.29 N 138.27 E
Rokugō ⬥[8] 268 35.33 N 139.43 E
Rokusei 94 36.58 N 136.52 E
Rokycany 60 49.45 N 13.36 E
Rokytná ≃ 61 49.05 N 16.22 E
Rolampont 58 47.57 N 5.16 E
Roland, Man., Can. 184 49.25 N 97.55 W
Roland, Ark., U.S. 194 34.54 N 92.30 W
Roland, Iowa, U.S. 190 42.10 N 93.30 W
Roland, Lake ⊜[1] 284b 39.23 N 76.38 W
Roland C. Nickerson State Park ♠ 207 41.46 N 70.03 W

Symbol	English	Deutsch	Español	Français	Português
≃	River	Fluss	Río	Rivière	Rio
≍	Canal	Kanal	Canal	Canal	Canal
⅃	Waterfall, Rapids	Wasserfall, Stromschnellen	Cascada, Rápidos	Chute d'eau, Rapides	Cascata, Rápidos
Ʉ	Strait	Meeresstrasse	Estrecho	Détroit	Estreito
C	Bay, Gulf	Bucht, Golf	Bahía, Golfo	Baie, Golfe	Baía, Golfo
⊜	Lake, Lakes	See, Seen	Lago, Lagos	Lac, Lacs	Lago, Lagos
≋	Swamp	Sumpf	Pantano	Marais	Pântano
⊼	Ice Features, Glacier	Eis- und Gletscherformen	Accidentes Glaciales	Formes glaciaires	Acidentes Glaciares
⊤	Other Hydrographic Features	Andere Hydrographische Objekte	Otros Elementos Hidrográficos	Autres données hydrographiques	Outros Elementos Hidrográficos
✢	Submarine Features	Untermeerische Objekte	Accidentes Submarinos	Formes de relief sous-marin	Acidentes Submarinos
□	Political Unit	Politische Einheit	Unidad Política	Entité politique	Unidade Política
ʊ	Cultural Institution	Kulturelle Institution	Institución Cultural	Institution culturelle	Instituição Cultural
⊥	Historical Site	Historische Stätte	Sitio Histórico	Site historique	Sítio Histórico
♠	Recreational Site	Erholungs- und Ferienort	Sitio de Recreo	Centre de loisirs	Sítio de Lazer
⊠	Airport	Flughafen	Aeropuerto	Aéroport	Aeroporto
■	Military Installation	Militäranlage	Instalación Militar	Installation militaire	Instalação Militar
⬥	Miscellaneous	Verschiedenes	Misceláneo	Divers	Miscelânea

Name	Page	Lat.°′	Long.°′
Rolândia	255	23.18 S	51.22 W
Roland Park •8	284b	39.22 N	76.39 W
Roland Run ≃	284b	39.23 N	76.39 W
Rolava ≃	54	50.15 N	12.51 E
Røldal	26	59.49 N	6.48 E
Roldán	252	32.54 S	60.54 W
Roldanillo	246	4.24 N	76.09 W
Rolde	52	52.58 N	6.38 E
Roldskov •3	26	56.48 N	9.50 E
Rolette	198	48.40 N	99.51 W
Roleystone	168a	32.08 S	116.04 E
Rolfe	198	42.49 N	94.31 W
Roll, Ariz., U.S.	200	32.45 N	113.59 W
Roll, Ind., U.S.	216	40.33 N	85.23 W
Rolla, B.C., Can.	182	55.54 N	120.09 W
Rolla, Kans., U.S.	198	37.07 N	101.38 W
Rolla, Mo., U.S.	194	37.57 N	91.46 W
Rolla, N. Dak., U.S.	198	48.52 N	99.37 W
Rolle	58	46.28 N	6.20 E
Rolle, Passo di)(	64	46.18 N	11.47 E
Rolleboise	261	49.01 N	1.36 E
Rolleston, Austl.	166	24.28 S	148.37 E
Rolleston, N.Z.	172	43.35 S	172.23 E
Rolling Acres	284b	39.17 N	76.52 W
Rollingbay	224	47.40 N	122.30 W
Rolling Fork	194	32.55 N	90.52 W
Rolling Fork ≃	194	37.55 N	85.50 W
Röllinghausen •8	263	51.31 N	7.08 E
Rolling Hills	280	33.46 N	118.21 W
Rolling Hills Estates	280	33.47 N	118.22 W
Rolling Meadows	216	42.04 N	88.01 W
Rolling Prairie	216	41.40 N	86.37 W
Rolling River Indian Reserve •4	184	50.27 N	100.00 W
Rollingstone	166	19.03 S	146.24 E
Rollingwood	226	37.57 N	122.20 W
Rolvsøya I	24	71.00 N	24.00 E
Rom → Roma	66	41.54 N	12.29 E
Roma, Austl.	166	26.35 S	148.47 E
Roma (Rome), It.	66 267a	41.54 N	12.29 E
Roma, Leso.	158	29.27 S	27.45 E
Roma □4	66	41.58 N	12.40 E
Romagna •1	64	44.30 N	12.15 E
Romagnano Sesia	62	45.38 N	8.23 E
Romagne-sous-Montfaucon	56	49.20 N	5.05 E
Romain, Cape ≻	192	33.00 N	79.22 W
Romaine ≃	176	50.18 N	63.47 W
Romainmôtier	58	46.42 N	6.29 E
Romainville	261	48.53 N	2.26 E
Romakloster	26	57.31 N	18.27 E
Roman, Blg.	38	43.09 N	23.55 E
Roman, Rom.	38	46.55 N	26.56 E
Roman ≃	42	51.51 N	0.57 E
Romanche ≃	62	45.05 N	5.43 E
Romanche Gap ✢1	10	0.10 S	18.15 W
Romang, Pulau I	164	7.35 S	127.26 E
Romang, Selat ⟗	164	7.30 S	127.00 E
Romania □1	22 38	46.00 N	25.30 E
Roman-Koš, Gora ∧	78	44.37 N	34.15 E
Romankovcy	78	48.29 N	27.13 E
Roman Nose Mountain ∧	202	43.55 N	123.44 W
Romano, Cape ≻	220	25.50 N	81.41 W
Romano, Cayo I	240p	22.04 N	77.50 W
Romano di Lombardia	62	45.31 N	9.45 E
Romanova	88	57.04 N	103.24 E
Romanovka, S.S.S.R.	80	49.47 N	45.05 E
Romanovka, S.S.S.R.	80	51.24 N	47.23 E
Romanovka, S.S.S.R.	80	51.45 N	42.45 E
Romanovka, S.S.S.R.	86	54.38 N	76.03 E
Romanovka, S.S.S.R.	88	53.14 N	112.46 E
Romanovka, S.S.S.R.	265a	60.03 N	30.42 E
Romanovo, S.S.S.R.	82	56.39 N	39.14 E
Romanovo, S.S.S.R.	86	53.58 N	80.30 E
Romanovo, S.S.S.R.	86	52.37 N	81.14 E
Romanovo, S.S.S.R.	86	59.09 N	61.30 E
Romans d'Isonzo	64	45.53 N	13.26 E
Romanshorn	58	47.34 N	9.22 E
Romans-sur-Isère	62	45.03 N	5.03 E
Romanzof Mountains ⛰	180	69.00 N	144.00 W
Romaški	80	50.13 N	46.41 E
Romaškino	80	52.29 N	51.48 E
Romaškovo	265b	55.44 N	37.20 E
Romayor	222	30.27 N	94.50 W
Rombari	154	4.33 N	31.02 E
Romblon	116	12.35 N	122.15 E
Romblon □4	116	12.30 N	122.10 E
Romblon Island I	116	12.33 N	122.17 E
Romblon Passage ⟗	116	12.27 N	122.12 E
Rombo, Ilhéus do II	150a	14.58 N	24.40 W
Rome → Roma, It.	66	41.54 N	12.29 E
Rome, Ga., U.S.	192	34.16 N	85.11 W
Rome, Ill., U.S.	190	40.53 N	89.30 W
Rome, Miss., U.S.	194	33.52 N	90.29 W
Rome, N.Y., U.S.	210	43.13 N	75.27 W
Rome, Ohio, U.S.	214	41.36 N	80.52 W
Rome, Pa., U.S.	210	41.51 N	76.21 W
Rome, Wis., U.S.	216	42.58 N	88.38 W
Rome City	216	41.30 N	85.23 W
Romeleåsen ⛰2	41	55.34 N	13.33 E
Romenay	58	46.30 N	5.04 E
Romeno	64	46.24 N	11.07 E
Romentino	62	45.28 N	8.42 E
Romeo	190	42.48 N	83.01 W
Romeoville	216	41.39 N	88.05 W
Rometan	128	39.56 N	64.23 E
Rometta	70	38.10 N	15.25 E
Romfartuna	40	59.44 N	16.35 E
Romford •8	260	51.35 N	0.11 E
Römhild	54	50.24 N	10.32 E
Romiley	262	53.25 N	2.05 W
Romilly, Mount ∧	162	20.27 S	126.34 E
Romilly-sur-Seine	50	48.31 N	3.43 E
Romita	234	20.52 N	101.31 W
Romitorio	267a	42.01 N	12.39 E
Rommani	148	34.34 N	6.37 W
Romme	40	60.26 N	15.30 E
Rommerskirchen	56	51.02 N	6.40 E
Romney, Ind., U.S.	216	40.15 N	86.54 W
Romney, W. Va., U.S.	188	39.21 N	78.45 W
Romney Marsh ☷	42	51.03 N	0.55 E
Romny, S.S.S.R.	78	50.45 N	33.30 E
Romny, S.S.S.R.	89	50.44 N	129.15 E
Rømø I	26	55.08 N	8.31 E
Romodan	78	49.59 N	33.19 E
Romodanovo	80	54.26 N	45.20 E
Romoland	228	33.45 N	117.10 W
Romont	58	46.42 N	6.55 E
Romorantin-Lanthenay	50	47.22 N	1.45 E
Rompin, Malay.	114	2.42 N	102.31 E
Rompin, Malay.	114	2.48 N	103.29 E
Rompin ≃	114	2.49 N	103.29 E
Romrod	56	50.43 N	9.13 E
Romsdalen ∨	26	62.15 N	8.05 E
Romsdalsfjorden C2	26	62.39 N	7.15 E
Romsey, Austl.	169	37.21 S	144.45 E
Romsey, Eng., U.K.	42	50.59 N	1.30 W
Romsø I	41	55.31 N	10.48 E
Romulus, Mich., U.S.	216	42.13 N	83.24 W
Romulus, N.Y., U.S.	210	42.45 N	76.50 W
Røn, Nor.	26	61.03 N	9.03 E
Ron, Viet.	110	17.53 N	106.27 E
Rona, Schw.	58	46.34 N	9.38 E
Rona, Zaïre	154	2.14 N	30.52 E
Rona I, Scot., U.K.	46	59.07 N	5.48 W
Rona I, Scot., U.K.	46	57.34 N	5.59 W
Ronald	224	47.14 N	121.01 W
Ronan	202	47.32 N	114.06 W
Ronas Hill ∧2	46a	60.31 N	1.28 W
Ronas Voe C	46	60.32 N	1.29 W
Ronay I	46	57.29 N	7.11 W
Roncade	64	45.38 N	12.22 E
Roncador, Serra do ⛰1	242	12.00 S	52.00 W
Roncador Bank ✢4	236	13.32 N	80.03 W
Roncador Reef ✢2	175e	6.13 S	159.22 E
Roncegno	64	46.03 N	11.25 E
Roncesvalles	34	43.01 N	1.19 W
Ronceverte	192	37.45 N	80.28 W
Ronchamp	58	47.42 N	6.39 E
Ronchi dei Legionari	64	45.50 N	13.30 E
Ronchin	50	50.36 N	3.06 E
Ronchis	64	45.49 N	13.00 E
Ronciglione	66	42.17 N	12.13 E
Ronco	58	46.08 N	8.44 E
Ronco Canavese	62	45.30 N	7.32 E
Roncofreddo	66	44.02 N	12.20 E
Roncone	64	45.59 N	10.40 E
Ronco Scrivia	62	44.37 N	8.59 E
Roncq	50	50.45 N	3.07 E
Ronda	34	36.44 N	5.10 W
Ronda, Serranía de ⛰	34	36.44 N	5.03 W
Rondane ∧	26	61.55 N	9.45 E
Rondane nasjonalpark ♠	26	61.50 N	9.50 E
Rønde	41	56.18 N	10.29 E
Rondeau Harbour C	214	42.18 N	81.53 W
Rondeau Provincial Park ♠	214	42.16 N	81.51 W
Rondebult	273d	26.18 S	28.14 E
Ronde Island I	241k	12.18 N	61.35 W
Rondissone	62	45.15 N	7.58 E
Rondon	255	23.23 S	52.48 W
Rondônia	248	10.52 S	61.57 W
Rondônia □8	248	11.00 S	63.00 W
Rondonópolis	255	16.28 S	54.38 W
Rondout	278	42.17 N	87.53 W
Rondout Creek ≃	210	41.55 N	73.53 W
Rondout Reservoir ⊜1	210	41.50 N	74.29 W
Rone ≃	50	50.46 N	3.27 E
Ronehamn	26	57.10 N	18.29 E
Ronga	80	56.43 N	48.32 E
Rongai	154	0.10 S	35.51 E
Rongan	102	25.10 N	109.20 E
Rongbacha	102	31.48 N	99.40 E
Rongchang	107	29.24 N	105.36 E
Rongcheng, Zhg.	98	37.08 N	122.23 E
Rongcheng, Zhg.	105	39.03 N	115.52 E
Rongding	107	28.57 N	103.40 E
Ronge, Lac la ⊜	184	55.10 N	105.00 W
Rongelap I1	14	11.20 N	166.50 E
Rongjiang	102	25.52 N	108.37 E
Rongjiatun	104	42.12 N	123.37 E
Rongkop	115a	8.10 S	110.45 E
Rongola	158	27.22 S	31.37 E
Rongotea	172	40.18 S	175.25 E
Rõngu	76	58.09 N	26.15 E
Rongui, Ilha I	154	10.50 S	40.40 E
Rongwanshi	100	28.10 N	112.57 E
Rongxian, Zhg.	102	22.50 N	110.38 E
Rongxian, Zhg.	107	29.28 N	104.25 E
Roniu ∧	174s	17.49 S	149.12 W
Ronkiti	174r	6.49 N	158.10 E
Ronkiti Harbor C	174r	6.48 N	158.10 E
Ronkonkoma	276	40.49 N	73.07 W
Ronkonkoma, Lake ⊜	276	40.50 N	73.07 W
Ron-ma, Mui ≻	110	18.07 N	106.22 E
Rønne	26	55.06 N	14.42 E
Rönne ≃	41	56.16 N	12.50 E
Ronneburg	54	50.51 N	12.10 E
Ronneby	26	56.12 N	15.18 E
Ronne Entrance C	9	72.30 S	74.00 W
Ronne Ice Shelf ▽	9	78.30 S	61.00 W
Ronnenberg	52	52.20 N	9.40 E
Rönneshytta	40	58.56 N	15.02 E
Rönninge	40	59.12 N	17.44 E
Ronroni	175e	9.37 S	159.58 E
Rönsahl	263	51.07 N	7.30 E
Ronsdorf •8	263	51.14 N	7.12 E
Ronse (Renaix-gleiche)	50	50.45 N	3.36 E
Röntgenmuseum υ	263	51.12 N	7.16 E
Ronuro ≃	255	11.56 S	53.33 W
Roodepoort-Maraisburg	158	26.11 S	27.54 E
Roodeschool	52	53.25 N	6.45 E
Roodhouse	219	39.29 N	90.22 W
Roof Butte ∧	200	36.28 N	109.05 W
Rooiberge ∧	158	28.27 S	28.26 E
Rooiboklaagte ≃	156	20.50 S	21.00 E
Rooidam	158	28.07 S	21.15 E
Rooiduinepunt ≻	158	31.57 S	18.17 E
Rooilyf	158	28.49 S	21.57 E
Rooks Creek ≃	216	40.57 N	88.44 W
Rookwood Cemetery •	274a	33.53 S	151.04 E
Roon, Pulau I	164	2.23 S	134.33 E
Roordahuizum	52	53.06 N	5.46 E
Roorkee	124	29.52 N	77.53 E
Roosendaal	52	51.32 N	4.28 E
Roosevelt, Ariz., U.S.	200	33.40 N	111.09 W
Roosevelt, Minn., U.S.	198	48.48 N	95.06 W
Roosevelt, N.J., U.S.	208	40.13 N	74.29 W
Roosevelt, N.Y., U.S.	276	40.41 N	73.36 W
Roosevelt, Okla., U.S.	196	34.51 N	99.01 W
Roosevelt, Utah, U.S.	200	40.18 N	109.59 W
Roosevelt ≃	248	7.35 S	60.20 W
Roosevelt Beach	210	43.19 N	78.52 W
Roosevelt-Campobello International Park ♠	186	44.52 N	66.58 W
Roosevelt Field •9	276	40.45 N	73.37 W
Roosevelt Island I	9	79.30 S	162.00 W
Roosevelt Park	216	43.11 N	86.16 W
Roosevelt Park ♠	276	40.33 N	74.21 W
Roosevelt Raceway ♠	276	40.44 N	73.36 W
Roosevelt Roads Naval Station ■	240m	18.15 N	65.38 W
Roosevelt Terrace	226	38.08 N	122.16 W
Root	58	47.07 N	8.23 E
Root ≃, N.W. Ter., Can.	180	62.50 N	123.40 W
Root ≃, Minn., U.S.	190	43.46 N	91.15 W
Root ≃, Wis., U.S.	216	42.44 N	87.47 W
Root, North Branch ≃	190	43.49 N	92.10 W
Root, South Branch ≃	190	43.44 N	91.58 W
Root Lake ⊜	184	54.04 N	101.24 W
Rootstown	214	41.06 N	81.15 W
Rooty Hill	170	33.46 S	150.50 E
Ropang	115b	8.52 S	117.29 E
Ropaži	76	57.08 N	24.30 E
Ropča	24	63.02 N	52.16 E
Ropczyce	30	50.03 N	21.37 E
Roper	192	35.53 N	76.37 W
Roper ≃	164	14.43 S	135.27 E
Roper River Mission	164	14.44 S	134.44 E
Roper Valley	164	14.56 S	134.00 E
Ropesville	196	33.26 N	102.09 W
Roppe	58	47.40 N	6.55 E
Ropša	265a	59.44 N	29.52 E
Roque	250	3.01 S	45.23 W
Roquebillière	62	44.01 N	7.18 E
Roquebrune-Cap-Martin	62	43.46 N	7.28 E
Roquebrune-sur-Argens	62	43.26 N	6.38 E
Roquefavour, Aqueduc de ≍1	62	43.31 N	5.19 E
Roquefort	32	44.02 N	0.19 W
Roquemaure	62	44.03 N	4.47 E
Roque Pérez	258	35.25 S	59.20 W
Roquestéron	62	43.52 N	7.00 E
Roquevaire	62	43.21 N	5.36 E
Rora Head ≻	46	58.52 N	3.25 W
Roraima □8	246	1.00 N	61.00 W
Roraima, Mount ∧	246	5.12 N	60.44 W
Rörbäcksnäs	26	61.08 N	12.49 E
Roreto Chisone	62	44.59 N	7.06 E
Rorey Lake ⊜	180	66.55 N	128.25 W
Rørholtfjorden ⊜	26	59.01 N	9.15 E
Rorke Lake ⊜	184	54.33 N	92.30 W
Rorke's Drift ⊥	158	28.20 S	30.32 E
Rorketon	184	51.26 N	99.32 W
Røros	26	62.35 N	11.20 E
Rorschach	58	47.29 N	9.30 E
Rørvig	41	55.57 N	11.46 E
Ros' ≃	78	49.39 N	31.35 E
Rosà, It.	64	45.43 N	11.45 E
Rosa, Zam.	154	9.38 S	31.21 E
Rosa, Cap ≻	148	36.57 N	8.14 E
Rosa, Lake ⊜	238	21.00 N	73.30 W
Rosa, Monte ∧	58	45.55 N	7.53 E
Rosairinho	266c	38.40 N	9.01 W
Rošal'	80	55.40 N	39.51 E
Rosales, Méx.	232	28.12 N	105.33 W
Rosales, Pil.	116	15.54 N	120.38 E
Rosalia	202	47.14 N	117.22 W
Rosalie, Lake ⊜	220	27.58 N	81.28 W
Rosamond, Calif., U.S.	228	34.52 N	118.10 W
Rosamond, Ill., U.S.	219	39.23 N	89.10 W
Rosamond Lake ⊜	228	34.50 N	118.04 W
Rosamorada	234	22.08 N	105.12 W
Rosander, Mount ∧	224	48.46 N	124.42 W
Rosanky	222	29.56 N	97.18 W
Rosanna	274b	37.45 S	145.04 E
Rosans	62	44.23 N	5.28 E
Rosario, Arg.	252	32.57 S	60.40 W
Rosário, Bra.	250	2.57 S	44.14 W
Rosario, Méx.	232	30.01 N	115.40 W
Rosario, Méx.	234	23.00 N	105.52 W
Rosario, Para.	252	24.27 S	57.03 W
Rosario, Pil.	116	16.14 N	120.29 E
Rosario, Pil.	116	13.51 N	121.12 E
Rosario, Ur.	258	34.19 S	57.21 W
Rosario, Ven.	246	10.19 N	72.19 W
Rosario ≃	252	24.50 S	65.43 W
Rosario, Bahía del C	232	29.52 N	115.45 W
Rosario, Cayo del I	240p	21.38 N	81.53 W
Rosario, Islas de II	246	10.10 N	75.46 W
Rosario, Laguna ⊜	234	17.52 N	93.48 W
Rosario Bank ✢4	238	18.30 N	84.00 W
Rosario de la Frontera	252	25.48 S	64.58 W
Rosario de Lerma	252	24.59 S	65.35 W
Rosario del Tala	252	32.18 S	59.09 W
Rosário de Minas	256	21.43 S	43.38 W
Rosário do Sul	252	30.15 S	54.55 W
Rosário Oeste	248	14.50 S	56.25 W
Rosarito, Méx.	204	32.20 N	117.02 W
Rosarito, Méx.	232	28.38 N	114.04 W
Rosarito, Méx.	232	26.27 N	111.38 W
Rosarito, Embalse de ⊜1	34	40.05 N	5.15 W
Rosarno	68	38.29 N	15.59 E
Rosas	196	26.09 N	103.27 W
Rosas, Golfo de C	34	42.10 N	3.15 E
Rosazza	62	45.41 N	7.58 E
Rosbach	56	50.48 N	7.37 E
Rosboom	158	28.36 S	29.44 E
Rošča	82	54.47 N	36.51 E
Roščino	76	60.15 N	29.37 E
Rosciolo	66	42.07 N	13.20 E
Roscoe, Ill., U.S.	216	42.25 N	89.01 W
Roscoe, N.Y., U.S.	210	41.56 N	74.55 W
Roscoe, Pa., U.S.	214	40.05 N	79.52 W
Roscoe, S. Dak., U.S.	198	45.27 N	99.20 W
Roscoe, Tex., U.S.	196	32.27 N	100.32 W
Roscoe Glacier ▽	9	66.30 S	95.20 E
Roscoe Village ⊥	214	40.18 N	81.54 W
Roscommon, Eire	48	53.38 N	8.11 W
Roscommon, Mich., U.S.	190	44.30 N	84.35 W
Roscommon □6	48	53.40 N	8.30 W
Roscrea	48	52.57 N	7.47 W
Rosdorf	52	51.30 N	9.53 E
Rose, It.	68	39.24 N	16.17 E
Rose, N.Y., U.S.	210	43.09 N	76.53 W
Rose, Monte ∧	70	37.39 N	13.25 E
Rose, Mount ∧	226	39.21 N	119.55 W
Rose, Pointe de la ≻	240e	14.40 N	60.53 W
Roseau, Dom.	240d	15.18 N	61.24 W
Roseau, Minn., U.S.	198	48.51 N	95.46 W
Roseau ≃, Dom.	240d	15.18 N	61.24 W
Roseau ≃, N.A.	198	49.08 N	97.15 W
Roseau ≃, St. Luc.	241f	13.58 N	61.02 W
Rosebank •8	273d	26.09 S	28.02 E
Rosebank Station	275b	43.47 N	79.07 W
Roseberry Lakes ⊜	184	52.40 N	92.30 W
Roseberth	166	25.47 S	139.37 E
Rosebery	166	41.46 S	145.32 E
Rosebery •8	274a	33.55 S	151.12 E
Rose-Blanche	186	47.37 N	58.41 W
Roseboom	210	42.45 N	74.47 W
Roseboro	192	34.58 N	78.31 W
Rose Bowl ♠	280	34.10 N	118.09 W
Rosebud, Austl.	169	38.21 S	144.54 E
Rosebud, Mo., U.S.	219	38.23 N	91.25 W
Rosebud, Mont., U.S.	202	46.16 N	106.27 W
Rose Bud, Pa., U.S.	214	40.45 N	78.33 W
Rosebud, S. Dak., U.S.	198	43.14 N	100.51 W
Rosebud, Tex., U.S.	222	31.04 N	96.59 W
Rosebud ≃	182	51.25 N	112.37 W
Rosebud Creek ≃	202	46.16 N	106.28 W
Rosebud Indian Reservation •4	198	43.25 N	100.28 W
Roseburg	202	43.13 N	123.20 W
Rosebush	190	43.42 N	84.46 W
Rose City	190	44.25 N	84.07 W
Rose Creek ≃, U.S.	198	40.04 N	97.07 W
Rose Creek ≃, Calif., U.S.	226	38.07 N	120.24 W
Rosecroft Raceway ♠	284c	38.48 N	76.58 W
Rosedale, Austl.	166	24.38 S	151.55 E
Rosedale, Alta., Can.	182	51.25 N	112.38 W
Rosedale, B.C., Can.	224	49.11 N	121.48 W
Rosedale, Ind., U.S.	194	39.37 N	87.17 W
Rosedale, La., U.S.	194	30.27 N	91.27 W
Rosedale, Md., U.S.	284b	39.19 N	76.31 W
Rosedale, Miss., U.S.	194	33.51 N	91.02 W
Rosedale •8, Ont., Can.	275b	43.41 N	79.22 W
Rosedale •8, N.Y., U.S.	276	40.39 N	73.45 W
Rosedale Hills	218	39.42 N	86.07 W
Rosedene	158	32.01 S	22.07 E
Rose Hall	246	6.16 N	57.21 W
Rosehearty	46	57.42 N	2.07 W
Rose Hill, Maus.	157c	20.14 S	57.27 E
Rose Hill, N.C., U.S.	192	34.50 N	78.02 W
Rose Hill, Va., U.S.	192	36.40 N	83.22 W
Rose Hill, Wash., U.S.	224	47.42 N	122.10 W
Rosehill Cemetery •	278	41.59 N	87.41 W
Rosehill Racecourse ♠	274a	33.49 S	151.02 E
Rose Hills Memorial Park •	280	34.01 N	118.02 W
Roseira	256	22.54 S	45.18 W
Roseiras	256	22.49 S	46.17 W
Rose Island I	192	25.06 N	77.14 W
Rose Lake	182	54.24 N	126.02 W
Roseland, Calif., U.S.	226	38.25 N	122.44 W
Roseland, Ind., U.S.	216	41.42 N	86.15 W
Roseland, La., U.S.	194	30.46 N	90.31 W
Roseland, N.J., U.S.	276	40.49 N	74.18 W
Roseland, Ohio, U.S.	214	40.47 N	82.32 W
Roseland •8	278	41.42 N	87.38 W
Roselawn	216	41.09 N	87.19 W
Roselle, Ill., U.S.	216	41.59 N	88.05 W
Roselle, N.J., U.S.	276	40.40 N	74.16 W
Roselle Field ⊠	278	41.59 N	88.06 W
Rosellen	263	51.08 N	6.43 E
Roselle Park	276	40.40 N	74.16 W
Rosellerheide	263	51.07 N	6.44 E
Rose Lodge	224	45.01 N	123.52 W
Rosemary	182	50.46 N	112.05 W
Rosemary Brook ≃	283	42.19 N	71.15 W
Rosemead	280	34.04 N	118.03 W
Rosemère	206	45.38 N	73.48 W
Rosemont, Calif., U.S.	226	38.34 N	121.20 W
Rosemont, Ill., U.S.	278	41.59 N	87.52 W
Rosemont, Ky., U.S.	218	38.01 N	84.32 W
Rosemont, Ohio, U.S.	214	41.03 N	80.53 W
Rosemont, Pa., U.S.	285	40.01 N	75.19 W
Rosenberg → Susz, Pol.	30	53.44 N	19.20 E
Rosenberg, Tex., U.S.	222	29.33 N	95.48 W
Rosendaël	50	51.02 N	2.24 E
Rosendal, Nor.	26	59.59 N	6.01 E
Rosendal, S. Afr.	158	28.30 S	27.55 E
Rosendale	210	41.51 N	74.05 W
Roseneath	273d	26.17 S	28.11 E
Rosenfeld	58	48.17 N	8.43 E
Rosenhayn	208	39.29 N	75.08 W
Rosenheim	64	47.51 N	12.07 E
Rosenhügel •8	263	51.10 N	7.12 E
Rosenthal, B.R.D.	56	50.58 N	8.52 E
Rosenthal, D.D.R.	54	50.51 N	14.04 E
Rosenthal •8	264a	52.36 N	13.23 E
Rose Peak ∧	200	33.26 N	109.22 W
Rosepine	194	30.55 N	93.17 W
Rose Point ≻	182	54.13 N	131.35 W
Rosersberg	40	59.35 N	17.53 E
Rosersberg ⊥	40	59.34 N	17.50 E
Roseto	210	40.53 N	75.15 W
Roseto Capo Spulico	68	39.59 N	16.36 E
Roseto degli Abruzzi	66	42.41 N	14.01 E
Roseto Valfortore	68	41.22 N	15.06 E
Rosetown	184	51.33 N	108.00 W
Rose Tree	285	39.56 N	75.23 W
Rosetta → Rashīd	142	31.24 N	30.25 E
Rosetta Mouth → Rashīd, Maṣabb ≃1	142	31.30 N	30.21 E
Rosettenville •8	273d	26.15 S	28.03 E
Rosevale	171a	27.51 S	152.29 E
Rose Valley, Sask., Can.	184	52.18 N	103.50 W
Rose Valley, Pa., U.S.	285	39.53 N	75.23 W
Rose Valley, Pa., U.S.	285	40.10 N	75.13 W
Rose Valley, Wash., U.S.	224	46.06 N	122.50 W
Roseville, Austl.	274a	33.47 S	151.11 E
Roseville, Calif., U.S.	226	38.45 N	121.17 W
Roseville, Ill., U.S.	190	40.44 N	90.40 W
Roseville, Mich., U.S.	214	42.30 N	82.56 W
Roseville, Minn., U.S.	190	45.01 N	93.09 W
Roseville, Ohio, U.S.	188	39.49 N	82.05 W
Roseville, Pa., U.S.	210	41.11 N	79.09 W
Roseville Park	285	39.42 N	75.43 W
Rosewood, Austl.	171a	27.39 S	152.35 E
Rosewood, Austl.	171b	35.41 S	147.52 E
Rosewood, Ohio, U.S.	216	40.13 N	83.58 W
Rosewood Heights	219	38.52 N	90.06 W
Roseworthy	168b	34.32 S	138.44 E
Roshanara Gardens ♠	272a	28.40 N	77.12 E
Rosharon	222	29.21 N	95.28 W
Rosheim	58	48.30 N	7.28 E
Rosherville Dam •6	273d	26.14 S	28.07 E
Rosh Ha'Ayin	132	32.06 N	34.57 E
Rosholt, S. Dak., U.S.	198	45.52 N	96.44 W
Rosholt, Wis., U.S.	190	44.38 N	89.18 W
Rosh Pinna	132	32.58 N	35.32 E
Rosh Pinna, Sede-Te'ufa ⊠	132	32.59 N	35.34 E
Rosica ≃	38	43.15 N	25.42 E
Rosice	30	49.11 N	16.23 E
Rosiclare	194	37.25 N	88.20 W
Rosières-aux-Salines	58	48.36 N	6.20 E
Rosières-en-Santerre	50	49.49 N	2.43 E
Rosiers, Rivière des ≃	206	45.59 N	72.07 W
Rosignano Marittimo	66	43.24 N	10.28 E
Rosignano Solvay	66	43.23 N	10.26 E
Rosignol	246	6.17 N	57.32 W
Roșiori-de-Vede	38	44.07 N	25.00 E
Rosita	236	13.53 N	84.24 W
Rositz	54	51.01 N	12.22 E
Ros'ka ≃	78	49.27 N	29.45 E
Roskilde	41	55.39 N	12.05 E
Roskilde □6	41	55.30 N	12.05 E
Roskilde Fjord C	41	55.56 N	12.00 E
Roskow	54	52.28 N	12.42 E
Roslagen □9	40	59.30 N	18.40 E
Roslags-Bro	40	59.50 N	18.44 E
Roslags-Näsby	40	59.26 N	18.04 E
Rosl'akovo	24	69.03 N	33.09 E
Rosl'atino	76	59.46 N	44.15 E
Roslavl'	76	53.57 N	32.52 E
Roslev	26	56.42 N	8.59 E
Roslindale •8	283	42.18 N	71.07 W
Roslyn, N.Y., U.S.	276	40.48 N	73.39 W
Roslyn, Pa., U.S.	285	40.07 N	75.08 W
Roslyn, Pa., U.S.	285	39.57 N	75.36 W
Roslyn, Wash., U.S.	224	47.13 N	120.59 W
Roslyn Estates	276	40.47 N	73.40 W
Roslyn Harbor	276	40.49 N	73.38 W
Roslyn Heights	276	40.47 N	73.39 W
Rosmalen	52	51.43 N	5.22 E
Rosman	192	35.03 N	82.49 W
Rosmarino ≃	70	38.05 N	14.40 E
Rosmead	158	31.29 S	25.08 E
Ros Mhic Treoin → New Ross	48	52.24 N	6.56 W
Røsnæs ≻1	41	55.44 N	10.59 E
Rosne, Ruisseau le ≃	261	48.58 N	2.25 E
Rosny-sous-Bois	261	48.53 N	2.29 E
Rosny-sur-Seine	50	49.00 N	1.38 E
Rosolina	64	45.05 N	12.15 E
Rosolini	70	36.49 N	14.57 E
Rošore	85	38.20 N	72.19 E
Rosporden	32	47.58 N	3.50 W
Rösrath	56	50.54 N	7.11 E
Ross, Austl.	166	42.02 S	147.29 E
Ross, N.Z.	172	42.54 S	170.49 E
Ross', S.S.S.R.	76	53.17 N	24.24 E
Ross, Calif., U.S.	226	37.55 N	122.32 W
Ross, Ind., U.S.	278	41.32 N	87.23 W
Ross, Ohio, U.S.	218	39.19 N	84.39 W
Ross □6	218	39.20 N	83.06 W
Ross ≃	180	61.59 N	132.26 W
Ross, Cape ≻	116	10.56 N	119.13 E
Ross, Mount ∧	172	41.28 S	175.21 E
Ross, Point ≻	174c	29.04 S	167.56 E
Ross, Pointe ≻	275a	45.21 N	73.48 W
Rossa	58	46.22 N	9.08 E
Rossach	56	50.09 N	10.56 E
Rossano	68	39.35 N	16.39 E
Rossan Point ≻	48	54.42 N	8.48 W
Rossasna	76	54.39 N	30.53 E
Rossau	54	52.47 N	11.38 E
Rossbach	54	51.15 N	11.53 E
Ross Barnett Reservoir ⊜1	194	32.30 N	90.00 W
Ross-Béthio	150	16.16 N	16.08 W
Rossburg	216	40.17 N	84.38 W
Rossburn	184	50.40 N	100.52 W
Rosscarbery	48	51.35 N	9.01 W
Ross Dam •6	224	48.44 N	121.04 W
Rossdorf	56	49.51 N	8.45 E
Rosseau	212	45.16 N	79.39 W
Rosseau, Lake ⊜	212	45.10 N	79.35 W
Rossel, Cap ≻	175f	20.23 S	166.36 E
Rossel Island I	160	11.21 S	154.09 E
Rossell y Rius	252	33.11 S	55.42 W
Rossen ⊜	40	60.19 N	16.26 E
Rossendale □8	262	53.43 N	2.14 W
Rossendale ∨	44	53.45 N	2.47 W
Rosser	222	32.28 N	96.27 W
Rosses Bay C	48	55.10 N	8.27 W
Rosses Point	48	54.18 N	8.33 W
Rossford	214	41.37 N	83.33 W
Ross Fork Creek ≃	202	47.05 N	109.43 W
Rosshaupten	58	47.39 N	10.43 E
Rosshyttan	40	60.04 N	16.21 E
Ross Ice Shelf ▽	9	81.30 S	175.00 W
Rossiglione	62	44.34 N	8.40 E
Rossignol, Lake ⊜	186	44.10 N	65.10 W
Rossijskaja Sovetskaja Federativnaja Socialističeskaja Respublika □3	74	60.00 N	100.00 E
Rössing	156	22.31 S	14.52 E
Rossio, Estação do •5	266c	38.43 N	9.09 W
Ross Island I, Ant.	9	77.30 S	168.00 E
Ross Island I, Man., Can.	184	54.14 N	97.45 W
Rossiter	214	40.53 N	78.56 W
Rossitten → Rybačij	76	55.09 N	20.51 E
Rossla	54	51.28 N	11.04 E
Ross Lake ⊜1	224	48.53 N	121.04 W
Ross Lake National Recreation Area ♠	224	48.45 N	121.00 W
Rossland	182	49.05 N	117.48 W
Rosslare	48	52.17 N	6.23 W
Rosslare Harbour	48	52.15 N	6.22 W
Rosslau	54	51.53 N	12.14 E
Rosslea	48	54.14 N	7.11 W
Rossleben	54	51.17 N	11.25 E
Rosslyn Farms	279b	40.26 N	80.05 W
Rossmoor	280	33.47 N	118.04 W
Rossmore	274a	33.57 S	150.46 E
Rossmoyne	208	40.13 N	76.57 W
Rosso	150	16.30 N	15.49 W
Rosso, Cap ≻	36	42.14 N	8.33 E
Rossön	26	63.55 N	16.21 E
Ross-on-Wye	42	51.55 N	2.35 W
Rossony	76	55.53 N	28.49 E
Rossoš', S.S.S.R.	78	50.12 N	39.34 E
Rossoš', S.S.S.R.	78	51.08 N	38.29 E
Rossouw	158	31.09 S	27.18 E
Ross River	180	61.59 N	132.27 W
Ross-Schelfeis → Ross Ice Shelf ▽	9	81.30 S	175.00 W
Ross Sea ⊤2	9	76.00 S	175.00 W
Rosstal	56	49.25 N	10.52 E
Rosston	218	40.03 N	86.17 W
Røssvatnet ⊜	24	65.45 N	14.00 E
Rossville, Ga., U.S.	192	34.59 N	85.16 W
Rossville, Ill., U.S.	216	40.23 N	87.40 W
Rossville, Ind., U.S.	216	40.25 N	86.36 W
Rossville, Kans., U.S.	198	39.08 N	95.57 W
Rossville, Md., U.S.	284b	39.20 N	76.29 W
Rosswein	54	51.03 N	13.10 E
Røst II	24	67.28 N	11.59 E
Rostāq	120	37.07 N	69.49 E
Röstånga	41	56.00 N	13.17 E
Rostavatn ⊜	24	68.45 N	20.30 E
Rosthern	184	52.40 N	106.17 W
Rostherne	262	53.21 N	2.23 W
Rostherne Mere ⊜	262	53.21 N	2.23 W
Roštkala	120	37.16 N	71.49 E
Rostock	54	54.05 N	12.07 E
Rostock □5	54	54.15 N	12.30 E
Rostov	80	57.11 N	39.25 E
Rostov □4	83	47.30 N	39.30 E
Rostov-na-Donu	83	47.14 N	39.42 E
Rostov-na-Donu, Aeroport ⊠	83	47.17 N	39.39 E
Rostraver Airport ⊠	279b	40.13 N	79.50 W
Rostraville	158	26.49 S	25.39 E
Rostrevor	48	54.06 N	6.12 W
Rosvinskoje	24	66.32 N	52.26 E
Roswell, Ga., U.S.	192	34.01 N	84.22 W
Roswell, N. Mex., U.S.	196	33.24 N	104.32 W
Roswell, Ohio, U.S.	214	40.28 N	81.21 W
Rosyth	46	56.03 N	3.26 W
Rot ≃	58	48.19 N	9.54 E
Rota	34	36.37 N	6.21 W
Rota I	108	14.10 N	145.12 E
Rot am See	56	49.15 N	10.01 E
Rotan	196	32.51 N	100.28 W
Rotanda	156	19.33 S	32.50 E
Rotary Island I	285	40.14 N	74.49 W
Rotbach ≃	263	51.34 N	6.41 E
Rotberg	264a	52.21 N	13.31 E
Rote-Erde, Stadion ♠	263	51.30 N	7.27 E
Rotem	56	51.03 N	5.44 E
Rotenburg	52	53.06 N	9.24 E
Rotenburg an der Fulda	56	51.00 N	9.45 E
Roter Main ≃	54	50.03 N	11.27 E
Rotes Meer → Red Sea ⊤2	136	20.00 N	38.00 E
Roth	56	50.46 N	7.42 E
Rötha	54	51.12 N	12.25 E
Rothaargebirge ⛰	56	51.05 N	8.15 E
Rothaargebirge, Naturpark ♠	56	51.05 N	8.15 E
Roth bei Nürnberg	60	49.14 N	11.04 E
Rothbury	44	55.19 N	1.55 W
Rothbury Forest •3	44	55.18 N	1.54 W
Rothemühl	54	53.36 N	13.49 E
Rothemühle	56	50.57 N	7.49 E
Röthenbach, B.R.D.	58	47.37 N	9.59 E
Röthenbach, Schw.	58	46.51 N	7.45 E
Röthenbach an der Pegnitz	60	49.29 N	11.15 E
Rothenburg	54	51.20 N	14.58 E
Rothenburg an der Oder → Czerwieńsk	30	52.01 N	15.25 E
Rothenburg ob der Tauber	56	49.23 N	10.10 E
Rothenkirchen	54	50.33 N	12.30 E
Rothenschirmbach	54	51.27 N	11.33 E
Rothenstadt	60	49.38 N	12.09 E
Rothenstein ∧2	263	51.07 N	7.41 E
Rother ≃	42	50.57 N	0.32 W
Rotherham, N.Z.	172	42.42 S	172.57 E
Rotherham, Eng., U.K.	44	53.26 N	1.20 W
Rothes	46	57.31 N	3.13 W
Rothesay, N.B., Can.	186	45.23 N	66.00 W
Rothesay, Scot., U.K.	46	55.51 N	5.03 W
Roth-neusiedl •8	264b	48.08 N	16.23 E
Rothrist	58	47.19 N	7.53 E
Rothsay, Austl.	162	29.17 S	116.53 E
Rothsay, Minn., U.S.	198	46.28 N	96.17 W
Rothschild	190	44.54 N	89.50 W
Rothsville	208	40.09 N	76.15 W
Rothwell, N.B., Can.	186	46.04 N	66.04 W
Rothwell, Eng., U.K.	42	52.25 N	0.48 W
Rothwell, Eng., U.K.	44	53.46 N	1.29 W
Roti, Pulau I	112	10.45 S	123.10 E
Roti, Selat ⟗	112	10.25 S	123.25 E
Roto	166	33.03 S	145.28 E
Rotoiti, Lake ⊜	172	38.02 S	176.25 E
Rotomanu	172	42.39 S	171.32 E
Rotonda	68	39.57 N	16.02 E
Rotondella	68	40.10 N	16.32 E
Rotondo, Monte ∧	36	42.13 N	9.03 E
Rotoroa, Lake ⊜	172	41.52 S	172.38 E
Rotorua	172	38.09 S	176.15 E
Rotorua, Lake ⊜	172	38.05 S	176.16 E
Rotowaro	172	37.36 S	175.05 E
Rott	64	47.54 N	10.59 E
Rott ≃	60	48.27 N	13.26 E
Rottach-Egern	64	47.41 N	11.46 E
Rott am Inn	64	47.59 N	12.07 E
Rotten ≃	58	46.17 N	7.33 E
Röttenbach	60	49.09 N	11.02 E
Rottenbach-Tremersdorf	56	50.21 N	10.56 E
Rottenbuch	64	47.44 N	10.58 E
Rottenburg am Neckar	58	48.28 N	8.56 E
Rottenburg an der Laaber	60	48.42 N	12.02 E
Rottenmann	61	47.31 N	14.22 E
Rottenmanner Tauern ⛰	61	47.24 N	14.22 E
Rotterdam, Ned.	52	51.55 N	4.28 E
Rotterdam, N.Y., U.S.	210	42.48 N	74.01 W
Rotterdam Junction	210	42.52 N	74.03 W
Rotthalmünster	60	48.21 N	13.12 E
Rotthausen •8	263	51.30 N	7.05 E
Rottingdean	42	50.48 N	0.04 W
Röttingen	56	49.30 N	9.58 E
Rottleberode	54	51.31 N	10.57 E
Rottnest Island I	168a	32.00 S	115.30 E
Rottofreno	62	45.03 N	9.34 E
Rottum	263	51.36 N	7.42 E
Rottumeroog I	52	53.30 N	6.30 E
Rottumerplaat I	52	53.32 N	6.30 E
Rottweil	58	48.10 N	8.37 E
Rotuma I	14	12.30 S	177.05 E
Rotwand •4	64	47.39 N	11.56 E
Rötz	60	49.21 N	12.32 E
Roubaix	50	50.42 N	3.10 E
Roubideau Creek ≃	200	38.44 N	108.10 W
Roubidoux Creek ≃	194	37.51 N	92.13 W
Roubion ≃	62	44.31 N	4.42 E
Rouceux	58	48.22 N	5.41 E
Roudnice [nad Labem]	54	50.22 N	14.16 E
Rouen	50	49.26 N	1.05 E
Rougé	32	47.47 N	1.27 W
Rouge ≃, Ont., Can.	212	43.47 N	79.01 W
Rouge ≃, Qué., Can.	206	45.39 N	74.42 W
Rouge → Red ≃, U.S.	178	31.00 N	91.40 W
Rouge, Bell Branch ≃	281	42.23 N	83.16 W
Rouge, Lac ⊜	206	46.56 N	74.38 W
Rouge, Mer → Red Sea ⊤2	136	20.00 N	38.00 E
Rouge, River ≃	281	42.17 N	83.06 W
Rougeau, Forêt de ♠	261	48.35 N	2.30 E
Rougemont, Fr.	58	47.29 N	6.21 E
Rougemont, Schw.	58	46.29 N	7.12 E
Rougemont-le-Château	58	47.44 N	6.58 E
Rough ≃	194	37.29 N	87.08 W
Rough And Ready	226	39.14 N	121.08 W
Rough River Lake ⊜1	194	37.40 N	86.25 W
Rouiba	34	36.44 N	3.17 E
Rouillac	32	45.47 N	0.04 W
Rouillon	261	48.33 N	2.00 E
Roujol, Pointe de ≻	241o	16.12 N	61.35 W
Rouku	164	8.40 S	141.35 E
Roulans	58	47.19 N	6.14 E
Rouleau	184	50.11 N	104.55 W
Roulers → Roeselare	50	50.57 N	3.08 E
Roulette	214	41.47 N	78.09 W
Roulo	281	42.12 N	83.29 W
Roumanie → Romania □1	38	46.00 N	25.30 E
Round, Point ≻	240d	15.33 N	61.29 W
Round Harbour	186	47.37 N	56.00 W
Roundhead	216	40.34 N	83.50 W
Round Hill Head ≻	166	24.10 S	151.53 E
Round Hill Regional Park ♠	279b	40.15 N	79.51 W
Round Island I	157c	19.51 S	57.48 E
Round Knowe ∧2	44	55.08 N	7.05 W
Round Lake, Ill., U.S.	278	42.21 N	88.05 W
Round Lake, Minn., U.S.	198	43.32 N	95.28 W
Round Lake, N.Y., U.S.	210	42.56 N	73.48 W
Round Lake ⊜, Newf., Can.	186	51.08 N	56.33 W
Round Lake ⊜, Ont., Can.	190	45.38 N	77.32 W
Round Lake ⊜, Ont., Can.	212	44.30 N	77.52 W
Round Lake ⊜, Ont., Can.	212	45.28 N	79.24 W
Round Lake ⊜, Sask., Can.	184	50.33 N	102.23 W
Round Lake ⊜, Mich., U.S.	216	41.58 N	84.17 W
Round Lake Beach	216	42.23 N	88.05 W
Round Lake Park	216	42.21 N	88.04 W
Round Mound ∧2	198	38.55 N	99.39 W
Round Mountain	204	38.43 N	117.04 W
Round Mountain ∧	171b	36.15 S	148.34 E
Round Mountain ∧2	166	30.27 S	152.14 E
Round Pond ⊜, Newf., Can.	186	48.10 N	56.00 W
Round Pond ⊜, Mass., U.S.	283	42.36 N	70.49 W
Round Rock	222	30.31 N	97.41 W
Roundstone	48	53.23 N	9.53 W
Round Top	210	42.16 N	74.02 W
Round Top ∧2	208	40.30 N	76.42 W
Roundtop Mountain ∧	206	45.05 N	72.33 W
Round Top Regional Park ♠	282	37.51 N	122.12 W
Roundup	202	46.27 N	108.33 W
Round Valley Indian Reservation •4	204	39.50 N	123.20 W
Round Valley Reservoir ⊜1	210	40.36 N	74.50 W
Roundwood	48	53.04 N	6.13 W
Roura	250	4.44 N	52.20 W
Rourkela → Raurkela	124	22.13 N	84.53 E
Rousay I	46	59.10 N	3.02 W
Rouse Hill	274a	33.41 S	150.56 E
Rouses Point	206	44.59 N	73.22 W
Rouseville	214	41.28 N	79.42 W
Rousies	50	50.16 N	4.00 E
Rousset, Col de)(	62	44.50 N	5.24 E
Roussigny	261	48.39 N	2.06 E
Roussillon, Fr.	62	43.54 N	5.17 E
Roussillon, Fr.	62	45.22 N	4.49 E
Roussillon □9	32	42.30 N	2.30 E
Roussy-le-Village	56	49.27 N	6.10 E
Routhierville	186	48.11 N	67.09 W
Routot	50	49.23 N	0.44 E
Rouveen	52	52.36 N	6.11 E
Rouvignies	50	50.20 N	3.26 E
Rouville □6	206	45.23 N	73.04 W
Rouvray	50	47.25 N	4.06 E
Rouvray, Lac ⊜	186	49.18 N	70.49 W
Rouxville	158	30.29 S	26.46 E
Rouyn	190	48.15 N	79.01 W
Rouzerville	208	39.44 N	77.32 W
Rovaniemi	24	66.34 N	25.48 E
Rovasenda	62	45.32 N	8.19 E
Rovato	64	45.34 N	10.00 E
Rovbick	76	52.40 N	24.05 E
Rove, Tunnel du •5	62	43.22 N	5.17 E
Rovegno	62	44.35 N	9.17 E
Rovellasca	62	45.40 N	9.03 E
Rovello Porro	62	45.39 N	9.02 E
Roven'ki, S.S.S.R.	78	49.56 N	38.54 E
Roven'ki, S.S.S.R.	83	48.05 N	39.21 E
Rovenskaja Sloboda	78	52.13 N	30.19 E
Roverbella	64	45.16 N	10.46 E
Rovere	66	42.10 N	13.31 E
Roverè della Luna	64	46.15 N	11.10 E

Symbols in the index entries represent the broad categories identified in the key at the right. Symbols with superior numbers (⛰2) identify subcategories (see complete key on page *I · 30*).

Kartensymbole in dem Registerverzeichnis stellen die rechts in Schlüssel erklärten Kategorien dar. Symbole mit hochgestellten Ziffern (⛰2) bezeichnen Unterabteilungen einer Kategorie (vgl. vollständiger Schlüssel auf Seite *I · 30*).

Los símbolos incluidos en el texto del índice representan las grandes categorias identificadas con la clave a la derecha. Los símbolos con numeros en su parte superior (⛰2) identifican las subcategorías (véase la clave completa en la página *I · 30*).

Les symboles de l'index représentent les catégories indiquées dans la légende à droite. Les symboles suivis d'un indice (⛰2) représentent des sous-catégories (voir légende complète à la page *I · 30*).

Os símbolos incluídos no texto do índice representam as grandes categorias identificadas com a chave à direita. Os símbolos com números em sua parte superior (⛰2) identificam as subcategorias (veja-se a chave completa à página *I · 30*).

	English	Deutsch	Español	Français	Português
∧	Mountain	Berg	Montaña	Montagne	Montanha
⛰	Mountains	Berge	Montañas	Montagnes	Montanhas
)(	Pass	Pass	Paso	Col	Passo
∨	Valley, Canyon	Tal, Cañon	Valle, Cañón	Vallée, Canyon	Vale, Canhão
≚	Plain	Ebene	Llano	Plaine	Planície
≻	Cape	Kap	Cabo	Cap	Cabo
I	Island	Insel	Isla	Île	Ilha
II	Islands	Inseln	Islas	Îles	Ilhas
•	Other Topographic Features	Andere Topographische Objekte	Otros Elementos Topográficos	Autres données topographiques	Outros Elementos Topográficos

ESPAÑOL

Nombre	Página	Lat.°′	Long.°′ W=Oeste
Roveredo	58	46.14 N	9.08 E
Rovereto	64	45.53 N	11.02 E
Roverè Veronese	64	45.36 N	11.03 E
Rövershagen	54	54.10 N	12.15 E
Roversi	252	27.35 S	61.57 W
Roverud	26	60.15 N	12.03 E
Roviano	66	42.01 N	13.00 E
Rovigo	64	45.04 N	11.47 E
Rovigo □[4]	64	45.02 N	11.50 E
Rovinj	36	45.05 N	13.38 E
Rovira	246	4.14 N	75.14 W
Rovno	78	50.37 N	26.15 E
Rovnoje, S.S.S.R.	78	48.15 N	31.45 E
Rovnoje, S.S.S.R.	80	50.47 N	46.05 E
Rovnoje, S.S.S.R.	85	42.53 N	73.32 E
Rovuma (Ruvuma) ≃	154	10.29 S	40.28 E
Rów	54	52.58 N	14.45 E
Rowan □[6]	218	38.17 N	83.26 W
Rowan Lake ◎	184	49.18 N	93.32 W
Rowanty Creek ≃	208	36.58 N	77.21 W
Rowena, Austl.	166	29.49 S	148.54 E
Rowena, Tex., U.S.	196	31.39 N	100.03 W
Rowe Park ♠	273a	6.30 N	3.23 E
Rowhill	273d	26.14 S	28.26 E
Rowland, N.C., U.S.	192	34.32 N	79.18 W
Rowland, Pa., U.S.	210	41.28 N	75.03 W
Rowland Flat	168b	34.35 S	138.56 E
Rowland Heights	280	33.59 N	117.54 W
Rowlands Gill	44	54.54 N	1.45 W
Rowlesburg	188	39.21 N	79.40 W
Rowlett	222	32.54 N	96.34 W
Rowlett, Isla ❙	254	44.48 S	74.25 W
Rowlett Creek ≃	222	32.49 N	96.31 W
Rowley	207	42.43 N	70.53 W
Rowley ≃, N.W. Ter., Can.	176	70.16 N	77.45 W
Rowley ≃, Mass., U.S.	283	42.43 N	70.49 W
Rowley Island ❙	176	69.08 N	78.50 W
Rowley Regis	42	52.29 N	2.03 W
Rowley Shoals ✣[2]	162	17.30 S	119.00 E
Rowntree Mill Park ♠	275b	43.45 N	79.35 W
Rowsburg	214	40.52 N	82.10 W
Rowville	274b	37.56 S	145.14 E
Roxa, Ilha ❙	150	11.15 N	15.40 W
Roxana	219	38.50 N	90.04 W
Roxas (Capiz), Pil.	108	11.35 N	122.45 E
Roxas, Pil.	116	12.35 N	121.31 E
Roxas, Pil.	116	10.20 N	119.21 E
Roxas (Capiz), Pil.	116	11.35 N	122.45 E
Roxas, Pil.	116	17.08 N	121.36 E
Roxboro, Qué., Can.	275a	45.31 N	73.48 W
Roxboro, N.C., U.S.	192	36.24 N	78.59 W
Roxborough	241r	11.15 N	60.35 W
Roxborough ◆[8]	285	40.02 N	75.13 W
Roxborough Downs	166	22.30 S	138.50 E
Roxburgh, N.Z.	172	45.32 S	169.19 E
Roxburgh, Scot., U.K.	46	55.34 N	2.30 W
Roxbury, Conn., U.S.	207	41.45 N	73.11 W
Roxbury, N.Y., U.S.	210	42.17 N	74.34 W
Roxbury, Pa., U.S.	214	40.07 N	77.40 W
Roxbury, Va., U.S.	208	37.28 N	77.09 W
Roxbury ◆[8], Mass., U.S.	283	42.20 N	71.06 W
Roxbury ◆[8], N.Y., U.S.	276	40.34 N	73.54 W
Roxel	52	51.57 N	7.32 E
Roxen ◎	26	58.30 N	15.41 E
Roxie	194	31.30 N	91.04 W
Roxo, Cap ≻	150	12.20 N	16.43 W
Roxton	196	33.33 N	95.44 W
Roxton Pond (Sainte-Pudentienne)	206	45.29 N	72.40 W
Roxwell	260	51.45 N	0.23 E
Roy, N. Mex., U.S.	196	35.57 N	104.12 W
Roy, Utah, U.S.	200	41.10 N	112.02 W
Roy, Wash., U.S.	224	47.00 N	122.33 W
Roya (Roia) ≃	62	43.48 N	7.35 E
Royal	198	43.04 N	95.17 W
Royal Albert Hall ♥	260	51.30 N	0.11 W
Royal Bangkok Sports Club ♠	269a	13.44 N	100.33 E
Royal Botanic Gardens ♠, Austl.	274a	33.52 S	151.13 E
Royal Botanic Gardens ♠, Austl.	274b	37.50 S	144.59 E
Royal Canal ≊	48	53.21 N	6.15 W
Royal Center	216	40.52 N	86.30 W
Royal City	202	46.54 N	119.38 W
Royale, Isle ❙	190	48.00 N	89.00 W
Royal Festival Hall ♥	260	51.30 N	0.07 W
Royal Island ❙	192	25.31 N	76.51 W
Royalla	171b	35.31 S	149.09 E
Royal Leamington Spa	42	52.18 N	1.31 W
Royal Natal National Park ♠	158	28.45 S	28.57 E
Royal Naval College ♥[2]	170	35.07 S	150.42 E
Royal Naval College ■	260	51.29 N	0.01 W
Royal Oak, B.C., Can.	224	48.30 N	123.23 W
Royal Oak, Md., U.S.	208	38.44 N	76.11 W
Royal Oak, Mich., U.S.	216	42.30 N	83.08 W
Royal Oak Township	281	42.27 N	83.10 W
Royal Observatory ♥[3]	271d	22.18 N	114.10 E
Royal Ontario Museum ♥	275b	43.40 N	79.24 W
Royal Opera House ♥	260	51.30 N	0.08 W
Royal Palms State Beach ♠	280	33.44 N	118.19 W
Royal Park ♠	274b	37.47 S	144.57 E
Royal Roads ⊂	224	48.26 N	123.26 W
Royalton, Ind., U.S.	218	39.56 N	86.21 W
Royalton, Minn., U.S.	190	45.50 N	94.18 W
Royalton, Pa., U.S.	208	40.11 N	76.44 W
Royal Tunbridge Wells → Tunbridge Wells	42	51.08 N	0.16 E
Royal Turf Club ♠	269a	13.46 N	100.32 E
Royan	32	45.37 N	1.01 W
Royaume-Uni → United Kingdom □[1]	28	54.00 N	2.00 W
Roybon	62	45.15 N	5.15 E
Royce Brook ≃	276	40.32 N	70.35 W
Roydon	42	51.46 N	0.03 E
Roye	50	49.42 N	2.48 E
Royersford	208	40.11 N	75.32 W
Royerton	216	40.16 N	85.22 W
Roy Hill	162	22.38 S	119.57 E
Royse City	222	32.59 N	96.20 W
Royston, Eng., U.K.	42	52.03 N	0.01 W
Royston, Eng., U.K.	44	53.37 N	1.27 W
Royston, Ga., U.S.	192	34.17 N	83.06 W
Royton	44	53.34 N	2.08 W
Rožaj	38	42.50 N	20.10 E
Różan	30	52.53 N	21.25 E
Rozay-en-Brie	50	48.41 N	2.58 E
Roždestvenka, S.S.S.R.	86	55.21 N	77.29 E
Roždestvenka, S.S.S.R.	86	50.52 N	71.22 E
Roždestvenka, S.S.S.R.	86	55.42 N	70.00 E
Roždestveno, S.S.S.R.	76	57.44 N	37.57 E
Roždestveno, S.S.S.R.	80	53.15 N	50.04 E
Roždestveno, S.S.S.R.	82	56.51 N	36.33 E
Roždestveno, S.S.S.R.	82	55.57 N	36.23 E
Roždestvenskaja Chava	78	51.38 N	39.40 E

FRANÇAIS

Nom	Page	Lat.°′	Long.°′ W=Ouest
Roždestvenskoje, S.S.S.R.	80	58.09 N	45.35 E
Roždestvenskoje, S.S.S.R.	80	52.47 N	42.10 E
Roždestvenskoje, S.S.S.R.	80	51.14 N	42.10 E
Roždestvo	76	57.36 N	33.48 E
Rozel	43b	49.14 N	2.03 W
Rozelle	274a	33.52 S	151.10 E
Roželov	60	49.33 N	13.48 E
Rozewie, Przylądek ≻	30	54.51 N	18.21 E
Rozhnof, Cape ≻	180	55.58 N	160.58 W
Rožišče	78	50.54 N	25.15 E
Rožki	80	56.41 N	50.31 E
Rožkov	80	51.39 N	52.19 E
Rožmberk	61	49.04 N	14.47 E
Rožmitál pod Třemšínem	60	49.36 N	13.52 E
Rožn'atov	78	48.56 N	24.09 E
Rožňava	30	48.40 N	20.32 E
Roznov	38	46.50 N	26.31 E
Rožnov pod Radhoštěm	30	49.28 N	18.10 E
Rożnów	30	49.46 N	20.42 E
Rozovka	78	47.23 N	37.04 E
Rozoy-sur-Serre	50	49.43 N	4.08 E
Roztocze ∧	30	50.30 N	23.20 E
Roztoky	54	50.09 N	14.22 E
Rrëshen	38	41.47 N	19.54 E
Rrogozhinë	38	41.05 N	19.40 E
Rtiščevo	80	52.16 N	43.47 E
Ru, Tanjong ≻	114	2.50 N	101.17 E
Ruabon	42	52.59 N	3.02 W
Ruacaná	152	17.25 S	14.12 E
Ruacana Falls ↳	152	17.22 S	14.12 E
Ruaha National Park ♠	154	7.30 S	34.40 E
Ruahine Range ⩘	172	40.00 S	176.06 E
Ruahmi, Ra's ≻	142	28.44 N	32.50 E
Ruanda	154	10.33 S	34.57 E
Ruanda → Rwanda □[1]	154	2.30 S	30.00 E
Ruango	164	5.35 S	150.10 E
Ruapehu, Mount ∧	172	39.17 S	175.34 E
Ruapuke Island ❙	172	46.47 S	168.30 E
Rua Sura ❙	175e	9.30 S	160.37 E
Ruatahuna	172	38.33 S	176.57 E
Ruatapu	172	42.48 S	170.53 E
Ruathair, Lochan ◎	46	58.18 N	3.56 W
Ruatoria	172	37.53 S	178.20 E
Ruaus, Wādī ∨	146	30.26 N	15.24 E
Ruawai	172	36.08 S	174.02 E
Ruba	76	26.08 N	30.19 E
Rub' al Khali → Ar-Rub' al-Khālī ◆[2]	136	20.00 N	51.00 E
Rubanovka	78	47.00 N	34.10 E
Rubbestadneset	26	59.49 N	5.17 E
Rubcovsk	86	51.33 N	81.10 E
Rubcy	83	49.12 N	37.33 E
Rubeho Mountains ⩘	154	6.55 S	36.30 E
Rubel'	78	51.58 N	27.04 E
Rübeland	54	51.45 N	10.50 E
Rubelles	261	48.34 N	2.41 E
Rubery	42	52.24 N	2.00 W
Rubeshibe	92a	43.47 N	143.38 E
Rubežka	80	51.26 N	51.59 E
Rubežnoje	83	49.01 N	38.23 E
Rubí, Esp.	266d	41.29 N	2.02 E
Rubi, Zaïre	154	2.49 N	25.14 E
Rubi ≃	152	2.48 N	23.54 E
Rubiana	62	45.08 N	7.23 E
Rubiataba	255	15.08 S	49.48 W
Rubicon ≃	226	39.00 N	120.44 W
Rubicone ≃	66	44.08 N	12.28 E
Rubidoux	228	34.00 N	117.25 W
Rubiera	64	44.39 N	10.45 E
Rubim	255	16.23 S	40.32 W
Rubio	246	7.43 N	72.22 W
Rubio Woods ♠	278	41.38 N	87.46 W
Rubl'ovka	78	49.15 N	33.19 E
Rubl'ovo	82	55.47 N	37.21 E
Ruboani	140	8.06 N	30.45 E
Rubona	154	0.33 N	30.10 E
Rubondo Island ❙	154	2.20 S	31.52 E
Rubtsovsk → Rubcovsk	86	51.33 N	81.10 E
Ruby, Alaska, U.S.	180	64.44 N	155.30 W
Ruby, N.Y., U.S.	210	42.01 N	74.01 W
Ruby ≃	202	45.34 N	112.21 W
Ruby Creek ≃	224	48.43 N	120.59 W
Ruby Dome ∧	204	40.37 N	115.28 W
Ruby Lake ☷	204	40.10 N	115.30 W
Ruby Mountains ⩘	204	40.25 N	115.35 W
Ruby Range ⩘	202	45.15 N	112.15 W
Ruby Valley ∨	204	40.30 N	115.15 W
Rucava	76	56.09 N	21.10 E
Ruchan'	76	53.33 N	32.48 E
Rucheng	100	25.34 N	113.41 E
Ruciane-Nida	30	53.39 N	21.35 E
Ručji ◆[8]	265a	60.01 N	30.24 E
Ručjuvom	24	66.42 N	61.08 E
Rucphen	52	51.32 N	4.34 E
Ruda	64	45.50 N	13.24 E
Rudall	166	33.41 S	136.16 E
Rudall ≃	162	22.16 S	122.47 E
Ruda Śląska	30	50.18 N	18.51 E
Rudauli	124	26.45 N	81.45 E
Ruḑaymah Lioûa	132	33.01 N	36.35 E
Rūdbār, Afg.	128	30.09 N	62.36 E
Rūdbar, Īrān	128	33.35 N	47.00 E
Rūdbār, Īrān	128	36.48 N	49.24 E
Rudbøl	41	54.54 N	8.45 E
Ruddervoorde	50	51.06 N	3.12 E
Ruddiman Terrace	216	43.12 N	86.17 W
Rudelsburg ⊥	54	51.07 N	11.43 E
Ruden ❙	54	54.12 N	13.46 E
Rudensk	76	53.36 N	27.52 E
Rüdersdorf	54	52.29 N	13.47 E
Rüdersdorf, Forst ◆[3]	264a	52.26 N	13.50 E
Rüdesheim am Rheim	56	49.59 N	7.56 E
Rudeville	276	41.09 N	74.33 W
Rudewa	154	10.06 S	34.39 E
Rudge Ramos	287b	23.41 S	46.34 W
Rüdinghausen ◆[8]	263	51.27 N	7.25 E
Rūdiškės	76	54.31 N	24.50 E
Rudki	78	49.39 N	23.29 E
Rudkino	78	51.27 N	39.01 E
Rudkøbing	41	54.56 N	10.43 E
Rudn'a, S.S.S.R.	76	54.57 N	31.06 E
Rudn'a, S.S.S.R.	80	50.48 N	44.33 E
Rudnevka ≃	265b	55.43 N	37.56 E
Rudnevo	82	54.44 N	38.09 E
Rudnica	78	48.15 N	28.55 E
Rudničnyj, S.S.S.R.	24	59.38 N	52.27 E
Rudničnyj, S.S.S.R.	86	59.42 N	60.18 E
Rudničnyj, S.S.S.R.	86	56.08 N	86.12 E
Rudničnyj, S.S.S.R.	86	44.40 N	78.55 E
Rudnik	30	50.28 N	22.15 E
Rüdnitz	54	52.43 N	13.37 E
Rudnyj	86	52.57 N	63.07 E
Rudo	38	43.37 N	19.22 E
Rudolf, Lake ◎	144	3.30 N	36.05 E
Rudolph	216	41.18 N	83.40 W
Rudolstadt	54	50.43 N	11.20 E
Rudong, Zhg.	102	21.39 N	111.23 E
Rudong, Zhg.	106	32.19 N	121.12 E
Rudovka, S.S.S.R.	80	53.07 N	42.23 E
Rudovka, S.S.S.R.	83	49.24 N	38.27 E
Rudow ◆[8]	264a	52.25 N	13.30 E
Rudrón ≃	34	42.47 N	3.45 W
Rūd Sar	128	37.08 N	50.18 E
Ruds Vedby	41	55.33 N	11.23 E
Rudyard, Mich., U.S.	190	46.14 N	84.36 W
Rudyard, Mont., U.S.	202	48.34 N	110.33 W
Rudyerd Bay ⊂	182	55.35 N	130.44 W
Rue, Fr.	50	50.16 N	1.40 E

PORTUGUÊS

Nome	Página	Lat.°′	Long.°′ W=Oeste
Rue, Schw.	58	46.37 N	6.50 E
Ruecas ≃	34	39.00 N	5.55 W
Rueil-Malmaison	261	48.53 N	2.11 E
Ruen ∧	38	42.10 N	22.31 E
Ruenya (Luenha) ≃	154	16.24 S	33.48 E
Rufā'ah	140	14.46 N	33.22 E
Ruffano	68	39.59 N	18.15 E
Ruffec	32	46.02 N	0.42 E
Ruffieu	58	46.00 N	5.40 E
Ruffieux	62	45.51 N	5.50 E
Ruffin	192	33.00 N	80.49 W
Ruffle Bar ❙	276	40.36 N	46.51 W
Rufford	262	53.38 N	2.49 W
Rufford Old Hall ⊥	262	53.38 N	2.49 W
Ruffs Dale	279b	40.10 N	79.37 W
Rufidschi → Rufiji ≃	154	8.00 S	39.20 E
Rufiji ≃	154	8.00 S	39.20 E
Rufina	66	43.49 N	11.29 E
Rufino	252	34.16 S	62.42 W
Rufisque	150	14.43 N	17.17 W
Rufunsa	154	15.05 S	29.40 E
Rufus	224	45.42 N	120.44 W
Rufus, Mount ∧	168b	34.20 S	139.07 E
Rugāji	76	57.00 N	27.08 E
Rugao	100	32.25 N	120.36 E
Rugby, Eng., U.K.	42	52.23 N	1.15 W
Rugby, N. Dak., U.S.	198	48.22 N	100.00 W
Rugeley	42	52.46 N	1.55 W
Rügen ❙	54	54.25 N	13.24 E
Rügenwalde → Darłowo	30	54.26 N	16.23 E
Rüggeberg	263	51.16 N	7.22 E
Rugged Mountain ∧	182	50.02 N	126.41 W
Ruggles Beach	214	41.22 N	82.29 W
Rugles	50	48.49 N	0.42 E
Ruguj	76	59.28 N	32.50 E
Ruḩama	132	31.30 N	34.42 E
Ruhea	124	26.10 N	88.25 E
Ruhengeri	154	1.30 S	29.38 E
Ruhla	54	50.53 N	10.22 E
Ruhland	54	51.27 N	13.52 E
Ruhlsdorf	264a	52.23 N	13.16 E
Ruhmannsfelden	60	48.59 N	12.59 E
Ruhner Berge ⩘[2]	54	53.17 N	11.55 E
Ruhnu Saar ❙	76	57.48 N	23.15 E
Ruhpolding	64	47.45 N	12.38 E
Ruhr ≃	52	51.27 N	6.44 E
Ruhr, Universität ♥[2]	263	51.27 N	7.16 E
Ruhrort ◆[8]	263	51.26 N	6.45 E
Ruhstorf an der Rott	60	48.26 N	13.20 E
Ruhudji ≃	154	8.52 S	36.01 E
Ruhuhu ≃	154	10.31 S	34.34 E
Ruian	100	27.49 N	120.38 E
Ruichang	100	29.41 N	115.40 E
Ruicheng	102	34.45 N	110.45 E
Ruidoso	200	33.20 N	105.40 W
Ruidoso, Rio ≃	200	33.23 N	105.16 W
Ruifengsha ❙	106	31.25 N	121.36 E
Ruijin	100	25.50 N	116.00 E
Ruinen	52	52.46 N	6.22 E
Ruinforme de l'Isalo, Massif ⩘	157b	22.45 S	45.15 E
Ruiselede	50	51.03 N	3.24 E
Ruislip ◆[8]	260	51.34 N	0.25 W
Ruit	56	48.43 N	9.14 E
Ruivos, Angra de los ⊂	148	24.45 N	15.05 W
Ruiz	234	21.57 N	105.09 W
Ruiz de Montoya	252	26.59 S	55.03 W
Rūjiena	76	57.54 N	25.21 E
Rujm ar-Rashīd, Jabal ∧	132	31.53 N	36.18 E
Rujm aş-Şakhrī	132	31.02 N	35.43 E
Rukan-shō ✣[2]	174m	26.06 N	127.32 E
Rukatunturi ∧[2]	26	66.09 N	29.10 E
Ruki ≃	152	0.05 N	18.17 E
Rukni	126	23.33 N	86.33 E
Rukungiri	154	0.48 S	29.55 E
Rukuruku Bay ⊂	175g	16.42 S	178.33 E
Rukwa, Lake ◎	154	8.00 S	32.25 E
Rule	196	33.11 N	99.54 W
Rule Creek ≃	198	38.02 N	103.02 W
Ruleville	194	33.44 N	90.33 W
Rulle	52	52.20 N	8.04 E
Rully	58	46.52 N	4.45 E
Rulo	198	40.03 N	95.26 W
Rum	61	47.08 N	16.51 E
Rum ≃	190	45.11 N	93.23 W
Ruma	38	45.00 N	19.49 E
Rumaat	164	5.49 S	132.48 E
Rumahtinggih	164	6.23 S	140.17 E
Rum'ancevo, S.S.S.R.	82	55.58 N	36.32 E
Rum'ancevo, S.S.S.R.	82	55.38 N	37.26 E
Rum'ancevo ◆[8]	83	48.21 N	38.06 E
Rumänien → Romania □[1]	38	46.00 N	25.30 E
Rumaysh	132	33.05 N	35.22 E
Rumbalara	162	25.20 S	134.29 E
Rumbek	140	6.48 N	29.41 E
Rumbeke	50	50.56 N	3.10 E
Rumberpon, Pulau ❙	164	1.50 S	134.15 E
Rumbling Bridge	46	56.10 N	3.35 W
Rumburk	54	50.57 N	14.32 E
Rum Cay ❙	238	23.40 N	74.53 W
Rumelange	56	49.28 N	6.02 E
Rumelifeneri	267b	41.14 N	29.06 E
Rumelihisarı ◆[8]	267b	41.05 N	29.03 E
Rumelihisarı ⊥	267b	41.05 N	29.02 E
Rumelikavağı ◆[8]	267b	41.11 N	29.04 E
Rumeln-Kaldenhausen	56	51.23 N	6.40 E
Rumford	188	44.33 N	70.33 W
Rumford ≃	283	41.58 N	71.11 W
Rumia	30	54.35 N	18.25 E
Rumigny	50	49.48 N	4.16 E
Rumilly	62	45.52 N	5.57 E
R'uminskoje	82	56.31 N	38.47 E
Rum Jungle	164	13.01 S	131.00 E
R'umki	265a	59.47 N	30.02 E
Rumkiğ	130	39.00 N	39.18 E
Rümlang	58	47.27 N	8.32 E
Rummah, Wādī ar- ∨	128	26.12 N	44.04 E
Rummān, Wādī ∨	132	29.43 N	35.23 E
Rummānah	142	31.01 N	32.40 E
Rummānah, Bi'r ar- ⊤[4]	142	31.00 N	32.40 E
Rummel	214	40.13 N	78.48 W
Rummelsburg → Miastko	30	54.01 N	17.00 E
Rummelsburg ◆[8]	264a	52.30 N	13.29 E
Rummenohl	263	51.17 N	7.32 E
Rumney	42	51.31 N	3.07 W
Rumoi	92a	43.56 N	141.39 E
Rumont	56	48.50 N	5.17 E
Rumphi	154	11.01 S	33.52 E
Rump Mountain ∧	188	45.12 N	71.04 W
Rumson	208	40.22 N	74.00 W
Rumst	50	51.05 N	4.25 E
Rumula	164	16.35 S	145.20 E
Rumung ❙	174q	9.37 N	138.10 E
Rumuruti	154	0.16 N	36.32 E
Runan	100	33.01 N	114.22 E
Runanga	172	42.24 S	171.16 E
Runaway, Cape ≻	172	37.32 S	177.59 E
Runazi	154	2.47 S	31.28 E
Runcorn	44	53.20 N	2.44 W
Rundeng	114	2.39 N	97.52 E
Rundēni	76	56.16 N	27.50 E
Ründeroth	56	50.59 N	7.28 E
Rundvik	26	63.32 N	19.26 E
Runere	154	3.06 S	33.16 E
Rŭng, Kaôh ❙	110	10.44 N	103.14 E
Rungāni	120	26.38 N	65.43 E
Runge	222	28.54 N	97.43 W
Rungis	261	48.45 N	2.21 E
Rungis-Halles, Marché de ♥	261	48.46 N	2.21 E
Rungsted	41	55.53 N	12.33 E
Rungus Point ≻	116	13.43 N	123.58 E
Rungwa, Tan.	154	7.21 S	31.40 E
Rungwa, Tan.	154	6.57 S	33.31 E
Rungwa ≃	154	7.36 S	31.50 E
Rungwa River Game Reserve ◆[4]	154	7.00 S	34.10 E
Rungwe	154	9.10 S	33.36 E
Runhällen	40	60.02 N	16.49 E
Runheji	100	32.30 N	116.05 E
Runkel	56	50.24 N	8.10 E
Runmarö ❙	40	59.17 N	18.46 E
Runn ◎	40	60.33 N	15.40 E
Runnemede	285	39.51 N	75.04 W
Running Springs	228	34.12 N	117.07 W
Running Water Draw ∨	196	33.58 N	101.30 W
Runnymede □[8]	260	51.24 N	0.32 W
Runnymede ⊥	260	51.26 N	0.34 W
Rünthe	263	51.39 N	7.39 E
Runtu	156	17.52 S	19.43 E
Runu	174q	9.35 N	138.09 E
Runwell	260	51.37 N	0.32 E
Ruo'ergai	102	33.16 N	102.55 E
Ruoheng	100	28.24 N	121.31 E
Ruokolahti	26	61.17 N	28.50 E
Ruoms	62	44.27 N	4.21 E
Ruoqiang	90	38.30 N	88.05 E
Ruoshui ≃	102	41.00 N	100.10 E
Ruoti	68	40.43 N	15.41 E
Ruovesi	26	61.59 N	24.05 E
Ruoxi	100	29.18 N	115.20 E
Rupanco	254	40.46 S	72.42 W
Rupanco, Lago ◎	254	40.49 S	72.28 W
Rūpar	123	30.59 N	76.31 E
Rupari	168b	35.37 S	139.09 E
Rupat, Pulau ❙	114	1.50 N	101.35 E
Rupat, Selat ⋓	114	1.50 N	101.25 E
Rupdia	126	23.08 N	89.18 E
Rupea	38	46.02 N	25.13 E
Rupert, Idaho, U.S.	202	42.37 N	113.41 W
Rupert, Vt., U.S.	210	43.16 N	73.13 W
Rupert, W. Va., U.S.	188	37.58 N	80.41 W
Rupert, Rivière de ≃	176	51.29 N	78.45 W
Rupert Creek ≃	166	20.53 S	142.23 E
Rupert House	176	51.30 N	78.45 W
Rupganj	126	23.48 N	90.31 E
Rūpnārāyan ≃	126	22.13 N	88.03 E
Ruponda	154	10.15 S	38.42 E
Ruppertenrod	56	50.37 N	9.05 E
Ruppiner See ◎	54	52.48 N	12.50 E
Rupprechteck ∧	61	47.14 N	14.00 E
Rupt de Mad ≃	56	49.01 N	6.02 E
Rupt-sur-Moselle	58	47.56 N	6.40 E
Rupununi □[5]	246	3.00 N	59.00 W
Rupununi ≃	246	4.03 N	58.34 W
Rur (Roer) ≃	56	51.12 N	5.59 E
Rural Hall	192	36.15 N	80.18 W
Rural Ridge	279b	40.35 N	79.50 W
Rural Valley	214	40.48 N	79.18 W
Rurberg	56	50.37 N	6.22 E
Ruri-kei ♠	96	35.04 N	135.28 E
Rurrenabaque	248	14.28 S	67.34 W
Rurstausee ◎[1]	56	50.36 N	6.22 E
Rurutu ❙	14	22.26 S	151.20 W
Rusambo	154	16.35 S	32.12 E
Rušan	120	37.58 N	71.30 E
Rusanov	78	50.29 N	31.09 E
Rusanovka	78	50.32 N	33.44 E
Rusape	154	18.32 S	32.07 E
Rusavkina-Popovščina	265b	55.42 N	38.04 E
Ruşayriş, Khazzān ar- ◎[1]	140	11.40 N	34.20 E
Ruschuk → Ruse	38	43.50 N	25.57 E
Ruscom ≃	214	42.18 N	82.38 W
Ruscom Station	214	42.13 N	82.39 W
Ruse	38	43.50 N	25.57 E
Rusera	124	25.45 N	86.02 E
Rusfontein	158	30.28 S	29.17 E
Rush, Eire	48	53.32 N	6.06 W
Rush, N.Y., U.S.	210	42.59 N	77.39 W
Rush, Pa., U.S.	210	41.47 N	76.03 W
Rush □[6]	218	39.37 N	85.27 W
Rush ≃, N. Dak., U.S.	198	47.00 N	96.54 W
Rush ≃, Wis., U.S.	190	44.34 N	92.19 W
Rushan (Xiacun)	98	36.54 N	121.29 E
Rush Center	198	38.28 N	99.19 W
Rush City	190	45.41 N	92.58 W
Rush Creek ≃, Colo., U.S.	198	38.22 N	102.32 W
Rush Creek ≃, Nebr., U.S.	198	41.27 N	102.32 W
Rush Creek ≃, N.Y., U.S.	284a	42.00 N	78.52 W
Rush Creek ≃, Ohio, U.S.	188	39.38 N	82.33 W
Rush Creek ≃, Ohio, U.S.	214	40.34 N	83.20 W
Rush Creek ≃, Okla., U.S.	196	34.42 N	97.10 W
Rushden	42	52.17 N	0.36 W
Rushford, Minn., U.S.	190	43.49 N	91.46 W
Rushford, N.Y., U.S.	210	42.24 N	78.15 W
Rush Hill	219	39.13 N	91.43 W
Rush Lake ◎, Ont., Can.	190	47.48 N	82.12 W
Rush Lake ◎, Wis., U.S.	190	43.49 N	89.00 W
Rushland	285	40.15 N	75.02 W
Rushmore	198	43.37 N	95.48 W
Rusholme ◆[8]	262	53.27 N	2.12 W
Rush Springs	196	34.47 N	97.58 W
Rushsylvania	216	40.28 N	83.41 W
Rushville, Ill., U.S.	219	40.07 N	90.34 W
Rushville, Ind., U.S.	218	39.37 N	85.27 W
Rushville, Nebr., U.S.	198	42.43 N	102.28 W
Rushville, N.Y., U.S.	210	42.46 N	77.14 W
Rusinga Island ❙	154	0.24 S	34.10 E
Rusizi (Ruzizi) ≃	154	3.16 S	29.14 E
Rusk	222	31.48 N	95.09 W
Rusk □[6]	222	32.10 N	94.50 W
Rusken ◎	26	57.17 N	14.20 E
Ruskin, B.C., Can.	224	49.12 N	122.28 W
Ruskin, Fla., U.S.	220	27.43 N	82.26 W
Rusnė	76	55.18 N	21.22 E
Rušonu Ezers ◎	76	56.11 N	27.02 E
Rusovce	61	48.04 N	17.10 E
Russa	272b	22.29 N	88.21 E
Russas	250	4.56 S	37.58 W
Russbach ≃	264b	48.17 N	16.35 E
Russee	41	54.18 N	10.04 E
Russel	150	8.15 N	13.05 W
Russell, Man., Can.	184	50.47 N	101.15 W
Russell, Ont., Can.	212	45.17 N	75.17 W
Russell, N.Z.	172	35.16 S	174.07 E
Russell, Calif., U.S.	226	37.39 N	122.08 W
Russell, Iowa, U.S.	190	40.59 N	93.12 W
Russell, Kans., U.S.	198	38.54 N	98.52 W
Russell, Ky., U.S.	188	38.32 N	82.42 W
Russell, Mass., U.S.	207	42.11 N	72.51 W
Russell, Minn., U.S.	198	44.19 N	95.57 W
Russell, Pa., U.S.	214	41.56 N	79.08 W
Russell □[6]	212	45.25 N	75.15 W
Russell, Cape ≻	176	75.15 N	117.35 W
Russell, Mount ∧	180	62.48 N	151.52 W
Russell Cave National Monument ♠	194	34.54 N	85.48 W
Russell Creek ≃	194	37.14 N	85.30 W
Russell Gardens	276	40.47 N	73.43 W
Russell Island ❙	176	73.55 N	98.25 W
Russell Islands ❙❙	175e	9.04 S	159.12 E
Russellkonda	120	19.56 N	84.35 E
Russell Lake ◎	184	56.15 N	101.30 W
Russell Point ≻	176	73.30 N	115.00 W
Russell Range ⩘	162	33.24 S	123.28 E
Russells Point	216	40.28 N	83.54 W
Russell Springs	194	37.03 N	85.05 W
Russellton	214	40.37 N	79.50 W
Russellville, Ala., U.S.	194	34.30 N	87.44 W
Russellville, Ark., U.S.	194	35.17 N	93.08 W
Russellville, Ky., U.S.	194	36.51 N	86.53 W
Russellville, Mo., U.S.	194	38.31 N	92.26 W
Russellville, Ohio, U.S.	218	38.52 N	83.47 W
Russellville, Oreg., U.S.	224	45.31 N	122.32 W
Rüsselsheim	56	50.00 N	8.25 E
Russi	66	44.22 N	12.02 E
Russia	216	40.14 N	84.24 W
Russian ≃	204	38.27 N	123.08 W
Russian Mission	180	61.34 N	159.34 W
Russian Soviet Federated Socialist Republic → Rosstjskaja Sovetskaja Federativnaja Socialističeskaja Respublica □[3]	74	60.00 N	100.00 E
Russiaville	216	40.25 N	86.16 W
Russka	76	58.59 N	28.30 E
Russkaja Bujlovka	78	50.22 N	40.03 E
Russkaja Gavan'	74	76.10 N	62.35 E
Russkaja Pol'ana	86	53.47 N	73.53 E
Russkaja Ţalovka	80	49.59 N	49.05 E
Russkaja Žuravka	80	50.21 N	40.33 E
Russkij	89	43.03 N	131.50 E
Russkij, Ostrov ❙	74	77.00 N	96.00 E
Russkij Aktaš	80	55.02 N	52.07 E
Russkij Brod	76	52.36 N	37.22 E
Russkij Kameškir	80	52.52 N	46.06 E
Russkij Pervyj	84	43.50 N	44.37 E
Russkij Turek	80	57.03 N	50.13 E
Russkij Vožoj	80	56.57 N	53.22 E
Russkij Zavorot, Mys ≻	24	68.58 N	54.34 E
Russkoje	83	47.45 N	38.56 E
Russkoje-Dobrino	80	54.22 N	52.28 E
Russko-Vysockoje	265a	59.42 N	29.56 E
Rust, B.R.D.	58	48.16 N	7.43 E
Rust, Öst.	61	47.48 N	16.41 E
Rustajskij	80	56.31 N	44.49 E
Rustam	123	34.21 N	72.17 E
Rustavi	84	41.33 N	45.02 E
Rustburg	192	37.17 N	79.06 W
Rustenburg	158	25.37 S	27.08 E
Rustic Canyon ∨	280	34.04 N	118.31 W
Rustington	42	50.48 N	0.31 W
Ruston, La., U.S.	194	32.32 N	92.38 W
Ruston, Wash., U.S.	224	47.19 N	122.32 W
Rusville	273d	26.10 S	28.18 E
Rutaki Passage ⋓	174k	21.15 S	159.48 W
Rutana	154	3.55 S	30.00 E
Rutčenkovo	83	47.57 N	37.44 E
Rute	34	37.19 N	4.22 W
Rütenbrock	52	52.50 N	7.10 E
Ruteng	115b	8.36 S	120.27 E
Rutenga	154	21.08 S	30.45 E
Rutersville	222	29.57 N	96.48 W
Rutgers University (Newark) ♥[2], N.J., U.S.	276	40.44 N	74.10 W
Rutgers University ♥[2], N.J., U.S.	276	40.30 N	74.27 W
Rutgers University (Camden) ♥[2], N.J., U.S.	285	39.56 N	75.07 W
Ruth, Miss., U.S.	194	31.23 N	90.19 W
Ruth, Nev., U.S.	204	39.17 N	114.59 W
Rüthen	52	51.29 N	8.25 E
Rutherford, Calif., U.S.	226	38.28 N	122.25 W
Rutherford, N.J., U.S.	210	40.49 N	74.07 W
Rutherford, Tenn., U.S.	194	36.08 N	88.59 W
Rutherfordton	192	35.22 N	81.57 W
Rutherglen, Scot., U.K.	46	55.50 N	4.12 W
Ruther Glen, Va., U.S.	208	37.56 N	77.27 W
Ruthin	44	53.07 N	3.18 W
Ruthton	198	44.11 N	96.06 W
Ruthven, Ont., Can.	214	42.03 N	82.40 W
Ruthven, Iowa, U.S.	198	43.08 N	94.54 W
Rüti	58	47.16 N	8.51 E
Rutig	158	27.22 S	27.09 E
Rutigliano	68	41.01 N	17.00 E
Rutino	68	40.18 N	15.04 E
Rutka ≃	80	56.22 N	46.38 E
Rutland, B.C., Can.	182	49.53 N	119.24 W
Rutland, Fla., U.S.	220	28.51 N	82.13 W
Rutland, Ill., U.S.	216	40.59 N	89.03 W
Rutland, Mass., U.S.	207	42.23 N	71.57 W
Rutland, N. Dak., U.S.	198	46.03 N	97.30 W
Rutland, Vt., U.S.	188	43.36 N	72.59 W
Rutland □[6]	210	43.21 N	73.15 W
Rutland Island ❙	110	11.25 N	92.40 E
Rutland State Park ♠	207	42.23 N	72.01 W
Rutledge, Ga., U.S.	192	33.38 N	83.37 W
Rutledge, Pa., U.S.	285	39.54 N	75.20 W
Rutledge, Tenn., U.S.	192	36.17 N	83.31 W
Rütli ⊥	58	46.58 N	8.36 E
Rutshuru	154	1.11 S	29.27 E
Rüttenscheid ◆[8]	263	51.26 N	7.00 E
Rutter	190	46.06 N	80.40 W
Rutul	84	41.33 N	47.25 E
Ruukki	26	64.40 N	25.06 E
Ruurlo	52	52.05 N	6.26 E
Ruvo del Monte	68	40.51 N	15.32 E
Ruvo di Puglia	68	41.07 N	16.29 E
Ruvu	154	6.48 S	38.39 E
Ruvu ≃	154	6.23 S	38.52 E
Ruvubu ≃	154	2.23 S	30.47 E
Ruvuma □[4]	154	11.00 S	36.00 E
Ruvuma (Rovuma) ≃	154	10.29 S	40.28 E
Ruwayān, Wādī ar- ⊤[7]	142	29.07 N	30.10 E
Ruwaybah ⊤[4]	140	15.39 N	28.45 E
Ruwayfī, Jabal ar- ∧	132	31.12 N	36.00 E
Ruwenzori ⩘	154	0.23 N	29.54 E
Ruwer	56	49.47 N	6.43 E
Ruwer ≃	56	49.47 N	6.42 E
Ruya (Luia) ≃	154	16.34 S	33.12 E
Ruyang	100	34.10 N	112.26 E
Ruy Barbosa	255	12.18 S	40.27 W
Ruyigi	154	3.29 S	30.15 E
Ruyton-Eleven-Towns	42	52.48 N	2.54 W
Ruza	82	55.42 N	36.12 E
Ruza ≃	82	55.38 N	36.17 E
Ruzajevka, S.S.S.R.	80	54.04 N	44.57 E
Ruzajevka, S.S.S.R.	86	52.49 N	66.57 E
Ružany	76	52.52 N	24.53 E
Ružičnaja	78	49.24 N	26.58 E
Ružin	78	49.43 N	29.14 E
Ruzizi (Rusizi) ≃	154	3.16 S	29.14 E
Ružomberok	30	49.06 N	19.18 E
Ruzyně ⊠	54	50.06 N	14.17 E
Ruzzah, Jabal ∧[2]	142	30.01 N	30.26 E
Rwanda □[1]	138		
	154	2.30 S	30.00 E
Rwashamaire	154	0.49 S	30.08 E
Ry	41	56.05 N	9.46 E
Ryal Fold	262	53.41 N	2.30 W
Ryan	196	34.01 N	97.57 W
Ryan ≃	182	50.25 N	122.43 W
Ryan, Loch ⊂	44	54.58 N	5.02 W
Ryan Peak ∧	202	43.54 N	114.25 W
Ryarsh	260	51.19 N	0.24 E
Ryazan' → R'azan'	80	54.38 N	39.44 E
Ryazovo	130	41.59 N	28.02 E
Rybačij (Rossitten)	76	55.09 N	20.51 E
Rybačij, Poluostrov ≻[1]	24	69.42 N	32.36 E
Rybačje, S.S.S.R.	85	42.28 N	76.10 E
Rybačje, S.S.S.R.	86	46.27 N	81.32 E
Rybackaja ◆[8]	265a	60.00 N	30.30 E
Rybackoje ◆[8]	265a	59.50 N	30.30 E
Rybakovka	78	46.37 N	31.20 E
Rybinsk	76	58.03 N	38.52 E
Rybinsker Stausee → Rybinskoje Vodochranilišče ◎[1]	76	58.30 N	38.25 E
Rybinskije Budy	78	51.13 N	35.57 E
Rybinskoje	86	55.47 N	94.47 E
Rybinskoje Vodochranilišče ◎[1]	76	58.30 N	38.25 E
Rybkino	80	54.15 N	43.46 E
Rybnaja Sloboda	80	55.28 N	50.09 E
Rybnica	78	47.45 N	29.01 E
Rybnik	30	50.06 N	18.32 E
Rybnoje, S.S.S.R.	76	54.44 N	39.30 E
Rybnoje, S.S.S.R.	86	58.08 N	94.30 E
Rybnovsk	89	53.12 N	141.50 E
Ryburn ≃	262	53.43 N	1.54 W
Rybuška	80	51.17 N	45.26 E
Rychnov nad Kněžnou	30	50.10 N	16.17 E
Rychwał	30	52.05 N	18.09 E
Ryčkovo	86	58.09 N	61.43 E
Rycroft	182	55.45 N	118.43 W
Ryd	26	56.28 N	14.41 E
Rydaholm	26	56.59 N	14.16 E
Rydal, Austl.	170	33.29 S	150.02 E
Rydal, Pa., U.S.	285	40.06 N	75.06 W
Rydalmere	274a	33.49 S	151.02 E
Rydbo	40	59.28 N	18.11 E
Ryde, Austl.	170	33.49 S	151.06 E
Ryde, Eng., U.K.	42	50.44 N	1.10 W
Ryder	198	47.55 N	101.40 W
Ryder's Hill ∧[2]	42	50.31 N	3.53 W
Ryderwood	224	46.23 N	123.03 W
Rydsgård	41	55.28 N	13.35 E
Rydzyna	30	51.48 N	16.40 E
Rye, Austl.	169	38.23 S	144.49 E
Rye, Eng., U.K.	42	50.57 N	0.44 E
Rye, N.Y., U.S.	210	40.59 N	73.41 W
Rye, Tex., U.S.	222	30.27 N	94.46 W
Rye ≃	44	54.10 N	0.45 W
Ryegate	202	46.18 N	109.15 W
Rye Hills-Rye Brook	276	41.00 N	73.41 W
Rye Lake ◎	276	41.04 N	73.43 W
Ryeosu → Yŏsu	98	34.46 N	127.44 E
Rye Patch Reservoir ◎[1]	204	40.38 N	118.18 W
Ryer Island ❙	282	38.05 N	122.01 W
Ryes	32	49.19 N	0.37 W
Ryfoss	26	61.09 N	8.49 E
Ryfylke ◆[1]	26	59.30 N	5.30 E
Rygge	26	59.23 N	10.43 E
Rygnestad	26	59.16 N	7.29 E
Ryhope	44	54.52 N	1.21 W
Rykaartspos	158	26.32 S	26.39 E
Ryker Lake ◎	276	41.03 N	74.33 W
Rykerts	182	49.00 N	116.35 W
Ryki	30	51.39 N	21.56 E
Rykonec	76	59.33 N	36.34 E
Ryley	182	53.17 N	112.26 W
Rylovići	76	52.31 N	32.04 E
Ryl'sk	78	51.36 N	34.43 E
Rylstone	170	32.48 S	149.58 E
Rymanów	30	49.34 N	21.53 E
Rýmařov	30	49.56 N	17.16 E
Ryn	30	53.56 N	21.33 E
Rynfield	273d	26.09 S	28.20 E
Rynok	80	45.39 N	47.34 E
Ryn-Peski ◆[2]	80	48.24 N	49.00 E
Ryō	270	34.44 N	135.55 E
Ryōhaku-sanchi ⩘	94	36.09 N	136.45 E
Ryojun → Lüshun	98	38.48 N	121.16 E
Ryōkami	94	36.00 N	138.58 E
Ryōke	268	35.58 N	139.33 E
Ryōnan	96	33.15 N	133.55 E
Ryōtsu	92	38.05 N	138.26 E
Rypin	30	53.05 N	19.25 E
Ryškany	78	47.58 N	27.32 E
Ryslinge	41	55.15 N	10.33 E
Rysy ∧	30	49.12 N	20.04 E
Ryton	44	54.59 N	1.46 W
Ryton ≃	44	53.25 N	1.00 W
Ryton-on-Dunsmore	42	52.22 N	1.26 W
Ryūga-do ⊤[5]	96	33.39 N	133.45 E
Ryūgasaki	94	35.54 N	140.11 E
Ryūjin	96	33.53 N	135.29 E
Ryukyu Islands → Nansei-shotō ❙❙	90	26.30 N	128.00 E
Ryukyu Trench ✣[1]	12	27.00 N	127.00 E
Ryūmon-dake ∧	270	34.26 N	135.53 E
Ryūō, Nihon	94	35.04 N	136.07 E
Ryūō, Nihon	94	35.39 N	138.30 E
Ryūsen	270	34.28 N	135.37 E
Ryūyō	94	34.40 N	137.48 E
Ržaksa-Vyselki	80	52.09 N	42.02 E
Ržanica	76	53.26 N	33.55 E
Ržava	78	51.14 N	36.43 E
Rzepin	30	52.22 N	14.50 E
Rzeszów	30	50.03 N	22.00 E
Ržev	76	56.16 N	34.20 E
Rżiščov	78	49.58 N	31.03 E
Ržovka ◆[8]	265a	59.58 N	30.30 E
S			
Sa	110	18.34 N	100.45 E
Saa	152	4.22 N	11.27 E
Sa'ad	132	31.28 N	34.32 E
Sa'ādatābād	128	30.06 N	53.08 E
Sääksjärvi ◎	26	61.24 N	22.24 E
Saal	54	54.19 N	12.29 E
Saalach ≃	64	47.51 N	13.00 E
Saal an der Donau	60	48.54 N	11.56 E
Saal an der Saale	56	50.19 N	10.21 E
Saalbach	64	47.23 N	12.38 E
Saalburg	54	50.30 N	11.43 E
Saaldorf	54	50.27 N	11.41 E
Saale ≃	54	51.57 N	11.55 E
Saaler Bodden ⊂	54	54.20 N	12.28 E
Saales	58	48.21 N	7.07 E
Saaletalsperre ◆[6]	54	50.30 N	11.35 E
Saalfeld	54	50.39 N	11.22 E
Saalfelden	64	47.25 N	12.51 E
Şā al-Ḩajar	142	30.58 N	30.46 E
Šaamar	88	50.08 N	106.10 E
Saâne ≃, Fr.	50	49.54 N	0.56 E
Saane ≃, Schw.	58	46.59 N	7.16 E
Saanen	58	46.29 N	7.16 E
Saanenmöser	58	47.32 N	7.18 E
Saanich Inlet ⊂	224	48.38 N	123.30 W
Saar → Saarland □[3]	56	49.20 N	7.00 E
Saar (Sarre) ≃	56	49.42 N	6.34 E
Saarbrücken	56	49.14 N	6.59 E
Saarburg	56	49.36 N	6.33 E
Sääre	76	57.56 N	22.02 E
Saarelouis → Saarlouis	56	49.21 N	6.45 E
Saaremaa ❙	76	58.25 N	22.30 E
Saarijärvi	26	62.43 N	25.16 E
Saarland □[3]	56	49.20 N	7.00 E
Saarlautern → Saarlouis	56	49.21 N	6.45 E
Saarlouis	56	49.21 N	6.45 E
Saarmund	264a	52.19 N	13.07 E
Saarn ◆[8]	263	51.24 N	6.53 E
Saarnberg ◆[8]	263	51.25 N	6.53 E
Saas Almagell	58	46.07 N	7.58 E
Saas Fee	58	46.07 N	7.55 E

Symbol	English	Deutsch	Español	Français	Português
≃	River	Fluss	Río	Rivière	Rio
≊	Canal	Kanal	Canal	Canal	Canal
↳	Waterfall, Rapids	Wasserfall, Stromschnellen	Cascada, Rápidos	Chute d'eau, Rapides	Cascata, Rápidos
⋓	Strait	Meeresstrasse	Estrecho	Détroit	Estreito
⊂	Bay, Gulf	Bucht, Golf	Bahía, Golfo	Baie, Golfe	Baía, Golfo
◎	Lake, Lakes	See, Seen	Lago, Lagos	Lac, Lacs	Lago, Lagos
☷	Swamp	Sumpf	Pantano	Marais	Pântano
⍓	Ice Features, Glacier	Eis- und Gletscherformen	Accidentes Glaciales	Formes glaciaires	Acidentes Glaciares
⊤	Other Hydrographic Features	Andere Hydrographische Objekte	Otros Elementos Hidrográficos	Autres données hydrographiques	Outros Elementos Hidrográficos
✣	Submarine Features	Untermeerische Objekte	Accidentes Submarinos	Formes de relief sous-marin	Acidentes Submarinos
□	Political Unit	Politische Einheit	Unidad Politica	Entité politique	Unidade Política
♥	Cultural Institution	Kulturelle Institution	Institución Cultural	Institution culturelle	Instituição Cultural
⊥	Historical Site	Historische Stätte	Sitio Histórico	Site historique	Sitio Histórico
♠	Recreational Site	Erholungs- und Ferienort	Sitio de Recreo	Centre de loisirs	Sítio de Lazer
⊠	Airport	Flughafen	Aeropuerto	Aéroport	Aeroporto
■	Military Installation	Militäranlage	Instalación Militar	Installation militaire	Instalação Militar
◆	Miscellaneous	Verschiedenes	Misceláneo	Divers	Miscelânea

Name	Page	Lat.	Long.
Saas Grund	58	46.08 N	7.56 E
Saastal V	58	46.10 N	7.56 E
Saatly	84	39.56 N	48.23 E
Saavedra	252	37.45 S	62.22 W
Saavedra •[8]	288	34.33 S	58.28 W
Sab, Tônlé ⊜	110	13.00 N	104.00 E
Saba	152	7.50 N	17.49 E
Saba I	238	17.38 N	63.10 W
Saba ≃, Nihon	96	34.02 N	131.30 E
Saba ≃, S.S.S.R.	76	59.08 N	29.00 E
Saba Bank ⊹[4]	238	17.25 N	63.30 W
Šabac	38	44.45 N	19.42 E
Sabadell	34		
	266d	41.33 N	2.06 E
Sabae	94	35.57 N	136.11 E
Sabah □[3]	112	5.20 N	117.10 E
Sa'Bah, Qārat as- ∧[2]	146	27.20 N	17.10 E
Sabajevo	80	53.59 N	45.43 E
Sabak, Cape ≻	181a	52.20 N	173.45 E
Sabak Bernam	114	3.46 N	100.59 E
Sabal	112	0.59 S	123.14 E
Sabalān, Kūhhā-ye ∧	128	38.15 N	47.49 E
Sabalgarh	124	26.15 N	77.24 E
Sabana	240m	18.20 N	65.44 W
Sabana ≃	196	32.03 N	98.34 W
Sabana, Archipiélago de II	240p	23.00 N	80.00 W
Sabana-Camagüey, Archipiélago de II	240p	22.30 N	79.00 W
Sabana de la Mar	238	19.04 N	69.23 W
Sabana de Mendoza	246	9.26 N	70.46 W
Sabanagrande, Hond.	236	13.50 N	87.15 W
Sabana Grande, P.R.	240m	18.05 N	66.58 W
Sabanalamar, Ensenada C	240p	21.36 N	78.44 W
Sabanalarga	246	10.38 N	74.55 W
Sabana Llana	240m	18.02 N	66.15 W
Sabancuy	232	18.58 N	91.11 W
Sabaneta, Rep. Dom.	238	19.30 N	71.21 W
Sabaneta, Ven.	246	8.46 N	69.56 W
Sābang, Bhārat	126	22.11 N	87.36 E
Sabang (Dampelas), Indon.	112	0.11 N	119.51 E
Sabang, Indon.	114	5.55 N	95.19 E
Sabanilla	232	25.08 N	101.44 W
Šabanovo	82	55.38 N	38.43 E
Şabanözü	130	40.29 N	33.18 E
Sabará	255	19.54 S	43.48 W
Sabarei	154	4.20 N	36.55 E
Sābari ≃	122	17.34 N	81.15 E
Sābarmati ≃	120	22.18 N	72.22 E
Sabasṭīyah (Samaria)	132	32.17 N	35.12 E
Sab'atayn, Ramlat as- ⊥[8]	144	15.30 N	46.20 E
Sabathu	123	30.59 N	76.59 E
Sabatini, Monti ⛰	66	42.10 N	12.15 E
Sabato ≃	66	41.08 N	14.45 E
Sabaudia	66	41.18 N	13.01 E
Sabaudia, Lago di C	66	41.16 N	13.02 E
Sabaúna	256	23.29 S	46.05 W
Saba Wanak	144	10.33 N	44.09 E
Sabaya	248	19.01 S	68.23 W
Sabažo	84	42.14 N	41.48 E
Sabbioneta	64	45.00 N	10.39 E
Şabe	272c	19.11 N	73.02 E
Šabel'kovka	83	48.45 N	37.29 E
Šabel'sk	83	46.51 N	38.29 E
Şāberī, Hāmūn-e ⊜	128	31.30 N	61.20 E
Sabetha	198	39.54 N	95.48 W
Şabḩā	132	32.20 N	36.30 E
Sabhah	146	27.03 N	14.26 E
Sabhah □[4]	146	28.00 N	14.00 E
Sābhār	126	23.51 N	90.15 E
Sabi (Save) ≃, Afr.	156	21.00 S	35.02 E
Sabi ≃, Nihon	94	36.48 N	140.04 E
Sabicy	76	58.50 N	29.18 E
Sabidana, Jabal ∧	140	18.04 N	36.50 E
Sabie	156	25.10 S	30.48 E
Sabie (Sábiè) ≃	156	25.19 S	32.18 E
Sabile	76	57.03 N	22.35 E
Sabillasville	208	39.42 N	77.27 W
Sabina	218	39.29 N	83.38 W
Sabina •[1]	36	42.15 N	12.42 E
Sabinal	196	29.19 N	99.28 W
Sabinal ≃	196	29.06 N	99.27 W
Sabinal, Península de ≻[1]	240p	21.40 N	77.18 W
Sabiñánigo	34	42.31 N	0.22 W
Sabinas	232	27.51 N	101.07 W
Sabinas ≃, Méx.	232	26.51 N	99.34 W
Sabinas ≃, Méx.	232	27.37 N	100.42 W
Sabinas ≃, Méx.	234	22.59 N	98.58 W
Sabinas Hidalgo	232	26.30 N	100.10 W
Sabine ≃	178	30.00 N	93.45 W
Sabine, Mount ∧, Ant.	9	71.55 S	169.33 E
Sabine, Mount ∧, Austl.	169	38.38 S	143.44 E
Sabine, South Fork ≃	222	32.52 N	96.10 W
Sabine Bay C	176	75.35 N	109.30 W
Sabine Lake ⊜	194	29.50 N	93.50 W
Sabine Pass C	194	29.44 N	93.52 W
Sabine Peninsula ≻[1]	176	76.20 N	109.30 W
Sabini, Monti ⛰	66	42.13 N	12.50 E
Sabinópolis	255	18.40 S	43.06 W
Sabinov	30	49.06 N	21.06 E
Şabinsville	210	41.52 N	77.31 W
Šabla	38	43.32 N	28.32 E
Sabl'a, Gora ∧	24	64.48 N	58.50 E
Sablayan	116	12.50 N	120.46 E
Sable, Anse au C	275a	45.21 N	73.56 W
Sable, Anse de C	241o	16.07 N	61.34 W
Sable, Cape ≻, N.S., Can.	186	43.25 N	65.35 W
Sable, Cape ≻, Fla., U.S.	220	25.12 N	81.05 W
Sable, Île de I, N. Cal.	160	19.15 S	159.56 E
Sable, Île de I, N. Cal.	175f	19.15 S	163.48 E
Sable, Rivière du ≃	176	55.30 N	68.21 W
Sable Island I	186	43.55 N	59.50 W
Sables, Lac aux ⊜	206	46.53 N	72.22 W
Sables, River aux ≃	190	46.13 N	82.04 W
Sablé-sur-Sarthe	32	47.50 N	0.20 W
Saboeiro	250	6.32 S	39.54 W
Sabogal ≃	236	10.55 N	84.43 W
Sāboli •[8]	272a	28.43 N	77.18 E
Sabonkafi	150	14.38 N	8.45 E
Sabor ≃	34	41.10 N	7.07 W
Sabou	150	12.04 N	2.14 W
Sabourin, Lac ⊜	190	47.58 N	77.41 W
Sabra, Tanjung ≻	164	2.17 S	132.19 E
Sabrata ⊥	146	32.47 N	12.29 E
Sabres	32	44.09 N	0.44 W
Sabrevois	206	45.12 N	73.14 W
Sabrina Coast ⊥[2]	9	67.00 S	119.30 E
Sabuda, Pulau I	164	2.38 S	131.36 E
Sabugal	34	40.21 N	7.05 W
Sabugo	266c	38.49 N	9.18 W
Sabuka	273b	4.27 S	15.10 E
Sabula	190	42.04 N	90.10 W
Sabuncu	130	39.33 N	30.12 E
Saburovo •[8]	265b	55.38 N	37.42 E
Sabyin	110	19.06 N	94.11 E
Sabzevār	128	36.13 N	57.42 E
Sac ≃	194	38.01 N	93.43 W
Sacaba	248	17.23 S	66.02 W
Sacaca	248	18.05 S	66.26 W
Sacacomie, Lac ⊜	206	46.31 N	73.14 W
Sacajawea Peak ∧	202	45.15 N	117.17 W
Sacanche	248	7.05 S	76.44 W
Sacandaga ≃	210	43.19 N	73.50 W
Sacandaga, West Branch ≃	210	43.22 N	74.17 W
Sacandica	152	5.58 S	15.56 E
Sacaola	152	12.57 S	22.25 E
Sacaton	200	33.05 N	111.44 W
Sacavém	266c	38.47 N	9.06 W
Sac City	198	42.25 N	95.00 W
Sacco ≃	66	41.31 N	13.32 E
Sacedón	34	40.29 N	2.43 W
Săcele	38	45.37 N	25.42 E
Šacha ≃	82	56.45 N	39.10 E
Sachalin □[4]	89	50.00 N	143.00 E
Sachalin, Ostrov I	89	51.00 N	143.00 E
Sachalinskij Zaliv C	89	53.45 N	141.30 E
Šachand	85	40.54 N	71.28 E
Sachayoj	252	26.41 S	61.50 W
Šachdagskij Chrebet ⛰	84	40.24 N	45.35 E
Saché	50	47.14 N	0.33 E
Šache ≃	84	43.47 N	39.27 E
Sachicapa	152	10.21 S	19.59 E
Sachigo ≃	176	55.06 N	88.58 W
Sachigo Lake ⊜	184	53.49 N	92.08 W
Sachimbo	152	9.14 S	20.16 E
Sachnovščina	78	49.08 N	35.53 E
Šachovskaja	76	56.02 N	35.29 E
Sachrang	64	47.41 N	12.15 E
Šachristan, Pereval)(	85	39.33 N	68.33 E
Šachrovka	80	58.34 N	52.12 E
Sachse	222	32.59 N	96.36 W
Sachseln	58	46.52 N	8.15 E
Sachsen □[9]	54	51.00 N	13.30 E
Sachsen-Anhalt □[9]	54	52.20 N	11.40 E
Sachsenbrunn	54	50.27 N	10.56 E
Sachsenburg	64	46.50 N	13.21 E
Sachsenhagen	52	52.24 N	9.16 E
Sachsenhausen, B.R.D.	56	51.15 N	9.00 E
Sachsenhausen, D.D.R.	54	52.47 N	13.14 E
Sachs Harbour	176	72.00 N	125.00 W
Sächsische Schweiz •[1]	54	50.55 N	14.10 E
Šachterskij	180	64.42 N	177.40 E
Šachtinsk	86	49.40 N	72.37 E
Šachtnoje	83	47.57 N	38.17 E
Šacht'orsk, S.S.S.R.	83	48.03 N	38.28 E
Šacht'orsk, S.S.S.R.	89	49.11 N	142.07 E
Šacht'orskij •[8]	83	48.09 N	39.08 E
Šachty	83	47.42 N	40.13 E
Šachunja	80	57.40 N	46.37 E
Sachy	56	49.40 N	5.08 E
Sacile	64	45.57 N	12.30 E
Sacır (Sājūr) ≃	130	36.40 N	38.05 E
Šack, S.S.S.R.	76	53.25 N	27.41 E
Šack, S.S.S.R.	78	51.31 N	23.57 E
Šack, S.S.S.R.	80	54.01 N	41.43 E
Sackets Harbor	212	43.57 N	76.07 W
Säckingen	58	47.33 N	7.56 E
Sackville	186	45.54 N	64.22 W
Saclay	261	48.44 N	2.10 E
Saclay, Étang de ⊜	261	48.45 N	2.10 E
Saco, Maine, U.S.	188	43.29 N	70.28 W
Saco, Mont., U.S.	202	48.28 N	107.21 W
Saco ≃	186	43.27 N	70.22 W
Saco Bay C	188	43.30 N	70.15 W
Sacol Island I	116	6.58 N	122.13 E
Sacotes	266c	38.48 N	9.20 W
Sacra, Isola I	267a	41.45 N	12.15 E
Sacra Família do Tinguá	256	22.29 S	43.36 W
Sacramento, Bra.	255	19.53 S	47.27 W
Sacramento, Calif., U.S.	226	38.35 N	121.30 W
Sacramento □[6]	226	38.35 N	121.30 W
Sacramento ≃	204	38.03 N	121.56 W
Sacramento, Pampa del ≍	248	8.00 S	75.50 W
Sacramento Deep Water Channel ≋	226	38.15 N	121.40 W
Sacramento Metropolitan Airport ⊠	226	38.42 N	121.37 W
Sacramento Mountains ⛰	200	33.10 N	105.50 W
Sacramento South	226	38.32 N	121.26 W
Sacramento Valley V	204	39.15 N	122.00 W
Sacramento Wash V	200	34.43 N	114.28 W
Sacre ≃	248	12.56 S	58.18 W
Sacré-Cœur ⛪[1]	261	48.53 N	2.21 E
Sacred Heart	198	44.47 N	95.21 W
Sacro, Monte ∧	68	40.13 N	15.20 E
Sacro Monte ⛪[1]	62	45.49 N	8.15 E
Sacrow •[8]	264a	52.26 N	13.06 E
Sacrower See ⊜	264a	52.27 N	13.06 E
Săcueni	38	47.21 N	22.06 E
Sacul	222	31.50 N	94.56 W
Sacupana	246	8.35 N	61.39 W
Sacuriuiná ≃	248	12.52 S	57.22 W
Sada, Esp.	34	43.21 N	8.15 W
Sada, Nihon	96	35.15 N	132.43 E
Sádaba	34	42.17 N	1.16 W
Sadābād, Bhārat	124	27.27 N	78.03 E
Sa'dābād, Īrān	128	29.23 N	51.07 E
Şadad	130	34.18 N	36.56 E
Şa'dah	144	16.52 N	43.37 E
Sadaik Taung ∧	110	15.09 N	98.12 E
Sadali	71	39.49 N	9.16 E
Sada-misaki ≻	96	33.20 N	132.01 E
Sada-misaki-hantō ≻[1]	96	33.26 N	132.13 E
Sadamitsu	96	34.02 N	134.04 E
Sadane ≃	115a	6.01 S	106.37 E
Sadang ≃	112	3.43 S	119.27 E
Sadanga	116	17.09 N	121.02 E
Sadani	154	6.03 S	38.47 E
Sadao	110	6.38 N	100.26 E
Sādarpur, Bhārat	272a	28.33 N	77.21 E
Sadarpur, Bngl.	126	23.28 N	90.02 E
Sadčikovka	86	53.01 N	63.27 E
Sadda	120	33.42 N	70.20 E
Saddle ≃	276	40.52 N	74.07 W
Saddleback ∧	44	54.38 N	3.03 W
Saddle Brook	276	40.54 N	74.06 W
Saddlebunch Keys II	220	24.37 N	81.37 W
Saddle Island I	175f	13.40 S	167.40 E
Saddle Lake Indian Reserve •[4]	182	54.00 N	111.40 W
Saddle Mountain ∧, Colo., U.S.	200	38.50 N	105.28 W
Saddle Mountain ∧, Oreg., U.S.	224	45.58 N	123.41 W
Saddle Mountains ⛰	202	46.50 N	119.55 W
Saddle Mountain State Park ♣	224	45.58 N	123.41 W
Saddle Peak ∧	110	13.09 N	93.01 E
Saddle River	276	41.02 N	74.06 W
Saddle Rock	276	40.48 N	73.45 W
Saddleworth, Austl.	168b	34.05 S	138.47 E
Saddleworth, Eng., U.K.	44	53.33 N	1.59 W
Saddleworth Moor •[3]	262	53.33 N	1.57 W
Sa-dec	110	10.18 N	105.46 E
Sadelkow	54	53.36 N	13.26 E
Sādhaura	124	30.23 N	77.13 E
Sādhuhāti	126	23.34 N	89.01 E
Sadieville	218	38.23 N	84.32 W
Sadiola	150	13.53 N	11.42 W
Sādiqābad	120	28.18 N	70.08 E
Sadiya	120	27.50 N	95.40 E
Sa'dīyah, Wādī V	144	20.35 N	39.38 E
Sa'dīyāt, Ra's as- ≻	132	33.41 N	35.25 E
Sadler Lake ⊜	184	55.17 N	103.45 W
Sado I	92	38.00 N	138.25 E
Sado ≃	34	38.29 N	8.55 W
Sado-kaikyō ⊔	92	37.50 N	138.40 E
Sadovoje Pervoje	78	51.33 N	40.29 E
Sadowara	92	32.02 N	131.26 E
Šādri	120	25.11 N	73.26 E
Šadrinsk	86	56.05 N	63.38 E
Sadsburyville	208	39.59 N	75.53 W
Sadulgarh	123	29.35 N	74.19 E
Sadulpur	123	28.38 N	75.24 E
Sädvaluspen	24	66.24 N	16.51 E
Sæby, Dan.	26	57.20 N	10.32 E
Sæby, Dan.	41	55.33 N	11.19 E
Saegertown	214	41.43 N	80.09 W
Sae Islands II	164	0.45 S	145.15 E
Saeki → Saiki, Nihon	96	32.57 N	131.54 E
Saeki, Nihon	96	34.22 N	132.11 E
Saeki, Nihon	96	34.51 N	134.06 E
Saerbeck	52	52.10 N	7.38 E
Saerluojiahu ⊜	120	33.55 N	86.55 E
Særslev, Dan.	41	55.43 N	11.23 E
Særslev, Dan.	41	55.31 N	10.11 E
Saeul	56	49.44 N	5.59 E
Şafā, Tulul aş- ∧[1]	132	33.02 N	37.12 E
Safad → Ẓefat	132	32.58 N	35.30 E
Safājah, Jazīrat I	140	26.45 N	33.59 E
Safakulevo	86	54.59 N	62.33 E
Şafānīyah	142	28.49 N	30.48 E
Şafarābād	128	38.59 N	47.27 E
Šafárikovo	30	48.27 N	20.20 E
Safata Bay C	175a	14.00 S	171.50 W
Safdar Jang Airport ⊠	272a	28.37 N	77.13 E
Safdar Jang's Tomb ⊥	272a	28.36 N	77.13 E
Safed Koh Range ⛰	123	33.58 N	70.25 E
Safe Harbor Dam •[6]	208	39.59 N	76.28 W
Safenbach ≃	61	47.06 N	16.05 E
Safety Bay	168a	32.18 S	115.43 E
Safety Harbor	220	27.59 N	82.42 W
Säffle	26	59.08 N	12.56 E
Safford	200	32.50 N	109.43 W
Saffron Walden	42	52.01 N	0.15 E
Safi	148	32.20 N	9.17 W
Safia	164	9.35 S	148.40 E
Safia, Hamada •[2]	148	23.10 N	4.15 W
Şafīābād	128	36.45 N	57.58 E
Safīd ≃, Afg.	120	36.44 N	65.38 E
Safīd ≃, Īrān	128	37.26 N	49.55 E
Safīdābeh	128	30.56 N	60.35 E
Safīd Kūh, Selseleh-ye ⛰	128	34.30 N	63.30 E
Safidon	124	29.25 N	76.40 E
Safiental V	58	46.40 N	9.18 E
Safioune, Sebkret ☷	148	32.16 N	5.27 E
Safipur	126	23.01 N	90.22 E
Safonovo, S.S.S.R.	24	65.42 N	47.39 E
Safonovo, S.S.S.R.	76	55.06 N	33.15 E
Safonovo, S.S.S.R.	82	55.33 N	38.17 E
Safraköy	267b	41.00 N	28.47 E
Safranbolu	130	41.15 N	32.45 E
Şafţ al-'Inab	142	30.49 N	30.41 E
Şafţ al-Khammār	142	28.02 N	30.42 E
Şafţ al-Laban	273c	30.02 N	31.10 E
Şafţ al-Mulūk	142	30.49 N	30.41 E
Şafţ Rāshīn	142	28.58 N	30.55 E
Şafţ Turāb	142	30.54 N	31.07 E
Şafwān	128	30.07 N	47.43 E
Saga, Nihon	92	33.15 N	130.18 E
Saga, Nihon	96	33.05 N	133.06 E
Saga □[5]	96	33.21 N	130.28 E
Sagaba	152	11.17 S	23.07 E
Sagae	92	38.22 N	140.17 E
Sagaing	110	21.52 N	95.59 E
Sagaing □[8]	110	24.00 N	95.00 E
Sagak, Cape ≻	180	52.48 N	169.08 W
Şagalaherang	115a	6.40 S	107.39 E
Šagalakasa	80	46.54 N	50.43 E
Sagami ≃	94	35.14 N	139.23 E
Sagamihara	94	35.32 N	139.23 E
Sagamihara-daichi ⛰[1]	268	35.25 N	139.27 E
Sagamiko	94	35.37 N	139.12 E
Sagami-ko ⊜	94	35.35 N	139.16 E
Sagami-nada C	94	35.00 N	139.30 E
Sagami-wan C	94	35.14 N	139.24 E
Sagamore, Mass., U.S.	207	41.45 N	70.33 W
Sagamore, Pa., U.S.	214	40.47 N	79.14 W
Sagamore Beach	207	41.48 N	70.32 W
Sagamore Hill National Historic Site ⊥	276	40.53 N	73.30 W
Sagamore Hills	214	41.19 N	81.34 W
Sagan → Żagań	30	51.37 N	15.19 E
Šagan ≃, S.S.S.R.	86	50.37 N	79.15 E
Sagån ≃, Sve.	40	59.35 N	16.54 E
Sagan ≃, Yai.	144	4.28 N	36.04 E
Saganaga Lake ⊜	190	48.14 N	90.52 W
Saganashkee Slough ≃	278	41.41 N	87.53 W
Saganash Lake ⊜	190	49.04 N	82.35 W
Saganoseki	96	33.15 N	131.53 E
Şaganthit Kyun I	110	11.56 N	98.29 E
Šagany, Ozero ⊜	78	45.43 N	29.53 E
Sagaon	272c	19.12 N	73.06 E
Sāgar, Bhārat	122	14.10 N	75.02 E
Sāgar, Bhārat	124	23.50 N	78.43 E
Sagara	94	34.41 N	138.12 E
Sagaranten	115a	7.13 S	106.52 E
Sagard	54	54.31 N	13.33 E
Sāgardīghi	126	24.17 N	88.06 E
Sagaredžo	84	41.44 N	45.20 E
Sāgar Island I	126	21.43 N	88.06 E
Sāgar Plateau ⛰[1]	124	23.30 N	78.30 E
Sagavanirktok ≃	180	70.20 N	148.00 W
Sage, Mount ∧	240m	18.25 N	64.39 W
Sage Creek ≃, N.A.	202	48.58 N	110.06 W
Sage Creek ≃, U.S.	202	44.50 N	108.26 W
Sage Creek ≃, Mont., U.S.	202	48.20 N	110.03 W
Sage Creek ≃, Mont., U.S.	202	47.16 N	109.43 W
Sagerton	196	33.05 N	99.58 W
Saggaubach ≃	61	46.43 N	15.24 E
Sag Harbor	207	41.00 N	72.18 W
Şaghbīn	132	33.37 N	35.42 E
Sagil	86	50.20 N	91.40 E
Saginaw, Mich., U.S.	190	43.25 N	83.58 W
Saginaw, Tex., U.S.	222	32.52 N	97.22 W
Saginaw ≃	190	43.39 N	83.51 W
Saginaw Bay C	190	43.50 N	83.40 W
Sagiz, S.S.S.R.	80	47.31 N	53.16 E
Sagiz, S.S.S.R.	86	48.12 N	54.56 E
Sagiz ≃	86	47.32 N	53.20 E
Sagleipie	150	7.00 N	8.52 W
Saglek Bay C	176	58.35 N	63.00 W
Saglouc	176	62.14 N	75.38 W
Šaglyteniz, Ozero ⊜	86	54.08 N	69.52 E
Šagonar	86	51.32 N	92.48 E
Sagra di San Michele ⛪[1]	62	45.11 N	7.21 E
Sagrado	64	45.52 N	13.29 E
Sagres	34	37.00 N	8.56 W
Sag Sag	164	5.35 S	148.20 E
Sagsaj	86	48.54 N	89.37 E
Sagu, Indon.	112	8.15 S	123.13 E
Şagu, Rom.	38	46.03 N	21.17 E
Saguache	200	38.05 N	106.08 W
Saguache Creek ≃	200	37.52 N	105.51 W
Sagua de Tánamo	240p	20.35 N	75.14 W
Sagua la Chica ≃	240p	22.45 N	79.39 W
Sagua la Grande	240p	22.49 N	80.05 W
Sagua la Grande ≃	240p	22.56 N	80.01 W
Saguaro National Monument ♣	200	32.12 N	110.38 W
Saguenay ≃	176	48.08 N	69.44 W
Saguna	272b	22.59 N	88.29 E
Sagunay Lake	216	41.43 N	86.34 W
Sagunovka	78	49.17 N	32.23 E
Sagunto	34	39.41 N	0.16 W
Saguny	78	50.36 N	39.43 E
Sagutjevo	76	52.28 N	33.28 E
Sāgwāra	120	23.41 N	74.01 E
Sagy	261	49.03 N	1.57 E
Sagyndyk, Mys ≻	84	44.02 N	50.52 E
Sah	150	15.38 N	4.03 W
Saḩāb	132	31.53 N	36.00 E
Sahaba	140	18.55 N	30.28 E
Sahagún, Col.	246	8.57 N	75.27 W
Sahagún, Esp.	34	42.22 N	5.02 W
Saḩam	132	32.42 N	35.47 E
Saḩam al-Jawlān	132	32.46 N	35.56 E
Sahana Ambodipont	157b	14.37 S	50.11 E
Sahand, Kūh-e ∧	128	37.44 N	46.27 E
Sahara •[2]	136	26.00 N	13.00 E
Sahāranpur	124	29.58 N	77.33 E
Saharānpur □[5]	124	30.00 N	77.35 E
Sahara Occidental → Western Sahara □[2]	148	24.30 N	13.00 W
Sahara Occidentale → Western Sahara □[2]	148	24.30 N	13.00 W
Saharsa	124	25.53 N	86.36 E
Sahasinaka	157b	21.49 S	47.49 E
Sahasrail	126	23.19 N	89.43 E
Sahaswān	124	28.05 N	78.45 E
Sahe ≃	105	40.22 N	117.58 E
Sahel, Canal du ≋	150	13.44 N	6.05 W
Sahel, Oued ≃	34	36.45 N	5.04 E
Sāhibabad	272a	28.40 N	77.22 E
Sāhibābad •[8]	272a	28.45 N	77.05 E
Sāhibganj	124	25.15 N	87.39 E
Şahin	130	41.01 N	26.50 E
Sāhiwāl, Pāk.	123	31.58 N	72.20 E
Sāhiwāl (Montgomery), Pāk.	123	30.40 N	73.06 E
Sahlenburg	52	53.52 N	8.38 E
Şaḩneh	128	34.29 N	47.41 E
Şaḩrā', Bi'r ⊤[4]	140	22.52 N	28.37 E
Şaḩrā', Jabal ∧	140	28.00 N	34.08 E
Şahrajat al-Kubrā wa Kafr Jirjis Yūsuf	142	30.38 N	31.17 E
Sahtlam	224	48.48 N	123.54 W
Sahuaripa	232	29.03 N	109.14 W
Sahuarita	200	31.57 N	110.58 W
Sahuayo	234	20.04 N	102.43 W
Sahul Shelf ⊹[4]	14	12.00 S	127.00 E
Şahwat al-Qamḩ	132	32.36 N	36.23 E
Šahy	30	48.05 N	18.57 E
Saï	150	13.50 N	5.00 W
Sai ≃, Bhārat	124	25.39 N	82.47 E
Sai ≃, Nihon	94	36.36 N	136.35 E
Sai ≃, Nihon	94	36.37 N	138.14 E
Saibai Island I	164	9.24 S	142.40 E
Sai Buri	110	6.42 N	101.37 E
Sai Buri ≃	110	6.43 N	101.39 E
Saïda	148	34.50 N	0.09 E
Saidābād, Bngl.	126	24.18 N	89.43 E
Sa'īdābād, Īrān	267d	35.40 N	51.11 E
Saidaiji	96	34.39 N	134.02 E
Saïdia	148	35.04 N	2.15 W
Saido	268	35.52 N	139.41 E
Saidor	164	5.35 S	146.30 E
Saidpur, Bhārat	124	25.33 N	83.11 E
Saidpur, Bngl.	124	25.47 N	88.54 E
Saidu	123	34.45 N	72.21 E
Saigawa	96	33.39 N	130.57 E
Saignelégier	58	47.15 N	7.00 E
Saignon	62	43.52 N	5.26 E
Saigō	92	36.12 N	133.20 E
Sai-gon → Thanh-pho Ho Chi Minh	269c	10.45 N	106.40 E
Sai-gon ≃	269c	10.45 N	106.45 E
Saihaku	96	35.20 N	133.20 E
Saijō, Nihon	96	33.55 N	133.11 E
Saijō, Nihon	96	34.25 N	132.45 E
Saijō ≃	96	34.48 N	132.51 E
Sai-kai-kokuritsu-kōen ♣	92	32.12 N	129.22 E
Sai Kang	271d	22.26 N	114.16 E
Saiki	96	32.57 N	131.54 E
Saiki-wan C	96	33.00 N	131.58 E
Sailimuhu ⊜	86	44.36 N	81.13 E
Sailkupa	126	23.41 N	89.15 E
Saillans	62	44.42 N	5.11 E
Sailly	261	49.02 N	1.48 E
Sailmouille, Ruisseau ≃	261	48.37 N	2.17 E
Sailor Creek ≃	202	42.56 N	115.29 W
Şail-sous-Couzan	62	45.44 N	3.57 E
Šaim	86	60.21 N	64.14 E
Saimaa ⊜	26	61.15 N	28.15 E
Saimaan kanava (Saimaa Canal) ≋	26	61.05 N	28.18 E
Saimbeyli	130	38.00 N	36.06 E
Saín Alto	234	23.35 N	103.15 W
Sain-Bel	58	45.49 N	4.36 E
Saindak	128	29.17 N	61.34 E
Sainghin-en-Weppes	50	50.33 N	2.54 E
Sainjang	98	39.15 N	125.51 E
Sainō-ha'iji ⊥	96	35.29 N	133.39 E
Sains-du-Nord	50	50.06 N	4.00 E
Sains-en-Gohelle	50	50.27 N	2.41 E
Sains-Richaumont	50	49.49 N	3.42 E
Saint Abb's Head ≻	46	55.54 N	2.09 W
Sainte-Adèle	206	45.57 N	74.07 W
Sainte-Adresse	50	49.30 N	0.05 E
Saint-Adrien	206	45.49 N	71.43 W
Saint-Affrique	32	43.57 N	2.53 E
Saint-Agapit	206	46.34 N	71.27 W
Saint Agatha	212	43.26 N	80.36 W
Sainte-Agathe, Man., Can.	184	49.34 N	97.10 W
Sainte-Agathe, Fr.	62	45.49 N	3.37 E
Sainte-Agathe [-de-Lotbinière]	206	46.23 N	71.24 W
Sainte-Agathe-des-Monts	206	46.03 N	74.17 W
Sainte-Agnès, Fr.	62	43.48 N	7.28 E
Saint Agnes, Eng., U.K.	42	50.18 N	5.13 W
Saint Agnes I	42a	49.54 N	6.20 W
Saint-Agrève	62	45.01 N	4.24 E
Saint-Aimé (Massueville)	206	45.55 N	72.56 W
Saint Albans, Austl.	169	37.44 S	144.48 E
Saint Albans, Austl.	170	33.17 S	150.59 E
Saint Alban's, Newf., Can.	186	47.52 N	55.51 W

ENGLISH

Name	Page	Lat.°′	Long.°′
Saint Albans, Eng., U.K.	42	51.46 N	0.21 W
Saint Albans, Mo., U.S.	219	38.35 N	90.46 W
Saint Albans, Vt., U.S.	188	44.49 N	73.05 W
Saint Albans, W. Va., U.S.	188	38.23 N	81.49 W
Saint Albans □[8]	260	51.45 N	0.20 W
Saint Albans •[8]	276	40.42 N	73.46 W
Saint Albans, Cape ≻	168b	35.49 S	138.07 E
Saint Albans Cathedral ⛪[1]	260	51.45 N	0.20 W
Saint Albert, Alta., Can.	182	53.38 N	113.38 W
Saint-Albert, Qué., Can.	206	46.00 N	72.05 W
Saint Aldhelm's Head ≻	42	50.34 N	2.04 W
Saint-Alexandre-de-Kamouraska	186	47.41 N	69.38 W
Saint-Alexis-des-Monts	206	46.28 N	73.08 W
Saint-Amand	56	48.49 N	4.36 E
Saint-Amand-en-Puisaye	50	47.31 N	3.04 E
Saint-Amand-les-Eaux	50	50.26 N	3.26 E
Saint-Amand-Longpré	50	47.41 N	1.01 E
Saint-Amand-Mont-Rond	32	46.44 N	2.30 E
Saint-Amant-Roche-Savine	62	45.34 N	3.38 E
Saint-Amarin	58	47.53 N	7.01 E
Saint-Ambroix	62	44.15 N	4.11 E
Sainte-Amélie	184	50.59 N	99.21 W
Saint-Amour	58	46.26 N	5.21 E
Saint-André	157c	20.57 S	55.39 E
Saint-André ≃	206	45.33 N	74.20 W
Saint-André, Cap ≻	157b	16.11 S	44.27 E
Saint-André, Ruisseau ≃	275a	45.22 N	73.29 W
Saint-André-Avellin	206	45.43 N	75.03 W
Saint-André-de-Cubzac	32	45.00 N	0.27 W
Saint-André-de-l'Eure	50	48.54 N	1.17 E
Saint-André-de-Valborgne	62	44.09 N	3.41 E
St.-André-Est	206	45.34 N	74.20 W
Saint-André-les-Alpes	62	43.58 N	6.30 E
Saint-André-les-Vergers	50	48.17 N	4.03 E
Saint Andrew	241g	13.15 N	59.33 W
Saint Andrew, Mount ∧	241h	13.11 N	61.13 W
Saint Andrew Lakes ⊜	212	44.36 N	76.40 W
Saint Andrews, Scot., U.K.	46	56.20 N	2.48 W
Saint Andrews, S.C., U.S.	192	32.47 N	80.00 W
Saint Andrews Bay C	46	56.22 N	2.50 W
Saint Andrew's Cathedral ⛪[1]	271c	1.18 N	103.51 E
Saint Andrew's Channel ⊔	186	46.03 N	60.38 W
Saint Ann	219	38.43 N	90.23 W
Sainte-Anne, Guad.	241o	16.14 N	61.23 W
Saint Anne, Guer.	43b	49.42 N	2.12 W
Sainte-Anne, Mart.	240e	14.26 N	60.53 W
Saint Anne, Ill., U.S.	216	41.01 N	87.43 W
Sainte-Anne ≃	206	46.33 N	72.12 W
Saint Anne, Cathedral of ⛪[1]	273b	4.18 S	15.19 E
Sainte-Anne, Lac ⊜, Alta., Can.	182	53.43 N	114.27 W
Sainte-Anne, Lac ⊜, Qué., Can.	186	50.05 N	67.50 W
Sainte-Anne-de-Beaupré	186	47.02 N	70.56 W
Sainte-Anne-de-Bellevue	275a	45.24 N	73.57 W
Sainte-Anne-de-la-Pérade	206	46.35 N	72.12 W
Sainte-Anne-de-Madawaska	186	47.15 N	68.02 W
Sainte-Anne-des-Chênes	184	49.40 N	96.40 W
Sainte-Anne-des-Monts	186	49.08 N	66.30 W
Sainte-Anne-des-Plaines	206	46.46 N	73.48 W
Saint Anne of the Congo ⛪[1]	273b	4.16 S	15.17 E
Saint Anne's	44	53.45 N	3.02 W
Saint Ann's Bay	241q	18.26 N	77.08 W
Saint Ann's Bay C	186	46.20 N	60.30 W
Saint Ann's Head ≻	42	51.41 N	5.10 W
Saint-Anselme	186	46.37 N	70.58 W
Saint Ansgar	190	43.23 N	92.55 W
Saint-Anthème	62	45.31 N	3.55 E
Saint Anthony, Newf., Can.	186	51.22 N	55.35 W
Saint Anthony, Idaho, U.S.	202	43.58 N	111.41 W
St.-Antoine, N.B., Can.	186	46.22 N	64.45 W
Saint-Antoine, Qué., Can.	206	45.46 N	73.59 W
Saint-Antoine, Fr.	62	45.10 N	5.13 E
Saint-Antonin	32	44.09 N	1.45 E
Saint-Apollinaire (Francoeur)	206	46.37 N	71.31 W
Saint Arnaud	166	36.37 S	143.15 E
Saint-Arnoult, Forêt de ♣	261	48.35 N	1.55 E
Saint-Arnoult-en-Yvelines	50	48.34 N	1.56 E
Saint Arvans	42	51.40 N	2.41 W
Saint Asaph	44	53.16 N	3.26 W
Saint-Astier	32	45.09 N	0.32 E
Saint Athan	42	51.24 N	3.25 W
Saint-Auban	62	43.51 N	6.44 E
Saint-Aubert, Mont ∧[2]	50	59.30 N	3.24 E
Saint Aubert Island I	219	38.40 N	91.52 W
Saint-Aubin, Fr.	50	49.53 N	0.53 E
Saint-Aubin, Fr.	58	47.02 N	5.20 E
Saint Aubin, Jersey	43b	49.11 N	2.10 W
Saint-Aubin, Schw.	58	46.54 N	6.47 E
Saint-Aubin-d'Aubigné	32	48.15 N	1.36 W
Saint-Aubin-lès-Elbeuf	50	49.18 N	1.01 E
Saint-Aubin-sur-Aire	58	48.42 N	5.27 E
St.-Augustin	157b	23.33 S	43.46 E
Saint-Augustin ≃	176	51.14 N	58.41 W
Saint-Augustin-Deux-Montagnes	275a	45.38 N	73.59 W
Saint Augustine	192	29.54 N	81.19 W
Saint-Augustin-Nord-Ouest ≃	186	51.16 N	58.42 W
Saint-Augustin-Saguenay	186	51.14 N	58.39 W
Saint-Aulaye	32	45.12 N	0.08 E
Saint Austell	42	50.20 N	4.48 W
Saint-Avertin	50	47.22 N	0.44 E
Saint-Avold	56	49.06 N	6.42 E

DEUTSCH

Name	Seite	Breite°′	Länge°′ E=Ost
Saint-Ay	50	47.51 N	1.45 E
Saint-Aygulf	62	43.23 N	6.44 E
Saint-Barthélemy I	238	17.54 N	62.50 W
Saint-Basile	186	47.21 N	68.14 W
Saint-Basile-de-Portneuf	206	46.45 N	71.49 W
Saint-Basile-le-Grand	206	45.32 N	73.17 W
Saint Bathans, Mount ∧	172	44.44 S	169.46 E
Sainte-Baume, Chaîne de la ⛰	62	43.20 N	5.45 E
Saint-Béat	32	42.55 N	0.42 E
Saint Bees Head ≻	44	54.32 N	3.38 W
Saint Benedict	214	40.38 N	78.44 W
Saint-Benoît, Fr.	261	48.40 N	1.55 E
Saint-Benoît, Réu.	157c	21.02 S	55.43 E
Saint-Benoît-du-Sault	32	46.27 N	1.23 E
Saint-Benoît-en-Woëvre	56	48.59 N	5.47 E
Saint Bernard	218	39.10 N	84.30 W
Saint-Bernard, Île I	275a	45.23 N	73.45 W
Saint-Bernard-de-Dorchester	206	46.30 N	71.08 W
Saint-Béron	62	45.30 N	5.43 E
Saint-Blaise, Qué., Can.	206	45.13 N	73.17 W
Saint-Blaise, Schw.	58	47.01 N	6.59 E
Saint-Blaise-la-Roche	58	48.24 N	7.10 E
Saint Blaize, Cape ≻	158	34.11 S	22.10 E
Saint Blazey	42	50.22 N	4.43 W
Saint-Blin	58	48.16 N	5.25 E
Saint-Bonaventure, Qué., Can.	206	45.58 N	72.41 W
Saint Bonaventure, N.Y., U.S.	210	42.05 N	78.28 W
Saint Boniface	184	49.55 N	97.06 W
Saint-Boniface-de-Shawinigan	206	46.30 N	72.49 W
Saint-Bonnet	62	44.41 N	6.05 E
Saint-Bonnet-de-Joux	58	46.29 N	4.27 E
Saint-Bonnet-le-Château	62	45.25 N	4.04 E
Saint-Bonnet-le-Froid	62	45.09 N	4.27 E
Saint Brendan's	186	48.52 N	53.40 W
Saint-Brice-sous-Forêt	261	49.00 N	2.21 E
Saint Bride, Mount ∧	182	51.30 N	115.57 W
Saint Bride's	186	46.55 N	54.10 W
Saint Brides Bay C	42	51.48 N	5.15 W
Saint Bride's Major	42	51.28 N	3.38 W
Saint-Brieuc	32	48.31 N	2.47 W
Saint-Brieux	184	52.38 N	104.52 W
Saint-Broing-les-Moines	58	47.41 N	4.50 E
Saint-Bruno	206	45.32 N	73.21 W
Saint-Bruno, Mont ∧[2]	275a	45.33 N	73.19 W
Saint-Calais	50	47.55 N	0.45 E
Saint-Calixte-de-Kilkenny	206	45.57 N	73.51 W
Saint-Cannat	62	43.37 N	5.18 E
Saint-Casimir	206	46.40 N	72.08 W
Saint Catharines	212		
	284a	43.10 N	79.15 W
Saint Catharines Airport ⊠	284a	43.11 N	79.10 W
Saint Catherine	220	28.37 N	82.08 W
Saint Catherine, Monastery of ⛪[1]	140	28.29 N	34.01 E
Saint Catherine, Mount ∧	241k	12.10 N	61.40 W
Sainte-Catherine-de-Fierbois	50	47.09 N	0.39 E
Saint Catherines Island I	192	31.38 N	81.10 W
Saint Catherine's Point ≻	42	50.34 N	1.15 W
Saint-Célestin (Annaville)	206	46.13 N	72.26 W
Saint-Céré	32	44.52 N	1.53 E
Saint-Cergue	58	46.27 N	6.09 E
Saint-Césaire	206	45.25 N	73.00 W
Saint-Cézaire-sur-Siagne	62	43.39 N	6.48 E
Saint-Chamas	62	43.33 N	5.02 E
Saint-Chamond	62	45.28 N	4.30 E
Saint-Chaptes	62	43.58 N	4.17 E
Saint Charles, Ark., U.S.	194	34.22 N	91.08 W
Saint Charles, Idaho, U.S.	202	42.07 N	111.23 W
Saint Charles, Ill., U.S.	216	41.54 N	88.19 W
Saint Charles, Mich., U.S.	190	43.18 N	84.09 W
Saint Charles, Minn., U.S.	190	43.58 N	92.04 W
Saint Charles, Mo., U.S.	219	38.47 N	90.29 W
Saint Charles □[6]	219	38.47 N	90.43 W
Saint-Charles ≃	275a	45.40 N	73.27 W
Saint-Charles, Lac ⊜	206	46.55 N	71.23 W
Saint-Charles-de-Drummond	206	45.54 N	72.28 W
Saint-Charles-Richelieu	206	45.41 N	73.11 W
Saint-Chef	62	45.38 N	5.22 E
Saint-Chély-d'Apcher	32	44.48 N	3.17 E
Saint-Chéron	261	48.33 N	2.07 E
Saint-Christophe-en-Bazelle	50	47.11 N	1.43 E
Saint-Christophe-Nevis → Saint Kitts-Nevis □[2]	238	17.20 N	62.45 W
Saint Christopher (Saint Kitts) I	238	17.20 N	62.45 W
Saint-Chrysostome	206	45.06 N	73.46 W
Saint-Ciers-sur-Gironde	32	45.18 N	0.37 W
Saint Clair, Mich., U.S.	190	42.49 N	82.30 W
Saint Clair, Mo., U.S.	219	38.20 N	90.59 W
Saint Clair, Pa., U.S.	208	40.43 N	76.11 W
Saint Clair, Pa., U.S.	279b	40.16 N	79.33 W
Saint Clair □[6], Ill., U.S.	219	38.31 N	90.00 W
Saint Clair □[6], Mich., U.S.	214	42.50 N	82.42 W
Saint Clair ≃	214	42.37 N	82.31 W
Saint Clair, Lake ⊜	214	42.25 N	82.41 W
Saint Clair Beach	281	42.19 N	82.51 W
Saint Clair Flats	214	42.32 N	82.37 W
Saint Clair Flats ≍	281	42.35 N	82.36 W
Saint Clair Flats Canal ≋	214	42.20 N	82.58 W
Saint Clair Flats State Wildlife Area •[4]	281	42.36 N	82.40 W
Saint Clair Haven	214	42.34 N	82.47 W
Saint Clair Shores	214	42.30 N	82.54 W
Saint-Clair-sur-Epte	50	49.12 N	1.41 E
Saint Clairsville, Ohio, U.S.	214	40.05 N	80.54 W
Saint Clairsville, Pa., U.S.	214	40.09 N	78.31 W

Symbols in the index entries represent the broad categories identified in the key at the right. Symbols with superior numbers (⛰[2]) identify subcategories (see complete key on page I · 30).

Kartensymbole in dem Registerverzeichnis stellen die rechts in Schlüssel erklärten Kategorien dar. Symbole mit hochgestellten Ziffern (⛰[2]) bezeichnen Unterabteilungen einer Kategorie (vgl. vollständiger Schlüssel auf Seite I · 30).

Los símbolos incluídos en el texto del índice representan las grandes categorías identificadas con la clave a la derecha. Los símbolos con numeros en su parte superior (⛰[2]) identifican las subcategorías (véase la clave completa en la página I · 30).

Les symboles de l'index représentent les catégories indiquées dans la légende à droite. Les symboles suivis d'un indice (⛰[2]) représentent des sous-catégories (voir légende complète à la page I · 30).

Os símbolos incluídos no texto do índice representam as grandes categorias identificadas com a chavé à direita. Os símbolos com números em sua parte superior (⛰[2]) identificam as subcategorias (veja-se a chave completa à página I · 30).

	English	Deutsch	Español	Français	Português
∧	Mountain	Berg	Montaña	Montagne	Montanha
⛰	Mountains	Berge	Montañas	Montagnes	Montanhas
)(	Pass	Pass	Paso	Col	Passo
V	Valley, Canyon	Tal, Cañon	Valle, Cañón	Vallée, Canyon	Vale, Canhão
≍	Plain	Ebene	Llano	Plaine	Planície
≻	Cape	Kap	Cabo	Cap	Cabo
I	Island	Insel	Isla	Île	Ilha
II	Islands	Inseln	Islas	Îles	Ilhas
⊥	Other Topographic Features	Andere Topographische Objekte	Otros Elementos Topográficos	Autres données topographiques	Outros Elementos Topográficos

ESPAÑOL · **FRANÇAIS** · **PORTUGUÊS**

Nombre / Nom / Nome	Página / Page / Página	Lat.°′	Long.°′ W=Oeste / W=Ouest / W=Oeste
Saint Clair Tunnel ⬥[5]	214	42.57 N	82.25 W
Saint-Claud	32	45.53 N	0.23 E
Saint-Claude, Man., Can.	184	49.40 N	98.22 W
Saint-Claude, Fr.	58	46.23 N	5.52 E
Saint-Claude, Guad.	241o	16.02 N	61.42 W
Saint Clears	42	51.50 N	4.30 W
Saint-Clément	58	48.32 N	6.36 E
Saint Clements	212	43.31 N	80.39 W
Saint Clements Bay C	208	38.17 N	76.42 W
Sainte-Clothilde	206	45.59 N	72.14 W
Saint-Cloud, Fr.	50	48.50 N	2.11 E
Saint Cloud, Fla., U.S.	220	28.15 N	81.17 W
Saint Cloud, Minn., U.S.	190	45.33 N	94.10 W
Saint-Cloud, Parc de ♠	261	48.50 N	2.13 E
Saint-Cloud, Ruisseau ≃	275a	45.25 N	73.28 W
Saint-Colomban-des-Villards	62	45.18 N	6.14 E
Sainte-Colombe	58	47.52 N	4.32 E
Saint Columb Major	42	50.26 N	5.03 W
Saint Combs	46	57.39 N	1.54 W
Saint-Constant	206	45.22 N	73.37 W
Saint-Cosme-en-vairais	50	48.16 N	0.28 E
Sainte-Croix, Qué., Can.	206	46.38 N	71.44 W
Sainte-Croix, Schw.	58	46.49 N	6.31 E
Saint Croix I	241n	17.45 N	64.45 W
Saint Croix ≃, N.A.	186	45.10 N	67.10 W
Saint Croix ≃, U.S.	190	44.45 N	92.49 W
Sainte-Croix-aux-Mines	58	48.16 N	7.13 E
Saint Croix Falls	190	45.24 N	92.38 W
Saint Croix Island I	158	33.48 S	25.45 E
Saint Croix Island National Monument ♠	186	45.08 N	67.08 W
Saint Croix National Scenic Riverway ♠	208	46.00 N	92.25 W
Saint Croix State Park ♠	190	46.00 N	92.40 W
Sainte-Croix-Vallée-Francaise	62	44.11 N	3.44 E
Saint-Cuthbert	206	46.09 N	73.14 W
Saint-Cyprien	32	44.52 N	1.02 E
Saint-Cyrille-de-Wendover	206	45.56 N	72.26 W
Sainte-Cyr-l'École	50	48.48 N	2.04 E
Saint-Cyr-l'École, Aérodrome de ⊠	261	48.49 N	2.04 E
Saint Cyr Range ⩓	180	61.10 N	131.10 W
Saint-Cyr-sous-Dourdan	261	48.34 N	2.02 E
Saint-Cyr-sur-Loire	50	47.24 N	0.40 E
Saint-Cyr-sur-Mer	62	43.11 N	5.43 E
Saint-Dalmas-de-Tende	62	44.03 N	7.35 E
Saint-Damien-de-Brandon	206	46.20 N	73.29 W
Saint David, Ariz., U.S.	200	31.54 N	110.13 W
Saint David, Ill., U.S.	190	40.30 N	90.03 W
Saint David's, Newf., Can.	186	48.12 N	58.52 W
Saint Davids, Ont., Can.	284a	43.10 N	79.06 W
Saint David's, Wales, U.K.	42	51.54 N	5.16 W
Saint Davids, Pa., U.S.	285	40.02 N	75.22 W
Saint David's Cathedral ʊ[1]	42	51.54 N	5.16 W
Saint David's Head ≻	42	51.55 N	5.19 W
Saint David's Island I	240a	32.22 N	64.39 W
Saint-Denis, Fr.	50	48.56 N	2.22 E
Saint-Denis, Réu.	157c	20.52 S	55.28 E
Saint-Denis, Basilique ʊ[1]	261	48.56 N	2.22 E
Saint-Denis-de-l'Hôtel	50	47.52 N	2.07 E
Saint-Denis-en-Bugey	58	45.57 N	5.20 E
Saint-Denis-Rivière-Richelieu	206	45.47 N	73.09 W
Saint Dennis	42	50.23 N	4.53 W
Saint-Didier-en-Velay	62	45.18 N	4.17 E
Saint-Didier-les-Bains	62	44.00 N	5.07 E
Saint-Dié	58	48.17 N	6.57 E
Saint-Disdier	62	44.44 N	5.54 E
Saint-Dizier	58	48.38 N	4.57 E
Saint Dogmaels	42	52.05 N	4.40 W
Saint-Donat-de-Montcalm	206	46.19 N	74.13 W
Saint-Donat-sur-l'Herbasse	62	45.07 N	5.00 E
Sainte-Dorothée ⬥[8]	275a	45.32 N	73.49 W
Saint-Dyé-sur-Loire	50	47.39 N	1.29 E
Sainte → Saint			
Saint-Édouard-de-Maskinongé	206	46.20 N	73.09 W
Saint Edward	198	41.34 N	97.52 W
Saint-Égrève	62	45.14 N	5.41 E
Saint Eleanor's	186	46.25 N	63.49 W
Saint-Éleuthère	186	47.29 N	69.17 W
Saint Elias, Cape ≻	180	59.52 N	144.30 W
Saint Elias, Mount ∧	180	60.18 N	140.55 W
Saint Elias Mountains ⩓	180	60.30 N	139.30 W
Saint-Élie	250	4.50 N	53.17 W
Saint Elmo	219	39.02 N	88.51 W
Saint-Éloi	186	48.02 N	69.14 W
Saint-Émile-de-Montcalm	206	46.06 N	74.00 W
Saint-Émile-de-Québec	206	46.52 N	71.20 W
Saint-Émile-de-Suffolk	206	45.56 N	74.55 W
Sainte-Enimie	32	44.22 N	3.26 E
Saint-Épain	50	47.08 N	0.32 E
Saint-Esprit ≃	206	45.52 N	73.27 W
Saint-Étienne	62	45.26 N	4.24 E
Saint-Étienne-de-Lugdarès	62	44.39 N	3.57 E
Saint-Étienne-de-Saint-Geoirs	62	45.20 N	5.21 E
Saint-Étienne-des-Grès	206	46.26 N	72.46 W
Saint-Étienne-de-Tinée	62	44.15 N	6.55 E
Saint-Étienne-du-Rouveray	50	49.23 N	1.06 E
Saint-Étienne-en-Dévoluy	62	44.42 N	5.56 E
Saint-Étienne-le-Laus	62	44.30 N	6.10 E
Saint-Étienne-les-Orgues	62	44.03 N	5.47 E
Saint-Étienne-lès-Remiremont	58	48.02 N	6.37 E
Saint-Eugène	206	45.30 N	74.28 W
Saint-Eustache	206	45.33 N	73.54 W
Saint-Evroult-Notre-Dame-du-Bois	50	48.48 N	0.28 E
Saint-Fabien	186	48.18 N	68.52 W
Saint Faith's	158	30.30 S	30.12 E
Saint-Fargeau	50	47.38 N	3.04 E
Saint-Fargeau-Ponthierry	261	48.33 N	2.32 E
Saint-Félicien, Qué., Can.	176	48.39 N	72.26 W
Saint-Félicien, Fr.	62	45.05 N	4.38 E
Sainte-Félicité	186	48.54 N	67.20 W
Saint-Félix	62	45.48 N	5.58 E
Saint-Félix-de-Kingsey	206	45.48 N	72.12 W
Saint-Félix-de-Valois	206	46.10 N	73.26 W
Saint-Ferdinand (Bernierville)	206	46.06 N	71.34 W
Saintfield	48	54.28 N	5.47 W
Saint Fillans	46	56.23 N	4.07 W
Saint-Firmin	62	44.47 N	6.02 E
Saint-Firmin-sur-Loire	50	47.37 N	2.44 E
Saint-Flavien	206	46.31 N	71.36 W
Saint-Florentin	50	48.00 N	3.44 E
Saint-Florent-sur-Cher	32	46.59 N	2.15 E
Saint-Floris, Parc National de ♠	146	9.40 N	21.35 E
Saint-Flour	32	45.02 N	3.05 E
Saint-Fons	62	45.42 N	4.52 E
Saint-Fortunat	206	45.58 N	71.36 W
Sainte-Foy	206	46.47 N	71.17 W
Sainte-Foy-la-Grande	32	44.50 N	0.13 E
Sainte-Foy-l'Argentière	62	45.42 N	4.28 E
Sainte-Foy-lès-Lyon	62	45.44 N	4.48 E
Sainte-Foy-Tarentaise	62	45.35 N	6.53 E
Saint Francis, Kans., U.S.	198	39.46 N	101.48 W
Saint Francis, S. Dak., U.S.	198	43.09 N	100.54 W
Saint Francis, Wis., U.S.	216	42.58 N	87.52 W
Saint Francis ≃, N.A.	186	47.10 N	68.57 W
Saint Francis ≃, U.S.	194	34.38 N	90.35 W
Saint Francis, Cape ≻, Newf., Can.	186	47.50 N	52.47 W
Saint Francis, Cape ≻, S. Afr.	158	34.14 S	24.49 E
Saint Francis, Lake ⊜	206	45.08 N	74.25 W
Saint Francis Bay C	158	34.35 S	25.10 E
Saint Francisville	194	30.47 N	91.23 W
Saint-François	241o	16.15 N	61.17 W
Saint-François ≃	206	46.07 N	72.55 W
Saint-François, Lac ⊜	206	45.55 N	71.10 W
Saint-François de Boundji	152	1.03 S	15.22 E
Saint-François-de-Laval ⬥[8]	275a	45.40 N	73.34 W
Saint-François-du-Lac	206	46.04 N	72.50 W
Saint Francois Mountains ⩓[2]	194	37.30 N	90.35 W
Saint-François-sur-Bugeon	62	45.24 N	6.21 E
Saint-Front	62	44.59 N	4.08 E
Saint-Gabriel	206	46.17 N	73.23 W
Saint Gabriel-deGaspé	186	48.31 N	64.32 W
Saint-Gabriel-de-Rimouski	186	48.25 N	68.10 W
Saint-Gall → Sankt Gallen	58	47.25 N	9.23 E
Saint-Galmier	62	45.35 N	4.19 E
Sainte-Gauburge-Sainte-Colombe	50	48.42 N	0.26 E
Saint-Gaudens	32	43.07 N	0.44 E
Saint-Gaudens National Historic Site ⊥	188	43.29 N	72.19 W
Saint-Gaultier	32	46.38 N	1.25 E
Saint-Gély-du-Fesc	62	43.42 N	3.48 E
Saint-Genest-Lerpt	62	45.27 N	4.20 E
Saint-Genest-Malifaux	62	45.20 N	4.25 E
Sainte-Geneviève, Qué., Can.	275a	45.29 N	73.52 W
Sainte Genevieve, Mo., U.S.	194	37.59 N	90.03 W
Sainte-Geneviève-de-Batiscan	206	46.32 N	72.20 W
Sainte-Geneviève-des-Bois	50	48.38 N	2.20 E
Saint-Gengoux-le-National	58	46.37 N	4.39 E
Saint-Genis-de-Saintonge	32	45.29 N	0.34 W
Saint-Genis-Laval	62	45.41 N	4.48 E
Saint-Genis-Pouilly	58	46.15 N	6.01 E
Saint-Genix-sur-Guiers	62	45.36 N	5.38 E
Saint-Geoire-en-Valdaine	62	45.27 N	5.38 E
Saint George, Austl.	166	28.02 S	148.35 E
Saint George, Ber.	240a	32.22 N	64.40 W
Saint George, N.B., Can.	186	45.08 N	66.49 W
Saint George, Ont., Can.	212	43.15 N	80.15 W
Saint George, Alaska, U.S.	180	56.36 N	169.32 W
Saint George, Pa., U.S.	214	41.15 N	79.47 W
Saint George, S.C., U.S.	192	33.11 N	80.35 W
Saint George, Utah, U.S.	200	37.06 N	113.35 W
Saint George ⬥[8]	276	40.39 N	74.05 W
Saint George, Cape ≻, Newf., Can.	186	48.27 N	59.15 W
Saint George, Cape ≻, Pap. N. Gui.	164	4.52 S	152.52 E
Saint George, Cape ≻, Fla., U.S.	192	29.35 N	85.04 W
Saint George, Point ≻	204	41.47 N	124.15 W
Saint George Island	208	38.07 N	76.29 W
Saint George Island I, Alaska, U.S.	180	56.35 N	169.35 W
Saint George Island I, Fla., U.S.	192	29.39 N	84.55 W
Saint George's, Newf., Can.	186	48.26 N	58.29 W
Saint-Georges, Qué., Can.	206	46.37 N	72.40 W
Saint-Georges, Fr.	58	48.40 N	6.56 E
Saint George's, Gren.	241k	12.03 N	61.45 W
Saint-Georges, Guy. fr.	250	3.54 N	51.48 W
Saint Georges, Del., U.S.	208	39.33 N	75.39 W
Saint Georges Basin C	170	35.07 S	150.36 E
Saint George's Bay C, Newf., Can.	186	48.20 N	59.00 W
Saint Georges Bay C, N.S., Can.	186	45.50 N	61.45 W
Saint George's Channel ɯ, Eur.	28	52.00 N	6.00 W
Saint George's Channel ɯ, Pap. N. Gui.	164	4.30 S	152.30 E
Saint-Georges-de-Reneins	58	46.04 N	4.43 E
Saint-Georges-de-Windsor	206	45.42 N	71.50 W
Saint-Georges-en-Couzan	62	45.42 N	3.56 E
Saint Georges Head ≻	170	35.12 S	150.42 E
Saint George's Island I	240a	32.22 N	64.40 W
Saint George Sound ɯ	192	29.47 N	84.42 W
Saint Georges Ranges ⩓	162	18.40 S	125.00 E
Saint-Gérard, Bel.	56	50.21 N	4.45 E
Saint-Gérard, Qué., Can.	206	45.46 N	71.25 W
Saint-Germain	32	48.54 N	2.05 E
Saint-Germain ≃	206	45.55 N	72.30 W
Saint-Germain, Forêt de ♠	261	48.55 N	2.05 E
Saint-Germain-de-Calberte	62	44.13 N	3.48 E
Saint-Germain-de-Grantham	206	45.50 N	72.34 W
Saint-Germain-de-Joux	58	46.11 N	5.44 E
Saint-Germain-des-Champs	50	47.25 N	3.55 E
Saint-Germain-du-Bois	58	46.45 N	5.15 E
Saint-Germain-du-Plain	58	46.42 N	4.58 E
Saint-Germain-en-Laye	50	48.54 N	2.05 E
Saint-Germain-en-Laye, Château de ⊥	261	48.54 N	2.06 E
Saint-Germain-Laval	62	45.50 N	4.01 E
Saint-Germain-Laxis	261	48.35 N	2.43 E
Saint-Germain-Lembron	32	45.28 N	3.14 E
Saint-Germain-lès-Arlay	58	46.46 N	5.34 E
Saint-Germain-lès-Corbeil	261	48.37 N	2.29 E
Saint-Germain-l'Herm	32	45.28 N	3.33 E
Saint-Germain-sur-Morin	261	48.53 N	2.51 E
Saint Germans	42	50.24 N	4.18 W
Saint-Germer-de-Fly	50	49.27 N	1.47 E
Saint-Gervais-d'Auvergne	32	46.02 N	2.49 E
Saint-Gervais-les-Bains	62	45.54 N	6.43 E
Saint-Gervasy	62	43.53 N	4.29 E
Saint-Géry	32	44.29 N	1.35 E
Saint-Gilles, Bel.	50	50.49 N	4.20 E
Saint-Gilles, Qué., Can.	206	46.31 N	71.22 W
Saint-Gilles, Fr.	62	43.41 N	4.26 E
Saint-Gilles-croix-de-Vie	32	46.42 N	1.57 W
Saint-Gingolph	58	46.24 N	6.52 E
Saint-Girons	32	42.59 N	1.09 E
Saint-Gobain	50	49.36 N	3.23 E
Saint Gotthard Pass → San Gottardo, Passo del)(	58	46.33 N	8.34 E
Saint Govan's Head ≻	42	51.36 N	4.55 W
Saint-Gratien	261	48.58 N	2.17 E
Saint-Grégoire (Larochelle)	206	46.16 N	72.30 W
Saint Gregory, Mount ∧	186	49.19 N	58.13 W
Saint-Guénolé	32	47.49 N	4.20 W
Saint-Guillaume-d'Upton	206	45.53 N	72.46 W
Saint-Héand	62	45.31 N	4.22 E
Saint Helena	226	38.30 N	122.28 W
Saint Helena □[2]	8	15.57 S	5.42 W
Saint Helena I	8	15.57 S	5.42 W
Saint Helena, Mount ∧	226	38.40 N	122.38 W
Saint Helenabaai C	158	32.43 S	18.05 E
Saint Helena Sound ɯ	192	32.27 N	80.25 W
Sainte-Hélène, Île I	275a	45.31 N	73.32 W
Sainte-Hélène-de-Bagot	206	45.44 N	72.44 W
Saint Helens, Austl.	166	41.20 S	148.15 E
Saint Helens, Eng., U.K.	42	50.42 N	1.06 W
Saint Helens, Eng., U.K.	44 / 262	53.28 N	2.44 W
Saint Helens, Oreg., U.S.	224	45.52 N	122.48 W
Saint Helens □[8]	262	53.28 N	2.45 W
Saint Helens, Mount ∧	224	46.12 N	122.11 W
Saint Helens Canal Ξ	262	53.27 N	2.42 W
Saint Helier	43b	49.12 N	2.37 W
Saint Henry	216	40.25 N	84.38 W
Sainte-Hermine	32	46.33 N	1.04 W
Sainthia	126	23.57 N	87.40 E
Saint-Hilaire-du-Harcouët	32	48.35 N	1.06 W
Saint-Hilaire-Est	206	45.34 N	73.11 W
Saint-Hilarion	261	48.37 N	1.44 E
Saint-Hippolyte, Fr.	58	47.19 N	6.49 E
Saint-Hippolyte, Fr.	62	43.38 N	4.45 E
Saint-Hippolyte-de-Kilkenny	206	45.56 N	74.01 W
Saint-Hippolyte-du-Fort	62	43.58 N	3.51 E
Saint-Honorat, Mont ∧	62	44.05 N	6.46 E
Saint-Hubert, Bel.	56	50.01 N	5.23 E
Saint-Hubert, Qué., Can.	206	45.30 N	73.25 W
Saint-Hubert, Étang de ⊜	261	48.43 N	1.51 E
Saint-Hubert-le-Roi	261	48.43 N	1.52 E
Saint-Hugues	206	45.48 N	72.52 W
Saint-Hyacinthe	206	45.37 N	72.57 W
Saint-Hyacinthe □[6]	206	45.40 N	73.05 W
Saint-Ignace, N.B., Can.	186	46.42 N	65.05 W
Saint Ignace, Mich., U.S.	190	45.52 N	84.43 W
Saint Ignace Island I	190	48.48 N	87.55 W
Saint Ignatius, Guy.	246	3.20 N	59.47 W
Saint Ignatius, Mont., U.S.	202	47.19 N	114.06 W
Saint-Imier	58	47.09 N	7.00 E
Saint-Imier, Vallon de V	58	47.10 N	7.00 E
Saint-Isidore	186	47.33 N	65.03 W
Saint-Isidore-d'Auckland	206	45.16 N	71.31 W
Saint-Isidore-de-Laprairie	275a	45.18 N	73.41 W
Saint Ives, Austl.	274a	33.44 S	151.10 E
Saint Ives, Eng., U.K.	32	50.12 N	5.29 W
Saint Ives, Eng., U.K.	42	52.20 N	0.05 W
Saint Ives Bay C	42	50.14 N	5.28 W
Saint Jacob	219	38.43 N	89.46 W
Saint Jacobs	212	43.32 N	80.33 W
Saint-Jacques	206	45.57 N	73.34 W
Saint-Jacques ≃	275a	45.26 N	73.29 W
Saint James, Ill., U.S.	219	38.57 N	88.51 W
Saint James, Mich., U.S.	190	45.45 N	85.31 W
Saint James, Minn., U.S.	198	43.59 N	94.38 W
Saint James, Mo., U.S.	194	38.00 N	91.37 W
Saint James, N.Y., U.S.	210	40.53 N	73.09 W
Saint James, Cape ≻	182	51.56 N	131.01 W
Saint James City	220	26.30 N	82.04 W
Saint James Islands II	240m	18.19 N	64.50 W
Saint James Palace ʊ	260	51.30 N	0.08 W
Saint-Jean	206	45.19 N	73.16 W
Saint-Jean □[6]	206	45.15 N	73.20 W
Saint-Jean ≃, Qué., Can.	186	48.46 N	64.26 W
Saint-Jean ≃, Qué., Can.	186	50.17 N	64.20 W
Saint-Jean, Île I	275a	45.41 N	73.39 W
Saint-Jean, Lac ⊜	176	48.35 N	72.05 W
Saint-Jean, Rapides de ∟	275a	45.19 N	73.15 W
Saint-Jean Airport ⊠	275a	45.18 N	73.17 W
Saint-Jean-aux-Bois	50	49.21 N	2.55 E
Saint-Jean-Baptiste	184	49.16 N	97.21 W
Saint-Jean-Baptiste-de-Rouville	206	45.31 N	73.07 W
Saint-Jean-Cap-Ferrat	62	43.41 N	7.20 E
Saint-Jean-d'Angély	32	45.57 N	0.31 W
Saint-Jean-d'Assé	50	48.09 N	0.07 E
Saint-Jean-de-Bournay	62	45.29 N	5.08 E
Saint-Jean-de-Braye	50	47.54 N	1.58 E
Saint-Jean-de-Losne	58	47.06 N	5.15 E
Saint-Jean-de-Luz	32	43.23 N	1.40 W
Saint-Jean-de-Maurienne	62	45.17 N	6.21 E
Saint-Jean-de-Monts	32	46.48 N	2.03 W
Saint-Jean-des-Piles	206	46.41 N	72.45 W
Saint-Jean-du-Gard	62	44.06 N	3.53 E
Saint-Jean-en-Royans	62	45.01 N	5.18 E
Saint-Jean-Pied-de-Port	32	43.10 N	1.14 W
Saint-Jean-Port-Joli	186	47.13 N	70.16 W
Saint-Jean-Soleymieux	62	45.30 N	4.02 E
Saint-Jeoire	58	46.09 N	6.28 E
Saint-Jérôme	206	45.47 N	74.00 W
Saint Jo	196	33.42 N	97.31 W
Saint Joachim	214	42.16 N	82.38 W
Saint Joe	216	41.19 N	84.54 W
Saint Joe ≃	202	47.21 N	116.42 W
Saint John, N.B., Can.	186	45.16 N	66.03 W
Saint John, Jersey	43b	49.15 N	2.08 W
Saint John, Ind., U.S.	216	41.27 N	87.28 W
Saint John, Kans., U.S.	198	38.00 N	98.46 W
Saint John, N. Dak., U.S.	198	48.57 N	99.43 W
Saint John, Wash., U.S.	202	47.05 N	117.35 W
Saint John I	240m	18.20 N	64.45 W
Saint John ≃, Liber.	150	6.40 N	9.10 W
Saint John ≃, N.A.	186	45.15 N	66.04 W
Saint John, Cape ≻	186	50.00 N	55.32 W
Saint John, Lake ⊜, Newf., Can.	186	48.23 N	54.41 W
Saint John, Lake ⊜, Ont., Can.	212	44.41 N	79.20 W
Saint John Bay C	186	50.54 N	57.08 W
Saint John Island I	186	50.49 N	57.14 W
Saint Johns, Antig.	240c	17.06 N	61.51 W
Saint John's, Newf., Can.	186	47.34 N	52.43 W
Saint Johns → Saint-Jean, Qué., Can.	206	45.19 N	73.16 W
Saint Johns, Ariz., U.S.	200	34.30 N	109.22 W
Saint Johns, Mich., U.S.	216	43.00 N	84.33 W
Saint Johns, Mo., U.S.	219	38.43 N	90.22 W
Saint Johns, Ohio, U.S.	216	40.33 N	84.05 W
Saint Johns ≃, Calif., U.S.	226	36.25 N	119.25 W
Saint Johns ≃, Fla., U.S.	192	30.24 N	81.24 W
Saint Johnsburg	210	43.05 N	78.53 W
Saint Johnsbury	188	44.25 N	72.01 W
Saint Johns Creek ≃	219	38.34 N	91.01 W
Saint John's Jerusalem ⊥	260	51.25 N	0.14 E
Saint Johns Marsh ☷	220	27.40 N	80.35 W
Saint John's Point ≻	44	54.13 N	5.40 W
Saint John's University ʊ[2]	276	40.43 N	73.48 W
Saint Johnsville	210	43.00 N	74.41 W
Saint Joseph, N.B., Can.	186	45.59 N	64.34 W
Saint Joseph, Dom.	240d	15.26 N	61.26 W
Saint-Joseph, Mart.	240e	14.40 N	61.03 W
Saint-Joseph, Réu.	157c	21.22 S	55.36 E
Saint Joseph, Ill., U.S.	194	40.07 N	88.02 W
Saint Joseph, La., U.S.	194	31.55 N	91.14 W
Saint Joseph, Mich., U.S.	216	42.06 N	86.29 W
Saint Joseph, Minn., U.S.	190	45.34 N	94.19 W
Saint Joseph, Mo., U.S.	194	39.46 N	94.51 W
Saint Joseph □[6], Ind., U.S.	216	41.41 N	86.15 W
Saint Joseph □[6], Mich., U.S.	216	41.55 N	85.31 W
Saint Joseph ≃, U.S.	216	42.07 N	86.29 W
Saint Joseph ≃, U.S.	216	41.05 N	85.08 W
Saint-Joseph, Île I	275a	45.41 N	73.42 W
Saint-Joseph, Lac ⊜	206	46.54 N	71.38 W
Saint Joseph, Lake ⊜	176	51.05 N	90.35 W
Saint Joseph, West Branch ≃	216	41.39 N	84.34 W
Saint Joseph Bay C	192	29.47 N	85.21 W
Saint Joseph Channel ɯ	190	46.16 N	83.51 W
Saint Joseph d'Alma → Alma	186	48.33 N	71.39 W
Saint-Joseph-de-Beauce	186	46.18 N	70.53 W
Saint-Joseph-de-Mékinac	206	46.55 N	72.42 W
Saint-Joseph-de-Sorel	206	46.02 N	73.07 W
Saint-Joseph-du-Lac	275a	45.32 N	74.00 W
Saint Joseph Island I	190	46.13 N	83.57 W
Saint Joseph's College ʊ[2]	285	40.00 N	75.14 W
Saint-Jouin-Bruneval	50	49.39 N	0.10 E
Saint-Jovite	206	46.07 N	74.36 W
Sainte-Julie	206	45.35 N	73.19 W
Saint-Julien	58	46.23 N	5.27 E
Saint-Julien-Chapteuil	62	45.02 N	4.04 E
Saint-Julien-du-Sault	50	48.02 N	3.18 E
Saint-Julien-du-Verdon	62	43.55 N	6.32 E
Saint-Julien-en-Beauchêne	62	44.37 N	5.42 E
Saint-Julien-en-Born	32	44.04 N	1.14 W
Saint-Julien-en-Genevois	58	46.08 N	6.05 E
Saint-Julien-en-Jarez	62	45.28 N	4.31 E
Saint-Julien-les-Villas	50	48.16 N	4.06 E
Saint-Julien-Molin-Molette	62	45.19 N	4.37 E
Sainte-Julienne	206	45.58 N	73.43 W
Saint-Junien	32	45.53 N	0.54 E
Saint Just, P.R.	240m	18.23 N	66.00 W
Saint Just, Eng., U.K.	42	50.07 N	5.42 W
Saint-Just-en-Chaussée	50	49.30 N	2.26 E
Saint-Just-en-Chevalet	32	45.55 N	3.50 E
Saint-Justin	206	46.15 N	73.05 W
Saint-Just-Malmont	62	45.20 N	4.19 E
Saint-Just-sur-Loire	62	45.29 N	4.16 E
Saint Keverne	42	50.03 N	5.06 W
Saint Kilda, Austl.	168b	34.44 S	138.32 E
Saint Kilda, Austl.	169	37.52 S	144.59 E
Saint Kilda, N.Z.	172	45.54 S	170.30 E
Saint Kilda I	46	57.49 N	8.36 W
Saint Kitts → Saint Christopher I	238	17.20 N	62.45 W
Saint Kitts-Nevis □[2]	238	17.20 N	62.45 W
Saint-Lambert, Qué., Can.	188	45.30 N	73.30 W
Saint-Lambert, Fr.	261	48.44 N	2.01 E
Saint Landry	194	30.51 N	92.15 W
Saint-Laurent, Man., Can.	184	50.24 N	97.56 W
Saint-Laurent, Qué., Can.	206	45.30 N	73.40 W
Saint-Laurent, Fr.	58	48.09 N	6.27 E
Saint-Laurent → Saint Lawrence ≃	176	49.30 N	67.00 W
Saint-Laurent-Blangy	50	50.18 N	2.48 E
Saint-Laurent-de-Chamousset	62	45.44 N	4.28 E
Saint-Laurent-du-Maroni	250	5.30 N	54.02 W
Saint-Laurent du Maroni □[8]	250	4.00 N	53.30 W
Saint-Laurent-du-Var, Fr.	62	45.23 N	5.44 E
Saint-Laurent-du-Var, Fr.	62	43.40 N	7.11 E
Saint-Laurent-en-Caux	50	49.45 N	0.53 E
Saint-Laurent-en-Grandvaux	58	46.35 N	5.57 E
Saint-Laurent-et-Benon	32	45.09 N	0.49 W
Saint-Laurent-les-Bains	62	44.37 N	3.58 E
Saint-Laurent-sur-Saône	58	46.18 N	4.50 E
Saint Lawrence, Austl.	166	22.21 S	149.31 E
Saint Lawrence, Newf., Can.	186	46.55 N	55.24 W
Saint Lawrence □[6]	212	44.30 N	75.27 W
Saint Lawrence ≃	176	49.30 N	67.00 W
Saint Lawrence, Cape ≻	186	47.03 N	60.37 W
Saint Lawrence, Gulf of C	186	48.00 N	62.00 W
Saint Lawrence Island I	180	63.30 N	170.30 W
Saint Lawrence Islands National Park ♠	212	44.18 N	76.08 W
Saint-Lazare	184	50.26 N	101.16 W
Saint-Lazare ⬥[5]	261	48.53 N	2.20 E
Saint-Léandre	186	48.44 N	67.36 W
Saint-Léger-en-Yvelines	261	48.43 N	1.46 E
Saint-Léger-sur-Dheune	58	46.51 N	4.38 E
Saint Leo	220	28.21 N	82.14 W
Saint Leon	218	39.17 N	84.57 W
Saint-Léonard, N.B., Can.	186	47.10 N	67.56 W
Saint-Léonard, Qué., Can.	206	45.35 N	73.35 W
Saint Leonard, Md., U.S.	208	38.28 N	76.30 W
Saint-Léonard-d'Aston	206	46.06 N	72.22 W
Saint-Léonard-de-Noblat	32	45.50 N	1.29 E
Saint Leonards	42	50.51 N	0.34 E
Saint-Leu-d'Esserent	50	49.13 N	2.25 E
Saint-Leu-la-Forêt	50	49.01 N	2.15 E
Saint-Liboire	206	45.39 N	72.46 W
Saint-Lô	32	49.07 N	1.05 W
Saint-Louis, Sask., Can.	184	52.56 N	105.49 W
Saint-Louis, Fr.	58	47.35 N	7.34 E
Saint-Louis, Guad.	241o	15.57 N	61.19 W
Saint-Louis, Réu.	157c	21.16 S	55.25 E
Saint-Louis, Sén.	150	16.02 N	16.30 W
Saint Louis, Mich., U.S.	190	43.25 N	84.36 W
Saint Louis, Mo., U.S.	219	38.38 N	90.11 W
Saint Louis, Tex., U.S.	222	32.18 N	95.20 W
Saint Louis □[6]	219	38.39 N	90.25 W
Saint-Louis ≃	275a	45.19 N	73.53 W
Saint-Louis, Baie de C	241o	15.57 N	61.20 W
Saint-Louis, Lac ⊜	206	45.24 N	73.48 W
Saint-Louis, Pointe ≻	275a	45.19 N	73.53 W
Saint Louis Crossing	218	39.19 N	85.51 W
Saint-Louis-de-Champlain	206	46.25 N	72.36 W
Saint-Louis-de-Kent	186	46.44 N	64.58 W
Saint Louis Park	190	44.56 N	93.22 W
Saint Louisville	214	40.10 N	82.25 W
Saint-Loup-sur-Aujon	58	47.53 N	5.05 E
Saint-Loup-sur-Semouse	58	47.53 N	6.16 E
Saint-Luc, Qué., Can.	206	45.22 N	73.18 W
Saint-Luc, Schw.	58	46.13 N	7.36 E
Sainte-Luce	240e	14.28 N	60.56 W
Saint Lucia □[1]	230 / 241f	13.53 N	60.58 W
Saint Lucia, Cape ≻	158	28.25 S	32.25 E
Saint Lucia, Lake ⊜	158	28.05 S	32.26 E
Saint Lucia Bay C	158	28.25 S	32.25 E
Saint Lucia Channel ɯ	238	14.09 N	60.57 W
Saint Lucia Estuary	158	28.22 S	32.25 E
Saint Lucia Game Reserve ⬥[4]	158	28.10 S	32.28 E
Sainte-Lucie, Fr.	36	41.42 N	9.22 E
Saint Lucie, Fla., U.S.	220	27.30 N	80.20 W
Saint Lucie □[6]	220	27.23 N	80.26 W
Saint Lucie ≃	220	27.10 N	80.11 W
Saint Lucie Canal Ξ	220	27.10 N	80.15 W
Saint Lucie Inlet C	220	27.10 N	80.10 W
Saint Lucie Lock ⬥[5]	220	27.07 N	80.17 W
Saint-Lucien	261	48.39 N	1.38 E
Saint-Lupicin	58	46.24 N	5.47 E
Sainte-Magnance	50	47.27 N	4.04 E
Saint Magnus Bay C	46a	60.24 N	1.34 W
Saint Magnus Cathedral ʊ[1]	46	58.58 N	2.57 W
Saint-Malo, Qué., Can.	206	45.12 N	71.30 W
Saint-Malo, Fr.	32	48.39 N	2.01 W
Saint-Malo, Golfe de C	32	48.45 N	2.00 W
Saint-Mamert-du-Gard	62	43.53 N	4.12 E
Saint-Mammès	50	48.23 N	2.49 E
Saint-Mandé	261	48.50 N	2.25 E
Saint-Mandrier-sur-Mer	62	43.04 N	5.56 E
Saint-Marc, Qué., Can.	275a	45.41 N	73.12 W
Saint-Marc, Haï.	238	19.07 N	72.42 W
Saint-Marc, Canal de ɯ	238	18.50 N	72.45 W
Saint-Marc-des-Carrières	206	46.41 N	72.03 W
Saint-Marcel	58	46.47 N	4.54 E
Saint-Marcellin	62	45.09 N	5.19 E
Saint-Marcelline-de-Kildare	206	46.07 N	73.36 W
Saint-Mard	261	49.02 N	2.42 E
Saint Margaret Bay C	186	51.01 N	56.58 W
Saint Margaret's at Cliffe	42	51.09 N	1.24 E
Saint Margaret's Bay C	186	44.35 N	64.00 W
Saint Margaret's Hope	46	58.49 N	2.57 W
Sainte-Marguerite ≃	176	50.09 N	66.36 W
Sainte-Marguerite, Baie C	186	50.06 N	66.36 W
Sainte-Marguerite-sur-Mer	50	49.55 N	0.57 E
Sainte-Marie	240e	14.47 N	61.00 W
Sainte-Marie, Cap ≻	157b	25.36 S	45.08 E
Sainte-Marie, Île I	157b	16.50 S	49.55 E
Sainte-Marie-aux-Mines (Markirch)	58	48.15 N	7.11 E
Saint Maries	202	47.19 N	116.35 W
Saint Maries ≃	202	47.19 N	116.33 W
Saint-Marin → San Marino □[1]	66	43.56 N	12.25 E
Saint Marks, S. Afr.	158	32.01 S	27.22 E
Saint Marks, Fla., U.S.	192	30.09 N	84.12 W
Saint Marks ≃	192	30.08 N	84.12 W
Sainte-Marthe-de-Gaspé	186	49.12 N	66.10 W
Saint-Martin (Sint Maarten) I	238	18.04 N	63.04 W
Saint-Martin, Cap ≻	240e	14.52 N	61.13 W
Saint Martin, Lake ⊜	184	51.37 N	98.29 W
Saint-Martin-Boulogne	50	50.43 N	1.38 E
Saint-Martin-d'Ardèche	62	44.18 N	4.35 E
Saint-Martin-d'Auxigny	50	47.12 N	2.25 E
Saint-Martin-de-Belleville	62	45.23 N	6.30 E
Saint-Martin-de-Bossenay	50	48.26 N	3.41 E
Saint-Martin-de-Bréthencourt	261	48.31 N	1.56 E
Saint-Martin-de-Crau	62	43.38 N	4.49 E
Saint-Martin-de-Londres	62	43.47 N	3.44 E
Saint-Martin-de-Nigelles	261	48.37 N	1.37 E
Saint-Martin-d'Entraunes	62	44.08 N	6.46 E
Saint-Martin-des-Champs	261	48.53 N	1.43 E
Saint-Martin-de-Valamas	62	44.56 N	4.22 E
Saint-Martin-d'Hères	62	45.10 N	5.46 E
Saint-Martin-du-Puy	50	47.20 N	3.52 E
Saint-Martin-du-Tertre	261	49.06 N	2.21 E
Saint-Martin-du-Var	62	43.49 N	7.12 E
Sainte-Martine	206	45.15 N	73.48 W
Saint-Martin-en-Bresse	58	46.49 N	5.04 E
Saint-Martin-la-Garenne	261	49.02 N	1.41 E
Saint-Martin-la-Plaine	62	45.32 N	4.36 E
Saint Martins	186	45.21 N	65.32 W
Saint Martin's I	42a	49.58 N	6.20 W
Saint Martins Keys II	220	28.47 N	82.44 W
Saint-Martin-Vésubie	62	44.04 N	7.15 E
Saint Martinville	194	30.07 N	91.50 W
Saint Mary ≃, B.C., Can.	182	49.37 N	115.38 W
Saint Mary ≃, N.A.	182	49.37 N	112.52 W
Saint Mary, Cape ≻, N.S., Can.	186	44.05 N	66.13 W
Saint Mary, Cape ≻, Gam.	150	13.28 N	16.40 W
Saint Mary, Mount ∧	164	8.10 S	147.00 E
Saint Mary Bourne	42	51.16 N	1.24 W
Saint Mary Cray ⬥[8]	260	51.23 N	0.07 E
Saint Mary Lake ⊜	202	48.40 N	113.30 W
Saint Marylebone ⬥[8]	260	51.31 N	0.10 W
Saint Mary of the Lake Seminary ʊ[2]	278	42.17 N	88.00 W
Saint Mary Peak ∧	166	31.30 S	138.33 E
Saint Mary Reservoir ⊜[1]	182	49.19 N	113.12 W
Saint Marys, Austl.	166	41.35 S	148.10 E
Saint Marys, Austl.	170	33.47 S	150.47 E
Saint Mary's, Newf., Can.	186	46.55 N	53.34 W
Saint Mary's, Ont., Can.	212	43.16 N	81.08 W
Saint Marys, Alaska, U.S.	180	62.04 N	163.10 W
Saint Marys, Ga., U.S.	192	30.44 N	81.33 W
Saint Marys, Kans., U.S.	198	39.12 N	96.04 W
Saint Marys, Ohio, U.S.	216	40.33 N	84.23 W
Saint Marys, Pa., U.S.	214	41.26 N	78.34 W

≃ River	Fluss	Río	Rivière	Rio
Ξ Canal	Kanal	Canal	Canal	Canal
∟ Waterfall, Rapids	Wasserfall, Stromschnellen	Cascada, Rápidos	Chute d'eau, Rapides	Cascata, Rápidos
ɯ Strait	Meeresstrasse	Estrecho	Détroit	Estreito
C Bay, Gulf	Bucht, Golf	Bahía, Golfo	Baie, Golfe	Baía, Golfo
⊜ Lake, Lakes	See, Seen	Lago, Lagos	Lac, Lacs	Lago, Lagos
☷ Swamp	Sumpf	Pantano	Marais	Pântano
⛛ Ice Features, Glacier	Eis- und Gletscherformen	Accidentes Glaciales	Formes glaciaires	Acidentes Glaciares
⊤ Other Hydrographic Features	Andere Hydrographische Objekte	Otros Elementos Hidrográficos	Autres données hydrographiques	Outros Elementos Hidrográficos

⌖ Submarine Features	Untermeerische Objekte	Accidentes Submarinos	Formes de relief sous-marin	Acidentes Submarinos
□ Political Unit	Politische Einheit	Unidad Politica	Entité politique	Unidade Política
ʊ Cultural Institution	Kulturelle Institution	Institución Cultural	Institution culturelle	Instituição Cultural
⊥ Historical Site	Historische Stätte	Sitio Histórico	Site historique	Sitio Histórico
♠ Recreational Site	Erholungs- und Ferienort	Sitio de Recreo	Centre de loisirs	Sítio de Lazer
⊠ Airport	Flughafen	Aeropuerto	Aéroport	Aeroporto
■ Military Installation	Militäranlage	Instalación Militar	Installation militaire	Instalação Militar
⬥ Miscellaneous	Verschiedenes	Misceláneo	Divers	Miscelânea

Name	Page	Lat.°′	Long.°′
Saint Marys, W. Va., U.S.	188	39.23 N	81.12 W
Saint Marys □[6]	208	38.17 N	76.38 W
Saint Mary's I	42a	49.55 N	6.18 W
Saint Mary's ≃, N.S., Can.	186	45.02 N	61.54 W
Saint Marys ≃, U.S.	192	30.43 N	81.27 W
Saint Marys ≃, U.S.	216	41.05 N	85.08 W
Saint Marys ≃, Md., U.S.	208	38.06 N	76.26 W
Saint Mary's, Cape ≻	186	46.49 N	54.12 W
Saint Marys, North Prong ≃	192	30.22 N	82.06 W
Saint Marys, South Prong ≃	192	30.22 N	82.06 W
Saint Mary's Bay	42	51.00 N	0.58 E
Saint Mary's Bay C, Newf., Can.	186	46.50 N	53.47 W
Saint Mary's Bay C, N.S., Can.	186	44.25 N	66.10 W
Saint Marys City	208	38.11 N	76.26 W
Saint Mary's Hoo	260	51.28 N	0.36 E
Saint Marys Lake ⊜	278	42.17 N	87.59 W
Saint Mary's Marshes ≋	260	51.28 N	0.35 E
Saint-Mathieu	32	45.42 N	0.46 E
Saint-Mathieu, Pointe de ≻	32	48.20 N	4.46 W
Saint-Mathieu-de-Laprairie	275a	45.19 N	73.31 W
Saint Matthew Island I	180	60.30 N	172.45 W
Saint Matthews, Ky., U.S.	218	38.15 N	85.39 W
Saint Matthews, S.C., U.S.	192	33.40 N	80.46 W
Saint Matthias Group II	164	1.30 S	149.40 E
Saint-Maur-des-Fossés	50	48.48 N	2.30 E
Sainte-Maure-du-Touraine	32	47.07 N	0.37 E
Saint-Maurice, Fr.	261	48.49 N	2.25 E
Saint-Maurice, Schw.	58	46.13 N	7.00 E
Saint-Maurice □[6]	206	46.35 N	73.00 W
Saint-Maurice ≃	176	46.21 N	72.31 W
Saint-Maurice, Parc de ♠	206	46.52 N	73.10 W
Saint-Maurice-de-Beynost	62	45.50 N	5.00 E
Saint-Maurice-en-Montagne	58	46.34 N	5.50 E
Saint-Maurice-Montcouronne	261	48.35 N	2.07 E
Saint Mawes	42	50.09 N	5.01 W
Saint Mawgan	42	50.28 N	4.58 W
Saint-Max	58	48.42 N	6.13 E
Sainte-Maxime	62	43.18 N	6.38 E
Saint-Maximin-la-Sainte-Baume	62	43.27 N	5.52 E
Saint-Méen-le-Grand	32	48.11 N	2.12 W
Saint Meinrad	194	38.10 N	86.49 W
Sainte-Menehould	56	49.05 N	4.54 E
Saint-Menges	56	49.44 N	4.56 E
Sainte-Mère-Église	32	49.25 N	1.19 W
Saint Merryn	42	50.31 N	4.58 W
Saint-Méry	261	48.35 N	2.50 E
Sainte-Mesme	261	48.32 N	1.58 E
Saint-Mesmes	261	48.59 N	2.42 E
Saint Michael, Alaska, U.S.	180	63.29 N	162.02 W
Saint Michael, Pa., U.S.	214	40.20 N	78.46 W
Saint Michaels	188	38.47 N	76.14 W
Saint-Michel, Fr.	50	49.55 N	4.08 E
Saint-Michel, Fr.	62	45.13 N	6.28 E
Saint-Michel-de-Napierville	206	45.14 N	73.34 W
Saint-Michel-des-Saints	206	46.41 N	73.55 W
Saint-Michel-sur-Meurthe	58	48.19 N	6.54 E
Saint-Michel-sur-Orge	261	48.38 N	2.18 E
Saint-Mihiel	56	48.54 N	5.33 E
Saint Monance	46	56.12 N	2.46 W
Sainte-Montaine	50	47.29 N	2.19 E
Saint-Moritz → Sankt Moritz	58	46.30 N	9.50 E
Saint-Narcisse	206	46.34 N	72.28 W
Saint-Nazaire	32	47.17 N	2.12 W
Saint-Nazaire-en-Royans	62	45.04 N	5.15 E
Saint-Nazaire-le-Désert	62	44.34 N	5.17 E
Saint Nazianz	190	44.00 N	87.55 W
Saint Neots	42	52.14 N	0.17 W
Saint-Nicéphore	206	45.50 N	72.25 W
Saint-Nicolas → Sint-Niklaas, Bel.	50	51.10 N	4.08 E
Saint-Nicolas, Qué., Can.	206	46.42 N	71.24 W
Saint-Nicolas-aux-Bois	50	49.36 N	3.25 E
Saint-Nicolas-d'Aliermont	50	49.53 N	1.13 E
Saint-Nicolas-de-Port	58	48.38 N	6.18 E
Saint-Nizier-du-Moucherotte	62	45.10 N	5.38 E
Saint-Nom-la-Bretèche	261	48.51 N	2.01 E
Saint Nora Lake ⊜	212	45.08 N	78.49 W
Saint-Norbert-d'Arthabaska	206	46.07 N	71.50 W
Sainte Odile ⚜[1]	58	48.26 N	7.24 E
Saint-Omer	50	50.45 N	2.15 E
Saintonge □[9]	32	45.30 N	0.30 W
Saint-Ouen, Fr.	50	50.02 N	2.03 E
Saint-Ouen, Fr.	261	48.54 N	2.20 E
Saint-Ouen-l'Aumône	50	49.03 N	2.06 E
Saint-Pacôme	186	47.24 N	69.57 W
Saint-Pamphile	186	46.58 N	69.47 W
Saint Pancras ⬥[8]	260	51.32 N	0.07 W
Saint Pancras Station ⬥[5]	260	51.32 N	0.08 W
Saint Paris	218	40.07 N	83.58 W
Saint-Pascal	186	47.32 N	69.49 W
Saint-Paterne	50	48.24 N	0.07 E
Saint-Pathus	261	49.04 N	2.48 E
Saint-Patrick, Lac ⊜	188	46.22 N	77.21 W
Saint Paul, Alta., Can.	182	53.59 N	111.17 W
Saint-Paul, Fr.	62	43.42 N	7.07 E
Saint-Paul, Fr.	62	44.31 N	6.45 E
Saint-Paul, Réu.	157c	21.00 S	55.16 E
Saint Paul, Ind., U.S.	218	39.26 N	85.38 W
Saint Paul, Minn., U.S.	190	44.58 N	93.07 W
Saint Paul, Nebr., U.S.	198	41.13 N	98.27 W
Saint Paul, Oreg., U.S.	224	45.12 N	122.58 W
Saint Paul, Va., U.S.	192	36.54 N	82.19 W
Saint-Paul ≃, Can.	176	51.26 N	57.40 W
Saint Paul ≃, Liber.	150	7.10 N	10.00 W
Saint Paul, Cape ≻	150	5.49 N	0.57 E
Saint-Paul, Lac ⊜	206	46.18 N	72.29 W
Saint Paul Bay C	116	10.14 N	118.54 E
Saint-Paul-de-Chester (Chesterville)	206	45.57 N	71.49 W
Saint-Paul-en-Jarez	62	45.29 N	4.35 E
Saint-Paul-et-Valmalle	62	43.38 N	3.40 E
Saint-Paulien	62	45.08 N	3.49 E
Saint-paulin	206	46.25 N	73.01 W
Saint Paul Island	180	57.07 N	170.17 W
Saint Paul Island I, N.S., Can.	186	47.15 N	60.10 W
Saint Paul Island I, Alaska, U.S.	180	57.10 N	170.15 W
Saint-Paul-l'Ermite	206	45.45 N	73.28 W
Saint Pauls	192	34.48 N	78.58 W
Saint Paul's Cathedral ⚜[1]	260	51.31 N	0.06 W
Saint Paul's Cray ⬥[8]	260	51.24 N	0.07 E
Saint Pauls Inlet C	186	49.50 N	57.45 W
Saint Paul's Point ≻	174e	25.04 S	130.05 W
Saint-Paul-Trois-Châteaux	62	44.21 N	4.46 E
Saint-péravy-la-Colombe	50	48.00 N	1.42 E
Saint-Péray	62	44.57 N	4.50 E
Saint-Père	50	47.28 N	3.46 E
Saint Peter, Ill., U.S.	219	38.52 N	88.51 W
Saint Peter, Minn., U.S.	190	44.17 N	93.57 W
Saint Peter, Lake ⊜	212	45.18 N	78.02 W
Saint Peter Island I	162	32.17 S	133.35 E
Saint Peter Port	43b	49.27 N	2.32 W
Saint Peters, N.S., Can.	186	45.40 N	60.52 W
Saint Peters, Mo., U.S.	219	38.48 N	90.38 W
Saint Peters, Pa., U.S.	285	40.11 N	75.44 W
Saint Peters Bay	186	46.25 N	62.35 W
Saint Petersburg → Leningrad, S.S.S.R.	76	59.55 N	30.15 E
Saint Petersburg, Fla., U.S.	220	27.46 N	82.38 W
Saint Petersburg, Pa., U.S.	214	41.10 N	79.37 W
Saint Petersburg Beach	220	27.45 N	82.45 W
Saint Peter's College ⚜[2]	276	40.44 N	74.05 W
Saint Philip and Saint James Bay C	175f	15.06 S	166.54 E
Saint-Philippe-d'Argenteuil	206	45.37 N	74.25 W
Saint-Philippe-de-Laprairie	275a	45.21 N	73.28 W
Saint-Pie	206	45.30 N	72.54 W
Saint-Pierre, It.	62	45.42 N	7.14 E
Saint-Pierre, Mart.	240e	14.45 N	61.11 W
Saint-Pierre, Réu.	157c	21.19 S	55.29 E
Saint-Pierre, St. P./M.	186	46.40 N	56.00 W
Saint-Pierre I	186	46.47 N	56.11 W
Saint-Pierre ≃	275a	45.23 N	73.34 W
Saint-Pierre, Lac ⊜	206	46.12 N	72.52 W
Saint-Pierre, Rade de ⚓[3]	240e	14.44 N	61.11 W
Saint Pierre and Miquelon □[2]	176		
	186	46.55 N	56.10 W
Saint-Pierre-d'Albigny	62	45.34 N	6.09 E
Saint-Pierre-de-Bœuf	62	45.22 N	4.45 E
Saint-Pierre-de-Broughton	206	46.15 N	71.12 W
Saint-Pierre-de-Chartreuse	62	45.20 N	5.49 E
Saint-Pierre-des-Corps	50	47.23 N	0.44 E
Saint-Pierre-de-Vacquière	62	43.52 N	4.13 E
Saint-Pierre-du-Vauvray	50	49.14 N	1.13 E
Saint-Pierre-Église	32	49.40 N	1.24 W
Saint-Pierre-en-Port	50	49.48 N	0.29 E
Saint-Pierre-et-Miquelon → Saint Pierre and Miquelon □[2]	186	46.55 N	56.10 W
Saint Pierre Island I	138	9.19 S	50.43 E
Saint-Pierre-Jolys	184	49.26 N	96.59 W
Saint-Pierre-la-Bourlhonne	62	45.40 N	3.45 E
Saint Pierre-le-Moûtier	32	46.48 N	3.07 E
Saint-Pierre-lès-Elbeuf	50	49.16 N	1.03 E
Saint-Pierreville	62	44.49 N	4.29 E
Saint-Point, Lac de ⊜	58	46.49 N	6.19 E
Saint-Pol-de-Léon	32	48.41 N	3.59 W
Saint-Pol-sur-Mer	50	51.02 N	2.21 E
Saint-Pol-sur-Ternoise	50	50.23 N	2.20 E
Saint-Polycarpe	206	45.18 N	74.18 W
Saint-Pons	32	43.29 N	2.46 E
Saint-Pourçain-sur-Sioule	32	46.19 N	3.17 E
Saint-Prex	58	46.29 N	6.28 E
Saint-Priest	62	45.42 N	4.57 E
Saint-Priest-en-Jarez	62	45.28 N	4.22 E
Saint-Prix	261	49.01 N	2.16 E
Saint-Prosper-de-Dorchester	188	46.13 N	70.29 W
Saint-Quentin, N.B., Can.	186	47.30 N	67.23 W
Saint-Quentin, Fr.	50	49.51 N	3.17 E
Saint-Quentin, Canal de ≋	50	49.36 N	3.11 E
Saint-Quentin, Étang de ⊜	261	48.47 N	2.01 E
Saint-Rambert-d'Albon	62	45.17 N	4.49 E
Saint-Rambert-en-Bugey	58	45.57 N	5.26 E
Saint-Rambert-sur-Loire	62	45.30 N	4.15 E
Saint-Raphaël	62	43.25 N	6.46 E
Saint-Raymond	206	46.54 N	71.50 W
Saint-Rédempter-de-Lévis	206	46.42 N	71.17 W
Saint Regis	202	47.18 N	115.06 W
Saint-Régis ≃, Qué., Can.	275a	45.24 N	73.34 W
Saint Regis ≃, Mont., U.S.	202	47.18 N	115.05 W
Saint Regis Falls	188	44.40 N	74.33 W
Saint Regis Indian Reservation ⬥[4]	206	44.58 N	74.39 W
Saint-Rémi	206	45.16 N	73.37 W
Saint-Rémi-d'Amherst	206	46.01 N	74.46 W
Saint-Rémy (lès-Chevreuse), Fr.	50	48.42 N	2.05 E
Saint-Rémy, Fr.	58	46.46 N	4.50 E
Saint Remy, N.Y., U.S.	210	41.54 N	74.01 W
Saint-Rémy-de-Provence	62	43.47 N	4.50 E
Saint-Rémy-en-Bouzemont	58	48.38 N	4.39 E
Saint-Rémy-l'Honoré	261	48.45 N	1.53 E
Saint-Rémy-sur-Avre	50	48.46 N	1.15 E
Saint-Renan	32	48.26 N	4.37 W
Saint-Révérien	50	47.13 N	3.30 E
Saint-Rhémy	62	45.50 N	7.11 E
Saint-Riquier	50	50.08 N	1.57 E
Saint-Roch-de-l'Achigan	206	45.51 N	73.36 W
Saint-Romain-de-Colbosc	50	49.32 N	0.22 E
Saint-Romain-le-Puy	62	45.33 N	4.07 E
Saint-Romans	62	45.07 N	5.19 E
Saint-Romuald-d'Etchemin	206	46.45 N	71.14 W
Sainte-Rosalie	206	45.38 N	72.54 W
Sainte-Rose	241o	16.20 N	61.42 W
Sainte-Rose ⬥[8]	275a	45.36 N	73.47 W
Sainte-Rose-du-Lac	184	51.03 N	99.32 W
Saintry-sur-Seine	261	48.36 N	2.30 E
Saintes, Bel.	50	50.42 N	4.10 E
Saintes, Fr.	32	45.45 N	0.52 W
Saintes, Îles des II	241o	15.52 N	61.37 W
Saint-Saëns	50	49.40 N	1.17 E
Saint Sampson	43b	49.29 N	2.31 W
Saint-Saturnin-d'Apt	62	43.56 N	5.23 E
Saint-Sauveur, Fr.	50	47.37 N	3.12 E
Saint-Sauveur, Fr.	58	47.48 N	6.23 E
Saint-Sauveur-des-Monts	206	45.52 N	74.10 W
Saint-Sauveur-sur-Tinée	62	44.05 N	7.06 E
Saint-Savin	32	46.34 N	0.52 E
Sainte-Savine	50	48.18 N	4.03 E
Saint Saviour	43b	49.11 N	2.06 W
Sainte-Scholastique	206	45.39 N	74.05 W
Saint Sebastian Bay C	158	34.25 S	21.00 E
Saint-Sébastien	206	45.07 N	73.09 W
Saint-Sébastien, Cap ≻	157b	12.26 S	48.44 E
Saint-Seine-l'Abbaye	58	47.26 N	4.47 E
Saint Servan	32	48.38 N	2.01 W
Saint Séverin	56	50.32 N	5.25 E
Saint Shotts	186	46.38 N	53.35 W
Sainte-Sigolène	62	45.14 N	4.15 E
Saint-Simon	50	49.45 N	3.10 E
Saint Simons Island	192	31.08 N	81.24 W
Saint Simons Island I	192	31.14 N	81.21 W
Saint-Sixte ≃	206	45.39 N	75.08 W
Saintes-Maries, Golfe des C	62	43.25 N	4.31 E
Saintes-Maries-de-la-Mer	62	43.27 N	4.26 E
Sainte-Sophie-de-Mégantic	206	46.09 N	71.42 W
Saint-Soupplets	261	49.02 N	2.48 E
Saint Stanislas Bay C	174o	1.53 N	157.30 W
Saint-Stanislas-de-Kosta	206	45.11 N	74.08 W
Saint Stephen, N.B., Can.	186	45.12 N	67.17 W
Saint Stephen, S.C., U.S.	192	33.24 N	79.55 W
Saint-Sulpice-de-Favières	261	48.33 N	2.11 E
Saint-Sulpice-les-Feuilles	32	46.19 N	1.22 E
Sainte-Suzanne	58	47.30 N	6.46 E
Saint-Sylvestre	206	46.22 N	71.14 W
Saint-Symphorien, Fr.	32	44.26 N	0.30 W
Saint-Symphorien, Fr.	261	48.31 N	1.46 E
Saint-Symphorien-d'Ozon	62	45.38 N	4.52 E
Saint-Symphorien-sur-Coise	62	45.38 N	4.27 E
Sainte-Thècle	206	46.49 N	72.31 W
Saint-Théodore-d'Acton	206	45.41 N	72.35 W
Sainte-Thérèse, Île I, Qué., Can.	275a	45.41 N	73.28 W
Sainte-Thérèse, Île I, Qué., Can.	275a	45.22 N	73.15 W
Sainte-Thérèse-de-Blainville	206	45.38 N	73.51 W
Saint-Thibault-des-Vignes	261	48.52 N	2.41 E
Saint Thomas, Ont., Can.	212	42.47 N	81.12 W
Saint Thomas, Mo., U.S.	219	38.23 N	92.13 W
Saint Thomas, N. Dak., U.S.	198	48.37 N	97.27 W
Saint Thomas → Charlotte Amalie, Vir. Is., U.S.	240m	18.21 N	64.56 W
Saint Thomas I	240m	18.21 N	64.55 W
Saint Timothée	206	45.18 N	74.02 W
Saint-Tite	206	46.44 N	72.34 W
Saint-Tite-des-Caps	186	47.08 N	70.47 W
Saint Tome et Principauté → Sao Tome and Principe □[1]	152	1.00 N	7.00 E
Saint-Trivier-de-Courtes	58	46.28 N	5.05 E
Saint-Trivier-sur-Moignans	58	46.04 N	4.54 E
Saint-Tropez	62	43.16 N	6.38 E
Saint Tudy	42	50.33 N	4.43 W
Sainte-Tulle	62	43.47 N	5.46 E
Saint-Ubald	206	46.45 N	72.16 W
Saint-Urbain-de-Charlevoix	186	47.33 N	70.32 W
Saint-Ursanne	58	47.22 N	7.10 E
Saint-Uze	62	45.11 N	4.52 E
Saint-Valérien	50	48.11 N	3.06 E
Saint-Valéry-en-Caux	50	49.52 N	0.44 E
Saint-Valéry-sur-Somme	50	50.11 N	1.38 E
Saint-Vallier, Fr.	58	46.38 N	4.22 E
Saint-Vallier, Fr.	62	45.10 N	4.49 E
Saint-Vallier-de-Thiey	62	43.42 N	6.51 E
Saint-Varent	32	46.53 N	0.14 W
Saint-Venant	50	50.37 N	2.33 E
Saint-Véran	62	44.42 N	6.52 E
Sainte-Victoire, Montagne ∧	62	43.32 N	5.39 E
Saint-Victoret	62	43.25 N	5.14 E
Saint Vincent	198	48.58 N	97.14 W
Saint Vincent □[1]	230		
	241h	13.15 N	61.12 W
Saint-Vincent, Baie de C	175f	22.00 S	166.05 E
Saint-Vincent, Cap ≻	157b	21.57 S	43.16 E
Saint Vincent, Cape ≻	166	43.18 S	145.50 E
Saint Vincent, Gulf C	168b	35.00 S	138.05 E
Saint Vincent Cape → São Vicente, Cabo de ≻	34	37.01 N	9.00 W
Saint-Vincent-de-Paul ⬥[8]	275a	45.37 N	73.39 W
Saint-Vincent-de-Tyrosse	32	43.40 N	1.18 W
Saint Vincent Passage ⩌	238	13.30 N	61.00 W
Saint Vincent's	186	46.48 N	53.38 W
Saint-Vit	58	47.11 N	5.49 E
Saint-Vith	56	50.17 N	6.08 E
Saint-Vivien-de-Médoc	32	45.26 N	1.02 W
Saint-Vrain	261	48.33 N	2.20 E
Saint Walburg	184	53.39 N	109.12 W
Saint-Wandrille-Rançon	50	49.32 N	0.46 E
Saint-Wenceslas ≃	206	46.18 N	72.23 W
Saint Williams	212	42.40 N	80.25 W
Saint-Witz	261	49.05 N	2.34 E
Saint-Yrieix-la-Perche	32	45.31 N	1.12 E
Saint-Yvon	186	49.10 N	64.48 W
Saint-Zacharie	62	43.23 N	5.43 E
Saint-Zénon	206	46.33 N	73.49 W
Saipan	175b	6.54 N	134.08 E
Saipan I	174n	15.12 N	145.45 E
Saipan Channel ⩌	174n	15.05 N	145.41 E
Saiqi	100	27.00 N	119.43 E
Sa'īr	132	31.35 N	35.09 E
Sairecábur, Cerro ∧	248	22.43 S	67.54 W
Saishu-to → Cheju-do I	90	33.20 N	126.30 E
Saita	96	34.08 N	133.49 E
Saita ≃	96	34.08 N	133.38 E
Saitama □[5]	94	36.00 N	139.30 E
Saitama University ⚜[2]	268	35.52 N	139.38 E
Saito	92	32.06 N	131.24 E
Saitula	120	36.21 N	78.02 E
Saiyidān ⬥[8]	272a	28.40 N	77.05 E
Sai Yok	110	14.07 N	99.08 E
Sajam	164	0.53 S	132.41 E
Sajama	248	18.07 S	69.00 W
Sajama, Nevado ∧	248	18.06 S	68.54 W
Sajan → Sayan Mountains ∧∧	88	52.45 N	96.00 E
Sajchan	88	48.40 N	102.39 E
Sajchandulaan	102	44.42 N	109.01 E
Sajen	115a	7.40 S	112.31 E
Šajgino	80	57.46 N	46.51 E
Sajhan-Ovoo	102	45.27 N	103.52 E
Sajīd I	144	16.52 N	41.50 E
Šajmak'	120	37.27 N	74.44 E
Sajnšand	102	44.55 N	110.11 E
Sajó ≃	30	47.56 N	21.08 E
Sajószentpéter	30	48.13 N	20.44 E
Sājūr (Sacır) ≃	130	36.40 N	38.05 E
Sak ≃	158	30.52 S	20.25 E
Saka	154	0.09 S	39.20 E
Sakado	94	35.57 N	139.24 E
Sakae, Nihon	94	35.50 N	140.15 E
Sakae, Nihon	94	36.58 N	138.35 E
Sa Kaeo	110	13.49 N	102.04 E
Sakahogi	94	35.26 N	136.59 E
Sakai, Nihon	94	36.10 N	136.14 E
Sakai, Nihon	94	36.16 N	139.15 E
Sakai, Nihon	94	36.06 N	139.48 E
Sakai, Nihon	96	34.35 N	135.28 E
Sakai, Nihon	268	35.25 N	139.22 E
Sakai ≃	94	35.18 N	139.29 E
Sakaide	96	34.19 N	133.52 E
Sakaigawa	94	35.35 N	138.37 E
Sakai-minato	96	35.33 N	133.15 E
Sakākah	128	29.59 N	40.06 E
Sakakawea, Lake ⊜[1]	198	47.50 N	102.20 W
Sakaki	94	36.28 N	138.11 E
Sakakita	94	36.25 N	138.01 E
Sakala, Pulau I	112	6.54 S	116.15 E
Sakami ≃	176	53.40 N	76.40 W
Sakami, Lac ⊜	176	53.15 N	76.45 W
Sakania	154	12.45 S	28.34 E
Sakar	128	38.56 N	63.45 E
Sakar ∧∧	38	41.59 N	26.16 E
Sakaraha	157b	22.55 S	44.32 E
Sakar-Čaga	128	37.38 N	61.40 E
Sakar Island I	164	5.25 S	148.05 E
Sakarya □[4]	130	40.45 N	30.35 E
Sakashita	94	35.34 N	137.32 E
Sakasso	150	7.27 N	5.18 W
Sakata	92	38.55 N	139.50 E
Sakau	175f	16.49 S	168.24 E
Sakau I	175f	14.57 S	167.08 E
Sakauchi	94	35.36 N	136.25 E
Sakawa	96	33.30 N	133.17 E
Sakawa ≃	94	35.15 N	139.11 E
Sakchu	98	40.23 N	125.01 E
Sakesar	123	32.33 N	71.56 E
Sakété	150	6.43 N	2.40 E
Sakhā	142	31.05 N	30.57 E
Sakhalin → Sachalin, Ostrov I	89	51.00 N	143.00 E
Sākhar	120	32.57 N	65.32 E
Sakhi Sarwar	120	29.59 N	70.18 E
Sakhnīn	132	32.52 N	35.17 E
Şakhrīyāt, Jabal aş- ∧	132	31.01 N	36.21 E
Saki	78	45.09 N	33.35 E
Şāki ⬥[8]	272c	19.06 N	72.53 E
Šakiai	76	54.57 N	23.03 E
Sākib	132	32.17 N	35.49 E
Sakiet Sidi Youssef	36	36.13 N	8.22 E
Sakijang Bendera, Pulau I	271c	1.13 N	103.51 E
Sakijang Pelepah, Pulau I	271c	1.13 N	103.52 E
Sakishima-guntō I	175d	24.46 N	124.00 E
Sakito	92	33.02 N	129.32 E
Sakkara → Şaqqārah	142	29.51 N	31.13 E
Sakleshpur	122	12.58 N	75.47 E
Sakmara ≃	86	51.46 N	55.01 E
Sako	270	34.53 N	135.47 E
Sākoli	120	21.05 N	79.59 E
Sakon Nakhon	110	17.10 N	104.09 E
Sakonnet	207	41.28 N	71.12 W
Sakoyra	150	14.17 N	1.24 E
Sakra, Pulau I	271c	1.16 N	103.42 E
Sakrān, Wādī V	142	30.22 N	31.53 E
Sakrand	120	26.08 N	68.16 E
Sakri	120	20.59 N	74.19 E
Sakrivier	158	30.54 S	20.28 E
Sakrow-Paretzer Kanal ≋	264a	52.28 N	12.55 E
Saksagan' ≃	78	47.53 N	33.18 E
Saksauldala ⬥[2]	86	44.30 N	73.00 E
Sakskøbing	41	54.48 N	11.39 E
Sakti	124	22.02 N	82.58 E
Saku	94	36.09 N	138.26 E
Sakubva	154	19.00 S	32.10 E
Sakugi	96	34.52 N	132.43 E
Sakuma	94	35.05 N	137.48 E
Sakuma-dam ⬥[6]	94	35.05 N	137.47 E
Sakuma-ko ⊜[1]	94	35.08 N	137.47 E
Sakura	94	35.43 N	140.14 E
Sakura ≃	94	36.05 N	140.14 E
Sakurae	96	34.57 N	132.20 E
Sakurai	96	34.30 N	135.51 E
Sakura-tōge)(	270	34.36 N	135.53 E
Saku-shima I	94	34.43 N	137.03 E
Sakutō	96	35.01 N	134.14 E
Sakwaso Lake ⊜	184	53.01 N	91.55 W
Säkylä	26	61.02 N	22.20 E
Sakyō ⬥[8]	270	35.02 N	135.48 E
Sal I	150a	16.45 N	22.55 W
Sal ≃	80	47.31 N	40.45 E
Sal, Cay I	238	23.42 N	80.24 W
Sal, Ponta do ≻	266c	38.41 N	9.22 W
Sal, Punta ≻	236	15.53 N	87.37 W
Šal'a, Česko.	30	48.09 N	17.52 E
Šal'a, S.S.S.R.	86	57.15 N	58.43 E
Sala, Sve.	40	59.55 N	16.36 E
Sala, Yai.	144	16.58 N	37.27 E
Sala, Ouadi V	146	17.00 N	20.53 E
Sala Baganza	64	44.43 N	10.14 E
Salabangka, Kepulauan II	112	3.02 S	122.25 E
Salaberry, Île de I	206	45.17 N	74.07 W
Salaca ≃	76	57.45 N	24.21 E
Salacgrīva	76	57.45 N	24.21 E
Sala Consilina	68	40.24 N	15.36 E
Salada, Laguna ⊜	232	32.20 N	115.40 W
Saladas	252	28.15 S	58.38 W
Saladillo	252	35.38 S	59.46 W
Saladillo ≃	252	29.05 S	63.25 W
Saladillo, Arroyo ≃	258	35.33 S	59.04 W
Saladillo Dulce, Arroyo ≃	252	31.25 S	60.33 W
Salado, Arg.	252	28.18 S	67.15 W
Salado, Tex., U.S.	222	30.57 N	97.32 W
Salado ≃, Arg.	252	31.42 S	60.44 W
Salado ≃, Arg.	252	35.44 S	57.21 W
Salado ≃, Arg.	252	38.49 S	64.57 W
Salado ≃, Cuba	240p	20.36 N	76.56 W
Salado ≃, Méx.	232	26.52 N	99.19 W
Salado ≃, Méx.	234	18.44 N	103.36 W
Salado, Arroyo ≃, Arg.	254	41.37 S	65.02 W
Salado, Arroyo ≃, Arg.	254	40.35 S	66.33 W
Salado, Arroyo ≃, Méx.	232	24.25 N	111.34 W
Salado, Rio ≃	200	34.16 N	106.52 W
Salado Creek ≃, N. Mex., U.S.	196	34.35 N	104.25 W
Salado Creek ≃, Tex., U.S.	196	29.14 N	98.25 W
Salado Creek ≃, Tex., U.S.	222	30.59 N	97.25 W
Salaga	150	8.33 N	0.31 W
Salagle	144	1.50 N	42.18 E
Sālah	132	32.38 N	36.46 E
Salahin	144	2.58 N	46.45 E
Salailua	175a	13.41 S	172.34 W
Salair	86	54.13 N	85.47 E
Salairskij Kr'až ∧	86	54.15 N	85.30 E
Sălaj □[4]	38	47.15 N	23.00 E
Salak, Gunung ∧	115a	6.42 S	106.44 E
Salakas	76	55.35 N	26.08 E
Šalakuša	24	62.15 N	40.17 E
Salal	146	14.51 N	17.13 E
Salala, Chile	252	30.41 S	71.32 W
Salala, Liber.	150	6.40 N	10.05 W
Salālah, Sūd.	140	21.19 N	36.13 E
Şalālah, 'Umān	118	17.00 N	54.06 E
Salamá, Guat.	236	15.06 N	90.16 W
Salamá, Hond.	236	14.50 N	86.36 W
Salaman	115a	7.35 S	110.08 E
Salamanca, Chile	252	31.47 S	70.58 W
Salamanca, Esp.	34	40.58 N	5.39 W
Salamanca, Méx.	234	20.34 N	101.12 W
Salamanca, Perú	248	15.31 S	72.50 W
Salamanca, Perú	286d	12.05 S	77.00 W
Salamanca, N.Y., U.S.	210	42.09 N	78.43 W
Salamanga	158	26.28 S	32.39 E
Salamat □[5]	146	11.00 N	20.30 E
Salamat, Bahr ≃	146	9.27 N	18.06 E
Salāmbek	120	28.16 N	65.08 E
Salamina	246	5.25 N	75.29 W
Salamínos, Órmos C	267c	37.56 N	23.27 E
Salamís	38	37.59 N	23.28 E
Salamís I	38	37.54 N	23.26 E
Salamis ⊥	130	35.10 N	33.54 E
Salām Khān	120	31.47 N	66.45 E
Salamonia	216	40.23 N	84.52 W
Salamonie ≃	216	40.50 N	85.43 W
Salamonie Lake ⊜[1]	216	40.46 N	85.37 W
Salāmūn	142	31.04 N	31.28 E
Salanda	130	38.50 N	34.32 E
Salandra	68	40.31 N	16.19 E
Salani	175a	14.00 S	171.33 W
Salantai	76	56.04 N	21.32 E
Salapaly, Baie de C	157b	24.40 S	43.55 E
Salaparuta	70	37.47 N	13.00 E
Salaquí	246	7.18 N	77.33 W
Salaquí ≃	246	7.27 N	77.07 W
Salāqūs	142	28.44 N	30.50 E
Salara	64	44.59 N	11.25 E
Salard	38	47.13 N	22.03 E
Salarjovo	265b	55.37 N	37.26 E
Salas	248	6.16 S	79.37 W
Salas de los Infantes	34	42.01 N	3.17 W
Salat ≃	32	43.10 N	0.58 E
Salatiga	115a	7.19 S	110.30 E
Salauš	80	55.59 N	52.53 E
Salavat, S.S.S.R.	86	53.21 N	55.55 E
Salavat, Tür.	130	41.53 N	34.55 E
Salavaux	58	46.55 N	7.02 E
Salaverry	248	8.14 S	78.58 W
Salavina	252	28.48 S	63.25 W
Salawati I	164	1.07 S	130.52 E
Salawe	154	3.19 S	32.52 E
Salay	116	8.52 N	124.47 E
Salāya	120	22.19 N	69.35 E
Sala y Gómez, Isla I	18	26.28 S	105.28 W
Sala y Gomez Ridge ⬥[3]	18	26.00 S	95.00 W
Salazgor'	80	54.07 N	43.09 E
Salba	88	53.14 N	92.36 E
Sālbani	126	22.38 N	87.20 E
Salbohed	40	59.55 N	16.19 E
Salbosjön ⊜	40	59.50 N	14.54 E
Salbris	50	47.26 N	2.03 E
Šalbuzdag, Gora ∧	84	41.19 N	47.48 E
Salcajá	236	14.53 N	91.27 W
Salcantay, Nevado ∧	248	13.20 S	72.33 W
Salcedo, Pil.	116	11.09 N	125.40 E
Salcedo, Rep. Dom.	238	19.23 N	70.25 W
Salcha ≃	180	64.29 N	147.00 W
Salching	60	48.49 N	12.34 E
Salcia	38	43.57 N	24.56 E
Šalčininkai	76	54.18 N	25.23 E
Salcombe	42	50.13 N	3.47 W
Salda ≃	86	58.48 N	61.20 E
Salda Gölü ⊜	130	37.33 N	29.42 E
Šaldaj	86	51.56 N	78.48 E
Saldaña	34	42.31 N	4.44 W
Saldaña ≃	246	4.01 N	74.52 W
Saldanha	158	33.00 S	17.56 E
Saldanhabaai C	158	33.04 S	18.00 E
Šaldež	80	56.52 N	44.46 E
Saldungaray	252	38.12 S	61.47 W
Saldus	76	56.40 N	22.30 E
Sale, Austl.	166	38.06 S	147.04 E
Sale, It.	62	44.59 N	8.48 E
Salé, Magreb	148	34.04 N	6.50 W
Sale, Eng., U.K.	44	53.26 N	2.19 W
Sale ≃	184	49.45 N	97.08 W
Salebabu, Pulau I	108	3.55 N	126.40 E
Salechard	74	66.33 N	66.40 E
Sale Creek	194	35.23 N	85.07 W
Salée, Rivière ⩌	241o	16.17 N	61.33 W
Saleh, Teluk C	115b	8.34 S	117.57 E
Salelologa	175a	13.44 S	172.10 W
Salem, Bhārat	122	11.39 N	78.10 E
Salem, B.R.D.	58	47.46 N	9.16 E
Salem, Ont., Can.	212	43.42 N	80.27 W
Salem, S. Afr.	158	33.28 S	26.29 E
Salem, Sve.	40	59.13 N	17.44 E
Salem, Ark., U.S.	194	36.22 N	91.49 W
Salem, Ill., U.S.	219	38.38 N	88.57 W

Name	Seite	Breite°′	Länge°′ E=Ost
Salem, Ind., U.S.	218	38.36 N	86.06 W
Salem, Iowa, U.S.	190	40.51 N	91.38 W
Salem, Mass., U.S.	207		
	283	42.31 N	70.55 W
Salem, Mich., U.S.	281	42.24 N	83.35 W
Salem, Mo., U.S.	194	37.39 N	91.32 W
Salem, N.H., U.S.	188	42.47 N	71.12 W
Salem, N.J., U.S.	208	39.34 N	75.28 W
Salem, N.Y., U.S.	210	43.10 N	73.20 W
Salem, Ohio, U.S.	214	40.54 N	80.52 W
Salem, Oreg., U.S.	224	44.57 N	123.01 W
Salem, S. Dak., U.S.	198	43.44 N	97.23 W
Salem, Utah, U.S.	200	40.03 N	111.40 W
Salem, Va., U.S.	192	37.17 N	80.03 W
Salem, W. Va., U.S.	188	39.17 N	80.34 W
Salem, Wis., U.S.	216	42.33 N	88.07 W
Salem □[6]	208	39.34 N	75.20 W
Salem ≃	208	39.34 N	75.31 W
Salem Airfield ⊠	281	42.25 N	83.34 W
Sale Marasino	64	45.43 N	10.06 E
Salem Canal ≋	285	39.41 N	75.31 W
Salem Depot	283	42.47 N	71.12 W
Salem Harbor C	283	42.31 N	70.53 W
Salem Heights	214	40.54 N	80.53 W
Salemi	70	37.49 N	12.48 E
Salem Maritime National Historic Site ▪	207	42.31 N	70.53 W
Salem Upland ∧∧[1]	194	37.25 N	91.30 W
Sälen, Sve.	26	61.10 N	13.16 E
Salen, Scot., U.K.	46	56.43 N	5.47 W
Salen, Scot., U.K.	46	56.31 N	5.57 W
Salentina, Penisola ≻[1]	68	40.25 N	18.00 E
Salentine, Murge ⬥[1]	68	40.02 N	18.13 E
Salento	68	40.15 N	15.11 E
Salernes	62	43.33 N	6.14 E
Salerno	68	40.41 N	14.47 E
Salerno □[4]	68	40.27 N	15.16 E
Salerno, Golfo di C	68	40.32 N	14.42 E
Salers	32	45.08 N	2.30 E
Salesbury	262	53.47 N	2.30 W
Salesópolis	256	23.32 S	45.51 W
Salève, Mont ∧	58	46.07 N	6.10 E
Salford	44	53.28 N	2.18 W
Salford □[8]	262	53.28 N	2.23 W
Salfords	260	51.12 N	0.10 W
Šalgačova	24	62.19 N	39.35 E
Salgado	250	11.02 S	37.28 W
Salgan	80	55.14 N	45.30 E
Salgar	246	5.58 N	75.59 W
Šalgija	86	47.35 N	70.36 E
Salgir ≃	78	45.38 N	35.01 E
Salgótarján	30	48.07 N	19.48 E
Salgueiro	250	8.04 S	39.06 W
Salher ∧	122	20.43 N	73.56 E
Sali, Alg.	148	26.58 N	0.01 W
Sali, Jugo.	36	43.56 N	15.10 E
Šali, S.S.S.R.	80	55.41 N	49.40 E
Šali, S.S.S.R.	84	43.08 N	45.54 E
Salí ≃	252	27.33 S	64.57 W
Salice Salentino	68	40.23 N	17.58 E
Salice Terme	62	44.55 N	9.01 E
Salici, Monte ∧	70	37.44 N	14.38 E
Salida, Calif., U.S.	226	37.42 N	121.05 W
Salida, Colo., U.S.	200	38.32 N	106.00 W
Salies-de-Béarn	32	43.29 N	0.55 W
Salignac-Eyvignes	32	44.59 N	1.19 E
Salihli	130	38.29 N	28.09 E
Sālikha	126	23.18 N	89.22 E
Šalikovo	82	55.30 N	36.13 E
Salim	140	12.52 N	28.40 E
Salima	154	13.47 S	34.26 E
Salīmah, Wāḩat ⚓[4]	140	21.22 N	29.19 E
Salimani	157a	11.47 S	43.17 E
Salimbatu	112	2.57 N	117.21 E
Salimi	152	9.24 S	23.35 E
Salin	110	20.35 N	94.39 E
Salina, Kans., U.S.	198	38.50 N	97.37 W
Salina, Pa., U.S.	214	40.31 N	79.30 W
Salina, Utah, U.S.	200	38.58 N	111.51 W
Salina, Canale di ≋	70	38.32 N	14.54 E
Salina, Isola I	70	38.34 N	14.50 E
Salina Cruz	234	16.10 N	95.12 W
Salina Point ≻	238	22.13 N	74.18 W
Salinas, Bra.	255	16.10 S	42.17 W
Salinas, Ec.	246	2.13 S	80.58 W
Salinas, P.R.	240m	17.59 N	66.18 W
Salinas, Calif., U.S.	226	36.40 N	121.38 W
Salinas ≃, Bra.	255	16.37 S	42.18 W
Salinas ≃, N.A.	236	16.28 N	90.33 W
Salinas ≃, Calif., U.S.	226	36.45 N	121.48 W
Salinas, Cabo de ≻	34	39.16 N	3.03 E
Salinas, Sierra de ∧∧	226	36.18 N	121.20 W
Salinas de Garci Mendoza	248	19.38 S	67.43 W
Salinas de Hidalgo	234	22.38 N	101.43 W
Salinas del Rey	196	27.38 N	102.24 W
Salinas Municipal Airport ⊠	226	36.40 N	121.40 W
Salinas Valley V	226	36.15 N	121.15 W
Salinas Victoria	196	25.53 N	100.19 W
Salin-de-Giraud	62	43.25 N	4.44 E
Salindres	62	44.10 N	4.10 E
Saline, La., U.S.	194	32.10 N	92.58 W
Saline, Mich., U.S.	216	42.10 N	83.47 W
Saline ≃, Ark., U.S.	194	33.10 N	92.08 W
Saline ≃, Ark., U.S.	194	33.44 N	93.58 W
Saline ≃, Ill., U.S.	194	37.35 N	88.08 W
Saline ≃, Kans., U.S.	198	38.51 N	97.30 W
Saline ≃, Mich., U.S.	216	41.59 N	83.37 W
Saline, North Fork ≃	194	37.44 N	88.19 W
Saline Bayou ≃	194	31.45 N	92.58 W
Saline di Volterra	66	43.22 N	10.49 E
Saline Lake ⊜[1]	194	31.55 N	92.55 W
Salines, Point ≻	241k	12.00 N	61.48 W
Salines, Pointe des ≻	240e	14.24 N	60.53 W
Salineville	214	40.37 N	80.51 W
Salingyi	110	21.58 N	95.03 E
Salinópolis	250	0.37 S	47.20 W
Šalinskoje	86	55.43 N	93.46 E
Salins-les-Bains	58	46.57 N	5.53 E
Salins-les-Thermes	62	45.28 N	6.32 E
Salıpazarı	130	40.54 N	31.58 E
Salipolo	112	3.45 S	119.29 E
Salisbury, Austl.	168b	34.46 S	138.38 E
Salisbury, Dom.	240d	15.26 N	61.27 W
Salisbury, Eng., U.K.	42	51.05 N	1.48 W
Salisbury, Conn., U.S.	207	41.59 N	73.25 W
Salisbury, Md., U.S.	208	38.22 N	75.36 W
Salisbury, Mass., U.S.	207	42.51 N	70.49 W
Salisbury, Mo., U.S.	194	39.25 N	92.48 W
Salisbury, N.C., U.S.	192	35.40 N	80.29 W
Salisbury, Pa., U.S.	188	39.45 N	79.05 W
Salisbury, Zimb.	154	17.50 S	31.03 E
Salisbury, Lake ⊜	154	1.38 N	33.56 E
Salisbury Cathedral ⚜[1]	42	51.05 N	1.48 W
Salisbury Center	210	43.09 N	74.47 W
Salisbury Hall ⊥	260	51.43 N	0.16 W
Salisbury Island I, Austl.	162	34.21 S	123.32 E
Salisbury Island I, N.W. Ter., Can.	176	63.30 N	77.00 W
Salisbury Mills	210	41.26 N	74.08 W
Salisbury Plain ⌣	42	51.12 N	1.55 W
Salisbury Plain ≃	283	42.02 N	70.58 W
Salish Mountains ∧∧	202	48.15 N	114.45 W
Salito ≃	70	37.29 N	13.46 E
Salitpa	194	31.37 N	88.01 W

Symbols in the index entries represent the broad categories identified in the key at the right. Symbols with superior numbers (∧∧[2]) identify subcategories (see complete key on page *I* · *30*).

Kartensymbole in dem Registerverzeichnis stellen die rechts in Schlüssel erklärten Kategorien dar. Symbole mit hochgestellten Ziffern (∧∧[2]) bezeichnen Unterabteilungen einer Kategorie (vgl. vollständiger Schlüssel auf Seite *I* · *30*).

Los símbolos incluídos en el texto del índice representan las grandes categorias identificadas con la clave a la derecha. Los símbolos con numeros en su parte superior (∧∧[2]) identifican las subcategorías (véase la clave completa en la página *I* · *30*).

Les symboles de l'index représentent les catégories indiquées dans la légende à droite. Les symboles suivis d'un indice (∧∧[2]) représentent des sous-catégories (voir légende complète à la page *I* · *30*).

Os símbolos incluídos no texto do índice representam as grandes categorias identificadas com a chave à direita. Os símbolos com números em sua parte superior (∧∧[2]) identificam as subcategorias (veja-se a chave completa à página *I* · *30*).

	English	Deutsch	Español	Français	Português
∧	Mountain	Berg	Montaña	Montagne	Montanha
∧∧	Mountains	Berge	Montañas	Montagnes	Montanhas
)(	Pass	Pass	Paso	Col	Passo
V	Valley, Canyon	Tal, Cañon	Valle, Cañón	Vallée, Canyon	Vale, Canhão
⌣	Plain	Ebene	Llano	Plaine	Planície
≻	Cape	Kap	Cabo	Cap	Cabo
I	Island	Insel	Isla	Île	Ilha
II	Islands	Inseln	Islas	Îles	Ilhas
⊥	Other Topographic Features	Andere Topographische Objekte	Otros Elementos Topográficos	Autres données topographiques	Outros Elementos Topográficos

ESPAÑOL — Nombre / Página / Lat.°′ / Long.°′ W=Oeste

Salitre ≃ 250 9.29 S 40.39 W
Salix 214 40.18 N 78.46 W
Saljany 84 39.34 N 48.58 E
Šalkar, S.S.S.R. 80 50.32 N 51.51 E
Šalkar, S.S.S.R. 80 48.03 N 48.56 E
Šalkar, Ozero ◎ 80 50.33 N 51.40 E
Šalkar-Jega-Kara, Ozero ◎ 86 50.45 N 60.54 E
Salkehatchie ≃ 192 32.37 N 80.53 W
Šalkhad 132 32.29 N 36.43 E
Salkhia 272b 22.35 N 88.21 E
Salkum 224 46.32 N 122.38 W
Salladasburg 210 41.17 N 77.14 W
Sallagriffon 62 43.53 N 6.54 E
Sallanches 58 45.56 N 6.38 E
Salland ◆^{1} 52 52.20 N 6.20 E
Salles-Curan 32 44.11 N 2.47 E
Salles-sous-Bois 62 44.27 N 4.56 E
Sallgast 54 51.35 N 13.51 E
Salling ◆^{1} 26 56.40 N 9.00 E
Salliqueló 252 36.45 S 62.56 W
Sallisaw 196 35.28 N 94.47 W
Sallisaw Creek ≃ 194 35.23 N 94.52 W
Sallūm 140 19.23 N 37.06 E
Sallūm, Khalīj as- C 146 31.41 N 25.21 E
Salluyo, Nevado ∧ 248 14.38 S 69.14 W
Sallyāna 124 28.22 N 82.10 E
Salm ≃, Bel. 56 50.22 N 5.52 E
Salm ≃, B.R.D. 56 49.51 N 6.51 E
Salmanlı 130 40.55 N 30.18 E
Salme 76 58.10 N 22.15 E
Salmehâteau 56 50.16 N 5.54 E
Salmi 24 61.22 N 31.50 E
Salmo 182 49.12 N 117.17 W
Salmon 202 45.11 N 113.54 W
Salmon ≃, B.C., Can. 182 54.05 N 122.34 W
Salmon ≃, N.B., Can. 186 46.06 N 65.56 W
Salmon ≃, Ont., Can. 212 44.11 N 77.15 W
Salmon ≃, N.A. 188 45.02 N 74.31 W
Salmon ≃, Calif., U.S. 204 41.23 N 123.29 W
Salmon ≃, Conn., U.S. 207 41.29 N 72.29 W
Salmon ≃, Idaho, U.S. 202 45.51 N 116.46 W
Salmon ≃, N.Y., U.S. 212 43.35 N 76.12 W
Salmon ≃, Oreg., U.S. 224 45.22 N 122.02 W
Salmon ≃, Oreg., U.S. 224 45.03 N 124.00 W
Salmon, East Fork ≃ 202 44.16 N 114.19 W
Salmon, Middle Fork ≃ 202 45.18 N 114.36 W
Salmon, North Fork ≃ 204 41.16 N 123.18 W
Salmon, South Fork ≃, Calif., U.S. 204 41.16 N 123.18 W
Salmon, South Fork ≃, Idaho, U.S. 202 45.23 N 115.31 W
Salmon Arm 182 50.42 N 119.16 W
Salmon-Bay 186 51.26 N 57.36 W
Salmon Creek ≃, N.Y., U.S. 210 43.19 N 77.43 W
Salmon Creek ≃, N.Y., U.S. 210 43.16 N 77.02 W
Salmon Creek ≃, Wash., U.S. 224 45.44 N 122.45 W
Salmon Creek ≃, Wash., U.S. 224 46.26 N 122.52 W
Salmon Falls Creek ≃ 202 42.43 N 114.51 W
Salmon Gums 162 32.59 S 121.38 E
Salmon Lake ◎ 212 44.49 N 78.28 W
Salmon Mountain ∧ 188 45.14 N 71.08 W
Salmon Mountains ⩚ 204 41.00 N 123.00 W
Salmon Peak ∧ 196 29.28 N 100.10 W
Salmon Point > 212 43.52 N 77.14 W
Salmon River Mountains ⩚ 202 44.45 N 115.30 W
Salmon River Reservoir ◎^{1} 212 43.32 N 75.52 W
Salmon Valley 182 54.05 N 122.41 W
Salmünster 56 50.16 N 9.22 E
Salmyš ≃ 86 52.01 N 55.21 E
Sal'nica 78 49.44 N 28.02 E
Salo, Centraf. 152 3.12 N 16.07 E
Salò, It. 64 45.36 N 10.31 E
Salo, Suomi 26 60.23 N 23.08 E
Salo ≃ 188 43.27 N 70.22 W
Salobel'ak 80 57.07 N 48.05 E
Salobra ≃ 248 20.12 S 56.29 W
Salomatino 80 50.01 N 44.50 E
Salome 200 33.47 N 113.37 W
Salomon, Cap > 240e 14.30 N 61.06 W
Salomon, Îles → Solomon Islands □^{1} 175e 8.00 S 159.00 E
Salomón, Islas → Solomon Islands □^{1} 175e 8.00 S 159.00 E
Salomone, Monte 267a 41.47 N 12.44 E
Salomon-Inseln → Solomon Islands □^{1} 175e 8.00 S 159.00 E
Salon ≃ 58 47.32 N 5.41 E
Salona 210 41.05 N 77.28 W
Salon-de-Provence 62 43.38 N 5.06 E
Salonga ≃ 152 0.10 S 19.50 E
Salonika → Thessaloniki 38 40.38 N 22.56 E
Salonta 38 46.48 N 21.40 E
Salop □^{6} 42 52.40 N 2.40 W
Salor ≃ 34 39.39 N 7.03 W
Salorno (Salurn) 64 46.14 N 11.13 E
Saloslovo 265b 55.42 N 37.09 E
Salouël 150 13.50 N 16.45 W
Šalovka ≃ 265b 55.47 N 38.12 E
Salpausselkä ∧ 26 61.00 N 26.30 E
Salqīn 130 36.08 N 36.27 E
Sal Rei 150a 16.11 N 22.55 W
Salsacate 252 31.19 S 65.05 W
Salsette Island I 272c 19.10 N 72.53 E
Salsilgo, Qawz ◆^{8} 140 10.49 N 22.54 E
Salsipuedes, Canal de ꓘ 232 28.37 N 113.00 W
Salsipuedes, Punta >, C.R. 236 8.28 N 83.37 W
Salsipuedes, Punta >, Méx. 232 32.05 N 116.53 W
Sal'sk 80 46.28 N 41.33 E
Šal'skij 24 61.48 N 35.58 E
Sal'sko-Manyčskaja Gr'ada ∧ 80 46.40 N 42.30 E
Salso ≃ 70 37.06 N 13.57 E
Salsomaggiore Terme 64 44.49 N 9.59 E
Salt ≃, U.S. 202 43.08 N 111.02 W
Salt ≃, Ariz., U.S. 200 33.23 N 112.18 W
Salt ≃, Ky., U.S. 194 38.00 N 85.57 W
Salt ≃, Mich., U.S. 281 42.39 N 82.47 W
Salt ≃, Mo., U.S. 219 39.28 N 91.04 W
Salt, Elk Fork ≃ 219 39.28 N 91.49 W
Salt, Middle Fork ≃ 219 39.28 N 91.49 W
Salt, North Fork ≃ 219 39.30 N 91.47 W
Salt, South Fork ≃ 219 39.28 N 91.49 W
Salta 252 24.47 S 65.25 W
Salta □^{4} 252 25.00 S 64.30 W
Saltaim, Ozero ◎ 86 56.10 N 71.45 E
Saltair 224 48.57 N 123.46 W

FRANÇAIS — Nom / Page / Lat.°′ / Long.°′ W=Ouest

Saltaire 276 40.39 N 73.12 W
Saltara 66 43.45 N 12.54 E
Salt Ash, Austl. 170 32.47 S 151.55 E
Saltash, Eng., U.K. 42 50.24 N 4.12 W
Salt Basin ◎ 196 31.50 N 105.00 W
Saltburn-by-the-Sea 44 54.35 N 0.58 W
Salt Cay I 240b 25.06 N 77.18 W
Saltcoats, Sask., Can. 184 51.03 N 102.12 W
Saltcoats, Scot., U.K. 46 55.38 N 4.47 W
Salt Creek ≃, Ont., Can. 275b 43.48 N 79.42 W
Salt Creek ≃, Calif., U.S. 204 36.15 N 116.49 W
Salt Creek ≃, Ill., U.S. 194 40.08 N 89.50 W
Salt Creek ≃, Ill., U.S. 278 41.49 N 87.50 W
Salt Creek ≃, Ind., U.S. 216 41.37 N 87.09 W
Salt Creek ≃, Ind., U.S. 218 38.50 N 86.32 W
Salt Creek ≃, Ind., U.S. 218 39.27 N 85.09 W
Salt Creek ≃, Kans., U.S. 198 39.06 N 97.44 W
Salt Creek ≃, N. Mex., U.S. 196 33.35 N 104.23 W
Salt Creek ≃, Okla., U.S. 196 36.32 N 96.43 W
Salt Creek ≃, Oreg., U.S. 202 43.43 N 122.26 W
Salt Creek ≃, Oreg., U.S. 224 45.09 N 123.13 W
Salt Creek ≃, Wyo., U.S. 202 43.41 N 106.20 W
Salt Creek, Lake Fork ≃ 219 40.05 N 89.25 W
Salt Creek, Lake Fork, North Fork ≃ 219 39.56 N 89.14 W
Salt Creek, Middle Fork ≃ 218 39.04 N 86.15 W
Salt Creek, North Fork ≃, Ill., U.S. 216 40.13 N 88.50 W
Salt Creek, North Fork ≃, Ind., U.S. 218 39.08 N 86.21 W
Salt Creek South Fork ≃ 218 39.02 N 86.16 W
Salt Draw ∨ 196 31.19 N 103.28 W
Saltee Islands II 48 52.07 N 6.36 W
Salten 41 56.05 N 9.35 E
Saltfjellet Nasjonalpark ◆ 24 66.40 N 14.40 E
Salt Fork Lake ◎^{1} 214 41.07 N 81.30 W
Salt Fork State Park ◆ 214 40.06 N 81.29 W
Saltholm I 41 55.38 N 12.46 E
Saltillo, Méx. 232 25.25 N 101.00 W
Saltillo, Miss., U.S. 194 34.23 N 88.41 W
Saltillo, Pa., U.S. 214 40.13 N 78.01 W
Saltillo, Tenn., U.S. 194 35.23 N 88.13 W
Saltillo, Tex., U.S. 222 33.11 N 95.20 W
Salt Island I 240m 18.23 N 64.31 W
Salt Lake 158 29.16 S 24.00 E
Salt Lake ◎ 196 34.05 N 103.05 W
Salt Lake City 200 40.46 N 111.53 W
Salto, Arg. 252 34.17 S 60.15 W
Salto, Bra. 255 23.12 S 47.17 W
Salto, Ur. 252 31.23 S 57.58 W
Salto ≃ 66 42.23 N 12.54 E
Salto, Lago del ◎ 66 42.15 N 13.02 E
Salto da Divisa 255 16.00 S 39.57 W
Salto de las Rosas 252 34.43 S 68.14 W
Salto del Fraile > 286d 12.11 S 77.03 W
Salto del Ojo, Arroyo de ≃ 200 31.13 N 107.58 W
Salto Grande 255 22.54 S 49.59 W
Salton City 204 33.19 N 115.59 W
Salton Sea ◎ 204 33.19 N 115.50 W
Salton Sea State Recreation Area ◆ 204 33.29 N 115.53 W
Saltonstall, Lake ◎ 283 42.47 N 71.04 W
Saltora 126 23.32 N 86.56 E
Saltoro ∧ 123 35.25 N 76.54 E
Saltos del Guaira 252 24.03 S 54.17 W
Salt Pan Creek ≃ 274a 33.59 S 151.02 E
Saltpeter Creek C 284b 39.20 N 76.22 W
Salt Point 210 41.44 N 73.42 W
Saltpond 150 5.12 N 1.04 W
Salt Range ⩚ 123 32.40 N 72.35 E
Salt River Indian Reservation ◆^{4} 200 33.31 N 111.48 W
Saltsburg 214 40.29 N 79.26 W
Saltsjöbaden 40 59.17 N 18.18 E
Salt Slough ≃ 226 37.18 N 120.54 W
Saltspring Island I 224 48.47 N 123.30 W
Salt Springs Reservoir ◎^{1} 226 38.30 N 120.11 W
Saltville 192 36.53 N 81.46 W
Salt Wells Creek ≃ 200 41.39 N 108.59 W
Saltykovka, S.S.S.R. 80 52.07 N 44.05 E
Saltykovka, S.S.S.R. 265b 55.46 N 37.55 E
Saluafata Harbour C 175a 13.50 S 171.34 W
Saluda, S.C., U.S. 192 34.00 N 81.46 W
Saluda, Va., U.S. 208 37.36 N 76.36 W
Saluda ≃ 192 34.00 N 81.04 W
Saludecio 66 43.52 N 12.40 E
Saluēn → Salween ≃ 12 16.31 N 97.37 E
Salue Timpuas, Selat ꓘ 112 1.55 S 124.00 E
Salug 116 8.07 N 122.47 E
Saluggia 62 45.14 N 8.00 E
Salūmbar 120 24.08 N 74.03 E
Salunga 208 40.06 N 76.26 W
Saluping Island I 116 6.20 N 122.02 E
Salūq 'Atīq 130 36.36 N 39.07 E
Salūr 122 18.32 N 83.13 E
Salurn → Salorno 64 46.14 N 11.13 E
Salussola 62 45.27 N 8.07 E
Salutāris 256 22.10 S 43.17 W
Saluzzo 62 44.39 N 7.29 E
Salvación, Bahía C 254 50.55 S 75.05 W
Salvado, Mount ∧ 162 25.15 S 121.01 E
Salvador, Bra. 255 12.59 S 38.31 W
Salvador, Pil. 116 7.54 N 123.50 E
Salvador, Calif., U.S. 226 38.20 N 122.18 W
Salvador, El → El Salvador □^{1} 236 13.50 N 88.55 W
Salvador, Lake ◎ 194 29.45 N 90.15 W
Salvador Mariá 258 35.18 S 59.10 W
Salvador Mazza 252 22.04 S 63.43 W
Salvage 186 48.41 N 53.38 W
Salvail ≃ 206 45.49 N 72.58 W
Salvaleón de Higüey 238 18.37 N 68.42 W
Salvaterra 250 0.46 S 48.31 W
Salvaterra de Magos 34 39.01 N 8.48 W
Salvatierra 234 20.13 N 100.53 W
Salvatore Rosa National Park ◆ 166 24.50 S 147.15 E
Salve 68 39.51 N 18.17 E
Salviac 32 44.41 N 1.16 E
Salwā, Bahr as- C 128 25.30 N 50.40 E
Salwā Bahrī 140 24.44 N 32.56 E
Salween ≃ 12 16.31 N 97.37 E
Salyer 204 40.54 N 123.35 W
Salyersville 192 37.45 N 83.04 W
Salygino 78 51.34 N 34.07 E
Salza ≃, D.D.R. 54 51.23 N 11.50 E

PORTUGUÊS — Nome / Página / Lat.°′ / Long.°′ W=Oeste

Salza ≃, Öst. 61 47.40 N 14.43 E
Salzach ≃ 30 48.12 N 12.56 E
Salza Irpina 68 40.55 N 14.53 E
Salzberg 64 47.38 N 13.02 E
Salzbergen 52 52.19 N 7.20 E
Salzböde ≃ 56 50.40 N 8.42 E
Salzbrunn 156 24.23 S 18.00 E
Salzburg 64 47.48 N 13.02 E
Salzburg □^{3} 64 47.25 N 13.15 E
Salzgitter 54 52.10 N 10.25 E
Salzgitter-Bad ◆^{8} 52 52.04 N 10.23 E
Salzgitter-Barum ◆^{8} 52 52.07 N 10.25 E
Salzgitter-Immendorf ◆^{8} 52 52.09 N 10.26 E
Salzgitter-Lebenstedt ◆^{8} 52 52.09 N 10.20 E
Salzgitter-Thiede ◆^{8} 52 52.11 N 10.29 E
Salzgitter-Watenstedt ◆^{8} 52 52.06 N 10.22 E
Salzhaff C 54 54.06 N 11.36 E
Salzhausen 52 53.13 N 10.09 E
Salzhemmendorf 52 52.04 N 9.35 E
Salzkammergut ◆^{1} 64 47.45 N 13.30 E
Salzkotten 52 51.40 N 8.36 E
Salzmünde 54 51.31 N 11.49 E
Salzwedel 54 52.51 N 11.09 E
Sam, Bhārat 120 26.50 N 70.31 E
Sam, Gabon 152 0.58 N 11.16 E
Samā 132 32.28 N 36.14 E
Sama ≃ 248 18.10 S 70.40 W
Sam A. Baker State Park ◆ 194 37.16 N 90.34 W
Samacá 246 5.29 N 73.29 W
Samacimbo 152 13.33 S 16.59 E
Sama [de Langreo] 34 43.18 N 5.41 W
Samādūn 142 30.20 N 30.57 E
Samagaltaj 88 50.36 N 95.03 E
Samah 146 28.12 N 19.09 E
Samāika ◆^{8} 272a 28.32 N 77.05 E
Samaipata 248 18.09 S 63.52 W
Samal (Peñaplata) 116 7.05 N 125.42 E
Samalá ≃ 236 14.11 N 91.47 W
Samalanga 114 5.13 N 96.22 E
Samalayuca 200 31.21 N 106.28 W
Samalayuca, Médanos de ◆^{8} 200 31.15 N 106.30 W
Šamaldy-Saj 85 41.12 N 72.11 E
Samales Group II 116 6.00 N 121.45 E
Samalga Pass ꓘ 180 52.48 N 169.25 W
Samal Island I 116 7.03 N 125.44 E
Sāmalkot 122 17.03 N 82.11 E
Samālūt 142 28.18 N 30.42 E
Samambaia ≃ 255 22.45 S 53.21 W
Samāna 124 30.09 N 76.12 E
Samaná, Bahía de C 238 19.10 N 69.25 W
Samaná, Cabo > 238 19.18 N 69.09 W
Samana Cay I 238 23.06 N 73.42 W
Samandağı 130 36.07 N 35.56 E
Samandira 130 40.59 N 29.13 E
Samandıra ≃ 267b 40.59 N 29.15 E
Samangān □^{4} 120 36.15 N 67.40 E
Samangwa 152 4.24 S 24.10 E
Samani 92a 42.07 N 142.56 E
Samaniego 246 1.20 N 77.35 W
Samannūd 142 30.58 N 31.15 E
Samar I 116 12.00 N 125.00 E
Samara → Kujbyšev 80 53.12 N 50.09 E
Samara ≃, S.S.S.R. 78 48.27 N 35.07 E
Samara ≃, S.S.S.R. 80 53.10 N 50.04 E
Samarai 164 10.37 S 150.40 E
Samarate 62 45.38 N 8.47 E
Samar del Norte □^{4} 116 12.30 N 124.30 E
Samarga 89 47.17 N 138.48 E
Samarga ≃ 89 47.15 N 138.46 E
Samaria, Idaho, U.S. 202 42.07 N 112.20 W
Samaria, Mich., U.S. 216 41.48 N 83.35 W
Samaria (As-Sāmirah) □^{9} 132 32.15 N 35.10 E
Samaria, Mount ∧ 169 36.52 S 146.03 E
Samariapo 246 5.15 N 67.48 W
Samarinda 112 0.30 S 117.09 E
Samarka 89 44.44 N 134.13 E
Samarkand 85 39.40 N 66.48 E
Samar Occidental □^{4} 116 11.50 N 125.00 E
Samar Oriental □^{4} 116 12.00 N 125.00 E
Sāmarrā' 128 34.12 N 43.52 E
Samar Sea ▽^{2} 116 12.15 N 124.15 E
Samasata 123 29.21 N 71.33 E
Samaso 144 3.12 N 43.44 E
Samassi 71 39.29 N 8.54 E
Samāstipur 124 25.51 N 85.47 E
Samatlar 130 41.14 N 33.07 E
Samatya ◆^{8} 267b 41.00 N 28.56 E
Samāwārī 120 28.34 N 66.46 E
Samba, Bhārat 123 32.34 N 75.07 E
Samba, Zaïre 152 0.14 N 21.19 E
Samba, Zaïre 154 4.38 S 26.22 E
Samba Caju 152 8.46 S 15.24 E
Sambaetiba 256 22.41 S 42.48 W
Sambaíba 250 7.08 S 45.21 W
Sambalpur 120 21.27 N 83.58 E
Sambalpur □^{5} 124 22.00 N 84.20 E
Sambar, Tanjung > 112 2.59 S 110.19 E
Sambas 112 1.20 N 109.15 E
Sambava 157b 14.16 S 50.10 E
Sambawizi 154 18.21 S 26.16 E
Sambayat 130 37.41 N 38.03 E
Sambāza 120 31.49 N 69.20 E
Sambek ≃ 83 47.16 N 39.01 E
Sambe-san ∧ 96 35.08 N 132.37 E
Sambesi → Zambezi ≃ 138 18.55 S 36.04 E
Sambe-yama ∧ 92 35.08 N 132.37 E
Sambhal 124 28.35 N 78.33 E
Sāmbhar 120 26.55 N 75.12 E
Sāmbhar Lake ◎ 120 26.58 N 75.05 E
Sambia → Zambia □^{1} 138 15.00 S 30.00 E
Sambiase 68 38.58 N 16.17 E
Sambit, Pulau I 112 1.46 N 119.03 E
Sambito ≃ 250 5.40 S 42.10 W
Sambo 152 12.57 S 16.05 E
Samboan 116 9.32 N 123.18 E
Samboja 112 1.02 S 117.02 E
Sambolabbo 152 7.05 N 11.59 E
Sambong-san ∧ 98 40.30 N 126.09 E
Sambon'yari-dake ∧ 94 37.09 N 139.58 E
Sâmbor, Kam. 110 12.46 N 105.58 E
Sambor, S.S.S.R. 78 49.32 N 23.11 E
Samborombón ≃ 252 35.43 S 57.20 W
Samborombón, Bahía C 252 36.00 S 57.12 W
Samborondón 246 1.57 S 79.44 W
Sambre ≃ 32 50.28 N 4.52 E
Sambre à l'Oise, Canal de la ≅ 50 49.39 N 3.20 E
Sambrial 123 32.28 N 74.21 E
Sambú ≃ 246 8.05 N 78.18 W
Sambuca di Sicilia 70 37.39 N 13.07 E
Sambuca Pistoiese 66 44.06 N 11.00 E
Sambughetti, Monte ∧ 70 37.50 N 14.22 E
Sambungo 152 8.39 S 20.43 E
Samburu Game Reserve ◆^{4} 154 0.45 N 37.30 E
Sambusu 156 17.50 S 19.20 E
Samch'ŏk 98 37.27 N 129.10 E
Sam Chom, Khao ∧ 110 8.07 N 99.26 E
Samchong Park ◆ 271b 37.36 N 126.59 E
Samch'ŏnp'o 98 34.57 N 128.03 E
Samchor 84 40.50 N 46.02 E
Samdari 120 25.49 N 72.35 E
Samdžir, Gora ∧ 88 52.32 N 93.53 E
Same 154 4.04 S 37.44 E
Same ≃ 94 36.54 N 140.49 E
Samedan 58 46.33 N 9.52 E
Samekawa 94 37.02 N 140.31 E
Samen 128 34.12 N 48.42 E
Samene, Oued ∨ 148 26.49 N 7.08 E
Samer 50 50.38 N 1.45 E
Sameru Dando ∧ 124 27.02 N 90.20 E
Samet' 80 57.49 N 40.44 E
Samford 171a 27.23 S 152.53 E
Samfya 154 11.21 S 29.32 E
Samga 98 35.25 N 128.05 E
Samho 98 39.56 N 127.53 E
Saminka ≃ 265b 55.45 N 37.17 E
Samiria ≃ 246 4.42 S 74.13 W
Samish 224 48.35 N 122.33 W
Samish ≃ 224 48.38 N 122.29 W
Samish Bay C 224 48.36 N 122.28 W
Samish Lake ◎ 224 48.39 N 122.24 W
Samj 132 32.27 N 36.30 E
Samka 110 20.09 N 96.57 E
Sam Kong I 271d 22.11 N 114.17 E
Samlesbury 262 53.46 N 2.38 W
Samlesbury Aerodrome ⊠ 262 53.47 N 2.34 W
Samlesbury Bottoms 262 53.45 N 2.34 W
Samlesbury Higher Hall ⊥ 262 53.46 N 2.34 W
Şamlı 130 39.48 N 27.51 E
Sammamish Lake ◎ 224 47.36 N 122.22 W
Sammichele di Bari 68 40.53 N 16.57 E
Samnangjin 98 35.23 N 128.50 E
Samnaun 58 46.56 N 10.22 E
Samnaungruppe ⩚ 58 47.00 N 10.25 E
Sam Ngao 110 17.15 N 99.01 E
Samnū 146 27.17 N 14.53 E
Samnye-ri 98 35.55 N 127.05 E
Samo 164 3.58 S 152.51 E
Samoa → American Samoa □^{2}, Oc. 14
175a 14.20 S 170.00 W
Samoa americane → American Samoa □^{2} 175a 14.20 S 170.00 W
Samoa Islands II 175a 14.00 S 171.00 W
Samo Alto 252 30.25 S 70.58 W
Samoa Occidental → Western Samoa □^{1} 175a 13.55 S 172.00 W
Samoa Occidentales → Western Samoa □^{1} 175a 13.55 S 172.00 W
Samobor 36 45.48 N 15.43 E
Samoded 24 63.38 N 40.29 E
Samoëns 58 46.05 N 6.44 E
Samofalovka 80 48.57 N 44.13 E
Samoggia ≃ 64 44.41 N 11.15 E
Samojlovka 80 51.12 N 43.43 E
Samokov 38 42.20 N 23.33 E
Samolaco 58 46.15 N 9.21 E
Samora ≃ 266c 38.50 N 8.57 W
Sámos 38 37.45 N 27.00 E
Sámos I 38 37.48 N 26.44 E
Samosdelka 80 46.02 N 47.53 E
Samoset 220 27.28 N 82.33 W
Samosir, Pulau I 114 2.35 N 98.50 E
Samotevići 76 53.13 N 31.50 E
Samothrace → Samothráki I 38 40.30 N 25.32 E
Samothráki 38 40.28 N 25.31 E
Samothráki I 38 40.30 N 25.32 E
Samouco 266c 38.43 N 9.00 W
Samovo 76 54.12 N 31.22 E
Samovol'no-Ivanovka 80 52.33 N 50.53 E
S'amozero 24 61.54 N 33.18 E
Sampacho 252 33.23 S 64.43 W
Sampaga 112 2.19 S 119.07 E
Sampaio Correia 256 22.52 S 42.36 W
Sampalan 115b 8.41 S 115.34 E
Sampaloc Point > 116 14.44 N 120.09 E
Sampanahan 112 2.38 S 116.11 E
Sampang 115a 7.12 S 113.14 E
Sampara ≃ 112 3.49 S 122.28 E
Sampawams Creek ≃ 276 40.41 N 73.19 W
Sam Pervyj 86 45.28 N 56.06 E
Sampéyre 62 44.34 N 7.11 E
Sampford Peverell 42 50.56 N 3.22 W
Sampieri 70 36.43 N 14.44 E
Sampit 112 2.32 S 112.57 E
Sampit ≃ 112 2.44 S 112.54 E
Sampit, Teluk C 112 3.05 S 113.03 E
Sampolawa 112 5.36 S 122.43 E
Sampson State Park ◆ 210 42.44 N 76.55 W
Sampués 246 9.11 N 75.23 W
Sampur 80 52.19 N 41.37 E
Sampwe 154 9.20 S 27.26 E
Samrah 130 37.30 N 40.30 E
Samrajevka 78 49.46 N 29.49 E
Samrala 123 30.51 N 76.11 E
Sam Rayburn Reservoir ◎^{1} 194 31.27 N 94.37 W
Samre 144 13.07 N 39.10 E
Samreboi 150 5.36 N 2.34 W
Samro, Ozero ◎ 76 58.57 N 28.49 E
Samrong, Khlong ≅ 269a 13.39 N 100.34 E
Sams ≃ 224 47.38 N 124.01 W
Samsat 130 37.30 N 38.31 E
Samsø I 41 55.52 N 10.37 E
Samsø Bælt ꓘ 41 55.48 N 10.47 E
Samson, Ala., U.S. 194 31.07 N 86.09 W
Sam-son, Viet. 110 19.44 N 105.54 E
Samson I 42a 49.56 N 6.22 W
Samson Indian Reserve ◆^{4} 182 52.48 N 113.10 W
Samsonovka 85 42.44 N 70.32 E
Samsonville 210 41.53 N 74.18 W
Sams Point ∧ 210 41.40 N 74.22 W
Samsu 98 41.19 N 128.02 E
Samsun 130 41.17 N 36.20 E
Samsun □^{4} 130 41.15 N 36.00 E
Samsun Limani C 130 41.18 N 36.21 E
Samtens 54 54.21 N 13.17 E
Samthar 124 25.51 N 78.55 E
Samtown 194 31.20 N 92.26 W
Samtredia 84 42.10 N 42.20 E
Samu 112 2.01 S 115.57 E
Samudragarh 126 23.21 N 88.20 E
Samuel, Mount ∧ 162 19.41 S 134.09 E
Samuel Alfred Ross Port 150 4.58 N 8.57 W
Samuel P. Taylor State Park ◆ 226 38.01 N 122.44 W
Samugheo 71 39.57 N 8.56 E
Samuhú 252 27.31 S 60.24 W
Samui, Ko I 110 9.30 N 100.00 E
Samukawa 94 35.22 N 139.23 E
Samundri 123 31.04 N 72.58 E
Samur ≃ 84 41.53 N 48.32 E
Samur-Divičinskij Kanal ≅ 84 41.38 N 48.25 E
Samurskij Chrebet ⩚ 84 41.35 N 47.35 E
Samusele 152 10.06 S 24.05 E
Samutlu 130 39.44 N 32.22 E
Samut Prakan 110 13.36 N 100.36 E
Samut Sakhon 110 13.32 N 100.17 E
Samut Songkhram 110 13.24 N 100.00 E
San 150 13.18 N 4.54 W
San ≃, As. 110 13.32 N 105.58 E
San ≃, Eur. 30 50.45 N 21.51 E
Saña, Perú 248 6.55 S 79.35 W
Şan'ā', Yaman 144 15.23 N 44.12 E
Sana ≃, Jugo. 36 45.03 N 16.23 E
San'a ≃, S.S.S.R. 82 54.41 N 35.55 E
Sanaba 150 12.25 N 3.49 W
Şanabū 142 27.30 N 30.47 E
Sanada 94 36.27 N 138.20 E
Sanae ◆^{3} 9 70.30 S 2.30 W
Sanafā 142 30.47 N 31.21 E
Şanāfīr I 128 27.55 N 34.40 E
Sanaga ≃ 152 3.35 N 9.38 E
Sanage-yama ∧ 94 35.12 N 137.10 E
Sanagōchi 96 33.59 N 134.28 E
San Agustín, Cape > 116 6.16 N 126.11 E
San Agustin, Plains of ≋ 200 33.50 N 108.00 W
San Agustín Atenango 234 17.38 N 97.59 W
San Agustín Loxicha 234 16.01 N 96.38 W
San Agustín Oapan 234 17.58 N 99.27 W
San Agustín Tlaxiaca 234 20.07 N 98.53 W
Sanak Islands II 180 54.25 N 162.35 W
San Alberto 196 27.30 N 101.20 W
San Alejo 236 13.26 N 87.58 W
Şān al-Ḥajar, Birkat ◎ 142 31.03 N 31.54 E
Şān al-Ḥajar al-Qiblīyah 142 30.58 N 31.52 E
Sanalona, Presa ◎^{1} 232 24.53 N 107.00 W
San Ambrosio, Isla I 244 26.21 S 79.52 W
Sanam Chai, Khlong ≅ 269a 13.38 N 100.27 E
Sanana 112 2.04 S 125.58 E
Sanana, Pulau I 112 2.12 S 125.55 E
Sānand 120 22.59 N 72.23 E
Sanandaj 128 35.19 N 47.00 E
Sanandita 248 21.40 S 63.35 W
San Andreas 226 38.12 N 120.41 W
San Andreas Lake ◎ 282 37.36 N 122.26 W
San Andreas Rift Zone ∨ 282 37.25 N 122.15 W
San Andrés, Col. 236 12.35 N 81.42 W
San Andrés, Col. 246 6.49 N 72.52 W
San Andrés, Méx. 232 27.14 N 114.14 W
San Andrés, Pan. 236 8.36 N 82.44 W
San Andrés, Cerro ∧ 234 19.48 N 100.36 W
San Andrés, Isla de I 236 12.32 N 81.42 W
San Andrés, Laguna de C 234 22.40 N 97.52 W
San Andrés Cohamiata 234 22.12 N 104.03 W
San Andrés de la Barca 266d 41.27 N 1.59 E
San Andres Mountains ⩚ 200 32.55 N 106.45 W
San Andres Point > 116 13.34 N 121.52 E
San Andrés Sajcabajá 236 15.13 N 90.55 W
San Andrés Totoltepec ◆^{8} 286a 19.15 N 99.10 W
San Andrés Tuxtla 234 18.27 N 95.13 W
San Andrés y Providencia □^{8} 238 12.30 N 81.45 W
San Angel → Villa Obregón ◆^{8} 286a 19.21 N 99.12 W
San Angelo 196 31.28 N 100.26 W
San Anselmo 226 37.59 N 122.34 W
San Antero 246 9.23 N 75.46 W
San Antonio, Belize 236 16.15 N 89.02 W
San Antonio, Chile 252 33.35 S 71.38 W
San Antonio, Chile 252 27.53 S 70.03 W
San Antonio, Col. 246 3.55 N 75.28 W
San Antonio, C.R. 236 10.12 N 85.26 W
San Antonio, Perú 248 6.22 S 76.21 W
San Antonio, P.R. 240m 18.30 N 67.07 W
San Antonio, Fla., U.S. 220 28.21 N 82.17 W
San Antonio, N. Mex., U.S. 200 33.55 N 106.52 W
San Antonio, Tex., U.S. 196 29.28 N 98.31 W
San Antonio, Ur. 252 31.22 S 57.48 W
San Antonio, Ur. 258 34.27 S 56.05 W
San Antonio □^{7} 286b 22.55 N 82.29 W
San Antonio ≃, Méx. 196 29.13 N 103.47 W
San Antonio ≃, Méx. 232 31.00 N 116.15 W
San Antonio ≃, Méx. 234 18.14 N 101.52 W
San Antonio ≃, Calif., U.S. 226 35.52 N 120.48 W
San Antonio ≃, Tex., U.S. 196 28.30 N 96.50 W
San Antonio ◆^{1} 288 34.24 S 58.31 W
San Antonio, Cabo >, Arg. 252 36.40 S 56.42 W
San Antonio, Cabo >, Cuba 240p 21.52 N 84.57 W
San Antonio, Mount ∧ 228 34.17 N 117.39 W
San Antonio, Punta > 232 29.46 N 115.42 W
San Antonio, Rio ≃ 200 37.11 N 105.55 W
San Antonio Abad 34 38.58 N 1.18 E
San Antonio Bay C, Pil. 116 8.38 N 117.35 E
San Antonio Bay C, Tex., U.S. 196 28.20 N 96.45 W
San Antonio Canyon ∨ 280 34.12 N 117.40 W
San Antonio Creek ≃ 226 38.09 N 122.33 W
San Antonio Dam ◆^{6} 280 34.09 N 117.41 W
San Antonio de Bravo 232 30.10 N 104.42 W
San Antonio de Galipán 286c 10.33 N 66.53 W
San Antonio de las Alazanas 232 25.16 N 100.36 W
San Antonio del Golfo 246 10.27 N 63.50 W
San Antonio de los Baños 240p 22.53 N 82.30 W
San Antonio del Táchira 246 7.50 N 72.27 W
San Antonio de Padua, Mission ✝^{1} 226 36.01 N 121.15 W
San Antonio de Tamanaco 246 9.41 N 66.03 W
San Antonio Eloxochitlán 234 18.11 N 96.52 W
San Antonio Heights 228 34.10 N 117.40 W
San Antonio Mountain ∧ 200 36.52 N 106.02 W
San Antonio Nogalar 234 23.04 N 98.22 W
San Antonio Reservoir ◎^{1}, Calif., U.S. 226 35.55 N 121.00 W
San Antonio Reservoir ◎^{1}, Calif., U.S. 226 37.35 N 121.50 W
San Antonio Suchitepéquez 236 14.32 N 91.25 W
San Antonio Tecómitl ◆^{8} 286a 19.13 N 98.59 W
San Antonio Ticino 266b 45.35 N 8.46 E
San Antonio Zomeyucan 286a 19.27 N 99.16 W
San'anzhuling 120 28.33 N 93.00 E
San Ardo 226 36.07 N 120.54 W
Sanaroa Island I 164 9.35 S 151.00 E
Sanary-sur-Mer 62 43.07 N 5.48 E
Sanatoga 285 40.15 N 75.36 W
Sanatoga Creek ≃ 285 40.14 N 75.36 W
San Augustine 194 31.32 N 94.07 W
San Augustin Pass ꓘ 200 32.26 N 106.34 W
Sanaur 124 30.18 N 76.27 E
Sanāw 144 17.50 N 51.00 E
Sanāwad 120 22.11 N 76.04 E
Sanāwān 123 30.19 N 70.59 E
San Bartolomé Ayautla 234 18.02 N 96.40 W
San Bartolomé de la Cuadra 266d 41.26 N 2.02 E
San Bartolomeo in Galdo 68 41.24 N 15.01 E
San Bartolo Morelos 234 19.41 N 99.29 W
San Basilio 71 39.32 N 9.11 E
San Baudilio de Llobregat 34 41.21 N 2.03 E
San Benedetto, Alpe di ⩚ 66 43.53 N 11.43 E
San Benedetto del Tronto 66 42.57 N 13.53 E
San Benedetto in Alpe 66 43.59 N 11.41 E
San Benedetto Po 64 45.02 N 10.55 E
San Benedicto, Isla I 232 19.18 N 110.49 W
San Benigno Canavese 62 45.13 N 7.46 E
San Benito, Bol. 248 17.31 S 65.55 W
San Benito, Guat. 232 16.55 N 89.54 W
San Benito, Tex., U.S. 196 26.08 N 97.38 W
San Benito □^{6} 226 36.51 N 121.24 W
San Benito ≃ 226 36.53 N 121.34 W
San Benito Mountain ∧ 226 36.22 N 120.38 W
San Bernard ≃ 222 28.52 N 95.27 W
San Bernardino, Schw. 58 46.28 N 9.12 E
San Bernardino, Calif., U.S. 228 34.06 N 117.17 W
San Bernardino □^{6} 228 34.40 N 117.17 W
San Bernardino, Passo del ꓘ 58 46.30 N 9.11 E
San Bernardino, Río de ≃ 200 30.48 N 109.11 W
San Bernardino Mountains ⩚ 204 34.10 N 117.00 W
San Bernardino National Forest ◆ 280 34.12 N 117.38 W
San Bernardino Strait ꓘ 116 12.32 N 124.10 E
San Bernardo, Chile 252 33.36 S 70.43 W
San Bernardo, Méx. 232 25.59 N 105.33 W
San Bernardo, Canal ≅ 286e 33.36 S 70.41 W
San Bernardo, Isla I 236 11.32 N 85.06 W
San Bernardo, Islas de II 246 9.45 N 75.50 W
San Bernardo del Viento 246 9.21 N 75.57 W
San Biagio 66 44.35 N 11.52 E
San Biagio di Callalta 64 45.41 N 12.22 E
San Biagio Platani 70 37.31 N 13.32 E
San Biagio Saracinisco 66 41.37 N 13.55 E
San Blas, Méx. 232 26.05 N 108.46 W
San Blas, Méx. 234 21.31 N 105.16 W
San Blas, Cape > 192 29.40 N 85.22 W
San Blas, Cordillera de ⩚ 246 9.18 N 79.00 W
San Blas, Golfo de C 246 9.30 N 79.00 W
San Blas Atempa 234 16.16 N 95.10 W
San Bonifacio 64 45.24 N 11.16 E
San Borja 248 14.49 S 66.51 W
Sanborn, Iowa, U.S. 198 43.11 N 95.39 W
Sanborn, Minn., U.S. 198 44.13 N 95.08 W
Sanborn, N. Dak., U.S. 198 46.57 N 98.13 W
Sanborn, N.Y., U.S. 210 43.08 N 78.53 W
San Bovio 266b 45.28 N 9.19 E
San Bruno 226 37.37 N 122.25 W
San Bruno, Point > 282 37.39 N 122.22 W
San Bruno Mountain ∧ 282 37.42 N 122.25 W
Sanbu 94 35.39 N 140.23 E
San Buena Ventura, Bol. 248 14.28 S 67.35 W
San Buenaventura, Méx. 232 27.05 N 101.32 W
San Buenaventura → Ventura, Calif., U.S. 228 34.17 N 119.18 W
San Buono 66 41.59 N 14.34 E
San Calogero 68 38.34 N 16.01 E
San Calogero, Monte ∧ 70 37.57 N 13.44 E
San Candido (Innichen) 64 46.44 N 12.17 E
San Carlo 58 46.25 N 8.32 E
San Carlos, Chile 252 36.25 S 71.58 W
San Carlos, Chile 286e 33.36 S 70.35 W
San Carlos, Gui. Ecu. 152 3.27 N 8.33 E
San Carlos, Méx. 232 29.01 N 100.51 W
San Carlos, Méx. 232 24.35 N 98.56 W
San Carlos, Nic. 236 11.07 N 84.47 W
San Carlos, Pan. 236 8.29 N 79.57 W
San Carlos, Para. 252 22.16 S 57.18 W
San Carlos, Pil. 116 10.30 N 123.25 E
San Carlos, Pil. 116 15.55 N 120.20 E
San Carlos, Ariz., U.S. 200 33.21 N 110.27 W
San Carlos, Calif., U.S. 226 37.31 N 122.16 W
San Carlos, Ur. 252 34.48 S 54.55 W
San Carlos, Ven. 246 9.40 N 68.36 W
San Carlos ≃, C.R. 236 10.47 N 84.12 W
San Carlos ≃, Ariz., U.S. 200 33.16 N 110.27 W
San Carlos ≃, Ven. 246 9.07 N 68.25 W
San Carlos, Canal ≅ 286e 33.25 S 70.38 W
San Carlos, Riacho ≃ 252 22.51 S 57.51 W
San Carlos Airport ⊠ 282 37.31 N 122.15 W
San Carlos Bay C 220 26.28 N 82.03 W
San Carlos Borromeo, Mission ✝^{1} 226 36.34 N 121.55 W
San Carlos Centro 252 31.44 S 61.06 W
San Carlos de Bariloche 254 41.09 S 71.18 W
San Carlos de Chena 286e 33.35 S 70.44 W
San Carlos de Guaroa 246 3.44 N 73.14 W
San Carlos de la Rápita 34 40.37 N 0.36 E
San Carlos del Zulia 246 9.01 N 71.55 W
San Carlos de Río Negro 246 1.55 N 67.04 W

≃ River	Fluss	Río	Rivière	Rio
≅ Canal	Kanal	Canal	Canal	Canal
Waterfall, Rapids	Wasserfall, Stromschnellen	Cascada, Rápidos	Chute d'eau, Rapides	Cascata, Rápidos
ꓘ Strait	Meeresstrasse	Estrecho	Détroit	Estreito
C Bay, Gulf	Bucht, Golf	Bahía, Golfo	Baie, Golfe	Baía, Golfo
◎ Lake, Lakes	See, Seen	Lago, Lagos	Lac, Lacs	Lago, Lagos
Swamp	Sumpf	Pantano	Marais	Pântano
Ice Features, Glacier	Eis- und Gletscherformen	Accidentes Glaciales	Formes glaciaires	Acidentes Glaciares
Other Hydrographic Features	Andere Hydrographische Objekte	Otros Elementos Hidrográficos	Autres données hydrographiques	Outros Elementos Hidrográficos
Submarine Features	Untermeerische Objekte	Accidentes Submarinos	Formes de relief sous-marin	Acidentes Submarinos
□ Political Unit	Politische Einheit	Unidad Política	Entité politique	Unidade Política
✝ Cultural Institution	Kulturelle Institution	Institución Cultural	Institution culturelle	Instituição Cultural
⊥ Historical Site	Historische Stätte	Sitio Histórico	Site historique	Sítio Histórico
◆ Recreational Site	Erholungs- und Ferienort	Sitio de Recreo	Centre de loisirs	Sítio de Lazer
⊠ Airport	Flughafen	Aeropuerto	Aéroport	Aeroporto
Military Installation	Militäranlage	Instalación Militar	Installation militaire	Instalação Militar
Miscellaneous	Verschiedenes	Misceláneo	Divers	Miscelânea

ENGLISH — Name / Page / Lat.°′ / Long.°′ DEUTSCH — Name / Seite / Breite°′ / Länge°′ E=Ost

Name	Page	Lat.°′	Long.°′
San Carlos Indian Reservation ⬥[4]	200	33.23 N	110.09 W
San Carlos Reservoir ⊖[1]	200	33.13 N	110.24 W
San Carpoforo Creek ≃	226	35.47 N	121.19 W
San Casciano dei Bagni	66	42.52 N	11.53 E
San Casciano in Val di Pesa	66	43.39 N	11.11 E
San Cataldo, It.	68	40.23 N	18.17 E
San Cataldo, It.	70	37.29 N	13.59 E
Sancergues	50	47.09 N	2.55 E
Sancerre	50	47.20 N	2.51 E
Sancerrois, Collines du ⩓[2]	50	47.25 N	2.45 E
San Cesario di Lecce	68	40.18 N	18.10 E
San Cesario sul Panaro	64	44.34 N	11.02 E
Sancey-le-Grand	58	47.18 N	6.35 E
Sanch'a, T'aiwan	100	24.25 N	120.46 E
Sánchez	238	19.14 N	69.36 W
Sanchez Creek ≃	222	32.36 N	97.50 W
Sánchez Magallanes	234	18.14 N	93.52 W
Sānchi	124	23.29 N	77.44 E
Sanchih	100	25.14 N	121.37 E
San Chirico Raparo	68	40.11 N	16.05 E
Sanch'ŏng	98	35.26 N	127.54 E
Sanchung	269d	25.04 N	121.29 E
Sanch'ungch'iao	269d	25.11 N	121.35 E
San Cipirello	70	37.58 N	13.10 E
San Cipriano Picentino	68	40.43 N	14.52 E
San Ciro de Acosta	234	21.38 N	99.49 W
San Clemente, Esp.	34	39.24 N	2.26 W
San Clemente, Calif., U.S.	228	33.26 N	117.37 W
San Clemente, Arroyo de ≃	266d	41.20 N	2.00 E
San Clemente a Casauria ʊ[1]	66	42.14 N	13.55 E
San Clemente de Llobregat	266d	41.20 N	2.00 E
San Clemente Island I	228	32.54 N	118.29 W
Sancoins	32	46.50 N	2.55 E
San Colombano al Lambro	62	45.11 N	9.29 E
San Cono	70	37.17 N	14.22 E
Sanco Point >	116	8.15 N	126.27 E
San Cosme	252	27.22 S	58.31 W
San Cosme Xalostoc	234	19.24 N	98.03 W
San Cosmo Albanese	68	39.35 N	16.25 E
San Costantino Albanese	68	40.02 N	16.18 E
San Cristóbal, Cuba	240p	22.43 N	83.03 W
San Cristóbal, Ven.	246	7.46 N	72.14 W
San Cristóbal I	175e	10.36 S	161.45 E
San Cristóbal ≃	234	18.02 N	96.12 W
San Cristóbal, Bahía de C	232	27.23 N	114.38 W
San Cristóbal, Cerro ∧, Chile	286e	33.25 S	70.39 W
San Cristóbal, Cerro ∧, Perú	286d	12.02 S	77.01 W
San Cristóbal, Isla I	246a	0.50 S	89.26 W
San Cristóbal, Nevis → Saint Kitts-Nevis □[2]	238	17.20 N	62.45 W
San Cristóbal, Volcán ∧[1]	236	12.42 N	87.01 W
San Cristóbal de la Barranca	234	21.03 N	103.26 W
San Cristóbal de la Laguna	148	28.29 N	16.19 W
San Cristóbal de las Casas	234	16.45 N	92.38 W
San Cristóbal Totonicapán	236	14.55 N	91.26 W
San Cristobal Trench ⬥[1]	14	11.00 S	161.00 E
San Cristóbal Verapaz	236	15.23 N	90.24 W
San Cristobal Wash ∨	200	32.47 N	113.44 W
Sancti-Spíritus	240p	21.56 N	79.27 W
Sancti-Spíritus □[4]	240p	22.00 N	79.20 W
San Cugat, Riera de ≃	266d	41.29 N	2.11 E
San Cugat del Vallés	266d	41.28 N	2.05 E
Sančursk	80	56.57 N	47.15 E
Sand, B.R.D.	56	48.32 N	7.55 E
Sand, Nor.	26	59.29 N	6.15 E
Sand ≃, Alta., Can.	184	54.22 N	111.05 W
Sand ≃, S. Afr.	156	22.25 S	30.05 E
Sand ≃, S. Afr.	158	28.05 S	26.25 E
Sanda, Nihon	96	34.53 N	135.14 E
Sanda, Nihon	268	35.28 N	139.21 E
Sandafā al-Fa'r	142	28.32 N	30.40 E
Sandagou	89	43.43 N	134.52 E
Sandai	112	1.15 S	110.31 E
Sanda Island I	44	55.18 N	5.34 W
Sandakan	112	5.50 N	118.07 E
Sandakan Harbour C	116	5.45 N	118.05 E
Sandal, Baie du C	175f	20.50 S	167.05 E
San Damián	248	12.02 S	76.24 W
San Damiano d'Asti	62	44.50 N	8.04 E
San Damiano Macra	62	44.29 N	7.16 E
Sândăn	110	12.42 N	106.01 E
Sandan, Chāh ⬥[4]	128	28.59 N	63.27 E
Sandane	26	61.46 N	6.13 E
San Daniele del Friuli	64	46.09 N	13.00 E
Sandan-kyō ♠	96	34.38 N	132.13 E
Sandanski	38	41.34 N	23.17 E
Sandaré	150	14.42 N	10.18 W
Sandared	26	57.43 N	12.47 E
Sandarne	26	61.16 N	17.10 E
Sand Arroyo Creek ≃	196	37.29 N	101.29 W
Sandata	80	46.16 N	41.46 E
Sandau	54	52.47 N	12.02 E
Sanday I	46	59.15 N	2.35 W
Sanday Sound C	46	59.11 N	2.31 W
Sandbach	44	53.09 N	2.22 W
Sandbank	46	55.59 N	4.58 W
Sandbanks Provincial Park ♠	212	43.55 N	77.17 W
Sandbochum	263	51.40 N	7.41 E
Sand City	226	36.37 N	121.51 W
Sand Coulee	202	47.24 N	111.10 W
Sand Coulee Creek ≃	202	47.27 N	111.18 W
Sand Creek ≃, U.S.	200	41.13 N	105.43 W
Sand Creek ≃, Ariz., U.S.	200	35.46 N	112.27 W
Sand Creek ≃, Ind., U.S.	218	39.03 N	85.51 W
Sand Creek ≃, Minn., U.S.	190	45.56 N	92.39 W
Sand Creek ≃, Mont., U.S.	202	47.18 N	106.45 W
Sand Creek ≃, S. Dak., U.S.	198	44.02 N	98.05 W
Sand Creek ≃, Wyo., U.S.	200	41.02 N	107.52 W
Sand Creek ≃, Wyo., U.S.	202	44.16 N	107.55 W
Sand Cut	220	26.56 N	80.35 W
Sande, B.R.D.	52	51.45 N	8.39 E
Sande, B.R.D.	52	53.30 N	8.01 E
Sandefjord	26	59.08 N	10.14 E
San Demetrio Corone	68	39.34 N	16.22 E
San Demetrio ne'Vestini	66	42.17 N	13.34 E
Sanders, Ariz., U.S.	200	35.13 N	109.20 W
Sanders, Ky., U.S.	218	38.39 N	84.57 W
Sandersdorf, B.R.D.	60	48.54 N	11.37 E
Sandersdorf, D.D.R.	54	51.37 N	12.15 E
Sandersleben	54	51.40 N	11.34 E
Sanderson	196	30.09 N	102.24 W
Sanderstead ⬥[8]	260	51.20 N	0.05 W
Sanderston	168b	34.46 S	139.13 E
Sandersville, Ga., U.S.	192	32.59 N	82.48 W
Sandersville, Miss., U.S.	194	31.47 N	89.02 W
Sandeshkhali	126	22.22 N	88.53 E
Sandesneben	52	53.41 N	10.30 E
Sandfly Lake ⊖	184	55.45 N	106.05 W
Sand Fork	188	38.55 N	80.45 W
Sandgate, Austl.	171a	27.20 S	153.05 E
Sandgate, Eng., U.K.	42	51.05 N	1.08 E
Sandhammaren >	26	55.23 N	14.12 E
Sandhamn	40	59.17 N	18.55 E
Sandhead	44	54.48 N	4.58 W
Sandheuwel	158	31.46 S	20.48 E
Sandhill, Ont., Can.	275b	43.50 N	79.49 W
Sand Hill, Mass., U.S.	207	42.13 N	70.44 W
Sand Hill ∧[2]	210	42.31 N	77.37 W
Sand Hill ≃	198	47.36 N	96.52 W
Sand Hills ⩓[2]	198	42.00 N	101.00 W
Sandhorst	52	53.29 N	7.29 E
Sandhurst	42	51.19 N	0.48 W
Sāndi	124	27.18 N	79.57 E
Sandia	248	14.17 S	69.26 W
Sandia Crest ∧	200	35.13 N	106.27 W
San Diego, Calif., U.S.	228	32.43 N	117.09 W
San Diego, Tex., U.S.	196	27.46 N	98.14 W
San Diego □[6]	228	33.00 N	117.05 W
San Diego ≃, Cuba	240p	22.20 N	83.16 W
San Diego ≃, Calif., U.S.	204	32.46 N	117.13 W
San Diego, Cabo >	254	54.38 S	65.07 W
San Diego Aqueduct ⩧[1]	228	32.55 N	116.55 W
San Diego Bay C	228	32.37 N	117.07 W
San Diego Creek ≃	196	27.47 N	98.03 W
San Diego de Alcala, Mission ʊ[1]	228	32.48 N	117.06 W
San Diego de la Unión	234	21.28 N	100.52 W
San Diego Naval Air Station ■	228	32.42 N	117.12 W
San Diego Naval Training Center ■	228	32.44 N	117.13 W
San Dieguito ≃	228	32.58 N	117.16 W
Sandies Creek ≃	222	29.06 N	97.20 W
Sandıklı	130	38.28 N	30.17 E
Sandīla	124	27.05 N	80.31 E
Sandilands	168b	34.31 S	137.46 E
Sandilands Village	240b	25.02 N	77.18 W
San Dimas	228	34.06 N	117.49 W
San Dimas Canyon ∨	280	34.10 N	117.46 W
San Dimas Reservoir ⊖[1]	280	34.09 N	117.43 W
San Dionisio, Nic.	236	12.45 N	85.51 W
San Dionisio, Pil.	116	11.16 N	123.06 E
Sand Island I	174g	28.12 N	177.23 W
Sand Islet I	174g	28.16 N	177.23 W
Sandiway	262	53.14 N	2.36 W
Sandizell	60	48.35 N	11.11 E
Sand Key I	220	27.53 N	82.51 W
Sandkrug	54	52.53 N	13.52 E
Sandl	61	48.33 N	14.38 E
Sand Lake	210	42.38 N	73.32 W
Sand Lake ⊖, Ont., Can.	184	50.05 N	94.39 W
Sand Lake ⊖, Ont., Can.	212	44.34 N	76.15 W
Sand Lake ⊖, Ont., Can.	212	44.56 N	77.02 W
Sandling ∧	64	47.39 N	13.43 E
Sandnes	26	58.51 N	5.44 E
Sandness	46a	60.17 N	1.38 W
Sandoa	152	9.41 S	22.52 E
Sandogora	80	58.12 N	40.59 E
Sandomierz	30	50.41 N	21.45 E
San Domingo Creek ≃	226	38.07 N	120.40 W
San Domino, Isola I	68	42.07 N	15.29 E
Sandon	260	51.43 N	0.32 E
Sandoná	246	1.17 N	77.28 W
San Donaci	68	40.27 N	17.55 E
San Donà di Piave	64	45.38 N	12.34 E
San Donato di Lecce	68	40.15 N	18.10 E
San Donato di Ninea	68	39.42 N	16.03 E
San Donato Milanese	62	45.24 N	9.16 E
San Donato Val di Comino	66	41.42 N	13.49 E
Sandongo	152	15.30 S	21.28 E
San Dorligo della Valle	64	45.36 N	13.51 E
Sandouping	102	30.48 N	110.49 E
Sandoval	219	38.37 N	89.07 W
Sandover ≃	162	21.43 S	136.32 E
Sandovo	76	58.28 N	36.25 E
Sandoway	110	18.28 N	94.22 E
Sandown	42	50.39 N	1.09 W
Sandown Park Racecourse ♠, Austl.	274b	37.57 S	145.10 E
Sandown Park Race Course ♠, Eng., U.K.	260	51.22 N	0.22 W
Sand Point, Alaska, U.S.	180	55.20 N	160.30 W
Sandpoint, Idaho, U.S.	202	48.16 N	116.33 W
Sand Point >	214	41.30 N	82.43 W
Sandrancourt	261	49.02 N	1.39 E
Sandray I	46	56.53 N	7.30 W
Sandridge, Eng., U.K.	260	51.47 N	0.18 W
Sand Ridge, N.Y., U.S.	210	43.15 N	76.14 W
Sandrigo	64	45.39 N	11.36 E
Sandringham, Austl.	166	24.05 S	139.04 E
Sandringham, Austl.	169	37.57 S	145.00 E
Sandringham, Eng., U.K.	42	52.50 N	0.30 E
Sandringham ⬥[8]	273d	26.09 S	28.07 E
Sandringham House ⊥	42	52.50 N	0.30 E
Sand River Valley	158	28.28 S	29.33 E
Šandrovka	78	48.57 N	35.46 E
Sands Key I	220	25.30 N	80.11 W
Sandslån	26	63.01 N	17.47 E
Sandspit	182	53.14 N	131.50 W
Sands Point	276	40.51 N	73.43 W
Sands Point >	276	40.52 N	73.44 W
Sand Springs	196	36.09 N	96.07 W
Sandspruit	158	27.18 S	29.48 E
Sandspruit ≃	273d	26.07 S	28.04 E
Sandstedt	52	53.21 N	8.31 E
Sandston	208	37.31 N	77.19 W
Sandstone, Austl.	162	27.59 S	119.17 E
Sandstone, Minn., U.S.	190	46.08 N	92.52 W
Sandstone Creek ≃	216	42.23 N	84.33 W
Sandūb	142	31.01 N	31.23 E
Sandugan Point >	116	9.18 N	123.36 E
Sandumba	152	13.45 S	17.29 E
Sandusky, Ind., U.S.	218	39.25 N	85.29 W
Sandusky, Mich., U.S.	190	43.25 N	82.50 W
Sandusky, N.Y., U.S.	210	42.30 N	78.23 W
Sandusky, Ohio, U.S.	214	41.27 N	82.42 W
Sandusky □[6]	214	41.21 N	83.07 W
Sandusky ≃	214	41.27 N	83.00 W
Sandusky Bay C	214	41.27 N	82.52 W
Sandvig	26	55.17 N	14.47 E
Sandvika	26	59.54 N	10.31 E
Sandviken	40	60.37 N	16.46 E
Sandweiler	56	49.37 N	6.13 E
Sandwich, Eng., U.K.	42	51.17 N	1.20 E
Sandwich, Ill., U.S.	216	41.39 N	88.37 W
Sandwich, Mass., U.S.	207	41.46 N	70.30 W
Sandwich, Port C	175f	16.27 S	167.46 E
Sandwich Bay C, Newf., Can.	176	53.35 N	57.15 W
Sandwich Bay C, Namibia	156	23.22 S	14.30 E
Sandwich del Sur, Islas → South Sandwich Islands II	18	57.45 S	26.30 W
Sandwick, B.C., Can.	182	49.42 N	124.59 W
Sandwick, Scot., U.K.	46a	60.00 N	1.15 W
Sand Wick C	46	60.42 N	0.52 W
Sandwīp	124	22.29 N	91.26 E
Sandwīp Channel Ų	124	22.30 N	91.35 E
Sandwīp Island I	124	22.30 N	91.25 E
Sandy, Eng., U.K.	42	52.08 N	0.18 W
Sandy, Oreg., U.S.	224	45.24 N	122.16 W
Sandy, Pa., U.S.	214	41.07 N	78.47 W
Sandy ≃, Maine, U.S.	188	44.45 N	69.52 W
Sandy ≃, Oreg., U.S.	224	45.34 N	122.24 W
Sandy ≃, Va., U.S.	192	36.35 N	79.25 W
Sandy Bay C, Nic.	236	14.28 N	83.16 W
Sandy Bay C, Mass., U.S.	283	42.40 N	70.37 W
Sandy Bay Indian Reserve ⬥[4]	184	50.33 N	98.40 W
Sandy Bay Mountain ∧	188	45.47 N	70.25 W
Sandy Beach	210	43.04 N	78.55 W
Sandy Branch ≃	284c	39.03 N	77.16 W
Sandy Cape >, Austl.	166	41.25 S	144.45 E
Sandy Cape >, Austl.	166	24.42 S	153.17 E
Sandy Creek	212	43.39 N	76.05 W
Sandy Creek ≃, U.S.	196	36.50 N	98.10 W
Sandy Creek ≃, U.S.	196	34.25 N	99.35 W
Sandy Creek ≃, Ill., U.S.	219	39.34 N	90.35 W
Sandy Creek ≃, N.C., U.S.	192	36.08 N	78.02 W
Sandy Creek ≃, N.Y., U.S.	212	43.20 N	77.55 W
Sandy Creek ≃, N.Y., U.S.	212	43.44 N	76.15 W
Sandy Creek ≃, Ohio, U.S.	214	40.38 N	81.26 W
Sandy Creek ≃, Pa., U.S.	214	41.18 N	79.51 W
Sandy Creek ≃, Tex., U.S.	196	30.34 N	98.26 W
Sandy Creek ≃, Tex., U.S.	222	29.02 N	96.33 W
Sandy Creek, East Branch ≃	210	43.17 N	78.03 W
Sandy Creek, West Branch ≃	210	43.17 N	78.03 W
Sandy Desert ⬥[2], Pāk.	120	28.40 N	62.30 E
Sandy Desert ⬥[2], Pāk.	128	28.15 N	64.30 E
Sandy Hook, Conn., U.S.	207	41.25 N	73.17 W
Sandy Hook, Ky., U.S.	192	38.05 N	83.08 W
Sandy Hook, Miss., U.S.	194	31.02 N	89.48 W
Sandy Hook >[2]	208	40.27 N	74.00 W
Sandy Hook Bay C	276	40.26 N	74.03 W
Sandykači	128	36.33 N	62.34 E
Sandy Key I	220	25.02 N	81.01 W
Sandy Lake	214	41.22 N	80.05 W
Sandy Lake ⊖, Newf., Can.	186	49.16 N	57.00 W
Sandy Lake ⊖, Ont., Can.	184	53.00 N	93.07 W
Sandy Lake ⊖, Ont., Can.	212	44.33 N	78.24 W
Sandy Lick Creek ≃	214	41.09 N	79.05 W
Sandy Point	238	17.22 N	62.50 W
Sandy Point >, Austl.	168b	34.16 S	138.09 E
Sandy Point >, R.I., U.S.	207	41.14 N	71.35 W
Sandy Pond ⊖	283	42.26 N	71.19 W
Sandy Ridge	214	40.49 N	78.14 W
Sandy Springs	192	33.55 N	84.23 W
Sandyville, Md., U.S.	208	39.31 N	76.55 W
Sandyville, Ohio, U.S.	214	40.38 N	81.23 W
Sandžak ⬥[1]	38	43.10 N	19.30 E
San Elizario	200	31.35 N	106.16 W
San Emigdio Creek ≃	228	35.02 N	119.11 W
Sanen ≃	115a	8.23 S	113.37 E
San Estanislao, Col.	246	10.24 N	75.09 W
San Estanislao, Para.	252	24.39 S	56.26 W
San Esteban	236	15.17 N	85.52 W
San Esteban, Bahía C	232	25.38 N	109.14 W
San Esteban, Isla I	232	28.42 N	112.36 W
San Esteban de Gormaz	34	41.35 N	3.12 W
San Fausto de Campcentellas	266d	41.31 N	2.14 E
San Fele	68	40.49 N	15.32 E
San Felice (Sankt Felix)	64	46.30 N	11.08 E
San Felice Circeo	66	41.14 N	13.05 E
San Felice sul Panaro	64	44.50 N	11.08 E
San Felipe, Chile	252	32.45 S	70.44 W
San Felipe, Col.	246	1.55 N	67.06 W
San Felipe, Méx.	232	31.00 N	114.52 W
San Felipe, Méx.	234	21.29 N	101.13 W
San Felipe, Tex., U.S.	222	29.48 N	96.06 W
San Felipe, Ven.	246	10.20 N	68.44 W
San Felipe, Castillo de ⊥	236	15.39 N	89.01 W
San Felipe, Cayos de II	240p	21.58 N	83.30 W
San Felipe, Punta >	200	31.03 N	114.51 W
San Felipe Aztatán	234	22.23 N	105.24 W
San Felipe Creek ≃	204	33.09 N	115.46 W
San Felipe de Puerto Plata → Puerto Plata, Rep. Dom.	238	19.48 N	70.41 W
San Felipe de Puerto Plata, Rep. Dom.	238	19.48 N	70.41 W
San Felipe de Vichayal	248	4.52 S	81.05 W
San Felipe Nuevo Mercurio	232	24.22 N	102.06 W
San Felipe Pueblo	200	35.27 N	106.28 W
San Felíu de Guixols	34	41.47 N	3.02 E
San Felíu de Llobregat	266d	41.23 N	2.03 E
San Félix ≃	236	8.10 N	81.51 W
San Félix, Isla I	244	26.17 S	80.05 W
San Ferdinando di Puglia	68	41.18 N	16.04 E
San Fermín	196	26.20 N	104.49 W
San Fermín, Punta >	232	30.25 N	114.40 W
San Fernando, Arg.	258	34.26 S	58.34 W
San Fernando, Chile	252	34.35 S	71.00 W
San Fernando, Esp.	34	36.28 N	6.12 W
San Fernando, Méx.	196	28.32 N	100.54 W
San Fernando, Méx.	200	31.16 N	110.36 W
San Fernando, Méx.	232	24.50 N	98.10 W
San Fernando, Méx.	234	16.52 N	93.13 W
San Fernando, Pil.	116	16.37 N	120.19 E
San Fernando, Pil.	116	15.01 N	120.41 E
San Fernando, Pil.	116	12.30 N	123.46 E
San Fernando, Trin.	241r	10.17 N	61.28 W
San Fernando, Calif., U.S.	228	34.17 N	118.26 W
San Fernando □[5]	288	34.28 S	58.34 W
San Fernando ≃	232	24.55 N	97.40 W
San Fernando, Aeródromo ⊠	288	34.27 S	58.35 W
San Fernando Airport ⊠	280	34.17 N	118.25 W
San Fernando Creek ≃	196	27.28 N	97.46 W
San Fernando de Apure	246	7.54 N	67.28 W
San Fernando de Atabapo	246	4.03 N	67.42 W
San Fernando de Henares	266a	40.25 N	3.32 W
San Fernando Mission ʊ[1]	280	34.16 N	118.28 W
San Fernando Point >	116	16.38 N	120.17 E
San Fernando Valley ∨	280	34.13 N	118.27 W
San Fili	68	39.20 N	16.09 E
San Filippo del Mela	70	38.10 N	15.17 E
Sånfjället ∧	26	62.17 N	13.32 E
Sånfjallets Nationalpark ♠	26	62.20 N	13.40 E
San Floriano	64	46.02 N	12.18 E
Sanford, Colo., U.S.	200	37.16 N	105.54 W
Sanford, Fla., U.S.	220	28.48 N	81.16 W
Sanford, Maine, U.S.	188	43.26 N	70.46 W
Sanford, Mich., U.S.	190	43.40 N	84.23 W
Sanford, N.C., U.S.	192	35.29 N	79.10 W
Sanford, Tex., U.S.	196	35.42 N	101.32 W
Sanford ≃	162	27.22 S	115.53 E
Sanford, Mount ∧	180	62.13 N	144.09 W
San Francesco, Convento ʊ[1]	267a	42.03 N	12.46 E
San Francisco, Arg.	252	31.26 S	62.05 W
San Francisco, Col.	246	1.11 N	76.53 W
San Francisco, C.R.	236	9.49 N	85.15 W
San Francisco, Pan.	236	8.15 N	80.58 W
San Francisco, Calif., U.S.	226		
	282	37.48 N	122.24 W
San Francisco □[6]	226	37.45 N	122.22 W
San Francisco ≃, Arg.	252	23.16 S	64.03 W
San Francisco → São Francisco ≃, Bra.	242	10.30 S	36.24 W
San Francisco ≃, U.S.	200	32.59 N	109.22 W
San Francisco, Arroyo ≃	288	34.43 S	58.19 W
San Francisco, La Cadena ⩓	240m	18.19 N	67.10 W
San Francisco, Paso de)(	252	26.53 S	68.19 W
San Francisco, University of ʊ[2]	282	37.46 N	122.26 W
San Francisco Bay C	226	37.43 N	122.17 W
San Francisco Creek ≃	196	29.53 N	102.19 W
San Francisco Culhuacán ⬥[8]	286a	19.20 N	99.08 W
San Francisco de Arriba	232	26.15 N	102.50 W
San Francisco de Borja	232	27.53 N	106.41 W
San Francisco de Horizonte	196	25.56 N	103.26 W
San Francisco de la Paz	236	14.55 N	86.14 W
San Franciscó del Carnicero	236	12.30 N	86.18 W
San Francisco del Chañar	252	29.47 S	63.56 W
San Francisco del Mar	234	16.14 N	94.39 W
San Francisco del Monte de Oro	252	32.36 S	66.08 W
San Francisco del Oro	232	26.52 N	105.51 W
San Francisco del Rincón	234	21.01 N	101.51 W
San Francisco de Macorís	238	19.18 N	70.15 W
San Francisco de Mostazal	252	33.59 S	70.43 W
San Francisco el Grande, Iglesia de ʊ[1]	266a	40.25 N	3.43 W
San Francisco Gotera	236	13.42 N	88.06 W
San Francisco International Airport ⊠	226	37.37 N	122.23 W
San Francisco Ixhuatán	234	16.22 N	94.29 W
San Francisco Maritime State Historical Park ♠	282	37.48 N	122.27 W
San Francisco Mountains ⩓	200	33.45 N	109.00 W
San Francisco-Oakland Bay Bridge ⬥[5]	282	37.48 N	122.22 W
San Francisco State Beach ♠	282	37.47 N	122.29 W
San Francisco State Fish and Game Refuge ⬥[4]	282	37.35 N	122.25 W
San Francisco State University ʊ[2]	282	37.43 N	122.28 W
San Francisco Tlalcilalcalpa	234	19.18 N	99.46 W
San Francisquito Creek ≃	282	37.28 N	122.07 W
San Fratello	70	38.01 N	14.36 E
San Fratello ≃	70	38.02 N	14.34 E
Sanga, Ang.	152	11.07 S	15.22 E
Sanga, H. Vol.	150	11.10 N	0.10 E
Sanga, Mali	150	14.28 N	3.19 W
Sanga, Zaïre	154	7.02 S	28.21 E
San Gabriel, Ec.	246	0.36 N	77.49 W
San Gabriel, Calif., U.S.	228	34.07 N	118.06 W
San Gabriel ≃, Calif., U.S.	280	33.45 N	118.07 W
San Gabriel ≃, Tex., U.S.	222	30.46 N	97.01 W
San Gabriel, Isla I	258	34.28 S	57.54 W
San Gabriel, North Fork ≃, Calif., U.S.	280	34.15 N	117.52 W
San Gabriel, North Fork ≃, Tex., U.S.	222	30.38 N	97.40 W
San Gabriel, South Fork ≃	196	30.38 N	97.41 W
San Gabriel Arcangel, Mission ʊ[1]	280	34.06 N	118.06 W
San Gabriel Chilac	234	18.19 N	97.21 W
San Gabriel Dam ⬥[6]	280	34.13 N	117.52 W
San Gabriel Mountains ⩓	228	34.20 N	118.00 W
San Gabriel Peak ∧	280	34.15 N	118.06 W
San Gabriel Reservoir ⊖[1]	228	34.13 N	117.51 W
Sangačal, Mys >	84	40.07 N	49.30 E
San Galgano, Abbazia di ʊ[1]	66	43.10 N	11.10 E
Šangaly	24	61.08 N	43.19 E
Sangamankanda Point >	122	7.01 N	81.52 E
Sangamner	122	19.34 N	74.13 E
Sangamon □[6]	219	39.47 N	89.40 W
Sangamon ≃	194	40.07 N	90.20 W
Sangamon, South Fork ≃	219	39.48 N	89.32 W
Sangamon, South Fork, Flat Branch ≃	219	39.33 N	89.16 W
Sangāreddi	122	17.38 N	78.07 E
Sangar Sarāy	120	34.24 N	70.38 E
Sangasanga-dalam	112	0.40 S	117.14 E
Sanga Sanga Island I	116	5.04 N	119.47 E
Sangat	123	30.05 N	74.50 E
Sangatte	50	50.56 N	1.45 E
San Gavino Monreale	71	39.33 N	8.47 E
Sangay, Volcán ∧[1]	246	2.00 S	78.20 W
Sangayán, Isla de I	248	13.51 S	76.28 W
Sang Bast	128	35.59 N	59.46 E
Sangbé	152	6.03 N	12.28 E
Sangchris Lake State Park ♠	219	39.38 N	89.28 W
Sangchungshih	100	25.04 N	121.29 E
Sangeang, Pulau I	115b	8.12 S	119.04 E
Sang-e Māsheh	120	33.08 N	67.27 E
San Gemini	66	42.37 N	12.33 E
San Genesio Atesino	64	46.32 N	11.20 E
Sangenjaya ⬥[8]	268	35.38 N	139.40 E
Sanger, Calif., U.S.	226	36.42 N	119.27 W
Sanger, Tex., U.S.	196	33.22 N	97.10 W
Sangerhausen	54	51.28 N	11.17 E
San Germán, Cuba	240p	20.36 N	76.08 W
San Germán, P.R.	240m	18.05 N	67.03 W
San Germano Vercellese	62	45.21 N	8.15 E
San Geronimo	226	38.01 N	122.39 W
San Gerónimo, Arroyo ≃	258	33.57 S	56.05 W
Sangerville	188	45.10 N	69.21 W
Sangganhe ≃	105	40.21 N	115.21 E
Sanggar, Teluk C	115b	8.20 S	118.18 E
Sanggau	112	0.08 N	110.36 E
Sangge-ri ⬥[8]	271b	37.41 N	127.05 E
Sanggi	112	5.27 S	104.30 E
Sanggona	112	3.52 S	121.46 E
Sangha □[5]	152	2.00 N	15.00 E
Sangha ≃	152	1.13 S	16.49 E
Sanghar	120	26.02 N	68.57 E
San Giacomo (Sankt Jakob in Pfitsch)	64	46.57 N	11.36 E
San Giacomo Filippo	58	46.20 N	9.21 E
Sangihe, Kepulauan II	112	3.00 N	125.30 E
Sangihe, Pulau I	112	3.35 N	125.32 E
Sangijn Dalaj Nuur ⊖	88	49.17 N	99.00 E
San Gil	246	6.33 N	73.08 W
Sangilen, Chrebet ⩓	88	50.18 N	96.30 E
San Gimignano	66	43.28 N	11.02 E
San Ginês de Vilasar	266d	41.31 N	2.22 E
San Ginesio	66	43.06 N	13.19 E
San Gion	58	46.38 N	8.50 E
San Giorgio Canavese	62	45.20 N	7.48 E
San Giorgio della Richinvelda	64	46.03 N	12.52 E
San Giorgio del Sannio	68	41.04 N	14.51 E
San Giorgio di Lomellina	62	45.10 N	8.47 E
San Giorgio di Nogaro	64	45.50 N	13.13 E
San Giorgio di Piano	64	44.39 N	11.22 E
San Giorgio Ionico	68	40.27 N	17.23 E
San Giorgio la Molara	68	41.16 N	14.55 E
San Giorgio Lucano	68	40.07 N	16.23 E
San Giorgio Monferrato	62	45.07 N	8.23 E
San Giorgio Morgeto	68	38.23 N	16.06 E
San Giorgio Piacentino	62	44.57 N	9.44 E
San Giorgio su Legnano	266b	45.34 N	8.55 E
San Giovanni (Sankt Johann)	64	46.38 N	11.44 E
San Giovanni al Timavo (Sankt Johann in Ahrn)	64	46.58 N	11.57 E
San Giovanni a Piro	68	40.03 N	15.27 E
San Giovanni-Bianco	58	45.52 N	9.39 E
San Giovanni d'Asso	66	43.09 N	11.35 E
San Giovanni Gemini	70	37.38 N	13.39 E
San Giovanni Ilarione	64	45.30 N	11.15 E
San Giovanni in Croce	64	45.05 N	10.22 E
San Giovanni in Fiore	68	39.15 N	16.42 E
San Giovanni in Laterano ʊ[1]	267a	41.53 N	12.30 E
San Giovanni in Persiceto	64	44.38 N	11.11 E
San Giovanni la Punta	70	37.35 N	15.07 E
San Giovanni Lupatoto	64	45.23 N	11.03 E
San Giovanni Rotondo	68	41.42 N	15.44 E
San Giovanni Suergiu	71	39.07 N	8.31 E
San Giovanni Valdarno	66	43.34 N	11.32 E
San Giuliano, Lago di ⊖	68	40.37 N	16.30 E
San Giuliano Milanese	266b	45.24 N	9.17 E
San Giuliano Terme	66	43.46 N	10.26 E
San Giuseppe, It.	62	44.22 N	8.18 E
San Giuseppe, It.	70	37.58 N	13.11 E
San Giuseppe Vesuviano	68	40.50 N	14.30 E
San Giustino	66	43.33 N	12.10 E
San Giusto, Aeroporto di ⊠	66	43.11 N	10.21 E
San Giusto Canavese	62	45.19 N	7.49 E
Sangjiatun	104	42.24 N	122.42 E
Sangju	98	36.26 N	128.09 E
Sangkapura	115a	5.52 S	112.40 E
Sângkê ≃	110	13.13 N	103.41 E
Sangkhai	110	14.39 N	103.52 E
Sangkhla	110	15.07 N	98.28 E
Sangkulirang	112	0.59 N	117.58 E
Sāngla	123	31.43 N	73.23 E
Sangley Point Naval Station (United States) ■	116	14.30 N	120.54 E
Sāngli	122	16.52 N	74.34 E
Sangmélima	152	2.56 N	11.59 E
Sangnyŏng-ni	98	38.14 N	126.54 E
Sango	270	34.36 N	135.42 E
San Godenzo	66	43.55 N	11.37 E
Sāngola	122	17.26 N	75.12 E
Sangolquí	246	0.19 S	78.27 W
San Gorgonio Mountain ∧	204	34.06 N	116.50 W
San Gottardo, Passo del)(	58	46.33 N	8.34 E
Sangre de Cristo Mountains ⩓	200	37.30 N	105.15 W
San Gregorio, It.	66	42.19 N	13.29 E
San Gregorio, Calif., U.S.	226	37.20 N	122.23 W
San Gregorio, Arroyo ≃	258	33.59 S	56.50 W
San Gregorio Atlapulco ⬥[8]	286a	19.15 N	99.03 W
San Gregorio Beach ♠	282	37.19 N	122.24 W
San Gregorio Creek ≃	282	37.19 N	122.25 W
San Gregorio Magno	68	40.39 N	15.24 E
Sangre Grande	241r	10.35 N	61.07 W
Sangro ≃	66	42.14 N	14.32 E
Sangrūr	123	30.14 N	75.50 E
Sangrūr ⬥[1]	123	30.16 N	75.52 E
Sangsues, Lac aux ⊖	190	46.29 N	77.57 W
Sanguandian	100	31.19 N	118.05 E
Sangudo	182	53.53 N	114.54 W
Sangue, Rio do ≃	248	11.01 S	58.39 W
Sangüesa	34	42.35 N	1.17 W
Sanguinetto	64	45.11 N	11.09 E
Sāngurli	272c	18.56 N	73.07 E
Sangwa	154	5.30 S	26.00 E
Sanhala	150	10.03 N	6.51 W
San Hipólito, Punta >	232	26.59 N	113.59 W
Sanhsient'ai I	100	23.08 N	121.26 E
Sanhsing	100	24.40 N	121.39 E
Sanhūr	142	29.25 N	30.46 E
Sanhūr al-Madīnah	142	31.07 N	30.44 E
Sanibel	220	26.27 N	82.01 W
Sanibel Island I	220	26.27 N	82.06 W
San Ignacio, Bol.	248	16.23 S	60.59 W
San Ignacio, Bol.	248	14.53 S	65.36 W
San Ignacio, C.R.	236	9.48 N	84.09 W
San Ignacio, Hond.	236	14.38 N	87.02 W
San Ignacio, Méx.	232	27.27 N	112.51 W
San Ignacio, Méx.	234	23.55 N	106.25 W
San Ignacio, Méx.	234	23.12 N	100.12 W
San Ignacio, Para.	252	26.52 S	57.03 W
San Ignacio, Isla de I	232	25.25 N	108.54 W
San Ignacio, Laguna ⊖	232	26.54 N	113.13 W
San Ildefonso, Cape >	116	16.02 N	121.59 E
San Ildefonso, Cerro ∧	236	15.31 N	88.17 W
San Ildefonso o La Granja	34	40.54 N	4.00 W
San Ildefonso Peninsula >[1]	116	16.10 N	122.05 E
San'in-kaigan-kokuritsu-kōen ♠	96	35.38 N	134.38 E
Sanino	265a	59.50 N	29.54 E
Sani Pass)(	158	29.34 S	29.19 E
San Isabel Creek ≃	196	27.39 N	99.38 W
San Isidro, Arg.	252	28.27 S	65.44 W
San Isidro, Arg.	258	34.27 S	58.30 W
San Isidro, Méx.	200	31.31 N	106.18 W
San Isidro, Méx.	234	21.55 N	100.15 W
San Isidro, Nic.	236	12.56 N	86.12 W
San Isidro, Perú	286d	12.07 S	77.03 W
San Isidro, Tex., U.S.	196	26.43 N	98.27 W
San Isidro □[5]	288	34.29 S	58.33 W
San Isidro del General	236	9.22 N	83.42 W
San Isidro el Real, Catedral de ʊ[1]	266a	40.25 N	3.42 W
Sanitaria Springs	210	42.09 N	75.46 W
Sanitz	54	54.04 N	12.22 E
San Jacinto, Col.	246	9.50 N	75.08 W
San Jacinto, Méx.	196	25.29 N	103.44 W
San Jacinto, Calif., U.S.	228	33.47 N	116.57 W
San Jacinto □[6]	222	30.35 N	95.10 W
San Jacinto ≃, Calif., U.S.	228	33.43 N	117.16 W
San Jacinto ≃, Tex., U.S.	222	29.46 N	95.05 W
San Jacinto, East Fork ≃	222	30.05 N	95.09 W
San Jacinto, West Fork ≃	222	30.02 N	95.15 W
San Jacinto Monument ⊥	222	29.45 N	95.01 W
San Jacinto Peak ∧	204	33.49 N	116.41 W
San Jacinto Valley ∨	228	33.50 N	117.05 W
Sanjahā	142	30.50 N	31.38 E
San Javier, Bol.	248	14.34 S	64.42 W
San Javier, Bol.	248	16.20 S	62.38 W
San Javier, Méx.	196	26.16 N	99.27 W
San Javier, Ur.	252	32.41 S	58.08 W
San Javier ≃	252	31.30 S	60.20 W
San Javier de Loncomilla	252	35.35 S	71.45 W
Sanjāwi	120	30.17 N	68.21 E
Sanje	154	0.46 S	31.30 E
San Jerónimo	236	15.03 N	90.12 W
San Jerónimo de Juárez	234	17.08 N	100.28 W
San Jerónimo Norte	252	31.33 S	61.05 W
Sanjō	92	37.37 N	138.57 E
San Joaquín, Bol.	248	13.04 S	64.49 W
San Joaquín, Para.	252	24.57 S	56.07 W
San Joaquin, Pil.	116	10.35 N	122.08 E
San Joaquin, Calif., U.S.	226	36.36 N	120.11 W
San Joaquin □[6]	226	37.57 N	121.17 W
San Joaquín ≃, Bol.	248	13.08 S	63.41 W
San Joaquin ≃, Calif., U.S.	226	38.03 N	121.50 W
San Joaquin, Middle Fork ≃	226	37.32 N	119.11 W
San Joaquin, North Fork ≃	226	37.32 N	119.11 W
San Joaquin, South Fork ≃	226	37.26 N	119.14 W
San Joaquin Valley ∨	204	36.50 N	120.10 W
San Jon	196	35.06 N	103.20 W
San Jorge, El Sal.	236	13.25 N	88.21 W
San Jorge, Nic.	236	11.27 N	85.48 W
San Jorge ≃	246	9.07 N	74.44 W
San Jorge, Bahía de C	232	31.12 N	113.15 W
San Jorge, Cabo >	254	45.47 S	67.21 W
San Jorge, Canal de → Saint George's Channel Ų	28	52.00 N	6.00 W
San Jorge, Golfo C	254	46.00 S	67.00 W
San Jorge, Golfo de C	34	40.53 N	1.00 E
San Jorge Island I	175e	8.27 S	159.35 E
San José, Bol.	248	14.13 S	68.05 W
San José, C.R.	236	9.56 N	84.05 W
San José, Ec.	246	1.42 S	79.01 W
San José, Hond.	236	14.54 N	88.44 W
San José, Méx.	196	28.16 N	100.15 W
San José, Méx.	232	27.32 N	110.09 W

Symbols in the index entries represent the broad categories identified in the key at the right. Symbols with superior numbers (⩓[2]) identify subcategories (see complete key on page *I · 30*).

Kartensymbole in dem Registerverzeichnis stellen die rechts in Schlüssel erklärten Kategorien dar. Symbole mit hochgestellten Ziffern (⩓[2]) bezeichnen Unterabteilungen einer Kategorie (vgl. vollständiger Schlüssel auf Seite *I · 30*).

Los símbolos incluídos en el texto del índice representan las grandes categorias identificadas con la clave a la derecha. Los símbolos con numeros en su parte superior (⩓[2]) identifican las subcategorías (véase la clave completa en la página *I · 30*).

Les symboles de l'index représentent les catégories indiquées dans la légende à droite. Les symboles suivis d'un indice (⩓[2]) représentent des sous-catégories (voir légende complète à la page *I · 30*).

Os símbolos incluídos no texto do índice representam as grandes categorias identificadas com a chave à direita. Os símbolos com números em sua parte superior (⩓[2]) identificam as subcategorias (veja-se a chave completa à página *I · 30*).

Symbol	English	Deutsch	Español	Français	Português
∧	Mountain	Berg	Montaña	Montagne	Montanha
⩓	Mountains	Berge	Montañas	Montagnes	Montanhas
)(	Pass	Pass	Paso	Col	Passo
∨	Valley, Canyon	Tal, Cañon	Valle, Cañón	Vallée, Canyon	Vale, Canhão
≍	Plain	Ebene	Llano	Plaine	Planície
>	Cape	Kap	Cabo	Cap	Cabo
I	Island	Insel	Isla	Île	Ilha
II	Islands	Inseln	Islas	Îles	Ilhas
⬥	Other Topographic Features	Andere Topographische Objekte	Otros Elementos Topográficos	Autres données topographiques	Outros Elementos Topográficos

ESPAÑOL

Nombre	Página	Lat.°′	Long.°′ W=Oeste
San José, Para.	252	25.33 S	56.45 W
San Jose, Calif., U.S.	226		
	282	37.20 N	121.53 W
San Jose, Fla., U.S.	192	30.15 N	81.36 W
San Jose, Ill., U.S.	194	40.18 N	89.36 W
San Jose, N. Mex., U.S.	200	35.24 N	105.29 W
San José, Ven.	286c	10.34 N	66.57 W
San José □[4]	236	9.40 N	84.00 W
San José □[5]	258	34.15 S	56.45 W
San José □[7]	286b	22.57 N	82.14 W
San Jose ≃, B.C., Can.	182	52.14 N	122.15 W
San José ≃, Ur.	258	34.38 S	56.29 W
San Jose, Arroyo ≃	282	38.03 N	122.30 W
San José, Golfo C	254	42.20 S	64.18 W
San José, Isla I	232	25.00 N	110.38 W
San José, Isla de I	246	8.15 N	79.07 W
San José, Laguna C	240m	18.25 N	66.01 W
San Jose, Mission ψ[1]	282	37.32 N	121.55 W
San José Ayuquila	234	17.58 N	97.57 W
San Jose Creek ≃	280	34.01 N	118.03 W
San José de Achuapa	236	13.03 N	86.35 W
San José de Aura	196	27.34 N	101.23 W
San José de Chiquitos	248	17.51 S	60.47 W
San José de Galipán	286c	10.35 N	66.54 W
San José de Galipán, Quebrada ≃	286c	10.37 N	66.54 W
San José de Gauribe	246	9.52 N	65.48 W
San José de Gracia	234	20.40 N	102.35 W
San José de Guanipa	246	8.54 N	64.09 W
San José de Jáchal	252	30.14 S	68.45 W
San José de la Esquina	252	33.06 S	61.42 W
San José de la Parilla	234	23.44 N	104.07 W
San José de la Popa	196	26.10 N	100.47 W
San José de las Flores	234	17.20 N	95.24 W
San José de las Lajas	240p	22.58 N	82.09 W
San José del Cabo	232	23.03 N	109.41 W
San José del Guaviare	246	2.35 N	72.38 W
San José de Llanetes	234	22.55 N	103.16 W
San José de los Molinos	248	13.57 S	75.41 W
San José de Lourdes	234	23.18 N	103.01 W
San José de Mayo	258	34.20 S	56.42 W
San José de Ocoa	238	18.33 N	70.30 W
San José de Ocuné	246	4.15 N	70.20 W
San José de Raíces	232	24.35 N	100.14 W
San José de Río Chico	246	10.18 N	65.59 W
San José de Sisa	248	6.37 S	76.39 W
San José de Tiznados	246	9.23 N	67.33 W
San Jose Hills ⛰[2]	280	34.04 N	117.49 W
San Jose Island I	196	28.10 N	96.45 W
San José Iturbide	234	21.00 N	100.23 W
San Jose Municipal Airport ⊠	226	37.22 N	121.56 W
San Jose State University ψ[2]	282	37.20 N	121.53 W
San Juan, Arg.	252	31.32 S	68.31 W
San Juan, Guat.	236	15.52 N	88.53 W
San Juan, Méx.	196	29.34 N	104.36 W
San Juan, Méx.	232	27.47 N	103.57 W
San Juan, Perú	248	15.21 S	75.10 W
San Juan, P.R.	240m	18.28 N	66.07 W
San Juan □[4]	252	31.00 S	69.00 W
San Juan □[6]	224	48.34 N	122.59 W
San Juan ≃, Arg.	252	32.17 S	67.22 W
San Juan ≃, B.C., Can.	224	48.34 N	124.24 W
San Juan ≃, Col.	246	4.03 N	77.27 W
San Juan ≃, Méx.	232	26.22 N	98.51 W
San Juan ≃, N.A.	236	10.56 N	83.42 W
San Juan ≃, Perú	248	13.27 S	76.11 W
San Juan ≃, Pil.	269f	14.35 N	121.01 E
San Juan ≃, S.A.	246	1.11 N	78.33 W
San Juan ≃, U.S.	200	37.18 N	110.28 W
San Juan ≃, Ven.	246	10.14 N	62.38 W
San Juan, Bahía de C	240m	18.27 N	66.07 W
San Juan, Cabezas de ≻	240m	18.23 N	65.37 W
San Juan, Cabo ≻, Arg.	254	54.44 S	63.44 W
San Juan, Cabo ≻, Gui. Ecu.	152	1.08 N	9.23 E
San Juan, Embalse de ⊛[1]	34	40.30 N	4.15 W
San Juan, Pasaje de Џ	240m	18.24 N	65.37 W
San Juan, Pico ▲	240p	21.59 N	80.09 W
San Juan, Port C	224	48.34 N	124.27 W
San Juan, Punta ≻	174z	27.03 S	109.22 W
San Juan Basin ⊻[1]	200	36.15 N	108.20 W
San Juan Bautista, Esp.	34	39.05 N	1.30 E
San Juan Bautista, Méx.	196	26.58 N	101.24 W
San Juan Bautista, Para.	252	26.38 S	57.10 W
San Juan Bautista, Calif., U.S.	226	36.51 N	121.32 W
San Juan Bautista Cuicatlán	234	17.48 N	96.58 W
San Juan Bautista State Historical Park ♠	226	36.51 N	121.31 W
San Juan Capistrano	228	33.30 N	117.40 W
San Juan Capistrano Mission ψ[1]	228	33.31 N	117.40 W
San Juan Colorado	234	16.32 N	97.55 W
San Juan Cotzal	236	15.26 N	91.01 W
San Juan Creek ≃, Calif., U.S.	226	35.40 N	120.22 W
San Juan Creek ≃, Calif., U.S.	228	33.28 N	117.41 W
San Juan de Abajo	234	20.48 N	105.13 W
San Juan de Aragón, Bosque ♠	286a	19.28 N	99.04 W
San Juan de Aragón, Zoológico de ♠	286a	19.28 N	99.05 W
San Juan de Colón	246	8.02 N	72.16 W
San Juan de Dios	286c	10.35 N	66.55 W
San Juan de Guadalupe	232	24.38 N	102.44 W
San Juan [de la Maguana]	238	18.48 N	71.14 W
San Juan de la Vega	234	20.38 N	100.46 W
San Juan del César	246	10.46 N	73.01 W
San Juan de Lima, Punta ≻	234	18.36 N	103.42 W
San Juan de Limay	236	13.10 N	86.37 W
San Juan del Monte	269f	14.36 N	121.02 E
San Juan del Norte	236	10.55 N	83.42 W
San Juan del Oro ≃	248	21.02 S	65.19 W
San Juan de los Cayos	246	11.10 N	68.25 W
San Juan de los Lagos	234	21.15 N	102.18 W
San Juan de los Lagos ≃	234	21.18 N	102.33 W
San Juan de los Morros	246	9.55 N	67.21 W
San Juan del Piray	248	20.27 S	64.09 W
San Juan del Río, Méx.	232	24.47 N	104.27 W
San Juan del Río, Méx.	234	20.23 N	100.00 W

FRANÇAIS

Nom	Page	Lat.°′	Long.°′ W=Ouest
San Juan del Río ≃	234	20.40 N	99.30 W
San Juan del Salado	234	23.18 N	101.56 W
San Juan del Sur	236	11.15 N	85.52 W
San Juan de Micay ≃	246	3.05 N	77.32 W
San Juan de Payara	246	7.39 N	67.36 W
San Juan de Pirque	286e	33.38 S	70.30 W
San Juan de Sabinas	196	27.55 N	101.18 W
San Juan Despí	266d	41.22 N	2.04 E
San Juan de Vilasar	266d	41.30 N	2.24 E
San Juan Evangelista	234	17.54 N	95.08 W
San Juanico, Isla I	234	21.43 N	106.38 W
San Juanillo	236	10.02 N	85.44 W
San Juan Island I	224	48.32 N	123.05 W
San Juan Islands II	224	48.36 N	122.50 W
San Juan Islands National Historical Park ♠	224	48.28 N	123.00 W
San Juan Ixcaquixtla	234	18.27 N	97.49 W
San Juan Ixtayopan ➔[8]	286a	19.14 N	99.00 W
San Juan Lachao	234	16.14 N	97.09 W
San Juan Mazatlán	234	17.02 N	95.25 W
San Juan Mountains ⛰	200	37.35 N	107.10 W
San Juan Naval Station ■	240m	18.28 N	66.06 W
San Juan Nepomuceno, Col.	246	9.57 N	75.05 W
San Juan Nepomuceno, Para.	252	26.06 S	55.58 W
San Juan Peyotán	234	22.24 N	104.21 W
San Juan Quiahije	234	16.17 N	97.20 W
San Juan Sacatepéquez	236	14.43 N	90.39 W
San Juan Sayultepec	234	17.27 N	97.17 W
San Juan y Martínez	240p	22.16 N	83.50 W
San Judas	234	23.15 N	100.52 W
San Julián, Arg.	254	49.18 S	67.43 W
San Julián, Méx.	234	21.01 N	102.10 W
San Julian, Quebrada ≃	286c	10.37 N	66.51 W
San Justo, Arg.	252	30.47 S	60.35 W
San Justo, Arg.	258	34.40 S	58.33 W
San Justo, Aeródromo ⊠	288	34.44 S	58.36 W
San Justo Desvern	266d	41.23 N	2.05 E
Sankanbiriwa ▲	150	8.56 N	10.48 W
Sankaranayinārkovil	122	9.10 N	77.33 E
Sankarani ≃	150	12.01 N	8.19 W
Sankarpur	272b	22.51 N	88.27 E
Sānkdaha	126	22.46 N	89.10 E
Sankertown	214	40.28 N	78.35 W
Sankeshwar	122	16.16 N	74.29 E
Sankey Brook ≃	262	53.22 N	2.38 W
Sankh ≃	124	22.15 N	84.48 E
Sankheda	120	22.10 N	73.35 E
Sankosh ≃	124	26.24 N	89.47 E
Sānkrāil	272b	22.34 N	88.14 E
Sankt Aegyd am Neuwalde	61	47.52 N	15.35 E
Sankt Andrä	61	46.46 N	14.49 E
Sankt Andrä vor dem Hagenthale	264b	48.19 N	16.13 E
Sankt Andreasberg	54	51.43 N	10.31 E
Sankt Anton am Arlberg	58	47.08 N	10.16 E
Sankt Antönien	58	46.58 N	9.49 E
Sankt Bartholomä ψ[1]	64	47.32 N	12.58 E
Sankt Blasien	58	47.46 N	8.07 E
Sankt Christopher-Nevis → Saint Kitts-Nevis □[2]	238	17.20 N	62.45 W
Sankt Egidien	54	50.47 N	12.36 E
Sankt Gallen, Öst.	61	47.41 N	14.37 E
Sankt Gallen, Schw.	58	47.25 N	9.23 E
Sankt Gallen □[3]	58	47.10 N	9.08 E
Sankt Gallenkirch	58	47.01 N	9.59 E
Sankt Georgen, B.R.D.	58	47.59 N	7.47 E
Sankt Georgen, B.R.D.	58	48.07 N	8.20 E
Sankt Georgen, Öst.	61	46.43 N	14.55 E
Sankt Georgen im Attergau	64	47.56 N	13.29 E
Sankt Gertraud → Santa Gertrude	64	46.29 N	10.53 E
Sankt Gertrud ➔[8]	54	53.52 N	10.47 E
Sankt Gilgen	64	47.46 N	13.22 E
Sankt Goar	56	50.09 N	7.43 E
Sankt Goarshausen	56	50.09 N	7.44 E
Sankt Helena → Saint Helena □[2]	8	15.57 S	5.42 W
Sankt Hubert	56	51.23 N	6.26 E
Sankt Ingbert	56	49.17 N	7.06 E
Sankt Jakob → San Giacomo	64	46.57 N	11.36 E
Sankt Jakob im Lesachtal	64	46.41 N	12.56 E
Sankt Jakob in Defereggen	64	46.55 N	12.20 E
Sankt Johann → San Giovanni	64	46.38 N	11.44 E
Sankt Johann am Tauern	61	47.22 N	14.29 E
Sankt Johann im Pongau	64	47.21 N	13.12 E
Sankt Johann im Walde	64	46.54 N	12.37 E
Sankt Johann in Tirol	64	47.31 N	12.26 E
Sankt Leonhard → San Leonardo	64	46.49 N	11.15 E
Sankt Leonhard im Pitztal	58	47.04 N	10.51 E
Sankt Lorenz ➔[8]	52	53.51 N	10.40 E
Sankt Lorenz → Saint Lawrence ≃	176	49.30 N	67.00 W
Sankt Lorenzen → San Lorenzo di Sebato	64	46.47 N	11.54 E
Sankt Lorenzen im Lesachtal	64	46.42 N	12.47 E
Sankt Lorenz-Golf → Saint Lawrence, Gulf of C	186	48.00 N	62.00 W
Sankt Lorenz-Insel → Saint Lawrence Island I	180	63.30 N	170.30 W
Sankt Mang	58	47.44 N	10.21 E
Sankt Märgen	58	48.00 N	8.05 E
Sankt Margrethen	58	47.27 N	9.36 E
Sankt Martin	64	47.28 N	13.23 E
Sankt Martin in Gsies → San Martino in Casies	64	46.49 N	12.14 E
Sankt Mauritz	52	51.57 N	7.39 E
Sankt Michael im Lungau	64	47.06 N	13.38 E
Sankt Michel → Mikkeli	26	61.41 N	27.15 E
Sankt Moritz	58	46.30 N	9.50 E
Sankt Niklaus → San Nicolò d'Ultimo, It.	64	46.30 N	10.55 E
Sankt Niklaus, Schw.	58	46.11 N	7.48 E
Sankt Oswald	60	48.54 N	13.25 E
Sankt Paul im Lavanttal	61	46.42 N	14.52 E
Sankt Peter, B.R.D.	30	54.18 N	8.38 E
Sankt Peter, B.R.D.	58	48.01 N	8.01 E

PORTUGUÊS

Nome	Página	Lat.°′	Long.°′ W=Oeste
Sankt Peter ψ[1]	263	51.37 N	7.12 E
Sankt Peterzell	58	47.19 N	9.11 E
Sankt Pölten	61	48.12 N	15.37 E
Sankt-Quirinus-Dom ψ[1]	263	51.12 N	6.42 E
Sankt Stefan an der Gail	64	46.37 N	13.31 E
Sankt Ulrich → Ortisei	64	46.34 N	11.40 E
Sankt Valentin	61	48.10 N	14.32 E
Sankt Veit an der Glan	61	46.46 N	14.21 E
Sankt Veit im Pongau	64	47.20 N	13.09 E
Sankt-Viktors-Dom ψ[1]	263	51.40 N	6.27 E
Sankt Vincent → Saint Vincent □[1]	241h	13.15 N	61.12 W
Sankt Wallburg → Santa Valburga	64	46.33 N	11.00 E
Sankt Wendel	56	49.28 N	7.10 E
Sankt-Willibrodi-Dom ψ[1]	263	51.40 N	6.37 E
Sankt Wolfgang im Salzkammergut	64	47.44 N	13.27 E
Sankuru ≃	152	4.17 S	20.25 E
San Lázaro	252	22.10 S	57.55 W
San Lázaro, Cabo ≻	232	24.48 N	112.19 W
San Lazzaro di Savena	64	44.28 N	11.25 E
San Leandro	226	37.43 N	122.09 W
San Leandro Creek ≃	282	37.45 N	122.12 W
San Leo	66	43.54 N	12.21 E
San Leon	222	29.29 N	94.55 W
San Leonardo (Sankt Leonhard), It.	64	46.49 N	11.15 E
San Leonardo, Méx.	196	27.28 N	104.55 W
San Leonardo ≃	70	37.59 N	13.41 E
San Leone	70	37.16 N	13.35 E
San Lope	246	6.12 N	71.56 W
San Lorenzo, Arg.	252	28.08 S	58.46 W
San Lorenzo, Arg.	252	32.45 S	60.44 W
San Lorenzo, Bol.	248	21.26 S	64.47 W
San Lorenzo, Ec.	246	1.17 N	78.50 W
San Lorenzo, Hond.	236	13.25 N	87.27 W
San Lorenzo, It.	68	38.01 N	15.50 E
San Lorenzo, Méx.	196	25.37 N	97.35 W
San Lorenzo, Méx.	232	25.32 N	102.11 W
San Lorenzo, Nic.	236	12.23 N	85.40 W
San Lorenzo, P.R.	240m	18.11 N	65.58 W
San Lorenzo, Calif., U.S.	226	37.41 N	122.08 W
San Lorenzo, Ven.	246	9.47 N	71.04 W
San Lorenzo ≃, Méx.	232	24.15 N	107.24 W
San Lorenzo ≃, Méx.	286a	19.28 N	99.16 W
San Lorenzo → Saint Lawrence ≃, N.A.	176	49.30 N	67.00 W
San Lorenzo ≃, Calif., U.S.	226	36.58 N	122.01 W
San Lorenzo, Bahía C	236	13.19 N	87.30 W
San Lorenzo, Cabo ≻	246	1.04 S	80.56 W
San Lorenzo, Cerro ▲	254	47.37 S	72.19 W
San Lorenzo, Golfo del → Saint Lawrence, Gulf of C	186	48.00 N	62.00 W
San Lorenzo, Isla I, Méx.	232	28.38 N	112.51 W
San Lorenzo, Isla I, Perú	248	12.05 S	77.15 W
San Lorenzo Bellizzi	68	39.53 N	16.20 E
San Lorenzo Creek ≃, Calif., U.S.	226	36.12 N	120.38 W
San Lorenzo Creek ≃, Calif., U.S.	282	37.39 N	122.09 W
San Lorenzo de El Escorial	34	40.35 N	4.09 W
San Lorenzo de la Parrilla	34	39.51 N	2.22 W
San Lorenzo del Vallo	68	39.40 N	16.18 E
San Lorenzo di Sebato (Sankt Lorenzen)	64	46.47 N	11.54 E
San Lorenzo in Campo	66	43.36 N	12.56 E
San Lorenzo Nuovo	66	42.41 N	11.54 E
San Lorenzo Tenoxtitlan ⊥	234	17.44 N	94.45 W
San Lorenzo Tezonco ➔[8]	286a	19.18 N	99.04 W
San Luca	68	38.09 N	16.04 E
Sanlúcar de Barrameda	34	36.47 N	6.21 W
Sanlúcar la Mayor	34	37.23 N	6.12 W
San Lucas, Bol.	248	20.06 S	65.07 W
San Lucas, Ec.	246	3.45 S	79.15 W
San Lucas, Méx.	232	24.13 N	103.04 W
San Lucas, Méx.	232	22.53 N	109.54 W
San Lucas, Calif., U.S.	226	36.08 N	121.01 W
San Lucas, Cabo ≻	232	22.52 N	109.53 W
San Lucas, Serranía de ⛰	246	8.00 N	74.20 W
San Luis, Arg.	252	33.18 S	66.21 W
San Luis, Cuba	240p	22.17 N	83.46 W
San Luis, Cuba	240p	20.12 N	75.51 W
San Luis, Guat.	236	16.14 N	89.27 W
San Luis, Ariz., U.S.	200	32.29 N	114.47 W
San Luis, Colo., U.S.	200	37.12 N	105.25 W
San Luis, Ven.	246	11.07 N	69.42 W
San Luis □[4]	252	34.00 S	66.00 W
San Luis ➔[8]	286b	23.05 N	82.20 W
San Luis, Arroyo ≃	258	34.10 S	57.44 W
San Luis, Laguna ⊛	248	13.45 S	64.00 W
San Luis, Sierra de ⛰	252	32.40 S	65.50 W
San Luis Acatlán	234	16.48 N	98.45 W
San Luis Creek ≃	200	37.42 N	105.44 W
San Luis de la Loma	234	17.18 N	100.55 W
San Luis de la Paz	234	21.18 N	100.31 W
San Luis del Cordero	232	25.26 N	104.18 W
San Luis del Palmar	252	27.31 S	58.34 W
San Luis Gonzaga	232	24.55 N	111.16 W
San Luis Gonzaga, Bahía C	232	29.48 N	114.22 W
San Luis Jilotepeque	236	14.39 N	89.44 W
San Luis Obispo	226	35.17 N	120.40 W
San Luis Obispo □[6]	226	35.30 N	120.30 W
San Luis Pass C	222	29.05 N	95.08 W
San Luis Peak ▲	200	37.59 N	106.56 W
San Luis Potosí	234	22.09 N	100.59 W
San Luis Potosí □[3]	234	22.30 N	100.30 W
San Luis Reservoir ⊛[1]	226	37.07 N	121.05 W
San Luis Rey	228	33.14 N	117.20 W
San Luis Rey ≃	204	33.12 N	117.24 W
San Luis Rey, Mission ψ[1]	228	33.14 N	117.20 W
San Luis Río Colorado	232	32.29 N	114.48 W
San Luis Soyatlán	234	20.12 N	103.18 W
San Luis State Recreation Area ♠	226	37.04 N	121.05 W
San Luis Valley V	200	37.25 N	106.00 W
Sanluri	71	39.34 N	8.54 E
San Macario	266b	45.36 N	8.47 E
Sanmaiden	270	34.39 N	135.51 E
San Mamete	58	46.02 N	9.04 E
San Mango d'aquino	68	39.03 N	16.11 E
San Manuel, Méx.	234	17.37 N	93.24 W
San Manuel, Ariz., U.S.	200	32.36 N	110.38 W
San Marcello Pistoiese	66	44.03 N	10.47 E
San Marcial, Punta ≻	232	25.30 N	111.01 W
San Marco, Chile	286e	33.37 S	70.38 W
San Marco, Esp.	34	43.13 N	8.17 W
San Marco, Capo ≻	70	37.30 N	13.01 E
San Marco Argentano	68	39.33 N	16.07 E
San Marco dei Cavoti	68	41.18 N	14.53 E
San Marco in Lamis	68	41.43 N	15.38 E
San Marco la Catola	68	41.31 N	15.00 E
San Marcos, Chile	252	30.56 S	71.03 W
San Marcos, Col.	246	8.39 N	75.08 W
San Marcos, C.R.	236	9.40 N	84.01 W
San Marcos, El Sal.	236	13.39 N	89.11 W
San Marcos, Guat.	236	14.58 N	91.48 W
San Marcos, Hond.	236	14.24 N	88.56 W
San Marcos, Hond.	236	15.17 N	88.23 W
San Marcos, Méx.	234	20.02 N	99.20 W
San Marcos, Méx.	234	16.48 N	99.21 W
San Marcos, Méx.	234	20.47 N	104.11 W
San Marcos, Calif., U.S.	228	33.09 N	117.10 W
San Marcos, Tex., U.S.	196	29.53 N	97.57 W
San Marcos □[5]	236	15.00 N	91.55 W
San Marcos ≃	196	29.29 N	97.28 W
San Marcos, Estadio de ♠	286d	12.04 S	77.05 W
San Marcos, Isla I	232	27.13 N	112.06 W
San Marcos, Laguna de ⊛	234	20.17 N	103.33 W
San Marcos, Universidad de ψ[2]	286d	12.03 S	77.05 W
San Marcos Arteaga	234	17.45 N	97.58 W
San Marcos de Colón	236	13.26 N	86.48 W
San Marino, S. Mar.	66	43.55 N	12.28 E
San Marino, Calif., U.S.	280	34.07 N	118.07 W
San Marino □[1]	22		
	66	43.56 N	12.25 E
San Martín, Arg.	252	33.04 S	68.28 W
San Martín, Arg.	252	29.14 S	65.46 W
San Martín → General San Martín, Arg.	258	34.34 S	58.32 W
San Martín, Col.	246	3.42 N	73.42 W
San Martin, Calif., U.S.	226	37.05 N	121.37 W
San Martín, Ur.	258	33.45 S	57.37 W
San Martín □[5]	248	7.00 S	76.50 W
San Martín ≃	248	13.08 S	63.43 W
San Martín, Arroyo ≃	258	33.49 S	57.44 W
San Martín, Cerro ▲[1]	234	18.19 N	94.48 W
San Martín, Cuchilla ⛰[2]	258	33.45 S	57.54 W
San Martín, Lago (Lago O'Higgins) ⊛	254	49.00 S	72.40 W
San Martín, Volcán ▲[1]	234	18.33 N	95.12 W
San Martín de Bolaños	234	21.29 N	103.58 W
San Martín [de las Pirámides]	234	19.42 N	98.50 W
San Martín de las Vacas	196	25.30 N	101.20 W
San Martín del Boracho, Sierra ⛰	200	30.45 N	105.42 W
San Martín de los Andes	254	40.10 S	71.21 W
San Martín de Valdeiglesias	34	40.21 N	4.24 W
San Martín Hidalgo	234	20.27 N	103.57 W
San Martino, It.	62	45.27 N	8.47 E
San Martino (Sankt Martin), It.	64	46.47 N	11.13 E
San Martino Buon Albergo	64	45.25 N	11.05 E
San Martino d'agri	68	40.14 N	16.04 E
San Martino di Castrozza	64	46.16 N	11.48 E
San Martino di Lupari	64	45.39 N	11.51 E
San Martino in Badia (Saint Martin)	64	46.41 N	11.52 E
San Martino in Casies (Sankt Martin in Gsies)	64	46.49 N	12.14 E
San Martino in Rio	64	44.44 N	10.48 E
San Martino Valle Caudina	68	41.01 N	14.39 E
San Martín Peras	234	17.19 N	98.15 W
San Marzano di San Giuseppe	68	40.27 N	17.30 E
San Marzano sul Sarno	66	40.46 N	14.35 E
San Mateo, Esp.	34	40.28 N	0.11 E
San Mateo, Méx.	234	22.59 N	103.30 W
San Mateo, Calif., U.S.	226	37.35 N	122.19 W
San Mateo, Fla., U.S.	192	29.36 N	81.35 W
San Mateo, N. Mex., U.S.	200	35.20 N	107.39 W
San Mateo, Ven.	246	9.45 N	64.33 W
San Mateo □[6]	226	37.25 N	122.20 W
San Mateo ≃	286a	19.30 N	99.17 W
San Mateo Atenco	234	19.16 N	99.32 W
San Mateo Bridge ➔[5]	282	37.36 N	122.13 W
San Mateo Canyon V	228	33.23 N	117.36 W
San Mateo Creek ≃	282	37.34 N	122.18 W
San Mateo del Mar	234	16.12 N	95.00 W
San Mateo Ixtatán	236	15.50 N	91.29 W
San Mateo Memorial Park ♠	282	37.17 N	122.18 W
San Mateo Point ≻	228	33.23 N	117.36 W
San Matías	248	16.22 S	58.24 W
San Matías, Golfo C	254	41.30 S	64.15 W
San Mauro Castelverde	70	37.55 N	14.11 E
San Mauro Forte	68	40.29 N	16.15 E
San Mauro la Bruca	68	40.07 N	15.17 E
San Mauro Marchesato	68	39.06 N	16.56 E
San Mauro Torinese	62	45.06 N	7.46 E
San Medi, Arroyo de ≃	266d	41.28 N	2.06 E
Sanmen I	100	22.26 N	114.38 E
San Menaio	68	41.56 N	15.58 E
Sanmendao I	100	29.55 N	121.52 E
Sanmenwan C	100	29.08 N	121.44 E
Sanmenxia (Shanxian)	102	34.45 N	111.05 E
San Michele all'Adige	64	46.12 N	11.08 E
San Michele al Tagliamento	64	45.46 N	12.59 E
San Michele di Ganzaria	70	37.17 N	14.26 E
San Michele Mondovì	62	44.23 N	7.54 E
San Michele Salentino	68	40.38 N	17.37 E
San Miguel → General Sarmiento, Arg.	258	34.33 S	58.43 W
San Miguel, Bol.	248	16.42 S	61.01 W
San Miguel, Chile	286e	33.30 S	70.40 W
San Miguel, Ec.	246	1.44 S	79.01 W
San Miguel, El Sal.	236	13.29 N	88.11 W
San Miguel, Esp.	148	28.05 N	16.37 W
San Miguel, Méx.	234	23.23 N	98.10 W
San Miguel, Pan.	246	8.27 N	78.56 W
San Miguel, Calif., U.S.	226	35.45 N	120.42 W
San Miguel ≃, Bol.	248	13.52 S	63.56 W
San Miguel ≃, Méx.	200	30.51 N	110.45 W
San Miguel ≃, Méx.	232	29.16 N	110.53 W
San Miguel ≃, Méx.	234	18.16 N	100.40 W
San Miguel ≃, S.A.	248	19.15 S	59.20 W
San Miguel ≃, Colo., U.S.	200	38.23 N	108.48 W
San Miguel, Cerro ▲[2]	248	19.19 S	60.36 W
San Miguel, Golfo de C	246	8.22 N	78.17 W
San Miguel, Volcán de ▲[1]	236	13.26 N	88.16 W
San Miguel Arcángel, Mission ψ[1]	226	35.44 N	120.42 W
San Miguel Bay C	116	13.50 N	123.10 E
San Miguel Canoa	234	19.09 N	98.05 W
San Miguel Chimalapa	234	16.43 N	94.41 W
San Miguel Creek ≃	196	28.30 N	98.25 W
San Miguel de Allende	234	20.55 N	100.45 W
San Miguel de Cruces	232	24.25 N	105.51 W
San Miguel del Monte	258	35.27 S	58.48 W
San Miguel de Pallaques	248	7.00 S	78.51 W
San Miguel de Salcedo	246	1.02 S	78.34 W
San Miguel de Tucumán	252	26.49 S	65.13 W
San Miguel el Alto	234	21.01 N	102.21 W
San Miguel Island I, Pil.	116	13.23 N	123.48 E
San Miguel Island I, Calif., U.S.	204	34.02 N	120.22 W
San Miguel Islands II	116	7.45 N	118.28 E
San Miguelito	236	11.24 N	84.54 W
San Miguel Ixtahuacán	236	15.15 N	91.45 W
San Miguel Mountain ▲	228	32.42 N	116.56 W
San Miguel Octopan	234	20.34 N	100.44 W
San Miguel [o San Graciano]	232	29.10 N	101.28 W
San Miguel Talea de Castro	234	17.22 N	96.15 W
San Miguel Tenango	234	16.16 N	95.36 W
San Miguel Totolapan	234	18.08 N	100.23 W
San Miniato	66	43.41 N	10.51 E
San Murezzan → Sankt Moritz	58	46.30 N	9.50 E
Sannahed	40	59.06 N	15.09 E
Sannan	96	35.04 N	135.02 E
Sannār	140	13.33 N	33.38 E
Sannazzaro de'Burgondi	62	45.06 N	8.54 E
Sannicandro di Bari	68	41.00 N	16.48 E
Sannicandro Garganico	68	41.50 N	15.34 E
Sannicola	68	40.05 N	18.04 E
San Nicola, Isola I	68	42.07 N	15.30 E
San Nicola, Monte ▲	68	38.35 N	16.24 E
San Nicola Arcella	68	39.51 N	15.48 E
San Nicola da Crissa	68	38.40 N	16.17 E
San Nicolás, Esp.	148	27.59 N	15.46 W
San Nicolás, Hond.	236	15.00 N	88.45 W
San Nicolás, Méx.	234	16.26 N	98.32 W
San Nicolas, Méx.	234	19.05 N	101.07 W
San Nicolás ≃	234	19.40 N	105.14 W
San Nicolás de Bari	240p	22.47 N	81.55 W
San Nicolás de los Arroyos	252	33.20 S	60.13 W
San Nicolás de los Garzas	196	25.45 N	100.18 W
San Nicolas Island I	204	33.15 N	119.31 W
San Nicolò di Comelico	64	46.35 N	12.31 E
San Nicolò d'Ultimo (Sankt Nikolaus)	64	46.30 N	10.55 E
San Nicolò Ferrarese	64	44.42 N	11.42 E
San Nicolò Gerrei	71	39.30 N	9.18 E
Sannieshof	158	26.30 S	25.47 E
Sannikova, Proliv Џ	74	74.30 N	140.00 E
Şannīn, Jabal ▲	132	33.57 N	35.52 E
Sannio, Monti del ⛰	66	41.30 N	14.45 E
Sanniquellie	150	7.22 N	8.43 W
Sannohe	92	40.22 N	141.15 E
Sannois	261	48.58 N	2.15 E
Sannō-tōge ⋈	94	37.04 N	139.45 E
Sannūr, Wādī V	142	28.58 N	31.03 E
Sano	94	36.19 N	139.35 E
Sanok	30	49.34 N	22.13 E
Sânon ≃	58	48.38 N	6.20 E
San Onofre	246	9.44 N	75.32 W
San Onofre Mountain ▲	228	33.22 N	117.30 W
San Pablo, Chile	254	40.24 S	73.01 W
San Pablo, Col.	246	1.40 N	77.00 W
San Pablo, Pil.	116	14.04 N	121.19 E
San Pablo, Pil.	116	7.40 N	123.27 E
San Pablo, Calif., U.S.	226	37.57 N	122.21 W
San Pablo ≃	236	7.51 N	81.10 W
San Pablo, Point ≻	282	37.58 N	122.26 W
San Pablo, Punta ≻	232	27.14 N	114.29 W
San Pablo Autopan	234	19.21 N	99.40 W
San Pablo Balleza	232	26.57 N	106.21 W
San Pablo Bay C	226	38.06 N	122.22 W
San Pablo Creek ≃	282	37.58 N	122.30 W
San Pablo de Tiquina	248	16.13 S	68.52 W
San Pablo Huitzo	234	17.15 N	96.52 W
San Pablo Huixtepec	234	16.50 N	96.46 W
San Pablo Ostotepec ➔[8]	286a	19.11 N	99.04 W
San Pablo Reservoir ⊛[1]	282	37.56 N	122.15 W
San Pablo Ridge ▲	282	37.55 N	122.15 W
San Pablo Strait Џ	282	37.58 N	122.26 W
San Pablo Villa de Mitla	234	16.55 N	96.24 W
Sanpāda	272c	19.04 N	73.01 E
San Pancrazio Salentino	68	40.25 N	17.50 E
San Paolo	64	46.29 N	11.15 E
San Paolo di Civitate	68	41.44 N	15.15 E
San Pasqual Indian Reservation ➔[4]	228	33.12 N	116.58 W
San Pedrillo, Punta ≻	236	8.39 N	83.45 W
San Pedro, Bol.	248	14.20 S	64.50 W
San Pedro, Chile	252	33.54 S	71.28 W
San Pedro, Chile	252	21.57 S	68.34 W
San Pedro, Col.	246	9.24 N	75.04 W
San Pedro, C.R.	236	9.56 N	84.03 W
San Pedro, Para.	252	24.07 S	56.59 W
San Pedro, Tex., U.S.	196	27.48 N	97.41 W
San Pedro, Ur.	258	34.21 S	57.51 W
San Pedro, Ven.	246	8.50 N	71.58 W
San Pedro □[5]	252	24.15 S	56.30 W
San Pedro ➔[8], Cuba	286b	23.03 N	82.27 W
San Pedro ➔[8], Calif., U.S.	228	33.44 N	118.18 W
San Pedro ≃, Cuba	240p	21.09 N	78.30 W
San Pedro ≃, Méx.	234	21.45 N	105.30 W
San Pedro ≃, N.A.	200	32.59 N	110.47 W
San Pedro ≃, N.A.	232	17.45 N	91.25 W
San Pedro ≃, Ven.	286c	10.35 N	66.48 W
San Pedro, Arroyo ≃	258	34.21 S	57.56 W
San Pedro, Point ≻, Calif., U.S.	282	37.35 N	122.31 W
San Pedro, Point ≻, Calif., U.S.	282	37.59 N	122.27 W
San Pedro, Punta ≻	252	25.30 S	70.38 W
San Pedro, Volcán ▲[1]	252	21.53 S	68.25 W
San Pedro Apóstol	234	16.44 N	96.44 W
San Pedro Ayampuc	236	14.47 N	90.27 W
San Pedro Bay C, Pil.	116	11.11 N	125.05 E
San Pedro Bay C, Calif., U.S.	228	33.45 N	118.11 W
San Pedro Breakwater ➔[5]	280	33.42 N	118.16 W
San Pedro Carchá	236	15.29 N	90.16 W
San Pedro Channel Џ	228	33.35 N	118.25 W
San Pedro Creek ≃, Calif., U.S.	282	37.36 N	122.30 W
San Pedro Creek ≃, Tex., U.S.	222	31.34 N	95.14 W
San Pedro de Arriba	258	34.18 S	57.47 W
San Pedro de Atacama	252	22.55 S	68.13 W
San Pedro de Buena Vista	248	18.13 S	65.59 W
San Pedro de la Cueva	232	29.18 N	109.44 W
San Pedro de las Colonias	232	25.45 N	102.59 W
San Pedro del Gallo	232	25.33 N	104.18 W
San Pedro de Lloc	248	7.26 S	79.31 W
San Pedro del Norte	236	13.04 N	84.33 W
San Pedro del Paraná	252	26.46 S	56.15 W
San Pedro de Macorís	238	18.27 N	69.18 W
San Pedro de Premiá	266d	41.31 N	2.21 E
San Pedro El Alto	234	16.01 N	96.28 W
San Pedro Huamelula	234	16.02 N	95.40 W
San Pedro Jicayán	234	16.25 N	97.59 W
San Pedro Juchatengo	234	16.21 N	97.06 W
San Pedro Mártir ➔[8]	286a	19.16 N	99.10 W
San Pedro Mártir, Sierra ⛰	232	30.45 N	115.13 W
San Pedro Mixtepec	234	16.00 N	97.07 W
San Pedro Peaks ⛰	200	36.07 N	106.49 W
San Pedro Piedra Gorda	234	22.27 N	102.21 W
San Pedro Pinula	236	14.40 N	89.51 W
San Pedro Sacatepéquez	236	14.58 N	91.46 W
San Pedro Sula	236	15.27 N	88.02 W
San Pedro Tapanatepec	234	16.21 N	94.12 W
San Pedro Xalostoc	286a	19.32 N	99.05 W
San Pedro y Miquelón → Saint Pierre and Miquelon □[2]	186	46.55 N	56.10 W
San Pelayo	246	8.58 N	75.51 W
San Pellegrino Terme	62	45.50 N	9.40 E
San Piero a Grado	66	43.41 N	10.21 E
San Piero in Bagno	66	43.51 N	11.58 E
San Pierre	216	41.12 N	86.53 W
San Pietro (Sankt Peter)	64	47.01 N	12.03 E
San Pietro, Isola di I	71	39.08 N	8.17 E
San Pietro a Maida	68	38.50 N	16.20 E
San Pietro di Cadore	64	46.34 N	12.35 E
San Pietro in Casale	64	44.42 N	11.24 E
San Pietro in Gu	64	45.37 N	11.40 E
San Pietro in Guarano	68	39.20 N	16.19 E
San Pietro in Palazzi	66	43.20 N	10.30 E
San Pietro in Vaticano ψ[1]	267a	41.54 N	12.28 E
San Pietro Vara	62	44.20 N	9.35 E
San Pietro Vernotico	68	40.29 N	18.00 E
San Pitch ≃	200	39.03 N	111.51 W
Sanpoil ≃	202	47.53 N	118.41 W
San Polo d'Enza	64	44.38 N	10.26 E
San Quentin	282	37.56 N	122.29 W
San Quentin State Prison ψ	282	37.56 N	122.28 W
Sanquhar	44	55.22 N	3.56 W
San Quintín, Bahía de C	232	30.22 N	115.55 W
San Quintín, Cabo ≻	232	30.21 N	116.00 W
San Quintín, Ventisquero ⛉	254	46.52 S	74.05 W
San Quírico de Tarrasa	266d	41.32 N	2.05 E
San Quirico d'Orcia	66	43.03 N	11.36 E
Sanqutan	100	27.17 N	115.04 E
San Rafael, Arg.	252	34.36 S	68.20 W
San Rafael, Chile	252	35.19 S	71.32 W
San Rafael, Méx.	232	25.01 N	100.33 W
San Rafael, Méx.	232	28.34 N	111.42 W
San Rafael, Méx.	234	20.12 N	96.51 W
San Rafael, Calif., U.S.	226	37.59 N	122.31 W
San Rafael, N. Mex., U.S.	200	35.06 N	107.53 W
San Rafael, Ven.	246	10.58 N	71.44 W
San Rafael ≃	200	38.47 N	110.07 W
San Rafael Bay C	282	37.58 N	122.28 W
San Rafael de Arriba	232	31.05 N	116.05 W
San Rafael de las Tortillas	196	26.49 N	99.32 W
San Rafael del Norte	236	13.12 N	86.06 W
San Rafael del Sur	236	11.51 N	86.27 W
San Rafael Hills ⛰[2]	280	34.10 N	118.12 W
San Rafael Mountains ⛰	204	34.45 N	119.50 W
San Rafael Oriente	236	13.23 N	88.21 W
San Rafael Swell ⛰[1]	200	38.40 N	110.45 W
San Ramón, Arg.	252	27.42 S	64.17 W
San Ramón, Bol.	248	13.17 S	64.43 W
San Ramón, C.R.	236	10.06 N	84.28 W
San Ramon, Calif., U.S.	282	37.47 N	121.59 W
San Ramón, Ur.	252	34.18 S	55.58 W
San Ramón, Bahía C	232	30.45 N	116.03 W
San Ramon Creek ≃	282	37.54 N	122.03 W
San Ramón de la Nueva Orán	252	23.08 S	64.20 W
San Ramon Valley V	282	37.46 N	121.58 W
San-rei ▲	96	33.50 N	133.59 E
San Remo, Austl.	169	38.31 S	145.22 E
San Remo, It.	62	43.49 N	7.46 E
San Remo, N.Y., U.S.	210	40.54 N	73.13 W

≃ River	Fluss	Río	Rivière	Rio	
≍ Canal	Kanal	Canal	Canal	Canal	
Waterfall, Rapids	Wasserfall, Stromschnellen	Cascada, Rápidos	Chute d'eau, Rapides	Cascata, Rápidos	
Џ Strait	Meeresstrasse	Estrecho	Détroit	Estreito	
C Bay, Gulf	Bucht, Golf	Bahía, Golfo	Baie, Golfe	Baía, Golfo	
⊛ Lake, Lakes	See, Seen	Lago, Lagos	Lac, Lacs	Lago, Lagos	
Swamp	Sumpf	Pantano	Marais	Pântano	
⛉ Ice Features, Glacier	Eis- und Gletscherformen	Accidentes Glaciales	Formes glaciaires	Acidentes Glaciares	
Other Hydrographic Features	Andere Hydrographische Objekte	Otros Elementos Hidrográficos	Autres données hydrographiques	Outros Elementos Hidrográficos	
✦ Submarine Features	Untermeerische Objekte	Accidentes Submarinos	Formes de relief sous-marin	Acidentes Submarinos	
□ Political Unit	Politische Einheit	Unidad Política	Entité politique	Unidade Política	
ψ Cultural Institution	Kulturelle Institution	Institución Cultural	Institution culturelle	Instituição Cultural	
⊥ Historical Site	Historische Stätte	Sitio Histórico	Site historique	Sítio Histórico	
♠ Recreational Site	Erholungs- und Ferienort	Sitio de Recreo	Centre de loisirs	Sítio de Lazer	
⊠ Airport	Flughafen	Aeropuerto	Aéroport	Aeroporto	
■ Military Installation	Militäranlage	Instalación Militar	Installation militaire	Instalação Militar	
➔ Miscellaneous	Verschiedenes	Misceláneo	Divers	Miscelânea	

Name	Page	Lat.	Long.
San Roberto	68	38.18 N	15.44 E
San Rodrigo ≃	196	28.54 N	100.37 W
San Román ≃	236	16.21 N	90.22 W
San Román, Cabo ≻	246	12.12 N	70.00 W
San Roque, Arg.	252	28.34 S	58.43 W
San Roque, Arg.	252	30.17 S	68.41 W
San Roque, Esp.	34	36.13 N	5.24 W
San Roque, Cabo → São Roque, Cabo de ≻	250	5.29 S	35.16 W
San Rosendo	252	37.16 S	72.43 W
San Rufo	68	40.26 N	15.28 E
San Saba	196	31.12 N	98.43 W
San Saba ≃	196	31.15 N	98.35 W
San Saep, Khlong ≅	269a	13.45 N	100.36 E
San Salvador, Arg.	252	31.37 S	58.30 W
San Salvador, Arg.	252	29.16 S	57.31 W
San Salvador, El Sal.	236	13.42 N	89.12 W
San Salvador (Watling Island) I	238	24.02 N	74.28 W
San Salvador ≃	258	33.37 S	58.06 W
San Salvador, Cuchilla de ⋀[2]	258	33.56 S	57.45 W
San Salvador, Isla I	246a	0.14 S	90.45 W
San Salvador, Volcán de ∧[1]	236	13.44 N	89.17 W
San Salvador de Jujuy	252	24.11 S	65.18 W
San Salvador el Seco	234	19.08 N	97.39 W
San Salvatore, Monte ∧	70	37.50 N	14.03 E
San Salvatore Monferrato	62	44.59 N	8.34 E
San Salvatore Telesino	68	41.14 N	14.30 E
San Salvo	66	42.03 N	14.44 E
Sansanding Dam ◆[6]	150	13.44 N	6.00 W
Sansanné-Mango	150	10.21 N	0.28 E
Sans Bois Creek ≃	196	35.20 N	94.50 W
San Sebastián, El Sal.	236	13.44 N	88.50 W
San Sebastián, Esp.	34	43.19 N	1.59 W
San Sebastián, Guat.	236	14.34 N	91.39 W
San Sebastián, Hond.	236	14.24 N	88.42 W
San Sebastián, Méx.	234	20.47 N	104.51 W
San Sebastián, Méx.	234	21.26 N	102.21 W
San Sebastián, Méx.	234	22.10 N	104.19 W
San Sebastián, P.R.	240m	18.20 N	66.59 W
San Sebastián, Bahía C	254	53.12 S	68.20 W
San Sebastián de la Gomera	148	28.06 N	17.06 W
San Sebastián de los Reyes	266a	40.33 N	3.38 W
San Sebastián de Yalí	236	13.18 N	86.11 W
San Sebastiano Curone	62	44.47 N	9.04 E
San Secondo Parmense	64	44.55 N	10.14 E
Sansepolcro	66	43.34 N	12.08 E
Sanserre	50	47.22 N	2.50 E
San Severino Lucano	68	40.01 N	16.08 E
San Severino Marche	66	43.13 N	13.10 E
San Severo	68	41.41 N	15.23 E
Sanshawan C	100	26.35 N	119.50 E
San Sigismondo (Sankt Sigmund)	64	46.49 N	11.46 E
San Simeon	226	35.39 N	121.11 W
San Simon, Méx.	204	30.30 N	115.58 W
San Simon, Ariz., U.S.	200	32.16 N	109.14 W
San Simón ≃, Bol.	248	13.13 S	63.31 W
San Simon ≃, Ariz., U.S.	200	32.50 N	109.39 W
San Simon Wash ∨	200	31.45 N	112.25 W
San Siro ◆[8]	266b	45.29 N	9.07 E
Sanski Most	36	44.46 N	16.40 E
Sanso	150	11.43 N	6.51 W
San Solano	252	31.29 S	65.55 W
Sansom Park Village	222	32.48 N	97.24 W
Sanson	172	40.13 S	175.25 E
San Sosti	68	39.40 N	16.02 E
Sanspareil	60	49.59 N	11.19 E
San Sperate	71	39.21 N	9.00 E
Sans Souci.	274a	33.59 S	151.08 E
Sans-Souci ⊥	238	19.37 N	72.12 W
Sanssouci, Schloss ʊ	54	52.24 N	13.02 E
San Stefano Ticino	266b	45.29 N	8.55 E
Santa ≃	248	8.58 S	78.39 W
Santa, Isla de I	248	9.02 S	78.40 W
Santa Adélia	255	21.16 S	48.48 W
Santa Albertina	255	20.02 S	50.44 W
Santa Amalia	34	39.01 N	6.01 W
Santa Ana, Arg.	252	27.22 S	55.34 W
Santa Ana, Bol.	248	18.43 S	58.44 W
Santa Ana, Bol.	248	13.45 S	65.35 W
Santa Ana, Bol.	248	15.31 S	67.30 W
Santa Ana, Col.	246	9.19 N	74.35 W
Santa Ana, Ec.	246	1.13 S	80.23 W
Santa Ana, El Sal.	236	13.59 N	89.34 W
Santa Ana, Méx.	232	30.33 N	111.07 W
Santa Ana, Méx.	232	24.04 N	100.30 W
Santa Ana, Méx.	234	19.19 N	98.11 W
Santa Ana, Méx.	234	18.15 N	93.28 W
Santa Ana, Calif., U.S.	228		
	280	33.43 N	117.54 W
Santa Ana ≃	228	33.38 N	117.57 W
Santa Ana, Volcán de ∧[1]	236	13.50 N	89.38 W
Santa Ana Canyon ∨	280	33.53 N	117.43 W
Santa Ana de Barcelona	246	9.19 N	64.39 W
Santa Ana de Chena	286e	33.34 S	70.47 W
Santa Ana Heights	228	33.39 N	117.54 W
Santa Ana Island I	175e	10.50 S	162.28 E
Santa Ana Marine Corps Air Facility ■	280	33.43 N	117.50 W
Santa Ana Mountains ⋀	228	33.45 N	117.35 W
Santa Ana Pacueco	234	20.22 N	102.00 W
Santa Anita	234	20.33 N	103.27 W
Santa Anita Canyon ∨	280	34.12 N	118.01 W
Santa Anita Park ♠	280	34.08 N	118.03 W
Santa Anna	196	31.45 N	99.19 W
Santa Apolonia	196	25.38 N	97.59 W
Santa Bábara	255	11.57 S	38.58 W
Santa Bárbara, Chile	252	37.40 S	72.01 W
Santa Bárbara, Col.	246	5.53 N	75.35 W
Santa Bárbara, Hond.	236	14.53 N	88.14 W
Santa Bárbara, Méx.	232	26.48 N	105.49 W
Santa Bárbara, Méx.	234	18.52 N	101.07 W
Santa Barbara, Calif., U.S.	204	34.25 N	119.42 W
Santa Bárbara, Ven.	246	7.47 N	71.10 W
Santa Bárbara, Ven.	246	3.57 N	67.06 W
Santa Bárbara □[5]	236	15.10 N	88.20 W
Santa Barbara □[6]	228	33.28 N	119.02 W
Santa Bárbara ≃	248	16.58 S	61.39 W
Santa Bárbara, Morro de ∧	287a	22.57 S	43.28 W
Santa Bárbara, Ribeirão ≃	256	22.00 S	45.43 W
Santa Bárbara, Túnel ◆[5]	287a	22.56 S	43.12 W
Santa Barbara Channel U	204	34.15 N	119.55 W
Santa Bárbara de Samaná	238	19.13 N	69.19 W
Santa Bárbara do Monte Verde	256	21.58 S	43.42 W
Santa Bárbara do Sul	252	28.22 S	53.15 W
Santa Barbara Island I	228	33.28 N	119.02 W
Santa Branca	256	23.24 S	45.53 W
Santaca	158	26.36 S	32.32 E
Santa Catalina, Arg.	252	21.57 S	66.04 W
Santa Catalina, Pan.	236	8.47 N	81.20 W
Santa Catalina, Pil.	116	9.20 N	122.51 E
Santa Catalina, Ur.	258	33.49 S	57.29 W
Santa Catalina, Arroyo ≃	288	34.46 S	58.27 W
Santa Catalina, Gulf of C	228	33.20 N	117.45 W
Santa Catalina, Isla I	232	25.40 N	110.47 W
Santa Catalina, Laguna @	288	34.46 S	58.27 W
Santa Catalina de Armara	34	43.02 N	8.49 W
Santa Catalina Island I	228	33.23 N	118.24 W
Santa Catarina, Méx.	204	31.37 N	115.48 W
Santa Catarina, Méx.	232	25.41 N	100.28 W
Santa Catarina, Méx.	234	19.18 N	101.10 W
Santa Catarina □[3]	252	27.00 S	50.00 W
Santa Catarina, Ilha de I	252	27.36 S	48.30 W
Santa Catarina Yosonotú	234	16.59 N	97.39 W
Santa Caterina di Pittinuri	71	40.06 N	8.30 E
Santa Caterina Valfurva	64	46.25 N	10.29 E
Santa Caterina Villarmosa	70	37.35 N	14.02 E
Santa Cecília	252	26.56 S	50.27 W
Santa Cesarea Terme	68	40.02 N	18.29 E
Santa Clara, Arg.	252	29.33 S	68.31 W
Santa Clara, Col.	246	2.43 S	69.43 W
Santa Clara, Cuba	240p	22.24 N	79.58 W
Santa Clara, Méx.	232	29.17 N	107.01 W
Santa Clara, Méx.	234	19.41 N	102.30 W
Santa Clara, Calif., U.S.	226	37.21 N	121.57 W
Santa Clara, Utah, U.S.	200	37.08 N	113.39 W
Santa Clara □[6]	226	37.20 N	121.53 W
Santa Clara ≃, Calif., U.S.	228	34.14 N	119.16 W
Santa Clara ≃, Utah, U.S.	200	37.05 N	113.36 W
Santa Clara, Bahía de C	240p	23.05 N	80.30 W
Santa Clara, University of ʊ[2]	282	37.21 N	121.56 W
Santa Clara Coatitla	286a	19.34 N	99.04 W
Santa Clara de Olimar	252	32.55 S	54.58 W
Santa Clara Valley ∨	226	37.10 N	121.40 W
Santa Coloma de Cervelló	266d	41.22 N	2.01 E
Santa Coloma de Farnés	34	41.52 N	2.40 E
Santa Coloma de Gramanet	266d	41.27 N	2.13 E
Santa Comba Dão	34	40.24 N	8.08 W
Santa Cristina	64	46.34 N	11.43 E
Santa Cristina d'aspromonte	68	38.15 N	15.58 E
Santa Croce	64	46.05 N	12.18 E
Santa Croce, Capo ≻	70	37.14 N	15.15 E
Santa Croce, Lago di @	64	46.10 N	12.20 E
Santa Croce Camerina	70	36.50 N	14.31 E
Santa Croce del Sannio	68	41.23 N	14.43 E
Santa Croce di Magliano	66	41.42 N	14.59 E
Santa Cruz, Arg.	254	50.01 S	68.31 W
Santa Cruz, Bol.	248	17.48 S	63.10 W
Santa Cruz, Bra.	250	6.13 S	36.01 W
Santa Cruz, Bra.	255	19.56 S	40.09 W
Santa Cruz, Chile	252	34.38 S	71.22 W
Santa Cruz, C.R.	236	10.16 N	85.36 W
Santa Cruz, Méx.	200	31.14 N	110.35 W
Santa Cruz, Méx.	234	23.05 N	97.50 W
Santa Cruz, Perú	248	6.37 S	78.57 W
Santa Cruz, Pil.	116	15.46 N	119.55 E
Santa Cruz, Pil.	116	13.29 N	122.02 E
Santa Cruz, Pil.	116	13.04 N	120.43 E
Santa Cruz (Tubajon), Pil.	116	10.19 N	125.33 E
Santa Cruz, Pil.	116	14.17 N	121.25 E
Santa Cruz, Pil.	116	6.50 N	125.25 E
Santa Cruz, Calif., U.S.	226	36.58 N	122.01 W
Santa Cruz □[4]	254	49.00 S	70.00 W
Santa Cruz □[5]	248	17.30 S	61.30 W
Santa Cruz □[6]	226	36.58 N	122.01 W
Santa Cruz ◆[8], Bhārat	272c	19.05 N	72.50 E
Santa Cruz ◆[8], Bra.	256	22.56 S	43.41 W
Santa Cruz ≃, Arg.	254	50.08 S	68.20 W
Santa Cruz ≃, Cuba	286b	23.04 N	82.29 W
Santa Cruz, Ilha I	287a	22.52 S	43.07 W
Santa Cruz, Isla I	246a	0.38 S	90.23 W
Santa Cruz, Sierra de ⋀	236	15.40 N	89.15 W
Santa Cruz Basin ✣[1]	14	13.00 S	163.00 E
Santa Cruz Cabrália	255	16.17 S	39.02 W
Santa Cruz da Graciosa	148a	39.05 N	28.01 W
Santa Cruz das Flores	148a	39.27 N	31.07 W
Santa Cruz da Vitória	255	14.57 S	39.48 W
Santa Cruz de el Seibo	238	18.46 N	69.02 W
Santa Cruz de Goiás	255	17.19 S	48.30 W
Santa Cruz de Juventino Rosas	234	20.39 N	101.00 W
Santa Cruz de la Palma	148	28.41 N	17.45 W
Santa Cruz de la Zarza	34	39.58 N	3.10 W
Santa Cruz del Norte	240p	23.09 N	81.55 W
Santa Cruz del Quiché	236	15.02 N	91.08 W
Santa Cruz del Sur	240p	20.43 N	78.00 W
Santa Cruz de Mudela	34	38.38 N	3.28 W
Santa Cruz de Tenerife	148	28.27 N	16.14 W
Santa Cruz International Airport ⊠	272c	19.05 N	72.52 E
Santa Cruz Island I	204	34.01 N	119.45 W
Santa Cruz Islands II	14	11.00 S	166.15 E
Santa Cruz Meyehualco ◆[8]	286a	19.20 N	99.03 W
Santa Cruz Mountains ⋀	226	37.15 N	122.00 W
Santa Cruz Point ≻	116	15.44 N	119.52 E
Santa Cruz Tacache Mina	234	17.51 N	98.07 W
Santadang ≅	106	31.23 N	119.15 E
Santadi	71	39.05 N	8.43 E
Santa Domenica Talao	68	39.49 N	15.51 E
Santa Domenica Vittoria	70	37.55 N	14.58 E
Santa Eduviges	286e	33.33 S	70.39 W
Santa Elena, Arg.	252	30.57 S	59.48 W
Santa Elena, Ec.	246	2.14 S	80.51 W
Santa Elena, El Sal.	236	13.22 N	88.25 W
Santa Elena, Méx.	196	27.59 N	103.56 W
Santa Elena, Méx.	232	27.28 N	102.33 W
Santa Elena, Méx.	234	18.39 N	101.34 W
Santa Elena, Bahía de C	246	2.06 S	80.53 W
Santa Elena, Golfo De C	236	10.59 N	85.50 W
Santa Elena, Punta ≻, C.R.	236	10.54 N	85.57 W
Santa Elena, Punta ≻, Ec.	246	2.11 S	81.00 W
Santa Elena del Gomero	286e	33.29 S	70.46 W
Santa Elena de Uairén	246	4.37 N	61.08 W
Santa Elisabetta	70	37.26 N	13.33 E
Santa Emilia	286e	33.23 S	70.39 W
Santa Eugenia	34	42.33 N	9.00 W
Santa Eulalia, Esp.	34	40.34 N	1.19 W
Santa Eulalia, Guat.	236	15.45 N	91.29 W
Santa Eulalia del Río	34	38.59 N	1.31 E
Santa Fe, Arg.	252	31.38 S	60.42 W
Santa Fé, Bra.	255	15.40 S	51.16 W
Santa Fé, Bra.	255	23.01 S	51.48 W
Santa Fé, Cuba	240p	21.45 N	82.45 W
Santa Fe, Esp.	34	37.11 N	3.43 W
Santa Fé, Hond.	236	15.55 N	86.05 W
Santa Fe, Pan.	236	8.31 N	81.05 W
Santa Fe, Mo., U.S.	219	39.22 N	91.49 W
Santa Fe, N. Mex., U.S.	200	35.42 N	106.57 W
Santa Fe □[4]	252	31.00 S	61.00 W
Santa Fé ◆[8]	286b	23.05 N	82.31 W
Santa Fe ≃, Fla., U.S.	192	29.53 N	82.53 W
Santa Fe ≃, N. Mex., U.S.	200	35.36 N	106.20 W
Santa Fé, Aeropuerto ⊠	286b	23.04 N	82.28 W
Santa Fe, Isla I	246a	0.49 S	90.04 W
Santa Fé, Ribeirão ≃	287b	23.24 S	46.48 W
Santa Fe Baldy ∧	200	35.50 N	105.46 W
Santa Fe Dam ◆[6]	280	34.07 N	117.58 W
Santa Fé do Sul	255	20.13 S	50.56 W
Santa Fe Flood Control Basin ≚[1]	280	34.07 N	117.58 W
Santa Fe Springs	280	33.56 N	118.04 W
Santa Filomena	250	9.07 S	45.56 W
Santa Fiora	66	42.50 N	11.35 E
Santa Flavia	70	38.05 N	13.31 E
Sant'Agata Bolognese	64	44.40 N	11.08 E
Sant'Agata de'Goti	68	41.05 N	14.30 E
Sant'Agata del Bianco	68	38.05 N	16.05 E
Sant'Agata di Militello	70	38.04 N	14.38 E
Sant'Agata di Puglia	68	41.09 N	15.23 E
Sant'Agata Feltria	66	43.52 N	12.12 E
Sant'Agata sul Santerno	66	44.26 N	11.51 E
Santa Gertrude (Sankt Gertraud)	64	46.29 N	10.53 E
Santa Gertrudis	196	26.09 N	98.44 W
Santa Giusta, Stagno di @	71	39.52 N	8.35 E
Sant'Agostino	64	44.48 N	11.23 E
Sāntāhār	124	24.48 N	88.59 E
Santa Helena	250	2.14 S	45.18 W
Santa Helena de Goiás	255	17.43 S	50.35 W
Santa Inês	255	13.17 S	39.48 W
Santa Inés, Bahía C	232	26.59 N	111.59 W
Santa Inés, Isla I	254	53.45 S	72.45 W
Santa Inés Ahuatempan	234	18.25 N	98.01 W
Santa Inés Zacatelco	234	19.13 N	98.14 W
Santa Iria de Azóia	266c	38.51 N	9.05 W
Santa Isabel, Ec.	246	3.21 S	79.19 W
Santa Isabel → Malabo, Gui. Ecu.	152	3.45 N	8.47 E
Santa Isabel, P.R.	240m	17.58 N	66.24 W
Santa Isabel I	175e	8.00 S	159.00 E
Santa Isabel ≃	236	15.59 N	90.00 W
Santa Isabel, Pico de ∧	152	3.35 N	8.46 E
Santa Isabel de las Lajas	240p	22.25 N	80.18 W
Santa Isabel de Sihuas	248	16.20 S	72.06 W
Santa Isabel do Araguaia	250	6.07 S	48.19 W
Santa Isabel do Rio Prêto	256	22.14 S	44.05 W
Santa Julia	286e	33.30 S	70.38 W
Santa Juliana	255	19.19 S	47.32 W
Sant'Alberto	66	44.32 N	12.09 E
Santa Leopoldina	255	20.06 S	40.32 W
Sant'Alfio	70	37.44 N	15.08 E
Santāl Parganas □[5]	124	24.30 N	87.20 E
Sāntalpur	120	23.45 N	71.10 E
Santa Luce	66	43.28 N	10.34 E
Santa Lucía, Arg.	252	28.59 S	59.06 W
Santa Lucía, Arg.	252	31.32 S	68.29 W
Santa Lucía, Cuba	240p	22.40 N	83.58 W
Santa Lucía, Cuba	240p	20.59 N	77.25 W
Santa Lucía, Cuba	240p	21.02 N	76.00 W
Santa Lucia, It.	64	46.28 N	10.21 E
Santa Lucía, Ur.	258	34.27 S	56.24 W
Santa Lucía, Ven.	246	8.07 N	69.46 W
Santa Lucía → Saint Lucia □[1]	241f	13.53 N	60.58 W
Santa Lucía ≃	258	34.48 S	56.22 W
Santa Lucia,, Cabo → Saint Lucia, Cape ≻	158	28.25 S	32.25 E
Santa Lucía, Cuchilla ⋀[2]	258	34.09 S	56.11 W
Santa Lucía Chico ≃	258	34.21 S	56.20 W
Santa Lucía Cotzumalguapa	236	14.20 N	91.01 W
Santa Lucia Creek ≃	226	36.13 N	121.30 W
Santa Lucia del Mela	70	38.09 N	15.17 E
Santa Lucia di Piave	64	45.51 N	12.17 E
Santa Lucia Range ⋀	226	36.00 N	121.20 W
Santa Lugarda, Punta ≻	232	26.44 N	109.48 W
Santa Luísa de Baixo	256	22.46 S	45.49 W
Santaluz	250	11.15 S	39.22 W
Santa Luzia, Bra.	250	6.53 S	36.56 W
Santa Luzia, Port.	34	37.44 N	8.24 W
Santa Luzia I	150a	16.46 N	24.45 W
Santa Magdalena	252	34.30 S	63.56 W
Santa Magdalena, Isla I	232	24.55 N	112.15 W
Santa Margarita	226	35.23 N	120.37 W
Santa Margarita ≃	228	33.14 N	117.25 W
Santa Margarita, Isla de I	232	24.27 N	111.50 W
Santa Margarita Lake @[1]	226	35.20 N	120.28 W
Santa Margarita Mountains ⋀	228	33.30 N	117.25 W
Santa Margherita di Belice	70	37.41 N	13.01 E
Santa Margherita Ligure	62	44.20 N	9.12 E
Santa María, Arg.	252	26.41 S	66.02 W
Santa Maria, Bra.	252	29.41 S	53.48 W
Santa María, C.R.	236	9.39 N	83.57 W
Santa Maria, C.V.	150a	16.36 N	22.54 W
Santa María, Méx.	196	28.02 N	101.38 W
Santa María, Pan.	236	8.07 N	80.40 W
Santa María, Perú	286d	11.59 S	77.00 W
Santa María, P.R.	240m	18.09 N	65.26 W
Santa Maria, Schw.	58	46.36 N	10.24 E
Santa Maria, Schw.	58	46.16 N	9.09 E
Santa Maria, Calif., U.S.	204	34.57 N	120.26 W
Santa Maria I	148a	36.58 N	25.06 W
Santa Maria ≃, Bra.	252	21.50 S	54.53 W
Santa Maria ≃, Bra.	252	29.48 S	54.56 W
Santa María ≃, Méx.	232	31.00 N	107.14 W
Santa María ≃, Méx.	234	21.48 N	99.10 W
Santa María ≃, Pan.	236	8.06 N	80.29 W
Santa Maria ≃, Ariz., U.S.	200	34.19 N	34.31 W
Santa María, Bahía de C	232	25.04 N	108.06 W
Santa Maria, Cabo → Sainte-Marie, Cap ≻, Madag.	157b	25.36 S	45.08 E
Santa María, Cabo ≻, Ur.	252	34.40 S	54.10 W
Santa Maria, Cabo de ≻, Ang.	152	13.25 S	12.32 E
Santa Maria, Cabo de ≻, Moç.	158	26.05 S	32.58 E
Santa Maria, Cabo de ≻, Port.	34	36.58 N	7.54 W
Santa Maria, Cape ≻	238	23.41 N	75.19 W
Santa María, Cayo I	240p	22.40 N	79.00 W
Santa María, Cerro ∧	286d	11.56 S	76.57 W
Santa Maria, Giogo di (Pass Umbrail))(	64	46.34 N	10.25 E
Santa María, Isla I, Chile	252	37.02 S	73.33 W
Santa María, Isla I, Ec.	246a	1.17 S	90.26 W
Santa Maria, Isola I	71	41.17 N	9.22 E
Santa María, Laguna de @	232	31.07 N	107.16 W
Santa Maria, Ribeirão ≃, Bra.	250	7.10 S	49.13 W
Santa Maria, Ribeirão ≃, Bra.	250	8.08 S	43.02 W
Santa María, Volcán ∧[1]	236	14.45 N	91.33 W
Santa María Ajoloapan	234	19.58 N	99.03 W
Santa Maria a Monte	66	43.42 N	10.42 E
Santa Maria a Vico	68	41.02 N	14.29 E
Santa Maria Capua Vetere	68	41.05 N	14.15 E
Santa María Chimalapa	234	16.55 N	94.41 W
Santa María Colotepec	234	15.53 N	96.55 W
Santa Maria da Boa Vista	250	8.49 S	39.49 W
Santa Maria da Vitória	255	13.24 S	44.12 W
Santa María de Barbará	266d	41.31 N	2.08 E
Santa Maria degli Angeli	66	43.03 N	12.34 E
Santa María de Ipire	246	8.49 N	65.19 W
Santa Maria de Itabira	255	19.27 S	43.08 W
Santa Maria del Cedro	68	39.45 N	15.50 E
Santa Maria della Versa	62	44.59 N	9.18 E
Santa Maria delle Grazie ʊ[1]	266b	45.27 N	9.10 E
Santa María del Oro	232	25.56 N	105.22 W
Santa María de los Ángeles	234	22.11 N	103.14 W
Santa María del Refugio	234	23.44 N	101.14 W
Santa María del Río	234	21.48 N	100.45 W
Santa María del Valle	234	20.54 N	102.22 W
Santa Maria di Galeria ◆[8]	267a	42.01 N	12.19 E
Santa Maria di Leuca, Capo ≻	68	39.47 N	18.22 E
Santa Maria di Licodia	70	37.37 N	14.53 E
Santa Maria do Suaçuí	255	18.12 S	42.25 W
Santa Maria Island I	175f	14.15 S	167.30 E
Santa María Jalapa [del Marqués]	234	16.30 N	95.28 W
Santa María la Real de Nieva	34	41.04 N	4.24 W
Santa Maria Madalena	255	21.57 S	42.01 W
Santa María Magdalena [Cahuacán]	234	19.38 N	99.25 W
Santa Maria Maggiore	58	46.08 N	8.28 E
Santa Maria Maggiore ʊ[1]	267a	41.53 N	12.30 E
Santa Maria Nuova	66	43.29 N	13.18 E
Santa-Maria-Siché	36	41.52 N	8.59 E
Santa María Tulpetlac	286a	19.34 N	99.03 W
Santa María Zoquitlán	234	16.33 N	96.23 W
Santa Marinella	66	42.02 N	11.51 E
Santa Marta, Col.	246	11.15 N	74.13 W
Santa Marta, Guat.	236	13.58 N	91.18 W
Santa Marta, Cabo de ≻	152	13.52 S	12.25 E
Santa Marta Grande, Cabo de ≻	252	28.38 S	48.45 W
Sant'Ambrogio	64	45.31 N	10.50 E
Santa Mónica, Méx.	196	28.12 N	100.37 W
Santa Monica, Calif., U.S.	228	34.01 N	118.30 W
Santa Mónica ◆[8]	286c	10.29 N	66.53 W
Santa Monica Bay C	228	33.54 N	118.25 W
Santa Monica Mountains ⋀	228	34.05 N	118.40 W
Santa Monica Municipal Airport ⊠	280	34.01 N	118.27 W
Santa Monica State Beach ♠	280	34.01 N	118.30 W
Santan	112	0.03 S	117.28 E
Santana ◆[8]	287b	23.29 S	46.38 W
Santana ≃, Bra.	250	8.35 S	44.01 W
Santana ≃, Bra.	255	19.43 S	51.02 W
Santana, Cachoeira L	255	14.45 S	49.10 W
Santana, Coxilha de ⋀[2]	252	31.15 S	55.15 W
Santana, Ribeirão ≃	250	9.47 S	50.13 W
Santana, Serra de ∧	256	22.30 S	42.35 W
Santana de Parnáiba □[7]	287b	23.27 S	46.54 W
Santana do Livramento	252	30.53 S	55.31 W
Sant'Anastasia	68	40.52 N	14.24 E
Santander, Col.	246	3.01 N	76.28 W
Santander, Esp.	34	43.28 N	3.48 W
Santander □[5]	246	7.00 N	73.15 W
Santander, Norte de □[3]	238	9.15 N	73.00 W
Santander Jiménez	232	24.13 N	98.28 W
Sant'andrea, Isola I	68	40.03 N	17.57 E
Sant'Andrea Frius	71	39.29 N	9.10 E
Santa Nella	226	37.03 N	121.02 W
Santanésia	256	22.30 S	43.49 W
Santang	100	28.44 N	116.32 E
Sant'angelo, Castel ⊥	267a	41.55 N	12.28 E
Sant'Angelo, Monte ∧	267a	41.56 N	12.49 E
Sant'Angelo dei Lombardi	68	40.56 N	15.11 E
Sant'Angelo in Vado	66	43.40 N	12.25 E
Sant'Angelo Lodigiano	62	45.14 N	9.24 E
Sant'Angelo Muxard	70	37.28 N	13.32 E
Sant'Angelo Romano	267a	42.02 N	12.42 E
Santanghu	102	44.13 N	93.22 E
Santanilla, Islas II	238	17.25 N	83.55 W
Santa Ninfa	70	37.46 N	12.53 E
Sant'Antimo	68	40.56 N	14.14 E
Sant'antine, Nuraghe ⊥	71	40.29 N	8.46 E
Sant'Antioco	71	39.04 N	8.27 E
Sant'antioco, Isola di I	71	39.02 N	8.25 E
Sant'Antonio Abate	68	40.43 N	14.32 E
Sant'Antonio di Santadi	71	39.43 N	8.29 E
Sant'Antonio Morignone	64	46.24 N	10.21 E
Santañy	34	39.22 N	3.07 E
Santa Panagia, Capo ≻	70	37.07 N	15.18 E
Santa Paula	228	34.21 N	119.04 W
Santa Paula Creek ≃	228	34.21 N	119.03 W
Santa Perpetua de Moguda	266d	41.32 N	2.11 E
Santapogue Creek ≃	276	40.40 N	73.21 W
Santa Pola, Cabo de ≻	34	38.12 N	0.31 W
Sant'Apollinare in Classe ʊ[1]	66	44.22 N	12.15 E
Santaquin	200	39.59 N	111.47 W
Santa Quitéria, Bra.	250	4.20 S	40.10 W
Santa Quiteria, Esp.	266d	41.34 N	2.19 E
Santa Quitéria do Maranhão	250	3.31 S	42.32 W
Sant'Arcangelo	68	40.15 N	16.17 E
Santarcangelo di Romagna	66	44.04 N	12.27 E
Sant'Arcangelo Trimonte	68	41.10 N	14.56 E
Santarém, Bra.	250	2.26 S	54.42 W
Santarém, Port.	34	39.14 N	8.41 W
Santarém □[5]	266c	38.50 N	8.56 W
Santarém Novo	250	0.56 S	47.23 W
Santa Rita, Bra.	250	7.08 S	34.58 W
Santa Rita, Bra.	287a	22.41 S	43.28 W
Santa Rita, Col.	246	1.04 N	73.58 W
Santa Rita, Hond.	236	15.09 N	87.53 W
Santa Rita, Méx.	196	27.29 N	100.33 W
Santa Rita, Pil.	116	11.27 N	124.56 E
Santa Rita, Ven.	246	10.32 N	71.32 W
Santa Rita, Riacho ≃	255	12.49 S	43.21 W
Santa Rita de Caldas	256	22.02 S	46.20 W
Santa Rita de Catuna	252	30.57 S	66.13 W
Santa Rita de Jacutinga	256	22.09 S	44.06 W
Santa Rita del Rucio	234	23.04 N	100.19 W
Santa Rita Park	226	37.03 N	120.36 W
Santa Rosa, Arg.	252	23.22 S	64.30 W
Santa Rosa, Arg.	252	28.02 S	67.37 W
Santa Rosa, Arg.	252	36.37 S	64.17 W
Santa Rosa, Arg.	252	32.20 S	65.12 W
Santa Rosa, Bol.	248	14.10 S	66.53 W
Santa Rosa, Bol.	248	17.07 S	63.35 W
Santa Rosa, Bol.	248	10.36 S	67.25 W
Santa Rosa, Col.	246	2.31 N	68.13 W
Santa Rosa, C.R.	236	10.51 N	85.38 W
Santa Rosa, Ec.	246	3.27 S	79.58 W
Santa Rosa, Méx.	204	31.59 N	116.45 W
Santa Rosa, Méx.	234	22.18 N	104.24 W
Santa Rosa, Méx.	234	19.41 N	100.02 W
Santa Rosa, Para.	248	21.46 S	61.43 W
Santa Rosa, Para.	252	26.52 S	56.49 W
Santa Rosa, Calif., U.S.	226	38.26 N	122.43 W
Santa Rosa, N. Mex., U.S.	196	34.57 N	104.41 W
Santa Rosa, Tex., U.S.	196	26.15 N	97.50 W
Santa Rosa, Ur.	258	34.30 S	56.03 W
Santa Rosa, Ven.	246	8.26 N	69.24 W
Santa Rosa, Ven.	286c	10.30 N	66.46 W
Santa Rosa □[5]	236	14.10 N	90.18 W
Santa Rosa, Mount ∧[2]	174p	13.32 N	144.55 E
Santa Rosa, Presa @[1]	234	20.58 N	103.35 W
Santa Rosa Beach	194	30.23 N	86.14 W
Santa Rosa Creek ≃	226	35.34 N	121.06 W
Santa Rosa de Aguán	236	15.57 N	85.43 W
Santa Rosa de Amanadona	246	1.29 N	66.55 W
Santa Rosa de Cabal	246	4.52 N	75.38 W
Santa Rosa [de Copán]	236	14.47 N	88.46 W
Santa Rosa de Huechuraba	286e	33.21 S	70.41 W
Santa Rosa de la Roca	248	16.04 S	61.32 W
Santa Rosa de Leales	252	27.09 S	65.15 W
Santa Rosa de Lima	236	13.37 N	87.53 W
Santa Rosa de Locobe	286e	33.26 S	70.33 W
Santa Rosa del Palmar	248	16.54 S	62.24 W
Santa Rosa de Osos	246	6.39 N	75.28 W
Santa Rosa de Río Primero	252	31.09 S	63.23 W
Santa Rosa de Sucumbíos	246	0.22 N	77.10 W
Santa Rosa de Viterbo	246	5.53 N	72.59 W
Santa Rosa Indian Reservation ◆[4]	204	33.35 N	116.35 W
Santa Rosa Island I, Calif., U.S.	204	33.58 N	120.06 W
Santa Rosa Island I, Fla., U.S.	194	30.22 N	86.55 W
Santa Rosa Jáuregui	234	20.44 N	100.27 W
Santa Rosalía, Méx.	196	26.08 N	98.59 W
Santa Rosalía, Méx.	232	27.19 N	112.17 W
Santa Rosalía, Ven.	246	9.02 N	69.01 W
Santa Rosalía, Bahía C	232	28.37 N	114.13 W
Santa Rosa Range ⋀	204	41.00 N	117.40 W
Santa Rosa Wash ∨	200	33.00 N	112.00 W
Santa Rosita	286d	12.03 S	76.59 W
Sant'Arsenio	68	40.28 N	15.29 E
Šantarskije Ostrova II	89	55.00 N	137.36 E
Santa Severa	66	42.02 N	11.57 E
Santa Severina	68	39.09 N	16.55 E
Santa Sofia	66	43.57 N	11.54 E
Santa Susana	228	34.16 N	118.43 W
Santa Susana Mountains ⋀	228	34.20 N	118.42 W
Santa Sylvina	252	27.49 S	61.09 W
Santa Tecla → Nueva San Salvador	236	13.41 N	89.17 W
Santa Teresa, Arg.	252	33.26 S	60.47 W
Santa Teresa, Bra.	255	19.55 S	40.36 W
Santa Teresa, Méx.	196	29.34 N	104.39 W
Santa Teresa, Méx.	200	30.52 N	111.33 W
Santa Teresa, Méx.	234	22.28 N	104.44 W
Santa Teresa ≃	255	11.47 S	48.37 W
Santa Teresa, Embalse de @[1]	34	40.40 N	5.30 W
Santa Teresa de Goiás	255	13.38 S	49.01 W
Santa Teresa de lo Ovalle	286e	33.23 S	70.47 W
Santa Teresa del Tuy	246	10.14 N	66.40 W
Santa Teresa di Riva	70	37.57 N	15.22 E
Santa Teresa Gallura	71	41.14 N	9.11 E
Santa Teresinha	255	12.45 S	39.32 W
Santa Valburga (Sankt Wallburg)	64	46.33 N	11.00 E
Santa Venerina	70	37.41 N	15.08 E
Santa Venetia	226	38.01 N	122.31 W
Santa Vitória	255	18.50 S	50.08 W
Santa Vitória do Palmar	252	33.31 S	53.21 W
Santa Vittoria, Monte ∧	71	39.45 N	9.18 E
Santa Vittoria in Matenano	66	43.01 N	13.29 E
Santa Ynez ≃	204	35.41 N	120.36 W
Santa Ynez Canyon ∨	280	34.04 N	118.34 W
Santa Ysabel Indian Reservation ◆[4]	204	33.11 N	116.41 W
Santee	228	32.50 N	116.58 W
Santee ≃	192	33.14 N	79.28 W
Santee Dam ◆[6]	192	33.24 N	80.12 W
Santee Indian Reservation ◆[4]	198	42.45 N	97.50 W
Sant'Egidio alla Vibrata	66	42.49 N	13.42 E
Sant'Elena	64	45.12 N	11.43 E
Sant'Elia a Pianisi	66	41.38 N	14.52 E
Sant'Elia Fiumerapido	66	41.32 N	13.52 E
San Telmo, Bahía de C	234	18.38 N	103.42 W
San Telmo, Cerro ∧	234	18.37 N	103.37 W
Sant'Elpidio a Mare	66	43.14 N	13.41 E
Santena	62	44.57 N	7.45 E
Santenay	58	46.55 N	4.41 E
Santeny	261	48.43 N	2.34 E
San Teodoro, It.	70	37.51 N	14.42 E
San Teodoro, It.	71	40.46 N	9.39 E
Santermo in Colle	68	40.48 N	16.45 E
Santerno ≃	66	44.34 N	11.58 E
Santerre □[9]	50	49.40 N	2.40 E
Sant'eufemia, Golfo di C	68	38.50 N	16.00 E
Sant'Eufemia a Maiella	66	42.07 N	14.02 E
Sant'Eufemia d'Aspromonte	68	38.16 N	15.52 E
Sant'Eufemia Lamezia	68	38.55 N	16.15 E
Sānthia, Bngl.	126	24.03 N	89.33 E
Santhià, It.	62	45.22 N	8.10 E
Santiago, Bol.	248	18.19 S	59.34 W
Santiago, Bra.	252	29.11 S	54.53 W
Santiago, Chile	252		
	286e	33.27 S	70.40 W
Santiago, C.R.	236	9.51 N	84.18 W
Santiago → Santiago de Compostela, Esp.	34	42.53 N	8.33 W
Santiago, Méx.	232	23.28 N	109.43 W
Santiago, Méx.	232	25.25 N	100.09 W
Santiago, Pan.	236	8.06 N	80.59 W
Santiago ≃	246	4.27 S	77.38 W
Santiago, Cape ≻	116	13.46 N	120.39 E
Santiago, Cerro ∧	236	8.33 N	81.44 W
Santiago, Isla I	288	34.50 S	57.53 W
Santiago, Río de ≃	232	25.11 N	105.26 W
Santiago, Serranía de ⋀	248	18.25 S	59.25 W
Santiago Apóstol	234	16.49 N	96.42 W
Santiago Atitlán	236	14.38 N	91.14 W
Santiago Creek ≃, Calif., U.S.	228	33.46 N	117.54 W
Santiago Creek ≃, Calif., U.S.	228	35.06 N	119.17 W
Santiago Dam ◆[6]	280	33.47 N	117.43 W
Santiago de Cao	248	7.58 S	79.15 W
Santiago de Chocorvos	248	13.50 S	75.16 W
Santiago de Chuco	248	8.09 S	78.11 W
Santiago de Compostela	34	42.53 N	8.33 W
Santiago de Cuba	240p	20.01 N	75.49 W
Santiago de Cuba □[4]	240p	20.10 N	75.55 W
Santiago de Huata	248	16.06 S	68.53 W
Santiago de la Peña	234	20.57 N	97.24 W
Santiago de las Vegas ◆[8]	286b	22.58 N	82.23 W
Santiago del Estero	252	27.47 S	64.16 W
Santiago del Estero □[4]	252	28.00 S	63.30 W
Santiago [de los Caballeros]	238	19.27 N	70.42 W
Santiago de Machaca	248	17.05 S	69.16 W
Santiago do Cacém	34	38.01 N	8.42 W
Santiago Island I	116	16.24 N	119.56 E
Santiago Ixcuintla	234	21.49 N	105.13 W
Santiago Ixtayutla	234	16.33 N	97.39 W
Santiago Lachiguirí	234	16.41 N	95.32 W
Santiago Larre	258	35.34 S	59.10 W
Santiago Maravatío	234	20.10 N	101.00 W
Santiago Papasquiaro	232	25.03 N	105.25 W
Santiago Peak ∧, Calif., U.S.	228	33.42 N	117.32 W
Santiago Peak ∧, Tex., U.S.	196	29.47 N	103.25 W
Santiago Reservoir @[1]	228	33.47 N	117.43 W
Santiago Tepalcatlapan ◆[8]	286a	19.15 N	99.08 W
Santiago Tulantepec	234	20.02 N	98.22 W
Santiago Tutla	234	17.10 N	95.26 W
Santiago Tuxtla	234	18.28 N	95.18 W
Santiago Vázquez	258	34.48 S	56.21 W

Symbols in the index entries represent the broad categories identified in the key at the right. Symbols with superior numbers (⋀[2]) identify subcategories (see complete key on page *I · 30*).

Kartensymbole in dem Registerverzeichnis stellen die rechts in Schlüssel erklärten Kategorien dar. Symbole mit hochgestellten Ziffern (⋀[2]) bezeichnen Unterabteilungen einer Kategorie (vgl. vollständiger Schlüssel auf Seite *I · 30*).

Los símbolos incluídos en el texto del índice representan las grandes categorias identificadas con la clave a la derecha. Los símbolos con numeros en su parte superior (⋀[2]) identifican las subcategorías (véase la clave completa en la página *I · 30*).

Les symboles de l'index représentent les catégories indiquées dans la légende à droite. Les symboles suivis d'un indice (⋀[2]) représentent des sous-catégories (voir légende complète à la page *I · 30*).

Os símbolos incluídos no texto do índice representam as grandes categorias identificadas com a chave à direita. Os símbolos com números em sua parte superior (⋀[2]) identificam as subcategorias (veja-se a chave completa à página *I · 30*).

	English	Deutsch	Español	Français	Português
∧	Mountain	Berg	Montaña	Montagne	Montanha
⋀	Mountains	Berge	Montañas	Montagnes	Montanhas
)(	Pass	Pass	Paso	Col	Passo
∨	Valley, Canyon	Tal, Cañon	Valle, Cañón	Vallée, Canyon	Vale, Canhão
≚	Plain	Ebene	Llano	Plaine	Planície
≻	Cape	Kap	Cabo	Cap	Cabo
I	Island	Insel	Isla	Île	Ilha
II	Islands	Inseln	Islas	Îles	Ilhas
◆	Other Topographic Features	Andere Topographische Objekte	Otros Elementos Topográficos	Autres données topographiques	Outros Elementos Topográficos

ESPAÑOL Nombre	Página	Lat.°′	Long.°′ W=Oeste
FRANÇAIS Nom	Page	Lat.°′	Long.°′ W=Ouest
PORTUGUÊS Nome	Página	Lat.°′	Long.°′ W=Oeste

Santiago Yaveo 234 17.19 N 95.42 W
Santiago Zacatepec 234 17.11 N 95.51 W
Santiaguillo, Laguna de ⊜ 232 24.48 N 104.48 W
Santiam Pass)(202 44.25 N 121.51 W
Santianzhu (Three Indian Temples) ♥1 106 30.15 N 120.08 E
Santiao Chiao ≻ 100 25.02 N 121.59 E
Santiaoqiao 106 31.36 N 121.22 E
Santi Filippo e Giacomo 70 37.51 N 12.31 E
Santigi 112 1.20 N 120.54 E
Santiguila 150 12.42 N 7.26 W
Sant'Ilario d'Enza 64 44.46 N 10.27 E
San Timoteo 246 9.48 N 71.04 W
San Timoteo Canyon V 228 34.04 N 117.17 W
Sāntipur 126 23.15 N 88.26 E
Säntis ʌ 58 47.15 N 9.21 E
Santissima Trinita di Saccargia ♥1 71 40.41 N 8.42 E
Santissimo ✦8 287a 22.53 S 43.31 W
Santisteban del Puerto 34 38.15 N 3.12 W
Santō, Nihon 94 35.21 N 136.22 E
Santō, Nihon 96 35.19 N 134.53 E
Santo, Tex., U.S. 196 32.36 N 98.13 W
Santo Aleixo 256 22.34 S 43.04 W
Santo Amaro, Bra. 250 2.33 S 43.14 W
Santo Amaro, Bra. 255 12.32 S 38.43 W
Santo Amaro ✦8 287b 23.39 S 46.42 W
Santo Amaro, Ilha de I 256 23.57 S 46.14 W
Santo Amaro das Brotas 250 10.47 S 37.04 W
Santo Anastácio 255 21.58 S 51.39 W
Santo Anastácio ≃ 255 21.49 S 52.11 W
Santo André 256 23.40 S 46.31 W
Santo Ângelo 252 28.18 S 54.16 W
Santo Antão I 150a 17.05 N 25.10 W
Santo Antônio, Bra. 250 6.18 S 35.27 W
Santo Antônio, Bra. 252 29.50 S 50.32 W
Santo Antônio, S. Tom./P. 152 1.39 N 7.26 E
Santo Antônio ≃, Bra. 250 11.31 S 48.37 W
Santo Antônio ≃, Bra. 255 17.30 S 45.37 W
Santo Antônio ≃, Bra. 287a 22.42 S 43.37 W
Santo Antônio, Cachoeira ⌊ 248 9.46 S 60.35 W
Santo Antônio, Igarapé ≃ 246 1.32 S 59.48 W
Santo Antônio da Boa Vista 255 15.52 S 44.09 W
Santo Antônio da Charneca 266c 38.37 N 9.02 W
Santo Antônio do Zaire 152 6.07 S 12.18 E
Santo Augusto 252 27.51 S 53.47 W
Santo Corazón 248 17.59 S 58.51 W
Santo Cristo 252 27.50 S 54.40 W
Santo Domingo, Arg. 252 29.16 S 63.56 W
Santo Domingo, Cuba 240p 22.35 N 80.15 W
Santo Domingo, Méx. 196 25.38 N 101.05 W
Santo Domingo, Méx. 196 25.48 N 104.28 W
Santo Domingo, Méx. 232 25.32 N 112.02 W
Santo Domingo, Méx. 234 23.20 N 101.44 W
Santo Domingo, Nic. 236 12.16 N 85.05 W
Santo Domingo, Rep. Dom. 238 18.28 N 69.54 W
Santo Domingo ≃, Méx. 234 17.40 N 98.07 W
Santo Domingo ≃, Méx. 234 18.10 N 96.08 W
Santo Domingo ≃, Méx. 234 16.41 N 93.00 W
Santo Domingo ≃, Méx. 236 16.15 N 91.17 W
Santo Domingo, Arroyo ≃, Méx. 204 30.43 N 116.03 W
Santo Domingo, Arroyo ≃, Méx. 232 25.29 N 112.05 W
Santo Domingo, Isla → Hispaniola I 238 19.00 N 71.00 W
Santo Domingo de la Calzada 34 42.26 N 2.57 W
Santo Domingo de los Colorados 246 0.15 S 79.09 W
Santo Domingo Nuxaá 234 17.08 N 97.02 W
Santo Domingo Pueblo 200 35.31 N 106.22 W
Santo Domingo Teojomulco 234 16.36 N 97.14 W
Santo Estevão 255 12.26 S 39.13 W
Sant'Olcese 62 44.30 N 8.58 E
Santolea, Embalse de ⊜1 34 40.47 N 0.19 W
San Tomé 246 8.58 N 64.08 W
San Tommaso 66 42.11 N 13.58 E
Sant'Omobono Imagna 62 45.48 N 9.32 E
Santoña 34 43.27 N 3.27 W
Santonghe ≃ 98 42.39 N 126.03 E
Santo Nino Island I 116 11.55 N 124.27 E
Sant' Onofrio ✦8 267a 41.56 N 12.25 E
Santo Onofre ≃ 255 12.34 S 43.12 W
Santo Peak ʌ 175f 15.27 S 166.48 E
Sant'Oreste 66 42.14 N 12.32 E
Santorini → Thira I 38 36.24 N 25.29 E
Santorso 64 45.44 N 11.23 E
Santos 256 23.57 S 46.20 W
Santos, Arroyo de los ≃ 258 35.28 S 57.29 W
Santos, Baía de C 256 24.00 S 46.21 W
Santos Dumont 256 21.28 S 43.34 W
Santos Dumont, Aeroporto ⊠ 256 22.55 S 43.10 W
Santoshpur 272b 22.40 N 88.10 E
Santo Stefano, Isola I 66 40.47 N 13.27 E
Santo Stefano Belbo 62 44.43 N 8.14 E
Santo Stefano d'Aveto 62 44.35 N 9.27 E
Santo Stefano di Cadore 64 46.33 N 12.32 E
Santo Stefano di Camastra 70 38.01 N 14.21 E
Santo Stefano di Magra 64 44.10 N 9.55 E
Santo Stefano Quisquina 70 37.37 N 13.29 E
Santo Stino di Livenza 64 45.44 N 12.41 E
Santo Tirso 34 41.21 N 8.28 W
Santo Tomás, Col. 246 10.46 N 74.45 W
Santo Tomás, Méx. 232 31.33 N 116.24 W
Santo Tomás, Nic. 236 12.04 N 85.05 W
Santo Tomás, Ven. 246 8.53 N 64.33 W
Santo Tomás ≃, Méx. 204 31.32 N 116.40 W
Santo Tomás ≃, Perú 248 13.47 S 72.09 W
Santo Tomás, Punta ≻ 232 31.34 N 116.42 W
Santo Tomás, University of ♥2 269f 14.37 N 120.59 E
Santo Tomás, Volcán ʌ1 246a 0.48 S 91.07 W
Santo Tomás de Nance 236 13.11 N 86.56 W
Santo Tomás Ocotepec 234 17.08 N 97.46 W
Santo Tomás y Principe → Sao Tome and Principe □1 152 1.00 N 7.00 E
Santo Tomé, Arg. 252 28.33 S 56.03 W
Santo Tomé, Arg. 252 31.40 S 60.46 W
Santo Tomé de Guayana → Ciudad Guayana 246 8.22 N 62.40 W
Santouwan 102 38.06 N 100.33 E
Sant' Pietro, Lago di ⊜ 68 41.01 N 15.30 E
Santpoort 52 52.25 N 4.38 E
Santuanjiang 106 30.54 N 121.43 E
Santuario di Oropa ♥1 62 45.38 N 7.58 E
Santu Lussurgiu 71 40.08 N 8.39 E
Santunying 105 40.14 N 118.12 E
San Ubaldo 236 11.51 N 85.20 W
Sanuki 268 35.55 N 139.53 E
Sanuki-sammyaku ᴬ 96 34.09 N 134.11 E
Šanūr 132 32.21 N 35.15 E
San Valentín, Cerro ʌ 254 46.36 S 73.20 W
San Valentino in Abruzzo Citeriore 66 42.14 N 13.59 E
San Valentino Torio 68 40.48 N 14.36 E
San Venanzo 66 42.52 N 12.16 E
San Vendemiano 64 45.54 N 12.20 E
San Vicente, El Sal. 236 13.38 N 88.48 W
San Vicente, Méx. 232 31.20 N 116.15 W
San Vicente □5 288 34.56 S 58.24 W
San Vicente → Saint Vincent □1 241h 13.15 N 61.12 W
San Vicente, Cabo → São Vicente, Cabo de ≻ 34 37.01 N 9.00 W
San Vicente, Volcán de ʌ1 236 13.36 N 88.51 W
San Vicente Creek ≃ 282 37.32 N 122.31 W
San Vicente de Alcántara 34 39.21 N 7.08 W
San Vicente de Baracaldo 34 43.18 N 2.59 W
San Vicente de Cañete 248 13.05 S 76.24 W
San Vicente de Chucurí 246 6.54 N 73.25 W
San Vicente de la Barquera 34 43.26 N 4.24 W
San Vicente del Caguán 246 2.07 N 74.46 W
San Vicente dels Horts 266d 41.24 N 2.01 E
San Vicente de Tagua-Tagua 252 34.26 S 71.05 W
San Vicente Mountain ʌ 280 34.08 N 118.31 W
San Vicente Reservoir ⊜1 228 32.55 N 116.55 W
San Vicente Tancuayalab 234 21.44 N 98.34 W
San Vigilio 64 45.34 N 10.41 E
San Vigilio ♥1 64 46.37 N 11.07 E
San Vincenzo 66 43.06 N 10.32 E
San Vito, C.R. 236 8.50 N 82.58 W
San Vito, It. 71 39.26 N 9.32 E
San Vito, Capo ≻ 70 38.11 N 12.44 E
San Vito, Serralta di ʌ 68 38.46 N 16.22 E
San Vito al Tagliamento 64 45.54 N 12.52 E
San Vito Chietino 66 42.18 N 14.27 E
San Vito dei Normanni 68 40.39 N 17.42 E
San Vito lo Capo 70 38.10 N 12.45 E
San Vito Romano 66 41.53 N 12.59 E
San Vito sullo Ionio 68 38.43 N 16.25 E
Sanwa, Nihon 94 37.07 N 138.21 E
Sanwa, Nihon 96 34.42 N 133.15 E
Sanwa, Nihon 96 34.39 N 132.51 E
San Xavier Indian Reservation ✦4 200 32.05 N 111.08 W
San Ygnacio 196 27.03 N 99.27 W
Sanyō, Nihon 96 34.02 N 131.10 E
Sanyō, Nihon 96 34.45 N 134.01 E
Sanza 68 40.15 N 15.33 E
Sanzaodao I 100 22.03 N 113.21 E
Sanza Pombo 152 7.19 S 15.59 E
Sanzar ≃ 85 40.00 N 67.40 E
San Zeno di Montagna 64 45.37 N 10.43 E
Sanzha 98 41.44 N 114.39 E
São Benedito ≃ 250 9.11 S 57.02 W
São Bento ≃ 256 21.42 S 45.18 W
São Bento, Mosteiro e Igreja de ♥1 287a 22.54 S 43.11 W
São Bernardo do Campo 256 23.42 S 46.33 W
São Bernardo do Campo □7 287b 23.44 S 46.33 W
São Brás de Alportel 34 37.09 N 7.53 W
São Braz, Cabo de ≻ 152 9.59 S 13.19 E
São Caetano de Odivelas 250 0.45 S 48.02 W
São Caetano do Sul 256 23.36 S 46.34 W
São Caetano do Sul □7 287b 23.37 S 46.33 W
São Caitano 250 8.21 S 36.06 W
São Carlos, Bra. 252 27.04 S 52.59 W
São Carlos, Bra. 255 22.01 S 47.54 W
São Cristóvão 250 11.01 S 37.12 W
São Cristóvão ✦8 287a 22.54 S 43.14 W
Saodatun 104 42.02 N 123.31 E
São Domingos, Bra. 252 26.34 S 52.32 W
São Domingos, Bra. 255 13.24 S 46.19 W
São Domingos, Bra. 256 21.41 S 42.47 W
São Domingos, Gui. B. 150 12.22 N 16.08 W
São Domingos ≃, Bra. 248 12.28 S 64.13 W
São Domingos ≃, Bra. 255 19.13 S 50.44 W
São Domingos ≃, Bra. 255 13.24 S 47.12 W
São Domingos ≃, Bra. 255 20.03 S 53.13 W
São Domingos da Bocaina 256 21.50 S 44.01 W
São Domingos do Capim 250 1.41 S 47.47 W
São Domingos do Maranhão 250 5.42 S 44.22 W
São Félix 250 11.36 S 50.39 W
São Félix de Balsas 250 7.08 S 44.52 W
São Félix do Piauí 250 5.56 S 42.07 W
São Filipe, Bra. 255 14.49 S 41.23 W
São Filipe, C.V. 150a 14.54 N 24.31 W
São Francisco ≃, Bra. 242 10.30 S 36.24 W
São Francisco ≃, Bra. 255 16.09 S 40.39 W
São Francisco ≃, Bra. 255 11.45 S 43.20 W
São Francisco ≃, Bra. 256 21.50 S 42.42 W
São Francisco ≃, Bra. 287a 22.57 S 43.20 W
São Francisco, Baía de C 252 26.10 S 48.34 W
São Francisco, Ilha de I 252 26.18 S 48.37 W
São Gabriel 252 30.20 S 54.19 W
São Gabriel da Palha 255 19.01 S 40.32 W
São Gabriel de Goiás 255 15.12 S 47.34 W
São Gonçalo, Bra. 256 21.36 S 46.19 W
São Gonçalo, Bra. 256 22.51 S 43.04 W
São Gonçalo □7 287a 22.48 S 43.01 W
São Gonçalo do Abaeté 255 18.20 S 45.49 W
São Gonçalo do Amarante 250 3.36 S 38.58 W
São Gonçalo do Pará 255 19.59 S 44.51 W
São Gonçalo do Sapucaí 256 21.54 S 45.36 W
São Gonçalo dos Campos 255 12.25 S 38.58 W
Sao Hill 154 8.20 S 35.12 E
São Jerônimo, Serra de ᴬ1 255 17.00 S 54.50 W
São Jerônimo da Serra 255 23.43 S 50.44 W
São Joana ≃ 255 19.31 S 40.43 W
São João 150 11.32 N 15.26 W
São João ≃, Bra. 255 12.27 S 51.07 W
São João ≃, Bra. 256 22.33 S 42.29 W
São João ≃, Bra. 287b 23.31 S 46.51 W
São João, Ribeirão ≃ 256 21.28 S 42.49 W
São João da Aliança 255 14.42 S 47.32 W
São João da Madeira 34 40.54 N 8.30 W
São João das Lampas 266c 38.52 N 9.24 W
São João de Côrtes 250 2.12 S 44.32 W
São João del Rei 255 21.09 S 44.16 W
São João de Meriti 256 22.48 S 43.22 W
São João de Meriti □7 287a 22.48 S 43.21 W
São João de Meriti ≃ 287a 22.48 S 43.18 W
São João de Pirabas 250 0.46 S 47.10 W
São Joaquim 252 28.18 S 49.56 W
São Joaquim, Parque Nacional de ♠ 252 28.15 S 49.57 W
São Joaquim da Barra 255 20.35 S 47.53 W
São Joaquim dos Melos 250 5.48 S 44.44 W
São Jorge 255 23.24 S 52.17 W
São Jorge I 148a 38.38 N 28.03 W
São Jorge, Castelo de ⊥ 266c 38.43 N 9.08 W
São José 252 27.38 S 48.39 W
São José ≃ 287a 22.39 S 43.27 W
São José, Ponta de ≻ 152 12.36 S 13.12 E
São José da Lagoa Tapada 250 6.57 S 38.10 W
São José da Laje 250 9.01 S 36.03 W
São José das Palmeiras 256 22.33 S 47.12 W
São José de Anauá 246 1.00 N 61.23 W
São José de Encoge 152 7.38 S 14.41 E
São José de Mipibu 250 6.05 S 35.15 W
São José de Piranhas 250 7.07 S 38.30 W
São José do Alegre 256 22.19 S 45.32 W
São José do Barreiro 256 22.38 S 44.35 W
São José do Belmonte 250 7.52 S 38.46 W
São José do Calçado 255 21.02 S 41.40 W
São José do Campestre 250 6.18 S 35.42 W
São José do Cedro 252 26.30 S 53.30 W
São José do Egito 250 7.28 S 37.16 W
São José do Goiabal 255 19.56 S 42.42 W
São José do Gurupi 250 1.36 S 46.13 W
São José do Norte 252 32.01 S 52.03 W
São José do Peixe 250 7.24 S 42.34 W
São José do Piriá 250 1.17 S 46.18 W
São José do Rio Pardo 256 21.36 S 46.54 W
São José do Rio Prêto, Bra. 255 20.48 S 49.23 W
São José do Rio Prêto, Bra. 256 22.10 S 42.57 W
São José dos Campos, Bra. 256 23.11 S 45.53 W
São José dos Campos, Bra. 256 22.10 S 45.06 W
São Julião da Barra 266c 38.40 N 9.21 W
São Julião do Tojal 266c 38.51 N 9.08 W
São Leopoldo 252 29.46 S 51.09 W
São Lourenço 256 22.07 S 45.03 W
São Lourenço ≃ 248 17.53 S 57.27 W
São Lourenço, Pantanal de ☷ 248 17.30 S 56.30 W
São Luís 250 2.31 S 44.16 W
São Luís de Montes Belos 255 16.32 S 50.20 W
São Luís do Curu 250 3.40 S 39.14 W
São Luís Do Paraitinga 256 23.14 S 45.20 W
São Luís do Quitunde 250 9.20 S 35.33 W
São Luís do Tocantins 255 14.17 S 47.59 W
São Luís Gonzaga 252 28.24 S 54.58 W
São Manuel ≃ 248 7.21 S 58.03 W
São Mateus, Bra. 256 22.49 S 43.23 W
São Mateus, Port. 148a 38.26 N 28.27 W
São Mateus ≃ 255 13.48 S 46.54 W
São Miguel I 148a 37.47 N 25.30 W
São Miguel ≃ 255 16.26 S 41.00 W
São Miguel Paulista (Baquiriru) ✦8 256 23.30 S 46.26 W
Saona, Isla I 238 18.09 N 68.40 W
Saonara 64 45.22 N 11.59 E
Saône ≃ 62 45.44 N 4.50 E
Saône-et-Loire □5 32 46.42 N 4.45 E
Saonek 164 0.28 S 130.47 E
Saoner 120 21.23 N 78.54 E
São Nicolau 152 14.15 S 12.21 E
São Nicolau I 150a 16.35 N 24.15 W
São Nicolau ≃ 250 5.45 S 42.02 W
São Paulo 256
São Paulo 287b 23.32 S 46.37 W
São Paulo □3 255 22.00 S 49.00 W
São Paulo □7 287b 23.33 S 46.38 W
São Paulo, Ribeirão de ≃ 256 22.16 S 46.37 W
São Paulo de Olivença 246 3.27 S 68.48 W
São Paulo do Potengi 250 5.55 S 35.45 W
São Pedro ≃ 255 16.30 S 41.17 W
São Pedro de Viseu 250 2.33 S 49.03 W
São Pedro do Estoril 266c 38.42 N 9.22 W
São Pedro do Ivaí 255 23.51 S 51.51 W
São Pedro do Piauí 250 5.56 S 42.43 W
São Pedro do Sul, Bra. 252 29.37 S 54.10 W
São Pedro do Sul, Port. 34 40.45 N 8.04 W
São Rafael 250 5.47 S 36.55 W
São Raimundo das Mangabeiras 250 7.01 S 45.29 W
São Raimundo de Codó 250 4.21 S 43.37 W
São Raimundo Nonato 250 9.01 S 42.42 W
Saorge 62 43.59 N 7.33 E
Saori 94 35.11 N 136.44 E
São Romão 255 16.22 S 45.04 W
São Roque 256 23.32 S 47.08 W
São Roque, Cabo de ≻ 250 5.29 S 35.16 W
São Roque da Fartura 256 21.51 S 46.45 W
São Roque do Paraguaçu 255 12.51 S 38.51 W
Saorre, Mount ʌ 176 64.27 N 84.30 W
São Salvador → Salvador 255 12.59 S 38.31 W
São Salvador do Congo 152 6.16 S 14.15 E
São Sebastião 256 23.48 S 45.25 W
São Sebastião, Canal de ⩫ 256 23.48 S 45.23 W
São Sebastião, Ilha de I 256 23.50 S 45.18 W
São Sebastião, Pico de ʌ 256 23.52 S 45.23 W
São Sebastião, Ponta ≻ 156 22.07 S 35.30 E
São Sepé 252 30.10 S 53.34 W
São Simão ≃ 248 12.40 S 63.04 W
São Tiago I 150a 15.05 N 23.40 W
São Timóteo 255 13.51 S 42.11 W
São Tomé, Bra. 250 5.58 S 36.04 W
São Tomé, S. Tom./P. 152 0.20 N 6.44 E
São Tomé I 152 0.12 N 6.39 E
São Tomé ≃ 250 8.10 S 58.13 W
São Tomé, Cabo de ≻ 255 21.59 S 40.59 W
São Tomé, Pico de ʌ 152 0.16 N 6.33 E
São Tomé, Ribeirão ≃ 256 21.26 S 46.02 W
Sao Tome and Principe □1 138
152 1.00 N 7.00 E
São Tomé das Letras 256 21.43 S 44.59 W
Saou 62 44.39 N 5.04 E
Saoura, Oued V 148 29.00 N 0.55 W
São Valério ≃ 250 11.20 S 48.28 W
São Vicente, Bra. 250 6.13 S 36.41 W
São Vicente, Bra. 256 23.58 S 46.23 W
São Vicente I 150a 16.50 N 25.00 W
São Vicente, Cabo de ≻ 34 37.01 N 9.00 W
São Vicente, Ribeirão ≃ 256 21.59 S 45.40 W
São Vicente de Minas 256 21.42 S 44.27 W
São Vicente Ferrer, Bra. 250 2.53 S 44.52 W
São Vicente Ferrer, Bra. 250 7.35 S 35.30 W
Šápai 38 41.02 N 25.41 E
Sapallanga 248 12.09 S 75.11 W
Sapanca 130 40.41 N 30.16 E
Sapang Baho ≃ 269f 14.33 N 121.06 E
Sapao 116 10.01 N 126.02 E
Sapão ≃ 250 11.01 S 45.32 W
Saparua, Pulau I 164 3.34 S 128.40 E
Sapatgrām 124 26.20 N 90.08 E
Sape, Indon. 115b 8.34 S 118.59 E
Sapé ≃ 287a 22.52 S 43.02 W
Sape, Selat ⩫ 115b 8.39 S 119.18 E
Sapeaçu 255 12.44 S 39.13 W
Sapele 150 5.54 N 5.41 E
Sapello ≃ 200 35.47 N 104.59 W
Sapelo Island I 192 31.28 N 81.15 W
Saphane 130 39.01 N 29.14 E
Sapian Bay C 116 11.33 N 122.37 E
Sapindji 152 9.39 S 23.12 E
Sapitwa ʌ 154 15.57 S 35.36 E
Sapkina ≃ 24 66.44 N 52.25 E
Sapodilla Cays I 236 16.08 N 88.15 W
Saponara 70 38.11 N 15.26 E
Saponé 150 12.03 N 1.36 W
Sap'o-ri 98 40.49 N 129.31 E
Saporoschje → Zaporožje 78 47.50 N 35.10 E
Saposoa 248 6.56 S 76.48 W
Sappa Creek ≃ 198 40.07 N 99.38 W
Sappa Creek, South Fork ≃ 198 39.47 N 100.35 W
Sappada 64 46.34 N 12.41 E
Sappemeer 52 53.09 N 6.50 E
Sapphire Mountains ᴬ 202 46.20 N 113.45 W
Sappho 182 48.04 N 124.16 W
Sappington 219 38.32 N 90.23 W
Sapporo 92a 43.03 N 141.21 E
Sapri 68 40.04 N 15.38 E
Šapša 76 60.34 N 34.01 E
Sap Songkhla, Thale C 110 7.13 N 100.30 E
Šapsugskaja 78 44.45 N 38.05 E
Sapta-ri 271b 37.43 N 126.44 E
Sapt Kosi ≃ 124 26.30 N 86.55 E
Sapu 152 12.29 S 19.26 E
Sapucaí ≃ 256 22.19 S 46.42 W
Sapucaí ≃ 256 21.33 S 45.40 W
Sapucaia 256 22.00 S 42.54 W
Sapucaí-Mirim 256 22.44 S 45.45 W
Sapucaí-Mirim ≃ 256 22.12 S 45.53 W
Sapudi, Pulau I 115a 7.06 S 114.20 E
Sapulpa 196 36.00 N 96.06 W
Sapulu 115a 6.54 S 112.57 E
Sapuran 115a 7.28 S 109.58 E
Sapwe 154 10.57 S 28.10 E
Sāq, Jabal ʌ2 128 26.17 N 43.16 E
Saqīat al-'Abd 140 20.48 N 30.19 E
Saqiqiao 100 27.19 N 117.35 E
Saqishanling ᴬ 89 48.55 N 122.45 E
Saqiyat Makkī 142 30.00 N 31.13 E
Saqqārah 142 29.51 N 31.13 E
Saqqez 128 36.14 N 46.16 E
Saquarema 256 22.56 S 42.30 W
Saquarema, Lagoa de C 256 22.55 S 42.33 W
Saquena 248 4.40 S 73.31 W
Saquish Neck ≻1 283 42.00 N 70.37 W
Saquisilí 246 0.51 S 78.40 W
Sara, Bngl. 126 24.07 N 89.02 E
Sara, H. Vol. 150 11.43 N 3.50 W
Sara, Niger 146 20.46 N 12.28 E
Sara, Pil. 116 11.16 N 123.01 E
Šaraargun ≃ 84 43.02 N 45.44 E
Sarāb 128 37.56 N 47.32 E
Sarabia 234 20.31 N 101.05 W
Sarabia ≃ 234 17.11 N 94.56 W
Sarābiyūm 142 30.23 N 32.17 E
Sara Buri 110 14.32 N 100.55 E
Saracen 158 27.16 S 24.02 E
Saracena 68 39.46 N 16.09 E
Saraceno, Monte ʌ 66 41.27 N 14.44 E
Saracura ≃ 255 12.18 S 40.07 W
Saracuruna ≃ 287a 22.41 S 43.13 W
Saraferé 150 15.50 N 3.42 W
Saragosa 196 31.01 N 103.39 W
Saragossa → Zaragoza 34 41.38 N 0.53 W
Saraguay ✦8 275a 45.31 N 73.45 W
Saraguro 246 3.36 S 79.13 W
Saraikela 124 22.43 N 85.57 E
Sarāi Naurang 123 32.50 N 70.47 E
Saraipali 120 21.20 N 83.00 E
Säräisniemi 26 64.27 N 26.47 E
Sarajas de Madrid ✦8 266a 40.28 N 3.35 W
Sarajevo 38 43.52 N 18.25 E
Sarakhs 128 36.32 N 61.11 E
Saraland 194 30.49 N 88.04 W
Saramacca □5 250 4.45 N 56.00 W
Saramacca ≃ 250 5.51 N 55.53 W
Saramaguacán ≃ 240p 21.30 N 77.17 W
Saran □5 124 26.00 N 84.30 E
Saran, Gunung ʌ 112 0.25 S 111.18 E
Saranac 216 42.56 N 85.13 W
Saranac ≃ 188 44.42 N 73.27 W
Saranac Lake 188 44.20 N 74.08 W
Saranakan, Gora ʌ 88 52.35 N 113.50 E
Saranap 226 37.53 N 122.06 W
Šaranbaš-Kn'azevo 80 54.58 N 54.09 E
Saranda 154 5.43 S 34.59 E
Sarandapótamos ≃ 267c 38.26 N 23.54 E
Sarandë 38 39.52 N 20.00 E
Sarandi 252 27.56 S 52.55 W
Sarandí ✦8 258 34.40 S 58.21 W
Sarandí del Yi 252 33.21 S 55.38 W
Sarandí Grande 258 33.44 S 56.20 W
Sarandira 256 21.50 S 43.11 W
Šaranga 80 57.11 N 46.34 E
Sarangani Bay C 116 5.57 N 125.11 E
Sarangani Island I 116 5.27 N 125.28 E
Sarangani Islands II 116 5.25 N 125.26 E
Sarangani Strait ⩫ 116 5.31 N 125.23 E
Sārangarh 120 21.36 N 83.05 E
Sārangpur 124 23.34 N 76.28 E
Sārankhola 126 22.18 N 89.47 E
Saranpaul' 24 64.14 N 60.53 E
Saransk 80 54.11 N 45.11 E
Sarantina, Valle V 64 46.35 N 11.25 E
Saraphi 110 18.43 N 99.03 E
Sarapiquí ≃ 236 10.43 N 83.56 W
Sarapó ≃ 287a 22.46 S 43.37 W
Sarapuí ≃ 287a 22.46 S 43.24 W
Sarapuí, Canal ⩦ 287a 22.44 S 43.16 W
Sarapul 80 56.28 N 53.48 E
Sarapul'skaja Vozvyšennost' ᴬ1 80 56.15 N 53.30 E
Sarāqib 130 35.52 N 36.48 E
Sarare 246 9.47 N 69.10 W
Sarar Plain ⊻ 144 9.35 N 46.15 E
Sarā-Sarā 256 23.40 S 47.05 W
Sara Sara, Nevado ʌ 248 15.19 S 73.27 W
Sarasota 220 27.20 N 82.34 W
Sarasota □6 220 27.10 N 82.21 W
Sarasota Bay C 220 27.23 N 82.39 W
Sarasota-Bradenton Airport ⊠ 220 27.24 N 82.33 W
Sarasota Springs 220 27.17 N 82.28 W
Saraswati ≃ 272b 22.59 N 88.22 E
Sarath 126 24.14 N 86.50 E
Saratoga, Austl. 170 33.28 S 151.21 E
Saratoga, Calif., U.S. 226 37.16 N 122.02 W
Saratoga, Ind., U.S. 216 40.14 N 84.55 W
Saratoga, Tex., U.S. 222 30.17 N 94.31 W
Saratoga, Wyo., U.S. 200 41.27 N 106.48 W
Saratoga □6 210 43.00 N 73.51 W
Saratoga Battle Monument ⊥ 210 43.05 N 75.36 W
Saratoga Creek ≃ 282 37.25 N 121.58 W
Saratoga Lake ⊜ 210 43.01 N 73.39 W
Saratoga National Historical Park ♠ 210 43.00 N 73.38 W
Saratoga Passage ⩫ 224 48.10 N 122.30 W
Saratoga Spa State Park ♠ 210 43.03 N 73.50 W
Saratoga Springs 210 43.05 N 73.47 W
Šara Togot 88 53.01 N 106.43 E
Saratok 112 1.44 N 111.20 E
Saratov 80 51.34 N 46.02 E
Saratov □4 76 52.00 N 42.40 E
Saratovka 86 51.12 N 54.54 E
Saratovskoje Vodochranilišče ⊜1 80 52.45 N 48.30 E
Saraurcu ʌ 246 0.06 S 77.55 W
Sarāvān, Īrān 128 27.15 N 62.40 E
Saravan, Lao 110 15.43 N 106.25 E
Sarawak □3 112 2.30 N 113.30 E
Saray 130 41.26 N 27.55 E
Saraya, Guinée 150 10.46 N 10.24 W
Saraya, Sén. 150 12.50 N 11.45 W
Sarayakpınar 130 41.46 N 26.29 E
Sarāyān 128 33.51 N 58.31 E
Saraycık 130 40.57 N 35.08 E
Sarayevo → Sarajevo 38 43.52 N 18.25 E
Sarayköy 130 37.55 N 28.58 E
Sarayönü 130 38.17 N 32.25 E
Sarbāz 128 26.39 N 61.15 E
Sarbinowo 54 52.40 N 14.40 E
Sárbogárd 30 46.53 N 18.38 E
Sarca ≃ 64 45.52 N 10.52 E
Sarce ≃ 50 48.09 N 4.18 E
Sarcee Indian Reserve ✦4 182 50.58 N 114.06 W
Sarcelle, Passe de la ⩫ 175f 22.29 S 167.12 E
Sarcelles 50 49.00 N 2.23 E
Sarche di Calavino 64 46.03 N 10.57 E
Sarcidano ✦1, It. 71 39.55 N 9.05 E
Sarcidano ✦1, It. 71 39.49 N 9.10 E
Sarclet 46 58.22 N 3.07 W
Sarcoxie 194 37.03 N 94.07 W
Sārda (Kāli) ≃ 124 27.22 N 81.23 E
Sard Āb)(123 36.40 N 71.32 E
Sārda Canal ⩦ 124 28.59 N 80.07 E
Sardagna 64 46.03 N 11.06 E
Sardah 124 24.18 N 88.44 E
Sardalas 146 25.46 N 10.34 E
Sardanyola 266d 41.30 N 2.09 E
Sardaq 128 34.48 N 58.07 E
Sardara 71 39.37 N 8.49 E
Sardār Chāh 128 27.58 N 64.50 E
Sardārpur 120 22.39 N 74.59 E
Sardārshahr 120 28.26 N 74.29 E
Sar Dasht, Īrān 128 36.09 N 45.28 E
Sar Dasht, Īrān 128 32.32 N 48.52 E
Sardegna □4 71 40.00 N 9.00 E
Sardegna (Sardinia) I 71 40.00 N 9.00 E
Sardhana 124 29.09 N 77.37 E
Sardiha 126 22.22 N 87.09 E
Sardinal 236 10.31 N 85.39 W
Sardinata 246 8.05 N 72.48 W
Sardinia, N.Y., U.S. 210 42.32 N 78.31 W
Sardinia, Ohio, U.S. 218 39.05 N 83.49 W
Sardinia → Sardegna I 71 40.00 N 9.00 E
Sardinien → Sardegna I 71 40.00 N 9.00 E
Sardis, B.C., Can. 224 49.08 N 121.57 W
Sardis, Ala., U.S. 194 32.17 N 86.59 W
Sardis, Ga., U.S. 192 32.58 N 81.46 W
Sardis, Ky., U.S. 218 38.32 N 83.57 W
Sardis, Miss., U.S. 194 34.26 N 89.55 W
Sardis, Pa., U.S. 279b 40.29 N 79.42 W
Sardis, Tenn., U.S. 194 35.27 N 88.18 W
Sardona, Piz ʌ 58 46.55 N 9.15 E
Sareks Nationalpark ♠ 24 67.15 N 17.30 E
Sarektjåkkå ʌ 24 67.25 N 17.46 E
Sārenga, Bhārat 126 22.46 N 87.02 E
Sārenga, Bhārat 272b 22.31 N 88.13 E
Sarentino (Sarnthein) 64 46.38 N 11.21 E
Sar-e Pol-e Žahāb 128 34.28 N 45.52 E
Sarepta 194 32.54 N 93.27 W
Sarezskoje, Ozero ⊜ 85 38.13 N 72.45 E
Sarezzo 64 45.39 N 10.12 E
Sargans 58 47.03 N 9.26 E
Sargé-lès-le-Mans 50 48.02 N 0.14 E
Sargent 198 41.38 N 99.22 W
Sargent Creek ≃ 226 35.57 N 120.52 W
Sargodha 123 32.05 N 72.40 E
Sargou ≃ 85 43.25 N 73.50 E
Šargul', Ozero ⊜ 86 54.35 N 78.51 E
Šargun 85 38.37 N 67.53 E
Sarh 146 9.09 N 18.23 E
Sarhli, Djebel ʌ 34 36.06 N 0.40 E
Sarhro, Jbel ᴬ 148 31.00 N 5.55 W
Sārī 128 36.34 N 53.04 E
Saria I 38 35.50 N 27.15 E
Saribi, Tanjung ≻ 164 1.36 S 135.25 E
Sáric 232 31.08 N 111.23 W
Saricumbe 152 12.12 S 19.46 E
Sarigan I 108 16.42 N 145.47 E
Sarıgazi 267b 41.01 N 29.12 E
Sarıgöl 130 38.14 N 28.43 E
Sarıkamış 130 40.20 N 42.35 E
Sarıkaya 130 38.47 N 32.15 E
Sarikei 112 2.07 N 111.31 E
Sarıköy 130 40.12 N 27.36 E
Sarilhos Grandes 266c 38.41 N 8.58 W
Sarilhos Pequenos 266c 38.41 N 8.59 W
Sarim 154 0.23 S 40.58 E
Sarimbun, Pulau I 271c 1.26 N 103.41 E
Sarina 166 21.26 S 149.13 E
Sarine ≃ 58 46.54 N 7.14 E
Sariñena 34 41.48 N 0.10 W
Sarıoğlan, Tür. 130 39.05 N 35.59 E
Sarıoğlan, Tür. 130 37.12 N 32.33 E
Sarīr 146 27.36 N 22.32 E
Sarısu 84 39.01 N 42.55 E
Sarita 196 27.13 N 97.47 W
Sariwŏn 98 38.31 N 125.44 E
Sarıyar Gölü ⊜1 130 40.02 N 31.40 E
Sarıyer 130 41.10 N 29.03 E
Sarju (Babai) ≃ 124 27.42 N 81.16 E
Sark I 43b 49.26 N 2.21 W
Sark ≃ 44 54.58 N 3.04 W
Sarkad 30 46.44 N 21.23 E
Şarkîkaraağaç 130 38.04 N 31.23 E
Şarkışla 130 39.21 N 36.26 E
Şarköy 130 40.37 N 27.06 E
Sarlat-la-Canéda 32 44.53 N 1.13 E
Sarles 198 48.57 N 99.00 W
Sărmașu 38 46.46 N 24.11 E
Sarmatskaja ≃ 83 47.20 N 38.48 E
Sármellék 30 46.44 N 17.10 E
Sarmi 164 1.51 S 138.44 E
Sarmiento 254 45.36 S 69.05 W
Sarmiento ≃ 288 34.25 S 58.35 W
Sarmiento, Cerro ʌ 254 54.27 S 70.50 W
Sarmiento, Lago ⊜ 254 51.04 S 72.45 W
Särna 26 61.41 N 13.08 E
Sarna, Ozero ⊜ 80 48.24 N 44.38 E
Sarnano 66 43.02 N 13.18 E
Sārnāth ⊥ 124 25.24 N 83.01 E
Sarnen 58 46.54 N 8.15 E
Sărnena ᴬ 38 42.35 N 25.10 E
Sarner See ⊜ 58 46.52 N 8.13 E
Sarnia 214 42.58 N 82.23 W
Sarnico 64 45.40 N 9.57 E
Sarno 68 40.49 N 14.37 E
Sarnow 54 53.45 N 13.37 E
Sarnowa 30 51.38 N 16.54 E
Sarnthein → Sarentino 64 46.38 N 11.21 E
Saroako 112 2.31 S 121.22 E
Sarolangun 112 2.18 S 102.42 E
Saroma-ko ⊜ 92a 44.08 N 143.50 E
Saron 158 33.11 S 19.01 E
Saronikós Kólpos C 38 37.54 N 23.12 E
Saronno 62 45.38 N 9.02 E
Saros Körfezi C 130 40.30 N 26.20 E
Sárospatak 30 48.19 N 21.34 E
Šarovka 78 50.01 N 35.27 E
Šarpa 80 47.07 N 45.29 E
Šarpajevka 78 48.34 N 40.59 E
Sar Passage ⩫ 175b 7.12 N 134.23 E
Sarpinskaja Nizmennost' ⊻ 80 47.30 N 45.30 E
Sarpinskije Ozera ⊜ 80 47.30 N 45.00 E
Šar Planina ᴬ 38 42.05 N 20.50 E
Sarpsborg 26 59.17 N 11.07 E
Sarpy Creek ≃ 202 46.15 N 107.09 W
Sarrabus ✦1 71 39.23 N 9.21 E
Sarralbe 56 49.00 N 7.01 E
Sarras 62 45.11 N 4.48 E
Sarrath, Oued V 36 35.59 N 8.23 E
Sarratt 260 51.41 N 0.29 W
Sarre 62 45.43 N 7.15 E
Sarre (Saar) ≃ 56 49.42 N 6.34 E
Sarre Blanche ≃ 56 48.41 N 7.01 E
Sarrebourg 58 48.44 N 7.03 E
Sarrebruck → Saarbrücken 56 49.14 N 6.59 E
Sarreguemines 56 49.06 N 7.03 E
Sarre Rouge ≃ 56 48.41 N 7.01 E
Sarre-Union 56 48.56 N 7.05 E
Sarria 34 42.47 N 7.24 W
Sarrià ✦8 266d 41.24 N 2.08 E
Sarro 150 13.43 N 5.15 W
Sarroch 71 39.04 N 9.00 E
Sarsfield 212 45.27 N 75.21 W
Sarsina 66 43.55 N 12.08 E
Sarsol 272c 19.02 N 73.01 E
Sarstedt 52 52.14 N 9.51 E
Sarstein ʌ 64 47.36 N 13.41 E
Sarstoon ≃ 236 15.53 N 88.55 W
Sarsuna 272b 22.28 N 88.18 E
Sart 56 50.31 N 5.56 E
Sartang ≃ 74 67.44 N 133.12 E
Sarteano 66 42.59 N 11.52 E
Sartell 190 45.37 N 94.12 W
Sartène 36 41.36 N 8.59 E
Sarthe □5 32 48.00 N 0.05 E
Sarthe ≃ 32 47.30 N 0.32 W
Sartilly 32 48.45 N 1.27 W
Sartirana Lomellina 62 45.07 N 8.39 E
Sartlan, Ozero ⊜ 86 55.00 N 78.35 E
Sartol'gen 80 48.57 N 47.03 E
Sartrouville 261 48.57 N 2.10 E
Saru 85 42.20 N 77.55 E
Saru ≃ 92a 42.30 N 142.00 E
Sarufutsu 92a 45.16 N 142.12 E
Saruhanlı 130 38.44 N 27.34 E
Sarūr 128 23.22 N 58.07 E
Šar Us ≃ 88 47.08 N 97.38 E
Saru-shima I 268 35.17 N 139.42 E
Sarvadyk 80 46.07 N 44.07 E
Sárvár 30 47.15 N 16.57 E
Sarver 214 40.44 N 79.45 W
Sarvestān 128 29.16 N 53.13 E
Sárvíz ≃ 30 46.24 N 18.41 E
Saryagač 85 41.27 N 69.10 E
Saryassija 85 38.25 N 67.57 E
Sarybarak 85 43.24 N 71.30 E
Sarybasat 86 46.38 N 60.27 E
Sarybulak, S.S.S.R. 85 40.54 N 73.49 E
Sarybulak, S.S.S.R. 86 49.27 N 76.27 E
Saryč, Mys ≻ 78 44.23 N 33.45 E
Sary-Išikotrau ✦2 86 45.30 N 76.00 E

Symbol	English	Deutsch	Español	Français	Português
≃	River	Fluss	Río	Rivière	Rio
⩦	Canal	Kanal	Canal	Canal	Canal
⌊	Waterfall, Rapids	Wasserfall, Stromschnellen	Cascada, Rápidos	Chute d'eau, Rapides	Cascata, Rápidos
⩫	Strait	Meeresstrasse	Estrecho	Détroit	Estreito
C	Bay, Gulf	Bucht, Golf	Bahía, Golfo	Baie, Golfe	Baía, Golfo
⊜	Lake, Lakes	See, Seen	Lago, Lagos	Lac, Lacs	Lago, Lagos
☷	Swamp	Sumpf	Pantano	Marais	Pântano
⊼	Ice Features, Glacier	Eis- und Gletscherformen	Accidentes Glaciales	Formes glaciaires	Acidentes Glaciares
⊤	Other Hydrographic Features	Andere Hydrographische Objekte	Otros Elementos Hidrográficos	Autres données hydrographiques	Outros Elementos Hidrográficos
✦	Submarine Features	Untermeerische Objekte	Accidentes Submarinos	Formes de relief sous-marin	Acidentes Submarinos
□	Political Unit	Politische Einheit	Unidad Política	Entité politique	Unidade Política
♥	Cultural Institution	Kulturelle Institution	Institución Cultural	Institution culturelle	Instituição Cultural
⊥	Historical Site	Historische Stätte	Sitio Histórico	Site historique	Sitio Histórico
♠	Recreational Site	Erholungs- und Ferienort	Sitio de Recreo	Centre de loisirs	Sítio de Lazer
⊠	Airport	Flughafen	Aeropuerto	Aéroport	Aeroporto
■	Military Installation	Militäranlage	Instalación Militar	Installation militaire	Instalação Militar
✦	Miscellaneous	Verschiedenes	Misceláneo	Divers	Miscelânea

Sarykol'skij Chrebet ⛰ 120 38.00 N 74.30 E
Sarykopa, Ozero ⊜ 86 50.22 N 64.08 E
Sarymoin, Ozero ⊜ 86 51.36 N 64.30 E
Sarysu ≃ 86 45.12 N 66.36 E
Sary-Taš 85 39.44 N 73.15 E
Sarytau 86 49.54 N 76.41 E
Saryžaz 72 42.55 N 79.38 E
Sarzana 64 44.07 N 9.58 E
Sarzanello, Fortezza di ⊥ 64 44.08 N 9.58 E
Sarzeau 32 47.32 N 2.46 W
S'as' ≃ 76 60.09 N 32.30 E
Sasa, Nihon 92 33.14 N 129.39 E
Sa' sa', Sūrīy 132 33.17 N 36.02 E
Sasa, Yis. 132 33.02 N 35.24 E
Sasabe 200 31.27 N 111.31 W
Sasabeneh 144 7.55 N 43.39 E
Sasaga-mine ∧ 96 33.49 N 133.17 E
Sasaginnigak Lake ⊜ 184 51.36 N 95.40 W
Sasago-tunnel ✦[5] 94 35.38 N 138.47 E
Sasaguri 96 33.37 N 130.32 E
Sasak 110 0.01 S 99.42 E
Sasakwa 196 34.57 N 96.31 W
Sasamungga 175e 7.02 S 156.47 E
Sasao 270 34.57 N 135.20 E
Sasar, Tanjung ≻ 115b 9.17 S 119.56 E
Sasarām 124 24.57 N 84.02 E
Sasayama 96 35.04 N 135.13 E
Sasa-yama ∧ 96 33.03 N 132.40 E
Sasbach 58 48.08 N 7.37 E
Sasco Brook ≃ 276 41.07 N 73.18 W
Sásd 30 46.15 N 18.06 E
Sasebo 92 33.10 N 129.43 E
Sasebo Naval Base (United States) ■ 92 33.09 N 129.45 E
Saseenos 224 48.24 N 123.40 W
Saseginaga, Lac ⊜ 190 47.06 N 78.35 W
Sashalom ✦[8] 264c 47.31 N 19.11 E
Sas-hegy ∧[2] 264c 47.23 N 19.18 E
Sashima 94 36.08 N 139.58 E
Sasiki 174m 26.10 N 127.47 E
Saskatchewan □[4] 184
176 54.00 N 105.00 W
Saskatchewan ≃ 184 53.12 N 99.16 W
Saskatoon 184 52.07 N 106.38 W
Saskylach 74 71.55 N 114.01 E
Sasmik, Cape ≻ 180 51.36 N 177.55 W
Sāsni 124 27.43 N 78.05 E
Sasolburg 158 26.48 S 27.45 E
Sason Dağları ⛰ 130 38.15 N 41.32 E
Sasovo 80 54.21 N 41.54 E
Saspamco 196 29.14 N 98.18 W
Saspul Gompa 123 34.15 N 77.09 E
Sassafras 274b 37.52 S 145.21 E
Sassafras ≃ 208 39.23 N 76.02 W
Sassafras Mountain ∧ 192 35.03 N 82.48 W
Sassandra 150 4.58 N 6.05 W
Sassandra □[5] 150 5.20 N 6.40 W
Sassandra ≃ 150 4.58 N 6.05 W
Sassano 68 40.20 N 15.33 E
Sassari 71 40.43 N 8.34 E
Sassari □[4] 71 40.40 N 9.00 E
Sassbach ≃ 61 46.43 N 15.48 E
Sasse ≃ 62 44.15 N 5.55 E
Sassello 62 44.29 N 8.30 E
Sassenage 62 45.12 N 5.40 E
Sassenberg 52 51.59 N 8.02 E
Sassenheim 52 52.13 N 4.31 E
Sassnitz 54 54.31 N 13.38 E
Sassocorvaro 66 43.47 N 12.30 E
Sasso di Castalda 68 40.30 N 15.40 E
Sassoferrato 66 43.26 N 12.51 E
Sasso Marconi 64 44.24 N 11.15 E
S'as'stroj 76 60.08 N 32.34 E
Sassuolo 64 44.33 N 10.47 E
Sas-Tobe 85 42.34 N 70.00 E
Sastown 150 4.40 N 8.26 W
Sastre 252 31.45 S 61.50 W
Sasumua Dam ⊜ 154 0.45 S 36.40 E
Sas van Gent 52 51.14 N 3.47 E
Sasyk, Ozero ⊜ 78 45.12 N 33.31 E
Sasykkol', Ozero ⊜ 86 46.35 N 81.00 E
Sasykoli 80 47.33 N 47.00 E
Šat ≃ 82 54.08 N 37.47 E
Satadougou 150 12.21 N 10.07 W
Satah Mountain ∧ 182 52.29 N 124.41 W
Satakunta ✦[1] 26 61.30 N 23.00 E
Šatalovka 78 51.09 N 38.16 E
Šatalovo 76 54.20 N 32.27 E
Sata-misaki ≻ 92 30.59 N 130.40 E
Satāna 122 20.35 N 74.12 E
Satanov 78 49.15 N 26.16 E
Satanta 198 37.26 N 100.59 W
Sátão 34 40.44 N 7.44 W
Sātāra, Bhārat 122 17.41 N 73.59 E
Satara, S. Afr. 156 24.29 S 31.47 E
Sataua 175a 13.28 S 172.40 W
Sātbāria, Bhārat 272b 22.25 N 88.33 E
Sātbāria, Bngl. 126 23.52 N 89.26 E
Satellite Beach 220 28.11 N 80.35 W
Satellite Channel ⋃ 224 48.43 N 123.30 W
Satema 152 4.18 N 21.42 E
Säter 40 60.21 N 15.45 E
Sātgāchia 126 23.16 N 88.08 E
Sātghara 272b 22.44 N 88.21 E
Saticoy 228 34.17 N 119.09 W
Satilla ≃ 192 30.59 N 81.28 W
Satilpa Creek ≃ 194 31.39 N 88.05 W
Satin 222 31.21 N 97.02 W
Satipo 248 11.16 S 74.37 W
Satırlar 130 37.30 N 29.46 E
Sátiro Dias 250 11.36 S 38.36 W
Satis 80 55.02 N 43.48 E
Satīt (Tekeze) ≃ 140 14.20 N 35.50 E
Satka 86 55.03 N 59.01 E
Satkānia 120 22.04 N 92.03 E
Sātkhira 124 22.43 N 89.06 E
Šatki 80 55.11 N 44.08 E
Satla Bīl ☵ 126 22.54 N 90.04 E
Satluj → Sutlej ≃ 120 29.23 N 71.02 E
Satna 124 24.35 N 80.50 E
Satna □[5] 124 24.30 N 80.50 E
Sato, Cañada de ≃ 288 34.35 S 58.38 W
Satomi 94 36.43 N 140.30 E
Satoou 150 13.38 N 6.58 E
Sátoraljaújhely 30 48.24 N 21.39 E
Šatovo 82 54.56 N 37.14 E
Satow 54 53.59 N 11.51 E
Sātpura Range ⛰ 122 22.00 N 78.00 E
Sätrabrunn 40 59.51 N 16.27 E
Satriano di Lucania 68 40.33 N 15.33 E
Šatrovo 86 56.31 N 64.38 E
Satrup 41 54.41 N 9.35 E
Satsop ≃ 224 47.03 N 123.30 W
Satsop, Middle Fork ≃ 224 47.05 N 123.30 W
Satsop, West Fork ≃ 224 47.02 N 123.32 W
Satsuma 194 30.51 N 88.03 W
Satsuma-hantō ≻[1] 92 31.25 N 130.25 E
Satsunan-shotō II 93b 29.00 N 130.00 E
Sattahip 110 12.40 N 100.54 E
Sattānkulam 122 8.27 N 77.56 E
Satte 94 36.04 N 139.43 E
Sattel 58 47.05 N 8.42 E
Sattenapalle 122 16.24 N 80.11 E
Satthwa 110 17.46 N 94.30 E
Sattledt 61 48.04 N 14.03 E
Satui 112 3.47 S 115.27 E
Sātuli 272b 22.33 N 88.34 E
Satu Mare 38 47.48 N 22.53 E
Satu Mare □[5] 38 47.40 N 23.00 E
Satun 110 6.37 N 100.04 E
Saturna 224 48.43 N 123.11 W
Saturna Island I 224 48.47 N 123.08 W
Saturnino M. Laspiur 252 31.42 S 62.29 W
Šaturtorf 76 55.34 N 39.26 E
Satus Creek ≃ 202 46.16 N 120.07 W
Satus Peak ∧ 224 46.15 N 120.45 W
Satyamangalam 122 11.31 N 77.15 E
Satzkorn 264a 52.29 N 12.59 E
Sau ≃ 269c 10.46 N 106.48 E
Sauble ≃ 212 44.40 N 81.17 W
Sauce, Arg. 252 30.05 S 58.46 W
Sauce, Perú 248 6.44 S 76.10 W
Sauce, Ur. 258 34.39 S 56.04 W
Sauce, Arroyo del ≃, Arg. 288 34.41 S 58.50 W
Sauce, Arroyo del ≃, Ur. 258 34.26 S 57.28 W
Sauce Chico ≃ 252 38.47 S 62.18 W
Sauce Corto, Arroyo ≃ 252 36.55 S 61.48 W
Sauce Grande ≃ 252 38.59 S 61.07 W
Saucier 194 30.38 N 89.08 W
Saucillo 232 28.01 N 105.17 W
Sauda 26 59.39 N 6.20 E
Saudade 256 21.56 S 43.03 W
Sauðárkrókur 24a 65.46 N 19.41 W
Saúde 250 10.56 S 40.24 W
Saúde ✦[8] 287b 23.37 S 46.37 W
Saudi Arabia □[1] 118 25.00 N 45.00 E
Saudi-Arabien → Saudi Arabia □[1] 118 25.00 N 45.00 E
Saudron 58 48.30 N 5.20 E
Sauer (Sûre) ≃ 56 49.44 N 6.31 E
Sauerkohl-Berge ⛰[2] 264a 52.20 N 13.45 E
Sauerlach 64 47.58 N 11.38 E
Sauerland ✦[1] 52 51.10 N 8.00 E
Sauêruiná ≃ 248 12.00 S 58.43 W
Sauêuiná ≃ 248 12.24 S 58.40 W
Saug ≃ 116 7.27 N 125.44 E
Saugatuck 216 42.40 N 86.12 W
Saugatuck ≃ 276 41.07 N 73.22 W
Saugatuck Reservoir ⊜[1] 207 41.16 N 73.22 W
Saugeen ≃ 190 44.30 N 81.22 W
Saugerties 210 42.05 N 73.57 W
Saughall 262 53.13 N 2.58 W
Saugor → Sāgar 124 23.50 N 78.43 E
Saugor □[5] 124 24.00 N 78.50 E
Saugstad, Mount ∧ 182 52.15 N 126.31 W
Saugus, Calif., U.S. 228 34.25 N 118.32 W
Saugus, Mass., U.S. 207 42.27 N 71.01 W
Saugus ≃ 283 42.28 N 70.58 W
Sauh, Tanjong ≻ 114 3.46 N 100.49 E
Saujil 252 28.11 S 66.14 W
Saujon 32 45.40 N 0.56 W
Sauk ≃, Minn., U.S. 198 45.36 N 94.10 W
Sauk ≃, Wash., U.S. 224 48.30 N 121.37 W
Sauk Centre 198 45.44 N 94.57 W
Sauk City 190 43.17 N 89.43 W
Sauk Rapids 190 45.34 N 94.09 W
Sauksaj ≃ 85 39.11 N 72.15 E
Sauk Village 216 41.30 N 87.34 W
Saukville 190 43.23 N 87.55 W
Saül 250 3.37 N 53.12 W
Şaulape ⛰ 61 46.55 N 14.40 E
Šaul'der 85 42.47 N 68.24 E
Sauldre ≃ 50 47.16 N 1.30 E
Sauldre, Canal de la ≍ 50 47.36 N 2.06 E
Saulgau 58 48.01 N 9.30 E
Saulgrub 64 47.40 N 11.01 E
Saulieu 50 47.16 N 4.14 E
Saulkrasti 76 57.17 N 24.25 E
Saulnot 58 47.34 N 6.38 E
Sault-au-Mouton 186 48.33 N 69.15 W
Sault au Récollet ✦[8] 275a 45.34 N 73.39 W
Sault aux Cochons, Rivière du ≃ 186 48.44 N 69.04 W
Sault-de-Vaucluse 62 44.05 N 5.25 E
Saulteaux ≃ 182 55.16 N 114.25 W
Saulteaux Indian Reserve ✦[4] 184 53.08 N 108.18 W
Sault-lès-Rethel 50 49.30 N 4.22 E
Sault Sainte Marie, Ont., Can. 190 46.31 N 84.20 W
Sault Sainte Marie, Mich., U.S. 190 46.30 N 84.21 W
Saulx ≃, Fr. 56 48.45 N 4.35 E
Saulx ≃, Fr. 261 48.41 N 2.19 E
Saulx-de-Vesoul 58 47.42 N 6.17 E
Saulx-les-Chartreux 261 48.42 N 2.16 E
Saulxures-sur-Moselotte 58 47.57 N 6.46 E
Šaum'ani 84 41.23 N 44.45 E
Šaum'anovsk 84 40.26 N 46.34 E
Saumarez Reef ✢[2] 166 21.50 S 153.40 E
Saumlaki 164 7.57 S 131.19 E
Saumon, Rivière au ≃ 206 45.41 N 71.27 W
Saumons, Rivíere aux ≃ 186 49.25 N 62.15 W
Saumur 32 47.16 N 0.05 W
Saundatti 122 15.47 N 75.07 E
Saundersfoot 42 51.43 N 4.43 W
Saunders Island I 18 57.47 S 26.27 W
Saunders Point ∧[2] 162 27.52 S 125.38 E
Saunderstown 207 41.30 N 71.25 W
Saunemin 216 40.54 N 88.24 W
Saupite 152 13.54 S 17.43 E
Sauquoit 210 43.00 N 75.16 W
Sauquoit Creek ≃ 210 43.08 N 75.16 W
Saurimo 152 9.39 S 20.24 E
Saur-Mogila ⊥ 83 47.56 N 38.46 E
Sausalito 226 37.51 N 122.29 W
Sausar 120 21.39 N 78.47 E
Sausset-les-Pins 62 43.20 N 5.07 E
Saussy 58 47.28 N 4.57 E
Sausu 112 1.00 S 120.30 E
Saútar 152 11.06 S 18.27 E
Sauteurs 241k 12.14 N 61.38 W
Sauteurs Bay C 241k 12.14 N 61.38 W
Sauvas 62 44.19 N 4.09 E
Sauve 62 43.56 N 3.57 E
Sauveterre 62 44.02 N 4.48 E
Sauveterre, Causse ⛰[1] 32 44.20 N 3.10 E
Sauveterre-de-Béarn 34 43.29 N 0.06 W
Sauveterre-de-Guyenne 32 44.42 N 0.05 W
Sauvie Island I 224 45.41 N 122.49 W
Sauvo 26 60.21 N 22.42 E
Sauwald ✦[3] 60 48.28 N 13.40 E
Sauzal 200 31.37 N 106.18 W
Sauze di Cesana 62 44.56 N 6.51 E
Sauze d'Oulx 62 45.02 N 6.52 E
Sava, It. 68 40.24 N 17.34 E
S'ava, S.S.S.R. 80 58.01 N 46.22 E
Sava ≃ 38 44.50 N 20.26 E
Sävaån ≃ 40 59.45 N 17.24 E
Savage, Md., U.S. 208 39.08 N 76.49 W
Savage, Mont., U.S. 202 47.27 N 104.21 W
Savai'i I 175a 13.35 S 172.25 W
Savala ≃ 80 51.03 N 41.30 E
Savalen ⊜ 26 62.15 N 10.29 E
Savalou 150 7.56 N 1.58 E
Savana Island I 240m 18.20 N 65.05 W
Savana Passage ⋃ 240m 18.21 N 65.04 W
Savane ≃ 186 51.08 N 71.26 W
Savanna, Ill., U.S. 190 42.05 N 90.08 W
Savanna, Okla., U.S. 196 34.50 N 95.51 W
Savannah, Ga., U.S. 192 32.04 N 81.05 W
Savannah, Mo., U.S. 194 39.56 N 94.50 W
Savannah, N.Y., U.S. 210 43.04 N 76.46 W
Savannah, Ohio, U.S. 214 40.58 N 82.22 W
Savannah, Tenn., U.S. 194 35.14 N 88.14 W
Savannah ≃ 192 32.02 N 80.53 W
Savannah Beach 192 32.01 N 80.51 W
Savannah Sound 192 25.06 N 76.09 W
Savannakhét 110 16.33 N 104.45 E
Savanna-la-Mar 241q 18.13 N 78.08 W
Savanna Portage State Park ♦ 190 46.51 N 93.10 W
Sāvantvādi 122 15.54 N 73.49 E
Savanūr 122 14.58 N 75.21 E
Sävar 26 63.54 N 20.34 E
Savara ≃ 62 45.42 N 7.12 E
Savasse ≃ 62 45.03 N 5.02 E
Savaştepe 130 39.22 N 27.40 E
Savcılıbüyükoba 130 39.14 N 33.41 E
Savé 150 8.02 N 2.29 E
Save (Sabi) ≃, Afr. 156 21.00 S 35.02 E
Save ≃, Fr. 32 43.47 N 1.17 E
Sāveh 128 35.01 N 50.20 E
Savelli 68 39.19 N 16.47 E
Savelovskij Vokzal ✦[5] 265b 55.48 N 37.35 E
Savelugu 150 9.37 N 0.49 W
Savenay 32 47.22 N 1.57 W
Săveni 38 47.57 N 26.52 E
Saverdun 32 43.14 N 1.35 E
Savernake Forest ✦[3] 42 51.24 N 1.38 W
Saverne 56 48.44 N 7.22 E
Savery Creek ≃ 200 41.01 N 107.27 W
Saviano 68 40.54 N 14.30 E
Savick Brook ≃ 262 53.49 N 2.37 W
Savièse 58 46.16 N 7.20 E
Savigliano 62 44.38 N 7.40 E
Savignano Irpino 68 41.14 N 15.11 E
Savignano sul Panaro 64 44.29 N 11.02 E
Savignano sul Rubicone 66 44.05 N 12.24 E
Savignone 62 44.34 N 8.58 E
Savigny-lès-Beaune 58 47.04 N 4.49 E
Savigny-le-Temple 261 48.35 N 2.35 E
Savigny-sur-Braye 50 47.53 N 0.49 E
Savigny-sur-Orge 50 48.40 N 2.21 E
Savill Gardens ♦ 260 51.27 N 0.36 E
Savines 62 44.32 N 6.24 E
Savinjske Alpe ⛰ 61 46.23 N 14.35 E
Savio 66 44.18 N 12.18 E
Savio ≃ 66 44.19 N 12.20 E
Saviore dell'Adamello 64 46.05 N 10.24 E
Săvîrsin 38 46.01 N 22.14 E
Savitaipale 26 61.12 N 27.42 E
Šavnik 38 42.57 N 19.05 E
Savo I 175e 9.08 S 159.49 E
Savognin 58 40.36 N 9.36 E
Savoie □[5] 32 45.30 N 6.25 E
Savolaks ✦[1] 26 62.00 N 28.00 E
Savona, B.C., Can. 182 50.45 N 120.50 W
Savona, It. 62 44.17 N 8.30 E
Savona, N.Y., U.S. 210 42.17 N 77.13 W
Savona □[4] 62 44.18 N 8.16 E
Savonlinna 26 61.52 N 28.53 E
Savonnières 50 47.21 N 0.33 E
Savonranta 26 62.11 N 29.12 E
Savoonga 180 63.42 N 170.27 W
Savory Creek ≃ 162 23.22 S 122.37 E
Savoureuse ≃ 58 47.31 N 6.51 E
Savran 78 48.09 N 30.04 E
Savruši 80 55.02 N 50.40 E
Sävsjö 26 57.25 N 14.40 E
S'avta 24 67.08 N 61.45 E
Savu Basin ✢[1] 14 9.30 S 122.00 E
Savudrija 64 45.30 N 13.30 E
Savur 130 37.33 N 40.53 E
Savusavu 175g 16.16 S 179.21 E
Savusavu Bay C 175g 16.45 S 179.15 E
Savu Sea → Sawu, Laut ⊤[2] 112 9.40 S 122.00 E
Savuto ≃ 68 39.02 N 16.06 E
Savvatejevka 88 52.20 N 103.39 E
Şawāb, Wādī aş- ∨ 130 34.36 N 40.25 E
Sawada 175d 24.50 N 125.09 E
Sawah 112 2.23 N 115.14 E
Sawahlunto 112 0.40 S 100.47 E
Sawai 164 2.58 S 129.09 E
Sawai, Teluk C 164 2.52 S 129.12 E
Sawai Mādhopur 124 25.59 N 76.22 E
Sawai Madhopur □[5] 124 26.15 N 74.45 E
Sawākin 140 19.07 N 37.20 E
Sawal, Gunung ∧ 115a 7.12 S 108.16 E
Sawan, Indon. 115b 8.08 S 115.11 E
Sawan, Mya. 110 24.30 N 96.19 E
Sawang 114 0.45 N 103.21 E
Sawankhalok 110 17.19 N 99.50 E
Sawara 94 35.53 N 140.30 E
Sawata 92 38.00 N 138.16 E
Sawatch Range ⛰ 200 39.10 N 106.25 W
Sawbridgeworth 42 51.50 N 0.09 E
Sawdā', Jabal as- ⛰[2] 146 28.40 N 15.30 E
Sawdā', Qurnat as- ∧ 130 34.18 N 36.07 E
Sawdirī 140 14.25 N 29.05 E
Sawel Mountain ∧ 48 54.49 N 7.02 W
Sawhāj 140 26.33 N 31.42 E
Sawi 110 10.14 N 99.07 E
Sawin, Lac ⊜ 206 46.32 N 73.54 W
Sawknah 146 29.04 N 15.47 E
Şawl 142 29.21 N 31.14 E
Sawla 150 9.17 N 2.25 W
Saw Log Creek ≃ 198 38.07 N 99.42 W
Saw Mill ≃ 276 40.56 N 73.53 W
Sawmill Brook ≃, Mass., U.S. 283 42.34 N 70.46 W
Sawmill Brook ≃, N.J., U.S. 276 40.28 N 74.26 W
Sawmill Creek ≃, N.J., U.S. 276 40.46 N 74.05 W
Sawmill Creek ≃, Pa., U.S. 279b 40.10 N 79.58 W
Sawmill Pond Brook ≃ 276 41.10 N 74.23 W
Sawmill Run ≃ 285 40.07 N 75.21 W
Sawmills 154 19.31 S 28.02 E
Sawqarah, Dawḩat C 118 18.35 N 57.15 E
Sawston 42 52.07 N 0.10 E
Sawţayr ⊤[4] 140 17.03 N 30.24 E
Sawtooth National Recreation Area ♦ 202 44.00 N 114.55 W
Sawtry 42 52.27 N 0.17 W
Sawu, Laut (Savu Sea) ⊤[2] 112 9.40 S 122.00 E
Sawu, Pulau I 112 10.30 S 121.54 E
Şawwān, Arḑ aş- ≚ 128 30.45 N 37.15 E
Sawyer, Mich., U.S. 216 41.53 N 86.35 W
Sawyer, N. Dak., U.S. 198 48.05 N 101.03 W
Sawyers Hill ∧[2] 186 47.11 N 53.52 W
Sawyers Valley 168a 31.54 S 116.13 E
Sawyerville, Qué., Can. 206 45.20 N 71.34 W
Sawyerville, Ill., U.S. 219 39.05 N 89.48 W
Sawyerwood 214 41.02 N 81.27 W
Saxby ≃ 166 18.25 S 140.53 E
Saxdalen 40 60.09 N 14.57 E
Saxen ⊜ 40 59.46 N 14.25 E
Saxike 120 30.44 N 86.22 E
Saxilby 44 53.17 N 0.40 W
Saxis 208 37.55 N 75.43 W
Saxmundham 42 52.13 N 1.29 E
Saxon, Schw. 58 46.09 N 7.11 E
Saxon, Wis., U.S. 190 46.29 N 90.25 W
Saxonburg 214 40.45 N 79.49 W
Saxon Woods Park ♦ 276 40.59 N 73.45 W
Saxony → Sachsen □[9] 54 51.00 N 13.30 E
Saxton 214 40.13 N 78.15 W
Say 150 13.07 N 2.21 E
Sāy, Jazīrat I 140 20.42 N 30.20 E
Saya 150 9.28 N 3.11 E
Saya de Malha Bank ✢[4] 12 10.30 S 61.00 E
Sayama, Nihon 94 35.51 N 139.24 E
Sayama, Nihon 270 34.31 N 135.34 E
Sayán 248 11.08 S 77.12 W
Sayan Mountains ⛰ 88 52.45 N 96.00 E
Sayaxché 232 16.31 N 90.10 W
Saybrook, Ill., U.S. 216 40.26 N 88.32 W
Saybrook, Ohio, U.S. 214 41.50 N 80.51 W
Saybrook Manor 207 41.17 N 72.24 W
Sayda, D.D.R. 54 50.43 N 13.25 E
Şaydā (Sidon), Lubnān 132 33.33 N 35.22 E
Şaydnāyā 132 33.42 N 36.22 E
Sayghān 120 35.11 N 67.42 E
Sayḩūt 144 15.12 N 51.14 E
Sayil ⊥ 232 20.16 N 89.42 W
Saylah 142 29.21 N 30.58 E
Saylorsburg 210 40.54 N 75.19 W
Saylorville Lake ⊜[1] 190 41.48 N 93.46 W
Säynätsalo 26 62.08 N 25.46 E
Sayō 96 35.00 N 134.22 E
Şayq, Wādī ∨ 144 14.36 N 47.47 E
Şayqal, Baḩr ⊜ 132 33.40 N 37.06 E
Sayre, Okla., U.S. 196 35.18 N 99.38 W
Sayre, Pa., U.S. 210 41.59 N 76.32 W
Sayreville 208 40.28 N 74.21 W
Sayula, Méx. 232 29.22 N 111.33 W
Sayula, Méx. 234 19.52 N 103.37 W
Sayula, Laguna de ⊜ 234 20.03 N 103.31 W
Sayula de Alemán 234 17.52 N 94.57 W
Say'ūn 144 15.56 N 48.47 E
Sayville 210 40.44 N 73.05 W
Sayward 182 50.22 N 125.55 W
Sazanit I 38 40.30 N 19.16 E
Sázava ≃ 30 49.53 N 14.24 E
Sazdy, S.S.S.R. 80 46.57 N 49.19 E
Sazdy, S.S.S.R. 86 47.22 N 61.48 E
Saze 62 43.56 N 4.41 E
Sažino 86 56.20 N 58.11 E
Sazlijka ≃ 38 42.02 N 25.52 E
Sazykul', Ozero ⊜ 86 55.22 N 67.34 E
Sba 148 28.13 N 0.08 W
Sbeïtla 148 35.14 N 9.08 E
Sbiba 36 35.33 N 9.05 E
Scaddan 162 33.27 S 121.43 E
Scaër 32 48.02 N 3.42 E
Scafati 68 40.45 N 14.31 E
Scafell Pikes ∧ 44 54.27 N 3.12 W
Scaggsville 208 39.09 N 76.54 W
Scajaquada Creek ≃ 284a 42.56 N 78.53 W
Scala, Teatro alla ✪ 266b 45.28 N 9.11 E
Scala Coeli 68 39.27 N 16.53 E
Scalasaig 46 56.04 N 6.11 W
Scalby 44 54.18 N 0.27 W
Scalea 68 39.49 N 15.48 E
Scaletta Zanclea 70 38.03 N 15.28 E
Scalloway 46a 60.08 N 1.18 W
Scalpay I, Scot., U.K. 46 57.17 N 5.59 W
Scalpay I, Scot., U.K. 46 57.52 N 6.40 W
Scalp Level 214 40.15 N 78.51 W
Scalp Mountain ∧[2] 44 55.04 N 7.24 W
Scammon 198 37.17 N 94.49 W
Scammon Bay 180 61.53 N 165.38 W
Scammon Bay C 180 61.53 N 165.54 W
Scammonden Water ⊜[1] 262 53.38 N 1.56 W
Scandale 68 39.07 N 16.57 E
Scandia 198 39.48 N 97.47 W
Scandiano 64 44.36 N 10.43 E
Scandicci 66 43.45 N 11.11 E
Scandinavian Peninsula ≻[1] 4 65.00 N 16.00 E
Scanlon 190 46.42 N 92.23 W
Scanno 66 41.54 N 13.53 E
Scansano 66 42.41 N 11.20 E
Scantic ≃ 207 41.52 N 72.38 W
Scapa 182 51.52 N 111.59 W
Scapa Flow C 46 58.55 N 3.06 W
Scapegoat Mountain ∧ 202 47.19 N 112.50 W
Ščapino 74 55.19 N 159.25 E
Ščapov 80 51.01 N 51.11 E
Ščapovo 82 55.09 N 38.11 E
Scappoose 224 45.45 N 122.53 W
Ščara ≃ 76 53.27 N 24.45 E
Scaramia o Scalambri, Capo ≻ 70 36.47 N 14.29 E
Scarba I 46 56.11 N 5.43 W
Scarborough, Austl. 168a 31.54 S 115.45 E
Scarborough, Ont., Can. 212 43.44 N 79.16 W
Scarborough, Trin. 241r 11.11 N 60.44 W
Scarborough, Eng., U.K. 44 54.17 N 0.24 W
Scarborough Bluffs ✦[8] 275b 43.42 N 79.14 W
Scarborough Centre ✦[9] 275b 43.47 N 79.16 W
Scarborough Point ≻ 171a 27.12 S 153.07 E
Scarborough Shoal I[1] 116 15.08 N 117.46 E
Scardroy 46 57.31 N 4.59 W
Scargill 172 42.56 S 172.57 E
Scarinish 46 56.29 N 6.48 W
Scarisbrick 262 53.37 N 2.56 W
Scărişoara 38 44.00 N 24.35 E
Scarlino 66 42.54 N 10.51 E
Scarp I 46 58.02 N 7.08 W
Scarpe ≃ 50 50.30 N 3.27 E
Scarperia 66 44.00 N 11.21 E
Scarper Peak ∧ 282 37.32 N 122.26 W
Scarriff 48 52.55 N 8.31 W
Scarsdale, Austl. 169 37.40 S 143.40 E
Scarsdale, N.Y., U.S. 210 40.59 N 73.49 W
Scartaglin 48 52.10 N 9.26 W
Scarth Hill 262 53.33 N 2.52 W
Ščastje 83 48.44 N 39.14 E
Scatarie Island I 186 46.00 N 59.44 W
Scatter Creek ≃ 224 46.48 N 123.06 W
Scauri, It. 66 41.15 N 13.42 E
Scauri, It. 70 36.45 N 11.58 E
Scavaig, Loch C 46 57.09 N 6.10 W
Scawfell Island I 166 20.52 S 149.36 E
Sceale Bay 162 33.01 S 134.12 E
Sceaux 50 48.47 N 2.17 E
Sceaux, Château de ⊥ 261 48.46 N 2.18 E
Ščedrin 76 52.53 N 29.33 E
Ščedro, Otok I 36 43.05 N 16.42 E
Ščedrovka 83 49.30 N 40.17 E
Ščeglovo 265a 60.02 N 30.46 E
Ščeljajur 24 65.21 N 53.21 E
Ščelkovo 76 55.55 N 38.00 E
Ščemilovo 265b 55.48 N 38.05 E

ENGLISH Name	Page	Lat.°′	Long.°′

Scena 64 46.41 N 11.12 E
Scenery Hill 214 40.05 N 80.04 W
Scenic 224 47.43 N 121.09 W
Sceptre 184 50.51 N 109.15 W
Ščerbakovo, S.S.S.R. 74 65.15 N 160.30 E
Ščerbakovo, S.S.S.R. 86 57.04 N 73.47 E
Ščerbakty 86 52.29 N 78.09 E
Ščerbinka 82 55.31 N 37.35 E
Ščerbinovka 83 48.26 N 37.50 E
Scerni 66 42.07 N 14.34 E
Scey-sur-Saône-et-Saint-Albin 58 47.40 N 5.58 E
Schaale ≃ 54 53.21 N 10.49 E
Schaalsee ⊜ 54 53.35 N 10.57 E
Schaan 58 47.10 N 9.31 E
Schabs → Sciaves 64 46.46 N 11.40 E
Schaefferstown 208 40.18 N 76.18 W
Schaephuysen 263 51.26 N 6.29 E
Schaerbeek 50 50.51 N 4.23 E
Schaf-Berg ∧ 64 47.47 N 13.27 E
Schäferberg ∧[2] 264a 52.25 N 13.08 E
Schaffhausen 58 47.42 N 8.38 E
Schaffhausen □[3] 58 47.40 N 8.35 E
Schafstädt 54 51.23 N 11.46 E
Schäftlarn 64 47.59 N 11.28 E
Schagen 52 52.46 N 4.47 E
Schaghticoke 210 42.54 N 73.35 W
Schalchen 60 48.07 N 13.10 E
Schale 52 52.26 N 7.37 E
Schalkau 54 50.24 N 11.00 E
Schalke ✦[8] 263 51.31 N 7.05 E
Schälker Heide ✦[3] 263 51.24 N 7.36 E
Schalksmühle 56 51.14 N 7.31 E
Schaller 198 42.30 N 95.18 W
Schanck, Cape ≻ 169 38.30 S 144.53 E
Schandelah 54 52.16 N 10.41 E
S-Chane 58 46.36 N 9.59 E
Schanfigg ∨ 58 46.51 N 9.38 E
Schanghai → Shanghai 106 31.14 N 121.28 E
Schangnau 58 46.50 N 7.52 E
Schapbach 58 48.22 N 8.17 E
Schapen 52 52.24 N 7.33 E
Schapenrust 273d 26.16 S 28.22 E
Schaprode 54 54.31 N 13.10 E
Schardenberg 60 48.32 N 13.30 E
Schardenberg ∧[2] 263 51.27 N 6.28 E
Schärding 60 48.27 N 13.26 E
Scharfling 64 47.48 N 13.25 E
Schari → Chari ≃ 146 12.58 N 14.31 E
Scharl 263 51.06 N 7.40 E
Scharmützelsee ⊜ 54 52.15 N 14.03 E
Scharnhörn I 52 53.57 N 8.25 E
Scharnhorst ✦[8] 263 51.32 N 7.32 E
Scharnitz 64 47.23 N 11.17 E
Scharrel 52 53.04 N 7.42 E
Scharzfeld 52 51.37 N 10.22 E
Schässburg → Sighişoara 38 46.13 N 24.48 E
Schauinsland ∧ 58 47.55 N 7.54 E
Schaumburg 216 42.02 N 88.05 W
Schaut 84 43.43 N 42.32 E
Schebeli → Shebele ≃ 144 0.01 S 42.45 E
Scheessel 52 53.10 N 9.29 E
Scheffau an der Lammer 64 47.35 N 13.12 E
Schefferville 176 54.48 N 66.50 W
Scheggia 66 43.24 N 12.40 E
Scheggino 66 42.43 N 12.50 E
Scheibbs 61 48.00 N 15.10 E
Scheibenberg 54 50.32 N 12.55 E
Scheiblingstein 264b 48.16 N 16.13 E
Scheidegg 58 47.35 N 9.51 E
Scheifling 61 47.09 N 14.24 E
Scheinfeld 56 49.40 N 10.27 E
Schelde (Escaut) ≃ 50 51.22 N 4.15 E
Schelklingen 58 48.22 N 9.44 E
Schell Creek Range ⛰ 204 39.10 N 114.40 W
Schellenberg ∧ 60 48.18 N 13.03 E
Schellsburg 214 40.03 N 78.39 W
Schelsen ✦[8] 263 51.09 N 6.31 E
Schenectady 210 42.47 N 73.53 W
Schenectady □[6] 210 42.47 N 73.53 W
Schenefeld 52 53.36 N 9.49 E
Schenevus 210 42.33 N 74.50 W
Schenevus Creek ≃ 210 42.29 N 74.59 W
Schenkendorf 264a 52.16 N 13.35 E
Schenkenhorst 264a 52.20 N 13.12 E
Schenklengsfeld 56 50.49 N 9.50 E
Schenley 214 40.41 N 79.40 W
Schenley Park ♦ 279b 40.26 N 79.56 W
Schepsdorf-Lohne 52 52.30 N 7.16 E
Schererville 216 41.30 N 87.27 W
Scherfede 52 51.32 N 9.02 E
Scherlebeck 263 51.37 N 7.08 E
Schermbeck 52 51.41 N 6.52 E
Schermerhorn 52 52.36 N 4.52 E
Schermützelsee ⊜ 54 52.34 N 14.04 E
Scherpenheuve 56 50.59 N 4.59 E
Scherpenzeel 52 52.05 N 5.30 E
Schertz 196 29.33 N 98.16 W
Schesch, Erg → Chech, Erg ✦[2] 148 25.00 N 2.15 W
Schesslitz 60 49.59 N 11.01 E
Schevelinge-Stausee ⊜[1] 263 51.08 N 7.26 E
Scheveningen ✦[8] 52 52.06 N 4.18 E
Schichallion ∧ 46 56.40 N 4.06 W
Schiedam 52 51.55 N 4.24 E
Schieder 52 51.55 N 9.09 E
Schiefbahn 56 51.14 N 6.31 E
Schierke 54 51.46 N 10.40 E
Schierling 60 48.50 N 12.08 E
Schiermonnikoog 52 53.24 N 6.10 E
Schiermonnikoog I 52 53.28 N 6.15 E
Schiers 58 46.59 N 9.41 E
Schiessen 58 48.18 N 10.14 E
Schiffdorf 52 53.32 N 8.39 E
Schiffenensee ⊜ 58 46.50 N 7.10 E
Schifferstadt 56 49.23 N 8.22 E
Schiffshebewerk ✦[5] 263 51.37 N 7.19 E
Schihkiatschwang → Shijiazhuang 98 38.03 N 114.28 E
Schijndel 52 51.37 N 5.25 E
Schikoku → Shikoku I 92 33.45 N 133.30 E
Schildau 54 51.27 N 12.56 E
Schilde 56 51.14 N 4.34 E
Schilde ≃ 54 53.26 N 10.53 E
Schildow 54 52.38 N 13.23 E
Schildwolde 52 53.14 N 6.49 E
Schiller Park 216 41.58 N 87.52 W
Schillingsfürst 56 49.17 N 10.15 E
Schillingstedt 54 51.14 N 11.11 E
Schilpario 64 46.01 N 10.09 E
Schiltach 58 48.17 N 8.20 E
Schiltigheim 58 48.36 N 7.45 E
Schimborn 56 50.03 N 9.11 E
Schimmert 56 50.55 N 5.50 E
Schinveld 56 50.57 N 5.59 E
Schinznach Bad 58 47.27 N 8.10 E
Schio 64 45.43 N 11.21 E
Schiphol, Luchthaven ⊠ 52 52.17 N 4.40 E
Schipkau 54 51.31 N 13.53 E
Schippenbeil → Sępopol 30 54.15 N 21.00 E
Schirgiswalde 54 51.05 N 14.27 E

DEUTSCH Name	Seite	Breite°′	Länge°′ E=Ost

Schirmeck 58 48.29 N 7.13 E
Schirnding 54 50.05 N 12.13 E
Schisuoka → Shizuoka 94 34.58 N 138.23 E
Schivelbein → Świdwin 30 53.47 N 15.47 E
Schjetman Reef ✢[2] 14 15.10 N 178.40 W
Schkeuditz 54 51.24 N 12.13 E
Schkoder-See → Scutari, Lake ⊜ 38 42.12 N 19.18 E
Schkölen 54 51.02 N 11.49 E
Schkopau 54 51.23 N 11.59 E
Schladen 54 52.01 N 10.32 E
Schladming 64 47.23 N 13.41 E
Schlanders → Silandro 64 46.38 N 10.46 E
Schlangen 52 51.49 N 8.50 E
Schlangenbad 56 50.05 N 8.05 E
Schlänitz-See ⊜ 264a 52.27 N 12.57 E
Schlanstedt 54 52.00 N 11.02 E
Schlater 194 33.38 N 90.21 W
Schlegel Lake ⊜ 276 40.59 N 74.03 W
Schlei C 41 54.36 N 9.51 E
Schleiden 56 50.31 N 6.28 E
Schleife 54 51.32 N 14.32 E
Schleinitz Range ⛰ 164 3.10 S 151.40 E
Schleithal 56 48.59 N 8.02 E
Schleitheim 58 47.45 N 8.29 E
Schleiz 54 50.34 N 11.49 E
Schlema 54 50.40 N 12.40 E
Schlepzig 54 52.01 N 13.53 E
Schlesien → Silesia □[9] 30 51.00 N 16.45 E
Schlesischer (Ost) Bahnhof ✦[5] 264a 52.30 N 13.26 E
Schleswig, B.R.D. 41 54.31 N 9.33 E
Schleswig, Iowa, U.S. 198 42.10 N 95.26 W
Schleswig-Holstein □[3] 30 54.00 N 10.30 E
Schlettau 54 50.33 N 12.56 E
Schlettstadt → Sélestat 58 48.16 N 7.27 E
Schleusingen 54 50.31 N 10.45 E
Schlichtingsheim → Szlichtyngowa 30 51.43 N 16.15 E
Schlicke ∧ 58 47.31 N 10.37 E
Schlieben 54 51.43 N 13.23 E
Schliengen 58 47.46 N 7.35 E
Schlieren 58 47.24 N 8.27 E
Schliersee 64 47.44 N 11.51 E
Schlitz 56 50.40 N 9.33 E
Schlochau → Człuchów 30 53.41 N 17.21 E
Schloppe → Człopa 30 53.06 N 16.08 E
Schloss Holte 52 51.52 N 8.35 E
Schloss Neuhaus 52 51.44 N 8.43 E
Schlossvippach 54 51.06 N 11.08 E
Schloss Zeil 64 47.52 N 10.00 E
Schlotheim 54 51.14 N 10.39 E
Schluchsee 58 47.49 N 8.10 E
Schluchsee ⊜ 58 47.49 N 8.10 E
Schlucht, Col de la)(58 48.04 N 7.02 E
Schlüchtern 56 50.20 N 9.31 E
Schluderns → Sluderno 64 46.40 N 10.35 E
Schlüsselburg 52 52.29 N 9.04 E
Schlüsselfeld 56 49.45 N 10.37 E
Schlutup ✦[8] 54 53.53 N 10.48 E
Schmachtendorf ✦[8] 263 51.32 N 6.49 E
Schmalfeld 52 53.52 N 9.58 E
Schmalkalden 54 50.43 N 10.26 E
Schmallenberg 56 51.09 N 8.17 E
Schmalnau 56 50.27 N 9.47 E
Schmannewitz 54 51.24 N 12.58 E
Schmarsau 54 52.54 N 11.21 E
Schmelz 56 49.27 N 6.51 E
Schmida ≃ 61 48.21 N 16.09 E
Schmidmühlen 60 49.16 N 11.56 E
Schmidt 56 50.39 N 6.25 E
Schmidtsdrif 158 28.41 S 24.02 E
Schmiedeberg 54 50.50 N 13.40 E
Schmiedefeld 54 50.37 N 10.49 E
Schmilka 54 50.53 N 14.14 E
Schmöckwitz ✦[8] 264a 52.23 N 13.39 E
Schmölln 54 50.53 N 12.20 E
Schmutter ≃ 58 48.42 N 10.46 E
Schnabelwaid 60 49.49 N 11.35 E
Schnackenburg 54 53.02 N 11.32 E
Schnait 56 48.47 N 9.23 E
Schnaitsee 60 48.04 N 12.22 E
Schnaittach 60 49.31 N 11.19 E
Schnaittenbach 60 49.33 N 12.01 E
Schnakenbek 52 53.23 N 10.30 E
Schnecksville 208 40.41 N 75.36 W
Schneealpe ⛰ 61 47.41 N 15.36 E
Schneeberg 54 50.36 N 12.38 E
Schneeberg ∧, B.R.D. 54 50.03 N 11.51 E
Schneeberg ∧, Öst. 61 47.47 N 15.47 E
Schneegattern 60 48.01 N 13.18 E
Schneidemühl → Piła 30 53.10 N 16.44 E
Schneider 216 41.11 N 87.27 W
Schneifel ⛰[1] 56 50.15 N 6.25 E
Schneverdingen 52 53.07 N 9.47 E
Schney 56 50.10 N 11.04 E
Schober Gruppe ⛰ 64 46.55 N 12.42 E
Schobüll 41 54.30 N 9.00 E
Schöckl ∧ 61 47.11 N 15.28 E
Schodn'a 82 55.57 N 37.18 E
Schodn'a ≃ 265b 55.50 N 37.25 E
Schoenbrunn Village State Memorial ⊥ 214 40.27 N 81.24 W
Schofield 190 44.54 N 89.36 W
Schofield Barracks ■ 229c 21.30 N 158.04 W
Schofields 274a 33.42 S 150.52 E
Schöftland 58 47.18 N 8.03 E
Schoharie 210 42.40 N 74.19 W
Schoharie □[6] 210 42.40 N 74.19 W
Schoharie Creek ≃ 210 42.57 N 74.18 W
Schoharie Reservoir ⊜[1] 210 42.22 N 74.26 W
Scholen 52 52.44 N 8.46 E
Schollene 54 52.41 N 12.13 E
Schöllenen ∨ 58 46.40 N 8.35 E
Schöller 263 51.14 N 7.01 E
Schöllkrippen 56 50.05 N 9.14 E
Schöllnach 60 48.45 N 13.11 E
Scholls 224 45.24 N 122.56 W
Scholven ✦[8] 263 51.36 N 7.01 E
Schömberg, B.R.D. 56 48.47 N 8.38 E
Schömberg, B.R.D. 58 48.13 N 8.46 E
Schomberg, Ont., Can. 212 44.00 N 79.41 W
Schonach 58 48.08 N 8.11 E
Schönaich 56 48.39 N 9.03 E
Schönau, B.R.D. 56 49.26 N 8.49 E
Schönau, B.R.D. 58 47.47 N 7.53 E
Schönau, B.R.D. 64 47.37 N 12.59 E
Schönau → Świerzawa, Pol. 30 51.01 N 15.54 E
Schönbeck 54 53.34 N 13.34 E
Schönberg, B.R.D. 54 54.23 N 10.22 E
Schönberg, B.R.D. 60 48.50 N 13.20 E
Schönberg, D.D.R. 54 53.50 N 11.38 E
Schönberg, D.D.R. 54 50.11 N 12.19 E
Schönberg, D.D.R. 54 50.31 N 11.57 E
Schönberg, Öst. 60 48.43 N 13.52 E
Schönberger Strand 54 54.25 N 10.24 E

Symbols in the index entries represent the broad categories identified in the key at the right. Symbols with superior numbers (⛰[2]) identify subcategories (see complete key on page *I* · *30*).

Kartensymbole in dem Registerverzeichnis stellen die rechts in Schlüssel erklärten Kategorien dar. Symbole mit hochgestellten Ziffern (⛰[2]) bezeichnen Unterabteilungen einer Kategorie (vgl. vollständiger Schlüssel auf Seite *I* · *30*).

Los símbolos incluídos en el texto del índice representan las grandes categorias identificadas con la clave a la derecha. Los símbolos con numeros en su parte superior (⛰[2]) identifican las subcategorías (véase la clave completa en la página *I* · *30*).

Les symboles de l'index représentent les catégories indiquées dans la légende à droite. Les symboles suivis d'un indice (⛰[2]) représentent des sous-catégories (voir légende complète à la page *I* · *30*).

Os símbolos incluídos no texto do índice representam as grandes categorias identificadas com a chave à direita. Os símbolos com números em sua parte superior (⛰[2]) identificam as subcategorias (veja-se a chave completa à página *I* · *30*).

	English	Deutsch	Español	Français	Português
∧	Mountain	Berg	Montaña	Montagne	Montanha
⛰	Mountains	Berge	Montañas	Montagnes	Montanhas
)(	Pass	Pass	Paso	Col	Passo
∨	Valley, Canyon	Tal, Cañon	Valle, Cañón	Vallée, Canyon	Vale, Canhão
≚	Plain	Ebene	Llano	Plaine	Planície
≻	Cape	Kap	Cabo	Cap	Cabo
I	Island	Insel	Isla	Île	Ilha
II	Islands	Inseln	Islas	Îles	Ilhas
⊥	Other Topographic Features	Andere Topographische Objekte	Otros Elementos Topográficos	Autres données topographiques	Outros Elementos Topográficos

ESPAÑOL

Nombre	Página	Lat.°′	Long.°′ W=Oeste
Schönberg im Stubaital	64	47.11 N	11.25 E
Schönbrunn, B.R.D.	60	48.33 N	12.12 E
Schönbrunn, D.D.R.	54	50.32 N	10.53 E
Schönbrunn, Schloss ʊ	264b	48.11 N	16.19 E
Schönbrunner Schlosspark ♠	264b	48.11 N	16.19 E
Schondra ≃	56	50.07 N	9.44 E
Schönebeck, D.D.R.	54	52.01 N	11.44 E
Schönebeck, D.D.R.	54	53.03 N	12.13 E
Schönebeck ◆[8]	263	51.28 N	6.56 E
Schöneberg ◆[8]	264a	52.29 N	13.21 E
Schöneck	54	50.23 N	12.20 E
Schönecken	56	50.09 N	6.27 E
Schönefeld	264a	52.23 N	13.30 E
Schönefeld, Zentralflughafen ⊠	54	52.23 N	13.31 E
Schöneiche	54	52.28 N	13.41 E
Schönenwerd	58	47.22 N	8.00 E
Schönerlinde	264a	52.39 N	13.27 E
Schönewalde	54	51.49 N	13.13 E
Schönfeld	264a	52.41 N	13.44 E
Schönficht	60	49.49 N	12.15 E
Schönfliess	264a	52.39 N	13.20 E
Schongau	58	47.49 N	10.54 E
Schönhagen, B.R.D.	41	54.38 N	10.01 E
Schönhagen, B.R.D.	52	51.41 N	9.33 E
Schönhaid	60	49.54 N	12.12 E
Schönhausen, B.R.D.	263	51.37 N	7.38 E
Schönhausen, D.D.R.	54	52.35 N	12.02 E
Schönheide	54	50.30 N	12.31 E
Schönholthausen	56	51.11 N	8.00 E
Schöningen	54	52.08 N	10.58 E
Schönkirchen	54	54.20 N	10.15 E
Schönlanke → Trzcianka	30	53.03 N	16.28 E
Schönmünzach	56	48.36 N	8.22 E
Schonnebeck ◆[8]	263	51.29 N	7.04 E
Schönningstedt	52	53.32 N	10.15 E
Schönow	54	52.40 N	13.32 E
Schönsee	60	49.31 N	12.33 E
Schönthal	60	49.21 N	12.36 E
Schonungen	56	50.03 N	10.18 E
Schönwald	58	48.06 N	8.11 E
Schönwalde, B.R.D.	54	54.11 N	10.45 E
Schönwalde, D.D.R.	54	52.37 N	13.07 E
Schönwalde, D.D.R.	54	52.40 N	13.26 E
Schönwalde, Forst ◆[3]	264a	52.42 N	13.28 E
Schönwies	58	47.11 N	10.39 E
Schoodic Lake ⊜	186	45.21 N	68.54 W
Schoolcraft	216	42.07 N	85.38 W
Schoolhouse Run ≃	285	40.13 N	75.27 W
Schoombee	158	31.28 S	25.30 E
Schoondijke	52	51.21 N	3.32 E
Schoonebeek	52	52.29 N	6.52 E
Schoonhoven	52	51.56 N	4.51 E
Schoorl	52	52.42 N	4.41 E
Schopfheim	58	47.39 N	7.49 E
Schopfloch	56	49.07 N	10.18 E
Schopp	56	49.21 N	7.41 E
Schöppenstedt	54	52.08 N	10.46 E
Schöppingen	52	52.05 N	7.14 E
Schorfheide	54	52.56 N	13.43 E
Schorfheide ◆[3]	54	52.55 N	13.35 E
Schörfling	64	47.56 N	13.36 E
Schorndorf	56	48.48 N	9.31 E
Schortens	52	53.31 N	7.56 E
Schoten	50	51.15 N	4.30 E
Schötmar	52	52.04 N	8.45 E
Schotten	56	50.30 N	9.07 E
Schottland → Scotland □[8]	28	57.00 N	4.00 W
Schouten, Kepulauan II	164	0.55 S	135.55 E
Schouten Island I	166	42.19 S	148.17 E
Schouten Islands II	164	3.30 S	144.40 E
Schouwen I	52	51.43 N	3.50 E
Schrader Creek ≃	210	41.43 N	76.30 W
Schrader Range ⋀	164	5.05 S	144.15 E
Schramberg	58	48.13 N	8.23 E
Schram City	219	39.10 N	89.27 W
Schrankogel ∧	64	47.02 N	11.06 E
Schraplau	54	51.26 N	11.40 E
Schreiber	190	48.48 N	87.15 W
Schrems	61	48.47 N	15.04 E
Schrick	61	48.30 N	16.37 E
Schriever	194	29.45 N	90.49 W
Schrobenhausen	60	48.33 N	11.17 E
Schröcken	58	47.15 N	10.05 E
Schroon ≃	188	43.29 N	73.49 W
Schroon Lake ⊜	188	43.47 N	73.46 W
Schrozberg	56	49.20 N	9.59 E
Schruns	58	47.04 N	9.55 E
Schulenburg, B.R.D.	52	52.12 N	9.47 E
Schulenburg, Tex., U.S.	222	29.41 N	96.54 W
Schull	48	51.32 N	9.33 W
Schuls → Scuol	58	46.48 N	10.18 E
Schultz Lake ⊜	176	64.45 N	97.30 W
Schulzendorf	54	52.22 N	13.35 E
Schulzenhöhe	264a	52.29 N	13.47 E
Schumacher	190	48.28 N	81.18 W
Schüpfheim	58	46.57 N	8.01 E
Schüren ◆[8]	263	51.30 N	7.32 E
Schussen ≃	58	47.37 N	9.32 E
Schussenried	58	48.00 N	9.40 E
Schutter ≃	58	48.34 N	7.50 E
Schüttorf	52	52.19 N	7.13 E
Schützenbruch → Kalety	30	50.34 N	18.54 E
Schuyler, Nebr., U.S.	198	41.27 N	97.04 W
Schuyler, Va., U.S.	192	37.47 N	78.42 W
Schuyler □[6], Ill., U.S.	219	40.07 N	90.34 W
Schuyler □[6], N.Y., U.S.	210	42.23 N	76.52 W
Schuyler Lake	210	42.47 N	75.02 W
Schuylerville	210	43.06 N	73.35 W
Schuylkill □[6]	210	40.41 N	76.12 W
Schuylkill ≃	208	39.53 N	75.12 W
Schuylkill Canal ≡	285	40.14 N	75.42 W
Schuylkill Haven	208	40.38 N	76.10 W
Schwaan	54	53.56 N	12.06 E
Schwabach	60	49.20 N	11.01 E
Schwaben □[5]	58	48.15 N	10.30 E
Schwaben □[9]	58	48.20 N	10.30 E
Schwabing ◆[8]	60	48.10 N	11.34 E
Schwäbische Alb ⋀	58	48.25 N	9.30 E
Schwäbisch Gmünd	56	48.48 N	9.47 E
Schwäbisch Hall	56	49.07 N	9.44 E
Schwabmünchen	58	48.11 N	10.45 E
Schwabstedt	41	54.23 N	9.11 E
Schwadorf	264b	48.04 N	16.35 E
Schwafheim	263	51.25 N	6.39 E
Schwagstorf	52	52.31 N	7.45 E
Schwaigern	56	49.08 N	9.03 E
Schwalenberg	52	51.52 N	9.11 E
Schwalm ≃	56	51.10 N	9.25 E
Schwalm-Nette, Naturpark ♠	56	51.15 N	6.15 E
Schwalmtal	56	51.13 N	6.16 E
Schwanden	58	47.00 N	9.04 E
Schwandorf in Bayern	60	49.20 N	12.08 E
Schwanebeck, D.D.R.	54	52.37 N	13.32 E
Schwanebeck, D.D.R.	54	51.58 N	11.07 E
Schwanenstadt	60	48.03 N	13.46 E
Schwanenwerder ◆[8]	264a	52.27 N	13.10 E

FRANÇAIS

Nom	Page	Lat.°′	Long.°′ W=Ouest
Schwaner, Pegunungan ⋀	112	0.40 S	112.40 E
Schwanewede	52	53.14 N	8.35 E
Schwangau	58	47.35 N	10.44 E
Schwansen ◆[1]	41	54.35 N	9.50 E
Schwante	264a	52.44 N	13.05 E
Schwarme	52	52.54 N	9.01 E
Schwarmstedt	52	52.40 N	9.37 E
Schwartau ≃	54	53.56 N	10.41 E
Schwarza, D.D.R.	54	50.38 N	10.32 E
Schwarza, D.D.R.	54	50.41 N	11.19 E
Schwarza ≃, D.D.R.	54	50.41 N	11.19 E
Schwarza ≃, Öst.	61	47.43 N	16.13 E
Schwarzach, B.R.D.	60	48.55 N	12.49 E
Schwarzach, Öst.	58	47.27 N	9.45 E
Schwarzach ≃	60	49.36 N	12.08 E
Schwarzach im Pongau	64	47.19 N	13.09 E
Schwarzbach	64	47.46 N	12.55 E
Schwarzbach ≃, B.R.D.	56	49.16 N	7.18 E
Schwarzbach ≃, B.R.D.	263	51.19 N	6.44 E
Schwarzburg	54	50.38 N	11.12 E
Schwarze Elster ≃	54	51.49 N	12.51 E
Schwarze Laaber ≃	60	49.00 N	12.03 E
Schwarzenbach am Wald	54	50.17 N	11.37 E
Schwarzenbach an der Saale	54	50.13 N	11.56 E
Schwarzenbek	52	53.30 N	10.29 E
Schwarzenberg, B.R.D.	263	51.24 N	6.42 E
Schwarzenberg, D.D.R.	54	50.32 N	12.47 E
Schwarzenberg Park ♠	264b	48.14 N	16.15 E
Schwarzenborn	56	50.37 N	9.58 E
Schwarzenbruck	60	49.21 N	11.14 E
Schwarzenburg	58	46.49 N	7.21 E
Schwarzenfeld	60	49.23 N	12.08 E
Schwarze Pumpe	54	51.32 N	14.20 E
Schwarzer Berg ∧[2]	263	51.41 N	7.12 E
Schwarzer Mann ∧	56	50.15 N	6.21 E
Schwarzer Regen ≃	60	49.10 N	12.50 E
Schwarzes Meer → Black Sea ⊤[2]	22	43.00 N	35.00 E
Schwarzheide	54	51.29 N	13.51 E
Schwarzkogel ∧	61	47.25 N	15.25 E
Schwarzrand ⋀	156	25.37 S	16.50 E
Schwarzriegel ∧	60	49.14 N	12.56 E
Schwarzsee	58	46.40 N	7.20 E
Schwarzwald (Black Forest) ⋀	58	48.00 N	8.15 E
Schwarzwälder Hochwald ◆[3]	56	49.39 N	6.55 E
Schwatka Mountains ⋀	180	67.25 N	157.00 W
Schwaz	64	47.20 N	11.42 E
Schwechat	264b	48.08 N	16.29 E
Schwechat ≃	264b	48.08 N	16.34 E
Schweden → Sweden □[1]	24	62.00 N	15.00 E
Schwedeneck	41	54.27 N	10.05 E
Schwedt	54	53.03 N	14.17 E
Schweez	54	53.53 N	12.24 E
Schweflinghausen	263	51.16 N	7.25 E
Schwegenheim	56	49.16 N	8.20 E
Schwei	52	53.24 N	8.21 E
Schweich	56	49.49 N	6.45 E
Schweidnitz → Świdnica	30	50.51 N	16.29 E
Schweighausen	58	48.13 N	7.57 E
Schweighausen-sur-Moder	56	48.49 N	7.44 E
Schweinfurt	56	50.03 N	10.14 E
Schweinitz	54	51.48 N	13.01 E
Schweinrich	54	53.10 N	12.37 E
Schweiz → Switzerland □[1]	58	47.00 N	8.00 E
Schweizer-Reneke	158	27.11 S	25.18 E
Schwelm	56	51.17 N	7.17 E
Schwendi	58	48.10 N	9.58 E
Schwenke	263	51.11 N	7.26 E
Schwenksville	285	40.16 N	75.28 W
Schwepnitz	54	51.20 N	13.57 E
Schwerin	54	53.38 N	11.25 E
Schwerin □[5]	54	53.30 N	11.30 E
Schwerin ◆[8]	263	51.33 N	7.20 E
Schwerin an der Warthe → Skwierzyna	30	52.36 N	15.30 E
Schweriner See ⊜	54	53.45 N	11.28 E
Schwerte	56	51.26 N	7.34 E
Schwerting	60	48.01 N	12.57 E
Schwetzingen	56	49.23 N	8.34 E
Schweyen	56	49.10 N	7.24 E
Schwieberdingen	56	48.52 N	9.04 E
Schwiebus → Świebodzin	30	52.15 N	15.32 E
Schwielochsee ⊜	54	52.03 N	14.12 E
Schwielowsee ⊜, D.D.R.	54	52.20 N	12.57 E
Schwielow-See ⊜, D.D.R.	264a	52.20 N	12.57 E
Schwitten	263	51.27 N	7.48 E
Schwyz	58	47.02 N	8.40 E
Schwyz □[3]	58	47.05 N	8.40 E
Sciacca	70	37.31 N	13.03 E
Sciara	70	37.55 N	13.45 E
Sciaves (Schabs)	64	46.46 N	11.40 E
Scicli	70	36.47 N	14.42 E
Scie ≃	50	49.55 N	1.02 E
Science and Industry, Museum of ʊ	278	41.47 N	87.35 W
Sciez	58	46.20 N	6.23 E
Scigliano	68	39.08 N	16.19 E
Ščigry	78	51.53 N	36.55 E
Scilla	68	38.15 N	15.44 E
Scilly I[1]	14	16.30 S	154.40 W
Scilly, Isles of II	42a	49.55 N	6.20 W
Ścinawa	30	51.25 N	16.27 E
Scio, N.Y., U.S.	210	42.10 N	77.59 W
Scio, Ohio, U.S.	214	40.24 N	81.05 W
Scio, Oreg., U.S.	202	44.42 N	122.51 W
Scionzier	58	46.03 N	6.34 E
Sciota	210	40.56 N	75.19 W
Scioto □[6]	218	38.48 N	83.01 W
Scioto ≃	188	38.44 N	83.01 W
Scioto Brush Creek ≃	218	38.50 N	83.01 W
Scipio, Ind., U.S.	218	39.05 N	85.43 W
Scipio, Utah, U.S.	200	39.15 N	112.06 W
Scipio Center	210	42.47 N	76.34 W
Scippo Creek ≃	218	39.31 N	82.59 W
Ščit ∧	36	44.02 N	17.47 E
Ščitkoviči	76	53.13 N	27.59 E
Scituate	207	42.12 N	70.44 W
Scituate Reservoir ⊜[1]	207	41.47 N	71.36 W
Sciuēref	146	29.53 N	14.08 E
Sclafani Bagni	70	37.49 N	13.51 E
Scobey	202	48.47 N	105.25 W
Scoffera, Passo della)(	62	44.29 N	9.07 E
Scofield Reservoir ⊜[1]	200	39.47 N	111.09 W
Scoglitti ◆[8]	70	36.53 N	14.26 E
Ščokino	76	54.01 N	37.31 E
Scole	42	52.22 N	1.10 E
Ščolkovo	82	55.55 N	38.00 E
Scoltenna ≃	64	44.15 N	10.50 E

PORTUGUÊS

Nome	Página	Lat.°′	Long.°′ W=Oeste
Scolt Head ≻	42	52.58 N	0.42 E
Scone	166	32.03 S	150.52 E
Scooba	194	32.50 N	88.29 W
Scopello	62	45.46 N	8.06 E
Scordia	70	37.18 N	14.51 E
Scoresby	274b	37.54 S	145.14 E
Scorno Punta di ≻	71	41.07 N	8.19 E
Scorrano, It.	66	42.35 N	13.49 E
Scorrano, It.	68	40.05 N	18.18 E
Ščors	78	51.49 N	31.59 E
Ščorsk	78	48.22 N	34.06 E
Scorzè	64	45.34 N	12.06 E
Scotch ≃	206	45.27 N	74.59 W
Scotch Plains	210	40.37 N	74.24 W
Scotchtown	210	41.29 N	74.21 W
Scotia, Nebr., U.S.	198	41.28 N	98.42 W
Scotia, N.Y., U.S.	210	44.54 N	73.33 W
Scotia Lake ⊜	190	47.05 N	81.23 W
Scotia Ridge ✢[3]	9	57.00 S	27.00 W
Scotia Sea ⊤[2]	9	56.00 S	40.00 W
Scotland, Ont., Can.	212	43.01 N	80.22 W
Scotland, Pa., U.S.	208	39.58 N	77.35 W
Scotland, S. Dak., U.S.	198	43.09 N	97.43 W
Scotland, Tex., U.S.	196	33.40 N	98.28 W
Scotland □[8]	28	57.00 N	4.00 W
Scotland Neck	192	36.02 N	77.32 W
Scotland Run ≃	285	39.39 N	75.03 W
Scotlandville	194	30.31 N	91.11 W
Ščot'ovo	83	48.09 N	39.04 E
Scotrun	210	41.04 N	75.19 W
Scotsburn	186	45.39 N	62.51 W
Scotstown	206	45.32 N	71.17 W
Scott, Sask., Can.	184	52.23 N	108.50 W
Scott, Miss., U.S.	194	33.36 N	91.04 W
Scott, Ohio, U.S.	216	40.59 N	84.35 W
Scott □[6], Ill., U.S.	219	39.38 N	90.27 W
Scott □[6], Ind., U.S.	218	38.41 N	85.46 W
Scott □[6], Ky., U.S.	218	38.18 N	84.35 W
Scott ≃	204	41.48 N	123.02 W
Scott, Cape ≻	182	50.47 N	128.26 W
Scott, Mount ∧, Okla., U.S.	196	34.44 N	98.32 W
Scott, Mount ∧, Oreg., U.S.	202	42.56 N	122.01 W
Scott Air Force Base ■	219	38.32 N	89.52 W
Scott Base ʊ[3]	9	77.50 S	166.25 E
Scottburgh	158	30.19 S	30.40 E
Scott City	198	38.29 N	100.54 W
Scott Cove C	276	41.03 N	73.28 W
Scott Creek ≃	226	37.02 N	122.13 W
Scottdale, Mich., U.S.	216	42.03 N	86.27 W
Scottdale, Pa., U.S.	214	40.06 N	79.35 W
Scott Glacier ⊼, Ant.	9	66.15 S	100.05 E
Scott Glacier ⊼, Ant.	9	85.45 S	153.00 W
Scott Haven	279b	40.15 N	79.47 W
Scott Island I	212	44.36 N	76.20 W
Scott Islands II	182	50.48 N	128.40 W
Scott Mountain ∧	202	44.11 N	115.47 W
Scott Peak ∧	202	44.21 N	112.50 W
Scott Reef ✢[2]	160	14.00 S	121.50 E
Scott Run ≃	284c	38.58 N	77.12 W
Scotts	216	42.11 N	85.25 W
Scottsbluff	198	41.52 N	103.40 W
Scotts Bluff National Monument ♠	198	41.49 N	103.41 W
Scottsboro	194	34.40 N	86.02 W
Scottsburg, Ind., U.S.	218	38.41 N	85.46 W
Scottsburg, N.Y., U.S.	210	42.40 N	77.43 W
Scottsdale, Austl.	166	41.10 S	147.31 E
Scottsdale, Ariz., U.S.	200	33.30 N	111.56 W
Scotts Flat Reservoir ⊜[1]	226	39.17 N	120.55 W
Scotts Head ≻	240d	15.13 N	61.23 W
Scotts Level Branch ≃	284b	39.22 N	76.45 W
Scottsmoor	220	28.46 N	80.53 W
Scott State Park ♠	198	38.40 N	100.54 W
Scotts Valley	226	37.03 N	122.02 W
Scottsville, Ky., U.S.	194	36.45 N	86.11 W
Scottsville, N.Y., U.S.	210	43.01 N	77.45 W
Scott Township	279b	40.24 N	80.06 W
Scottville, Ill., U.S.	219	39.29 N	90.06 W
Scottville, Mich., U.S.	190	43.57 N	86.17 W
Scour ≃	44	55.13 N	3.46 W
Scourie	46	58.20 N	5.08 W
Scout Lake	184	49.22 N	106.00 W
Scranton, Iowa, U.S.	198	42.01 N	94.33 W
Scranton, N. Dak., U.S.	198	46.09 N	103.09 W
Scranton, N.Y., U.S.	210	42.44 N	78.50 W
Scranton, Pa., U.S.	210	41.24 N	75.40 W
Scremerston	44	55.44 N	1.59 W
Screven	192	31.29 N	82.01 W
Screw ≃	164	3.55 S	142.50 E
Scribner	198	41.40 N	96.40 W
Scridain, Loch C	46	56.21 N	6.07 W
Scripps Institution of Oceanography ʊ[3]	228	32.52 N	117.15 W
Scrivia ≃	62	45.03 N	8.54 E
Scroggins	222	32.58 N	95.11 W
Scrooby	44	53.25 N	1.01 W
Scrub Island I	240m	18.28 N	64.31 W
Ščučin	76	53.36 N	24.45 E
Ščučinsk	86	52.56 N	70.12 E
Ščučje, S.S.S.R.	80	51.46 N	40.29 E
Ščučje, S.S.S.R.	86	55.17 N	63.59 E
Ščučje Ozero	86	56.28 N	56.38 E
Scugog ≃	212	44.24 N	78.45 W
Scugog, Lake ⊜	212	44.10 N	78.51 W
Scugog Indian Reserve ◆[4]	212	44.11 N	78.54 W
Scugog Island I	212	44.10 N	78.53 W
Ščukino	82	54.28 N	37.01 E
Scunthorpe	44	53.36 N	0.38 W
Scuol (Schuls)	58	46.48 N	10.18 E
Scuppernong ≃	216	42.54 N	88.42 W
Scurcola Marsicana	66	42.03 N	13.20 E
Ščurovo	82	55.03 N	38.49 E
Scurrival Point ≻	46	57.04 N	7.31 W
Scurry	222	32.31 N	96.23 W
Scutari → Shkodër, Shq.	38	42.05 N	19.30 E
Scutari → Üsküdar, Tür.	130	41.01 N	29.01 E
Scutari, Lake ⊜	38	42.12 N	19.18 E
Sé ◆[8]	287b	23.33 S	46.37 W
Seabeck	224	47.38 N	122.51 W
Sea Bird Island I	224	49.15 N	121.45 W
Seabird Island Indian Reserve ◆[4]	182	49.17 N	121.42 W
Seaboard	192	36.24 N	77.26 W
Sea Bright	276	40.22 N	73.59 W
Seabrook, Md., U.S.	284c	38.58 N	76.51 W
Seabrook, N.J., U.S.	208	39.30 N	74.14 W
Seabrook, Tex., U.S.	222	29.34 N	95.02 W
Seabrook, Lake ⊜	162	30.56 S	119.40 E
Sea Cliff	210	40.51 N	73.38 W
Seacock Swamp ≋	208	36.48 N	76.51 W
Seacombe	262	53.25 N	3.01 W
Sea Dog Island I	276	40.36 N	73.35 W
Seadrift	196	28.30 N	96.47 W
Seaford, Eng., U.K.	42	50.46 N	0.06 E
Seaford, Del., U.S.	208	38.39 N	75.37 W
Seaford, N.Y., U.S.	276	40.40 N	73.30 W
Seaford, Va., U.S.	208	37.12 N	76.26 W
Seaford Creek ≃	276	40.38 N	73.29 W
Seaforth, Austl.	274a	33.48 S	151.15 E
Seaforth, Ont., Can.	190	43.33 N	81.24 W
Seaforth, Eng., U.K.	262	53.28 N	3.01 W
Seaforth, Loch C	46	57.54 N	6.40 W
Seafox Seamount ✢[3]	14	30.30 S	172.40 W
Seager Wheeler Lake ⊜	184	54.27 N	103.30 W
Seagoville	222	32.38 N	96.32 W
Seagraves	196	32.57 N	102.34 W
Seaham	44	54.52 N	1.21 W
Seaholme	274b	37.52 S	144.50 E
Seahorse Point ≻	176	63.47 N	80.09 W
Seahorse Shoal ✢[2]	112	5.30 N	112.37 E
Seahouses	44	55.35 N	1.38 W
Seahurst	224	47.28 N	122.22 W
Sea Island I	224	49.12 N	123.10 W
Sea Islands II	192	31.20 N	81.20 W
Sea Isle City	208	39.09 N	74.42 W
Seal	260	51.17 N	0.14 E
Seal ≃	176	59.04 N	94.48 W
Seal, Cape ≻	158	34.07 S	23.25 E
Sea Lake	166	35.30 S	142.51 E
Sealand	262	53.12 N	2.58 W
Sealark Channel ⋃	175e	9.18 S	160.20 E
Seal Bay C	9	71.40 S	12.25 W
Seal Beach	228	33.44 N	118.06 W
Seal Beach Naval Weapons Station ■	280	33.45 N	118.03 W
Seal Cove, N.B., Can.	186	44.39 N	66.51 W
Seal Cove, Newf., Can.	186	47.28 N	53.05 W
Sealdah Railroad Station ◆[5]	272b	22.34 N	88.23 E
Seale	194	32.18 N	85.10 W
Sealevel	192	34.52 N	76.23 W
Seal Harbor	188	44.18 N	68.14 W
Seal Islands II	282	38.03 N	122.03 W
Seal Lake ⊜	176	54.18 N	61.40 W
Seal Rocks II[1]	282	37.47 N	122.31 W
Sealston	208	38.16 N	77.20 W
Sealy	222	29.47 N	96.09 W
Seaman	218	38.56 N	83.34 W
Seanor	214	40.13 N	78.54 W
Seara	252	27.07 S	52.17 W
Searchlight	204	35.28 N	114.55 W
Searcy	194	35.15 N	91.44 W
Searles Lake ⊜	204	35.43 N	117.20 W
Sears Lake ⊜	281	42.35 N	83.39 W
Searsport	188	44.28 N	68.56 W
Searsville Lake ⊜	282	37.24 N	122.14 W
Seascale	44	54.24 N	3.29 W
Seashore State Park ♠	208	36.54 N	76.02 W
Seaside, Calif., U.S.	226	36.37 N	121.50 W
Seaside, Oreg., U.S.	224	46.02 N	123.55 W
Seaside Park	208	39.55 N	74.05 W
Seaside Park ♠	276	41.10 N	73.12 W
Seaton, Eng., U.K.	42	50.43 N	3.05 W
Seaton, Eng., U.K.	44	54.41 N	3.33 W
Seaton, Eng., U.K.	44	53.54 N	0.14 W
Seaton ≃	42	50.22 N	4.22 W
Seaton Delaval	44	55.04 N	1.31 W
Seat Pleasant	284c	38.53 N	76.52 W
Seattle	224	47.36 N	122.20 W
Seattle, Mount ∧	180	60.06 N	139.11 W
Seattle Heights	224	47.48 N	122.20 W
Seattle-tacoma International Airport ⊠	224	47.27 N	122.18 W
Seatuck National Wildlife Refuge ◆[4]	276	40.43 N	73.13 W
Sea View, Mass., U.S.	283	42.08 N	70.43 W
Seaview, N.Y., U.S.	276	40.39 N	73.09 W
Seaview, Wash., U.S.	224	46.20 N	124.03 W
Seaward Kaikoura Range ⋀	172	42.14 S	173.39 E
Seaward Roads ⋃	174g	28.13 N	177.25 W
Seawell Airport ⊠	241g	13.04 N	59.29 W
Sea World ♠, Fla., U.S.	220	28.25 N	81.28 W
Sea World ♠, Ohio, U.S.	214	41.21 N	81.23 W
Seba	112	10.29 S	121.50 E
Sébaco	236	12.51 N	86.06 W
Sebago Lake ⊜	188	43.50 N	70.35 W
Se Bai ≃	110	15.13 N	104.47 E
Sebakor, Teluk C	164	3.35 S	132.50 E
Sebakung	112	1.37 S	116.26 E
Sebakwe National Park ♠	154	19.00 S	30.14 E
Šebalin	80	47.22 N	43.36 E
Šebalino, S.S.S.R.	80	48.16 N	43.21 E
Šebalino, S.S.S.R.	86	51.17 N	85.40 E
Sebanga	114	1.24 N	101.10 E
Sebangan, Teluk C	112	3.15 S	113.30 E
Sébaou, Oued ≃	34	36.55 N	3.55 E
Sebarok, Pulau I	271c	1.13 N	103.48 E
Sebastian, Fla., U.S.	220	27.49 N	80.28 W
Sebastian, Tex., U.S.	196	26.20 N	97.47 W
Sebastian, Cape ≻	202	42.19 N	124.26 W
Sebastian Inlet C	220	27.51 N	80.26 W
Sebastián Vizcaíno, Bahía C	232	28.00 N	114.30 W
Sebastião de Lacerda	256	22.17 S	43.35 W
Sebastopol, Austl.	169	37.36 S	143.51 E
Sebastopol, Calif., U.S.	204	38.24 N	122.49 W
Sebastopol, Miss., U.S.	194	32.34 N	89.27 W
Sebatik, Pulau I	112	4.08 N	117.47 E
Sebba	150	13.26 N	0.32 E
Sebderat	144	15.26 N	36.40 E
Sébé ≃	152	1.02 S	13.06 E
Sebec Lake ⊜	186	45.18 N	69.18 W
Sebei □[5]	154	1.25 N	34.25 E
Sebeka	198	46.38 N	95.05 W
Šebekino	78	50.25 N	36.56 E
Sébékoro	150	12.57 N	8.59 W
Seben	130	40.24 N	31.34 E
Sebenico → Šibenik	36	43.44 N	15.54 E
Seberi	252	27.29 S	53.24 W
Seberida	112	0.43 S	102.31 E
Sebeș	38	45.58 N	23.34 E
Sebesi, Pulau I	115a	5.57 S	105.30 E
Sebes Körös (Crișu Repede) ≃	38	46.55 N	20.59 E
Sebeșului, Munții ⋀	38	45.38 N	23.27 E
Sebewaing	190	43.44 N	83.27 W
Sebidiro	164	9.00 S	142.15 E
Sebille Manor	281	42.39 N	82.49 W
Şebinkarahisar	130	40.18 N	38.26 E
Sebiș	38	46.23 N	22.08 E
Sebnitz	54	50.58 N	14.16 E
Sebou, Oued ≃	148	34.15 N	6.40 W
Sebree	194	37.36 N	87.32 W
Sebrell	208	36.47 N	77.07 W
Sebring, Fla., U.S.	220	27.30 N	81.26 W
Sebring, Ohio, U.S.	214	40.55 N	81.02 W
Sebringville	212	43.24 N	81.04 W
Sebseb, Oued V	148	32.04 N	4.19 E
Sebuku	112	4.03 N	116.56 E
Sebuku, Pulau I, Indon.	112	3.30 S	116.22 E
Sebuku, Pulau I, Indon.	115a	5.53 S	105.31 E
Šebunino	89	46.27 N	141.51 E
Seč	60	49.36 N	13.30 E
Sêca, Ilha I	287a	22.50 S	43.11 W
Secane	208	39.55 N	75.18 W
Secang	115a	7.23 S	110.15 E
Secas, Islas II	236	7.58 N	82.02 W
Secaucus	276	40.47 N	74.04 W
Secchia ≃	64	45.04 N	11.00 E
Sečenovo	80	55.13 N	45.54 E
Secesh ≃	202	45.02 N	115.43 W
Séchault	56	49.16 N	4.44 E
Sechelt	182	49.28 N	123.45 W
Šechman'	76	52.32 N	40.29 E
Sechura	248	5.33 S	80.51 W
Sechura, Bahía de C	248	5.42 S	81.00 W
Sechura, Desierto de ◆[2]	248	5.50 S	80.40 W
Seckach	56	49.26 N	9.20 E
Seckau	61	47.16 N	14.47 E
Seckau ʊ[1]	61	47.16 N	14.47 E
Seckauer Tauern ⋀	61	47.20 N	14.40 E
Seclantas	252	25.18 S	66.15 W
Seclin	50	50.33 N	3.02 E
Seco ≃, Esp.	266d	41.30 N	2.09 E
Seco ≃, Méx.	200	30.41 N	111.56 W
Seco, Arroyo ≃, Calif., U.S.	226	36.25 N	121.20 W
Seco, Arroyo ≃, Calif., U.S.	280	34.05 N	118.13 W
Seco Creek ≃, N. Mex., U.S.	200	32.59 N	107.18 W
Seco Creek ≃, Tex., U.S.	196	29.02 N	99.08 W
Seco Island I	116	11.19 N	121.40 E
Second ≃	276	40.47 N	74.09 W
Second Cliff ●[4]	283	42.12 N	70.43 W
Second Herring Brook ≃	283	42.09 N	70.47 W
Second Lake ⊜	206	45.09 N	71.10 W
Second Mountain ∧	208	40.33 N	76.30 W
Second Swamp ≃	208	37.08 N	77.12 W
Second Valley	168b	35.33 S	138.14 E
Second Watchung Mountain ∧	276	40.55 N	74.13 W
Sečovce	30	48.43 N	21.40 E
Sečovská Polianka	30	48.47 N	21.42 E
Secretário, Ribeirão do ≃	256	22.14 S	43.25 W
Secretary	208	38.37 N	75.57 W
Secretary Island I	172	45.15 S	166.55 E
Section	194	34.35 N	85.59 W
Secubun Island I	116	5.06 N	120.18 E
Sécure ≃	248	15.10 S	64.52 W
Security	198	38.45 N	104.44 W
Séd ≃	30	47.00 N	18.31 E
Seda ≃	76	57.47 N	25.15 E
Sedah	112	10.46 S	123.12 E
Sedalia, Alta., Can.	184	51.41 N	110.40 W
Sedalia, Ind., U.S.	216	40.25 N	86.31 W
Sedalia, Mo., U.S.	194	38.42 N	93.14 W
Sedalia, Ohio, U.S.	218	39.44 N	83.29 W
Sedan, Austl.	168b	34.35 S	139.18 E
Sedan, Fr.	56	49.42 N	4.57 E
Sedan, Kans., U.S.	198	37.08 N	96.11 W
Sedanka, Cape ≻	180	53.49 N	166.06 W
Sedanka Island I	180	53.50 N	166.10 W
Sedano	34	42.43 N	3.45 W
Sedano, Tanjung ≻	115a	7.49 S	114.27 E
Sedanovo	88	56.58 N	101.22 E
Sedari, Tanjung ≻	115a	5.57 S	107.18 E
Sedayu	115a	6.59 S	112.33 E
Sedbergh	44	54.20 N	2.31 W
Sedco Hills	228	33.39 N	117.24 W
Seddin	54	52.16 N	13.01 E
Seddin-Berg ∧[2]	264a	52.24 N	13.40 E
Seddinsee ⊜	264a	52.23 N	13.41 E
Seddon	172	41.40 S	174.05 E
Seddonville	172	41.33 S	171.59 E
Sede Boqer	132	30.52 N	34.47 E
Sede Dov, Sede-Te'ufa ⊠	132	32.06 N	34.47 E
Sedel'nikovo	86	56.57 N	75.18 E
Sederberge ⋀	158	32.23 S	19.20 E
Séderon	62	44.12 N	5.32 E
Sederot	132	31.31 N	34.35 E
Sedgefield, Eng., U.K.	44	54.39 N	1.26 W
Sedgefield, N.J., U.S.	276	40.51 N	74.28 W
Sedgefield, N.C., U.S.	192	35.10 N	80.51 W
Sedge Island I	276	40.21 N	73.59 W
Sedgewick	182	52.46 N	111.41 W
Sedgewick, Mount ∧	200	35.11 N	108.06 W
Sedgley	42	52.33 N	2.08 W
Sedgwick, Colo., U.S.	198	40.56 N	102.31 W
Sedgwick, Kans., U.S.	198	37.55 N	97.25 W
Sedgwick, Maine, U.S.	188	44.18 N	68.37 W
Sédhiou	150	12.44 N	15.33 W
Sedico	64	46.06 N	12.06 E
Sedilo	71	40.10 N	8.55 E
Sedini	71	40.51 N	8.49 E
Sedlčany	30	49.40 N	14.26 E
Sedley	208	36.46 N	76.59 W
Sedlice	60	49.23 N	13.56 E
Sedlitz	54	51.33 N	14.03 E
Sedlo ∧	54	50.36 N	14.17 E
Sedn'ov	78	51.39 N	31.34 E
Šedok	84	44.13 N	40.52 E
Sedom	132	31.04 N	35.24 E
Sedom (Sodom) ⊥	132	31.04 N	35.23 E
Sedona	200	34.52 N	111.46 W
Sedot Yam	132	32.29 N	34.53 E
Sedova, Pik ∧	72	73.29 N	54.58 E
Sedovo	83	47.03 N	38.10 E
Sedovo-Vasiljevka	83	47.14 N	38.08 E
Sedrata	36	36.08 N	7.32 E
Sedriano	62	45.29 N	8.58 E
Sedrina	62	45.47 N	9.38 E
Sedro Woolley	224	48.30 N	122.14 W
Sedrun	58	46.41 N	8.46 E
Sedtim	24	66.25 N	56.20 E
Šeduva	76	55.46 N	23.46 E
Sędziszów	30	50.04 N	21.41 E
See, Öst.	58	47.05 N	10.28 E
See, Öst.	64	47.48 N	13.27 E
Seebad Ahlbeck	54	53.56 N	14.11 E
Seebad Bansin	54	53.57 N	14.07 E
Seebad Heringsdorf	54	53.56 N	14.08 E
Seeberg, D.D.R.	264a	52.33 N	13.41 E
Seeberg, Schw.	58	47.09 N	7.40 E
Seeberg Sattel)(	61	47.38 N	15.18 E
Seeber Lake ⊜	184	53.52 N	93.03 W
Seeboden	64	46.49 N	13.30 E
Seebruck	64	47.56 N	12.28 E
Seebrugg	58	47.49 N	8.13 E
Seeburg, D.D.R.	264a	52.31 N	13.07 E
Seeburg → Jeziorany, Pol.	30	53.58 N	20.46 E
Seefeld, B.R.D.	52	53.27 N	8.21 E
Seefeld, D.D.R.	54	52.37 N	13.40 E
Seefeld in Tirol	64	47.20 N	11.11 E
Seeg	58	47.38 N	10.36 E
Seegatterl	64	47.39 N	12.32 E
Seehaus	64	47.45 N	13.57 E
Seehausen, D.D.R.	54	52.06 N	11.17 E
Seehausen, D.D.R.	54	52.53 N	11.45 E
Seeheim	156	26.50 S	17.45 E
Seehof	264a	52.24 N	13.17 E
Seeis	156	22.29 S	17.39 E
Seekaskootch Indian Reserve ◆[4]	184	53.43 N	109.55 W
Seekirchen Markt	64	47.54 N	13.08 E
Seekoegat	158	33.03 S	22.31 E
Seekoei ≃	158	30.18 S	25.01 E
Seekonk	207	41.49 N	71.20 W
Seelbach	58	48.18 N	7.56 E
Seeley Lake	202	47.11 N	113.29 W
Seeleys Bay	212	44.29 N	76.14 W
Seelingstädt	54	50.46 N	12.14 E
Seelow	54	52.32 N	14.23 E
Seelyville, Ind., U.S.	194	39.30 N	87.16 W
Seelyville, Pa., U.S.	210	41.35 N	75.17 W
Seelze	52	52.24 N	9.35 E
Seemalik Butte ∧	180	60.09 N	167.08 W
Seemenbach ≃	56	50.17 N	8.59 E
Seemore Downs	162	30.42 S	125.15 E
Seen	58	47.29 N	8.46 E
Seengen	58	47.19 N	8.13 E
Seeon	64	47.58 N	12.26 E
Seer Green	260	51.37 N	0.36 W
Seergu	102	32.00 N	103.33 E
Seerhausen	54	51.16 N	13.15 E
Sées	50	48.36 N	0.10 E
Seesen	52	51.53 N	10.10 E
Seeshaupt	64	47.49 N	11.18 E
Seest	41	55.29 N	9.27 E
Seetal	61	47.09 N	13.57 E
Seetaler Alpen ⋀	61	47.05 N	14.35 E
Seevetal	52	53.23 N	9.59 E
Seewalchen am Attersee	64	47.57 N	13.35 E
Seewiesen	61	47.37 N	15.16 E
Seewinkel ◆[1]	61	47.48 N	16.49 E
Seewis	58	47.00 N	9.32 E
Séez	62	45.37 N	6.48 E
Seez ≃	58	47.07 N	9.18 E
Şefaatlı	130	39.31 N	34.46 E
Sefadu	150	8.39 N	10.59 W
Seferihisar	130	38.11 N	26.51 E
Séféto	150	14.08 N	9.49 W
Seffern	56	50.04 N	6.30 E
Seffner	220	27.59 N	82.17 W
Sefhare	156	23.02 S	27.28 E
Sefrou	148	33.50 N	4.50 W
Sefton, N.Z.	172	43.15 S	172.40 E
Sefton, Eng., U.K.	262	53.30 N	2.58 W
Sefton □[8]	262	53.34 N	3.14 W
Sefton, Mount ∧	172	43.41 S	170.03 E
Sefton Park ♠	262	53.23 N	2.56 W
Segaliud ≃	116	5.43 N	117.55 E
Segama ≃	112	5.27 N	118.48 E
Segamat	114	2.30 N	102.49 E
Segang	100	31.58 N	114.18 E
Segangane	34	35.09 N	3.00 W
Şegarcea	38	44.06 N	23.45 E
Šegarka ≃	86	57.16 N	84.05 E
Segbana	150	10.56 N	3.42 E
Segbwema	150	8.00 N	10.57 W
Segeg	144	7.42 N	42.50 E
Ségélo-Koro	150	9.25 N	7.09 W
Segera	164	8.15 S	143.30 E
Segeri	112	4.39 S	119.33 E
Segesta ⊥	70	37.56 N	12.50 E
Segesvár → Sighișoara	38	46.13 N	24.48 E
Segeža	24	63.44 N	34.19 E
Seggeuer, Oued es V	148	31.39 N	2.26 E
Seggiano	66	42.56 N	11.33 E
Šegmas	24	64.43 N	49.14 E
Segni	66	41.41 N	13.01 E
Segno	222	30.35 N	94.41 W
Segorbe	34	39.51 N	0.29 W
Ségou	150	13.27 N	6.16 W
Ségou □[4]	150	14.00 N	6.20 W
Šegovary	24	62.23 N	42.57 E
Segovia, Col.	246	7.07 N	74.42 W
Segovia, Esp.	34	40.57 N	4.07 W
Segozero, Ozero ⊜	24	63.18 N	33.45 E
Segrate	266b	45.29 N	9.19 E
Segré	32	47.41 N	0.53 W
Seguam Island I	180	52.17 N	172.30 W
Seguam Pass ⋃	180	52.08 N	172.45 W
Séguédine	146	20.12 N	12.59 E
Séguéla, C. Iv.	150	7.57 N	6.40 W
Séguéla, Mali	150	14.07 N	6.44 W
Séguéla □[5]	150	8.30 N	6.30 W
Séguénéga	150	13.27 N	1.58 W
Seguí	252	31.57 S	60.08 W
Seguin	196	29.34 N	97.58 W
Seguin ≃	212	45.21 N	80.01 W
Seguine Point ≻	276	40.31 N	74.12 W
Segula Island I	181a	52.01 N	178.07 E
Segundo	198	37.07 N	104.45 W
Segundo ≃	252	31.21 S	62.59 W
Seguntur	112	1.54 N	117.47 E
Segura	34	39.50 N	6.59 W
Segura ≃	34	38.06 N	0.38 W
Segura, Sierra de ⋀	34	38.00 N	2.43 W
Sehāni Kalān	272a	28.41 N	77.25 E
Sehāni Khurd	272a	28.42 N	77.25 E
Sehāra Bāzār	126	23.06 N	87.49 E
Sehithwa	156	20.23 S	22.45 E
Sehlaba-Thebe	158	29.53 S	29.05 E
Sehma	54	50.32 N	13.00 E
Sehnde	52	52.18 N	9.57 E
Sehnkwehn	150	5.13 N	9.12 W
Sehnkwehn ≃	150	5.12 N	9.21 W
Sehore	124	23.12 N	77.05 E
Sehore □[5]	124	23.00 N	77.00 E
Sehwān	120	26.26 N	67.52 E
Sehyŏn-ni	98	38.20 N	127.41 E
Seia	34	40.25 N	7.42 W
Seibeeshiden	268	35.34 N	139.22 E
Seibert	198	39.18 N	102.52 W
Seiches-sur-le-Loir	32	47.35 N	0.22 W
Seidan	96	34.19 N	134.45 E
Seidersville	210	40.35 N	75.23 W
Seiffen	54	50.39 N	13.26 E
Seifhennersdorf	54	50.56 N	14.36 E
Seignelay	50	47.54 N	3.36 E
Seigneurial, Lac ⊜	275a	45.33 N	73.20 W
Seika	270	34.46 N	135.48 E
Seikpyu	110	20.55 N	94.47 E
Seil I	46	56.18 N	5.39 W
Seiland I	24	70.25 N	23.15 E
Seilhac	32	45.22 N	1.42 E
Seiling	196	36.09 N	98.56 W
Seillans	62	43.38 N	6.38 E
Seille ≃, Fr.	56	49.07 N	6.11 E
Seille ≃, Fr.	58	46.31 N	4.56 E
Seilo	140	12.20 N	23.50 E
Seim → Sejm ≃	78	51.27 N	32.34 E
Sein, Île de I	32	48.02 N	4.51 W
Seinaiji	94	35.30 N	137.42 E
Seinäjoki	26	62.47 N	22.50 E
Seine □[5]	50	48.50 N	2.10 E
Seine ≃, Man., Can.	184	49.54 N	97.07 W
Seine ≃, Ont., Can.	190	48.40 N	92.49 W
Seine ≃, Fr.	32	49.26 N	0.26 E
Seine, Baie de la C[1]	50	49.25 N	0.15 E
Seine, Baie de la ≃	32	49.30 N	0.30 W
Seine-et-Marne □[5]	50	48.30 N	3.00 E
Seine-et-Oise □[5]	50	48.45 N	2.00 E
Seine-Maritime □[5]	50	49.45 N	1.00 E
Seine-Port	50	48.33 N	2.33 E
Seine-Saint-Denis □[5]	261	48.55 N	2.30 E
Seip Mound State Memorial ⊥	218	39.15 N	83.13 W
Seipstown	208	40.35 N	75.40 W
Seis de Septiembre → Morón	258	34.39 S	58.37 W
Seishin → Ch'ŏngjin	98	41.47 N	129.50 E
Seitenstetten	61	48.02 N	14.39 E
Seitovka	80	46.43 N	48.03 E
Seiwa, Nihon	94	35.15 N	140.00 E
Seiwa, Nihon	94	34.29 N	136.30 E
Seixal	34	38.38 N	9.06 W
Seiz	61	47.23 N	14.55 E

Symbol	English	Deutsch	Español	Français	Português
≃	River	Fluss	Río	Rivière	Rio
≡	Canal	Kanal	Canal	Canal	Canal
ʟ	Waterfall, Rapids	Wasserfall, Stromschnellen	Cascada, Rápidos	Chute d'eau, Rapides	Cascata, Rápidos
⋃	Strait	Meeresstrasse	Estrecho	Détroit	Estreito
C	Bay, Gulf	Bucht, Golf	Bahía, Golfo	Baie, Golfe	Baía, Golfo
⊜	Lake, Lakes	See, Seen	Lago, Lagos	Lac, Lacs	Lago, Lagos
≋	Swamp	Sumpf	Pantano	Marais	Pântano
⊼	Ice Features, Glacier	Eis- und Gletscherformen	Accidentes Glaciales	Formes glaciaires	Acidentes Glaciares
⊤	Other Hydrographic Features	Andere Hydrographische Objekte	Otros Elementos Hidrográficos	Autres données hydrographiques	Outros Elementos Hidrográficos
✢	Submarine Features	Untermeerische Objekte	Accidentes Submarinos	Formes de relief sous-marin	Acidentes Submarinos
□	Political Unit	Politische Einheit	Unidad Política	Entité politique	Unidade Política
ʊ	Cultural Institution	Kulturelle Institution	Institución Cultural	Institution culturelle	Instituição Cultural
⊥	Historical Site	Historische Stätte	Sitio Histórico	Site historique	Sítio Histórico
♠	Recreational Site	Erholungs- und Ferienort	Sitio de Recreo	Centre de loisirs	Sítio de Lazer
⊠	Airport	Flughafen	Aeropuerto	Aéroport	Aeroporto
■	Military Installation	Militäranlage	Instalación Militar	Installation militaire	Instalação Militar
◆	Miscellaneous	Verschiedenes	Misceláneo	Divers	Miscelânea

ENGLISH: Name — Page — Lat.°′ — Long.°′
DEUTSCH: Name — Seite — Breite°′ — Länge°′ E=Ost

Seize-Îles, Lac des @ 206 45.54 N 74.28 W
Sejaka 112 3.34 S 116.12 E
Sejerø I 41 55.53 N 11.09 E
Sejerø Bugt C 41 55.50 N 11.15 E
Sejm ≃ 78 51.27 N 32.34 E
Šejmčan 74 62.53 N 152.26 E
Šejno 80 53.22 N 43.12 E
Sejny 30 54.07 N 23.20 E
Sejorong 115b 9.02 S 116.48 E
Sejs 41 56.09 N 9.36 E
Seka 144 8.12 N 36.55 E
Sekači 80 50.30 N 43.37 E
Sekadau 112 0.01 S 110.54 E
Sekake's 158 29.58 S 28.27 E
Sekampung ≃ 115a 5.36 S 105.50 E
Sekayam ≃ 112 0.07 N 110.38 E
Sekayu 112 2.51 S 103.51 E
Seke 154 3.20 S 33.31 E
Seke-Banza 152 5.20 S 13.16 E
Sekeladi 112 2.38 S 102.14 E
Sekenke 154 4.16 S 34.10 E
Seki, Nihon 94 34.51 N 136.24 E
Seki, Nihon 94 35.29 N 136.55 E
Šeki (Nucha), S.S.S.R. 84 41.12 N 47.12 E
Seki, Tür. 130 36.24 N 29.13 E
Sekidō-san ▲ 94 36.58 N 136.59 E
Sekigahara 94 35.22 N 136.28 E
Sekigane 96 35.22 N 133.46 E
Sekijō 94 36.14 N 139.55 E
Sekima 112 1.41 S 111.31 E
Sekinomiya 96 35.22 N 134.38 E
Sekiu 182 48.16 N 124.18 W
Sekiya 270 34.27 N 135.42 E
Sekiyado 94 36.06 N 139.47 E
Sek Kong 271d 22.26 N 114.06 E
Sek Kong Airfield ⊠ 271d 22.27 N 114.05 E
Sekoma 156 24.41 S 23.50 E
Sekondi-Takoradi 150 4.59 N 1.43 W
Sekong Bay C 116 5.45 N 118.00 E
Sekota 144 12.38 N 39.03 E
Sekpiegu 150 9.33 N 0.02 W
Sekretaris ≃ 269e 6.10 S 106.47 E
Sekretarka 80 52.36 N 44.11 E
Šekšema 80 58.22 N 45.11 E
Šeksna 76 59.13 N 38.30 E
Sekudai 114 1.32 N 103.40 E
Sela ≃[1] 126 21.54 N 89.39 E
Sela, Ponta da ➤ 256 23.54 S 45.27 W
Šelabolicha 86 53.25 N 82.37 E
Sela Dingay 144 9.59 N 39.33 E
Šelagskij, Mys ➤ 74 70.06 N 170.26 E
Selah 202 46.39 N 120.32 W
Selai ≃ 114 2.13 N 103.26 E
Šelajevo 88 56.56 N 97.42 E
Selama 114 5.13 N 100.42 E
Šelanger 80 56.13 N 48.16 E
Selangor □3 114 3.20 N 101.30 E
Selangor ≃ 114 3.20 N 101.15 E
Selaön I 40 59.24 N 17.12 E
Selaphum 110 16.02 N 103.57 E
Selargius 71 39.16 N 9.10 E
Selaru, Pulau I 164 8.09 S 131.00 E
Selatan, Tanjung ➤ 112 4.10 S 114.38 E
Sel'atin 78 47.53 N 25.12 E
Selatpanjang 114 1.00 N 102.43 E
Selawik 180 66.37 N 160.03 W
Selawik ≃ 180 66.36 N 160.20 W
Selawik Lake @ 180 66.30 N 160.40 W
Selayar, Pulau I 112 6.05 S 120.30 E
Selayar, Selat ⊔ 112 5.42 S 120.28 E
Selb 54 50.10 N 12.08 E
Selbach 56 49.32 N 7.02 E
Selbeck ◆8 263 51.22 N 6.50 E
Selbecke ◆8 263 51.20 N 7.28 E
Selbitz 54 50.19 N 11.44 E
Selborne 42 51.06 N 0.56 W
Selbu 26 63.13 N 11.02 E
Selbusjøen @ 26 63.14 N 10.54 E
Selby, Austl. 274b 37.55 S 145.22 E
Selby, Eng., U.K. 44 53.48 N 1.04 W
Selby, S. Dak., U.S. 198 45.31 N 100.02 W
Selby ◆8 273d 26.13 S 28.02 E
Selby Creek ≃ 212 44.09 N 77.08 W
Selbyville 208 38.28 N 75.13 W
Selchow 264a 52.21 N 13.28 E
Sel'co, S.S.S.R. 24 63.18 N 41.22 E
Sel'co, S.S.S.R. 76 53.22 N 34.06 E
Selcourt 273d 26.18 S 28.27 E
Selčuga ≃ 89 49.42 N 133.20 E
Selçuk 130 37.56 N 27.22 E
Sel'cy, S.S.S.R. 76 57.57 N 35.59 E
Sel'cy, S.S.S.R. 265a 59.57 N 30.43 E
Selden, Kans., U.S. 198 39.33 N 100.34 W
Selden, N.Y., U.S. 210 40.51 N 73.02 W
Seldovia 180 59.27 N 151.43 W
Sele ≃ 68 40.29 N 14.56 E
Sele, Piana del ≃ 68 40.33 N 14.57 E
Sele, Selat ⊔ 164 1.10 S 131.05 E
Sele, Tanjung ➤ 164 1.26 S 130.55 E
Selec 76 52.33 N 33.35 E
Selec-Cholopejev 76 53.23 N 30.24 E
Selecn'a 76 52.23 N 34.23 E
Selection Park 273d 26.18 S 28.27 E
Selegas 71 39.34 N 9.06 E
Selemadeg 115b 8.29 S 115.02 E
Selembao 273b 4.22 S 15.17 E
Selemdža ≃ 89 51.42 N 128.53 E
Selemdžinsk 89 52.36 N 131.08 E
Šelemeti 80 57.27 N 48.07 E
Selendi 130 38.46 N 27.53 E
Selenduma 88 50.55 N 106.10 E
Selenga (Selenge Mörön) ≃ 88 52.16 N 106.16 E
Selenge, Mong. 88 49.25 N 103.59 E
Selenge, Zaïre 152 1.58 S 18.11 E
Selenge □4 88 50.15 N 106.12 E
Selenge Mörön (Selenga) ≃ 88 52.16 N 106.16 E
Selenginsk 88 52.06 N 107.01 E
Seleniće 38 40.32 N 19.38 E
Selenn'ach ≃ 74 67.48 N 144.54 E
Selent 54 54.17 N 10.26 E
Selenter See @ 54 54.17 N 10.28 E
Selepür 84 39.36 N 39.54 E
Sélestat (Schlettstadt) 58 48.16 N 7.27 E
Seletar 271c 1.25 N 103.53 E
Seletar ≃ 271c 1.25 N 103.52 E
Seletar, Pulau I 271c 1.27 N 103.52 E
Seletar Airfield ⊠ 271c 1.16 N 103.53 E
Seletar Reservoir @[1] 271c 1.24 N 103.48 E
Selety ≃ 86 53.06 N 73.22 E
Seletyteniz, Ozero @ 86 53.15 N 73.15 E
Selezen'ovo 76 59.12 N 42.18 E
Selezni, S.S.S.R. 76 55.39 N 31.29 E
Selezni, S.S.S.R. 80 52.48 N 41.15 E
Selezn'ovo 76 60.45 N 28.39 E
Self Defense Fleet Headquarters ■ 268 35.18 N 139.38 E
Selfoss 24a 63.56 N 20.57 W
Selfridge 198 46.02 N 100.56 W
Selghar 272c 18.57 N 73.02 E
Sel'gon 89 49.36 N 135.26 E
Sélibaby 150 15.13 N 12.11 W
Šelichino 89 50.22 N 137.38 E
Šelichov 88 52.13 N 104.08 E
Šelichova, Zaliv C 74 60.00 N 158.00 E
Šelichovo 89 55.42 N 97.41 E
Selidovo 83 48.08 N 37.18 E
Seligenporten 60 49.16 N 11.19 E
Seligenstadt 56 50.02 N 8.58 E
Seligenthal 54 50.45 N 10.28 E
Seliger, Ozero @ 76 57.13 N 33.05 E
Seligman, Ariz., U.S. 200 35.20 N 112.53 W
Seligman, Mo., U.S. 194 36.31 N 93.56 W
Seliksa 80 53.13 N 45.18 E
Selim 114 3.51 N 101.29 E
Selimbau 112 0.37 N 112.08 E
Selimiye 130 37.24 N 27.40 E
Selim River 114 3.50 N 101.24 E
Selinia 267c 37.56 N 23.32 E
Selinsgrove 208 40.48 N 76.52 W
Selinunte ⊥ 70 37.35 N 12.49 E
Selinus ⊥ 36 37.35 N 12.49 E
Selišče, S.S.S.R. 24 64.58 N 46.18 E
Selišče, S.S.S.R. 76 56.53 N 33.16 E
Selitrennoje 80 47.11 N 47.27 E
Selivanovskaja 80 48.52 N 41.42 E
Seližarovo 76 56.51 N 33.27 E
Selje 26 62.03 N 5.22 E
Seljord 26 59.29 N 8.37 E
Selkämeri (Bottenhavet) C 26 62.00 N 20.00 E
Šelkan ≃ 80 50.47 N 43.33 E
Selke ≃ 54 51.52 N 11.14 E
Selkirk, Man., Can. 184 50.09 N 96.52 W
Selkirk, Ont., Can. 212 42.49 N 79.56 W
Selkirk, Scot., U.K. 46 55.33 N 2.50 W
Selkirk, N.Y., U.S. 210 42.32 N 73.48 W
Selkirk Mountains ⩕ 182 51.00 N 117.40 W
Selkirk Shores State Park ♠ 212 43.33 N 76.12 W
Šelkovka 82 55.32 N 36.22 E
Šelkovskaja 84 43.30 N 46.22 E
Sella 64 46.00 N 11.25 E
Sella, Monte ▲ 64 46.40 N 12.02 E
Sella, Paso di)(64 46.30 N 11.45 E
Sella di Corno 66 42.21 N 13.14 E
Sellam, Oued Bou ≃ 34 36.12 N 5.00 E
Sellano 66 42.54 N 12.55 E
Selle ≃ 50 49.54 N 2.17 E
Selle, Chaîne de la ▲ 238 18.22 N 71.59 W
Seller Lake @ 184 55.00 N 94.32 W
Sellero 64 46.03 N 10.20 E
Sellers 192 34.17 N 79.28 W
Sellersburg 218 38.24 N 85.45 W
Sellersville 208 40.22 N 75.19 W
Selles-sur-Cher 50 47.16 N 1.33 E
Sellia Marina 68 38.55 N 16.45 E
Sellières 58 46.50 N 5.34 E
Sellin 54 54.22 N 13.41 E
Sells 200 31.55 N 111.53 W
Selly Oak ◆8 42 52.25 N 1.52 W
Selm 52 51.42 N 7.28 E
Selma, Ala., U.S. 194 32.25 N 87.01 W
Selma, Calif., U.S. 226 36.34 N 119.37 W
Selma, Ind., U.S. 218 40.12 N 85.16 W
Selma, N.C., U.S. 192 35.32 N 78.17 W
Selman City 222 32.11 N 94.58 W
Selmer 194 35.11 N 88.36 W
Selmigerheide 263 51.38 N 7.47 E
Selmsdorf 54 53.48 N 10.50 E
Selommes 50 47.45 N 1.12 E
Šelon' ≃ 76 58.14 N 30.50 E
Seloncourt 58 47.28 N 6.52 E
Selong 115b 8.39 S 116.32 E
Selongey 58 47.35 N 5.10 E
Šelopugino 88 51.39 N 117.33 E
Selouane 34 35.04 N 2.58 W
Selous, Mount ▲ 180 62.57 N 132.31 W
Selous Game Reserve ♠4 154 9.10 S 37.10 E
Selsdon ◆8 260 51.21 N 0.04 W
Selsey 42 50.44 N 0.48 W
Selsey Bill ➤ 42 50.43 N 0.48 W
Selsingen 52 53.22 N 9.13 E
Selston 42 53.04 N 1.20 W
Selters 56 50.32 N 7.44 E
Selty 80 57.19 N 52.10 E
Seltz 58 48.53 N 8.06 E
Seltzer 208 40.42 N 76.14 W
Selu, Pulau I 164 7.32 S 130.54 E
Selukwe 154 19.40 S 30.00 E
Selva, Arg. 252 29.46 S 62.03 W
Selva, It. 64 46.33 N 11.46 E
Sel'vačevo 82 55.25 N 37.57 E
Selva di Cadore 64 46.27 N 12.02 E
Selvagens, Ilhas II 148 30.05 N 15.55 W
Selvānā 128 37.25 N 44.51 E
Selvas ◆3 242 5.00 S 68.00 W
Selvino 62 45.48 N 9.45 E
Selway ≃ 202 46.08 N 115.36 W
Selwyn 166 21.32 S 140.30 E
Selwyn, Mount ▲ 182 55.59 N 123.36 W
Selwyn Lake @ 176 59.55 N 104.35 W
Selwyn Mountains ⩕ 180 63.10 N 130.20 W
Selwyn Range ⩕ 166 21.35 S 140.35 E
Selwyn Strait ⊔ 175f 16.03 S 168.12 E
Selz ≃ 56 49.59 N 8.02 E
Šemacha, S.S.S.R. 84 40.38 N 48.39 E
Šemacha, S.S.S.R. 86 56.15 N 59.16 E
Semai, Pulau I 164 3.08 S 132.30 E
Semakau, Pulau I 271c 1.12 N 103.46 E
Semal ≃ 38 40.56 N 19.24 E
Semanggol 114 4.57 N 100.38 E
Semangka, Teluk C 112 5.36 S 104.42 E
Šemanicha 80 57.18 N 45.24 E
Semans 184 51.25 N 104.44 W
Semanu 115a 8.00 S 110.39 E
Semara 148 26.44 N 11.41 W
Semarang 115a 6.58 S 110.25 E
Semaria 124 24.16 N 79.54 E
Sematan 112 1.48 N 109.46 E
Semau, Pulau I 112 10.13 S 123.22 E
Semayang, Danau @ 112 0.14 S 116.28 E
Sembabule 154 0.05 S 31.27 E
Sembadel 62 45.16 N 3.41 E
Sembakung ≃ 112 3.47 N 117.30 E
Sembawang 271c 1.27 N 103.50 E
Sembawang Airfield ⊠ 271c 1.25 N 103.49 E
Sembé 152 1.39 N 14.36 E
Semberong ≃ 114 2.30 N 103.08 E
Sembilan, Selat ⊔ 271c 1.18 N 103.42 E
Semblançay 50 47.30 N 0.35 E
Sembo ≃ 152 7.42 S 13.01 E
Semcy 76 52.51 N 33.28 E
Semejkino 83 48.19 N 39.32 E
Semeliškės 76 54.40 N 24.40 E
Semena ≃ 158 29.33 S 28.42 E
Semendua 152 3.11 S 18.05 E
Semène ≃ 62 45.23 N 4.13 E
Semenic, Munții ⩕ 38 45.12 N 22.05 E
Semenovka 78 49.36 N 33.10 E
Semenyih 114 2.57 N 101.51 E
Semertak 89 52.57 N 132.34 E
Semeru, Gunung ▲ 115a 8.06 S 112.55 E
Šemetovo 82 54.28 N 38.30 E
Semeževo 76 52.58 N 27.00 E
Semiahmoo Bay C 224 48.58 N 122.48 W
Semibalki 83 47.00 N 39.03 E
Semibratovo 80 57.18 N 39.32 E
Semibugry 80 46.11 N 48.16 E
Semichi Islands II 181a 52.42 N 174.00 E
Semides'atnoje 78 51.21 N 38.44 E
Semidi Islands II 180 56.07 N 156.44 W
Semien National Park ♠ 144 13.08 N 38.15 E
Semijarka 86 50.54 N 78.20 E
Semikarakorskij 80 47.31 N 40.48 E
Semilej 80 53.57 N 45.21 E
Semilovo 80 55.04 N 42.10 E
Semiluki 78 51.41 N 39.02 E
Semily 30 50.36 N 15.20 E
Seminara 68 38.20 N 15.52 E
Seminary 194 31.34 N 89.30 W
Seminoe Reservoir @[1] 200 42.00 N 106.50 W
Seminoe State Park ♠ 202 42.05 N 106.55 W
Seminole, Fla., U.S. 220 27.50 N 82.47 W
Seminole, Okla., U.S. 196 35.14 N 96.41 W
Seminole, Tex., U.S. 196 32.43 N 102.39 W
Seminole □6 228 28.45 N 81.13 W
Seminole, Lake @[1] 192 30.46 N 84.50 W
Seminole Draw V 196 32.26 N 102.10 W
Seminole Park 220 27.52 N 82.45 W
Seminskij Chrebet ⩕ 86 51.05 N 85.50 E
Semiozerje 88 49.52 N 110.23 E
Semioz'ornoje 86 52.22 N 64.08 E
Semioz'ornyj 88 53.44 N 120.25 E
Semipalatinsk 86 50.28 N 80.13 E
Semipolka 86 54.07 N 67.16 E
Semipolki 78 50.43 N 30.56 E
Semirara Island I 116 12.04 N 121.23 E
Semisopochnoi Island I 181a 52.00 N 179.35 E
Semitau 112 0.33 N 111.58 E
Semizbugy 86 50.12 N 74.48 E
Semjany 80 56.02 N 45.59 E
Semli Kalān 124 24.10 N 76.39 E
Semliki ≃ 154 1.14 N 30.28 E
Seml'ovo 76 55.03 N 33.58 E
Semmade 144 7.10 N 48.39 E
Semmens Lake @ 184 55.03 N 94.11 W
Semmering 61 47.38 N 15.49 E
Semnān 128 35.33 N 53.24 E
Semnān □8 128 35.30 N 54.00 E
Semois ≃ 56 49.53 N 4.45 E
Šemonaicha 86 50.39 N 81.54 E
Sem'ono-Aleksandrovka 78 51.03 N 40.12 E
Sem'onov 24 56.48 N 44.30 E
Sem'onovka, S.S.S.R. 78 52.10 N 32.35 E
Sem'onovka, S.S.S.R. 85 42.43 N 77.32 E
Sem'onovka, S.S.S.R. 86 51.20 N 70.46 E
Sem'onovskoje, S.S.S.R. 82 55.03 N 37.46 E
Sem'onovskoje, S.S.S.R. 82 55.18 N 38.21 E
Šemordan 80 56.11 N 50.26 E
Semouse ≃ 58 47.49 N 6.12 E
Sempach 58 47.08 N 8.11 E
Sempacher See @ 58 47.09 N 8.09 E
Sempang Mengayau, Tanjong ➤ 112 7.02 N 116.45 E
Semple Lake @ 184 55.02 N 95.38 W
Sempol 115a 8.01 S 114.08 E
Semporna 112 4.28 N 118.36 E
Sempu, Pulau I 115a 8.26 S 112.42 E
Semuda 112 2.51 S 112.58 E
Semur-en-Auxois 50 47.29 N 4.20 E
Šemurša 80 54.53 N 47.32 E
Šemyšejka 80 52.54 N 45.24 E
Semža 24 66.09 N 44.08 E
Sên ≃ 110 12.32 N 104.28 E
Sena, Bol. 248 11.32 S 67.11 W
Seňa, Česko. 30 48.34 N 21.15 E
Sena, Moç. 154 17.27 S 35.00 E
Sena → Seine ≃ 32 49.26 N 0.26 E
Senador Amaral 256 22.35 S 46.11 W
Senador Canedo 255 16.43 S 49.05 W
Senador Côrtes 256 21.48 S 42.56 W
Senador Firmino 255 20.55 S 43.06 W
Senador José Bento 256 22.10 S 46.10 W
Senador José Porfírio 250 2.39 S 51.55 W
Senador Pompeu 250 5.35 S 39.22 W
Senago 266b 45.35 N 9.07 E
Senahú 236 15.24 N 89.50 W
Senai 114 1.36 N 103.39 E
Senainville 261 48.30 N 1.37 E
Senaja 112 6.45 N 117.03 E
Senale 64 46.31 N 11.06 E
Senales, Val di V 64 46.45 N 10.50 E
Sena Madureira 248 9.04 S 68.40 W
Senamanik 114 0.45 N 100.47 E
Senanayake Samudra @[1] 122 7.11 N 81.29 E
Senang, Pulau I 271c 1.11 N 103.44 E
Senanga 152 16.06 S 23.16 E
Sénart, Forêt de ♠ 261 48.40 N 2.30 E
Sénas 62 43.45 N 5.05 E
Senate 184 49.18 N 109.41 W
Senath 194 36.08 N 90.10 W
Senatobia 194 34.39 N 89.58 W
Šenber 86 49.46 N 66.09 E
Šenbertal 86 48.43 N 60.20 E
Senča 78 50.16 N 33.20 E
Send 260 51.17 N 0.31 W
Sendafa 144 9.07 N 39.00 E
Sendai, Nihon 92 31.49 N 130.18 E
Sendai, Nihon 92 38.15 N 140.53 E
Sendai ≃, Nihon 92 31.51 N 130.12 E
Sendai ≃, Nihon 96 35.02 N 134.11 E
Sendai-heiya ≃ 92 38.15 N 141.00 E
Sendai-wan C 92 38.18 N 141.18 E
Sendamangalam 122 11.18 N 78.14 E
Senden, B.R.D. 52 51.51 N 7.29 E
Senden, B.R.D. 58 48.19 N 10.03 E
Sendenhorst 52 51.50 N 7.49 E
Sendhwa 120 21.41 N 75.06 E
Sendlingsdrift 156 28.12 S 16.53 E
Sendurjana 120 21.32 N 78.17 E
Senduruhan 112 1.00 S 110.46 E
Sene ≃ 150 7.30 N 0.33 W
Senec 30 48.14 N 17.24 E
Seneca, Ill., U.S. 216 41.19 N 88.36 W
Seneca, Kans., U.S. 198 39.50 N 96.04 W
Seneca, Md., U.S. 284c 39.04 N 77.17 W
Seneca, Mo., U.S. 194 36.51 N 94.37 W
Seneca, Oreg., U.S. 202 44.08 N 118.58 W
Seneca, Pa., U.S. 214 41.23 N 79.42 W
Seneca, S.C., U.S. 192 34.41 N 82.57 W
Seneca □6, N.Y., U.S. 210 42.54 N 76.52 W
Seneca □6, Ohio, U.S. 214 41.07 N 83.11 W
Seneca ≃ 210 43.12 N 76.17 W
Seneca, Mount ▲ 210 42.01 N 78.49 W
Seneca Castle 210 42.53 N 77.06 W
Seneca Caverns ◆5 214 41.11 N 82.53 W
Seneca Creek C 284b 39.19 N 76.22 W
Seneca Creek ≃ 196 36.36 N 102.52 W
Seneca Falls 210 42.55 N 76.48 W
Seneca Lake @ 210 42.40 N 76.57 W
Seneca State Park ♠ 208 39.08 N 77.15 W
Senecaville Lake @[1] 188 39.55 N 81.25 W
Senecú 232 31.43 N 106.23 W
Seneffe 50 50.31 N 4.15 E
Senegal □1 134 14.00 N 14.00 W
Sénégal ≃ 150 15.48 N 16.32 W
Sénégal Oriental □4 150 14.00 N 13.00 W
Seneghe 71 40.05 N 8.36 E
Senekal 158 28.30 S 27.32 E
Senerchia 68 40.44 N 15.12 E
Senetosa, Punta di ➤ 71 41.33 N 8.47 E
Sénez 62 43.55 N 6.24 E
Senežskoje, Ozero @ 82 56.12 N 37.00 E
Senftenberg 54 51.31 N 14.00 E
Senga Hill 154 9.22 S 31.12 E
Sengbachstausee @[1] 263 51.08 N 7.09 E
Sengejskij, Ostrov I 24 68.27 N 51.05 E
Šengel'šij 86 48.33 N 57.28 E
Sengés 255 24.06 S 49.29 W
Senggarang 114 1.45 N 103.03 E
Senghenydd 42 51.36 N 3.16 W
Sengilej 80 53.58 N 48.46 E
Sengkamang 114 0.42 N 101.55 E
Sengsengbirge ⩕ 61 47.47 N 14.15 E
Senguerr ≃ 254 45.32 S 68.54 W
Sengwa ≃ 154 17.07 S 28.05 E
Sengwarden 52 53.35 N 8.02 E
Senhāti 126 22.53 N 89.33 E
Senhora do Pôrto 255 18.53 S 43.06 W
Senhor do Bonfim 250 10.27 S 40.11 W
Senica 30 48.41 N 17.22 E
Senigallia 66 43.43 N 13.13 E
Senirkent 130 38.07 N 30.33 E
Senise 68 40.09 N 16.18 E
Senj 36 44.59 N 14.54 E
Senja I 24 69.20 N 17.30 E
Senjō-san ▲ 96 35.26 N 133.36 E
Senkevičevka 78 50.32 N 25.02 E
Senkobo 154 17.38 S 25.58 E
Sen'kovo 83 49.31 N 37.43 E
Şenköy 130 36.05 N 36.05 E
Šenkursk 24 62.08 N 42.53 E
Senlac 184 52.29 N 109.41 W
Şenlikköy ◆8 267b 40.59 N 28.47 E
Senlis 50 49.12 N 2.35 E
Senlisse 261 48.41 N 1.59 E
Senmonorom 110 12.27 N 107.12 E
Sennaja 78 45.15 N 37.01 E
Sennan 96 34.22 N 135.17 E
Senne ≃ 50 51.04 N 4.26 E
Sennecey-le-Grand 58 46.39 N 4.52 E
Senne I 52 51.57 N 8.31 E
Senne II → Sennestadt 52 51.59 N 8.37 E
Sennen 42 50.04 N 5.42 W
Sennestadt (Senne II) 52 51.59 N 8.37 E
Senneterre 190 48.23 N 77.15 W
Senneville 275a 45.27 N 73.57 W
Sennevoy-le-Bas 58 47.48 N 4.17 E
Senno 76 54.49 N 29.43 E
Sennoj, S.S.S.R. 80 52.11 N 46.57 E
Sennoj, S.S.S.R. 80 50.16 N 43.37 E
Sennokura-yama ▲ 94 36.49 N 138.50 E
Sennori 71 40.47 N 8.35 E
Sennwald 58 47.16 N 9.30 E
Sennybridge 42 51.57 N 3.34 W
Senogawa 96 34.25 N 132.35 E
Senoia 192 33.18 N 84.33 W
Senonches 50 48.33 N 1.02 E
Senones 58 48.24 N 6.59 E
Senorbì 71 39.32 N 9.08 E
Sénou 150 12.31 N 6.56 W
Sénouire ≃ 62 45.16 N 3.25 E
Senqu → Orange ≃ 156 28.41 S 16.28 E
Senriyama 270 34.47 N 135.30 E
Sens 50 48.12 N 3.17 E
Sensburg → Mrągowo 30 53.52 N 21.19 E
Sense ≃ 58 46.54 N 7.14 E
Sensée ≃ 50 50.16 N 3.06 E
Sensée, Canal de la ≃ 50 50.14 N 3.17 E
Sensuntepeque 236 13.52 N 88.38 W
Senta 38 45.56 N 20.04 E
Šentala 80 54.27 N 51.29 E
Sentani, Danau @ 164 2.36 S 140.34 E
Sentarum, Danau @ 112 0.51 N 112.06 E
Sentas 86 49.19 N 82.28 E
Šentelek 86 51.13 N 83.44 E
Sentery 154 5.22 S 25.45 E
Sentinel 196 35.09 N 99.10 W
Sentinel Butte ▲ 198 46.53 N 103.50 W
Sentinel Peak ▲ 182 54.54 N 121.57 W
Sentinel Plain ≃ 200 32.45 N 113.15 W
Sentinel Range ⩕ 9 78.10 S 85.30 W
Sentino ≃ 66 43.24 N 12.59 E
Šentjur 36 46.13 N 15.24 E
Sentolo 115a 7.50 S 110.13 E
Sentosa I 271c 1.15 N 103.50 E
Sento Sé 250 9.40 S 41.18 W
Sentsū-zan ▲ 96 35.09 N 133.11 E
Senyavin Islands II 14 6.55 N 158.00 E
Senye 152 1.34 N 9.50 E
Senza 154 3.02 N 26.19 E
Senzaki-wan C 96 34.24 N 131.15 E
Sen-zan ▲ 96 34.21 N 134.51 E
Senzig 54 52.17 N 13.39 E
Senzō Camp ■ 270 34.47 N 135.24 E
Senzu-dake ▲ 270 34.57 N 135.52 E
Seo de Urgel 34 42.21 N 1.28 E
Seohāra 124 29.13 N 78.35 E
Seon 58 47.21 N 8.10 E
Seonāth ≃ 122 21.44 N 82.28 E
Seoni 124 22.05 N 79.32 E
Seoni Mālwa 124 22.27 N 77.28 E
Seorīnārāyan 120 21.44 N 82.35 E
Seoul → Sŏul 98 37.33 N 126.58 E
Seoul Airport ⊠ 271b 37.32 N 126.56 E
Seoul National University ◆2 271b 37.28 N 126.57 E
Seoul Stadium ◆ 271b 37.35 N 127.02 E
Seoul Station ◆5 271b 37.34 N 126.58 E
Sepahat 114 1.59 N 102.47 E
Sepang 114 2.42 N 101.45 E
Sepanjang, Pulau I 112 7.10 S 115.50 E
Separation Creek ≃ 200 41.59 N 107.28 W
Separation Point ➤ 172 40.47 S 173.00 E
Sepasu 112 0.43 N 117.35 E
Sepatini ≃ 248 7.36 S 65.24 W
Sépeaux 50 47.57 N 3.14 E
Sepetiba ◆8 256 22.58 S 43.42 W
Sepetiba, Baía de C 256 23.00 S 43.42 W
Šepetovka 78 50.11 N 27.04 E
Sepi 175e 8.33 S 159.50 E
Sepino 66 41.24 N 14.37 E
Sep'o 98 38.39 N 127.22 E
Sępólno Krajeńskie 30 53.28 N 17.32 E
Sépone → Muang Xépôn 110 16.41 N 106.14 E
Sepopa 156 18.13 S 22.13 E
Sepopol 30 54.15 N 21.00 E
Sepoti ≃ 248 5.36 S 60.21 W
Sepotuba ≃ 248 15.56 S 57.39 W
Seppenrade 52 51.46 N 7.23 E
Sepphoris → Zippori 132 32.45 N 35.17 E
Seppois-le-Bas 58 47.33 N 7.10 E
Septeuil 261 48.54 N 1.41 E
Sept-Frères, Lac des @ 206 46.20 N 75.10 W
Sept-Îles (Seven Islands) 186 50.12 N 66.23 W
Septvaux 50 49.34 N 3.23 E
Sepulga ≃ 194 31.11 N 86.46 W
Sepúlveda 34 41.18 N 3.45 W
Sepulveda ◆8 280 34.13 N 118.28 W
Sepulveda Dam ◆6 280 34.10 N 118.29 W
Sepulveda Flood Control Basin ≃[1] 228 34.11 N 118.29 W
Seputih ≃ 112 4.40 S 105.51 E
Sepyč 80 58.11 N 54.08 E
Sequals 64 46.10 N 12.50 E
Sequatchie ≃ 192 35.02 N 85.38 W
Sequeros 34 40.31 N 6.01 W
Sequillo ≃ 34 41.45 N 5.30 W
Sequim 224 48.05 N 123.06 W
Sequim Bay C 224 48.03 N 123.02 W
Sequoia National Park ♠ 204 36.30 N 118.30 W
Sera 96 34.36 N 133.03 E
Sera, Pulau I 164 7.40 S 131.05 E
Šerabad 128 37.40 N 67.01 E
Serafeddin Dağları ⩕ 130 39.05 N 41.10 E
Serafimovič 80 49.36 N 42.43 E
Šeragul 88 54.29 N 100.56 E
Seraidi 36 36.55 N 7.41 E
Seraing 56 50.36 N 5.29 E
Seraja ≃ 82 56.15 N 38.45 E
Seram (Ceram) I 164 3.00 S 129.00 E
Seram, Laut (Ceram Sea) ⩕2 108 2.30 S 128.00 E
Serampore 126 22.45 N 88.21 E
Serang 115a 6.07 S 106.09 E
Serang ≃ 115a 6.43 S 110.35 E
Serangoon 271c 1.22 N 103.54 E
Serangoon ≃ 271c 1.24 N 103.56 E
Serangoon, Pulau I 271c 1.25 N 103.56 E
Serangoon Harbour C 271c 1.23 N 103.57 E
Serapo 66 41.13 N 13.34 E
Serasan, Pulau I 112 2.30 N 109.03 E
Serasan, Selat ⊔ 112 2.20 N 109.00 E
Seravalle Sesia 62 45.41 N 8.19 E
Seravezza 64 43.59 N 10.13 E
Seraya, Pulau I 271c 1.16 N 103.43 E
Serayevo → Sarajevo 38 43.52 N 18.25 E
Serayu ≃ 115a 7.41 S 109.06 E
Šerbakul' 86 54.38 N 72.24 E
Serbeulangit, Pegunungan ⩕ 114 3.45 N 97.50 E
Serbia → Srbija □3 38 44.00 N 21.00 E
Serchio ≃ 64 43.47 N 10.16 E
Serdar 130 37.08 N 36.27 E
Serdce-Kamen', Mys ➤ 180 66.57 N 171.40 W
Serdež 80 57.17 N 48.17 E
Serditoje 83 48.02 N 38.24 E
Serdoba ≃ 80 52.34 N 44.01 E
Serdobsk 80 52.28 N 44.13 E
Serebr'anka, S.S.S.R. 83 48.55 N 38.08 E
Serebr'anka, S.S.S.R. 86 57.13 N 70.42 E
Serebr'anka, S.S.S.R. 265b 55.45 N 37.55 E
Serebr'anka ≃ 265b 55.47 N 37.42 E
Serebr'ansk 86 49.43 N 83.20 E
Serebr'anyj Bor ◆8 265b 55.48 N 37.30 E
Serebr'anyje Prudy 82 54.28 N 38.44 E
Serebrovo 88 55.24 N 97.52 E
Serechoviči 78 51.25 N 24.40 E
Sered' 30 48.17 N 17.44 E
Sereda, S.S.S.R. 76 55.54 N 35.31 E
Sereda, S.S.S.R. 80 58.00 N 40.27 E
Šeredar' 82 55.56 N 39.04 E
Seredejskij 76 54.03 N 35.14 E
Seredići 76 53.35 N 35.51 E
Seredina-Buda 78 52.11 N 34.01 E
Serednikovo, S.S.S.R. 80 55.15 N 39.40 E
Serednikovo, S.S.S.R. 265b 55.56 N 37.14 E
Seredn'ovo 265b 55.35 N 37.18 E
Seredžius 76 55.05 N 23.25 E
Şereflikoçhisar 130 38.56 N 33.33 E
Šereges 86 52.57 N 88.02 E
Seregno 62 45.39 N 9.12 E
Serein ≃ 50 47.55 N 3.31 E
Seremban 114 2.43 N 101.56 E
Šeremetjevka 80 55.23 N 51.32 E
Šeremetjevo, Aeroport ⊠ 82 55.59 N 37.24 E
Šeremetjevskij 82 55.59 N 37.30 E
Serena 216 41.29 N 88.44 W
Seren del Grappa 64 45.59 N 11.51 E
Serengeti National Park ♠ 154 2.20 S 34.50 E
Serengeti Plain ≃ 154 2.50 S 35.00 E
Serengka 112 1.40 S 110.40 E
Serenje 154 13.15 S 30.14 E
Serenli 144 2.22 N 42.20 E
Sereno 256 21.19 S 42.39 W
Šereševo 76 52.33 N 24.13 E
Seret ≃ 78 48.38 N 25.52 E
Serfaus 58 47.02 N 10.36 E
Ser'ga 86 57.46 N 56.52 E
Sergeant 214 41.38 N 78.45 W
Sergeant Bluff 198 42.24 N 96.22 W
Sergeja Kirova, Ostrova II 74 77.12 N 89.30 E
Sergejeviči 76 53.30 N 27.45 E
Sergejevka, S.S.S.R. 83 48.40 N 37.22 E
Sergejevka, S.S.S.R. 86 53.51 N 67.25 E
Sergejevka, S.S.S.R. 86 51.39 N 68.13 E
Sergejevka, S.S.S.R. 89 43.23 N 133.22 E
Sergejevka, S.S.S.R. 89 44.22 N 131.39 E
Sergejevo 86 57.18 N 86.02 E
Sergen 38 41.42 N 27.42 E
Sergijevka 78 51.16 N 33.16 E
Sergijevskaja, S.S.S.R. 76 60.16 N 43.54 E
Sergijevskaja, S.S.S.R. 80 50.16 N 43.47 E
Sergijevskij 80 51.56 N 51.24 E
Sergili 85 41.13 N 69.14 E
Sergines 50 48.20 N 3.15 E
Sergipe □3 250 10.30 S 37.30 W
Sergokala 84 42.27 N 47.40 E
Sergozero, Ozero @ 24 66.47 N 36.42 E
Seria 112 4.39 N 114.23 E
Serian 112 1.10 N 110.34 E
Seriana, Valle V 64 45.55 N 9.55 E
Seriate 62 45.41 N 9.43 E
Seribu, Kepulauan II 115a 5.36 S 106.33 E
Seribudolok, Indon. 114 2.51 N 99.04 E
Seribudolok, Indon. 114 2.56 N 98.37 E
Sericho 154 2.30 N 40.10 E
Seridó ≃ 250 6.12 S 37.10 W
Sérifontaine 50 49.21 N 1.46 E
Sérifos 38 37.09 N 24.31 E
Sérifos I 38 37.11 N 24.31 E
Sérignan-du-Comtat 62 44.11 N 4.51 E
Sérigny ≃ 176 56.47 N 66.00 W
Seringa, Serra da ⩕[1] 250 7.00 S 50.40 W
Seringapatam 122 12.25 N 76.42 E
Serino 68 40.51 N 14.52 E
Serio ≃ 62 45.16 N 9.45 E
Serir Daği ▲ 130 39.39 N 42.41 E
Seritinga 256 21.54 S 44.30 W
Serjol 24 60.02 N 48.58 E
Serkhe, Cerro ▲ 248 17.22 S 69.22 W
Serkout, Djebel ▲ 148 23.30 N 6.48 E
Serkovo 82 54.28 N 38.46 E
Serles ▲ 64 47.08 N 11.23 E
Šerlovaja Gora 88 50.34 N 116.15 E
Serm ◆8 263 51.21 N 6.42 E
Sermaise 261 48.32 N 2.05 E
Sermaises 50 48.18 N 2.12 E
Sermaize-les-Bains 56 48.47 N 4.55 E
Serman 80 53.34 N 46.22 E
Sermata, Kepulauan II 164 8.10 S 128.40 E
Sermide 64 45.00 N 11.18 E
Sermizelles 50 47.32 N 3.48 E
Sermoneta 66 41.33 N 12.59 E
Šerna ≃ 82 55.51 N 38.34 E
Sernambitiba 287a 22.41 S 42.59 W
Sernambitiba, Pontal de ➤ 287a 23.02 S 43.27 W
Serniki 78 51.49 N 26.14 E
Sernovodsk 80 53.56 N 51.17 E
Sernur 80 56.56 N 49.09 E
Sernyy Zavod 128 39.59 N 58.50 E
Séro 150 14.48 N 11.04 W
Serock 30 52.31 N 21.03 E
Serodino 252 32.37 S 60.57 W
Ser'odka 76 58.10 N 28.12 E
Seroglazka 80 47.01 N 47.29 E
Ser'ogovo 24 62.20 N 50.36 E
Serooskerke 52 51.42 N 3.50 E
Seropédica 256 22.44 S 43.43 W
Serov 86 59.29 N 60.31 E
Serovo 85 40.27 N 71.12 E
Serowe 156 22.25 S 26.44 E
Ser'oža ≃ 80 55.34 N 42.29 E
Serpa 34 37.56 N 7.36 W
Serpejsk 76 54.20 N 34.59 W
Serpent, Lac du @ 186 49.50 N 71.37 W
Serpent, Rivière au ≃ 186 49.33 N 71.14 W
Serpentine 168a 32.22 S 115.59 E
Serpentine ≃, Austl. 168a 32.33 S 115.46 E
Serpentine ≃, B.C., Can. 224 49.05 N 122.50 W
Serpentine Dam ◆6 168a 32.25 S 116.08 E
Serpentine Lakes @ 162 28.32 S 129.09 E
Serpent Mound State Memorial ⊥ 218 39.02 N 83.26 W
Serpents Mouth ⊔ 241r 10.00 N 62.00 W
Serpis ≃ 34 38.59 N 0.09 W
Serpnevoje 78 46.18 N 29.02 E
Serpuchov 82 54.55 N 37.25 E
Serpukhov → Serpuchov 82 54.55 N 37.25 E
Serqo → Sark I 43b 49.26 N 2.21 W
Serra 255 20.07 S 40.18 W
Serra, Monte ▲ 66 43.46 N 10.33 E
Serra Branca 250 7.29 S 36.40 W
Serracapriola 68 41.48 N 15.09 E
Serrada 64 45.53 N 11.09 E
Serra d'aiello 68 39.05 N 16.08 E
Serra de'Conti 66 43.33 N 13.02 E
Serradifalco 70 37.27 N 13.53 E
Serra do Navio 250 0.59 N 52.03 W
Serra do Salitre 255 19.06 S 46.41 W
Serra dos Órgãos, Parque Nacional da ♠ 256 22.26 S 43.02 W
Serra Grande 250 7.15 S 38.19 W
Sérrai 38 41.05 N 23.32 E
Serramanna 71 39.25 N 8.55 E
Serramazzoni 64 44.25 N 10.47 E
Serramonte Center ◆9 282 37.40 N 122.28 W
Serrana 255 21.14 S 47.36 W
Serrana Bank ◆4 236 14.23 N 80.12 W
Serra Negra 256 22.36 S 46.42 W
Serra Negra do Norte 250 6.40 S 37.24 W
Serrania 255 21.33 S 46.03 W
Serranilla Bank ◆4 236 15.50 N 79.50 W
Serrano, Isla I 254 48.30 S 74.45 W
Serranópolis 255 18.16 S 52.00 W
Serranos 256 21.51 S 44.30 W
Serra Preta 255 12.09 S 39.20 W
Serrara 68 40.42 N 13.54 E
Serraria, Bra. 250 6.49 S 35.38 W
Serraria, Bra. 256 22.01 S 43.12 W
Serra San Bruno 68 38.35 N 16.20 E
Serra San Quirico 66 43.27 N 13.01 E
Serrastretta 68 39.01 N 16.25 E
Serrat, Cap ➤ 36 37.14 N 9.13 E
Serra Talhada 250 7.59 S 38.18 W
Serravalle, It. 66 42.47 N 13.01 E
Serravalle, It. 66 43.57 N 12.30 E
Serravalle all'Adige 64 45.49 N 11.01 E
Serravalle Pistoiese 66 43.54 N 10.49 E
Serravalle Scrivia 62 44.43 N 8.51 E
Serre 68 40.35 N 15.11 E
Serre ≃ 50 49.41 N 3.23 E
Serrenti 71 39.29 N 8.58 E
Serre Ponçon, Barrage de ◆6 62 44.33 N 6.30 E
Serre-Ponçon, Lac de @[1] 62 44.30 N 6.17 E
Serres 62 44.26 N 5.43 E
Serrezuela 252 30.38 S 65.23 W
Serri 71 39.42 N 9.08 E
Serrières 62 45.19 N 4.45 E
Serrinha 250 11.39 S 39.00 W
Serriola, Bocca)(66 43.31 N 12.21 E
Serris 261 48.51 N 2.47 E
Serrita 250 7.56 S 39.19 W
Serro 255 18.37 S 43.23 W
Sersale 68 39.01 N 16.44 E
Šerstin 76 52.39 N 31.03 E
Šerstobitovo 86 57.16 N 78.52 E
Sertã 34 39.48 N 8.06 W
Sertaneja 255 23.03 S 50.50 W
Sertânia 250 8.05 S 37.16 W
Sertãozinho 256 22.19 S 46.03 W
Sertig-Dörfli 58 46.44 N 9.51 E
Sertung, Pulau I 115a 6.06 S 105.24 E
Seru 144 7.50 N 40.28 E
Serua, Pulau I 164 6.18 S 130.01 E
Serubaj-Nura ≃ 86 49.54 N 72.31 E
Serui 164 1.53 S 136.14 E
Seruini ≃ 248 7.42 S 66.42 W
Serule 156 21.58 S 27.20 E
Serutu, Pulau I 112 1.42 S 108.45 E
Seruwai 114 4.21 N 98.10 E
Sérvia 38 40.11 N 22.00 E
Servi Burnu ➤ 130 41.40 N 28.06 E
Service Creek Reservoir @[1] 214 40.34 N 80.21 W
Servigliano 66 43.05 N 13.29 E
Servon 261 48.43 N 2.35 E
Servoz 58 45.56 N 6.46 E
Serwaru 112 8.10 S 127.42 E
Seryševo 89 51.08 N 128.20 E
Šes, Munții ⩕ 38 47.05 N 22.30 E
Šešan 180 66.46 N 171.26 W
Sesayap ≃ 112 3.36 N 117.15 E
Sesayap-lama 112 3.36 N 117.03 E
Šeščinskij 76 53.45 N 33.23 E
Sese Islands II 154 0.20 S 32.20 E
Seseke ≃ 263 51.37 N 7.32 E
Sesfontein 156 19.07 S 13.39 E
Sesheke 152 17.29 S 24.18 E
Seshu 105 39.33 N 115.37 E
Sesia ≃ 62 45.05 N 8.37 E
Sesia, Val V 62 45.47 N 8.05 E
Sesibu 112 4.02 N 116.33 E
Seskar, Ostrov I 76 60.02 N 28.22 E
Seskarön 26 65.44 N 23.44 E
Šešma ≃ 80 55.27 N 51.05 E
Sesmarias ≃ 256 22.28 S 44.27 W

Symbols in the index entries represent the broad categories identified in the key at the right. Symbols with superior numbers (⩕[2]) identify subcategories (see complete key on page I · 30).

Kartensymbole in dem Registerverzeichnis stellen die rechts in Schlüssel erklärten Kategorien dar. Symbole mit hochgestellten Ziffern (⩕[2]) bezeichnen Unterabteilungen einer Kategorie (vgl. vollständiger Schlüssel auf Seite I · 30).

Los símbolos incluidos en el texto del índice representan las grandes categorías identificadas con la clave a la derecha. Los símbolos con numeros en su parte superior (⩕[2]) identifican las subcategorías (véase la clave completa en la página I · 30).

Les symboles de l'index représentent les catégories indiquées dans la légende à droite. Les symboles suivis d'un indice (⩕[2]) représentent des sous-catégories (voir légende complète à la page I · 30).

Os símbolos incluídos no texto do índice representam as grandes categorias identificadas com a chave à direita. Os símbolos com números em sua parte superior (⩕[2]) identificam as subcategorias (veja-se a chave completa à página I · 30).

Symbol	English	Deutsch	Español	Français	Português
▲	Mountain	Berg	Montaña	Montagne	Montanha
⩕	Mountains	Berge	Montañas	Montagnes	Montanhas
)(	Pass	Pass	Paso	Col	Passo
V	Valley, Canyon	Tal, Cañon	Valle, Cañón	Vallée, Canyon	Vale, Canhão
≃	Plain	Ebene	Llano	Plaine	Planície
➤	Cape	Kap	Cabo	Cap	Cabo
I	Island	Insel	Isla	Île	Ilha
II	Islands	Inseln	Islas	Îles	Ilhas
◆	Other Topographic Features	Andere Topographische Objekte	Otros Elementos Topográficos	Autres données topographiques	Outros Elementos Topográficos

ESPAÑOL Nombre	Página	Lat.°′	Long.°′ W = Oeste
FRANÇAIS Nom	Page	Lat.°′	Long.°′ W = Ouest
PORTUGUÊS Nome	Página	Lat.°′	Long.°′ W = Oeste

Seso-jima I 174m 26.38 N 127.52 E
Sespe 228 34.23 N 118.58 W
Sespe Creek ≃ 204 34.23 N 118.57 W
Sessa 152 13.56 S 20.38 E
Sessa Aurunca 68 41.14 N 13.56 E
Sessenheim 56 48.48 N 7.59 E
Sesta Godano 62 44.17 N 9.40 E
Šestakovka 78 48.32 N 31.58 E
Šestakovo, S.S.S.R. 82 56.21 N 35.49 E
Šestakovo, S.S.S.R. 88 56.29 N 103.59 E
Sestao 34 43.18 N 3.00 W
Šestern'a 78 47.33 N 33.16 E
Sestino 66 43.42 N 12.18 E
Sesto (Sexten) 64 46.42 N 12.21 E
Sesto Calende 62 45.44 N 8.38 E
Sesto Fiorentino 66 43.50 N 11.12 E
Sestola 64 44.14 N 10.46 E
Sesto San Giovanni 62 45.32 N 9.14 E
Sestra ≃, S.S.S.R. 80 52.11 N 49.36 E
Sestra ≃, S.S.S.R. 82 56.43 N 37.14 E
Sestriere 62 44.57 N 6.53 E
Sestri Levante 62 44.16 N 9.24 E
Sestri Ponente 62 44.25 N 8.51 E
Sestroreck 76 60.06 N 29.58 E
Sestroreckij Razliv, Ozero ⊜ 265a 60.04 N 30.00 E
Sestu 71 39.18 N 9.05 E
Šešupe ≃ 76 55.30 N 22.12 E
Šešurga 80 57.29 N 47.35 E
Šešuvis ≃ 76 55.13 N 22.15 E
Seta, Nihon 270 34.58 N 135.55 E
Šeta, S.S.S.R. 76 55.17 N 24.15 E
Seta ≃ 270 34.56 N 135.54 E
Setagaya ➔8 268 35.39 N 139.40 E
Setail ≃ 115a 8.30 S 114.21 E
Setaka 96 33.09 N 130.28 E
Setana 92a 42.26 N 139.51 E
Setapak 114 3.11 N 101.42 E
Setauket 210 40.57 N 73.07 W
Sète 62 43.24 N 3.41 E
Sete Barras 252 24.23 S 47.55 W
Sete Cidades, Parque Nacional de ♠ 250 3.50 S 41.40 W
Sete de Setembro ≃ 255 12.56 S 52.51 W
Sete Lagoas 255 19.27 S 44.14 W
Sete Pontes 256 22.51 S 43.05 W
Sete Quedas, Cachoeira das ⌊ 250 9.27 S 56.41 W
Sete Quedas, Parque Nacional de ♠ 252 24.02 S 54.12 W
Sete Quedas, Salto das ⌊ 252 24.02 S 54.16 W
Sete Rios ➔8 266c 38.45 N 9.10 W
Setesdal V 26 59.25 N 7.25 E
Seth Ward 196 34.13 N 101.42 W
Seti ≃ 124 28.58 N 81.06 E
Sétif 148 36.09 N 5.26 E
Setlagodi 158 26.16 S 25.06 E
Seto, Nihon 94 35.14 N 137.06 E
Seto, Nihon 96 33.27 N 132.15 E
Seto, Nihon 96 34.44 N 134.02 E
Setoda 96 34.18 N 133.05 E
Seto-naikai ▾2 92 34.20 N 133.30 E
Seto-naikai-kokuritsu-kōen ♠ 96 34.15 N 133.28 E
Seton Hall University ⊍2 276 40.45 N 74.15 W
Seton Lake ⊜ 182 50.45 N 122.05 W
Seton Portage 182 50.43 N 122.18 W
Seto-saki ≻ 174m 26.51 N 128.18 E
Setouchi 93b 28.10 N 129.15 E
Seto-zaki ≻ 96 33.40 N 135.20 E
Setraki 78 49.23 N 40.49 E
Setta ≃ 64 44.22 N 11.14 E
Settat 148 33.04 N 7.37 W
Sette Bagni ➔8 267a 42.00 N 12.31 E
Sette Cama 152 2.32 S 9.45 E
Settecamini ➔8 267a 41.56 N 12.37 E
Sette-Daban, Chrebet ⋀ 74 62.00 N 138.00 E
Settee Lake ⊜ 184 57.03 N 96.55 W
Settepani, Monte ⋀ 62 44.15 N 8.12 E
Settimo Milanese 266b 45.29 N 9.03 E
Settimo San Pietro 71 39.17 N 9.11 E
Settimo Torinese 62 45.09 N 7.46 E
Settimo Vittone 62 45.33 N 7.50 E
Settingiano 68 38.55 N 16.31 E
Setting Lake ⊜ 184 55.00 N 98.38 W
Settle 44 54.04 N 2.16 W
Settlement Point ≻ 169 38.25 S 145.25 E
Settlers 156 25.02 S 28.30 E
Settlers Cabin Regional Park ♠ 279b 40.26 N 80.10 W
Settons, Lac des ⊜ 50 41.11 N 4.04 E
Settsu 96 34.46 N 135.33 E
Setúbal 34 38.32 N 8.54 W
Setúbal □5 266c 38.37 N 9.00 W
Setúbal, Baía de C 34 38.27 N 8.53 W
Setun' ≃ 265b 55.44 N 37.33 E
Seui 71 39.50 N 9.19 E
Seŭl → Sŏul 98 37.33 N 126.58 E
Seul, Lac ⊜ 184 50.20 N 92.30 W
Seul Choix Point ≻ 190 45.56 N 85.52 W
Seulimeum 114 5.22 N 95.35 E
Seulo 71 39.52 N 9.14 E
Seurre 58 47.00 N 5.09 E
Seutakan ≃ 180 65.38 N 176.58 W
Seuversholz 60 48.57 N 11.11 E
Seuzach 58 47.32 N 8.44 E
Sev ≃ 76 52.24 N 34.10 E
Sevagram 122 20.45 N 78.30 E
Sevan 84 40.34 N 44.57 E
Sevan, Ozero ⊜ 84 40.20 N 45.20 E
Sévaré 150 14.32 N 4.06 W
Sevastopol' 78 44.36 N 33.32 E
Sevastopol'skij 86 53.08 N 65.44 E
Ševčenko 72 43.35 N 51.05 E
Ševčenkovo, S.S.S.R. 78 51.40 N 33.39 E
Ševčenkovo, S.S.S.R. 78 45.33 N 29.20 E
Ševčenkovo, S.S.S.R. 78 49.41 N 37.10 E
Ševčenkovo Vtoroje 78 47.29 N 36.08 E
Sevelen, B.R.D. 52 51.29 N 6.25 E
Sevelen, Schw. 58 47.07 N 9.29 E
Ševelevskaja 24 60.52 N 44.12 E
Ševelevskij Majdan 80 54.25 N 42.15 E
Seven ≃ 44 54.11 N 0.52 W
Seven Caves ⊥5 218 39.13 N 83.23 W
Seven Harbors 216 42.40 N 83.34 W
Sevenhill 168b 33.53 S 138.38 E
Seven Hills, Austl. 274a 33.46 S 150.57 E
Seven Hills, Ohio, U.S. 214 41.22 N 81.41 W
Seven Islands → Sept-Îles 186 50.12 N 66.23 W
Seven Kings ➔8 260 51.34 N 0.05 E
Seven Mile 218 39.29 N 84.33 W
Sevenmile Bridge ➔5 220 24.41 N 81.11 W
Sevenmile Creek ≃ 218 39.28 N 84.33 W
Sevenoaks, Eng., U.K. 42 51.16 N 0.12 E
Seven Oaks, Tex., U.S. 222 30.51 N 94.51 W
Sevenoaks □8 260 51.18 N 0.10 E
Sevenoaks Weald 260 51.14 N 0.12 E
Seven Palm Lake ⊜ 220 25.12 N 80.44 W
Seven Persons 184 49.52 N 110.54 W
Seven Sisters 42 51.46 N 3.43 W
Seven Sisters Peaks ⋀ 182 54.58 N 128.10 W
Seventy Mile House 182 51.18 N 121.24 W
Seven Valleys 208 39.51 N 76.46 W
Sévérac-le-château 32 44.19 N 3.04 E
Severance Center ➔9 279a 41.31 N 81.33 W
Sever'anskij Les ♠ 83 48.55 N 38.00 E
Severka ≃ 82 55.10 N 38.45 E
Severn, S. Afr. 158 26.36 S 22.52 E
Severn, N.C., U.S. 208 36.31 N 77.11 W
Severn, Va., U.S. 208 37.18 N 76.25 W
Severn ≃, Ont., Can. 176 56.02 N 87.36 W
Severn ≃, Ont., Can. 212 44.52 N 79.41 W
Severn ≃, Eng., U.K. 42 51.35 N 2.40 W
Severn ≃, Md., U.S. 208 38.58 N 76.28 W
Severn, Mouth of the ≃ 42 51.25 N 3.00 W
Severnaja Dvina ≃ 24 64.32 N 40.30 E
Severnaja Sos'va ≃ 72 64.10 N 65.28 E
Severnaja Zeml'a II 74 79.30 N 98.00 E
Severna Park 208 39.04 N 76.33 W
Severn Bridge ➔5 42 51.39 N 2.42 W
Severnoje, S.S.S.R. 80 54.06 N 52.32 E
Severnoje, S.S.S.R. 80 58.02 N 41.26 E
Severnoje, S.S.S.R. 83 48.04 N 38.44 E
Severnoje, S.S.S.R. 84 44.49 N 42.51 E
Severnoje, S.S.S.R. 86 56.21 N 78.23 E
Severn River C 208 37.19 N 76.25 W
Severn Tunnel ➔5 42 51.35 N 2.44 W
Severnyj, S.S.S.R. 24 67.38 N 64.06 E
Severnyj, S.S.S.R. 265b 55.56 N 37.33 E
Severnyje Uvaly ⋀2 24 59.30 N 49.00 E
Severnyj Kommunar 80 58.23 N 54.02 E
Severnyj Prijut 84 43.16 N 41.51 E
Severnyj Sučan 89 43.13 N 133.11 E
Severnyj Ural ⋀ 24 63.00 N 59.00 E
Severo-Bajkal'skoje Nagorje ⋀1 88 57.00 N 111.00 E
Severočeský Kraj □4 60 50.08 N 13.20 E
Severodoneck 83 48.58 N 38.27 E
Severodvinsk 24 64.34 N 39.50 E
Severo-Dvinskij Kanal ≊ 76 59.45 N 38.22 E
Severo-Jenisejskij 74 60.22 N 93.01 E
Severo-Kazachstanskaja Oblast' □4 86 54.30 N 69.00 E
Severo-Kuril'sk 74 50.40 N 156.08 E
Severomoravský Kraj □4 30 49.45 N 17.50 E
Severomorsk 24 69.05 N 33.24 E
Severo-Mujskij Chrebet ⋀ 88 56.30 N 114.00 E
Severo-Osetinskaja Avtonomnaja Sovetskaja Socialističeskaja Respublika □3 84 43.00 N 44.15 E
Severo-Sibirskaja Nizmennost' ≚ 74 73.00 N 100.00 E
Severoural'sk 86 60.09 N 59.57 E
Severo-Zadonsk 82 54.00 N 38.23 E
Severskaja 78 44.51 N 38.42 E
Severskij Donec ≃ 72 48.20 N 40.15 E
Severskij Donec-Donbass, Kanal ≊ 83 48.55 N 37.45 E
Severucha 86 58.28 N 63.25 E
Severy 198 37.37 N 96.14 W
Seveso 62 45.39 N 9.09 E
Seveso ≃ 266b 45.30 N 9.12 E
Sevettijärvi 24 69.26 N 28.38 E
Sevier 200 39.04 N 113.06 W
Sevier, East Fork ≃ 200 38.14 N 112.12 W
Sevier Bridge Reservoir ⊜1 200 39.21 N 111.57 W
Sevier Desert ➔2 200 39.25 N 112.50 W
Sevier Lake ⊜ 200 38.55 N 113.09 W
Sevierville 192 35.52 N 83.34 W
Sevilla, Col. 246 4.16 N 75.57 W
Sevilla, Esp. 34 37.23 N 5.59 W
Sevilla, Isla I 236 8.14 N 82.24 W
Seville → Sevilla, Esp. 34 37.23 N 5.59 W
Seville, Fla., U.S. 192 29.19 N 81.30 W
Seville, Ohio, U.S. 214 41.01 N 81.52 W
Sevir 130 39.12 N 38.13 E
Şevketiye 130 40.05 N 27.51 E
Ševli ≃ 89 54.08 N 133.04 E
Sevlievo 38 43.01 N 25.06 E
Sevran 50 48.56 N 2.32 E
Sevrej 102 43.31 N 102.35 E
Sèvres 50 48.49 N 2.12 E
Sévrier 58 45.52 N 6.08 E
Sevsk 78 52.09 N 34.30 E
Ševykan 88 54.20 N 106.49 E
Sewa ≃ 150 7.18 N 12.08 W
Sewanee 194 35.12 N 85.55 W
Seward, Alaska, U.S. 180 60.06 N 149.26 W
Seward, Nebr., U.S. 198 40.55 N 97.06 W
Seward, N.Y., U.S. 210 42.43 N 74.37 W
Seward, Pa., U.S. 214 40.25 N 79.01 W
Seward Glacier ⊓ 180 60.22 N 140.15 W
Seward Peninsula ≻1 180 65.00 N 164.00 W
Sewaren 276 40.33 N 74.16 W
Sewekow 54 53.15 N 12.39 E
Sewell, Chile 252 34.05 S 70.23 W
Sewell, N.J., U.S. 208 39.46 N 75.09 W
Sewen 58 47.48 N 5.54 E
Sewernaja-Semlja → Severnaja Zeml'a II 74 79.30 N 98.00 E
Seweweekspoort 158 33.22 S 21.25 E
Sewickley 214 40.33 N 80.11 W
Sewickley Creek ≃ 279b 40.14 N 79.47 W
Sewickley Heights 279b 40.33 N 80.09 W
Sewickley Hills 279b 40.34 N 80.08 W
Sewri ➔8 272c 19.00 N 72.51 E
Sewu, Pegunungan ⋀ 115a 8.05 S 110.35 E
Sexcello 152 3.58 S 11.38 E
Sexsmith 182 55.21 N 118.47 W
Sexten → Sesto 64 46.42 N 12.21 E
Sexton 218 39.42 N 85.27 W
Sexton Island I 206 40.39 N 73.14 W
Seya 268 35.29 N 139.29 E
Seybaplaya 232 19.39 N 90.40 W
Seybaplaya, Punta ≻ 232 19.39 N 90.42 W
Seybothenreuth 60 49.54 N 11.43 E
Seybouse, Oued ≃ 148 36.54 N 7.47 E
Seychellen → Seychelles □1 138 4.35 S 55.40 E
Seychelles □1 138 4.35 S 55.40 E
Seychelles-Mauritius Ridge ➔3 12 14.00 S 61.00 E
Seyches 32 44.33 N 0.18 E
Seyda 54 51.53 N 12.53 E
Seydābād 128 34.51 N 50.36 E
Seydim 130 40.33 N 34.45 E
Seydişehir 130 37.25 N 31.51 E
Seydisfjördur 24a 65.16 N 14.00 W
Seyfe Gölü ⊜ 130 39.13 N 34.23 E
Seyhan ≃ 130 36.43 N 34.53 E
Seyhan Gölü ⊜1 130 37.05 N 35.13 E
Seyitgazi 130 39.27 N 30.43 E
Seymour, Austl. 169 37.02 S 145.08 E
Seymour, S. Afr. 158 32.33 S 26.46 E
Seymour, Conn., U.S. 207 41.24 N 73.04 W
Seymour, Ind., U.S. 218 38.58 N 85.53 W
Seymour, Iowa, U.S. 190 40.44 N 93.07 W
Seymour, Mo., U.S. 194 37.09 N 92.46 W
Seymour, Tex., U.S. 196 33.35 N 99.16 W
Seymour, Wis., U.S. 190 44.31 N 88.20 W
Seymour ≃ 182 51.05 N 126.50 W
Seymour Inlet C 182 51.03 N 127.10 W
Seymour Range ⋀ 224 48.40 N 124.00 W
Seyne-les-Alpes 62 44.21 N 6.21 E
Seyring 264b 48.20 N 16.29 E
Seyringer Graben ≊ 264b 48.18 N 16.33 E
Seyssel 58 45.57 N 5.49 E
Şeytan ≃ 267b 41.06 N 28.59 E
Sežana 36 45.42 N 13.52 E
Sézanne 50 48.43 N 3.43 E
Sezela 158 30.24 S 30.42 E
Sezimbra 34 38.26 N 9.06 W
Sezimovo Ústí 30 49.23 N 14.42 E
Sezze 66 41.30 N 13.03 E
Sfax 148 34.44 N 10.46 E
Sferracavallo ➔8 70 38.12 N 13.17 E
Sfîntu-Gheorghe 38 45.52 N 25.47 E
Sfîntu Gheorghe, Braţul ≃1 38 44.53 N 29.36 E
Sfîntu Gheorghe, Ostrovul I 38 45.07 N 29.22 E
Sforzesco, Castello ⊥ 266b 45.28 N 9.11 E
's-Gravendeel 52 51.46 N 4.37 E
's-Gravenhage (The Hague) 52 52.06 N 4.18 E
's-Gravenzande 52 52.00 N 4.10 E
Sgritheall, Beinn ⋀ 46 57.08 N 5.35 W
Sguè ▾4 150 17.45 N 7.43 W
Sgurgola 66 41.40 N 13.09 E
Sha'alav, Har ⋀ 132 30.04 N 35.06 E
Sha'alvim 132 31.52 N 34.59 E
Sha'ar HaGolan 132 32.41 N 35.36 E
Sha'ar Menashe 132 32.27 N 35.01 E
Shab'ā 132 33.21 N 35.45 E
Shaba □4 154 8.00 S 27.00 E
Shābah 142 31.11 N 30.46 E
Shabakunk Creek ≃ 285 40.15 N 74.43 W
Shabani 154 20.20 S 30.02 E
Shabbona 216 41.46 N 88.52 W
Shabestar 128 38.11 N 45.42 E
Shabomeka Lake ⊜ 212 44.54 N 77.09 W
Shabotik ≃ 190 48.50 N 85.34 W
Shabqadar 123 34.13 N 71.34 E
Shabunda 154 2.42 S 27.20 E
Shabwah 144 15.22 N 47.01 E
Shackan Indian Reserve ➔4 182 50.17 N 112.10 W
Shackleton Glacier ⊓ 9 84.35 S 176.15 W
Shackleton Ice Shelf ⊓ 9 66.00 S 100.00 E
Shackleton Range ⋀ 9 80.40 S 26.00 W
Shaddādī 130 36.02 N 40.45 E
Shādegān 128 30.40 N 48.38 E
Shade Gap 214 40.11 N 77.52 W
Shadehill Reservoir ⊜1 198 45.45 N 102.15 W
Shade Mountain ⋀ 208 40.34 N 77.30 W
Shades Creek ≃ 194 33.11 N 87.02 W
Shades Glen 210 41.11 N 75.42 W
Shading 102 31.20 N 94.40 E
Shadow Lake ⊜, Ont., Can. 212 44.43 N 78.48 W
Shadow Lake ⊜, Mass., U.S. 283 42.50 N 71.14 W
Shadow Lake ⊜, N.J., U.S. 276 40.21 N 74.06 W
Shadow Mountain National Recreation Area ♠ 200 40.07 N 105.48 W
Shado-Wood Village 214 40.35 N 79.12 W
Shadrinsk → Šadrinsk 86 56.05 N 63.38 E
Shadwān, Jazīrat I 140 27.30 N 33.59 E
Shady Cove 202 42.37 N 122.49 W
Shady Grove, Fla., U.S. 192 30.17 N 83.38 W
Shady Grove, Tex., U.S. 222 32.48 N 97.01 W
Shady Hills 216 40.36 N 85.41 W
Shady Shores 222 33.10 N 97.02 W
Shadyside 188 39.58 N 80.45 W
Sha'f 132 32.38 N 36.51 E
Shafer, Lake ⊜ 216 40.47 N 86.46 W
Shafer Butte ⋀ 202 43.47 N 116.05 W
Shafir 132 31.42 N 34.44 E
Shaft 128 37.12 N 49.24 E
Shaftesbury 42 51.01 N 2.12 W
Shafton 279b 40.20 N 79.42 W
Shaftsburg 216 42.48 N 84.18 W
Shaftsbury 210 42.57 N 73.13 W
Shafu 100 22.25 N 113.01 E
Shagamu 150 6.51 N 3.39 E
Shageluk 180 62.36 N 159.32 W
Shag Rocks II1 244 53.33 S 42.02 W
Shaguotun 104 41.10 N 120.38 E
Shāhābād, Īrān 128 37.32 N 56.54 E
Shāhābād, Īrān 128 34.06 N 46.31 E
Shāhābād, Īrān 267d 35.49 N 51.29 E
Shāhābād □5 124 25.10 N 84.00 E
Shāhāda 120 21.28 N 74.18 E
Shahba 132 32.51 N 36.37 E
Shāhbandar 120 24.10 N 67.54 E
Shāhbāz Kalāt 128 26.42 N 63.58 E
Shāhbāzpur ⊔ 124 22.05 N 90.50 E
Shāhdādkot 120 27.51 N 67.54 E
Shāhdādpur 120 25.56 N 68.37 E
Shāhdara 123 31.38 N 74.18 E
Shāhdara ➔8 272a 28.30 N 77.25 E
Shāhdol 124 23.17 N 81.21 E
Shāhdol □5 124 23.30 N 81.10 E
Shahe ≃, Zhg. 98 38.20 N 115.22 E
Shahe ≃, Zhg. 98 37.31 N 117.50 E
Shahe ≃, Zhg. 100 33.38 N 114.36 E
Shāhganj 124 26.03 N 82.41 E
Shāhgarh, Bhārat 124 27.07 N 69.54 E
Shāhgarh, Bhārat 124 24.19 N 79.08 E
Shahhat 146 32.49 N 21.52 E
Shāhī 128 36.28 N 52.53 E
Shāhī Kowt 123 34.16 N 70.34 E
Shāh-i-Mashhad 128 35.03 N 63.58 E
Shāhīn Dezh 128 36.40 N 46.33 E
Shāhjahānpur 124 27.53 N 79.55 E
Shāhjahānpur □5 124 28.00 N 79.55 E
Shāh Jūy 120 32.31 N 67.25 E
Shāh Kot 123 31.34 N 73.29 E
Shāh Mosque ⊍1 267d 35.40 N 51.25 E
Shāh Pasand 120 31.10 N 62.58 E
Shāhpur, Bhārat 122 16.42 N 76.50 E
Shāhpūr, Īrān 128 38.11 N 44.47 E
Shāhpur, Pāk. 120 28.43 N 68.25 E
Shāhpur, Pāk. 123 32.16 N 72.28 E
Shāhpura, Bhārat 120 25.38 N 74.56 E
Shāhpura, Bhārat 120 27.23 N 75.58 E
Shāhpura, Bhārat 124 23.11 N 80.42 E
Shāhpur Chākar 120 26.09 N 68.39 E
Shahrak 120 34.06 N 64.18 E
Shahr-e Bābak 128 30.07 N 55.09 E
Shahr-e Monjān 120 36.02 N 70.46 E
Shahr-e Şafā 128 31.50 N 66.22 E
Shahrestān 120 34.22 N 66.47 E
Shahreẕā 128 32.01 N 51.52 E
Shahr Kord 128 32.19 N 50.50 E
Shāhrūd 128 36.25 N 55.01 E
Shāhrūd ≃ 128 37.17 N 48.43 E
Shahsavār 128 36.49 N 50.53 E
Shāhzādpur 124 24.10 N 89.36 E
Shā'ib al-Banāt, Jabal ⋀ 140 26.59 N 33.29 E
Shaighālu 120 31.11 N 68.49 E
Sha'īrah, Jabal ⋀2 132 30.06 N 34.17 E
Sha'īrah, Jabal ash- ⋀ 132 29.31 N 34.29 E
Shājāpur 124 23.26 N 76.16 E
Shājāpur □5 124 23.45 N 76.15 E
Shajianzi 98 41.01 N 125.26 E
Shakaga-hana ≻ 96 34.25 N 134.14 E
Shakaga-take ⋀ 96 33.11 N 130.53 E
Shakaga-take-tunnel ➔5 96 33.27 N 130.52 E
Shakardarra 123 33.14 N 71.30 E
Shakargarh 123 32.16 N 75.10 E
Shakarpura 272a 28.46 N 77.21 E
Shakarpur Khās ➔8 272a 28.38 N 77.17 E
Shakaskraal 158 29.26 S 31.14 E
Shakawe 156 18.23 S 21.50 E
Shakeng 98 42.13 N 116.35 E
Shaker Heights 214 41.29 N 81.36 W
Shaker Heights Park ♠ 279a 41.29 N 81.33 W
Shakespeare 212 43.22 N 80.49 W
Shākhen 128 33.22 N 59.32 E
Shakhty → Šachty 83 47.42 N 40.13 E
Shaki 150 8.39 N 3.25 E
Shakopee 190 44.48 N 93.32 W
Shakotan-hantō ≻1 92a 43.20 N 140.30 E
Shakou 100 24.25 N 113.32 E
Shakshūk 142 29.28 N 30.42 E
Shaktoolik 180 64.20 N 161.09 W
Shakūrpur ➔8 272a 28.41 N 77.09 E
Shala, Lake ⊜ 144 7.25 N 38.30 E
Shalalth 182 50.44 N 122.13 W
Shalamulunhe ≃ 102 43.02 N 111.20 E
Shalatayn, Bi'r ▾4 140 23.08 N 35.36 E
Shaleitiandao I 98 39.03 N 118.44 E
Shaler Mountains ⋀ 176 72.35 N 110.45 W
Shaleshanto 156 19.09 S 23.58 E
Shalford 260 51.13 N 0.34 W
Shālimah 142 31.14 N 30.52 E
Shalimar Railroad Station ➔5 272b 22.33 N 88.19 E
Shallotte 192 33.58 N 78.23 W
Shallowater 196 33.41 N 101.59 W
Shallow Brook ≃ 276 40.21 N 74.35 W
Shallow Lake 212 44.36 N 81.05 W
Shaluhe 89 51.08 N 126.00 E
Shām, Bādiyat ash- ➔2 128 32.00 N 40.00 E
Shām, Jabal ash- ⋀ 128 23.13 N 57.16 E
Shamattawa 184 55.52 N 92.05 W
Shambat 140 15.40 N 32.32 E
Shambe 140 7.07 N 30.46 E
Shambi 152 1.49 S 22.39 E
Shambu 144 9.40 N 37.03 E
Shambuanda 152 6.38 S 20.13 E
Shām Churasi 123 31.30 N 75.45 E
Shamei 100 24.32 N 118.25 E
Shamerpur ➔8 272a 28.45 N 77.09 E
Shamīl 128 27.30 N 56.53 E
Shāmli 124 29.27 N 77.19 E
Shammākh 132 30.30 N 35.30 E
Shammar, Jabal ⋀ 128 27.20 N 41.45 E
Shamo, Lake ⊜ 144 5.49 N 37.35 E
Shamokin 208 40.47 N 76.34 W
Shamokin Dam 210 40.51 N 76.49 W
Shamona Creek ≃ 285 40.02 N 75.43 W
Shamrock, Fla., U.S. 192 29.39 N 83.08 W
Shamrock, Tex., U.S. 196 35.13 N 100.15 W
Shamsābād 124 27.01 N 78.08 E
Shamsher 272a 28.44 N 77.24 E
Shamsol Emareh Palace ♠ 267d 35.41 N 51.25 E
Shamva 154 17.18 S 31.34 E
Shan □3 110 22.00 N 98.00 E
Shanchengzi 104 42.02 N 123.47 E
Shandaken 210 42.07 N 74.24 W
Shandan 102 38.48 N 101.20 E
Shandatgyi 110 19.37 N 94.43 E
Shandī 140 16.42 N 33.26 E
Shandianhe ≃ 98 42.22 N 116.15 E
Shandianhe ≃ 98 42.23 N 116.21 E
Shandīd 142 30.55 N 30.40 E
Shandon 226 35.39 N 120.22 W
Shandong 107 29.31 N 106.25 E
Shandong □4 98 36.00 N 118.00 E
Shandongbandao ≻1 98 37.00 N 121.00 E
Shaner 279b 40.17 N 79.47 W
Shanesville 214 40.31 N 81.39 W
Shangani 154 19.47 S 29.22 E
Shangani ≃ 154 18.41 S 27.10 E
Shang'ao 106 30.41 N 119.25 E
Shangbahe 100 30.40 N 115.05 E
Shangbai 106 30.29 N 119.58 E
Shangbancheng 105 40.50 N 118.03 E
Shangbatang 102 32.46 N 96.20 E
Shangcai 100 33.16 N 114.15 E
Shangcang 105 39.54 N 117.23 E
Shangchen 106 30.07 N 119.53 E
Shangcheng 100 31.48 N 115.24 E
Shangchewan 100 29.48 N 113.01 E
Shangch'iu → Shangqiu 98 34.27 N 115.42 E
Shangchuandao I 102 21.40 N 112.48 E
Shangdang 102 32.06 N 119.24 E
Shangdayangqi 89 51.09 N 124.02 E
Shangdian 100 34.07 N 112.23 E
Shangdianmiao 106 30.56 N 120.51 E
Shangdouying 102 40.36 N 115.33 E
Shangdu 98 41.29 N 113.34 E
Shangduichunshi 104 41.00 N 123.02 E
Shangdundu 100 27.56 N 116.15 E
Shangduxiang-huangqi 98 42.27 N 113.55 E
Shangfu 100 28.40 N 114.59 E
Shanggaixin 102 23.25 N 100.02 E
Shanggan 100 25.56 N 119.22 E
Shanggang 100 33.30 N 120.04 E
Shanggangzi 104 42.26 N 123.03 E
Shanggao 100 28.18 N 114.54 E
Shanggecun 106 31.49 N 119.07 E
Shanggu 98 40.47 N 118.28 E
Shangguan 106 31.39 N 119.15 E
Shangguanying 98 41.18 N 117.07 E
Shanghai, Va., U.S. 208 37.37 N 76.47 W
Shanghai, Zhg. 106 31.01 N 121.25 E
Shanghai, Zhg. 106
269b 31.14 N 121.28 E
Shanghailingao 104 41.57 N 120.55 E
Shanghai Museum ⊍ 269b 31.13 N 121.28 E
Shanghai Shih □7 106 31.10 N 121.30 E
Shanghai Station ➔5 269b 31.15 N 121.28 E
Shanghang 100 25.06 N 116.25 E
Shanghe 98 37.19 N 117.07 E
Shanghekou 98 40.26 N 124.47 E
Shanghetou 105 39.12 N 116.59 E
Shanghewantun 104 41.42 N 123.23 E
Shanghu ⊜ 106 31.39 N 120.41 E
Shanghuang 106 31.33 N 119.34 E
Shanghuangqi 98 41.29 N 116.31 E
Shanghucun 105 40.45 N 115.45 E
Shangjao → Shangrao 100 28.26 N 117.58 E
Shangjiafen 104 41.18 N 121.18 E
Shangjiahe 98 41.51 N 124.28 E
Shangjialin 98 38.19 N 116.05 E
Shangjiaodao 100 29.00 N 119.54 E
Shangjiatai 104 40.53 N 123.35 E
Shangjie 100 27.06 N 116.06 E
Shangjiuwu 100 33.59 N 113.01 E
Shangkasa 120 33.45 N 80.12 E
Shangkou 98 37.03 N 118.45 E
Shanglanjiagou 104 40.52 N 120.37 E
Shanglin, Zhg. 102 23.28 N 108.33 E
Shanglin, Zhg. 104 41.31 N 122.14 E
Shanglishi 100 27.52 N 113.46 E
Shangliuhezicun 104 41.28 N 123.32 E
Shangliulinzi 104 41.02 N 120.13 E
Shangmagushan 104 41.41 N 124.10 E
Shangmatai 105 39.22 N 117.15 E
Shangmatun 104 40.57 N 123.22 E
Shangmengyun 102 23.01 N 99.50 E
Shangmingdian 106 31.12 N 120.57 E
Shangmingju 105 39.41 N 115.12 E
Shangnan 102 33.31 N 110.45 E
Shangpan I 106 30.31 N 121.18 E
Shangpandaoling 104 41.42 N 121.14 E
Shangping, Zhg. 100 25.57 N 117.33 E
Shangping, Zhg. 100 24.43 N 115.27 E
Shangping, Zhg. 100 24.29 N 114.38 E
Shangpufou 106 31.28 N 119.13 E
Shangpuzi 104 41.37 N 121.35 E
Shangqianbu 106 30.27 N 120.04 E
Shangqiao 100 31.02 N 117.42 E
Shangqikou 100 29.44 N 118.02 E
Shangqing, Zhg. 100 28.02 N 117.00 E
Shangqing, Zhg. 100 25.53 N 118.36 E
Shangqingshuicun 105 39.56 N 115.38 E
Shangqitai 104 41.14 N 121.14 E
Shangqiu, Zhg. 98 34.27 N 115.42 E
Shangqiu, Zhg. 98 34.23 N 115.37 E
Shangrao 100 28.26 N 117.58 E
Shangshe 102 38.15 N 113.20 E
Shangshibatai 104 42.02 N 120.51 E
Shangshui 100 33.39 N 114.39 E
Shangsi 102 22.09 N 107.57 E
Shangtai 100 28.34 N 118.37 E
Shangtan 106 30.27 N 118.42 E
Shangtang 100 33.23 N 118.02 E
Shangtuan ⤫ 100 27.30 N 117.06 E
Shangweiniuchang 104 40.54 N 120.44 E
Shangxian 102 33.51 N 109.54 E
Shangxingbu 106 31.32 N 119.15 E
Shangxinhe 106 32.02 N 118.43 E
Shangxinqiu 104 42.27 N 121.37 E
Shangyangbao 98 42.30 N 124.14 E
Shangyangcun 106 30.48 N 118.40 E
Shangye 98 35.26 N 117.59 E
Shangyi 98 41.04 N 114.03 E
Shangying 89 44.10 N 127.17 E
Shangyinkou 102 32.52 N 103.04 E
Shangyou 100 25.51 N 114.30 E
Shangyoushui ≃ 100 25.55 N 113.56 E
Shangyu 100 30.02 N 120.54 E
Shangyuan 104 41.39 N 120.55 E
Shangzhai 98 39.13 N 114.17 E
Shangzhaoshugou 104 42.12 N 121.58 E
Shangzhazi 105 40.52 N 117.42 E
Shangzhenzhuang 105 40.20 N 117.06 E
Shangzhi 89 45.13 N 127.59 E
Shangzhuang 98 37.01 N 122.15 E
Shangzhuangtai 105 39.41 N 115.25 E
Shanhaiguan 98 40.01 N 119.44 E
Shanhaikwan → Shanhaiguan 98 40.01 N 119.44 E
Shanhe 120 33.38 N 79.50 E
Shanhecun 89 45.38 N 128.27 E
Shanhetun 89 44.44 N 127.12 E
Shanjiang 100 27.32 N 115.08 E
Shanjiazhuang 105 38.52 N 115.45 E
Shanklin 42 50.38 N 1.10 W
Shankou, Zhg. 100 26.40 N 117.46 E
Shankou, Zhg. 100 28.58 N 115.12 E
Shankou, Zhg. 100 28.48 N 114.29 E
Shankou, Zhg. 102 21.38 N 109.43 E
Shanlenggang 102 28.33 N 103.23 E
Shanli 100 29.52 N 117.21 E
Shanlian 106 30.42 N 120.19 E
Shanmenjie 106 30.40 N 118.52 E
Shanmulong 102 24.39 N 98.05 E
Shannanguan 100 31.36 N 116.52 E
Shannock 207 41.27 N 71.38 W
Shannon, N.Z. 172 40.33 S 175.25 E
Shannon, S. Afr. 158 29.08 S 26.18 E
Shannon, Ga., U.S. 192 34.20 N 85.04 W
Shannon, Ill., U.S. 190 42.09 N 89.44 W
Shannon, Miss., U.S. 194 34.07 N 88.43 W
Shannon ≃ 48 52.36 N 9.41 W
Shannon, Lake ⊜ 224 48.37 N 121.42 W
Shannon, Mouth of the ≃1 48 52.30 N 9.50 W
Shannon Airport ⊠ 48 52.41 N 8.55 W
Shannons Flat 171b 35.54 S 148.58 E
Shannontown 192 33.53 N 80.21 W
Shannonville 212 44.12 N 77.13 W
Shanpo 100 30.06 N 114.20 E
Shanrendong 89 46.50 N 123.08 E
Shanrenqiao 106 31.16 N 120.27 E
Shanshan 86 42.52 N 90.10 E
Shanshenmiao 105 40.45 N 116.47 E
Shanshūr 142 30.21 N 31.00 E
Shansi → Shanxī □4 102 37.00 N 112.00 E
Shanting 98 35.09 N 117.29 E
Shantou (Swatow) 100 23.23 N 116.41 E
Shantouguan ⤫ 100 27.54 N 117.26 E
Shantung → Shandong □4 98 36.00 N 118.00 E
Shantung Peninsula → Shandongbandao ≻1 98 37.00 N 121.00 E
Shanty Bay 212 44.25 N 79.36 W
Shanwa 154 3.10 S 33.46 E
Shanwangchang 107 29.38 N 104.38 E
Shanwei, Zhg. 100 22.47 N 115.21 E
Shanwei, Zhg. 102 22.21 N 107.58 E
Shānxī □4, Zhg. 102 37.00 N 112.00 E
Shǎnxī □4, Zhg. 102 35.00 N 109.00 E
Shanxian → Sanmenxia 102 34.45 N 111.05 E
Shanxiawu 100 28.52 N 113.52 E
Shanyang, Zhg. 100 26.43 N 119.13 E
Shanyang, Zhg. 102 33.35 N 109.49 E
Shanyang, Zhg. 106 31.19 N 120.16 E
Shanyao 100 25.08 N 118.53 E
Shanyaqiao 106 31.15 N 119.33 E
Shanyin 102 39.35 N 112.58 E
Shanzhijiafen 105 40.37 N 116.44 E
Shanzui 105 40.48 N 118.13 E
Shanzuizi 104 41.55 N 120.30 E
Shaobo 100 32.30 N 119.32 E
Shaodenggao 104 42.13 N 121.47 E
Shaodian, Zhg. 98 34.05 N 118.30 E
Shaodian, Zhg. 100 33.10 N 114.18 E
Shaoguan 100 24.50 N 113.37 E
Shaogudian 98 36.57 N 115.32 E
Shaoguoyingzi 104 41.33 N 120.27 E
Shaohing → Shaoxing 100 30.00 N 120.35 E
Shaohsing → Shaoxing 100 30.00 N 120.35 E
Shaohuyingzi 104 41.46 N 121.35 E
Shaojiaolou 106 31.05 N 121.32 E
Shaokuan → Shaoguan 100 24.50 N 113.37 E
Shaowu 100 27.20 N 117.28 E
Shaoxing 100 30.00 N 120.35 E
Shaoyang, Zhg. 100 27.06 N 111.25 E
Shaoyang, Zhg. 102 26.53 N 111.13 E
Shaozihe 98 40.13 N 123.33 E
Shap 44 54.32 N 2.41 W
Shapinsay I 46 59.03 N 2.53 W
Shāpūr ≃ 128 29.39 N 51.03 E
Shaq'ah, Ra's ash- ≻ 130 34.19 N 35.41 E
Shaqqā 132 32.53 N 36.42 E
Shaqq al-Ju'ayfir, Wādī V 140 15.16 N 26.00 E
Shaqrā, Lubnān 132 33.12 N 35.28 E
Shaqrā', Sūrīy. 132 32.54 N 36.14 E
Shaquan 86 44.33 N 83.25 E
Shaquzhen 107 30.33 N 103.45 E
Shār ≃ 128 34.50 N 58.32 E
Sharafābād 272a 28.36 N 77.23 E
Sharafkhāneh 128 38.11 N 45.29 E
Sha'rah, Khabrat ⊜ 132 33.52 N 37.02 E
Sharan Jogīzai 120 31.02 N 68.33 E
Sharatin Mountain ⋀ 180 57.49 N 152.41 W
Sharbatāt, Ra's ash- ≻ 118 17.52 N 56.22 E
Sharbīn, Jabal ⋀ 132 33.43 N 36.21 E
Sharbot Lake 212 44.46 N 76.41 W
Sharbot Lake ⊜ 212 44.46 N 76.41 W
Share 150 8.50 N 4.56 E
Shari 92a 43.55 N 144.50 E
Shari-dake ⋀ 92a 43.46 N 144.43 E
Shark ≃ 220 25.21 N 81.05 W
Shark Bay C 162 25.30 S 113.30 E
Shark Point ≻, Austl. 274a 33.55 S 151.17 E
Shark Point ≻, Fla., U.S. 220 25.23 N 81.09 W
Shark River Hills 208 40.12 N 74.03 W
Sharnūb 142 31.01 N 30.35 E
Sharon, Ont., Can. 212 44.06 N 79.26 W
Sharon, Ont., Can. 214 42.53 N 81.22 W
Sharon, Conn., U.S. 207 41.53 N 73.29 W
Sharon, Mass., U.S. 207 42.05 N 71.11 W
Sharon, N. Dak., U.S. 198 47.36 N 97.54 W
Sharon, Pa., U.S. 214 41.14 N 80.31 W
Sharon, Wis., U.S. 216 42.30 N 88.44 W
Sharon Center 214 41.06 N 81.44 W
Sharon Hill 285 39.55 N 75.16 W
Sharon Park 218 39.23 N 84.35 W
Sharon Springs, Kans., U.S. 198 38.54 N 101.45 W
Sharon Springs, N.Y., U.S. 210 42.48 N 74.37 W
Sharon Valley 207 41.54 N 73.30 W
Sharonville 218 39.16 N 84.25 W
Sharpe Lake ⊜ 184 54.24 N 93.30 W
Sharpes 220 28.26 N 80.46 W
Sharp Park ♠ 282 37.37 N 122.29 W
Sharp Peak ⋀ 116 5.58 N 125.31 E
Sharpsburg, Ill., U.S. 219 39.37 N 89.21 W
Sharpsburg, Ky., U.S. 218 38.12 N 83.56 W
Sharps Hill 279b 40.30 N 79.56 W
Sharps Run ≃ 285 39.54 N 74.49 W
Sharpsville, Ind., U.S. 216 40.23 N 86.05 W
Sharpsville, Pa., U.S. 214 41.15 N 80.29 W
Sharptown 285 39.39 N 74.22 W
Sharqpur 123 31.28 N 74.06 E
Sharshar, Jabal ⋀2 140 23.52 N 30.20 E
Shartlesville 208 40.31 N 76.06 W
Sharūnah 142 28.36 N 30.51 E
Shārūnah, Wādī V 142 28.36 N 30.52 E
Shasha 144 6.20 N 35.57 E
Shashi 102 30.19 N 112.14 E
Shashi ≃ 156 22.14 S 29.20 E
Shashibu 100 25.48 N 114.54 E
Shasi → Shashi 102 30.19 N 112.14 E
Shasta 204 40.36 N 122.29 W
Shasta ≃ 204 41.50 N 122.35 W
Shasta, Mount ⋀1 204 41.20 N 122.20 W
Shasta Lake ⊜1 204 40.50 N 122.25 W
Shatangjiang 106 31.25 N 120.01 E
Shaṭānūf 142 30.14 N 31.04 E
Shatawī 140 14.39 N 32.06 E
Shāti', Wādī ash- V 146 27.30 N 13.15 E
Shatian, Zhg. 100 25.53 N 113.44 E
Shatian, Zhg. 100 23.59 N 113.56 E
Sha Tin Hoi C 271d 22.24 N 114.12 E
Sha Tin New Town 271d 22.23 N 114.11 E
Shattuck 196 36.16 N 99.53 W
Shatuji 98 35.18 N 115.45 E
Shatuosi 102 31.20 N 108.51 E
Shauck 214 40.37 N 82.40 W
Shaunavon 184 49.40 N 108.25 W
Shaver Lake 226 37.09 N 119.18 W
Shaver Lake ⊜1 226 37.08 N 119.17 W
Shavertown 210 41.19 N 75.55 W
Shave Ziyyon 132 32.59 N 35.05 E
Shaw, Eng., U.K. 262 53.35 N 2.06 W
Shaw, Miss., U.S. 194 33.36 N 90.46 W
Shaw ≃ 162 20.20 S 119.17 E
Shaw Air Force Base ⊞ 192 33.58 N 80.29 W
Shawan, Zhg. 86 44.34 N 85.48 E
Shawan, Zhg. 100 27.52 N 114.52 E
Shawan, Zhg. 107 29.25 N 103.33 E
Shawanaga Inlet C 190 45.32 N 80.24 W
Shawangunk Kill ≃ 210 41.41 N 74.10 W
Shawangunk Mountains ⋀ 210 41.35 N 74.30 W
Shawano 190 44.47 N 88.36 W
Shawbridge 206 45.52 N 74.05 W
Shawbury 42 52.47 N 2.39 W
Shaw Creek ≃ 192 33.34 N 81.30 W
Shawhan 218 38.18 N 84.16 W
Shawinigan 206 46.33 N 72.45 W
Shawinigan ≃ 206 46.32 N 72.46 W
Shawinigan, Lac ⊜ 206 46.41 N 73.10 W
Shawinigan Falls → Shawinigan 206 46.33 N 72.45 W
Shawinigan-Sud 206 46.31 N 72.45 W
Shaw Island I 224 48.34 N 122.57 W
Shawmere ≃ 190 48.40 N 82.29 W
Shawnee, Kans., U.S. 190 39.01 N 94.43 W
Shawnee, Ohio, U.S. 188 39.36 N 82.13 W
Shawnee, Okla., U.S. 196 35.20 N 96.55 W
Shawnee, Lake ⊜ 276 40.58 N 74.35 W
Shawnee Hills 214 40.07 N 83.09 W
Shawnee On Delaware 210 41.01 N 75.07 W
Shawnee State Park ♠ 218 38.43 N 83.10 W
Shawneetown 194 37.42 N 88.08 W
Shawnī 142 30.45 N 30.55 E
Shawnigan Lake 224 48.38 N 123.35 W
Shawnigan Lake ⊜ 224 48.37 N 123.37 W
Shawo, Som. 144 3.26 N 45.22 E
Shawo, Zhg. 98 34.28 N 114.37 E
Shawo, Zhg. 100 28.52 N 114.47 E
Shawo, Zhg. 100 31.44 N 115.08 E
Shaw River 162 20.43 S 119.20 E
Shawsheen ≃ 283 42.42 N 71.11 W
Shawtown 279b 40.20 N 79.42 W
Shawville 188 45.36 N 76.30 W
Shaxi, Zhg. 100 24.38 N 113.42 E
Shaxi, Zhg. 100 28.34 N 118.06 E
Shaxi, Zhg. 100 26.53 N 115.34 E
Shaxi, Zhg. 106 31.34 N 121.04 E
Shaxi ≃ 100 26.34 N 118.02 E
Shaxian 100 26.24 N 117.47 E
Shaxikou 100 26.33 N 118.02 E
Shaximiao 107 29.57 N 106.19 E
Shayangzhen 100 30.42 N 112.33 E
Shaybārā I 128 25.27 N 36.48 E

Symbol	English	Deutsch	Español	Français	Português
≃	River	Fluss	Río	Rivière	Rio
≊	Canal	Kanal	Canal	Canal	Canal
⌊	Waterfall, Rapids	Wasserfall, Stromschnellen	Cascada, Rápidos	Chute d'eau, Rapides	Cascata, Rápidos
⊔	Strait	Meeresstrasse	Estrecho	Détroit	Estreito
C	Bay, Gulf	Bucht, Golf	Bahía, Golfo	Baie, Golfe	Baía, Golfo
⊜	Lake, Lakes	See, Seen	Lago, Lagos	Lac, Lacs	Lago, Lagos
≚	Swamp	Sumpf	Pantano	Marais	Pântano
⊓	Ice Features, Glacier	Eis- und Gletscherformen	Accidentes Glaciales	Formes glaciaires	Acidentes Glaciares
▾	Other Hydrographic Features	Andere Hydrographische Objekte	Otros Elementos Hidrográficos	Autres données hydrographiques	Outros Acidentes Hidrográficos
➔	Submarine Features	Untermeerische Objekte	Accidentes Submarinos	Formes de relief sous-marin	Acidentes Submarinos
□	Political Unit	Politische Einheit	Unidad Política	Entité politique	Unidade Política
⊍	Cultural Institution	Kulturelle Institution	Institución Cultural	Institution culturelle	Instituição Cultural
⊥	Historical Site	Historische Stätte	Sitio Histórico	Site historique	Sitio Histórico
♠	Recreational Site	Erholungs- und Ferienort	Sitio de Recreo	Centre de loisirs	Sítio de Lazer
⊠	Airport	Flughafen	Aeropuerto	Aéroport	Aeroporto
⊞	Military Installation	Militäranlage	Instalación Militar	Installation militaire	Instalação Militar
➔	Miscellaneous	Verschiedenes	Misceláneo	Divers	Miscelânea

Name	Page	Lat.°′	Long.°′
Shaykh, Jabal ash- (Mount Hermon) ∧	132	33.26 N	35.51 E
Shaykh, Wādī ash- V	142	28.48 N	30.55 E
Shaykh al-Ḥadīd	130	36.30 N	36.35 E
Shaykh Sa'd	128	32.34 N	46.17 E
Shaykh 'Uthmān	144	12.52 N	44.59 E
Shayuan	100	27.45 N	120.38 E
Shazhen	98	36.23 N	115.47 E
Shazihe	102	32.12 N	106.42 E
Shchekino → Ščokino	76	54.01 N	37.31 E
Shchelkovo → Ščelkovo	76	55.55 N	38.00 E
Shcherbakov → Rybinsk	76	58.03 N	38.52 E
Sheaf ≃	44	53.23 N	1.26 W
Shea Island I	276	41.03 N	73.24 W
Sheakhala	126	22.46 N	88.10 E
Sheakleyville	214	41.27 N	80.13 W
Shea Stadium ♠	276	40.45 N	73.51 W
Shebele	144	9.43 N	42.43 E
Shebele (Shebelle) ≃	144	0.01 S	42.45 E
Sheberghān	120	36.41 N	65.45 E
Shebeshekong ≃	212	45.26 N	80.19 W
Sheboygan	190	43.46 N	87.36 W
Sheboygan ≃	190	43.45 N	87.42 W
Sheboygan Falls	190	43.44 N	87.49 W
Shebu	100	27.40 N	112.48 E
Shechem → Nābulus	132	32.13 N	35.16 E
Shechem ⊥	132	32.13 N	35.15 E
Shecheng	102	37.14 N	113.05 E
Shedden	214	42.44 N	81.21 W
Shedfield	42	50.55 N	1.12 W
Shediac	186	46.13 N	64.32 W
Shedin Peak ∧	182	55.55 N	127.32 W
Sheelin, Lough ⊜	48	53.48 N	7.22 W
Sheenjek ≃	180	66.45 N	144.33 W
Sheep ≃	182	50.44 N	113.51 W
Sheep Creek ≃, Alta., Can.	182	54.04 N	119.00 W
Sheep Creek ≃, U.S.	202	42.27 N	115.36 W
Sheep Creek ≃, Wyo., U.S.	200	42.03 N	106.04 W
Sheep Haven C	48	55.10 N	7.52 W
Sheepmoor	158	26.42 S	30.13 E
Sheep Mountain ∧, Ariz., U.S.	200	32.32 N	114.14 W
Sheep Mountain ∧, Wyo., U.S.	200	43.33 N	110.32 W
Sheep Peak ∧	196	31.14 N	104.59 W
Sheepranch	226	38.13 N	120.28 W
Sheep Range ⋀	204	36.45 N	115.05 W
Sheepscot ≃	188	44.00 N	69.50 W
Sheepshead Bay •[8]	276	40.35 N	73.56 W
's-Heerenberg	52	51.53 N	6.15 E
's-Heerenhoek	52	51.27 N	3.46 E
Sheerness	42	51.27 N	0.45 E
Sheet Harbour	186	44.55 N	62.32 W
Shefar'am	132	32.48 N	35.10 E
Sheffield, N.Z.	172	43.23 S	172.01 E
Sheffield, Eng., U.K.	44	53.23 N	1.30 W
Sheffield, Ala., U.S.	194	34.46 N	87.40 W
Sheffield, Ill., U.S.	190	41.21 N	89.44 W
Sheffield, Iowa, U.S.	190	42.54 N	93.13 W
Sheffield, Mass., U.S.	207	42.05 N	73.21 W
Sheffield, Ohio, U.S.	214	41.28 N	82.03 W
Sheffield, Pa., U.S.	214	41.42 N	79.02 W
Sheffield, Tex., U.S.	196	30.41 N	101.49 W
Sheffield Island I	276	41.03 N	73.25 W
Sheffield Island Harbor C	276	41.03 N	73.25 W
Sheffield Lake	214	41.29 N	82.07 W
Sheffield Lake ⊜	186	49.20 N	56.35 W
Shefford	42	52.02 N	0.20 W
Shefford □[6]	206	45.25 N	72.30 W
Shefuwei	100	26.11 N	115.22 E
Shegangshi	100	28.32 N	113.36 E
Shegaon	122	20.47 N	76.41 E
Sheho	184	51.38 N	103.12 W
Shehojele	144	10.40 N	35.09 E
Shehong (Taihezhon)	102	30.56 N	105.22 E
Shehongmiao	107	30.44 N	106.03 E
Shehuen ≃	254	49.35 S	69.34 W
Shehy Mountains ⋀	48	51.48 N	3.15 W
Shekatika Bay	186	51.17 N	58.20 W
Shēkhābād	120	34.05 N	68.45 E
Shek Hasan	144	12.09 N	35.54 E
Shekhūpura	123	31.42 N	73.59 E
Sheki → Šeki	84	41.12 N	47.12 E
Shekki → Zhongshan	100	22.31 N	113.22 E
Shek Ku Chau I	271d	22.12 N	113.59 E
Shekou	100	30.44 N	114.20 E
Shelagyote Peak ∧	182	55.58 N	127.12 W
Shelbina	219	39.47 N	92.02 W
Shelbourne	169	36.52 S	144.01 E
Shelburn	194	39.11 N	87.24 W
Shelburne, N.S., Can.	186	43.46 N	65.19 W
Shelburne, Ont., Can.	212	44.04 N	80.12 W
Shelburne Bay C	164	11.49 S	143.00 E
Shelburne Falls	207	42.36 N	72.44 W
Shelby, Ind., U.S.	216	41.12 N	87.21 W
Shelby, Iowa, U.S.	198	41.31 N	95.27 W
Shelby, Mich., U.S.	190	43.37 N	86.22 W
Shelby, Miss., U.S.	194	33.57 N	90.46 W
Shelby, Mont., U.S.	202	48.30 N	111.51 W
Shelby, Nebr., U.S.	198	41.12 N	97.26 W
Shelby, N.C., U.S.	192	35.17 N	81.32 W
Shelby, Ohio, U.S.	214	40.53 N	82.40 W
Shelby □[6], Ill., U.S.	219	39.24 N	88.48 W
Shelby □[6], Ind., U.S.	218	39.31 N	85.47 W
Shelby □[6], Ky., U.S.	218	38.15 N	85.13 W
Shelby □[6], Mo., U.S.	219	39.49 N	92.03 W
Shelby □[6], Ohio, U.S.	216	40.17 N	84.09 W
Shelby Village	214	42.38 N	83.04 W
Shelbyville, Ill., U.S.	219	39.24 N	88.48 W
Shelbyville, Ind., U.S.	218	39.31 N	85.47 W
Shelbyville, Ky., U.S.	218	38.13 N	85.14 W
Shelbyville, Mo., U.S.	219	39.48 N	92.02 W
Shelbyville, Tenn., U.S.	194	35.29 N	86.27 W
Shelbyville, Lake ⊜[1]	219	39.30 N	88.40 W
Sheldon, Ill., U.S.	216	40.46 N	87.34 W
Sheldon, Iowa, U.S.	198	43.11 N	95.51 W
Sheldon, Mich., U.S.	216	42.17 N	83.28 W
Sheldon, Mo., U.S.	194	37.40 N	94.18 W
Sheldon, Tex., U.S.	222	29.52 N	95.08 W
Sheldon Brook ≃	276	41.03 N	73.52 W
Sheldon Creek ≃	212	44.07 N	79.53 W
Sheldon Point	180	62.32 N	164.52 W
Sheldon Reservoir ⊜[1]	222	29.52 N	95.10 W
Sheldonville	283	42.02 N	71.23 W
Sheldrake ≃	276	40.57 N	73.44 W
Sheldrake Lake ⊜, Ont., Can.	212	44.49 N	77.16 W
Sheldrake Lake ⊜, N.Y., U.S.	276	40.57 N	73.46 W
Shelikof Strait Ц	180	57.30 N	155.00 W
Shell ≃	184	50.58 N	101.24 W
Shell, Loch C	46	58.00 N	6.30 W
Shellbrook	184	53.13 N	106.24 W
Shell Creek ≃, U.S.	200	40.56 N	108.37 W
Shell Creek ≃, Nebr., U.S.	198	41.27 N	96.58 W
Shell Creek ≃, N. Dak., U.S.	198	47.59 N	102.17 W
Shell Creek ≃, Wyo., U.S.	202	44.31 N	108.03 W
Shelley, B.C., Can.	182	54.00 N	122.37 W
Shelley, Idaho, U.S.	202	43.23 N	112.07 W
Shellharbour	170	34.35 S	150.52 E
Shell Lake, Sask., Can.	184	53.18 N	107.07 W
Shell Lake, Wis., U.S.	190	45.45 N	91.55 W
Shell Lakes ⊜	162	29.21 S	127.25 E
Shellman	192	31.46 N	84.37 W
Shellow Bowells	260	51.45 N	0.20 E
Shell Rock	190	42.43 N	92.35 W
Shell Rock ≃	190	42.38 N	92.30 W
Shellrock Peak ∧	224	46.43 N	121.14 W
Shellsburg	190	42.06 N	91.52 W
Shelocta	214	40.39 N	79.18 W
Shelter, Port C	271d	22.21 N	114.17 E
Shelter Island	207	41.05 N	72.21 W
Shelter Island I	271d	22.20 N	114.17 E
Shelter Island Heights	207	41.05 N	72.21 W
Shelter Island Sound Ц	207	41.03 N	72.22 W
Shelton, Conn., U.S.	207	41.19 N	73.05 W
Shelton, Nebr., U.S.	198	40.47 N	98.44 W
Shelton, Wash., U.S.	224	47.13 N	123.06 W
Shemanker ≃	150	8.12 N	9.45 E
Shemogue	186	46.09 N	64.11 W
Shemya Station	180	52.43 N	174.05 E
Shenandoah, Iowa, U.S.	198	40.46 N	95.22 W
Shenandoah, Pa., U.S.	208	40.49 N	76.12 W
Shenandoah, Va., U.S.	188	38.29 N	78.37 W
Shenandoah ≃	188	39.19 N	92.03 W
Shenandoah, North Fork ≃	188	38.57 N	78.12 W
Shenandoah, South Fork ≃	188	38.57 N	78.12 W
Shenandoah Heights	210	40.49 N	76.12 W
Shenandoah National Park ♠	188	38.48 N	78.12 W
Shenango	214	41.23 N	80.24 W
Shenango ≃	214	40.57 N	80.23 W
Shenango River Lake ⊜[1]	214	41.22 N	80.28 W
Shenchi	102	39.09 N	112.19 E
Shencottah	122	8.58 N	77.16 E
Shencun	106	31.04 N	118.51 E
Shendam	150	8.53 N	9.32 E
Shendang	106	30.34 N	120.49 E
Shenduncun	106	30.48 N	120.25 E
Shenfield	260	51.38 N	0.19 E
Shengang, Zhg.	100	27.20 N	116.18 E
Shen'gang, Zhg.	106	31.54 N	120.08 E
Shengcitang	106	32.03 N	120.10 E
Shenge	150	7.55 N	12.57 W
Shengsi I	100	30.41 N	122.28 E
Shengsiqundao II	100	30.42 N	122.20 E
Shenhuwan C	100	24.40 N	118.42 E
Shenipsit Lake ⊜	207	41.53 N	72.26 W
Shenk'eng	269d	25.00 N	121.36 E
Shenkou	100	28.42 N	116.02 E
Shenley	260	51.41 N	0.17 W
Shenmu	102	38.56 N	110.19 E
Shennanling	105	39.01 N	114.50 E
Shenorock	210	41.20 N	73.44 W
Shenqiu	100	33.24 N	115.02 E
Shenquan	100	22.59 N	116.20 E
Shenquangang C	100	22.54 N	116.18 E
Shensi → Shănxī □[4]	102	35.00 N	109.00 E
Shenton, Mount ∧	162	28.00 S	123.22 E
Shentuan	98	35.30 N	119.17 E
Shenxian	98	38.01 N	115.33 E
Shenxian'gou ≃	98	37.53 N	118.47 E
Shenyang (Mukden)	104	41.48 N	123.27 E
Shenze	98	38.11 N	115.11 E
Shenzha	120	30.57 N	88.38 E
Sheo	120	26.11 N	71.15 E
Sheoganj	120	25.09 N	73.04 E
Sheopur	124	25.40 N	76.42 E
Shepard	182	50.57 N	113.55 W
Shepard Island I	9	74.25 S	132.30 W
Shepards Brook ≃	283	42.08 N	71.25 W
Shepaug ≃	207	41.28 N	73.19 W
Shepherd, Mich., U.S.	190	43.32 N	84.41 W
Shepherd, Tex., U.S.	222	30.30 N	95.00 W
Shepherd Bay C	176	68.56 N	93.40 W
Shepherd Islands II	175f	16.55 S	168.36 E
Shepherdstown	188	39.26 N	77.48 W
Shepherdsville	194	37.59 N	85.43 W
Sheppard Air Force Base ■	196	33.58 N	98.30 W
Sheppard Peak ∧	180	57.41 N	132.37 W
Sheppard Pond ⊜	276	41.08 N	74.13 W
Shepparton	166	36.23 S	145.25 E
Shepperd, Lake ⊜	162	29.55 S	123.09 E
Shepperton	260	51.24 N	0.27 W
Sheppey, Isle of I	42	51.24 N	0.50 E
Sheppler Hill ∧[2]	279b	40.09 N	79.49 W
Sheppton	210	40.54 N	76.07 W
Shepshed	42	52.47 N	1.18 W
Shepton Mallet	42	51.12 N	2.33 W
Shepway	260	51.15 N	0.33 E
Sheqizhen	100	33.03 N	112.57 E
Sherab	140	10.43 N	24.47 E
Sherada	144	7.21 N	36.32 E
Sheraden •[8]	279b	40.28 N	80.05 W
Sherard, Cape ≻	176	74.36 N	80.25 W
Sherborn	283	42.14 N	71.22 W
Sherborne	42	50.57 N	2.31 W
Sherborne Lake ⊜	212	45.11 N	78.47 W
Sherborne Saint John	42	51.18 N	1.07 W
Sherbro ≃	150	7.45 N	12.55 W
Sherbro Island I	150	7.45 N	12.55 W
Sherbrooke, N.S., Can.	186	45.08 N	61.59 W
Sherbrooke, Qué., Can.	206	45.24 N	71.54 W
Sherbrooke □[6]	206	45.25 N	71.55 W
Sherbrooke Forest Park ♠	169	37.53 S	145.22 E
Sherbrooke Lake ⊜	186	44.40 N	64.35 W
Sherburn	198	43.39 N	94.43 W
Sherburne	210	42.41 N	75.30 W
Sherburne Reef ✣[2]	164	3.20 S	148.00 E
Shercock	48	54.00 N	6.54 W
Shere	260	51.13 N	0.28 W
Sheridan, Ark., U.S.	194	34.19 N	92.24 W
Sheridan, Calif., U.S.	226	38.59 N	121.22 W
Sheridan, Ill., U.S.	216	41.32 N	88.41 W
Sheridan, Ind., U.S.	218	40.08 N	86.13 W
Sheridan, Mont., U.S.	202	45.27 N	112.12 W
Sheridan, Oreg., U.S.	202	45.06 N	123.24 W
Sheridan, Pa., U.S.	208	40.21 N	76.14 W
Sheridan, Tex., U.S.	222	29.29 N	96.40 W
Sheridan, Wyo., U.S.	202	44.48 N	106.58 W
Sheridan, Mount ∧	202	44.16 N	110.32 W
Sheridan Park ♠	284a	42.59 N	78.54 W
Sheringa	162	33.51 S	135.15 E
Sheringham	42	52.57 N	1.12 E
Sherkston	284a	42.53 N	79.08 W
Sherlock ≃	162	20.44 S	117.35 E
Sherman, Conn., U.S.	207	41.35 N	73.30 W
Sherman, Ill., U.S.	219	39.54 N	89.36 W
Sherman, Ky., U.S.	218	38.44 N	84.36 W
Sherman, Miss., U.S.	194	34.22 N	88.57 W
Sherman, N.Y., U.S.	214	42.10 N	79.36 W
Sherman, Tex., U.S.	196	33.38 N	96.36 W
Sherman □[6]	224	45.25 N	120.49 W
Sherman Creek ≃	208	40.23 N	77.02 W
Sherman Mills	188	45.52 N	68.23 W
Sherman Mountain ∧	194	36.01 N	93.17 W
Sherman Oaks •[8]	280	34.09 N	118.26 W
Sherman Reservoir ⊜[1]	198	41.20 N	98.55 W
Sherman Station	188	45.54 N	68.26 W
Sherpur, Bngl.	124	25.01 N	90.01 E
Sherpur, Bngl.	124	24.41 N	89.25 E
Sher Qila	123	36.06 N	74.03 E
Sherrard	190	41.19 N	90.31 W
Sherridon	184	55.07 N	101.05 W
Sherrill	210	43.04 N	75.35 W
Sherri Park	278	42.02 N	87.51 W
Sherrodsville	214	40.30 N	81.15 W
Sher Shāh	123	30.06 N	71.21 E
Shertallai	122	9.42 N	76.20 E
's-Hertogenbosch	52	51.41 N	5.19 E
Sherwood, Ont., Can.	275b	43.50 N	79.31 W
Sherwood, P.E.I., Can.	186	46.17 N	63.08 W
Sherwood, Md., U.S.	208	38.36 N	76.19 W
Sherwood, Mich., U.S.	216	42.00 N	85.14 W
Sherwood, N. Dak., U.S.	198	48.58 N	101.38 W
Sherwood, Ohio, U.S.	216	41.17 N	84.33 W
Sherwood, Oreg., U.S.	224	45.21 N	122.50 W
Sherwood, Tenn., U.S.	194	35.05 N	85.56 W
Sherwood, Lake ⊜	281	42.36 N	83.33 W
Sherwood Forest, Calif., U.S.	226	37.57 N	122.17 W
Sherwood Forest, Md., U.S.	284c	39.05 N	77.01 W
Sherwood Forest •[3]	44	53.08 N	1.08 W
Sherwood Island State Park ♠	276	41.07 N	73.20 W
Sherwood Manor	207	42.01 N	72.38 W
Sherwood Park, Alta., Can.	182	53.31 N	113.19 W
Sherwood Park, N.Y., U.S.	210	42.36 N	73.43 W
Sherwood Park ♠	275b	43.43 N	79.24 W
Sherwood Point ≻	276	41.07 N	73.20 W
Sheshan ∧[2]	106	31.06 N	121.11 E
Sheshan I	100	28.26 N	121.53 E
Sheshea ≃	248	9.36 S	74.10 W
Shesh Gāv	120	33.45 N	68.33 E
Shet Bandar	272c	18.58 N	72.56 E
Shetland del Sur, Islas → South Shetland Islands II	9	62.00 S	58.00 W
Shetland Islands □[4]	46a	60.30 N	0.15 W
Shetland Islands II	46a	60.30 N	1.00 W
Shetou	106	31.39 N	119.27 E
Shetrunji ≃	120	21.19 N	72.07 E
Shetucket ≃	207	41.31 N	72.05 W
Sheva	272c	18.56 N	72.57 E
Sheva Nhava	272c	18.58 N	72.58 E
Shevaroy Hills ⋀[2]	122	11.50 N	78.16 E
Shevington	262	53.34 N	2.42 W
Shevington Moor	262	53.35 N	2.41 W
Shevut 'Am	132	32.19 N	34.55 E
Shewa □[4]	144	9.00 N	39.00 E
Shewa Gimira	144	7.00 N	35.50 E
Shexian	100	29.53 N	118.26 E
Sheyang (Hede), Zhg.	100	33.46 N	120.18 E
Sheyang, Zhg.	100	33.20 N	119.38 E
Sheyanghu ⊜	100	33.19 N	119.46 E
Sheyenne	198	47.39 N	99.07 W
Sheyenne ≃	198	47.05 N	96.50 W
Shezhu	106	31.19 N	119.16 E
Shḥīm	132	33.37 N	35.29 E
Shiant, Sound of Ц	46	57.55 N	6.25 W
Shiant Islands II	46	57.53 N	6.21 W
Shiawassee □[6]	216	42.56 N	84.09 W
Shiawassee ≃	216	43.06 N	84.10 W
Shiawassee, South Branch ≃	216	42.49 N	83.56 W
Shiba	100	32.45 N	118.07 E
Shiba ≃	268	35.37 N	139.44 E
Shibadu	102	28.01 N	110.51 E
Shibakawa	94	35.13 N	138.33 E
Shibām	144	15.56 N	48.38 E
Shibandeng	107	30.18 N	104.28 E
Shibanxi	107	29.17 N	103.51 E
Shibaocheng	102	39.48 N	96.10 E
Shibarni	140	14.50 N	24.25 E
Shibasaki	268	35.39 N	139.34 E
Shibata	92	37.57 N	139.20 E
Shibayama	94	35.41 N	140.25 E
Shibayama-gata ⊜	94	36.21 N	136.23 E
Shibden Hall	262	53.44 N	1.51 W
Shibecha	92a	43.17 N	144.36 E
Shibetsu, Nihon	92a	44.10 N	142.23 E
Shibetsu, Nihon	92a	43.40 N	145.08 E
Shibi	100	26.43 N	120.02 E
Shibīn al-Kawm	142	30.33 N	31.01 E
Shibīn al-Qanāṭir	142	30.19 N	31.19 E
Shibing	102	26.50 N	108.04 E
Shiblanjah	142	30.28 N	31.16 E
Shibotsu-tō I	92a	43.30 N	146.09 E
Shibu, Zhg.	98	36.25 N	119.44 E
Shibu, Zhg.	98	36.09 N	119.06 E
Shibukawa	94	36.29 N	139.00 E
Shibure-yama ∧[2]	270	34.45 N	135.05 E
Shibushi	92	31.28 N	131.07 E
Shibutsu-san ∧	94	36.54 N	139.11 E
Shibuya •[8]	268	35.40 N	139.42 E
Shicha	100	28.24 N	115.50 E
Shichangyu	104	41.12 N	123.14 E
Shicheng, Zhg.	98	40.39 N	124.17 E
Shicheng, Zhg.	100	25.18 N	119.21 E
Shicheng, Zhg.	100	26.22 N	116.22 E
Shichengdao I	98	39.31 N	123.02 E
Shichisō	94	35.33 N	137.07 E
Shichiyo I	175c	7.23 N	151.40 E
Shichuan	102	36.10 N	103.57 E
Shickley	198	40.25 N	97.43 W
Shickshinny	210	41.09 N	76.09 W
Shicun	106	31.09 N	119.20 E
Shidai	100	30.20 N	117.56 E
Shidao	98	36.53 N	122.23 E
Shideng	102	26.44 N	99.11 E
Shidler	196	36.47 N	96.40 W
Shido	96	34.19 N	134.10 E
Shidong, Zhg.	107	30.25 N	105.20 E
Shidong, Zhg.	107	28.59 N	105.27 E
Shidongzigou	105	40.41 N	118.23 E
Shiducun	98	39.37 N	115.36 E
Shiel, Loch ⊜	46	56.47 N	5.35 W
Shiel Bridge	46	57.12 N	5.25 W
Shieldaig	46	57.31 N	5.39 W
Shields ≃	202	45.43 N	110.28 W
Shiercun	106	30.31 N	119.34 E
Shiershan ∧	100	29.18 N	118.08 E
Shierwei, Zhg.	106	31.59 N	120.43 E
Shierwei, Zhg.	106	32.15 N	119.14 E
Shierzhan	89	51.13 N	125.52 E
Shifang	100	25.01 N	116.14 E
Shifengxi ≃	100	28.52 N	121.04 E
Shifnal	42	52.40 N	2.21 W
Shifo	107	29.58 N	103.50 E
Shifobao	104	41.28 N	121.27 E
Shifochang	107	30.19 N	105.07 E
Shifodian	100	32.06 N	115.46 E
Shifosi	104	42.08 N	123.20 E
Shifoya	98	40.12 N	123.10 E
Shifuhu ⊜	120	31.20 N	83.25 E
Shiga, Nihon	94	36.20 N	137.59 E
Shiga, Nihon	94	35.09 N	135.55 E
Shiga □[5]	96	35.15 N	136.00 E
Shigaib	140	15.01 N	23.36 E
Shigaise → Rikaze	120	29.17 N	88.53 E
Shigang	100	32.16 N	121.00 E
Shigaopu	107	30.16 N	104.01 E
Shigar ≃	123	34.39 N	75.51 E
Shigaraki	94	34.52 N	136.03 E
Shigaraki-gū ☧[1]	94	34.54 N	136.04 E
Shiga University ☧[2]	270	35.00 N	135.53 E
Shigenobu	96	33.48 N	132.50 E
Shigenobu ≃	96	33.48 N	132.41 E
Shigezhuang, Zhg.	105	39.18 N	116.53 E
Shigezhuang, Zhg.	105	38.57 N	116.19 E
Shigezhuang, Zhg.	105	38.59 N	115.36 E
Shiggar ≃	123	34.35 N	75.59 E
Shigoubao	102	37.44 N	106.26 E
Shigu, Zhg.	100	29.27 N	117.14 E
Shigu, Zhg.	100	34.10 N	113.39 E
Shigu, Zhg.	102	26.50 N	99.55 E
Shiguantun	104	41.38 N	123.39 E
Shigulingyu	105	40.38 N	116.54 E
Shīḥān ∧	132	31.23 N	35.44 E
Shihch'i → Zhongshan	100	22.31 N	113.22 E
Shihchiachuang → Shijiazhuang	98	38.03 N	114.28 E
Shihe	98	39.19 N	121.52 E
Shihe ≃	100	32.18 N	114.31 E
Shihengyuanyu	106	31.50 N	121.45 E
Shihkiachwang → Shijiazhuang	98	38.03 N	114.28 E
Shihlin	269d	25.05 N	121.31 E
Shihti	269d	25.02 N	121.44 E
Shihting	269d	24.59 N	121.39 E
Shihu, Zhg.	98	41.29 N	126.18 E
Shihu, Zhg.	105	40.04 N	117.17 E
Shihuajie	102	32.20 N	111.25 E
Shihudang	106	30.58 N	121.07 E
Shihuiqiao	100	26.58 N	114.23 E
Shihuixi	107	29.02 N	105.04 E
Shihuiyaozi	104	42.08 N	123.47 E
Shihuxia	105	40.48 N	117.22 E
Shiida	96	33.39 N	131.04 E
Shijiaba	107	30.18 N	104.46 E
Shijiagang	100	30.41 N	114.32 E
Shijiagangzi	104	42.19 N	123.34 E
Shijiagou	104	42.27 N	123.28 E
Shijiao	100	23.36 N	112.59 E
Shijiaqiao	106	32.18 N	119.26 E
Shijiawu	105	39.21 N	116.15 E
Shijiaxiang	107	29.38 N	104.59 E
Shijiayaozhuang	106	32.13 N	120.29 E
Shijiazhai	98	38.56 N	114.18 E
Shijiazhen	106	31.51 N	121.10 E
Shijiazhuang	98	38.03 N	114.28 E
Shijiazi, Zhg.	104	42.12 N	122.14 E
Shijiazi, Zhg.	104	42.39 N	122.06 E
Shijiedu	106	30.57 N	119.13 E
Shijing, Zhg.	100	24.40 N	118.24 E
Shijing, Zhg.	105	39.54 N	114.58 E
Shijingshan	105	39.56 N	116.07 E
Shijiuhu ⊜	106	31.28 N	118.53 E
Shijiusuo	98	35.24 N	119.29 E
Shijiutuo I	98	39.11 N	118.56 E
Shijōnawate	270	34.45 N	135.39 E
Shijūmagari-tōge)(	96	35.11 N	133.32 E
Shijushan	102	39.20 N	106.50 E
Shika	94	37.01 N	136.47 E
Shikami-yama ∧	270	34.47 N	135.10 E
Shikano	96	35.28 N	134.04 E
Shikārpur, Bhārat	122	14.16 N	75.21 E
Shikārpur, Bhārat	124	28.17 N	78.01 E
Shikārpur, Pāk.	120	27.57 N	68.38 E
Shikata	96	34.49 N	134.49 E
Shikatsu	94	35.14 N	136.53 E
Shikewusumiao	102	40.13 N	108.52 E
Shiki	268	35.50 N	139.35 E
Shiki I	175c	7.24 N	151.53 E
Shikishima	94	35.41 N	138.32 E
Shikohābād	124	27.06 N	78.36 E
Shikoku I	92	33.45 N	133.30 E
Shikoku-sanchi ⋀	96	33.47 N	133.30 E
Shikoma	268	35.11 N	139.56 E
Shikongling ∧	100	24.56 N	113.00 E
Shikotsu-ko ⊜	92a	42.45 N	141.20 E
Shikotsu-tōya-kokuritsu-kōen ♠	92a	42.47 N	141.00 E
Shikuang	106	31.54 N	121.24 E
Shil	272c	19.09 N	73.03 E
Shilabo	144	6.05 N	44.48 E
Shilbottle	44	55.23 N	1.42 W
Shildon	44	54.38 N	1.39 W
Shiliangji	100	33.54 N	115.14 E
Shilibao	105	39.55 N	116.29 E
Shilihe	104	41.31 N	123.22 E
Shiling	106	30.26 N	119.35 E
Shilipeng	106	31.14 N	119.35 E
Shilipu, Zhg.	105	39.11 N	115.59 E
Shilipu, Zhg.	105	39.29 N	116.18 E
Shilipu, Zhg.	105	40.15 N	117.58 E
Shiliuban	100	24.11 N	117.31 E
Shiliugu	98	34.14 N	115.52 E
Shillelagh	48	52.45 N	6.32 W
Shillingstone	42	50.54 N	2.14 W
Shillington	208	40.18 N	75.58 W
Shillong	120	25.34 N	91.53 E
Shiloh, Ill., U.S.	219	38.34 N	89.54 W
Shiloh, N.J., U.S.	208	39.27 N	75.18 W
Shiloh, Ohio, U.S.	214	40.58 N	82.36 W
Shiloh, Pa., U.S.	208	39.59 N	76.49 W
Shiloh National Military Park ♠	194	35.06 N	88.21 W
Shilong	100	23.07 N	113.48 E
Shilongchang	107	30.15 N	106.34 E
Shilou	100	22.58 N	113.29 E
Shima, Nihon	92	34.13 N	136.51 E
Shima, Nihon	270	34.59 N	135.20 E
Shima, Zhg.	100	24.27 N	117.49 E
Shimabara	92	32.47 N	130.22 E
Shimachang, Zhg.	107	28.59 N	105.55 E
Shimachang, Zhg.	107	29.03 N	105.36 E
Shimada, Nihon	94	34.49 N	138.11 E
Shimada, Nihon	268	35.59 N	139.25 E
Shimagahara	94	34.46 N	136.03 E
Shima-hantō ≻[1]	94	34.26 N	136.33 E
Shimamiao	106	32.08 N	119.20 E
Shimamoto	96	34.53 N	135.40 E
Shimane □[5]	96	35.00 N	132.30 E
Shimane-hantō ≻[1]	96	35.30 N	133.00 E
Shimantan	100	33.17 N	113.28 E
Shimanto ≃	96	32.56 N	133.00 E
Shimata ≃	96	33.57 N	131.55 E
Shimba Hills National Reserve •[4]	154	4.15 S	39.25 E
Shimei	106	32.14 N	120.10 E
Shimen, Zhg.	98	39.44 N	118.52 E
Shimen, Zhg.	102	29.28 N	111.17 E
Shimen, Zhg.	105	40.06 N	117.42 E
Shimen, Zhg.	107	29.36 N	106.27 E
Shimencun, Zhg.	106	31.21 N	119.34 E
Shimencun, Zhg.	106	30.23 N	119.41 E
Shimendong	100	28.16 N	120.07 E
Shimengou	104	40.40 N	123.43 E
Shimenjie	100	29.34 N	116.44 E
Shimenlou	100	28.58 N	114.51 E
Shimenwan	106	30.37 N	120.26 E
Shimenzi	89	48.30 N	121.31 E
Shimian (Nongchang)	102	29.18 N	102.22 E
Shimiaozi	104	40.39 N	123.31 E
Shimizu, Nihon	92	35.01 N	138.29 E
Shimizu → Tosa-shimizu, Nihon	92	32.46 N	132.57 E
Shimizu, Nihon	92a	43.01 N	142.53 E
Shimizu, Nihon	94	36.02 N	136.09 E
Shimizu, Nihon	94	35.01 N	138.29 E
Shimizu, Nihon	96	34.05 N	135.26 E
Shimizu-tunnel •[5]	94	36.52 N	138.55 E
Shimminato	94	36.47 N	137.04 E
Shimobe	94	35.27 N	138.29 E
Shimoda	94	34.40 N	138.57 E
Shimodate	94	36.18 N	139.59 E
Shimofusa	94	35.52 N	140.21 E
Shimofusa-daichi ⋀[1]	268	35.45 N	139.58 E
Shimoga	122	13.55 N	75.34 E
Shimogawara	268	35.56 N	139.21 E
Shimogōri	268	35.21 N	140.03 E
Shimogyō •[8]	270	34.59 N	135.45 E
Shimohōya	268	35.45 N	139.34 E
Shimoichi	96	34.22 N	135.47 E
Shimoigusa •[8]	268	35.43 N	139.37 E
Shimoji-shima I	175d	24.49 N	125.09 E
Shimojō	94	35.24 N	137.47 E
Shimokawa	92a	44.18 N	142.39 E
Shimokita-hantō ≻[1]	92	41.15 N	141.00 E
Shimomatsu	270	34.27 N	135.23 E
Shimomizo	268	35.31 N	139.23 E
Shimoni	154	4.39 S	39.23 E
Shimoniikura	268	35.47 N	139.38 E
Shimonita	94	36.13 N	138.47 E
Shimonoseki	96	33.57 N	130.57 E
Shimookudomi	268	35.53 N	139.26 E
Shimosakamoto	270	35.03 N	135.53 E
Shimoshakujii •[8]	268	35.45 N	139.37 E
Shimosuwa	94	36.04 N	138.05 E
Shimotajiri	270	34.57 N	135.28 E
Shimotomi	268	35.50 N	139.29 E
Shimotsu	96	34.10 N	135.08 E
Shimotsuchidana	268	35.24 N	139.27 E
Shimotsuma	94	36.11 N	139.58 E
Shimotsuruma	268	35.29 N	139.28 E
Shimoya	268	35.23 N	139.21 E
Shimoyama	94	35.02 N	137.19 E
Shimoyugi	268	35.38 N	139.23 E
Shimpuru Rapids ⌊	156	17.50 S	19.56 E
Shimura •[8]	268	35.46 N	139.41 E
Shin, Loch ⊜	46	58.06 N	4.34 W
Shinagawa •[8]	268	35.37 N	139.45 E
Shinan	102	22.43 N	109.54 E
Shinano	94	36.48 N	138.13 E
Shinano ≃	92	37.56 N	139.03 E
Shinarā	142	28.47 N	30.46 E
Shināṣ	128	24.46 N	56.28 E
Shināwari	123	33.32 N	70.48 E
Shinbārī	273c	30.07 N	31.09 E
Shīndand	128	33.18 N	62.08 E
Shindo	268	35.21 N	139.21 E
Shiner	222	29.26 N	97.10 W
Shingbwiyang	110	26.41 N	96.13 E
Shingishū → Sinŭiju	98	40.05 N	124.24 E
Shinglehouse	214	41.58 N	78.12 W
Shingle Springs	226	38.40 N	120.56 W
Shingō	96	34.54 N	133.29 E
Shingū, Nihon	92	33.44 N	135.59 E
Shingū, Nihon	96	34.55 N	134.33 E
Shingwidzi	156	23.05 S	31.25 E
Shinichi	96	34.33 N	133.16 E
Shining Tor ∧	262	53.16 N	2.01 W
Shinīrah	132	32.22 N	36.45 E
Shiniujie	100	28.26 N	119.48 E
Shinji	96	35.24 N	132.54 E
Shinji-ko ⊜	96	35.27 N	132.58 E
Shinjō, Nihon	92	38.46 N	140.18 E
Shinjō, Nihon	270	34.30 N	135.44 E
Shinjuku •[8]	268	35.41 N	139.42 E
Shinkawa	94	35.09 N	136.50 E
Shīnkay	120	31.57 N	67.26 E
Shinkolobwe	154	11.02 S	26.35 E
Shinmachi	94	36.16 N	139.07 E
Shinminato ≃	270	34.38 N	135.09 E
Shinnārah, Minqār ⊥[4]	142	28.52 N	30.38 E
Shīn Naray	120	31.19 N	66.43 E
Shinnecock Bay C	207	40.52 N	72.28 W
Shinnel Water ≃	44	55.13 N	3.49 W
Shinness	46	58.05 N	4.28 W
Shinnston	188	39.24 N	80.18 W
Shino-jima I	94	34.39 N	137.00 E
Shinshār	130	34.36 N	36.44 E
Shinshiro	94	34.54 N	137.30 E
Shinshū-shinmachi	94	36.34 N	138.01 E
Shintone	94	35.50 N	140.20 E
Shinyanga	154	3.40 S	33.26 E
Shinyanga □[4]	154	3.45 S	33.00 E
Shin-yōdo ≃[1]	270	34.41 N	135.26 E
Shio	94	36.52 N	136.48 E
Shiobara	94	36.58 N	139.49 E
Shiocton	190	44.27 N	88.35 W
Shioda	94	36.21 N	138.12 E
Shiogama	92	38.19 N	141.01 E
Shiojiri	94	36.06 N	137.58 E
Shiojiri-tōge)(	94	36.05 N	138.02 E
Shiokawa	175d	24.40 N	124.41 E
Shiomi-dake ∧	94	35.34 N	138.12 E
Shionoe	96	34.10 N	134.05 E
Shiono-misaki ≻	90	33.26 N	135.45 E
Shiono-zaki ≻	92	33.26 N	135.45 E
Shioya	94	36.46 N	139.51 E
Shioya •[8]	270	34.38 N	135.06 E
Shioya-zaki ≻, Nihon	92	33.26 N	135.45 E
Shioya-zaki ≻, Nihon	94	37.00 N	140.59 E
Shiozawa	94	37.02 N	138.51 E
Shipai, Zhg.	100	23.08 N	113.21 E
Shipai, Zhg.	106	31.30 N	120.55 E
Shipanpu	107	30.28 N	104.23 E
Shipantuo	107	30.25 N	106.13 E
Ship Bottom	208	39.39 N	74.11 W
Shipbourne	260	51.15 N	0.17 E
Ship Cove	186	47.06 N	54.05 W
Shipdham	42	52.37 N	0.53 E
Shiping, Zhg.	102	28.20 N	107.42 E
Shiping, Zhg.	102	23.47 N	102.30 E
Ship Island I	194	30.13 N	88.55 W
Shipley	44	53.50 N	1.47 W
Shipman, Ill., U.S.	219	39.07 N	90.03 W
Shipman, Va., U.S.	192	37.43 N	78.51 W
Shippan Point ≻	276	41.01 N	73.32 W
Shippegan	186	47.45 N	64.42 W
Shippegan Island I	186	47.48 N	64.36 W
Shippensburg	208	40.03 N	77.31 W
Shippenville	214	41.15 N	79.28 W
Shippingport	214	40.38 N	80.25 W
Shippō	94	35.40 N	136.47 E
Shiprock	200	36.47 N	108.41 W
Ship Rock ∧	200	36.42 N	108.50 W
Shipshewana	216	41.41 N	85.35 W
Shipston-on-Stour	42	52.04 N	1.37 W
Shipu, Zhg.	100	29.13 N	121.55 E
Shipu, Zhg.	106	31.15 N	121.03 E
Shiqi → Zhongshan	100	22.31 N	113.22 E
Shiqian	102	27.31 N	108.20 E
Shiqiao, Zhg.	106	30.31 N	119.11 E
Shiqiao, Zhg.	107	30.25 N	104.31 E
Shiqiaopu	107	30.05 N	105.23 E
Shiqiaozhen	100	33.12 N	112.36 E
Shiqiaozi, Zhg.	104	41.18 N	123.17 E
Shiqiaozi, Zhg.	104	41.27 N	123.43 E
Shiqma ≃	132	31.36 N	34.30 E
Shiqu	102	33.04 N	97.45 E
Shiquan, Zhg.	102	32.55 N	108.33 E
Shiquan, Zhg.	106	30.30 N	120.48 E
Shira ≃	92	32.12 N	130.37 E
Shirahama, Nihon	94	34.54 N	139.54 E
Shirahama, Nihon	96	33.40 N	135.20 E
Shirahata-yama ∧	96	34.54 N	134.23 E
Shiraitono-taki ⌊	94	35.18 N	138.38 E
Shirakami-saki ≻	92a	41.24 N	140.12 E
Shirakawa, Nihon	94	37.07 N	140.13 E
Shirakawa, Nihon	94	36.16 N	136.54 E
Shirakawa, Nihon	94	35.35 N	137.12 E
Shirakawano-seki ⊥	94	37.03 N	140.15 E
Shirakawa-tōge ∧[2]	270	34.42 N	135.07 E
Shiraki	96	34.33 N	132.40 E
Shirako	94	35.26 N	140.23 E
Shirākol	126	22.18 N	88.16 E
Shirakura-yama ∧	94	35.00 N	137.46 E
Shirama-yama ∧	96	34.01 N	135.23 E
Shiramine	94	36.10 N	136.37 E
Shirane	94	35.38 N	138.28 E
Shirane-san ∧, Nihon	94	36.38 N	138.32 E
Shirane-san ∧, Nihon	94	36.48 N	139.22 E
Shirane-san (Kita-dake) ∧, Nihon	94	35.40 N	138.15 E
Shiranuka, Nihon	92a	42.57 N	144.05 E
Shiranuka, Nihon	92a	41.08 N	141.24 E
Shiraoi	92a	42.33 N	141.21 E
Shiraoka	94	36.01 N	139.40 E
Shiraone	272c	19.03 N	73.01 E
Shirasawa	94	36.40 N	139.08 E
Shirase Glacier ⛋	9	70.10 S	38.35 E
Shīrāz	128	29.36 N	52.32 E
Shirbīn	142	31.11 N	31.32 E
Shirdley Hill	262	53.36 N	2.58 W
Shire (Chire) ≃	154	17.42 S	35.19 E
Shirebrook	44	53.12 N	1.13 W
Shiremanstown	208	40.13 N	76.57 W
Shiretoko-hantō ≻[1]	92a	44.00 N	145.00 E
Shiretoko-kokuritsu-kōen ♠	92a	44.08 N	145.10 E
Shiretoko-misaki ≻[1]	92a	44.14 N	145.17 E
Shīrīn ≃	120	36.49 N	65.01 E
Shiriya-saki ≻	92	41.26 N	141.28 E
Shīr Kūh ∧	128	31.37 N	54.04 E
Shirland	216	42.27 N	89.12 W
Shirley, B.C., Can.	224	48.23 N	123.54 W
Shirley, Ill., U.S.	216	40.24 N	89.04 W
Shirley, Ind., U.S.	218	39.53 N	85.35 W
Shirley, Mass., U.S.	207	42.33 N	71.39 W
Shirley Plantation ⊥	208	37.21 N	77.15 W
Shirleysburg	214	40.18 N	77.53 W
Shīr Manṣūr, Jabal ⋀	132	33.41 N	36.02 E
Shiro	222	30.37 N	95.53 W
Shiroi	94	35.48 N	140.04 E
Shiroishi	92	38.00 N	140.37 E
Shirokawa	96	33.23 N	132.46 E
Shirone	92	37.46 N	139.01 E
Shirotori, Nihon	94	35.53 N	136.52 E
Shirotori, Nihon	96	34.15 N	134.20 E
Shirouma-dake ∧	94	36.45 N	137.46 E
Shiroyama	94	35.35 N	139.19 E
Shiro-yama ∧	270	34.38 N	135.53 E
Shirpur	120	21.21 N	74.53 E
Shirrell Heath	42	50.55 N	1.12 W
Shirshābah	142	30.47 N	31.10 E
Shīrvān	128	37.24 N	57.55 E
Shisaka-jima I	96	34.07 N	133.11 E
Shisanling	105	40.17 N	116.11 E
Shisanzhan	89	51.21 N	125.43 E
Shishaldin Volcano ∧[1]	180	54.45 N	163.57 W
Shishanshan	104	41.16 N	121.30 E
Shishikui	96	33.34 N	134.18 E
Shishishan ∧	100	24.44 N	117.54 E
Shishmaref	180	66.14 N	166.09 W
Shishmaref Inlet C	180	66.07 N	165.50 W
Shishou	102	29.43 N	112.19 E
Shisht al-An'ām	142	30.52 N	30.44 E
Shisixian	104	40.53 N	122.59 E
Shisler Point ≻	284a	42.52 N	79.08 W
Shisui	94	35.43 N	140.16 E
Shitan, Zhg.	100	23.10 N	113.47 E
Shitan, Zhg.	100	27.44 N	112.42 E
Shitang, Zhg.	100	28.16 N	121.36 E
Shitang, Zhg.	102	25.38 N	110.50 E
Shitangwan	106	31.40 N	120.13 E
Shitara	94	35.05 N	137.35 E
Shithāthah	128	32.33 N	43.29 E
Shiting, Zhg.	100	27.36 N	113.16 E
Shiting, Zhg.	105	39.31 N	115.41 E
Shitoufangzi	89	48.38 N	126.08 E
Shitougouzi	89	49.19 N	125.55 E
Shitouhe	89	44.50 N	128.44 E
Shitoumiao	102	41.41 N	106.50 E
Shitoumiaozi	104	41.38 N	121.26 E
Shitouqiao	98	41.51 N	119.04 E
Shitoushan	105	40.27 N	116.13 E
Shitoushuangmiao	98	41.28 N	118.55 E
Shituanzhen	107	30.09 N	105.01 E
Shitunwei	104	41.07 N	121.31 E
Shiva, Ḫorvot (Subeita) ⊥	132	30.53 N	34.38 E
Shively	218	38.11 N	85.49 W
Shivering, Mount ∧	170	34.08 S	150.02 E
Shivpuri	124	25.26 N	77.39 E
Shivpuri □[5]	124	25.20 N	77.40 E
Shiwa	96	34.29 N	132.41 E
Shiwaku-shotō II	96	34.20 N	133.45 E
Shiwan, Zhg.	100	27.17 N	112.57 E
Shiwan, Zhg.	100	28.12 N	113.49 E
Shiwan, Zhg.	100	23.01 N	113.04 E
Shiwanzhen	102	37.35 N	109.01 E
Shiwenchang	104	41.43 N	123.54 E
Shiwu	89	43.48 N	124.13 E
Shiwudu	100	29.44 N	119.10 E
Shixi, Zhg.	100	28.16 N	117.45 E
Shixi, Zhg.	100	28.16 N	115.36 E
Shixia, Zhg.	98	40.15 N	114.54 E
Shixia, Zhg.	105	40.32 N	117.01 E
Shixia, Zhg.	105	40.20 N	114.59 E
Shixian	89	43.05 N	129.47 E
Shixiancun	106	31.12 N	120.29 E
Shixiechang	107	29.51 N	106.41 E
Shixing	100	24.58 N	114.03 E
Shixun	100	24.44 N	118.11 E
Shiyachang	107	30.27 N	106.31 E
Shiyan, Zhg.	102	32.38 N	110.44 E
Shiyan, Zhg.	107	30.22 N	104.27 E
Shiyangchang, Zhg.	107	30.42 N	105.57 E
Shiyangchang, Zhg.	107	29.56 N	105.37 E
Shiyanqiao	107	29.19 N	105.22 E
Shiyu	107	29.46 N	106.06 E
Shizhangzi	98	40.24 N	119.48 E
Shizhen	100	22.37 N	113.11 E
Shizheng	100	24.32 N	115.50 E
Shizhenjie	100	28.51 N	116.56 E
Shizhong, Zhg.	100	24.58 N	117.04 E
Shizhong, Zhg.	106	30.44 N	120.16 E
Shizhongtan	107	30.26 N	104.35 E
Shizhu	102	30.07 N	108.08 E
Shizhuang	106	32.08 N	120.31 E
Shizhuangzi, Zhg.	104	42.24 N	122.53 E
Shizhuangzi, Zhg.	105	40.38 N	116.59 E
Shizhuzi	104	41.18 N	121.35 E
Shizichang	107	29.32 N	106.14 E
Shizigu	105	39.23 N	118.08 E
Shizihe	98	34.07 N	115.33 E
Shizikou	100	24.12 N	113.38 E
Shizilin	106	31.26 N	121.25 E

Symbols in the index entries represent the broad categories identified in the key at the right. Symbols with superior numbers (⋀[2]) identify subcategories (see complete key on page *I* · 30).

Kartensymbole in dem Registerverzeichnis stellen die rechts in Schlüssel erklärten Kategorien dar. Symbole mit hochgestellten Ziffern (⋀[2]) bezeichnen Unterabteilungen einer Kategorie (vgl. vollständiger Schlüssel auf Seite *I* · 30).

Los símbolos incluídos en el texto del índice representan las grandes categorias identificadas con la clave a la derecha. Los símbolos con numeros en su parte superior (⋀[2]) identifican las subcategorías (véase la clave completa en la página *I* · 30).

Les symboles de l'index représentent les catégories indiquées dans la légende à droite. Les symboles suivis d'un indice (⋀[2]) représentent des sous-catégories (voir légende complète à la page *I* · 30).

Os símbolos incluídos no texto do índice representam as grandes categorias identificadas com a chave à direita. Os símbolos com números em sua parte superior (⋀[2]) identificam as subcategorias (veja-se a chave completa à página *I* · 30).

Symbol	English	Deutsch	Español	Français	Português
∧	Mountain	Berg	Montaña	Montagne	Montanha
⋀	Mountains	Berge	Montañas	Montagnes	Montanhas
)(	Pass	Pass	Paso	Col	Passo
V	Valley, Canyon	Tal, Cañon	Valle, Cañón	Vallée, Canyon	Vale, Canhão
⌣	Plain	Ebene	Llano	Plaine	Planície
≻	Cape	Kap	Cabo	Cap	Cabo
I	Island	Insel	Isla	Île	Ilha
II	Islands	Inseln	Islas	Îles	Ilhas
⊥	Other Topographic Features	Andere Topographische Objekte	Otros Elementos Topográficos	Autres données topographiques	Outros Elementos Topográficos

ESPAÑOL — Nombre | Página | Lat.°′ | Long.°′ W=Oeste
FRANÇAIS — Nom | Page | Lat.°′ | Long.°′ W=Ouest
PORTUGUÊS — Nome | Página | Lat.°′ | Long.°′ W=Oeste

Shizipo 105 40.21 N 115.07 E
Shizipu 106 30.59 N 119.07 E
Shizugawa 92 38.40 N 141.27 E
Shizui 98 38.52 N 113.42 E
Shizuizi 89 43.08 N 126.06 E
Shizuma ≃ 96 35.12 N 132.28 E
Shizunai 92a 42.20 N 142.22 E
Shizuoka 94 34.58 N 138.23 E
Shizuoka □[5] 94 35.00 N 138.00 E
Shizushan 104 41.47 N 121.17 E
Shkodër 38 42.05 N 19.30 E
Shkumbin ≃ 38 41.01 N 19.26 E
Shō ≃ 94 36.47 N 137.04 E
Shoal ≃ 194 30.41 N 86.39 W
Shoal Cape > 162 33.53 S 121.07 E
Shoal Creek ≃, U.S. 194 40.28 N 92.42 W
Shoal Creek ≃, U.S. 194 37.05 N 94.42 W
Shoal Creek ≃, Ill., U.S. 219 38.28 N 89.35 W
Shoal Creek ≃, Mo., U.S. 194 39.44 N 93.32 W
Shoal Creek, East Fork ≃ 219 38.51 N 89.30 W
Shoal Harbour 186 48.11 N 53.59 W
Shoalhaven ≃ 170 34.52 S 150.44 E
Shoalhaven Bight C 170 34.52 S 150.47 E
Shoal Lake 184 50.26 N 100.34 W
Shoal Lake ⊜ 184 49.32 N 95.00 W
Shoal Point > 276 41.08 N 73.15 W
Shoals 194 38.40 N 86.47 W
Shoals, Bay of C 168b 35.37 S 137.37 E
Shoalwater Bay C 166 22.02 S 150.25 E
Shobonier 219 38.52 N 89.05 W
Shōdai 270 34.51 N 135.42 E
Shōdo-shima I 96 34.30 N 134.17 E
Shoeburyness 42 51.32 N 0.48 E
Shoe Cove 186 47.45 N 52.44 W
Shoemakersville 208 40.30 N 75.58 W
Shōgawa 94 36.34 N 136.59 E
Shogunle 273a 6.35 N 3.21 E
Shohola 210 41.28 N 74.55 W
Shohola Creek ≃ 210 41.28 N 74.55 W
Shokan 210 41.58 N 74.13 W
Sholāpur 122 17.41 N 75.55 E
Sholinghur 122 13.07 N 79.25 E
Shomera 132 33.05 N 35.17 E
Shomolu 273a 6.32 N 3.23 E
Shōmyō-no-taki L 94 36.35 N 137.31 E
Shona, Eilean I 46 56.47 N 5.52 W
Shōnai ≃ 94 35.04 N 136.50 E
Shongum 276 40.50 N 74.33 W
Shongum Lake ⊜ 276 40.51 N 74.32 W
Shongwe 158 27.24 S 32.25 E
Shooters Hill 170 33.54 S 149.52 E
Shooters Island I 276 40.39 N 74.10 W
Shopiere 216 42.34 N 88.57 W
Shoranūr 122 10.46 N 76.17 E
Shorāpur 122 16.31 N 76.45 E
Shoreacres, B.C., Can. 182 49.26 N 117.32 W
Shore Acres, Calif., U.S. 226 38.02 N 121.58 W
Shore Acres, Mass., U.S. 207 42.13 N 70.44 W
Shore Acres, N.J., U.S. 208 40.02 N 74.06 W
Shoreacres, Tex., U.S. 222 29.37 N 95.01 W
Shoreditch ◆[8] 260 51.32 N 0.05 W
Shoreham, Eng., U.K. 260 51.20 N 0.11 E
Shoreham, Mich., U.S. 216 42.04 N 86.30 W
Shoreham-by-Sea 42 50.49 N 0.16 W
Shorewood, Ill., U.S. 216 41.32 N 88.12 W
Shorewood, Wis., U.S. 216 43.05 N 87.53 W
Shorewood Hills 216 43.03 N 89.27 W
Shorkot 123 30.50 N 72.04 E
Shorkot Road 123 30.47 N 72.15 E
Shorne 260 51.25 N 0.26 E
Short Acres 226 36.21 N 119.38 W
Short Beach 207 41.15 N 72.52 W
Short Creek 214 40.11 N 80.55 W
Shortland Island I 175e 7.02 S 155.47 E
Short Mountain ∧ 192 36.23 N 83.10 W
Shortsville 210 42.57 N 77.14 W
Shoshone 202 42.56 N 114.24 W
Shoshone ≃ 202 44.52 N 108.11 W
Shoshone, North Fork ≃ 202 44.29 N 109.18 W
Shoshone, South Fork ≃ 202 44.27 N 109.14 W
Shoshone Basin ≋[1] 202 43.05 N 108.05 W
Shoshone Lake ⊜ 202 44.22 N 110.43 W
Shoshone Mountains ∧ 204 39.25 N 117.15 W
Shoshone Peak ∧ 204 36.56 N 116.16 W
Shoshone Range ∧ 204 40.20 N 116.50 W
Shoshong 156 22.59 S 26.30 E
Shoshoni 200 43.14 N 108.07 W
Shostka → Šostka 78 51.52 N 33.30 E
Shotley Gate 42 51.58 N 1.15 E
Shotton 262 53.12 N 3.02 W
Shotton Colliery 44 54.44 N 1.20 W
Shotts 46 55.49 N 3.48 W
Shotwick 262 53.14 N 2.59 W
Shouanzhen 107 30.16 N 103.36 E
Shouchang 100 29.22 N 119.13 E
Shoufeng 100 23.52 N 121.30 E
Shouguang 98 36.53 N 118.42 E
Shoultes 224 48.07 N 122.09 W
Shouning 100 27.27 N 119.30 E
Shournagh ≃ 48 51.53 N 8.35 W
Shoushan 104 41.12 N 123.03 E
Shouxian 100 32.35 N 116.47 E
Shouyang 102 37.59 N 113.09 E
Shōwa, Nihon 94 36.37 N 139.04 E
Shōwa, Nihon 96 34.43 N 133.39 E
Showa ♥[3] 9 69.00 S 39.35 E
Showell 208 38.24 N 75.13 W
Show Low 200 34.15 N 110.02 W
Shqipëri → Albania □[1] 38 41.00 N 20.00 E
Shreve 214 40.41 N 82.01 W
Shreveport 194 32.30 N 93.45 W
Shrewsbury, Eng., U.K. 42 52.43 N 2.45 W
Shrewsbury, Mass., U.S. 207 42.18 N 71.43 W
Shrewsbury, N.J., U.S. 208 40.19 N 74.04 W
Shrewsbury, Pa., U.S. 208 39.46 N 76.41 W
Shrewsbury River C 276 40.21 N 74.00 W
Shrewton 42 51.12 N 1.55 W
Shri Lakshmi Narayan Temple ♥[1] 272a 28.38 N 77.12 E
Shriner Mountain ∧ 210 40.56 N 77.20 W
Shrivenham 42 51.36 N 1.39 W
Shropshire Union Canal ≅ 262 53.17 N 2.53 W
Shrub Oak 210 41.20 N 73.49 W
Shrule 48 53.30 N 9.08 W
Shuajingsi 102 32.00 N 103.05 E
Shuangbai 102 24.54 N 101.32 E
Shuangcheng 89 45.26 N 126.18 E
Shuangchengzi 105 40.11 N 118.03 E
Shuang Ch'i ≃ 269d 25.02 N 121.29 E
Shuangdian 100 32.23 N 120.51 E
Shuangdun 106 32.13 N 121.08 E
Shuangfeng, Zhg. 102 27.24 N 112.05 E
Shuangfeng, Zhg. 106 31.31 N 121.01 E
Shuangfengchang 107 30.02 N 106.24 E
Shuangfengdao I 100 26.35 N 120.08 E
Shuangfengshan ∧, Zhg. 100 24.28 N 114.43 E
Shuangfengshan ∧, Zhg. 107 29.26 N 105.47 E
Shuangfengyi 107 29.27 N 105.09 E
Shuangfu 105 39.48 N 117.44 E
Shuangfuchang, Zhg. 107 30.08 N 103.32 E
Shuangfuchang, Zhg. 107 29.41 N 103.31 E
Shuanggang, Zhg. 89 45.07 N 122.59 E
Shuanggang, Zhg. 100 28.11 N 117.30 E
Shuanggetun 89 48.58 N 129.57 E
Shuanggou, Zhg. 98 34.03 N 117.37 E
Shuanggou, Zhg. 100 33.16 N 118.10 E
Shuanggou, Zhg. 100 32.12 N 112.21 E
Shuanggufen 107 29.38 N 104.11 E
Shuanghe, Zhg. 100 31.41 N 112.46 E
Shuanghe, Zhg. 100 31.33 N 116.46 E
Shuanghe, Zhg. 107 30.07 N 105.10 E
Shuanghe, Zhg. 107 30.15 N 104.44 E
Shuanghe, Zhg. 107 29.41 N 105.31 E
Shuanghe, Zhg. 107 29.40 N 104.48 E
Shuanghechang, Zhg. 107 29.18 N 105.36 E
Shuanghechang, Zhg. 107 28.51 N 104.51 E
Shuanghechang, Zhg. 107 29.25 N 106.17 E
Shuanghechang, Zhg. 107 29.12 N 105.43 E
Shuanghezhen 107 29.38 N 103.48 E
Shuang-hsi 269d 25.01 N 121.39 E
Shuangjiang, Zhg. 100 26.48 N 116.28 E
Shuangjiang, Zhg. 102 23.37 N 99.41 E
Shuangjiangqiao 102 25.19 N 98.51 E
Shuangjiangzhen 107 30.13 N 105.45 E
Shuangjihe ≃ 100 34.05 N 114.24 E
Shuangjingzi 104 42.28 N 123.42 E
Shuangkou 105 39.15 N 117.02 E
Shuangliao 89 43.31 N 123.30 E
Shuanglin 106 30.47 N 120.19 E
Shuanglingzi, Zhg. 104 40.54 N 124.10 E
Shuanglingzi, Zhg. 104 40.50 N 123.06 E
Shuangliu 107 30.34 N 103.55 E
Shuangliushu 100 31.56 N 115.12 E
Shuanglongtai 104 40.56 N 122.39 E
Shuangmiao 100 28.24 N 120.45 E
Shuangmiaoxian 100 32.09 N 116.52 E
Shuangmiaozi, Zhg. 104 42.25 N 122.17 E
Shuangmiaozi, Zhg. 104 42.02 N 121.52 E
Shuangpai 110 25.57 N 111.32 E
Shuangpaishi 106 31.24 N 118.59 E
Shuangqiao, Zhg. 105 39.54 N 116.37 E
Shuangqiao, Zhg. 106 30.59 N 118.47 E
Shuangqiaoji 100 32.28 N 116.11 E
Shuangquanzhen 89 47.32 N 127.22 E
Shuangrgun 100 33.12 N 116.40 E
Shuangshanzi 98 40.21 N 119.08 E
Shuangshipu 107 29.14 N 104.42 E
Shuangshiqiao, Zhg. 107 29.23 N 104.29 E
Shuangshiqiao, Zhg. 107 29.22 N 105.51 E
Shuangshu 105 39.34 N 117.01 E
Shuangshutai 89 43.50 N 121.15 E
Shuangtaizi, Zhg. 104 41.34 N 121.12 E
Shuangtaizi, Zhg. 104 41.00 N 122.34 E
Shuangtaizi, Zhg. 104 42.25 N 123.11 E
Shuangtaizi, Zhg. 104 41.11 N 121.14 E
Shuangtaizi, Zhg. 104 42.21 N 124.10 E
Shuangtang, Zhg. 100 28.01 N 116.44 E
Shuangtang, Zhg. 105 39.03 N 116.17 E
Shuangtang, Zhg. 105 38.53 N 116.54 E
Shuangtangdian 106 30.59 N 118.51 E
Shuangtuo 105 39.14 N 117.20 E
Shuangtuozhen 105 39.29 N 118.23 E
Shuangxi 106 30.24 N 119.50 E
Shuangxi ≃ 100 25.56 N 119.12 E
Shuangyang 89 43.32 N 125.42 E
Shuangyangdian 104 41.07 N 121.16 E
Shuangyaocun 105 38.55 N 117.03 E
Shuangyashan 89 46.37 N 131.22 E
Shu'ayb, Wādī V 132 31.54 N 35.38 E
Shu'ayt, Wādī V 144 17.30 N 52.00 E
Shubenacadie ≃ 186 45.20 N 63.30 W
Shubenacadie Lake ⊜ 186 44.55 N 63.36 W
Shublik Mountains ∧ 180 69.31 N 145.40 W
Shubrā al-Khaymah 142 30.06 N 31.15 E
Shubrā Bābil 142 30.54 N 31.11 E
Shubrā Khalfūn 142 30.29 N 31.05 E
Shubrā Khīt 142 31.02 N 30.43 E
Shubrāwīt, Jabal ∧[2] 142 30.17 N 32.17 E
Shubuta 194 31.52 N 88.42 W
Shucheng 100 31.27 N 116.57 E
Shueib Dam ◆[6] 132 31.54 N 35.39 E
Shufu → Kashi 85 39.29 N 75.59 E
Shufukashan ∧ 89 50.28 N 123.10 E
Shugudali 89 52.47 N 124.02 E
Shuhe ≃ 98 34.08 N 118.29 E
Shuheyingzi 104 42.18 N 122.16 E
Shuhezhen 106 31.35 N 121.35 E
Shuhō 96 34.13 N 131.18 E
Shuhong 100 28.39 N 120.09 E
Shuibatang 102 28.39 N 107.03 E
Shuibei 100 28.04 N 115.01 E
Shuichaoyang 100 26.22 N 117.57 E
Shuicheng 102 26.41 N 104.50 E
Shuidiangou 89 47.43 N 122.40 E
Shuidong 106 31.23 N 119.37 E
Shuidongjie 106 31.07 N 119.33 E
Shuidongzhen 106 30.47 N 115.07 E
Shuiduixia 106 30.17 N 118.50 E
Shuihai 100 33.02 N 120.26 E
Shuihouling 100 30.43 N 116.26 E
Shuiji 100 27.26 N 118.20 E
Shuijiahu 100 32.27 N 117.09 E
Shuijiahuangdi 104 42.14 N 123.28 E
Shuijian 105 40.09 N 115.58 E
Shuijing 102 26.10 N 99.09 E
Shuijingtang 102 28.50 N 108.11 E
Shuikou, Zhg. 100 26.59 N 117.41 E
Shuikou, Zhg. 100 24.00 N 115.55 E
Shuikou, Zhg. 100 26.22 N 118.44 E
Shuikou, Zhg. 100 25.09 N 114.28 E
Shuikou, Zhg. 106 31.51 N 118.12 E
Shuikou, Zhg. 107 29.29 N 103.42 E
Shuikouchang 107 29.33 N 103.40 E
Shuikouguan 102 22.30 N 106.34 E
Shuikoushan 102 26.30 N 112.30 E
Shuiliandong 98 42.12 N 125.09 E
Shuilipu 98 36.24 N 116.35 E
Shuimenzi 98 39.36 N 122.19 E
Shuimingqiao 106 31.03 N 119.09 E
Shuimoqipan 85 39.51 N 76.42 E
Shuiquan'gou 104 41.58 N 121.50 E
Shuiquanzi, Zhg. 104 40.53 N 121.05 E
Shuiquanzi, Zhg. 104 42.15 N 121.32 E
Shuitangzi 102 29.18 N 101.10 E
Shuiting 100 29.10 N 119.14 E
Shuitou, Zhg. 100 24.43 N 118.25 E
Shuitou, Zhg. 100 23.53 N 113.37 E
Shuitoujie 100 27.38 N 120.16 E
Shuitouwei 100 26.06 N 115.28 E
Shuiwei 100 26.18 N 113.46 E
Shuiyang 106 31.14 N 118.47 E
Shuiye 98 36.08 N 114.07 E
Shuizhai 98 36.54 N 117.24 E
Shuizhuyang 100 26.59 N 119.13 E
Shujāābād 123 29.53 N 71.18 E
Shujālpur 124 23.24 N 76.43 E
Shujiawazi 104 42.20 N 121.57 E
Shuksan, Mount ∧ 224 48.50 N 121.36 W
Shulan 89 44.27 N 126.57 E
Shulaps Peak ∧ 182 50.57 N 122.31 W
Shule 85 39.23 N 76.06 E
Shulehe ≃ 102 40.50 N 94.10 E
Shullsburg 190 42.34 N 90.14 W
Shulu (Xinji) 98 37.54 N 115.13 E
Shumagin Islands II 180 55.07 N 159.45 W
Shumatuscacant ≃ 283 42.03 N 70.51 W
Shumen → Šumen 38 43.16 N 26.55 E
Shūnah, Wādī ash- V 142 29.38 N 32.13 E
Shun'an 100 30.59 N 118.03 E
Shūnat Nimrīn 132 31.54 N 35.37 E
Shunchang 100 26.50 N 117.48 E
Shunde 100 22.50 N 113.14 E
Shundian 100 34.15 N 113.20 E
Shundianqiao 106 31.24 N 120.41 E
Shunge 102 37.25 N 95.27 E
Shungnak 180 66.53 N 157.02 W
Shunhechang 107 29.57 N 104.42 E
Shunlongchang 107 30.04 N 103.27 E
Shunshanpu 104 42.08 N 122.21 E
Shuntianhu 100 24.08 N 114.48 E
Shunyi 105 40.08 N 116.38 E
Shuoduzong 102 30.48 N 95.47 E
Shuojiaji 100 33.42 N 119.44 E
Shupīyan 123 33.43 N 74.50 E
Shuqayyiqah, Nafūd ◆[8] 128 25.45 N 43.55 E
Shuqrā' 144 13.21 N 45.42 E
Shuqualak 194 32.59 N 88.34 W
Shūr ≃ 128 34.38 N 51.46 E
Shūrāb, Īrān 128 33.43 N 56.29 E
Shūrāb, Īrān 128 28.09 N 60.18 E
Shūrāb ≃ 128 32.40 N 54.50 E
Shuraytah, Ra's > 128 26.24 N 56.22 E
Shurhabil Ben Hasna Dam ◆[6] 132 32.32 N 35.36 E
Shuri 174m 26.13 N 127.43 E
Shurkhua 110 22.15 N 93.38 E
Shūsf 128 31.48 N 60.01 E
Shūsh 128 32.11 N 48.15 E
Shushan, N.Y., U.S. 210 43.05 N 73.21 W
Shushan, Zhg. 106 31.18 N 119.51 E
Shushanhu ⊜ 98 35.36 N 116.27 E
Shūshtar 128 32.03 N 48.51 E
Shuswap ≃ 182 50.50 N 119.00 W
Shuswap Lake ⊜ 182 50.57 N 119.15 W
Shuṭab 142 27.08 N 31.14 E
Shutendōji-yama ∧ 96 33.06 N 130.54 E
Shuteye Peak ∧ 226 37.21 N 119.25 W
Shutlingsloe ∧ 262 53.13 N 2.02 W
Shūtō 96 34.05 N 132.05 E
Shuwak 140 14.23 N 35.52 E
Shuwaykah 132 32.20 N 35.02 E
Shuwaysh, Rujm ash- ∧ 132 32.30 N 36.27 E
Shuya, Nihon 174m 26.40 N 128.06 E
Shuya → Šuja, S.S.S.R. 24 61.55 N 34.12 E
Shuyak Island I 180 58.35 N 152.30 W
Shuyang 98 34.08 N 118.47 E
Shuyūkh al-Fawqanī 130 36.46 N 38.03 E
Shwangliao → Liaoyuan 89 42.54 N 125.07 E
Shwebo 110 22.34 N 95.42 E
Shwegun 110 17.09 N 97.39 E
Shwegyin 110 17.55 N 96.53 E
Shwenyaung 110 20.46 N 96.57 E
Shyamdih 126 23.47 N 86.56 E
Shyok 120 34.11 N 78.08 E
Shyok ≃ 120 35.13 N 75.53 E
Siachen Glacier ⊓ 123 35.30 N 77.00 E
Siagne ≃ 62 43.32 N 6.57 E
Siāhān Range ∧ 120 27.25 N 64.30 E
Siak ≃ 114 1.13 N 102.09 E
Siak-kecil ≃ 114 1.16 N 102.08 E
Siaksriinderapura 114 0.46 N 102.04 E
Sialang 114 1.31 N 99.27 E
Sialejevskaja P'atina 80 53.49 N 44.32 E
Siālghuni 126 22.33 N 90.27 E
Siālkot 123 32.30 N 74.31 E
Sialsūk 120 23.24 N 92.45 E
Siam → Thailand □[1] 110 15.00 N 100.00 E
Siam, Gulf of → Thailand, Gulf of C 110 10.00 N 101.00 E
Siamanna 71 39.55 N 8.46 E
Sian → Xi'an, Zhg. 102 34.15 N 108.52 E
Sian, Zhg. 106 30.54 N 119.39 E
Siangtan → Xiangtan 102 27.51 N 112.54 E
Sianów 30 54.15 N 16.16 E
Siantan, Pulau I 112 3.10 N 106.15 E
Sianzhuang 100 33.05 N 119.13 E
Siapa ≃ 246 2.07 N 66.28 W
Siargao Island I 116 9.53 N 126.02 E
Siari 123 34.56 N 76.44 E
Siasconset 207 41.16 N 69.58 W
Siasi 116 5.33 N 120.49 E
Siaškotan, Ostrov I 74 48.49 N 154.06 E
Siātista 38 40.16 N 21.33 E
Siaton 116 9.04 N 123.02 E
Siaton ≃ 116 9.02 N 123.02 E
Siaton Point > 116 9.03 N 123.01 E
Siau, Pulau I 112 2.42 N 125.24 E
Siauges-Saint-Romain 62 45.06 N 3.38 E
Šiauliai 76 55.56 N 23.19 E
Siazan' 84 41.05 N 49.06 E
Sibago Island I 116 6.45 N 122.24 E
Sibā'ī, Jabal as- ∧ 140 25.43 N 34.09 E
Sibaj 86 52.42 N 58.39 E
Sibālay 126 23.50 N 89.47 E
Sibalom 116 10.47 N 122.01 E
Sibanicú 240p 21.14 N 77.31 W
Sibari 100 25.55 N 116.42 E
Sibari, Piana di ≋ 68 39.45 N 16.25 E
Sibasa 156 22.53 S 30.33 E
Sibayi, Lake ⊜ 158 27.20 S 32.40 E
Sibay Island I 116 11.51 N 121.29 E
Sibbald 184 51.23 N 110.09 W
Sibbe 85 39.53 N 72.05 E
Sibbo 26 60.22 N 25.16 E
Sibchar 126 23.21 N 90.09 E
Šibenik 36 43.44 N 15.54 E
Siberia → Sibir' ◆[1] 74 65.00 N 110.00 E
Siberia Occidental, Llanura de → Zapadno-Sibirskaja Nizmennost' ≋ 72 60.00 N 75.00 E
Sibérie Occidentale, Dépression de la → Zapadno-Sibirskaja Nizmennost' ≋ 72 60.00 N 75.00 E
Siberut, Pulau I 108 1.20 S 98.55 E
Sibi 120 29.33 N 67.53 E
Sibiči 89 46.04 N 135.22 E
Sibigo 114 2.51 N 95.55 E
Sibillini, Monti ∧ 66 42.54 N 13.13 E
Sibir' (Siberia) ◆[1] 74 65.00 N 110.00 E
Sibir'akova, Ostrov I 74 72.50 N 79.00 E
Sibirbāy 142 30.49 N 31.01 E
Sibiti 152 3.41 S 13.21 E
Sibiti ≃ 154 3.49 S 34.46 E
Sibiu 38 45.48 N 24.09 E
Sibiu □[4] 38 46.00 N 24.15 E
Sible Hedingham 42 51.58 N 0.35 E
Sibley, Ill., U.S. 216 40.35 N 88.23 W
Sibley, La., U.S. 194 32.33 N 93.18 W
Sibley, Miss., U.S. 194 31.23 N 91.24 W
Sibley Provincial Park ♠ 190 48.30 N 88.30 W
Siboa 112 0.30 N 120.02 E
Sibochi 107 28.50 N 104.32 E
Siboga, Teluk C 114 1.38 N 98.45 E
Sibotu 86 47.12 N 88.15 E
Sibpur, Bhārat 272b 22.24 N 88.33 E
Sibpur, Bhārat 272b 22.34 N 88.19 E
Sibpur, Bngl. 124 24.02 N 90.44 E
Sibsa ≃[1] 126 22.01 N 89.30 E
Sibsāgar 120 26.59 N 94.38 E
Sibu 112 2.18 N 111.49 E
Sibu, Pulau I 114 2.13 N 104.04 E
Sibuatan, Gunung ∧ 114 2.56 N 98.24 E
Sibuguey ≃ 116 7.38 N 122.48 E
Sibuguey Bay C 116 7.30 N 122.40 E
Sibuko, Teluk C 112 4.00 N 118.26 E
Sibuti 112 4.03 N 113.48 E
Sibutu Island I 112 4.46 N 119.29 E
Sibutu Passage ‖ 116 4.50 N 119.35 E
Sibuyan Island I 116 12.25 N 122.34 E
Sibuyan Sea ⊹[2] 116 12.50 N 122.40 E
Siby 150 12.23 N 8.20 W
Sicamous 182 50.50 N 119.00 W
Sicapoo, Mount ∧ 116 18.01 N 120.56 E
Sicasica 248 17.22 S 67.45 W
Siccus ≃ 166 31.26 S 139.30 E
Sichany 80 52.07 N 47.13 E
Sichifulo ≃ 154 17.26 S 25.02 E
Si Chon 110 9.00 N 99.54 E
Sichote-Alin' ∧ 89 48.00 N 138.00 E
Sichtovo 76 55.43 N 32.18 E
Sichuan □[4] 102 31.00 N 105.00 E
Sichuanzhai 102 23.02 N 101.44 E
Sicié, Cap > 62 43.03 N 5.51 E
Sicignano degli Alburni 68 40.34 N 15.18 E
Sicilia □[4] 36 37.30 N 14.00 E
Sicilia (Sicily) I 70 37.30 N 14.00 E
Sicilia, Isla de → Sicilia I 70 37.30 N 14.00 E
Sicily → Sicilia I 70 37.30 N 14.00 E
Sicily, Strait of ‖ 36 37.20 N 11.20 E
Sicily Island 194 31.51 N 91.40 W
Sickingmühle 263 51.42 N 7.07 E
Sicklerville 208 39.43 N 74.58 W
Sicogon Island I 116 11.27 N 123.16 E
Sico Tinto ≃ 236 15.58 N 84.58 W
Sicuani 248 14.16 S 71.13 W
Siculiana 70 37.20 N 13.25 E
Sicun 106 31.55 N 119.18 E
Šid 38 45.08 N 19.13 E
Sīdah, Qārat ∧[2] 142 30.16 N 29.58 E
Sidamo □[4] 144 5.00 N 39.00 E
Sidao 271a 39.51 N 116.26 E
Sidaohe 105 40.24 N 117.17 E
Şidarah, Wādī V 144 16.40 N 48.20 E
Sidareja 115a 7.29 S 108.47 E
Sidas 112 0.24 N 109.46 E
Sidcup ◆[8] 260 51.25 N 0.06 E
Siddeburen 52 53.25 N 6.52 E
Siddinghausen 263 51.32 N 7.48 E
Siddington 262 53.14 N 2.14 W
Siddipet 122 18.06 N 78.51 E
Sideia Island I 164 10.35 S 150.50 E
Sidel'kino 80 54.32 N 51.08 E
Sidenreng 112 4.03 S 119.38 E
Sidéradougou 150 10.40 N 4.15 W
Siderno 68 38.16 N 16.18 E
Siderópolis 252 28.35 S 49.26 W
Šiderty ≃, S.S.S.R. 80 50.10 N 52.20 E
Šiderty ≃, S.S.S.R. 86 52.32 N 74.50 E
Sidhauli 124 27.17 N 80.50 E
Sídheros, Ákra > 38 35.19 N 26.19 E
Sidhi 124 24.25 N 81.53 E
Sidhirókastron 38 41.14 N 23.22 E
Sidhpur 120 23.55 N 72.23 E
Sīdī 'Abd ar-Raḥmān 140 30.58 N 29.44 E
Sidi Aïch 34 36.37 N 4.42 E
Sidi Aïssa 148 35.53 N 3.48 E
Sidi Akacha 34 36.28 N 1.18 E
Sidi Ali 34 36.06 N 0.25 E
Sidi Ali, Oued V 148 34.07 N 2.05 W
Sidi Ali Ben Nasrallah 36 35.15 N 9.50 E
Sīdī Barrānī 140 31.36 N 25.55 E
Sidi bel Abbès 148 35.13 N 0.10 W
Sidi-Bennour 148 32.30 N 8.30 W
Sidi Bou Zid 148 35.02 N 9.30 E
Sidi Daoud 36 37.00 N 10.55 E
Sidi el Hani, Sebkra de ⊜ 36 35.33 N 10.25 E
Sīdī Ghāzī 142 31.12 N 31.03 E
Sīdī Ḥunaysh 142 31.10 N 27.37 E
Sidi Ifni 148 29.24 N 10.12 W
Sidi-Kacem 148 34.15 N 5.39 W
Sidikalang 114 2.45 N 98.19 E
Sidimo 144 2.28 N 41.58 E
Sidi Mohammed Ben Ali 34 36.09 N 0.51 E
Sidi Moussa, Oued V 148 26.58 N 3.54 E
Sidi Okba 148 34.48 N 5.54 E
Sīdī Sālim 142 31.17 N 30.48 E
Sidi-Slimane 148 34.15 N 5.49 W
Sidi-Smaïl 148 32.49 N 8.30 W
Sīdī Tha'am 144 16.14 N 44.41 E
Sidlaghatta 122 13.23 N 77.52 E
Sidlaw Hills ∧[2] 46 56.30 N 3.10 W
Sidley, Mount ∧ 9 77.02 S 126.00 W
Sidli 124 26.33 N 90.28 E
Sidman 214 40.20 N 78.45 W
Sidmouth 42 50.41 N 3.15 W
Sidnaw 190 46.30 N 88.43 W
Sidney, B.C., Can. 182 48.39 N 123.24 W
Sidney, Ill., U.S. 194 40.01 N 88.04 W
Sidney, Ind., U.S. 216 41.06 N 85.45 W
Sidney, Iowa, U.S. 198 40.45 N 95.39 W
Sidney, Mont., U.S. 198 47.43 N 104.09 W
Sidney, Nebr., U.S. 198 41.09 N 102.59 W
Sidney, N.Y., U.S. 210 42.19 N 75.24 W
Sidney, Ohio, U.S. 216 40.17 N 84.09 W
Sidney Center 210 42.17 N 75.16 W
Sidney Island I 224 48.37 N 123.18 W
Sidney Lanier, Lake ⊜[1] 192 34.15 N 83.57 W
Sido, Centraf. 146 8.13 N 18.43 E
Sido, Mali 150 11.40 N 7.36 W
Sidoan 112 0.16 N 120.12 E
Sidoarjo 115a 7.27 S 112.43 E
Sidon → Şaydā, Lubnān 132 33.33 N 35.22 E
Sidon, Miss., U.S. 194 33.25 N 90.12 W
Sidorovo 76 58.48 N 40.58 E
Sidory 80 50.08 N 43.19 E
Sidr, Ra's as- > 142 29.35 N 32.42 E
Sidr, Wādī V 142 29.40 N 32.41 E
Sidra, Gulf of → Surt, Khalīj C 146 31.30 N 18.00 E
Sidrolândia 255 20.55 S 54.58 W
Sidu, Zhg. 100 23.48 N 117.18 E
Sidu, Zhg. 100 24.12 N 115.15 E
Siduan 106 30.59 N 121.48 E
Siebengebirge ∧[2] 56 50.40 N 7.14 E
Siebenlehn 54 51.01 N 13.18 E
Sieber 52 51.42 N 10.25 E
Siebnen 58 47.11 N 8.54 E
Siedenbollentin 54 53.44 N 13.23 E
Siedenburg 52 52.41 N 8.56 E
Siedlce 30 52.11 N 22.16 E
Sieg ≃ 56 50.45 N 7.05 E
Siegburg 56 50.47 N 7.12 E
Siegen 56 50.52 N 8.02 E
Siegenburg 60 48.45 N 11.51 E
Siegenfeld 264b 48.02 N 16.10 E
Sieglar 56 50.48 N 7.08 E
Siegler Springs 226 38.54 N 122.39 W
Siegsdorf 64 47.46 N 12.39 E
Sielbeck 54 54.11 N 10.37 E
Sielenbach 60 48.24 N 11.10 E
Siemens, Cape > 164 1.21 S 149.34 E
Siemensstadt ◆[8] 264a 52.32 N 13.17 E
Siemianowice Śląskie 30 50.19 N 19.01 E
Siemiatycze 30 52.26 N 22.53 E
Siĕmpang 110 14.07 N 106.23 E
Siĕmréab 110 13.22 N 103.51 E
Siems-Dänischburg ◆[8] 54 53.55 N 10.44 E
Siena 66 43.19 N 11.21 E
Siena □[4] 66 43.13 N 11.24 E
Sieniawa 30 50.11 N 22.36 E
Sienna → Siena 66 43.19 N 11.21 E
Sienyang → Xianyang 102 34.22 N 108.42 E
Sieradz 30 51.36 N 18.45 E
Sieraków 30 52.39 N 16.04 E
Sierbao 104 40.47 N 120.41 E
Sierck-les-Bains 56 49.26 N 6.21 E
Sierksdorf 54 54.04 N 10.46 E
Sierpc 30 52.52 N 19.41 E
Sierra □[6] 226 39.30 N 120.30 W
Sierra Blanca 200 31.11 N 105.21 W
Sierra Blanca Peak ∧ 200 33.23 N 105.48 W
Sierra-Bullones 116 9.51 N 124.20 E
Sierra Chica 252 36.50 S 60.13 W
Sierra City 226 39.34 N 120.38 W
Sierra Colorada 254 40.35 S 67.48 W
Sierra de Agua 232 17.32 N 88.54 W
Sierra del Carmen, Parque Nacional ♠ 232 29.15 N 102.42 W
Sierra de Outes 34 42.51 N 8.54 W
Sierra de San Pedro Mártir, Parque Nacional ♠, Méx. 204 31.00 N 115.30 W
Sierra Gorda 252 22.54 S 69.19 W
Sierra Leona → Sierra Leone □[1] 150 8.30 N 11.30 W
Sierra Leone □[1] 134
150 8.30 N 11.30 W
Sierra Leone Basin ✦[1] 10 5.00 N 16.00 W
Sierra Leone Rise ✦[3] 10 6.00 N 24.00 W
Sierra Madre 228 34.10 N 118.03 W
Sierra Mojada 196 27.17 N 103.42 W
Sierra Nevada, Parque Nacional ♠ 246 8.36 N 70.50 W
Sierra Peak ∧ 280 33.51 N 117.39 W
Sierras Bayas 252 36.57 S 60.09 W
Sierraville 226 39.36 N 120.22 W
Sierra Vista 200 31.33 N 110.18 W
Sierre 58 46.18 N 7.32 E
Siersleben 54 51.36 N 11.32 E
Siesta Key 220 27.19 N 82.34 W
Siesta Key I 220 27.16 N 82.33 W
Siete Puntas ≃ 252 23.34 S 57.20 W
Siethen 264a 52.17 N 13.13 E
Siethener See ⊜ 264a 52.17 N 13.12 E
Sietow 54 53.26 N 12.35 E
Sieve ≃ 66 43.46 N 11.26 E
Sievering ◆[8] 264b 48.15 N 16.20 E
Siezenheim 64 47.48 N 12.59 E
Sifangtai, Zhg. 89 46.55 N 128.00 E
Sifangtai, Zhg. 104 41.02 N 122.46 E
Sifangtai, Zhg. 104 41.33 N 121.19 E
Sifangtai, Zhg. 104 41.35 N 122.57 E
Sifani 144 12.20 N 40.24 E
Sifen 100 27.32 N 113.30 E
Sifentoudun 106 32.18 N 121.21 E
Siffu ≃ 116 17.12 N 121.48 E
Sifié 150 7.59 N 6.55 W
Sífnos I 38 36.59 N 24.40 E
Sifón Villanueva 196 27.17 N 100.17 W
Sifton 184 51.21 N 100.07 W
Sig, Alg. 148 35.32 N 0.11 W
Sig, S.S.S.R. 24 65.35 N 34.13 E
Si Galangang 114 1.15 N 99.20 E
Šigali 80 55.33 N 48.02 E
Sigean 32 43.02 N 2.59 E
Sigel 214 41.17 N 79.07 W
Sigep 110 1.02 S 98.49 E
Siggebohyttan 40 59.37 N 15.01 E
Sighetul Marmaţiei 38 47.56 N 23.54 E
Sighişoara 38 46.13 N 24.48 E
Sighty Crag ∧ 44 55.07 N 2.37 W
Sigillo 66 43.20 N 12.44 E
Sigiriya 122 7.57 N 80.45 E
Sigl 60 49.37 N 11.45 E
Siglan 74 59.02 N 152.25 E
Siglerville 208 40.44 N 77.31 W
Sigli 114 5.23 N 95.57 E
Sigli, Cap > 148 36.54 N 4.46 E
Sigloy 50 47.50 N 2.14 E
Siglufjördur 24a 66.10 N 18.56 W
Sigmaringen 58 48.05 N 9.13 E
Sigmaringendorf 58 48.04 N 9.15 E
Signa 66 43.47 N 11.05 E
Signachi 84 41.37 N 45.54 E
Signalberg ∧ 60 49.28 N 12.32 E
Signal Hill, Calif., U.S. 280 33.48 N 118.11 W
Signal Hill, Ill., U.S. 219 38.34 N 90.05 W
Signal Hill National Historic Park ♠ 186 47.30 N 52.42 W
Signal Mountain 194 35.07 N 85.21 W
Signal Mountain ∧ 188 44.12 N 72.20 W
Signal Peak ∧ 200 37.19 N 113.29 W
Signau 58 46.55 N 7.43 E
Signes 62 43.18 N 5.52 E
Signy-l'Abbaye 50 49.42 N 4.25 E
Signy-le-Petit 50 49.54 N 4.17 E
Šigony 80 53.23 N 48.42 E
Sigourney 190 41.20 N 92.12 W
Sigras 60 49.36 N 11.43 E
Sigre ≃ 236 15.49 N 84.38 W
Sigriswil 58 46.43 N 7.42 E
Sigsbee Deep ✦[1] 16 23.54 N 91.51 W
Sigsig 246 3.01 S 78.45 W
Sigtuna 40 59.37 N 17.43 E
Siguanea, Ensenada de la C 240p 21.38 N 83.05 W
Siguas ≃ 248 16.37 S 72.19 W
Siguatepeque 236 14.32 N 87.49 W
Siguel ≃ 116 5.58 N 125.06 E
Sigüenza 34 41.04 N 2.38 W
Sigües 34 42.38 N 1.00 W
Siguiri 150 11.25 N 9.10 W
Siguiri □[4] 150 11.30 N 9.15 W
Sigulda 76 57.09 N 24.51 E
Siguliduogantuola 89 49.43 N 122.03 E
Sigurd 200 38.50 N 111.58 W
Siguri Falls L 154 8.31 S 37.23 E
Sihabuhabu, Dolok ∧ 114 2.10 N 99.21 E
Sihaibao 105 40.33 N 116.24 E
Sihala → Sri Lanka □[1] 122 7.00 N 81.00 E
Sihanoukville → Kâmpóng Saôm 110 10.38 N 103.30 E
Sihaus 248 8.34 S 77.37 W
Sihecun 105 39.56 N 117.07 E
Sihepeng 114 1.06 N 99.27 E
Sihiyan 130 37.53 N 41.46 E
Sihl ≃ 58 47.23 N 8.32 E
Şıhlar 130 40.43 N 38.21 E
Sihlepu 158 27.42 S 32.06 E
Sihlsee ⊜ 58 47.07 N 8.47 E
Sihong 100 33.28 N 118.11 E
Sihor 120 21.42 N 71.58 E
Sihorā 124 23.29 N 80.07 E
Şıhraş 130 37.28 N 42.13 E
Sihu 98 34.38 N 117.59 E
Sihui 102 23.19 N 112.40 E
Sihŭng ◆[8] 271b 37.28 N 126.54 E
Siiči 78 52.15 N 29.14 E
Siikajoki ≃ 26 64.50 N 24.44 E
Siilinjärvi 26 63.05 N 27.40 E
Siirt 130 37.56 N 41.57 E
Siirt □[4] 130 38.00 N 42.00 E
Sija 24 63.38 N 41.38 E
Sijbekarspel 52 52.43 N 4.59 E
Sijerdero 144 8.47 N 48.02 E
Sijia 106 32.02 N 121.18 E
Sijianfang 104 42.29 N 122.17 E
Sijiao I 100 30.39 N 122.25 E
Sijiazi 98 41.47 N 120.06 E
Sijing 106 31.07 N 121.16 E
Sijunjung 112 0.42 S 100.58 E
Sijupu 107 30.02 N 106.18 E
Sik 114 5.49 N 100.44 E
Sika 115b 8.45 S 122.12 E
Sikaiana I 175e 8.25 S 162.52 E
Sikalongo 154 16.46 S 27.07 E
Sikandarābād 124 28.27 N 77.42 E
Sikandarpur, Bhārat 272a 28.42 N 77.21 E
Sikandarpur, Bhārat 272b 22.57 N 88.12 E
Sikandra 124 24.57 N 86.02 E
Sikandra Rao 124 27.42 N 78.24 E
Sikao 110 7.34 N 99.21 E
Šikaochskij Zapovednik ♠ 84 39.05 N 46.30 E
Sīkar 120 27.37 N 75.09 E
Sikaram ∧ 118 34.50 N 69.55 E
Sikarpur 272b 22.36 N 88.32 E
Sikasso 150 11.19 N 5.40 W
Sikasso □[4] 150 10.55 N 7.00 W
Sikéai 38 36.46 N 22.56 E
Sikelenge 152 14.50 S 24.14 E
Sikeli 112 5.16 S 121.48 E
Sikerete 156 19.03 S 20.50 E
Sikeshu 86 44.25 N 84.14 E
Sikeston 194 36.53 N 89.35 W
Sikfors 40 59.48 N 14.35 E
Si Khiu 110 14.53 N 101.44 E
Sikiá 38 40.02 N 23.56 E
Sikiang → Xijiang ≃ 102 22.25 N 113.23 E
Sikijang 114 4.22 N 98.02 E
Siking → Xi'an 102 34.15 N 108.52 E
Síkinos 38 25.07 N 26.43 E
Síkinos I 38 36.39 N 25.06 E
Sikinssi 150 5.40 N 4.34 W
Sikión ⊥ 38 37.59 N 22.44 E
Sikkim □[3] 124 27.35 N 88.35 E
Siklós ⊥ 30 45.52 N 18.28 E
Sikonge 154 5.38 S 32.46 E
Şikosi 156 17.59 S 23.19 E
Šikotan, Ostrov (Shikotan-tō) I 92a 43.48 N 146.45 E
Sikrod 272a 28.43 N 77.11 E
Sikt'ach 74 69.55 N 125.02 E
Sikuati 112 6.53 N 116.40 E
Sikutu 112 0.53 N 120.37 E
Şil ≃ 34 42.27 N 7.43 W
Šila 86 56.33 N 93.02 E
Silacayoapan 234 17.30 N 98.09 W
Sila Grande ∧ 68 39.22 N 16.30 E
Sila Greca ∧ 68 39.30 N 16.30 E
Silai ≃ 126 22.41 N 87.46 E
Silalahi 114 2.48 N 98.32 E
Silalė 76 55.28 N 22.12 E
Silam, Mount ∧ 116 4.58 N 118.10 E
Silāmpur ◆ 272a 28.40 N 77.16 E
Silandro (Schlanders) 64 46.38 N 10.46 E
Silang 116 14.14 N 120.58 E
Silangcheng 98 42.19 N 115.43 E
Silanus 71 40.17 N 8.53 E
Silao 234 20.56 N 101.26 W
Sila Piccola ∧ 68 39.05 N 16.35 E
Silas 194 31.46 N 88.20 W
Silat 112 0.21 N 111.47 E
Silat az-Zahr 132 32.19 N 35.11 E
Silau ≃ 114 2.58 N 99.48 E
Silaut 112 2.22 S 101.08 E
Silaw Aihagam, Gunung ∧ 114 5.25 N 95.40 E
Silay 116 10.48 N 122.58 E
Silay, Mount ∧ 116 10.47 N 123.14 E
Silba 36 44.23 N 14.42 E
Silba, Otok I 36 44.24 N 14.42 E
Silbertal 58 47.05 N 9.59 E
Silchar 120 24.49 N 92.48 E
Silda 126 22.37 N 86.49 E
Şile 130 41.11 N 29.36 E
Sile ≃ 64 45.33 N 12.27 E
Silenrieux 50 50.14 N 4.24 E
Silent Lake ⊜ 212 44.55 N 78.04 W
Siler City 192 35.44 N 79.28 W
Sileru ≃ 122 17.47 N 81.24 E
Silesia □[9] 30 51.00 N 16.45 E
Silet 148 22.44 N 4.37 E
Siletz 202 44.43 N 123.55 W
Siletz ≃ 202 44.54 N 124.00 W
Silex 219 39.07 N 91.03 W
Silgarhi-Doti 124 29.16 N 80.59 E
Silghāt 120 26.37 N 92.56 E
Silhouette I 138 4.29 S 55.14 E
Siliana 148 36.05 N 9.22 E
Siliana, Oued ≃ 36 36.33 N 9.25 E
Silifke 130 36.22 N 33.56 E
Silīguri 124 26.42 N 88.26 E
Şilijiang 105 39.43 N 117.28 E
Šilikty 86 47.10 N 84.32 E
Silil 144 10.59 N 43.31 E
Silingan, Mount ∧ 116 7.46 N 122.30 E
Siliqua 71 39.18 N 8.48 E
Silistra 38 44.07 N 27.16 E
Şilivri 130 41.04 N 28.15 E
Šiljak ∧ 38 43.45 N 21.50 E
Siljan ⊜ 26 60.50 N 14.45 E
Siljansnäs 26 60.45 N 14.42 E
Šilka 88 51.51 N 116.02 E
Šilka ≃ 74 53.22 N 121.32 E
Silkāripāra 126 24.14 N 87.28 E
Silkeborg 41 56.10 N 9.34 E
Silkworth 210 41.16 N 76.05 W
Sill ≃ 64 47.16 N 11.25 E
Sillamäe 76 59.24 N 27.45 E
Sillānwāli 123 31.50 N 72.33 E
Sillaro ≃ 66 44.34 N 11.51 E
Sille 130 37.56 N 32.26 E
Sillé-le-Guillaume 32 48.12 N 0.08 W
Sillem Island I 176 70.55 N 71.30 W
Sillen ⊜ 40 58.59 N 17.22 E

Symbol	English	Deutsch	Español	Français	Português
≃	River	Fluss	Río	Rivière	Rio
≅	Canal	Kanal	Canal	Canal	Canal
L	Waterfall, Rapids	Wasserfall, Stromschnellen	Cascada, Rápidos	Chute d'eau, Rapides	Cascata, Rápidos
‖	Strait	Meeresstrasse	Estrecho	Détroit	Estreito
C	Bay, Gulf	Bucht, Golf	Bahía, Golfo	Baie, Golfe	Baía, Golfo
⊜	Lake, Lakes	See, Seen	Lago, Lagos	Lac, Lacs	Lago, Lagos
≋	Swamp	Sumpf	Pantano	Marais	Pântano
⊓	Ice Features, Glacier	Eis- und Gletscherformen	Accidentes Glaciales	Formes glaciaires	Acidentes Glaciares
⊹	Other Hydrographic Features	Andere Hydrographische Objekte	Otros Elementos Hidrográficos	Autres données hydrographiques	Outros Elementos Hidrográficos

Symbol	English	Deutsch	Español	Français	Português
✦	Submarine Features	Untermeerische Objekte	Accidentes Submarinos	Formes de relief sous-marin	Acidentes Submarinos
□	Political Unit	Politische Einheit	Unidad Política	Entité politique	Unidade Política
♥	Cultural Institution	Kulturelle Institution	Institución Cultural	Institution culturelle	Instituição Cultural
⊥	Historical Site	Historische Stätte	Sitio Histórico	Site historique	Sitio Histórico
♠	Recreational Site	Erholungs- und Ferienort	Sitio de Recreo	Centre de loisirs	Sitio de Lazer
⊠	Airport	Flughafen	Aeropuerto	Aéroport	Aeroporto
■	Military Installation	Militäranlage	Instalación Militar	Installation militaire	Instalação Militar
◆	Miscellaneous	Verschiedenes	Misceláneo	Divers	Miscelânea

Sillenstede 52 53.34 N 7.59 E
Sillery, Qué., Can. 206 46.46 N 71.15 W
Sillery, Fr. 50 49.12 N 4.08 E
Silli 150 11.36 N 2.30 W
Sillian 64 46.45 N 12.25 E
Sillon de Talbert ≻[1] 32 48.53 N 3.05 W
Silloth 44 54.52 N 3.23 W
Sillustani ⊥ 248 15.45 S 70.05 W
Silly-le-Long 261 49.06 N 2.48 E
Šil'naja Balka 80 50.34 N 49.01 E
Silnice 60 48.54 N 13.44 E
Siloam Springs 194 36.11 N 94.32 W
Siloam Springs State Park ♠ 219 39.53 N 90.54 W
Siloana Plains ⊻ 152 17.00 S 23.15 E
Silogui 110 1.14 S 99.00 E
Silong 102 23.54 N 109.40 E
Šilovići 76 55.24 N 32.33 E
Šilovka 80 54.03 N 48.40 E
Šilovo, S.S.S.R. 76 55.00 N 33.46 E
Šilovo, S.S.S.R. 80 54.19 N 40.53 E
Silphuh 126 23.44 N 86.22 E
Silsbee 194 30.21 N 94.11 W
Silsby Lake ⊜ 184 55.29 N 95.46 W
Silschede 263 51.21 N 7.19 E
Silsden 44 53.55 N 1.55 W
Sils im Engadin 58 46.22 N 9.46 E
Silton 184 50.48 N 104.55 W
Siluas 112 1.17 N 109.51 E
Siluko 150 6.31 N 5.09 E
Šilutė 76 55.21 N 21.29 E
Silvacane, Abbaye de ♥[1] 62 43.44 N 5.20 E
Silva Jardim 255 22.39 S 42.23 W
Silvan (Miyafarkin) 130 38.08 N 41.01 E
Silvana 224 48.12 N 122.15 W
Silvânia 255 16.42 S 48.38 W
Silvano d'Orba 62 44.41 N 8.40 E
Silvan Reservoir ⊜[1] 169 37.50 S 145.25 E
Silvaplana 58 46.26 N 9.47 E
Silvassa 122 20.17 N 73.00 E
Silveiras, Bra. 256 22.33 S 46.55 W
Silveiras, Bra. 256 22.40 S 44.52 W
Silver 196 32.04 N 100.40 W
Silverado 228 33.45 N 117.35 W
Silver Bank ◆[4] 238 20.30 N 69.40 W
Silver Bank Passage ⊔ 238 20.45 N 70.15 W
Silver Bay 190 47.17 N 91.16 W
Silver Bell 200 32.23 N 111.30 W
Silver Bow Park 202 46.01 N 112.28 W
Silver City 200 32.46 N 108.17 W
Silver Creek, Miss., U.S. 194 31.36 N 89.59 W
Silver Creek, Nebr., U.S. 198 41.19 N 97.40 W
Silver Creek, N.Y., U.S. 214 42.33 N 79.10 W
Silver Creek ≃, Ariz., U.S. 200 34.44 N 110.02 W
Silver Creek ≃, Calif., U.S. 226 38.47 N 120.35 W
Silver Creek ≃, Calif., U.S. 226 36.36 N 120.41 W
Silver Creek ≃, Ill., U.S. 219 38.20 N 89.52 W
Silver Creek ≃, Ill., U.S. 278 41.54 N 87.50 W
Silver Creek ≃, Ind., U.S. 218 39.36 N 84.59 W
Silver Creek ≃, Ind., U.S. 218 38.17 N 85.47 W
Silver Creek ≃, Ky., U.S. 192 37.48 N 84.30 W
Silver Creek ≃, Oreg., U.S. 202 43.16 N 119.13 W
Silver Creek ≃, Wash., U.S. 224 46.32 N 121.55 W
Silver Creek, Muddy Fork ≃ 218 38.25 N 86.44 W
Silver Creek, South Fork ≃ 226 38.49 N 120.27 W
Silverdale, B.C., Can. 224 49.09 N 122.24 W
Silverdale, N.Z. 172 36.37 S 174.40 E
Silverdale, Pa., U.S. 208 40.21 N 75.16 W
Silverdale, Wash., U.S. 224 47.39 N 122.42 W
Silverdalen 26 57.32 N 15.44 E
Silver Falls State Park ♠ 202 44.48 N 122.50 W
Silverfields 273d 26.07 S 27.49 E
Silver Fork ≃ 219 39.06 N 92.21 W
Silver Grove 218 39.02 N 84.24 W
Silver Hills ∧[2] 275b 43.46 N 79.22 W
Silverhope Creek ≃ 224 49.18 N 121.27 W
Silver Lake, Calif., U.S. 226 38.38 N 120.07 W
Silver Lake, Ind., U.S. 216 41.04 N 85.53 W
Silver Lake, Kans., U.S. 198 39.06 N 95.52 W
Silver Lake, Mass., U.S. 207 42.34 N 70.44 W
Silver Lake, Mass., U.S. 283 42.00 N 70.48 W
Silver Lake, Minn., U.S. 190 44.54 N 94.12 W
Silver Lake, Ohio, U.S. 214 41.09 N 81.27 W
Silver Lake, Oreg., U.S. 202 43.08 N 120.56 W
Silverlake, Wash., U.S. 224 46.18 N 122.49 W
Silver Lake, Wis., U.S. 216 42.33 N 88.10 W
Silver Lake ⊜, Calif., U.S. 226 38.39 N 120.07 W
Silver Lake ⊜, Del., U.S. 208 39.11 N 75.32 W
Silver Lake ⊜, Mass., U.S. 283 42.01 N 70.48 W
Silver Lake ⊜, N.Y., U.S. 210 42.42 N 78.02 W
Silver Lake ⊜, N.Y., U.S. 276 41.03 N 73.45 W
Silver Lake ⊜, Oreg., U.S. 202 43.06 N 120.53 W
Silver Lake ⊜, Oreg., U.S. 202 43.22 N 119.24 W
Silver Lake ⊜, Wash., U.S. 224 46.17 N 122.47 W
Silver Lake ⊜, Wash., U.S. 224 48.58 N 122.04 W
Silver Lake Park ♠ 276 41.03 N 73.45 W
Silver Lake Reservoir ⊜[1], Calif., U.S. 280 34.06 N 118.16 W
Silver Lake Reservoir ⊜[1], N.Y., U.S. 276 40.37 N 74.06 W
Silvermine ≃ 276 41.08 N 73.26 W
Silvermine Brook ≃ 276 41.08 N 73.27 W
Silvermine Mountains ⩕ 48 52.45 N 8.15 W
Silvermines 48 52.47 N 8.13 W
Silver Mountain ∧ 280 34.12 N 117.52 W
Silver Peak ∧ 228 33.28 N 118.35 W
Silver Peak Range ⩕ 204 37.35 N 117.45 W
Silver Spring, Md., U.S. 284c 39.02 N 77.03 W
Silver Spring, Pa., U.S. 208 40.04 N 76.26 W
Silver Springs, Nev., U.S. 226 39.25 N 119.13 W
Silver Springs, N.Y., U.S. 210 42.40 N 78.05 W
Silver Springs State Park ♠ 216 41.38 N 88.32 W
Silver Star Mountain ∧ 202 48.33 N 120.35 W
Silver Star Provincial Park ♠ 182 50.22 N 119.05 W
Silverstone 42 52.05 N 1.02 W
Silver Streams 158 28.20 S 23.33 E
Silverthrone Mountain ∧ 182 51.31 N 126.06 W
Silvertip Mountain ∧ 202 47.47 N 113.15 W
Silverton, Austl. 166 31.53 S 141.13 E
Silverton, B.C., Can. 182 49.57 N 117.21 W
Silverton, Eng., U.K. 42 50.48 N 3.28 W
Silverton, Colo., U.S. 200 37.49 N 107.40 W
Silverton, N.J., U.S. 208 40.01 N 74.10 W
Silverton, Ohio, U.S. 218 39.12 N 84.24 W
Silverton, Oreg., U.S. 224 45.01 N 122.47 W
Silverton, Tex., U.S. 196 34.28 N 101.19 W
Silverton, Wash., U.S. 224 48.05 N 121.34 W
Silves 34 37.11 N 8.26 W
Silvi 66 42.34 N 14.05 E
Silvia 246 2.37 N 76.21 W
Silvianópolis 256 22.02 S 45.50 W
Silvícola 164 8.39 S 126.59 E
Silvies ≃ 202 43.22 N 118.48 W
Silview 285 39.43 N 75.37 W
Silvolde 52 51.54 N 6.53 E
Silvretta Gruppe ⩕ 58 46.50 N 10.15 E
Sim 86 54.59 N 57.41 E
Sim, Cap ≻ 148 31.23 N 9.51 W
Sima, Comores 157a 12.11 S 44.17 E
Sima, S.S.S.R. 80 56.41 N 39.33 E
Simaltala 124 24.43 N 86.33 E
Simanggang 112 1.15 N 111.26 E
Simanoviči 76 53.05 N 28.38 E
Šimanovsk 89 52.00 N 127.42 E
Simao 102 22.50 N 101.00 E
Simão Dias 250 10.44 S 37.49 W
Simão Pereira 256 21.58 S 43.19 W
Simara Island I 116 12.48 N 122.03 E
Simard, Lac ⊜ 190 47.37 N 78.41 W
Simatang, Pulau I 112 1.04 N 120.23 E
Simav 130 39.05 N 28.59 E
Simav ≃ 130 40.23 N 28.31 E
Simav Gölü ⊜ 130 39.09 N 28.55 E
Simaxis 71 39.56 N 8.41 E
Simba, Kenya 154 2.10 S 37.36 E
Simba, Zaïre 152 0.36 N 22.55 E
Simbach 60 48.34 N 12.45 E
Simbach am Inn 60 48.16 N 13.01 E
Simbal 248 7.58 S 78.49 W
Simbario 68 38.37 N 16.20 E
Simba Sirori 154 1.44 S 34.13 E
Simberi Island I 164 2.40 S 152.00 E
Simbirsk → Uljanovsk 80 54.20 N 48.24 E
Simbo, Tan. 154 4.40 S 33.27 E
Simbo, Tan. 154 4.53 S 29.44 E
Simbo I 175e 8.17 S 156.33 E
Simbruini, Monti ⩕ 66 41.55 N 13.15 E
Simcoe 212 42.50 N 80.18 W
Simcoe □[6] 212 44.25 N 79.50 W
Simcoe, Lake ⊜ 212 44.20 N 79.20 W
Simcoe Creek ≃ 224 46.22 N 120.36 W
Simcoe Island I 212 44.10 N 76.31 W
Simcoe Point ≻ 275b 43.49 N 79.03 W
Simdega 124 22.37 N 84.31 E
Simeiz 78 44.26 N 34.01 E
Simen 104 40.44 N 123.49 E
Simengzhen 107 29.56 N 103.44 E
Simenti 150 13.00 N 13.25 W
Simeri ≃ 68 38.52 N 16.43 E
Simeria 38 45.51 N 23.01 E
Simeto ≃, It. 70 37.24 N 15.06 E
Simeulue, Pulau I 114 2.35 N 96.00 E
Simferopol' 78 44.57 N 34.06 E
Sími 38 36.36 N 27.50 E
Sími I 38 36.35 N 27.52 E
Simi, Arroyo ≃ 228 34.16 N 118.39 W
Simiane 62 43.25 N 5.26 E
Simianshan 107 28.49 N 105.09 E
Simikot 124 29.58 N 81.50 E
Similkameen ≃, B.C., Can. 224 49.18 N 120.32 W
Similkameen ≃, N.A. 182 48.56 N 119.26 W
Simingchang 107 29.02 N 105.45 E
Simingshan ⩕ 100 29.50 N 121.00 E
Simiri 150 14.08 N 2.08 E
Simisa Island I 116 5.57 N 121.35 E
Simití 246 7.58 N 73.57 W
Simi Valley 228 34.16 N 118.47 W
Şimiz 130 37.49 N 41.22 E
Simizu → Shimizu 94 35.01 N 138.29 E
Simkwe 156 19.41 S 20.30 E
Simla, Bhārat 123 31.06 N 77.10 E
Simla, Bhārat 272b 22.47 N 88.16 E
Simla, Bhārat 272b 22.54 N 88.22 E
Simla, Colo., U.S. 198 39.09 N 104.05 W
Simla ◆[8] 272b 22.35 N 88.22 E
Simlāpāl 126 22.55 N 87.05 E
Şimleul Silvaniei 38 47.14 N 22.48 E
Simlipālgarh 126 21.51 N 86.23 E
Simme ≃ 58 46.41 N 7.38 E
Simmelsdorf 60 49.36 N 11.21 E
Simmental V 58 46.37 N 7.25 E
Simmerath 56 50.36 N 6.18 E
Simmerberg 58 47.35 N 9.56 E
Simmering ◆[8] 264b 48.11 N 16.25 E
Simmern 56 49.59 N 7.31 E
Simmesport 194 30.59 N 91.49 W
Simmie 184 49.57 N 108.06 W
Simmons Island I 282 38.06 N 121.58 W
Simmons Point ≻ 282 38.03 N 121.56 W
Simmonswood Moss ◆[3] 262 53.30 N 2.50 W
Simms 202 47.30 N 111.55 W
Simnas 76 54.24 N 23.39 E
Simoca 252 27.16 S 65.21 W
Simões 250 7.36 S 40.49 W
Simojärvi ⊜ 26 66.06 N 27.03 E
Simojoki ≃ 26 65.37 N 25.03 E
Simojovel de Allende 234 17.12 N 92.38 W
Simon 273b 4.15 S 15.11 E
Simon, Lac ⊜ 206 45.58 N 75.05 W
Simón Bolívar, Parque Nacional → Sierra Nevada, Parque Nacional ♠ 246 8.36 N 70.50 W
Simoneti 84 42.14 N 42.52 E
Simonette ≃ 182 55.07 N 118.00 W
Simonhouse Lake ⊜ 184 54.30 N 101.10 W
Simonicha 80 56.31 N 53.50 E
Simoniči 78 51.53 N 28.04 E
Šimonka ∧ 30 48.58 N 21.27 E
Simonoseki → Shimonoseki 96 33.57 N 130.57 E
Simonsbath 42 51.09 N 3.45 W
Simonson Brook ≃ 276 40.26 N 74.37 W
Simonstone 262 53.48 N 2.20 W
Simonstorp 40 58.47 N 16.09 E
Simonstown 158 34.14 S 18.26 E
Simonton Lake 216 41.44 N 85.59 W
Simoom Sound 182 50.45 N 126.45 W
Šimorskoje 80 55.19 N 42.02 E
Simpang, Indon. 112 1.16 S 104.05 E
Simpang, Indon. 112 1.03 S 110.06 E
Simpang, Indon. 112 0.09 N 103.15 E
Simpang Empat 114 6.20 N 100.11 E
Simpang-kanan ≃ 114 2.21 N 97.51 E
Simpangkawat 114 2.55 N 99.43 E
Simpang-kiri ≃ 114 2.21 N 97.51 E
Simpang Rengam 114 1.50 N 103.19 E
Simpangtiga 114 2.23 N 99.47 E
Simpangulim 114 5.06 N 97.32 E
Simpele 26 61.26 N 29.22 E
Simplon Pass)(58 46.15 N 8.02 E
Simplon Tunnel ◆[5] 58 46.15 N 8.05 E
Simpnäs 40 59.52 N 19.04 E
Simp'o-ri 98 38.36 N 127.41 E
Simpson, La., U.S. 194 31.16 N 93.00 W
Simpson, Pa., U.S. 210 41.35 N 75.29 W
Simpson ≃ 254 45.25 S 72.32 W
Simpson, Isla I 254 45.53 S 73.48 W
Simpson Desert ◆[2] 162 25.00 S 137.00 E
Simpson Island I 190 48.48 N 87.40 W
Simpson Lake ⊜, N.W. Ter., Can. 176 68.39 N 91.19 W
Simpson Lake ⊜, N.W. Ter., Can. 180 68.10 N 126.35 W
Simpson Peak ∧ 180 59.44 N 131.27 W
Simpson Peninsula ≻[1] 176 68.34 N 88.45 W
Simpson Strait ⊔ 176 68.27 N 97.45 W
Simpsonville, Ky., U.S. 218 38.13 N 85.22 W
Simpsonville, Md., U.S. 208 39.11 N 76.52 W
Simpsonville, S.C., U.S. 192 34.44 N 82.15 W
Simrishamn 26 55.33 N 14.20 E
Sims 216 40.30 N 85.51 W
Şimsbury 207 41.52 N 72.48 W
Šimsk 76 58.13 N 30.43 E
Simssee ⊜ 64 47.52 N 12.14 E
Simunjan 112 1.23 N 110.45 E
Simurāli 126 23.03 N 88.30 E
Simušir, Ostrov I 74 46.58 N 152.02 E
Sīnā' □[4] 142 30.15 N 32.40 E
Sīna ≃ 122 17.22 N 75.54 E
Sīnā', Shibh Jazīrat (Sinai Peninsula) ≻[1] 140 29.30 N 34.00 E
Sinabang 114 2.29 N 96.23 E
Sinabung, Gunung ∧ 114 3.10 N 98.24 E
Sinadogo 144 5.22 N 46.22 E
Şināfīr, Jazīrat I 140 27.55 N 34.40 E
Sinagra 70 38.05 N 14.51 E
Sinai, Mount → Mūsā, Jabal ∧ 140 28.32 N 33.59 E
Sinaia 38 45.21 N 25.33 E
Sinai Peninsula → Sīnā', Shibh Jazīrat ≻[1] 140 29.30 N 34.00 E
Sin'aja ≃, S.S.S.R. 74 61.06 N 126.50 E
Sin'aja ≃, S.S.S.R. 76 57.10 N 28.31 E
Sinajana 174p 13.28 N 144.45 E
Sinako, Mount ∧ 116 7.30 N 125.17 E
Sinaloa □[3] 232 25.00 N 107.30 W
Sinaloa ≃ 232 25.18 N 108.30 W
Sinalunga 66 43.12 N 11.44 E
Sinamaica 246 11.05 N 71.51 W
Sinan, Tür. 130 37.52 N 41.00 E
Sinan, Tür. 130 38.06 N 38.45 E
Sinan, Zhg. 102 27.54 N 108.18 E
Sinanča 89 44.42 N 135.43 E
Sinanju 98 39.36 N 125.36 E
Sinanpaşa 130 38.45 N 30.15 E
Sīnarū 142 29.22 N 30.45 E
Sinatle 84 42.28 N 43.04 E
Sin'avka, S.S.S.R. 76 52.58 N 26.29 E
Sin'avka, S.S.S.R. 83 47.17 N 39.17 E
Sīnāwan 146 31.02 N 10.36 E
Sinbad Creek ≃ 282 37.35 N 121.53 W
Sinbaungwe 110 19.43 N 95.10 E
Sinbo 110 24.46 N 97.03 E
Sinbokchang 98 41.01 N 128.54 E
Sincan 130 39.28 N 37.54 E
Sincé 246 9.15 N 75.09 W
Sincelejo 246 9.18 N 75.24 W
Sinch'ang, C.M.I.K. 98 40.19 N 125.27 E
Sinch'ang, C.M.I.K. 98 40.07 N 128.28 E
Sinch'ŏn 98 38.22 N 125.28 E
Sinch'ŏn-ni 271b 37.27 N 126.48 E
Sinclair, S. Afr. 273d 26.07 S 28.24 E
Sinclair, Wyo., U.S. 200 41.47 N 107.07 W
Sinclair, Lake ⊜[1] 192 33.11 N 83.16 W
Sinclair, Point ≻ 162 32.06 S 133.00 E
Sinclair Island I 224 48.37 N 122.40 W
Sinclair Mills 182 54.02 N 121.41 W
Sinclair's Bay C 46 58.30 N 3.07 W
Sinclairville 214 42.16 N 79.16 W
Sincovo 82 56.26 N 36.04 E
Sind □[4] 120 26.00 N 69.00 E
Sind ≃ 124 26.26 N 79.13 E
Şinda 89 48.57 N 136.18 E
Šinda ≃ 86 54.10 N 93.35 E
Sindal 26 57.28 N 10.13 E
Sindangan 116 8.14 N 123.00 E
Sindangan ≃ 116 8.13 N 123.00 E
Sindangan Bay C 116 8.11 N 122.50 E
Sindangan Point ≻ 116 8.10 N 122.40 E
Sindangbarang 115a 7.27 S 107.08 E
Sindara 152 1.02 S 10.40 E
Sindari 120 25.35 N 71.55 E
Sindelfingen 56 48.42 N 9.00 E
Sindhnūr 122 15.47 N 76.46 E
Sindhūli Garhi 124 27.16 N 85.58 E
Sindi 76 58.24 N 24.40 E
Sindia 71 40.18 N 8.39 E
Sindingale 110 18.17 N 94.25 E
Sındıran 130 39.17 N 32.41 E
Sındırgı 130 39.14 N 28.10 E
Sindiyūn 142 30.15 N 31.12 E
Sin-do I 98 39.48 N 124.14 E
Sindŏk 98 36.47 N 126.10 E
Sindor 24 62.50 N 51.57 E
Sindou 150 10.40 N 5.10 W
Sindou, Réserve de Faune ◆[4] 150 11.35 N 1.00 E
Sindri 126 23.45 N 86.42 E
Sind Sāga Doāb ⩕[1] 123 31.30 N 71.30 E
Siné V 150 14.10 N 16.28 W
Sinegorje 24 59.42 N 50.40 E
Sinegorsk 89 47.10 N 142.30 E
Sinegorskij 78 48.00 N 40.53 E
Šine-Ider 88 48.56 N 99.33 E
Sinekçi 130 40.16 N 27.24 E
Sinekli 130 41.14 N 28.12 E
Sinel'nikovo 78 48.20 N 35.31 E
Sinen'kije 80 51.15 N 45.46 E
Sinepuxent Bay C 208 38.16 N 75.09 W
Sines 34 37.57 N 8.52 W
Sines, Cabo de ≻ 34 37.57 N 8.53 W
Sine-Saloum □[4] 150 14.00 N 15.50 W
Sinevir 78 48.30 N 23.38 E
Sinevka 78 50.33 N 34.06 E
Sinewit, Mount ∧ 164 4.40 S 152.00 E
Sinez'orki 76 53.02 N 34.26 E
Sinfães 34 41.04 N 8.05 W
Sinfra 150 6.37 N 5.55 W
Singa (North) 126 23.16 N 89.30 E
Singair 126 23.49 N 90.08 E
Singako 146 9.50 N 19.29 E
Singal 123 36.06 N 73.53 E
Singalamwe 156 17.41 S 23.23 E
Singālila ∧ 124 27.13 N 88.01 E
Singālila Range ⩕ 124 27.25 N 88.05 E
Singānallūr 122 11.00 N 77.01 E
Singaparna 115a 7.21 S 108.06 E
Singapore 114; 271c 1.17 N 103.51 E
Singapore □[1] 108; 271c 1.22 N 103.48 E
Singapore I 271c 1.23 N 103.48 E
Singapore ≃ 271c 1.17 N 103.51 E
Singapore, University of ♥[2] 271c 1.19 N 103.49 E
Singapore Polytechnic ♥[2] 271c 1.16 N 103.51 E
Singapore Station ◆[5] 271c 1.17 N 103.50 E
Singapore Strait ⊔ 112 1.15 N 104.00 E
Singapour → Singapore □[1] 271c 1.22 N 103.48 E
Singapur → Singapore 114 1.17 N 103.51 E
Singapur → Singapore □[1] 271c 1.22 N 103.48 E
Singaraja 115b 8.07 S 115.06 E
Singarka ≃ 265a 59.53 N 29.54 E
Singāti 126 22.44 N 89.43 E
Singatoka 175g 18.08 S 177.30 E
Singatoka ≃ 175g 18.11 S 177.31 E
Sing Buri 110 14.53 N 100.25 E
Singe 272b 22.57 N 88.26 E
Singen (Hohentwiel) 58 47.46 N 8.50 E
Singer 194 30.39 N 93.25 W
Singhbhūm □[5] 124 22.30 N 85.30 E
Singhi 126 23.37 N 87.48 E
Singida 154 4.49 S 34.45 E
Singida □[4] 154 5.30 S 34.30 E
Singing 120 28.53 N 94.47 E
Singing Tower ♠ 220 27.57 N 81.34 W
Singkaling Hkāmti 110 26.00 N 95.42 E
Singkang 112 4.08 S 120.01 E
Singkawang 112 0.54 N 109.00 E
Singkep, Pulau I 112 0.30 S 104.25 E
Singkil 114 2.17 N 97.49 E
Singkuang 114 1.03 N 98.56 E
Singleton, Austl. 170 32.34 S 151.10 E
Singleton, Eng., U.K. 42 50.55 N 0.46 W
Singleton, Mount ∧, Austl. 162 29.28 S 117.18 E
Singleton, Mount ∧, Austl. 162 22.00 S 130.49 E
Singleton Ditch ≅ 216 41.10 N 87.37 W
Singlewell or Ifield 260 51.25 N 0.23 E
Singö 40 60.10 N 18.44 E
Singö I 40 60.11 N 18.46 E
Singora → Songkhla 110 7.12 N 100.36 E
Singorkai 164 5.55 S 146.55 E
Šingoža 86 47.45 N 80.40 E
Singpāra 272b 22.40 N 88.31 E
Singrāmau 124 25.57 N 82.23 E
Singuédeze (Groot Shingwidzi) ≃ 156 23.53 S 32.17 E
Singur 126 22.49 N 88.14 E
Sin'gye 98 38.36 N 126.30 E
Sinhai → Xinhailian 98 34.39 N 119.16 E
Sinhŭng 98 40.11 N 127.34 E
Siniaka-Minia, Réserve de ■ 146 10.30 N 18.00 E
Sinicha 83 49.31 N 37.34 E
Sinička ≃ 265b 55.50 N 37.19 E
Sinij, Chrebet ⩕ 89 45.12 N 133.51 E
Sinije Gory ⩕[2] 80 51.10 N 49.25 E
Sinije Lip'agi 78 51.23 N 38.29 E
Siniloan 116 14.25 N 121.27 E
Sinindé 150 10.21 N 2.23 E
Sining → Xining 102 36.38 N 101.55 E
Siniscola 71 40.34 N 9.41 E
Sinj 36 43.42 N 16.38 E
Sinjah 140 13.09 N 33.56 E
Sinjai 112 5.07 S 120.15 E
Sinjang-ni 98 39.04 N 127.46 E
Sinjār 128 36.19 N 41.52 E
Sinkan 110 24.08 N 97.01 E
Sinkāt 140 18.50 N 36.50 E
Sinkiang → Xinjiang Weiwuer Zizhiqu □[4] 90 40.00 N 85.00 E
Sinking ≃ 48 53.37 N 8.52 W
Sinking Creek ≃, Ky., U.S. 194 37.55 N 86.31 W
Sinking Creek ≃, Pa., U.S. 210 40.51 N 77.34 W
Sinking Spring, Ohio, U.S. 218 39.04 N 83.23 W
Sinking Spring, Pa., U.S. 208 40.19 N 76.02 W
Sin'kok-ni 271b 37.37 N 126.46 E
Šinkovo, S.S.S.R. 76 56.03 N 31.31 E
Sin'kovo, S.S.S.R. 82 54.37 N 38.56 E
Sin'kovo, S.S.S.R. 82 56.23 N 37.19 E
Sin'kovo, S.S.S.R. 82 55.30 N 38.06 E
Sin-le-Noble 50 50.22 N 3.07 E
Sinmak 98 38.25 N 126.14 E
Sinmi-do I 98 39.33 N 124.53 E
Sinn ≃ 56 50.03 N 9.42 E
Sinnahwā 142 30.25 N 31.21 E
Sinnai 71 39.18 N 9.12 E
Sinnamahoning 214 41.19 N 78.06 W
Sinnamary 250 5.23 N 52.57 W
Sinnamary ≃ 250 5.27 N 53.00 W
Sinnar 122 19.51 N 74.00 E
Sinnersdorf 56 51.01 N 6.49 E
Sinnes 26 58.56 N 6.50 E
Sinni ≃, It. 68 40.09 N 16.42 E
Sînnicolau Mare 38 46.05 N 20.38 E
Sinnūris 142 29.25 N 30.52 E
Sinnyŏng 98 36.04 N 128.46 E
Sinoe □[6] 150 5.10 N 9.00 W
Sinoe, Lacul ⊜ 38 44.38 N 28.53 E
Sinoia 154 17.22 S 30.12 E
Sinop 130 42.01 N 35.09 E
Sinop □[4] 130 41.40 N 34.50 E
Sinop ≻ 130 42.02 N 35.12 E
Sinop Limanı C 130 41.50 N 35.15 E
Sino-Soviet Friendship, Palace of ♥ 269b 31.14 N 121.25 E
Sinp'a 98 41.24 N 127.46 E
Sinp'o 98 40.03 N 128.12 E
Sins 58 47.11 N 8.23 E
Sinsang 98 39.38 N 127.25 E
Sinsen 263 51.40 N 7.11 E
Sinsheim 56 49.15 N 8.53 E
Sinsiang → Xinxiang 98 35.20 N 113.51 E
Sinsin 56 50.17 N 5.15 E
Sinsi-ri 98 39.59 N 124.58 E
Sinskoje 74 61.08 N 126.48 E
Sinspelt 56 49.58 N 6.19 E
Sint-Amandsberg 50 51.04 N 3.45 E
Sîntana 38 46.21 N 21.30 E
Sint-Andries 50 51.12 N 3.10 E
Sintang 112 0.04 N 111.30 E
Sint Annaland 52 51.36 N 4.06 E
Sint Annaparochie 52 53.16 N 5.39 E
Sint Anthonis 52 51.37 N 5.52 E
Sint Christoffelberg ∧ 241s 12.20 N 69.08 W
Sint-Denijs-Westrem 50 51.01 N 3.40 E
Sint Eustatius I 238 17.30 N 62.59 W
Sint-Gillis-Waas 50 51.13 N 4.08 E
Sint-Joris-Weert 56 50.48 N 4.39 E
Sint-Joris-Winge 56 50.55 N 4.52 E
Sint-Katelijne-Waver 56 51.04 N 4.32 E

ENGLISH

Name Page Lat.°' Long.°'

Sint-Kruis, Bel. 50 51.13 N 3.15 E
Sint Kruis, Ned. Ant. 241s 12.18 N 69.08 W
Sint-Lenaarts 56 51.21 N 4.41 E
Sint Maarten 52 52.46 N 4.44 E
Sint Maartensdijk 52 51.33 N 4.05 E
Sint Marten (Saint-Martin) I 238 18.04 N 63.04 W
Sint-Michiels 50 51.11 N 3.12 E
Sint Michielsgestel 52 51.38 N 5.21 E
Sint Nicolaas 241s 12.27 N 69.52 W
Sint-Niklaas (Saint-Nicolas) 50 51.10 N 4.08 E
Sint-Oedenrode 52 51.34 N 5.27 E
Sinton 196 29.41 N 95.58 W
Sintong 114 1.31 N 100.58 E
Sint Pancras 52 52.39 N 4.46 E
Sint-Pieters-Leeuw 50 50.47 N 4.14 E
Sintra 34 38.48 N 9.23 W
Sintra, Paço do ♥ 266c 38.48 N 9.23 W
Sintra, Serra de ⩕[2] 266c 38.47 N 9.25 W
Sintra Granjo do Marquez, Aeroporto ⊠ 266c 38.49 N 9.20 W
Sint-Truiden 56 50.48 N 5.12 E
Sint Willebrord 52 51.33 N 4.35 E
Sinú ≃ 246 9.24 N 75.49 W
Sin'ucha ≃, S.S.S.R. 78 48.03 N 30.51 E
Sin'ucha ≃, S.S.S.R. 84 45.47 N 41.00 E
Sin'uga 88 57.45 N 115.13 E
Sinŭiju 98 40.05 N 124.24 E
Sinujif 144 8.30 N 48.59 E
Sinŭp, C.M.I.K. 98 39.54 N 126.47 E
Sinŭp, Taehan 98 37.54 N 127.12 E
Sinwŏn-ni 98 38.13 N 125.44 E
Sinzig 56 50.32 N 7.15 E
Sinzing 60 49.00 N 12.02 E
Sió ≃, Magy. 30 46.20 N 18.55 E
Sio ≃, Togo 150 6.17 N 1.13 E
Siocon 116 7.42 N 122.08 E
Siófok 30 46.54 N 18.04 E
Sioma 152 16.39 S 23.30 E
Sion (Sitten) 58 46.14 N 7.21 E
Sionascaig, Loch ⊜ 46 58.04 N 5.11 W
Sioule ≃ 32 46.22 N 3.19 W
Sioux Center 198 43.05 N 96.10 W
Sioux City 198 42.30 N 96.23 W
Sioux Falls 198 43.32 N 96.44 W
Sioux Lookout 184 50.06 N 91.55 W
Sioux Narrows 190 49.25 N 94.06 W
Sioux Rapids 198 42.53 N 95.09 W
Sipalay 116 9.45 N 122.24 E
Sipalay ≃ 116 9.46 N 122.24 E
Sipaliwini ≃ 250 2.22 N 56.50 W
Sipaozi 104 41.26 N 122.13 E
Sipapo ≃ 246 5.03 N 67.48 W
Siparia 241r 10.08 N 61.30 W
Şipek 130 40.14 N 41.29 E
Sipes 220 28.48 N 81.14 W
Sipesville 214 40.06 N 79.06 W
Šipicyno, S.S.S.R. 24 61.17 N 46.28 E
Šipicyno, S.S.S.R. 86 56.04 N 77.18 E
Šipilovo 82 54.49 N 37.32 E
Siping 89 43.12 N 124.20 E
Sipingjie 98 42.31 N 125.08 E
Sipirok 114 1.37 N 99.16 E
Sipitang 112 5.05 N 115.33 E
Sipiwesk 184 55.27 N 97.24 W
Sipiwesk Lake ⊜ 184 55.05 N 97.35 W
Siple, Mount ∧ 9 73.15 S 126.06 W
Siple Coast •[2] 9 82.00 S 153.00 W
Sipocot 116 13.46 N 122.58 E
Sipofaneni 158 26.41 S 31.41 E
Sipolilo 154 16.39 S 30.42 E
Siponto ⊥ 68 41.40 N 15.51 E
Sipot 114 4.31 N 96.02 E
Şipoteny 78 47.18 N 28.11 E
Šipovatoje 78 49.56 N 37.24 E
Sipplingen 58 47.47 N 9.05 E
Si Prachan 110 14.37 N 100.09 E
Sipsey ≃ 194 33.00 N 88.10 W
Sipsey Creek ≃ 194 33.53 N 88.17 W
Sipu 98 40.48 N 113.43 E
Şipul 164 5.50 S 148.45 E
Šipunovo 86 52.13 N 82.17 E
Sipupus 114 1.25 N 99.31 E
Sipura, Pulau I 112 2.12 S 99.40 E
Siqian, Zhg. 100 22.31 N 112.52 E
Siqian, Zhg. 100 24.40 N 114.06 E
Siqueira Campos 255 23.42 S 49.50 W
Siquia ≃ 236 12.09 N 84.13 W
Siquijor Island I 116 9.11 N 123.34 E
Siquirres 236 10.06 N 83.30 W
Siquisique 246 10.34 N 69.42 W
Sīra, Bhārat 122 13.45 N 76.54 E
Şira, Nor. 26 58.25 N 6.38 E
Šira, S.S.S.R. 86 54.29 N 89.56 E
Sira ≃ 26 58.17 N 6.24 E
Si Racha 110 13.10 N 100.56 E
Siracuas 248 21.03 S 61.46 W
Siracusa (Syracuse) 70 37.04 N 15.18 E
Siracusa □[4] 70 37.03 N 15.00 E
Sir Adam Beck II Reservoir ⊜[1] 284a 43.08 N 79.04 W
Şīr aḍ-Ḍinnīyah 130 34.23 N 36.02 E
Šir'aj 80 49.34 N 44.07 E
Šir'ajevo 78 47.23 N 30.13 E
Şirājganj 124 24.27 N 89.43 E
Širakskaja Step' ⊻ 84 41.25 N 46.15 E
Sir Alexander, Mount ∧ 182 53.56 N 120.23 W
Sirāmpur 126 24.08 N 86.20 E
Sirasso 150 9.16 N 6.06 W
Sirault 50 50.30 N 3.47 E
Siraway 116 7.34 N 122.08 E
Sirba ≃ 150 13.46 N 1.40 E
Şīr Banī Yās I 128 24.20 N 52.37 E
Sir Colin Mackenzie Wildlife Sanctuary ◆[4] 169 37.40 S 145.32 E
Sirdalsvatn ⊜ 26 58.33 N 6.41 E
Sīrdān 128 36.39 N 49.12 E
Şirdar 182 49.15 N 116.37 W
Širdkoje 78 48.08 N 34.49 E
Sir Douglas, Mount ∧ 182 50.44 N 115.20 W
Sire 144 9.00 N 36.55 E
Sir Edward Pellew Group II 164 15.40 S 136.48 E
Širega 76 60.10 N 41.15 E
Sireniki 180 64.25 N 173.57 W
Sirente, Monte ∧ 66 42.09 N 13.36 E
Siret 38 47.57 N 26.04 E
Siret ≃ 38 45.24 N 28.01 E
Sirevåg 26 58.30 N 5.47 E
Sir Francis Drake Channel ⊔ 240m 18.25 N 64.30 W
Sirghāyā 132 33.48 N 36.09 E
Sirha 124 26.39 N 86.12 E
Sirḥān, Wādī as- V 128 30.30 N 38.00 E
Sirhind 124 30.39 N 76.23 E
Sirhind Canal ≅ 123 30.59 N 76.31 E
Siria → Syria □[1] 128 35.00 N 38.00 E
Sirik, Tanjong ≻ 112 2.46 N 111.19 E
Sírina I 130 36.21 N 26.42 E
Širinquši 80 53.51 N 42.46 E
Sirino, Monte ∧ 68 40.08 N 15.50 E
Sir James MacBrien, Mount ∧ 180 62.07 N 127.41 W
Sir Joseph Banks Group II 166 34.32 S 136.17 E
Sirkābād 126 23.16 N 86.12 E
Sirkeli 130 40.09 N 32.52 E

DEUTSCH

Name Seite Breite°' Länge°' E=Ost

Sirmaur 124 24.51 N 81.23 E
Sirmione 64 45.30 N 10.36 E
Širmovka 78 49.34 N 29.06 E
Sirmūr □[5] 123 30.40 N 77.20 E
Sir Muttra 124 26.31 N 77.22 E
Sirnach 58 47.28 N 9.00 E
Siro, Jabal ∧ 140 14.23 N 24.23 E
Sirohi 120 24.53 N 72.52 E
Širokaja Pad' 89 50.14 N 142.09 E
Širokij 89 49.45 N 129.30 E
Širokij Bujerak 80 52.07 N 47.46 E
Širokino 83 47.06 N 37.49 E
Širokoje, S.S.S.R. 78 47.41 N 33.14 E
Širokoje, S.S.S.R. 83 47.58 N 38.13 E
Širokolanovka 78 47.10 N 31.24 E
Širokovo 88 55.27 N 99.23 E
Sirolo 66 43.32 N 13.37 E
Sirombu 114 0.57 N 97.25 E
Sironj 124 24.06 N 77.42 E
Síros → Ermoúpolis 38 37.26 N 24.56 E
Síros I 38 37.26 N 24.54 E
Sirotino, S.S.S.R. 76 55.23 N 29.37 E
Sirotino, S.S.S.R. 83 48.55 N 38.31 E
Sirotinskaja 80 49.16 N 43.39 E
Siroua, Jbel ∧ 148 30.41 N 7.37 W
Sirrah, Nafūd as- •[8] 128 25.15 N 44.45 E
Sīrrī, Jazīreh-ye I 128 25.55 N 54.32 E
Sirsa, Bhārat 123 29.32 N 75.01 E
Sirsa, Bhārat 126 22.14 N 86.38 E
Sirsāganj 124 27.03 N 78.42 E
Sirs al-Layyānah 142 30.26 N 30.58 E
Sir Sandford, Mount ∧ 182 51.40 N 117.52 W
Sirsi 122 14.37 N 74.51 E
Sirsilla 122 18.23 N 78.50 E
Sirsinā, Mişr 142 29.24 N 30.58 E
Sirsinā, Mişr 142 30.36 N 30.54 E
Sirsiri 154 4.24 N 31.53 E
Sir Thomas, Mount ∧ 162 27.10 S 129.45 E
Siruma 116 14.00 N 123.15 E
Sīrvān (Diyālā) ≃ 128 33.14 N 44.31 E
Širvanskaja Step' ⊻ 84 40.15 N 48.00 E
Širvintos 76 55.03 N 24.57 E
Sir Wilfrid Laurier, Mount ∧ 182 52.47 N 119.45 W
Sir Wilfrid Laurier's Birthplace National Historic Site ⊥ 206 45.51 N 73.45 W
Siryāqūs 142 30.12 N 31.19 E
Sís ≃, Guat. 236 14.09 N 91.39 W
Šiš ≃, S.S.S.R. 86 57.19 N 73.23 E
Sisaiya Thana 124 27.35 N 81.20 E
Sisak 36 45.29 N 16.23 E
Sisaket 110 15.07 N 104.20 E
Šišaki 78 49.53 N 34.00 E
Šišakovo 76 60.02 N 41.30 E
Si Satchanalai 110 17.31 N 99.46 E
Šišchid ≃ 88 51.27 N 98.03 E
Šiševka 76 58.52 N 38.52 E
Sishangcun 105 40.16 N 116.33 E
Sishen 158 27.55 S 22.59 E
Sishibadu 100 28.14 N 118.02 E
Sishili 106 32.09 N 120.45 E
Sishilijie 100 29.08 N 116.44 E
Sishilipu 105 40.12 N 118.08 E
Sishuangdao I 100 26.42 N 120.24 E
Sishui 98 35.39 N 117.15 E
Sisian 84 39.32 N 46.02 E
Şisib Lake ⊜ 184 52.35 N 99.22 W
Šišicy 76 53.13 N 27.32 E
Sisikon 58 46.57 N 8.42 E
Sisili ≃ 150 10.16 N 1.15 W
Sisim ≃ 88 55.09 N 91.54 E
Şisipuk Lake ⊜ 184 55.45 N 101.50 W
Šiškejevo 80 54.12 N 44.45 E
Šiškino 88 52.18 N 113.35 E
Siskiyou Mountains ⩕ 204 41.55 N 123.15 W
Siskiyou Pass)(202 42.03 N 122.36 W
Şişli ◆[8] 267b 41.04 N 28.59 E
Šišlovo 82 54.14 N 38.33 E
Sison 116 9.40 N 125.31 E
Sisŏphŏn 110 13.35 N 102.59 E
Sisquoc ≃ 204 34.54 N 120.18 W
Sissa ≃ 115b 8.29 S 121.18 E
Sissach 58 47.28 N 7.49 E
Sissano 164 3.00 S 142.05 E
Sissela 150 10.49 N 10.37 W
Sisseton 198 45.40 N 97.03 W
Sisseton Indian Reservation ◆[4] 198 45.40 N 97.02 W
Sisson Branch Reservoir ⊜[1] 186 47.16 N 67.20 W
Sissonne 50 49.34 N 3.54 E
Sissonville 188 38.32 N 81.38 W
Sister Bay 190 45.11 N 87.07 W
Sister Lakes 216 42.05 N 86.12 W
Sisteron 62 44.12 N 5.56 E
Sisters 202 44.17 N 121.33 W
Sistersville 188 39.34 N 81.00 W
Sistig 56 50.29 N 6.30 E
Sisto ≃ 66 41.18 N 13.10 E
Sistranda 26 63.43 N 8.50 E
Sit' ≃, S.S.S.R. 76 58.16 N 37.54 E
Sit' ≃, S.S.S.R. 76 59.59 N 40.10 E
Sitabamba 248 8.02 S 77.44 W
Sitai, Zhg. 85 39.23 N 77.56 E
Sitai, Zhg. 98 41.16 N 114.13 E
Sitaizi, Zhg. 104 42.29 N 123.20 E
Sitaizi, Zhg. 104 41.17 N 122.16 E
Sitaizui 105 40.49 N 115.20 E
Sitakili 150 13.07 N 11.14 W
Sitalike 154 6.38 S 31.08 E
Sitalkuchi 124 26.10 N 89.11 E
Sītāmarhi 124 26.36 N 85.29 E
Sitampiky 157b 16.41 S 46.06 E
Si Tangkay 112 4.40 N 119.24 E
Sītāpur 124 27.34 N 80.41 E
Sītāpur □[5] 124 27.30 N 80.50 E
Sitārāmpur 126 23.43 N 86.53 E
Sites 226 39.19 N 122.20 W
Sithoniá 38 35.12 N 26.07 E
Sithoniá ≻[1] 38 40.10 N 23.47 E
Sitidgi Lake ⊜ 180 68.32 N 132.42 W
Sítio da Abadia 255 14.48 S 46.16 W
Sítio Nôvo do Grajaú 250 5.51 S 46.43 W
Sitionuevo 246 10.47 N 74.43 W
Sitka 180 57.03 N 135.14 W
Sitkalidak Island I 180 57.10 N 153.14 W
Sitka National Monument ♠ 180 57.05 N 135.15 W
Sitka Point ≻ 180 57.00 N 135.49 W
Sitka Sound ⊔ 180 57.00 N 135.30 W
Sitkinak Island I 180 56.35 N 154.12 W
Sitkinak Strait ⊔ 180 56.39 N 154.06 W
Šitkino 88 56.23 N 98.21 E
Sitkovcy 78 48.54 N 29.12 E
Sitna ≃ 38 47.37 N 27.08 E
Sitn'a-Ščelkanovo 82 54.58 N 37.59 E
Sitnica ≃ 38 42.45 N 21.01 E
Sitniki 80 56.27 N 44.06 E
Sitnikovo 86 56.23 N 67.53 E
Sitobela 158 26.53 S 31.36 E
Sitona 144 14.28 N 37.27 E
Sitrah 128 26.09 N 50.38 E
Sitrah ◆[4] 140 28.42 N 26.54 E
Sittang ≃ 110 17.10 N 96.58 E
Sittard 56 51.00 N 5.53 E
Sitten → Sion 58 46.14 N 7.21 E
Sittendorf 264b 48.05 N 16.10 E

Symbols in the index entries represent the broad categories identified in the key at the right. Symbols with superior numbers (⩕[2]) identify subcategories (see complete key on page *I · 30*).

Kartensymbole in dem Registerverzeichnis stellen die rechts in Schlüssel erklärten Kategorien dar. Symbole mit hochgestellten Ziffern (⩕[2]) bezeichnen Unterabteilungen einer Kategorie (vgl. vollständiger Schlüssel auf Seite *I · 30*).

Los símbolos incluídos en el texto del índice representan las grandes categorias identificadas con la clave a la derecha. Los símbolos con numeros en su parte superior (⩕[2]) identifican las subcategorías (véase la clave completa en la página *I · 30*).

Les symboles de l'index représentent les catégories indiquées dans la légende à droite. Les symboles suivis d'un indice (⩕[2]) représentent des sous-catégories (voir légende complète à la page *I · 30*).

Os símbolos incluídos no texto do índice representam as grandes categorias identificadas com a chave à direita. Os símbolos com números em sua parte superior (⩕[2]) identificam as subcategorias (veja-se a chave completa à página *I · 30*).

	English	Deutsch	Español	Français	Português
∧	Mountain	Berg	Montaña	Montagne	Montanha
⩕	Mountains	Berge	Montañas	Montagnes	Montanhas
)(	Pass	Pass	Paso	Col	Passo
V	Valley, Canyon	Tal, Cañon	Valle, Cañón	Vallée, Canyon	Vale, Canhão
⊻	Plain	Ebene	Llano	Plaine	Planície
≻	Cape	Kap	Cabo	Cap	Cabo
I	Island	Insel	Isla	Île	Ilha
II	Islands	Inseln	Islas	Îles	Ilhas
•	Other Topographic Features	Andere Topographische Objekte	Otros Elementos Topográficos	Autres données topographiques	Outros Elementos Topográficos

ESPAÑOL

Nombre	Página	Lat.°′	Long.°′ W=Oeste
Sittensen	52	53.17 N	9.30 E
Sitter ≃	58	47.29 N	9.14 E
Sittingbourne	42	51.21 N	0.44 E
Sittwe (Akyab)	110	20.09 N	92.54 E
Situ	105	39.20 N	115.39 E
Situbondo	115a	7.42 S	114.00 E
Siufaalele Point ≻	174y	14.17 S	169.29 W
Siufaga	174y	14.14 S	169.32 W
Siulakderas	112	1.55 S	101.18 E
Siu Lek Yuen	271d	22.23 N	114.12 E
Siumbatu	112	2.45 S	122.03 E
Siumpu, Pulau I	112	5.40 S	122.31 E
Siuna	236	13.44 N	84.46 W
Siurgus Donigala	71	39.35 N	9.12 E
Siusi (Seis)	64	46.32 N	11.34 E
Siuslaw ≃	202	44.01 N	124.08 W
Siva ≃	80	56.48 N	53.55 E
Sivaganga	122	9.52 N	78.29 E
Sivakāsi	122	9.27 N	77.49 E
Sivaki	89	52.39 N	126.45 E
Sīvan ≃	128	29.51 N	52.46 E
Sivas	130	39.45 N	37.02 E
Sivas □[4]	130	39.30 N	37.15 E
Sivaš, Ozero ⋓	78	46.00 N	34.30 E
Sivaslı	130	38.30 N	29.42 E
Sivašskoje	78	46.23 N	34.34 E
Sivé	150	15.42 N	13.12 W
Siverek	130	37.45 N	39.19 E
Siverskij	76	59.21 N	30.05 E
Sivkovo	82	55.26 N	35.53 E
Sivomaskinskij	24	66.40 N	62.35 E
Sivriada I	267b	40.54 N	28.59 E
Sivrice	130	38.27 N	39.19 E
Sivrihisar	130	39.27 N	31.34 E
Sivry-Courtry	261	48.32 N	2.45 E
Sivry-sur-Meuse	56	49.19 N	5.16 E
Sīwah	140	29.12 N	25.31 E
Sīwah, Wāḥat ⊤[4]	140	29.12 N	25.31 E
Siwalik Range ⩕	120	31.00 N	78.00 E
Siwān	124	26.13 N	84.22 E
Siwangxi ≃	107	29.25 N	103.50 E
Siwāni	123	28.55 N	75.37 E
Six Flags over Mid-America ♠	219	38.31 N	90.40 W
Six Flags Over Texas ♠	222	32.45 N	97.05 W
Six-Fours-la-Plage	62	43.06 N	5.51 E
Sixian	100	33.30 N	117.56 E
Sixitou	100	27.31 N	119.57 E
Six Mile Creek ≃, Ont., Can.	284a	43.15 N	79.10 W
Sixmile Creek ≃, Ky., U.S.	218	38.26 N	84.58 W
Sixmile Creek ≃, N.Y., U.S.	284a	43.17 N	78.58 W
Sixmile Creek ≃, N.Y., U.S.	284a	43.02 N	79.01 W
Sixmilecross	48	54.34 N	7.08 W
Six Mile Lake ⊜	212	44.55 N	79.45 W
Sixmile Run ≃	276	40.28 N	74.35 W
Six Mile Water ≃	44	54.42 N	6.14 W
Six Nations Indian Reserve ⬩[4]	212	43.03 N	80.07 W
Sixshooter Draw ∨	196	30.51 N	102.33 W
Sixteenmile Creek ≃	202	46.06 N	111.23 W
Sixth Cataract → Ash-Shallāl as-Sablūkah ↳	140	16.20 N	32.42 E
Siyāl, Jazā'ir II	140	22.47 N	36.12 E
Siyāna	124	28.38 N	78.03 E
Siyang	100	33.43 N	118.41 E
Si Yat ≃	110	13.42 N	101.26 E
Siyeteb	140	18.00 N	35.01 E
Siz'absk	24	65.05 N	53.49 E
Sizaja	88	58.07 N	100.38 E
Sizhijian	98	42.25 N	114.36 E
Siziano	62	45.20 N	9.12 E
Sizilien → Sicilia I	70	37.30 N	14.00 E
Siziman	89	50.43 N	140.26 E
Siziwangqi	102	41.33 N	111.31 E
Sizun	32	48.24 N	4.05 W
Sizuoka → Shizuoka	94	34.58 N	138.23 E
Sjælland I	41	55.30 N	11.45 E
Sjællands Odde ≻[1]	41	55.58 N	11.22 E
Själevad	26	63.18 N	18.36 E
Sjanovo	82	54.59 N	37.25 E
Sjenica	38	43.16 N	20.00 E
Sjeništa ∧	38	43.42 N	18.37 E
Sjoa ≃	26	61.41 N	9.33 E
Sjöbo	41	55.38 N	13.42 E
Sjøholt	26	62.29 N	6.48 E
Sjösa	40	58.46 N	17.04 E
Sjötorp	40	58.50 N	13.59 E
Sjujutlijka ≃	38	42.17 N	25.55 E
Skaby	264a	52.19 N	13.51 E
Skaby-Berge ⩕[2]	264a	52.19 N	13.49 E
Skåde	41	56.06 N	10.13 E
Skadovsk	78	46.08 N	32.54 E
Skælskør	41	55.15 N	11.19 E
Skærbæk, Dan.	41	55.09 N	8.46 E
Skærbæk, Dan.	41	55.31 N	9.38 E
Skævinge	41	55.55 N	12.10 E
Skaftung	26	62.07 N	21.22 E
Skagafjörður C	24a	65.55 N	19.35 W
Skagen	26	57.44 N	10.36 E
Skagern ⊜	40	58.59 N	14.17 E
Skagerrak ⋓	26	57.45 N	9.00 E
Skagersvik	40	58.58 N	14.06 E
Skaggs Creek ≃	194	36.54 N	86.04 W
Skagit □[6]	224	48.29 N	121.45 W
Skagit ≃	224	48.20 N	122.25 W
Skagit Bay C	224	48.19 N	122.24 W
Skagway	180	59.28 N	135.19 W
Skaidi	24	70.25 N	24.30 E
Skaistkalne	76	56.23 N	24.39 E
Skála Oropoú	38	38.20 N	23.46 E
Skala-Podol'skaja	78	48.51 N	26.12 E
Skalat	78	49.26 N	25.59 E
Skalbmierz	30	50.19 N	20.25 E
Skälderviken	41	56.17 N	12.50 E
Skälderviken C	41	56.18 N	12.38 E
Skalica	30	48.51 N	17.14 E
Skalino	76	58.32 N	40.13 E
Skalistyj Chrebet ⩕	84	43.40 N	42.30 E
Skalka ⊜	24	66.50 N	18.46 E
Skalka, údolní nádrž ⊜[1]	60	50.06 N	12.19 E
Skalká přehradová nádrž ⊜[1]	54	50.05 N	12.15 E
Skalná	54	50.07 N	12.23 E
Skal'nij	86	58.22 N	57.59 E
Skamania	224	45.37 N	122.03 W
Skamania □[6]	224	45.58 N	121.53 W
Skamlingsbanke ∧[2]	41	55.25 N	9.34 E
Skamokawa	224	46.16 N	123.27 W
Skanderborg	41	56.02 N	9.56 E
Skanderborg Sø ⊜	41	56.01 N	9.56 E
Skåne □[9]	41	55.59 N	13.30 E
Skaneateles	210	42.57 N	76.26 W
Skaneateles Falls	210	43.00 N	76.27 W
Skaneateles Lake ⊜	210	42.53 N	76.24 W
Skånevik	26	59.44 N	5.59 E
Skänninge	26	58.24 N	15.05 E
Skanör	26	55.25 N	12.52 E
Skara	26	58.22 N	13.25 E
Skaraborgs Län □[6]	26	58.20 N	13.30 E
Skaramagás	267c	38.01 N	23.36 E
Skärblacka	40	58.34 N	15.54 E
Skarđ	24a	64.03 N	19.50 W

FRANÇAIS

Nom	Page	Lat.°′	Long.°′ W=Ouest
Skārdu	123	35.18 N	75.37 E
Skärhamn	26	58.00 N	11.33 E
Skarhult	41	55.49 N	13.23 E
Skarnes	26	60.15 N	11.41 E
Skarø I	41	55.00 N	10.29 E
Skärplinge	40	60.28 N	17.46 E
Skarszewy	30	54.05 N	18.27 E
Skårup	41	55.05 N	10.42 E
Skaryszew	30	51.19 N	21.15 E
Skarżysko-Kamienna	30	51.08 N	20.53 E
Skášov	60	49.31 N	13.26 E
Skate Creek ≃	224	46.37 N	121.41 W
Skattkärr	40	59.25 N	13.41 E
Skaudvilė	76	55.24 N	22.35 E
Skaugum	26	59.51 N	10.26 E
Skawina	30	49.59 N	19.49 E
Skebobruk	40	59.58 N	18.36 E
Skebokvarn	40	59.04 N	16.42 E
Skedviken ⊜	40	59.46 N	18.16 E
Skedvisjön ⊜	40	59.35 N	15.40 E
Skeena ≃	182	54.09 N	130.02 W
Skeena Crossing	182	55.06 N	127.49 W
Skeen Peak ∧	222	32.59 N	97.48 W
Skegness	44	53.10 N	0.21 E
Skegrie	41	55.24 N	13.04 E
Skei	26	61.38 N	6.30 E
Skeikampen	26	61.20 N	10.07 E
Skelde	41	54.51 N	9.44 E
Skeldon	246	5.53 N	57.08 W
Skeleton Creek ≃	196	35.58 N	97.25 W
Skeleton Lake ⊜	212	45.15 N	79.27 W
Skellefteå	26	64.46 N	20.57 E
Skellefteälven ≃	26	64.42 N	21.06 E
Skelleftehamn	26	64.41 N	21.14 E
Skellig Rocks II[1]	48	51.48 N	10.31 W
Skellytown	196	35.34 N	101.11 W
Skelmersdale	44	53.33 N	2.48 W
Skelmorlie	46	55.51 N	4.53 W
Skelton, Eng., U.K.	44	54.43 N	2.51 W
Skelton, Eng., U.K.	44	54.33 N	0.59 W
Skene	26	57.29 N	12.38 E
Skene, Mount ∧	169	37.25 S	146.23 E
Skepptuna	40	59.43 N	18.05 E
Skerne ≃	44	54.29 N	1.34 W
Skerpioensdrif	158	31.05 S	21.33 E
Skerryvore II[1]	46	56.19 N	7.07 W
Skewen	42	51.40 N	3.51 W
Skhíza I	38	36.44 N	21.46 E
Ski	26	59.43 N	10.50 E
Skíathos	38	39.10 N	23.29 E
Skiatook	196	36.22 N	96.01 W
Skibbereen	48	51.33 N	9.15 W
Skibby	41	55.45 N	11.58 E
Skibotn	24	69.24 N	20.16 E
Skiddaw ∧	44	54.38 N	3.08 W
Skidegate	182	53.15 N	132.00 W
Skidegate Inlet C	182	53.14 N	132.00 W
Skidel'	76	53.34 N	24.15 E
Skidmore	196	28.15 N	97.41 W
Skien	26	59.12 N	9.36 E
Skierniewice	30	51.58 N	20.08 E
Skiftet ⋓	26	60.15 N	21.05 E
Skihist Mountain ∧	182	50.11 N	121.54 W
Skikda (Philippeville)	148	36.50 N	6.58 E
Skilak Lake ⊜	180	60.25 N	150.25 W
Skillet Fork ≃	194	38.08 N	88.07 W
Skillingaryd	26	57.26 N	14.05 E
Skillman	276	40.25 N	74.43 W
Škin'	82	55.11 N	38.30 E
Skinnastaður	24a	66.07 N	16.24 W
Skinner Reservoir ⊜[1]	228	33.35 N	117.03 W
Skinnskatteberg	40	59.50 N	15.41 E
Skippack Creek ≃	285	40.09 N	75.27 W
Skippack Creek, West Branch ≃	285	40.14 N	75.23 W
Skippers	208	36.37 N	77.38 W
Skipskop	158	34.33 S	20.25 E
Skipton, Austl.	169	37.41 S	143.22 E
Skipton, Eng., U.K.	44	53.58 N	2.01 W
Skirfare ≃	44	54.07 N	2.01 W
Skirmish Point ≻	171a	27.05 S	153.13 E
Skíros	38	38.53 N	24.33 E
Skíros I	38	38.53 N	24.32 E
Skivarp	41	55.25 N	13.34 E
Skive	26	56.34 N	9.02 E
Skjálfandafljót ≃	24a	65.57 N	17.38 W
Skjálfandi C	24a	66.08 N	17.38 W
Skjeberg	26	59.14 N	11.12 E
Skjern	26	55.57 N	8.30 E
Skjern Å ≃	41	55.57 N	8.40 E
Sklad	74	71.55 N	123.33 E
Šklov	76	54.13 N	30.18 E
Skobeleva, Pik ∧	85	39.49 N	72.44 E
Skoby	40	60.02 N	18.01 E
Škocjanske Jame ●[7]	36	45.40 N	14.00 E
Skodborg	41	55.25 N	9.09 E
Skodsborg	41	55.49 N	12.34 E
Skoenmakerskop	158	34.02 S	25.33 E
Škofije	64	45.34 N	13.48 E
Škofja Loka	36	46.10 N	14.18 E
Skoganvarre	24	69.47 N	25.06 E
Skoghall	40	59.19 N	13.26 E
Skogstorp	40	59.20 N	16.28 E
Skokholm Island I	42	51.42 N	5.16 W
Skoki	30	52.41 N	17.10 E
Skokie	216	42.02 N	87.46 W
Skokie ≃	216	42.05 N	87.46 W
Skokie Lagoons C	278	42.07 N	87.47 W
Skokloster ⊥	40	59.42 N	17.37 E
Skokomish, North Fork ≃	224	47.18 N	123.14 W
Skokomish, South Fork ≃	224	47.18 N	123.14 W
Skokomish Indian Reservation ⬩[4]	224	47.21 N	123.12 W
Sköldinge	40	59.02 N	16.26 E
Skole	78	49.02 N	23.29 E
Sköllersta	40	59.09 N	15.20 E
Skolsta	40	59.40 N	17.14 E
Skolwin	54	53.32 N	14.35 E
Skomer Island I	42	51.44 N	5.17 W
Skomoroški, S.S.S.R.	78	49.20 N	29.26 E
Skomoroški, S.S.S.R.	82	54.05 N	36.57 E
Skón	110	12.04 N	105.04 E
Skookumchuck ≃	224	46.41 N	123.00 W
Skoonspruit ≃	158	27.00 S	25.38 E
Skootamatta ≃	212	44.32 N	77.20 W
Skootamatta Lake ⊜	212	44.50 N	77.15 W
Skópelos	38	39.07 N	23.43 E
Skópelos I	38	39.10 N	23.40 E
Skopin	76	53.51 N	39.33 E
Skopje	38	41.59 N	21.26 E
Skórcz	30	53.48 N	18.32 E
Skorodnoje, S.S.S.R.	78	51.05 N	37.14 E
Skorodnoje, S.S.S.R.	78	51.38 N	28.49 E
Skørping	26	56.50 N	9.53 E
Skotfoss	26	59.12 N	9.30 E
Skotovataja	83	48.13 N	37.54 E
Škotovo	89	43.20 N	132.21 E
Skotterud	26	59.59 N	12.07 E
Skovby	41	54.53 N	10.00 E
Skövde	26	58.24 N	13.50 E
Skovlund	41	55.44 N	8.43 E
Skovorodino	89	53.59 N	123.55 E
Skowhegan	188	44.46 N	69.43 W
Skownan	184	51.57 N	99.36 W
Skradin	36	43.49 N	15.56 E
Skreen	48	54.15 N	8.45 W
Skreia	26	60.39 N	10.56 E
Skriplivka	76	57.32 N	30.38 E
Skrīveri	76	56.39 N	25.08 E

PORTUGUÊS

Nome	Página	Lat.°′	Long.°′ W=Oeste
Skromberga	26	56.00 N	12.58 E
Skrudaļiena	76	55.49 N	26.43 W
Skrunda	76	56.41 N	22.01 E
Skruv	26	56.41 N	15.22 E
Skrydstrup	41	55.14 N	9.15 E
Skudeneshavn	26	59.09 N	5.17 E
Skuilte	273d	26.07 S	28.19 E
Skukuza	156	25.01 S	31.38 E
Skuleberget ∧[2]	26	63.05 N	18.21 E
Skulforp	26	58.21 N	13.49 E
Skull Creek ≃	222	29.32 N	96.24 W
Skull Valley	200	34.30 N	112.41 W
Skull Valley Indian Reservation ⬩[4]	200	40.24 N	112.45 W
Skultuna	40	59.43 N	16.25 E
Skuna ≃	194	33.54 N	89.41 W
Skunk ≃	190	40.42 N	91.07 W
Škunovka	86	50.45 N	55.27 E
Skuodas	76	56.16 N	21.32 E
Skuratovskij	82	54.07 N	37.36 E
Škurinskaja	78	46.35 N	39.22 E
Skurišenskaja	80	49.52 N	42.57 E
Skurup	41	55.28 N	13.30 E
Skutskär	40	60.38 N	17.25 E
Skvira	78	49.44 N	29.40 E
Skwentna	180	61.58 N	151.11 W
Skwentna ≃	180	62.00 N	151.08 W
Skwierzyna	30	52.36 N	15.30 E
Skye I	46	57.15 N	6.10 W
Skye, Island of I	46	57.18 N	6.15 W
Sky Harbor Airport ⊠	278	42.09 N	87.51 W
Skykomish	224	47.42 N	121.22 W
Skykomish ≃	224	47.50 N	122.03 W
Skykomish, North Fork ≃	224	47.47 N	121.33 W
Skykomish, South Fork ≃	224	47.47 N	121.33 W
Sky Lake	220	28.28 N	81.24 W
Sky Lake ⊜	212	44.48 N	81.15 W
Skyland, Nev., U.S.	226	39.01 N	119.57 W
Skyland, N.C., U.S.	192	35.29 N	82.31 W
Skylight	218	38.26 N	85.32 W
Skyline Lakes ⊜	276	41.04 N	74.16 W
Skyllberg	40	58.57 N	14.59 E
Skyring, Península ≻[1]	254	45.58 S	74.53 W
Skyring, Seno ⋓	254	52.35 S	72.00 W
Sky Sailing Airport ⊠	282	37.30 N	121.58 W
Skytop	210	41.14 N	75.15 W
Skyttorp	40	60.05 N	17.44 E
Skyway	224	47.29 N	122.14 W
Slabce	60	50.00 N	13.44 E
Slackhall	262	53.20 N	1.53 W
Slackwood	208	40.15 N	74.44 W
Slade Green ⬩[8]	260	51.28 N	0.12 E
Sladkij	80	46.10 N	42.17 E
Sladkovo	86	55.32 N	70.20 E
Slagelse	41	55.24 N	11.22 E
Slagnäs	24	65.34 N	18.05 E
Slagovišči	76	53.57 N	35.54 E
Slaithwaite	262	53.37 N	1.53 W
Slamet, Gunung ∧	115a	7.14 S	109.12 E
Slancy	76	59.06 N	28.04 E
Slaney ≃	48	52.21 N	6.30 W
Slangerup	41	55.51 N	12.11 E
Slănic	38	45.15 N	25.57 E
Slănic Moldova	38	46.13 N	26.26 E
Slano	36	42.47 N	17.54 E
Slanské Vrchy ⩕	30	48.50 N	21.30 E
Slaný	54	50.11 N	14.04 E
Šlapanice	30	49.10 N	16.44 E
Slaščevskaja	80	49.52 N	42.21 E
Śląsk → Silesia □[9]	30	51.00 N	16.45 E
Slastucha	80	51.57 N	44.32 E
Slate Bottom Creek ≃	284a	42.53 N	78.45 W
Slate Creek ≃, Kans., U.S.	198	37.08 N	97.09 W
Slate Creek ≃, Pa., U.S.	279b	40.28 N	79.32 W
Slatedale	208	40.45 N	75.40 W
Slate Hill	210	41.23 N	74.29 W
Slater, Iowa, U.S.	190	41.53 N	93.41 W
Slater, Mo., U.S.	194	39.13 N	93.04 W
Slatersville	207	42.00 N	71.35 W
Slaterville Springs	210	42.24 N	76.21 W
Slatina	38	44.26 N	24.22 E
Slatington	208	40.45 N	75.37 W
Slatino	78	50.12 N	36.11 E
Slaton	196	33.26 N	101.39 W
Slattocks	262	53.35 N	2.10 W
Slaung	115a	8.02 S	111.24 E
Slautnoje	74	63.00 N	167.59 E
Slava	89	52.08 N	129.24 E
Slav'anka, S.S.S.R.	78	48.24 N	36.43 E
Slav'anka, S.S.S.R.	85	40.40 N	68.32 E
Slav'anka, S.S.S.R.	89	42.53 N	131.21 E
Slav'anka ≃	265a	59.50 N	30.32 E
Slav'anogorsk	83	49.02 N	37.31 E
Slav'anoserbsk	83	48.42 N	38.59 E
Slav'ansk	83	48.52 N	37.37 E
Slav'ansk-na-Kubani	78	45.15 N	38.08 E
Slave ≃	176	61.18 N	113.39 W
Slave Coast ●[2]	150	6.25 N	3.00 E
Slave Lake	182	55.17 N	114.46 W
Slavgorod, S.S.S.R.	76	53.27 N	31.00 E
Slavgorod, S.S.S.R.	78	48.06 N	35.31 E
Slavgorod, S.S.S.R.	78	50.36 N	35.21 E
Slavgorod, S.S.S.R.	86	53.00 N	78.40 E
Slavitino	82	56.41 N	39.13 E
Slavkino	80	52.58 N	47.11 E
Slavkoviči	76	57.39 N	29.05 E
Slavkovský les ⩕	54	50.07 N	12.45 E
Slavkov u Brna	30	49.09 N	16.52 E
Slavnoje	76	54.18 N	29.27 E
Slavonia → Slavonija ⬩[1]	36	45.00 N	18.00 E
Slavonice	61	49.00 N	15.21 E
Slavonija ⬩[1]	36	45.00 N	18.00 E
Slavonska Požega	36	45.20 N	17.41 E
Slavonski Brod	38	45.10 N	18.01 E
Slavsk (Heinrichswalde)	76	55.03 N	21.41 E
Slavskoje	78	48.49 N	23.24 E
Slavuta	78	50.18 N	26.52 E
Sławа	30	51.53 N	16.04 E
Slawi	115a	6.59 S	109.08 E
Sławno	30	54.22 N	16.40 E
Slayton	198	43.59 N	95.45 W
Slea ≃	42	53.03 N	0.12 W
Sleaford	42	53.00 N	0.24 W
Slea Head ≻	48	52.06 N	10.27 W
Sleat, Point of ≻	46	57.01 N	6.02 W
Sleat, Sound of ⋓	46	57.06 N	5.49 W
Sledge	194	34.26 N	90.13 W
Sledge Island I	180	64.29 N	166.13 W
Sled Lake ⊜	184	54.27 N	107.25 W
Sledmere	44	54.04 N	0.35 W
Slednevo	82	56.25 N	38.36 E
Sled'uki	76	53.35 N	30.22 E
Sleen	52	52.46 N	6.48 E
Sleeping Bear Dunes National Lakeshore ♠	190	44.50 N	86.08 W
Sleeping Giant State Park ♠	207	41.25 N	72.53 W
Sleepy Eye	198	44.18 N	94.43 W
Sleepy Hollow, Calif., U.S.	226	38.00 N	122.34 W
Sleepy Hollow, Calif., U.S.	280	33.57 N	117.47 W
Sleepy Hollow, Ill., U.S.	216	42.06 N	88.24 W
Sleetmute	180	61.42 N	157.11 W
Sleidinge	50	51.08 N	3.41 E
Sleman	115a	7.42 S	110.20 E
Slepino	76	59.11 N	29.02 E
Ślesin	30	52.23 N	18.19 E
Slessor Glacier ⍓	9	79.50 S	28.30 W
Sliabh Gaoil ∧	46	55.55 N	5.28 W
Slickville	214	40.28 N	79.32 W
Slidell	194	30.17 N	89.47 W
Slide Mountain ∧	210	42.00 N	74.23 W
Sliderock Mountain ∧	202	46.35 N	113.33 W
Sliedrecht	52	51.49 N	4.45 E
Slievenaman ∧	48	52.25 N	7.34 W
Sligeach → Sligo	48	54.17 N	8.28 W
Sligo, Eire	48	54.17 N	8.28 W
Sligo, Pa., U.S.	214	41.07 N	79.29 W
Sligo □[6]	48	54.10 N	8.40 W
Sligo Bay C	48	54.20 N	8.40 W
Sligo Creek ≃	284c	38.57 N	76.58 W
Slikkerveer	52	51.53 N	4.37 E
Slinger	190	43.20 N	88.17 W
Šlino, Ozero ⊜	76	57.40 N	33.23 E
Slioch ∧	46	57.41 N	5.22 W
Slippery Rock	214	41.04 N	80.03 W
Slippery Rock Creek ≃	214	40.51 N	80.15 W
Slite	26	57.43 N	18.48 E
Slīteres Rezervāts ♠	76	57.38 N	22.25 E
Sliven	38	42.40 N	26.19 E
Slivnica	38	42.51 N	23.02 E
Sloan, Iowa, U.S.	198	42.14 N	96.14 W
Sloan, Nev., U.S.	204	35.57 N	115.13 W
Sloan, N.Y., U.S.	210	42.54 N	78.47 W
Sloan Peak ∧	224	48.03 N	121.20 W
Sloansville	210	42.46 N	74.20 W
Sloatsburg	210	41.09 N	74.12 W
Sloboda, S.S.S.R.	76	55.30 N	31.51 E
Sloboda, S.S.S.R.	76	53.58 N	28.08 E
Sloboda, S.S.S.R.	78	51.09 N	40.17 E
Sloboda, S.S.S.R.	78	51.11 N	33.37 E
Slobodka, S.S.S.R.	76	55.41 N	27.11 E
Slobodka, S.S.S.R.	78	47.53 N	29.21 E
Slobodka, S.S.S.R.	82	54.22 N	37.33 E
Slobodskoj	86	58.24 N	50.12 E
Slobodzeja	78	46.44 N	29.43 E
Slobodzeja-Prut	78	45.34 N	28.12 E
Slobozia	38	44.34 N	27.23 E
Slocan	182	49.46 N	117.28 W
Slocan Lake ⊜	182	49.56 N	117.22 W
Slochteren	52	53.12 N	6.47 E
Slocomb	194	31.06 N	85.36 W
Slocum	207	41.32 N	71.31 W
Slocum Mountain ∧	228	35.18 N	117.13 W
Słomniki	30	50.15 N	20.06 E
Slonim	76	53.06 N	25.19 E
Slonovka	78	50.39 N	37.45 E
Słońsk	54	52.35 N	14.50 E
Sloop Channel ⋓	276	40.36 N	73.31 W
Sloping Hills	276	40.42 N	74.34 W
Slosh Indian Reserve ⬩[4]	182	50.44 N	122.13 W
Sloten	52	52.54 N	5.38 E
Sloten ⬩[8]	52	52.21 N	4.48 E
Sloter Meer ⊜	52	52.55 N	5.40 E
Slough	42	51.31 N	0.36 W
Slough □[8]	260	51.32 N	0.35 W
Slough Brook ≃	276	40.45 N	74.21 W
Sloughhouse	226	38.30 N	121.12 W
Slovakia → Slovensko □[9]	30	48.50 N	20.00 E
Slovan	214	40.22 N	80.23 W
Slovečna ≃	78	51.41 N	29.41 E
Slovečno	78	51.23 N	28.21 E
Slovenia → Slovenija □[3]	36	46.15 N	15.10 E
Slovenija □[3]	36	46.15 N	15.10 E
Slovenjgradec	61	46.31 N	15.05 E
Slovenska Bistrica	61	46.23 N	15.34 E
Slovenská Socialistická Republika □[3]	30	48.30 N	20.00 E
Slovenske Gorice ⩕[2]	61	46.35 N	15.55 E
Slovenské rudohorie ⩕	30	48.45 N	20.00 E
Slovensko □[9]	30	48.50 N	20.00 E
Slovinka	80	58.02 N	43.07 E
Slowakei → Slovensko □[9]	30	48.50 N	20.00 E
Słowiński Park Narodowy ♠	30	54.40 N	17.25 E
Słubice	54	52.20 N	14.32 E
Sluč' ≃, S.S.S.R.	76	52.08 N	27.31 E
Sluč' ≃, S.S.S.R.	78	51.37 N	26.38 E
Sluck	76	53.01 N	27.33 E
Sl'ud'anka	88	51.38 N	103.42 E
Sluderno (Schluderns)	64	46.40 N	10.35 E
Sludy	76	58.52 N	36.52 E
Sluis	52	51.18 N	3.24 E
Sluiskil	52	51.16 N	3.50 E
Šluknov	54	51.00 N	14.27 E
Slunj	36	45.07 N	15.35 E
Słupca	30	52.19 N	17.52 E
Słupia ≃	30	54.35 N	16.50 E
Słupsk (Stolp)	30	54.28 N	17.01 E
Slurry	156	25.49 S	25.52 E
Šl'uz-Mokr'aki	86	59.17 N	88.50 E
Slyne Head ≻	48	53.24 N	10.13 W
Smachtino	82	54.51 N	36.25 E
Smackover	194	33.22 N	92.44 W
Smackover Creek ≃	194	33.22 N	92.24 W
Småland □[9]	26	57.20 N	15.00 E
Smålandsfarvandet ⋓	41	55.05 N	11.20 E
Smålandsstenar	26	57.10 N	13.24 E
Smalininkai	76	55.05 N	22.35 E
Smallbridge	262	53.38 N	2.08 W
Smalleytown	276	40.39 N	74.28 W
Smallwood	210	41.40 N	74.49 W
Smallwood State Park ♠	208	38.33 N	77.12 W
Smara → Semara	148	26.44 N	11.41 W
Smartt Syndicate Reservoir ⊜[1]	158	30.40 S	23.18 E
Smartville	226	39.12 N	121.18 W
Smeaton	184	53.30 N	104.49 W
Smeaton Bay C	182	55.20 N	130.50 W
Smečno	54	50.10 N	14.03 E
Smedby	40	58.33 N	16.16 E
Smědeč	61	48.56 N	14.09 E
Smederevo	38	44.40 N	20.56 E
Smederevska Palanka	38	44.22 N	20.58 E
Smedjebacken	40	60.08 N	15.25 E
Smela	78	49.14 N	31.53 E
Smeloje	78	50.55 N	33.36 E
Šmel'ovka	80	54.47 N	49.11 E
Smelt Brook ≃, Mass., U.S.	283	42.13 N	70.58 W
Smelt Brook ≃, Mass., U.S.	283	42.00 N	70.43 W
Smelt Pond ⊜	283	41.58 N	70.43 W
Smeralda, Costa ●[2]	71	41.04 N	9.30 E
Smerwick Harbour C	48	52.12 N	10.24 W
Smethport	214	41.49 N	78.27 W
Smethwick (Warley)	42	52.30 N	1.58 W
Smicksburg	214	40.52 N	79.10 W
Smidovič	89	48.36 N	133.49 E
Šmidta → Mys Šmidta	180	68.56 N	179.26 W
Šmidta, Mys ≻	180	68.56 N	179.30 W
Šmidta, Ostrov I	74	81.08 N	90.48 E
Šmidta, Poluostrov ≻[1]	89	54.10 N	142.40 E
Śmigiel	30	52.01 N	16.32 E
Smilde	52	52.56 N	5.27 E
Smile	218	38.15 N	83.29 W
Smiley, Sask., Can.	184	51.37 N	109.29 W
Smiley, Tex., U.S.	222	29.16 N	97.38 W
Smiloviči	76	53.45 N	28.01 E
Smiltene	76	57.26 N	25.56 E
Smirnovskij	86	54.31 N	69.25 E
Smirnych	89	49.43 N	142.38 E
Smite ≃	42	52.57 N	0.53 W
Smith	182	55.10 N	114.02 W
Smith □[6]	222	32.20 N	95.15 W
Smith ≃, Calif., U.S.	204	41.56 N	124.12 W
Smith ≃, Mont., U.S.	202	47.25 N	111.29 W
Smith ≃, Oreg., U.S.	202	43.43 N	124.05 W
Smith, Cape ≻	190	45.48 N	81.35 W
Smith Arm C	180	66.15 N	124.00 W
Smith Bay C	180	70.51 N	154.25 W
Smithboro, Ill., U.S.	219	38.54 N	89.20 W
Smithboro, N.Y., U.S.	210	42.02 N	76.24 W
Smith Canyon ∨	198	37.46 N	103.26 W
Smith Center	198	39.47 N	98.47 W
Smith Creek ≃, S. Dak., U.S.	198	43.58 N	99.20 W
Smith Creek ≃, Wash., U.S.	224	46.45 N	123.53 W
Smithdale	279b	40.14 N	79.48 W
Smithers, B.C., Can.	182	54.47 N	127.10 W
Smithers, W. Va., U.S.	188	38.11 N	81.18 W
Smithfield, Austl.	168b	34.41 S	138.41 E
Smithfield, Austl.	274a	33.51 S	150.57 E
Smithfield, Ont., Can.	212	44.04 N	77.41 W
Smithfield, S. Afr.	158	30.09 S	26.30 E
Smithfield, Eng., U.K.	44	54.59 N	2.52 W
Smithfield, N.C., U.S.	192	35.30 N	78.21 W
Smithfield, Ohio, U.S.	214	40.16 N	80.47 W
Smithfield, Pa., U.S.	214	40.29 N	78.01 W
Smithfield, Utah, U.S.	200	41.50 N	111.50 W
Smithfield, Va., U.S.	208	36.59 N	76.38 W
Smithflat	226	38.44 N	120.45 W
Smith Haven Mall ⬩[9]	276	40.52 N	73.08 W
Smithills Hall ⊥	262	53.36 N	2.27 W
Smith Island I, B.A.T.	9	62.59 S	62.32 W
Smith Island I, N.C., U.S.	192	33.52 N	77.59 W
Smith Island I, Va., U.S.	208	37.10 N	75.51 W
Smith Island I, Wash., U.S.	224	48.19 N	122.50 W
Smith Island II	208	38.01 N	76.02 W
Smithland	194	37.09 N	88.24 W
Smithmill	214	40.46 N	78.25 W
Smith Mountain ∧	280	34.17 N	117.52 W
Smith Mountain Lake ⊜[1]	192	37.10 N	79.40 W
Smith Peak ∧	202	48.50 N	116.39 W
Smith Peninsula ≻[1]	9	74.25 S	61.15 W
Smith Point	222	29.27 N	94.45 W
Smith Point ≻, N.S., Can.	186	45.51 N	63.25 W
Smith Point ≻, Tex., U.S.	222	29.32 N	94.46 W
Smith Point ≻, Va., U.S.	208	37.53 N	76.14 W
Smithport	214	40.50 N	78.52 W
Smith River	204	41.56 N	124.09 W
Smiths	194	32.32 N	85.06 W
Smiths Creek	214	42.55 N	82.36 W
Smiths Falls	212	44.54 N	76.01 W
Smiths Grove	194	37.03 N	86.12 W
Smiths Mills	276	41.01 N	74.22 W
Smith Sound ⋓	182	51.18 N	127.48 W
Smithton, Austl.	166	40.51 S	145.07 E
Smithton, Mo., U.S.	194	38.41 N	93.05 W
Smithton, Pa., U.S.	279b	40.09 N	79.44 W
Smithtown	210	40.52 N	73.13 W
Smith Valley	218	39.36 N	86.12 W
Smithville, Ont., Can.	212	43.06 N	79.33 W
Smithville, Ga., U.S.	192	31.54 N	84.15 W
Smithville, Ind., U.S.	218	39.04 N	86.30 W
Smithville, Miss., U.S.	194	33.59 N	88.23 W
Smithville, Mo., U.S.	194	39.23 N	94.35 W
Smithville, N.J., U.S.	208	39.31 N	74.27 W
Smithville, N.J., U.S.	285	39.59 N	74.45 W
Smithville, Ohio, U.S.	214	40.52 N	81.51 W
Smithville, Tenn., U.S.	194	35.58 N	85.49 W
Smithville, Tex., U.S.	222	30.00 N	97.09 W
Smithville Flats	210	42.24 N	75.49 W
Smögen	26	58.21 N	11.13 E
Smoke Creek ≃, Mont., U.S.	198	48.18 N	104.41 W
Smoke Creek ≃, N.Y., U.S.	284a	42.49 N	78.52 W
Smoke Creek, South Branch ≃	284a	42.49 N	78.49 W
Smoke Creek Desert ⬩[2]	204	40.30 N	119.40 W
Smoke Lake ⊜	212	45.32 N	78.41 W
Smokeless	214	40.24 N	76.02 W
Smokerun	214	40.48 N	78.26 W
Smoketown	208	40.02 N	76.12 W
Smokey Dome ∧	202	43.29 N	114.56 W
Smoky ≃	182	56.10 N	117.21 W
Smoky, Cape ≻	186	46.38 N	60.21 W
Smoky Bay	162	32.22 S	133.56 E
Smoky Cape ≻	166	30.56 S	153.05 E
Smoky Hill ≃	198	39.03 N	96.48 W
Smoky Hill, North Fork ≃	198	39.28 N	98.26 W
Smoky Hills ⩕[2]	198	39.15 N	99.00 W
Smoky Lake	182	54.07 N	112.28 W
Smøla I, Nor.	24		
	26	63.24 N	8.00 E
Smol'anica	76	52.42 N	24.38 E
Smol'aninovo	89	43.19 N	132.28 E
Smol'any	76	54.36 N	30.04 E
Smolensk	76	54.47 N	32.03 E
Smolenskoje	86	52.20 N	85.05 E
Smolensko-Moskovskaja Vozvyšennost' ⩕[1]	76	55.00 N	34.00 E
Smoleviči	76	54.02 N	28.05 E
Smólikas ∧	38	40.06 N	20.52 E
Smoljan	38	41.35 N	24.41 E
Smol'nyj ʊ	265a	59.57 N	30.24 E
Smolovka	76	55.33 N	30.13 E
Smoot	200	42.37 N	110.55 W
Smoothstone ≃	184	55.20 N	106.39 W
Smoothstone Lake ⊜	184	54.40 N	106.50 W
Smorgon'	76	54.29 N	26.24 E
Smorodovka	76	57.08 N	29.52 E
Smotrič	78	48.56 N	26.34 E
Smotrič ≃	78	48.34 N	26.38 E
Smuskovoje	80	47.19 N	46.02 E
Smyčka	82	56.04 N	35.56 E
Smygehamn	41	55.21 N	13.22 E
Smygehuk ≻	41	55.21 N	13.23 E
Smyley, Cape ≻	9	72.26 S	78.10 W
Smyrna → İzmir, Tür.	130	38.25 N	27.09 E
Smyrna, Del., U.S.	208	39.18 N	75.36 W
Smyrna, Ga., U.S.	192	33.53 N	84.31 W
Smyrna, N.Y., U.S.	210	42.41 N	75.34 W
Smyrna, Tenn., U.S.	194	35.59 N	86.31 W
Smyrna ≃	208	39.22 N	75.31 W
Smyrna Mills	188	46.08 N	68.10 W
Smyšl'ajevka	80	53.15 N	50.22 E
Smyth, Canal ⋓	254	52.15 S	73.40 W
Smythe Park ♠	275b	43.41 N	79.30 W
Smythesdale	169	37.38 S	143.41 E
Sn'adin	78	52.04 N	28.19 E
Snæfell ∧, Ísland	24a	64.48 N	15.32 W
Snaefell ∧, I. of Man	44	54.16 N	4.27 W
Snæfellness ≻[1]	24a	64.50 N	23.00 W
Snag	180	62.24 N	140.22 W
Snaght, Slieve ∧	44	55.12 N	7.20 W
Snagost'	78	51.21 N	34.54 E
Snahapish ≃	224	47.38 N	124.11 W
Šn'ajevo	80	52.34 N	46.11 E
Snake ≃, Yukon, Can.	180	65.58 N	134.10 W
Snake ≃, U.S.	202	46.12 N	119.02 W
Snake ≃, Calif., U.S.	226	39.07 N	121.43 W
Snake ≃, Minn., U.S.	190	45.49 N	92.46 W
Snake ≃, Minn., U.S.	198	48.26 N	97.07 W
Snake ≃, Nebr., U.S.	198	42.47 N	100.48 W
Snake Brook ≃	283	42.18 N	71.22 W
Snake Creek ≃, Mont., U.S.	202	48.32 N	108.53 W
Snake Creek ≃, Nebr., U.S.	198	42.01 N	102.45 W
Snake Creek ≃, S. Dak., U.S.	198	44.58 N	98.29 W
Snake Creek Canal ≅	220	25.57 N	80.11 W
Snake Indian ≃	182	53.11 N	118.00 W
Snake Range ⩕	204	39.00 N	114.15 W
Snake Rapids ↳	212	45.14 N	77.20 W
Snake River Plain ⊻	202	43.00 N	113.00 W
Snake Valley ∨	204	39.20 N	113.55 W
Snaptun	41	55.49 N	10.04 E
Snare Islands II	9	48.00 S	166.30 E
Snasahögarna ∧	26	63.13 N	12.21 E
Sn'atyn	78	48.28 N	25.34 E
Snay Pôl	110	11.40 N	105.13 E
Sneads	192	30.42 N	84.56 W
Snedsted	26	56.54 N	8.32 E
Sneedville	192	36.32 N	83.13 W
Sneek	52	53.02 N	5.40 E
Sneekermeer ⊜	52	53.02 N	5.45 E
Snee-oosh-Beach	224	48.24 N	122.33 W
Sneeuberg ⩕	158	31.46 S	24.20 E
Snekkersten	41	56.00 N	12.36 E
Snelgrove	275b	43.44 N	79.49 W
Snelling	204	37.31 N	120.26 W
Snettisham	42	52.53 N	0.30 E
Snežnaja ≃	88	51.28 N	104.38 E
Snežnik ∧	36	45.35 N	14.27 E
Snežnoje	83	48.01 N	38.46 E
Śniardwy, Jezioro ⊜	30	53.46 N	21.44 E
Snicarte	219	40.07 N	90.14 W
Snicarte Island I	219	40.08 N	90.12 W
Sniga ≃	82	54.53 N	37.24 E
Snigir'ovka	78	47.06 N	32.47 E
Snina	30	48.59 N	22.07 E
Snipe Keys II	220	24.40 N	81.38 W
Snipe Lake ⊜	182	55.07 N	116.46 W
Snizort, Loch C	46	57.34 N	6.28 W
Snøde	41	55.05 N	10.55 E
Snodland	42	51.20 N	0.27 E
Snoghøj	41	55.31 N	9.43 E
Snøhetta ∧	26	62.20 N	9.17 E
Snohomish	224	47.55 N	122.06 W
Snohomish □[6]	224	48.02 N	121.41 W
Snohomish ≃	224	48.01 N	122.13 W
Snønipa ⍓	26	61.42 N	6.41 E
Snook	222	30.29 N	96.28 W
Snoqualmie	224	47.32 N	121.50 W
Snoqualmie ≃	224	47.50 N	122.03 W
Snoqualmie, Middle Fork ≃	224	47.49 N	122.02 W
Snoqualmie, North Fork ≃	224	47.31 N	121.46 W
Snoqualmie, South Fork ≃	224	47.49 N	122.02 W
Snoqualmie Falls	224	47.32 N	121.49 W
Snoqualmie Mountain ∧	224	47.27 N	121.25 W
Snoqualmie Pass)(	224	47.25 N	121.25 W
Snøtinden ∧	24	66.38 N	14.00 E
Snov	76	53.13 N	26.24 E
Snov ≃	78	51.45 N	31.45 E
Snover	190	43.28 N	82.58 W
Snowbird Lake ⊜	176	60.41 N	103.00 W
Snow Canyon State Park ♠	200	37.11 N	113.42 W
Snow Creek ≃	224	47.59 N	122.53 W
Snowden, Sask., Can.	184	53.30 N	104.41 W
Snowden, Pa., U.S.	279b	40.16 N	79.58 W
Snowdenville	285	40.11 N	75.36 W
Snowdon ∧	44	53.04 N	4.05 W
Snowdonia National Park ♠	44	53.09 N	3.57 W
Snowdoun	194	32.15 N	86.18 W
Snowdrift	176	62.23 N	110.47 W
Snowflake	200	34.30 N	110.05 W
Snow Hill, Md., U.S.	208	38.11 N	75.24 W
Snow Hill, N.C., U.S.	192	35.27 N	77.40 W
Snow Hill Island I	18	64.00 S	57.30 W
Snowking Mountain ∧	224	48.24 N	121.17 W
Snow Lake	184	54.53 N	100.02 W
Snow Lakes ⊜	224	47.29 N	120.45 W
Snowmass Mountain ∧	200	39.07 N	107.04 W
Snow Mountain ∧	226	39.23 N	122.45 W
Snow Peak ∧	202	48.35 N	118.29 W
Snows Brook ≃	283	42.47 N	71.06 W
Snow Shoe	214	41.02 N	77.57 W
Snowshoe Butte ∧	224	47.13 N	121.22 W
Snowshoe Peak ∧	202	48.13 N	115.41 W
Snowtown	166	33.47 S	138.13 E
Snow Water Lake ⊜	204	41.07 N	115.00 W
Snowy ≃	166	37.48 S	148.32 E
Snowy Mountain ∧	188	43.42 N	74.23 W
Snowy Mountains ⩕	166	36.30 S	148.20 E
Snowyside Peak ∧	202	43.57 N	114.58 W
Snubba Range ⩕	171b	35.40 S	148.10 E
Snuŏl	110	12.04 N	106.26 E
Snyder, Okla., U.S.	196	34.40 N	98.57 W
Snyder, Tex., U.S.	196	32.44 N	100.55 W
Snyder □[6]	210	40.47 N	77.03 W
Snydertown	210	40.53 N	76.40 W
So ≃	150	6.28 N	2.25 E
Soacha	246	4.35 N	74.13 W
Soahanina	157b	18.42 S	44.13 E
Soaker, Mount ∧	172	45.23 S	167.15 E
Soalala	157b	16.06 S	45.20 E
Soalary	157b	23.36 S	43.44 E
Soaloka	157b	18.32 S	45.15 E
Sŏam	98	38.01 N	126.43 E
Soamanonga	157b	23.52 S	44.47 E
Soān ≃	123	33.01 N	71.44 E
Soanierana Ivongo	157b	16.55 S	49.35 E
Soanindrariny	157b	19.54 S	47.14 E
Soap Creek ≃	194	40.55 N	92.14 W
Soap Lake	202	47.23 N	119.29 W

Symbol	English	Deutsch	Español	Français	Português
≃	River	Fluss	Río	Rivière	Rio
≅	Canal	Kanal	Canal	Canal	Canal
↳	Waterfall, Rapids	Wasserfall, Stromschnellen	Cascada, Rápidos	Chute d'eau, Rapides	Cascata, Rápidos
⋓	Strait	Meeresstrasse	Estrecho	Détroit	Estreito
C	Bay, Gulf	Bucht, Golf	Bahía, Golfo	Baie, Golfe	Baía, Golfo
⊜	Lake, Lakes	See, Seen	Lago, Lagos	Lac, Lacs	Lago, Lagos
⊻	Swamp	Sumpf	Pantano	Marais	Pântano
⍓	Ice Features, Glacier	Eis- und Gletscherformen	Accidentes Glaciales	Formes glaciaires	Acidentes Glaciares
⊤	Other Hydrographic Features	Andere Hydrographische Objekte	Otros Elementos Hidrográficos	Autres données hydrographiques	Outros Elementos Hidrográficos
✣	Submarine Features	Untermeerische Objekte	Accidentes Submarinos	Formes de relief sous-marin	Acidentes Submarinos
□	Political Unit	Politische Einheit	Unidad Política	Entité politique	Unidade Política
ʊ	Cultural Institution	Kulturelle Institution	Institución Cultural	Institution culturelle	Instituição Cultural
⊥	Historical Site	Historische Stätte	Sitio Histórico	Site historique	Sítio Histórico
♠	Recreational Site	Erholungs- und Ferienort	Sitio de Recreo	Centre de loisirs	Sítio de Lazer
⊠	Airport	Flughafen	Aeropuerto	Aéroport	Aeroporto
●	Military Installation	Militäranlage	Instalación Militar	Installation militaire	Instalação Militar
⬩	Miscellaneous	Verschiedenes	Misceláneo	Divers	Miscelânea

Name	Page	Lat.	Long.
Soasiu			
→ Tidore	108	0.40 N	127.26 E
Soatá	246	6.20 N	72.41 W
Soave	64	45.25 N	11.15 E
Soavina	157b	20.23 S	46.56 E
Soavinandriana	157b	19.09 S	46.45 E
Soay I	46	57.08 N	6.14 W
Soazza	58	46.22 N	9.13 E
Sob ≃	78	48.42 N	29.17 E
Sobaco, Sierra del			
∧∧	196	26.15 N	103.00 W
Sobaek-sanmaek ∧∧	98	36.00 N	128.00 E
Sobat ≃	140	9.22 N	31.33 E
Sobernheim	56	49.47 N	7.38 E
Soběšice	60	49.12 N	13.41 E
Soběslav	30	49.15 N	14.44 E
Sobger ≃	164	3.44 S	140.20 E
Sobič	78	51.52 N	33.14 E
Sobinka	80	55.59 N	40.01 E
Soboba Indian			
Reservation ◆[4]	228	33.47 N	116.54 W
Soboko	140	6.49 N	24.50 E
Sobolekovo	80	55.39 N	51.53 E
Sobolev	80	51.56 N	51.43 E
Sobolevka	78	48.36 N	29.30 E
Sobolevo	82	55.31 N	38.43 E
Sobolino	88	53.23 N	119.42 E
Sobótka	30	50.55 N	16.45 E
Sobradinho	252	29.24 S	53.03 W
Sobrado	34	41.02 N	8.16 W
Sobral	250	3.42 S	40.21 W
Sobrance	30	48.45 N	22.11 E
Sobrante Ridge ∧	282	37.58 N	122.15 W
Sobrarbe ◆[1]	34	42.22 N	0.10 E
Sobue	94	35.15 N	136.43 E
Søby	41	54.56 N	10.16 E
Soča	64	46.20 N	13.39 E
Soča (Isonzo) ≃	64	45.47 N	13.32 E
Socaire	252	23.36 S	67.51 W
Socamirim	256	23.37 S	47.12 W
Socchieve	64	46.25 N	12.52 E
Soc-giang	110	22.54 N	106.01 E
Socgorodok	78	50.11 N	38.09 E
Soch	85	39.57 N	71.08 E
Soch ≃	85	40.20 N	71.02 E
Sochaczew	30	52.14 N	20.14 E
Sochaux	58	47.31 N	6.50 E
Soch'e			
→ Suoche	120	38.25 N	77.16 E
Sochi			
→ Soči	84	43.35 N	39.45 E
Sŏch'ŏn	98	36.05 N	126.41 E
Sochondo	88	51.49 N	112.32 E
Sochondo, Gora ∧	88	49.44 N	111.05 E
Sochor, Gora ∧	88	51.18 N	105.15 E
Soči	84	43.35 N	39.45 E
Social Circle	192	33.39 N	83.43 W
Sociedade Hípica			
Paulista ♠	287b	23.36 S	46.41 W
Société, Îles de la II	14	17.00 S	150.00 W
Society Hill	192	34.31 N	79.51 W
Society Islands			
→ Société, Îles de			
la II	14	17.00 S	150.00 W
Society Ridge ⊹[3]	14	17.00 S	152.00 W
Soco ≃	238	18.27 N	69.12 W
Socoltenango	232	16.13 N	92.15 W
Socompa, Paso)(	252	24.27 S	68.18 W
Soconusco, Sierra de			
→ Madre, Sierra			
∧∧	236	15.20 N	92.20 W
Socorro, Bra.	256	22.36 S	46.32 W
Socorro, Col.	246	6.29 N	73.16 W
Socorro, Pil.	116	9.37 N	125.58 E
Socorro, N. Mex.,			
U.S.	200	34.04 N	106.54 W
Socorro, Tex., U.S.	200	31.39 N	106.18 W
Socorro ◆[8]	287b	23.39 S	46.42 W
Socorro, Isla I	232	18.45 N	110.58 W
Sócota	248	6.18 S	78.44 W
Socotora, Isla			
→ Suquṭrā I	118	12.30 N	54.00 E
Socotra			
→ Suquṭrā I	118	12.30 N	54.00 E
Socuéllamos	34	39.17 N	2.48 W
Soda Creek	182	52.21 N	122.18 W
Soda Creek ≃	226	38.48 N	122.29 W
Soda Lake ⊜, Calif.,			
U.S.	204	35.08 N	116.04 W
Soda Lake ⊜, Calif.,			
U.S.	226	35.15 N	119.53 W
Sodankylä	24	67.29 N	26.32 E
Soda Springs	202	42.39 N	111.36 W
Soddy-Daisy	194	35.17 N	85.10 W
Sodegaura	94	35.26 N	139.57 E
Södel	56	50.23 N	8.48 E
Söderälgen ⊜	40	59.43 N	14.35 E
Söderåsen ∧∧[2]	41	56.04 N	13.05 E
Söderbärke	40	60.05 N	15.33 E
Söderby-Karl	40	59.53 N	18.41 E
Söderfors	40	60.23 N	17.14 E
Söderhamn	26	61.18 N	17.03 E
Söderköping	26	58.29 N	16.18 E
Södermanland □[9]	41	59.12 N	16.49 E
Södermanlands Län			
□[6]	40	59.15 N	16.40 E
Södernmanland □[9]	40	59.12 N	16.49 E
Söderslätt □[9]	41	55.29 N	13.15 E
Södertälje	40	59.12 N	17.37 E
Södertörn ≻[1]	40	59.05 N	18.00 E
Sodhra	123	32.28 N	74.11 E
Sodingen ◆[8]	263	51.32 N	7.15 E
Sodium	158	30.11 S	23.09 E
Sodo	144	6.52 N	37.47 E
Sodpur	272b	22.42 N	88.23 E
Södra Åby	41	55.23 N	13.18 E
Södra Björkfjärden			
C	40	59.18 N	17.32 E
Södra Hörken ⊜	40	60.02 N	15.02 E
Södra Kvarken ⊔	26	60.15 N	19.05 E
Södra Råda	40	59.01 N	14.10 E
Södra Sandby	41	55.43 N	13.20 E
Södra Vi	26	57.45 N	15.48 E
Sodražica	36	45.46 N	14.38 E
Sodus	210	43.14 N	77.04 W
Sodus Bay C	210	43.15 N	76.58 W
Sodus Creek ≃	210	43.13 N	76.56 W
Sodus Point	210	43.16 N	76.59 W
Sodwalls	170	33.31 S	149.59 E
Soe	112	9.52 S	124.17 E
Soeda	96	33.34 N	130.52 E
Soekmekaar	156	23.28 S	29.58 E
Soela Väin ⊔	76	58.40 N	22.35 E
Soerabaja			
→ Surabaya	115a	7.15 S	112.45 E
Soest, B.R.D.	52	51.34 N	8.07 E
Soest, Ned.	52	52.09 N	5.18 E
Soestdijk	52	52.11 N	5.18 E
Soestdijk, Paleis ♥	52	52.12 N	5.16 E
Soeste ≃	52	53.10 N	7.44 E
Soesterberg	52	52.07 N	5.17 E
Soeurs, Île des I	275a	45.28 N	73.33 W
Sofádhes	38	39.20 N	22.06 E
Sofala	170	33.05 S	149.42 E
Sofia			
→ Sofija	38	42.41 N	23.19 E
Sofia ≃	157b	15.27 S	47.23 E
Sofiero	41	56.05 N	12.39 E
Sofija (Sofia)	38	42.41 N	23.19 E
Sofijevka, S.S.S.R.	78	48.04 N	33.52 E
Sofijevka, S.S.S.R.	78	46.33 N	34.03 E
Sofijevskij	83	48.12 N	38.52 E
Sofijsk, S.S.S.R.	89	51.34 N	139.52 E
Sofijsk, S.S.S.R.	89	52.15 N	133.58 E
Sofjanga	24	65.52 N	31.15 E
Sofje-Kondratjevka	83	48.18 N	38.12 E
Sofjino	82	55.30 N	38.11 E
Sofrino	82	56.09 N	37.56 E
Sofronovo	76	59.48 N	36.54 E
Sogakofe	150	6.00 N	0.36 E
Sogamoso	246	5.43 N	72.56 W
Sogamoso ≃	246	7.13 N	73.56 W
Soğanlı	267b	40.55 N	29.12 E
Soğanlı Dağları ∧∧	130	40.30 N	40.30 E
Soğanlı Geçidi)(	130	40.33 N	40.16 E
Sogcho			
→ Sŏkch'o	98	38.12 N	128.36 E
Sogda	89	50.24 N	132.12 E
Sögel	52	52.50 N	7.31 E
Sogliano al Rubicone	66	44.00 N	12.18 E
Sognafjorden C[2]	26	61.06 N	5.10 E
Søgne	26	58.05 N	7.49 E
Sogne Fjord			
→ Sognafjorden			
C[2]	26	61.06 N	5.10 E
Sogn og Fjordane			
□[6]	26	61.30 N	6.50 E
Sogod, Pil.	116	10.45 N	124.00 E
Sogod, Pil.	116	10.23 N	124.59 E
Sogod Bay C	116	10.15 N	125.02 E
Sogoža ≃	76	58.28 N	39.06 E
Söğüt	130	40.00 N	30.11 E
Söğütalan	130	40.03 N	28.34 E
Söğüt Gölü ⊜	130	37.03 N	29.53 E
Söğütlü	130	40.54 N	30.29 E
Sohāg			
→ Sawhāj	140	26.33 N	31.42 E
Sohāgpur, Bhārat	124	23.19 N	81.21 E
Sohāgpur, Bhārat	124	22.42 N	78.12 E
Soham	42	52.20 N	0.20 E
Sohano	175e	5.27 S	154.40 E
Soharkha	272a	28.35 N	77.24 E
Soheit-tinlot	56	50.29 N	5.22 E
Sohland	54	51.02 N	14.25 E
Söhlde	52	52.11 N	10.14 E
Sohna	124	28.15 N	77.04 E
Sŏhŭng	98	38.27 N	126.10 E
Sŏhwa-ri	98	38.15 N	128.13 E
Soignes, Forêt de			
◆[3]	56	50.47 N	4.25 E
Soignies (Zinnik)	50	50.35 N	4.04 E
Soignolles-en-Brie	261	48.39 N	2.42 E
Soin	150	12.47 N	3.49 W
Soindres	261	48.57 N	1.40 E
Soini	26	62.52 N	24.13 E
Sointula	182	50.38 N	127.01 W
Soisalo ∧	26	62.40 N	28.10 E
Soissons	50	49.22 N	3.20 E
Soisy-sous-			
Montmorency	261	48.59 N	2.18 E
Soisy-sur-Seine	261	48.39 N	2.27 E
Sōja	96	34.40 N	133.45 E
Sojat	120	25.55 N	73.40 E
Sojiji Temple ♥[1]	268	35.31 N	139.41 E
Sojitra	120	22.33 N	72.43 E
Sŏjosŏn-man C	98	39.20 N	124.50 E
Sojoton Point ≻	116	9.58 N	122.27 E
Sojuz Sovetskich			
Socialističeskich			
Respublik → Union			
of Soviet Socialist			
Republics □[1]	72	60.00 N	80.00 E
Sok ≃	80	53.24 N	50.08 E
Sōka, Nihon	94	35.49 N	139.48 E
Soka, Taehan	271b	37.30 N	126.48 E
Šokal'skogo, Proliv			
⊔	74	79.00 N	100.25 E
Sŏkch'o	98	38.12 N	128.36 E
Söke	130	37.45 N	27.24 E
Sokele	154	9.55 S	24.36 E
Sokhós	38	40.49 N	23.21 E
Sokna	26	60.14 N	9.54 E
Sokodé	150	8.59 N	1.08 E
Soko Islands II	100	22.10 N	113.54 E
Sokol, S.S.S.R.	76	59.28 N	40.10 E
Sokol, S.S.S.R.	89	47.14 N	142.45 E
Sokol ∧	60	49.03 N	13.31 E
Sokółka, Pol.	30	53.25 N	23.31 E
Sokolka, S.S.S.R.	80	55.34 N	51.30 E
Sokol'niki ◆[8]	265b	55.48 N	37.41 E
Sokol'niki, Park ♠	265b	55.48 N	37.41 E
Sokolo	150	14.44 N	6.08 W
Sokolov	54	50.09 N	12.40 E
Sokołów	30	50.14 N	22.07 E
Sokołów Podlaski	30	52.25 N	22.15 E
Sokone	150	13.53 N	16.22 W
Sokoto	150	13.04 N	5.16 E
Sokoto ≃	150	11.20 N	4.10 E
Sŏkp'o-ri	98	37.46 N	125.27 E
Soksa-ri	98	40.40 N	127.17 E
Sokskije Jary ∧∧[2]	80	54.10 N	51.30 E
Sol', Česko.	30	48.56 N	21.36 E
Sol, Costa del ●[2]	34	36.30 N	4.30 W
Sol, Rio do ≃	248	6.45 S	67.05 W
Sola, Nor.	26	58.53 N	5.36 E
Sola, Zaïre	154	5.09 S	27.06 E
Soła ≃	30	50.04 N	19.13 E
Solacolu	38	44.23 N	26.34 E
Sola de Vega	234	16.31 N	96.59 W
Solai	154	0.02 N	36.09 E
Solana	220	26.57 N	82.01 W
Solana Beach	228	32.59 N	117.16 W
Solander, Cape ≻	274a	34.01 S	151.14 E
Solander Island I	172	46.34 S	166.53 E
Solânea	250	6.45 S	35.39 W
Solangāri	272b	22.36 N	88.27 E
Sol'anka ≃	80	50.10 N	51.20 E
Solano	116	16.31 N	121.11 E
Solano □[6]	226	38.15 N	121.52 W
Solar, Morro ∧[2]	286d	12.11 S	77.02 W
Solarino	70	37.06 N	15.07 E
Solaro	266b	45.37 N	9.05 E
Solaro, Monte ∧	68	40.33 N	14.13 E
Solbad Hall in Tirol	64	47.17 N	11.31 E
Solberg	26	63.47 N	17.38 E
Solbiate Arno	62	45.42 N	8.48 E
Solbiate Olona	266b	45.39 N	8.53 E
Solca, Arg.	252	30.46 S	66.28 W
Solca, Rom.	38	47.42 N	25.50 E
Soldados, Cerro ∧	246	2.54 S	79.10 W
Sölde ◆[8]	263	51.31 N	7.35 E
Sol de Julio	252	29.33 S	63.27 W
Sölden	64	46.58 N	11.00 E
Sölderholz ◆[8]	263	51.29 N	7.35 E
Soldier Creek ≃	198	39.04 N	95.39 W
Soldier Field ♠	278	41.52 N	87.37 W
Soldier Key I	220	25.35 N	80.10 W
Soldier Point ≻	240c	17.02 N	61.41 W
Soldier Pond	186	47.09 N	68.35 W
Soldiers Grove	190	43.24 N	90.47 W
Soldin			
→ Myślibórz	30	52.55 N	14.52 E
Soldotna	180	60.29 N	151.04 W
Sole, Val di ∨	64	46.20 N	10.45 E
Solebury	208	40.23 N	75.02 W
Solec Kujawski	30	53.06 N	18.14 E
Soledad, Col.	246	10.55 N	74.46 W
Soledad, Calif., U.S.	226	36.26 N	121.19 W
Soledad, Ven.	246	8.10 N	63.34 W
Soledad, Cerro ∧	196	26.29 N	103.23 W
Soledad de Doblado	234	19.03 N	96.25 W
Soledad Díez			
Gutiérrez	234	22.12 N	100.57 W
Soledade	252	28.50 S	52.30 W
Soledade de Minas	256	22.04 S	45.03 W
Soledad Pass)(	228	34.30 N	118.07 W
Soleduck ≃	224	47.55 N	124.35 W
Solen	198	46.23 N	100.48 W
Solenoje, Ozero ⊜	86	55.20 N	70.05 E
Solentiname,			
Archipiélago de			
II	236	11.10 N	85.00 W
Solenzara	36	41.51 N	9.23 E
Solenzo	150	12.11 N	4.05 W
Solero	62	44.55 N	8.30 E
Solers	261	48.40 N	2.43 E
Solesmes	50	50.11 N	3.30 E
Soleure			
→ Solothurn	58	47.13 N	7.32 E
Solferino	64	45.23 N	10.34 E
Solgne	56	48.58 N	6.18 E
Solgonskij Kr'až ∧	86	55.30 N	91.00 E
Solhan Dağı ∧	84	39.46 N	43.45 E
Solheim, Nor.	26	60.53 N	5.27 E
Solheim, S. Afr.	273d	26.11 S	28.10 E
Soliera	64	44.45 N	10.55 E
Solignac-sur-Loire	62	44.58 N	3.53 E
Soligny-la-Trappe	50	48.37 N	0.32 E
Soligorsk	76	52.48 N	27.32 E
Solihull	42	52.25 N	1.45 W
Solikamsk	86	59.39 N	56.47 E
Solila	157b	21.25 S	46.37 E
Sol'-Ileck	86	51.10 N	54.59 E
Soliman	148	36.42 N	10.30 E
Solimões			
→ Amazon ≃	242	0.05 S	50.00 W
Solin ≃	50	48.02 N	2.43 E
Solingen	56		
	263	51.10 N	7.05 E
Solís, Arg.	258	34.18 S	59.20 W
Solís, Ur.	252	34.36 S	55.29 W
Solís, Presa ⊜[1]	234	20.05 N	100.36 W
Soliseño	196	26.01 N	97.48 W
Söll	64	47.30 N	12.11 E
Šollar	84	41.40 N	48.38 E
Sollas	46	57.39 N	7.21 W
Sollefteå	26	63.10 N	17.16 E
Sollenau	61	47.53 N	16.15 E
Sollentuna	40	59.28 N	17.54 E
Sóller	34	39.46 N	2.42 E
Søllerød	41	55.49 N	12.31 E
Sollerön I	26	60.55 N	14.37 E
Søllested	41	54.49 N	11.17 E
Solliès-Pont	62	43.11 N	6.03 E
Solling ∧∧	52	51.45 N	9.35 E
Söllingen	54	52.05 N	10.55 E
Solling-Vogler,			
Naturpark ♠	52	51.45 N	9.40 E
Solln ◆[8]	60	48.05 N	11.31 E
Sollom	262	53.40 N	2.50 W
Sollstedt	54	51.25 N	10.31 E
Søln ∧	26	61.55 N	11.30 E
Solna	40	59.22 N	18.01 E
Solncevo	265b	55.39 N	37.24 E
Solnhofen	56	48.53 N	10.59 E
Solo			
→ Surakarta	115a	7.35 S	110.50 E
Solo ≃	115a	6.47 S	112.33 E
Solofra	68	40.50 N	14.51 E
Sologne ◆[1]	50	47.50 N	2.00 E
Solok	112	0.48 S	100.39 E
Sololá, Guat.	236	14.46 N	91.11 W
Solola, Som.	144	0.08 N	41.30 E
Sololá □[5]	236	14.40 N	91.15 W
Solomennoje	24	61.51 N	34.19 E
Solomon, Ariz., U.S.	200	32.49 N	109.38 W
Solomon, Kans., U.S.	198	38.55 N	97.22 W
Solomon ≃	198	38.54 N	97.22 W
Solomon, North Fork			
≃	198	39.29 N	98.26 W
Solomon, South Fork			
≃	198	39.29 N	98.26 W
Solomon Basin ⊹[1]	14	7.30 S	152.00 E
Solomon Islands □[1]	14		
	175e	8.00 S	159.00 E
Solomon Islands II	14	8.00 S	159.00 E
Solomon Sea ⊤[2]	14	8.00 S	155.00 E
Solon, Bhārat	123	30.55 N	77.07 E
Solon, Iowa, U.S.	190	41.48 N	91.30 W
Solon, Maine, U.S.	188	44.57 N	69.52 W
Solon, Ohio, U.S.	214	41.22 N	81.55 W
Solonešnoje	86	51.40 N	84.21 E
Solonka	80	50.13 N	41.28 E
Sol'onoje, S.S.S.R.	78	48.13 N	34.52 E
Sol'onoje, S.S.S.R.	83	49.18 N	37.39 E
Sol'onoje, S.S.S.R.	84	44.03 N	40.53 E
Sol'onoje Ozero	78	45.53 N	34.27 E
Solonópole	250	5.44 S	39.01 W
Solon Springs	190	46.22 N	91.48 W
Solopaca	68	41.11 N	14.33 E
Solor, Kepulauan II	112	8.25 S	123.30 E
Solor, Pulau I	112	8.27 S	123.05 E
Solotča	80	54.48 N	39.51 E
Solothurn	58	47.13 N	7.32 E
Solothurn □[3]	58	47.25 N	7.35 E
Solotobe	86	44.38 N	66.05 E
Solotvin	78	48.42 N	24.25 E
Solotvina	78	47.57 N	23.52 E
Soloveckije Ostrova			
II, S.S.S.R.	24	65.05 N	35.40 E
Soloveckije Ostrova			
II, S.S.S.R.	24	65.07 N	35.53 E
Solovjevsk, S.S.S.R.	88	49.55 N	115.42 E
Solovjevsk, S.S.S.R.	89	54.14 N	124.26 E
Solovjovka	76	60.46 N	30.09 E
Sol'oy	24	58.08 N	30.20 E
Solre-le-Château	50	50.10 N	4.05 E
Solre-sur-Sambre	50	50.18 N	4.08 E
Solsona	34	41.59 N	1.31 E
Solt	30	46.48 N	19.00 E
Šolta, Otok I	36	43.23 N	16.15 E
Solṭānābād	128	36.23 N	58.02 E
Solṭānīyeh	128	36.26 N	48.48 E
Soltau	52	52.59 N	9.49 E
Solton	86	52.50 N	86.28 E
Solunto ⊥	70	38.06 N	13.32 E
Solus, Mount ∧	168a	32.28 S	116.13 E
Solutré-Pouilly	58	46.18 N	4.43 E
Solva	42	51.52 N	5.11 W
Solva ≃	42	51.52 N	5.17 W
Solvang	204	34.36 N	120.08 W
Solvarbo	40	60.24 N	15.40 E
Solvay	210	43.04 N	76.12 W
Sölvesborg	26	56.03 N	14.33 E
Sol'vyčegodsk	24	61.21 N	46.52 E
Solway Firth C[1]	44	54.50 N	3.35 W
Solwezi	154	12.11 S	26.25 E
Soly	76	54.31 N	26.11 E
Solymár	264c	47.36 N	18.56 E
Solza	24	64.33 N	39.29 E
Sōma, Nihon	92	37.48 N	140.57 E
Soma, Tür.	130	39.10 N	27.36 E
Somabula	154	19.41 S	29.41 E
Somain	50	50.22 N	3.17 E
Somalia □[1]	10		
Somali Basin ⊹[1]	12	5.00 N	53.00 E
Somalie			
→ Somalia □[1]	144	10.00 N	49.00 E
Somaliland			
→ Somalia □[1]	144	10.00 N	49.00 E
Somali Republic			
→ Somalia □[1]	144	10.00 N	49.00 E
Somaliya			
→ Somalia □[1]	144	10.00 N	49.00 E
Somalomo	152	3.23 N	12.44 E
Somang	98	41.20 N	128.54 E
Somanga	154	8.24 S	39.17 E
Sombernon	58	47.18 N	4.42 E
Sombo	152	8.42 S	20.57 E
Sombor	38	45.46 N	19.07 E
Somborn	56	50.08 N	9.07 E
Sombra	214	42.43 N	82.29 W
Sombrerete	234	23.38 N	103.39 W
Sombreretillo	196	26.19 N	99.58 W
Sombrero I	238	18.36 N	63.26 W
Sombrero Channel			
⊔	110	7.41 N	93.35 E
Sombrio	252	29.07 S	49.40 W
Sombrio, Lagoa do			
C	252	29.12 S	49.42 W
Şomcuta-Mare	38	47.31 N	23.29 E
Somenos	224	48.49 N	123.44 W
Somerdale, N.J., U.S.	208	39.51 N	75.01 W
Somerdale, Ohio,			
U.S.	214	40.34 N	81.22 W
Someren	52	51.24 N	5.44 E
Somero	26	60.37 N	23.32 E
Sõmerpalu	76	57.51 N	26.48 E
Somers, Conn., U.S.	207	41.59 N	72.27 W
Somers, Mont., U.S.	202	48.05 N	114.13 W
Somers, Wis., U.S.	216	42.38 N	87.55 W
Somersby	170	33.25 S	151.17 E
Somerset, Man., Can.	184	49.24 N	98.39 W
Somerset, Colo., U.S.	200	38.56 N	107.16 W
Somerset, Ky., U.S.	192	37.05 N	84.36 W
Somerset, Md., U.S.	284c	38.58 N	77.05 W
Somerset, Mass., U.S.	207	41.45 N	71.09 W
Somerset, N.J., U.S.	208	40.29 N	74.29 W
Somerset, Ohio, U.S.	188	39.48 N	82.18 W
Somerset, Pa., U.S.	188	40.01 N	79.05 W
Somerset, Tex., U.S.	196	29.13 N	98.40 W
Somerset, Wis., U.S.	190	45.08 N	92.40 W
Somerset □[6], Eng.,			
U.K.	42	51.08 N	3.00 W
Somerset □[6], Md.,			
U.S.	208	38.12 N	75.41 W
Somerset □[6], N.J.,			
U.S.	208	40.34 N	74.37 W
Somerset □[6], Pa.,			
U.S.	214	40.09 N	79.00 W
Somerset Airport ⊠	276	40.37 N	74.40 W
Somerset Center	216	42.03 N	84.25 W
Somerset East	158	32.42 S	25.35 E
Somerset Hills			
Airport ⊠	276	40.41 N	74.32 W
Somerset Island I,			
Ber.	240a	32.17 N	64.52 W
Somerset Island I,			
N.W. Ter., Can.	176	73.15 N	93.30 W
Somerset West	158	34.08 S	18.50 E
Somersham	42	52.23 N	0.01 E
Somers Point	208	39.20 N	74.36 W
Somersworth	188	43.16 N	70.52 W
Somerton, Eng., U.K.	42	51.03 N	2.44 W
Somerton, Ariz., U.S.	200	32.36 N	114.43 W
Somerton ◆[8]	285	40.06 N	75.01 W
Somerton Creek ≃	208	36.32 N	76.55 W
Somervell □[6]	222	32.15 N	97.45 W
Somerville, Austl.	169	38.13 S	145.10 E
Somerville, Mass.,			
U.S.	207	42.23 N	71.06 W
Somerville, N.J., U.S.	210	40.34 N	74.37 W
Somerville, Ohio,			
U.S.	218	39.34 N	84.38 W
Somerville, Tenn.,			
U.S.	194	35.15 N	89.21 W
Somerville, Tex., U.S.	222	30.21 N	96.32 W
Somerville Lake ⊜[1]	222	30.18 N	96.40 W
Someș (Szamos) ≃	38	48.07 N	22.22 E
Someșu Cald ≃	38	46.44 N	23.22 E
Someșu Mare ≃	38	47.12 N	24.12 E
Someșu Mic ≃	38	47.09 N	23.55 E
Someșu Rece ≃	38	46.44 N	23.22 E
Somino	76	59.21 N	34.52 E
Somis	228	34.16 N	119.00 W
Sŏmjin-gang ≃	98	34.58 N	127.46 E
Somma, It.	66	42.40 N	12.44 E
Somma, It.	266b	45.41 N	8.42 E
Sommacampagna	64	45.24 N	10.50 E
Somma Lombardo	62	45.41 N	8.42 E
Sommariva	166	26.24 S	146.36 E
Sommariva del Bosco	62	44.46 N	7.47 E
Sommatino	70	37.20 N	13.59 E
Somma Vesuviana	68	40.52 N	14.26 E
Somme □[5]	50	49.55 N	2.30 E
Somme ≃, Fr.	50	49.01 N	4.12 E
Somme ≃, Fr.	50	50.11 N	1.39 E
Somme, Baie de la			
C	50	50.14 N	1.33 E
Somme, Canal de la			
≍	50	50.11 N	1.39 E
Sommedieue	56	49.05 N	5.28 E
Sommelsdijk	52	51.45 N	4.09 E
Sommen ⊜	26	58.01 N	15.15 E
Sommepy-Tahure	56	49.15 N	4.33 E
Sommerberg	263	51.27 N	7.32 E
Sömmerda	54	51.10 N	11.07 E
Sommerfeld			
→ Lubsko	30	51.46 N	14.59 E
Sommersdorf	54	53.17 N	14.11 E
Sommersted	41	55.19 N	9.19 E
Sommesous	50	48.44 N	4.12 E
Somme Woods ♠	278	42.09 N	87.49 W
Somnitel'nyj	89	52.12 N	139.04 E
Somo ≃	190	45.29 N	89.48 W
Somogy □[6]	30	46.25 N	17.35 E
Somonauk	216	41.38 N	88.41 W
Somonauk Creek ≃	216	41.32 N	88.41 W
Somosierra, Puerto			
de)(	34	41.09 N	3.35 W
Somosomo	175g	16.46 S	179.58 W
Somosomo Strait ⊔	175g	16.47 S	179.58 E
Somotillo	236	13.02 N	86.55 W
Somoto	236	13.28 N	86.35 W
Somovo, S.S.S.R.	76	52.53 N	34.58 E
Somovo, S.S.S.R.	78	51.44 N	39.23 E
Sompeta	122	18.56 N	84.36 E
Somplago	64	46.21 N	13.04 E
Sompolno	30	52.24 N	18.31 E
Somport, Puerto de			
)(	34	42.48 N	0.31 W
Sompuis	50	48.41 N	4.23 E
Somuncurá, Meseta			
de ∧∧[1]	254	41.30 S	67.15 W
Somvix	58	46.44 N	8.56 E
Šomyškol'	86	46.30 N	59.53 E
Son, Ned.	52	51.31 N	5.30 E
Son, Nor.	26	59.31 N	10.42 E
Son ≃	124	25.42 N	84.52 E
Soná	236	8.01 N	81.19 W
Sona-Bata	152	4.54 S	15.09 E
Sonādugi	126	22.47 N	90.40 E
Sonaguera	236	15.38 N	86.20 W
Sonahula	124	25.05 N	87.09 E
Sonāmarg	123	34.18 N	75.18 E
Sonāmukhi	126	23.18 N	87.25 E
Sonāmura	120	23.29 N	91.17 E
Sonāpur	120	23.42 N	89.30 E
Sonar	164	2.33 S	133.00 E
Sonār ≃	124	24.24 N	79.56 E
Sonari	272c	18.52 N	72.59 E
Sonārpur	272b	22.26 N	88.25 E
Sonātikri	272b	22.57 N	88.20 E
Sonceboz	58	47.11 N	7.11 E
Sonchamp	261	48.35 N	1.53 E
Sŏnch'ŏn	98	39.48 N	124.55 E
Soncino	62	45.24 N	9.52 E
Sondags ≃	158	33.44 S	25.51 E
Sondalo	64	46.20 N	10.19 E
Sønderå ≃	41	54.53 N	8.59 E
Sønderborg	41	54.55 N	9.47 E
Sønderby	41	55.47 N	10.01 E
Sønder Felding	41	55.57 N	8.47 E
Sønderhav	41	54.51 N	9.30 E
Sønderjylland □[6]	41	55.10 N	9.15 E
Sønder Nærå	41	55.18 N	10.30 E
Sønder Omme	41	55.50 N	8.54 E
Sondershausen	54	51.22 N	10.52 E
Søndersø	41	55.29 N	10.16 E
Sondi	114	2.58 N	98.52 E
Søndre Strømfjord	176	66.59 N	50.40 W
Søndre Strømfjord			
C[2]	176	67.30 N	52.00 W
Sondrio	64	46.10 N	9.52 E
Sondrio □[4]	58	46.10 N	10.03 E
Sonduga	76	60.08 N	41.55 E
Sone ≃	126	21.34 N	86.54 E
Sonepur	120	20.50 N	83.55 E
Sonestown	210	41.21 N	76.33 W
Song, Malay.	112	2.01 N	112.33 E
Song, Nig.	146	9.50 N	12.38 E
Song, Thai	110	18.28 N	100.11 E
Songbahutun	104	41.28 N	121.11 E
Song-bay-hap, Cua			
C	110	8.46 N	104.52 E
Songbu	100	31.05 N	114.48 E
Sŏngbyŏn-ni	98	38.03 N	125.18 E
Song-cau	110	13.27 N	109.13 E
Sŏng-ch'ŏn-gang			
≃	98	39.48 N	127.35 E
Songcun	106	30.26 N	119.43 E
Songe	26	58.41 N	9.00 E
Songea	154	10.41 S	35.39 E
Songeons	50	49.33 N	1.52 E
Songfengchang	107	29.44 N	104.13 E
Songgai	107	29.03 N	105.54 E
Songgao	100	29.36 N	121.41 E
Songgato ≃	164	3.26 S	140.22 E
Songhe	100	31.10 N	113.20 E
Songhuahu ⊜	89	43.20 N	127.07 E
Songhuajiang	89	44.46 N	125.54 E
Songhuajiang ≃	89	47.44 N	132.32 E
Songhwa	98	38.21 N	125.08 E
Songino	88	48.54 N	95.49 E
Sŏngjang-ni	98	41.02 N	126.50 E
Songjiachang	107	28.47 N	104.55 E
Songjiacun	107	29.01 N	103.46 E
Songjiang	106	31.01 N	121.14 E
Songjiangzhen	98	42.12 N	126.56 E
Songjiawa	98	37.24 N	122.07 E
Songjiaying	105	40.38 N	115.14 E
Songjiayu	105	38.55 N	114.49 E
Sŏngjin			
→ Kimch'aek	98	40.41 N	129.12 E
Songjŏng	98	35.10 N	126.46 E
Sŏngju	98	35.55 N	128.16 E
Songkan	102	28.27 N	106.50 E
Songkhla	110	7.12 N	100.36 E
Songkou, Zhg.	100	24.32 N	116.24 E
Songkou, Zhg.	100	25.48 N	118.36 E
Songlinba	100	24.00 N	115.59 E
Songlindian	105	39.25 N	115.54 E
Songlingshan ∧∧	104	41.30 N	120.30 E
Songlukelujia	120	29.15 N	84.49 E
Songmen	100	28.19 N	121.34 E
Songmenshan I	100	28.18 N	121.37 E
Sŏngnae-ri	98	39.28 N	126.59 E
Sŏng-ni	98	39.38 N	127.06 E
Songnim	98	38.44 N	125.38 E
Songo	152	7.22 S	14.51 E
Songololo	152	5.42 S	14.02 E
Songot ∧	154	3.59 N	34.28 E
Songpan	102	32.40 N	103.24 E
Song Phi Nong	110	14.13 N	100.03 E
Songqigang C	100	26.25 N	119.43 E
Sŏngsa-ri	271b	37.38 N	126.52 E
Songsha	100	30.07 N	120.51 E
Songshancun	104	41.02 N	121.09 E
Songshu	98	39.50 N	122.06 E
Songshugou	105	41.02 N	117.49 E
Songtangmiao	106	31.08 N	119.16 E
Songtao	102	28.06 N	109.05 E
Songtun	98	39.54 N	123.56 E
Šonguj	24	68.47 N	33.00 E
Songu-ri	98	37.49 N	127.09 E
Songwe, Zaïre	154	12.25 S	29.40 E
Songwe, Zaïre	154	3.24 S	26.16 E
Songxi	100	26.16 N	116.59 E
Songxia	100	25.44 N	119.36 E
Songxian	102	34.10 N	112.05 E
Songyan	98	37.13 N	113.43 E
Songyang	100	28.27 N	119.29 E
Songyangzhen	102	25.24 N	102.59 E
Songyin	106	30.54 N	121.13 E
Songyinxi ≃	100	28.18 N	119.44 E
Songzhangzi	98	41.13 N	119.08 E
Songzheng	100	27.33 N	118.46 E
Songzhuang	106	32.06 N	121.17 E
Songziguan)(	100	31.17 N	115.31 E
Songzong	102	29.45 N	96.10 E
Son-ha	110	15.03 N	108.34 E
Son-hoa	110	13.02 N	108.58 E
Soni, Ehi ∧	146	20.49 N	17.23 E
Sonico	64	46.10 N	10.21 E
Soninho ≃	250	10.13 S	46.56 W
Sonīpat	124	28.59 N	77.01 E
Sonkach	124	22.59 N	76.21 E
Sonk'ol', Ozero ⊜	85	41.50 N	75.08 E
Sonkovo	76	57.47 N	37.09 E
Son-la	110	21.19 N	103.54 E
Sonmiāni	120	25.26 N	66.36 E
Sonmiāni Bay C	120	25.15 N	66.30 E
Sonnberg ∧	264b	48.20 N	16.15 E
Sonneberg	54	50.22 N	11.10 E
Sonnefeld	56	50.13 N	11.08 E
Sonnen	60	48.41 N	13.43 E
Sonnenberg ∧[2]	61	47.52 N	16.28 E
Sonnewalde	54	51.42 N	13.38 E
Sonning	42	51.29 N	0.55 W
Sonningdale	184	52.24 N	107.40 W
Sonnino	66	41.25 N	13.14 E
Sonntagberg	61	47.59 N	14.45 E
Sono	270	34.48 N	135.55 E
Sono, Rio do ≃, Bra.	250	8.58 S	48.11 W
Sono, Rio do ≃, Bra.	255	17.02 S	45.32 W
Sonobe	96	35.06 N	135.28 E
Sonogno	58	46.21 N	8.47 E
Sonoita	232	31.51 N	112.50 W
Sonoita Creek ≃	200	31.30 N	110.58 W
Sonoma	226	38.17 N	122.28 W
Sonoma □[6]	226	38.26 N	122.35 W
Sonoma Creek ≃	226	38.10 N	122.24 W
Sonoma Mountains			
∧∧	226	38.17 N	122.35 W
Sonoma Peak ∧	204	40.52 N	117.36 W
Sonoma State			
Historical Park ♠	226	38.18 N	122.28 W
Sononder	158	29.43 S	21.51 E
Sonop	158	25.39 S	27.42 E
Sonora, Calif., U.S.	226	37.59 N	120.23 W
Sonora, Tex., U.S.	196	30.34 N	100.39 W
Sonora □[3]	232	29.20 N	110.40 W
Sonora ≃	232	28.48 N	111.33 W
Sonora Desert ◆[2]	200	33.00 N	114.00 W
Sonora Pass)(	226	38.19 N	119.37 W
Sonostrov	24	66.09 N	34.10 E
Sonoyta ≃	200	31.16 N	113.26 W
Sonpăr Hills ∧∧[2]	124	24.20 N	82.15 E
Sonqor	128	34.47 N	47.36 E
Sŏnsan	98	36.16 N	128.17 E
Sonsbeck	263	51.37 N	6.22 E
Sonseca	34	39.42 N	3.57 W
Sonskyn	158	30.47 S	26.28 E
Sonsón	246	5.42 N	75.18 W
Sonsonate	236	13.43 N	89.44 W
Sonsorol Islands II	108	5.20 N	132.13 E
Sonstorp	40	58.45 N	15.36 E
Sonstraal	158	27.07 S	22.28 E
Sontag	194	31.39 N	90.12 W
Son-tay	110	21.08 N	105.30 E
Sontheim	56	49.07 N	9.11 E
Sonthofen	58	47.31 N	10.17 E
Sontra	56	51.04 N	9.56 E
Sonwān	124	27.40 N	81.45 E
Sonyea	210	42.41 N	77.50 W
Soo			
→ Sault Sainte			
Marie	190	46.30 N	84.21 W
Soochow			
→ Suzhou	106	31.18 N	120.37 E
Sooke	182	48.23 N	123.43 W
Sooke ≃	224	48.23 N	123.42 W
Sooke Basin C	224	48.23 N	123.40 W
Sooke Lake ⊜	224	48.33 N	123.42 W
Soonwald ∧∧	56	49.55 N	7.40 E
Sopachuy	248	19.29 S	64.31 W
Sopa Sopa Head ≻	164	1.58 S	146.35 E
Sopchoppy	192	30.04 N	84.29 W
Soperton	192	32.23 N	82.35 W
Sopetrán	246	6.30 N	75.46 W
Sop Hao	110	20.33 N	104.27 E
Sophia	192	37.43 N	81.15 W
Sopot	30	54.28 N	18.34 E
Sop Pong	110	22.04 N	102.03 E
Sop Prap	110	17.53 N	99.20 E
Soprabolzano	64	46.32 N	11.24 E
Sopron	61	47.41 N	16.36 E
Sopur	123	34.18 N	74.28 E
Sŏp'yŏng-ni	98	35.01 N	127.24 E
Soquel	226	36.59 N	121.57 W
Soquel Creek ≃	226	36.58 N	121.57 W
Sor, Ribeira de ≃	34	39.00 N	8.17 W
Sora	66	41.43 N	13.37 E
Sorada	122	19.45 N	84.26 E
Sorae-san ∧	271b	37.27 N	126.47 E
Soraga	64	46.22 N	11.39 E
Soragna	64	44.56 N	10.07 E
Söråker	26	62.31 N	17.30 E
Sorano	66	42.41 N	11.43 E
Šorapani	84	42.05 N	43.05 E
Soras	248	14.07 S	73.37 W
Sorata	248	15.47 S	68.40 W
Soratte, Monte ∧	66	42.15 N	12.30 E
Sorau			
→ Żary	30	51.38 N	15.09 E
Soraya	248	14.10 S	73.19 W
Sorbas	34	37.07 N	2.07 W
Šorbas, Gora ∧	86	47.25 N	84.12 E
Sörberge	26	62.31 N	17.22 E
Sorbhog	120	26.30 N	90.52 E
Sorbie	44	54.48 N	4.26 W
Sorbo ≃	85	38.45 N	69.20 E
Sorbolo	64	44.51 N	10.28 E
Sorbonne ♥[2]	261	48.51 N	2.21 E
Sorcier, Lac au ⊜	206	46.42 N	73.24 W
Sordevolo	62	45.34 N	7.59 E
Sordo ≃	234	16.30 N	97.31 W
Sore	32	44.20 N	0.35 W
Sorel	206	46.02 N	73.07 W
Sorell	166	42.47 S	147.33 E
Sorell, Cape ≻	166	42.12 S	145.10 E
Sorel Point ≻	43b	49.16 N	2.10 W
Sörenberg	58	46.50 N	8.03 E
Sorento	219	39.00 N	89.34 W
Soreq ≃	132	31.56 N	34.42 E
Soresina	64	45.17 N	9.51 E
Sorezaru Point ≻	175e	7.34 S	156.36 E
Sörfjärden C	40	59.24 N	16.50 E
Sørfjorden C[2]	26	60.24 N	6.40 E
Sørfold	24	67.28 N	15.22 E
Sörforsa	26	61.40 N	17.00 E
Sorge ≃	41	54.21 N	9.25 E
Sorgono	71	40.01 N	9.06 E
Sorgues	62	44.00 N	4.52 E
Sori	62	44.22 N	9.06 E
Soria	34	41.46 N	2.28 W
Soriano	252	33.24 S	58.19 W
Soriano □[5]	258	33.45 S	57.45 W
Soriano Calabro	68	38.36 N	16.14 E
Soriano nel Cimino	66	42.25 N	12.14 E
Sorico	58	46.10 N	9.22 E
Sorido	164	1.09 S	136.03 E
Sørli	26	64.15 N	13.45 E
Sormonne ≃	56	49.46 N	4.40 E
Sorn	46	55.30 N	4.18 W
Sorne ≃	58	47.22 N	7.22 E
Soro, Bhārat	120	21.17 N	86.40 E
Sorø, Dan.	41	55.26 N	11.34 E
Sorocaba	255	23.29 S	47.27 W
Sorocá-Buçu ≃	256	23.38 S	47.13 W
Soročinka	80	47.30 N	51.44 E
Soročinsk	80	52.26 N	53.10 E
Soročkino	86	57.02 N	68.52 E
Soroco	240m	18.22 N	65.38 W
Sorok	88	52.20 N	100.12 E
Sorok ≃	61	47.07 N	16.50 E
Soroki	78	48.09 N	28.17 E
Sorokino, S.S.S.R.	86	53.45 N	84.58 E
Sorokino, S.S.S.R.	86	54.13 N	91.31 E
Sorokino, S.S.S.R.	86	55.52 N	93.15 E
Sorokošiči	78	51.12 N	30.35 E
Soroksár ◆[8]	264c	47.24 N	19.07 E
Soroksári-Duna ≃[1]	264c	47.19 N	19.02 E
Sorol I[1]	108	8.08 N	140.23 E
Soron	124	27.53 N	78.45 E
Sorong	164	0.53 S	131.15 E
Sororó ≃	250	5.24 S	49.07 W
Sorot' ≃	76	57.04 N	28.50 E
Soroti	154	1.43 N	33.37 E
Sorovskije	86	59.53 N	71.34 E
Sørøya I	24	70.36 N	22.46 E
Sorpestausee ⊜[1]	56	51.20 N	7.56 E
Sorraia ≃	34	38.56 N	8.53 W
Sorrento, Austl.	169	38.20 S	144.45 E
Sorrento, It.	68	40.37 N	14.22 E
Sorrento, Fla., U.S.	220	28.49 N	81.34 W
Sorrento, La., U.S.	194	30.11 N	90.51 W
Sorris Sorris	156	20.57 S	14.50 E
Sør Rondane			
Mountains ∧∧	9	72.00 S	25.00 E
Sorsakoski	26	62.27 N	27.39 E
Sorsatunturi ∧	24	67.24 N	29.38 E
Sorsele	24	65.30 N	17.30 E
Sorso	71	40.48 N	8.34 E
Sorsogon	116	12.58 N	124.00 E
Sorsogon □[4]	116	12.50 N	123.55 E
Sorsogon Bay C	116	12.55 N	123.55 E
Sörstafors	40	59.35 N	16.13 E
Šorsu	85	40.17 N	70.48 E
Sort	34	42.24 N	1.08 E
Sortandy	86	51.42 N	71.00 E
Sortat	46	58.33 N	3.13 W
Sortavala	24	61.42 N	30.41 E
Sortino	70	37.09 N	15.02 E
Sortland	24	68.40 N	15.20 E
Sør-Trøndelag □[6]	26	63.00 N	10.40 E
Sorūbī	120	34.36 N	69.43 E
Sorunda	40	59.01 N	17.48 E
Sörup	54	54.43 N	9.40 E
Sörvik	40	60.11 N	15.09 E
Sorviži	80	57.52 N	48.32 E
Sosa, D.D.R.	54	50.30 N	12.39 E
Sosa, Taehan	271b	37.29 N	126.47 E
Sosai	82	56.31 N	36.05 E
Sŏsan	98	36.47 N	126.26 E
Šošar ≃	84	39.22 N	40.59 E
Sösdala	41	56.02 N	13.40 E

Symbols in the index entries represent the broad categories identified in the key at the right. Symbols with superior numbers (∧∧[2]) identify subcategories (see complete key on page *I* · 30).

Kartensymbole in dem Registerverzeichnis stellen die rechts in Schlüssel erklärten Kategorien dar. Symbole mit hochgestellten Ziffern (∧∧[2]) bezeichnen Unterabteilungen einer Kategorie (vgl. vollständiger Schlüssel auf Seite *I* · 30).

Los símbolos incluidos en el texto del índice representan las grandes categorías identificadas con la clave a la derecha. Los símbolos con numeros en su parte superior (∧∧[2]) identifican las subcategorías (véase la clave completa en la página *I* · 30).

Les symboles de l'index représentent les catégories indiquées dans la légende à droite. Les symboles suivis d'un indice (∧∧[2]) représentent des sous-catégories (voir légende complète à la page *I* · 30).

Os símbolos incluídos no texto do índice representam as grandes categorias identificadas com a chave à direita. Os símbolos com números em sua parte superior (∧∧[2]) identificam as subcategorias (veja-se a chave completa à página *I* · 30).

Symbol	English	Deutsch	Español	Français	Português
∧	Mountain	Berg	Montaña	Montagne	Montanha
∧∧	Mountains	Berge	Montañas	Montagnes	Montanhas
)(	Pass	Pass	Paso	Col	Passo
∨	Valley, Canyon	Tal, Cañon	Valle, Cañón	Vallée, Canyon	Vale, Canhão
⌒	Plain	Ebene	Llano	Plaine	Planície
C	Cape	Kap	Cabo	Cap	Cabo
I	Island	Insel	Isla	Île	Ilha
II	Islands	Inseln	Islas	Îles	Ilhas
◆	Other Topographic Features	Andere Topographische Objekte	Otros Elementos Topográficos	Autres données topographiques	Outros Elementos Topográficos

ESPAÑOL

Nombre	Página	Lat.°′	Long.°′ W=Oeste
Sos del Rey Católico	34	42.30 N	1.13 W
Sosedka	80	53.15 N	42.40 E
Sosedno	76	58.14 N	28.42 E
Sosenka ≃	265b	55.35 N	37.23 E
Sosenki	82	55.34 N	37.26 E
Sösetalsperre ◂[6]	52	51.44 N	10.20 E
Soshigaya ◂[8]	268	35.39 N	139.36 E
Sösjöfjällen Ѧ	26	63.53 N	13.15 E
Šoška	24	62.42 N	50.40 E
Soskovo	76	52.45 N	35.23 E
Sosna ≃	76	52.42 N	38.55 E
Sosneado, Cerro ∧	252	34.45 S	69.59 W
Sosnica	78	51.32 N	32.28 E
Sosnicy	76	57.38 N	30.25 E
Sosnogorsk	24	63.37 N	53.51 E
Sosnovaja Maza	80	52.30 N	47.53 E
Sosnovaja Pol'ana ◂[8]	265a	59.50 N	30.09 E
Sosnovec	24	64.26 N	34.27 E
Sosnovica	76	60.21 N	40.50 E
Sosnowiec	30	50.18 N	19.08 E
Soso	194	31.45 N	89.16 W
Sosok	112	0.17 N	110.14 E
Sospel	62	43.53 N	7.27 E
Sospirolo	64	46.09 N	12.04 E
Sossusvlei @	156	24.40 S	15.23 E
Šoštanj	61	46.23 N	15.03 E
Šostka	78	51.52 N	33.30 E
Sõsura	98	42.16 N	130.37 E
Sos'va, S.S.S.R.	72	63.40 N	62.06 E
Sos'va, S.S.S.R.	86	59.10 N	61.50 E
Sos'va ≃	86	59.32 N	62.20 E
Sosyka ≃	78	46.35 N	39.05 E
Sot' ≃	80	58.00 N	40.39 E
Sota ≃	150	11.52 N	3.24 E
Sotério ≃	248	11.36 S	65.10 W
Sotkamo	26	64.08 N	28.25 E
Sotnicyno	80	54.17 N	41.49 E
Soto de Aldovea	266a	40.26 N	3.27 W
Soto de Pajares	266a	40.17 N	3.32 W
Soto la Marina	234	23.46 N	98.13 W
Soto la Marina ≃	234	23.45 N	97.45 W
Sotomayor	248	19.18 S	65.03 W
Sotonera, Embalse de la @[1]	34	42.05 N	0.48 W
Sotouboua	150	8.34 N	0.59 E
Sottens	58	46.39 N	6.44 E
Sottern @	40	59.02 N	15.29 E
Sotteville	50	49.25 N	1.06 E
Sottile, Punta ≻	71a	35.30 N	12.38 E
Sottomarina	64	45.13 N	12.17 E
Sottrum	52	53.06 N	9.14 E
Sottunga I	26	60.08 N	20.40 E
Sotuf, Adrar Ѧ	148	22.15 N	15.40 W
Souain-Perthes-lès-Hurlus	56	49.11 N	4.32 E
Souanké	152	2.05 N	14.03 E
Soubakaniédougou	150	10.28 N	5.01 W
Soubré	150	5.47 N	6.36 W
Soudan, Austl.	166	20.05 S	137.00 E
Soudan, Minn., U.S.	190	47.49 N	92.10 W
Soudan → Sudan □[1]	140	15.00 N	30.00 E
Soude ≃	50	48.52 N	4.10 E
Soudersburg	208	40.01 N	76.09 W
Souderton	208	40.19 N	75.19 W
Souesmes	50	47.27 N	2.10 E
Soufflay	152	2.01 N	14.54 E
Soufflenheim	56	48.50 N	7.58 E
Soufflot, Lac @	190	47.24 N	78.31 W
Souflion	38	41.12 N	26.18 E
Soufrière	241f	13.52 N	61.04 W
Soufrière ∧, Guad.	241o	16.03 N	61.40 W
Soufrière ∧, St. Vin.	241h	13.20 N	61.11 W
Soufrière Bay C, Dom.	240d	15.14 N	61.22 W
Soufrière Bay C, St. Luc.	241f	13.51 N	61.04 W
Sougahatchee Creek ≃	194	32.38 N	85.50 W
Sougne-Remouchamps	56	50.29 N	5.40 E
Sougueur	148	35.12 N	1.30 E
Souhegan ≃	188	42.51 N	71.29 W
Souillac	32	44.54 N	1.29 E
Souilly	56	49.01 N	5.17 E
Souk Ahras	148	36.23 N	8.00 E
Souk-el-Arba-des-Beni-Hassan	34	35.16 N	5.20 W
Souk-el-Arba-du-Rharb	148	34.43 N	6.01 W
Souk-Khemis-du-Sahel	34	35.17 N	6.05 W
Sŏul	98		
	271b	37.33 N	126.58 E
Sŏul □[8]	98	37.34 N	127.00 E
Soulac-sur-Mer	32	45.31 N	1.07 W
Soulaines-Dhuys	58	48.22 N	4.44 E
Soulanges □[6]	206	45.20 N	74.15 W
Soulanges, Canal de ⩸	275a	45.20 N	73.58 W
Soulougou	150	13.01 N	0.23 E
Soulsbyville	226	37.59 N	120.16 W
Soultzeren	58	48.04 N	7.06 E
Soultz-Haut-Rhin	58	47.53 N	7.14 E
Soultzmatt	58	47.58 N	7.14 E
Soultz-sous-Forêts	56	48.56 N	7.53 E
Soummam, Oued ≃	34	36.45 N	5.04 E
Sound Beach	210	40.58 N	72.58 W
Sounding Creek ≃	184	52.06 N	110.28 W
Sound View Park ♠	276	40.49 N	73.52 W
Soúnion, Ákra ≻	38	37.39 N	24.02 E
Soup Harbour C	212	43.51 N	77.11 W
Souppes-sur-Loing	50	48.11 N	2.44 E
Sources, Mount aux ∧	158	28.46 S	28.52 E
Soure, Bra.	250	0.44 S	48.31 W
Soure, Port.	34	40.03 N	8.38 W
Sour el Ghozlane	148	36.10 N	3.45 E
Souris, Man., Can.	184	49.38 N	100.15 W
Souris, P.E.I., Can.	186	46.21 N	62.15 W
Souris ≃	176	49.39 N	99.34 W
Souris Plain ⌣	198	48.15 N	100.15 W
Sourlake	194	30.09 N	94.25 W
Sourland Mountain ∧[2]	188	40.29 N	74.43 W
Sourou ≃	150	12.45 N	3.25 W
Souroukaha	150	8.13 N	5.08 W
Souš	54	50.32 N	13.34 E
Sous, Oued ∨	148	30.27 N	9.31 W
Sousa	250	6.45 S	38.14 W
Sousânia	255	16.11 S	49.05 W
Sousas	256	22.52 S	46.59 W
Sousel	34	38.57 N	7.40 W
Sous-le-Vent, Îles → Leeward Islands II	238	17.00 N	63.00 W
Sousse	148	35.49 N	10.38 E
Sousse □[8]	36	35.35 N	10.30 E
Sout ≃, S. Afr.	158	31.35 S	18.24 E
Sout ≃, S. Afr.	158	33.03 S	23.28 E
South ≃, Iowa, U.S.	194	41.29 N	93.20 W
South ≃, Md., U.S.	208	38.57 N	76.29 W
South ≃, Mass., U.S.	283	42.10 N	70.43 W
South ≃, Mo., U.S.	219	39.52 N	91.26 W
South ≃, N.J., U.S.	208	40.29 N	74.23 W
South ≃, N.C., U.S.	192	34.20 N	78.03 W
South ≃, Va., U.S.	188	38.18 N	78.49 W
South ≃, Va., U.S.	208	38.02 N	77.23 W
South Acton	207	42.28 N	71.27 W
South Africa □[1]	138		
	156	30.00 S	26.00 E
Southall ◂[8]	260	51.31 N	0.23 W

FRANÇAIS

Nom	Page	Lat.°′	Long.°′ W=Ouest
South Alligator ≃	164	12.15 S	132.24 E
Southam	42	52.15 N	1.23 W
South Amboy	208	40.29 N	74.17 W
South America •[1]	4		
	18	15.00 S	60.00 W
South Amherst, Mass., U.S.	207	42.21 N	72.30 W
South Amherst, Ohio, U.S.	214	41.22 N	82.14 W
Southampton, N.S., Can.	186	45.35 N	64.15 W
Southampton, Ont., Can.	212	44.29 N	81.23 W
Southampton, Eng., U.K.	42	50.55 N	1.25 W
Southampton, Mass., U.S.	207	42.14 N	72.44 W
Southampton, N.Y., U.S.	207	40.53 N	72.24 W
Southampton, Pa., U.S.	285	40.10 N	75.03 W
Southampton □[6]	208	36.42 N	77.05 W
Southampton (Eastleigh) Airport ⊠	42	50.57 N	1.21 W
Southampton, Cape ≻	176	62.09 N	83.40 W
Southampton Island I	176	64.20 N	84.40 W
South Andaman I	110	11.45 N	92.45 E
South Anna ≃	192	37.48 N	77.25 W
South Apopka	220	28.39 N	81.31 W
Southard	208	40.08 N	74.14 W
Southards Pond @	276	40.43 N	73.20 W
South Ashburnham	207	42.37 N	71.57 W
South Aulatsivik Island I	176	56.45 N	61.30 W
South Australia □[3]	162	30.00 S	135.00 E
South Australian Basin ✢[1]	14	38.00 S	125.00 E
South Bald Mountain ∧	200	40.45 N	105.41 W
South Baldy ∧	200	33.59 N	107.11 W
South Banda Basin ✢[1]	14	6.30 S	127.00 E
Southbank	182	54.02 N	125.46 W
South Barre	207	42.23 N	72.06 W
South Barrington	278	42.06 N	88.07 W
South Barrule ∧[2]	44	54.12 N	4.40 W
South Barwon	169	38.17 S	144.30 E
South Bass Island I	214	41.39 N	82.49 W
South Bay	220	26.40 N	80.43 W
South Bay C, Man., Can.	184	56.43 N	99.00 W
South Bay C, N.W. Ter., Can.	176	63.58 N	83.30 W
South Bay C, Ont., Can.	190	45.38 N	81.50 W
South Bay C, Ont., Can.	212	44.52 N	79.47 W
South Bay C, Ont., Can.	212	43.55 N	77.03 W
South Bay C, Fla., U.S.	220	26.42 N	80.45 W
South Bay C, Va., U.S.	208	37.14 N	75.52 W
South Bay C, Wash., U.S.	224	46.53 N	124.04 W
South Baymouth	190	45.33 N	82.01 W
South Beach ♠	276	40.35 N	74.05 W
South Beacon Mountain ∧	210	41.29 N	73.57 W
South Bedias Creek ≃	222	30.54 N	95.42 W
South Bellingham	207	42.03 N	71.28 W
South Belmar	208	40.10 N	74.02 W
South Beloit	216	42.29 N	89.02 W
South Bend, Ind., U.S.	216	41.41 N	86.15 W
South Bend, Wash., U.S.	224	46.40 N	123.48 W
South Benfleet	42	51.33 N	0.34 E
South Bentinck Arm C	182	52.15 N	126.15 W
South Bethlehem	214	41.00 N	79.20 W
South Bihar Plains ⌣	124	25.15 N	84.30 E
South Bloomfield	218	39.43 N	82.59 W
Southborough, Eng., U.K.	42	51.10 N	0.15 E
Southborough, Mass., U.S.	207	42.18 N	71.31 W
South Bosque ≃	222	31.29 N	97.16 W
South Boston	192	36.42 N	78.54 W
South Boston ◂[8]	283	42.20 N	71.03 W
South Bound Brook	276	40.33 N	74.32 W
South Branch, Newf., Can.	186	47.55 N	59.02 W
South Branch, N.J., U.S.	276	40.33 N	74.42 W
South Brent	42	50.25 N	3.50 W
Southbridge, N.Z.	172	43.49 S	172.15 E
Southbridge, Mass., U.S.	207	42.05 N	72.02 W
South Britain	207	41.28 N	73.15 W
Southbrook, Austl.	171a	27.41 S	151.43 E
Southbrook, N.Z.	172	43.20 S	172.36 E
South Brook ≃	285	39.52 N	75.44 W
South Brookfield	186	44.23 N	64.58 W
South Brooklyn ◂[8]	276	40.41 N	73.59 W
South Bruny I	166	43.23 S	147.17 E
South Burlington	188	44.28 N	73.13 W
Southbury	207	41.29 N	73.13 W
South Butler	210	43.08 N	76.46 W
South Byfield	283	42.45 N	70.54 W
South Byron	210	43.03 N	78.04 W
South Cairo	210	42.17 N	73.57 W
South Canaan	210	41.30 N	75.25 W
South Cape ≻	175g	17.01 S	179.55 E
South Carolina □[3]	178		
	192	34.00 N	81.00 W
South Carver	207	41.51 N	70.54 W
South Castor ≃	212	45.15 N	75.23 W
South Cave	44	53.46 N	0.35 W
South Chagrin Reservation ♠	279a	41.25 N	81.25 W
South Channel Ʉ	116	14.20 N	120.37 E
South Channel ≃[1]	281	42.32 N	82.40 W
South Chaplin	207	41.46 N	72.09 W
South Charleston, Ohio, U.S.	218	39.50 N	83.38 W
South Charleston, W. Va., U.S.	188	38.22 N	81.44 W
South Chatham	207	41.41 N	70.01 W
South Chelmsford	283	42.34 N	71.23 W
South Chicago ◂[8]	278	41.44 N	87.33 W
South China Basin ✢[1]	12	15.00 N	115.00 E
South China Sea ⊤[2]	108	10.00 N	113.00 E
South Cle Elum	224	47.10 N	120.56 W
South Coast Botanic Garden ♠	280	33.47 N	118.21 W
South Coatesville	208	39.58 N	75.49 W
South Concho ≃	196	31.21 N	100.28 W
South Corinth	210	43.12 N	73.51 W
South Corning	210	42.07 N	77.02 W
South Creek ≃	170	33.36 S	150.50 E
Southcrest	273d	26.15 S	28.07 E
South Dakota □[3]	178		
	198	44.15 N	100.00 W
South Dandalup ≃	168a	32.35 S	115.53 E
South Darenth	260	51.24 N	0.15 E

PORTUGUÊS

Nome	Página	Lat.°′	Long.°′ W=Oeste
South Dartmouth	207	41.36 N	70.57 W
South Dayton	210	42.22 N	79.03 W
South Deerfield	207	42.29 N	72.37 W
South Dennis, Mass., U.S.	207	41.41 N	70.09 W
South Dennis, N.J., U.S.	208	39.11 N	74.49 W
South Dorset	210	43.13 N	73.04 W
South Dorset Downs Ѧ[1]	42	50.40 N	2.25 W
South Dos Palos	226	36.58 N	120.39 W
South Downs Ѧ[1]	42	50.55 N	0.25 W
South Dum-Dum	126	22.37 N	88.25 E
South Duxbury	207	42.01 N	70.41 W
South East □[5]	156	25.00 S	25.45 E
Southeast Asia Treaty Organization Headquarters ⊽	269a	13.45 N	100.31 E
South East Cape ≻, Austl.	166	43.39 S	146.50 E
Southeast Cape ≻, Alaska, U.S.	180	62.55 N	169.42 W
South-Eastern □[3]	150	6.00 N	8.30 E
South East Mountain ∧	241k	12.05 N	61.40 W
Southeast Newfoundland Ridge ✢[3]	8	40.00 N	47.00 W
South Easton	207	42.03 N	71.05 W
Southeast Pacific Basin ✢[1]	6	60.00 S	115.00 W
South East Point ≻	174o	1.40 N	157.10 W
South Egg Harbor	208	39.31 N	74.39 W
South Egremont	207	42.10 N	73.25 W
South Elgin	216	41.59 N	88.18 W
South Elkhorn Creek ≃	218	38.13 N	84.48 W
South El Monte	280	34.03 N	118.02 W
Southend	44	55.20 N	5.38 W
Southend Municipal Airport ⊠	42	51.34 N	0.41 E
Southend-on-Sea	42		
	260	51.33 N	0.43 E
Southend-on-Sea □[8]	260	51.33 N	0.41 E
Southend Pier ◂[5]	260	51.31 N	0.44 E
South English ≃	190	41.30 N	91.56 W
Southern □[4], Malawi	154	15.30 S	35.00 E
Southern □[4], S.L.	150	8.00 N	12.15 W
Southern □[4], Zam.	154	16.00 S	27.00 E
Southern Alps Ѧ	172	43.30 S	170.30 E
Southern California, University of ⊽[2]	280	34.02 N	118.17 W
Southern Cross	162	31.13 S	119.19 E
Southern Division □[5]	175f	19.30 S	169.00 E
Southern Ghāts Ѧ	122	9.30 N	77.00 E
Southern Highlands □[5]	164	6.00 S	143.30 E
Southern Indian Lake @	176	57.10 N	98.40 W
Southern Leyte □[4]	116	10.50 N	124.55 E
Southern Lueti ≃	152	16.14 S	23.13 E
Southern Pines	192	35.11 N	79.24 W
Southern Ute Indian Reservation ◂[4]	200	37.05 N	107.45 W
Southern View	219	39.46 N	89.39 W
Southern Yemen → Yemen, People's Democratic Republic of □[1]	144	15.00 N	48.00 E
Southery	42	52.32 N	0.23 E
South Esk ≃, Austl.	166	41.25 S	147.08 E
South Esk ≃, Scot., U.K.	46	56.42 N	2.32 W
South Esk ≃, Scot., U.K.	46	55.53 N	3.04 W
Southesk Tablelands Ѧ[1]	162	20.50 S	126.40 E
South Essex	207	42.38 N	70.46 W
South Euclid	214	41.31 N	81.32 W
Southey	184	50.56 N	104.30 W
South Fabius ≃	219	39.54 N	91.30 W
South Fallsburg	210	41.43 N	74.38 W
South Farmbridge	260	51.38 N	0.41 E
South Farmingdale	276	40.44 N	73.27 W
Southfield, Mass., U.S.	207	42.06 N	73.14 W
Southfield, Mich., U.S.	216	42.29 N	83.17 W
Southfields	210	41.15 N	74.11 W
South Fiji Basin ✢[1]	14	27.00 S	176.00 E
South Fiji Ridge ✢[3]	14	23.00 S	179.00 W
Southfleet	260	51.25 N	0.19 E
South Floral Park	276	40.43 N	73.42 W
South Fontana	228	34.05 N	117.24 W
South Foreland ≻	42	51.09 N	1.23 E
South Fork, Colo., U.S.	200	37.40 N	106.37 W
South Fork, Pa., U.S.	214	40.22 N	78.48 W
South Fort George	182	53.54 N	122.45 W
South Forty Foot Drain ⩸	42	52.56 N	0.15 W
South Fox Island I	190	45.25 N	85.50 W
South Fulton	194	36.30 N	88.53 W
South Gate, Calif., U.S.	228	33.57 N	118.12 W
Southgate, Fla., U.S.	220	27.18 N	82.32 W
Southgate, Mich., U.S.	216	42.12 N	83.13 W
Southgate, Wash., U.S.	224	47.10 N	122.30 W
Southgate ◂[8]	260	51.38 N	0.08 W
Southgate ◂[9]	279a	41.25 N	81.32 W
South Georgia I	244	54.15 S	36.45 W
South Germiston	273d	26.15 S	28.10 E
South Gibson	210	41.44 N	75.38 W
South Glamorgan □[6]	42	51.30 N	3.25 W
South Glastonbury	207	41.40 N	72.36 W
South Glens Falls	210	43.18 N	73.39 W
South Grafton	207	42.11 N	71.42 W
South Grand ≃	194	38.18 N	93.28 W
South Grand Island Bridge ◂[5]	284a	43.00 N	78.56 W
South Green	260	51.37 N	0.26 E
South Greensburg	214	40.17 N	79.33 W
South Hackensack	276	40.52 N	74.03 W
South Hadley	207	42.16 N	72.35 W
South Hadley Falls	207	42.14 N	72.36 W
South Hamilton	207	42.37 N	70.53 W
South Hams ⌣	42	50.22 N	3.50 W
South Hanningfield	260	51.39 N	0.31 E
South Hanover	283	42.06 N	70.51 W
South Hartford	210	43.21 N	73.25 W
South Harwich	207	41.41 N	70.03 W
South Hātia Island I	124	22.19 N	91.07 E
South Haven, Ind., U.S.	216	41.33 N	87.08 W
South Haven, Kans., U.S.	198	37.03 N	97.24 W
South Haven, Mich., U.S.	216	42.24 N	86.16 W
South Hayling	42	50.47 N	0.59 W
South Head ≻	274a	33.50 S	151.17 E
South Heart ≃	182	55.34 N	116.11 W
South Hempstead	276	40.41 N	73.37 W
South Henderson	192	36.17 N	78.25 W
South Henik Lake @	176	61.30 N	97.30 W
South Hero	188	44.39 N	73.19 W
South Hill, N.Y., U.S.	210	42.25 N	76.33 W
South Hill, Va., U.S.	192	36.44 N	78.08 W
South Hills ◂[8]	273d	26.15 S	28.05 E
South Hills Village ◂[9]	279b	40.21 N	80.03 W
South Hingham	207	42.11 N	70.53 W
South Hogan Creek ≃	218	39.03 N	84.54 W
South Holland	216	41.37 N	87.37 W
South Holston Lake @[1]	192	36.35 N	82.00 W
South Honcut Creek ≃	226	39.19 N	121.35 W
South Honshu Ridge ✢[3]	14	18.00 N	143.00 E
South Hopkinton	207	41.24 N	71.45 W
South Horr	154	2.06 N	36.55 E
South Houston	222	29.40 N	95.14 W
South Huntington	276	40.49 N	73.26 W
South Indian Basin ✢[1]	9	60.00 S	120.00 E
South Indian Lake	184	56.46 N	98.57 W
Southington, Conn., U.S.	207	41.36 N	72.53 W
Southington, Ohio, U.S.	214	41.19 N	80.57 W
South International Falls	190	48.35 N	93.24 W
South Ionia	216	42.57 N	85.04 W
South Island I, Bhārat	122	10.03 N	72.17 E
South Island I, Kenya	154	2.38 N	36.36 E
South Island I, N.Z.	172	43.00 S	171.00 E
South Island I, P.I.T.T.	175c	6.59 N	151.59 E
South Islet I	116	8.44 N	119.49 E
South Jacksonville	219	39.44 N	90.12 W
South Kemptville Creek ≃	212	44.54 N	75.41 W
South Kenosha	216	42.33 N	87.51 W
South Kensington Museums ⊽	260	51.30 N	0.11 W
South Kent	207	41.41 N	73.28 W
South Kirkby	44	53.34 N	1.20 W
South Konkan Hills Ѧ[2]	122	17.00 N	73.30 E
South Korea → Korea, South □[1]	98	36.30 N	128.00 E
South Laguna	228	33.30 N	117.45 W
Southlake	222	32.57 N	97.09 W
South Lake @, Ont., Can.	212	44.26 N	76.13 W
South Lake @, Fla., U.S.	220	28.37 N	80.52 W
South Lake Tahoe	226	38.57 N	119.57 W
South Lancaster	207	42.27 N	71.41 W
Southland, Ky., U.S.	218	38.01 N	84.31 W
Southland, Mich., U.S.	216	42.13 N	84.24 W
Southland, Tex., U.S.	196	33.22 N	101.33 W
Southland ◂[9]	282	37.39 N	122.06 W
Southlawn, Ill., U.S.	219	39.45 N	89.37 W
South Lawn, Md., U.S.	284c	38.48 N	76.59 W
South Lebanon	218	39.22 N	84.13 W
South Lee	207	42.17 N	73.17 W
South Lima	210	42.51 N	77.41 W
South Line Island I	276	40.37 N	73.30 W
South Llano ≃	196	30.30 N	99.46 W
South Lockport	284a	43.09 N	78.42 W
South Loup ≃	198	41.04 N	98.40 W
South Luconia Shoals ✢[2]	112	5.03 N	112.33 E
South Lynnfield	283	42.31 N	71.00 W
South Lyon	216	42.28 N	83.39 W
South MacMillan ≃	180	63.03 N	133.18 W
South Magnetic Pole ◂	9	66.40 S	140.10 E
South Malosmadulu Atoll I[1]	122	5.10 N	72.58 E
South Manitou Island I	190	45.01 N	86.07 W
South Marsh Island I	208	38.06 N	76.02 W
South Medford	202	42.18 N	122.50 W
South Media	285	39.54 N	75.23 W
South Melbourne	274b	37.50 S	144.57 E
South Merrimack	207	42.49 N	71.34 W
South Miami	220	25.42 N	80.17 W
South Miami Heights	220	25.37 N	80.25 W
South Middleboro	207	41.45 N	70.50 W
South Milford	216	41.32 N	85.16 W
South Mills	192	36.27 N	76.20 W
South Milwaukee	216	42.55 N	87.52 W
South Mimms	260	51.42 N	0.14 W
Southminster	42	51.40 N	0.50 E
South Modesto	226	37.38 N	120.58 W
South Mokelumne ≃	226	38.08 N	121.35 W
South Molton	42	51.01 N	3.50 W
South Monroe	216	41.54 N	83.25 W
Southmont	214	40.18 N	78.56 W
South Montrose	210	41.48 N	75.53 W
South Moose Lake @	184	53.46 N	100.08 W
South Mountain	208	39.51 N	77.29 W
South Mountain ∧, U.S.	208	39.40 N	77.30 W
South Mountain ∧, Idaho, U.S.	202	42.44 N	116.54 W
South Mountain Reservation ♠	276	40.45 N	74.18 W
South Nahanni ≃	176	61.03 N	123.20 W
South Naknek	180	58.43 N	157.05 W
South Nation ≃	206	45.35 N	75.06 W
South Negril Point ≻	241q	18.15 N	78.22 W
South New Berlin	210	42.32 N	75.23 W
South New Castle	214	40.58 N	80.21 W
South New River Canal ⩸	220	26.04 N	80.12 W
South Ninepin Island I	271d	22.15 N	114.21 E
South Norfolk → Chesapeake	208	36.43 N	76.15 W
South Norwalk Reservoir @[1]	276	41.11 N	73.27 W
South Norwood ◂[8]	260	51.24 N	0.04 W
South Nutfield	260	51.14 N	0.08 W
South Nyack	276	41.05 N	73.55 W
South Ockendon	42	51.32 N	0.18 E
South Ogden	200	41.12 N	111.59 W
Southold	207	41.04 N	72.26 W
South Onondaga	210	42.56 N	76.13 W
South Orange	276	40.45 N	74.15 W
South Orkney Islands II	9	60.35 S	45.30 W
South Oroville	226	39.30 N	121.33 W
South Otselic	210	42.39 N	75.46 W
Southowram	262	53.43 N	1.50 W
South Oxhey	260	51.38 N	0.23 W
South Oyster Bay C	276	40.38 N	73.28 W
South Palo Duro Creek ≃	196	36.06 N	101.29 W
South Para ≃	168b	34.36 S	138.45 E
South Paris	188	44.13 N	70.31 W
South Park, Calif., U.S.	226	38.25 N	122.42 W
South Park, Ill., U.S.	216	41.44 N	88.18 W
South Park ♠, N.Y., U.S.	284a	42.50 N	78.50 W
South Park ♠, Pa., U.S.	279b	40.19 N	80.01 W
South Pasadena, Calif., U.S.	280	34.07 N	118.10 W
South Pasadena, Fla., U.S.	220	27.46 N	82.43 W
South Pass)(	200	42.22 N	108.55 W
South Pass Ʉ	175c	7.14 N	151.48 E
South Passage Ʉ	171a	27.22 S	153.26 E
South Patrick Shores	220	28.12 N	80.35 W
South Pekin	190	40.30 N	89.39 W
South Pender	224	48.45 N	123.14 W
South Pender Island I	224	48.45 N	123.10 W
South Perth	168a	31.59 S	115.52 E
South Petherton	42	50.58 N	2.49 W
South Philadelphia ◂[8]	285	39.56 N	75.10 W
South Philipsburg	214	40.53 N	78.13 W
South Pittsburg	194	35.01 N	85.42 W
South Plainfield	210	40.35 N	74.25 W
South Platte ≃	198	41.07 N	100.42 W
South Platte, North Fork ≃	200	39.25 N	105.10 W
South Point ≻, Ba.	238	22.50 N	74.52 W
South Point ≻, Barb.	241g	13.02 N	59.31 W
South Point ≻, Pil.	116	10.24 N	122.30 E
South Pole ◂	9	90.00 S	0.00
South Porcupine	190	48.28 N	81.13 W
Southport, Austl.	171a	27.58 S	153.25 E
Southport, Eng., U.K.	44	53.39 N	3.01 W
Southport, Conn., U.S.	207	41.08 N	73.17 W
Southport, Fla., U.S.	194	30.17 N	85.39 W
Southport, Ind., U.S.	218	39.40 N	86.09 W
Southport, N.C., U.S.	192	33.55 N	78.01 W
Southport, N.Y., U.S.	210	42.03 N	76.49 W
South Portland	188	43.38 N	70.15 W
South Portsmouth	218	38.44 N	83.00 W
South Pottstown	208	40.14 N	75.39 W
South Prairie Creek ≃	224	47.08 N	122.10 W
South Raisin ≃	206	45.08 N	74.35 W
South Range	190	47.04 N	88.39 W
South Renovo	214	41.19 N	77.45 W
South Reservoir @[1]	283	42.27 N	71.07 W
South Revelstoke	182	50.48 N	118.11 W
South Ribble □[8]	262	53.45 N	2.42 W
South River, Ont., Can.	190	45.45 N	79.25 W
South River, N.J., U.S.	208	40.27 N	74.23 W
South Rockwood	216	42.04 N	83.16 W
South Ronaldsay I	46	58.46 N	2.58 W
South Roxana	219	38.50 N	90.04 W
South Royalston	207	42.38 N	72.09 W
South Rukuru ≃	154	10.46 S	34.14 E
South Russell	214	41.25 N	81.21 W
South Salmara	124	25.55 N	90.01 E
South Salt Lake	200	40.43 N	111.53 W
South Sand Bluff ≻	158	31.19 S	30.01 E
South Sandwich Islands II	18	57.45 S	26.30 W
South Sandwich Trench ✢[1]	18	57.00 S	25.00 W
South Sandy Creek ≃	212	43.43 N	76.12 W
South San Francisco	226	37.39 N	122.24 W
South San Gabriel	280	34.04 N	118.05 W
South San Jose Hills	280	34.01 N	117.55 W
South San Ramon Creek ≃	282	37.42 N	121.55 W
South Santiam ≃	202	44.41 N	123.00 W
South Saskatchewan ≃	184	53.15 N	105.05 W
South Saugeen ≃	212	44.08 N	81.02 W
South Seaville	208	39.11 N	74.46 W
South Setauket	210	40.54 N	73.06 W
South Shafter	226	35.28 N	122.42 W
South Shetland Islands II	9	62.00 S	58.00 W
South Shields	44	55.00 N	1.25 W
South Shore	218	38.43 N	82.59 W
South Shore ◂[8]	278	41.46 N	87.35 W
South Shore Mall ◂[9]	276	40.44 N	73.15 W
South Shore Plaza ◂[9]	283	42.13 N	71.01 W
Southside	174h	2.49 S	171.43 W
South Side ◂[8]	279b	40.26 N	79.58 W
Southside Place	222	29.42 N	95.26 W
South Sioux City	198	42.28 N	96.24 W
South Skunk ≃	190	41.15 N	92.02 W
South Slocan	182	49.28 N	117.32 W
South Solon	218	39.44 N	83.37 W
South Sound Ʉ	48	53.02 N	9.28 W
South Spicer Island I	176	68.06 N	79.13 W
South Standard	219	39.21 N	89.47 W
South Sterling	210	41.17 N	75.21 W
South Stickney	278	41.45 N	87.46 W
South Stony Brook	276	40.53 N	73.07 W
South Stradbroke Island I	171a	27.51 S	153.25 E
South Streator	216	41.06 N	88.50 W
South Suburban → Behāla	126	22.31 N	88.19 E
South Sulphur ≃	196	33.23 N	95.18 W
South Sunday Creek ≃	202	46.27 N	105.54 W
South Superior	200	41.46 N	108.58 W
South Swansea	207	41.43 N	71.12 W
South Taranaki Bight C[3]	172	39.40 S	174.10 E
South Tasmania Rise ✢[3]	14	47.00 S	147.00 E
South Temple	208	40.24 N	75.55 W
South Thompson ≃	182	50.41 N	120.21 W
South Toms River	208	39.56 N	74.13 W
South Torrington	198	42.03 N	104.11 W
South Towanda	210	41.45 N	76.27 W
South Turkeyfoot Creek ≃	216	41.25 N	83.58 W
South Turlock	226	37.29 N	120.51 W
South Tuscon	200	32.12 N	110.58 W
South Twillingate Island I	186	49.37 N	54.47 W
South Tyne ≃	44	54.59 N	2.08 W
South Ubian	116	5.11 N	120.30 E
South Uist I	46	57.15 N	7.21 W
South Umpqua ≃	202	43.20 N	123.25 W
South Valley	210	42.42 N	74.43 W
South Valley Hills Ѧ[2]	285	40.00 N	75.40 W
South Valley Stream	276	40.38 N	73.44 W
South Venice	220	27.03 N	82.24 W
South Ventana Cone ∧	204	36.17 N	121.38 W
South Vernon	214	40.23 N	82.23 W
South Vestal	210	42.01 N	76.00 W
South Vietnam → Vietnam □[1]	108	16.00 N	108.00 E
Southview	214	40.20 N	80.16 W
South Vijayapuri	122	16.49 N	79.33 E
South Wabasca Lake @	182	55.54 N	113.45 W
South Wales	210	42.43 N	78.35 W
South Walpole	283	42.06 N	71.16 W
Southwark ◂[8]	42	51.30 N	0.06 W
South Warren Reservoir @[1]	168b	34.43 S	138.55 E
South Waverly	210	42.00 N	76.32 W
South Weald	260	51.37 N	0.16 E
South Wellfleet	207	41.55 N	69.58 W
South Wellington	224	49.06 N	123.53 W
Southwest	214	40.12 N	79.32 W
South West Bay C	240b	25.00 N	77.32 W
Southwest Branch ≃	284c	38.53 N	76.48 W
South Westbury	276	40.45 N	73.35 W
South West Cape ≻, Austl.	166	43.34 S	146.02 E
Southwest Cape ≻, N.Z.	172	47.17 S	167.28 E
Southwest Cape ≻, Alaska, U.S.	180	63.18 N	171.27 W
Southwest Cape ≻, Vir. Is., U.S.	241n	17.41 N	64.54 W
Southwest Channel Ʉ	220	27.34 N	82.45 W
South West City	194	36.31 N	94.37 W
South Westerlo	210	42.27 N	74.02 W
Southwest Greensburg	214	40.17 N	79.33 W
Southwest Harbor	188	44.17 N	68.20 W
Southwest Indian Ridge ✢[3]	10	32.00 S	58.00 E
Southwest Miramichi ≃	186	46.58 N	65.35 W
Southwest Museum ⊽	280	34.06 N	118.13 W
Southwest Pacific Basin ✢[1]	14	42.00 S	166.00 W
Southwest Point ≻, Ba.	238	25.51 N	77.13 W
South West Point ≻, Kiribati	174o	1.52 N	157.33 W
Southwest Point ≻, Pap. N. Gui.	164	2.14 S	146.34 E
Southwest Road Ʉ	240m	18.20 N	65.00 W
South Weymouth	283	42.10 N	70.57 W
South Weymouth Naval Air Station ■	207	42.09 N	70.57 W
South Whitley	216	41.05 N	85.38 W
South Whittier	280	33.56 N	118.03 W
South Wichita ≃	196	33.43 N	99.29 W
Southwick, Eng., U.K.	42	50.50 N	0.13 W
Southwick, Mass., U.S.	207	42.03 N	72.46 W
South Williamson	192	37.40 N	82.16 W
South Williamsport	210	41.14 N	77.01 W
South Wilmington	216	41.10 N	88.17 W
South Windham	188	43.44 N	70.26 W
South Windsor	207	41.49 N	72.37 W
Southwold	42	52.20 N	1.40 E
Southwood	210	42.59 N	76.08 W
Southwood Acres	207	41.59 N	72.32 W
South Woodham Ferrers	42	51.39 N	0.37 E
South Woodslee	214	42.14 N	82.43 W
South Woodstock	207	41.56 N	71.58 W
Southworth	224	47.31 N	122.30 W
South Yadkin ≃	192	35.45 N	80.27 W
South Yamhill ≃	224	45.13 N	123.08 W
South Yarmouth	207	41.40 N	70.10 W
South Yorkshire □[6]	44	53.30 N	1.15 W
South Yuba ≃	226	39.17 N	121.12 W
South Zeal	42	50.44 N	3.54 W
Soutpan	158	28.43 S	26.04 E
Soutpansberg Ѧ	156	22.55 S	29.30 E
Souvigny	32	46.32 N	3.11 E
Souzy-la-Briche	261	48.32 N	2.09 E
Sovata	38	46.35 N	25.04 E
Soverato	68	38.41 N	16.33 E
Sovere	64	45.49 N	10.01 E
Sovereign Mountain ∧	180	62.08 N	148.36 W
Soveria Mannelli	68	39.05 N	16.22 E
Sövestad	41	55.30 N	13.47 E
Sovetabad	85	40.14 N	69.44 E
Sovetašen, S.S.S.R.	84	40.06 N	44.33 E
Sovetašen, S.S.S.R.	84	39.50 N	45.03 E
Sovetka	83	47.30 N	39.15 E
Sovetsk, S.S.S.R.	76	53.56 N	37.39 E
Sovetsk (Tilsit), S.S.S.R.	76	55.05 N	21.53 E
Sovetsk, S.S.S.R.	80	57.37 N	48.58 E
Sovetskaja, S.S.S.R.	80	49.00 N	42.07 E
Sovetskaja, S.S.S.R.	84	44.46 N	41.11 E
Sovetskaja, S.S.S.R.	84	44.02 N	44.03 E
Sovetskaja Gavan'	89	48.58 N	140.18 E
Sovetskich Oficerov, Pik ∧	85	38.26 N	73.18 E
Sovetskij, S.S.S.R.	76	60.32 N	28.41 E
Sovetskij, S.S.S.R.	78	45.20 N	34.56 E
Sovetskij, S.S.S.R.	80	56.46 N	48.32 E
Sovetskij, S.S.S.R.	85	38.02 N	69.35 E
Sovetskij, S.S.S.R.	86	51.04 N	56.29 E
Sovetskoje, S.S.S.R.	78	50.21 N	39.01 E
Sovetskoje, S.S.S.R.	80	51.27 N	46.44 E
Sovetskoje, S.S.S.R.	84	43.19 N	43.36 E
Sovetskoje, S.S.S.R.	84	42.52 N	45.41 E
Sovetskoje, S.S.S.R.	85	42.17 N	70.15 E
Šovgenovskij	78	45.02 N	40.14 E
Sovicille	66	43.17 N	11.13 E
Sovico	266b	45.39 N	9.16 E
Soviet Union → Union of Soviet Socialist Republics □[1]	72	60.00 N	80.00 E
Søvik	26	62.33 N	6.18 E
Søvind	41	55.54 N	10.01 E
Sovpolje	24	65.18 N	43.55 E
Sow ≃	42	52.48 N	2.00 W
Sowek	164	0.49 S	135.30 E
Sowerby, Eng., U.K.	44	54.13 N	1.21 W
Sowerby, Eng., U.K.	262	53.42 N	1.56 W
Sowerby Bridge	44	53.43 N	1.54 W
Soweto ◂[8]	273d	26.14 S	27.54 E
Sowjetisches Ehrenmal ⊥	264a	52.29 N	13.28 E
Sowjetunion → Union of Soviet Socialist Republics □[1]	72	60.00 N	80.00 E
Soy	56	50.17 N	5.31 E
Soya'	144	0.01 N	42.20 E
Sōya-kaikyō → La Perouse Strait Ʉ	89	45.45 N	142.00 E
Sōya-misaki ≻	92a	45.31 N	141.56 E
Soyang-gang ≃	98	37.52 N	127.40 E
Soyapango	236	13.42 N	89.09 W
Soyers Lake @	212	45.02 N	78.37 W
Soyet	124	24.12 N	76.10 E
Soyland Moor ◂[3]	262	53.40 N	2.02 W
Soyons	62	44.53 N	4.51 E
Sož ≃, S.S.S.R.	78	51.57 N	30.48 E
Soz' ≃, S.S.S.R.	82	56.48 N	36.44 E
Sozimskij	24	59.44 N	52.16 E
Šožma	24	61.56 N	40.15 E
Sozopol	38	42.25 N	27.42 E
Sozzago	266b	45.24 N	8.43 E
Spa	56	50.30 N	5.52 E
Space Needle ⊽	224	47.38 N	122.23 W
Spadafora	70	38.13 N	15.22 E
Spada Lake @[1]	224	47.57 N	121.40 W
Spaden	52	53.34 N	8.38 E
Spahl	56	50.39 N	9.55 E
Spaichingen	58	48.04 N	8.44 E
Spain □[1]	22		
	34	40.00 N	4.00 W
Spakenburg	52	52.15 N	5.23 E
Spalato → Split	36	43.31 N	16.27 E
Spalding, Austl.	166	33.30 S	138.37 E
Spalding, Sask., Can.	184	52.20 N	104.30 W
Spalding, Eng., U.K.	42	52.47 N	0.10 W

Symbol	English	Deutsch	Español	Français	Português
≃	River	Fluss	Río	Rivière	Rio
⩸	Canal	Kanal	Canal	Canal	Canal
ʟ	Waterfall, Rapids	Wasserfall, Stromschnellen	Cascada, Rápidos	Chute d'eau, Rapides	Cascata, Rápidos
Ʉ	Strait	Meeresstrasse	Estrecho	Détroit	Estreito
C	Bay, Gulf	Bucht, Golf	Bahía, Golfo	Baie, Golfe	Baía, Golfo
@	Lake, Lakes	See, Seen	Lago, Lagos	Lac, Lacs	Lago, Lagos
≋	Swamp	Sumpf	Pantano	Marais	Pântano
ᴙ	Ice Features, Glacier	Eis- und Gletscherformen	Accidentes Glaciales	Formes glaciaires	Acidentes Glaciares
⊤	Other Hydrographic Features	Andere Hydrographische Objekte	Otros Elementos Hidrográficos	Autres données hydrographiques	Outros Elementos Hidrográficos
✢	Submarine Features	Untermeerische Objekte	Accidentes Submarinos	Formes de relief sous-marin	Acidentes Submarinos
□	Political Unit	Politische Einheit	Unidad Politica	Entité politique	Unidade Política
⊽	Cultural Institution	Kulturelle Institution	Institución Cultural	Institution culturelle	Instituição Cultural
⊥	Historical Site	Historische Stätte	Sitio Histórico	Site historique	Sitio Histórico
♠	Recreational Site	Erholungs- und Ferienort	Sitio de Recreo	Centre de loisirs	Sítio de Lazer
⊠	Airport	Flughafen	Aeropuerto	Aéroport	Aeroporto
■	Military Installation	Militäranlage	Instalación Militar	Installation militaire	Instalação Militar
◂	Miscellaneous	Verschiedenes	Misceláneo	Divers	Miscelânea

ENGLISH / DEUTSCH

Name	Page (Seite)	Lat.°′ (Breite°′)	Long.°′ (Länge°′ E=Ost)
Spalding, Mo., U.S.	219	39.38 N	91.32 W
Spalding, Nebr., U.S.	198	41.41 N	98.22 W
Spálené Poříčí	60	49.37 N	13.36 E
Spalt	56	49.10 N	10.55 E
Spam Island I	174h	2.48 S	171.43 W
Spanaway	224	47.06 N	122.26 W
Spandau ⇠[8]	264a	52.32 N	13.12 E
Spandau, Berliner Forst ⇠[3]	264a	52.35 N	13.11 E
Spang	41	54.56 N	9.50 E
Spangenberg	56	51.07 N	9.40 E
Spangler	214	40.39 N	78.47 W
Spaniard's Bay	186	47.37 N	53.17 W
Spanien → Spain □[1]	34	40.00 N	4.00 W
Spanish	190	46.12 N	82.21 W
Spanish ≃	190	46.11 N	82.19 W
Spanish Camp	222	29.23 N	96.10 W
Spanish Fork	200	40.07 N	111.39 W
Spanish Lake	219	38.47 N	90.13 W
Spanish North Africa □[2]	34		
	134	35.53 N	5.19 W
Spanish Peak ∧	202	44.24 N	119.46 W
Spanish Point ≻	240a	32.18 N	64.48 W
Spanish Sahara → Western Sahara □[2]	134	24.30 N	13.00 W
Spanish Town	241q	17.59 N	76.57 W
Spannberg	61	48.27 N	16.44 E
Sparbach	264b	48.04 N	16.11 E
Spargi, Isola I	71	41.14 N	9.21 E
Sparkford	42	51.02 N	2.34 W
Sparkill	276	41.02 N	73.56 W
Sparkle Lake	210	41.18 N	73.47 W
Sparkman	194	33.55 N	92.51 W
Sparks, Ga., U.S.	192	31.11 N	83.26 W
Sparks, Nev., U.S.	226	39.32 N	119.45 W
Sparland	190	41.02 N	89.26 W
Sparlingville	214	42.58 N	82.30 W
Sparneck	54	50.09 N	11.50 E
Sparreholm	40	59.04 N	16.49 E
Sparrow Bush	210	41.23 N	74.43 W
Sparrow Lake ⊜	212	44.49 N	79.24 W
Sparrowpit	262	53.19 N	1.52 W
Sparrows Point	208	39.14 N	76.29 W
Sparrows Point ≻	284b	39.12 N	76.30 W
Sparta, Ont., Can.	212	42.42 N	81.05 W
Sparta → Spárti, Ellás	38	37.05 N	22.27 E
Sparta, Ga., U.S.	192	33.17 N	82.58 W
Sparta, Ill., U.S.	194	38.07 N	89.42 W
Sparta, Ky., U.S.	218	38.41 N	84.55 W
Sparta, Mich., U.S.	190	43.10 N	85.42 W
Sparta, N.J., U.S.	210	41.02 N	74.38 W
Sparta, N.C., U.S.	192	36.30 N	81.07 W
Sparta, Ohio, U.S.	214	40.24 N	82.42 W
Sparta, Tenn., U.S.	194	35.56 N	85.29 W
Sparta, Wis., U.S.	190	43.57 N	90.47 W
Sparta Brook ≃	276	41.08 N	73.52 W
Spartak, Sad ♠	265a	59.51 N	30.30 E
Sparta Lake	210	41.03 N	74.34 W
Spartanburg, Ind., U.S.	218	40.04 N	84.51 W
Spartanburg, S.C., U.S.	192	34.57 N	81.55 W
Spartansburg	214	41.49 N	79.41 W
Spartel, Cap ≻	148	35.48 N	5.56 W
Spárti (Sparta)	38	37.05 N	22.27 E
Spartivento, Capo ≻, It.	68	37.55 N	16.04 E
Spartivento, Capo ≻, It.	71	38.53 N	8.50 E
Spass	82	55.55 N	35.55 E
Spassk-Dal'nij	89	44.37 N	132.48 E
Spasskij	86	53.42 N	59.12 E
Spasskij Zavod	86	49.32 N	73.17 E
Spasskoje, S.S.S.R.	76	53.06 N	36.24 E
Spasskoje, S.S.S.R.	80	55.52 N	45.42 E
Spasskoje, S.S.S.R.	82	54.05 N	38.28 E
Spassk-R'azanskij	80	54.24 N	40.23 E
Spas-Zaulok	82	56.29 N	36.34 E
Spáta	267c	38.00 N	21.31 E
Spátha, Ákra ≻	38	35.42 N	23.44 E
Spaulding	219	39.52 N	89.32 W
Spaulding, Lake ⊜[1]	226	39.20 N	120.37 W
Speaks	222	29.15 N	96.42 W
Spean, Glen ∨	46	56.53 N	4.45 W
Spean Bridge	46	56.53 N	4.54 W
Spear, Cape ≻	186	47.32 N	52.32 W
Spearfish	198	44.30 N	103.52 W
Spearman	196	36.12 N	101.12 W
Spearsville	218	39.21 N	86.11 W
Spearville	198	37.51 N	99.45 W
Spearwood	168a	32.07 S	115.47 E
Speas Artemidos (Rock Tombs) ⊥	142	27.54 N	30.52 E
Spechtsbrunn	54	50.30 N	11.14 E
Speckhorn ⇠[8]	263	51.39 N	7.11 E
Spectacle Island I	283	42.19 N	70.59 W
Spectrum ♠	285	39.54 N	75.10 W
Spectrum Range ⛰	180	57.30 N	130.40 W
Spednic Lake ⊜	186	45.36 N	67.35 W
Speed	218	38.25 N	85.45 W
Speed ≃	212	43.23 N	80.22 W
Speedway	218	39.47 N	86.15 W
Speicher	58	47.24 N	9.27 E
Speichersee ⊜	60	48.13 N	11.45 E
Speightstown	241g	13.15 N	59.39 W
Speigletown	210	42.48 N	73.38 W
Speikkogel ∧	61	47.14 N	15.03 E
Speinshart	60	49.47 N	11.49 E
Speising ⇠[8]	264b	48.10 N	16.17 E
Speke ⇠[8]	262	53.21 N	2.51 W
Speke Hall ⊥	262	53.20 N	2.52 W
Speldorf ⇠[8]	263	51.25 N	6.52 E
Spellen	263	51.37 N	6.37 E
Spello	66	42.59 N	12.40 E
Spelthorne □[8]	260	51.25 N	0.28 W
Spelve, Loch C	46	56.22 N	5.46 W
Spenard	180	61.11 N	149.55 W
Spence Bay	176	69.32 N	93.31 W
Spencer, Ind., U.S.	194	39.17 N	86.46 W
Spencer, Iowa, U.S.	198	43.09 N	95.09 W
Spencer, Mass., U.S.	207	42.15 N	71.59 W
Spencer, Nebr., U.S.	198	42.53 N	98.42 W
Spencer, N.C., U.S.	192	35.37 N	80.26 W
Spencer, N.Y., U.S.	210	42.13 N	76.30 W
Spencer, Ohio, U.S.	214	41.06 N	82.07 W
Spencer, S. Dak., U.S.	198	43.44 N	97.36 W
Spencer, Tenn., U.S.	194	35.45 N	85.28 W
Spencer, W. Va., U.S.	188	38.48 N	81.21 W
Spencer, Wis., U.S.	190	44.46 N	90.18 W
Spencer, Cape ≻, Austl.	166	35.18 S	136.53 E
Spencer, Cape ≻, N.B., Can.	186	45.12 N	65.55 W
Spencer, Cape ≻, Alaska, U.S.	180	58.14 N	136.40 W
Spencer, Mount ∧	224	49.03 N	124.38 W
Spencer, Point ≻	180	65.18 N	166.50 W
Spencer Brook ≃	283	42.28 N	71.22 W
Spencer Creek ≃, Ont., Can.	212	43.17 N	79.54 W
Spencer Creek ≃, Mo., U.S.	219	39.33 N	91.20 W
Spencer Field ⊠	281	42.31 N	83.33 W
Spencer Gulf C	166	34.00 S	137.00 E
Spencer Lake ⊜	224	47.16 N	122.57 W
Spencerport	210	43.11 N	77.48 W
Spencertown	210	42.20 N	73.33 W
Spencerville, Ont., Can.	212	44.51 N	75.33 W
Spencerville, Ind., U.S.	216	41.19 N	84.54 W
Spencerville, Ohio, U.S.	216	40.42 N	84.21 W
Spences Bridge	182	50.25 N	121.21 W
Spenge	52	52.08 N	8.28 E
Spennymoor	44	54.42 N	1.35 W
Spenser Mountains ⛰	172	42.15 S	172.30 E
Sperenberg	54	52.08 N	13.22 E
Sperillen ⊜	26	60.28 N	10.03 E
Sperkhiós ≃	38	38.52 N	22.34 E
Sperling	224	49.08 N	122.33 W
Sperlonga	66	41.15 N	13.26 E
Spermaceti Cove C	276	40.26 N	73.59 W
Sperone, Capo ≻	71	38.57 N	8.25 E
Sperrin Mountains ⛰	48	54.50 N	7.05 W
Sperry Creek ≃	279a	41.29 N	81.53 W
Sperry Rand Corporation ⊍[3]	276	40.45 N	73.42 W
Sperryville	188	38.39 N	78.14 W
Spessart ⇠[1]	56	50.10 N	9.20 E
Spessart, Naturpark ♠	56	49.50 N	9.25 E
Spesutie Island I	208	39.27 N	76.05 W
Spétsai I	38	37.16 N	23.08 E
Spevakovka	83	49.03 N	38.54 E
Spexard	52	51.52 N	8.24 E
Spey ≃	46	57.40 N	3.06 W
Spey Bay C	46	57.41 N	3.00 W
Speyer	56	49.19 N	8.26 E
Speyerbach ≃	56	49.19 N	8.27 E
Speyside	241r	11.18 N	60.32 W
Spezia → La Spezia	62	44.07 N	9.50 E
Spezzano Albanese	68	39.40 N	16.19 E
Spezzano della Sila	68	39.18 N	16.20 E
Spiazzo	64	46.07 N	10.40 E
Spiceland	218	39.50 N	85.26 W
Spicer	198	45.14 N	94.56 W
Spicer Creek ≃	284a	43.02 N	78.53 W
Spicer Meadow Reservoir ⊜[1]	226	38.23 N	119.59 W
Spicheren	56	49.12 N	6.58 E
Spickard	194	40.14 N	93.35 W
Spicket ≃	283	42.42 N	71.09 W
Spiegelau	60	48.55 N	13.22 E
Spieka	52	53.45 N	8.35 E
Spiekeroog I	52	53.46 N	7.42 E
Spiess Seamount ⇠[3]	8	54.40 S	0.15 E
Spiez	58	46.41 N	7.39 E
Spijkenisse	52	51.21 N	4.20 E
Špikov	78	48.46 N	28.35 E
Spilamberto	64	44.32 N	11.01 E
Spilimbergo	64	46.07 N	12.54 E
Spilinga	68	38.37 N	15.54 E
Spillersboda	40	59.42 N	18.51 E
Spillimacheen ≃	182	50.55 N	116.20 W
Spinazzola	68	40.58 N	16.06 E
Spīn Būldak	120	31.01 N	66.24 E
Spincourt	32	49.20 N	5.40 E
Spindale	192	35.22 N	81.55 W
Spindoli	66	43.12 N	12.54 E
Spinea	64	45.29 N	12.10 E
Spinetta Marengo	62	44.53 N	8.41 E
Spinnerstown	208	40.26 N	75.26 W
Spinoso	68	40.16 N	15.58 E
Spires → Speyer	56	49.19 N	8.26 E
Spirit Lake, Idaho, U.S.	202	47.58 N	116.52 W
Spirit Lake, Iowa, U.S.	198	43.26 N	95.06 W
Spirit Lake, Wash., U.S.	224	46.16 N	122.09 W
Spirit Lake ⊜	224	46.16 N	122.08 W
Spirit River	182	55.47 N	118.50 W
Spiritwood	184	53.22 N	107.31 W
Spiro	194	35.16 N	94.37 W
Spirovo	76	57.26 N	34.59 E
Spišská Nová Ves	30	48.57 N	20.34 E
Spitak	84	40.51 N	44.16 E
Spital am Pyhrn	61	47.39 N	14.20 E
Spithead ≻	42	50.45 N	1.05 W
Spit Point ≻	162	20.02 S	119.00 E
Spitsbergen I	12	78.45 N	16.00 E
Spitsbergen Bank ⇠[3]	10	76.00 N	23.00 E
Spittal an der Drau	64	46.48 N	13.30 E
Spittal of Glenshee	46	56.48 N	3.28 W
Spitz	61	48.22 N	15.25 E
Spitzbergen und Jan Mayen → Svalbard and Jan Mayen □[2]	10	78.00 N	20.00 E
Spitzer-Berg ∧[2]	264a	52.38 N	13.35 E
Spjelkavik	26	62.28 N	6.23 E
Splavnucha	80	51.05 N	45.22 E
Splendora	222	30.14 N	95.10 W
Split	36	43.31 N	16.27 E
Split, Cape ≻	186	45.20 N	64.30 W
Split Lake ⊜	184	56.08 N	96.15 W
Split Rock, Rapides ᒪ	275a	45.19 N	73.57 W
Split Rock Creek ≃	198	43.34 N	96.35 W
Splitrock Reservoir ⊜[1]	276	40.58 N	74.27 W
Spluga, Passo della (Splügenpass))(	58	46.30 N	9.20 E
Splügen	58	46.33 N	9.20 E
Splügenpass (Passo della Spluga))(	58	46.30 N	9.20 E
Spodsbjerg	41	54.56 N	10.50 E
Spofford	196	29.11 N	100.25 W
Spoģi	76	56.05 N	26.44 E
Spokane	202	47.40 N	117.23 W
Spokane ≃	202	47.44 N	118.20 W
Spokane, Mount ∧	202	47.55 N	117.07 W
Spokane Indian Reservation ⇠[4]	202	47.55 N	118.00 W
Spokojnaja	84	44.15 N	41.25 E
Špola	78	49.01 N	31.24 E
Spoleto	66	42.44 N	12.44 E
Spoltore	66	42.27 N	14.08 E
Spondigna	64	46.38 N	10.37 E
Spondon	42	52.54 N	1.25 W
Sponds Hill ∧[2]	262	53.19 N	2.03 W
Spóng	110	13.27 N	105.34 E
Spoon ≃	190	40.18 N	90.04 W
Spooner	190	45.50 N	91.53 W
Spořice	54	50.26 N	13.25 E
Spornitz	54	53.24 N	11.43 E
Spornoje	74	62.20 N	151.03 E
Sporovo	76	52.25 N	25.20 E
Spørring	41	56.18 N	10.09 E
Sportforum ♠	264a	52.33 N	13.29 E
Sport Hill	207	41.14 N	73.16 W
Sporting Hill	208	40.09 N	76.26 W
Sportsman's Park Race Track ♠	278	41.50 N	87.46 W
Spotorno	62	44.14 N	8.25 E
Spot Pond ⊜	283	42.27 N	71.06 W
Spotswood, Austl.	274b	37.50 S	144.53 E
Spotswood, N.J., U.S.	208	40.23 N	74.23 W
Spotsylvania	208	38.12 N	77.35 W
Spotsylvania □[6]	208	38.15 N	77.30 W
Spotsylvania Court House Battlefield (1864) ⊥	208	38.15 N	77.35 W
Sprague, Man., Can.	184	49.02 N	95.38 W
Sprague, Wash., U.S.	202	47.18 N	117.59 W
Sprague ≃	202	42.34 N	121.51 W
Sprague, North Fork ≃	202	42.26 N	121.07 W
Sprague, South Fork ≃	202	42.26 N	121.07 W
Spragueville	207	41.53 N	71.32 W
Sprain Ridge Park ♠	276	40.59 N	73.51 W
Sprankle Mills	214	41.00 N	79.07 W
Spratly Island I	108	8.38 N	111.55 E
Spratt Point ≻	212	44.36 N	80.01 W
Spray	202	44.50 N	119.48 W
Spray Lakes Reservoir ⊜[1]	182	50.55 N	115.20 W
Spreča ≃	38	44.45 N	18.06 E
Spreckels	226	36.36 N	121.34 W
Spreckelsville	229a	20.54 N	156.25 W
Spree ≃	54	52.32 N	13.13 E
Spreenhagen	54	52.20 N	13.52 E
Spreeufontein	158	33.22 S	20.45 E
Spremberg	54	51.34 N	14.22 E
Sprendlingen, B.R.D.	56	50.01 N	8.41 E
Sprendlingen, B.R.D.	56	49.51 N	7.59 E
Spresiano	64	45.46 N	12.16 E
Spring	222	30.09 N	95.25 W
Spring ≃, U.S.	194	36.52 N	94.44 W
Spring ≃, Ark., U.S.	194	36.08 N	91.05 W
Spring, South Fork ≃	194	36.19 N	91.30 W
Spring Arbor	216	42.12 N	84.34 W
Spring Bay C	200	41.40 N	112.50 W
Springbok	156	29.43 S	17.55 E
Springboro, Ohio, U.S.	218	39.33 N	84.15 W
Springboro, Pa., U.S.	214	41.48 N	80.22 W
Spring Branch ≃	284b	39.26 N	76.35 W
Springbrook, Ont., Can.	275b	43.39 N	79.47 W
Springbrook, Md., U.S.	284c	39.03 N	77.00 W
Spring Brook, N.Y., U.S.	210	42.49 N	78.40 W
Spring Brook ≃, Ill., U.S.	278	41.58 N	87.59 W
Spring Brook ≃, N.J., U.S.	276	40.53 N	74.35 W
Springburn	172	43.40 S	171.28 E
Spring City, Pa., U.S.	208	40.11 N	75.33 W
Spring City, Tenn., U.S.	192	35.42 N	84.52 W
Spring City, Utah, U.S.	200	39.29 N	111.30 W
Spring Coulee ∨	198	48.31 N	100.54 W
Spring Creek, N.Z.	172	41.28 S	173.58 E
Spring Creek, Pa., U.S.	214	41.53 N	79.32 W
Spring Creek ≃, Austl.	166	24.12 S	140.58 E
Spring Creek ≃, U.S.	198	40.30 N	101.21 W
Spring Creek ≃, Ga., U.S.	192	30.54 N	84.45 W
Spring Creek ≃, Ill., U.S.	216	40.49 N	87.50 W
Spring Creek ≃, Ill., U.S.	219	39.52 N	89.37 W
Spring Creek ≃, Ill., U.S.	278	41.32 N	88.04 W
Spring Creek ≃, Mo., U.S.	219	38.21 N	91.10 W
Spring Creek ≃, Nev., U.S.	204	39.55 N	117.50 W
Spring Creek ≃, N. Dak., U.S.	198	47.15 N	101.48 W
Spring Creek ≃, Pa., U.S.	214	40.56 N	77.47 W
Spring Creek ≃, Pa., U.S.	214	41.24 N	78.57 W
Spring Creek ≃, S. Dak., U.S.	198	43.52 N	113.00 W
Spring Creek ≃, S. Dak., U.S.	198	45.54 N	100.18 W
Spring Creek ≃, Tex., U.S.	222	30.02 N	95.16 W
Springdale, Newf., Can.	186	49.30 N	56.04 W
Springdale, Ark., U.S.	194	36.11 N	94.08 W
Springdale, Ohio, U.S.	218	39.17 N	84.28 W
Springdale, Pa., U.S.	214	40.33 N	79.46 W
Springdale, S.C., U.S.	192	33.57 N	81.06 W
Springdale, Utah, U.S.	200	37.11 N	113.00 W
Springdale, Wash., U.S.	202	48.04 N	117.45 W
Spring Dale, W. Va., U.S.	192	37.53 N	80.48 W
Springe	52	52.12 N	9.32 E
Springer	196	36.22 N	104.36 W
Springers Brook ≃	285	39.44 N	74.41 W
Springerville	200	34.08 N	109.17 W
Springfield, N.B., Can.	186	46.01 N	67.03 W
Springfield, Ont., Can.	212	42.50 N	80.56 W
Springfield, N.Z.	172	43.20 S	171.55 E
Springfield, S. Afr.	158	29.02 S	22.53 E
Springfield, Colo., U.S.	198	37.24 N	102.37 W
Springfield, Fla., U.S.	194	30.09 N	85.37 W
Springfield, Ga., U.S.	192	32.22 N	81.18 W
Springfield, Ill., U.S.	219	39.47 N	89.40 W
Springfield, Ky., U.S.	194	37.41 N	85.13 W
Springfield, Mass., U.S.	207	42.07 N	72.36 W
Springfield, Mich., U.S.	216	42.20 N	85.15 W
Springfield, Minn., U.S.	198	44.14 N	94.59 W
Springfield, Mo., U.S.	194	37.14 N	93.17 W
Springfield, N.J., U.S.	276	40.43 N	74.19 W
Springfield, Ohio, U.S.	218	39.56 N	83.49 W
Springfield, Oreg., U.S.	202	44.03 N	123.01 W
Springfield, Pa., U.S.	285	39.55 N	75.24 W
Springfield, S.C., U.S.	192	33.30 N	81.17 W
Springfield, S. Dak., U.S.	198	42.49 N	97.54 W
Springfield, Tenn., U.S.	194	36.31 N	86.52 W
Springfield, Vt., U.S.	188	43.18 N	72.29 W
Springfield, Va., U.S.	284c	38.45 N	77.13 W
Springfield, Lake ⊜[1]	219	39.44 N	89.36 W
Springfield Center	210	42.50 N	74.53 W
Springfield Lake ⊜	285	40.11 N	75.00 W
Springfield Lake ⊜[1]	222	31.36 N	96.33 W
Springfield Plateau ⛰[1]	194	37.10 N	93.30 W
Springfontein	158	30.19 S	25.36 E
Spring Garden	246	6.59 N	58.31 W
Spring Garden Brook ≃	276	40.46 N	74.23 W
Spring Garden Township	208	39.57 N	76.44 W
Spring Glen, Fla., U.S.	192	30.18 N	81.36 W
Spring Glen, N.Y., U.S.	210	41.40 N	74.26 W
Spring Glen, Pa., U.S.	208	40.38 N	76.37 W
Spring Green	190	43.11 N	90.04 W
Spring Grove, Ill., U.S.	216	42.26 N	88.13 W
Spring Grove, Minn., U.S.	190	43.33 N	91.38 W
Spring Grove, Pa., U.S.	208	39.52 N	76.52 W
Springhill, N.S., Can.	186	45.39 N	64.03 W
Spring Hill, Calif., U.S.	226	39.15 N	121.03 W
Spring Hill, Fla., U.S.	220	28.29 N	82.35 W
Springhill, La., U.S.	194	33.00 N	93.28 W
Spring Hill, Pa., U.S.	214	40.23 N	78.40 W
Spring Hill, Tenn., U.S.	194	35.45 N	86.56 W
Spring Hill, Tex., U.S.	222	32.34 N	94.48 W
Spring Hills	216	40.16 N	83.22 W
Spring Hope	192	35.57 N	78.06 W
Springhouse	182	51.55 N	122.07 W
Spring Lake, Mich., U.S.	216	43.04 N	86.11 W
Spring Lake, N.J., U.S.	208	40.09 N	74.02 W
Spring Lake, N.C., U.S.	192	35.10 N	78.58 W
Spring Lake ⊜, Mich., U.S.	216	43.06 N	86.11 W
Spring Lake ⊜, N.J., U.S.	276	40.35 N	74.25 W
Spring Lake Heights	208	40.09 N	74.04 W
Spring Mill, Ohio, U.S.	214	40.54 N	82.36 W
Spring Mill, Pa., U.S.	285	40.04 N	75.17 W
Spring Mill Reservoir ⊜[1]	262	53.39 N	2.13 W
Spring Mills	210	40.51 N	77.34 W
Spring Mill State Park ♠	218	38.43 N	86.25 W
Spring Mount	208	40.17 N	75.28 W
Spring Mountains ⛰	204	36.10 N	115.40 W
Spring Pond ⊜	283	42.30 N	70.57 W
Springport, Ind., U.S.	218	40.03 N	85.24 W
Springport, Mich., U.S.	216	42.22 N	84.42 W
Spring Run	214	40.09 N	83.47 W
Springs	158	26.13 S	28.25 E
Springs Aerodrome ⊠	273d	26.15 S	28.24 E
Springside	285	40.04 N	74.51 W
Springs Junction	172	42.19 S	172.11 E
Springs Stadium ♠	273d	26.15 S	28.26 E
Springsure	166	24.07 S	148.05 E
Springton	168b	34.43 S	139.05 E
Springtown	222	32.58 N	97.41 W
Springvale, Austl.	162	17.48 S	127.41 E
Springvale, Austl.	166	23.33 S	140.42 E
Springvale, Austl.	169	37.57 S	145.09 E
Springvale, Maine, U.S.	188	43.28 N	70.48 W
Springvale South	274b	37.58 S	145.09 E
Spring Valley, Calif., U.S.	228	32.45 N	116.59 W
Spring Valley, Ill., U.S.	190	41.20 N	89.12 W
Spring Valley, Minn., U.S.	190	43.41 N	92.23 W
Spring Valley, N.Y., U.S.	210	41.07 N	74.03 W
Spring Valley, Ohio, U.S.	218	39.37 N	84.01 W
Spring Valley, Tex., U.S.	222	29.47 N	95.31 W
Spring Valley, Wis., U.S.	190	44.51 N	92.14 W
Spring Valley ∨	204	39.15 N	114.25 W
Spring Valley Creek ≃	204	39.20 N	114.25 W
Springview	198	42.49 N	99.45 W
Springville, Ala., U.S.	194	33.46 N	86.30 W
Springville, Calif., U.S.	204	36.08 N	118.49 W
Springville, Iowa, U.S.	190	42.03 N	91.27 W
Springville, N.J., U.S.	285	39.56 N	74.52 W
Springville, N.Y., U.S.	210	42.31 N	78.40 W
Springville, Pa., U.S.	210	41.42 N	75.55 W
Springville, Utah, U.S.	200	40.10 N	111.37 W
Springwater	210	42.38 N	77.36 W
Springwood	170	33.42 S	150.33 E
Sprint ≃	44	54.22 N	2.45 W
Sprite Creek ≃	210	43.08 N	74.44 W
Sproat Lake ⊜	182	49.16 N	125.03 W
Sprockhövel	56	51.22 N	7.15 E
Sprogels Run ≃	285	40.14 N	75.37 W
Sprogø I	41	55.20 N	10.58 E
Sprottau → Szprotawa	30	51.34 N	15.33 E
Sprötze	52	53.18 N	9.49 E
Sproul	214	40.16 N	78.28 W
Sprout Brook ≃	276	40.54 N	74.05 W
Spruce Brook	186	48.45 N	58.11 W
Spruce Creek	214	40.37 N	78.08 W
Spruce Creek ≃	210	43.07 N	74.46 W
Spruce Grove	182	53.32 N	113.55 W
Spruce Knob ∧	188	38.42 N	79.32 W
Spruce Knob-Seneca Rocks National Recreation Area ♠	188	38.50 N	79.20 W
Spruce Lake	184	53.32 N	109.14 W
Spruce Mountain ∧, Ariz., U.S.	200	34.28 N	112.24 W
Spruce Mountain ∧, Nev., U.S.	204	40.33 N	114.49 W
Spruce Pine	192	35.55 N	82.04 W
Spruce Run Reservoir ⊜[1]	210	40.40 N	74.57 W
Spruce Run State Park ♠	210	40.40 N	74.56 W
Spruce Woods Provincial Park ♠	184	49.42 N	99.05 W
Spry	208	39.55 N	76.41 W
Spry Lake ⊜	212	44.44 N	81.15 W
Spulico, Capo ≻	68	39.58 N	16.39 E
Spurfield	182	55.13 N	114.16 W
Spurn Head ≻	44	53.34 N	0.07 E
Spurr, Mount ∧	180	61.18 N	152.15 W
Sputendorf	264a	52.20 N	13.13 E
Spuzzum	182	49.41 N	121.25 W
Spy Hill	184	50.36 N	101.41 W
Spy Pond ⊜	283	42.24 N	71.09 W
Squally Channel ⩌	182	53.10 N	129.15 W
Squamish	182	49.42 N	123.09 W
Squamish ≃	182	49.45 N	123.09 W
Squam Lake ⊜	188	43.45 N	71.32 W
Square Butte Creek ≃	198	46.55 N	100.55 W
Square Lake ⊜	186	47.03 N	68.20 W
Squatteck	186	47.53 N	68.43 W
Squaw Cap Mountain ∧	186	47.53 N	66.53 W
Squaw Creek ≃, Idaho, U.S.	202	43.51 N	116.22 W
Squaw Creek ≃, Ill., U.S.	278	42.21 N	88.07 W
Squaw Creek ≃, Oreg., U.S.	202	44.27 N	121.20 W
Squaw Harbor	180	55.11 N	160.30 W
Squaw Hill ∧	200	41.48 N	105.02 W
Squaw Island I	284a	42.56 N	78.54 W
Squaw Peak ∧, Calif., U.S.	226	39.11 N	120.16 W
Squaw Peak ∧, Mont., U.S.	202	47.10 N	114.21 W
Squaw Rapids	184	53.41 N	103.20 W
Squaw Rapids Dam ⇠[6]	184	53.40 N	103.25 W
Squaw Run ≃	279b	40.29 N	79.52 W
Squaw Valley State Recreation Area ♠	226	39.12 N	120.15 W
Squibnocket Point ≻	207	41.18 N	70.47 W
Squilax	182	50.52 N	119.35 W
Squillace	68	38.47 N	16.31 E
Squillace, Golfo di C	68	38.50 N	16.50 E
Squinzano	68	40.26 N	18.03 E
Squire	192	37.14 N	81.36 W
Squires, Mount ∧	162	26.12 S	127.28 E
Squirrel ≃	180	66.57 N	160.27 W
Squirrel Hill ⇠[8]	279b	40.26 N	79.55 W
Squirrel Hill Tunnel ⇠[5]	279b	40.26 N	79.55 W
Squirrel's Heath ⇠[8]	260	51.35 N	0.13 E
Sragen	115a	7.26 S	111.02 E
Šramkovka	78	50.10 N	32.05 E
Srbija □[3]	38	44.00 N	21.00 E
Srbija □[9]	38	43.00 N	21.00 E
Srbobran	38	45.33 N	19.48 E
Srê Âmběl	110	11.07 N	103.46 E
Sredinnyj Chrebet ⛰	74	56.00 N	158.00 E
Sredna Gora ⛰	38	42.30 N	25.00 E
Sredn'aja Achtuba	80	48.43 N	44.52 E
Sredn'aja Mokla ≃	88	55.01 N	119.37 E
Srednaja Nanaki, Golec ∧	89	52.26 N	132.50 E
Sredn'aja Ol'okma	88	55.26 N	120.33 E
Srednegorje	76	60.34 N	29.25 E
Sredneje Kujto, Ozero ⊜	24	65.08 N	31.15 E
Srednekolymsk	74	67.27 N	153.41 E
Srednerusskaja Vozvyšennost' ⛰[1]	72	52.00 N	38.00 E
Srednesibirskoje Ploskogorje ⛰[1]	74	65.00 N	105.00 E
Srednij Ikorec	78	51.05 N	39.45 E
Srednij Kalar	88	55.51 N	117.24 E
Srednij Oseredok, Ostrov I	80	45.50 N	48.30 E
Srednij Ural ⛰	86	58.00 N	59.00 E
Srednij Urgal	89	51.09 N	132.59 E
Srednij Vas'ugan	86	59.16 N	78.15 E
Srednyj	83	48.09 N	39.50 E
Srê Khtŭm	110	12.10 N	106.52 E
Śrem	30	52.08 N	17.01 E
Srê Moăt	110	13.18 N	107.10 E
Sremska Mitrovica	38	44.58 N	19.37 E
Sremski Karlovci	38	45.12 N	19.57 E
Srêng ≃	110	13.21 N	103.27 E
Srêpŏk ≃	110	13.33 N	106.16 E
Sretensk	88	52.15 N	117.43 E
Sretenskoje	88	56.28 N	96.25 E
Srīdharpur	126	23.04 N	89.25 E
Sri Dūngargarh	120	28.05 N	74.00 E
Sri Gangānagar	123	29.55 N	73.53 E
Sri Hargobindpur	123	31.41 N	75.39 E
Srīkākulam	122	18.18 N	83.54 E
Sri Karanpur	123	29.50 N	73.27 E
Sri Lanka □[1]	118		
	122	7.00 N	81.00 E
Sri Lanka I	122	7.00 N	81.00 E
Sri Mohangarh	120	27.17 N	71.14 E
Srīnagar, Bhārat	123	34.05 N	74.49 E
Srīnagar, Bhārat	124	30.13 N	78.47 E
Srīnagar, Bngl.	126	23.32 N	90.18 E
Srīnagar Airport ⊠	123	34.00 N	74.52 E
Srīpur, Bngl.	126	24.12 N	90.29 E
Srīpur, Bngl.	126	23.36 N	89.24 E
Srirāmpur	272b	22.49 N	88.29 E
Srīrangam	122	10.52 N	78.41 E
Sri Thep ⊥	110	16.25 N	101.04 E
Srīvardhan	122	18.02 N	73.01 E
Srīvilliputtūr	122	9.31 N	77.38 E
Srní	60	49.06 N	13.27 E
Środa Śląska	30	51.10 N	16.36 E
Środa Wielkopolski	30	52.14 N	17.17 E
Srostki	86	56.20 N	126.00 E
Srpska Crnja	38	45.43 N	20.42 E
Ssangmun-ni ⇠[8]	271b	37.39 N	127.02 E
Ssuch'ungch'i	100	22.06 N	120.46 E
Ssup'ing → Siping	89	43.12 N	124.20 E
St. → Saint, Sankt, Sint			
Staaken ⇠[8]	264a	52.32 N	13.08 E
Staaken, Flugplatz ⊠	264a	52.32 N	13.06 E
Staaten ≃	164	16.24 S	141.17 E
Staatsburg	210	41.51 N	73.56 W
Staatz	61	48.40 N	16.29 E
Stabbursdalen Nasjonalpark ♠	24	70.06 N	24.30 E
Staberhuk ≻	54	54.24 N	11.19 E
Stabroek	50	51.20 N	4.22 E
Stachy	60	49.06 N	13.40 E
Stack, Loch ⊜	46	58.20 N	4.55 W
Stackpoie Head ≻	42	51.37 N	4.54 W
Stack Skerry I[2]	46	59.01 N	4.31 W
Stacksteads	262	53.41 N	2.13 W
Stacyville	190	43.26 N	92.47 W
Stad-Delden	52	52.16 N	6.42 E
Stade	52	53.36 N	9.28 E
Stade □[6]	52	53.30 N	9.30 E
Staden, Bel.	50	50.59 N	3.01 E
Staden, B.R.D.	56	50.20 N	8.54 E
Städjan ∧	26	61.55 N	12.52 E
Stadl an der Mur	61	47.05 N	13.58 E
Stadlandet ≻[1]	26	62.07 N	5.18 E
Stadlau ⇠[8]	264b	48.14 N	16.28 E
Stadl-Paura	64	48.05 N	13.53 E
Stadskanaal	52	53.00 N	6.55 E
Stadt Allendorf	56	50.50 N	9.01 E
Stadtbergen	58	48.22 N	10.50 E
Stadt Haag	30	48.07 N	14.34 E
Stadthagen	52	52.19 N	9.13 E
Stadtilm	54	50.47 N	11.05 E
Städtische Rahmede	263	51.17 N	7.40 E
Stadtkyll	56	50.21 N	6.32 E
Stadtlauringen	56	50.11 N	10.22 E
Stadtlengsfeld	56	50.47 N	10.07 E
Stadtlohn	52	51.59 N	6.55 E
Stadtoldendorf	52	51.53 N	9.37 E
Stadtprozelten	56	49.47 N	9.25 E
Stadtroda	54	50.51 N	11.44 E
Stadtsteinach	54	50.09 N	11.30 E
Stadt Wehlen	54	50.58 N	14.02 E
Stadum	41	54.44 N	9.03 E
Stäfa	58	47.15 N	8.44 E
Staffa I	46	56.25 N	6.20 W
Staffanstorp	41	55.38 N	13.13 E
Staffelde	264a	52.44 N	13.00 E
Staffelsee ⊜	64	47.42 N	11.10 E
Staffelstein	56	50.06 N	11.00 E
Staffin	46	57.37 N	6.12 W
Staffora ≃	62	45.04 N	9.01 E
Stafford, Eng., U.K.	42	52.48 N	2.07 W
Stafford, Conn., U.S.	207	41.59 N	72.17 W
Stafford, Kans., U.S.	198	37.58 N	98.36 W
Stafford, N.Y., U.S.	210	42.59 N	78.04 W
Stafford, Tex., U.S.	222	29.37 N	95.34 W
Stafford, Va., U.S.	208	38.09 N	76.51 W
Stafford □[6]	208	38.25 N	77.30 W
Staffordshire □[6]	42	52.50 N	2.00 W
Stafford Springs	207	41.57 N	72.18 W
Staffordsville	188	37.50 N	82.50 W
Staffordville	207	42.00 N	72.16 W
Stagen	112	3.18 S	116.10 E
Stag Pond ⊜	276	40.59 N	74.42 W
Stahl-Berg ∧[2]	264a	52.21 N	13.46 E
Stahlbrode	54	54.14 N	13.17 E
Stahle	52	51.50 N	9.25 E
Stahnsdorf	54	52.23 N	13.13 E
Stahringen	58	47.47 N	8.58 E
Staicele	76	57.50 N	24.45 E
Staines	42	51.26 N	0.31 W
Staines Reservoirs ⊜[1]	260	51.27 N	0.30 W
Stainforth	44	53.36 N	1.01 W
Stainland	262	53.40 N	1.53 W
Stainmore Forest ⇠[3]	44	54.30 N	2.10 W
Stains	261	48.57 N	2.23 E
Stainz	61	46.54 N	15.16 E
Stairtown	222	29.43 N	97.44 W
Stajki	78	50.05 N	30.54 E
Staked Plain → Estacado, Llano ⌣	196	33.30 N	102.40 W
Stäket	40	59.28 N	17.48 E
Stakroge	41	55.53 N	8.51 E
Stalać	38	43.40 N	21.25 E
Stalbridge	42	50.58 N	2.23 W
Stalden	58	46.14 N	7.52 E
Staletti	68	38.46 N	16.32 E
Stalham	42	52.47 N	1.31 E
Stalheim	26	60.50 N	6.40 E
Stalin → Varna, Blg.	38	43.13 N	27.55 E
Stalin → Brașov, Rom.	38	45.39 N	25.37 E
Stalin (Kuçovë), Shq.	38	40.48 N	19.54 E
Stalinabad → Dušanbe	85	38.35 N	68.48 E
Stalino → Doneck	83	48.00 N	37.48 E
Stalinogorsk → Novomoskovsk	82	54.05 N	38.13 E
Stalinogród → Katowice	30	50.16 N	19.00 E
Stalinsk → Novokuzneck	86	53.45 N	87.06 E
Stallarholmen	40	59.22 N	17.12 E
Ställberg	40	59.59 N	14.55 E
Ställdalen	40	59.56 N	14.56 E
Stallwang	60	49.03 N	12.40 E
Stalowa Wola	30	50.35 N	22.02 E
Stalybridge	262	53.29 N	2.04 W
Stambaugh	190	46.04 N	88.38 W
Stamford, Austl.	166	21.16 S	143.49 E
Stamford, Eng., U.K.	42	52.39 N	0.29 W
Stamford, Conn., U.S.	207	41.03 N	73.32 W
Stamford, N.Y., U.S.	210	42.25 N	74.37 W
Stamford, Tex., U.S.	196	32.57 N	99.48 W
Stamford, Vt., U.S.	207	42.45 N	73.05 W
Stamford, Lake ⊜[1]	196	33.05 N	99.35 W
Stamford Bridge	44	53.59 N	0.55 W
Stamford Brige Stadium ♠	260	51.29 N	0.11 W
Stamford Harbor C	276	41.02 N	73.32 W
Stamford Museum ⊍	276	41.07 N	73.33 W
Stammbach	54	50.09 N	11.41 E
Stammersdorf ⇠[8]	264b	48.18 N	16.25 E
Stammham	60	48.15 N	12.53 E
Stammheim, B.R.D.	56	48.41 N	8.46 E
Stammheim, Schw.	58	47.38 N	8.47 E
Stampede Pass)(	224	47.17 N	121.21 W
Stampede Reservoir ⊜[1]	226	39.29 N	120.07 W
Stamping Ground	218	38.16 N	84.41 W
Stampriet	156	24.20 S	18.28 E
Stamps	194	33.22 N	93.30 W
Stams	64	47.16 N	10.59 E
Stanaford	188	37.49 N	81.10 W
Stanardsville	188	38.18 N	78.26 W
Stanberry	194	40.13 N	94.35 W
Stanborough	260	51.47 N	0.13 W
Stancija-Gorčakovo	85	40.27 N	71.42 E
Standard, Alta., Can.	182	51.07 N	112.59 W
Standard, Alaska, U.S.	180	64.47 N	148.32 W
Standard, Calif., U.S.	226	37.59 N	120.20 W
Standard, Pa., U.S.	214	40.10 N	79.32 W
Standard Oil Company Refinery ⊍[3]	282	37.57 N	122.24 W
Standard Shaft	279b	40.10 N	79.32 W
Standedge Canal Tunnel ⇠[5]	262	53.34 N	2.00 W
Standedge Railway Tunnel ⇠[5]	262	53.34 N	2.00 W
Standerton	158	26.58 S	29.07 E
Standiford Field ⊠	218	38.11 N	85.44 W
Standing Buffalo Indian Reserve ⇠[4]	184	50.53 N	103.54 W
Standing Rock Indian Reservation ⇠[4]	198	45.50 N	101.10 W
Standing Stone Creek ≃	214	40.30 N	78.00 W
Standing Stones ⊥	46	58.12 N	6.48 W
Standish, Eng., U.K.	44	53.36 N	2.41 W
Standish, Mich., U.S.	190	43.59 N	83.57 W
Standon	42	51.53 N	0.02 E
Stanfield, Ariz., U.S.	200	32.53 N	111.58 W
Stanfield, Oreg., U.S.	202	45.47 N	119.13 W
Stanford, S. Afr.	158	34.26 S	19.29 E
Stanford, Calif., U.S.	226	37.25 N	122.08 W
Stanford, Ky., U.S.	192	37.32 N	84.40 W
Stanford, Mont., U.S.	202	47.09 N	110.13 W
Stanford Center ⇠[9]	282	37.27 N	122.10 W
Stanford Heights	210	42.46 N	73.53 W
Stanford le Hope	42	51.31 N	0.26 E
Stanford Linear Accelerator ⊍[3]	282	37.25 N	122.12 W
Stanford Rivers	260	51.41 N	0.13 E
Stanford University ⊍[2]	282	37.26 N	122.10 W
Stanfordville	210	41.52 N	73.43 W
Stånga	26	57.17 N	18.28 E
Stångån ≃	26	58.27 N	15.37 E
Stångby	41	55.46 N	13.10 E
Stange	26	60.43 N	11.11 E
Stanger	158	29.27 S	31.14 E
Stanghella	64	45.08 N	11.45 E
Stanhope, Eng., U.K.	44	54.45 N	2.01 W
Stanhope, Iowa, U.S.	190	42.17 N	93.48 W
Stanhope, N.J., U.S.	210	40.54 N	74.43 W
Staničnο-Luganskoje	83	48.39 N	39.30 E
Stanislaus □[6]	226	37.39 N	121.00 W
Stanislaus ≃	226	37.40 N	121.14 W
Stanislaus, Clark Fork ≃	226	38.22 N	119.52 W
Stanislaus, Middle Fork ≃	226	38.09 N	120.21 W
Stanislaus, North Fork ≃	226	38.09 N	120.21 W
Stanislaus, South Fork ≃	226	38.04 N	120.25 W
Stanislav, S.S.S.R.	78	46.34 N	32.09 E
Stanislav → Ivano-Frankovsk, S.S.S.R.	78	48.55 N	24.43 E
Stanislavčik	78	48.58 N	28.07 E
Stanisławów → Ivano-Frankovsk	78	48.55 N	24.43 E
Stanke Dimitrov	38	42.16 N	23.07 E
Staňkov	60	49.34 N	13.04 E
Stanley, Austl.	166	40.46 S	145.18 E
Stanley, N.B., Can.	186	46.17 N	66.44 W

Symbols in the index entries represent the broad categories identified in the key at the right. Symbols with superior numbers (⛰[2]) identify subcategories (see complete key on page *I · 30*).

Kartensymbole in dem Registerverzeichnis stellen die rechts in Schlüssel erklärten Kategorien dar. Symbole mit hochgestellten Ziffern (⛰[2]) bezeichnen Unterabteilungen einer Kategorie (vgl. vollständiger Schlüssel auf Seite *I · 30*).

Los símbolos incluídos en el texto del índice representan las grandes categorias identificadas con la clave a la derecha. Los símbolos con numeros en su parte superior (⛰[2]) identifican las subcategorias (véase la clave completa en la página *I · 30*).

Les symboles de l'index représentent les catégories indiquées dans la légende à droite. Les symboles suivis d'un indice (⛰[2]) représentent des sous-catégories (voir légende complète à la page *I · 30*).

Os símbolos incluídos no texto do índice representam as grandes categorias identificadas com a chave à direita. Os símbolos com números em sua parte superior (⛰[2]) identificam as subcategorias (veja-se a chave completa à página *I · 30*).

	English	Deutsch	Español	Français	Português
∧	Mountain	Berg	Montaña	Montagne	Montanha
⛰	Mountains	Berge	Montañas	Montagnes	Montanhas
)(	Pass	Pass	Paso	Col	Passo
∨	Valley, Canyon	Tal, Cañon	Valle, Cañón	Vallée, Canyon	Vale, Canhão
⌣	Plain	Ebene	Llano	Plaine	Planície
≻	Cape	Kap	Cabo	Cap	Cabo
I	Island	Insel	Isla	Île	Ilha
II	Islands	Inseln	Islas	Îles	Ilhas
•	Other Topographic Features	Andere Topographische Objekte	Otros Elementos Topográficos	Autres données topographiques	Outros Elementos Topográficos

ESPAÑOL

Nombre	Página	Lat.°′	Long.°′ W=Oeste
Stanley, Falk. Is.	254	51.42 S	57.51 W
Stanley, H.K.	271d	22.13 N	114.12 E
Stanley, Eng., U.K.	44	54.52 N	1.42 W
Stanley, Scot., U.K.	46	56.28 N	3.27 W
Stanley, N.C., U.S.	192	35.21 N	81.06 W
Stanley, N. Dak., U.S.	198	48.19 N	102.23 W
Stanley, N.Y., U.S.	210	42.49 N	77.06 W
Stanley, Va., U.S.	188	38.34 N	78.31 W
Stanley, Wis., U.S.	190	44.58 N	90.56 W
Stanley ≃	171a	27.09 S	152.32 E
Stanley, Port ⊂	175f	16.06 S	167.27 E
Stanley Falls ᒪ	154	0.30 N	25.12 E
Stanley Mills	275b	43.46 N	79.44 W
Stanley Mound ∧[2]	271d	22.14 N	114.12 E
Stanley Park ♠, B.C., Can.	224	49.19 N	123.09 W
Stanley Park ♠, Eng., U.K.	262	53.26 N	2.57 W
Stanley Park ♠, Eng., U.K.	262	53.49 N	3.02 W
Stanley Pool ⊜	152	4.17 S	15.20 E
Stanley Reservoir ⊜[1]	122	11.54 N	77.50 E
Stanleyville → Kisangani	154	0.30 N	25.12 E
Stanlow	44	53.17 N	2.52 W
Stanmore ◆[8]	260	51.37 N	0.19 W
Stannards	210	42.05 N	77.55 W
Stann Creek	232	16.58 N	88.13 W
Stannington	44	55.06 N	1.40 W
Stanoionno-Ojašinskij	86	55.28 N	83.53 E
Stanovoj Chrebet ⋀⋀	74	56.20 N	126.00 E
Stanovoje Nagorje ⋀⋀	88	56.00 N	114.00 E
Stanovoj Kolodez'	76	52.51 N	36.16 E
Stanovoy Mountains → Stanovoje Nagorje ⋀⋀	88	56.00 N	114.00 E
Stans	58	46.57 N	8.22 E
Stansbury	168b	34.55 S	137.47 E
Stansmore Range ⋀⋀	162	21.23 S	128.33 E
Stansstad	58	46.59 N	8.20 E
Stanstead	206	45.01 N	72.05 W
Stanstead □[6]	206	45.10 N	72.00 W
Stanstead Abbots	42	51.47 N	0.01 E
Stansted	260	51.20 N	0.18 E
Stansted Mountfitchet	42	51.54 N	0.12 E
Stanthorpe	166	28.39 S	151.57 E
Stanton, Eng., U.K.	42	52.19 N	0.53 E
Stanton, Calif., U.S.	228	33.48 N	117.59 W
Stanton, Del., U.S.	208	39.43 N	75.37 W
Stanton, Iowa, U.S.	198	40.59 N	95.06 W
Stanton, Ky., U.S.	192	37.54 N	83.52 W
Stanton, Mich., U.S.	190	43.18 N	85.05 W
Stanton, Mo., U.S.	219	38.16 N	91.06 W
Stanton, Nebr., U.S.	198	41.57 N	97.14 W
Stanton, N. Dak., U.S.	198	47.19 N	101.23 W
Stanton, Tenn., U.S.	194	35.28 N	89.24 W
Stanton, Tex., U.S.	196	32.08 N	101.48 W
Stantonsburg	192	35.37 N	77.49 W
Stanwell	260	51.27 N	0.29 W
Stanwell Moor	260	51.28 N	0.30 W
Stanwix	44	54.54 N	2.55 W
Stanwood	224	48.15 N	122.23 W
Stanwood Gardens	285	40.07 N	74.57 W
Stanz	61	47.28 N	15.30
Stanzach	58	47.23 N	10.34 E
Stapelburg	54	51.53 N	10.40 E
Stapelfeld	52	53.36 N	10.13 E
Staphorst	52	52.37 N	6.12 E
Stapleford	42	52.56 N	1.16 W
Stapleford Abbotts	260	51.38 N	0.10 E
Stapleford Aerodrome ⊠	260	51.39 N	0.08 E
Stapleford Tawney	260	51.40 N	0.11 E
Staplehurst	42	51.10 N	0.33 E
Staples	198	46.21 N	94.48 W
Stapleton, Ala., U.S.	194	30.45 N	87.48 W
Stapleton, Nebr., U.S.	198	41.29 N	100.31 W
Stąporków	30	51.09 N	20.34 E
Star', S.S.S.R.	76	53.37 N	34.09 E
Star, Miss., U.S.	194	32.06 N	90.03 W
Star, N.C., U.S.	192	35.24 N	79.47 W
Stará Boleslav	54	50.12 N	14.42 E
Starachowice	30	51.03 N	21.04 E
Stara Fužina	64	46.17 N	13.54 E
Staraja	265a	59.55 N	30.38 E
Staraja Belica, S.S.S.R.	76	54.42 N	29.38 E
Staraja Belica, S.S.S.R.	78	51.59 N	35.13 E
Staraja Belogorka	80	52.05 N	53.17 E
Staraja Derevn'a ◆[8]	265a	59.59 N	30.15 E
Staraja Duginka	82	54.20 N	38.45 E
Staraja Kriuša	78	50.12 N	41.09 E
Staraja Kulatka	80	52.43 N	47.37 E
Staraja Kupavna	82	55.48 N	38.10 E
Staraja Majačka	78	46.30 N	33.11 E
Staraja Majna	80	54.36 N	48.57 E
Staraja Poltavka	80	50.28 N	46.28 E
Staraja Porubežka	80	52.03 N	49.11 E
Staraja Račejka	80	53.22 N	48.03 E
Staraja Rudn'a	76	52.50 N	30.17 E
Staraja Russa	76	58.00 N	31.23 E
Staraja Ruza	82	55.39 N	36.20 E
Staraja Sachča	80	54.25 N	49.58 E
Staraja Sin'ava	78	49.36 N	27.37 E
Staraja Sitn'a	82	54.56 N	38.09 E
Staraja Terizmorga	80	54.16 N	44.32 E
Staraja Toropa	76	56.17 N	31.40 E
Staraja Ušica	78	48.35 N	27.07 E
Staraja Veduga	78	51.48 N	38.31 E
Staraja Vičuga	80	57.16 N	41.53 E
Staraja Vyževka	78	51.27 N	24.24 E
Staranzano	64	45.49 N	13.30 E
Stara Pazova	38	44.59 N	20.10 E
Stara Planina (Balkan Mountains) ⋀⋀	38	43.15 N	25.00 E
Stará Role	54	50.14 N	12.47 E
Starav, Ben ∧	46	56.32 N	5.03 W
Stará Voda	60	50.00 N	12.36 E
Stara Zagora	38	42.25 N	25.38 E
Starbejevo	265b	55.55 N	37.28 E
Starbrick	214	41.50 N	79.12 W
Starbuck, Man., Can.	184	49.46 N	97.36 W
Starbuck, Minn., U.S.	198	45.37 N	95.32 W
Starbuck, Wash., U.S.	202	47.31 N	118.08 W
Starbuck Island ▮	14	5.37 S	155.53 W
Starčenkovo	78	47.17 N	36.59 E
Star City, Sask., Can.	184	52.53 N	104.21 W
Star City, Ark., U.S.	194	33.56 N	91.51 W
Star City, Ind., U.S.	216	40.58 N	86.33 W
Starcross	42	50.38 N	3.27 W
Stare Czarnowo	54	53.16 N	14.45 E
Staré Sedliště	60	49.45 N	12.42 E
Starford	214	40.42 N	78.58 W
Stargard Szczeciński (Stargard in Pommern)	30	53.20 N	15.02 E
Stargo	200	33.04 N	109.21 W
Star Harbour ⊂	175e	10.47 S	162.18 E
Stari Bar	38	42.06 N	19.08 E
Starica, S.S.S.R.	76	56.30 N	34.56 E
Starica, S.S.S.R.	76	59.04 N	29.30 E
Starica, S.S.S.R.	80	48.13 N	45.56 E
Stari Grad	36	43.11 N	16.36 E
Starij R'ad	76	58.05 N	34.54 E
Starina	76	59.37 N	44.42 E
Stari Vlah ◆[1]	38	43.35 N	20.15 E
Star Junction	214	40.04 N	79.46 W

FRANÇAIS

Nom	Page	Lat.°′	Long.°′ W=Ouest
Stark □[6]	214	40.48 N	81.22 W
Starke	192	29.57 N	82.07 W
Starke □[6]	216	41.18 N	86.37 W
Starkey	210	42.32 N	76.56 W
Starkville	194	33.28 N	88.48 W
Star Lake	224	47.22 N	122.18 W
Starnberg	60	48.00 N	11.20 E
Starnberger See ⊜	64	47.55 N	11.18 E
Starnikovo	82	55.22 N	38.24 E
Staroalejskoje	86	51.00 N	82.01 E
Starobačaty	86	54.14 N	86.07 E
Starobaltačevo	86	56.01 N	55.56 E
Starobel'sk	83	49.16 N	38.56 E
Starobeševo	83	47.44 N	38.03 E
Starobin	76	52.44 N	27.28 E
Staročerkasskaja	83	47.15 N	40.03 E
Starocuruchajtuj	88	50.12 N	119.15 E
Staroderev'ankovskaja	78	46.08 N	38.58 E
Starodub	76	52.35 N	32.46 E
Starod'umejevo	80	55.16 N	54.22 E
Starogan'kino	80	53.55 N	52.15 E
Starogard Gdański	30	53.59 N	18.33 E
Staroignatjevka	83	47.32 N	37.47 E
Staroje	76	59.16 N	40.40 E
Staroje Bojsarovo	80	55.31 N	53.54 E
Staroje Ibrajkino	80	54.52 N	51.02 E
Staroje Jaškino	80	52.49 N	52.57 E
Staroje Jermakovo	80	54.04 N	51.59 E
Staroje Oleničevo	80	45.34 N	47.11 E
Staroje Rachino	76	58.08 N	32.39 E
Staroje Šajgovo	80	54.18 N	44.26 E
Staroje Šajmurzino	80	54.45 N	47.58 E
Staroje Selo	76	55.14 N	29.54 E
Staroje Sindrovo	80	54.25 N	44.06 E
Staroje Slavkino	80	52.34 N	45.08 E
Staroje Ustje	80	53.28 N	41.51 E
Starojurjevo	80	53.21 N	40.42 E
Starokazačje	78	46.21 N	29.59 E
Starokonstantinov	78	49.46 N	27.13 E
Starokuručevo	80	55.09 N	54.04 E
Starolaspa	83	47.34 N	37.59 E
Staroleuškovskaja	78	45.59 N	39.44 E
Staromichajlovka	83	47.58 N	37.36 E
Starominskaja	78	46.31 N	39.04 E
Staromlinovka	78	47.42 N	36.49 E
Staromušta	80	55.49 N	54.14 E
Staronikolajevo	82	55.37 N	36.16 E
Staro-Podgorodneje	82	54.46 N	38.57 E
Staropokrovka	85	42.50 N	75.18 E
Staroščerbinovskaja	78	46.37 N	38.40 E
Staroseslavino	80	53.12 N	40.25 E
Starošešminsk	80	55.22 N	51.15 E
Starosiedle	54	51.50 N	14.50 E
Starosoldatskoje	86	56.12 N	72.37 E
Starosubchangulovo	86	53.06 N	57.26 E
Starotimoškino	24	53.43 N	47.32 E
Starotitarovskaja	78	45.14 N	37.09 E
Staroutkinsk	86	57.14 N	59.20 E
Staroverovka	78	49.33 N	35.42 E
Starožilovo	80	54.14 N	39.55 E
Starožil'skij	80	56.34 N	47.17 E
Star Peak ∧	204	40.32 N	118.10 W
Starr	214	41.32 N	79.22 W
Starrucca	210	41.54 N	75.28 W
Start Bay ⊂	42	50.17 N	3.36 W
Start Point ›	42	50.13 N	3.38 W
Startup	224	47.52 N	121.44 W
Starvation Reservoir ⊜[1]	200	40.15 N	110.30 W
Starved Rock State Park ♠	216	41.19 N	88.58 W
Staryj Ajbesi	80	54.57 N	47.03 E
Staryj-Ajdar	83	48.43 N	39.11 E
Staryj Bagr'až	80	54.54 N	51.39 E
Staryj Bir'uz'ak	84	44.47 N	46.54 E
Staryj Bol'ševik	265b	55.57 N	37.47 E
Staryj Čartorijsk	78	51.15 N	25.54 E
Staryj Chop'or	80	51.30 N	42.58 E
Staryj Čindant	88	50.33 N	115.33 E
Staryje Burasy	80	52.16 N	46.09 E
Staryje Dorogi	76	53.02 N	28.16 E
Staryje Maty	80	55.14 N	53.55 E
Staryje Popel'uchi	78	48.18 N	28.55 E
Staryje Senžary	78	49.25 N	34.27 E
Staryje Turdaki	80	53.55 N	45.29 E
Staryje Z'atcy	80	57.21 N	52.39 E
Staryj Kazangal	80	50.15 N	47.39 E
Staryj Krym, S.S.S.R.	78	45.03 N	35.05 E
Staryj Krym, S.S.S.R.	83	47.10 N	37.30 E
Staryj Lesken	84	43.20 N	43.55 E
Staryj Medved'	76	58.18 N	30.30 E
Staryj Merčik	78	49.58 N	35.46 E
Staryj Oskol	78	51.19 N	37.51 E
Staryj Sambor	78	49.27 N	22.59 E
Staryj Terek ≃	84	44.00 N	47.24 E
Staryj Tukšum	80	53.42 N	48.33 E
Starý Plzenec	60	49.42 N	13.28 E
Stary Sącz	30	49.34 N	20.38 E
Stassfurt	54	51.51 N	11.34 E
Staszów	30	50.34 N	21.20 E
State Center	190	42.01 N	93.10 W
State College, Miss., U.S.	194	33.26 N	88.47 W
State College, Pa., U.S.	214	40.48 N	77.52 W
Stateline, Calif., U.S.	226	38.57 N	119.57 W
State Line, Miss., U.S.	194	31.26 N	88.28 W
Stateline, Nev., U.S.	204	38.57 N	119.57 W
Staten Island ▮	276	40.35 N	74.09 W
Staten Island Mall ◆[9]	276	40.35 N	74.10 W
Statenville	192	30.42 N	83.02 W
State Park Place	219	38.40 N	90.03 W
State Road	192	36.19 N	80.52 W
Statesboro	192	32.27 N	81.47 W
Statesville	192	35.47 N	80.53 W
Stateville State Prison ■	278	41.35 N	88.06 W
Station Peak	162	21.10 S	118.11 E
Statue of Liberty National Monument ♠	210	40.41 N	74.03 W
Staufen	58	47.53 N	7.44 E
Staufenberg	56	50.40 N	8.43 E
Staughton Vale	169	37.51 S	144.17 E
Staunton, Ill., U.S.	219	39.01 N	89.47 W
Staunton, Va., U.S.	188	38.09 N	79.04 W
Staunton → Roanoke ≃	192	35.56 N	76.43 W
Stavanger	26	58.58 N	5.45 E
Stave ≃	224	49.10 N	122.26 W
Stave Lake ⊜	182	49.15 N	122.21 W
Staveley	44	53.16 N	1.20 W
Stavelot	56	50.23 N	5.56 E
Stavely	182	50.10 N	113.38 W
Staveren	52	52.53 N	5.22 E
Stavern	26	59.00 N	10.02 E
Stavišče	78	49.23 N	30.12 E
Stavnoje	78	48.59 N	22.40 E
Stavropol', S.S.S.R.	72	45.02 N	41.59 E
Stavropol → Toljatti, S.S.S.R.	80	53.31 N	49.26 E
Stavropol' □[8]	84	44.38 N	43.30 E
Stavrovo	80	56.08 N	40.00 E
Stavsnäs	40	59.17 N	18.41 E
Stawell	166	37.04 S	142.46 E
Stawell ≃	166	20.38 S	142.55 E
Stawiski	30	53.23 N	22.09 E
Stawiszyn	30	51.55 N	18.07 E
Staxigoe	46	58.28 N	3.04 W
Stayner	212	44.25 N	80.05 W
Stayton	202	44.48 N	122.48 W

PORTUGUÊS

Nome	Página	Lat.°′	Long.°′ W=Oeste
Stazzema	64	43.59 N	10.19 E
Ste. → Saint			
Steamboat	226	39.23 N	119.44 W
Steamboat Creek ≃	226	39.31 N	119.42 W
Steamboat Mountain ∧	200	41.58 N	108.58 W
Steamboat Slough ≃	226	38.11 N	121.40 W
Steamboat Springs	200	40.29 N	106.50 W
Steamburg	210	42.07 N	78.54 W
Stearns	192	36.42 N	84.28 W
Stearns Pond ⊜	283	42.37 N	71.04 W
Stebbins	180	63.32 N	162.18 W
Stebl'ov	78	49.24 N	31.06 E
Stechow	54	52.38 N	12.28 E
Steckborn	58	47.40 N	8.55 E
Stederdorf	52	52.21 N	10.15 E
Stedten	54	51.26 N	11.41 E
Stedum	52	53.18 N	6.41 E
Steeg	58	47.14 N	10.17 E
Steel ≃	190	48.46 N	86.54 W
Steel City	210	40.38 N	75.20 W
Steele, Mo., U.S.	194	36.05 N	89.50 W
Steele, N. Dak., U.S.	198	46.51 N	99.55 W
Steele ◆[8]	263	51.27 N	7.05 E
Steele, Mount ∧	200	41.50 N	107.00 W
Steele Creek ≃, Tex., U.S.	222	31.13 N	96.19 W
Steele Creek ≃, Tex., U.S.	222	32.01 N	97.28 W
Steeles Corners	275b	43.48 N	79.25 W
Steeleville	194	38.00 N	89.40 W
Steelhead	224	49.13 N	122.19 W
Steel's Drift	158	27.21 S	29.30 E
Steel's Point ›	174c	29.02 S	168.00 E
Steels Run ≃	279b	40.25 N	79.38 W
Steelton, N.Y., U.S.	284a	42.47 N	78.49 W
Steelton, Pa., U.S.	208	40.14 N	76.49 W
Steelville	194	37.58 N	91.22 W
Steenbergen	52	51.35 N	4.19 E
Steenburg Lake ⊜	212	44.50 N	77.41 W
Steenderen	52	52.04 N	6.11 E
Steenkool	164	2.07 S	133.32 E
Steens Mountain ⋀⋀	202	42.35 N	118.40 W
Steenvoorde	50	50.48 N	2.35 E
Steenwijk	52	52.47 N	6.08 E
Steephill Lake ⊜	184	55.58 N	103.08 W
Steep Holm ▮	42	51.21 N	3.07 W
Steeping ≃	44	53.06 N	0.18 E
Steep Point ›	162	26.08 S	113.08 E
Steep Rock	184	51.26 N	98.48 W
Stefanie, Lake (Chew Bahir) ⊜	144	4.40 N	36.50 E
Stefansson Island ▮	176	73.17 N	106.45 W
Ştefan Vodă	38	44.19 N	27.19 E
Steffisburg	58	46.47 N	7.39 E
Steg	58	47.21 N	8.56 E
Stegalovka	76	52.24 N	38.19 E
Stege	41	54.59 N	12.18 E
Stegeborg	26	58.26 N	16.35 E
Stege Bugt ⊂	41	55.01 N	12.50 E
Stegelitz	54	53.08 N	13.51 E
Steger	216	41.29 N	87.41 W
Stegersbach	61	47.10 N	16.10 E
Stegi	158	26.32 S	31.58 E
Steglitz ◆[8]	264a	52.28 N	13.19 E
Stehag	41	55.54 N	13.23 E
Stehekin	224	48.19 N	120.39 W
Stehekin ≃	224	48.21 N	120.40 W
Steiermark □[3]	61	47.10 N	15.10 E
Steigerwald ⋀⋀	56	49.40 N	10.20 E
Steigra	54	51.18 N	11.39 E
Steilacoom	224	47.10 N	122.36 W
Steimbke	52	52.40 N	9.22 E
Stein, B.R.D.	64	47.59 N	12.32 E
Stein, Ned.	56	50.57 N	5.46 E
Stein, Schw.	58	47.33 N	7.58 E
Steina	54	51.12 N	14.01 E
Steinach, B.R.D.	58	48.18 N	8.04 E
Steinach, D.D.R.	54	50.25 N	11.10 E
Steinach, Öst.	64	47.05 N	11.28 E
Steinach ≃	56	50.11 N	11.12 E
Steinamanger → Szombathely	61	47.14 N	16.38 E
Stein am Rhein	58	47.40 N	8.51 E
Steinau, B.R.D.	56	50.23 N	9.27 E
Steinau → Ścinawa, Pol.	30	51.25 N	16.27 E
Steinbach, B.R.D.	56	48.43 N	8.10 E
Steinbach, B.R.D.	56	50.01 N	9.36 E
Steinbach, Man., Can.	184	49.32 N	96.41 W
Steinbach-Hallenberg	54	50.42 N	10.34 E
Stein bei Nürnberg	60	49.25 N	11.01 E
Steinberg	60	48.34 N	12.35 E
Steinberg ∧[2]	263	51.05 N	7.27 E
Steinberger Slough ≃	282	37.33 N	122.13 W
Steinbourg	56	48.46 N	7.25 E
Steinen	58	47.38 N	7.44 E
Steinernes Meer ⋀⋀	64	47.30 N	12.58 E
Steinfeld, B.R.D.	52	52.35 N	8.12 E
Steinfeld, D.D.R.	54	50.22 N	10.44 E
Steinfeld, Öst.	64	46.45 N	13.15 E
Steinfort	56	49.40 N	5.55 E
Steinforth	263	51.09 N	6.32 E
Steingaden	58	47.42 N	10.51 E
Steinhagen, B.R.D.	52	52.00 N	8.24 E
Steinhagen, D.D.R.	54	54.13 N	12.59 E
Steinhatchie ≃	192	29.40 N	83.24 W
Steinhausen	156	21.49 S	18.20 E
Steinhausen ♉[1], B.R.D.	64	40.00 N	9.41 E
Steinhausen ♉[1], B.R.D.	64	48.01 N	9.41 E
Steinheid	54	50.28 N	11.04 E
Steinheim, B.R.D.	52	51.52 N	9.05 E
Steinheim, B.R.D.	56	48.58 N	9.16 E
Steinheim, B.R.D.	56	50.06 N	8.55 E
Steinheim, B.R.D.	58	48.01 N	10.09 E
Steinhöfel	54	52.24 N	14.10 E
Steinhöring	60	48.05 N	12.02 E
Steinhude	52	52.27 N	9.21 E
Steinhuder Meer ⊜	52	52.28 N	9.19 E
Steinkjer	26	64.01 N	11.30 E
Steinkopf	156	29.18 S	17.43 E
Steinloge	52	52.54 N	8.19 E
Stein-Neukirch	56	50.41 N	8.03 E
Steinpass)(	64	47.39 N	12.45 E
Steinpleis	54	50.43 N	12.23 E
Steinsdorf	54	52.02 N	14.40 E
Steinshamn	26	62.47 N	6.29 E
Steinstücken ◆[8]	264a	52.23 N	13.08 E
Steinwiesen	54	50.17 N	11.28 E
Stekene	50	51.12 N	4.02 E
Stekl'anka	76	59.08 N	41.37 E
Steklino	76	56.51 N	32.10 E
Steksovo	80	55.17 N	43.25 E
Stella, It.	62	44.24 N	8.30 E
Stella, S. Afr.	158	26.38 S	24.48 E
Stella, Nebr., U.S.	198	40.14 N	95.46 W
Stella Niagara	210	43.12 N	79.02 W
Stella-Plage	50	50.29 N	1.35 E
Stellaquo Indian Reserve ◆[4]	182	54.03 N	124.55 W
Stellarton	186	45.34 N	62.40 W
Stelle	52	53.23 N	10.06 E
Stellenbosch	158	33.58 S	18.50 E
Steller, Mount ∧	180	60.30 N	143.02 W
Stelvio, Parco Nazionale dello ♠	58	46.20 N	10.40 E
Stelvio, Passo dello)(	58	46.32 N	10.27 E
Stenay	56	49.29 N	5.11 E
Stendal	54	52.36 N	11.51 E
Stende	76	57.09 N	22.33 E
Stenden	263	51.25 N	6.27 E
Stenhammars slott ⊥	40	59.03 N	16.31 E
Stenhousemuir	46	56.02 N	3.48 W
Stenico	64	46.03 N	10.51 E
Stenlille	41	55.32 N	11.36 E
Stenløse	41	55.46 N	12.12 E
Stenness, Loch of ⊜	46	59.00 N	3.15 W
Stenón	267c	37.58 N	22.20 E
Stenón Návstathmou ⋓	267c	37.58 N	23.33 E
Stensätra	40	60.36 N	16.44 E
Stensele	24	65.05 N	17.09 E
Stenstorp	26	58.16 N	13.43 E
Stenstrup	41	55.07 N	10.31 E
Stentrop	263	51.30 N	7.49 E
Stenungsund	26	58.05 N	11.49 E
Stepan'	78	51.10 N	26.18 E
Stepanakert	84	39.49 N	46.44 E
Stepanavan	84	41.00 N	44.23 E
Stepancevo, S.S.S.R.	80	56.08 N	41.42 E
Stepancevo, S.S.S.R.	82	56.22 N	36.10 E
Stepancy	78	49.42 N	31.18 E
Stepano-Krynka	83	47.55 N	38.21 E
Stepanovka, S.S.S.R.	78	50.58 N	34.37 E
Stepanovka, S.S.S.R.	80	52.04 N	53.02 E
Stepanovka, S.S.S.R.	86	57.13 N	67.26 E
Stepanovo	82	55.43 N	38.28 E
Stepanovskoje	265b	55.47 N	37.10 E
Stepan Razin	84	40.24 N	49.59 E
Stepanščino	82	55.15 N	38.30 E
Stepenitz ≃	54	53.48 N	11.10 E
Stephans-Dom ♉[1]	264b	48.12 N	16.23 E
Stephanskirchen	64	47.51 N	12.11 E
Stephen	198	48.27 N	96.53 W
Stephen A. Forbes State Park ♠	219	38.44 N	88.46 W
Stephen F. Austin State Historic Park ♠	222	29.48 N	96.05 W
Stephens	194	33.25 N	93.04 W
Stephens, Cape ›	172	40.42 S	173.57 E
Stephens, Port ⊂	166	32.45 S	152.05 E
Stephens Brook ≃	276	40.54 N	74.35 W
Stephens City	188	39.05 N	78.13 W
Stephens Creek	166	31.50 S	141.30 E
Stephens Island ▮	182	54.10 N	130.45 W
Stephens Mills	210	42.23 N	77.38 W
Stephenson	190	45.20 N	87.38 W
Stephenson, Lake ⊜	222	29.35 N	94.40 W
Stephenson, Mount ∧	9	69.49 S	69.43 W
Stephens Passage ⋓	180	57.50 N	133.50 W
Stephentown	210	42.33 N	73.23 W
Stephentown Center	210	42.34 N	73.25 W
Stephenville, Newf., Can.	186	48.33 N	58.35 W
Stephenville, Tex., U.S.	196	32.13 N	98.12 W
Stephenville Crossing	186	48.30 N	58.26 W
Stepn'ak	86	52.50 N	70.50 E
Stepney ◆[8]	260	51.31 N	0.02 W
Stepnica	54	53.40 N	14.36 E
Stepnoj	80	48.56 N	45.36 E
Stepnoje, S.S.S.R.	80	51.24 N	46.52 E
Stepnoje, S.S.S.R.	84	44.17 N	44.36 E
Steps Point ›	174u	14.22 S	170.45 W
Steptoe Valley ∨	204	39.25 N	114.45 W
Stepurino	76	56.24 N	35.16 E
Sterdyń	30	52.35 N	22.18 E
Sterkaar	158	31.05 S	23.42 E
Sterkrade ◆[8]	263	51.31 N	6.51 E
Sterkspruit	158	30.32 S	27.22 E
Sterkstroom	158	31.32 S	26.32 E
Sterlibaševo	86	53.28 N	55.15 E
Sterling, S. Afr.	158	31.16 S	21.28 E
Sterling, Alaska, U.S.	180	60.28 N	150.08 W
Sterling, Colo., U.S.	198	40.37 N	103.13 W
Sterling, Conn., U.S.	207	41.42 N	71.50 W
Sterling, Ill., U.S.	190	41.48 N	89.42 W
Sterling, Kans., U.S.	198	38.13 N	98.12 W
Sterling, Mass., U.S.	207	42.26 N	71.46 W
Sterling, Mich., U.S.	190	44.02 N	84.02 W
Sterling, Nebr., U.S.	198	40.28 N	96.23 W
Sterling, N.Y., U.S.	210	43.20 N	76.39 W
Sterling, Ohio, U.S.	214	40.58 N	81.51 W
Sterling, Okla., U.S.	196	34.45 N	98.10 W
Sterling, Va., U.S.	208	39.00 N	77.26 W
Sterling City	196	31.50 N	100.59 W
Sterling Creek ≃	210	43.20 N	76.42 W
Sterling Forest Gardens ♠	210	41.14 N	74.16 W
Sterling Forest Lake ⊜	276	41.10 N	74.16 W
Sterling Heights	214	42.35 N	83.02 W
Sterling Junction	207	42.24 N	71.46 W
Sterling Park	282	37.41 N	122.26 W
Sterling Reservoir ⊜[1]	198	40.47 N	103.17 W
Sterling Run	214	41.25 N	78.12 W
Sterlington	194	32.42 N	92.05 W
Sterlitamak	86	53.37 N	55.58 E
Sternberg	54	53.43 N	11.49 E
Sternberg in der Neumark → Torzym	30	52.20 N	15.04 E
Šternberk	30	49.44 N	17.18 E
∧Ernstein	61	48.34 N	14.16
Šterovka	83	48.19 N	38.57 E
Sterup	41	54.44 N	9.44 E
Sterzing → Vipiteno	64	46.54 N	11.26 E
Stęszew	30	52.18 N	16.42 E
Štětí	54	50.25 N	14.23 E
Stetson Pond ⊜	283	42.02 N	70.50 W
Stetten am kalten Markt	58	48.07 N	9.04 E
Stettin → Szczecin	30	53.24 N	14.32 E
Stettler	182	52.19 N	112.43 W
Steuben □[6], Ind., U.S.	216	41.38 N	85.00 W
Steuben □[6], N.Y., U.S.	210	42.20 N	77.19 W
Steubenville	214	40.22 N	80.37 W
Stevenage	42	51.55 N	0.14 W
Stevens, N.J., U.S.	285	40.05 N	74.49 W
Stevens, Pa., U.S.	208	40.13 N	76.09 W
Stevens, Lake ⊜	224	48.01 N	122.05 W
Stevens, Mount ∧	172	40.48 S	172.27 E
Stevens Creek ≃, Calif., U.S.	282	37.26 N	122.05 W
Stevens Creek ≃, S.C., U.S.	192	33.34 N	82.03 W
Stevens Creek Park ♠	282	37.17 N	122.04 W
Stevens Creek Reservoir ⊜[1]	282	37.17 N	122.05 W
Stevens Institute of Technology ♉[2]	276	40.44 N	74.02 W
Stevenson, Ala., U.S.	194	34.52 N	85.50 W
Stevenson, Wash., U.S.	224	45.42 N	121.53 W
Stevenson Creek ≃	162	27.06 S	135.33 E
Stevenson Entrance ⋓	180	57.45 N	152.20 W
Stevenson Lake ⊜	184	53.56 N	96.09 W
Stevens Pass)(	224	47.45 N	121.04 W
Stevens Peak ∧	202	47.27 N	115.46 W
Stevens Point	190	44.31 N	89.34 W
Stevenston	46	55.39 N	4.45 W
Stevens Village	180	66.00 N	155.05 W
Stevensville, Ont., Can.	284a	42.57 N	79.04 W
Stevensville, Md., U.S.	208	38.59 N	76.19 W
Stevensville, Mich., U.S.	216	42.01 N	86.31 W
Stevensville, Mont., U.S.	202	46.30 N	114.05 W
Stevensville, Pa., U.S.	210	41.46 N	76.11 W
Stevinson	226	37.20 N	120.51 W
Stevns Klint •[4]	41	55.18 N	12.27 E
Steward	216	41.51 N	89.01 W
Stewardson	219	39.16 N	88.38 W
Stewart, B.C., Can.	182	55.56 N	129.59 W
Stewart, Minn., U.S.	190	44.43 N	94.29 W
Stewart ≃	180	63.18 N	139.25 W
Stewart, Cape ›	164	11.57 S	134.45 E
Stewart, Isla ▮	254	54.52 S	71.12 W
Stewart Island ▮	172	47.00 S	167.50 E
Stewart Lake ⊜	219	40.09 N	90.16 W
Stewart Manor	276	40.43 N	73.41 W
Stewarton	46	55.41 N	4.31 W
Stewartstown, N. Ire., U.K.	48	54.35 N	6.41 W
Stewartstown, Pa., U.S.	208	39.45 N	76.35 W
Stewartsville, Mo., U.S.	194	39.45 N	94.30 W
Stewartsville, N.J., U.S.	208	40.42 N	75.07 W
Stewartsville, Pa., U.S.	279b	40.21 N	79.46 W
Stewart Valley	184	50.36 N	107.50 W
Stewartville	190	43.51 N	92.29 W
Stewiacke	186	45.08 N	63.21 W
Steyerberg	52	52.34 N	9.01 E
Steyning	42	50.53 N	0.20 W
Steynsburg	158	31.15 S	25.49 E
Steynsrus	158	27.58 S	27.33 E
Steyr	61	48.03 N	14.25 E
Steyr ≃	61	48.02 N	14.25 E
Steytlerville	158	33.21 S	24.21 E
Stežki	80	53.06 N	41.13 E
Stezzano	62	45.38 N	9.39 E
Sthal	126	24.12 N	89.44 E
Ştia	66	43.48 N	11.42 E
Štiavnické vrchy ⋀⋀	30	48.40 N	18.45 E
Stickle Pond ⊜	276	40.59 N	74.25 W
Stickney, Ill., U.S.	216	41.49 N	87.47 W
Stickney, S. Dak., U.S.	198	43.35 N	98.26 W
Stidsvig	41	56.12 N	13.08 E
Stiefingbach ≃	61	46.47 N	15.35 E
Stiege	54	51.40 N	10.53 E
Stiene	76	57.26 N	24.34 E
Stienitzfliess ≃	264a	52.33 N	13.43 E
Stienitz-See ⊜	264a	52.30 N	13.49 E
Stiens	52	53.15 N	5.45 E
Stiepel ◆[8]	263	51.25 N	7.15 E
Stiftskirche ♉[1]	263	51.23 N	7.00 E
Stige	41	55.26 N	10.25 E
Stigler	196	35.15 N	95.08 W
Stigliano	68	40.24 N	16.14 E
Stigtomta	40	58.48 N	16.47 E
Stikine ≃	180	56.40 N	132.30 W
Stikine Ranges ⋀⋀	180	58.45 N	130.00 W
Stiklestad	26	63.48 N	11.33 E
Stilbaai	158	34.24 S	21.26 E
Stile	148	34.20 N	5.51 E
Stiles	210	40.40 N	75.30 W
Stiles Pond ⊜	283	42.41 N	71.02 W
Stilesville	210	42.05 N	75.24 W
Stilfontein	158	26.50 S	26.50 E
Stilís	38	38.55 N	22.36 E
Stillaguamish ≃	224	48.11 N	122.22 W
Stillaguamish, North Fork ≃	224	48.11 N	122.07 W
Stillaguamish, South Fork ≃	224	48.11 N	122.07 W
Stillhouse Hollow Lake ⊜[1]	222	31.00 N	97.35 W
Stilling	41	56.04 N	10.00 E
Stillman Valley	216	42.07 N	89.11 W
Stillmore	192	32.27 N	82.13 W
Still Pond	208	39.20 N	76.03 W
Still Run ≃	285	39.49 N	75.18 W
Stillwater, B.C., Can.	182	49.46 N	124.18 W
Stillwater, Minn., U.S.	190	45.04 N	92.49 W
Stillwater, N.J., U.S.	210	41.02 N	74.52 W
Stillwater, N.Y., U.S.	210	42.57 N	73.39 W
Stillwater, Ohio, U.S.	214	40.20 N	81.18 W
Stillwater, Okla., U.S.	196	36.07 N	97.04 W
Stillwater, Pa., U.S.	210	41.09 N	76.22 W
Stillwater ≃, Mont., U.S.	202	45.38 N	109.17 W
Stillwater ≃, Ohio, U.S.	218	39.47 N	84.12 W
Stillwater Creek ≃	214	40.25 N	81.22 W
Stillwater Range ⋀⋀	204	39.50 N	118.15 W
Stillwell, Ill., U.S.	219	40.13 N	91.11 W
Stillwell, Okla., U.S.	194	35.49 N	94.38 W
Stilo	68	38.29 N	16.28 E
Stilo, Punta ›	68	38.28 N	16.36 E
Stimberg ∧[2]	263	51.40 N	7.15 E
Stimigliano	66	42.18 N	12.34 E
Stimson, Mount ∧	202	48.31 N	113.36 W
Stinchar ≃	44	55.06 N	5.00 W
Stinear Nunataks ⋀⋀	9	69.42 S	64.40 E
Stine Canal ≊	226	35.15 N	119.08 W
Stine Mountain ∧	202	45.44 N	113.07 W
Stingray Point ›	208	37.33 N	76.18 W
Stînisoara, Munţii ⋀⋀	38	47.10 N	26.00 E
Stinking Water Creek ≃	198	40.22 N	101.07 W
Stinnett	196	35.50 N	101.27 W
Stintino	71	40.56 N	8.13 E
Stintonville	273d	26.14 S	28.13 E
Štip	38	41.44 N	22.12 E
Stiperstones ∧	42	52.35 N	2.56 W
Stiring-wendel	56	49.12 N	6.56 E
Stírka ∧	60	49.24 N	13.34 E
Stirling, Austl.	162	21.44 S	133.45 E
Stirling, Austl.	168b	35.00 S	138.43 E
Stirling, Alta., Can.	182	49.30 N	112.31 W
Stirling, Ont., Can.	212	44.18 N	77.33 W
Stirling, Scot., U.K.	46	56.07 N	3.57 W
Stirling, N.J., U.S.	210	40.41 N	74.30 W
Stirling, Mount ∧	162	31.50 S	117.38 E
Stirling Castle ⊥	46	56.07 N	3.57 W
Stirling City	204	39.54 N	121.32 W
Stirling Range ⋀⋀	162	34.23 S	117.50 E
Stirling Reservoir ⊜[1]	168a	33.08 S	116.03 E
Stirrat	192	37.44 N	82.00 W
Stissing Mountain ∧	210	41.57 N	73.42 W
Stittsville	212	45.15 N	75.55 W
Stittville	210	43.13 N	75.17 W
Stjärnhov	40	59.05 N	17.00 E
Stjärnsund, Sve.	40	58.51 N	14.55 E
Stjärnsund, Sve.	40	60.26 N	16.12 E
Stjernøya ▮	24	70.18 N	22.45 E
Stjørdalshalsen	26	63.28 N	10.56 E
Stöberhai ∧	54	51.39 N	10.34 E
Stobi ⊥	38	41.34 N	21.58 E
Stochod ≃	78	51.52 N	25.38 E
Stock	260	51.40 N	0.27 E
Stock, Étang du ⊜	56	48.45 N	6.55 E
Stockach	58	47.51 N	9.00 E
Stöckalp	58	46.48 N	8.17 E
Stockamöllan	41	55.57 N	13.22 E
Stockbridge, Eng., U.K.	42	51.07 N	1.29 W
Stockbridge, Ga., U.S.	192	33.33 N	84.14 W
Stockbridge, Mass., U.S.	207	42.17 N	73.19 W
Stockbridge, Mich., U.S.	216	42.27 N	84.11 W
Stockbridge Bowl ⊜	207	42.20 N	73.19 W
Stockbridge Indian Reservation ◆[4]	190	44.52 N	88.53 W
Stockbury	260	51.20 N	0.39 E
Stockby	40	59.20 N	17.41 E
Stockdale, Ohio, U.S.	218	38.57 N	82.51 W
Stockdale, Tex., U.S.	196	29.14 N	97.58 W
Stockelsdorf	52	53.54 N	10.38 E
Stöcken	54	53.00 N	10.40 E
Stockerau	61	48.23 N	16.13 E
Stockertown	208	40.45 N	75.16 W
Stockett	202	47.21 N	111.10 W
Stockheim	56	50.19 N	9.01 E
Stöckheim bei Braunschweig	52	52.12 N	10.31 E
Stockholm, Sve.	40	59.20 N	18.03 E
Stockholm, Maine, U.S.	186	47.03 N	68.08 W
Stockholm, N.J., U.S.	210	41.05 N	74.31 W
Stockholm, Lake ⊜	276	41.04 N	74.32 W
Stock Island	220	24.34 N	81.45 W
Stockland	216	40.37 N	87.36 W
Stockport, Eng., U.K.	44	53.25 N	2.10 W
Stockport, N.Y., U.S.	210	42.19 N	73.45 W
Stockport □[8]	262	53.23 N	2.08 W
Stocksbridge	44	53.27 N	1.34 W
Stockstadt	56	49.48 N	8.28 E
Stocksund	40	59.23 N	18.04 E
Stockton, Austl.	170	32.55 S	151.47 E
Stockton, Ala., U.S.	194	31.00 N	87.52 W
Stockton, Calif., U.S.	226	37.57 N	121.17 W
Stockton, Ill., U.S.	190	42.21 N	90.01 W
Stockton, Kans., U.S.	198	39.26 N	99.16 W
Stockton, Md., U.S.	208	38.03 N	75.25 W
Stockton, Mo., U.S.	194	37.42 N	93.48 W
Stockton, N.J., U.S.	208	40.24 N	74.58 W
Stockton, N.Y., U.S.	214	42.19 N	79.22 W
Stockton, Utah, U.S.	200	40.27 N	112.22 W
Stockton Heath	262	53.22 N	2.35 W
Stockton Metropolitan Airport ⊠	226	37.54 N	121.15 W
Stockton-on-Tees	44	54.34 N	1.19 W
Stockton Plateau ⋀⋀[1]	196	30.30 N	102.30 W
Stockton Reservoir ⊜[1]	194	37.40 N	93.45 W
Stockton Springs	188	44.29 N	68.52 W
Stockum, B.R.D.	52	51.40 N	7.42 E
Stockum, B.R.D.	263	51.36 N	6.39 E
Stockum, B.R.D.	263	51.32 N	7.47 E
Stockum ◆[8], B.R.D.	263	51.28 N	7.22 E
Stockum ◆[8], B.R.D.	263	51.16 N	6.44 E
Stockville	198	40.32 N	100.23 W
Stockwell	216	40.17 N	86.46 W
Stockwell, Lake ⊜	285	39.51 N	74.47 W
Stoco Lake ⊜	212	44.28 N	77.18 W
Stoczek Łukowski	30	51.58 N	21.58 E
Stod	60	49.39 N	13.10 E
Stoddard Mountain ∧	228	34.42 N	117.07 W
Stöde	26	62.25 N	16.35 E
Stodoliči	78	51.44 N	28.30 E
Stodolišče	76	54.11 N	32.39 E
Stœng Tréng	110	13.31 N	105.58 E
Stoer	46	58.12 N	.5.20 W
Stoer, Point of ›	46	58.15 N	5.21 W
Stoffberg	156	25.29 S	29.49 E
Stoj, Gora ∧	78	48.37 N	23.11 E
Stojba	89	52.49 N	131.43 E
Stoke	260	51.27 N	0.37 E
Stoke ≃	206	45.35 N	71.58 W
Stoke D'Abernon	260	51.19 N	0.23 W
Stoke Golding	42	52.34 N	1.24 W
Stoke Mountains ⋀⋀	206	45.33 N	71.42 W
Stokenchurch	42	51.40 N	0.55 W
Stoke Newington ◆[8]	260	51.34 N	0.05 W
Stoke-on-Trent	42	53.00 N	2.10 W
Stoke Poges	260	51.33 N	0.35 W
Stokes, Mount ∧	172	41.06 S	174.06 E
Stokes Inlet ⊂	162	33.50 S	121.08 E
Stokesley	44	54.28 N	1.11 W
Stokes Point ›	166	40.10 S	143.56 E
Stokes Range ⋀⋀[2]	164	15.46 S	130.57 E
Stokkemarke	41	54.50 N	11.23 E
Stokksnes ›	24a	64.17 N	14.54 W
Stol ∧	38	44.13 N	22.14 E
Stolac	36	43.05 N	17.58 E
Stolbcy	76	53.29 N	26.44 E
Stolberg, B.R.D.	56	50.46 N	6.13 E
Stolberg, D.D.R.	54	51.34 N	10.57 E
Stolbišči	80	55.39 N	49.14 E
Stolboucha	86	49.59 N	84.30 E
Stolbovo	76	52.38 N	34.47 E
Stolbovoj, Ostrov ▮	74	74.05 N	136.00 E
Stolbun	76	52.48 N	31.25 E
Stolby, Zapovednik ♠	88	55.45 N	92.45 E
Stolica ∧	30	48.48 N	20.11 E
Stolin	78	51.53 N	26.51 E
Stollberg	54	50.42 N	12.47 E
Stöllet	26	60.24 N	13.16 E
Stol'noje	78	51.31 N	31.55 E
Stolp → Słupsk	30	54.28 N	17.01 E
Stolpe	264a	52.40 N	13.16 E
Stolpen	54	51.05 N	14.04 E
Stolper Heide ◆[3]	264a	52.39 N	13.14 E
Stolpino	80	57.24 N	42.55 E
Stolpmünde → Ustka	30	54.35 N	16.50 E
Stolzenau	52	52.31 N	9.04 E
Ston	36	42.50 N	17.42 E
Stondon Massey	260	51.41 N	0.18 E
Stone, Eng., U.K.	42	52.54 N	2.10 W
Stone, Eng., U.K.	260	51.27 N	0.16 E
Stoneboro	214	41.20 N	80.07 W
Stone Canyon Reservoir ⊜[1]	280	34.07 N	118.28 W
Stone Corral Creek ≃	226	39.16 N	122.06 W
Stone Creek	214	40.24 N	81.34 W
Stonefort	194	37.37 N	88.42 W
Stoneham, Mass., U.S.	283	42.29 N	71.06 W
Stoneham, Pa., U.S.	214	41.49 N	79.07 W
Stone Harbor	208	39.03 N	74.45 W
Stonehaven	46	56.38 N	2.13 W
Stonehenge	166	24.22 S	143.17 E
Stonehenge ⊥	42	51.11 N	1.49 W
Stonehouse, Eng., U.K.	42	51.45 N	2.17 W
Stonehouse, Scot., U.K.	46	55.43 N	4.00 W

Symbol	English	Deutsch	Español	Français	Português
≃	River	Fluss	Río	Rivière	Rio
≊	Canal	Kanal	Canal	Canal	Canal
ᒪ	Waterfall, Rapids	Wasserfall, Stromschnellen	Cascada, Rápidos	Chute d'eau, Rapides	Cascata, Rápidos
⋓	Strait	Meeresstrasse	Estrecho	Détroit	Estreito
⊂	Bay, Gulf	Bucht, Golf	Bahía, Golfo	Baie, Golfe	Baía, Golfo
⊜	Lake, Lakes	See, Seen	Lago, Lagos	Lac, Lacs	Lago, Lagos
≡	Swamp	Sumpf	Pantano	Marais	Pântano
⍓	Ice Features, Glacier	Eis- und Gletscherformen	Accidentes Glaciales	Formes glaciaires	Acidentes Glaciares
⍑	Other Hydrographic Features	Andere Hydrographische Objekte	Otros Elementos Hidrográficos	Autres données hydrographiques	Outros Elementos Hidrográficos
✢	Submarine Features	Untermeerische Objekte	Accidentes Submarinos	Formes de relief sous-marin	Acidentes Submarinos
□	Political Unit	Politische Einheit	Unidad Politica	Entité politique	Unidade Política
♉	Cultural Institution	Kulturelle Institution	Institución Cultural	Institution culturelle	Instituição Cultural
⊥	Historical Site	Historische Stätte	Sitio Histórico	Site historique	Sitio Histórico
♠	Recreational Site	Erholungs- und Ferienort	Sitio de Recreo	Centre de loisirs	Sítio de Lazer
⊠	Airport	Flughafen	Aeropuerto	Aéroport	Aeroporto
■	Military Installation	Militäranlage	Instalación Militar	Installation militaire	Instalação Militar
◆	Miscellaneous	Verschiedenes	Misceláneo	Divers	Miscelânea

Name	Page	Lat.°′	Long.°′
Stone Indian Reserve ⊸[4]	182	51.54 N	123.12 W
Stoneleigh	42	52.21 N	1.31 W
Stonelick Creek ≃	218	39.07 N	84.13 W
Stonelick State Park ♠	218	39.13 N	84.04 W
Stone Mountain	192	33.49 N	84.10 W
Stone Mountain Λ	188	44.34 N	71.40 W
Stone Park	278	41.45 N	87.53 W
Stoner	182	53.36 N	122.40 W
Stoner Creek ≃	218	38.18 N	84.14 W
Stone Ridge	210	41.51 N	74.09 W
Stonerstown	214	40.13 N	78.16 W
Stones, East Fork ≃	194	35.59 N	86.27 W
Stones, West Fork ≃	194	35.59 N	86.27 W
Stonestown ⊸[9]	282	37.44 N	122.28 W
Stonevilla	279b	40.18 N	79.31 W
Stoneville	192	36.28 N	79.54 W
Stonewall, Man., Can.	184	50.09 N	97.21 W
Stonewall, Miss., U.S.	194	32.08 N	88.47 W
Stonewall, Okla., U.S.	196	34.39 N	96.31 W
Stoney Creek	212	43.13 N	79.46 W
Stoney Point ❯	214	42.18 N	82.34 W
Stonington, Conn., U.S.	207	41.20 N	71.54 W
Stonington, Ill., U.S.	219	39.44 N	89.12 W
Stonington, Maine, U.S.	188	44.09 N	68.40 W
Stony ≃, Alaska, U.S.	180	61.45 N	156.35 W
Stony ≃, Minn., U.S.	190	47.44 N	91.47 W
Stony Brook	210	40.56 N	73.09 W
Stony Brook ≃, Conn., U.S.	276	41.04 N	73.28 W
Stony Brook ≃, Conn., U.S.	276	41.08 N	73.22 W
Stony Brook ≃, Mass., U.S.	283	42.38 N	71.22 W
Stony Brook ≃, Mass., U.S.	283	42.22 N	71.16 W
Stony Brook ≃, N.J., U.S.	276	40.56 N	74.26 W
Stony Brook ≃, N.J., U.S.	276	40.19 N	74.41 W
Stony Brook Harbor C	276	40.54 N	73.10 W
Stony Brook Reservation ♠	283	42.16 N	71.09 W
Stony Creek, Conn., U.S.	207	41.16 N	72.45 W
Stony Creek, Mich., U.S.	281	42.42 N	83.07 W
Stony Creek, Va., U.S.	208	36.57 N	77.24 W
Stony Creek ≃, Calif., U.S.	204	39.41 N	121.58 W
Stony Creek ≃, Ill., U.S.	278	41.41 N	87.51 W
Stony Creek ≃, Mich., U.S.	216	41.57 N	83.18 W
Stony Creek ≃, Mich., U.S.	216	43.00 N	84.55 W
Stony Creek ≃, N.Y., U.S.	212	43.49 N	76.14 W
Stony Creek ≃, Pa., U.S.	214	40.20 N	78.55 W
Stony Creek ≃, Pa., U.S.	285	40.07 N	75.21 W
Stony Creek ≃, Va., U.S.	208	36.56 N	77.23 W
Stony Creek, Middle Fork ≃	226	39.25 N	122.31 W
Stony Creek, North Fork ≃	226	39.22 N	122.37 W
Stony Creek, South Fork ≃	226	39.22 N	122.39 W
Stony Creek Indian Reserve ⊸[4]	182	53.57 N	124.07 W
Stony Creek Mills	208	40.21 N	75.52 W
Stony Crossing	166	35.05 S	143.35 E
Stonyford	226	39.23 N	122.33 W
Stony Gorge Reservoir ⊜[1]	226	39.34 N	122.31 W
Stony Indian Reserve ⊸[4]	182	51.10 N	114.55 W
Stony Island I, Mich., U.S.	281	42.07 N	83.08 W
Stony Island I, N.Y., U.S.	212	43.53 N	76.25 W
Stony Kill ≃	210	42.24 N	73.38 W
Stony Lake ⊜, Man., Can.	176	58.51 N	98.35 W
Stony Lake ⊜, Ont., Can.	212	44.33 N	78.05 W
Stony Plain	182	53.02 N	114.00 W
Stony Plain Indian Reserve ⊸[4]	182	53.30 N	113.45 W
Stony Point, Mich., U.S.	216	41.57 N	83.16 W
Stony Point, N.C., U.S.	192	35.52 N	81.03 W
Stony Point, N.Y., U.S.	210	41.14 N	73.59 W
Stony Point ❯	284a	42.50 N	78.52 W
Stony Point ❯[1]	212	43.52 N	76.15 W
Stony Prairie	214	41.21 N	83.10 W
Stony Rapids	176	59.16 N	105.50 W
Stony Ridge	214	41.31 N	83.30 W
Stony River	180	61.47 N	156.41 W
Stony Run	284b	39.11 N	76.42 W
Stony Run ≃	285	40.09 N	75.32 W
Stony Stratford	42	52.04 N	0.52 W
Stooberbach ≃	61	47.27 N	16.35 E
Stop ≃	283	42.10 N	71.19 W
Stopnica	30	50.27 N	20.57 E
Stoppenberg ⊸[8]	263	51.29 N	7.02 E
Stör ≃	54	53.50 N	11.29 E
Storå	40	59.43 N	15.08 E
Storå ≃	26	56.19 N	8.19 E
Stora Alvaret ⏝	26	56.30 N	16.30 E
Stora Gla ⊜	26	59.30 N	12.30 E
Stora Kloten ⊜	40	59.52 N	15.16 E
Stora Le ⊜	26	59.05 N	11.53 E
Stora Lulevatten ⊜	24	67.10 N	19.16 E
Stora Mellösa	40	59.13 N	15.30 E
Stora Möja I	40	59.26 N	18.55 E
Stora Norn ⊜	40	60.14 N	15.42 E
Stora Sjöfallets Nationalpark ♠	24	67.44 N	18.16 E
Stora Skedvi	40	60.24 N	15.48 E
Stora Sotra I	26	60.18 N	5.05 E
Stora Sundby	40	59.16 N	16.07 E
Storavan ⊜	24	65.40 N	18.15 E
Stora Vika	40	58.56 N	17.48 E
Storby	26	60.13 N	19.34 E
Stord I	26	59.53 N	5.25 E
Store Andst	41	55.29 N	9.14 E
Store Bælt ⊔	41	55.30 N	11.00 E
Store Heddinge	41	55.19 N	12.25 E
Store Magleby	41	55.36 N	12.38 E
Store Merløse	41	55.33 N	11.40 E
Støren	26	63.02 N	10.18 E
Storeton	262	53.21 N	3.03 W
Storey □[6]	226	39.28 N	119.30 W
Storfjärden ⊜	40	60.30 N	17.23 E
Storfjorden C[2]	26	62.25 N	6.30 E
Storfors	40	59.32 N	14.16 E
Störitzsee ⊜	264a	52.23 N	13.51 E
Störkanal ≊	54	53.36 N	11.30 E
Storkerson Bay C	176	73.00 N	124.50 W
Storkerson Peninsula ❯[1]	176	72.30 N	106.30 W
Storkow, D.D.R.	54	53.19 N	14.17 E
Storkow, D.D.R.	54	52.15 N	13.56 E
Storlien	26	63.19 N	12.06 E
Stormarn ⊸[1]	52	53.45 N	10.20 E
Storm Bay C	166	43.10 S	147.32 E
Stormberg ⋀⋀	158	31.27 S	26.55 E
Storm King Mountain Λ	224	46.39 N	122.10 W
Storm Lake	198	42.39 N	95.13 W
Storm Mountain Λ	180	59.37 N	150.35 W
Stormont □[6]	206	45.10 N	75.00 W
Štormovo	83	49.06 N	38.55 E
Stormsrivier	158	33.59 S	23.52 E
Stormsvlei	158	34.05 S	20.06 E
Stormville	210	41.34 N	73.45 W
Stornara	68	41.17 N	15.46 E
Stornarella	68	41.15 N	15.44 E
Stornorrforsen	26	63.52 N	20.03 E
Stornoway	46	58.12 N	6.23 W
Storo	64	45.51 N	10.35 E
Storoževaja	84	43.53 N	41.27 E
Storoževsk	24	61.57 N	52.16 E
Storožinec	78	48.10 N	25.43 E
Storrensjön ⊜	26	63.38 N	12.34 E
Storrington	42	50.55 N	0.28 W
Storrs	207	41.48 N	72.15 W
Storsjøen ⊜, Nor.	26	61.35 N	11.12 E
Storsjøen ⊜, Nor.	26	60.23 N	11.40 E
Storsjön ⊜, Sve.	26	63.12 N	14.18 E
Storsjön ⊜, Sve.	26	62.48 N	13.07 E
Storsjön ⊜, Sve.	40	60.34 N	16.44 E
Storsjön ⊜, Sve.	40	59.04 N	17.12 E
Storskardhøa Λ	26	62.30 N	8.45 E
Storsteinsfjellet Λ	24	68.14 N	17.52 E
Storstrøm □[6]	41	55.00 N	11.55 E
Storstrømmen ⊔	41	54.58 N	11.55 E
Storstrømsbroen ⊸[5]	41	54.58 N	11.50 E
Stort ≃	260	51.46 N	0.01 E
Storthoaks	184	49.22 N	101.38 W
Storuman	24	65.06 N	17.06 E
Storuman-See → Storavan ⊜	24	65.40 N	18.15 E
Storvarts gruve	26	62.38 N	11.31 E
Storvätteshågna Λ	26	62.07 N	12.27 E
Storvik	40	60.35 N	16.32 E
Storvindeln ⊜	24	65.43 N	17.05 E
Storvreta	40	59.58 N	17.42 E
Story	202	44.35 N	106.53 W
Story City	190	42.11 N	93.36 W
Storytown, U.S.A. ♠	210	43.22 N	73.42 W
Stössen	54	51.06 N	11.55 E
Stotfold	42	52.01 N	0.14 W
Stotternheim	54	51.03 N	11.02 E
Stottville	210	42.17 N	73.45 W
Stouchsburg	208	40.23 N	76.14 W
Stough Park ♠	280	34.12 N	118.18 W
Stoughton, Sask., Can.	184	49.41 N	103.03 W
Stoughton, Eng., U.K.	260	51.15 N	0.35 W
Stoughton, Mass., U.S.	207	42.07 N	71.06 W
Stoughton, Wis., U.S.	216	42.55 N	89.13 W
Stoumont	56	50.25 N	5.48 E
Stoŭng ≃	110	12.50 N	104.19 E
Stour ≃, Eng., U.K.	42	52.20 N	2.15 W
Stour ≃, Eng., U.K.	42	51.18 N	1.22 E
Stour ≃, Eng., U.K.	42	51.52 N	1.16 E
Stour ≃, Eng., U.K.	42	50.43 N	1.46 W
Stourbridge	42	52.27 N	2.09 W
Stourport-on-Severn	42	52.21 N	2.16 W
Stout Lake ⊜	184	52.08 N	94.33 W
Stoutsville	219	39.33 N	91.51 W
Stover	194	38.27 N	92.59 W
Stow, Mass., U.S.	207	42.26 N	71.30 W
Stow, N.Y., U.S.	214	42.09 N	79.25 W
Stow, Ohio, U.S.	214	41.10 N	81.27 W
Stowe, Pa., U.S.	208	40.15 N	75.39 W
Stowe, Vt., U.S.	188	44.28 N	72.41 W
Stowe Township	279b	40.29 N	80.04 W
Stow Maries	260	51.40 N	0.39 E
Stowmarket	42	52.11 N	1.00 E
Stow-on-the-Wold	42	51.56 N	1.44 W
Stoyoma Mountain Λ	182	49.59 N	121.13 W
Stoystown	214	40.06 N	78.57 W
Stožec	60	48.51 N	13.50 E
Stra	64	45.25 N	12.00 E
Straach	54	51.57 N	12.35 E
Strabane, N. Ire., U.K.	48	54.49 N	7.27 W
Strabane, Pa., U.S.	214	40.08 N	80.10 W
Straberg	263	51.05 N	6.45 E
Strachan	46	57.01 N	2.32 W
Strachan Island I	164	9.00 S	142.10 E
Strachur	46	56.10 N	5.04 W
Stradbally	48	53.00 N	7.08 W
Stradbroke	42	52.19 N	1.16 E
Stradeč'	78	51.56 N	23.40 E
Stradella	62	45.05 N	9.18 E
Stradone	48	53.58 N	7.14 W
Stradovn'a, Ozero ⊜	82	56.53 N	36.18 E
Straelen	56	51.27 N	6.16 E
Strafford	285	40.03 N	75.25 W
Straffordville	212	42.45 N	80.47 W
Strahan	166	42.09 S	145.19 E
Straight Creek ≃	218	38.46 N	83.55 W
Strakonice	60	49.16 N	13.55 E
Stralsund	54	54.19 N	13.05 E
Strambino	62	45.23 N	7.53 E
Strand	158	34.06 S	18.50 E
Stranda	26	62.19 N	6.54 E
Strande	54	54.26 N	10.12 E
Strandhill	48	54.17 N	8.36 W
Stranger Creek ≃	198	39.00 N	95.01 W
Strangford	48	54.22 N	5.34 W
Strangford Lough ⊜	48	54.30 N	5.36 W
Strängnäs	40	59.23 N	17.02 E
Strångsjö	40	58.54 N	16.12 E
Strangways ≃	164	14.52 S	133.50 E
Strangways, Mount Λ	162	23.02 S	133.51 E
Stranorlar	48	54.48 N	7.46 W
Stranraer	44	54.55 N	5.02 W
Strasbourg, Sask., Can.	184	51.04 N	104.57 W
Strasbourg, Fr.	58	48.35 N	7.45 E
Strasburg, D.D.R.	54	53.30 N	13.44 E
Strasburg, Colo., U.S.	198	39.44 N	104.20 W
Strasburg, N. Dak., U.S.	198	46.08 N	100.10 W
Strasburg, Ohio, U.S.	214	40.36 N	81.32 W
Strasburg, Pa., U.S.	208	39.59 N	76.11 W
Strasburg, Va., U.S.	188	38.59 N	78.22 W
Strašeny	78	47.08 N	28.36 E
Straševiči	76	56.49 N	34.36 E
Strašice	60	49.44 N	13.46 E
Strašín	60	49.08 N	13.38 E
Stråssa	40	59.45 N	15.13 E
Strass bei Jenbach	64	47.23 N	11.49 E
Strassburg → Strasbourg	58	48.35 N	7.45 E
Strassgiech	60	49.58 N	11.00 E
Strasskirchen	60	48.50 N	12.43 E
Strasswalchen	64	47.59 N	13.15 E
Strat Florida Abbey ᵿ[1]	42	52.16 N	3.51 W
Stratford, Ont., Can.	212	43.22 N	80.57 W
Stratford, N.Z.	172	39.20 S	174.17 E
Stratford, Calif., U.S.	226	36.11 N	119.49 W
Stratford, Conn., U.S.	207	41.14 N	73.07 W
Stratford, Iowa, U.S.	190	42.16 N	93.56 W
Stratford, N.J., U.S.	208	39.50 N	75.01 W
Stratford, N.Y., U.S.	210	43.11 N	74.42 W
Stratford, Okla., U.S.	196	34.48 N	96.58 W
Stratford, Tex., U.S.	196	36.20 N	102.04 W
Stratford, Wis., U.S.	190	44.48 N	90.04 W
Stratford Centre	206	45.47 N	71.16 W
Stratford Hall ⊥	208	38.10 N	76.49 W
Stratford Point ❯	276	41.09 N	73.06 W
Stratford-upon-Avon	42	52.12 N	1.41 W
Strathalbyn	168b	35.16 S	138.54 E
Strathaven	46	55.40 N	4.04 W
Strathbogie Ranges ⋀⋀	169	36.55 S	145.45 E
Strathclair	184	50.24 N	100.24 W
Strathclyde □[4]	46	56.00 N	5.15 W
Strathcona Provincial Park ♠	182	49.40 N	125.50 W
Strathdearn ∨	46	57.15 N	4.05 W
Strathdon	46	57.11 N	3.02 W
Strathearn ∨	46	56.18 N	3.45 W
Strathfield	170	33.52 S	151.06 E
Strathkanaird	46	57.59 N	5.11 W
Strathlorne	186	46.11 N	61.17 W
Strathminglo	46	56.16 N	3.16 W
Strathmoor ⊸[8]	281	42.23 N	83.11 W
Strathmore, Alta., Can.	182	51.03 N	113.23 W
Strathmore, Calif., U.S.	204	36.09 N	119.04 W
Strathmore, N.J., U.S.	276	40.24 N	74.13 W
Strathmore ∨	46	56.39 N	3.00 W
Strathpeffer	46	57.35 N	4.33 W
Strathpine	171a	27.19 S	152.59 E
Strathroy	214	42.57 N	81.38 W
Strathy ≃	46	58.34 N	4.00 W
Strathy Point ❯	46	58.35 N	4.02 W
Strattanville	214	41.12 N	79.20 W
Stratton, Eng., U.K.	42	50.50 N	4.31 W
Stratton, Colo., U.S.	198	39.18 N	102.36 W
Stratton, Maine, U.S.	188	45.08 N	70.26 W
Stratton, Nebr., U.S.	198	40.09 N	101.14 W
Stratton, Ohio, U.S.	214	40.32 N	80.38 W
Stratton Mountain Λ	188	43.05 N	72.56 W
Stratton Saint Margaret	42	51.35 N	1.45 W
Straubing	60	48.53 N	12.34 E
Strauch	263	51.09 N	6.56 E
Straumen	26	63.52 N	11.18 E
Straupitz	54	51.54 N	14.07 E
Strausberg	54	52.35 N	13.53 E
Straus-Berger Stadtforst ♠	264a	52.34 N	13.52 E
Strausberg-Vorstadt	264a	52.32 N	13.51 E
Straussberg	54	51.23 N	10.44 E
Straussee ⊜	264a	52.35 N	13.53 E
Straussfurt	54	51.09 N	10.59 E
Strausstown	208	40.30 N	76.11 W
Stravignano	66	43.05 N	12.49 E
Strawberry	226	38.13 N	118.35 W
Strawberry ≃, Ark., U.S.	194	35.53 N	91.13 W
Strawberry ≃, Utah, U.S.	200	40.10 N	110.24 W
Strawberry Island I	284a	42.57 N	78.55 W
Strawberry Mountain Λ	202	44.19 N	118.43 W
Strawberry Point, Calif., U.S.	282	37.54 N	122.31 W
Strawberry Point, Iowa, U.S.	190	42.41 N	91.32 W
Strawberry Point ❯	283	42.15 N	70.46 W
Strawberry Reservoir ⊜[1]	200	40.11 N	111.08 W
Strawberry Valley	226	39.34 N	121.06 W
Strawbridge Lake ⊜	285	39.57 N	74.57 W
Strawn	196	32.33 N	98.30 W
Straw Pump	279b	40.19 N	79.40 W
Stráž	61	49.04 N	14.54 E
Strážnice	30	48.54 N	17.18 E
Strážný	60	48.54 N	13.42 E
Strážov	60	49.18 N	13.15 E
Strážske	30	48.53 N	21.50 E
Streaky Bay	162	32.48 S	134.13 E
Streaky Bay C	162	32.36 S	134.08 E
Streamwood	216	42.02 N	88.11 W
Streatham, Austl.	169	37.41 S	143.04 E
Streatham, B.C., Can.	182	53.52 N	126.12 W
Streatham ⊸[8]	260	51.26 N	0.08 W
Streator	216	41.07 N	88.50 W
Strebersdorf ⊸[8]	264b	48.18 N	16.23 E
Streda nad Bodrogem	30	48.23 N	21.46 E
Středočeský Kraj □[4]	30	49.55 N	14.30 E
Stredoslovenský Kraj □[4]	30	48.50 N	19.10 E
Street	42	51.07 N	2.42 W
Streeter	198	46.39 N	99.21 W
Streetman	222	31.53 N	96.19 W
Streetsboro	214	41.14 N	81.21 W
Streets Run ≃	279b	40.23 N	79.56 W
Streetsville	212	43.35 N	79.42 W
Strehaia	38	44.37 N	23.12 E
Strehla	54	51.21 N	13.13 E
Strehlen → Strzelin	30	50.47 N	17.03 E
Streitberg	60	49.49 N	11.13 E
Střela ≃	60	49.55 N	13.33 E
Strelasund ⊔	54	54.20 N	13.05 E
Strel'covka	83	49.18 N	39.52 E
Streleckaja Step', Zapovednik ♠	83	49.16 N	40.05 E
Streleckije Vyselki	82	54.12 N	38.57 E
Strelica	78	51.37 N	38.55 E
Strelitzalt	54	53.20 N	13.05 E
Strelka	86	58.05 N	93.01 E
Strelka ≃	265a	59.52 N	30.03 E
Strelka-Čun'a	74	61.45 N	102.48 E
Strelkovo	82	55.28 N	37.37 E
Strelkovoje	78	45.54 N	34.53 E
Strelkovskij, Porog ⌊	86	58.04 N	93.07 E
Strel'na, S.S.S.R.	24	66.06 N	38.40 E
Strel'na, S.S.S.R.	76	59.51 N	30.02 E
Strel'na ≃	24	66.04 N	38.39 E
Strel'skaja	24	59.28 N	47.47 E
Střelské Hoštice	60	49.18 N	13.46 E
Strem ≃	61	47.00 N	16.31 E
Strembo	64	46.09 N	10.44 E
Stremilovo	82	55.09 N	37.09 E
Strenči	76	57.37 N	25.41 E
Strengen	58	47.08 N	10.27 E
Stresa	62	45.53 N	8.32 E
Strešin	76	52.43 N	30.05 E
Stretford	44	53.27 N	2.19 W
Stretton, Austl.	162	32.32 S	117.41 E
Stretton, Eng., U.K.	42	52.44 N	0.35 W
Stretton, Eng., U.K.	44	53.21 N	2.35 W
Streu ≃	56	50.21 N	10.16 E
Strib	41	55.32 N	9.47 E
Striberg	40	59.33 N	14.56 E
Stříbro	60	49.46 N	13.00 E
Strichen	46	57.34 N	2.05 W
Strickherdicke	263	51.29 N	7.43 E
Strickland ≃	164	6.00 S	142.05 E
Striegau → Strzegom	30	50.57 N	16.21 E
Strigno	64	46.04 N	11.31 E
Strijen	52	51.45 N	4.33 E
Striker, Lake ⊜[1]	222	31.57 N	94.59 W
Strimón (Struma) ≃	38	40.47 N	23.51 E
Stringtown, Ind., U.S.	218	40.05 N	86.29 W
Stringtown, Okla., U.S.	196	34.28 N	96.03 W
Striven, Loch C	46	55.58 N	5.09 W
Strižament, Gora Λ	84	44.46 N	42.01 E
Strižavka	78	49.19 N	28.28 E
Striži	80	58.30 N	49.13 E
Strjama ≃	38	42.10 N	24.56 E
Strobel	252	32.03 S	60.37 W
Strobel, Lago ⊜	254	48.22 S	71.12 W
Strobl	64	47.43 N	13.29 E
Strobleton	214	41.22 N	79.25 W
Strøby	41	55.23 N	12.18 E
Stroeder	254	40.11 S	62.37 W
Strogino ⊸[8]	265b	55.49 N	37.25 E
Strogonof Point ❯	180	56.53 N	158.49 W
Stroh	216	41.35 N	85.12 W
Ströhen	52	52.32 N	8.41 E
Stroitel'	78	50.47 N	36.26 E
Strokestown	48	53.47 N	8.08 W
Strom ≃	54	53.15 N	13.50 E
Stroma I	46	58.41 N	3.08 W
Stromberg, B.R.D.	52	51.48 N	8.12 E
Stromberg, B.R.D.	56	49.57 N	7.46 E
Stromboli, Isola I	70	38.47 N	15.13 E
Strome	182	52.48 N	112.04 W
Stromeferry	46	57.21 N	5.34 W
Strömkendorf	54	53.58 N	11.29 E
Stromness	46	58.57 N	3.18 W
Strömsberg	40	60.24 N	17.35 E
Strömsbro	40	60.42 N	17.10 E
Strömsbruk	26	61.53 N	17.19 E
Stromsburg	198	41.07 N	97.36 W
Strömsholm	40	59.32 N	16.15 E
Strömsnäsbruk	26	56.33 N	13.43 E
Strömstad	26	58.56 N	11.10 E
Strömsund	26	63.51 N	15.35 E
Ströms Vattudal ∨	26	63.56 N	15.28 E
Stromyn'	82	56.03 N	38.29 E
Strong, Ark., U.S.	194	33.07 N	92.21 W
Strong, Maine, U.S.	188	44.48 N	70.13 W
Strong ≃	194	31.51 N	90.08 W
Strong City	198	38.24 N	96.32 W
Stronghurst	190	40.45 N	90.55 W
Strongoli	68	39.15 N	17.03 E
Strongs Creek ≃	276	40.40 N	73.22 W
Strongs Neck ❯[1]	276	40.58 N	73.07 W
Strongstown	214	40.33 N	78.55 W
Strongsville	214	41.19 N	81.50 W
Strongsville Air Park ⊠	279a	41.19 N	81.52 W
Stronsay I	46	59.07 N	2.37 W
Stronsay Firth ⊔	46	59.02 N	2.41 W
Strontian	46	56.41 N	5.44 W
Strood	42	51.24 N	0.28 E
Stropkov	30	49.12 N	21.40 E
Stropnice ≃	61	48.52 N	14.30 E
Stroppiana	62	45.14 N	8.27 E
Stroud, Eng., U.K.	42	51.45 N	2.12 W
Stroud, Okla., U.S.	196	35.45 N	96.40 W.
Stroud Road	166	32.20 S	151.56 E
Stroudsburg	210	40.59 N	75.12 W
Strövelstorp	41	56.09 N	12.49 E
Strubenvale	273d	26.16 S	28.28 E
Strücklingen	52	53.07 N	7.40 E
Struer	26	56.29 N	8.37 E
Struga	38	41.11 N	20.40 E
Strugi-Krasnyje	76	58.17 N	29.06 E
Struisbaai	158	34.49 S	20.04 E
Struisbelt	273d	26.19 S	28.29 E
Strule ≃	48	54.43 N	7.25 W
Strullendorf	60	49.50 N	10.59 E
Strum	190	44.33 N	91.24 W
Struma (Strimón) ≃	38	40.47 N	23.51 E
Strumble Head ❯	42	52.02 N	5.04 W
Strumica	38	41.26 N	22.38 E
Strümp	263	51.17 N	6.40 E
Strunino	82	56.23 N	38.34 E
Strupna	82	54.43 N	38.48 E
Struthers	214	41.04 N	80.38 W
Struy	46	57.24 N	4.39 W
Strydenburg	158	29.58 S	23.40 E
Strydomsvlei	158	33.10 S	23.03 E
Strydpoort	158	27.00 S	25.58 E
Stryj	78	49.15 N	23.51 E
Stryj ≃	78	49.24 N	24.13 E
Stryker	216	41.30 N	84.25 W
Strykersville	210	42.42 N	78.27 W
Stryków	30	51.55 N	19.37 E
Stryn	26	61.55 N	6.47 E
Strynø I	41	54.54 N	10.37 E
Strypa ≃	78	48.52 N	25.26 E
Strzegom	30	50.57 N	16.21 E
Strzegowo-Osada	30	52.55 N	20.18 E
Strzelce Krajeńskie	30	52.53 N	15.32 E
Strzelce Opolskie	30	50.31 N	18.19 E
Strzelecki, Mount Λ	162	21.10 S	133.53 E
Strzelecki Creek ≃	166	29.37 S	139.59 E
Strzelin	30	50.47 N	17.03 E
Strzelno	30	52.38 N	18.11 E
Strzyżów	30	49.52 N	21.47 E
Stuart, Fla., U.S.	220	27.12 N	80.15 W
Stuart, Iowa, U.S.	198	41.30 N	94.19 W
Stuart, Nebr., U.S.	198	42.36 N	99.08 W
Stuart, Va., U.S.	192	36.38 N	80.16 W
Stuart ≃	182	54.00 N	123.32 W
Stuart, Mount Λ	224	47.29 N	120.54 W
Stuart Bluff Range ⋀⋀	162	22.47 S	132.13 E
Stuart Channel ⊔	224	48.55 N	123.45 W
Stuart Island I, Alaska, U.S.	180	63.35 N	162.30 W
Stuart Island I, Wash., U.S.	224	48.42 N	123.12 W
Stuart Lake ⊜	182	54.32 N	124.35 W
Stuart Mountains ⋀⋀	172	45.00 S	167.37 E
Stuart Range ⋀⋀	162	29.10 S	134.56 E
Stuarts Draft	192	38.01 N	79.02 W
Stubai ∨	64	47.06 N	11.19 E
Stubaier Alpen ⋀⋀	64	47.10 N	11.05 E
Stubalpe ⋀⋀	61	47.06 N	14.54 E
Stübbecken	263	51.23 N	7.36 E
Stubbekøbing	41	54.53 N	12.03 E
Stubbenfelde	54	54.02 N	14.01 E
Stubbenkammer	54	54.35 N	13.40 E
Stubbins	262	53.39 N	2.19 W
Stubbs Bay C	241h	13.08 N	61.10 W
Stubbs Lake ⊜	212	45.29 N	77.44 W
Stubla ≃	78	50.50 N	26.04 E
Stubner Kogel Λ	64	47.07 N	13.06 E
Stučka	76	56.38 N	25.13 E
Studená	61	49.11 N	15.17 E
Studenec	80	54.52 N	48.16 E
Studenica, Manastir ᵿ[1]	38	43.21 N	20.35 E
Studénka	30	49.42 N	18.05 E
Studen Kladenec, Jazovir ⊜[1]	38	41.37 N	25.30 E
Studholme Junction	172	44.44 S	171.08 E
Studland	42	50.39 N	1.58 W
Studley	42	52.16 N	1.52 W
Stud'onoje, S.S.S.R.	80	51.36 N	53.10 E
Stud'onoje, S.S.S.R.	86	53.37 N	77.31 E
Stud'onok	78	51.42 N	34.07 E
Studsvik	40	58.46 N	17.23 E
Stugudal	26	62.54 N	11.52 E
Stugun	26	63.10 N	15.36 E
Stuhleck Λ	61	47.34 N	15.47 E
Stühlingen	58	47.44 N	8.26 E
Stuhlweissenburg → Székesfehérvár	30	47.12 N	18.25 E
Stuhm → Sztum	30	53.56 N	19.01 E
Stuhr	52	53.01 N	8.45 E
Stuie	182	52.22 N	126.02 W
Stukely Lake ⊜	206	45.22 N	72.15 W
Stukenbrock	52	51.54 N	8.39 E
Stull Lake ⊜	184	54.23 N	92.34 W
Stülpe	54	52.02 N	13.19 E
Stumm	64	47.17 N	11.53 E
Stump Creek	214	41.01 N	78.50 W
Stump Creek ≃	276	40.28 N	74.16 W
Stumpf	263	51.06 N	7.13 E
Stump Lake ⊜	198	47.54 N	98.24 W
Stumsdorf	54	51.37 N	12.03 E
Stuorre Tjõure Λ	26	63.56 N	13.30 E
Stupart ≃	184	56.00 N	93.22 W
Stupava	61	48.17 N	17.02 E
Stupino	82	54.53 N	38.05 E
Stuppach	56	49.27 N	9.44 E
Stura di Ala ≃	62	45.18 N	7.24 E
Stura di Demonte ≃	62	44.40 N	7.53 E
Stura di Lanzo ≃	62	45.06 N	7.44 E
Stura di Val Grande ≃	62	45.18 N	7.24 E
Stura di Viù ≃	62	45.16 N	7.26 E
Sturbridge	207	42.07 N	72.05 W
Sturdee	162	31.52 S	132.23 E
Sturge Island I	9	67.27 S	164.18 E
Sturgeon, Mo., U.S.	219	39.14 N	92.17 W
Sturgeon, Pa., U.S.	279b	40.23 N	80.13 W
Sturgeon ≃, Ont., Can.	190	46.19 N	79.58 W
Sturgeon ≃, Sask., Can.	184	53.12 N	105.53 W
Sturgeon ≃, Mich., U.S.	190	45.24 N	84.38 W
Sturgeon ≃, Mich., U.S.	190	47.02 N	88.30 W
Sturgeon ≃, Mich., U.S.	190	45.50 N	86.41 W
Sturgeon Bay	190	44.50 N	87.23 W
Sturgeon Bay C	184	52.00 N	97.50 W
Sturgeon Falls	190	46.22 N	79.55 W
Sturgeon Lake ⊜, Alta., Can.	182	55.06 N	117.30 W
Sturgeon Lake ⊜, Ont., Can.	184	55.25 N	90.55 W
Sturgeon Lake ⊜, Ont., Can.	212	44.28 N	78.42 W
Sturgeon Lake ⊜, Wash., U.S.	224	45.44 N	122.48 W
Sturgeon Lake Indian Reserve ⊸[4], Alta., Can.	182	55.04 N	117.29 W
Sturgeon Lake Indian Reserve ⊸[4], Sask., Can.	184	53.25 N	106.05 W
Sturgeon Landing	184	54.16 N	101.49 W
Sturgeon Point ❯	212	42.42 N	79.03 W
Sturgis, Sask., Can.	184	51.58 N	102.32 W
Sturgis, Ky., U.S.	194	37.33 N	87.59 W
Sturgis, Mich., U.S.	190	41.48 N	85.25 W
Sturgis, Miss., U.S.	194	33.21 N	89.03 W
Sturgis, S. Dak., U.S.	198	44.25 N	103.31 W
Sturla	62	44.24 N	8.59 E
Sturminster Newton	42	50.50 N	2.19 W
Štúrovo	30	47.48 N	18.49 E
Sturry	42	51.18 N	1.07 E
Sturt, Mount Λ	166	29.33 S	141.42 E
Sturt Creek	162	19.10 S	128.10 E
Sturt Creek ≃	162	20.08 S	127.24 E
Sturt Desert ⊸[2]	166	28.30 S	141.00 E
Sturtevant	216	42.42 N	87.54 W
Stürzelberg	263	51.08 N	6.49 E
Stutterheim	158	32.33 S	27.28 E
Stuttgart, B.R.D.	56	48.46 N	9.11 E
Stuttgart, Ark., U.S.	194	34.30 N	91.33 W
Stuttgart □[5]	56	49.00 N	9.45 E
Stuttgart-Echterdingen, Flughafen ⊠	56	48.41 N	9.12 E
Stützengrün	54	50.32 N	12.31 E
Stützerbach	54	50.38 N	10.51 E
Stuyvesant	210	42.24 N	73.47 W
Stuyvesant Falls	210	42.21 N	73.44 W
Stviga ≃	78	52.04 N	27.54 E
Stvolny	60	50.03 N	13.15 E
Styal	262	53.21 N	2.15 W
Stykkishólmur	24a	65.06 N	22.48 W
Styla	83	47.41 N	37.50 E
Styr' ≃	78	52.07 N	26.35 E
Styrum ⊸[8]	263	51.27 N	6.51 E
Styx ≃, Ont., Can.	212	44.11 N	80.57 W
Styx ≃, Ala., U.S.	194	30.31 N	87.27 W
Suaçuí Grande ≃	255	18.50 S	41.46 W
Suai	112	3.48 N	113.38 E
Suain	164	3.20 S	142.55 E
Suaita	246	6.07 N	73.27 W
Suakin Archipelago II	140	18.42 N	38.30 E
Sual	116	16.04 N	120.05 E
Suan	98	38.42 N	126.22 E
Suao, T'aiwan	100	24.36 N	121.51 E
Suao, Zhg.	100	25.38 N	119.42 E
Suaqui Grande	232	28.24 N	109.54 W
Suār	124	29.02 N	79.03 E
Suātala	124	23.09 N	79.02 E
Šubač	76	60.22 N	38.14 E
Subačius	76	55.46 N	24.47 E
Subah	115a	6.58 S	109.52 E
Subaio	256	22.35 S	42.52 W
Subang	115a	6.34 S	107.45 E
Subansiri ≃	120	26.48 N	93.50 E
Šubarkuduk	86	49.13 N	56.34 E
Subarnapur	272b	22.58 N	88.34 E
Subarnarekha ≃	126	21.34 N	87.24 E
Šubarši	86	48.35 N	57.12 E
Subashi	85	38.22 N	74.57 E
Subasio, Monte Λ	66	43.03 N	12.40 E
Subata	76	56.01 N	25.56 E
Subay', 'Irq as- ⊸[2]	144	22.15 N	43.05 E
Subbiano	66	43.34 N	11.52 E
Subbotino	86	53.04 N	91.55 E
Subchankulovo	80	54.34 N	53.49 E
Subei	102	39.27 N	95.03 E
Suben	60	48.25 N	13.26 E
Subhepur	272a	28.45 N	77.16 E
Subiaco	66	41.55 N	13.06 E
Subi Besar, Pulau I	112	2.55 N	108.50 E
Subic	116	14.53 N	120.14 E
Subic Bay C	116	14.45 N	120.13 E
Subic Bay Naval Station (United States) ■	116	14.47 N	120.16 E
Subipur	272b	22.54 N	88.08 E
Subk al-Ahad	142	30.18 N	31.02 E
Sublette	198	37.29 N	100.50 W
Sublett Range ⋀⋀	202	42.20 N	112.50 W
Sublime	222	29.29 N	96.48 W
Subotica	38	46.06 N	19.39 E
Şubr, Jabal Λ	144	13.25 N	44.06 E
Subugo Λ	154	1.40 N	35.49 E
Sučan	89	43.08 N	133.09 E
Sucarnoochee ≃	194	32.25 N	88.02 W
Succasunna	210	40.52 N	74.38 W
Succor Creek ≃	202	43.38 N	116.56 W
Suceava	38	47.39 N	26.19 E
Suceava □[4]	38	47.30 N	25.45 E
Suceava ≃	38	47.32 N	26.32 E
Sucha [beskidzka]	30	49.44 N	19.36 E
Suchaja	88	52.32 N	107.06 E
Suchaja Volnovacha ≃	83	47.37 N	38.01 E
Suchań, Pol.	30	53.17 N	15.19 E
Suchan → Sučan, S.S.S.R.	89	43.08 N	133.09 E
Suchana	74	68.45 N	118.00 E
Suchang	107	30.34 N	103.34 E
Süchbaatar	88	50.17 N	106.10 E
Süchbaatar □[4]	102	45.30 N	114.00 E
Suchdol ⊸[8]	54	50.08 N	14.21 E
Suchedniów	30	51.03 N	20.51 E
Suchetgarh	123	32.34 N	74.40 E
Suchiapa	234	16.37 N	93.05 W
Suchiapa ≃	234	16.36 N	93.01 W
Súchil	234	23.38 N	103.55 W
Suchilquitongo	234	17.15 N	96.53 W
Suchiniči	76	54.06 N	35.20 E
Suchitepéquez □[5]	236	14.25 N	91.20 W
Suchitlán	234	19.22 N	103.43 W
Suchitoto	236	13.56 N	89.02 W
Suchobezvodnoje	80	57.03 N	44.50 E
Suchoborka	24	59.06 N	49.58 E
Suchodol	82	54.27 N	37.22 E
Suchodol'skij	76	53.43 N	38.17 E
Suchodrev ≃	82	54.44 N	35.59 E
Suchoj	80	47.06 N	41.21 E
Suchoj Jelančik ≃	83	47.16 N	38.25 E
Suchoj Log	86	56.55 N	62.01 E
Suchoj Pit	86	58.48 N	92.49 E
Suchoj Sambek ≃	83	47.23 N	39.07 E
Suchoj Torec ≃	83	48.49 N	37.36 E
Suchona ≃	24	60.46 N	46.24 E
Suchorečka	80	52.49 N	52.27 E
Suchotinka	80	52.31 N	41.35 E
Suchotinskij	80	47.18 N	44.31 E
Suchou → Suzhou	106	31.18 N	120.37 E
Suchoverkovo	76	56.37 N	35.35 E
Suchov Pervyj	80	49.59 N	43.28 E
Süchow → Xuzhou	98	34.16 N	117.11 E
Süchteln	56	51.17 N	6.22 E
Suchumi	84	43.01 N	41.02 E
Sucio ≃, Col.	246	7.27 N	77.07 W
Sucio ≃, El Sal.	236	14.02 N	89.17 W
Šučje	78	51.45 N	40.29 E
Suck ≃	48	53.16 N	8.03 W
Sucker Creek Indian Reserve ⊸[4]	182	55.28 N	116.10 W
Sucker Lake ⊜	212	44.46 N	78.16 W
Suckling, Mount Λ	164	9.45 S	148.55 E
Sucre, Arg.	258	34.30 S	59.07 W
Sucre, Bol.	248	19.02 S	65.17 W
Sucre, Col.	246	8.49 N	74.44 W
Sucre, Ec.	246	1.16 S	80.26 W
Sucre □[3]	246	10.25 N	63.30 W
Sucre □[5], Col.	246	9.00 N	75.00 W
Sucre □[5], Ven.	286c	10.25 N	66.50 W
Sucúa	246	2.28 S	78.10 W
Sucuaro	246	4.34 N	68.50 W
Sucunduri ≃	248	5.50 S	59.32 W
Sucuriju	250	1.39 N	49.57 W
Sucuriú ≃	255	20.47 S	51.38 W
Sucy-en-Brie	50	48.46 N	2.32 E
Sud, Canal du ⊔	238	18.40 N	73.05 W
Sud, Pointe ❯	157a	11.53 S	43.49 E
Sud, Récif du ⊹[2]	175f	23.00 S	167.02 E
Sud, Rivière du ≃	206	45.08 N	73.15 W
Suda	76	59.09 N	37.33 E
Suda ≃	76	59.11 N	37.30 E
Südafrika → South Africa □[1]	156	30.00 S	26.00 E
Sudaj	76	58.58 N	43.08 E
Sudak	78	44.52 N	34.59 E
Sudalsvatnet ⊜	26	59.35 N	6.45 E
Südamerika → South America •[1]	18	15.00 S	60.00 W
Sudan	196	34.04 N	102.32 W
Sudan □[1]	136		
	140	15.00 N	30.00 E
Sudan ⊸[1]	134	10.00 N	20.00 E
Sudarsan	272b	22.59 N	88.17 E
Südbahnhof ⊸[5]	264b	48.11 N	16.23 E
Sudberg ⊸[8]	263	51.11 N	7.08 E
Sudbišči	76	52.57 N	37.39 E
Sud'bodarovka	80	52.19 N	54.07 E
Sudbury, Ont., Can.	190	46.30 N	81.00 W
Sudbury, Eng., U.K.	42	52.02 N	0.44 E
Sudbury, Mass., U.S.	207	42.23 N	71.25 W
Sudbury ≃	283	42.28 N	71.22 W
Sudbury Center	283	42.23 N	71.25 W
Sudbury Reservoir ⊜[1]	207	42.19 N	71.31 W
Südchinesisches Meer → South China Sea ⍑[2]	108	10.00 N	113.00 E
Sud Dakota → South Dakota □[3]	198	44.15 N	100.00 W
Sudd an-Na'ām, Jabal Λ	142	29.49 N	31.43 E
Suddie	246	7.07 N	58.29 W
Sude ≃	54	53.22 N	10.45 E
Süderbrarup	41	54.38 N	9.46 E
Süderlügum	41	54.52 N	8.55 E
Suderwich ⊸[8]	263	51.37 N	7.15 E
Sudeten → Sudety ⋀⋀	30	50.30 N	16.00 E
Sudety ⋀⋀	30	50.30 N	16.00 E
Süd-Georgien → South Georgia I	244	54.15 S	36.45 W
Südheide, Naturpark ♠	52	52.50 N	10.10 E
Sudi	154	10.06 S	39.57 E
Sudislavl'	80	57.53 N	41.43 E
Südkamen	263	51.35 N	7.39 E
Süd-Korea → Korea, South □[1]	98	36.30 N	128.00 E
Südlengern	52	52.11 N	8.38 E
Sudlersville	208	39.11 N	75.52 W
Südlicher Bug → Južnyj Bug ≃	78	46.59 N	31.58 E
Südlicher Indianer-See → Southern Indian Lake ⊜	176	57.10 N	98.40 W
Südlicher Teutoburger Wald, Naturpark ♠	52	52.10 N	8.15 E
Südlicher Teutoburger Wald-Eggegebirge, Naturpark ♠	52	51.50 N	8.50 E
Sudnikovo	82	55.53 N	36.02 E
Sudočje, Ozero ⊜	86	43.25 N	58.30 E
Sudogda	80	55.57 N	40.50 E
Sudomskaja Vozvyšennost' ⋀⋀[1]	76	57.25 N	29.25 E
Sudong, Pulau I	271c	1.13 N	103.44 E
Süd-Orkney-Inseln → South Orkney Islands II	9	60.35 S	45.30 W
Sudost' ≃	76	52.19 N	33.24 E
Sud-Ouest, Pointe du ❯	186	49.23 N	63.36 W
Sudovaja Višn'a	78	49.49 N	23.22 E
Südradde ≃	52	52.41 N	7.34 E
Süd-Sandwich-Inseln → South Sandwich Islands II	18	57.45 S	26.30 W

Symbols in the index entries represent the broad categories identified in the key at the right. Symbols with superior numbers (⋀⋀[2]) identify subcategories (see complete key on page *I* · *30*).

Kartensymbole in dem Registerverzeichnis stellen die rechts in Schlüssel erklärten Kategorien dar. Symbole mit hochgestellten Ziffern (⋀⋀[2]) bezeichnen Unterabteilungen einer Kategorie (vgl. vollständiger Schlüssel auf Seite *I* · *30*).

Los símbolos incluídos en el texto del índice representan las grandes categorias identificadas con la clave a la derecha. Los símbolos con numeros en su parte superior (⋀⋀[2]) identifican las subcategorías (véase la clave completa en la página *I* · *30*).

Les symboles de l'index représentent les catégories indiquées dans la légende à droite. Les symboles suivis d'un indice (⋀⋀[2]) représentent des sous-catégories (voir légende complète à la page *I* · *30*).

Os símbolos incluídos no texto do índice representam as grandes categorias identificadas com a chave à direita. Os símbolos com números em sua parte superior (⋀⋀[2]) identificam as subcategorias (veja-se a chave completa à página *I* · *30*).

Λ Mountain	Berg	Montaña	Montagne	Montanha
⋀⋀ Mountains	Berge	Montañas	Montagnes	Montanhas
)(Pass	Pass	Paso	Col	Passo
∨ Valley, Canyon	Tal, Cañon	Valle, Cañón	Vallée, Canyon	Vale, Canhão
⏝ Plain	Ebene	Llano	Plaine	Planície
❯ Cape	Kap	Cabo	Cap	Cabo
I Island	Insel	Isla	Île	Ilha
II Islands	Inseln	Islas	Îles	Ilhas
• Other Topographic Features	Andere Topographische Objekte	Otros Elementos Topográficos	Autres données topographiques	Outros Elementos Topográficos

ESPAÑOL
Nombre Página Lat.°′ Long.°′ W=Oeste

Süd-Shetland-Inseln → South Shetland Islands II 9 62.00 S 58.00 W
Sudūd 142 30.25 N 30.54 E
Sudupu 106 31.41 N 119.34 E
Südwest-Kap → South West Cape ≻ 166 43.34 S 146.02 E
Sudweyhe 52 52.59 N 8.53 E
Sudža 78 51.12 N 35.16 E
Sudzuche 89 42.52 N 133.45 E
Sue 96 33.35 N 130.30 E
Sue ≃ 140 7.41 N 28.03 E
Sueca 34 39.12 N 0.19 W
Suecia → Sweden □[1] 24 62.00 N 15.00 E
Sue Creek C 284b 39.17 N 76.24 W
Suedberg 208 40.32 N 76.28 W
Suède → Sweden □[1] 24 62.00 N 15.00 E
Suemez Island I 180 55.17 N 133.21 W
Suèvres 50 47.40 N 1.28 E
Suez → As-Suways 142 29.58 N 32.33 E
Suez, Gulf of → Suways, Khalīj as- C 140 29.00 N 32.50 E
Suez Canal → Suways, Qanāt as- ≍ 142 29.55 N 32.33 E
Sūf 132 32.19 N 35.50 E
Şufaynah 128 23.09 N 40.32 E
Suffern 210 41.07 N 74.09 W
Suffern Park 276 41.07 N 74.07 W
Suffield, Alta., Can. 184 50.12 N 111.10 W
Suffield, Conn., U.S. 207 41.59 N 72.39 W
Suffield, Ohio, U.S. 214 41.01 N 81.21 W
Suffolk 208 36.44 N 76.35 W
Suffolk □[6], Eng., U.K. 42 52.10 N 1.20 E
Suffolk □[6], Mass., U.S. 207 42.21 N 71.04 W
Suffolk □[6], N.Y., U.S. 210 40.55 N 72.40 W
Suffolk, Ruisseau ≃ 206 45.48 N 74.59 W
Suffolk Downs Race Track ♠ 283 42.23 N 71.00 W
Şūfīān 128 38.17 N 45.59 E
Sufi-Kurgan 85 40.02 N 73.30 E
Sufu → Kashi 85 39.29 N 75.59 E
Sugana, Val ∨ 64 46.00 N 11.40 E
Sugandha 272b 22.54 N 88.20 E
Sugandy 85 43.27 N 74.38 E
Suganhu ⊛ 102 38.50 N 94.00 E
Sugano 268 35.44 N 139.56 E
Sugar ≃, U.S. 190 42.26 N 89.12 W
Sugar ≃, N.H., U.S. 188 43.24 N 72.24 W
Sugar ≃, N.Y., U.S. 212 43.31 N 75.19 W
Sugar City 202 43.52 N 111.45 W
Sugarcreek, Ohio, U.S. 214 40.30 N 81.39 W
Sugar Creek, Pa., U.S. 214 41.26 N 79.53 W
Sugar Creek ≃, U.S. 216 40.47 N 87.45 W
Sugar Creek ≃, Ill., U.S. 194 40.09 N 89.38 W
Sugar Creek ≃, Ill., U.S. 219 38.28 N 89.37 W
Sugar Creek ≃, Ill., U.S. 219 39.48 N 89.32 W
Sugar Creek ≃, Ind., U.S. 194 39.51 N 87.21 W
Sugar Creek ≃, Ind., U.S. 218 39.21 N 86.00 W
Sugar Creek ≃, Iowa, U.S. 194 40.23 N 91.28 W
Sugar Creek ≃, Mich., U.S. 281 42.06 N 83.36 W
Sugar Creek ≃, N.Y., U.S. 210 42.38 N 77.09 W
Sugar Creek ≃, Ohio, U.S. 214 40.31 N 81.28 W
Sugar Creek ≃, Ohio, U.S. 216 40.57 N 84.11 W
Sugar Creek ≃, Ohio, U.S. 218 39.27 N 83.25 W
Sugar Creek ≃, Okla., U.S. 196 35.05 N 98.10 W
Sugar Creek ≃, Pa., U.S. 210 41.47 N 76.27 W
Sugar Creek ≃, Wis., U.S. 216 42.43 N 88.19 W
Sugar Grove, Ill., U.S. 216 41.45 N 88.27 W
Sugargrove, Pa., U.S. 214 41.59 N 79.21 W
Sugar Grove, Va., U.S. 192 36.47 N 81.25 W
Sugar Hill 192 34.07 N 84.02 W
Sugar Island I, Ont., Can. 212 44.26 N 77.17 W
Sugar Island I, Mich., U.S. 190 46.25 N 84.12 W
Sugar Land 222 29.37 N 95.38 W
Sugar Loaf 210 41.19 N 74.17 W
Sugar Loaf → Pão de Açúcar ∧ 287a 22.57 S 43.09 W
Sugarloaf ∧[2] 214 41.24 N 81.06 W
Sugarloaf Hill ∧[2] 274b 37.58 S 145.19 E
Sugarloaf Key I 220 24.40 N 81.32 W
Sugarloaf Mountain ∧, Ky., U.S. 218 38.13 N 83.32 W
Sugarloaf Mountain ∧, Maine, U.S. 188 45.01 N 70.22 W
Sugar Loaf Mountain ∧, Md., U.S. 208 39.16 N 77.23 W
Sugarloaf Mountain ∧, Okla., U.S. 194 35.02 N 94.28 W
Sugarloaf Mountain ∧[2] 220 28.39 N 81.44 W
Sugarloaf Peak ∧, Calif., U.S. 280 34.14 N 117.38 W
Sugarloaf Peak ∧, Wash., U.S. 224 47.45 N 120.32 W
Sugarloaf Point ≻, Austl. 166 32.26 S 152.33 E
Sugar Loaf Point ≻, Ont., Can. 284a 42.52 N 79.17 W
Sugarloaf Ridge State Park ♠ 226 38.26 N 122.29 W
Sugar Notch 210 41.12 N 75.56 W
Sugar Pine Point State Park ♠ 226 39.03 N 120.07 W
Sugartown 285 40.00 N 75.31 W
Suga-shima I 94 34.29 N 136.53 E
Sugauli Bazar 124 26.46 N 84.44 E
Sugbai Passage Џ 116 5.22 N 120.33 E
Sugbay 116 7.31 N 123.19 E
Sugbuhan Point ≻ 116 10.04 N 126.04 E
Suggi Lake ⊛ 184 54.22 N 102.47 W
Suginami ◆[8] 268 35.42 N 139.38 E
Sugita ◆[8] 268 35.23 N 139.38 E
Sugito 94 36.02 N 139.44 E
Şūğla Gölü ⊛ 130 37.20 N 32.02 E
Šugnou 85 38.35 N 70.20 E
Sugod 116 12.03 N 124.09 E
Sugoj ≃ 74 64.15 N 154.29 E
Sugonovo 82 54.41 N 36.41 E
Šugozero 76 59.55 N 34.12 E
Šugurovo, S.S.S.R. 80 53.26 N 46.29 E
Šugurovo, S.S.S.R. 80 54.31 N 52.06 E
Sugut ≃ 112 6.26 N 117.43 E
Suguta ≃ 154 2.03 N 36.33 E

FRANÇAIS
Nom Page Lat.°′ Long.°′ W=Ouest

Suguti 154 1.44 S 33.39 E
Suhaitu 102 44.50 N 93.39 E
Sūhānak 267d 35.48 N 51.32 E
Şuḩār 128 24.22 N 56.45 E
Suheli Par I[1] 122 10.03 N 72.17 E
Suhl 54 50.37 N 10.41 E
Suhl □[5] 54 50.40 N 10.30 E
Suhlendorf 54 52.55 N 10.46 E
Suhopolje 36 45.48 N 17.30 E
Suhr 58 47.22 N 8.05 E
Suhr ≃ 58 47.25 N 8.04 E
Suhum 150 6.05 N 0.27 W
Şuhut 130 38.32 N 30.33 E
Sūi 120 28.37 N 69.19 E
Suia-Miçu ≃ 250 11.13 S 53.15 W
Suian 100 29.28 N 118.44 E
Suianzhan 89 53.07 N 125.20 E
Suiattle ≃ 224 48.20 N 121.33 W
Suichang 100 28.34 N 119.14 E
Suichuan 100 26.26 N 114.32 E
Suid-Afrika → South Africa □[1] 156 30.00 S 26.00 E
Suide 102 37.33 N 110.04 E
Suiding 86 44.03 N 80.49 E
Suido-suigenchi ⊛[1] 270 34.54 N 135.17 E
Suidvaal 158 26.52 S 29.47 E
Suifenhe 89 44.24 N 131.10 E
Suifu, Nihon 94 36.37 N 140.29 E
Suifu → Yibin, Zhg. 107 28.47 N 104.38 E
Suigō-kokutei-kōen ♠ 94 36.05 N 140.20 E
Suihua 89 46.37 N 127.00 E
Suijiang 102 28.31 N 104.07 E
Suijiang ≃ 100 26.30 N 114.45 E
Sui Kau Island I 271d 22.16 N 114.03 E
Suileng 89 47.18 N 127.10 E
Suining, Zhg. 100 33.54 N 117.56 E
Suining, Zhg. 102 26.21 N 110.00 E
Suining, Zhg. 107 30.31 N 105.34 E
Suipacha 252 34.45 S 59.41 W
Suiping 100 33.10 N 113.57 E
Suippe ≃ 50 49.25 N 3.57 E
Suippes 56 49.08 N 4.32 E
Suir ≃ 48 52.15 N 7.00 W
Suisse → Switzerland □[1] 58 47.00 N 8.00 E
Suisun Bay C 226 38.06 N 122.00 W
Suisun City 226 38.15 N 122.02 W
Suisun Creek ≃ 226 38.12 N 122.06 W
Suita 96 34.45 N 135.32 E
Suitland 284c 38.51 N 76.56 W
Suixi, Zhg. 100 33.56 N 116.46 E
Suixi, Zhg. 102 21.25 N 110.15 E
Suixian 100 31.42 N 113.20 E
Suiyang, Zhg. 89 44.26 N 130.53 E
Suiyang, Zhg. 102 27.56 N 107.18 E
Suiyangdian 100 32.04 N 112.55 E
Suiza → Switzerland □[1] 58 47.00 N 8.00 E
Suize ≃ 58 48.08 N 5.08 E
Şuizhong 98 40.20 N 120.19 E
Šuja, S.S.S.R. 24 61.55 N 34.12 E
Šuja, S.S.S.R. 80 56.50 N 41.23 E
Šuja ≃, S.S.S.R. 24 61.54 N 34.15 E
Šuja ≃, S.S.S.R. 80 57.56 N 43.15 E
Sujānagar 126 23.57 N 89.25 E
Sūjāngarh 120 27.42 N 74.28 E
Sujāwal 120 24.36 N 68.05 E
Sujeticha 88 55.57 N 97.49 E
Sujfun ≃ 89 43.22 N 131.47 E
Suji 107 29.35 N 103.37 E
Sujiabu 100 31.38 N 116.22 E
Sujiaqiao 105 39.24 N 116.10 E
Sujiatun 104 41.40 N 123.22 E
Sujiawan 107 29.48 N 104.57 E
Sujiawu 105 39.17 N 115.55 E
Şujiazui 100 33.40 N 119.29 E
Šujskoje 76 59.22 N 40.59 E
Sujutkina Kosa, Mys ≻ 84 44.13 N 47.15 E
Sukabihanawa 112 9.30 S 124.57 E
Sukabumi 115a 6.55 S 106.56 E
Sukadana, Indon. 112 1.15 S 109.57 E
Sukadana, Indon. 115a 5.05 S 105.33 E
Sukadana, Teluk C 112 1.24 S 109.50 E
Sukagawa 92 37.17 N 140.23 E
Sukamandi 115a 6.20 S 107.39 E
Sukamara 112 2.43 S 111.11 E
Sukanegara 115a 7.06 S 107.07 E
Sukapura 115a 7.52 S 113.03 E
Sukaraja, Indon. 112 2.21 S 110.37 E
Sukaraja, Indon. 115a 7.27 S 108.12 E
Sukaraja, Indon. 115a 7.27 S 109.17 E
Sukarno, Pegunungan → Jaya, Puncak ∧ 164 4.05 S 137.11 E
Sukau 112 5.32 N 118.17 E
Sukchar 272b 22.42 N 88.22 E
Sukch'ŏn 98 39.24 N 125.38 E
Sukematsu 270 34.31 N 135.26 E
Sukeva 26 63.52 N 27.26 E
Sukhnah, 'Ayn ⊤[4] 142 29.35 N 32.15 E
Sukhothai 110 17.01 N 99.49 E
Sukhumi → Suchumi 84 43.01 N 41.02 E
Sukkertoppen 176 65.25 N 52.53 W
Sukkozero 24 63.11 N 32.18 E
Sukkur 120 27.42 N 68.52 E
Sukkwan Island I 180 55.05 N 132.45 W
Suklāra 126 23.11 N 86.21 E
Sukmanovka 78 51.47 N 41.34 E
Sukodadi 115a 7.06 S 112.19 E
Sukoharjo 115a 7.41 S 110.50 E
Sukovo 82 54.54 N 38.19 E
Sukroml'a 76 56.53 N 34.44 E
Sukses 156 21.01 S 16.52 E
Suksun 86 57.07 N 57.24 E
Sukumo 92 32.56 N 132.44 E
Sukun, Pulau I 115b 8.07 S 122.08 E
Sukunka ≃ 182 55.37 N 121.37 W
Sul, Baía do C 252 27.40 S 48.35 W
Sul, Canal do Џ 250 0.10 S 49.30 W
Sula I 26 61.08 N 4.55 E
Sula ≃, S.S.S.R. 24 67.16 N 52.07 E
Sula ≃, S.S.S.R. 78 49.40 N 32.41 E
Sula, Kepulauan II 112 1.52 S 125.22 E
Sulaco ≃ 236 14.58 N 87.45 W
Sulaimān Khel 123 33.41 N 71.01 E
Sulaimān Range ⋏ 120 30.30 N 70.10 E
Sulak, S.S.S.R. 80 51.52 N 48.21 E
Sulak, S.S.S.R. 84 43.16 N 47.32 E
Sulak ≃ 84 43.20 N 47.34 E
Sulak, Buchta C 84 43.18 N 47.31 E
Sulakyurt 130 40.10 N 33.44 E
Sulancheer 102 42.42 N 109.22 E
Sulang 115a 6.48 S 111.23 E
Sulat 116 11.49 N 125.27 E
Sulauan Point ≻ 116 8.37 N 124.29 E
Sulawesi (Celebes) I 112 2.00 S 121.00 E
Sulawesi Selatan □[4] 112 3.30 S 120.00 E
Sulawesi Tengah □[4] 112 1.00 N 123.00 E
Sulaymān, Birak (Solomon's Pools) ⊥ 132 31.41 N 35.10 E
Sulcis ◆[1] 71 39.04 N 8.41 E
Sūldeh 128 36.34 N 52.01 E
Sulechów 30 52.06 N 15.37 E
Sulęcin 30 52.26 N 15.08 E
Suleja 86 55.09 N 58.50 E
Sulejów 30 51.22 N 19.53 E
Sulejówek 30 52.14 N 21.17 E

PORTUGUÊS
Nome Página Lat.°′ Long.°′ W=Oeste

Sülemaniye Camii ♥[1] 267b 41.00 N 28.57 E
Sulen, Mount ∧ 164 3.25 S 142.15 E
Sule Skerry I[2] 46 59.05 N 4.26 W
Süleymanlı 130 37.54 N 36.50 E
Sülfeld 52 53.48 N 10.14 E
Şūlgan 267d 35.49 N 51.15 E
Šul'ginka 83 49.08 N 38.56 E
Šulğino, S.S.S.R. 82 55.50 N 35.55 E
Šul'gino, S.S.S.R. 82 54.33 N 37.35 E
Sulia 154 1.32 S 26.33 E
Suliki 112 0.06 S 100.27 E
Sulima 150 6.58 N 11.35 W
Sulin 83 48.54 N 40.07 E
Sulina 38 45.09 N 29.40 E
Sulina, Braţul ≃[1] 38 45.09 N 29.41 E
Sulingen 52 52.41 N 8.47 E
Sulinskij 83 47.52 N 40.06 E
Sulitelma ∧ 24 67.08 N 16.24 E
Sulkava 26 61.47 N 28.23 E
Sullana 248 4.53 S 80.41 W
Sullane ≃ 48 51.53 N 8.56 W
Sulligent 194 33.54 N 88.08 W
Sullivan, Ill., U.S. 194 39.36 N 88.37 W
Sullivan, Ind., U.S. 194 39.06 N 87.24 W
Sullivan, Mo., U.S. 219 38.13 N 91.10 W
Sullivan, Ohio, U.S. 214 41.02 N 82.13 W
Sullivan, Wis., U.S. 216 43.01 N 88.35 W
Sullivan □[6], N.Y., U.S. 210 41.39 N 74.42 W
Sullivan □[6], Pa., U.S. 210 41.25 N 76.29 W
Sullivan Canyon ∨ 280 34.03 N 118.30 W
Sullivan Creek ≃ 226 37.53 N 120.25 W
Sullivan Lake ⊛ 182 52.00 N 112.00 W
Sullivanville 210 42.14 N 76.46 W
Sully-sur-Loire 50 47.46 N 2.22 E
Sulm ≃ 61 46.45 N 15.34 E
Sulmona 66 42.03 N 13.55 E
Sulot' ≃ 82 56.41 N 38.01 E
Sulphur, Yukon, Can. 180 63.47 N 138.53 W
Sulphur, Ind., U.S. 218 38.14 N 86.28 W
Sulphur, Ky., U.S. 218 38.30 N 85.17 W
Sulphur, La., U.S. 194 30.14 N 93.23 W
Sulphur, Okla., U.S. 196 34.31 N 96.58 W
Sulphur ≃, Alta., Can. 182 53.50 N 119.10 W
Sulphur ≃, U.S. 194 33.07 N 93.52 W
Sulphur Creek ≃ 198 44.46 N 102.25 W
Sulphur Draw ∨ 196 33.12 N 102.17 W
Sulphur Springs, Ind., U.S. 218 40.00 N 85.27 W
Sulphur Springs, Ohio, U.S. 214 40.52 N 82.53 W
Sulphur Springs, Tex., U.S. 222 33.08 N 95.36 W
Sulphur Springs Draw ∨ 196 32.12 N 101.36 W
Sulsul 144 5.06 N 44.55 E
Sultan 224 47.51 N 121.49 W
Sultan ≃ 224 47.52 N 121.49 W
Sultana 226 36.33 N 119.20 W
Sultanahmet Camii ♥[1] 267b 41.00 N 28.58 E
Sultana Point ≻ 168b 35.08 S 137.45 E
Sulṭanatābād 267d 35.46 N 51.28 E
Sultançiftlikköy 267b 41.02 N 29.11 E
Sultandağı 130 38.32 N 31.14 E
Sultandağı ∧ 130 38.58 N 27.26 E
Sultanhanı 130 38.15 N 33.33 E
Sultanhisar 130 37.53 N 28.10 E
Sultan Mosque ♥[1] 271c 1.18 N 103.52 E
Sultānpur, Bhārat 123 31.13 N 75.11 E
Sultānpur, Bhārat 124 26.16 N 82.04 E
Sultānpur □[5] 124 26.20 N 82.00 E
Sultānpur Dabās ◆[8] 272a 28.46 N 77.03 E
Sultan sa Barongis 116 6.46 N 124.38 E
Sultan-Saly 83 47.21 N 39.35 E
Sulu 164 5.25 S 151.00 E
Sulu □[4] 116 5.30 N 120.30 E
Suluan Island I 116 10.46 N 125.57 E
Sulu Archipelago II 116 6.00 N 121.00 E
Sulu Basin ✣[1] 12 7.30 N 121.00 E
Suluchi ⊛ 124 30.12 N 86.20 E
Sülüklü 130 39.05 N 30.58 E
Sul'ukta 85 39.56 N 69.34 E
Sululta 144 9.10 N 38.48 E
Suluntah 146 32.36 N 21.43 E
Suluova (Suluca) 130 40.47 N 35.42 E
Sulūq 146 31.39 N 20.15 E
Sūlūru 122 13.42 N 80.01 E
Sulusaj 85 38.50 N 67.05 E
Sulusaray 130 40.00 N 36.06 E
Sulu Sea ⊤[2] 116 8.00 N 120.00 E
Sulusi 102 33.08 N 95.08 E
Suly 86 53.45 N 66.30 E
Sulz 58 48.18 N 7.51 E
Sulz ≃ 60 48.36 N 13.02 E
Sulz am Neckar 58 48.21 N 8.37 E
Sulzano 64 45.41 N 10.05 E
Sulzbach, B.R.D. 56 49.18 N 7.07 E
Sulzbach, B.R.D. 56 49.21 N 9.13 E
Sulzbach, B.R.D. 60 48.26 N 11.05 E
Sulzbach am Kocher 56 48.58 N 9.50 E
Sulzbach-Rosenberg 60 49.30 N 11.45 E
Sulzberger Bay C 9 77.00 S 152.00 W
Sulzbrunn 58 47.41 N 10.20 E
Sulzburg 58 47.50 N 7.42 E
Sülze 52 52.46 N 10.02 E
Šum, S.S.S.R. 76 59.52 N 31.46 E
Šum, S.S.S.R. 88 54.51 N 95.18 E
Suma ◆[8] 270 34.39 N 135.08 E
Šum'ači 76 53.52 N 32.25 E
Šumadija ◆[1] 38 44.10 N 20.50 E
Sumalata 112 0.59 N 122.30 E
Sumallo ≃ 224 49.14 N 121.05 W
Şumampa 252 29.22 S 63.28 W
Šumanaj 86 42.37 N 59.08 E
Sumangat, Tanjong ≻ 112 6.35 N 117.33 E
Sumano-ura (Suma Beach) •[2] 96 34.38 N 135.08 E
Sumano-ura ♠ 96 34.38 N 135.08 E
Sūmār 128 33.52 N 45.39 E
Sumarokovo 82 55.46 N 35.55 E
Sumas 202 49.00 N 122.13 W
Sumas ≃ 224 49.09 N 122.12 W
Sumatera (Sumatra) I 108 0.05 S 102.00 E
Sumatera Barat □[4] 112 0.30 S 100.30 E
Sumatera Selatan □[4] 112 3.00 S 104.00 E
Sumatera Utara □[4] 114 2.20 N 99.00 E
Sum'atino 82 55.00 N 36.21 E
Sumatou 107 30.28 N 104.03 E
Sumatra → Sumatera I 108 0.05 S 102.00 E
Sumaúma 248 7.50 S 60.02 W
Sumava Resorts 216 41.10 N 87.26 W
Sumayḩ 140 12.43 N 30.50 E
Sumba I 115b 10.00 S 120.00 E
Sumba, Île I 152 1.44 N 19.32 E
Sumba, Selat Џ 115b 9.05 S 120.00 E
Sumbang Point ≻ 116 5.50 N 125.11 E
Sumbar ≃ 128 38.00 N 55.17 E
Sumbawa I 115b 8.40 S 118.00 E
Sumbawa Besar 115b 8.30 S 117.26 E
Sumbawanga 154 7.58 S 31.37 E
Sumbay 248 15.58 S 71.23 W
Sümber 90 46.21 N 108.25 E
Sumbi Head ≻ 175e 7.18 S 157.01 E
Sumbilla 34 43.10 N 1.40 W

Sumbing, Gunung ∧ 115a 7.23 S 110.04 E
Sumbu Game Reserve ◆[4] 154 8.50 S 30.25 E
Sumburgh Head ≻ 46a 59.53 N 1.20 W
Sumburgh Roost Џ 46 59.49 N 1.19 W
Šumbut 80 55.33 N 50.41 E
Sumbuya 150 7.39 N 11.58 W
Sumdo 120 35.01 N 78.41 E
Sumé 250 7.39 S 36.55 W
Sumedang 115a 6.52 S 107.55 E
Sümeg 30 46.59 N 17.17 E
Šumek 86 48.42 N 85.32 E
Šumen 38 43.16 N 26.55 E
Sumène 62 43.59 N 3.43 E
Sumenep 115a 7.01 S 113.52 E
Šumerl'a 80 55.30 N 46.26 E
Sumgait, S.S.S.R. 84 40.36 N 49.38 E
Sumgait ≃ 84 40.37 N 49.37 E
Šumicha 86 55.14 N 63.19 E
Sumida ◆[8] 268 35.42 N 139.48 E
Sumida ≃ 268 35.40 N 139.47 E
Sumidouro 256 22.03 S 42.41 W
Sumilao 116 8.18 N 124.57 E
Šumilino 76 55.18 N 29.37 E
Šumilinskaja 80 49.58 N 41.26 E
Sumisu-jima I 90 31.27 N 140.03 E
Sumiswald 58 47.02 N 7.45 E
Sumiyoshi ◆[8] 270 34.36 N 135.31 E
Sumki 86 55.03 N 65.44 E
Sumkino 86 58.09 N 68.21 E
Sumlug ≃ 116 6.53 N 126.02 E
Summer Bridge 44 54.03 N 1.41 W
Summerdale 208 40.18 N 76.56 W
Summerfield, Fla., U.S. 220 29.00 N 82.02 W
Summerfield, Mo., U.S. 219 38.17 N 91.49 W
Summerfield, N.C., U.S. 192 36.12 N 79.54 W
Summerford, Newf., Can. 186 49.29 N 54.47 W
Summerford, Ohio, U.S. 218 39.55 N 83.29 W
Summerhill, Eire 48 53.29 N 6.44 W
Summerhill, Pa., U.S. 214 40.22 N 78.46 W
Summer Island I 190 45.34 N 86.39 W
Summer Isles II 46 58.02 N 5.28 W
Summer Lake ⊛ 202 42.50 N 120.45 W
Summerland 182 49.39 N 119.33 W
Summerland Reserve ◆[4] 169 38.31 S 145.10 E
Sümmern 56 51.25 N 7.43 E
Summerseat 262 53.38 N 2.19 W
Summerside 186 46.24 N 63.47 W
Summersville, Mo., U.S. 194 37.11 N 91.40 W
Summersville, W. Va., U.S. 188 38.17 N 80.51 W
Summerton 192 33.36 N 80.20 W
Summerville, Ont., Can. 275b 43.37 N 79.34 W
Summerville, Ga., U.S. 192 34.29 N 85.21 W
Summerville, Pa., U.S. 214 41.07 N 79.11 W
Summerville, S.C., U.S. 192 33.01 N 80.11 W
Summit, Eng., U.K. 262 53.40 N 2.05 W
Summit, Alaska, U.S. 180 63.20 N 149.08 W
Summit, Calif., U.S. 228 34.20 N 117.25 W
Summit, Ill., U.S. 216 41.47 N 87.48 W
Summit, Miss., U.S. 194 31.17 N 90.28 W
Summit, N.J., U.S. 210 40.43 N 74.22 W
Summit, N.Y., U.S. 210 42.35 N 74.35 W
Summit, S. Dak., U.S. 198 45.18 N 97.02 W
Summit, Wash., U.S. 224 47.10 N 122.21 W
Summit □[6] 214 41.05 N 81.31 W
Summit Creek ≃ 224 46.00 N 121.10 W
Summit Hill 210 40.50 N 75.53 W
Summit Lake 182 54.17 N 122.38 W
Summit Lake ⊛ 224 47.04 N 123.07 W
Summit Mountain ∧ 204 39.23 N 116.28 W
Summit Park 276 41.09 N 74.03 W
Summit Peak ∧ 200 37.21 N 106.42 W
Summit Rock ∧ 172 45.25 S 170.04 E
Summit Station 208 40.34 N 76.12 W
Summitville, Ind., U.S. 216 40.20 N 85.39 W
Summitville, N.Y., U.S. 210 41.37 N 74.27 W
Summitville, Ohio, U.S. 214 40.41 N 80.53 W
Summt 264a 52.41 N 13.22 E
Şummter See ⊛ 264a 52.42 N 13.23 E
Šumná 61 48.56 N 15.52 E
Sumnal 120 35.45 N 78.40 E
Sumner, Iowa, U.S. 190 42.51 N 92.06 W
Sumner, Miss., U.S. 194 33.58 N 90.22 W
Sumner, Wash., U.S. 224 47.12 N 122.14 W
Sumner, Lake ⊛ 172 42.42 S 172.13 E
Sumner, Lake ⊛[1] 196 34.38 N 104.25 W
Sumner Strait Џ 180 56.15 N 133.45 W
Sumoto 96 34.21 N 134.54 E
Şumpangbinangae 112 4.24 S 119.36 E
Šumperk 30 49.58 N 16.58 E
Sumpiuh 115a 7.37 S 109.21 E
Sumprabum 110 26.33 N 97.34 E
Sumpter 281 42.10 N 83.29 W
Sumrall 194 31.25 N 89.33 W
Sumsar 85 41.18 N 71.19 E
S'umsi 80 57.07 N 51.37 E
Šumskij 88 54.48 N 99.09 E
Šumskij Posad 24 64.15 N 35.25 E
Šumskoje 78 50.07 N 26.07 E
Šumšu, Ostrov I 74 50.45 N 156.20 E
Sumter 192 33.55 N 80.20 W
Sumter □[6] 220 28.38 N 82.08 W
Sumusṭā al-Waqf 142 28.55 N 30.51 E
Sumy, S.S.S.R. 78 50.55 N 34.45 E
Sumy, S.S.S.R. 86 54.48 N 80.26 E
Sumy □[4] 76 52.10 N 33.40 E
S'un' ≃, S.S.S.R. 86 55.43 N 54.17 E
Sun ≃, Mont., U.S. 202 48.29 N 111.55 W
Suna, Kenya 154 1.05 S 34.26 E
Suna, S.S.S.R. 80 57.51 N 50.05 E
Suna ≃ 24 62.08 N 34.12 E
Sunagawa 92a 43.29 N 141.55 E
Sun al-Heteimi ⊤[4] 132 31.05 N 34.00 E
Sun' al-Menī'i ⊤[4] 132 31.07 N 34.12 E
Sunām 123 30.08 N 75.48 E
Sunāmganj 120 25.04 N 91.24 E
Sunami 94 35.25 N 136.40 E
Sunan 98 39.13 N 125.41 E
Sunapee Lake ⊛ 188 43.23 N 72.03 W
Sunart, Loch ⊛ 46 56.41 N 5.43 W
Sunashinden 268 35.53 N 139.30 E
Sunaysilah ⊛ 128 35.35 N 41.53 E
Sunbāţ 142 30.48 N 31.12 E
Sunbright 192 36.15 N 84.40 W
Sunburst 202 48.53 N 111.55 W
Sunbury, Austl. 169 37.35 S 144.44 E
Sunbury, Eng., U.K. 260 51.25 N 0.26 W
Sunbury, N.C., U.S. 192 36.27 N 76.37 W
Sunbury, Ohio, U.S. 214 40.14 N 82.52 W
Sunbury, Pa., U.S. 210 40.52 N 76.47 W
Sunchales 252 30.56 S 61.34 W
Sunch'ang 98 35.23 N 127.07 E
Sunchild Indian Reserve ◆[4] 182 52.43 N 115.24 W
Sünching 60 48.53 N 12.21 E
Suncho Corral 252 27.56 S 63.27 W

Sunch'ŏn, C.M.I.K. 98 39.26 N 125.54 E
Sunch'ŏn, Taehan 98 34.57 N 127.28 E
Sun City, Ariz., U.S. 200 33.36 N 112.17 W
Sun City, Calif., U.S. 228 33.42 N 117.11 W
Sun City, Fla., U.S. 220 27.41 N 82.28 W
Sun City Center 220 27.43 N 82.21 W
Suncook 188 43.08 N 71.27 W
Suncook ≃ 188 43.08 N 71.28 W
Sunda, Selat (Sunda Strait) Џ 112 6.00 S 105.45 E
Sundance 198 44.24 N 104.23 W
Sundar 112 4.54 N 115.12 E
Sundar ∧ 124 28.26 N 84.20 E
Sundarbans ◆[1] 126 22.00 N 89.00 E
Sundargarh 124 22.07 N 84.02 E
Sundargarh □[5] 124 22.18 N 84.30 E
Sundarnagar 123 31.32 N 76.53 E
Sunda Strait → Sunda, Selat Џ 112 6.00 S 105.45 E
Sundby, Dan. 41 54.42 N 11.48 E
Sundby, Sve. 40 59.23 N 17.03 E
Sundbyberg 40 59.22 N 17.58 E
Sundbyholm 40 59.27 N 16.37 E
Sundbyholms slott ⊥ 40 59.27 N 16.37 E
Sunde 26 59.50 N 5.43 E
Sunderland, Ont., Can. 212 44.16 N 79.04 W
Sunderland, Eng., U.K. 44 54.55 N 1.23 W
Sunderland, Mass., U.S. 207 42.28 N 72.35 W
Sunderland, Vt., U.S. 210 43.08 N 73.08 W
Sundern 56 51.20 N 8.00 E
Sünderup 41 54.46 N 9.27 E
Sundhausen 54 50.56 N 10.40 E
Sundhouse 58 48.15 N 7.36 E
Sundi-Lutete 152 4.34 S 14.14 E
Sundown, Austl. 162 26.14 S 133.12 E
Sundown, N.Y., U.S. 210 41.53 N 74.28 W
Sundown, Tex., U.S. 196 33.27 N 102.29 W
Sundra 273d 26.11 S 28.33 E
Sundre 182 51.48 N 114.38 W
Sundridge, Ont., Can. 190 45.46 N 79.24 W
Sundridge, Eng., U.K. 260 51.17 N 0.18 E
Sunds 41 56.12 N 9.01 E
Sundsbruk 26 62.27 N 17.22 E
Sundsvall 26 62.23 N 17.18 E
Sundwig 263 51.23 N 7.47 E
Suneori 268 35.56 N 139.24 E
Sunfield 216 42.45 N 85.00 W
Sunfish Creek ≃ 218 39.01 N 83.03 W
Sunflower 194 33.33 N 90.32 W
Sunflower, Mount ∧ 198 39.04 N 102.01 W
Sungaianyar 112 2.55 S 116.18 E
Sungaibamban 114 3.26 N 99.09 E
Sungaibatu 112 0.48 N 110.45 E
Sungai Bayor 114 5.15 N 100.47 E
Sungaibuntu 112 6.03 S 107.24 E
Sungaidareh 112 0.58 S 101.30 E
Sungaigerong 112 2.59 S 104.52 E
Sungaiguntung 112 0.18 N 103.37 E
Sungaikakap 112 0.04 S 109.10 E
Sungai Kolok 114 6.02 N 101.58 E
Sungailangsat 112 0.52 S 101.18 E
Sungai Lembing 114 3.55 N 103.02 E
Sungailiat 112 1.51 S 106.08 E
Sungailimau 112 0.31 S 100.03 E
Sungaimanasip 114 1.49 N 100.54 E
Sungainipah 114 0.57 N 98.57 E
Sungaipenuh 112 2.05 S 101.23 E
Sungaipenyu 112 0.16 N 109.04 E
Sungai Petani 114 5.39 N 100.30 E
Sungaipinang 112 0.48 S 114.04 E
Sungairampah 114 3.29 N 99.09 E
Sungairotan, Indon. 112 1.39 S 102.51 E
Sungairotan, Indon. 112 3.06 S 104.18 E
Sungaisalak 112 0.27 S 102.59 E
Sungaiselan 112 2.24 S 105.59 E
Sungai Siput 114 4.49 N 101.04 E
Sungaitampang 114 2.20 N 100.07 E
Şungaitiram 112 0.47 S 117.12 E
Šungaj 80 48.32 N 46.46 E
Sungari → Songhuajiang ≃ 89 47.44 N 132.32 E
Sungchiang → Songjiang 106 31.01 N 121.14 E
Sungezhuang 105 40.15 N 116.39 E
Sungguminasa 112 5.12 S 119.27 E
Sungi ≃ 115b 8.38 S 115.06 E
Sungi Point ≻ 116 10.55 N 125.50 E
Sungkai 114 4.00 N 101.19 E
Sung Noen 110 14.54 N 101.50 E
Sungsang 112 2.22 S 104.56 E
Sungurlu 130 40.10 N 34.23 E
Sunharon Roads C 174n 14.57 N 145.36 E
Sunhezhen 105 40.03 N 116.31 E
Suni 71 40.17 N 8.33 E
Suning 98 38.25 N 115.50 E
Suniteyouqi 102 42.32 N 112.58 E
Sunitezouqi (Beilemiao) 102 43.57 N 113.52 E
Sunjiabu 106 30.55 N 118.54 E
Sunjiadizi 104 42.09 N 124.09 E
Sunjiagou 104 40.45 N 120.39 E
Sunjiajiang 105 40.10 N 115.32 E
Sunjiakanzi 104 40.42 N 123.02 E
Sunjiatai 104 42.32 N 124.01 E
Sunjiawan 104 41.59 N 121.42 E
Sunjiazhai 106 30.55 N 121.52 E
Sunjikāy 140 12.20 N 29.46 E
Sunkar, Gora ∧ 86 44.15 N 73.50 E
Sun Kosi ≃ 124 26.55 N 87.09 E
Sunland ◆[8] 280 34.16 N 118.19 W
Sunland Park 200 32.15 N 106.45 W
Sunlight Creek ≃ 202 44.47 N 109.23 W
Sunlongwan 104 41.19 N 122.57 E
Sunman 218 39.14 N 85.06 W
Sunnansjö 40 60.13 N 14.57 E
Sunndalsøra 26 62.40 N 8.33 E
Sunne 26 59.50 N 13.09 E
Sunnemo 40 59.53 N 13.43 E
Sunnersta 40 59.48 N 17.39 E
Sunnī, Khawr ∨ 140 7.09 N 28.41 E
Sunningdale 260 51.24 N 0.38 W
Sunninghill 42 51.25 N 0.40 W
Sunnybrae 186 45.24 N 62.30 W
Sunny Corner 170 33.23 S 149.53 E
Sunny Crest 278 41.33 N 87.42 W
Sunnydale 224 47.28 N 122.20 W
Sunnyland 220 27.17 N 82.29 W
Sunnylvsfjorden C[2] 26 62.17 N 7.01 E
Sunnymead 228 33.56 N 117.15 W
Sunnynook 182 51.17 N 111.40 W
Sunnyridge 273d 26.10 S 28.11 E
Sunnyside, Newf., Can. 186 47.51 N 53.55 W
Sunnyside, Calif., U.S. 226 32.40 N 117.01 W
Sunny Side, Tex., U.S. 222 29.54 N 96.04 W
Sunnyside, Utah, U.S. 200 39.33 N 110.24 W
Sunnyside, Wash., U.S. 202 46.20 N 120.00 W
Sunnyside ⊥ 276 41.03 N 73.52 W
Sunnyslope, Alta., Can. 182 51.40 N 113.32 W
Sunnyslope, Wash., U.S. 224 47.30 N 122.44 W

Sunnyvale, Calif., U.S. 226 37.23 N 122.01 W
Sunnyvale, Tex., U.S. 222 32.48 N 96.33 W
Sunol 282 37.36 N 121.53 W
Sunol Ridge ∧ 282 37.38 N 121.56 W
Sun Prairie 216 43.11 N 89.13 W
Sunray 196 36.01 N 101.49 W
Sunrise, Fla., U.S. 220 26.08 N 80.14 W
Sunrise, Ky., U.S. 218 38.33 N 84.14 W
Sunrise, Tex., U.S. 222 31.17 N 96.53 W
Sunrise, Wyo., U.S. 200 42.20 N 104.42 W
Sunrise Heights 216 42.18 N 85.09 W
Sunrise Mall ◆[9] 276 40.41 N 73.26 W
Sunrise Peak ∧ 224 46.20 N 121.46 W
Sunset, La., U.S. 194 30.25 N 92.04 W
Sunset, Tex., U.S. 196 33.27 N 97.46 W
Sunset ◆[8] 282 37.45 N 122.30 W
Sunset Bay 214 42.11 N 79.24 W
Sunset Beach, Calif., U.S. 280 33.43 N 118.04 W
Sunset Beach, Haw., U.S. 229c 21.40 N 158.03 W
Sunset Crater National Monument ♠ 200 35.18 N 111.21 W
Sunset Hill 276 40.26 N 74.35 W
Sunset Hills 279b 40.35 N 80.15 W
Sunset Peak ∧ 280 34.13 N 117.42 W
Sunset Prairie 182 55.50 N 120.48 W
Sunset Trailer Park 278 42.06 N 87.48 W
Sunset Valley 214 40.18 N 79.44 W
Sunshine, Austl. 169 37.47 S 144.50 E
Sunshine, Alaska, U.S. 180 62.10 N 150.04 W
Sunshine Point ≻ 281 42.36 N 82.47 W
Sunshine Skyway Bridge ◆[5] 220 27.37 N 82.39 W
Suntai ≃ 146 8.05 N 10.04 E
Suntar 74 62.10 N 117.40 E
Suntar-Chajata, Chrebet ⋏ 74 62.00 N 143.00 E
Suntaug Lake ⊛ 283 42.32 N 71.00 W
Süntel ⋏ 52 52.12 N 9.25 E
Sunter ◆[8] 269e 6.09 S 106.50 E
Sunter, Kali ≍ 269e 6.07 S 106.50 E
Sunti ≃ 272b 22.37 N 88.34 E
Suntrana 180 63.51 N 148.51 W
Suntsar 128 25.31 N 62.00 E
Sun Valley, Idaho, U.S. 202 43.42 N 114.21 W
Sun Valley, Nev., U.S. 226 39.34 N 119.47 W
Sun Valley ◆[8] 280 34.14 N 118.21 W
SunValley Center ◆[9] 282 37.58 N 122.03 W
Sunview 222 32.48 N 94.38 W
Sun Village 228 34.35 N 118.03 W
Sunwapta ≃ 182 52.32 N 117.41 W
Sunwu 89 49.27 N 127.20 E
Sunwui → Jiangmen 100 22.35 N 113.05 E
Sunxi ≃ 107 29.13 N 106.21 E
Sunyani 150 7.20 N 2.20 W
Sunying 98 34.30 N 114.21 E
Sunža ≃ 84 43.26 N 46.08 E
Sunženskij Chrebet ⋏ 84 43.21 N 45.00 E
Sunzhongshanling (Tomb of Sun Yat Sen) ⊥ 106 32.10 N 118.56 E
Suoche (Yarkand) 120 38.25 N 77.16 E
Suoguohu ⊛ 102 42.18 N 101.08 E
Suojarvi 24 62.05 N 32.21 E
Suolahti 26 62.34 N 25.52 E
Suolun 89 46.36 N 121.13 E
Suolunqi (Nantun) 89 49.07 N 119.40 E
Suomenlahti → Finland, Gulf of C 26 60.00 N 27.00 E
Suomenselkä ∧ 26 63.59 N 27.00 E
Suomi → Finland □[1] 24 64.00 N 26.00 E
Suomussalmi 26 64.53 N 29.05 E
Suō-nada ⊤[2] 96 33.50 N 131.30 E
Suonenjoki 26 62.37 N 27.08 E
Suonne ⊛ 26 61.40 N 26.30 E
Suordach 74 66.43 N 132.04 E
Suoshu 106 31.57 N 119.00 E
Suoxian 120 31.50 N 93.45 E
Supamo ≃ 246 6.48 N 61.50 W
Supaul 124 26.07 N 86.36 E
Supe 144 8.37 N 35.38 E
Superbe ≃ 50 48.35 N 3.53 E
Superga, Basilica di ♥[1] 62 45.05 N 7.46 E
Superior, Ariz., U.S. 200 33.18 N 111.06 W
Superior, Mont., U.S. 202 47.12 N 114.53 W
Superior, Nebr., U.S. 198 40.01 N 98.04 W
Superior, Wis., U.S. 190 46.44 N 92.05 W
Superior, Laguna C 234 16.20 N 94.55 W
Superior, Lake ⊛ 190 48.00 N 88.00 W
Superior Lake ⊛ 228 35.15 N 117.02 W
Superior Upland ⋏[1] 190 46.00 N 90.30 W
Superior Valley ∨ 228 35.16 N 117.00 W
Supersano 68 40.01 N 18.14 E
Supetar 36 43.23 N 16.33 E
Suphan Buri 110 14.28 N 100.07 E
Suphan Buri ≃ 110 13.29 N 100.17 E
Süphan Dağı ∧ 84 38.54 N 42.48 E
Supino 66 41.37 N 13.14 E
Sūpkhār 124 22.12 N 80.56 E
Supoj ≃ 78 49.38 N 31.48 E
Suponevo 76 53.12 N 34.18 E
Supoqiao 107 30.40 N 103.59 E
Süpplingen 54 52.14 N 10.54 E
Supraśl 30 53.13 N 23.20 E
Supraśl ≃ 30 53.04 N 22.56 E
Sup'ung 98 40.27 N 124.57 E
Sup'ung-chŏsuji ⊛[1] 98 40.30 N 125.05 E
Supur 126 23.01 N 86.52 E
Sūq ash-Shuyūkh 128 30.53 N 46.28 E
Suq'at al-Jamal 140 12.48 N 27.42 E
Suqian 100 33.59 N 118.18 E
Suqiao, Zhg. 100 34.08 N 113.47 E
Suqiao, Zhg. 105 39.03 N 116.29 E
Sūq Suwayq 128 24.23 N 38.27 E
Suquamish 224 47.44 N 122.33 W
Suquṭrā I 118 12.30 N 54.00 E
Şūr (Tyre), Lubnān 132 33.16 N 35.11 E
Şūr, 'Umān 118 22.35 N 59.31 E
Sur □[4] 148 23.40 N 14.15 W
Sur, Cabo ≻ 174z 27.12 S 109.26 W
Sur, Point ≻ 226 36.18 N 121.54 W
Sur, Punta ≻ 252 36.52 S 56.40 W
Sura 80 53.53 N 45.45 E
Sura ◆[8] 272b 22.33 N 88.25 E
Sura ≃ 80 56.06 N 46.00 E
Sura, Ras ≻ 144 11.10 N 47.32 E
Şūrāb, Pāk. 120 28.29 N 66.16 E
Šurab, S.S.S.R. 85 40.03 N 70.33 E
Surabaya 115a 7.15 S 112.45 E
S'urachi, Nuraghe ⊥ 71 40.01 N 8.33 E
Şurad 142 30.59 N 30.54 E
Surag-san ∧ 271b 37.42 N 127.04 E
Surahammar 40 59.43 N 16.13 E
Sūrak 128 25.43 N 58.48 E
Surakarta 115a 7.35 S 110.50 E
Suramana 112 0.50 S 119.33 E
Surami 84 42.01 N 43.34 E
Suramskij Chrebet ⋏ 84 42.12 N 43.36 E
Şūrān, Īrān 128 27.18 N 62.04 E
Šuran, S.S.S.R. 80 55.22 N 49.50 E
Şūrān, Sūrīy. 130 36.34 N 37.13 E

Symbol	English	Deutsch	Español	Français	Português
≃	River	Fluss	Río	Rivière	Rio
≍	Canal	Kanal	Canal	Canal	Canal
ʟ	Waterfall, Rapids	Wasserfall, Stromschnellen	Cascada, Rápidos	Chute d'eau, Rapides	Cascata, Rápidos
Џ	Strait	Meeresstrasse	Estrecho	Détroit	Estreito
C	Bay, Gulf	Bucht, Golf	Bahía, Golfo	Baie, Golfe	Baía, Golfo
⊛	Lake, Lakes	See, Seen	Lago, Lagos	Lac, Lacs	Lago, Lagos
≣	Swamp	Sumpf	Pantano	Marais	Pântano
⍓	Ice Features, Glacier	Eis- und Gletscherformen	Accidentes Glaciales	Formes glaciaires	Acidentes Glaciares
⊤	Other Hydrographic Features	Andere Hydrographische Objekte	Otros Elementos Hidrográficos	Autres données hydrographiques	Outros Elementos Hidrográficos

Symbol	English	Deutsch	Español	Français	Português
✣	Submarine Features	Untermeerische Objekte	Accidentes Submarinos	Formes de relief sous-marin	Acidentes Submarinos
□	Political Unit	Politische Einheit	Unidad Politica	Entité politique	Unidade Política
♥	Cultural Institution	Kulturelle Institution	Institución Cultural	Institution culturelle	Instituição Cultural
⊥	Historical Site	Historische Stätte	Sitio Histórico	Site historique	Sitio Histórico
♠	Recreational Site	Erholungs- und Ferienort	Sitio de Recreo	Centre de loisirs	Sítio de Lazer
⊠	Airport	Flughafen	Aeropuerto	Aéroport	Aeroporto
■	Military Installation	Militäranlage	Instalación Militar	Installation militaire	Instalação Militar
◆	Miscellaneous	Verschiedenes	Misceláneo	Divers	Miscelânea

Name	Page	Lat.°′	Long.°′
Şūrān, Sūrīy.	130	35.17 N	36.45 E
Suran ≃	58	46.02 N	5.19 E
Šurany	30	48.06 N	18.14 E
Surat, Austl.	166	27.09 S	149.04 E
Surat, Bhārat	120	21.10 N	72.50 E
Sūratgarh	123	29.19 N	73.54 E
Surat Thani (Ban Don)	110	9.08 N	99.19 E
Surava	80	52.57 N	41.18 E
Suraż, Pol.	30	52.58 N	22.58 E
Suraž, S.S.S.R.	76	55.25 N	30.44 E
Suraž, S.S.S.R.	76	53.01 N	32.24 E
Surbiton •[8]	260	51.24 N	0.18 W
Surbo	68	40.24 N	18.08 E
Surbourg	56	48.55 N	7.51 E
Surchan	80	46.39 N	49.38 E
Surchandarja ≃	85	37.58 N	67.50 E
Surchandarjinskaja Oblast' □[4]	85	38.00 N	67.30 E
Surchdara	85	38.37 N	69.55 E
Şurchob ≃	85	38.53 N	70.03 E
Šurči	85	37.59 N	67.47 E
Surco	286d	12.09 S	77.01 W
Surduleşti	38	44.23 N	24.57 E
Surdulica	38	42.41 N	22.10 E
Sûre (Sauer) ≃	56	49.44 N	6.31 E
Šureksor, Ozero ⊜	86	52.16 N	75.50 E
Surendorf	41	54.28 N	10.04 E
Surendranagar	120	22.42 N	71.41 E
Suresnes	261	48.52 N	2.14 E
Suretamati, Mount ∧	175f	13.47 S	167.29 E
Suretka	236	9.34 N	82.56 W
Surf City	208	39.40 N	74.10 W
Surfers Paradise	171a	28.00 S	153.26 E
Surfside, Fla., U.S.	220	25.53 N	80.07 W
Surfside, Tex., U.S.	222	28.57 N	95.17 W
Surgères	32	46.07 N	0.45 W
Surgidero	240p	22.41 N	82.18 W
Surgoinsville	192	36.27 N	82.59 W
Sürgü	130	38.01 N	37.59 E
Sürgücü	130	37.35 N	40.44 E
Surguja □[5]	124	23.15 N	83.00 E
Surgut, S.S.S.R.	74	61.14 N	73.20 E
Surgut, S.S.S.R.	80	53.55 N	51.14 E
Surhuisterveen	52	53.10 N	6.10 E
Sūri (Bīrbhūm), Bhārat	126	23.55 N	87.32 E
Suri, Pap. N. Gui.	164	7.10 S	143.55 E
Suria	272b	22.51 N	88.33 E
Suriāpet	122	17.09 N	79.37 E
Suribachi-yama ∧[2]	174f	24.45 N	141.17 E
Suribao ≃	116	11.33 N	125.28 E
Surigao	116	9.45 N	125.30 E
Surigao del Norte □[4]	116	9.35 N	125.36 E
Surigao del Sur □[4]	116	9.00 N	126.00 E
Surigao Strait Ʉ	116	10.15 N	125.23 E
Surin	110	14.53 N	103.29 E
Surinam → Suriname □[1]	250	4.00 N	56.00 W
Suriname □[5]	250	5.30 N	55.00 W
Suriname □[1]	242		
	250	4.00 N	56.00 W
Šurinda	88	55.13 N	113.23 E
Suring	190	44.59 N	88.22 W
Surkh Hisār	267d	35.43 N	51.33 E
Surkole	144	10.25 N	34.38 E
S'urkum	89	50.08 N	140.31 E
S'urkum, Mys ≻	89	50.05 N	140.41 E
Šurma	80	56.58 N	50.21 E
Sūrmaq	128	31.03 N	52.48 E
Surmelin ≃	50	49.04 N	3.13 E
Surnadalsøra	26	62.59 N	8.39 E
Surodadi	115a	6.53 S	109.15 E
Surovaticha	80	55.45 N	43.56 E
Surovikino	80	48.36 N	42.51 E
Surovo	88	55.37 N	105.36 E
Surprise	200	33.38 N	112.20 W
Surprise, Lake ⊜	222	29.33 N	94.41 W
Surprise Valley ∨	204	41.35 N	120.05 W
Surquillo	286d	12.07 S	77.02 W
Surrency	192	31.44 N	82.12 W
Surrey □[6]	42	51.10 N	0.20 W
Surrey, University of ʊ[2]	260	51.14 N	0.36 W
Surrey Heath □[8]	260	51.23 N	0.35 W
Surry	208	37.08 N	76.50 W
Surry □[6]	208	37.10 N	76.50 W
Sursee	58	47.10 N	8.06 E
Sursés ∨	58	46.34 N	9.38 E
Sursk	80	53.04 N	45.42 E
Surskij Majdan	80	55.01 N	46.32 E
Surskoje	80	54.30 N	46.44 E
Surt, Khalīj (Gulf of Sidra) C	146	31.30 N	18.00 E
Surtanāhu	120	26.22 N	70.00 E
Surte	26	57.49 N	12.01 E
Surtsey I	24a	63.16 N	20.32 W
Suru	164	6.50 S	144.45 E
Suru ≃	123	34.45 N	76.12 E
Surubim ≃	250	11.15 S	48.27 W
Surubiú ≃	250	3.58 S	48.52 W
Sürüç	130	36.58 N	38.24 E
Surud Ad ∧	144	10.41 N	47.18 E
Suruga-wan C	94	34.51 N	138.33 E
Suruí	256	22.40 S	43.07 W
Suruí ≃	287a	22.42 S	43.07 W
Surulangun	112	2.37 S	102.45 E
Suru-Lere •[8]	273a	6.31 N	3.22 E
Surumu ≃	246	3.22 N	60.19 W
Surveyor Point ≻	168b	34.47 S	137.51 E
Survey Pass)(	180	67.51 N	154.06 W
Survilliers	261	49.06 N	2.33 E
Surwold	52	53.00 N	7.30 E
Sury-le-Comtal	62	45.32 N	4.10 E
Šuryškary	74	65.54 N	65.22 E
Susa, It.	62	45.08 N	7.03 E
Susa, Nihon	96	34.37 N	131.36 E
Suså ≃	41	55.11 N	11.46 E
Susa, Valle di ∨	62	45.09 N	7.10 E
Susak, Otok I	36	44.31 N	14.18 E
Susaki	96	33.22 N	133.17 E
Susami	96	33.33 N	135.30 E
Susamyr	85	42.09 N	73.58 E
Susamyr ≃	85	42.08 N	74.03 E
Susamyrtau, Chrebet ∧∧	85	42.08 N	73.15 E
Susan	208	37.22 N	76.19 W
Susan ≃	204	40.19 N	120.17 W
Susan, Port C	224	48.10 N	122.25 W
Susana Knolls	228	34.16 N	118.41 W
Sūsangerd	128	31.34 N	48.11 E
Susanino, S.S.S.R.	76	59.30 N	30.22 E
Susanino, S.S.S.R.	80	58.09 N	41.36 E
Susanino, S.S.S.R.	89	52.47 N	140.06 E
Susanville	204	40.25 N	120.39 W
Šušary	265a	59.48 N	30.23 E
Susch	58	46.46 N	10.04 E
Susegana	64	45.51 N	12.15 E
Suşehri	130	40.11 N	38.06 E
Süsel	54	54.04 N	10.43 E
Šušenskoje	86	53.19 N	91.58 E
Sušice	60	49.14 N	13.32 E
Susitna	180	61.33 N	150.31 W
Susitna ≃	180	61.16 N	150.30 W
Susleny	78	47.25 N	28.59 E
Suslonger	80	56.18 N	48.13 E
Sušn'aki Pervoje	86	57.53 N	88.47 E
Susobana ≃	94	36.37 N	138.11 E
Susoh	114	3.43 N	96.50 E
Susong	100	30.09 N	116.06 E
Susono	94	35.09 N	138.54 E
Suspiro del Moro, Puerto)(	34	37.04 N	3.39 W
Susquehanna	210	41.57 N	75.36 W
Susquehanna ≃	188	39.33 N	76.05 W
Susquehanna, West Branch ≃	210	40.53 N	76.47 W
Susquehanna State Park ♣	208	39.36 N	76.09 W
Susques	252	23.25 S	66.29 W
Sussa ≃	152	7.22 S	17.05 E
Süssen	56	48.41 N	9.45 E
Süssenbrunn •[8]	264b	48.17 N	16.30 E
Süsser See ⊜	54	51.30 N	11.40 E
Sussex, N.B., Can.	186	45.43 N	65.31 W
Sussex, N.J., U.S.	210	41.13 N	74.36 W
Sussex, Va., U.S.	208	36.55 N	77.17 W
Sussex, Wis., U.S.	216	43.08 N	88.13 W
Sussex □[6], Del., U.S.	208	38.42 N	75.23 W
Sussex □[6], N.J., U.S.	210	41.08 N	74.41 W
Sussex □[6], Va., U.S.	208	36.50 N	77.15 W
Sussex, East □[6]	42	50.55 N	0.15 E
Sussex, Vale of ∨	42	50.57 N	0.17 W
Sussex Inlet	170	35.11 S	150.36 E
Sussey	50	47.13 N	4.22 E
Sustenhorn ∧	58	46.42 N	8.28 E
Susten Pass)(	58	46.44 N	8.27 E
Susteren	52	51.04 N	5.51 E
Šustikovo	82	55.17 N	35.59 E
Susu	174m	26.47 N	128.19 E
Susubona	175e	8.18 S	159.27 E
Susui	112	4.56 N	116.41 E
Susuman	74	62.47 N	148.10 E
Susurluk	130	39.54 N	28.10 E
Susuzmüsellim	130	41.06 N	27.03 E
Šušvė ≃	76	55.10 N	23.49 E
Susz	30	53.44 N	19.20 E
Sutāhāta	126	22.08 N	88.07 E
Sutak	123	33.12 N	77.28 E
Sutama	94	35.47 N	138.25 E
Sut-Chol'	86	51.24 N	91.17 E
Sütçüler	130	37.30 N	30.59 E
Sutera	70	37.31 N	13.44 E
Sutersville	214	40.14 N	79.48 W
Suthat, Wat ʊ[1]	269a	13.45 N	100.30 E
Sutherland, Austl.	170	34.02 S	151.04 E
Sutherland, S. Afr.	158	32.24 S	20.40 E
Sutherland, Iowa, U.S.	198	42.58 N	95.29 W
Sutherland, Nebr., U.S.	198	41.10 N	101.08 W
Sutherland ≃	182	54.29 N	125.05 W
Sutherland, Lake ⊜	224	48.05 N	123.42 W
Sutherlands	168b	34.10 S	139.13 E
Sutherlin	202	43.25 N	123.19 W
Suthiāna	272a	28.31 N	77.26 E
Sutlej (Satluj) (Langchuhe) ≃	120	29.23 N	71.02 E
Sutri	66	42.14 N	12.13 E
Sutrio	64	46.31 N	12.59 E
Sütschou → Xuzhou, Zhg.	98	34.16 N	117.11 E
Sutschou → Suzhou, Zhg.	106	31.18 N	120.37 E
Sutter	226	39.10 N	121.45 W
Sutter □[6]	226	39.08 N	121.37 W
Sutter Buttes ∧	226	39.12 N	121.50 W
Sutter Bypass ≃	226	38.47 N	121.38 W
Sutter Creek	226	38.23 N	120.48 W
Sutter Creek ≃	226	38.22 N	120.59 W
Sutton, Austl.	171b	35.10 S	149.15 E
Sutton, Qué., Can.	206	45.06 N	72.37 W
Sutton, Eng., U.K.	42	52.23 N	0.07 E
Sutton, Eng., U.K.	260	51.12 N	0.26 W
Sutton, Alaska, U.S.	180	61.43 N	148.53 W
Sutton, Mass., U.S.	207	42.09 N	71.45 W
Sutton, Nebr., U.S.	198	40.36 N	97.52 W
Sutton, W. Va., U.S.	188	38.40 N	80.43 W
Sutton •[8]	42	51.22 N	0.12 W
Sutton-at-Hone	260	51.25 N	0.14 E
Sutton Bridge	42	52.46 N	0.12 E
Sutton Coldfield	42	52.34 N	1.48 W
Sutton Courtenay	42	51.39 N	1.17 W
Sutton Forest	170	34.35 S	150.19 E
Sutton-in-Ashfield	44	53.08 N	1.15 W
Sutton Lake ⊜[1]	188	38.40 N	80.40 W
Sutton Lane Ends	262	53.14 N	2.06 W
Sutton Leach	262	53.26 N	2.42 W
Sutton Mountains ∧∧	206	45.05 N	72.30 W
Sutton-on-Sea	44	53.19 N	0.17 E
Sutton on Trent	44	53.10 N	0.49 W
Sutton Park	276	40.49 N	74.42 W
Sutton Place ⊥	260	51.16 N	0.33 W
Suttons Bay	190	44.59 N	85.39 W
Sutton Scotney	42	51.10 N	1.21 W
Sutton Valence	42	51.12 N	0.36 E
Sutton Veny	42	51.11 N	2.08 W
Sutton Weaver	262	53.18 N	2.41 W
Sutton West	212	44.18 N	79.22 W
Suttor ≃	166	21.25 S	147.45 E
Suttrop	56	51.27 N	8.22 E
Suttsu	92a	42.48 N	140.14 E
Sutwik Island I	180	56.34 N	157.05 W
Suunduk ≃	86	51.46 N	58.46 E
Suurbekom	273d	26.19 S	27.44 E
Suurberge ∧∧	158	33.18 S	25.32 E
Suurbraak	158	34.00 S	20.39 E
Suure-Jaani	76	58.33 N	25.28 E
Suur Pakri I	76	59.20 N	23.55 E
Suur Väin Ʉ	76	58.28 N	23.27 E
Suva	175g	18.08 S	178.25 E
Suvainiškis	76	56.10 N	25.17 E
Šuvalovo Oz'orki •[8]	265a	60.02 N	30.18 E
Suva Planina ∧∧	38	43.10 N	22.10 E
Suvarlı	130	37.32 N	37.38 E
Suvasvesi ⊜	26	62.39 N	28.12 E
Šuvel'an	84	40.30 N	50.09 E
Suvereto	66	43.05 N	10.40 E
Suvo	88	53.39 N	110.00 E
Suvorka	88	56.33 N	103.24 E
Suvorov	82	54.07 N	36.30 E
Suvorovo, S.S.S.R.	78	45.34 N	28.59 E
Suvorovo, S.S.S.R.	82	56.07 N	35.54 E
Suwa	94	36.02 N	138.08 E
Suwa-ko ⊜	94	36.05 N	138.05 E
Suwałki	30	54.07 N	22.56 E
Suwannaphum	110	15.33 N	103.47 E
Suwannee ≃	192	29.18 N	83.09 W
Suwannee Lake ⊜	184	56.08 N	100.10 W
Suwanose-jima I	93b	29.38 N	129.43 E
Suwanose-suidō Ʉ	93b	29.32 N	129.40 E
Suwarrow I[1]	14	13.15 S	163.05 W
Suwaydah	130	35.46 N	39.38 E
Şuwaylih	132	32.02 N	35.50 E
Suways, Khalīj as- C	140	29.00 N	32.50 E
Suways, Qanāt as- ≍	142	29.55 N	32.33 E
Suwŏn	98	37.17 N	127.01 E
Suwon-dong	98	41.54 N	129.43 E
Suxi	100	29.25 N	120.07 E
Suxian	100	33.38 N	116.58 E
Suykbulak	86	49.48 N	80.50 E
Suyo	246	4.30 S	80.00 W
Suzak	86	44.07 N	68.28 E
Suzaka	94	36.39 N	138.19 E
Suzano	256	23.32 S	46.20 W
Suzano □[7]	287b	23.35 S	46.18 W
Suzdal'	80	56.25 N	40.26 E
Suze ≃	58	47.08 N	7.14 E
Suze-la-Rousse	62	44.17 N	4.51 E
Suzhi	98	42.17 N	113.42 E
Suzhou (Soochow)	106	31.18 N	120.37 E
Suzhuang	105	40.04 N	116.44 E
Suzigou	98	40.25 N	123.25 E
Suzihe ≃	98	41.55 N	124.17 E
S'uzikozero	24	61.48 N	37.20 E
Suz'omka	76	52.19 N	34.05 E
Suzu	92	37.25 N	137.17 E
Suzuka	94	34.51 N	136.35 E
Suzuka ≃	94	34.54 N	136.39 E
Suzuka-sammyaku ∧∧	94	35.00 N	136.25 E
Suzuki-shinden	268	35.43 N	139.31 E
S'uz'um	80	58.02 N	47.32 E
Suzu-misaki ≻	92	37.31 N	137.21 E
Suzun	86	53.47 N	82.19 E
Suzzara	64	45.00 N	10.45 E
Sværdborg	41	55.05 N	11.54 E
Sval'ava	78	48.33 N	22.59 E
Svalbard II	4	78.00 N	20.00 E
Svalbard and Jan Mayen □[2]	10	78.00 N	20.00 E
Svalbard og Jan Mayen → Svalbard and Jan Mayen □[2]	10	78.00 N	20.00 E
Svalöv	41	55.55 N	13.06 E
Svaneholm	41	55.30 N	13.28 E
Svaneke	26	55.08 N	15.09 E
Svanetskij Chrebet ∧∧	84	42.55 N	42.42 E
Svängsta	26	56.16 N	14.46 E
Svanninge	41	55.07 N	10.15 E
Svanskog	26	59.11 N	12.33 E
Svapa ≃	78	51.44 N	34.56 E
Svappavaara	24	67.39 N	21.04 E
Švarcevskij	82	54.06 N	37.59 E
Svärdsjö	26	60.45 N	15.55 E
Švaricha	80	57.33 N	49.37 E
Svartå	40	59.08 N	14.31 E
Svartälven ≃	40	59.19 N	14.35 E
Svartån ≃	40	59.37 N	16.33 E
Svarte	41	55.25 N	13.43 E
Svartenhuk ≻[1]	176	71.55 N	55.00 W
Svärtinge	40	58.39 N	16.00 E
Svartisen ⩃	24	66.38 N	14.00 E
Svartlöga I	40	59.34 N	19.03 E
Svartsjölandet I	40	59.22 N	17.41 E
Svataj	74	67.57 N	151.54 E
Svatava	54	50.11 N	12.35 E
Svatava ≃	54	50.32 N	12.07 E
Sv'atica ≃	80	58.22 N	51.43 E
Sv'atogorskaja	83	49.04 N	37.32 E
Sv'atoj Nos, Mys ≻, S.S.S.R.	24	68.10 N	39.45 E
Sv'atoj Nos, Mys ≻, S.S.S.R.	74	72.52 N	140.42 E
Sv'atoj Nos, Poluostrov ≻[1]	88	53.40 N	108.50 E
Sv'atoslavka	80	51.20 N	43.26 E
Svatovo	83	49.23 N	38.13 E
Svay Chék	110	13.48 N	102.58 E
Svay Riĕng	110	11.05 N	105.48 E
Sveafallen └	40	59.10 N	14.22 E
Svebølle	41	55.38 N	11.20 E
Sveča	80	58.16 N	47.32 E
Svedala	41	55.30 N	13.14 E
Svėdasai	76	55.41 N	25.22 E
Sveg	26	62.02 N	14.21 E
Švėkšna	76	55.31 N	21.37 E
Svelgen	26	61.47 N	5.15 E
Svelvik	26	59.37 N	10.24 E
Sven'	76	53.09 N	34.21 E
Švenčionėliai	76	55.10 N	26.00 E
Švenčionys	76	55.07 N	26.10 E
Svendborg	41	55.03 N	10.37 E
Svenljunga	26	57.30 N	13.07 E
Svennevad	40	59.01 N	15.22 E
Svensen	224	46.10 N	123.40 W
Svenstorp	41	55.46 N	13.15 E
Svenstrup	26	56.59 N	9.52 E
Šventoji	76	56.02 N	21.05 E
Šventoji ≃	76	55.06 N	24.22 E
Sverbejevo	89	53.36 N	123.15 E
Sverdlovo, S.S.S.R.	80	51.16 N	44.34 E
Sverdlovo, S.S.S.R.	82	56.38 N	36.37 E
Sverdlovsk, S.S.S.R.	83	48.05 N	39.40 E
Sverdlovsk, S.S.S.R.	86	56.51 N	60.36 E
Sverdrup, Ostrov I	74	74.35 N	74.30 E
Sverige → Sweden □[1]	24	62.00 N	15.00 E
Sverkestaån ≃	40	59.28 N	15.28 E
Švermov	54	50.09 N	14.05 E
Svessa	78	51.57 N	33.54 E
Sveti Arhandjel Mihajlo ʊ[1]	38	42.07 N	21.28 E
Sveti Jovan Bigorski ʊ[1]	38	41.38 N	20.37 E
Svetilovići	76	52.48 N	31.19 E
Sveti Nikole	38	41.52 N	21.58 E
Sveti Petar u Šumi	64	45.11 N	13.52 E
Svetlaja	89	46.33 N	138.18 E
Světlá nad Sázavou	30	49.40 N	15.25 E
Svetlanovo	83	48.42 N	38.28 E
Svetlogorsk, S.S.S.R.	76	52.38 N	29.42 E
Svetlogorsk, S.S.S.R.	76	54.57 N	20.10 E
Svetlograd	72	45.20 N	42.40 E
Svetloje	80	57.03 N	53.38 E
Svetlyj, S.S.S.R.	76	54.41 N	20.08 E
Svetlyj, S.S.S.R.	86	50.47 N	60.53 E
Svetlyj, S.S.S.R.	88	58.26 N	115.55 E
Svetlyj Jar	80	48.29 N	44.46 E
Svetogorsk	24	61.07 N	28.51 E
Svetozarevo	38	43.58 N	21.16 E
Svežen'kaja	80	54.01 N	42.26 E
Svidník	30	49.18 N	21.35 E
Švihov	60	49.29 N	13.17 E
Svijaga ≃	80	55.47 N	48.40 E
Svilajnac	38	44.14 N	21.13 E
Svilengrad	38	41.46 N	26.12 E
Svindal	26	58.30 N	7.28 E
Svinecea ∧	38	44.48 N	22.09 E
Svinesund	26	59.06 N	11.16 E
Svinninge	41	55.43 N	11.28 E
Svir'	76	54.51 N	26.24 E
Svir' ≃	76	60.30 N	32.48 E
Svirica	76	60.29 N	32.51 E
Svirsk	88	53.04 N	103.21 E
Svir'stroj	76	60.48 N	33.43 E
Sviščovka	80	52.51 N	43.44 E
Svisloč', S.S.S.R.	76	53.02 N	24.06 E
Svisloč', S.S.S.R.	76	53.26 N	28.59 E
Svisloč' ≃	76	53.26 N	28.59 E
Svištov	38	43.37 N	25.20 E
Svistunovka	83	49.29 N	38.20 E
Svit	30	49.03 N	20.12 E
Svitávka	30	49.30 N	16.37 E
Svitavy	30	49.45 N	16.27 E
Svitino	82	54.54 N	35.49 E
Svoboda, S.S.S.R.	78	51.58 N	36.17 E
Svoboda, S.S.S.R.	78	47.12 N	40.39 E
Svobodnaja	89	46.48 N	143.23 E
Svobodnoje	83	47.32 N	37.34 E
Svobodnyj, S.S.S.R.	80	52.20 N	46.22 E
Svobodnyj, S.S.S.R.	89	51.24 N	128.07 E
Svobodnyj Port	78	46.20 N	31.51 E
Svoge	38	42.58 N	23.21 E
Svojna	82	54.09 N	36.39 E
Svol'na ≃	76	55.43 N	28.02 E
Svolvær	24	68.14 N	14.34 E
Svor	54	50.47 N	14.36 E
Svorkmo	26	63.10 N	9.45 E
Svratka ≃	61	49.11 N	16.38 E
Svržno	60	49.35 N	12.46 E
Svullrya	26	60.25 N	12.24 E
Svyataya Anna Trough ✣[1]	12	80.00 N	70.00 E
Swābi	123	34.07 N	72.28 E
Swadlincote	42	52.47 N	1.33 W
Swaffham	42	52.39 N	0.41 E
Swain	210	42.29 N	77.51 W
Swain Reefs ✣[2]	166	21.40 S	152.15 E
Swainsboro	192	32.36 N	82.20 W
Swains Island I[1]	14	11.03 S	171.05 W
Swakop ≃	156	22.38 S	14.36 E
Swakopmund	156	22.41 S	14.34 E
Swakopmund □[5]	156	22.00 S	14.30 E
Swale □[8]	260	51.21 N	0.41 E
Swale ≃	44	54.06 N	1.20 W
Swale Canyon ∨	224	45.49 N	121.05 W
Swale Creek ≃	224	45.49 N	121.05 W
Swaledale ∨	44	54.25 N	1.47 W
Swallowfield	218	38.21 N	84.51 W
Swalmen	52	51.15 N	6.02 E
Swamp City	222	32.29 N	94.56 W
Swampscott	207	42.28 N	70.55 W
Swan	222	32.26 N	95.22 W
Swan ≃, Austl.	168a	32.03 S	115.45 E
Swan ≃, Can.	184	52.30 N	100.47 W
Swan ≃, Alta., Can.	182	55.31 N	115.17 W
Swan ≃, Minn., U.S.	190	47.01 N	93.16 W
Swan Acres	279b	40.33 N	80.02 W
Swanage	42	50.37 N	1.58 W
Swan Bay C	169	38.14 S	144.40 E
Swan Creek ≃, Austl.	171a	28.08 S	152.13 E
Swan Creek ≃, Mich., U.S.	216	41.58 N	83.17 W
Swan Creek ≃, Mich., U.S.	216	41.58 N	85.19 W
Swan Creek ≃, Ohio, U.S.	216	41.39 N	83.32 W
Swan Creek ≃, S. Dak., U.S.	198	45.19 N	100.15 W
Swan Creek, North Branch ≃	281	42.06 N	83.23 W
Swan Creek Point ≻	281	42.40 N	82.39 W
Swan Hill	166	35.21 S	143.34 E
Swan Hills	182	54.52 N	115.45 W
Swan Hills ∧∧[2]	182	54.48 N	115.52 W
Swanington	216	40.35 N	87.17 W
Swan Island I	169	38.15 S	144.41 E
Swank Creek ≃	224	47.07 N	120.45 W
Swan Lake, Man., Can.	184	49.24 N	98.46 W
Swan Lake, Mont., U.S.	202	47.55 N	113.50 W
Swan Lake, N.Y., U.S.	210	41.45 N	74.47 W
Swan Lake ⊜, Man., Can.	184	52.30 N	100.45 W
Swan Lake ⊜, Ont., Can.	184	54.17 N	91.12 W
Swan Lake ⊜, Ill., U.S.	219	38.57 N	90.33 W
Swan Lake ⊜, Minn., U.S.	190	44.19 N	94.15 W
Swanley	42	51.24 N	0.12 E
Swanlinbar	48	54.10 N	7.42 W
Swannanda	192	35.36 N	82.23 W
Swannanoa, Lake ⊜	276	41.01 N	74.31 W
Swan Peak ∧	202	47.43 N	113.38 W
Swanquarter	192	35.24 N	76.20 W
Swan Range ∧∧	202	47.50 N	113.40 W
Swan River	184	52.06 N	101.16 W
Swansboro	192	34.36 N	77.07 W
Swanscombe	260	51.26 N	0.18 E
Swansea, Austl.	166	42.08 S	148.04 E
Swansea, Austl.	170	33.05 S	151.38 E
Swansea, Wales, U.K.	42	51.38 N	3.57 W
Swansea, Ill., U.S.	219	38.32 N	89.58 W
Swansea, Mass., U.S.	207	41.45 N	71.11 W
Swansea, S.C., U.S.	192	33.44 N	81.06 W
Swansea •[8]	275b	43.38 N	79.28 W
Swansea Bay C	42	51.35 N	3.52 W
Swans Island I	188	44.10 N	68.25 W
Swanson Lake ⊜[1]	198	40.09 N	101.06 W
Swanton, Ohio, U.S.	216	41.35 N	83.53 W
Swanton, Vt., U.S.	188	44.55 N	73.07 W
Swanville	190	45.55 N	94.38 W
Swanzey Center	207	42.52 N	72.17 W
Swartberg	158	30.15 S	29.23 E
Swarthmore	208	39.54 N	75.21 W
Swarthmore College ʊ[2]	285	39.54 N	75.21 W
Swart Kei ≃	158	32.09 S	27.24 E
Swartplaas	158	26.08 S	26.57 E
Swartruggens	156	25.40 S	26.42 E
Swartruggens ∧∧	158	33.02 S	19.35 E
Swartswood Lake	210	41.04 N	74.51 W
Swartswood State Park ♣	210	41.05 N	74.50 W
Swartz Creek	216	42.58 N	83.50 W
Swarupkāti	126	22.45 N	90.06 E
Swarupnagar	126	22.49 N	88.52 E
Swarzędz	30	52.26 N	17.05 E
Swasey Wash ∨	200	39.15 N	112.53 W
Swasiland → Swaziland □[1]	158	26.30 S	31.30 E
Swāt ≃	123	34.20 N	71.34 E
Swatara Creek ≃	208	40.11 N	76.44 W
Swa-Tenda	152	7.09 S	17.07 E
Swatow → Shantou	100	23.23 N	116.41 E
Swauger Creek ≃	226	38.16 N	119.16 W
Swauk Pass)(	224	47.21 N	120.40 W
Sway	42	50.47 N	1.37 W
Swayzee	216	40.30 N	85.49 W
Swaziland □[1]	138		
	158	26.30 S	31.30 E
Swea City	190	43.23 N	94.19 W
Swede Hill	279b	40.17 N	79.34 W
Sweden □[1]	22		
	24	62.00 N	15.00 E
Sweden Valley	214	41.45 N	77.56 W
Swede Run ≃	285	40.02 N	74.58 W
Swedesboro	208	39.45 N	75.15 W
Swedesburg	285	40.06 N	75.20 W
Swedru	150	5.32 N	0.43 W
Sweeney Plan	279b	40.11 N	79.48 W
Sweeny	222	29.02 N	85.42 W
Sweeny Park ♣	284a	43.02 N	78.52 W
Sweet Briar	192	37.33 N	79.04 W
Sweet Grass Creek ≃	202	45.47 N	109.47 W
Sweetgrass Hills ∧∧[2]	202	48.55 N	111.30 W
Sweet Grass Indian Reserve •[4]	184	52.44 N	108.45 W
Sweetheart Abbey ʊ[1]	44	54.59 N	3.38 W
Sweet Home, Oreg., U.S.	202	44.24 N	122.44 W
Sweet Home, Tex., U.S.	222	29.21 N	97.04 W
Sweetsers	216	40.34 N	85.46 W
Sweet Springs	194	38.58 N	93.25 W
Sweet Valley	210	41.17 N	76.09 W
Sweetwater, Fla., U.S.	220	25.46 N	80.21 W
Sweetwater, Ill., U.S.	219	40.03 N	89.42 W
Sweetwater, Tenn., U.S.	192	35.36 N	84.28 W
Sweetwater, Tex., U.S.	196	32.28 N	100.25 W
Sweetwater ≃	200	42.31 N	107.02 W
Sweetwater Creek	220	27.59 N	82.33 W
Sweetwater Creek ≃, U.S.	196	35.18 N	99.57 W
Sweetwater Creek ≃, Tex., U.S.	196	32.40 N	100.06 W
Sweetwater Mountains ∧∧	226	38.30 N	119.25 W
Swellendam	158	34.02 S	20.26 E
Swepsonville	192	36.01 N	79.22 W
Swerdlowsk → Sverdlovsk	86	56.51 N	60.36 E
Świdnica (Schweidnitz)	30	50.51 N	16.29 E
Świdnik	30	51.14 N	22.41 E
Świdwin	30	53.47 N	15.47 E
Świebodzice	30	50.52 N	16.19 E
Świebodzin	30	52.15 N	15.32 E
Świecie	30	53.25 N	18.28 E
Świerzawa	30	51.01 N	15.54 E
Świerzno	54	53.57 N	14.59 E
Święta	54	53.35 N	14.36 E
Świętokrzyskie, Góry ∧∧	30	50.55 N	21.00 E
Świętokrzyski Park Narodowy ♣	30	50.55 N	21.00 E
Swift ≃, Eng., U.K.	42	52.23 N	1.16 W
Swift ≃, Alaska, U.S.	180	61.53 N	156.18 W
Swift ≃, Mass., U.S.	207	42.12 N	72.22 W
Swift Creek ≃, Ala., U.S.	194	32.25 N	86.38 W
Swift Creek ≃, N.C., U.S.	192	35.12 N	77.05 W
Swift Creek ≃, N.C., U.S.	192	35.57 N	77.35 W
Swift Current	184	50.17 N	107.50 W
Swiftcurrent Creek ≃	184	50.40 N	107.44 W
Swifton	194	35.49 N	91.08 W
Swift Reservoir ⊜[1]	224	46.04 N	122.05 W
Swiftwater	210	41.06 N	75.20 W
Swilly ≃	48	54.57 N	7.42 W
Swilly, Lough C	48	55.10 N	7.38 W
Swimming ≃	276	40.21 N	74.05 W
Swimming River Reservoir ⊜[1]	276	40.19 N	74.07 W
Świna ≃[1]	54	53.55 N	14.17 E
Swinburne, Cape ≻	176	71.14 N	98.34 W
Swinden Reservoirs ⊜[1]	262	53.48 N	2.10 W
Swindle Island I	182	52.32 N	128.35 W
Swindon	42	51.34 N	1.47 W
Swinemünde → Świnoujście	30	53.53 N	14.14 E
Swinford	48	53.57 N	8.57 W
Swing Bridge •[5]	142	30.42 N	32.20 E
Swinging Bridge Reservoir ⊜[1]	210	41.37 N	74.48 W
Swinomish Indian Reservation •[4]	224	48.25 N	122.33 W
Świnoujście (Swinemünde)	30	53.53 N	14.14 E
Swinton, Eng., U.K.	44	53.28 N	1.20 W
Swinton, Eng., U.K.	262	53.31 N	2.20 W
Swinton, Scot., U.K.	46	55.43 N	2.15 W
Swissvale	279b	40.25 N	79.53 W
Switzerland □[6]	218	38.45 N	85.04 W
Switzerland □[1]	22		
	58	47.00 N	8.00 E
Swona I	46	58.45 N	3.03 W
Swordfish Seamount ✣[3]	14	18.30 N	158.25 W
Swords	48	53.28 N	6.13 W
Swords Range ∧∧	166	21.57 S	141.32 E
Swormville	212	43.02 N	78.42 W
Sworton Heath	262	53.21 N	2.28 W
Swoyerville	210	41.18 N	75.53 W
Syalach	74	66.12 N	124.00 E
Syam	58	46.42 N	5.57 E
Syāmnagar	126	22.21 N	89.07 E
Syāmpur, Bhārat	126	22.18 N	88.02 E
Syampur, Bhārat	272b	22.29 N	88.13 E
Sybille Creek ≃	198	42.07 N	105.02 W
Syburg •[8]	263	51.25 N	7.29 E
Sycamore, Ga., U.S.	192	31.40 N	83.38 W
Sycamore, Ill., U.S.	216	41.59 N	88.41 W
Sycamore, Ohio, U.S.	214	40.57 N	83.10 W
Sycamore Creek ≃, Ariz., U.S.	200	33.38 N	111.40 W
Sycamore Creek ≃, Ariz., U.S.	200	34.52 N	112.05 W
Sycamore Creek ≃, Mich., U.S.	216	42.43 N	84.32 W
Sycamore Creek ≃, Ohio, U.S.	214	40.59 N	83.12 W
Sycamore Creek ≃, Tex., U.S.	196	29.14 N	100.48 W
Sycamore Island I	279b	40.29 N	79.52 W
Sycamore Park ♣	280	33.52 N	117.42 W
Sycamore Slough ≃	226	38.48 N	121.44 W
Sycan ≃	202	42.27 N	121.15 W
Sycaway	210	42.44 N	73.39 W
Syčova	86	57.35 N	69.20 E
Syčovka	76	55.50 N	34.17 E
Syców	30	51.19 N	17.43 E
Syda ≃	86	54.22 N	91.23 E
Sydenham, Austl.	274b	37.42 S	144.46 E
Sydenham, Ont., Can.	212	44.25 N	76.36 W
Sydenham •[8], S. Afr.	273d	26.09 S	28.06 E
Sydenham •[8], Eng., U.K.	260	51.26 N	0.03 W
Sydenham ≃	212	44.35 N	80.57 W
Sydenham Lake ⊜	212	44.25 N	76.35 W
Sydenham West	274b	37.41 S	144.39 E
Sydney, Austl.	170		
	274a	33.52 S	151.13 E
Sydney, N.S., Can.	186	46.09 N	60.11 W
Sydney, Fla., U.S.	220	27.58 N	82.12 W
Sydney I[1]	14	4.27 S	171.15 W
Sydney, University of ʊ[2]	274a	33.53 S	151.11 E
Sydney Bay C, Ont., Can.	212	44.54 N	81.05 W
Sydney Bay C, Norf. I.	174c	29.04 S	167.57 E
Sydney Bay Bluff ⊥[4]	212	44.54 N	81.07 W
Sydney Harbour Bridge •[5]	170	33.52 S	151.12 E
Sydney Lake ⊜	184	50.40 N	94.24 W
Sydney Mines	186	46.14 N	60.14 W
Sydney Point ≻	174d	0.53 S	169.36 E
Syferbult	158	26.00 S	27.20 E
Sygan	279b	40.21 N	80.08 W
Syke	52	52.54 N	8.49 E
Sykesville, Md., U.S.	188	39.22 N	76.58 W
Sykesville, Pa., U.S.	214	41.03 N	78.49 W
Sykkylven	26	62.24 N	6.35 E
Syktyvkar	24	61.40 N	50.46 E
Sylacauga	194	33.10 N	86.15 W
Sylhet	120	24.54 N	91.52 E
Syloga	24	63.50 N	43.39 E
Sylsjön ⊜	26	62.56 N	12.11 E
Sylt I	30	54.54 N	8.20 E
Sylva	192	35.23 N	83.13 W
Sylvan	224	45.30 N	122.41 W
Sylvan Beach	210	43.12 N	75.44 W
Sylvan Grove	198	39.00 N	98.24 W
Sylvan Hills	194	34.51 N	92.12 W
Sylvania, Austl.	274a	34.01 S	151.07 E
Sylvania, Ga., U.S.	192	32.45 N	81.38 W
Sylvania, Ohio, U.S.	214	41.43 N	83.42 W
Sylvania, Pa., U.S.	210	41.48 N	76.51 W
Sylvania Heights	274a	34.02 S	151.06 E
Sylvan Lake, Alta., Can.	182	52.19 N	114.05 W
Sylvan Lake, Ill., U.S.	278	42.15 N	88.03 W
Sylvan Lake, Mich., U.S.	281	42.37 N	83.20 W
Sylvan Lake ⊜, Alta., Can.	182	52.21 N	114.10 W
Sylvan Lake ⊜, Ind., U.S.	216	41.29 N	85.20 W
Sylvan Lake ⊜, Mich., U.S.	281	42.37 N	83.20 W
Sylvan Pass)(	202	44.28 N	110.08 W
Sylvan Shores	220	28.49 N	81.41 W
Sylvensteinsee ⊜	64	47.34 N	11.32 E
Sylvester, Ga., U.S.	192	31.32 N	83.49 W
Sylvester, Tex., U.S.	196	32.43 N	100.15 W
Sylvester, Mount ∧[2]	186	48.11 N	55.04 W
Sylvia	198	37.57 N	98.24 W
Sylvia Grinnell Lake ⊜	176	64.10 N	69.25 W
Sym	74	60.20 N	88.23 E
Symmes Creek ≃	188	38.26 N	82.27 W
Syn'a	24	65.22 N	57.42 E
Syndal	274b	37.53 S	145.09 E
Synkovo	82	55.21 N	37.38 E
Synnyr, Chrebet ∧∧	88	56.50 N	111.10 E
Syntul	80	55.00 N	41.18 E
Synžereja	78	47.38 N	28.09 E
Syon House ⊥	260	51.29 N	0.19 W
Syosset	210	40.50 N	73.30 W
Syracuse → Siracusa, It.	70	37.04 N	15.18 E
Syracuse, Ind., U.S.	216	41.26 N	85.45 W
Syracuse, Kans., U.S.	198	37.59 N	101.45 W
Syracuse, Nebr., U.S.	198	40.39 N	96.11 W
Syracuse, N.Y., U.S.	210	43.03 N	76.09 W
Syrčan	80	57.22 N	50.15 E
Syrdarja	85	40.52 N	68.38 E
Syrdarja (Syr-Darya) ≃	72	46.03 N	61.00 E
Syrdarjinskaja Oblast' □[4]	85	40.40 N	67.40 E
Syrdarjinskij	85	41.15 N	68.00 E
Syr-Darya → Syrdarja ≃	72	46.03 N	61.00 E
Syre	46	58.22 N	4.14 W
Syre ≃	56	49.35 N	6.08 E
Syria □[1]	118		
	128	35.00 N	38.00 E
Syriam	110	16.46 N	96.15 E
Syrian Desert → Shām, Bādiyat ash- •[2]	128	32.00 N	40.00 E
Syrie → Syria □[1]	128	35.00 N	38.00 E
Syrien → Syria □[1]	128	35.00 N	38.00 E
Syrskij	76	52.34 N	39.29 E
Sysert'	86	56.29 N	60.49 E
Sysmä	26	61.30 N	25.41 E
Sysola ≃	24	61.42 N	50.53 E
Sysslebäck	26	60.44 N	12.52 E
Syston	42	52.42 N	1.04 W
Systyg Chem	88	52.40 N	95.30 E
Syt'kovo	76	56.31 N	34.01 E
Sytykanskij, Porog └	88	57.49 N	118.33 E
Syukunosho	270	34.50 N	135.32 E
Syväri ⊜	26	63.16 N	28.06 E
Syzran'	80	53.09 N	48.27 E
Syzran' ≃	80	53.04 N	48.26 E
Szabadka → Subotica	38	46.06 N	19.39 E
Szabolcs-Szatmár □[6]	30	48.00 N	22.10 E
Szada	264c	47.38 N	19.19 E
Szamocin	30	53.02 N	17.08 E
Szamos (Someş) ≃	38	48.07 N	22.20 E
Szamotuły	30	52.37 N	16.35 E
Szarvas	30	46.52 N	20.34 E
Szatmárnémeti → Satu Mare	38	47.48 N	22.53 E
Százhalombatta	264c	47.20 N	18.56 E
Szczawnica	30	49.26 N	20.30 E
Szczecin (Stettin)	30	53.24 N	14.32 E
Szczecin □[4]	54	53.15 N	14.45 E
Szczecinek (Neustettin)	30	53.43 N	16.42 E
Szczeciński, Zalew (Oderhaff) C	54	53.46 N	14.14 E
Szczekociny	30	50.38 N	19.50 E
Szczuczyn	30	53.34 N	22.18 E
Szczytno	30	53.34 N	21.00 E
Szechwan → Sichuan □[4]	102	31.00 N	105.00 E
Szécsény	30	48.06 N	19.31 E
Szeged	30	46.15 N	20.09 E
Szeghalom	30	47.01 N	21.11 E
Székesfehérvár	30	47.12 N	18.25 E
Szekszárd	30	46.21 N	18.42 E
Szentendre	30	47.40 N	19.05 E
Szentendrei-Duna ≃[1]	264c	47.36 N	19.05 E
Szentendrei-sziget I	264c	47.39 N	19.07 E
Szentes	30	46.39 N	20.16 E
Szentgotthárd	61	46.57 N	16.17 E
Szeping → Siping	89	43.12 N	124.20 E
Szépművészeti Múzeum ʊ	264c	47.31 N	19.05 E
Szerencs	30	48.09 N	21.13 E
Szigethalom	264c	47.20 N	19.00 E
Szigetszentmiklós	264c	47.21 N	19.03 E
Szilas (Palotai)-patak ≃	264c	47.36 N	19.06 E
Szlichtyngowa	30	51.43 N	16.15 E
Szob	30	47.50 N	18.52 E
Szolnok	30	47.10 N	20.12 E
Szolnok □[6]	30	47.12 N	20.11 E
Szombathely	61	47.14 N	16.38 E
Szprotawa	30	51.34 N	15.33 E
Sztum	30	53.56 N	19.01 E
Szubin	30	53.00 N	17.44 E
Szydłowiec	30	51.14 N	20.51 E
Szypliszki	30	54.15 N	23.05 E
Szzarvíz ≃	30	46.24 N	18.41 E
T			
Ta ≃	94	36.17 N	139.54 E
Taacyn Gol ≃	102	45.09 N	101.27 E
Taakoka I	174k	21.15 S	159.43 W
Taalintehdas → Dalsbruk	26	60.02 N	22.31 E
Taal Lake ⊜	116	13.55 N	121.00 E
Taancan Point ≻	116	10.00 N	125.01 E
Taan Ch'i ≃	100	24.22 N	120.42 E
Taavetti	26	60.55 N	27.34 E
Tabacal	252	23.16 S	64.15 W
Tabacal, Quebrada ≃	286c	10.31 N	67.02 W
Tabaco	116	13.23 N	123.44 E
Tabaco Bay C	116	13.20 N	123.47 E
Tabacundo	246	0.03 N	78.12 W
Tabai ≃	164	3.01 S	135.52 E
Tabalosos	248	6.21 S	76.41 W
Tabanan	115b	8.32 S	115.08 E
Tabango	116	11.19 N	124.22 E
Tabankulu	158	30.58 S	29.19 E
Tabaqah	130	35.52 N	38.34 E
Tábara	34	41.49 N	5.57 W
Tabar Island I	164	2.55 S	152.05 E
Tabar Islands II	164	2.50 S	152.00 E
Tabarka	148	36.57 N	8.45 E

Symbols in the index entries represent the broad categories identified in the key at the right. Symbols with superior numbers (∧∧[2]) identify subcategories (see complete key on page *I · 30*).

Kartensymbole in dem Registerverzeichnis stellen die rechts in Schlüssel erklärten Kategorien dar. Symbole mit hochgestellten Ziffern (∧∧[2]) bezeichnen Unterabteilungen einer Kategorie (vgl. vollständiger Schlüssel auf Seite *I · 30*).

Los símbolos incluídos en el texto del índice representan las grandes categorias identificadas con la clave a la derecha. Los símbolos con numeros en su parte superior (∧∧[2]) identifican las subcategorías (véase la clave completa en la página *I · 30*).

Les symboles de l'index représentent les catégories indiquées dans la légende à droite. Les symboles suivis d'un indice (∧∧[2]) représentent des sous-catégories (voir légende complète à la page *I · 30*).

Os símbolos incluídos no texto do índice representam as grandes categorias identificadas com a chave à direita. Os símbolos com números em sua parte superior (∧∧[2]) identificam as subcategorias (veja-se a chave completa à página *I · 30*).

Symbol	English	Deutsch	Español	Français	Português
∧	Mountain	Berg	Montaña	Montagne	Montanha
∧∧	Mountains	Berge	Montañas	Montagnes	Montanhas
)(	Pass	Pass	Paso	Col	Passo
∨	Valley, Canyon	Tal, Cañon	Valle, Cañón	Vallée, Canyon	Vale, Canhão
≚	Plain	Ebene	Llano	Plaine	Planície
≻	Cape	Kap	Cabo	Cap	Cabo
I	Island	Insel	Isla	Île	Ilha
II	Islands	Inseln	Islas	Îles	Ilhas
⊥	Other Topographic Features	Andere Topographische Objekte	Otros Elementos Topográficos	Autres données topographiques	Outros Elementos Topográficos

ESPAÑOL

Nombre — Página — Lat.°′ — Long.°′ W=Oeste

Tabarz 54 50.52 N 10.31 E
Ṭabas, Īrān 128 32.48 N 60.14 E
Ṭabas, Īrān 128 33.36 N 56.54 E
Tabasará ≃ 236 8.00 N 81.39 W
Tabasco 232 32.35 N 114.55 W
Tabasco □[3] 232 18.15 N 93.00 W
Tabat 86 52.57 N 90.43 E
Tabatinga ≃ 255 17.24 S 43.18 W
Tabayama 94 35.47 N 138.55 E
Tabayin 110 22.42 N 95.19 E
Tabb 208 37.08 N 76.29 W
Tabei 98 39.44 N 122.29 E
Tabelbala 148 29.23 N 3.15 W
Tabelbala, Kahal •[8] 148 28.30 N 2.00 W
Taber 182 49.47 N 112.08 W
Taberg, Sve. 26 57.41 N 14.05 E
Taberg, Sve. 40 59.50 N 14.08 E
Taberg, N.Y., U.S. 210 43.18 N 75.37 W
Tabernacle 285 39.50 N 74.43 W
Tabernes de Valldigna 34 39.04 N 0.16 W
Tabi 152 8.10 S 13.18 E
Tabiang, Kiribati 174d 0.52 S 169.35 E
Tabiang, Kiribati 174t 1.26 N 173.06 E
Tabiano Terme 64 44.48 N 10.21 E
Tabira 250 7.35 S 37.33 W
Tabiteuea 174t 1.25 N 173.07 E
Tabiteuea I[1] 14 1.20 S 174.50 E
Tabla 150 13.46 N 3.01 E
Tabla, Cerro de la ∧ 240m 18.03 N 66.08 W
Tablada 288 34.42 S 58.32 W
Tablas, Cabo ≻ 252 31.51 S 71.34 W
Tablas Island I 116 12.24 N 122.02 E
Tablas Plateau ⛰[1] 116 9.43 N 122.43 E
Tablas Strait ⊔ 116 12.40 N 121.48 E
Tablat 34 36.24 N 3.19 E
Table Bay C 158 33.53 S 18.27 E
Table Cape ≻ 172 39.06 S 178.00 E
Table Mountain ∧, Newf., Can. 186 47.43 N 59.13 W
Table Mountain ∧, S. Afr. 158 33.57 S 18.25 E
Table Mountain ∧, Ariz., U.S. 200 32.49 N 110.31 W
Table Rock 198 40.11 N 96.06 W
Table Rock Lake @[1] 194 36.35 N 93.30 W
Tabletop ∧, Austl. 162 22.32 S 123.55 E
Table Top ∧, Ariz., U.S. 200 32.46 N 112.07 W
Tabletop Mountain ∧ 171b 35.58 S 148.30 E
Tabley Mere @ 262 53.17 N 2.25 W
Tabligbo 150 6.35 N 1.30 E
Tablones 240m 18.15 N 65.45 W
Taboan ≃ 116 17.57 N 122.11 E
Taboão, Ribeirão do ≃ 287b 23.40 S 46.28 W
Taboão da Serra 256 23.38 S 46.46 W
Taboco ≃ 248 19.53 S 55.58 W
Taboga 236 8.48 N 79.33 W
Tabogon 116 10.57 N 124.02 E
Tábor, Česko. 30 49.25 N 14.41 E
Tabor, S.S.S.R. 74 71.16 N 150.12 E
Tabor, Iowa, U.S. 198 40.54 N 95.40 W
Tabor, N.J., U.S. 276 40.52 N 74.29 W
Tabor, S. Dak., U.S. 198 42.57 N 97.39 W
Tabor, Mount → Tavor, Har ∧ 132 32.41 N 35.23 E
Tabora 154 5.01 S 32.48 E
Tabora □[4] 154 6.00 S 32.00 E
Tabor City 192 34.09 N 78.52 W
Tabory 86 58.31 N 64.33 E
Tabou 150 4.25 N 7.21 W
Tabrīz 128 38.05 N 46.18 E
Tábua, Riacho da ≃ 250 9.12 S 44.25 W
Tabuaço 34 41.07 N 7.34 W
Tabuão 256 21.59 S 44.02 W
Tábuas 256 22.12 S 43.37 W
Tabu-dong 98 36.03 N 128.31 E
Tabuelan 116 10.49 N 123.52 E
Tabūk, Ar. Sa. 128 28.23 N 36.35 E
Tabuk, Pil. 116 17.24 N 121.25 E
Tabuleiro 256 21.22 S 43.15 W
Tabuleiro do Norte 250 5.15 S 38.07 W
Tabunifi 174q 9.28 N 138.05 E
Tabuny 86 52.46 N 78.45 E
Tabuse 96 33.57 N 132.03 E
Tabwemasana, Mount ∧ 175f 15.20 S 166.44 E
Täby 40 59.30 N 18.03 E
Tabyn-Bogdo-Ola ⛰ 86 49.08 N 87.45 E
Tacagua, Quebrada ≃ 286c 10.37 N 67.02 W
Tacámbaro ≃ 234 18.29 N 101.07 W
Tacámbaro de Codallos 234 19.14 N 101.28 W
Tacaná 236 15.14 N 92.05 W
Tacaná, Volcán ∧[1] 236 15.08 N 92.06 W
Tacañitas 252 28.38 S 62.36 W
Tacaratu 250 9.06 S 38.10 W
Taceno 58 46.02 N 9.21 E
T'ačev 78 48.02 N 23.34 E
Taché, Lac @ 176 64.00 N 120.00 W
Tacheng 86 46.45 N 82.57 E
Tacherting 60 48.05 N 12.34 E
Tach'i 100 24.57 N 121.53 E
Tachia 100 24.21 N 120.37 E
Tachia Ch'i ≃ 100 24.19 N 120.34 E
Tachiataš 72 42.25 N 59.35 E
Tachibana, Nihon 96 33.11 N 130.36 E
Tachibana, Nihon 96 33.54 N 132.17 E
Tachichilte, Isla de I 232 24.59 N 108.04 W
Tachie ≃ 182 54.40 N 124.50 W
Tachikawa 94 35.42 N 139.25 E
Tachikawa Air Base (United States) ■ 94 35.43 N 139.25 E
Táchira □[3] 246 7.50 N 72.05 W
Tachoshui 100 24.19 N 121.45 E
Tachov 60 49.48 N 12.38 E
Tachta, S.S.S.R. 80 45.54 N 42.07 E
Tachta, S.S.S.R. 89 53.08 N 139.53 E
Tachta-Bazar 128 35.57 N 62.50 E
Tachtakupyr 86 43.02 N 60.17 E
Tachtamygda 89 54.06 N 123.34 E
Tacima 250 6.30 S 35.39 W
Tacina ≃ 68 38.56 N 16.53 E
Tacinskij 80 48.13 N 41.17 E
Taciuã, Lago ≃ 246 4.29 S 60.35 W
Tacloban 116 11.15 N 125.00 E
Taclobo 116 12.20 N 122.34 E
Tacna, Perú 248 18.01 S 70.15 W
Tacna, Ariz., U.S. 200 32.41 N 114.01 W
Tacna □[5] 248 17.40 S 70.20 W
Tacoigmières 261 48.50 N 1.40 E
Tacoma 224 47.15 N 122.27 W
Tacoma Narrows Bridge ◆[5] 224 47.16 N 122.33 W
Taconic 207 42.02 N 73.25 W
Taconic Range ⛰ 210 42.30 N 73.20 W
Taconic State Park ♠ 210 42.05 N 73.34 W
Tacony ◆[8] 285 40.02 N 75.03 W
Tacony Creek ≃ 285 40.01 N 75.06 W
Tacony Creek Park ♠ 285 40.02 N 75.07 W
Tacony Palmyra Bridge ◆[5] 285 40.01 N 75.02 W
Taco Pozo 252 25.37 S 63.17 W
Tacotalpa 234 17.36 N 92.49 W
Tacotalpa ≃ 234 17.50 N 92.52 W

FRANÇAIS

Nom — Page — Lat.°′ — Long.°′ W=Ouest

Tacuarembó 252 31.44 S 55.59 W
Tacuarembó ≃ 252 32.25 S 55.29 W
Tacuarí ≃ 252 32.46 S 53.18 W
Tacuatí 252 23.27 S 56.35 W
Tacuba ◆[8] 286a 19.28 N 99.12 W
Tacubaya 232 28.20 N 104.34 W
Tacubaya ◆[8] 286a 19.25 N 99.12 W
Tacurong 116 6.42 N 124.42 E
Tacurú, Laguna @ 258 34.58 S 58.25 W
Tacutu (Takutu) ≃ 246 3.01 N 60.29 W
Tadain 270 34.52 N 135.24 E
Tadami 92 37.21 N 139.19 E
Tadaoka 96 34.29 N 135.24 E
Tadasuni 71 40.06 N 8.53 E
Tadcaster 44 53.53 N 1.16 W
Tademaït, Plateau du ⛰[1] 148 28.30 N 2.00 E
Tadenac Lake @ 212 45.03 N 79.56 W
Tādepallegūdem 122 16.50 N 81.30 E
Tadía, Ciénaga de @ 246 6.48 N 76.49 W
Tadinou 175f 21.33 S 167.52 E
Tadio, Lagune C 150 5.11 N 5.15 W
Tadjemout 148 25.37 N 3.48 E
Tadjenanet 34 36.08 N 5.59 E
Tadjeraout, Oued V 148 21.17 N 1.19 E
Tadjerouine 36 35.54 N 8.34 E
Tadjettaret, Oued V 148 21.20 N 7.22 E
Tadjoura 144 11.47 N 42.54 E
Tadjoura, Golfe de C 144 11.42 N 43.00 E
Tadley 42 51.21 N 1.08 W
Tado 94 35.08 N 136.38 E
Tadotsu 96 34.16 N 133.45 E
Tadoule Lake @ 176 58.36 N 98.20 W
Tadoussac 186 48.09 N 69.43 W
Tādpatri 122 14.55 N 78.01 E
Taduno 112 1.55 S 123.05 E
Tadworth 42 51.17 N 0.14 W
Tadzhik Soviet Socialist Republic → Tadžikskaja Sovetskaja Socialističeskaja Respublika □[3] 72 39.00 N 71.00 E
Tadžikabad 85 39.07 N 70.50 E
Tadžikskaja Sovetskaja Socialističeskaja Respublika □[3] 72 39.00 N 71.00 E
T'aean 98 36.46 N 126.16 E
T'aebaek-san ∧ 98 37.06 N 128.55 E
T'aebaek-sanmaek ⛰ 98 37.40 N 128.50 E
Taech'ŏn 98 36.22 N 126.34 E
Taedong 98 39.05 N 125.31 E
Taedong-gang ≃ 98 38.42 N 125.15 E
Taegu 98 35.52 N 128.35 E
Taegwan 98 40.13 N 125.12 E
Taehan-Min'guk → Korea, South □[1] 98 36.30 N 128.00 E
Taehŭksan-do I 98 34.40 N 125.25 E
Taehŭng 98 40.06 N 126.56 E
Taehwajŏn 271b 37.36 N 126.52 E
T'aein 98 35.40 N 126.55 E
Taejin 98 36.34 N 129.24 E
Taejŏn 98 36.20 N 127.26 E
Taejujŏm 98 38.24 N 127.58 E
T'aemo-san ∧ 271b 37.27 N 127.04 E
Taeng ≃ 110 19.06 N 98.57 E
Taer 102 34.09 N 98.50 E
Taerwan 100 31.49 N 113.25 E
Taeryanghwa 98 41.14 N 129.42 E
Tafahi I 14 15.51 S 173.43 W
Tafahnā al-'Azab 142 30.36 N 31.15 E
Tafalla 34 42.31 N 1.40 W
Ṭafas 132 32.44 N 36.04 E
Tafāsīkh, Ghurd at- •[8] 142 29.43 N 29.45 E
Tafassasset, Oued V, Afr. 148 21.20 N 10.10 E
Tafassasset, Oued V, Alg. 148 23.00 N 9.20 E
Tafassasset, Ténéré du ◆[2] 146 21.00 N 11.00 E
Tafelbaai → Table Bay C 158 33.53 S 18.27 E
Tafermaar 164 6.51 S 134.06 E
Taff ≃ 42 51.27 N 3.09 W
Tafiré 150 9.04 N 5.10 W
Tafí Viejo 252 26.44 S 65.16 W
Taflan 130 41.25 N 36.09 E
Tafna, Oued ≃ 34 35.17 N 1.30 W
Tafo 150 6.13 N 0.22 W
Tafraout 148 29.40 N 8.58 W
Taft, Īrān 128 31.45 N 54.14 E
Taft, Pil. 116 11.54 N 125.25 E
Taft, Calif., U.S. 204 35.08 N 119.28 W
Taft, Fla., U.S. 220 28.23 N 81.24 W
Taft, Okla., U.S. 196 35.46 N 95.32 W
Taft, Tex., U.S. 196 27.57 N 97.46 W
Taftān, Kūh-e ∧ 128 28.36 N 61.06 E
Tafton 210 41.25 N 75.11 W
Tafuna Airport ⊠ 174u 14.20 S 170.43 W
Taga, Nihon 94 35.13 N 136.17 E
Taga, Nihon 270 34.49 N 135.49 E
Taga, W. Sam. 175a 13.46 S 172.28 W
Tagabukid 116 7.00 N 126.21 E
Taga Dzong 124 27.04 N 89.53 E
Tagagawik ≃ 180 66.30 N 159.00 W
Tagaj 80 54.18 N 47.39 E
Tagajō 92 38.20 N 141.00 E
Tagama ◆[1] 150 15.50 N 8.12 E
Tagan 86 54.57 N 77.18 E
Tagana-an 116 9.42 N 125.35 E
Taganrog 83 47.12 N 38.56 E
Taganrogskij Zaliv C 78 47.00 N 38.23 E
Tagapula Island I 116 12.04 N 124.12 E
Tågarp 41 55.56 N 12.57 E
Tagauayan Island I 116 10.58 N 121.13 E
Tagaytay 116 14.06 N 120.56 E
Tagbilaran 116 9.39 N 123.51 E
Tagdempt → Tiaret 148 35.28 N 1.21 E
Tage 164 6.20 S 143.20 E
Tageren Canal ≅ 174q 9.33 N 138.09 E
Taggia 62 43.52 N 7.51 E
Taghkanic Creek ≃ 210 42.13 N 73.45 W
Taghmon 48 52.18 N 6.39 W
Taghrīfat 146 29.12 N 17.22 E
Tagig 269f 14.32 N 121.04 E
Tagig ≃ 269f 14.31 N 121.05 E
T'aginka 78 46.47 N 33.04 E
Tagish Lake @ 180 59.45 N 134.15 W
Tagliacozzo 66 42.04 N 13.14 E
Tagliamento ≃ 64 45.38 N 13.06 E
Tagliata, Monte della ∧ 64 44.34 N 9.48 E
Taglio di Po 64 45.00 N 12.12 E
Tagna 88 53.36 N 101.54 E
Tagna ≃ 88 53.38 N 101.53 E
Tagnant, Dhar •[4] 150 18.30 N 11.00 W
Tago 116 9.02 N 126.13 E
Tago ≃ 116 9.01 N 126.14 E
Tagoloan 116 8.32 N 124.45 E
Tagolo Point ≻ 116 8.44 N 123.23 E
Tagon Harbour C 162 33.53 S 123.00 E
Tagounit 148 29.58 N 5.36 W
Tagow Bāy 120 35.42 N 66.03 E
Tagrina, Oued V 148 21.00 N 6.16 E

PORTUGUÊS

Nome — Página — Lat.°′ — Long.°′ W=Oeste

Taguatinga 255 12.25 S 46.26 W
Tagubanhan Island I 116 11.08 N 123.07 E
Tagudin 116 16.56 N 120.27 E
Taguedoufat V 150 14.50 N 7.42 E
Taguke 120 32.07 N 84.35 E
Tagul ≃ 88 55.35 N 97.45 E
Tagula Island I 160 11.30 S 153.30 E
Tagum 116 7.28 N 125.48 E
T'agun 86 53.56 N 85.38 E
Tagun Bay C 116 13.55 N 123.46 E
Tagus (Tejo) (Tajo) ≃ 34 38.40 N 9.24 W
T'agyŏng-ni 98 38.04 N 126.03 E
Tah, Sebkha @ 148 27.45 N 12.42 W
Taha 89 47.33 N 124.14 E
Tahaa I 14 16.38 S 151.30 W
Tahakopa 172 46.31 S 169.23 E
Tahala 148 34.04 N 4.20 W
Tahan, Gunong ∧ 114 4.38 N 102.14 E
Tahāneh-ye Ney Basteh 128 32.59 N 60.53 E
Tahara 94 34.40 N 137.16 E
Tahart 148 22.51 N 5.12 E
Tahat ∧ 148 23.18 N 5.47 E
Taheke 172 35.27 S 173.39 E
Ṭāherī 128 27.42 N 52.21 E
Tahifet 148 22.58 N 5.55 E
Tahir 130 38.47 N 38.17 E
Tahir Geçidi)(130 39.54 N 42.22 E
Tahiryuak Lake @ 176 70.56 N 112.20 W
Tahiti I 174s 17.37 S 149.27 W
Tahkuna Nina ≻ 76 59.07 N 22.36 E
Tahlequah 196 35.55 N 94.58 W
Ṭahmā wa Minshāt 'Abd as-Sayyid 142 29.38 N 31.14 E
Tahmoor 170 34.13 S 150.36 E
Tahnaout 148 31.24 N 7.54 W
Tahneta Pass)(180 61.53 N 147.20 W
Tahoe, Lake @ 226 39.07 N 120.03 W
Tahoe City 226 39.10 N 120.09 W
Tahoe Lake @ 176 70.15 N 108.45 W
Tahoe Paradise 226 38.52 N 120.01 W
Tahoe Valley 226 38.55 N 120.00 W
Tahoka 196 33.10 N 101.48 W
Taholah 224 47.21 N 124.17 W
Tahoua 150 14.54 N 5.16 E
Tahoua □[5] 150 16.00 N 5.00 E
Tahquamenon ≃ 190 46.34 N 85.02 W
Tahquamenon Falls State Park ♠ 190 46.29 N 85.05 W
Tahsis 182 49.55 N 126.39 W
Ta Hsü I 100 23.10 N 119.32 E
Ṭahṭā 140 26.46 N 31.30 E
Tahtaköprü 130 39.57 N 29.39 E
Tahtsa Lake @ 182 53.42 N 127.26 W
Tahtsa Peak ∧ 182 53.33 N 127.47 W
Tahu 100 24.26 N 120.52 E
Tahuamanú ≃ 248 11.06 S 67.36 W
Tahuata I 174x 9.57 S 139.05 W
Tahulandang, Pulau I 112 2.20 N 125.25 E
Tahuna 112 3.37 N 125.29 E
Tahuofang @[1] 104 41.55 N 124.07 E
Tahuya ≃ 224 47.23 N 123.03 W
Ṭahwāy 142 30.22 N 30.52 E
Taḥwīṭat an-Nahr 132 33.52 N 35.31 E
Taï, C. Iv. 150 5.52 N 7.27 W
Tai, It. 64 46.25 N 12.20 E
Tai, Nihon 270 34.31 N 135.26 E
Tai ◆[8] 270 34.45 N 135.00 E
Taiaçupeba 256 23.40 S 46.11 W
Taian, Zhg. 98 36.12 N 117.07 E
Taian, Zhg. 104 41.23 N 122.27 E
Taianchang 107 30.05 N 105.47 E
Taian'gang 106 31.43 N 121.40 E
Taiarapu, Presqu'île de ≻[1] 174s 17.47 S 149.14 W
Taibaiqu 102 34.00 N 107.18 E
Taibaishan ∧, Zhg. 98 39.19 N 114.11 E
Taibaishan ∧, Zhg. 102 33.54 N 107.46 E
Taibilla, Sierra de ⛰ 34 38.10 N 2.10 W
Taibon Agordino 64 46.18 N 12.00 E
Taicang 106 31.26 N 121.07 E
T'aichou → Taizhou 100 32.30 N 119.58 E
Taichu → T'aichung 100 24.09 N 120.41 E
T'aichung 100 24.09 N 120.41 E
T'aichunghsien 100 24.15 N 120.43 E
Taicunzhen 106 31.27 N 119.03 E
Taiden → Taejŏn 98 36.20 N 127.26 E
Taiei 94 35.49 N 140.25 E
Taieri ≃ 172 46.03 S 170.11 E
Taif → Aṭ-Ṭā'if 144 21.16 N 40.24 E
Taigong 102 26.32 N 108.22 E
Taigu 102 37.28 N 112.30 E
Tai Hang 271d 22.17 N 114.11 E
Taihangshan ⛰ 102 36.00 N 113.35 E
Taihape 172 39.40 S 175.48 E
Taihe, Zhg. 100 26.49 N 114.55 E
Taihe, Zhg. 100 33.11 N 115.36 E
Taihechang 107 30.07 N 103.50 E
Taihezhen 89 44.47 N 123.29 E
Taihezhen ⊥ 110 25.41 N 100.07 E
Taiho 174m 26.39 N 128.07 E
Taihoku → T'aipei 100 25.03 N 121.30 E
T'aihsi 100 23.42 N 120.11 E
T'aihsien → Taizhou 100 32.30 N 119.58 E
Taihu 100 30.26 N 116.16 E
Taihu @ 106 31.15 N 120.10 E
Taihuaizhen 98 38.59 N 113.34 E
Taijimiao 98 40.55 N 113.46 E
Taijinai'erhu @ 120 37.15 N 93.20 E
Taijüan → Taiyuan 102 37.55 N 112.30 E
Taikang 98 34.04 N 114.50 E
Taikkyi 110 17.19 N 95.58 E
Taikou 102 31.53 N 111.07 E
Taiko-yama ∧ 96 35.46 N 135.12 E
Taikyu → Taegu 98 35.52 N 128.35 E
Tailai 89 46.23 N 123.27 E
Tai Lam Chung 271d 22.22 N 114.01 E
Tai Lam Chung Reservoir @[1] 271d 22.23 N 114.01 E
Tailem Bend 166 35.16 S 139.27 E
Tailfingen 58 48.15 N 9.01 E
Tai Long, H.K. 271d 22.13 N 113.59 E
Tai Long, H.K. 271d 22.25 N 114.23 E
Tai Long Head ≻ 271d 22.24 N 114.24 E
Tai Long Wan C 271d 22.24 N 114.24 E
Taima, Nihon 96 34.30 N 135.42 E
T'aima, T'aiwan 100 22.37 N 120.59 E
Taimba 74 60.18 N 98.58 E
Tai Mo Shan ∧ 271d 22.25 N 114.07 E
Taimyr-Halbinsel → Tajmyr, Poluostrov ≻[1] 74 76.00 N 104.00 E
Tain 46 57.48 N 4.04 W
Tainaka 270 34.36 N 135.37 E
T'ainan 100 23.00 N 120.11 E
T'ainanhsien 100 23.18 N 120.19 E
Taínaron, Ákra ≻ 38 36.22 N 22.30 E
Taining 100 26.54 N 117.09 E
Tain-l'Hermitage 62 45.04 N 4.51 E
Tai O, H.K. 100 22.15 N 113.51 E
Taio, It. 64 46.20 N 11.04 E

Taiobeiras 255 15.49 S 42.14 W
Taiof Island I 175e 5.31 S 154.39 E
Taipas 255 12.15 S 47.09 W
T'aipei 100; 269d 25.03 N 121.30 E
T'aipei □[6] 269d 25.00 N 121.40 E
Taipei Bridge ◆[5] 269d 24.04 N 121.30 E
T'aipeihsien 100 25.00 N 121.27 E
Taipei Institute of Technology ⊽[2] 269d 25.02 N 121.32 E
Taipei International Airport ⊠ 269d 25.04 N 121.33 E
Taipei Park ♠ 269d 25.03 N 121.31 E
T'aipei Shih □[7] 269d 25.03 N 121.30 E
Taiping, Malay. 114 4.51 N 100.44 E
Taiping, Zhg. 100 30.18 N 118.12 E
Taiping, Zhg. 102 22.34 N 107.30 E
Taipingchang, Zhg. 102 27.25 N 103.04 E
Taipingchang, Zhg. 107 29.33 N 103.33 E
Taipingchang, Zhg. 107 29.53 N 106.04 E
Taipingchang, Zhg. 107 30.10 N 106.21 E
Taipingchang, Zhg. 107 30.39 N 105.54 E
Taipingchang, Zhg. 107 29.55 N 103.49 E
Taipingchuan, Zhg. 89 44.23 N 123.11 E
Taipingchuan, Zhg. 98 42.36 N 127.20 E
Taipingdian 102 32.08 N 111.45 E
Taipingkou 100 29.50 N 113.35 E
Taipingling 89 43.26 N 128.09 E
Taipingqiao 106 31.26 N 120.42 E
Taipingshan, Zhg. 98 40.34 N 122.25 E
Taipingshan, Zhg. 104 41.36 N 123.41 E
T'aip'ing Shan ∧ 100 24.30 N 121.38 E
Taipingshao 98 40.54 N 125.08 E
Taipingsi 107 29.24 N 103.34 E
Taipingxigou 104 42.36 N 121.13 E
Taipingzhai 104 42.14 N 124.07 E
Taipingzhen, Zhg. 89 51.33 N 120.17 E
Taipingzhen, Zhg. 89 46.44 N 130.44 E
Taipingzhen, Zhg. 102 35.42 N 107.37 E
Taipingzhen, Zhg. 107 30.26 N 104.12 E
Taipingzhen, Zhg. 107 29.24 N 105.47 E
Taipingzhuang, Zhg. 104 42.38 N 123.45 E
Taipingzhuang, Zhg. 105 40.08 N 117.36 E
Taipingzhuang, Zhg. 105 40.03 N 116.24 E
Tai Po Hoi C 271d 22.26 N 114.12 E
Tai Po Tsai 271d 22.21 N 114.15 E
Taipu 250 5.37 S 35.36 W
Taipusiqi (Baochang) 98 41.56 N 115.22 E
Taira → Iwaki, Nihon 94 37.03 N 140.55 E
Taira, Nihon 94 36.26 N 136.57 E
Taira, Nihon 174m 26.38 N 128.09 E
Tairetá 256 22.36 S 43.42 W
Tairiqiao 106 30.59 N 121.33 E
Tais 112 4.06 S 102.34 E
Taisen-zan ∧ 96 33.06 N 131.17 E
Taisetsu-zan ∧ 90 43.30 N 142.57 E
Taisetsu-zan-kokuritsu-kōen ♠ 92a 43.30 N 142.57 E
Taisha, Nihon 96 35.24 N 132.40 E
Taisha → Izumo, Nihon 96 35.22 N 132.46 E
Taishaku-kyō ♠ 96 34.53 N 133.13 E
Taishaku-zan ∧, Nihon 94 36.58 N 139.28 E
Taishaku-zan ∧, Nihon 270 34.47 N 135.07 E
Taishan 102 22.16 N 112.44 E
Taishan I 100 26.59 N 120.37 E
Taishanchang 107 30.32 N 106.42 E
Taishi, Nihon 96 34.50 N 134.33 E
Taishi, Nihon 270 34.31 N 135.39 E
Taishō 96 33.12 N 132.58 E
Taishō ◆[8] 270 34.38 N 135.27 E
Taishun 100 27.33 N 119.43 E
Taita Hills ⛰[2] 154 3.25 S 38.20 E
Taitao, Península de ≻[1] 254 46.30 S 74.25 W
Taitapu 172 43.40 S 172.33 E
Taitō ◆[8] 268 35.43 N 139.47 E
Tai Tong 271d 22.25 N 114.01 E
Taitouying 98 40.02 N 119.12 E
Taitō-zaki ≻ 94 35.18 N 140.29 E
T'aitung 100 22.45 N 121.09 E
Taivalkoski 26 65.34 N 28.15 E
Taiwan (T'aiwan) □[1] 90; 100 23.30 N 121.00 E
T'aiwan (Formosa) I 100 23.30 N 121.00 E
Tai Wan Tau 271d 22.18 N 114.17 E
Tai Wan Tsun 271d 22.19 N 114.12 E
Taiwei 100 23.19 N 114.29 E
Taixi 100 24.42 N 116.56 E
Taixing 106 32.11 N 120.01 E
Taixinzhuang 105 38.57 N 115.44 E
Taixizhen 106 31.03 N 119.49 E
Taiyang 100 30.12 N 119.19 E
Taiyanggong 271a 39.58 N 116.25 E
Taiyanghekou 102 31.54 N 101.49 E
Taíyetos Óros ⛰ 38 37.16 N 22.12 E
Taiyuan 102 37.55 N 112.30 E
Taizhao 120 30.01 N 93.08 E
Taizhou 100 32.30 N 119.58 E
Taizhouwan C 100 28.38 N 121.40 E
Taizihe ≃ 98 41.00 N 122.26 E
Ta'izz 144 13.38 N 44.04 E
Tāj al-'Izz 142 30.57 N 31.35 E
Tajarḥī 146 24.21 N 14.28 E
Tajbola 24 68.26 N 33.19 E
Tajdakovo 82 54.29 N 37.32 E
Taježnyj 88 56.13 N 94.55 E
Tajga 86 56.04 N 85.37 E
Tajginka 86 55.37 N 60.30 E
Tajgonos, Poluostrov ≻[1] 74 61.20 N 161.00 E
Tajima 94 37.12 N 139.46 E
Tajimi 94 35.19 N 137.08 E
Tajique 200 34.45 N 106.17 W
Tajiri 270 34.24 N 135.18 E
Tajitos 232 30.58 N 112.18 W
Tajkanskij Chrebet ⛰ 89 54.15 N 134.50 E
Tajlakdžegen 86 43.54 N 60.29 E
Tajlakovy 86 59.20 N 74.04 E
Tajmyr, Ozero @ 74 74.30 N 102.30 E
Tajmyr, Poluostrov ≻[1] 74 76.00 N 104.00 E
Tajna 88 56.27 N 95.30 E
Tajninka 265b 55.54 N 37.45 E
Tajo → Tagus ≃ 34 38.40 N 9.24 W
Tajpur, Bhārat 124 29.10 N 78.29 E
Tajpur, Bhārat 124 25.51 N 85.41 E
Tājpur, Bhārat 272b 22.44 N 88.16 E
Tajpur Khurd ◆[8] 272a 28.35 N 77.03 E
Tajrīsh 128 35.48 N 51.25 E
Tajšet 88 55.57 N 98.00 E
Tajsojgan 80 48.19 N 53.29 E
Tajturka 88 52.51 N 103.28 E
Tajumulco, Volcán ∧[1] 236 15.02 N 91.55 W
Tajuña ≃ 34 40.07 N 3.35 W
Tājūrā', Lībīya 146 32.53 N 13.21 E
Tajura, S.S.S.R. 88 57.00 N 106.35 E
Tajura ≃ 88 57.00 N 106.35 E
Tajžina 86 53.38 N 87.28 E
Tak 110 16.52 N 99.08 E
Takāb 128 36.24 N 47.07 E
Takabanare-jima I 174m 26.22 N 127.59 E
Takabara 150 11.50 N 11.30 W
Takachiho 92 32.42 N 131.18 E
Takachu 156 22.37 S 21.58 E
Takada, Nihon 94 37.06 N 138.15 E

Takada, Nihon 96 33.06 N 130.28 E
Takada → Bungo-takada, Nihon 96 33.33 N 131.27 E
Takada → Yamato-takada, Nihon 96 34.31 N 135.45 E
Takagi 268 35.56 N 139.35 E
Takahagi 94 36.43 N 140.43 E
Takahama, Nihon 94 34.55 N 136.59 E
Takahama, Nihon 94 37.00 N 136.46 E
Takahama, Nihon 96 35.29 N 135.33 E
Takahara ≃ 94 36.28 N 137.15 E
Takahashi 96 34.47 N 133.37 E
Takahashi ≃ 96 34.31 N 133.42 E
Takahe, Mount ∧ 9 76.16 S 112.14 W
Takaido ◆[8] 268 35.40 N 139.37 E
Takaishi 96 34.32 N 135.26 E
Takaka 172 40.51 S 172.48 E
Takalar 112 5.28 S 119.24 E
Takamatsu, Nihon 94 36.46 N 136.43 E
Takamatsu, Nihon 96 34.20 N 134.03 E
Takamatsu, Nihon 96 34.41 N 133.49 E
Takami-shima I 96 34.19 N 133.41 E
Takamiya 96 34.47 N 132.44 E
Takami-yama ∧ 94 34.25 N 136.05 E
Takamori 94 35.33 N 137.53 E
Takanabe 92 32.08 N 131.30 E
Takanawa-hantō ≻[1] 96 33.58 N 132.56 E
Takanawa-san ∧ 96 33.56 N 132.51 E
Takane 94 35.50 N 138.25 E
Takanezawa 94 36.37 N 139.59 E
Takano 96 35.02 N 132.55 E
Takanosu 92 40.13 N 140.22 E
Takao → Kaohsiung 100 22.38 N 120.17 E
Takaoka 94 36.45 N 137.01 E
Takao-kokutei-kōen ♠ 94 35.38 N 139.15 E
Takao-san ∧ 94 35.38 N 139.15 E
Takao-san ∧[2] 270 34.49 N 135.51 E
Takapau 172 40.02 S 176.21 E
Takapoto I[1] 14 14.38 S 145.12 W
Takapuna 172 36.47 S 174.47 E
Takara-jima I 93b 29.09 N 129.13 E
Takarazuka 96 34.49 N 135.21 E
Takartibah 146 26.32 N 13.15 E
Takasago 96 34.45 N 134.48 E
Takasaki 94 36.20 N 139.01 E
Takase 96 34.10 N 133.45 E
Takase ≃ 94 36.28 N 137.52 E
Takashima, Nihon 92 32.39 N 129.45 E
Takashima, Nihon 94 35.18 N 136.01 E
Taka-shima I 96 34.50 N 131.50 E
Takashippu 174m 26.24 N 127.44 E
Takasu 94 35.57 N 136.53 E
Takata → Rikuzen-takata, Nihon 92 39.01 N 141.38 E
Takata → Takada, Nihon 94 37.06 N 138.15 E
Takatik I 174r 7.00 N 158.12 E
Takatō 94 35.50 N 138.04 E
Takatomi 94 35.29 N 136.47 E
Takatori 96 34.27 N 135.48 E
Takatori-yama ∧, Nihon 96 33.18 N 130.43 E
Takatori-yama ∧, Nihon 268 35.18 N 139.37 E
Takatsu ≃ 96 34.42 N 131.49 E
Takatsuki, Nihon 94 35.28 N 136.14 E
Takatsuki, Nihon 96 34.51 N 135.37 E
Takaungu 154 3.41 S 39.51 E
Ta-kaw 110 21.36 N 98.56 E
Takawa 96 33.38 N 130.49 E
Takaya 96 34.27 N 132.49 E
Takayama, Nihon 94 36.08 N 137.15 E
Takayama, Nihon 94 36.40 N 138.21 E
Takayama, Nihon 94 36.37 N 138.57 E
Takayama, Nihon 270 34.45 N 135.49 E
Takayanagi, Nihon 94 37.13 N 138.38 E
Takayanagi, Nihon 268 35.25 N 139.57 E
Tak Bai 114 6.16 N 102.03 E
Takčijan 85 38.32 N 68.03 E
Takefu 94 35.54 N 136.10 E
Takehara 96 34.21 N 132.55 E
Takela 120 37.54 N 76.44 E
Takeli 85 40.30 N 69.25 E
Takenake 120 34.11 N 81.20 E
Takeno ≃ 96 35.45 N 135.06 E
Takenotsuka ◆[8] 268 35.48 N 139.48 E
Takeo 92 33.12 N 130.01 E
Takeoka 268 35.12 N 139.51 E
Tåkern @ 26 58.21 N 14.48 E
Takeshi 94 36.17 N 138.14 E
Take-shima I 93b 30.49 N 130.26 E
Tākestān 128 36.04 N 49.43 E
Taketa 96 32.58 N 131.24 E
Taketoyo 94 34.51 N 136.55 E
Takêv 110 10.59 N 104.47 E
Take-yama ∧[2] 268 35.13 N 139.39 E
Takhādīd ⊤[4] 128 29.59 N 44.30 E
Takhār □[4] 120 36.30 N 69.30 E
Takhatpur 124 22.09 N 81.52 E
Ta Khli 110 15.15 N 100.21 E
Ta-khoa 110 21.13 N 104.18 E
Takht-e Jamshīd ⊥ 128 29.57 N 52.52 E
Takht-i-Bhāi 123 34.17 N 71.56 E
Takht-i-Sulaiman ∧ 123 35.29 N 75.18 E
Tāki, Bhārat 126 22.36 N 88.55 E
Taki, Nihon 94 34.30 N 136.33 E
Taki, Nihon 96 35.16 N 132.38 E
Taki, Pap. N. Gui. 175e 6.29 S 155.50 E
Takijuq Lake @ 176 66.15 N 113.05 W
Takikawa 92a 43.33 N 141.54 E
Takingeun 114 4.38 N 96.50 E
Takino 96 34.56 N 134.58 E
Takipur 126 24.19 N 87.58 E
Takitimu Mountains ⛰ 172 45.41 S 167.53 E
Takla Lake @ 182 55.25 N 125.53 W
Takla Landing 182 55.29 N 125.58 W
Takla Makan → Talimupendi ◆[2] 90 39.00 N 83.00 E
Tako 94 35.44 N 140.28 E
Takob 85 38.50 N 68.57 E
Tako-bana ≻ 96 35.36 N 133.06 E
Takolekaju, Pegunungan ⛰ 112 2.00 S 121.00 E
Takoma Park 284c 38.59 N 77.01 W
Takoradi → Sekondi-Takoradi 150 4.59 N 1.43 W
Takotna 180 62.56 N 156.04 W
Takow → Kaohsiung 100 22.38 N 120.17 E
Takrouna 36 36.09 N 10.20 E
Taksino 82 56.19 N 36.10 E
Takslesluk Lake @ 180 61.04 N 162.55 W
Taksony 264c 47.20 N 19.04 E
Taku 92 33.17 N 130.08 E
Taku ≃ 180 58.26 N 133.59 W
Takuam, Mount ∧ 175e 6.27 S 155.36 E
Takua Pa 110 8.53 N 98.21 E
Taku Arm @ 180 60.00 N 134.10 W
Taku Glacier ⊓ 180 58.35 N 134.10 W
Takum 150 7.17 N 9.59 E
Takuma 96 34.13 N 133.40 E
Takundi 152 4.45 S 16.34 E
Takutea I 14 19.49 S 158.18 W

Takut Tangug Bay C 116 6.33 N 122.15 E
Takutu (Tacutu) ≃ 246 3.01 N 60.29 W
Takysie Lake 182 53.54 N 125.53 W
Tāl 123 34.55 N 72.13 E
Tāla, Bhārat 124 23.43 N 81.02 E
Tala, Bngl. 126 22.46 N 89.16 E
Tala, Méx. 234 20.40 N 103.42 W
Talā, Miṣr 142 30.41 N 30.56 E
Tala, Ur. 252 34.21 S 55.46 W
Tala, Arroyo del ≃ 258 33.37 S 56.34 W
Talacogon 116 8.28 N 125.46 E
Talaga 112 2.11 S 125.53 E
Talagang 123 32.55 N 72.25 E
Talagante 252 33.40 S 70.56 W
Talagou 104 41.37 N 120.32 E
Talaimannar 122 9.05 N 79.44 E
Talāja 120 21.21 N 72.03 E
Talak ◆[1] 150 18.20 N 6.00 E
Talakag 116 8.16 N 124.37 E
Talakan 89 49.38 N 133.18 E
Talakovka 83 47.10 N 37.43 E
Tālāla 120 21.02 N 70.32 E
Talalajevka 78 50.51 N 33.08 E
Talamanca, Cordillera de ⛰ 236 9.30 N 83.40 W
Talamba 123 30.32 N 72.14 E
Talamone 66 42.33 N 11.08 E
Talana, It. 71 40.02 N 9.30 E
Talana, S. Afr. 158 28.10 S 30.15 E
Talandža 89 49.27 N 131.35 E
Talang, Gunung ∧ 112 1.11 S 100.43 E
Talangbatu 112 4.06 S 105.29 E
Talangbetutu 112 2.53 S 104.41 E
Talangpadang 112 5.21 S 104.11 E
Talangrimbo 112 3.29 S 105.25 E
Talant 58 47.19 N 5.00 E
Talap 80 48.26 N 48.03 E
Talara 246 4.34 S 81.17 W
Talarrubias 34 39.02 N 5.14 W
Talas 85 42.32 N 72.14 E
Talas ≃ 85 44.02 N 69.37 E
Talasea 164 5.20 S 150.05 E
Talatakoh, Pulau I 112 0.22 S 122.05 E
Tal'at al-Jamā'ah, Rujm ∧ 132 30.23 N 35.30 E
Talata Mafara 150 12.35 N 6.04 E
Talaud, Kepulauan II 108 4.20 N 126.50 E
Talavera 116 15.35 N 120.55 E
Talavera de la Reina 34 39.57 N 4.50 W
Talawanta 166 18.38 S 140.16 E
Talawdī 140 10.38 N 30.23 E
Talayan 116 6.55 N 124.24 E
Tālbāndh 126 22.03 N 86.20 E
Talbingo 171b 35.34 S 148.18 E
Talbingo Reservoir @[1] 171b 35.43 S 148.20 E
Talbot 169 37.11 S 143.43 E
Talbot ≃ 212 44.28 N 79.10 W
Talbot, Cape ≻ 164 13.48 S 126.43 E
Talbot Brook 168a 32.01 S 116.40 E
Talbot Islands II 164 9.15 S 142.08 E
Talbot Lake @, Man., Can. 184 54.00 N 99.55 W
Talbot Lake @, Ont., Can. 212 44.42 N 78.51 W
Talbotton 192 32.41 N 84.32 W
Talbotville Royal 214 42.48 N 81.15 W
Talbragar ≃ 166 32.12 S 148.37 E
Talca 252 35.26 S 71.40 W
Talcahuano 252 36.43 S 73.07 W
Tālcher 120 20.57 N 85.13 E
Talco 196 33.22 N 95.06 W
Talcottville 207 41.49 N 72.30 W
Talcy, Château de ⊥ 50 47.46 N 1.27 E
Taldan 89 53.40 N 124.48 E
Tāldāngra 126 23.02 N 87.06 E
Taldom 82 56.44 N 37.32 E
Taldyapan, S.S.S.R. 80 48.07 N 47.08 E
Taldyapan, S.S.S.R. 80 49.46 N 50.14 E
Taldyk, Pereval)(85 39.47 N 73.11 E
Taldykuduk 80 50.09 N 49.33 E
Taldy-Kurgan 86 45.00 N 78.23 E
Taldy-Kurgan Oblast' □[4] 85 44.00 N 78.00 E
Tale 150 9.26 N 1.07 W
Taleh 144 9.12 N 48.23 E
Tal-e Khosravī 128 30.37 N 51.35 E
Talent 202 42.15 N 122.47 W
Taley 152 6.40 N 16.23 E
Talgar 85 43.18 N 77.18 E
Talgar, Pik ∧ 85 43.05 N 77.20 E
Talgarreg 42 52.08 N 4.18 W
Talgarth 42 52.00 N 3.15 W
Ṭalḥ, 'Ilw aṭ- ∧[2] 142 28.30 N 29.38 E
Talhār 120 24.53 N 68.49 E
Tali, Pointe de ≻ 241o 15.56 N 61.12 W
Talia, Austl. 162 33.19 S 134.54 E
Talia, Méx. 196 25.44 N 102.26 W
Taliabu, Pulau I 112 1.48 S 124.48 E
Taliandao I 98 39.03 N 122.52 E
Talibon 116 10.09 N 124.19 E
Talibong, Ko I 110 7.15 N 99.23 E
Talica, S.S.S.R. 76 58.44 N 41.34 E
Talica, S.S.S.R. 80 58.01 N 51.30 E
Talica, S.S.S.R. 86 57.00 N 63.43 E
Talickij Čamlyk 80 52.02 N 40.32 E
Talien → Lüda 98 38.53 N 121.35 E
Talihina 196 34.45 N 95.03 W
Tālīkota 122 16.29 N 76.19 E
Talikud Island I 116 6.56 N 125.42 E
Talim Island I 116 14.21 N 121.14 E
Talimuashili 85 39.08 N 77.03 E
Talimuhe ≃ 90 41.05 N 86.40 E
Talimupendi (Takla Makan) ◆[2] 90 39.00 N 83.00 E
Taling Chan 269a 13.46 N 100.27 E
Taliouine 148 30.36 N 7.49 W
Taliparamba 122 12.03 N 75.21 E
Tali Post 140 5.54 N 30.47 E
Talisay, Pil. 116 14.08 N 122.55 E
Talisay, Pil. 116 10.44 N 122.58 E
Talisayan 116 9.00 N 124.55 E
Talisei, Pulau I 112 1.51 N 125.05 E
Talish-Mikeyli 84 39.23 N 48.22 E
Talish Mountains (Kūhhā-ye Ṭavālesh) ⛰ 128 38.42 N 48.18 E
Talisker 46 57.17 N 6.27 W
Taliwang 115b 8.44 S 116.52 E
Tal'ka 76 53.22 N 28.21 E
Talkeetna 180 62.20 N 150.07 W
Talkeetna Mountains ⛰ 180 62.10 N 148.15 W
Ṭalkhā 142 31.03 N 31.22 E
Talkheh ≃ 128 37.40 N 45.46 E
Tālkot 124 29.37 N 81.19 E
Talladale 46 57.42 N 5.29 W
Talladega 194 33.26 N 86.06 W
Tall 'Afar 128 36.22 N 42.27 E
Tallaght 48 53.26 N 6.21 W
Tal Lah, Bhārat 126 22.19 N 87.18 E
Tallah, Miṣr 142 28.05 N 30.44 E
Tallahaga Creek ≃ 194 32.55 N 88.58 W
Tallahala Creek ≃ 194 31.12 N 89.05 W
Tallahassee 192 30.25 N 84.16 W
Tall al-Abyaḍ 130 36.41 N 38.57 E
Tall al-'Amārnah (Akhetatem) ⊥ 142 27.38 N 30.54 E

Symbol	English	Deutsch	Español	Français	Português
≃	River	Fluss	Río	Rivière	Rio
≅	Canal	Kanal	Canal	Canal	Canal
⌊	Waterfall, Rapids	Wasserfall, Stromschnellen	Cascada, Rápidos	Chute d'eau, Rapides	Cascata, Rápidos
⊔	Strait	Meeresstrasse	Estrecho	Détroit	Estreito
C	Bay, Gulf	Bucht, Golf	Bahía, Golfo	Baie, Golfe	Baía, Golfo
@	Lake, Lakes	See, Seen	Lago, Lagos	Lac, Lacs	Lago, Lagos
≡	Swamp	Sumpf	Pantano	Marais	Pântano
⊓	Ice Features, Glacier	Eis- und Gletscherformen	Accidentes Glaciales	Formes glaciaires	Acidentes Glaciares
⊤	Other Hydrographic Features	Andere Hydrographische Objekte	Otros Elementos Hidrográficos	Autres données hydrographiques	Outros Elementos Hidrográficos
✢	Submarine Features	Untermeerische Objekte	Accidentes Submarinos	Formes de relief sous-marin	Acidentes Submarinos
□	Political Unit	Politische Einheit	Unidad Politica	Entité politique	Unidade Política
⊽	Cultural Institution	Kulturelle Institution	Institución Cultural	Institution culturelle	Instituição Cultural
⊥	Historical Site	Historische Stätte	Sitio Histórico	Site historique	Sitio Histórico
♠	Recreational Site	Erholungs- und Ferienort	Sitio de Recreo	Centre de loisirs	Sítio de Lazer
⊠	Airport	Flughafen	Aeropuerto	Aéroport	Aeroporto
■	Military Installation	Militäranlage	Instalación Militar	Installation militaire	Instalação Militar
◆	Miscellaneous	Verschiedenes	Misceláneo	Divers	Miscelânea

Name	Page	Lat.°′	Long.°′
Tall al-Maskhūtah (Succotah) ⊥	142	30.33 N	32.07 E
Tallanalla	168a	33.06 S	116.07 E
Tallangatta	166	36.13 S	147.15 E
Tallangatta Creek ≃	171b	36.15 S	147.13 E
Tallapoosa	194	33.45 N	85.17 W
Tallapoosa ≃	194	32.30 N	86.16 W
Tallard	62	44.28 N	6.03 E
Talla Reservoir @[1]	46	55.29 N	3.24 W
Tallarook, Mount ∧	169	37.22 S	145.19 E
Tall ar-Ratābah (Pithom) ⊥	142	30.32 N	32.06 E
Tall ar-Rub'(Mendes) ⊥	142	30.58 N	31.31 E
Tallassee	194	32.27 N	85.54 W
Tall as-Sulṭān ⊥	132	31.52 N	35.27 E
Tall Banī 'Umrān	142	27.40 N	30.54 E
Tall Basṭah (Bubastis) ⊥	142	30.34 N	31.31 E
Tällberg	26	60.49 N	15.00 E
Tall Bīsah	130	34.50 N	36.44 E
Talleyville	208	39.48 N	75.33 W
Tallinn	76	59.25 N	24.45 E
Tall Kalakh	130	34.40 N	36.15 E
Tall Kayf	128	36.29 N	43.08 E
Tall Kūshik	130	36.48 N	42.04 E
Tallmadge	214	41.06 N	81.27 W
Tallman	276	41.07 N	74.06 W
Tallman Mountain State Park ♠	276	41.01 N	73.54 W
Talloires	62	45.51 N	6.13 E
Tallong	170	34.44 S	150.05 E
Tallow	48	52.05 N	8.00 W
Tall Rāk	142	30.54 N	31.43 E
Tall Rif'at	130	36.28 N	37.06 E
Tall Salḥab	130	35.15 N	36.22 E
Tall Tamir	130	36.39 N	40.22 E
Tallula	219	39.56 N	89.56 W
Tallulah	194	32.25 N	91.11 W
Tally	80	53.08 N	53.04 E
Tally Ho	274b	37.52 S	145.09 E
Tālma	126	23.29 N	89.54 E
Talmage, Calif., U.S.	204	39.08 N	123.10 W
Talmage, Nebr., U.S.	198	40.32 N	96.01 W
Talmage, Pa., U.S.	208	40.07 N	76.13 W
Talmalmo	171b	35.56 S	147.30 E
Talmas	50	50.02 N	2.20 E
Talmazy	78	46.38 N	29.40 E
Tal'menka	86	53.51 N	83.35 E
Talmine	46	58.31 N	4.26 W
Talmont	32	46.28 N	1.37 W
Tal'niki	88	52.47 N	102.24 E
Tal'noje	78	48.53 N	30.42 E
Talo ∧	144	10.44 N	37.55 E
Taloda	120	21.34 N	74.13 E
Talofofo	174p	13.21 N	144.45 E
Talofofo Bay C	174p	13.20 N	144.46 E
Taloga	196	36.02 N	98.58 W
Taloje	88	55.24 N	95.40 E
Taloje Budrukh	272c	19.05 N	73.05 E
Talok	112	1.03 N	118.48 E
Talomako	175f	15.10 S	166.48 E
Talonan, Tano ≻	115b	9.07 S	117.02 E
Tāloqān	120	36.44 N	69.33 E
Taloro ≃	71	40.08 N	8.58 E
Talovaja	78	51.06 N	40.44 E
Talovka, S.S.S.R.	80	49.58 N	45.01 E
Talovka, S.S.S.R.	80	50.25 N	47.35 E
Talovka, S.S.S.R.	84	44.14 N	46.36 E
Talovka, S.S.S.R.	86	57.10 N	93.09 E
Talovka, S.S.S.R.	86	51.27 N	81.54 E
Talovoje	83	48.18 N	39.40 E
Talpa	196	31.47 N	99.43 W
Talpa de Allende	234	20.23 N	104.51 W
Talpaka Sar ∧	123	33.42 N	70.31 E
Talquin, Lake @[1]	192	30.26 N	84.33 W
Tālsa	272b	22.49 N	88.33 E
Talsarnau	42	52.54 N	4.03 W
Talsi	76	57.15 N	22.36 E
Talšik	86	53.42 N	71.53 E
Taltal	252	25.24 S	70.29 W
Taltapin Lake @	182	54.19 N	125.20 W
Taltson ≃	176	61.23 N	112.45 W
Talu	112	0.14 N	99.59 E
Taludaa	112	0.20 N	123.28 E
Taluk	112	0.32 S	101.35 E
Talumphuk, Laem ≻	110	8.30 N	100.10 E
Taluti, Teluk C	164	3.21 S	129.45 E
Talvik'ul'a	24	68.45 N	29.19 E
Talwandi Bhāi	123	30.51 N	74.56 E
Talwood	166	28.30 S	149.30 E
Taly	78	49.51 N	40.04 E
Ṭalyā	142	30.16 N	31.00 E
Talybont	42	52.29 N	3.59 W
Talyzino	80	55.06 N	45.49 E
Tama, Arg.	252	30.31 S	66.32 W
Tama, Nihon	94	35.37 N	139.27 E
Tama, Iowa, U.S.	190	41.58 N	92.35 W
Tama ≃	94	35.32 N	139.47 E
Tama Cemetery ◂	268	35.41 N	139.31 E
Tamacuarí, Pico ∧	246	1.15 N	64.45 W
Tamadjert	148	25.36 N	7.20 E
Tamagawa, Nihon	94	37.12 N	140.24 E
Tamagawa, Nihon	96	34.01 N	132.56 E
Tamagawa ◂[8]	268	35.37 N	139.39 E
Tamagawa-josui ≃	268	35.42 N	139.35 E
Tamakautoga	174v	19.05 S	169.55 W
Tamakawa	94	35.07 N	138.20 E
Tamaki ∧∧[2]-kyūryō	94	34.29 N	136.38 E
	268	35.35 N	139.30
Tamala, Austl.	162	26.42 S	113.45 E
Tamala, S.S.S.R.	80	52.33 N	43.16 E
Tamalameque	246	8.52 N	73.49 W
Ṭamalāy	142	30.30 N	30.51 E
Tamale	150	9.25 N	0.50 W
Tamalea	112	2.29 S	119.19 E
Tamalpais, Mount ∧	226	37.56 N	122.35 W
Tamalpais Valley	226	37.53 N	122.32 W
Tamamura	94	36.18 N	139.07 E
Taman, Indon.	115a	7.25 S	112.41 E
Taman', S.S.S.R.	78	45.13 N	36.43 E
Tamana	92	32.55 N	130.33 E
Tamana I	14	2.29 S	175.59 E
Tamaná, Cerro ∧	246	5.02 N	76.17 W
Tamana, Mount ∧[2]	241r	10.28 N	61.12 W
Tamanaco ≃	246	9.25 N	65.23 W
Tamanan	115a	8.01 S	113.49 E
Tamanar	148	31.00 N	9.35 W
Tamandaré	250	8.45 S	35.06 W
Tamandourirt, Oued ∨	150	19.39 N	2.04 W
Tamanduatei ≃	287b	23.36 S	46.35 W
Tamanhint	146	27.13 N	14.36 E
Tamani	150	13.20 N	6.50 W
Tamaniquá	246	2.38 S	65.44 W
Taman Negara ♠	114	4.43 N	102.23 E
Tamano	96	34.30 N	133.56 E
Tamanrasset	148	22.56 N	5.30 E
Tamanrasset □[5]	148	25.00 N	5.00 E
Tamanrasset, Oued ∨	148	22.10 N	0.10 E
Tamanskij Zaliv C	78	45.18 N	36.45 E
Tamanthi	110	25.19 N	95.18 E
Tamanusi	112	1.48 S	121.18 E
Tamapatz	234	21.35 N	99.09 W
Tamaqua	208	40.48 N	75.58 W
Tamaquari, Ilha I	246	0.28 S	64.55 W
Tamar	88	50.24 N	107.25 E
Tamar ≃, Austl.	166	41.04 S	146.47 E
Tamar ≃, Eng., U.K.	42	50.22 N	4.10 W
Támara	246	5.50 N	72.10 W
Tamarac ≃	198	48.29 N	97.07 W
Tamarack Lake @[1]	214	41.35 N	80.05 W
Tamarite de Litera	34	41.52 N	0.26 E
Tamaroa	194	38.08 N	89.14 W
Tamarome	164	2.54 S	133.38 E
Tamarugal, Pampa del ⊻	248	21.00 S	69.25 W
Tamashima	96	34.32 N	133.40 E
Tamási	30	46.38 N	18.18 E
Tamaské	150	14.49 N	5.39 E
Tamatave	157b	18.10 S	49.23 E
Tamatave □[4]	157b	18.00 S	48.40 E
Tamatsukuri	94	36.06 N	140.25 E
Tamaulipas □[3]	232	24.00 N	98.45 W
Tamaya ≃	248	8.31 S	74.13 W
Tamayu	96	35.25 N	133.01 E
Tamazula	232	24.57 N	106.57 W
Tamazula de Gordiano	234	19.38 N	103.15 W
Tamazulapan [del Progreso]	234	17.41 N	97.34 W
Tamazunchale	234	21.16 N	98.47 W
Tamba	96	35.09 N	135.25 E
Tambach-Dietharz	54	50.48 N	10.36 E
Tambacounda	150	13.47 N	13.40 W
Tamba Dabatou	150	11.48 N	10.40 W
Tambak	115a	5.45 S	112.37 E
Tambakboyo	115a	6.48 S	111.50 E
Tamba-kōchi ∧∧[1]	92	35.20 N	135.30 E
Tambakrejo	115a	7.16 S	111.36 E
Tambalan	112	3.08 N	115.34 E
Tambangsawah	112	3.02 S	102.11 E
Tambara	154	16.45 S	34.15 E
Tāmbaram	122	12.55 N	80.07 E
Tamba-sanchi ∧∧	270	34.58 N	135.25 E
Tambaú ≃	256	21.34 S	47.05 W
Tambault, Île à I	275a	45.20 N	73.51 W
També	250	7.25 S	35.06 W
Tambea	112	4.12 S	121.36 E
Tambej	74	71.30 N	71.50 E
Tambelan, Kepulauan II	112	1.00 N	107.30 E
Tambelan Besar, Pulau I	112	0.58 N	107.34 E
Tambellup	162	34.02 S	117.39 E
Tamberías	252	31.28 S	69.25 W
Tambisan, Pulau I	116	5.27 N	119.10 E
Tambler	116	6.03 N	125.09 E
Tambo, Austl.	166	24.53 S	146.15 E
Tambo, Perú	248	12.56 S	74.01 W
Tambo ≃, Austl.	166	37.51 S	147.48 E
Tambo ≃, Perú	248	17.10 S	71.51 W
Tambo ≃, Perú	248	10.43 S	73.45 W
Tamboara	255	23.09 S	52.33 W
Tambo Grande	248	4.56 S	80.21 W
Tambohorano	157b	17.30 S	43.58 E
Tamboli	112	3.57 S	121.20 E
Tambolongang, Pulau I	112	6.36 S	120.24 E
Tambor	236	9.43 N	85.01 W
Tambora, Gunung ∧	115b	8.14 S	117.55 E
Tamboril	250	4.50 S	40.20 W
Tamborine	171a	27.53 S	153.08 E
Tamboritha, Mount ∧	166	37.28 S	146.41 E
Tambov	80	52.43 N	41.25 E
Tambov □[4]	78	51.45 N	41.20 E
Tambovka, S.S.S.R.	80	47.18 N	47.23 E
Tambovka, S.S.S.R.	89	50.06 N	128.04 E
Tambo Yacu ≃	246	2.31 S	73.40 W
Tambre ≃	34	42.49 N	8.53 W
Tambu	112	0.02 S	119.52 E
Tambu, Teluk C	112	0.02 N	119.45 E
Tambulian Point ≻	116	7.22 N	123.27 E
Tambunan	112	5.40 N	116.22 E
Tambura	140	5.36 N	27.28 E
Tamchaket	150	17.15 N	10.40 W
Tam Chuak, Laem ≻	110	8.33 N	98.12 E
Tamčijn Davaa)(	102	45.50 N	94.01 E
Tame	246	6.28 N	71.44 W
Tame ≃, Eng., U.K.	42	52.44 N	1.43 W
Tame ≃, Eng., U.K.	262	53.25 N	2.09 W
Tameapa	232	25.39 N	107.22 W
Tamedda, Djebel ∧	148	32.48 N	0.05 E
Tâmega ≃	34	41.05 N	8.21 W
Tamel Aike	254	48.19 S	70.58 W
Tamelelt	148	31.50 N	7.29 W
Tamenuen	164	6.27 S	139.48 E
Tamerton Foliot	42	50.26 N	4.08 W
Tamerza	148	34.23 N	7.57 E
Tamesí ≃	234	22.13 N	97.52 W
Tameside □[8]	262	53.29 N	2.03 W
Tamga, S.S.S.R.	85	42.09 N	77.32 E
Tamga, S.S.S.R.	89	45.34 N	133.36 E
Tamgak, Monts ∧∧	150	19.11 N	8.42 E
Tamgué, Massif du ∧∧	150	12.00 N	12.18 W
Tamiahua	234	21.16 N	97.27 W
Tamiahua, Laguna de C	234	21.35 N	97.35 W
Tamiami Canal ≊	220	25.47 N	80.15 W
Tamica	24	64.10 N	38.05 E
Tamil Nadu □[3]	122	11.00 N	78.15 E
Tamiment	210	41.09 N	75.02 W
Tamina	222	30.11 N	96.26 W
Tamines	56	50.26 N	4.36 E
Tamiryn ≃	88	47.48 N	102.36 E
Tamiš (Timiș) ≃	38	44.51 N	20.39 E
Tamitatoala ≃	255	11.56 S	53.36 W
Ṭāmiyah	142	29.29 N	30.58 E
Tamkuhi	124	26.41 N	84.11 E
Tam-ky	110	15.34 N	108.29 E
Tamlūk	126	22.18 N	87.55 E
Tāmma	120	25.11 N	93.42 E
Tammaro ≃	66	41.09 N	14.50 E
Tammerfors → Tampere	26	61.30 N	23.45 E
Tammisaari → Ekenäs	26	59.58 N	23.26 E
Tamms	194	37.14 N	89.16 W
Ṭammūh	273c	29.56 N	31.16 E
Tāmna	126	23.15 N	86.21 E
Tämnarån ≃	40	60.31 N	17.39 E
Tämnaren @	40	60.10 N	17.20 E
Tamon ◂[8]	270	34.39 N	135.04 E
Ta Mong Tsai	271d	22.24 N	114.18 E
Tamoroi	174r	6.51 N	158.19 E
Tamós, Laguna de @	234	22.10 N	98.02 W
Tampa, Ang.	152	15.30 S	13.27 E
Tampa, Fla., U.S.	220	27.57 N	82.27 W
Tampa Bay C	220	27.45 N	82.35 W
Tampa International Airport ⊠	220	27.59 N	82.32 W
Tampamachoco, Laguna C	234	21.00 N	97.21 W
Tampang	112	5.54 S	104.43 E
Tampaon ≃	234	21.59 N	98.36 W
Tamparan	116	8.27 N	117.13 E
Tampere	26	61.30 N	23.45 E
Tampico, Méx.	234	22.13 N	97.51 W
Tampico, Ill., U.S.	190	41.38 N	89.47 W
Tampico, Ind., U.S.	218	38.48 N	85.58 W
Tampin	114	2.28 N	102.14 E
Tampoc ≃	250	3.27 N	54.00 W
Tampu-lunanjing, Dolok ∧	114	1.46 N	99.24 E
Tam-quan	110	14.35 N	109.03 E
Tamra	132	32.51 N	35.12 E
Tamrau, Pegunungan ∧∧	164	0.30 S	132.27 E
Tamri	148	30.43 N	9.43 W
Tamsagbulag	88	47.16 N	117.17 E
Tamsalu	76	59.10 N	26.06 E
Tamshiyacu	246	4.05 S	72.58 W
Tamsweg	64	47.08 N	13.48 E
Tamu	110	24.13 N	94.18 E
Tamuín	234	21.59 N	98.45 W
Tamuín ≃	234	21.59 N	98.36 W
Tamuk Island I	116	6.27 N	121.49 E
Tamulung Point ≻	116	17.15 N	120.25 E
Tamur ≃	124	26.55 N	87.10 E
Tamura	268	35.22 N	139.22 E
Tamusuke	85	38.03 N	76.53 E
Tamworth, Austl.	166	31.05 S	150.55 E
Tamworth, Ont., Can.	212	44.29 N	77.00 W
Tamyang	98	35.21 N	126.58 E
Tana, Chile	248	19.27 S	69.57 W
Tana, Nor.	24	70.28 N	28.18 E
Tana I	175f	19.30 S	169.20 E
Tana ≃, Cuba	240p	20.42 N	77.25 W
Tana ≃, Kenya	154	2.32 S	40.31 E
T'an'a ≃, S.S.S.R.	88	58.40 N	120.30 E
Tana, Lake @	144	12.00 N	37.20 E
Tanabe, Nihon	96	34.49 N	135.46 E
Tanabe, Nihon	96	33.44 N	135.22 E
Tanabi	255	20.37 S	49.37 W
Tanacross	180	63.23 N	143.21 W
Tanafjorden C[2]	24	70.54 N	28.40 E
Tanaga Island I	181a	51.50 N	178.00 W
Tanaga Volcano ∧[1]	181a	51.53 N	178.09 W
Tanagro ≃	68	40.38 N	15.14 E
Tanaguarena	286c	10.37 N	66.49 W
Tanagura	94	37.02 N	140.23 E
Tanah, Tanjung ≻	115a	6.29 S	108.32 E
Tanahbala, Pulau I	110	0.25 S	98.25 E
Tanahgrogot	112	1.55 S	116.12 E
Tanahjampea, Pulau I	112	7.05 S	120.42 E
Tanahmasa, Pulau I	110	0.12 S	98.27 E
Tanahmerah, Indon.	112	3.41 N	117.31 E
Tanahmerah, Indon.	164	6.05 S	140.17 E
Tanah Merah, Malay.	114	2.36 N	101.48 E
Tanah Merah, Malay.	114	5.48 N	102.09 E
Tanahputih	114	1.41 N	101.03 E
Tanaka ◂[8]	270	34.42 N	135.00 E
Tanaka Malai ∧	122	10.21 N	77.04 E
Tanakeke, Pulau I	112	5.30 S	119.16 E
Tanakpur	124	29.05 N	80.07 E
Tan'am	128	23.09 N	56.29 E
Tanami	162	19.59 S	129.43 E
Tanami Desert ◂[2]	162	20.00 S	129.30 E
Tanami Desert Wildlife Sanctuary ◂[4]	162	20.45 S	131.10 E
Ṭanān, Miṣr	142	30.15 N	31.14 E
Tan-an, Viet.	110	8.46 N	105.11 E
Tan-an, Viet.	110	10.32 N	106.25 E
Tanana	180	65.10 N	152.05 W
Tanana ≃	180	65.09 N	151.55 W
Tananarive → Antananarivo	157b	18.55 S	47.31 E
Tananarive □[4]	157b	19.00 S	47.00 E
Tanapag	174n	15.14 N	145.45 E
Tanapag Harbor C	174n	15.14 N	145.44 E
Tanaro ≃	62	45.01 N	8.47 E
Tanārūt, Wādī ∨	146	30.08 N	9.59 E
Tanashi	94	35.44 N	139.33 E
Tanat ≃	42	52.46 N	3.07 W
Tanauan	116	11.07 N	125.01 E
Tanay	116	14.30 N	121.17 E
Tanba-kōchi ∧∧[1]	96	35.17 N	135.30 E
Tanbar	166	25.50 S	141.55 E
Tanbara	96	33.54 N	133.04 E
Ṭanbidī	142	28.38 N	30.47 E
Tan-binh	269c	10.48 N	106.40 E
Tanbu, Zhg.	98	35.51 N	118.17 E
Tanbu, Zhg.	100	28.08 N	114.12 E
Tancarville	50	49.29 N	0.28 E
Tancarville, Canal de ≊	50	49.28 N	0.28 E
Tancha	174m	26.28 N	121.50 E
Tan-chau	110	10.48 N	105.15 E
Tancheng	98	34.37 N	118.23 E
Tanchipa, Sierra de ∧∧	234	22.20 N	98.50 W
Tanchoj	88	51.33 N	105.07 E
Tanch'ŏn	98	40.27 N	128.54 E
Tancítaro	234	19.20 N	102.22 W
Tancítaro, Pico de ∧	234	19.23 N	102.13 W
Tancochapa ≃	234	17.59 N	94.04 W
Tānda, Bhārat	124	26.33 N	82.39 E
Tānda, Bhārat	124	28.59 N	78.56 E
Tanda, C. Iv.	150	7.48 N	3.10 W
Tānda, Pāk.	123	32.42 N	74.22 E
Tandaai	154	19.36 S	32.48 E
Tandag	116	9.04 N	126.12 E
Tandah	142	27.41 N	30.46 E
Tandaj	80	47.33 N	51.30 E
Tandala	154	9.23 S	34.14 E
Tandaltī	140	13.01 N	31.52 E
Ţăndărei	38	44.38 N	27.40 E
Tandian	98	40.39 N	124.46 E
Tandil	252	37.19 S	59.09 W
Tandjiesberg ∧∧	158	32.12 S	25.00 E
Tandjilé □[5]	146	9.45 N	16.30 E
Tandjilé ≃	146	9.45 N	15.50 E
Tāndliānwāla	123	31.02 N	73.08 E
Tando Ādam	120	25.46 N	68.40 E
Tando Allāhyār	120	25.28 N	68.43 E
Tando Bāgo	120	24.47 N	68.58 E
Tando Muhammad Khān	120	25.08 N	68.32 E
Tandou Lake @	166	32.38 S	142.05 E
Tandovo, Ozero @	86	55.07 N	78.02 E
Tando Zinze	152	5.22 S	12.26 E
Tandragee	48	54.21 N	6.25 W
Tandridge	260	51.14 N	0.02 W
Tandridge □[8]	260	51.17 N	0.05 W
Tandslet	41	54.55 N	9.59 E
Tandubas	116	5.10 N	120.20 E
Tandubatu Island I	116	5.13 N	120.17 E
Tandula Tank @[1]	122	20.40 N	81.12 E
Tandun	112	0.36 N	100.38 E
Tāndūr	122	17.14 N	77.35 E
Tanduy ≃	115a	7.41 S	108.47 E
Taneatua	172	38.04 S	177.01 E
Tanega-shima I	93b	30.40 N	131.00 E
Taneichi	92	40.26 N	141.43 E
Tan Emellel	148	27.30 N	9.45 E
Tanete	112	4.32 S	119.36 E
Taneum Creek ≃	224	47.10 N	120.40 W
Tanew ≃	30	50.31 N	22.16 E
Taneytown	188	39.40 N	77.10 W
Tanezrouft ◂[2]	148	24.00 N	0.45 W
Tanezrouft ta n' Ahenet ◂[2]	148	22.15 N	1.30 E
Tanezzuft, Wādī ∨	146	25.51 N	10.19 E
Tanforan Park ◂[9]	282	37.38 N	122.25 W
Tanga, S.S.S.R.	88	51.02 N	111.33 E
Tånga, Sve.	41	56.12 N	12.46 E
Tanga, Tan.	154	5.04 S	39.06 E
Tanga □[4]	154	5.00 S	38.15 E
Tanga ≃	152	1.22 N	17.32 E
Tangail	124	24.15 N	89.55 E
Tangainony	157b	22.42 S	47.45 E
Tanga Islands II	14	3.30 S	153.15 E
Tangalla	122	6.01 N	80.48 E
Tangamandapio	232	19.57 N	102.26 W
Tangamong Lake @	212	44.43 N	77.51 W
Tangancícuaro [de Arista]	234	19.54 N	102.08 W
Tanganika, Lago → Tanganyika, Lake @	154	6.00 S	29.30 E
Tanganjika-See → Tanganyika, Lake @	154	6.00 S	29.30 E
Tanganyika, Lake @	154	6.00 S	29.30 E
Tangará	252	27.08 S	51.13 W
Tangarana ≃	246	3.02 S	75.08 W
Tangarare	175e	9.35 S	159.39 E
Tanga-shima I	96	34.40 N	134.35 E
Tangbazhen	107	30.00 N	105.46 E
Tangchi	89	47.00 N	123.46 E
Tangchigou	104	41.04 N	124.11 E
Tangcun, Zhg.	100	25.26 N	113.10 E
Tangcun, Zhg.	100	29.50 N	118.54 E
Tanger (Tangier)	148	35.48 N	5.45 W
Tanger ≃	54	52.33 N	11.59 E
Tangerang	115a	6.11 S	106.37 E
Tangerhütte	54	52.26 N	11.48 E
Tangerine	220	28.47 N	81.38 W
Tangerli	105	39.09 N	116.43 E
Tangermünde	54	52.32 N	11.58 E
Tangfang, Zhg.	102	27.00 N	101.08 E
Tangfang, Zhg.	104	41.20 N	120.34 E
Tangfang, Zhg.	105	39.29 N	118.01 E
Tangfangqiao	106	31.45 N	120.50 E
Tangfeng	98	38.07 N	115.30 E
Tanggangzi	104	41.01 N	122.54 E
Tanggeasinua, Pegunungan ∧∧	112	3.24 S	121.42 E
Tanggengtou	106	30.55 N	119.03 E
Tanggou	100	34.01 N	118.56 E
Tanggu	105	39.01 N	117.40 E
Tangguantun	98	38.43 N	116.55 E
Tanggul	115a	8.10 S	113.26 E
Tanggulahu @	120	31.00 N	86.20 E
Tanggulashan (Tuotuoheyan)	120	34.05 N	92.45 E
Tanggulashankou)(	120	32.59 N	91.45 E
Tanggulashanmai ∧∧	120	33.00 N	90.00 E
Tanggushiluke	120	38.45 N	80.55 E
Tangguxin'gang ≃	105	39.00 N	117.43 E
Tanghe	100	32.43 N	112.48 E
Tanghe ≃, Zhg.	98	38.45 N	115.35 E
Tanghe ≃, Zhg.	100	32.09 N	112.25 E
Tanghekou	105	40.44 N	116.38 E
Tanghuang	106	31.41 N	119.25 E
Tanghuzhen	105	39.11 N	115.24 E
Tāngi, Bhārat	120	19.56 N	85.24 E
Tangi, Pāk.	123	34.18 N	71.40 E
Tangier → Tanger, Magreb	148	35.48 N	5.45 W
Tangier, Va., U.S.	208	37.49 N	75.59 W
Tangier Island I	208	37.50 N	76.00 W
Tangier Sound ⋓	208	38.02 N	75.58 W
Tangijatuo	107	29.36 N	106.39 E
Tangipahoa ≃	194	30.20 N	90.18 W
Tangjia	104	41.40 N	122.14 E
Tangjiagou	100	30.48 N	117.28 E
Tangjiang	100	25.51 N	114.44 E
Tangjiapao	104	40.00 N	122.14 E
Tangjiaqiao	106	31.24 N	119.12 E
Tangjiazha	106	32.05 N	120.49 E
Tangjiazhen	100	22.23 N	113.36 E
Tangjin	98	36.54 N	126.37 E
Tangjiqiaozhen	106	31.13 N	121.31 E
Tangkahan	112	1.36 S	113.52 E
Tangkak	114	2.16 N	102.33 E
Tangkou	100	30.06 N	118.11 E
Tanglad	115b	8.47 S	115.35 E
Tanglewood	222	30.30 N	96.59 W
Tanglewood ♠	207	42.21 N	73.20 W
Tangling	100	26.14 N	119.24 E
Tanglitun	104	41.45 N	123.57 E
Tangmarg	123	34.02 N	74.26 E
Tangmazhai	104	41.10 N	122.44 E
Tangnang-ni	98	34.12 N	126.52 E
Tang-nhon-phu	269c	10.50 N	106.47 E
Tango	96	35.44 N	135.06 E
Tangowahine	172	35.52 S	173.56 E
Tangpu, Zhg.	100	28.28 N	114.58 E
Tangpu, Zhg.	100	29.51 N	120.47 E
Tangqi	106	30.29 N	120.11 E
Tangqian	100	25.53 N	119.07 E
Tangqiao	106	31.13 N	119.15 E
Tangqipu	104	40.39 N	122.20 E
Tangsanying	98	41.38 N	117.40 E
Tangschan → Tangshan	105	39.38 N	118.11 E
Tangse	114	5.01 N	95.55 E
Tangshan, Zhg.	105	39.38 N	118.11 E
Tangshan, Zhg.	105	40.10 N	116.22 E
Tangshan, Zhg.	106	32.05 N	119.03 E
Tangshan ∧	106	32.03 N	119.02 E
Tangtou, Zhg.	102	27.42 N	108.17 E
Tangtou, Zhg.	106	31.38 N	120.19 E
Tangtouxia	100	22.50 N	114.06 E
Tangtouzhen	98	35.16 N	118.35 E
Tangtse	120	34.02 N	78.11 E
Tanguá	256	22.44 S	42.43 W
Tangub	116	8.03 N	123.44 E
Tanguiéta	150	10.37 N	1.16 E
Tanguip Point ≻	116	7.43 N	126.32 E
Tanguisson Point ≻	174p	13.33 N	144.49 E
Tanguj	88	55.23 N	100.58 E
Tangulbei	154	0.48 N	36.17 E
Tangusu Bay C	116	5.27 N	119.03 E
Tangxi	100	29.04 N	119.23 E
Tangxian	98	38.45 N	114.58 E
Tangxianzhen	100	31.59 N	113.07 E
Tangyan	110	22.29 N	98.24 E
Tangyicheng	98	36.32 N	115.47 E
Tangyin, Zhg.	98	35.55 N	114.21 E
Tangyin, Zhg.	100	27.32 N	116.16 E
Tangyuan	89	46.42 N	129.55 E
Tanhu	124	28.02 N	84.20 E
Tanhuato	234	20.17 N	102.20 W
Tanhushan I	106	30.37 N	121.37 E
Taniantawengshan ∧∧	102	30.15 N	97.32 E
Tanigami ◂[8]	270	34.46 N	135.12 E
Tanigawa-dake ∧	94	36.50 N	138.56 E
Tanigumi	94	35.31 N	136.36 E
Tanimbar, Kepulauan II	164	7.30 S	131.30 E
Taninges	58	46.07 N	6.36 E
Tanır	130	38.26 N	36.55 E
Tanis (Zoan) ⊥	142	30.57 N	31.53 E
Tanishpa ∧	120	31.10 N	68.24 E
Tanjay	116	9.31 N	123.09 E
Tanjiafang	98	36.41 N	118.36 E
Tanjiahe	100	31.58 N	113.56 E
Tanjiang	100	24.07 N	116.32 E
Tanjiang ≃	100	23.57 N	115.47 E
Tanjiaqiao	100	30.11 N	118.15 E
Tanjil ≃	169	38.08 S	146.17 E
Tanjong Balai ≻	271c	1.19 N	103.47 E
Tanjong Dawai	114	5.41 N	100.22 E
Tanjong Malim	114	3.41 N	101.31 E
Tanjore → Thanjāvūr	122	10.48 N	79.09 E
Tanjung, Indon.	112	2.11 S	115.23 E
Tanjung, Indon.	115a	6.52 S	108.52 E
Tanjung, Indon.	115b	8.21 S	116.09 E
Tanjungbalai	114	2.58 N	99.48 E
Tanjungbatu, Indon.	112	0.45 N	117.26 E
Tanjungbatu, Indon.	112	0.38 N	103.26 E
Tanjungbatu, Indon.	112	2.17 N	118.05 E
Tanjungenim	112	3.45 S	103.48 E
Tanjungkarang	115a	5.25 S	105.16 E
Tanjunglabu	112	2.57 S	106.54 E
Tanjungmedan	114	1.26 N	100.34 E
Tanjungmengedar	114	2.39 N	100.01 E
Tanjungpandan	112	2.45 S	107.39 E
Tanjungpinang	112	0.55 N	104.27 E
Tanjungpriok ◂[8]	269e	6.06 S	106.53 E
Tanjungpura	114	3.54 N	98.26 E
Tanjungpusu	112	0.01 S	113.30 E
Tanjungraja	112	3.21 S	104.40 E
Tanjungredep	112	2.09 N	117.29 E
Tanjungselor	112	2.51 N	117.22 E
Tanjungslamat	114	3.49 N	98.20 E
Tanjunguban	112	1.03 N	104.14 E
Tānk	120	32.13 N	70.24 E
Tan Kena	148	26.33 N	9.35 E
Tan-kien	269c	10.42 N	106.35 E
Tankou	100	25.48 N	114.50 E
Tankwa ≃	158	32.20 S	19.33 E
Tanlay	50	47.50 N	4.05 E
Tann	56	50.38 N	10.01 E
Tanna	54	50.30 N	11.51 E
Tannan	96	35.05 N	135.10 E
Tännäs	26	62.27 N	12.40 E
Tanna-tunnel ◂[5]	94	35.06 N	139.00 E
Tannay	50	47.21 N	3.36 E
Tanne	54	51.41 N	10.42 E
Tannenbergsthal	54	50.26 N	12.27 E
Tanner, Mount ∧	182	49.40 N	118.34 W
Tannersville, N.Y., U.S.	210	42.12 N	74.08 W
Tannersville, Pa., U.S.	210	41.03 N	75.18 W
Tännesberg	60	49.32 N	12.20 E
Tännforsen ↳	26	63.27 N	12.44 E
Tannhausen	56	48.59 N	10.21 E
Tannheim	58	47.30 N	10.31 E
Tannila	26	65.29 N	25.59 E
Tannis Bugt C	26	57.40 N	10.15 E
Tannu-Ola, Chrebet ∧∧	74	51.00 N	94.00 E
Tannūrah, Ra's at- ≻	128	26.40 N	50.30 E
Tano, Nihon	96	33.26 N	134.00 E
Tano, Nihon	270	34.57 N	135.36 E
Tano ≃	150	5.07 N	2.56 W
Tanon Strait ⋓	116	10.20 N	123.30 E
Tanoriki	175f	14.59 S	168.09 E
Tânout	150	14.58 N	8.53 E
Tanque de Dolores	234	23.40 N	101.10 W
Tanque Grande, Ribeirão ≃	287b	23.25 S	46.28 W
Tan-qui-dong	269c	10.44 N	106.42 E
Tanquinho, Bra.	255	11.58 S	39.06 W
Tanquinho, Bra.	256	22.48 S	47.00 W
T'an'šan' → Tien Shan ∧∧	90	42.00 N	80.00 E
Tansania → Tanzania □[1]	154	6.00 S	35.00 E
Tansboro	285	39.46 N	74.55 W
Tanshui	100	25.10 N	121.26 E
Tanshui Ho ≃	100	25.11 N	121.25 E
Tanshui River Bridge ◂[5]	269d	25.03 N	121.29 E
Tansilla	150	12.26 N	4.23 W
Tánsin, Isla de I	236	15.17 N	83.54 W
Tánsin, Laguna de C	236	15.13 N	83.55 W
Tānsing	124	27.52 N	83.33 E
Tan Son Nhut Airport ⊠	269c	10.49 N	106.40 E
Tansyk	86	47.20 N	79.52 E
Ṭanṭā	142	30.47 N	31.00 E
Tantabogue Creek ≃	222	31.00 N	95.21 W
Tantangara Reservoir @[1]	171b	35.45 S	148.39 E
Tan-thoi-nhut	269c	10.50 N	106.36 E
Tan-thuan-dong	269c	10.45 N	106.44 E
Tāntipāra	126	23.54 N	87.22 E
Tantō	96	35.29 N	135.00 E
Tantonville	58	48.28 N	6.08 E
Tantou, Zhg.	100	26.53 N	115.26 E
Tantou, Zhg.	100	26.03 N	119.35 E
Tantou, Zhg.	100	29.07 N	121.09 E
Tantoushan I	100	23.11 N	122.01 E
Tantoyuca	234	21.21 N	98.14 W
Tanuku	122	16.45 N	81.42 E
Tanuma	94	36.22 N	139.35 E
Tanumshede	26	58.44 N	11.19 E
Tanunda	168b	34.32 S	138.57 E
Tanūr	122	10.58 N	75.52 E
Tan'urer ≃	180	64.44 N	174.15 E
Tanushimaru	96	33.21 N	130.41 E
Tanvald	30	50.45 N	15.19 E
Tanwax Creek ≃	224	46.52 N	122.27 W
Tanworth	42	52.20 N	1.50 W
Tanworth-in-Arden	42	52.39 N	1.40 W
Tanxi	100	28.58 N	115.38 E
Tanxia	100	23.58 N	115.34 E
Tanyang	98	36.57 N	128.21 E
Tanyeri	130	39.38 N	39.49 E
Tanyi	98	35.14 N	118.09 E
Tanymas ≃	85	38.25 N	72.39 E
Tanyp ≃	86	55.46 N	54.35 E
Tanza	116	14.24 N	120.51 E
Tanzania □[1]	154	6.00 S	35.00 E
Tanzanie → Tanzania □[1]	154	6.00 S	35.00 E
Tanzawa-ō-yama-kokuteikōen ♠	94	35.30 N	139.30 E
Tanzawa-san ∧	94	35.28 N	139.10 E
Tao, Ko I	110	10.05 N	99.52 E
Taoan	89	45.22 N	122.47 E
Taochong	100	31.04 N	118.06 E
Taocun, Zhg.	98	37.10 N	121.05 E
Taocun, Zhg.	100	28.44 N	119.36 E
Taodigou	105	40.52 N	116.14 E
Taoerdeng	98	40.44 N	119.02 E
Taoershan	89	44.42 N	120.30 E
Taohe	105	39.12 N	116.50 E
Taohe ≃	102	35.52 N	103.16 E
Taohua	106	31.23 N	120.04 E
Taohuabao	105	40.04 N	114.59 E
Taohuachiyingzi	104	42.18 N	121.06 E
Taohuadao I	100	29.48 N	122.17 E
Taohuanbuligai	104	42.13 N	122.14 E
Taohuatu	104	41.40 N	120.40 E
Taohuayuan	106	30.34 N	118.42 E
Taojiahe	100	30.55 N	115.56 E
Taojialiang	104	42.36 N	121.25 E
Taojiang ≃	100	25.56 N	115.06 E
Taojiayan	100	30.02 N	120.44 E
Taolahusu	98	42.34 N	116.48 E
Taolaizhao	89	44.51 N	125.57 E
Taolakepa	120	32.05 N	85.22 E
Taole	102	38.46 N	106.40 E
Taolimin	102	39.38 N	108.40 E
Taolin	98	34.30 N	118.30 E
Taoling	100	30.21 N	118.16 E
Taoluo	98	35.17 N	119.24 E
T'aonan → Taoan	89	45.22 N	122.47 E
Taongi I[1]	14	14.37 N	168.58 E
Taormina	70	37.51 N	15.17 E
Taos, Mo., U.S.	219	38.31 N	92.04 W
Taos, N. Mex., U.S.	200	36.24 N	105.34 W
T'aosai	100	24.16 N	121.30 E
Taouardeï ⊤[4]	150	16.56 N	1.19 E
Taoudenni	148	22.40 N	4.00 W
Taougrite	34	36.15 N	0.55 E
Taounate	148	34.25 N	4.39 W
Taoura	36	36.09 N	8.03 E
Taourirt	148	34.25 N	2.53 W
Taourirt ∧	148	23.55 N	4.50 E
Taoussa	150	16.55 N	0.35 W
Taowu	106	31.47 N	118.46 E
Taoxi, Zhg.	100	31.33 N	117.00 E
Taoxi, Zhg.	100	25.18 N	116.05 E
Taoxiantun	104	41.39 N	123.27 E
T'aoyüan, T'aiwan	100	25.00 N	121.18 E
Taoyuan, Zhg.	100	25.48 N	117.32 E
Taoyuan, Zhg.	102	28.46 N	111.20 E
Taozhuang	106	30.58 N	120.48 E
Taozhusuo	100	28.50 N	121.31 E
Taozikou ≃[1]	100	34.24 N	120.05 E
Taoziyu	106	31.04 N	121.41 E
Tap	130	38.29 N	41.49 E
Tapa, Bhārat	123	30.19 N	75.21 E
Tapa, S.S.S.R.	76	59.16 N	25.58 E
Tapaan Island I	116	5.28 N	120.44 E
Tapacarí	248	17.31 S	66.36 W
Tapachula	232	14.54 N	92.17 W
Tapaga, Cape ≻	175a	14.01 S	171.23 W
Tapah	114	4.11 N	101.16 E
Tapah Road	114	4.10 N	101.12 E
Tapaje ≃	246	2.44 N	78.07 W
Tapajós ≃	250	2.24 S	54.41 W
Tapak I	174r	6.57 N	158.18 E
Tapaktuan	114	3.16 N	97.11 E
Tapalpa	234	19.57 N	103.46 W
Tapalquén	252	36.21 S	60.01 W
Tapan	112	2.10 S	101.04 E
Tapanahony ≃	250	4.22 N	54.27 W
Tapanlieh	100	21.58 N	120.47 E
Tapanui	172	45.57 S	169.16 E
Tapasi	126	23.40 N	87.08 E
Tapauá	248	5.45 S	63.04 W
Tapauá ≃	248	5.40 S	64.21 W
Tapawera	172	41.24 S	172.49 E
Tapaz	116	11.16 N	122.32 E
Tapejara	252	28.04 S	52.00 W
Tapera	252	28.38 S	52.52 W
Taperoá, Bra.	250	7.12 S	36.49 W
Taperoá, Bra.	255	13.31 S	39.06 W
Tapes	252	30.40 S	51.23 W
Tapeta	150	6.29 N	8.51 W
Taphan Hin	110	16.13 N	100.26 E
Taphoen ≃	110	14.07 N	99.25 E
Tāpi ≃, Bhārat	120	21.06 N	72.41 E
Ta Pi ≃, Thai	110	9.05 N	99.12 E
Tapiales	288	34.42 S	58.31 W
Tapiantana Channel ⋓	116	6.23 N	122.00 E
Tapiantana Group II	116	6.20 N	122.00 E
Tapiantana Island I	116	6.18 N	121.59 E
Tapiau → Gvardejsk	76	54.39 N	21.05 E
Tapiche ≃	248	4.59 S	73.51 W
Tapili	154	3.25 N	27.40 E
Tapilula	234	17.14 N	93.02 W
Tapini	164	8.20 S	147.00 E
Tapiraí	255	19.52 S	46.01 W
Tapirapé ≃	250	10.41 S	50.38 W
Tapiratiba	256	21.28 S	46.45 W
Tapis, Gunong ∧	114	4.03 N	102.54 E
Tapiutan Island I	116	11.12 N	119.16 E
Tapiwa	174d	0.52 S	169.35 E
Tāplejung	124	27.21 N	87.40 E
Tapochau, Mount ∧	174n	15.11 N	145.45 E
Tapol	146	8.31 N	15.35 E
Tapolca	30	46.53 N	17.27 E
Tappahannock	208	37.56 N	76.52 W
Tappal	124	28.03 N	77.35 E
Tappan	210	41.01 N	73.57 W
Tappan, Lake @	276	41.01 N	73.59 W
Tappan Lake @[1]	214	40.21 N	81.11 W
Tappan Zee C	276	41.06 N	73.53 W
Tappan Zee Bridge ◂[5]	276	41.04 N	73.54 W
Tappen	198	46.52 N	99.38 W
Tappernøje	41	55.10 N	11.59 E
Tappi-zaki ≻	92	41.15 N	140.21 E
Tappo	150	10.12 N	2.38 W
Tapps, Lake @	224	47.13 N	122.09 W
Tapsiā ◂[8]	272b	22.32 N	88.22 E
Tapu, Motu I	174w	21.05 S	175.04 W
Tapuaenuku ∧	172	42.00 S	173.40 E
Tapuio ≃	250	3.41 S	44.16 W
Tapul Group II	116	5.30 N	121.00 E
Tapul Island I	116	5.43 N	120.55 E
Tapun	110	18.22 N	95.27 E
Tapurucuara	246	0.24 S	65.02 W
Taputapu, Cape ≻	174u	14.19 S	170.50 W
Taqāṭu' Hayyā	140	18.20 N	36.22 E
Taqian	100	29.03 N	117.03 E
Taqiao, Zhg.	100	31.28 N	118.25 E
Taqiao, Zhg.	100	28.24 N	117.02 E
Taqin	120	30.57 N	81.20 E
Ṭaqṭaq	128	35.53 N	44.35 E
Taquara	252	29.39 S	50.47 W
Taquara ◂[8]	287a	22.55 S	43.21 W
Taquara, Serra da ∧	256	22.12 S	43.53 W
Taquaral	255	16.01 S	49.38 W
Taquaras, Ponta das ≻	252	27.01 S	48.34 W
Taquari, Bra.	252	29.48 S	51.51 W
Taquari, Bra.	255	17.50 S	53.17 W
Taquari ≃, Bra.	248	19.15 S	57.17 W
Taquari ≃, Bra.	252	29.56 S	51.44 W
Taquari, Pantanal do ≡	248	18.20 S	56.30 W
Taquaritinga	255	21.24 S	48.30 W
Taquaruçu ≃	255	21.35 S	52.07 W
Taquaxiara, Ribeirão ≃	287b	23.44 S	46.47 W
Taquaxiara, Serra da ∧∧[2]	287b	23.46 S	46.52 W
Tar ≃, S.S.S.R.	85	40.38 N	73.26 E
Tar ≃, N.C., U.S.	192	35.33 N	77.05 W
Tara, Austl.	166	27.17 S	150.28 E
Tara, Ont., Can.	212	44.28 N	81.09 W
Tara, S.S.S.R.	86	56.54 N	74.22 E
Tara, Zam.	154	16.56 S	26.47 E
Tara ∧∧	38	43.55 N	19.25 E
Tara ≃, Jugo.	38	43.21 N	18.51 E
Tara ≃, S.S.S.R.	86	56.42 N	74.36 E
Taraba ≃	146	8.30 N	10.15 E
Tarabuco	248	19.10 S	64.57 W
Ṭarābulus (Tripoli), Lībīya	146	32.54 N	13.11 E
Ṭarābulus (Tripoli), Lubnān	130	34.26 N	35.51 E
Ṭarābulus (Tripolitania) □[4]	146	31.00 N	15.00 E
Ṭarābulus ◂[1]	146	31.00 N	15.00 E
Tarabya ◂[8]	267b	41.08 N	29.03 E
Tarach ≃	154	4.09 N	34.56 E
Taradale	172	39.32 S	176.51 E
Taragaj ≃	85	41.35 N	77.42 E
Tarago	170	35.04 S	149.39 E
Tara Hills	282	38.00 N	122.19 W
Tarai ⊻	124	26.35 N	86.40 E
Taraia	124	26.05 N	84.53 E
Taraira (Traíra) ≃	246	1.04 S	69.26 W
Tara Island I	116	12.17 N	120.22 E
Taraju	115a	7.27 S	107.59 E
Tarakan	112	3.18 N	117.38 E

Symbols in the index entries represent the broad categories identified in the key at the right. Symbols with superior numbers (∧∧[2]) identify subcategories (see complete key on page *I* · *30*).

Kartensymbole in dem Registerverzeichnis stellen die rechts in Schlüssel erklärten Kategorien dar. Symbole mit hochgestellten Ziffern (∧∧[2]) bezeichnen Unterabteilungen einer Kategorie (vgl. vollständiger Schlüssel auf Seite *I* · *30*).

Los símbolos incluídos en el texto del índice representan las grandes categorias identificadas con la clave a la derecha. Los símbolos con numeros en su parte superior (∧∧[2]) identifican las subcategorías (véase la clave completa en la página *I* · *30*).

Les symboles de l'index représentent les catégories indiquées dans la légende à droite. Les symboles suivis d'un indice (∧∧[2]) représentent des sous-catégories (voir légende complète à la page *I* · *30*).

Os símbolos incluídos no texto do índice representam as grandes categorias identificadas com a chave à direita. Os símbolos com números em sua parte superior (∧∧[2]) identificam as subcategorias (veja-se a chave completa à página *I* · *30*).

	English	Deutsch	Español	Français	Português
∧	Mountain	Berg	Montaña	Montagne	Montanha
∧∧	Mountains	Berge	Montañas	Montagnes	Montanhas
)(	Pass	Pass	Paso	Col	Passo
∨	Valley, Canyon	Tal, Cañon	Valle, Cañón	Vallée, Canyon	Vale, Canhão
⊻	Plain	Ebene	Llano	Plaine	Planície
≻	Cape	Kap	Cabo	Cap	Cabo
I	Island	Insel	Isla	Île	Ilha
II	Islands	Inseln	Islas	Îles	Ilhas
◂	Other Topographic Features	Andere Topographische Objekte	Otros Elementos Topográficos	Autres données topographiques	Outros Elementos Topográficos

ESPAÑOL

Nombre	Página	Lat.°′	Long.°′ W=Oeste
Tarakan, Pulau I	112	3.21 N	117.36 E
Tarakanovka	82	55.07 N	35.44 E
Tārakeswar	126	22.54 N	88.02 E
Taraklı	130	40.24 N	30.29 E
Taraklija, S.S.S.R.	78	46.34 N	29.06 E
Taraklija, S.S.S.R.	78	45.54 N	28.38 E
Taralga	170	34.24 S	149.49 E
Tarama-jima I	175d	24.39 N	124.42 E
Taramakau ≃	172	42.34 S	171.08 E
Taramana	112	8.10 S	124.51 E
Tarana	170	33.32 S	149.54 E
Tarancón	34	40.01 N	3.00 W
Tarandacuao	234	19.59 N	100.32 W
Taranga Island I	172	35.58 S	174.43 E
Tarangire National Park ♠	154	4.00 S	36.00 E
Tarangnan	116	11.54 N	124.45 E
Tarango, Presa ⊜[1]	286a	19.22 N	99.13 W
Taranovka	78	49.37 N	36.08 E
Taransay I	46	57.54 N	7.01 W
Taranta Peligna	66	42.01 N	14.10 E
Tarantine, Murge ⬥[1]	68	40.22 N	17.40 E
Taranto	68	40.28 N	17.15 E
Taranto, Golfo di C	68	40.10 N	17.20 E
Tarapacá	246	2.52 S	69.44 W
Tarapacá □[4]	248	20.00 S	69.20 W
Tarapoto	248	6.30 S	76.25 W
Ţaraq al-Hbâri ⬥[1]	130	34.17 N	39.16 E
Ţaraq an-Na'jah ⬥[1]	130	34.16 N	39.53 E
Ţaraq Sidâoui ⬥[1]	130	34.33 N	39.54 E
Taraquá	246	0.06 N	68.28 W
Tarara	175e	6.02 S	155.24 E
Tarare	58	45.54 N	4.26 E
Tarariras	258	34.17 S	57.37 W
Tararua Range ⩕	172	40.46 S	175.23 E
Tarāsa Dwīp I	110	8.15 N	93.10 E
Tarašča	78	49.34 N	30.29 E
Tarascon, Fr.	32	42.51 N	1.36 E
Tarascon, Fr.	62	43.48 N	4.40 E
Tarasht	267d	35.42 N	51.21 E
Tarasovka, S.S.S.R.	83	48.21 N	37.33 E
Tarasovka, S.S.S.R.	83	49.40 N	38.23 E
Tarasovka, S.S.S.R.	83	49.28 N	40.05 E
Tarasovka, S.S.S.R.	265b	55.58 N	37.50 E
Tarasovo, S.S.S.R.	24	66.13 N	46.39 E
Tarasovo, S.S.S.R.	24	62.49 N	41.10 E
Tarasovo, S.S.S.R.	80	58.18 N	48.45 E
Tarasovo, S.S.S.R.	88	55.52 N	107.48 E
Tarasovskij	78	48.43 N	40.22 E
Tarasp	58	46.38 N	10.25 E
Tarat	148	26.13 N	9.18 E
Tarat, Oued ∨	148	26.09 N	9.20 E
Tarata, Bol.	248	17.37 S	66.01 W
Tarata, Perú	248	17.28 S	70.02 W
Taratakbuluh	112	0.23 N	101.27 E
Tāratanr	126	23.58 N	86.29 E
Tarauacá	248	8.10 S	70.46 W
Tarauacá ≃	248	6.42 S	69.48 W
Taravao, Baie de C	174s	17.43 S	149.17 W
Taravao, Isthme de ⬥[3]	174s	17.43 S	149.19 W
Taravo ≃	36	41.42 N	8.49 E
Tarawa I	174t	1.25 N	173.00 E
Tarawera	172	39.02 S	176.35 E
Tarawera, Lake ⊜	172	38.12 S	176.27 E
Tarazit, Massif de ⩕	150	20.00 N	8.25 E
Tarazona	34	41.54 N	1.44 W
Tarazona de la Mancha	34	39.15 N	1.55 W
Tarba	144	0.48 N	42.42 E
Tårbæk	41	55.47 N	12.36 E
Tarbagataj, S.S.S.R.	88	51.12 N	109.05 E
Tarbagataj, S.S.S.R.	88	52.07 N	109.12 E
Tarbagataj, S.S.S.R.	88	51.30 N	107.22 E
Tarbagataj, Chrebet ⩕	86	47.12 N	83.00 E
Tarbat Ness ≻	46	57.51 N	3.47 W
Tarbela	123	34.08 N	72.49 E
Tarbert, Eire	48	52.32 N	9.23 W
Tarbert, Scot., U.K.	46	57.54 N	6.49 W
Tarbert, Scot., U.K.	46	55.52 N	5.26 W
Tarbert, Loch C	46	55.57 N	6.00 W
Tarbes	32	43.14 N	0.05 E
Tarbet	46	56.12 N	4.43 W
Tarbock Green	262	53.23 N	2.49 W
Tarbolton	46	55.31 N	4.29 W
Tarboro	192	35.54 N	77.32 W
Tarbū	146	26.02 N	15.10 E
Tarcăului, Munţii ⩕	38	46.45 N	26.20 E
Tarcento	64	46.13 N	13.13 E
Tarchankut, Mys ≻	78	45.21 N	32.30 E
Tarchankutskaja Vozvyšennost' ⩕[1]	78	45.30 N	33.10 E
Tarchov Cholm, Gora ∧[2]	76	57.11 N	38.25 E
Tarchovka	265a	60.04 N	29.58 E
Tarcoola	162	30.41 S	134.33 E
Tarcoon	166	30.16 S	146.43 E
Tarcutta	171b	35.17 S	147.44 E
Tarcutta Creek ≃	171b	35.08 S	147.36 E
Tārdah	272b	22.27 N	88.31 E
Tardajos	34	42.21 N	3.49 W
Tardoki-Jani, Gora ∧	89	48.55 N	138.04 E
Tardun	162	28.48 S	115.45 E
Taredo ⬥[8]	272c	19.58 N	72.49 E
Taree	166	31.54 S	152.28 E
Tareja	74	73.20 N	90.37 E
Taremert n' Akli, Oued ∨	148	25.49 N	5.17 E
Tärendö	24	67.10 N	22.38 E
Tarent, Golf von → Taranto, Golfo di C	68	40.10 N	17.20 E
Tarentaise ∨	62	45.30 N	6.30 E
Tarento, Golfo de → Taranto, Golfo di C	68	40.10 N	17.20 E
Tarentum	214	40.36 N	79.45 W
Tarf, Garaet et ⊜	148	35.40 N	7.10 E
Ţarfā', Baţn aţ- ☷	128	23.50 N	51.27 E
Ţarfā', Ra's ≻	144	17.05 N	42.24 E
Ţarfā', Wādī aţ- ∨	142	28.25 N	30.50 E
Ţarfāwī, Bi'r ⍑[4], Mişr	140	22.55 N	28.53 E
Tarfawi, Bi'r ⍑[4], Sūd.	140	21.04 N	34.08 E
Tarfaya	148	27.58 N	12.55 W
Tarfside	46	56.54 N	2.50 W
Tarf Water ≃	44	54.55 N	4.35 W
Targa	124	22.27 N	84.40 E
Targan ≃	85	43.38 N	75.58 E
Target Rock National Wildlife Refuge ⬥[4]	276	40.56 N	73.26 W
Targhee Pass)(	202	44.41 N	111.17 W
Targon	32	44.44 N	0.16 W
Târgovişte	38	43.15 N	26.34 E
Targuist	148	34.57 N	4.18 W
Târgu-Mureş → Tîrgu Mureş	38	46.33 N	24.33 E
Tarhaouaout	148	22.20 N	5.58 E
Tarhit	148	30.55 N	2.02 W
Tarhjicht	148	29.05 N	9.24 W
Tarhūnah	146	32.26 N	13.38 E
Tari	164	5.50 S	143.00 E
Tarialan	86	49.47 N	91.55 E
Tariat	88	48.06 N	99.32 E
Táriba	246	7.49 N	72.13 W
Tarifa	34	36.01 N	5.36 W
Tarifa, Punta de ≻	34	36.00 N	5.37 W
Tariffville	207	41.55 N	72.46 W
Tarija	248	21.31 S	64.45 W
Tarija □[5]	248	21.30 S	64.00 W
Tarikere	122	13.43 N	75.49 E

FRANÇAIS

Nom	Page	Lat.°′	Long.°′ W=Ouest
Tariki	172	39.14 S	174.15 E
Tariku ≃	164	3.04 S	138.09 E
Tarīm	144	16.03 N	48.59 E
Tarim → Talimuhe ≃	90	41.05 N	86.40 E
Tarimoro	234	20.17 N	100.45 W
Taring	114	3.50 N	97.33 E
Tarīn Kowt	120	32.52 N	65.38 E
Taritai	174t	1.32 N	173.00 E
Taritatu ≃	164	2.54 S	138.27 E
Tarituba	256	23.02 S	44.36 W
Tarka	150	14.37 N	7.55 E
Tarka, Vallée de ∨	150	14.00 N	6.00 E
Tarkastad	158	32.00 S	26.16 E
Tarkazy	80	53.52 N	53.39 E
Tarkhowrān	128	34.41 N	50.00 E
Tarki	84	42.56 N	47.30 E
Tarkiln	207	41.57 N	71.35 W
Tarkington Bayou ≃	222	30.10 N	94.59 W
Tarkio	194	40.27 N	95.23 W
Tarkio ≃	198	40.10 N	95.26 W
Tarko-Sale	74	64.55 N	77.49 E
Tarkwa	150	5.19 N	1.59 W
Tarlac	116	15.29 N	120.35 E
Tarlac □[4]	116	15.30 N	120.25 E
Tarlac ≃	116	15.45 N	120.27 E
Tarland	46	57.08 N	2.52 W
Tarlee	168b	34.16 S	138.46 E
Tarleton	44	53.41 N	2.50 W
T'arlevo	265a	59.42 N	30.27 E
Tarlscough	262	53.37 N	2.52 W
Tarm	26	55.55 N	8.32 E
Tarma	248	11.25 S	75.42 W
Tarmstedt	52	53.13 N	9.04 E
Tarn □[5]	32	43.50 N	2.00 E
Tarn ≃	32	44.05 N	1.06 E
Tarna ≃	30	47.31 N	19.59 E
Tärnaby	24	65.43 N	15.16 E
Tarnak ≃	120	31.26 N	65.31 E
Tarna Mare	38	47.29 N	26.20 E
Tårnby	41	55.38 N	12.36 E
Tarneit	274b	37.52 S	144.41 E
Tarn-et-Garonne □[5]	32	44.05 N	1.20 E
Tarnewitz	54	53.58 N	11.14 E
Tarnica ∧	30	49.05 N	22.42 E
Tarnobrzeg	30	50.35 N	21.41 E
Tarnogród	30	50.23 N	22.45 E
Tarnogskij Gorodok	24	60.29 N	43.33 E
Tarnopol → Ternopol'	78	49.34 N	25.36 E
Tarnów, Pol.	30	50.01 N	21.00 E
Tarnów, Pol.	54	52.47 N	14.58 E
Tarnowskie Góry	30	50.27 N	18.52 E
Tärnsjö	40	60.09 N	16.56 E
Tarn Tāran	123	31.27 N	74.55 E
Taro ≃	36	45.00 N	10.15 E
Taron	164	4.25 S	153.05 E
Tarong	166	26.46 S	151.51 E
Taronga Zoological Park ♠	274a	33.51 S	151.15 E
Taroom	166	25.39 S	149.49 E
Tarouadji, Massif de ⩕	150	17.15 N	8.33 E
Tarouca	34	41.00 N	7.40 W
Taroudant	148	30.31 N	8.55 W
Ta-roun, Co ∧	110	17.17 N	106.17 E
Tarp	41	54.40 N	9.23 E
Tarpey	226	36.47 N	119.42 W
Tarpon, Lake ⊜	220	28.07 N	82.44 W
Tarpon Springs	220	28.09 N	82.45 W
Tarporley	44	53.09 N	2.40 W
Tarqui	246	1.35 S	75.15 W
Tarquinia	66	42.15 N	11.45 E
Tarquinia (Tarquinii) ⊥	66	42.15 N	11.47 E
Tarqūmiyah	132	31.35 N	35.01 E
Tarra ≃	246	9.05 N	72.30 W
Tarrafal, C.V.	150a	15.17 N	23.46 W
Tarrafal, C.V.	150a	16.58 N	25.19 W
Tarragona	34	41.07 N	1.15 E
Tarrakoski ∟	24	68.10 N	20.00 E
Tarraleah	166	42.18 S	146.27 E
Tarran Hills ⩕[2]	166	32.27 S	146.27 E
Tarrant	194	33.34 N	86.46 W
Tarrant □[6]	222	32.47 N	97.18 W
Tarrant Hinton	42	50.53 N	2.05 W
Tarrara Creek ≃	208	36.33 N	77.10 W
Tarras	172	44.50 S	169.25 E
Tarrasa	34		
	266d	41.34 N	2.01 E
Tárrega	34	41.39 N	1.09 E
Tarri Mashen	144	0.45 N	41.50 E
Tarrs	214	40.10 N	79.35 W
Tarrtown	214	40.51 N	79.31 W
Tarryall Creek ≃	200	39.05 N	105.19 W
Tarrytown	210	41.05 N	73.52 W
Tarrytown Reservoir ⊜[1]	276	41.05 N	73.51 W
Tarsus	130	36.55 N	34.53 E
Tarta	128	40.02 N	52.46 E
Tartagal, Arg.	252	28.40 S	59.52 W
Tartagal, Arg.	252	22.32 S	63.49 W
Tartaro ≃	64	45.02 N	11.30 E
Tartas	32	43.50 N	0.48 W
Tartas ≃	86	55.37 N	76.44 E
Tartu	76	58.23 N	26.43 E
Ţarţūs	130	34.53 N	35.53 E
Taruaçu	256	21.37 S	42.56 W
Tarui	94	35.22 N	136.32 E
Tarum ≃	115a	5.59 S	107.03 E
Tarumi ⬥[8]	270	34.38 N	135.03 E
Tarumirim	255	19.16 S	41.59 W
Tarumizu	92	31.29 N	130.42 E
Tarumovka	84	44.03 N	46.33 E
Tarusa	82	54.43 N	37.11 E
Tarusa ≃	82	54.44 N	37.11 E
Ţārūţ	142	30.32 N	31.28 E
Tarutino, S.S.S.R.	78	46.12 N	29.09 E
Tarutino, S.S.S.R.	82	55.07 N	36.56 E
Tarutung	114	2.01 N	98.58 E
Tarvagatajn Nuruu ⩕	88	48.20 N	99.00 E
Tarves	46	57.22 N	2.13 W
Tarvisio	64	46.30 N	13.35 E
Tarvo ≃	248	14.47 S	61.03 W
Tarwin ≃	169	38.42 S	145.50 E
Tarza	24	62.30 N	40.25 E
Tarzan	196	32.18 N	101.58 W
Tarzana ⬥[8]	280	34.10 N	118.32 W
Tarzo	64	45.58 N	12.14 E
Tas	80	48.27 N	51.02 E
Tas ≃	42	52.36 N	1.18 E
Taşağıl, Tür.	130	36.55 N	31.14 E
Taşağıl, Tür.	130	41.31 N	27.07 E
Tašanta	86	49.43 N	89.11 E
Tasaral	86	46.20 N	73.58 E
Tašauz	72	41.50 N	59.58 E
Tašauz □[4]	128	50.15 N	59.00 E
Tasāwah	146	25.58 N	13.30 E
Tasbuget	86	44.48 N	65.33 E
Taschkent → Taškent	85	41.20 N	69.18 E
Taşcı	130	38.13 N	35.48 E
Tasejeva ≃	86	58.06 N	94.01 E
Tasejevo	86	57.12 N	94.54 E
Taseko ≃	182	52.00 N	123.40 W
Taseko Lakes ⊜	182	51.15 N	123.35 W
Taseko Mountain ∧	182	51.14 N	123.28 W
Tašelan	88	51.45 N	108.55 E
Tasendjanet, Oued ∨	148	24.36 N	1.07 E
Tāsgaon	122	17.02 N	74.36 E

PORTUGUÊS

Nome	Página	Lat.°′	Long.°′ W=Oeste
Tashan, Zhg.	104	40.48 N	122.39 E
Tashan, Zhg.	104	40.51 N	120.56 E
Tashibuhu ⊜	120	32.10 N	85.05 E
Tashi Gang Dzong	120	27.19 N	91.34 E
Tashikuergan	120	37.49 N	75.14 E
Tashimalike	85	39.06 N	75.41 E
Tashiyi	100	29.43 N	112.48 E
Ţashk, Daryācheh-ye ⊜	128	29.45 N	53.35 E
Tashkent → Taškent	85	41.20 N	69.18 E
Tāshkurghān → Kholm	120	36.42 N	67.41 E
Ta Shui Hang	271d	22.25 N	113.56 E
Tashuik'u	269d	25.14 N	121.31 E
Tasikmalaya	115a	7.20 S	108.12 E
Tasīl	132	32.50 N	35.58 E
Tåsinge I	41	55.00 N	10.36 E
Taširovo	82	55.25 N	36.39 E
Tasitan	85	39.17 N	76.07 E
Tåsjö	26	64.13 N	15.54 E
Tåsjön ⊜	26	64.15 N	15.47 E
Taskajevo	86	55.06 N	78.36 E
Taškent	85	41.20 N	69.18 E
Taškepri	128	36.18 N	62.38 E
Taşkesen	130	39.43 N	41.29 E
Taskesken	86	47.15 N	80.44 E
Tasköprü	130	41.30 N	34.14 E
Taskul	164	2.35 S	150.25 E
Taš-Kumyr	85	41.21 N	72.14 E
Taškyja	85	40.16 N	74.19 E
Tašla	80	51.47 N	52.46 E
Taslina	180	62.04 N	146.27 W
Tasman, Mount ∧	172	43.34 S	170.09 E
Tasman Basin ⊹[1]	14	44.00 S	157.00 E
Tasman Bay C	172	41.00 S	173.20 E
Tasmania □[3]	166	43.00 S	147.00 E
Tasmania I	166	42.00 S	147.00 E
Tasmanien → Tasmania I	166	42.00 S	147.00 E
Tasman Mountains ⩕	172	41.07 S	172.33 E
Tasman Peninsula ≻[1]	166	43.05 S	147.50 E
Tasman Sea ⍑[2]	14	40.00 S	163.00 E
Tăşnad	38	47.29 N	22.35 E
Tasoba	80	49.47 N	49.52 E
Taşova	130	40.46 N	36.20 E
Tasrār Sharīf	123	33.52 N	74.46 E
Taşrumi	84	38.48 N	44.04 E
Tassajara Creek ≃	282	37.41 N	121.53 W
Tassdorf	264a	52.30 N	13.47 E
Tassialouc, Lac ⊜	176	59.03 N	74.00 W
Tassin-la-Demi-Lune	62	45.46 N	4.47 E
Tasso Lake ⊜	212	45.27 N	78.56 W
Taštagol	86	52.47 N	87.53 E
Tastiota	232	28.22 N	111.23 W
Tåstrup	41	55.39 N	12.19 E
Taštyp	86	52.48 N	89.54 E
Tasucu	130	36.19 N	33.53 E
Tata, Magreb	148	29.44 N	7.56 W
Tata, Magy.	30	47.39 N	18.18 E
Tataa, Pointe ≻	174s	17.34 S	149.37 W
Tatabánya	30	47.34 N	18.26 E
Tatahuicapan	234	18.14 N	94.45 W
Tatal	80	47.17 N	46.16 E
Tata Mailau, Monte ∧	112	8.55 S	125.30 E
Tatamy	208	40.44 N	75.15 W
Tataouine	148	32.56 N	10.27 E
Tatarbunary	78	45.49 N	29.36 E
Tatarinka	76	55.58 N	33.54 E
Tatarino	78	50.36 N	39.07 E
Tatarinovo, S.S.S.R.	82	55.13 N	37.56 E
Tatarinovo, S.S.S.R.	82	56.34 N	38.25 E
Tatarischer Sund → Tatarskij Proliv ⊔	89	50.00 N	141.15 E
Tatarka, S.S.S.R.	76	53.16 N	28.48 E
Tatarka, S.S.S.R.	86	53.58 N	75.05 E
Tatarlar	130	41.46 N	26.55 E
Tatarovo ⬥[8]	265b	55.46 N	37.26 E
Tātārpur ⬥[8]	272a	28.39 N	77.07 E
Tatarsk	86	55.13 N	75.58 E
Tatarskaja Avtonomnaja Sovetskaja Socialističeskaja Respublika □[3]	80	55.00 N	51.00 E
Tatarskij Kandyz	80	54.07 N	53.07 E
Tatarskij Proliv ⊔	89	50.00 N	141.15 E
Tatarskij Sajman	80	53.18 N	47.07 E
Tatarskoje-Maklakovo	80	55.48 N	45.34 E
Tatar Strait → Tatarskij Proliv ⊔	89	50.00 N	141.15 E
Tatau ≃	112	3.07 N	112.49 E
Tatau Island I	164	2.50 S	152.00 E
Tataurovo, S.S.S.R.	76	58.44 N	43.20 E
Tataurovo, S.S.S.R.	80	57.48 N	49.34 E
Tataurovo, S.S.S.R.	88	51.37 N	112.56 E
Tate	192	34.25 N	84.23 W
Tate ≃	166	17.22 S	143.44 E
Tatebayashi	94	36.15 N	139.32 E
Tate Gallery ʊ	260	51.29 N	0.08 W
Tateishi-misaki ≻	94	35.46 N	136.01 E
Tateiwa	94	37.05 N	139.32 E
Tateiwa-chosuichi ⊜[1]	96	34.33 N	132.10 E
Tatelang	120	38.28 N	85.35 E
Tatelu	100	22.45 N	120.47 E
Tateshina	94	36.16 N	138.19 E
Tateyama, Nihon	94	36.40 N	137.19 E
Tateyama, Nihon	94	34.59 N	139.52 E
Tate-yama ∧	94	36.35 N	137.37 E
Tathlina Lake ⊜	176	60.32 N	117.32 W
Tathlīth, Wādī ∨	144	20.44 N	44.17 E
Tathong Channel ⊔	271d	22.15 N	114.15 E
Tathong Point ≻	271d	22.14 N	114.17 E
Tathra	166	36.44 S	149.59 E
Tatikawa → Tachikawa	94	35.42 N	139.25 E
Tatiščevo, S.S.S.R.	80	51.40 N	45.35 E
Tatiščevo, S.S.S.R.	82	56.24 N	37.31 E
Tatitlek	180	60.52 N	146.41 W
Tatla Lake	182	51.55 N	124.36 W
Tatlayoko Lake	182	51.39 N	124.24 W
Tatlayoko Lake ⊜	182	51.30 N	124.25 W
Tatlow, Mount ∧	182	51.23 N	123.52 W
Tatnam, Cape ≻	176	57.16 N	91.00 W
Tatomi	94	35.36 N	138.31 E
Tatoosh Island I	224	48.24 N	124.44 W
Tatos Dağları ⩕	130	40.55 N	41.10 E
Tatrzański Park Narodowy ♠	30	49.15 N	20.00 E
Tatsfield	260	51.18 N	0.02 E
Tatsuno, Nihon	94	35.59 N	137.59 E
Tatsuno, Nihon	96	34.52 N	134.33 E
Tatsunokuchi	94	36.27 N	136.35 E
Tatsuyama	94	34.58 N	137.49 E
Tatta	120	24.45 N	67.55 E
Tatton Hall ⊥	262	53.20 N	2.23 W
Tatton Mere ⊜	262	53.19 N	2.22 W
Tatton Park ♠	262	53.20 N	2.22 W
Tatty	85	43.12 N	73.19 E
Tatuapé ⬥[8]	287b	23.32 S	46.34 W
Tatu Ch'i ≃	100	24.12 N	120.29 E
Tatuk Lake ⊜	182	53.32 N	124.15 W
Tatum, N. Mex., U.S.	196	33.16 N	103.19 W
Tatum, Tex., U.S.	222	32.19 N	94.31 W
Tat'ung → Datong	102	40.08 N	113.13 E
Tat'un Shan ∧	100	25.10 N	121.31 E
Tatvan	130	38.30 N	42.16 E
Tatzuli Ch'i ≃	100	24.08 N	121.40 E
Tau, Nor.	26	59.04 N	5.54 E
Tau, S.S.S.R.	80	49.40 N	47.17 E
Tau I, Am. Sam.	174y	14.15 S	169.30 W
Tau I, Tonga	174w	21.01 S	175.00 W
Tauá	250	6.01 S	40.26 W
Tauak Passage ⊔	174r	6.55 N	158.06 E
Taualap Pass ⊔	175c	7.28 N	151.36 E
Tauari	250	1.07 S	47.04 W
Taubaté	256	23.02 S	45.33 W
Tauber ≃	56	49.46 N	9.31 E
Tauberbischofsheim	56	49.37 N	9.40 E
Taucha	54	51.23 N	12.30 E
Taučik	72	44.21 N	51.19 E
Tauern-Tunnel ⬥[5]	64	47.05 N	13.05 E
Täuffelen	58	47.04 N	7.12 E
Taufkirchen	60	48.21 N	12.08 E
Taufstein ∧	56	50.31 N	9.14 E
Taughannock Creek ≃	210	42.33 N	76.36 W
Taughannock Falls State Park ♠	210	42.32 N	76.35 W
Taujskaja Guba C	74	59.20 N	150.20 E
Taukum ⬥[2]	86	44.50 N	75.30 E
Taulabé	236	14.38 N	87.59 W
Taulihawa	124	27.32 N	83.03 E
Taulov	41	55.33 N	9.37 E
Taumarunui	172	38.52 S	175.17 E
Taumaturgo	248	8.57 S	72.48 W
Taum Sauk Mountain ∧	194	37.34 N	90.44 W
Taunay	248	20.18 S	56.05 W
Taung	158	27.33 S	24.47 E
Taungbon	110	15.25 N	97.50 E
Taungdwingyi	110	20.01 N	95.33 E
Taunggon	110	23.38 N	96.32 E
Taunggyi	110	20.47 N	97.02 E
Taungnyo Range ⩕	110	15.38 N	97.56 E
Taungup	110	18.51 N	94.14 E
Taungup Pass)(	110	18.40 N	94.45 E
Taunoa	174s	17.45 S	149.21 W
Taunsa	123	30.42 N	70.39 E
Taunton, Eng., U.K.	42	51.01 N	3.06 W
Taunton, Mass., U.S.	207	41.54 N	71.06 W
Taunton, N.Y., U.S.	210	43.01 N	76.13 W
Taunton ≃	207	41.42 N	71.10 W
Taunton, Vale of ∨	42	51.02 N	3.08 W
Taunton Lake ⊜	285	39.51 N	74.51 W
Taunton Lakes	285	39.51 N	74.51 W
Taunus ⩕	56	50.10 N	8.15 E
Taupiri	172	37.37 S	175.11 E
Tauplitz	61	47.33 N	14.00 E
Taupo	172	38.41 S	176.05 E
Taupo, Lake ⊜	172	38.49 S	175.55 E
Taura	54	50.55 N	12.50 E
Tauragė	76	55.15 N	22.17 E
Taurak	86	51.35 N	85.01 E
Tauranga	172	37.42 S	176.10 E
Taurasi	68	41.00 N	14.57 E
Taureau, Réservoir ⊜[1]	206	46.46 N	73.50 W
Tauri ≃	164	8.08 S	146.06 E
Taurianova	68	38.21 N	16.01 E
Tauripampa	248	12.35 S	76.07 W
Taurisano	68	39.57 N	18.13 E
Taurisma	248	15.10 S	72.51 W
Tauroa Point ≻	172	35.10 S	173.04 E
Taurovo	86	59.36 N	73.18 E
Taurus Mountains → Toros Dağları ⩕	130	37.00 N	33.00 E
Tauste	34	41.55 N	1.15 W
Tautara, Motu I[2]	174z	27.06 S	109.27 W
Tautira	174s	17.44 S	149.09 W
Tauu Islands II	14	4.45 S	157.00 E
Tauxigny	50	47.13 N	0.50 E
Tauz	84	41.00 N	45.38 E
Tavaí	252	26.07 S	55.32 W
Tavajvaam ≃	180	64.56 N	177.30 W
Tavajza	89	45.12 N	136.44 E
Ţavālesh, Kūhhā-ye → Talish Mountains ⩕	128	38.42 N	48.18 E
Tavanasa	58	46.45 N	9.04 E
Tavannes	58	47.13 N	7.12 E
Tavant	50	47.07 N	0.23 E
Tavares, Bra.	250	7.38 S	37.54 W
Tavares, Fla., U.S.	220	28.48 N	81.44 W
Tavares, Ilha dos I	287a	22.49 S	43.06 W
Tavarnelle Val di Pesa	66	43.33 N	11.10 E
Tavas	130	37.34 N	29.04 E
Tavastehus → Hämeenlinna	26	61.00 N	24.27 E
Tavaux	58	47.02 N	5.24 E
Tavda	86	58.03 N	65.15 E
Tavda ≃, S.S.S.R.	72	59.20 N	63.28 E
Tavda ≃, S.S.S.R.	86	57.47 N	67.16 E
Tave ≃	62	44.07 N	4.42 E
Tavera ≃	64	46.29 N	11.21 E
Taverna	68	39.01 N	16.35 E
Tavern Creek ≃	194	38.19 N	92.18 W
Tavernelle, It.	64	44.18 N	10.04 E
Tavernelle, It.	66	43.00 N	12.09 E
Tavernes	62	43.36 N	6.01 E
Tavernier	220	25.01 N	80.31 W
Tavernole sul Mella	64	45.45 N	10.14 E
Taverny	50	49.02 N	2.13 E
Taveta, Kenya	154	3.24 S	37.41 E
Taveta, Tan.	154	9.01 S	35.37 E
Taveuni I	175g	16.51 S	179.58 W
Taviano	68	39.59 N	18.05 E
Tavil'dara	85	38.43 N	70.28 E
Tavira	34	37.07 N	7.39 W
Tavistock, Ont., Can.	212	43.19 N	80.50 W
Tavistock, Eng., U.K.	42	50.33 N	4.08 W
Tavn-Gašun	80	46.01 N	45.55 E
Tavolara, Isola I	71	40.54 N	9.42 E
Tavoliere ⬥[1]	68	41.35 N	15.25 E
Tavolžan	86	52.44 N	77.27 E
Tavor, Har (Mount Tabor) ∧	132	32.41 N	35.23 E
Tavoy	110	14.05 N	98.12 E
Tavoy Point ≻	110	13.32 N	98.10 E
Tavričanka	89	43.22 N	131.52 E
Tavričeskij Dvorec ʊ	265a	59.57 N	30.23 E
Tavričeskoje	86	54.35 N	73.38 E
Tavry	265a	59.55 N	30.42 E
Tavsalayihüseyan	130	38.38 N	40.32 E
Tavşanlı	130	39.33 N	29.30 E
Tavsi	130	37.56 N	38.39 E
Tavua	175g	17.27 S	177.51 E
Tavy ≃	42	50.16 N	4.10 W
Taw ≃	42	51.04 N	4.11 W
Tawa	172	41.10 S	174.51 E
Tawa ≃	124	22.48 N	77.48 E
Tawaeli	112	0.43 S	119.51 E
Tawakoni, Lake ⊜[1]	222	32.55 N	96.00 W
Tawar, Laut ⊜	114	4.38 N	96.54 E
Tawara	270	34.27 N	135.57 E
Tawarada	268	35.19 N	140.04 E
Tawaramoto	96	34.33 N	135.48 E
Tawas City	190	44.16 N	83.31 W
Tawau	112	4.15 N	117.54 E
Tawd ≃	262	53.36 N	2.48 W
Tawe ≃	42	51.37 N	3.55 W
Tāwi ≃	123	32.40 N	74.41 E
Ţawīl, Jabal aţ- ∧[2]	142	27.22 N	31.07 E
Ţawīlah, Juzur II	140	27.35 N	33.46 E
Tawitawi Group II	116	5.10 N	120.15 E
Tawitawi Island I	116	5.10 N	120.00 E
Ţawkar	140	18.26 N	37.44 E
Tawu	100	22.22 N	120.54 E
Ţāwūq	128	35.08 N	44.27 E
Tāwurghā'	146	32.02 N	15.09 E
Tāwurghā', Sabkhat ☷	146	31.45 N	15.20 E
Ţawwah Banī Ibrāhīm	142	28.05 N	30.41 E
Taxco de Alarcón	234	18.33 N	99.36 W
Taxenbach	64	47.17 N	12.58 E
Taxi	89	49.26 N	126.08 E
Taxila	123	33.44 N	72.49 E
Taxisco	236	14.04 N	90.28 W
Taxusi	102	32.58 N	98.10 E
Tay ≃, Ont., Can.	212	44.53 N	76.07 W
Tay ≃, Scot., U.K.	46	56.22 N	3.21 W
Tay, Firth of C[1]	46	56.26 N	3.00 W
Tay, Lake ⊜	162	32.55 S	120.48 E
Tay, Loch ⊜	46	56.31 N	4.10 W
Tayabamba	248	8.17 S	77.18 W
Tayabas	116	14.01 N	121.35 E
Tayabas Bay C	116	13.45 N	121.45 E
Tayan	112	0.02 S	110.07 E
Tayandu, Kepulauan II	164	5.30 S	132.15 E
Tayangshan I	106	30.35 N	122.00 E
Tayegle	144	4.02 N	44.36 E
Tayin'gou	89	51.27 N	124.16 E
Taylor, B.C., Can.	182	56.10 N	120.41 W
Taylor, Ariz., U.S.	200	34.28 N	110.05 W
Taylor, Ark., U.S.	194	33.06 N	93.28 W
Taylor, Mich., U.S.	216	42.13 N	83.16 W
Taylor, Mo., U.S.	219	39.56 N	91.32 W
Taylor, Nebr., U.S.	198	41.46 N	99.23 W
Taylor, Pa., U.S.	210	41.24 N	75.35 W
Taylor, Tex., U.S.	222	30.34 N	97.25 W
Taylor, Mount ∧, N.Z.	172	43.30 S	171.19 E
Taylor, Mount ∧, N. Mex., U.S.	200	35.14 N	107.37 W
Taylor Creek ≃	219	39.13 N	90.18 W
Taylor Lake Village	222	29.36 N	95.03 W
Taylor Mountain ∧	202	44.53 N	114.13 W
Taylor Mountains ⩕	180	60.50 N	157.20 W
Taylor Run ≃	285	39.57 N	75.39 W
Taylors	192	34.55 N	82.18 W
Taylors Bush Park ♠	275b	43.42 N	79.19 W
Taylors Island	208	38.28 N	76.18 W
Taylor Springs	219	39.08 N	89.30 W
Taylors Run ≃	279b	40.11 N	79.57 W
Taylorstown	214	40.10 N	80.23 W
Taylorsville, Ind., U.S.	218	39.18 N	85.57 W
Taylorsville, Ky., U.S.	194	38.02 N	85.21 W
Taylorsville, Miss., U.S.	194	31.50 N	89.32 W
Taylorsville, N.C., U.S.	192	35.55 N	81.04 W
Taylorsville Reservoir ⊜[1]	218	40.00 N	84.10 W
Taylortown, N.J., U.S.	276	40.56 N	74.24 W
Taylortown, Ohio, U.S.	214	40.28 N	80.40 W
Taylortown Reservoir ⊜[1]	276	40.58 N	74.22 W
Taylorville	219	39.33 N	89.18 W
Taylorville, Lake ⊜[1]	219	39.30 N	89.15 W
Taymā'	128	27.38 N	38.29 E
Taymouth	186	46.11 N	66.37 W
Taymyr Peninsula → Tajmyr, Poluostrov ≻[1]	74	76.00 N	104.00 E
Tay-ninh	110	11.18 N	106.06 E
Taynuilf	46	56.25 N	5.14 W
Tayoltita	232	24.05 N	105.56 W
Tayport	46	57.27 N	2.53 W
Táyros	267c	37.58 N	23.42 E
Tayside □[4]	46	56.30 N	3.30 W
Taytay, Pil.	116	14.34 N	121.08 E
Taytay, Pil.	116	10.49 N	119.31 E
Taytay Bay C	116	10.55 N	119.35 E
Tayu	115a	6.32 S	111.02 E
Tayüan	100	25.06 N	121.14 E
Tayug	116	16.02 N	120.45 E
Tayyārah	140	13.12 N	30.47 E
Ţayyebāt	128	34.44 N	60.45 E
Taz ≃	72	67.32 N	78.40 E
Taza	148	34.16 N	4.01 W
Tazawa-ko ⊜	92	39.43 N	140.40 E
Tazenakht	148	30.35 N	7.12 W
Tazerbo ⍑[4]	146	25.45 N	21.00 E
Tazewell, Tenn., U.S.	192	36.27 N	83.34 W
Tazewell, Va., U.S.	192	37.07 N	81.31 W
Tazhuang	105	39.55 N	117.13 E
Tazicheng	89	46.35 N	123.06 E
Tazigouhe ≃	104	41.44 N	121.30 E
Tazin ≃	176	60.26 N	110.45 W
Tazin Lake ⊜	176	59.47 N	109.03 W
T'ažinskij	86	56.07 N	88.31 E
Tazishan	107	29.28 N	104.14 E
Tazlina Lake ⊜	180	61.50 N	146.30 W
Tazoult-Lambese	34	35.29 N	6.15 E
Tazovskaja Guba C	74	69.05 N	76.00 E
Tazovskij	74	67.28 N	78.42 E
Tazovskij Poluostrov ≻[1]	72	68.35 N	76.00 E
Tazrouk	148	23.25 N	6.16 E
Tazumal ⊥	236	13.59 N	89.41 W
Tāzumuddin	126	22.29 N	90.53 E
Tazuruhama	94	37.04 N	136.53 E
Tbilisi	84	41.43 N	44.49 E
Tbilisskaja	78	45.23 N	40.12 E
Tchaba	273b	4.06 S	15.16 E
Tchad → Chad □[1]	146	15.00 N	19.00 E
Tchad, Lac (Lake Chad) ⊜	146	13.20 N	14.00 E
Tchagin Golo	146	10.03 N	16.19 E
Tchamba	150	9.02 N	1.25 E
Tch'ang-Cha → Changsha	100	28.11 N	113.01 E
Tchaourou	150	8.53 N	2.36 E
Tchécoslovaquie → Czechoslovakia □[1]	30	49.30 N	17.00 E
Tchefuncta ≃	194	30.22 N	90.10 W
Tchékapika	152	1.17 S	16.11 E
Tcheliabinsk → Čel'abinsk	86	55.10 N	61.24 E
Tcheng-Tcheou → Zhengzhou	102	34.48 N	113.39 E
Tchentlo ⊜	182	55.11 N	125.00 W
Tchériba	150	12.16 N	3.05 W
Tchetti	150	7.50 N	1.40 E
Tchibanga	152	2.51 S	11.02 E
Tchien	150	6.04 N	8.08 W
Tchigaï, Plateau du ⩕[1]	146	21.30 N	14.50 E
Tchin Tabaraden	150	15.58 N	5.50 E
Tchitondi	152	4.33 S	12.08 E
Tchollíré	146	8.24 N	14.10 E
Tchong-K'ing → Chongqing	107	29.39 N	106.34 E
Tchořovice	60	49.27 N	13.48 E
Tchula	194	33.11 N	90.13 W
Tczew	30	54.06 N	18.47 E
Te, Kinh Ξ	269c	10.45 N	106.42 E
Tea ≃	246	0.30 S	65.09 W
Teaca	38	46.55 N	24.31 E
Teacapán	234	22.33 N	105.45 W
Teaehoa, Pointe ≻	174x	9.51 S	139.01 W
Teague	222	31.38 N	96.17 W
Te Anau	172	45.25 S	167.43 E
Te Anau, Lake ⊜	172	45.12 S	167.48 E
Teanaway ≃	224	47.10 N	120.50 W
Teanaway, Middle Fork ≃	224	47.15 N	120.53 W
Teanaway, North Fork ≃	224	47.22 N	120.53 W
Teaneck	210	40.53 N	74.01 W
Teangue	46	57.07 N	5.50 W
Teano	68	41.15 N	14.04 E
Teapa	234	17.33 N	92.57 W
Teapa ≃	234	17.58 N	92.54 W
Te Araroa	172	37.38 S	178.22 E
Tearinibai	174t	1.35 N	172.58 E
Te Aroha	172	37.33 S	175.43 E
Teaticket	207	41.34 N	70.36 W
Tea Tree	162	22.11 S	133.17 E
Teatree Gully	168b	34.49 S	138.44 E
Te Atukura ∧	174k	21.14 S	159.45 W
Teavaraa, Passe ⊔	174s	17.46 S	149.28 W
Te Awamutu	172	38.01 S	175.19 E
Teba, Esp.	34	36.58 N	4.56 W
Teba, Indon.	164	1.29 S	137.54 E
Tebakang	112	1.06 N	110.30 E
Tebas	256	21.35 S	42.44 W
Tebay	44	54.26 N	2.35 W
Tebbetts	219	38.37 N	91.58 W
Teberda	84	43.28 N	41.45 E
Teberdinskij Zapovednik ♠	84	43.20 N	41.45 E
Tebes	286d	12.07 S	77.00 W
Tébessa	148	35.28 N	8.09 E
Tébessa, Monts de ⩕	148	35.20 N	8.20 E
Tebicuary ≃	252	26.36 S	58.16 W
Tebicuary-mí ≃	252	26.26 S	56.51 W
Tebingbulan	112	3.03 S	103.44 E
Tebingtinggi, Indon.	112	3.36 S	103.05 E
Tebingtinggi, Indon.	112	0.36 N	101.36 E
Tebingtinggi, Indon.	114	3.20 N	99.09 E
Tebingtinggi, Pulau I	114	0.54 N	102.45 E
Tébourba	36	36.49 N	9.51 E
Téboursouk	148	36.28 N	9.15 E
Téboursouk, Monts de ⩕	36	36.30 N	9.10 E
Tebra ≃	76	56.51 N	21.12 E
Tebstrup	41	55.59 N	9.53 E
Tebulosmta, Gora ∧	84	42.33 N	45.19 E
Tebza ≃	80	58.23 N	41.19 E
Tecalitlán	234	19.26 N	103.15 W
Tecamachalco	234	18.53 N	97.44 W
Tecate	232	32.34 N	116.38 W
Tech ≃	32	42.36 N	3.03 E
Techendorf	64	46.43 N	13.17 E
Techiman	150	7.35 N	1.56 W
Techimentia	150	7.11 N	2.02 W
Techirghiol	38	44.03 N	28.36 E
Techny	278	42.07 N	87.49 W
Techou → Dezhou	98	37.27 N	116.18 E
Techtin	76	53.51 N	29.44 E
Tecka	254	43.29 S	70.48 W
Tecka ≃	254	42.37 S	70.25 W
Tecklenburg	52	52.13 N	7.48 E
Teckomatorp	41	55.52 N	13.05 E
Tecolote Creek ≃	200	35.22 N	105.15 W
Tecolotlán	234	20.13 N	104.03 W
Tecolutla ≃	234	20.29 N	97.00 W
Tecomán	234	18.55 N	103.53 W
Tecomate, Laguna C	234	16.35 N	99.25 W
Tecomaxtlahuaca	234	17.21 N	98.02 W
Tecominoacán	234	17.53 N	93.37 W
Tecopa	204	35.51 N	116.13 W
Tecozautla	234	20.32 N	99.38 W
Tecpan de Galeana	234	17.15 N	100.41 W
Tecpán Guatemala	236	14.46 N	91.00 W
Tecpatán	234	17.08 N	93.18 W
Tecuala	234	22.23 N	105.27 W
Tecuamburro, Volcán ∧[1]	236	14.09 N	90.24 W
Tecuantepec ≃	234	20.16 N	97.27 W
Tecuci	38	45.50 N	27.26 E
Tecumseh, Ont., Can.	214	42.19 N	82.54 W
Tecumseh, Mich., U.S.	216	42.00 N	83.57 W
Tecumseh, Nebr., U.S.	198	40.22 N	96.11 W
Tecumseh, Okla., U.S.	196	35.15 N	96.56 W
Ted	144	4.26 N	43.55 E
Teddington ⬥[8]	260	51.25 N	0.20 W
Tedesa	144	5.07 N	37.45 E
Tedori ≃	94	36.29 N	136.28 E
Tedrow	216	41.37 N	84.13 W
Tedžen	128	37.23 N	60.31 E
Tedžen (Harīrūd) ≃	128	37.24 N	60.38 E
Tedženstroj	128	36.55 N	60.53 E
Teec Nos Pos	200	36.55 N	109.07 W
Tee Creek ≃	284a	43.02 N	79.06 W
Teels Marsh ☷	204	38.12 N	118.21 W
Teen ⊜	40	59.07 N	14.40 E
Teerijärvi → Terjärv	26	63.32 N	23.30 E
Tees ≃	44	54.34 N	1.16 W
Tees Bay C	44	54.39 N	1.07 W
Teesdale ∨	44	54.38 N	2.07 W
Teesside → Middlesbrough	44	54.35 N	1.14 W
Teesside (Saint George) Airport ⊠	44	54.31 N	1.25 W
Teeswater	212	44.00 N	81.17 W
Teeswater ≃	212	44.18 N	81.17 W
Tefé	246	3.22 S	64.42 W
Tefé ≃	242	3.35 S	64.47 W
Tefé, Lago de ⊜	246	3.27 S	64.47 W
Tefen	130	41.19 N	32.08 E
Tefenni	130	37.18 N	29.47 E
Tefft	216	41.12 N	86.58 W
Tefle	150	5.59 N	0.35 E
Tegal	115a	6.52 S	109.08 E
Tegalombo	115a	8.04 S	111.17 E
Tega-numa ⊜	268	35.51 N	140.04 E
Tegel ⬥[8]	264a	52.35 N	13.17 E
Tegel, Berliner Forst ♠	264a	52.37 N	13.16 E
Tegelen	52	51.21 N	6.09 E
Tegeler See ⊜	264a	52.35 N	13.15 E
Tegernsee	64	47.43 N	11.45 E
Tegernsee ⊜	64	47.42 N	11.45 E
Teggiano	68	40.23 N	15.32 E
Teghra	124	25.29 N	85.57 E
Tegid, Llyn ⊜	42	52.53 N	3.36 W
Tegina	150	10.05 N	6.14 E
Tegineneng	112	5.12 S	105.10 E
Tegistyk	85	44.02 N	68.22 E
Teglio	64	46.10 N	10.04 E
Tegua I	175f	13.15 S	166.37 E
Tegualda	254	41.02 S	73.26 W
Tegucigalpa	236	14.06 N	87.13 W
Tehachapi	228	35.08 N	118.27 W
Tehachapi Creek ≃	228	35.17 N	118.38 W
Tehachapi Mountains ⩕	228	35.00 N	118.40 W
Tehachapi Pass)(	228	35.06 N	118.18 W
Tehamiyam	140	18.20 N	36.32 E
Te Hapua	172	34.31 S	172.54 E
Tehar ⬥[8]	272a	28.38 N	77.07 E
Te Haroto	172	39.08 S	176.36 E
Tehata	126	23.43 N	88.32 E
Tehek Lake ⊜	176	64.55 N	95.38 W

≃ River	Fluss	Río	Rivière	Rio
Ξ Canal	Kanal	Canal	Canal	Canal
∟ Waterfall, Rapids	Wasserfall, Stromschnellen	Cascada, Rápidos	Chute d'eau, Rapides	Cascata, Rápidos
⊔ Strait	Meeresstrasse	Estrecho	Détroit	Estreito
C Bay, Gulf	Bucht, Golf	Bahía, Golfo	Baie, Golfe	Baía, Golfo
⊜ Lake, Lakes	See, Seen	Lago, Lagos	Lac, Lacs	Lago, Lagos
☷ Swamp	Sumpf	Pantano	Marais	Pântano
⍓ Ice Features, Glacier	Eis- und Gletscherformen	Accidentes Glaciales	Formes glaciaires	Acidentes Glaciares
⍑ Other Hydrographic Features	Andere Hydrographische Objekte	Otros Elementos Hidrográficos	Autres données hydrographiques	Outros Elementos Hidrográficos

⊹ Submarine Features	Untermeerische Objekte	Accidentes Submarinos	Formes de relief sous-marin	Acidentes Submarinos
□ Political Unit	Politische Einheit	Unidad Politica	Entité politique	Unidade Política
ʊ Cultural Institution	Kulturelle Institution	Institución Cultural	Institution culturelle	Instituição Cultural
⊥ Historical Site	Historische Stätte	Sitio Histórico	Site historique	Sitio Histórico
♠ Recreational Site	Erholungs- und Ferienort	Sitio de Recreo	Centre de loisirs	Sítio de Lazer
⊠ Airport	Flughafen	Aeropuerto	Aéroport	Aeroporto
■ Military Installation	Militäranlage	Instalación Militar	Installation militaire	Instalação Militar
⬥ Miscellaneous	Verschiedenes	Misceláneo	Divers	Miscelânea

Name	Page	Lat.	Long.
Teheran → Tehrān	128	35.40 N	51.26 E
Téhini	150	9.36 N	3.40 W
Tehoohaivei, Cap ≻	174x	9.49 S	138.54 W
Te Hope O Te Keho, Cap ≻	174x	10.02 S	139.06 W
Tehoru	164	3.23 S	129.30 E
Tehrān	128		
	267d	35.40 N	51.26 E
Tehrān □[4]	128	35.30 N	51.00 E
Tehrān, University of ʊ[2]	267d	35.42 N	51.24 E
Tehrān Pars •[8]	267d	35.44 N	51.32 E
Tehri	124	30.23 N	78.29 E
Tehri Garhwāl □[5]	124	30.30 N	78.30 E
Tehri Sar ∧	123	36.48 N	74.48 E
Tehrthum	124	27.07 N	87.32 E
Tehuacán	234	18.27 N	97.23 W
Tehuacana	222	31.44 N	96.33 W
Tehuacana Creek ≃, Tex., U.S.	222	31.31 N	97.02 W
Tehuacana Creek ≃, Tex., U.S.	222	31.50 N	95.59 W
Tehuantepec, Méx.	234	18.41 N	103.17 W
Tehuantepec, Méx.	234	16.20 N	95.14 W
Tehuantepec ≃	234	16.10 N	95.07 W
Tehuantepec, Golfo de C	234	16.00 N	94.50 W
Tehuantepec, Istmo de •[3]	234	17.00 N	95.00 W
Tehuantepec Ridge ◆[3]	16	13.00 N	98.45 W
Tehuelches	254	46.56 S	67.27 W
Tehuipango	234	18.31 N	97.04 W
Tehuitzingo	234	18.21 N	98.17 W
Teichl ≃	61	47.46 N	14.10 E
Teichröda	54	50.45 N	11.18 E
Teichwolframsdorf	54	50.43 N	12.14 E
Teide, Pico de ∧	148	28.16 N	16.38 W
Teifi ≃	42	52.07 N	4.42 W
Teifiside •[1]	42	52.02 N	4.22 W
Teiga Plateau ⋀[1]	140	15.38 N	25.40 E
Teign ≃	42	50.33 N	3.29 W
Teignmouth	42	50.33 N	3.30 W
Teise ≃	260	51.13 N	0.25 E
Teisendorf	64	47.51 N	12.49 E
Teisnach	60	49.02 N	13.00 E
Teita	234	17.05 N	97.25 W
Teith ≃	46	56.08 N	3.59 W
Teitipac	234	16.54 N	96.34 W
Teixeira	250	7.13 S	37.15 W
Teixeira Pinto	150	12.10 N	13.55 W
Teixeiras	255	20.39 S	42.51 W
Teixeira Soares	252	25.22 S	50.27 W
Tejakula	115b	8.08 S	115.20 E
Tejamén	232	24.48 N	105.07 W
Tejkovo	80	56.52 N	40.34 E
Tejo → Tagus ≃	34	38.40 N	9.24 W
Tejon Creek ≃	228	35.08 N	118.53 W
Tejon Pass)(	228	34.48 N	118.52 W
Tejupan, Punta ≻	234	18.20 N	103.32 W
Tejupilco de Hidalgo	234	18.54 N	100.09 W
Te Kaha	172	37.44 S	177.41 E
Tekai ≃	114	4.14 N	102.23 E
Tekakwitha, Île I	275a	45.25 N	73.42 W
Tekam ≃	114	3.52 N	102.27 E
Tekamah	198	41.47 N	96.13 W
Te Kao	172	34.39 S	172.57 E
Tekapo, Lake ⊜	172	43.53 S	170.31 E
Te Karaka	172	38.28 S	177.52 E
Tekāri	124	24.56 N	84.50 E
Te Kauwhata	172	37.24 S	175.09 E
Tekax de Álvaro Obregón	232	20.12 N	89.17 W
Teke	130	41.04 N	29.39 E
Teke, Ozero ⊜	86	53.48 N	73.00 E
Teke Burnu ≻, Tür.	130	38.05 N	26.36 E
Teke Burnu ≻, Tür.	130	40.02 N	26.10 E
Tekeli	86	44.48 N	78.57 E
Tekesi	86	43.10 N	81.43 E
Tekesihe ≃	86	43.36 N	82.32 E
Tekeze (Satīt) ≃, Afr.	140	14.20 N	35.50 E
Tekeze ≃, Yai.	144	14.20 N	35.50 E
Tekirdağ	130	40.59 N	27.31 E
Tekirdağ □[4]	130	41.00 N	27.30 E
Tekkali	122	18.37 N	84.14 E
Tekke	130	40.43 N	36.12 E
Tekkiraz	130	40.59 N	37.08 E
Tekman	130	39.38 N	41.31 E
Tekoa	202	47.14 N	117.04 W
Tekong, Pulau I	271c	1.24 N	104.03 E
Tekong Kechil, Pulau I	271c	1.25 N	104.01 E
Tekonsha	216	42.05 N	84.59 W
Te Kopuru	172	36.02 S	173.56 E
Tekouiat, Oued ∨	148	22.25 N	2.35 E
Tekro ◆[4]	146	19.30 N	20.58 E
Tekstil'ščiki	82	55.57 N	37.49 E
Tekstil'ščiki •[8]	265b	55.42 N	37.44 E
Teku	112	0.46 S	123.26 E
Te Kuiti	172	38.20 S	175.10 E
Tekukor, Pulau I	271c	1.14 N	103.50 E
Tel ≃	122	20.50 N	83.54 E
Tela, Bhārat	272a	28.44 N	77.20 E
Tela, Hond.	236	15.44 N	87.27 W
Tela, Bahía de C	236	15.48 N	87.30 W
Teladuomu	120	29.38 N	84.13 E
Telaga	116	6.51 N	117.03 E
Telaga, Teluk C	114	2.10 N	98.00 E
Telaga-kulon	115a	6.58 S	108.18 E
Télagh	148	34.47 N	0.34 W
Telaopengshashan ∧	120	30.33 N	86.25 E
Tel Ashqelon ⊥	132	31.39 N	34.32 E
Telavåg	26	60.16 N	4.49 E
Telavi	84	41.55 N	45.28 E
Tel Aviv □[5]	132	32.05 N	34.48 E
Tel Aviv-Yafo	132	32.04 N	34.46 E
Telč	30	49.11 N	15.27 E
Tel'čje	76	53.21 N	36.20 E
Telde	148	28.00 N	15.25 W
Tele ≃	152	2.48 N	23.54 E
Telechany	76	52.31 N	25.51 E
Teleckoje, Ozero ⊜	86	51.35 N	87.40 E
Telefomin	164	5.10 S	141.35 E
Telegapulang	112	2.55 S	112.25 E
Telegino	80	52.55 N	44.34 E
Telegraph Canyon ∨	280	33.55 N	117.45 W
Telegraph Cove	182	50.33 N	126.50 W
Telegraph Creek	180	57.55 N	131.10 W
Telemark □[6]	26	59.30 N	8.40 E
Telemba	88	52.43 N	113.16 E
Telembí ≃	246	1.50 N	78.16 W
Telén	252	36.16 S	65.30 W
Telen ≃	112	0.26 S	116.42 E
Telenešty	78	47.30 N	28.22 E
Teleño ∧	34	42.21 N	6.23 W
Teleorman □[4]	38	44.00 N	25.15 E
Teleorman ≃	38	43.52 N	25.26 E
Téléphone, Île du I	273b	4.20 S	15.12 E
Telergma	148	36.07 N	6.21 E
Telerig	38	43.51 N	27.40 E
Telertheba, Djebel ∧	148	24.10 N	6.51 E
Telescope Peak ∧	204	36.10 N	117.05 W
Telescope Point ≻	241k	12.08 N	61.36 W
Telese	68	41.13 N	14.32 E
Telesterion ⊥	267c	38.02 N	23.32 E
Telferner	222	28.51 N	96.53 W
Telfes, Öst.	64	47.18 N	11.04 E
Telfes, Öst.	64	47.10 N	11.22 E
Telford	208	40.20 N	75.20 W
Telgte	52	51.59 N	7.47 E
Teli	86	51.07 N	90.14 E
Telica, Volcán ∧[1]	236	12.36 N	86.50 W
Telida	180	63.23 N	153.16 W
Telikovka	80	52.35 N	48.17 E
Télimélé	150	10.54 N	13.02 W
Télimélé □[4]	150	11.00 N	13.30 W
Telixtlahuaca	234	17.18 N	96.54 W
Telizi	265a	59.42 N	29.59 E
Teljo, Jabal ∧	140	14.42 N	25.56 E
Telkwa	182	54.42 N	127.03 W
Telkwa ≃	182	54.41 N	127.02 W
Tel Lakhish ⊥	132	31.34 N	34.51 E
Tellaro ≃	70	36.50 N	15.06 E
Tell City	194	37.57 N	86.46 W
Teller	180	65.16 N	166.22 W
Tellicherry	122	11.45 N	75.32 E
Tellico ≃	192	35.36 N	84.13 W
Tellico Plains	192	35.22 N	84.18 W
Tellier	254	47.39 S	66.03 W
Tellier, Lac ⊜	206	46.23 N	74.00 W
Tello	246	3.04 N	75.08 W
Telluride	200	37.56 N	107.49 W
Tel'ma	88	52.43 N	103.41 E
Tel'mana	83	48.30 N	39.18 E
Tel'manovo	83	47.24 N	38.02 E
Tel Megiddo ⊥	132	32.35 N	35.11 E
Telmen	88	48.38 N	97.37 E
Telmen Nuur ⊜	88	48.50 N	97.18 E
Tel Mond	132	32.15 N	34.56 E
Tel'novskij	89	49.22 N	142.05 E
Teloekbetoeng → Telukbetung	115a	5.27 S	105.16 E
Telogia Creek ≃	192	30.16 N	84.44 W
Telok Anson	114	4.02 N	101.01 E
Telok Datok	114	2.49 N	101.31 E
Teloloapan	234	18.21 N	99.51 W
Telpaneca	236	13.32 N	86.17 W
Telsen	254	42.24 S	66.57 W
Telsen, Arroyo ≃	254	42.51 S	66.48 W
Telšiai	76	55.59 N	22.15 E
Telti	71	40.52 N	9.21 E
Teltow	54	52.23 N	13.16 E
Teltower Hochfläche ⋀[1]	264a	52.22 N	13.20 E
Teltowkanal ≍	264a	52.26 N	13.35 E
Telukbatang	112	1.00 S	109.46 E
Telukbayur, Indon.	112	2.09 N	117.24 E
Telukbayur, Indon.	112	1.00 S	100.22 E
Telukbetung	115a	5.27 S	105.16 E
Telukbrombang	114	2.03 N	100.52 E
Telukbutun	112	4.13 N	108.12 E
Telukdalem	114	0.34 N	97.49 E
Teluklanjut	112	0.09 N	103.29 E
Teluklecah	114	1.51 N	101.44 E
Telukmerbau	114	2.04 N	100.38 E
Teluk Punggur, Ujung ≻	112	3.53 S	102.17 E
Teluksamak	114	0.52 N	103.03 E
Telumengtangshan ∧	120	30.33 N	86.27 E
Teluša	76	53.03 N	29.31 E
Tem'	88	55.21 N	100.44 E
Tema	150	5.38 N	0.01 E
Temae	174s	17.29 S	149.46 W
Temagami, Lake ⊜	190	47.00 N	80.05 W
Temaju, Pulau I	112	0.29 N	108.52 E
Temalacacingo	234	17.52 N	98.41 W
Te Manga ∧	174k	21.13 S	159.45 W
Temangan Baharu	114	5.42 N	102.09 E
Temangga	112	0.27 N	111.21 E
Temanggung	115a	7.18 S	110.10 E
Temascal, Méx.	234	18.15 N	96.20 W
Temascal, Méx.	234	23.24 N	104.14 W
Temascaltepec ≃	234	18.47 N	100.41 W
Tem'asovo	86	52.59 N	58.06 E
Temastián	234	21.53 N	103.28 W
Tematangi I[1]	14	21.41 S	140.40 W
Temax	232	21.09 N	88.56 W
Tembe	154	0.16 S	28.14 E
Tembe ≃	158	26.03 S	32.26 E
Tembeling	114	4.04 N	102.19 E
Tembeling ≃	114	4.04 N	102.20 E
Tembenči ≃	74	64.36 N	99.58 E
Tembesi ≃	112	1.43 S	103.06 E
Tembilahan	112	0.19 S	103.09 E
Tembisa	158	25.58 S	28.14 E
Temblador	246	8.59 N	62.44 W
Tembleque	34	39.42 N	3.30 W
Temblor Range ⋀	226	35.20 N	119.55 W
Tembo Aluma	152	7.42 S	17.17 E
Tembuè	154	14.52 S	32.58 E
Tembuland •[1]	158	31.30 S	28.20 E
Teme ≃	42	52.09 N	2.18 W
Temecula	228	33.46 N	117.29 W
Temecula Creek ≃	228	33.28 N	117.08 W
Temengor	114	5.19 N	101.22 E
Temerin	38	45.24 N	19.53 E
Temerloh	114	3.27 N	102.25 E
Temescal Canyon ∨	280	34.04 N	118.32 W
Temescal Wash ∨	228	33.40 N	117.20 W
Temesvár → Timişoara	38	45.45 N	21.13 E
Temiang, Pulau I	112	0.19 N	104.23 E
Teminabuan	164	1.26 S	132.01 E
Temir	86	49.08 N	57.06 E
Temir ≃	86	48.31 N	57.27 E
Temirgojevskaja	78	45.07 N	40.16 E
Temirlanovka	85	42.36 N	69.17 E
Temirtau, S.S.S.R.	86	50.05 N	72.56 E
Temirtau, S.S.S.R.	86	53.08 N	87.28 E
Témiscamie, Lac ⊜	186	51.11 N	72.12 W
Témiscaming	190	46.43 N	79.06 W
Témiscouata, Lac ⊜	186	47.41 N	68.47 W
Temixco	234	18.50 N	99.14 W
Temnik ≃	88	51.00 N	106.18 E
Temnikov	80	54.38 N	43.12 E
Temnikovo	265b	55.43 N	38.01 E
Temo ≃	71	40.21 N	8.47 E
Temoaya	234	19.28 N	99.35 W
Temora	166	34.26 S	147.32 E
Temósachic	232	28.57 N	107.51 W
Tempe	200	33.25 N	111.56 W
Tempe, Danau ⊜	112	4.06 S	119.57 E
Tempelburg → Czaplinek	30	53.34 N	16.14 E
Tempelfelde	264a	52.43 N	13.43 E
Tempelhof •[8]	264a	52.28 N	13.23 E
Temperance	216	41.47 N	83.34 W
Temperanceville	208	37.54 N	75.33 W
Temperley •[8]	258	34.47 S	58.24 W
Tempest, Mount ∧[2]	171a	27.10 S	153.26 E
Tempilang	112	2.07 S	105.40 E
Tempino	112	1.44 S	103.29 E
Tempio di Clitunno ⊥	66	42.48 N	12.45 E
Tempio Pausania	71	40.54 N	9.06 E
Tempisque ≃	236	10.12 N	85.14 W
Temple, Okla., U.S.	196	34.16 N	98.14 W
Temple, Pa., U.S.	208	40.25 N	75.56 W
Temple, Tex., U.S.	222	31.06 N	97.21 W
Temple City	228	34.07 N	118.03 W
Templecombe	42	51.00 N	2.25 W
Temple Ewell	42	51.09 N	1.16 E
Templemore	48	52.48 N	7.50 W
Templers	168b	34.28 S	138.45 E
Temple Sowerby	44	54.39 N	2.35 W
Templestowe	169	37.45 S	145.07 E
Temple Terrace	220	28.02 N	82.23 W
Templeton, Austl.	166	18.26 S	142.28 E
Templeton, Qué., Can.	212	45.29 N	75.36 W
Templeton, Calif., U.S.	226	35.33 N	120.42 W
Templeton, Ind., U.S.	216	40.31 N	87.12 W
Templeton, Mass., U.S.	207	42.33 N	72.04 W
Templeton, Pa., U.S.	214	40.55 N	79.28 W
Templeton ≃	166	21.14 S	138.13 E
Temple University ʊ[2]	285	39.59 N	75.09 W
Templeuve, Bel.	50	50.38 N	3.16 E
Templeuve, Fr.	50	50.32 N	3.10 E
Templi, Valle dei ⊥	70	37.17 N	13.35 E
Templin	54	53.07 N	13.30 E
Templiner See ⊜	264a	52.22 N	13.01 E
Templo Island I	116	13.09 N	122.52 E
Tempoal	234	21.31 N	98.23 W
Tempoal ≃	234	21.47 N	98.27 W
Tempy	82	56.38 N	37.18 E
Temr'uk	78	45.17 N	37.23 E
Temr'ukskij Zaliv C	78	45.24 N	37.20 E
Temse	50	51.08 N	4.13 E
Temù	64	46.15 N	10.28 E
Temuco	252	38.44 S	72.36 W
Temuka	172	44.15 S	171.17 E
Tena	246	0.59 S	77.49 W
Tenabo	232	20.03 N	90.14 W
Tenacatita, Bahía C	234	19.17 N	104.50 W
Tenafly	210	40.56 N	73.58 W
Tenaha	194	31.57 N	94.15 W
Tenakee Springs	180	57.47 N	135.13 W
Tenakill Brook ≃	276	40.59 N	73.58 W
Tenāli	122	16.15 N	80.35 E
Tenamaxtlán	234	20.13 N	104.10 W
Tenancingo [de Degollado]	234	18.58 N	99.36 W
Tenango del Valle	234	19.07 N	99.33 W
Tenantongo, Presa ⊜[1]	286a	19.28 N	99.16 W
Tenasillahe Island I	224	46.14 N	123.27 W
Tenasserim	110	12.05 N	99.01 E
Tenasserim □[8]	110	12.00 N	99.00 E
Tenay	58	45.55 N	5.30 E
Tenaya Creek ≃	226	37.44 N	119.35 W
Tenbury Wells	42	52.19 N	2.35 W
Tenby	42	51.41 N	4.43 W
Tence	62	45.07 N	4.17 E
Tench Island I	164	1.40 S	150.40 E
Tencin	62	45.19 N	5.58 E
Tenda, Colle di (Col de Tende))(	62	44.09 N	7.34 E
Tendaho	144	11.48 N	40.52 E
Tendai-san ∧	270	34.55 N	135.28 E
Tende	62	44.05 N	7.36 E
Tende, Col de (Colle di Tenda))(	62	44.09 N	7.34 E
Tende, Tunnel de •[5]	62	44.09 N	7.34 E
Ten Degree Channel ⋓	110	10.00 N	93.00 E
Tendeka	158	27.44 S	30.54 E
Tendō	92	38.21 N	140.22 E
Tendrara	148	33.04 N	1.59 W
Tendrovskaja Kosa ≻[2]	78	46.12 N	31.50 E
Tendrovskij Zaliv C	78	46.15 N	31.55 E
Tendürek Dağı ∧	84	39.22 N	43.52 E
Teneguiban	116	11.22 N	119.30 E
Ténenkou	150	14.28 N	4.55 W
Tenente Marques ≃	248	11.10 S	59.56 W
Tenente Portela	252	27.22 S	53.45 W
Tenentes	256	22.48 S	46.20 W
Ténéré •[2]	146	19.00 N	10.30 E
Ténéré, Erg du •[8]	146	17.35 N	10.55 E
Tenerife I	148	28.19 N	16.34 W
Ténès	148	36.31 N	1.14 E
Ténès, Cap ≻	34	36.33 N	1.21 E
Tenexpa	234	17.11 N	100.43 W
Tenextepango	234	18.43 N	98.57 W
Tengah, Kepulauan II	112	7.30 S	117.30 E
Tengah Airfield ⊠	271c	1.23 N	103.42 E
Tengaobao	104	41.05 N	122.49 E
Tengchong	102	25.04 N	98.29 E
Tengen	58	47.49 N	8.40 E
Tenggarong	112	0.24 S	116.58 E
Tenggol, Pulau I	114	4.48 N	103.38 E
Tenghilan	112	6.14 N	116.19 E
Tengi ≃	114	3.24 N	101.10 E
Tengiz, Ozero ⊜	86	50.24 N	68.57 E
Tengjiabao	100	31.10 N	115.29 E
Tengjiatun	104	41.10 N	121.32 E
Tengqiao	110	18.22 N	109.46 E
Tengra	272b	22.48 N	88.32 E
Tengtian	100	27.04 N	115.40 E
Ten'guševo	80	54.46 N	42.44 E
Tengxian, Zhg.	98	35.08 N	117.10 E
Tengxian, Zhg.	102	23.21 N	110.53 E
Teniente Matienzo ʊ[3]	9	64.58 S	60.02 W
Teniet el Had	148	35.47 N	2.01 E
Tenigerbad	58	46.42 N	8.57 E
Tenino	224	46.51 N	122.51 W
Tenis, Ozero ⊜	86	56.09 N	71.56 E
Teniz, Ozero ⊜	86	54.08 N	64.34 E
Tenjin ≃	96	35.30 N	133.53 E
Tenjo, Mount ∧	174p	13.25 N	144.42 E
Tenkāsi	122	8.58 N	77.18 E
Tenke, Zaïre	154	11.26 S	26.45 E
Tenke, Zaïre	154	10.35 S	26.07 E
Ten'ki	80	55.26 N	49.00 E
Tenkiller Ferry Lake ⊜[1]	196	35.43 N	95.00 W
Tenkodogo	150	11.47 N	0.22 W
Tenmile ≃, Mass., U.S.	283	41.58 N	71.20 W
Tenmile ≃, N.Y., U.S.	210	41.40 N	73.31 W
Ten Mile Creek ≃, Ont., Can.	284a	43.07 N	79.11 W
Ten Mile Creek ≃, Ky., U.S.	218	38.43 N	84.46 W
Tenmile Creek ≃, Ohio, U.S.	216	41.42 N	83.33 W
Tenmile Creek ≃, Pa., U.S.	188	40.08 N	80.22 W
Tenmile Creek ≃, Tex., U.S.	222	32.34 N	96.34 W
Ten Mile Lake ⊜	186	51.06 N	56.41 W
Tenmile Run ≃	276	40.27 N	74.35 W
Tenmoku-san ∧	94	35.52 N	139.03 E
Tenna ≃	66	43.14 N	13.47 E
Tennant Creek	162	19.40 S	134.10 E
Tennenbronn	58	48.11 N	8.20 E
Tennengau •[1]	64	47.40 N	13.15 E
Tennen-Gebirge ⋀	64	47.30 N	13.15 E
Tennent	208	40.17 N	74.20 W
Tennent Pond ⊜	276	40.26 N	74.20 W
Tennessee □[3]	178	35.50 N	85.30 W
Tennessee ≃	178	37.04 N	88.33 W
Tennessee Colony	222	31.50 N	95.50 W
Tenneville	56	50.06 N	5.32 E
Tennille	192	32.56 N	82.48 W
Tenno	64	45.55 N	10.49 E
Tennōji •[8]	270	34.39 N	135.31 E
Teno	252	34.52 S	71.11 W
Tenom	112	5.08 N	115.57 E
Ténos, Pointe ≻	240e	14.48 N	61.00 W
Tenosique de Pino Suárez	232	17.29 N	91.26 W
Tenri	96	34.36 N	135.51 E
Tenryū, Nihon	94	35.16 N	137.51 E
Tenryū, Nihon	94	34.52 N	137.49 E
Tenryū ≃	94	34.39 N	137.47 E
Tensed	202	47.10 N	116.55 W
Tensift, Oued ≃	148	32.02 N	9.22 W
Ten Sleep	202	44.02 N	107.27 W
Tensta	40	60.02 N	17.40 E
Tente	263	51.07 N	7.11 E
Tente •[8]	263	51.18 N	7.14 E
Tentena	112	1.47 S	120.39 E
Tenterden	42	51.05 N	0.42 E
Tenterfield	166	29.03 S	152.01 E
Tent Hill	171a	27.36 S	152.14 E
Ten Thousand Islands II	220	25.50 N	81.33 W
Tentugal	250	1.19 S	46.59 W
Tentulia	272b	22.50 N	88.28 E
Teocaltiche	234	21.26 N	102.35 W
Teocelo	234	19.23 N	96.58 W
Teocuitatlán de Corona	234	20.07 N	103.24 W
Teocuitlapa	234	17.22 N	98.58 W
Teodelina	252	34.11 S	61.32 W
Teófilo Cunha	287a	22.39 S	43.34 W
Teófilo Otoni	255	17.51 S	41.30 W
Teofipol'	78	49.50 N	26.25 E
Teohotepapa, Pointe ≻	174x	9.46 S	138.48 W
Teohotupa, Pointe ≻	174x	9.46 S	138.50 W
Teolo	64	45.21 N	11.40 E
Teomabal Island I	116	6.20 N	120.51 E
Teor	64	45.51 N	13.03 E
Teora	68	40.51 N	15.15 E
Teotihuacán ⊥	234	19.44 N	98.50 W
Teotitlán del Camino	234	18.08 N	97.05 W
Teotitlán del Valle	234	17.02 N	96.30 W
Tepa, Ghana	150	7.00 N	2.10 W
Tepa, Indon.	164	7.52 S	129.31 E
Tepalcatepec	234	19.11 N	102.51 W
Tepalcatepec ≃	234	18.50 N	102.05 W
Tepalcatepec, Arroyo ≃	234	17.25 N	100.40 W
Tepalcingo	234	18.36 N	98.51 W
Tepa Point ≻	174v	19.07 S	169.56 W
Tepatepec	234	20.14 N	99.05 W
Tepatitlán [de Morelos]	234	20.49 N	102.44 W
Tepatlaxco [de Hidalgo]	234	19.04 N	97.58 W
Tepe	130	37.48 N	40.47 E
Tepeaca	234	18.58 N	97.54 W
Tepeapulco	234	19.47 N	98.33 W
Tepechitlán	234	21.40 N	103.20 W
Tepecoacuilco [de Trujano]	234	18.18 N	99.29 W
Tepeguaje, Méx.	196	25.40 N	99.50 W
Tepeguaje, Méx.	234	23.30 N	97.50 W
Tepehuanes	232	25.21 N	105.44 W
Tepehuanes, Río los ≃	232	25.10 N	105.25 W
Tepeji del Río	232	19.54 N	99.21 W
Tepelenë	38	40.18 N	20.01 E
Tepelmeme [de Morelos]	234	17.51 N	97.21 W
Tepelská plošina ⋀[1]	60	50.00 N	13.00 E
Tepepan •[8]	286a	19.16 N	99.08 W
Tepetixtla	234	17.13 N	100.08 W
Tepetlixpa	234	19.02 N	98.49 W
Tepi	144	7.10 N	35.23 E
Tepic	234	21.30 N	104.54 W
Tepko	168b	34.58 S	139.11 E
Teplá	60	49.59 N	12.52 E
Teplá ≃	54	50.14 N	12.52 E
Teplice	54	50.39 N	13.48 E
Teplik	78	48.40 N	29.44 E
Teplitz → Teplice	54	50.39 N	13.48 E
Teplooz'orsk	89	49.00 N	131.48 E
Teplovka	80	51.33 N	51.33 E
Teplovo	80	55.25 N	42.56 E
Tepoca, Bahía de C	232	30.15 N	112.50 W
Te Pohue	172	39.15 S	176.41 E
Tepopa, Cabo ≻	232	29.22 N	112.27 W
Teposcolula	234	17.31 N	97.29 W
Te Puia	172	38.04 S	178.18 E
Te Puke	172	37.47 S	176.20 E
Tepuxtepec, Presa ⊜[1]	234	20.02 N	100.13 W
Tepuzhuacán	234	20.53 N	104.33 W
Tequepa, Bahía de C	234	17.17 N	101.05 W
Tequesquite Creek ≃	196	35.40 N	103.43 W
Tequila	234	20.54 N	103.47 W
Tequisquiac	234	19.55 N	99.09 W
Tequisquita Slough ≃	226	36.58 N	121.27 W
Tequma	132	31.27 N	34.35 E
Ter ≃, Esp.	34	42.01 N	3.12 E
Ter ≃, Eng., U.K.	42	51.50 N	0.36 E
Téra	150	14.01 N	0.45 E
Tera ≃	34	41.54 N	5.44 W
Teradomari	92	37.38 N	138.46 E
Terai	94	36.26 N	136.30 E
Ter'ajevo	82	56.11 N	36.07 E
Terakhāda	126	22.56 N	89.40 E
Teralba	170	32.58 S	151.37 E
Teramo	66	42.39 N	13.42 E
Teramo □[6]	66	42.39 N	13.41 E
Terampa	112	3.14 N	106.14 E
Terán	234	16.45 N	93.10 W
Terang	169	38.14 S	142.55 E
Teranum	114	3.44 N	101.49 E
Ter Apel	52	52.53 N	7.04 E
Terarama	164	8.00 S	141.50 E
Teras	114	3.45 N	101.49 E
Teratak	112	0.46 S	110.32 E
Terborg	52	51.55 N	6.21 E
Terbuny	76	52.08 N	38.17 E
Tercan	130	39.47 N	40.24 E
Terceira I	148a	38.43 N	24.13 W
Tercero ≃	252	32.55 S	62.19 W
Terdal	122	16.30 N	75.03 E
Terebovl'a	78	49.18 N	25.43 E
Terebuš	82	54.16 N	38.09 E
Terebutinec	76	59.01 N	33.39 E
Tere-Chol, Ozero ⊜	88	50.35 N	97.30 E
Terechovka	78	52.13 N	31.27 E
Terechovo	82	55.50 N	35.45 E
Te Rehunga	172	40.13 S	176.01 E
Tereida	140	10.35 N	31.17 E
Terek, S.S.S.R.	84	43.29 N	44.08 E
Terek, S.S.S.R.	85	40.01 N	73.33 E
Terek ≃	84	43.44 N	46.33 E
Terekli-Mekteb	84	44.10 N	45.53 E
Terek-Saj	85	41.32 N	71.09 E
Terektinskij Chrebet ⋀	86	50.30 N	86.00 E
Terekty	80	48.34 N	49.02 E
Terence Bay	186	44.28 N	63.43 W
Teren'ga	80	53.42 N	48.24 E
Terengganu □[3]	114	5.00 N	103.00 E
Terengganu ≃	114	5.17 N	103.05 E
Terenino	76	54.31 N	33.35 E
Terenkuduk	80	48.24 N	47.11 E
Terenni ⊥	150	16.30 N	9.35 W
Terenos	255	20.26 S	54.50 W
Terensaj	86	51.36 N	59.31 E
Terenuzek	86	45.05 N	64.59 E
Tereora College ʊ[2]	174k	21.12 S	159.49 W
Teresina	250	5.05 S	42.49 W
Tereška ≃	80	51.48 N	46.26 E
Teresópolis	256	22.26 S	42.59 W
Terespol	30	52.05 N	23.36 E
Teresva	78	48.01 N	23.42 E
Terevaka, Cerro ∧	174z	27.05 S	109.23 W
Terezín	54	50.31 N	14.08 E
Tergauči	85	41.11 N	71.30 E
Tergnier	50	49.39 N	3.18 E
Terhorne	52	53.02 N	5.46 E
Teriang	114	3.14 N	102.25 E
Teriang ≃	114	3.19 N	102.31 E
Terib'orka	24	69.08 N	35.08 E
Teripa ≃	114	3.53 N	96.23 E
Terjärv (Teerijärvi)	26	63.32 N	23.30 E
Terkos Gölü ⊜	130	41.20 N	28.35 E
Terlago	64	46.06 N	11.02 E
Terlano	64	46.32 N	11.15 E
Terlingua	196	29.19 N	103.37 W
Terlingua Creek ≃	196	29.10 N	103.36 W
Terlizzi	68	41.08 N	16.32 E
Terme	130	41.12 N	36.59 E
Terme del Brennero (Brennerbad)	64	46.58 N	11.29 E
Terme di Stigliano	66	42.09 N	12.01 E
Terme di Suio	68	41.18 N	13.51 E
Terme di Valdieri	62	44.12 N	7.16 E
Termeno (Tramin)	64	46.20 N	11.14 E
Termez	72	37.14 N	67.16 E
Termignon	62	45.17 N	6.49 E
Terminal	258	34.09 S	57.31 W
Terminal Island I	280	33.45 N	118.15 W
Terminal Island Coast Guard Base ■	280	33.43 N	118.17 W
Termini Imerese	70	37.59 N	13.42 E
Termini Imerese, Golfo di C	70	38.01 N	13.45 E
Terminillo, Monte ∧	66	42.28 N	13.00 E
Términos, Laguna de C	232	18.37 N	91.33 W
Termit, Massif de ⋀	146	16.15 N	11.17 E
Termoli	66	42.00 N	15.00 E
Termonde → Dendermonde	50	51.02 N	4.07 E
Termsdorf	264a	52.16 N	13.07 E
Tern ≃	42	52.47 N	2.32 W
Ternate, Indon.	108	0.48 N	127.24 E
Ternate, Pil.	116	14.17 N	120.43 E
Ternberg	61	47.58 N	14.22 E
Ternej	89	45.03 N	136.37 E
Terneuzen	52	51.20 N	3.50 E
Terni	66	42.34 N	12.37 E
Terni □[4]	66	42.41 N	12.19 E
Ternitz	61	47.44 N	16.03 E
Ternoise ≃	50	50.23 N	2.01 E
Ternopol'	78	49.34 N	25.36 E
Ternovatoje	78	47.50 N	36.09 E
Ternovka, S.S.S.R.	78	51.40 N	41.37 E
Ternovka, S.S.S.R.	78	47.02 N	32.01 E
Ternovka, S.S.S.R.	78	48.32 N	29.58 E
Ternovka, S.S.S.R.	80	51.19 N	42.56 E
Ternovka, S.S.S.R.	80	53.09 N	45.02 E
Ternovoje	80	51.03 N	43.43 E
Ternovskaja	78	45.53 N	40.24 E
Terolak	114	3.53 N	101.23 E
Terong	114	4.43 N	100.44 E
Terontola	66	43.13 N	12.02 E
Terpe	54	51.32 N	14.19 E
Terpenija, Mys ≻	89	48.39 N	144.44 E
Terpenija, Zaliv C	89	49.00 N	143.30 E
Terra Alta	188	39.27 N	79.31 W
Terra Bella	204	35.58 N	119.03 W
Terra Boa	255	23.45 S	52.27 W
Terrace	182	54.31 N	128.35 W
Terrace Bay	190	48.47 N	87.09 W
Terracina	66	41.17 N	13.15 E
Terra del Sole	66	44.11 N	11.57 E
Terra di Bari •[1]	36	41.10 N	16.50 E
Terral	196	33.54 N	97.57 W
Terralba	71	39.43 N	8.39 E
Terra Linda	226	38.00 N	122.32 W
Terra Nova	186	48.30 N	54.13 W
Terranova → Newfoundland □[4]	176	52.00 N	56.00 W
Terra Nova Bay C	9	74.45 S	164.30 E
Terranova da Sibari	68	39.39 N	16.20 E
Terranova di Pollino	68	39.59 N	16.18 E
Terranova di Sicilia → Gela	70	37.03 N	14.15 E
Terra Nova Lake ⊜	186	48.30 N	54.20 W
Terra Nova National Park ◆	186	48.37 N	53.56 W
Terranuova Bracciolini	66	43.33 N	11.35 E
Terra Rica	255	22.43 S	52.38 W
Terrarossa, Foce di)(	64	44.12 N	10.26 E
Terra Roxa d'Oeste	252	24.08 S	53.59 W
Terras, Pinhal do •[3]	266c	38.39 N	9.02 W
Terra Santa	250	2.06 S	56.29 W
Terrasini	70	38.09 N	13.05 E
Terrasse-Vaudreuil	206	45.24 N	73.59 W
Terrasson-la-Villedieu	32	45.08 N	1.18 E
Terravecchia	68	39.29 N	16.58 E
Terrebonne	206	45.42 N	73.38 W
Terrebonne □[6]	206	46.00 N	74.10 W
Terrebonne Bay C	194	29.09 N	90.35 W
Terre Ceia	220	27.35 N	82.35 W
Terre-de-Bas	241o	15.51 N	61.39 W
Terre-de-Bas I	241o	15.52 N	61.38 W
Terre de Feu → Tierra del Fuego, Isla Grande de I	254	54.00 S	69.00 W
Terre-de-Haut	241o	15.58 N	61.35 W
Terre-de-Haut I	241o	15.52 N	61.35 W
Terre des Hommes ◆	275a	45.31 N	73.32 W
Terre Haute	194	39.28 N	87.24 W
Terre Hill	208	40.10 N	76.03 W
Terrell	222	32.44 N	96.17 W
Terrell, Lake ⊜	224	48.52 N	122.41 W
Terrell Hills	196	29.29 N	98.27 W
Terrenceville	186	47.40 N	54.44 W
Terre-Neuve → Newfoundland □[4]	176	52.00 N	56.00 W
Terrenoire	62	45.26 N	4.26 E
Terre Noire Creek ≃	194	33.49 N	92.55 W
Terre Rouge Creek ≃	194	33.49 N	93.11 W
Terres australes et antarctiques françaises → French Southern and Antarctic Territories □[2]	6	49.30 S	69.30 E
Terrey Hills	170	33.41 S	151.14 E
Terrigal	170	33.27 S	151.27 E
Terrington Saint Clement	42	52.45 N	0.18 E
Territoires du Nord-Ouest → Northwest Territories □[4]	176	70.00 N	100.00 W
Territorio Británico de la Antártica → British Antarctic Territory □[2]	9	60.00 S	45.00 W
Territorio Británico del Oceano Índico → British Indian Ocean Territory □[2]	12	7.00 S	72.00 E
Territorios del Oroeste → Northwest Territories □[4]	176	70.00 N	100.00 W
Terror Point ≻	182	53.10 N	129.56 W
Terrugem	266c	38.51 N	9.20 W
Terry, Miss., U.S.	194	32.05 N	90.18 W
Terry, Mont., U.S.	198	46.47 N	105.19 W
Terry Peak ∧	198	44.19 N	103.50 W
Terryville, Conn., U.S.	207	41.41 N	73.01 W
Terryville, N.Y., U.S.	210	40.54 N	73.03 W
Tersa, S.S.S.R.	80	52.05 N	47.32 E
Tersa, S.S.S.R.	80	50.53 N	43.48 E
Tersa ≃	80	50.46 N	44.40 E
Tersakkan ≃	86	51.15 N	67.10 E
Terschelling I	52	53.24 N	5.20 E
Tersiva, Punta ∧	62	45.37 N	7.28 E
Terskej-Alatau, Chrebet ⋀	85	41.55 N	77.00 E
Terskij Chrebet ⋀	84	43.32 N	45.00 E
Terslev	41	55.22 N	11.59 E
Tersløse	41	55.31 N	11.30 E
Tertenia	71	39.42 N	9.34 E
Terter ≃	84	40.35 N	47.22 E
Teru	123	36.11 N	72.45 E
Teruapu, Passe ⋓	174s	17.34 S	149.47 W
Teruel, Col.	246	2.44 N	75.33 W
Teruel, Esp.	34	40.21 N	1.06 W
Terujak	114	4.23 N	97.31 E
Terutao, Ko I	114	6.35 N	99.40 E
Tervakoski	26	60.48 N	24.37 E
Tervel	38	43.45 N	27.24 E
Tervola	26	66.05 N	24.48 E
Tervuren	56	50.49 N	4.31 E
Terwagne	56	50.27 N	5.20 E
Terwolde	52	52.16 N	6.06 E
Terzaghi Dam •[5]	182	50.49 N	122.12 W
Terzigno	68	40.48 N	14.29 E
Teržola	84	42.12 N	42.59 E
Tes	88	50.31 N	93.36 E
Tésa, Magy.	30	48.02 N	18.51 E
Teša, S.S.S.R.	80	55.30 N	42.50 E
Teša ≃	80	55.38 N	42.09 E
Tesalia	246	2.29 N	75.44 W
Tešanj	38	44.37 N	18.00 E
Tesaret, Oued ∨	148	26.18 N	1.58 E
Tes-Chem (Tesijn) ≃	88	50.28 N	93.04 E
Teschen → Český Těšín	30	49.45 N	18.37 E
Teschendorf	54	52.51 N	13.10 E
Tescott	198	39.01 N	97.53 W
Tesdrero, Cerro ∧	234	22.47 N	103.04 W
Teseney	144	15.07 N	36.41 E
Tesero	64	46.17 N	11.31 E
Teshekpuk Lake ⊜	180	70.35 N	153.30 W
Teshi	150	5.35 N	0.05 W
Teshikaga	92a	43.29 N	144.28 E
Te-shima I, Nihon	96	34.24 N	133.40 E
Te-shima I, Nihon	96	34.29 N	134.05 E
Teshio	92a	44.53 N	141.44 E
Teshio ≃	92a	44.53 N	141.44 E
Teshio-sanchi ⋀	92a	44.15 N	142.05 E
Tešig	88	49.56 N	102.34 E
Tesimo (Tisens)	64	46.34 N	11.10 E
Teslić	38	44.37 N	17.51 E
Teslin	180	60.09 N	132.45 W
Teslin ≃	180	61.34 N	134.54 W
Teslin Lake ⊜	180	60.15 N	132.57 W
Teso □[5]	154	1.45 N	33.40 E
Tesouras ≃	255	14.36 S	50.51 W
Tesouro	255	16.04 S	53.34 W
Tesovo	82	55.34 N	36.05 E
Tesperhude	52	53.24 N	10.26 E
Tessa, Oued ≃	36	36.34 N	8.54 E
Tessala, Djebel ∧	34	35.17 N	0.48 W
Tessala, Monts du ⋀	34	35.25 N	0.45 W
Tessalit	150	20.12 N	1.00 E
Tessancourt-sur-Aubette	261	49.02 N	1.55 E
Tessaoua	150	13.45 N	7.59 E
Tessei	96	34.56 N	133.20 E
Tessenderlo	56	51.04 N	5.05 E
Tesserete	58	46.04 N	8.58 E
Tessik Lake ⊜	176	64.53 N	75.25 W
Tessin	54	54.01 N	12.28 E
Tessin → Ticino □[3]	58	46.20 N	8.45 E
Tessy-sur-Vire	32	48.58 N	1.04 W
Test ≃	42	50.55 N	1.29 W
Testa, Capo ≻	71	41.14 N	9.08 E
Teştik	130	40.08 N	38.45 E
Teston, Ont., Can.	275b	43.52 N	79.32 W
Teston, Eng., U.K.	260	51.15 N	0.26 E
Testour	36	36.33 N	9.27 E
Têt ≃	32	42.44 N	3.02 E
Tetachuck Lake ⊜	182	53.20 N	125.50 W
Tetagouche ≃	186	47.38 N	65.41 W
Tetas, Punta ≻	252	23.31 S	70.38 W
Tetbury	42	51.39 N	2.10 W
Tete	154	16.13 S	33.35 E
Tete □[5]	154	15.15 S	32.40 E
Tête-à-la-Baleine	186	50.41 N	59.20 W
Tête du Parmelan ∧	58	45.57 N	6.14 E
Tête-Jaune-Cache	182	52.57 N	119.26 W
Te Teko	172	38.02 S	176.48 E
Tétépisca, Lac ⊜	186	51.00 N	69.25 W
Teterboro	276	40.52 N	74.03 W
Teterboro Airport ⊠	276	40.51 N	74.04 W
Téterchen	56	49.14 N	6.34 E
Tetere ≃	88	59.30 N	105.00 E
Teterev ≃	78	51.01 N	30.05 E
Teterow	54	53.46 N	12.34 E
Teteven	38	42.55 N	24.16 E
Tetiaroa I[1]	14	17.05 S	149.32 W
Tetijev	78	49.23 N	29.41 E
Tetipari I	175e	8.43 S	157.33 E
Tetla	234	19.26 N	98.06 W
Tetlin	180	63.08 N	142.31 W
Tetlin Lake ⊜	180	63.05 N	142.45 W
Teton	202	43.59 N	111.40 W
Teton ≃, Idaho, U.S.	202	43.54 N	111.51 W
Teton ≃, Mont., U.S.	202	47.56 N	110.31 W
Tetonia	202	43.49 N	111.10 W
Tétouan	148	35.34 N	5.23 W
Tetovo	38	42.01 N	20.58 E
Tétreauville •[8]	275a	45.36 N	73.32 W
Tetri-Ckaro	84	41.34 N	44.28 E
Tetschen → Děčín	54	50.48 N	14.13 E
Tetsuta	96	34.56 N	133.28 E
Tettau	54	50.28 N	11.15 E
Tettenhall	42	52.36 N	2.09 W
Tettens	52	53.38 N	7.53 E
Tettnang	58	47.40 N	9.35 E
Tetuán → Tétouan	148	35.34 N	5.23 W
Tet'uche	89	44.35 N	135.35 E
Tet'uche-Pristan'	89	44.22 N	135.48 E
Tetufera, Mont ∧	174s	17.40 S	149.26 W
Tetulbăria	126	21.58 N	90.03 E
Tetulia ≃[1]	126	22.15 N	90.37 E
Teturi	154	1.04 N	29.08 E
Tet'uši	80	54.57 N	48.50 E
Tet'usskoje	80	54.18 N	48.03 E
Teublitz	60	49.13 N	12.05 E

Symbols in the index entries represent the broad categories identified in the key at the right. Symbols with superior numbers (⋀[2]) identify subcategories (see complete key on page I · 30).

Kartensymbole in dem Registerverzeichnis stellen die rechts in Schlüssel erklärten Kategorien dar. Symbole mit hochgestellten Ziffern (⋀[2]) bezeichnen Unterabteilungen einer Kategorie (vgl. vollständiger Schlüssel auf Seite I · 30).

Los símbolos incluidos en el texto del índice representan las grandes categorias identificadas con la clave a la derecha. Los símbolos con numeros en su parte superior (⋀[2]) identifican las subcategorias (véase la clave completa en la página I · 30).

Les symboles de l'index représentent les catégories indiquées dans la légende à droite. Les symboles suivis d'un indice (⋀[2]) représentent des sous-catégories (voir légende complète à la page I · 30).

Os símbolos incluídos no texto do índice representam as grandes categorias identificadas com a chave à direita. Os símbolos com números em sua parte superior (⋀[2]) identificam as subcategorias (veja-se a chave completa à página I · 30).

∧ Mountain	Berg	Montaña	Montagne	Montanha
⋀ Mountains	Berge	Montañas	Montagnes	Montanhas
)(Pass	Pass	Paso	Col	Passo
∨ Valley, Canyon	Tal, Cañon	Valle, Cañón	Vallée, Canyon	Vale, Canhão
⌣ Plain	Ebene	Llano	Plaine	Planície
≻ Cape	Kap	Cabo	Cap	Cabo
I Island	Insel	Isla	Île	Ilha
II Islands	Inseln	Islas	Îles	Ilhas
◆ Other Topographic Features	Andere Topographische Objekte	Otros Elementos Topográficos	Autres données topographiques	Outros Elementos Topográficos

ESPAÑOL

Nombre	Página	Lat.°′	Long.°′ W=Oeste
Teuchern	54	51.07 N	12.01 E
Teuco ≃	252	25.38 S	60.12 W
Teufelshöhle •[5]	60	49.45 N	11.25 E
Teufels-Insel → Diable, Île du I	250	5.17 N	52.35 W
Teufelsmoor ◆[3]	52	53.15 N	8.50 E
Teufen	58	47.23 N	9.23 E
Teufenbach	61	47.08 N	14.21 E
Teulada	71	38.58 N	8.46 E
Teulada, Capo ≻	71	38.52 N	8.38 E
Teúl de González Ortega	234	21.28 N	103.29 W
Teulon	184	50.23 N	97.16 W
Teun, Pulau I	164	6.59 S	129.08 E
Teunom ≃	114	4.26 N	95.48 E
Teunz	60	49.29 N	12.23 E
Teupitz	54	52.08 N	13.36 E
Teuplitz → Tuplice	30	51.41 N	14.50 E
Teureubangan Cut	114	3.12 N	97.18 E
Teuri-tō I	92a	44.25 N	141.19 E
Teuschnitz	54	50.24 N	11.23 E
Teutleben	54	50.57 N	10.33 E
Teutli, Cerro del Λ	286a	19.14 N	99.01 W
Teutoburger Wald ◆[3]	52	52.10 N	8.15 E
Teutopolis	194	39.08 N	88.29 W
Teutschenthal	54	51.27 N	11.46 E
Teuva	26	62.29 N	21.44 E
Tevere ≃	66	41.44 N	12.14 E
Teverya (Tiberias)	132	32.47 N	35.32 E
Teviot ≃	46	55.35 N	2.26 W
Teviot Brook ≃	171a	27.51 S	152.57 E
Teviotdale V	44	55.25 N	2.50 W
Teviothead	44	55.21 N	2.56 W
Tevli	76	52.20 N	24.15 E
Tevriz	86	57.34 N	72.24 E
Te Waewae Bay ⊂	172	46.15 S	167.30 E
Tewah	112	1.05 S	113.42 E
Te Whaiti	172	38.35 S	176.47 E
Tewkesbury	42	51.59 N	2.09 W
Tewksbury	207	42.37 N	71.14 W
Tew-Mac Airport ⊠	283	42.36 N	71.12 W
Texada Island I	182	49.40 N	124.24 W
Texarkana, Ark., U.S.	194	33.26 N	94.02 W
Texarkana, Tex., U.S.	194	33.26 N	94.03 W
Texas, Austl.	166	28.51 S	151.11 E
Texas, Ohio, U.S.	216	41.26 N	83.57 W
Texas □[3]	178		
	196	31.30 N	99.00 W
Texas City	222	29.23 N	94.54 W
Texcaltitlán	234	18.54 N	99.55 W
Texcoco □[7]	286a	19.28 N	99.01 W
Texcoco, Lago de ⊜	234	19.30 N	99.00 W
Texcoco [de Mora]	234	19.31 N	98.53 W
Texel I	52	53.05 N	4.45 E
Texhoma	196	36.30 N	101.47 W
Texico	196	34.23 N	103.03 W
Texistepec	234	17.53 N	94.47 W
Texline	196	36.23 N	103.01 W
Texoma, Lake ⊜[1]	196	33.55 N	96.37 W
Teyá	266d	41.30 N	2.19 E
Teyateyaneng	158	29.07 S	27.34 E
Teyéa ⊥	38	37.29 N	22.24 E
Teylān	120	35.32 N	64.47 E
Teynham	42	51.20 N	0.50 E
Teyvareh	120	33.21 N	64.25 E
Teza ≃	80	56.32 N	41.53 E
Teziutlán	234	19.49 N	97.21 W
Težler, Gora Λ	84	40.42 N	44.37 E
Tezoatlán [de Segura y Luna]	234	17.42 N	97.49 W
Tezpur	120	26.38 N	92.48 E
Tezzeron Lake ⊜	182	54.41 N	124.25 W
Tha ≃	110	20.07 N	100.36 E
Tha-anne ≃	176	60.31 N	94.37 W
Thabana Ntlenyana Λ	158	29.28 S	29.17 E
Thaba Nchu	158	29.17 S	26.52 E
Thabankulu Λ	158	27.30 S	30.20 E
Thaba Putsoa Range ⩕	158	29.45 S	27.55 E
Thabaung	110	17.02 N	94.48 E
Thabawleikkyi	110	12.01 N	99.12 E
Thabazimbi	156	24.41 S	27.21 E
Thabor, Mont Λ	62	45.07 N	6.34 E
Thabyu	110	15.36 N	98.29 E
Thach-by	110	14.40 N	109.04 E
Thacher Island I	207	42.38 N	70.35 W
Thādiq	128	25.18 N	45.52 E
Thagyettaw	110	13.45 N	98.09 E
Thai-binh	110	20.27 N	106.20 E
Thailand □[1]	108		
	110	15.00 N	100.00 E
Thailand, Gulf of ⊂	110	10.00 N	101.00 E
Thaïlande → Thailand □[1]	110	15.00 N	100.00 E
Thailandia → Thailand □[1]	110	15.00 N	100.00 E
Thai Muang	110	8.24 N	98.16 E
Thai-nguyen	110	21.36 N	105.50 E
Thak	120	30.32 N	70.13 E
Thakhek → Muang Khammouan	110	17.24 N	104.48 E
Thākurdwāra	124	29.12 N	78.51 E
Thākurdwāri	272b	22.34 N	88.28 E
Thākurgaon	124	26.02 N	88.28 E
Thākurpukur	272b	22.28 N	88.19 E
Thākurvādi	272c	18.54 N	73.04 E
Thal, D.D.R.	54	50.55 N	10.23 E
Thal, Pāk.	123	33.22 N	70.33 E
Tha'l, Jabal Λ	140	14.13 N	24.14 E
Thala	36	35.35 N	8.40 E
Thalang	110	8.01 N	98.19 E
Thal-Assling	64	46.47 N	12.38 E
Thal Desert ◆[2]	123	31.30 N	71.40 E
Thale	54	51.45 N	11.02 E
Thalfang	56	49.45 N	6.59 E
Thalgau	64	47.50 N	13.15 E
Thalheim, B.R.D.	60	49.28 N	11.33 E
Thalheim, D.D.R.	54	50.42 N	12.51 E
Tha Li	110	17.37 N	101.25 E
Thalia	196	33.59 N	99.32 W
Thalitter	56	51.13 N	8.53 E
Thalkirch	58	46.38 N	9.16 E
Thallon	166	28.38 S	148.52 E
Thallwitz	54	51.26 N	12.40 E
Thalmah, Jabal Λ	142	29.00 N	32.34 E
Thalmah, Marsā ⊂	142	29.03 N	32.38 E
Thalmässing	60	49.05 N	11.13 E
Thalwil	58	47.17 N	8.34 E
Thambach	60	48.25 N	12.32 E
Thame	42	51.45 N	0.59 W
Thames	172	37.08 S	175.33 E
Thames ≃, Ont., Can.	190	42.19 N	82.28 W
Thames ≃, Eng., U.K.	42	51.28 N	0.43 E
Thames ≃, Conn., U.S.	207	41.18 N	72.05 W
Thames, Firth Of ⊂	172	37.00 S	175.25 E
Thames Ditton	260	51.23 N	0.21 W
Thames Estuary ⊂[1]	260	51.30 N	0.40 W
Thamesford	212	43.04 N	81.00 W
Thames Haven	260	51.30 N	0.31 E
Thamesville	214	42.33 N	81.59 W
Thāmir, Jabal Λ	144	13.53 N	45.30 E
Thāmit, Wādī V	146	31.15 N	16.06 E
Thammasat, University of ♁[2]	269a	13.45 N	100.30 E
Thamnūn	144	15.07 N	50.49 E

FRANÇAIS

Nom	Page	Lat.°′	Long.°′ W=Ouest
Thamūd ⍑[4]	144	17.15 N	49.54 E
Thāna, Bhārat	122		
	272c	19.12 N	72.58 E
Thāna, Pāk.	128	28.55 N	63.45 E
Thāna □[5]	272c	19.12 N	73.05 E
Thāna Creek ⊂	272c	19.00 N	72.57 E
Thāna Ghāzi	124	27.25 N	76.19 E
Thāna Kasba	124	25.13 N	77.20 E
Thanbyuzayat	110	15.58 N	97.44 E
Thandaung	110	19.04 N	96.41 E
Thānedārwāla	123	32.36 N	71.07 E
Thānesar	124	29.59 N	76.49 E
Thanet, Isle of I	42	51.22 N	1.20 E
Thanet Lake ⊜	212	44.47 N	77.46 W
Thang-binh	110	15.44 N	108.22 E
Thangoo	162	18.10 S	122.22 E
Thangool	166	24.29 S	150.35 E
Thanh-hoa	110	19.48 N	105.46 E
Thanh-my-tay	269c	10.49 N	106.46 E
Thanh-pho Ho Chi Minh	110		
	269c	10.45 N	106.40 E
Thanjāvūr	122	10.48 N	79.09 E
Thānkot	124	27.41 N	85.11 E
Thann	58	47.49 N	7.05 E
Thannhausen	58	48.17 N	10.28 E
Thāno Bula Khān	120	25.22 N	67.50 E
Than-uyen	110	22.00 N	103.54 E
Thaon-les-Vosges	58	48.15 N	6.25 E
Tha Pla	110	17.48 N	100.32 E
Thap Than ≃	110	15.21 N	104.06 E
Tharabwin West	110	12.17 N	99.03 E
Tharād	120	24.24 N	71.38 E
Tharandt	54	50.59 N	13.35 E
't Harde	52	52.25 N	5.53 E
Thar Desert (Great Indian Desert) ◆[2]	120	27.00 N	71.00 E
Thargomindah	166	28.00 S	143.49 E
Thāri Pātan Λ	124	28.58 N	82.04 E
Thar Nhom	140	7.26 N	30.29 E
Tharptown	210	40.48 N	76.34 W
Tharr, Wüste → Thar Desert ◆[2]	120	27.00 N	71.00 E
Tharrawaddy	110	17.39 N	95.48 E
Tharrawaw	110	17.41 N	95.28 E
Tharros ⊥	71	39.52 N	8.26 E
Tharsuinn, Beinn Λ	46	57.47 N	4.21 W
Tharthār, Wādī ath- V	128	33.59 N	43.12 E
Tharwa	171b	35.31 S	149.04 E
Tha Sala	110	8.40 N	99.56 E
Thásos	38	40.47 N	24.42 E
Thásos I	38	40.41 N	24.47 E
Thásos ⊥	38	40.46 N	24.33 E
Tha Tako	110	15.38 N	100.29 E
Thatcham	42	51.25 N	1.15 W
Thatch Cay I	240m	18.22 N	64.52 W
Thatcher	200	32.51 N	109.46 W
Thatch Island I	276	40.38 N	73.23 W
That-khe	110	22.16 N	106.28 E
Thaton	110	16.55 N	97.22 E
That Phanom	110	16.57 N	104.44 E
Thatto Heath	262	53.26 N	2.45 W
Tha Tum	110	15.19 N	103.41 E
Thau, Bassin de ⊂	32	43.23 N	3.36 E
Thaungdut	110	24.26 N	94.42 E
Thaungyin ≃	110	17.50 N	97.42 E
Tha Uthen	110	17.34 N	104.36 E
Thawville	216	40.41 N	88.07 W
Thaxted	42	51.57 N	0.20 E
Thaya (Dyje) ≃	30	48.37 N	16.56 E
Thayawthadangyi Kyun I	110	12.20 N	98.00 E
Thayer, Ill., U.S.	219	39.32 N	89.46 W
Thayer, Ind., U.S.	216	41.10 N	87.20 W
Thayer, Kans., U.S.	198	37.30 N	95.28 W
Thayer, Mo., U.S.	194	36.31 N	91.33 W
Thayetchaung	110	13.52 N	98.16 E
Thayetmyo	110	19.19 N	95.11 E
Thayngen	58	47.45 N	8.42 E
Thazi	110	20.51 N	96.05 E
Theale	42	51.27 N	1.04 W
Thealka	192	37.49 N	82.47 W
The Basin	274b	37.51 S	145.19 E
Thebes	194	37.13 N	89.28 W
Thebes ⊥	140	25.42 N	32.37 E
The Bight	238	24.19 N	75.24 W
The Birket ≃	262	53.24 N	3.01 W
The Bluffs •[4]	210	43.22 N	76.40 W
The Bourne ≃	260	51.22 N	0.29 W
The Calvados Chain II	164	11.10 S	152.40 E
The Capital ♁	284c	38.53 N	77.00 W
The Cheviot Λ	44	55.28 N	2.09 W
The Church of the Holy Sepulchre ♁[1]	132	31.46 N	35.14 E
The Coorong ⊂	168b	35.40 S	139.15 E
The Coteau ⩕[2]	184	51.10 N	107.30 W
The Coves Palisades State Park ♠	202	44.34 N	121.15 W
The Curragh ♠	48	53.10 N	6.52 W
The Dalles	224	45.36 N	121.10 W
The Dalles Dam ◆[6]	224	45.37 N	121.08 W
The Deeps ⊂	46a	60.09 N	1.23 W
Thedford	198	41.59 N	100.35 W
Thedinghausen	52	52.58 N	9.01 E
The Dome of the Rock (Mosque of Omar) ♁[1]	132	31.47 N	35.13 E
The Downs ⍑[3]	42	51.13 N	1.27 E
Theebine	166	25.57 S	152.33 E
The English Companys Islands II	164	11.50 S	136.32 E
The Entrance	170	33.21 S	151.30 E
Theessen	54	52.14 N	12.02 E
The Everglades ☷	220	26.00 N	80.40 W
The Father Λ	164	5.03 S	151.20 E
The Fens ☷	42	52.38 N	0.02 E
The Fiery Range ⩕	171b	35.30 S	148.40 E
The Flash ⊜	262	53.29 N	2.33 W
The Flat Tops ⩕	200	40.00 N	107.10 W
The Forest of Nisene Marks State Park ♠	226	37.03 N	121.53 W
The Glenkens ◆[1]	44	55.10 N	4.15 W
Thègon	110	18.39 N	95.25 E
The Granites	162	20.35 S	130.21 E
The Granites Λ	162	20.35 S	130.20 E
The Graves II	283	42.22 N	70.52 W
The Grove	222	31.16 N	97.32 W
The Hague → 's-Gravenhage	52	52.06 N	4.18 E
The Heads ≻	202	42.44 N	124.31 W
The Home Park ♠	260	51.28 N	0.36 W
The Hunters Hills ⩕[2]	172	44.30 S	170.50 E
Theinkun	110	11.53 N	99.09 E
The Isles Lagoon ⊂	174o	1.50 N	157.23 W
Theiss → Tisa ≃	38	45.15 N	20.17 E
Theissen	54	51.05 N	12.06 E
The Key Indian Reserve ◆[4]	184	51.45 N	102.08 W
The Lake Fleet Islands II	212	44.18 N	76.07 W
Thelon ≃	176	64.16 N	96.05 W
The Long Mynd Λ	42	52.35 N	2.48 W
The Lower Hope ≃[1]	260	51.28 N	0.28 E
Thelwall	262	53.23 N	2.32 W
The Lynd	166	18.56 S	144.30 E
Them	41	56.06 N	9.33 E
The Machars □[8]	44	54.50 N	4.30 W
The Machars ◆[1]	44	55.20 N	4.33 W

PORTUGUÊS

Nome	Página	Lat.°′	Long.°′ W=Oeste
Themar	54	50.30 N	10.37 E
The Meadows Race Track ♠	279b	40.13 N	80.12 W
The Mere ⊜	262	53.20 N	2.24 W
Théméricourt	261	49.05 N	1.54 E
The Minch ⋓	46	58.10 N	5.50 W
The Moors ◆[1]	44	54.56 N	4.40 W
The Mumbles	42	51.34 N	4.00 W
Then	123	32.26 N	75.44 E
The Narrows ⋓	276	40.37 N	74.03 W
The Navy Islands II	212	44.21 N	76.03 W
The Naze ≻	42	51.53 N	1.16 E
The Needles ≻	42	50.39 N	1.34 W
Thénezay	32	46.43 N	0.02 W
Thenia	148	36.43 N	3.34 E
The Oa ◆[1]	46	55.37 N	6.16 W
The Oaks, Austl.	170	34.04 S	150.34 E
The Oaks, Calif., U.S.	226	39.13 N	121.05 W
Theodore, Austl.	166	24.57 S	150.05 E
Theodore, Sask., Can.	184	51.25 N	102.54 W
Theodore, Ala., U.S.	194	30.33 N	88.10 W
Theodore Francis Green Airport ⊠	207	41.44 N	71.26 W
Theodore Roosevelt Island I	284c	38.54 N	77.03 W
Theodore Roosevelt Lake ⊜[1]	200	33.42 N	111.07 W
Theodore Roosevelt National Park (North Unit) ♠, N. Dak., U.S.	198	47.34 N	103.24 W
Theodore Roosevelt National Park (South Unit) ♠, N. Dak., U.S.	198	46.55 N	103.26 W
Theodor-Heuss-Brücke ◆[5]	263	51.15 N	6.45 E
Theog	123	31.07 N	77.21 E
Theólogos	38	40.39 N	24.41 E
Théoule-sur-Mer	62	43.31 N	6.57 E
The Oval ⊥	260	51.29 N	0.07 W
The Pages II	168b	35.47 S	138.17 E
The Paps Λ	48	52.00 N	9.17 W
The Pas	184	53.50 N	101.15 W
The Peak Λ	192	36.24 N	81.39 W
Thepha	110	6.52 N	100.58 E
The Pilot Λ	166	36.45 S	148.13 E
The Pinnacle Λ[2]	219	39.22 N	90.55 W
Thérain ≃	50	49.15 N	2.27 E
The Rajah Λ	182	53.15 N	118.31 W
The Rand → Witwatersrand ◆[1]	158	26.00 S	27.00 E
The Range	154	19.00 S	31.04 E
Theresa	212	44.13 N	75.48 W
Theresa Creek ≃	166	23.26 S	148.09 E
Theresa Park	274a	34.01 S	150.39 E
Theresienstadt → Terezín	54	50.31 N	14.08 E
The Rhins ≻[1]	44	54.50 N	5.00 W
The Rip ⊂	169	38.17 S	144.37 E
The Riverstone Wildlife Refuge ◆[4]	274a	33.42 S	150.51 E
Thermaïkós Kólpos ⊂	38	40.23 N	22.47 E
Thermalito	226	39.31 N	121.36 W
Thermopílai ⊥	38	38.48 N	22.33 E
Thermopolis	200	43.39 N	108.13 W
Thermopylae → Thermopílai ⊥	38	38.48 N	22.33 E
The Road ⊂	42a	49.56 N	6.20 W
The Rock	166	35.16 S	147.07 E
The Rockies Λ	224	46.39 N	122.22 W
Theron Mountains ⩕	9	79.05 S	28.15 W
The Rope •[4]	174e	25.04 S	130.05 W
Thérouanne	50	50.38 N	2.15 E
The Royal National Park ♠	170	34.10 S	151.05 E
The Savannahs ⊜	220	27.19 N	80.17 W
Theseion ⊥	267c	37.58 N	23.43 E
Thesiger Bay ⊂	176	71.30 N	124.05 W
The Sisters Λ[2]	162	26.17 S	126.40 E
The Slot ⋓	175e	8.00 S	158.10 E
The Sluice ≊	262	53.41 N	2.57 W
The Sny ≃	219	39.16 N	90.44 W
The Solent ⋓	42	50.46 N	1.20 W
The Sound ⋓, Austl.	274a	33.49 S	151.17 E
The Sound (Øresund) ⋓, Eur.	41	55.50 N	12.40 E
The Springs	207	41.01 N	72.09 W
Thesprotikón	38	39.15 N	20.47 E
Thessalía ◆[1]	38	39.30 N	22.00 E
Thessalon	190	46.15 N	83.34 W
Thessaloníki (Salonika)	38	40.38 N	22.56 E
Thessalonique → Thessaloníki	38	40.38 N	22.56 E
The Storr Λ	46	57.31 N	6.12 W
The Swale ⋓	42	51.22 N	0.56 E
Thet ≃	42	52.27 N	0.33 E
The Terraces •[4]	162	28.40 S	121.30 E
Thetford	42	52.25 N	0.45 E
Thetford Mines	206	46.05 N	71.18 W
The Thumbs Λ	172	43.36 S	170.44 E
Thetis Island	224	49.59 N	123.40 W
Thetis Island I	224	49.00 N	123.41 W
The Twelve Pins Λ	48	53.31 N	9.50 W
The Twins Λ	172	41.14 S	172.39 E
Theuern	60	49.22 N	11.55 E
Theunissen	158	28.30 S	26.41 E
Theux	56	50.32 N	5.49 E
The Valley	238	18.13 N	63.04 W
Thevenard	162	32.09 S	133.38 E
Thevenard Island I	162	21.27 S	115.00 E
The Village	196	35.35 N	97.33 W
The Wash ⊂	42	52.55 N	0.15 E
The Weald ◆[1]	42	51.05 N	0.05 E
The Whirlpool ≃	284a	43.07 N	79.04 W
The Winehead Λ	210	40.58 N	77.28 W
The Wrekin Λ[2]	42	52.41 N	2.34 W
Theydon Bois	260	51.40 N	0.06 E
Theys	62	45.18 N	6.00 E
Thiais	261	48.46 N	2.23 E
Thiant	50	50.18 N	3.27 E
Thiaucourt-Regniéville	56	48.57 N	5.52 E
Thibaudeau	184	57.05 N	94.08 W
Thiberville	50	49.08 N	0.27 E
Thibodaux	194	29.48 N	90.49 W
Thicket	222	30.24 N	94.38 W
Thicket Portage	184	55.19 N	97.42 W
Thiéblemont-Farémont	58	48.41 N	4.44 E
Thief ≃	198	48.08 N	96.10 W
Thief River Falls	198	48.07 N	96.10 W
Thièle ≃	58	47.03 N	7.05 E
Thiel Mountains ⩕	9	85.15 S	91.00 W
Thielsen, Mount Λ	202	43.09 N	122.04 W
Thiendorf	54	51.17 N	13.44 E
Thiene	64	45.42 N	11.29 E
Thiensville	216	43.14 N	87.58 W
Thier	263	51.05 N	7.22 E
Thiérache, Collines de la ⩕[2]	50	49.50 N	3.50 E
Thierhaupten	56	48.34 N	10.54 E
Thiers	62	45.51 N	3.34 E
Thiersheim	54	50.04 N	12.07 E
Thierville-sur-Meuse	56	49.10 N	5.21 E
Thiès	150	14.48 N	16.56 W
Thiès □[4]	150	14.45 N	16.50 W
Thiesi	71	40.31 N	8.43 E
Thiessow	54	54.16 N	13.43 E
Thieux	261	49.01 N	2.40 E
Thieveley Pike Λ[2]	262	53.45 N	2.12 W
Thika	154	1.03 S	37.05 E
Thikombia I	175g	15.44 S	179.55 W
Thilay	56	49.52 N	4.49 E
Thilenius, Cape ≻	164	1.35 S	149.57 E
Thimbu	124	27.28 N	89.39 E
Thines	62	44.29 N	4.03 E
Thingvallavatn ⊜	24a	64.12 N	21.10 W
Thingvellir	24a	64.17 N	21.07 W
Thio	175f	21.37 S	166.14 E
Thionville	56	49.22 N	6.10 E
Thiou	150	13.48 N	2.40 W
Thíra	38	36.25 N	25.26 E
Thíra I	38	36.24 N	25.29 E
Third ≃	276	40.49 N	74.08 W
Third Cataract → Ash-Shallāl ath-Thālith ⌊	140	19.49 N	30.19 E
Third Cliff •[4]	283	42.11 N	70.43 W
Third Creek ≃, Mo., U.S.	219	38.26 N	91.40 W
Third Creek ≃, N.C., U.S.	192	35.47 N	80.31 W
Third Herring Brook ≃	283	42.07 N	70.48 W
Third Lake ⊜	206	45.14 N	71.12 W
Third Street Station ◆[5]	282	37.46 N	122.23 W
Thirlmere	170	34.12 S	150.34 E
Thirlmere ⊜	44	54.33 N	3.04 W
Thiron	50	48.19 N	0.59 E
Thironne ≃	50	48.17 N	1.15 E
Thirroul	170	34.19 S	150.56 E
Thirsk	44	54.14 N	1.20 W
Thirtieth Street Station ◆[5]	285	39.57 N	75.11 W
Thirtymile Creek ≃	198	46.22 N	102.03 W
Thirtymile Point ≻	210	43.22 N	78.29 W
Thisted	26	56.57 N	8.42 E
Thistilfjördur ⊂	24a	66.20 N	15.25 W
Thistledown Race Track ♠	279a	41.26 N	81.32 W
Thistle Island I	166	35.00 S	136.09 E
Thistletown ◆[8]	275b	43.44 N	79.33 W
Thithia I	175g	17.45 S	179.18 W
Thívai (Thebes)	38	38.21 N	23.19 E
Thiverval-Grignon	261	48.51 N	1.55 E
Thiviers	32	45.25 N	0.56 E
Thizy	32	46.02 N	4.19 E
Thjórsá ≃	24a	63.47 N	20.48 W
Thlewiaza ≃	176	60.28 N	94.45 W
Thoa ≃	176	60.30 N	109.47 W
Thoen	110	17.36 N	99.12 E
Thoi-binh	110	9.21 N	105.05 E
Thoirette	58	46.16 N	5.32 E
Thoiry	261	48.52 N	1.48 E
Thoissey	58	46.10 N	4.48 E
Tholen	52	51.32 N	4.12 E
Tholen I	52	51.35 N	4.05 E
Tholey	56	49.29 N	7.02 E
Thollon	58	46.23 N	6.43 E
Thomas, Okla., U.S.	196	35.45 N	98.45 W
Thomas, Pa., U.S.	279b	40.15 N	80.06 W
Thomas, Wash., U.S.	224	47.21 N	122.14 W
Thomas, W. Va., U.S.	188	39.09 N	79.30 W
Thomasboro	216	40.15 N	88.11 W
Thomas J. O'Brien Lock and Dam ◆[5]	278	41.39 N	87.35 W
Thomas Lake ⊜	184	57.00 N	96.43 W
Thomas Mountains ⩕	9	75.32 S	70.57 W
Thomas Point ≻	208	38.54 N	76.28 W
Thomaston, Ala., U.S.	194	32.11 N	87.37 W
Thomaston, Conn., U.S.	207	41.40 N	73.04 W
Thomaston, Ga., U.S.	192	32.54 N	84.20 W
Thomaston, Maine, U.S.	188	44.05 N	69.10 W
Thomaston, N.Y., U.S.	276	40.47 N	73.43 W
Thomaston, Tex., U.S.	222	28.60 N	97.09 W
Thomastown, Austl.	274b	37.41 S	145.01 E
Thomastown, Eire	48	52.31 N	7.08 W
Thomasville, Ala., U.S.	194	31.55 N	87.51 W
Thomasville, Ga., U.S.	192	30.50 N	83.59 W
Thomasville, N.C., U.S.	192	35.53 N	80.05 W
Thomasville, Pa., U.S.	208	39.56 N	76.51 W
Thom Bay ⊂	176	70.09 N	92.00 W
Thomes Creek ≃	204	39.59 N	122.06 W
Thom Lake ⊜	184	55.24 N	96.08 W
Thomlinson, Mount Λ	182	55.33 N	127.29 W
Thompson, Man., Can.	184	55.45 N	97.45 W
Thompson, Conn., U.S.	207	41.57 N	71.52 W
Thompson, Iowa, U.S.	190	43.22 N	93.46 W
Thompson, Mo., U.S.	219	39.11 N	91.59 W
Thompson, Ohio, U.S.	214	41.41 N	81.03 W
Thompson, Pa., U.S.	210	41.52 N	75.31 W
Thompson ≃, B.C., Can.	182	50.15 N	121.33 W
Thompson ≃, U.S.	194	39.45 N	93.36 W
Thompson Creek ≃, U.S.	198	45.04 N	104.25 W
Thompson Creek ≃, Miss., U.S.	194	31.10 N	88.54 W
Thompson Falls	202	47.36 N	115.21 W
Thompson Island I	283	42.23 N	71.01 W
Thompson Lake ⊜[1]	184	49.45 N	106.35 W
Thompson Pass)(	180	61.08 N	145.45 W
Thompson Peak Λ	204	41.00 N	123.03 W
Thompson Place	224	47.03 N	122.45 W
Thompson Ridge	210	41.34 N	74.20 W
Thompson Run ≃	279b	40.24 N	79.50 W
Thompsons	222	29.30 N	95.36 W
Thompsons Creek ≃	284a	43.03 N	79.08 W
Thompson Sound ⋓	172	45.09 S	166.57 E
Thompsontown	208	40.33 N	77.14 W
Thompsonville	190	44.31 N	85.56 W
Thomsen ≃	176	74.08 N	119.35 W
Thomson, Ga., U.S.	192	33.28 N	82.30 W
Thomson, Ill., U.S.	190	41.58 N	90.06 W
Thomson, N.Y., U.S.	210	43.07 N	73.35 W
Thomson ≃, Austl.	166	25.11 S	142.53 E
Thomson ≃, Austl.	169	37.58 S	146.32 E
Thomson's Falls	154	0.02 N	36.22 E
Thon ≃	50	49.53 N	3.55 E
Thon Buri	110	13.43 N	100.29 E
Thônes	62	45.53 N	6.20 E
Thong	260	51.24 N	0.24 E
Thong Hoe	271c	1.25 N	103.42 E
Thong Pha Phum	110	14.44 N	98.38 E
Thong-tay-hoi	269c	10.50 N	106.39 E
Thongwa	110	16.46 N	96.32 E
Thon-lac-nghiep	110	11.20 N	108.54 E
Thonnance-lès-Joinville	58	48.27 N	5.10 E
Thonon-les-Bains	58	46.22 N	6.29 E
Thonotosassa	220	28.03 N	82.18 W
Thonze	110	17.38 N	95.47 E
Thorah Island I	212	44.27 N	79.14 W
Thorame-Haute	62	44.06 N	6.33 E
Thorburn	186	45.34 N	62.33 W
Thoreau	200	35.24 N	108.13 W
Thorembais-les-Béguines	56	50.40 N	4.49 E
Thorenc	62	43.48 N	6.49 E
Thorens-Glières	58	45.59 N	6.15 E
Thorez → Torez	83	48.01 N	38.37 E
Thorhild	182	54.10 N	113.07 W
Thorial	140	8.40 N	29.56 E
Thorigny	50	48.17 N	3.24 E
Thorigny-sur-Marne	261	48.53 N	2.42 E
Thorigny-sur-Oreuse	50	48.17 N	3.24 E
Thórisvatn ⊜	24a	64.50 N	19.26 W
Thörl	61	47.31 N	15.13 E
Thorlákshöfn	24a	63.53 N	21.18 W
Thormanby	44	54.10 N	1.14 W
Thorn, Ned.	52	51.10 N	5.50 E
Thorn → Toruń, Pol.	30	53.02 N	18.35 E
Thornaby-on-Tees	44	54.34 N	1.18 W
Thornapple ≃, Mich., U.S.	216	42.56 N	85.28 W
Thornapple ≃, Wis., U.S.	190	45.28 N	91.16 W
Thornapple Lake ⊜	216	42.37 N	85.11 W
Thornburg	279b	40.26 N	80.05 W
Thornbury, Austl.	274b	37.45 S	145.00 E
Thornbury, Ont., Can.	212	44.34 N	80.26 W
Thornbury, N.Z.	172	46.17 S	168.06 E
Thornbury, Eng., U.K.	42	51.37 N	2.32 W
Thorn Creek ≃	278	41.36 N	87.35 W
Thorndale, Ont., Can.	212	43.06 N	81.08 W
Thorndale, Tex., U.S.	222	30.37 N	97.12 W
Thorndike	207	42.11 N	72.20 W
Thorndon	42	52.17 N	1.08 E
Thorne	44	53.37 N	0.58 W
Thorne ≃	184	54.56 N	90.35 W
Thorne Bay	182	55.44 N	132.32 W
Thorney	42	52.37 N	0.07 W
Thornhill, S. Afr.	273d	26.07 S	28.09 E
Thornhill, Scot., U.K.	44	55.15 N	3.46 W
Thornhurst	210	41.11 N	75.35 W
Thornleigh	274a	33.44 S	151.05 E
Thornton, Austl.	171a	27.49 S	152.23 E
Thornton, Eng., U.K.	44	53.53 N	3.02 W
Thornton, Eng., U.K.	262	53.47 N	1.51 W
Thornton, Ark., U.S.	194	33.47 N	92.29 W
Thornton, Calif., U.S.	226	38.14 N	121.25 W
Thornton, Colo., U.S.	200	39.51 N	104.59 W
Thornton, Pa., U.S.	285	39.54 N	75.32 W
Thornton, Tex., U.S.	222	31.24 N	96.34 W
Thornton Beach ♠	282	37.42 N	122.30 W
Thornton Dale	44	54.14 N	0.43 W
Thornton Hough	262	53.19 N	3.03 W
Thornton-le-Moors	262	53.16 N	2.50 W
Thornwood	210	41.07 N	73.47 W
Thornwood Common	260	51.43 N	0.08 E
Thorny Mountain Λ	194	37.06 N	91.10 W
Thorofare	285	39.51 N	75.12 W
Thorold	212	43.07 N	79.12 W
Thorold South	284a	43.06 N	79.12 W
Thoronet, Abbaye du ♁[1]	62	43.28 N	6.16 E
Thorp, Wash., U.S.	224	47.04 N	120.40 W
Thorp, Wis., U.S.	190	44.58 N	90.48 W
Thorpe	260	51.24 N	0.32 W
Thorpe-le-Soken	42	51.52 N	1.10 E
Thorpe Saint Andrew	42	52.38 N	1.20 E
Thorp Spring	222	32.28 N	97.49 W
Thorsby, Alta., Can.	182	53.14 N	114.03 W
Thorsby, Ala., U.S.	194	32.55 N	86.43 W
Thorshavn → Tórshavn	22	62.01 N	6.46 W
Thórshöfn	24a	66.13 N	15.17 W
Thorsø	41	56.18 N	9.48 E
Thorsteinson Lake ⊜	184	57.15 N	97.30 W
Thorton Moor Reservoir ⊜[1]	262	53.47 N	1.55 W
Thot-not	110	10.16 N	105.32 E
Thouars	32	46.59 N	0.13 W
Thouin, Cape ≻	162	20.20 S	118.12 E
Thoune → Thun	58	46.45 N	7.37 E
Thourotte	50	49.29 N	2.53 E
Thousand Islands II	212	44.15 N	76.12 W
Thousand Islands International Bridge ◆[5]	212	44.20 N	75.58 W
Thousand Lake Mountain Λ	200	38.25 N	111.29 W
Thousand Oaks	228	34.10 N	118.50 W
Thousand Ships Bay ⊂	175e	8.25 S	159.40 E
Thousand Springs Creek ≃	200	41.17 N	113.51 W
Thowa ≃	154	1.33 S	40.03 E
Thowgla Creek ≃	171b	36.10 S	147.57 E
Thrace □[9]	38	41.20 N	26.45 E
Thrakikón Pélagos ⍑[2]	38	40.15 N	24.28 E
Thrall	222	30.35 N	97.18 W
Thrapston	42	52.24 N	0.32 W
Thrasher Lake ⊜	212	44.55 N	78.58 W
Thread Creek ≃	216	43.01 N	83.42 W
Thredbo Village	171b	36.29 S	148.19 E
Three Bridges, Eng., U.K.	42	51.07 N	0.09 W
Three Bridges, N.J., U.S.	208	40.31 N	74.48 W
Three Brothers Λ	224	47.23 N	120.45 W
Three Brothers Mountain Λ	224	49.10 N	120.46 W
Three Creek ≃	208	36.47 N	77.10 W
Three Fingered Jack Λ	202	44.29 N	121.50 W
Three Fingers Λ	224	48.10 N	121.41 W
Three Fools Creek ≃	224	48.53 N	120.57 W
Three Forks	202	45.54 N	111.33 W
Three Hills	182	51.42 N	113.16 W
Three Hummock Island I	166	40.26 S	144.55 E
Three Kings Islands II	172	34.10 S	172.05 E
Three Lakes	190	45.48 N	89.10 W
Three M Airport ⊠	285	40.08 N	74.51 W
Three Mile Bay	212	44.05 N	76.12 W
Three Mile Plains	186	44.58 N	64.07 W
Three Oaks	216	41.48 N	86.36 W
Three Pagodas Pass)(	110	15.18 N	98.23 E
Threepoint Lake ⊜	184	55.41 N	98.56 W
Three Points, Cape ≻	150	4.45 N	2.06 W
Three Rivers, Austl.	162	25.07 S	119.09 E
Three Rivers → Trois-Rivières, Qué., Can.	206	46.21 N	72.33 W
Three Rivers, Mass., U.S.	207	42.11 N	72.22 W
Three Rivers, Mich., U.S.	216	41.57 N	85.38 W
Three Rivers, Tex., U.S.	196	28.28 N	98.11 W
Three Rivers □[8]	260	51.40 N	0.27 W
Three Sisters	158	31.54 S	23.06 E
Three Sisters Λ	202	44.10 N	121.46 W
Three Sisters Pass)(	158	30.08 S	28.32 E
Three Springs, Austl.	162	29.32 S	115.45 E
Three Springs, Pa., U.S.	214	40.12 N	77.59 W
Threlkeld	44	54.38 N	3.03 W
Throat ≃	184	51.48 N	93.30 W
Throckley	44	54.59 N	1.45 W
Throckmorton	196	33.11 N	99.11 W
Throgs Neck ◆[8]	276	40.49 N	73.49 W
Throgs Neck Bridge ◆[5]	276	40.48 N	73.48 W
Throgs Point ≻	276	40.48 N	73.48 W
Throop	210	41.26 N	75.36 W
Throssel, Lake ⊜	162	27.27 S	124.16 E
Throssel Range ⩕	162	22.03 S	121.43 E
Thrushel ≃	42	50.39 N	4.15 W
Thruway Plaza ◆[9]	284a	42.55 N	78.46 W
Thuan-chau	110	21.26 N	103.41 E
Thu-duc	269c	10.51 N	106.45 E
Thueyts	62	44.41 N	4.13 E
Thuilley-aux-Groseilles	58	48.34 N	5.58 E
Thuin	50	50.20 N	4.17 E
Thul	120	28.14 N	68.46 E
Thulaythiwāt, Tilāl ath- Λ	132	30.58 N	36.40 E
Thulba ≃	56	50.11 N	9.52 E
Thule	16	76.34 N	68.47 W
Thum	54	50.40 N	12.57 E
Thumaymah, Jabal Λ[2]	142	30.21 N	30.37 E
Thumb Peak Λ	116	9.48 N	118.36 E
Thumby	41	54.35 N	9.54 E
Thun	58	46.45 N	7.37 E
Thun Chang	110	19.25 N	100.53 E
Thunder Bay	190	48.23 N	89.15 W
Thunder Bay ⊂, Ont., Can.	190	48.24 N	89.00 W
Thunder Bay ⊂, Ont., Can.	212	44.48 N	80.03 W
Thunder Bay ≃	190	45.04 N	83.25 W
Thunder Bay, North Branch ≃	190	45.08 N	83.35 W
Thunderbird, Lake ⊜[1]	196	35.15 N	97.20 W
Thunderbolt	192	32.03 N	81.04 W
Thunder Butte Λ	198	45.19 N	101.53 W
Thunder Butte Creek ≃	198	45.13 N	101.42 W
Thunder Creek ≃	224	48.40 N	121.05 W
Thunder Hills ⩕[2]	184	54.30 N	106.00 W
Thunder Mountain Λ[2]	216	42.16 N	86.20 W
Thundersley	260	51.34 N	0.35 E
Thunersee ⊜	58	46.40 N	7.45 E
Thüngen	56	49.56 N	9.51 E
Thung Song	110	8.09 N	99.41 E
Thung Wa	110	7.06 N	99.46 E
Thur ≃, Fr.	58	48.05 N	7.23 E
Thur ≃, Schw.	58	47.36 N	8.35 E
Thurgau □[3]	58	47.35 N	9.00 E
Thurgovie → Thurgau □[3]	58	47.35 N	9.00 E
Thüringen	58	47.12 N	9.45 E
Thüringen □[9]	54	51.00 N	11.00 E
Thüringer Wald ⩕	54	50.30 N	11.00 E
Thürkow	54	53.50 N	12.33 E
Thurles	48	52.41 N	7.49 W
Thurmont	188	39.37 N	77.25 W
Thurn, Pass)(	64	47.19 N	12.24 E
Thurnham	260	51.17 N	0.36 E
Thurnscoe	44	53.31 N	1.19 W
Thurnwald Range ⩕	164	4.45 S	141.15 E
Thurø	41	55.03 N	10.40 E
Thurrock □[8]	260	51.30 N	0.21 E
Thursby	44	54.51 N	3.03 W
Thursday Island	164	10.35 S	142.13 E
Thurso, Qué., Can.	206	45.36 N	75.15 W
Thurso, Scot., U.K.	46	58.35 N	3.32 W
Thurso ≃	46	58.36 N	3.30 W
Thurstaston	262	53.21 N	3.08 W
Thurston □[6]	224	46.59 N	122.42 W
Thurston Island I	9	72.20 S	99.00 W
Thury-Harcourt	32	48.59 N	0.29 W
Thusis	58	46.42 N	9.26 E
Thwaites Ice Tongue ⍓	9	74.45 S	106.30 W
Thy ◆[1]	26	57.00 N	8.30 E
Thyborøn	26	56.42 N	8.13 E
Thylungra	166	26.04 S	143.28 E
Thyregod	41	55.54 N	9.16 E
Thysville → Mbanza-Ngungu	138	5.15 S	14.52 E
Tiadiaye	150	14.25 N	16.42 W
Tiahuanacu	248	16.33 S	68.42 W
Tía Juana	246	10.16 N	71.22 W
Tiana, Esp.	266d	44.29 N	2.16 E
Tiana, It.	71	40.04 N	9.08 E
Tiananmen ♠	271a	39.55 N	116.23 E
Tian'aoshan I	100	28.48 N	121.51 E
Tianban	100	29.20 N	116.50 E
Tianbao	100	24.36 N	117.35 E
Tiancang	102	41.09 N	100.17 E
Tianchang	100	32.41 N	119.01 E
Tiancunpu	105	39.06 N	115.41 E
Tiandeng	102	23.09 N	107.10 E
Tiandong	102	23.40 N	106.57 E
Tian'e	102	25.01 N	107.20 E
Tianeti	84	42.07 N	44.59 E
Tiangang, Zhg.	89	43.24 N	125.54 E
Tiangang, Zhg.	89	43.55 N	127.00 E
Tiangongsi	105	39.14 N	115.53 E
Tianguá	250	3.44 S	40.59 W
Tianhe	100	27.01 N	114.30 E
Tianhekou	100	32.08 N	113.25 E
Tianhelong	89	43.56 N	120.39 E
Tianhengdao I	98	36.14 N	120.46 E
Tianhuang	98	35.29 N	117.18 E
Tianjara Mountain Λ	170	35.11 S	150.18 E
Tianjia, Zhg.	104	41.07 N	122.03 E
Tianjia, Zhg.	107	29.40 N	105.08 E
Tianjiaba	102	32.08 N	110.03 E
Tianjiatun	104	41.39 N	123.44 E
Tianjiawopu	104	42.28 N	122.38 E
Tianjiazhen	100	29.56 N	115.26 E
Tianjin (Tientsin)	105	39.08 N	117.12 E
Tianjing	106	31.27 N	120.46 E
Tianjin Shi (Tientsin Shih) □[7]	98	39.30 N	117.15 E
Tianjun (Tangnaihai)	102	37.25 N	98.58 E
Tiankai	105	39.38 N	115.51 E
Tiankoura	150	10.46 N	3.16 W
Tiankoye	150	12.35 N	12.40 W
Tianlin, Zhg.	102	24.14 N	106.03 E
Tianlin, Zhg.	107	29.49 N	105.19 E
Tianling Λ	89	44.22 N	129.52 E
Tianmashan	106	31.04 N	121.08 E
Tianmen	100	30.40 N	113.08 E
Tianmushan ⩕	100	30.25 N	119.30 E
Tianpu	106	31.56 N	121.07 E
Tianqiaochang	104	40.52 N	121.02 E
Tianqiaoling	89	43.26 N	129.38 E
Tianqiao Theatre ♁	271a	39.53 N	116.23 E
Tianquan	102	30.10 N	102.48 E
Tianshanmai → Tien Shan ⩕	90	42.00 N	80.00 E
Tianshenggang, Zhg.	106	32.14 N	121.00 E
Tianshenggang, Zhg.	106	32.03 N	120.45 E
Tianshifu	98	41.17 N	124.21 E
Tianshui	102	34.30 N	105.58 E
Tianshuijing, Zhg.	102	40.17 N	95.21 E
Tianshuijing, Zhg.	104	41.19 N	121.48 E
Tianshuituo	105	39.20 N	118.12 E

Symbol	English	Deutsch	Español	Français	Português
≃	River	Fluss	Río	Rivière	Rio
≊	Canal	Kanal	Canal	Canal	Canal
⌊	Waterfall, Rapids	Wasserfall, Stromschnellen	Cascada, Rápidos	Chute d'eau, Rapides	Cascata, Rápidos
⋓	Strait	Meeresstrasse	Estrecho	Détroit	Estreito
⊂	Bay, Gulf	Bucht, Golf	Bahía, Golfo	Baie, Golfe	Baía, Golfo
⊜	Lake, Lakes	See, Seen	Lago, Lagos	Lac, Lacs	Lago, Lagos
☷	Swamp	Sumpf	Pantano	Marais	Pântano
⍓	Ice Features, Glacier	Eis- und Gletscherformen	Accidentes Glaciales	Formes glaciaires	Acidentes Glaciares
⍑	Other Hydrographic Features	Andere Hydrographische Objekte	Otros Elementos Hidrográficos	Autres données hydrographiques	Outros Elementos Hidrográficos

Symbol	English	Deutsch	Español	Français	Português
✢	Submarine Features	Untermeerische Objekte	Accidentes Submarinos	Formes de relief sous-marin	Acidentes Submarinos
□	Political Unit	Politische Einheit	Unidad Politica	Entité politique	Unidade Política
♁	Cultural Institution	Kulturelle Institution	Institución Cultural	Institution culturelle	Instituição Cultural
⊥	Historical Site	Historische Stätte	Sitio Histórico	Site historique	Sitio Histórico
♠	Recreational Site	Erholungs- und Ferienort	Sitio de Recreo	Centre de loisirs	Sítio de Lazer
⊠	Airport	Flughafen	Aeropuerto	Aéroport	Aeroporto
■	Military Installation	Militäranlage	Instalación Militar	Installation militaire	Instalação Militar
◆	Miscellaneous	Verschiedenes	Misceláneo	Divers	Miscelânea

Tianshuizhan 104 41.00 N 123.34 E
Tianshuizhen 102 34.18 N 105.57 E
Tiantai 100 29.09 N 121.02 E
Tiantaishan ⛰ 100 29.22 N 121.10 E
Tiantang 102 22.32 N 111.55 E
Tiantou, Zhg. 100 28.48 N 120.39 E
Tiantou, Zhg. 100 26.19 N 115.57 E
Tianwangsi 106 31.45 N 119.12 E
Tianweijiao ❯ 100 22.45 N 115.49 E
Tianxin 102 27.21 N 111.00 E
Tianxinduan 100 27.53 N 113.06 E
Tianxingqiao 106 32.05 N 119.57 E
Tianxinwei 100 28.11 N 114.35 E
Tianxiyang 100 26.31 N 118.33 E
Tianyang 102 23.51 N 106.34 E
Tianyangping 107 29.11 N 105.16 E
Tianyar 115b 8.12 S 115.30 E
Tianzhen 98 40.28 N 114.06 E
Tianzhongying 100 33.13 N 115.22 E
Tianzhu (Anyuanyi), Zhg. 102 37.14 N 102.59 E
Tianzhu, Zhg. 102 26.50 N 109.00 E
Tianzhuang, Zhg. 100 25.43 N 113.40 E
Tianzhuang, Zhg. 105 39.25 N 117.54 E
Tianzhuangtai 104 40.50 N 122.08 E
Tiaodengchang 107 30.47 N 106.22 E
Tiaohe ≃ 107 29.53 N 106.10 E
Tiarei 174s 17.32 S 149.20 W
Tiaret 148 35.28 N 1.21 E
Tiarno 64 45.53 N 10.40 E
Tiaro 166 25.44 S 152.35 E
Tiassalé 150 5.54 N 4.50 W
Tiati ∧ 154 1.19 N 35.56 E
Tiavea 175a 13.57 S 171.24 W
Tiawichi Creek ≃ 222 32.19 N 94.44 W
Tiba
→ Chiba 94 35.36 N 140.07 E
Ṭibābī, Jabal aṭ- ∧[2] 142 30.28 N 30.28 E
Tibagi 252 24.30 S 50.24 W
Tibaji ≃ 252 22.47 S 51.01 W
Tibari 154 5.01 N 31.43 E
Tibasti, Sarīr •[2] 146 24.15 N 17.15 E
Tibati 152 6.27 N 12.38 E
Tibbermore 46 56.22 N 3.32 W
Tibbie 194 31.16 N 88.15 W
Tibe 144 9.03 N 37.08 E
Tibel'ti 88 51.46 N 103.11 E
Tiber
→ Tevere ≃ 66 41.44 N 12.14 E
Tiberias
→ Teverya 132 32.47 N 35.32 E
Tiberias, Lake
→ Kinneret, Yam ◎ 132 32.48 N 35.35 E
Tiberina, Val ∨ 66 43.31 N 12.10 E
Tiber Reservoir ◎[1] 202 48.22 N 111.17 W
Tibesti ⛰ 146 21.30 N 17.30 E
Tibet, Lake ◎ 220 28.27 N 81.31 W
Tibiao 116 11.17 N 122.02 E
Tibiao Point ❯ 116 11.18 N 122.02 E
Tibidabo ∧ 266d 41.25 N 2.07 E
Tibiri 150 13.06 N 4.00 E
Tibiriçá ≃ 255 21.43 S 50.15 W
Tibirke 41 56.03 N 12.07 E
Tiblawan 116 6.29 N 126.06 E
Tiblemont, Lac ◎ 190 48.14 N 77.18 W
Ţibleş, Munţii ⛰ 38 47.38 N 24.05 E
Tibnah 132 32.59 N 36.13 E
Tibnīn 132 33.12 N 35.25 E
Tibro 26 58.26 N 14.10 E
Tiburon 226 36.04 N 119.19 W
Tiburón, Cabo ❯ 246 8.42 N 77.24 W
Tiburón, Isla I 232 29.00 N 112.23 W
Tiburon Peninsula ❯[1] 282 37.53 N 122.28 W
Ticao Island I 116 12.31 N 123.42 E
Ticao Pass ⊔ 116 12.38 N 123.47 E
Tice 220 26.41 N 81.49 W
Tice Creek ≃ 282 37.53 N 122.03 W
Ticehurst 42 51.03 N 0.25 E
Tichigan 216 42.50 N 88.12 W
Tichigan Lake ◎ 216 42.49 N 88.13 W
Tîchît 150 18.28 N 9.30 W
Tîchît, Dhar •[4] 150 18.30 N 9.25 W
Tichla 148 21.35 N 14.58 W
Tichmenevo, S.S.S.R. 76 58.00 N 38.36 E
Tichmenevo, S.S.S.R. 89 49.12 N 142.54 E
Ticho 144 7.50 N 39.32 E
Tichon 24 59.23 N 46.38 E
Tichonova Pustyn' 82 54.38 N 36.09 E
Tichonoviči 78 51.56 N 32.09 E
Tichonovka 88 53.13 N 104.13 E
Tichoreck 78 45.51 N 40.09 E
Tichtozero 24 65.35 N 30.27 E
Tichvin 76 59.39 N 33.31 E
Tichvinskaja Gr'ada ∧ 76 59.30 N 34.30 E
Tichvinskij Kanal ≋ 76 59.30 N 34.29 E
Ticino □[3] 58 46.20 N 8.45 E
Ticino ≃ 36 45.09 N 9,14 E
Tickfaw 194 30.35 N 90.29 W
Tickfaw ≃ 194 30.20 N 90.28 W
Tickhill 44 53.26 N 1.06 W
Ticomán •[8] 286a 19.31 N 99.08 W
Ticul 232 20.24 N 89.32 W
Tīdah 142 31.15 N 30.50 E
Tidaholm 26 58.11 N 13.57 E
Tidan ≃ 40 58.42 N 13.58 E
Tiddim 110 23.23 N 93.39 E
Tide Lake ◎ 182 50.33 N 111.20 W
Tidewater 208 37.51 N 76.42 W
Tidewater •[1] 208 37.45 N 77.00 W
Tidikelt, Plaine du ≚ 148 26.54 N 1.20 E
Tidioute 214 41.41 N 79.24 W
Tidirhine, Jbel ∧ 148 34.50 N 4.30 W
Tidjenaouine 148 22.33 N 5.15 E
Tidjidit, Erg •[2] 148 23.30 N 1.00 E
Tidjikdja 150 18.33 N 11.25 W
Tidö 40 59.30 N 16.28 E
Tidone ≃ 62 45.04 N 9.32 E
Tidore 108 0.40 N 127.26 E
Tidra, Île I 150 19.44 N 16.24 W
Tiébissou 150 7.10 N 5.13 W
Tiechang, Zhg. 98 41.44 N 126.11 E
Tiechang, Zhg. 100 24.10 N 115.30 E
Tiechang, Zhg. 102 26.34 N 103.58 E
Tiechang, Zhg. 105 40.04 N 118.12 E
Tiechangpu 107 29.29 N 104.20 E
Tiefenbach 60 49.26 N 12.35 E
Tiefenbroich 263 51.18 N 6.49 E
Tiefencastel 58 46.40 N 9.35 E
Tiefensee 54 52.41 N 13.50 E
Tiefo 107 29.45 N 104.33 E
Tiegenhof
→ Nowy Dwór Gdański 30 54.13 N 19.06 E
T'iehling
→ Tieling 104 42.18 N 123.49 E
Tiekou 98 37.16 N 121.13 E
Tiel, Ned. 52 51.54 N 5.25 E
Tièl, Sén. 150 14.56 N 15.04 W
Tielelihu ◎ 90 44.30 N 85.15 E
Tieli 89 46.59 N 128.02 E
Tielinanmuhu ◎ 120 31.05 N 85.35 E
Tieling 104 42.18 N 123.49 E
Tielt 50 51.00 N 3.19 E
Tielutou 100 27.49 N 115.48 E
T'ienching
→ Tianjin 105 39.08 N 117.12 E
T'ienchung 100 23.53 N 120.34 E
Tienen 56 50.48 N 4.57 E
Tiengen 58 47.38 N 8.16 E
Tiénigbé 150 8.11 N 5.43 W
Tienko 150 10.14 N 7.29 W
Tien Shan ⛰ 90 42.00 N 80.00 E
T'ienshui
→ Tianshui 102 34.30 N 105.58 E
Tientsin
→ Tianjin 105 39.08 N 117.12 E
Tien-yen 110 21.20 N 107.24 E
Tiepido ≃ 64 44.30 N 10.59 E
Tie Plant 194 33.44 N 89.47 W
Tierga 34 41.37 N 1.36 W
Tiergarten •[8] 264a 52.31 N 13.21 E
Tiergarten ♠ 264a 52.31 N 13.21 E
Tieroko ∧ 146 20.45 N 17.52 E
Tierp 40 60.20 N 17.30 E
Tierpark ♠ 264a 52.30 N 13.32 E
Tierra Amarilla, Chile 252 27.29 S 70.17 W
Tierra Amarilla, N. Mex., U.S. 200 36.42 N 106.33 W
Tierra Blanca, Méx. 196 27.12 N 104.53 W
Tierra Blanca, Méx. 234 18.25 N 96.20 W
Tierra Blanca ≃ 234 21.02 N 99.50 W
Tierra Blanca Creek ≃ 196 34.58 N 101.55 W
Tierra Buena 226 39.09 N 121.40 W
Tierra Colorada, Méx. 234 17.56 N 92.39 W
Tierra Colorada, Méx. 234 17.10 N 99.35 W
Tierra Colorada, Bajo de la ≚[1] 254 42.52 S 66.48 W
Tierra de Campos •[1] 34 42.10 N 4.50 W
Tierra del Fuego □[8] 254 54.00 S 67.00 W
Tierra del Fuego, Isla Grande de I 254 54.00 S 69.00 W
Tierra del Norte
→ Severnaja Zeml'a II 74 79.30 N 98.00 E
Tierralta 246 8.11 N 76.04 W
Tierra Nueva 234 17.47 N 93.28 W
Tierra Redonda Mountain ∧ 226 35.47 N 120.59 W
Tierras Australes y Antárticas Francesas → French Southern and Antarctic Territories □[2] 6 49.30 S 69.30 E
Tierras Coloradas 234 22.24 N 104.35 W
Tieshan 100 30.14 N 114.52 E
Tieshanguan 100 23.30 N 113.54 E
Tietar ≃ 34 39.50 N 6.01 W
Tietê 255 23.07 S 47.43 W
Tietê ≃ 255 20.40 S 51.35 W
Tiéti 175f 20.57 S 165.19 E
Tieton 224 46.42 N 120.46 W
Tieton ≃ 224 46.45 N 120.45 W
Tieton, South Fork ≃ 224 46.38 N 121.08 W
Tietzow 264a 52.43 N 12.56 E
Tiffany Mountain ∧ 202 48.40 N 119.56 W
Tiffin 214 41.07 N 83.11 W
Tiffin ≃ 216 41.17 N 84.23 W
Tifi 144 6.15 N 37.00 E
Tiflis
→ Tbilisi 84 41.43 N 44.49 E
Tifton 192 31.27 N 83.31 W
Tiftona 192 35.05 N 85.10 W
Tiga, Île I 175f 21.07 S 167.49 E
Tiga, Pulau I 112 5.43 N 115.39 E
Tigalda Island I 180 54.05 N 165.05 W
Tigapuluh, Pegunungan ⛰ 112 1.05 S 102.30 E
Tigard 224 45.26 N 122.46 W
Tigasaki
→ Chigasaki 94 35.19 N 139.24 E
Tigbauan 116 10.41 N 122.22 E
Tigeaux 261 48.50 N 2.54 E
Tiger Lake ◎ 220 27.53 N 81.22 W
Tiger Stadium ♠ 281 42.20 N 83.04 W
Tigery 261 48.38 N 2.31 E
Tighennif 148 35.20 N 0.21 E
Tighina
→ Bendery 78 46.48 N 29.29 E
Tighvein ∧[2] 46 55.30 N 5.10 W
Tigil' 74 57.48 N 158.40 E
Tiglione ≃ 62 44.48 N 8.27 E
Tiglit 148 28.31 N 10.15 W
Tignale 64 45.44 N 10.44 E
Tignall 192 33.52 N 82.44 W
Tignère 152 7.22 N 12.39 E
Tignes 62 45.30 N 6.55 E
Tignish 186 46.57 N 64.02 W
Tignousti, Jbel ∧ 148 31.31 N 6.44 W
Tigoda ≃ 76 59.22 N 31.54 E
Tigre 258 34.25 S 58.34 W
Tigre □[4] 144 13.40 N 40.00 E
Tigre □[5] 288 34.24 S 58.37 W
Tigre ∧ 234 19.53 N 102.59 W
Tigre ≃, Arg. 288 34.25 S 58.35 W
Tigre
→ Tigris ≃, As. 128 31.00 N 47.25 E
Tigre ≃, Méx. 234 22.43 N 97.51 W
Tigre ≃, Perú 246 4.26 S 74.05 W
Tigre ≃, Ven. 246 9.20 N 62.30 W
Tigre, Cerro ∧ 236 8.31 N 83.28 W
Tigre, Isla del I 258 34.47 S 56.23 W
Tigre, Punta del ❯ 258 34.46 S 56.33 W
Tigris (Dicle) (Dijlah) ≃ 128 31.00 N 47.25 E
Tiguabos 240p 20.14 N 75.21 W
Tiguentourine 148 27.50 N 9.18 E
Tiguesmat ⛰[2] 148 24.54 N 8.14 W
Tigui ⊤[4] 146 18.38 N 18.47 E
Tigy 50 47.48 N 2.12 E
Tigyaing 110 23.46 N 96.08 E
Tigzert, Oued ∨ 148 28.20 N 9.35 W
Tigzirt 34 36.54 N 4.08 E
Tīh, Jabal at- ⛰[1] 140 29.30 N 34.00 E
Tihany ⊥ 30 46.54 N 17.53 E
Ṭihnāwī, Wādī aṭ- ∨ 142 28.11 N 30.46 E
Tihua
→ Wulumuqi 86 43.48 N 87.35 E
Tihuatlán 234 20.43 N 97.32 W
Tijamuchi ≃ 248 14.10 S 64.58 W
Tijesno 36 43.48 N 15.39 E
Tijī 146 32.01 N 11.22 E
Tijirît, Oued ∨ 150 20.01 N 15.29 W
Tijuana 232 32.32 N 117.01 W
Tijuana ≃ 204 32.33 N 117.07 W
Tijuca •[8] 287a 22.56 S 43.14 W
Tijuca, Barra da ⊔ 287a 23.01 S 43.18 W
Tijuca, Floresta da ♠ 287a 22.56 S 43.17 W
Tijuca, Lagoa da C 287a 22.59 S 43.20 W
Tijuca, Pico da ∧ 287a 22.56 S 43.17 W
Tijucas 252 27.14 S 48.38 W
Tijucas do Sul 252 25.55 S 49.12 W
Tijuco ≃ 255 18.40 S 50.05 W
Tijuco Prêto 256 22.56 S 46.40 W
Tikal ⊥ 232 17.20 N 89.39 W
Tīkamgarh 124 24.44 N 78.50 E
Tīkamgarh □[5] 124 25.00 N 79.00 E
Tikaré 150 13.17 N 1.43 W
Tikchik Lakes ◎ 180 60.07 N 158.35 W
Tikei I 14 14.58 S 144.32 W
Tikhand •[8] 272a 28.31 N 77.17 E
Tikhoretsk
→ Tichoreck 78 45.51 N 40.09 E
Tikitiki 172 37.48 S 178.24 E
Tiko 152 4.05 N 9.22 E
Tikokino 172 39.49 S 176.27 E
Tikrīt 128 34.36 N 43.42 E
Tikša 24 64.07 N 32.27 E
Tikšeozero, Ozero ◎ 24 66.16 N 31.53 E
Tiksi 74 71.36 N 128.48 E
Tiku 112 0.24 S 99.56 E
Til 130 38.44 N 41.49 E
Tila ≃ 124 29.08 N 81.35 E
Tiladummati Atoll I[1] 122 6.50 N 73.05 E
Tilamuta 112 0.30 N 122.20 E
Tilape ≃ 234 18.06 N 94.31 W
Tilarán 236 10.28 N 84.59 W
Tilbalakan, Laguna C 236 15.30 N 84.17 W
Tilbānah 142 30.59 N 31.27 E
Tilburg 52 51.34 N 5.05 E
Tilbury, Ont., Can. 214 42.16 N 82.26 W
Tilbury, Eng., U.K. 42 51.28 N 0.23 E
Tilcara 252 23.34 S 65.22 W
Tilcha 166 29.36 S 140.54 E
Til-Châtel 58 47.31 N 5.10 E
Tilden, Ill., U.S. 219 38.13 N 89.41 W
Tilden, Nebr., U.S. 198 42.03 N 97.50 W
Tilden, Tex., U.S. 196 28.28 N 98.33 W
Tilden Lake ◎ 226 38.07 N 119.36 W
Tilemsi, Vallée du ∨ 150 16.15 N 0.02 E
Tilff 56 50.34 N 5.35 E
Tilghman Island I 208 38.42 N 76.20 W
Tilhar 124 27.59 N 79.44 E
Tilia, Oued ∨ 148 27.27 N 0.01 W
Tiligul ≃ 78 47.04 N 30.57 E
Tiligulo-Berezanka 78 46.52 N 31.24 E
Tiligul'skij Liman ◎ 78 46.48 N 31.08 E
Tiliktino 82 56.06 N 36.36 E
Tilin 110 21.42 N 94.04 E
Tilisarao 252 32.44 S 65.18 W
Till ≃, Eng., U.K. 44 53.16 N 0.37 W
Till ≃, Eng., U.K. 44 55.41 N 2.12 W
Tillabéry 150 14.13 N 1.27 E
Tillamook 202 45.27 N 123.51 W
Tillamook □[6] 224 45.25 N 123.39 W
Tillamook ≃ 224 45.28 N 123.53 W
Tillamook Bay C 224 45.30 N 123.53 W
Tillamook Head ❯ 224 45.57 N 124.00 W
Tillanchāng Dwīp I 110 8.30 N 93.37 E
Tillberga 40 59.41 N 16.37 E
Tille ≃ 58 47.07 N 5.21 E
Tillé, Aéroport de ⊠ 50 49.28 N 2.07 E
Tillery, Lake ◎[1] 192 35.17 N 80.05 W
Tilley 182 50.27 N 111.39 W
Tilli 126 23.57 N 89.57 E
Tillia 150 16.08 N 4.47 E
Tillicoultry 46 56.09 N 3.45 W
Tillicum 224 47.08 N 122.33 W
Tillières-sur-Avre 50 48.46 N 1.04 E
Tilling Bourne ≃ 260 51.13 N 0.34 W
Tillmans Corner 194 30.46 N 88.08 W
Tillson 210 41.50 N 74.04 W
Tillsonburg 212 42.51 N 80.44 W
Tillyfourie 46 57.11 N 2.35 W
Tilogne 150 15.58 N 13.36 W
Tilomar 112 9.21 S 125.08 E
Tílos I 38 36.25 N 27.25 E
Tilpa 166 30.57 S 144.24 E
Tilrhemt 148 33.10 N 3.21 E
Tilsit
→ Sovetsk 76 55.05 N 21.53 E
Tilt ≃ 46 56.46 N 3.50 W
Tilton, Ky., U.S. 218 38.22 N 83.45 W
Tilton, N.H., U.S. 188 43.27 N 71.35 W
Tilton ≃ 224 46.33 N 122.33 W
Tiltonsville 214 40.10 N 80.42 W
Tilzapotla 234 18.29 N 99.16 W
Tim 78 51.37 N 37.07 E
Tim ≃ 76 52.15 N 37.22 E
Ṭimā 140 26.54 N 31.26 E
Timahoe 44 53.20 N 6.49 W
Timaná 246 1.58 N 75.56 W
Timane ≃ 248 20.34 S 59.15 W
Timanskij Kr'až ∧ 24 65.00 N 51.00 E
Timar 84 38.49 N 43.27 E
Timaricha 80 57.33 N 44.47 E
Timarni Muafi 124 22.22 N 77.22 E
Timaru 172 44.24 S 171.15 E
Timaševo, S.S.S.R. 80 53.21 N 51.12 E
Timaševo, S.S.S.R. 82 55.08 N 36.29 E
Timaševskaja 78 45.37 N 38.57 E
Timau, It. 64 46.35 N 13.00 E
Timau, Kenya 154 0.05 N 37.14 E
Timavo San Giovanni 64 45.48 N 13.37 E
Timay al-Amdīd 142 30.57 N 31.32 E
Timbákion 38 35.04 N 24.46 E
Timbalier Bay C 194 29.10 N 90.20 W
Timbaúba 250 7.31 S 35.19 W
Timbédra 150 16.15 N 8.10 W
Timber 224 45.43 N 123.18 W
Timber Creek ≃ 198 44.49 N 98.17 W
Timber Lake, Ill., U.S. 278 42.14 N 88.07 W
Timberlake, Ohio, U.S. 214 41.41 N 81.25 W
Timber Lake, S. Dak., U.S. 198 45.26 N 101.04 W
Timber Run ≃ 284b 39.27 N 76.52 W
Timber Trails 278 41.52 N 87.57 W
Timberview 284b 39.13 N 76.45 W
Timbío 246 2.20 N 76.40 W
Timbira ≃ 287a 22.41 S 43.13 W
Timbiras 250 4.15 S 43.57 W
Timblin 214 40.58 N 79.12 W
Timbó, Bra. 252 26.50 S 49.18 W
Timbo, Guinée 150 10.38 N 11.50 W
Timbo, Liber. 150 5.37 N 9.43 W
Timbó ≃ 287a 22.52 S 43.16 W
Timboon 169 38.29 S 142.59 E
Timbuctoo 285 40.00 N 74.49 W
Timbuktu
→ Tombouctou 150 16.46 N 3.01 W
Timbun Mata, Pulau I 112 4.39 N 118.28 E
Timel'ga 86 58.53 N 76.42 E
Timelkam 60 48.00 N 13.36 E
Timellouline 148 29.15 N 8.54 E
Times Square ♠ 276 40.45 N 74.00 W
Timétrine 150 19.27 N 0.26 W
Timétrine Monts ⛰ 150 19.20 N 0.42 W
Timeu Creek ≃ 182 54.28 N 114.27 W
Timewell 219 40.00 N 90.52 W
Timi, Ehi ∧ 146 21.08 N 16.31 E
Timilpan 234 19.52 N 99.45 W
Timimoun 148 29.14 N 0.16 E
Timimoun, Sebkha de ◎ 148 29.00 N 0.05 E
Timinar 140 19.02 N 30.29 E
Timir'azevo 76 55.05 N 21.37 E
Timir'azevskij 86 56.29 N 84.54 E
Timirevo 82 55.08 N 39.10 E
Timiris, Cap ❯ 150 19.23 N 16.32 W
Timiş □[5] 38 45.40 N 21.20 E
Timiş (Tamiš) ≃ 38 44.51 N 20.39 E
Timiskaming, Lake ◎ 190 47.35 N 79.35 W
Timişoara 38 45.45 N 21.13 E
Timkoviči 76 53.03 N 27.00 E
Timkovo 82 55.56 N 38.37 E
Timmendorfer Strand 54 54.00 N 10.46 E
Timmernabben 26 56.58 N 16.26 E
Timmins 190 48.28 N 81.20 W
Timmonsville 192 34.08 N 79.57 W
Timmoudi 148 29.19 N 1.09 W
Timms Hill ∧[2] 190 45.27 N 90.11 W
Timok ≃ 38 44.13 N 22.40 E
Timon 250 5.06 S 42.49 W
Timoneng 174p 13.29 N 144.46 E
Timonovo 82 56.13 N 37.02 E
Timor Sea ⊤[2] 14 11.00 S 128.00 E
Timor Timur □[4] 112 8.35 S 126.00 E
Timor Trough ⊹[1] 14 10.00 S 126.00 E
Timošino, S.S.S.R. 76 60.05 N 36.10 E
Timošino, S.S.S.R. 80 57.50 N 44.25 E
Timotes 246 8.59 N 70.44 W
Timothy Lake ◎[1] 224 45.07 N 121.47 W
Timousserarène ≃ 150 16.21 N 8.07 E
Timovo 80 53.17 N 43.41 E
Timpanogos Cave National Monument ♠ 200 40.18 N 111.52 W
Timpas Creek ≃ 198 38.02 N 103.38 W
Timpaus, Pulau I 112 1.51 S 124.01 E
Timperley 262 53.24 N 2.19 W
Timpia ≃ 248 11.35 S 72.58 W
Timpson 194 31.54 N 94.24 W
Timpton ≃ 74 58.43 N 127.12 E
Timsāh, Buḥayrat at- (Lake Timsah) ◎ 142 30.34 N 32.17 E
Timsah, Lake
→ Timsāh, Buḥayrat at- ◎ 142 30.34 N 32.17 E
Timšer 24 62.06 N 54.40 E
Tims Ford Lake ◎[1] 194 35.15 N 86.10 W
Timur 85 42.50 N 68.26 E
Tina ≃ 158 31.18 S 29.14 E
Tinaca Point ❯ 116 5.33 N 125.20 E
Tinaco 246 9.42 N 68.26 W
Tinaga Island I 116 14.28 N 122.56 E
Ṭīnah, Khalīj aṭ- C 140 31.08 N 32.40 E
Tinahely 48 52.47 N 7.26 W
Tinaja, Punta ❯ 248 16.14 S 73.39 W
Tinajas, Cerro de las ∧ 232 29.57 N 112.12 W
Tinalmud 116 13.36 N 122.53 E
Tinambac 116 13.49 N 123.19 E
Tinambung 112 3.31 S 119.01 E
Tin Amzi, Oued ∨ 148 20.30 N 4.35 E
Tinapagee 166 29.28 S 144.23 E
Tinaquillo 246 9.55 N 68.18 W
Tindari, Capo ❯ 70 38.10 N 15.03 E
Tindila 150 10.16 N 8.15 W
Tindis 126 21.35 N 86.44 E
Tindivanam 122 12.15 N 79.39 E
Tindouf 148 27.50 N 8.04 W
Tindouf, Sebkha de ≚ 148 27.45 N 7.15 W
Tineba, Pegunungan ⛰ 112 1.40 S 120.25 E
Tinée ≃ 62 43.55 N 7.11 E
Tineg ≃ 116 17.38 N 120.37 E
Tineo 34 43.20 N 6.25 W
Tingambato 234 19.30 N 101.52 W
Tinganbao 105 40.39 N 116.09 E
Tinggi, Pulau I 114 2.18 N 104.07 E
Tingha 166 29.57 S 151.13 E
Tinghert, Ḥammādat (Plateau du Tinrhert) ⛰[1] 148 29.00 N 9.00 E
Tinghsien
→ Dingxian 98 38.32 N 114.59 E
Tinghuanghsi 100 25.01 N 121.52 E
Tingi Mountains ⛰[2] 150 8.55 N 10.47 W
Tingjiang ≃ 100 24.24 N 116.35 E
Tingka, Batu ∧ 116 5.20 N 117.06 E
Ting Kau 271d 22.23 N 114.04 E
Tingkawk Sakan 110 26.04 N 96.44 E
Tingkou 98 36.34 N 119.46 E
Tinglev 41 54.56 N 9.15 E
Tinglin 106 30.53 N 121.17 E
Tingliuhe 98 39.34 N 118.49 E
Tingloy 116 13.40 N 120.52 E
Tingmerkpuk Mountain ∧ 180 68.34 N 162.28 W
Tingo de Saposoa 248 7.07 S 76.38 W
Tingo María 248 9.09 S 75.56 W
Tingqianyi 100 30.10 N 115.54 E
Tingréla 150 10.29 N 6.24 W
Tingsiqiao 100 29.50 N 114.12 E
Tingsryd 26 56.32 N 14.59 E
Tingstäde 26 57.44 N 18.36 E
Tingsted 41 54.49 N 11.56 E
Tinguá 256 22.36 S 43.26 W
Tingüindín 234 19.45 N 102.29 W
Tinguipaya 248 19.11 S 65.51 W
Tingvoll 26 62.54 N 8.12 E
Tingvollfjorden C[2] 26 62.50 N 8.11 E
Tingwick 206 45.50 N 71.58 W
Tingwon Group II 164 2.35 S 149.45 E
Tingzitou 106 30.12 N 119.46 E
Tinharé, Ilha de I 255 13.30 S 38.58 W
Tinh-bien 110 10.36 N 104.57 E
Tinian 174n 14.58 N 145.38 E
Tinian I 174n 15.00 N 145.38 E
Tinié 150 14.20 N 1.28 W
Tinitian 116 10.04 N 119.12 E
Tinjar ≃ 112 4.04 N 114.18 E
Tin Jedane, Oued ∨ 148 24.55 N 6.30 E
Tinjil, Pulau I 115a 6.58 S 105.47 E
Tinker Air Force Base ■ 196 35.25 N 97.24 W
Tinkers Creek ≃, Md., U.S. 284c 38.46 N 76.57 W
Tinkers Creek ≃, Ohio, U.S. 214 41.22 N 81.37 W
Tinkertown 283 42.01 N 70.44 W
Tinkisso ≃ 150 11.21 N 9.10 W
Tinley Creek ≃ 278 41.39 N 87.45 W
Tinley Creek Woods ♠ 278 41.39 N 87.47 W
Tinley Park 216 41.35 N 87.47 W
Tinniswood, Mount ∧ 182 50.19 N 123.50 W
Tinnoset 26 59.43 N 9.02 E
Tinnsjø ◎ 26 59.54 N 8.55 E
Tinogasta 252 28.04 S 67.34 W
Tinompo 112 2.09 S 121.17 E
Tínos 38 37.32 N 25.10 E
Tínos I 38 37.38 N 25.10 E
Tin Rerhoh, Tassili ⛰ 150 19.40 N 4.00 E
Tinrhert, Plateau du (Ḥammādat Tinghert) ⛰[1] 148 29.00 N 9.00 E
Tinrhir 148 31.28 N 5.30 W
Tin Sam 271d 22.22 N 114.11 E
Tinskoj 88 56.10 N 96.55 E
Tinsley 194 32.44 N 90.28 W
Tinsukia 120 27.30 N 95.22 E
Tintagel, B.C., Can. 182 54.12 N 125.35 W
Tintagel, Eng., U.K. 42 50.40 N 4.45 W
Tintagel Head ❯ 42 50.41 N 4.46 W
Tintaldra 171b 36.03 S 147.56 E
Tin Tarabine, Oued ∨, Afr. 148 20.50 N 7.25 E
Tin Tarabine, Oued ∨, Alg. 148 22.45 N 6.58 E
Tintas, Rio das ≃ 287a 22.52 S 43.28 W
Tinte, Cerro ∧ 248 22.40 S 67.02 W
Tintern Abbey ʋ[1] 42 51.41 N 2.40 W
Tintern Parva 42 51.42 N 2.40 W
Tintigny 56 49.41 N 5.31 E
Tintina 252 27.02 S 62.43 W
Tintinara 166 35.54 S 140.03 E
Tintioulé 150 10.13 N 9.12 W
Tinto ∧ 46 55.36 N 3.39 W
Tinto ≃ 34 37.12 N 6.55 W
Ti-n-Toumma •[1] 146 16.04 N 12.40 E
Tintwistle 262 53.28 N 1.58 W
Tinui 172 40.53 S 176.04 E
Tinwald 172 43.55 S 171.43 E

ENGLISH Name	Page	Lat.°′	Long.°′

Tin-Zaouaten 150 19.55 N 2.52 E
Tioga, Ill., U.S. 219 40.13 N 91.21 W
Tioga, N. Dak., U.S. 198 48.24 N 102.56 W
Tioga, Pa., U.S. 210 41.55 N 77.08 W
Tioga □[6], N.Y., U.S. 210 42.06 N 76.16 W
Tioga □[6], Pa., U.S. 210 41.45 N 77.17 W
Tioga •[8] 285 40.00 N 75.10 W
Tioga ≃ 210 42.09 N 77.05 W
Tioga Center 210 42.04 N 76.21 W
Tioga Pass)(226 37.54 N 119.16 W
Tioga Terrace 210 42.03 N 76.07 W
Tiojala 24 61.10 N 23.52 E
Tioman, Pulau I 114 2.48 N 104.10 E
Tiona 214 41.45 N 79.03 W
Tione di Trento 64 46.02 N 10.43 E
Tionesta 214 41.30 N 79.27 W
Tionesta Creek ≃ 214 41.28 N 79.22 W
Tionesta Lake ◎[1] 214 41.28 N 79.28 W
Tior 140 6.23 N 31.11 E
Tioro 112 4.41 S 122.36 E
Tioughnioga ≃ 210 42.14 N 75.51 W
Tioughnioga, East Branch ≃ 210 42.36 N 76.10 W
Tipasa 34 36.35 N 2.27 E
Tipitapa 236 12.12 N 86.06 W
Tipp City 218 39.58 N 84.10 W
Tippecanoe, Ind., U.S. 216 41.12 N 86.07 W
Tippecanoe, Ohio, U.S. 214 40.16 N 81.17 W
Tippecanoe □[6] 216 40.25 N 86.53 W
Tippecanoe ≃ 216 40.31 N 86.47 W
Tippecanoe, Lake ◎ 216 41.20 N 85.46 W
Tippecanoe Battlefield State Memorial ⊥ 216 40.31 N 86.52 W
Tippecanoe River State Park ♠ 216 41.07 N 86.36 W
Tipperary, Austl. 164 13.44 S 131.02 E
Tipperary, Eire 48 52.29 N 8.10 W
Tipperary □[6] 48 52.40 N 8.20 W
Tipton, Eng., U.K. 42 52.32 N 2.05 W
Tipton, Calif., U.S. 226 36.04 N 119.19 W
Tipton, Ind., U.S. 216 40.17 N 86.02 W
Tipton, Iowa, U.S. 190 41.46 N 91.08 W
Tipton, Mich., U.S. 216 42.01 N 84.04 W
Tipton, Mo., U.S. 194 38.39 N 92.47 W
Tipton, Okla., U.S. 196 34.30 N 99.08 W
Tipton, Pa., U.S. 214 40.38 N 78.18 W
Tipton □[6] 216 40.17 N 86.02 W
Tipton, Mount ∧ 200 35.32 N 110.12 W
Tiptonville 194 36.23 N 89.29 W
Tip Top Mountain ∧ 190 48.16 N 85.59 W
Tiptree 42 51.49 N 0.45 E
Tiptūr 122 13.16 N 76.29 E
Tiputini ≃ 246 0.47 S 75.32 W
Tiquicheo 234 18.53 N 100.44 W
Tiquisate 236 14.17 N 91.22 W
Tiracambu, Serra do ⛰[1] 250 3.15 S 46.30 W
Tira Chapéu, Morro ∧ 256 22.45 S 44.39 W
Tiradentes 255 21.07 S 44.11 W
Tiradero 232 17.47 N 91.10 W
Tīrah 142 31.05 N 31.14 E
Tīrah, Baḥr ≋ 142 31.03 N 31.15 E
Tirahart, Oued ∨ 148 23.45 N 3.10 E
Tīrān, Jazīrat I 128 27.56 N 34.34 E
Tīrān, Maḍīq ⊔ 140 27.58 N 34.28 E
Tiran, Strait of
→ Tīrān, Maḍīq ⊔ 140 27.58 N 34.28 E
Tirana
→ Tiranë 38 41.20 N 19.50 E
Tiranë 38 41.20 N 19.50 E
Tirano 64 46.13 N 10.10 E
Tiraque 248 17.37 S 65.04 W
Tiraspol' 78 46.51 N 29.38 E
Tirat Karmel 132 32.46 N 34.58 E
Tirat Ẕevi 132 32.25 N 35.32 E
Tirau 172 37.59 S 175.45 E
Tire 130 38.04 N 27.45 E
Tirebolu 130 41.00 N 38.48 E
Tiree I 46 56.30 N 6.55 W
Tire Hill 214 40.16 N 78.55 W
Tires (Tiers), It. 64 46.28 N 11.31 E
Tires, Port. 266c 38.43 N 9.21 W
Tîrgovişte 38 44.56 N 25.27 E
Tîrgu Bujor 38 45.52 N 27.54 E
Tîrgu-Cărbuneşti 38 44.58 N 23.31 E
Tîrgu-Frumos 38 47.13 N 27.00 E
Tîrgu-Jiu 38 45.02 N 23.17 E
Tîrgu-Lăpuş 38 47.27 N 23.52 E
Tîrgu Mureş 38 46.33 N 24.33 E
Tîrgu-Neamţ 38 47.12 N 26.22 E
Tîrgu-Ocna 38 46.15 N 26.37 E
Tîrgu-Secuiesc 38 46.00 N 26.08 E
Tîrgusor 38 44.28 N 28.25 E
Tirich Mīr ∧ 123 36.15 N 71.50 E
Tirilye 130 40.23 N 28.47 E
Tirins ⊥ 38 37.36 N 22.48 E
Tirio 164 8.25 S 143.00 E
Tiriro 150 10.27 N 8.39 W
Tiris •[1] 148 23.30 N 13.10 W
Tirl'anskij 86 54.14 N 58.35 E
Tirna ≃ 122 18.04 N 76.57 E
Tîrnava Mare ≃ 38 46.09 N 23.42 E
Tîrnava Mică ≃ 38 46.11 N 23.55 E
Tîrnăveni 38 46.20 N 24.17 E
Tírnavos 38 39.45 N 22.17 E
Tirnovo
→ Veliko Târnovo 38 43.04 N 25.39 E
Tiro 214 40.54 N 82.46 W
Tirodi 120 21.41 N 79.42 E
Tirol □[3] 64 47.15 N 11.20 E
Tiroler Ache ≃ 64 47.51 N 12.30 E
Tirolo (Tirol) 64 46.42 N 11.10 E
Tirón ≃ 34 41.23 N 4.31 W
Tiros 255 19.00 S 45.58 W
Tiroungoulou 146 9.34 N 22.09 E
Tīr Pol 128 34.36 N 61.15 E
Tirrenia 66 43.38 N 10.17 E
Tirreno, Mare
→ Tyrrhenian Sea ⊤[2] 36 40.00 N 12.00 E
Tirry ≃ 46 58.02 N 4.26 W
Tirsā, Miṣr 142 29.25 N 30.49 E
Tirsā, Miṣr 273c 29.58 N 31.12 E
Tirschenreuth 60 49.53 N 12.21 E
Tirschtiegel
→ Trzciel 30 52.23 N 15.52 E
Tirso ≃ 71 39.53 N 8.32 E
Tirsted 41 54.44 N 11.21 E
Tirstrup 41 56.18 N 10.42 E
Tīrthahalli 122 13.42 N 75.14 E
Tirua Point ❯ 172 38.23 S 174.38 E
Tiruchchirāppalli 122 10.49 N 78.41 E
Tiruchendūr 122 8.29 N 78.07 E
Tiruchengodu 122 11.23 N 77.56 E
Tirukkalukkunram 122 12.37 N 80.04 E
Tirukkoyilūr 122 11.57 N 79.12 E
Tiruliai 76 55.47 N 23.22 E
Tirumangalam 122 9.50 N 77.59 E
Tirunelveli 122 8.44 N 77.42 E
Tirupati 122 13.39 N 79.25 E
Tirupparangunram 122 9.53 N 78.05 E
Tiruppattūr, Bhārat 122 12.30 N 78.34 E
Tiruppattūr, Bhārat 122 10.08 N 78.37 E
Tiruppur 122 11.06 N 77.21 E
Tirūr 122 10.54 N 75.55 E
Tiruttani 122 13.11 N 79.38 E

DEUTSCH Name	Seite	Breite°′	Länge°′ E=Ost

Tirutturaippūndi 122 10.32 N 79.39 E
Tiruvalla 122 9.23 N 76.34 E
Tiruvallūr 122 13.09 N 79.55 E
Tiruvālūr 122 10.46 N 79.39 E
Tiruvannāmalai 122 12.13 N 79.04 E
Tiruvettipuram 122 12.40 N 79.33 E
Tiruvottiyūr 122 13.09 N 80.18 E
Tiruvur 122 17.06 N 80.38 E
Tisa (Tisza) ≃ 38 45.15 N 20.17 E
Tisaiyanvilai 122 8.20 N 77.53 E
Tisaren ◎ 40 59.00 N 15.08 E
Tisbury 42 51.04 N 2.03 W
Tisdale 184 52.51 N 104.04 W
Tishomingo, Miss., U.S. 194 34.38 N 88.14 W
Tishomingo, Okla., U.S. 196 34.14 N 96.40 W
Ṭīsīyah 132 32.24 N 36.27 E
Tisjön ◎ 26 60.55 N 12.58 E
Tiskilwa 190 41.18 N 89.30 W
Tiskino 86 58.05 N 83.10 E
Tiškovka 78 48.29 N 30.56 E
Tiškovo, S.S.S.R. 80 46.02 N 48.36 E
Tiškovo, S.S.S.R. 82 56.05 N 37.44 E
Tisma 236 12.05 N 86.01 W
Tisnaren ◎ 40 58.57 N 15.57 E
Tišnevo 82 55.10 N 36.17 E
Tišnov 30 49.21 N 16.25 E
Tisovec 30 48.43 N 19.57 E
Tissa 146 7.26 N 10.16 E
Tissemsilt 148 35.35 N 1.50 E
Tissø ◎ 41 55.35 N 11.18 E
Tīsta ≃ 124 25.23 N 89.43 E
Tisul' 86 55.45 N 88.19 E
Tisvildeleje 41 56.03 N 12.05 E
Tisza (Tisa) ≃ 38 45.15 N 20.17 E
Tiszaföldvár 30 46.59 N 20.15 E
Tiszafüred 30 47.37 N 20.46 E
Tiszavasvári 30 47.58 N 21.22 E
Tit 148 27.00 N 1.37 E
Titaf 148 27.26 N 0.13 W
Titāgarh 126 22.45 N 88.22 E
Titano, Monte ∧ 66 43.55 N 12.28 E
Titao 150 13.46 N 2.04 W
Tit-Ary 74 71.58 N 127.01 E
Titchfield 42 50.51 N 1.13 W
Titel 38 45.12 N 20.18 E
Tithwal 123 34.24 N 73.47 E
Titicaca, Lago ◎ 248 15.50 S 69.20 W
Titicus 207 41.18 N 73.30 W
Titi Karangan 114 5.31 N 100.37 E
Titikaveka 174k 21.15 S 159.45 W
Titisee-Neustadt 58 47.54 N 8.13 E
Titlagarh 122 20.18 N 83.09 E
Titlis ∧ 58 46.47 N 8.25 E
Tito 68 40.35 N 15.40 E
Tito, Lagh ≃ 154 1.34 N 39.24 E
Titograd 38 42.26 N 19.14 E
Titonka 190 43.14 N 94.03 W
Titou 100 29.52 N 112.42 E
Titova Korenica 36 44.45 N 15.43 E
Titovka 83 48.59 N 39.44 E
Titovo, S.S.S.R. 82 55.35 N 39.07 E
Titovo, S.S.S.R. 82 54.19 N 36.56 E
Titovo Užice 38 43.51 N 19.51 E
Titov Veles 38 41.41 N 21.48 E
Titov vrh ∧ 38 42.00 N 20.51 E
Titran 26 63.40 N 8.18 E
Tittabawassee ≃ 190 43.23 N 83.59 W
Titteri ⛰ 34 36.00 N 3.30 E
Titterstone Clee Hill ∧[2] 42 52.23 N 2.35 W
Titting 60 49.00 N 11.13 E
Tittling 60 48.44 N 13.23 E
Tittmoning 60 48.04 N 12.46 E
Titu 38 44.41 N 25.32 E
Titule 154 3.17 N 25.32 E
Titus □[6] 222 33.05 N 94.58 W
Titusville, Fla., U.S. 220 28.37 N 80.49 W
Titusville, N.J., U.S. 208 40.18 N 74.53 W
Titusville, Pa., U.S. 214 41.38 N 79.41 W
Titz 56 51.01 N 6.25 E
Tiu Chung Chau I 271d 22.20 N 114.19 E
Tiu Keng Wan 271d 22.18 N 114.15 E
Tiumpan Head ❯ 46 58.16 N 6.09 W
Tiuni 120 30.57 N 77.51 E
Tiva ≃ 154 2.20 S 38.48 E
Tivaouane 150 14.57 N 16.49 W
Tiveden ⛰[2] 40 58.45 N 14.40 E
Tiverton, Eng., U.K. 42 50.55 N 3.29 W
Tiverton, R.I., U.S. 207 41.38 N 71.12 W
Tivoli, Gren. 241k 12.10 N 61.37 W
Tivoli, It. 66 41.58 N 12.48 E
Tivoli, N.Y., U.S. 210 42.04 N 73.55 W
Tivoli, Tex., U.S. 196 28.27 N 96.53 W
Tivoli ♠ 41 55.40 N 12.34 E
Ṭiwāl, Wādī ∨ 146 10.22 N 22.43 E
Tiwi, Pil. 116 13.27 N 123.41 E
Ṭīwī, 'Umān 128 22.49 N 59.16 E
Tiwuronto 115b 8.48 S 120.09 E
Tixtla [de Guerrero] 234 17.35 N 99.26 W
Tiyās 130 34.33 N 37.40 E
Tiyo 144 14.40 N 40.15 E
Tiyo, Pegunungan ⛰ 164 4.00 S 135.30 E
Tiyunhe ≋ 105 39.07 N 117.43 E
Tizapán •[8] 286a 19.20 N 99.13 W
Tizapán el Alto 234 20.10 N 103.04 W
Tizatlán ⊥ 234 19.21 N 98.15 W
Tizayuca 234 19.50 N 98.59 W
Tizimín 232 21.10 N 88.10 W
Tizi-Ouzou 148 36.48 N 4.02 E
Tizmant ash-Sharqīyah 142 29.03 N 31.03 E
Tiznados ≃ 246 8.16 N 67.47 W
Tiznit 148 29.43 N 9.44 W
Tizoc 196 25.41 N 101.59 W
Tizzeine 148 25.21 N 8.50 E
Tjällmo 40 58.43 N 15.21 E
Tjeuke Meer ◎ 52 52.54 N 5.50 E
Tjolotjo 154 19.47 S 27.46 E
Tjøme I 26 59.07 N 10.24 E
Tjörn I 26 58.00 N 11.38 E
Tjörnarp 41 56.00 N 13.37 E
Tkibuli 84 42.21 N 42.59 E
Tkvarčeli 84 42.51 N 41.41 E
Tlachichuca 234 19.06 N 97.25 W
Tlacoapa 234 17.09 N 98.52 W
Tlacolula [de Matamoros] 234 16.57 N 96.29 W
Tlacotalpan 234 18.37 N 95.40 W
Tlacotepec 234 17.46 N 99.59 W
Tlacuitapa 234 21.14 N 102.12 W
Tláhuac □[7] 286a 19.17 N 99.00 W
Tláhuac •[8] 286a 19.16 N 99.00 W
Tlahualilo de Zaragoza 232 26.07 N 103.27 W
Tlahuelilpa de Ocampo 234 20.08 N 99.14 W
Tlahuitoltepec 234 17.04 N 95.59 W
Tlajomulco de Zúñiga 234 20.28 N 103.27 W
Tlalamabele 156 21.16 S 26.20 E
Tlalchapa 234 18.24 N 100.28 W
Tlalcozotitlán 234 17.54 N 99.15 W
Tlalixtac de Cabrera 234 17.04 N 96.39 W
Tlalixtaquilla 234 17.21 N 98.28 W
Tlalnepantla 286a 19.33 N 99.12 W
Tlalnepantla □[7] 286a 19.32 N 99.12 W
Tlalnepantla ≃ 286a 19.31 N 99.16 W
Tláloc, Cerro ∧ 234 19.25 N 98.42 W
Tlalpan □[7] 286a 19.13 N 99.12 W
Tlalpujahua 234 19.48 N 100.10 W

Symbols in the index entries represent the broad categories identified in the key at the right. Symbols with superior numbers (⛰[2]) identify subcategories (see complete key on page I · 30).

Kartensymbole in dem Registerverzeichnis stellen die rechts in Schlüssel erklärten Kategorien dar. Symbole mit hochgestellten Ziffern (⛰[2]) bezeichnen Unterabteilungen einer Kategorie (vgl. vollständiger Schlüssel auf Seite I · 30).

Los símbolos incluídos en el texto del índice representan las grandes categorias identificadas con la clave a la derecha. Los símbolos con numeros en su parte superior (⛰[2]) identifican las subcategorías (véase la clave completa en la página I · 30).

Les symboles de l'index représentent les catégories indiquées dans la légende à droite. Les symboles suivis d'un indice (⛰[2]) représentent des sous-catégories (voir légende complète à la page I · 30).

Os símbolos incluídos no texto do índice representam as grandes categorias identificadas com a chave à direita. Os símbolos com números em sua parte superior (⛰[2]) identificam as subcategorias (veja-se a chave completa à página I · 30).

	English	Deutsch	Español	Français	Português
∧	Mountain	Berg	Montaña	Montagne	Montanha
⛰	Mountains	Berge	Montañas	Montagnes	Montanhas
)(	Pass	Pass	Paso	Col	Passo
∨	Valley, Canyon	Tal, Cañon	Valle, Cañón	Vallée, Canyon	Vale, Canhão
≚	Plain	Ebene	Llano	Plaine	Planície
❯	Cape	Kap	Cabo	Cap	Cabo
I	Island	Insel	Isla	Île	Ilha
II	Islands	Inseln	Islas	Îles	Ilhas
•	Other Topographic Features	Andere Topographische Objekte	Otros Elementos Topográficos	Autres données topographiques	Outros Elementos Topográficos

Tlaltenango de Sánchez Román 234 21.47 N 103.19 W
Tlaltenco ⬥8 286a 19.17 N 99.01 W
Tl'ančetamak 80 55.28 N 52.37 E
Tlanyuku Pass)(158 29.04 S 29.15 E
Tlapa 234 17.33 N 98.33 W
Tlapacoyan 234 19.58 N 97.13 W
Tlapaneco ≃ 234 18.05 N 98.48 W
Tlapehuala 234 18.13 N 100.31 W
Tlapeng 156 23.15 S 21.49 E
Tlaquepaque 234 20.39 N 103.19 W
Tl'arata 84 42.07 N 46.22 E
Tlatlauqui 234 19.51 N 97.29 W
Tlaxcala □3 234 19.25 N 98.10 W
Tlaxcala [de Xicoténcatl] 234 19.19 N 98.14 W
Tlaxcoapan 234 20.05 N 99.13 W
Tlaxco [de Morelos] 234 19.37 N 98.07 W
Tlaxiaco 234 17.16 N 97.41 W
Tlaxmalac 234 18.21 N 99.25 W
Tlazazalca 234 19.58 N 102.04 W
Tlemcen 148 34.52 N 1.15 W
Tletat ed Douair 34 35.59 N 2.55 E
Tlētē Ouāte Gharbī, Jabal ∧ 130 35.20 N 39.13 E
Tlevak Strait ⩌ 182 55.03 N 132.58 W
Tlhakmeng 158 26.27 S 24.21 E
Tloch 84 42.38 N 46.28 E
Tlučiná 60 49.44 N 13.14 E
Tlumač 78 48.52 N 25.01 E
Tłuszcz 30 52.26 N 21.26 E
Tmassah 146 26.22 N 15.47 E
Tmīšān 146 27.32 N 13.19 E
Tnâot ≃ 110 11.29 N 104.57 E
Tnekvejem ≃ 180 65.51 N 177.30 E
Toa ≃ 240p 20.23 N 74.32 W
Toa, Cuchillas de ⩘ 240p 20.27 N 74.58 W
Toa Alta 240m 18.23 N 66.15 W
Toa Baja 240m 18.27 N 66.15 W
Toabré ≃ 236 8.56 N 80.33 W
Toaca ∧ 38 46.59 N 25.57 E
Toachi ≃ 246 0.08 N 79.18 W
Toahayanā 232 26.08 N 107.44 W
Toandos Peninsula ≻1 224 47.43 N 122.47 W
Toano, It. 64 44.23 N 10.34 E
Toano, Va., U.S. 208 37.23 N 76.48 W
Toanoano 174s 17.51 S 149.13 W
Toano Draw V 204 41.27 N 114.35 W
Toano Range ⩘ 204 40.50 N 114.20 W
Toast 182 36.30 N 80.38 W
Toay 252 36.40 S 64.21 W
Toba, Mali 150 11.52 N 7.28 W
Toba, Nihon 94 34.29 N 136.51 E
Toba ≃ 182 50.30 N 124.15 W
Toba, Danau ⊛ 114 2.35 N 98.50 E
Tobacco ≃ 190 43.49 N 84.24 W
Tobacco Plains Indian Reserve ⬥4 182 49.04 N 115.06 W
Tobacco Root Mountains ⩘ 202 45.35 N 112.00 W
Tobago I 241r 11.15 N 60.40 W
Toba Inlet C 182 50.20 N 124.50 W
Toba Kākar Range ⩘ 120 31.15 N 68.00 E
Tobalai, Pulau I 164 1.37 S 128.20 E
Tobarra 34 38.35 N 1.41 W
Tobas 252 28.08 S 62.42 W
Toba Tek Singh 123 30.58 N 72.29 E
Tobe 96 33.44 N 132.47 E
Tobe Jube, Bahía C 246 9.15 N 60.45 W
Tobekuduk 86 49.50 N 54.15 E
Tobelo 108 1.44 N 128.01 E
Tobelombang 112 0.57 S 122.00 E
Tobercurry 48 54.03 N 8.43 W
Tobermorey 166 22.15 S 138.00 E
Tobermory, Austl. 166 27.17 S 143.41 E
Tobermory, Scot., U.K. 46 56.37 N 6.05 W
Toberonochy 46 56.13 N 5.38 W
Tōbetsu 92a 43.13 N 141.31 E
Tobi I 108 3.00 N 131.10 E
Tobias 198 40.25 N 97.20 W
Tobias Barreto 250 11.11 S 38.01 W
Tobiishi-bana ≻ 174f 24.45 N 141.17 E
Tobin, Mount ∧ 204 40.22 N 117.32 W
Tobin Lake ⊛, Austl. 162 21.45 S 125.49 E
Tobin Lake ⊛, Sask., Can. 184 53.40 N 103.35 W
Tobique ≃ 186 46.46 N 67.42 W
Tobi-shima I 92 39.12 N 139.34 E
Toblach → Dobbiaco 64 46.44 N 12.14 E
Tobo, Indon. 164 3.34 S 130.11 E
Tobo, Sve. 40 60.16 N 17.39 E
Toboali 112 3.00 S 106.30 E
Tobol 86 52.40 N 62.39 E
Tobol ≃ 86 58.10 N 68.12 E
Toboli 112 0.43 S 120.05 E
Tobol'sk 86 58.12 N 68.16 E
Tobong-san ∧ 271b 37.42 N 127.01 E
Tobor 150 12.39 N 16.16 W
Toboso 116 10.43 N 123.31 E
Tobré 150 10.12 N 2.08 E
Tobruk → Ţubruq 146 32.05 N 23.59 E
Tobseda 24 68.36 N 52.14 E
Tōbu 94 36.21 N 138.20 E
Toburdanovo 80 55.22 N 47.38 E
Toby, Mount ∧ 207 42.29 N 72.32 W
Tobyhanna 210 41.11 N 75.25 W
Tobyhanna Creek ≃ 210 41.07 N 75.39 W
Tobyhanna State Park ♠ 210 41.13 N 75.25 W
Tobyš ≃ 24 65.30 N 51.00 E
Tocaima 246 4.28 N 74.38 W
Tocantínia 250 9.33 S 48.22 W
Tocantinópolis 250 6.20 S 47.25 W
Tocantins ≃ 242 1.45 S 49.10 W
Tocantins, Parque Nacional do ♠ 255 13.42 S 47.37 W
Tocantinzinho ≃ 255 13.57 S 48.20 W
Toccoa 192 34.35 N 83.19 W
Toccoa ≃ 192 34.59 N 84.23 W
Toce ≃ 58 45.56 N 8.29 E
Tochcha Lake ⊛ 182 54.56 N 125.54 W
Tochigi 94 36.23 N 139.44 E
Tochigi □5 94 36.45 N 139.45 E
Tochimilco 234 18.54 N 98.34 W
Tochio 92 37.28 N 139.00 E
Tochoj 88 50.30 N 105.00 E
Tochta 24 62.14 N 48.48 E
Tochtamyš 120 37.50 N 74.39 E
Tockholes 262 53.42 N 2.31 W
Tockoje 80 52.32 N 52.45 E
Töcksfors 26 59.30 N 11.50 E
Točnik 60 49.27 N 13.19 E
Toco, Chile 252 22.05 S 69.35 W
Toco, Trin. 241r 10.50 N 60.57 W
Tocoa 236 15.41 N 86.03 W
Tócome ≃ 286c 10.29 N 66.49 W
Toconao 252 23.11 S 68.01 W
Tocopilla 252 22.05 S 70.12 W
Tocos do Mogi 256 22.22 S 46.06 W
Tocumwal 166 35.49 S 145.34 E
Tocuyo ≃ 246 11.03 N 68.23 W
Tocuyo de la Costa 246 11.02 N 68.23 W
Toda 94 35.48 N 139.41 E
Toda Bhīm 124 26.55 N 76.49 E
Todaiji Temple ɣ1 270 34.42 N 135.51 E
Todang-ni 271b 37.37 N 126.50 E
Toda Rai Singh 120 26.01 N 75.29 E
Todd 214 40.16 N 78.04 W
Todd ≃ 162 24.52 S 135.48 E
Todd Estates 285 39.40 N 75.43 W
Toddington 42 51.57 N 0.32 W
Todd Point ≻ 284b 39.15 N 76.27 W
Toddville, Md., U.S. 208 38.18 N 76.04 W
Toddville, N.Y., U.S. 210 41.17 N 73.53 W
Todeli 112 1.40 S 124.29 E
Todenyang 154 4.32 N 35.56 E
Todi 66 42.47 N 12.24 E
Tödi ∧ 58 46.49 N 8.56 E
Todmorden, Austl. 162 27.08 S 134.48 E
Todmorden, Eng., U.K. 44 53.43 N 2.05 W
Todoromi 270 34.53 N 135.28 E
Todo-saki ≻ 92 39.33 N 142.05 E
Todos Santos, Bol. 248 16.48 S 65.08 W
Todos Santos, Méx. 232 23.27 N 110.13 W
Todos Santos, Bahía C 232 31.48 N 116.42 W
Todro 154 3.21 N 30.14 E
Todtenhausen 52 52.20 N 8.56 E
Todtmoos 58 47.44 N 8.00 E
Todtmoos Au 58 47.42 N 7.58 E
Todtnau 58 47.50 N 7.56 E
Todža, Ozero ⊛ 88 52.22 N 96.30 E
Toécé 150 11.50 N 1.16 W
Toe Head ≻ 46 57.50 N 7.08 W
Tōei 94 35.04 N 137.41 E
T'oejo-dong 98 39.54 N 127.46 E
Toetoes Bay C 172 46.38 S 168.43 E
Tofield 182 53.22 N 112.40 W
Tofino 182 49.09 N 125.54 W
Töfsingdalens Nationalpark ♠ 26 62.09 N 12.30 E
Tofte 26 59.33 N 10.34 E
Toften ⊛ 40 59.03 N 14.36 E
Tofterup 41 55.39 N 8.50 E
Toftlund 41 55.11 N 9.04 E
Toga 94 36.27 N 137.02 E
Toga I 175f 13.26 S 166.42 E
Togakushi 94 36.44 N 138.05 E
Togakushi-yama ∧ 94 36.46 N 138.04 E
Toganas 80 50.49 N 52.02 E
Tōgane 94 35.33 N 140.22 E
Toggenburg V 58 47.45 N 9.10 E
Togi 94 37.08 N 136.44 E
Togiak 180 59.04 N 160.24 W
Togiak Bay C 180 59.00 N 160.30 W
Togiak Lake ⊛ 180 59.38 N 159.35 W
Togian, Kepulauan II 112 0.20 S 122.00 E
Togian, Pulau I 112 0.22 S 121.56 E
Töging am Inn 60 48.15 N 12.35 E
Togliatti → Toljatti 80 53.31 N 49.26 E
Togni 140 18.04 N 35.13 E
Tōgō, Nihon 94 35.05 N 137.03 E
Tōgō, Nihon 96 35.28 N 133.53 E
Togo □1 134 8.00 N 1.10 E
Togochale 144 9.33 N 43.18 E
Tōgō-ike ⊛ 96 35.28 N 133.54 E
Togoron 116 12.35 N 123.27 E
Togouchi 96 34.34 N 132.13 E
Tögrög, Mong. 102 45.31 N 102.59 E
Tögrög, Mong. 102 45.46 N 94.55 E
Toguchi 174m 26.39 N 127.54 E
Toguchin 86 55.16 N 84.23 E
Togur 86 58.24 N 82.49 E
Togura 94 36.29 N 138.09 E
Toguzak ≃ 86 54.06 N 62.50 E
Toguzbulak 85 42.06 N 76.44 E
Togwotee Pass)(202 43.45 N 110.04 W
Tŏgyu-san ∧ 98 36.48 N 127.23 E
Togyz 86 47.34 N 60.33 E
Tōhaku 96 35.30 N 133.40 E
Tohakum Peak ∧ 204 40.11 N 119.27 W
Tohāna 124 29.42 N 75.54 E
Tohen 144 11.42 N 51.17 E
Tohivea ∧ 174s 17.33 S 149.49 W
Tohma ≃ 130 38.31 N 37.38 E
Toholampi 26 63.46 N 24.15 E
Tohopekaliga, Lake ⊛ 220 28.12 N 81.23 W
Tohor, Tanjong ≻ 114 1.51 N 102.42 E
T'ohyŏn-ni 98 39.53 N 124.52 E
Toi, Nihon 94 34.54 N 138.47 E
Toi, Niue 174v 18.57 S 169.51 W
Toijala 26 61.10 N 23.52 E
Toili 112 1.27 S 122.24 E
Toi-misaki ≻ 92 31.20 N 131.22 E
Tōin 94 35.05 N 136.35 E
Toinya 140 6.17 N 29.44 E
Toi Sar 120 31.06 N 69.54 E
Toiyabe Range ⩘ 204 39.10 N 117.10 W
Tojg 128 32.04 N 61.48 E
To-jima I 96 33.12 N 132.22 E
Tojo, Indon. 112 1.17 S 121.11 E
Tōjō, Nihon 96 34.53 N 133.16 E
Tōjō, Nihon 270 34.55 N 135.04 E
Tojtepa 85 41.03 N 69.22 E
Tōju-in ɣ1 94 35.19 N 136.04 E
Tok 180 63.20 N 142.59 W
Tok ≃ 80 52.46 N 52.22 E
Tokaanu 172 38.58 S 175.46 E
Tokachi ≃ 92a 42.44 N 143.42 E
Tokachi-dake ∧ 92a 43.25 N 142.41 E
Tokachi-heiya ≚ 92a 43.00 N 143.30 E
Tōkagi 268 35.42 N 139.56 E
Tokai, Malay. 114 6.01 N 100.24 E
Tōkai, Nihon 94 36.27 N 140.34 E
Tokaj ≃ 78 51.18 N 41.04 E
Tokala 112 1.47 S 121.43 E
Tōkamachi 94 37.08 N 138.46 E
Tokanui 172 46.34 S 168.56 E
Tokara-kaikyō ⩌ 93b 30.10 N 130.10 E
Tokara-rettō II 93b 29.36 N 129.43 E
Tokarevka 86 50.08 N 73.12 E
Tokaris 130 37.45 N 38.50 E
Tokar'ovka 80 51.59 N 41.09 E
Tokar'ovo, S.S.S.R. 76 55.17 N 35.04 E
Tokar'ovo, S.S.S.R. 265b 55.38 N 37.55 E
Tokashiki-shima I 93b 26.11 N 127.21 E
Tokat 130 40.19 N 36.34 E
Tokat □4 130 40.25 N 36.30 E
Tŏkchŏk-kundo II 98 37.14 N 126.07 E
Tŏkch'ŏn 98 39.46 N 126.19 E
Tok-dŏ I 92 37.17 N 131.53 E
Toke 98 35.32 N 140.17 E
Tokeland 224 46.42 N 123.59 W
Tokelau-Inseln → Tokelau Islands □2 14 9.00 S 171.45 W
Tokelau Islands □2 14 9.00 S 171.45 W
Tokelau Islands II 4 9.00 S 171.45 W
Tokeneke Brook ≃ 276 41.03 N 73.28 W
Tŏkhŭng-ni 98 40.02 N 127.08 E
Toki 94 35.21 N 137.11 E
Toki ≃ 94 35.12 N 136.52 E
Tokio → Tōkyō 94 35.42 N 139.46 E
Toki Point ≻ 174a 19.19 N 166.35 E
Tokko 74 59.59 N 119.52 E
Tokko ≃ 88 58.42 N 119.50 E
Toklar 130 38.26 N 36.01 E
Toklat ≃ 180 64.27 N 150.17 W
Tokma 88 58.13 N 105.42 E
Tokmak, S.S.S.R. 78 47.15 N 35.43 E
Tokmak, S.S.S.R. 85 42.55 N 75.18 E
Toko 172 39.20 S 174.24 E
Tököl 264c 47.19 N 18.58 E
Tokolimbu 112 2.48 S 121.34 E
Tokomaru 172 40.28 S 175.30 E
Tokomaru Bay 172 38.08 S 178.18 E
Tokoname 94 34.53 N 136.51 E
Toko Range ⩘ 166 23.05 S 138.20 E
Tokoro ≃ 92a 44.07 N 144.05 E
Tokoroa 172 38.14 S 175.52 E
Tokorozawa 94 35.47 N 139.28 E
Tokovskoje 78 47.38 N 33.59 E
Toksook Bay 180 60.32 N 165.06 W
Toksovo 76 60.09 N 30.31 E
Toksu Palace ɣ 271b 37.35 N 126.58 E
Toktogul 85 41.50 N 72.50 E
Toktogul'skoje Vodochranilišče ⊛1 85 41.50 N 72.55 E
Toku I 14 18.10 S 174.11 W
Tokuji 96 34.09 N 131.45 E
Tokul Creek ≃ 224 47.35 N 121.50 W
Tokung 112 0.18 S 114.28 E
Tokuno-shima I 93b 27.45 N 128.58 E
Tokur 89 53.10 N 132.53 E
Tokura 270 34.58 N 135.18 E
Tokura-tōge)(96 35.17 N 134.31 E
Tokusaga-mine ∧ 96 34.26 N 131.41 E
Tokushima 96 34.04 N 134.34 E
Tokushima □5 96 33.45 N 134.00 E
Tokuyama, Nihon 94 35.42 N 136.29 E
Tokuyama, Nihon 96 34.03 N 131.49 E
Tokwe ≃ 154 21.09 S 31.30 E
Tōkyō 94
268 35.42 N 139.46 E
Tōkyō □5 94 35.45 N 139.30 E
Tokyo, University of ɣ2 268 35.42 N 139.46 E
Tokyo Bay → Tōkyō-wan C 94 35.30 N 139.54 E
Tōkyō-daigaku-uchūkūkan-kenkyūsho ɣ3 92 31.17 N 131.05 E
Tōkyō-kō C 268 35.37 N 139.47 E
Tōkyō-kokusai-kūkō ⊠ 94 35.45 N 140.21 E
Tokyo University of Education ɣ2 268 35.43 N 139.44 E
Tōkyō-wan (Tokyo Bay) C 94 35.30 N 139.54 E
Tokzār 120 35.52 N 66.26 E
Tol I 175c 7.22 N 151.37 E
Tolaga Bay 172 38.22 S 178.18 E
Tolala 112 2.56 S 121.06 E
Tolang 114 1.56 N 99.26 E
Tolbert 52 53.10 N 6.21 E
Tolbonuur 86 48.25 N 90.17 E
Tolbuchino 80 57.51 N 40.03 E
Tolbuhin 38 43.34 N 27.50 E
Tolderol Point ≻ 168b 35.22 S 139.10 E
Tolé, Pan. 236 8.14 N 81.41 W
Tole, S.S.S.R. 85 42.40 N 70.08 E
Toledo, Bol. 248 18.10 S 67.25 W
Toledo, Bra. 252 24.44 S 53.45 W
Toledo, Bra. 256 22.44 S 46.23 W
Toledo, Col. 246 7.19 N 72.28 W
Toledo, Esp. 34 39.52 N 4.01 W
Toledo, Pil. 116 10.23 N 123.38 E
Toledo, Ill., U.S. 194 39.16 N 88.15 W
Toledo, Iowa, U.S. 190 42.00 N 92.35 W
Toledo, Ohio, U.S. 214 41.39 N 83.32 W
Toledo, Oreg., U.S. 202 44.37 N 123.56 W
Toledo, Wash., U.S. 224 46.26 N 122.51 W
Toledo, Ur. 258 34.45 S 56.05 W
Toledo □5 236 16.20 N 88.55 W
Toledo, Montes de ⩘ 34 39.33 N 4.20 W
Toledo Bend Reservoir ⊛1 194 31.30 N 93.45 W
Toledo Express Airport ⊠ 216 41.35 N 83.49 W
Tolentino 66 43.12 N 13.17 E
Tolfa 66 42.09 N 11.56 E
Tolfa, Monti della ⩘ 66 42.08 N 11.54 E
Tolga, Alg. 148 34.46 N 5.22 E
Tolga, Nor. 26 62.25 N 11.00 E
Tolima □5 246 3.45 N 75.15 W
Tolima, Nevado del ∧ 246 4.40 N 75.19 W
Tolimán, Méx. 234 20.55 N 99.56 W
Tolimán, Méx. 234 19.36 N 103.55 W
Tolitoli 112 1.02 N 120.49 E
Toljatti (Togliatti) 80 53.31 N 49.26 E
Tol'ka 74 64.02 N 81.55 E
Tolkmicko 30 54.20 N 19.31 E
Tolland 207 41.52 N 72.22 W
Tolland □6 207 41.52 N 72.22 W
Tollarp 26 55.56 N 13.59 E
Tollense ≃ 54 53.54 N 13.02 E
Tollensesee ⊛ 54 53.30 N 13.11 E
Tollesboro 218 38.34 N 83.35 W
Tollesbury 42 51.46 N 0.50 E
Tolleson 200 33.27 N 112.16 W
Tollhouse 226 37.01 N 119.24 W
Tolloche 252 25.30 S 63.32 W
Tølløse 41 55.37 N 11.45 E
Tollygunge ⬥8 272b 22.30 N 88.21 E
Tolmači 76 57.26 N 35.41 E
Tolmačovo 76 58.52 N 29.55 E
Tolmezzo 64 46.24 N 13.01 E
Tolmin 36 46.11 N 13.44 E
Tolna 30 46.26 N 18.46 E
Tolna □6 30 46.30 N 18.35 E
Tolo 152 2.56 S 18.34 E
Tolo, Teluk C 112 2.00 S 122.30 E
Toloa, Houma ≻ 174w 21.17 S 175.08 W
Tolob 46a 59.53 N 1.19 W
Toločin 76 54.25 N 29.42 E
Tolokiwa Island I 164 5.20 S 147.40 E
Tolomo 89 50.03 N 137.45 E
Tolong Bay C 116 9.20 N 122.49 E
Tolongoina 157b 21.33 S 47.31 E
Tolono 194 39.59 N 88.16 W
Tolosa 34 43.08 N 2.04 W
Tolosa, Aeródromo ⊠ 288 34.53 S 57.58 W
Tolovana ≃ 180 64.51 N 149.45 W
Tolpuddle 42 50.45 N 2.18 W
Tol'skij Majdan 80 54.57 N 44.39 E
Tolsta Head ≻ 46 58.20 N 6.10 W
Tolstoj, Mys ≻ 74 59.10 N 155.12 E
Tolstoje 78 48.50 N 25.44 E
Tolstopal'cevo 265b 55.38 N 37.13 E
Tolt, North Fork ≃ 224 47.42 N 121.49 W
Toltén 254 39.13 S 73.14 W
Tolten ≃ 254 39.15 S 73.14 W
Tolti 123 35.02 N 76.06 E
Toltry ⩘1 78 49.00 N 26.10 E
Tolt-Seattle Water Supply Reservoir ⊛1 224 47.42 N 121.39 W
Tolú 246 9.31 N 75.35 W
Toluca 216 41.00 N 89.08 W
Toluca, Nevado de ∧1 234 19.08 N 99.44 W
Toluca [de Lerdo] 234 19.17 N 99.40 W
Tolvajarvi 24 62.17 N 31.27 E
Tolvdalselva ≃ 26 58.10 N 8.00 E
Tolve 68 40.42 N 16.01 E
Tolwa 140 6.38 N 32.37 E
Tolworth ⬥8 260 51.23 N 0.17 W
Tolyatti → Toljatti 80 53.31 N 49.26 E
Tolybaj 86 50.31 N 62.19 E
Tom' ≃, S.S.S.R. 86 56.50 N 84.27 E
Tom' ≃, S.S.S.R. 89 51.00 N 127.54 E
Toma 150 12.46 N 2.53 W
Tomah 190 43.59 N 90.30 W
Tomahawk 190 45.28 N 89.44 W
Tomakomai 92a 42.38 N 141.36 E
Tomakovka 78 47.48 N 34.44 E
Tomani 112 4.50 N 115.55 E
Tomaniivi, Mount ∧ 175g 17.37 S 178.01 E
Tomar, Port. 34 39.36 N 8.25 W
Tomar, S.S.S.R. 86 46.24 N 75.03 E
Tomara 174r 6.54 N 158.08 E
Tomari 89 47.47 N 142.03 E
Tomarovka 78 50.41 N 36.14 E
Tomarza 130 38.27 N 35.49 E
Tomás Barrón (Eucaliptus) 248 17.35 S 67.31 W
Tomasboda ∧2 40 59.24 N 14.58 E
Tomás Gomensoro 252 30.26 S 57.26 W
Tomašgorod 78 51.19 N 27.02 E
Tomasina ≃ 190 46.40 N 76.16 W
Tomás Jofré 258 34.43 S 59.19 W
Tomašpol' 78 48.33 N 28.31 E
Tomaszów Lubelski 30 50.28 N 23.25 E
Tomaszów Mazowiecki 30 51.32 N 20.01 E
Tomatin 46 57.20 N 3.59 W
Tomatlán 234 19.56 N 105.15 W
Tomatlán ≃ 234 19.50 N 105.23 W
Tomave 248 20.06 S 66.35 W
Tomazina 255 23.46 S 49.58 W
Tomba di Nerone ⬥8 267a 41.57 N 12.27 E
Tombadonkéa 150 11.00 N 14.23 W
Tombador, Serra do ⩘ 248 12.00 S 57.40 W
Tomball 222 30.06 N 95.37 W
Tombara 96 35.05 N 132.47 E
Tombe 140 5.49 N 31.41 E
Tombigbee ≃ 194 31.04 N 87.58 W
Tomboco 152 6.48 S 13.18 E
Tombolo 64 45.38 N 11.50 E
Tombos 255 20.55 S 42.02 W
Tombouctou (Timbuktu) 150 16.46 N 3.01 W
Tombs of the Caliphs ⊥ 273c 30.03 N 31.17 E
Tombstone 200 31.43 N 110.04 W
Tombstone Mountain ∧ 180 64.25 N 138.30 W
Tom Burke 156 23.05 S 28.00 E
Tomdoun 46 57.04 N 5.03 W
Tomé 252 36.37 S 72.57 W
Tomea, Pulau I 112 5.45 S 123.56 E
Tomé-Açu 250 2.25 S 48.09 W
Tomek 130 38.02 N 32.41 E
Tomelilla 26 55.33 N 13.57 E
Tomelloso 34 39.10 N 3.01 W
Tomerong 170 35.04 S 150.35 E
Tomhannock Reservoir ⊛1 210 42.51 N 73.33 W
Tomi ≃ 152 5.07 N 19.19 E
Tomich 46 57.18 N 4.48 W
Tomichi Creek ≃ 200 38.31 N 106.58 W
Tomifobia ≃ 206 45.11 N 72.02 W
Tomiko Lake ⊛ 190 46.32 N 79.49 W
Tomil 174q 9.31 N 138.09 E
Tomil Harbor C 174q 9.30 N 138.09 E
Tomilino 265b 55.39 N 37.57 E
Tomini 112 0.30 N 120.32 E
Tomini, Teluk C 112 0.20 S 121.00 E
Tominian 150 13.17 N 4.35 W
Tomintoul 46 57.14 N 3.22 W
Tomio ≃ 270 34.35 N 135.44 E
Tomioka 94 36.15 N 138.54 E
Tomisato 94 35.44 N 140.19 E
Tomiura 94 35.03 N 139.50 E
Tomiyama, Nihon 94 35.11 N 137.48 E
Tomiyama, Nihon 94 35.05 N 139.51 E
Tomizawa 94 35.14 N 138.29 E
T'omkino 76 55.05 N 35.01 E
Tomkins Cove 210 41.15 N 73.59 W
Tomkinson Ranges ⩘ 162 26.11 S 129.05 E
Tomlinson Run State Park ♠ 214 40.33 N 80.34 W
Tommerup Stationsby 41 55.19 N 10.13 E
Tommot 74 58.58 N 126.19 E
Tomnavoulin 46 57.18 N 3.19 W
T'omnyj 88 53.24 N 118.31 E
Tomo ≃ 246 5.20 N 67.48 W
Tomobe 94 36.20 N 140.20 E
Tomohon 112 1.19 N 124.49 E
Tömörbulag 88 49.16 N 100.15 E
Tomori 174m 26.08 N 127.44 E
Tomori, Teluk C 112 1.58 S 121.28 E
Tomorolong 174r 6.51 N 158.10 E
Tompa 88 55.08 N 109.47 E
Tompkins, Newf., Can. 186 47.48 N 59.13 W
Tompkins, Sask., Can. 184 50.04 N 108.47 W
Tompkins □6 210 42.27 N 76.30 W
Tompkins County Airport ⊠ 210 42.29 N 76.57 W
Tompkinsville 194 36.42 N 85.41 W
Tompo 112 0.56 N 120.20 E
Tom Price, Mount ∧ 162 22.39 S 117.40 E
Tomptokan 74 57.06 N 133.59 E
Tomra 26 62.35 N 6.56 E
Toms ≃ 208 39.57 N 74.07 W
Toms, Ridgeway Branch ≃ 208 40.00 N 74.14 W
Toms Cove C 208 37.53 N 75.22 W
Toms Creek ≃ 208 39.38 N 77.17 W
Tomsk 86 56.30 N 84.58 E
Toms River 208 39.58 N 74.12 W
Tomtabacken ∧2 26 57.30 N 14.28 E
Tömük 130 36.41 N 34.22 E
Tomuzlovka ≃ 84 44.46 N 44.10 E
Ton 64 46.15 N 11.04 E
Tonadico 64 46.11 N 11.50 E
Tonalá, Méx. 234 20.37 N 103.14 W
Tonalá, Méx. 234 16.04 N 93.45 W
Tonale, Passo del)(64 46.16 N 10.35 E
Tonami 94 36.38 N 136.54 E
Tonantins 246 2.47 S 67.47 W
Tonantins ≃ 246 2.47 S 67.47 W
Tonara 71 40.02 N 9.10 E
Tonasket 202 48.42 N 119.26 W
Tonatico 234 18.47 N 99.41 W
Tonawanda 210 43.01 N 78.53 W
Tonawanda, Town of 210 42.59 N 78.52 W
Tonawanda Channel ≃1 284a 43.04 N 79.00 W
Tonawanda Creek ≃ 210 43.02 N 78.53 W
Tonawanda Indian Reservation ⬥4 210 43.05 N 78.27 W
Tonawanda Island I 284a 43.02 N 78.53 W
Tonbo 110 18.31 N 95.05 E
Tonbridge 42 51.12 N 0.16 E
Tonbridge and Malling □8 260 51.16 N 0.20 E
Tonda 270 34.50 N 135.36 E
Tonda ≃ 96 33.38 N 135.24 E
Tondabayashi 96 34.30 N 135.36 E
Tondano 112 1.19 N 124.54 E
Tønder 41 54.56 N 8.54 E
Tondhre 272c 19.05 N 73.08 E
Tondi 122 9.44 N 79.01 E
Tondibi 150 16.39 N 0.14 W
Tondidji 150 13.06 N 10.20 W
Tondi Kiwindi 150 14.28 N 2.02 E
Tondoro 156 17.45 S 18.50 E
Tondou, Massif du ⩘ 146 7.50 N 23.45 E
Tone, Nihon 94 35.51 N 140.09 E
Tone, Nihon 94 36.42 N 139.13 E
Tone ≃ 94 35.44 N 140.51 E
Tone-unga ☰ 268 35.54 N 139.53 E
Toněž 78 51.49 N 27.48 E
Tonga, Cam. 152 4.58 N 10.42 E
Tonga, Sūd. 140 9.28 N 31.03 E
Tonga □1 14 20.00 S 175.00 W
Tongaat 158 29.37 S 31.03 E
Tonga Islands II 14 20.00 S 175.00 W
Tong'an, Zhg. 100 24.46 N 118.08 E
Tongan, Zhg. 102 26.23 N 102.18 E
Tonganoxie 198 39.07 N 95.05 W
Tonganqiao 106 31.22 N 120.27 E
Tonga Ridge ✢3 14 22.00 S 175.00 W
Tongariki I 175f 17.01 S 168.38 E
Tongariro, Mount ∧ 172 39.08 S 175.38 E
Tongariro National Park ♠ 172 39.15 S 175.30 E
Tongas 115a 7.44 S 113.06 E
Tongatapu I 174w 21.10 S 175.10 W
Tongatapu Group II 14 21.10 S 175.10 W
Tonga Trench ✢1 14 22.00 S 173.00 W
Tongbai, Zhg. 100 32.22 N 113.24 E
Tongbai, Zhg. 105 39.35 N 116.44 E
Tongbaishan ⩘ 100 32.20 N 113.15 E
Tongcheng, Zhg. 100 32.53 N 118.58 E
Tongcheng, Zhg. 100 29.11 N 113.49 E
Tongcheng, Zhg. 100 31.03 N 116.58 E
Tongchengzha 100 31.30 N 118.07 E
Tongchengzhuang 105 39.22 N 117.36 E
T'ongch'ŏn 98 38.54 N 127.54 E
Tongchuan 102 35.01 N 109.01 E
Tongdao 102 26.23 N 109.23 E
Tongde 102 35.17 N 100.42 E
Tongerbao 104 41.26 N 123.02 E
Tongeren 56 50.47 N 5.28 E
Tongerlo 56 51.07 N 4.54 E
Tonggou 98 41.53 N 125.46 E
Tonggu, Zhg. 100 28.33 N 114.21 E
Tonggu, Zhg. 100 21.53 N 112.55 E
Tongguan, Zhg. 100 28.29 N 112.48 E
Tongguan, Zhg. 102 34.38 N 110.20 E
Tongguan, Zhg. 102 23.18 N 101.23 E
Tongguanyi 107 29.20 N 106.23 E
Tongguye 120 37.22 N 78.48 E
Tonghai 102 24.07 N 102.49 E
Tonghaikou 100 30.14 N 113.08 E
Tonghe, Zhg. 89 45.59 N 128.45 E
Tonghe, Zhg. 100 32.56 N 112.45 E
Tongho-ri 98 35.49 N 127.54 E
Tonghua 98 41.50 N 125.55 E
Tong Island I 164 2.05 S 147.50 E
Tongjiang 102 31.58 N 107.14 E
Tongjiangchang 107 29.37 N 103.43 E
Tongjiangkou 104 42.37 N 123.41 E
Tongjing 100 31.47 N 118.33 E
Tongjosŏn-man C 98 39.30 N 128.00 E
Tongjuzhen 98 38.36 N 117.11 E
Tongkenhe ≃ 89 46.31 N 126.22 E
Tongli 106 31.10 N 120.43 E
Tongliang 107 29.51 N 106.03 E
Tongliao 89 43.39 N 122.14 E
Tongling, Zhg. 100 30.53 N 117.46 E
Tongling, Zhg. 102 23.28 N 109.40 E
Tonglingzhen 100 30.56 N 117.47 E
Tonglu 100 29.48 N 119.40 E
Tongmai 102 30.08 N 95.11 E
Tongmang-ni 98 37.37 N 126.26 E
Tongmu, Zhg. 100 27.57 N 113.55 E
Tongmu, Zhg. 102 24.09 N 110.04 E
Tongnae 98 35.12 N 129.05 E
Tongnan 107 30.11 N 105.48 E
Tongo, Austl. 166 30.30 S 143.45 E
Tongo, Cam. 152 5.11 N 14.00 E
Tong O, H.K. 271d 22.12 N 114.08 E
Tongoa I 175f 16.54 S 168.34 E
Tongobory 157b 23.32 S 44.20 E
Tongololo Creek ≃ 162 22.06 S 121.08 E
Tongoy 252 30.15 S 71.30 W
Tongpanshan I 100 27.43 N 120.55 E
Tongqin 100 28.52 N 119.56 E
Tongquansi 107 30.23 N 104.50 E
Tongquil Island I 116 6.02 N 121.51 E
Tongren, Zhg. 102 27.38 N 109.03 E
Tongren, Zhg. 102 35.32 N 101.54 E
Tongrenchang 107 30.02 N 106.42 E
Tongsa ≃ 124 26.52 N 90.57 E
Tongsa Dzong 124 27.31 N 90.30 E
Tongsan-ni 271b 37.38 N 126.53 E
Tongshan, Zhg. 98 34.17 N 117.03 E
Tongshan, Zhg. 100 29.38 N 114.29 E
Tongshi 98 35.26 N 117.43 E
Tongshuping 100 27.17 N 114.54 E
Tongta 110 21.20 N 99.16 E
Tongtai 100 32.38 N 120.47 E
Tongtan 107 28.56 N 105.17 E
Tongtianhe ≃ 102 33.25 N 96.32 E
Tongtianheyan 120 33.50 N 92.28 E
Tongue 46 58.28 N 4.25 W
Tongue ≃, U.S. 202 46.24 N 105.52 W
Tongue ≃, N. Dak., U.S. 198 48.56 N 97.18 W
Tongue ≃, Tex., U.S. 196 34.07 N 100.25 W
Tongue, Kyle of C 46 58.30 N 4.26 W
Tongue of the Ocean ✢1 238 24.00 N 77.20 W
Tongue River Reservoir ⊛1 202 45.06 N 106.47 W
Tongwei 102 35.07 N 105.27 E
Tongxi 107 30.01 N 106.07 E
Tongxi ≃ 100 29.49 N 119.41 E
Tongxian, Zhg. 105 39.55 N 116.39 E
Tongxian, Zhg. 107 30.15 N 105.23 E
Tongxiang 106 30.38 N 120.32 E
Tongxin 102 37.02 N 106.09 E
Tongxinchang 107 29.42 N 106.26 E
Tongxing 89 47.45 N 126.46 E
Tongxingchang 107 30.35 N 106.12 E
Tongxu 98 34.29 N 114.28 E
Tongyu 89 44.48 N 123.05 E
Tongyuan 106 30.28 N 120.52 E
Tongyuanbao 104 40.49 N 123.54 E
Tongyuanwei 100 28.04 N 116.03 E
Tongzhaipu 100 32.48 N 112.44 E
Tongzi 102 28.08 N 106.49 E
Tongzidixia 104 41.08 N 120.34 E
Tonica 216 41.13 N 89.04 W
Tónichi 232 28.35 N 109.34 W
Tonila 234 19.26 N 103.31 W
Tönisberg 263 51.25 N 6.30 E
Tönisheide 263 51.19 N 7.03 E
Tönisvort 56 51.19 N 6.29 E
Tonj 140 7.17 N 28.45 E
Tonk 120 26.10 N 75.47 E
Tonk □5 124 25.55 N 76.10 E
Tonkawa 196 36.41 N 97.18 W
Tonkin, Gulf of C 110 20.00 N 108.00 E
Tonkino 80 57.23 N 46.28 E
Tonkwa 110 23.36 N 96.58 E
Tonle Sap → Sab, Tônlé ⊛ 110 13.00 N 104.00 E
Tonnay-Boutonne 32 45.58 N 0.42 W
Tonneins 32 44.23 N 0.19 E
Tonner Canyon V 280 33.58 N 117.48 W
Tonnerre 50 47.51 N 3.58 E
Tönnet 40 60.14 N 13.30 E
Tönning 41 54.19 N 8.56 E
Tōno 92 39.19 N 141.32 E
Tonogaya 268 35.46 N 139.22 E
Tonopah 204 38.04 N 117.14 W
Tōnoshō, Nihon 94 35.49 N 140.42 E
Tonoshō, Nihon 96 34.29 N 134.11 E
Tonosí 246 7.24 N 80.27 W
Tonota 156 21.29 S 27.29 E
Tonquish Creek ≃ 281 42.21 N 83.22 W
Tons ≃ 124 25.17 N 82.04 E
Tonšajevo 80 57.44 N 47.00 E
Tønsberg 26 59.17 N 10.25 E
Tönsholt 263 51.38 N 6.58 E
Tonstad 26 58.40 N 6.43 E
Tonto ≃ 234 18.10 N 96.08 W
Tonto Creek ≃ 200 33.46 N 111.15 W
Tontogany 216 41.25 N 83.44 W
Tonto National Monument ♠ 200 33.34 N 111.02 W
Tonya 130 40.53 N 39.16 E
Tonyrefail 42 51.36 N 3.25 W
Toobeah 166 28.25 S 149.52 E
Toodyay 168a 31.33 S 116.28 E
Tooele 200 40.32 N 112.18 W
Toogoolawah 171a 27.06 S 152.23 E
Tool 222 32.16 N 96.10 W
Toolik ≃ 180 69.55 N 149.30 W
Tooma 171b 35.58 S 148.03 E
Tooma ≃ 171b 36.04 S 148.00 E
Tooma Reservoir ⊛1 171b 36.04 S 148.16 E
Toomebridge 44 54.45 N 6.27 W
Toomevara 48 52.50 N 8.02 W
Toompine 166 27.13 S 144.22 E
Toomsboro 192 32.50 N 83.05 W
Toongabbie 274a 33.47 S 150.57 E
Toora 169 38.40 S 146.20 E
Toora-Chem 88 52.28 N 96.17 E
Toormakeady 48 53.39 N 9.24 W
Toosey Indian Reserve ⬥4 182 51.56 N 122.29 W
Toot Hill 260 51.42 N 0.12 E
Tootie, Mount ∧ 170 33.28 S 150.30 E
Tootsi 76 58.34 N 24.47 E
Toowoomba 171a 27.33 S 151.57 E
Topanga 228 34.06 N 118.36 W
Topanga Canyon V 280 34.05 N 118.36 W
Topar 86 49.32 N 72.50 E
Topawa 200 31.48 N 111.51 W
Topaz Lake ⊛ 226 38.41 N 119.32 W
Topchānchi 126 23.54 N 86.12 E
Töpchin 54 52.10 N 13.34 E
Topčicha 86 52.49 N 83.10 E
Topeka, Ind., U.S. 216 41.32 N 85.32 W
Topeka, Kans., U.S. 198 39.03 N 95.41 W
Töpen 54 50.23 N 11.52 E
Topia 232 25.13 N 106.34 W
Topilejo ⬥8 286a 19.12 N 99.09 W
Topino ≃ 66 43.02 N 12.30 E
Topka, Gora ∧ 74 57.08 N 137.24 E
Topkanovo 82 54.43 N 38.29 E
Topkapı ⬥8 267b 41.02 N 28.54 E
Topkapı Müzesi ɣ1 267b 41.00 N 28.59 E
Topki 86 55.16 N 85.36 E
Topl'a ≃ 30 48.45 N 21.45 E
Topley 182 54.49 N 126.18 W
Toplica ≃ 38 43.13 N 21.49 E
Toplița 38 46.55 N 25.21 E
T'oploje, S.S.S.R. 76 53.37 N 37.36 E
T'oploje, S.S.S.R. 76 51.13 N 38.53 E
T'oploje ≃ 83 48.47 N 39.19 E
T'oplyj Stan, S.S.S.R. 80 53.58 N 50.10 E
T'oplyj Stan, S.S.S.R. 82 55.37 N 37.30 E
T'oplyj Stan ⬥8 265b 55.37 N 37.30 E
Topo, Quebrada ≃ 286c 10.33 N 67.00 W
Topocalma, Punta ≻ 252 34.08 S 72.01 W
Top of Hebers 262 53.34 N 2.12 W
Topo Infiernito ∧ 286c 10.33 N 66.55 W
Topol'čany 30 48.34 N 18.10 E
Topoli 80 47.59 N 51.36 E
Topolnica ≃ 38 42.11 N 24.18 E
Topolobampo 232 25.36 N 109.03 W
Topolog 38 44.53 N 28.22 E
Topolovățu Mare 38 45.46 N 21.37 E
Topolovgrad 38 42.05 N 26.20 E
Toporok 76 58.33 N 33.28 E
Topozero, Ozero ⊛ 24 65.40 N 32.00 E
Toppenish 202 46.23 N 120.19 W
Toppenish Creek ≃ 202 46.20 N 120.11 W
Toppenish Ridge ⩘ 224 46.18 N 120.40 W
Toppings 262 53.37 N 2.25 W
Toprakkale 130 37.06 N 36.07 E
Tops, Mount ∧ 162 21.50 S 134.00 E
Topsa 24 62.39 N 43.34 E
Topsfield 207 42.38 N 70.57 W
Topsham, Eng., U.K. 42 50.41 N 3.27 W
Topsham, Maine, U.S. 188 43.56 N 69.58 W
Top Springs 164 16.38 S 131.50 E
Topton 208 40.30 N 75.42 W
Toquima Range ⩘ 204 39.00 N 117.00 W
Toquop Wash V 204 36.45 N 114.11 W
Torahime 94 35.25 N 136.16 E
Torano Castello 68 39.30 N 16.08 E
Torari 175f 17.39 S 168.32 E
Torawitan, Tanjung ≻ 112 1.46 N 124.58 E
Toraya 248 14.03 S 73.18 W
Torbalı 130 38.10 N 27.21 E
Torbat-e Heydarīyeh 128 35.16 N 59.13 E
Torbat-e Jām 128 35.14 N 60.36 E
Torbay, Newf., Can. 186 47.40 N 52.44 W
Torbay → Torquay, Eng., U.K. 42 50.28 N 3.30 W
Tor Bay C 42 50.25 N 3.30 W
Torbejevo, S.S.S.R. 80 54.05 N 43.15 E
Torbejevo, S.S.S.R. 82 54.44 N 36.11 E
Torbert, Mount ∧ 180 61.25 N 152.24 W
Torbino 76 58.35 N 32.53 E
Torbole 64 45.52 N 10.52 E
Torbreck, Mount ∧ 169 37.21 S 145.57 E
Torbrook 186 44.55 N 64.59 W
Torch ≃ 184 53.50 N 103.05 W
Torchany 80 55.34 N 46.36 E
Torchiarolo 68 40.29 N 18.03 E
Torch Lake ⊛ 190 45.00 N 85.19 W
Torčin 78 50.46 N 24.59 E
Torcy 261 48.51 N 2.39 E
Torda → Turda 38 46.34 N 23.47 E
Tordera ≃ 34 41.39 N 2.47 E
Tordesillas 34 41.30 N 5.00 W
Tordino ≃ 66 42.44 N 13.59 E
Tor di Quinto ⬥8 267a 41.56 N 12.28 E
Töre 26 65.54 N 22.39 E
Töreboda 40 58.43 N 14.08 E
Torej 88 50.33 N 104.50 E
Torekov 26 56.26 N 12.37 E
Toreno 34 42.42 N 6.30 W
Torez 83 48.01 N 38.37 E
Torfou 261 48.32 N 2.14 E
Torgau 54 51.34 N 13.00 E
Torgelow 54 53.37 N 14.00 E
Torgelower See ⊛ 54 53.34 N 12.47 E
Torgo 88 58.28 N 119.50 E
Torgun ≃ 80 50.15 N 46.18 E
Torhamn 26 56.05 N 15.50 E
Torhout 50 51.04 N 3.06 E
Tori 144 7.53 N 33.40 E
Toribero ≃ 250 10.59 S 49.48 W
Toribulu 112 0.19 S 120.01 E

Symbol	English	Deutsch	Español	Français	Português
≃	River	Fluss	Rio	Rivière	Rio
☰	Canal	Kanal	Canal	Canal	Canal
⋃	Waterfall, Rapids	Wasserfall, Stromschnellen	Cascada, Rápidos	Chute d'eau, Rapides	Cascata, Rápidos
⩌	Strait	Meeresstrasse	Estrecho	Détroit	Estreito
C	Bay, Gulf	Bucht, Golf	Bahía, Golfo	Baie, Golfe	Baía, Golfo
⊛	Lake, Lakes	See, Seen	Lago, Lagos	Lac, Lacs	Lago, Lagos
☷	Swamp	Sumpf	Pantano	Marais	Pântano
⊼	Ice Features, Glacier	Eis- und Gletscherformen	Accidentes Glaciales	Formes glaciaires	Acidentes Glaciares
⊽	Other Hydrographic Features	Andere Hydrographische Objekte	Otros Elementos Hidrográficos	Autres données hydrographiques	Outros Elementos Hidrográficos
✢	Submarine Features	Untermeerische Objekte	Accidentes Submarinos	Formes de relief sous-marin	Acidentes Submarinos
□	Political Unit	Politische Einheit	Unidad Politica	Entité politique	Unidade Política
ɣ	Cultural Institution	Kulturelle Institution	Institución Cultural	Institution culturelle	Instituição Cultural
⊥	Historical Site	Historische Stätte	Sitio Histórico	Site historique	Sitio Histórico
♠	Recreational Site	Erholungs- und Ferienort	Sitio de Recreo	Centre de loisirs	Sítio de Lazer
⊠	Airport	Flughafen	Aeropuerto	Aéroport	Aeroporto
■	Military Installation	Militäranlage	Instalación Militar	Installation militaire	Instalação Militar
⬥	Miscellaneous	Verschiedenes	Misceláneo	Divers	Miscelânea

ENGLISH — Name, Page, Lat.°′, Long.°′ / DEUTSCH — Name, Seite, Breite°′, Länge°′ E=Ost

Name	Page	Lat.	Long.
Toride	94	35.53 N	140.04 E
Torigakubi-misaki ≻	94	37.10 N	138.06 E
Torigoe	94	36.21 N	136.36 E
Toriido	270	34.25 N	135.43 E
Torii-tōge)(	94	36.29 N	138.24 E
Toriki	265a	59.47 N	30.07 E
Torín	232	27.34 N	110.14 W
Torino (Turin)	62	45.03 N	7.40 E
Torino □[4]	62	45.08 N	7.22 E
Torino di Sangro Marina	66	42.11 N	14.32 E
Torio ≃	34	42.35 N	5.34 W
Toriparu	255	16.20 S	53.55 W
Torit	154	4.24 N	32.34 E
Toritto	68	41.00 N	16.41 E
Toriya	94	36.59 N	136.54 E
Torjun	115a	7.10 S	113.13 E
Torkamān	128	37.35 N	47.23 E
Torkestān, Selseleh-ye Band-e ⋀	128	35.25 N	64.15 E
Torkoviči	76	58.52 N	30.20 E
Torlino	86	58.53 N	63.46 E
Torment, Point ≻	162	17.02 S	123.36 E
Tormes ≃	34	41.18 N	6.29 W
Tormestorp	41	56.07 N	13.44 E
Tormey	282	38.03 N	122.15 W
Tormini	64	45.36 N	10.29 E
Tormosin	80	48.12 N	42.42 E
Torna	24	68.04 N	44.10 E
Torna ∧	122	18.16 N	73.37 E
Tornado Mountain ∧	182	49.58 N	114.39 W
Tornareccio	66	42.02 N	14.24 E
Tornberget ∧[2]	40	59.08 N	18.01 E
Torne ≃	44	53.36 N	0.44 W
Torneälven ≃	24	65.48 N	24.08 E
Torne Brook ≃	276	41.08 N	74.10 W
Tornesch	52	53.41 N	9.43 E
Torneträsk ⊜	24	68.20 N	19.10 E
Torngat Mountains ⋀	176	59.00 N	64.00 W
Tornillo	200	31.27 N	106.05 W
Tornillo Creek ≃	196	29.11 N	103.00 W
Tornimparte	66	42.17 N	13.18 E
Torning	41	56.17 N	9.20 E
Tornio	26	65.51 N	24.08 E
Tornquist	252	38.06 S	62.14 W
T'orny, S.S.S.R.	78	48.09 N	33.33 E
T'orny, S.S.S.R.	78	50.59 N	33.59 E
T'orny, S.S.S.R.	83	49.05 N	37.57 E
Toro	34	41.31 N	5.24 W
Toro □[5]	154	0.30 N	30.30 E
Torö I	40	58.50 N	17.50 E
Toro, Arroyo ≃	288	34.27 S	58.52 W
Toro, Cañada del ≃	258	35.16 S	59.05 W
Toro, Lago del ⊜	254	51.14 S	72.45 W
Toro, Punta ≻	252	33.47 S	71.49 W
Torobuku	112	4.25 S	122.26 E
Torodi	150	13.18 N	1.40 E
Toro-iseki ⊥	94	34.57 N	138.24 E
Torok	146	10.03 N	14.33 E
Torokina	175e	6.14 S	155.03 E
Törökszentmiklós	30	47.11 N	20.25 E
Torola ≃	236	13.52 N	88.30 W
Torom	89	54.32 N	135.50 E
Torom ≃	89	54.36 N	135.46 E
Toroni, Nevado ∧	248	19.43 S	68.41 W
Toronto, Austl.	170	33.01 S	151.36 E
Toronto, Ont., Can.	212		
	275b	43.39 N	79.23 W
Toronto, Kans., U.S.	198	37.48 N	95.57 W
Toronto, Ohio, U.S.	214	40.28 N	80.36 W
Toronto, S. Dak., U.S.	198	44.34 N	96.39 W
Toronto □[6]	275b	43.44 N	79.24 W
Toronto, University of ♥[2]	275b	43.40 N	79.24 W
Toronto Harbour C	275b	43.38 N	79.22 W
Toronto International Airport ⊠	212	43.41 N	79.38 W
Toronto Island Airport ⊠	275b	43.38 N	79.24 W
Toronto Lake ⊜[1]	198	37.46 N	95.57 W
Toronto Reservoir ⊜[1]	210	41.38 N	74.51 W
Toro Peak ∧	204	33.32 N	116.25 W
Toropec	76	56.30 N	31.39 E
Toropovo	82	54.21 N	36.07 E
Tororo	154	0.42 N	34.11 E
Toros Dağı ∧	130	37.23 N	34.34 E
Toros Dağları ⋀	130	37.00 N	33.00 E
Torošino	76	57.56 N	28.36 E
Torosozero	24	62.30 N	38.10 E
Torotoro	248	18.07 S	65.46 W
Toroume ∧	174k	21.15 S	159.45 W
Torpa ⊥	26	57.39 N	13.16 E
Torpè	71	40.38 N	9.40 E
Torphins	46	57.06 N	2.37 W
Tor Pignatara ◆[8]	267a	41.52 N	12.32 E
Torpo	26	60.40 N	8.43 E
Torpoint	42	50.22 N	4.11 W
Torquay, Austl.	169	38.21 S	144.19 E
Torquay, Sask., Can.	184	49.08 N	103.31 W
Torquay (Torbay), Eng., U.K.	42	50.28 N	3.30 W
Torquemada	34	42.02 N	4.19 W
Torraca	68	40.07 N	15.38 E
Torraccia, Fosso ≃	267a	42.00 N	12.30 E
Torrance, Calif., U.S.	228	33.50 N	118.19 W
Torrance, Pa., U.S.	214	40.25 N	79.14 W
Torrance Lake ⊜	184	57.04 N	98.12 W
Torrance Municipal Airport ⊠	280	33.48 N	118.20 W
Torrão	34	38.18 N	8.13 W
Torre Annunziata	68	40.45 N	14.27 E
Torre Astura ⊥	66	41.24 N	12.46 E
Torre Baja	34	40.07 N	1.15 W
Torrebelvicino	64	45.43 N	11.18 E
Torre Beretti	62	45.04 N	8.40 E
Torreblanca	34	40.13 N	0.12 E
Torrebruna	66	41.52 N	14.33 E
Torrecilla ∧	34	37.36 N	2.31 W
Torrecilla en Cameros	34	42.16 N	2.37 W
Torre del Campo	34	37.46 N	3.53 W
Torre del Greco	68	40.47 N	14.22 E
Torre del Lago Puccini	66	43.50 N	10.17 E
Torre de Moncorvo	34	41.10 N	7.03 W
Torre de'Passeri	66	42.14 N	13.56 E
Torre di Mosto	64	45.41 N	12.43 E
Torre di Santa Maria	64	46.14 N	9.51 E
Torredonjimeno	34	37.46 N	3.57 W
Torre Faro ◆[8]	70	38.16 N	15.39 E
Torre Gaia ◆[8]	267a	41.51 N	12.39 E
Torregrotta	70	38.11 N	15.21 E
Torrejón, Embalse de ⊜[1]	34	39.50 N	5.50 W
Torrejon Air Base ■	266a	40.28 N	3.28 W
Torrejoncillo	34	39.54 N	6.28 W
Torrejón de Ardoz	34	40.27 N	3.29 W
Torrelaguna	34	40.50 N	3.32 W
Torrelavega	34	43.21 N	4.03 W
Torrellas, Riera de ≃	266d	41.23 N	2.01 E
Torrellas de Llobregat	266d	41.21 N	1.59 E
Torremaggiore	68	41.41 N	15.17 E
Torremolinos	34	36.37 N	4.30 W
Torrenieri	66	43.05 N	11.33 E
Torrens ≃	168b	34.56 S	138.30 E
Torrens, Lake ⊜	166	31.00 S	137.50 E
Torrens Creek	166	20.46 S	145.02 E
Torrens Creek ≃	166	22.22 S	145.09 E
Torrens Island I	168b	34.48 S	138.32 E
Torrent	252	28.50 S	56.28 W
Torrente	34	39.26 N	0.28 W
Torreões	256	21.52 S	43.33 W
Torreón	232	25.33 N	103.26 W
Torre Orsaia	68	40.08 N	15.28 E
Torre Pedrera	66	44.06 N	12.31 E
Torre Pellice	62	44.49 N	7.13 E
Torreperogil	34	38.02 N	3.17 W
Torres, Arg.	258	34.26 S	59.08 W
Tôrres, Bra.	252	29.21 S	49.44 W
Torres, Arroyo ≃	288	34.39 S	58.45 W
Torre Santa Susanna	68	40.28 N	17.44 E
Torresdale ◆[8]	285	40.03 N	75.00 W
Torres de Alcalá	34	35.10 N	4.16 W
Torres Islands II	175f	13.15 S	166.37 E
Torres Martinez Indian Reservation ◆[4]	204	33.35 N	116.02 W
Torres Novas	34	39.29 N	8.32 W
Torres Strait Ц	164	10.25 S	142.10 E
Torres Vedras	34	39.06 N	9.16 W
Torretta	68	38.08 N	13.14 E
Torrette di Fano	66	43.47 N	13.07 E
Torrevieja	34	37.59 N	0.41 W
Torricella	68	40.21 N	17.29 E
Torricella in Sabina	66	42.16 N	12.52 E
Torricella Peligna	66	42.01 N	14.15 E
Torricella Sicura	66	42.39 N	13.39 E
Torricelli Mountains ⋀	164	3.25 S	142.20 E
Torridge ≃	42	51.03 N	4.11 W
Torridon	46	57.33 N	5.31 W
Torridon, Loch C	46	57.35 N	5.46 W
Torriglia	62	44.31 N	9.10 E
Torrijos, Esp.	34	39.59 N	4.17 W
Torrijos, Pil.	116	13.19 N	122.05 E
Torrild	41	55.59 N	10.04 E
Torrimpietra ◆[8]	267a	41.56 N	12.13 E
Torrin	46	57.12 N	6.02 W
Tørring	41	55.51 N	9.29 E
Torrington, Conn., U.S.	207	41.48 N	73.08 W
Torrington, Wyo., U.S.	198	42.04 N	104.11 W
Torrinha	255	22.26 S	48.09 W
Torrita di Siena	66	43.10 N	11.46 E
Torröjen ⊜	26	63.55 N	12.56 E
Torrox	34	36.46 N	3.58 W
Torrvarpen ⊜	40	59.42 N	14.30 E
Torsåker	40	60.31 N	16.29 E
Tor Sapienza ◆[8]	267a	41.54 N	12.35 E
Torsås	26	56.24 N	16.00 E
Torsburgen ⊥	26	57.25 N	18.43 E
Torsby	26	60.08 N	13.00 E
Tors Cove	186	47.13 N	52.51 W
Torshälla	40	59.25 N	16.28 E
Tórshavn	22	62.01 N	6.46 W
Torside Reservoir ⊜[1]	262	53.29 N	1.54 W
Torsö	40	58.47 N	13.48 E
Torsö I	40	58.48 N	13.50 E
Torteval	43b	49.27 N	2.38 W
Torto ≃	70	37.58 N	13.46 E
Tortola I	240m	18.27 N	64.36 W
Tortolì	71	39.55 N	9.39 E
Tortona	62	44.54 N	8.52 E
Tortora	68	39.56 N	15.48 E
Tortoreto	66	42.48 N	13.55 E
Tortorici	70	38.02 N	14.49 E
Tortosa	34	40.48 N	0.31 E
Tortosa, Cabo de ≻	34	40.43 N	0.55 E
Tortue, Île de la I	238	20.04 N	72.49 W
Tortue, Rivière de la ≃	206	45.24 N	73.32 W
Tortugas, Laguna ⊜	234	22.20 N	98.07 W
Tortuguero ≃	236	10.34 N	83.31 W
Tortuguero, Laguna C	240m	18.28 N	66.26 W
Tortuguero, Puerto del C	240m	18.29 N	66.28 W
Tortuguitas	288	34.28 S	58.46 W
Tortum	130	40.19 N	41.35 E
Toru ≃	114	1.26 N	98.46 E
Toruajgyr	85	42.32 N	76.26 E
Torue	112	0.58 S	120.18 E
Torugart, Pereval)(	85	40.33 N	75.20 E
Toruń	30	53.02 N	18.35 E
Torunos	246	8.30 N	70.04 W
Torup, Sve.	26	56.58 N	13.05 E
Torup, Sve.	41	55.34 N	13.12 E
Tõrva	76	58.00 N	25.56 E
Tory	88	51.47 N	103.00 E
Tory Island I	48	55.16 N	8.14 W
Torysa ≃	30	48.39 N	21.21 E
Tory Sound Ц	48	55.14 N	8.14 W
Toržkovskaja Gr'ada ∧	76	57.00 N	34.44 E
Toržok	76	57.03 N	34.58 E
Torzym	30	52.20 N	15.04 E
Tosa	96	33.29 N	133.25 E
T'osan	98	38.18 N	126.43 E
Tosari	115a	7.53 S	112.54 E
Tosas, Puerto de)(	34	42.19 N	2.01 E
Tosa-shimizu	92	32.46 N	132.57 E
Tosa-wan C	96	33.20 N	133.40 E
Tosayama	96	33.38 N	133.32 E
Tosa-yamada	96	33.36 N	133.41 E
Tosca	156	25.53 S	23.58 E
Toscaig	46	57.24 N	5.50 W
Toscana □[4]	36	43.25 N	11.00 E
Toscolano	64	45.38 N	10.37 E
Tösens	58	47.01 N	10.36 E
Tōshi-jima I	94	34.31 N	136.53 E
Toshima ◆[8]	268	35.44 N	139.43 E
To-shima I, Nihon	92	32.12 N	130.05 E
To-shima I, Nihon	94	34.31 N	139.17 E
Tōshō-gū ♥[1]	94	36.46 N	139.36 E
Tosi	66	43.45 N	11.31 E
Tosilei	144	1.24 N	41.23 E
Toškalykaja, Gora ∧	86	50.38 N	89.30 E
Toškovskij	83	48.46 N	38.34 E
Tosköy	130	41.27 N	35.54 E
Tosna ≃	265a	59.46 N	30.46 E
Tosno	76	59.33 N	30.53 E
Tosoncengel	88	48.47 N	98.15 E
T'osovo	76	55.37 N	34.30 E
T'osovo-Netyl'skij	76	58.57 N	31.04 E
T'osovskij	76	58.48 N	30.52 E
Töss ≃	58	47.33 N	8.33 E
Tossens	52	53.34 N	8.16 E
Tossi	115b	9.35 S	118.57 E
Tossicia	66	42.33 N	13.39 E
Tost → Toszek	30	50.28 N	18.32 E
Tostado	252	29.14 S	61.46 W
Tõstamaa	76	58.20 N	24.00 E
Tostedt	52	53.17 N	9.42 E
Tosterön I	40	59.25 N	17.00 E
Tostu	85	41.34 N	71.34 E
Tost Uul ⋀	102	43.15 N	100.30 E
Tosu	96	33.22 N	130.31 E
Tosya	130	41.01 N	34.02 E
Toszek	30	50.28 N	18.32 E
Totagatic ≃	190	46.05 N	92.11 W
Totak ⊜	26	59.42 N	7.57 E
Totana	34	37.46 N	1.30 W
Totānāla	126	22.05 N	87.40 E
Totatiche	234	21.56 N	103.27 W
Totban	80	46.47 N	49.06 E
Toteng	156	20.22 S	22.58 E
Tôtes	50	49.41 N	1.03 E
Totes Gebirge ⋀	30	47.42 N	13.55 E
Totias	144	3.57 N	43.58 E
T'otkino	78	51.17 N	34.16 E
Tot'ma	76	59.57 N	42.45 E
Totnes	42	50.25 N	3.41 W
Totness	250	5.53 N	56.19 W
Totolom ∧	174r	6.52 N	158.14 E
Totonicapán	236	14.55 N	91.22 W
Totonicapán □[5]	236	15.00 N	91.20 W
Totopotomoy Creek ≃	208	37.41 N	77.13 W
Totora, Bol.	248	17.49 S	68.07 W
Totora, Bol.	248	17.42 S	65.09 W
Totora Palca	248	19.55 S	65.26 W
Totoras	252	32.35 S	61.11 W
Totos	248	13.31 S	74.30 W
Tototlán	234	20.33 N	102.48 W
Totowa	210	40.54 N	74.13 W
Totoya I	175g	18.57 S	179.50 W
Totson Mountain ∧	180	64.26 N	157.15 W
Totsuka ◆[8]	268	35.24 N	139.32 E
Totten Glacier ⊓	9	66.45 S	116.10 E
Tottenham, Austl.	166	32.14 S	147.21 E
Tottenham, Ont., Can.	212	44.01 N	79.49 W
Tottenham ◆[8]	260	51.35 N	0.04 W
Tottenham Hotspur Football Ground ♠	260	51.36 N	0.04 W
Totten Inlet C	224	47.07 N	123.02 W
Tottenville ◆[8]	276	40.31 N	74.15 W
Totteridge ◆[8]	260	51.38 N	0.12 W
Tottington	44	53.37 N	2.20 W
Totton	42	50.56 N	1.29 W
Tottori	96	35.30 N	134.14 E
Tottori □[5]	96	35.30 N	134.00 E
Tottori-sakyū ∧[2]	96	35.31 N	134.25 E
Totuskey Creek ≃	208	37.52 N	76.45 W
Tou, Motu I	174k	21.11 S	159.48 W
Touba, C. Iv.	150	8.17 N	7.41 W
Touba, Sén.	150	14.51 N	15.53 W
Touba □[5]	150	8.20 N	7.30 W
Toubéré Bafal	150	14.23 N	13.32 W
Toubkal, Jbel ∧	148	31.05 N	7.55 W
T'ouch'eng	100	24.51 N	121.49 E
Touchet ≃	202	46.02 N	118.41 W
Touchwood Hills ⋀[2]	184	51.35 N	104.17 W
Touchwood Lake ⊜, Alta., Can.	182	54.50 N	111.23 W
Touchwood Lake ⊜, Man., Can.	184	54.29 N	95.00 W
Toucy	50	47.44 N	3.18 E
Toudaogou, Zhg.	98	42.46 N	129.12 E
Toudaogou, Zhg.	104	41.37 N	121.40 E
Toudaogou, Zhg.	105	40.58 N	117.59 E
Toudaojiang ≃	98	42.36 N	127.11 E
Touët-sur-Var	62	43.57 N	7.00 E
Tougaloo	194	32.24 N	90.09 W
Tougan	150	13.04 N	3.04 W
Touggourt	148	33.10 N	6.00 E
Toughkenamon	285	39.50 N	75.46 W
Tougouri	150	13.19 N	0.31 W
Tougué	150	11.27 N	11.41 W
Tougué □[4]	150	11.28 N	11.36 W
Touho	175f	20.47 S	165.14 E
Touïel, Oued ∨	148	31.30 N	4.46 E
Touil, Oued ∨	148	35.30 N	2.33 E
Touisset	207	41.43 N	71.14 W
Toukansi	100	29.22 N	119.06 E
Toukley	170	33.16 S	151.33 E
Toukoto	150	13.27 N	9.53 W
Toul	58	48.41 N	5.54 E
Toulépleu	150	6.35 N	8.25 W
Toulnustouc ≃	186	49.35 N	68.24 W
Toulnustouc-Nord-Est ≃	186	50.56 N	67.44 W
Toulon, Fr.	62	43.07 N	5.56 E
Toulon, Ill., U.S.	190	41.06 N	89.52 W
Toulon Lake ⊜	204	40.01 N	118.40 W
Toulon-sur-Arroux	32	46.42 N	4.08 E
Touloubre ≃	62	43.33 N	5.02 E
Toulourenc ≃	62	44.14 N	5.09 E
Toulouse	32	43.36 N	1.26 E
Toumenshan I	100	28.41 N	121.46 E
Toumfafi	150	15.02 N	5.38 E
Toumodi	150	7.26 N	5.37 W
Tounan	100	23.41 N	120.28 E
Tounassine, Hamada ◆[2]	148	28.30 N	5.00 W
Toungoo	110	18.56 N	96.26 E
Toupeng	106	30.19 N	120.31 E
Toupi	100	26.44 N	116.05 E
Touques	50	49.22 N	0.06 E
Touques ≃	50	49.22 N	0.06 E
Tour, Étang de la ⊜	261	48.40 N	1.53 E
Toura, Monts du ⋀	150	7.40 N	7.25 W
Touraine	188	45.34 N	75.47 W
Touraine □[9]	50	47.12 N	1.30 E
Tourakom	110	18.26 N	102.32 E
Tourane → Da-nang	110	16.04 N	108.13 E
Tourbe ≃	56	49.10 N	4.52 E
Tourcoing	50	50.43 N	3.09 E
Tourinan, Cabo ≻	34	43.03 N	9.18 W
Tournai	50	50.36 N	3.23 E
Tournan-en-Brie	50	48.44 N	2.46 E
Tournesac ≃	50	47.15 N	4.12 E
Tournhout	56	51.19 N	4.57 E
Tournon	62	45.04 N	4.50 E
Tournus	58	46.34 N	4.54 E
Touros	250	5.12 S	35.28 W
Tou-rout	110	16.24 N	107.00 E
Tourouvre	50	48.35 N	0.40 E
Tourrette-Levens	62	43.47 N	7.16 E
Tours	50	47.23 N	0.41 E
Tours-sur-Marne	50	49.03 N	4.07 E
Tours-sur-Meymont	62	45.40 N	3.35 E
Tourteron	56	49.32 N	4.39 E
Tourves	62	43.24 N	5.56 E
Toury	50	48.12 N	1.56 E
Touside, Pic ∧	146	21.02 N	16.25 E
Toussaint Creek ≃	214	41.35 N	83.04 W
Toussus-le-Noble	261	48.45 N	2.07 E
Toussus-le-Noble, Aéroport de ⊠	261	48.45 N	2.10 E
Toustain	36	36.40 N	8.15 E
Toutai, Zhg.	89	45.40 N	124.50 E
Toutai, Zhg.	104	41.41 N	121.11 E
Toutaizi	104	42.19 N	122.49 E
Toutle	224	46.20 N	122.41 W
Toutle ≃	224	46.17 N	122.55 W
Toutle, North Fork ≃	224	46.23 N	122.34 W
Toutle, South Fork ≃	224	46.20 N	122.44 W
Toutle Mountain Range ⋀	224	46.20 N	122.30 W
Toutuohe	100	31.06 N	116.25 E
Touws ≃	158	33.45 S	21.11 E
Touwsrivier	158	33.20 S	20.00 E
Touzhan	89	49.27 N	129.41 E
Toužim	60	50.04 N	13.00 E
Töv □[4]	88	47.30 N	106.30 E
Tova	24	65.58 N	40.45 E
Tovar	246	8.20 N	71.46 W
Tovarkovo	82	54.42 N	35.57 E
Tovarkovskij	76	53.40 N	38.14 E
Tove ≃	42	52.05 N	0.38 W
Tovey	219	39.35 N	89.27 W
Tow	196	30.53 N	98.28 W
Tōwa	96	33.13 N	132.53 E
Towaco	210	40.56 N	74.21 W
Towada	92	40.37 N	141.13 E
Towada-hachimantai-kokuritsu-kōen ♠	92	40.35 N	140.53 E
Towada-ko ⊜	92	40.28 N	140.55 E
Towai	172	35.29 S	174.08 E
Towamencin Creek ≃	285	40.13 N	75.23 W
Towanda, Ill., U.S.	216	40.34 N	88.54 W
Towanda, Kans., U.S.	198	37.48 N	97.02 W
Towanda, Pa., U.S.	210	41.46 N	76.27 W
Towanda Creek ≃	210	41.45 N	76.26 W
Towan Head ≻	42	50.25 N	5.07 W
Towar Gardens	216	42.45 N	84.28 W
Towari	112	4.36 S	121.29 E
Towcester	42	52.08 N	1.00 W
Tower	190	47.48 N	92.17 W
Tower City, N. Dak., U.S.	198	46.55 N	97.40 W
Tower City, Pa., U.S.	208	40.35 N	76.33 W
Tower Hamlets ◆[8]	42	51.32 N	0.03 W
Tower Hill, Austl.	166	22.03 S	144.36 E
Tower Hill, Ill., U.S.	219	39.23 N	88.58 W
Towerhill Creek ≃	166	22.29 S	144.39 E
Tower of London ⊥	260	51.30 N	0.05 W
Tower Peak ∧	226	38.09 N	119.33 W
Towers of Silence ♥[1]	272c	18.58 N	72.48 E
Tower Soudan State Park ♠	190	47.50 N	92.15 W
Towla, Mount ∧	154	21.22 S	29.52 E
Tow Law	44	54.44 N	1.49 W
Towlī	84	39.11 N	47.32 E
Town ≃	283	42.00 N	70.57 W
Town Bank	208	39.00 N	74.56 W
Town Creek ≃, Ala., U.S.	194	34.24 N	86.11 W
Town Creek ≃, Ala., U.S.	194	32.34 N	89.14 W
Town Creek ≃, Ohio, U.S.	216	41.05 N	84.25 W
Town Creek Manor	208	38.19 N	76.27 W
Towneley Hall ⊥	262	53.46 N	2.13 W
Towner	198	48.21 N	100.25 W
Town Estates	285	40.04 N	74.52 W
Town Hill ∧[2]	240a	32.19 N	64.44 W
Town of Pines	216	41.41 N	86.58 W
Townsend, Del., U.S.	208	39.24 N	75.41 W
Townsend, Mass., U.S.	207	42.40 N	71.42 W
Townsend, Mont., U.S.	202	46.19 N	111.31 W
Townsend, Va., U.S.	208	37.11 N	75.57 W
Townsend, Mount ∧	171b	36.25 S	148.15 E
Townsend Island I	276	40.38 N	73.26 W
Townsends Inlet C	208	39.07 N	74.43 W
Townshend Island I	166	22.15 S	150.30 E
Township Line Run ≃	279b	40.13 N	79.33 W
Townsville	166	19.16 S	146.48 E
Townville	214	41.41 N	79.53 W
Towrang	170	34.42 S	149.51 E
Towrang ∧	170	34.46 S	149.51 E
Towra Point ≻	274a	34.00 S	151.10 E
Towr Kham	123	34.08 N	71.05 E
Towrzī, Afg.	120	30.11 N	65.59 E
Towrzī, Afg.	128	32.38 N	65.53 E
Towson	284b	39.24 N	76.36 W
Towson State College ♥[2]	284b	39.24 N	76.37 W
Towuti, Danau ⊜	112	2.45 S	121.32 E
Toyah	196	31.19 N	103.47 W
Toyah Creek ≃	196	31.18 N	103.27 W
Tōya-ko ⊜	92a	42.35 N	140.51 E
Toyama	94	36.41 N	137.13 E
Toyama □[5]	94	36.30 N	137.30 E
Toyama-heiya ≚	94	36.40 N	137.15 E
Toyama-wan C	94	36.50 N	137.10 E
Toyapakeh	115b	8.41 S	115.29 E
Tōyō	96	33.22 N	134.18 E
Toyo ≃	94	34.47 N	137.20 E
Toyoake	94	35.03 N	137.01 E
Toyoda, Nihon	94	34.45 N	137.49 E
Toyoda, Nihon	268	35.39 N	139.23 E
Toyofuta	268	35.54 N	139.56 E
Toyohama	96	34.04 N	133.38 E
Toyohashi	94	34.46 N	137.23 E
Toyohira	96	34.40 N	132.24 E
Toyokawa	94	34.49 N	137.24 E
Toyo-kawa-yōsui ≊	94	34.35 N	137.03 E
Toyonaka, Nihon	96	34.47 N	135.28 E
Toyonaka, Nihon	96	34.09 N	133.42 E
Toyone	94	35.09 N	137.43 E
Toyono	94	36.43 N	138.16 E
Toyooka, Nihon	94	34.50 N	137.52 E
Toyooka, Nihon	94	35.33 N	137.54 E
Toyooka, Nihon	96	35.32 N	134.50 E
Toyooka, Nihon	268	35.11 N	139.58 E
Toyosaka	96	34.34 N	132.50 E
Toyosato	94	36.06 N	140.02 E
Toyoshina	94	36.18 N	137.54 E
Toyota, Nihon	94	35.05 N	137.09 E
Toyota, Nihon	94	36.46 N	138.19 E
Toyota, Nihon	96	34.12 N	131.04 E
Toyota-ko ⊜	96	34.14 N	131.08 E
Toyotomi	94	35.34 N	138.33 E
Toyotsu	96	33.40 N	130.58 E
Toyoura	96	34.08 N	130.58 E
Toy's Hill	260	51.14 N	0.06 E
Tozer, Mount ∧	164	12.45 S	143.13 E
Tozeur	148	33.55 N	8.08 E
Tozi, Mount ∧	180	65.41 N	150.58 W
Tozitna ≃	180	65.08 N	152.23 W
Tpig	84	41.47 N	47.36 E
Traar ◆[8]	263	51.23 N	6.36 E
Trabaria, Bocca)(	66	43.36 N	12.14 E
Traben-Trarbach	56	49.57 N	7.06 E
Trabia	70	37.59 N	13.39 E
Trabiju	255	22.03 S	48.18 W
Trabuco, Arroyo ≃	228	33.31 N	117.40 W
Trabzon	130	41.00 N	39.43 E
Trabzon □[4]	130	40.50 N	39.50 E
Tracadie	186	47.31 N	64.54 W
Tracajá, Cachoeira ↳	248	10.29 S	64.05 W
Trachenberg → Żmigród	30	51.29 N	16.55 E
Trachselwald	58	47.01 N	7.45 E
Tra-cu	110	9.42 N	106.16 E
Tracuateua	250	1.05 S	46.54 W
Tracy, Qué., Can.	206	46.01 N	73.09 W
Tracy, Calif., U.S.	226	37.44 N	121.25 W
Tracy, Minn., U.S.	198	44.14 N	95.37 W
Tracy City	194	35.16 N	85.44 W
Tracyton	224	47.37 N	122.39 W
Tradate	62	45.43 N	8.54 E
Trade Lake ⊜	184	55.22 N	103.44 W
Tradewater ≃	194	37.31 N	88.03 W
Trading Bay C	212	45.15 N	78.55 W
Trælleborg ⊥	41	55.23 N	11.17 E
Traer	190	42.12 N	92.28 W
Traessu, Monte ∧	71	40.28 N	8.40 E
Trafalgar, Austl.	169	38.12 S	146.09 E
Trafalgar, Ont., Can.	275b	43.29 N	79.43 W
Trafalgar, Ind., U.S.	218	39.25 N	86.09 W
Trafalgar, Cabo ≻	34	36.11 N	6.02 W
Trafaria	266c	38.40 N	9.14 W
Trafford	214	40.23 N	79.45 W
Trafford □[8]	262	53.24 N	2.21 W
Trafford, Lake ⊜	220	26.25 N	81.30 W
Trafford Park	262	53.28 N	2.20 W
Trafoi	64	46.33 N	10.31 E
Tragacete	34	40.21 N	1.51 W
Trāghan	146	25.59 N	14.26 E
Tragliata ◆[8]	267a	41.58 N	12.15 E
Traição, Córrego ≃	287b	23.36 S	46.41 W
Traid	34	40.40 N	1.49 W
Traíghlí → Tralee	48	52.16 N	9.42 W
Traiguén	252	38.15 S	72.41 W
Traiguén, Isla I	254	45.35 S	73.42 W
Trail	182	49.06 N	117.42 W
Trail Creek	216	41.42 N	86.52 W
Trailer Estates	220	27.24 N	82.34 W
Traînel	50	48.25 N	3.27 E
Trainer	285	39.50 N	75.25 W
Traipu	250	9.58 S	37.01 W
Traíra (Taraira) ≃	246	1.04 S	69.26 W
Trairão ≃	250	7.20 S	51.14 W
Traíras ≃	255	14.07 S	48.31 W
Trairi	250	3.17 S	39.15 W
Traisen ≃	61	48.22 N	15.46 E
Traiskirchen	264b	48.01 N	16.18 E
Traismauer	61	48.21 N	15.44 E
Traîtres, Baie des C	174x	9.50 S	139.02 W
Trajouce	266c	38.44 N	9.20 W
Trakai	76	54.38 N	24.56 E
Trakt	24	62.44 N	51.11 E
Träkvista	40	59.16 N	17.47 E
Tralee	48	52.16 N	9.42 W
Tralee Bay C	48	52.15 N	9.59 W
Tramatza	71	40.00 N	8.39 E
Tramayes	58	46.18 N	4.36 E
Tramelan	58	47.13 N	7.06 E
Tramin → Termeno	64	46.20 N	11.14 E
Trammel	192	37.01 N	82.18 W
Trammel Creek ≃	194	36.52 N	86.23 W
Tramonti di sopra	64	46.18 N	12.47 E
Tramore	48	52.10 N	7.10 W
Tramperos Creek ≃	196	36.05 N	103.15 W
Tramutola	68	40.19 N	15.47 E
Trân	38	42.50 N	22.39 E
Tranås	26	58.03 N	14.59 E
Trancão ≃	266c	38.48 N	9.06 W
Trancas	252	26.13 S	65.17 W
Trancoso, Méx.	234	22.44 N	102.22 W
Trancoso, Port.	34	40.47 N	7.21 W
Trand	123	34.38 N	72.59 E
Tranderup	41	54.52 N	10.22 E
Tranebjerg	41	55.50 N	10.36 E
Tranekær	41	55.00 N	10.51 E
Tranemo	26	57.29 N	13.21 E
Tranent	46	55.57 N	2.58 W
Tränental	158	27.09 S	19.33 E
Trang	110	7.33 N	99.36 E
Trangahy	157b	19.07 S	44.43 E
Trangan, Pulau I	164	6.35 S	134.20 E
Trangie	166	32.02 S	147.59 E
Tran Grande ≃	116	6.43 N	124.01 E
Trängslet	26	61.25 N	13.40 E
Trani	68	41.17 N	16.26 E
Tranmere	262	53.23 N	3.01 W
Trannon ≃	42	52.31 N	3.25 W
Tranoroa	157b	24.42 S	45.04 E
Tranquebar	122	11.02 N	79.51 E
Tranqueira ≃	250	7.15 S	42.12 W
Tranqueras	252	31.12 S	55.45 W
Tranquility	218	38.58 N	83.32 W
Tranquilla	236	8.30 N	80.14 W
Tranquillity	226	36.39 N	120.15 W
Trans-en-Provence	62	43.30 N	6.29 E
Transfer	214	41.20 N	80.26 W
Transit Airport ⊠	284a	43.06 N	78.44 W
Transkei □[9]	158	31.20 S	29.00 E
Transquaking ≃	208	38.22 N	76.00 W
Transsylvanische Alpen → Carpaţii Meridionali ⋀	38	45.30 N	24.15 E
Transtrand	26	61.05 N	13.19 E
Transtrandsfjällen ∧	26	61.17 N	13.00 E
Transvaal □[3]	156	25.00 S	29.00 E
Transylvania □[9]	38	46.30 N	24.00 E
Transylvanian Alps → Carpaţii Meridionali ⋀	38	45.30 N	24.15 E
Tranters Creek ≃	192	35.33 N	77.05 W
Traona	58	46.09 N	9.31 E
Trapalcó, Salinas de ≚	254	39.45 S	66.45 W
Trapani	70	38.01 N	12.29 E
Trapani □[4]	70	37.50 N	12.40 E
Traphole Brook ≃	283	42.10 N	71.11 W
Trappe, Md., U.S.	208	38.40 N	76.04 W
Trappe, Pa., U.S.	208	40.12 N	75.29 W
Trappenkamp	54	54.03 N	10.16 E
Trapper Peak ∧	202	45.54 N	114.18 W
Trappes	50	48.47 N	2.00 E
Trappeto	70	38.04 N	13.03 E
Trapuá ≃	287b	23.36 S	46.17 W
Traralgon	169	38.12 S	146.32 E
Traras, Monts des ⋀	34	35.10 N	1.40 W
Trarza ◆[1]	150	18.00 N	15.00 W
Trasacco	66	41.57 N	13.32 E
Trasadingen	58	47.40 N	8.26 E
Trăscau, Munţii ⋀	38	46.23 N	23.33 E
Trasching	60	49.09 N	12.28 E
Trasimeno, Lago ⊜	66	43.08 N	12.06 E
Trask ≃	224	45.28 N	123.53 W
Träslövsläge	26	57.04 N	12.16 E
Trasna	82	54.45 N	38.42 E
Trás-os-Montes □[9]	34	41.30 N	7.15 W
Trassem	56	49.34 N	6.31 E
Trasslberg	60	49.29 N	11.50 E
Trâstenik	38	43.31 N	24.28 E
Trat	110	12.14 N	102.30 E
Tratalias	71	39.06 N	8.34 E
Tratzberg, Schloss ⊥	64	47.23 N	11.44 E
Trauchgau	58	47.38 N	10.49 E
Traun	61	48.13 N	14.14 E
Traun ≃, B.R.D.	60	48.00 N	12.32 E
Traun ≃, Öst.	64	48.09 N	14.01 E
Traunkirchen	64	47.50 N	13.47 E
Traunreut	64	47.56 N	12.35 E
Traun-See ⊜	64	47.51 N	13.48 E
Traunstein	64	47.52 N	12.38 E
Traunstein ∧	64	47.52 N	13.50 E
Traunwalchen	64	47.56 N	12.36 E
Trautenstein	54	51.41 N	10.43 E
Travagliato	64	45.31 N	10.05 E
Trave ≃	54	53.54 N	10.50 E
Travedona	62	45.48 N	8.40 E
Travellers Lake ⊜	166	33.18 S	142.00 E
Travemünde ◆[8]	54	53.57 N	10.52 E
Traver	226	36.27 N	119.29 W
Travers, Mount ∧	172	42.01 S	172.44 E
Travers, Val de ∨	58	46.57 N	6.38 E
Traverse, Lake ⊜	198	45.43 N	96.40 W
Traverse Bay C	184	50.40 N	96.25 W
Traverse City	190	44.46 N	85.37 W
Traversella	62	45.30 N	7.45 E
Traverse Peak ∧	180	65.10 N	159.12 W
Traversetolo	64	44.38 N	10.23 E
Travers Reservoir ⊜[1]	182	50.14 N	112.51 W
Travesía ⊥	236	15.20 N	87.53 W
Travis	222	31.08 N	97.00 W
Travis □[6]	222	30.18 N	97.40 W
Travis, Lake ⊜[1]	196	30.27 N	98.00 W
Travis Air Force Base ■	226	38.16 N	121.55 W
Travnik	36	44.14 N	17.40 E
Trawalla	169	37.26 S	143.29 E
Trawbreaga Bay C	48	55.17 N	7.18 W
Trawick	222	31.46 N	94.45 W
Trawsfynydd	42	52.54 N	3.55 W
Trayning	162	31.07 S	117.48 E
Trazegnies	50	50.28 N	4.19 E
Trbovlje	36	46.10 N	15.03 E
Treadwell	210	42.21 N	75.03 W
Treales	262	53.47 N	2.51 W
Treasure Island	220	27.46 N	82.46 W
Treasure Island I	226	37.48 N	122.22 W
Treasure Island Naval Station ■	282	37.49 N	122.22 W
Treasury Islands II	175e	7.22 S	155.34 E
Trebatsch	54	52.05 N	14.09 E
Trebbia ≃	62	45.04 N	9.41 E
Trebbin	54	52.13 N	13.13 E
Třebechovice pod Orebem	30	50.12 N	16.00 E
Trebel	54	52.59 N	11.20 E
Trebel ≃	54	53.55 N	13.01 E
Trebelsee ⊜	54	52.28 N	12.47 E
Třebenice	54	50.29 N	14.00 E
Třebíč	30	49.13 N	15.53 E
Trebinje	38	42.43 N	18.20 E
Trebisacce	68	39.52 N	16.32 E
Trebitz	54	51.45 N	12.44 E
Trebizond → Trabzon	130	41.00 N	39.43 E
Trebjerg ∧[2]	41	55.10 N	10.14 E
Treble Mountain ∧	182	55.50 N	129.51 W
Treblinka	30	52.39 N	22.03 E
Trebnitz → Trzebnica	30	51.19 N	17.03 E
Třeboň	61	49.00 N	14.47 E
Třeboňská pánev ≚[1]	30	49.00 N	14.50 E
Třebouň ∧	60	50.01 N	12.59 E
Trebsen	54	51.17 N	12.45 E
Trecastagni	70	37.37 N	15.05 E
Trecate	62	45.26 N	8.44 E
Trecchina	68	40.02 N	15.46 E
Trece Martires	116	14.16 N	120.50 E
Trecenta	64	45.02 N	11.28 E
Tred Avon River C	208	38.42 N	76.08 W
Tredegar	42	51.47 N	3.16 W
Tredici Archi, Ponte ◆[5]	66	41.32 N	14.57 E
Treene ≃	41	54.22 N	9.05 E
Trees Mills	279b	40.23 N	80.13 W
Treffen	64	46.40 N	13.52 E
Treffort	58	46.16 N	5.22 E
Treffurt	56	51.08 N	10.14 E
Trèfle, Lac ⊜	206	46.36 N	73.55 W
Tregaron	42	52.13 N	3.55 W
Tregnago	64	45.31 N	11.10 E
Tregosse Islets II	166	17.41 S	150.43 E
Tregubovo	76	58.59 N	31.33 E
Tréguier	32	48.47 N	3.14 W
Treharris	42	51.41 N	3.16 W
Treherne	184	49.38 N	98.41 W
Trehörningsjö	26	63.42 N	18.48 E
Treia, B.R.D.	41	54.30 N	9.17 E
Treia, It.	66	43.19 N	13.19 E
Treig, Loch ⊜[1]	46	56.50 N	4.44 W
Treinta y Tres	252	33.14 S	54.23 W
Treis	56	50.10 N	7.17 E
Trekkopje	156	22.18 S	14.53 E
Trélazé	32	47.27 N	0.28 W
Trelde Næs ≻	41	55.37 N	9.52 E
Trelew	254	43.15 S	65.18 W
Trelleborg	41	55.22 N	13.10 E
Treloar	219	38.39 N	91.10 W
Trélon	50	50.04 N	4.06 E
Tremadoc	42	52.56 N	4.09 W
Tremadoc Bay C	42	52.52 N	4.15 W
Tremblant, Lac ⊜	206	46.15 N	74.38 W
Tremblant, Mont ∧	206	46.16 N	74.35 W
Tremblay, Hippodrome du ♠	261	48.50 N	2.29 E
Tremblay, Île du I	275a	45.31 N	73.45 W
Tremblay-lès-Gonesse	261	48.59 N	2.34 E
Trembleur Lake ⊜	182	54.51 N	125.07 W
Tremedal	255	14.58 S	41.24 W
Tremembé	256	22.58 S	45.33 W
Tremezzo	58	45.59 N	9.15 E
Tremino	88	56.42 N	98.04 E
Tremiti, Isole II	68	42.07 N	15.30 E
Tremo La)(	124	27.44 N	89.12 E
Tremont, Ill., U.S.	190	40.28 N	89.29 W
Tremont, Ind., U.S.	216	41.39 N	87.02 W
Tremont, Pa., U.S.	208	40.38 N	76.23 W
Tremont ◆[8]	276	40.51 N	73.55 W
Tremont City	218	40.01 N	83.50 W
Tremonton	200	41.43 N	112.10 W
Třemošna	60	49.49 N	13.20 E
Třemošná ≃	60	49.52 N	13.32 E
Tremp	34	42.10 N	0.54 E
Trempealeau	190	44.00 N	91.26 W
Trempealeau ≃	190	44.02 N	91.32 W
Trempen → Novostrojevo	76	54.27 N	21.50 E
Tremsbüttel	52	53.44 N	10.18 E
Trena	144	10.45 N	40.38 E
Trenčín	30	48.54 N	18.04 E
Trendelburg	52	51.34 N	9.25 E
Trenel	252	35.42 S	64.08 W
Trêng	110	12.49 N	102.54 E
Trenggalek	115a	8.03 S	111.43 E
Trenque Lauquen	252	35.58 S	62.42 W
Trent, D.D.R.	54	54.31 N	13.15 E
Trent → Trento, It.	64	46.04 N	11.08 E
Trent ≃, Ont., Can.	212	44.06 N	77.34 W
Trent ≃, Eng., U.K.	44	53.42 N	0.41 W
Trent ≃, N.C., U.S.	192	35.05 N	77.02 W
Trent, Vale of ∨	42	52.44 N	1.50 W
Trent and Mersey Canal ≊	262	53.19 N	2.39 W
Trente-et-un-Milles, Lac des ⊜	188	46.12 N	75.49 W
Trentham	169	37.23 S	144.19 E
Trentino-Alto Adige □[4]	64	46.30 N	11.20 E
Trento	64	46.04 N	11.08 E
Trento □[4]	64	46.08 N	11.07 E
Trentola-Ducenta	68	40.59 N	14.10 E
Trenton, N.S., Can.	186	45.37 N	62.38 W
Trenton, Ont., Can.	212	44.06 N	77.35 W
Trenton, Fla., U.S.	192	29.37 N	82.49 W
Trenton, Ga., U.S.	192	34.52 N	85.31 W
Trenton, Ill., U.S.	219	38.36 N	89.41 W
Trenton, Ky., U.S.	194	36.43 N	87.16 W
Trenton, Mich., U.S.	216	42.09 N	83.11 W
Trenton, Mo., U.S.	194	40.05 N	93.37 W
Trenton, Nebr., U.S.	198	40.11 N	101.01 W
Trenton, N.J., U.S.	208		
	285	40.13 N	74.45 W
Trenton, N.C., U.S.	192	35.04 N	77.21 W
Trenton, Ohio, U.S.	218	39.29 N	84.28 W
Trenton, Tenn., U.S.	194	35.59 N	88.56 W
Trenton, Tex., U.S.	196	33.26 N	96.20 W
Trenton Channel ≃[1]	281	42.06 N	83.11 W
Trentwood	202	47.42 N	117.13 W
Trepalade	64	45.34 N	12.24 E
Trepassey	186	46.44 N	53.22 W
Trepassey Bay C	186	46.40 N	52.20 W
Treptow ◆[8]	54	52.29 N	13.29 E

Symbols in the index entries represent the broad categories identified in the key at the right. Symbols with superior numbers (⋀[2]) identify subcategories (see complete key on page I · 30).

Kartensymbole in dem Registerverzeichnis stellen die rechts in Schlüssel erklärten Kategorien dar. Symbole mit hochgestellten Ziffern (⋀[2]) bezeichnen Unterabteilungen einer Kategorie (vgl. vollständiger Schlüssel auf Seite I · 30).

Los símbolos incluídos en el texto del índice representan las grandes categorias identificadas con la clave a la derecha. Los símbolos con numeros en su parte superior (⋀[2]) identifican las subcategorías (véase la clave completa en la página I · 30).

Les symboles de l'index représentent les catégories indiquées dans la légende à droite. Les symboles suivis d'un indice (⋀[2]) représentent des sous-catégories (voir légende complète à la page I · 30).

Os símbolos incluídos no texto do índice representam as grandes categorias identificadas com a chave à direita. Os símbolos com números em sua parte superior (⋀[2]) identificam as subcategorias (veja-se a chave completa à página I · 30).

Symbol	English	Deutsch	Español	Français	Português
∧	Mountain	Berg	Montaña	Montagne	Montanha
⋀	Mountains	Berge	Montañas	Montagnes	Montanhas
)(	Pass	Pass	Paso	Col	Passo
∨	Valley, Canyon	Tal, Cañon	Valle, Cañón	Vallée, Canyon	Vale, Canhão
≚	Plain	Ebene	Llano	Plaine	Planície
≻	Cape	Kap	Cabo	Cap	Cabo
I	Island	Insel	Isla	Île	Ilha
II	Islands	Inseln	Islas	Îles	Ilhas
⊥	Other Topographic Features	Andere Topographische Objekte	Otros Elementos Topográficos	Autres données topographiques	Outros Elementos Topográficos

ESPAÑOL — Nombre | Página | Lat.°′ | Long.°′ W=Oeste

FRANÇAIS — Nom | Page | Lat.°′ | Long.°′ W=Ouest

PORTUGUÊS — Nome | Página | Lat.°′ | Long.°′ W=Oeste

Treptow an der Rega → Trzebiatów 30 54.04 N 15.14 E
Trepuzzi 68 40.24 N 18.05 E
Trequanda 66 43.11 N 11.40 E
Tresa ≏ 58 46.00 N 8.43 E
Tres Algarrobos 252 35.12 S 62.46 W
Tres Árboles 252 32.24 S 56.43 W
Tres Arroyos 252 38.23 S 60.17 W
Tres Cerros 254 48.13 S 67.33 W
Treščevo 82 54.11 N 37.55 E
Tresckow 210 40.55 N 75.58 W
Tresco I 42a 49.57 N 6.19 W
Três Corações 256 21.42 S 45.16 W
Trescore Balneario 62 45.41 N 9.50 E
Três Coroas 252 29.32 S 50.48 W
Tres de Febrero → Caseros 258 34.36 S 58.33 W
Tres de Febrero □[5] 288 34.36 S 58.35 W
Tres de Febrero, Parque ♠ 288 34.34 S 58.25 W
Três de Maio 252 27.47 S 54.14 W
Tresenda 64 46.10 N 10.05 E
Tres Esquinas 246 0.43 N 75.16 W
Três Fronteiras 255 20.13 S 50.55 W
Treshnish Isles II 46 56.30 N 6.24 W
Treshnish Point ≻ 46 56.33 N 6.21 W
Três Ilhas 256 22.04 S 43.29 W
Tresinaro ≏ 64 44.39 N 10.47 E
Tres Isletas 252 26.21 S 60.26 W
Treskino 80 52.40 N 44.40 E
Três Lagoas 255 20.48 S 51.43 W
Tres Lagos 254 49.37 S 71.30 W
Três Marias, Represa @[1] 255 18.12 S 45.15 W
Tres Montes, Golfo C 254 46.54 S 75.00 W
Tres Montes, Península ≻[1] 254 46.50 S 75.30 W
Tres Montosas ∧ 200 34.06 N 107.28 W
Tresnuraghes 71 40.15 N 8.31 E
Tres Palacio ≏ 196 28.45 N 96.09 W
Três Passos 252 27.27 S 53.56 W
Tres Picos 234 15.52 N 93.32 W
Tres Picos, Cerro ∧, Arg. 252 38.09 S 61.57 W
Tres Picos, Cerro ∧, Méx. 234 16.36 N 94.13 W
Tres Pinos 226 36.48 N 121.19 W
Tres Pinos Creek ≏ 226 36.47 N 121.21 W
Três Pontas 256 21.22 S 45.31 W
Três Pontas, Cabo das ≻ 152 10.23 S 13.32 E
Tres Puntas, Cabo ≻ 254 47.06 S 65.53 W
Três Ranchos 255 18.22 S 47.47 W
Tres Reyes Islands II 116 13.14 N 121.51 E
Três Rios, Bra. 256 22.07 S 43.12 W
Tres Ríos, C.R. 236 9.54 N 83.58 W
Tressancourt 261 48.55 N 2.00 E
Třešť 30 49.18 N 15.30 E
Tresta 46 60.14 N 1.21 W
Tres Valles 234 18.15 N 96.08 W
Tres Zapotes ⊥ 234 18.28 N 95.24 W
Tret'akovskaja Galereja ✤ 265b 55.45 N 37.37 E
Tretet 114 4.40 N 96.51 E
Trets 62 43.27 N 5.41 E
Tretten 26 61.19 N 10.19 E
Treuburg → Olecko 30 54.03 N 22.30 E
Treuchtlingen 56 48.57 N 10.54 E
Treuen 54 50.32 N 12.18 E
Treuenbrietzen 54 52.06 N 12.52 E
Treuhandgebiet Pazifische Inseln → Pacific Islands Trust Territory □[2] 14 10.00 N 155.00 E
Trevelín 254 43.04 S 71.28 W
Trèves → Trier 56 49.45 N 6.38 E
Trevi 66 42.52 N 12.45 E
Treviglio 62 45.31 N 9.35 E
Trevignano Romano 66 42.09 N 12.15 E
Treviño 34 42.44 N 2.45 W
Treviso 64 45.40 N 12.15 E
Treviso □[4] 64 45.50 N 12.13 E
Trevor 216 42.31 N 88.07 W
Trevorton 208 40.47 N 76.41 W
Trevose 208 40.09 N 74.59 W
Trevose Head ≻ 42 50.33 N 5.01 W
Trévoux 58 45.56 N 4.46 E
Trexlertown 208 40.33 N 75.36 W
Treysa 56 50.55 N 9.11 E
Treze Quedas Ⳑ 250 0.07 N 56.55 W
Trezevant 194 36.01 N 88.37 W
Trezzano 266b 45.25 N 9.04 E
Trezzo sull'Adda 62 45.36 N 9.31 E
Trgovište 38 42.21 N 22.05 E
Trhomné 60 49.55 N 13.05 E
Trhové Sviny 61 48.51 N 14.39 E
Triabunna 166 42.30 S 147.55 E
Triadelphia Reservoir @[1] 208 39.13 N 77.01 W
Trialeti 84 41.33 N 44.07 E
Trialetskij Chrebet ⩕ 84 41.45 N 43.50 E
Triana 66 42.47 N 11.33 E
Triánda 38 36.24 N 28.10 E
Triangle, Eng., U.K. 262 53.42 N 1.56 W
Triangle, Va., U.S. 208 38.33 N 77.20 W
Triangle Lake 210 42.32 N 74.13 W
Triángulos, Arrecifes ✢[2] 232 20.57 N 92.16 W
Triaucourt-en-Argonne 56 48.59 N 5.04 E
Tribeni 126 22.59 N 88.24 E
Triberg 58 48.08 N 8.13 E
Tribes Hill 210 42.57 N 74.17 W
Tribobó 287a 22.52 S 43.01 W
Triborough Bridge ◂[5] 276 40.47 N 73.55 W
Tri Brata, Porog Ⳑ 86 57.25 N 95.39 E
Tribsees 54 54.05 N 12.45 E
Tribugá, Golfo de C 246 5.45 N 77.20 W
Tribune, Sask., Can. 184 49.15 N 103.50 W
Tribune, Kans., U.S. 198 38.28 N 101.45 W
Tribune Channel Џ 182 50.50 N 126.16 W
Tribuswinkel 264b 48.00 N 16.16 E
Tricao Malal 252 37.03 S 70.19 W
Tricarico 68 40.37 N 16.09 E
Tricase 68 39.56 N 18.22 E
Tricesimo 64 46.10 N 13.13 E
Trichardt 158 26.28 S 29.13 E
Trichiana 64 46.05 N 12.07 E
Trichinopoly → Tiruchchirāppalli 122 10.49 N 78.41 E
Trichūr 122 10.31 N 76.13 E
Tri Cities 222 32.09 N 95.56 W
Tricot 50 49.34 N 2.35 E
Tri County Supply Canal ≊ 198 40.49 N 100.06 W
Trida 166 33.01 S 145.01 E
Trident Peak ∧ 204 41.54 N 118.25 W
Triduby 78 48.06 N 30.24 E
Trieben 61 47.29 N 14.30 E
Triebes 54 50.41 N 12.01 E
Trieching 60 48.45 N 12.40 E
Triel-sur-Seine 261 48.59 N 2.00 E
Trient → Trento 64 46.04 N 11.08 E

Triepkendorf 54 53.17 N 13.20 E
Trier 56 49.45 N 6.38 E
Trier □[5] 56 50.00 N 6.40 E
Triesen 58 47.06 N 9.31 E
Trieste (Triest) 64 45.40 N 13.46 E
Trieste □[4] 64 45.30 N 13.50 E
Trieste, Gulf of C 64 45.40 N 13.35 E
Trieste Depth ✢[1] 14 11.21 N 142.12 E
Triesting ≏ 264b 48.05 N 16.24 E
Trieux 56 49.20 N 5.56 E
Triftern 60 48.24 N 13.01 E
Trigal 248 18.17 S 64.08 W
Triggiano 68 41.04 N 16.55 E
Triglav ∧ 64 46.23 N 13.50 E
Triglitz 54 53.12 N 12.05 E
Trigna, Pizzo ∧ 70 37.58 N 13.34 E
Trigno ≏ 66 42.04 N 14.48 E
Trigo Mountains ⩕ 200 33.15 N 114.35 W
Trigueros 34 37.23 N 6.50 W
Trijangul'atoroje, Pik ∧ 88 53.45 N 97.00 E
Tríkala 38 39.34 N 21.46 E
Trikhonís, Límni @ 38 38.34 N 21.28 E
Tríkomon 130 35.17 N 33.52 E
Trikora, Puncak (Wilhelmina Peak) ∧ 164 4.15 S 138.45 E
Tri Lakes 216 41.15 N 85.27 W
Trilbardou 261 48.57 N 2.48 E
Trilby 220 28.28 N 82.12 W
Trilesy 78 49.59 N 29.50 E
Trillick 48 54.27 N 7.30 W
Trilport 50 48.57 N 2.57 E
Trim 48 53.34 N 6.47 W
Triman 120 29.38 N 69.05 E
Trimbach 58 47.22 N 7.54 E
Trimble □[6] 218 38.37 N 85.20 W
Trim Creek ≏ 216 41.10 N 87.38 W
Trimonte 256 21.43 S 42.35 W
Trin 58 46.50 N 9.22 E
Trinchera Creek ≏ 200 37.19 N 105.45 W
Trincheras, Méx. 196 25.37 N 101.55 W
Trincheras, Méx. 232 30.24 N 111.32 W
Trincomalee 122 8.34 N 81.14 E
Trincomali Channel Џ 224 48.02 N 123.30 W
Trindade 255 16.40 S 49.30 W
Trindade I 244 20.31 S 29.19 W
Třinec 30 49.41 N 18.40 E
Tring 42 51.48 N 0.40 W
Trinidad, Bol. 248 14.47 S 64.47 W
Trinidad, Col. 246 5.25 N 71.40 W
Trinidad, Cuba 240p 21.48 N 79.59 W
Trinidad, Hond. 236 14.57 N 88.45 W
Trinidad, Colo., U.S. 198 37.10 N 104.31 W
Trinidad, Tex., U.S. 222 32.09 N 96.06 W
Trinidad, Ur. 252 33.32 S 56.54 W
Trinidad I 241r 10.30 N 61.15 W
Trinidad, Golfo C 254 49.55 S 75.25 W
Trinidad, Isla I 252 39.08 S 61.58 W
Trinidad, Río la ≏ 234 17.49 N 95.09 W
Trinidad and Tobago □[1] 230 / 241r 11.00 N 61.00 W
Trinità 62 44.30 N 7.45 E
Trinità, Lago @ 70 37.43 N 12.46 E
Trinità d'agultu 71 40.59 N 8.54 E
Trinitapoli 68 41.21 N 16.05 E
Trinitaria 232 16.07 N 92.03 W
Trinité, Havre de la C 240e 14.44 N 60.58 W
Trinity, Newf., Can. 186 48.59 N 53.55 W
Trinity, Tex., U.S. 222 30.57 N 95.22 W
Trinity □[6] 222 31.07 N 95.10 W
Trinity ≏, Calif., U.S. 204 41.11 N 123.42 W
Trinity ≏, Tex., U.S. 222 29.47 N 94.42 W
Trinity, Clear Fork ≏ 196 32.46 N 97.21 W
Trinity, East Fork ≏ 222 32.30 N 96.30 W
Trinity, Elm Fork ≏ 222 32.47 N 96.54 W
Trinity, South Fork ≏ 204 40.54 N 123.35 W
Trinity, West Fork ≏ 196 32.48 N 96.51 W
Trinity Bay C, Newf., Can. 186 48.00 N 53.40 W
Trinity Bay C, Tex., U.S. 222 29.40 N 94.45 W
Trinity Islands II 180 56.33 N 154.25 W
Trinity Mountain ∧ 202 43.36 N 115.26 W
Trinity Mountains ⩕ 204 41.00 N 122.30 W
Trinity Park ♠ 275b 43.39 N 79.25 W
Trinity Peak ∧ 204 40.14 N 118.45 W
Trinkat Island I 110 8.05 N 93.30 E
Trinkitat 140 18.41 N 37.43 E
Trino 62 45.12 N 8.18 E
Trins 64 47.05 N 11.25 E
Trinway 214 40.09 N 82.01 W
Triolet 157c 20.03 S 57.32 E
Triolo ≏ 66 41.40 N 15.34 E
Trion 192 34.33 N 85.19 W
Trionto ≏ 68 39.37 N 16.45 E
Trionto, Capo ≻ 68 39.37 N 16.45 E
Triora 62 43.59 N 7.46 E
Tripi 70 38.03 N 15.06 E
Triplett Creek ≏ 218 38.10 N 83.27 W
Triplett Creek, North Fork ≏ 218 38.10 N 83.31 W
Tripoli → Ṭarābulus, Lībīya 146 32.54 N 13.11 E
Tripoli → Ṭarābulus, Lubnān 130 34.26 N 35.51 E
Tripoli, Iowa, U.S. 190 42.48 N 92.16 W
Trípolis, Ellás 38 37.31 N 22.21 E
Tripolis → Ṭarābulus, Lībīya 146 32.54 N 13.11 E
Tripolitania → Ṭarābulus □[4] 146 31.00 N 15.00 E
Tripolitania → Ṭarābulus ◂[1] 146 31.00 N 15.00 E
Tripolje 78 50.07 N 30.46 E
Triponzo 66 42.50 N 12.56 E
Tripp 198 43.13 N 97.58 W
Trips Subdivision 281 42.34 N 83.25 W
Triptis 54 50.44 N 11.52 E
Tripura □[4] 120 24.00 N 92.00 E
Trisanna ≏ 58 47.07 N 10.30 E
Tristan da Cunha Group II 10 37.15 S 12.30 W
Tristan Island I 10 37.05 S 12.17 W
Tristán Suárez 258 34.53 S 58.34 W
Tristao, Îles II 150 10.53 N 14.58 W
Tristate Village 278 41.44 N 87.57 W
Triste 34 42.23 N 0.43 W
Triste, Golfo C 246 10.40 N 68.10 W
Trisūli ≏ 124 27.49 N 84.47 E
Tri-ton 110 10.25 N 105.00 E
Triton Island I 108 15.47 N 111.12 E
Tritriva 157b 22.46 S 46.07 E
Trittau 52 53.37 N 10.25 E
Trittenheim 56 49.49 N 6.54 E
Triuggio 266b 45.40 N 9.16 E
Triumph 194 29.20 N 89.30 W
Triunfo 250 7.50 S 38.07 W
Triunfo, Igarapé ≏ 250 6.22 S 52.25 W
Triunfo de Madero 234 16.52 N 93.48 W
Trivandrum 122 8.29 N 76.55 E
Trivento 66 41.47 N 14.33 E
Trivero 62 45.40 N 8.10 E

Trivigno 68 40.35 N 15.59 E
Trnava 30 48.23 N 17.35 E
Trnovo → Veliko Târnovo 38 43.04 N 25.39 E
Troarn 32 49.11 N 0.11 W
Trobriand Island I 164 8.35 S 151.05 E
Trobriand Islands II 164 8.35 S 151.05 E
Tr'ochgolovyj Golec, Gora ∧ 88 53.22 N 107.03 E
Tr'ochizbenka 83 48.45 N 38.58 E
Tr'ochsv'atskoje 82 56.29 N 37.03 E
Trochtelfingen 58 48.18 N 9.14 E
Trochu 182 51.50 N 113.13 W
Troense 41 55.02 N 10.39 E
Trofa, Arroyo de ≏ 266a 40.30 N 3.45 W
Trofaich 61 47.25 N 15.00 E
Trofarello 62 44.59 N 7.44 E
Trögd ≻[1] 40 59.31 N 17.15 E
Trogen 58 47.24 N 9.28 E
Trogir 36 43.31 N 16.15 E
Troglav ∧ 36 43.57 N 16.36 E
Tröglitz 54 51.04 N 12.11 E
Troia 68 41.22 N 15.18 E
Troica 80 54.24 N 40.14 E
Troice-Lykovo ◂[8] 265b 55.47 N 37.24 E
Troick, S.S.S.R. 86 54.06 N 61.35 E
Troick, S.S.S.R. 88 57.25 N 94.50 E
Troickaja 78 45.08 N 38.07 E
Troickij, S.S.S.R. 80 50.14 N 43.05 E
Troickij, S.S.S.R. 86 50.41 N 54.38 E
Troickij, S.S.S.R. 86 57.03 N 63.43 E
Troickij, S.S.S.R. 88 54.36 N 113.09 E
Troickije Rosl'ai 80 53.21 N 41.24 E
Troickij Sungur 80 53.17 N 47.37 E
Troickij Zavod 88 53.27 N 102.09 E
Troicko-Charcyzsk 83 47.58 N 38.16 E
Troickoje, S.S.S.R. 78 47.38 N 30.19 E
Troickoje, S.S.S.R. 78 51.17 N 41.28 E
Troickoje, S.S.S.R. 78 49.55 N 38.19 E
Troickoje, S.S.S.R. 80 53.22 N 48.23 E
Troickoje, S.S.S.R. 80 46.26 N 44.15 E
Troickoje, S.S.S.R. 80 53.23 N 52.48 E
Troickoje, S.S.S.R. 80 53.06 N 52.32 E
Troickoje, S.S.S.R. 82 54.52 N 37.07 E
Troickoje, S.S.S.R. 82 55.23 N 37.25 E
Troickoje, S.S.S.R. 83 48.32 N 38.23 E
Troickoje, S.S.S.R. 83 47.22 N 38.53 E
Troickoje, S.S.S.R. 86 52.58 N 84.40 E
Troickoje, S.S.S.R. 86 59.07 N 58.25 E
Troickoje, S.S.S.R. 86 52.19 N 56.23 E
Troickoje, S.S.S.R. 89 49.27 N 136.36 E
Troicko-Pečorsk 24 62.44 N 56.06 E
Troina 70 37.47 N 14.36 E
Troina ≏ 70 37.49 N 14.46 E
Troisdorf 56 50.49 N 7.08 E
Trois Fourches, Cap des ≻ 148 35.26 N 2.58 W
Trois-Îlets 240e 14.32 N 61.02 W
Trois-Montagnes, Lac des @ 206 46.10 N 74.45 W
Trois Pitons, Morne ∧ 240d 15.22 N 61.20 W
Trois Ponts 56 50.22 N 5.52 E
Trois-Rivières, Qué., Can. 206 46.21 N 72.33 W
Trois-Rivières, Guad. 241o 15.59 N 61.39 W
Troisvierges 56 50.08 N 6.00 E
Trojan 38 42.51 N 24.43 E
Trojanov 78 50.07 N 28.31 E
Trojanova Tabla ⊥ 38 44.37 N 22.20 E
Trojanovka 78 51.20 N 25.17 E
Trojanski prohod)(38 42.47 N 24.37 E
Trojebratskij 86 54.28 N 66.01 E
Trojekurovo, S.S.S.R. 76 53.00 N 38.58 E
Trojekurovo, S.S.S.R. 76 53.25 N 39.43 E
Troldhede 41 55.59 N 8.45 E
Trolleholm 41 55.54 N 13.15 E
Trollhättan 26 58.16 N 12.18 E
Trollheimen ∧ 26 62.51 N 9.05 E
Trombay ◂[8] 272c 19.02 N 72.57 E
Trombetas ≏ 250 1.55 S 55.35 W
Trombudo Central 252 27.18 S 49.47 W
Tromelin I 138 15.52 S 54.25 E
Tromello 62 45.12 N 8.52 E
Tromper Wiek C 54 54.37 N 13.24 E
Trompia, Val ∨ 64 45.44 N 10.12 E
Trompsburg 158 30.01 S 25.46 E
Troms □[6] 24 69.15 N 19.40 E
Tromsø 24 69.40 N 18.58 E
Trona 204 35.45 N 117.23 W
Tronador, Monte ∧ 254 41.10 S 71.54 W
Trondheim 26 63.25 N 10.25 E
Trondheimsfjorden C[2] 26 63.39 N 10.49 E
Trondheimsleia Џ 26 63.30 N 9.00 E
Tronto ≏ 66 42.54 N 13.55 E
Tronville-en-Barrois 56 48.43 N 5.17 E
Tronzano Vercellese 62 45.21 N 8.10 E
Troo 50 47.47 N 0.47 E
Troödos 130 34.55 N 32.53 E
Trooilapspan 158 28.40 S 21.25 E
Troon 46 55.32 N 4.40 W
Trooper 285 40.09 N 75.24 W
Troparevo 82 55.23 N 35.54 E
Tropar'ovo ◂[8] 265b 55.39 N 37.29 E
Tropas, Rio das ≏ 250 6.07 S 57.28 W
Tropea 68 38.41 N 15.54 E
Trophy Mountain ∧ 182 51.47 N 119.48 W
Tropic 200 37.37 N 112.05 W
Tropojë 38 42.24 N 20.10 E
Troppau → Opava 30 49.56 N 17.54 E
Trosa 40 58.54 N 17.33 E
Troškovo 80 57.19 N 46.05 E
Troškūnai 76 55.36 N 24.51 E
Trosna 76 52.26 N 35.46 E
Trossingen 58 48.04 N 8.38 E
Trostan ∧ 48 55.03 N 6.10 W
Trost'anec, S.S.S.R. 78 50.28 N 34.59 E
Trost'anec, S.S.S.R. 78 48.31 N 29.12 E
Trostberg 60 48.01 N 12.32 E
Trostenskoje Ozero @ 82 55.52 N 36.29 E
Trotha ◂[8] 54 51.31 N 11.58 E
Trottiscliffe 260 51.19 N 0.21 E
Trotuș ≏ 38 46.03 N 27.14 E
Trotwood 218 39.48 N 84.18 W
Troublesome Creek ≏, Ky., U.S. 192 37.29 N 83.21 W
Troublesome Creek ≏, Mo., U.S. 219 39.54 N 91.37 W
Troubridge Point ≻ 168b 35.11 S 137.41 E
Trou-du-Nord 238 19.38 N 72.01 W
Troumasse C 241f 13.49 N 60.54 W
Troup 222 32.09 N 95.07 W
Troup Head ≻ 46 57.41 N 2.18 W
Troupsburg 210 42.03 N 77.33 W
Trout 194 31.42 N 92.11 W
Trout ≏, N.W. Ter., Can. 176 61.19 N 119.51 W
Trout ≏, N.A. 206 45.05 N 74.10 W
Trout Brook ≏, Mass., U.S. 283 42.39 N 71.16 W
Trout Brook ≏, Mass., U.S. 283 42.16 N 71.18 W
Trout Creek, Mich., U.S. 190 46.28 N 89.01 W
Trout Creek, N.Y., U.S. 210 42.12 N 75.17 W
Trout Creek ≏, Ariz., U.S. 200 34.56 N 113.36 W

Trout Creek ≏, Oreg., U.S. 202 44.48 N 121.03 W
Trout Creek ≏, Oreg., U.S. 202 42.23 N 118.36 W
Trout Creek ≏, Pa., U.S. 285 40.07 N 75.24 W
Trout Creek ≏, Wash., U.S. 224 46.02 N 121.12 W
Trout Creek Pass)(200 38.54 N 105.58 W
Troutdale 224 45.32 N 116.23 W
Trout Lake 224 46.00 N 121.32 W
Trout Lake @, B.C., Can. 182 50.35 N 117.26 W
Trout Lake @, N.W. Ter., Can. 176 60.35 N 121.10 W
Trout Lake @, Ont., Can. 184 51.13 N 93.20 W
Trout Lake @, Ont., Can. 190 46.18 N 79.20 W
Trout Lake @, Ont., Can. 190 46.13 N 80.35 W
Trout Lake Creek ≏ 224 46.00 N 121.30 W
Trout Peak ∧ 202 44.36 N 109.32 W
Trout River 186 49.29 N 58.08 W
Trout Run 210 41.23 N 77.03 W
Troutville, Pa., U.S. 214 41.02 N 78.47 W
Troutville, Va., U.S. 192 37.25 N 79.53 W
Trouville-sur-Mer 50 49.22 N 0.05 E
Trowbridge 42 51.20 N 2.13 W
Troxelville 210 40.48 N 77.12 W
Troy, Ala., U.S. 194 31.48 N 85.58 W
Troy, Idaho, U.S. 202 46.44 N 116.46 W
Troy, Ill., U.S. 219 38.44 N 89.53 W
Troy, Kans., U.S. 198 39.47 N 95.05 W
Troy, Mich., U.S. 214 42.36 N 83.09 W
Troy, Mo., U.S. 219 38.59 N 90.59 W
Troy, Mont., U.S. 202 48.28 N 115.53 W
Troy, N.H., U.S. 188 42.50 N 72.11 W
Troy, N.C., U.S. 192 35.22 N 79.53 W
Troy, N.Y., U.S. 210 42.43 N 73.40 W
Troy, Ohio, U.S. 218 40.02 N 84.13 W
Troy, Pa., U.S. 210 41.47 N 76.47 W
Troy, Tenn., U.S. 194 36.20 N 89.10 W
Troy ⊥ 130 39.57 N 26.15 E
Troy Brook ≏ 276 40.50 N 74.22 W
Troyes 50 48.18 N 4.05 E
Troy Grove 216 41.28 N 89.05 W
Troy Hills 210 40.51 N 74.23 W
Troy Lake @ 204 34.49 N 116.33 W
Troy Meadows ☵ 276 40.50 N 74.22 W
Troy Peak ∧ 204 38.19 N 115.30 W
Troyville ◂[8] 273d 26.12 S 28.04 E
Trpanj 36 43.00 N 17.17 E
Trst → Trieste 64 45.40 N 13.46 E
Trstená 30 49.22 N 19.37 E
Trstenik 38 43.37 N 21.00 E
Truax 184 49.55 N 104.58 W
Trubč'ovsk 76 52.37 N 33.44 E
Trubetčino 76 52.53 N 39.33 E
Trubino, S.S.S.R. 82 55.59 N 38.08 E
Trubino, S.S.S.R. 82 54.58 N 36.42 E
Trub'ož ≏ 82 56.44 N 38.51 E
Truc-giang 110 10.14 N 106.23 E
Truchas 200 36.03 N 105.49 W
Truchas Peak ∧ 200 35.58 N 105.39 W
Truchtersheim 58 48.40 N 7.36 E
Trucial States → United Arab Emirates □[1] 128 24.00 N 54.00 E
Truckee 226 39.20 N 120.11 W
Truckee ≏ 204 39.51 N 119.24 W
Trucksville 210 41.18 N 75.56 W
Trud 76 57.37 N 33.58 E
Trudfront 80 45.56 N 47.41 E
Trudnovo 86 56.39 N 91.30 E
Trudovaja 83 48.21 N 38.04 E
Trudovoj, S.S.S.R. 80 51.42 N 52.43 E
Trudovoj, S.S.S.R. 86 53.15 N 66.51 E
Trues Creek ≏ 276 40.41 N 73.17 W
Truganina 274b 37.49 S 144.43 E
Truim ≏ 46 57.02 N 4.10 W
Truite, Lac à la @ 190 47.16 N 78.17 W
Trujillo, Col. 246 4.10 N 76.19 W
Trujillo, Esp. 34 39.28 N 5.53 W
Trujillo, Hond. 236 15.55 N 86.00 W
Trujillo, Perú 248 8.07 S 79.02 W
Trujillo, Ven. 246 9.22 N 70.26 W
Trujillo □[3] 246 9.25 N 70.30 W
Trujillo Alto 240m 18.22 N 66.01 W
Truk □[5] 175c 7.28 N 151.50 E
Truk Islands II 175c 7.25 N 151.47 E
Trull Brook ≏ 283 42.39 N 71.15 W
Truman 198 43.50 N 94.26 W
Trumann 194 35.41 N 90.31 W
Trumansburg 210 42.33 N 76.40 W
Trumbauersville 208 40.25 N 75.23 W
Trumbull 207 41.15 N 73.12 W
Trumbull □[6] 214 41.14 N 80.52 W
Trumbull, Mount ∧ 200 36.25 N 113.10 W
Trumon 114 2.49 N 97.38 E
Trun, Fr. 50 48.51 N 0.02 E
Trun, Schw. 58 46.45 N 8.58 E
Trundle 166 32.55 S 147.43 E
Trung-luong 110 13.57 N 109.15 E
Trunovskoje 80 45.29 N 42.08 E
Truro, Austl. 168b 34.25 S 139.07 E
Truro, N.S., Can. 186 45.22 N 63.16 W
Truro, Eng., U.K. 42 50.16 N 5.03 W
Truro, Mass., U.S. 207 42.00 N 70.03 W
Trusan ≏ 112 4.58 N 115.11 E
Truscott 196 33.45 N 99.49 W
Trušeny 78 47.04 N 28.41 E
Trușești 38 47.46 N 27.01 E
Trusetal 54 50.47 N 10.25 E
Truskavec 78 49.16 N 23.33 E
Truslejka 80 53.54 N 46.24 E
Truth or Consequences (Hot Springs) 200 33.08 N 107.15 W
Trutnov 30 50.34 N 15.55 E
Truxall 279b 40.33 N 79.33 W
Truxton, Mo., U.S. 219 39.00 N 91.14 W
Truxton, N.Y., U.S. 210 42.43 N 76.02 W
Truxton Wash ∨ 200 35.38 N 114.04 W
Truyère ≏ 32 44.39 N 2.34 E
Trwyn Cilan ≻ 42 52.46 N 4.30 W
Tryon, Nebr., U.S. 198 41.33 N 100.57 W
Tryon, N.C., U.S. 192 35.13 N 82.14 W
Tryonville 214 41.42 N 79.47 W
Trysil 26 61.19 N 12.16 E
Trysilelva (Klarälven) ≏ 26 59.23 N 13.32 E
Tryškiai 76 56.04 N 22.35 E
Tryweryn ≏ 42 52.24 N 3.35 W
Trzcianka 30 53.03 N 16.28 E
Trzciel 30 52.23 N 15.52 E
Trzcińsko-Zdrój 30 52.58 N 14.35 E
Trzebiatów 30 54.04 N 15.14 E
Trzebiel 54 51.37 N 14.50 E
Trzebież 30 53.42 N 14.31 E
Trzebinia 30 50.10 N 19.18 E
Trzebnica 30 51.19 N 17.03 E
Trzemeszno 30 52.35 N 17.50 E
Trzęsacz 54 54.05 N 14.58 E
Tržič 61 46.22 N 14.19 E
Tsacha Lake @ 182 53.05 N 124.40 W
Tsala Apopka Lake @ 220 28.52 N 82.20 W
Tsamkong → Zhanjiang 102 21.16 N 110.28 E
Tsangano 154 15.08 S 34.32 E

Ts'anghsien → Cangzhou 98 38.19 N 116.51 E
T'sangwu → Wuzhou 102 23.30 N 111.27 E
Ts'aot'un 100 23.59 N 120.40 E
Tsarabaria 157b 13.46 S 49.58 E
Tsaramandroso 157b 16.22 S 47.02 E
Tsaratanana 157b 16.47 S 47.39 E
Tsaratanana, Massif du ⩕ 157b 14.00 S 49.00 E
Tsaraxaibis 158 27.25 S 19.22 E
Tsaritsyn → Volgograd 80 48.44 N 44.25 E
Tsau 156 20.12 S 22.22 E
Tsaukaib 156 26.37 S 15.31 E
Tsavo 154 2.59 S 38.28 E
Tsavo National Park ♠ 154 3.00 S 38.40 E
Tsawwassen 224 49.01 N 123.06 W
Tsaydaychuz Peak ∧ 182 53.02 N 126.35 W
Tschad → Chad □[1] 146 15.00 N 19.00 E
Tschad-See → Chad, Lake @ 146 13.20 N 14.00 E
Tschagguns 58 47.05 N 9.54 E
Tschamut 58 46.40 N 8.42 E
Tschangscha → Changsha 100 28.11 N 113.01 E
Tschangtschun → Changchun 89 43.53 N 125.19 E
Tschechoslowakei → Czechoslovakia □[1] 30 49.30 N 17.00 E
Tscheljuskin, Kap → Čel'uskin, Mys ≻ 74 77.45 N 104.20 E
Tschengtu → Chengdu 107 30.39 N 104.04 E
Tschenstochau → Częstochowa 30 50.49 N 19.06 E
Tschernitz 54 51.35 N 14.37 E
Tscheschkaja-Bucht → Češskaja Guba C 24 67.30 N 46.30 E
Tschida, Lake @[1] 198 46.36 N 101.54 W
Tschingtau → Qingdao 98 36.06 N 120.19 E
Tschittagong → Chittagong 120 22.20 N 91.50 E
Tschuktschen-Meer → Chukchi Sea ₸[2] 16 69.00 N 171.00 W
Tschungking → Chongqing 107 29.39 N 106.34 E
Tščikskoje Vodochranilišče @[1] 78 45.06 N 39.31 E
Tsekanyani 156 19.52 S 26.39 E
Tsembeyi 158 31.36 S 27.03 E
Ts'engwen Ch'i ≏ 100 23.04 N 120.04 E
Tsenke ≏ 273b 4.24 S 15.26 E
Tses 156 25.58 S 18.08 E
Tsethang → Zedang 120 29.16 N 91.46 E
Tsévié 150 6.25 N 1.13 E
Tshabong 156 26.03 S 22.29 E
Tshabuta 152 7.47 S 23.16 E
Tshandi 156 17.42 S 14.50 E
Tshane 156 24.05 S 21.54 E
Tshaneni 158 26.00 S 31.47 E
Tshangalele, Lac @ 154 10.55 S 27.03 E
Tshela 152 4.59 S 12.56 E
Tshesebe 156 21.51 S 27.35 E
Tshibeke 154 2.44 S 28.36 E
Tshibinda 154 2.19 S 28.45 E
Tshibomba 152 9.02 S 22.34 E
Tshidilamolomo 156 25.50 S 24.41 E
Tshikapa 152 6.25 S 20.48 E
Tshilenge 152 6.15 S 23.46 E
Tshimbulu 152 6.29 S 22.51 E
Tshimhaka 152 17.20 S 13.51 E
Tshindjamba 152 10.54 S 22.41 E
Tshinota 152 7.01 S 20.57 E
Tshinsenda 154 12.18 S 27.58 E
Tshisuku 152 6.26 S 19.55 E
Tshitadi 152 6.45 S 21.45 E
Tshoa 152 5.34 S 12.41 E
Tshofa 154 5.14 S 25.15 E
Tshopo ≏ 154 0.33 N 25.07 E
Tshougu ≏ 273b 4.25 S 15.23 E
Tshuapa ≏ 152 0.14 S 20.42 E
Tshukudu 156 22.30 S 23.22 E
Tshumbiri 152 2.39 S 16.14 E
Tshwaane 156 22.29 S 22.03 E
Tsiafajavona ∧ 157b 19.21 S 47.15 E
Tsiama ≏ 273b 4.15 S 15.18 E
Tsianaloka 157b 18.08 S 44.50 E
Tsigara 156 20.10 S 25.18 E
Tsihombe 157b 25.18 S 45.29 E
Tsilmamo 144 6.01 N 35.17 E
Tsimanampetsotsa, Lac @ 157b 24.08 S 43.46 E
Tsimilofo 157b 24.59 S 45.10 E
Tsimpsean Indian Reserve ◂[4] 182 54.30 N 130.22 W
Tsinan → Jinan 98 36.40 N 116.57 E
Tsineng 158 27.06 S 23.04 E
Tsinghai → Qinghai □[4] 90 36.00 N 96.00 E
Tsing Island I 271d 22.21 N 114.05 E
Tsingkiang → Huaiyin 100 33.35 N 119.02 E
Tsingtao → Qingdao 98 36.06 N 120.19 E
Tsingyuan → Baoding 105 38.52 N 115.29 E
Tsinh-ho 110 22.22 N 103.14 E
Tsining → Jining 98 35.25 N 116.36 E
Tsinjoarivo 157b 19.37 S 47.40 E
Tsinjomitondraka 157b 15.36 S 47.08 E
Tsinling Shan → Qinlingshanmai ⩕ 102 34.00 N 108.00 E
Tsin Shui Wan C 271d 22.13 N 114.10 E
Tsintsabis 156 18.45 S 17.51 E
Tsiribihina ≏ 157b 19.42 S 44.31 E
Tsiroanomandidy 157b 18.46 S 46.02 E
Tsitondroina 157b 21.19 S 46.00 E
Tsitsihar → Qiqihaer 89 47.19 N 123.55 E
Tsitsikama Forest and Coastal National Park ♠ 158 34.00 S 23.36 E
Tsitsikammaberge ⩕ 158 33.54 S 23.42 E
Tsitsutl Peak ∧ 182 52.44 N 125.47 W
Tsivory 157b 24.04 S 46.05 E
Tskhinvali → Cchinvali 84 42.13 N 43.56 E
Tsna → Cna ≏ 80 54.32 N 42.05 E
Tsobis 156 19.27 S 17.30 E
Tsodilo Hill ∧[2] 156 18.45 S 21.45 E
Tsolo 158 31.18 S 28.37 E
Tsomo 158 32.00 S 27.42 E
Tsomo ≏ 158 32.25 S 27.50 E
Tsowkêy 123 34.41 N 70.56 E
Tsoying 100 22.41 N 120.17 E
Tsu 94 34.43 N 136.31 E
Tsubakuro-dake ∧ 94 36.24 N 137.42 E

Tsubame 92 37.39 N 138.56 E
Tsubata 94 36.40 N 136.44 E
Tsuboro-suigenchi @ 270 34.24 N 135.54 E
Tsuchiura 94 36.05 N 140.12 E
Tsuchiyama 94 34.56 N 136.17 E
Tsuda, Nihon 96 34.17 N 134.15 E
Tsuda, Nihon 270 34.49 N 135.43 E
Tsudaka 96 34.44 N 133.55 E
Tsugaru-hantō ≻[1] 92 41.00 N 140.30 E
Tsugaru-heiya ⏝ 92 40.49 N 140.27 E
Tsugaru-kaikyō Џ 92a 41.35 N 141.00 E
Tsuge 94 34.35 N 135.57 E
Tsugu 94 35.10 N 137.37 E
Tsuha 174m 26.14 N 127.47 E
Tsuiki 96 33.40 N 131.03 E
Tsujidō 268 35.20 N 139.27 E
Tsukahara 268 35.18 N 139.58 E
Tsukechi 94 35.38 N 137.26 E
Tsuken-jima I 174m 26.15 N 127.57 E
Tsukinowa-kofun ⊥ 96 34.55 N 134.11 E
Tsukise 94 34.42 N 136.02 E
Tsukiyono 94 36.41 N 138.59 E
Tsukuba 94 36.13 N 140.06 E
Tsukuba-san ∧ 94 36.13 N 140.06 E
Tsukude 94 34.59 N 137.25 E
Tsukui 94 35.35 N 139.16 E
Tsukumi 96 33.04 N 131.52 E
Tsukumono ◂[8] 270 34.50 N 135.11 E
Tsukushi-heiya ⩕ 96 33.40 N 130.25 E
Tsukushi-sanchi ⩕ 96 33.30 N 130.30 E
Tsumagoi 94 36.31 N 138.32 E
Tsumeb 156 19.13 S 17.42 E
Tsumeb □[5] 156 19.00 S 17.30 E
Tsumeki-zaki ≻ 94 34.39 N 138.59 E
Tsumis Park 156 23.43 S 17.28 E
Tsuna 96 34.26 N 134.54 E
Tsunan 94 37.01 N 138.39 E
Tsunashima ◂[8] 268 35.32 N 139.38 E
Tsunekami-misaki ≻ 94 35.38 N 135.49 E
Tsuni → Zunyi 102 27.39 N 106.57 E
Tsuno-shima I 96 34.12 N 130.58 E
Tsun Wan (Quanwan) 271d 22.22 N 114.07 E
Tsuru 94 35.30 N 138.56 E
Tsuruga 94 35.39 N 136.04 E
Tsurugaoka-hachimangu Shrine ✤[1] 268 35.19 N 139.33 E
Tsurugashima 268 35.56 N 139.24 E
Tsuruga-wan C 94 35.45 N 136.04 E
Tsurugi 94 36.27 N 136.38 E
Tsurugi-dake ∧ 94 36.37 N 137.37 E
Tsurugi-saki ≻ 268 35.08 N 139.41 E
Tsurugi-san ∧ 96 33.51 N 134.06 E
Tsurugi-san-kokutei-kōen ♠ 96 33.50 N 134.06 E
Tsuruhara 270 34.26 N 135.20 E
Tsuruma 268 35.51 N 139.33 E
Tsurumi ◂[8] 268 35.30 N 139.41 E
Tsurumi ≏ 94 35.29 N 139.41 E
Tsurumi-dake ∧ 96 33.17 N 131.26 E
Tsuruoka 92 38.44 N 139.50 E
Tsushima, Nihon 94 35.10 N 136.43 E
Tsushima, Nihon 96 33.05 N 132.30 E
Tsushima II 92 34.30 N 129.22 E
Tsushima-kaikyō Џ 92 34.00 N 129.00 E
Tsuwano 96 34.28 N 131.46 E
Tsuyama 96 35.03 N 134.00 E
Tsuyazaki 96 33.47 N 130.28 E
Tu → Tsu 94 34.43 N 136.31 E
Tua 152 3.38 S 16.36 E
Tua ≏ 34 41.13 N 7.26 W
Tua, Tanjung ≻ 112 5.54 S 105.44 E
Tua-chua 110 21.55 N 103.21 E
Tuakau 172 37.16 S 174.57 E
Tual 164 5.40 S 132.45 E
Tualatin 224 45.23 N 122.46 W
Tualatin ≏ 224 45.20 N 122.39 W
Tuam 48 53.31 N 8.50 W
Tuamarina 172 41.26 S 173.57 E
Tuamotu, Îles II 14 19.00 S 142.00 W
Tuan, Tanjong ≻ 114 2.23 N 101.52 E
Tuanan 112 2.07 S 114.24 E
Tuanfeng 100 30.38 N 114.51 E
Tuan-giao 110 21.35 N 103.25 E
Tuangku, Pulau I 114 2.10 N 97.18 E
Tuanpi 100 30.44 N 115.13 E
Tuanshan 98 40.02 N 123.34 E
Tuanwang 98 36.45 N 120.38 E
Tuanxi 102 27.26 N 106.54 E
Tuapa 174v 18.57 S 169.54 W
Tuapeka Mouth 172 46.01 S 169.31 E
Tuapse 84 44.07 N 39.05 E
Tuaran 112 6.11 N 116.14 E
Tuas 114 1.19 N 103.38 E
Tuasivi 175a 13.40 S 172.07 W
Tuasivi, Cape ≻ 175a 13.40 S 172.07 W
Tuatapere 172 46.08 S 167.41 E
Tuath, Loch Џ 46 56.30 N 6.12 W
Tuba 88 57.24 N 102.48 E
Tuba ≏ 86 53.57 N 91.31 E
Tubac 200 31.37 N 111.03 W
Tuba City 200 36.08 N 111.14 W
T'ub'ak-Čekurča 80 56.05 N 49.56 E
Tubalan Head ≻ 116 6.30 N 125.35 E
Tuban 115a 6.54 S 112.03 E
Tubarão 252 28.30 S 49.01 W
Ṭūbās 132 32.19 N 35.22 E
Tubas ≏ 156 22.55 S 14.37 E
Tubau 112 3.08 N 113.42 E
Ṭubayq, Jabal aṭ- ⩕ 128 29.40 N 37.15 E
Tubbataha Reefs ✢[2] 116 8.51 N 119.56 E
Tubbergen 52 52.25 N 6.46 E
Tubbs Island I 282 38.08 N 122.26 W
Ṭubhār 142 29.19 N 30.42 E
Tubig ≏ 116 11.54 N 125.25 E
Tubigan Island I 116 6.26 N 120.47 E
Tubingantan Point ≻ 116 5.54 N 120.55 E
Tübingen 58 48.31 N 9.02 E
Tübingen □[5] 58 48.10 N 9.30 E
Tubinskij 86 52.53 N 58.13 E
Tubize 50 50.41 N 4.12 E
T'ub-Karagan, Mys ≻ 84 44.39 N 50.18 E
T'ub-Karagan, Poluostrov ≻[1] 84 44.30 N 50.30 E
Tubli 116 13.56 N 124.09 E
Tubod 116 8.03 N 123.48 E
Tubre 64 46.39 N 10.27 E
Ṭubruq (Tobruk) 146 32.05 N 23.59 E
Tuburan, Pil. 116 6.39 N 122.16 E
Tuburan, Pil. 116 10.44 N 123.49 W
Tubutama 200 30.53 N 111.29 W
Tucacas 246 10.48 N 68.19 W
Tucacas, Punta ≻ 246 10.50 N 68.14 W
Tucalota Creek ≏ 228 33.32 N 117.10 W
Tucannon ≏ 202 46.33 N 118.11 W
Tucano 250 10.58 S 38.48 W
Tucavaca ≏ 248 18.37 S 58.59 W
T'uch'ang 100 24.34 N 121.29 E
Tucheim 54 52.17 N 12.11 E
Tüchen 54 53.04 N 12.05 E
T'uch'eng, T'aiwan 269d 24.59 N 121.26 E
Tucheng, Zhg. 98 38.53 N 121.15 E
Tuchengchang 102 28.12 N 105.58 E
Tuchengzi, Zhg. 98 40.29 N 124.24 E
Tuchengzi, Zhg. 98 41.20 N 116.29 E
Tuchengzi, Zhg. 104 42.27 N 122.44 E

≏ River	Fluss	Río	Rivière	Rio	
≊ Canal	Kanal	Canal	Canal	Canal	
Ⳑ Waterfall, Rapids	Wasserfall, Stromschnellen	Cascada, Rápidos	Chute d'eau, Rapides	Cascata, Rápidos	
Џ Strait	Meeresstrasse	Estrecho	Détroit	Estreito	
C Bay, Gulf	Bucht, Golf	Bahía, Golfo	Baie, Golfe	Baía, Golfo	
@ Lake, Lakes	See, Seen	Lago, Lagos	Lac, Lacs	Lago, Lagos	
☵ Swamp	Sumpf	Pantano	Marais	Pântano	
Ѫ Ice Features, Glacier	Eis- und Gletscherformen	Accidentes Glaciales	Formes glaciaires	Acidentes Glaciares	
₸ Other Hydrographic Features	Andere Hydrographische Objekte	Otros Elementos Hidrográficos	Autres données hydrographiques	Outros Elementos Hidrográficos	

✢ Submarine Features	Untermeerische Objekte	Accidentes Submarinos	Formes de relief sous-marin	Acidentes Submarinos
□ Political Unit	Politische Einheit	Unidad Politica	Entité politique	Unidade Política
✤ Cultural Institution	Kulturelle Institution	Institución Cultural	Institution culturelle	Instituição Cultural
⊥ Historical Site	Historische Stätte	Sitio Histórico	Site historique	Sitio Histórico
♠ Recreational Site	Erholungs- und Ferienort	Sitio de Recreo	Centre de loisirs	Sítio de Lazer
⊠ Airport	Flughafen	Aeropuerto	Aéroport	Aeroporto
■ Military Installation	Militäranlage	Instalación Militar	Installation militaire	Instalação Militar
◂ Miscellaneous	Verschiedenes	Misceláneo	Divers	Miscelânea

ENGLISH — Name | Page | Lat.°′ | Long.°′
DEUTSCH — Name | Seite | Breite°′ | Länge°′ E=Ost

Name	Page	Lat.	Long.
Tuchengzicun	104	41.52 N	120.41 E
Tuchengziwuhao	98	40.56 N	113.58 E
Tuchlovice	54	50.06 N	14.00 E
Tuchola	30	53.35 N	17.50 E
Tuchów	30	49.54 N	21.03 E
T'uchtet	86	56.32 N	89.19 E
Tuckahoe, N.J., U.S.	208	39.17 N	74.45 W
Tuckahoe, N.Y., U.S.	207	40.54 N	72.25 W
Tuckahoe, N.Y., U.S.	276	40.57 N	73.50 W
Tuckahoe ≃	208	39.17 N	74.39 W
Tuckahoe Creek ≃	208	38.49 N	75.53 W
Tuckanarra	162	27.07 S	118.05 E
Tucker Heights	210	42.55 N	73.55 W
Tuckerman	194	35.44 N	91.12 W
Tuckernuck Island I	207	41.18 N	70.15 W
Tuckerton, N.J., U.S.	208	39.36 N	74.20 W
Tuckerton, Pa., U.S.	208	40.25 N	75.57 W
Tuckfield, Mount ∧	162	18.44 S	124.54 E
Tučkovo	82	55.36 N	36.28 E
Tucson	200	32.13 N	110.58 W
Tucumã, Paraná ≃[1]	246	3.58 S	66.26 W
Tucumán → San Miguel de Tucumán	252	26.49 S	65.13 W
Tucumán □[4]	252	27.00 S	65.30 W
Tucumcari	196	35.10 N	103.44 W
Tucunduva	252	27.39 S	54.27 W
Tucunuco	252	30.36 S	68.38 W
Tucuparé, Cachoeira do ʟ	250	5.20 S	55.50 W
Tucupido	246	9.17 N	65.47 W
Tucupita	246	9.04 N	62.03 W
Tucuruí	250	3.42 S	49.27 W
Tucuruvi ⬥[8]	287b	23.28 S	46.35 W
Tuczna	30	51.54 N	23.26 E
Tud ≃	42	52.38 N	1.15 E
Tudameda	112	10.52 S	122.55 E
Tudcum	252	30.14 S	69.15 W
Tude Å ≃	41	55.23 N	11.13 E
Tudela, Esp.	34	42.05 N	1.36 W
Tudela, Pil.	116	8.15 N	123.50 E
Tudela de Duero	34	41.35 N	4.35 W
Tudian	106	30.35 N	120.37 E
Tudichang	107	30.06 N	103.56 E
Tuditang	100	30.12 N	114.18 E
Tudmur (Palmyra)	130	34.33 N	38.17 E
Tudu	76	59.11 N	26.51 E
Tudweiliog	42	52.54 N	4.35 W
Tuela ≃	34	41.30 N	7.12 W
Tuenno	64	46.20 N	11.01 E
Tueré ≃	250	2.48 S	50.59 W
Tuergate	85	40.28 N	75.21 E
Tufānganj	124	26.19 N	89.40 E
Tuffé	50	48.07 N	0.31 E
Tufi	164	9.05 S	149.20 E
Tufo	68	41.00 N	14.47 E
Tufts University ᵿ[2]	283	42.24 N	71.07 W
Tufukia	174v	19.02 S	169.56 W
Tufu Point ≻	174y	14.13 S	169.32 W
Tug	130	38.27 N	42.16 E
Tugaske	184	50.53 N	106.16 W
Tug Der ≃	144	9.20 N	46.20 E
Tugela	158	29.09 S	31.29 E
Tugela ≃	158	29.14 S	31.30 E
Tugela Beach	158	29.12 S	31.31 E
Tugela Ferry	158	28.44 S	30.27 E
Tuggerah Lake C	170	33.18 S	151.30 E
Tughlakābād ⬥[8]	272a	28.31 N	77.16 E
Tugidak Island I	180	56.30 N	154.36 W
Tuglie	68	40.04 N	18.05 E
Tugolesskij Bor	80	55.33 N	39.49 E
Tugolukovo	80	51.56 N	41.40 E
Tugubun Point ≻	116	7.00 N	126.27 E
Tuguegarao	116	17.37 N	121.44 E
Tugulym	86	57.04 N	64.39 E
Tugun	171a	28.09 S	153.30 E
Tugur	89	53.48 N	136.48 E
Tugur ≃	89	53.48 N	136.44 E
Tugúrio	256	21.15 S	43.35 W
Tugurskij Poluostrov ≻[1]	89	54.00 N	137.24 E
Tuguša	88	55.57 N	96.26 E
Tugutuj	88	52.40 N	104.50 E
Tuguwa	156	17.25 S	18.25 E
Tuhaihe ≃	98	37.55 N	118.05 E
Tuhepu	104	40.54 N	122.49 E
Tuht	130	40.46 N	33.47 E
Tuhuangba	102	31.40 N	108.21 E
Tuibo	89	44.01 N	127.47 E
Tuichi ≃	248	14.36 S	67.35 W
Tuim	86	54.20 N	89.55 E
Tuineje	148	28.19 N	14.03 W
Tuirc, Beinn an ∧[2]	46	55.34 N	5.34 W
Tuitán	234	21.08 N	103.48 W
Tuitui	256	22.47 S	46.42 W
Tuj ≃	86	57.33 N	72.31 E
T'ujabuguz	85	40.58 N	69.15 E
Tujemojnak	86	49.20 N	62.55 E
Tuji-ri	98	41.31 N	127.12 E
Tujmazy	80	54.36 N	53.42 E
Tüjn Gol ≃	102	45.04 N	100.46 E
Tujunga ⬥[8]	280	34.15 N	118.17 W
Tujunga Valley V	280	34.17 N	118.20 W
Tujunga Wash V	280	34.09 N	118.24 W
Tuka ∧	144	9.07 N	36.47 E
Tukaj	86	55.24 N	90.49 E
T'ukalinsk	86	55.52 N	72.12 E
Tukan	86	53.50 N	57.26 E
Tukangbesi, Kepulauan II	112	5.40 S	123.50 E
Tukayyid	128	29.47 N	45.36 E
Ṭūkh, Miṣr	142	30.21 N	31.12 E
Ṭūkh, Miṣr	142	27.41 N	30.49 E
Ṭūkh al-Aqlām	142	30.52 N	31.26 E
Ṭūkh al-Khayl	142	28.06 N	30.40 E
Ṭūkh Dalakah	142	30.39 N	30.55 E
Tukituki ≃	172	39.36 S	176.57 E
Tuk Méas	110	10.40 N	104.34 E
Tukolon'	88	55.24 N	107.42 E
Tukpo	154	4.25 N	25.52 E
Tūkrah	146	32.32 N	20.34 E
Tuktoyaktuk	180	69.27 N	133.02 W
Tukuj-Mekteb	84	44.20 N	45.11 E
Tukums	76	57.00 N	23.10 E
Tukuran	116	7.51 N	123.35 E
Tukuringra, Chrebet ⋀	89	54.20 N	126.20 E
Tukuyu	154	9.15 S	33.39 E
T'uk'u Yüeh ∧	269d	25.01 N	121.38 E
Tukwila	224	47.29 N	122.16 W
Tula, Am. Sam.	174u	14.15 S	170.34 W
Tula, It.	71	40.44 N	8.59 E
Tula, Méx.	234	23.00 N	99.43 W
Tula, S.S.S.R.	82	54.12 N	37.37 E
Tula □[4]	82	54.23 N	37.47 E
Tula ≃	234	20.40 N	99.30 W
Tula ⊥	234	20.06 N	99.19 W
Tula de Allende	234	20.03 N	99.21 W
Tulagi	175e	9.06 S	160.09 E
Tūlāk	128	33.58 N	63.44 E
Tulalip Indian Reservation ⬥[4]	224	48.06 N	122.15 W
Tulancingo	234	20.05 N	98.22 W
Tulangbawang ≃	112	4.24 S	105.52 E
Tulaodian	104	41.13 N	121.27 E
T'ul'apsy	88	57.28 N	89.38 E
Tulare, Calif., U.S.	226	36.13 N	119.21 W
Tulare, S. Dak., U.S.	198	44.44 N	98.31 W
Tulare □[6]	226	36.20 N	119.18 W
Tulare Canal ≍	226	36.08 N	119.25 W
Tulare Lake Bed ⊜	226	36.03 N	119.49 W
Tulare Lake Canal ≍	226	36.04 N	119.39 W
Tularosa	200	33.04 N	106.01 W
Tularosa ≃	200	33.41 N	108.46 W
Tularosa Valley ≚[1]	200	32.45 N	106.10 W
Tulbagh	158	33.17 S	19.09 E
Tulbing	264b	48.16 N	16.09 E
Tulbinger Kogel ∧	264b	48.17 N	16.09 E
Tulcán	246	0.48 N	77.43 W
Tulcea	38	45.11 N	28.48 E
Tulcea □[4]	38	45.00 N	29.00 E
Tul'čin	78	48.39 N	28.52 E
Tulcingo de Valle	234	18.03 N	98.26 W
Tule ≃, Nic.	236	11.20 N	84.52 W
Tule ≃, Calif., U.S.	226	36.03 N	119.50 W
Tule, North Branch ≃	226	36.06 N	119.22 W
Tule, South Branch ≃	226	36.05 N	119.29 W
Tuléar	157b	23.21 S	43.40 E
Tuléar □[4]	157b	24.00 S	45.00 E
Tule Canal ≍	226	38.37 N	121.35 W
Tule Creek ≃	196	34.40 N	101.14 W
T'ulek	85	41.56 N	75.41 E
Tulelake	204	41.57 N	121.29 W
Tule Lake Sump ⊜	204	41.54 N	121.32 W
T'ulenij, Mys ≻	84	40.12 N	50.22 E
T'ulenij, Ostrov I	84	44.28 N	47.30 E
Tule River Indian Reservation ⬥[4]	204	36.02 N	118.42 W
Tulette	62	44.17 N	4.56 E
T'ul'gan	86	52.22 N	56.12 E
Tul'goviči	78	51.47 N	29.38 E
Tuli	154	21.59 S	29.15 E
Tuli ≃	154	21.48 S	29.04 E
Tulia	196	34.32 N	101.46 W
Tulica ≃	82	54.12 N	37.37 E
Tulik Volcano ∧[1]	180	53.22 N	168.03 W
Tulillo	234	22.30 N	104.05 W
Tuling	100	25.11 N	118.50 E
Tuliszków	30	52.05 N	18.17 E
T'uljapsy	86	57.28 N	89.38 E
Ṭūlkarm	132	32.19 N	35.02 E
T'ul'kino	86	59.49 N	56.30 E
T'ul'kubas	85	42.28 N	70.02 E
Tulla	48	52.52 N	8.45 W
Tullahoma	194	35.22 N	86.11 W
Tullamarine	274b	37.41 S	144.52 E
Tullamarine Airport ⊠	169	37.40 S	144.50 E
Tullamore, Austl.	166	32.38 S	147.34 E
Tullamore, Ont., Can.	275b	43.47 N	79.46 W
Tullamore, Eire	48	53.16 N	7.30 W
Tullaroop Creek ≃	169	36.53 S	143.53 E
Tull Bay C	208	36.30 N	76.04 W
Tulle	32	45.16 N	1.46 E
Tullgarn	40	58.57 N	17.35 E
Tullibigeal	166	33.25 S	146.44 E
Tullinge	40	59.12 N	17.53 E
Tullins	62	45.18 N	5.29 E
Tulln	61	48.20 N	16.03 E
Tullner Feld ⬥[1]	264b	48.19 N	16.10 E
Tulloch Lake ⊜[1]	226	37.53 N	120.35 W
Tullock Creek ≃	202	46.08 N	107.27 W
Tullos	194	31.49 N	92.19 W
Tullow	48	52.48 N	6.44 W
Tullus	140	11.03 N	24.33 E
Tully, Austl.	166	17.56 S	145.56 E
Tully, N.Y., U.S.	210	42.48 N	76.07 W
Tully Lake ⊜[1]	207	42.42 N	72.14 W
Tullytown	208	40.09 N	74.49 W
Ṭulmaythah	146	32.43 N	20.57 E
Tuloma ≃	24	68.52 N	32.49 E
Tulpehocken Creek ≃	208	40.21 N	75.57 W
Tulpfontein	158	32.44 S	19.43 E
Tulsa	196	36.09 N	95.58 W
Tulsequah	176	58.35 N	133.35 W
Tulsī Lake ⊜	272c	19.11 N	72.55 E
Tulsk	48	53.47 N	8.16 W
Tul'skij	84	44.31 N	40.10 E
Tulstrup	41	56.07 N	9.46 E
Tultepec	234	19.41 N	99.08 W
Tultitlán □[7]	286a	19.39 N	99.09 W
Tultitlán de Mariano Escobedo	286a	19.39 N	99.09 W
Tuluá	246	4.06 N	76.11 W
Tulufan	86	42.56 N	89.10 E
Tulufanpendi ⍛[7]	86	42.40 N	89.10 E
Tuluksak	180	61.06 N	160.58 W
Tulum	232	20.13 N	87.28 W
Tulum ⊥	232	20.12 N	87.26 W
Tulumaya (Lavalle)	252	32.43 S	68.35 W
Tulumayo ≃	248	11.10 S	75.16 W
Tulun	88	54.35 N	100.33 E
Tulungagung	115a	8.04 S	111.54 E
Tulungselapan	112	3.15 S	105.19 E
Tuluran Island I	116	10.59 N	119.17 E
Tulu Welel ∧	144	8.53 N	34.47 E
Tulyehualco ⬥[8]	286a	19.15 N	99.01 W
Tum	164	3.38 S	130.23 E
Tuma	80	55.09 N	40.34 E
Tuma ≃	236	13.03 N	84.44 W
Tumacacori National Monument ♠	200	31.25 N	111.01 W
Tumaco	246	1.49 N	78.46 W
Tumaco, Ensenada de C	246	1.55 N	78.45 W
Tumak	80	46.14 N	48.31 E
Tumalykol'	86	48.21 N	60.03 E
Tuman'an	84	41.00 N	44.40 E
Tuman-gang (Tumenjiang) ≃	98	42.18 N	130.41 E
Tumannaja, Gora ∧	180	66.33 N	179.43 E
Tumanovo	76	55.25 N	34.39 E
Tumanšet ≃	88	55.53 N	97.30 E
Tumanskij	180	63.58 N	178.12 E
Tumany	74	60.56 N	155.56 E
Tumarbong	116	10.23 N	119.27 E
T'um'ati → Sklad	74	71.55 N	123.33 E
Tumatumari	246	5.22 N	59.00 W
Tumauini	116	17.17 N	121.49 E
Tumba	40	59.12 N	17.49 E
Tumba, Lac ⊜	152	0.48 S	18.03 E
Tumbagaan Island I	116	5.22 N	120.19 E
Tumbarumba	171b	35.47 S	148.01 E
Tumbarumba Creek ≃	171b	35.58 S	148.03 E
Tumbaya	252	23.51 S	65.28 W
Tumbes	246	3.34 S	80.28 W
Tumbes □[4]	246	3.50 N	80.30 W
Tumbes, Punta ≻	252	36.37 S	73.07 W
Tumbiscatio de Ruiz	234	18.31 N	102.21 W
Tumble Mountain ∧	202	45.19 N	110.02 W
Tumblong	171b	35.09 S	148.00 E
Tumbotino	80	55.59 N	43.02 E
Tumbur	154	4.20 N	31.34 E
Tumby Bay	166	34.22 S	136.06 E
Tumča ≃	24	66.36 N	30.48 E
Tŭmch'on-ni ⬥[8]	271b	37.34 N	126.51 E
T'umen', S.S.S.R.	86	57.09 N	65.32 E
Tumen, Zhg.	98	42.58 N	129.49 E
T'umen'-Aryk	86	44.02 N	67.01 E
T'umencevo	86	53.20 N	81.31 E
T'umenec, Porog ʟ	88	56.38 N	99.00 E
Tumenjiang (Tuman-gang) ≃	98	42.18 N	130.41 E
Tumenpu	107	29.49 N	103.39 E
T'umenskaja Oblast' □[4]	24	65.00 N	62.00 E
Tumenskoje	82	55.00 N	38.32 E
Tumenzi	102	37.43 N	103.09 E
Tumeremo	246	7.18 N	61.30 W
Tumin ≃	89	49.18 N	140.22 E
Tumiritinga	255	18.58 S	41.38 W
Tumkūr	122	13.21 N	77.05 E
Tummel ≃	46	56.38 N	3.40 W
Tummo	146	22.40 N	14.10 E
Tumon Bay C	174p	13.31 N	144.48 E
Tumoteqi	102	40.52 N	111.28 E
Tumpang	115a	8.00 S	112.46 E
Tumpat	114	6.12 N	102.10 E
Tumsar	120	21.23 N	79.44 E
Tumu	150	10.52 N	1.59 W
Tumuc-Humac Mountains ⋀	250	2.20 N	55.00 W
Tumupasa	248	14.09 S	67.55 W
Tumu Point ≻	174r	6.56 N	158.07 E
Tumupu	105	40.23 N	115.36 E
Tumut	171b	35.18 S	148.13 E
Tumut ≃	171b	35.07 S	148.13 E
Tumut Pond Reservoir ⊜[1]	171b	35.59 S	148.25 E
Tumutuk	80	55.02 N	53.19 E
Tumwater	224	47.01 N	122.54 W
Tun ≃	110	17.25 N	98.42 E
Tuna Canyon V	280	34.03 N	118.36 W
Tunago Lake ⊜	180	66.18 N	125.50 W
Tuna-Hästberg	40	60.20 N	15.11 E
Tunapuna	241r	10.38 N	61.23 W
Tunari, Cerro ∧	248	17.18 S	66.22 W
Tunas Creek ≃	196	31.01 N	102.11 W
Tunas de Zaza	240p	21.38 N	79.33 W
Tūnat al-Jabal	142	27.46 N	30.44 E
Tunaydah	140	25.31 N	29.21 E
Tunbridge Wells	42	51.08 N	0.16 E
Tunca (Tundža) ≃	38	41.40 N	26.34 E
Tunçbilek	130	39.37 N	29.29 E
Tunceli	130	39.07 N	39.32 E
Tunceli □[4]	130	39.10 N	39.30 E
Tunchang	110	19.28 N	110.08 E
T'unch'i → Tunxi	100	29.44 N	118.18 E
Tunda, Pulau I	115a	5.49 S	106.16 E
Tundazi ∧	154	17.33 S	28.05 E
Tündern	52	52.04 N	9.22 E
Tūndla	124	27.12 N	78.17 E
Tundubai ⊤[4]	140	18.31 N	28.33 E
Tunduru	154	11.07 S	37.21 E
Tundža (Tunca) ≃	38	41.40 N	26.34 E
Tune	41	55.36 N	12.11 E
Tunesien → Tunisia □[1]	148	34.00 N	9.00 E
T'unež, S.S.S.R.	82	54.37 N	38.29 E
Túnez → Tunis, Tun.	148	36.48 N	10.11 E
Túnez → Tunisia □[1]	148	34.00 N	9.00 E
T'ung ≃	74	63.46 N	121.35 E
Tunga	150	8.00 N	9.19 E
Tunga ≃	122	14.00 N	75.41 E
Tungabhadra ≃	122	15.57 N	78.15 E
Tungabhadra Reservoir ⊜[1]	122	15.16 N	76.21 E
Tungaru	140	10.14 N	30.42 E
Tungauan Bay C	116	7.28 N	122.21 E
Tungchiang	100	22.28 N	120.26 E
Tungchi Hsü I	100	23.15 N	119.40 E
Tungchi University ᵿ[2]	269b	31.18 N	121.10 E
T'ungchou → Tongxian	105	39.55 N	116.39 E
T'ungch'uan → Tongchuan	102	35.01 N	109.01 E
Tungch'üan Tao I	100	25.58 N	119.58 E
Tungelsta	40	59.06 N	18.02 E
Tung Hai → East China Sea ⊤[2]	90	30.00 N	126.00 E
Tungho	100	22.58 N	121.18 E
T'unghsien → Tongxian	105	39.55 N	116.39 E
T'unghua → Tonghua	98	41.50 N	125.55 E
Tunghwa → Tonghua	98	41.50 N	125.55 E
Tungi	126	23.53 N	90.24 E
Tungir ≃	88	55.24 N	120.32 E
Tungirskij Chrebet ⋀	88	54.40 N	119.40 E
Tungkal ≃	112	0.48 S	103.29 E
Tungkillo	168b	34.49 S	139.04 E
Tungku	112	5.01 N	118.53 E
Tungla	236	13.18 N	84.26 W
T'ungliao → Tongliao	89	43.39 N	122.14 E
Tung Lung I	271d	22.15 N	114.17 E
Tungokočen	88	53.33 N	115.36 E
Tungshih	100	24.16 N	120.50 E
Tungsten	180	62.00 N	127.40 W
Tungsunga, Jabal ∧	140	11.29 N	23.21 E
Tungting Hsü I	100	24.10 N	118.14 E
Tungurahua □[4]	246	1.15 S	78.35 W
Tungyin Shan I	100	26.22 N	120.30 E
Tuni	122	17.21 N	82.33 E
Tunica	194	34.41 N	90.23 W
Tunis	148	36.48 N	10.11 E
Tunis, Golfe de C	148	37.00 N	10.30 E
Tunis Et Banlieue □[8]	36	36.48 N	10.10 E
Tunisia □[1]	134		
	148	34.00 N	9.00 E
Tunisie → Tunisia □[1]	148	34.00 N	9.00 E
Tunitas Creek ≃	282	37.21 N	122.24 W
Tunja	246	5.31 N	73.22 W
Tunjang	114	6.16 N	100.21 E
Tunka	88	51.45 N	102.32 E
Tunkás	232	20.54 N	88.45 W
Tunkhannock	210	41.32 N	75.57 W
Tunkhannock Creek ≃	210	41.32 N	75.57 W
Tunkhannock Creek, East Branch ≃	210	41.38 N	75.43 W
Tunkinskije Gol'cy ⋀	88	51.50 N	101.40 E
Tunliu	102	36.19 N	112.54 E
Tunnel	210	42.13 N	75.44 W
Tunnelhill	214	40.29 N	78.33 W
Tunnelton, Ind., U.S.	218	38.46 N	86.21 W
Tunnelton, W. Va., U.S.	188	39.24 N	79.45 W
Tunnsjøen ⊜	24	64.43 N	13.24 E
Tunø I	41	55.57 N	10.26 E
Tunstall	42	53.05 N	2.13 W
Tuntenhausen	64	47.56 N	12.01 E
Tuntum	250	5.14 S	44.39 W
Tuntutuliak	180	60.22 N	162.38 W
Tununak	180	60.35 N	165.16 W
Tunungayualok Island I	176	56.05 N	61.05 W
Tunuyán	252	33.34 S	69.01 W
Tunuyán ≃	252	34.03 S	66.45 W
Tunxi	100	29.44 N	118.18 E
Tuoba	102	31.18 N	97.40 E
Tuobalage	120	31.37 N	88.10 E
Tuobuja	74	62.00 N	122.02 E
Tuocheng	100	24.05 N	115.13 E
Tuoeshan ∧	102	24.20 N	103.32 E
Tuohe	100	33.26 N	117.26 E
Tuohu ⊜	100	33.11 N	117.49 E
Tuoj-Chaja	74	62.32 N	111.18 E
Tuojiang ≃	102	28.57 N	105.27 E
Tuojidao I	98	38.09 N	120.14 E
Tuokedingling	120	32.45 N	84.55 E
Tuoketuo	102	40.22 N	111.11 E
Tuokexun	86	42.47 N	88.38 E
Tuokusidawanling ∧	120	37.14 N	85.47 E
Tuoli, Zhg.	86	45.57 N	83.37 E
Tuoli, Zhg.	105	39.46 N	116.01 E
Tuolumne	226	37.58 N	120.14 W
Tuolumne □[6]	226	37.59 N	120.23 W
Tuolumne ≃	226	37.36 N	121.10 W
Tuolumne, Lyell Fork ≃	226	37.53 N	119.23 W
Tuolumne, North Fork ≃	226	37.54 N	120.15 W
Tuolumne, South Fork ≃	226	37.50 N	120.03 W
Tuolunduo	89	50.35 N	120.05 E
Tuoningdao I	100	22.28 N	114.38 E
Tuorong (Tuoyang)	100	27.16 N	119.54 E
Tuoshihanhe (Aksaj) ≃	85	40.55 N	78.16 E
Tuosuohu ⊜, Zhg.	102	35.18 N	98.54 E
Tuosuohu ⊜, Zhg.	102	37.10 N	96.55 E
Tuowu	102	28.58 N	102.13 E
T'up	85	42.44 N	78.22 E
Tupã	255	21.56 S	50.30 W
Tupaciguara	255	18.35 S	48.42 W
Tupa Creek ≃	170	33.05 S	150.37 E
Tupana ≃	246	4.25 S	60.05 W
Tupanciretã	252	29.05 S	53.51 W
Tupelo, Miss., U.S.	194	34.16 N	88.43 W
Tupelo, Okla., U.S.	196	34.37 N	96.26 W
Tupelo National Battlefield ⊥	194	34.13 N	88.44 W
Tupi	116	6.19 N	124.57 E
Tupičov	78	51.46 N	31.26 E
Tupik	88	54.26 N	119.57 E
Tupilac	116	7.40 N	122.30 E
Tupi Paulista	255	21.24 S	51.34 W
Tupiraçaba	255	14.29 S	48.34 W
Tupirama	250	8.58 S	48.12 W
Tupiza	248	21.27 S	65.43 W
Tuplice	30	51.41 N	14.50 E
Tupman	226	35.18 N	119.21 W
Tupper	182	55.31 N	120.02 W
Tupper Lake	188	44.13 N	74.29 W
Tupperville	214	42.36 N	82.16 W
Tupuai, Île I	14	23.18 S	149.30 W
Tupungato	252	33.22 S	69.08 W
Tupungato, Cerro ∧	252	33.22 S	69.47 W
Tupuseleia	164	9.33 S	147.18 E
Tuqiao, Zhg.	106	31.39 N	120.24 E
Tuqiao, Zhg.	106	31.56 N	119.03 E
Tuqiao, Zhg.	107	30.32 N	104.50 E
Tuqiao, Zhg.	107	30.24 N	105.28 E
Tuqiaochang	107	29.47 N	106.01 E
Tuquan	89	45.26 N	121.50 E
Túquerres	246	1.05 N	77.37 W
Tura, Bhārat	124	25.31 N	90.13 E
Ṭurā, Miṣr	142	29.56 N	31.16 E
Tura, S.S.S.R.	74	64.17 N	100.15 E
Tura ≃, S.S.S.R.	86	57.12 N	66.56 E
Tura ≃, S.S.S.R.	88	51.36 N	114.09 E
Turabah	144	21.13 N	41.39 E
Turabah ⊤[4]	128	28.15 N	42.55 E
Turābah, 'Ayn at- ⊤[4]	132	31.36 N	35.25 E
Turabah, Wādī V	144	21.36 N	41.52 E
Turāg ≃	126	23.45 N	90.21 E
Turaiyūr	122	11.10 N	78.37 E
Turakina	172	40.02 S	175.13 E
Turakina ≃	172	40.04 S	175.08 E
Turama ≃	164	6.50 S	143.05 E
Turambhe	272c	19.04 N	73.01 E
Turan, S.S.S.R.	88	51.38 N	101.40 E
Turan, S.S.S.R.	88	52.08 N	93.55 E
Turangi	172	39.00 S	175.49 E
Turano ≃	66	42.26 N	12.47 E
Turanskaja Nizmennost' ≚	86	44.30 N	63.00 E
Turate	266b	45.39 N	9.00 E
Tur'at Ghunaym	142	31.16 N	31.29 E
Turbaco	246	10.20 N	75.25 W
Turbacz ∧	30	49.33 N	20.08 E
Turbah	144	12.40 N	43.30 E
Turbat	128	25.59 N	63.04 E
Turbenthal	58	47.27 N	8.51 E
Turbigo	62	45.32 N	8.44 E
Turbio ≃	234	20.19 N	101.37 W
Turbo	246	8.06 N	76.43 W
Turbotville	210	41.06 N	76.46 W
Turbov	78	49.21 N	28.44 E
Turčasovo	24	63.06 N	39.12 E
Turchi, Balata dei ≻	70	36.43 N	12.02 E
Turčiansky Svätý Martin → Martin	30	49.05 N	18.55 E
Turckheim	58	48.05 N	7.17 E
Turda	38	46.34 N	23.47 E
Turdej	76	53.22 N	38.01 E
Turee Creek	162	23.37 S	118.39 E
Turee Creek ≃	162	23.35 S	117.25 E
Turek	30	52.02 N	18.30 E
Turen	115a	8.10 S	112.41 E
Turenki	26	60.55 N	24.38 E
Turfan → Tulufan	86	42.56 N	89.10 E
Turfan Depression → Tulufanpendi ⍛[7]	86	42.40 N	89.10 E
Turffontein ⬥[8]	273d	26.15 S	28.02 E
Turffontein Race Course ♠	273d	26.14 S	28.03 E
Turgaj, S.S.S.R.	86	49.38 N	63.28 E
Turgaj, S.S.S.R.	86	51.46 N	72.44 E
Turgaj ≃	86	48.01 N	62.45 E
Turgajskaja Dolina V	86	51.00 N	64.30 E
Turgajskaja Stolovaja Strana ⋀[1]	86	51.00 N	64.00 E
Türgen, Mong.	86	50.04 N	91.36 E
Turgen', S.S.S.R.	85	43.24 N	77.36 E
Turgen' ≃	85	43.50 N	77.38 E
Turgenevka	88	53.02 N	105.41 E
Turgenevo	80	54.50 N	46.19 E
Turginovo	82	56.30 N	36.00 E
Turgojak	86	55.10 N	60.07 E
Turgoš	76	59.18 N	35.10 E
Tŭrgovishte → Târgovište	38	43.15 N	26.34 E
Turgut	130	38.37 N	31.49 E
Turgutlu	130	38.30 N	27.43 E
Turgwe ≃	154	20.28 S	32.18 E
Turhal	130	40.24 N	36.06 E
Turi, It.	68	40.55 N	17.01 E
Türi, S.S.S.R.	76	58.48 N	25.26 E
Turia ≃	34	39.27 N	0.19 W
Turiaçu	250	1.41 S	45.21 W
Turiaçu ≃	250	1.36 S	45.19 W
Turiančajskij Zapovednik ♠	84	40.40 N	47.35 E
Turijsk	78	51.07 N	24.31 E
Turij Tog	89	45.14 N	131.58 E
Turilovka	83	49.06 N	40.13 E
Turimetta Head ≻	274a	33.42 S	151.19 E
Turimiquire, Cerro ∧	246	10.07 N	63.53 W
Turin, Alta., Can.	182	49.58 N	112.31 W
Turin → Torino, It.	62	45.03 N	7.40 E
Turin, N.Y., U.S.	212	43.38 N	75.25 W
Turinge	40	59.12 N	17.27 E
Turinsk	86	58.03 N	63.42 E
Turinskaja Sloboda	86	57.37 N	64.25 E
Turja ≃	78	51.48 N	24.52 E
Turka, S.S.S.R.	78	49.10 N	23.02 E
Turka, S.S.S.R.	88	52.57 N	108.13 E
Turka ≃	88	52.56 N	108.13 E
Türkei → Turkey □[1]	22	39.00 N	35.00 E
Türkeli Adası I	130	40.30 N	27.30 E
Turkestan	85	43.18 N	68.15 E
Turkestanskij Chrebet ⋀	85	39.35 N	69.15 E
Túrkeve	30	47.06 N	20.45 E
Turkey	196	34.23 N	100.54 W
Turkey □[1], As., Eur.	22	39.00 N	35.00 E
Turkey ≃	190	42.43 N	91.01 W
Turkey Branch ≃	284c	38.52 N	76.48 W
Turkey City	214	41.11 N	79.37 W
Turkey Creek	164	17.02 S	128.12 E
Turkey Creek ≃, U.S.	198	39.58 N	96.02 W
Turkey Creek ≃, Ind., U.S.	278	41.31 N	87.18 W
Turkey Creek ≃, Iowa, U.S.	198	41.20 N	95.05 W
Turkey Creek ≃, Kans., U.S.	198	38.53 N	97.11 W
Turkey Creek ≃, Nebr., U.S.	198	40.23 N	96.53 W
Turkey Creek ≃, Okla., U.S.	196	35.58 N	97.56 W
Turkey Creek ≃, Tex., U.S.	196	28.42 N	99.58 W
Turkey Creek ≃, Tex., U.S.	222	30.39 N	97.05 W
Turkey Island I	284c	38.58 N	77.12 W
Turkey Point ≻, Ont., Can.	212	42.40 N	80.21 W
Turkey Point ≻, Fla., U.S.	220	25.26 N	80.19 W
Turkey Point Provincial Park ♠	212	42.40 N	80.22 W
Turkey Run State Park ♠	194	39.54 N	87.13 W
Turkeytown	279b	40.12 N	79.44 W
Türkheim	58	48.03 N	10.38 E
Turki	80	51.59 N	43.16 E
Türkiye → Turkey □[1]	22	39.00 N	35.00 E
Turkmān Deh	267d	35.40 N	51.36 E
Turkmen-Kala	128	37.26 N	62.20 E
Turkmenskaja Sovetskaja Socialističeskaja Respublika □[3]	72	40.00 N	60.00 E
Turkmen Soviet Socialist Republic → Turkmenskaja Sovetskaja Socialističeskaja Respublika □[3]	72	40.00 N	60.00 E
Turk Mine	154	19.45 S	28.50 E
Turkoğlu	130	37.31 N	36.49 E
Turks and Caicos Islands □[2]	230		
	238	21.45 N	71.35 W
Turks Island Passage ⊔	238	21.25 N	71.19 W
Turks Islands II	238	21.24 N	71.07 W
Turks- und Caicos-Inseln → Turks and Caicos Islands □[2]	238	21.45 N	71.35 W
Turku (Åbo)	26	60.27 N	22.17 E
Turkwel ≃	154	3.06 N	36.06 E
Turlan	85	43.36 N	69.03 E
Turley	196	36.14 N	95.58 W
Turlock	226	37.30 N	120.51 W
Turlock Lake ⊜[1]	226	42.17 N	73.21 W
Turmalina	255	17.17 S	42.45 W
Turmantas	76	55.42 N	26.27 E
Turmerito, Quebrada ≃	286c	10.26 N	66.55 W
Turnagain ≃	180	59.06 N	127.35 W
Turnagain, Cape ≻	172	40.29 S	176.37 E
Turnagain Arm C	180	61.00 N	150.00 W
Turnagain Island I	164	9.34 S	142.18 E
Turna nad Bodvou	30	48.37 N	20.53 E
Turnau	61	47.33 N	15.20 E
Turnbull, Mount ∧	200	33.04 N	110.16 W
Turnbull, Mount ∧[2]	162	21.03 S	131.57 E
Turnbull Dry Lake ⊜	202	43.10 N	118.00 W
Turneffe Islands II	232	17.22 N	87.51 W
Turner, Austl.	162	17.50 S	128.17 E
Turner, Mont., U.S.	202	48.51 N	108.24 W
Turner, Oreg., U.S.	202	44.51 N	122.57 W
Turner ≃	162	20.21 S	118.25 E
Turner Field ⊠	285	40.13 N	75.13 W
Turners Falls	207	42.36 N	72.33 W
Turners Peninsula ≻[1]	150	7.22 N	12.22 W
Turnersville, N.J., U.S.	285	39.46 N	75.03 W
Turnersville, Tex., U.S.	222	31.37 N	97.44 W
Turner Valley	182	50.40 N	114.17 W
Turnhout	52	51.19 N	4.57 E
Türnitz	61	47.57 N	15.30 E
Turnor Lake ⊜	184	56.32 N	108.38 W
Turnov	30	50.35 N	15.10 E
Tŭrnovo → Veliko Târnovo	38	43.04 N	25.39 E
Turnpike Lake ⊜	283	42.01 N	71.19 W
Turnu-Măgurele	38	43.45 N	24.53 E
Turnu Roşu, Pasul)(	38	45.33 N	24.16 E
Turnu-Severin → Drobeta-Turnu-Severin	38	44.38 N	22.39 E
Turobin	30	50.50 N	22.45 E
Turočak	86	52.16 N	87.08 E
Turon	198	37.48 N	98.26 W
Turon ≃	170	33.03 S	149.43 E
Turopin	78	51.00 N	24.27 E
Turopolje ≚	36	45.40 N	16.05 E
Tuross ≃	171b	36.09 S	149.39 E
Turov	78	52.04 N	27.44 E
Turovo	82	54.52 N	37.49 E
Turques et Caicos Îles → Turks and Caicos Islands □[2]	238	21.45 N	71.35 W
Turquía → Turkey □[1]	22	39.00 N	35.00 E
Turquie → Turkey □[1]	22	39.00 N	35.00 E
Turquino, Pico ∧	240p	19.59 N	76.50 W
Turrach	64	46.57 N	13.52 E
Turramurra	274a	33.44 S	151.08 E
Turrell	194	35.23 N	90.15 W
Turret Peak ∧	200	34.15 N	111.53 W
Turriaco	64	45.49 N	13.26 E
Turrialba	236	9.54 N	83.41 W
Turrialba, Volcán ∧[1]	236	10.02 N	83.46 W
Turriers	62	44.24 N	6.10 E
Turriff	46	57.32 N	2.28 W
Turritano ⬥[1]	71	40.45 N	8.35 E
Turrubares, Cerro ∧	236	9.47 N	84.28 W
Turša	80	56.56 N	47.40 E
Tursi	68	40.15 N	16.28 E
Turtas ≃	86	59.06 N	68.52 E
Turtipār	124	26.10 N	83.54 E
Turtle ≃, Man., Can.	184	51.07 N	99.39 W
Turtle ≃, Ont., Can.	184	48.51 N	92.45 W
Turtle ≃, N. Dak., U.S.	198	48.20 N	97.08 W
Turtle, North Branch ≃	198	47.57 N	97.35 W
Turtle Creek, N.B., Can.	186	45.58 N	64.53 W
Turtle Creek, Pa., U.S.	214	40.25 N	79.49 W
Turtle Creek ≃, Pa., U.S.	279b	40.23 N	79.51 W
Turtle Creek ≃, S. Dak., U.S.	198	44.55 N	98.29 W
Turtle Creek ≃, Wis., U.S.	216	42.29 N	89.03 W
Turtle Flambeau Flowage ⊜[1]	190	46.05 N	90.11 W
Turtleford	184	53.23 N	108.56 W
Turtle Harbor Channel ⊔	220	25.15 N	80.18 W
Turtle Islands II	150	7.37 N	13.02 W
Turtle Lake, N. Dak., U.S.	198	47.31 N	100.53 W
Turtle Lake, Wis., U.S.	190	45.24 N	92.08 W
Turtle Lake ⊜	184	53.35 N	108.40 W
Turtle Mountain Indian Reservation ⬥[4]	198	48.51 N	99.45 W
Turtle Mountain Provincial Park ♠	184	49.03 N	100.15 W
Turtmann	58	46.18 N	7.41 E
Turton and Entwistle Reservoir ⊜[1]	262	53.39 N	2.25 W
Turton Bottoms	262	53.38 N	2.24 W
Turton Moor ⬥[3]	262	53.40 N	2.29 W
Turton Tower	262	53.38 N	2.25 W
Turu ≃	74	64.38 N	100.00 E
Turua	172	37.14 S	175.34 E
Turuchan ≃	74	65.56 N	87.42 E
Turuchansk	74	65.49 N	87.59 E
Turuntajevo, S.S.S.R.	86	56.38 N	85.59 E
Turuntajevo, S.S.S.R.	88	52.12 N	107.37 E
Türüşmek	130	39.03 N	39.32 E
Turvânia	255	16.39 S	50.09 W
Turvo	252	28.56 S	49.41 W
Turvo ≃, Bra.	255	17.46 S	50.12 W
Turvo ≃, Bra.	255	19.56 S	49.55 W
Turvo ≃, Bra.	256	22.04 S	45.42 W
Turvo ≃, Bra.	256	21.32 S	44.26 W
Turvo ≃, Bra.	256	22.29 S	44.15 W
Turvo Grande ≃	256	21.42 S	44.22 W
Turvo Pequeno ≃	256	21.42 S	44.22 W
Turyu-san ∧	98	41.10 N	128.47 E
Turzovka	30	49.25 N	18.39 E
Tusa	70	37.59 N	14.14 E
Tusa ≃	70	38.01 N	14.16 E
Tusas, Rio ≃	200	36.23 N	106.03 W
Tuscaloosa	194	33.13 N	87.33 W
Tuscania	66	42.25 N	11.52 E
Tuscarawas	214	40.24 N	81.25 W
Tuscarawas □[6]	214	40.30 N	81.27 W
Tuscarawas ≃	214	40.17 N	81.52 W
Tuscarora, N.Y., U.S.	210	42.38 N	77.52 W
Tuscarora, Pa., U.S.	208	40.46 N	76.02 W
Tuscarora Creek ≃, N.Y., U.S.	210	42.07 N	77.14 W
Tuscarora Creek ≃, Pa., U.S.	208	40.32 N	77.23 W
Tuscarora Creek, North Branch ≃	210	42.05 N	77.18 W
Tuscarora Indian Reservation ⬥[4]	210	43.09 N	78.57 W
Tuscarora Mountain ∧	188	40.10 N	77.45 W
Tuscarora Mountains ⋀	204	41.00 N	116.20 W
Tuscarora State Park ♠	208	40.48 N	76.01 W
Tuscarora Tunnel ⬥[5]	214	40.05 N	77.50 W
Tuscola, Ill., U.S.	194	39.48 N	88.17 W
Tuscola, Tex., U.S.	196	32.12 N	99.48 W
Tuscolo ⊥	267a	41.48 N	12.42 E
Tuscumbia, Ala., U.S.	194	34.44 N	87.42 W
Tuscumbia, Mo., U.S.	194	38.14 N	92.28 W
Tuse	41	55.43 N	11.37 E
Tushanzhen	98	34.14 N	117.51 E
Tušino ⬥[8]	265b	55.50 N	37.26 E
Tuskegee	194	32.26 N	85.42 W
Tusker Rock II[1]	42	51.27 N	3.40 W
Tussey Mountain ∧	214	40.25 N	78.07 W
Tüssling	60	48.13 N	12.36 E
Tustin	228	33.45 N	117.49 W
Tustumena Lake ⊜	180	60.12 N	150.50 W
Tuszyn	30	51.37 N	19.34 E
Tut	130	37.48 N	37.55 E
Tuta	152	14.37 S	20.45 E
Tutaekuri ≃	172	39.30 S	176.54 E
Tutaizi	104	41.01 N	122.38 E
Tutajev	80	57.53 N	39.32 E
Tutak	84	39.32 N	42.46 E
Tutang	100	29.21 N	116.24 E
Tuthills Creek ≃	276	40.45 N	73.02 W
Tuticorin	122	8.47 N	78.08 E
Tutin	38	42.59 N	20.20 E
Tutkaul	85	38.18 N	69.17 E
T'ut'kovo	82	54.37 N	38.32 E
Tutóia	250	2.45 S	42.16 W
Tutoko, Mount ∧	172	44.36 S	168.00 E
Tutong	112	4.50 N	114.40 E
Tutova ≃	38	46.06 N	27.32 E
Tutrakan	38	44.03 N	26.37 E
Tuttle	198	47.09 N	100.00 W
Tuttle Creek Lake ⊜[1]	198	39.22 N	96.40 W
Tuttlingen	58	47.59 N	8.49 E
Tutuala	164	8.24 S	127.15 E
Tutuba I	175f	15.34 S	167.16 E
Tutuban Station ⬥[5]	269f	14.37 N	120.58 E
Tutu Bay C	116	5.55 N	121.12 E
Tutubu	154	5.30 S	32.41 E
Tutuila I	174u	14.18 S	170.42 W
Tuṭūn	142	29.09 N	30.46 E
Tutupaca, Volcán ∧[1]	248	17.01 S	70.22 W
Tutura	88	54.46 N	105.15 E
Tutura ≃	88	54.47 N	105.12 E
Tututalak Mountain ∧	180	67.46 N	161.10 W
Tututepec	234	16.09 N	97.38 W
Tutwiler	194	34.01 N	90.26 W
Tutzing	64	47.54 N	11.17 E
Tuul ≃	88	48.57 N	104.48 E
Tuupovaara	26	62.29 N	30.36 E
Tuurun ja Poorin lääni □[4]	26	61.20 N	22.30 E
Tuusniemi	26	62.49 N	28.30 E
Tuutapu, Cerro ∧	174z	27.08 S	109.24 W
T'uva-Guba	24	69.08 N	33.32 E
Tuvalu □[1]	14	8.00 S	178.00 E
Tuvinskaja Avtonomnaja Sovetskaja Socialističeskaja Respublika □[3]	88	53.00 N	96.00 E
Tuvutha I	175g	17.40 S	178.48 W
Tuwang	107	29.06 N	105.48 E
Ṭuwayq, Jabal ⋀	118	23.00 N	46.00 E
Tuxedo Park, Del., U.S.	285	39.43 N	75.37 W

Symbols in the index entries represent the broad categories identified in the key at the right. Symbols with superior numbers (⋀[2]) identify subcategories (see complete key on page *I · 30*).

Kartensymbole in dem Registerverzeichnis stellen die rechts in Schlüssel erklärten Kategorien dar. Symbole mit hochgestellten Ziffern (⋀[2]) bezeichnen Unterabteilungen einer Kategorie (vgl. vollständiger Schlüssel auf Seite *I · 30*).

Los símbolos incluídos en el texto del índice representan las grandes categorias identificadas con la clave a la derecha. Los símbolos con numeros en su parte superior (⋀[2]) identifican las subcategorías (véase la clave completa en la página *I · 30*).

Les symboles de l'index représentent les catégories indiquées dans la légende à droite. Les symboles suivis d'un indice (⋀[2]) représentent des sous-catégories (voir légende complète à la page *I · 30*).

Os símbolos incluídos no texto do índice representam as grandes categorias identificadas com a chave à direita. Os símbolos com números em sua parte superior (⋀[2]) identificam as subcategorias (veja-se a chave completa à página *I · 30*).

Symbol	English	Deutsch	Español	Français	Português
∧	Mountain	Berg	Montaña	Montagne	Montanha
⋀	Mountains	Berge	Montañas	Montagnes	Montanhas
)(	Pass	Pass	Paso	Col	Passo
V	Valley, Canyon	Tal, Cañon	Valle, Cañón	Vallée, Canyon	Vale, Canhão
≚	Plain	Ebene	Llano	Plaine	Planície
≻	Cape	Kap	Cabo	Cap	Cabo
I	Island	Insel	Isla	Île	Ilha
II	Islands	Inseln	Islas	Îles	Ilhas
⍛	Other Topographic Features	Andere Topographische Objekte	Otros Elementos Topográficos	Autres données topographiques	Outros Elementos Topográficos

ESPAÑOL — Nombre · Página · Lat. · Long. W=Oeste

Tuxedo Park, N.Y., U.S. 210 41.11 N 74.11 W
Tuxer Hauptkamm 64 47.10 N 11.45 E
Tuxer Vorberge 64 47.10 N 11.45 E
Tuxford 184 50.35 N 105.35 W
Tuxiaqiao 100 28.47 N 121.29 E
Tuxpan, Méx. 234 19.33 N 103.24 W
Tuxpan, Méx. 234 21.37 N 104.07 W
Tuxpan, Méx. 234 19.34 N 100.28 W
Tuxpan, Méx. 234 21.57 N 105.18 W
Tuxpan 234 20.59 N 97.18 W
Tuxpan de Rodríguez Cano 234 20.57 N 97.24 W
Tuxtepec 234 18.06 N 96.07 W
Tuxtla Chico 232 14.57 N 92.10 W
Tuxtla Gutiérrez 234 16.45 N 93.07 W
Túy 34 42.03 N 8.38 W
Tuy 246 10.24 N 65.59 W
Tuy-an 110 13.17 N 109.16 E
Tuyen-hoa 110 17.50 N 106.10 E
Tuy-hoa 110 13.05 N 109.18 E
Tūysarkān 128 34.33 N 48.27 E
Tuyün → Duyun 102 26.12 N 107.31 E
Ţuyūr, Burj aţ- 140 20.55 N 27.55 E
Tuża 80 57.37 N 47.57 E
Tuzamapan 234 19.24 N 96.51 W
T'uzašu, Pereval 85 42.21 N 73.48 E
T'uzbel' 85 40.34 N 73.21 E
Tuzdykol', Ozero 80 49.36 N 52.20 E
Tuz Gölü 130 38.45 N 33.25 E
Tuzigoot National Monument 200 34.40 N 111.52 W
Tuzkan, Ozero 85 40.35 N 67.28 E
Ţūz Khurmātū 128 34.53 N 44.38 E
Tuzla, Jugo. 38 44.32 N 18.41 E
Tuzla, Tür. 130 36.42 N 35.05 E
Tuzla 84 39.43 N 40.18 E
Tuzla Gölü 130 39.02 N 35.50 E
Tuzlov 83 47.23 N 40.08 E
Tuzluca 84 40.03 N 43.40 E
Tuzlukçu 130 38.28 N 31.38 E
Tuzly 78 45.52 N 30.05 E
Tvârdica, Blg. 38 43.42 N 25.52 E
Tvardica, S.S.S.R. 78 46.09 N 28.58 E
Tvedestrand 26 58.37 N 8.55 E
Tveitsund 26 59.01 N 8.32 E
Tver → Kalinin 82 56.52 N 35.55 E
Tverca 76 56.52 N 35.55 E
Twain Harte 226 38.02 N 120.14 W
Twann 58 47.06 N 7.10 E
Twante 110 16.43 N 95.56 E
Twardogóra 30 51.22 N 17.28 E
Tweed 212 44.29 N 77.19 W
Tweed 44 55.46 N 2.00 W
Tweeddale 46 55.37 N 2.55 W
Tweede Exloërmond 52 52.55 N 6.58 E
Tweed Heads 171a 28.10 S 153.31 E
Tweedmouth 44 55.45 N 2.01 W
Tweedsmuir Provincial Park 182 52.55 N 126.05 W
Tweedy Mountain 202 45.29 N 112.58 W
Tweeling 158 27.38 S 28.31 E
Tweespruit 158 29.11 S 27.01 E
Twello 52 52.14 N 6.06 E
Twelve Mile 216 40.52 N 86.13 W
Twelve Mile Creek, Ont., Can. 212 43.11 N 79.16 W
Twelvemile Creek, N.Y., U.S. 210 43.18 N 78.51 W
Twelvemile Island 279b 40.32 N 79.51 W
Twelve Mile Lake, Ont., Can. 212 45.02 N 78.43 W
Twelve Mile Lake, Sask., Can. 184 49.29 N 106.14 W
Tweng 64 47.11 N 13.36 E
Twente 52 52.17 N 6.40 E
Twentekanaal 52 52.15 N 6.40 E
Twentieth Century Fox Studios 280 34.03 N 118.25 W
25 de Abril, Ponte 266c 38.41 N 9.11 W
Twentyfive Mile Wash 200 37.33 N 111.07 W
24-Parganas 126 22.15 N 88.30 E
Twenty Mile Creek 212 43.11 N 79.26 W
Twentynine Palms 204 34.08 N 116.03 W
Twentynine Palms Marine Corps Base 204 34.25 N 116.10 W
Tweya 152 0.54 S 19.05 E
Twickenham 260 51.27 N 0.20 W
Twilight Cove 162 32.16 S 126.03 E
Twilight Park 210 42.11 N 74.05 W
Twillingate 186 49.39 N 54.46 W
Twin Beach 216 42.34 N 83.24 W
Twinberg 61 46.55 N 14.50 E
Twin Bridges 202 45.33 N 112.20 W
Twin Butte Creek 198 38.46 N 100.56 W
Twin Buttes 202 44.20 N 122.15 W
Twin Buttes Reservoir 196 31.20 N 100.35 W
Twin City 192 32.35 N 82.10 W
Twin Creek 218 39.33 N 84.21 W
Twin Falls 202 42.34 N 114.28 W
Twin Heads 162 20.13 S 126.30 E
Twin Hills 180 59.23 N 159.58 W
Twin Lakes, Calif., U.S. 226 36.58 N 122.00 W
Twin Lakes, Ind., U.S. 216 41.19 N 86.23 W
Twin Lakes, Mich., U.S. 216 43.22 N 86.10 W
Twin Lakes, Ohio, U.S. 214 41.11 N 81.21 W
Twin Lakes, Pa., U.S. 210 41.24 N 74.54 W
Twin Lakes, Wis., U.S. 216 42.32 N 88.15 W
Twin Lakes, Calif., U.S. 226 38.09 N 119.21 W
Twin Lakes, Conn., U.S. 207 42.02 N 73.26 W
Twin Lakes, Wash., U.S. 224 47.55 N 120.51 W
Twin Oaks, Ill., U.S. 278 42.03 N 87.50 W
Twin Oaks, Pa., U.S. 208 39.51 N 75.26 W
Twin Peak Islands 162 34.00 S 122.50 E
Twin Peaks 228 34.12 N 117.12 W
Twin Peaks, Calif., U.S. 282 37.45 N 122.27 W
Twin Peaks, Idaho, U.S. 202 44.35 N 114.29 W
Twin Rocks, Oreg., U.S. 224 45.36 N 123.57 W
Twin Rocks, Pa., U.S. 214 40.30 N 78.52 W
Twinsburg 214 41.19 N 81.27 W
Twin Valley 198 47.16 N 96.16 W
Twisp 202 48.22 N 120.07 W
Twiss Green 262 53.27 N 2.32 W
Twist 52 52.38 N 7.03 E
Twiste 52 51.29 N 9.09 E
Twistringen 52 52.48 N 8.38 E
Twitchell Reservoir 204 35.00 N 120.19 W
Twitya 180 64.10 N 128.12 W
Two, Channel 220 24.50 N 80.45 W
Two Butte Creek 198 38.02 N 102.08 W
Twofold Bay 166 37.06 S 149.55 E

FRANÇAIS — Nom · Page · Lat. · Long. W=Ouest

Two Harbors 190 47.01 N 91.40 W
Two Hills 182 53.43 N 111.45 W
Two Lakes 224 46.22 N 121.27 W
Two Medicine 202 48.29 N 112.14 W
Two Mile Creek, Ont., Can. 284a 43.16 N 79.06 W
Twomile Creek, N.Y., U.S. 284a 43.01 N 78.55 W
Twong 140 8.18 N 28.20 E
Two Penny Run 285 39.41 N 75.26 W
Two River Lake 184 53.52 N 91.27 W
Two Rivers, Bots. 158 26.27 S 20.37 E
Two Rivers, Wis., U.S. 190 44.09 N 87.34 W
Two Rivers 198 48.49 N 97.09 W
Two Rivers Reservoir 196 33.17 N 104.45 W
Two Thumb Range 172 43.45 S 170.43 E
Two Wells 168b 34.36 S 138.30 E
Twrch, Wales, U.K. 42 51.46 N 3.46 W
Twrch, Wales, U.K. 42 52.42 N 3.29 W
Twyford, Eng., U.K. 42 51.29 N 0.53 W
Twyford, Eng., U.K. 42 51.01 N 1.19 W
Twymyn 42 52.38 N 3.44 W
Tyabb 169 38.16 S 145.11 E
Tybju 24 60.37 N 50.20 E
Tybkino 24 54.15 N 43.46 E
Tychy 30 50.09 N 18.59 E
Tyczyn 30 49.58 N 22.02 E
Tydal 26 63.04 N 11.34 E
Tye 196 32.27 N 99.52 W
Tyémé 150 9.33 N 7.19 W
Tyende Creek 200 36.50 N 109.43 W
Tyendinaga Indian Reserve 212 44.11 N 77.07 W
Tyfors 40 60.09 N 14.12 E
Tygarts Creek 218 38.43 N 82.57 W
Tygda 89 53.07 N 126.20 E
Tygda 89 52.35 N 127.55 E
Tygelsjö 41 55.31 N 13.00 E
Tygh Valley 224 45.15 N 121.10 W
Tyin 26 61.17 N 8.13 E
Tyja 88 55.36 N 109.20 E
Tylden 158 32.07 S 27.05 E
Tyldesley 44 53.31 N 2.28 W
Tyler, Minn., U.S. 198 44.17 N 96.08 W
Tyler, Pa., U.S. 214 41.14 N 78.32 W
Tyler, Tex., U.S. 222 32.21 N 95.18 W
Tyler 222 30.47 N 94.32 W
Tyler, Lake 222 32.13 N 95.10 W
Tyler East, Lake 222 32.15 N 95.10 W
Tyler Park 284c 38.52 N 77.12 W
Tylersburg 214 41.23 N 79.19 W
Tyler State Park, Pa., U.S. 208 40.14 N 74.59 W
Tyler State Park, Tex., U.S. 222 32.29 N 95.14 W
Tylersville 210 40.60 N 77.25 W
Tylerton 208 37.58 N 76.01 W
Tylertown 194 31.07 N 90.09 W
Tylla 40 60.28 N 15.33 E
Tylösand 26 56.39 N 12.44 E
Tylöskog 40 58.45 N 15.20 E
Tylovaj 80 57.30 N 53.47 E
Tym, S.S.S.R. 74 59.25 N 80.04 E
Tym', S.S.S.R. 89 51.51 N 143.10 E
Tymna, Laguna 180 64.00 N 178.30 E
Tymochtee Creek 214 40.57 N 83.16 W
Tymovskoje 89 50.51 N 142.39 E
Tymsk 86 59.24 N 80.18 E
Tynagh 48 53.09 N 8.22 W
Tyndall 198 42.59 N 97.52 W
Tyndaris 70 38.09 N 15.03 E
Tyndinskij 74 55.10 N 124.43 E
Tyndrum 46 56.27 N 4.44 W
Tyne, Eng., U.K. 44 55.01 N 1.26 W
Tyne, Scot., U.K. 44 56.00 N 2.31 W
Tyne and Wear 44 54.55 N 1.35 W
Tynemouth 44 55.01 N 1.24 W
Tyner 216 41.25 N 86.24 W
Tyngsboro 283 42.41 N 71.26 W
Tyngsjö 40 60.18 N 13.53 E
Tynica 78 51.08 N 32.54 E
Týn nad Vltavou 30 49.14 N 14.26 E
Tynnelsö 40 59.25 N 17.06 E
Tynset 26 62.17 N 10.47 E
Tyonek 180 61.02 N 151.17 W
Tyoronyaradougou 150 9.21 N 5.38 W
Typta 88 54.35 N 104.31 E
Tyr 89 52.57 N 139.48 E
Tyre → Şūr, Lubnān 132 33.16 N 35.11 E
Tyre, Pa., U.S. 214 40.26 N 80.16 W
Tyresö 40 59.14 N 18.18 E
Tyret' 88 53.41 N 102.19 E
Tyrgetuj 88 51.27 N 113.46 E
Tyrifjorden 26 60.02 N 10.08 E
Tyringe 41 56.10 N 13.35 E
Tyringham 207 42.15 N 73.12 W
Tyrka 88 54.30 N 107.09 E
Tyrma 89 50.03 N 132.12 E
Tyrma 89 50.29 N 131.18 E
Tyrnovo 78 48.10 N 27.40 E
Tyrnyauz 84 43.23 N 42.56 E
Tyrone, Ky., U.S. 218 38.02 N 84.51 W
Tyrone, N.Y., U.S. 210 42.25 N 77.03 W
Tyrone, Okla., U.S. 196 36.57 N 101.04 W
Tyrone, Pa., U.S. 214 40.40 N 78.14 W
Tyrone Lake 281 42.42 N 83.43 W
Tyrrell, Lake 166 35.21 S 142.50 E
Tyrrellspass 48 53.23 N 7.22 W
Tyrrhenian Sea (Mare Tirreno) 36 40.00 N 12.00 E
Tyrrhenisches Meer → Tyrrhenian Sea 36 40.00 N 12.00 E
Tysmenica 78 48.54 N 24.49 E
Tysnesøy 26 60.00 N 5.35 E
Tysons Corner 284c 38.55 N 77.14 W
Tysons Corner Center 284c 38.55 N 77.13 W
Tysse 26 60.22 N 5.45 E
Tyssedal 26 60.07 N 6.34 E
Tysslingen 40 59.19 N 15.02 E
Tystberga 40 58.52 N 17.15 E
Tystrup Sø 41 55.22 N 11.35 E
Tytherington 262 53.17 N 2.08 W
Tytuvėnai 76 55.36 N 23.12 E
Ty Ty 192 31.28 N 83.39 W
Tyumen' → T'umen' 86 57.09 N 65.32 E
Tyurginpil'gyn, Laguna 180 68.30 N 178.00 W
Tyvrov 78 49.01 N 28.30 E
Tywa 54 53.13 N 14.29 E
Tywardreath 42 50.22 N 4.41 W
Tywi 42 51.46 N 4.22 W
Tywyn 42 52.35 N 4.05 W
Tzanconeja 232 16.35 N 91.35 W
Tzaneen 156 23.50 S 30.09 E
Tzekung → Zigong 107 29.22 N 104.46 E
Tzeliutsing → Zigong 107 29.22 N 104.46 E
Tzimol 236 16.16 N 92.16 W
Tzintzuntzan 234 19.38 N 101.34 W
Tzucacab 232 20.04 N 89.03 W
Tzukung → Zigong 107 29.22 N 104.46 E
Tzupo → Boshan, Zhg. 98 36.29 N 117.50 E

PORTUGUÊS — Nome · Página · Lat. · Long. W=Oeste

Tzupo → Zibo, Zhg. 98 36.47 N 118.01 E

U

Uac, Mount 116 12.12 N 123.40 E
Uaçá 250 4.13 N 51.32 W
Uagadugu → Ouagadougou 150 12.22 N 1.31 W
Uamba 152 7.12 S 16.25 E
Uamba (Wamba) 152 3.56 S 17.12 E
Uampochane 158 26.23 S 32.41 E
Uaoa Bay 229a 20.56 N 156.16 W
Uapao, Cap 175f 21.35 S 167.50 E
Uaran → Ouarane 134 21.00 N 10.30 W
Uatumã 246 2.26 S 57.37 W
Uauá 250 9.50 S 39.28 W
Uaupés (Vaupés) 246 0.02 N 67.16 W
Uaxactún 232 17.24 N 89.39 W
Ubá 255 21.07 S 42.56 W
Uba 86 50.15 N 81.41 E
Übach-Palenberg 56 50.55 N 6.07 E
Ubagan 86 54.24 N 64.45 E
Ubai 164 5.40 S 150.40 E
Ubaidullāhganj 124 22.59 N 77.36 E
Ubaíra 255 13.16 S 39.39 W
Ubaitaba 255 14.18 S 39.20 W
Ubajara 250 3.51 S 40.56 W
Ubajara, Parque Nacional de 250 3.47 S 40.56 W
Ubangi (Oubangui) 152 0.30 S 17.42 E
Ubatã 255 14.12 S 39.31 W
Ubaté 246 5.19 N 73.49 W
Ubatuba 256 23.26 S 45.04 W
Ubatuba, Baía de 256 23.27 S 45.02 W
Ubauro 120 28.10 N 69.44 E
Ubay 116 10.03 N 124.28 E
Ubaye 62 44.28 N 6.22 E
Ubaye 62 44.28 N 6.18 E
Ubayyiḍ, Wādī al- 128 32.34 N 43.48 E
Ubby 41 55.37 N 11.13 E
Ube 96 33.56 N 131.15 E
Ubed' 78 51.27 N 32.29 E
Úbeda 34 38.01 N 3.22 W
Uberaba 255 19.45 S 47.55 W
Uberaba 255 20.07 S 48.31 W
Uberaba, Lagoa 248 17.30 S 57.45 W
Überackern 60 48.11 N 12.52 E
Über dem Wind, Inseln → Leeward Islands 238 17.00 N 63.00 W
Uberlândia 255 18.56 S 48.18 W
Überlingen 58 47.46 N 9.10 E
Überlinger See 58 47.45 N 9.09 E
Übersee 64 47.49 N 12.28 E
Ubiaja 150 6.38 N 6.21 E
Ubili 154 1.07 S 26.55 E
Ubin, Pulau 271c 1.24 N 103.58 E
Ubinskoje 86 55.19 N 79.41 E
Ubinskoje, Ozero 86 55.30 N 80.05 E
Ubl'a 30 48.55 N 22.23 E
Ubly 190 43.43 N 82.56 W
Uboldo 266b 45.37 N 9.00 E
Ubombo 158 27.33 S 32.00 E
Ubondo 154 0.52 S 25.37 E
Ubon Ratchathani 110 15.14 N 104.54 E
Úborsko 60 49.20 N 13.09 E
Ubort' 78 52.06 N 28.28 E
Ubrique 34 36.41 N 5.27 W
Ubudiah, Masjid 114 4.46 N 100.56 E
Ubundu (Ponthierville) 154 0.21 S 25.29 E
Ubur-Tochtor 88 50.06 N 113.37 E
Uča 82 56.02 N 37.37 E
Ucacha 252 33.02 S 63.31 W
Uč-Adži 128 38.05 N 62.48 E
Učami 74 63.50 N 96.29 E
Učaral 86 46.10 N 80.56 E
Ucayali 242 4.30 S 73.27 W
Uccellina, Monti dell' 66 42.38 N 11.05 E
Uccle 50 50.48 N 4.19 E
Uch 123 29.14 N 71.03 E
Uchab 156 19.47 S 17.42 E
Uchāna 124 29.28 N 76.10 E
Uchaud 62 43.45 N 4.16 E
Uchee Creek 192 32.18 N 84.57 W
Uchihara 94 36.22 N 140.21 E
Uchihata 270 34.25 N 135.27 E
Uchiko 96 33.33 N 132.39 E
Uchi Lake 184 51.05 N 92.35 W
Uchinada 94 36.39 N 136.39 E
Uchinomi 96 34.30 N 134.20 E
Uchinoura 92 31.16 N 131.05 E
Uchiumi 96 33.01 N 132.30 E
Uchiura-wan 92a 42.20 N 140.40 E
Uchiza 248 8.29 S 76.23 W
Uchoa 255 20.56 S 49.13 W
Ucholovo 80 53.47 N 40.29 E
Uchra 80 58.20 N 39.00 E
Uchta, S.S.S.R. 24 63.33 N 53.38 E
Uchta, S.S.S.R. 24 61.12 N 38.32 E
Uchte 52 52.30 N 8.54 E
Uchte 54 52.46 N 11.45 E
Uchtoma 76 60.10 N 38.02 E
Uchtspringe 54 52.32 N 11.36 E
Učinskij Ryboučastok 86 60.02 N 65.10 E
Učinskoje Vodochranilišče 82 56.02 N 37.45 E
Uckange 56 49.18 N 6.09 E
Ückendorf 263 51.30 N 7.07 E
Uckermark 54 53.10 N 13.35 E
Uckfield 42 50.58 N 0.06 E
Üçköşe 130 40.13 N 41.00 E
Uckro 54 51.51 N 13.37 E
Učkupr'uk 85 40.33 N 71.04 E
Učkurgan 85 41.07 N 72.05 E
Ucluelet 182 48.57 N 125.33 W
Ucon 202 43.36 N 111.58 W
Ucria 70 38.03 N 14.53 E
Učterek 85 41.45 N 73.12 E
Úcua 152 8.35 S 13.40 E
Učujevskij Majdan 80 54.33 N 44.30 E
Učur 74 58.48 N 130.35 E
Uda, S.S.S.R. 88 56.05 N 99.34 E
Uda, S.S.S.R. 88 51.47 N 107.33 E
Uda, S.S.S.R. 89 54.42 N 135.14 E
Udaipur 120 24.35 N 73.41 E
Udaj 78 50.05 N 33.07 E
Udala 126 21.35 N 86.34 E
Udalguri 120 26.46 N 92.08 E
Udall 198 37.23 N 97.07 W
Udamalpet 122 10.35 N 77.15 E
Udankudi 122 8.26 N 78.01 E
Udaquiola 252 36.34 S 58.31 W
Udarnyj 89 49.07 N 142.09 E
Udaypur 124 26.56 N 86.31 E
Udbina 36 44.32 N 15.46 E
Udby 41 55.05 N 11.57 E
Uddeholm 40 60.01 N 13.37 E
Uddel 52 52.15 N 5.46 E
Uddevalla 26 58.21 N 11.55 E
Uddingston 46 55.50 N 4.06 W
Uddjaur 24 65.55 N 17.49 E
Udel'naja 82 55.38 N 38.03 E
Udel'naja 265a 60.01 N 30.19 E
Uden 52 51.40 N 5.36 E
Udenhout 52 51.37 N 5.08 E
Uder 56 51.22 N 10.05 E

Udgīr 122 18.23 N 77.07 E
Udhampur 123 32.56 N 75.08 E
Udhruḥ 132 30.20 N 35.36 E
Udi 150 6.19 N 7.25 E
Udimskij 24 61.09 N 45.52 E
Udine 64 46.03 N 13.14 E
Udine 64 46.10 N 13.00 E
Udinskij Chrebet 88 53.20 N 97.50 E
Udipi 122 13.21 N 74.45 E
Udjung-kulon, Menandjung 112 6.45 S 105.20 E
Udmurtskaja Avtonomnaja Sovetskaja Socialističeskaja Respublika 80 57.00 N 53.00 E
Udokan, Chrebet 88 56.20 N 118.10 E
Udoml'a 76 57.52 N 35.01 E
Udone-jima 94 34.28 N 139.18 E
Udono 92 33.44 N 136.01 E
Udon Thani 110 17.26 N 102.46 E
Udor, Mount 162 23.30 S 131.01 E
Udot 175c 7.23 N 151.43 E
Udskaja Guba 89 54.50 N 135.45 E
Udskoje 89 54.32 N 134.26 E
Udy 78 50.24 N 36.03 E
Udyl', Ozero 89 52.06 N 139.48 E
Udža 74 71.14 N 117.10 E
Udžary 84 40.31 N 47.39 E
Uebaru 175d 24.25 N 123.46 E
Uebigau 54 51.35 N 13.18 E
Uebonti 112 0.55 S 121.38 E
Uebonti, Teluk 112 0.50 S 121.45 E
Uecker 54 53.45 N 14.04 E
Ueckeritz 54 54.00 N 14.02 E
Ueckermünde 54 53.44 N 14.03 E
Ueckermünder Heide 54 53.40 N 14.10 E
Ueda 94 36.24 N 138.16 E
Uedem 52 51.40 N 6.16 E
Uedesheim 263 51.10 N 6.48 E
Uegō 268 35.10 N 139.56 E
Uehlfeld 56 49.40 N 10.43 E
Uele 136 4.09 N 22.26 E
Uelen 180 66.10 N 169.48 W
Uel'kal' 180 65.32 N 179.17 E
Uelsen 52 52.30 N 6.53 E
Uelzen, B.R.D. 52 52.58 N 10.33 E
Uelzen, B.R.D. 263 51.33 N 7.44 E
Ueno, Nihon 94 36.05 N 138.47 E
Ueno, Nihon 94 35.02 N 136.54 E
Ueno, Nihon 94 34.45 N 136.08 E
Ueno, Nihon 270 34.57 N 135.14 E
Uenohara 94 35.37 N 139.07 E
Ueno Park 268 35.43 N 139.46 E
Uenoshiba 270 34.33 N 135.28 E
Uerdingen 263 51.21 N 6.39 E
Uere 154 3.42 N 25.24 E
Uetersen 52 53.41 N 9.39 E
Uettingen 56 49.48 N 9.43 E
Uetz 264a 52.28 N 12.56 E
Uetze 52 52.28 N 10.11 E
Ueza 152 8.03 S 13.11 E
Ufa 86 54.44 N 55.56 E
Ufa 86 54.40 N 56.00 E
Ufala, Punta 70 38.22 N 14.59 E
Uffculme 42 50.54 N 3.20 W
Uffenheim 56 49.32 N 10.14 E
Ufita, It. 66
68 41.09 N 14.56 E
Ufra 128 40.00 N 53.02 E
Uft'uga 76 59.46 N 39.21 E
Ugab 156 21.08 S 13.40 E
Ugak Bay 180 57.25 N 152.45 W
Ugāle 76 57.16 N 22.02 E
Ugalla 154 5.08 S 30.42 E
Ugamskij Chrebet 85 42.00 N 70.20 E
Uganda 10
154 1.00 N 32.00 E
Uganik Island 180 57.53 N 153.28 W
Ugârčin 38 43.06 N 24.25 E
Ugarit 130 35.35 N 35.45 E
Ugashik 180 57.32 N 157.25 W
Ugashik Bay 180 57.34 N 157.38 W
Ugatkyn 180 68.24 N 171.30 W
Ugento 68 39.56 N 18.10 E
Ugep 150 5.50 N 8.05 E
Ugerløse 41 55.35 N 11.40 E
Uggiano la Chiesa 68 40.06 N 18.27 E
Ughaybish 140 10.52 N 31.05 E
Ughelli 150 5.29 N 5.59 E
Ugi 175e 10.15 S 161.45 E
Ugie 158 31.10 S 28.13 E
Ugie 46 57.30 N 1.47 W
Ugíjar 34 36.57 N 3.03 W
Ugimi 174m 26.42 N 128.07 E
Ugine 62 45.45 N 6.25 E
Uglegorsk, S.S.S.R. 83 48.19 N 38.17 E
Uglegorsk, S.S.S.R. 89 49.02 N 142.03 E
Uglezavodsk 89 47.21 N 142.38 E
Uglič 76 57.32 N 38.19 E
Ugličskaja Vozvyšennost' 76 57.20 N 38.51 E
Ugljan, Otok 36 44.05 N 15.10 E
Uglovaja 80 57.01 N 52.57 E
Uglovka 76 58.14 N 33.31 E
Uglovoje 89 43.20 N 132.06 E
Uglovskoje 86 51.23 N 80.12 E
Ugly-Zavod 78 52.11 N 32.53 E
Ugnev 78 50.23 N 23.44 E
Ugodiči 80 57.10 N 39.30 E
Ugodskij Zavod 82 55.02 N 36.45 E
Ugol'naja, Buchta 180 63.00 N 179.20 E
Ugolnyy 180 63.03 N 179.03 E
Ugoma 154 4.00 S 28.45 E
Ugovizza 64 46.31 N 13.29 E
Ugra 76 54.47 N 34.17 E
Ugra 82 54.30 N 36.07 E
Ugrojedy 78 50.52 N 35.17 E
Ugr'umovo 82 55.09 N 37.40 E
Ugtaalcajdam 88 48.17 N 105.20 E
Uguj 86 56.02 N 76.03 E
Ug'ut 85 41.24 N 74.50 E
Ugyak, Cape 180 58.17 N 154.04 W
Uh (Už) 30 48.34 N 22.00 E
Uha-dong 98 40.41 N 125.38 E
Uḥayjibah, Jabal al- 132 30.11 N 34.33 E
Uherské Hradiště 30 49.05 N 17.28 E
Uherský Brod 30 49.02 N 17.39 E
Uhingen 56 48.42 N 9.35 E
Úhlava 60 49.43 N 13.23 E
Uhlenhorst 156 23.45 S 17.55 E
Ühlingen 58 47.43 N 8.19 E
Uhlman Lake 184 56.40 N 98.23 W
Uhlstädt 54 50.44 N 11.28 E
Uhrichsville 214 40.24 N 81.20 W
Uhyst, D.D.R. 54 51.24 N 14.30 E
Uhyst, D.D.R. 54 51.11 N 14.13 E
Uiche 152 12.03 S 21.02 E
Uig, Scot., U.K. 46 58.12 N 7.00 W
Uig, Scot., U.K. 46 57.35 N 6.22 W
Uíge 152 7.37 S 15.03 E
Uíge 152 7.00 S 15.30 E
Ŭijŏngbu 98 37.44 N 127.03 E
Ŭiju 98 40.12 N 124.32 E
Uil 86 49.05 N 54.40 E
Uil 80 48.36 N 52.30 E
Uilpata, Gora 84 42.48 N 43.48 E
Uimaharju 26 62.55 N 30.15 E
Uina 146 7.45 N 15.36 E

Uiñaimarca, Lago 248 16.20 S 68.50 W
Uinebona 246 5.04 N 63.01 W
Uinskoje 86 56.53 N 56.35 E
Uinta 200 40.14 N 109.51 W
Uintah and Ouray Indian Reservation 200 40.20 N 110.20 W
Uinta Mountains 200 40.45 N 110.05 W
Uiraúna 250 6.31 S 38.25 W
Uis 156 21.08 S 14.49 E
Ŭisŏng 98 36.22 N 128.41 E
Uitenhage 158 33.40 S 25.28 E
Uitgeest 52 52.32 N 4.43 E
Uithoorn 52 52.14 N 4.50 E
Uithuizen 52 53.24 N 6.40 E
Uithuizermeeden 52 53.24 N 6.42 E
Uitspanning 158 26.46 S 29.56 E
Uj 86 54.17 N 64.58 E
Ujae 14 9.05 N 165.40 E
Ujaly 86 44.37 N 60.57 E
Ujandina 74 68.23 N 145.50 E
Ujar 86 55.48 N 94.20 E
Ujarrás 236 9.51 N 83.50 W
Ujazd 30 50.24 N 18.22 E
Ujedinenija, Ostrov 72 77.28 N 82.28 E
Ujelang 14 9.49 N 160.55 E
Ujemskij 24 64.29 N 40.50 E
Újezd, Česko. 54 50.03 N 14.44 E
Ujęzd, Česko. 60 49.26 N 13.27 E
Újfehértó 30 47.48 N 21.40 E
Ujgursaj 85 40.53 N 71.03 E
Ujhāni 124 28.01 N 79.01 E
Uji 96 34.53 N 135.48 E
Uji 96 34.51 N 135.42 E
Uji-guntō 92 31.11 N 129.27 E
Ujiie 94 36.41 N 139.58 E
Ujiji 154 4.55 S 29.41 E
Uji-tawara 96 34.51 N 135.31 E
Uji-yamada → Ise 94 34.29 N 136.42 E
Ujjain 120 23.11 N 75.46 E
'Ujmān 128 25.25 N 55.27 E
Ujongtankayji 114 3.32 N 97.13 E
Újpest 264c 47.34 N 19.06 E
Ujście 30 53.04 N 16.43 E
Ujskoje 86 54.22 N 60.00 E
Ujum 85 38.22 N 70.51 E
Ujung 112 7.04 S 120.46 E
Ujungbatu 114 0.43 N 100.31 E
Ujungberung 115a 6.55 S 107.42 E
Ujunggading 110 0.16 N 99.33 E
Ujunggenteng 115a 7.22 S 106.24 E
Ujunglamuru 112 4.40 S 119.58 E
Ujung Pandang (Makasar) 112 5.07 S 119.24 E
Újvidék → Novi Sad 38 45.15 N 19.50 E
Uk 88 55.04 N 98.52 E
Uka, Nihon 174m 26.48 N 128.14 E
Uka, S.S.S.R. 74 57.50 N 162.06 E
Ukamas 158 28.02 S 19.45 E
Ukara Island 154 1.50 S 33.03 E
'Ukāsh, Wādī 128 34.18 N 40.42 E
Ukaturaka, Île 152 1.55 N 20.15 E
Ukerewe Island 154 2.03 S 33.00 E
Ukhayḍir, Jabal 142 29.44 N 32.11 E
Ukhayḍir, Wādī 132 30.55 N 37.01 E
Ukhra 126 23.39 N 87.14 E
Ukhrul 120 25.07 N 94.22 E
Ukhta → Uchta 24 63.33 N 53.38 E
Ukiah, Calif., U.S. 204 39.09 N 123.13 W
Ukiah, Oreg., U.S. 202 45.08 N 118.56 W
Ukibaru-jima 174m 26.18 N 128.00 E
Ukiha 96 33.19 N 130.47 E
Ukita 268 35.40 N 139.52 E
Ukmergė 76 55.15 N 24.45 E
Ukolnoi Island 180 55.14 N 161.34 W
Ukrainian Soviet Socialist Republic → Ukrainskaja Sovetskaja Socialističeskaja Respublika 78 49.00 N 32.00 E
Ukrainka 86 54.39 N 71.20 E
Ukrainsk 83 48.06 N 37.18 E
Ukrainskaja Sovetskaja Socialističeskaja Respublika 78 49.00 N 32.00 E
Ukrina 36 45.05 N 17.56 E
Uks'anskoje 86 55.57 N 63.01 E
Uktuz 86 55.38 N 68.30 E
Uktym 24 62.38 N 48.52 E
Uku 174m 26.50 N 128.17 E
Ukui 112 0.09 S 102.11 E
Ukurejskij 88 52.24 N 116.49 E
Ukuti 154 3.39 N 33.32 E
Ukyō 270 35.03 N 135.42 E
Ukyr 88 49.28 N 108.52 E
Ula, Bhārat 272b 22.43 N 88.33 E
Ula, Tür. 130 37.05 N 28.26 E
Ula 86 54.40 N 56.00 E
Ulaan Baatar 88 47.55 N 106.53 E
Ulaanbaatar 88 47.55 N 106.53 E
Ulaanbadrach 102 43.38 N 110.30 E
Ulaanchus 86 49.02 N 89.23 E
Ulaangom 86 49.58 N 92.02 E
Ulaan Nuur 102 44.30 N 103.35 E
Ulaan Tajga 88 50.45 N 98.30 E
'Ulab, Ţaraq al- 130 33.55 N 38.18 E
Ulache 89 44.54 N 133.35 E
Ula-Chuduk 80 47.39 N 45.34 E
Ulak Island 181a 51.22 N 179.00 W
Ulakmedan 114 2.43 N 99.38 E
Ulamba 152 9.07 S 23.40 E
Ulamona 164 5.00 S 151.15 E
Ulan Bator → Ulaan Baatar 88 47.55 N 106.53 E
Ulanbel' 86 44.48 N 71.10 E
Ulan-Burgasy, Chrebet 88 52.45 N 109.00 E
Ulan-Erge 80 46.19 N 44.53 E
Ulang 236 14.27 N 83.14 W
Ulanhot → Wulanhaote 89 46.05 N 122.05 E
Ulānia 126 22.12 N 90.29 E
Ulanov 78 49.42 N 28.08 E
Ulanovo 78 51.46 N 34.18 E
Ulanovskij 82 54.04 N 37.51 E
Ulanów 30 50.30 N 22.16 E
Ulan-Ude 88 51.50 N 107.37 E
Ulan-Ušotej 88 50.45 N 105.29 E
Ulāpāra 126 24.19 N 89.34 E
Ulaş 130 39.27 N 37.03 E
Ul'ašovo 24 65.27 N 56.57 E
Ulatis Creek 226 38.18 N 121.00 W
Ul'atuj 88 51.09 N 116.14 E
Ulawa 175e 9.46 S 161.57 E
Ulaya 154 7.04 S 36.54 E
Ułazów 30 50.17 N 23.00 E
Ul'ba 86 50.16 N 83.22 E
Ul'banskij Zaliv 89 53.45 N 137.50 E
Ulchin 98 36.59 N 129.23 E
Ul'chun-Partija 88 49.56 N 112.46 E
Ulcinj 38 41.55 N 19.11 E
Ulco 158 28.21 S 24.15 E
Ulcombe 260 51.12 N 0.39 E
Ulcumayo 248 11.01 S 75.55 W
Uldum 41 55.51 N 9.36 E
Uldz 88 49.56 N 115.31 E

Uleåborg → Oulu 26 65.01 N 25.28 E
Ulefoss 26 59.17 N 9.16 E
Ulen 198 47.05 N 96.16 W
Ulety 88 51.22 N 112.29 E
Ulfborg 26 56.16 N 8.20 E
Ulft 52 51.54 N 6.23 E
Ulgajsyn 86 49.38 N 60.17 E
Ulgueira 266c 38.47 N 9.28 W
Ulhās 272c 19.13 N 73.01 E
Ulhāsnagar 122 19.13 N 73.07 E
Uliast 86 48.57 N 91.17 E
Uliastaj (Dżavchlant) 88 47.45 N 96.49 E
Úlice 60 49.45 N 13.09 E
Ulindi 154 1.40 S 25.52 E
Ulingan 164 4.30 S 145.25 E
Ulithi 108 9.58 N 139.40 E
Ulja 74 58.51 N 141.50 E
Uljanino 82 55.21 N 38.26 E
Uljanovka, S.S.S.R. 76 59.38 N 30.46 E
Uljanovka, S.S.S.R. 78 50.58 N 34.18 E
Uljanovka, S.S.S.R. 78 48.20 N 30.13 E
Uljanovo 76 53.43 N 35.32 E
Uljanovsk 80 54.20 N 48.24 E
Uljanovskoje, S.S.S.R. 86 50.02 N 73.42 E
Uljanovskoje, S.S.S.R. 89 46.17 N 142.13 E
Ul'kajak 86 48.54 N 62.00 E
Ul'kan 88 57.14 N 107.19 E
Ul'kan 88 55.53 N 107.45 E
Ul'ken-Karoj, Ozero 86 54.00 N 71.58 E
Ulla 76 55.14 N 29.15 E
Ulla, Esp. 34 42.39 N 8.44 W
Ulla, S.S.S.R. 76 55.14 N 29.14 E
Ulladulla 170 35.21 S 150.29 E
Ulladulla Trough 14 34.00 S 154.00 E
Ullapool 46 57.54 N 5.10 W
Ullastrell 266d 41.31 N 1.58 E
Üllendahl 263 51.19 N 7.18 E
Ullerslev 41 55.22 N 10.40 E
Ullervad 40 58.40 N 13.52 E
Ullin 194 37.17 N 89.11 W
Üllő 264c 47.23 N 19.21 E
Ullswater 44 54.34 N 2.54 W
Ullučaj 84 42.18 N 48.08 E
Ullún 252 31.28 S 68.42 W
Ullŭng-do 92 37.29 N 130.52 E
Ullvettern 40 59.27 N 14.16 E
Ullvi 40 59.42 N 16.37 E
Ulm, B.R.D. 58 48.24 N 10.00 E
Ulm, Mont., U.S. 202 47.26 N 111.30 W
Ulma 38 47.53 N 25.18 E
Ulmarra 166 29.37 S 153.02 E
Ulmeni 38 45.04 N 26.39 E
Ulmer, Mount 9 77.35 S 86.09 W
Ulmeu-Meisereich 56 50.13 N 6.58 E
Ulpur 126 23.04 N 89.50 E
Ulricehamn 26 57.47 N 13.25 E
Ulrichberg 60 48.41 N 13.54 E
Ulrichstein 56 50.34 N 9.11 E
Ulrum 52 53.22 N 6.20 E
Ulsan 98 35.34 N 129.19 E
Ulsta 46 60.30 N 1.09 W
Ulsteinvik 26 62.20 N 5.53 E
Ulster 210 41.51 N 76.30 W
Ulster 210 41.56 N 74.00 W
Ulster 48 54.37 N 7.15 W
Ulster 56 50.51 N 9.59 E
Ulster Canal 48 54.08 N 7.22 W
Ultimo, Val D' 64 46.35 N 11.00 E
Ultraoriental, Cordillera (Serra do Divisor) 248 8.20 S 73.30 W
Ulu, Indon. 112 2.45 N 125.24 E
Ulu, S.S.S.R. 74 60.19 N 127.24 E
Ulu, Sūd. 140 10.43 N 33.29 E
Ulúa 236 15.53 N 87.44 W
Ulubāria 126 22.28 N 88.06 E
Ulubat Gölü 130 40.10 N 28.35 E
Ulubey 130 38.25 N 29.18 E
Uluborlu 130 38.05 N 30.28 E
Ulu Dağ 130 40.04 N 29.13 E
Uludāngar 272b 22.51 N 88.31 E
Ulugan Bay 116 10.07 N 118.47 E
Ulug-Chol', Ozero 88 52.43 N 97.20 E
Uluguru Mountains 154 7.10 S 37.40 E
Uluinggalau 175g 16.54 S 179.59 E
Ulu-Jul 86 57.46 N 85.30 E
Ulukışla 130 37.33 N 34.30 E
Ulul 14 8.35 N 149.40 E
Ulu Laho, Bukit 114 5.43 N 101.27 E
Ulunchan 88 54.51 N 111.02 E
Ulundi 158 28.17 S 31.26 E
Ulunga 89 46.31 N 136.56 E
Ulurijskij-Golec, Gora 88 50.12 N 111.45 E
Ulus 130 41.35 N 32.39 E
Ulusara 126 24.16 N 90.36 E
Ulut 116 12.00 N 125.27 E
Ulutau 86 48.39 N 67.01 E
Ulu Tiram 114 1.36 N 103.49 E
Ulu Yam 114 3.27 N 101.38 E
Ulva 272c 18.59 N 73.02 E
Ulva 46 56.29 N 6.14 W
Ulvenhout 52 51.34 N 4.48 E
Ulverston 44 54.12 N 3.06 W
Ulverstone 166 41.09 S 146.10 E
Ulvöarna 26 63.01 N 18.40 E
Ulvshale 41 55.02 N 12.16 E
Ulvshyttan 40 60.18 N 15.22 E
Ulvsund 41 54.59 N 12.11 E
Ulyanovsk → Uljanovsk 80 54.20 N 48.24 E
Ulysses, Kans., U.S. 198 37.35 N 101.22 W
Ulysses, Nebr., U.S. 198 41.04 N 97.12 W
Ulysses, Pa., U.S. 214 41.54 N 77.46 W
Uly-Žilanšik 86 48.51 N 63.47 E
Ulzë 38 41.41 N 19.54 E
Umag 64 45.25 N 13.32 E
Umaji 96 34.00 N 133.44 E
Umal'tinskij 89 51.56 N 133.36 E
Umán, Méx. 232 20.53 N 89.45 W
Uman', S.S.S.R. 78 48.44 N 30.14 E
'Umān → Oman 118 22.00 N 58.00 E
Uman 175c 7.18 N 151.53 E
Umanak 176 70.40 N 52.07 W
Umanak Fjord 176 70.55 N 53.00 W
Umancevo 80 47.44 N 44.16 E
Umaralla 171b 36.10 S 149.20 E
Umari 250 6.38 S 38.42 W
'Umarī, Qā' al- 132 31.42 N 36.57 E
Umaria, Bhārat 124 23.32 N 80.50 E
Umaria, Bhārat 124 23.48 N 80.56 E
Umarizal 250 5.59 S 37.49 W
Umarkot 120 25.22 N 69.44 E
Umatac 174p 13.18 N 144.39 E
Umatilla, Fla., U.S. 220 28.55 N 81.40 W
Umatilla, Oreg., U.S. 202 45.55 N 119.21 W
Umatilla 202 45.55 N 119.20 W
Umatilla Indian Reservation 202 45.41 N 118.31 W
Umayan 116 8.13 N 125.50 E
Umaze 270 34.57 N 135.03 E
Umba 24 66.41 N 34.15 E
Umbai 114 2.10 N 102.20 E
Umbargaon 122 20.12 N 72.45 E
Umbaúba 250 11.22 S 37.39 W
Umbelasha 140 9.51 N 24.50 E

River	Fluss	Río	Rivière	Rio
Canal	Kanal	Canal	Canal	Canal
Waterfall, Rapids	Wasserfall, Stromschnellen	Cascada, Rápidos	Chute d'eau, Rapides	Cascata, Rápidos
Strait	Meeresstrasse	Estrecho	Détroit	Estreito
Bay, Gulf	Bucht, Golf	Bahía, Golfo	Baie, Golfe	Baía, Golfo
Lake, Lakes	See, Seen	Lago, Lagos	Lac, Lacs	Lago, Lagos
Swamp	Sumpf	Pantano	Marais	Pântano
Ice Features, Glacier	Eis- und Gletscherformen	Accidentes Glaciales	Formes glaciaires	Acidentes Glaciares
Other Hydrographic Features	Andere Hydrographische Objekte	Otros Elementos Hidrográficos	Autres données hydrographiques	Outros Elementos Hidrográficos

Submarine Features	Untermeerische Objekte	Accidentes Submarinos	Formes de relief sous-marin	Acidentes Submarinos
Political Unit	Politische Einheit	Unidad Política	Entité politique	Unidade Política
Cultural Institution	Kulturelle Institution	Institución Cultural	Institution culturelle	Instituição Cultural
Historical Site	Historische Stätte	Sitio Histórico	Site historique	Sítio Histórico
Recreational Site	Erholungs- und Ferienort	Sitio de Recreo	Centre de loisirs	Sítio de Lazer
Airport	Flughafen	Aeropuerto	Aéroport	Aeroporto
Military Installation	Militäranlage	Instalación Militar	Installation militaire	Instalação Militar
Miscellaneous	Verschiedenes	Misceláneo	Divers	Miscelânea

Umbertide 66 43.18 N 12.20 E
Umbogintwini 158 30.00 S 30.58 E
Umboi Island 164 5.36 S 148.00 E
Umbozero, Ozero 24 67.43 N 34.25 E
Umbrail, Pass (Giogo di Santa Maria) 64 46.34 N 10.25 E
Umbria 66 43.00 N 12.30 E
Umbriatico 68 39.21 N 16.55 E
Umbroli 272c 19.11 N 73.06 E
Umbukul 164 2.30 S 150.00 E
Umbuzeiro 250 7.41 S 35.40 W
Ume 154 16.40 S 28.26 E
Umeå 26 63.50 N 20.15 E
Umeälven 24 63.47 N 20.16 E
Umedani 270 34.44 N 135.51 E
Umedpur 126 22.31 N 89.59 E
Umegashima 94 35.14 N 138.21 E
Umfolozi Game Reserve 158 28.19 S 31.50 E
Umfors 24 65.56 N 15.00 E
Umfreville Lake 184 50.18 N 94.45 W
Umfuli 154 17.30 S 29.23 E
Umgungundhlovu 158 28.27 S 31.28 E
Umguza 154 19.25 S 27.51 E
Umhausen 64 47.08 N 10.56 E
Umhlanga Rocks 158 29.43 S 31.06 E
Umhlatuzi 158 28.47 S 32.06 E
Umi 96 33.34 N 130.30 E
Umingan 116 15.56 N 120.50 E
Umiray 116 15.13 N 121.25 E
Umkomaas 158 30.15 S 30.42 E
Umm ad-Daraj, Jabal 132 32.19 N 35.48 E
Umm 'Ajārim 142 30.50 N 32.49 E
Umm Al-'Abīd 146 27.31 N 15.02 E
Umm al-'Arā'is, Wādī 146 26.26 N 13.55 E
Umm al-Arānib 146 26.08 N 14.45 E
Umm al-Birak 128 23.25 N 39.13 E
Umm al-Hawāyā, Jabal 142 28.41 N 31.06 E
Umm al-Jimāl, Khirbat 132 32.20 N 36.22 E
Umm al-Khashab 144 17.21 N 42.32 E
Umm al-Qaywayn 128 25.35 N 55.34 E
Umm al-Qiṭṭayn 132 32.19 N 36.38 E
Umm al-Quṣūr 142 27.23 N 30.54 E
Ummanz 54 54.28 N 13.10 E
Umm Artah, Wādī 142 28.41 N 32.37 E
Umm as-Sa'd 132 33.16 N 36.47 E
Umm Badr 140 14.14 N 27.57 E
Umm Balad, Wādī 142 27.40 N 32.39 E
Umm Bayyū'd 140 12.05 N 31.40 E
Umm Bel 140 13.32 N 28.04 E
Umm Boim 140 11.43 N 25.57 E
Umm Dabbī 140 14.37 N 30.23 E
Umm Dam 140 13.45 N 30.59 E
Umm Dhibbān, Sūd. 140 14.14 N 29.37 E
Umm Dhibbān, Sūd. 140 15.26 N 32.51 E
Umm Digulgulaya 140 10.29 N 24.57 E
Umm Dīnār 142 30.12 N 31.04 E
Umm Durmān (Omdurman) 140 15.38 N 32.30 E
Umm el Faḥm 132 32.31 N 35.09 E
Ummeln 52 51.58 N 8.27 E
Ummendorf 54 52.09 N 11.11 E
Umm Habwah, Jabal 142 27.23 N 31.29 E
Umm Hamāṭ 132 31.02 N 35.46 E
Umm Jamālah 140 11.27 N 28.12 E
Umm Jurdī, Jabal 142 29.49 N 32.39 E
Umm Kaddādah 140 13.36 N 26.42 E
Umm Khunān 273c 29.55 N 31.15 E
Umm Khushayb, Wādī 142 30.24 N 32.43 E
Umm Kuwaykah 140 13.00 N 32.17 E
Umm Lajj 128 25.04 N 37.13 E
Umm Marahik, Jabal 140 13.40 N 26.53 E
Umm Mirdī 140 18.59 N 33.32 E
Umm Mitmān 142 30.41 N 32.30 E
Umm Qantur 140 14.17 N 31.22 E
Umm Qurayn 140 9.58 N 28.55 E
Umm Quṣayr 132 31.40 N 35.53 E
Umm Raqabah, Jabal 142 28.58 N 31.08 E
Umm Raqm, Jabal 142 30.14 N 31.52 E
Umm Rīshah, Birkat 142 30.21 N 30.22 E
Umm Rubūl, Jabal 142 28.20 N 32.37 E
Umm Rumaylah 140 16.55 N 31.40 E
Umm Ruwābah 140 12.54 N 31.13 E
Umm Saggāt, Wādī 140 15.15 N 23.12 E
Umm Saysabān, Jabal 132 29.45 N 35.10 E
Umm Sayyālah 140 14.25 N 31.10 E
Umm Shalīl 140 10.51 N 23.42 E
Umm Shanqah 140 13.14 N 27.14 E
Umm Shuṭūr 140 7.17 N 33.14 E
Umm Sidr, Wādī 142 27.54 N 32.33 E
Umm Sughra 140 15.03 N 27.12 E
Umm 'Umayd, Khashm 142 27.39 N 32.37 E
Umm 'Umayd, Ra's 142 27.50 N 32.19 E
Umm 'Umayyid, Bi'r 142 27.53 N 32.30 E
Umm 'Umayyid, Wādī 142 27.37 N 32.41 E
Umm Urūmah 128 25.46 N 36.32 E
Umm Walad 132 32.39 N 36.26 E
Umm Zaytah, Jabal 142 29.49 N 32.16 E
Umnak Island 180 53.25 N 168.10 W
Umnak Pass 180 53.20 N 167.45 W
Umnäs 24 65.24 N 16.10 E
Umniati 154 18.39 S 29.49 E
Umniati 154 16.49 S 28.45 E
Um'ot, S.S.S.R. 80 52.31 N 42.58 E
Um'ot, S.S.S.R. 80 54.08 N 42.42 E
Umpferstedt 54 50.59 N 11.25 E
Umpqua 202 43.42 N 124.03 W
Umpulo 152 12.38 S 17.42 E
'Umrān 144 15.50 N 43.56 E
'Umrānī, Wādī al- 142 27.37 N 30.53 E
Umraniye, Tür. 130 38.37 N 30.48 E
Umraniye, Tür. 267b 41.01 N 29.05 E
Umrer 122 20.51 N 79.20 E
Umreth 120 22.42 N 73.07 E
Umsŏng 98 36.56 N 127.41 E
Umtali 154 18.58 S 32.40 E
Umtanum Creek 224 46.52 N 120.35 W
Umtata 158 31.35 S 28.47 E
Umtentweni 158 30.42 S 30.28 E
Umuahia 150 5.33 N 7.29 E
Umuarama 255 23.45 S 53.20 W
Umurlu 130 37.50 N 27.58 E
Umvukwe Range 154 17.20 S 30.40 E
Umvuma 154 19.19 S 30.35 E
Umzimkulu 158 30.16 S 29.56 E
Umzingwane 154 22.12 S 29.56 E
Umzinto 158 30.22 S 30.33 E
Una, Bhārat 120 20.49 N 71.02 E
Una, Bhārat 123 31.29 N 76.17 E
Una, Bra. 255 15.18 S 39.04 W
Una 36 45.16 N 16.55 E
Una, Ribeirão 287b 23.31 S 46.18 W
Unac 36 44.30 N 16.09 E
Uña de Gato 196 25.58 N 99.41 W
Unadilla, Ga., U.S. 192 32.16 N 83.44 W
Unadilla, N.Y., U.S. 210 42.20 N 75.19 W
Unadilla 210 42.20 N 75.25 W
Unaí 255 16.23 S 46.53 W
Unakami 94 35.46 N 140.45 E
Unalakleet 180 63.53 N 160.47 W
Unalaska 180 53.52 N 166.32 W
Unalaska Island 180 53.45 N 166.45 W
Unanderra 170 34.27 S 150.52 E
Unango 154 12.50 S 35.20 E
Unao 124 25.35 N 78.36 E
Unare 246 10.03 N 65.14 W
Unauna, Pulau 112 0.10 S 121.35 E
Unayyir, Harrat al- 128 25.20 N 37.45 E
'Unayzah 128 26.06 N 43.56 E
'Unayzah, Jabal 132 30.30 N 35.47 E
Unazuki 94 36.49 N 137.35 E
Uncasville 207 41.26 N 72.07 W
Unchahra 124 24.23 N 80.47 E
Ŭnch'ŏn 98 38.34 N 125.26 E
Uncia 248 18.27 S 66.37 W
Uncompahgre 200 38.45 N 108.06 W
Uncompahgre Peak 200 38.04 N 107.28 W
Uncompahgre Plateau 200 38.30 N 108.25 W
Uncukul' 84 42.42 N 46.48 E
Unda 88 51.42 N 116.56 E
Unda 88 51.25 N 116.05 E
Unden 40 58.47 N 14.26 E
Undenäs 40 58.39 N 14.25 E
Underberg 158 29.50 S 29.22 E
Under River 260 51.15 N 0.14 E
Undersåker 26 63.20 N 13.23 E
Ündersdorf 56 50.09 N 6.49 E
Underwood, Ind., U.S. 218 38.36 N 85.46 W
Underwood, N. Dak., U.S. 198 47.27 N 101.08 W
Underwood, Wash., U.S. 224 45.44 N 121.32 W
Undløse 41 55.36 N 11.35 E
Undory 80 54.37 N 48.25 E
Undu, Tanjung 115b 10.05 S 120.51 E
Undu Cape 175g 16.08 S 179.57 W
Undva Nina 76 58.32 N 21.55 E
Unea Island 164 4.55 S 149.10 E
Uneča 76 52.50 N 32.40 E
Uneča 76 52.50 N 31.56 E
Uneiuxi 246 0.37 S 65.34 W
Unèšov 60 49.53 N 13.09 E
Unga Island 180 55.15 N 160.45 W
Ungaran 115a 7.07 S 110.24 E
Ungarie 166 33.38 S 146.58 E
Ungarn → Hungary 30 47.00 N 20.00 E
Ungava, Péninsule d' 176 60.00 N 74.00 W
Ungava Bay 176 59.30 N 67.30 W
Ungay Point 116 13.11 N 124.13 E
Ungch'ŏn 98 35.07 N 128.44 E
Ungeny 78 47.12 N 27.48 E
Unggi 98 42.20 N 130.24 E
Ungurkuj 88 50.27 N 106.58 E
Ungvár → Užgorod 78 48.37 N 22.18 E
Unhos 266c 38.50 N 9.07 W
Unhošt' 54 50.04 N 14.08 E
Uni 80 57.46 N 51.30 E
União 250 4.35 S 42.52 W
União da Vitória 252 26.13 S 51.05 W
União dos Palmares 250 9.10 S 36.02 W
Unica 24 62.38 N 34.38 E
Unicoi 192 36.12 N 82.21 W
Unicorn Branch 208 39.15 N 75.52 W
Unicorn Ridge 271d 22.22 N 114.11 E
Unidad Santa Fe 286a 19.23 N 99.15 W
Uniejów 30 51.58 N 18.49 E
Unieux 62 45.24 N 4.16 E
Unije, Otok 36 44.38 N 14.15 E
Unimak Island 180 54.50 N 164.00 W
Unimak Pass 180 54.35 N 164.43 W
Unini 246 1.41 S 61.31 W
Unión 258 34.53 S 56.08 W
Unión, Arg. 252 35.09 S 65.57 W
Union, Ont., Can. 212 42.42 N 81.12 W
Unión, Para. 252 24.48 S 56.33 W
Union, Ill., U.S. 216 42.14 N 88.33 W
Union, Iowa, U.S. 190 42.15 N 93.04 W
Union, Ky., U.S. 218 38.57 N 84.41 W
Union, Maine, U.S. 188 44.13 N 69.17 W
Union, Miss., U.S. 194 32.34 N 89.14 W
Union, Mo., U.S. 219 38.27 N 91.00 W
Union, N.J., U.S. 210 40.42 N 74.16 W
Union, Ohio, U.S. 218 39.54 N 84.18 W
Union, Oreg., U.S. 202 45.13 N 117.52 W
Union, S.C., U.S. 192 34.43 N 81.37 W
Union, Wash., U.S. 224 47.21 N 123.06 W
Union, W. Va., U.S. 192 37.36 N 80.33 W
Union, Ind., U.S. 218 39.38 N 84.56 W
Union, N.J., U.S. 208 40.40 N 74.11 W
Union, Ohio, U.S. 214 40.18 N 83.19 W
Union, Pa., U.S. 208 40.58 N 76.54 W
Unión 8On 258 34.53 S 56.08
Union Bay 182 49.35 N 124.53 W
Union Beach 208 40.27 N 74.10 W
Union Bridge 208 39.34 N 77.11 W
Union Center 210 42.09 N 76.04 W
Union City, Calif., U.S. 226 37.36 N 122.01 W
Union City, Ga., U.S. 192 33.35 N 84.33 W
Union City, Ind., U.S. 194 40.12 N 84.49 W
Union City, Mich., U.S. 216 42.04 N 85.08 W
Union City, N.J., U.S. 276 40.46 N 74.02 W
Union City, Ohio, U.S. 216 40.10 N 84.48 W
Union City, Pa., U.S. 214 41.54 N 79.51 W
Union City, Tenn., U.S. 194 36.26 N 89.03 W
Union City Reservoir 214 41.56 N 79.52 W
Uniondale, S. Afr. 158 33.40 S 23.08 E
Uniondale, Ind., U.S. 216 40.50 N 85.15 W
Uniondale, N.Y., U.S. 276 40.43 N 73.36 W
Union Dale, Pa., U.S. 210 41.43 N 75.30 W
Unión de Repúblicas Socialistas Soviéticas → Union of Soviet Socialist Republics 72 60.00 N 80.00 E
Unión de Reyes 240p 22.48 N 81.32 W
Unión de San Antonio 234 21.06 N 101.58 W
Union des Émirats Arabes → United Arab Emirates 128 24.00 N 54.00 E
Union des Républiques socialistes soviétiques → Union of Soviet Socialist Republics 72 60.00 N 80.00 E
Unión de Tula 234 19.58 N 104.16 W
Union Gap 202 46.34 N 120.34 W
Union Grove, Tex., U.S. 222 32.34 N 94.55 W
Union Grove, Wis., U.S. 216 42.41 N 88.03 W
Unión Hidalgo 234 16.28 N 94.50 W
Union Hill 210 43.13 N 77.23 W
Union Lake 216 42.37 N 83.27 W
Union Lake, Mich., U.S. 216 42.03 N 85.11 W
Union Lake, Mich., U.S. 281 42.37 N 83.26 W
Union Lake, N.J., U.S. 208 39.25 N 75.03 W
Union Mills 216 41.30 N 86.47 W
Union of Soviet Socialist Republics, As., Eur. 12 60.00 N 80.00 E
Union Park 220 28.30 N 81.15 W
Union Pier 216 41.50 N 86.42 W
Union Point 192 33.37 N 83.04 W
Unionport, Ind., U.S. 218 40.07 N 85.06 W
Unionport, Ohio, U.S. 214 40.21 N 80.51 W
Union Seamount 16 49.35 N 132.40 W
Union Springs, Ala., U.S. 194 32.09 N 85.49 W
Union Springs, N.Y., U.S. 210 42.50 N 76.42 W
Union Station, Calif., U.S. 280 34.04 N 118.14 W
Union Station, D.C., U.S. 284c 38.54 N 77.00 W
Union Stock Yards 278 41.49 N 87.40 W
Uniontown, Ala., U.S. 194 32.22 N 87.31 W
Uniontown, Ky., U.S. 194 37.46 N 87.56 W
Uniontown, Md., U.S. 208 39.36 N 77.07 W
Uniontown, Ohio, U.S. 214 40.59 N 81.25 W
Uniontown, Pa., U.S. 188 39.54 N 79.44 W
Union Valley Reservoir 226 38.50 N 120.26 W
Union Village 207 42.00 N 71.32 W
Unionville, Ont., Can. 275b 43.52 N 79.18 W
Unionville, Conn., U.S. 207 41.45 N 72.53 W
Unionville, Ind., U.S. 218 39.14 N 86.25 W
Unionville, Mich., U.S. 190 43.39 N 83.28 W
Unionville, Mo., U.S. 194 40.29 N 93.01 W
Unionville, N.J., U.S. 285 40.01 N 74.46 W
Unionville, N.Y., U.S. 210 41.18 N 74.34 W
Unionville, Ohio, U.S. 214 41.47 N 81.00 W
Unionville, Pa., U.S. 285 39.54 N 75.44 W
Unionville Center 214 40.08 N 83.21 W
Uniopolis 216 40.36 N 84.05 W
Unipouheos Indian Reserve 184 53.52 N 110.21 W
Unisan 116 13.51 N 121.59 E
United 214 40.13 N 79.31 W
United Arab Emirates 118
128 24.00 N 54.00 E
United Arab Republic → Egypt 140 27.00 N 30.00 E
United Kingdom 22 54.00 N 2.00 W
United Nations Headquarters 276 40.45 N 73.58 W
United Nations Military Headquarters 271b 37.33 N 126.59 E
United States 178 38.00 N 97.00 W
United States Air Force Academy 200 39.00 N 104.55 W
United States Coast Guard Academy 207 41.22 N 72.06 W
United States Merchant Marine Academy 276 40.48 N 73.46 W
United States Military Academy 210 41.23 N 73.28 W
United States Naval Academy 208 38.59 N 76.30 W
United States Steel Corporation (Lorain Plant), Ohio, U.S. 279a 41.27 N 82.07 W
United States Steel Corporation, Pa., U.S. 279b 40.25 N 79.54 W
United States Steel Corporation, Pa., U.S. 279b 40.20 N 79.54 W
United States Steel Corporation Fairless Works 285 40.09 N 74.45 W
Unity, Sask., Can. 184 52.27 N 109.10 W
Unity, Maine, U.S. 188 44.40 N 69.14 W
Unity Reservoir 279b 40.17 N 79.30 W
Universal City 196 29.33 N 98.17 W
Universal City 280 34.09 N 118.21 W
Universal Mall 281 42.30 N 83.05 W
Università Degli Studi 266b 45.28 N 9.14 E
University 194 34.21 N 89.32 W
University City 219 38.39 N 90.19 W
University Gardens 276 40.46 N 73.44 W
University Heights, Calif., U.S. 226 37.27 N 122.14 W
University Heights, Ohio, U.S. 279a 41.30 N 81.32 W
University Park, Md., U.S. 284c 38.58 N 76.57 W
University Park, N. Mex., U.S. 200 32.17 N 106.45 W
University Park, Tex., U.S. 222 32.52 N 96.47 W
University Place 224 47.14 N 122.34 W
University View 218 40.00 N 83.03 W
Unjha 120 23.48 N 72.24 E
Unkel 56 50.35 N 7.13 E
Unken 64 47.39 N 12.43 E
Unkurda 86 55.48 N 59.24 E
Unley 168b 34.57 S 138.35 E
Un'ma 89 51.54 N 129.18 E
Unna 52 51.32 N 7.41 E
Unna 263 51.34 N 7.42 E
'Unnāb, Jabal al- 132 29.57 N 36.55 E
'Unnāb, Wādī al- 132 30.11 N 36.39 E
Unnão 124 26.32 N 80.30 E
Unnão 124 26.30 N 80.30 E
Uno, Ilha de 150 11.12 N 16.15 W
Unoke 94 36.43 N 136.42 E
Ŭnp'a 98 38.26 N 125.46 E
Unpenji-san 96 34.02 N 133.44 E
Unqua Point 276 40.39 N 73.26 W
Unquillo 252 31.14 S 64.19 W
Unsan 98 39.25 N 126.01 E
Unseburg 54 51.56 N 11.30 E
Unserfrau → Madonna 64 46.43 N 10.52 E
Unsleben 56 50.22 N 10.15 E
Unst 46a 60.45 N 0.53 W
Unstrut 54 51.10 N 11.48 E
Un't 88 49.07 N 102.50 E
Unten 174m 26.41 N 128.00 E
Unterägeri 58 47.08 N 8.35 E
Unterbach, B.R.D. 263 51.12 N 6.54 E
Unterbäch, Schw. 58 46.17 N 7.48 E
Unter dem Wind, Inseln → Windward Islands 238 13.00 N 61.00 W
Unterelchingen 58 48.27 N 10.07 E
Unterföhring 60 48.12 N 11.38 E
Unterfranken 56 50.10 N 10.00 E
Untergermaringen 58 47.56 N 10.40 E
Untergloltertal 58 48.03 N 7.56 E
Untergriesbach 60 48.35 N 13.40 E
Untergröningen 58 48.55 N 9.53 E
Untergrüne 263 51.22 N 7.39 E
Unterhaching 60 48.04 N 11.38 E
Unterhausen 58 48.26 N 9.16 E
Unter-Inn-Tal 64 47.24 N 11.47 E
Unterjettenberg 64 47.41 N 12.49 E
Unterkirchen 64 47.25 N 11.12 E
Unterlaa 264b 48.08 N 16.25 E
Unterlüss 52 52.50 N 10.17 E
Untermauerbach 264b 48.14 N 16.12 E
Untermünkheim 56 49.09 N 9.44 E
Untermünstertal 58 47.51 N 7.46 E
Unterneuses 56 50.05 N 10.58 E
Unteröwisheim 56 49.08 N 8.40 E
Unterrath 263 51.16 N 6.47 E
Unterschächen 58 46.52 N 8.47 E
Unterschwaningen 56 49.04 N 10.37 E
Unterseen 58 46.41 N 7.51 E
Unterspreewald 54 52.05 N 13.50 E
Untertauern 64 47.18 N 13.30 E
Unterterzen 58 47.07 N 9.15 E
Unterthingau 58 47.46 N 10.31 E
Unterueckersee 54 53.17 N 13.51 E
Unteruhldingen 58 47.43 N 9.14 E
Unterwalden 58 46.55 N 8.20 E
Unterwasser 58 47.12 N 9.19 E
Unterweissbach 54 50.37 N 11.10 E
Unterwellenborn 54 50.39 N 11.26 E
Unterwössen 64 47.44 N 12.27 E
Unterzeiring 61 47.15 N 14.31 E
Untraverket 40 60.25 N 17.18 E
Unūf, Ra's al- 146 30.31 N 18.34 E
Ünye 130 41.08 N 37.17 E
Unža 80 58.01 N 44.01 E
Unža 80 57.20 N 43.08 E
Unzen-amakusa-kokuritsu-kōen 92 32.45 N 130.17 E
Unzen-dake 92 32.45 N 130.17 E
Unže-Pavinskaja 86 58.53 N 64.02 E
Uojan 88 56.07 N 111.38 E
Uo-shima 96 34.11 N 133.19 E
Uozu 94 36.48 N 137.24 E
Upa 76 54.02 N 36.15 E
Upala 236 10.47 N 85.02 W
Upanema 250 5.38 S 37.15 W
Upano 246 2.45 S 78.12 W
Upardāng Garhi 124 27.46 N 84.34 E
Upata 246 8.01 N 62.24 W
Upatoi Creek 192 32.22 N 84.58 W
Upavon 260 51.18 N 1.49 W
Upch'o-ri 98 37.53 N 125.09 E
Upchurch 260 51.23 N 0.39 E
Upemba, Lac 154 8.36 S 26.26 E
Upemba, Parc National de l' 154 9.10 S 26.35 E
Upernavik 176 72.47 N 56.10 W
Upgant-Schott 52 53.30 N 7.16 E
Uphal 140 6.58 N 34.16 E
Upham 198 48.35 N 100.44 W
Up Holland 44 53.33 N 2.44 W
Uphusen 52 53.01 N 8.58 E
Upi 116 6.57 N 124.09 E
Upía 246 4.18 N 72.45 W
Upington 158 28.25 S 21.15 E
Upire 246 11.27 N 68.58 W
Upland, Calif., U.S. 228 34.06 N 117.39 W
Upland, Ind., U.S. 216 40.28 N 85.30 W
Upland, Nebr., U.S. 198 40.19 N 98.54 W
Upland, Pa., U.S. 285 39.51 N 75.23 W
Upleta 120 21.44 N 70.17 E
Upnuk Lake 180 60.21 N 158.58 W
Upolu 175a 13.55 S 171.45 W
Upolu Point 229d 20.16 N 155.51 W
Uporovo 86 56.18 N 66.17 E
Upper 150 10.30 N 1.30 W
Upper Aetna Lake 285 39.51 N 74.48 W
Upper Arlington 218 40.00 N 83.03 W
Upper Arrow Lake 182 50.30 N 117.55 W
Upper Artichoke Reservoir 283 42.48 N 70.57 W
Upper Beaconsfield 274b 38.01 S 145.25 E
Upper Berkshire Valley 276 40.56 N 74.35 W
Upper Beverley Lake 212 44.37 N 76.05 W
Upper Black Eddy 210 40.35 N 75.07 W
Upper Blackville 186 46.39 N 65.52 W
Upper Brookville 276 40.51 N 73.34 W
Upper Canada Village 206 44.57 N 75.03 W
Upper Castlereagh 274a 33.43 S 150.40 E
Upperco 208 39.34 N 76.50 W
Upper Crystal Springs Reservoir 282 37.30 N 122.20 W
Upper Darby 208 39.58 N 75.16 W
Upper End 262 53.17 N 1.52 W
Upper Erskine Lake 276 41.06 N 74.15 W
Upper Fairmount 208 38.06 N 75.47 W
Upper Falls 284b 39.26 N 76.24 W
Upper Ferntree Gully 274b 37.54 S 145.19 E
Upper Fraser 182 54.07 N 121.56 W
Upper Ganga Canal 124 29.57 N 78.12 E
Upper Gap 212 44.06 N 76.50 W
Upper Goose Lake 184 51.44 N 92.44 W
Upper Greenwood Lake 276 41.11 N 74.24 W
Upper Greenwood Lake 276 41.11 N 74.23 W
Upper Hat Creek 182 50.38 N 121.35 W
Upper Humber 186 49.10 N 57.28 W
Upper Hutt 172 41.08 S 175.04 E
Upper Iowa 190 43.29 N 91.14 W
Upper Island Cove 186 47.39 N 53.12 W
Upper Juba 144 3.00 N 43.00 E
Upper Keechi Creek 222 31.23 N 95.42 W
Upper Klamath Lake 202 42.23 N 122.55 W
Upper Lake 204 39.10 N 122.54 W
Upper Lake 204 41.44 N 120.08 W
Upper Lehigh 210 41.02 N 75.55 W
Upper Liard 180 60.02 N 128.55 W
Upper Machodoc Creek 208 38.18 N 77.02 W
Upper Manitou Lake 184 49.24 N 92.48 W
Upper Matecumbe Key 220 24.55 N 80.39 W
Upper Moutere 172 41.16 S 173.00 E
Upper Musquodoboit 186 45.08 N 62.57 W
Upper Mystic Lake 283 42.27 N 71.09 W
Upper New York Bay 276 40.41 N 74.03 W
Upper Nyack 210 41.07 N 73.55 W
Upper Red Lake 198 48.10 N 94.40 W
Upper Rideau Lake 212 44.41 N 76.20 W
Upper River Rouge 281 42.23 N 83.16 W
Upper Saddle River 276 41.04 N 74.06 W
Upper Saint Clair 279b 40.21 N 80.05 W
Upper Sandusky 214 40.50 N 83.17 W
Upper San Leandro Reservoir 226 37.47 N 122.07 W
Upper Sheila 186 47.28 N 64.56 W
Upper Straits Lake 281 42.35 N 83.24 W
Upper Sumas 224 49.01 N 122.12 W
Upper Takaka 172 41.02 S 172.50 E
Upper Tean 42 52.57 N 1.58 W
Upper Tooting 260 51.26 N 0.10 W
Upper Ugashik Lake 180 57.40 N 156.43 W
Upper Volta 134
150 13.00 N 2.00 W
Upper Windigo Lake 184 52.30 N 91.35 W
Upper Yarra Reservoir 169 37.41 S 145.56 E
Upper Yosemite Fall 226 37.45 N 119.36 W
Uppingham 42 52.35 N 0.43 W
Uppland 40 59.59 N 17.48 E
Upplanda 40 60.14 N 17.44 E
Upplands Väsby 40 59.31 N 17.54 E
Uppsala 40 59.52 N 17.38 E
Uppsala Län 40 60.00 N 17.50 E
Upright, Cape 180 60.17 N 172.15 W
Upsala → Uppsala 40 59.52 N 17.38 E
Upshi 120 33.50 N 77.49 E
Upshur 222 32.45 N 94.55 W
Upstart, Cape 166 19.42 S 147.45 E
Upton, Qué., Can. 206 45.39 N 72.41 W
Upton, Eng., U.K. 44 53.13 N 2.52 W
Upton, Eng., U.K. 260 51.30 N 0.35 W
Upton, Mass., U.S. 207 42.11 N 71.36 W
Upton, Wyo., U.S. 198 44.06 N 104.38 W
Upton upon Severn 42 52.04 N 2.13 W
Uptown 278 41.58 N 87.40 W
Upwell 42 52.36 N 0.12 E
Upwey 274b 37.54 S 145.20 E
Ur 128 30.57 N 46.09 E
Urabá, Golfo de 246 8.25 N 76.53 W
Urach 58 48.29 N 9.23 E
Urachi 84 42.21 N 47.36 E
Uracoa 246 9.00 N 62.21 W
Urad 54 52.15 N 14.45 E
Uradome-kaigan 96 35.35 N 134.21 E
Uraga 268 35.15 N 139.43 E
Uraga-kō 268 35.14 N 139.44 E
Uraga-suido 94 35.13 N 139.45 E
Uragawara 94 37.09 N 138.26 E
Urahoro 92a 42.48 N 143.39 E
Uraj 86 60.08 N 64.48 E
Urakan 88 58.38 N 106.01 E
Urakawa 92a 42.09 N 142.47 E
Ural 72 47.00 N 51.48 E
Uralla 166 30.39 S 151.30 E
Ural Mountains → Ural'skije Gory 72 60.00 N 60.00 E
Uralo-Kl'uči 88 56.03 N 97.28 E
Uralovo 78 52.11 N 33.34 E
Ural'sk 80 51.14 N 51.22 E
Ural'skij 80 51.36 N 51.40 E
Ural'skije Gory (Ural Mountains) 72 60.00 N 60.00 E
Uraltau 86 54.00 N 59.00 E
Urambo 154 5.04 S 32.03 E
Uran 272c 18.52 N 72.56 E
Urana 166 35.20 S 146.16 E
Urandangi 166 21.36 S 138.18 E
Urandi 255 14.46 S 42.38 W
Urangan 166 25.18 S 152.54 E
Urania, Austl. 168b 34.31 S 137.36 E
Urania, La., U.S. 194 31.52 N 92.18 W
Uranium City 176 59.34 N 108.36 W
Uranquinty 171b 35.12 S 147.15 E
Urarey 162 27.26 S 122.18 E
Urariá, Paraná 246 3.03 S 57.43 W
Uraricaá 246 3.20 N 61.56 W
Uraricoera 246 3.27 N 60.59 W
Uraricoera 246 3.02 N 60.30 W
Uras 71 39.42 N 8.42 E
Urasaki 174m 26.40 N 127.53 E
Ura-T'ube 85 39.55 N 68.59 E
Uravakonda 122 14.57 N 77.16 E
Uravan 200 38.22 N 108.44 W
Urawa 94 35.51 N 139.39 E
Urayasu 94 35.39 N 139.54 E
'Urayfān Nāqah, Jabal 132 30.22 N 34.27 E
'Urayyiḍah, Bi'r 142 29.00 N 31.58 E
Urazmetovo 86 53.49 N 55.25 E
Urazovka 80 55.24 N 45.38 E
Urazovo 78 50.07 N 38.04 E
Urbach 56 50.53 N 7.05 E
Urban 224 48.38 N 122.40 W
Urbana, Ill., U.S. 194 40.07 N 88.12 W
Urbana, Ind., U.S. 216 40.54 N 85.47 W
Urbana, Mo., U.S. 194 37.51 N 93.10 W
Urbana, Ohio, U.S. 218 40.07 N 83.45 W
Urbancrest 218 39.54 N 83.05 W
Urbandale, Iowa, U.S. 190 41.38 N 93.48 W
Urbandale, Mich., U.S. 216 44.09 N 85.11 W
Urbania 66 43.40 N 12.31 E
Urbanización Feliú 266d 41.16 N 1.58 E
Urbanización La Pineda 266d 41.16 N 2.00 E
Urbanización Lluminetas 266d 41.16 N 1.59 E
Urbanna 208 37.38 N 76.35 W
Urbano Santos 250 3.12 S 43.23 W
Urbe 62 44.29 N 8.36 E
Urbe, Aeroporto dell' 267a 41.57 N 12.30 E
Urbiña, Peña 34 43.01 N 5.57 W
Urbino 66 43.43 N 12.38 E
Urbisaglia 66 43.12 N 13.23 E
Urcos 248 13.42 S 71.38 W
Urda 80 48.47 N 47.26 E
Urdaneta 116 15.59 N 120.34 E
Urdenbach 263 51.09 N 6.53 E
Urdinarrain 252 32.41 S 58.53 W
Urdoma 24 61.47 N 48.32 E
Urdžar 86 47.05 N 81.38 E
Urè 246 7.46 N 75.31 W
Ure, Fr. 50 48.45 N 0.11 E
Ure, Eng., U.K. 44 54.01 N 1.12 W
Urečje 76 52.57 N 27.54 E
Ūrein 142 30.58 N 30.42 E
Ureki 84 41.59 N 41.46 E
Ureliki 180 64.25 N 172.20 W
Uren' 80 57.28 N 45.49 E
Uren 40 58.59 N 16.44 E
Urén 236 9.33 N 82.55 W
Ureña 246 7.55 N 72.28 W
Urenui 172 39.00 S 174.23 E
Urepara 175f 13.32 S 167.20 E
Ures 232 29.26 N 110.24 W
Ureshino, Nihon 92 33.06 N 129.59 E
Ureshino, Nihon 94 34.37 N 136.29 E
Ureterp 52 53.05 N 6.10 E
Urewera National Park 172 38.40 S 177.00 E
Urfa 130 37.08 N 38.46 E
Urfa 130 37.20 N 39.15 E
Urft 56 50.35 N 6.30 E
Urga → Ulaan Baatar, Mong. 88 47.55 N 106.53 E
Urga, S.S.S.R. 86 43.35 N 58.30 E
Urgamal 88 48.34 N 94.16 E
Urgenč 72 41.33 N 60.38 E
Urgnano 62 45.35 N 9.41 E
Ürgüp 130 38.38 N 34.56 E
Urgut 85 39.23 N 67.15 E
Uri, Bhārat 123 34.05 N 74.02 E
Uri, It. 71 40.38 N 8.29 E
Uri 58 46.50 N 8.40 E
Uriage-les-Bains 62 45.09 N 5.50 E
Uriah 194 31.18 N 87.30 W
Uriangato 234 20.09 N 101.11 W
Uribe 246 3.13 N 74.24 W
Uribelarrea 258 35.09 S 58.54 W
Uribia 246 11.43 N 72.16 W
Urich 194 38.28 N 94.02 W
Uričkoje, S.S.S.R. 78 52.02 N 38.11 E
Uričkoje, S.S.S.R. 86 53.19 N 65.34 E
Urie 46 57.19 N 2.30 W
Uri-Hauchab 156 25.20 S 15.15 E
Urimba 152 10.56 S 16.32 E
Urión, Canal 288 34.24 S 58.31 W
Urique 232 27.13 N 107.55 W
Urique 232 26.29 N 107.58 W
Uri-Rotstock 58 46.52 N 8.33 E
Urituyacu 246 4.45 S 75.28 W
Uriuana 250 2.47 S 50.29 W
Urizura 94 36.30 N 140.27 E
Urjala 26 61.05 N 23.32 E
Urk 52 52.39 N 5.36 E
Urkan 89 53.27 N 126.56 E
Urkarach 84 42.11 N 47.38 E
Urla 130 38.18 N 26.46 E
Urlaţi 38 44.59 N 26.14 E
Urlingford 48 52.42 N 7.35 W
Urlins 240c 17.02 N 61.52 W
Urluk 88 50.03 N 107.55 E
Urma 126 23.10 N 86.15 E
Urman, S.S.S.R. 86 54.52 N 56.52 E
'Urmān, Sūrīy. 132 32.30 N 36.45 E
Urmar Tanda 123 31.42 N 75.38 E
Urmary 80 55.42 N 47.57 E
Ürmeli 130 40.55 N 37.32 E
Urmetan 85 39.27 N 68.17 E
Urmi 89 48.44 N 134.16 E
Urmia → Reẕā'īyeh 128 37.33 N 45.04 E
Urmia, Lake → Reẕā'īyeh, Daryācheh-ye 128 37.40 N 45.30 E
Urmston 44 53.27 N 2.21 W
Urnäsch 58 47.19 N 9.17 E
Urnersee 58 46.55 N 8.37 E
Üröm 264c 47.36 N 19.01 E
Uromi 150 6.44 N 6.18 E
Uroševac 38 42.22 N 21.09 E
Uroyán, Montañas de 240m 18.14 N 67.02 W
Urožajnoje, S.S.S.R. 84 43.42 N 44.13 E
Urožajnoje, S.S.S.R. 84 44.47 N 44.55 E
Urquhart, Glen 46 57.20 N 4.35 W
Urrao 246 6.20 N 76.11 W
Urr Water 44 54.53 N 3.49 W
Ursa 219 40.04 N 91.22 W
Uršel'skij 80 55.41 N 40.13 E
Ursensollen 60 49.24 N 11.46 E
Ursk 86 54.27 N 85.24 E
Urspring 56 48.33 N 9.53 E
Ursus 30 52.12 N 20.53 E
Urtak Sari 86 45.05 N 81.30 E
Urtazym 86 52.12 N 58.50 E
Uru 255 15.24 S 49.36 W
Uruaçu 255 14.30 S 49.10 W
Uruana 255 15.30 S 49.41 W
Uruapan 204 31.38 N 116.15 W
Uruapan [del Progreso] 234 19.25 N 102.04 W
Uruará 250 2.06 S 53.38 W
Urubamba 248 13.18 S 72.07 W
Urubamba 248 10.44 S 73.45 W
Urubaxi 246 0.31 S 64.50 W
Urubu 246 2.55 S 58.25 W
Urubu, Cachoeira do 255 12.52 S 48.13 W
Urubu Grande 250 10.51 S 49.47 W
Uruburetama 250 3.38 S 39.30 W
Urucará 250 2.32 S 57.45 W
Uruch 84 43.28 N 44.06 E
Urucu 246 4.11 S 63.36 W
Uruçuca 255 14.35 S 39.16 W
Uruçuí 250 7.14 S 44.33 W
Uruçuí, Serra da 250 9.00 S 44.45 W
Urucuia 255 16.08 S 45.05 W
Uruçuí-Prêto 250 7.20 S 44.38 W
Urucurituba 250 2.41 S 57.40 W
Urugi 94 35.16 N 137.42 E
Uruguaiana 252 29.45 S 57.05 W
Uruguay 244
252 33.00 S 56.00 W
Uruguay (Uruguai) 252 34.12 S 58.18 W
Urugudejevskij Golec, Gora 88 51.25 N 102.09 E
Urukthapel 175b 7.15 N 134.24 E
Urul'ga 88 51.45 N 114.47 E
Urul'unguj 88 50.24 N 119.08 E
Ur'um, Ozero 86 54.33 N 78.30 E
Urumchi → Wulumuqi 86 43.48 N 87.35 E
Ur'umkan 88 52.35 N 120.08 E
Urumkuvejem 180 66.14 N 173.35 E
Urundel 252 23.33 S 64.25 W
Urung-Chaja 74 72.48 N 113.23 E
Urun-Islāmpur 122 17.03 N 74.16 E
Uruoca 250 3.20 S 40.32 W
Urup 84 43.52 N 41.09 E
Urup 84 44.49 N 41.04 E
Urup, Gora 84 43.38 N 40.58 E
Urup, Ostrov 74 46.00 N 150.00 E
Urupá 248 10.54 S 61.57 W
Urupadi 250 3.51 S 57.21 W
Urupês 255 21.13 S 49.17 W
Ur'upino 88 52.46 N 120.00 E
Ur'upinsk 80 50.47 N 41.59 E
Uruša 89 54.03 N 122.54 E
Urus-Martan 84 43.08 N 45.32 E
Urusovo 82 54.15 N 38.26 E
Urussanga 252 28.31 S 49.19 W
Urussu 80 54.36 N 53.24 E
Urutaí 255 17.28 S 48.12 W
Urutaí, Ilha 250 1.07 S 51.17 W
Urutaú 252 25.42 S 63.04 W
Uruti 172 38.57 S 174.32 E
Uruwira 154 6.27 S 31.21 E
Urwi 156 23.22 S 20.30 E
Uryl' 86 49.15 N 86.20 E
Uryū-san 270 35.03 N 135.48 E
Uryv 78 51.07 N 39.10 E
Urzabaš 80 54.43 N 54.23 E
Urziceni 38 44.43 N 26.38 E
Ürzig 56 49.59 N 7.01 E
Urzulei 71 40.06 N 9.30 E
Uržum 80 57.08 N 50.00 E
Us 261 49.06 N 1.58 E
Us 86 52.07 N 92.15 E
Usa, Nihon 96 33.31 N 131.22 E
Usa, S.S.S.R. 86 54.03 N 88.45 E
Usa, S.S.S.R. 24 65.57 N 56.55 E
Uša, S.S.S.R. 76 54.00 N 28.55 E
Ušač 76 55.32 N 28.20 E
Ušači 76 55.11 N 28.37 E
Usada Island 116 6.08 N 120.33 E
Usadel 54 53.26 N 13.11 E
Uşak 130 38.41 N 29.25 E
Uşak 130 38.35 N 29.20 E
Ušaki 76 59.29 N 30.59 E
Usakos 156 22.01 S 15.32 E
Ušakovka 83 48.48 N 39.48 E

Symbols in the index entries represent the broad categories identified in the key at the right. Symbols with superior numbers (★²) identify subcategories (see complete key on page *I · 30*).

Kartensymbole in dem Registerverzeichnis stellen die rechts in Schlüssel erklärten Kategorien dar. Symbole mit hochgestellten Ziffern (★²) bezeichnen Unterabteilungen einer Kategorie (vgl. vollständiger Schlüssel auf Seite *I · 30*).

Los símbolos incluidos en el texto del índice representan las grandes categorías identificadas con la clave a la derecha. Los símbolos con numeros en su parte superior (★²) identifican las subcategorías (véase la clave completa en la página *I · 30*).

Les symboles de l'index représentent les catégories indiquées dans la légende à droite. Les symboles suivis d'un indice (★²) représentent des sous-catégories (voir légende complète à la page *I · 30*).

Os símbolos incluídos no texto do índice representam as grandes categorias identificadas com a chave à direita. Os símbolos com números em sua parte superior (★²) identificam as subcategorias (veja-se a chave completa à página *I · 30*).

English	Deutsch	Español	Français	Português
Mountain	Berg	Montaña	Montagne	Montanha
Mountains	Berge	Montañas	Montagnes	Montanhas
Pass	Pass	Paso	Col	Passo
Valley, Canyon	Tal, Cañon	Valle, Cañón	Vallée, Canyon	Vale, Canhão
Plain	Ebene	Llano	Plaine	Planície
Cape	Kap	Cabo	Cap	Cabo
Island	Insel	Isla	Île	Ilha
Islands	Inseln	Islas	Îles	Ilhas
Other Topographic Features	Andere Topographische Objekte	Otros Elementos Topográficos	Autres données topographiques	Outros Elementos Topográficos

ESPAÑOL: Nombre, Página, Lat.°′, Long.°′ W=Oeste
FRANÇAIS: Nom, Page, Lat.°′, Long.°′ W=Ouest
PORTUGUÊS: Nome, Página, Lat.°′, Long.°′ W=Oeste

Ušakovo, S.S.S.R. 86 56.22 N 75.41 E
Ušakovo, S.S.S.R. 89 51.55 N 126.34 E
Usambara Mountains ∧ 154 4.45 S 38.30 E
Usangu Flats ≃ 154 8.30 S 34.15 E
Usanovy 86 59.28 N 73.24 E
Ušaral 85 43.54 N 70.42 E
Usarp Mountains ∧ 9 71.10 S 160.00 E
Ušava 60 49.46 N 12.40 E
Usaymir, Wādī al- ∨ 273c 30.04 N 31.23 E
Ušba, Gora ∧ 84 43.08 N 42.40 E
Ušbas ≃ 85 43.55 N 69.39 E
Usborne, Mount ∧ 254 51.41 S 58.50 W
Ušće 38 43.28 N 20.37 E
Uščerpje 76 52.43 N 31.53 E
Uscio 62 44.25 N 9.10 E
Usedom 54 53.52 N 13.55 E
Useldange 56 49.47 N 5.59 E
Usellus 71 39.48 N 8.51 E
Usen' ≃ 80 54.44 N 53.38 E
'Usfān 144 21.55 N 39.21 E
Ushaa 152 14.55 S 23.18 E
Ushashi 154 2.00 S 33.57 E
'Ushayrah 144 21.46 N 40.38 E
Ushetu 154 4.10 S 32.16 E
Ushibuka 92 32.11 N 130.01 E
Ushiku 94 35.58 N 140.08 E
Ushimado 96 34.37 N 134.10 E
Ushi Point ≻ 174n 15.06 N 145.39 E
Ushuaia 254 54.48 S 68.18 W
Usibelli 180 63.51 N 148.47 W
Ušica ≃ 78 48.35 N 27.08 E
Usingen 56 50.20 N 8.32 E
Usini 71 40.40 N 8.32 E
Usisya 154 11.09 S 34.11 E
Usk, B.C., Can. 182 54.38 N 128.25 W
Usk, Wales, U.K. 42 51.43 N 2.54 W
Usk, Wash., U.S. 202 48.19 N 117.17 W
Usk ≃ 42 51.36 N 2.58 W
Uškakij Kr'až ∧ 180 65.15 N 178.35 E
Uskedal 26 59.56 N 5.52 E
Usken ◎ 40 59.39 N 15.01 E
Uskovo 265b 55.56 N 37.19 E
Üsküb → Skopje 38 41.59 N 21.26 E
Üsküdar 130 41.01 N 29.01 E
Uskumuruköy 267b 41.12 N 29.01 E
Uslar 52 51.39 N 9.38 E
Uslava ≃ 60 49.45 N 13.24 E
Usmajac 234 19.52 N 103.34 W
Usman', S.S.S.R. 76 52.02 N 39.44 E
Usman', S.S.S.R. 89 51.29 N 134.00 E
Usmanka 80 52.49 N 51.42 E
Usmānpur ✦8 272a 28.41 N 77.15 E
Usmas Ezers ◎ 76 57.11 N 22.10 E
Usmate Velate 62 45.39 N 9.21 E
Usmyn' 76 55.52 N 31.09 E
Ušna ≃ 80 55.43 N 42.12 E
Usoke 154 5.06 S 32.20 E
Usolje, S.S.S.R. 80 53.23 N 49.05 E
Usolje, S.S.S.R. 82 56.49 N 38.40 E
Usolje, S.S.S.R. 86 59.25 N 56.41 E
Usolje-Sibirskoje 88 52.47 N 103.38 E
Usolka ≃ 86 57.47 N 94.35 E
Uson 116 12.13 N 123.47 E
Usoro 150 5.34 N 6.13 E
Usovo 265b 55.44 N 37.13 E
Uspallata 252 32.35 S 69.20 W
Uspanapa ≃ 234 17.58 N 94.29 W
Uspenka, S.S.S.R. 80 50.38 N 41.28 E
Uspenka, S.S.S.R. 83 48.23 N 39.10 E
Uspenka, S.S.S.R. 83 47.43 N 38.42 E
Uspenka, S.S.S.R. 86 52.54 N 77.25 E
Uspenovka 80 51.16 N 53.36 E
Uspenskij 86 48.42 N 72.40 E
Uspenskoje 82 55.43 N 37.04 E
Usri ≃ 126 24.03 N 86.23 E
Ussaj 86 43.50 N 58.53 E
Ussassai 71 39.49 N 9.23 E
Usseglio 62 45.14 N 7.13 E
Ussel 32 45.33 N 2.18 E
Ussel ≃ 56 48.44 N 11.04 E
Usshers Creek ≃ 284a 43.03 N 79.02 W
Usson-en-Forez 62 45.23 N 3.56 E
Ussure 154 4.39 S 34.23 E
Ussuri (Wusulijiang) ≃ 89 48.27 N 135.04 E
Ussurijsk 89 43.48 N 131.59 E
Ussurka 89 45.12 N 133.31 E
Üst 123 36.56 N 72.53 E
Usta 80 57.26 N 45.40 E
Usta ≃ 80 56.53 N 45.28 E
Ust'-Ajsk 86 56.07 N 57.40 E
Ustaoset 26 60.30 N 8.04 E
Ustaritz 32 43.24 N 1.27 W
Ust'-Bagar'ak 86 56.08 N 61.52 E
Ust'-Barguzin 88 53.27 N 108.59 E
Ust'-Belaja 74 65.30 N 173.20 E
Ust'-Bol'šereck 74 52.48 N 156.14 E
Ust'-B'ur' 86 53.49 N 90.15 E
Ust'-Buzulukskaja 80 50.12 N 42.10 E
Ust'-Bystr'anskaja 80 47.49 N 41.03 E
Ust'-Čaja 86 58.17 N 82.38 E
Ust'-Čaryšskaja Pristan' 86 52.24 N 83.39 E
Ust'-Čaun 74 68.47 N 170.30 E
Ust'-Choperskaja 80 49.36 N 42.24 E
Ust'-Cil'ma 24 65.27 N 52.06 E
Ust'-Čižapka 86 59.02 N 79.37 E
Ust'-Čorna 78 48.18 N 23.56 E
Ust'-Čornaja 88 52.57 N 119.02 E
Ust'-Dolgaja 86 59.56 N 57.21 E
Ust'-Dolyssy 76 56.09 N 29.39 E
Ust'-Doneckij 80 47.39 N 40.52 E
Ust'-Dżegutinskaja 84 44.05 N 41.58 E
Uštěk 54 50.36 N 14.20 E
Ust'-Elegest 88 51.32 N 94.05 E
Uster 58 47.21 N 8.43 E
Ust' Gr'aznucha 80 50.28 N 45.26 E
Ustica 70 38.42 N 13.11 E
Ustica, Isola di ❙ 70 38.42 N 13.11 E
Ust'-Il'a 88 50.25 N 113.41 E
Ust'ilga 88 55.00 N 105.02 E
Ust'-Ilimsk 88 58.03 N 102.43 E
Ust'-Ilimskoje Vodochranilišče ◎ 88 57.00 N 102.15 E
Ustilug 78 50.51 N 24.09 E
Ust'-Ilyč 24 62.32 N 56.41 E
Ustí nad Labem 54 50.40 N 14.02 E
Ustí nad Orlicí 30 49.58 N 16.24 E
Ustinovka, S.S.S.R. 78 47.57 N 32.32 E
Ustinovka, S.S.S.R. 83 48.49 N 38.34 E
Ust'-Išim 86 57.44 N 71.10 E
Ust'-Izes 86 55.56 N 76.56 E
Ust'-Ižora 265a 59.48 N 30.36 E
Ustja ≃ 24 61.30 N 42.36 E
Ust'-Javron'ga 24 63.25 N 44.21 E
Ustje, S.S.S.R. 76 60.49 N 32.49 E
Ustje, S.S.S.R. 76 59.38 N 39.43 E
Ustje, S.S.S.R. 80 57.47 N 39.47 E
Ustje, S.S.S.R. 82 55.16 N 36.20 E
Ustje, S.S.S.R. 86 57.46 N 94.42 E
Ustje-Grivas, Porog ⌐ 24 68.05 N 30.20 E
Ustje-Kirovskoje 76 58.45 N 35.55 E
Ustka 30 54.35 N 16.50 E
Ust'-K'achta 88 50.32 N 106.16 E
Ust'-Kajtym 86 57.23 N 95.28 E
Ust'-Kalmanka 86 52.07 N 83.19 E
Ust'-Kamčatsk 74 56.15 N 162.30 E
Ust'-Kamenogorsk 86 49.58 N 82.38 E
Ust'-Kan, S.S.S.R. 86 56.31 N 93.48 E

Ust'-Kan, S.S.S.R. 86 50.57 N 84.45 E
Ust'-Karenga 88 54.26 N 116.30 E
Ust'-Karsk 88 52.43 N 118.48 E
Ust'-Katav 86 54.56 N 58.10 E
Ust'-Kemčug 86 57.13 N 90.30 E
Ust'-Kil'mez' 80 56.57 N 50.30 E
Ust'-Kišert' 86 57.22 N 57.15 E
Ust'-Koksa 86 50.18 N 85.36 E
Ust'-Kulom 24 61.42 N 53.40 E
Ust'-Kurd'um 80 51.39 N 46.12 E
Ust'-Kurenga 86 57.27 N 75.34 E
Ust'-Kut 88 56.46 N 105.40 E
Ust'-Labinsk 78 45.13 N 39.42 E
Ust'-Lubija 88 52.36 N 120.16 E
Ust'-Luga 76 59.40 N 28.15 E
Ust'-Lyža 24 65.44 N 56.36 E
Ust'-Maja 74 60.25 N 134.32 E
Ust'-Manja 72 62.11 N 60.20 E
Ust'-Naryk 86 54.20 N 87.25 E
Ust'-Nemda 80 57.03 N 50.22 E
Ust'-Nera 74 64.34 N 143.12 E
Ust'-Niman 89 51.23 N 132.42 E
Ust'-N'ukža 88 56.34 N 121.37 E
Uštobe 86 45.16 N 78.00 E
Ust'-Omčug 74 61.09 N 149.38 E
Ust'-Ordynskij 88 52.48 N 104.45 E
Ust'-Ordynskij Bur'atskij Nacional'nyj Okrug □8 88 53.30 N 104.00 E
Ust'-Oz'ornaja 88 50.42 N 117.06 E
Ust'-Oz'ornoje 86 58.54 N 87.48 E
Ust'-Paden'ga 24 61.53 N 42.36 E
Ust'-Pečengskoje 76 59.47 N 42.37 E
Ust'-Pinega 24 64.11 N 41.56 E
Ust'-Pit 86 58.59 N 91.44 E
Ust'-Pogožje 80 49.28 N 44.38 E
Ustreka 76 58.38 N 34.33 E
Ust'-Reki 24 62.12 N 46.45 E
Ustroń 30 49.43 N 18.49 E
Ustrzyki Dolne 30 49.26 N 22.37 E
Ust'-Šara 76 60.13 N 33.57 E
Ust'-Ščerbedino 80 51.53 N 42.52 E
Ust'-Šlav'anka ✦8 265a 59.50 N 30.32 E
Ust'-Šonoša 24 61.10 N 41.18 E
Ust'-Tara 86 56.41 N 74.39 E
Ust'-Tarka 86 55.34 N 75.42 E
Ust'-Tašino 89 51.07 N 129.35 E
Ust'-Tygda 89 52.35 N 127.53 E
Ust'-Tym 86 59.26 N 80.08 E
Ust'-Tyrma 89 50.29 N 131.18 E
Ust'uckoje 76 58.32 N 35.20 E
Ust'-Uda 88 54.10 N 103.03 E
Ust'-Ulagan 86 50.38 N 87.58 E
Ust'-Umal'ta 89 51.39 N 133.18 E
Ust'-Undurga 89 53.07 N 118.04 E
Ust'-Unja 24 61.48 N 57.48 E
Ustupo Yantupo 246 9.27 N 78.34 W
Ust'-Urgal 89 51.09 N 132.33 E
Ust'urt, Plato ∧1 72 43.00 N 56.00 E
Ust'-Us 86 52.07 N 92.17 E
Ust'-Usa 24 65.59 N 56.54 E
Ust'-Uza 80 52.58 N 45.17 E
Ust'užna 76 58.51 N 36.26 E
Ust'-Vichoreva 88 56.47 N 101.24 E
Ust'-Voja 24 64.27 N 57.40 E
Ust'-Vyjskaja 24 62.57 N 46.41 E
Ust'-Vym' 24 62.14 N 50.24 E
Ust'-Zaza 88 53.10 N 111.40 E
Ust'-Žuja 88 58.48 N 118.12 E
Usuch-Čaj 84 41.25 N 47.53 E
Usuda 94 36.12 N 138.29 E
Usu-dake ∧ 92a 42.32 N 140.51 E
Usugli 88 52.39 N 115.16 E
Usui 96 33.34 N 130.42 E
Usuki 96 33.08 N 131.49 E
Usuki-wan C 96 33.10 N 131.52 E
Usulután 236 13.21 N 88.27 W
Usumacinta ≃ 232 18.24 N 92.38 W
Usumbura → Bujumbura 154 3.23 S 29.22 E
Ušumun 89 52.49 N 126.27 E
Ušur 80 57.47 N 52.58 E
Usuyōng 98 34.35 N 126.18 E
Usv'aty 76 55.45 N 30.45 E
Uta 71 39.17 N 8.57 E
Utah □3 178
Utah ≃ 200 39.30 N 111.30 W
Utah Lake ◎ 200 40.13 N 111.49 W
Utajärvi 26 64.45 N 26.23 E
Utamba 154 1.06 S 26.50 E
Utamboni ≃ 152 1.00 N 9.48 E
Utan 115b 8.24 S 117.07 E
Utano 94 34.28 N 135.59 E
Utapi 156 17.31 S 15.08 E
Utashinai 92a 43.31 N 142.03 E
Utata 88 50.51 N 102.45 E
'Utaybah, Buḥayrat al- ◎ 132 33.31 N 36.37 E
Ute 198 42.03 N 95.42 W
Ute Creek ≃ 196 35.21 N 103.50 W
Utegi 154 1.20 S 34.35 E
Utelle 62 43.55 N 7.15 E
Utembo ≃ 152 17.06 S 22.01 E
Ute Mountain Indian Reservation ✦4 200 37.10 N 108.35 W
Utena 76 55.30 N 25.36 E
Utengule 154 8.57 S 35.50 E
Ute Reservoir ◎1 196 35.21 N 103.31 W
Utersky potok ≃ 60 49.48 N 13.06 E
Utersum 30 54.43 N 8.24 E
Utery 60 49.57 N 13.01 E
Utete 154 7.59 S 38.47 E
Utevka 80 52.57 N 50.58 E
Utfort 263 51.28 N 6.38 E
Uthai Thani 110 15.22 N 100.03 E
Uthal 120 25.48 N 66.37 E
U Thong 110 14.22 N 99.54 E
Uthumphon Phisai 110 15.05 N 104.08 E
Utiariti 248 13.02 S 58.17 W
Utica, Ill., U.S. 216 41.21 N 89.01 W
Utica, Ind., U.S. 218 38.20 N 85.39 W
Utica, Kans., U.S. 198 38.39 N 100.10 W
Utica, Mich., U.S. 214 42.38 N 83.02 W
Utica, Miss., U.S. 194 32.07 N 90.37 W
Utica, Mo., U.S. 198 40.54 N 97.21 W
Utica, N.Y., U.S. 210 43.05 N 75.14 W
Utica, Ohio, U.S. 214 40.14 N 82.27 W
Utica, Pa., U.S. 214 41.26 N 79.58 W
Utica → Utique ⊥ 36 37.03 N 10.03 E
Utiel 34 39.34 N 1.12 W
Utik Lake ◎ 184 55.16 N 96.00 W
Utikoomak Indian Reserve ✦4 182 55.57 N 115.30 W
Utikuma Lake ◎ 182 55.50 N 115.25 W
Utila 236 16.06 N 86.54 W
Utila, Isla de ❙ 236 16.06 N 86.56 W
Utinga 287b 23.38 S 46.32 W
Utinga ≃ 255 12.34 S 41.20 W
Utique 36 37.03 N 10.03 E
Utique ⊥ 36 37.03 N 10.03 E
Utirik ❙1 148 11.15 N 169.48 E
Utlängan ❙ 26 56.01 N 15.47 E
Utl'ukskij Liman C1 78 46.15 N 35.12 E
Ut'ma 88 57.35 N 71.45 E
Utmānzai 123 34.11 N 71.46 E
Uto 92 32.41 N 130.40 E
Utö ❙ 40 58.56 N 18.16 E
Utokota 152 17.50 S 20.22 E
Utonde 152 1.56 N 9.49 E
Utopia, Austl. 162 22.14 S 134.33 E
Utopia, Tex., U.S. 196 29.37 N 99.32 W

Utorgoš 76 58.17 N 30.15 E
Utraula 124 27.19 N 82.25 E
Utrecht, Ned. 52 52.05 N 5.08 E
Utrecht, S. Afr. 158 27.38 S 30.20 E
Utrecht □4 52 52.05 N 5.08 E
Utrera 34 37.11 N 5.47 W
Utroja ≃ 76 57.23 N 28.09 E
Utsaladdy 224 48.15 N 122.30 W
Utsira 26 59.18 N 4.54 E
Utsjoki 24 69.53 N 27.00 E
Utsumi 96 34.21 N 133.17 E
Utsunomiya 94 36.33 N 139.52 E
Utta 80 46.23 N 46.01 E
Uttamapālaiyam 122 9.48 N 77.20 E
Uttaradit 110 17.38 N 100.06 E
Uttarkāshi 120 30.44 N 78.27 E
Uttarpara-Kotrung 272b 22.40 N 88.21 E
Uttar Pradesh □3 124 27.00 N 80.00 E
Uttendorf, Öst. 60 48.09 N 13.07 E
Uttendorf, Öst. 64 47.17 N 12.34 E
Uttenweiler 58 48.09 N 9.36 E
Ütterlingsen 263 51.15 N 7.45 E
Utting 60 48.02 N 11.05 E
Uttlesford □8 260 51.47 N 0.19 E
Uttoxeter 42 52.54 N 1.51 W
Utu 154 1.45 S 27.54 E
Utuado 240m 18.16 N 66.42 W
Utukok ≃ 180 70.04 N 162.18 W
Utunomiya → Utsunomiya 94 36.33 N 139.52 E
Utupua ❙ 14 11.16 S 166.29 E
Utva ≃ 80 51.28 N 52.40 E
Utzenstorf 58 47.08 N 7.33 E
Uudenmaan lääni □4 26 60.30 N 25.00 E
Uulu 76 58.17 N 24.35 E
Üür ≃ 88 50.18 N 101.54 E
Uusikaarlepyy (Nykarleby) 26 63.32 N 22.32 E
Uusikaupunki (Nystad) 26 60.48 N 21.25 E
Uusimaa ✦1 26 60.30 N 25.00 E
Uvá, Bra. 255 15.53 S 50.25 W
Uva, S.S.S.R. 80 56.59 N 52.13 E
Uvá ≃ 246 3.41 N 70.03 W
Uvalda 192 32.02 N 82.31 W
Uvalde 196 29.13 N 99.47 W
Uvaly 54 50.03 N 14.47 E
Uvån ≃ 40 60.01 N 13.37 E
Uvaroviči 76 52.36 N 30.44 E
Uvarovka 76 55.32 N 35.37 E
Uvarovo 80 51.59 N 42.15 E
Uvas Creek ≃ 226 36.58 N 121.33 W
Uvas Reservoir ◎1 226 37.05 N 121.42 W
Uvat 86 59.09 N 68.54 E
Uvdal 26 60.16 N 8.44 E
Uvéa ❙ 175f 20.27 S 166.36 E
Uvéa, Baie de C 175f 20.33 S 166.27 E
Uvéa, Île ❙ 175f 20.30 S 166.35 E
Uvel'skij 86 54.26 N 61.22 E
Uvernet 62 44.22 N 6.38 E
Uvero, Punta ≻ 241s 11.21 N 68.41 W
Uvinza 154 5.06 S 30.22 E
Uvira 154 3.24 S 29.08 E
Uvod' ≃ 80 56.26 N 41.26 E
Uvongo Beach 158 30.51 S 30.23 E
Uvs □4 86 47.00 N 90.30 E
Uvs Nuur ◎ 74 50.20 N 92.45 E
Uwa 96 33.20 N 132.30 E
Uwajima 96 33.13 N 132.34 E
Uwak 114 4.23 N 97.07 E
Uwa-kai ⊤2 96 33.15 N 132.15 E
Uwaumi 96 33.11 N 132.27 E
'Uwaybid, Jabal ∧ 142 30.06 N 32.09 E
Uwayl 140 8.46 N 27.24 E
'Uwaynāt 130 35.43 N 36.05 E
'Uwaynāt, Jabal al- ∧ 140 21.54 N 24.58 E
'Uwayriḍ, Ḥarrat al- ✦9 128 27.00 N 37.30 E
Uwchland 285 40.05 N 75.42 W
Uwi, Pulau ❙ 112 1.05 N 107.24 E
Uxbridge, Ont., Can. 212 44.06 N 79.07 W
Uxbridge, Mass., U.S. 207 42.05 N 71.38 W
Uxbridge ✦8 260 51.33 N 0.29 W
Uxmal 232 20.22 N 89.46 W
Uxmal ⊥ 232 20.22 N 89.46 W
Uyak 180 57.38 N 154.00 W
Uyak Bay C 180 57.36 N 153.57 W
Uyama 270 34.50 N 135.41 E
U-yin 110 22.53 N 95.13 E
Uyo 150 5.03 N 7.56 E
Uyuni 248 20.28 S 66.50 W
Uyuni, Salar de ≃ 248 20.20 S 67.42 W
Už (Uh) ≃, Eur. 30 48.34 N 22.00 E
Už ≃, S.S.S.R. 78 51.15 N 30.12 E
Uza ≃, S.S.S.R. 76 57.48 N 29.31 E
Uza ≃, S.S.S.R. 80 53.02 N 45.18 E
Užanicha 86 54.41 N 81.02 E
Uzas 86 57.04 N 76.55 E
Užava 76 57.14 N 21.27 E
Uzbekskaja Sovetskaja Socialističeskaja Respublika □3 72 41.00 N 64.00 E
Uzbek Soviet Socialist Republic → Uzbekskaja Sovetskaja Socialističeskaja Respublika □3 72 41.00 N 64.00 E
Uzda 76 53.27 N 27.13 E
Uzdin 38 45.12 N 20.38 E
Uzerche 32 45.26 N 1.34 E
Uzès 62 44.01 N 4.25 E
Uzgen 85 40.46 N 73.18 E
Užgorod 78 48.37 N 22.18 E
Užice → Titovo Užice 38 43.51 N 19.51 E
Uzin 78 49.50 N 30.24 E
Uzkij Lug 88 50.42 N 108.01 E
Uzkoje ✦8 265b 55.37 N 37.32 E
Uzlovaja 76 53.59 N 38.10 E
Uzmorje 80 51.15 N 45.55 E
Uznach 58 47.14 N 9.00 E
Užokskij, Pereval)(78 49.02 N 22.54 E
Uzola ≃ 80 56.32 N 43.38 E
Uz'ukovo 80 53.38 N 49.43 E
Üzümlü, Tür. 130 36.44 N 29.14 E
Üzümlü, Tür. 130 37.32 N 31.37 E
Uzun 85 38.22 N 68.03 E
Uzun Ada ❙ 130 38.28 N 26.42 E
Uzun-Agač 85 43.36 N 76.19 E
Uzunca ≃ 267b 40.58 N 28.50 E
Uzunköprü 130 41.16 N 26.41 E
Uzunkuduk 85 41.33 N 67.11 E
Uzunovo 82 54.32 N 38.37 E
Užur 86 55.20 N 89.50 E
Užventis 76 55.47 N 22.39 E

V

V □4 150 18.30 N 11.30 E
Vä 26 55.59 N 14.05 E
Vaajakoski 26 62.16 N 25.54 E
Vääksy 26 61.11 N 25.33 E
Vaal ≃ 158 29.04 S 23.38 E
Vaala 26 64.26 N 26.48 E
Vaaldam ✦6 158 26.55 S 28.40 E
Vaals 56 50.46 N 6.01 E
Vaalserberg ∧ 56 50.46 N 6.01 E
Vaalwater 156 24.20 S 28.03 E

Vaanta (Vanda) 26 60.16 N 25.03 E
Vaasa (Vasa) 26 63.06 N 21.36 E
Vaasan lääni □4 26 63.00 N 23.00 E
Vaassen 52 52.17 N 5.57 E
Vabalninkas 76 55.58 N 24.45 E
Vabkent 128 40.02 N 64.30 E
Vác 30 47.47 N 19.08 E
Vača 80 55.48 N 42.46 E
Vaca, Mount ∧ 226 38.24 N 122.06 W
Vacacaí ≃ 252 29.55 S 53.06 W
Vaca Key ❙ 220 24.43 N 81.04 W
Vacaria 252 28.30 S 50.56 W
Vacaria ≃, Bra. 255 21.55 S 53.59 W
Vacaria ≃, Bra. 255 16.39 S 42.45 W
Vacas, Arroyo de las ≃ 258 34.00 S 58.18 W
Vacaville 226 38.21 N 121.59 W
Vacca, Kaap ≻ 158 34.21 S 21.53 E
Vaccarès, Étang de C 62 43.32 N 4.34 E
Vach ≃ 74 60.45 N 76.45 E
Vacha 56 50.50 N 10.01 E
Vache, Île à ❙ 238 18.05 N 73.38 W
Vaches, Île aux ❙ 275a 45.41 N 73.40 W
Vaches, Rivière aux ≃ 206 46.02 N 72.46 W
Vachruševo 89 48.59 N 142.58 E
Vachruševo 83 48.10 N 38.46 E
Vachš ≃ 72 37.06 N 68.18 E
Vachšskij Chrebet ∧ 85 38.35 N 69.45 E
Vachtan 80 57.58 N 46.42 E
Vači 84 42.05 N 47.13 E
Vacía Talega, Punta ≻ 240m 18.27 N 65.54 W
Vacoas 157c 20.18 S 57.29 E
Vacov 60 49.09 N 13.45 E
Vad, S.S.S.R. 80 55.32 N 44.12 E
Vad, Sve. 40 60.02 N 15.39 E
Vad ≃ 80 54.33 N 42.37 E
Väddö ❙ 40 60.00 N 18.50 E
Vådeni 38 45.22 N 27.56 E
Vader 224 46.24 N 122.58 W
Vadheim 26 61.13 N 5.49 E
Vādi 272c 18.56 N 73.06 E
Vadino 76 55.16 N 33.16 E
Vadinsk 80 53.43 N 43.04 E
Vadnagar 120 23.47 N 72.38 E
Vado de Cedillos 200 31.05 N 105.50 W
Vado de Piedra 196 29.50 N 104.40 W
Vado Hondo 200 31.09 N 111.22 W
Vado Ligure 62 44.17 N 8.27 E
Vadret, Piz ∧ 58 46.41 N 9.57 E
Vadsbro 40 58.58 N 16.36 E
Vadsø 24 70.05 N 29.46 E
Vadstena 26 58.27 N 14.54 E
Vaduz 58 47.09 N 9.31 E
Vadvetjåkko Nationalpark ♦ 24 68.35 N 18.20 E
Væggerløse 41 54.42 N 11.56 E
Værøy ❙ 24 67.40 N 12.39 E
Vaga ≃ 24 62.48 N 42.56 E
Vagaj, S.S.S.R. 86 56.28 N 67.18 E
Vagaj, S.S.S.R. 86 57.56 N 69.01 E
Vagaj ≃ 86 57.59 N 69.01 E
Vågåmo 26 61.53 N 9.06 E
Vaganski Vrh ∧ 36 44.22 N 15.31 E
Vaggeryd 26 57.30 N 14.07 E
Vaglia 66 43.54 N 11.17 E
Vaglio Basilicata 68 40.40 N 15.55 E
Vagney 58 48.01 N 6.43 E
Vagnhärad 40 58.55 N 17.30 E
Vagues 258 34.19 S 59.26 W
Våh ≃ 30 47.55 N 18.00 E
Vahsel Bay C 9 77.48 S 34.39 W
Vaiano 66 43.58 N 11.07 E
Vaiau, Passe Џ 174s 17.52 S 149.11 W
Vaich, Loch ◎ 46 57.43 N 4.46 W
Vaiden 194 33.20 N 89.45 W
Vaiere, Baie C 174s 17.31 S 149.46 W
Vaigai ≃ 122 9.21 N 79.00 E
Vaihingen an der Enz 56 48.56 N 8.58 E
Vaihingen auf den Fildern 56 48.44 N 9.07 E
Vaihiria, Lac ◎ 174s 17.40 S 149.25 W
Vaijāpur 122 19.55 N 74.44 E
Vaikam 122 9.45 N 76.24 E
Väike-Maarja 76 59.08 N 26.15 E
Väike Pakri ❙ 76 59.20 N 24.00 E
Väike Väin Џ 76 58.32 N 23.18 E
Vail 198 42.04 N 95.12 W
Vaila ❙ 46a 60.12 N 1.37 W
Vailala ≃ 164 7.25 S 145.25 E
Vaileka 175g 17.23 S 178.09 E
Vail Lake ◎1 228 33.29 N 116.58 W
Vailly-sur-Aisne 50 49.25 N 3.31 E
Vailly-sur-Sauldre 50 47.27 N 2.39 E
Vail Mills 210 43.03 N 74.13 W
Vail Point ≻ 212 44.43 N 80.45 W
Vails Gate 210 41.27 N 74.04 W
Vainode 76 56.26 N 21.50 E
Vaiont, Lago di ◎ 64 46.21 N 10.21 E
Vaippār ≃ 122 9.01 N 78.17 E
Vair ≃ 58 48.27 N 5.42 E
Vairano Scalo 68 41.20 N 14.08 E
Vairao 174s 17.47 S 149.17 W
Vaires-sur-Marne 261 48.52 N 2.39 E
Vaison-la-Romaine 62 44.14 N 5.04 E
Vaitahu 174x 9.56 S 139.06 W
Vaïte 58 47.35 N 5.44 E
Vaitogi 174u 14.21 S 170.44 W
Vaitoto 174s 17.46 S 149.07 W
Vaitown 150 6.52 N 10.52 W
Vaitupu ❙ 14 7.28 S 178.41 E
Vaja ≃ 80 57.27 N 46.00 E
Vajgač 72 70.25 N 58.46 E
Vajgač, Ostrov ❙ 72 70.00 N 59.30 E
Vakaga □5 146 10.00 N 22.30 E
Vakaga ≃ 146 9.48 N 21.32 E
Vakhān ≃ 120 37.00 N 72.40 E
Vakhān ✦1 120 37.00 N 73.00 E
Vaklan 272c 19.07 N 73.06 E
Vaksdal 26 60.29 N 5.44 E
Vakš ≃ 89 45.57 N 133.45 E
Vala ≃ 80 56.59 N 51.16 E
Valaam 24 61.23 N 30.57 E
Vålådalen 26 63.10 N 12.57 E
Valadeces 196 26.14 N 98.40 W
Valadim 154 12.22 S 36.10 E
Valais (Wallis) □3 58 46.10 N 7.30 E
Valaisannes, Alpes ∧ 58 46.00 N 7.30 E
Val-Alain 206 46.24 N 71.45 W
Valamaz 80 57.35 N 52.07 E
Valandovo 38 41.19 N 22.34 E
Valangin 58 47.01 N 6.54 E
Valap 272c 19.03 N 73.08 E
Valašské Klobouky 30 49.08 N 18.01 E
Valašské Meziříčí 30 49.28 N 17.58 E
Valatie 210 42.25 N 73.41 W
Vala Ull 272c 19.02 N 73.07 E
Valbaai C 158 34.12 S 18.40 E
Valbella 58 46.45 N 9.33 E
Vålberg 26 59.24 N 13.12 E
Valbert 56 51.07 N 7.44 E
Valbo 40 60.40 N 17.04 E
Valbondione 64 46.02 N 10.00 E
Valbonnais 62 44.54 N 5.54 E
Valcanuta ✦8 267a 41.53 N 12.25 E
Valcēdrām 38 43.42 N 23.27 E
Valcheta 254 40.42 S 66.09 W
Valcheta, Arroyo ≃ 254 40.35 S 66.03 W
Valchetta ≃ 267a 41.58 N 12.30 E

Valchiusella 62 45.32 N 7.42 E
Valcivières 62 45.35 N 3.48 E
Valcourt 206 45.29 N 72.18 W
Valdagno 64 45.39 N 11.18 E
Valdahon 58 47.09 N 6.21 E
Valdai Hills → Valdajskaja Vozvyšennost' ∧2 24 57.00 N 33.30 E
Valdaj, S.S.S.R. 24 63.26 N 35.30 E
Valdaj, S.S.S.R. 76 57.59 N 33.14 E
Valdajskaja Vozvyšennost' ∧2 24 57.00 N 33.30 E
Valdarno ∨ 66 43.45 N 11.15 E
Valdavia ≃ 34 42.24 N 4.16 W
Val-David 206 46.01 N 74.12 W
Valdebeba, Arroyo de ≃ 266a 41.23 N 2.10 E
Valdeblore 62 44.04 N 7.12 E
Val-de-Cães 250 1.23 S 48.29 W
Valdecañas, Embalse de ◎1 34 39.45 N 5.30 W
Valdelândia 255 15.11 S 50.02 W
Val-de-Marne □5 261 48.47 N 2.29 E
Valdemārpils 76 57.22 N 22.35 E
Valdemarsvik 26 58.12 N 16.36 E
Valdepeñas 34 38.46 N 3.23 W
Valderaduey ≃ 34 41.31 N 5.42 W
Valderas 34 42.05 N 5.27 W
Valderice 70 38.03 N 12.38 E
Valderrama 116 11.00 N 122.08 E
Valderrobres 34 40.53 N 0.09 E
Valders 190 44.09 N 87.53 W
Valdés, Península ≻1 254 42.30 S 64.00 W
Val-des-Bois 188 45.54 N 75.35 W
Valdese 192 35.44 N 81.34 W
Valdes Island ❙ 224 49.04 N 123.38 W
Valdez, Ec. 246 1.15 N 79.00 W
Valdez, Alaska, U.S. 180 61.07 N 146.16 W
Valdieri 62 44.17 N 7.24 E
Val-d'Isère 62 45.27 N 6.59 E
Valdivia, Chile 254 39.48 S 73.14 W
Valdivia, Col. 246 7.11 N 75.27 W
Valdobbiadene 64 45.54 N 12.00 E
Valdoie 58 47.40 N 6.51 E
Val-d'Oise □5 50 49.10 N 2.10 E
Val-d'Or 190 48.07 N 77.47 W
Valdorf 52 52.09 N 8.51 E
Valdosta 192 30.50 N 83.17 W
Valdoviño 34 43.36 N 8.08 W
Valdres ∨ 26 60.55 N 9.10 E
Valdurna (Durnholz) 64 46.44 N 11.26 E
Vale, Guer. 43b 49.29 N 2.31 W
Vale, Oreg., U.S. 202 43.59 N 117.15 W
Valea lui Mihai 38 47.31 N 22.09 E
Vale de Lobos 266c 38.49 N 9.17 W
Valeene 218 38.26 N 86.24 W
Valeggio sul Mincio 64 45.21 N 10.44 E
Valehouse Reservoir ◎1 262 53.29 N 1.57 W
Valemount 182 52.50 N 119.15 W
Valença, Bra. 255 13.22 S 39.05 W
Valença, Bra. 256 22.15 S 43.43 W
Valença, Port. 34 42.02 N 8.38 W
Valença do Piauí 250 6.24 S 41.45 W
Valençay 50 47.09 N 1.34 E
Valence → Valencia, Esp. 34 39.28 N 0.22 W
Valence, Fr. 62 44.56 N 4.54 E
Valencia, Esp. 34 39.28 N 0.22 W
Valencia, Hond. 236 14.47 N 85.18 W
Valencia, Pil. 116 7.57 N 125.03 E
Valencia, Pa., U.S. 214 40.40 N 79.59 W
Valencia, Ven. 246 10.11 N 68.00 W
Valencia □9 34 39.30 N 0.40 W
Valencia, Golfo de C 34 39.50 N 0.30 E
Valencia, Lago de ◎ 246 10.15 N 67.45 W
Valencia, Quebrada ≃ 286c 10.30 N 66.46 W
Valencia de Alcántata 34 39.25 N 7.14 W
Valencia de Don Juan 34 42.18 N 5.31 W
Valencia Island ❙ 48 51.52 N 10.20 W
Valenciennes 50 50.21 N 3.32 E
Valenii-de-Munte 38 45.12 N 26.03 E
Valensole 62 43.50 N 5.59 E
Valentano 66 42.34 N 11.49 E
Valente 250 11.34 S 39.27 W
Valentigney 58 47.28 N 6.50 E
Valentin 89 43.08 N 134.17 E
Valentín Alsina ✦8 288 34.40 S 58.25 W
Valentine, Nebr., U.S. 198 42.52 N 100.33 W
Valentine, Tex., U.S. 196 30.34 N 104.29 W
Valentine Mountain ∧ 224 48.32 N 123.56 W
Valentinovka 265b 55.55 N 37.56 E
Valenton 261 48.45 N 2.28 E
Valenza 62 45.01 N 8.38 E
Valenzano 68 41.02 N 16.53 E
Valepp 64 47.37 N 11.53 E
Våler 26 60.40 N 11.50 E
Valera 246 9.19 N 70.37 W
Valérien, Mont ∧2 261 48.53 N 2.13 E
Vale Royal □8 262 53.17 N 2.37 W
Valets, Lac ◎ 190 48.32 N 76.30 W
Valette, La → Valletta 36 35.54 N 14.31 E
Valfabbrica 66 43.09 N 12.36 E
Valflaunès 62 43.48 N 3.52 E
Valfurva 64 46.27 N 10.25 E
Valfurva ∨ 64 46.26 N 10.26 E
Valga 76 57.47 N 26.02 E
Valgejõgi ≃ 76 59.35 N 25.42 E
Valgorge 62 44.35 N 4.07 E
Valgrisanche 62 45.38 N 7.04 E
Valguarnera Caropepe 70 37.30 N 14.23 E
Valhalla, S. Afr. 158 25.49 S 28.08 E
Valhalla, N.Y., U.S. 210 41.04 N 73.46 W
Valhalla, Lake ◎ 276 40.56 N 74.22 W
Válicka ≃ 61 46.52 N 16.53 E
Valiente, Península ≻1 236 9.05 N 81.51 W
Valiente, Punta ≻ 236 9.11 N 81.55 W
Valier, Ill., U.S. 194 38.01 N 89.03 W
Valier, Mont., U.S. 202 48.18 N 112.15 W
Valier, Pa., U.S. 214 40.55 N 79.03 W
Valili ∧ 175g 16.39 S 179.10 E
Valinda 280 34.03 N 117.57 W
Valinhos 256 22.57 S 47.01 W
Valir 130 38.48 N 40.41 E
Valjevo 38 44.16 N 19.53 E
Valka 76 57.46 N 26.00 E
Valkeakoski 26 61.16 N 24.02 E
Valkenburg 56 50.52 N 5.50 E
Valkenswaard 52 51.21 N 5.28 E
Valki, S.S.S.R. 78 49.50 N 35.37 E
V'alki, S.S.S.R. 82 55.39 N 38.05 E
Valkininkas 76 54.21 N 24.50 E
Valla 40 59.02 N 16.23 E
Vallabhbhai Patel Stadium ♦ 272c 18.59 N 72.49 E
Valladares 196 26.53 N 100.37 W
Valladolid, Ec. 246 4.33 S 79.08 W
Valladolid, Esp. 34 41.39 N 4.43 W
Valladolid, Méx. 232 20.41 N 88.12 W
Vallage ✦1 58 48.24 N 5.00 E
Vallåkra 41 55.58 N 12.52 E
Vallarsa 64 45.47 N 11.07 E
Vallata 68 41.02 N 15.15 E
Vallauris 62 43.35 N 7.03 E

Vallco Fashion Park ✦9 282 37.19 N 122.01 W
Valldal 26 62.20 N 7.21 E
Vall de Uxó 34 39.49 N 0.14 W
Valldoreix 266d 41.28 N 2.04 E
Valle, Esp. 34 43.14 N 4.18 W
Valle, It. 64 46.04 N 10.25 E
Valle, S.S.S.R. 76 56.30 N 24.44 E
Valle □5 236 13.30 N 87.35 W
Valle, Arroyo ≃ 226 37.39 N 121.54 W
Valle, Lake del ◎1 226 37.35 N 121.43 W
Vallecas ✦8 266a 40.23 N 3.37 W
Valle Castellana 66 42.44 N 13.29 E
Vallecillo 196 26.40 N 99.58 W
Vallecito 226 38.07 N 120.27 W
Vallecitos 200 36.30 N 106.01 W
Vallecitos Creek ≃ 282 37.36 N 121.53 W
Vallecorsa 66 41.27 N 13.24 E
Valle Crucis Abby ⊥1 42 52.59 N 3.12 W
Valle d'Aosta □4 62 45.45 N 7.25 E
Valle de Bravo 234 19.11 N 100.08 W
Valle de Guadalupe 234 21.00 N 102.37 W
Valle de Guanape 246 9.54 N 65.41 W
Valle de Juárez 234 19.53 N 102.51 W
Valle de la Pascua 246 9.13 N 66.00 W
Valle del Cauca □5 246 3.45 N 76.30 W
Valle de Olivos 232 27.12 N 106.17 W
Valle de San José 234 23.20 N 98.24 W
Valle de Santiago 234 20.23 N 101.12 W
Valle de Zaragoza 232 27.28 N 105.49 W
Valle di Cadore 64 46.24 N 12.20 E
Valle di Sotto 64 46.25 N 10.21 E
Valledolmo 70 37.45 N 13.49 E
Valledupar 246 10.29 N 73.15 W
Valle Edén 252 31.50 S 56.09 W
Vallefiorita 68 38.46 N 16.27 E
Vallegrande 248 18.29 S 64.06 W
Valle Hermoso, Arg. 252 31.07 S 64.29 W
Valle Hermoso, Méx. 196 25.39 N 97.52 W
Vallehermoso, Pil. 116 10.20 N 123.19 E
Vallejo 226 38.07 N 122.14 W
Valle Lomellina 62 45.09 N 8.40 E
Vallelunga Pratameno 70 37.41 N 13.50 E
Valle Mosso 62 45.38 N 8.09 E
Vällen ◎ 40 60.03 N 18.20 E
Vallenar 252 28.35 S 70.46 W
Vallendar 56 50.24 N 7.37 E
Vallensbæk 41 55.38 N 12.22 E
Vallentuna 40 59.32 N 18.05 E
Vallepietra 66 41.55 N 13.14 E
Valleraugue 62 44.05 N 3.38 E
Valle Redondo 204 32.31 N 116.46 W
Vallerotonda 66 41.33 N 13.55 E
Valley 66 49.12 N 5.55 E
Valles → Ciudad de Valles 234 21.59 N 99.01 W
Vallet 32 47.10 N 1.16 W
Valletta 36 35.54 N 14.31 E
Valley 198 41.19 N 96.21 W
Valley Bend 188 38.46 N 79.56 W
Valley Center, Calif., U.S. 228 33.13 N 117.02 W
Valley Center, Kans., U.S. 198 37.50 N 97.22 W
Valley City, N. Dak., U.S. 198 46.55 N 97.59 W
Valley City, Ohio, U.S. 214 41.14 N 81.56 W
Valley Cottage 210 41.07 N 73.57 W
Valley Creek ≃, Pa., U.S. 285 39.58 N 75.40 W
Valley Creek ≃, Pa., U.S. 285 40.06 N 75.28 W
Valley Creek ≃, Tex., U.S. 196 31.43 N 100.02 W
Valleydale 280 34.06 N 117.56 W
Valley Falls, Kans., U.S. 198 39.21 N 95.28 W
Valley Falls, N.Y., U.S. 210 42.54 N 73.34 W
Valley Falls, R.I., U.S. 207 41.54 N 71.24 W
Valley Farms 200 32.59 N 111.27 W
Valleyfield, Newf., Can. 186 49.08 N 53.37 W
Valleyfield, Qué., Can. 206 45.15 N 74.08 W
Valley Forge 208 40.06 N 75.28 W
Valley Forge National Historical Park ♦ 208 40.06 N 75.27 W
Valley Grove 214 40.05 N 80.34 W
Valley Head, Ala., U.S. 194 34.34 N 85.37 W
Valley Head, W. Va., U.S. 188 38.33 N 80.02 W
Valley Home 226 37.50 N 120.55 W
Valley Mede 284b 39.17 N 76.50 W
Valley Mills 222 31.39 N 97.28 W
Valley of Desolation National Monument ⊥ 158 32.17 S 24.30 E
Valley of Fire State Park ♦ 204 36.26 N 114.30 W
Valley of the Kings ⊥ 140 25.45 N 32.37 E
Valley Park 219 38.33 N 90.30 W
Valley Plaza ✦9 280 34.11 N 118.24 W
Valley Springs, Calif., U.S. 226 38.12 N 120.50 W
Valley Springs, S. Dak., U.S. 198 43.35 N 96.28 W
Valley Station 194 38.06 N 85.52 W
Valley Stream 210 40.40 N 73.42 W
Valley Stream ≃ 276 40.39 N 73.45 W
Valley Stream State Park ♦ 276 40.41 N 73.42 W
Valleyview, Alta., Can. 182 55.04 N 117.17 W
Valley View, Ill., U.S. 216 41.50 N 88.03 W
Valley View, Ohio, U.S. 279a 41.23 N 81.37 W
Valley View, Pa., U.S. 210 40.39 N 76.32 W
Valley View, Tex., U.S. 196 33.29 N 97.10 W
Valley View Park 228 34.13 N 117.20 W
Valleywood 218 39.41 N 84.03 W
Vallgrund ❙ 26 63.12 N 21.14 E
Valli del Pasubio 64 45.41 N 11.15 E
Vallières 58 45.54 N 5.56 E
Vallimanca, Arroyo ≃ 252 35.40 S 60.02 W
Vallio 64 45.38 N 10.23 E
Vallirana 266d 41.23 N 1.56 E
Vallø 41 55.24 N 12.15 E
Vallo della Lucania 68 40.14 N 15.17 E
Valloire 62 45.10 N 6.26 E
Vallombrosa 64 43.44 N 11.32 E
Vallonia 218 38.51 N 86.06 W
Vallon-Pont-d'Arc 62 44.24 N 4.24 E
Vallorbe 58 46.43 N 6.22 E
Vallorcine 58 46.02 N 6.56 E
Vallouise 62 44.51 N 6.29 E
Vallromanas 266d 41.32 N 2.18 E
Valls 34 41.17 N 1.15 E
Valluga ∧ 58 47.09 N 10.12 E
Vallvidrera ✦8 266d 41.25 N 2.07 E
Vallvidrera, Riera de ≃ 266d 41.25 N 2.01 E
Val-Marie 184 49.14 N 107.44 W
Valmaseda 34 43.12 N 3.12 W
Valmeyer 219 38.18 N 90.19 W
Valmiera 76 57.33 N 25.24 E
Valmondois 261 49.06 N 2.12 E

≃ River — Fluss — Rio — Rivière — Rio
⊤ Canal — Kanal — Canal — Canal — Canal
⌐ Waterfall, Rapids — Wasserfall, Stromschnellen — Cascada, Rápidos — Chute d'eau, Rapides — Cascata, Rápidos
Џ Strait — Meeresstrasse — Estrecho — Détroit — Estreito
C Bay, Gulf — Bucht, Golf — Bahía, Golfo — Baie, Golfe — Baía, Golfo
◎ Lake, Lakes — See, Seen — Lago, Lagos — Lac, Lacs — Lago, Lagos
≛ Swamp — Sumpf — Pantano — Marais — Pântano
❖ Ice Features, Glacier — Eis- und Gletscherformen — Accidentes Glaciales — Formes glaciaires — Acidentes Glaciares
≂ Other Hydrographic Features — Andere Hydrographische Objekte — Otros Elementos Hidrográficos — Autres données hydrographiques — Outros Elementos Hidrográficos

✦ Submarine Features — Untermeerische Objekte — Accidentes Submarinos — Formes de relief sous-marin — Acidentes Submarinos
□ Political Unit — Politische Einheit — Unidad Política — Entité politique — Unidade Política
▼ Cultural Institution — Kulturelle Institution — Institución Cultural — Institution culturelle — Instituição Cultural
⊥ Historical Site — Historische Stätte — Sitio Histórico — Site historique — Sitio Histórico
♦ Recreational Site — Erholungs- und Ferienort — Sitio de Recreo — Centre de loisirs — Sitio de Lazer
⊠ Airport — Flughafen — Aeropuerto — Aéroport — Aeroporto
■ Military Installation — Militäranlage — Instalación Militar — Installation militaire — Instalação Militar
✦ Miscellaneous — Verschiedenes — Misceláneo — Divers — Miscelânea

Valmont 50 49.44 N 0.31 E
Valmontone 66 41.46 N 12.57 E
Valmy 56 49.05 N 4.46 E
Valognes 32 49.31 N 1.28 W
Valois 210 42.32 N 76.53 W
Valois, Baie de ⊂ 275a 45.26 N 73.47 W
Valok 78 45.47 N 34.57 E
Valona
→ Vlorë 38 40.27 N 19.30 E
Valongo 34 41.11 N 8.30 W
Valoria la Buena 34 41.48 N 4.32 W
Valparai 122 10.22 N 76.58 E
Valparaíso, Bra. 255 21.13 S 50.51 W
Valparaíso, Chile 252 33.02 S 71.38 W
Valparaíso, Méx. 234 22.46 N 103.34 W
Valparaiso, Fla., U.S. 194 30.29 N 86.30 W
Valparaiso, Ind., U.S. 216 41.28 N 87.03 W
Valparaiso, Nebr., U.S. 198 41.05 N 96.50 W
Valparaíso ≃ 234 22.33 N 103.39 W
Valpelline ∨ 62 45.50 N 7.25 E
Valpolicella •[1] 64 45.25 N 10.52 E
Valpovo 38 45.39 N 18.26 E
Valprato Soana 62 45.31 N 7.33 E
Valréas 62 44.23 N 4.59 E
Valrico 220 27.57 N 82.16 W
Val Roveto ∨ 66 41.52 N 13.30 E
Vals ≃ 158 27.23 S 26.30 E
Vals, Tanjung ≻ 164 8.26 S 137.38 E
Val-Saint-Michel 206 46.52 N 71.27 W
Valsequillo, Presa ⊜[1] 234 18.55 N 98.10 W
Valserine ≃ 58 46.06 N 5.50 E
Valserrhein ≃ 58 46.42 N 9.10 E
Valsertal ∨ 58 46.37 N 9.10 E
Valsetz 202 44.50 N 123.39 W
Valsinni 68 40.10 N 16.26 E
Valsjöbyn 26 64.04 N 14.08 E
Valskog 40 59.27 N 15.57 E
Vals-les-Bains 62 44.40 N 4.22 E
Vals Platz 58 46.37 N 9.11 E
Vals-près-le-Puy 62 45.01 N 3.52 E
Valstagna 64 45.51 N 11.39 E
Valstruisleegte 158 33.05 S 23.28 E
Val-Suzon 58 47.25 N 4.54 E
Valtellina ∨ 64 46.11 N 9.55 E
Valthermond 52 52.53 N 6.59 E
Valtice 61 48.44 N 16.45 E
Valtierrilla 234 20.32 N 101.08 W
Valtimo 26 63.40 N 28.48 E
Valtorta 58 45.59 N 9.32 E
Valtournanche 62 45.53 N 7.37 E
Valujec 76 52.46 N 33.23 E
Valujevka 80 46.44 N 43.43 E
Valujevo 265b 55.35 N 37.21 E
Valujki 78 50.13 N 38.08 E
Valvasone 64 45.59 N 12.52 E
Valverde 148 27.48 N 17.55 W
Valverde del Camino 34 37.34 N 6.45 W
Val Verde Park 228 34.27 N 118.40 W
Valyermo 228 34.26 N 117.50 W
Vamba ≃ 152 7.27 S 14.17 E
Vamdrup 41 55.25 N 9.17 E
Våmhus 26 61.08 N 14.28 E
Vamizi, Ilha I 154 11.02 S 40.40 E
Vammala 26 61.20 N 22.54 E
Vamsadhāra ≃ 122 18.21 N 84.08 E
Van, Tür. 128 38.28 N 43.20 E
Van, Pa., U.S. 214 41.19 N 79.40 W
Van, Tex., U.S. 222 32.31 N 95.38 W
Van □[4] 84 39.00 N 43.45 E
Vanajanselkä ⊜ 26 61.09 N 24.15 E
Vanak 267d 35.45 N 51.23 E
Van Alstyne 196 33.25 N 96.35 W
Vanån ≃ 40 60.31 N 14.14 E
Vananda 182 49.45 N 124.33 W
Vanapa ≃ 164 9.05 S 147.10 E
Vanault-les-Dames 56 48.51 N 4.46 E
Vanavana I[1] 14 20.47 S 139.09 W
Vanavara 74 60.22 N 102.16 E
Van Buren, Ark., U.S. 194 35.26 N 94.21 W
Van Buren, Ind., U.S. 216 40.37 N 85.30 W
Van Buren, Maine, U.S. 186 47.09 N 67.56 W
Van Buren, Mo., U.S. 194 37.00 N 91.01 W
Van Buren, Ohio, U.S. 216 41.08 N 83.39 W
Van Buren □[6] 216 42.14 N 86.04 W
Van Buren Point 214 42.27 N 79.25 W
Vanč 85 38.23 N 71.26 E
Vanč ≃ 85 38.18 N 71.19 E
Vance Air Force Base ■ 196 36.21 N 97.55 W
Vanceboro 188 45.34 N 67.26 W
Vanceburg 218 38.36 N 83.19 W
Vancleave 194 30.32 N 88.46 W
Van Cortlandt Park ♠ 276 40.54 N 73.53 W
Van Cortlandtville 210 41.19 N 73.54 W
Vancouver, B.C., Can. 182 49.16 N 123.07 W
Vancouver, Wash., U.S. 224 45.39 N 122.40 W
Vancouver, Cape ≻, Austl. 162 35.01 S 118.12 E
Vancouver, Cape ≻, Alaska, U.S. 180 60.33 N 165.27 W
Vancouver, Mount ∧ 180 60.20 N 139.40 W
Vancouver International Airport ⊠ 224 48.39 N 123.26 W
Vancouver Island I 182 49.45 N 126.00 W
Vancouver Island Ranges ⋏ 182 49.25 N 125.25 W
Vancouver Lake ⊜ 224 45.41 N 122.44 W
Van Daalen ≃ 164 3.05 S 138.09 E
Vandalia, Ill., U.S. 219 38.58 N 89.06 W
Vandalia, Mich., U.S. 216 41.55 N 85.55 W
Vandalia, Mo., U.S. 219 39.19 N 91.29 W
Vandalia, Ohio, U.S. 218 39.53 N 84.12 W
Vandam 84 40.57 N 47.57 E
Vandavāsi 122 12.30 N 79.37 E
Vandekerckhove Lake ⊜ 184 57.02 N 101.25 W
Vandel 41 55.42 N 9.13 E
Vandenberg Air Force Base ■ 204 34.43 N 120.33 W
Van den Bosch, Tanjung ≻ 164 4.06 S 132.55 E
Vandenesse 58 47.98 N 4.37 E
Vanderbijlpark 158 26.42 S 27.54 E
Vanderbilt, Mich., U.S. 190 45.09 N 84.40 W
Vanderbilt, Tex., U.S. 196 28.49 N 96.37 W
Vanderbilt Mansion National Historic Site ⊥ 210 41.47 N 73.56 W
Vanderbilt Museum ◇ 276 40.54 N 73.22 W
Vandercook Lake 216 42.12 N 84.24 W
Vandergrift 214 40.36 N 79.34 W
Vanderhoof 182 54.01 N 124.01 W
Van der Kloof Dam •[6] 158 30.00 S 24.46 E
Vanderlin Island I 164 15.44 S 137.02 E
Vandervoort 194 34.23 N 94.22 W
Van Diemen, Cape ≻, Austl. 164 11.10 S 130.23 E
Van Diemen, Cape ≻, Austl. 164 16.31 S 139.41 E
Van Diemen Gulf ⊂ 164 11.50 S 132.00 E
Vandling 210 41.38 N 75.29 W
Vandoies (Vintl) 64 46.49 N 11.43 E
Vändra 76 58.39 N 25.02 E
Van Duzen ≃ 204 40.33 N 124.08 W
Vandúzi 156 18.57 S 33.16 E
Vandžiogala 76 55.07 N 23.58 E
Vanegas 234 23.51 N 100.52 W
Vänern ⊜ 26 58.55 N 13.30 E
Vänersborg 26 58.22 N 12.19 E
Van Etten 210 42.12 N 76.33 W
Vang, Mount ∧ 9 73.56 S 68.39 W
Vanga 154 4.39 S 39.13 E
Vangaindrano 157b 23.21 S 47.36 E
Vängelälven ≃ 26 63.41 N 16.25 E
Van Gölü ⊜ 128 38.33 N 42.46 E
Vangsnes 26 61.11 N 6.38 E
Vanguard 184 49.55 N 107.20 W
Vangunu I 175e 8.38 S 158.00 E
Vangunu, Mount ∧ 175e 8.42 S 158.00 E
Van Horn 196 31.03 N 104.50 W
Van Horne 190 42.01 N 92.05 W
Van Hornesville 210 42.54 N 74.50 W
Vani 84 42.06 N 42.30 E
Vanier 212 45.26 N 75.40 W
Vanikoro I 14 11.39 S 166.54 E
Vaniköy •[8] 267b 41.04 N 29.04 E
Vanimo 164 2.40 S 141.20 E
Vanino 89 49.05 N 140.15 E
Vānīvilāsa Sāgara ⊜[1] 122 13.52 N 76.26 E
Vāniyambādi 122 12.41 N 78.37 E
Vankarem 180 67.51 N 175.50 W
Vankarem ≃ 180 68.10 N 177.40 W
Vankarem, Laguna ⊂ 180 67.40 N 176.00 W
Vankaremskaja Nizmennost' ≍ 180 67.30 N 176.00 W
Vankleek Hill 206 45.31 N 74.39 W
Vanlay 50 48.02 N 4.01 E
Van Lear 192 37.46 N 82.46 W
Vanlue 216 40.59 N 83.29 W
Vanna I 24 70.09 N 19.51 E
Vännäs 26 63.55 N 19.45 E
Vanndale 194 35.19 N 90.46 W
Vanne ≃ 50 48.12 N 3.16 E
Vanne et du Loing, Aqueduc de la ≖[1] 261 48.36 N 2.26 E
Vannes 32 47.39 N 2.46 W
Vannes-sur-Cosson 50 47.43 N 2.13 E
Van-ninh (Van-gia) 110 12.42 N 109.14 E
Van Norman Lakes ⊜[1] 228 34.18 N 118.28 W
Vannovka 85 42.32 N 70.21 E
Van Nuys •[8] 228 34.11 N 118.26 W
Van Nuys Airport ⊠ 280 34.12 N 118.29 W
Van Nuys-Sherman Oaks Park ♠ 280 34.10 N 118.27 W
Vanoi ≃ 64 46.06 N 11.45 E
Vanoise, Massif de la ⋏ 62 45.20 N 6.40 E
Vanoise, Parc National de la ♠ 62 45.20 N 6.45 E
Van Ormer 214 40.41 N 78.30 W
Van-phong, Vung ⊂ 110 12.33 N 109.18 E
Vanport 214 40.41 N 80.20 W
Van Reenen 158 28.22 S 29.24 E
Van Reenen's Plaats 158 30.55 S 21.14 E
Van Rees, Pegunungan ⋏ 164 2.35 S 138.15 E
Vanrhyn Dam •[6] 273d 26.09 S 28.21 E
Vanrhynsdorp 158 31.36 S 18.44 E
Vanrook 166 16.57 S 141.57 E
Vansant 192 37.14 N 82.06 W
Van Saun Mill Brook ≃ 276 40.55 N 74.03 W
Vansbro 40 60.31 N 14.13 E
Van Sciver Lake ⊜ 285 40.09 N 74.48 W
Van Sickle Island I 282 38.04 N 121.53 W
Vansittart Island I 176 65.50 N 84.00 W
Vansjön ⊜ 40 59.59 N 16.57 E
Vanskoje 76 58.56 N 36.52 E
Vanstadensrus 158 29.59 S 27.02 E
Vantaa ≃ 26 60.13 N 24.59 E
Vanthali 120 21.29 N 70.20 E
Vanua Lava I 175f 13.48 S 167.28 E
Vanua Levu I 175g 16.33 S 179.15 E
Vanua Mbalavu I 175g 17.40 S 178.57 W
Vanua Vatu I 175g 18.22 S 179.16 E
Van Vleck 222 29.01 N 95.53 W
Van Voorhis 279b 40.10 N 79.58 W
Van Wert 216 40.52 N 84.35 W
Van Wert □[6] 216 40.52 N 84.35 W
Van Winkle 194 32.17 N 90.15 W
Vanwyksdorp 158 33.46 S 21.28 E
Vanwyksvlei 158 30.18 S 21.49 E
Vanzaghello 266b 45.35 N 8.47 E
Vanzago 266b 45.32 N 9.00 E
Van Zandt □[6] 222 32.35 N 95.50 W
Vanzylsrus 158 26.52 S 22.04 E
Vao 175f 22.39 S 167.32 E
Vapn'arka 78 48.32 N 28.44 E
Vaprio d'Adda 62 45.35 N 9.31 E
Vaqueros Creek ≃ 226 36.16 N 121.20 W
Var □[5] 62 43.30 N 6.20 E
Var ≃ 62 43.39 N 7.12 E
Vara 26 58.16 N 12.57 E
Vara ≃ 64 44.09 N 9.53 E
Vara, Pico da ∧ 148 32.45 N 16.56 W
Varada ≃ 122 14.55 N 75.40 E
Varadero 240p 23.09 N 81.16 W
Varades 32 47.23 N 1.02 W
Varages 62 43.36 N 5.58 E
Varaita ≃ 62 44.49 N 7.36 E
Varaita, Valle ∨ 62 44.35 N 7.10 E
Varaklāni 76 56.37 N 26.44 E
Varallo, It. 62 45.49 N 8.15 E
Varallo, It. 266b 45.40 N 8.38 E
Varāmīn 128 35.20 N 51.39 E
Vārānasi (Benares) 124 25.20 N 83.00 E
Vārānasi □[5] 124 25.20 N 83.00 E
Varandej 24 68.48 N 58.00 E
Varangerfjorden ⊂[2] 24 70.00 N 30.00 E
Varangerhalvøya ≻[1] 24 70.25 N 29.30 E
Varangéville 56 48.38 N 6.19 E
Varano, Lago Di ⊂ 68 41.53 N 15.45 E
Varano de'Melegari 64 44.41 N 10.01 E
Varapodio 68 38.19 N 15.59 E
Varaždin 36 46.19 N 16.20 E
Varazze 62 44.22 N 8.34 E
Varberg 26 57.06 N 12.15 E
Varces 62 45.05 N 5.41 E
Varciche 84 42.08 N 42.43 E
Vardak □[4] 120 34.15 N 68.00 E
Vardaman 194 33.47 N 89.10 W
Vardar (Axiós) ≃ 38 40.31 N 22.43 E
Varde 26 55.38 N 8.29 E
Vardenik 84 40.08 N 45.27 E
Vardenisskij Chrebet ⋏ 84 39.58 N 45.25 E
Vardhoúsia Óri ⋏ 38 38.44 N 22.07 E
Vardø 24 70.21 N 31.02 E
Varedo 62 45.36 N 9.09 E
Varegovo 80 57.47 N 39.17 E
Varel 52 53.22 N 8.10 E
Varela 252 34.07 S 66.27 W
Varėna 76 54.13 N 24.34 E
Varengeville-sur-Mer 50 49.55 N 0.59 E
Varenikovskaja 78 45.07 N 37.37 E
Varenna 58 46.01 N 9.17 E
Varenne ≃ 50 49.53 N 1.08 E
Varennes, Qué., Can. 206 45.41 N 73.26 W
Varennes, Fr. 50 50.03 N 2.32 E
Varennes, Îles de II 275a 45.40 N 73.27 W
Varennes-en-Argonne 56 49.14 N 5.02 E
Varennes-Jarcy 261 48.41 N 2.34 E
Varennes-Saint-Sauveur 58 46.29 N 5.15 E
Varennes-sur-Allier 32 46.19 N 3.24 E
Varennes-sur-Amance 58 47.54 N 5.37 E
Varenovka 83 47.18 N 39.02 E
Vareš 38 44.09 N 18.19 E
Varese 62 45.48 N 8.48 E
Varese □[4] 58 45.55 N 8.45 E
Varese, Lago di ⊜ 62 45.49 N 8.45 E
Varese Ligure 62 44.22 N 9.37 E
Varèze ≃ 62 45.25 N 4.45 E
Varfolomejevka, S.S.S.R. 80 50.01 N 48.12 E
Varfolomejevka, S.S.S.R. 89 44.18 N 133.30 E
Vårgårda 26 58.02 N 12.48 E
Vargas □[5] 286c 10.34 N 66.52 W
Vargaši 86 55.23 N 65.48 E
Vargem 256 22.53 S 46.25 W
Vargem, Riacho da ≃ 250 8.42 S 39.09 W
Vargem Alegre 256 22.30 S 43.55 W
Vargem do Laje 256 22.08 S 44.49 W
Vargem Grande, Bra. 250 3.33 S 43.56 W
Vargem Grande, Bra. 256 22.59 S 45.17 W
Vargem Grande •[8] 287a 22.59 S 43.29 W
Vargem Grande ≃ 256 22.17 S 45.40 W
Vargem Grande do Sul 256 21.50 S 46.53 W
Varginha 256 21.33 S 45.26 W
Vargön 26 58.22 N 12.22 E
Varigotti 62 44.11 N 8.24 E
Väringen ⊜ 40 59.26 N 15.23 E
Varjão 255 17.03 S 49.37 W
Varkaus 26 62.19 N 27.55 E
Varkhān ≃ 128 32.55 N 65.30 E
Varkkallai 122 8.40 N 76.50 E
Varlamovo 86 54.38 N 60.40 E
Värmdölandet I 40 59.20 N 18.33 E
Värmeln ⊜ 26 59.32 N 12.54 E
Värmland □[9] 26 59.48 N 13.03 E
Värmlands Län □[6] 26 59.45 N 13.15 E
Värmlandsnäs ≻[1] 26 59.00 N 13.10 E
Varna, Blg. 38 43.13 N 27.55 E
Varna (Vahrn), It. 64 46.44 N 11.38 E
Varna, S.S.S.R. 86 53.24 N 60.58 E
Varna, N.Y., U.S. 210 42.27 N 76.26 W
Värnamo 26 57.11 N 14.02 E
Varnavino 80 57.24 N 45.04 E
Varnenski zaliv ⊂ 38 43.11 N 27.56 E
Varner-Hogg Plantation State Historic Park ♠ 222 29.09 N 95.37 W
Varnhem 26 58.23 N 13.39 E
Varniai 76 55.45 N 22.22 E
Varnsdorf 54 50.52 N 14.40 E
Varnville 192 32.51 N 81.05 W
Värö 26 57.16 N 12.11 E
Városliget ♠ 264c 47.31 N 19.06 E
Varpaisjärvi 26 63.22 N 27.45 E
Várpalota 30 47.12 N 18.09 E
Várpalota ⊥ 264c 47.30 N 19.02 E
Varpan ⊜ 40 60.38 N 15.36 E
Varresbeck •[8] 263 51.15 N 7.06 E
Vars, Ont., Can. 212 45.21 N 75.21 W
Vars, Fr. 62 44.37 N 6.41 E
Vars, Col de)(62 44.32 N 6.42 E
Varšavskij Vokzal •[5] 265a 59.54 N 30.19 E
Vârşec 38 43.12 N 23.17 E
Varsi 62 44.40 N 9.51 E
Varsinais-Suomi •[1] 26 60.40 N 22.30 E
Värska 76 57.58 N 27.38 E
Varsovie
→ Warszawa 30 52.15 N 21.00 E
Varsseveld 52 51.57 N 6.28 E
Vårsta 40 59.10 N 17.48 E
Vartašen 84 41.06 N 47.28 E
Varto 130 39.10 N 41.28 E
V'artsil'a, S.S.S.R. 24 62.11 N 30.41 E
Värtsilä, Suomi 26 62.15 N 30.40 E
Varty Lake ⊜ 212 44.23 N 76.48 W
Varunga Point ≻ 175e 7.11 S 157.17 E
Varva 78 50.31 N 32.41 E
Varvarin 38 43.43 N 21.19 E
Varvarovka, S.S.S.R. 78 48.42 N 36.02 E
Varvarovka, S.S.S.R. 78 49.33 N 35.12 E
Varvarovka, S.S.S.R. 83 49.05 N 38.24 E
Varysburg 210 42.46 N 78.19 W
Várzea 256 22.30 S 44.46 W
Várzea, Rio da ≃ 252 27.13 S 53.19 W
Várzea Alegre 250 6.47 S 39.17 W
Várzea da Palma 255 17.36 S 44.44 W
Várzea das Moças 287a 22.57 S 42.58 W
Varzea de Sintra 266c 38.49 N 9.24 W
Várzea Grande 248 15.39 S 56.08 W
Varzeão 252 24.34 S 49.26 W
Várzea Paulista 256 23.12 S 46.50 W
Varzi, It. 62 44.49 N 9.12 E
Varzi, S.S.S.R. 80 56.03 N 52.50 E
Varzino 24 68.19 N 38.19 E
Varzo 36 46.12 N 8.15 E
Varzob 85 38.46 N 68.49 E
Varzob ≃ 85 38.30 N 68.45 E
Varzuga 24 67.24 N 36.32 E
Varzy 50 47.22 N 3.23 E
Varzyk 85 41.07 N 71.14 E
Vas 64 45.56 N 11.56 E
Vas □[6] 61 47.05 N 16.45 E
Vasa
→ Vaasa 26 63.06 N 21.36 E
Vasai (Bassein) 122 19.21 N 72.48 E
Vasalemma 76 59.14 N 24.18 E
Vašana ≃ 82 54.36 N 37.10 E
Vasar 272c 19.11 N 73.09 E
Vascão ≃ 34 37.31 N 7.31 W
Vaşcău 38 46.28 N 22.28 E
Vascongadas □[9] 34 43.00 N 2.45 W
Väse 40 59.23 N 13.57 E
Vāshi 272c 19.04 N 72.59 E
Vashon 224 47.27 N 122.28 W
Vashon Heights 224 47.30 N 122.28 W
Vashon Island I 224 47.24 N 122.27 W
Vasile Roaită 38 44.03 N 28.38 E
Vasileviči 78 52.14 N 29.49 E
Vasilija, Mys ≻ 180 64.34 N 178.33 W
Vasiliká 38 40.28 N 23.08 E
Vasiliški 76 53.47 N 24.51 E
Vasiljevka, S.S.S.R. 78 47.26 N 35.16 E
Vasiljevka, S.S.S.R. 78 52.15 N 31.31 E
Vasiljevka, S.S.S.R. 89 46.52 N 134.03 E
Vasiljevo, S.S.S.R. 24 60.46 N 38.59 E
Vasiljevo, S.S.S.R. 80 55.52 N 48.42 E
Vasiljevskij, Ostrov I 265a 59.56 N 30.15 E
Vasiljevskij Moch 76 57.01 N 35.55 E
Vasiljevskoje, S.S.S.R. 80 56.56 N 41.40 E
Vasiljevskoje, S.S.S.R. 80 56.31 N 45.49 E
Vasiljevskoje, S.S.S.R. 82 56.20 N 37.54 E
Vasiljevskoje, S.S.S.R. 82 55.00 N 37.25 E
Vasil'kov 78 50.12 N 60.19 E
Vasil'kovka 78 48.13 N 36.02 E
Vasil'sursk 80 56.08 N 46.01 E
Vasis 86 57.22 N 74.44 E
Vaška ≃ 24 64.53 N 45.47 E
Vaskelovo 76 60.22 N 30.22 E
Vaskess Bay ⊂ 174o 1.51 N 157.31 W
Vas'kin Bor 86 58.20 N 65.28 E
Vaskovan 130 38.57 N 38.57 E
Vaškovci 78 48.24 N 27.08 E
Vaškovcy 78 48.23 N 25.30 E
Vaslui 38 46.38 N 27.44 E
Vaslui □[4] 38 46.30 N 27.45 E
Väsman ⊜ 40 60.11 N 15.04 E
Vass 192 35.15 N 79.17 W
Vassar 190 43.22 N 83.35 W
Vassdalsegga ∧ 26 59.46 N 7.10 E
Vassieux-en-Vercors 62 44.53 N 5.22 E
Vassouras 256 22.25 S 43.40 W
Vassy-sur-Pizy 50 44.34 N 4.10 E
Västanfors 40 59.59 N 15.49 E
Västerås 40 59.37 N 16.33 E
Västeråsfjärden ⊂ 40 59.34 N 16.34 E
Västerbotten □[9] 26 64.36 N 20.04 E
Västerbottens Län □[6] 24 64.00 N 17.30 E
Västerby 40 60.19 N 15.55 E
Västerdalälven ≃ 40 60.33 N 15.08 E
Västerfärnebo 40 59.57 N 16.17 E
Västergötland □[9] 26 58.01 N 13.03 E
Västerhaninge 40 59.07 N 18.06 E
Västernorrlands Län □[6] 26 63.00 N 17.30 E
Västervik 26 57.45 N 16.38 E
Västmanland □[9] 40 59.38 N 15.15 E
Västmanlands Län □[6] 40 59.45 N 16.20 E
Vasto 66 42.07 N 14.42 E
Västra Laxsjön ⊜ 40 58.54 N 14.38 E
Västra Torup 41 56.09 N 13.29 E
Vastseliina 76 57.44 N 27.17 E
Vas'ugan ≃ 86 59.07 N 80.46 E
Vas'uganje ≡ 86 58.00 N 77.00 E
Vas'unino 82 55.15 N 37.01 E
Vašutino 265b 55.56 N 37.26 E
Vašutkiny Ozera ⊜ 24 68.06 N 61.18 E
Vasvár 61 47.03 N 16.49 E
Vát 61 47.17 N 16.47 E
Vaţa de Jos 38 46.10 N 22.35 E
Vatan 32 47.05 N 1.48 E
Vaternish Point ≻ 46 57.36 N 6.38 W
Vatersay I 46 56.55 N 7.32 W
Vatganai I 175f 13.15 S 167.39 E
Vathí 38 37.45 N 26.59 E
Vatia 174u 14.15 S 170.40 W
Vatican (Cité du)
→ Vatican City □[1] 267a 41.54 N 12.27 E
Vatican City □[1] 267a 41.54 N 12.27 E
Vaticano, Capo ≻ 68 38.38 N 15.50 E
Vatikanstadt
→ Vatican City □[1] 267a 41.54 N 12.27 E
Vatilau I 175e 8.53 S 160.01 E
V'atka
→ Kirov 80 58.38 N 49.42 E
V'atka ≃ 80 55.36 N 51.30 E
Vatlirchvin, Gora ∧ 180 68.08 N 179.52 W
Vatnajökull ⊓ 24a 64.25 N 16.50 W
Vatneyri 24a 65.38 N 23.57 W
Vätö I 40 59.49 N 18.57 E
Vatoa I 175g 19.50 S 178.13 W
Vatoloha ∧ 157b 17.52 S 47.48 E
Vatomandry 157b 19.20 S 48.59 E
Vatra Dornei 38 47.21 N 25.21 E
V'atskije Pol'any 80 56.14 N 51.04 E
V'atskij Uval ⋏[2] 80 57.00 N 49.00 E
V'atskoje, S.S.S.R. 80 57.52 N 40.16 E
V'atskoje, S.S.S.R. 89 48.44 N 135.43 E
Vattalkundu 122 10.10 N 77.46 E
Vättern ⊜ 26 58.24 N 14.36 E
Vättersee
→ Vättern ⊜ 26 58.24 N 14.36 E
Vattholma 40 60.01 N 17.44 E
Vättis 58 46.55 N 9.27 E
Vatu-i-Ra Channel ⊔ 175g 17.17 S 178.31 E
Vatukoula 175g 17.31 S 177.51 E
Vatulele I 175g 18.33 S 177.37 E
Vatulino 82 55.39 N 36.09 E
Vatutino 78 49.02 N 31.04 E
Vaubecourt 56 48.56 N 5.07 E
Vauclaix 50 47.14 N 3.49 E
Vauclin, Montagne du ∧ 240e 14.33 N 60.53 W
Vaucluse 274a 33.51 S 151.17 E
Vaucluse □[5] 62 44.00 N 5.10 E
Vaucluse, Fontaine de ⊥ 62 43.55 N 5.08 E
Vaucluse, Plateau de ⋏[1] 62 44.00 N 5.22 E
Vaucouleurs 58 48.36 N 5.40 E
Vaucouleurs ≃ 261 48.59 N 1.44 E
Vaucresson 261 48.50 N 2.09 E
Vaud □[3] 58 46.40 N 6.30 E
Vaudherland 261 49.00 N 2.29 E
Vaudoy-en-Brie 50 48.41 N 3.05 E
Vaudreuil (Saint-Michel-de-Vaudreuil) 206 45.24 N 74.01 W
Vaudreuil □[6] 206 45.26 N 74.15 W
Vaudreuil, Baie de ⊂ 275a 45.24 N 74.00 W
Vaufrey 58 47.21 N 6.55 E
Vaughan 212 43.47 N 79.36 W
Vaughn, N. Mex., U.S. 200 34.36 N 105.13 W
Vaughn, Wash., U.S. 224 47.21 N 122.46 W
Vaughnsville 216 40.53 N 84.09 W
Vaugneray 62 45.44 N 4.39 E
Vaugrigneuse 261 48.36 N 2.07 E
Vauhallan 261 48.44 N 2.12 E
Vaujours 261 48.56 N 2.35 E
Vaulovo 82 56.09 N 39.17 E
Vaulruz 58 46.37 N 6.59 E
Vaulx-en-Velin 62 45.47 N 4.56 E
Vaupés □[8] 246 1.00 N 71.00 W
Vaupés (Uaupés) ≃ 246 0.02 N 67.16 W
Vauréal 261 49.02 N 2.02 E
Vauvenargues 62 43.33 N 5.36 E
Vauvert 62 43.42 N 4.17 E
Vauvillers 58 47.55 N 6.06 E
Vauvilliers, Île I 175f 21.08 S 167.35 E
Vauvise ≃ 50 47.18 N 2.57 E
Vaux ≃ 50 49.03 N 4.17 E
Vaux, Rû des ≃ 261 48.42 N 2.00 E
Vauxhall 182 50.04 N 112.07 W
Vaux-le-Compte, Château-de- ⊥ 50 48.35 N 2.42 E
Vaux-le-Pénil 261 48.32 N 2.41 E
Vaux-lès-Saint-Claude 58 46.22 N 5.44 E
Vaux-le-Vicomte, Château de ⊥ 261 48.34 N 2.43 E
Vaux-sous-Aubigny 58 47.39 N 5.17 E
Vaux-sur-Seine 261 49.00 N 1.58 E
Vavatenina 157b 17.28 S 49.12 E
Vavau I 14 18.36 S 174.00 W
Vavau Group II 14 18.40 S 174.00 W
Vavincourt 56 48.49 N 5.13 E
Vavoua 150 7.23 N 6.29 W
Vavož 80 56.47 N 51.55 E
Vavuniya 122 8.45 N 80.30 E
Vaxholm 40 59.24 N 18.20 E
Växjö 26 56.52 N 14.49 E
V'aža 78 49.16 N 41.01 E
Vaza-Barris ≃ 250 11.10 S 37.10 W
Vazante 255 18.00 S 46.54 W
Vazante Grande ≃ 248 19.21 S 56.53 W
V'azemskij 89 47.32 N 134.48 E
Važgort 24 64.01 N 47.02 E
V'az'ma 76 55.13 N 34.18 E
V'az'ma ≃, S.S.S.R. 76 55.28 N 33.34 E
V'az'ma ≃, S.S.S.R. 82 56.29 N 35.49 E
V'azniki 80 56.15 N 42.10 E
Vazobe ∧ 157b 18.25 S 47.18 E
V'azovaja 80 57.39 N 45.44 E
V'azovka, S.S.S.R. 80 48.19 N 45.36 E
V'azovka, S.S.S.R. 80 51.48 N 45.47 E
V'azovka, S.S.S.R. 80 50.52 N 43.57 E
V'azovka, S.S.S.R. 80 52.52 N 48.24 E
V'azovoje, S.S.S.R. 78 51.54 N 36.59 E
V'azovoje, S.S.S.R. 78 51.09 N 37.01 E
V'azovok 78 49.11 N 31.25 E
Vazuza ≃ 76 56.10 N 34.35 E
V'azyn' 76 54.25 N 27.10 E
Vazzola 64 45.50 N 12.23 E
Veachland 218 38.14 N 85.12 W
Veado, Ilha do I 287a 22.57 S 43.06 W
Veazie 188 44.51 N 68.42 W
Veberöd 41 55.38 N 13.29 E
Veblen 198 45.52 N 97.17 W
Vecchiano 66 43.47 N 10.23 E
Vechelde 52 52.16 N 10.22 E
Vechta 52 52.43 N 8.16 E
Vechte (Vecht) ≃ 52 52.35 N 6.05 E
Veckerhagen 52 51.30 N 9.35 E
Vecpiėbalga 76 57.08 N 25.50 E
Vecsés 30 47.25 N 19.16 E
Vecumnieki 76 56.36 N 24.31 E
Vedado •[8] 286b 23.08 N 82.24 W
Vedano al Lambro 266b 45.37 N 9.16 E
Vedano Olona 62 45.46 N 8.53 E
Vedāranniyam 122 10.22 N 79.51 E
Vedbæk 41 55.51 N 12.34 E
Vedder Crossing 224 49.06 N 121.57 W
Veddige 26 57.16 N 12.19 E
Vedea 38 44.47 N 24.37 E
Vedea ≃ 38 43.53 N 25.59 E
Vedelago 64 45.41 N 12.01 E
Vedène 62 43.59 N 4.54 E
Vedeno 84 42.58 N 46.05 E
Vedeseta 58 45.53 N 9.32 E
Vedevåg 40 59.32 N 15.17 E
Vedi 84 39.56 N 44.42 E
Vedia 252 34.30 S 61.32 W
Vednoje 76 57.08 N 36.10 E
Vedomša 82 56.44 N 38.21 E
Vedrovo 80 57.33 N 42.52 E
Veedersburg 194 40.07 N 87.16 W
Veen 263 51.37 N 6.27 E
Veendam 52 53.06 N 6.58 E
Veenendaal 52 52.02 N 5.34 E
Veenhuizen 52 53.03 N 6.24 E
Veenoord 52 52.43 N 6.50 E
Veere 52 51.34 N 3.40 E
Veert 52 51.33 N 6.17 E
Vefsna ≃ 24 65.50 N 13.12 E
Vega 196 35.15 N 102.26 W
Vega I 24 65.39 N 11.50 E
Vega, Arroyo de la ≃ 266a 40.31 N 3.33 W
Vega Alta 240m 18.25 N 66.20 W
Vega Baja 240m 18.27 N 66.23 W
Vega Island I 18 63.00 S 57.00 W
Vega Point ≻ 181a 51.49 N 177.16 E
Vegesack •[8] 52 53.10 N 8.37 E
Veghel 52 51.37 N 5.33 E
Veglie 68 40.20 N 17.58 E
Vegreville 182 53.30 N 112.03 W
Veguita 200 34.31 N 106.46 W
Vehār Lake ⊜ 272c 19.09 N 72.55 E
Vehlefanz 264a 52.43 N 13.06 E
Vehnemoor •[3] 52 53.05 N 8.00 E
Veigné 50 47.17 N 0.44 E
Veil, Loch ⊜ 46 56.20 N 4.25 W
Veilsdorf 54 50.24 N 10.48 E
Veinticinco de Agosto 258 34.24 S 56.25 W
Veinticinco de Mayo, Arg. 252 35.26 S 60.10 W
Veinticinco de Mayo, Arg. 252 34.35 S 68.33 W
Veinticinco de Mayo, Ur. 258 34.12 S 56.22 W
Veintiocho de Mayo 246 3.50 S 78.52 W
Veintisiete de Abril 236 10.15 N 85.45 W
Veio ⊥ 66 42.02 N 12.24 E
Veiros 250 2.05 S 52.10 W
Veisiejai 76 54.06 N 23.42 E
Veitsbronn 56 49.31 N 10.53 E
Veitsch 61 47.35 N 15.30 E
Veitschalpe ⋏ 61 47.39 N 15.30 E
Veitshöchheim 56 49.50 N 9.52 E
Vejbystrand 41 56.19 N 12.45 E
Vejčin 76 52.27 N 28.10 E
Vejdelevka 78 50.09 N 38.27 E
Vejen 41 55.29 N 9.09 E
Vejer de la Frontera 34 36.15 N 5.58 W
Vejlby 41 56.12 N 10.13 E
Vejle 41 55.42 N 9.32 E
Vejle □[6] 41 55.45 N 9.30 E
Vejle Fjord ⊂ 41 55.40 N 9.50 E
Vejprty 54 50.30 N 13.02 E
Vejrhøj ∧[2] 41 55.47 N 11.24 E
Vejrø I 41 55.02 N 11.22 E
Veksor 24 60.33 N 49.22 E
Vel'a ≃ 82 56.31 N 37.41 E
Veladero, Cerro ∧ 234 16.55 N 99.54 W
Vela Luka 36 42.58 N 16.43 E
Velapāda 272c 18.59 N 73.04 E
Velardeña 232 25.04 N 103.44 W
Velas 148a 38.41 N 28.13 W
Velas, Cabo ≻ 236 10.22 N 85.53 W
Velázquez 252 34.02 S 54.17 W
Velbert 56 51.20 N 7.02 E
Velburg 60 49.14 N 11.41 E
Velddrif 158 32.47 S 18.11 E
Velden, B.R.D. 60 48.19 N 12.16 E
Velden, B.R.D. 60 49.37 N 11.31 E
Velden, Öst. 61 46.37 N 14.03 E
Veldhoven 52 51.24 N 5.24 E
Velebit ⋏ 36 44.38 N 15.03 E
Velebitski Kanal ⊔ 36 45.00 N 14.50 E
Velegož 82 54.42 N 37.16 E
Veleka ≃ 38 42.04 N 27.58 E
Velemín 54 50.33 N 13.59 E
Velen 52 51.53 N 6.59 E
Velencei-tó ⊜ 30 47.12 N 18.35 E
Velenje 36 46.21 N 15.06 E
Velesa ≃ 76 56.03 N 31.58 E
Velešin 61 48.50 N 14.28 E
Velestínon 38 39.23 N 22.45 E
Velet'ma 80 55.20 N 42.25 E
Velevščina 76 54.44 N 28.35 E
Vélez 246 6.01 N 73.41 W
Velez de la Gomera, Peñon de I 34 35.11 N 4.21 W
Vélez-Málaga 34 36.47 N 4.06 W
Vélez Rubio 34 37.39 N 2.04 W
Velgast 54 54.16 N 12.48 E
Vel'gija 76 58.23 N 33.59 E
Velhartice 60 49.16 N 13.23 E
Velhas, Canal do ≖ 287a 22.42 S 43.22 W
Velhas, Rio das ≃ 255 17.13 S 44.49 W
Veličkovo 82 54.59 N 36.46 E
Velika Gorica 36 45.43 N 16.05 E
Velika Gubavica ⌊ 36 43.26 N 16.54 E
Velikaja, S.S.S.R. 24 59.13 N 49.04 E
Velikaja, S.S.S.R. 180 64.04 N 176.12 E
Velikaja ≃, S.S.S.R. 76 57.48 N 28.20 E
Velikaja ≃, S.S.S.R. 180 64.40 N 176.20 E
Velikaja Aleksandrovka 78 47.20 N 33.18 E
Velikaja Bagačka 78 49.47 N 33.43 E
Velikaja Beloz'orka 78 47.16 N 34.42 E
Velikaja Danilovka 78 50.04 N 36.19 E
Velikaja Dymerka 78 50.36 N 30.55 E
Velikaja Gluša 78 51.49 N 25.02 E
Velikaja Kema 89 45.30 N 137.12 E
Velikaja Kochnovka 78 49.07 N 33.27 E
Velikaja Korenicha 78 46.57 N 31.54 E
Velikaja Kosnica 78 48.09 N 28.27 E
Velikaja Lepeticha 78 47.11 N 33.56 E
Velikaja Michajlovka 78 47.04 N 29.52 E
Velikaja Novos'olka 78 47.50 N 36.50 E
Velikaja Pisarevka 78 50.26 N 35.28 E
Velikaja Rublevka 78 49.53 N 34.49 E
Velikaja Vradijevka 78 47.52 N 30.35 E
Velika Kapela ⋏ 36 45.15 N 15.00 E
Velika Morava ≃ 38 44.43 N 21.03 E
Velika Plana 38 44.20 N 21.04 E
Velike Lašče 36 45.50 N 14.38 E
Veliki Bečkerek
→ Zrenjanin 38 45.23 N 20.24 E
Velikij Agar, Gora ∧ 88 50.21 N 94.31 E
Velikij Ber'oznyj 78 48.53 N 22.27 E
Velikij Bor 78 52.02 N 29.56 E
Velikij Buruluk 78 50.05 N 37.24 E
Velikij Byčkov 78 47.58 N 24.03 E
Velikij Chutor 78 49.52 N 32.06 E
Velikij Dvor 82 56.46 N 37.25 E
Velikije Borki 78 49.32 N 25.45 E
Velikije Dederkaly 78 50.02 N 26.07 E
Velikije Kopani 78 46.29 N 32.59 E
Velikije Korovincy 78 49.59 N 28.17 E
Velikije Krynki 78 49.27 N 33.29 E
Velikije Lučki 78 48.26 N 22.35 E
Velikije Luki 76 56.20 N 30.32 E
Velikije Mosty 78 50.14 N 24.06 E
Velikije Soročincy 78 50.03 N 33.56 E
Velikij Glubočok 78 49.37 N 25.32 E
Velikij Log 83 48.15 N 39.33 E
Velikij Žvančik 78 48.46 N 26.59 E
Veliki kanal ≖ 38 45.45 N 18.50 E
Veliki Vitorog ∧ 36 44.07 N 17.03 E
Velikoanadol'skij Les ♠ 83 47.42 N 37.23 E
Velikoarchangel'skoje 78 50.51 N 40.46 E
Velikockoje 83 49.21 N 40.02 E
Velikodolinskoje 78 46.21 N 30.35 E
Velikodvorskaja 76 60.18 N 41.58 E
Velikodvorskij 80 55.15 N 40.41 E
Veliko Gradište 38 44.45 N 21.32 E
Velikoje, S.S.S.R. 76 59.32 N 36.59 E
Velikoje, S.S.S.R. 80 57.21 N 39.47 E
Velikoje, Ozero ⊜, S.S.S.R. 76 57.02 N 36.34 E
Velikoje, Ozero ⊜, S.S.S.R. 80 55.13 N 40.10 E
Velikonda Hills ⋏[2] 122 14.45 N 79.10 E
Velikookt'abr'skij 76 57.26 N 33.49 E
Velikopoloskoje 78 47.01 N 29.40 E
Velikorusskoje 86 54.39 N 74.38 E
Veliko Târnovo 38 43.04 N 25.39 E
Velikovisočnoje 24 67.16 N 52.01 E
Velikovo 76 59.18 N 42.08 E
Velilla de San Antonio 266a 40.22 N 3.29 W
Veli Lošinj 36 44.31 N 14.30 E
Velimče 78 51.36 N 24.44 E
Vélingara, Sén. 150 15.00 N 14.40 W
Vélingara, Sén. 150 13.09 N 14.07 W
Velingrad 38 42.04 N 24.00 E
Velino ≃ 66 42.33 N 12.43 E
Velino, Monte ∧ 66 42.09 N 13.23 E
Veli Stol (Hochstuhl) ∧ 61 46.26 N 14.10 E
Veliž 76 55.38 N 31.12 E
Veližany 86 57.34 N 65.49 E
Veljaminovo, S.S.S.R. 82 55.12 N 37.52 E
Veljaminovo, S.S.S.R. 82 55.53 N 36.52 E
Velká Bíteš 30 49.17 N 16.13 E
Velká Deštná ∧ 30 50.18 N 16.24 E
Vel'ká Fatra ⋏ 30 49.00 N 19.05 E
Vel'ké Kapušany 30 48.33 N 22.04 E
Velké Meziříčí 30 49.21 N 16.00 E
Velké Němčie 61 48.59 N 16.40 E
Velké Pavlovice 61 48.54 N 16.19 E
Velký Bor 60 49.22 N 13.42 E
Velký Šenov 54 51.00 N 14.25 E
Vellach ≃ 61 46.35 N 14.29 E
Vella Gulf ⊔ 175e 8.00 S 156.50 E
Vella Lavella I 175e 7.45 S 156.40 E
Vellano 66 43.57 N 10.43 E
Vellār ≃ 122 11.29 N 79.46 E
Vellberg 56 49.05 N 9.53 E
Vellechevreux-et-Courbenans 58 47.33 N 6.32 E
Velletri 66 41.41 N 12.47 E
Vellinge 41 55.28 N 13.01 E
Vellmar 56 51.21 N 9.28 E
Vellore, Bhārat 122 12.56 N 79.08 E
Vellore, Ont., Can. 275b 43.50 N 79.34 W
Velm 264b 48.03 N 16.27 E
Velmede 56 51.21 N 8.22 E
Velo d'Astico 64 45.43 N 11.23 E
Velp 52 52.00 N 5.59 E
Velp ≃ 56 50.58 N 5.05 E
Velpke 54 52.24 N 10.56 E
Velsen 52 52.27 N 4.39 E
Vel'sk 24 61.05 N 42.05 E
Vel't 24 68.03 N 49.55 E
Velten 54 52.41 N 13.10 E
Veltheim 52 52.11 N 8.58 E
Veltrusy 54 50.14 N 14.18 E
Veltrusy ⊥ 32 50.14 N 14.18 E
Veluwe •[1] 52 52.12 N 5.45 E
Veluwemeer ⊜ 52 52.22 N 5.38 E
Velva, It. 62 44.16 N 9.33 E
Velva, N. Dak., U.S. 198 48.04 N 100.56 W
Velvary 54 50.15 N 14.15 E
Vémars 261 49.04 N 2.34 E
Vembādi Shola ∧ 122 10.12 N 77.24 E
Vembanād Lake ⊜ 122 9.35 N 76.25 E
Vemdalen 26 62.27 N 13.52 E
Vemmenæs 41 54.59 N 10.40 E
Vempalle 122 14.22 N 78.28 E
Ven I 41 55.54 N 12.41 E
Venachar, Loch ⊜ 46 56.13 N 4.19 W
Venaco 36 42.14 N 9.10 E
Venadillo 246 4.43 N 74.55 W
Venado 234 22.56 N 101.05 W
Venado, Isla I 241r 10.00 N 62.25 W
Venado Tuerto 252 33.45 S 61.58 W
Venafiorita, Aeroporto di ⊠ 71 40.53 N 9.30 E
Venafro 66 41.29 N 14.02 E
Venalzio 62 45.09 N 7.01 E
Venâncio Aires 252 29.36 S 52.11 W
Venango 214 41.46 N 80.07 W
Venango □[6] 214 41.24 N 79.50 W
Venanson 62 44.03 N 7.15 E
Venant 261 48.30 N 2.06 E
Venarey-les-Laumes 58 47.32 N 4.26 E
Venaria 62 45.08 N 7.38 E
Venasca 62 44.33 N 7.24 E
Venasque 62 43.59 N 5.09 E
Vence 62 43.43 N 7.07 E
Venceslau Brás 255 23.51 S 49.48 W
Vencimont 56 50.02 N 4.55 E
Venda Nova 34 41.40 N 7.58 W
Vendargues 62 43.39 N 3.58 E
Vendas Novas 34 38.41 N 8.28 W
Vendée □[5] 32 46.40 N 1.20 W
Vendée •[1] 32 46.40 N 1.10 W
Vendel 40 60.10 N 17.36 E

Symbols in the index entries represent the broad categories identified in the key at the right. Symbols with superior numbers (⋏[2]) identify subcategories (see complete key on page I · 30).

Kartensymbole in dem Registerverzeichnis stellen die rechts in Schlüssel erklärten Kategorien dar. Symbole mit hochgestellten Ziffern (⋏[2]) bezeichnen Unterabteilungen einer Kategorie (vgl. vollständiger Schlüssel auf Seite I · 30).

Los símbolos incluidos en el texto del indice representan las grandes categorias identificadas con la clave a la derecha. Los símbolos con números en su parte superior (⋏[2]) identifican las subcategorias (véase la clave completa en la página I · 30).

Les symboles de l'index représentent les catégories indiquées dans la légende à droite. Les symboles suivis d'un indice (⋏[2]) représentent des sous-catégories (voir légende complète à la page I · 30).

Os símbolos incluídos no texto do índice representam as grandes categorias identificadas com a chave à direita. Os símbolos com números em sua parte superior (⋏[2]) identificam as subcategorias (veja-se a chave completa à página I · 30).

English	Deutsch	Español	Français	Português
∧ Mountain	Berg	Montaña	Montagne	Montanha
⋏ Mountains	Berge	Montañas	Montagnes	Montanhas
)(Pass	Pass	Paso	Col	Passo
∨ Valley, Canyon	Tal, Cañon	Valle, Cañón	Vallée, Canyon	Vale, Canhão
≍ Plain	Ebene	Llano	Plaine	Planície
≻ Cape	Kap	Cabo	Cap	Cabo
I Island	Insel	Isla	Île	Ilha
II Islands	Inseln	Islas	Îles	Ilhas
♠ Other Topographic Features	Andere Topographische Objekte	Otros Elementos Topográficos	Autres données topographiques	Outros Elementos Topográficos

ESPAÑOL: Nombre | Página | Lat.°′ | Long.°′ W=Oeste
FRANÇAIS: Nom | Page | Lat.°′ | Long.°′ W=Ouest
PORTUGUÊS: Nome | Página | Lat.°′ | Long.°′ W=Oeste

Vendelsö 40 59.12 N 18.12 E
Vendeuvre-sur-Barse 58 48.14 N 4.28 E
Vendičany 78 48.37 N 27.48 E
Vendin-lès-Béthune 50 50.32 N 2.37 E
Vendin-le-Vieil 50 50.28 N 2.52 E
Vendôme 50 47.48 N 1.04 E
Vendrell 34 41.13 N 1.32 E
Vendsyssel ✦[1] 26 57.20 N 10.00 E
Venecia, C.R. 236 10.22 N 84.17 W
Venecia
→ Venezia, It. 64 45.27 N 12.21 E
Venedig
→ Venezia 64 45.27 N 12.21 E
Venedocia 216 40.44 N 84.25 W
Venedy 219 38.24 N 89.39 W
Veneta, Laguna C 64 45.25 N 12.19 E
Venetia 214 40.15 N 80.03 W
Venetian Village 216 42.24 N 88.02 W
Venetie 180 66.30 N 147.26 W
Veneto □[4] 64 45.30 N 11.45 E
Venev 82 54.21 N 38.16 E
Venezia (Venice) 64 45.27 N 12.21 E
Venezia □[4] 64 45.35 N 12.34 E
Venezuela □[1] 242
246 8.00 N 66.00 W
Venezuela, Golfo de
C 246 11.30 N 71.00 W
Venezuelan Basin
✣[1] 16 14.30 N 68.00 W
Veng 41 56.07 N 9.53 E
Vengerovka 83 48.43 N 38.24 E
Vengerovo 86 55.41 N 76.45 E
Vengurla 122 15.52 N 73.38 E
Veniaminof, Mount
∧ 180 56.13 N 159.18 W
Venice
→ Venezia, It. 64 45.27 N 12.21 E
Venice, Fla., U.S. 220 27.06 N 82.27 W
Venice, Ill., U.S. 219 38.40 N 90.11 W
Venice, La., U.S. 194 29.17 N 89.21 W
Venice, Ohio, U.S. 214 41.27 N 82.46 W
Venice, Pa., U.S. 279b 40.19 N 80.14 W
Venice ✦[8] 228 34.00 N 118.29 W
Venice, Gulf of C 64 45.15 N 13.00 E
Venise
→ Venezia 64 45.27 N 12.21 E
Vénissieux 62 45.41 N 4.53 E
Venjan 26 60.57 N 13.55 E
Venjansjön ⊜ 26 60.54 N 14.00 E
Venkatagiri 122 13.58 N 79.35 E
Venlo 52 51.24 N 6.10 E
Vennesla 26 58.17 N 7.59 E
Vennhausen ✦[8] 263 51.13 N 6.51 E
Venosa 68 40.57 N 15.49 E
Vénosc 62 44.59 N 6.07 E
Venosta, Val ∨ 64 46.40 N 10.35 E
Venoste, Alpi
(Ötztaler Alpen)
⩓ 64 46.45 N 10.55 E
Venraij 52 51.32 N 5.59 E
Vent 64 46.52 N 10.56 E
Vent, Îles du
→ Windward
Islands II 238 13.00 N 61.00 W
Venta ≃ 76 57.24 N 21.33 E
Venta, Río de la ≃ 234 16.59 N 93.46 W
Ventanas 246 1.23 S 79.25 W
Ventasso, Monte ∧ 64 44.23 N 10.17 E
Ventenat, Cape ≻ 164 10.10 S 151.15 E
Ventersburg 158 28.09 S 27.08 E
Ventersdorp 158 26.17 S 26.48 E
Venterspos 273d 26.18 S 27.39 E
Venterspos Location 273d 26.18 S 27.42 E
Venterspos West 273d 26.16 S 27.38 E
Venterstad 158 30.47 S 25.48 E
Venticano 68 41.05 N 14.50 E
Ventimiglia 62 43.47 N 7.36 E
Ventimiglia di Sicilia 70 37.55 N 13.34 E
Ventnor 42 50.36 N 1.11 W
Ventnor City 208 39.20 N 74.29 W
Ventotene 66 40.48 N 13.26 E
Ventotene, Isola di
I 66 40.47 N 13.25 E
Ventoux, Mont ∧ 62 44.10 N 5.17 E
Ventry 48 52.08 N 10.22 W
Ventspils 76 57.24 N 21.36 E
Ventuari ≃ 246 3.58 N 67.02 W
Ventura (San
Buenaventura) 228 34.17 N 119.18 W
Ventura □[6] 228 34.30 N 119.00 W
Ventura ≃ 228 34.16 N 119.18 W
Venturina 66 43.02 N 10.36 E
Venus, Fla., U.S. 220 27.04 N 81.21 W
Venus, Pa., U.S. 214 41.22 N 79.29 W
Venus, Tex., U.S. 222 32.26 N 97.06 W
Vénus, Pointe ≻ 174s 17.29 S 149.29 W
Venus Bay C 169 38.40 S 145.43 E
Venustiano Carranza,
Méx. 232 16.21 N 92.33 W
Venustiano Carranza,
Méx. 234 19.44 N 103.47 W
Venustiano Carranza,
Presa ⊜[1] 232 27.30 N 100.40 W
Venzone 64 46.20 N 13.09 E
Veprik 78 50.23 N 34.11 E
Vepsovskaja
Vozvyšennost' ⩓[1] 76 60.20 N 35.15 E
Ver 175f 14.11 S 167.34 E
Ver ≃ 42 51.42 N 0.20 W
Vera (Jobson), Arg. 252 29.28 S 60.13 W
Vera, Esp. 34 37.15 N 1.52 W
Vera, Ill., U.S. 219 39.02 N 89.07 W
Veracruz, Méx. 200 32.25 N 115.05 W
Vera Cruz, Pa., U.S. 208 40.30 N 75.30 W
Veracruz □[3] 234 19.20 N 96.40 W
Veracruz [Llave] 234 19.12 N 96.08 W
Veraguas □[4] 236 8.30 N 81.00 W
Verano Brianza 266b 45.41 N 9.14 E
Veranópolis 252 28.57 S 51.33 W
Verao I 175f 17.30 S 168.15 E
Verava 256 23.47 S 47.05 W
Verāval 120 20.54 N 70.22 E
Verba 78 50.17 N 25.37 E
Verbania 58 45.56 N 8.33 E
Verbank 210 41.44 N 73.43 W
Verbeek,
Pegunungan ⩓ 112 2.35 S 121.25 E
Verberg ✦[8] 263 51.22 N 6.36 E
Verberie 50 49.19 N 2.44 E
Verbicaro 68 39.45 N 15.55 E
Verbier 58 46.06 N 7.13 E
Verbilki 82 56.32 N 37.36 E
Verbinskij 83 47.53 N 40.02 E
Verbl'užka 78 48.23 N 32.54 E
Verbovskij 80 55.32 N 42.00 E
Vercelli 62 45.19 N 8.25 E
Vercelli □[4] 62 45.37 N 8.10 E
Vercel-Villedieu-le-
Camp 58 47.11 N 6.24 E
Verchazovka 80 50.56 N 48.46 E
Verchères 206 45.47 N 73.21 W
Verchères □[6] 206 45.45 N 73.20 W
Verchn'ačka 78 48.49 N 30.02 E
Verchn'aja Amga 74 59.30 N 126.08 E
Verchn'aja Angara
≃ 88 55.42 N 109.54 E
Verchnaja Balkarija 84 43.06 N 43.24 E
Verchnaja Buzinovka 80 49.04 N 43.12 E
Verchn'aja Čebula 86 56.02 N 87.36 E
Verchn'aja Chava 78 51.50 N 39.56 E
Verchn'aja Chila 88 52.06 N 115.54 E
Verchn'aja Chortica 78 47.51 N 35.01 E
Verchn'aja Čuginka 83 48.55 N 39.39 E
Verchnaja Dobrinka 80 50.46 N 45.03 E
Verchn'aja Gniluša 78 50.16 N 40.23 E
Verchn'aja
Grajvoronka 78 51.41 N 37.46 E
Verchn'aja Inta 24 66.00 N 60.20 E
Verchn'aja Irmen' 86 54.35 N 82.14 E
Verchnaja Maza 80 52.58 N 47.56 E
Verchn'aja Orl'anka 80 53.44 N 51.04 E
Verchn'aja Pyšma 86 56.55 N 60.37 E
Verchn'aja Salda 86 58.02 N 60.33 E
Verchn'aja
Serebr'akovka 80 47.21 N 42.14 E
Verchn'aja Sin'āčicha 86 57.59 N 61.40 E
Verchn'aja Sysert' 86 56.26 N 60.46 E
Verchn'aja Tajmyra
≃ 74 74.15 N 99.48 E
Verchn'aja Tarka 86 56.37 N 77.30 E
Verchnaja Tereška 80 52.54 N 47.24 E
Verchn'aja Tišanka 78 51.20 N 40.33 E
Verchn'aja Tojma 24 62.13 N 45.00 E
Verchn'aja Troica 76 57.15 N 37.08 E
Verchn'aja Tura 86 58.22 N 59.49 E
Verchn'aja Zaimka 88 55.51 N 110.09 E
Verchn'aja Zima 88 53.48 N 101.47 E
Verchneaks'onovskij 80 48.21 N 42.38 E
Verchne-Angarskij
Chrebet ⩓ 88 56.20 N 111.30 E
Verchne-Anikin 83 48.09 N 39.59 E
Verchnebakanskij 78 44.52 N 37.39 E
Verchneber'ozovskij 86 50.17 N 82.13 E
Verchnebuzanskij 80 46.38 N 48.02 E
Verchnecaricynskij 80 48.23 N 43.57 E
Verchnedneprovsk 78 48.39 N 34.21 E
Verchnedneprovskij 76 54.59 N 33.21 E
Verchneduvannyj 78 48.20 N 39.48 E
Verchneduvannyj ✦[8] 83 48.20 N 39.48 E
Verchnedvinsk 76 55.47 N 27.56 E
Verchneimbatskoje 74 63.11 N 87.58 E
Verchnejarkejev 80 55.27 N 54.19 E
Verchneje 78 48.51 N 38.28 E
Verchneje ✦[8] 83 48.53 N 38.28 E
Verchneje Šachlovo 82 55.02 N 37.15 E
Verchneje
Sinevidnoje 78 49.06 N 23.34 E
Verchne-Kamskaja
Vozvyšennost' ⩓[1] 80 58.15 N 52.30 E
Verchne Karabachskij
Kanal ☲ 84 39.44 N 47.57 E
Verchnemakejevka 78 49.10 N 41.03 E
Verchnesadovoje 78 44.42 N 33.42 E
Verchnesjezžeje 80 52.44 N 51.15 E
Verchnespasskoje 80 52.29 N 41.47 E
Verchne-T'oploje 83 48.51 N 39.26 E
Verchnetulomskij 24 68.38 N 31.45 E
Verchneural'sk 86 53.53 N 59.13 E
Verchneusinskoje 86 52.14 N 93.01 E
Verchnevil'ujsk 74 63.27 N 120.18 E
Verchnevolynskoje 85 40.43 N 68.51 E
Verchnij Amyl 88 53.08 N 94.30 E
Verchnij Avz'an 86 53.32 N 57.33 E
Verchnij Balyklej 80 49.34 N 45.10 E
Verchnij Baskunčak 80 48.14 N 46.44 E
Verchnij Byk 78 50.43 N 41.14 E
Verchnije Dvoriki 82 56.28 N 38.22 E
Verchnije Kigi 86 55.28 N 58.37 E
Verchnije Korobki 80 50.19 N 44.38 E
Verchnije Lipki 80 49.38 N 43.51 E
Verchnije Tatyšly 86 56.17 N 55.52 E
Verchnij Ikorec 78 51.11 N 39.46 E
Verchnij-Karačan 80 51.24 N 41.46 E
Verchnij Krasnyj
Pereval 89 46.33 N 134.37 E
Verchnij Kužebar 86 53.22 N 93.15 E
Verchnij Landech 80 56.51 N 42.36 E
Verchnij Leb'ažinskij 80 46.45 N 47.50 E
Verchnij Lomov 80 53.28 N 43.34 E
Verchnij Lomovec 76 52.13 N 38.37 E
Verchnij Mamon 78 50.10 N 40.23 E
Verchnij Most 76 57.31 N 28.50 E
Verchnij Nejvinskij 86 57.17 N 60.09 E
Verchnij Petr'ak 86 57.29 N 77.30 E
Verchnij Rogačik 78 47.14 N 34.21 E
Verchnij Šergol'džin 88 50.12 N 108.20 E
Verchnij Tagil 86 57.22 N 59.56 E
Verchnij Takermen' 80 55.39 N 52.43 E
Verchnij Trojanov Val
(Upper Trajan's
Wall) ⊥ 78 46.35 N 29.00 E
Verchnij Ufalej 86 56.04 N 60.14 E
Verchnij Ul'chun 88 49.34 N 112.32 E
Verchnij Uslon 80 55.47 N 48.57 E
Verchnij Zub, Gora
∧ 86 53.45 N 89.15 E
Verchnyje Nikul'asy 76 60.25 N 30.45 E
Verchnyj Nagol'čik 83 48.05 N 39.06 E
Verchojansk 74 67.35 N 133.27 E
Verchojanskij
Chrebet ⩓ 74 67.00 N 129.00 E
Vercholensk 88 54.06 N 105.35 E
Verchopuja 24 61.34 N 41.31 E
Verchošižemje 80 58.01 N 49.07 E
Verchososna 78 50.44 N 38.14 E
Verchoturje 86 58.52 N 60.48 E
Verchoturovo 86 58.22 N 95.21 E
Verchovažje 24 60.45 N 42.00 E
Verchovcevo 78 48.29 N 34.14 E
Verchovino 76 59.33 N 43.19 E
Verchovje 76 52.49 N 37.14 E
Verchovl'an' 82 55.03 N 38.21 E
Verchozim 80 52.56 N 46.23 E
Verchubinka 86 50.29 N 82.26 E
Verclause 62 44.23 N 5.26 E
Vercors □[9] 62 44.57 N 5.25 E
Verdalsøra 26 63.48 N 11.29 E
Verde ≃, Bra. 248 13.33 S 58.01 W
Verde ≃, Bra. 248 11.54 S 55.48 W
Verde ≃, Bra. 250 10.11 S 42.24 W
Verde ≃, Bra. 255 18.01 S 50.14 W
Verde ≃, Bra. 255 17.05 S 46.05 W
Verde ≃, Bra. 255 21.12 S 51.53 W
Verde ≃, Bra. 255 15.07 S 48.40 W
Verde ≃, Bra. 255 19.55 S 49.45 W
Verde ≃, Bra. 255 19.11 S 50.44 W
Verde ≃, Bra. 256 21.38 S 47.03 W
Verde ≃, Bra. 256 21.34 S 45.31 W
Verde ≃, Méx. 234 20.42 N 103.14 W
Verde ≃, Méx. 234 21.37 N 99.15 W
Verde ≃, Para. 252 23.09 S 57.37 W
Verde ≃, S.A. 248 13.59 S 60.24 W
Verde ≃, Ariz., U.S. 200 33.33 N 111.40 W
Verde, Arroyo ≃,
Arg. 254 41.56 S 65.03 W
Verde, Arroyo ≃, Bol. 248 11.25 S 66.20 W
Verde, Costa ▪[2] 71 39.34 N 8.28 E
Verde Grande ≃ 255 14.35 S 43.53 W
Verde Island I 116 13.33 N 121.05 E
Verde Island Passage
⊔ 116 13.34 N 120.51 E
Verdello 62 45.36 N 9.37 E
Verden, B.R.D. 52 52.55 N 9.13 E
Verden, Okla., U.S. 196 35.05 N 98.05 W
Verde Pequeno ≃ 255 14.48 S 43.31 W
Verdesela, Pinhal da
♠ 266c 38.37 N 9.08 W
Verdi 226 39.31 N 119.59 W
Verdigre 198 42.36 N 98.02 W
Verdigre Creek ≃ 198 42.42 N 98.03 W
Verdinho ≃ 255 17.29 S 50.27 W
Verdon 198 40.08 N 95.48 W
Verdon ≃ 62 43.43 N 5.46 E
Verdon, Canal du ☲ 62 43.43 N 5.57 E
Verdoy 210 42.46 N 73.48 W
Verduga 76 58.46 N 29.12 E
Verdugo Mountains
⩓ 280 34.13 N 118.18 W
Verdun, Qué., Can. 206 45.27 N 73.34 W
Verdun, Fr. 32 43.52 N 1.14 E
Verdun, Fr. 56 49.10 N 5.23 E
Verdun-sur-le-Doubs 58 46.54 N 5.01 E
Verdura ≃ 70 37.28 N 13.12 E
Vereb'jo 76 58.41 N 32.42 E
Vereeniging 158 26.38 S 27.57 E
Vereinigte Arabische
Emirate → United
Arab Emirates □[1] 128 24.00 N 54.00 E
Vereinigte Königreich
→ United Kingdom
□[1] 28 54.00 N 2.00 W
Vereinigte Staaten
→ United States
□[1] 178 38.00 N 97.00 W
Vereja, S.S.S.R. 82 55.46 N 39.06 E
Vereja, S.S.S.R. 82 55.21 N 36.11 E
Vereja, S.S.S.R. 265b 55.37 N 38.02 E
Veremejki 76 53.46 N 31.15 E
Vereščagino, S.S.S.R. 74 64.14 N 87.37 E
Vereščagino, S.S.S.R. 80 58.05 N 54.40 E
Veresegyház 264c 47.39 N 19.17 E
Veresoč' 78 51.19 N 31.46 E
Veretje 82 54.08 N 36.17 E
Véretz 50 47.22 N 0.48 E
Verga 285 39.52 N 75.10 W
Verga, Cap ≻ 150 10.12 N 14.27 W
Vergara, Esp. 34 43.07 N 2.25 W
Vergara, Ur. 252 32.56 S 53.57 W
Vergato 64 44.17 N 11.07 E
Vergel 196 25.39 N 103.32 W
Vergeletto 58 46.14 N 8.36 E
Vergemont Creek
≃ 166 24.12 S 143.17 E
Vergennes 188 44.10 N 73.15 W
Verghereto 66 43.47 N 12.00 E
Vergiate 62 45.43 N 8.42 E
Vergons 62 43.55 N 6.35 E
Vergt 32 45.02 N 0.43 E
Vergulevka 83 48.24 N 38.32 E
Verigin 184 51.35 N 102.08 W
Verigino 82 56.42 N 38.08 E
Verín 34 41.56 N 7.26 W
Veringenstadt 58 48.11 N 9.12 E
Verin Talin 84 40.23 N 43.53 E
Veriora 76 58.00 N 27.21 E
Veríssimo 255 19.42 S 48.18 W
Veríssimo Sarmento 152 8.10 S 20.39 E
Verkeerdevlei 158 28.48 S 26.48 E
Verkhneudinsk
→ Ulan-Ude 88 51.50 N 107.37 E
Verkhniy Ufaley
→ Verchnij Ufalej 86 56.04 N 60.14 E
Verkhnyaya Salda
→ Verchn'aja Salda 86 58.02 N 60.33 E
Verkhoyansk
→ Verchojansk 74 67.35 N 133.27 E
Verkykerskop 158 27.54 S 29.17 E
Verl (Senne I) 52 51.53 N 8.31 E
Vermaaklikheid 158 34.19 S 21.01 E
Vermaas 158 26.30 S 25.59 E
Vermand 50 49.52 N 3.09 E
Verme Falls ⌊ 144 5.20 N 40.16 E
Vermejo ≃ 196 36.30 N 104.33 W
Vermelho ≃, Bra. 250 9.16 S 47.23 W
Vermelho ≃, Bra. 250 7.44 S 47.17 W
Vermelho ≃, Bra. 250 5.33 S 49.14 W
Vermelho ≃, Bra. 255 14.54 S 51.06 W
Vermenton 50 47.40 N 3.44 E
Vermette Lake ⊜ 184 55.40 N 109.05 W
Vermezzo 266b 45.24 N 8.59 E
Vermiglio 64 46.18 N 10.42 E
Vermilion, Alta., Can. 182 53.22 N 110.51 W
Vermilion, Ohio, U.S. 214 41.25 N 82.22 W
Vermilion □[6] 216 40.08 N 87.37 W
Vermilion ≃, Alta.,
Can. 184 53.44 N 110.18 W
Vermilion ≃, Ont.,
Can. 190 46.16 N 81.41 W
Vermilion ≃, Ill., U.S. 216 41.19 N 89.04 W
Vermilion ≃, Minn.,
U.S. 190 48.16 N 92.30 W
Vermilion ≃, Ohio,
U.S. 214 41.26 N 82.22 W
Vermilion, Middle
Fork ≃ 216 40.12 N 87.45 W
Vermilion, South
Fork ≃ 216 40.49 N 88.30 W
Vermilion Bay 184 49.51 N 93.24 W
Vermilion Bay C 194 29.40 N 92.00 W
Vermilion Hills ⩓[2] 184 50.43 N 106.50 W
Vermilion Lake ⊜,
Ont., Can. 184 50.03 N 92.13 W
Vermilion Lake ⊜,
Minn., U.S. 190 47.53 N 92.25 W
Vermilion Range ⩓[2] 190 47.50 N 92.00 W
Vermillion 198 42.47 N 96.56 W
Vermillion ≃, Minn.,
U.S. 190 44.45 N 92.51 W
Vermillion ≃, S.
Dak., U.S. 198 42.44 N 96.53 W
Vermillion, East Fork
≃ 198 43.44 N 97.03 W
Vermillion, West Fork
≃ 198 43.44 N 97.03 W
Vermillion Creek ≃,
U.S. 200 40.46 N 108.53 W
Vermillion Creek ≃,
Kans., U.S. 198 39.12 N 96.13 W
Vermont 274b 37.50 S 145.12 E
Vermont □[3] 178
188 43.50 N 72.45 W
Vermontville 216 42.38 N 85.02 W
Vernà, Pizzo di ∧ 70 38.01 N 15.15 E
Vernaison 62 45.39 N 4.49 E
Vernal 200 40.27 N 109.32 W
Vernalis 226 37.38 N 121.17 W
Vernante 62 44.15 N 7.32 E
Vernayaz 58 46.08 N 7.02 E
Vernazza 62 44.08 N 9.41 E
Verndale 198 46.24 N 95.01 W
Verne 52 51.41 N 8.34 E
Verner 190 46.25 N 80.07 W
Verneuil 32 48.44 N 0.56 E
Verneuil-l'Étang 261 48.39 N 2.50 E
Verneuil-sur-Avre 50 48.44 N 0.56 E
Verneuil-sur-Seine 50 48.59 N 1.59 E
Verneukpan 158 30.00 S 21.00 E
Verneukpan ⊜ 158 29.58 S 21.10 E
Vernier 58 46.13 N 6.06 E
Verninge 41 55.18 N 10.13 E
Vernio 66 44.03 N 11.09 E
Vernole 68 40.17 N 18.18 E
Vernon, B.C., Can. 182 50.16 N 119.16 W
Vernon, Ont., Can. 212 45.10 N 75.28 W
Vernon, Fr. 32 47.48 N 1.38 E
Vernon, Fr. 50 49.05 N 1.29 E
Vernon, Ala., U.S. 194 33.45 N 88.07 W
Vernon, Calif., U.S. 280 34.01 N 118.13 W
Vernon, Conn., U.S. 207 41.50 N 72.28 W
Vernon, Fla., U.S. 194 30.37 N 85.43 W
Vernon, Ill., U.S. 219 38.48 N 89.05 W
Vernon, Ind., U.S. 218 38.59 N 85.36 W
Vernon, Mich., U.S. 216 42.56 N 84.02 W
Vernon, N.J., U.S. 210 41.12 N 74.29 W
Vernon, N.Y., U.S. 210 43.05 N 75.32 W
Vernon, Ohio, U.S. 214 41.23 N 80.34 W
Vernon, Tex., U.S. 196 34.09 N 99.17 W
Vernon, Utah, U.S. 200 40.06 N 112.26 W
Vernon, Lake ⊜ 212 45.20 N 79.17 W
Vernon Dam ✦[6] 207 42.46 N 72.31 W
Vernon Hills 278 42.13 N 87.58 W
Vernonia 224 45.52 N 123.11 W
Vernon Lake ⊜[1] 194 31.15 N 93.25 W
Vernon River 186 46.12 N 62.50 W
Vernouillet 261 48.58 N 1.59 E
Vernoux-en-Vivarais 62 44.54 N 4.39 E
Verny 56 49.01 N 6.12 E
Vero ≃ 34 42.00 N 0.10 E
Vero Beach 220 27.38 N 80.24 W
Véroia 38 40.31 N 22.12 E
Verolanuova 64 45.19 N 10.04 E
Verolavecchia 64 45.19 N 10.03 E
Veroli 66 41.41 N 13.25 E
Verona, Ont., Can. 212 44.29 N 76.42 W
Verona, It. 64 45.27 N 11.00 E
Verona, Ky., U.S. 218 38.49 N 84.40 W
Verona, Miss., U.S. 194 34.12 N 88.43 W
Verona, N.J., U.S. 276 40.50 N 74.12 W
Verona, N.Y., U.S. 210 43.08 N 75.34 W
Verona, Ohio, U.S. 218 39.54 N 84.29 W
Verona, Wis., U.S. 216 42.59 N 89.32 W
Verona □[4] 64 45.25 N 11.02 E
Verona Beach 210 43.12 N 75.44 W
Verona Beach State
Park ♠ 210 43.14 N 75.44 W
Verona Park 216 42.21 N 85.09 W
Verónica 258 35.22 S 57.20 W
Verperluda, Ostrov
I 265a 59.59 N 30.01 E
Verplanck 210 41.15 N 73.58 W
Verran 166 33.51 S 136.18 E
Verrazano-Narrows
Bridge ✦[5] 210 40.36 N 74.03 W
Verrès 62 45.40 N 7.42 E
Verrettes 238 19.03 N 72.28 W
Verrey-sous-
Salmaise 58 47.26 N 4.40 E
Verrières, Bois de
♠ 261 48.45 N 2.15 E
Verrières-le-Buisson 261 48.45 N 2.16 E
Versa ≃ 62 44.54 N 8.16 E
Versailles, Fr. 50 48.48 N 2.08 E
Versailles, Ill., U.S. 194 39.53 N 90.39 W
Versailles, Ind., U.S. 218 39.04 N 85.15 W
Versailles, Ky., U.S. 218 38.03 N 84.44 W
Versailles, Mo., U.S. 194 38.26 N 92.51 W
Versailles, N.Y., U.S. 210 42.31 N 78.59 W
Versailles, Ohio, U.S. 216 40.13 N 84.29 W
Versailles, Pa., U.S. 279b 40.21 N 79.51 W
Versailles ✦[8] 288 34.38 S 58.31 W
Versailles, Château
de ⊥ 261 48.48 N 2.07 E
Versailles, Parc de
♠ 261 48.49 N 2.06 E
Versailles State Park
♠ 218 39.04 N 85.13 W
Verse ≃ 263 51.15 N 7.46 E
Versec
→ Vršac 38 45.07 N 21.18 E
Versestausee ⊜[1] 263 51.11 N 7.41 E
Versien 158 27.05 S 27.52 E
Veršina Tei 86 53.20 N 89.36 E
Veršino-Darasunskij 88 52.20 N 115.32 E
Veršino-
Šachtaminskij 88 51.21 N 117.50 E
Versmold 52 52.02 N 8.09 E
Versoix 58 46.16 N 6.10 E
Ver-sur-Launette 261 49.06 N 2.41 E
Vert 261 48.57 N 1.41 E
Vert, Cap ≻ 150 14.43 N 17.30 W
Vert'ačij 80 48.57 N 43.53 E
Verte, Île I 275a 45.34 N 73.30 W
Vertedero 240m 18.05 N 66.15 W
Verteillac 32 45.21 N 0.22 E
Vertentes 250 7.54 S 35.59 W
Vertientes 240p 21.16 N 78.09 W
Vertijevka 78 51.10 N 31.51 E
Vertkovo 82 56.07 N 36.25 E
Vert-le-Grand 261 48.34 N 2.22 E
Vert-le-Petit 261 48.33 N 2.22 E
Vertlinskoje 82 56.14 N 36.58 E
Vertou 32 47.10 N 1.29 W
Vertova 62 45.48 N 9.50 E
Vert-Saint-Denis 261 48.34 N 2.37 E
Vertus 50 48.54 N 4.00 E
Verucchio 66 43.59 N 12.25 E
Verulam 158 29.45 S 31.02 E
Verulamium ⊥ 260 51.45 N 0.22 W
Verviers 56 50.35 N 5.52 E
Vervins 50 49.50 N 3.54 E
Verwall Gruppe ⩓ 58 47.02 N 10.10 E
Verwoerd Reservoir
⊜[1] 158 30.40 S 25.40 E
Verwood 42 50.53 N 1.52 W
Veryan 42 50.13 N 4.54 W
Verzasca ≃ 58 46.09 N 8.52 E
Verzegnis 64 46.25 N 12.59 E
Verzenay 50 49.10 N 4.09 E
Verzino 68 39.19 N 16.51 E
Verzuolo 62 44.36 N 7.29 E
Verzy 50 49.09 N 4.10 E
Vesanto 26 62.56 N 26.25 E
Vesava ✦[8] 272c 19.08 N 72.48 E
Vescovato, Fr. 36 42.30 N 9.26 E
Vescovato, It. 64 45.10 N 10.10 E
Vescovo di Squillace,
Roccelletta del ⊥ 68 38.48 N 16.35 E
Vesdre ≃ 56 50.37 N 5.37 E
Veseja 76 53.04 N 27.41 E
Veselí nad Lužnicí 30 49.11 N 14.43 E
Veselí nad Moravou 30 48.58 N 17.22 E
Veselinovo 78 47.21 N 31.14 E
Veselovskoje 86 54.00 N 78.43 E
Veselovskoje
Vodochranilišče
⊜[1] 80 47.00 N 41.18 E
Vésenaz 58 46.14 N 6.12 E
Vešenskaja 80 49.38 N 41.43 E
Vesgre ≃ 50 48.53 N 1.28 E
Vesijärvi ⊜ 26 61.06 N 25.32 E
Vesjegonsk 76 58.40 N 37.16 E
Veškajma, S.S.S.R. 80 54.03 N 47.08 E
Veškajma, S.S.S.R. 80 54.04 N 47.02 E
Veški 265b 55.56 N 37.37 E
Vesle ≃ 50 49.23 N 3.38 E
Vešn'aki ✦[8] 265b 55.44 N 37.49 E
Ves'olaja Gora 83 48.43 N 39.16 E
Ves'olaja Rošča 86 53.47 N 76.22 E
Ves'oloje, S.S.S.R. 78 47.01 N 34.55 E
Ves'oloje, S.S.S.R. 80 50.17 N 45.15 E
Ves'oloje, S.S.S.R. 83 47.10 N 38.45 E
Ves'oloje, S.S.S.R. 85 43.19 N 77.06 E
Ves'olo-Voznesenka 83 47.09 N 38.20 E
Ves'olyj, S.S.S.R. 80 47.06 N 40.45 E
Ves'olyj, S.S.S.R. 83 47.20 N 39.18 E
Ves'olyje Terny 78 48.07 N 33.32 E
Ves'olyj Jar, S.S.S.R. 86 51.18 N 81.07 E
Ves'olyj Jar, S.S.S.R. 89 43.57 N 135.28 E
Ves'olyj Podol,
S.S.S.R. 78 49.36 N 33.16 E
Ves'olyj Podol,
S.S.S.R. 86 53.31 N 65.54 E
Ves'olyj Pos'olok ✦[8] 265a 59.54 N 30.28 E
Vesoul 58 47.38 N 6.10 E
Vespasiano 255 19.40 S 43.55 W
Vespolate 62 45.21 N 8.40 E
Vesta 236 9.43 N 83.03 W
Vest-Agder □[6] 26 58.30 N 7.10 E
Vestal 210 42.05 N 76.03 W
Vestal Center 210 42.02 N 76.01 W
Vestavia Hills 194 33.27 N 86.47 W
Vestbygd 26 58.06 N 6.35 E
Vesterålen II 24 68.45 N 15.00 E
Vester Egede 41 55.16 N 11.59 E
Vesterø Havn 26 57.18 N 10.56 E
Vester Skerninge 41 55.03 N 10.28 E
Vester Sottrup 41 54.57 N 9.43 E
Vestfjorden C[2] 24 68.08 N 15.00 E
Vestfold □[6] 26 59.15 N 10.10 E
Vestmannaeyjar 24a 63.26 N 20.12 W
Vestone 64 45.42 N 10.24 E
Vestreno 58 46.06 N 9.18 E
Vestsjælland □[6] 41 55.35 N 11.30 E
Vestvågøya I 24 68.15 N 13.50 E
Vésubie ≃ 62 43.52 N 7.12 E
Vesubio
→ Vesuvio ∧[1] 68 40.49 N 14.26 E
Vesuv
→ Vesuvio ∧[1] 68 40.49 N 14.26 E
Vesuvio ∧[1] 68 40.49 N 14.26 E
Vesuvius
→ Vesuvio ∧[1] 68 40.49 N 14.26 E
Vesuvius Bay 224 48.53 N 123.35 W
Veszprém 30 47.06 N 17.55 E
Veszprém □[6] 30 46.50 N 17.30 E
Vésztő 30 46.55 N 21.16 E
Vet ≃ 158 27.40 S 25.40 E
Vetapālem 122 15.47 N 80.19 E
Vétheuil 50 49.04 N 1.42 E
Vetju 24 62.57 N 50.44 E
Vetka 76 52.33 N 31.10 E
Vetlanda 26 57.26 N 15.04 E
Vetl'anka 80 52.52 N 51.09 E
Vetluga 80 57.51 N 45.47 E
Vetluga ≃ 80 56.18 N 46.24 E
Vetlužskij, S.S.S.R. 80 57.11 N 45.07 E
Vetlužskij, S.S.S.R. 80 58.23 N 45.26 E
Vetoškino 80 57.18 N 49.44 E
Vetovo 38 43.42 N 26.16 E
Vetralla 66 42.19 N 12.03 E
Vetren 38 42.16 N 24.03 E
Vetrino 76 55.25 N 28.28 E
Vetriolo 64 46.02 N 11.18 E
Vetrişoaia 38 46.26 N 28.13 E
Vetschau 54 51.47 N 14.04 E
Vettaikkāranpudūr 122 10.34 N 76.56 E
Vettisfossen ⌊ 26 61.22 N 7.55 E
Vetto 64 44.29 N 10.20 E
Vettore, Monte ∧ 66 42.49 N 13.16 E
Vetulonia 66 42.51 N 10.58 E
Veules-les-Roses 50 49.52 N 0.48 E
Veulettes-sur-Mer 50 49.51 N 0.36 E
Veurne (Furnes) 50 51.04 N 2.40 E
Vevay 218 38.45 N 85.04 W
Vevelstad 24 65.43 N 12.30 E
Veveno, Khawr ∨ 140 6.40 N 32.58 E
Vevey 58 46.28 N 6.51 E
Vex 58 46.13 N 7.24 E
Veyle ≃ 58 46.18 N 4.50 E
Veynes 62 44.32 N 5.49 E
Veyrier 62 45.53 N 6.10 E
Vézelay 50 47.28 N 3.44 E
Vézelise 58 48.29 N 6.05 E
Vézénobres 62 44.03 N 4.09 E
Vézère ≃ 32 44.53 N 0.53 E
Vezirköprü 130 41.09 N 35.28 E
Vezouze ≃ 58 48.35 N 6.29 E
Vezza d'Oglio 64 46.14 N 10.24 E
Vezzana, Cima della
∧ 64 46.17 N 11.50 E
Vezzano 64 46.05 N 11.00 E
Vezzano Ligure 64 44.09 N 9.52 E
VI □[4] 150 19.00 N 15.00 W
Viacha 248 16.39 S 68.18 W
Viadana 64 44.56 N 10.31 E
Viadutos 252 27.34 S 52.01 W
Viai Island I 164 3.20 S 144.25 E
Viale 252 31.53 S 60.01 W
Vialonga 266c 38.52 N 9.05 W
Via Mala ∨ 58 46.40 N 9.26 E
Viamão 252 30.05 S 51.02 W
Viamonte 252 33.44 S 63.06 W
Vian 196 35.30 N 94.58 W
Viana 250 3.13 S 45.00 W
Viana, Ilha do I 287a 22.52 S 43.08 W
Viana del Bollo 34 42.11 N 7.06 W
Viana do Alentejo 34 38.20 N 8.00 W
Viana do Castelo 34 41.42 N 8.50 W
Vianden 56 49.57 N 6.11 E
Vianen 52 52.00 N 5.05 E
Viangchan
(Vientiane) 110 17.58 N 102.36 E
Viangphoukha 110 20.41 N 101.04 E
Viar ≃ 34 37.36 N 5.50 W
Viareggio 64 43.52 N 10.14 E
Viarmes 50 49.08 N 2.22 E
Viatka
→ Kirov 80 58.38 N 49.42 E
Viaur ≃ 32 44.08 N 2.23 E
Vibank 184 50.20 N 103.55 W
Víboras, Arroyo de las
≃ 258 33.57 S 58.21 W
Viborg, Dan. 26 56.26 N 9.24 E
Viborg
→ Vyborg, S.S.S.R. 76 60.42 N 28.45 E
Viborg, S. Dak., U.S. 198 43.10 N 97.05 W
Viborg □[6] 41 56.18 N 9.27 E
Vibo Valentia 68 38.40 N 16.06 E
Vibraye 50 48.03 N 0.44 E
Viburnum 194 37.43 N 91.08 W
Viby 41 55.33 N 12.02 E
Viby ✦[8] 41 56.07 N 10.10 E
Vic, Étang de C 62 43.29 N 3.50 E
Vicálvaro ✦[8] 266a 40.24 N 3.36 W
Vicarello 66 42.10 N 12.12 E
Vicari 70 37.49 N 13.34 E
Vicchio 66 43.56 N 11.28 E
Vicco 192 37.13 N 83.04 W
Vic-en-Bigorre 32 43.06 N 0.05 E
Vicência 250 7.40 S 35.20 W
Vicente, Point ≻ 280 33.44 N 118.25 W
Vicente Casares 258 34.57 S 58.38 W
Vicente de Carvalho 256 23.56 S 46.19 W
Vicente Guerrero,
Méx. 232 30.45 N 116.00 W
Vicente Guerrero,
Méx. 234 18.24 N 92.53 W
Vicente Guerrero,
Méx. 234 19.08 N 98.10 W
Vicente López 258 34.32 S 58.28 W
Vicente López □[5] 288 34.32 S 58.30 W
Vicente Noble 238 18.23 N 71.11 W
Vicenza 64 45.33 N 11.33 E
Vicenza □[4] 64 45.40 N 11.27 E
Viceroy 184 49.27 N 105.22 W
Vich 34 41.56 N 2.15 E
Vichada □[5] 246 5.00 N 69.30 W
Vichada ≃ 246 4.55 N 67.50 W
Vichadero 252 31.48 S 54.43 W
Vichigasta 252 29.29 S 67.31 W
Vichoreva ≃ 88 56.47 N 101.22 E
Vichorevka 88 56.12 N 101.09 E
Vichra ≃ 76 54.01 N 31.52 E
Vichuga
→ Vičuga 80 57.13 N 41.56 E
Vichun 100 27.49 N 114.23 E
Vichuquén 252 34.53 S 72.00 W
Vichy 32 46.08 N 3.26 E
Vici 196 36.09 N 99.18 W
Vickery 214 41.23 N 82.56 W
Vickie 46 59.53 N 1.18 W
Vicksburg, Mich.,
U.S. 216 42.06 N 85.32 W
Vicksburg, Miss., U.S. 194 32.14 N 90.56 W
Vicksburg, Pa., U.S. 210 40.56 N 76.59 W
Vicksburg National
Military Park ♠ 194 32.24 N 90.52 W
Vico 36 42.10 N 8.48 E
Vico, Lago di ⊜ 66 42.19 N 12.10 E
Vico Canavese 62 45.30 N 7.47 E
Vico del Gargano 68 41.54 N 15.57 E
Vico Equense 68 40.40 N 14.25 E
Vicoforte 62 44.21 N 7.54 E
Vicopisano 66 43.42 N 10.35 E
Viçosa, Bra. 250 9.24 S 36.14 W
Viçosa, Bra. 255 20.45 S 42.53 W
Viçosa do Ceará 250 3.34 S 41.05 W
Vicosoprano 58 46.22 N 9.37 E
Vicovaro 66 42.01 N 12.54 E
Vicq 261 48.49 N 1.50 E
Vic-sur-Aisne 50 49.24 N 3.07 E
Vic-sur-Cère 32 44.59 N 2.37 E
Vic-sur-Seille 56 48.47 N 6.32 E
Victor, Calif., U.S. 226 38.08 N 121.12 W
Victor, Idaho, U.S. 202 43.36 N 111.07 W
Victor, Iowa, U.S. 190 41.44 N 92.18 W
Victor, Mont., U.S. 202 46.25 N 114.09 W
Victor, N.Y., U.S. 210 42.59 N 77.24 W
Victor, Lac ⊜ 186 50.35 N 61.50 W
Victorbur 52 53.29 N 7.20 E
Victor Harbor 168b 35.34 S 138.37 E
Victoria, Arg. 252 32.37 S 60.10 W
Victoria
→ Vitória, Bra. 255 20.19 S 40.21 W
Victoria, Cam. 152 4.01 N 9.12 E
Victoria, B.C., Can. 182 48.25 N 123.22 W
Victoria, P.E.I., Can. 186 46.13 N 63.29 W
Victoria, Chile 252 38.13 S 72.20 W
Victoria, Gren. 241k 12.12 N 61.42 W
Victoria, Guinée 150 10.50 N 14.33 W
Victoria (Xianggang),
H.K. 271d 22.17 N 114.09 E
Victoria, Malay. 112 5.17 N 115.15 E
Victoria
→ Ciudad Victoria,
Méx. 234 23.44 N 99.08 W
Victoria, Pil. 116 15.35 N 120.41 E
Victoria, Pil. 116 13.12 N 121.15 E
Victoria, Rom. 38 45.45 N 24.41 E
Victoria, Sey. 138 4.38 S 55.27 E
Victoria, Kans., U.S. 198 38.52 N 99.09 W
Victoria, Tex., U.S. 196 28.48 N 97.00 W
Victoria, Va., U.S. 192 36.59 N 78.14 W
Victoria □[3] 166 38.00 S 145.00 E
Victoria □[4] 154 20.54 S 31.21 E
Victoria □[6], Ont.,
Can. 212 44.35 N 78.50 W
Victoria □[6], Tex.,
U.S. 222 28.55 N 97.00 W
Victoria ✦[8] 288 34.28 S 58.31 W
Victoria ≃, Austl. 160 15.12 S 129.43 E
Victoria ≃, Newf.,
Can. 186 48.45 N 56.40 W
Victoria, Isla I 254 45.18 S 73.58 W
Victoria, Lake ⊜, Afr. 154 1.00 S 33.00 E
Victoria, Lake ⊜,
Austl. 166 34.00 S 141.16 E
Victoria, Mount ∧,
Mya. 110 21.14 N 93.55 E
Victoria, Mount ∧,
Pap. N. Gui. 164 8.55 S 147.35 E
Victoria, Pont ✦[5] 275a 45.29 N 73.32 W
Victoria and Albert
Museum ⊍ 272c 18.59 N 72.50 E
Victoria Beach 184 50.43 N 96.33 W
Victoria de Durango
→ Durango 234 24.02 N 104.40 W
Victoria de las Tunas 240p 20.58 N 76.57 W
Victoria Falls 154 17.56 S 25.50 E
Victoria Falls ⌊ 154 17.55 S 25.51 E
Victoria Falls
National Park ♠ 154 17.55 S 25.40 E
Victoria Gardens ♠ 272c 18.59 N 72.50 E
Victoria Harbour 212 44.45 N 79.46 W
Victoria International
Airport ⊠ 224 48.39 N 123.26 W
Victoria Island I,
N.W. Ter., Can. 176 71.00 N 114.00 W
Victoria Island I, Nig. 273a 6.26 N 3.26 E
Victoria Lake ⊜ 273d 26.14 S 28.09 E
Victoria Lake ⊜[1] 186 48.18 N 57.30 W
Victoria Land ✦[1] 9 75.00 S 163.00 E
Victoria Lawn Tennis
Association Courts
♠ 274b 37.51 S 145.02 E
Victoria Memorial
⊥ 272b 22.33 N 88.21 E
Victoria Memorial
Hall ⊍ 271c 1.17 N 103.51 E
Victoria Nile ≃ 154 2.14 N 31.26 E
Victoria Park 168a 31.58 S 115.55 E
Victoria Park ♠, H.K. 271d 22.17 N 114.07 E
Victoria Park ♠, Eng.,
U.K. 262 53.23 N 2.34 W
Victoria Peak ∧,
Belize 232 16.48 N 88.37 W
Victoria Peak ∧,
B.C., Can. 182 50.03 N 126.06 W
Victoria Peak ∧, H.K. 271d 22.17 N 114.08 E
Victoria Peaks ⩓ 116 9.22 N 118.20 E
Victoria Point 171a 27.35 S 153.18 E
Victoria Range ⩓,
N.Z. 172 42.09 S 172.08 E
Victoria Range ⩓,
Pil. 116 9.32 N 118.23 E
Victoria River Downs 164 16.24 S 131.00 E
Victorias 116 10.54 N 123.05 E
Victoria State Car
Club Race Circuit
♠ 274b 37.45 S 145.11 E
Victoria Station ✦[5],
Eng., U.K. 260 51.29 N 0.09 W
Victoria Station ✦[5],
Eng., U.K. 262 53.29 N 2.15 W
Victoria Strait ⊔ 176 69.15 N 100.30 W
Victoria University of
Manchester ⊍[2] 262 53.28 N 2.14 W
Victoriaville 206 46.03 N 71.57 W
Victoria West 158 31.25 S 23.04 E
Victorica 252 36.13 S 65.27 W
Victorino 246 2.48 N 67.50 W
Victorino de la Plaza 252 36.36 S 62.40 W
Victor Manuel Bueno 232 24.20 N 98.58 W
Victorville 228 34.32 N 117.18 W
Victory, Mount ∧ 164 9.10 S 149.05 E
Victory Gardens 276 40.52 N 74.32 W
Victory Heights 214 41.22 N 79.46 W
Victory Hills 279b 40.11 N 79.53 W
Victory Mills 210 43.05 N 73.36 W
Victory Monument
⊥ 269a 13.46 N 100.33 E
Vičuga 80 57.13 N 41.56 E
Vicuña 252 30.02 S 70.44 W
Vicuña Mackenna 252 33.54 S 64.23 W
Vidal, Cape ≻ 158 28.09 S 32.33 E
Vidalia, Ga., U.S. 192 32.13 N 82.25 W
Vidalia, La., U.S. 194 31.34 N 91.26 W
Vidal Ramos 252 27.23 S 49.22 W
Vidauban 62 43.26 N 6.26 E
Videbæk 26 56.05 N 8.38 E
Videira 252 27.00 S 51.08 W
Videle 38 44.16 N 25.31 E
Vidigueira 34 38.13 N 7.48 W
Vidim, Česko. 54 50.28 N 14.31 E
Vidim, S.S.S.R. 88 56.29 N 103.09 E
Vidin 38 43.59 N 22.52 E
Vidisha 124 23.32 N 77.49 E
Vidlica 24 61.10 N 32.21 E

	English	Deutsch	Español	Français	Português
≃	River	Fluss	Río	Rivière	Rio
☲	Canal	Kanal	Canal	Canal	Canal
⌊	Waterfall, Rapids	Wasserfall, Stromschnellen	Cascada, Rápidos	Chute d'eau, Rapides	Cascata, Rápidos
⊔	Strait	Meeresstrasse	Estrecho	Détroit	Estreito
C	Bay, Gulf	Bucht, Golf	Bahía, Golfo	Baie, Golfe	Baía, Golfo
⊜	Lake, Lakes	See, Seen	Lago, Lagos	Lac, Lacs	Lago, Lagos
☷	Swamp	Sumpf	Pantano	Marais	Pântano
⍓	Ice Features, Glacier	Eis- und Gletscherformen	Accidentes Glaciales	Formes glaciaires	Acidentes Glaciares
⊤	Other Hydrographic Features	Andere Hydrographische Objekte	Otros Elementos Hidrográficos	Autres données hydrographiques	Outros Elementos Hidrográficos

	English	Deutsch	Español	Français	Português
✣	Submarine Features	Untermeerische Objekte	Accidentes Submarinos	Formes de relief sous-marin	Acidentes Submarinos
□	Political Unit	Politische Einheit	Unidad Politica	Entité politique	Unidade Política
⊍	Cultural Institution	Kulturelle Institution	Institución Cultural	Institution culturelle	Instituição Cultural
⊥	Historical Site	Historische Stätte	Sitio Histórico	Site historique	Sitio Histórico
♠	Recreational Site	Erholungs- und Ferienort	Sitio de Recreo	Centre de loisirs	Sítio de Lazer
⊠	Airport	Flughafen	Aeropuerto	Aéroport	Aeroporto
▪	Military Installation	Militäranlage	Instalación Militar	Installation militaire	Instalação Militar
✦	Miscellaneous	Verschiedenes	Misceláneo	Divers	Miscelânea

Vidnoje 82 55.34 N 37.41 E
Vidogošči 82 56.42 N 36.23 E
Vidor 194 30.07 N 94.01 W
Vidos ≐ 267b 40.58 N 28.53 E
Vidöstern @ 26 57.04 N 14.01 E
Vidourle ≐ 62 43.32 N 4.08 E
Vidra, Rom. 38 45.55 N 26.54 E
Vidra, Rom. 38 44.16 N 26.11 E
Vidsel 24 65.51 N 20.24 E
Vidzeme ✦[1] 76 57.10 N 25.30 E
Vidzy 76 55.24 N 26.38 E
Vie ≐ 50 49.05 N 0.04 E
Viecht 60 48.30 N 12.04 E
Viechtach 60 49.05 N 12.53 E
Viechtwang 64 47.55 N 13.57 E
Viedma 254 40.48 S 63.00 W
Viedma, Lago @ 254 49.35 S 72.35 W
Viehberg ∧ 61 48.33 N 14.37 E
Viehhausen 60 48.59 N 11.58 E
Vieil Armand ✦ 58 47.52 N 7.10 E
Vieillard, Lac du @ 190 47.23 N 78.02 W
Vieille Case 240d 15.36 N 61.24 W
Vieira do Minho 34 41.39 N 8.09 W
Viejo ≐ 236 12.28 N 86.21 W
Viejo, Cerro ∧ 246 4.49 S 79.27 W
Viekšniai 76 56.16 N 22.31 E
Viel, Lac @ 206 46.40 N 74.32 W
Vielank 54 53.15 N 11.08 E
Viella 34 42.42 N 0.48 E
Vielle-Eglise-en-Yvelines 261 48.40 N 1.53 E
Vielsalm 56 50.17 N 5.55 E
Viels-Maisons 50 48.54 N 3.24 E
Viena
→ Vienne ≐ 32 47.13 N 0.05 E
Vienenburg 54 51.57 N 10.34 E
Vienna, Ont., Can. 212 42.41 N 80.48 W
Vienna
→ Wien, Öst. 61 48.13 N 16.20 E
Vienna, Ga., U.S. 192 32.06 N 83.47 W
Vienna, Ill., U.S. 194 37.25 N 88.54 W
Vienna, Ind., U.S. 218 38.39 N 85.46 W
Vienna, Md., U.S. 208 38.29 N 75.49 W
Vienna, Mo., U.S. 194 38.11 N 91.57 W
Vienna, N.J., U.S. 210 40.52 N 74.54 W
Vienna, Ohio, U.S. 214 41.14 N 80.40 W
Vienna, S. Dak., U.S. 198 44.42 N 97.30 W
Vienna, Va., U.S. 208 38.54 N 77.16 W
Vienna, W. Va., U.S. 188 39.20 N 81.26 W
Vienne, Fr. 62 45.31 N 4.52 E
Vienne
→ Wien, Öst. 61 48.13 N 16.20 E
Vienne □[5] 32 46.35 N 0.30 E
Vienne ≐ 32 47.13 N 0.05 E
Vienne-en-Arthies 261 49.04 N 1.44 E
Vienne-le-Château 56 49.11 N 4.53 E
Vientos, Paso de los
→ Windward Passage ⋓ 238 20.00 N 73.50 W
Vieques 240m 18.09 N 65.27 W
Vieques, Isla de I 240m 18.08 N 65.25 W
Vieques, Pasaje de ⋓ 240m 18.11 N 65.37 W
Vieques, Sonda de ⋓ 240m 18.15 N 65.23 W
Vière ≐ 56 48.46 N 4.41 E
Viereck 54 53.32 N 14.02 E
Vieremä 26 63.45 N 27.01 E
Vierfontein 158 27.03 S 26.46 E
Vierhouten 52 52.20 N 5.50 E
Vieringhausen ✦[8] 263 51.11 N 7.10 E
Vierlande ✦[1] 52 53.26 N 10.14 E
Viernau 54 50.40 N 10.32 E
Viernheim 56 49.32 N 8.34 E
Vierraden 54 53.06 N 14.17 E
Viersen 56 51.15 N 6.23 E
Vierumäki 26 61.06 N 25.57 E
Vierwaldstättersee @ 58 47.00 N 8.28 E
Vierzehn-Heiligen ✝[1] 56 50.08 N 11.02 E
Vierzon 50 47.13 N 2.05 E
Viesca 232 25.21 N 102.48 W
Viesecke 54 53.01 N 12.01 E
Vieselbach 54 51.00 N 11.08 E
Viesīte 76 56.21 N 25.33 E
Vieste 68 41.53 N 16.10 E
Vietgest 54 53.45 N 12.20 E
Vietnam □[1] 108 16.00 N 108.00 E
Viet-nam
→ Vietnam □[1], As. 108 16.00 N 108.00 E
Viet-nam
→ Vietnam □[1], As. 108 16.00 N 108.00 E
Vietnam □[1] 110 16.00 N 108.00 E
Vietri di Potenza 68 40.36 N 15.30 E
Vietri sul Mare 68 40.40 N 14.44 E
Viet-tri 110 21.18 N 105.26 E
Vietz
→ Witnica 30 52.40 N 14.55 E
Vieux-Condé 50 50.27 N 3.34 E
Vieux-Ferette 58 47.30 N 7.18 E
Vieux-Fort, Guad. 241f 15.57 N 61.43 W
Vieux Fort, St. Luc. 241f 13.44 N 60.57 W
Vieux-Fort, Pointe du ≻ 241o 15.57 N 61.43 W
Vieux Fort Bay ⊂ 241f 13.44 N 60.58 W
Vieux-Habitants 241o 16.04 N 61.46 W
Vieux-Thann 58 47.48 N 7.08 E
Vievis 76 54.46 N 24.48 E
View Park 280 34.00 N 118.21 W
Vieytes 258 35.16 S 57.35 W
Vif 62 45.03 N 5.40 E
Vig 41 55.51 N 11.36 E
Viga ≐ 76 59.14 N 43.41 E
Vigala 76 58.43 N 24.22 E
Vigan 116 17.34 N 120.23 E
Vigarano Mainarda 64 44.50 N 11.30 E
Vigatto 64 44.43 N 10.20 E
Vigeland 26 58.05 N 7.18 E
Vigentino ✦[8] 266b 45.25 N 9.11 E
Vigersted 41 55.29 N 11.54 E
Vigese, Monte ∧ 64 44.12 N 11.06 E
Vigevano 62 45.19 N 8.51 E
Viggianello 68 39.58 N 16.05 E
Viggiano 68 40.20 N 15.54 E
Viggiù 62 45.52 N 8.54 E
Vigia 250 0.48 S 48.08 W
Vigie Airport ⊠ 241f 14.01 N 60.59 W
Vignacourt 50 50.01 N 2.12 E
Vignale 62 45.01 N 8.24 E
Vignanello 66 42.23 N 12.17 E
Vigneulles-lès-Hattonchâtel 56 48.59 N 5.43 E
Vigneux-sur-Seine 261 48.42 N 2.25 E
Vignola 64 44.29 N 11.00 E
Vignory 58 48.17 N 5.06 E
Vignot 56 48.46 N 5.36 E
Vigny 261 49.05 N 1.56 E
Vigo 34 42.14 N 8.43 W
Vigo, Ría de ⊂[1] 34 42.15 N 8.45 W
Vigodarzere 64 45.27 N 11.53 E
Vigo di Fassa 64 46.25 N 11.40 E
Vigolzone 62 44.55 N 9.40 E
Vigone 62 44.51 N 7.30 E
Vigonovo 64 45.23 N 12.00 E
Vigo-Rendena 64 46.05 N 10.43 E
Vigrestad 26 58.34 N 5.42 E
Viguzzolo 62 44.54 N 8.55 E
Vigy 56 49.12 N 6.18 E
Vihanti 26 64.29 N 25.00 E
Vihāri 123 30.02 N 72.21 E
Vihiers 32 47.09 N 0.32 W
Vihorlat ⩕ 30 48.55 N 22.10 E
Vihowa 123 31.08 N 70.30 E
Vihren ∧ 38 41.46 N 23.24 E
Vihti 26 60.25 N 24.20 E
VII □[4] 148 22.30 N 10.00 W
Viiala 26 61.13 N 23.47 E
Viinijärvi 26 62.39 N 29.14 E
Viinijärvi @ 26 62.44 N 29.17 E
Viipuri
→ Vyborg 76 60.42 N 28.45 E
Viitasaari 26 63.04 N 25.52 E
Viivikonna 76 59.19 N 27.42 E
Vijāpur 120 23.34 N 72.45 E
Vijayapuri 118 16.52 N 79.35 E
Vijayawāda 122 16.31 N 80.37 E
Vijosë (Aóös) ≐ 38 40.37 N 19.20 E
Vik 40 59.44 N 17.28 E
Vik ⊥ 40 59.44 N 17.27 E
Vika 40 60.31 N 15.42 E
Vikajärvi 24 66.37 N 26.12 E
Vikārābad 122 17.20 N 77.54 E
Vikbolandet ≻[1] 41 58.32 N 16.40 E
Viken 41 56.09 N 12.34 E
Viken @ 26 58.39 N 14.20 E
Vikern @ 40 59.30 N 14.55 E
Vikersund 26 59.59 N 10.02 E
Vikhroli ✦[8] 272c 19.07 N 72.56 E
Viking 182 53.06 N 111.46 W
Viking Village 218 39.05 N 84.18 W
Vikmanshyttan 40 60.17 N 15.49 E
Vikna 24 64.57 N 10.58 E
Vikna I 22 64.57 N 10.58 E
Vikramasingapuram 122 8.43 N 77.24 E
Viksøyri 26 61.05 N 6.35 E
Viktor 24 66.09 N 58.07 E
Viktorovka 86 52.51 N 62.32 E
Viktring 61 46.35 N 14.16 E
Vikulovo 86 56.49 N 70.37 E
Vila, N. Heb. 175f 17.44 S 168.19 E
Vil'a, S.S.S.R. 80 55.15 N 42.13 E
Vila Alferes Chamusca 156 24.55 S 33.00 E
Vila Armindo Monteiro 112 9.02 S 125.22 E
Vila Arriaga 152 14.46 S 13.21 E
Vila Augusta 287b 23.28 S 46.32 W
Vila Boacaya ✦[8] 287b 23.29 S 46.44 W
Vila Cabral 154 13.18 S 35.14 E
Vila Caldas Xavier 154 14.28 S 33.00 E
Vila Coutinho 154 14.37 S 34.19 E
Vila da Maganja 154 17.18 S 37.30 E
Vila da Ribeira Brava 150a 16.37 N 24.18 W
Viladecaballs 266d 41.33 N 1.58 E
Viladecáns 266d 41.19 N 2.01 E
Vila de Manabuto 112 8.30 S 126.01 E
Vila de Manica 156 18.56 S 32.53 E
Vila de Rei 34 39.40 N 8.09 W
Vila do Bispo 34 37.05 N 8.55 W
Vila do Conde 34 41.21 N 8.45 W
Vila do Porto 148a 36.56 N 25.09 W
Vila Flor 34 41.18 N 7.09 W
Vila Fontes 156 17.50 S 35.21 E
Vila Formosa ✦[8] 287b 23.34 S 46.33 W
Vilafranca del Panadés 34 41.21 N 1.42 E
Vila Franca de Xira 34 38.57 N 8.59 W
Vila Galvão 287b 23.27 S 46.33 W
Vila Gamito 154 14.12 S 33.00 E
Vila General Carmona 112 8.43 S 125.34 E
Vila Gomes da Costa 156 24.19 S 33.38 E
Vila Gouveia 156 18.03 S 33.11 E
Vila Guilherme ✦[8] 287b 23.30 S 46.36 W
Vilaine ≐ 32 47.30 N 2.27 W
Vila Isabel ✦[8] 287a 22.55 S 43.15 W
Vila Jaguára ✦[8] 287b 23.31 S 46.45 W
Vila Junqueiro 154 15.25 S 36.58 E
Viļaka 76 57.11 N 27.41 E
Vila Luísa 156 25.44 S 32.40 E
Vilama, Laguna de @ 252 22.36 S 66.55 W
Vila Machado 156 19.18 S 34.11 E
Vila Madalena ✦[8] 287b 23.33 S 46.42 W
Vila Maria ✦[8] 287b 23.31 S 46.34 W
Vila Mariana ✦[8] 287b 23.35 S 46.38 W
Vila Matilde ✦[8] 287b 23.32 S 46.31 W
Vila Muriqui 256 22.56 S 43.57 W
Vilanculos 156 22.01 S 35.19 E
Viļāni 76 56.33 N 26.57 E
Vila Nova 152 12.38 S 16.03 E
Vila Nova ≐ 250 0.04 S 51.13 W
Vila Nova de Famalicão 34 41.25 N 8.32 W
Vila Nova de Foz Côa 34 41.05 N 7.12 W
Vila Nova de Gaia 34 41.08 N 8.37 W
Vilanova de la Roca 266d 41.33 N 2.17 E
Vila Nova de Malaca 112 8.22 S 126.54 E
Vila Nova do Seles 152 11.24 S 14.15 E
Vila Nova de Ourém 34 39.39 N 8.35 W
Vila Paiva de Andrada 156 18.44 S 34.03 E
Vila Pery 156 19.08 S 33.29 E
Vila Progresso 287a 22.55 S 43.03 W
Vila Prudente ✦[8] 287b 23.35 S 46.34 W
Vila Real 34 41.18 N 7.45 W
Vila Real de Santo António 34 37.12 N 7.25 W
Vilar Formoso 34 40.37 N 6.50 W
Vila Rica 246 3.40 S 61.02 W
Vilarinho do Monte 250 1.37 S 52.01 W
Vila Salazar 112 8.27 S 126.27 E
Vila Trigo de Morais 156 24.36 S 33.00 E
Vila Vasco da Gama 154 14.54 S 32.14 E
Vila Velha, Bra. 250 3.13 N 51.13 W
Vila Velha, Bra. 255 20.20 S 40.17 W
Vila Velha de Ródão 34 39.38 N 7.40 W
Vila Verde, Port. 34 41.39 N 8.26 W
Vila Verde, Port. 266c 38.50 N 9.22 W
Vila Viçosa 34 38.47 N 8.13 W
Vil'ča 78 51.22 N 29.24 E
Vîlcea □[4] 38 45.19 N 24.00 E
Vildbjerg 41 56.12 N 8.46 E
Vilejka 76 54.30 N 26.53 E
Vilelas 252 27.57 S 62.38 W
Vilenki 82 54.16 N 38.55 E
Vil'gort, S.S.S.R. 24 61.35 N 50.40 E
Vil'gort, S.S.S.R. 24 60.34 N 56.24 E
Vilhelmina 26 64.37 N 16.39 E
Vilhena 248 12.43 S 60.07 W
Vilija ≐ 76 55.54 N 23.53 E
Viljandi 76 58.22 N 25.36 E
Viljoensdrif 158 26.44 S 27.55 E
Viljoenshof 158 34.40 S 19.42 E
Viljoenskroon 158 27.12 S 27.00 E
Viljoenspos 158 25.44 S 28.05 E
Vilkaviškis 76 54.39 N 23.02 E
Vil'kickogo, Ostrov I, S.S.S.R. 72 73.29 N 75.06 E
Vil'kickogo, Ostrov I, S.S.S.R. 74 75.44 N 152.20 E
Vil'kickogo, Proliv ⋓ 74 77.55 N 103.00 E
Vilkija 76 55.03 N 23.35 E
Vilkovo 78 45.25 N 29.35 E
Villa Abecia 248 21.00 S 65.23 W
Villa Aberastain 252 31.39 S 68.35 W
Villa Acuña
→ Ciudad Acuña 232 29.18 N 100.55 W
Villa Adelina ✦[8] 288 34.31 S 58.32 W
Villa Adriana ⊥ 66 41.56 N 12.45 E
Villa Ahumada 232 30.37 N 106.31 W
Villa Alberdi 252 27.35 S 65.37 W
Villa Alejandrina 288 33.46 S 58.21 W
Villa Alemana 252 33.03 S 71.23 W
Villa Allende 252 31.18 S 64.18 W
Villa Alta 234 17.21 N 96.09 W
Villa Ana 252 28.29 S 59.37 W
Villa Ángela 252 27.35 S 60.43 W
Villa Atamisqui 252 28.29 S 63.48 W
Villa Atuel 252 34.50 S 67.54 W
Villaba 116 11.13 N 124.23 E
Villa Ballester ✦[8] 288 34.32 S 58.33 W
Villabassa (Niederdorf) 64 46.44 N 12.10 E
Villabate 70 38.04 N 13.26 E
Villabé 261 48.35 N 2.27 E
Villa Bella 248 10.23 S 65.24 W
Villa Berthet 252 27.17 S 60.25 W
Villablino 34 42.56 N 6.19 W
Villa Borghese ✝ 267a 41.55 N 12.29 E
Villa Bruzual 246 9.20 N 69.06 W
Villa Bustos 252 29.17 S 67.02 W
Villa Cañás, Arg. 252 34.00 S 61.36 W
Villacañas, Esp. 34 39.38 N 3.20 W
Villa Carlos Paz 252 31.24 S 64.31 W
Villacarriedo 34 43.14 N 3.48 W
Villacarrillo 34 38.07 N 3.05 W
Villa Castelli, Arg. 252 29.00 S 68.11 W
Villa Castelli, It. 68 40.35 N 17.28 E
Villacastín 34 40.47 N 4.25 W
Villach 64 46.36 N 13.50 E
Villacidro 71 39.27 N 8.44 E
Villa Ciudadela ✦[8] 288 34.38 S 58.34 W
Villa Clara □[4] 240p 22.30 N 80.00 W
Villa Colón (Caucete), Arg. 252 31.39 S 68.17 W
Villa Colón, Méx. 234 20.48 N 100.03 W
Villa Concepción del Tío 252 31.19 S 62.50 W
Villa Constitución 252 33.14 S 60.20 W
Villa Corona 234 20.25 N 103.41 W
Villa Cortese 266b 45.34 N 8.53 E
Villacoublay, Aérodrome de ⊠ 261 48.45 N 2.10 E
Villa Creek ≐ 226 35.27 N 120.58 W
Villa Cuauhtémoc, Méx. 234 22.11 N 97.50 W
Villa Cuauhtémoc, Méx. 234 19.24 N 99.34 W
Villada 34 42.15 N 4.58 W
Villa de Apaseo el Alto 234 20.27 N 100.37 W
Villa de Arriaga 234 21.54 N 101.23 W
Villadeati 62 45.04 N 8.10 E
Villa de Comaltitlán 236 15.13 N 92.35 W
Villa de Cos 234 23.17 N 102.21 W
Villa de Cura 246 10.02 N 67.29 W
Villa de García 196 25.49 N 100.35 W
Villa de Guadalupe 234 23.22 N 100.46 W
Villa del Carmen 252 32.57 S 65.03 W
Villa Delgado 236 13.43 N 89.10 W
Villa del Pueblito 234 20.32 N 100.27 W
Villa del Río 34 37.59 N 4.17 W
Villa del Rosario, Arg. 252 30.47 S 57.55 W
Villa del Rosario, Arg. 252 31.35 S 63.32 W
Villa de María 252 29.54 S 63.43 W
Villa de Mayo 258 34.30 S 58.41 W
Villa de Méndez 232 25.07 N 98.34 W
Villa de Nova Sintra 150a 14.52 N 24.43 W
Villa de Reyes 234 21.48 N 100.56 W
Villa de San Antonio 236 14.16 N 87.36 W
Villa de San Francisco 236 14.10 N 86.58 W
Villa de Soto 252 30.51 S 64.59 W
Villa d'Este ⊥ 267a 41.57 N 12.48 E
Villa Devoto ✦[8] 288 34.36 S 58.31 W
Villa Diamante ✦[8] 288 34.41 S 58.26 W
Villa di Chiavenna 58 46.20 N 9.29 E
Villa Diego, Arg. 252 33.01 S 60.37 W
Villadiego, Esp. 34 42.31 N 4.00 W
Villa Dolores 252 31.56 S 65.12 W
Villa Dominico ✦[8] 288 34.41 S 58.19 W
Villadose 64 45.04 N 11.53 E
Villadossola 58 46.04 N 8.16 E
Villa El Alto 252 28.18 S 65.22 W
Villa el Carmen 236 11.59 N 86.31 W
Villa Elisa 252 32.10 S 58.24 W
Villa Elisa ✦[8] 258 34.50 S 58.05 W
Villa Escalante 234 19.24 N 101.39 W
Villa Eufronio Viscarra 248 17.59 S 65.36 W
Villa Flores 234 16.14 N 93.14 W
Villa Florida 252 26.23 S 57.09 W
Villafranca d'Asti 62 44.55 N 8.02 E
Villafranca del Bierzo 34 42.36 N 6.48 W
Villafranca de los Barros 34 38.34 N 6.20 W
Villafranca di Verona 64 45.21 N 10.50 E
Villafranca in Lunigiana 64 44.17 N 9.57 E
Villafranca Piemonte 62 44.47 N 7.33 E
Villafranca Sicula 70 37.35 N 13.17 E
Villafranca Tirrena 70 38.14 N 15.26 E
Villafrati 70 37.54 N 13.29 E
Villa Frontera 232 26.56 N 101.27 W
Villagaracía 34 42.36 N 8.45 W
Villa García 234 22.10 N 101.57 W
Village Creek ≐ 194 35.28 N 91.19 W
Village Green 285 39.52 N 75.26 W
Villa General Roca 252 32.39 S 66.28 W
Village of the Branch 276 40.51 N 73.11 W
Villa González 234 22.50 N 98.27 W
Villa González Ortega 234 22.30 N 101.55 W
Villagrán, Méx. 234 24.29 N 99.29 W
Villagrán, Méx. 234 20.31 N 100.59 W
Villagrande Strisaili 71 39.58 N 9.30 E
Villa Grazia 70 38.09 N 13.10 E
Villagrazia ✦[8] 70 38.05 N 13.20 E
Villa Grove 194 39.52 N 88.10 W
Villaguay 252 31.51 S 59.01 W
Villa Guerrero, Méx. 234 18.52 N 99.39 W
Villa Guerrero, Méx. 234 21.59 N 103.36 W
Villa Guillermina 252 28.14 S 59.28 W
Villa Hayes 252 25.06 S 57.34 W
Villahermosa 234 17.59 N 92.55 W
Villa Hernandarias 252 31.13 S 59.59 W
Villa Hidalgo, Méx. 204 30.59 N 116.10 W
Villa Hidalgo, Méx. 234 21.40 N 102.36 W
Villa Hidalgo, Méx. 234 21.44 N 105.15 W
Villa Huidobro (Cañada Verde) 252 34.50 S 64.35 W
Villa Imeriale ⊥ 70 37.22 N 14.20 E
Villaines-la-Juhel 32 48.21 N 0.17 W
Villa Iris 252 38.10 S 63.15 W
Villa Jiménez 234 19.55 N 101.35 W
Villajoyosa 34 38.30 N 0.14 W
Villa Juárez, Méx. 232 27.10 N 109.50 W
Villa Juárez, Méx. 234 22.20 N 100.17 W
Villa Krause 252 31.34 S 68.32 W
Villa La Angostura 254 40.47 S 71.40 W
Villa Lagarina 64 45.55 N 11.01 E
Villalago 66 41.56 N 13.50 E
Villa La Paz 252 33.27 S 67.38 W
Villa Larca 252 32.37 S 64.59 W
Villa Larroque 252 33.02 S 59.01 W
Villalba, Esp. 34 43.18 N 7.41 W
Villalba, It. 70 37.39 N 13.50 E
Villalba, P.R. 240m 18.08 N 66.30 W
Villa Lía 258 34.07 S 59.26 W
Villalon 116 11.31 N 124.22 E
Villalon ✦[8] 286b 23.03 N 82.26 W
Villalón de Campos 34 42.06 N 5.02 W
Villalonga 254 39.53 S 62.35 W
Villa López 232 27.00 N 105.02 W
Villalpando 34 41.52 N 5.24 W
Villa Lugano ✦[8] 288 34.41 S 58.28 W
Villalvernia 62 44.49 N 8.51 E
Villa Madero, Arg. 288 34.42 S 58.30 W
Villa Madero, Méx. 234 19.24 N 101.16 W
Villa Mainero 232 24.32 N 99.38 W
Villamar 71 39.37 N 8.59 E
Villa María, Arg. 252 32.25 S 63.15 W
Villa Maria, Pa., U.S. 214 41.05 N 80.30 W
Villa María Grande 252 31.39 S 59.54 W
Villa Martín, Bol. 248 20.46 S 67.47 W
Villamartín, Esp. 34 36.52 N 5.38 W
Villamarzana 64 45.01 N 11.41 E
Villamassargia 71 39.16 N 8.38 E
Villa Matoque 252 25.49 S 63.49 W
Villa Mazán 252 28.40 S 66.34 W
Villa Mercedes 252 30.07 S 68.42 W
Villamil 246a 0.56 S 91.01 W
Villa Minozzo 64 44.22 N 10.28 E
Villa Montes 248 21.15 S 63.30 W
Villa Morelos 234 20.00 N 101.25 W
Villandraut 32 44.28 N 0.23 W
Villandry 50 47.20 N 0.31 E
Villa Nova, Md., U.S. 284b 39.21 N 76.44 W
Villa Nova, Ohio, U.S. 216 40.33 N 84.26 W
Villanova, Pa., U.S. 208 40.02 N 75.21 W
Villanova d'Asti 62 44.57 N 7.56 E
Villanova Mondovì 62 44.21 N 7.45 E
Villanova Monferrato 62 45.11 N 8.28 E
Villanova Monteleone 71 40.30 N 8.28 E
Villanova sull'Arda 64 45.01 N 10.00 E
Villanova Tulo 71 39.47 N 9.13 E
Villanova University ✝[2] 285 40.02 N 75.21 W
Villa Nueva, Arg. 252 32.54 S 68.47 W
Villa Nueva, Arg. 252 32.26 S 63.15 W
Villanueva, Col. 246 10.37 N 72.59 W
Villa Nueva, Guat. 236 14.31 N 90.35 W
Villanueva, Hond. 236 15.17 N 88.00 W
Villanueva, Méx. 234 22.21 N 102.53 W
Villanueva, Nic. 236 12.58 N 86.49 W
Villanueva, N. Mex., U.S. 200 35.17 N 105.23 W
Villanueva de Córdoba 34 38.20 N 4.37 W
Villa Nueva de Guaymallén → Guaymallén 252 32.54 S 68.47 W
Villanueva de la Serena 34 38.58 N 5.48 W
Villanueva de la Sierra 34 40.12 N 6.24 W
Villanueva de los Infantes 34 38.44 N 2.59 W
Villanueva del Río y Minas 34 37.39 N 5.42 W
Villanueva y Geltrú 34 41.14 N 1.44 E
Villa Numancia 288 34.55 S 58.24 W
Villa Obregón 234 21.07 N 102.42 W
Villa Obregón ✦[8] 286a 19.21 N 99.12 W
Villa Ocampo 252 28.28 S 59.22 W
Villa Ojo de Agua 252 29.31 S 63.42 W
Villa Oliva 252 26.01 S 57.53 W
Villa Opicina 64 45.40 N 13.49 E
Villa Orestes Pereyra 232 26.31 N 105.40 W
Villa Ottone (Uttenheim) 64 46.52 N 11.57 E
Villa Park, Calif., U.S. 228 33.49 N 117.49 W
Villa Park, Ill., U.S. 278 41.53 N 87.59 W
Villa Park Dam ✦[6] 280 33.48 N 117.46 W
Villa Pérez 240m 18.12 N 66.47 W
Villapiana 68 39.51 N 16.28 E
Villapiana Lido 68 39.48 N 16.29 E
Villapinzón 246 5.13 N 73.36 W
Villa Potenza 66 43.19 N 13.25 E
Villaputzu 71 39.26 N 9.34 E
Villa Quinteros 252 27.14 S 65.33 W
Villa Quintilio Varo ⊥ 267a 41.58 N 12.47 E
Villa Ramírez 252 32.11 S 60.12 W
Villarcayo 34 42.56 N 3.34 W
Villar-d'Arêne 62 45.02 N 6.20 E
Villard-Bonnot 62 45.14 N 5.53 E
Villard-de-Lans 62 45.04 N 5.33 E
Villardefrades 34 41.43 N 5.15 W
Villar del Arzobispo 34 39.44 N 0.49 W
Villareal 116 11.34 N 124.56 E
Villa Real ✦[8] 288 34.37 S 58.31 W
Villa Regina 252 39.06 S 67.04 W
Villa Reynolds 252 33.43 S 65.23 W
Villa Rica 192 33.44 N 84.55 W
Villa Rivero 248 17.37 S 65.48 W
Villaroche 261 48.37 N 2.39 E
Villa Rosa, Arg. 258 34.25 S 58.52 W
Villarosa, It. 70 37.35 N 14.10 E
Villar Pellice 62 44.48 N 7.09 E
Villar Perosa 62 44.56 N 7.15 E
Villarreal 34 39.56 N 0.06 W
Villarreales 196 26.07 N 100.20 W
Villarrica, Chile 254 39.16 S 72.13 W
Villarrica, Col. 246 3.58 N 74.37 W
Villarrica, Para. 252 25.45 S 56.26 W
Villarrica, Lago @ 254 39.15 S 72.06 W
Villarrobledo 34 39.16 N 2.36 W
Villarrubia de los Ojos 34 39.13 N 3.36 W
Villars, Arg. 258 34.50 S 58.56 W
Villars, Schw. 58 46.18 N 7.04 E
Villars-Colmars 62 44.10 N 6.36 E
Villars-en-Azois 58 48.04 N 4.45 E
Villars-les-Dombes 58 46.00 N 5.01 E
Villars-sur-Var 62 43.56 N 7.06 E
Villa Ruiz 258 34.25 S 59.15 W
Villas 208 39.02 N 74.56 W
Villa Sáenz Peña ✦[8] 288 34.36 S 58.31 W
Villa San Andrés ✦[8] 288 34.33 S 58.32 W
Villa San Giovanni 68 38.13 N 15.38 E
Villa San José 252 32.12 S 58.13 W
Villa San Martín 252 28.18 S 64.12 W
Villasanta 62 45.37 N 9.18 E
Villa Santa, Montaña ∧ 236 14.12 N 86.27 W
Villa Santa Maria 66 41.57 N 14.21 E
Villa Santina 64 46.24 N 12.55 E
Villa Santos Lugares ✦[8] 288 34.36 S 58.32 W
Villasayas 34 41.21 N 2.37 W
Villa Serrano 248 19.06 S 64.22 W
Villasimius 71 39.08 N 9.31 E
Villasis 116 15.54 N 120.35 E
Villa Somoza 236 12.03 N 84.59 W
Villasor 71 39.23 N 8.56 E
Villa Tunari 248 16.55 S 65.25 W
Villa Turdera ✦[8] 288 34.48 S 58.25 W
Villa Unión, Arg. 252 29.24 S 62.47 W
Villa Unión, Arg. 252 29.18 S 68.12 W
Villa Unión, Méx. 232 28.15 N 100.43 W
Villa Unión, Méx. 234 23.12 N 106.14 W
Villa Unión, Méx. 234 23.58 N 104.02 W
Villa Vaca Guzmán 248 19.54 S 63.48 W
Villa Valeria 252 34.20 S 64.55 W
Villa Vallelonga 66 41.52 N 13.37 E
Villa Vázquez 238 19.45 N 71.27 W
Villaverde ✦[8] 266a 40.21 N 3.42 W
Villaverla 64 45.39 N 11.29 E
Villa Verona 226 39.28 N 121.33 W
Villavicencio 246 4.09 N 73.37 W
Villa Vicente Guerrero 234 23.45 N 103.59 W
Villaviciosa 34 43.29 N 5.26 W
Villaviciosa de Córdoba 34 38.05 N 5.01 W
Villa Victoria 234 19.26 N 100.00 W
Villa Vomano 66 42.37 N 13.46 E
Villazón 248 22.06 S 65.36 W
Villa Zorraquín 252 31.19 S 58.02 W
Villé 58 48.20 N 7.18 E

ENGLISH: Name — Page — Lat.°′ — Long.°′
DEUTSCH: Name — Seite — Breite°′ — Länge°′ E = Ost

Villebon, Lac @ 190 47.58 N 77.17 W
Villebon-sur-Yvette 261 48.42 N 2.15 E
Villeconin 261 48.31 N 2.08 E
Villecresnes 261 48.43 N 2.32 E
Villecroze 62 43.35 N 6.16 E
Ville-d'Avray 261 48.50 N 2.11 E
Ville-de-laval
→ Laval 206 45.35 N 73.45 W
Villedieu 32 48.50 N 1.13 W
Ville-en-Tardenois 50 49.11 N 3.48 E
Villefort 62 44.26 N 3.56 E
Villefranche 58 45.59 N 4.43 E
Villefranche-de-Rouergue 32 44.21 N 2.02 E
Villefranche-du-Périgord 32 44.38 N 1.05 E
Villefranche-sur-Cher 50 47.18 N 1.46 E
Villefranche-sur-Mer 62 43.42 N 7.19 E
Villejuif 50 48.48 N 2.22 E
Villejust 261 48.41 N 2.14 E
Ville-Marie 190 47.19 N 79.26 W
Villemaur-sur-Vanne 50 48.15 N 3.44 E
Villemeux-sur-Eure 50 48.40 N 1.28 E
Villemoisson-sur-Orge 261 48.40 N 2.19 E
Villemomble 261 48.53 N 2.31 E
Villena 34 38.38 N 0.51 W
Villenauxe-la-Grande 50 48.35 N 3.33 E
Villeneuve, It. 62 45.42 N 7.14 E
Villeneuve, Schw. 58 46.24 N 6.55 E
Villeneuve-d'Ascq 50 50.37 N 3.10 E
Villeneuve-d'Aveyron 32 44.26 N 2.02 E
Villeneuve-de-Berg 62 44.33 N 4.30 E
Villeneuve-la-Garenne 261 48.56 N 2.20 E
Villeneuve-la-Guyard 50 48.20 N 3.04 E
Villeneuve-l'Archevêque 50 48.14 N 3.33 E
Villeneuve-le-Comte 261 48.49 N 2.50 E
Villeneuve-le-Roi 50 48.44 N 2.25 E
Villeneuve-lès-Avignon 62 43.58 N 4.48 E
Villeneuve-lès-Maguelonne 62 43.32 N 3.52 E
Villeneuve-Saint-Denis 261 48.49 N 2.48 E
Villeneuve-Saint-Georges 50 48.44 N 2.27 E
Villeneuve-sous-Dammartin 261 49.02 N 2.39 E
Villeneuve-sur-Lot 32 44.25 N 0.42 E
Villeneuve-sur-Yonne 50 48.05 N 3.18 E
Villennes-sur-Seine 261 48.56 N 2.00 E
Villenoy 50 48.57 N 2.52 E
Villeny 50 47.37 N 1.45 E
Villeparisis 50 48.56 N 2.37 E
Villepinte 261 48.58 N 2.32 E
Ville Platte 194 30.42 N 92.16 W
Villepreux 261 48.50 N 2.01 E
Villequier 50 49.31 N 0.40 E
Villeron 261 49.03 N 2.33 E
Villeroy 50 48.59 N 2.47 E
Villers-Bocage, Fr. 32 49.05 N 0.39 W
Villers-Bocage, Fr. 50 49.59 N 2.20 E
Villers-Bretonneux 50 49.52 N 2.31 E
Villers-Carbonnel 50 49.52 N 2.54 E
Villers-Cotterêts 50 49.15 N 3.05 E
Villers-devant-Orval 56 49.37 N 5.19 E
Villers-en-Arthies 261 49.05 N 1.44 E
Villersexel 58 47.33 N 6.26 E
Villers-Farlay 58 47.00 N 5.45 E
Villers-la-Ville 50 50.35 N 4.32 E
Villers-le-Lac 58 47.04 N 6.40 E
Villers-lès-Nancy 58 48.40 N 6.09 E
Villers-lès-Pots 58 47.13 N 5.21 E
Villers-Outréaux 50 50.02 N 3.18 E
Villers-Saint-Paul 50 49.17 N 2.29 E
Villers-Semeuse 56 49.44 N 4.45 E
Villerupt 56 49.28 N 5.56 E
Villerville 50 49.24 N 0.08 E
Ville-Saint-Georges 188 46.07 N 70.40 W
Villes-sur-Auzon 62 44.03 N 5.14 E
Ville-sur-Tourbe 56 49.11 N 4.47 E
Villeta 246 5.01 N 74.28 W
Villetta Barrea 66 41.47 N 13.56 E
Villeurbanne 62 45.46 N 4.53 E
Villevaudé 261 48.55 N 2.39 E
Villeziers 261 48.40 N 2.10 E
Villiers 158 27.03 S 28.35 E
Villiers-Adam 261 49.04 N 2.14 E
Villiersdorp 158 34.00 S 19.19 E
Villiers-le-Bâcle 261 48.44 N 2.08 E
Villiers-le-Bel 261 49.00 N 2.23 E
Villiers-le-Sec 261 49.04 N 2.23 E
Villiers-Saint-Frédéric 261 48.49 N 1.54 E
Villiers-Saint-Georges 50 48.39 N 3.25 E
Villiers-sur-Marne 50 48.50 N 2.33 E
Villiers-sur-Morin 261 48.52 N 2.53 E
Villigst 263 51.26 N 7.35 E
Villingen-Schwenningen 58 48.04 N 8.28 E
Villisca 198 40.56 N 94.59 W
Villmanstrand
→ Lappeenranta 26 61.04 N 28.11 E
Villmergen 58 47.21 N 8.15 E
Villorba 64 45.44 N 12.14 E
Villoresi, Canale ≚ 62 45.33 N 9.31 E
Villotta 64 45.52 N 12.45 E
Villupuram 122 11.56 N 79.29 E
Vilm I 54 54.19 N 13.32 E
Vilmnitz 54 54.21 N 13.31 E
Vilna, Alta., Can. 182 54.07 N 111.55 W
Vilna
→ Vilnius, S.S.S.R. 76 54.41 N 25.19 E
Vilnius 76 54.41 N 25.19 E
Vilosnes-sur-Meuse 56 49.20 N 5.14 E
Vilppula 26 62.01 N 24.31 E
Vils 58 47.33 N 10.38 E
Vils ≐, B.R.D. 60 49.09 N 11.58 E
Vils ≐, B.R.D. 60 48.37 N 13.11 E
Vils ≐, Eur. 58 47.33 N 10.40 E
Vilsandi I 76 58.23 N 21.52 E
Vilsbiburg 60 48.27 N 12.12 E
Vilseck 60 49.37 N 11.48 E
Vilsheim 60 48.27 N 12.07 E
Vilshofen 60 48.39 N 13.12 E
Vil'uj ≐ 74 64.24 N 126.26 E
Vil'ujsk 74 63.45 N 121.35 E
Vil'ujskoje Vodochranilišče @[1] 74 62.30 N 111.00 E
Vil'va 86 58.37 N 56.52 E
Vilvoorde 50 50.56 N 4.26 E
Vilzing 60 49.11 N 12.41 E
Vimercate 62 45.37 N 9.22 E
Vimianzo 34 43.07 N 9.02 W
Vimmerby 26 57.40 N 15.51 E
Vimodrone 266b 45.31 N 9.17 E
Vimoutiers 50 48.55 N 0.12 E
Vimpeli 26 63.09 N 23.48 E
Vimperk 60 49.03 N 13.47 E
Vimy 50 50.22 N 2.49 E
Vina 204 39.56 N 122.03 W
Vina ≐ 152 7.45 N 15.36 E
Viñac 248 12.56 S 75.47 W
Viña del Mar 252 33.02 S 71.34 W
Vinadi 58 46.55 N 10.29 E
Vinadio 62 44.18 N 7.10 E
Viñales 240p 22.37 N 83.43 W
Vinalhaven 188 44.03 N 68.50 W
Vinalhaven Island I 188 44.05 N 68.52 W
Vina Roni, Mount ∧ 175e 8.10 S 157.28 E
Vinaroz 34 40.28 N 0.29 E
Vinay 62 45.13 N 5.24 E
Vinazco ≐ 234 20.56 N 97.44 W
Vincennes, Fr. 50 48.51 N 2.26 E
Vincennes, Ind., U.S. 194 38.41 N 87.32 W
Vincennes, Bois de ✦ 261 48.50 N 2.25 E
Vincennes, Château de ⊥ 261 48.51 N 2.26 E
Vincennes, Étang de @ 261 48.47 N 2.45 E
Vincennes Bay ⊂ 9 66.30 S 109.30 E
Vincent, Ala., U.S. 194 33.23 N 86.25 W
Vincent, Ohio, U.S. 214 39.23 N 81.40 W
Vincent, Point ≻ 174c 29.00 S 167.55 E
Vincentown 208 39.56 N 74.45 W
Vinces 246 1.32 S 79.45 W
Vinces ≐ 246 1.39 S 79.47 W
Vincey 58 48.20 N 6.20 E
Vinchiaturo 66 41.29 N 14.35 E
Vinchina 252 28.46 S 68.10 W
Vinchos 248 13.16 S 74.21 W
Vinci 66 43.47 N 10.55 E
Vinco 214 40.25 N 78.52 W
Vindeby 41 55.03 N 10.38 E
Vindelälven ≐ 24 63.54 N 19.52 E
Vindeln 26 64.12 N 19.44 E
Vinden, Mount ∧ 162 27.01 S 115.38 E
Vinderslev 41 56.15 N 9.26 E
Vinderup 26 56.29 N 8.47 E
Vindhya Range ⩕ 120 23.00 N 77.00 E
Vinding 41 55.41 N 9.35 E
Vindinge 41 55.19 N 10.45 E
Vine Brook ≐ 283 42.27 N 71.13 W
Vinegar Hill ∧ 202 44.43 N 118.34 W
Vine Grove 194 37.49 N 85.59 W
Vine Hill 282 38.00 N 122.06 W
Vineland, Fla., U.S. 220 28.24 N 81.31 W
Vineland, Mich., U.S. 216 42.03 N 86.30 W
Vineland, N.J., U.S. 208 39.29 N 75.02 W
Vinemont 194 34.10 N 86.52 W
Vine Valley 210 42.43 N 77.20 W
Vineyard Canyon ∨ 226 35.46 N 120.41 W
Vineyard Haven 207 41.27 N 70.36 W
Vineyard Lake @ 216 42.05 N 84.13 W
Vineyard Sound ⋓ 207 41.25 N 70.46 W
Vingåker 40 59.02 N 15.52 E
Vingeanne ≐ 58 47.21 N 5.29 E
Ving Ngün 110 22.37 N 99.16 E
Vinh 110 18.40 N 105.40 E
Vinhais 34 41.50 N 7.00 W
Vinhas, Ribeira das ≐ 266c 38.42 N 9.25 W
Vinh-chau 110 9.19 N 105.59 E
Vinhedo 256 23.01 S 46.59 W
Vinh-linh 110 17.04 N 107.02 E
Vinh-loc 269c 10.49 N 106.34 E
Vinh-long 110 10.15 N 105.58 E
Vinh-tuy, Viet. 110 17.24 N 106.36 E
Vinh-tuy, Viet. 110 9.37 N 105.22 E
Vinica 36 45.28 N 15.15 E
Vinita 196 36.39 N 95.09 W
Vinju Mare 38 44.26 N 22.52 E
Vinkekuil 158 32.42 S 20.27 E
Vinkeveen 52 52.13 N 4.54 E
Vinkovci 38 45.17 N 18.49 E
Vin'kovcy 78 49.02 N 27.14 E
Vinnhorst 52 52.25 N 9.43 E
Vinnica 78 49.14 N 28.29 E
Vinnica □[4] 78 48.30 N 28.30 E
Vinniki 78 49.48 N 24.08 E
Vinnitsa
→ Vinnica 78 49.14 N 28.29 E
Vinnum 263 51.41 N 7.24 E
Vinogradov 78 48.09 N 23.02 E
Vinogradovo, S.S.S.R. 82 55.25 N 38.23 E
Vinogradovo, S.S.S.R. 82 55.57 N 37.32 E
Vinogrobol' 78 51.51 N 36.26 E
Vinön I 40 59.12 N 15.43 E
Vinon-sur-Verdon 62 43.43 N 5.48 E
Vinovo 62 44.57 N 7.38 E
Vinslöv 26 56.06 N 13.55 E
Vinson Massif ∧ 9 78.35 S 85.25 W
Vinstra 26 61.36 N 9.45 E
Vintilă Vodă 38 45.28 N 26.44 E
Vinton, Iowa, U.S. 190 42.10 N 92.01 W
Vinton, Va., U.S. 192 37.17 N 80.01 W
Vintondale 214 40.29 N 78.55 W
Vintrosa 40 59.15 N 14.57 E
Viñuelas, Arroyo de ≐ 266a 40.33 N 3.33 W
Viny 76 58.22 N 32.13 E
Vinzelberg 54 52.33 N 11.40 E
Vinzili 86 56.58 N 65.46 E
Viola, Ill., U.S. 190 41.12 N 90.35 W
Viola, N.Y., U.S. 276 41.08 N 74.05 W
Viola, Wis., U.S. 190 43.31 N 90.40 W
Viola, Val ∨ 64 46.27 N 10.15 E
Violin, Isla I 236 8.51 N 83.39 W
Viols-le-Fort 62 43.45 N 3.42 E
Viosne ≐ 261 49.03 N 2.06 E
Vipava 36 45.51 N 13.58 E
Vipava ≐ 64 45.54 N 13.33 E
Vipiteno (Sterzing) 64 46.54 N 11.26 E
Vipos 252 26.29 S 65.22 W
Vipperow 54 53.19 N 12.41 E
Viquique 112 8.52 S 126.22 E
Vir, Otok I 36 44.18 N 15.04 E
Vira 58 46.08 N 8.51 E
Virac, Pil. 116 13.35 N 124.15 E
Virac, Pil. 116 12.16 N 120.39 E
Viracopos, Aeroporto de ⊠ 256 23.00 S 47.08 W
Virac Point ≻ 116 13.31 N 124.13 E
Viradouro 255 20.53 S 48.18 W
Virago Sound ⋓ 182 54.00 N 132.36 W
Viramgām 120 23.07 N 72.02 E
Virandozero 24 64.05 N 35.58 E
Viranşehir, Tür. 130 39.00 N 36.39 E
Viranşehir, Tür. 130 37.13 N 39.45 E
Vīrarājendrapet 122 12.12 N 75.48 E
Virbalis 76 54.38 N 22.49 E
Virden, Man., Can. 184 49.51 N 100.55 W
Virden, Ill., U.S. 219 39.30 N 89.46 W
Virden, N. Mex., U.S. 200 32.42 N 109.00 W
Vire 32 48.50 N 0.53 W
Vire ≐ 32 49.20 N 1.07 W
Virelles 50 50.04 N 4.20 E
Virelles, Étang de @ 50 50.04 N 4.21 E
Vireši 76 57.27 N 26.23 E
Vireux-Molhain 56 50.05 N 4.43 E
Vîrful, Muntelui ∧ 78 46.29 N 23.14 E
Vîrfurile 38 46.19 N 22.31 E
Virgem da Lapa 255 16.49 S 42.21 W
Virgen 64 47.00 N 12.27 E
Vírgen del San Cristóbal ✝[1] 286e 33.26 S 70.39 W
Vírgenes, Cabo ≻ 254 52.22 S 68.20 W
Vírgenes, Islas
→ Virgin Islands □[2], N.A. 240m 18.20 N 64.50 W
Vírgenes, Islas
→ British Virgin Islands □[2], N.A. 240m 18.30 N 64.30 W
Virgen Tal ∨ 64 47.00 N 12.25 E
Virgil, Ont., Can. 284a 43.13 N 79.08 W
Virgil, Kans., U.S. 198 37.59 N 96.01 W

Symbols in the index entries represent the broad categories identified in the key at the right. Symbols with superior numbers (⩕[2]) identify subcategories (see complete key on page I · 30).

Kartensymbole in dem Registerverzeichnis stellen die rechts in Schlüssel erklärten Kategorien dar. Symbole mit hochgestellten Ziffern (⩕[2]) bezeichnen Unterabteilungen einer Kategorie (vgl. vollständiger Schlüssel auf Seite I · 30).

Los símbolos incluidos en el texto del índice representan las grandes categorías identificadas con la clave a la derecha. Los símbolos con números en su parte superior (⩕[2]) identifican las subcategorías (véase la clave completa en la página I · 30).

Les symboles de l'index représentent les catégories indiquées dans la légende à droite. Les symboles suivis d'un indice (⩕[2]) représentent des sous-catégories (voir légende complète à la page I · 30).

Os símbolos incluídos no texto do índice representam as grandes categorias identificadas com a chave à direita. Os símbolos com números em sua parte superior (⩕[2]) identificam as subcategorias (veja-se a chave completa à página I · 30).

	English	Deutsch	Español	Français	Português
∧	Mountain	Berg	Montaña	Montagne	Montanha
⩕	Mountains	Berge	Montañas	Montagnes	Montanhas
≻	Pass	Pass	Paso	Col	Passo
∨	Valley, Canyon	Tal, Cañon	Valle, Cañón	Vallée, Canyon	Vale, Canhão
≐	Plain	Ebene	Llano	Plaine	Planície
⊂	Cape	Kap	Cabo	Cap	Cabo
I	Island	Insel	Isla	Île	Ilha
II	Islands	Inseln	Islas	Îles	Ilhas
✦	Other Topographic Features	Andere Topographische Objekte	Otros Elementos Topográficos	Autres données topographiques	Outros Elementos Topográficos

ESPAÑOL — Nombre | Página | Lat.°′ | Long.°′ W=Oeste
FRANÇAIS — Nom | Page | Lat.°′ | Long.°′ W=Ouest
PORTUGUÊS — Nome | Página | Lat.°′ | Long.°′ W=Oeste

Virgil, N.Y., U.S. 210 42.31 N 76.12 W
Virgilina 192 36.33 N 78.52 W
Virgilio 64 45.07 N 10.47 E
Virgin ≃ 200 36.31 N 114.20 W
Virginal-Samme 50 50.38 N 4.12 E
Virgin Gorda I 240m 18.30 N 64.24 W
Virgin Gorda Peak ∧ 240m 18.30 N 64.24 W
Virginia, Austl. 168b 34.40 S 138.34 E
Virgínia, Bra. 256 22.20 S 45.06 W
Virginia, Eire 48 53.49 N 7.04 W
Virginia, S. Afr. 158 28.12 S 26.49 E
Virginia, Ill., U.S. 219 39.57 N 90.13 W
Virginia, Minn., U.S. 190 47.31 N 92.32 W
Virginia □[3] 178 37.30 N 78.45 W
Virginia Beach 208 36.51 N 75.58 W
Virginia City, Mont., U.S. 202 45.18 N 111.56 W
Virginia City, Nev., U.S. 226 39.19 N 119.39 W
Virginia Creek ≃ 226 38.13 N 119.14 W
Virginia Falls ʟ 180 61.38 N 125.42 W
Virginia Gardens 220 25.49 N 80.17 W
Virginia Hills 208 38.47 N 77.06 W
Virginia Key I 220 25.44 N 80.09 W
Virginia Peak ∧ 204 39.45 N 119.28 W
Virginia Ranch Reservoir ◎[1] 226 39.20 N 121.19 W
Virginia Range ⋏ 226 39.18 N 119.30 W
Virginiatown 190 48.08 N 79.35 W
Virginia Water 260 51.24 N 0.34 W
Virginie occidentale → West Virginia □[3] 188 38.45 N 80.30 W
Virgin Islands □[2] 240m 18.20 N 64.50 W
Virgin Islands II 240m 18.00 N 64.40 W
Virgin Islands National Park ♠ 240m 18.20 N 64.45 W
Virginópolis 255 18.45 S 42.45 W
Virgin Passage C[1] 240m 18.20 N 65.10 W
Virginville 208 40.31 N 75.52 W
Virgolândia 255 18.27 S 42.18 W
Virieu 62 45.29 N 5.28 E
Virieux-le-Grand 62 45.51 N 5.39 E
Virihaure ◎ 24 67.20 N 16.35 E
Virje 36 46.04 N 16.59 E
Virkkala 26 60.12 N 24.01 E
Virklund 41 56.07 N 9.34 E
Virneburg 56 50.20 N 7.04 E
Virôchey 110 13.59 N 106.49 E
Viroflay 50 48.48 N 2.10 E
Viroin ≃ 56 50.05 N 4.43 E
Virojoki 26 60.35 N 27.42 E
Víron 267c 37.57 N 23.45 E
Vironvay 50 49.12 N 1.13 E
Viroqua 190 43.34 N 90.53 W
Virovitica 36 45.50 N 17.23 E
Virpazar 38 42.15 N 19.05 E
Virrat 26 62.14 N 23.47 E
Virsbo 40 59.52 N 16.02 E
Virserum 26 57.19 N 15.35 E
Virtaniemi 24 68.53 N 28.27 E
Virton 56 49.34 N 5.32 E
Vîrtopu 38 44.12 N 23.21 E
Virtsu 76 58.34 N 23.31 E
Virú 248 8.25 S 78.45 W
Virudunagar 122 9.36 N 77.58 E
Viru-Jaagupi 76 59.15 N 26.28 E
Virulento 196 28.52 N 104.21 W
Virungu 154 7.04 S 29.46 E
Viru-Nigula 76 59.27 N 26.41 E
Virvyčia ≃ 76 56.13 N 22.34 E
Viry-Châtillon 50 48.40 N 2.23 E
Vis 36 43.03 N 16.12 E
Vis ≃, Fr. 62 43.56 N 3.42 E
Vis ≃, S. Afr. 158 33.30 S 27.08 E
Vis, Otok I 36 43.02 N 16.11 E
Visale 175e 9.15 S 159.42 E
Visalia 226 36.20 N 119.18 W
Visalia Airport ⊠ 226 36.19 N 119.23 W
Visayan Sea ⊤[2] 116 11.35 N 123.51 E
Visbaai C 158 34.16 S 21.57 E
Visbek 52 52.48 N 8.19 E
Visby 26 57.38 N 18.18 E
Viscaya, Bahía de → Biscay, Bay of C 32 44.00 N 4.00 W
Viscount 184 51.57 N 105.39 W
Viscount Melville Sound Ʉ 176 74.10 N 113.00 W
Visé 56 50.44 N 5.42 E
Višegrad 38 43.47 N 19.17 E
Vis-en-Artois 50 50.15 N 2.56 E
Višera ≃ 76 58.34 N 31.24 E
Viserba 66 44.05 N 12.32 E
Viseu, Bra. 250 1.12 S 46.07 W
Viseu, Port. 34 40.39 N 7.55 W
Vişeu ≃ 38 46.55 N 23.47 E
Vişeu de Sus 38 47.44 N 24.22 E
Vishākhapatnam 122 17.42 N 83.18 E
Vishoek 158 34.07 S 18.27 E
Visim 86 57.39 N 59.30 E
Visingsö I 26 58.03 N 14.20 E
Visitation, Île de la I 275a 45.35 N 73.40 W
Viskafors 26 57.38 N 12.50 E
Viskan ≃ 26 57.14 N 12.12 E
Viškil' 80 58.05 N 48.19 E
Viskinge 41 55.40 N 11.16 E
Visl'ajevo 82 54.25 N 36.43 E
Vislanda 26 56.47 N 14.27 E
Vislinskij Zaliv C 30 54.27 N 19.40 E
Vismen ◎ 40 59.17 N 14.17 E
Visnagar 120 23.42 N 72.33 E
Visn'aki 265b 55.47 N 37.54 E
Višn'akovo 82 55.45 N 38.10 E
Višnevčik 78 49.02 N 26.28 E
Visnevo 76 54.08 N 26.14 E
Višnevoje, S.S.S.R. 78 48.27 N 33.56 E
Višnevoje, S.S.S.R. 80 52.38 N 43.26 E
Višňové 61 48.59 N 16.09 E
Višn'ovec 78 49.54 N 25.45 E
Višn'ovka, S.S.S.R. 78 46.20 N 28.26 E
Višn'ovka, S.S.S.R. 86 50.49 N 72.12 E
Viso, Monte ∧ 62 44.40 N 7.07 E
Visoki Dečani, Manastir ♉[1] 38 42.30 N 20.31 E
Visoko 38 43.59 N 18.11 E
Visokoi Island I 18 56.42 S 27.12 W
Visp 58 46.18 N 7.53 E
Vispa ≃ 58 46.18 N 7.52 E
Vissefjärda 26 56.32 N 15.35 E
Visselhövede 52 52.59 N 9.35 E
Vissenbjerg 41 55.23 N 10.08 E
Visso 66 42.56 N 13.05 E
Vissoie 58 46.13 N 7.36 E
Vista, Calif., U.S. 228 33.12 N 117.15 W
Vista, N.Y., U.S. 210 41.12 N 73.31 W
Vista Alegre, Arg. 252 38.45 S 68.11 W
Vista Alegre, Bra. 256 21.27 S 42.35 W
Vista Alegre, Chile 286e 33.30 S 70.43 W
Vista Alegre, Perú 286d 12.09 S 77.00 W
Vista Flores 252 33.38 S 69.09 W
Vista Hermosa, Méx. 234 19.38 N 103.22 W
Vista Hermosa, Méx. 234 20.16 N 102.29 W
Vista La Mesa 228 32.35 N 117.01 W
Vista Park 228 35.21 N 118.55 W
Vistina 76 59.47 N 28.29 E
Vistre ≃ 62 43.40 N 4.15 E
Vistula → Wisła ≃ 30 54.22 N 18.55 E
Visun' ≃ 78 47.07 N 35.53 E
Vit ≃ 38 43.41 N 24.45 E
Vita, Man., Can. 184 49.08 N 96.34 W
Vita, It. 70 37.52 N 12.49 E
Vitacura 286e 33.24 S 70.36 W
Vitali 116 7.22 N 122.18 E
Vitanje 36 46.23 N 15.18 E
Vitarte 248 12.02 S 76.56 W
Vit'azevka 78 48.01 N 31.53 E
Vite 122 17.17 N 74.33 E
Vitebsk 76 55.12 N 30.11 E
Vitebskij Vokzal ◆[5] 265a 59.55 N 30.21 E
Viterbo 66 42.25 N 12.06 E
Viterbo □[4] 66 42.25 N 12.05 E
Vitiaz Strait Ʉ 164 5.50 S 147.20 E
Vitichi 248 20.13 S 65.29 W
Vitigudino 34 41.01 N 6.26 W
Viti Levu I 175g 18.00 S 178.00 E
Viti Levu Bay C 175g 17.26 S 178.15 E
Vitim 74 59.28 N 112.34 E
Vitim ≃ 74 59.26 N 112.34 E
Vitimskij 88 58.14 N 113.18 E
Vitimskoje Ploskogorje ⋏[1] 88 54.00 N 113.30 E
Vitinia ◆[8] 267a 41.47 N 12.24 E
Vitis 61 48.45 N 15.10 E
Vítkov 30 49.46 N 17.45 E
Vítor 248 16.26 S 71.49 W
Vitor ≃ 248 16.37 S 72.19 W
Vitória, Bra. 250 2.54 S 52.01 W
Vitória, Bra. 255 20.19 S 40.21 W
Vitoria, Esp. 34 42.51 N 2.40 W
Vitória, Ilha da I 256 23.45 S 45.01 W
Vitória da Conquista 255 14.51 S 40.51 W
Vitória de Santo Antão 250 8.07 S 35.18 W
Vitória do Mearim 250 3.28 S 44.53 W
Vitorino Freire 250 4.04 S 45.10 W
Vitravo ≃ 68 39.11 N 17.05 E
Vitré 28 48.08 N 1.12 W
Vitrey-sur-Mance 58 47.49 N 5.45 E
Vitry-en-Artois 50 50.20 N 2.59 E
Vitry-la-Ville 50 48.50 N 4.28 E
Vitry-le-François 56 48.44 N 4.35 E
Vitry[-sur-Seine] 50 48.48 N 2.24 E
Vitshumbi 154 0.41 S 29.23 E
Vitte 54 54.34 N 13.06 E
Vitteaux 58 47.24 N 4.32 E
Vittel 58 48.12 N 5.57 E
Vittinge 40 59.54 N 17.04 E
Vittoria, Ont., Can. 212 42.46 N 80.19 W
Vittoria, It. 70 36.57 N 14.32 E
Vittorio Veneto 64 45.59 N 12.18 E
Vittsjö 26 56.20 N 13.40 E
Vitulano 68 41.10 N 14.38 E
Vitznau 58 47.01 N 8.29 E
Viù 62 45.14 N 7.22 E
Vivarais □[9] 62 44.40 N 4.30 E
Vivarais, Monts du ⋏ 62 44.55 N 4.15 E
Viver 34 39.55 N 0.36 W
Vivero 34 43.38 N 7.35 W
Viverols 62 45.26 N 3.53 E
Viverone, Lago di ◎ 62 45.25 N 8.02 E
Vivi ≃ 74 63.52 N 97.50 E
Vivian 194 32.53 N 93.59 W
Viviers 62 44.29 N 4.41 E
Viviers-du-Lac 62 45.39 N 5.54 E
Vivione, Passo del)(64 46.02 N 10.12 E
Vivonne 32 46.26 N 0.16 E
Vivoratá 252 37.40 S 57.39 W
Vivorillo, Cayos II 236 15.50 N 83.18 W
Vivsta 26 62.29 N 17.19 E
Viwa I 175g 17.08 S 176.54 E
Vizagapatam → Vishākhapatnam 122 17.42 N 83.18 E
Vizcaíno, Desierto de ◆[2] 232 27.40 N 114.40 W
Vizcaya □[4] 34 43.20 N 2.45 W
Vize 130 41.34 N 27.45 E
Vize, Ostrov I 72 79.30 N 77.00 E
Vizianagaram 122 18.07 N 83.25 E
Vizille 62 45.05 N 5.46 E
Vižinada 36 45.20 N 13.46 E
Vizinga 24 61.05 N 50.04 E
Vižnica 78 48.15 N 25.12 E
Vizzini 36 37.09 N 14.46 E
Vizzola 266b 45.38 N 8.42 E
Vjulka ≃ 82 56.53 N 37.57 E
Vjunka ≃ 265b 55.42 N 38.01 E
Vjuny 86 55.31 N 82.55 E
Vḱ 24a 63.25 N 19.00 W
Vlaanderen → Flanders □[9] 50 51.00 N 3.00 E
Vlaardingen 52 51.54 N 4.21 E
Vlachovo Březí 60 49.05 N 13.57 E
Vladař ∧ 54 50.05 N 13.14 E
Vlădeasa ∧ 38 46.45 N 22.48 E
Vlădeni 38 47.25 N 27.20 E
Vladičin Han 38 42.42 N 22.04 E
Vladikavkaz → Ordžonikidze 84 43.03 N 44.40 E
Vladimir 80 56.10 N 40.25 E
Vladimir □[4] 82 56.15 N 39.00 E
Vladimirec 78 51.25 N 26.08 E
Vladimirovka, S.S.S.R. 78 47.32 N 32.55 E
Vladimirovka, S.S.S.R. 80 50.51 N 51.08 E
Vladimirovka, S.S.S.R. 83 47.44 N 37.23 E
Vladimirovka, S.S.S.R. 86 53.28 N 64.02 E
Vladimirskij Tupik 76 55.42 N 33.18 E
Vladimirskoje 80 56.49 N 45.07 E
Vladimir-Volynskij 78 50.51 N 24.20 E
Vladivostok 89 43.10 N 131.56 E
Vladyčnoje 76 58.49 N 39.29 E
Vladykino ◆[8] 265b 55.52 N 37.36 E
Vlárský priesmyk)(30 49.03 N 18.02 E
Vlasenica 38 44.11 N 18.56 E
Vlašim 30 49.42 N 14.54 E
Vlasinsko Jezero ◎ 38 42.42 N 22.22 E
Vlaskovo 82 56.11 N 36.31 E
Vlasotince 38 42.58 N 22.08 E
Vlasovo 82 56.38 N 38.14 E
Vlatten 56 50.39 N 6.32 E
Vlazoviči 76 53.01 N 32.18 E
Vledder 52 52.52 N 6.12 E
Vleikolk 158 29.43 S 20.50 E
Vleuten 52 52.05 N 5.02 E
Vlieland I 52 53.15 N 5.00 E
Vlijmen 52 51.42 N 5.15 E
Vlissingen (Flushing) 52 51.26 N 3.35 E
Vlodrop 52 51.08 N 6.05 E
Vloesberg → Flobecq 50 50.44 N 3.44 E
Vlonë → Vlorë 38 40.27 N 19.30 E
Vloorskop ∧ 156 25.45 S 20.50 E
Vlorë 38 40.27 N 19.30 E
Vlorës, Gji i C 38 40.25 N 19.25 E
Vlotho 52 52.10 N 8.51 E
Vltava ≃ 30 50.21 N 14.30 E
Vluyn 52 51.26 N 6.32 E
Vnukovo 82 55.38 N 37.16 E
Vnukovo, Aeroport ⊠ 82 55.37 N 37.17 E
Vobarno 64 45.39 N 10.30 E
Voca 196 31.01 N 99.11 W
Vočaž, Porog ʟ 24 64.55 N 34.22 E
Vochrinka 82 55.24 N 38.18 E
Vochtoga 76 58.47 N 41.07 E
Počin 36 45.37 N 17.32 E
Vöckla ≃ 64 48.00 N 13.36 E
Vöcklabruck 60 48.01 N 13.39 E
Vöcklamarkt 60 48.00 N 13.29 E
Vodla ≃ 24 61.49 N 36.00 E
Vodlozero, Ozero ◎ 24 62.20 N 36.55 E
Vodňany 30 49.09 N 14.11 E
Vodnjan 64 44.57 N 13.51 E
Vodnyj 24 63.32 N 53.18 E
Vodo 64 46.25 N 12.14 E
Vodosalma 24 64.29 N 30.44 E
Vodovatovo 80 55.24 N 43.34 E
Vodzimonje 80 56.49 N 51.38 E
Voerde, B.R.D. 52 51.35 N 6.41 E
Voerde, B.R.D. 263 51.18 N 7.24 E
Voesch 263 51.24 N 6.26 E
Vogelenzang 52 52.19 N 4.35 E
Vogelheim ◆[8] 263 51.29 N 6.59 E
Vogelkop → Doberai, Jazirah ≻[1] 164 1.30 S 132.30 E
Vogel Peak → Dimlang ∧ 146 8.24 N 11.47 E
Vogelsang, B.R.D. 56 50.35 N 6.27 E
Vogelsang, D.D.R. 54 53.43 N 14.09 E
Vogelsberg ⋏ 56 50.30 N 9.15 E
Vogelsberg, Naturpark ♠ 56 50.35 N 9.15 E
Vogesen → Vosges ⋏ 58 48.30 N 7.10 E
Voghera 62 44.59 N 9.01 E
Vognema 76 59.59 N 38.10 E
Vogogna 58 46.01 N 8.17 E
Vogtland ◆[1] 54 50.30 N 12.05 E
Voh 175f 20.58 S 164.42 E
Vohburg an der Donau 60 48.46 N 11.37 E
Vohémar 157b 13.21 S 50.02 E
Vohenstrauss 60 49.37 N 12.21 E
Vohilava 157b 21.04 S 48.00 E
Vohipeno 157b 22.22 S 47.51 E
Vohitsora 157b 23.54 S 44.17 E
Võhma 76 58.38 N 25.33 E
Vöhringen, B.R.D. 58 48.02 N 8.18 E
Vöhringen, B.R.D. 58 48.20 N 8.40 E
Vöhringen, B.R.D. 58 48.16 N 10.04 E
Vöhrum 52 52.20 N 10.10 E
Vohwinkel ◆[8] 263 51.14 N 7.09 E
Voi 154 3.23 S 38.34 E
Void 58 48.41 N 5.37 E
Voight Creek ≃ 224 47.06 N 122.10 W
Voikkaa 26 60.56 N 26.37 E
Voineşti 38 47.05 N 27.26 E
Voinjama 150 8.25 N 9.45 W
Voinka 78 45.52 N 33.59 E
Voiotía □[5] 38 38.20 N 23.30 E
Voire ≃ 58 48.27 N 4.25 E
Voiron 62 45.22 N 5.35 E
Voise 50 48.24 N 1.43 E
Voise ≃ 50 48.35 N 1.35 E
Voisenon 261 48.34 N 2.40 E
Voisin, Lac ◎ 184 54.13 N 107.15 W
Voisins-le-Bretonneux 50 48.45 N 2.03 E
Voiteur 58 46.45 N 5.37 E
Voitsberg 61 47.03 N 15.10 E
Voja ≃ 80 57.23 N 49.55 E
Vojens 41 55.15 N 9.19 E
Vojevodskoje 86 52.47 N 85.35 E
Vojkovice 54 50.15 N 13.02 E
Vojkovo, S.S.S.R. 78 45.31 N 33.52 E
Vojkovo, S.S.S.R. 83 48.00 N 38.02 E
Vojkovskij 83 47.46 N 38.20 E
Vojmsjön ◎ 26 64.55 N 16.40 E
Vojnić 36 45.19 N 15.42 E
Vojnica 24 65.12 N 30.15 E
Vojnilov 78 49.08 N 24.30 E
Vojtanov 54 50.06 N 12.19 E
Voj-Vož, S.S.S.R. 24 64.20 N 55.03 E
Voj-Vož, S.S.S.R. 24 62.56 N 54.56 E
Vokeo Island I 164 3.10 S 144.05 E
Volano 66 45.55 N 11.03 E
Volant 214 41.07 N 80.16 W
Volary 60 48.55 N 13.54 E
Volcán 252 23.54 S 65.27 W
Volcancillo ∧ 234 19.02 N 103.36 W
Volcán de Colima, Parque Nacional ♠ 234 19.30 N 103.35 W
Volčanka 80 52.33 N 49.59 E
Volcano, Calif., U.S. 226 38.26 N 120.37 W
Volcano, Haw., U.S. 229d 19.26 N 155.14 W
Volcano Islands → Kazan-rettō II 14 25.00 N 141.00 E
Volčansk, S.S.S.R. 78 50.18 N 36.57 E
Volčansk, S.S.S.R. 86 59.56 N 60.04 E
Volčejarovka 83 48.50 N 38.22 E
Volčenskij 83 48.14 N 40.07 E
Volchonka-Zil ◆[8] 265b 55.40 N 37.37 E
Volchov 76 59.55 N 32.20 E
Volchov ≃ 76 60.08 N 32.20 E
Volčicha 86 52.02 N 80.23 E
Volčij Nos, Mys ≻ 76 60.31 N 32.35 E
Volčja ≃ 78 48.00 N 36.08 E
Volčje 78 49.14 N 22.53 E
Volčki 80 52.29 N 40.42 E
Volda 26 62.09 N 6.06 E
Volders 64 47.17 N 11.34 E
Volendam 52 52.30 N 5.04 E
Volga, S.S.S.R. 76 57.57 N 38.24 E
Volga, Iowa, U.S. 190 42.48 N 91.33 W
Volga, S. Dak., U.S. 198 44.19 N 96.56 W
Volga ≃, S.S.S.R. 22 45.55 N 47.52 E
Volga ≃, Iowa, U.S. 190 42.45 N 91.17 W
Volga-Baltic Canal → Volgo-Baltijskij Vodnyj Put' ≡ 24 59.00 N 38.00 E
Volga-Donskoj Kanal ≡ 80 48.40 N 43.37 E
Volgino 76 58.27 N 33.52 E
Volgo, Ozero ◎ 76 56.55 N 33.10 E
Volgo-Baltijskij Vodnyj Put' ≡ 24 59.00 N 38.00 E
Volgodonsk 80 47.33 N 42.08 E
Volgograd (Stalingrad) 80 48.44 N 44.25 E
Volgogradskoje Vodochranilišče ◎[1] 80 49.20 N 45.00 E
Volissós 38 38.29 N 25.58 E
Vol'ka 76 52.47 N 25.39 E
Volkach 56 49.52 N 10.13 E
Volkel 52 51.38 N 5.40 E
Völkermarkt 61 46.39 N 14.38 E
Völkerschlachtdenkmal ⊥ 54 51.18 N 12.24 E
Völklingen 56 49.15 N 6.50 E
Volkmarsen 56 51.24 N 9.07 E
Volkovincy 78 49.13 N 27.39 E
Volkovo, S.S.S.R. 76 59.15 N 41.27 E
Volkovo, S.S.S.R. 82 55.46 N 36.15 E
Volkovo, Kladbišče ◆ 265a 59.54 N 30.22 E
Volkovskoje 82 54.49 N 37.13 E
Volkovysk 76 53.10 N 24.28 E
Volksdorf ◆[8] 52 53.39 N 11.00 E
Völksen 52 52.13 N 9.37 E
Volksrust 158 27.24 S 29.53 E
Vollenhove 52 52.41 N 5.58 E
Vollersode 52 53.18 N 8.56 E
Vollme 263 51.10 N 7.36 E
Vollore-Montagne 62 45.47 N 3.41 E
Vollore-Ville 62 45.47 N 3.36 E
Vollsjö 41 55.42 N 13.46 E
Volma ≃ 76 53.35 N 28.19 E
Volmarstein 56 51.22 N 7.23 E
Volme ≃ 263 51.24 N 7.27 E
Volmerange-les-Mines 56 49.27 N 6.05 E
Volmerswerth ◆[8] 263 51.11 N 6.46 E
Volmunster 56 49.07 N 7.21 E
Vol'naja Gorka 76 58.43 N 30.51 E
Volnay 58 47.00 N 4.47 E
Vol'nogorsk 78 48.29 N 34.01 E
Vol'noje, S.S.S.R. 80 47.09 N 47.38 E
Vol'noje, S.S.S.R. 86 54.17 N 71.21 E
Volnovacha 83 47.36 N 37.31 E
Vol'nyj 80 45.55 N 45.14 E
Vol'nyj, Ostrov I 265a 59.58 N 30.14 E
Voločajevkall-ja 89 48.34 N 134.34 E
Voločanka 74 71.00 N 94.28 E
Voločisk 78 49.32 N 26.11 E
Volockaja 76 60.17 N 42.59 E
Volodarka, S.S.S.R. 78 49.31 N 29.55 E
Volodarka, S.S.S.R. 86 52.43 N 83.38 E
Volodarsk, S.S.S.R. 76 56.13 N 43.10 E
Volodarsk, S.S.S.R. 83 48.06 N 39.35 E
Volodarskij, S.S.S.R. 80 46.24 N 48.32 E
Volodarskij, S.S.S.R. 82 55.30 N 37.57 E
Volodarskij ◆[8] 265a 59.49 N 30.05 E
Volodarskoje, S.S.S.R. 83 47.12 N 37.20 E
Volodarskoje, S.S.S.R. 86 53.18 N 68.08 E
Volodarsk-Volynskij 78 50.37 N 28.25 E
Volodino 86 57.06 N 83.54 E
Vologda 76 59.12 N 39.55 E
Vologda ≃ 76 59.17 N 40.13 E
Voloje 76 54.09 N 34.35 E
Volokolamsk 82 56.02 N 35.57 E
Volokonovka 78 50.29 N 37.51 E
Volokovaja 24 66.28 N 48.10 E
Volonga 24 67.07 N 47.41 E
Volonne 62 44.07 N 6.01 E
Volontirovka 78 46.26 N 29.37 E
Vólos 38 39.21 N 22.56 E
Vološino, S.S.S.R. 83 47.31 N 39.40 E
Vološino, S.S.S.R. 83 48.55 N 39.56 E
Vološka 24 61.20 N 40.06 E
Vološn'a ≃ 82 55.51 N 35.54 E
Vološno 76 58.29 N 28.29 E
Volosoviči 76 54.46 N 28.50 E
Volosovo 76 59.26 N 29.29 E
Volosskaja Balaklejka 83 49.37 N 37.20 E
Volot 76 57.56 N 30.42 E
Volovec 78 48.43 N 23.11 E
Volovo, S.S.S.R. 76 53.35 N 38.02 E
Volovo, S.S.S.R. 78 52.03 N 37.53 E
Vložin 76 54.05 N 26.32 E
Volpago del Montello 64 45.47 N 12.07 E
Volpedo 62 44.53 N 8.59 E
Volpiano 62 45.12 N 7.46 E
Völpke 54 52.08 N 11.09 E
Völs → Fiè 64 46.31 N 11.30 E
Volsini, Monti ⋏ 66 42.40 N 11.55 E
Vol'sk 80 52.02 N 47.23 E
Volta □[4] 150 7.00 N 0.30 E
Volta ≃ 150 5.46 N 0.41 E
Volta, Lake ◎[1] 150 7.30 N 0.15 E
Volta, Riacho da ≃ 250 7.24 S 44.51 W
Volta Blanche (White Volta) ≃ 150 9.10 N 1.15 W
Voltaggio 62 44.37 N 8.50 E
Voltago 64 46.16 N 12.00 E
Volta Grande 256 21.46 S 42.32 W
Volta Mantovana 64 45.19 N 10.39 E
Volta-Noire □[5] 150 11.00 N 4.00 W
Volta Noire (Black Volta) ≃ 150 8.38 N 1.40 W
Volta Redonda 256 22.32 S 44.07 W
Volta Rouge ≃ 150 10.34 N 0.30 W
Volterra 66 43.24 N 10.51 E
Vol'teva 24 64.30 N 44.12 E
Voltri 62 44.26 N 8.45 E
Volturara Appula 68 41.30 N 15.03 E
Volturara Irpina 68 40.53 N 14.55 E
Volturino 68 41.28 N 15.07 E
Volturino, Monte ∧ 68 40.25 N 15.49 E
Volturno ≃ 68 41.01 N 13.55 E
Volubilis ⊥ 148 34.00 N 5.30 W
Voluntown 207 41.34 N 71.52 W
Volusia □[6] 220 28.51 N 81.05 W
Vólvi, Límni ◎ 38 40.41 N 23.23 E
Volx 62 43.53 N 5.51 E
Volyncy, S.S.S.R. 76 55.42 N 28.11 E
Volyncy, S.S.S.R. 80 57.48 N 45.28 E
Volyně 60 49.10 N 13.53 E
Volynka 78 51.37 N 32.26 E
Volyňka ≃ 60 49.16 N 13.54 E
Volynskaja Oblast' □[4] 78 51.00 N 25.00 E
Volynskaya Vozvyšennost' ⋏[1] 78 50.35 N 25.10 E
Volynskoje Polesje ◆[1] 78 51.10 N 26.00 E
Volzhskiy → Volžskij 80 48.50 N 44.44 E
Volžsk 80 55.53 N 48.21 E
Volžskij, S.S.S.R. 80 53.27 N 50.07 E
Volžskij, S.S.S.R. 80 48.50 N 44.44 E
Vom 150 9.41 N 8.42 E
Vomano ≃ 66 42.39 N 14.02 E
Vombsjön ◎ 41 55.41 N 13.36 E
Vomp 64 47.20 N 11.41 E
Vonda 184 52.19 N 106.06 W
Vondanka 24 59.07 N 47.49 E
Vondrozo 157b 22.49 S 47.20 E
Von Frank Mountain ∧ 180 63.33 N 154.20 W
Võnnu 76 58.17 N 27.05 E
Vonozero 76 60.22 N 34.26 E
Vonsild 41 55.27 N 9.29 E
Von Treuer Tableland ⋏[1] 162 26.38 S 122.53 E
Voorburg 52 52.05 N 4.23 E
Voordeelspan 158 29.05 S 21.32 E
Voorheesville 210 42.39 N 73.56 W
Voorne I 52 51.55 N 4.00 E
Voorschoten 52 52.07 N 4.27 E
Voorst 52 52.10 N 6.09 E
Voorthuizen 52 52.12 N 5.35 E
Vop' ≃ 76 54.56 N 32.44 E
Vopnafjördur 24a 65.47 N 14.44 W
Vopnafjördur C 24a 65.52 N 14.40 W
Vörå (Vöyri) 26 63.09 N 22.15 E
Vor'a ≃, S.S.S.R. 76 54.54 N 35.01 E
Vor'a ≃, S.S.S.R. 82 55.52 N 38.13 E
Vorarlberg □[3] 64 47.15 N 9.55 E
Vorau 61 47.25 N 15.54 E
Vorbach 60 49.49 N 11.45 E
Vorbasse 41 55.38 N 9.05 E
Vorchdorf 60 48.00 N 13.55 E
Vörden, B.R.D. 52 52.28 N 8.05 E
Vorden, Ned. 52 52.07 N 6.18 E
Vorder-Grauspitz ∧ 58 47.03 N 9.36 E
Vordernberg 61 47.28 N 15.00 E
Vorderrhein ≃ 58 46.49 N 9.25 E
Vorderriss 64 47.33 N 11.26 E
Vordingborg 41 55.01 N 11.55 E
Voreifel ⋏ 56 50.15 N 7.10 E
Voreppe 62 45.18 N 5.38 E
Vorey 62 45.11 N 3.54 E
Vorga 76 53.45 N 32.45 E
Vorhalle ◆[8] 263 51.23 N 7.28 E
Vorhelm 52 51.48 N 7.56 E
Voríai Sporádhes II 38 39.17 N 23.23 E
Vøringsfossen ʟ 26 60.26 N 7.15 E
Vórios Evvoïkós Kólpos C 38 38.40 N 23.15 E
Vorkuta 24 67.27 N 63.58 E
Vorlich, Ben ∧ 46 56.20 N 4.14 W
Vorma ≃ 26 60.09 N 11.27 E
Vormholz 263 51.24 N 7.18 E
Vormsi I 76 59.00 N 23.20 E
Vorn'any 76 54.44 N 26.01 E
Vornbach 60 48.29 N 13.27 E
Vorobjevka 80 50.39 N 40.56 E
Vorobjevo, S.S.S.R. 82 56.11 N 35.45 E
Vorobjevo, S.S.S.R. 86 56.08 N 76.32 E
Vorobjevo, S.S.S.R. 88 57.23 N 102.18 E
Vorobji 82 55.09 N 36.48 E
Vorobjovka 78 50.38 N 40.56 E
Vorob'jovo, S.S.S.R. 76 59.38 N 40.53 E
Vorobjovo, S.S.S.R. 78 45.19 N 33.15 E
Vorochta 78 48.18 N 24.36 E
Voron' 76 55.00 N 28.39 E
Voron, Porog ʟ 88 57.05 N 98.40 E
Vorona ≃ 80 51.22 N 42.03 E
Voroncovka, S.S.S.R. 78 45.51 N 33.47 E
Voroncovka, S.S.S.R. 78 50.37 N 40.21 E
Voroncovka, S.S.S.R. 86 48.49 N 81.32 E
Voroncovka, S.S.S.R. 86 59.39 N 60.14 E
Voroncovka, S.S.S.R. 88 58.51 N 112.56 E
Voroncovo, S.S.S.R. 76 57.18 N 28.42 E
Voroncovo, S.S.S.R. 80 55.16 N 40.27 E
Voronej → Voronež 78 51.40 N 39.10 E
Voronež, S.S.S.R. 78 51.40 N 39.10 E
Voronež, S.S.S.R. 78 51.46 N 33.28 E
Voronež □[4], S.S.S.R. 76 51.55 N 40.00 E
Voronež □[4], S.S.S.R. 83 49.53 N 40.00 E
Voronež ≃ 76 51.56 N 39.17 E
Voronezh → Voronež 78 51.40 N 39.10 E
Voronežskij Zapovednik ◆[4] 76 51.56 N 39.37 E
Voronino 82 56.24 N 36.52 E
Voronin Trough ✢[1] 12 82.00 N 85.00 E
Voronja ≃ 24 69.10 N 35.50 E
Voronjo, S.S.S.R. 24 68.27 N 35.21 E
Voronjo, S.S.S.R. 80 58.00 N 42.01 E
Voron'ki, S.S.S.R. 78 50.14 N 33.02 E
Voronki, S.S.S.R. 82 55.48 N 37.16 E
Voronkovo 78 47.43 N 29.08 E
Voronok 76 52.23 N 32.40 E
Voronov, Mys ≻ 76 60.15 N 32.05 E
Voronovica 78 49.06 N 28.41 E
Voronovkova Niva 76 57.04 N 29.16 E
Voronovo, S.S.S.R. 76 54.09 N 25.19 E
Voronovo, S.S.S.R. 82 55.19 N 37.10 E
Voronovo, S.S.S.R. 86 56.01 N 83.52 E
Voropajevo 76 55.09 N 27.13 E
Voroshilov → Ussurijsk 89 43.48 N 131.59 E
Voroshilovsk → Stavropol', S.S.S.R. 72 45.02 N 41.59 E
Voroshilovsk → Kommunarsk, S.S.S.R. 83 48.30 N 38.47 E
Vorošilovgrad 83 48.34 N 39.20 E
Vorošilovgrad Avtonomnaja Sovetskaja Socialističeskaja Respublika □[4] 83 49.00 N 39.00 E
Vorotajevka 80 51.56 N 47.16 E
Vorotynec 80 56.04 N 45.52 E
Vorotynsk 82 54.25 N 36.05 E
Vorovskolesskaja 84 44.23 N 42.25 E
Vorožba 78 51.12 N 34.14 E
Vorožejka 86 58.12 N 90.02 E
Vorpommern □[9] 54 53.40 N 13.45 E
Vorra 60 49.33 N 11.30 E
Vorsfelde 54 52.26 N 10.49 E
Vorskla ≃ 78 48.53 N 34.06 E
Vorsma 80 55.59 N 43.16 E
Vorst, Bel. 56 51.04 N 5.01 E
Vorst, B.R.D. 56 51.18 N 6.25 E
Vørterkaka Nunatak ∧ 9 72.20 S 27.29 E
Võrtsjärv ◎ 76 58.16 N 26.03 E
Võru 76 57.50 N 27.01 E
Voruch 85 39.52 N 70.35 E
Vorzel' 78 50.33 N 30.09 E
Vosburg 158 30.33 S 22.52 E
Voschod 80 47.24 N 41.50 E
Vösendorf 264b 48.07 N 16.20 E
Vosges □[5] 58 48.10 N 6.20 E
Vosges ⋏ 58 48.30 N 7.10 E
Vosja 76 59.01 N 41.11 E
Voskresenka, S.S.S.R. 80 51.01 N 46.28 E
Voskresenka, S.S.S.R. 88 53.15 N 119.31 E
Voskresenki 82 54.57 N 38.04 E
Voskresenovskoje 265a 59.43 N 30.47 E
Voskresensk 82 55.19 N 38.42 E
Voskresenskoje, S.S.S.R. 76 53.12 N 38.43 E
Voskresenskoje, S.S.S.R. 76 59.26 N 37.56 E
Voskresenskoje, S.S.S.R. 76 57.49 N 37.40 E
Voskresenskoje, S.S.S.R. 76 58.54 N 38.36 E
Voskresenskoje, S.S.S.R. 78 47.02 N 32.09 E
Voskresenskoje, S.S.S.R. 80 56.51 N 45.26 E
Voskresenskoje, S.S.S.R. 80 51.51 N 46.56 E
Voskresenskoje, S.S.S.R. 82 56.20 N 38.29 E
Voskresenskoje, S.S.S.R. 82 54.07 N 37.07 E
Voskresenskoje, S.S.S.R. 86 53.08 N 56.10 E
Voslapp 52 53.36 N 8.05 E
Voss 26 60.39 N 6.26 E
Vosselaar 56 51.19 N 4.53 E
Vossijatskoje 78 47.41 N 32.07 E
Vossman's Beacon 158 26.11 S 30.40 E
Vostočnaja Kambal'nica 24 68.18 N 46.00 E
Vostočno-Kazachstanskaja Oblast' □[4] 86 49.00 N 84.00 E
Vostočno-Kounradskij 86 47.02 N 75.07 E
Vostočno-Sibirskoje More ⊤[2] 12 74.00 N 166.00 E
Vostočnyj, S.S.S.R. 82 55.47 N 37.49 E
Vostočnyj, S.S.S.R. 86 58.48 N 61.52 E
Vostočnyj, S.S.S.R. 89 53.29 N 143.03 E
Vostočnyj, S.S.S.R. 89 48.17 N 142.34 E
Vostočnyj Sajan ⋏ 88 53.00 N 97.00 E
Vostočnyj Tannu-Ola, Chrebet ⋏ 88 50.54 N 94.30 E
Vostok ♉[3] 9 78.30 S 106.50 E
Vostok Island I 14 10.06 S 152.23 W
Vostr'akovo 82 55.23 N 37.49 E
Vostrovo 86 52.09 N 80.38 E
Vosves 261 48.31 N 2.36 E
Votaw 222 30.26 N 94.41 W
Votice 30 49.38 N 14.39 E
Votkinsk 80 57.03 N 53.59 E
Votkinskoje Vodochranilišče ◎[1] 80 56.45 N 54.08 E
Vot'pa 86 60.13 N 62.57 E
Votuporanga 255 20.24 S 49.59 W
Voué 50 48.28 N 4.07 E
Vouga 152 12.11 S 16.47 E
Vouga ≃ 34 40.41 N 8.40 W
Vougeot 58 47.10 N 4.58 E
Vouillé 32 46.39 N 0.10 E
Voujeaucourt 58 47.28 N 6.46 E
Voulangis 261 48.51 N 2.54 E
Voulou 146 8.33 N 22.36 E
Voulx 50 48.17 N 2.58 E
Voulzie ≃ 50 48.25 N 3.12 E
Voutenay-sur-Cure 50 47.33 N 3.47 E
Vouvray 50 47.25 N 0.48 E
Vouvry 58 46.20 N 6.53 E
Vouziers 56 49.24 N 4.42 E
Voves 50 48.16 N 1.38 E
Vovodo ≃ 140 5.40 N 24.21 E
Vowinckel 214 41.25 N 79.14 W
Voxnan ≃ 26 61.17 N 16.26 E
Voxtrup 52 52.14 N 8.07 E
Voyageurs National Park ♠ 190 48.30 N 93.00 W
Voyeykov Ice Shelf ⊼ 9 66.20 S 124.38 E
Vöyri → Vörå 26 63.09 N 22.15 E
Voža ≃ 82 54.38 N 39.10 E
Vožajol' 24 62.50 N 51.17 E
Vožd' Proletariata 76 55.26 N 39.19 E
Vozdviženka, S.S.S.R. 78 47.46 N 36.05 E
Vozdviženka, S.S.S.R. 80 53.10 N 54.14 E
Vozdviženskoje, S.S.S.R. 80 56.58 N 45.37 E
Vozdviženskoje, S.S.S.R. 80 45.50 N 43.40 E
Vozdviženskoje, S.S.S.R. 82 56.12 N 38.04 E
Vože, Ozero ◎ 24 60.30 N 39.00 E
Vožega 76 60.29 N 40.12 E
Vožega ≃ 76 60.33 N 39.11 E
Vožgaly 80 58.09 N 50.11 E
Vožgora 24 64.32 N 48.25 E
Voznesenje 24 61.01 N 35.27 E
Voznesenka, S.S.S.R. 78 46.51 N 35.26 E
Voznesenka, S.S.S.R. 86 52.24 N 70.12 E
Voznesenovka 80 46.16 N 44.21 E
Voznesensk 78 47.34 N 31.20 E
Voznesenskoje, S.S.S.R. 80 45.49 N 43.25 E
Voznesenskoje, S.S.S.R. 80 54.54 N 42.46 E
Vozroždenija, Ostrov I 86 45.03 N 59.12 E
Vozroždenije 80 52.42 N 48.12 E
Vozžajevka 89 50.44 N 128.41 E
Vrå 26 57.21 N 9.57 E
Vráble 30 48.15 N 18.19 E
Vraca 38 43.12 N 23.33 E
Vračevo 82 54.53 N 39.10 E
Vrådal 26 59.20 N 8.25 E
Vrancea □[4] 38 45.45 N 27.00 E
Vrancei, Munţii ⋏ 38 46.00 N 26.30 E
Vrangel'a, Mys ≻ 89 54.17 N 138.39 E
Vrangel'a, Ostrov I 74 71.00 N 179.30 W
Vranje 38 42.33 N 21.54 E
Vranov [nad Topl'ou] 30 48.54 N 21.41 E
Vrbas 38 45.35 N 19.39 E
Vrbas ≃ 36 45.06 N 17.31 E
Vrbovec 36 45.53 N 16.25 E
Vrbovsko 36 45.23 N 15.05 E
Vrchlabí 30 50.38 N 15.37 E
Vrede 158 27.30 S 29.06 E
Vredefort 158 27.05 S 27.16 E
Vreden 52 52.02 N 6.52 E
Vredenburg 158 32.54 S 17.59 E
Vredendal 158 31.41 S 18.35 E
Vreed en Hoop 246 6.48 N 58.11 W
Vreeswijk 52 52.01 N 5.05 E
Vrena 40 58.52 N 16.41 E
Vresse 56 49.52 N 4.56 E
Vreta Kloster ♉[1] 26 58.28 N 15.29 E
Vretstorp 40 59.02 N 14.52 E
Vrginmost 36 45.21 N 15.52 E
Vrhnika 36 45.58 N 14.18 E
Vriddhāchalam 122 11.30 N 79.20 E
Vriendschaaps ≃ 164 5.28 S 138.53 E
Vries 52 53.04 N 6.35 E
Vriezenveen 52 52.25 N 6.38 E
Vrigne-Meuse 56 49.42 N 4.51 E
Vrigstad 26 57.21 N 14.28 E
Vrilissia 267c 38.02 N 23.50 E
Vrille ≃ 50 47.31 N 2.52 E
Vrin 58 46.39 N 9.06 E
Vrin ≃ 50 48.00 N 3.20 E
Vrindāvan 124 27.35 N 77.42 E
Vrlika 36 43.55 N 16.24 E
Vrnograč 36 45.10 N 15.57 E
Vroeggedeel 158 28.02 S 22.32 E
Vroeunspan 158 27.50 S 20.24 E
Vron 50 50.19 N 1.45 E
Vrondádhes 38 38.24 N 26.08 E
Vroomshoop 52 52.27 N 6.34 E
Vroutek 54 50.08 N 13.24 E
Vršac 38 45.07 N 21.18 E
Vrsar 64 45.08 N 13.37 E
Vršič)(64 46.26 N 13.44 E
Vrubovka 83 48.44 N 38.20 E
Vrubovskij 83 48.26 N 39.07 E
Vrútky 30 49.07 N 18.55 E
Vryburg 158 26.55 S 24.45 E
Vryheid 158 27.52 S 30.38 E
Vschody 76 54.42 N 34.06 E
Vselug, Ozero ◎ 76 57.03 N 32.42 E
Všepadly 60 49.28 N 13.06 E
Všeruby 60 49.51 N 13.14 E
Vsetín 30 49.21 N 17.59 E
Vsevidof, Mount ∧ 180 53.07 N 168.43 W
Vsevoložsk 76 60.01 N 30.40 E
Vtoryje Levyje Lamki 80 53.17 N 41.04 E
Vuadil' 85 40.11 N 71.43 E
Vučitrn 38 42.49 N 20.58 E
Vue-des-Alpes)(58 47.04 N 6.53 E
Vught 52 51.40 N 5.17 E
Vuillafans 58 47.04 N 6.13 E
Vuimasia ∧ 175g 17.59 S 178.07 E
Vuitebœuf 58 46.37 N 6.34 E
Vukovar 38 45.21 N 19.00 E
Vulcan, Alta., Can. 182 50.24 N 113.15 W
Vulcan, Rom. 38 45.23 N 23.17 E
Vulcan, Mich., U.S. 190 45.47 N 87.53 W
Vulcano, Bocche di Ʉ 70 38.26 N 14.57 E
Vulcano, Isola I 70 38.24 N 14.58 E
Vulcano, Monte ∧ 71a 35.51 N 12.52 E
Vulci ⊥ 66 42.25 N 11.35 E
Vu-liet 110 18.43 N 105.23 E
Vulkanešty 78 45.41 N 28.24 E
Vulture, Monte ∧ 68 40.57 N 15.38 E
Vul'vyvejem ≃ 180 66.58 N 179.10 E
Vundúzi ≃ 154 18.56 S 34.01 E
Vung-tau (Cap-Saint-Jacques) 110 10.21 N 107.04 E
Vunindawa 175g 17.49 S 178.19 E
Vunisea 175g 19.03 S 178.09 E
Vunmarama 175f 15.29 S 168.10 E
Vuoggatjålme 24 66.36 N 16.22 E
Vuohijärvi 26 61.05 N 26.48 E

Symbol	English	Deutsch	Español	Français	Português
≃	River	Fluss	Río	Rivière	Rio
≡	Canal	Kanal	Canal	Canal	Canal
ʟ	Waterfall, Rapids	Wasserfall, Stromschnellen	Cascada, Rápidos	Chute d'eau, Rapides	Cascata, Rápidos
Ʉ	Strait	Meeresstrasse	Estrecho	Détroit	Estreito
C	Bay, Gulf	Bucht, Golf	Bahía, Golfo	Baie, Golfe	Baía, Golfo
◎	Lake, Lakes	See, Seen	Lago, Lagos	Lac, Lacs	Lago, Lagos
☷	Swamp	Sumpf	Pantano	Marais	Pântano
⊼	Ice Features, Glacier	Eis- und Gletscherformen	Accidentes Glaciales	Formes glaciaires	Acidentes Glaciares
⊤	Other Hydrographic Features	Andere Hydrographische Objekte	Otros Elementos Hidrográficos	Autres données hydrographiques	Outros Elementos Hidrográficos
✢	Submarine Features	Untermeerische Objekte	Accidentes Submarinos	Formes de relief sous-marin	Acidentes Submarinos
□	Political Unit	Politische Einheit	Unidad Politica	Entité politique	Unidade Política
♉	Cultural Institution	Kulturelle Institution	Institución Cultural	Institution culturelle	Instituição Cultural
⊥	Historical Site	Historische Stätte	Sitio Histórico	Site historique	Sitio Histórico
♠	Recreational Site	Erholungs- und Ferienort	Sitio de Recreo	Centre de loisirs	Sítio de Lazer
⊠	Airport	Flughafen	Aeropuerto	Aéroport	Aeroporto
■	Military Installation	Militäranlage	Instalación Militar	Installation militaire	Instalação Militar
◆	Miscellaneous	Verschiedenes	Misceláneo	Divers	Miscelânea

Name	Page	Lat.	Long.
Vuohijärvi ⊜	26	61.12 N	26.42 E
Vuokatti ∧[2]	26	64.07 N	28.14 E
Vuoksa, Ozero ⊜	76	60.40 N	29.50 E
Vuoksenniska	26	61.13 N	28.49 E
Vuoksi ≃	26	61.03 N	30.11 E
Vuotso	24	68.08 N	27.08 E
Vurnary	80	55.29 N	46.58 E
Vuturu, Pizzo ∧	70	37.56 N	14.13 E
Vuya	154	5.21 N	29.40 E
Vuyyūru	122	16.22 N	80.51 E
Vvedenka	86	54.03 N	63.45 E
Vvedenovka	89	51.19 N	128.12 E
Vvedenskoje	82	55.42 N	36.54 E
Vyāra	120	21.07 N	73.24 E
Vyatka → Kirov	80	58.38 N	49.42 E
Vyaz'ma → V'az'ma	76	55.13 N	34.18 E
Vyazniki → V'azniki	80	56.15 N	42.10 E
Vyborg	76	60.42 N	28.45 E
Vyborgskij Zaliv C	76	60.35 N	28.24 E
Vyčegda ≃	24	61.18 N	46.36 E
Vyčegodskij	24	61.16 N	46.48 E
Vychino •[8]	265b	55.43 N	37.48 E
Východočeský Kraj □[4]	30	50.10 N	16.00 E
Východoslovenský Kraj □[4]	30	49.00 N	21.15 E
Vydrino, S.S.S.R.	88	56.50 N	99.02 E
Vydrino, S.S.S.R.	88	51.27 N	104.39 E
Vygoda	78	48.56 N	23.55 E
Vygoniči	76	53.08 N	34.05 E
Vygonišči	76	52.37 N	25.55 E
Vygor'	76	54.49 N	33.59 E
Vygozero, Ozero ⊜	24	63.35 N	34.42 E
Vyjezdnoje	80	55.23 N	43.47 E
Vyježžij Log	86	54.58 N	93.57 E
Vyksa	80	55.18 N	42.11 E
Vylkovo	86	53.05 N	81.26 E
Vym' ≃	24	62.13 N	50.25 E
Vyntja	86	60.31 N	67.18 E
Vypolzovo	76	57.53 N	33.42 E
Vyrica	76	59.25 N	30.21 E
Vyrnwy, Lake ⊜	42	52.47 N	3.30 W
Vyša	80	53.52 N	42.24 E
Vyša ≃	80	54.02 N	42.06 E
Vyšehrad •[8]	54	50.01 N	14.27 E
Vyšelej	80	53.26 N	45.29 E
Vyselki	78	45.35 N	39.38 E
Vyšesteblijevskaja	78	45.12 N	37.00 E
Vyšgorodok	76	57.02 N	28.01 E
Vyška, S.S.S.R.	76	57.31 N	35.57 E
Vyška, S.S.S.R.	128	39.20 N	54.08 E
Vyskod'	76	57.46 N	30.04 E
Vyškov	76	52.29 N	31.41 E
Vyškovskij, Pereval)(	78	48.42 N	23.38 E
Vyšná Radvaň	30	49.07 N	21.56 E
Vyšneol'šanoje	76	52.08 N	37.39 E
Vyšnevolockoje Vodochranilišče ⊜[1]	76	57.35 N	34.28 E
Vyšnij Voločok	76	57.35 N	34.34 E
Vysočany •[8]	54	50.05 N	14.31 E
Vysock, S.S.S.R.	76	60.36 N	28.34 E
Vysock, S.S.S.R.	78	51.43 N	26.39 E
Vysokaja, Gora ∧	89	45.59 N	136.35 E
Vysokaja Gora	80	55.56 N	49.19 E
Vysoké Mýto	30	49.57 N	16.10 E
Vysoké Tatry ⩕	30	49.12 N	20.05 E
Vysokiniči	82	54.54 N	36.55 E
Vysokogornyj	89	50.09 N	139.09 E
Vysokogorsk	89	44.23 N	135.23 E
Vysokoje, S.S.S.R.	76	52.22 N	23.22 E
Vysokoje, S.S.S.R.	76	54.02 N	33.44 E
Vysokoje, S.S.S.R.	76	56.43 N	34.55 E
Vysokoje, S.S.S.R.	82	54.30 N	37.03 E
Vysokoje, S.S.S.R.	85	42.30 N	70.32 E
Vysokoje, S.S.S.R.	265b	55.59 N	37.09 E
Vysokopolje	78	47.29 N	33.32 E
Vysokovsk	82	56.19 N	36.33 E
Vysoký kámen ∧	61	49.06 N	15.13 E
Vyssšaja Dubečn'a	78	50.44 N	30.40 E
Vyšší Brod	61	48.37 N	14.19 E
Vystavka Dostiženij Narodnogo Choz'ajstva S.S.R. ʊ	265b	55.50 N	37.37 E
Vystupoviči	78	51.34 N	29.04 E
Vytebet' ≃	76	53.53 N	35.38 E
Vytegra	24	61.00 N	36.24 E
Vyževka ≃	78	51.41 N	24.35 E
Vzmorje	89	47.51 N	142.31 E
Vzvad	76	58.10 N	31.29 E
W			
W, Parcs Nationaux du ♠	150	12.50 N	2.30 W
Wa	150	10.04 N	2.29 W
Waabs	41	54.32 N	9.58 E
Waackaack Creek ≃	276	40.27 N	74.08 W
Waadt → Vaud □[3]	58	46.40 N	6.30 E
Waakirchen	64	47.46 N	11.40 E
Waal	58	48.00 N	10.46 E
Waal ≃	52	51.55 N	4.30 E
Waalre	52	51.24 N	5.26 E
Waalwijk	52	51.42 N	5.04 E
Waao	102	24.20 N	104.40 E
Waar, Pulau I	164	2.05 S	134.23 E
Waarschoot	50	51.09 N	3.36 E
Waasmunster	50	51.06 N	4.05 E
Wabag	164	5.30 S	143.40 E
Wabamun	182	53.33 N	114.28 W
Wabamun Indian Reserve •[4]	182	53.30 N	114.30 W
Wabamun Lake ⊜	182	53.33 N	114.35 W
Waban	283	42.20 N	71.14 W
Waban, Lake ⊜	283	42.17 N	71.17 W
Wabana	186	47.38 N	52.57 W
Wabasca	182	56.00 N	113.53 W
Wabasca ≃	176	58.22 N	115.20 W
Wabasca Indian Reserve •[4]	182	55.53 N	113.32 W
Wabash, Ind., U.S.	216	40.48 N	85.49 W
Wabash, Ohio, U.S.	216	40.33 N	84.45 W
Wabash □[6]	216	40.48 N	85.49 W
Wabash ≃	194	37.46 N	88.02 W
Wabasha	190	44.23 N	92.02 W
Wabasso	220	27.45 N	80.26 W
Wabatongushi Lake ⊜	190	48.26 N	84.15 W
Wabeno	190	45.26 N	88.39 W
Wabern	56	51.06 N	9.20 E
Wabigoon Lake ⊜	184	49.44 N	92.44 W
Waboe	174b	0.31 S	166.55 E
Wabowden	184	54.55 N	98.38 W
Wabrah ⫪[4]	128	27.26 N	47.22 E
Wąbrzeźno	30	53.17 N	18.57 E
Wabuhu	100	32.17 N	116.55 E
Wabuska	226	39.09 N	119.11 W
W.A.C. Bennett Dam •[6]	182	56.01 N	122.10 W
Waccamaw ≃	192	33.21 N	79.16 W
Waccamaw, Lake ⊜	192	34.17 N	78.30 W
Waccasassa Bay C	192	29.06 N	82.52 W
Wachapreague	208	37.36 N	75.41 W
Wachapreague Inlet C	208	37.35 N	75.36 W
Wachau •[1]	61	48.18 N	15.24 E
Wachenheim	56	49.26 N	8.10 E
Wachenzell	60	48.58 N	11.14 E
Wachi	96	35.15 N	135.24 E
Wąchock, Klasztory ʊ[1]	30	51.05 N	21.01 E
Wachtendonk	56	51.24 N	6.20 E
Wächtersbach	56	50.15 N	9.17 E
Wachusett Mountain ∧	207	42.29 N	71.53 W
Wachusett Reservoir ⊜[1]	207	42.23 N	71.43 W
Wachusett Shoal ✣[2]	14	32.10 S	151.05 W
Wacissa	192	30.21 N	83.59 W
Wackersdorf	60	49.19 N	12.11 E
Waco	222	31.55 N	97.08 W
Waco Lake ⊜[1]	222	31.34 N	97.13 W
Waconda Lake ⊜[1]	198	39.30 N	98.35 W
Waconia	190	44.51 N	93.47 W
Wacouno ≃	186	50.54 N	65.57 W
Wacousta	216	42.49 N	84.42 W
Wad	120	27.21 N	66.22 E
Wada, Nihon	94	36.12 N	138.13 E
Wada, Nihon	94	35.02 N	140.01 E
Wada, Nihon	268	35.12 N	139.38 E
Wada, Nihon	270	34.33 N	135.55 E
Wadagou	104	42.27 N	120.58 E
Wad al-Ḥaddād	140	13.49 N	33.32 E
Wadamago	144	8.54 N	46.18 E
Wada-misaki ≻	96	34.39 N	135.11 E
Wādat Ga	120	26.00 N	97.00 E
Wadayama	96	35.19 N	134.52 E
Wad Bandah	140	13.06 N	27.57 E
Wad Ban Naqa	140	16.30 N	33.08 E
Waddān	146	29.10 N	16.08 E
Waddān, Jabal ∧	146	29.20 N	16.20 E
Waddeneilanden II	52	53.26 N	5.30 E
Waddenzee ⫪[2]	52	53.15 N	5.15 E
Wadderin Hill	162	32.00 S	118.27 E
Waddesdon	42	51.51 N	0.56 W
Waddingham	44	53.27 N	0.31 W
Waddington	212	44.52 N	75.12 W
Waddington, Mount ∧	182	51.23 N	125.15 W
Waddinxveen	52	52.03 N	4.40 E
Waddy	218	38.08 N	85.04 W
Wade, Mount ∧	9	84.51 S	174.15 W
Wadebridge	42	50.32 N	4.50 W
Wadena, Sask., Can.	184	51.57 N	103.47 W
Wadena, Ind., U.S.	216	40.43 N	87.16 W
Wadena, Minn., U.S.	198	46.26 N	95.08 W
Wädenswil	58	47.14 N	8.40 E
Wadern	56	49.32 N	6.53 E
Wadersloh	52	51.44 N	8.15 E
Wadesboro	192	34.58 N	80.04 W
Wadeville	273d	26.16 S	28.11 E
Wad Ḥāmid	140	16.30 N	32.48 E
Wadham Islands II	186	49.34 N	53.50 W
Wadhams	182	51.30 N	127.31 W
Wadhurst	42	51.04 N	0.21 E
Wadi	120	28.02 N	96.59 E
Wadian	100	32.48 N	112.30 E
Wādī as-Sīr	132	31.57 N	35.49 E
Wādī Ḥalfā'	140	21.56 N	31.20 E
Wādī Jimāl, Jazīrat I	140	24.40 N	35.10 E
Wādī Mūsā	132	30.19 N	35.29 E
Wading ≃, Mass., U.S.	283	41.56 N	71.13 W
Wading ≃, N.J., U.S.	208	39.33 N	74.28 W
Wading, West Branch ≃	208	39.40 N	74.32 W
Wading River	207	40.57 N	72.51 W
Wādī Rashrāsh, Bi'r ⫪[4]	142	29.26 N	31.31 E
Wadley, Ala., U.S.	194	33.07 N	85.34 W
Wadley, Ga., U.S.	192	32.52 N	82.24 W
Wad Madanī	140	14.25 N	33.28 E
Wadowice	30	49.53 N	19.30 E
Wadsworth, Ill., U.S.	216	42.26 N	87.56 W
Wadsworth, Nev., U.S.	204	39.38 N	119.17 W
Wadsworth, N.Y., U.S.	210	42.49 N	77.54 W
Wadsworth, Ohio, U.S.	214	41.02 N	81.44 W
Wadsworth Moor •[3]	262	53.48 N	2.02 W
Wadu I	122	5.51 N	72.58 E
Waegwan	98	35.58 N	128.24 E
Waelder	222	29.42 N	97.18 W
Waenhuiskrans	158	34.41 S	20.14 E
Wafang	98	41.44 N	118.54 E
Wafania	152	1.21 S	20.20 E
Wafrah	128	28.33 N	48.02 E
Wagadugu → Ouagadougou	150	12.22 N	1.31 W
Wāgah	123	31.36 N	74.33 E
Wagait Aboriginal Reserve •[4]	164	13.00 S	130.20 E
Wagang	102	28.04 N	103.10 E
Wagenborgen	52	53.15 N	6.56 E
Wagenfeld-Hasslingen	52	52.33 N	8.34 E
Wageningen, Ned.	52	51.58 N	5.40 E
Wageningen, Sur.	250	5.46 N	56.41 W
Wager Bay C	176	65.26 N	88.40 W
Wagerup	168a	32.55 S	115.54 E
Wagga Wagga	171b	35.07 S	147.22 E
Waggoner	219	39.23 N	89.39 W
Wagin	162	33.18 S	117.21 E
Wagina I	175e	7.26 S	157.46 E
Waging am See	64	47.56 N	12.43 E
Waginger See ⊜	64	47.56 N	12.47 E
Wägitaler See ⊜	58	47.06 N	8.55 E
Wagner	198	43.05 N	98.18 W
Wagner College ʊ[2]	276	40.37 N	74.07 W
Wagoner	196	35.58 N	95.22 W
Wagon Mound	196	36.01 N	104.42 W
Wagontire Mountain ∧	202	43.21 N	119.53 W
Wagontown	208	40.01 N	75.51 W
Wagrain	64	47.20 N	13.18 E
Wagrien •[1]	54	54.15 N	10.45 E
Wągrowiec	30	52.49 N	17.11 E
Wah	123	33.48 N	72.42 E
Waha	146	28.16 N	19.54 E
Wahai	164	2.48 S	129.30 E
Waharoa	172	37.46 S	175.46 E
Wahiawa	229c	21.30 N	158.01 W
Wahkiakum □[6]	224	46.16 N	123.28 W
Wahlen	56	49.37 N	8.51 E
Wahlstedt	54	53.57 N	10.12 E
Wahn	56	50.52 N	7.05 E
Wahnbachstausee ⊜[1]	56	50.48 N	7.19 E
Wahneta	220	27.57 N	81.44 W
Wahoo	198	41.13 N	96.37 W
Wahpeton	198	46.16 N	96.36 W
Wahrenbrück	54	51.33 N	13.22 E
Wahrenholz	54	52.36 N	10.36 E
Währing •[8]	264b	48.14 N	16.21 E
Wahroonga	274a	33.43 S	151.07 E
Wahweap Creek ≃	200	36.57 N	111.29 W
Wai, Bhārat	122	17.56 N	73.54 E
Wai, Indon.	164	1.42 S	127.59 E
Waialailing ⩕	85	39.35 N	74.10 E
Waialeale ∧	229b	22.04 N	159.30 W
Waialua	229c	21.34 N	158.08 W
Waialua Bay C	229c	21.36 N	158.07 W
Waianae	229c	21.27 N	158.11 W
Waianae Mountains ⩕	229c	21.30 N	158.10 W
Waianapanapa Caves State Park ♠	229a	20.47 N	156.01 W
Waiapu ≃	172	37.47 S	178.29 E
Waiatoto ≃	172	43.59 S	168.47 E
Waiau	172	42.39 S	173.03 E
Waiau ≃, N.Z.	172	38.58 S	177.24 E
Waiau ≃, N.Z.	172	46.12 S	167.38 E
Waiau ≃, N.Z.	172	42.47 S	173.22 E
Waibakul	115b	9.36 S	119.35 E
Waibeem	164	0.28 S	132.58 E
Waiblingen	56	48.50 N	9.19 E
Waibstadt	56	49.18 N	8.54 E
Waichagoumen	98	40.54 N	125.45 E
Waidbruck → Ponte Gardena	64	46.36 N	11.32 E
Waidhān	124	24.04 N	82.20 E
Waidhofen an der Thaya	61	48.49 N	15.18 E
Waidhofen an der Ybbs	61	47.58 N	14.47 E
Waidmannslust •[8]	264a	52.36 N	13.20 E
Waidring	64	47.35 N	12.34 E
Waiehu	229a	20.55 N	156.30 W
Waigang	106	31.22 N	121.11 E
Waigatsch → Vajgač, Ostrov I	72	70.00 N	59.30 E
Waigeo, Pulau I	164	0.14 S	130.45 E
Waigoumen	98	41.56 N	116.25 E
Waihao Downs	172	44.48 S	170.55 E
Waihee	229a	20.56 N	156.31 W
Waihee Point ≻	229a	20.57 N	156.31 W
Waiheke Island I	172	36.48 S	175.06 E
Waihi	172	37.24 S	175.51 E
Waihola	172	46.02 S	170.06 E
Waihopai ≃	172	41.31 S	173.44 E
Waihou ≃	172	37.10 S	175.32 E
Waihuantan	106	30.25 N	118.40 E
Waika	154	2.21 S	25.43 E
Waikabubak	115b	9.38 S	119.25 E
Waikaia	172	45.44 S	168.51 E
Waikaia ≃	172	45.53 S	168.48 E
Waikanae	172	40.53 S	175.04 E
Waikane	229c	21.30 N	157.51 W
Waikapu	229a	20.51 N	156.30 W
Waikare, Lake ⊜	172	37.26 S	175.13 E
Waikaremoana, Lake ⊜	172	38.46 S	177.07 E
Waikari	172	42.58 S	172.41 E
Waikato ≃	172	37.23 S	174.43 E
Waikelo	115b	9.24 S	119.14 E
Waikerie	166	34.11 S	139.59 E
Waikiki Beach ♠	229c	21.17 N	157.50 W
Waikino	172	37.25 S	175.46 E
Waikouaiti	172	45.36 S	170.41 E
Waikuatang	106	31.20 N	120.41 E
Wailingding I	100	22.07 N	114.05 E
Wailing Wall, The (Kotel Hama'aravi) ⊥	132	31.46 N	35.14 E
Wailua	229b	22.03 N	159.19 W
Wailua River State Park ♠	229b	22.02 N	159.21 W
Wailuku	229a	20.53 N	156.30 W
Waimahaka	172	46.31 S	168.49 E
Waimakariri ≃	172	43.24 S	172.42 E
Waimamaku	172	35.33 S	173.29 E
Waimana	172	38.09 S	177.05 E
Waimana ≃	172	38.04 S	177.00 E
Waimanalo	229c	21.21 N	157.42 W
Waimangaroa	172	41.43 S	171.46 E
Waimangura	115b	9.30 S	119.14 E
Waimarama	172	39.48 S	176.59 E
Waimate	172	44.44 S	171.02 E
Waimea, Haw., U.S.	229c	21.39 N	158.04 W
Waimea, Haw., U.S.	229d	21.58 N	159.42 W
Waimea Canyon V	229b	22.04 N	159.39 W
Waimea Canyon State Park ♠	229b	22.04 N	159.40 W
Waimes	56	50.25 N	6.07 E
Wainfleet All Saints	44	53.07 N	0.14 E
Wainganga ≃	122	18.50 N	79.55 E
Waingapu	115b	9.39 S	120.16 E
Waini ≃	246	8.24 N	59.51 W
Wainscott	260	51.25 N	0.31 E
Wainstalls	262	53.45 N	1.56 W
Wainuiomata	172	41.16 S	174.57 E
Wainunu Bay C	175g	16.55 S	178.53 E
Wainwright, Alta., Can.	182	52.49 N	110.52 W
Wainwright, Alaska, U.S.	180	70.38 N	160.01 W
Wainwright, Ohio, U.S.	214	40.25 N	81.26 W
Waiohau	172	38.14 S	176.51 E
Waiotira	172	35.56 S	174.12 E
Waiouru	172	39.29 S	175.40 E
Waipahi	172	46.07 S	169.15 E
Waipahu	229c	21.23 N	158.01 W
Waipaoa	172	38.32 S	177.54 E
Waipara	172	43.04 S	172.45 E
Waipara ≃	172	43.09 S	172.48 E
Waipawa	172	39.56 S	176.36 E
Waipiata	172	45.11 S	170.10 E
Waipio Acres	229c	21.28 N	158.01 W
Waipio Bay C	229a	20.55 N	156.13 W
Waipiqundao II	100	23.57 N	117.55 E
Waipiro	172	38.01 S	178.20 E
Waipu	172	35.59 S	174.27 E
Waipukurau	172	40.00 S	176.34 E
Wairakei	172	38.38 S	176.06 E
Wairarapa, Lake ⊜	172	41.13 S	175.15 E
Wairau ≃	172	41.30 S	174.04 E
Wairau Valley	172	41.34 S	173.32 E
Wairio	172	46.00 S	168.02 E
Wairoa	172	39.02 S	177.25 E
Wairoa ≃	172	39.04 S	177.26 E
Waisanzao	106	30.57 N	121.52 E
Waischenfeld	60	49.51 N	11.21 E
Waitahanui	172	38.47 S	176.05 E
Waitahuna	172	45.59 S	169.46 E
Waitakaruru	172	37.15 S	175.23 E
Waitara, Austl.	274a	33.43 S	151.07 E
Waitara, N.Z.	172	39.00 S	174.13 E
Waitara ≃	172	38.59 S	174.14 E
Waitarere	172	40.33 S	175.12 E
Waita Reservoir ⊜[1]	229b	21.55 N	159.27 W
Waitati	172	45.45 S	170.34 E
Waita-zan ∧	96	33.08 N	131.10 E
Waite Hill	214	41.37 N	81.22 W
Waite Park	190	45.33 N	94.14 W
Waitoa	172	37.37 S	175.38 E
Waitotara	172	39.48 S	174.44 E
Waitotara ≃	172	39.51 S	174.41 E
Waitpinga	168b	35.37 S	138.29 E
Waitsburg	202	46.16 N	118.09 W
Waitzen → Vác	30	47.47 N	19.08 E
Waiuku	172	37.15 S	174.45 E
Waiuta	172	42.18 S	171.49 E
Waiwera South	172	46.13 S	169.30 E
Waiwo	164	0.56 S	131.03 E
Waiya	164	3.13 S	128.55 E
Waizenkirchen	60	48.20 N	13.52 E
Wajid	144	3.50 N	43.14 E
Wajima	92	37.24 N	136.54 E
Wajir	154	1.45 N	40.04 E
Waka, Tex., U.S.	196	36.17 N	101.03 W
Waka, Yai.	144	7.07 N	37.26 E
Waka, Zaïre	152	1.01 N	20.13 E
Waka, Zaïre	152	0.48 S	20.10 E
Wakajabi	164	5.38 S	134.24 E
Wakakusa	94	35.36 N	138.29 E
Wakakusa-yama ∧[2]	270	34.42 N	135.52 E
Wakalla Wen	144	2.00 N	42.30 E
Wakalla Yero	144	1.47 N	42.42 E
Wakamatsu → Aizu-wakamatsu	92	37.30 N	139.56 E
Wakami ≃	190	47.43 N	82.22 W
Wakami Lake ⊜	190	47.29 N	82.51 W
Wakamiya	96	33.44 N	130.37 E
Wakano-ura ♠	96	34.11 N	135.11 E
Wakarusa	216	41.32 N	86.01 W
Wakarusa ≃	198	38.57 N	95.05 W
Wakasa	96	35.20 N	134.24 E
Wakasa-wan C	96	35.45 N	135.40 E
Wakasa-wan-kokutei-kōen ♠	96	35.35 N	135.30 E
Wakatipu, Lake ⊜	172	45.05 S	168.34 E
Wakatomika Creek ≃	214	40.07 N	82.00 W
Wakato-ohashi •[5]	96	33.54 N	130.49 E
Wakaw	184	52.39 N	105.44 W
Wakaya I	175g	17.37 S	179.00 E
Wakayama	96	34.13 N	135.11 E
Wakayama □[5]	96	34.00 N	135.20 E
Wakayanagi	92	38.46 N	141.08 E
Wake	96	34.48 N	134.08 E
Wake Airport ⊠	174a	19.17 N	166.37 E
Wa Keeney	198	39.01 N	99.53 W
Wakefield, N.Z.	172	41.24 S	173.03 E
Wakefield, Eng., U.K.	44	53.42 N	1.29 W
Wakefield, Kans., U.S.	198	39.13 N	97.01 W
Wakefield, Mass., U.S.	207	42.30 N	71.04 W
Wakefield, Nebr., U.S.	198	42.16 N	96.52 W
Wakefield, Ohio, U.S.	218	38.59 N	83.01 W
Wakefield, R.I., U.S.	207	41.26 N	71.30 W
Wakefield, Va., U.S.	192	36.58 N	76.59 W
Wakefield ≃	168b	34.10 S	138.10 E
Wake Forest	192	35.59 N	78.30 W
Wake Island □[2]	14, 174a	19.17 N	166.36 E
Wakema	110	16.36 N	95.11 E
Wakeman	214	41.15 N	82.24 W
Wakeman ≃	182	51.00 N	126.30 W
Wakenda Creek ≃	194	39.19 N	93.16 W
Wake Village	194	33.26 N	94.07 W
Wakhān → Vākhān •[1]	120	37.00 N	73.00 E
Waki	96	34.04 N	134.09 E
Wakis	164	6.13 S	150.17 E
Wakita	196	36.53 N	97.55 W
Wakkanai	92a	45.25 N	141.40 E
Wakkerstroom	158	27.24 S	30.10 E
Wakomata Lake ⊜	190	46.34 N	83.22 W
Wakonassin ≃	190	46.28 N	81.51 W
Wakonda	198	43.00 N	97.06 W
Wakre	164	0.19 S	131.09 E
Waku	164	6.05 S	149.05 E
Wakunai	175e	5.52 S	155.13 E
Wālājāpet	122	12.56 N	79.23 E
Walamba	154	13.29 S	28.45 E
Walamo	234	23.07 N	106.15 W
Walanae ≃	112	4.08 S	119.58 E
Walang	102	28.33 N	100.54 E
Wal Athiang	140	7.42 N	29.40 E
Walawe ≃	122	6.06 N	81.01 E
Walbeck	52	51.30 N	6.15 E
Walberswick	42	52.19 N	1.39 E
Walbran Creek ≃	224	48.34 N	124.40 W
Walbridge	214	41.35 N	83.29 W
Wałbrzych (Waldenburg)	30	50.46 N	16.17 E
Walburg	222	30.44 N	97.35 W
Walbury Hill ∧[2]	42	51.21 N	1.30 W
Walcha	166	30.59 S	151.36 E
Walchensee	64	47.35 N	11.19 E
Walchensee ⊜	64	47.36 N	11.20 E
Walcheren I	52	51.33 N	3.35 E
Walcheren, Kanaal door ≍	50	51.26 N	3.35 E
Walchsee	64	47.39 N	12.19 E
Walcott, B.C., Can.	182	54.31 N	126.51 W
Walcott, Iowa, U.S.	190	41.35 N	90.47 W
Walcott, N. Dak., U.S.	198	46.33 N	90.56 W
Walcott, Lake ⊜[1]	202	42.40 N	113.23 W
Walcourt	50	50.15 N	4.25 E
Wałcz	30	53.17 N	16.28 E
Wald, Öst.	61	47.27 N	14.40 E
Wald, Schw.	58	47.17 N	8.55 E
Wald •[8]	263	51.11 N	7.03 E
Walda	60	48.37 N	11.06 E
Waldai → Valdajskaja Vozvyšennost' ⩕[2]	24	57.00 N	33.30 E
Waldaist ≃	61	48.19 N	14.34 E
Waldangelloch	56	49.12 N	8.47 E
Waldbauer •[8]	263	51.18 N	7.28 E
Waldbillig	56	49.47 N	6.18 E
Waldböckelheim	56	49.49 N	7.43 E
Waldbröl	56	50.53 N	7.37 E
Waldburg	58	47.45 N	9.43 E
Waldeck, B.R.D.	56	51.12 N	9.04 E
Waldeck, B.R.D.	60	49.52 N	11.57 E
Walden, Colo., U.S.	200	40.44 N	106.17 W
Walden, N.Y., U.S.	210	41.34 N	74.11 W
Waldenbuch	56	48.38 N	9.07 E
Waldenburg, B.R.D.	56	49.11 N	9.38 E
Waldenburg, D.D.R.	54	50.52 N	12.36 E
Waldenburg → Wałbrzych, Pol.	30	50.46 N	16.17 E
Waldenburg, Schw.	58	47.23 N	7.45 E
Walden Pond ⊜	283	42.28 N	71.00 W
Walden Ridge ∧	194	35.30 N	85.15 W
Waldershof	60	49.59 N	12.04 E
Walderslade	260	51.21 N	0.32 E
Waldfischbach	56	49.17 N	7.40 E
Waldheim, Sask., Can.	184	52.37 N	106.38 W
Waldheim, D.D.R.	54	51.04 N	13.01 E
Waldighoffen	58	47.33 N	7.19 E
Wald im Pinzgau	64	47.15 N	12.14 E
Waldkappel	56	51.08 N	9.52 E
Waldkirch	58	48.05 N	7.57 E
Waldkirchen	60	48.44 N	13.37 E
Waldkirchen am Wesen	60	48.26 N	13.49 E
Waldkraiburg	60	48.12 N	12.28 E
Waldmünchen	60	49.23 N	12.43 E
Waldnaab ≃	60	49.36 N	12.08 E
Waldo, B.C., Can.	182	49.13 N	115.13 W
Waldo, Ark., U.S.	194	33.21 N	93.18 W
Waldo, Ohio, U.S.	214	40.28 N	83.05 W
Waldoboro	188	44.06 N	69.23 W
Waldo Lake ⊜	283	42.07 N	71.03 W
Waldon ≃	42	50.22 N	4.14 W
Waldorf	188	38.37 N	76.54 W
Waldport	202	44.26 N	124.04 W
Waldron, Sask., Can.	184	50.51 N	102.30 W
Waldron, Ark., U.S.	194	34.54 N	94.05 W
Waldron, Ind., U.S.	218	39.27 N	85.40 W
Waldron, Mich., U.S.	216	41.44 N	84.25 W
Waldron Island I	224	48.43 N	123.02 W
Waldsassen	60	50.00 N	12.18 E
Waldshut	58	47.37 N	8.13 E
Waldstatt	58	47.21 N	9.17 E
Waldthurn	60	49.40 N	12.20 E
Waldviertel •[1]	61	48.40 N	15.40 E
Waldwick	276	41.01 N	74.08 W
Walembele	150	10.30 N	1.58 W
Walensee ⊜	58	47.07 N	9.12 E
Walenstadt	58	47.07 N	9.19 E
Wales, Alaska, U.S.	180	65.36 N	168.05 W
Wales, Mass., U.S.	207	42.04 N	72.13 W
Wales, Wis., U.S.	216	43.00 N	88.23 W
Wales □[8]	28	52.30 N	3.30 W

ENGLISH / DEUTSCH

Name / Name	Page / Seite	Lat.°′ / Breite°′	Long.°′ / Länge°′ E=Ost
Wales Center	210	42.46 N	78.32 W
Wales Island I, N.W. Ter., Can.	176	61.50 N	72.05 W
Wales Island I, N.W. Ter., Can.	176	68.00 N	86.43 W
Walewale	150	10.21 N	0.48 W
Walgett	166	30.01 S	148.07 E
Walgreen Coast ⫠[2]	9	75.15 S	105.00 W
Walhachin	182	50.45 N	120.59 W
Walhalla, N. Dak., U.S.	198	48.55 N	97.55 W
Walhalla, S.C., U.S.	192	34.46 N	83.04 W
Walhalla ⊥	60	49.03 N	12.14 E
Walheim	56	50.42 N	6.10 E
Walhonding	214	40.22 N	82.09 W
Walhonding ≃	214	40.18 N	81.53 W
Wali	105	39.42 N	118.20 E
Walia	164	3.47 S	138.32 E
Walikale	154	1.25 S	28.03 E
Walincourt	50	50.04 N	3.20 E
Walis Island I	164	3.15 S	143.20 E
Walkaway	162	28.57 S	114.48 E
Walkden	44	53.32 N	2.24 W
Walkenried	54	51.35 N	10.37 E
Walker, Iowa, U.S.	190	42.17 N	91.47 W
Walker, Mich., U.S.	216	42.58 N	85.46 W
Walker, Minn., U.S.	190	47.06 N	94.35 W
Walker, N.Y., U.S.	210	43.18 N	77.52 W
Walker □[6]	222	30.42 N	95.35 W
Walker ≃	204	38.54 N	118.47 W
Walker, Lac ⊜	186	50.16 N	67.09 W
Walker, Mount ∧[2]	171a	27.48 S	152.34 E
Walker Basin Creek ≃	228	35.20 N	118.47 W
Walker Bay C	158	34.30 S	19.20 E
Walker Creek ≃, Ariz., U.S.	200	36.58 N	109.42 W
Walker Creek ≃, Mass., U.S.	283	42.38 N	70.44 W
Walker Creek ≃, Wyo., U.S.	198	43.09 N	104.52 W
Walker Lake ⊜, Man., Can.	184	54.42 N	96.57 W
Walker Lake ⊜, Alaska, U.S.	180	67.10 N	154.26 W
Walker Lake ⊜, Nev., U.S.	204	38.44 N	118.43 W
Walker Point ≻	158	34.05 S	22.57 E
Walker River Indian Reservation •[4]	204	39.00 N	118.40 W
Walkers Mill	279b	40.24 N	80.08 W
Walkersville	188	39.29 N	77.21 W
Walkerton, Ont., Can.	212	44.07 N	81.09 W
Walkerton, Ind., U.S.	216	41.28 N	86.29 W
Walkerton, Va., U.S.	208	37.43 N	77.01 W
Walkertown	192	36.10 N	80.10 W
Walker Valley	210	41.38 N	74.23 W
Walkerville	202	46.01 N	112.30 W
Walk Mill	262	53.46 N	2.12 W
Wall, Pa., U.S.	279b	40.24 N	79.47 W
Wall, S. Dak., U.S.	198	43.59 N	102.14 W
Wallace, Calif., U.S.	226	38.12 N	120.59 W
Wallace, Idaho, U.S.	202	47.28 N	115.56 W
Wallace, Nebr., U.S.	198	40.50 N	101.10 W
Wallace, N.C., U.S.	192	34.44 N	77.59 W
Wallace, N.Y., U.S.	210	42.26 N	77.28 W
Wallaceburg	214	42.36 N	82.23 W
Wallace Lake ⊜	279a	41.22 N	81.52 W
Wallaceton	214	40.57 N	78.17 W
Wallacetown	214	42.38 N	81.28 W
Wallach	263	51.35 N	6.34 E
Wallachia □[9]	38	44.00 N	25.00 E
Wallacia	170	33.52 S	150.39 E
Wallal Downs	162	19.47 S	120.40 E
Wallangarra	166	28.56 S	151.56 E
Wallaroo	168b	33.56 S	137.38 E
Wallaroo Mines	168b	33.57 S	137.41 E
Wallasey	44	53.26 N	3.03 W
Wallau	56	50.56 N	8.28 E
Walla Walla	202	46.08 N	118.20 W
Walla Walla Plateau ⩕[1]	202	46.20 N	117.45 W
Walldorf, B.R.D.	56	49.18 N	8.38 E
Walldorf, D.D.R.	54	50.36 N	10.23 E
Walldürn	56	49.35 N	9.22 E
Walled Lake	216	42.32 N	83.29 W
Walled Lake ⊜	281	42.31 N	83.29 W
Wallen	216	41.10 N	85.11 W
Wallend	260	51.27 N	0.42 E
Wallenfels	54	50.16 N	11.28 E
Wallenpaupack, Lake ⊜	210	41.25 N	75.12 W
Waller	222	30.04 N	95.56 W
Waller □[6]	222	30.00 N	96.00 W
Wallerawang	170	33.25 S	150.04 E
Wallern	61	47.43 N	16.56 E
Wallers	50	50.22 N	3.24 E
Wallersdorf	60	48.44 N	12.45 E
Wallersee ⊜	64	47.55 N	13.11 E
Wallerstein	56	48.53 N	10.28 E
Wallgau	64	47.31 N	11.16 E
Wallgrove	274a	33.47 S	150.51 E
Wallhead Airport ⊠	279a	41.21 N	82.09 W
Wallibou	241h	13.19 N	61.15 W
Wallingford, Eng., U.K.	42	51.37 N	1.08 W
Wallingford, Conn., U.S.	207	41.27 N	72.50 W
Wallingford, Pa., U.S.	285	39.54 N	75.22 W
Wallingford, Vt., U.S.	188	43.28 N	72.59 W
Wallington	276	40.51 N	74.07 W
Wallington •[8]	260	51.21 N	0.09 W
Wallis	222	29.38 N	96.04 W
Wallis → Valais □[3]	58	46.10 N	7.30 E
Wallis, Îles II	14	13.18 S	176.10 W
Wallis and Futuna □[2]	14	14.00 S	177.00 W
Wallisellen	58	47.25 N	8.36 E
Wallisville	222	29.50 N	94.44 W
Wallisville Lake ⊜[1]	222	29.50 N	94.45 W
Wallkill	210	41.36 N	74.11 W
Wallkill ≃, U.S.	210	41.51 N	74.03 W
Wallkill ≃, U.S.	276	41.11 N	74.35 W
Wallkill, Wildcat Branch ≃	276	41.07 N	74.36 W
Wall Lake, Iowa, U.S.	198	42.16 N	95.05 W
Wall Lake, Mich., U.S.	216	42.31 N	85.24 W
Wall Lake ⊜	216	42.31 N	85.23 W
Wallmer Bridge	262	53.43 N	2.48 W
Wallmerod	56	50.29 N	7.56 E
Wallops Island I	208	37.52 N	75.27 W
Wallowa	202	45.34 N	117.32 W
Wallowa ≃	202	45.43 N	117.47 W
Wallowa Mountains ⩕	202	45.10 N	117.30 W
Walls, Scot., U.K.	46a	60.14 N	1.35 W
Walls, Miss., U.S.	194	34.58 N	90.16 W
Wallsbüll	41	54.47 N	9.14 E
Wallsend, Austl.	170	32.55 S	151.40 E
Wallsend, Eng., U.K.	44	55.00 N	1.31 W
Wallstawe	54	52.47 N	11.01 E
Wall Town Drainage Ditch ≍	216	40.26 N	88.10 W
Wallula, Lake ⊜[1]	202	46.07 N	119.58 W
Walmer	42	51.13 N	1.24 E
Walmersley	262	53.37 N	2.18 W
Walney, Isle of I	44	54.07 N	3.15 W
Walnut, Calif., U.S.	228	34.01 N	117.51 W
Walnut, Ill., U.S.	190	41.33 N	89.36 W
Walnut, Kans., U.S.	198	37.36 N	95.05 W
Walnut, Miss., U.S.	194	34.57 N	88.54 W
Walnut, N.C., U.S.	192	35.51 N	82.44 W
Walnut ≃	196	37.03 N	97.00 W
Walnut Canyon National Monument ♠	200	34.59 N	111.10 W
Walnut Canyon Reservoir ⊜[1]	280	33.50 N	117.45 W
Walnut Cove	192	36.18 N	80.09 W
Walnut Creek, Calif., U.S.	226	37.55 N	122.04 W
Walnut Creek, Ohio, U.S.	214	40.33 N	81.43 W
Walnut Creek ≃, Calif., U.S.	280	34.03 N	118.01 W
Walnut Creek ≃, Calif., U.S.	282	37.54 N	122.03 W
Walnut Creek ≃, Kans., U.S.	198	38.21 N	98.41 W
Walnut Creek ≃, Ohio, U.S.	188	39.41 N	82.59 W
Walnut Creek ≃, Tex., U.S.	222	32.38 N	97.00 W
Walnut Creek, Middle Fork ≃	198	38.32 N	100.08 W
Walnut Grove, B.C., Can.	224	49.11 N	122.39 W
Walnut Grove, Calif., U.S.	226	38.15 N	121.31 W
Walnut Grove, Minn., U.S.	198	44.13 N	95.28 W
Walnut Grove, Miss., U.S.	194	32.36 N	89.28 W
Walnut Heights	282	37.53 N	122.08 W
Walnut Hill	219	38.29 N	89.03 W
Walnut Lake	281	42.33 N	83.19 W
Walnut Lake ⊜	281	42.33 N	83.20 W
Walnut Park	280	33.58 N	118.13 W
Walnutport	208	40.45 N	75.36 W
Walnut Ridge	194	36.04 N	90.57 W
Walnut Springs	222	32.03 N	97.45 W
Walpert Ridge ∧	282	37.38 N	122.00 W
Walpeup	166	35.08 S	142.02 E
Walpole, Austl.	162	34.57 S	116.44 E
Walpole, Mass., U.S.	207	42.08 N	71.15 W
Walpole, N.H., U.S.	188	43.05 N	72.26 W
Walpole, Île I	175f	22.37 S	168.57 E
Walpole Island I	214	42.34 N	82.30 W
Walpole Island Indian Reserve •[4]	214	42.32 N	82.37 W
Walpole Saint Peter	42	52.42 N	0.15 E
Walsall	42	52.35 N	1.58 W
Walschleben	54	51.04 N	10.56 E
Walsden	262	53.42 N	2.06 W
Walsenburg	200	37.37 N	104.47 W
Walsh, Austl.	164	16.39 S	143.54 E
Walsh, Alta., Can.	184	49.57 N	110.03 W
Walsh, Colo., U.S.	198	37.23 N	102.17 W
Walsh, Ky., U.S.	218	38.41 N	82.58 W
Walsh ≃	164	16.31 S	143.42 E
Walshaw Dean Reservoirs ⊜[1]	262	53.48 N	2.03 W
Walshville	219	39.04 N	89.37 W
Walsingham	212	42.41 N	80.32 W
Walsoken	42	52.41 N	0.12 E
Walsoorden	52	51.23 N	4.02 E
Walsrode	52	52.52 N	9.35 E
Walston	214	40.58 N	79.01 W
Walsum	52	51.32 N	6.41 E
Walt Disney World ♠	220	28.26 N	81.35 W
Waltenhofen	64	47.40 N	10.17 E
Walterboro	192	32.55 N	80.39 W
Walter F. George Lake ⊜[1]	192	31.49 N	85.08 W
Walter Reed Army Medical Center ʊ	284c	38.58 N	77.02 W
Walters	196	34.22 N	98.19 W
Waltersdorf, D.D.R.	54	50.52 N	14.38 E
Waltersdorf, D.D.R.	264a	52.22 N	13.35 E
Waltershausen	54	50.53 N	10.33 E
Waltershofen	58	47.46 N	9.55 E
Waltersville	194	32.22 N	90.52 W
Walthall	194	33.31 N	89.16 W
Waltham	207	42.23 N	71.14 W
Waltham Abbey	42	51.42 N	0.01 E
Waltham Forest •[8]	42	51.35 N	0.01 W
Waltham on the Wolds	42	52.49 N	0.49 W
Walthamstow •[8]	260	51.35 N	0.01 W
Walthill	198	42.09 N	96.30 W
Walton, N.S., Can.	186	45.14 N	64.00 W
Walton, Eng., U.K.	42	51.24 N	0.25 W
Walton, Eng., U.K.	42	51.58 N	1.21 E
Walton, Fla., U.S.	220	27.18 N	80.14 W
Walton, Ind., U.S.	216	40.40 N	86.15 W
Walton, Ky., U.S.	218	38.52 N	84.37 W
Walton, N.Y., U.S.	210	42.10 N	75.08 W
Walton Hills	214	41.22 N	81.32 W
Walton-le-Dale	44	53.45 N	2.39 W
Walton on the Hill	260	51.17 N	0.15 W
Walton-on-the-Naze	42	51.51 N	1.16 E
Walton Run ≃	285	40.05 N	74.59 W
Waltonville	219	38.13 N	89.02 W
Waltrop	52	51.37 N	7.23 E
Walt Whitman Center •[9]	276	40.50 N	73.25 W
Walt Whitman Homes	285	39.52 N	75.11 W
Walt Whitman House ⊥	276	40.49 N	73.25 W
Waltz	216	42.06 N	83.23 W
Walupt Lake ⊜	224	46.25 N	121.28 W
Walurigi	175f	15.21 S	167.50 E
Walvisbaai (Walvis Bay)	156	22.59 S	14.31 E
Walvis Bay → Walvisbaai	156	22.59 S	14.31 E
Walvis Bay □[8]	156	22.59 S	14.31 E
Walvis Bay C	156	22.57 S	14.30 E
Walvis Ridge ✣[3]	10	30.00 S	3.00 E
Walwa	171b	35.58 S	147.45 E
Walwen	262	53.14 N	3.15 W
Walworth, N.Y., U.S.	210	43.08 N	77.17 W
Walworth, Wis., U.S.	216	42.32 N	88.36 W
Walworth □[6]	216	42.41 N	88.32 W
Walyungup, Lake ⊜	168a	32.21 S	115.47 E
Walze	263	51.16 N	7.31 E
Walzin, Château de ⊥	56	50.13 N	4.55 E
Wamac	219	38.31 N	89.08 W
Wamba, Kenya	154	0.59 N	37.19 E
Wamba, Nig.	150	8.58 N	8.36 E
Wamba, Zaïre	154	2.09 N	28.00 E
Wamba (Uamba) ≃	152	3.56 S	17.12 E
Wambel •[8]	263	51.32 N	7.32 E
Wamego	198	39.12 N	96.18 W
Wamel	52	51.53 N	5.28 E
Wamesit	283	42.37 N	71.16 W
Wami ≃	154	6.08 S	38.49 E
Wamiao	100	30.49 N	112.56 E
Wamic	224	45.14 N	121.21 W
Wamma ≃	164	3.23 S	135.13 E
Wamme ≃	56	50.10 N	5.16 E
Wamplers Lake ⊜	216	42.05 N	84.09 W
Wampool ≃	44	54.54 N	3.14 W
Wampsville	210	43.05 N	75.42 W
Wampú ≃	236	14.59 N	85.03 W
Wampum	214	40.54 N	80.21 W
Wampus ≃	276	41.07 N	73.43 W
Wampus Lake Reservoir ⊜[1]	276	41.09 N	73.43 W
Wamsasi	112	3.33 S	126.10 E
Wamsutter	200	41.40 N	107.58 W
Wamuran	171a	27.02 S	152.52 E
Wanaaring	166	29.42 S	144.09 E

Symbols in the index entries represent the broad categories identified in the key at the right. Symbols with superior numbers (⩕[2]) identify subcategories (see complete key on page *I* · *30*).

Kartensymbole in dem Registerverzeichnis stellen die rechts in Schlüssel erklärten Kategorien dar. Symbole mit hochgestellten Ziffern (⩕[2]) bezeichnen Unterabteilungen einer Kategorie (vgl. vollständiger Schlüssel auf Seite *I* · *30*).

Los símbolos incluídos en el texto del índice representan las grandes categorias identificadas con la clave a la derecha. Los símbolos con numeros en su parte superior (⩕[2]) identifican las subcategorías (véase la clave completa en la página *I* · *30*).

Les symboles de l'index représentent les catégories indiquées dans la légende à droite. Les symboles suivis d'un indice (⩕[2]) représentent des sous-catégories (voir légende complète à la page *I* · *30*).

Os símbolos incluídos no texto do índice representam as grandes categorias identificadas com a chave à direita. Os símbolos com números em sua parte superior (⩕[2]) identificam as subcategorias (veja-se a chave completa à página *I* · *30*).

	English	Deutsch	Español	Français	Português
∧	Mountain	Berg	Montaña	Montagne	Montanha
⩕	Mountains	Berge	Montañas	Montagnes	Montanhas
)(	Pass	Pass	Paso	Col	Passo
V	Valley, Canyon	Tal, Cañon	Valle, Cañón	Vallée, Canyon	Vale, Canhão
⊻	Plain	Ebene	Llano	Plaine	Planície
≻	Cape	Kap	Cabo	Cap	Cabo
I	Island	Insel	Isla	Île	Ilha
II	Islands	Inseln	Islas	Îles	Ilhas
⫠	Other Topographic Features	Andere Topographische Objekte	Otros Elementos Topográficos	Autres données topographiques	Outros Elementos Topográficos

ESPAÑOL — Nombre / Página / Lat.°′ / Long.°′ W=Oeste
FRANÇAIS — Nom / Page / Lat.°′ / Long.°′ W=Ouest
PORTUGUÊS — Nome / Página / Lat.°′ / Long.°′ W=Oeste

Wanaka 172 44.42 S 169.09 E
Wanaka, Lake ⊜ 172 44.30 S 169.08 E
Wanakah 210 42.45 N 78.54 W
Wanamassa 208 40.14 N 74.02 W
Wanamie 210 41.10 N 76.02 W
Wanamingo 190 44.18 N 92.47 W
Wan'an, Zhg. 100 26.30 N 114.49 E
Wanan, Zhg. 100 26.56 N 117.22 E
Wan'anchang 107 30.39 N 104.25 E
Wanapiri 164 4.33 S 135.59 E
Wanapitei ≃ 190 46.02 N 80.51 W
Wanapitei Lake ⊜ 190 46.45 N 80.45 W
Wanapum Lake ⊜[1] 202 47.00 N 120.00 W
Wanaque 210 41.03 N 74.17 W
Wanaque ≃ 276 40.58 N 74.17 W
Wanaque Reservoir ⊜[1] 210 41.05 N 74.17 W
Wanatah 216 41.26 N 86.54 W
Wanau 164 1.22 S 132.42 E
Wanawana I 175e 8.15 S 157.05 E
Wanbaoshan 89 44.12 N 125.11 E
Wanbasha 100 22.44 N 113.33 E
Wanbi 166 34.46 S 140.19 E
Wanblee 198 43.34 N 101.40 W
Wanborough 42 51.33 N 1.42 W
Wanchese 192 35.51 N 75.38 W
Wanda 158 29.36 S 24.28 E
Wandai 164 3.41 S 136.41 E
Wandana 162 32.04 S 133.49 E
Wandawega 216 42.45 N 88.40 W
Wande 98 36.21 N 116.56 E
Wanderer 154 19.37 S 29.59 E
Wandering 168a 32.40 S 116.40 E
Wandering ≃ 182 55.05 N 112.30 W
Wanderup 41 54.41 N 9.20 E
Wandhofen 263 51.26 N 7.33 E
Wandingzhen 102 24.10 N 98.04 E
Wandlitz 54 52.45 N 13.26 E
Wandlitzer See ⊜ 264a 52.46 N 13.27 E
Wando 98 34.18 N 126.47 E
Wandoan 166 26.08 S 149.57 E
Wandsbek ⊸[8] 52 53.34 N 10.04 E
Wandsworth ⊸[8] 42 51.27 N 0.11 W
Waneta Lake ⊜ 210 42.27 N 77.06 W
Wanette 196 34.58 N 97.02 W
Wanfang 104 41.57 N 122.52 E
Wanfoxia 102 40.04 N 95.55 E
Wanfried 56 51.10 N 10.10 E
Wang ≃ 110 17.08 N 99.02 E
Wanga 154 2.58 N 29.13 E
Wangal 164 6.10 S 134.12 E
Wanga Mountains ⩕ 146 7.06 N 10.22 E
Wanganderry, Mount ∧ 170 34.20 S 150.15 E
Wanganella Bank ✦[4] 14 32.30 S 168.00 E
Wanganui 172 39.56 S 175.03 E
Wanganui ≃ 172 39.56 S 175.00 E
Wang'anzhen 105 39.18 N 114.50 E
Wangaratta 166 36.22 S 146.20 E
Wangary 166 34.33 S 135.29 E
Wangbaotaicun 104 41.10 N 123.18 E
Wangbayan ∧ 107 28.52 N 106.16 E
Wangbenying 105 40.28 N 116.06 E
Wangbintun 104 41.58 N 123.43 E
Wangchang, Zhg. 107 29.29 N 103.36 E
Wangchang, Zhg. 107 28.52 N 105.55 E
Wangchang, Zhg. 107 30.37 N 103.36 E
Wangchang, Zhg. 107 29.05 N 104.40 E
Wangchangtuizigou 104 41.14 N 120.32 E
Wangcheng, Zhg. 100 28.23 N 112.48 E
Wangcheng, Zhg. 100 29.45 N 120.40 E
Wang Chin 110 17.53 N 99.37 E
Wangcunkou 100 28.22 N 118.59 E
Wangdalong 102 29.25 N 99.03 E
Wangdian 106 30.37 N 120.44 E
Wangdu 98 38.43 N 115.09 E
Wangdu Phodrang 124 27.29 N 89.54 E
Wangels 54 54.16 N 10.45 E
Wangen 60 48.01 N 11.24 E
Wangen an der Aare 58 47.14 N 7.39 E
Wangenbourg 58 48.37 N 7.19 E
Wangen im Allgäu 58 47.41 N 9.50 E
Wangerin → Węgorzyno 30 53.32 N 15.33 E
Wangerooge I 52 53.46 N 7.55 E
Wangersen 52 53.22 N 9.25 E
Wangfu 104 42.05 N 121.29 E
Wanggameti, Gunung ∧ 115b 10.07 S 120.14 E
Wanggangpu 104 41.38 N 123.09 E
Wangganji 100 33.11 N 116.04 E
Wanggao 102 24.38 N 111.30 E
Wanggava I 175g 18.52 S 178.54 W
Wanggezhuang 105 40.00 N 117.52 E
Wanggil-li 271b 37.36 N 126.39 E
Wanggoutun 104 41.40 N 121.53 E
Wanggucun 98 39.47 N 113.54 E
Wanghai 98 40.26 N 120.30 E
Wanghechenggou 104 41.52 N 121.13 E
Wang Hin, Khlong ☰ 269a 13.48 N 100.35 E
Wanghongbao 102 38.20 N 106.17 E
Wanghuzhuang 105 38.50 N 117.05 E
Wangi, Kenya 154 2.00 S 40.55 E
Wängi, Schw. 58 47.30 N 8.57 E
Wangi Wangi 170 33.04 S 151.35 E
Wangiwangi, Pulau I 112 5.20 S 123.35 E
Wangji 100 33.52 N 118.44 E
Wangjia, Zhg. 106 31.59 N 121.13 E
Wangjia, Zhg. 106 32.07 N 120.59 E
Wangjiachang 107 29.44 N 104.18 E
Wangjiadian, Zhg. 100 31.26 N 113.58 E
Wangjiadian, Zhg. 105 40.03 N 117.29 E
Wangjiagou 104 42.33 N 123.16 E
Wangjiajing 98 39.56 N 122.11 E
Wangjiang 100 30.09 N 116.41 E
Wangjiangjing 106 30.53 N 120.43 E
Wangjianmu (Tomb of Wangjian) ⊥ 107 29.51 N 106.31 E
Wangjiaputun 104 40.39 N 122.50 E
Wangjiapuzi, Zhg. 104 40.41 N 122.24 E
Wangjiapuzi, Zhg. 104 41.05 N 123.34 E
Wangjiaqiao 106 30.50 N 119.18 E
Wangjiashan 105 40.19 N 114.45 E
Wangjiashao 102 23.57 N 102.18 E
Wangjiatai 105 39.17 N 117.29 E
Wangjiaying, Zhg. 105 39.06 N 115.59 E
Wangjiaying, Zhg. 105 40.36 N 116.34 E
Wangjiazhai, Zhg. 105 39.31 N 116.43 E
Wangjiazhai, Zhg. 106 31.21 N 121.37 E
Wangjiazui 106 31.16 N 120.18 E
Wangkantou 100 29.12 N 120.09 E
Wangkouzhen 105 38.56 N 116.44 E
Wangkui 89 46.50 N 126.30 E
Wang Lan I 271d 22.11 N 114.18 E
Wanglanzhuang 105 39.26 N 118.01 E
Wangling 100 27.13 N 113.26 E
Wangliuji 100 32.25 N 115.40 E
Wanglongji 98 34.02 N 114.51 E
Wangmiao 100 26.50 N 112.52 E
Wangmulazi 104 41.42 N 124.02 E
Wang Noi 110 14.13 N 100.44 E
Wangong 89 49.10 N 118.53 E
Wangpingchang 107 29.17 N 105.45 E
Wangqing 89 43.20 N 129.48 E
Wangqingmen 98 41.42 N 125.23 E
Wangqingtuo 105 39.11 N 116.53 E
Wangqinzhuang 105 39.15 N 117.05 E
Wangqucun 106 31.22 N 120.19 E
Wangs 58 47.02 N 9.26 E
Wang Saphung 110 17.18 N 101.46 E
Wangshanhutun 104 42.03 N 122.37 E
Wangsi 98 38.00 N 116.55 E
Wangsim-ni ⊸[8] 271b 37.36 N 127.03 E
Wangsiying 107 30.34 N 103.29 E
Wangtai, Zhg. 98 36.05 N 119.59 E
Wangtai, Zhg. 100 26.39 N 117.57 E
Wang Thong 110 16.50 N 100.26 E
Wangtian 100 25.59 N 116.04 E
Wangting 106 31.26 N 120.26 E
Wangtong 100 33.12 N 116.21 E
Wangtongshitai 104 42.05 N 123.11 E
Wangtuan, Zhg. 98 37.32 N 116.08 E
Wangtuan, Zhg. 98 37.17 N 122.04 E
Wanguchang 107 29.41 N 105.57 E
Wangwan 106 30.22 N 120.48 E
Wangwenzhuang 105 38.53 N 117.15 E
Wangxiangshang 106 31.29 N 120.15 E
Wangxiangtai 105 40.02 N 115.09 E
Wangxiuqiao 106 31.38 N 121.03 E
Wangyedian 98 41.36 N 118.17 E
Wangyefu 98 41.50 N 118.23 E
Wangyehmiao → Wulanhaote 89 46.05 N 122.05 E
Wangyiguantun 104 42.36 N 123.19 E
Wangzhai 98 34.09 N 116.47 E
Wangzhimawo 105 39.39 N 117.40 E
Wangzhong 98 35.08 N 116.58 E
Wangzhuang, Zhg. 98 34.09 N 118.23 E
Wangzhuang, Zhg. 100 33.07 N 117.29 E
Wangzhuang, Zhg. 105 38.55 N 115.36 E
Wangzhuangbao 98 39.27 N 113.56 E
Wangzhuangzi 105 39.17 N 118.14 E
Wanham 182 55.44 N 118.24 W
Wanhedian 100 32.16 N 113.16 E
Wanheimerort ⊸[8] 263 51.24 N 6.46 E
Wanhsien → Wanxian 102 30.52 N 108.22 E
Wanhuyu 102 38.24 N 110.40 E
Wani 122 20.04 N 78.57 E
Wani, Gunung ∧ 112 4.29 S 123.01 E
Wani, Laguna C 236 14.45 N 83.20 W
Wanie-Rukula 154 0.15 N 25.32 E
Wanigela 164 9.22 S 149.10 E
Wanipigow ≃ 184 51.11 N 96.18 W
Wanjiabu 100 28.51 N 115.39 E
Wanjiaqiao 106 30.25 N 119.07 E
Wanjiatun 98 40.03 N 119.51 E
Wanjindian 100 32.50 N 114.46 E
Wānkāner 120 22.37 N 70.56 E
Wankendorf 54 54.07 N 10.13 E
Wankie 154 18.22 S 26.29 E
Wankie National Park ♠ 154 19.00 S 26.35 E
Wankum 56 51.24 N 6.20 E
Wanle Iten 144 2.38 N 44.55 E
Wanli, T'aiwan 269d 25.11 N 121.41 E
Wanli, Zhg. 106 31.06 N 120.16 E
Wanna 52 53.44 N 8.46 E
Wanna Lakes ⊜ 162 28.30 S 128.27 E
Wān Namton 110 22.03 N 99.33 E
Wanne-Eickel 52 51.32 N 7.09 E
Wanneroo 168a 31.45 S 115.48 E
Wannery Creek ≃ 162 22.47 S 115.43 E
Wannian 100 28.40 N 116.55 E
Wanning 110 18.53 N 110.26 E
Wannsee ⊸[8] 264a 52.25 N 13.09 E
Wanon Niwat 110 17.38 N 103.46 E
Wanouchi 94 35.17 N 136.38 E
Wānow 120 32.38 N 65.54 E
Wanparti 122 16.22 N 78.04 E
Wanquan 98 40.52 N 114.45 E
Wansbeck 28 55.08 N 1.35 W
Wansbeck ≃ 44 55.10 N 1.34 W
Wansdorf 264a 52.38 N 13.05 E
Wan-See → Van Gölü ⊜ 128 38.33 N 42.46 E
Wansen → Wiązów 30 50.49 N 17.11 E
Wanshan 107 30.23 N 106.06 E
Wanshanqundao II 100 22.02 N 113.45 E
Wanshouchang 107 29.26 N 105.55 E
Wansleben 54 51.27 N 11.45 E
Wanstead 172 40.08 S 176.32 E
Wanstead ⊸[8] 260 51.34 N 0.02 E
Wantage 42 51.36 N 1.25 W
Wantagh 210 40.40 N 73.30 W
Wantan 102 30.03 N 110.18 E
Wantirna 274b 37.51 S 145.14 E
Wantirna South 274b 37.52 S 145.14 E
Wanxian, Zhg. 102 30.52 N 108.22 E
Wanxian, Zhg. 105 38.50 N 115.09 E
Wanyangshan ⩕ 100 26.30 N 114.00 E
Wanyuan 102 32.03 N 108.08 E
Wanzai 100 28.06 N 114.27 E
Wanzarīk 146 27.31 N 13.29 E
Wanzhizhen 100 31.11 N 118.35 E
Wanzhuang 105 39.35 N 116.33 E
Wanzleben 54 52.03 N 11.26 E
Wapack Range ⩕ 207 42.48 N 71.52 W
Wapakoneta 216 40.34 N 84.12 W
Wapanucka 196 34.22 N 96.25 W
Wapato 202 46.27 N 120.25 W
Wapawekka Hills ⩕[2] 184 54.45 N 104.20 W
Wapawekka Lake ⊜ 184 54.55 N 104.40 W
Wapella, Sask., Can. 184 50.15 N 102.00 W
Wapella, Ill., U.S. 219 40.13 N 88.58 W
Wapello 190 41.11 N 91.11 W
Wapenamanda 164 5.35 S 143.55 E
Wapesi Lake ⊜ 184 50.34 N 92.21 W
Wāpi 122 20.22 N 72.54 E
Wapinda 152 3.41 N 22.48 E
Wapinitia Pass)(224 45.14 N 121.42 W
Wapisu Lake ⊜ 184 55.47 N 99.11 W
Wapiti ≃ 182 55.08 N 118.18 W
Wapizagonka, Lac ⊜ 206 46.43 N 73.03 W
Waples 222 32.29 N 97.43 W
Wapoga ≃ 164 2.42 S 136.06 E
Wappapello, Lake ⊜[1] 194 36.58 N 90.20 W
Wapping 207 41.50 N 72.33 W
Wappinger Creek ≃ 210 41.35 N 73.57 W
Wappingers Falls 210 41.36 N 73.55 W
Wapsipinicon ≃ 190 41.44 N 90.20 W
Waptus Lake ⊜ 224 47.30 N 121.10 W
Wapus ≃ 190 47.11 N 76.06 W
Wapus Lake ⊜ 184 56.27 N 102.12 W
Waqf aṣ-Ṣiwwān, Jibāl ⩕ 132 31.04 N 36.53 E
Wāqid 142 30.42 N 30.44 E
Waqqāṣ 132 32.33 N 35.36 E
War 192 37.18 N 81.41 W
Wara 94 35.45 N 137.05 E
Warabi 94 35.49 N 139.41 E
Wārāh 120 27.27 N 67.48 E
Warakaraket I 164 2.15 S 130.36 E
Waramaug, Lake ⊜ 207 41.42 N 73.22 W
Warangal 122 18.00 N 79.35 E
Wararisbari, Tanjung ≻ 164 1.05 S 136.23 E
Wārāseoni 120 21.45 N 80.02 E
Waratah, Austl. 166 41.27 S 145.32 E
Waratah, Austl. 170 32.54 S 151.44 E
Waratah Bay C 166 38.51 S 146.04 E
Warbreccan 166 24.18 S 142.51 E
Warburg 52 51.29 N 9.08 E
Warburton, Austl. 169 37.46 S 145.41 E
Warburton, Pāk. 123 31.33 N 73.50 E
Warburton, Eng., U.K. 262 53.24 N 2.27 W
Warburton Bay C 176 63.50 N 111.30 W
Warburton Creek ≃ 166 27.55 S 137.28 E
Warburton Range ⩕ 162 26.09 S 126.38 E
Warcha 123 32.25 N 71.59 E
Ward, Īrān 267d 35.48 N 51.10 E
Ward, N.Z. 172 41.50 S 174.08 E
Ward, Pa., U.S. 285 39.53 N 75.31 W
Ward ≃ 166 26.32 S 146.06 E
Ward, Mount ∧, Ant. 9 71.55 S 66.00 W
Ward, Mount ∧, N.Z. 172 43.52 S 169.50 E
Warda 222 30.03 N 96.55 W
Wardcliff 216 42.43 N 84.28 W
Ward Cove 182 55.24 N 131.43 W
Warden, S. Afr. 158 27.56 S 29.00 E
Warden, Wash., U.S. 202 46.58 N 119.02 W
Wardenburg 52 53.04 N 8.11 E
Warden Head ≻ 170 35.22 S 150.30 E
Warder, B.R.D. 54 53.59 N 10.22 E
Warder, Yai. 144 6.58 N 45.21 E
Wardersee ⊜ 54 53.58 N 10.26 E
Wardha 122 20.45 N 78.37 E
Wardha ≃ 122 19.38 N 79.48 E
Ward Hill ∧[2], Scot., U.K. 46 58.54 N 3.20 W
Ward Hill ∧[2], Scot., U.K. 46 58.57 N 3.09 W
Ward Hunt, Cape ≻ 164 8.05 S 149.55 E
Ward Hunt Strait ⊔ 164 9.25 S 149.55 E
Wardle 44 53.39 N 2.08 W
Wardlow 182 50.54 N 111.33 W
Ward Mountain ∧ 202 46.10 N 114.17 W
Wardner 182 49.25 N 115.26 W
Wardour, Vale of ∨ 42 51.05 N 2.00 W
Wards Chapel 284b 39.24 N 76.52 W
Wards Island I 276 40.47 N 73.56 W
Ward's Stone ∧ 44 54.02 N 2.38 W
Wardsville, Ont., Can. 214 42.39 N 81.45 W
Wardsville, Mo., U.S. 219 38.29 N 92.10 W
Wardt 52 51.41 N 6.25 E
Wardūj ≃ 123 37.01 N 70.47 E
Ware, Eng., U.K. 42 51.49 N 0.02 W
Ware, Mass., U.S. 207 42.16 N 72.15 W
Ware ≃ 207 42.11 N 72.22 W
War Eagle Creek ≃ 194 36.14 N 94.00 W
Waregem 50 50.53 N 3.25 E
Wareham, Eng., U.K. 42 50.41 N 2.07 W
Wareham, Mass., U.S. 207 41.46 N 70.43 W
Warehouse Point 207 41.56 N 72.37 W
Waremme 56 50.41 N 5.15 E
Waren 54 53.31 N 12.40 E
Warenda 166 22.37 S 140.32 E
Warendorf 52 51.57 N 7.59 E
Ware River C 208 37.23 N 76.27 W
Ware Shoals 192 34.24 N 82.15 W
Waretown 208 39.47 N 74.12 W
Warffum 52 53.23 N 6.34 E
Warfusée-Abancourt 50 49.52 N 2.35 E
Warga 52 53.08 N 5.51 E
War Galla 144 1.10 N 41.11 E
Wargalo 144 6.15 N 47.42 E
Warialda 166 29.32 S 150.34 E
Wariap 164 1.34 S 134.11 E
Warilau 164 5.24 S 134.30 E
Warilau, Pulau I 164 5.23 S 134.33 E
Warin 54 53.48 N 11.42 E
Warinanco Park ♠ 276 40.39 N 74.14 W
Warin Chamrap 110 15.12 N 104.53 E
Warinchiui 144 3.29 N 42.43 E
Waring Mountains ⩕ 180 66.50 N 159.00 W
Wāris Alīganj 124 25.01 N 85.38 E
Warka 30 51.47 N 21.10 E
Warkopi 164 1.08 S 134.07 E
Warks Burn ≃ 44 55.03 N 2.08 W
Warkworth, Ont., Can. 212 44.12 N 77.53 W
Warkworth, N.Z. 172 36.24 S 174.40 E
Warkworth, Eng., U.K. 44 55.21 N 1.36 W
Warland 262 53.41 N 2.05 W
Warland Reservoir ⊜[1] 262 53.41 N 2.04 W
Warley → Smethwick 42 52.30 N 1.58 W
Warley Moor Reservoir ⊜[1] 262 53.47 N 1.57 W
Warlingham 42 51.19 N 0.04 W
Warlington 42 51.39 N 1.01 W
Warman 184 52.20 N 106.34 W
Warmandi 164 0.22 S 132.39 E
Warmbad, Namibia 156 28.29 S 18.41 E
Warmbad, S. Afr. 156 24.55 S 28.15 E
Warmbad □[5] 156 28.00 S 18.45 E
Warm Baths → Warmbad 156 24.55 S 28.15 E
Warm Beach 224 48.16 N 122.21 W
War Memorial Cross ⊥ 169 37.20 S 144.36 E
Warmenhuizen 52 52.43 N 4.44 E
Warmensteinach 60 49.59 N 11.47 E
Warmeriville 50 49.21 N 4.13 E
Warmington 42 52.08 N 1.24 W
Warminster, Eng., U.K. 42 51.13 N 2.12 W
Warminster, Pa., U.S. 208 40.12 N 75.06 W
Warminster Naval Air Development Center ■ 285 40.12 N 75.09 W
Warm Springs, Ga., U.S. 192 32.54 N 84.41 W
Warm Springs, Mont., U.S. 202 46.11 N 112.48 W
Warm Springs, Oreg., U.S. 202 44.46 N 121.16 W
Warm Springs, Va., U.S. 192 38.03 N 79.47 W
Warm Springs ≃ 202 44.52 N 121.04 W
Warm Springs Indian Reservation ⊸[4] 224 45.00 N 121.25 W
Warm Springs Reservoir ⊜[1] 202 43.37 N 118.14 W
Warnbro Sound ⊔ 168a 32.20 S 115.40 E
Warnemünde 54 54.10 N 12.04 E
Warner, Alta., Can. 182 49.17 N 112.12 W
Warner, N.H., U.S. 188 43.17 N 71.49 W
Warner Lakes ⊜ 202 42.25 N 119.50 W
Warner Mountains ⩕ 204 41.40 N 120.20 W
Warner Peak ∧ 202 42.27 N 119.44 W
Warner Ranch 228 33.56 N 117.13 W
Warner Robins 192 32.37 N 83.36 W
Warners 210 43.05 N 76.20 W
Warners Pond ⊜ 283 42.28 N 71.24 W
Warnerville 210 42.34 N 74.30 W
Warnes, Arg. 252 34.55 S 60.31 W
Warnes, Bol. 248 17.30 S 63.10 W
Warnes Brook ≃ 276 40.25 N 74.18 W
Warneton 50 50.45 N 2.57 E
Warngau 64 47.50 N 11.41 E
Warnicken → Primorje 76 54.57 N 20.02 E
Warnkenhagen 54 54.00 N 11.04 E
Warnow ≃ 54 54.06 N 12.09 E
Warns 52 52.52 N 5.25 E
Warnsveld 52 52.08 N 6.13 E
Waroona 168a 32.50 S 115.55 E
Warpath ≃ 184 52.21 N 98.26 W
Warra 166 26.56 S 150.55 E
Warracknabeal 166 36.15 S 142.24 E
Warr Acres 196 35.31 N 97.37 W
Warragamba Dam ⊸[6] 170 33.54 S 150.36 E
Warragul 169 38.10 S 145.56 E
Warrandyte 274b 37.45 S 145.13 E
Warrandyte South 274b 37.46 S 145.14 E
Warrāq al-'Arab 142 30.06 N 31.12 E
Warrāq al-Ḥaḍar 273c 30.06 N 31.13 E
Warrāq al-Ḥaḍar, Jazīrat I 273c 30.07 N 31.13 E
Warrāq al-Hadar wa Ambūtbah wa Mīt an-Naṣārā 273c 30.06 N 31.13 E
Warrawagine 162 20.51 S 120.42 E
Warrawee 274a 33.44 S 151.07 E
Warrawong 170 34.29 S 150.53 E
Warrego ≃ 166 30.24 S 145.21 E
Warrego Range ⩕ 166 25.00 S 146.30 E
Warren, Austl. 166 31.42 S 147.50 E
Warren, Eng., U.K. 262 53.14 N 2.10 W
Warren, Ark., U.S. 194 33.37 N 92.04 W
Warren, Ind., U.S. 216 40.41 N 85.26 W
Warren, Mass., U.S. 207 42.13 N 72.12 W
Warren, Mich., U.S. 216 42.28 N 83.01 W
Warren, Minn., U.S. 198 48.12 N 96.46 W
Warren, Mo., U.S. 219 39.47 N 91.45 W
Warren, N.J., U.S. 276 40.37 N 74.30 W
Warren, Ohio, U.S. 214 41.14 N 80.52 W
Warren, Oreg., U.S. 224 45.49 N 122.51 W
Warren, Pa., U.S. 214 41.51 N 79.08 W
Warren, R.I., U.S. 207 41.43 N 71.17 W
Warren □[6], Ind., U.S. 216 40.21 N 87.17 W
Warren □[6], Mo., U.S. 219 38.45 N 91.09 W
Warren □[6], N.J., U.S. 210 40.49 N 75.05 W
Warren □[6], N.Y., U.S. 210 43.26 N 73.43 W
Warren □[6], Ohio, U.S. 218 39.26 N 84.13 W
Warren □[6], Pa., U.S. 214 41.51 N 79.08 W
Warren ≃ 162 34.35 S 115.50 E
Warren City 222 32.33 N 94.54 W
Warrendale 214 40.39 N 80.05 W
Warren Dunes State Park ♠ 216 41.56 N 86.36 W
Warren H. Manning State Park ♠ 283 42.34 N 71.18 W
Warren Park 218 39.48 N 86.03 W
Warren Peaks ⩕ 198 44.29 N 104.28 W
Warrenpoint 48 54.06 N 6.15 W
Warren Point ≻ 180 69.44 N 132.30 W
Warrens 190 44.08 N 90.30 W
Warrensburg, Ill., U.S. 219 39.56 N 89.04 W
Warrensburg, Mo., U.S. 194 38.46 N 93.44 W
Warrensburg, N.Y., U.S. 188 43.30 N 73.46 W
Warrensville 210 41.19 N 76.57 W
Warrensville Heights 214 41.26 N 81.29 W
Warrenton, S. Afr. 158 28.09 S 24.47 E
Warrenton, Ga., U.S. 192 33.24 N 82.40 W
Warrenton, Mo., U.S. 219 38.49 N 91.08 W
Warrenton, N.C., U.S. 192 36.24 N 78.09 W
Warrenton, Oreg., U.S. 224 46.10 N 123.56 W
Warrenton, Tex., U.S. 222 30.01 N 96.44 W
Warrenton, Va., U.S. 188 38.43 N 77.48 W
Warrenville 216 41.49 N 88.11 W
Warrenzin 54 53.54 N 12.57 E
Warri 150 5.31 N 5.45 E
Warriedar Hill ∧[2] 162 29.06 S 117.06 E
Warriewood 274a 33.42 S 151.18 E
Warrill Creek ≃ 171a 27.39 S 152.44 E
Warrina 166 28.12 S 135.50 E
Warringah War Memorial ⊥ 274a 33.46 S 151.15 E
Warrington, N.Z. 172 45.43 S 170.35 E
Warrington, Eng., U.K. 44 / 262 53.24 N 2.37 W
Warrington, Fla., U.S. 194 30.23 N 87.16 W
Warrington, Pa., U.S. 285 40.15 N 75.08 W
Warrington □[8] 262 53.24 N 2.33 W
Warrington Airport ⊠ 285 40.16 N 75.09 W
Warrior 194 33.49 N 86.49 W
Warrior Creek ≃ 192 31.15 N 83.34 W
Warrior Reefs ✦[2] 164 9.35 S 143.10 E
Warriors Mark 214 40.42 N 78.08 W
Warrnambool 166 38.23 S 142.29 E
Warroad 198 48.54 N 95.19 W
Warrumbungle National Park ♠ 166 31.20 S 149.00 E
Warsak 123 34.10 N 71.25 E
Warsaw → Warszawa, Pol. 30 52.15 N 21.00 E
Warsaw, Ill., U.S. 190 40.22 N 91.26 W
Warsaw, Ind., U.S. 216 41.14 N 85.51 W
Warsaw, Ky., U.S. 218 38.47 N 84.54 W
Warsaw, Mo., U.S. 194 38.15 N 93.23 W
Warsaw, N.C., U.S. 192 35.00 N 78.05 W
Warsaw, N.Y., U.S. 210 42.44 N 78.08 W
Warsaw, Ohio, U.S. 214 40.20 N 82.00 W
Warsaw, Va., U.S. 208 37.57 N 76.46 W
Warschau → Warszawa 30 52.15 N 21.00 E
Warscheneck ∧ 61 47.39 N 14.14 E
Warshikh 144 2.19 N 45.50 E
Warsingsfehn 52 53.20 N 7.28 E
Warsop 44 53.13 N 1.09 W
Warspite 182 54.06 N 112.37 W
Warstein 56 51.26 N 8.21 E
Warszawa (Warsaw) 30 52.15 N 21.00 E
Warta 30 51.42 N 18.38 E
Warta ≃ 30 52.35 N 14.39 E
Wartburg, S. Afr. 158 29.25 S 30.35 E
Wartburg, Tenn., U.S. 192 36.06 N 84.36 W
Wartburg ⊥ 54 50.58 N 10.18 E
Wartenberg 60 48.24 N 11.59 E
Wartenberg ⊸[8] 264a 52.34 N 13.31 E
Warth 58 47.15 N 10.11 E
Warthan Creek ≃ 226 36.08 N 120.20 W
Warthe → Warta ≃ 30 52.35 N 14.39 E
Warti Kogon 144 3.10 N 45.02 E
Wartin 54 53.15 N 14.09 E
Warton, Eng., U.K. 44 54.09 N 2.47 W
Warton, Eng., U.K. 262 53.45 N 2.54 W
Warton Aerodrome ⊠ 262 53.45 N 2.54 W
Wartrace 194 35.32 N 86.19 W
Wartsberg ∧[2] 263 51.25 N 6.29 E
Waru 164 3.24 S 130.40 E
Warud 120 21.28 N 78.16 E
Warumi 175d 24.45 N 125.26 E
Warunta, Laguna ⊜ 236 15.22 N 84.09 W
Waruta ≃ 164 3.18 S 140.08 E
Warwick, Austl. 171a 28.13 S 152.02 E
Warwick, Qué., Can. 206 45.56 N 71.59 W
Warwick, Eng., U.K. 42 52.17 N 1.34 W
Warwick, Md., U.S. 208 39.25 N 75.47 W
Warwick, N.Y., U.S. 210 41.16 N 74.22 W
Warwick, R.I., U.S. 207 41.43 N 71.28 W
Warwick ≃ 208 37.05 N 76.33 W
Warwick Castle ⊥ 42 52.17 N 1.34 W
Warwick Channel ⊔ 164 13.51 S 136.16 E
Warwick Farm Racecourse and Motor Race Track ♠ 274a 33.55 S 150.57 E
Warwickshire □[6] 42 52.13 N 1.37 W
Warza 54 51.00 N 10.41 E
Wasaga Beach 212 44.31 N 80.01 W
Wasagu 150 11.25 N 5.49 E
Wasatch Plateau ⩕[1] 200 39.20 N 111.30 W
Wasatch Range ⩕ 200 41.15 N 111.30 W
Wasāwewāla 123 30.28 N 73.40 E
Wasbank 158 28.24 S 30.05 E
Wasbister 46 59.10 N 3.07 W
Wascana Creek ≃ 184 50.20 N 104.25 W
Wäschenbeuren 56 48.46 N 9.41 E
Wasco, Calif., U.S. 226 35.36 N 119.20 W
Wasco, Oreg., U.S. 224 45.35 N 120.42 W
Wasco □[6] 224 45.10 N 121.12 W
Wase 150 9.06 N 9.59 E
Waseca 190 44.05 N 93.30 W
Waseda University ⊍[2] 268 35.42 N 139.43 E
Wasekamio Lake ⊜ 184 56.45 N 108.45 W
Wasen 58 47.03 N 7.48 E
Wasfanārd 267d 35.39 N 51.21 E
Washademoak Lake ⊜ 186 45.48 N 65.58 W
Washago 212 44.45 N 79.20 W
Washburn, Ill., U.S. 190 40.55 N 89.17 W
Washburn, Maine, U.S. 186 46.47 N 68.09 W
Washburn, N. Dak., U.S. 198 47.17 N 101.02 W
Washburn, Wis., U.S. 190 46.41 N 90.52 W
Washburn, Mount ∧ 202 44.48 N 110.25 W
Washburn Lake ⊜ 176 70.03 N 106.50 W
Washdyke 172 44.21 S 171.14 E
Washicoutai 186 50.17 N 60.42 W
Washiga-take ∧ 94 35.56 N 136.58 E
Washiki 96 33.51 N 134.30 E
Wāshim 122 20.06 N 77.09 E
Washimiya 94 36.06 N 139.40 E
Washington, Eng., U.K. 44 54.55 N 1.30 W
Washington, Calif., U.S. 226 39.22 N 120.48 W
Washington, Conn., U.S. 207 41.39 N 73.19 W
Washington, D.C., U.S. 208 / 284c 38.54 N 77.01 W
Washington, Ga., U.S. 192 33.44 N 82.44 W
Washington, Ill., U.S. 190 40.42 N 89.24 W
Washington, Ind., U.S. 194 38.40 N 87.10 W
Washington, Iowa, U.S. 190 41.18 N 91.42 W
Washington, Kans., U.S. 198 39.49 N 97.03 W
Washington, Ky., U.S. 218 38.37 N 83.49 W
Washington, La., U.S. 194 30.37 N 92.03 W
Washington, Mich., U.S. 214 42.44 N 83.02 W
Washington, Mo., U.S. 219 38.33 N 91.01 W
Washington, N.J., U.S. 210 40.46 N 74.59 W
Washington, N.C., U.S. 192 35.33 N 77.03 W
Washington, Pa., U.S. 214 40.10 N 80.15 W
Washington, Tex., U.S. 222 30.20 N 96.10 W
Washington, Va., U.S. 188 38.43 N 78.10 W
Washington □[6], Ill., U.S. 219 38.21 N 89.23 W
Washington □[6], Ind., U.S. 218 38.36 N 86.06 W
Washington □[6], N.Y., U.S. 210 43.15 N 73.27 W
Washington □[6], Oreg., U.S. 224 45.33 N 123.07 W
Washington □[6], Pa., U.S. 214 40.10 N 80.15 W
Washington □[6], R.I., U.S. 207 41.28 N 71.35 W
Washington □[6], Tex., U.S. 222 30.15 N 96.20 W
Washington □[6], Wis., U.S. 216 43.14 N 88.15 W
Washington □[3] 178 / 202 47.30 N 120.30 W
Washington, Lake ⊜, Fla., U.S. 220 28.07 N 80.45 W
Washington, Lake ⊜, Wash., U.S. 224 47.37 N 122.15 W
Washington, Mount ∧ 188 44.15 N 71.15 W
Washington Court House 218 39.32 N 83.26 W
Washington Crossing 208 40.18 N 74.52 W
Washington Crossing State Park ♠ 208 40.17 N 74.53 W
Washington D.C. → District of Columbia □[5] 284c 38.54 N 77.01 W
Washington Depot 207 41.38 N 73.19 W
Washington Island 190 45.23 N 86.55 W
Washington Island I, Oc. 14 4.43 N 160.24 W
Washington Island I, Wis., U.S. 190 45.23 N 86.55 W
Washington Memorial Chapel ⊍[1] 285 40.06 N 75.26 W
Washington Mills 210 43.03 N 75.16 W
Washington Monument ♠ 284c 38.53 N 77.03 W
Washington Monument State Park ♠ 208 39.30 N 77.38 W
Washington National Airport ⊠ 208 38.51 N 77.02 W
Washington-on-the-Brazos State Historic Park ♠ 222 30.20 N 96.09 W
Washington Park 219 38.38 N 90.05 W
Washington Park ♠, Ill., U.S. 278 41.48 N 87.37 W
Washington Park ♠, Ohio, U.S. 279a 41.27 N 81.40 W
Washington Park Race Track ♠ 278 41.34 N 87.38 W
Washington Place 218 39.47 N 86.01 W
Washington Rock State Park ♠ 276 40.37 N 74.28 W
Washington Terrace 200 41.12 N 111.59 W
Washington Township 276 41.00 N 74.04 W
Washington Valley 276 40.48 N 74.32 W
Washington Valley Reservoir ⊜[1] 276 40.36 N 74.34 W
Washingtonville, N.Y., U.S. 210 41.26 N 74.10 W
Washingtonville, Ohio, U.S. 214 40.54 N 80.46 W
Washingtonville, Pa., U.S. 210 41.03 N 76.40 W
Washita ≃ 196 34.12 N 96.50 W
Washoe □[6] 226 39.22 N 119.43 W
Washoe Lake ⊜ 226 39.16 N 119.48 W
Washougal 224 45.35 N 122.21 W
Washougal ≃ 224 45.35 N 122.23 W
Washow Bay C 184 51.22 N 96.47 W
Washtenaw □[6] 216 42.15 N 83.50 W
Washtucna 202 46.45 N 118.19 W
Wāshuk 128 27.44 N 64.48 E
Washurn ≃ 44 53.54 N 1.39 W
Wasian 164 1.54 S 133.17 E
Wasilków 30 53.12 N 23.12 E
Wasilla 180 61.35 N 149.26 W
Wasior 164 2.43 S 134.30 E
Waskada 184 49.06 N 100.46 W
Waskahigan ≃ 182 54.45 N 117.12 W
Waskaiowaka Lake ⊜ 184 56.30 N 96.20 W
Waskatenau 182 54.07 N 112.47 W
Waskesiu Lake ⊜ 184 53.56 N 106.10 W
Waskom 194 32.29 N 94.04 W
Wasmes 50 50.33 N 3.32 E
Wąsosz 30 51.34 N 16.42 E
Waspam 236 14.44 N 83.58 W
Waspuk ≃ 236 14.38 N 84.26 W
Wasquehal 50 50.40 N 3.09 E
Wassage 144 2.56 N 46.02 E
Wassaic 210 41.48 N 73.35 W
Wasselonne 58 48.38 N 7.27 E
Wassen 58 46.42 N 8.36 E
Wassenaar 52 52.07 N 4.24 E
Wassenberg 56 51.06 N 6.08 E
Wasseralfingen 56 48.52 N 10.06 E
Wasserbillig 56 49.44 N 6.30 E
Wasserburg am Inn 60 48.04 N 12.13 E
Wasserkuppe ∧ 56 50.30 N 9.56 E
Wasserkurl 263 51.33 N 7.38 E
Wasserleben 54 51.55 N 10.44 E
Wassertrüdingen 56 49.02 N 10.35 E
Wassigny 50 50.01 N 3.36 E
Wass Lake ⊜ 184 53.40 N 95.25 W
Wassmannsdorf 264a 52.22 N 13.28 E
Wassou 150 10.02 N 13.39 W
Wassy 58 48.30 N 4.57 E
Wast Water ⊜ 44 54.26 N 3.18 W
Wasu 164 6.00 S 147.15 E
Wasum 164 6.05 S 149.20 E
Wasungen 54 50.40 N 10.22 E
Watabeag Lake ⊜ 190 48.14 N 80.32 W
Watampone (Bone) 112 4.32 S 120.20 E
Watamu Marine National Park ♠ 154 3.23 S 40.00 E
Waṭan, Wādī al- ∨ 142 30.26 N 31.49 E
Watansoppeng 112 4.21 S 119.53 E
Watarai 94 34.26 N 136.37 E
Watarase ≃ 94 36.13 N 139.42 E
Wataru I 122 5.43 N 73.23 E
Watatic, Mount ∧ 188 42.42 N 71.53 W
Watchet 42 51.12 N 3.20 W
Watch Hill 207 41.18 N 71.51 W
Watchung Reservation ♠ 276 40.41 N 74.23 W
Water 262 53.44 N 2.14 W
Waterbeach 42 52.16 N 0.11 E
Waterberg 156 20.28 S 17.13 E
Waterberge ⩕ 156 20.30 S 17.18 E
Waterbury, Conn., U.S. 207 41.33 N 73.02 W
Waterbury, Vt., U.S. 188 44.20 N 72.46 W
Waterdale 158 30.40 S 24.02 E
Waterdown 212 43.20 N 79.53 W
Wateree ≃ 192 33.45 N 80.37 W
Wateree Lake ⊜[1] 192 34.25 N 80.50 W
Waterend, Eng., U.K. 260 51.47 N 0.30 W
Water End, Eng., U.K. 262 53.41 N 2.15 W
Waterfall 214 40.08 N 78.04 W
Waterfall Gully Reserve ♠ 168b 34.58 S 138.40 E
Waterford, Ont., Can. 212 42.56 N 80.17 W
Waterford, Eire 48 52.15 N 7.06 W
Waterford, S. Afr. 158 33.05 S 25.00 E
Waterford, Calif., U.S. 226 37.38 N 120.46 W
Waterford, Conn., U.S. 207 41.20 N 72.09 W
Waterford, Ind., U.S. 216 41.40 N 86.50 W
Waterford, Mich., U.S. 216 42.42 N 83.24 W
Waterford, N.Y., U.S. 210 42.47 N 73.41 W
Waterford, Pa., U.S. 214 41.57 N 79.59 W
Waterford, Wis., U.S. 216 42.46 N 88.13 W
Waterford □[6] 48 52.10 N 7.40 W
Waterford Harbour C 48 52.10 N 6.55 W
Waterford Mills 216 41.33 N 85.50 W
Waterford Works 208 39.43 N 74.51 W
Watergate Bay C 42 50.27 N 5.05 W
Watergrasshill 48 52.01 N 8.21 W
Watergrove Reservoir ⊜[1] 262 53.39 N 2.08 W
Waterhen ≃ 184 54.38 N 107.47 W
Waterhen Lake ⊜, Man., Can. 184 52.06 N 99.34 W
Waterhen Lake ⊜, Sask., Can. 184 54.28 N 108.25 W
Waterhouse Range ⩕ 162 24.01 S 133.25 E
Wateringbury 260 51.15 N 0.25 E
Wateringen 52 52.02 N 4.16 E
Water Island 276 40.41 N 73.02 W
Waterkloof 158 30.19 S 25.18 E
Waterloo, Austl. 164 16.38 S 129.18 E
Waterloo, Austl. 168a 33.20 S 115.47 E
Waterloo, Austl. 168b 33.59 S 138.53 E
Waterloo, Bel. 50 50.43 N 4.23 E
Waterloo, Ont., Can. 212 43.28 N 80.31 W
Waterloo, Qué., Can. 206 45.21 N 72.31 W
Waterloo, S.L. 150 8.20 N 13.04 W
Waterloo, Eng., U.K. 44 53.28 N 3.02 W
Waterloo, Ala., U.S. 194 34.55 N 88.04 W
Waterloo, Ill., U.S. 219 38.20 N 90.09 W
Waterloo, Ind., U.S. 216 41.26 N 85.01 W
Waterloo, Iowa, U.S. 190 42.30 N 92.20 W
Waterloo, N.Y., U.S. 210 42.54 N 76.52 W
Waterloo, Wis., U.S. 216 43.11 N 88.59 W
Waterloo □[6] 212 43.30 N 80.30 W
Waterloo State Recreation Area ♠ 216 42.22 N 84.20 W
Waterloo Station ⊸[5] 260 51.30 N 0.07 W
Waterlooville 42 50.53 N 1.02 W
Waterman, Ill., U.S. 216 41.46 N 88.46 W
Waterman, Wash., U.S. 224 47.34 N 122.35 W
Waterman Mountain ∧ 228 34.20 N 117.56 W
Waterman Wash ∨ 200 33.21 N 112.31 W
Water Mill 207 40.55 N 72.21 W
Waterport 210 43.20 N 78.16 W
Waterproof 194 31.48 N 91.23 W
Waterside, Scot., U.K. 44 55.21 N 4.28 W
Waterside, Pa., U.S. 214 40.11 N 78.23 W
Waterside Park 276 40.56 N 73.20 W
Watersmeet 190 46.13 N 89.11 W
Waterton-Glacier International Peace Park ♠ 202 48.47 N 113.45 W
Waterton Lakes National Park ♠ 182 49.05 N 113.50 W
Watertown, Conn., U.S. 207 41.36 N 73.07 W
Watertown, Mass., U.S. 207 42.22 N 71.11 W
Watertown, N.Y., U.S. 212 43.59 N 75.55 W
Watertown, S. Dak., U.S. 198 44.54 N 97.07 W
Watertown, Wis., U.S. 216 43.12 N 88.43 W
Waterval-Boven 156 25.40 S 30.20 E
Watervale 168b 33.57 S 138.38 E
Water Valley, Miss., U.S. 194 34.09 N 89.38 W
Water Valley, N.Y., U.S. 284a 42.42 N 78.51 W
Water View 208 37.43 N 76.37 W
Waterville, N.S., Can. 186 45.03 N 64.41 W
Waterville, Qué., Can. 206 45.16 N 71.54 W
Waterville, Eire 48 51.49 N 10.13 W
Waterville, Kans., U.S. 198 39.42 N 96.45 W

	English	Deutsch	Español	Français	Português
≃	River	Fluss	Río	Rivière	Rio
☰	Canal	Kanal	Canal	Canal	Canal
↳	Waterfall, Rapids	Wasserfall, Stromschnellen	Cascada, Rápidos	Chute d'eau, Rapides	Cascata, Rápidos
⊔	Strait	Meeresstrasse	Estrecho	Détroit	Estreito
C	Bay, Gulf	Bucht, Golf	Bahía, Golfo	Baie, Golfe	Baía, Golfo
⊜	Lake, Lakes	See, Seen	Lago, Lagos	Lac, Lacs	Lago, Lagos
☷	Swamp	Sumpf	Pantano	Marais	Pântano
⊼	Ice Features, Glacier	Eis- und Gletscherformen	Accidentes Glaciales	Formes glaciaires	Acidentes Glaciares
⊤	Other Hydrographic Features	Andere Hydrographische Objekte	Otros Elementos Hidrográficos	Autres données hydrographiques	Outros Elementos Hidrográficos

	English	Deutsch	Español	Français	Português
✦	Submarine Features	Untermeerische Objekte	Accidentes Submarinos	Formes de relief sous-marin	Acidentes Submarinos
□	Political Unit	Politische Einheit	Unidad Politica	Entité politique	Unidade Política
⊍	Cultural Institution	Kulturelle Institution	Institución Cultural	Institution culturelle	Instituição Cultural
⊥	Historical Site	Historische Stätte	Sitio Histórico	Site historique	Sitio Histórico
♠	Recreational Site	Erholungs- und Ferienort	Sitio de Recreo	Centre de loisirs	Sítio de Lazer
⊠	Airport	Flughafen	Aeropuerto	Aéroport	Aeroporto
■	Military Installation	Militäranlage	Instalación Militar	Installation militaire	Instalação Militar
⊸	Miscellaneous	Verschiedenes	Misceláneo	Divers	Miscelânea

Name	Page	Lat.°′	Long.°′
Waterville, Maine, U.S.	**188**	44.33 N	69.38 W
Waterville, Mass., U.S.	**207**	42.40 N	72.05 W
Waterville, Minn., U.S.	**190**	44.13 N	93.34 W
Waterville, N.Y., U.S.	**210**	42.56 N	75.23 W
Waterville, Ohio, U.S.	**216**	41.30 N	83.43 W
Waterville, Pa., U.S.	**210**	41.19 N	77.22 W
Waterville, Wash., U.S.	**202**	47.39 N	120.04 W
Watervliet, Mich., U.S.	**216**	42.11 N	86.16 W
Watervliet, N.Y., U.S.	**210**	42.44 N	73.42 W
Watervliet Reservoir ⊜[1]	**210**	42.43 N	73.58 W
Wates, Indon.	**114**	1.00 N	100.16 E
Wates, Indon.	**115a**	7.55 S	112.07 E
Wates, Indon.	**115a**	7.51 S	110.10 E
Watford, Ont., Can.	**214**	42.57 N	81.53 W
Watford, Eng., U.K.	**42**	51.40 N	0.25 W
Watford □[8]	**260**	51.40 N	0.25 W
Watford City	**198**	47.48 N	103.17 W
Wa'th	**140**	8.10 N	32.07 E
Wathaman ≃	**184**	57.16 N	102.52 W
Wathaman Lake ⊜	**184**	56.55 N	103.43 W
Watheroo	**162**	30.17 S	116.04 E
Wathlingen	**52**	52.32 N	10.09 E
Wath upon Dearne	**44**	53.29 N	1.20 W
Wati	**120**	28.02 N	96.59 E
Watino	**182**	55.43 N	117.37 W
Watkins Glen	**210**	42.23 N	76.52 W
Watkins Glen Grand Prix Course ♠	**210**	42.20 N	76.55 W
Watkins Glen State Park ♠	**210**	42.22 N	76.55 W
Watkins Island I	**284c**	39.02 N	77.17 W
Watkins Lake ⊜	**281**	42.40 N	83.22 W
Watkinsville	**192**	33.52 N	83.25 W
Watlaar	**164**	5.28 S	133.07 E
Watling Island → San Salvador I	**238**	24.02 N	74.28 W
Watlington	**42**	51.37 N	1.00 W
Watoga State Park ♠	**188**	38.07 N	80.05 W
Watonga	**196**	35.51 N	98.25 W
Watonwan ≃	**198**	44.04 N	94.07 W
Watopeka ≃	**206**	45.34 N	72.00 W
Watou	**50**	50.51 N	2.37 E
Wat Phai Tan, Khlong ☲	**269a**	13.48 N	100.33 E
Watrous, Sask., Can.	**184**	51.40 N	105.28 W
Watrous, N. Mex., U.S.	**200**	35.48 N	104.59 W
Watsa	**154**	3.03 N	29.32 E
Watseka	**216**	40.47 N	87.44 W
Watsi Kengo	**152**	0.48 S	20.33 E
Watson, Austl.	**162**	30.29 S	131.31 E
Watson, Sask., Can.	**184**	52.07 N	104.31 W
Watson, Ind., U.S.	**218**	38.22 N	85.41 W
Watsonia	**274b**	37.43 S	145.05 E
Watson Lake	**180**	60.07 N	128.48 W
Watsons Bay	**274a**	33.51 S	151.17 E
Watsons Creek	**274b**	37.40 S	145.13 E
Watsontown	**210**	41.05 N	76.52 W
Watsonville	**226**	36.55 N	121.45 W
Watt	**222**	31.39 N	96.51 W
Watten	**50**	50.50 N	2.13 E
Watten, Loch ⊜	**46**	58.29 N	3.19 W
Wattens	**64**	47.17 N	11.36 E
Wattenscheid	**56**	51.29 N	7.08 E
Wattenwil	**58**	46.46 N	7.30 E
Wattignies	**50**	50.35 N	3.03 E
Wattiwarriganna ≃	**162**	28.57 S	136.10 E
Wattle Flat	**170**	33.08 S	149.41 E
Wattle Glen	**274b**	37.40 S	145.11 E
Wattle Park ♠	**274b**	37.50 S	145.07 E
Watton	**42**	52.35 N	0.48 E
Wattrelos	**50**	50.42 N	3.13 E
Watts ◆[8]	**280**	33.56 N	118.15 W
Watts Bar Lake ⊜[1]	**192**	35.48 N	84.39 W
Watts Branch ≃	**284c**	39.03 N	77.15 W
Wattsburg	**214**	42.00 N	79.49 W
Watts Island I	**208**	37.48 N	75.53 W
Wattsville	**192**	34.31 N	82.02 W
Wattville	**273d**	26.13 S	28.18 E
Wattwil	**58**	47.18 N	9.06 E
Watu	**152**	3.18 S	20.03 E
Watubela, Kepulauan II	**164**	4.35 S	131.40 E
Watudirang	**115b**	8.40 S	122.34 E
Watukancoa	**112**	1.36 S	121.48 E
Watuppa Pond ⊜	**207**	41.42 N	71.06 W
Wat Wat	**164**	4.29 S	152.21 E
Watzekopf ∧	**58**	46.59 N	10.48 E
Watzmann ∧	**64**	47.33 N	12.55 E
Wau	**164**	7.20 S	146.45 E
Waubach	**56**	50.55 N	6.03 E
Waubaushene	**212**	44.45 N	79.42 W
Waubaushene Channel)(	**212**	44.46 N	79.45 W
Waubay	**198**	45.20 N	97.18 W
Waubay Lake ⊜	**198**	45.25 N	97.25 W
Waubesa, Lake ⊜	**216**	43.01 N	89.20 W
Waubra	**169**	37.21 S	143.39 E
Waubuno Creek ≃	**212**	42.58 N	81.08 W
Wauchope, Austl.	**162**	20.36 S	134.15 E
Wauchope, Austl.	**166**	31.27 S	152.44 E
Wauchula	**220**	27.33 N	81.49 W
Wauconda	**216**	42.16 N	88.08 W
Waugh	**184**	49.40 N	95.13 W
Waugh Mountain ∧	**202**	45.29 N	114.47 W
Waukaringa	**166**	32.18 S	139.26 E
Waukarlycarly, Lake ⊜	**162**	21.25 S	121.50 E
Waukegan	**216**	42.22 N	87.50 W
Waukena	**226**	36.08 N	119.31 W
Waukesha	**216**	43.01 N	88.14 W
Waukesha □[6]	**216**	43.02 N	88.20 W
Waukon	**190**	43.16 N	91.29 W
Waulsort	**56**	50.13 N	4.52 E
Wauna	**224**	47.23 N	122.39 W
Waunakee	**216**	43.11 N	89.27 W
Wauneta	**198**	40.25 N	101.23 W
Waupaca	**190**	44.21 N	89.05 W
Waupecan Creek ≃	**216**	41.20 N	88.28 W
Waupoos Island I	**212**	43.59 N	76.58 W
Waupun	**190**	43.38 N	88.44 W
Wauregan	**207**	41.45 N	71.55 W
Waurika	**196**	34.10 N	98.00 W
Wausa	**198**	42.30 N	97.32 W
Wausau	**190**	44.59 N	89.39 W
Wausaukee	**190**	45.23 N	87.57 W
Wauseon	**216**	41.33 N	84.09 W
Wautoma	**190**	44.04 N	89.17 W
Wauwa	**154**	3.27 N	27.21 E
Wauwatosa	**216**	43.03 N	88.00 W
Wauzeka	**190**	43.05 N	90.52 W
Wave Hill	**162**	17.29 S	130.57 E
Waveland, Mass., U.S.	**283**	42.17 N	70.53 W
Waveland, Miss., U.S.	**194**	30.16 N	89.29 W
Waveney ≃	**42**	52.28 N	1.45 E
Waver ≃	**44**	54.52 N	3.17 W
Waverley, Austl.	**274a**	33.54 S	151.16 E
Waverley, N.Z.	**172**	39.46 S	174.38 E
Waverley, S. Afr.	**158**	31.58 S	26.28 E
Waverley, Mass., U.S.	**283**	42.23 N	71.11 W
Waverley ◆[8]	**273d**	26.08 S	28.04 E
Waverly, Ala., U.S.	**194**	32.44 N	85.35 W
Waverly, Fla., U.S.	**220**	28.01 N	81.37 W
Waverly, Ill., U.S.	**219**	39.36 N	89.57 W
Waverly, Iowa, U.S.	**190**	42.44 N	92.29 W
Waverly, Kans., U.S.	**198**	38.23 N	95.36 W
Waverly, Mich., U.S.	**216**	42.44 N	84.33 W
Waverly, Minn., U.S.	**190**	45.04 N	93.57 W
Waverly, Mo., U.S.	**194**	39.12 N	93.31 W
Waverly, Nebr., U.S.	**198**	40.55 N	96.32 W
Waverly, N.Y., U.S.	**210**	42.00 N	76.32 W
Waverly, Ohio, U.S.	**218**	39.07 N	82.59 W
Waverly, Pa., U.S.	**210**	41.32 N	75.42 W
Waverly, Tenn., U.S.	**194**	36.05 N	87.48 W
Waverly, Va., U.S.	**208**	37.02 N	77.06 W
Waverly Hall	**192**	32.41 N	84.44 W
Wavre	**56**	50.43 N	4.37 E
Wavrin	**50**	50.34 N	2.55 E
Wāw	**140**	7.42 N	28.00 E
Wāw ≃	**140**	7.03 N	27.13 E
Wawa, Ont., Can.	**190**	47.59 N	84.47 W
Wawa, Nig.	**150**	9.55 N	4.25 E
Wawa, Sūd.	**140**	20.26 N	30.21 E
Wawa ≃	**236**	13.53 N	83.28 W
Wawaka	**216**	41.28 N	85.29 W
Wāw al-Kabīr	**146**	25.20 N	16.43 E
Wawanesa	**184**	49.36 N	99.41 W
Wawarsing	**210**	41.46 N	74.21 W
Wawasee, Lake ⊜	**216**	41.24 N	85.41 W
Wawayanda State Park ♠	**276**	41.11 N	74.26 W
Wawiag ≃	**190**	48.25 N	91.07 W
Wawoi ≃	**164**	8.01 S	143.33 E
Waworada, Teluk C	**115b**	8.44 S	118.51 E
Wawota	**184**	49.55 N	102.00 W
Waxahachie	**222**	32.24 N	96.51 W
Waxahachie, Lake ⊜[1]	**222**	32.20 N	96.49 W
Waxhaw	**192**	34.55 N	80.45 W
Waxuecun	**106**	31.07 N	121.38 E
Waxweiler	**56**	50.05 N	6.22 E
Way, Lake ⊜	**162**	26.48 S	120.18 E
Waya I	**175g**	17.18 S	177.08 E
Wayabula	**108**	2.17 N	128.12 E
Wayao	**98**	34.23 N	118.11 E
Wayaopu	**106**	30.33 N	118.53 E
Waycross	**192**	31.13 N	82.21 W
Wayi	**154**	5.11 N	30.10 E
Wayland, Iowa, U.S.	**190**	41.08 N	91.40 W
Wayland, Ky., U.S.	**192**	37.27 N	82.48 W
Wayland, Mass., U.S.	**283**	42.22 N	71.22 W
Wayland, Mich., U.S.	**216**	42.40 N	85.39 W
Wayland, N.Y., U.S.	**210**	42.34 N	77.35 W
Wayland, Ohio, U.S.	**214**	41.10 N	81.04 W
Waymansville	**218**	39.04 N	86.03 W
Waymart	**210**	41.35 N	75.25 W
Wayne, Alta., Can.	**182**	51.23 N	112.39 W
Wayne, Mich., U.S.	**216**	42.17 N	83.23 W
Wayne, Nebr., U.S.	**198**	42.14 N	97.01 W
Wayne, N.J., U.S.	**210**	40.55 N	74.17 W
Wayne, N.Y., U.S.	**210**	42.28 N	77.06 W
Wayne, Ohio, U.S.	**214**	41.18 N	83.28 W
Wayne, Okla., U.S.	**196**	34.55 N	97.19 W
Wayne, Pa., U.S.	**208**	40.03 N	75.23 W
Wayne, W. Va., U.S.	**188**	38.13 N	82.27 W
Wayne □[6], Ill., U.S.	**219**	38.25 N	88.40 W
Wayne □[6], Ind., U.S.	**218**	39.50 N	84.54 W
Wayne □[6], Mich., U.S.	**216**	42.14 N	83.12 W
Wayne □[6], N.Y., U.S.	**210**	43.04 N	77.00 W
Wayne □[6], Ohio, U.S.	**214**	40.48 N	81.56 W
Wayne □[6], Pa., U.S.	**210**	41.34 N	75.16 W
Waynesboro, Ga., U.S.	**192**	33.06 N	82.01 W
Waynesboro, Miss., U.S.	**194**	31.40 N	88.39 W
Waynesboro, Pa., U.S.	**208**	39.45 N	77.35 W
Waynesboro, Tenn., U.S.	**194**	35.19 N	87.45 W
Waynesboro, Va., U.S.	**192**	38.04 N	78.53 W
Waynesburg, Ohio, U.S.	**214**	40.40 N	81.16 W
Waynesburg, Pa., U.S.	**188**	39.54 N	80.11 W
Waynesfield	**216**	40.36 N	83.59 W
Wayne State University ʊ[2]	**281**	42.21 N	83.04 W
Waynesville, Ill., U.S.	**194**	40.15 N	89.08 W
Waynesville, Mo., U.S.	**194**	37.50 N	92.12 W
Waynesville, N.C., U.S.	**192**	35.29 N	83.00 W
Waynesville, Ohio, U.S.	**218**	39.32 N	84.05 W
Waynoka	**196**	36.35 N	98.53 W
Wayoh Reservoir ⊜[1]	**262**	53.39 N	2.24 W
Waza, Parc National de ♠	**146**	11.20 N	13.40 E
Waza Garou	**146**	11.25 N	14.34 E
Wazay	**120**	33.22 N	69.26 E
Waziers	**50**	50.23 N	3.07 E
Wāzin	**146**	31.57 N	10.40 E
Wazīrābād	**123**	32.27 N	74.07 E
Wazīrābād ◆[8]	**272a**	28.43 N	77.14 E
Wāzīrpur ◆[8]	**272a**	28.41 N	77.10 E
Wazuka	**96**	34.47 N	135.55 E
Wazuka ≃	**270**	34.45 N	135.53 E
Wda ≃	**30**	53.25 N	18.29 E
We, Pulau I	**114**	5.51 N	95.18 E
Wea Creek ≃	**216**	40.24 N	86.57 W
Weagamow Lake ⊜	**184**	52.53 N	91.22 W
Weald Park ♠	**260**	51.38 N	0.14 E
Wealdstone ◆[8]	**260**	51.36 N	0.20 W
Weam	**164**	8.40 S	141.08 E
Wear ≃	**44**	54.55 N	1.22 W
Wearhead	**44**	54.45 N	2.13 W
Wearyan ≃	**164**	15.57 S	136.51 E
Weatherford, Okla., U.S.	**196**	35.32 N	98.42 W
Weatherford, Tex., U.S.	**222**	32.46 N	97.48 W
Weatherford, Lake ⊜[1]	**222**	32.47 N	97.41 W
Weatherly	**210**	40.57 N	75.50 W
Weatogue	**207**	41.51 N	72.49 W
Weaubleau	**194**	37.54 N	93.32 W
Weaver, Ala., U.S.	**194**	33.45 N	85.49 W
Weaver, Tex., U.S.	**222**	33.10 N	95.25 W
Weaver ≃	**44**	53.19 N	2.44 W
Weaver ☲	**262**	53.19 N	2.45 W
Weaverham	**44**	53.16 N	2.35 W
Weaver Lake ⊜	**184**	52.45 N	96.35 W
Weavertown	**279b**	40.16 N	80.11 W
Weaverville, Calif., U.S.	**204**	40.44 N	122.56 W
Weaverville, N.C., U.S.	**192**	35.42 N	82.34 W
Webau	**54**	51.10 N	12.04 E
Webb, Sask., Can.	**184**	50.11 N	108.12 W
Webb, Miss., U.S.	**194**	33.57 N	90.21 W
Webb Air Force Base ■	**196**	32.14 N	101.31 W
Webb Brook ≃	**283**	42.32 N	71.14 W
Webb City	**194**	37.09 N	94.28 W
Webber Lake ⊜	**184**	54.28 N	94.00 W
Webberville	**216**	42.40 N	84.11 W
Webbwood	**190**	41.16 N	81.53 W
Weber, Mount ∧	**182**	55.32 N	128.31 W
Webera, Yai.	**144**	9.44 N	39.02 E
Webera, Yai.	**144**	6.25 N	40.45 E
Weber City	**192**	36.37 N	82.34 W
Weber Creek ≃	**226**	38.46 N	121.00 W
Weber Hill	**219**	38.27 N	90.34 W
Webi Gof ≃	**144**	1.07 N	43.45 E
Webi Haharro ≃	**144**	1.12 N	43.43 E
Webling	**60**	48.17 N	11.25 E
Webster, Alta., Can.	**182**	55.26 N	118.42 W
Webster, Fla., U.S.	**220**	28.37 N	82.03 W
Webster, Ind., U.S.	**218**	39.54 N	84.57 W
Webster, Mass., U.S.	**207**	42.03 N	71.53 W
Webster, N.Y., U.S.	**210**	43.13 N	77.26 W
Webster, Pa., U.S.	**214**	40.11 N	79.51 W
Webster, S. Dak., U.S.	**198**	45.20 N	97.31 W
Webster, Wis., U.S.	**190**	45.53 N	92.22 W
Webster City	**190**	42.28 N	93.49 W
Webster Crossing	**210**	42.40 N	77.38 W
Webster Groves	**219**	38.35 N	90.21 W
Webster Lake ⊜	**216**	41.19 N	85.41 W
Websters Corners, B.C., Can.	**224**	49.13 N	122.30 W
Websters Corners, N.Y., U.S.	**284a**	41.47 N	78.45 W
Webster Springs	**188**	38.29 N	80.25 W
Weches	**222**	31.33 N	95.14 W
Wechmar	**54**	50.53 N	10.47 E
Wechselburg	**54**	51.00 N	12.47 E
Weda	**108**	0.21 N	127.52 E
Wedau ◆[8]	**263**	51.24 N	6.48 E
Wedau, Sportpark ♠	**263**	51.25 N	6.47 E
Weddell Island I	**254**	51.55 S	61.00 W
Weddell Sea ⊤[2]	**9**	72.00 S	45.00 W
Wedderburn	**166**	36.25 S	143.37 E
Wedding ◆[8]	**264a**	52.33 N	13.22 E
Weddinghofen	**263**	51.36 N	7.37 E
Wedel	**52**	53.35 N	9.41 E
Wedge Mountain ∧	**182**	50.10 N	122.50 W
Wedgeport	**186**	43.44 N	65.59 W
Wedgewood	**219**	38.47 N	90.17 W
Wedmore	**42**	51.14 N	2.49 W
Wednesbury	**42**	52.34 N	2.00 W
Wednesfield	**42**	52.36 N	2.04 W
Wedowee	**194**	33.19 N	85.29 W
Wedron	**216**	41.26 N	88.46 W
Weduar, Tanjung ≻	**164**	6.00 S	132.50 E
Wedweil	**140**	9.00 N	27.12 E
Wedza	**154**	18.35 S	31.35 E
Weebo	**162**	28.01 S	121.03 E
Weed	**204**	41.25 N	122.23 W
Weed Heights	**226**	38.59 N	119.11 W
Weedon	**206**	45.42 N	71.28 W
Weedon Beck	**42**	52.14 N	1.05 W
Weedon Island I	**220**	27.51 N	82.36 W
Weedon Lake ⊜	**206**	45.43 N	71.25 W
Weed Patch	**226**	30.19 N	118.55 W
Weed Patch Hill ∧[2]	**218**	39.10 N	86.13 W
Weedsport	**210**	43.03 N	76.34 W
Weedville	**214**	41.17 N	78.30 W
Weehawken	**276**	40.46 N	74.01 W
Weeim, Pulau I	**164**	1.29 S	130.14 E
Wee Jasper	**171b**	35.09 S	148.41 E
Weekapauq	**207**	41.20 N	71.45 W
Weeki Wachee Spring ♠	**220**	28.32 N	82.35 W
Weeki Wachee Swamp ☷	**220**	28.31 N	82.37 W
Weeks Point ≻	**276**	40.53 N	73.39 W
Weekstown	**208**	39.37 N	74.37 W
Weelde	**56**	51.25 N	5.00 E
Weems	**208**	37.39 N	76.27 W
Weende	**52**	51.33 N	9.55 E
Weenen	**158**	28.57 S	30.03 E
Weener	**52**	53.10 N	7.21 E
Weeney Bay C	**274a**	34.01 S	151.10 E
Weeping Water	**198**	40.52 N	96.08 W
Weequahic Lake ⊜	**276**	40.42 N	74.12 W
Weert	**52**	51.15 N	5.43 E
Weesatche	**222**	28.51 N	97.27 W
Weesby	**41**	54.50 N	9.08 E
Weesow	**264a**	52.39 N	13.43 E
Weesp	**52**	52.17 N	5.02 E
Weetfeld	**263**	51.38 N	7.49 E
Weethalle	**166**	33.53 S	146.38 E
Weeton	**262**	53.48 N	2.56 W
Wee Waa	**166**	30.14 S	149.26 E
Weeze	**52**	51.37 N	6.12 E
Wefensleben	**54**	52.11 N	11.09 E
Weferlingen	**54**	52.19 N	11.02 E
Wegberg	**56**	51.08 N	6.16 E
Wegdras	**158**	28.50 S	21.52 E
Wegeleben	**54**	51.53 N	11.10 E
Wegendorf	**264a**	52.36 N	13.45 E
Wegenstedt	**54**	52.23 N	11.11 E
Wegeringhausen	**56**	51.02 N	7.45 E
Weggis	**58**	47.02 N	8.26 E
Węgliniec	**30**	51.17 N	15.13 E
Węgorzewo	**30**	54.14 N	21.44 E
Węgorzyno	**30**	53.32 N	15.33 E
Węgrów	**30**	52.25 N	22.01 E
Wegscheid	**60**	48.36 N	13.48 E
Wehdel	**52**	53.30 N	8.48 E
Wehingen	**58**	48.08 N	8.47 E
Wehofen ◆[8]	**263**	51.32 N	6.46 E
Wehr	**58**	47.37 N	7.54 E
Wehringhausen ◆[8]	**263**	51.21 N	7.27 E
Wehrsdorf	**54**	51.03 N	14.22 E
Weichang	**98**	42.00 N	117.32 E
Weichsel → Wisła ≃	**30**	54.22 N	18.55 E
Weichselboden	**61**	47.40 N	15.10 E
Weichshofen	**60**	48.43 N	12.26 E
Weichuan	**98**	34.17 N	113.58 E
Weicun	**106**	31.59 N	119.55 E
Weida	**54**	50.45 N	12.04 E
Weida ≃	**54**	50.47 N	12.06 E
Weiden am See	**61**	47.55 N	16.52 E
Weidenberg	**60**	49.57 N	11.43 E
Weiden in der Oberpfalz	**60**	49.41 N	12.10 E
Weidenstetten	**56**	48.33 N	9.59 E
Weidhausen	**56**	50.12 N	11.08 E
Weiding	**60**	49.16 N	12.46 E
Weidling	**264b**	48.17 N	16.19 E
Weidlingau ◆[8]	**264b**	48.13 N	16.13 E
Weidlingbach	**264b**	48.16 N	16.15 E
Weidlinger Bach ≃	**264b**	48.18 N	16.20 E
Weifang	**98**	36.42 N	119.04 E
Weigelstown	**208**	39.59 N	76.49 W
Weihai	**98**	37.28 N	122.07 E
Weihaiwei → Weihai	**98**	37.28 N	122.07 E
Weihe ≃, Zhg.	**98**	37.05 N	119.28 E
Weihe ≃, Zhg.	**98**	36.51 N	115.43 E
Weihe ≃, Zhg.	**102**	34.30 N	110.20 E
Weihmichl	**60**	48.36 N	12.03 E
Weihnachtsinsel → Christmas Island □[2]	**112**	10.30 S	105.40 E
Weijiagou	**105**	40.28 N	115.08 E
Weijiatang	**106**	31.25 N	118.55 E
Weijiawan	**98**	36.43 N	115.54 E
Weijiazhuang	**105**	39.37 N	116.22 E
Weijiazui	**100**	30.29 N	117.20 E
Weijingtang	**106**	31.27 N	120.39 E
Weikersheim	**56**	49.29 N	9.54 E
Weil ≃	**56**	50.28 N	8.16 E
Weil am Rhein	**58**	47.37 N	7.38 E
Weilbach	**56**	50.03 N	8.26 E
Weilburg	**56**	50.29 N	8.15 E
Weil der Stadt	**56**	48.45 N	8.52 E
Weiler	**58**	47.36 N	9.55 E
Weilerbach	**56**	49.29 N	7.37 E
Weilerswist	**56**	50.45 N	6.50 E
Weilheim	**64**	47.50 N	11.08 E
Weilheim an der Teck	**56**	48.37 N	9.32 E
Weilmoringle	**166**	29.15 S	146.51 E
Weilmünster	**56**	50.26 N	8.22 E
Weimar, B.R.D.	**56**	51.22 N	9.23 E
Weimar, D.D.R.	**54**	50.59 N	11.19 E
Weimar, Calif., U.S.	**226**	39.02 N	120.58 W
Weimar, Tex., U.S.	**222**	29.42 N	96.47 W
Weinan	**102**	34.29 N	109.29 E
Weinböhla	**54**	51.10 N	13.34 E
Weinel Cross Roads	**279b**	40.37 N	79.37 W
Weiner	**194**	35.37 N	90.54 W
Weinfelden	**58**	47.34 N	9.06 E
Weingarten, B.R.D.	**56**	49.05 N	8.31 E
Weingarten, B.R.D.	**58**	47.48 N	9.38 E
Weinheim	**56**	49.33 N	8.39 E
Weining	**102**	26.43 N	104.18 E
Weiningying	**104**	41.21 N	123.49 E
Weinsberg	**56**	49.10 N	9.17 E
Weinsberger Wald ◆[3]	**61**	48.30 N	14.50 E
Weinviertel ◆[1]	**61**	48.38 N	16.25 E
Weipa	**164**	12.41 S	141.52 E
Weiping	**100**	29.43 N	118.45 E
Weir, Bhārat	**124**	27.01 N	77.11 E
Weir, Kans., U.S.	**198**	37.19 N	94.46 W
Weir, Miss., U.S.	**194**	33.16 N	89.17 W
Weir ≃, Austl.	**166**	28.50 S	149.06 E
Weir ≃, Man., Can.	**184**	56.54 N	93.21 W
Weir ≃, Mass., U.S.	**283**	42.16 N	70.53 W
Weir, Lake ⊜	**220**	29.00 N	81.57 W
Weir River	**184**	56.49 N	94.04 W
Weirsdale	**220**	28.59 N	81.55 W
Weirton	**214**	40.25 N	80.35 W
Weisberg → Monguelfo	**64**	46.45 N	12.06 E
Weisburd	**252**	27.18 S	62.36 W
Weisburg	**218**	39.13 N	85.03 W
Weischlitz	**54**	50.26 N	12.02 E
Weisendorf	**56**	49.37 N	10.49 E
Weiser	**202**	44.15 N	116.58 W
Weiser ≃	**202**	44.15 N	116.59 W
Weishan, Zhg.	**98**	34.52 N	117.09 E
Weishan, Zhg.	**100**	29.20 N	120.25 E
Weishan, Zhg.	**102**	25.15 N	100.20 E
Weishancheng	**100**	32.34 N	113.24 E
Weishanhe	**104**	40.47 N	123.31 E
Weishanhu ⊜	**98**	34.40 N	117.15 E
Weishanzhuang	**105**	39.40 N	116.25 E
Weishi	**98**	34.25 N	114.11 E
Weismain	**54**	50.05 N	11.14 E
Weisner Mountain ∧	**194**	34.02 N	85.40 W
Weissach, B.R.D.	**56**	48.50 N	8.55 E
Weissach, B.R.D.	**64**	47.41 N	11.45 E
Weissbach bei Lofer	**64**	47.31 N	12.45 E
Weissbriach	**64**	46.41 N	13.15 E
Weisse Elster ≃	**54**	51.26 N	11.57 E
Weissenbach	**264b**	48.05 N	16.13 E
Weissenbach am Attersee	**64**	47.48 N	13.32 E
Weissenbach am Lech	**58**	47.26 N	10.39 E
Weissenberg	**54**	51.11 N	14.40 E
Weissenborn	**54**	50.52 N	13.25 E
Weissenbrunn	**54**	50.12 N	11.20 E
Weissenburg	**58**	46.39 N	7.28 E
Weissenburg in Bayern	**56**	49.01 N	10.58 E
Weissenfels	**54**	51.12 N	11.58 E
Weissenhorn	**58**	48.18 N	10.09 E
Weissensee	**54**	51.11 N	11.04 E
Weissensee ◆[8]	**264a**	52.33 N	13.27 E
Weissensee ⊜	**64**	46.42 N	13.22 E
Weissenstadt	**54**	50.06 N	11.53 E
Weissenstein, B.R.D.	**56**	48.42 N	9.53 E
Weissenstein, Öst.	**64**	46.41 N	13.44 E
Weissenstein ∧	**58**	47.15 N	7.31 E
Weissenstein Tunnel ◆[5]	**58**	47.12 N	7.23 E
Weissenthurm	**56**	50.24 N	7.27 E
Weisser Main ≃	**54**	50.05 N	11.24 E
Weisser Nil → White Nile ≃	**140**	15.38 N	32.31 E
Weisser See → Beloje, Ozero ⊜	**76**	60.11 N	37.37 E
Weisser Stein ∧	**56**	50.23 N	6.20 E
Weisses Meer → Beloje More ⊤[2]	**24**	65.30 N	38.00 E
Weisse Spitze ∧	**64**	46.52 N	12.21 E
Weissfluh ∧	**58**	46.50 N	9.48 E
Weisshorn ∧	**58**	46.06 N	7.42 E
Weissig	**54**	51.05 N	13.52 E
Weisskugel (Palla Bianca) ∧	**64**	46.48 N	10.44 E
Weiss Lake ⊜[1]	**192**	34.15 N	85.35 W
Weissmeer-Ostsee Kanal → Belomorsko-Baltijskij Kanal ☲	**24**	62.48 N	34.48 E
Weissport	**210**	40.50 N	75.42 W
Weisstannen	**58**	46.59 N	9.21 E
Weisswasser	**54**	51.30 N	14.38 E
Weisweiler	**56**	50.50 N	6.19 E
Weitang, Zhg.	**105**	40.24 N	117.24 E
Weitang, Zhg.	**106**	31.57 N	119.59 E
Weitendorf	**54**	53.54 N	12.16 E
Weitensfeld	**61**	46.51 N	14.11 E
Weitian	**100**	27.43 N	118.46 E
Weitin	**54**	53.34 N	13.12 E
Weiting	**106**	31.22 N	120.47 E
Weitmar ◆[8]	**263**	51.27 N	7.12 E
Weitnau	**58**	47.38 N	10.07 E
Weitou	**100**	24.34 N	118.34 E
Weitouwan C	**100**	24.34 N	118.30 E
Weitra	**61**	48.42 N	14.54 E
Weituo	**107**	30.03 N	106.08 E
Weitzgrund	**54**	52.11 N	12.32 E
Weixdorf	**54**	51.09 N	13.48 E
Weixi	**102**	27.14 N	99.12 E
Weixian, Zhg.	**98**	36.57 N	115.15 E
Weixian, Zhg.	**98**	36.52 N	119.07 E
Weixian, Zhg.	**98**	36.22 N	114.56 E
Weixin	**102**	27.48 N	105.06 E
Weiyuan, Zhg.	**100**	30.09 N	115.15 E
Weiyuan, Zhg.	**107**	29.33 N	104.39 E
Weiyuanbao	**98**	42.39 N	124.16 E
Weiz	**61**	47.13 N	15.37 E
Weizhoudao I	**102**	21.03 N	109.04 E
Weizhuang	**105**	39.02 N	115.20 E
Weizi	**98**	40.04 N	123.10 E
Weizigou, Zhg.	**104**	42.05 N	120.34 E
Weizigou, Zhg.	**104**	42.25 N	122.47 E
Weizigou, Zhg.	**104**	41.05 N	120.38 E
Weizigoumen	**98**	41.58 N	116.49 E
Weizixi	**107**	30.11 N	106.03 E
Weiziyu	**98**	41.29 N	124.31 E
Wejherowo	**30**	54.37 N	18.15 E
Wekiva ≃	**220**	28.52 N	81.23 W
Wekiwa Springs State Park ♠	**220**	28.43 N	81.27 W
Wekoewa Punt ≻	**241s**	12.14 N	68.24 W
Wekusko Lake ⊜	**184**	54.45 N	99.50 W
Welaka	**192**	29.29 N	81.40 W
Welbourn Hill	**162**	27.21 S	134.06 E
Welch, Okla., U.S.	**196**	36.52 N	95.06 W
Welch, Tex., U.S.	**196**	32.56 N	102.08 W
Welch, W. Va., U.S.	**192**	37.25 N	81.31 W
Welch Creek ≃	**282**	37.32 N	121.51 W
Welches	**224**	45.20 N	121.58 W
Welch Peak ∧	**224**	49.10 N	121.36 W
Welcome, Ont., Can.	**212**	43.58 N	78.21 W
Welcome, Minn., U.S.	**198**	43.40 N	94.37 W
Welcome, S.C., U.S.	**192**	34.49 N	82.26 W
Welcome Lake ⊜	**212**	45.25 N	78.25 W

ENGLISH

Name	Page	Lat.°′	Long.°′
Welcome Monument ⊥	**269e**	6.11 S	106.49 E
Welden	**58**	48.27 N	10.40 E
Weldon, Sask., Can.	**184**	53.00 N	105.08 W
Weldon, Ill., U.S.	**219**	40.07 N	88.45 W
Weldon, N.C., U.S.	**192**	36.25 N	77.36 W
Weldon, Tex., U.S.	**222**	31.01 N	95.34 W
Weldon ≃	**194**	40.06 N	93.38 W
Weldona	**198**	40.21 N	103.58 W
Weldon Brook ≃	**276**	40.58 N	74.35 W
Weldya	**144**	11.50 N	39.36 E
Weleetka	**196**	35.20 N	96.08 W
Welega □[4]	**144**	9.40 N	35.50 E
Weleri	**115a**	6.58 S	110.04 E
Welfare Island I	**276**	40.45 N	73.57 W
Welgedag	**273d**	26.12 S	28.30 E
Welhamgreen	**260**	51.44 N	0.13 W
Welheim ◆[8]	**263**	51.32 N	6.59 E
Weligama	**122**	5.58 N	80.25 E
Welikaja → Velikaja ≃	**76**	57.48 N	28.20 E
Welkenraedt	**56**	50.40 N	5.59 E
Welker Seamount ⊹[3]	**16**	55.10 N	140.20 W
Welkite	**144**	8.15 N	37.50 E
Wel Koban	**144**	2.33 N	44.20 E
Welkom	**158**	27.59 S	26.45 E
Well	**52**	51.34 N	6.06 E
Welland	**212**	42.59 N	79.15 W
Welland ≃, Ont., Can.	**212**	43.04 N	79.03 W
Welland ≃, Eng., U.K.	**42**	52.53 N	0.02 E
Welland Canal ☲	**212**	43.14 N	79.13 W
Welland Junction	**284a**	42.57 N	79.14 W
Wellard	**168a**	32.19 S	115.50 E
Wellaune	**54**	51.34 N	12.33 E
Wellborn, Fla., U.S.	**192**	30.14 N	82.49 W
Wellborn, Tex., U.S.	**222**	30.32 N	96.18 W
Wellerode	**56**	51.14 N	9.34 E
Wellers Bay C	**212**	44.00 N	77.34 W
Wellers Creek ≃	**278**	42.03 N	87.53 W
Wellesbourne	**42**	52.12 N	1.35 W
Welles Harbor C	**174g**	28.12 N	177.26 W
Wellesley, Ont., Can.	**212**	43.28 N	80.45 W
Wellesley, Mass., U.S.	**207**	42.18 N	71.17 W
Wellesley College ʊ[2]	**283**	42.18 N	71.19 W
Wellesley Hills	**283**	42.19 N	71.17 W
Wellesley Island I	**212**	44.19 N	75.58 W
Wellesley Islands II	**164**	16.42 S	139.30 E
Wellesley Island State Park ♠	**212**	44.19 N	76.01 W
Wellesley Lake ⊜	**180**	62.30 N	139.50 W
Wellfleet	**207**	41.56 N	70.02 W
Wellheim	**60**	48.48 N	11.06 E
Well Hill	**260**	51.21 N	0.09 E
Wellin	**56**	50.05 N	5.07 E
Welling ◆[8]	**260**	51.28 N	0.07 E
Wellingborough	**42**	52.19 N	0.42 W
Wellinghofen ◆[8]	**263**	51.28 N	7.29 E
Wellington, Austl.	**166**	32.33 S	148.57 E
Wellington, B.C., Can.	**224**	49.13 N	124.01 W
Wellington, Ont., Can.	**212**	43.57 N	77.21 W
Wellington, N.Z.	**172**	41.18 S	174.47 E
Wellington, S. Afr.	**158**	33.38 S	18.57 E
Wellington, Eng., U.K.	**42**	52.43 N	2.31 W
Wellington, Eng., U.K.	**42**	50.59 N	3.14 W
Wellington, Colo., U.S.	**200**	40.42 N	105.00 W
Wellington, Ill., U.S.	**216**	40.32 N	87.41 W
Wellington, Kans., U.S.	**198**	37.16 N	97.24 W
Wellington, Mo., U.S.	**194**	39.08 N	93.59 W
Wellington, Nev., U.S.	**226**	38.45 N	119.22 W
Wellington, Ohio, U.S.	**214**	41.10 N	82.13 W
Wellington, Tex., U.S.	**196**	34.51 N	100.13 W
Wellington, Utah, U.S.	**200**	39.32 N	110.44 W
Wellington □[6]	**212**	43.50 N	80.30 W
Wellington, Isla I	**254**	49.20 S	74.40 W
Wellington Bay C, N.W. Ter., Can.	**176**	69.30 N	106.30 W
Wellington Bay C, Ont., Can.	**212**	43.56 N	77.21 W
Wellington Channel)(	**176**	75.00 N	93.00 W
Wellington Point	**171a**	27.29 S	153.15 E
Wellington Reservoir ⊜[1]	**168a**	33.24 S	116.01 E
Wellington Station	**186**	46.27 N	64.00 W
Wellman, Iowa, U.S.	**190**	41.28 N	91.50 W
Wellman, Tex., U.S.	**196**	33.03 N	102.26 W
Wells, B.C., Can.	**182**	53.06 N	121.34 W
Wells, Eng., U.K.	**42**	51.13 N	2.39 W
Wells, Mich., U.S.	**190**	45.47 N	87.04 W
Wells, Minn., U.S.	**190**	43.44 N	93.44 W
Wells, Nev., U.S.	**204**	41.07 N	114.58 W
Wells, N.Y., U.S.	**210**	43.24 N	74.17 W
Wells, Tex., U.S.	**222**	31.29 N	94.56 W
Wells □[6]	**216**	40.44 N	85.11 W
Wells, Lake ⊜	**162**	26.43 S	123.10 E
Wells, Mount ∧[2]	**162**	17.26 S	127.14 E
Wellsboro	**210**	41.45 N	77.18 W
Wells Bridge	**210**	42.22 N	75.15 W
Wellsburg, Iowa, U.S.	**190**	42.26 N	92.56 W
Wellsburg, N.Y., U.S.	**210**	42.01 N	76.44 W
Wellsburg, W. Va., U.S.	**214**	40.16 N	80.37 W
Wells Cathedral ʊ[1]	**42**	51.13 N	2.39 W
Wellsford	**172**	36.17 S	174.31 E
Wells Gray Provincial Park ♠	**182**	52.20 N	120.00 W
Wells Lake ⊜	**184**	57.15 N	101.00 W
Wells-next-the-Sea	**42**	52.58 N	0.51 E
Wells Point ≻	**284b**	39.17 N	76.23 W
Wells State Park ♠	**207**	42.09 N	72.05 W
Wells Tannery	**214**	40.05 N	78.10 W
Wellston	**188**	39.07 N	82.32 W
Wellsville, Kans., U.S.	**198**	38.43 N	95.05 W
Wellsville, Mo., U.S.	**219**	39.04 N	91.34 W
Wellsville, N.Y., U.S.	**210**	42.07 N	77.57 W
Wellsville, Ohio, U.S.	**214**	40.36 N	80.39 W
Wellsville, Pa., U.S.	**208**	40.03 N	76.56 W
Wellsville, Utah, U.S.	**200**	41.38 N	111.56 W
Wellton	**200**	32.40 N	114.08 W
Welmel ≃	**144**	5.38 N	40.47 E
Welmen	**263**	51.39 N	6.41 E
Welney	**42**	52.31 N	0.15 E
Welo	**144**	9.27 N	48.57 E
Welo □[4]	**144**	11.50 N	40.20 E
Wels	**61**	48.10 N	14.02 E
Welschbillig	**56**	49.51 N	6.34 E
Welse ≃	**54**	53.10 N	14.18 E
Welsford	**186**	45.27 N	66.20 W
Welsh	**194**	30.14 N	92.49 W
Wel Shimbiro	**144**	2.22 N	44.20 E
Welshpool, Austl.	**169**	38.39 S	146.26 E
Welshpool, Wales, U.K.	**42**	52.40 N	3.09 W
Welsickendorf	**54**	51.54 N	13.08 E
Welsleben	**54**	52.00 N	11.38 E
Weltenburg	**60**	48.54 N	11.50 E
Welverdiend	**158**	26.23 S	27.16 E
Welwitschia	**156**	20.21 S	14.57 E
Welwyn Garden City	**42**	51.50 N	0.13 W
Welwyn Hatfield □[8]	**260**	51.47 N	0.12 W
Welzheim	**56**	48.53 N	9.38 E

DEUTSCH

Name	Seite	Breite°′	Länge°′ E=Ost
Welzow	**54**	51.34 N	14.10 E
Wem	**42**	52.51 N	2.44 W
Wema	**152**	0.26 S	21.38 E
Wembere ≃	**154**	4.10 S	34.11 E
Wembley	**182**	55.09 N	119.08 W
Wembley ◆[8]	**260**	51.33 N	0.18 W
Wembley Stadium ♠, S. Afr.	**273d**	26.14 S	28.03 E
Wembley Stadium ♠, Eng., U.K.	**260**	51.33 N	0.17 W
Wemding	**56**	48.52 N	10.43 E
Wemeldinge	**52**	51.31 N	4.00 E
Wemme	**224**	45.21 N	121.58 W
Wemmetsweiler	**56**	49.22 N	7.05 E
Wemperhardt	**56**	50.09 N	6.05 E
Wen'an	**105**	38.52 N	116.28 E
Wenas Creek ≃	**224**	46.42 N	120.35 W
Wenatchee	**202**	47.25 N	120.19 W
Wenatchee ≃	**202**	47.27 N	120.19 W
Wenatchee Lake ⊜	**224**	47.49 N	120.47 W
Wenatchee Mountains ⩕	**202**	47.20 N	120.45 W
Wenchang	**110**	19.41 N	110.48 E
Wencheng	**100**	27.50 N	120.05 E
Wenchi	**150**	7.42 N	2.07 W
Wenchow → Wenzhou	**100**	28.01 N	120.39 E
Wendaohezi	**104**	41.46 N	124.09 E
Wendel	**279b**	40.18 N	79.41 W
Wendell, Idaho, U.S.	**202**	42.46 N	114.42 W
Wendell, N.C., U.S.	**192**	35.47 N	78.22 W
Wendelsheim	**56**	49.46 N	7.59 E
Wendelstein	**60**	49.21 N	11.08 E
Wendelstein ∧	**64**	47.42 N	12.00 E
Wendelville	**284a**	43.04 N	78.47 W
Wenden, B.R.D.	**52**	52.19 N	10.30 E
Wenden, Ariz., U.S.	**200**	33.49 N	113.32 W
Wendeng	**98**	37.12 N	122.04 E
Wendesi	**164**	2.25 S	134.13 E
Wendilou	**104**	41.13 N	121.08 E
Wendisch Rietz	**54**	52.13 N	14.01 E
Wendish Baggendorf	**54**	54.04 N	12.56 E
Wendji	**152**	0.04 S	18.10 E
Wendlingen am Neckar	**56**	48.40 N	9.23 E
Wendo	**144**	6.38 N	38.27 E
Wendover, Eng., U.K.	**42**	51.46 N	0.46 W
Wendover, Utah, U.S.	**200**	40.44 N	114.02 W
Wenduine	**50**	51.18 N	3.05 E
Wenebegon ≃	**190**	46.53 N	83.12 W
Wenebegon Lake ⊜	**190**	47.24 N	83.08 W
Wenfang	**100**	28.02 N	117.19 E
Weng	**60**	48.40 N	12.23 E
Weng'an	**102**	26.53 N	107.22 E
Wengbo	**120**	31.23 N	86.40 E
Wengcheng	**100**	24.23 N	113.51 E
Wengdang	**124**	28.50 N	90.03 E
Wenge	**152**	0.03 N	24.01 E
Wengen, B.R.D.	**58**	47.41 N	10.09 E
Wengen, Schw.	**58**	46.36 N	7.56 E
Wengern	**263**	51.24 N	7.21 E
Wengjiafou	**106**	30.23 N	120.21 E
Wengjiang ≃	**100**	24.10 N	113.24 E
Wengongchang	**107**	30.11 N	104.09 E
Wenguantun	**104**	41.53 N	123.30 E
Wengyang	**100**	28.03 N	120.58 E
Wengyuan (Longxianwei)	**100**	24.21 N	114.08 E
Wenham	**207**	42.36 N	70.53 W
Wenham Lake ⊜	**283**	42.35 N	70.53 W
Wenham Swamp ☷	**283**	42.37 N	70.55 W
Wenhe ≃	**98**	36.38 N	119.22 E
Wenheng	**100**	25.42 N	116.45 E
Wenjiachang	**107**	30.41 N	103.55 E
Wenjiang	**107**	30.42 N	103.49 E
Wenjiangban	**100**	26.01 N	117.51 E
Wenjiazhen	**100**	28.20 N	116.05 E
Wenling	**100**	28.22 N	121.20 E
Wenlock	**164**	13.06 S	142.58 E
Wenlock ≃	**164**	12.02 S	141.55 E
Wenlock Edge ⊥[4]	**42**	52.30 N	2.40 W
Wenlong	**100**	24.48 N	114.54 E
Wenmingsi	**100**	25.33 N	113.20 E
Wennigsen	**52**	52.16 N	9.34 E
Wenning ≃	**44**	54.07 N	2.39 W
Wennington ◆[8]	**260**	51.30 N	0.13 E
Wenniu	**102**	24.18 N	104.31 E
Wenns	**58**	47.10 N	10.44 E
Wenona, Ill., U.S.	**216**	41.03 N	89.03 W
Wenona, Md., U.S.	**208**	38.08 N	75.57 W
Wenonah	**208**	39.48 N	75.09 W
Wenquan, Zhg.	**86**	44.59 N	81.04 E
Wenquan, Zhg.	**100**	23.37 N	113.43 E
Wenquansi	**104**	41.20 N	124.04 E
Wenshan	**102**	23.30 N	104.20 E
Wenshang	**98**	35.44 N	116.29 E
Wenshui, Zhg.	**102**	28.28 N	106.30 E
Wenshui, Zhg.	**102**	37.28 N	112.01 E
Wensickendorf	**264a**	52.45 N	13.23 E
Wensleydale ∨	**44**	54.19 N	2.00 W
Wensum ≃	**42**	52.37 N	1.19 E
Went ≃	**44**	53.39 N	0.59 W
Wentorf	**52**	53.30 N	10.15 E
Wentworth, Austl.	**166**	34.07 S	141.55 E
Wentworth, N.C., U.S.	**192**	36.24 N	79.53 W
Wentworth, S. Dak., U.S.	**198**	44.00 N	96.58 W
Wentworth □[6]	**212**	43.15 N	80.00 W
Wentworth Falls	**170**	33.43 S	150.22 E
Wentworth Park	**273d**	26.07 S	27.48 E
Wentworthville	**274a**	33.48 S	150.58 E
Wentzville	**219**	38.49 N	90.51 W
Wenxi	**102**	35.26 N	111.11 E
Wenxian	**102**	32.58 N	104.46 E
Wenxiang	**102**	34.37 N	110.45 E
Wenxingchang	**107**	29.52 N	106.29 E
Wenyuhe ≃	**105**	39.59 N	116.38 E
Wenzenbach	**60**	49.05 N	12.12 E
Wenzhou	**100**	28.01 N	120.39 E
Wenzhouwan C	**100**	27.56 N	121.00 E
Wenzhu	**100**	26.58 N	114.04 E
Wenzhuangzicun	**104**	42.16 N	123.51 E
Weobley	**42**	52.09 N	2.51 W
Weohyakapka, Lake ⊜	**220**	27.49 N	81.25 W
Wepener	**158**	29.46 S	27.00 E
Wépion	**56**	50.25 N	4.52 E
Weppersdorf	**61**	47.35 N	16.26 E
Wequetequock	**207**	41.22 N	71.52 W
Wera ≃	**115b**	8.20 S	120.43 E
Werbellin	**54**	52.53 N	13.41 E
Werbellinsee ⊜	**54**	52.54 N	13.40 E
Werben	**54**	52.52 N	11.58 E
Werbomont	**56**	50.23 N	5.41 E
Werchojansker Gebirge → Verchojanskij Chrebet ⩕	**74**	67.00 N	129.00 E
Werda	**156**	25.15 S	23.16 E
Werdau	**54**	50.44 N	12.22 E
Werden ◆[8]	**263**	51.23 N	7.00 E
Werder	**54**	52.23 N	12.56 E
Werder ◆[1]	**54**	53.40 N	13.25 E
Werdohl	**56**	51.15 N	7.45 E
Weregta	**144**	1.30 N	42.28 E
Were Ilu	**144**	10.37 N	39.28 E
Werfen	**64**	47.28 N	13.11 E
Weri	**164**	3.12 S	132.38 E
Werkel	**56**	51.09 N	9.18 E
Werkendam	**52**	51.49 N	4.53 E
Werl	**52**	51.33 N	7.54 E
Werlaburgdorf	**54**	52.04 N	10.31 E
Werl-Aspe	**52**	52.04 N	8.43 E

Symbols in the index entries represent the broad categories identified in the key at the right. Symbols with superior numbers (⩕[2]) identify subcategories (see complete key on page *I* · *30*).

Kartensymbole in dem Registerverzeichnis stellen die rechts in Schlüssel erklärten Kategorien dar. Symbole mit hochgestellten Ziffern (⩕[2]) bezeichnen Unterabteilungen einer Kategorie (vgl. vollständiger Schlüssel auf Seite *I* · *30*).

Los símbolos incluídos en el texto del índice representan las grandes categorias identificadas con la clave a la derecha. Los símbolos con numeros en su parte superior (⩕[2]) identifican las subcategorías (véase la clave completa en la página *I* · *30*).

Les symboles de l'index représentent les catégories indiquées dans la légende à droite. Les symboles suivis d'un indice (⩕[2]) représentent des sous-catégories (voir légende complète à la page *I* · *30*).

Os símbolos incluídos no texto do índice representam as grandes categorias identificadas com a chave à direita. Os símbolos com números em sua parte superior (⩕[2]) identificam as subcategorias (veja-se a chave completa à página *I* · *30*).

Symbol	English	Deutsch	Español	Français	Português
∧	Mountain	Berg	Montaña	Montagne	Montanha
⩕	Mountains	Berge	Montañas	Montagnes	Montanhas
)(	Pass	Pass	Paso	Col	Passo
∨	Valley, Canyon	Tal, Cañon	Valle, Cañón	Vallée, Canyon	Vale, Canhão
≚	Plain	Ebene	Llano	Plaine	Planície
≻	Cape	Kap	Cabo	Cap	Cabo
I	Island	Insel	Isla	Île	Ilha
II	Islands	Inseln	Islas	Îles	Ilhas
⊥	Other Topographic Features	Andere Topographische Objekte	Otros Elementos Topográficos	Autres données topographiques	Outros Elementos Topográficos

ESPAÑOL · FRANÇAIS · PORTUGUÊS

Nombre / Nom / Nome	Página / Page	Lat.°	Long.° W=Oeste / W=Ouest
Werleshausen	56	51.19 N	9.54 E
Werlte	52	52.51 N	7.41 E
Wermelskirchen	56	51.08 N	7.13 E
Wermsdorf	54	51.17 N	12.56 E
Wern ≃	56	50.02 N	9.44 E
Wernadinga	166	18.07 S	139.58 E
Wernau	56	48.41 N	9.25 E
Wernberg, B.R.D.	60	49.32 N	12.10 E
Wernberg, Öst.	64	46.37 N	13.56 E
Werne ↞8	263	51.29 N	7.18 E
Werne an der Lippe	52	51.40 N	7.38 E
Werneck, Bra.	256	22.13 S	43.19 W
Werneck, B.R.D.	56	49.59 N	10.05 E
Werneuchen	54	52.38 N	13.44 E
Wernigerode	54	51.50 N	10.47 E
Wernitz ≃	264a	52.34 N	12.55 E
Wernsdorf	264a	52.22 N	13.43 E
Wernsdorfer See @	264a	52.23 N	13.42 E
Wernshausen	54	50.43 N	10.21 E
Wernstein	60	48.30 N	13.28 E
Werra ≃	30	51.26 N	9.39 E
Werribee	169	37.54 S	144.40 E
Werribee ≃	169	37.59 S	144.41 E
Werribee Gorge National Park ♠	169	37.40 S	144.21 E
Werribee South	169	37.56 S	144.42 E
Werries	52	51.41 N	7.53 E
Werrimull	166	34.24 S	141.26 E
Werrington	274a	33.45 S	150.46 E
Werris Creek	166	31.21 S	150.39 E
Werschweiler	56	49.27 N	7.13 E
Wersen	52	52.18 N	7.56 E
Wersten ↞8	263	51.11 N	6.49 E
Wertach	58	47.36 N	10.25 E
Wertach ≃	58	48.24 N	10.53 E
Wertheim	56	49.46 N	9.31 E
Werther, B.R.D.	52	52.04 N	8.24 E
Werther, D.D.R.	54	51.29 N	10.46 E
Wertingen	56	48.34 N	10.41 E
Wervershoof	52	52.44 N	5.09 E
Wervik	50	50.47 N	3.02 E
Wervin	262	53.15 N	2.52 W
Werwaru	164	8.13 S	128.11 E
Weschnitz ≃	56	49.43 N	8.24 E
Wesconnett	192	30.14 N	81.44 W
Weseke	52	51.54 N	6.51 E
Wesel	52	51.40 N	6.38 E
Wesel-Datteln-Kanal ☲	263	51.38 N	6.36 E
Wesenberg	54	53.17 N	12.58 E
Wesendahl	264a	52.36 N	13.49 E
Wesendorf	52	52.35 N	10.31 E
Wesenufer	60	48.27 N	13.49 E
Weser ≃	52	53.32 N	8.34 E
Wesergebirge ⩘	52	52.15 N	9.10 E
Wesham	262	53.48 N	2.53 W
Wesickaman Creek ≃	285	39.44 N	74.43 W
Wesiri	112	7.35 S	126.38 E
Weskan	198	38.41 N	101.57 W
Weslaco	196	26.09 N	97.59 W
Weslemkoon Lake @	212	45.02 N	77.25 W
Wesley, Dom.	240d	15.34 N	61.19 W
Wesley, Iowa, U.S.	190	43.05 N	93.59 W
Wesleyville, Newf., Can.	186	49.09 N	53.34 W
Wesleyville, Pa., U.S.	214	42.08 N	80.01 W
Wessel, Cape ≻	164	10.59 S	136.46 E
Wesseling	56	50.49 N	6.58 E
Wessel Islands II	164	11.30 S	136.25 E
Wesselsbron	158	27.50 S	26.23 E
Wesselsvlei	158	27.23 S	23.47 E
Wessington	198	44.27 N	98.42 W
Wessington Springs	198	44.05 N	98.34 W
Wessobrunn	64	47.52 N	11.01 E
Wesson	194	31.42 N	90.23 W
Wessum	52	52.05 N	6.58 E
West, Miss., U.S.	194	33.12 N	89.47 W
West, Tex., U.S.	222	31.48 N	97.06 W
West ≃, N.Y., U.S.	210	42.41 N	77.22 W
West ≃, Vt., U.S.	188	42.52 N	72.33 W
West Abington	207	42.08 N	70.59 W
Westacres	216	42.35 N	83.26 W
West Acton	207	42.29 N	71.28 W
West Alexander	214	40.06 N	80.31 W
West Alexandria	218	39.45 N	84.32 W
Westall, Point ≻	162	32.55 S	134.04 E
West Allen ≃	44	54.55 N	2.19 W
West Allis	216	43.01 N	88.00 W
Westalton	219	38.52 N	90.13 W
West Amityville	276	40.41 N	73.26 W
West Andover	207	42.39 N	71.10 W
West Athens	280	33.55 N	118.18 W
West Atlantic City	208	39.23 N	74.28 W
West Auckland	44	54.38 N	1.43 W
West Australian Basin ↞1	12	20.00 S	100.00 E
West Babylon	210	40.43 N	73.22 W
Westbahnhof ↞5	264b	48.11 N	16.20 E
West Baines ≃	164	15.36 S	129.58 E
West Bangor	210	40.52 N	75.14 W
Westbank	182	49.50 N	119.38 W
West Barnstable	207	41.42 N	70.23 W
West Barrington	207	41.45 N	71.21 W
West Bay, N.S., Can.	186	45.43 N	61.10 W
Westbay, Fla., U.S.	194	30.17 N	85.52 W
West Bay C, Fla., U.S.	194	30.16 N	85.47 W
West Bay C, Tex., U.S.	222	29.15 N	94.57 W
West Bay Shore	276	40.42 N	73.17 W
West Belmar	208	40.10 N	74.02 W
West Bend, Iowa, U.S.	198	42.57 N	94.27 W
West Bend, Wis., U.S.	190	43.25 N	88.11 W
West Bengal □3	124	24.00 N	88.00 E
West Bergholt	42	51.55 N	0.51 E
West-Berlin → Berlin (West), B.R.D.	264a	52.31 N	13.24 E
West Berlin, N.J., U.S.	208	39.49 N	74.57 W
West-Berlin □3	264a	52.30 N	13.15 E
West Bernard Creek ≃	222	29.23 N	95.58 W
Westbevern	52	52.01 N	7.47 E
West Bhāgīrath Plain ≃	126	23.30 N	88.00 E
West Bijou Creek ≃	198	39.51 N	104.08 W
West Billerica	283	42.33 N	71.19 W
West Blocton	194	33.07 N	87.07 W
West Bloomfield	210	42.54 N	77.32 W
West Bolivar	214	40.23 N	79.10 W
Westborough	207	42.16 N	71.37 W
Westbourne	184	50.09 N	98.35 W
West Bow Creek ≃	198	42.46 N	97.08 W
West Boxford	283	42.42 N	71.04 W
West Boylston	207	42.22 N	71.47 W
West Bradenton	220	27.30 N	82.37 W
West Branch, Iowa, U.S.	190	41.40 N	91.20 W
West Branch, Mich., U.S.	190	44.17 N	84.14 W
West Branch Reservoir @1	210	41.25 N	73.42 W
West Branch State Park ♠	214	41.07 N	81.05 W
Westbridge	182	49.10 N	118.59 W
West Bridgewater	207	42.01 N	71.00 W
West Bridgford	42	52.56 N	1.08 W
West Bristol	285	40.06 N	74.53 W
West Bromwich	42	52.31 N	1.56 W
Westbrook, Austl.	171a	27.36 S	151.52 E
Westbrook, Ont., Can.	212	44.16 N	76.38 W
Westbrook, Conn., U.S.	207	41.17 N	72.27 W
Westbrook, Maine, U.S.	188	43.41 N	70.21 W
Westbrook, Minn., U.S.	198	44.03 N	95.26 W
Westbrook, Tex., U.S.	196	32.21 N	101.01 W
West Brook ≃	276	41.04 N	74.18 W
West Brookfield	207	42.14 N	72.09 W
Westbrookville	210	41.30 N	74.34 W
West Burlington, Iowa, U.S.	190	40.49 N	91.09 W
West Burlington, N.Y., U.S.	210	42.42 N	75.11 W
West Burra I	46a	60.05 N	1.21 W
Westbury, Eng., U.K.	42	52.41 N	2.57 W
Westbury, Eng., U.K.	42	51.16 N	2.11 W
Westbury, N.Y., U.S.	276	40.45 N	73.35 W
Westbury-on-Severn	42	51.50 N	2.24 W
West Butte Λ	202	48.57 N	111.32 W
Westby, Austl.	171b	35.30 S	147.25 E
Westby, Mont., U.S.	198	48.52 N	104.03 W
Westby, Wis., U.S.	190	43.39 N	90.51 W
West Cache Creek ≃	196	34.13 N	98.23 W
West Caicos I	238	21.39 N	72.28 W
West Calder	46	55.52 N	3.35 W
West Caldwell	276	40.51 N	74.17 W
West Cameron	208	40.45 N	76.58 W
West Camp	210	42.07 N	73.56 W
West Canada Creek ≃	210	43.01 N	74.58 W
West Cape ≻	172	45.54 S	166.26 E
West Cape Howe ≻	162	35.08 S	117.36 E
West Cape May	208	38.56 N	74.56 W
West Caroline Basin ↞1	14	5.00 N	139.00 E
West Carrollton	218	39.40 N	84.15 W
West Carson	280	33.50 N	118.18 W
West Carthage	212	43.59 N	75.38 W
West Catfish Creek ≃	212	42.46 N	81.04 W
West Channel ≃1	180	68.51 N	136.10 W
Westchester, Ill., U.S.	216	41.51 N	87.53 W
West Chester, Pa., U.S.	285	39.58 N	75.36 W
Westchester, Va., U.S.	284c	38.51 N	77.16 W
Westchester □6	210	41.02 N	73.46 W
Westchester ↞8, Calif., U.S.	280	33.55 N	118.25 W
Westchester ↞8, N.Y., U.S.	276	40.51 N	73.52 W
West Chester Airport ⊠	285	39.59 N	75.35 W
Westchester County Airport ⊠	207	41.04 N	73.43 W
Westchester Creek ≃	276	40.48 N	73.51 W
West Chester State College ʊ2	285	39.57 N	75.36 W
West Chicago	216	41.53 N	88.12 W
West Clandon	260	51.15 N	0.30 W
West Clarksville	210	42.08 N	78.15 W
West Clear Creek ≃	200	34.34 N	111.51 W
West Cleddau ≃	42	51.46 N	4.54 W
Westcliff ↞8	273d	26.11 S	28.02 E
Westcliffe	200	38.08 N	105.28 W
Westcliff-on-Sea	260	51.32 N	0.41 E
West College Corner	218	39.34 N	84.49 W
West Collingswood Heights	285	39.59 N	75.07 W
West Columbia, S.C., U.S.	192	34.00 N	81.04 W
West Columbia, Tex., U.S.	222	29.09 N	95.39 W
West Concord, Mass., U.S.	207	42.27 N	71.24 W
West Concord, Minn., U.S.	190	44.09 N	92.54 W
West Conshohocken	285	40.04 N	75.19 W
West Cote Blanche Bay C	194	29.40 N	91.45 W
Westcott	260	51.13 N	0.22 W
Westcott Cove C	276	41.02 N	73.30 W
West Covina	228	34.05 N	117.58 W
West Creek	208	39.38 N	74.18 W
West Creek ≃, Ind., U.S.	216	41.12 N	87.30 W
West Creek ≃, Pa., U.S.	214	41.30 N	78.15 W
Westdale, Ill., U.S.	278	41.56 N	87.55 W
Westdale, Mass., U.S.	283	42.01 N	70.59 W
Westdale, N.Y., U.S.	210	43.23 N	75.49 W
West Danby	210	42.19 N	76.32 W
West Davenport	210	42.27 N	74.58 W
West Deane Park ♠	275b	43.40 N	79.34 W
West Decatur	214	40.56 N	78.17 W
West Demerara-Essequibo Coast □5	246	7.00 N	58.40 W
Westdene ↞8	273d	26.11 S	27.59 E
West Dennis	207	41.40 N	70.10 W
West Derby ↞8	262	53.26 N	2.54 W
West Derry	214	40.20 N	79.20 W
West Des Moines	190	41.35 N	93.43 W
West Dināipur □5	124	25.30 N	88.20 E
West Ditch ☲	276	40.56 N	74.19 W
West Dolores ≃	200	37.35 N	108.21 W
West Don ≃	275b	43.43 N	79.20 W
West Drayton ↞8	260	51.30 N	0.29 W
West Duffin Creek ≃	212	43.51 N	79.04 W
West Duxbury	283	42.03 N	70.47 W
West Eaton	210	42.51 N	75.39 W
Westecunk Creek ≃	208	39.37 N	74.16 W
West Edmeston	210	42.46 N	75.17 W
West Elk Mountains ⩘	200	38.40 N	107.15 W
West Elk Peak Λ	200	38.43 N	107.13 W
West Elkton	218	39.35 N	84.33 W
West Ellicott	214	42.05 N	79.16 W
West Elmira	210	42.05 N	76.51 W
West End, Ba.	238	26.41 N	78.58 W
West End, Eng., U.K.	260	51.44 N	0.04 W
West End, Eng., U.K.	260	51.20 N	0.38 W
West End, Ark., U.S.	194	34.13 N	92.03 W
West End, Ill., U.S.	216	42.17 N	89.09 W
West End, N.C., U.S.	192	35.15 N	79.33 W
West End, N.Y., U.S.	210	42.28 N	75.05 W
West End ↞8, Eng., U.K.	260	51.32 N	0.24 W
West End ↞8, Pa., U.S.	279b	40.27 N	80.02 W
Westende, Bel.	50	51.10 N	2.46 E
Westende, B.R.D.	263	51.25 N	7.24 E
Westendorf	64	47.26 N	12.13 E
Westenfeld ↞8	263	51.28 N	7.09 E
Westenholz	52	51.45 N	8.28 E
Westenschouwen	52	51.41 N	3.42 E
Westerbauer ↞8	263	51.20 N	7.23 E
Westerblokker	52	52.39 N	5.08 E
Westerbönen	263	51.36 N	7.46 E
Westerbork	52	52.51 N	6.37 E
Westerburg	56	50.33 N	7.58 E
Westercelle	52	52.36 N	10.05 E
Westerdale	46	58.27 N	3.30 W
Westeregeln	54	51.57 N	11.23 E
Westerham	42	51.16 N	0.05 E
Westerhausen	54	51.48 N	11.03 E
Westerholt	52	51.36 N	7.05 E
Westerholz ↞3	263	51.32 N	7.28 E
Westerich □9	56	49.15 N	7.20 E
Westerkappeln	52	52.18 N	7.52 E
Westerland	30	54.54 N	8.18 E
Westerlo, Bel.	56	51.05 N	4.55 E
Westerlo, N.Y., U.S.	210	42.31 N	74.03 W
Westerly	207	41.22 N	71.50 W
Western	198	40.24 N	97.12 W
Western □3	150	7.45 N	4.00 E
Western □4, Ghana	150	5.30 N	2.30 W
Western □4, Kenya	154	0.30 N	34.35 E
Western (Area) □4, S.L.	150	8.20 N	13.00 W
Western □4, Zam.	152	16.00 S	24.00 E
Western □5	164	7.00 S	142.00 E
Western ≃	166	22.22 S	142.25 E
Western Australia □3	160	25.00 S	122.00 E
Western Branch ≃	284c	38.55 N	76.48 W
Western Canal ☲	226	39.28 N	121.35 W
Western Channel ⊔	98	34.40 N	129.00 E
Western Cove C	168b	35.43 S	137.38 E
Western Desert → al-Gharbīyah, Aṣ-Ṣaḥrā' ↞2	140	27.00 N	27.00 E
Western Division □5, Fiji	175g	18.00 S	177.30 E
Western Division □5, Sol.is.	175e	8.00 S	157.00 E
Western Ghāts ⩘	122	14.00 N	75.00 E
Western Highlands □5	164	5.30 S	143.30 E
Western Isles Islands □4	46	57.40 N	7.00 W
Westernport	188	39.29 N	79.03 W
Western Port C	169	38.25 S	145.10 E
Western Sahara □2	134 / 148	24.30 N	13.00 W
Western Samoa □1	14 / 175a	13.55 S	172.00 W
Western Sayans → Zapadnyj Sajan ⩘	74	53.00 N	94.00 E
Western Shore	186	44.32 N	64.19 W
Western Springs	278	41.47 N	87.53 W
Westernville	210	43.18 N	75.23 W
Westerschelde C1	52	51.25 N	3.45 E
Westerstede	52	53.15 N	7.55 E
Westervelt	219	39.29 N	88.52 W
Westerville	214	40.08 N	82.56 W
Westerwald ⩘	56	50.40 N	7.55 E
West European Basin ↞1	10	46.00 N	15.00 W
West Exeter	210	42.48 N	75.09 W
West Fairview	208	40.17 N	76.55 W
Westfalen ↞1	52	51.50 N	7.30 E
Westfalenhalle ʊ	263	51.30 N	7.27 E
Westfalenpark ♠	263	51.30 N	7.28 E
West Falkland I	254	51.50 S	60.00 W
West Falls	210	42.42 N	78.41 W
West Falmouth	207	41.36 N	70.38 W
West Farleigh	260	51.15 N	0.27 E
West Farmington, Maine, U.S.	188	44.40 N	70.10 W
West Farmington, Ohio, U.S.	214	41.23 N	80.59 W
Westfield, Eng., U.K.	42	50.55 N	0.35 E
Westfield, Ill., U.S.	194	39.27 N	88.01 W
Westfield, Ind., U.S.	218	40.02 N	86.08 W
Westfield, Mass., U.S.	207	42.08 N	72.45 W
Westfield, N.J., U.S.	210	40.39 N	74.21 W
Westfield, N.Y., U.S.	214	42.19 N	79.35 W
Westfield, Pa., U.S.	210	41.55 N	77.32 W
Westfield, Tex., U.S.	222	30.01 N	95.24 W
Westfield, Wis., U.S.	190	43.53 N	89.30 W
Westfield ≃	207	42.05 N	72.35 W
Westfield, Middle Branch ≃	207	42.16 N	72.52 W
Westfield, West Branch ≃	207	42.13 N	72.52 W
Westfield Center	214	41.06 N	81.56 W
West Fiord C2	176	76.02 N	90.00 W
Westford, Mass., U.S.	283	42.35 N	71.26 W
Westford, N.Y., U.S.	210	42.39 N	74.48 W
West Foxboro	283	42.05 N	71.17 W
West Frankfort	194	37.54 N	88.55 W
West Friesland ↞1	52	52.45 N	4.50 E
West Frisian Islands → Waddeneilanden II	52	53.26 N	5.30 E
West Fulton	210	42.34 N	74.28 W
Westgate, Austl.	166	26.35 S	146.12 E
Westgate, Fla., U.S.	220	26.47 N	80.06 W
Westgate, Mich., U.S.	216	43.03 N	85.42 W
Westgate ↞9	279a	41.27 N	81.51 W
Westgate-on-Sea	42	51.23 N	1.21 E
West Genesee Terrace	210	43.03 N	76.16 W
West Germany → Germany, Federal Republic Of □1	30	51.00 N	9.00 E
West-Ghats → Western Ghāts ⩘	122	14.00 N	75.00 E
West Gilgo Beach	276	40.37 N	73.25 W
West Glacier	202	48.30 N	113.59 W
West Glamorgan □6	42	51.35 N	3.35 W
West Glens Falls	210	43.18 N	73.43 W
West Glenville	210	42.56 N	74.04 W
West Goshen	207	41.50 N	73.15 W
West Granby	207	41.57 N	72.50 W
West Groton	207	42.36 N	71.38 W
West Grove	208	39.49 N	75.50 W
Westham	208	37.35 N	77.33 W
West Ham ↞8	260	51.31 N	0.01 E
West Hamburg	208	40.33 N	76.00 W
West Ham Football Club ♠	260	51.32 N	0.02 E
Westham Island I	224	49.05 N	123.10 W
West Hamlin	188	38.17 N	82.12 W
Westhampton, N.Y., U.S.	207	40.49 N	72.39 W
Westhampton, Va., U.S.	284c	38.54 N	77.11 W
West Hanningfield	260	51.40 N	0.30 E
West Hanover	283	42.07 N	70.53 W
West Harbour	172	45.51 S	170.35 E
West Harrison	218	39.16 N	84.50 W
West Hartford	207	41.46 N	72.45 W
West Hartland	207	42.00 N	72.58 W
Westhausen	56	48.53 N	10.11 E
Westhaven, Calif., U.S.	204	41.03 N	124.06 W
West Haven, Conn., U.S.	207	41.16 N	72.57 W
Westhaven, Ill., U.S.	278	41.35 N	87.51 W
West Haverstraw	210	41.12 N	74.00 W
West Hazleton	210	40.58 N	76.00 W
Westhead	262	53.34 N	2.51 W
West Hebron	210	43.14 N	73.22 W
West Heidelberg	274b	37.45 S	145.02 E
Westheim	56	49.03 N	9.44 E
West Helena	194	34.33 N	90.39 W
Westhemmerde	263	51.33 N	7.47 E
West Hempstead	276	40.42 N	73.39 W
West Henrietta	210	43.02 N	77.40 W
West Hickory	214	41.34 N	79.25 W
West Highland	281	42.38 N	83.39 W
West Highland Creek ≃	275b	43.46 N	79.08 W
West Hill ↞8	275b	43.46 N	79.11 W
West Hills	228	34.27 N	119.17 W
Westhofen	263	51.25 N	7.31 E
Westhoff	222	29.12 N	97.28 W
Westhoffen	58	48.36 N	7.26 E
West Hollywood, Calif., U.S.	228	34.05 N	118.24 W
West Hollywood, Fla., U.S.	220	26.01 N	80.10 W
Westholme	224	49.52 N	123.42 W
West Homestead	279b	40.24 N	79.55 W
Westhope, N. Dak., U.S.	198	48.55 N	101.01 W
Westhope, Ohio, U.S.	216	41.18 N	83.57 W
West Horndon	260	51.34 N	0.21 E
West Horsley	260	51.16 N	0.27 W
Westhoughton	262	53.33 N	2.32 W
West Hoxton	274a	33.55 S	150.49 E
West Humber ≃	212	43.44 N	79.33 W
West Humble	260	51.15 N	0.20 W
West Huntington	276	40.51 N	73.27 W
West Hurley	210	42.00 N	74.06 W
Westhuyzen	158	27.30 S	25.27 E
West Hyde	260	51.37 N	0.30 W
West Ice Shelf ⍓	9	67.00 S	85.00 E
Westick	263	51.35 N	7.38 E
Westig	263	51.22 N	7.45 E
West-Indian Ridge ↞3	6	26.00 S	50.00 E
West Indies II	230	19.00 N	70.00 W
West Island I, Austl.	164	15.36 S	136.34 E
West Island I, Mass., U.S.	207	41.36 N	70.50 W
West Islip	210	40.42 N	73.19 W
West Jan Mayen Ridge ↞3	10	71.00 N	15.00 W
West Jefferson, N.C., U.S.	192	36.24 N	81.30 W
West Jefferson, Ohio, U.S.	218	39.57 N	83.16 W
Westkapelle, Bel.	50	51.19 N	3.18 E
Westkapelle, Ned.	52	51.32 N	3.27 E
West Keansburg	276	40.27 N	74.09 W
West Kettle ≃	182	49.07 N	119.00 W
West Kilbride	46	55.42 N	4.51 W
West Kildonan	184	49.56 N	97.07 W
West Kill	210	42.13 N	74.31 W
West Kingsdown	260	51.21 N	0.17 E
West Kingston	207	41.29 N	71.34 W
West Kirby	44	53.22 N	3.10 W
Westkirchen	52	51.53 N	8.02 E
West Kittanning	214	40.49 N	79.32 W
West Lafayette, Ind., U.S.	216	40.27 N	86.55 W
West Lafayette, Ohio, U.S.	214	40.17 N	81.45 W
Westlake, La., U.S.	194	30.15 N	93.15 W
Westlake, Ohio, U.S.	214	41.27 N	81.55 W
Westlake, Tex., U.S.	222	32.59 N	97.12 W
West Lake □4	154	2.00 S	31.30 E
West Lake @, Ont., Can.	212	43.56 N	77.17 W
West Lake @, Fla., U.S.	220	25.12 N	80.49 W
West Lake @, N.J., U.S.	276	40.58 N	74.22 W
West Lamma Channel ⊔	271d	22.13 N	114.04 E
West Lancashire □8	262	53.35 N	2.50 W
Westland, Mich., U.S.	216	42.19 N	83.23 W
Westland, Pa., U.S.	214	40.17 N	80.16 W
Westland Center ↞9	281	42.20 N	83.23 W
Westland National Park ♠	172	43.30 S	170.10 E
Westlands	207	42.37 N	71.20 W
West Lawn	284c	38.52 N	77.11 W
West Lebanon, Ind., U.S.	216	40.16 N	87.23 W
West Lebanon, Pa., U.S.	214	40.35 N	79.22 W
West Leechburg	214	40.37 N	79.37 W
Westleigh, S. Afr.	158	27.31 S	27.21 E
Westleigh, Eng., U.K.	262	53.30 N	2.31 W
West Leipsic	216	41.07 N	84.00 W
Westley	226	37.33 N	121.12 W
West Leyden	212	43.28 N	75.28 W
West Liberty, Iowa, U.S.	190	41.34 N	91.16 W
West Liberty, Ky., U.S.	192	37.55 N	83.16 W
West Liberty, Ohio, U.S.	216	40.15 N	83.46 W
West Liberty, Pa., U.S.	214	41.00 N	80.03 W
West Liberty, W. Va., U.S.	214	40.10 N	80.36 W
West Liberty ↞8	279b	40.24 N	80.01 W
Westliche Sahara → Western Sahara □2	148	24.30 N	13.00 W
Westliche Sierra Madre → Madre Occidental, Sierra ⩘	232	25.00 N	105.00 W
Westline	214	41.47 N	78.46 W
West Linn	224	45.21 N	122.36 W
West Linton	46	55.46 N	3.22 W
West Little Owyhee ≃	202	42.28 N	117.15 W
West Loch Roag C	46	58.13 N	6.53 W
West Loch Tarbert C, Scot., U.K.	46	55.48 N	5.32 W
West Loch Tarbert C, Scot., U.K.	46	57.55 N	6.54 W
Westlock	182	54.09 N	113.52 W
West Looe	42	50.21 N	4.28 W
West Lorne	214	42.36 N	81.36 W
West Los Angeles ↞8	280	34.03 N	118.28 W
West Lubec	188	44.49 N	67.05 W
West Lulworth	42	50.38 N	2.15 W
West Lunga ≃	154	13.06 S	24.39 E
Westmalle	56	51.18 N	4.41 E
West Malling	42	51.18 N	0.25 E
West Malling Aerodrome ⊠	260	51.16 N	0.24 E
West Manayunk	285	40.01 N	75.14 W
West Manchester	218	39.54 N	84.38 W
West Mansfield, Mass., U.S.	207	41.59 N	71.15 W
West Mansfield, Ohio, U.S.	216	40.24 N	83.33 W
West Mayfield	214	40.47 N	80.20 W
West Meadowview	216	41.08 N	87.52 W
Westmeath □6	48	53.30 N	7.30 W
West Medway	207	42.09 N	71.26 W
West Melbourne	220	28.04 N	80.38 W
West Memphis	194	35.08 N	90.11 W
West Mengo □5	154	0.30 N	32.10 E
West Meon	42	51.01 N	1.05 W
Westmere	210	42.42 N	73.52 W
West Mersea	42	51.47 N	0.55 E
West Miami	220	25.45 N	80.18 W
West Middlesex	214	41.10 N	80.27 W
West Middletown	214	40.15 N	80.25 W
West Midlands □6	42	52.30 N	2.00 W
West Mifflin	214	40.22 N	79.52 W
West Milford	210	41.08 N	74.22 W
West Milton, Ohio, U.S.	218	39.58 N	84.20 W
West Milton, Pa., U.S.	210	41.01 N	76.52 W
West Milwaukee	216	42.57 N	87.58 W
West Mineola	222	32.41 N	95.31 W
Westminster, Calif., U.S.	228	33.46 N	118.01 W
Westminster, Colo., U.S.	200	39.50 N	105.02 W
Westminster, Md., U.S.	188	39.35 N	77.00 W
Westminster, Ohio, U.S.	216	40.42 N	83.58 W
Westminster, S.C., U.S.	192	34.40 N	83.06 W
Westminster Abbey ʊ1	260	51.30 N	0.07 W
Westminster Mall ↞9	280	33.45 N	118.01 W
West Modesto	226	37.37 N	121.02 W
West Monroe	194	32.31 N	92.09 W
Westmont, Calif., U.S.	280	33.56 N	118.18 W
Westmont, Ill., U.S.	278	41.48 N	87.57 W
Westmont, N.J., U.S.	285	39.55 N	75.03 W
Westmont, Pa., U.S.	214	40.19 N	78.57 W
West Monterey	214	41.03 N	79.39 W
West Montreal ≃	190	47.56 N	80.39 W
West Moors	42	50.49 N	1.55 W
Westmoreland, Kans., U.S.	198	39.24 N	96.25 W
Westmoreland, N.Y., U.S.	210	43.07 N	75.24 W
Westmoreland, Tenn., U.S.	194	36.34 N	86.15 W
Westmoreland, Va., U.S.	208	38.04 N	76.34 W
Westmoreland □6, Pa., U.S.	214	40.18 N	79.33 W
Westmoreland □6, Va., U.S.	208	38.10 N	76.50 W
Westmoreland City	214	40.20 N	79.41 W
Westmoreland State Park ♠	208	38.09 N	76.50 W
Westmorland	204	33.02 N	115.37 W
Westmount	206	45.29 N	73.36 W
West Mountain Λ	188	43.51 N	74.43 W
West Mud Creek ≃	222	32.07 N	95.10 W
West Mustang Creek ≃	222	29.04 N	96.26 W
West Nab Λ	262	53.35 N	1.53 W
West Nanticoke	210	41.13 N	76.01 W
West New Britain □5	164	5.45 S	149.30 E
West Newbury	207	42.48 N	71.00 W
West Newton, Mass., U.S.	283	42.21 N	71.14 W
West Newton, Pa., U.S.	214	40.13 N	79.46 W
West New York	276	40.47 N	74.04 W
West Nicholson	154	21.06 S	29.25 E
West Nile □5	154	3.00 N	31.10 E
West Nishnabotna ≃	198	40.39 N	95.37 W
West Nodaway ≃	194	40.38 N	95.01 W
West Norriton	208	40.08 N	75.22 W
West Norwood ↞8	260	51.26 N	0.06 W
West Novaya Zemlya Trough ↞1	10	73.30 N	50.00 E
West Nueces ≃	196	29.16 N	99.56 W
West Nyack	210	41.06 N	73.58 W
West Okaw ≃	219	39.32 N	88.42 W
Weston, Austl.	170	32.49 S	151.28 E
Weston, Malay.	112	5.13 N	115.36 E
Weston, Eng., U.K.	262	53.19 N	2.44 W
Weston, Colo., U.S.	200	37.08 N	104.48 W
Weston, Conn., U.S.	207	41.12 N	73.22 W
Weston, Idaho, U.S.	202	42.02 N	111.59 W
Weston, Mass., U.S.	207	42.22 N	71.18 W
Weston, Mich., U.S.	216	41.46 N	84.06 W
Weston, Mo., U.S.	194	39.25 N	94.54 W
Weston, Nebr., U.S.	198	41.12 N	96.45 W
Weston, Ohio, U.S.	216	41.21 N	83.48 W
Weston, Oreg., U.S.	202	45.49 N	118.26 W
Weston, Pa., U.S.	210	40.57 N	76.09 W
Weston, W. Va., U.S.	188	39.02 N	80.28 W
Weston □8	275b	43.43 N	79.31 W
Westonaria	158	26.19 S	27.41 E
West Oneonta	210	42.28 N	75.07 W
Westönnen	52	51.33 N	7.58 E
Weston Reservoir @1	283	42.21 N	71.18 W
Westons Mill Pond @	276	40.28 N	74.25 W
Weston Mills	210	42.04 N	78.23 W
Weston-super-Mare	42	51.21 N	2.59 W
Weston upon Trent	42	52.45 N	2.02 W
West Orange, N.J., U.S.	276	40.47 N	74.14 W
West Orange, Tex., U.S.	194	30.05 N	93.46 W
Westover, Md., U.S.	208	38.07 N	75.42 W
Westover, Pa., U.S.	214	40.45 N	78.40 W
Westover, W. Va., U.S.	188	39.38 N	79.58 W
Westover Air Force Base ■	207	42.12 N	72.33 W
West Palm Beach	220	26.43 N	80.04 W
West Palm Beach Canal ☲	220	26.38 N	80.03 W
West Paris	188	44.20 N	70.35 W
West Park	210	41.48 N	73.58 W
West Paterson	276	40.54 N	74.12 W
West Pawlet	210	43.21 N	73.15 W
West Peckham	260	51.15 N	0.22 E
West Pembroke	188	44.57 N	67.11 W
West Pensacola	194	30.27 N	87.15 W
West Petersburg	180	56.49 N	132.57 W
Westphalia, Kans., U.S.	198	38.11 N	95.29 W
Westphalia, Mich., U.S.	216	42.56 N	84.48 W
Westphalia, Mo., U.S.	219	38.26 N	92.00 W
West Pittsburg, Calif., U.S.	226	38.02 N	121.54 W
West Pittsburg, Pa., U.S.	214	40.56 N	80.22 W
West Pittston	210	41.20 N	75.49 W
West Plains	194	36.44 N	91.51 W
West Point, Calif., U.S.	226	38.24 N	120.32 W
West Point, Ga., U.S.	192	32.52 N	85.10 W
Westpoint, Ind., U.S.	216	40.21 N	87.03 W
West Point, Iowa, U.S.	190	40.43 N	91.27 W
West Point, Ky., U.S.	194	37.59 N	85.57 W
West Point, Miss., U.S.	194	33.36 N	88.39 W
West Point, Nebr., U.S.	198	41.51 N	96.43 W
West Point, N.Y., U.S.	210	41.23 N	73.57 W
West Point, Ohio, U.S.	214	40.42 N	80.42 W
West Point, Pa., U.S.	285	40.12 N	75.18 W
West Point, Va., U.S.	208	37.32 N	76.48 W
West Point Λ	180	64.57 N	144.40 W
West Point ≻, P.E.I., Can.	186	46.37 N	64.25 W
West Point ≻, N. Heb.	175f	16.30 S	167.25 E
West Pond @	276	40.53 N	73.38 W
Westport, Newf., Can.	186	49.47 N	56.38 W
Westport, N.S., Can.	186	44.16 N	66.21 W
Westport, Ont., Can.	212	44.41 N	76.26 W
Westport, Eire	48	53.48 N	9.32 W
Westport, N.Z.	172	41.45 S	171.36 E
Westport, Conn., U.S.	207	41.09 N	73.22 W
Westport, Ind., U.S.	218	39.11 N	85.34 W
Westport, Ky., U.S.	218	38.29 N	85.29 W
Westport, Mass., U.S.	207	41.37 N	71.04 W
Westport, Oreg., U.S.	224	46.10 N	123.23 W
Westport, Pa., U.S.	214	41.18 N	77.51 W
Westport, Wash., U.S.	224	46.53 N	124.06 W
Westport ≃	207	41.32 N	71.04 W
West Portland	224	45.25 N	122.45 W
West Portland Park	224	45.21 N	122.37 W
Westport Point	207	41.31 N	71.05 W
West Portsmouth	218	38.46 N	83.02 W
West Prairie ≃	182	55.30 N	116.31 W
West Puente Valley	280	34.04 N	117.59 W
West Pullman ↞8	278	41.41 N	87.39 W
Westpunt ≻	241s	12.37 N	70.03 W
West Pymble	274a	33.46 S	151.08 E
West Quoddy Head ≻	186	44.49 N	66.57 W
West Rand	273d	26.07 S	27.45 E
Westray I	46	59.18 N	3.00 W
Westray Firth ⊔	46	59.12 N	2.55 W
West Redding	207	41.20 N	73.26 W
Westrem	50	50.58 N	3.52 E
Westrhauderfehn	52	53.08 N	7.34 E
West Richfield	214	41.14 N	81.39 W
West Richland	202	46.18 N	119.20 W
West River C	208	38.52 N	76.31 W
West Road ≃	182	53.19 N	122.52 W
West Rosebud Creek ≃	202	45.29 N	109.27 W
West Roxbury ↞8	283	42.17 N	71.09 W
West Rupert	210	43.14 N	73.15 W
West Rutland	188	43.36 N	73.03 W
West Ryde	274a	33.48 S	151.05 E
West Sacramento	226	38.34 N	121.32 W
West Saint Mary's ≃	186	45.15 N	62.04 W
West Saint Modeste	186	51.36 N	56.42 W
West Salem, Ill., U.S.	194	38.31 N	88.01 W
West Salem, Ohio, U.S.	214	40.58 N	82.06 W
West Salem, Wis., U.S.	190	43.54 N	91.05 W
West Salt Creek ≃	200	39.13 N	108.54 W
Westsamoa → Western Samoa □1	175a	13.55 S	172.00 W
West Sand Lake	210	42.39 N	73.37 W
West Saugerties	210	42.07 N	74.03 W
West Sayville	276	40.44 N	73.06 W
West Sayville County Park ♠	276	40.43 N	73.06 W
West Scenic Park	220	27.55 N	81.39 W
West Scotia Basin ↞1	9	57.00 S	53.00 W
West Seneca	210	42.50 N	78.45 W
West Sepik □5	164	4.00 S	141.30 E
West Shoal Lake @	184	50.20 N	97.41 W
West Siberian Plain → Zapadno-Sibirskaja Nizmennost' ≃	72	60.00 N	75.00 E
Westsibirisches Flachland → Zapadno-Sibirskaja Nizmennost' ≃	72	60.00 N	75.00 E
West Side Canal ☲	226	35.19 N	119.23 W
West Side Tennis Club ♠	276	40.43 N	73.51 W
West Simsbury	207	41.52 N	72.51 W
West Sister Island I	166	39.42 S	147.55 E
West Slope	224	45.31 N	122.46 W
West Spanish Peak Λ	200	37.23 N	104.59 W
West Springfield, Mass., U.S.	207	42.06 N	72.38 W
West Springfield, Pa., U.S.	214	41.57 N	80.29 W
West Springfield, Va., U.S.	208	38.47 N	77.13 W
West Stewartstown	206	44.59 N	71.32 W
West Stockbridge	207	42.20 N	73.22 W
West Stony Creek ≃	210	43.15 N	74.13 W
West Suffield	207	41.59 N	72.42 W
West Sunbury	214	41.00 N	79.54 W
West Sussex □6	42	50.55 N	0.35 W
West Swanzey	207	42.52 N	72.20 W
West Terre Haute	194	39.28 N	87.27 W
West-Terschelling	52	53.21 N	5.13 E
West Thompson Lake @1	207	41.57 N	71.54 W
West Thurrock	260	51.29 N	0.16 E
West Tiana	207	40.52 N	72.33 W
West Tilbury	260	51.29 N	0.24 E
West Tisbury	207	41.23 N	70.41 W
West Toodyay	168a	31.33 S	116.27 E
West Torrens	168b	34.56 S	138.32 E
Westtown, N.Y., U.S.	210	41.20 N	74.32 W
Westtown, Pa., U.S.	285	39.56 N	75.33 W
West Townsend	207	42.41 N	71.44 W
West Turffontein ↞8	273d	26.16 S	28.02 E
West Twin ≃	190	44.08 N	87.34 W
West Union, Iowa, U.S.	190	42.57 N	91.49 W
West Union, Ohio, U.S.	218	38.48 N	83.32 W
West Union, W. Va., U.S.	188	39.18 N	80.47 W
West Union Creek ≃	282	37.25 N	122.16 W
West Unity	216	41.35 N	84.26 W
West University Place	222	29.43 N	95.26 W
West Upton	207	42.10 N	71.37 W
Westvale	210	43.02 N	76.13 W
West Valley, Mont., U.S.	202	46.08 N	113.01 W
West Valley, N.Y., U.S.	210	42.24 N	78.37 W
West Vancouver	182	49.22 N	123.12 W
West View	214	40.31 N	80.02 W
West View Amusement Park ♠	279b	40.31 N	80.02 W
Westview Heights	207	41.33 N	73.05 W
Westville, N.S., Can.	186	45.34 N	62.43 W
Westville, Ind., U.S.	216	41.33 N	86.54 W
Westville, N.H., U.S.	207	42.49 N	71.07 W
Westville, N.J., U.S.	285	39.52 N	75.08 W
Westville, Ohio, U.S.	218	40.07 N	83.51 W
Westville, Okla., U.S.	194	35.59 N	94.34 W
Westville, Pa., U.S.	214	41.13 N	78.50 W
Westville Center	206	44.57 N	74.24 W
Westville Grove	285	39.51 N	75.07 W
Westville Lake @1	207	42.05 N	72.05 W
Westville Oaks	285	39.51 N	75.08 W
West Virginia □3	178 / 188	38.45 N	80.30 W
West-Vlaanderen □4	50	51.00 N	3.00 E
West Walker ≃	226	38.53 N	119.10 W
West Wallsend	170	32.54 S	151.35 E
Westward Ho	42	51.02 N	4.15 W
West Wareham	207	41.47 N	70.46 W
West Warren	207	42.13 N	72.14 W
West Warwick	207	41.42 N	71.32 W
West Water ≃	46	56.47 N	2.38 W
West Webster	210	43.12 N	77.30 W
Westwego	194	29.55 N	90.09 W
West Wellow	42	50.58 N	1.35 W
West Whittier	280	33.59 N	118.04 W
West Wickham ↞8	260	51.22 N	0.01 W
West Willington	207	41.53 N	72.18 W
West Willow, Mich., U.S.	216 / 281	42.14 N	83.34 W
West Windsor	210	42.06 N	74.46 W

Symbol	English	Deutsch	Español	Français	Português
≃	River	Fluss	Río	Rivière	Rio
☲	Canal	Kanal	Canal	Canal	Canal
⌊	Waterfall, Rapids	Wasserfall, Stromschnellen	Cascada, Rápidos	Chute d'eau, Rapides	Cascata, Rápidos
⊔	Strait	Meeresstrasse	Estrecho	Détroit	Estreito
C	Bay, Gulf	Bucht, Golf	Bahía, Golfo	Baie, Golfe	Baía, Golfo
@	Lake, Lakes	See, Seen	Lago, Lagos	Lac, Lacs	Lago, Lagos
☵	Swamp	Sumpf	Pantano	Marais	Pântano
⍓	Ice Features, Glacier	Eis- und Gletscherformen	Accidentes Glaciales	Formes glaciaires	Acidentes Glaciares
⊹	Other Hydrographic Features	Andere Hydrographische Objekte	Otros Elementos Hidrográficos	Autres données hydrographiques	Outros Acidentes Hidrográficos
↞	Submarine Features	Untermeerische Objekte	Accidentes Submarinos	Formes de relief sous-marin	Acidentes Submarinos
□	Political Unit	Politische Einheit	Unidad Política	Entité politique	Unidade Política
ʊ	Cultural Institution	Kulturelle Institution	Institución Cultural	Institution culturelle	Instituição Cultural
⊥	Historical Site	Historische Stätte	Sitio Histórico	Site historique	Sítio Histórico
♠	Recreational Site	Erholungs- und Ferienort	Sitio de Recreo	Centre de loisirs	Sítio de Lazer
⊠	Airport	Flughafen	Aeropuerto	Aéroport	Aeroporto
■	Military Installation	Militäranlage	Instalación Militar	Installation militaire	Instalação Militar
▲	Miscellaneous	Verschiedenes	Misceláneo	Divers	Miscelânea

Name	Page	Lat.	Long.
West Winfield, N.Y., U.S.	210	42.53 N	75.12 W
West Winfield, Pa., U.S.	214	40.48 N	79.42 W
Westwold	182	50.28 N	119.45 W
Westwood, Calif., U.S.	204	40.18 N	121.00 W
Westwood, Ind., U.S.	218	39.55 N	85.25 W
Westwood, Mass., U.S.	207	42.12 N	71.14 W
Westwood, Mich., U.S.	216	42.19 N	85.38 W
Westwood, N.J., U.S.	210	41.59 N	74.02 W
Westwood, Pa., U.S.	214	40.18 N	78.56 W
Westwood ♦[8]	280	34.04 N	118.27 W
Westwood Lakes	220	25.44 N	80.22 W
Westworth Village	222	32.45 N	97.25 W
West Wyalong	166	33.55 S	147.13 E
West Wycombe	42	51.39 N	0.49 W
West Yarmouth	207	41.39 N	70.15 W
West Yegua Creek ≃	222	30.20 N	96.52 W
West Yellow Creek ≃	194	39.38 N	93.04 W
West Yellowstone	202	44.30 N	111.05 W
West York	208	39.57 N	76.46 W
West Yorkshire □[6]	44	53.45 N	1.40 W
Wetan, Pulau ❙	164	7.54 S	129.32 E
Wetar, Pulau ❙	112	7.48 S	126.18 E
Wetaskiwin	182	52.58 N	113.22 W
Wete	154	5.04 S	39.43 E
Wethau	54	51.08 N	11.52 E
Wetherby	44	53.56 N	1.23 W
Wetherill Park	274a	33.51 S	150.54 E
Wethersfield	207	41.43 N	72.40 W
Wethmar	263	51.37 N	7.33 E
Wetiko Hills ⛰[2]	184	54.30 N	92.20 W
Wetluga → Vetluga ≃	80	56.18 N	46.24 E
Wetmore	198	39.38 N	95.49 W
Wet Mountains ⛰	200	38.00 N	105.10 W
Weto	152	7.57 N	7.50 E
Wetten	52	51.34 N	6.17 E
Wetter, B.R.D.	56	51.23 N	7.23 E
Wetter, B.R.D.	56	50.54 N	8.43 E
Wetter ≃	56	50.18 N	8.49 E
Wetterau □[9]	56	50.15 N	8.50 E
Wetteren	50	51.00 N	3.53 E
Wetterhorn ∧	58	46.39 N	8.08 E
Wetterstein Gebirge ⛰	64	47.25 N	11.05 E
Wettigan	110	18.57 N	95.21 E
Wettin	54	51.35 N	11.48 E
Wettingen	58	47.28 N	8.19 E
Wettringen	52	52.12 N	7.19 E
Wetumka	196	35.14 N	96.15 W
Wetumpka	194	32.27 N	86.13 W
Wetwang	44	54.01 N	0.34 W
Wetzikon	58	47.19 N	8.47 E
Wetzlar	56	50.33 N	8.29 E
Wetzstein ∧[2]	54	50.27 N	11.27 E
Wevelgem	50	50.48 N	3.10 E
Wevelinghoven	56	51.06 N	6.37 E
Wewahitchka	192	30.07 N	85.12 W
Wewak	164	3.35 S	143.40 E
Wewelsfleth	52	53.50 N	9.24 E
Wewer	52	51.41 N	8.42 E
Wewoka	196	35.09 N	96.30 W
Wexford, Eire	48	52.20 N	6.27 W
Wexford, Pa., U.S.	214	40.38 N	80.03 W
Wexford □[6]	48	52.20 N	6.40 W
Wexford ♦[8]	275b	43.45 N	79.18 W
Wexford Harbour ⊂	48	52.20 N	6.55 W
Wey ≃	42	51.23 N	0.28 W
Weyakwin Lake ⊜	184	54.30 N	106.00 W
Weyanoke	284c	38.48 N	77.09 W
Weyarn	64	47.51 N	11.48 E
Weyauwega	190	44.19 N	88.56 W
Weybridge	42	51.23 N	0.28 W
Weyburn	184	49.41 N	103.52 W
Weyer ♦[8]	263	51.10 N	7.01 E
Weyersheim	56	48.43 N	7.48 E
Weyhausen	52	52.47 N	10.23 E
Weyib ≃	144	4.11 N	42.09 E
Weymouth, N.S., Can.	186	44.25 N	66.00 W
Weymouth, Eng., U.K.	42	50.36 N	2.28 W
Weymouth, Mass., U.S.	207	42.13 N	70.58 W
Weymouth, N.J., U.S.	208	39.31 N	74.47 W
Weymouth Back ≃	283	42.15 N	70.55 W
Weymouth Fore ≃	283	42.16 N	70.56 W
Weymouth Great Pond ⊜	283	42.12 N	71.02 W
Wezemaal	56	50.57 N	4.46 E
Wezep	52	52.27 N	6.00 E
Whakatane	172	37.58 S	177.00 E
Whakatane ≃	172	37.57 S	177.00 E
Whalan	274a	33.45 S	150.49 E
Whale Creek ≃	276	40.27 N	74.13 W
Whales, Bay of ⊂	9	78.30 S	164.20 W
Whaley Bridge	44	53.20 N	1.59 W
Whaley Lake	210	41.33 N	73.40 W
Whaleysville	208	38.24 N	75.18 W
Whaleyville	208	36.37 N	76.41 W
Whalley	44	53.50 N	2.24 W
Whalom	207	42.34 N	71.45 W
Whalsay ❙	46a	60.20 N	0.59 W
Whangaehu ≃	172	40.03 S	175.06 E
Whangamata	172	37.12 S	175.52 E
Whangamomona	172	39.09 S	174.44 E
Whangara	172	38.34 S	178.13 E
Whangarei	172	35.43 S	174.19 E
Whangaruru Harbour ⊂	172	35.22 S	174.21 E
Whaplode	42	52.48 N	0.02 W
Wharfe ≃	44	53.51 N	1.07 W
Wharfedale ∨	44	54.01 N	1.56 W
Wharles	262	53.49 N	2.50 W
Wharton, N.J., U.S.	210	40.54 N	74.35 W
Wharton, Ohio, U.S.	214	40.52 N	83.21 W
Wharton, Tex., U.S.	222	29.19 N	96.06 W
Wharton, W. Va., U.S.	188	37.55 N	81.40 W
Wharton □[6]	222	29.17 N	96.13 W
Wharton Basin ⊹[4]	14	14.30 S	105.40 E
Wharton Lake ⊜	176	64.00 N	99.55 W
Wharton State Forest ♣	285	39.45 N	74.40 W
Whataroa	172	43.17 S	170.25 E
Whatatutu	172	38.23 S	177.50 E
What Cheer	190	41.24 N	92.21 W
Whatcom □[6]	224	48.48 N	121.59 W
Whatcom, Lake ⊜	224	48.43 N	122.20 W
Whately	207	42.26 N	72.38 W
Whatley	194	31.39 N	87.42 W
Whatshan Lake ⊜	182	50.00 N	118.03 W
Whauphill	44	54.49 N	4.29 W
Wheao ≃	172	38.34 S	176.39 E
Wheatfield	216	41.12 N	87.03 W
Wheathampstead	42	51.49 N	0.17 W
Wheatland, Calif., U.S.	226	39.01 N	121.25 W
Wheatland, Iowa, U.S.	190	41.50 N	90.51 W
Wheatland, Pa., U.S.	214	41.12 N	80.28 W
Wheatland, Wyo., U.S.	200	42.03 N	104.57 W
Wheatland Hills	208	40.02 N	76.21 W
Wheatland Reservoir ⊜[1]	200	41.52 N	105.36 W
Wheatley	214	42.06 N	82.27 W
Wheatley Hill	44	54.45 N	1.23 W
Wheaton, Ill., U.S.	216	41.52 N	88.06 W
Wheaton, Md., U.S.	284c	39.03 N	77.03 W
Wheaton, Minn., U.S.	198	45.48 N	96.30 W
Wheaton Plaza ♦[9]	284c	39.02 N	77.03 W
Wheaton Regional Park ♣	284c	39.03 N	77.02 W
Wheat Ridge	200	39.46 N	105.07 W
Wheelbarrow Peak ∧	204	37.27 N	116.05 W
Wheeler, Ind., U.S.	216	41.31 N	87.11 W
Wheeler, Tex., U.S.	196	35.27 N	100.16 W
Wheeler ≃, Qué., Can.	176	57.02 N	67.13 W
Wheeler ≃, Sask., Can.	184	57.25 N	105.30 W
Wheeler Air Force Base ■	229c	21.29 N	158.03 W
Wheeler Dam ♦[6]	283	42.48 N	71.12 W
Wheeler Island ❙	282	38.05 N	121.56 W
Wheeler Lake ⊜[1]	194	34.40 N	87.05 W
Wheeler Peak ∧, Calif., U.S.	226	38.25 N	119.17 W
Wheeler Peak ∧, Nev., U.S.	204	38.59 N	114.19 W
Wheeler Peak ∧, N. Mex., U.S.	200	36.34 N	105.25 W
Wheeler Ridge	228	35.06 N	119.01 W
Wheelersburg	218	38.44 N	82.51 W
Wheelers Hill	274b	37.55 S	145.11 E
Wheeling, Ill., U.S.	216	42.09 N	87.55 W
Wheeling, W. Va., U.S.	214	40.05 N	80.42 W
Wheeling Creek ≃	214	40.03 N	80.41 W
Wheelock	222	30.54 N	96.24 W
Wheelock ≃	44	53.12 N	2.26 W
Wheelton	262	53.41 N	2.36 W
Wheelwright, Arg.	252	33.47 S	61.13 W
Wheelwright, Ky., U.S.	192	37.20 N	82.43 W
Whela Creek ≃	162	26.17 S	116.50 E
Whelan, Mount ∧[2]	166	23.25 S	138.54 E
Whelpleyhill	260	51.44 N	0.33 W
Whernside ∧	44	54.14 N	2.23 W
Whetstone Creek ≃	214	40.23 N	83.03 W
Whetstone Gulf State Park ♣	212	43.44 N	75.27 W
Whidbey Island ❙	224	48.15 N	122.40 W
Whidbey Island Naval Air Station ■	224	48.17 N	122.37 W
Whidbey Islands ❙❙	162	34.45 S	135.04 E
Whiddon Down	42	50.43 N	3.51 W
Whigham	192	30.53 N	84.19 W
Whigville	207	41.44 N	72.57 W
Whim Creek	162	20.50 S	117.50 E
Whinham, Mount ∧	162	26.04 S	130.15 E
Whippany	210	40.49 N	74.25 W
Whippany ≃	276	40.51 N	74.21 W
Whirl Creek ≃	212	43.28 N	81.12 W
Whirlwind Reefs ⊹[2]	164	4.42 S	148.16 E
Whiskey Peak ∧	200	42.18 N	107.35 W
Whiskeytown-Shasta-Trinity National Recreation Area ♣	204	40.45 N	122.15 W
Whisky Chitto Creek ≃	194	30.31 N	92.55 W
Whiston	44	53.25 N	2.50 W
Whitacres	207	42.02 N	72.34 W
Whitaker	279b	40.24 N	79.53 W
Whitakers	192	36.06 N	77.43 W
Whitbourne	186	47.25 N	53.32 W
Whitburn	46	55.52 N	3.42 W
Whitby, Ont., Can.	212	43.52 N	78.56 W
Whitby, Eng., U.K.	44	54.29 N	0.37 W
Whitby, Eng., U.K.	262	53.17 N	2.54 W
Whitby Abbey ʋ[1]	44	54.28 N	0.38 W
Whitchurch, Eng., U.K.	42	52.58 N	2.41 W
Whitchurch, Eng., U.K.	42	51.14 N	1.20 W
Whitchurch, Eng., U.K.	42	51.53 N	0.51 W
Whitchurch, Eng., U.K.	42	51.52 N	2.39 W
Whitchurch, Wales, U.K.	42	51.33 N	3.14 W
Whitchurch-Stouffville	212	43.58 N	79.15 W
Whitcombe, Mount ∧	172	43.13 S	170.55 E
White, Ga., U.S.	192	34.17 N	84.45 W
White, S. Dak., U.S.	198	44.26 N	96.39 W
White □[6]	216	40.45 N	86.46 W
White ≃, B.C., Can.	182	50.23 N	115.35 W
White ≃, Ont., Can.	190	48.33 N	86.16 W
White ≃, N.A.	180	63.11 N	139.36 W
White ≃, U.S.	194	33.53 N	91.03 W
White ≃, U.S.	198	43.45 N	99.30 W
White ≃, U.S.	200	40.04 N	109.41 W
White ≃, Ariz., U.S.	200	33.44 N	110.13 W
White ≃, Ind., U.S.	194	38.25 N	87.44 W
White ≃, Nev., U.S.	204	37.42 N	115.10 W
White ≃, Oreg., U.S.	224	45.14 N	121.04 W
White ≃, Tex., U.S.	196	33.14 N	100.56 W
White ≃, Vt., U.S.	188	43.37 N	72.20 W
White ≃, Wash., U.S.	224	47.12 N	122.15 W
White ≃, Wash., U.S.	224	47.50 N	120.49 W
White ≃, Wis., U.S.	190	46.36 N	90.42 W
White ≃, Wis., U.S.	216	42.41 N	88.17 W
White, East Fork ≃, Ariz., U.S.	200	33.47 N	110.00 W
White, East Fork ≃, Ind., U.S.	194	38.33 N	87.14 W
White, Lake ⊜	162	21.05 S	129.00 E
White, Lake ⊜[1]	218	39.07 N	83.02 W
White, North Fork ≃, Ariz., U.S.	200	33.47 N	110.00 W
White, North Fork ≃, Colo., U.S.	200	39.58 N	107.38 W
White, South Fork ≃	200	39.58 N	107.38 W
White, West Fork ≃	224	47.07 N	121.37 W
White Bay ⊂	186	50.00 N	56.30 W
White Bear Indian Reserve ♦[4]	184	49.15 N	102.15 W
White Bear Lake	190	45.05 N	93.01 W
White Bluff	194	36.06 N	87.13 W
White Breast Creek ≃	194	41.24 N	93.02 W
White Butte ∧	198	46.23 N	103.19 W
Whitecap Lake ⊜	184	56.54 N	95.14 W
White Cap Mountain ∧	188	45.35 N	69.13 W
White Castle	194	30.10 N	91.09 W
White Center	224	47.31 N	122.21 W
White Chuck ≃	224	48.11 N	121.27 W
White City, Fla., U.S.	220	27.18 N	80.15 W
White City, Kans., U.S.	198	38.48 N	96.44 W
White City Stadium ♣	260	51.31 N	0.14 W
White Clay Creek ≃	198	43.12 N	102.48 W
White Cliffs, Austl.	162	28.26 S	122.57 E
White Cliffs, Austl.	166	30.51 S	143.05 E
White Cloud	190	43.33 N	85.46 W
White Cloud Island ❙	212	44.50 N	80.58 W
Whitecoomb ∧, N.Z.	172	45.36 S	169.05 E
White Coomb ∧, Scot., U.K.	44	55.26 N	3.20 W
Whitecourt	182	54.09 N	115.41 W
White Creek	210	42.58 N	73.18 W
White Creek ≃, Ind., U.S.	218	38.58 N	86.01 W
White Creek ≃, Wash., U.S.	224	46.01 N	121.08 W
White Deer, Pa., U.S.	210	41.05 N	76.52 W
White Deer, Tex., U.S.	196	35.26 N	101.10 W
White Deer Creek ≃	210	41.05 N	76.53 W
White Earth ≃	198	48.09 N	102.42 W
White Earth Indian Reservation ♦[4]	198	47.18 N	95.50 W
White Esk ≃	44	55.12 N	3.10 W
Whiteface	196	33.36 N	102.37 W
Whiteface ≃	190	46.58 N	92.48 W
Whiteface Mountain ∧	188	44.22 N	73.54 W
Whitefield, Eng., U.K.	262	53.33 N	2.18 W
Whitefield, Maine, U.S.	188	44.10 N	69.38 W
Whitefield, N.H., U.S.	188	44.22 N	71.36 W
Whitefish	202	48.25 N	114.20 W
Whitefish ≃	190	45.55 N	86.57 W
Whitefish, East Branch ≃	190	46.05 N	86.52 W
Whitefish, West Branch ≃	190	46.05 N	86.52 W
Whitefish Bay	216	43.07 N	87.55 W
Whitefish Bay ⊂, Ont., Can.	184	49.26 N	94.14 W
Whitefish Bay ⊂, N.A.	190	46.40 N	84.50 W
Whitefish Lake ⊜, Alta., Can.	182	54.22 N	111.55 W
Whitefish Lake ⊜, N.W. Ter., Can.	176	62.41 N	106.48 W
Whitefish Lake ⊜, Ont., Can.	190	48.03 N	84.29 W
Whitefish Lake ⊜, Ont., Can.	212	45.18 N	79.47 W
Whitefish Lake ⊜, Ont., Can.	212	44.31 N	76.14 W
Whitefish Lake ⊜, Alaska, U.S.	180	61.21 N	160.00 W
Whitefish Lake ⊜, Mont., U.S.	202	48.27 N	114.22 W
White Fish Lake Indian Reserve ♦[4]	182	54.39 N	111.51 W
Whitefish Point	190	46.45 N	84.59 W
Whitefish Point ≻	190	46.45 N	85.00 W
Whitefish Range ⛰	202	48.40 N	114.26 W
Whiteford	208	39.42 N	76.21 W
White Fox	184	53.27 N	104.05 W
Whitefox ≃	184	53.32 N	104.00 W
Whitegate	48	51.50 N	8.14 W
White Gull Creek ≃	184	53.44 N	104.20 W
Whitehall, Scot., U.K.	46	59.07 N	2.37 W
White Hall, Ill., U.S.	219	39.26 N	90.24 W
White Hall, Md., U.S.	208	39.37 N	76.38 W
Whitehall, Mich., U.S.	190	43.24 N	86.21 W
Whitehall, Mont., U.S.	202	45.52 N	112.06 W
Whitehall, N.Y., U.S.	188	43.33 N	73.25 W
Whitehall, Ohio, U.S.	218	39.58 N	82.54 W
White Hall, Pa., U.S.	210	41.07 N	76.38 W
Whitehall, Pa., U.S.	214	40.22 N	79.59 W
Whitehall, Wis., U.S.	190	44.22 N	91.19 W
Whitehaven, Eng., U.K.	44	54.33 N	3.35 W
White Haven, Pa., U.S.	210	41.04 N	75.47 W
Whitehead	48	54.46 N	5.43 W
White Holme Reservoir ⊜[1]	262	53.41 N	2.02 W
Whitehorse, Yukon, Can.	180	60.43 N	135.03 W
White Horse, N.J., U.S.	208	40.11 N	74.22 W
White Horse, Vale of ∨	42	51.37 N	1.37 W
Whitehorse Hill ∧[2]	42	51.34 N	1.34 W
Whitehouse, Scot., U.K.	46	57.13 N	2.37 W
Whitehouse, N.J., U.S.	210	40.37 N	74.46 W
Whitehouse, Ohio, U.S.	216	41.31 N	83.48 W
Whitehouse, Tex., U.S.	222	32.13 N	95.14 W
White House ʋ	284c	38.54 N	77.02 W
White House Station	210	40.37 N	74.46 W
White Island ❙, Ant.	9	66.44 S	48.35 E
White Island ❙, N.W. Ter., Can.	176	65.50 N	84.50 W
White Island ❙, N.Z.	172	37.31 S	177.11 E
White Lake, Mich., U.S.	281	42.41 N	83.33 W
White Lake, N.Y., U.S.	210	41.40 N	74.50 W
White Lake, S. Dak., U.S.	198	43.44 N	98.43 W
White Lake, Wis., U.S.	190	45.09 N	88.46 W
White Lake ⊜, Ont., Can.	190	48.48 N	85.36 W
White Lake ⊜, Ont., Can.	212	45.18 N	76.31 W
White Lake ⊜, Ont., Can.	212	44.47 N	76.45 W
White Lake ⊜, La., U.S.	194	29.45 N	92.30 W
White Lake ⊜, Mich., U.S.	216	42.40 N	83.34 W
Whiteland	218	39.33 N	86.05 W
Whitelaw	182	56.07 N	118.04 W
Whiteley Village	260	51.21 N	0.26 W
White Lick Creek ≃	218	39.30 N	86.23 W
White Lick Creek, East Fork ≃	218	39.35 N	86.22 W
White Lick Creek, West Fork ≃	218	39.38 N	86.23 W
Whiteman Air Force Base ■	194	38.44 N	93.34 W
Whiteman Airpark ⊠	280	34.15 N	118.25 W
Whiteman Range ⛰	164	5.50 S	149.55 E
Whitemans Creek ≃	212	43.10 N	80.21 W
Whitemark	166	40.07 S	148.01 E
White Marsh	284b	39.23 N	76.26 W
Whitemarsh Run ≃	284b	39.22 N	76.25 W
White Meadow Lake	210	40.55 N	74.31 W
White Meadow Lake ⊜	276	40.55 N	74.31 W
White Mills	210	41.32 N	75.12 W
White Mountain	180	64.40 N	162.12 W
White Mountain Peak ∧	204	37.38 N	118.15 W
White Mountains ⛰, U.S.	204	37.30 N	118.15 W
White Mountains ⛰, Alaska, U.S.	180	65.30 N	147.00 W
White Mountains ⛰, Ariz., U.S.	200	33.45 N	109.40 W
White Mountains ⛰, N.H., U.S.	188	44.10 N	71.35 W
Whitemouth	184	49.57 N	95.59 W
Whitemouth ≃	184	50.07 N	96.02 W
Whitemouth Lake ⊜	184	49.14 N	95.40 W
Whitemud ≃	184	50.15 N	98.37 W
Whiten Head ≻	46	58.34 N	4.36 W
White Nile (Al-Baḥr al-Abyaḍ) ≃	140	15.38 N	32.31 E
White Nossob ≃	156	23.05 S	18.45 E
White Oak, Pa., U.S.	279b	40.21 N	79.48 W
White Oak, Tex., U.S.	222	32.32 N	94.52 W
White Oak ≃	192	34.40 N	77.07 W
White Oak Creek ≃	194	33.16 N	94.39 W
White Oak Creek, East Fork ≃	218	39.00 N	83.53 W
White Oak Creek, North Fork ≃	218	39.00 N	83.53 W
White Oak Lake ⊜[1]	194	33.40 N	93.10 W
White Oak Regional Park ♣	279a	40.21 N	79.47 W
White Pass)(, N.A.	180	59.38 N	135.05 W
White Pass)(, Wash., U.S.	224	46.38 N	121.24 W
White Pigeon	216	41.48 N	85.38 W
White Pine, Mich., U.S.	190	46.44 N	89.35 W
White Pine, Tenn., U.S.	192	36.07 N	83.17 W
White Pines, Calif., U.S.	226	38.18 N	120.21 W
White Pines, Ill., U.S.	278	41.57 N	87.57 W
White Plains, N.C., U.S.	192	36.27 N	80.38 W
White Plains, N.Y., U.S.	210	41.02 N	73.46 W
White Pond ⊜	283	42.26 N	71.23 W
White River, Ont., Can.	190	48.35 N	85.15 W
Whiteriver, Ariz., U.S.	200	33.50 N	109.58 W
White River, S. Dak., U.S.	198	43.34 N	100.45 W
White River Junction	188	43.39 N	72.19 W
White Rock	182	49.02 N	122.49 W
White Rock Creek ≃, Kans., U.S.	198	39.55 N	97.51 W
White Rock Creek ≃, Tex., U.S.	222	32.43 N	96.44 W
White Rock Lake ⊜[1]	222	32.50 N	96.44 W
White Rocks ∧	192	36.40 N	83.27 W
Whiterocks ≃	200	40.26 N	109.55 W
White Roding	260	51.48 N	0.16 E
Whitesail Lake ⊜	182	53.30 N	127.00 W
White Salmon	224	45.44 N	121.29 W
White Salmon ≃	224	45.43 N	121.31 W
Whitesand ≃	184	51.34 N	101.55 W
Whitesands	175f	19.28 S	169.25 E
White Sands Beach	207	41.18 N	72.09 W
White Sands Missile Range ■	200	32.23 N	106.28 W
White Sands National Monument ♣	200	32.46 N	106.20 W
Whitesboro, N.J., U.S.	208	39.03 N	74.51 W
Whitesboro, N.Y., U.S.	210	43.07 N	75.18 W
Whitesboro, Tex., U.S.	196	33.39 N	96.54 W
Whitesburg	192	37.07 N	82.49 W
White Sea → Beloje More ▾[2]	24	65.30 N	38.00 E
White Settlement	222	32.45 N	97.27 W
Whiteshell Provincial Park ♣	184	50.00 N	95.25 W
Whiteside	219	39.11 N	91.01 W
Whiteside, Canal ⊔	254	53.55 S	70.15 W
White's Landing	214	41.25 N	82.54 W
White Springs	192	30.20 N	82.45 W
White Stone	208	37.39 N	76.23 W
Whitestone ♦[8]	276	40.47 N	73.49 W
White Stone Lake ⊜	184	56.25 N	97.31 W
Whitestown	218	38.59 N	86.21 W
White Sulphur Springs, Mont., U.S.	202	46.33 N	110.54 W
White Sulphur Springs, N.Y., U.S.	210	41.48 N	74.50 W
White Sulphur Springs, W. Va., U.S.	192	37.48 N	80.18 W
Whites Valley	210	41.42 N	75.22 W
Whitesville, Ky., U.S.	194	37.41 N	86.52 W
Whitesville, N.Y., U.S.	210	42.02 N	77.46 W
Whitesville, W. Va., U.S.	188	37.59 N	81.32 W
White Swan	224	46.23 N	120.44 W
White Umbeluzi ≃	158	26.08 S	31.52 E
White Umfolozi ≃	158	28.22 S	31.58 E
Whitevale	212	43.53 N	79.09 W
White Valley	214	40.25 N	79.36 W
Whiteville, N.C., U.S.	192	34.20 N	78.42 W
Whiteville, Tenn., U.S.	194	35.20 N	89.11 W
White Volta (Volta Blanche) ≃	150	9.10 N	1.15 W
Whitewater, Kans., U.S.	198	37.58 N	97.09 W
Whitewater, Mont., U.S.	202	48.46 N	107.38 W
Whitewater, Wis., U.S.	216	42.50 N	88.44 W
Whitewater ≃, U.S.	218	39.10 N	84.47 W
Whitewater ≃, Calif., U.S.	204	33.30 N	116.03 W
Whitewater ≃, Mo., U.S.	194	37.01 N	89.43 W
Whitewater, Dry Fork ≃	218	39.11 N	84.47 W
Whitewater, East Fork ≃	218	39.24 N	85.01 W
Whitewater, Greens Fork ≃	218	39.45 N	85.07 W
Whitewater, Nolands Fork ≃	218	39.41 N	85.07 W
Whitewater Baldy ∧	200	33.20 N	108.39 W
Whitewater Bay ⊂	220	25.16 N	81.00 W
Whitewater Creek ≃, N.A.	202	48.30 N	107.11 W
Whitewater Creek ≃, Ala., U.S.	194	31.25 N	86.04 W
Whitewater Creek ≃, Ga., U.S.	192	32.21 N	84.03 W
Whitewater Creek ≃, Wis., U.S.	216	42.52 N	88.45 W
Whitewater Lake ⊜, Man., Can.	184	49.15 N	100.20 W
Whitewater Lake ⊜, Wis., U.S.	216	42.47 N	88.42 W
Whitewater State Park ♣	218	39.36 N	84.58 W
White Woman Creek ≃	198	38.25 N	100.54 W
Whitewood, Austl.	166	21.28 S	143.36 E
Whitewood, Sask., Can.	184	50.20 N	102.15 W
Whitewood, Lake ⊜	198	44.20 N	97.18 W
Whitewright	196	33.31 N	96.24 W
Whitford Point ≻	42	51.38 N	4.14 W
Whithorn, Jam.	241q	18.15 N	78.02 W
Whithorn, Scot., U.K.	44	54.44 N	4.25 W
Whitianga	172	36.50 S	175.42 E
Whiting, Ind., U.S.	216	41.40 N	87.29 W
Whiting, Iowa, U.S.	198	42.08 N	96.09 W
Whiting, Kans., U.S.	198	39.35 N	95.37 W
Whiting, N.J., U.S.	208	39.57 N	74.23 W
Whiting, Wis., U.S.	190	44.29 N	89.33 W
Whiting Bay	44	55.29 N	5.06 W
Whitingham	207	42.47 N	72.53 W
Whitinsville	207	42.07 N	71.40 W
Whitland	42	51.50 N	4.37 W
Whitley □[6]	216	41.10 N	85.29 W
Whitley Bay	44	55.03 N	1.25 W
Whitley City	192	36.43 N	84.28 W
Whitley Row	260	51.15 N	0.09 E
Whitman	207	42.05 N	70.56 W
Whitman Mission National Historic Site ⊥	202	46.01 N	118.30 W
Whitmans Pond ⊜	283	42.12 N	70.57 W
Whitman Square	208	39.45 N	75.03 W
Whitmire	192	34.30 N	81.37 W
Whitmore Lake	216	42.25 N	83.46 W

ENGLISH

Name	Page	Lat.°′	Long.°′
Whitmore Lake ⊜	281	42.26 N	83.45 W
Whitmore Mountains ⛰	9	82.35 S	104.30 W
Whitmore Village	229c	21.31 N	158.01 W
Whitner Heights	226	36.37 N	119.32 W
Whitney, Ont., Can.	212	45.30 N	78.14 W
Whitney, Pa., U.S.	214	40.15 N	79.25 W
Whitney, Tex., U.S.	222	31.57 N	97.19 W
Whitney, Lake ⊜[1]	222	31.55 N	97.23 W
Whitney, Mount ∧	204	36.35 N	118.18 W
Whitney Point	210	42.20 N	75.58 W
Whitney Point Lake ⊜[1]	210	42.25 N	75.55 W
Whitney Woods Reservation ♣	283	42.13 N	70.51 W
Whitstable	42	51.22 N	1.02 E
Whitsunday Island ❙	166	20.17 S	148.59 E
Whittaker	216	42.08 N	83.36 W
Whittemore, Iowa, U.S.	198	43.04 N	94.25 W
Whittemore, Mich., U.S.	190	44.14 N	83.48 W
Whittier, Alaska, U.S.	180	60.46 N	148.41 W
Whittier, Calif., U.S.	228	33.59 N	118.02 W
Whittier, N.C., U.S.	192	35.26 N	83.22 W
Whittier Narrows Dam ♦[6]	280	34.01 N	118.04 W
Whittier Narrows Flood Control Basin ⊜[1]	280	34.02 N	118.04 W
Whittier South	280	33.57 N	118.01 W
Whittingham	44	55.24 N	1.54 W
Whittington	42	52.52 N	3.00 W
Whittle, Cap ≻	186	50.11 N	60.08 W
Whittle Hill ∧[2]	262	53.40 N	2.16 W
Whittle-le-Woods	262	53.41 N	2.38 W
Whittlesea, Austl.	169	37.31 S	145.07 E
Whittlesea, S. Afr.	158	32.10 S	26.50 E
Whittlesey	42	52.34 N	0.08 W
Whittlesey, Mount ∧[2]	190	46.18 N	90.37 W
Whitwell	194	35.12 N	85.31 W
Whitwick	42	52.44 N	1.21 W
Whitworth	44	53.40 N	2.10 W
Whitworth Peak ∧	224	49.05 N	121.13 W
Wholdaia Lake ⊜	176	60.43 N	104.10 W
Whonock	224	49.11 N	122.28 W
W. Howard Frankland Bridge ♦[5]	220	27.56 N	82.35 W
Whyalla	166	33.02 S	137.35 E
Whycocomagh	186	45.59 N	61.07 W
Whymper, Mount ∧	224	48.57 N	124.10 W
Wiang Pa Pao	110	19.22 N	99.30 E
Wiang Phan	110	20.26 N	99.53 E
Wiarton	212	44.45 N	81.09 W
Wiasi	150	10.21 N	1.20 W
Wiau Lake ⊜	182	55.23 N	111.18 W
Wiawso	150	6.12 N	2.29 W
Wiay ❙	46	57.23 N	7.13 W
Wiązów	30	50.49 N	17.11 E
Wibaux	198	46.59 N	104.11 W
Wiblingen ♦[8]	58	48.21 N	9.58 E
Wichian Buri	110	15.39 N	101.07 E
Wichita	198	37.41 N	97.20 W
Wichita Falls	196	33.54 N	98.30 W
Wichita Mountain ∧	196	34.52 N	99.17 W
Wichita Mountains ⛰	196	34.45 N	98.40 W
Wichlinghofen ♦[8]	263	51.27 N	7.30 E
Wick	46	58.26 N	3.06 W
Wick ≃	46	58.27 N	3.05 W
Wickatunk	276	40.21 N	74.15 W
Wickede	52	51.29 N	7.52 E
Wickede ♦[8]	263	51.32 N	7.37 E
Wickenburg	200	33.58 N	112.44 W
Wickepin	162	32.46 S	117.30 E
Wicker Memorial Park ♣	278	41.34 N	87.28 W
Wickett	196	31.34 N	102.59 W
Wickford	42	51.38 N	0.31 E
Wickham, Qué., Can.	206	45.45 N	72.30 W
Wickham, Eng., U.K.	42	50.54 N	1.10 W
Wickham ≃	164	16.22 S	131.06 E
Wickham, Cape ≻	166	39.36 S	143.57 E
Wickham Bishops	260	51.47 N	0.40 E
Wickham Market	42	52.09 N	1.22 E
Wickiup Reservoir ⊜[1]	202	43.40 N	121.43 W
Wickliffe, Ky., U.S.	194	36.58 N	89.05 W
Wickliffe, Ohio, U.S.	214	41.07 N	80.44 W
Wickliffe, Ohio, U.S.	214	41.36 N	81.28 W
Wicklow	48	52.59 N	6.03 W
Wicklow □[6]	48	53.00 N	6.30 W
Wicklow Head ≻	48	52.58 N	6.00 W
Wicklow Mountains ⛰	48	53.02 N	6.24 W
Wickrath	56	51.07 N	6.24 E
Wicksteed Lake ⊜	190	46.46 N	79.40 W
Wicomico	208	37.17 N	76.31 W
Wicomico □[6]	208	38.22 N	75.36 W
Wicomico ≃	208	38.13 N	75.55 W
Wicomico Church	208	37.49 N	76.23 W
Wiconisco	208	40.34 N	76.41 W
Wiconisco Creek ≃	208	40.32 N	76.58 W
Wid ≃	262	51.45 N	0.27 E
Widas ≃	115a	7.30 S	112.08 E
Widawa ≃	30	51.13 N	16.55 E
Widdern	56	49.19 N	9.25 E
Widdert ♦[8]	263	51.08 N	7.04 E
Widdop Reservoir ⊜[1]	262	53.48 N	2.06 W
Wide Bay ⊂, Pap. N. Gui.	164	5.05 S	152.05 E
Wide Bay ⊂, Alaska, U.S.	180	57.20 N	156.25 W
Widecombe in the Moor	42	50.35 N	3.48 W
Widemouth Bay	42	50.47 N	4.32 W
Widen	188	38.28 N	80.52 W
Widerøe, Mount ∧	9	72.08 S	23.30 E
Wide Ruin Wash ∨	200	35.13 N	109.52 W
Widford	260	51.43 N	0.27 E
Widgeegoara Creek ≃	166	27.30 S	145.55 E
Widgiemooltha	162	31.30 S	121.34 E
Widnes	44	53.22 N	2.44 W
Widodaren	115a	7.25 S	111.14 E
Widuchowa	54	53.10 N	14.25 E
Wiebelskirchen	56	49.22 N	7.11 E
Więcbork	30	53.22 N	17.30 E
Wieck	54	54.06 N	13.26 E
Wied	222	29.26 N	97.04 W
Wied ≃	56	50.26 N	7.27 E
Wieda	54	51.38 N	10.34 E
Wiederitzsch	54	51.24 N	12.22 E
Wiedlisbach	58	47.15 N	7.39 E
Wiefelstede	52	53.15 N	8.07 E
Wiehe	54	51.16 N	11.25 E
Wiehengebirge ⛰	52	52.20 N	8.40 E
Wiehengebirge, Naturpark ♣	52	52.20 N	8.20 E
Wiehl	56	50.57 N	7.31 E
Wiek	54	54.37 N	13.17 E
Wieleń	30	52.54 N	16.10 E
Wielichowo	30	52.08 N	16.21 E
Wieliczka	30	49.59 N	20.04 E
Wielkopolska ♦[1]	30	51.50 N	17.20 E
Wielkopolski Park Narodowy ♣	30	52.15 N	16.50 E
Wieluń	30	51.14 N	18.34 E
Wiemelhausen ♦[8]	263	51.28 N	7.13 E

DEUTSCH

Name	Seite	Breite°′	Länge°′ E=Ost
Wien	30		
	264b	48.13 N	16.20 E
Wien □[3]	264b	41.10 N	16.22 E
Wien ≃	264b	48.13 N	16.23 E
Wien, Universität ʋ[2]	264b	48.13 N	16.22 E
Wiener Berg ∧[2]	264b	48.10 N	16.22 E
Wienerherberg	264b	48.03 N	16.33 E
Wiener Hochquellen Leitung ≍[1]	61	48.10 N	16.14 E
Wiener Neudorf	264b	48.05 N	16.19 E
Wiener Neustadt	61	47.49 N	16.15 E
Wiener Neustädterkanal	61	48.05 N	16.22 E
Wiener Neustädter Kanal	61	48.05 N	16.22 E
Wienerwald ⛰	61	48.10 N	16.00 E
Wienhagen ∧[2]	263	51.08 N	7.33 E
Wienhausen	52	52.35 N	10.11 E
Wien-Schwechat, Flughafen ⊠	264b	48.07 N	16.33 E
Wiepke	54	52.36 N	11.20 E
Wieprz ≃	30	51.34 N	21.49 E
Wieprza ≃	30	54.26 N	16.22 E
Wieprz-Krzna, Kanał ≍	30	51.56 N	22.56 E
Wiera ≃	56	50.55 N	9.10 E
Wierden	52	52.22 N	6.35 E
Wieren	54	52.53 N	10.39 E
Wiergate	194	31.00 N	93.42 W
Wieringermeer ♦[1]	52	52.45 N	5.00 E
Wieringerwerf	52	52.51 N	5.02 E
Wieruszów	30	51.18 N	18.08 E
Wierzyca ≃	30	53.51 N	18.50 E
Wies	61	46.43 N	15.16 E
Wies ʋ[1]	58	47.40 N	10.53 E
Wiesa	54	50.36 N	13.01 E
Wiesau	60	49.55 N	12.11 E
Wiesbaden	56	50.05 N	8.14 E
Wiesbaden □[5]	56	50.20 N	8.20 E
Wiescheid ♦[8]	263	51.08 N	6.59 E
Wiese ≃	58	47.35 N	7.35 E
Wiesede	52	53.27 N	7.46 E
Wieselburg	61	48.08 N	15.09 E
Wiesen	58	46.43 N	9.43 E
Wiesenburg	54	52.07 N	12.26 E
Wiesenfeld	56	51.16 N	10.06 E
Wiesenfelden	60	49.02 N	12.32 E
Wiesensteig	56	48.34 N	9.37 E
Wiesent ≃	60	49.42 N	11.05 E
Wiesental	56	49.14 N	8.31 E
Wiesentheid	56	49.47 N	10.20 E
Wieseth ≃	56	49.10 N	10.39 E
Wiesloch	56	49.17 N	8.42 E
Wiesmoor	52	53.25 N	7.43 E
Wieting	61	46.52 N	14.32 E
Wietmarschen	52	52.31 N	7.07 E
Wietze	52	52.39 N	9.50 E
Wietzen	52	52.43 N	9.04 E
Wigan	44		
	262	53.33 N	2.38 W
Wigan □[8]	262	53.32 N	2.35 W
Wiggensbach	58	47.44 N	10.14 E
Wigger ≃	58	47.18 N	7.53 E
Wiggington	260	51.47 N	0.38 W
Wiggins, Colo., U.S.	198	40.14 N	104.04 W
Wiggins, Miss., U.S.	194	30.51 N	89.08 W
Wigglesworth	44	54.01 N	2.17 W
Wight, Isle of ❙	42	50.40 N	1.20 W
Wigmore, Eng., U.K.	42	52.19 N	2.51 W
Wigmore, Eng., U.K.	260	51.21 N	0.35 E
Wignehies	50	50.01 N	4.00 E
Wigston Magna	42	52.36 N	1.05 W
Wigton	44	54.49 N	3.09 W
Wigtown	44	54.52 N	4.26 W
Wigtown Bay ⊂	44	54.46 N	4.15 W
Wijchen	52	51.48 N	5.43 E
Wijhe	52	52.24 N	6.07 E
Wijk aan Zee	52	52.29 N	4.35 E
Wijk bij Duurstede	52	51.58 N	5.20 E
Wil	58	47.27 N	9.03 E
Wilbarger Creek ≃	222	30.11 N	97.23 W
Wilber	198	40.29 N	96.58 W
Wilberforce, Austl.	170	33.33 S	150.50 E
Wilberforce, Ohio, U.S.	218	39.43 N	83.53 W
Wilberforce Falls ⌊	176	67.07 N	108.47 W
Wilbraham	207	42.07 N	72.26 W
Wilbur	202	47.46 N	118.42 W
Wilburton	196	34.55 N	95.19 W
Wilcannia	166	31.34 S	143.23 E
Wilcock, Península ≻[1]	254	50.40 S	74.00 W
Wilcox, Sask., Can.	184	50.07 N	104.44 W
Wilcox, Nebr., U.S.	198	40.22 N	99.10 W
Wilcox, Pa., U.S.	214	41.35 N	78.41 W
Wilcox, Tex., U.S.	222	30.27 N	96.22 W
Wilcox, Mount ∧	207	42.13 N	73.16 W
Wildalpen	61	47.39 N	14.59 E
Wildau	54	52.19 N	13.38 E
Wildbad im Schwarzwald	56	48.45 N	8.32 E
Wildberg, B.R.D.	56	48.37 N	8.44 E
Wildberg, D.D.R.	54	52.52 N	12.37 E
Wildboarclough	262	53.13 N	2.02 W
Wildcat Canyon Regional Park ♣	282	37.56 N	122.17 W
Wildcat Creek ≃, Calif., U.S.	282	37.57 N	122.23 W
Wildcat Creek ≃, Ind., U.S.	216	40.28 N	86.52 W
Wildcat Creek, Middle Fork ≃	216	40.25 N	86.46 W
Wildcat Creek, South Fork ≃	216	40.26 N	86.48 W
Wildcat Hill ∧[2]	184	53.17 N	102.30 W
Wilde ♦[8]	288	34.42 S	58.20 W
Wildegg	58	47.25 N	8.11 E
Wildeman ≃	164	5.33 S	139.13 E
Wildemann	52	51.49 N	10.17 E
Wildenbruch	264a	52.17 N	13.04 E
Wildenfels	54	50.40 N	12.35 E
Wildenranna	60	48.35 N	13.44 E
Wildenstein	58	47.59 N	6.58 E
Wildenthal	54	50.27 N	12.37 E
Wilder	202	43.40 N	116.55 W
Wilderness	158	34.00 S	22.36 E
Wilderness of Judæa (Midbar Yehuda) ♦[2]	132	31.30 N	35.18 E
Wilderness State Park ♣	190	45.42 N	84.57 W
Wilder Shoal ⊹[2]	14	8.30 N	174.05 W
Wildersville	194	35.48 N	88.22 W
Wildervank	52	53.04 N	6.51 E
Wildeshausen	52	52.54 N	8.26 E
Wildfield	212	43.49 N	79.44 W
Wildflecken	56	50.23 N	9.54 E
Wildfontein	158	31.04 S	24.50 E
Wildhaus	58	47.12 N	9.22 E
Wildhay ≃	182	54.02 N	117.20 W
Wildhorn ∧	58	46.21 N	7.22 E
Wildhorse Creek ≃, Okla., U.S.	196	34.32 N	97.10 W
Wild Horse Creek ≃, Wyo., U.S.	198	44.39 N	106.08 W
Wild Horse Draw ∨	196	31.11 N	104.50 W
Wild Horse Lake ⊜	202	48.58 N	110.00 W
Wildnest Lake ⊜	184	55.00 N	102.20 W
Wildon	61	46.53 N	15.31 E
Wild Rice ≃, Minn., U.S.	198	47.20 N	96.50 W
Wild Rice ≃, N. Dak., U.S.	198	46.45 N	96.47 W

Symbols in the index entries represent the broad categories identified in the key at the right. Symbols with superior numbers (⛰[2]) identify subcategories (see complete key on page *I* · 30).

Kartensymbole in dem Registerverzeichnis stellen die rechts in Schlüssel erklärten Kategorien dar. Symbole mit hochgestellten Ziffern (⛰[2]) bezeichnen Unterabteilungen einer Kategorie (vgl. vollständiger Schlüssel auf Seite *I* · 30).

Los símbolos incluídos en el texto del índice representan las grandes categorias identificadas con la clave a la derecha. Los símbolos con numeros en su parte superior (⛰[2]) identifican las subcategorías (véase la clave completa en la página *I* · 30).

Les symboles de l'index représentent les catégories indiquées dans la légende à droite. Les symboles suivis d'un indice (⛰[2]) représentent des sous-catégories (voir légende complète à la page *I* · 30).

Os símbolos incluídos no texto do índice representam as grandes categorias identificadas com a chave à direita. Os símbolos com números em sua parte superior (⛰[2]) identificam as subcategorias (veja-se a chave completa à página *I* · 30).

∧ Mountain	Berg	Montaña	Montagne	Montanha
⛰ Mountains	Berge	Montañas	Montagnes	Montanhas
)(Pass	Pass	Paso	Col	Passo
∨ Valley, Canyon	Tal, Cañon	Valle, Cañón	Vallée, Canyon	Vale, Canhão
═ Plain	Ebene	Llano	Plaine	Planície
≻ Cape	Kap	Cabo	Cap	Cabo
❙ Island	Insel	Isla	Île	Ilha
❙❙ Islands	Inseln	Islas	Îles	Ilhas
⊥ Other Topographic Features	Andere Topographische Objekte	Otros Elementos Topográficos	Autres données topographiques	Outros Elementos Topográficos

ESPAÑOL / FRANÇAIS / PORTUGUÊS

Nombre / Nom / Nome	Página / Page	Lat.	Long. W=Oeste / W=Ouest
Wild Rice, South Branch ≃	198	47.12 N	96.38 W
Wildrose, N. Dak., U.S.	198	48.38 N	103.11 W
Wild Rose, Wis., U.S.	190	44.11 N	89.15 W
Wildseeloder Λ	64	47.26 N	12.32 E
Wildspitze Λ	58	46.53 N	10.52 E
Wildstrubel Λ	58	46.24 N	7.32 E
Wildwood, Alta., Can.	182	53.37 N	115.14 W
Wildwood, Fla., U.S.	220	28.52 N	82.02 W
Wildwood, Ill., U.S.	216	42.21 N	88.00 W
Wildwood, N.J., U.S.	208	38.59 N	74.49 W
Wildwood, Pa., U.S.	214	40.36 N	79.58 W
Wildwood, Lake ⊜	276	41.09 N	74.32 W
Wild Wood Beach	284b	39.15 N	76.25 W
Wildwood Canyon Park ♠	280	34.13 N	118.17 W
Wildwood Crest	208	38.58 N	74.50 W
Wiley	224	46.33 N	120.39 W
Wilferdingen	56	48.56 N	8.35 E
Wilfersdorf	61	48.35 N	16.38 E
Wilge ≃	158	27.03 S	28.20 E
Wilgena	162	30.46 S	134.44 E
Wilgersdorf	56	50.49 N	8.09 E
Wilhelm, Lake ⊜[1]	214	41.23 N	80.08 W
Wilhelm, Mount Λ	164	5.45 S	145.05 E
Wilhelmina Gebergte Ѧ	250	3.45 N	56.30 W
Wilhelminakanaal Ξ	52	51.47 N	4.51 E
Wilhelminaoord	52	52.53 N	6.10 E
Wilhelmina Peak → Trikora, Puncak Λ	164	4.15 S	138.45 E
Wilhelm-Pieck-Stadt Guben	54	51.57 N	14.43 E
Wilhelmsburg	61	48.06 N	15.36 E
Wilhelmsburg ◆[8]	52	53.30 N	10.00 E
Wilhelmshaven	52	53.31 N	8.08 E
Wilhelmshöhe, Schloss ⊥	56	51.21 N	9.22 E
Wilhelmshorst	54	52.19 N	13.03 E
Wilhelmstadt ◆[8]	264a	52.31 N	13.11 E
Wilhelmstal	156	21.54 S	16.19 E
Wilhelmstein, Schloss ⊥	52	52.28 N	9.18 E
Wilis, Gunung Λ	115a	7.48 S	111.45 E
Wilkau-Hasslau	54	50.40 N	12.31 E
Wilkerson Pass)(	200	39.02 N	105.32 W
Wilkes ʋ[3]	9	66.15 S	110.35 E
Wilkes-Barre	210	41.14 N	75.53 W
Wilkes-Barre Scranton Airport ⊠	210	41.20 N	75.45 W
Wilkesboro	192	36.09 N	81.09 W
Wilkes Island I	174a	19.18 N	166.34 E
Wilkes Lake ⊜	190	46.01 N	79.00 W
Wilkes Land ◆[1]	9	69.00 S	120.00 E
Wilkeson	224	47.06 N	122.03 W
Wilket Creek ≃	275b	43.43 N	79.21 W
Wilket Creek Park ♠	275b	43.43 N	79.21 W
Wilkhaven	46	57.52 N	3.45 W
Wilkie	184	52.25 N	108.43 W
Wilkinsburg	214	40.27 N	79.53 W
Wilkinson	218	39.53 N	85.36 W
Wilkinson Basin ✢[1]	16	42.30 N	69.30 W
Wilkinson Lakes ⊜	162	29.40 S	132.39 E
Wilkins Sound Ш	9	70.15 S	73.00 W
Wilkins Township	279b	40.25 N	79.50 W
Will □[6]	216	41.32 N	88.05 W
Will, Mount Λ	180	57.31 N	128.46 W
Willacoochee	192	31.20 N	83.03 W
Willacoochee ≃	192	31.21 N	83.06 W
Willamette ≃	202	45.39 N	122.46 W
Willamette, Middle Fork ≃	202	44.01 N	123.01 W
Willamette, North Fork ≃	202	43.46 N	122.32 W
Willamina	224	45.05 N	123.29 W
Willamina Creek ≃	224	45.05 N	123.28 W
Willandra Billabong Creek ≃	166	33.08 S	144.06 E
Willapa	224	46.40 N	123.40 W
Willapa ≃	224	46.42 N	123.50 W
Willapa Bay C	224	46.37 N	124.00 W
Willard, N. Mex., U.S.	200	34.36 N	106.02 W
Willard, N.Y., U.S.	210	42.41 N	76.52 W
Willard, Ohio, U.S.	214	41.03 N	82.44 W
Willard, Utah, U.S.	200	41.25 N	112.02 W
Willard, Wash., U.S.	224	45.48 N	121.38 W
Willaston, Austl.	168b	34.36 S	138.45 E
Willaston, Eng., U.K.	262	53.18 N	3.00 W
Willaumez Peninsula >[1]	164	5.05 S	150.05 E
Willcox	200	32.15 N	109.50 W
Willcox Playa ⊜	200	32.08 N	109.51 W
Willebadessen	52	51.37 N	9.02 E
Willebroek	50	51.04 N	4.22 E
Willem Pretorius Game Reserve ◆[4]	156	28.16 S	27.13 E
Willemsoord	52	52.49 N	6.05 E
Willemstad, Ned.	52	51.42 N	4.26 E
Willemstad, Ned. Ant.	241s	12.06 N	68.56 W
Willenhall	42	52.36 N	2.02 W
Willerburn Acres	284c	39.03 N	77.10 W
Willerby	44	53.46 N	0.27 W
Willeroo	164	15.17 S	131.35 E
Willer-sur-Thur	58	47.51 N	7.05 E
Willerswalde	54	54.07 N	13.08 E
Willesden ◆[8]	260	51.33 N	0.14 W
Willet	210	42.28 N	75.55 W
Willett Pond ⊜	283	42.11 N	71.14 W
Willey Creek ≃	279a	41.25 N	81.25 W
William, Lac ⊜	206	46.07 N	71.34 W
William, Mount Λ, Austl.	166	37.17 S	142.36 E
William, Mount Λ, Austl.	169	37.13 S	144.47 E
William Boyce Regional Park ♠	279b	40.28 N	79.45 W
William Creek	166	28.55 S	136.21 E
William Girling Reservoir ⊜[1]	260	51.37 N	0.02 W
William Lake ⊜	184	53.50 N	99.25 W
William Patterson College ʋ[2]	276	40.56 N	74.12 W
William P. Gleason Park ♠	278	41.33 N	87.21 W
William Preston Lane Jr. Memorial Bridge ◆[5]	208	39.00 N	76.28 W
Williams, Austl.	168a	33.01 S	116.52 E
Williams, Ariz., U.S.	200	35.15 N	112.11 W
Williams, Calif., U.S.	226	39.09 N	122.09 W
Williams, Iowa, U.S.	190	42.29 N	93.33 W
Williams, Minn., U.S.	198	48.45 N	94.54 W
Williams □[6]	216	41.35 N	84.33 W
Williams ≃, Austl.	166	20.04 S	141.08 E
Williams ≃, Austl.	168a	32.59 S	116.24 E
Williams ≃, Austl.	170	32.45 S	151.45 E
Williams, Cape >	9	70.29 S	164.05 E
Williams, Mount Λ	175f	18.39 S	169.03 E
Williams Bay	216	42.35 N	88.33 W
Williamsburg, Ont., Can.	212	44.58 N	75.15 W
Williamsburg, Ind., U.S.	218	39.57 N	85.01 W
Williamsburg, Iowa, U.S.	190	41.40 N	92.01 W
Williamsburg, Ky., U.S.	192	36.44 N	84.10 W
Williamsburg, Mass., U.S.	207	42.23 N	72.44 W
Williamsburg, Mo., U.S.	219	38.55 N	91.42 W
Williamsburg, Ohio, U.S.	218	39.03 N	84.04 W
Williamsburg, Pa., U.S.	214	40.28 N	78.12 W
Williamsburg, Va., U.S.	208	37.16 N	79.43 W
Williamsburg ◆[8]	276	40.42 N	73.57 W
Williamsburg Bridge ◆[5]	276	40.43 N	73.58 W
Williams Center	216	41.26 N	84.36 W
Williams Creek ≃, Austl.	274a	33.57 S	150.58 E
Williams Creek ≃, Ind., U.S.	218	39.36 N	85.09 W
Williamsdale	171b	35.35 S	149.09 E
Williamsfield, Jam.	241q	17.56 N	77.46 W
Williamsfield, Ohio, U.S.	214	41.32 N	80.32 W
Williams Lake	182	52.08 N	122.09 W
Williams Lake Indian Reserve ◆[4]	182	52.07 N	122.00 W
Williamson, N.Y., U.S.	210	43.13 N	77.11 W
Williamson, W. Va., U.S.	192	37.41 N	82.17 W
Williamson □[6]	222	30.40 N	97.32 W
Williamson ≃	202	42.28 N	121.57 W
Williamson Head >	9	69.09 S	157.49 E
Williamsport, Newf., Can.	186	50.32 N	56.19 W
Williamsport, Ind., U.S.	216	40.17 N	87.17 W
Williamsport, Ohio, U.S.	214	39.35 N	83.07 W
Williamsport, Pa., U.S.	210	41.14 N	77.00 W
Williamston, Mich., U.S.	216	42.41 N	84.17 W
Williamston, S.C., U.S.	192	34.37 N	82.29 W
Williamstown, Austl.	168b	34.40 S	138.53 E
Williamstown, Austl.	169	37.52 S	144.54 E
Williamstown, Ont., Can.	206	45.08 N	74.35 W
Williamstown, Ky., U.S.	218	38.38 N	84.34 W
Williamstown, Mass., U.S.	207	42.43 N	73.12 W
Williamstown, N.J., U.S.	208	39.41 N	75.01 W
Williamstown, Pa., U.S.	208	40.35 N	76.37 W
Williamstown, Vt., U.S.	188	44.07 N	72.33 W
Williamstown, W. Va., U.S.	188	39.24 N	81.27 W
Williamstown Junction	285	39.45 N	74.56 W
Williamstown Lake ⊜[1]	218	38.41 N	84.32 W
Williamsville, Ill., U.S.	219	39.57 N	89.33 W
Williamsville, N.Y., U.S.	210	42.59 N	78.43 W
Williamtown	170	32.49 S	151.50 E
Willich	56	51.16 N	6.33 E
Willikies	240c	17.05 N	61.42 W
Willimantic	207	41.43 N	72.13 W
Willimantic ≃	207	41.43 N	72.12 W
Willingale	260	51.44 N	0.19 E
Willingboro	208	40.03 N	74.53 W
Willingboro Plaza ◆[9]	285	40.03 N	74.53 W
Willingdon, Alta., Can.	182	53.50 N	112.08 W
Willingdon, Eng., U.K.	42	50.47 N	0.15 E
Willingdon, Mount Λ	182	51.45 N	116.15 W
Willingen	56	51.17 N	8.37 E
Willingham	42	52.19 N	0.04 E
Willington	44	54.43 N	1.41 W
Willis, Mich., U.S.	216	42.09 N	83.34 W
Willis, Tex., U.S.	222	30.25 N	95.29 W
Willis ≃	192	37.41 N	78.07 W
Willisau	58	47.07 N	8.00 E
Willis Group II	164	16.18 S	150.00 E
Willis Island I	186	48.48 N	53.42 W
Williston, S. Afr.	158	31.20 S	20.53 E
Williston, Fla., U.S.	192	29.23 N	82.27 W
Williston, N. Dak., U.S.	198	48.09 N	103.37 W
Williston, Ohio, U.S.	214	41.36 N	83.20 W
Williston, S.C., U.S.	192	33.24 N	81.25 W
Williston Basin ⌣[1]	198	48.15 N	105.00 W
Williston Lake ⊜[1]	182	56.00 N	124.00 W
Williston Park	276	40.45 N	73.39 W
Willisville	194	37.59 N	89.35 W
Willis Wharf	208	37.31 N	75.48 W
Williton	42	51.10 N	3.20 W
Willits	204	39.25 N	123.21 W
Willmar	198	45.07 N	95.03 W
Willmersdorf	264a	52.40 N	13.41 E
Willmore Wilderness Provincial Park ♠	182	53.45 N	119.00 W
Willoughby, Austl.	170	33.48 S	151.12 E
Willoughby, Ohio, U.S.	214	41.38 N	81.25 W
Willoughby, Cape >	166	35.51 S	138.07 E
Willoughby Bay C	240c	17.02 N	61.44 W
Willoughby Hills	214	41.35 N	81.27 W
Willow, Alaska, U.S.	180	61.45 N	150.03 W
Willow, Mich., U.S.	216	42.07 N	83.24 W
Willow, N.Y., U.S.	210	42.05 N	74.14 W
Willow ≃, Alta., Can.	182	55.58 N	113.55 W
Willow ≃, B.C., Can.	182	54.03 N	122.21 W
Willow ≃, Minn., U.S.	190	46.40 N	93.35 W
Willow ≃, Wis., U.S.	190	44.59 N	92.46 W
Willowbrook, Sask., Can.	184	51.13 N	102.47 W
Willow Brook, Calif., U.S.	280	33.55 N	118.14 W
Willowbrook, Ill., U.S.	278	41.46 N	87.56 W
Willow Brook ≃, Ont., Can.	212	43.53 N	80.16 W
Willow Brook ≃, Eng., U.K.	42	52.32 N	0.24 W
Willow Brook ≃, N.J., U.S.	276	40.20 N	74.10 W
Willowbrook Mall ◆[9]	276	40.53 N	74.15 W
Willowbrook Park ♠	276	40.36 N	74.09 W
Willow Bunch	184	49.24 N	105.37 W
Willow Bunch Lake ⊜	184	49.27 N	105.28 W
Willow City	198	48.36 N	100.18 W
Willow Creek, Calif., U.S.	204	40.56 N	123.38 W
Willow Creek, Mont., U.S.	202	45.49 N	111.39 W
Willow Creek ≃, Alta., Can.	182	49.46 N	113.21 W
Willow Creek ≃, Ont., Can.	212	44.25 N	79.53 W
Willow Creek ≃, Calif., U.S.	226	37.09 N	119.27 W
Willow Creek ≃, Calif., U.S.	226	39.22 N	122.05 W
Willow Creek ≃, Ill., U.S.	216	41.42 N	89.10 W
Willow Creek ≃, Ind., U.S.	216	41.15 N	85.08 W
Willow Creek ≃, Mich., U.S.	281	42.20 N	83.25 W
Willow Creek ≃, Mont., U.S.	202	46.28 N	108.28 W
Willow Creek ≃, Mont., U.S.	202	48.10 N	111.11 W
Willow Creek ≃, Mont., U.S.	202	48.09 N	106.38 W
Willow Creek ≃, Nev., U.S.	204	38.10 N	116.35 W
Willow Creek ≃, Ohio, U.S.	279a	41.20 N	82.03 W
Willow Creek ≃, Oreg., U.S.	202	44.00 N	117.13 W
Willow Creek ≃, Oreg., U.S.	202	45.48 N	120.01 W
Willow Creek ≃, Utah, U.S.	200	40.02 N	109.45 W
Willow Creek, North Fork ≃	226	37.13 N	119.30 W
Willow Creek, South Fork ≃	226	39.32 N	122.10 W
Willowdale ◆[8]	275b	43.47 N	79.26 W
Willowdale State Forest ♠	283	42.40 N	70.54 W
Willowdene	273d	26.18 S	29.57 E
Willowemac	210	41.55 N	74.41 W
Willow Glen ◆[8]	282	37.18 N	121.53 W
Willow Grove	208	40.08 N	75.06 W
Willow Grove Naval Air Station ■	208	40.12 N	75.08 W
Willow Grove Park ♠	285	40.08 N	75.08 W
Willow Hill	214	40.06 N	77.48 W
Willowick	214	41.38 N	81.28 W
Willow Lake	198	44.38 N	97.38 W
Willow Lake ⊜, N.W. Ter., Can.	176	62.11 N	119.10 W
Willow Lake ⊜, N.Y., U.S.	276	40.43 N	73.50 W
Willowlake ≃	176	62.52 N	123.08 W
Willowmac Creek ≃	210	41.53 N	74.48 W
Willow Metropolitan Park ♠	281	42.08 N	83.22 W
Willowmore	158	33.17 S	23.29 E
Willow Park	222	32.45 N	97.39 W
Willowra	162	21.15 S	132.35 E
Willow Reservoir ⊜[1]	190	45.45 N	89.50 W
Willow River	182	54.04 N	122.28 W
Willow Run, Mich., U.S.	216	42.16 N	83.34 W
Willow Run, Va., U.S.	284c	38.49 N	77.10 W
Willows	226	39.31 N	122.12 W
Willow Springs, Calif., U.S.	228	34.53 N	118.18 W
Willow Springs, Mo., U.S.	194	36.59 N	91.58 W
Willow Springs, Pa., U.S.	279b	40.19 N	79.44 W
Willow Street	208	39.59 N	76.17 W
Willowvale	158	32.16 S	28.30 E
Willow Wall ⊥	104	42.10 N	122.30 E
Will Rogers State Beach ♠	280	34.01 N	118.30 W
Will Rogers State Historical Park ♠	280	34.03 N	118.31 W
Wills Creek ≃, Austl.	166	22.43 S	140.02 E
Wills Creek ≃, Ohio, U.S.	188	40.09 N	81.55 W
Wills Creek Lake ⊜[1]	214	40.08 N	81.45 W
Willseyville	210	42.17 N	76.23 W
Willshire	216	40.45 N	84.48 W
Wills Point	222	32.43 N	96.01 W
Willunga	168b	35.17 S	138.33 E
Wilmar	194	33.38 N	91.56 W
Wilmer, Ala., U.S.	194	30.44 N	88.28 W
Wilmer, Pa., U.S.	285	40.07 N	75.32 W
Wilmer, Tex., U.S.	222	32.35 N	96.41 W
Wilmerding	279b	40.24 N	79.48 W
Wilmersdorf ◆[8]	264a	52.30 N	13.19 E
Wilmette	216	42.04 N	87.43 W
Wilmington, Austl.	166	32.39 S	138.07 E
Wilmington, Eng., U.K.	260	51.26 N	0.12 E
Wilmington, Del., U.S.	208		
	285	39.44 N	75.33 W
Wilmington, Ill., U.S.	216	41.18 N	88.09 W
Wilmington, Mass., U.S.	207	42.33 N	71.10 W
Wilmington, N.C., U.S.	192	34.13 N	77.55 W
Wilmington, Ohio, U.S.	218	39.27 N	83.50 W
Wilmington, Vt., U.S.	188	42.52 N	72.52 W
Wilmington ◆[8]	280	33.47 N	118.16 W
Wilmington Manor	285	39.41 N	75.35 W
Wilmore, Ky., U.S.	192	37.52 N	84.40 W
Wilmore, Pa., U.S.	214	40.23 N	78.43 W
Wilmot, Ark., U.S.	194	33.04 N	91.34 W
Wilmot, Ohio, U.S.	214	40.39 N	81.38 W
Wilmot, S. Dak., U.S.	198	45.25 N	96.52 W
Wilmot, Wis., U.S.	216	42.31 N	88.11 W
Wilmot Woods ♠	278	42.18 N	87.56 W
Wilmslow	44	53.20 N	2.15 W
Wilna → Vilnius	76	54.41 N	25.19 E
Wilpen	214	40.17 N	79.12 W
Wilpoort	158	27.10 S	26.08 E
Wilpshire	262	53.47 N	2.28 W
Wilrijk	50	51.10 N	4.24 E
Wilsall	202	46.00 N	110.40 W
Wilsdruff	54	51.05 N	13.32 E
Wilseder Berg Λ[2]	52	53.10 N	9.56 E
Wilseyville	226	38.23 N	120.31 W
Wilshamstead	42	52.05 N	0.27 W
Wilson, Austl.	166	32.00 S	138.22 E
Wilson, Ark., U.S.	194	35.34 N	90.03 W
Wilson, Conn., U.S.	207	41.48 N	72.38 W
Wilson, Ill., U.S.	278	42.21 N	87.54 W
Wilson, Kans., U.S.	198	38.50 N	98.29 W
Wilson, N.C., U.S.	192	35.44 N	77.55 W
Wilson, N.Y., U.S.	210	43.19 N	78.50 W
Wilson, Okla., U.S.	196	34.10 N	97.26 W
Wilson, Pa., U.S.	208	40.41 N	75.15 W
Wilson, Tex., U.S.	196	33.19 N	101.44 W
Wilson ≃, Austl.	164	16.47 S	128.17 E
Wilson ≃, Austl.	166	27.38 S	141.24 E
Wilson ≃, Oreg., U.S.	224	45.28 N	123.53 W
Wilson, Cape >	176	66.59 N	81.28 W
Wilson, Mount Λ, Calif., U.S.	280	34.13 N	118.04 W
Wilson, Mount Λ, Colo., U.S.	200	37.51 N	107.59 W
Wilson, Mount Λ, Nev., U.S.	204	38.15 N	114.23 W
Wilson, Mount Λ, Oreg., U.S.	224	45.04 N	121.39 W
Wilson, Mount Λ[2]	162	20.14 S	127.39 E
Wilson, Point >	224	48.08 N	122.45 W
Wilson Cliffs •[4]	162	22.03 S	127.09 E
Wilson Creek ≃, Tex., U.S.	222	33.07 N	96.35 W
Wilson Creek ≃, Wash., U.S.	202	47.25 N	119.07 W
Wilson Lake ⊜[1], Ala., U.S.	194	34.49 N	87.30 W
Wilson Lake ⊜[1], Kans., U.S.	198	38.57 N	98.40 W
Wilson Range Ѧ	162	28.50 S	124.25 E
Wilson Run ≃, Del., U.S.	285	39.48 N	75.35 W
Wilson Run ≃, Pa., U.S.	279b	40.13 N	79.37 W
Wilsons Beach	186	44.56 N	66.56 W
Wilson's Creek National Battlefield ♠	194	37.06 N	93.27 W
Wilsons Promontory >	166	38.55 S	146.20 E
Wilsons Promontory National Park ♠	166	39.00 S	146.25 E
Wilsonville, Ill., U.S.	219	39.04 N	89.51 W
Wilsonville, Nebr., U.S.	198	40.07 N	100.07 W
Wilsonville, Oreg., U.S.	224	45.18 N	122.46 W
Wilster	52	53.55 N	9.22 E
Wilthen	54	51.06 N	14.24 E
Wilton, Eng., U.K.	42	51.05 N	1.52 W
Wilton, Conn., U.S.	207	41.12 N	73.26 W
Wilton, Maine, U.S.	188	44.35 N	70.14 W
Wilton, N.H., U.S.	188	42.51 N	71.44 W
Wilton, N. Dak., U.S.	198	47.10 N	100.47 W
Wilton, N.Y., U.S.	210	43.11 N	73.45 W
Wilton, Wis., U.S.	190	43.48 N	90.32 W
Wilton ≃	164	14.45 S	134.33 E
Wilton Creek ≃	212	44.12 N	76.56 W
Wilton Farm Acres	284b	39.18 N	76.50 W
Wilton Junction	194	41.35 N	91.01 W
Wilton Manors	220	26.10 N	80.07 W
Wiltshire □[6]	42	51.15 N	1.50 W
Wiltz	56	49.48 N	5.55 E
Wiluna	162	26.36 S	120.13 E
Wimapedi Lake ⊜	184	55.11 N	99.46 W
Wimauma	220	27.43 N	82.18 W
Wimberley	196	30.00 N	98.06 W
Wimbledon	198	47.10 N	98.28 W
Wimbledon ◆[8]	260	51.25 N	0.12 W
Wimbledon Common ♠	260	51.26 N	0.14 W
Wimborne Minster	42	50.48 N	1.59 W
Wimereux	50	50.46 N	1.37 E
Wimmelburg	54	51.31 N	11.30 E
Wimmenau	56	48.55 N	7.25 E
Wimmera ≃	169	36.55 S	142.56 E
Wimmis	58	46.41 N	7.38 E
Wimsbach	60	48.04 N	13.54 E
Winagami Lake ⊜	182	55.38 N	116.45 W
Winam C	154	0.15 S	34.35 E
Winamac	216	41.03 N	86.36 W
Winburg	158	28.37 S	27.00 E
Winburne	214	40.58 N	78.08 W
Wincanton	42	51.04 N	2.25 W
Wincham	262	53.16 N	2.29 W
Winchcombe	42	51.57 N	1.58 W
Winchelsea, Austl.	169	38.15 S	143.59 E
Winchelsea, Eng., U.K.	42	50.55 N	0.42 E
Winchendon	207	42.41 N	72.03 W
Winchester, Ont., Can.	212	45.06 N	75.21 W
Winchester, N.Z.	172	44.12 S	171.17 E
Winchester, Eng., U.K.	42	51.04 N	1.19 W
Winchester, Calif., U.S.	228	33.42 N	117.05 W
Winchester, Idaho, U.S.	202	46.14 N	116.38 W
Winchester, Ill., U.S.	219	39.38 N	90.27 W
Winchester, Ind., U.S.	218	40.10 N	84.59 W
Winchester, Ky., U.S.	192	37.59 N	84.11 W
Winchester, Mass., U.S.	283	42.28 N	71.10 W
Winchester, N.H., U.S.	188	42.46 N	72.23 W
Winchester, Ohio, U.S.	218	38.57 N	83.39 W
Winchester, Tenn., U.S.	194	35.10 N	86.01 W
Winchester, Tex., U.S.	222	30.01 N	97.01 W
Winchester, Va., U.S.	188	39.11 N	78.10 W
Winchester Cathedral ʋ[1]	42	51.04 N	1.19 W
Winchmore Hill	260	51.39 N	0.39 W
Winchmore Hill ◆[8]	260	51.38 N	0.06 W
Wind ≃, Yukon, Can.	180	65.49 N	135.18 W
Wind ≃, Wash., U.S.	224	45.43 N	121.47 W
Wind ≃, Wyo., U.S.	202	43.35 N	108.13 W
Wind, North Fork ≃	202	43.27 N	109.28 W
Windang	170	34.32 S	150.53 E
Windau → Ventspils	76	57.24 N	21.36 E
Windber	214	40.14 N	78.50 W
Wind Cave National Park ♠	198	43.32 N	103.25 W
Windecken	56	50.13 N	8.52 E
Winder	192	32.59 N	83.43 W
Winder, Lake ⊜	220	28.15 N	80.51 W
Windera	166	26.03 S	151.50 E
Windermere, B.C., Can.	182	50.30 N	115.58 W
Windermere, Eng., U.K.	44	54.23 N	2.54 W
Windermere, Fla., U.S.	220	28.30 N	81.32 W
Windermere ⊜	44	54.22 N	2.56 W
Windermere Lake ⊜	190	47.56 N	83.47 W
Winder Village	285	40.06 N	74.52 W
Windfall, Alta., Can.	182	54.11 N	116.15 W
Windfall, Ind., U.S.	216	40.22 N	85.57 W
Windgap	210	40.51 N	75.18 W
Windham, Conn., U.S.	207	41.42 N	72.10 W
Windham, N.H., U.S.	283	42.49 N	71.19 W
Windham, N.Y., U.S.	210	42.19 N	74.15 W
Windham, Ohio, U.S.	214	41.14 N	81.03 W
Windham □[6], Conn., U.S.	207	41.55 N	71.55 W
Windham □[6], Vt., U.S.	207	42.50 N	72.43 W
Windhoek	156	22.34 S	17.06 E
Windhoek □[5]	156	22.30 S	17.00 E
Windigo ≃	184	53.22 N	91.48 W
Windigo Lake ⊜	184	52.35 N	91.32 W
Windisch	58	47.29 N	8.13 E
Windischeschenbach	60	49.48 N	12.09 E
Windischgarsten	61	47.44 N	14.20 E
Wind Lake	216	42.50 N	88.09 W
Wind Lake ⊜	216	42.50 N	88.09 W
Windlass Run ≃	284b	39.24 N	76.24 W
Windleite Λ	54	51.22 N	10.56 E
Windlesham	260	51.22 N	0.40 W
Windley Key I	220	24.57 N	80.35 W
Windmill Point >, Ont., Can.	284a	42.52 N	79.01 W
Windmill Point >, Mich., U.S.	281	42.22 N	82.55 W
Windmill Point >, Va., U.S.	208	37.37 N	76.17 W
Windom, Minn., U.S.	198	43.52 N	95.07 W
Windom, N.Y., U.S.	210	42.47 N	78.48 W
Windom Peak Λ	200	37.37 N	107.35 W
Windorah	166	25.26 S	142.39 E
Windorf, B.R.D.	60	48.37 N	13.13 E
Windorf, Öst.	61	48.27 N	14.02 E
Window Rock	200	35.41 N	109.03 W
Wind Point	216	42.47 N	87.46 W
Wind River Indian Reservation ◆[4]	202	43.26 N	109.00 W
Wind River Peak Λ	200	42.42 N	109.07 W
Wind River Range Ѧ	200	43.05 N	109.25 W
Windrush ≃	42	51.42 N	1.25 W
Windsbach	56	49.14 N	10.50 E
Windsor, Austl.	168b	34.25 S	138.20 E
Windsor, Austl.	170	33.37 S	150.49 E
Windsor, N.B., Can.	186	48.57 N	55.40 W
Windsor, N.S., Can.	186	44.59 N	64.08 W
Windsor, Ont., Can.	214		
	281	42.18 N	83.01 W
Windsor, Qué., Can.	206	45.34 N	72.00 W
Windsor, Eng., U.K.	42	51.29 N	0.38 W
Windsor, Calif., U.S.	204	38.33 N	122.49 W
Windsor, Colo., U.S.	200	40.29 N	104.54 W
Windsor, Conn., U.S.	207	41.51 N	72.39 W
Windsor, Ill., U.S.	194	39.26 N	88.36 W
Windsor, Ind., U.S.	218	40.09 N	85.12 W
Windsor, Mo., U.S.	194	38.32 N	93.31 W
Windsor, N.J., U.S.	208	40.15 N	74.35 W
Windsor, N.C., U.S.	192	36.00 N	76.57 W
Windsor, N.Y., U.S.	210	42.05 N	75.39 W
Windsor, Ohio, U.S.	214	41.32 N	80.56 W
Windsor, Pa., U.S.	208	39.55 N	76.35 W
Windsor, Vt., U.S.	188	43.29 N	72.23 W
Windsor, Va., U.S.	208	36.48 N	76.45 W
Windsor, Wis., U.S.	216	43.13 N	89.20 W
Windsor, Gare ◆[5]	275a	45.30 N	73.34 W
Windsor, University of ʋ[2]	281	42.18 N	83.04 W
Windsor Airport ⊠	214	42.17 N	82.58 W
Windsor and Maidenhead □[8]	260	51.28 N	0.37 W
Windsor Castle ⊥	42	51.29 N	0.36 W
Windsor Dam ◆[6]	188	42.29 N	72.42 W
Windsor Forest ◆[3]	42	51.27 N	0.43 W
Windsor Great Park ♠	260	51.27 N	0.37 W
Windsor Heights	214	40.12 N	80.40 W
Windsor Hills	280	33.59 N	118.21 W
Windsor Locks	207	41.56 N	72.38 W
Windsor Race Course ♠	260	51.29 N	0.39 W
Windsor Raceway ♠	281	42.15 N	83.05 W
Windsorton	158	28.16 S	24.44 E
Windsorville	207	41.53 N	72.32 W
Windthorst	196	33.34 N	98.26 W
Windward Islands II	238	13.00 N	61.00 W
Windward Passage Ш	238	20.00 N	73.50 W
Windy Hills	285	39.41 N	75.43 W
Windy Lake ⊜	184	54.22 N	102.35 W
Windy Peak Λ	202	48.56 N	119.58 W
Windy Run ≃	284c	38.54 N	77.05 W
Winefred ≃	184	56.02 N	110.36 W
Winefred Lake ⊜	182	55.30 N	110.35 W
Winejok	140	9.01 N	27.34 E
Winesburg	214	40.37 N	81.42 W
Winfield, Alta., Can.	182	52.58 N	114.26 W
Winfield, Ala., U.S.	194	33.56 N	87.49 W
Winfield, Ill., U.S.	216	41.52 N	88.10 W
Winfield, Iowa, U.S.	190	41.07 N	91.26 W
Winfield, Kans., U.S.	198	37.15 N	96.59 W
Winfield, Mo., U.S.	219	38.59 N	90.44 W
Winfield, N.J., U.S.	276	40.39 N	74.17 W
Winfield, Tex., U.S.	222	33.10 N	95.07 W
Winfield, W. Va., U.S.	188	38.32 N	81.53 W
Wing	198	47.09 N	100.17 W
Wing ≃	198	46.29 N	94.58 W
Wingan National Park ♠	166	37.43 S	149.30 E
Wingate, Md., U.S.	208	38.18 N	76.06 W
Wingate, N.C., U.S.	192	34.59 N	80.27 W
Wingate Mountains Ѧ	164	14.29 S	130.42 E
Wingates	262	53.34 N	2.32 W
Wingdale	210	41.39 N	73.34 W
Wingecarribee ≃	170	34.23 S	150.07 E
Wingello	170	34.42 S	150.09 E
Wingene	50	51.04 N	3.16 E
Wingen-sur-Moder	56	48.55 N	7.22 E
Wingham, Austl.	166	31.52 S	152.22 E
Wingham, Ont., Can.	212	43.53 N	81.19 W
Wingham, Eng., U.K.	42	51.17 N	1.13 E
Wing Lake Shores	281	42.33 N	83.17 W
Wingles	50	50.29 N	2.51 E
Wings Airport ⊠	285	40.08 N	75.16 W
Wingst	52	53.43 N	9.03 E
Winhole Channel Ш	276	43.37 N	73.48 W
Winhöring	60	48.16 N	12.39 E
Winifred	202	47.04 N	109.23 W
Winifreda	252	36.15 S	64.14 W
Winisk	176	55.15 N	85.12 W
Winisk ≃	176	55.17 N	85.05 W
Winisk Lake ⊜	176	52.55 N	87.22 W
Wink	196	31.45 N	103.09 W
Winkana	110	15.44 N	98.01 E
Winkelman	200	32.59 N	110.46 W
Winkelpos	158	27.35 S	26.49 E
Winkler, Man., Can.	184	49.11 N	97.56 W
Winkler, Tex., U.S.	222	31.56 N	96.13 W
Winklern	64	46.52 N	12.52 E
Winlaw	182	49.37 N	117.34 W
Winlock	224	46.29 N	122.56 W
Winneba	150	5.25 N	0.36 W
Winnebago, Ill., U.S.	190	42.16 N	89.15 W
Winnebago, Minn., U.S.	190	43.46 N	94.10 W
Winnebago, Nebr., U.S.	198	42.14 N	96.28 W
Winnebago □[6]	216	42.17 N	89.06 W
Winnebago ≃	190	43.03 N	92.57 W
Winnebago, Lake ⊜	190	44.00 N	88.25 W
Winnebago Indian Reservation ◆[4], Nebr., U.S.	198	42.15 N	96.31 W
Winnebago Indian Reservation ◆[4], Wis., U.S.	190	44.15 N	90.38 W
Winnecke, Mount Λ[2]	162	18.47 S	130.20 E
Winnecke Creek ≃	162	18.35 S	131.34 E
Winneconne	190	44.07 N	88.43 W
Winneconnet	283	41.59 N	71.08 W
Winneconnet Pond ⊜	283	41.58 N	71.08 W
Winnekendonk	52	51.36 N	6.17 E
Winnemucca	204	40.58 N	117.44 W
Winnemucca Lake ⊜	204	40.09 N	119.20 W
Winnenden	56	48.53 N	9.24 E
Winner	198	43.22 N	99.51 W
Winnetka	216	42.07 N	87.44 W
Winnetka ◆[8]	280	34.13 N	118.35 W
Winnett	202	47.00 N	108.21 W
Winnfield	194	31.55 N	92.38 W
Winnibigoshish, Lake ⊜	190	47.27 N	94.12 W
Winnie	194	29.49 N	94.23 W
Winning	162	23.09 S	114.32 E
Winningen, B.R.D.	56	50.18 N	7.31 E
Winningen, D.D.R.	54	51.49 N	11.26 E
Winnipeg	184	49.53 N	97.09 W
Winnipeg ≃	184	50.38 N	96.19 W
Winnipeg, Lake ⊜	184	52.00 N	97.00 W
Winnipeg Beach	184	50.31 N	96.58 W
Winnipegosis	184	51.39 N	99.56 W
Winnipegosis, Lake ⊜	184	52.30 N	100.00 W
Winnipesaukee, Lake ⊜	188	43.35 N	71.20 W
Winnsboro, La., U.S.	194	32.10 N	91.43 W
Winnsboro, S.C., U.S.	192	34.22 N	81.05 W
Winnsboro, Tex., U.S.	222	32.58 N	95.17 W
Winnsboro Mills	192	34.22 N	81.06 W
Winnweiler	56	49.34 N	7.51 E
Winona, Kans., U.S.	198	39.04 N	101.15 W
Winona, Mich., U.S.	190	46.52 N	88.55 W
Winona, Minn., U.S.	190	44.03 N	91.39 W
Winona, Miss., U.S.	194	33.29 N	89.44 W
Winona, Mo., U.S.	194	37.06 N	91.19 W
Winona, Ohio, U.S.	214	40.50 N	80.54 W
Winona, Tex., U.S.	222	32.29 N	95.10 W
Winona Lake, Ind., U.S.	216	41.14 N	85.49 W
Winona Lake, N.Y., U.S.	210	41.31 N	74.03 W
Winona Lake ⊜	216	41.13 N	85.50 W
Winooski	188	44.29 N	73.11 W
Winooski ≃	188	44.30 N	73.15 W
Winooski, North Branch ≃	188	44.15 N	72.35 W
Winschoten	52	53.08 N	7.02 E
Winsen, B.R.D.	52	52.41 N	9.54 E
Winsen, B.R.D.	52	53.22 N	10.12 E
Winsford, Eng., U.K.	42	51.06 N	3.33 W
Winsford, Eng., U.K.	44	53.12 N	2.32 W
Winshill	42	52.48 N	1.36 W
Winside	198	42.11 N	97.10 W
Winslow, Eng., U.K.	42	51.57 N	0.54 W
Winslow, Ariz., U.S.	200	35.01 N	110.42 W
Winslow, Maine, U.S.	188	44.32 N	69.38 W
Winslow, N.J., U.S.	285	39.39 N	74.52 W
Winslow, Wash., U.S.	224	47.37 N	122.31 W
Winslow Seamount ✢[3]	14	1.35 N	174.55 W
Winsted, Conn., U.S.	207	41.55 N	73.04 W
Winsted, Minn., U.S.	190	44.58 N	94.03 W
Winston, Fla., U.S.	220	28.02 N	82.01 W
Winston, Oreg., U.S.	202	45.07 N	123.25 W
Winston Churchill Memorial ʋ	219	38.52 N	91.58 W
Winston Creek ≃	224	46.30 N	122.40 W
Winston-Salem	192	36.06 N	80.15 W
Winsum	52	53.19 N	6.31 E
Wintego Lake ⊜	184	55.33 N	102.52 W
Winter	190	45.49 N	91.01 W
Winter Beach	220	27.43 N	80.25 W
Winterberg, B.R.D.	56	51.11 N	8.32 E
Winterberg, B.R.D.	263	51.17 N	7.18 E
Winterberg Λ[2]	263	51.20 N	7.13 E
Winterberge Ѧ	158	32.28 S	26.15 E
Winterbourne Abbas	42	50.43 N	2.34 W
Winter Creek ≃	280	34.12 N	118.02 W
Winterfeld	54	52.44 N	11.14 E
Winter Garden	220	28.34 N	81.35 W
Winter Gardens	228	32.50 N	116.56 W
Winter Harbor	188	44.24 N	68.05 W
Winter Harbour	182	50.31 N	128.02 W
Winterhaven, Calif., U.S.	204	32.44 N	114.38 W
Winter Haven, Fla., U.S.	220	28.01 N	81.44 W
Winter Hill Λ[2]	262	53.38 N	2.31 W
Wintering ≃	198	48.12 N	100.34 W
Wintering Lake ⊜	184	55.24 N	97.42 W
Winter Island I, N.W. Ter., Can.	176	66.14 N	83.04 W
Winter Island I, Calif., U.S.	282	38.03 N	121.51 W
Winter Island I, Mass., U.S.	283	42.32 N	70.52 W
Winterlingen	58	48.11 N	9.07 E
Winter Park	220	28.36 N	81.20 W
Winterport	188	44.38 N	68.51 W
Winters, Calif., U.S.	226	38.31 N	121.58 W
Winters, Tex., U.S.	196	31.57 N	99.58 W
Winters Bayou ≃	222	30.22 N	95.06 W
Winters Canal Ξ	226	38.32 N	121.58 W
Wintersdorf	54	51.03 N	12.21 E
Winterset, Iowa, U.S.	190	41.20 N	94.01 W
Winterset, Ohio, U.S.	214	40.06 N	81.25 W
Winter Springs	220	28.42 N	81.19 W
Winters Run ≃	208	39.26 N	76.18 W
Winterstown	208	39.50 N	76.37 W
Wintersville	214	40.23 N	80.42 W
Winterswijk	52	51.58 N	6.44 E
Winterthur, Schw.	58	47.30 N	8.43 E
Winterthur, Del., U.S.	285	39.48 N	75.36 W
Winterton, Newf., Can.	186	47.58 N	53.20 W
Winterton, S. Afr.	158	28.46 S	29.35 E
Winterton-on-Sea	42	52.43 N	1.42 E
Winterville, Miss., U.S.	194	33.30 N	91.10 W
Winterville, N.C., U.S.	192	35.32 N	77.24 W
Winthrop, Conn., U.S.	207	41.22 N	72.30 W
Winthrop, Iowa, U.S.	190	42.28 N	91.44 W
Winthrop, Maine, U.S.	188	44.18 N	69.59 W
Winthrop, Mass., U.S.	283	42.23 N	70.59 W
Winthrop, Minn., U.S.	190	44.32 N	94.22 W
Winthrop, Lake ⊜	283	42.11 N	71.25 W
Winthrop Harbor	216	42.29 N	87.49 W
Wintinna	162	27.44 S	134.07 E
Wintinna Creek ≃	162	27.47 S	134.14 E
Winton, Austl.	166	22.23 S	143.02 E
Winton, N.Z.	172	46.09 S	168.20 E
Winton, S. Afr.	158	27.29 S	22.34 E
Winton, Calif., U.S.	226	37.23 N	120.37 W
Winton, N.C., U.S.	192	36.24 N	76.56 W
Winton, Wash., U.S.	224	47.44 N	120.44 W
Wintzenheim	58	48.04 N	7.17 E
Winwick	262	53.26 N	2.36 W
Winzenberg	263	51.06 N	7.38 E
Winzer	60	48.44 N	13.04 E
Winzermark	263	51.23 N	7.08 E
Wipper ≃, B.R.D.	263	51.07 N	7.24 E
Wipper ≃, D.D.R.	54	51.47 N	11.42 E
Wipperdorf	54	51.28 N	10.42 E
Wipperfeld	263	51.05 N	7.19 E
Wipperfürth	56	51.07 N	7.23 E
Wippra	54	51.34 N	11.16 E
Wireton, Ill., U.S.	278	41.40 N	87.42 W
Wireton, Pa., U.S.	279b	40.34 N	80.14 W
Wiriaga ≃	164	2.17 S	132.52 E
Wirosari	115a	7.05 S	111.05 E
Wirral □[8]	262	53.22 N	3.05 W
Wirraminna	166	31.12 S	136.15 E
Wirrulla	162	32.24 S	134.31 E
Wisbech	42	52.40 N	0.10 E
Wisby → Visby	26	57.38 N	18.18 E
Wiscasset	188	44.00 N	69.40 W
Wische ◆[1]	54	52.50 N	11.55 E
Wischhafen	52	53.46 N	9.19 E
Wisconsin □[3]	178		
	190	44.45 N	89.30 W
Wisconsin ≃	190	43.00 N	91.15 W
Wisconsin, Lake ⊜[1]	190	43.24 N	89.43 W
Wisconsin Dells	190	43.38 N	89.46 W
Wisconsin Dells V	190	43.41 N	89.49 W
Wisconsin Rapids	190	44.23 N	89.49 W
Wiscoy	210	42.30 N	78.05 W
Wisdom	202	45.37 N	113.27 W
Wisdom, Lake ⊜	164	5.20 S	147.05 E
Wise	192	36.59 N	82.34 W
Wise □[6]	222	33.07 N	97.40 W
Wise ≃	202	45.48 N	112.57 W
Wiseman	180	67.25 N	150.06 W
Wisemans Ferry	170	33.24 S	150.59 E
Wises Landing	218	38.35 N	85.25 W
Wishart	184	51.34 N	104.00 W

Symbol	English	Deutsch	Español	Français	Português
≃	River	Fluss	Río	Rivière	Rio
Ξ	Canal	Kanal	Canal	Canal	Canal
↳	Waterfall, Rapids	Wasserfall, Stromschnellen	Cascada, Rápidos	Chute d'eau, Rapides	Cascata, Rápidos
Ш	Strait	Meeresstrasse	Estrecho	Détroit	Estreito
C	Bay, Gulf	Bucht, Golf	Bahía, Golfo	Baie, Golfe	Baía, Golfo
⊜	Lake, Lakes	See, Seen	Lago, Lagos	Lac, Lacs	Lago, Lagos
☰	Swamp	Sumpf	Pantano	Marais	Pântano
⍓	Ice Features, Glacier	Eis- und Gletscherformen	Accidentes Glaciales	Formes glaciaires	Acidentes Glaciares
⍑	Other Hydrographic Features	Andere Hydrographische Objekte	Otros Elementos Hidrográficos	Autres données hydrographiques	Outros Elementos Hidrográficos
✢	Submarine Features	Untermeerische Objekte	Accidentes Submarinos	Formes de relief sous-marin	Acidentes Submarinos
□	Political Unit	Politische Einheit	Unidad Política	Entité politique	Unidade Política
ʋ	Cultural Institution	Kulturelle Institution	Institución Cultural	Institution culturelle	Instituição Cultural
⊥	Historical Site	Historische Stätte	Sitio Histórico	Site historique	Sitio Histórico
♠	Recreational Site	Erholungs- und Ferienort	Sitio de Recreo	Centre de loisirs	Sítio de Lazer
⊠	Airport	Flughafen	Aeropuerto	Aéroport	Aeroporto
■	Military Installation	Militäranlage	Instalación Militar	Installation militaire	Instalação Militar
◆	Miscellaneous	Verschiedenes	Misceláneo	Divers	Miscelânea

ENGLISH — Name | Page | Lat.°′ | Long.°′
DEUTSCH — Name | Seite | Breite°′ | Länge°′ E=Ost

Wishaw 46 55.47 N 3.56 W
Wishek 198 46.16 N 99.33 W
Wishkah ≃ 224 46.58 N 123.45 W
Wishram 224 45.40 N 120.58 W
Wisła 30 49.40 N 18.52 E
Wisła ≃ 30 54.22 N 18.55 E
Wisley Aerodrome ⊠ 260 51.18 N 0.28 W
Wisley Gardens ♠ 260 51.19 N 0.29 W
Wisłok ≃ 30 50.13 N 22.32 E
Wisłoka ≃ 30 50.27 N 21.23 E
Wismar, D.D.R. 54 53.53 N 11.28 E
Wismar, Guy. 246 6.00 N 58.18 W
Wismarbucht ⊂ 54 53.57 N 11.25 E
Wisner, La., U.S. 194 31.59 N 91.39 W
Wisner, Nebr., U.S. 198 41.59 N 96.55 W
Wissahickon Creek ≃ 285 40.01 N 75.12 W
Wissant 50 50.53 N 1.40 E
Wissembourg 56 49.02 N 7.57 E
Wissen 56 50.47 N 7.43 E
Wissenkerke 52 51.35 N 3.45 E
Wissey ≃ 42 52.33 N 0.21 E
Wissinoming ✦[8] 285 40.01 N 75.04 W
Wissmar 56 50.38 N 8.41 E
Wissous 261 48.44 N 2.20 E
Wister 194 34.58 N 94.43 W
Wisznice 30 51.48 N 23.12 E
Witbank 158 25.56 S 29.07 E
Witbooisvlei 156 25.04 S 18.27 E
Witchekan Lake ⊜ 184 53.25 N 107.35 W
Witch Hazel 224 45.30 N 122.46 W
Witdraai 158 26.58 S 20.45 E
Witfield 273d 26.11 S 28.12 E
Witham 42 51.48 N 0.38 E
Witham ≃ 44 53.06 N 0.13 W
Withamsville 218 39.03 N 84.16 W
Withens Clough Reservoir ⊜[1] 262 53.42 N 2.02 W
Witheridge 42 50.55 N 3.42 W
Withernsea 44 53.44 N 0.02 E
Witherspoon, Mount ∧ 180 61.23 N 147.12 W
Withington ✦[8] 262 53.26 N 2.14 W
Withington Green 262 53.14 N 2.18 W
Withlacoochee ≃, U.S. 192 30.24 N 83.10 W
Withlacoochee ≃, Fla., U.S. 192 29.00 N 82.45 W
Withnell 262 53.42 N 2.34 W
Withok 273d 26.18 S 28.23 E
Withokspruit ≃ 273d 26.19 S 28.21 E
Wit Kei ≃ 158 32.09 S 27.24 E
Witkoppies ∧ 158 27.44 S 29.20 E
Witkowo 30 52.27 N 17.47 E
Witless Bay 186 47.16 N 52.50 W
Witley 42 51.09 N 0.38 W
Witney 42 51.48 N 1.29 W
Witnica 30 52.40 N 14.55 E
Witpoortje 273d 26.08 S 27.50 E
Witrivier 156 24.40 S 31.00 E
Witry-lès-Reims 50 49.18 N 4.07 E
Witsand 158 34.24 S 20.50 E
Witt 219 39.15 N 89.21 W
Wittabrenna Creek ≃ 166 29.20 S 142.43 E
Witteberg ⛰ 158 33.15 S 23.15 E
Witteberge ∧ 158 28.40 S 28.02 E
Witteberge ⛰, S. Afr. 158 30.45 S 27.32 E
Witteberge ⛰, S. Afr. 158 33.18 S 20.36 E
Wittelsheim 58 47.49 N 7.15 E
Witten 56 51.26 N 7.20 E
Wittenau ✦[8] 264a 52.35 N 13.20 E
Wittenberg, D.D.R. 54 51.52 N 12.39 E
Wittenberg, Wis., U.S. 190 44.49 N 89.10 W
Wittenberge 54 53.00 N 11.44 E
Wittenburg 54 53.31 N 11.04 E
Wittenheim 58 47.49 N 7.20 E
Wittenoom 162 22.17 S 118.19 E
Wittensee ⊜ 41 54.23 N 9.45 E
Wittgensdorf 54 50.53 N 12.52 E
Wittichenau 54 51.23 N 14.14 E
Wittingen 54 52.43 N 10.44 E
Wittislingen 56 48.37 N 10.25 E
Wittlaer 56 51.19 N 6.44 E
Wittlich 56 49.59 N 6.53 E
Wittmar 54 52.07 N 10.38 E
Wittmund 52 53.34 N 7.47 E
Witton Park ♠ 262 53.45 N 2.31 W
Wittow ≻[1] 54 54.38 N 13.19 E
Wittstock 54 53.10 N 12.29 E
Witu 154 2.23 S 40.26 E
Witu Islands II 164 4.40 S 149.25 E
Witvlei 156 22.23 S 18.32 E
Witwatersrand ✦[1] 158 26.00 S 27.00 E
Witwatersrand, University of ʋ[2] 273d 26.12 S 28.02 E
Witwatersrand Gold Mine ✦[7] 273d 26.12 S 28.15 E
Witzenhausen 56 51.20 N 9.51 E
Witzhelden 263 51.07 N 7.06 E
Witzputz 156 27.25 S 17.43 E
Wiveliscombe 42 51.03 N 3.19 W
Wivenhoe 42 51.52 N 0.58 E
Wiwa Creek ≃ 184 50.02 N 106.31 W
Wixom 216 42.31 N 83.32 W
Wiżajny 30 54.23 N 22.51 E
Wizernes 50 50.43 N 2.14 E
Wjatka → V'atka ≃ 80 55.36 N 51.30 E
W. J. van Blommestein Meer ⊜[1] 250 4.45 N 55.00 W
Wkra ≃ 30 52.27 N 20.44 E
Wladiwostok → Vladivostok 89 43.10 N 131.56 E
Władysławowo 30 54.49 N 18.25 E
Wleń 30 51.01 N 15.40 E
Wlingi 115a 8.05 S 112.19 E
Włocławek 30 52.39 N 19.02 E
Włodawa 30 51.34 N 23.32 E
Włoszczowa 30 50.52 N 19.59 E
Wnion ≃ 42 52.45 N 3.54 W
Woady Yaloak ≃ 169 38.06 S 143.33 E
Wobaer 85 39.19 N 75.32 E
Wöbbelin 54 53.24 N 11.30 E
Woburn 207 42.29 N 71.09 W
Woburn ✦[8] 275b 43.46 N 79.13 W
Woburn Sands 42 52.01 N 0.39 W
Woden, Austl. 171b 35.22 S 149.08 E
Woden, Tex., U.S. 222 31.30 N 94.32 W
Wodgina 162 21.11 S 118.40 E
Wodonga 166 36.07 S 146.54 E
Wodzisław Śląski 30 50.00 N 18.28 E
Woensdrecht 52 51.26 N 4.18 E
Woerdeke 85 39.41 N 77.53 E
Woerden 52 52.05 N 4.54 E
Woerth 56 48.56 N 7.45 E
Woëvre □[9] 56 49.27 N 5.17 E
Wofosi 105 40.09 N 115.18 E
Wofosi (Temple of the Sleeping Buddha) ʋ[1] 105 40.01 N 116.12 E
Wognum 52 52.41 N 5.01 E
Wohlau → Wołów 30 51.21 N 16.39 E
Wohlde 41 54.24 N 9.17 E
Wohlen 58 47.21 N 8.17 E
Wohlensee ⊜ 58 46.58 N 7.20 E
Wohlford, Lake ⊜[1] 228 33.10 N 116.59 W
Wohlthat Mountains ⛰ 9 71.35 S 12.20 E
Wohra ≃ 56 50.49 N 8.55 E
Woi 140 7.53 N 31.10 E
Woincourt 50 50.04 N 1.32 E
Wojcieszów 30 50.58 N 15.56 E
Wokalup 168a 33.06 S 115.53 E
Wokam, Pulau I 164 5.37 S 134.30 E
Wokha 120 26.06 N 94.16 E
Woking, Alta., Can. 182 55.35 N 118.46 W
Woking, Eng., U.K. 42 51.20 N 0.34 W
Woking □[8] 260 51.19 N 0.32 W
Wokingham 42 51.25 N 0.51 W
Wokingham Creek ≃ 166 22.19 S 142.30 E
Wolbach 198 41.24 N 98.24 W
Wolbeck 52 51.55 N 7.43 E
Wolbrom 30 50.24 N 19.46 E
Wolcott, Conn., U.S. 207 41.36 N 72.59 W
Wolcott, Ind., U.S. 216 40.46 N 87.03 W
Wolcott, N.Y., U.S. 210 43.13 N 76.49 W
Wolcott Creek ≃ 210 43.17 N 76.50 W
Wolcottsburg 210 43.04 N 78.38 W
Wolcottsville 210 43.07 N 78.31 W
Wolcottville 194 41.32 N 85.22 W
Wołczyn 30 51.01 N 18.03 E
Woldberg ⛰[1] 52 52.25 N 5.55 E
Woldegk 54 53.27 N 13.35 E
Woldenburg → Dobiegniew 30 52.59 N 15.47 E
Woldingham 260 51.17 N 0.02 W
Woleai I[1] 108 7.21 N 143.52 E
Woleu-Ntem □[4] 152 2.00 N 12.00 E
Wolf ≃, U.S. 194 35.09 N 90.04 W
Wolf ≃, Kans., U.S. 198 39.54 N 95.11 W
Wolf ≃, Miss., U.S. 194 30.21 N 89.18 W
Wolf ≃, Wis., U.S. 190 44.11 N 88.48 W
Wolf, Isla I 246a 1.23 N 91.49 W
Wolf, Volcán ∧[1] 246a 0.02 N 91.20 W
Wolfach 58 48.17 N 8.13 E
Wolf Bay 186 50.16 N 60.08 W
Wolf Creek, Mont., U.S. 202 47.00 N 112.04 W
Wolf Creek, Oreg., U.S. 202 42.42 N 123.24 W
Wolf Creek ≃, U.S. 196 36.35 N 99.30 W
Wolf Creek ≃, Calif., U.S. 226 39.02 N 121.08 W
Wolf Creek ≃, Ind., U.S. 216 41.15 N 87.07 W
Wolf Creek ≃, Iowa, U.S. 190 42.20 N 92.09 W
Wolf Creek ≃, Mont., U.S. 198 48.05 N 105.40 W
Wolf Creek ≃, Mont., U.S. 202 46.50 N 112.20 W
Wolf Creek ≃, Mont., U.S. 202 47.37 N 109.38 W
Wolf Creek ≃, Ohio, U.S. 214 41.16 N 83.11 W
Wolf Creek ≃, Pa., U.S. 214 41.03 N 80.07 W
Wolf Creek ≃, S. Dak., U.S. 198 44.42 N 98.40 W
Wolf Creek ≃, S. Dak., U.S. 198 43.21 N 97.37 W
Wolf Creek Pass)(200 37.29 N 106.48 W
Wolf Creek State Park ♠ 219 39.30 N 88.41 W
Wolfdale 214 40.12 N 80.17 W
Wolfe □[6] 206 45.45 N 71.30 W
Wolfeboro 188 43.35 N 71.12 W
Wolfegg 58 47.49 N 9.47 E
Wolfe Island 212 44.12 N 76.26 W
Wolfe Island I 212 44.12 N 76.26 W
Wolfe Lake ⊜ 212 44.40 N 76.30 W
Wolfen 54 51.40 N 12.16 E
Wolfenbüttel 52 52.10 N 10.32 E
Wolfenden, Mount ∧ 182 50.26 N 127.33 W
Wolfenschiessen 58 46.55 N 8.24 E
Wolfertschwenden 58 47.53 N 10.16 E
Wolfforth 196 33.30 N 102.01 W
Wolfhagen 56 51.19 N 9.10 E
Wölfis 54 50.48 N 10.46 E
Wolf Island I 212 44.33 N 78.15 W
Wolflake, Ind., U.S. 216 41.20 N 85.30 W
Wolf Lake, Mich., U.S. 216 43.14 N 86.10 W
Wolf Lake ⊜, Alta., Can. 182 54.42 N 110.59 W
Wolf Lake ⊜, Ont., Can. 212 44.44 N 78.11 W
Wolf Lake ⊜, Yukon, Can. 180 60.40 N 131.40 W
Wolf Lake ⊜, U.S. 278 41.40 N 87.31 W
Wolf Lake ⊜, N.J., U.S. 276 40.57 N 74.42 W
Wolf Mountain ∧ 180 65.17 N 154.02 W
Wolfpassing 264b 48.19 N 16.11 E
Wolf Point 202 48.05 N 105.39 W
Wolframs-Eschenbach 56 49.14 N 10.43 E
Wolfratshausen 64 47.54 N 11.25 E
Wolf Rock I[2] 28 49.57 N 5.49 W
Wolf Run 214 40.30 N 80.54 W
Wolfsberg 61 46.51 N 14.51 E
Wolfsberg ∧[2] 263 51.38 N 6.27 E
Wolfsburg 54 52.25 N 10.47 E
Wolf's Castle 42 51.54 N 4.58 W
Wolfsegg am Hausruck 60 48.06 N 13.40 E
Wolfskehlen 56 49.51 N 8.30 E
Wolfstein 56 49.35 N 7.36 E
Wolftrap Creek ≃ 284c 38.58 N 77.17 W
Wolfurt 58 47.28 N 9.45 E
Wolfville 186 45.05 N 64.22 W
Wolga → Volga ≃ 22 45.55 N 47.52 E
Wolgan ≃ 170 33.12 S 150.28 E
Wolgast 54 54.03 N 13.46 E
Wolgograd → Volgograd 80 48.44 N 44.25 E
Wolgograder Stausee → Volgogradskoje Vodochranilišče ⊜[1] 80 49.20 N 45.00 E
Wolhusen 58 47.04 N 8.04 E
Wolin 30 53.50 N 14.35 E
Wolin I 54 53.55 N 14.31 E
Woliński Park Narodowy ♠ 30 53.55 N 14.30 E
Wolkenstein 54 50.39 N 13.04 E
Wolkersdorf 61 48.23 N 16.31 E
Wölkisch 54 51.13 N 13.21 E
Wolkramshausen 54 51.25 N 10.44 E
Wollangambe Creek ≃ 170 33.21 S 150.35 E
Wollaston, Cape ≻ 176 71.04 N 118.07 W
Wollaston, Islas II 254b 55.40 S 67.30 W
Wollaston Lake ⊜, Ont., Can. 212 44.50 N 77.50 W
Wollaston Lake ⊜, Sask., Can. 176 58.15 N 103.20 W
Wollaston Peninsula ≻[1] 176 70.00 N 115.00 W
Wollemi Creek ≃ 170 33.13 S 150.31 E
Wollogorang 166 17.13 S 137.57 E
Wollombi 170 32.56 S 151.09 E
Wollombi Brook ≃ 170 32.33 S 151.04 E
Wollondilly ≃ 170 33.57 S 150.26 E
Wollongong 170 34.25 S 150.54 E
Wöllstein 56 49.49 N 7.58 E
Wolmaransstad 158 27.12 S 26.13 E
Wolmirsleben 54 51.57 N 11.29 E
Wolmirstedt 54 52.15 N 11.37 E
Wolnzach 60 48.36 N 11.37 E
Wołomin 30 52.21 N 21.14 E
Wołów 30 51.21 N 16.39 E
Wolowaru 115b 8.46 S 121.54 E
Wolseley, Sask., Can. 184 50.25 N 103.19 W
Wolseley, S. Afr. 158 33.26 S 19.12 E
Wölserbach ≃ 61 47.08 N 14.23 E
Wolsey 198 44.25 N 98.28 W
Wolsingham 44 54.44 N 1.52 W
Wolsztyn 30 52.08 N 16.06 E
Wolterdingen 52 53.02 N 9.50 E
Woltersdorf, D.D.R. 54 52.24 N 12.22 E
Woltersdorf, D.D.R. 54 52.26 N 13.45 E
Woluogu 105 39.40 N 117.46 E
Woluwe-Saint-Pierre 50 50.50 N 4.25 E
Wolvega 52 52.53 N 6.00 E
Wolvenspruit 158 28.50 S 25.32 E
Wolverhampton 42 52.36 N 2.08 W
Wolverine 190 45.16 N 84.36 W
Wolverine Lake 281 42.33 N 83.29 W
Wolverine Loon Lake ⊜ 281 42.33 N 83.30 W
Wolverine Mountain ∧ 180 65.20 N 149.51 W
Wolvertem 50 50.57 N 4.18 E
Wolverton 42 52.04 N 0.50 W
Wolwehoek 158 26.55 S 27.48 E
Wolziger See ⊜ 54 52.16 N 13.50 E
Woman ≃ 190 47.57 N 82.19 W
Wombarra 170 34.16 S 150.58 E
Wombat, Mount ∧ 169 36.51 S 145.40 E
Wombeyan Caves •[5] 170 34.18 S 149.56 E
Wombwell 44 53.31 N 1.24 W
Womelsdorf 208 40.22 N 76.11 W
Womerah Range ⛰ 170 33.16 S 150.46 E
Wommels 52 53.06 N 5.36 E
Wonarah 162 19.55 S 136.20 E
Wondai 166 26.19 S 151.52 E
Wondelgem 50 51.05 N 3.43 E
Wonderkop 158 27.50 S 27.26 E
Wonder Lake 216 42.25 N 88.21 W
Wonderland 204 40.24 N 121.19 W
Wonderland Center ✦[9] 281 42.22 N 83.20 W
Wondinong 162 27.52 S 118.25 E
Wŏndong-ni 98 34.23 N 126.40 E
Wonersh 260 51.12 N 0.33 W
Wonewoc 190 43.39 N 90.14 W
Wong ≃ 124 27.10 N 89.30 E
Wongan Hills 162 30.53 S 116.42 E
Wonga Park 274b 37.44 S 145.16 E
Wonggarasi 112 0.33 N 121.36 E
Wong Ka Wai 271d 22.24 N 113.58 E
Woniushi 104 42.31 N 123.03 E
Wŏnjang-ni 98 39.05 N 125.32 E
Wŏnju 98 37.22 N 127.58 E
Wono 144 8.31 N 37.30 E
Wonogiri 115a 7.49 S 110.55 E
Wonokromo 115a 7.18 S 112.44 E
Wonosari 115a 7.58 S 110.35 E
Wonosegoro 115a 7.18 S 110.39 E
Wonosobo 115a 7.22 S 109.54 E
Wonreli 112 8.05 S 127.09 E
Wŏnsan 98 39.09 N 127.25 E
Wonthaggi 169 38.36 S 145.35 E
Woocalla 166 31.42 S 137.13 E
Wood, Pa., U.S. 214 40.10 N 78.08 W
Wood, S. Dak., U.S. 198 43.30 N 100.29 W
Wood □[6], Ohio, U.S. 216 41.22 N 83.39 W
Wood □[6], Tex., U.S. 222 32.48 N 95.20 W
Wood ≃, B.C., Can. 182 52.10 N 118.30 W
Wood ≃, Sask., Can. 184 50.08 N 106.10 W
Wood ≃, U.S. 207 41.26 N 71.43 W
Wood ≃, Nebr., U.S. 198 41.02 N 98.05 W
Wood ≃, Wyo., U.S. 202 44.07 N 108.58 W
Wood, Mount ∧, Yukon, Can. 180 61.14 N 140.31 W
Wood, Mount ∧, Mont., U.S. 202 45.17 N 109.49 W
Woodacre 226 38.05 N 122.36 W
Woodall Mountain ∧[2] 194 34.45 N 88.11 W
Wood Bay ⊂ 180 69.45 N 129.00 W
Woodbine, Ga., U.S. 192 30.58 N 81.43 W
Woodbine, Iowa, U.S. 198 41.44 N 95.43 W
Woodbine, Md., U.S. 208 39.22 N 77.04 W
Woodbine, N.J., U.S. 208 39.14 N 74.49 W
Woodbourne, N.Y., U.S. 210 41.46 N 74.35 W
Woodbourne, Ohio, U.S. 218 39.38 N 84.10 W
Woodbourne, Pa., U.S. 285 40.12 N 74.53 W
Woodbridge, Eng., U.K. 42 52.06 N 1.19 E
Woodbridge, Calif., U.S. 226 38.09 N 121.18 W
Woodbridge, Conn., U.S. 207 41.21 N 73.02 W
Woodbridge, N.J., U.S. 210 40.33 N 74.17 W
Woodbridge, Va., U.S. 208 38.39 N 77.15 W
Woodbridge Center ✦[9] 276 40.33 N 74.18 W
Woodbridge Creek ≃ 276 40.32 N 74.15 W
Woodbridge Island I 283 42.48 N 70.50 W
Woodburn, Ill., U.S. 219 39.03 N 90.00 W
Woodburn, Ind., U.S. 216 41.08 N 84.51 W
Woodburn, Oreg., U.S. 224 45.09 N 122.51 W
Woodbury, Eng., U.K. 42 50.41 N 3.24 W
Woodbury, Conn., U.S. 207 41.33 N 73.13 W
Woodbury, Ga., U.S. 192 32.59 N 84.35 W
Woodbury, Mich., U.S. 216 42.46 N 85.05 W
Woodbury, N.J., U.S. 208 39.50 N 75.10 W
Woodbury, N.Y., U.S. 276 40.49 N 73.28 W
Woodbury, Pa., U.S. 214 40.14 N 78.22 W
Woodbury, Tenn., U.S. 194 35.50 N 86.04 W
Woodbury Creek ≃ 285 39.52 N 75.11 W
Woodbury Heights 285 39.49 N 75.09 W
Woodchester 168b 35.13 S 138.57 E
Woodchopper 180 65.03 N 151.00 W
Woodchurch 42 51.05 N 0.46 E
Woodcliff Lake 276 41.01 N 74.03 W
Woodcliff Lake ⊜ 276 41.01 N 74.03 W
Woodcock 214 41.45 N 80.05 W
Woodcock, Mount ∧ 162 19.16 S 134.02 E
Woodcrest 228 33.52 N 117.21 W
Wood Dale 278 41.58 N 87.58 W
Wooded Bluff •[4] 166 29.22 S 153.22 E
Woodenbong 166 28.23 S 152.37 E
Woodend 169 37.22 S 144.32 E
Woodfibre 182 49.40 N 123.15 W
Woodford, Austl. 171a 26.57 S 152.47 E
Woodford, Eire 48 53.03 N 8.23 W
Woodford, Eng., U.K. 262 53.21 N 2.10 W
Woodford □[6], Ill., U.S. 216 40.43 N 89.16 W
Woodford □[6], Ky., U.S. 218 38.06 N 84.15 W
Woodford ✦[8] 260 51.36 N 0.02 E
Woodford Aerodrome ⊠ 262 53.20 N 2.09 W
Woodford Bridge ✦[8] 260 51.36 N 0.04 E
Woodford Halse 42 52.10 N 1.12 W
Wood Green ✦[8] 260 51.36 N 0.07 W
Woodham 260 51.21 N 0.30 W
Woodham Ferrers 260 51.40 N 0.36 E
Woodham Mortimer 260 51.43 N 0.37 E
Woodham Walter 260 51.44 N 0.37 E
Woodhaven 216 42.08 N 83.14 W
Woodhaven ✦[8] 276 40.41 N 73.51 W
Woodhead Reservoir ⊜[1] 262 53.30 N 1.52 W
Woodhill 275b 43.45 N 79.41 W
Wood Hill ∧[2] 283 42.39 N 71.13 W
Woodhull, Ill., U.S. 190 41.11 N 90.20 W
Woodhull, N.Y., U.S. 210 42.05 N 77.25 W
Woodinville 224 47.45 N 122.09 W
Wood Islands 186 45.58 N 62.45 W
Woodlake, Calif., U.S. 204 36.25 N 119.06 W
Wood Lake, Nebr., U.S. 198 42.38 N 100.14 W
Woodlake, Tex., U.S. 222 31.01 N 95.02 W
Wood Lake ⊜, Ont., Can. 212 45.01 N 79.05 W
Wood Lake ⊜, Sask., Can. 184 55.17 N 103.17 W
Woodland, Calif., U.S. 226 38.41 N 121.46 W
Woodland, Ill., U.S. 216 40.43 N 87.44 W
Woodland, Maine, U.S. 188 45.09 N 67.24 W
Woodland, Mich., U.S. 216 42.43 N 85.08 W
Woodland, Pa., U.S. 214 41.00 N 78.21 W
Woodland, Wash., U.S. 224 45.54 N 122.45 W
Woodland Acres 228 34.24 N 119.18 W
Woodland Beach 216 41.57 N 83.19 W
Woodland Heights 214 41.25 N 79.43 W
Woodland Hills 222 32.39 N 96.55 W
Woodland Hills ✦[8] 280 34.11 N 118.35 W
Woodland Hills Park ♠ 279a 41.28 N 81.36 W
Woodland Park, Colo., U.S. 200 39.00 N 105.03 W
Woodland Park, Pa., U.S. 210 41.18 N 77.03 W
Woodlands, N.Z. 172 46.22 S 168.33 E
Woodlands, Sing. 271c 1.27 N 103.46 E
Woodlands, N.Y., U.S. 276 41.01 N 73.50 W
Woodlark Island I 164 9.05 S 152.50 E
Woodlawn, Ill., U.S. 219 38.20 N 89.02 W
Woodlawn, Ky., U.S. 194 37.04 N 85.04 W
Woodlawn, Md., U.S. 284b 39.19 N 76.43 W
Woodlawn, Md., U.S. 284c 38.57 N 76.53 W
Woodlawn, Wash., U.S. 224 47.01 N 123.48 W
Woodlawn ✦[8] 278 41.47 N 87.36 W
Woodlawn Beach 210 42.48 N 78.51 W
Woodlawn Heights 284b 39.11 N 76.39 W
Woodley 42 51.28 N 0.54 W
Woodlyn 285 39.52 N 75.21 W
Woodlynne 285 39.55 N 75.05 W
Woodmansey 44 53.50 N 0.29 W
Woodmansterne 260 51.19 N 0.10 W
Woodmere, N.Y., U.S. 210 40.38 N 73.43 W
Woodmere, Ohio, U.S. 279a 41.28 N 81.29 W
Woodmoor 284b 39.20 N 76.44 W
Wood Mountain ∧ 184 49.14 N 106.20 W
Woodplumpton 44 53.48 N 2.47 W
Woodport 276 40.59 N 74.36 W
Woodrarung Range ⛰ 162 27.10 S 115.30 E
Woodridge, Austl. 171a 27.38 S 153.06 E
Woodridge, Man., Can. 184 49.17 N 96.09 W
Woodridge, Ill., U.S. 216 41.46 N 88.04 W
Wood-Ridge, N.J., U.S. 276 40.51 N 74.05 W
Woodridge, N.Y., U.S. 210 41.43 N 74.34 W
Wood River, Alaska, U.S. 180 59.04 N 158.26 W
Wood River, Ill., U.S. 219 38.52 N 90.05 W
Wood River, Nebr., U.S. 198 40.49 N 98.36 W
Wood River Indian Reserve ✦[4] 184 49.21 N 106.24 W
Wood River Lakes ⊜ 180 59.30 N 158.45 W
Wood River Mountains ⛰ 180 59.32 N 159.30 W
Woodroffe ≃ 166 21.28 S 137.58 E
Woodroffe, Mount ∧ 162 26.20 S 131.45 E
Woodrow Wilson Memorial Bridge ✦[5] 284c 38.48 N 77.02 W
Woodruff, Ariz., U.S. 200 34.47 N 110.03 W
Woodruff, S.C., U.S. 192 34.45 N 82.02 W
Woodruff, Wis., U.S. 190 45.54 N 89.42 W
Woodruff Creek ≃ 281 42.21 N 83.43 W
Woods 168b 34.15 S 138.31 E
Woods, Lake ⊜ 162 17.50 S 133.30 E
Woods, Lake of the ⊜ 184 49.15 N 94.45 W
Woods Bay ⊂ 212 45.08 N 80.00 W
Woodsboro, Md., U.S. 208 39.32 N 77.19 W
Woodsboro, Tex., U.S. 196 28.14 N 97.20 W
Woodsburgh 276 40.37 N 73.42 W
Woods Creek ≃, N.Y., U.S. 276 40.39 N 73.24 W
Woods Creek ≃, N.Y., U.S. 284a 43.04 N 78.58 W
Woodsfield 188 39.46 N 81.07 W
Woods Hole 207 41.31 N 70.40 W
Woodside, Austl. 166 38.31 S 146.52 E
Woodside, Austl. 168b 34.57 S 138.52 E
Woodside, Eng., U.K. 260 51.45 N 0.11 W
Woodside, Calif., U.S. 226 37.26 N 122.15 W
Woodside, Del., U.S. 208 39.04 N 75.34 W
Woodside, Pa., U.S. 285 40.13 N 74.53 W
Woodside ✦[8] 276 40.45 N 73.55 W
Woodside National Historic Park ♠ 212 43.26 N 80.08 W
Woodson, Ill., U.S. 219 39.38 N 90.13 W
Woodson, Tex., U.S. 196 33.01 N 99.03 W
Woods Point 169 37.35 S 146.15 E
Woodstock, Austl. 166 22.15 S 141.57 E
Woodstock, N.B., Can. 186 46.09 N 67.34 W
Woodstock, Ont., Can. 212 43.08 N 80.45 W
Woodstock, Eng., U.K. 42 51.52 N 1.21 W
Woodstock, Conn., U.S. 207 41.57 N 71.59 W
Woodstock, Ill., U.S. 216 42.19 N 88.27 W
Woodstock, Md., U.S. 284b 39.20 N 76.52 W
Woodstock, N.Y., U.S. 210 42.02 N 74.07 W
Woodstock, Ohio, U.S. 218 40.10 N 83.32 W
Woodstock, Vt., U.S. 188 43.37 N 72.31 W
Woodstock, Va., U.S. 188 38.53 N 78.31 W
Woodstown 208 39.39 N 75.19 W
Wood Street 260 51.15 N 0.38 W
Woodsville 188 44.09 N 72.02 W
Woodvale Airfield ⊠ 262 53.35 N 3.03 W
Woodview Manor 278 42.06 N 87.53 W
Wood Village 224 45.32 N 122.19 W
Woodville, Austl. 168b 34.53 S 138.32 E
Woodville, Ont., Can. 212 44.24 N 78.59 W
Woodville, N.Z. 172 40.20 S 175.52 E
Woodville, Ala., U.S. 194 34.38 N 86.16 W
Woodville, Calif., U.S. 226 36.06 N 119.12 W
Woodville, Fla., U.S. 192 30.20 N 84.15 W
Woodville, Ga., U.S. 192 33.40 N 83.06 W
Woodville, Mass., U.S. 207 42.14 N 71.34 W
Woodville, Mich., U.S. 216 42.16 N 84.30 W
Woodville, Miss., U.S. 194 31.01 N 91.18 W
Woodville, N.Y., U.S. 210 42.40 N 77.22 W
Woodville, Ohio, U.S. 214 41.27 N 83.22 W
Woodville, Tex., U.S. 194 30.46 N 94.25 W
Woodward, Iowa, U.S. 190 41.51 N 93.55 W
Woodward, Okla., U.S. 196 36.26 N 99.24 W
Woodward, Pa., U.S. 210 40.54 N 77.21 W
Woodward Reservoir ⊜[1] 226 37.51 N 120.52 W
Woodway, Tex., U.S. 222 31.30 N 97.13 W
Woodway, Wash., U.S. 224 47.47 N 122.23 W
Woodworth, Ohio, U.S. 214 40.59 N 80.40 W
Woodworth, Wis., U.S. 216 42.34 N 88.00 W
Woody ≃ 184 52.30 N 100.51 W
Woody Creek ≃ 202 47.27 N 106.21 W
Woody Island 180 57.47 N 152.22 W
Wool 42 50.41 N 2.14 W
Woolacombe 42 51.10 N 4.13 W
Woolamai, Cape ≻ 169 38.34 S 145.21 E
Wool Bay 168b 35.00 S 137.45 E
Wooldridge 158 33.13 S 27.15 E
Wooler 44 55.33 N 2.01 W
Woolford 208 38.30 N 76.11 W
Woolgangie 162 31.10 S 120.32 E
Woolgoolga 166 30.07 S 153.12 E
Woollahra 274a 33.53 S 151.15 E
Woolooware Bay ⊂ 274a 34.02 S 151.09 E
Woolpit 42 52.13 N 0.54 E
Woolrich 210 41.12 N 77.23 W
Woolsey Peak ∧ 200 33.10 N 112.53 W
Woolston 262 53.24 N 2.32 W
Woolton ✦[8] 262 53.23 N 2.52 W
Woolwich ✦[8] 260 51.29 N 0.04 E
Woomargama 171b 35.50 S 147.15 E
Woomera 166 31.31 S 137.10 E
Woonona 170 34.21 S 150.55 E
Woonsocket, R.I., U.S. 207 42.00 N 71.31 W
Woonsocket, S. Dak., U.S. 198 44.03 N 98.16 W
Woorabinda 166 24.08 S 149.28 E
Wooramel 162 25.44 S 114.17 E
Wooramel ≃ 162 25.47 S 114.10 E
Woorim 171b 27.08 S 153.12 E
Wooroloo 168a 31.48 S 116.19 E
Wooster 214 40.48 N 81.56 W
Wootton Bassett 42 51.33 N 1.54 W
Wootton Wawen 42 52.16 N 1.47 W
Worb 58 46.56 N 7.34 E
Worbis 54 51.25 N 10.21 E
Worcester, S. Afr. 158 33.39 S 19.27 E
Worcester, Eng., U.K. 42 52.11 N 2.13 W
Worcester, Mass., U.S. 207 42.16 N 71.48 W
Worcester, N.Y., U.S. 210 42.36 N 74.45 W
Worcester, Pa., U.S. 285 40.12 N 75.21 W
Worcester □[6], Md., U.S. 208 38.11 N 75.24 W
Worcester □[6], Mass., U.S. 207 42.16 N 71.48 W
Worcester Municipal Airport ⊠ 207 42.16 N 71.52 W
Worden, Ill., U.S. 219 38.56 N 89.50 W
Worden, Mont., U.S. 202 45.58 N 108.10 W
Worden Pond ⊜ 207 41.26 N 71.35 W
Wördern 264b 48.20 N 16.13 E
Wörgl 64 47.29 N 12.04 E
Workai, Pulau I 164 6.40 S 134.40 E
Work Channel Џ 182 54.30 N 130.15 W
Workers' Cultural Palace ʋ 269b 31.14 N 121.28 E
Working People's Cultural Palace ʋ 271a 39.55 N 116.23 E
Workington 44 54.39 N 3.35 W
Worksop 44 53.18 N 1.07 W
Workum 52 52.57 N 5.26 E
Worland 202 44.01 N 107.57 W
Worli ✦[8] 272c 19.01 N 72.50 E
Wörlitz 54 51.50 N 12.25 E
Wormditt → Orneta 30 54.08 N 20.08 E
Wormerveer 52 52.28 N 4.46 E
Wormhoudt 50 50.53 N 2.28 E
Wormit 46 56.25 N 2.59 W
Wormley 260 51.44 N 0.01 W
Worms 56 49.38 N 8.22 E
Worms Head ≻ 42 51.34 N 4.20 W
Wormshill 260 51.17 N 0.42 E
Wörnitz ≃ 56 48.42 N 10.45 E
Woronesch → Voronež 78 51.40 N 39.10 E
Woronoco 207 42.10 N 72.50 W
Woronora 274a 34.01 S 151.03 E
Woronora ≃ 274a 34.00 S 151.04 E
Worplesdon 260 51.16 N 0.37 W
Worpswede 52 53.13 N 8.56 E
Wörrstadt 56 49.50 N 8.07 E
Wörsbach ≃ 56 50.22 N 8.09 E
Worsley 262 53.30 N 2.23 W
Worsthorne 262 53.47 N 2.11 W
Wörth, B.R.D. 56 49.48 N 9.09 E
Worth, B.R.D. 263 51.13 N 7.39 E
Worth, Ill., U.S. 216 41.41 N 87.48 W
Worth, Lake ⊜[1] 222 32.48 N 97.28 W
Wortham 222 31.47 N 96.28 W
Wörth am Rhein 56 49.03 N 8.16 E
Wörth an der Donau 60 49.00 N 12.25 E
Worthen 42 52.38 N 3.00 W
Wörther See ⊜ 61 46.37 N 14.10 E
Worthing 42 50.48 N 0.23 W
Worthington, Ind., U.S. 194 39.07 N 86.59 W
Worthington, Md., U.S. 284b 39.14 N 76.47 W
Worthington, Minn., U.S. 198 43.37 N 95.36 W
Worthington, N.Y., U.S. 276 41.02 N 73.50 W
Worthington, Ohio, U.S. 214 40.05 N 83.01 W
Worthington, Pa., U.S. 214 40.50 N 79.38 W
Worthington Peak ∧ 204 37.55 N 115.37 W
Wörthsee ⊜ 60 48.03 N 11.10 E
Worthville, Ky., U.S. 218 38.37 N 85.04 W
Worthville, Pa., U.S. 214 41.02 N 79.08 W
Worton 208 39.17 N 76.06 W
Wŏrun-dong 98 39.36 N 125.20 E
Wosimi 164 2.54 S 134.31 E
Wostok → Vostok ʋ[3] 9 78.30 S 106.50 E
Wosu 112 2.21 S 121.50 E
Wotap, Pulau I 164 7.21 S 131.16 E
Wotho I[1] 14 10.06 N 165.59 E
Wotje I[1] 14 9.27 N 170.02 E
Wotton, Qué., Can. 206 45.44 N 71.48 W
Wotton, Eng., U.K. 260 51.13 N 0.23 W
Wotton-under-Edge 42 51.39 N 2.21 W
Wotu 112 2.35 S 120.48 E
Woudenberg 52 52.05 N 5.25 E
Woudrichem 52 51.49 N 5.00 E
Woudsend 52 52.56 N 5.36 E
Wouldham 260 51.21 N 0.28 E
Wounded Knee Creek ≃ 198 43.26 N 102.32 W
Wounta 236 13.33 N 83.32 W
Wounta, Laguna de ⊂ 236 13.38 N 83.34 W
Wour 146 21.21 N 15.57 E
Wouri ≃ 152 4.06 N 9.43 E
Woutchaba 152 5.13 N 13.05 E
Wouw 52 51.32 N 4.24 E
Wowan 166 23.55 S 150.12 E
Wowoni, Pulau I 112 4.08 S 123.06 E
Woy Woy 170 33.30 S 151.20 E
Woźniki 30 50.36 N 19.03 E
Wragby 44 53.18 N 0.19 W
Wrangel Island → Vrangel'a, Ostrov I 74 71.00 N 179.30 W
Wrangell 180 56.28 N 132.23 W
Wrangell, Cape ≻ 181a 52.50 N 172.26 E
Wrangell, Mount ∧ 180 62.00 N 144.06 W
Wrangell Island I 180 56.15 N 132.10 W
Wrangell Mountains ⛰ 180 62.00 N 143.00 W
Wrath, Cape ≻ 46 58.37 N 5.01 W
Wray 198 40.05 N 102.13 W
Wraysbury 260 51.27 N 0.33 W
Wrea Green 262 53.46 N 2.55 W
Wreck Bay ⊂ 170 35.11 S 150.40 E
Wreck Island I 208 37.16 N 75.48 W
Wreck Reef ✢[2] 166 22.13 S 155.17 E
Wrecks, Bay of ⊂ 174o 1.52 N 157.17 W
Wredenhagen 54 53.17 N 12.31 E
Wremen 52 53.39 N 8.30 E
Wren 216 40.48 N 84.46 W
Wrens 192 33.12 N 82.23 W
Wrentham, Alta., Can. 182 49.32 N 112.10 W
Wrentham, Eng., U.K. 42 52.23 N 1.40 E
Wrentham, Mass., U.S. 207 42.04 N 71.20 W
Wrentham State Forest ♠ 283 42.02 N 71.20 W
Wrexham 44 53.03 N 3.00 W
Wriezen 54 52.43 N 14.08 E
Wright 278 41.31 N 87.21 W
Wright, Mount ∧, Austl. 166 31.12 S 142.26 E
Wright, Mount ∧, Mont., U.S. 202 47.58 N 112.49 W
Wright Brothers National Memorial ⊥ 192 35.55 N 75.50 W
Wright City, Mo., U.S. 219 38.50 N 91.01 W
Wright City, Okla., U.S. 194 34.03 N 95.01 W
Wright City, Tex., U.S. 222 32.12 N 94.59 W
Wrightington Bar 262 53.37 N 2.42 W
Wright Patman Lake ⊜[1] 194 33.16 N 94.14 W
Wright-Patterson Air Force Base ■ 218 39.49 N 84.03 W
Wright Peak ∧ 204 38.59 N 122.46 W
Wrights 219 39.23 N 90.18 W
Wrightsboro 222 29.22 N 97.34 W
Wrights Corners 210 43.13 N 78.46 W
Wrightson, Mount ∧ 200 31.42 N 110.50 W
Wrightstown, N.J., U.S. 208 40.02 N 74.37 W
Wrightstown, Pa., U.S. 208 40.17 N 74.58 W
Wrightstown, Wis., U.S. 190 44.19 N 88.09 W
Wrightsville, Ga., U.S. 192 32.44 N 82.43 W
Wrightsville, Pa., U.S. 214 40.02 N 76.32 W
Wrightwood 228 34.21 N 117.38 W
Wrigley 180 63.16 N 123.37 W
Wrigley Field ♠ 278 41.57 N 87.39 W
Wrigley Gulf ⊂ 9 74.00 S 129.00 W
Writtle 42 51.44 N 0.26 E
Wrocław (Breslau) 30 51.06 N 17.00 E
Wrong Lake ⊜ 184 52.38 N 96.10 W
Wronki 30 52.43 N 16.23 E
Wrotham 42 51.19 N 0.19 E
Wrotham Heath 260 51.18 N 0.21 E
Wroughton 42 51.31 N 1.46 W
Wroxham 42 52.42 N 1.24 E
Wroxton 184 51.14 N 101.53 W
Września 30 52.20 N 17.34 E
Wschowa 30 51.48 N 16.19 E
Wuan 98 36.40 N 114.12 E
Wubao 102 37.33 N 110.39 E
Wubaozhen 107 29.14 N 104.29 E
Wubin 162 30.06 S 116.38 E
Wuchang → Wuhan 100 30.36 N 114.17 E
Wuchang ✦[8] 100 44.54 N 127.08 E
Wucheng, Zhg. 98 37.09 N 115.53 E
Wucheng, Zhg. 100 33.28 N 113.44 E
Wucheng, Zhg. 100 29.36 N 118.10 E
Wuchengzhen 100 29.10 N 115.59 E
Wuch'i 100 24.13 N 120.31 E
Wuchin → Changzhou 106 31.47 N 119.57 E
Wuch'iu Hsü I 100 25.00 N 119.27 E
Wuchow → Wuzhou 102 23.30 N 111.27 E
Wuchuan, Zhg. 102 21.25 N 110.40 E
Wuchuan, Zhg. 102 41.05 N 111.23 E
Wuchuan, Zhg. 102 28.25 N 107.56 E
Wuchung → Wuzhong 102 37.57 N 106.10 E
Wucun 105 38.57 N 115.19 E
Wuda 102 39.30 N 105.56 E
Wudangshan ⛰ 102 32.30 N 110.50 E
Wudaogou, Zhg. 98 42.08 N 125.51 E
Wudaogou, Zhg. 98 41.43 N 127.05 E
Wudaogou, Zhg. 98 41.13 N 116.07 E
Wudaohe ≃ 104 42.03 N 122.58 E
Wudaolianggou 104 40.59 N 120.35 E
Wudi 98 37.44 N 117.35 E
Wudian 100 32.42 N 117.18 E
Wuding 102 25.32 N 102.23 E
Wudinna 166 33.03 S 135.28 E
Wudu, Zhg. 100 28.23 N 118.14 E
Wudu, Zhg. 102 33.21 N 105.00 E
Wuduhe 102 31.03 N 111.03 E
Wuerqihan 89 49.37 N 121.45 E
Wuershunhe ≃ 88 49.00 N 117.41 E
Wufeng 102 30.11 N 110.33 E
Wufengshan I 106 31.07 N 120.16 E
Wufengxi 107 30.37 N 104.29 E
Wufu 100 30.06 N 120.58 E
Wugang 102 26.40 N 110.31 E
Wugong 102 34.20 N 108.04 E
Wugonghe ≃ 105 39.20 N 117.29 E
Wugongshan ∧ 100 27.21 N 113.50 E
Wugouying 100 33.28 N 114.08 E
Wugunuoer 89 49.10 N 119.19 E
Wuhan 100 30.36 N 114.17 E
Wuhe, Zhg. 100 33.10 N 117.54 E
Wuhe, Zhg. 100 24.26 N 115.25 E
Wuhe ≃ 98 34.25 N 117.55 E
Wuhle ≃ 264a 52.29 N 13.34 E
Wuhsi → Wuxi 106 31.35 N 120.18 E
Wuhsing → Huzhou 106 30.52 N 120.06 E
Wuhu 100 31.21 N 118.22 E

Symbols in the index entries represent the broad categories identified in the key at the right. Symbols with superior numbers (⛰[2]) identify subcategories (see complete key on page *I · 30*).

Kartensymbole in dem Registerverzeichnis stellen die rechts in Schlüssel erklärten Kategorien dar. Symbole mit hochgestellten Ziffern (⛰[2]) bezeichnen Unterabteilungen einer Kategorie (vgl. vollständiger Schlüssel auf Seite *I · 30*).

Los símbolos incluídos en el texto del índice representan las grandes categorias identificadas con la clave a la derecha. Los símbolos con numeros en su parte superior (⛰[2]) identifican las subcategorías (véase la clave completa en la página *I · 30*).

Les symboles de l'index représentent les catégories indiquées dans la légende à droite. Les symboles suivis d'un indice (⛰[2]) représentent des sous-catégories (voir légende complète à la page *I · 30*).

Os símbolos incluídos no texto do índice representam as grandes categorias identificadas com a chave à direita. Os símbolos com números em sua parte superior (⛰[2]) identificam as subcategorias (veja-se a chave completa à página *I · 30*).

	English	Deutsch	Español	Français	Português
∧	Mountain	Berg	Montaña	Montagne	Montanha
⛰	Mountains	Berge	Montañas	Montagnes	Montanhas
)(	Pass	Pass	Paso	Col	Passo
∨	Valley, Canyon	Tal, Cañon	Valle, Cañón	Vallée, Canyon	Vale, Canhão
≚	Plain	Ebene	Llano	Plaine	Planície
≻	Cape	Kap	Cabo	Cap	Cabo
I	Island	Insel	Isla	Île	Ilha
II	Islands	Inseln	Islas	Îles	Ilhas
•	Other Topographic Features	Andere Topographische Objekte	Otros Elementos Topográficos	Autres données topographiques	Outros Elementos Topográficos

ESPAÑOL

Nombre	Página	Lat.°′	Long.°′ W=Oeste
Wuhua (Shuizhai)	100	23.57 N	115.48 E
Wuhuanchi	104	42.20 N	121.51 E
Wuhuangchang	107	29.58 N	104.46 E
Wuhudongmiao	102	38.19 N	107.20 E
Wuhushui ≃	100	30.41 N	114.32 E
Wuji, Zhg.	98	34.12 N	119.02 E
Wuji, Zhg.	98	38.13 N	114.57 E
Wuji, Zhg.	100	27.03 N	112.57 E
Wujiabeigou	104	40.57 N	123.50 E
Wujiadian	100	31.57 N	112.46 E
Wujiagou	104	42.01 N	123.52 E
Wujiahe ≃	102	41.10 N	108.45 E
Wujiaku	106	31.06 N	121.11 E
Wujiang, Zhg.	100	31.52 N	118.28 E
Wujiang, Zhg.	100	27.14 N	115.15 E
Wujiang, Zhg.	106	31.10 N	120.38 E
Wujiang ≃, Zhg.	100	27.14 N	115.05 E
Wujiang ≃, Zhg.	100	28.57 N	116.39 E
Wujiangdu	102	27.16 N	106.48 E
Wujianpu	107	29.10 N	105.50 E
Wujiapai	105	39.32 N	117.18 E
Wujiapu, Zhg.	105	38.52 N	117.07 E
Wujiapu, Zhg.	107	29.38 N	105.24 E
Wujiazhuang, Zhg.	105	40.35 N	115.20 E
Wujiazhuang, Zhg.	106	32.18 N	120.10 E
Wujiazi, Zhg.	89	46.27 N	123.34 E
Wujiazi, Zhg.	104	42.30 N	121.10 E
Wujiazi, Zhg.	104	42.13 N	122.08 E
Wujieqiao	106	32.05 N	120.33 E
Wujing	100	25.16 N	114.36 E
Wukang	106	30.33 N	119.58 E
Wukari	150	7.51 N	9.47 E
Wukeshu, Zhg.	89	46.02 N	123.45 E
Wukeshu, Zhg.	89	44.48 N	126.08 E
Wulai	100	24.52 N	121.33 E
Wulajia	89	48.23 N	129.58 E
Wulan	102	36.59 N	98.26 E
Wulandabanshan ⩕	102	38.53 N	96.11 E
Wulanhaote	89	46.05 N	122.05 E
Wulanheduojia	102	42.40 N	113.20 E
Wulanhutong	98	41.44 N	114.49 E
Wulanmuluhne ≃	120	34.15 N	93.11 E
Wulanmutou	104	42.23 N	121.21 E
Wulanwusu, Zhg.	86	44.20 N	85.50 E
Wulanwusu, Zhg.	102	41.39 N	107.48 E
Wular Lake ◎	123	34.20 N	74.33 E
Wulasitai	89	43.15 N	121.27 E
Wulateqianqi	102	40.39 N	109.05 E
Wulatezhonghouqi	102	41.42 N	108.49 E
Wulaxi	102	28.38 N	101.40 E
Wuleidaowan C	98	36.55 N	122.00 E
Wulfen	52	51.43 N	7.00 E
Wülfrath	56	51.17 N	7.02 E
Wulfsen	52	53.18 N	10.08 E
Wulfsode	52	53.04 N	10.13 E
Wulften	52	51.40 N	10.10 E
Wulian (Hongning)	98	35.47 N	119.15 E
Wulianfeng ⩕	102	28.03 N	103.57 E
Wuliangdian	104	41.52 N	122.16 E
Wuliangshan ⩕	102	24.30 N	100.45 E
Wuliaru, Pulau ▮	164	7.27 S	131.04 E
Wulichuan	102	33.49 N	111.08 E
Wuling	98	35.53 N	114.36 E
Wuling ⩕	102	27.10 N	108.06 E
Wulingshan ⩕	102	28.48 N	110.15 E
Wulitaizi	104	41.28 N	123.21 E
Wulizhuang	100	33.49 N	118.57 E
Wulka ≃	61	47.52 N	16.40 E
Wüllen	52	52.04 N	6.58 E
Wullwye Creek ≃	171b	36.30 S	148.49 E
Wulong, Zhg.	102	29.14 N	107.59 E
Wulong, Zhg.	104	41.39 N	124.13 E
Wulongbei	98	40.21 N	124.16 E
Wulonghe ≃	98	36.35 N	120.56 E
Wulsdorf ◆[8]	52	53.30 N	8.35 E
Wuluhan	115a	8.21 S	113.33 E
Wuluhayingzi	104	42.20 N	121.34 E
Wulumuch'i → Wulumuqi	86	43.48 N	87.35 E
Wulumuqi (Urumchi)	86	43.48 N	87.35 E
Wulunguhe ≃	86	46.59 N	87.27 E
Wuluo	102	26.09 N	108.15 E
Wulur	164	7.09 S	128.39 E
Wulushui ≃	85	39.38 N	74.38 E
Wum	152	6.23 N	10.04 E
Wuma	89	52.36 N	120.37 E
Wumangdao ▮	98	39.14 N	123.03 E
Wumiaoxiang	107	30.23 N	104.17 E
Wuming	102	23.10 N	108.18 E
Wümme ≃	52	53.10 N	8.44 E
Wunamu	86	46.06 N	85.44 E
Wundowie	168a	31.46 S	116.22 E
Wundwin	110	21.05 N	96.02 E
Wuneba	154	4.50 N	30.20 E
Wuning	100	29.17 N	115.06 E
Wünnenberg	52	51.31 N	8.42 E
Wunnummin Lake ◎	176	52.55 N	89.10 W
Wun Rog	140	9.00 N	28.21 E
Wünschendorf	54	50.48 N	12.05 E
Wünsdorf	54	52.10 N	13.28 E
Wunstorf	52	52.25 N	9.26 E
Wuntho	110	23.54 N	95.41 E
Wunuer	89	48.53 N	121.15 E
Wupaowan	107	29.50 N	103.59 E
Wupatki National Monument ▲	200	35.24 N	111.14 W
Wuping	100	25.08 N	116.06 E
Wupper ≃	263	51.05 N	7.00 E
Wuppertal, B.R.D.	56		
	263	51.16 N	7.11 E
Wuppertal, S. Afr.	158	32.15 S	19.15 E
Wuqi, Zhg.	100	27.10 N	120.23 E
Wuqi, Zhg.	102	37.08 N	108.10 E
Wuqia	85	39.42 N	75.13 E
Wuqiagou	86	46.48 N	89.45 E
Wuqiang	98	38.03 N	115.58 E
Wuqiangxi ≃	100	29.33 N	118.57 E
Wuqiao	98	37.36 N	116.30 E
Wuqiluofu	89	52.10 N	120.48 E
Wuqing (Yangcun)	105	39.23 N	117.04 E
Wuraming	168a	32.48 S	116.16 E
Wurarga	162	28.25 S	116.17 E
Würenlingen	58	47.32 N	8.16 E
Wurgwitz	54	51.01 N	13.37 E
Wurm ≃, B.R.D.	56	51.08 N	6.10 E
Würm ≃, B.R.D.	60	48.10 N	11.28 E
Wurmannsquick	60	48.21 N	12.47 E
Wurmberg ∧	54	51.45 N	10.37 E
Wurno	150	13.17 N	5.24 E
Würnsdorf	61	48.18 N	15.10 E
Wurong	164	6.07 S	140.47 E
Würselen	56	50.49 N	6.08 E
Wurtsboro	210	41.35 N	74.29 W
Wurtsboro Hills	210	41.36 N	74.30 W
Wurtsmith Air Force Base ■	190	44.27 N	83.23 W
Wuruf	164	6.43 S	146.25 E
Wuryantoro	115a	7.54 S	110.51 E
Wurzbach	54	50.28 N	11.32 E
Würzburg	56	49.48 N	9.56 E
Wurzen	54	51.22 N	12.44 E
Wusanga	152	3.22 S	22.50 E
Wusha	100	30.39 N	117.18 E
Wushan, Zhg.	102	31.05 N	109.48 E
Wushan, Zhg.	102	34.38 N	105.04 E
Wushan, Zhg.	106	31.44 N	118.58 E
Wushanmiao	100	32.04 N	117.03 E
Wushe	100	24.02 N	121.08 E
Wusheng	107	30.21 N	106.17 E
Wushengchang	107	29.00 N	103.43 E
Wushenqi	102	38.58 N	109.01 E
Wushi, Zhg.	102	22.11 N	110.11 E

FRANÇAIS

Nom	Page	Lat.°′	Long.°′ W=Ouest
Wushi, Zhg.	106	31.44 N	120.59 E
Wushishi	150	9.46 N	6.07 E
Wushonkou C[1]	106	31.23 N	121.30 E
Wushui ≃, Zhg.	100	24.48 N	113.35 E
Wushui ≃, Zhg.	102	27.03 N	109.53 E
Wusih → Wuxi	106	31.35 N	120.18 E
Wuskwatim Lake ◎	184	55.32 N	98.32 W
Wusong	106	31.23 N	121.29 E
Wusongjiang ≃	106	31.15 N	121.29 E
Wusongkou ≃[1]	269b	31.23 N	121.30 E
Wust	54	52.33 N	12.07 E
Wüsten	52	52.06 N	8.47 E
Wüstensachsen	56	50.30 N	10.00 E
Wusterhausen	54	52.54 N	12.28 E
Wusterhusen	54	54.07 N	13.37 E
Wustermark	54	52.33 N	12.56 E
Wüstermarke	54	51.49 N	13.36 E
Wusterwitz	54	52.22 N	12.18 E
Wüsting	52	53.07 N	8.20 E
Wustrow, B.R.D.	54	52.55 N	11.07 E
Wustrow, D.D.R.	54	54.05 N	11.34 E
Wustrow ≻[1]	54	54.05 N	11.34 E
Wusu	86	44.27 N	84.37 E
Wusulijiang (Ussuri) ≃	89	48.27 N	135.04 E
Wusuo, Zhg.	100	25.02 N	116.02 E
Wusuo, Zhg.	100	26.20 N	114.56 E
Wutach ≃	58	47.37 N	8.15 E
Wutai, Zhg.	85	39.28 N	78.09 E
Wutai, Zhg.	86	44.36 N	82.06 E
Wutai, Zhg.	98	41.18 N	113.59 E
Wutai, Zhg.	102	38.44 N	113.17 E
Wutaishan ∧	98	39.04 N	113.35 E
Wutaishan ⩕	102	39.06 N	113.30 E
Wutaizi	104	42.27 N	123.17 E
Wutan	102	28.29 N	111.40 E
Wutanchang	107	29.15 N	106.04 E
Wutang	106	31.31 N	119.10 E
Wutangdun	106	30.38 N	120.08 E
Wutangjie	100	29.59 N	122.22 E
Wutashi	106	31.31 N	120.39 E
Wutianzhen	100	30.23 N	117.12 E
Wutong	102	25.18 N	110.01 E
Wutonghaolai	89	42.55 N	120.15 E
Wutongqiao	107	29.26 N	103.51 E
Wutongwozi	102	42.27 N	95.17 E
Wutsin → Changzhou	106	31.47 N	119.57 E
Wutun	100	27.51 N	118.04 E
Wut'ungch'iao → Wutongqiao	107	29.26 N	103.51 E
Wutuohuo	102	40.51 N	101.48 E
Wuustwezel	50	51.23 N	4.36 E
Wuvulu Island ▮	164	1.45 S	142.50 E
Wuwei, Zhg.	100	31.18 N	117.54 E
Wuwei (Liangzhou), Zhg.	102	37.58 N	102.49 E
Wuxi, Zhg.	102	31.25 N	109.34 E
Wuxi, Zhg.	106	31.20 N	118.39 E
Wuxi (Wuhsi), Zhg.	106	31.35 N	120.18 E
Wuxi ≃	100	29.00 N	118.56 E
Wuxiang	102	36.51 N	113.00 E
Wuxingchang	106	31.13 N	119.23 E
Wuxuan	102	23.36 N	109.42 E
Wuyang, Zhg.	100	33.26 N	113.34 E
Wuyang, Zhg.	102	26.41 N	110.20 E
Wuyangyuan	100	25.41 N	115.55 E
Wuyi, Zhg.	98	37.49 N	115.54 E
Wuyi, Zhg.	100	28.54 N	119.48 E
Wuyi, Zhg.	100	32.13 N	118.26 E
Wuying	89	48.05 N	129.15 E
Wuyishan ∧	100	27.50 N	117.45 E
Wuyishan ⩕	90	27.52 N	117.40 E
Wuyou ≃	100	33.28 N	120.41 E
Wuyuan, Zhg.	100	29.15 N	117.49 E
Wuyuan, Zhg.	102	41.06 N	108.29 E
Wuyun	89	46.16 N	129.37 E
Wuyunqiao	100	26.02 N	114.52 E
Wuzaizi	104	42.28 N	123.57 E
Wuzhai	102	38.58 N	111.55 E
Wuzhan	89	45.51 N	126.17 E
Wuzhen	106	30.46 N	120.29 E
Wuzhishan ∧	110	18.57 N	109.43 E
Wuzhong	102	37.57 N	106.10 E
Wuzhou (Wuchow)	102	23.30 N	111.27 E
Wuzongbu	106	32.14 N	121.03 E
Wyaaba Creek ≃	164	16.27 S	141.35 E
Wyaconda	194	40.24 N	91.55 W
Wyaconda ≃	194	40.04 N	91.30 W
Wyalkatchem	162	31.10 S	117.22 E
Wyalusing	210	41.40 N	76.16 W
Wyalusing Creek ≃	210	41.40 N	76.16 W
Wyandanch	276	40.45 N	73.22 W
Wyandot	214	40.44 N	83.08 W
Wyandot □[6]	214	40.50 N	83.17 W
Wyandotte	216	42.12 N	83.10 W
Wyandotte Cave ●[5]	218	38.14 N	86.18 W
Wyandotte National Wildlife Refuge ◆[4]	281	42.14 N	83.08 W
Wyandra	166	27.15 S	145.59 E
Wyangala Reservoir ◎[1]	166	33.58 S	148.55 E
Wyano	214	40.12 N	79.42 W
Wyatt, Ind., U.S.	216	41.32 N	86.10 W
Wyatt, Mo., U.S.	194	36.55 N	89.13 W
Wycheproof	166	36.05 S	143.14 E
Wyckoff	210	41.01 N	74.10 W
Wydegeleë	158	34.23 S	20.26 E
Wydgee	162	28.51 S	117.49 E
Wy-dit-Joli-Village	261	49.06 N	1.50 E
Wye	42	51.11 N	0.56 E
Wye ≃, Ont., Can.	212	44.44 N	79.52 W
Wye ≃, Eng., U.K.	42	51.37 N	2.39 W
Wye ≃, Eng., U.K.	44	53.12 N	1.37 W
Wyee	170	33.11 S	151.29 E
Wye Lake ◎	212	44.43 N	79.52 W
Wyemandoo ∧	162	28.31 S	118.32 E
Wyeville	190	44.01 N	90.23 W
Wyhl	58	48.09 N	7.39 E
Wyhra ≃	54	51.09 N	12.27 E
Wyk	30	54.42 N	8.34 E
Wyke Regis	42	50.36 N	2.29 W
Wykoff	190	43.42 N	92.16 W
Wylandville	279b	40.12 N	80.08 W
Wyleswood Lake ◎	279a	41.20 N	81.55 W
Wylie, Pa., U.S.	279b	40.27 N	79.59 W
Wylie, Tex., U.S.	222	33.01 N	96.32 W
Wylie, Lake ◎[1]	192	35.07 N	81.02 W
Wylye ≃	42	51.04 N	1.52 W
Wymah	171b	36.02 S	147.17 E
Wymark	184	50.07 N	107.44 W
Wymondham	42	52.34 N	1.07 E
Wymore	198	40.07 N	96.40 W
Wynantskill	210	42.42 N	73.39 W
Wynberg	158	34.02 S	18.28 E
Wynbring	162	30.33 S	133.32 E
Wyncote	285	40.05 N	75.09 W
Wyndham, Austl.	164	15.28 S	128.06 E
Wyndham, N.Z.	172	46.20 S	168.51 E
Wyndmere	198	46.16 N	97.08 W
Wyndmoor	285	40.05 N	75.12 W
Wynigen	58	47.06 N	7.40 E
Wynne	194	35.14 N	90.47 W
Wynnewood, Okla., U.S.	196	34.39 N	97.10 W
Wynnewood, Pa., U.S.	285	40.01 N	75.17 W
Wynniatt Bay C	176	72.55 N	110.30 W
Wynnum	171a	27.27 S	153.10 E
Wynona	196	36.33 N	96.20 W
Wynoochee ≃	224	46.58 N	123.35 W
Wynoochee Lake ◎[1]	224	47.25 N	123.35 W

PORTUGUÊS

Nome	Página	Lat.°′	Long.°′ W=Oeste
Wynot	198	42.45 N	97.10 W
Wynyard, Austl.	166	40.59 S	145.41 E
Wynyard, Sask., Can.	184	51.47 N	104.10 W
Wyocena	190	43.30 N	89.19 W
Wyodak	198	44.18 N	105.24 W
Wyola Lake ◎	162	29.08 S	130.17 E
Wyoming, Ont., Can.	190	42.57 N	82.07 W
Wyoming, Del., U.S.	208	39.12 N	75.34 W
Wyoming, Ill., U.S.	190	41.04 N	89.47 W
Wyoming, Iowa, U.S.	190	42.04 N	91.00 W
Wyoming, Mich., U.S.	216	42.54 N	85.42 W
Wyoming, N.Y., U.S.	210	42.50 N	78.05 W
Wyoming, Ohio, U.S.	218	39.14 N	84.27 W
Wyoming, Pa., U.S.	210	41.19 N	75.50 W
Wyoming, R.I., U.S.	207	41.31 N	71.42 W
Wyoming □[6], N.Y., U.S.	210	42.44 N	78.08 W
Wyoming □[6], Pa., U.S.	210	41.32 N	75.57 W
Wyoming □[3]	178	43.00 N	107.30 W
Wyoming Peak ∧	200	42.36 N	110.37 W
Wyoming Range ⩕	200	42.00 N	111.00 W
Wyomissing	208	40.20 N	75.58 W
Wyong	170	33.17 S	151.25 E
Wyong Creek ≃	170	33.18 S	151.28 E
Wyperfeld National Park ▲	166	35.30 S	142.00 E
Wyre ≃	44	53.55 N	3.00 W
Wyreema	171a	27.39 S	151.52 E
Wyre Forest ◆[3]	42	52.23 N	2.23 W
Wyrzysk	30	53.10 N	17.15 E
Wyśmierzyce	30	51.38 N	20.49 E
Wysoka	30	53.11 N	17.05 E
Wysokie Mazowieckie	30	52.56 N	22.32 E
Wysox	210	41.46 N	76.24 W
Wyszków	30	52.36 N	21.28 E
Wyszogród	30	52.23 N	20.11 E
Wythenshawe ◆[8]	262	53.24 N	2.17 W
Wythenshawe Hall ⊥	262	53.24 N	2.17 W
Wytheville	192	36.57 N	81.05 W
Wytopitlock	188	45.38 N	68.05 W
Wytschegda → Vyčegda ≃	24	61.18 N	46.36 E
Wyvis, Ben ∧	46	57.42 N	4.35 W
X			
Xabregas ◆[8]	266c	38.44 N	9.07 W
Xá-Cassau	152	9.02 S	20.14 E
Xaclbal ≃	236	16.06 N	90.58 W
Xadani	234	15.56 N	96.04 W
Xalpatláhuac	234	17.01 N	99.18 W
Xaltianguis	234	17.04 N	99.50 W
Xambioá	250	6.25 S	48.40 W
Xambrê ≃	255	24.02 S	53.59 W
Xamindele	152	7.08 S	14.16 E
Xam Nua	110	20.25 N	104.02 E
Xa-muong-man	110	10.58 N	108.01 E
Xanten	52	51.39 N	6.26 E
Xánthi	38	41.08 N	24.53 E
Xanxerê	252	26.53 S	52.23 W
Xapecó ≃	252	27.06 S	53.01 W
Xapuri	248	10.39 S	68.31 W
Xapuri ≃	248	10.39 S	68.30 W
Xarrama ≃	34	38.14 N	8.20 W
Xau, Lake ◎	156	21.15 S	24.38 E
Xauen → Chechaouene	148	35.10 N	5.16 W
Xavantina	255	21.15 S	52.48 W
Xa-vo-dat	110	11.09 N	107.31 E
Xaxim	252	26.56 S	52.31 W
X-Can	232	20.50 N	87.43 W
Xenia, Ill., U.S.	219	38.38 N	88.38 W
Xenia, Ohio, U.S.	218	39.41 N	83.56 W
Xénô	110	16.35 N	104.50 E
Xercavins, Arroyo de ≃	266d	41.30 N	2.02 E
Xerém	256	22.33 S	43.18 W
Xeres → Jerez de la Frontera	34	36.41 N	6.08 W
Xertigny	58	48.03 N	6.24 E
Xhumo	156	21.07 S	24.42 E
Xiaang	106	30.45 N	120.07 E
Xiaba, Zhg.	100	24.54 N	116.06 E
Xiaba, Zhg.	106	31.18 N	119.05 E
Xiabai, Zhg.	106	31.12 N	119.50 E
Xiabai, Zhg.	106	30.29 N	120.00 E
Xiabancheng	105	40.47 N	118.08 E
Xiabanghu	100	30.31 N	112.38 E
Xiabaocun	106	30.44 N	119.58 E
Xiabeiwo	106	30.06 N	120.02 E
Xiabian	104	40.51 N	120.30 E
Xiabu	100	28.19 N	116.20 E
Xiacang	105	39.47 N	117.24 E
Xiache	100	24.40 N	115.08 E
Xiachengzi	89	44.41 N	130.27 E
Xiachuandao ▮	102	21.40 N	112.30 E
Xiacun	105	40.21 N	116.14 E
Xiadao	100	26.34 N	118.16 E
Xiadian, Zhg.	98	37.06 N	120.19 E
Xiadian, Zhg.	100	31.26 N	114.17 E
Xiadian, Zhg.	105	39.57 N	116.55 E
Xiadianjie	100	25.13 N	118.27 E
Xiafeidi	98	42.18 N	124.21 E
Xiafu, Zhg.	100	25.01 N	113.41 E
Xiafu, Zhg.	100	23.52 N	115.45 E
Xiagaixin	102	22.36 N	99.59 E
Xiagang	106	31.55 N	120.13 E
Xiage	100	28.52 N	120.52 E
Xiagezhuang	98	36.41 N	120.25 E
Xiaguan, Zhg.	98	39.07 N	114.09 E
Xiaguan, Zhg.	102	25.34 N	100.14 E
Xiaguan, Zhg.	106	32.06 N	118.44 E
Xiaguanjunchang	104	41.28 N	121.40 E
Xiaguanpi	100	24.04 N	117.06 E
Xiagucheng	102	36.47 N	102.53 E
Xiagucun	106	30.56 N	119.09 E
Xiahada	104	41.58 N	124.08 E
Xiahailangzhai	104	41.35 N	123.46 E
Xiahe, Zhg.	98	34.39 N	114.46 E
Xiahe, Zhg.	102	35.06 N	102.40 E
Xiahuangjintun	104	41.57 N	123.48 E
Xiahuayuan	105	40.29 N	115.17 E
Xiajiabaozi	98	42.16 N	124.37 E
Xiajialou	104	42.25 N	123.39 E
Xiajiangdun	106	31.14 N	120.24 E
Xiajiangwu	106	30.29 N	119.00 E
Xiajiayuan	106	32.13 N	120.38 E
Xiajiezi	102	27.28 N	101.35 E
Xiajin	98	36.55 N	115.57 E
Xiakou	100	28.28 N	118.31 E
Xialianggang	105	39.14 N	115.07 E
Xialufang	102	31.11 N	103.38 E
Xiamaguan	102	37.14 N	106.28 E
Xiamen (Amoy)	100	24.28 N	118.07 E
Xiamengang C	100	24.24 N	118.10 E
Xiamin'ansutai	104	41.54 N	120.53 E
Xiamocun	106	31.09 N	119.22 E
Xi'an (Sian)	102	34.15 N	108.52 E
Xianchenggu	98	36.53 N	115.17 E
Xiandu	100	25.04 N	117.44 E
Xianfeng, Zhg.	100	25.42 N	117.53 E
Xianfeng, Zhg.	102	29.41 N	109.02 E
Xianfengpo	105	39.33 N	115.58 E
Xiang'an	100	31.12 N	117.46 E
Xiangcheng, Zhg.	100	33.28 N	114.53 E
Xiangcheng, Zhg.	100	33.53 N	113.29 E
Xiangcheng, Zhg.	102	28.59 N	99.45 E
Xiangcheng, Zhg.	106	31.29 N	120.44 E
Xiangfan	102	32.03 N	112.01 E
Xiangfuguan	100	28.30 N	115.26 E
Xiangfusi	107	30.06 N	104.24 E
Xianggang → Victoria	271d	22.17 N	114.09 E
Xianggongshi	100	28.25 N	113.32 E
Xianggongzhuang	105	39.48 N	118.19 E
Xianghe	105	39.46 N	116.59 E
Xiangheguan	100	33.08 N	113.26 E
Xianghua	106	31.31 N	121.43 E
Xiangjia, Zhg.	106	31.19 N	120.23 E
Xiangjia, Zhg.	106	31.20 N	120.31 E
Xiangjiachang	107	30.08 N	104.18 E
Xiangjiang ≃	102	29.00 N	112.56 E
Xiangkhoang	110	19.20 N	103.22 E
Xiangkhoang, Plateau de ⩕[1]	110	19.30 N	103.10 E
Xianglushan	107	30.17 N	106.09 E
Xiangning	102	36.01 N	110.45 E
Xiangride	102	36.02 N	98.08 E
Xiangshan, Zhg.	98	36.14 N	116.16 E
Xiangshan, Zhg.	100	29.28 N	121.51 E
Xiangshan, Zhg.	105	39.59 N	116.10 E
Xiangshangang C	100	29.38 N	121.48 E
Xiangshanzicun	104	41.06 N	123.13 E
Xiangshishan	107	29.17 N	105.09 E
Xiangshui	100	23.15 N	114.10 E
Xiangshui ≃	100	25.35 N	115.49 E
Xiangshuikou	100	34.13 N	119.37 E
Xiangtan	100	27.51 N	112.54 E
Xiangtang	100	28.26 N	115.58 E
Xiangxiang	102	27.43 N	112.27 E
Xiangyang	105	39.13 N	115.25 E
Xiangyangkou	105	40.06 N	115.47 E
Xiangyin	100	28.40 N	112.53 E
Xiangyuan	102	36.32 N	113.00 E
Xiangyun	102	25.30 N	100.30 E
Xiangzhenpu	100	30.52 N	117.21 E
Xiangzhou, Zhg.	98	36.12 N	119.24 E
Xiangzhou, Zhg.	102	23.55 N	109.49 E
Xiangzhu	100	29.02 N	120.04 E
Xianhe ≃	107	29.22 N	104.44 E
Xianinggang	100	28.20 N	112.56 E
Xianjiang	100	27.48 N	120.30 E
Xianju	100	28.51 N	120.44 E
Xianmübu	100	25.36 N	114.40 E
Xianning	100	29.53 N	114.17 E
Xianru	89	43.11 N	128.02 E
Xianshichang	107	28.43 N	105.44 E
Xianshuigu	105	38.59 N	117.23 E
Xiantan	107	29.21 N	104.53 E
Xiantanchang	107	28.50 N	106.12 E
Xiantang	100	23.48 N	114.46 E
Xianxialing ⩕	100	28.30 N	118.46 E
Xianyang, Zhg.	100	28.02 N	118.30 E
Xianyang, Zhg.	102	34.22 N	108.42 E
Xianyou	100	25.23 N	118.40 E
Xianzhong	100	28.36 N	113.48 E
Xiaoao	100	26.14 N	119.39 E
Xiaoazhang	102	23.42 N	104.58 E
Xiaoba	98	34.32 N	115.29 E
Xiaobangniulu	104	41.34 N	122.46 E
Xiaobazi	98	41.24 N	116.13 E
Xiaobeigou	104	41.55 N	120.46 E
Xiaobeihe, Zhg.	104	42.39 N	123.58 E
Xiaobeihe, Zhg.	104	41.22 N	122.50 E
Xiaocaohu	86	43.06 N	88.30 E
Xiaochangshandao ▮	98	39.12 N	122.41 E
Xiaocheng	100	26.20 N	119.47 E
Xiaochengdu	106	30.59 N	120.04 E
Xiaochengshan ▮	98	37.27 N	122.39 E
Xiaochengzi, Zhg.	89	42.56 N	123.12 E
Xiaochengzi, Zhg.	89	46.33 N	122.54 E
Xiaochikou	100	29.46 N	115.59 E
Xiaochiyi	100	30.33 N	116.23 E
Xiaodanyang	106	31.38 N	118.43 E
Xiaodong	102	22.14 N	108.39 E
Xiaoeguan ▮	100	28.51 N	121.50 E
Xiaofangshen	104	42.13 N	123.54 E
Xiaofangtang	106	31.04 N	118.40 E
Xiaofanshan	105	40.16 N	115.19 E
Xiaofen	106	31.45 N	119.39 E
Xiaofeng	106	30.36 N	119.32 E
Xiaogan	100	30.55 N	113.54 E
Xiaogang	100	28.14 N	115.50 E
Xiaogaojiatun	104	41.02 N	121.59 E
Xiaogencaigangzi	104	41.48 N	122.42 E
Xiaoguai	86	45.13 N	85.02 E
Xiaoguhe ≃	98	36.42 N	120.16 E
Xiaogushan	98	39.49 N	123.12 E
Xiaohai	106	31.58 N	120.59 E
Xiaohaladaokou	98	42.37 N	119.32 E
Xiaohan	98	35.48 N	114.52 E
Xiaohe	106	32.01 N	119.52 E
Xiaoheishan ∧	102	24.42 N	98.55 E
Xiaohekou	102	33.19 N	107.25 E
Xiaoheyan	98	42.26 N	119.38 E
Xiaoheying	102	32.37 N	104.23 E
Xiaohongmen	271a	39.49 N	116.26 E
Xiaohu	100	27.20 N	118.14 E
Xiaohuying	98	41.09 N	117.13 E
Xiaoji, Zhg.	98	36.45 N	121.01 E
Xiaoji, Zhg.	100	27.08 N	113.15 E
Xiaoji, Zhg.	100	32.38 N	119.48 E
Xiaojiachang	107	30.18 N	106.28 E
Xiaojiagang	100	31.06 N	113.55 E
Xiaojialing	100	29.35 N	116.32 E
Xiaojiang	100	25.08 N	114.59 E
Xiaojiawu	105	39.36 N	116.36 E
Xiaojiayingzi	98	40.17 N	118.47 E
Xiaojieling	100	31.36 N	115.09 E
Xiaojin	102	31.00 N	102.21 E
Xiaojingfang	105	39.22 N	116.34 E
Xiaojiu	89	45.15 N	127.47 E
Xiaokaoshantun	104	42.10 N	123.53 E
Xiaokuli	89	50.18 N	120.20 E
Xiaokunshan	106	31.02 N	121.07 E
Xiaolan	100	22.41 N	113.14 E
Xiaoling, Zhg.	89	45.20 N	127.18 E
Xiaoling, Zhg.	104	42.18 N	123.23 E
Xiaolinghe ≃	104	41.06 N	121.07 E
Xiaolingzi	104	41.07 N	123.19 E
Xiaolinzhuang	104	41.36 N	124.01 E
Xiaolongtan	102	23.51 N	103.10 E
Xiaolüzhuang	106	31.57 N	119.25 E
Xiaomei	100	27.50 N	118.58 E
Xiaomeiguan)(	100	25.17 N	114.17 E
Xiaomianxi	107	30.08 N	106.32 E
Xiaomiaozi, Zhg.	98	41.40 N	115.21 E
Xiaomiaozi, Zhg.	98	41.24 N	114.25 E
Xiaonanhai	107	29.23 N	106.27 E
Xiaoniuqun	98	41.59 N	118.20 E
Xiaopikou	98	35.47 N	115.53 E
Xiaopingyang	102	23.22 N	109.13 E
Xiaoqiao	100	26.57 N	118.30 E
Xiaoqiaotou	106	30.43 N	119.27 E
Xiaoqingchuizi	104	42.30 N	123.39 E
Xiaoqinghe ≃, Zhg.	98	37.17 N	118.52 E
Xiaoqinghe ≃, Zhg.	105	39.32 N	116.08 E
Xiaoquan	102	41.14 N	95.26 E
Xiaorun	100	33.23 N	116.29 E
Xiaosanjiazi	104	42.34 N	123.23 E
Xiaosanxia ≃	107	29.34 N	106.35 E
Xiaoshachang	100	29.58 N	113.16 E
Xiaoshan	106	30.10 N	120.15 E
Xiaoshangqiao	100	33.43 N	113.58 E
Xiaoshi, Zhg.	100	27.27 N	116.49 E
Xiaoshi, Zhg.	104	41.17 N	124.06 E
Xiaoshixiang	100	30.36 N	116.38 E
Xiaoshu	106	30.48 N	119.46 E
Xiaoshun	100	29.11 N	119.51 E
Xiaosigou	98	40.53 N	118.33 E
Xiaosijia	104	42.24 N	120.46 E
Xiaotang	98	41.38 N	119.33 E
Xiaotanghe	98	42.04 N	127.10 E
Xiaotao	100	25.46 N	117.08 E
Xiaotianshi	100	32.45 N	115.36 E
Xiaotianzhen	100	31.12 N	116.33 E
Xiaotun	104	42.24 N	123.44 E
Xiaotunzicun	104	41.14 N	123.20 E
Xiaowa	104	41.03 N	122.04 E
Xiaowan	100	26.53 N	116.36 E
Xiaowangmiao	100	29.41 N	121.21 E
Xiaowenhe ≃	98	35.59 N	117.11 E
Xiaowugonghe ≃	105	39.21 N	117.32 E
Xiaowutaishan ∧	105	39.51 N	115.09 E
Xiaoxi	100	25.48 N	115.21 E
Xiaoxian	98	34.11 N	116.56 E
Xiaoxihe ≃	106	32.15 N	120.24 E
Xiaoxincheng	105	39.24 N	115.11 E
Xiaoxing'anling-shanmai ⩕	89	50.00 N	126.25 E
Xiaoxingshan ▮	100	22.31 N	114.51 E
Xiaoxintian	271a	39.58 N	116.22 E
Xiaoxizhen	106	30.51 N	119.50 E
Xiaoyangjiadian	104	42.23 N	122.24 E
Xiaoyangkou ≃[1]	100	32.38 N	121.02 E
Xiaoyangqi	89	50.48 N	124.12 E
Xiaoyantai	104	41.26 N	123.10 E
Xiaoyaozhen	100	33.46 N	114.16 E
Xiaoyi	102	37.10 N	111.46 E
Xiaoying, Zhg.	98	37.18 N	118.04 E
Xiaoying, Zhg.	105	40.12 N	116.33 E
Xiaoyingcun	105	39.28 N	116.41 E
Xiaoyushan ▮	106	30.19 N	121.55 E
Xiaozhanghe ≃	105	39.47 N	117.22 E
Xiaozhongdian	102	27.40 N	99.46 E
Xiaozhonghe ≃	271a	39.54 N	116.41 E
Xiaozhuang	104	41.30 N	121.27 E
Xiaozhujiawan	106	31.24 N	121.01 E
Xiapan ▮	106	30.30 N	121.20 E
Xiapu, Zhg.	100	26.52 N	120.01 E
Xiapu, Zhg.	100	27.49 N	114.26 E
Xiaqialafangzi	104	41.48 N	121.44 E
Xiaqiupu	98	36.59 N	119.55 E
Xiasantumen	105	38.50 N	114.48 E
Xiashe	106	30.33 N	120.11 E
Xiashesi	100	27.46 N	112.57 E
Xiashi	106	30.32 N	120.42 E
Xiashu	106	32.11 N	119.10 E
Xiashuerfowei	89	50.23 N	120.47 E
Xiashuiquan	104	41.52 N	123.38 E
Xiataizi	105	40.37 N	117.45 E
Xiatang, Zhg.	100	33.45 N	112.39 E
Xiatang, Zhg.	106	31.29 N	118.41 E
Xiatangtian	106	30.55 N	120.12 E
Xiataohuatu	104	41.42 N	120.36 E
Xiawa	98	42.39 N	120.35 E
Xiawajiang	106	30.59 N	121.51 E
Xiawaziyu	104	41.15 N	123.38 E
Xiaxi	106	31.43 N	119.45 E
Xiaxian	102	35.11 N	111.15 E
Xiaxiangcheng	102	28.42 N	99.59 E
Xiaxinhe	106	31.40 N	119.31 E
Xiayang, Zhg.	100	28.48 N	119.41 E
Xiayang, Zhg.	100	26.46 N	117.59 E
Xiayang, Zhg.	100	24.39 N	116.52 E
Xiayi	98	34.14 N	116.06 E
Xiaying, Zhg.	98	37.03 N	119.25 E
Xiaying, Zhg.	105	40.10 N	117.25 E
Xiayunling	105	39.43 N	115.44 E
Xiazhang	98	36.08 N	116.57 E
Xiazhen	100	28.39 N	118.21 E
Xiazhi ▮	100	29.42 N	122.15 E
Xiazhuang, Zhg.	98	35.28 N	118.43 E
Xiazhuang, Zhg.	100	27.22 N	119.01 E
Xiazhuang, Zhg.	105	40.18 N	116.21 E
Xiazhuang, Zhg.	105	39.54 N	117.01 E
Xiazhuang, Zhg.	105	39.38 N	115.26 E
Xiazhuangzhen	98	34.56 N	118.44 E
Xiazikou	105	39.01 N	115.25 E
Xibanchang	107	30.32 N	106.12 E
Xibaqianmou	104	40.59 N	121.35 E
Xibeiyingzi	104	41.55 N	121.38 E
Xibu	100	31.46 N	118.17 E
Xicang	106	31.34 N	120.29 E
Xichang, Zhg.	100	23.53 N	114.29 E
Xichang, Zhg.	102	27.58 N	102.13 E
Xichang, Zhg.	104	42.15 N	124.12 E
Xicheng, Zhg.	89	48.10 N	125.29 E
Xicheng, Zhg.	102	24.09 N	102.39 E
Xichengsi	105	39.36 N	115.45 E
Xichong	102	31.00 N	105.52 E
Xichuan	102	33.02 N	111.30 E
Xicicun	105	39.29 N	116.08 E
Xico	234	19.25 N	97.00 W
Xicoténcatl	234	23.00 N	98.56 W
Xicotepec de Juárez	234	20.17 N	97.57 W
Xicun	100	27.46 N	114.14 E
Xidachuan	98	41.46 N	127.34 E
Xidapo	89	43.12 N	130.02 E
Xidaying	105	39.41 N	116.14 E
Xidazhen	98	36.27 N	113.50 E
Xidian	100	29.32 N	121.26 E
Xié ≃	246	0.54 N	67.11 W
Xiecun	105	39.00 N	115.31 E
Xiedian	100	33.27 N	113.28 E
Xiefang	100	26.12 N	116.41 E
Xiegeer	120	28.38 N	87.04 E
Xiehejian	105	39.58 N	116.03 E
Xiejia	98	42.24 N	125.42 E
Xiejiagangzi	104	41.55 N	122.20 E
Xiejiapu	106	31.15 N	119.09 E
Xiejiaqiao	106	31.44 N	120.45 E
Xiejunmiao	107	30.15 N	103.40 E
Xielipuke	120	31.30 N	82.45 E
Xiemachang	107	29.46 N	106.22 E
Xiemaqiao	106	31.13 N	121.03 E
Xiematashan ∧	89	50.28 N	120.47 E
Xiepu	100	30.02 N	121.37 E
Xieqiao, Zhg.	106	30.29 N	120.34 E
Xieqiao, Zhg.	106	32.03 N	120.22 E
Xietang	106	31.18 N	120.44 E
Xiexi	106	31.54 N	118.54 E
Xiexinggou	104	41.51 N	121.05 E
Xieyujiangkou C[1]	106	32.10 N	121.23 E
Xiezhen	106	31.35 N	118.38 E
Xifeng, Zhg.	98	42.43 N	124.40 E
Xifeng, Zhg.	102	27.02 N	106.30 E
Xifengkou	105	40.24 N	118.19 E
Xifocun	104	41.26 N	122.33 E
Xigangzi	89	49.58 N	127.20 E
Xigaolizhuangzi	104	41.40 N	122.55 E
Xigaotan	98	38.18 N	116.13 E
Xigaotun	98	40.27 N	122.36 E
Xigouzi	89	53.06 N	120.40 E
Xiguanjiatun	104	42.35 N	123.10 E
Xiguanyingzi	104	41.50 N	120.37 E
Xigui ◎	106	31.23 N	119.45 E
Xiguituqi (Yakeshi)	89	49.17 N	120.41 E
Xihaikou	104	40.50 N	121.01 E
Xihamaling ⩕	104	42.03 N	124.00 E
Xihe, Zhg.	100	31.01 N	118.28 E
Xihe, Zhg.	102	34.01 N	105.17 E
Xihe ≃	104	41.44 N	121.30 E
Xiheying	98	39.53 N	114.42 E
Xihezhen	100	31.41 N	113.27 E
Xihezhuang	105	39.20 N	118.02 E
Xihu ◎	106	30.15 N	120.08 E
Xihua	100	33.47 N	114.31 E
Xihuangcang	106	31.43 N	121.40 E
Xihuanzidong	104	41.31 N	122.28 E
Xihuashan, Zhg.	100	25.28 N	114.20 E
Xihuashan, Zhg.	105	40.07 N	116.54 E
Xihuishan	104	41.41 N	122.38 E
Xiji, Zhg.	102	35.48 N	105.43 E
Xiji, Zhg.	105	39.49 N	116.52 E
Xijialong	102	23.31 N	103.51 E
Xijiang	100	25.50 N	115.49 E
Xijiang ≃	102	22.25 N	113.23 E
Xijianshanzi	104	40.47 N	120.48 E
Xijiao Jichang ⊠	105	39.57 N	116.20 E
Xijiapuzitun	104	41.26 N	123.50 E
Xikou, Zhg.	89	46.40 N	120.40 E
Xikou, Zhg.	100	29.14 N	114.24 E
Xikou, Zhg.	100	28.52 N	119.11 E
Xikou, Zhg.	100	25.26 N	118.45 E
Xikou, Zhg.	100	25.24 N	117.03 E
Xikou, Zhg.	100	26.15 N	118.59 E
Xikou, Zhg.	106	30.40 N	118.41 E
Xilaichang	107	30.20 N	103.29 E
Xilaiqiao	106	32.03 N	119.54 E
Xilaizhen	106	32.07 N	120.25 E
Xilanmulunhe ≃	102	41.40 N	106.15 E
Xiliaohe ≃	89	43.10 N	123.37 E
Xilin	120	28.33 N	87.48 E
Xiling ⊥	105	39.19 N	115.15 E
Xilinhaote	102	43.58 N	116.04 E
Xilintuo	120	30.08 N	88.04 E
Xilitla	234	21.20 N	98.58 W
Xiliuhe	105	38.58 N	116.32 E
Xiliushuyingzi	104	42.25 N	121.54 E
Xilókastron	38	38.05 N	22.38 E
Xiluncun	89	47.08 N	126.26 E
Ximagou	105	40.16 N	117.50 E
Ximakou	100	30.33 N	113.47 E
Ximalatu	89	47.00 N	122.01 E
Ximalin	98	40.48 N	114.29 E
Ximenqiao	106	30.58 N	119.30 E
Ximucheng	104	40.42 N	122.54 E
Xin'an, Zhg.	89	43.46 N	125.40 E
Xi'nan, Zhg.	100	25.26 N	117.35 E
Xin'an, Zhg.	100	26.44 N	116.13 E
Xin'an, Zhg.	105	39.09 N	116.38 E
Xin'an, Zhg.	105	39.45 N	117.32 E
Xin'an, Zhg.	106	31.47 N	120.09 E
Xin'an, Zhg.	106	31.30 N	120.22 E
Xin'andian	100	32.37 N	114.03 E
Xin'andu	100	30.54 N	116.59 E
Xin'anji	100	33.22 N	115.13 E
Xin'anjiang ≃, Zhg.	100	29.12 N	119.27 E
Xin'anjiang ≃, Zhg.	100	29.33 N	118.58 E
Xin'anpu	104	42.39 N	123.27 E
Xin'anqiao	106	32.16 N	121.07 E
Xin'ansuo	102	23.16 N	103.27 E
Xin'anzhen	89	44.06 N	123.46 E
Xi'nanzhuang	105	40.48 N	118.23 E
Xinavane	156	25.02 S	32.47 E
Xinba, Zhg.	98	34.27 N	119.39 E
Xinba, Zhg.	100	30.24 N	116.52 E
Xinba, Zhg.	106	32.08 N	120.39 E
Xinba, Zhg.	106	32.16 N	119.45 E
Xinbaerhuyouqi (Alatan'aola)	88	48.41 N	116.53 E
Xinbaerhuzuoqi (Amugulang)	88	48.14 N	118.18 E
Xinbaoan	105	40.27 N	115.24 E
Xinbin, Zhg.	98	41.42 N	125.02 E
Xinbin, Zhg.	106	30.56 N	121.04 E
Xinbo	98	42.16 N	117.34 E
Xincai	100	32.44 N	114.59 E
Xincang, Zhg.	106	30.25 N	120.42 E
Xincang, Zhg.	106	30.44 N	121.11 E
Xinchang, Zhg.	100	29.30 N	120.53 E
Xinchang, Zhg.	102	25.10 N	104.18 E
Xinchang, Zhg.	102	28.03 N	103.46 E
Xinchang, Zhg.	106	31.42 N	121.46 E
Xinchang, Zhg.	106	31.02 N	121.38 E
Xinchang, Zhg.	107	30.29 N	106.21 E
Xinchang, Zhg.	107	30.16 N	104.29 E
Xinchang, Zhg.	107	29.20 N	104.15 E
Xinchang, Zhg.	107	29.38 N	104.33 E
Xinchang, Zhg.	107	30.31 N	104.56 E
Xinchangzi	107	29.40 N	103.46 E
Xincheng, Zhg.	98	40.37 N	120.43 E
Xincheng, Zhg.	100	25.34 N	114.36 E
Xincheng, Zhg.	102	24.09 N	108.46 E
Xincheng, Zhg.	105	39.15 N	115.59 E
Xincheng, Zhg.	105	38.59 N	117.33 E
Xincheng, Zhg.	106	30.48 N	120.36 E
Xinchengzi	104	42.03 N	123.30 E
Xincunji	100	32.53 N	115.31 E
Xindai	106	30.49 N	121.05 E
Xindeng	100	29.59 N	119.44 E
Xindi	104	42.21 N	120.35 E
Xindian, Zhg.	89	45.55 N	127.50 E
Xindian, Zhg.	98	37.29 N	118.28 E
Xindian, Zhg.	98	37.07 N	114.49 E
Xindian, Zhg.	100	31.33 N	115.16 E
Xindian, Zhg.	100	33.07 N	112.38 E
Xindian, Zhg.	100	33.38 N	113.51 E
Xindian, Zhg.	100	29.40 N	113.40 E
Xindian, Zhg.	105	39.10 N	116.27 E
Xindian, Zhg.	105	40.47 N	116.49 E
Xindian, Zhg.	105	40.11 N	116.11 E
Xindian, Zhg.	107	29.19 N	105.40 E
Xindianbu	100	32.24 N	116.22 E
Xindianji	100	33.33 N	114.50 E
Xindianzhen	107	29.19 N	104.57 E
Xindianzi, Zhg.	105	40.04 N	118.01 E
Xindianzi, Zhg.	107	29.46 N	105.11 E
Xindianzi, Zhg.	107	29.03 N	103.46 E
Xindianzi, Zhg.	107	29.43 N	104.01 E
Xindianzi, Zhg.	107	29.52 N	106.06 E
Xindianzi, Zhg.	107	28.49 N	103.35 E
Xindu	102	23.59 N	111.46 E
Xindukou	102	24.06 N	100.30 E
Xinfatuncun	104	41.13 N	122.28 E
Xinfeng, Zhg.	100	33.19 N	120.30 E
Xinfeng, Zhg.	100	24.04 N	114.12 E
Xinfeng, Zhg.	100	25.24 N	114.56 E
Xinfeng, Zhg.	100	27.26 N	116.40 E
Xinfeng, Zhg.	100	24.05 N	116.53 E
Xinfeng, Zhg.	106	32.05 N	119.34 E
Xinfeng, Zhg.	106	30.43 N	120.55 E
Xinfeng, Zhg.	106	31.09 N	118.40 E
Xinfengshui ≃	100	23.42 N	114.42 E
Xing'an, Zhg.	89	48.49 N	121.45 E
Xing'an, Zhg.	102	25.37 N	110.31 E
Xin'gang	106	31.56 N	120.57 E
Xing'anlingzhan	89	51.37 N	125.38 E
Xing'antun	89	51.31 N	120.08 E
Xingcheng	104	40.37 N	120.43 E
Xingguo	100	26.21 N	115.19 E
Xinghai	102	35.31 N	99.36 E
Xinghe	98	40.48 N	113.58 E
Xinghua	100	32.57 N	119.50 E
Xinghuawan C	100	25.20 N	119.20 E
Xingkathu (Ozero Chanka) ◎	89	45.00 N	132.24 E
Xingliuji	100	33.04 N	115.41 E
Xinglong, Zhg.	105	40.26 N	117.34 E
Xinglong, Zhg.	107	30.36 N	106.20 E
Xinglongchang, Zhg.	107	29.34 N	106.09 E
Xinglongchang, Zhg.	107	29.54 N	105.26 E
Xinglongchang, Zhg.	107	30.06 N	105.55 E
Xinglongchang, Zhg.	107	30.25 N	104.06 E
Xinglongchang, Zhg.	107	30.20 N	106.07 E
Xinglongcun	89	48.50 N	125.12 E
Xinglongdian, Zhg.	104	42.16 N	124.00 E
Xinglongdian, Zhg.	104	41.59 N	123.03 E
Xinglonggou, Zhg.	104	40.45 N	123.08 E
Xinglonggou, Zhg.	104	41.46 N	120.38 E
Xinglongji	100	32.05 N	112.51 E
Xinglongpao	89	46.27 N	125.47 E
Xinglongtai	104	42.30 N	123.48 E
Xinglongtang	105	40.41 N	117.42 E
Xinglongzhen	102	35.38 N	106.08 E

Symbol	English	Deutsch	Español	Français	Português
≃	River	Fluss	Río	Rivière	Rio
☲	Canal	Kanal	Canal	Canal	Canal
⌊	Waterfall, Rapids	Wasserfall, Stromschnellen	Cascada, Rápidos	Chute d'eau, Rapides	Cascata, Rápidos
⋃	Strait	Meeresstrasse	Estrecho	Détroit	Estreito
C	Bay, Gulf	Bucht, Golf	Bahía, Golfo	Baie, Golfe	Baía, Golfo
◎	Lake, Lakes	See, Seen	Lago, Lagos	Lac, Lacs	Lago, Lagos
☷	Swamp	Sumpf	Pantano	Marais	Pântano
⍓	Ice Features, Glacier	Eis- und Gletscherformen	Accidentes Glaciales	Formes glaciaires	Acidentes Glaciares
⍑	Other Hydrographic Features	Andere Hydrographische Objekte	Otros Elementos Hidrográficos	Autres données hydrographiques	Outros Elementos Hidrográficos
◆	Submarine Features	Untermeerische Objekte	Accidentes Submarinos	Formes de relief sous-marin	Acidentes Submarinos
□	Political Unit	Politische Einheit	Unidad Política	Entité politique	Unidade Política
▾	Cultural Institution	Kulturelle Institution	Institución Cultural	Institution culturelle	Instituição Cultural
⊥	Historical Site	Historische Stätte	Sitio Histórico	Site historique	Sitio Histórico
▲	Recreational Site	Erholungs- und Ferienort	Sitio de Recreo	Centre de loisirs	Sítio de Lazer
⊠	Airport	Flughafen	Aeropuerto	Aéroport	Aeroporto
■	Military Installation	Militäranlage	Instalación Militar	Installation militaire	Instalação Militar
◆	Miscellaneous	Verschiedenes	Misceláneo	Divers	Miscelânea

Xingning 100 24.09 N 115.45 E
Xingningjiang ≃ 100 24.00 N 115.54 E
Xin'gou 100 30.41 N 113.57 E
Xin'gouzui 100 30.08 N 112.56 E
Xingren 102 25.27 N 105.13 E
Xingrenbao 102 37.06 N 105.12 E
Xingshanbao 89 45.30 N 125.45 E
Xingtai 98 37.04 N 114.29 E
Xingtan 100 22.46 N 113.07 E
Xingtang 98 38.26 N 114.33 E
Xingtian 100 27.30 N 118.02 E
Xingu ≃ 242 1.30 S 51.53 W
Xinguan 100 33.38 N 118.05 E
Xingwenping 102 29.24 N 103.23 E
Xingxian 102 38.36 N 111.15 E
Xingxing 106 30.39 N 121.09 E
Xingyi, Zhg. 98 38.19 N 114.59 E
Xingyi, Zhg. 102 25.06 N 104.58 E
Xingzhuangzi 105 40.34 N 115.00 E
Xingzi 100 29.28 N 116.01 E
Xinhailian 98 34.39 N 119.16 E
Xinhe, Zhg. 98 37.32 N 115.14 E
Xinhe, Zhg. 100 28.30 N 121.27 E
Xinhe, Zhg. 105 39.03 N 117.37 E
Xinhe, Zhg. 106 31.59 N 121.21 E
Xinhe ≃ 98 35.06 N 116.39 E
Xinhekou 89 48.22 N 130.45 E
Xinheng 100 23.38 N 116.18 E
Xinhezhuang 106 31.09 N 118.45 E
Xinhua 102 27.37 N 111.02 E
Xinhuang 106 30.37 N 120.55 E
Xinhuanghekou ≃[1] 98 38.00 N 119.00 E
Xinhui 100 22.32 N 113.02 E
Xining (Sining) 102 36.38 N 101.55 E
Xiniu 106 31.25 N 120.07 E
Xiniuguchengzi 104 41.01 N 122.24 E
Xiniutan 100 24.10 N 113.07 E
Xinjeji 89 52.08 N 126.24 E
Xinji, Zhg. 98 35.19 N 115.36 E
Xinji, Zhg. 100 33.24 N 114.44 E
Xinji, Zhg. 105 39.52 N 117.10 E
Xinjiaji 98 36.56 N 116.59 E
Xinjian (Shengmi), Zhg. 100 28.34 N 115.47 E
Xinjian, Zhg. 100 28.46 N 120.02 E
Xinjian, Zhg. 106 31.33 N 119.39 E
Xinjiang, Zhg. 100 24.29 N 113.52 E
Xinjiang, Zhg. 102 35.40 N 111.11 E
Xinjiang, Zhg. 106 32.05 N 120.40 E
Xinjiang ≃ 100 28.38 N 116.39 E
Xinjianglang 106 30.58 N 120.54 E
Xinjiang Weiwuer Zizhiqu (Sinkiang) □[4] 90 40.00 N 85.00 E
Xinjiapu 105 40.32 N 115.57 E
Xinjiazhuang 105 40.31 N 114.58 E
Xinjie 102 26.48 N 101.15 E
Xinjin, Bhārat 102 28.59 N 94.50 E
Xinjin, Zhg. 98 39.24 N 121.58 E
Xinjin, Zhg. 107 30.25 N 103.49 E
Xinjingzi 86 42.13 N 87.36 E
Xinkaihe 106 31.35 N 121.31 E
Xinkaihe ≃, Zhg. 89 43.37 N 123.36 E
Xinkaihe ≃, Zhg. 98 41.52 N 122.50 E
Xinkaijing 106 31.09 N 121.00 E
Xinkengdong 100 26.09 N 113.46 E
Xinle 98 38.24 N 114.47 E
Xinlitun, Zhg. 89 44.41 N 126.45 E
Xinlitun, Zhg. 104 42.00 N 122.09 E
Xinlizhuang 105 39.17 N 116.10 E
Xinmin 104 42.00 N 122.48 E
Xinmintun 104 41.39 N 123.02 E
Xinning 102 26.19 N 110.45 E
Xinnongzhen (Xiaozhan) 105 38.55 N 117.25 E
Xinping 102 24.06 N 101.58 E
Xinpu, Zhg. 100 24.31 N 116.08 E
Xinpu, Zhg. 100 32.50 N 118.45 E
Xinqianghe ≃ 100 29.12 N 113.03 E
Xinqianzhen 98 37.59 N 118.15 E
Xinqiao, Zhg. 106 31.32 N 119.04 E
Xinqiao, Zhg. 106 31.04 N 121.18 E
Xinqiao, Zhg. 107 30.33 N 105.33 E
Xinqiao, Zhg. 107 29.32 N 106.28 E
Xinqiao, Zhg. 107 30.10 N 103.50 E
Xinqiaotou 106 31.00 N 119.24 E
Xinqiu 98 41.53 N 119.41 E
Xinqizhou 100 28.56 N 115.50 E
Xinqu 86 44.57 N 85.15 E
Xinquan 100 25.23 N 116.38 E
Xinsanyu 106 31.58 N 120.07 E
Xinshao 102 27.11 N 111.20 E
Xinshenggang 106 32.03 N 120.25 E
Xinshengzhen 107 29.29 N 104.39 E
Xinshi 106 30.37 N 120.19 E
Xinshizhen 107 30.20 N 104.35 E
Xinshuhe ≃ 98 34.41 N 119.12 E
Xintai 98 35.54 N 117.44 E
Xintaimen 98 40.50 N 120.23 E
Xintaizi 104 42.07 N 123.36 E
Xintang, Zhg. 100 23.08 N 113.36 E
Xintang, Zhg. 102 30.13 N 109.30 E
Xintang, Zhg. 106 31.02 N 119.59 E
Xintangcun 106 31.53 N 119.31 E
Xintanpu 100 29.43 N 114.54 E
Xintian 102 25.53 N 112.05 E
Xintun 104 42.11 N 123.45 E
Xinwei, Zhg. 100 22.52 N 114.20 E
Xinwei, Zhg. 100 25.21 N 115.48 E
Xinwei, Zhg. 100 24.57 N 117.34 E
Xinxian, Zhg. 98 36.15 N 115.41 E
Xinxian, Zhg. 100 31.38 N 114.51 E
Xinxian, Zhg. 102 38.25 N 112.48 E
Xinxiang 98 35.20 N 113.51 E
Xinxim ≃ 250 7.57 S 53.20 W
Xinxing, Zhg. 89 43.16 N 129.48 E
Xinxing, Zhg. 100 22.40 N 112.52 E
Xinxing, Zhg. 102 19.57 N 109.32 E
Xinyang 100 32.19 N 114.01 E
Xinyao 100 27.39 N 118.52 E
Xinye 100 32.33 N 112.21 E
Xinyi (Xin'anzhen), Zhg. 98 34.22 N 118.21 E
Xinyi (Dongzhen), Zhg. 102 22.13 N 110.50 E
Xinying 102 36.04 N 105.30 E
Xinyu 100 27.49 N 114.57 E
Xinyuan 86 43.08 N 82.31 E
Xinzao 100 23.02 N 113.26 E
Xinzha 102 23.41 N 101.09 E
Xinzhai, Zhg. 98 39.24 N 118.46 E
Xinzhai, Zhg. 98 36.24 N 118.37 E
Xinzhai, Zhg. 102 24.33 N 99.08 E
Xinzhang 105 39.05 N 116.46 E
Xinzhangzi 105 40.47 N 117.52 E
Xinzhao 102 39.32 N 107.52 E
Xinzhazhen 106 31.50 N 119.52 E
Xinzhen, Zhg. 98 35.37 N 114.03 E
Xinzhen, Zhg. 105 39.01 N 116.22 E
Xinzhen, Zhg. 106 31.24 N 121.24 E
Xinzheng 100 34.25 N 113.43 E
Xinzhenshi 106 32.04 N 120.02 E
Xinzhou, Zhg. 100 30.50 N 114.47 E
Xinzhou, Zhg. 102 19.48 N 109.18 E
Xinzhuang, Zhg. 98 35.05 N 117.56 E
Xinzhuang, Zhg. 106 31.07 N 121.22 E
Xinzhuang, Zhg. 271a 39.56 N 116.31 E
Xinzhuangtou 105 39.25 N 115.45 E
Xinzhuangzi, Zhg. 104 41.05 N 121.23 E
Xinzhuangzi, Zhg. 105 39.20 N 118.25 E
Xinzhuangzi, Zhg. 105 40.14 N 116.59 E
Xinzhuangzi, Zhg. 105 40.32 N 115.10 E
Xinzhuangzi, Zhg. 105 38.52 N 117.21 E
Xinzhuntun 105 39.39 N 117.57 E
Xiongdidao II 100 23.33 N 117.40 E
Xiongershan ⩕ 102 34.08 N 111.40 E
Xiongjiachang 102 26.31 N 105.39 E
Xiongjiaping 107 29.55 N 106.03 E
Xiongxian 105 38.59 N 116.05 E
Xiongyuecheng 98 40.10 N 122.08 E
Xipamanu ≃ 248 10.43 S 67.50 W
Xiping 100 33.23 N 114.02 E
Xiping'anhe 104 40.47 N 122.01 E
Xipu 100 23.42 N 117.24 E
Xiqi 100 26.45 N 118.42 E
Xiqi ≃ 100 25.14 N 118.03 E
Xiqia 106 31.03 N 119.37 E
Xiqilichiquan 89 49.59 N 119.27 E
Xiqin 100 26.33 N 118.06 E
Xiqingshan ⩕ 102 35.16 N 101.30 E
Xiqu ≃ 102 31.29 N 100.48 E
Xique-Xique 250 10.50 S 42.44 W
Xiriri, Lago ⊜ 250 1.37 S 55.56 W
Xiruá ≃ 248 6.03 S 67.50 W
Xisanshilipu 100 32.40 N 117.31 E
Xishan, Zhg. 100 28.34 N 115.37 E
Xishan, Zhg. 105 39.38 N 118.10 E
Xishanqiao 106 31.57 N 118.43 E
Xishanxicun 105 40.01 N 116.50 E
Xishijiazi 104 41.46 N 120.55 E
Xishiqiao 106 31.53 N 120.06 E
Xishui 100 30.27 N 115.13 E
Xishui ≃ 100 30.21 N 115.06 E
Xishuiyu 105 40.25 N 116.16 E
Xisuhupu 104 41.41 N 123.14 E
Xitai 98 40.37 N 120.12 E
Xitaihu C 106 31.12 N 120.25 E
Xitan 100 23.47 N 117.08 E
Xitang 106 30.57 N 120.53 E
Xitangqiao, Zhg. 106 31.49 N 120.38 E
Xitangqiao, Zhg. 106 30.37 N 121.01 E
Xitaoyuan 104 40.57 N 122.11 E
Xiti 120 33.27 N 82.48 E
Xitianmushan ∧ 106 30.21 N 119.25 E
Xitiaoxi ≃ 106 30.56 N 120.11 E
Xiting 106 32.08 N 121.02 E
Xititou 105 39.16 N 117.21 E
Xitole 150 11.43 N 14.50 W
Xituan 105 39.29 N 115.47 E
Xiujiangpu 104 41.17 N 123.02 E
Xiuning 100 29.47 N 118.10 E
Xiushan 102 28.29 N 108.52 E
Xiushui 100 29.04 N 114.33 E
Xiushui ≃ 100 29.13 N 115.56 E
Xiushuihe 104 42.22 N 123.01 E
Xiuyan 98 40.17 N 123.18 E
Xiwei 100 25.22 N 117.46 E
Xiweizigou 104 42.01 N 121.59 E
Xiwenquan 107 29.42 N 106.07 E
Xiwu 100 29.40 N 121.30 E
Xiwukou 106 30.24 N 118.54 E
Xixia 102 33.22 N 111.28 E
Xixian, Zhg. 100 32.21 N 114.44 E
Xixian, Zhg. 102 36.43 N 110.52 E
Xixiang 102 32.48 N 107.55 E
Xixiangyang 105 39.33 N 116.02 E
Xixiaojie 104 40.42 N 122.12 E
Xixiaosanjiazi 104 41.22 N 122.32 E
Xixiashu 106 31.57 N 119.49 E
Xixing 106 30.11 N 120.13 E
Xiyang, Zhg. 98 37.37 N 113.42 E
Xiyang, Zhg. 100 25.50 N 117.25 E
Xiyang, Zhg. 100 33.25 N 116.22 E
Xiyang, Zhg. 106 31.52 N 119.23 E
Xiyang, Zhg. 106 31.49 N 120.43 E
Xiyangjiao 106 31.43 N 120.23 E
Xiyangshugou 104 40.41 N 122.44 E
Xiyangzhuang 106 31.50 N 119.22 E
Xiyingzi 104 41.55 N 122.34 E
Xiyinhe ≍ 105 39.08 N 117.43 E
Xiyou 98 37.24 N 119.56 E
Xiyuqiaozhai 104 41.45 N 123.40 E
Xiyushi 106 30.36 N 119.26 E
Xizang Zizhiqu □[4] 90 32.00 N 88.00 E
Xizhou 100 29.29 N 121.39 E
Xizhoushan ⩕ 102 38.20 N 113.00 E
Xkalak 232 18.16 N 87.50 W
Xlukehu ⊜ 120 31.42 N 89.30 E
Xochapa 234 17.39 N 95.46 W
Xochimilco □[7] 286a 19.14 N 99.05 W
Xochimilco, Lago de ⊜ 286a 19.16 N 99.06 W
Xochipala 234 17.48 N 99.39 W
Xochistlahuaca 234 16.47 N 98.15 W
Xochitlán 234 19.59 N 97.36 W
Xom-binh-phuoc 269c 10.40 N 106.47 E
Xom-long-moc 110 18.51 N 105.01 E
Xom-xoai-minh 269c 10.42 N 106.50 E
Xoxocotla 234 18.41 N 99.15 W
Xuancheng 106 30.58 N 118.45 E
Xuan'en 102 30.00 N 109.20 E
Xuanfeng 100 27.42 N 114.08 E
Xuang ≃ 110 19.58 N 102.15 E
Xuanhan 102 31.24 N 107.43 E
Xuanhua 105 40.37 N 115.03 E
Xuanhuadian 100 31.42 N 114.29 E
Xuanjiabao 106 32.17 N 120.01 E
Xuanjiangying 98 41.25 N 116.45 E
Xuan-loc 110 10.56 N 107.14 E
Xuanping 100 28.36 N 119.34 E
Xuantanchang 107 29.12 N 105.34 E
Xuan-thoi-thuong 269c 10.52 N 106.34 E
Xuanwei 102 26.07 N 104.05 E
Xuanzhuang 105 39.29 N 118.07 E
Xuchang, Zhg. 100 34.03 N 113.49 E
Xuchang, Zhg. 107 29.06 N 104.31 E
Xucheng 98 35.56 N 116.27 E
Xucun 106 30.27 N 120.22 E
Xudazhuang 100 33.44 N 117.53 E
Xueao 100 29.27 N 121.30 E
Xueba 120 29.58 N 93.48 E
Xuebu 106 31.43 N 119.22 E
Xuecheng 98 34.50 N 117.16 E
Xuedian 100 34.30 N 113.44 E
Xuefanggou 104 41.57 N 121.01 E
Xuefeng 100 33.21 N 118.22 E
Xuefengshan ⩕ 102 27.44 N 111.00 E
Xuejiahu 98 34.08 N 116.27 E
Xueshanzhang 100 24.47 N 113.37 E
Xueshanzhang ∧ 100 24.24 N 113.37 E
Xueshuiwen 89 49.10 N 129.45 E
Xuetangpuzi 104 40.38 N 123.53 E
Xueyanqiao 106 31.30 N 120.06 E
Xuguichenxiaodian 106 32.07 N 121.20 E
Xujiabao 98 40.00 N 113.43 E
Xujiabu 100 29.27 N 116.18 E
Xujiadong 100 25.54 N 113.02 E
Xujiadu 100 28.18 N 114.44 E
Xujiagou 104 42.17 N 124.04 E
Xujiaji 100 31.50 N 116.22 E
Xujiang ≃ 100 28.17 N 116.05 E
Xujiapuzi 104 40.44 N 123.18 E
Xujiatou 106 31.19 N 119.25 E
Xujiazhai 106 31.11 N 121.46 E
Xuliying 105 39.28 N 116.02 E
Xunhe 89 49.18 N 128.04 E
Xunhua 102 35.49 N 102.26 E
Xunjiansi 105 40.50 N 116.04 E
Xunke 89 49.35 N 128.25 E
Xunle 102 25.17 N 108.12 E
Xunmukou 98 34.03 N 114.42 E
Xunshansuo 98 37.10 N 122.29 E
Xunwu 100 24.58 N 115.38 E
Xunwushui ≃ 100 24.28 N 115.26 E
Xunyangba 102 33.19 N 108.49 E
Xupu 102 27.44 N 110.24 E
Xushe 106 31.24 N 119.39 E
Xushui 105 39.02 N 115.39 E
Xutian 98 34.10 N 114.03 E
Xuwen 102 20.21 N 110.11 E
Xuxiandai 106 30.40 N 120.47 E
Xuxiang 106 31.33 N 120.13 E
Xuyen-moc 110 10.34 N 107.25 E
Xuyi 100 33.01 N 118.29 E
Xuyong 102 28.10 N 105.24 E
Xuzhou (Süchow) 98 34.16 N 117.11 E
Xuzhuang, Zhg. 98 35.07 N 117.42 E
Xuzhuang, Zhg. 106 31.09 N 120.32 E

Y

Yaan 102 30.03 N 103.02 E
Yaapeet 166 35.46 S 142.03 E
Ya'aqov Housman, Sede-Te'ufa ⊠ 132 29.33 N 34.59 E
Yaba ➳[8] 273a 6.30 N 3.23 E
Yaba College of Technology ❦[2] 273a 6.32 N 3.23 E
Ya'bad 132 32.27 N 35.10 E
Yabakei 96 33.27 N 131.07 E
Yabassi 152 4.28 N 9.58 E
Yabe 96 33.09 N 130.49 E
Yabe ≃ 96 33.06 N 130.26 E
Yabelo 144 4.54 N 38.05 E
Yablis 236 14.10 N 83.49 W
Yablonovy Range → Jablonovyj Chrebet ⩕ 88 53.30 N 115.00 E
Yabrīn ⫪[4] 128 23.17 N 48.58 E
Yabrūd 130 33.58 N 36.40 E
Yabu, Nihon 96 35.22 N 134.47 E
Yabu, Nihon 174m 26.36 N 127.57 E
Yabucoa 240m 18.03 N 65.53 W
Yabuki 94 37.12 N 140.19 E
Yabuluoni 89 44.55 N 128.35 E
Yacambu, Parque Nacional ♠ 246 9.40 N 68.39 W
Yacaré Norte, Riacho ≃ 252 22.43 S 58.14 W
Yachengzhen 110 18.25 N 109.11 E
Yachimata 94 35.39 N 140.19 E
Yachiyo, Nihon 94 36.10 N 139.53 E
Yachiyo, Nihon 94 35.43 N 140.07 E
Yaciretá, Isla I 252 27.25 S 56.30 W
Yaco 248 17.09 S 67.24 W
Yaco (Iaco) ≃ 248 9.03 S 68.34 W
Yacolt 224 45.52 N 122.25 W
Yacuiba 248 22.02 S 63.45 W
Yacuma ≃ 248 13.38 S 65.23 W
Yādgīr 122 16.46 N 77.08 E
Yadkin ≃ 192 35.23 N 80.03 W
Yadkinville 192 36.08 N 80.39 W
Yad Mordekhay 132 31.35 N 34.34 E
Yadong 124 27.29 N 88.55 E
Yādūdah 132 32.40 N 36.04 E
Yaenengu 152 2.28 N 23.15 E
Yaeyama-rettō II 175d 24.20 N 124.00 E
Yāfā 132 32.41 N 35.17 E
Yafran 146 32.04 N 12.31 E
Yaftābād 267d 35.39 N 51.19 E
Yafuquan 85 39.12 N 76.09 E
Yagachi-shima I 174m 26.40 N 128.01 E
Yağcılar 130 39.25 N 28.23 E
Yageg 144 3.24 N 44.00 E
Yageying 98 37.32 N 114.34 E
Yagi 96 35.04 N 135.32 E
Yago 234 21.50 N 105.04 W
Yagonde 152 0.02 N 22.41 E
Yagoona 274a 33.55 S 151.02 E
Yagoua 146 10.20 N 15.14 E
Yaguachi 246 2.07 S 79.41 W
Yaguachi ≃ 246 2.02 S 79.44 W
Yaguajay 240p 22.19 N 79.14 W
Yaguará 246 2.40 N 75.31 W
Yaguaraparo 246 10.34 N 62.49 W
Yaguarí 252 31.31 S 54.58 W
Yaguarón (Jaguarão) ≃ 252 32.39 S 53.12 W
Yaguas ≃ 246 2.45 S 70.04 W
Yaguhu ⊜ 120 28.40 N 91.45 E
Yagur 132 32.44 N 35.04 E
Yahagi ≃ 94 34.50 N 136.59 E
Yahagong 102 28.24 N 99.11 E
Yahara ≃ 190 42.48 N 89.07 W
Yahata → Kitakyūshū 96 33.53 N 130.50 E
Yahe, Zhg. 89 45.24 N 130.24 E
Yahe, Zhg. 106 31.44 N 119.52 E
Yaheladazeshan ∧ 120 35.12 N 95.20 E
Yahila 152 0.13 N 24.28 E
Yahk 182 49.05 N 116.05 W
Yahmūm al-Asmar, Jabal ∧ 142 29.56 N 31.38 E
Yaho 268 35.41 N 139.27 E
Yahōga-take ∧ 96 33.04 N 130.50 E
Yahongqiao 105 39.45 N 117.51 E
Yahualica 234 21.08 N 102.51 W
Yahuma 152 1.05 N 23.13 E
Yahyalı 130 38.07 N 35.22 E
Yai ≃ 114 5.02 N 101.47 E
Yai, Khao ∧ 110 15.25 N 99.20 E
Yainax Butte ∧ 202 42.20 N 121.16 W
Yaita, Nihon 94 36.48 N 139.56 E
Yaita, Nihon 268 35.57 N 140.03 E
Yaitopya → Ethiopia □[1] 144 9.00 N 39.00 E
Yaizu 94 34.52 N 138.20 E
Yajiang 102 30.02 N 101.05 E
Yaka 130 41.15 N 34.01 E
Yakacık 267b 40.55 N 29.13 E
Yakage 96 34.37 N 133.35 E
Yakak, Cape ≻ 180 51.38 N 177.00 W
Yakapınar 130 37.00 N 35.36 E
Yakarta → Jakarta 115a 6.10 S 106.48 E
Yakchāl 128 31.47 N 64.41 E
Yake-dake ∧ 94 36.14 N 137.35 E
Yakehu ⊜ 120 34.55 N 87.20 E
Yake-yama ∧ 94 36.55 N 138.03 E
Yakhchāl 120 31.47 N 64.41 E
Yakima 202 46.36 N 120.31 W
Yakima □[6] 224 46.34 N 121.03 W
Yakima ≃ 202 46.15 N 119.02 W
Yakima Indian Reservation ➳[4] 224 46.16 N 121.03 W
Yakishiri-jima I 92a 44.26 N 141.25 E
Yakkan ≃ 96 33.34 N 131.22 E
Yakmach 128 28.45 N 63.51 E
Yak Monis 144 0.37 N 41.25 E
Yako 150 12.58 N 2.16 W
Yakō ➳[8] 268 35.32 N 139.41 E
Yakobi Island I 180 58.00 N 136.30 W
Yakoma 152 4.05 N 22.27 E
Yakotoko 154 5.20 N 25.20 E
Yakou 100 24.46 N 118.46 E
Yakounga ⩕ 152 5.04 N 11.19 E
Yakuendai 268 35.43 N 140.03 E
Yakuluku 154 4.20 N 28.48 E
Yakumo 92a 42.15 N 140.16 E
Yakuno 96 35.19 N 135.00 E
Yakushi-dake ∧ 94 36.28 N 137.33 E
Yakushi-ji ❦[1] 94 36.25 N 139.53 E
Yaku-shima I 93b 30.20 N 130.30 E
Yakutat 180 59.33 N 139.44 W
Yakutat Bay C 180 59.45 N 140.45 W
Yakutat Seamount ⟡[3] 16 35.15 N 48.00 W
Yakutsk → Jakutsk 74 62.13 N 129.49 E
Yala, Ghana 150 10.07 N 1.52 W
Yala, Thai 110 6.33 N 101.18 E
Yalaha 220 28.44 N 81.49 W
Yalahán, Laguna de C 232 21.30 N 87.15 W
Yalakdereköy 130 40.36 N 29.33 E
Yalata 162 31.29 S 131.52 E
Yalca, Laguna ⊜ 258 35.34 S 57.55 W
Yalding 260 51.13 N 0.26 E
Yale, B.C., Can. 182 49.34 N 121.26 W
Yale, Mich., U.S. 190 43.08 N 82.48 W
Yale, Va., U.S. 208 36.34 N 77.17 W
Yale, Lake ⊜ 220 28.54 N 81.45 W
Yale, Mount ∧ 200 38.51 N 106.18 W
Yale Lake ⊜[1] 224 46.00 N 122.12 W
Yalgoo 162 28.20 S 116.41 E
Yali, Zaïre 152 0.04 N 21.03 E
Yali, Zhg. 102 24.43 N 106.48 E
Yaliji 98 36.06 N 114.56 E
Yalikomba 152 1.17 S 22.30 E
Yalinga 152 6.31 N 23.15 E
Yalisere 152 0.11 N 22.33 E
Yalleroi 166 24.04 S 145.45 E
Yallourn 169 38.11 S 146.21 E
Yallourn North 169 38.09 S 146.22 E
Yalnızçam Dağları ⩕ 84 41.10 N 42.25 E
Yalnızçam Geçidi)(130 41.03 N 42.20 E
Yaloke 152 5.19 N 17.05 E
Yalongjiang ≃ 102 30.01 N 101.07 E
Yalova 130 40.39 N 29.15 E
Yalta → Jalta 78 44.30 N 34.10 E
Yalu 89 48.34 N 122.09 E
Yalufi 152 0.45 N 24.26 E
Yalujiang (Amnok-kang) ≃ 98 39.55 N 124.22 E
Yaluzangbujiang → Brahmaputra ≃ 120 24.02 N 90.59 E
Yalvaç 130 38.17 N 31.11 E
Yamachiche 206 46.16 N 72.50 W
Yamachiche ≃ 206 46.16 N 72.48 W
Yamada, Nihon 92 39.28 N 141.57 E
Yamada, Nihon 94 36.34 N 137.05 E
Yamada, Nihon 94 35.49 N 140.36 E
Yamada → Tosa-yamada, Nihon 96 33.36 N 133.41 E
Yamada, Nihon 96 33.33 N 130.47 E
Yamada, Nihon 174m 26.26 N 127.47 E
Yamada, Nihon 270 34.31 N 135.41 E
Yamada ≃ 270 34.47 N 135.04 E
Yamaga, Nihon 96 33.27 N 131.30 E
Yamaga, Nihon 96 33.01 N 130.41 E
Yamagata, Nihon 92 38.15 N 140.15 E
Yamagata, Nihon 94 36.38 N 140.24 E
Yamagata, Nihon 94 36.10 N 137.52 E
Yamagawa 92 31.12 N 130.39 E
Yamaguchi, Nihon 94 35.33 N 137.33 E
Yamaguchi, Nihon 96 34.10 N 131.29 E
Yamaguchi, Nihon 270 34.50 N 135.15 E
Yamaguchi □[5] 96 34.20 N 131.30 E
Yamaguchi-chosuichi ⊜[1] 268 35.46 N 139.25 E
Yamaguni ≃ 96 33.37 N 131.12 E
Yama-hita-hiko-san-kokutei-kōen ♠ 96 33.25 N 131.02 E
Yamakawa 96 34.04 N 134.15 E
Yamakita 94 35.21 N 139.05 E
Yamakuni 96 33.24 N 131.02 E
Yamām, Jabal al- ∧ 132 30.02 N 35.28 E
Yamamoto, Nihon 96 34.07 N 133.44 E
Yamamoto, Nihon 270 34.38 N 135.38 E
Yamanaka 94 36.15 N 136.22 E
Yamanakako 94 35.24 N 138.52 E
Yamanakā-ko ⊜ 94 35.25 N 138.52 E
Yamanashi 94 35.40 N 138.40 E
Yamanashi □[5] 94 35.30 N 138.30 E
Yamanouchi 94 36.44 N 138.25 E
Yamasaki 96 35.00 N 134.33 E
Yamashiro, Nihon 96 34.45 N 135.49 E
Yamashiro, Nihon 96 33.57 N 133.45 E
Yamaska (Saint-Michel) 206 46.00 N 72.55 W
Yamaska □[6] 206 46.00 N 72.45 W
Yamaska ≃ 206 46.06 N 72.56 W
Yamaska Mountain ∧[2] 206 45.27 N 72.52 W
Yamaska-Nord ≃ 206 45.17 N 72.51 W
Yamaska-Sud-Est ≃ 206 45.17 N 72.55 W
Yamate 270 34.30 N 135.27 E
Yamatengwumulu 102 38.38 N 97.05 E
Yamato, Nihon 94 35.48 N 136.54 E
Yamato, Nihon 94 35.29 N 139.29 E
Yamato, Nihon 94 37.10 N 138.56 E
Yamato, Nihon 96 33.08 N 130.30 E
Yamato, Nihon 268 35.47 N 139.37 E
Yamato, Nihon 268 35.44 N 139.26 E
Yamato ≃ 96 34.36 N 135.26 E
Yamato Air Station (United States) ■ 268 35.44 N 139.25 E
Yamato-Kōriyama 96 34.38 N 135.47 E
Yamato-takada 96 34.31 N 135.45 E
Yamatsuri 94 36.52 N 140.25 E
Yamazaki 268 35.56 N 139.54 E
Yamba 166 29.26 S 153.22 E
Yambata 152 2.26 N 21.58 E
Yambéring 150 11.49 N 12.21 W
Yambio 154 4.34 N 28.23 E
Yambol → Jambol 38 42.29 N 26.30 E
Yambou Head ≻ 241h 13.09 N 61.09 W
Yamboyo 152 0.40 N 22.18 E
Yambrasbamba 248 5.45 S 77.54 W
Yambuya 154 1.16 N 24.33 E
Yamdena, Pulau I 164 7.36 S 131.25 E
Yame 96 33.10 N 130.36 E
Yamen C 100 22.08 N 113.06 E
Yamenkou 105 39.53 N 116.12 E
Yamenying 89 43.25 N 122.19 E
Yamethin 110 20.26 N 96.09 E
Yamhill 224 45.21 N 123.11 W
Yamhill □[6] 224 45.15 N 123.20 W
Yamhill ≃ 224 45.14 N 123.00 W
Yamia 150 13.24 N 10.18 E
Y'Ami Island I 108 21.07 N 121.57 E
Yamizo-san ∧ 94 36.56 N 140.17 E
Yamma Yamma, Lake ⊜ 166 26.20 S 141.25 E
Yamoussoukro 150 6.49 N 5.17 W
Yampa 200 40.09 N 106.55 W
Yampa ≃ 200 40.32 N 108.59 W
Yampa, Williams Fork ≃ 200 40.26 N 107.39 W
Yampa Plateau ⩕[1] 200 40.25 N 109.00 W
Yamparáez 248 19.10 S 65.10 W
Yampi Sound 160 15.15 S 123.30 E
Yamsay Mountain ∧ 202 42.56 N 121.22 W
Yamu 102 43.48 N 94.48 E
Yamuna ≃ 120 25.25 N 81.50 E
Yamuna Bridge ➳[5] 272a 28.40 N 77.14 E
Yamunānagar 124 30.07 N 77.18 E
Yan 114 5.48 N 100.22 E
Yan ≃ 122 8.55 N 81.01 E
Yanac 166 36.08 S 141.26 E
Yanacachi 248 16.23 S 67.43 W
Yanadani 96 33.32 N 133.01 E
Yanagawa 96 33.10 N 130.24 E
Yanagi 270 34.25 N 135.56 E
Yanagimoto 270 34.34 N 135.51 E
Yanahara 96 34.55 N 134.05 E
Yanaha-shima I 174m 26.54 N 127.56 E
Yanahuara 248 16.24 S 71.33 W
Yanai 96 33.58 N 132.07 E
Yanaka 268 35.24 N 140.01 E
Yanam 122 16.44 N 82.13 E
Yan'an (Yenan) 102 36.41 N 109.19 E
Yanaoca 248 14.13 S 71.26 W
Yanbian 102 26.55 N 101.30 E
Yanbu' 128 24.05 N 38.03 E
Yanbutou 100 29.52 N 115.04 E
Yanceyville 192 36.24 N 79.20 W
Yanchang 102 36.35 N 110.15 E
Yancheng, Zhg. 98 36.48 N 116.44 E
Yancheng, Zhg. 100 33.24 N 120.09 E
Yancheng, Zhg. 100 33.36 N 113.57 E
Yanchep 168a 31.33 S 115.41 E
Yanchep Park and Caves ♠ 168a 31.32 S 115.40 E
Yanchi (Huamachi), Zhg. 102 37.52 N 107.22 E
Yanchi, Zhg. 105 40.02 N 115.53 E
Yanchuan 102 36.56 N 110.05 E
Yanco 166 34.36 S 146.25 E
Yandal 162 27.33 S 121.07 E
Yandama Creek ≃ 166 30.00 S 140.10 E
Yandé, Île I 175f 20.03 S 163.49 E
Yandev 150 7.20 N 9.01 E
Yandina 175e 9.07 S 159.13 E
Yandja 152 1.41 S 17.43 E
Yandongi 152 2.51 N 22.16 E
Yandoon 110 17.02 N 95.39 E
Yandua I 175g 16.49 S 178.18 E
Yandun 102 42.20 N 94.09 E
Yanfeng 102 25.53 N 101.01 E
Yanfolila 150 11.11 N 8.09 W
Yang ≃ 110 15.44 N 104.00 E
Yanga 234 18.50 N 96.48 W
Yangambi 154 0.47 N 24.28 E
Yangan, Austl. 171a 28.12 S 152.13 E
Yang'an, Zhg. 98 37.38 N 117.09 E
Yan'gang 100 26.02 N 116.22 E
Yangarakata 154 3.01 N 30.28 E
Yangasa Levu I 175g 18.57 S 178.26 W
Yangbajing 120 30.06 N 90.33 E
Yangce 100 32.58 N 113.14 E
Yangcha 98 41.11 N 126.15 E
Yangchang 107 30.22 N 103.42 E
Yangcheng, Zhg. 102 35.29 N 112.25 E
Yangcheng, Zhg. 106 31.24 N 120.47 E
Yangchenghu ⊜ 106 31.26 N 120.47 E
Yangchengzi 89 43.59 N 124.25 E
Yangchiang → Yangjiang 102 21.51 N 111.56 E
Yangch'ŏn ➳[8] 271b 37.34 N 126.51 E
Yangchow → Yangzhou 100 32.24 N 119.26 E
Yangchu 98 37.11 N 120.47 E
Yangch'üan → Yangquan 98 37.52 N 113.36 E
Yangchun 102 22.10 N 111.46 E
Yangcun, Zhg. 100 23.26 N 114.30 E
Yangcun, Zhg. 100 28.07 N 117.40 E
Yangcun, Zhg. 105 39.09 N 115.50 E
Yangcunqiao 100 29.36 N 119.28 E
Yangdalinzi 98 42.38 N 125.07 E
Yangdian 106 31.08 N 119.45 E
Yang'erzhuang 98 38.18 N 117.30 E
Yangfangpu 105 40.48 N 115.01 E
Yangfangzhen 105 40.07 N 116.07 E
Yangfen'gang 105 39.07 N 116.52 E
Yangfenzhen 106 30.28 N 120.03 E
Yangganga I 175g 16.35 S 178.35 E
Yanggang Do □[4] 98 41.15 N 128.00 E
Yangganzhen 106 31.00 N 119.15 E
Yanggezhuang 105 40.09 N 116.48 E
Yanggong-ni 271b 37.39 N 126.37 E
Yanggu, Taehan 98 38.06 N 127.59 E
Yanggu, Zhg. 98 34.44 N 114.48 E
Yanggu, Zhg. 98 36.08 N 115.48 E
Yangguan)(102 39.58 N 94.25 E
Yangguanpu 100 32.13 N 115.31 E
Yanghang 106 31.22 N 121.26 E
Yanghe 100 33.47 N 118.23 E
Yanghe ≃ 105 40.24 N 115.20 E
Yanghexi 102 29.39 N 108.40 E
Yanghu 100 32.34 N 116.30 E
Yanghua 107 30.11 N 104.45 E
Yangi-Yul' → Jangijul' 85 41.07 N 69.03 E
Yangji, Zhg. 98 36.44 N 113.56 E
Yangji, Zhg. 98 34.00 N 116.13 E
Yangjia 106 30.41 N 120.15 E
Yangjiachang, Zhg. 107 29.56 N 104.41 E
Yangjiachang, Zhg. 107 29.45 N 105.21 E
Yangjiachang, Zhg. 107 29.23 N 104.21 E
Yangjiadang 100 32.23 N 112.39 E
Yangjiagou, Zhg. 98 37.16 N 118.50 E
Yangjiagou, Zhg. 105 39.18 N 117.54 E
Yangjiaji, Zhg. 98 34.28 N 119.19 E
Yangjiaji, Zhg. 100 34.19 N 119.28 E
Yangjiajiang 100 30.49 N 112.47 E
Yangjiajie 107 30.18 N 104.39 E
Yangjian 106 31.39 N 120.33 E
Yangjiang 102 21.51 N 111.56 E
Yangjiang ≃ 100 33.37 N 120.33 E
Yangjiaqiao, Zhg. 100 27.44 N 112.46 E
Yangjiaqiao, Zhg. 106 32.02 N 121.26 E
Yangjiaqiao, Zhg. 106 31.53 N 121.42 E
Yangjiatao 105 39.49 N 117.51 E
Yangjiatun 104 40.57 N 121.41 E
Yangjiawopu 104 42.21 N 122.57 E
Yangjiazeng 105 40.12 N 117.04 E
Yangjiazhangzi 104 40.48 N 120.33 E
Yangjie 102 24.49 N 100.22 E
Yangjishi 100 26.39 N 113.14 E
Yangkou, Zhg. 100 28.39 N 118.53 E
Yangkou, Zhg. 100 26.47 N 117.51 E
Yanglinjie 100 29.07 N 113.27 E
Yangliupu, Zhg. 100 30.52 N 118.37 E
Yangliupu, Zhg. 107 30.09 N 104.03 E
Yangliuqing 105 39.08 N 116.59 E
Yangloudong 100 29.31 N 113.44 E
Yanglousi 100 29.30 N 113.38 E
Yangluomayu 104 40.47 N 122.54 E
Yangmachang 107 30.39 N 103.45 E
Yangmadatun 104 42.35 N 124.13 E
Yangmahe 107 30.29 N 104.31 E
Yangmeisi 100 25.42 N 114.30 E
Yangmiao, Zhg. 98 34.11 N 114.53 E
Yangmiao, Zhg. 106 30.51 N 120.49 E
Yangmingshan 269d 25.09 N 121.33 E
Yangmingshan □[5] 269d 25.09 N 121.32 E
Yangmingshan ∧ 102 26.03 N 111.56 E
Yangmugou, Zhg. 98 40.36 N 124.28 E
Yangmugou, Zhg. 104 41.11 N 123.50 E
Yangmulin 105 40.06 N 115.12 E
Yangon → Rangoon 110 16.47 N 96.10 E
Yangor 174b 0.31 S 166.54 E
Yangpingguan 102 32.51 N 106.09 E
Yangpu 100 27.14 N 119.08 E
Yangp'yŏng 98 37.30 N 127.29 E
Yangp'yŏng-ni 98 40.53 N 127.58 E
Yangqi 106 31.23 N 119.57 E
Yangquan 98 37.52 N 113.36 E
Yangquanzi 98 41.17 N 121.39 E
Yangriwan 102 31.37 N 110.49 E
Yangsan 98 35.21 N 129.03 E
Yangshan, Zhg. 98 41.13 N 120.24 E
Yangshan, Zhg. 102 24.28 N 112.38 E
Yangshanji 98 35.13 N 116.13 E
Yangsheying 106 31.52 N 120.32 E
Yangshigangzi 104 41.42 N 122.59 E
Yangshitun 104 42.06 N 123.44 E
Yangshugemen 105 40.55 N 118.18 E
Yangshugoudonggou 104 41.43 N 120.41 E
Yangshuling 98 41.02 N 118.47 E
Yangshuo 102 24.45 N 110.24 E
Yangtianzhang ∧ 100 24.37 N 115.38 E
Yangtou 100 23.26 N 115.24 E
Yangtze → Changjiang ≃ 90 31.48 N 121.10 E
Yanguan 106 30.26 N 120.32 E
Yangwan, Zhg. 100 28.22 N 116.46 E
Yangwan, Zhg. 106 31.03 N 120.22 E
Yangxi, Zhg. 100 30.11 N 118.39 E
Yangxi, Zhg. 100 29.31 N 119.18 E
Yangxi, Zhg. 100 27.18 N 114.10 E
Yangxian 102 33.03 N 107.47 E
Yangxiang 106 31.29 N 119.35 E
Yangxiangjing 106 31.12 N 121.01 E
Yangxiangtun 104 40.58 N 122.48 E
Yangxiaodian 100 31.46 N 116.45 E
Yangxin, Zhg. 98 37.39 N 117.34 E
Yangxin, Zhg. 100 29.51 N 115.12 E
Yangxing 106 31.37 N 120.34 E
Yangxiudian 271a 39.44 N 116.32 E
Yang Yang, Sén. 150 15.35 N 15.21 W
Yangyang, Taehan 98 38.04 N 128.36 E
Yangyuan 98 40.01 N 114.10 E
Yangze 100 26.57 N 118.23 E
Yangzhong (Sanmaozhen) 106 32.16 N 119.49 E
Yangzhou 100 32.24 N 119.26 E
Yangzhuang, Zhg. 98 34.02 N 117.14 E
Yangzhuang, Zhg. 100 33.36 N 118.58 E
Yangzhujuanzi 104 41.38 N 122.46 E
Yangzhuoyonghu ⊜ 120 28.58 N 90.44 E
Yangzishao 98 42.28 N 126.09 E
Yangzizhen 100 31.19 N 112.36 E
Yanhaiyingzi 104 41.52 N 123.05 E
Yanhe 102 28.37 N 108.35 E
Yanhecheng 105 40.04 N 115.43 E
Yanheying 98 40.02 N 119.03 E
Yanhui 98 37.54 N 113.51 E
Yanina → Ioánnina 38 39.40 N 20.50 E
Yanji (Longjing), Zhg. 98 42.47 N 129.26 E
Yanji, Zhg. 98 34.41 N 115.27 E
Yanji, Zhg. 98 42.57 N 129.32 E
Yanjiabao 106 32.19 N 120.07 E
Yanjiahe, Zhg. 100 31.48 N 114.50 E
Yanjiahe, Zhg. 100 31.16 N 115.07 E
Yanjiajie 104 41.02 N 121.32 E
Yanjiao 105 39.56 N 116.48 E
Yanjiatuozi 104 42.27 N 123.47 E
Yanjiawopeng 104 40.59 N 121.17 E
Yanjin 98 35.11 N 114.11 E
Yanjingchi 107 29.56 N 106.21 E
Yankalilla 168b 35.28 S 138.21 E
Yankalilla Bay C 168b 35.28 S 138.15 E
Yankari Game Reserve ➳[4] 150 9.30 N 10.20 E
Yankdŏk 98 39.14 N 126.41 E
Yankee Lake 210 41.35 N 74.33 W
Yankee Springs State Recreation Area ♠ 216 42.38 N 85.30 W
Yankee Stadium ♠ 276 40.50 N 73.56 W
Yankeetown 220 29.02 N 82.43 W
Yan Kit 271c 1.22 N 103.58 E
Yankton 198 42.53 N 97.23 W
Yankton Indian Reservation ➳[4] 198 43.10 N 98.22 W
Yanling, Zhg. 98 34.07 N 114.11 E
Yanling, Zhg. 106 31.54 N 119.30 E
Yanliuji 100 32.01 N 116.52 E
Yanmeimeizi 105 39.42 N 115.03 E
Yanna 166 26.56 S 146.03 E
Yannarie ≃ 162 22.28 S 114.48 E
Yanqi 90 42.00 N 86.15 E
Yanqian, Zhg. 100 24.54 N 116.14 E
Yanqian, Zhg. 100 26.15 N 117.28 E
Yanqianhu 104 42.16 N 123.12 E
Yanqiao 106 31.41 N 120.17 E
Yanqidoumen 106 31.17 N 118.42 E
Yanqing 105 40.28 N 115.58 E
Yanque 248 15.39 S 71.39 W
Yanrey 162 22.31 S 114.48 E
Yanshan, Zhg. 98 38.05 N 117.13 E
Yanshan, Zhg. 102 23.41 N 104.21 E
Yanshankou 105 39.59 N 117.42 E
Yanshi 100 25.17 N 117.10 E
Yanshixi ≃ 100 25.20 N 117.17 E
Yanshou 89 45.28 N 128.20 E
Yansi 100 29.48 N 118.20 E
Yanṭā 132 33.36 N 35.57 E
Yantabulla 166 29.21 S 145.00 E
Yantai (Chefoo), Zhg. 98 37.33 N 121.20 E
Yantai, Zhg. 105 39.47 N 116.38 E
Yantan, Zhg. 100 28.55 N 120.11 E
Yantan, Zhg. 100 28.28 N 120.44 E
Yantan, Zhg. 107 29.17 N 104.52 E
Yantian, Zhg. 100 27.21 N 114.22 E
Yantian, Zhg. 100 26.53 N 119.53 E
Yantic ≃ 207 41.31 N 72.05 W
Yantietang ≍ 106 31.49 N 120.46 E
Yanting 102 31.19 N 105.23 E
Yantis 222 32.56 N 95.35 W
Yantongshan, Zhg. 89 43.17 N 126.00 E
Yantongshan, Zhg. 105 40.42 N 115.06 E
Yanwangshan 104 41.36 N 123.57 E
Yanweixiang 98 34.30 N 119.48 E
Yanxi 100 24.46 N 117.47 E
Yanxia 100 29.31 N 114.52 E
Yanxidu 100 26.51 N 114.58 E
Yanxing 102 25.23 N 101.42 E
Yan Yean Reservoir ⊜[1] 169 37.33 S 145.08 E
Yanyegongsi 106 32.02 N 121.41 E
Yanyuan 102 27.29 N 101.32 E
Yanzhou 98 35.33 N 116.50 E
Yanziji 106 32.09 N 118.49 E
Yanzijiao 102 23.38 N 100.12 E
Yanzikou 102 27.31 N 105.21 E
Yao, Nihon 96 34.37 N 135.36 E
Yao, Tchad 146 12.51 N 17.34 E
Yao Airport ⊠ 270 34.36 N 135.36 E
Yaoan 102 25.32 N 101.12 E
Yaoba 107 28.45 N 105.39 E
Yaocun, Zhg. 98 35.41 N 116.57 E
Yaocun, Zhg. 98 36.12 N 113.50 E
Yaocun, Zhg. 105 39.09 N 115.32 E
Yaodafangshen 104 42.27 N 122.59 E
Yaoerwan 105 40.49 N 115.27 E
Yaogongbu 100 29.51 N 120.18 E
Yaogutuo 107 29.08 N 104.01 E
Yaohongcaopao 104 40.55 N 122.26 E
Yaohuamen 106 32.08 N 118.52 E
Yaohuangdi 104 41.32 N 122.48 E
Yaojiadian 100 31.14 N 114.22 E
Yaojiaqiao 106 32.10 N 119.46 E
Yaojiatun 104 41.18 N 121.47 E
Yaojiawopeng 104 41.47 N 122.25 E
Yaojie 102 36.26 N 102.59 E
Yaoling 100 24.49 N 113.58 E
Yaolugou 98 40.34 N 119.24 E
Yaoluzi 104 41.26 N 121.34 E
Yao Malikidza 152 5.19 N 19.36 E
Yaopi 100 26.52 N 113.38 E
Yaopu 100 32.14 N 118.20 E
Yaoqianhutun 104 41.32 N 123.36 E

Symbols in the index entries represent the broad categories identified in the key at the right. Symbols with superior numbers (⩕[2]) identify subcategories (see complete key on page *I · 30*).

Kartensymbole in dem Registerverzeichnis stellen die rechts in Schlüssel erklärten Kategorien dar. Symbole mit hochgestellten Ziffern (⩕[2]) bezeichnen Unterabteilungen einer Kategorie (vgl. vollständiger Schlüssel auf Seite *I · 30*).

Los símbolos incluídos en el texto del índice representan las grandes categorias identificadas con la clave a la derecha. Los símbolos con numeros en su parte superior (⩕[2]) identifican las subcategorías (véase la clave completa en la página *I · 30*).

Les symboles de l'index représentent les catégories indiquées dans la légende à droite. Les symboles suivis d'un indice (⩕[2]) représentent des sous-catégories (voir légende complète à la page *I · 30*).

Os símbolos incluídos no texto do índice representam as grandes categorias identificadas com a chave à direita. Os símbolos com números em sua parte superior (⩕[2]) identificam as subcategorias (veja-se a chave completa à página *I · 30*).

	English	Deutsch	Español	Français	Português
∧	Mountain	Berg	Montaña	Montagne	Montanha
⩕	Mountains	Berge	Montañas	Montagnes	Montanhas
)(	Pass	Pass	Paso	Col	Passo
∨	Valley, Canyon	Tal, Cañon	Valle, Cañón	Vallée, Canyon	Vale, Canhão
⌣	Plain	Ebene	Llano	Plaine	Planície
≻	Cape	Kap	Cabo	Cap	Cabo
I	Island	Insel	Isla	Île	Ilha
II	Islands	Inseln	Islas	Îles	Ilhas
⊥	Other Topographic Features	Andere Topographische Objekte	Otros Elementos Topográficos	Autres données topographiques	Outros Elementos Topográficos

ESPAÑOL Nombre	Página	Lat.°′	Long.°′ W=Oeste
Yaoshizhen	107	30.11 N	105.30 E
Yaotou	100	26.38 N	114.48 E
Yaotsu	94	35.28 N	137.09 E
Yaotun, Zhg.	89	48.28 N	127.30 E
Yaotun, Zhg.	104	40.59 N	122.18 E
Yaotutun	104	42.06 N	123.29 E
Yaoundé	152	3.52 N	11.31 E
Yaowan	98	34.12 N	118.03 E
Yaowangmiao	98	40.47 N	120.10 E
Yaoxian	102	34.56 N	108.53 E
Yaoya ≃	236	13.28 N	84.14 W
Yao Yai, Ko I	110	8.00 N	98.35 E
Yaozhan, Zhg.	89	52.53 N	125.13 E
Yaozhan, Zhg.	98	37.02 N	116.14 E
Yap	174q	9.31 N	138.08 E
Yap □[5]	174q	9.30 N	138.10 E
Yap I	174q	9.31 N	138.06 E
Yapacani ≃	248	16.00 S	64.25 W
Yapakopra	164	4.24 S	135.05 E
Yapehe	152	0.13 S	24.27 E
Yapei (Tamale Port)	150	9.10 N	1.10 W
Yapen, Pulau I	164	1.45 S	136.15 E
Yapen, Selat ⩌	164	1.30 S	136.10 E
Yapero	164	4.59 S	137.11 E
Yapeyú	252	29.28 S	56.49 W
Yaphank	207	40.50 N	72.56 W
Yappar ≃	166	18.22 S	141.16 E
Yaq Braway	144	2.00 N	43.45 E
Yaqian	100	26.38 N	114.30 E
Ya'qūb	140	12.29 N	25.11 E
Yaque del Norte ≃	238	19.51 N	71.41 W
Yaqui	232	27.19 N	110.01 W
Yaqui ≃	232	27.37 N	110.39 W
Yaquina ≃	202	44.37 N	124.04 W
Yara	240p	20.16 N	76.57 W
Yaracuy □[3]	246	10.20 N	69.10 W
Yaraka	166	24.53 S	144.04 E
Yaratuar	164	2.58 S	134.40 E
Yarbasan	130	38.59 N	28.49 E
Yarcombe	42	50.52 N	3.05 W
Yardea	166	32.23 S	135.32 E
Yardley	208	40.15 N	74.50 W
Yardville	208	40.11 N	74.40 W
Yare ≃	42	52.35 N	1.44 E
Yari	146	13.59 N	12.18 E
Yarí ≃	246	0.23 S	72.16 W
Yariga-take ∧	94	36.20 N	137.39 E
Yārik	123	32.06 N	70.47 E
Yarīm	144	14.29 N	44.21 E
Yaring	110	6.52 N	101.22 E
Yaritagua	246	10.05 N	69.08 W
Yarkand → Suoche	120	38.25 N	77.16 E
Yarkand → Yeerqianghe ≃	90	40.28 N	80.52 E
Yarker	212	44.23 N	76.46 W
Yarkhūn ≃	123	36.17 N	72.30 E
Yarlarweelor	162	25.35 S	117.59 E
Yarle Lakes ⊜	162	30.15 S	131.27 E
Yarloop	168a	32.57 S	115.54 E
Yarma	130	37.49 N	32.54 E
Yarmouth, N.S., Can.	186	43.50 N	66.07 W
Yarmouth → Great Yarmouth, Eng., U.K.	42	52.37 N	1.44 E
Yarmouth, Eng., U.K.	42	50.42 N	1.29 W
Yarmouth, Maine, U.S.	188	43.48 N	70.12 W
Yarmouth, Mass., U.S.	207	41.40 N	70.11 W
Yarmu	164	4.18 S	142.17 E
Yarmuk, Nahr al- ≃	132	32.38 N	35.34 E
Yaroupi ≃	250	2.47 N	52.28 W
Yarra ≃	169	37.51 S	144.54 E
Yarra Bend National Park ♠	274b	37.48 S	145.01 E
Yarra Glen	169	37.40 S	145.23 E
Yarragon	169	38.12 S	146.04 E
Yarraloola	162	21.34 S	115.52 E
Yarram	166	38.33 S	146.41 E
Yarraman	171a	26.50 S	151.59 E
Yarrangobilly	171b	35.39 S	148.28 E
Yarrangobilly Caves ⬥[5]	171b	35.44 S	148.29 E
Yarraville	274b	37.49 S	144.53 E
Yarrawonga	166	36.01 S	146.00 E
Yarra Yarra Lakes ⊜	162	29.40 S	115.47 E
Yarrow, B.C., Can.	224	49.05 N	122.02 W
Yarrow, Scot., U.K.	46	55.32 N	3.01 W
Yarrow ≃	262	53.40 N	2.49 W
Yarrowee ≃	169	38.07 S	144.04 E
Yarrow Point	224	47.39 N	122.13 W
Yarrow Reservoir ⊜[1]	262	53.38 N	2.34 W
Yarrow Water ≃	44	55.34 N	2.51 W
Yarty ≃	42	50.47 N	3.01 W
Yarumal	246	6.58 N	75.24 W
Yarvicoya, Cerro ∧	248	20.07 S	69.00 W
Yasa	152	3.42 S	21.24 E
Yasaka, Nihon	96	34.46 N	132.04 E
Yasaka, Nihon	96	35.39 N	135.07 E
Yasa-Lokwa	152	5.15 S	19.24 E
Yasato	94	36.14 N	140.12 E
Yasawa I	175g	16.47 S	177.31 E
Yasawa Group II	175g	17.00 S	177.23 E
Yasendu	152	0.27 N	24.20 E
Yashanjie	106	30.51 N	119.03 E
Yashbum	144	14.19 N	46.56 E
Yashi	150	12.23 N	7.54 E
Yashikera	150	9.46 N	3.28 E
Ya-shima I	96	33.44 N	132.09 E
Yashio	268	35.49 N	139.51 E
Yashiro	96	34.55 N	134.58 E
Yashiro-jima I	96	33.55 N	132.15 E
Yāsīn	123	33.57 N	72.30 E
Yasku	146	12.20 N	12.30 E
Yasothon	110	15.45 N	104.08 E
Yass	166	34.50 S	148.55 E
Yassy → Iaşi	38	47.10 N	27.35 E
Yasu, Nihon	94	35.03 N	136.01 E
Yasu, Nihon	96	33.32 N	133.45 E
Yasuda	96	33.26 N	133.59 E
Yasufuruichi	96	34.27 N	132.28 E
Yasugi	96	35.26 N	133.15 E
Yasun Burnu ≻	130	41.09 N	37.41 E
Yasuni ≃	246	0.56 S	75.23 W
Yasuoka	94	35.22 N	137.50 E
Yasuura	96	34.15 N	132.50 E
Yasuzuka	94	37.08 N	138.28 E
Yata	248	13.20 S	66.35 W
Yata ≃, Bol.	248	10.29 S	65.26 W
Yata ≃, Nihon	96	35.38 N	134.37 E
Yatabe	94	36.02 N	140.04 E
Yatağan	130	37.20 N	28.09 E
Yatakala	150	14.48 N	0.22 E
Yāṭar	132	33.09 N	35.20 E
Yatate-yama ∧	92	34.10 N	129.10 E
Yaté, N. Cal.	175f	22.09 S	166.57 E
Yate, Eng., U.K.	42	51.32 N	2.25 W
Yates □[6]	210	42.40 N	77.03 W
Yatesboro	214	40.48 N	79.20 W
Yates Center	198	37.53 N	95.44 W
Yates City	190	40.47 N	90.01 W
Yathata I	175g	17.15 S	179.32 W
Yathkyed Lake ⊜	176	62.41 N	98.00 W
Yating	102	25.03 N	106.05 E
Yatomi	94	35.06 N	136.43 E
Yatsuga-take ∧	94	35.59 N	138.23 E
Yatsuga-take-chūshin-kōgen-kokutei-kōen ♠	94	36.03 N	138.20 E

FRANÇAIS Nom	Page	Lat.°′	Long.°′ W=Ouest
Yatsuka	96	35.17 N	133.52 E
Yatsuo	94	36.34 N	137.08 E
Yatsushiro	92	32.30 N	130.36 E
Yatsushiro-wan C	92	32.20 N	130.25 E
Yaṭṭah	132	31.27 N	35.05 E
Yatta Plateau ⛰[1]	154	2.00 S	38.00 E
Yatton	42	51.24 N	2.49 W
Yatua ≃	246	1.43 N	66.30 W
Yatusiro → Yatsushiro	92	32.30 N	130.36 E
Yauca	248	15.40 S	74.32 W
Yauca ≃	248	15.41 S	74.31 W
Yauco	240m	18.02 N	66.51 W
Yauco ≃	240m	17.59 N	66.48 W
Yauco, Embalse de ⊜[1]	240m	18.07 N	66.50 W
Yauli	248	11.41 S	76.06 W
Yaundé → Yaoundé	152	3.52 N	11.31 E
Yaupi	246	2.59 S	77.50 W
Yautepec	234	18.53 N	99.04 W
Yauyos	248	12.24 S	75.57 W
Yāval	120	21.10 N	75.42 E
Yavarí (Javari) ≃	242	4.21 S	70.02 W
Yavarí Mirim ≃	246	4.31 S	71.44 W
Yavaros	232	26.42 N	109.31 W
Yavatmāl	122	20.24 N	78.08 E
Yaven Yaven Creek ≃	171b	35.06 S	147.46 E
Yavero ≃	248	12.06 S	72.57 W
Yavi	130	39.48 N	36.13 E
Yaví, Cerro ∧	246	5.32 N	65.59 W
Yavita	246	2.55 N	67.26 W
Yaviza	246	8.11 N	77.41 W
Yavne	132	31.53 N	34.45 E
Yawahara	268	35.59 N	140.01 E
Yawata, Nihon	96	34.52 N	135.42 E
Yawata → Kitakyūshū, Nihon	96	33.53 N	130.50 E
Yawata, Nihon	268	35.32 N	140.08 E
Yawatahama	96	33.27 N	132.24 E
Yawosha I	106	31.23 N	121.41 E
Yaxchilan ⊥	232	16.54 N	90.58 W
Yaxi, Zhg.	102	27.32 N	106.45 E
Yaxi, Zhg.	106	31.23 N	119.10 E
Yaxian	110	18.20 N	109.30 E
Yaxierhu ⊜	120	34.59 N	81.35 E
Yaxley	42	52.31 N	0.16 W
Yayama	152	1.16 S	23.07 E
Yaylak	130	37.23 N	38.20 E
Yayouta	150	8.11 N	8.30 W
Yayuan	98	41.47 N	126.11 E
Yazd	128	31.53 N	54.25 E
Yazi	98	37.04 N	121.17 E
Yazichangcun	104	41.16 N	122.26 E
Yazıhan	130	38.36 N	38.11 E
Yazikou	85	39.48 N	74.21 E
Yazmān	123	29.08 N	71.45 E
Yazoo ≃	194	32.22 N	91.00 W
Yazoo City	194	32.51 N	90.28 W
Ybbs ≃	61	48.10 N	15.06 E
Ybbs an der Donau	61	48.11 N	15.05 E
Ybbsitz	61	47.56 N	14.53 E
Ybor City	220	27.57 N	82.27 W
Ybycuí	252	26.01 S	57.03 W
Yding Skovhøj ∧[2]	41	56.00 N	9.48 E
Ydstebøhavn	26	59.08 N	5.15 E
Ydžid Parma ⛰	24	63.06 N	58.15 E
Ye	110	15.15 N	97.51 E
Yé ≃	152	1.25 N	13.14 E
Yea	169	37.13 S	145.26 E
Yea ≃	169	37.11 S	145.23 E
Yeading ⬥[8]	260	51.32 N	0.24 W
Yeadon, Eng., U.K.	44	53.52 N	1.41 W
Yeadon, Pa., U.S.	285	39.56 N	75.15 W
Yeagertown	208	40.39 N	77.35 W
Yealm ≃	42	50.18 N	4.03 W
Yealmpton	42	50.21 N	3.59 W
Yebawgyi	110	18.40 N	94.35 E
Yebbi Bou	146	20.58 N	18.04 E
Yebbi Souma	146	21.08 N	17.56 E
Yébigé, Enneri ∨	146	22.04 N	17.49 E
Yebyu	110	14.15 N	98.12 E
Yecapixtla	234	18.53 N	98.52 W
Yecheng	120	37.54 N	77.25 E
Yech'ŏn	98	36.40 N	128.26 E
Yecla	34	38.37 N	1.07 W
Yécora	232	28.20 N	108.58 W
Yedashe	110	19.09 N	96.21 E
Yedikule ⬥[8]	267b	40.59 N	28.55 E
Yedikule Suriarı ⊥	267b	40.59 N	28.55 E
Yédinga, Ouadi ∨	146	15.46 N	20.05 E
Yedseram ≃	146	12.30 N	14.05 E
Yeeda	162	17.36 S	123.39 E
Yeelanna	166	34.09 S	135.45 E
Yeelirrie	162	27.17 S	120.06 E
Yeernuozhahu ⊜	120	32.30 N	89.30 E
Yeerqianghe (Yarkand) ≃	90	40.28 N	80.52 E
Yegor'yevsk → Jegorjevsk	82	55.23 N	39.02 E
Yegros	252	26.24 S	56.25 W
Yegua Creek ≃	222	30.23 N	96.18 W
Yeguas, Río de las ≃	34	37.22 N	4.45 W
Yehliu	269d	25.12 N	121.41 E
Yehliu Chia ≻	269d	25.13 N	121.42 E
Yehud	132	32.02 N	34.53 E
Yei	154	4.05 N	30.40 E
Yei ≃	140	6.15 N	30.13 E
Yeji	150	8.13 N	0.39 W
Yejiaji	100	31.52 N	115.55 E
Yekaterinburg → Sverdlovsk	86	56.51 N	60.36 E
Yekaterinodar → Krasnodar	78	45.02 N	39.00 E
Yekaterinoslav → Dnepropetrovsk	78	48.27 N	34.59 E
Yekokora ≃	152	1.20 N	20.21 E
Yekumbo	152	1.02 S	23.27 E
Ye Kyun I	110	18.37 N	93.47 E
Yelarbon	166	28.34 S	150.45 E
Yele	150	8.25 N	11.50 W
Yelets → Jelec	76	52.37 N	38.30 E
Yélimané	150	15.08 N	10.34 W
Yell I	46a	60.36 N	1.06 W
Yellandu	122	17.36 N	80.20 E
Yellow ≃, U.S.	194	30.33 N	87.00 W
Yellow ≃, Ind., U.S.	216	41.16 N	86.50 W
Yellow ≃, Iowa, U.S.	190	43.05 N	91.11 W
Yellow ≃, Wis., U.S.	190	43.59 N	90.03 W
Yellow ≃, Wis., U.S.	190	46.01 N	92.22 W
Yellow ≃, Wis., U.S.	190	44.58 N	91.18 W
Yellow → Huanghe ≃, Zhg.	90	37.32 N	118.19 E
Yellow Breeches Creek ≃	208	40.13 N	76.51 W
Yellow Creek ≃, U.S.	194	33.34 N	88.20 W
Yellow Creek ≃, Colo., U.S.	200	40.10 N	108.24 W
Yellow Creek ≃, Ohio, U.S.	214	40.34 N	80.40 W
Yellow Creek ≃, Tenn., U.S.	194	36.26 N	87.34 W
Yellow Creek, North Fork ≃	214	40.33 N	80.42 W
Yellow Creek State Park ♠	214	40.35 N	79.02 W
Yellowdine	162	31.18 S	119.39 E
Yellow Grass	184	49.49 N	104.08 W

PORTUGUÊS Nome	Página	Lat.°′	Long.°′ W=Oeste
Yellowhead Pass)(	182	52.53 N	118.28 W
Yellow Housedraw ∨	196	33.35 N	101.50 W
Yellowknife	176	62.27 N	114.21 W
Yellowknife ≃	176	62.31 N	114.19 W
Yellow Lake ⊜	212	44.20 N	75.36 W
Yellow Medicine ≃	198	44.44 N	95.25 W
Yellow Mountain ∧	166	32.30 S	146.51 E
Yellow Sea ⍑[2]	90	36.00 N	123.00 E
Yellow Springs	218	39.48 N	83.53 W
Yellowstone ≃	178	47.58 N	103.59 W
Yellowstone, Clarks Fork ≃	202	45.39 N	108.43 W
Yellowstone Falls ᒪ	202	44.43 N	110.30 W
Yellowstone Lake ⊜	202	44.25 N	110.22 W
Yellowstone National Park	202	44.58 N	110.42 W
Yellowstone National Park ♠	202	44.30 N	110.35 W
Yellowtail Dam ⬥[6]	202	45.12 N	107.57 W
Yell Sound ⩌	46a	60.32 N	1.15 W
Yellville	194	36.14 N	92.41 W
Yelm	224	46.56 N	122.36 W
Yelma	162	26.30 S	121.40 E
Yelusuhu ⊜	120	35.11 N	92.15 E
Yelvertoft	166	20.13 S	138.53 E
Yelverton	42	50.30 N	4.05 W
Yelwa	150	10.51 N	4.46 E
Yemadu	86	43.36 N	81.50 E
Yemagong	124	29.28 N	89.06 E
Yemaoba	107	30.10 N	105.56 E
Yemassee	192	32.41 N	80.51 W
Yematan	102	34.40 N	98.16 E
Yemen □[1]	118		
	144	15.00 N	44.00 E
Yemen, People's Democratic Republic of □[1]	144		
	118	15.00 N	48.00 E
Yemen, República Popular Democrática del → Yemen, People's Democratic Republic of □[1]	144	15.00 N	48.00 E
Yémen, République démocratique populaire du → Yemen, People's Democratic Republic of □[1]	144	15.00 N	48.00 E
Yemesguida ∧	148	29.12 N	9.58 W
Yenagoa	150	4.55 N	6.19 E
Yenakiyevo → Jenakijevo	83	48.14 N	38.13 E
Yenangyaung	110	20.28 N	94.52 E
Yenanma	110	19.46 N	94.48 E
Yen-bai	110	21.42 N	104.52 E
Yen-chau	110	21.03 N	104.18 E
Yench'eng → Yancheng	100	33.24 N	120.09 E
Yenchi → Yanji	98	42.57 N	129.32 E
Yenda	166	34.15 S	146.11 E
Yende Millimou	150	8.53 N	10.11 W
Yendéré	150	10.12 N	4.58 W
Yendi	150	9.26 N	0.01 W
Ye-ngan	110	21.09 N	96.27 E
Yenge ≃	152	0.55 S	20.40 E
Yengo	152	0.22 N	15.29 E
Yengo, Mount ∧	170	32.59 S	150.51 E
Yéni	150	13.26 N	2.59 E
Yeniçağa	130	40.46 N	32.02 E
Yenice, Tür.	130	39.45 N	28.55 E
Yenice, Tür.	130	36.59 N	35.03 E
Yenice, Tür.	130	39.55 N	27.18 E
Yenice ≃	130	37.36 N	35.35 E
Yenicekale	130	37.37 N	36.37 E
Yeniceoba	130	38.53 N	32.48 E
Yenifoça	130	38.44 N	26.51 E
Yenikapı ⬥[8]	267b	41.00 N	28.57 E
Yeniköy, Tür.	130	39.46 N	28.00 E
Yeniköy, Tür.	130	37.04 N	30.36 E
Yeniköy ⬥[8]	267b	41.07 N	29.04 E
Yenimehmetli	130	39.26 N	32.10 E
Yenipazar, Tür.	130	40.11 N	30.31 E
Yenipazar, Tür.	130	37.48 N	28.12 E
Yenişehir	130	40.16 N	29.39 E
Yenisey → Jenisej ≃	72	71.50 N	82.40 E
Yennadon	224	49.14 N	122.34 W
Yenne	62	45.42 N	5.46 E
Yennora	274a	33.52 S	150.58 E
Yenshui	100	23.20 N	120.16 E
Yentna ≃	180	61.34 N	150.28 W
Yeo ≃	42	51.02 N	2.49 W
Yeola	122	20.02 N	74.29 E
Yeo Lake ⊜	162	28.04 S	124.23 E
Yeoman	216	40.40 N	86.43 W
Yeoval	166	32.45 S	148.40 E
Yeovil	42	50.57 N	2.39 W
Yeoville ⬥[8]	273d	26.12 S	28.04 E
Yepachic	232	28.26 N	108.23 W
Yeppoon	166	23.08 S	150.45 E
Yerba Buena, Montaña ∧	236	14.05 N	87.26 W
Yerba Buena Island I	282	37.48 N	122.22 W
Yères ≃	50	50.02 N	1.19 E
Yerevan → Jerevan	84	40.11 N	44.30 E
Yerilla	162	29.28 S	121.49 E
Yering	274b	37.41 S	145.23 E
Yerington	226	38.59 N	119.10 W
Yerington Indian Reservation ⬥[4]	226	39.05 N	119.12 W
Yerkes	285	40.10 N	75.27 W
Yerkes Astronomical Observatory ⊍[3]	216	42.34 N	88.34 W
Yerkesik	130	37.07 N	28.17 E
Yerköy	130	39.38 N	34.29 E
Yermasóyia	130	34.43 N	33.05 E
Yermenonville	261	48.33 N	1.37 E
Yermo	204	34.54 N	116.50 W
Yeroḥam	132	31.00 N	34.55 E
Yerolimín	38	36.28 N	22.24 E
Yèrre ≃	50	48.01 N	1.16 E
Yerres	50	48.43 N	2.30 E
Yerres ≃	50	48.43 N	2.27 E
Yerseke	52	51.29 N	4.02 E
Yerupaja, Nevado ∧	248	10.16 S	76.54 W
Yerushalayim (Al-Quds) (Jerusalem)	132	31.46 N	35.14 E
Yerushalayim □[5]	132	31.45 N	35.00 E
Yerushalayim, Sede-Te'ufa ⊠	132	31.52 N	35.12 E
Yerville	50	49.40 N	0.54 E
Yesa, Embalse de ⊜[1]	34	42.36 N	1.09 W
Yesan	98	36.41 N	126.50 E
Yeshenpu	104	40.51 N	122.32 E
Yeshui ≃	98	38.17 N	114.09 E
Yeshvi	272c	18.55 N	73.03 E
Yeşil ≃	130	41.24 N	36.35 E
Yeşilhisar	130	38.21 N	35.06 E
Yeşilkent	130	36.59 N	36.10 E
Yeşilköy	130	40.57 N	28.49 E
Yeşilköy Burnu ≻	267b	40.57 N	28.50 E
Yeşilyurt	130	38.18 N	38.15 E
Yeso	196	34.26 N	104.37 W

Name	Page	Lat.	Long.
Yeso Creek ≃	196	34.13 N	104.15 W
Yesŏng-gang ≃	98	37.53 N	126.24 E
Yessentuki → Jessentuki	84	44.03 N	42.51 E
Yeste	34	38.22 N	2.18 W
Yes Tor ∧	42	50.42 N	4.00 W
Yesud HaMa'ala	132	33.03 N	35.36 E
Yet	144	4.48 N	43.02 E
Yetholme	170	33.27 S	149.49 E
Yetman	166	28.54 S	150.46 E
Yetminster	42	50.53 N	2.33 W
Yetsou	152	2.08 S	10.42 E
Yettem	226	36.29 N	119.16 W
Yetti	164	3.00 S	140.53 E
Yetti ⬥[1]	148	26.10 N	7.50 W
Ye-u	110	22.46 N	95.26 E
Yeu, Île d' I	32	46.42 N	2.20 W
Yevpatoriya → Jevpatorija	78	45.12 N	33.22 E
Yexian, Zhg.	98	37.13 N	119.54 E
Yexian, Zhg.	100	33.37 N	113.20 E
Yexie	106	30.56 N	121.19 E
Yextla ≃	234	18.00 N	100.06 W
Yeysk → Jejsk	78	46.42 N	38.16 E
Yeyuan	98	36.22 N	118.27 E
Yeyupan I	106	30.35 N	121.34 E
Yeywa	110	21.41 N	96.24 E
Yezd → Yazd	128	31.53 N	54.25 E
Yezehu ⊜	106	31.08 N	120.40 E
Yezhuang	105	39.10 N	116.18 E
Yezhuhe	105	40.53 N	118.13 E
Ygatimí	252	24.05 S	55.30 W
Ygnacio Canal ≚	282	37.55 N	122.03 W
Yguazú ≃	252	25.20 S	55.00 W
Yhú	252	24.59 S	55.59 W
Yi ≃	252	33.07 S	57.08 W
Yian	89	47.55 N	125.20 E
Yiannitsá	38	40.48 N	22.25 E
Yibao	106	30.25 N	119.53 E
Yibin (Ipin)	107	28.47 N	104.38 E
Yicanghe	100	32.47 N	120.43 E
Yichang (Ichang)	102	30.42 N	111.11 E
Yichefan	102	26.50 N	103.28 E
Yicheng, Zhg.	98	36.48 N	114.17 E
Yicheng, Zhg.	102	31.43 N	112.07 E
Yichuan, Zhg.	100	34.26 N	112.24 E
Yichuan, Zhg.	102	36.14 N	110.05 E
Yichun, Zhg.	90	47.42 N	128.55 E
Yichun, Zhg.	100	27.50 N	114.23 E
Yicun	105	38.57 N	115.37 E
Yidan	89	43.24 N	125.25 E
Yidiezhen	102	37.08 N	110.30 E
Yidu, Zhg.	98	36.41 N	118.28 E
Yidu, Zhg.	102	30.22 N	111.22 E
Yidun	102	29.56 N	99.22 E
Yiershi	89	47.20 N	119.45 E
Yiewsley ⬥[8]	260	51.31 N	0.28 W
Yifag	144	12.02 N	37.44 E
Yifeng, Zhg.	100	28.26 N	114.46 E
Yifeng, Zhg.	100	33.19 N	113.47 E
Yigaolou	106	30.56 N	120.20 E
Yiğitaliler	130	39.52 N	26.37 E
Yigongzong	102	30.17 N	94.51 E
Yigou	98	35.51 N	114.20 E
Yiguqihu ⊜	120	31.05 N	86.55 E
Yihe, Zhg.	98	42.08 N	118.48 E
Yihe, Zhg.	100	23.50 N	114.53 E
Yihe ≃, Zhg.	98	34.13 N	118.03 E
Yihe ≃, Zhg.	100	34.10 N	112.10 E
Yihechang	107	30.23 N	106.24 E
Yiheyuan	271a	40.00 N	116.16 E
Yiheyuan (Summer Palace) ⊍	105	4.00 N	116.16 E
Yihezhen	98	37.53 N	118.23 E
Yihezhuang	104	41.15 N	122.57 E
Yihuang	100	27.34 N	116.10 E
Yihuta	89	43.13 N	122.15 E
Yijiawan	100	27.58 N	113.01 E
Yijiazi	104	42.29 N	122.41 E
Yijin	100	30.54 N	117.12 E
Yijingpu	105	40.08 N	117.47 E
Yijitathu ⊜	120	35.00 N	87.00 E
Yijun	102	35.24 N	109.00 E
Yikechaidamuhu ⊜	102	37.50 N	95.00 E
Yikengaolu	102	42.17 N	98.19 E
Yikou	100	26.45 N	117.00 E
Yilaha	89	48.50 N	125.14 E
Yilan	89	46.19 N	129.34 E
Yilaxi	89	43.47 N	126.08 E
Yıldızdağı ∧	130	40.08 N	36.56 E
Yıldızeli	130	39.52 N	36.38 E
Yilehulishan ⛰	89	51.20 N	124.30 E
Yili	107	30.45 N	105.58 E
Yiliang, Zhg.	102	24.58 N	103.07 E
Yiliang, Zhg.	102	27.32 N	104.13 E
Yiliekede	89	48.51 N	121.37 E
Yilin	100	33.36 N	119.37 E
Yiling	100	32.30 N	119.46 E
Yiliping	120	37.55 N	93.30 E
Yili Zizhizhou □[4]	86	45.00 N	89.00 E
Yilliminning	162	32.54 S	117.22 E
Yilong, Zhg.	89	47.28 N	125.23 E
Yilong, Zhg.	102	31.34 N	106.19 E
Yilong, Zhg.	102	25.20 N	103.14 E
Yimachi	104	42.11 N	122.15 E
Yimatu	104	41.55 N	121.25 E
Yimen, Zhg.	100	33.39 N	116.02 E
Yimen, Zhg.	102	24.43 N	102.10 E
Yimuhe	89	52.45 N	120.07 E
Yin ≃	110	20.04 N	95.01 E
Yinan	98	35.37 N	118.30 E
Yinbaing	110	17.25 N	97.46 E
Yinchuan	102	38.30 N	106.18 E
Yindarlgooda, Lake ⊜	162	30.45 S	121.55 E
Yindi	154	1.35 N	27.40 E
Yinfang	105	39.07 N	114.52 E
Yingcheng	100	30.57 N	113.32 E
Yingchengzi, Zhg.	89	44.08 N	125.56 E
Yingchengzi, Zhg.	98	38.58 N	121.23 E
Yingchengzi, Zhg.	104	42.22 N	124.14 E
Yingchengzi, Zhg.	104	41.50 N	124.04 E
Yingde	100	24.12 N	113.24 E
Yingen	102	41.09 N	104.45 E
Yingfang	105	40.14 N	116.17 E
Yinggehai	110	18.31 N	108.44 E
Yinggen	110	19.04 N	109.48 E
Yinghe ≃	100	32.30 N	116.32 E
Yingheji	100	32.16 N	116.31 E
Yingjisha	85	38.57 N	76.03 E
Yingkou, Zhg.	104	40.40 N	122.14 E
Yingkou (Dashiqiao), Zhg.	104	40.38 N	122.30 E
Yingnahe ≃	98	39.42 N	123.20 E
Yingpan, Zhg.	98	41.54 N	124.15 E
Yingpan, Zhg.	102	25.48 N	106.18 E
Yingpan, Zhg.	102	24.44 N	99.38 E
Yingpanjie	102	25.27 N	98.24 E
Yingqiao	100	33.58 N	113.39 E
Yingshan, Zhg.	100	30.45 N	115.39 E
Yingshan, Zhg.	100	31.38 N	113.50 E
Yingshan, Zhg.	102	31.08 N	106.31 E
Yingshang	100	32.38 N	116.15 E
Yingshouyingzi, Zhg.	105	40.33 N	117.40 E
Yingshouyingzi, Zhg.	105	40.49 N	117.55 E
Yingtan	100	28.14 N	117.00 E
Yingtaogou	104	42.08 N	121.57 E
Yingtaoyuan	104	41.10 N	123.05 E
Yingtian	100	28.50 N	112.56 E
Yingxiangjie	107	29.24 N	105.11 E
Yingxianpu	104	41.20 N	121.31 E

Name	Page	Lat.	Long.
Yining (Kuldja)	86	43.55 N	81.14 E
Yinjia	107	29.34 N	106.01 E
Yinjiadai	106	32.03 N	120.07 E
Yinjiang	102	28.02 N	108.28 E
Yinjiawopeng	104	42.34 N	121.01 E
Yinkanie	166	34.20 S	140.19 E
Yinkeng	100	26.14 N	115.34 E
Yinliu	105	39.59 N	117.23 E
Yinmabin	110	22.05 N	94.54 E
Yinmahe	89	44.07 N	125.44 E
Yinmatuhe ≃	98	40.57 N	117.43 E
Yinnietharra	162	24.39 S	116.11 E
Yinnyein	110	16.48 N	97.23 E
Yinong	102	30.19 N	101.01 E
Yinping	98	34.15 N	118.39 E
Yinqiaotou	106	31.52 N	119.13 E
Yinshanmai ⛰	102	41.48 N	109.00 E
Yinshanzhen	107	29.41 N	104.59 E
Yinwogou	98	41.55 N	117.55 E
Yinxian (Qiuai)	100	29.50 N	121.38 E
Yinxiang	106	31.55 N	118.49 E
Yinxianji	100	32.07 N	116.32 E
Yinyangjie	104	42.16 N	121.23 E
Yinyuan	102	23.26 N	101.54 E
Yinzhan'ao	100	23.33 N	113.07 E
Yio Chu Kang	271c	1.23 N	103.51 E
Yipinchang	107	29.17 N	106.34 E
Yipinglang	102	25.11 N	101.51 E
Yiqian	100	26.34 N	116.11 E
Yirba Moda	144	6.12 N	38.47 E
Yirga Alem	144	6.52 N	38.22 E
Yirkā	132	32.57 N	35.13 E
Yirol	140	6.33 N	30.30 E
Yirrkala Mission	164	12.14 S	136.56 E
Yirwa	140	7.47 N	27.15 E
Yisaduo	102	28.50 N	96.44 E
Yishan, Zhg.	100	27.32 N	120.32 E
Yishan, Zhg.	102	24.40 N	108.35 E
Yishui	98	35.50 N	118.41 E
Yishui ≃, Zhg.	98	35.34 N	116.52 E
Yishui ≃, Zhg.	100	28.05 N	116.18 E
Yishui ≃, Zhg.	105	39.14 N	115.45 E
Yisikan	89	49.09 N	124.47 E
Yisra'el → Israel □[1]	132	31.30 N	35.00 E
Yisuhe	100	27.46 N	112.54 E
Yitajing	102	42.32 N	94.12 E
Yitangji	98	35.10 N	118.16 E
Yitangzhen	100	31.06 N	113.42 E
Yíthion	38	36.45 N	22.34 E
Yiting	100	29.15 N	119.57 E
Yitong	89	43.20 N	125.17 E
Yitonghe ≃	98	42.40 N	125.58 E
Yitulihe	89	50.38 N	121.57 E
Yiwu, Zhg.	100	29.18 N	120.04 E
Yiwu, Zhg.	102	43.15 N	94.45 E
Yiwu, Zhg.	102	22.00 N	101.28 E
Yiwulüshan ⛰	104	41.42 N	121.42 E
Yixi	100	23.45 N	116.38 E
Yixian, Zhg.	98	34.46 N	117.37 E
Yixian, Zhg.	100	29.55 N	117.56 E
Yixian, Zhg.	104	41.32 N	121.15 E
Yixian, Zhg.	105	39.21 N	115.29 E
Yixiken	89	52.57 N	125.40 E
Yixing	106	31.22 N	119.50 E
Yixingbu	105	39.12 N	117.12 E
Yixingchang	107	30.37 N	106.38 E
Yixu	100	26.02 N	119.16 E
Yixunhe ≃	98	41.16 N	117.35 E
Yiyang, Zhg.	100	28.23 N	117.25 E
Yiyang, Zhg.	102	34.30 N	112.10 E
Yiyang, Zhg.	102	28.36 N	112.20 E
Yiyuan	98	36.11 N	118.08 E
Yiyuankou	98	40.13 N	119.32 E
Yizhang	100	25.26 N	112.56 E
Yizheng	106	32.16 N	119.12 E
Yizikong	102	25.38 N	104.28 E
Yizre'el	132	32.33 N	35.20 E
Yizre'el, 'Emeq ⩡	132	32.36 N	35.14 E
Ylakiai	76	56.17 N	21.51 E
Yläne	26	60.53 N	22.55 E
Ylig Bay C	174p	13.24 N	144.46 E
Ylihärmä	26	63.09 N	22.47 E
Ylikitka ⊜	26	66.08 N	28.30 E
Ylimarkku → Övermark	26	62.38 N	21.30 E
Ylistaro	26	62.57 N	22.31 E
Ylivieska	26	64.05 N	24.33 E
Ylöjärvi	26	61.33 N	23.36 E
Ymeray	261	48.31 N	1.42 E
Ymir	182	49.17 N	117.13 W
Yndin	24	61.24 N	55.10 E
Yngaren ⊜	40	58.52 N	16.35 E
Yngen ⊜	40	59.44 N	14.18 E
Yngern ⊜	40	59.09 N	17.22 E
Yntaly	86	48.58 N	70.55 E
Ynykčanskij	74	60.15 N	137.43 E
Yoakum	222	29.17 N	97.09 W
Yobi, Indon.	164	1.43 S	138.04 E
Yobi, Indon.	164	1.42 S	136.27 E
Yockanookany ≃	194	32.40 N	89.40 W
Yoco	246	10.36 N	62.24 W
Yōda	268	35.24 N	139.25 E
Yoder	216	40.56 N	85.11 W
Yodo ≃	96	34.41 N	135.25 E
Yodoe	96	35.28 N	133.26 E
Yoe	208	39.55 N	76.39 W
Yōga ⬥[8]	268	35.38 N	139.38 E
Yogo	94	35.33 N	136.12 E
Yog Point ≻	116	14.06 N	124.12 E
Yogyakarta	115a	7.48 S	110.22 E
Yogyakarta □[4]	115a	7.45 S	110.30 E
Yoho National Park ♠	182	51.26 N	116.30 W
Yoichi	92a	43.12 N	140.41 E
Yojoa, Lago de ⊜	236	14.50 N	88.00 W
Yŏju	98	37.18 N	127.37 E
Yōka	96	35.24 N	134.46 E
Yokadouma	152	3.31 N	15.03 E
Yōkaichi	94	35.06 N	136.12 E
Yōkaichiba	94	35.42 N	140.33 E
Yokamba	152	0.01 N	22.17 E
Yokana	152	0.45 N	22.53 E
Yokawa	96	34.52 N	135.06 E
Yoko, Cam.	152	5.32 N	12.19 E
Yoko, Zaïre	152	2.36 S	20.06 E
Yokohama	94		
	268	35.27 N	139.39 E
Yokohama-kō C	268	35.27 N	139.39 E
Yokohama National University ⊍[2]	268	35.25 N	139.36 E
Yokohama Park Baseball Ground ♠	268	35.26 N	139.39 E
Yokolo	152	0.36 S	23.04 E
Yokonuma	268	35.58 N	139.21 E
Yokoshiba	94	35.40 N	140.28 E
Yokosuka, Nihon	94	35.00 N	136.53 E
Yokosuka, Nihon	94	35.18 N	139.40 E
Yokosuka District Naval Headquarters ■	268	35.17 N	139.39 E
Yokosuka-kō C	268	35.18 N	139.39 E
Yokosuka Naval Base (United States) ■	94	35.18 N	139.41 E
Yokota, Nihon	96	35.10 N	133.06 E
Yokota, Nihon	268	35.23 N	140.01 E
Yokota, Nihon	270	34.40 N	135.55 E
Yokota Air Base (United States) ■	268	35.45 N	139.21 E
Yokote	92	39.18 N	140.34 E
Yola	146	9.12 N	12.29 E

Name	Page	Lat.	Long.
Yolaina, Serranías de ⛰	236	11.40 N	84.20 W
Yolo	226	38.44 N	121.48 W
Yolo □[6]	226	38.41 N	121.46 W
Yolo ≃	273b	4.19 S	15.20 E
Yolo Bypass ≃	226	38.25 N	121.40 W
Yolombó, Col.	246	6.36 N	75.01 W
Yolombo, Zaïre	152	1.32 S	23.15 E
Yolonga	152	1.36 S	23.12 E
Yom ≃	110	15.52 N	100.16 E
Yombi	152	1.26 S	10.37 E
Yomou	150	7.34 N	9.16 W
Yona	174p	13.25 N	144.47 E
Yonabaru	174m	26.12 N	127.45 E
Yonago	96	35.26 N	133.20 E
Yonaguni-jima I	175d	24.27 N	123.00 E
Yonaha	175d	24.45 N	125.16 E
Yonaha-dake ∧[2]	174m	26.43 N	127.45 E
Yŏnan	98	37.55 N	126.10 E
Yoncalla	202	43.36 N	123.17 W
Yŏnch'on ⬥[8]	271b	37.38 N	127.04 E
Yŏndŏk	98	36.26 N	129.23 E
Yoneshiro ≃	92	40.13 N	140.01 E
Yonezawa	92	37.55 N	140.07 E
Yŏngam	98	34.48 N	126.40 E
Yongamp'o	98	39.55 N	124.24 E
Yŏngan, C.M.I.K.	98	41.15 N	129.30 E
Yongan, Zhg.	100	25.58 N	117.22 E
Yongan, Zhg.	107	30.44 N	106.16 E
Yonganbao	98	40.15 N	119.52 E
Yonganchang	107	30.24 N	103.58 E
Yonganshi	100	28.13 N	113.19 E
Yong'anxi ≃	100	28.52 N	121.04 E
Yŏngbyŏn	98	39.49 N	125.48 E
Yongchang, Zhg.	100	29.13 N	119.20 E
Yongchang, Zhg.	102	39.15 N	102.09 E
Yongchangzhen	106	31.42 N	121.44 E
Yongcheng, Zhg.	98	34.26 N	115.05 E
Yongcheng, Zhg.	100	33.58 N	116.21 E
Yongch'ŏn, C.M.I.K.	98	39.59 N	124.28 E
Yŏngch'ŏn, Taehan	98	35.58 N	128.56 E
Yongch'ŏn-dong	98	41.18 N	129.40 E
Yongchuan	107	29.21 N	105.54 E
Yongchun	100	25.21 N	118.21 E
Yongdeng	102	36.48 N	103.14 E
Yongdian	98	40.34 N	124.48 E
Yongding	100	24.46 N	116.43 E
Yongdinghe ≃	98	39.39 N	116.13 E
Yongdingxi ≃	100	24.42 N	116.34 E
Yongdingzhen	102	26.08 N	101.40 E
Yŏngdong	98	36.10 N	127.48 E
Yŏngdŏngp'o ⬥[8]	271b	37.31 N	126.57 E
Yŏngdungp'o	98	37.31 N	126.54 E
Yŏngdŭngp'o ⬥[8]	271b	37.32 N	126.54 E
Yongfeng, Zhg.	100	29.44 N	116.49 E
Yongfeng, Zhg.	100	27.19 N	115.24 E
Yongfengchang	107	30.33 N	105.05 E
Yongfu	100	25.05 N	117.20 E
Yonggangonch'ŏn	98	38.53 N	125.14 E
Yonggi	98	36.24 N	128.24 E
Yongguzhai	98	34.05 N	116.50 E
Yongheshi	100	28.18 N	113.51 E
Yonghŭng	98	39.32 N	127.13 E
Yŏnghŭng-man C	98	39.15 N	127.30 E
Yŏngil-man C	98	36.02 N	129.26 E
Yongji	102	34.51 N	110.29 E
Yongjia	100	28.11 N	120.42 E
Yongjiang ≃	100	29.58 N	121.44 E
Yŏngju	98	36.50 N	128.37 E
Yongkang, Zhg.	100	32.32 N	117.24 E
Yongkang, Zhg.	100	28.53 N	120.02 E
Yongkou	100	26.16 N	118.19 E
Yongle, Zhg.	89	45.45 N	125.12 E
Yongle, Zhg.	105	39.32 N	115.59 E
Yongledian	105	39.43 N	116.46 E
Yonglong	106	31.34 N	121.48 E
Yonglonghe	100	30.46 N	112.48 E
Yŏngmi-dong	98	39.40 N	125.31 E
Yongnian	98	36.43 N	114.46 E
Yongnianchang	107	29.08 N	104.51 E
Yongning, Zhg.	100	24.43 N	118.42 E
Yongning, Zhg.	102	22.42 N	108.50 E
Yongning, Zhg.	102	27.47 N	100.38 E
Yongningcheng	105	40.34 N	116.11 E
Yongningjiang ≃	100	28.42 N	121.19 E
Yong Peng	114	2.01 N	103.04 E
Yongping	102	25.28 N	99.33 E
Yongpingzhen	100	28.12 N	117.45 E
Yongqing	105	39.19 N	116.29 E
Yongqingchang	107	30.01 N	105.27 E
Yongquan	100	28.46 N	121.19 E
Yŏngsan-gang ≃	98	34.54 N	126.32 E
Yongsan-ni	98	38.52 N	125.56 E
Yŏngsanp'o	98	34.58 N	126.44 E
Yongshan	102	28.15 N	103.24 E
Yongshanqiao	100	29.06 N	117.17 E
Yongsheng	102	26.42 N	100.43 E
Yongshou	102	34.43 N	108.05 E
Yongshun	102	28.57 N	109.41 E
Yongshunchang	107	30.06 N	105.26 E
Yongtai	100	25.54 N	118.58 E
Yŏngwŏl	98	37.12 N	128.28 E
Yongwŏn-ni	98	40.41 N	128.42 E
Yongxin	100	26.56 N	114.18 E
Yongxing, Zhg.	98	40.11 N	123.52 E
Yongxing, Zhg.	100	26.08 N	113.06 E
Yongxing, Zhg.	106	31.56 N	120.55 E
Yongxing, Zhg.	107	30.13 N	105.06 E
Yongxingbao	102	39.08 N	110.31 E
Yongxingchang, Zhg.	107	29.37 N	106.23 E
Yongxingchang, Zhg.	107	28.59 N	106.23 E
Yongxingchang, Zhg.	107	29.02 N	104.34 E
Yongxingchang, Zhg.	107	30.34 N	105.35 E
Yongxingchang, Zhg.	107	30.20 N	103.44 E
Yongxiu	100	29.04 N	115.49 E
Yŏngyang, Taehan	98	36.40 N	129.07 E
Yongyang, Zhg.	100	26.57 N	114.46 E
Yŏngyn	98	39.18 N	125.34 E
Yongyŏn-ni	98	40.44 N	126.09 E
Yongzhai	100	27.59 N	115.26 E
Yŏnhŭi-ri	271b	37.33 N	126.41 E
Yŏnhwa-san ∧	98	40.46 N	127.23 E
Yonibana	150	8.26 N	12.14 W
Yonkers	210	40.55 N	73.52 W
Yonkers Raceway ♠	276	40.55 N	73.52 W
Yonne □[5]	50	47.55 N	3.45 E
Yonne ≃	32	48.23 N	2.58 E
Yono	94	35.53 N	139.38 E
Yonsei University ⊍[2]	271b	37.34 N	126.56 E
Yoo, Enneri ∨	146	19.24 N	16.38 E
Yop'o-ri	98	38.50 N	125.33 E
Yoqne'am	132	32.39 N	35.07 E
Yorba Linda	228	33.53 N	117.49 W
Yorii	94	36.07 N	139.12 E
Yorishima	96	34.29 N	133.35 E
York, Austl.	168a	31.53 S	116.46 E
York, Ont., Can.	212	43.41 N	79.29 W
York, S.L.	150	8.17 N	13.11 W
York, Eng., U.K.	44	53.58 N	1.05 W
York, Ala., U.S.	194	32.29 N	88.18 W
York, Ind., U.S.	216	41.41 N	84.49 W
York, Nebr., U.S.	198	40.52 N	97.36 W
York, N. Dak., U.S.	198	48.19 N	99.34 W
York, N.Y., U.S.	210	42.52 N	77.53 W
York, Pa., U.S.	208	39.58 N	76.44 W
York, S.C., U.S.	192	35.00 N	81.14 W
York □[6], Ont., Can.	212	43.55 N	79.25 W
York □[6], Pa., U.S.	208	39.58 N	76.44 W
York □[6], Va., U.S.	208	37.15 N	76.40 W
York ≃, Ont., Can.	212	45.20 N	77.35 W
York ≃, Qué., Can.	186	48.49 N	64.34 W
York ≃, Va., U.S.	208	37.15 N	76.23 W

Symbol	English	Deutsch	Español	Français	Português
≃	River	Fluss	Río	Rivière	Rio
≚	Canal	Kanal	Canal	Canal	Canal
ᒪ	Waterfall, Rapids	Wasserfall, Stromschnellen	Cascada, Rápidos	Chute d'eau, Rapides	Cascata, Rápidos
⩌	Strait	Meeresstrasse	Estrecho	Détroit	Estreito
C	Bay, Gulf	Bucht, Golf	Bahía, Golfo	Baie, Golfe	Baía, Golfo
⊜	Lake, Lakes	See, Seen	Lago, Lagos	Lac, Lacs	Lago, Lagos
☷	Swamp	Sumpf	Pantano	Marais	Pântano
⍓	Ice Features, Glacier	Eis- und Gletscherformen	Accidentes Glaciales	Formes glaciaires	Acidentes Glaciares
⍑	Other Hydrographic Features	Andere Hydrographische Objekte	Otros Elementos Hidrográficos	Autres données hydrographiques	Outros Elementos Hidrográficos
✢	Submarine Features	Untermeerische Objekte	Accidentes Submarinos	Formes de relief sous-marin	Acidentes Submarinos
□	Political Unit	Politische Einheit	Unidad Politica	Entité politique	Unidade Política
⊍	Cultural Institution	Kulturelle Institution	Institución Cultural	Institution culturelle	Instituição Cultural
⊥	Historical Site	Historische Stätte	Sitio Histórico	Site historique	Sitio Histórico
♠	Recreational Site	Erholungs- und Ferienort	Sitio de Recreo	Centre de loisirs	Sítio de Lazer
⊠	Airport	Flughafen	Aeropuerto	Aéroport	Aeroporto
■	Military Installation	Militäranlage	Instalación Militar	Installation militaire	Instalação Militar
⬥	Miscellaneous	Verschiedenes	Misceláneo	Divers	Miscelânea

ENGLISH — Name, Page, Lat.°′, Long.°′
DEUTSCH — Name, Seite, Breite°′, Länge°′ E=Ost

York, Cape ≻ 164 10.42 S 142.31 E
York, Kap ≻ 16 75.53 N 66.12 W
York, Vale of ∨ 44 54.10 N 1.20 W
Yorkana 208 39.59 N 76.35 W
York Center, Ill., U.S. 278 41.52 N 87.59 W
York Center, Ohio, U.S. 216 40.24 N 83.27 W
York College ʊ[2] 276 40.42 N 73.48 W
Yorkdale Centre ◆[9] 275b 43.44 N 79.27 W
Yorke Peninsula ≻[1] 166 35.00 S 137.30 E
Yorketown 168b 35.02 S 137.36 E
York Factory 184 57.00 N 92.18 W
Yorkfield 278 41.52 N 87.56 W
York Haven 208 40.07 N 76.43 W
Yorklyn 285 39.48 N 75.41 W
York Minster ʊ[1] 44 53.57 N 1.04 W
York New Salem 208 39.54 N 76.47 W
Yorkshire, N.Y., U.S. 210 42.32 N 78.28 W
Yorkshire, Pa., U.S. 208 39.59 N 76.41 W
Yorkshire, Va., U.S. 208 38.47 N 77.27 W
Yorkshire Dales National Park ♠ 44 54.13 N 2.10 W
Yorkshire Wolds ∧∧[2] 44 54.00 N 0.40 W
York Sound ⋃ 160 14.50 S 125.05 E
York Springs 208 40.00 N 77.07 W
Yorkton 184 51.13 N 102.28 W
Yorktown, Ind., U.S. 218 40.10 N 85.30 W
Yorktown, Tex., U.S. 222 28.59 N 97.30 W
Yorktown, Va., U.S. 208 37.14 N 76.30 W
Yorktown ◆[9] 278 41.51 N 88.01 W
Yorktown Battlefield (1781) ⊥ 208 37.13 N 76.31 W
Yorktown Heights 210 41.16 N 73.47 W
Yorktown Manor 207 41.38 N 71.26 W
York Township Airport ⊠ 278 41.51 N 88.02 W
York University ʊ[2] 275b 43.47 N 79.30 W
Yorkville, Ill., U.S. 216 41.38 N 88.27 W
Yorkville, Mich., U.S. 216 42.23 N 85.24 W
Yorkville, N.Y., U.S. 210 43.07 N 75.16 W
Yorkville, Ohio, U.S. 214 40.09 N 80.43 W
Yorkville ◆[8] 275b 43.40 N 79.24 W
Yoro, Hond. 236 15.09 N 87.07 W
Yoro, Mali 150 14.17 N 2.08 W
Yōrō, Nihon 94 35.18 N 136.33 E
Yoro □[5] 236 15.15 N 87.15 W
Yōrō ≃ 94 35.32 N 140.04 E
Yoroi-zaki ≻ 94 34.24 N 136.55 E
Yoron-jima I 93b 27.02 N 128.26 E
Yōrō-no-taki ⌊ 94 35.17 N 136.32 E
Yorosso 150 12.22 N 4.47 W
Yŏryang-ni 98 37.30 N 128.43 E
Yosemite Creek ≃ 226 37.44 N 119.36 W
Yosemite National Park 204 37.45 N 119.35 W
Yosemite National Park ♠ 226 37.51 N 119.33 W
Yoshida, Nihon 94 34.46 N 138.15 E
Yoshida, Nihon 94 36.02 N 139.02 E
Yoshida, Nihon 96 35.10 N 132.51 E
Yoshida, Nihon 96 34.40 N 132.42 E
Yoshida, Nihon 96 33.16 N 132.33 E
Yoshida ≃ 96 34.03 N 131.02 E
Yoshii, Nihon 94 36.15 N 138.59 E
Yoshii, Nihon 96 34.38 N 133.26 E
Yoshii, Nihon 96 34.55 N 134.06 E
Yoshii, Nihon 96 33.20 N 130.45 E
Yoshii, Nihon 270 34.53 N 135.03 E
Yoshii ≃ 96 34.36 N 134.03 E
Yoshikawa, Nihon 94 37.13 N 138.25 E
Yoshikawa, Nihon 94 35.53 N 139.51 E
Yoshikawa, Nihon 270 34.55 N 135.28 E
Yoshimi 94 36.02 N 139.27 E
Yoshino, Nihon 96 34.21 N 135.51 E
Yoshino, Nihon 96 34.06 N 134.23 E
Yoshino ≃, Nihon 94 34.22 N 135.40 E
Yoshino ≃, Nihon 96 34.05 N 134.36 E
Yoshinodani 94 36.17 N 136.39 E
Yoshino-kumano-kokuritsu-kōen ♠ 92 34.07 N 135.55 E
Yoshioka 94 36.27 N 139.01 E
Yoshiumi 96 34.09 N 133.03 E
Yoshiwa 96 34.29 N 132.09 E
Yoshkar-Ola → Joškar-Ola 80 56.38 N 47.52 E
Yosowilangun 115a 8.15 S 113.18 E
Yos Sudarsa, Pulau (Frederik Hendrik-Eiland) I 164 7.50 S 138.30 E
Yŏsu 98 34.46 N 127.44 E
Yotala 248 19.10 S 65.17 W
Yotaú 248 16.03 S 63.03 W
Yōtei-zan ∧ 92a 42.49 N 140.49 E
Yotsukaidō 94 35.39 N 140.10 E
Yotvata 132 29.53 N 35.03 E
Youanmi 162 28.37 S 118.49 E
Youbou 182 48.53 N 124.13 W
Youcheng 100 29.14 N 116.48 E
Youfang 106 32.09 N 119.50 E
Youfangling 100 30.27 N 114.27 E
Youghal 48 51.51 N 7.50 W
Youghal Bay C 48 51.52 N 7.50 W
Youghiogheny ≃ 214 40.22 N 79.52 W
Yougoslavie → Yugoslavia □[1] 22 44.00 N 19.00 E
Youhe 100 32.19 N 113.50 E
Youhuangge 104 40.44 N 120.53 E
Youjiang ≃ 102 22.50 N 108.06 E
Youjidong 104 42.12 N 121.07 E
Youkounkoun 150 12.32 N 13.08 W
Youlantang 100 28.34 N 116.10 E
Young, Austl. 166 34.19 S 148.18 E
Young, Sask., Can. 184 51.47 N 105.46 W
Young, Ariz., U.S. 200 34.06 N 110.57 W
Young, Ur. 252 32.41 S 57.38 W
Young America 216 40.34 N 86.21 W
Younghusband Peninsula ≻[1] 166 36.00 S 139.30 E
Youngs ≃ 224 46.10 N 123.49 W
Youngs, Lake ◎ 224 47.25 N 122.07 W
Youngs Creek 218 38.29 N 86.30 W
Youngs Creek ≃ 219 39.21 N 91.51 W
Youngs Rock I[2] 174e 25.03 S 130.07 W
Youngstown, Alta., Can. 182 51.32 N 111.13 W
Youngstown, Fla., U.S. 192 30.22 N 85.27 W
Youngstown, N.Y., U.S. 210 43.15 N 79.03 W
Youngstown, Ohio, U.S. 214 41.06 N 80.39 W
Youngstown Municipal Airport ⊠ 214 41.15 N 80.41 W
Youngsville, La., U.S. 194 30.06 N 92.00 W
Youngsville, N.C., U.S. 192 36.01 N 78.29 W
Youngsville, N.Y., U.S. 210 41.48 N 74.54 W
Youngsville, Pa., U.S. 214 41.51 N 79.19 W
Youngwood 214 40.14 N 79.35 W
Youngwood Park ♠ 279b 40.14 N 79.36 W
Yountville 226 38.24 N 122.22 W
Youssoufia 148 32.16 N 8.33 W
Youtingpu 107 29.26 N 105.45 E
Youville ◆[8] 275a 45.33 N 73.39 W
Youxi, Zhg. 100 28.45 N 121.06 E
Youxi, Zhg. 100 26.11 N 118.09 E
Youxi, Zhg. 107 29.12 N 106.09 E
Youxian 100 27.00 N 113.21 E
Youxisi 107 30.35 N 106.18 E
Youyang 102 28.58 N 108.41 E
Youyi 89 46.44 N 131.44 E
Youyu 102 40.09 N 112.32 E
Youzhou 105 40.09 N 115.42 E
Yoweragabbie 162 28.13 S 117.39 E
Yozgat 130 39.50 N 34.48 E
Yozgat □[4] 130 39.40 N 35.10 E
Ypacaraí 252 25.23 S 57.16 W
Ypané ≃ 252 23.29 S 57.19 W
Ypé Jhu 252 23.54 S 55.20 W
Yport 50 49.44 N 0.19 E
Ypres → Ieper 50 50.51 N 2.53 E
Ypsilanti 216 42.15 N 83.36 W
Ypsilanti East 216 42.15 N 83.35 W
Yreka 204 41.44 N 122.38 W
Yrgajty ≃ 85 43.03 N 74.43 E
Yron ≃ 56 49.10 N 5.52 E
Ysabel Channel ⋃ 164 2.00 S 150.00 E
Ysbyty Ystwyth 42 52.20 N 3.48 W
Yscir ≃ 42 51.57 N 3.27 W
Yser (IJzer) ≃ 50 51.09 N 2.43 E
Ysieux, Ruisseau l' ≃ 261 49.09 N 2.22 E
Yssche ≃ 56 50.49 N 4.38 E
Yssel → Issel ≃ 52 52.00 N 6.10 E
Ysselmeer → IJsselmeer ⊤[2] 52 52.45 N 5.25 E
Yssingeaux 62 45.08 N 4.07 E
Ystad 41 55.25 N 13.49 E
Ystalyfera 42 51.47 N 3.47 W
Ysterfonteinpunt ≻ 158 33.22 S 18.09 E
Ystrad ≃ 44 53.13 N 3.20 W
Ystrad Aeron 42 52.11 N 4.11 W
Ystradfellte 42 51.48 N 3.34 W
Ystradgynlais 42 51.47 N 3.45 W
Ystwyth ≃ 42 52.24 N 4.05 W
Ytambey ≃ 252 24.46 S 54.24 W
Ythan ≃ 46 57.18 N 2.00 W
Ytre Arna 26 60.26 N 5.30 E
Ytterharnäs 40 60.39 N 17.21 E
Ytterhogdal 26 62.12 N 14.51 E
Yttermalung 40 60.35 N 13.50 E
Ytterselö 40 59.23 N 17.15 E
Yū 96 34.02 N 132.13 E
Yu, Pulau I 164 0.03 S 129.36 E
Yu'alliq, Jabal ∧ 140 30.22 N 33.31 E
Yuam ≃ 110 17.47 N 97.45 E
Yuan'an 102 31.04 N 111.26 E
Yuanao 100 26.29 N 119.48 E
Yuanbachang 107 29.44 N 105.27 E
Yuanchengzhen 102 36.43 N 107.52 E
Yuanhua 106 30.25 N 120.46 E
Yuan Huan ◆[9] 269d 25.03 N 121.31 E
Yuanjiang, Zhg. 98 34.14 N 115.19 E
Yuanjiang, Zhg. 102 23.34 N 102.03 E
Yuanjiang → Red ≃ 110 20.17 N 106.34 E
Yuanjiazao 106 32.05 N 121.35 E
Yuankeng 100 26.48 N 117.44 E
Yüanli 100 24.28 N 120.41 E
Yüanlin 100 23.58 N 120.34 E
Yuanling 102 28.20 N 110.16 E
Yuanmou 102 25.38 N 101.54 E
Yuanshancun 106 31.08 N 120.20 E
Yuanshi 98 37.45 N 114.32 E
Yuanshui ≃ 100 28.09 N 115.34 E
Yuantan, Zhg. 100 32.47 N 112.53 E
Yuantan, Zhg. 100 23.39 N 113.12 E
Yuantongsi 107 30.13 N 104.15 E
Yuantouzhu 106 31.32 N 120.14 E
Yuanxing 107 30.36 N 104.59 E
Yuanyang, Zhg. 98 35.04 N 113.57 E
Yuanyang, Zhg. 102 23.12 N 102.52 E
Yuanyangchang 107 29.41 N 106.33 E
Yuanyangpu 107 30.10 N 105.15 E
Yuanyuansha I 106 31.21 N 121.45 E
Yuanzhuang 100 26.52 N 116.58 E
Yuasa 96 34.02 N 135.11 E
Yuat ≃ 164 4.25 S 143.55 E
Yuba 102 29.27 N 97.42 E
Yuba □[6] 226 39.16 N 121.17 W
Yuba ≃ 226 39.07 N 121.36 W
Yuba City 226 39.08 N 121.37 W
Yubara 96 35.12 N 133.45 E
Yubara-chosuichi ◎ 96 35.13 N 133.43 E
Yubara-dam ◆[6] 96 35.13 N 133.44 E
Yūbari 92a 43.04 N 141.59 E
Yubari-sanchi ∧∧ 92a 43.15 N 142.20 E
Yubdo 144 9.00 N 35.22 E
Yūbetsu 92a 43.13 N 144.05 E
Yūbetsu ≃ 92a 44.14 N 143.37 E
Yucaipa 228 34.02 N 117.02 W
Yucatán □[3] 232 20.50 N 89.00 W
Yucatan Channel ⋃ 238 21.45 N 85.45 W
Yucatan Peninsula ≻[1] 232 19.30 N 89.00 W
Yucca 200 34.52 N 114.09 W
Yucca Lake ◎ 204 36.59 N 116.01 W
Yucca Valley 204 34.07 N 116.35 W
Yuchaozhuang 105 39.35 N 117.50 E
Yucheng, Zhg. 98 34.24 N 115.52 E
Yucheng, Zhg. 98 36.56 N 116.39 E
Yucheng, Zhg. 106 30.32 N 120.51 E
Yuci 102 37.45 N 112.41 E
Yucuyácua, Cerro ∧ 234 17.07 N 97.40 W
Yuda 92 39.20 N 140.50 E
Yudaokou 98 42.14 N 116.48 E
Yudong 106 32.02 N 121.22 E
Yudu 100 25.59 N 115.24 E
Yuebo 107 29.03 N 104.12 E
Yuecheng 100 32.39 N 114.49 E
Yuechi 107 30.33 N 106.26 E
Yuejiatun 104 41.10 N 120.43 E
Yuejiawopeng 104 41.35 N 122.20 E
Yuekou 100 30.32 N 113.03 E
Yuelai 106 31.56 N 121.27 E
Yuelaichang 107 29.44 N 106.32 E
Yuemenpu 107 30.28 N 106.34 E
Yuendumu 162 22.16 S 131.49 E
Yuepu 106 31.25 N 121.26 E
Yuepuhu 85 39.15 N 76.45 E
Yuewangshi 106 31.33 N 121.09 E
Yuexi, Zhg. 100 30.50 N 116.24 E
Yuexi, Zhg. 102 28.42 N 102.28 E
Yueyang 100 29.23 N 113.06 E
Yuezijiang 100 24.54 N 115.02 E
Yufa 105 39.31 N 116.19 E
Yufeng 107 30.37 N 105.11 E
Yufu-dake ∧ 96 33.17 N 131.24 E
Yufuin 96 33.15 N 131.20 E
Yugan 100 28.41 N 116.41 E
Yugawara 94 35.09 N 139.04 E
Yuge 96 34.15 N 133.12 E
Yugoslavia □[1] 22 44.00 N 19.00 E
Yugou 100 33.42 N 118.55 E
Yuguanzhen 98 39.56 N 119.22 E
Yuguo 104 41.52 N 123.15 E
Yuhang 106 30.17 N 119.56 E
Yuhebao 102 38.01 N 109.37 E
Yuhu 100 27.53 N 120.08 E
Yuhuaizhuang 105 39.24 N 117.40 E
Yui 94 35.06 N 138.34 E
Yuin 162 27.58 S 116.02 E
Yujiachang 107 29.57 N 104.04 E
Yujiang ≃ 102 23.24 N 110.05 E
Yujiaqiao 106 31.30 N 119.25 E
Yujiawan 86 44.32 N 86.45 E
Yukarıbey 130 39.15 N 27.06 E
Yukarı Ezbider 130 40.06 N 38.21 E
Yuke 98 37.56 N 115.39 E
Yūki, Nihon 94 36.18 N 139.53 E
Yuki, Nihon 96 34.29 N 132.16 E
Yuki, Nihon 96 34.46 N 133.17 E
Yuki, Nihon 96 33.46 N 134.36 E
Yukon 214 40.13 N 79.41 W
Yukon □[4] 176
180 64.00 N 135.00 W
Yukon ≃ 180 62.33 N 163.59 W
Yukou 105 40.12 N 117.00 E
Yukuhashi 96 33.44 N 130.59 E
Yulan 210 41.31 N 74.56 W
Yulao 102 23.31 N 111.46 E
Yule ≃ 162 20.41 S 118.17 E
Yule Bay C 9 70.44 S 166.40 E
Yule Island I 164 8.50 S 146.30 E
Yüli 100 23.20 N 121.19 E
Yuliang 100 29.52 N 118.30 E
Yuliangbao 89 43.26 N 121.55 E
Yulin, Zhg. 102 38.20 N 109.29 E
Yulin, Zhg. 102 22.36 N 110.07 E
Yulin, Zhg. 110 18.16 N 109.32 E
Yulincun 105 40.12 N 116.42 E
Yuling ∧∧ 100 29.35 N 118.25 E
Yul-li 98 38.52 N 126.13 E
Yulong 107 29.58 N 104.22 E
Yulongkashihe ≃ 120 37.00 N 79.55 E
Yuma, Ariz., U.S. 200 32.43 N 114.37 W
Yuma, Colo., U.S. 198 40.08 N 102.43 W
Yuma, Bahía de C 238 18.21 N 68.35 W
Yumare 246 10.37 N 68.41 W
Yumbel 252 37.08 S 72.32 W
Yumbi, Zaïre 152 1.53 S 16.32 E
Yumbi, Zaïre 154 1.14 S 26.14 E
Yumbo 246 3.35 N 76.28 W
Yumen (Laojunmiao) 102 39.56 N 97.51 E
Yumenzhen 102 40.17 N 97.07 E
Yumesaki 96 34.58 N 134.42 E
Yumesaki ≃ 96 34.47 N 134.39 E
Yumin 86 46.02 N 82.37 E
Yumurtalık 130 36.49 N 35.45 E
Yuna, Austl. 162 28.20 S 115.00 E
Yuna, Nihon 174m 26.46 N 128.12 E
Yuna ≃ 238 19.12 N 69.37 W
Yunak 130 38.49 N 31.45 E
Yunan (Ducheng) 102 23.11 N 111.29 E
Yunaska Island I 180 52.40 N 170.50 W
Yuncao 100 31.26 N 118.04 E
Yuncheng, Zhg. 98 35.35 N 115.54 E
Yuncheng, Zhg. 102 35.00 N 110.59 E
Yunchuanbao 98 41.01 N 115.44 E
Yundamindra 162 29.07 S 122.02 E
Yundanyingzi 104 42.00 N 121.34 E
Yunderup 168a 32.35 S 115.46 E
Yunfengding ∧ 106 30.56 N 120.02 E
Yungas •[1] 248 16.00 S 67.45 W
Yungay, Chile 252 37.07 S 72.01 W
Yungay, Perú 248 9.09 S 77.44 W
Yungchi → Jilin 89 43.51 N 126.33 E
Yungchia → Wenzhou 100 28.01 N 120.39 E
Yungho 269d 25.01 N 121.31 E
Yungning → Nanning 102 22.48 N 108.20 E
Yung Shu Wan 271d 22.14 N 114.06 E
Yunhe → Peixian, Zhg. 98 34.21 N 117.59 E
Yunhe, Zhg. 107 30.31 N 104.46 E
Yunhe (Grand Canal) ≋ 90 32.12 N 119.31 E
Yunjiguan)(100 27.50 N 117.40 E
Yunjinchang 107 29.06 N 105.40 E
Yunlian 102 28.08 N 104.35 E
Yünlin 100 23.43 N 120.33 E
Yunling ∧∧ 102 27.20 N 99.20 E
Yunlinhe ≋ 100 30.15 N 120.11 E
Yunlong 102 25.50 N 99.17 E
Yunluchang 107 29.45 N 105.57 E
Yunmeng 100 31.02 N 113.41 E
Yunmenling 100 25.15 N 115.49 E
Yunmenzhen 107 30.06 N 106.20 E
Yunnan □[4] 102 24.00 N 101.00 E
Yunnanfu → Kunming 102 25.05 N 102.40 E
Yunotani 94 37.14 N 139.01 E
Yunotsu 96 35.05 N 132.21 E
Yunshui ≃ 100 30.43 N 114.04 E
Yunta 166 32.35 S 139.33 E
Yunting 106 31.53 N 120.19 E
Yunwushan ∧ 98 41.07 N 116.34 E
Yunxi, Zhg. 100 29.28 N 113.16 E
Yunxi, Zhg. 102 32.49 N 110.13 E
Yunxian, Zhg. 102 24.30 N 100.03 E
Yunxian (Yunyang), Zhg. 102 32.49 N 110.49 E
Yunxiao 100 24.04 N 117.20 E
Yunyang 100 33.28 N 112.42 E
Yunyanhe ≃ 106 32.02 N 120.48 E
Yunzalin Chaung ≃ 110 17.23 N 97.40 E
Yunzhong 100 29.13 N 117.40 E
Yunzhongshan ∧∧ 102 38.30 N 112.30 E
Yupanshan II 106 30.30 N 121.15 E
Yupanyang C 100 30.30 N 121.46 E
Yuping 102 27.07 N 108.47 E
Yuqi 106 31.43 N 120.11 E
Yuqia 102 38.07 N 94.35 E
Yuqian 100 30.11 N 119.25 E
Yuqian'gou 104 41.41 N 121.28 E
Yuqing 102 27.05 N 107.44 E
Yuqizhen 107 30.19 N 105.47 E
Yura, Nihon 96 34.17 N 134.57 E
Yura, Perú 248 16.11 S 71.40 W
Yura ≃ 96 35.31 N 135.17 E
Yurano-hana ≻ 96 33.01 N 132.23 E
Yurécuaro 234 20.20 N 102.18 W
Yurga → Jurga 86 55.42 N 84.51 E
Yuri-jima I 96 33.51 N 132.32 E
Yurimaguas 248 5.54 S 76.05 W
Yuriria 234 20.12 N 101.09 W
Yuriria, Laguna de ◎ 234 20.15 N 101.06 W
Yuruarí ≃ 246 6.44 N 61.40 W
Yurubí, Parque Nacional ♠ 246 10.25 N 68.42 W
Yürük 130 40.56 N 27.04 E
Yurumanguí ≃ 246 3.27 N 77.21 W
Yuryev → Tartu 76 58.23 N 26.43 E
Yusala, Laguna ◎ 248 14.05 S 67.12 W
Yuşa Tepesi ∧[2] 267b 41.09 N 29.05 E
Yuscarán 236 13.55 N 86.51 W
Yushan, Zhg. 100 26.54 N 118.36 E
Yushan, Zhg. 100 28.41 N 118.15 E
Yushan ∧ 100 26.06 N 115.20 E
Yushanji 98 35.17 N 116.12 E
Yushanzhai 100 33.19 N 113.41 E
Yushanzhen 102 29.38 N 108.19 E
Yushu, Zhg. 89 44.46 N 126.34 E
Yushu (Jiegu), Zhg. 102 33.28 N 96.18 E
Yushugou 86 44.07 N 87.05 E
Yushulinzi, Zhg. 98 40.59 N 125.57 E
Yushulinzi, Zhg. 98 41.30 N 119.07 E
Yushupu 104 41.10 N 122.08 E
Yushutai, Zhg. 89 43.30 N 124.17 E
Yushutai, Zhg. 104 41.42 N 123.26 E
Yushuwan 105 40.04 N 115.35 E
Yusichang 107 29.14 N 105.25 E
Yūsofābād 267d 35.44 N 51.25 E
Yuste, Monasterio de ʊ[1] 34 40.08 N 5.45 W
Yūsuf, Baḥr ≋ 142 29.18 N 30.50 E
Yusuhara 96 33.23 N 132.55 E
Yusuhara ≃ 96 33.11 N 132.58 E
Yutian, Zhg. 100 26.27 N 114.36 E
Yutian, Zhg. 105 39.53 N 117.45 E
Yutian, Zhg. 120 36.51 N 81.40 E
Yuting 100 29.50 N 117.57 E
Yūtō 94 34.42 N 137.38 E
Yutou 100 28.36 N 118.30 E
Yuty 252 26.32 S 56.18 W
Yütz'u → Yuci 102 37.45 N 112.41 E
Yūwan-dake ∧ 93b 28.18 N 129.21 E
Yuwangcheng 100 31.31 N 114.29 E
Yüweng Tao I 100 23.35 N 119.30 E
Yuwŏnjin 98 40.18 N 126.37 E
Yuxi, Zhg. 100 25.36 N 119.18 E
Yuxi, Zhg. 102 24.21 N 102.34 E
Yuxi, Zhg. 106 32.03 N 121.11 E
Yuxian, Zhg. 98 39.48 N 114.33 E
Yuxian, Zhg. 100 34.10 N 113.28 E
Yuxian, Zhg. 102 38.09 N 113.25 E
Yuxiangpu 98 34.27 N 114.57 E
Yuxiangtou 106 31.14 N 120.53 E
Yuyao 100 30.04 N 121.10 E
Yuyŏn-ni 98 38.42 N 127.10 E
Yuza 92 39.01 N 139.54 E
Yuzawa, Nihon 92 39.10 N 140.30 E
Yuzawa, Nihon 94 36.56 N 138.49 E
Yuzhagou 106 31.04 N 118.46 E
Yuzhno-Sakhalinsk → Južno-Sachalinsk 89 46.58 N 142.42 E
Yuzovka → Doneck 83 48.00 N 37.48 E
Yuzuruha-yama ∧ 96 34.14 N 134.49 E
Yvelines □[5] 50 48.50 N 1.50 E
Yvelines, Forêt des ♠ 261 48.40 N 1.55 E
Yverdon 58 46.47 N 6.39 E
Yvetot 50 49.37 N 0.46 E
Yvette 261 48.43 N 1.55 E
Yvette ≃ 50 48.40 N 2.20 E
Yvoir 56 50.20 N 4.53 E
Yvoire 58 46.22 N 6.20 E
Yvonand 58 46.48 N 6.45 E
Yvron ≃ 50 48.39 N 2.56 E
Ywamun 110 20.31 N 95.25 E
Ywathagyi 110 22.18 N 95.42 E
Ywathit 110 19.10 N 97.30 E
Yxlan I 40 59.38 N 18.52 E
Yxsjöberg 40 60.03 N 14.46 E
Yzeron 62 45.42 N 4.35 E

Z

Za, Oued ≃ 148 34.34 N 3.03 W
Zaachila 234 16.57 N 96.45 W
Zaaimansdal 158 33.35 S 23.22 E
Zaajatskaja 86 52.53 N 61.35 E
Zaalajskij Chrebet ∧∧ 85 39.40 N 72.05 E
Zaamin 85 39.58 N 68.24 E
Zaandam 52 52.26 N 4.49 E
Žabaj ≃ 86 51.42 N 68.22 E
Zabajkal'sk 88 49.38 N 117.19 E
Zăbala ≃ 38 45.51 N 26.46 E
Zăbalț 38 46.01 N 21.55 E
Žabari 38 44.21 N 21.13 E
Zabarjad, Jazīrat I 140 23.37 N 36.12 E
Žabasak 86 50.21 N 61.40 E
Zāb-e Kūchek → Little Zab ≃ 128 35.12 N 43.25 E
Zaberfeld 56 49.03 N 8.55 E
Zabīd 144 14.10 N 43.17 E
Zabīd, Wādī ∨ 144 14.07 N 43.05 E
Žabinka 76 52.12 N 24.01 E
Zabituj 88 53.16 N 102.50 E
Žabje 78 48.11 N 24.46 E
Ząbkowice Śląskie 30 50.36 N 16.53 E
Žabljak 38 43.09 N 19.07 E
Zabłudów 30 53.01 N 23.20 E
Žabno 30 50.09 N 20.53 E
Zābol 128 31.02 N 61.30 E
Zābol □[4] 120 32.00 N 67.15 E
Zābolī 128 27.07 N 61.40 E
Zabolotje, S.S.S.R. 76 52.40 N 28.34 E
Zabolotje, S.S.S.R. 76 53.56 N 24.46 E
Zabolotje, S.S.S.R. 78 51.38 N 24.15 E
Zabolotje, S.S.S.R. 82 55.32 N 38.12 E
Zabolotje, S.S.S.R. 82 54.24 N 38.54 E
Zabolotje, S.S.S.R. 82 56.40 N 38.06 E
Zabolotov 78 48.29 N 25.16 E
Zaborje, S.S.S.R. 76 55.55 N 29.19 E
Zaborje, S.S.S.R. 76 54.51 N 32.41 E
Zaborje, S.S.S.R. 76 55.24 N 31.34 E
Zaborje, S.S.S.R. 76 53.06 N 31.42 E
Zaborje, S.S.S.R. 82 55.23 N 37.47 E
Zabory 76 55.58 N 32.17 E
Zabré 150 11.10 N 0.38 W
Zábřeh 30 49.53 N 16.52 E
Zabrze 30 50.18 N 18.46 E
Zaburunje 80 46.44 N 50.09 E
Zabyčanje 76 53.25 N 31.52 E
Zabzugu 150 9.17 N 0.22 E
Zacapa 236 14.58 N 89.32 W
Zacapa □[5] 236 15.00 N 89.30 W
Zacapoaxtla 234 19.53 N 97.35 W
Zacapu 234 19.50 N 101.43 W
Zacata 208 38.07 N 76.47 W
Zacatecas 234 22.47 N 102.35 W
Zacatecas □[3] 234 23.00 N 103.00 W
Zacatecoluca 236 13.30 N 88.52 W
Zacatepec 234 18.39 N 99.12 W
Zacatlán 234 19.56 N 97.58 W
Zacatongo 234 20.49 N 104.33 W
Začepilovka 78 49.12 N 35.14 E
Zachan → Suchań 30 53.17 N 15.19 E
Zacharias Creek ≃ 285 40.11 N 75.23 W
Zacharkovo 265b 55.47 N 37.19 E
Zacharovo, S.S.S.R. 76 54.22 N 39.17 E
Zacharovo, S.S.S.R. 82 56.31 N 36.44 E
Zacharvan' 24 66.21 N 55.48 E
Zachary 194 30.39 N 91.09 W
Zachidnoje 78 51.29 N 31.15 E
Zachmet 128 37.43 N 62.30 E
Zachožje 265a 59.44 N 30.51 E
Zachrebetnoje 24 69.00 N 36.25 E
Začistje 76 54.24 N 28.45 E
Zacks Bay C 276 40.36 N 73.29 W
Zacoalco de Torres 234 20.14 N 103.35 W
Zacualpa 236 15.05 N 90.50 W
Zacualpan, Méx. 234 21.15 N 105.10 W
Zacualpan, Méx. 234 20.28 N 98.22 W
Zacualtipán 234 20.39 N 98.36 W
Zaculeu ⊥ 236 15.21 N 91.29 W
Zadar 36 44.07 N 15.14 E
Zadetkale Kyun I 110 10.08 N 98.12 E
Zadetkyi Kyun I 110 9.58 N 98.13 E
Zadi (Inkisi) ≃ 152 4.46 S 14.52 E
Zadní Chodov 60 49.54 N 12.44 E
Zadonsk 76 52.23 N 38.57 E
Zadorra ≃ 34 42.40 N 2.54 W
Žadovo 78 52.03 N 32.39 E
Zaerap 76 59.18 N 36.37 E
Ẓafar al-Qadīmah 142 30.58 N 31.37 E
Za'farānah, Bi'r ⊤[4] 142 29.07 N 32.33 E
Za'farānah, Ra's ≻ 142 29.06 N 32.40 E
Zafarobod 85 40.11 N 68.51 E
Zafarwāl 123 32.21 N 74.54 E
Zafferana Etnea 70 37.41 N 15.06 E
Zafirovo 38 44.00 N 26.50 E
Zafra 34 38.25 N 6.25 W
Žaga 64 46.18 N 13.29 E
Zagabria → Zagreb 36 45.48 N 15.58 E
Żagań 30 51.37 N 15.19 E
Žagarė 76 56.21 N 23.15 E
Zagarise 68 39.00 N 16.39 E
Zagarolo 66 41.50 N 12.50 E
Zagazig → Az-Zaqāzīq 142 30.35 N 31.31 E
Zāgheh 128 33.30 N 48.42 E
Zaghouan 148 36.24 N 10.09 E
Zaghouan, Djebel ∧ 36 36.21 N 10.08 E
Zagnanado 150 7.16 N 2.21 E
Zagnitkov 78 48.03 N 28.54 E
Zagora 148 30.22 N 5.50 W
Zagora ∧∧ 36 43.40 N 16.15 E
Zagor'anskij 265b 55.55 N 37.55 E
Zagórów 30 52.11 N 17.55 E
Zagorsk 82 56.18 N 38.08 E
Zagorskij 89 47.19 N 142.28 E
Zagórz 30 49.31 N 22.17 E
Zagreb 36 45.48 N 15.58 E
Zāgros, Kūhhā-ye ∧∧ 128 33.40 N 47.00 E
Zagros Mountains → Zāgros, Kūhhā-ye ∧∧ 128 33.40 N 47.00 E
Zagryzovo 83 49.31 N 37.43 E
Žagubica 38 44.13 N 21.48 E
Zagustaj 88 51.58 N 110.45 E
Zagyva ≃ 30 47.10 N 20.13 E
Zahana 34 35.32 N 0.25 W
Zāhedān 128 29.30 N 60.52 E
Zahirābād 122 17.41 N 77.37 E
Zaḥlah 130 33.51 N 35.53 E
Zahna 54 51.54 N 12.47 E
Zahns Airport ⊠ 276 40.42 N 73.24 W
Záhony 30 48.25 N 22.11 E
Ẓahrān 144 17.40 N 43.30 E
Zahrensdorf 54 53.45 N 11.40 E
Zaidpur 124 26.50 N 81.20 E
Zaigrajevo 88 51.50 N 108.16 E
Zaijiafangzi 104 41.17 N 122.39 E
Zailijskij-Alatau, Chrebet ∧∧ 85 43.00 N 77.00 E
Žailma, S.S.S.R. 85 39.32 N 69.30 E
Žailma, S.S.S.R. 86 51.32 N 61.37 E
Zaimka 88 58.41 N 100.40 E
Zaimokuza 268 35.18 N 139.33 E
Zainsk 80 55.18 N 52.06 E
Zaire □[5] 152 7.00 S 13.30 E
Zaire □[1] 10 0.00 S 25.00 E
Zaïre → Congo ≃ 138 6.04 S 12.24 E
Zaizhuangzi 105 40.02 N 117.43 E
Zaj ≃ 80 55.36 N 51.40 E
Zajarsk 88 56.10 N 103.08 E
Zajcevka 83 49.41 N 40.00 E
Zajcevo, S.S.S.R. 82 54.48 N 37.33 E
Zajcevo, S.S.S.R. 83 48.24 N 38.02 E
Zajcevo, S.S.S.R. 83 48.32 N 38.04 E
Zajcevo, S.S.S.R. 265b 55.39 N 37.11 E
Zaječar 38 43.54 N 22.17 E
Zajkany 78 47.59 N 27.22 E
Zaj-Karataj 80 54.42 N 52.22 E
Zajmo-Obryv 83 47.02 N 39.19 E
Zajsan 86 47.28 N 84.55 E
Zajsan, Ozero ◎ 86 48.00 N 84.00 E
Žajsk 80 55.54 N 42.32 E
Zajukovo 84 43.37 N 43.19 E
Zaka 154 20.20 S 31.29 E
Zakamensk 88 50.23 N 103.17 E
Zakarpatskaja Oblast' □[4] 78 48.30 N 23.00 E
Zákas 38 40.02 N 21.16 E
Zakatal'skij Zapovednik ♠ 84 41.48 N 46.38 E
Zakataly 84 41.38 N 46.39 E
Zakatnyj 80 46.32 N 44.04 E
Zakfero 140 12.10 N 27.35 E
Zākhū 128 37.08 N 42.41 E
Zákinthos 38 37.47 N 20.53 E
Zákinthos I 38 37.52 N 20.44 E
Zakínthou, Porthmós ⋃ 38 37.50 N 21.00 E
Zakīyah 132 33.20 N 36.08 E
Zakliczyn 30 49.51 N 20.48 E
Zaklików 30 50.47 N 22.06 E
Zákolany 54 50.10 N 14.14 E
Zakopane 30 49.19 N 19.57 E
Zakotnoje, S.S.S.R. 83 49.28 N 38.58 E
Zakotnoje, S.S.S.R. 83 48.54 N 37.58 E
Zakouma 146 10.54 N 19.49 E
Zakouma, Parc National de ♠ 146 10.45 N 19.30 E
Zakroczym 30 52.26 N 20.37 E
Žaksy 86 51.55 N 67.20 E
Žaksybaj ≃ 80 49.24 N 53.18 E
Zákupy 54 50.42 N 14.40 E
Zala 144 6.28 N 37.20 E
Zala □[6] 61 46.45 N 16.50 E
Zala ≃ 61 46.43 N 17.16 E
Zalaegerszeg 30 46.51 N 16.51 E
Zalai-Dombság ∧∧[2] 61 46.37 N 16.48 E
Zalalövő 61 46.51 N 16.35
Zalamea de la Serana 34 38.39 N 5.39 W
Žalanaš 86 51.12 N 65.02 E
Zalanga 150 10.37 N 10.10 E
Žalany 54 50.35 N 13.55 E
Zalari 88 53.34 N 102.32 E
Zalaszentgrót 30 46.59 N 17.02 E
Zalau, Nig. 150 10.20 N 9.00 E
Zalău, Rom. 38 47.11 N 23.03 E
Žalauly, Ozero ◎ 86 52.53 N 74.10 E
Zaldívar, Laguna ◎ 286b 22.58 N 82.27 W
Žalec 36 46.15 N 15.10 E
Zalegošč' 76 52.56 N 36.53 E
Zaleščiki 78 48.38 N 25.44 E
Zalesje, S.S.S.R. 76 58.42 N 36.10 E
Zalesje, S.S.S.R. 76 54.51 N 21.32 E
Zalesovo 86 54.00 N 84.47 E
Zalingei 140 12.54 N 23.29 E
Zalizničnoje 78 47.53 N 33.29 E
Zallāf, Wādī ∨ 146 27.22 N 14.22 E
Záložcy 78 49.48 N 25.24 E
Zalṭan 146 32.57 N 11.52 E
Zaltbommel 52 51.48 N 5.15 E
Žaltyr 86 51.40 N 69.50 E
Žaltyr, Ozero ◎ 80 47.24 N 51.07 E
Zalučje 76 57.40 N 31.46 E
Zalukokoaže 84 43.54 N 43.13 E
Zalun 110 17.29 N 95.34 E
Zama, Nihon 268 35.29 N 139.24 E
Zama, Miss., U.S. 194 32.53 N 89.23 W
Zama, Camp ■ 268 35.30 N 139.24 E
Zama-iriya 268 35.29 N 139.24 E
Zamakh 144 16.30 N 47.35 E
Zamālik, Jazīrat az- I 273c 30.03 N 31.13 E
Žaman-Akkol', Ozero ◎ 86 48.58 N 63.30 E
Žamankak 80 48.56 N 48.45 E
Žamantau, Gora ∧[2] 80 48.20 N 51.50 E
Zamarino 82 54.18 N 37.11 E
Žambaj 80 47.11 N 50.34 E
Zambales □[4] 116 15.20 N 120.05 E
Zambales Mountains ∧∧ 116 15.45 N 120.05 E
Žamberk 30 50.05 N 16.28 E
Zambezi (Zambeze) ≃ 138 18.55 S 36.04 E
Zambézia □[5] 156 16.15 S 37.30 E
Zambezi Escarpment •[4] 154 16.20 S 30.00 E
Zambia □[1] 138 15.00 S 30.00 E
Zambie → Zambia □[1] 138 15.00 S 30.00 E
Zamboanga 116 6.54 N 122.04 E
Zamboanga del Norte □[4] 116 8.00 N 123.00 E
Zamboanga del Sur □[4] 116 7.50 N 123.00 E
Zamboanga Peninsula ≻[1] 116 7.32 N 122.16 E
Zamboanguita 116 9.06 N 123.12 E
Zambrano 246 9.45 N 74.49 W
Zambrone 68 38.42 N 15.59 E
Zambrów 30 53.00 N 22.15 E
Zâmbuè 154 15.10 S 30.50 E
Zambujal 266c 38.52 N 9.07 W
Zamch 30 50.20 N 23.00 E
Zamežnaja 24 65.02 N 51.50 E
Zamfara ≃ 150 12.05 N 4.02 E
Zamglaj 78 51.49 N 31.13 E
Zami ≃ 110 16.09 N 97.58 E
Zamjany 80 46.50 N 47.40 E
Zamkova, Gora ∧[2] 76 53.30 N 25.43 E
Zamora, Ec. 246 4.04 S 78.58 W
Zamora, Esp. 34 41.30 N 5.45 W
Zamora, Calif., U.S. 226 38.48 N 121.53 W
Zamora ≃ 246 2.59 S 78.13 W
Zamora-Chinchipe □[4] 246 4.15 S 78.50 W
Zamora de Hidalgo 234 19.59 N 102.16 W
Zamość 30 50.44 N 23.15 E
Zamožnoje 83 47.19 N 37.49 E
Zampa-misaki ≻ 174m 26.26 N 127.43 E
Zams 58 47.09 N 10.35 E
Zamševa 86 59.07 N 89.14 E
Zamuro, Punta ≻ 246 11.26 N 68.50 W
Zamzam, Wādī ∨ 146 31.26 N 15.27 E
Zamzor 88 55.21 N 98.35 E
Zana ⊥ 34 35.45 N 6.05 E
Žanadarja 86 44.45 N 64.40 E
Zanaga 152 2.51 S 13.50 E
Zanapa 130 37.25 N 34.13 E
Zanapa ≃ 234 17.58 N 94.06 W
Žanašu 80 47.27 N 48.31 E
Žanatalap, S.S.S.R. 86 47.06 N 84.13 E
Žanatalap, S.S.S.R. 86 47.11 N 61.52 E
Žanatarlyk 86 44.16 N 73.12 E
Zanatepec 234 16.29 N 94.21 W
Záncara ≃ 34 39.18 N 3.18 W
Žandov 54 50.44 N 14.24 E
Zandvoort 52 52.22 N 4.32 E
Zandvoort, Circuit Autorace ♠ 52 52.24 N 4.32 E
Zane Hills ∧∧[2] 180 66.10 N 156.00 W
Zanesfield 216 40.20 N 83.41 W
Zanesville, Ind., U.S. 216 40.55 N 85.17 W
Zanesville, Ohio, U.S. 188 39.56 N 82.01 W
Zanevka 265a 59.56 N 30.31 E
Zangasso 150 12.09 N 5.37 W
Zangelan 84 39.06 N 46.39 E
Zangenstein 60 49.24 N 12.19 E
Zangezurskij Chrebet ∧∧ 84 39.30 N 45.54 E
Žangiztobe 86 49.16 N 81.18 E
Zangji 100 33.01 N 113.52 E
Zangjiaqiao 98 38.13 N 116.06 E
Zangjiazhuang 98 37.28 N 120.57 E
Zangmār ≃ 84 39.17 N 44.50 E
Zânguè ≃ 154 17.50 S 35.21 E
Zangwan 100 29.27 N 117.23 E
Zanhuang 98 37.38 N 114.26 E
Zaniasand 156 23.28 S 18.26 E
Zanjān 128 36.40 N 48.29 E
Zanjānrūd ≃ 128 37.08 N 47.47 E
Zanjón 252 27.55 S 64.15 W
Zanjón ≃ 252 31.16 S 67.41 W
Žankala ⊥ 86 44.29 N 64.05 E
Žannetty, Ostrov I 74 76.43 N 158.00 E
Zannone, Isola I 66 40.58 N 13.03 E
Zanri 102 28.58 N 100.50 E
Zante → Zákinthos I 38 37.52 N 20.44 E
Žanterek 86 47.57 N 54.21 E
Zanthus 162 31.02 S 123.34 E
Zantiébougou 150 11.24 N 7.15 W
Zanzibar 154 6.10 S 39.11 E
Zanzibar I 154 6.10 S 39.20 E
Zanzibar Channel ⋃ 154 6.00 S 39.00 E
Zanzibar Mjini □[4] 154 6.10 S 39.11 E
Zanzibar Shambini □[4] 154 6.08 S 39.14 E
Zaohe 98 34.03 N 118.07 E
Zaoheshi 100 26.53 N 114.41 E
Zaojiang 98 37.30 N 115.43 E
Zaojiaochang 107 29.58 N 106.11 E
Zaojiatuo 105 39.23 N 118.11 E
Zaokskoje 82 54.44 N 37.24 E
Zaolin 100 26.24 N 114.24 E
Zaorosongou 152 5.02 N 16.13 E
Zaō-san ∧ 92 38.08 N 140.26 E
Zaoshi, Zhg. 100 30.51 N 113.20 E
Zaoshi, Zhg. 100 26.22 N 112.50 E
Zaostroviči 76 52.54 N 26.47 E
Zaostrovje, S.S.S.R. 24 60.50 N 30.22 E
Zaostrovje, S.S.S.R. 76 60.38 N 33.16 E
Zaouia Bouhamed 148 35.25 N 5.00 W
Zaouia el Kahla (Fort Flatters) 148 28.09 N 6.43 E
Zaouiet Azmour 36 36.55 N 11.01 E
Zaouiet el Mgaïz 36 36.56 N 10.50 E
Zaoxi 100 30.13 N 119.30 E
Zaoyang 100 32.10 N 112.43 E
Zaozhuang 98 34.53 N 117.34 E
Zaoz'orje, S.S.S.R. 76 57.12 N 38.15 E
Zaoz'orje, S.S.S.R. 265b 55.34 N 38.02 E
Zaoz'ornyj 86 55.58 N 94.42 E
Zap 198 47.17 N 101.55 W
Zapadnaja Dvina 76 56.16 N 32.04 E
Zapadnaja Dvina (Daugava) ≃ 76 57.04 N 24.03 E
Zapadna Morava ≃ 38 43.42 N 21.23 E
Zapadno-Sibirskaja Nizmennost' ⌣ 72 60.00 N 75.00 E
Zapadnyj Alamedin, Pik ∧ 85 42.32 N 74.34 E
Zapadnyj Chrebet ∧∧ 89 50.00 N 142.25 E
Zapadnyj Karakol ≃ 85 42.08 N 74.05 E
Zapadnyj Sajan ∧∧ 74 53.00 N 94.00 E
Západočeský Kraj □[4] 30 49.45 N 13.00 E
Západoslovenský Kraj □[4] 30 48.20 N 18.00 E
Zapala 252 38.54 S 70.04 W
Zapardiel ≃ 34 41.29 N 5.02 W
Zapata 196 26.52 N 99.19 W
Zapata, Península de ≻[1] 240p 22.20 N 81.35 W
Zapatera, Isla I 236 11.45 N 85.50 W
Zapatoca 246 6.49 N 73.17 W
Zapato Chino Creek ≃ 226 36.09 N 120.11 W
Zapatosa, Ciénaga de ◎ 246 9.05 N 73.50 W
Zapfendorf 56 50.01 N 10.56 E
Zapiola 258 35.03 S 59.03 W
Zaplavnoje, S.S.S.R. 80 52.58 N 51.44 E
Zaplavnoje, S.S.S.R. 80 48.43 N 45.01 E
Zapl'usje 76 58.26 N 29.43 E
Zapokrovskij 88 50.50 N 119.05 E

Symbols in the index entries represent the broad categories identified in the key at the right. Symbols with superior numbers (∧∧[2]) identify subcategories (see complete key on page I · 30).

Kartensymbole in dem Registerverzeichnis stellen die rechts in Schlüssel erklärten Kategorien dar. Symbole mit hochgestellten Ziffern (∧∧[2]) bezeichnen Unterabteilungen einer Kategorie (vgl. vollständiger Schlüssel auf Seite I · 30).

Los símbolos incluídos en el texto del índice representan las grandes categorias identificadas con la clave a la derecha. Los símbolos con numeros en su parte superior (∧∧[2]) identifican las subcategorías (véase la clave completa en la página I · 30).

Les symboles de l'index représentent les catégories indiquées dans la légende à droite. Les symboles suivis d'un indice (∧∧[2]) représentent des sous-catégories (voir légende complète à la page I · 30).

Os símbolos incluídos no texto do índice representam as grandes categorias identificadas com a chave à direita. Os símbolos com números em sua parte superior (∧∧[2]) identificam as subcategorias (veja-se a chave completa à página I · 30).

Symbol	English	Deutsch	Español	Français	Português
∧	Mountain	Berg	Montaña	Montagne	Montanha
∧∧	Mountains	Berge	Montañas	Montagnes	Montanhas
)(	Pass	Pass	Paso	Col	Passo
∨	Valley, Canyon	Tal, Cañon	Valle, Cañón	Vallée, Canyon	Vale, Canhão
⌣	Plain	Ebene	Llano	Plaine	Planície
≻	Cape	Kap	Cabo	Cap	Cabo
I	Island	Insel	Isla	Île	Ilha
II	Islands	Inseln	Islas	Îles	Ilhas
•	Other Topographic Features	Andere Topographische Objekte	Otros Elementos Topográficos	Autres données topographiques	Outros Elementos Topográficos

ESPAÑOL

Nombre	Página	Lat.°′	Long.°′ W=Oeste
Zapol'arnyj, S.S.S.R.	24	69.26 N	30.48 E
Zapol'arnyj, S.S.S.R.	24	67.30 N	63.42 E
Zapolje	76	58.23 N	29.41 E
Zapopan	234	20.43 N	103.24 W
Zaporojie → Zaporožje	78	47.50 N	35.10 E
Zaporozh'ye → Zaporožje	78	47.50 N	35.10 E
Zaporožje, S.S.S.R.	78	47.50 N	35.10 E
Zaporožje, S.S.S.R.	83	48.14 N	38.41 E
Zaporožskaja	78	45.23 N	36.52 E
Zapotal	246	1.40 S	79.28 W
Zapotillo	246	4.25 S	80.31 W
Zapotiltic	234	19.37 N	103.26 W
Zapotitlán	234	19.31 N	103.44 W
Zapotitlán [8]	286a	19.18 N	99.02 W
Zapotitlán, Punta	234	18.33 N	94.49 W
Zapotitlán Tablas	234	17.25 N	98.45 W
Zapotlán, Laguna	234	19.45 N	103.30 W
Zapotlanejo	234	20.38 N	103.04 W
Zapovednoje	76	55.04 N	21.24 E
Zaprudn'a	82	56.34 N	37.26 E
Zaqqūṭ	146	28.29 N	19.37 E
Zara → Zadar, Jugo.	36	44.07 N	15.14 E
Zara, Tür.	130	39.55 N	37.46 E
Zarāf, Baḥr az-	140	9.25 N	31.10 E
Zaragoza, Col.	246	7.30 N	74.52 W
Zaragoza, Esp.	34	41.38 N	0.53 W
Zaragoza, Méx.	232	31.39 N	106.20 W
Zaragoza, Méx.	232	28.29 N	100.55 W
Zaragoza, Méx.	234	23.58 N	99.46 W
Zaragoza, Méx.	234	22.02 N	100.44 W
Zaragoza, Méx.	234	19.46 N	97.33 W
Zaragoza [7]	286a	19.34 N	99.15 W
Zarajsk	82	54.46 N	38.53 E
Zaramag	84	42.43 N	43.57 E
Zarand	128	30.48 N	56.35 E
Zarand, Munții	38	46.10 N	22.15 E
Zaranda Hill [2]	150	10.15 N	9.35 E
Zarand-e Kohneh	128	35.17 N	50.30 E
Zaranj	128	31.06 N	61.53 E
Zarasai	76	55.44 N	26.15 E
Zárate	258	34.06 S	59.02 W
Zaratí	236	8.28 N	80.26 W
Zarauz	34	43.17 N	2.10 W
Zaraza	246	9.21 N	65.19 W
Žarbulak	86	46.05 N	82.04 E
Zarcero	236	10.11 N	84.23 W
Zardaly	85	39.38 N	70.57 E
Zard Kūh	128	32.22 N	50.04 E
Zardob	84	40.13 N	47.43 E
Zarečensk	24	66.41 N	33.18 E
Zarečje, S.S.S.R.	24	63.08 N	44.46 E
Zarečje, S.S.S.R.	76	56.52 N	33.50 E
Zarečje, S.S.S.R.	76	58.56 N	39.40 E
Zarečje, S.S.S.R.	265b	55.41 N	37.23 E
Zarečnoje	78	51.48 N	26.06 E
Zarečnyj, S.S.S.R.	76	53.45 N	39.35 E
Zarečnyj, S.S.S.R.	80	57.28 N	42.18 E
Zarečnyj, S.S.S.R.	80	53.13 N	45.13 E
Zarembo Island	180	56.20 N	132.50 W
Zarephath	276	40.32 N	74.35 W
Zarezskoje, Ozero	120	38.12 N	72.45 E
Zarghūn Shahr	120	32.51 N	68.25 E
Zari	146	13.04 N	12.43 E
Zaria	150	11.07 N	7.44 E
Zarīneh	128	37.05 N	45.54 E
Zarinskaja	86	53.43 N	84.58 E
Žarkamys	86	47.56 N	56.26 E
Žarki	30	50.38 N	19.22 E
Žarkova	86	58.00 N	87.17 E
Žarkovskij	76	55.52 N	32.17 E
Žarma	86	48.48 N	80.50 E
Zarnān	267d	35.41 N	51.09 E
Zărnești	38	45.34 N	25.19 E
Žarnovica	30	48.29 N	18.44 E
Zarow	54	53.46 N	14.02 E
Zarqā', Nahr az-	132	32.07 N	35.33 E
Zarqā', Raqabat az-	140	9.14 N	29.44 E
Zarqān	128	29.46 N	52.43 E
Zarqūn	142	31.07 N	30.28 E
Zarrentin	54	53.35 N	10.55 E
Žarsuat	86	46.27 N	80.48 E
Zarten	58	47.58 N	7.56 E
Zarubino, S.S.S.R.	76	58.44 N	33.28 E
Zarubino, S.S.S.R.	89	42.40 N	131.04 E
Zaruma	246	3.41 S	79.37 W
Zarumilla	246	3.30 S	80.16 W
Żary (Sorau)	30	51.38 N	15.09 E
Žaryk	86	48.52 N	72.51 E
Žaryn'	76	53.47 N	33.04 E
Zarzaïtine	148	28.18 N	9.48 E
Zarzal	246	4.24 N	76.04 W
Zarzis	148	33.30 N	11.07 E
Zarzuela, Arroyo de la	266a	40.29 N	3.45 W
Zarzuela, Hipodromo de la	266a	40.28 N	3.45 W
Zasa	76	56.17 N	25.58 E
Zaschendorf	54	53.42 N	11.37 E
Zaschwitz	54	51.10 N	13.02 E
Zašejek	24	67.25 N	32.28 E
Zasenbeck	54	52.40 N	10.51 E
Zasieki	54	51.43 N	14.43 E
Zāskār	123	34.10 N	77.20 E
Zāskār Mountains	120	33.00 N	78.00 E
Žaškov	78	49.15 N	30.06 E
Zaslavl'	76	54.01 N	27.15 E
Zasosna	78	50.37 N	38.23 E
Žastalap	80	49.11 N	50.24 E
Zastava	24	59.12 N	46.46 E
Zastavna	78	48.31 N	25.50 E
Zastron	158	30.18 S	27.07 E
Zasulje, S.S.S.R.	24	64.41 N	47.48 E
Zasulje, S.S.S.R.	76	53.34 N	26.50 E
Žatec	54	50.18 N	13.32 E
Zaterečnyj	84	44.47 N	43.12 E
Zatišje	78	47.19 N	29.51 E
Z'at'kovo	86	53.36 N	80.20 E
Zatobol'sk	86	53.12 N	63.43 E
Zaton	86	53.18 N	83.49 E
Zauche [1]	54	52.15 N	12.35 E
Zauchwitz	54	52.12 N	13.02 E
Zaural'skoje Plato [1]	86	53.00 N	62.00 E
Zavalje	78	48.13 N	30.01 E
Zavalla	194	31.09 N	94.26 W
Zaval'noje	76	52.02 N	39.51 E
Zaventem	50	50.53 N	4.28 E
Zavet	38	43.46 N	26.40 E
Zavetnoje	80	47.07 N	43.52 E
Zavety Iljiča	89	49.02 N	140.17 E
Zavidovići	38	44.27 N	18.09 E
Zavidovka	82	54.16 N	38.49 E
Zavidovo	82	56.32 N	36.32 E
Zavitinsk	89	50.07 N	129.27 E
Zavjalovo, S.S.S.R.	80	56.47 N	53.23 E
Zavjalovo, S.S.S.R.	86	54.30 N	82.27 E
Zavlekov	60	49.20 N	13.30 E
Zavod Michajlovskij	80	56.32 N	54.17 E
Zavodo-Petrovskij	86	56.50 N	66.45 E
Zavodoukovsk	86	56.33 N	66.32 E
Zavodouspenskoje	86	56.51 N	65.00 E
Zavodovski Island	18	56.20 S	27.35 W
Zavodskoj, S.S.S.R.	78	48.24 N	40.19 E
Zavodskoj, S.S.S.R.	86	53.04 N	84.25 E
Zavolžje	80	56.37 N	43.26 E
Zavolžsk	80	57.30 N	42.10 E

FRANÇAIS

Nom	Page	Lat.°′	Long.°′ W=Ouest
Zavolžskoje	80	46.59 N	47.37 E
Zavoronežskoje	80	52.53 N	40.33 E
Zavorovo	82	55.20 N	38.13 E
Zāwa	120	28.04 N	66.23 E
Zawadzkie	30	50.37 N	18.29 E
Zawel	144	3.33 N	43.47 E
Zawi	154	17.13 S	30.02 E
Zawichost	30	50.49 N	21.52 E
Zawiercie	30	50.30 N	19.25 E
Zawīlah	146	26.10 N	15.07 E
Zāwiyat 'Abd al-Qādir	142	31.02 N	29.49 E
Zāwiyat Abū Musallam	273c	29.56 N	31.10 E
Zāwiyat al-Amwāt	142	28.04 N	30.50 E
Zāwiyat al-Bayḍā' (Beida)	146	32.46 N	21.43 E
Zawiyat al-Judhāmī	142	28.42 N	30.54 E
Zāwiyat Masūs	146	31.33 N	21.03 E
Zāwiyat Nābit	273c	30.07 N	31.09 E
Zāwiyat Razīn	142	30.25 N	30.51 E
Zāwiyat Saqr	142	30.56 N	30.12 E
Zawiyat Shammās	140	31.31 N	26.24 E
Zāwiyat Sīdī Ghāzī	142	31.03 N	30.05 E
Zāwiyet an-Najjār	273c	30.11 N	31.17 E
Zawr, Ra's az-, Ar. Sa.	128	27.25 N	49.20 E
Zawr, Ra's az-, Ar. Sa.	128	28.44 N	48.24 E
Zāyandeh	128	32.20 N	52.50 E
Zaydābād	120	34.17 N	69.07 E
Zaza	240p	21.37 N	79.32 W
Zaza del Medio	240p	22.00 N	79.23 W
Zazafotsy	157b	22.13 S	46.26 E
Zāzamt, Wādī	146	30.58 N	14.49 E
Zazir, Oued	148	20.25 N	5.30 E
Zban	86	48.53 N	63.58 E
Zbaraž	78	49.39 N	25.47 E
Zbąszyń	30	52.16 N	15.55 E
Zbąszynek	30	52.15 N	15.50 E
Zbiroh	60	49.52 N	13.47 E
Zborov	78	49.39 N	25.08 E
Zborovy	60	49.23 N	13.31 E
Zbraslav	30	49.59 N	14.24 E
Zbruč	78	48.32 N	26.26 E
Zbůch	60	49.41 N	13.14 E
Ždanov	83	47.06 N	37.33 E
Ždanova	86	58.37 N	88.58 E
Ždanovo	78	48.14 N	34.44 E
Ždanovsk	84	39.47 N	47.37 E
Ždany	78	50.12 N	33.13 E
Žd'ár, Česko.	60	50.03 N	13.28 E
Žd'ár, Česko.	60	49.52 N	12.35 E
Žd'ár nad Sazavou	30	49.34 N	15.57 E
Ždiar	30	49.17 N	20.16 E
Zdice	60	49.55 N	13.59 E
Zdíkovec	60	49.05 N	13.42 E
Zdolbunov	78	50.31 N	26.15 E
Zdroje [8]	54	53.20 N	14.40 E
Zduńska Wola	30	51.36 N	18.57 E
Zduny	30	51.39 N	17.24 E
Zdvuž	78	51.01 N	30.02 E
Zealandia	184	51.37 N	107.45 W
Zearing	190	42.10 N	93.18 W
Zeballos	182	49.49 N	126.50 W
Zeballos, Monte	254	47.01 S	71.42 W
Zebila	150	10.56 N	0.29 W
Zebl'aki	80	58.23 N	45.45 E
Žebrák	60	49.52 N	13.56 E
Zebulon, Ga., U.S.	192	33.06 N	84.21 W
Zebulon, N.C., U.S.	192	35.49 N	78.19 W
Zechlinerhütte	54	53.09 N	12.51 E
Zeda, Monte	58	46.03 N	8.32 E
Zedang	120	29.16 N	91.46 E
Zeddine, Oued	34	36.15 N	1.48 E
Zedelgem	50	51.09 N	3.08 E
Zederhaus	64	47.09 N	13.30 E
Zeebrugge	50	51.20 N	3.12 E
Zeehan	166	41.53 S	145.20 E
Zeeland, Ned.	52	51.42 N	5.40 E
Zeeland, Mich., U.S.	216	42.49 N	86.01 W
Zeeland, N. Dak., U.S.	198	45.58 N	99.50 W
Zeeland [4]	52	51.27 N	3.45 E
Zeelandbrug [5]	52	51.37 N	3.53 E
Zeerust	156	25.33 S	26.06 E
Zeesen	54	52.16 N	13.38 E
Zeestow	264a	52.34 N	12.58 E
Zeeuws-Vlaanderen [1]	52	51.19 N	3.45 E
Zefat (Safad)	132	32.58 N	35.30 E
Žegalovo, S.S.S.R.	80	54.43 N	43.25 E
Žegalovo, S.S.S.R.	265b	55.54 N	37.59 E
Žegdoči	89	53.20 N	120.49 E
Zege	144	11.42 N	37.23 E
Zegher, Hamada	146	27.18 N	11.30 E
Zégoua	150	10.30 N	5.40 W
Zegrir, Oued	148	32.43 N	5.00 E
Zeguo	100	28.32 N	121.20 E
Zehden → Cedynia	30	52.50 N	14.14 E
Zehdenick	54	52.59 N	13.20 E
Zehlendorf	54	52.47 N	13.23 E
Zehlendorf [8]	264a	52.26 N	13.15 E
Zeigler	194	37.54 N	89.03 W
Zeil	56	50.01 N	10.35 E
Zeil, Mount	162	23.24 S	132.23 E
Zeila	144	11.21 N	43.30 E
Zeiselmauer	264b	48.20 N	16.11 E
Zeist	52	52.05 N	5.15 E
Zeithain	54	51.19 N	13.19 E
Zeitlarn	60	49.05 N	12.06 E
Zeitz	54	51.03 N	12.08 E
Zeja	89	53.45 N	127.15 E
Zeja	89	50.13 N	127.35 E
Zekeriyaköy	267b	41.11 N	29.01 E
Zekiah Swamp Run	208	38.25 N	76.57 W
Žel'abino	265b	55.52 N	37.11 E
Žel'abužskaja	82	54.36 N	36.32 E
Želannoje	83	48.13 N	37.25 E
Zelaya	258	34.21 S	58.52 W
Zelaya [5]	236	13.00 N	84.00 W
Želča	76	58.19 N	27.40 E
Žel'dyadyr [1]	86	49.30 N	68.30 E
Želdybino	82	56.14 N	39.02 E
Zele	50	51.04 N	4.02 E
Żelechów	30	51.49 N	21.54 E
Zelee, Cape	175e	9.45 S	161.34 E
Zelená Lhota	60	49.14 N	13.10 E
Zelencovo	76	59.52 N	44.59 E
Zelenčukskaja	84	43.52 N	41.36 E
Zelenec	24	62.29 N	55.16 E
Zelenga	80	46.11 N	48.37 E
Zelengora	38	43.15 N	18.45 E
Zelenoborskij	24	66.49 N	32.18 E
Zelenogorsk	76	60.12 N	29.42 E
Zelenogradsk	76	54.58 N	20.29 E
Zelenokumsk	84	44.24 N	43.53 E
Zelenovka	78	46.59 N	36.14 E
Zeletin	38	46.03 N	27.23 E
Železinka	86	53.32 N	75.18 E
Železn'a	82	54.31 N	37.28 E
Železná Ruda	60	49.09 N	13.14 E
Železnik	38	44.43 N	20.23 E
Železnodorožnyj, S.S.S.R.	24	67.58 N	64.38 E
Železnodorožnyj, S.S.S.R.	24	62.37 N	50.55 E
Železnodorožnyj, S.S.S.R.	76	54.22 N	21.19 E
Železnodorožnyj, S.S.S.R.	82	55.45 N	38.01 E
Železnodorožnyj, S.S.S.R.	86	43.04 N	58.50 E

PORTUGUÊS

Nome	Página	Lat.°′	Long.°′ W=Oeste
Železnogorsk	76	52.22 N	35.23 E
Železnogorsk-Ilimskij	88	56.37 N	104.08 E
Železnoje	83	48.19 N	37.51 E
Železnovodsk	84	44.08 N	43.02 E
Zelienople	214	40.48 N	80.08 W
Zeligar	130	38.04 N	41.49 E
Zelina	36	45.58 N	16.15 E
Zell, B.R.D.	56	50.01 N	7.10 E
Zell, B.R.D.	58	47.42 N	7.51 E
Zell, Schw.	58	47.09 N	7.55 E
Zella-Mehlis	54	50.39 N	10.39 E
Zell am Harmersbach	58	48.21 N	8.04 E
Zell am Moos	64	47.54 N	13.19 E
Zell am See	64	47.19 N	12.47 E
Zell am Ziller	64	47.14 N	11.53 E
Zellersee	58	47.42 N	9.03 E
Zeller See	64	47.19 N	12.48 E
Zellingen	56	49.53 N	9.43 E
Zellwood	220	28.44 N	81.36 W
Želon'	78	51.33 N	29.51 E
Zel'onaja Rošča, S.S.S.R.	76	60.10 N	29.08 E
Zel'onaja Rošča, S.S.S.R.	80	54.29 N	52.02 E
Zel'onaja Rošča, S.S.S.R.	83	47.07 N	40.13 E
Zel'onodol'sk	80	55.51 N	48.33 E
Zel'onoje	78	47.43 N	33.12 E
Zel'onoje Ozero	88	53.40 N	116.36 E
Zel'onyj, S.S.S.R.	80	48.07 N	51.31 E
Zel'onyj, S.S.S.R.	80	51.10 N	50.41 E
Zel'onyj, Ostrov (Shibotsu-tō)	92a	43.30 N	146.09 E
Zel'onyj Bor	76	54.01 N	28.28 E
Zelo Surrigone	266b	45.23 N	8.59 E
Zelów	30	51.28 N	19.13 E
Žel'tau Ajtau	86	44.30 N	74.00 E
Zeltiņi	76	57.22 N	26.46 E
Zeltweg	61	47.11 N	14.45 E
Želudok	76	53.36 N	24.59 E
Zel'va, S.S.S.R.	76	53.08 N	24.48 E
Želva, S.S.S.R.	76	55.13 N	25.06 E
Zel'v'anka	76	53.24 N	24.32 E
Zelzate	50	51.12 N	3.49 E
Žemaičių Naumiestis	76	55.22 N	21.42 E
Žemaitija [1]	76	55.45 N	23.00 E
Žembejtinskij	80	50.30 N	52.39 E
Zembin	76	54.22 N	28.13 E
Zembla Septentrional → Severnaja Zeml'a	74	79.30 N	98.00 E
Zembra, Île	148	37.08 N	10.48 E
Žemčug	88	51.41 N	102.24 E
Zemcy	76	56.15 N	32.23 E
Zemetčino	80	53.30 N	42.38 E
Zemgale [9]	76	56.30 N	25.00 E
Zemio	154	5.02 N	25.08 E
Zeml'a Franca-Iosifa	12	81.00 N	55.00 E
Zeml'ansk	78	51.54 N	38.44 E
Zemmer	56	49.53 N	6.41 E
Zemmora	34	35.44 N	0.45 E
Zemmur [1]	148	24.50 N	12.15 W
Zemo-Kedi	84	41.26 N	46.24 E
Zemoul, Oued	148	29.12 N	7.52 W
Žemovo	82	54.45 N	38.49 E
Zempin	54	54.04 N	13.57 E
Zempoala	234	19.24 N	96.24 W
Zempoala	234	19.27 N	96.23 W
Zempoala, Punta	234	19.28 N	96.19 W
Zemst	50	50.59 N	4.28 E
Zenas	218	39.07 N	85.29 W
Zendeh Jān	128	34.21 N	61.45 E
Zeneta	184	50.44 N	102.02 W
Zengcheng	100	23.19 N	113.49 E
Zengjiang	100	23.09 N	113.46 E
Zengjiawan	105	39.22 N	118.24 E
Zengkouhe	105	39.19 N	117.37 E
Zenica	38	44.12 N	17.55 E
Zenifim, Har [2]	132	30.06 N	34.51 E
Zenith	224	47.23 N	122.19 W
Zen'kov	78	50.13 N	34.22 E
Zenn	56	49.31 N	10.58 E
Zenna	58	46.06 N	8.45 E
Zenon Park	184	53.04 N	103.45 W
Zenon Videla Dorna	258	35.33 S	58.53 W
Zenson di Piave	64	45.41 N	12.29 E
Zentralafrikanische Republik → Central African Republic [1]	136	7.00 N	21.00 E
Zentral-Friedhof	264b	48.10 N	16.16 E
Zentral-Massiv → Central, Massif	32	45.00 N	3.10 E
Zentsūji	96	34.14 N	133.47 E
Zenza do Itombe	152	9.16 S	14.13 E
Zenzeli	80	45.56 N	47.03 E
Zepernick	54	52.39 N	13.32 E
Zephyr	196	31.41 N	98.48 W
Zephyr Cove	226	39.00 N	119.57 W
Zephyrhills	220	28.14 N	82.11 W
Zepu	120	38.13 N	77.16 E
Zeralda	34	36.41 N	2.53 E
Zeravšan	85	39.11 N	68.40 E
Zeravšan	72	39.22 N	63.45 E
Zeravšanskij Chrebet	85	39.15 N	68.30 E
Zerbst	54	51.58 N	12.04 E
Žerdevka	80	51.51 N	41.28 E
Žerebec	83	48.57 N	38.03 E
Zereh, Gowd-e	128	29.45 N	61.50 E
Zerenda	86	52.55 N	69.10 E
Zerenik	130	39.20 N	39.05 E
Žerev	78	51.12 N	29.04 E
Zerf	56	49.36 N	6.41 E
Zerga, Merja	34	34.51 N	6.17 W
Zergenta	80	47.42 N	45.12 E
Zeri	62	44.21 N	9.46 E
Zerind	38	46.37 N	21.31 E
Żerków	30	52.05 N	17.34 E
Zermatt	58	46.02 N	7.45 E
Zernez	58	46.43 N	10.05 E
Zernograd	78	46.50 N	40.19 E
Žernovka	82	54.49 N	37.46 E
Zernsdorf	54	52.18 N	13.41 E
Zero	64	45.32 N	12.22 E
Zeroud, Oued	36	35.50 N	10.13 E
Zerqan	38	41.30 N	20.21 E
Žertv 9-go Janvar'a 1905, Kladbišče	265a	55.51 N	30.27 E
Žešart	24	62.05 N	49.34 E
Zestafoni	84	42.07 N	43.02 E
Žest'anka	80	51.36 N	49.24 E
Zestienhoven, Luchthaven	52	51.58 N	4.30 E
Žestoki	82	56.19 N	36.22 E
Žestylevo	82	56.24 N	37.39 E
Zetel	52	53.25 N	7.58 E
Žetybaj	80	48.51 N	48.04 E
Žetykol', Ozero	86	51.02 N	60.54 E
Žetysaj	85	40.47 N	68.16 E
Zeulenroda	54	50.39 N	11.58 E
Zeuthen	54	52.20 N	13.37 E
Zeuthener See	264a	52.21 N	13.39 E
Zeven	52	53.18 N	9.16 E
Zevenaar	52	51.56 N	6.05 E
Zevenbergen	52	51.38 N	4.36 E
Zevenbergschen Hoek	52	51.41 N	4.40 E
Zevenwouden [1]	52	52.57 N	6.00 E
Zevio	64	45.22 N	11.08 E
Zevker	130	40.00 N	38.51 E
Zeyādah Kot	272b	22.27 N	88.20 E
Zeyawadi	110	18.33 N	96.26 E
Zeyse	144	5.46 N	37.22 E
Zeytinburnu [8]	267b	40.59 N	28.54 E
Zeytindağ	130	38.58 N	27.04 E
Zeyveh	84	39.07 N	47.42 E
Zeze	270	35.00 N	135.54 E
Zêzere	34	39.28 N	8.20 W
Zghartā	130	34.24 N	35.54 E
Zgierz	30	51.52 N	19.25 E
Zgorzelec	30	51.12 N	15.01 E
Zgurovka	78	50.31 N	31.46 E
Zhabuchakahu	120	31.30 N	84.00 E
Zhada	120	31.30 N	79.30 E
Zhage	102	26.20 N	103.51 E
Zhagenasongduo	102	33.12 N	93.33 E
Zhaha	102	36.20 N	94.37 E
Zhahasutai	86	42.58 N	85.20 E
Zhaihe	100	31.10 N	114.52 E
Zhaili, Zhg.	98	35.30 N	118.57 E
Zhaili, Zhg.	100	27.42 N	117.22 E
Zhailing	98	40.59 N	116.53 E
Zhaiqiao	106	31.35 N	119.55 E
Zhaitang	105	39.57 N	115.42 E
Zhaitun	104	41.46 N	122.06 E
Zhakou, Zhg.	102	29.59 N	112.10 E
Zhakou, Zhg.	106	30.23 N	120.47 E
Zhakou, Zhg.	106	30.13 N	120.08 E
Zhalaiteqi (Yindeer)	89	46.40 N	122.55 E
Zhalantun → Butehaqi	89	48.02 N	122.43 E
Zhalanyingzi	104	41.29 N	120.37 E
Zhalinghu	102	34.53 N	97.58 E
Zhalinhu	120	31.10 N	88.15 E
Zhalun	120	32.25 N	81.35 E
Zhaluomude	89	49.13 N	120.22 E
Zhaluteqi (Lubei)	89	44.37 N	120.58 E
Zhangbei	98	41.04 N	114.48 E
Zhangcang	98	35.54 N	119.57 E
Zhangcun, Zhg.	100	33.20 N	115.59 E
Zhangcun, Zhg.	106	30.40 N	119.57 E
Zhangcun, Zhg.	106	30.28 N	119.22 E
Zhangcunjie	100	28.50 N	117.57 E
Zhangdang	104	41.54 N	124.05 E
Zhangdatun	98	34.14 N	116.38 E
Zhangde	100	34.07 N	113.27 E
Zhangdian	100	34.14 N	119.19 E
Zhangdiying	89	50.30 N	127.16 E
Zhangduhu	100	30.40 N	114.42 E
Zhangfang	105	39.38 N	115.34 E
Zhangfengji	98	35.14 N	116.01 E
Zhanggao	98	40.38 N	113.44 E
Zhanggezhuang, Zhg.	98	36.47 N	119.47 E
Zhanggezhuang, Zhg.	105	40.17 N	116.42 E
Zhanggezhuang, Zhg.	105	40.08 N	116.56 E
Zhanggou	104	42.07 N	124.06 E
Zhangguangcailing	89	45.25 N	129.20 E
Zhangguizhuang	105	39.07 N	117.18 E
Zhanggutai	98	42.40 N	122.28 E
Zhanghe	98	36.10 N	115.05 E
Zhanghezhuang	105	38.56 N	114.56 E
Zhanghuang	102	22.03 N	109.24 E
Zhanghuanggang	106	32.07 N	120.30 E
Zhanghuban	100	26.23 N	118.29 E
Zhangji	98	34.08 N	117.24 E
Zhangjiachang, Zhg.	107	29.33 N	104.54 E
Zhangjiachang, Zhg.	107	29.26 N	104.34 E
Zhangjiachang, Zhg.	107	29.57 N	103.48 E
Zhangjiacun	106	31.08 N	119.42 E
Zhangjiadian	105	39.44 N	114.54 E
Zhangjiadu	100	30.38 N	118.13 E
Zhangjiagou	100	30.18 N	113.22 E
Zhangjiaji	100	32.09 N	112.23 E
Zhangjiajie	104	41.28 N	124.08 E
Zhangjiakou (Kalgan)	105	40.50 N	114.53 E
Zhangjiapang	100	30.25 N	115.47 E
Zhangjiapu	104	41.18 N	122.02 E
Zhangjiaqiao, Zhg.	106	31.36 N	120.36 E
Zhangjiaqiao, Zhg.	107	29.56 N	106.12 E
Zhangjiaqiao, Zhg.	107	30.02 N	104.15 E
Zhangjiatou	106	31.38 N	119.05 E
Zhangjiatun, Zhg.	104	41.05 N	121.44 E
Zhangjiatun, Zhg.	105	40.37 N	114.57 E
Zhangjiawa	105	40.10 N	117.52 E
Zhangjiawan	105	39.51 N	116.41 E
Zhangjiawopu	104	41.10 N	122.17 E
Zhangjiayingzi	104	42.04 N	120.57 E
Zhangjiegang	100	30.34 N	112.51 E
Zhangjingqiao	106	31.39 N	120.27 E
Zhangjinhe	100	30.14 N	112.35 E
Zhangliangdian	100	33.42 N	113.02 E
Zhangliantang	106	31.01 N	121.02 E
Zhangling	98	36.32 N	119.29 E
Zhangluji	98	36.16 N	115.33 E
Zhangmang	100	32.03 N	114.32 E
Zhangming	102	31.49 N	104.51 E
Zhangmu	100	27.01 N	112.38 E
Zhangmuqiao	100	31.26 N	116.44 E
Zhangmutou	100	22.55 N	114.05 E
Zhangping	100	25.19 N	117.25 E
Zhangpu, Zhg.	100	24.09 N	117.36 E
Zhangpu, Zhg.	106	31.17 N	120.57 E
Zhangqiangzhen	98	42.39 N	122.59 E
Zhangqiao	100	32.21 N	117.38 E
Zhangqiu	98	36.48 N	117.28 E
Zhangsanta	102	39.37 N	110.14 E
Zhangsanying	98	41.34 N	117.39 E
Zhangshitai	104	41.50 N	122.51 E
Zhangshui, Zhg.	100	25.51 N	114.46 E
Zhangshui, Zhg.	100	31.05 N	113.11 E
Zhangshuping	102	31.20 N	111.02 E
Zhangshuxia	100	25.54 N	112.45 E
Zhangtaitai	104	40.59 N	121.05 E
Zhangtaizi	104	41.22 N	123.16 E
Zhangting	100	30.02 N	121.19 E
Zhangwan	100	26.43 N	119.36 E
Zhangwenpu	105	40.26 N	116.04 E
Zhangwu	104	42.22 N	122.31 E
Zhangwucun	106	30.47 N	119.33 E
Zhangwutaimen	104	42.16 N	122.42 E
Zhangxinliuji	100	33.43 N	115.48 E
Zhangyan, Zhg.	106	31.48 N	119.44 E
Zhangyan, Zhg.	106	30.48 N	121.16 E
Zhangyangongtun	104	40.58 N	120.46 E
Zhangye (Ganzhou)	102	38.57 N	100.37 E
Zhangze	106	30.55 N	121.15 E
Zhangzhishan	106	31.56 N	121.01 E
Zhangzhou (Longxi)	100	24.33 N	117.39 E
Zhangzhu	106	31.16 N	119.37 E
Zhangzhuang, Zhg.	98	37.03 N	116.32 E
Zhangzhuang, Zhg.	106	31.57 N	119.52 E
Zhangzidao	98	39.00 N	122.44 E
Zhanhua	98	37.41 N	117.46 E
Zhanjiajing	107	29.15 N	104.55 E
Zhanjiang	102	21.16 N	110.28 E
Zhanjiaqiao, Zhg.	100	29.19 N	113.34 E
Zhanjiaqiao, Zhg.	106	30.25 N	120.08 E
Zhanyang	100	25.30 N	119.28 E
Zhanyi	102	25.38 N	103.43 E
Zhanyu	89	44.31 N	122.37 E
Zhanzhai	98	35.45 N	118.09 E
Zhaoan	100	23.44 N	116.11 E
Zhaoanwan	100	23.38 N	117.19 E
Zhaoanxi	100	23.42 N	117.13 E
Zhaobeikou	105	38.55 N	116.06 E
Zhaochuanbao	105	40.41 N	115.18 E
Zhaocun	105	39.35 N	116.14 E
Zhaodong	89	46.05 N	125.59 E
Zhaogezhuang, Zhg.	98	37.27 N	120.37 E
Zhaogezhuang, Zhg.	105	39.45 N	118.24 E
Zhaoguang	89	48.07 N	126.43 E
Zhaohezhen	100	33.12 N	112.49 E
Zhaohuazhen	107	29.02 N	105.08 E
Zhaojiagou	104	40.47 N	123.27 E
Zhaojiapuzi, Zhg.	104	40.51 N	123.49 E
Zhaojiapuzi, Zhg.	104	40.43 N	122.41 E
Zhaojiaqiao	106	30.44 N	121.12 E
Zhaojiatangfang	104	42.07 N	122.57 E
Zhaojiatun	104	41.24 N	121.53 E
Zhaojiawopeng	104	42.30 N	123.06 E
Zhaojiaying	105	38.58 N	116.42 E
Zhaojue	102	28.15 N	102.50 E
Zhaoling [1]	104	41.51 N	123.53 E
Zhaomaozhuang	105	39.28 N	117.59 E
Zhaomutun	104	41.10 N	121.38 E
Zhaoping	102	24.03 N	110.52 E
Zhaoqiao	100	28.42 N	114.45 E
Zhaoqing (Gaoyao)	102	23.03 N	112.27 E
Zhaosu	86	43.06 N	81.08 E
Zhaosuhe	98	42.34 N	119.38 E
Zhaotanjie	100	29.42 N	116.48 E
Zhaotong	102	27.19 N	103.48 E
Zhaotun	104	41.54 N	121.59 E
Zhaoxian, Zhg.	98	37.45 N	114.46 E
Zhaoxian, Zhg.	98	35.44 N	118.55 E
Zhaoxing	89	47.43 N	131.19 E
Zhaoyachang	107	29.00 N	105.35 E
Zhaoyi	105	39.55 N	116.43 E
Zhaoyuan, Zhg.	89	45.31 N	125.09 E
Zhaoyuan, Zhg.	98	37.22 N	120.24 E
Zhaozhou	89	45.41 N	125.21 E
Zhaozhuang	98	34.45 N	116.27 E
Zhaozhuangzi	105	39.10 N	117.20 E
Zhapu	106	30.36 N	121.05 E
Zhasakeqi	102	39.27 N	109.40 E
Zhaxigang	120	32.32 N	79.41 E
Zhayi	102	28.34 N	99.09 E
Zhaze	106	32.09 N	119.29 E
Zhdanov → Ždanov	83	47.06 N	37.33 E
Zhecheng	98	34.06 N	115.19 E
Zheduoshankou	102	30.05 N	101.44 E
Zhegao	100	31.46 N	117.45 E
Zhegu	120	28.43 N	91.43 E
Zhejiang [4]	100	29.00 N	120.00 E
Zhelang	100	22.43 N	115.32 E
Zhelin, Zhg.	100	29.14 N	115.30 E
Zhelin, Zhg.	106	30.50 N	121.29 E
Zhen'an	102	33.27 N	109.01 E
Zhenbeikou	102	39.15 N	106.17 E
Zhenbiancheng	105	40.10 N	115.49 E
Zhenchang	106	32.04 N	121.02 E
Zheng'an	102	28.31 N	107.29 E
Zheng'anbao	104	41.43 N	121.56 E
Zhengcun	105	39.13 N	115.40 E
Zhengding	98	38.10 N	114.34 E
Zhengdongyu	106	31.59 N	120.10 E
Zhengfeng	102	25.23 N	105.41 E
Zhengguanchang	107	29.54 N	106.35 E
Zhengguo	100	23.25 N	113.53 E
Zhenghe	100	27.22 N	118.50 E
Zhengjiadiancun	104	41.05 N	122.20 E
Zhengjiafang	100	28.42 N	117.53 E
Zhengjiawu	100	29.29 N	120.05 E
Zhengjiayao	98	39.54 N	114.14 E
Zhenglanqi (Huangqidayingzi)	98	42.16 N	115.49 E
Zhengluqiao	106	31.50 N	120.05 E
Zhengning	102	35.21 N	108.13 E
Zhengping	100	25.22 N	114.46 E
Zhen'guosi	271a	39.51 N	116.21 E
Zhengxiangbaiqi	98	42.16 N	114.52 E
Zhengyang	100	32.37 N	114.23 E
Zhengyangguan	100	32.28 N	116.32 E
Zhengyi	106	31.23 N	120.52 E
Zhengzhou (Chengchow)	102	34.48 N	113.39 E
Zhengzhuang	100	28.11 N	119.01 E
Zhengzichang	107	29.08 N	106.38 E
Zhenhai, Zhg.	100	24.16 N	118.06 E
Zhenhai, Zhg.	100	29.52 N	121.48 E
Zhenhai, Zhg.	100	29.57 N	121.42 E
Zhenhai, Zhg.	102	21.53 N	112.25 E
Zhenhaijiao	100	24.16 N	118.08 E
Zhenjiang, Zhg.	98	40.44 N	125.28 E
Zhenjiang (Chinkiang), Zhg.	106	32.13 N	119.26 E
Zhenjiangguan	102	32.25 N	103.35 E
Zhenjiaqiao	106	32.08 N	120.49 E
Zhenjinqiao	107	30.12 N	104.22 E
Zhenkang	102	24.06 N	99.16 E
Zhenlai	89	45.52 N	123.14 E
Zhenning	102	26.05 N	105.46 E
Zhenping	102	33.08 N	112.19 E
Zhenru	106	31.15 N	121.24 E
Zhenshui	100	24.55 N	113.44 E
Zhentong	100	32.39 N	120.08 E
Zhentou	100	27.04 N	114.56 E
Zhentoudian	100	29.10 N	117.29 E
Zhentouhe	100	32.58 N	114.24 E
Zhentoushi	100	28.01 N	113.20 E
Zhenxiaguan	100	27.12 N	120.28 E
Zhenxichang	107	29.29 N	104.33 E
Zhenxingjie	98	42.38 N	124.53 E
Zhenyu	100	27.08 N	120.18 E
Zhenyuan, Zhg.	102	35.46 N	107.18 E
Zhenyuan, Zhg.	102	26.53 N	108.19 E
Zhenze, Zhg.	106	30.55 N	120.30 E
Zhenze (Dongshan), Zhg.	106	31.04 N	120.24 E
Zhenzhumen	98	41.53 N	126.45 E
Zhenzichang, Zhg.	107	29.52 N	104.12 E
Zhenzichang, Zhg.	107	30.38 N	104.20 E
Zhenzichang, Zhg.	107	29.59 N	105.11 E
Zhenzijie	107	28.48 N	106.40 E
Zhenziling	104	42.10 N	124.12 E
Zhenzizhen	105	39.50 N	118.20 E
Zheqiao	100	26.27 N	112.48 E
Zheshan	106	30.15 N	120.24 E
Zhetang	106	31.45 N	118.55 E
Zhidan	102	37.00 N	108.40 E
Zhide	100	30.04 N	116.58 E
Zhierling	98	40.26 N	114.16 E
Zhigou	98	35.55 N	119.13 E
Zhijiang, Zhg.	102	30.19 N	111.26 E
Zhijiang, Zhg.	102	26.54 N	109.31 E
Zhijin	102	26.41 N	105.37 E
Zhili, Zhg.	106	30.52 N	120.16 E
Zhili, Zhg.	106	31.09 N	120.16 E
Zhitan	100	29.35 N	117.16 E
Zhitang, Zhg.	106	31.33 N	121.01 E
Zhitang, Zhg.	106	31.36 N	120.58 E
Zhitomir → Žitomir	78	50.16 N	28.40 E
Zhitouji	100	33.28 N	118.18 E
Zhiwucun	106	30.38 N	119.47 E
Zhixi	100	23.57 N	114.33 E
Zhixia	100	29.42 N	119.36 E
Zhixiqiao	106	31.49 N	119.29 E
Zhiyang	100	33.47 N	113.07 E
Zhizhudao	100	26.02 N	120.04 E
Zhizushan	104	41.50 N	121.24 E
Zhob	120	32.04 N	69.50 E
Zhonganpu	104	41.37 N	121.58 E
Zhongaochang	107	29.46 N	105.41 E
Zhongba	120	29.54 N	83.40 E
Zhongbu, Zhg.	100	28.50 N	117.16 E
Zhongbu, Zhg.	100	31.40 N	117.45 E
Zhongbu, Zhg.	100	31.25 N	117.45 E
Zhongchuan	100	26.58 N	119.27 E
Zhongchuanhe	102	22.58 N	101.44 E
Zhongcun	102	33.27 N	110.05 E
Zhongcungang	100	32.38 N	115.45 E
Zhongdai	106	30.46 N	120.59 E
Zhongdian	102	27.50 N	99.40 E
Zhongdiquan	98	34.45 N	115.34 E
Zhongdu, Zhg.	100	33.04 N	118.46 E
Zhongdu, Zhg.	107	28.46 N	103.58 E
Zhongduan	100	25.17 N	116.41 E
Zhongerchong	104	41.58 N	123.58 E
Zhongfang	98	34.36 N	118.10 E
Zhongfengsi	107	28.53 N	106.25 E
Zhonggang	89	43.41 N	127.29 E
Zhonggong	98	36.30 N	117.01 E
Zhonggoumen	98	41.00 N	116.26 E
Zhonggu	104	42.27 N	124.00 E
Zhongguan	106	30.39 N	120.11 E
Zhongguanyi	100	31.08 N	114.52 E
Zhongguo → China [1]	90	35.00 N	105.00 E
Zhonghe	102	27.11 N	103.52 E
Zhonghechang, Zhg.	107	30.12 N	104.49 E
Zhonghechang, Zhg.	107	30.35 N	104.05 E
Zhongheying	102	23.48 N	103.36 E
Zhonghezhen	102	25.44 N	100.08 E
Zhonghuamen	106	32.01 N	118.46 E
Zhonghuopu	100	29.44 N	113.59 E
Zhongjianchang	107	28.46 N	106.13 E
Zhongjiatai	104	40.48 N	122.46 E
Zhonglou	98	35.24 N	119.02 E
Zhongluotan	100	23.23 N	113.23 E
Zhongluyantai	104	41.32 N	123.17 E
Zhongmeihe	100	31.19 N	116.45 E
Zhongmou	98	34.46 N	114.01 E
Zhongning (Ninganbao)	102	37.27 N	105.38 E
Zhongpingchang	102	31.15 N	110.10 E
Zhongqiao	106	31.11 N	119.11 E
Zhongsha	100	26.24 N	116.36 E
Zhongshan, Zhg.	100	26.12 N	117.26 E
Zhongshan (Shiqi), Zhg.	100	22.31 N	113.22 E
Zhongshanhe	100	34.23 N	120.05 E
Zhongshan Park	269b	31.13 N	121.25 E
Zhongshi	100	25.24 N	115.28 E
Zhongtiao	102	35.12 N	111.35 E
Zhongtou	100	34.00 N	113.21 E
Zhongwei	102	37.33 N	105.10 E
Zhongwopu	102	38.30 N	102.59 E
Zhongxian, Zhg.	100	27.17 N	116.47 E
Zhongxian, Zhg.	102	30.29 N	108.05 E
Zhongxiang	100	31.11 N	112.33 E
Zhongxiangchang	107	29.50 N	104.08 E
Zhongxin, Zhg.	100	23.16 N	113.38 E
Zhongxin, Zhg.	100	24.14 N	114.44 E
Zhongxin, Zhg.	104	40.47 N	124.08 E
Zhongxinba	100	23.43 N	115.22 E
Zhongxing	106	32.17 N	119.34 E
Zhongxingchang, Zhg.	107	29.07 N	105.18 E
Zhongxingchang, Zhg.	107	30.12 N	103.32 E
Zhongxingzhen	107	30.31 N	104.03 E
Zhongxinzhen	107	30.16 N	106.15 E
Zhongyangqu	104	40.47 N	122.05 E
Zhongyaozhan	89	50.39 N	125.44 E
Zhongying	105	39.38 N	117.06 E
Zhongzangcun	105	38.52 N	115.38 E
Zhongzhan	100	25.16 N	114.24 E
Zhongzhuang	105	39.25 N	114.47 E
Zhouba	107	29.06 N	103.43 E
Zhoubachang	107	29.59 N	103.52 E
Zhoucun	98	36.47 N	117.48 E
Zhoudangfan	100	31.54 N	114.31 E
Zhouhe	105	39.47 N	117.23 E
Zhoujiachang	107	30.33 N	104.25 E
Zhoujiadai	106	32.12 N	120.26 E
Zhoujiadu	106	31.11 N	121.29 E
Zhoujiagou	107	30.08 N	104.30 E
Zhoujiapo	107	29.48 N	104.01 E
Zhoujiapuzi	104	40.56 N	123.33 E
Zhoujiatun, Zhg.	104	41.16 N	120.58 E
Zhoujiatun, Zhg.	104	41.29 N	121.50 E
Zhoujiatun, Zhg.	104	41.04 N	120.47 E
Zhoujiawopu	104	42.31 N	122.45 E
Zhoujiayao	104	41.19 N	122.48 E
Zhoujingxiang	106	31.32 N	120.23 E
Zhoukoudian	105	39.41 N	115.56 E
Zhoulichang	107	29.55 N	105.09 E
Zhouning	100	27.16 N	119.12 E
Zhoupu	106	31.07 N	121.34 E
Zhouqu	102	33.43 N	104.10 E
Zhouquan	106	30.35 N	120.21 E
Zhoushan	100	30.02 N	122.06 E
Zhoushang	100	29.18 N	119.31 E
Zhoushanqundao	100	30.00 N	122.00 E
Zhoushu	106	31.28 N	120.59 E
Zhoushuizi	98	38.57 N	121.34 E
Zhoutian	100	24.59 N	113.50 E
Zhoutieqiao	106	31.26 N	120.00 E
Zhouwangmiao	106	30.28 N	120.29 E
Zhouxi	100	29.13 N	116.20 E
Zhouxiang, Zhg.	100	30.10 N	121.08 E
Zhouxiang, Zhg.	106	31.19 N	120.57 E
Zhouxin	106	31.30 N	120.18 E
Zhouxing	107	29.24 N	105.22 E
Zhouzhai	106	32.02 N	121.31 E
Zhouzhi	102	34.12 N	108.10 E
Zhouzhuang, Zhg.	105	39.09 N	115.18 E
Zhouzhuang, Zhg.	106	31.06 N	120.51 E
Zhouzhuang, Zhg.	106	32.15 N	120.08 E
Zhuangaerpendi [1]	86	45.00 N	88.00 E
Zhuanghang	106	30.54 N	121.23 E
Zhuanghe	98	39.43 N	123.01 E
Zhuangji	98	34.20 N	115.15 E
Zhuangtou	105	40.55 N	117.57 E
Zhuangtouyingzi, Zhg.	104	41.43 N	120.32 E
Zhuangtouyingzi, Zhg.	104	41.50 N	120.43 E
Zhuangxi	107	30.33 N	104.31 E
Zhuangyuanqiao	100	27.54 N	120.48 E
Zhuanmiaoji	98	34.57 N	115.24 E
Zhuanpingshan	107	29.07 N	103.37 E
Zhuanqiao	106	31.04 N	121.23 E
Zhuantouwan	100	31.29 N	112.24 E
Zhuanwantai	104	41.20 N	122.22 E
Zhuao	100	29.05 N	121.16 E
Zhuchang	102	27.18 N	107.26 E
Zhuchen	98	34.57 N	118.17 E
Zhucheng	98	36.00 N	119.24 E
Zhucikou	100	29.17 N	112.41 E
Zhudian	100	30.33 N	115.12 E
Zhuergan	89	52.04 N	120.48 E
Zhufeng	106	30.35 N	118.56 E
Zhuganhe	100	32.18 N	114.42 E
Zhuganpu	100	32.13 N	114.39 E
Zhugaosi	107	30.37 N	104.40 E
Zhuge	100	29.15 N	119.18 E
Zhugentan	107	29.25 N	103.50 E
Zhugou, Zhg.	98	36.52 N	120.15 E
Zhugou, Zhg.	100	32.47 N	113.42 E
Zhuguangshan	100	26.00 N	114.00 E
Zhugusi	102	37.01 N	102.27 E
Zhuhonggang	100	32.52 N	119.58 E
Zhuhongyu	104	40.48 N	123.00 E
Zhuimuhu	120	34.30 N	87.00 E
Zhuji	100	29.43 N	120.14 E
Zhujiabeng	106	31.21 N	120.41 E
Zhujiabian	106	31.38 N	119.11 E
Zhujiachang, Zhg.	107	30.03 N	104.13 E
Zhujiachang, Zhg.	107	29.48 N	104.20 E
Zhujiafang	104	41.20 N	122.40 E

River	Fluss	Río	Rivière	Rio
Canal	Kanal	Canal	Canal	Canal
Waterfall, Rapids	Wasserfall, Stromschnellen	Cascada, Rápidos	Chute d'eau, Rapides	Cascata, Rápidos
Strait	Meeresstrasse	Estrecho	Détroit	Estreito
Bay, Gulf	Bucht, Golf	Bahía, Golfo	Baie, Golfe	Baía, Golfo
Lake, Lakes	See, Seen	Lago, Lagos	Lac, Lacs	Lago, Lagos
Swamp	Sumpf	Pantano	Marais	Pântano
Ice Features, Glacier	Eis- und Gletscherformen	Accidentes Glaciales	Formes glaciaires	Acidentes Glaciares
Other Hydrographic Features	Andere Hydrographische Objekte	Otros Elementos Hidrográficos	Autres données hydrographiques	Outros Elementos Hidrográficos

Submarine Features	Untermeerische Objekte	Accidentes Submarinos	Formes de relief sous-marin	Acidentes Submarinos
Political Unit	Politische Einheit	Unidad Politica	Entité politique	Unidade Política
Cultural Institution	Kulturelle Institution	Institución Cultural	Institution culturelle	Instituição Cultural
Historical Site	Historische Stätte	Sitio Histórico	Site historique	Sítio Histórico
Recreational Site	Erholungs- und Ferienort	Sitio de Recreo	Centre de loisirs	Sítio de Lazer
Airport	Flughafen	Aeropuerto	Aéroport	Aeroporto
Military Installation	Militäranlage	Instalación Militar	Installation militaire	Instalação Militar
Miscellaneous	Verschiedenes	Misceláneo	Divers	Miscelânea

Name (ENGLISH) / Name (DEUTSCH)	Page / Seite	Lat.°′ / Breite°′	Long.°′ / Länge°′ E=Ost
Zhujiahang	106	30.51 N	121.19 E
Zhujiahe, Zhg.	100	29.44 N	113.06 E
Zhujiahe, Zhg.	106	31.08 N	120.53 E
Zhujiajian I	100	29.54 N	122.24 E
Zhujiajiao	106	31.06 N	121.02 E
Zhujiajiaotou	106	31.24 N	121.11 E
Zhujiangkou C[1]	100	23.36 N	113.44 E
Zhujiangkou ≃	100	23.36 N	113.44 E
Zhujiangqing	100	27.18 N	114.44 E
Zhujiaqiao, Zhg.	106	30.26 N	119.03 E
Zhujiaqiao, Zhg.	106	31.07 N	121.44 E
Zhujiatuo	107	29.02 N	105.51 E
Zhujiawan, Zhg.	100	30.56 N	114.10 E
Zhujiawan, Zhg.	100	32.28 N	117.29 E
Zhujiawan, Zhg.	105	40.08 N	114.56 E
Zhujiawopeng	104	42.27 N	122.13 E
Zhujiesi	102	33.34 N	97.21 E
Zhukeng	100	23.49 N	112.55 E
Zhukou, Zhg.	98	34.07 N	115.04 E
Zhukou, Zhg.	100	26.58 N	117.16 E
Zhukou, Zhg.	100	27.41 N	118.53 E
Zhukovskiy → Žukovskij	82	55.35 N	38.08 E
Zhukuiqiao	106	31.34 N	119.20 E
Zhulanbu	100	25.36 N	115.46 E
Zhulin	106	31.45 N	119.27 E
Zhulinzong	100	32.20 N	113.38 E
Zhulonghe ≃	98	38.47 N	115.59 E
Zhulongqiao	100	32.21 N	118.09 E
Zhuluke	98	41.36 N	119.54 E
Zhumadian	100	33.00 N	114.01 E
Zhumulangmafeng → Everest, Mount ∧	124	27.59 N	86.56 E
Zhungeerqi	102	39.49 N	111.10 E
Zhuolu (Baoan)	105	40.22 N	115.12 E
Zhuoni	102	34.32 N	103.24 E
Zhuotian	100	25.38 N	116.13 E
Zhuoxian	105	39.30 N	115.58 E
Zhuozhanghe ≃	102	36.15 N	115.10 E
Zhuozi	102	40.51 N	112.41 E
Zhuqianzongpuzi	104	42.17 N	123.18 E
Zhuqiao, Zhg.	98	37.22 N	120.05 E
Zhuqiao, Zhg.	106	30.26 N	120.36 E
Zhurushan	100	30.26 N	113.48 E
Zhushan, Zhg.	100	28.43 N	117.01 E
Zhushan, Zhg.	102	32.10 N	110.19 E
Zhusigang	100	31.14 N	118.23 E
Zhutan	100	28.04 N	114.10 E
Zhutang	106	31.06 N	118.39 E
Zhutangqiao	106	31.47 N	120.24 E
Zhuting, Zhg.	100	27.48 N	114.02 E
Zhuting, Zhg.	100	27.24 N	113.04 E
Zhuwasi	102	28.48 N	97.27 E
Zhuwo, Zhg.	102	31.41 N	100.24 E
Zhuwo, Zhg.	105	40.02 N	115.48 E
Zhuwotuo	107	30.31 N	104.34 E
Zhuwumiao	100	30.54 N	116.19 E
Zhuxi, Zhg.	100	28.10 N	118.53 E
Zhuxi, Zhg.	102	32.09 N	109.42 E
Zhuxiang	100	32.19 N	117.12 E
Zhuxianzhen	98	34.37 N	114.16 E
Zhuxichang	100	28.58 N	114.06 E
Zhuya	98	36.38 N	118.12 E
Zhuyang	98	36.16 N	117.22 E
Zhuyangxi	107	29.06 N	105.58 E
Zhuyangzhen	102	34.20 N	110.44 E
Zhuyoucun	98	37.20 N	119.53 E
Zhuyuanpu	107	29.34 N	104.08 E
Zhuzhen	100	32.31 N	118.42 E
Zhuzhou	100	27.50 N	113.09 E
Ziama Mansouria	34	36.40 N	5.29 E
Ziano	64	46.17 N	11.34 E
Ziārat	120	30.23 N	67.43 E
Zīārat-e Shāh Maqṣūd	120	31.59 N	65.30 E
Ziārat Gali Chāh ⊤[4]	128	28.20 N	63.38 E
Žiar nad Hronom	30	48.36 N	18.52 E
Ẕibā'	128	27.21 N	35.40 E
Zībāk	120	36.32 N	71.21 E
Zibdīn	132	33.22 N	35.28 E
Zibo (Tzupo)	98	36.47 N	118.01 E
Zicapa	234	17.57 N	99.02 W
Zicavo	36	41.54 N	9.08 E
Zicheng	98	36.38 N	117.55 E
Žichovice	60	49.16 N	13.37 E
Žičicy	76	55.07 N	31.17 E
Zickhusen	54	53.45 N	11.25 E
Židačov	78	49.23 N	24.08 E
Ziddi	85	39.03 N	68.48 E
Žideli	86	48.40 N	70.29 E
Zid'ki	78	49.42 N	36.21 E
Židlochovice	61	49.02 N	16.37 E
Ziębice	30	50.37 N	17.00 E
Ziegelroda	54	51.20 N	11.28 E
Ziegendorf	54	53.18 N	11.49 E
Ziegenhain	56	50.55 N	9.15 E
Ziegenhals, D.D.R.	264a	52.21 N	13.40 E
Ziegenhals → Głuchołazy, Pol.	30	50.20 N	17.22 E
Ziegenort → Trzebież	30	53.42 N	14.31 E
Ziegenrück	54	50.37 N	11.38 E
Zielenzig → Sulęcin	30	52.26 N	15.08 E
Zielona Góra (Grünberg)	30	51.56 N	15.31 E
Ziemetshausen	58	48.18 N	10.31 E
Zierenberg	56	51.22 N	9.18 E
Zierikzee	52	51.38 N	3.55 E
Ziersdorf	61	48.31 N	15.55 E
Ziesar	54	52.16 N	12.17 E
Ziesendorf	54	54.00 N	12.02 E
Ziethen	54	53.53 N	13.40 E
Žiežmariai	76	54.48 N	24.27 E
Ziftā	142	30.43 N	31.15 E
Zifta Barrage ➛[6]	142	30.43 N	31.15 E
Žigajlovka	78	50.38 N	35.07 E
Žigalgan	84	44.36 N	50.46 E
Žigalovo	88	54.48 N	105.08 E
Zigana Dağları ⛰	130	40.37 N	39.30 E
Žigansk	74	66.45 N	123.20 E
Zigazinskij	86	53.50 N	57.20 E
Zigey	146	14.43 N	15.47 E
Zīghan ⊤[4]	146	25.30 N	22.25 E
Zigong (Tzukung)	107	29.22 N	104.46 E
Zigui	102	31.00 N	110.31 E
Ziguinchor	150	12.35 N	16.16 W
Žigulevsk	80	53.25 N	49.27 E
Žiguli	80	53.22 N	49.19 E
Žiguli ⛰	80	53.30 N	49.40 E
Zīguri	76	57.16 N	27.40 E
Zigutaicun	104	42.01 N	121.16 E
Zihe ≃	98	37.12 N	118.34 E
Zihedian	98	36.48 N	118.22 E
Žihle	60	50.03 N	13.22 E
Zihuatanejo	234	17.38 N	101.33 W
Zihukou, Zhg.	100	28.44 N	112.33 E
Zihukou, Zhg.	100	28.55 N	118.08 E
Ziichang	102	37.19 N	109.33 E
Ziiyang	102	32.31 N	108.48 E
Ziizhou	102	37.37 N	109.41 E
Zijančurino	86	51.33 N	56.55 E
Žijenkum	85	42.50 N	69.00 E
Zijiao	98	37.21 N	117.25 E
Zijin	100	23.40 N	115.11 E
Zijingguan	105	39.23 N	115.08 E
Zijinshan ∧	106	32.04 N	118.51 E
Zikejevo	76	53.44 N	34.52 E
Zikhron Ya'aqov	132	32.34 N	34.57 E
Zikoufang	100	26.22 N	117.24 E
Zilair	86	52.14 N	57.30 E
Žilaja Kosa	86	46.49 N	53.12 E
Žilaja Tambica	24	62.32 N	36.09 E
Zile	130	40.18 N	35.54 E
Zili	102	26.50 N	100.27 E
Žilina	30	49.14 N	18.46 E
Žilino	76	54.54 N	21.56 E
Zillah, Lībīya	146	28.33 N	17.35 E
Zillah, Wash., U.S.	202	46.24 N	120.16 W
Ziller ≃	64	47.24 N	11.50 E
Ziller-Tal ∨	64	47.20 N	11.50 E
Zillertaler Alpen (Alpi Aurine) ⛰	64	47.00 N	11.55 E
Zillis	58	46.38 N	9.27 E
Zillisheim	58	47.41 N	7.16 E
Zilly	54	51.56 N	10.49 E
Zilme	144	16.25 N	43.49 E
Žiloj, Ostrov I	128	40.19 N	50.36 E
Žiloj Bor	76	59.06 N	34.37 E
Žil'ovo	82	54.59 N	38.02 E
Ziltendorf	54	52.12 N	14.37 E
Zilupe	76	56.23 N	28.07 E
Zilwaukee	190	43.28 N	83.55 W
Zima	88	53.55 N	102.04 E
Zima ≃	88	53.52 N	102.02 E
Zimapán	234	20.45 N	99.21 W
Zimatlán de Alvarez	234	16.52 N	96.47 W
Zimba	154	17.19 S	26.13 E
Zimbabwe □[1]	138		
	154	20.00 S	30.00 E
Zimbabwe National Park ♠	154	20.17 S	30.57 E
Zimbor	38	47.00 N	23.16 E
Zimella	64	45.20 N	11.22 E
Zimi	150	7.19 N	11.18 W
Zimljansker-Stausee → Ciml'anskoje Vodochranilišče ⊜[1]	80	48.00 N	43.00 E
Zimmerman	218	39.42 N	84.02 W
Zimn'ackij	80	49.44 N	42.53 E
Zimnicea	38	43.39 N	25.21 E
Zimogorje	83	48.35 N	38.56 E
Zimonino	76	53.47 N	31.52 E
Zimovniki	80	47.08 N	42.28 E
Zimovskoje	86	57.31 N	86.52 E
Zin	60	47.17 N	11.14 E
Ẕin, Naḥal ∨	132	30.57 N	35.19 E
Zina	146	11.16 N	14.58 E
Zinacatepec	234	18.20 N	97.15 W
Zinal	58	46.08 N	7.38 E
Zinapécuaro [de Figueroa]	234	19.52 N	100.49 W
Zinder	150	13.48 N	8.59 E
Zinder □[5]	146	15.00 N	10.30 E
Zinga	152	3.43 N	18.35 E
Zinga Mulike	154	9.09 S	38.44 E
Zingaro, Passo dello)(	70	37.43 N	14.50 E
Zingst	54	54.26 N	12.41 E
Zingst ≻[1]	54	54.25 N	12.50 E
Zingwanda	140	7.10 N	27.56 E
Ziniaré	150	12.35 N	1.18 W
Žiniške ≃	85	43.14 N	78.30 E
Zinken ∧	61	47.20 N	14.44 E
Zinkenbach	64	47.44 N	13.25 E
Zinkgruvan	40	58.49 N	15.05 E
Zin'kov	78	49.04 N	27.04 E
Zinnik → Soignies	50	50.35 N	4.04 E
Zinnowitz	54	54.04 N	13.55 E
Zinnwald-Georgenfeld	54	50.44 N	13.46 E
Zinswiller	56	48.55 N	7.35 E
Zion	216	42.27 N	87.50 W
Zionhill	208	40.29 N	75.24 W
Zion National Park ♠	200	37.10 N	113.00 W
Zionsville	218	39.57 N	86.16 W
Zionz Lake ⊜	184	51.25 N	91.52 W
Zipaquirá	246	5.02 N	74.00 W
Žipkovšino	88	51.52 N	112.59 E
Ẕippori	132	32.45 N	35.17 E
Žipsendorf	54	51.02 N	12.16 E
Ziqlāb, Wādī ∨	132	32.30 N	35.34 E
Zir	130	39.59 N	33.21 E
Zira	123	30.58 N	74.59 E
Zirahuén, Laguna ⊜	234	19.27 N	101.44 W
Žir'akovo	86	57.53 N	65.37 E
Zirándaro	234	18.27 N	100.59 W
Zirāpur	124	24.01 N	76.22 E
Žir'atino	76	53.15 N	33.44 E
Zirbitzkogel ∧, Öst.	30		
	61	47.04 N	14.34 E
Zirchow	54	53.53 N	14.08 E
Zirgan	86	53.14 N	55.55 E
Žirje, Otok I	36	43.40 N	15.39 E
Zirl	64	47.17 N	11.14 E
Zirndorf	56	49.26 N	10.58 E
Žirnov	80	48.13 N	41.06 E
Žirnovsk	80	51.00 N	44.46 E
Ziro	120	27.38 N	93.42 E
Žiroškino	82	55.22 N	38.03 E
Žirovnice	30	49.15 N	15.11 E
Zishan	100	25.57 N	115.35 E
Zishui ≃, Zhg.	102	28.45 N	112.25 E
Zishui ≃, Zhg.	107	30.09 N	104.42 E
Zisterzinser Abtei ʋ[1]	56	49.01 N	8.47 E
Zisuntang	106	30.38 N	118.42 E
Zitácuaro	234	19.24 N	100.22 W
Zitácuaro ≃	234	18.51 N	100.44 W
Zitadelle ⊥	264a	52.33 N	13.13 E
Žiteli	24	65.04 N	47.26 E
Žitenice	54	50.35 N	14.08 E
Žitjevo	76	59.54 N	41.06 E
Žitkoviči	78	52.14 N	27.54 E
Žitkovo	76	60.42 N	29.20 E
Žitkur	80	48.57 N	46.17 E
Zitlala	234	17.38 N	99.05 W
Zitlaltepec	234	19.12 N	97.54 W
Žitnoje	80	45.49 N	47.41 E
Žitomir	78	50.16 N	28.40 E
Žitomirskoje Polesje ➛[1]	78	50.40 N	28.00 E
Zitong	102	31.43 N	105.10 E
Zittau	54	50.54 N	14.47 E
Zitundo	156	26.45 S	32.50 E
Živa, Gora ∧	88	53.18 N	107.38 E
Zıvarık	130	38.19 N	32.53 E
Zivint	130	37.13 N	30.18 E
Ziway, Lake ⊜	144	8.00 N	38.50 E
Ziwuji	100	32.55 N	115.58 E
Zixi	100	27.42 N	117.02 E
Zixing	100	26.00 N	113.23 E
Ziyahe ≃	105	39.11 N	117.08 E
Ziyang	107	30.07 N	104.39 E
Ziyuan	102	26.01 N	110.31 E
Ziyun	102	25.43 N	106.05 E
Žizdra	76	53.45 N	34.44 E
Žizdra ≃	82	54.14 N	36.12 E
Zizers	58	46.56 N	9.34 E
Zizhong	107	29.48 N	104.51 E
Zizi	100	28.01 N	117.46 E
Žižica	76	56.17 N	31.21 E
Žižickoje, Ozero ⊜	76	56.14 N	31.15 E
Žižma ≃	76	53.54 N	25.36 E
Zlarin	36	43.42 N	15.50 E
Zlatá Koruna ʋ[1]	61	48.52 N	14.22 E
Zlatar	36	46.06 N	16.05 E
Zlaté Moravce	30	48.25 N	18.24 E
Zlatica	38	42.43 N	24.08 E
Zlatograd	38	41.23 N	25.06 E
Zlatoust	86	55.10 N	59.40 E
Zlatoustovsk	89	52.58 N	133.38 E
Zlín → Gottwaldov	30	49.13 N	17.41 E
Ẕlītan	146	32.28 N	14.34 E
Žlobin	76	52.54 N	30.03 E
Złocieniec	30	53.33 N	16.01 E
Złoczew	30	51.25 N	18.36 E
Zlonice	54	50.15 N	14.07 E
Złotoryja	30	51.08 N	15.55 E
Złotów	30	53.22 N	17.02 E
Žlutice	54	50.03 N	13.10 E
Zlydnev	80	48.46 N	45.48 E
Zlynka, S.S.S.R.	76	52.25 N	31.44 E
Zlynka, S.S.S.R.	78	48.28 N	31.32 E
Zmeinogorsk	86	51.10 N	82.13 E
Zmeinyj, Ostrov I	78	45.15 N	30.12 E
Žmerinka	78	49.02 N	28.06 E
Żmigród	30	51.29 N	16.55 E
Zmijov	78	49.40 N	36.19 E
Zmijovka	76	52.40 N	36.23 E
Žminj	36	45.09 N	13.55 E
Zna → Cna ≃	80	54.32 N	42.05 E
Znaim → Znojmo	61	48.52 N	16.02 E
Znamenka, S.S.S.R.	76	54.54 N	34.34 E
Znamenka, S.S.S.R.	78	48.43 N	32.40 E
Znamenka, S.S.S.R.	80	52.24 N	41.26 E
Znamenka, S.S.S.R.	83	48.51 N	37.22 E
Znamenka, S.S.S.R.	86	50.05 N	79.32 E
Znamenka, S.S.S.R.	86	53.32 N	91.54 E
Znamenka, S.S.S.R.	86	53.10 N	79.30 E
Znamenka, S.S.S.R.	88	54.42 N	104.50 E
Znamenka Vtoraja	78	48.43 N	32.35 E
Znamensk	76	54.37 N	21.13 E
Znamenskoje, S.S.S.R.	76	53.17 N	35.41 E
Znamenskoje, S.S.S.R.	80	53.19 N	42.57 E
Znamenskoje, S.S.S.R.	86	57.08 N	73.55 E
Znamenskoje, S.S.S.R.	265b	55.45 N	37.09 E
Żnin	30	52.52 N	17.43 E
Znob'-Novgorodskoje	78	52.16 N	33.36 E
Znojmo	61	48.52 N	16.02 E
Zoadiba	152	3.04 N	14.02 E
Zoagli	62	44.20 N	9.16 E
Zoar	158	33.30 S	21.28 E
Zoar Village State Memorial ⊥	214	40.36 N	81.27 W
Zoarville	214	40.35 N	81.24 W
Zobia	154	2.58 N	25.56 E
Zöblitz	54	50.39 N	13.14 E
Zóbuè	154	15.38 S	34.26 E
Zocca	64	44.21 N	10.59 E
Žochova, Ostrov I	74	76.04 N	152.40 E
Zódhia	130	35.10 N	33.00 E
Žodino	76	54.06 N	28.21 E
Žodiški	76	54.38 N	26.26 E
Zoétélé	152	3.15 N	11.53 E
Zoetermeer	52	52.03 N	4.30 E
Zofingen	58	47.18 N	7.57 E
Zogno	62	45.48 N	9.40 E
Zográfos	267c	37.59 N	23.46 E
Zohar	132	31.36 N	34.42 E
Zohreh ≃	128	30.04 N	49.34 E
Zok	130	38.02 N	41.33 E
Zola Predosa	64	44.29 N	11.12 E
Zolder	56	51.01 N	5.18 E
Zoldo Alto	64	46.22 N	12.06 E
Zolfo Springs	220	27.30 N	81.48 W
Zolka ≃	84	44.17 N	43.51 E
Żółkiewka	30	50.55 N	22.51 E
Zollhaus	56	50.17 N	8.04 E
Zollikofen	58	47.00 N	7.28 E
Zollikon	58	47.20 N	8.35 E
Zolling	60	48.27 N	11.46 E
Zol'noje	80	53.27 N	49.48 E
Zoločov, S.S.S.R.	78	50.17 N	35.59 E
Zoločov, S.S.S.R.	78	49.47 N	24.52 E
Zolotaja Gora	89	54.16 N	126.36 E
Zolotaja Lipa ≃	78	48.59 N	25.04 E
Zolotari	80	49.46 N	46.21 E
Zolotar'ovka	80	53.04 N	45.20 E
Zolotkovo	80	55.32 N	41.06 E
Zolotniki	78	49.17 N	25.23 E
Zolotoje, S.S.S.R.	80	50.51 N	45.53 E
Zolotoje, S.S.S.R.	83	48.41 N	38.31 E
Zolotoj Kolodec	83	48.32 N	37.15 E
Zolotoj Potok	78	48.54 N	25.20 E
Zolotonoša	78	49.40 N	32.02 E
Zolotucha	80	47.49 N	46.44 E
Zolotuchino	78	52.05 N	36.23 E
Žoltoje, S.S.S.R.	78	47.47 N	33.50 E
Žoltoje, S.S.S.R.	78	48.30 N	33.31 E
Ž'oltoje, S.S.S.R.	83	48.39 N	39.07 E
Žoltyje Vody	78	48.21 N	33.31 E
Žolymbet	86	51.45 N	71.44 E
Zomba	154	15.23 S	35.18 E
Zomergem	50	51.07 N	3.33 E
Zone Point ≻	42	50.08 N	5.00 W
Zongchang	107	28.52 N	104.36 E
Zongo	152	4.21 N	18.36 E
Zonguldak	130	41.27 N	31.49 E
Zonguldak □[4]	130	41.30 N	32.15 E
Zongwe	154	5.05 S	27.55 E
Zonhoven	56	50.59 N	5.21 E
Zonnebeke	50	50.52 N	2.59 E
Zons	56	51.07 N	6.50 E
Zontehuitz, Cerro ∧	232	16.50 N	92.38 W
Zonza	36	41.45 N	9.10 E
Zoo, Bahnhof ➛[5]	264a	52.30 N	13.20 E
Zooafskolk	158	29.56 S	20.24 E
Zoom ≃	52	51.30 N	4.14 E
Zoppot → Sopot	30	54.28 N	18.34 E
Zopten am Berge → Sobótka	30	50.55 N	16.45 E
Zopui	120	23.39 N	92.14 E
Zörbig	54	51.37 N	12.07 E
Zorge	54	51.38 N	10.38 E
Zorge ≃	54	51.27 N	10.54 E
Zorgo	150	12.15 N	0.36 W
Zorgongo	150	12.16 N	0.48 W
Zorikovka	83	49.24 N	39.51 E
Zorinsk	83	48.25 N	38.34 E
Zorita	34	39.17 N	5.42 W
Zorkul', Ozero ⊜	120	37.27 N	73.40 E
Zorn ≃	56	48.45 N	7.55 E
Zorneding	60	48.05 N	11.49 E
Zornica	38	42.23 N	26.56 E
Zorra, Arroyo de la ≃	196	29.31 N	101.13 W
Zorritos	246	3.40 S	80.40 W
Zorzor	150	7.46 N	9.28 W
Zöschen	54	51.21 N	12.07 E
Zossen	54	52.13 N	13.27 E
Zoti	84	41.53 N	42.28 E
Zottegem	50	50.52 N	3.48 E
Zou □[5]	150	8.00 N	2.15 E
Zouan-Hounien	150	6.55 N	8.13 W
Zouar	146	20.27 N	16.32 E
Zoug → Zug	58	47.10 N	8.31 E
Zouginindja	152	5.24 N	21.40 E
Zouîrât	148	22.42 N	12.30 W
Zoulabot	152	3.17 N	14.02 E
Zoumagang	107	29.28 N	106.18 E
Zoumatang ≃	269b	31.18 N	121.23 E
Zoumayi	98	39.07 N	114.34 E
Zouping	98	36.53 N	117.42 E
Zourma	150	11.22 N	0.49 W
Zousfana, Oued ∨	148	30.29 N	2.17 W
Zoutelande	52	51.30 N	3.30 E
Zoutkamp	52	53.20 N	6.18 E
Zouxian	98	35.24 N	117.00 E
Zovka	76	58.26 N	28.52 E
Žovnino	78	49.23 N	32.41 E
Žovten', S.S.S.R.	78	47.14 N	30.20 E
Žovten', S.S.S.R.	78	49.03 N	24.45 E
Žovtnevoje, S.S.S.R.	78	51.15 N	28.07 E
Žovtnevoje, S.S.S.R.	78	50.57 N	34.22 E
Žovtnevoje, S.S.S.R.	78	49.39 N	34.09 E
Žovtnevoje, S.S.S.R.	78	46.52 N	32.02 E
Zozaya, Picacho de ∧	232	27.10 N	102.34 W
Zozov	78	49.19 N	29.01 E
Zreïgat, Bir ⊤[4]	148	22.27 N	8.53 W
Zrenjanin	38	45.23 N	20.24 E
Zriba	36	36.20 N	10.16 E
Zrmanja ≃	36	44.15 N	15.32 E
Zruč nad Sázavou	30	49.45 N	15.07 E
Zscherndorf	54	51.36 N	12.15 E
Zschieren ➛[8]	54	51.00 N	13.52 E
Zschopau	54	50.44 N	13.04 E
Zschopau ≃	54	51.08 N	13.03 E
Zschorlau	54	50.34 N	12.38 E
Zschornewitz	54	51.43 N	12.25 E
Zschortau	54	51.28 N	12.21 E
Žuanbalyk	86	45.04 N	61.51 E
Žuantobe	86	44.45 N	68.54 E
Zuarungu	150	10.47 N	0.48 W
Zuata ≃	246	7.52 N	65.22 W
Zubaydīyah, Jabal az- ∧	132	33.48 N	37.02 E
Zubayr, Jazā'ir az- II	144	15.05 N	42.05 E
Zubayr, Wādī ∨	142	27.27 N	32.41 E
Zubcov	76	56.10 N	34.34 E
Zubkoviči	78	51.02 N	27.41 E
Zubova Pol'ana	80	54.04 N	42.51 E
Zubovka	80	54.16 N	51.06 E
Zubovo, S.S.S.R.	76	54.33 N	35.29 E
Zubovo, S.S.S.R.	76	60.19 N	36.57 E
Zubovo, S.S.S.R.	80	56.52 N	44.08 E
Zuccarello	62	44.07 N	8.07 E
Zuccone, Monte ∧	62	44.26 N	9.37 E
Zuchering	60	48.43 N	11.24 E
Zuchwil	58	47.12 N	7.33 E
Zuckerhütl ∧	64	46.58 N	11.09 E
Zudañez	248	19.06 S	64.44 W
Zudar	54	54.15 N	13.20 E
Z'udev, Ostrov I	80	45.35 N	47.58 E
Z'udostinskij, Ostrov I	80	45.58 N	48.50 E
Zuel	64	46.31 N	12.08 E
Zuénoula	150	7.26 N	6.03 W
Zuera	34	41.52 N	0.47 W
Zufaytat Mashtūl	142	30.20 N	31.21 E
Zug	58	47.10 N	8.31 E
Zug □[3]	58	47.00 N	8.30 E
Zugdeli	88	55.03 N	111.10 E
Zugdidi	84	42.30 N	41.53 E
Zugersee ⊜	58	47.08 N	8.30 E
Zug Island I	281	42.17 N	83.07 W
Zugló ➛[8]	264c	47.31 N	19.08 E
Zugres	83	48.01 N	38.15 E
Zugspitze ∧	64	47.25 N	10.59 E
Zühlsdorf	264a	52.44 N	13.24 E
Zui	76	57.06 N	31.37 E
Zuid-Beijerland	52	51.45 N	4.22 E
Zuid-Beveland I	52	51.25 N	3.45 E
Zuidbroek	52	53.10 N	6.52 E
Zuidelijk Flevoland ➛[1]	52	52.22 N	5.20 E
Zuiderzee → IJsselmeer ⊤[2]	52	52.45 N	5.25 E
Zuidholland □[4]	52	52.00 N	4.30 E
Zuidhorn	52	53.14 N	6.24 E
Zuidland	52	51.48 N	4.15 E
Zuidlaren	52	53.05 N	6.41 E
Zuid-Willemsvaart ≍	52	51.12 N	5.52 E
Zuidwolde	52	53.15 N	6.35 E
Zuja	78	45.03 N	34.20 E
Žuja ≃	88	58.45 N	118.11 E
Zújar ≃	34	39.01 N	5.47 W
Zújar, Embalse del ⊜[1]	34	38.50 N	5.20 W
Zujevka, S.S.S.R.	80	58.25 N	51.10 E
Zujevka, S.S.S.R.	83	48.04 N	38.15 E
Z'ukajka	80	58.12 N	54.43 E
Žukopa	76	56.33 N	32.42 E
Žukopa ≃	76	56.54 N	32.46 E
Žukovka, S.S.S.R.	76	53.32 N	33.44 E
Žukovka, S.S.S.R.	86	56.05 N	91.42 E
Žukovka, S.S.S.R.	265b	55.44 N	37.15 E
Žukovskaja	80	47.37 N	42.28 E
Žukovskij	82	55.35 N	38.08 E
Žukovskoje	80	46.05 N	41.21 E
Żukowo	30	54.21 N	18.22 E
Zula	144	15.11 N	39.41 E
Zula ≃	234	20.21 N	102.46 W
Žulanka	86	54.22 N	80.36 E
Ẕulayl, Wādī aẓ- ∨	132	32.09 N	36.03 E
Žuldyz	80	49.16 N	49.30 E
Žulebino	265b	55.42 N	37.51 E
Zulia	154	4.10 N	34.01 E
Zulia □[3]	246	10.00 N	72.10 W
Zulia □[5]	154	3.00 N	32.30 E
Zulia ∧	154	4.07 N	33.58 E
Zulia ≃	246	9.04 N	72.18 W
Zulia, Jabal ∧	154	4.07 N	33.58 E
Züllichau → Sulechów	30	52.06 N	15.37 E
Zülpich	56	50.41 N	6.39 E
Züls → Biała	30	50.23 N	17.40 E
Zulueta	240p	22.22 N	79.34 W
Zululand □[9]	158	28.10 S	32.00 E
Z'ul'z'a	88	52.33 N	116.13 E
Žumala	80	50.29 N	49.47 E
Zumarraga	116	11.38 N	124.50 E
Zumate, Cerro ∧	234	20.10 N	98.40 W
Zumba	246	4.52 S	79.09 W
Zumbo	154	15.36 S	30.25 E
Zumbro ≃	190	44.18 N	91.56 W
Zumbro, North Fork ≃	190	44.15 N	92.29 W
Zumbro, South Fork ≃	190	44.15 N	92.29 W
Zumbrota	190	44.17 N	92.40 W
Zumpango	234	19.48 N	99.06 W
Zumpango, Lago de ⊜	234	19.46 N	99.09 W
Zumpango del Río	234	17.39 N	99.30 W
Zundert	52	51.28 N	4.40 E
Zundi	152	10.28 S	16.48 E
Zune	156	18.59 S	35.18 E
Zungeru	150	9.48 N	6.09 E
Zungri	68	38.39 N	15.59 E
Zungur	150	9.58 N	9.47 E
Zungwini	158	27.34 S	30.53 E
Zunhua	105	40.12 N	117.58 E
Zuni, N. Mex., U.S.	200	35.04 N	108.51 W
Zuni, Va., U.S.	208	36.52 N	76.50 W
Zuni ≃	200	34.39 N	109.40 W
Zuni Indian Reservation ➛[4]	200	35.15 N	108.20 W
Zuni Mountains ⛰	200	35.10 N	108.15 W
Zun-Murin ≃	88	51.47 N	102.55 E
Zunsuzhi	102	44.40 N	112.50 E
Zunyi	102	27.39 N	106.57 E
Zuoan	100	26.10 N	114.16 E
Zuodengwei	102	23.27 N	106.57 E
Zuogezhuang	105	39.01 N	116.37 E
Zuojiang ≃	102	22.50 N	108.06 E
Zuojiazhuang	98	37.40 N	118.35 E
Zuomaozigou	104	42.12 N	120.41 E
Zuomuchedonghu ⊜	120	28.25 N	88.15 E
Zuoquan	102	37.03 N	113.30 E
Zuoshui	102	33.40 N	109.01 E
Zuosuo	102	27.45 N	100.54 E
Zuotema	120	35.50 N	80.45 E
Zuowei	105	40.41 N	114.43 E
Zuoxiunulemiao	88	48.08 N	115.38 E
Zuoyun	102	40.02 N	112.54 E
Zuoz	58	46.36 N	9.58 E
Županja	38	45.04 N	18.42 E
Zuqar, Jazīrat I	144	14.00 N	42.45 E
Zūq Mīkhā'īl	132	33.58 N	35.37 E
Žura, S.S.S.R.	78	47.31 N	29.04 E
Zura, S.S.S.R.	80	57.37 N	53.26 E
Zūrābād	128	38.49 N	44.35 E
Žuraviči, S.S.S.R.	76	53.15 N	30.33 E
Žuraviči, S.S.S.R.	78	50.59 N	25.43 E
Žuravl'ovka, S.S.S.R.	83	48.13 N	38.58 E
Žuravl'ovka, S.S.S.R.	86	51.57 N	69.56 E
Zurayghiṭ	128	26.29 N	40.33 E
Žurban	89	54.12 N	127.56 E
Zurich, Ont., Can.	190	43.26 N	81.37 W
Zurich, Ned.	52	53.06 N	5.23 E
Zürich, Schw.	58	47.23 N	8.32 E
Zürich □[3]	58	47.25 N	8.40 E
Zurich, Lake ⊜	278	42.12 N	88.06 W
Zürich-Kloten, Flughafen ☒	58	47.27 N	8.33 E
Zürichsee ⊜	58	47.13 N	8.45 E
Zurigo → Zürich	58	47.23 N	8.32 E
Zurmi	150	12.46 N	6.48 E
Żuromin	30	53.04 N	19.55 E
Zürs	58	47.10 N	10.10 E
Zuru	150	11.27 N	5.12 E
Zurzach	58	47.35 N	8.18 E
Zuša ≃	76	53.27 N	36.23 E
Zusam ≃	56	48.42 N	10.45 E
Žusandala ➛[2]	86	44.20 N	75.00 E
Zushi	94	35.18 N	139.35 E
Zusmarshausen	58	48.24 N	10.35 E
Züssow	54	53.59 N	13.32 E
Žut, Otok I	36	43.52 N	15.19 E
Zutiua ≃	250	3.43 S	45.29 W
Žutovo Vtoroje	80	47.49 N	43.51 E
Zutphen	52	52.08 N	6.12 E
Zützen	54	51.57 N	13.38 E
Zuurbekom	273d	26.19 S	27.49 E
Zuwārah	146	32.56 N	12.06 E
Zuwayzā	132	31.42 N	35.55 E
Z'uzel'skij	86	56.29 N	60.07 E
Žužemberk	36	45.50 N	14.56 E
Z'uzino	265b	55.40 N	38.07 E
Z'uzino ➛[8]	265b	55.39 N	37.35 E
Žuzymdyk	85	43.05 N	69.08 E
Zv'agino	265b	55.59 N	37.48 E
Zvannoje	78	51.23 N	34.33 E
Zvenigorod	82	55.44 N	36.51 E
Zvenigorodka	78	49.04 N	30.57 E
Zvenigovo	80	55.58 N	48.02 E
Zverevo	83	48.01 N	40.07 E
Zverinogolovskoje	86	54.28 N	64.50 E
Zvezdec	38	42.07 N	27.25 E
Zvíkovec	60	49.56 N	13.42 E
Zvolen	30	48.35 N	19.08 E
Zvon ∧	60	49.33 N	12.39 E
Zvornik	38	44.23 N	19.06 E
Zwaag	52	52.40 N	5.05 E
Zwaagwesteinde	52	53.15 N	6.04 E
Zwanenburg	52	52.23 N	4.45 E
Zwartemeer	52	52.43 N	7.03 E
Zwarte Meer ⊜	52	52.37 N	5.57 E
Zwartsluis	52	52.37 N	6.04 E
Zweckel ➛[8]	263	51.36 N	6.59 E
Zweibrücken	56	49.15 N	7.21 E
Zweifall	56	50.43 N	6.15 E
Zweisimmen	58	46.33 N	7.22 E
Zwenkau	54	51.13 N	12.19 E
Zwesten	56	51.03 N	9.10 E
Zwettl	61	48.37 N	15.10 E
Zwevegem	50	50.48 N	3.20 E
Zwevezele	50	51.02 N	3.12 E
Zwickau	54	50.44 N	12.29 E
Zwickauer Mulde ≃	54	51.10 N	12.48 E
Zwiefalten	58	48.14 N	9.28 E
Zwiefaltendorf	58	48.13 N	9.31 E
Zwierzyniec	30	50.37 N	22.58 E
Zwiesel	60	49.01 N	13.14 E
Zwieselstein	64	46.56 N	11.02 E
Zwijndrecht	52	51.49 N	4.39 E
Zwillbrock	52	52.04 N	6.42 E
Zwingenberg, B.R.D.	56	49.43 N	8.37 E
Zwingenberg, B.R.D.	56	49.25 N	9.02 E
Zwischenahn	52	53.11 N	8.00 E
Zwischenahner Meer ⊜	52	53.12 N	8.01 E
Zwochau	54	51.28 N	12.16 E
Zwoleń	30	51.22 N	21.35 E
Zwölfaxing	264b	48.06 N	16.28 E
Zwolle, Ned.	52	52.30 N	6.05 E
Zwolle, La., U.S.	194	31.38 N	93.38 W
Zwönitz	54	50.38 N	12.49 E
Zwota	54	50.21 N	12.25 E
Żychlin	30	52.15 N	19.39 E
Zymoetz ≃	182	54.33 N	128.26 W
Zyr'anka	74	65.45 N	150.51 E
Zyr'anovsk	86	49.43 N	84.20 E
Zyr'anovskij	86	57.46 N	61.42 E
Zyr'anskoje	86	56.50 N	86.38 E
Żyrardów	30	52.04 N	20.25 E
Zyryanovsk → Zyr'anovsk	86	49.43 N	84.20 E
Żyrzyn	30	51.30 N	22.07 E
Żywiec	30	49.41 N	19.12 E

Symbols in the index entries represent the categories identified in the key on page I · 30

Kartensymbole in dem Registerverzeichnis stellen die auf Seite I · 30 im Schlüssel erklärten Kategorien dar.

Los símbolos incluídos en el texto del índice representan las categorías identificadas con la clave en la página I · 30

Les symboles de l'index représentent les catégories indiquées dans la légende à la page I · 30

Os símbolos incluídos no texto do índice representam as categorias identificadas com a chave na página I · 30

Printed in the United States of America